Collins Cobuild

# Advanced Learner's

## ENGLISH DICTIONARY

COLLINS COBUILD

# Advanced Learner's

## ENGLISH DICTIONARY

THE UNIVERSITY OF BIRMINGHAM

COLLINS COBUILD

HarperCollins*Publishers*

fourth edition 2003



**latest reprint 2004**

HarperCollins Publishers
Westerhill Road, Bishopbriggs, Glasgow G64 2QT,
Great Britain

**www.cobuild.collins.co.uk**



ISBN 0-00-715800-9 paperback with CD-ROM
ISBN 0-00-715799-1 hardback with CD-ROM
ISBN 0-00-768394-4 paperback without CD-ROM
ISBN 0-00-768395-2 hardback without CD-ROM

---

Published in Germany by:
Ernst Klett Sprachen GmbH
Rotebühlstraße 77
70178 Stuttgart
Internet: www.pons.de
Email: info@pons.de
ISBN 3-12-517908-4

Distributed in Greece by:
Express Publishing –
Andrew Betsis ELT
31, Pyrgou Street
Pireas 18542
abetsis@hol.gr
ISBN 0-00-768750-8

Distributed in Poland by:
Express Publishing – EGIS
31-462 Kraków
ul. Pilotów 71
egis@egis.com.pl
ISBN 1-84466-083-4 paperback
ISBN 1-84466-082-6 hardback

---



A catalogue record for this book is available from the British Library

Computer typeset by Morton Word Processing Ltd, Scarborough

Printed and bound in Great Britain by William Clowes Ltd, Beccles and London

# Contents




## Corpus Acknowledgements

We would like to acknowledge the assistance of the many hundreds of individuals and companies who have kindly given permission for copyright material to be used in the Bank of English. The written sources include many national and regional newspapers in Britain and overseas; magazines and periodical publishers; and book publishers in Britain, the United States and Australia. Extensive spoken data has been provided by radio and television broadcasting companies; research workers at many universities and other institutions; and numerous individual contributors. We are grateful to them all.


## Note

Entered words that we have reason to believe constitute trademarks have been designated as such. However, neither the presence nor absence of such designation should be regarded as affecting the legal status of any trademark.

**FOURTH/THIRD EDITION**

**Founding Editor-in-Chief**
John Sinclair

**Publishing Director**
Lorna Sinclair Knight

**Editorial Director**
Michela Clari

**Managing Editor**
Maree Airlie

**Project Manager**
Carol McCann

**Lexicographers**
Elizabeth Potter    Bob Grossmith    Jane Bradbury    Laura Wedgeworth    Rosalind Combley
Duncan Marshall    Isabel Griffiths    Daphne Day
Rosamund Moon    Gill Francis    Elizabeth Manning

**Editors**
Alison Macaulay    Maggie Seaton

**Editorial Assistance**
Susanne Ogden    Moira MacDonald    Cindy Mitchell

**US Consultant**
John Wright

**Computing**
Mark Taylor    Ray Carrick
Jeremy Clear

**Illustrations**
Ela Bullon    Anthony Boswell

**SECOND EDITION**

**Editor in Chief**
John Sinclair

**Editorial Director**
Gwyneth Fox

**Editorial Manager**
Stephen Bullon

**Senior Editor**
Elizabeth Manning

**Editors**
Jane Bradbury    Rosalind Combley    Ramesh Krishnamurthy
Carole Murphy    Michael Murphy    Elizabeth Potter
Christina Rammell    Jenny Watson    Laura Wedgeworth    John Williams

**Assistant Editors**
Michael Lax    Dawn McKen    Deborah Oprin
Luisa Plaja    Jim Ronald    Miranda Timewell

**Grammar**
Gill Francis
Susan Hunston

**Pragmatics**
Joanna Channell
Alice Deignan

**Pronunciation**
Jonathan Payne

**The Bank of English**
Sue Smith

**Computer Staff**
Jeremy Clear    Zoe James
Tim Lane    Andrea Lewis

**Secretarial Staff**
Sue Crawley
Michelle Devereux

**Design and Production**
Ted Carden
Jill McNair

**Publishing Manager**
Debbie Seymour

**Managing Director, Collins Dictionaries**
Richard Thomas

**FIRST EDITION**

**Editor in Chief**
John Sinclair

**Managing Editor**
Patrick Hanks

**Editors**
Gwyneth Fox    Rosamund Moon    Penny Stock

**Senior Compilers**
Andrew Delahunty    Sheila Dignen
Ramesh Krishnamurthy    Elaine Pollard

**Compilers**
Stephen Bullon    Deborah Kirby
Helen Liebeck    Elizabeth Manning    John Todd

**Senior Computing Officer**
Jeremy Clear

**Computing Officer**
Eileen Fitzgerald

**Clerical Staff**
Lynne Farrow    Janice Johnson
Brenda Nicholls    Pat Smith

**Collins Publishing Director**
Richard Thomas

# Introduction

I am proud to present the Fourth Edition of the Cobuild Advanced Learner's English Dictionary, which continues the distinctive Cobuild tradition established sixteen years ago. This new edition updates the "snapshot" of current English, and adds some attractive features to make the book even easier to use.

The new edition of the dictionary is also available on CD-ROM. It is difficult to say whether the electronic dictionary will ever replace our familiar paper dictionaries; for a quick check on a meaning or usage a paper dictionary on your desk is simple and final, while the electronic version has a flexibility that the paper one cannot compete with. I would urge you to try out the electronic Cobuild, because when you become familiar with its structure and what it can do, you will find it very easy to consult, and you will be able to flick from place to place and reorganize the information in all sorts of ways.

The basis for the authority of Cobuild is the *Bank of English®*, still the largest collection of data of its kind in any language, and now containing 520,000,000 words. Decisions about which words to include as headwords in the dictionary, which meanings to draw attention to, which phrases to recognize as settled expressions in the language, and many other issues, are directly informed by the *Bank of English®*. The regular updating of this *corpus* ensures that this edition is up-to-date; new words and phrases constantly creep into the language, and sometimes establish themselves quickly, so the lexicographers keep a careful watch for them.

All the examples in this book are quoted from the rich selection that the corpus offers, and normally they are printed exactly as they occur in the text. In the choice of examples, we pay careful attention to *collocation* – the significant co-occurrence of words – so that the examples are not only natural forms of expression, but also are reliable models of usage. Important collocations are also highlighted in the definitions, giving help with set lexical and grammatical patterns.

The Cobuild defining style is modelled on the way people explain the meanings of words to each other, and it is refreshingly direct, because the definitions are just normal sentences of English with the headword in bold face. This style is not only easier to understand than the usual way definitions are written, it also allows a lot of extra information to be presented in a natural way. Please read the definitions carefully and learn to take from them all the information that they provide.

Cobuild was the first dictionary to stress the importance of the commoner words for a learner. Dictionaries traditionally try to pack as many headwords in as possible, without always indicating which are the ones that keep coming up in speech and writing. The common vocabulary words often have several senses and are found in phrase patterns which help to distinguish the senses, and all this is carefully set out in this dictionary. Common words have diamond symbols, with a simple code to tell you approximately how common they are.

This dictionary has the unique Cobuild feature of the "Extra Column", which contains a lot of information that does not fit easily into the defining text. This includes information about the grammatical patterns associated with each sense, and some semantic relations like synonyms and antonyms. The information is coded for brevity, and every effort is made to keep the coding clear and easily memorable. This edition makes the Extra Column even easier to use.

The authority of a very large corpus, and the experience of many years in using this corpus to get from it accurate and important information about today's English, makes me very confident that this will be a valuable resource. I know that many native speakers of English, and many whose English, although not native, is extremely fluent, use Cobuild as their dictionary of preference. So while it is primarily aimed at the needs of advanced learners, it does not matter how advanced they are!

Cobuild is always keen to know how the dictionaries and other books are appreciated, and we have set up an e-mail address (cobuild@ref.collins.co.uk) for your comments and criticisms, so that future editions can continue to meet your needs.

John Sinclair
*Founding Editor-in-Chief*
*Emeritus Professor of Modern English Language, University of Birmingham*
*President, The Tuscan Word Centre*

# Guide to the Dictionary Entries

COLOUR HEADWORDS

FULL SENTENCE DEFINITIONS

IMPORTANT GRAMMATICAL STRUCTURES

PRONUNCIATION

HYPHENATION POINTS

REGIONAL AND REGISTER LABELS

CORPUS EXAMPLES

INFLECTED FORMS

MEANING SPLITS

ALTERNATIVE SPELLINGS

NOTES ON ALTERNATIVE FORMS

**after|life** /ɑːftəʳlaɪf, æf-/ **(afterlives)** also **after-life.** The **afterlife** is a life that some people believe begins when you die, for example a life in heaven or as another person or animal. N-COUNT: usu sing

**after|market** /ɑːftəʳmɑːʳkɪt, æf-/ 1 The **aftermarket** is all the related products that are sold after an item, especially a car, has been bought. [BUSINESS] N-SING 2 The **aftermarket** in shares and bonds is the buying and selling of them after they have been issued. [BUSINESS] N-SING

**after|math** /ɑːftəʳmɑːθ, æftəʳmæθ/ The **aftermath of** an important event, especially a harmful one, is the situation that results from it. ❑ *In the aftermath of the coup, the troops opened fire on the demonstrators.* N-SING: with supp, oft *the* N *of* n

**after|noon** /ɑːftəʳnuːn, æf-/ **(afternoons)** ◆◆◇ The **afternoon** is the part of each day which begins at lunchtime and ends at about six o'clock. ❑ *He's arriving in the afternoon... He had stayed in his room all afternoon. ...an afternoon news conference.* N-VAR

**after|noon tea** **(afternoon teas)** **Afternoon tea** is a small meal you can have in the afternoon. It includes a cup of tea and food such as sandwiches and cakes. [BRIT] N-VAR

**after-sales ser|vice** **(after-sales services)** A company's **after-sales service** is all the help and information that it provides to customers after they have bought a particular product. [BUSINESS] ❑ *...a local retailer who offers a good after-sales service... They are also attempting to keep the car buyer as a long-term customer by offering after-sales service.* N-VAR

**after-school** **After-school** activities are those that are organized for children in the afternoon or evening after they have finished school. ❑ *...an after-school childcare scheme.* ADJ: ADJ n

**after|shave** /ɑːftəʳʃeɪv, æf-/ **(aftershaves)** also **after-shave. Aftershave** is a liquid with a pleasant smell that men sometimes put on their faces after shaving. N-MASS

**after|shock** /ɑːftəʳʃɒk, æf-/ **(aftershocks)** 1 **Aftershocks** are smaller earthquakes which occur after a large earthquake. N-COUNT 2 People sometimes refer to the effects of an important event, especially a bad one, as the **aftershock.** [mainly JOURNALISM] ❑ *They were already under stress, thanks to the aftershock of last year's drought.* N-COUNT: usu with supp

**after|taste** /ɑːftəʳteɪst, æf-/ also **after-taste.** An **aftertaste** is a taste that remains in your mouth after you have finished eating or drinking something. N-SING: usu with supp

**after|thought** /ɑːftəʳθɔːt, æf-/ **(afterthoughts)** If you do or say something as **an afterthought**, you do or say it after something else as an addition, perhaps without careful thought. ❑ *Almost as an afterthought he added that he missed her.* N-COUNT: usu sing, usu *a* N

**after|wards** /ɑːftəʳwəʳdz, æf-/ ◆◇◇

> ✓ The form **afterward** is also used, mainly in American English.

If you do something or if something happens **afterwards**, you do it or it happens after a particular event or time that has already been mentioned. ❑ *Shortly afterwards, police arrested four suspects... James was taken to hospital but died soon afterwards.* ADV: ADV with cl

# Guide to the Dictionary Entries

MENU TO HELP NAVIGATE LONGER ENTRIES

FREQUENCY INFORMATION

GRAMMATICAL INFORMATION AND PATTERNS

CLEAR SENSE SPLITS

INFORMATION ON PRAGMATICS

SYNONYMS AND ANTONYMS

DERIVED WORDS

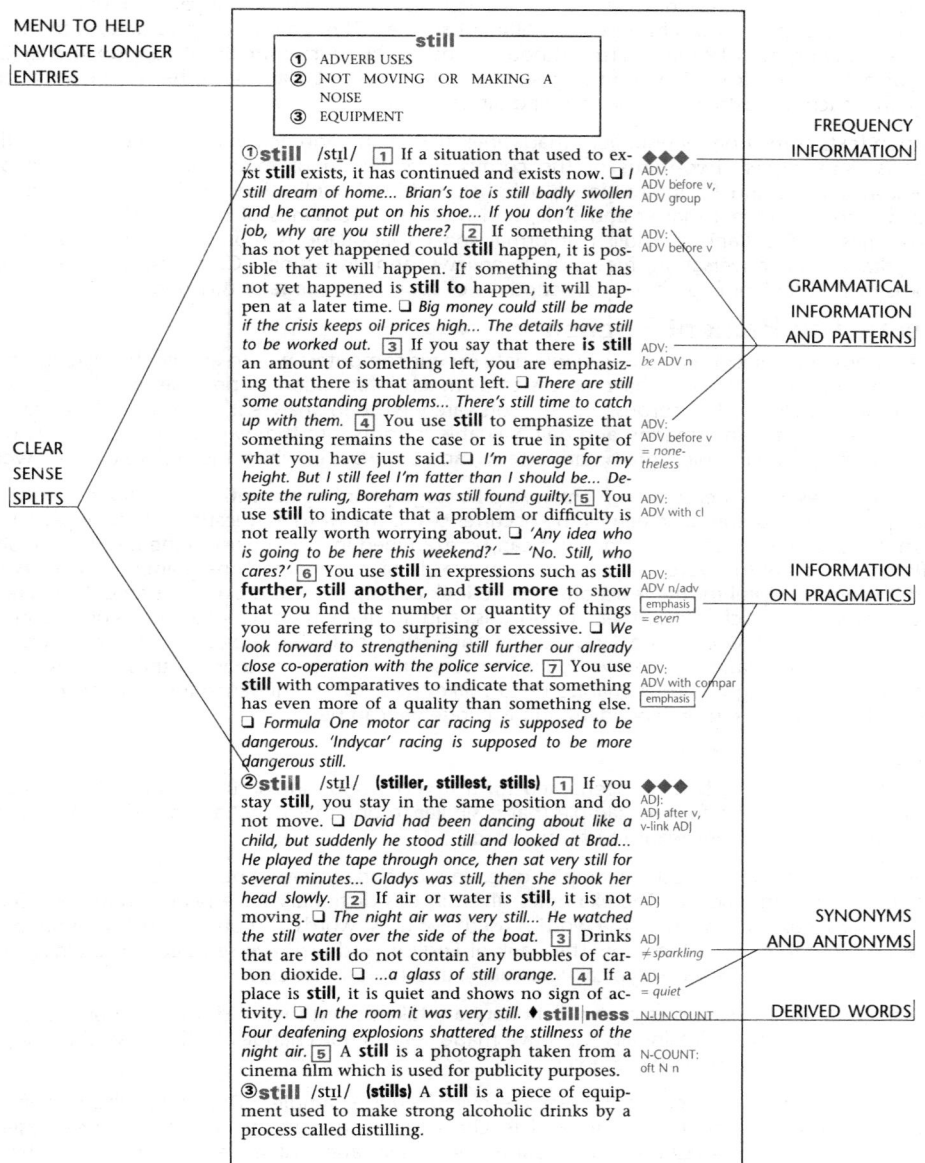

**still**

① ADVERB USES

② NOT MOVING OR MAKING A NOISE

③ EQUIPMENT

①**still** /stɪl/ ◆◆◆ [1] If a situation that used to exist **still** exists, it has continued and exists now. ❑ *I still dream of home... Brian's toe is still badly swollen and he cannot put on his shoe... If you don't like the job, why are you still there?* ADV: ADV before v, ADV group

[2] If something that has not yet happened could **still** happen, it is possible that it will happen. If something that has not yet happened is **still to** happen, it will happen at a later time. ❑ *Big money could still be made if the crisis keeps oil prices high... The details have still to be worked out.* ADV: ADV before v

[3] If you say that there **is still** an amount of something left, you are emphasizing that there is that amount left. ❑ *There are still some outstanding problems... There's still time to catch up with them.* ADV: *be* ADV n

[4] You use **still** to emphasize that something remains the case or is true in spite of what you have just said. ❑ *I'm average for my height. But I still feel I'm fatter than I should be... Despite the ruling, Boreham was still found guilty.* ADV: ADV before v = *nonetheless*

[5] You use **still** to indicate that a problem or difficulty is not really worth worrying about. ❑ *'Any idea who is going to be here this weekend?' — 'No. Still, who cares?'* ADV: ADV with cl

[6] You use **still** in expressions such as **still further**, **still another**, and **still more** to show that you find the number or quantity of things you are referring to surprising or excessive. ❑ *We look forward to strengthening still further our already close co-operation with the police service.* ADV: ADV n/adv [emphasis] = *even*

[7] You use **still** with comparatives to indicate that something has even more of a quality than something else. ❑ *Formula One motor car racing is supposed to be dangerous. 'Indycar' racing is supposed to be more dangerous still.* ADV: ADV with compar [emphasis]

②**still** /stɪl/ ◆◆◆ (**stiller, stillest, stills**) [1] If you stay **still**, you stay in the same position and do not move. ❑ *David had been dancing about like a child, but suddenly he stood still and looked at Brad... He played the tape through once, then sat very still for several minutes... Gladys was still, then she shook her head slowly.* ADJ: ADJ after v, v-link ADJ

[2] If air or water is **still**, it is not moving. ❑ *The night air was very still... He watched the still water over the side of the boat.* ADJ

[3] Drinks that are **still** do not contain any bubbles of carbon dioxide. ❑ *...a glass of still orange.* ADJ ≠ *sparkling*

[4] If a place is **still**, it is quiet and shows no sign of activity. ❑ *In the room it was very still.* ADJ = *quiet* ♦ **still|ness** N-UNCOUNT *Four deafening explosions shattered the stillness of the night air.*

[5] A **still** is a photograph taken from a cinema film which is used for publicity purposes. N-COUNT: oft N n

③**still** /stɪl/ (**stills**) A **still** is a piece of equipment used to make strong alcoholic drinks by a process called distilling.

# The Bank of English

The Bank of English is a collection, or corpus, of around *520 million* words of written and spoken English held on computer for the study of language use. It contains a wide range of different types of writing and speech from hundreds of different sources. The material is up to date, with most of the texts dating from 1990 onwards. Although most of the sources are British, approximately 25% of our data comes from American English sources, and about 5% from other native varieties of English – such as Australian, Canadian, and Singaporean.

Written texts come from newspapers, magazines, fiction and non-fiction books, brochures, leaflets, reports, and letters. Two-thirds of the corpus is made up of media language: newspapers, magazines, radio and TV. International, national, and local publications are included to capture a broad range of subject matter and style, and there are thousands of books and special interest magazines in The Bank of English. Informal spoken language is represented by recordings of everyday casual conversation, meetings, interviews, and discussions. Currently, about 20 million words of The Bank of English are transcriptions of spoken language of this kind.

## Using The Bank of English

The purpose of collecting all this valuable data on our computers was to enable the lexicographers – the dictionary writers – to have access to as much information as possible about each of the words being defined. The corpus, and the software we use to analyse it, helps the COBUILD team to sort through the information and gain valuable insights into the way words are actually used: their meanings, their typical grammar patterns, and the ways in which they relate to other words.

The corpus lies at the heart of each entry. As a lexicographer begins writing an entry, he or she can call up onto the computer screen all the occurrences of the word in question. These appear in the form of concordance lines, and the lines can be examined in a number of different ways to show different aspects of the word's behaviour. Many words have more than one grammatical word class and it is often helpful for the lexicographers to look at only one word class at a time. Software has been developed which allows them to do this, and so helps them to make decisions about the different senses of words, the language of the definitions, the choice of examples, and the grammatical information given. We could, of course, make statements about these things without a corpus, but having a corpus enables us to make them with confidence and accuracy. And the larger the corpus, the more confident and accurate we can be.

## Examples

Examples of how words have been used form a very important part of COBUILD dictionaries. Users are often looking for an example that is similar to one that they have heard or read, or that will confirm the way they want to use the word.

This means, of course, that the examples given in a dictionary should be characteristic of the ones that users will come across. The examples given in this dictionary have been carefully chosen to show typical contexts in which the word is used. For most words and phrases, we have hundreds, or even thousands, of instances in The Bank of English, and we have selected those which show typical grammatical patterns, typical vocabulary, and typical contexts.

The majority of the examples in the dictionary are taken word for word from one of the texts in The Bank of English. Occasionally, we have made very minor changes to them, so that they are more successful as dictionary examples.

Throughout the whole dictionary, there are over 75,000 examples. This makes the dictionary a valuable resource for both students and teachers, showing how the words have been used in books, newspapers, magazines, broadcasting, and conversation. All the examples in the dictionary have been chosen with care, and contain important information about the typical patterning associated with a word. In the case of verbs, we give examples for all the main grammatical structures in which they are used. The examples are given in the same order as the patterns shown in the Extra Column. These patterns are explained in the **Grammar** section on pages xv-xxii.

At COBUILD, great emphasis is placed on describing and explaining the English language accurately, through the evidence in our corpus. The Bank of English helps our dictionaries to be more effective and reliable. Our choices of representative examples, taken from the corpus, will give students and teachers information which, we believe, they will find very useful.

# Definitions

One of the features of the Collins COBUILD Advanced Learner's English Dictionary is that the definitions (or explanations) are written in full sentences, using vocabulary and grammatical structures that occur naturally with the word being explained. This enables us to give a lot of information about the way a word or meaning is used by speakers of the language. Whenever possible, words are explained using simpler and more common words. This gives us a natural defining vocabulary with most words in our definitions being amongst the 2,500 commonest words of English.

## Information about collocates and structures

In our definitions, we try to show the typical collocates of a word: that is, the other words that are used with the word we are defining. For example, the definition of meaning 1 of the adjective **savoury** says:

> **Savoury** food has a salty or spicy flavour rather than a sweet one.

This shows that you use the adjective **savoury** to describe food, rather than other things.

Meaning 1 of the verb **wag** says:

> When a dog **wags** its tail, it repeatedly waves its tail from side to side.

This shows that the subject of meaning 1 of **wag** refers to a dog, and the object of the verb is 'tail'.

## Information about grammar

The definitions also give information about the grammatical structures that a word is used with. For example, meaning 1 of the adjective **candid** says:

> When you are **candid** about something or with someone, you speak honestly.

This shows that you use **candid** with the preposition 'about' with something and 'with' with someone.

Other definitions show other kinds of structure. Meaning 1 of the verb **soften** says:

> If you **soften** something or if it **softens**, it becomes less hard, stiff, or firm.

This shows that the verb is used both transitively and intransitively. In the transitive use, you have a human subject and a non-human object. In the intransitive use, you have a non-human subject.

Finally, meaning 1 of **compel** says:

> If a situation, a rule, or a person **compels** you to do something, they force you to do it.

This shows you what kinds of subject and object to use with **compel**, and it also shows that you typically use the verb in a structure with a to-infinitive.

## Information about context and usage

In addition to information about collocation and grammar, definitions can also be used to convey your evaluation of something, for example to express your approval or disapproval. For example, here is a definition of **awful**:

> If you say that something is **awful**, you mean that it is extremely unpleasant, shocking, or bad.

In this definition, the expressions 'if you say that', and 'you mean that' indicate that these words are used subjectively, rather than objectively.

## Other kinds of definition

We sometimes explain grammatical words and other function words by paraphrasing the word in context. For example, meaning 3 of **through** says:

> To go **through** a town, area, or country means to travel across it or in it.

In many cases, it is impossible to paraphrase the word, and so we explain its function instead. For example, the definition of **unfortunately** says:

> You can use **unfortunately** to introduce or refer to a statement when you consider that it is sad or disappointing, or when you want to express regret.

Lastly, some definitions are expressed as if they are cross-references. For example:

> **hr** is a written abbreviation for **hour**.
>
> A **banker's draft** is the same as a **bank draft**.

If you need to know more about the words **hour** or **bank draft**, you look at those entries.

# Style and Usage

Some words or meanings are used mainly by particular groups of people, or in particular social contexts. In this dictionary, when it is relevant, the definitions also give information about the kind of people who are likely to use a word or expression, and the type of social situation in which it is used. This information is usually placed at the end of the definition, in small caps and within square brackets.

Although English is spoken as a first language in many parts of the world, two groups of speakers are especially important; those who speak British English, and those who speak American English. Most of the books, newspapers, radio and TV programmes, and teaching materials for international use are produced in Britain or the USA.

This dictionary focuses on both British and American English using evidence from The Bank of English. Where relevant, the British or American form is shown at its equivalent word or meaning; this information is given after the examples in a ticked box.

## Geographical labels

BRIT: used mainly by speakers and writers in Britain, and in other places where British English is used or taught. Where relevant the American equivalent is provided.

AM: used mainly by speakers and writers in the USA, and in other places where American English is used or taught. Where relevant the British equivalent is provided.

Other geographical labels are used in the text to refer to English as it is spoken in other parts of the world, eg AUSTRALIAN, IRISH, NORTHERN ENGLISH, SCOTTISH.

## Style labels

BUSINESS: used mainly when talking about the field of business, e.g. **annuity**

COMPUTING: used mainly when talking about the field of computing, e.g. **chat room**

DIALECT: used in some dialects of English, e.g. **ain't**

FORMAL: used mainly in official situations, or by political and business organizations, or when speaking or writing to people in authority, e.g. **gratuity**

HUMOROUS: used mainly to indicate that a word or expression is used in a humorous way, e.g. **gents**

INFORMAL: used mainly in informal situations, conversations, and personal letters, e.g. **pep talk**

JOURNALISM: used mainly in journalism, e.g. **glass ceiling**

LEGAL: used mainly in legal documents, in law courts, and by the police in official situations, e.g. **manslaughter**

LITERARY: used mainly in novels, poetry, and other forms of literature, e.g. **plaintive**

MEDICAL: used mainly in medical texts, and by doctors in official situations, e.g. **psychosis**

MILITARY: used mainly when talking or writing about military terms, e.g. **armour**

OFFENSIVE: likely to offend people, or to insult them; words labelled OFFENSIVE should therefore usually be avoided, e.g. **cripple**

OLD-FASHIONED: generally considered to be old-fashioned, and no longer in common use, e.g. **dashing**

RUDE: used mainly to describe words which could be considered taboo by some people; words labelled RUDE should therefore usually be avoided, e.g. **bloody**

SPOKEN: used mainly in speech rather than in writing, e.g. **pardon**

TECHNICAL: used mainly when talking or writing about objects, events, or processes in a specialist subject, such as business, science, or music, e.g. **biotechnology**

TRADEMARK: used to show a designated trademark, e.g. **hoover**

VERY OFFENSIVE: highly likely to offend people, or to insult them; words labelled ⚠ VERY OFFENSIVE should be avoided, e.g. **wog**

VERY RUDE: used mainly to describe words which most people consider taboo; words labelled ⚠ VERY RUDE should be avoided, e.g. **fuck**

WRITTEN: used mainly in writing rather than in speech, e.g. **avail**

# Pragmatics

People use language to achieve different goals – they invite, give compliments, give warnings, show their emotions, tell lies, and make commitments. The ability to use language effectively to fulfil intentions and goals is known as pragmatic competence, and the study of this ability is called pragmatics. The analysis of language which has been used to prepare this dictionary is based on the idea that speakers and writers plan and fulfil goals as they use language. This in turn entails choices. Speakers choose their goals and they choose appropriate language for their goals.

Different languages use different pragmatic strategies. In order to use a language effectively, and be successful in achieving your goals, you need to know what the pragmatic conventions are for that particular language. It is therefore important that learners of English are given as much information as possible about the ways in which English speakers use their language to communicate.

Because of the large amounts of data in The Bank of English, COBUILD is uniquely placed to help learners with pragmatics. We have analyzed the data and have found, for example, the ways in which English speakers express approval and disapproval, show their emotions, or emphasize what they are saying.

In the dictionary, we draw attention to certain pragmatic aspects of words and phrases of English, paying special attention to those that, for cultural and linguistic reasons, we feel may be confusing to learners. We do this by having a label in the Extra Column to show the type of pragmatic information being given. The following labels are used in the dictionary.

## approval

You can choose words and expressions to show that you approve of the person or thing you are talking about, e.g. **angelic**.

## disapproval

You can choose words and expressions to show that you disapprove of the person or thing you are talking about, e.g. **brat**.

## emphasis

Many words and expressions are used to emphasize the point you are making, e.g. **never-ending**.

## feelings

Another function of pragmatics is to express your feelings about something, or towards someone, e.g. **unfortunately**.

## formulae

There are many words and expressions in English which are fairly set, and are used in particular situations such as greeting and thanking people, or acknowledging something, e.g. **hi**, **congratulations**.

## politeness

Certain words and expressions in English are used to express politeness, sometimes even to the point of being euphemistic, e.g. **elderly**.

## vagueness

Speakers and writers use many words and expressions in English to show how certain they are about the truth or validity of their statements. We have called this type of pragmatic information 'vagueness', though it is sometimes also called 'hedging' or 'modality', e.g. **presumably**.

We hope that you will enjoy learning about pragmatics in the English language. Pragmatics, in any language, is central to communication. When you can understand the context and subtle meanings of a word, you can give and receive accurate messages. This should enable you to achieve your pragmatic goals whether you are intending to criticize, to praise, to persuade, and so on. Good communication is vital. We hope that by giving you a great deal of pragmatic information in this dictionary, we will encourage you to improve your communication skills.

# List of Grammatical Notations

## Word classes

| | |
|---|---|
| **ADJ** | adjective |
| **ADV** | adverb |
| **AUX** | auxiliary verb |
| **COLOUR** | colour word |
| **COMB** | combining form |
| **CONJ** | conjunction |
| **CONVENTION** | convention |
| **DET** | determiner |
| **EXCLAM** | exclamation |
| **FRACTION** | fraction |
| **LINK** | see V-LINK |
| **MODAL** | modal verb |
| **N-COUNT** | count noun |
| **N-COUNT-COLL** | collective count noun |
| **N-FAMILY** | family noun |
| **N-IN-NAMES** | noun in names |
| **N-MASS** | mass noun |
| **N-PLURAL** | plural noun |
| **N-PROPER** | proper noun |
| **N-PROPER-COLL** | collective proper noun |
| **N-PROPER-PLURAL** | plural proper noun |
| **N-SING** | singular noun |
| **N-SING-COLL** | collective singular noun |
| **N-TITLE** | title noun |
| **N-UNCOUNT** | uncount noun |
| **N-UNCOUNT-COLL** | collective uncount noun |
| **N-VAR** | variable noun |
| **N-VAR-COLL** | collective variable noun |
| **N-VOC** | vocative noun |
| **NEG** | negative |
| **NUM** | number |
| **ORD** | ordinal |
| **PASSIVE** | see V-PASSIVE |
| **PHRASAL VERB** | phrasal verb |
| **PHRASE** | phrase |
| **PREDET** | predeterminer |
| **PREFIX** | prefix |
| **PREP** | preposition |
| **PREP-PHRASE** | phrasal preposition |
| **PRON** | pronoun |
| **QUANT** | quantifier |
| **QUANT-PLURAL** | plural quantifier |
| **QUEST** | question word |
| **RECIP** | see V-RECIP |
| **SOUND** | sound word |
| **SUFFIX** | suffix |
| **VERB** | verb |
| **V-LINK** | link verb |
| **V-PASSIVE** | passive verb |
| **V-RECIP** | reciprocal verb |
| **V-RECIP-PASSIVE** | passive reciprocal verb |

## Words and abbreviations used in patterns

| | |
|---|---|
| **adj** | adjective group |
| **adj-compar** | comparative form |
| **adj-superl** | superlative form |
| **adv** | adverb group |
| **amount** | word or phrase indicating an amount of something |
| **as if** | clause beginning with *as if* or *as though* |
| **brd-neg** | broad negative |
| **cl** | clause |
| **colour** | colour word |
| **compar** | comparative form |
| **cont** | continuous |
| **def-n** | definite noun group |
| **def-n-uncount** | definite noun group with an uncount noun |
| **def-pl-n** | definite noun group with a noun in the plural |
| **det** | determiner |
| **det-poss** | possessive determiner |
| **-ed** | past participle of a verb |
| **group** | noun group, adjective, adverb, or prepositional phrase |
| **imper** | imperative |
| **inf** | infinitive form of a verb |
| **-ing** | present participle of a verb |
| ***it*** | 'introductory' or 'dummy' *it* |
| **like** | clause beginning with *like* |
| **n** | noun or noun group |
| **n (not pron)** | noun group, but not a personal pronoun |
| **names** | names of places or institutions |
| **neg** | negative word |
| **non-recip** | verb pattern with no reciprocal meaning |
| **n-proper** | proper noun |
| **num** | number |
| **n-uncount** | uncount noun or noun group with an uncount noun |
| **oft** | often |
| **ord** | ordinal |
| **P** | particle, part of a phrasal verb |
| **passive** | passive voice |
| **pl** | plural |
| **pl-n** | noun in the plural, plural noun group, co-ordinated noun group |
| **pl-num** | plural number |
| **poss** | possessive |
| **prep** | prepositional phrase or preposition |
| **pron** | pronoun |
| **pron-indef** | indefinite pronoun |
| **pron-recip** | reciprocal pronoun |
| **pron-refl** | reflexive pronoun |
| **pron-rel** | relative pronoun |
| **quest** | question word |
| **quote** | direct speech |
| **sing** | singular |
| **sing-n** | noun in the singular |
| **supp** | supplementary information accompanying a noun |
| **that** | 'that'-clause |
| **to-inf** | the to-infinitive form of a verb |
| **usu** | usually |
| **v** | verb or verb group |
| **v-cont** | continuous verb |
| **V-ed** | past participle of the verb |
| **V-ing** | present participle of the verb |
| **v-link** | link verb |
| ***way*** | *way* preceded by a possessive determiner |
| **wh** | wh-word, clause beginning with a wh-word |

# Explanation of Grammatical Notations

## Introduction

For each use of each word in this dictionary, there is grammar information in the Extra Column. For a very few words, such as abbreviations, contractions and some words of foreign origin, no grammar is given, because the words do not belong to any word class, or are used so freely that every example could be given a different word class, e.g. *AD, ditto, mpg, must've.*

The grammar information that is given is of three types:
1. the word class of the word: e.g. **VERB, N-COUNT, ADJ, QUANT**
2. restrictions or extensions to its behaviour, compared to other words of that word class: e.g. **usu passive, usu sing, also no det**
3. the patterns that the word most frequently occurs in: e.g. **V n, N *of* n, ADJ that, ADV with v**

For all word classes except verbs, the patterns are given immediately after the word class and any restrictions or extensions. For verbs, the patterns are given next to the examples and in the same order as the examples, so that they are easier to see and understand.

The word class of the word being explained is in CAPITAL LETTERS. The order of items in a pattern is the order in which they normally occur in a sentence. Words in *italics* are words (not word classes) that occur in the pattern. Alternatives are separated by a slash (/).

## Word classes

**ADJ** An **adjective** can be in the comparative or the superlative form. e.g. *He has been absent from his desk for two weeks. ...the most accurate description of the killer to date... The eldest child was a daughter called Fiona.*

### Adjective patterns

**ADJ n** The adjective is always used before a noun, e.g. *...a governmental agency.*

**usu ADJ n** The adjective is usually used before a noun. It is sometimes used after a link verb.

**v-link ADJ** The adjective is used after a link verb such as *be* or *feel*, e.g. *She was feeling unwell.* Adjectives with this label are sometimes used in other positions such as after the object of a verb such as *make* or *keep*, but never before a noun.

**usu v-link ADJ** The adjective is usually used after a link verb. It is sometimes used before a noun.

**ADJ after v** The adjective is used after a verb that is not a link verb, e.g. *Alan came running barefoot through the house.*

**n ADJ** The adjective comes immediately after a noun, e.g. *...a trade union leader not a politician proper.*

**det ADJ** The adjective comes immediately after a determiner and before any other adjectives, and sometimes comes before numbers, e.g. *...a certain limited geographic area.*

If the dictionary does not show that an adjective is used only or mainly in the pattern **ADJ n** and **v-link ADJ**, this means that the adjective is used freely in both patterns.

These main adjective patterns are sometimes combined with other patterns, see pages xix-xxii.

**ADV** An **adverb** can be in the comparative or the superlative form. e.g. *Much of our behaviour is biologically determined... She blinked hard... Inflation is below 5% and set to fall further. ...those areas furthest from the coast.*

### Adverb patterns

For some adverbs in this dictionary, you will see two sets of patterns, the second set introduced by *usu* or *oft*, e.g. everywhere 1: **n ADV, ADV after V, *be* ADV, oft *from* ADV, ADV cl/group**. This means that any of the patterns in the second set can occur in combination with any of the patterns in the first set.

**AUX** An **auxiliary verb** is used with another verb to add particular meanings to that verb, for example, to form the continuous aspect or the passive voice, or to form negatives and interrogatives. The verbs *be, do, get* and *have* have some senses in which they are auxiliary verbs.

**COLOUR** A **colour word** refers to a colour. It is like an adjective, e.g. *the blue sky... The sky was blue,* and also like a noun, e.g. *She was dressed in red. ...several shades of yellow.*

**COMB** A **combining form** is a word which is joined with another word, usually with a hyphen, to form compounds, e.g. *grey-haired, lemon-flavoured, heat-resistant.* The word class of the compound is also given, e.g. **COMB in ADJ, COMB in N-UNCOUNT.**

**CONJ** A **conjunction** usually links elements of the same grammatical type, such as two clauses, two groups, or two words, e.g. *She and Simon had already gone... It is completely waterproof, yet light and comfortable... Racing was halted for an hour while the track was repaired.*

**CONVENTION** A **convention** is a word or a fixed phrase which is used in conversation, for example when greeting someone, apologizing, or replying, e.g. *hello, sorry, no comment.*

**DET** A **determiner** is a word that is used at the beginning of a noun group, e.g. *a tray, more time, some books, this amount.* It can also be used to say who or what something belongs or relates to e.g. *his face, my flat*, or to begin a question e.g. *Whose care are they in?*

**EXCLAM** An **exclamation** is a word or phrase which is spoken suddenly, loudly, or emphatically in order to express a strong emotion such as shock or anger. Exclamations are often followed by exclamation marks, e.g. *good heavens!, Ouch!*

**FRACTION** A **fraction** is used in numbers, e.g. *three and a half, two and two thirds;* before *of* and a noun group, e.g. *half of the apple, a third of the biscuits, three eighths of the pie;* after *in* or *into,* e.g. *in half, into thirds.* A fraction is also used like a count noun, e.g. *two halves, the first quarter of the year.*

**LINK** see **V-LINK**

**MODAL** A **modal** is used before the infinitive form of a verb, e.g. *You may go.* In questions, it comes before the subject, e.g. *Must you speak?* In negatives, it comes before the negative word, e.g. *They would not like this.* It does not inflect, for example, it does not take an *-s* in the third person singular, e.g. *She can swim.*

**N-COUNT** A **count noun** has a plural form, usually made by adding *-s*. When it is singular, it must have a determiner in front of it, such as *the, her,* or *such,* e.g. *My cat is getting fatter... She's a good friend.*

**N-COUNT-COLL** A **collective count noun** is a count noun which refers to a group of people or things. It behaves like a count noun, but when it is in the singular form it can be used with either a singular or plural verb, e.g. *Their audience are much younger than the average... The British audience has a huge appetite for serials... Audiences are becoming more selective.*

**N-FAMILY** A **family noun** refers to a member of a family, e.g. *father, mummy,* and *granny.* Family nouns are count nouns which are typically used in the singular, and usually follow a possessive determiner. They are also vocative nouns. They are also proper nouns, used with no determiner, e.g. *My mummy likes marzipan... Tell them I didn't do it, Mummy... Mummy's always telling me I'm too old for dolls.*

**N-IN-NAMES** The **noun** occurs **in names** of people, things, or institutions.

**N-MASS** A **mass noun** typically combines the behaviour of both count and uncount nouns in the same sense. It is used like an uncount noun to refer to a substance. It is used like a count noun to refer to a brand or type, e.g. *Rinse in cold water to remove any remaining detergent... Wash it in hot water with a good detergent... We used several different detergents in our stain-removal tests.* Other examples of mass nouns are: *bleach, butter, shampoo.*

**N-PLURAL** A **plural noun** is always plural, and is used with plural verbs. If a pronoun is used to stand for the noun, it is a plural pronoun such as *they* or *them,* e.g. *These clothes are ready to wear... He expressed his condolences to the families of people who died in the incident.* Plural nouns which end in *-s* usually lose the *-s* when they come in front of another noun, e.g. *trousers, trouser pocket.* If they refer to a single object which has two main parts, such as *jeans* and *glasses,* the expression *a pair of* is sometimes used, e.g. *a pair of jeans* or *a pair of glasses.* This is shown as **N-PLURAL: also *a pair of* N.**

**N-PROPER** A **proper noun** refers to one person, place, thing, or institution, and begins with a capital letter. Many proper nouns are used without a determiner, e.g. *...higher education in America ... Father Christmas;* some must be used with *the,* and this is indicated: **N PROPER, *the* N**, e.g. *the Ice Age.*

**N-PROPER-COLL** A **collective proper noun** is a proper noun which refers to a group of people or things. It can be used with either a singular or a plural verb, e.g. *The Boy Scouts is sending a message to all of these kids... The Boy Scouts have a different view.*

**N-PROPER-PLURAL** A **plural proper noun** is a proper noun which is always used in the plural with a plural verb, e.g. *... a salesman from the Home Counties.*

**N-SING** A **singular noun** is always singular, and needs a determiner, e.g. *...damage to the environment... He looks the epitome of personal and professional contentment.* When only *a* or *the* is used, this is indicated: **N-SING: a N** or **N-SING: *the* N**, e.g. *Production is more or less at a standstill. ...a come-down, the vicinity.*

**N-SING-COLL** A **collective singular noun** is a singular noun which refers to a group of people or things. It behaves like a singular noun, but can be used with either a singular or plural verb, e.g. *Her shop clientele are mostly women with babies... The clientele is a mixed bunch.*

**N-TITLE** A **title noun** is used to refer to someone who has a particular role or position. Titles come before the name of the person and begin with a capital letter, e.g. *Sir Isaac Newton, Lady Macbeth.*

**N-UNCOUNT** An **uncount noun** refers to things that are not normally counted or considered to be individual items. Uncount nouns do not have a plural form, and are used with a singular verb. They do not need determiners, e.g. *...an area of outstanding natural beauty.*

**N-UNCOUNT-COLL** A **collective uncount noun** is an uncount noun which refers to a group of people or things. It behaves like an uncount noun, but can be used with either a singular or plural verb, e.g. *...in a country where livestock outnumber people by ten to one... Any kind of livestock is totally dependent on its owner for all its needs.*

**N-VAR** A **variable noun** typically combines the behaviour of both count and uncount nouns in the same sense (see **N-COUNT, N-UNCOUNT**). The singular form occurs freely both with and without determiners. Variable nouns also have a plural form, usually made by adding *-s*. Some variable nouns when used like uncount nouns refer to abstract things like *hardship* and *injustice,* and when used like count nouns refer to individual examples or instances of that thing, e.g. *He is not afraid to protest against injustice... It is never too late to correct an injustice. ...the injustices of world poverty.* Others refer to objects which can be mentioned either individually or generally, like *potato* and *salad:* you can talk about *a potato, potatoes,* or *potato.*

**N-VAR-COLL** A **collective variable noun** is a variable noun which refers to a group of people or things. It behaves like a variable noun, but when it is singular it can be used with either a singular or a plural verb, e.g. *...the recent fall in party membership.*

**N-VOC** A **vocative noun** is used when speaking directly to someone or writing to them. Vocative nouns do not need a determiner, but some may be used with a possessive determiner, e.g. *I want you to enjoy yourself darling... How are you, my darling?*

**NEG** A **negative** word indicates the absence or opposite of something, or is used to say that something is not the case, e.g. *I was not in Britain at the time.*

**NUM** A **number** is a word such as *three* and *hundred.* Numbers such as *one, two, three* are used like determiners, e.g. *three bears;* like adjectives, e.g. *the four horsemen;* like pronouns, e.g. *She has three cases and I have two;* and like quantifiers, e.g. *Six of the boys stayed behind.* Numbers such as *hundred, thousand, million* always follow a determiner or another number, e.g. *two hundred bears, the thousand horsemen, She has a thousand dollars and I have a million, A hundred of the boys stayed behind.*

**ORD** An **ordinal** is a type of number. Ordinals are used like adjectives, e.g. *He was the third victim;* like pronouns, e.g. *She took the first place and I took the second... the second of the two teams;* like adverbs, e.g. *The other team came first;* and like determiners, e.g. *Fourth place goes to Timmy.*

**PASSIVE** see **V-PASSIVE**

**PHRASAL VERB** A **phrasal verb** consists of a verb and one or more particles e.g. *look after, look back, look down on.* Some phrasal verbs are reciprocal, link or passive verbs. See **V-RECIP, V-LINK** and **V-PASSIVE.**

**PHRASE** **Phrases** are groups of words which are used together with little variation and which have a meaning of their own, e.g. *They are reluctant to upset the applecart.*

**PREDET** A **predeterminer** is used in a noun group before *a, the,* or another determiner, e.g. *What a busy day! ...both the parents. ...all his skill.*

**PREFIX** A **prefix** is a letter or group of letters, such as *un-* or *multi-*, which is added to the beginning of a word in order to form another word. For example, the prefix *un-* is added to *happy* to form *unhappy.*

**PREP** A **preposition** begins a prepositional phrase and is followed by a noun group or a present participle. Patterns for prepositions are shown in the dictionary only if they are restricted in some way. For example, if a preposition occurs only before a present participle, it is shown as **PREP -ing**.

**PREP-PHRASE** A **phrasal preposition** is a phrase which behaves like a preposition, e.g. *Prices vary according to the quantity ordered.*

**PRON** **Pronouns** are used like noun groups, to refer to someone or something that has already been mentioned or whose identity is known, e.g. *They produced their own shampoos and hair-care products, all based on herbal recipes... She began to consult doctors, and each had a different diagnosis.*

**QUANT** A **quantifier** comes before *of* and a noun group, e.g. *most of the house.* If there are any restrictions on the type of noun group, this is indicated: **QUANT *of* def-n** means that the quantifier occurs before *of* and a definite noun group, e.g. *Most of the houses in the capital have piped water.*

**QUANT-PLURAL** **Plural quantifiers** are words like *billions* and *millions* which are followed by *of* and a noun group, e.g. *...for billions of years.*

**QUEST** A **question word** is a wh-word that is used to begin a question, e.g. *Why do you say that?*

**RECIP** see **V-RECIP**

**SOUND** **Sound words** are used before or after verbs such as *go* and *say*, e.g. *Bang went the door... It went bang.*

**SUFFIX** A **suffix** is a letter or group of letters such as *-ly* or *-ness*, which is added to the end of a word in order to form a new word, usually of a different word class, e.g. *quick, quickly.*

**V-LINK** A **link verb** connects a subject and a complement. Link verbs most commonly occur in the patterns **V adj** and **V n**. Most link verbs do not occur in the passive voice, e.g. *be, become, taste, feel.*

Some phrasal verbs are link verbs, e.g. *I was sure things were going to turn out fine* (**V adj**); *Sometimes things don't turn out the way we think they are going to* (**V n**).

**V-PASSIVE** A **passive verb** occurs in the passive voice only, e.g. *His parents are rumoured to be on the verge of splitting up.* Some phrasal verbs are passive verbs, e.g. *The civilians were just caught up in the conflict.*

**V-RECIP** **Reciprocal verbs** describe processes in which two or more people, groups, or things interact mutually: they do the same thing to each other, or participate jointly in the same action or event. Reciprocal verbs are used in the pattern **pl-n V**, e.g. *Fred and Sally met,* where the subject is both participants. The participants can also be referred to separately in other patterns, e.g. **V n** *Fred met Sally,* and **V *with* n** *Fred argued with Sally.* These patterns are reciprocal because they also mean that *Sally met Fred* and *Sally argued with Fred.* Note that many reciprocal verbs can also be used in a way that is not reciprocal. For example, *Fred and Sally kissed* is reciprocal, but *Fred kissed Sally* is not reciprocal (because it does not mean that Sally also kissed Fred). Non-reciprocal uses of reciprocal verbs are shown as **non-recip**.

Some phrasal verbs are reciprocal verbs, e.g. *He felt appalled by the idea of marriage so we broke up.* (**pl-n V P**); *My girlfriend broke up with me.* (**V P *with* n**).

**V-RECIP-PASSIVE** A **passive reciprocal verb** behaves like both a passive verb and a reciprocal verb, e.g. *She was reconciled with her mother.*

## Words and abbreviations used in patterns

In a pattern, the element in capital letters represents the word in the entry. All the other elements are in small letters. Items in *italics* show the actual word that is used, such as ***of***. Items in roman print show the word class or type of clause that is used. For example:

**V n** means that the word being explained is a verb (**V**), and it is followed in the sentence by a noun or noun group (**n**).
**N *of* n** means that the word being explained is a noun (**N**), and it is followed in the sentence by the word *of* and another noun or noun group (**n**).
**ADV adj/adv** means that the word being explained is an adverb (**ADV**), and it is followed in the sentence by an adjective (**adj**) or (/) another adverb (**adv**).

When the word in the entry occurs in a pattern, the element in capital letters is **V** for a verb, **N** for any kind of noun, **ADJ** for any kind of adjective, and so on. **PHR** is used for a phrase, and **V** and **N** are used to represent verbs and nouns in phrases. For phrasal verbs, **V** and **P** are used to represent the verb and the particle(s) respectively.

## Words used to structure information in patterns

**after:** **after v** means after a verb. The word is used either immediately after the verb, or after the verb and another word or phrase, or in a marked position at the beginning of the clause. For example, the adverb **nowhere** is used:

immediately after a verb: *He had nowhere to call home;*
at the beginning of a clause: *Nowhere is language a more serious issue than in Hawaii.*

The adverb **orally** is used:

immediately after a verb: ... *antibiotic tablets taken orally;*
after a verb and its object: ... *their ability to present ideas orally and in writing.*

**also:** used with some nouns to show that the word is used in a way that is not typical of that type of noun. For example, **N-UNCOUNT: also N in pl** means that unlike most uncount nouns, this noun also has a plural form and use. **Also** is used with some adverbs and adjectives to show a pattern that is less common than the other patterns mentioned. For example, **ADV: usu ADV with V, also ADV adj** means that the adverb is usually used with a verb but is also used before an adjective. **Also** is used before less common verb patterns which do not have examples.

**before:** **before v** means before a verb. The word is used before the main element in a verb group. For example, the adverb **already** is used:

before the whole verb group: *I already told you not to come over;*
immediately before the main element in the group: *They had already voted for him at the first ballot.*

**inflects:** used to show that an element in a phrase inflects. **V inflects** means that the form of the verb in the phrase is not fixed but changes according to the subject of the verb or its tense. **N inflects** means that the noun in the phrase is used in the singular and the plural forms. If a phrase has two verbs, but only one inflects, or two nouns, but only one inflects, that verb or noun is given in italics, e.g. for the phrase 'a change of heart' the Extra Column says: ***change* inflects**.

**no:** used to indicate that a verb is not used in a particular way, for example **no passive**, or that a singular noun is also used without a determiner: **N-SING: also no det**.

**oft:** used to indicate that a word or phrase often occurs in a particular pattern or behaves in a particular way.

**only:** used to indicate that a verb is always used in a particular way, for example **only cont**.

**usu:** used to indicate that a word or phrase usually occurs in a particular pattern or behaves in a particular way.

**with:** **with** is used when the position of a word or phrase is not fixed. This means that the word or phrase sometimes comes before the named word class and sometimes comes after it. For example, **quickly** has the pattern **ADV with v**. It occurs:

after the verb: *Cussane worked quickly and methodically;*
before the verb: *It quickly became the most popular men's fragrance in the world.*

**bring** has the pattern **V n with adv.** The adverb occurs:

after the noun group: *Her mother brought her hands up to her face;*
before the noun group: *Reaching into her pocket, she brought out a cigarette.*

In addition, **with cl** and **with quote** are used when the word sometimes occurs at the beginning of the clause or quote, sometimes at the end, and sometimes in the middle. For example, **please** has the pattern **V with cl.** It occurs:

after the clause: *Can you help us please?;*
before the clause: *Please come in;*
in the middle of the clause: *Would you please open the door?*

## Elements used in patterns

**adj:** stands for **adjective group.** This may be one word, such as 'happy', or a group of words, such as 'very happy'or 'as happy as I have ever been'.

e.g. **adj N: read** 8 ... *Ben Okri's latest novel is a good read.*

**adj-compar:** stands for **comparative adjective.** This is used to indicate an adjective group with the comparative form of the adjective.

e.g. **V adj-compar:** ① **close** 10 ... *The US dollar closed higher in Tokyo today.*

**adj-superl:** stands for **superlative adjective**. It is used to indicate an adjective group with the superlative form of the adjective.

e.g. **PREP poss adj-superl: at** 15 ... *He was at his happiest whilst playing cricket.*

**adv:** stands for **adverb group.** This may be one word, such as 'slowly', or a group of words, such as 'extremely slowly' or 'more slowly than ever'.

e.g. **adv ADV: else** 1 ... *I never wanted to live anywhere else.*

**amount:** means **word or phrase indicating an amount of something,** such as 'a lot', 'nothing', 'three percent', 'four hundred pounds', 'more', or 'much'.

e.g. **V amount *for* n: budget** 4 ... *The company has budgeted $10 million for advertising.*

**as if:** stands for **clause beginning with 'as if' or 'as though'**.

e.g. **V as if:** ② **look** 1 ... *He looked as if he was going to smile.*

***be*:** stands for any form of the verb 'be'. It is used in passive verb patterns.

e.g. ***be* V-ed to-inf: think** 2 ... *The storm is thought to be responsible for as many as four deaths.*

**brd-neg:** stands for **broad negative,** that is, a clause which is negative in meaning. It may contain a negative element such as 'no-one', 'never', or 'hardly', or may show that it is negative in some other way.

e.g. **VERB: with brd-neg: budge** 1 ... *They will not budge on this.*

**cl:** stands for **clause.**

e.g. **cl ADV: anyway** 4 ... *What do you want from me, anyway?*

**colour:** means **colour word**, such as 'red', 'green', or 'blue'.

e.g. **V colour: blush** ... *I blushed scarlet at my stupidity.*

**compar:** stands for **comparative form of an adjective or adverb.**

e.g. **ADV compar:** ① **even** 2 ... *Stan was speaking even more slowly than usual.*

**cont:** stands for **continuous**. It is used when indicating that a verb is always, usually, or never used in the continuous.

e.g. **VERB: only cont: die** 6 ... *I'm dying for a breath of fresh air.*
**VERB: no cont: adore** 2 ... *My mother adores bananas.*

**def-n:** stands for **definite noun group.** A definite noun group is a noun group that refers to a specific person or thing, or a specific group of people or things, that is known and identified.

e.g. **QUANT *of* def-n: whole** 1 ... *I was cold throughout the whole of my body.*

**def-n-uncount:** stands for **definite noun group with an uncount noun.** An uncount noun is a noun which has no plural form and which is sometimes used without a determiner.

e.g. **QUANT *of* def-n-uncount: much** 5 ... *She does much of her work abroad.*

**def-pl-n:** stands for **definite noun group with a noun in the plural**.

e.g. **QUANT *of* def-pl-n: a few** at **few** 1 ... *a little tea-party I'm giving for a few of the teachers.*

**det:** stands for **determiner.** A determiner is a word that comes at the beginning of a noun group, such as 'the', 'her', or 'those'.

e.g. **det ADJ: final** 1 ... *On the last Saturday in September, I received a final letter from Clive.*

**det-poss:** stands for **possessive determiner.** A possessive determiner is a determiner which is only used in the possessive form.

e.g. **det-poss N: grace** 8 ... *Your Grace, I have a great favour to ask of you.*

**-ed:** stands for **past participle of a verb,** such as 'decided', 'gone', or 'taken'.

e.g. **V n -ed: hear** 2 ... *I'd love to hear it played by a professional orchestra.*
**AUX -ed:** ① **be** 2 ... *Her husband was killed in a car crash.*

***get*:** stands for any form of the verb 'get'. It is used in passive verb patterns.

e.g. ***get* V-ed: change** 6 ... *I've got to get changed first.*

**group:** stands for **noun group, adjective, adverb, or prepositional phrase**.

e.g. **ADV group: altogether** 3 ... *We were not altogether sure that the comet would miss the Earth.*

**imper:** stands for **imperative.** It is used when indicating that a verb is always or usually used in the imperative.

e.g. **only imper** and **inf: beware** ... *Beware of being too impatient with others.*

**inf:** stands for **infinitive form of a verb,** such as 'decide', 'go', or 'sit'.

e.g. **V n inf:** ② **make** 1 ... *Grit from the highway made him cough.*

**-ing:** stands for **present participle of a verb,** such as 'deciding', 'going', or 'taking'.

e.g. **V n -ing: catch** 7 ... *He caught a youth breaking into a car.*
**V n *into* -ing: nudge** 3 ... *Bit by bit Bob had nudged Fritz into selling his controlling interest.*

***it*:** means an 'introductory' or 'dummy' *it. It* does not refer to anything in a previous sentence or in the world; it may refer to what is coming later in the clause or it may refer to things in general.

e.g. **oft *it* v-link ADJ to-inf: time-consuming** ... *It's just very time consuming to get such a large quantity of data.*

**like:** means **clause beginning with 'like'.**

e.g. **V like: feel** 1 ... *I felt like I was being kicked in the teeth every day.*

**n:** stands for **noun** or **noun group**. If the **n** element occurs in a pattern with something that is part of a noun group, such as an adjective or another noun, it represents a noun. If the **n** element occurs in a pattern with something that is not part of a noun group, such as a verb or preposition, it represents a noun group. The noun group can be of any kind, including a pronoun.

e.g. **V *for* n: advertise** 2 ... *We advertised for staff in a local newspaper.*

**n (not pron):** stands for a **noun group** of some kind, but **not a personal pronoun.** It is used in phrasal verb patterns where the particle is an adverb.

e.g. **V P n (not pron): burn down** ... *Anarchists burnt down a restaurant.*

**names:** means **names of places or institutions.**

e.g. **N-COUNT: oft in names, also** *by* **N: road** 1 ... *We just go straight up the Bristol Road.*

**neg:** stands for **negative word,** such as 'not', or 'never'.

e.g. **VERB: with neg: dream** 9 ... *I wouldn't dream of making fun of you.*

**non-recip:** stands for **verb pattern with no reciprocal meaning.** It is used when the verb is a reciprocal verb (see the explanation for **V-RECIP** in **Word classes** on page xxxii).

e.g. **V n (non-recip): hug** 1 ... *She had hugged him exuberantly.*

**n-proper:** stands for **proper noun.** A proper noun is the name of a particular person or thing.

e.g. *the* **ADJ n-proper: honourable** 2 ... *the Honourable Mr Justice Swinton Thomas.*

**num:** stands for **number**.

e.g. **num ADV: odd** 3 ... *He has now appeared in sixty odd films.*

**n-uncount:** stands for **uncount noun** or **noun group with an uncount noun.** An uncount noun is a noun which has no plural form and which is sometimes used with no determiner.

e.g. **QUANT** *of* **n-uncount: touch** 16 ... *She thought she just had a touch of flu.*

**ord:** stands for **ordinal**, such as 'first', or 'second'.

e.g. **ord ADJ n: generation** 4 ... *second generation Asians in Britain.*

**P:** stands for **particle**. It is used in phrasal verb patterns to represent the particle. Particles may be either adverbs or prepositions.

e.g. **V P n: look after** 1 ... *I love looking after the children.*

**passive:** stands for **passive voice**. It is used when indicating that a verb usually or never occurs in the passive voice.

e.g. **VB: usu passive: expel** 1 ... *More than five-thousand secondary school students have been expelled for cheating.*

**pl:** stands for **plural**.

**pl-n:** stands for **noun in the plural, plural noun group**, or **co-ordinate noun group** (two or more noun groups joined by a co-ordinating conjunction).

e.g. **pl-n V: argue** 1 ... *They were still arguing; I could hear them down the road.*

**pl-num:** stands for **plural number**. A plural number is a number which is used only in the plural.

e.g. **PREP poss pl-num:** ③ **in** 5 ... *young people in their twenties.*

**poss:** stands for **possessive.** Possessives which come before the noun may be a possessive determiner, such as 'my', 'her', or 'their', or a possessive formed from a noun group, such as 'the horse's'. Possessives which come after the noun are of the form '*of* n', such as 'of the horse'.

e.g. **with poss: ancestor** 1 ... *He could trace his ancestors back seven hundred years.*

**prep:** stands for **prepositional phrase** or **preposition.**
e.g. **V prep: advance** 1 ... *Rebel forces are advancing on the capital.*
**prep PRON: him** 1 ... *Is Sam there? Let me talk to him.*

**pron:** stands for **pronoun.** A pronoun is a word such as 'I', 'it', or 'them' which is used like a noun group. It refers to someone or something that has already been mentioned or whose identity is known.
e.g. **PREP pron: before** 12 ... *Everyone in the room knew it was the single hardest task before them.*
**V pron: kill** 5 ... *My feet are killing me.*

**pron-indef:** stands for **indefinite pronoun.** An indefinite pronoun is a word like *anyone, anything, everyone* and *something.*
e.g. **pron-indef ADJ: else** 2 ... *I expect everyone else to be truthful.*

**pron-recip:** stands for **reciprocal pronoun.** The reciprocal pronouns are 'each other' and 'one another'.
e.g. **pl-n V *with* pron-recip: compete** 1 ... *The stores will inevitably end up competing with each other.*

**pron-refl:** stands for **reflexive pronoun,** such as 'yourself', 'herself', or 'ourselves'.
e.g. **PREP pron-refl: among** 9 ... *European farm ministers disagree among themselves.*

**pron-rel:** stands for **relative pronoun.** A relative pronoun is a word such as 'which' or 'who', that introduces a relative clause.
e.g. **PRON pron-rel: those** 4 ... *The interests he is most likely to enjoy will be those which enable him to show off himself or his talents.*

**quest:** stands for **question word.** A question word is a wh-word such as 'what', 'how', or 'why' which is used to begin a question.
e.g. **quest ADV: ever** 6 ... *Why ever didn't you tell me?*

**quote** means **direct speech.** Direct speech is often found in quotation marks.
e.g. **V with quote: announce** 2 ... *'I'm having a bath and going to bed', she announced.*

**sing:** stands for **singular.**

**sing-n:** stands for **noun in the singular.**
e.g. **PREDET det sing-n: all** 2 ... *She's worked all her life.*

**supp:** stands for **supplementary information accompanying a noun.** Supplementary information that comes before a noun may be given by a determiner, possessive, adjective, or noun modifier. Supplementary information that comes after the noun may be given by a prepositional phrase or a clause.
e.g. **supp N: park** 3 ... *a science and technology park.*

**that:** stands for **'that'-clause.** The clause may begin with the word 'that', but does not necessarily do so.
e.g. **V n that: tell** 1 ... *I returned to tell Phyllis our relationship was over.*

**to-inf:** stands for **to-infinitive form of a verb.**
e.g. **V to-inf: want** 1 ... *People wanted to know who this talented designer was.*

**v:** stands for **verb or verb group.** It is not used to represent a link verb. See also the explanations of **after, before** and **with.**
e.g. **v PRON: her** 1 ... *I told her I had something to say.*
**v PREP n: at** 10 ... *She opened the door and stood there, frowning at me.*

**v-cont:** stands for **continuous verb.** It is used to show a verb which is used in the continuous.
e.g. **ADV before v-cont: always** 3 ... *She was always moving things around.*

**V-ed:** stands for **past participle** of the verb explained in the entry.

**V-ing:** stands for **present participle** of the verb explained in the entry.

**v-link:** stands for **link verb.** A link verb is a verb such as 'be' which connects a subject and a complement.
e.g. **v-link ADJ:** ② **down** 3 ... *The computer's down again.*

***way*:** means the noun 'way' preceded by a possessive determiner.
e.g. **V *way* prep/adv: push** 2 ... *He pushed his way towards her.*

**wh:** stands for **wh-word,** or **clause beginning with a wh-word,** such as 'what', 'why', 'when', 'how', 'if', or 'whether'.
e.g. **V wh to-inf: know** 7 ... *We know what to do to make it work.*
**V wh: ask** 1 ... *If Daniel asks what happened in court we will tell him.*

# Pronunciation

The basic principle underlying the suggested pronunciations is 'If you pronounce it like this, most people will understand you'. The pronunciations are therefore broadly based on the two most widely taught accents of English, RP or Received Pronunciation for British English, and GenAm or General American for American English.

For the majority of words, a single pronunciation is given, as most differences between British and American pronunciation are systematic. Where the usual American pronunciation differs from the usual British pronunciation more significantly, a separate transcription is given of the part of the word that is pronounced differently in American English after the code AM. Where more than one pronunciation is common in British English, alternative pronunciations are also given.

The pronunciations are the result of a programme of monitoring spoken English and consulting leading reference works. For American English, the advice and helpful criticism of Debbie Posner is gratefully acknowledged.

The transcription system has developed from original work by Dr David Brazil for the Collins COBUILD English Language Dictionary. The symbols used in the dictionary are adapted from those of the International Phonetic Alphabet (IPA), as standardized in the English Pronouncing Dictionary by Daniel Jones (14th Edition, revised by AC Gimson and SM Ramsaran 1988), for representing RP.

## IPA symbols

| Vowel Sounds | | | | Consonant Sounds | | | |
|---|---|---|---|---|---|---|---|
| ɑː | calm, ah | ɒ | lot, spot | b | bed, rub | s | soon, bus |
| ɑːʳ | heart, far | oʊ | note, coat | d | done, red | t | talk, bet |
| æ | act, mass | ɔː | claw, maul | f | fit, if | v | van, love |
| aɪ | dive, cry | ɔʳ | more, cord | g | good, dog | w | win, wool |
| aɪəʳ | fire, tyre | ɔɪ | boy, joint | h | hat, horse | ʰw | why, wheat |
| aʊ | out, down | ʊ | could, stood | j | yellow, you | x | loch |
| aʊəʳ | flour, sour | uː | you, use | k | king, pick | z | zoo, buzz |
| e | met, lend, pen | ʊəʳ | lure, pure | l | lip, bill | ʃ | ship, wish |
| eɪ | say, weight | ɜːʳ | turn, third | ᵊl | handle, panel | ʒ | measure, leisure |
| eəʳ | fair, care | ʌ | fund, must | m | mat, ram | ŋ | sing, working |
| ɪ | fit, win | ə | the first vowel in about | n | not, tin | tʃ | cheap, witch |
| iː | feed, me | əʳ | the first vowel in forgotten | ᵊn | hidden, written | θ | thin, myth |
| ɪəʳ | near, beard | i | the second vowel in very | p | pay, lip | ð | then, bathe |
| | | u | the second vowel in actual | r | run, read | dʒ | joy, bridge |

## Notes

/ɑː/ or /æ/

There are a number of words which are shown in the dictionary with alternative pronunciations with /ɑː/ and /æ/, such as 'path' /pɑːθ, pæθ/. In this case, /pɑːθ/ is the RP pronunciation. However, in most other accents of English, including GenAm, the pronunciation is /pæθ/.

/ʳ/

One of the main ways in which RP differs from most other accents of English is that 'r' is only pronounced as /r/ when the next sound is a vowel. Thus, in RP, 'far gone' is pronounced /fɑː gɒn/ but 'far out' is pronounced /fɑːr aʊt/. In other accents of English, including GenAm, the 'r' in 'far' is always pronounced. The /ʳ/ superscript shows that:

1) in RP, /r/ is pronounced only when it is followed by a vowel;
2) in GenAm, /r/ is always pronounced

Some of the complex vowel sounds shown in the table above are simplified in GenAm. The vowel sound in 'fire' is shown as /aɪəʳ/. This represents the pronunciation /aɪə/ in RP, but in GenAm the pronunciation is not /aɪər/, but /aɪr/. So 'fire', 'flour', 'fair', 'near' and 'lure' are pronounced /faɪə/, /flaʊə/, /feə/, /nɪə/ and /lʊə/ in RP, but /faɪr/, /flaʊr/, /fer/, /nɪr/ and /lʊr/ in GenAm.

/ɒ/

In GenAm, this symbol represents the same sound as the symbol /ɑː/, so that the first syllable of 'common' sounds like 'calm'. In RP, the sounds are different.

/oʊ/

This symbol is used to represent the sound /əʊ/ in RP, and also the sound /o/ in GenAm, as these sounds are almost entirely equivalent.

/i/ and /u/

These are short vowels which only occur in unstressed syllables:

/i/ has a sound like /iː/, but is short like /ɪ/: **very** /veri/ **create** /krieɪt/
/u/ has a sound like /uː/, but is short like /ʊ/: **actual** /æktʃuəl/

/ᵊl/ and /ᵊn/

These show that /l/ and /n/ are pronounced as separate syllables:
**handle** /hændᵊl/ **hidden** /hɪdᵊn/

/ʰw/

This shows that some people say /w/, and others, including many American speakers, say /hw/: **why** /ʰwaɪ/

# Stress

Stress is shown by underlining the vowel in the stressed syllable:

**two** /tuː/ **result** /rɪzʌlt/ **disappointing** /dɪsəpɔɪntɪŋ/

When a word is spoken in isolation, stress falls on the syllables which have vowels which are underlined. If there is one syllable underlined, it will have primary stress.

'TWO' 'reSULT'

If two syllables are underlined, the first will have secondary stress, and the second will have primary stress:

'DISapPOINTing'

A few words are shown with three underlined syllables, for example 'disqualification' /dɪskwɒlɪfɪkeɪʃᵊn/. In this case, the third underlined syllable will have primary stress, while the secondary stress may be on the first or second syllable:

'DISqualifiCAtion' or 'disQUALifiCAtion'

RP tends to prefer 'DIS-', while GenAm usually prefers 'dis-'.

In the case of compound words, where the pronunciation of each part is given separately, the stress pattern is shown by underlining the headword: 'off-peak', 'first-class', but 'off day'.

## Stressed syllables

When words are used in context, the way in which they are pronounced depends upon the information units that are constructed by the speaker. For example, a speaker could say:

1) 'the reSULT was disapPOINTing'
2) 'it was a DISappointing reSULT'
3) 'it was VERy disappointing inDEED'

In (3), neither of the two underlined syllables in disappointing /dɪsəpɔɪntɪŋ/ receives either primary or secondary stress. This shows that it is not possible for a dictionary to predict whether a particular syllable will be stressed in context.

It should be noted, however, that in the case of adjectives with two stressed syllables, the second syllable often loses its stress when it is used before a noun:

'an OFF-peak FARE'
'a FIRST-class SEAT'

Two things should be noted about the marked syllables:

1) They can take primary or secondary stress in a way that is not shared by the other syllables.
2) Whether they are stressed or not, the vowel must be pronounced distinctly; it cannot be weakened to /ə/, /ɪ/, or /ʊ/.

These features are shared by most of the one-syllable words in English, which are therefore transcribed in this dictionary as stressed syllables:

**two** /tuː/ **inn** /ɪn/ **tree** /triː/

## Unstressed syllables

It is an important characteristic of English that vowels in unstressed syllables tend not to be pronounced clearly. Many unstressed syllables contain the vowel /ə/, a neutral vowel which is not found in stressed syllables. The vowels /ɪ/ and /ʊ/, which are relatively neutral in quality, are also common in unstressed syllables.

Single-syllable grammatical words such as 'shall' and 'at' are often pronounced with a weak vowel such as /ə/. However some of them are pronounced with a more distinct vowel under certain circumstances, for example when they occur at the end of a sentence. This distinct pronunciation is generally referred to as the strong form, and is given in this dictionary after the word STRONG.

**shall** /ʃəl, STRONG ʃæl/ **at** /ət, STRONG æt/

# A a

**A, a** /eɪ/ **(A's, a's)** 1 **A** is the first letter of the English alphabet. N-VAR 2 In music, **A** is the sixth note in the scale of C major. N-VAR 3 If you get an **A** as a mark for a piece of work or in an exam, your work is extremely good. N-VAR 4 **A** or **a** is used as an abbreviation for words beginning with a, such as 'acceleration', 'ampère', or 'answer'. 5 People talk about getting **from A to B** when they are referring generally to journeys they need to make, without saying where the journeys will take them. PHRASE: PHR after v ❑ *Cars are for getting people from A to B in maximum safety.*

**a** /ə, STRONG eɪ/ or **an** /ən, STRONG æn/ ◆◆◆

> **A** or **an** is the indefinite article. It is used at the beginning of noun groups which refer to only one person or thing. The form **an** is used in front of words that begin with vowel sounds.

1 You use **a** or **an** when you are referring to someone or something for the first time or when people may not know which particular person or thing you are talking about. DET: DET sing-n ❑ *A waiter entered with a tray... He started eating an apple... Today you've got a new teacher taking you... I manage a hotel.* 2 You use **a** or **an** when you are referring to any person or thing of a particular type and do not want to be specific. DET: DET sing-n ❑ *I suggest you leave it to an expert... Bring a sleeping bag... I was waiting for a bus.* 3 You use **a** or **an** in front of an uncount noun when that noun follows an adjective, or when the noun is followed by words that describe it more fully. DET: DET n-uncount with supp ❑ *There was a terrible sadness in her eyes.* 4 You use **a** or **an** in front of a mass noun when you want to refer to a single type or make of something. DET: DET n-mass ❑ *Bollinger 'RD' is a rare, highly prized wine.* 5 You use **a** in quantifiers such as **a lot**, **a little**, and **a bit**. DET: DET in quant ❑ *I spend a lot on expensive jewelry and clothing... I've come looking for a bit of advice.* 6 You use **a** or **an** to refer to someone or something as a typical member of a group, class, or type. DET: DET sing-n ❑ *Some parents believe a boy must learn to stand up and fight like a man.* 7 You use **a** or **an** in front of the names of days, months, or festivals when you are referring to one particular instance of that day, month, or festival. DET: DET sing-n ❑ *The interview took place on a Friday afternoon.* 8 You use **a** or **an** when you are saying what someone is or what job they have. DET: DET sing-n ❑ *I explained that I was an artist... He was now a teacher and a respectable member of the community.* 9 You use **a** or **an** in front of the names of artists to refer to one individual painting or sculpture created by them. DET: DET n-proper ❑ *Most people have very little difficulty in seeing why a Van Gogh is a work of genius.* 10 You use **a** or **an** instead of the number 'one', especially with words of measurement such as 'hundred', 'hour', and 'metre', and with fractions such as 'half', 'quarter', and 'third'. DET: DET sing-n ❑ *...more than a thousand acres of land. ...a quarter of an hour.* 11 You use **a** or **an** in expressions such as **eight hours a day** to express a rate or ratio. DET: num DET sing-n ❑ *Prices start at £13.95 a metre for printed cotton... The helicopter can zip along at about 150 kilometres an hour.*

**a-** /eɪ-/ **A-** is added to the beginning of some adjectives in order to form adjectives that describe someone or something that does not have the feature or quality indicated by the original word. PREFIX ❑ *I'm a completely apolitical man. ...asymmetrical shapes.*

**aah** /ɑː/ → see **ah**.

**A & E** /eɪ ən iː/ In Britain, **A & E** is the part of a hospital that deals with accidents and emergencies. **A & E** is an abbreviation for 'accident and emergency'. [BRIT] N-UNCOUNT

> ✓ in AM, use **ER**

**AB** /eɪ biː/ **(ABs)** In some American universities, an **AB** is the same as a **BA**. N-COUNT

**aback** /əbæk/ If you are **taken aback by** something, you are surprised or shocked by it and you cannot respond at once. PHRASE: usu v-link PHR, oft PHR *by* n ❑ *Roland was taken aback by our strength of feeling.*

**aba|cus** /æbəkəs/ **(abacuses)** An **abacus** is a frame used for counting. It has rods with sliding beads on them. N-COUNT

**aba|lo|ne** /æbəlouni/ **(abalones) Abalone** is a shellfish that you can eat and that has a shiny substance called mother-of-pearl inside its shell. N-VAR

**aban|don** /əbændən/ **(abandons, abandoning, abandoned)** ◆◇◇ 1 If you **abandon** a place, thing, or person, you leave the place, thing, or person permanently or for a long time, especially when you should not do so. VERB ❑ *He claimed that his parents had abandoned him...* V n *The road is strewn with abandoned vehicles.* V-ed 2 If you **abandon** an activity or piece of work, you stop doing it before it is finished. VERB = give up ≠ continue ❑ *The authorities have abandoned any attempt to distribute food.* V n 3 If you **abandon** an idea or way of thinking, you stop having that idea or thinking in that way. VERB = give up ❑ *Logic had prevailed and he had abandoned the idea.* V n 4 If you say that someone does something **with abandon**, you mean that they behave in a wild, uncontrolled way and do not think or care about how they should behave. N-UNCOUNT: usu *with* N [disapproval] ❑ *He has spent money with gay abandon.* 5 → See also **abandoned**. 6 If people **abandon ship**, they get off a ship because it is sinking. PHRASE: v inflects

**aban|doned** /əbændənd/ ◆◇◇ An **abandoned** place or building is no longer used or occupied. ADJ: usu ADJ n ❑ *All that digging had left a network of abandoned mines and tunnels.*

**aban|don|ment** /əbændənmənt/ 1 The **abandonment of** a place, thing, or person is the act of leaving it permanently or for a long time, especially when you should not do so. N-UNCOUNT: oft N *of* n ❑ *...memories of her father's complete abandonment of her.* 2 The **abandonment of** a piece of work or activity is the act of stopping doing it before it is finished. N-UNCOUNT: oft N *of* n ❑ *Constant rain forced the abandonment of the next day's competitions.* 3 The **abandonment of** an idea or way of thinking is the act of stopping having the idea or of stopping thinking in that way. N-UNCOUNT: oft N *of* n

**abashed** /əbæʃt/ If you are **abashed**, you feel embarrassed and ashamed. [WRITTEN] ADJ: usu v-link ADJ ❑ *He looked abashed, uncomfortable.*

**abate** /əbeɪt/ **(abates, abating, abated)** If something bad or undesirable **abates**, it becomes much less strong or severe. [FORMAL] VERB ❑ *The storms had abated by the time they rounded Cape Horn.* V

**abate|ment** /əbeɪtmənt/ **Abatement** means a reduction in the strength or power of N-UNCOUNT: also *a* N something or the reduction of it. [FORMAL] ❑ *...the abatement of carbon dioxide emissions. ...noise abatement.*

**ab|at|toir** /æbətwɑːʳ/ **(abattoirs)** An **abattoir** is a place where animals are killed in order to provide meat. [BRIT] N-COUNT = *slaughterhouse*

☑ in AM, use **slaughterhouse**

**ab|bess** /æbes/ **(abbesses)** An **abbess** is the nun who is in charge of the other nuns in a convent. N-COUNT

**ab|bey** /æbi/ **(abbeys)** An **abbey** is a church with buildings attached to it in which monks or nuns live or used to live. N-COUNT

**ab|bot** /æbət/ **(abbots)** An **abbot** is the monk who is in charge of the other monks in a monastery or abbey. N-COUNT

**ab|bre|vi|ate** /əbriːvieɪt/ **(abbreviates, abbreviating, abbreviated)** If you **abbreviate** something, especially a word or a piece of writing, you make it shorter. ❑ *He abbreviated his first name to Alec.* VERB = *shorten* V n *to* n Also V n

**ab|bre|via|tion** /əbriːvieɪʃᵊn/ **(abbreviations)** An **abbreviation** is a short form of a word or phrase, made by leaving out some of the letters or by using only the first letter of each word. ❑ *The postal abbreviation for Kansas is KS.* N-COUNT

**ABC** /eɪ biː siː/ **(ABCs)** [1] The **ABC of** a subject or activity is the parts of it that you have to learn first because they are the most important and basic. ❑ *...the ABC of Marxism.* N-SING: N *of* n [2] Children who have learned their **ABC** or their **ABCs** have learned to recognize, write, or say the alphabet. [INFORMAL] N-COUNT: poss N

**ab|di|cate** /æbdɪkeɪt/ **(abdicates, abdicating, abdicated)** [1] If a king or queen **abdicates**, he or she gives up being king or queen. ❑ *The last French king was Louis Philippe, who abdicated in 1848.* VERB V Also V n ♦ **ab|di|ca|tion** /æbdɪkeɪʃᵊn/ *...the most serious royal crisis since the abdication of Edward VIII.* N-UNCOUNT: usu with poss [2] If you say that someone has **abdicated** responsibility for something, you disapprove of them because they have refused to accept responsibility for it any longer. [FORMAL] ❑ *Many parents simply abdicate all responsibility for their children.* VERB [disapproval] V n ♦ **ab|di|ca|tion** *There had been a complete abdication of responsibility.* N-UNCOUNT: N *of* n

**ab|do|men** /æbdəmən, AM æbdoʊ-/ **(abdomens)** Your **abdomen** is the part of your body below your chest where your stomach and intestines are. [FORMAL] ❑ *He was suffering from pains in his abdomen.* N-COUNT: oft poss N

**ab|domi|nal** /æbdɒmɪnᵊl/ **Abdominal** is used to describe something that is situated in the abdomen or forms part of it. [FORMAL] ❑ *...vomiting, diarrhoea and abdominal pain.* ADJ: ADJ n

**ab|domi|nals** /æbdɒmɪnᵊlz/ You can refer to your abdominal muscles as your **abdominals** when you are talking about exercise. N-PLURAL

**ab|duct** /æbdʌkt/ **(abducts, abducting, abducted)** If someone **is abducted** by another person, he or she is taken away illegally, usually using force. ❑ *His car was held up and he was abducted by four gunmen... She was charged with abducting a six-month-old child.* VERB = *kidnap* *be* V-ed V n ♦ **ab|duc|tion** /æbdʌkʃᵊn/ **(abductions)** *...the abduction of four youths.* N-VAR ♦ **ab|duc|tor (abductors)** *She co-operated with her abductor.* N-COUNT

**ab|er|rant** /æberənt/ **Aberrant** means unusual and not socially acceptable. [FORMAL] ❑ *Ian's rages and aberrant behavior worsened.* ADJ: usu ADJ n

**ab|er|ra|tion** /æbəreɪʃᵊn/ **(aberrations)** An **aberration** is an incident or way of behaving that is not typical. [FORMAL] ❑ *It became very clear that the incident was not just an aberration, it was not just a single incident.* N-VAR

**abet** /əbet/ **(abets, abetting, abetted)** If one person **abets** another, they help or encourage them to do something criminal or wrong. **Abet** is often used in the legal expression 'aid and abet'. [LEGAL, FORMAL] ❑ *His wife was sentenced to seven years imprisonment for aiding and abetting him.* VERB V n

**abey|ance** /əbeɪəns/ If something is **in abeyance**, it is not operating or being used at the present time. [FORMAL] ❑ *The Russian threat is, at the least, in abeyance.* PHRASE: v-link PHR, PHR after v

**ab|hor** /æbhɔːʳ/ **(abhors, abhorring, abhorred)** If you **abhor** something, you hate it very much, especially for moral reasons. [FORMAL] ❑ *He was a man who abhorred violence and was deeply committed to reconciliation.* VERB = *detest* V n

**ab|hor|rence** /æbhɒrəns, AM -hɔːr-/ Someone's **abhorrence** of something is their strong hatred of it. [FORMAL] ❑ *They are anxious to show their abhorrence of racism.* N-UNCOUNT: usu with supp, oft poss N, N *of* n = *hatred*

**ab|hor|rent** /æbhɒrənt, AM -hɔːr-/ If something is **abhorrent to** you, you hate it very much or consider it completely unacceptable. [FORMAL] ❑ *Racial discrimination is abhorrent to my council and our staff.* ADJ: usu v-link ADJ, oft ADJ *to* n

**abide** /əbaɪd/ **(abides, abiding, abided)** If you **can't abide** someone or something, you dislike them very much. ❑ *I can't abide people who can't make up their minds.* → See also **abiding**, **law-abiding**. PHRASE: with brd-neg = *can't stand*

♦ **abide by** If you **abide by** a law, agreement, or decision, you do what it says you should do. ❑ *They have got to abide by the rules.* PHRASAL VERB = *observe* V P n

**abid|ing** /əbaɪdɪŋ/ An **abiding** feeling, memory, or interest is one that you have for a very long time. ❑ *He has a genuine and abiding love of the craft.* ADJ: ADJ n = *lasting* ≠ *short-lived*

**abil|ity** /əbɪlɪti/ **(abilities)** ◆◆◇ [1] Your **ability to** do something is the fact that you can do it. ❑ *The public never had faith in his ability to handle the job... He has the ability to bring out the best in others.* N-SING: N to-inf, oft with poss = *capability* [2] Your **ability** is the quality or skill that you have which makes it possible for you to do something. ❑ *Her drama teacher spotted her ability... They repeatedly questioned his leadership abilities... Does the school cater for all abilities?* N-VAR: oft with poss [3] If you do something **to the best of** your **abilities** or **to the best of** your **ability**, you do it as well as you can. ❑ *I take care of them to the best of my abilities.* PHRASE

**-ability** /-əbɪlɪti/ **(-abilities)** **-ability** replaces '-able' at the end of adjectives to form nouns. Nouns formed in this way refer to the state or quality described by the adjectives. ❑ *...the desirability of global co-operation... No one ever questioned her capability.* SUFFIX

**ab|ject** /æbdʒekt/ You use **abject** to emphasize that a situation or quality is extremely bad. ❑ *Both of them died in abject poverty... This scheme was an abject failure.* ADJ: usu ADJ n [emphasis] = *total* ♦ **ab|ject|ly** *Both have failed abjectly.* ADV

**ab|jure** /æbdʒʊəʳ/ **(abjures, abjuring, abjured)** If you **abjure** something such as a belief or way of life, you state publicly that you will give it up or that you reject it. [FORMAL] ❑ *...a formal statement abjuring military action.* VERB V n

**ablaze** /əbleɪz/ [1] Something that is **ablaze** is burning very fiercely. ❑ *Shops, houses, and vehicles were set ablaze.* ADJ: v n ADJ, v-link ADJ [2] If a place is **ablaze with** lights or colours, it is very bright because of them. ❑ *The chamber was ablaze with light.* ADJ: v-link ADJ, usu ADJ *with* n

**able** /eɪbᵊl/ **(abler** /eɪblәʳ/, **ablest** /eɪblɪst/**)** ◆◆◆ [1] If you **are able to** do something, you have skills or qualities which make it possible for you to do it. ❑ *The older child should be able to prepare a simple meal... The company say they're able to keep pricing competitive... They seemed able to work together very efficiently.* PHRASE = *can* [2] If you **are able to** do something, you have enough freedom, power, time, or money to do it. ❑ *You'll be able to read in peace... It would be nice to be able to afford to retire earlier.* PHRASE = *can* [3] Someone who is **able** is very clever or very good at doing something. ❑ *...one of the brightest and ablest members of the government.* ADJ = *capable*

**-able** /-əbᵊl/ **-able** combines with verbs to form adjectives. Adjectives formed in this way de- SUFFIX scribe someone or something that can have a particular thing done to them. For example, if something is avoidable, it can be avoided. ❑ *These injuries were avoidable... He was an admirable chairman.*

**able-bodied** /eɪbəl bɒdid/ An **able-bodied** person is physically strong and healthy, rather than weak or disabled. ❑ *The gym can be used by both able-bodied and disabled people.* ♦ **The able-bodied** are people who are able-bodied. ADJ ≠ disabled; N-PLURAL: the N

**ab|lu|tions** /əbluːʃənz/ Someone's **ablutions** are all the activities that are involved in washing himself or herself. [FORMAL or HUMOROUS] N-PLURAL: oft poss N

**ably** /eɪbli/ **Ably** means skilfully and successfully. ❑ *He was ably assisted by a number of other members.* ADV: ADV with v

**ab|nor|mal** /æbnɔːʳməl/ Someone or something that is **abnormal** is unusual, especially in a way that is worrying. [FORMAL] ❑ *...abnormal heart rhythms and high anxiety levels. ...a child with an abnormal fear of strangers.* ♦ **ab|nor|mal|ly** *...abnormally high levels of glucose.* ADJ; ADV: usu ADV adj/adv, also ADV with v

**ab|nor|mal|ity** /æbnɔːʳmælɪti/ **(abnormalities)** An **abnormality** in something, especially in a person's body or behaviour, is an unusual part or feature of it that may be worrying or dangerous. [FORMAL] ❑ *Further scans are required to confirm the diagnosis of an abnormality.* N-VAR

**aboard** /əbɔːʳd/ If you are **aboard** a ship or plane, you are on it or in it. ❑ *She invited 750 people aboard the luxury yacht, the Savarona... They said goodbye to him as he got aboard the train at Union Station.* ♦ **Aboard** is also an adverb. ❑ *It had taken two hours to load all the people aboard.* PREP = on board; ADV: ADV after v = on board

**abode** /əboʊd/ **(abodes)** 1 Your **abode** is the place where you live. [FORMAL] ❑ *I went round the streets and found his new abode.* 2 If someone has **no fixed abode**, they are homeless. [LEGAL] ❑ *30 per cent of psychiatric hospital beds are occupied by people of no fixed abode.* N-COUNT: usu poss N; PHRASE: oft of PHR

**abol|ish** /əbɒlɪʃ/ **(abolishes, abolishing, abolished)** If someone in authority **abolishes** a system or practice, they formally put an end to it. ❑ *The following year Parliament voted to abolish the death penalty for murder.* VERB; V n

**abo|li|tion** /æbəlɪʃən/ The **abolition of** something such as a system or practice is its formal ending. ❑ *...the abolition of slavery in Brazil and the Caribbean.* N-UNCOUNT: also a N, usu with supp, oft N of n

**abo|li|tion|ist** /æbəlɪʃənɪst/ **(abolitionists)** An **abolitionist** is someone who campaigns for the abolition of a particular system or practice. ❑ *As long as most people are happy to have the monarchy, the abolitionist position is an arrogant fantasy.* N-COUNT: oft N n

**A-bomb** /eɪ bɒm/ **(A-bombs)** An **A-bomb** is an atomic bomb. N-COUNT

**abomi|nable** /əbɒmɪnəbəl/ Something that is **abominable** is very unpleasant or bad. ❑ *The President described the killings as an abominable crime.* ♦ **abomi|nably** /əbɒmɪnəbli/ *Chloe has behaved abominably... Wallis was often abominably rude.* ADJ; ADV: ADV after v, ADV -ed/adj

**abom|ina|tion** /əbɒmɪneɪʃən/ **(abominations)** If you say that something is an **abomination**, you think that it is completely unacceptable. [FORMAL] N-COUNT [disapproval] = outrage

**abo|rigi|nal** /æbərɪdʒɪnəl/ **(aboriginals)** 1 An **Aboriginal** is an Australian Aborigine. ❑ *He remained fascinated by the Aboriginals' tales.* 2 **Aboriginal** means belonging or relating to the Australian Aborigines. ❑ *...Aboriginal art.* 3 The **aboriginal** people or animals of a place are ones that have been there from the earliest known times or that were there before people or animals from other countries arrived. N-COUNT = Aborigine; ADJ: ADJ n; ADJ: ADJ n = native, indigenous

**Abo|rigi|ne** /æbərɪdʒɪni/ **(Aborigines)** **Aborigines** are members of the tribes that were living in Australia when Europeans arrived there. N-COUNT: usu pl

**abort** /əbɔːʳt/ **(aborts, aborting, aborted)** 1 If an unborn baby **is aborted**, the pregnancy is ended deliberately and the baby is not born alive. [FORMAL] ❑ *Her lover walked out on her after she had aborted their child. ...tissue from aborted fetuses.* 2 If someone **aborts** a process, plan, or activity, they stop it before it has been completed. ❑ *The decision was made to abort the mission.* VERB; V n; V-ed; VERB; V n

**abor|tion** /əbɔːʳʃən/ **(abortions)** If a woman has an **abortion**, she ends her pregnancy deliberately so that the baby is not born alive. ❑ *His girlfriend had an abortion.* ♦◇◇ N-VAR

**abor|tion|ist** /əbɔːʳʃənɪst/ **(abortionists)** An **abortionist** is someone who performs abortions, usually illegally. → See also **anti-abortionist**. N-COUNT

**abor|tive** /əbɔːʳtɪv/ An **abortive** attempt or action is unsuccessful. [FORMAL] ❑ *...an abortive attempt to prevent the current President from taking office.* ADJ: usu ADJ n = unsuccessful

**abound** /əbaʊnd/ **(abounds, abounding, abounded)** If things **abound**, or if a place **abounds with** things, there are very large numbers of them. [FORMAL] ❑ *Stories abound about when he was in charge... The book abounds with close-up images from space.* VERB; V; V with/in n

**about** /əbaʊt/ ♦♦♦

> In addition to the uses shown below, **about** is used after some verbs, nouns, and adjectives to introduce extra information. **About** is also often used after verbs of movement, such as 'walk' and 'drive', and in phrasal verbs such as 'mess about' and 'set about', especially in British English.

1 You use **about** to introduce who or what something relates to or concerns. ❑ *She came in for a coffee, and told me about her friend Shona... She knew a lot about food... He never complains about his wife.* PREP

2 When you mention the things that an activity or institution is **about**, you are saying what it involves or what its aims are. ❑ *Leadership is about the ability to implement change.* PREP

3 You use **about** after some adjectives to indicate the person or thing that a feeling or state of mind relates to. ❑ *'I'm sorry about Patrick,' she said... I feel so guilty and angry about the whole issue.* PREP

4 If you do something **about** a problem, you take action in order to solve it. ❑ *Rachel was going to do something about Jacob.* PREP

5 When you say that there is a particular quality **about** someone or something, you mean that they have this quality. ❑ *I think there's something a little peculiar about the results of your test.* PREP

6 **About** is used in front of a number to show that the number is not exact. ❑ *In my local health centre there's about forty parking spaces... The rate of inflation is running at about 2.7 percent.* ADV: ADV num = approximately, around ≠ precisely

7 If someone or something moves **about**, they keep moving in different directions. ❑ *Everyone was running about.* ♦ **About** is also a preposition. ❑ *From 1879 to 1888 he wandered about Germany, Switzerland, and Italy.* ADV: ADV after v = around; PREP: v PREP n = around

8 If you put something **about** a person or thing, you put it around them. ❑ *Helen threw her arms about him.* PREP = round, around

9 If someone or something is **about**, they are present or available. ❑ *There's lots of money about these days for schemes like this.* ADJ: v-link ADJ

10 If you are **about to** do something, you are going to do it very soon. If something is **about to** happen, it will happen very soon. ❑ *I think he's about to leave... The film was about to start.* ADJ: v-link ADJ to-inf

11 **how about** → see **how**. **what about** → see **what**. **just about** → see **just**.

PHRASES 12 If someone is **out and about**, they are going out and doing things, especially after they have been unable to for a while. ❑ *Despite considerable pain she has been getting out and about almost as normal.* PHRASE: usu PHR after v, also v-link PHR

13 If someone is **out and about**, they are going to a lot of different places, often as part of their job. ❑ *They often saw me out and about.* PHRASE: usu PHR after v, also v-link PHR

**about-face** **(about-faces)** An **about-face** is a complete change of attitude or opinion. ❑ *Few observers believe the president will do an about-face and start spending more.* N-COUNT = U-turn, volte-face

**about-turn** **(about-turns)** An **about-turn** is the same as an **about-face**. [BRIT] N-COUNT

in AM, use **about-face**

**above** /əbʌv/ ◆◆◇ 1 If one thing is **above** another one, it is directly over it or higher than it. ❑ *He lifted his hands above his head... Apartment 46 was a quiet apartment, unlike the one above it... He was staring into the mirror above him.* PREP ≠ below ♦ **Above** is also an adverb. ❑ *A long scream sounded from somewhere above. ...a picture of the new plane as seen from above.* ADV: ADV after v, *from* ADV ≠ below 2 In writing, you use **above** to refer to something that has already been mentioned or discussed. ❑ *Several conclusions could be drawn from the results described above.* ADV: ADV after v, n ADV ≠ below ♦ **Above** is also a noun. ❑ *For additional information, contact any of the above.* N-SING-COLL: *the* N ♦ **Above** is also an adjective. ❑ *For a copy of their brochure, write to the above address.* ADJ: ADJ n 3 If an amount or measurement is **above** a particular level, it is greater than that level. ❑ *The temperature crept up to just above 40 degrees... Victoria Falls has had above average levels of rainfall this year... Government spending is planned to rise 3 per cent above inflation.* PREP ≠ below ♦ **Above** is also an adverb. ❑ *Banks have been charging 25 percent and above for unsecured loans.* ADV: amount *and* ADV 4 If you hear one sound **above** another, it is louder or clearer than the second one. ❑ *Then there was a woman's voice, rising shrilly above the barking.* PREP = over 5 If someone is **above** you, they are in a higher social position than you or in a position of authority over you. ❑ *I married above myself – rich county people.* PREP ≠ below ♦ **Above** is also an adverb. ❑ *The policemen admitted beating the student, but said they were acting on orders from above.* ADV: *from* ADV 6 If you say that someone thinks they are **above** something, you mean that they act as if they are too good or important for it. ❑ *I'm not above doing my own cleaning.* PREP disapproval 7 If someone is **above** criticism or suspicion, they cannot be criticized or suspected because of their good qualities or their position. ❑ *He was a respected academic and above suspicion.* PREP: v-link PREP n = beyond 8 If you value one person or thing **above** any other, you value them more or consider that they are more important. ❑ *...his tendency to put the team above everything.* PREP 9 **over and above** → see **over**. **above the law** → see **law**. **above board** → see **board**.

**above-the-line promotion** **(above-the-line promotions)** **Above-the-line promotion** is the use of promotional methods that cannot be directly controlled by the company selling the goods or service, such as television or press advertising. Compare **below-the-line promotion**. [BUSINESS] ❑ *For all maternity clothing retailers, most above-the-line promotion is conducted through focused sources such as mother and baby magazines.* N-VAR

**abracadabra** /æbrəkədæbrə/ **Abracadabra** is a word that someone says when they are performing a magic trick in order to make the magic happen. EXCLAM

**abrade** /əbreɪd/ **(abrades, abrading, abraded)** To **abrade** something means to scrape or wear down its surface by rubbing it. [FORMAL] ❑ *My skin was abraded and very tender.* VERB be V-ed

**abrasion** /əbreɪʒən/ **(abrasions)** An **abrasion** is an area on a person's body where the skin has been scraped. [FORMAL] ❑ *He had severe abrasions to his right cheek.* N-COUNT = graze, cut

**abrasive** /əbreɪsɪv/ 1 Someone who has an **abrasive** manner is unkind and rude. ❑ *His abrasive manner has won him an unenviable notoriety.* ADJ 2 An **abrasive** substance is rough and can be used to clean hard surfaces. ❑ *...a new all-purpose, non-abrasive cleaner.* ADJ

**abreast** /əbrest/ 1 If people or things walk or move **abreast**, they are next to each other, side by side, and facing in the same direction. ❑ *The steep pavement was too narrow for them to walk abreast.* ADV: ADV after v, num ADV

**PHRASES** 2 If you are **abreast of** someone or something, you are level with them or in line with them. ❑ *As he drew abreast of the man he pretended to stumble.* PREP-PHRASE 3 If you **keep abreast of** a subject, you know all the most recent facts about it. ❑ *He will be keeping abreast of the news.* PREP-PHRASE

**abridged** /əbrɪdʒd/ An **abridged** book or play has been made shorter by removing some parts of it. ❑ *This is an abridged version of her new novel 'The Queen and I'.* ADJ: usu ADJ n = shortened

**abroad** /əbrɔːd/ ◆◇◇ If you go **abroad**, you go to a foreign country, usually one which is separated from the country where you live by an ocean or a sea. ❑ *I would love to go abroad this year, perhaps to France. ...public opposition here and abroad... About 65 per cent of its sales come from abroad.* ADV: ADV after v, n ADV, *be* ADV, *from* ADV = overseas

**abrogate** /æbrəgeɪt/ **(abrogates, abrogating, abrogated)** If someone in a position of authority **abrogates** something such as a law, agreement, or practice, they put an end to it. [FORMAL] ❑ *The next prime minister could abrogate the treaty.* VERB = revoke V n

**abrupt** /əbrʌpt/ 1 An **abrupt** change or action is very sudden, often in a way which is unpleasant. ❑ *Rosie's idyllic world came to an abrupt end when her parents' marriage broke up.* ADJ ♦ **abruptly** *He stopped abruptly and looked my way.* ADV 2 Someone who is **abrupt** speaks in a rather rude, unfriendly way. ❑ *He was abrupt to the point of rudeness... Cross was a little taken aback by her abrupt manner.* ADJ = brusque ♦ **abruptly** *'Good night, then,' she said abruptly.* ADV

**abs** /æbz/ **Abs** are the same as **abdominals**. [INFORMAL] ❑ *Throughout the exercise, focus on keeping your abs tight.* N-PLURAL

**abscess** /æbses/ **(abscesses)** An **abscess** is a painful swelling containing pus. N-COUNT

**abscond** /æbskɒnd/ **(absconds, absconding, absconded)** 1 If someone **absconds from** somewhere such as a prison, they escape from it or leave it without permission. [FORMAL] ❑ *He was ordered to appear the following day, but absconded... A dozen inmates have absconded from Forest Jail.* VERB = run away V V *from* n 2 If someone **absconds with** something, they leave and take it with them, although it does not belong to them. [FORMAL] ❑ *Unfortunately, his partners were crooks and absconded with the funds.* VERB = run off V *with* n

**abseil** /æbseɪl/ **(abseils, abseiling, abseiled)** To **abseil down** a cliff or rock face means to slide down it in a controlled way using a rope, with your feet against the cliff or rock. [BRIT] VERB

in AM, use **rappel**

**absence** /æbsəns/ **(absences)** ◆◇◇ 1 Someone's **absence** from a place is the fact that they are not there. ❑ *...a bundle of letters which had arrived for me in my absence... Eleanor would later blame her mother-in-law for her husband's frequent absences.* N-VAR: with supp ≠ presence 2 The **absence** of something from a place is the fact that it is not there or does not exist. ❑ *The presence or absence of clouds can have an important impact on heat transfer... In the absence of a will the courts decide who the guardian is.* N-SING: with supp = lack ≠ presence 3 → See also **leave of absence**. **conspicuous by** one's **absence** → see **conspicuous**.

**absent** /æbsənt/ 1 If someone or something is **absent from** a place or situation where they should be or where they usually are, they are not there. ❑ *He has been absent from his desk for two weeks... Any soldier failing to report would be considered absent without leave and punished accordingly.* ADJ: usu v-link ADJ, oft ADJ *from* n 2 If someone appears **absent**, they are not paying attention because they are thinking about something else. ❑ *'Nothing,' Rosie said in an absent way.* ADJ ♦ **absently** /æbsəntli/ *He nodded absently.* ADV 3 An **absent** parent does not live with his or her children. ❑ *...absent fathers who fail to pay towards the costs of looking after their children.* ADJ: ADJ n 4 If you say that **absent** one thing, another thing will happen, you mean that if the first thing does not happen, the second thing will happen. [AM, FORMAL] ❑ *Absent a solution, people like Sue Godfrey will just keep on fighting.* PREP = without

**ab|sen|tee** /æbsəntiː/ **(absentees)** [1] An **absentee** is a person who is expected to be in a particular place but who is not there. N-COUNT [2] **Absentee** is used to describe someone who is not there to do a particular job in person. ❑ *Absentee fathers will be forced to pay child maintenance.* ADJ: ADJ n [3] In elections in the United States, if you vote by **absentee** ballot or if you are an **absentee** voter, you vote in advance because you will be away. [AM] ADJ: ADJ n

**ab|sen|tee|ism** /æbsəntiːɪzəm/ **Absenteeism** is the fact or habit of frequently being away from work or school, usually without a good reason. N-UNCOUNT ≠ *attendance*

**ab|sen|tia** /æbsentiə, AM -senʃə/ If something is done to you **in absentia**, it is done to you when you are not present. [FORMAL] ❑ *He was tried in absentia and sentenced to seven years in prison.* PHRASE: PHR after v

**absent-minded** Someone who is **absent-minded** forgets things or does not pay attention to what they are doing, often because they are thinking about something else. ❑ *In his later life he became even more absent-minded.* ADJ = *forgetful* ♦ **absent-mindedly** *Elizabeth absent-mindedly picked a thread from his lapel.* ADV: ADV with v

**ab|sinthe** /æbsɪnθ/ **Absinthe** is a very strong alcoholic drink that is green and tastes bitter. N-UNCOUNT

**ab|so|lute** /æbsəluːt/ **(absolutes)** ◆◇◇ [1] **Absolute** means total and complete. ❑ *It's not really suited to absolute beginners... A sick person needs absolute confidence and trust in a doctor.* ADJ: usu ADJ n = *complete* [2] You use **absolute** to emphasize something that you are saying. ❑ *About 12 inches wide is the absolute minimum you should consider... I think it's absolute nonsense.* ADJ: ADJ n [emphasis] = *complete* [3] An **absolute** ruler has complete power and authority over his or her country. ❑ *He ruled with absolute power.* ADJ: ADJ n [4] **Absolute** is used to say that something is definite and will not change even if circumstances change. ❑ *They had given an absolute assurance that it would be kept secret.* ADJ: usu ADJ n [5] An amount that is expressed in **absolute** terms is expressed as a fixed amount rather than referring to variable factors such as what you earn or the effects of inflation. ❑ *In absolute terms British wages remain low by European standards.* ADJ: ADJ n ≠ *real* [6] **Absolute** rules and principles are believed to be true, right, or relevant in all situations. ❑ *There are no absolute rules.* ADJ: usu ADJ n ≠ *relative* [7] An **absolute** is a rule or principle that is believed to be true, right, or relevant in all situations. N-COUNT [8] ➔ See also **decree absolute**.

**ab|so|lute|ly** /æbsəluːtli/ ◆◆◇ [1] **Absolutely** means totally and completely. ❑ *Jill is absolutely right... I absolutely refuse to get married... There is absolutely no difference!* ADV [emphasis] [2] Some people say **absolutely** as an emphatic way of saying yes or of agreeing with someone. They say **absolutely not** as an emphatic way of saying no or of disagreeing with someone. ❑ *'It's worrying, isn't it?' — 'Absolutely.'* ADV: ADV as reply [emphasis]

**ab|so|lute ma|jor|ity** **(absolute majorities)** If a political party wins an **absolute majority**, they obtain more seats or votes than the total number of seats or votes gained by their opponents in an election. N-COUNT: usu sing

**ab|so|lute ze|ro** **Absolute zero** is a theoretical temperature that is thought to be the lowest possible temperature. N-UNCOUNT

**ab|so|lu|tion** /æbsəluːʃən/ If someone is given **absolution**, they are forgiven for something wrong that they have done. [FORMAL] ❑ *She felt as if his words had granted her absolution.* N-UNCOUNT = *forgiveness*

**ab|so|lut|ism** /æbsəluːtɪzəm/ [1] **Absolutism** is a political system in which one ruler or leader has complete power and authority over a country. ❑ *...royal absolutism.* N-UNCOUNT [2] You can refer to someone's beliefs as **absolutism** if they think that their beliefs are true, right, or relevant in all situations, especially if you think they are wrong to behave in this way. N-UNCOUNT [disapproval] ♦ **ab|so|lut|ist** ❑ *This absolutist belief is replaced by an appreciation that rules can vary.* ADJ

**ab|solve** /æbzɒlv/ **(absolves, absolving, absolved)** If a report or investigation **absolves** someone from blame or responsibility, it formally states that he or she is not guilty or is not to blame. ❑ *A police investigation yesterday absolved the police of all blame in the incident. ...the inquiry which absolved the soldiers.* VERB = *excuse* V n *of/from* n, V n

**ab|sorb** /əbzɔːʳb/ **(absorbs, absorbing, absorbed)** [1] If something **absorbs** a liquid, gas, or other substance, it soaks it up or takes it in. ❑ *Plants absorb carbon dioxide from the air and moisture from the soil... Refined sugars are absorbed into the bloodstream very quickly.* VERB = *soak up* V n, *be* V-ed *into* n [2] If something **absorbs** light, heat, or another form of energy, it takes it in. ❑ *A household radiator absorbs energy in the form of electric current and releases it in the form of heat.* VERB V n [3] If a group **is absorbed into** a larger group, it becomes part of the larger group. ❑ *The Colonial Office was absorbed into the Foreign Office. ...an economy capable of absorbing thousands of immigrants.* VERB *be* V-ed *into* n, V n [4] If something **absorbs** a force or shock, it reduces its effect. ❑ *...footwear which does not absorb the impact of the foot striking the ground.* VERB V n [5] If a system or society **absorbs** changes, effects, or costs, it is able to deal with them. ❑ *The banks would be forced to absorb large losses.* VERB V n [6] If something **absorbs** something valuable such as money, space, or time, it uses up a great deal of it. ❑ *It absorbed vast amounts of capital that could have been used for investment.* VERB = *consume* V n [7] If you **absorb** information, you learn and understand it. ❑ *Too often he only absorbs half the information given in the manual.* VERB = *digest, assimilate* V n [8] If something **absorbs** you, it interests you a great deal and takes up all your attention and energy. ❑ *...a second career which absorbed her more completely than her acting ever had.* VERB V n ➔ See also **absorbed**, **absorbing**.

**ab|sorbed** /əbzɔːʳbd/ If you are **absorbed in** something or someone, you are very interested in them and they take up all your attention and energy. ❑ *They were completely absorbed in each other.* ADJ: v-link ADJ, usu ADJ *in/by* n = *engrossed*

**ab|sor|bent** /əbzɔːʳbənt/ **Absorbent** material soaks up liquid easily. ❑ *The towels are highly absorbent.* ADJ

**ab|sorb|er** /əbzɔːʳbəʳ/ ➔ see **shock absorber**.

**ab|sorb|ing** /əbzɔːʳbɪŋ/ An **absorbing** task or activity interests you a great deal and takes up all your attention and energy. ❑ *'Two Sisters' is an absorbing read.* ADJ

**ab|sorp|tion** /əbzɔːʳpʃən/ [1] The **absorption of** a liquid, gas, or other substance is the process of it being soaked up or taken in. ❑ *Vitamin C increases the absorption of iron from food.* N-UNCOUNT: oft N *of* n [2] The **absorption** of a group **into** a larger group is the process of it becoming part of the larger group. N-UNCOUNT: usu with poss, oft N *into/by* n

**ab|stain** /æbsteɪn/ **(abstains, abstaining, abstained)** [1] If you **abstain from** something, usually something you want to do, you deliberately do not do it. [FORMAL] ❑ *Abstain from sex or use condoms... Do you drink alcohol, smoke, or abstain?* VERB V *from* n, V [2] If you **abstain** during a vote, you do not use your vote. ❑ *Three Conservative MPs abstained in the vote.* VERB V

**ab|ste|mi|ous** /æbstiːmiəs/ Someone who is **abstemious** avoids doing too much of something enjoyable such as eating or drinking. [FORMAL] ADJ

**ab|sten|tion** /æbstenʃən/ **(abstentions)** **Abstention** is a formal act of not voting either for or against a proposal. ❑ *...a vote of sixteen in favor, three against, and one abstention.* N-VAR

**ab|sti|nence** /æbstɪnəns/ **Abstinence** is the practice of abstaining from something such as alcoholic drink or sex, often for health or religious N-UNCOUNT = *abstention* reasons. ❑ *...six months of abstinence. ...total abstinence from alcohol.*

**ab|stract** /æbstrækt/ **(abstracts)** [1] An **abstract** idea or way of thinking is based on general ideas rather than on real things and events. ❑ *...abstract principles such as justice... It's not a question of some abstract concept.* ♦ **ab|stract|ly** *It is hard to think abstractly in these conditions.* [2] When you talk or think about something **in the abstract**, you talk or think about it in a general way, rather than considering particular things or events. ❑ *Money was a commodity she never thought about except in the abstract.* [3] In grammar, an **abstract** noun refers to a quality or idea rather than to a physical object. ❑ *...abstract words such as glory, honor, and courage.* [4] **Abstract** art makes use of shapes and patterns rather than showing people or things. ❑ *...a modern abstract painting.* [5] An **abstract** is an abstract work of art. [6] An **abstract of** an article, document, or speech is a short piece of writing that gives the main points of it.
ADJ = theoretical; ADV; PHRASE: PHR with cl/group; ADJ: ADJ n ≠ concrete; ADJ: usu ADJ n ≠ figurative; N-COUNT; N-COUNT: oft N *of* n = summary

**ab|stract|ed** /æbstræktɪd/ Someone who is **abstracted** is thinking so deeply that they are not fully aware of what is happening around them. [WRITTEN] ❑ *The same abstracted look was still on his face.* ♦ **ab|stract|ed|ly** *She nodded abstractedly.*
ADJ = preoccupied; ADV: ADV with v

**ab|strac|tion** /æbstrækʃᵊn/ **(abstractions)** An **abstraction** is a general idea rather than one relating to a particular object, person, or situation. [FORMAL] ❑ *Is it worth fighting a big war, in the name of an abstraction like sovereignty?*
N-VAR

**ab|struse** /æbstruːs/ You can describe something as **abstruse** if you find it difficult to understand, especially when you think it could be explained more simply. [FORMAL] ❑ *...fruitless discussions about abstruse resolutions.*
ADJ [disapproval]

**ab|surd** /æbsɜːʳd/ If you say that something is **absurd**, you are criticizing it because you think that it is ridiculous or that it does not make sense. ❑ *It is absurd to be discussing compulsory redundancy policies for teachers... I've known clients of mine go to absurd lengths, just to avoid paying me a few pounds.* ♦ **The absurd** is something that is absurd. [FORMAL] ❑ *Parkinson had a sharp eye for the absurd.* ♦ **ab|surd|ly** *Prices were still absurdly low, in his opinion.* ♦ **ab|surd|ity** /æbsɜːʳdɪti/ **(absurdities)** *I find myself growing increasingly angry at the absurdity of the situation.*
ADJ: oft *it* v-link ADJ to-inf/that [disapproval] = ridiculous; N-SING: *the* N; ADV; N-VAR

**ab|surd|ist** /æbsɜːʳdɪst/ An **absurdist** play or other work shows how absurd some aspect of society or human behaviour is.
ADJ: usu ADJ n

**abun|dance** /əbʌndəns/ An **abundance of** something is a large quantity of it. ❑ *The area has an abundance of wildlife... Food was in abundance.*
N-SING-COLL: usu N *of* n, also *in* N = wealth

**abun|dant** /əbʌndənt/ Something that is **abundant** is present in large quantities. ❑ *There is an abundant supply of cheap labour... Birds are abundant in the tall vegetation.*
ADJ = plentiful

**abun|dant|ly** /əbʌndəntli/ [1] If something is **abundantly** clear, it is extremely obvious. ❑ *He made it abundantly clear that anybody who disagrees with his policies will not last long.* [2] Something that occurs **abundantly** is present in large quantities. ❑ *...a plant that grows abundantly in the United States.*
ADV: ADV adj; ADV: usu ADV with v, also ADV adj

**abuse** **(abuses, abusing, abused)** ◆◆◇

> ✔ The noun is pronounced /əbjuːs/. The verb is pronounced /əbjuːz/.

[1] **Abuse** of someone is cruel and violent treatment of them. ❑ *...investigation of alleged child abuse. ...victims of sexual and physical abuse. ...controversy over human rights abuses.* [2] **Abuse** is extremely rude and insulting things that people say when they are angry. ❑ *I was left shouting abuse as the car sped off.* [3] **Abuse** of something is the use of it in a wrong way or for a bad purpose. ❑ *What went on here was an abuse of power. ...drug and alcohol abuse.* [4] If someone **is abused**, they are treated cruelly and violently. ❑ *Janet had been abused by her father since she was eleven. ...parents who feel they cannot cope or might abuse their children. ...those who work with abused children.* ♦ **abus|er** **(abusers)** *...a convicted child abuser.* [5] You can say that someone **is abused** if extremely rude and insulting things are said to them. ❑ *He alleged that he was verbally abused by other soldiers.* [6] If you **abuse** something, you use it in a wrong way or for a bad purpose. ❑ *He showed how the rich and powerful can abuse their position.* ♦ **abus|er** *...the treatment of alcohol and drug abusers.*
N-UNCOUNT: also N in pl, usu with supp; N-UNCOUNT; N-VAR: with supp; VERB: *be* V-ed, V n, V-ed; N-COUNT; VERB = insult: *be* V-ed, Also V n; VERB: V n; N-COUNT

**abu|sive** /əbjuːsɪv/ [1] Someone who is **abusive** behaves in a cruel and violent way towards other people. ❑ *He became violent and abusive toward Ben's mother... One in eight women lives in an abusive relationship.* [2] **Abusive** language is extremely rude and insulting.
ADJ; ADJ = insulting

**abut** /əbʌt/ **(abuts, abutting, abutted)** When land or a building **abuts** something or **abuts on** something, it is next to it. [FORMAL]
VERB = adjoin

**abuzz** /əbʌz/ If someone says that a place is **abuzz with** rumours or plans, they mean that everyone there is excited about them. [JOURNALISM]
ADJ: v-link ADJ, usu ADJ *with* n

**abys|mal** /əbɪzmᵊl/ If you describe a situation or the condition of something as **abysmal**, you think that it is very bad or poor in quality. ❑ *...our abysmal record at producing a scientifically trained workforce... The general standard of racing was abysmal.* ♦ **abys|mal|ly** *The standard of education was abysmally low... As the chart shows, it has failed abysmally.*
ADJ = dismal; ADV: ADV adj, ADV after v

**abyss** /əbɪs/ **(abysses)** [1] An **abyss** is a very deep hole in the ground. [LITERARY] [2] If someone is on the edge or brink of an **abyss**, they are about to enter into a very frightening or threatening situation. [LITERARY]
N-COUNT: usu sing; N-COUNT: usu sing

**AC** /eɪ siː/ **AC** is used to refer to an electric current that continually changes direction as it flows. **AC** is an abbreviation for 'alternating current'.
N-UNCOUNT: oft N n

**aca|cia** /əkeɪʃə/ **(acacias** or **acacia)** An **acacia** or an **acacia tree** is a tree which grows in warm countries and which usually has small yellow or white flowers.
N-COUNT

**aca|deme** /ækədiːm/ The academic world of universities is sometimes referred to as **academe**. [FORMAL]
N-UNCOUNT

**aca|demia** /ækədiːmiə/ **Academia** refers to all the academics in a particular country or region, the institutions they work in, and their work. ❑ *...the importance of strong links between industry and academia.*
N-UNCOUNT

**aca|dem|ic** /ækədemɪk/ **(academics)** ◆◇◇
[1] **Academic** is used to describe things that relate to the work done in schools, colleges, and universities, especially work which involves studying and reasoning rather than practical or technical skills. ❑ *Their academic standards are high... I was terrible at school and left with few academic qualifications.* ♦ **aca|dem|ical|ly** /ækədemɪkli/ *He is academically gifted.* [2] **Academic** is used to describe things that relate to schools, colleges, and universities. ❑ *...the start of the last academic year... I'd had enough of academic life.* [3] **Academic** is used to describe work, or a school, college, or university, that places emphasis on studying and reasoning rather than on practical or technical skills. ❑ *The author has settled for a more academic approach.* [4] Someone who is **academic** is good at studying. ❑ *The system is failing most disastrously among less academic children.* [5] An **academic** is a member of a university or college who teaches or does research. [6] You can say that a discussion or situation is **academic** if you think it is not important because it has no real effect or cannot happen. ❑ *Such is the size of the problem that these arguments are purely academic.*
ADJ: ADJ n; ADV; ADJ: ADJ n; ADJ; ADJ; N-COUNT = scholar; ADJ = theoretical

**acad|emi|cian** /əkædəmɪʃən, AM ækədə-/ **(academicians)** An **academician** is a member of an academy, usually one which has been formed to improve or maintain standards in a particular field. [N-COUNT]

**acad|emy** /əkædəmi/ **(academies)** 1 **Academy** is sometimes used in the names of schools and colleges, especially those specializing in particular subjects or skills, or private high schools in the United States. ❑ *...the Royal Academy of Music. ...her experience as a police academy instructor.* [N-COUNT: usu with supp, oft in names] 2 **Academy** appears in the names of some societies formed to improve or maintain standards in a particular field. ❑ *...the American Academy of Psychotherapists.* [N-IN-NAMES]

**ac|cede** /æksiːd/ **(accedes, acceding, acceded)** 1 If you **accede to** someone's request, you do what they ask. [FORMAL] ❑ *Britain would not accede to France's request.* [VERB] [V to n] 2 When a member of a royal family **accedes to** the throne, they become king or queen. [FORMAL] [VERB]

**ac|cel|er|ate** /ækseləreɪt/ **(accelerates, accelerating, accelerated)** 1 If the process or rate of something **accelerates** or if something **accelerates** it, it gets faster and faster. ❑ *Growth will accelerate to 2.9 per cent next year... The government is to accelerate its privatisation programme.* [VERB] [V] [V n] 2 When a moving vehicle **accelerates**, it goes faster and faster. ❑ *Suddenly the car accelerated... She accelerated away from the kerb.* [VERB] [V] [V prep/adv]

**ac|cel|era|tion** /ækseləreɪʃən/ 1 The **acceleration of** a process or change is the fact that it is getting faster and faster. ❑ *He has also called for an acceleration of political reforms.* [N-UNCOUNT: oft N *of/in* n] 2 **Acceleration** is the rate at which a car or other vehicle can increase its speed, often seen in terms of the time that it takes to reach a particular speed. ❑ *Acceleration to 60 mph takes a mere 5.7 seconds.* [N-UNCOUNT] 3 **Acceleration** is the rate at which the speed of an object increases. [TECHNICAL] [N-UNCOUNT]

**ac|cel|era|tor** /ækseləreɪtəʳ/ **(accelerators)** The **accelerator** in a car or other vehicle is the pedal which you press with your foot in order to make the vehicle go faster. ➔ See picture on page 1708. ❑ *He eased his foot off the accelerator.* [N-COUNT]

**ac|cent** /æksənt/ **(accents)** 1 Someone who speaks with a particular **accent** pronounces the words of a language in a distinctive way that shows which country, region, or social class they come from. ❑ *He had developed a slight American accent.* [N-COUNT] 2 An **accent** is a short line or other mark which is written above certain letters in some languages and which indicates the way those letters are pronounced. [N-COUNT] 3 If you put the **accent on** a particular feature of something, you emphasize it or give it special importance. ❑ *He is putting the accent on military readiness.* [N-SING: oft N *on* n = emphasis]

**ac|cent|ed** /æksentɪd/ Language or speech that is **accented** is spoken with a particular accent. ❑ *I spoke rather good, but heavily accented English.* ➔ See also **accent**. [ADJ]

**ac|cen|tu|ate** /æksentʃueɪt/ **(accentuates, accentuating, accentuated)** To **accentuate** something means to emphasize it or make it more noticeable. ❑ *His shaven head accentuates his large round face.* [VERB] [V n]

**ac|cept** /æksept/ **(accepts, accepting, accepted)** ◆◆◆ 1 If you **accept** something that you have been offered, you say yes to it or agree to take it. ❑ *Eventually Sam persuaded her to accept an offer of marriage... All those invited to next week's peace conference have accepted.* [VERB] [V n] [V] 2 If you **accept** an idea, statement, or fact, you believe that it is true or valid. ❑ *I do not accept that there is any kind of crisis in British science... I don't think they would accept that view... He did not accept this reply as valid. ...a workforce generally accepted to have the best conditions in Europe.* [VERB = acknowledge] [V that] [V n] [V n *as* adj/n] [V-ed] 3 If you **accept** a plan or an intended action, you agree to it and allow it to happen. ❑ *The Council will meet to decide if it should accept his resignation.* [VERB ≠ reject] [V n] 4 If you **accept** an unpleasant fact or situation, you get used to it or recognize that it is necessary or cannot be changed. ❑ *People will accept suffering that can be shown to lead to a greater good... Urban dwellers often accept noise as part of city life... I wasn't willing to accept that her leaving was a possibility.* [VERB] [V n] [V n *as* n/adj] [V that] 5 If a person, company, or organization **accepts** something such as a document, they recognize that it is genuine, correct, or satisfactory and agree to consider it or handle it. ❑ *We advised newspapers not to accept the advertising... Cheques can only be accepted up to the value guaranteed on the card.* [VERB ≠ reject] [V n] [V n] 6 If an organization or person **accepts** you, you are allowed to join the organization or use the services that are offered. ❑ *All-male groups will not be accepted. ...incentives to private landlords to accept young people as tenants.* [VERB ≠ reject] [V n] [V n *as* n] 7 If a person or a group of people **accepts** you, they begin to be friendly towards you and are happy with who you are or what you do. ❑ *My grandparents have never had a problem accepting me... Many men still have difficulty accepting a woman as a business partner... Stephen Smith was accepted into the family like an adopted brother.* [VERB ≠ reject] [V n] [V n *as* n] [V n *into* n] 8 If you **accept** the responsibility or blame for something, you recognize that you are responsible for it. ❑ *The company cannot accept responsibility for loss or damage.* [VERB ≠ deny] [V n] 9 If you **accept** someone's advice or suggestion, you agree to do what they say. ❑ *The army refused to accept orders from the political leadership.* [VERB ≠ reject] [V n] 10 If a machine **accepts** a particular kind of thing, it is designed to take it and deal with it or process it. ❑ *The telephone booths accept 10 and 20 pence coins.* [VERB] [V n] 11 ➔ See also **accepted**.

**ac|cept|able** /ækseptəbəl/ ◆◇◇ 1 **Acceptable** activities and situations are those that most people approve of or consider to be normal. ❑ *It is becoming more acceptable for women to drink alcohol... The air pollution exceeds most acceptable levels by 10 times or more.* [ADJ ≠ unacceptable] ♦ **ac|cept|abil|ity** /ækseptəbɪlɪti/ *...an increase in the social acceptability of divorce.* [N-UNCOUNT: usu N *of* n] ♦ **ac|cept|ably** /ækseptəbli/ *The aim of discipline is to teach children to behave acceptably.* [ADV] 2 If something is **acceptable to** someone, they agree to consider it, use it, or allow it to happen. ❑ *They have thrashed out a compromise formula acceptable to Moscow... They recently failed to negotiate a mutually acceptable new contract.* [ADJ: oft ADJ *to* n ≠ unacceptable] 3 If you describe something as **acceptable**, you mean that it is good enough or fairly good. ❑ *On the far side of the street was a restaurant that looked acceptable.* [ADJ] ♦ **ac|cept|ably** *...a method that provides an acceptably accurate solution to a problem.* [ADV: ADV adj, ADV with v]

**ac|cept|ance** /ækseptəns/ **(acceptances)** 1 **Acceptance of** an offer or a proposal is the act of saying yes to it or agreeing to it. ❑ *The Party is being degraded by its acceptance of secret donations. ...a letter of acceptance. ...his acceptance speech for the Nobel Peace Prize.* [N-VAR: usu with supp, oft poss N, N *of* n ≠ rejection] 2 If there is **acceptance** of an idea, most people believe or agree that it is true. ❑ *...a theory that is steadily gaining acceptance... There was a general acceptance that the defence budget would shrink.* [N-UNCOUNT] 3 Your **acceptance of** a situation, especially an unpleasant or difficult one, is an attitude or feeling that you cannot change it and that you must get used to it. ❑ *...his calm acceptance of whatever comes his way.* [N-UNCOUNT: usu N *of* n ≠ rejection] 4 **Acceptance** of someone into a group means beginning to think of them as part of the group and to act in a friendly way towards them. ❑ *...an effort to ensure that the disabled achieve real acceptance.* [N-UNCOUNT = recognition ≠ rejection]

**ac|cept|ed** /ækseptɪd/ ◆◆◇ **Accepted** ideas are agreed by most people to be correct or reasonable. ❑ *There is no generally accepted definition of life... It is accepted wisdom that science has been partly responsible for the decline of religion.* ➔ See also **accept**. [ADJ: oft adv ADJ]

**ac|cess** /ækses/ **(accesses, accessing, accessed)** ◆◇◇ 1 If you have **access to** a building or other place, you are able or allowed to go into it. ❑ *The facilities have been adapted to give access to* [N-UNCOUNT: usu N *to* n] *wheelchair users... Scientists have only recently been able to gain access to the area... The Mortimer Hotel offers easy access to central London.* [2] If you have **access to** something such as information or equipment, you have the opportunity or right to see it or use it. ❑ *...a Code of Practice that would give patients right of access to their medical records.* [3] If you have **access to** a person, you have the opportunity or right to see them or meet them. ❑ *He was not allowed access to a lawyer.* [4] If you **access** something, especially information held on a computer, you succeed in finding or obtaining it. ❑ *You've illegally accessed and misused confidential security files.* N-UNCOUNT: usu N *to* n / N-UNCOUNT: usu N *to* n / VERB / V n

**ac|cess course (access courses)** An **access course** is an educational course which prepares adults with few or no qualifications for study at a university or other place of higher education. [BRIT] N-COUNT

**ac|ces|sible** /æksesɪbᵊl/ [1] If a place or building is **accessible to** people, it is easy for them to reach it or get into it. If an object is **accessible**, it is easy to reach. ❑ *The Centre is easily accessible to the general public... The premises are wheelchair accessible.* ♦ **ac|ces|sibil|ity** /æksesɪbɪlɪti/ *...the easy accessibility of the area.* [2] If something is **accessible to** people, they can easily use it or obtain it. ❑ *The legal aid system should be accessible to more people.* ♦ **ac|ces|sibil|ity** *...the quality and accessibility of health care.* [3] If you describe a book, painting, or other work of art as **accessible**, you think it is good because it is simple enough for people to understand and appreciate easily. ❑ *...literary books that are accessible to a general audience.* ♦ **ac|ces|sibil|ity** *Seminar topics are chosen for their accessibility to a general audience.* ADJ: oft ADJ *to* n / N-UNCOUNT / ADJ: oft ADJ *to* n / N-UNCOUNT / ADJ: oft ADJ *to* n [approval] / N-UNCOUNT

**ac|ces|sion** /æksеʃᵊn/ **Accession** is the act of taking up a position as the ruler of a country. [FORMAL] ❑ *...the 50th anniversary of the Queen's accession to the throne.* N-UNCOUNT: with poss, oft N *to* n

**ac|ces|so|rize** /æksesəraɪz/ **(accessorizes, accessorizing, accessorized)**

> in BRIT, also use **accessorise**

To **accessorize** something such as a set of furniture or clothing means to add other things to it in order to make it look more attractive. ❑ *Use a belt to accessorise a plain dress.* VERB / V n / Also V n *with* n

**ac|ces|so|ry** /æksesəri/ **(accessories)** [1] **Accessories** are items of equipment that are not usually essential, but which can be used with or added to something else in order to make it more efficient, useful, or decorative. ❑ *...an exclusive range of hand-made bedroom and bathroom accessories.* [2] **Accessories** are articles such as belts and scarves which you wear or carry but which are not part of your main clothing. [3] If someone is guilty of being an **accessory to** a crime, they helped the person who committed it, or knew it was being committed but did not tell the police. [LEGAL] ❑ *She was charged with being an accessory to the embezzlement of funds.* N-COUNT: usu pl / N-COUNT: usu pl / N-COUNT: usu N *to* n = accomplice

**ac|cess road (access roads)** An **access road** is a road which enables traffic to reach a particular place or area. ❑ *...the access road to the airport.* N-COUNT

**ac|cess time (access times)** **Access time** is the time that is needed to get information that is stored in a computer. [COMPUTING] ❑ *This system helps speed up access times.* N-COUNT

**ac|ci|dent** /æksɪdənt/ **(accidents)** [1] An **accident** happens when a vehicle hits a person, an object, or another vehicle, causing injury or damage. ❑ *She was involved in a serious car accident last week... Six passengers were killed in the accident.* [2] If someone has an **accident**, something unpleasant happens to them that was not intended, sometimes causing injury or death. ❑ *5,000 people die every year because of accidents in the home... The police say the killing of the young man was an accident.* [3] If something happens **by accident**, it happens completely by chance. ❑ *She discovered the problem by accident.* ◆◇◇ N-COUNT / N-COUNT / N-VAR: usu *by* N = chance

**ac|ci|den|tal** /æksɪdentᵊl/ An **accidental** event happens by chance or as the result of an accident, and is not deliberately intended. ❑ *The jury returned a verdict of accidental death... His hand brushed against hers; it could have been either accidental or deliberate.* ♦ **ac|ci|den|tal|ly** /æksɪdentli/ *A policeman accidentally killed his two best friends with a single bullet... A special locking system means the door cannot be opened accidentally.* ADJ ≠ deliberate / ADV: ADV with v ≠ deliberately

**ac|ci|dent and emer|gen|cy** The **accident and emergency** is the room or department in a hospital where people who have severe injuries or sudden illness are taken for emergency treatment. The abbreviation **A & E** is also used. [BRIT] N-COUNT = A & E, casualty

> in AM, use **emergency room**

**ac|ci|dent prone** also **accident-prone.** If you describe someone or something as **accident prone**, you mean that a lot of accidents or other unpleasant things happen to them. ADJ

**ac|claim** /əkleɪm/ **(acclaims, acclaiming, acclaimed)** [1] If someone or something **is acclaimed**, they are praised enthusiastically. [FORMAL] ❑ *She has been acclaimed for the TV drama 'Prime Suspect'... He was acclaimed as England's greatest modern painter... The group's debut album was immediately acclaimed a hip hop classic.* ♦ **ac|claimed** *She has published six highly acclaimed novels.* [2] **Acclaim** is public praise for someone or something. [FORMAL] ❑ *Angela Bassett has won critical acclaim for her excellent performance.* VERB: usu passive / *be* V-ed *for* n/-ing / *be* V-ed *as* n / *be* V-ed n / ADJ / N-UNCOUNT: usu with supp, oft adj N = praise

**ac|cla|ma|tion** /ækləmeɪʃᵊn/ [1] **Acclamation** is a noisy or enthusiastic expression of approval for someone or something. [FORMAL] ❑ *The news was greeted with considerable popular acclamation.* [2] If someone is chosen or elected **by acclamation**, they are elected without a written vote. [FORMAL] ❑ *At first it looked like I was going to win by acclamation.* N-UNCOUNT = praise / N-UNCOUNT

**ac|cli|ma|tize** /əklaɪmətaɪz/ **(acclimatizes, acclimatizing, acclimatized)**

> in BRIT, also use **acclimatise**

When you **acclimatize** or **are acclimatized to** a new situation, place, or climate, you become used to it. [FORMAL] ❑ *The athletes are acclimatising to the heat by staying in Monte Carlo... This year he has left for St Louis early to acclimatise himself... They have been travelling for two days and will need some time to acclimatise.* ♦ **ac|cli|ma|ti|za|tion** /əklaɪmətaɪzeɪʃᵊn, AM -tɪz-/ *Acclimatization to higher altitudes may take several weeks.* ♦ **ac|cli|ma|tized** *It took her a while to get acclimatized to her new surroundings.* VERB / V *to* n / V pron-refl / V / N-UNCOUNT / ADJ: usu v-link ADJ, oft ADJ *to* n

**ac|co|lade** /ækəleɪd/ **(accolades)** If someone is given an **accolade**, something is done or said about them which shows how much people admire them. [FORMAL] ❑ *The Nobel prize has become the ultimate accolade in the sciences.* N-COUNT = tribute

**ac|com|mo|date** /əkɒmədeɪt/ **(accommodates, accommodating, accommodated)** [1] If a building or space can **accommodate** someone or something, it has enough room for them. ❑ *The school in Poldown was not big enough to accommodate all the children.* [2] To **accommodate** someone means to provide them with a place to live or stay. ❑ *...a hotel built to accommodate guests for the wedding of King Alfonso... Students are accommodated in homes nearby.* [3] If something is planned or changed to **accommodate** a particular situation, it is planned or changed so that it takes this situation into account. [FORMAL] ❑ *The roads are built to accommodate gradual temperature changes.* [4] If you do something to **accommodate** someone, you do it with the main purpose of pleasing or satisfying them. ❑ *He has never put an arm around his wife to accommodate photographers.* VERB: no cont / V n / VERB / V n / *be* V-ed prep/adv / VERB / V n / VERB = oblige / V n

**ac|com|mo|dat|ing** /əkɒmədeɪtɪŋ/ If you describe someone as **accommodating**, you like the fact that they are willing to do things in order to please you or help you. [ADJ] [approval] [= obliging]

**ac|com|mo|da|tion** /əkɒmədeɪʃᵊn/ **(accommodations)** [◆◇◇] 1 **Accommodation** is used to refer to buildings or rooms where people live or stay. [BRIT] ❑ *The government will provide temporary accommodation for up to three thousand people... Rates are higher for deluxe accommodations.* [N-UNCOUNT: also N in pl]

☑ in AM, use **accommodations**

2 **Accommodation** is space in buildings or vehicles that is available for certain things, people, or activities. [FORMAL] ❑ *The school occupies split-site accommodation on the main campus.* [N-UNCOUNT]

**ac|com|pa|ni|ment** /əkʌmpnɪmənt/ **(accompaniments)** 1 The **accompaniment** to a song or tune is the music that is played at the same time as it and forms a background to it. ❑ *He sang 'My Funny Valentine' to a piano accompaniment.* [N-COUNT: usu with supp] 2 An **accompaniment** is something which goes with another thing. ❑ *This recipe makes a good accompaniment to ice-cream.* [N-COUNT: usu with supp] ● If one thing happens **to the accompaniment of** another, they happen at the same time. ❑ *The team came out to the accompaniment of fireworks.* [PREP-PHRASE]

**ac|com|pa|nist** /əkʌmpənɪst/ **(accompanists)** An **accompanist** is a musician, especially a pianist, who plays one part of a piece of music while someone else sings or plays the main tune. [N-COUNT]

**ac|com|pa|ny** /əkʌmpəni/ **(accompanies, accompanying, accompanied)** [◆◇◇] 1 If you **accompany** someone, you go somewhere with them. [FORMAL] ❑ *Ken agreed to accompany me on a trip to Africa... The Prime Minister, accompanied by the governor, led the President up to the house.* [VERB] [V n] [V-ed] 2 If one thing **accompanies** another, it happens or exists at the same time, or as a result of it. [FORMAL] ❑ *This volume of essays was designed to accompany an exhibition in Cologne.* [VERB] [V n] 3 If you **accompany** a singer or a musician, you play one part of a piece of music while they sing or play the main tune. ❑ *He sang and Alice accompanied him on the piano.* [VERB] [V n]

**ac|com|pli** /ækɒmpliː/ → see **fait accompli**.

**ac|com|plice** /əkʌmplɪs, AM əkɒm-/ **(accomplices)** Someone's **accomplice** is a person who helps them to commit a crime. ❑ *The gunman escaped on a motorcycle being ridden by an accomplice.* [N-COUNT: oft poss N]

**ac|com|plish** /əkʌmplɪʃ, AM əkɒm-/ **(accomplishes, accomplishing, accomplished)** If you **accomplish** something, you succeed in doing it. ❑ *If we'd all work together, I think we could accomplish our goal... They are skeptical about how much will be accomplished by legislation.* [VERB] [= achieve] [V n] [V n]

**ac|com|plished** /əkʌmplɪʃt, AM əkɒm-/ If someone is **accomplished** at something, they are very good at it. [FORMAL] ❑ *She is an accomplished painter.* [ADJ]

**ac|com|plish|ment** /əkʌmplɪʃmənt, AM əkɒm-/ **(accomplishments)** 1 An **accomplishment** is something remarkable that has been done or achieved. ❑ *For a novelist, that's quite an accomplishment... By any standards, the accomplishments of the past year are extraordinary.* [N-COUNT] [= achievement] 2 Your **accomplishments** are the things that you can do well or the important things that you have done. [FORMAL] [N-COUNT: usu pl, oft poss N]

**ac|cord** /əkɔːʳd/ **(accords, according, accorded)** [◆◆◆] 1 An **accord** between countries or groups of people is a formal agreement, for example to end a war. ❑ *...a fitting way to celebrate the peace accord.* [N-COUNT: usu with supp, oft n N] 2 If you **are accorded** a particular kind of treatment, people act towards you or treat you in that way. [FORMAL] ❑ *His predecessor was accorded an equally tumultuous welcome... The government accorded him the rank of Colonel... The treatment accorded to a United Nations official was little short of insulting.* [VERB] [= grant] [*be* V-ed n] [V n n] [V-ed] [Also V n *to* n] 3 If one fact, idea, or condition **accords with** another, they are in agreement and there is no conflict between them. [FORMAL] ❑ *Such an approach accords with the principles of socialist ideology. ...scientific evidence that did not fully accord with the facts uncovered by the police.* [VERB] [= correspond] [V *with* n] [V *with* n] 4 → See also **according to**.

PHRASES 5 If one person, action, or fact is **in accord with** another, they are in agreement and there is no conflict between them. You can also say that two people or things are **in accord**. [FORMAL] ❑ *...this military action, taken in accord with United Nations resolutions.* [PHRASE: v-link PHR, PHR after v, oft PHR *with* n] 6 If something happens **of its own accord**, it seems to happen by itself, without anyone making it happen. ❑ *In many cases the disease will clear up of its own accord.* [PHRASE: PHR after v] 7 If you do something **of** your **own accord**, you do it because you want to, without being asked or forced. ❑ *He did not quit as France's prime minister of his own accord.* [PHRASE: PHR after v] [= voluntarily] 8 If a number of people do something **with one accord**, they do it together or at the same time, because they agree about what should be done. [LITERARY] ❑ *With one accord they turned and walked back over the grass.* [PHRASE]

**ac|cord|ance** /əkɔːʳdəns/ If something is done **in accordance with** a particular rule or system, it is done in the way that the rule or system says that it should be done. ❑ *Entries which are not in accordance with the rules will be disqualified.* [PREP-PHRASE]

**ac|cord|ing|ly** /əkɔːʳdɪŋli/ 1 You use **accordingly** to introduce a fact or situation which is a result or consequence of something that you have just referred to. ❑ *We have a different background, a different history. Accordingly, we have the right to different futures.* [ADV: usu ADV with cl, also ADV with v] [= therefore, consequently] 2 If you consider a situation and then act **accordingly**, the way you act depends on the nature of the situation. ❑ *It is a difficult job and they should be paid accordingly.* [ADV: ADV after v]

**ac|cord|ing to** [◆◆◆] 1 If someone says that something is true **according to** a particular person, book, or other source of information, they are indicating where they got their information. ❑ *Philip stayed at the hotel, according to Mr Hemming... He and his father, according to local gossip, haven't been in touch for years.* [PREP-PHRASE] 2 If something is done **according to** a particular set of principles, these principles are used as a basis for the way it is done. ❑ *They both played the game according to the rules.* [PREP-PHRASE] 3 If something varies **according to** a changing factor, it varies in a way that is determined by this factor. ❑ *Prices vary according to the quantity ordered.* [PREP-PHRASE] 4 If something happens **according to plan**, it happens in exactly the way that it was intended to happen. ❑ *If all goes according to plan, the first concert will be Tuesday evening.* [PHRASE: usu PHR after v]

**ac|cor|di|on** /əkɔːʳdiən/ **(accordions)** An **accordion** is a musical instrument in the shape of a fairly large box which you hold in your hands. You play the accordion by pressing keys or buttons on either side while moving the two sides together and apart. Accordions are used especially to play traditional popular music. [N-COUNT]

**ac|cost** /əkɒst, AM əkɔːst/ **(accosts, accosting, accosted)** If someone **accosts** another person, especially a stranger, they stop them or go up to them and speak to them in a way that seems rude or threatening. [FORMAL] ❑ *A man had accosted me in the street.* [VERB] [disapproval] [V n]

**ac|count** /əkaʊnt/ **(accounts, accounting, accounted)** [◆◆◆] 1 If you have an **account** with a bank or a similar organization, you have an arrangement to leave your money there and take some out when you need it. ❑ *Some banks make it difficult to open an account... I had two accounts with Natwest, a savings account and a current account.* [N-COUNT] 2 In business, a regular customer of a company can be referred to as an **account**, especially when the customer is another company. [BUSINESS] ❑ *Biggart Donald, the Glasgow-based marketing agency, has won two Edinburgh accounts.* [N-COUNT] 3 **Accounts** are detailed records of all the money that a person or business receives and spends. [BUSINESS] ❑ *He kept detailed accounts. ...an account book.* [N-COUNT: usu pl] 4 An [N-COUNT:]

**account** is a written or spoken report of something that has happened. ❑ *He gave a detailed account of what happened on the fateful night.* [5] → See also **accounting**, **bank account**, **current account**, **deposit account**, **joint**.
with supp, usu N *of* n = report

PHRASES [6] If you say that something is true **by all accounts** or **from all accounts**, you believe it is true because other people say so. ❑ *He is, by all accounts, a superb teacher.*
PHRASE: PHR with cl

[7] If you say that someone **gave a good account of** themselves in a particular situation, you mean that they performed well, although they may not have been completely successful. ❑ *The team fought hard and gave a good account of themselves.*
PHRASE: V inflects

[8] If you say that something is **of no account** or **of little account**, you mean that it is very unimportant and is not worth considering. [FORMAL] ❑ *These obscure groups were of little account in national politics.*
PHRASE: v-link PHR

[9] If you buy or pay for something **on account**, you pay nothing or only part of the cost at first, and pay the rest later. ❑ *He bought two bottles of vodka on account.*
PHRASE: PHR after v

[10] You use **on account of** to introduce the reason or explanation for something. ❑ *The President declined to deliver the speech himself, on account of a sore throat.*
PREP-PHRASE

[11] Your feelings **on** someone's **account** are the feelings you have about what they have experienced or might experience, especially when you imagine yourself to be in their situation. ❑ *Mollie told me what she'd done and I was really scared on her account.*
PHRASE: usu adj/n PHR

[12] If you tell someone not to do something **on** your **account**, you mean that they should do it only if they want to, and not because they think it will please you. [SPOKEN] ❑ *Don't leave on my account.*
PHRASE: PHR after v

[13] If you say that something should **on no account** be done, you are emphasizing that it should not be done under any circumstances. ❑ *On no account should the mixture boil.*
PHRASE [emphasis]

[14] If you do something **on** your **own account**, you do it because you want to and without being asked, and you take responsibility for your own action. ❑ *I told him if he withdrew it was on his own account.*
PHRASE: PHR after v

[15] If you **take** something **into account**, or **take account of** something, you consider it when you are thinking about a situation or deciding what to do. ❑ *The defendant asked for 21 similar offences to be taken into account... Urban planners in practice have to take account of many interest groups in society.*
PHRASE: V inflects = consider

[16] If someone **is called, held,** or **brought to account** for something they have done wrong, they are made to explain why they did it, and are often criticized or punished for it. ❑ *Ministers should be called to account for their actions.*
PHRASE: V inflects, oft PHR *for* n

♦ **account for** [1] If a particular thing **accounts for** a part or proportion of something, that part or proportion consists of that thing, or is used or produced by it. ❑ *Computers account for 5% of the country's commercial electricity consumption.*
PHRASAL VERB
V P n

[2] If something **accounts for** a particular fact or situation, it causes or explains it. ❑ *Now, the gene they discovered today doesn't account for all those cases.*
PHRASAL VERB = explain
V P n

[3] If you can **account for** something, you can explain it or give the necessary information about it. ❑ *How do you account for the company's alarmingly high staff turnover?... He said only 200 of the train's 600 passengers had been accounted for.*
PHRASAL VERB = explain
V P n
V P n

[4] If someone has to **account for** an action or policy, they are responsible for it, and may be required to explain it to other people or be punished if it fails. ❑ *The President and the President alone must account for his government's reforms.*
PHRASAL VERB = answer for
V P n

[5] If a sum of money **is accounted for** in a budget, it has been included in that budget for a particular purpose. ❑ *The really heavy redundancy costs have been accounted for.*
PHRASAL VERB = budget for
*be* V-ed P

**ac|count|able** /əkaʊntəbᵊl/ If you are **accountable to** someone **for** something that you do, you are responsible for it and must be prepared to justify your actions to that person. ❑ *Public officials can finally be held accountable for their actions.* ♦ **ac|count|abil|ity** /əkaʊntəbɪlɪti/ *...an impetus towards democracy and greater accountability.*
ADJ: usu v-link ADJ, oft ADJ *to/for* n
N-UNCOUNT

**ac|count|an|cy** /əkaʊntənsi/ **Accountancy** is the theory or practice of keeping financial accounts.
N-UNCOUNT

**ac|count|ant** /əkaʊntənt/ **(accountants)** An **accountant** is a person whose job is to keep financial accounts.
N-COUNT

**ac|count|ing** /əkaʊntɪŋ/ **Accounting** is the activity of keeping detailed records of the amounts of money a business or person receives and spends. ❑ *...the accounting firm of Leventhal & Horwath.* → See also **account**.
N-UNCOUNT

**ac|cou|tre|ment** /əkuːtrəmənt/ **(accoutrements)**

in AM, also use **accouterment**

**Accoutrements** are all the things you have with you when you travel or when you take part in a particular activity. [HUMOROUS or OLD-FASHIONED]
N-COUNT: usu pl, usu with supp, oft N *of* n

**ac|cred|it** /əkredɪt/ **(accredits, accrediting, accredited)** If an educational qualification or institution **is accredited**, it is officially declared to be of an approved standard. [FORMAL] ❑ *This degree programme is fully accredited by the Institution of Electrical Engineers. ...an accredited college of Brunel University.* ♦ **ac|credi|ta|tion** /əkredɪteɪʃᵊn/ *...the Council for the Accreditation of Teacher Education.*
VERB: usu passive = endorse
*be* V-ed
V-ed
N-UNCOUNT

**ac|cre|tion** /əkriːʃᵊn/ **(accretions)** [1] An **accretion** is an addition to something, usually one that has been added over a period of time. [FORMAL] ❑ *The script has been gathering editorial accretions for years.*
N-COUNT

[2] **Accretion** is the process of new layers or parts being added to something so that it increases in size. [FORMAL] ❑ *A coral reef is built by the accretion of tiny, identical organisms.*
N-UNCOUNT

**ac|cru|al** /əkruːəl/ **(accruals)** In finance, the **accrual** of something such as interest or investments is the adding together of interest or different investments over a period of time. [BUSINESS]
N-COUNT: usu sing, oft N n = accumulation

**ac|crue** /əkruː/ **(accrues, accruing, accrued)** [1] If money or interest **accrues** or if you **accrue** it, it gradually increases in amount over a period of time. [BUSINESS] ❑ *I owed £5,000 – part of this was accrued interest... If you do not pay within 28 days, interest will accrue... Officials say the options will offer investors a longer time in which to accrue profits.*
VERB = accumulate
V-ed
V
V n

[2] If things such as profits or benefits **accrue to** someone, they are added to over a period of time. [FORMAL] ❑ *...the expectation that profits will accrue. ...a project from which considerable benefit will accrue to the community.*
VERB
V
V *to* n

**ac|cu|mu|late** /əkjuːmjʊleɪt/ **(accumulates, accumulating, accumulated)** When you **accumulate** things or when they **accumulate**, they collect or are gathered over a period of time. ❑ *Households accumulate wealth across a broad spectrum of assets... Lead can accumulate in the body until toxic levels are reached.*
VERB = build up
V n
V

**ac|cu|mu|la|tion** /əkjuːmjʊleɪʃᵊn/ **(accumulations)** [1] An **accumulation of** something is a large number of things which have been collected together or acquired over a period of time. ❑ *...an accumulation of experience and knowledge.*
N-COUNT: oft N *of* n

[2] **Accumulation** is the collecting together of things over a period of time. ❑ *...the accumulation of capital and the distribution of income.*
N-UNCOUNT: oft N *of* n

**ac|cu|mu|la|tive** /əkjuːmjʊlətɪv, AM -leɪtɪv/ If something is **accumulative**, it becomes greater in amount, number, or intensity over a period of time. ❑ *The consensus is that risk factors have an accumulative effect.*
ADJ = cumulative

**ac|cu|ra|cy** /ækjʊrəsi/ [1] The **accuracy of** information or measurements is their quality of being true or correct, even in small details. ❑ *We cannot guarantee the accuracy of these figures.*
N-UNCOUNT: oft N *of* n ≠ inaccuracy

[2] If someone or something performs a task, for example hitting a target, **with accuracy**, they do it in an exact way without making a mistake.
N-UNCOUNT: oft *with* N ≠ inaccuracy

❑ *...weapons that could fire with accuracy at targets 3,000 yards away.*

**ac|cu|rate** /ækjʊrət/ ◆◇◇ [1] ADJ = *precise* ≠ *inaccurate* **Accurate** information, measurements, and statistics are correct to a very detailed level. An **accurate** instrument is able to give you information of this kind. ❑ *Police have stressed that this is the most accurate description of the killer to date... Quartz timepieces are very accurate, to a minute or two per year.* ♦ **ac|cu|rate|ly** ADV *The test can accurately predict what a bigger explosion would do.* [2] ADJ ≠ *inaccurate* An **accurate** statement or account gives a true or fair judgment of something. ❑ *Joseph Stalin gave an accurate assessment of the utility of nuclear weapons... They were accurate in their prediction that he would change her life drastically.* ♦ **ac|cu|rate|ly** ADV: ADV with v *What many people mean by the word 'power' could be more accurately described as 'control'.* [3] ADJ ≠ *inaccurate* You can use **accurate** to describe the results of someone's actions when they do or copy something correctly or exactly. ❑ *Marks were given for accurate spelling and punctuation.* [4] ADJ ≠ *inaccurate* An **accurate** weapon or throw reaches the exact point or target that it was intended to reach. You can also describe a person as **accurate** if they fire a weapon or throw something in this way. ❑ *The rifle was extremely accurate.* ♦ **ac|cu|rate|ly** ADV: ADV with v = *precisely* *...the technology to aim bombs accurately from aircraft.*

**ac|curs|ed** /əkɜ͟ːʳsɪd, əkɜ͟ːʳst/ [1] ADJ: ADJ n [feelings] = *damned* Some people use **accursed** to describe something which they are very annoyed about. [OLD-FASHIONED] [2] ADJ: v-link ADJ If a person is **accursed**, they have been cursed. [LITERARY]

**ac|cu|sa|tion** /ækjʊzeɪʃᵊn/ **(accusations)** [1] N-VAR: oft N that, N of n/-ing = *charge* If you make an **accusation** against someone, you criticize them or express the belief that they have done something wrong. ❑ *Kim rejects accusations that Country music is over-sentimental.* [2] N-COUNT: oft N of n, N that An **accusation** is a statement or claim by a witness or someone in authority that a particular person has committed a crime, although this has not yet been proved. ❑ *...people who have made public accusations of rape.*

**ac|cu|sa|tive** /əkju͟ːzətɪv/ N-SING: the N In the grammar of some languages, **the accusative**, or **the accusative case**, is the case used for a noun when it is the direct object of a verb, or the object of some prepositions. In English, only the pronouns 'me', 'him', 'her', 'us', and 'them' are in the accusative. Compare **nominative**.

**ac|cu|sa|tory** /əkju͟ːzətəri, AM -tɔːri/ ADJ = *accusing* An **accusatory** look, remark, or tone of voice suggests blame or criticism. [WRITTEN] ❑ *...the accusatory tone of the questions.*

**ac|cuse** /əkju͟ːz/ **(accuses, accusing, accused)** ◆◆◇ [1] VERB If you **accuse** someone **of** doing something wrong or dishonest, you say or tell them that you believe that they did it. ❑ *He was accusing my mum of having an affair with another man...* (V n of n/-ing) *Talk things through in stages. Do not accuse or apportion blame.* (V) [2] VERB If you **are accused of** a crime, a witness or someone in authority states or claims that you did it, and you may be formally charged with it and put on trial. ❑ *Her assistant was accused of theft and fraud by the police...* (be V-ed of n) *All seven charges accused him of lying in his testimony...* (V n of n) *The accused men have been given relatively light sentences.* (V-ed) [3] ➔ See also **accused**, **accusing**. [4] PHRASE: V inflects, PHR of n/-ing If someone **stands accused of** something, they have been accused of it. ❑ *The candidate stands accused of breaking promises even before he's in office.*

**ac|cused** /əkju͟ːzd/ **(accused)** N-COUNT: the N = *defendant* You can use **the accused** to refer to a person or a group of people charged with a crime or on trial for it. [LEGAL] ❑ *The accused is alleged to be a member of a right-wing gang.*

**ac|cus|er** /əkju͟ːzəʳ/ **(accusers)** N-COUNT: usu poss N An **accuser** is a person who says that another person has done something wrong, especially that he or she has committed a crime. ❑ *...a criminal proceeding where defendants have the right to confront their accusers.*

**ac|cus|ing** /əkju͟ːzɪŋ/ ADJ If you look at someone with an **accusing** expression or speak to them in an **accusing** tone of voice, you are showing that you think they have done something wrong. ❑ *The accusing look in her eyes conveyed her sense of betrayal.* ♦ **ac|cus|ing|ly** ADV: ADV after v *'Where have you been?' he asked Blake accusingly.* ➔ See also **accuse**.

**ac|cus|tom** /əkʌ͟stəm/ **(accustoms, accustoming, accustomed)** VERB = *familiarize* If you **accustom yourself** or another person **to** something, you make yourself or them become used to it. [FORMAL] ❑ *The team has accustomed itself to the pace of first division rugby...* (V pron-refl to n) *Shakespeare has accustomed us to a mixture of humor and tragedy in the same play.* (V n to n) ➔ See also **accustomed**.

**ac|cus|tomed** /əkʌ͟stəmd/ [1] ADJ: v-link ADJ to n/-ing = *used* If you are **accustomed to** something, you know it so well or have experienced it so often that it seems natural, unsurprising, or easy to deal with. ❑ *I was accustomed to being the only child at a table full of adults.* [2] ADJ: v-link ADJ to n When your eyes become **accustomed to** darkness or bright light, they adjust so that you start to be able to see things, after not being able to see properly at first. ❑ *My eyes were becoming accustomed to the gloom.* [3] ADJ: poss ADJ n = *usual, habitual* You can use **accustomed** to describe an action that someone usually does, a quality that they usually show, or an object that they usually use. ❑ *He took up his accustomed position with his back to the fire... Freed acted with his accustomed shrewdness. ...his accustomed glass of whisky.*

**ace** /eɪs/ **(aces)** [1] N-COUNT: oft N of n An **ace** is a playing card with a single symbol on it. In most card games, the ace of a particular suit has either the highest or the lowest value of the cards in that suit. ❑ *...the ace of hearts.* [2] N-COUNT: usu with supp, oft n N If you describe someone such as a sports player as an **ace**, you mean that they are very good at what they do. [JOURNALISM] ❑ *...former motor-racing ace Stirling Moss.* ♦ **Ace** ADJ: ADJ n is also an adjective. ❑ *...ace horror-film producer Lawrence Woolsey.* [3] ADJ [approval] If you say that something is **ace**, you think that it is good and you like it a lot. [INFORMAL] ❑ *...a really ace film.* [4] N-COUNT In tennis, an **ace** is a serve which is so fast that the other player cannot reach the ball. [5] PHRASE: V inflects If you say that someone **holds all the aces**, you mean that they have all the advantages in a contest or situation.

**acer|bic** /əsɜ͟ːʳbɪk/ ADJ = *acid* **Acerbic** humour is critical and direct. [FORMAL] ❑ *He was acclaimed for his acerbic wit and repartee.*

**acer|bity** /əsɜ͟ːʳbɪti/ N-UNCOUNT **Acerbity** is a kind of bitter, critical humour. [FORMAL]

**ac|etate** /æ͟sɪteɪt/ N-UNCOUNT **Acetate** is a shiny artificial material, sometimes used for making clothes or records.

**acetic acid** /əsi͟ːtɪk æ͟sɪd/ N-UNCOUNT **Acetic acid** is a colourless acid. It is the main substance in vinegar.

**ac|etone** /æ͟sɪtoʊn/ N-UNCOUNT **Acetone** is a type of solvent.

**acety|lene** /əse͟tɪliːn/ N-UNCOUNT: oft N n **Acetylene** is a colourless gas which burns with a very hot bright flame. It is often used in lamps and for cutting and welding metal.

**ache** /e͟ɪk/ **(aches, aching, ached)** [1] VERB If you **ache** or a part of your body **aches**, you feel a steady, fairly strong pain. ❑ *Her head was throbbing and she ached all over...* (V adv/prep) *My leg still aches when I sit down...* (V) *The weary walkers soothed their aching feet in the sea.* (V-ing) [2] N-COUNT: usu with supp, oft N in n, n N An **ache** is a steady, fairly strong pain in a part of your body. ❑ *Poor posture can cause neck ache, headaches and breathing problems.* ➔ See also **backache**, **headache**, **heartache**, **stomach ache**. [3] VERB = *long, yearn* If you **ache for** something or your heart **aches**, you want something very much, and feel very unhappy because you cannot have it. [WRITTEN] ❑ *She still ached for the lost intimacy and sexual contact of marriage...* (V for n) *It was quite an achievement to keep smiling when his heart must have been aching.* (V) [4] PHRASE You can use **aches and pains** to refer in a general way to any minor pains that you feel in your body. ❑ *It seems to ease all the aches and pains of a hectic and tiring day.*

**achiev|able** /ətʃiːvəbəl/ If you say that something you are trying to do is **achievable**, you mean that it is possible for you to succeed in doing it. ❑ *A 50% market share is achievable... It is often a good idea to start with smaller, easily achievable goals.* — ADJ = attainable

**achieve** /ətʃiːv/ **(achieves, achieving, achieved)** If you **achieve** a particular aim or effect, you succeed in doing it or causing it to happen, usually after a lot of effort. ❑ *There are many who will work hard to achieve these goals... We have achieved what we set out to do.* — ◆◆◇ VERB = accomplish; V n; V n

**achieve|ment** /ətʃiːvmənt/ **(achievements)** ◆◇◇ 1 An **achievement** is something which someone has succeeded in doing, especially after a lot of effort. ❑ *Reaching this agreement so quickly was a great achievement.* — N-COUNT = accomplishment. 2 **Achievement** is the process of achieving something. ❑ *Only the achievement of these goals will bring lasting peace.* — N-UNCOUNT: oft N *of* n

**achiev|er** /ətʃiːvəʳ/ **(achievers)** A high **achiever** is someone who is successful in their studies or their work, usually as a result of their efforts. A low **achiever** is someone who achieves less than those around them. ❑ *High achievers will receive cash bonuses.* — N-COUNT

**Achilles heel** /əkɪliːz hiːl/ Someone's **Achilles heel** is the weakest point in their character or nature, where it is easiest for other people to attack or criticize them. ❑ *Horton's Achilles heel was that he could not delegate.* — N-SING: usu poss N

**Achilles ten|don** /əkɪliːz tendən/ **(Achilles tendons)** Your **Achilles tendon** or your **Achilles** is the tendon inside the back of your leg just above your heel. — N-COUNT

**ach|ing|ly** /eɪkɪŋli/ You can use **achingly** for emphasis when you are referring to things that create feelings of wanting something very much, but of not being able to have it. [WRITTEN] ❑ *...three achingly beautiful ballads.* — ADV: ADV adj/adv [emphasis]

**achy** /eɪki/ If you feel **achy**, your body hurts. [INFORMAL, SPOKEN] ❑ *I feel achy all over.* — ADJ: usu v-link ADJ

**acid** /æsɪd/ **(acids)** ◆◇◇ 1 An **acid** is a chemical substance, usually a liquid, which contains hydrogen and can react with other substances to form salts. Some acids burn or dissolve other substances that they come into contact with. ❑ *...citric acid.* — N-MASS. 2 An **acid** substance contains acid. ❑ *These shrubs must have an acid, lime-free soil.* — ADJ ♦ **acid|ity** /æsɪdɪti/ *...the acidity of rainwater.* — N-UNCOUNT: oft N *of* n. 3 The drug **LSD** is sometimes referred to as **acid**. [INFORMAL] — N-UNCOUNT. 4 → See also **amino acid**, **hydrochloric acid**, **nitric acid**, **nucleic acid**, **sulphuric acid**.

**acid house** **Acid house** is a type of electronic dance music with a strong, repeated rhythm. — N-UNCOUNT

**acid|ic** /əsɪdɪk/ **Acidic** substances contain acid. ❑ *Dissolved carbon dioxide makes the water more acidic.* — ADJ

**acid rain** **Acid rain** is rain polluted by acid that has been released into the atmosphere from factories and other industrial processes. Acid rain is harmful to the environment. — N-UNCOUNT

**acid test** **The acid test** of something is an important aspect or result that it might have, which allows you to decide whether it is true or successful. ❑ *The acid test of a school is 'would you send your own children there?'* — N-SING: *the* N

**ac|knowl|edge** /æknɒlɪdʒ/ **(acknowledges, acknowledging, acknowledged)** ◆◇◇ 1 If you **acknowledge** a fact or a situation, you accept or admit that it is true or that it exists. [FORMAL] ❑ *Naylor acknowledged, in a letter to the judge, that he was a drug addict... Belatedly, the government has acknowledged the problem... There is an acknowledged risk of lung cancer from radon.* — VERB = recognize; V that; V n; V-ed. 2 If someone's achievements, status, or qualities **are acknowledged**, they are known about and recognized by a lot of people, or by a particular group of people. ❑ *He is also acknowledged as an excellent goalkeeper... Some of the clergy refused to acknowledge the new king's legitimacy.* — VERB = recognize; *be* V-ed *as* n; V n. 3 If you **acknowledge** a message or letter, you write to the person who sent it in order to say that you have received it. ❑ *The army sent me a postcard acknowledging my request.* — VERB; V n. 4 If you **acknowledge** someone, for example by moving your head or smiling, you show that you have seen and recognized them. ❑ *He saw her but refused to even acknowledge her.* — VERB; V n

**ac|knowl|edge|ment** /æknɒlɪdʒmənt/ **(acknowledgements)** also **acknowledgment.** 1 An **acknowledgement** is a statement or action which recognizes that something exists or is true. ❑ *The President's resignation appears to be an acknowledgment that he has lost all hope of keeping the country together.* — N-SING: also no det, usu with supp, oft N that, N *of* n = recognition. 2 The **acknowledgements** in a book are the section in which the author thanks all the people who have helped him or her. — N-PLURAL. 3 A gesture of **acknowledgement**, such as a smile, shows someone that you have seen and recognized them. ❑ *Farling smiled in acknowledgement and gave a bow.* — N-UNCOUNT: also *a* N. 4 An **acknowledgement** is a letter or message that you receive from someone, telling you that something you have sent to them has arrived. ❑ *I have received neither an acknowledgment nor a reply.* — N-COUNT

**acme** /ækmi/ **The acme of** something is its highest point of achievement or excellence. [FORMAL] ❑ *His work is considered the acme of cinematic art.* — N-SING: usu *the* N *of* n = pinnacle

**acne** /ækni/ If someone has **acne**, they have a skin condition which causes a lot of spots on their face and neck. — N-UNCOUNT

**aco|lyte** /ækəlaɪt/ **(acolytes)** An **acolyte** is a follower or assistant of an important person. [FORMAL] ❑ *To his acolytes, he is known simply as 'the Boss'.* — N-COUNT

**acorn** /eɪkɔːʳn/ **(acorns)** An **acorn** is a pale oval nut that is the fruit of an oak tree. — N-COUNT

**acous|tic** /əkuːstɪk/ **(acoustics)** 1 An **acoustic** guitar or other instrument is one whose sound is produced without any electrical equipment. ♦ **acous|ti|cal|ly** /əkuːstɪkli/ ❑ *...acoustically based music.* — ADJ: ADJ n; ADV: oft ADV with cl. 2 If you refer to the **acoustics** or the **acoustic** of a space, you are referring to the structural features which determine how well you can hear music or speech in it. ♦ **acous|ti|cal|ly** ❑ *The church is acoustically perfect.* — N-COUNT; ADV: ADV adj. 3 **Acoustics** is the scientific study of sound. — N-UNCOUNT. 4 **Acoustic** means relating to sound or hearing. Compare **aural**. ❑ *...acoustic signals.* — ADJ: ADJ n

**ac|quaint** /əkweɪnt/ **(acquaints, acquainting, acquainted)** If you **acquaint** someone **with** something, you tell them about it so that they know it. If you **acquaint yourself with** something, you learn about it. [FORMAL] ❑ *...efforts to acquaint the public with their rights under the new law... I want to acquaint myself with your strengths and weaknesses.* → See also **acquainted**. — VERB = familiarize; V n *with* n; V pron-refl *with* n

**ac|quaint|ance** /əkweɪntəns/ **(acquaintances)** 1 An **acquaintance** is someone who you have met and know slightly, but not well. ❑ *The proprietor was an old acquaintance of his.* — N-COUNT: oft with poss. 2 If you have an **acquaintance with** someone, you have met them and you know them. ❑ *...a writer who becomes involved in a real murder mystery through his acquaintance with a police officer.* — N-VAR: oft poss N, N *with* n, *on* N. 3 Your **acquaintance with** a subject is your knowledge or experience of it. [FORMAL] ❑ *They had little or no acquaintance with philosophy or history.* — N-UNCOUNT: usu with supp, oft N *with* n. 4 When you **make** someone's **acquaintance**, you meet them for the first time and get to know them a little. [FORMAL] ❑ *I first made his acquaintance in the early 1960s.* — PHRASE: V inflects

**ac|quaint|ed** /əkweɪntɪd/ 1 If you are **acquainted with** something, you know about it because you have learned it or experienced it. [FORMAL] ❑ *He was well acquainted with the literature of France, Germany and Holland.* — ADJ: v-link ADJ *with* n = familiar. 2 If you are **ac-** — ADJ:

**quainted with** someone, you have met them and you know them. You can also say that two people are **acquainted**. [FORMAL] ❑ *No-one personally acquainted with the couple was permitted to talk to the Press... It's true we were acquainted, but no more than that.* [3] If you get or become **acquainted with** someone that you do not know, you talk to each other or do something together so that you get to know each other. You can also say that two people get or become **acquainted**. ❑ *The meetings were a way to get acquainted with each other.* [4] → See also **acquaint**.

v-link ADJ, usu ADJ *with* n
ADJ: v-link ADJ, oft ADJ *with* n

**ac|qui|esce** /ækwies/ **(acquiesces, acquiescing, acquiesced)** If you **acquiesce in** something, you agree to do what someone wants or to accept what they do. [FORMAL] ❑ *Steve seemed to acquiesce in the decision... When her mother suggested that she stay, Alice willingly acquiesced.*

VERB = submit
V *in/to* n
V

**ac|qui|es|cence** /ækwiesᵊns/ **Acquiescence** is agreement to do what someone wants, or acceptance of what they do even though you do not agree with it. [FORMAL] ❑ *Deirdre smiled her acquiescence.*

N-UNCOUNT: with supp, oft N *in/to* n

**ac|qui|es|cent** /ækwiesᵊnt/ Someone who is **acquiescent** is ready to agree to do what someone wants, or to accept what they do. [FORMAL] ❑ *Perhaps you are too acquiescent.*

ADJ

**ac|quire** /əkwaɪəʳ/ **(acquires, acquiring, acquired)** [1] If you **acquire** something, you buy or obtain it for yourself, or someone gives it to you. [FORMAL] ❑ *General Motors acquired a 50% stake in Saab for about $400m... I recently acquired some wood from a holly tree.* [2] If you **acquire** something such as a skill or a habit, you learn it, or develop it through your daily life or experience. ❑ *I've never acquired a taste for wine.* [3] If someone or something **acquires** a certain reputation, they start to have that reputation. ❑ *He has acquired a reputation as this country's premier solo violinist.* [4] If you describe something as an **acquired taste**, you mean that a lot of people do not like it when they first experience it, but often start to like it more when they get to know it better. ❑ *Broad beans are very much an acquired taste.*

◆◇◇
VERB
V n
V n *from* n
VERB
V n
VERB
V n
PHRASE: usu v-link PHR

**ac|quired im|mune de|fi|cien|cy syn|drome** **Acquired immune deficiency syndrome** is the same as **AIDS**.

N-UNCOUNT

**ac|quir|er** /əkwaɪərəʳ/ **(acquirers)** In business, an **acquirer** is a company or person who buys another company. [BUSINESS]

N-COUNT

**ac|qui|si|tion** /ækwɪzɪʃᵊn/ **(acquisitions)** [1] If a company or business person makes an **acquisition**, they buy another company or part of a company. [BUSINESS] ❑ *...the acquisition of a profitable paper recycling company.* [2] If you make an **acquisition**, you buy or obtain something, often to add to things that you already have. ❑ *...the President's recent acquisition of a helicopter.* [3] The **acquisition** of a skill or a particular type of knowledge is the process of learning it or developing it. ❑ *...language acquisition.*

◆◇◇
N-VAR: oft N *of* n
N-COUNT: oft N *of* n = purchase
N-UNCOUNT: n N, N *of* n

**ac|quisi|tive** /əkwɪzɪtɪv/ If you describe a person or an organization as **acquisitive**, you do not approve of them because you think they are too concerned with getting new possessions. ❑ *We live in an acquisitive society.*

ADJ: usu ADJ n [disapproval]

**ac|quit** /əkwɪt/ **(acquits, acquitting, acquitted)** [1] If someone **is acquitted of** a crime in a court of law, they are formally declared not to have committed the crime. ❑ *Mr Ling was acquitted of disorderly behaviour by magistrates.* [2] If you **acquit yourself** well or admirably in a particular situation, other people feel that you have behaved well or admirably. [FORMAL] ❑ *Most officers and men acquitted themselves well throughout the action.*

VERB: usu passive = clear ≠ convict
*be* V-ed *of* n
VERB
V pron-refl adv

**ac|quit|tal** /əkwɪtᵊl/ **(acquittals)** **Acquittal** is a formal declaration in a court of law that someone who has been accused of a crime is innocent. ❑ *...the acquittal of six police officers charged with beating a suspect... The jury voted 8-to-4 in favor of acquittal.*

N-VAR ≠ conviction

**acre** /eɪkəʳ/ **(acres)** An **acre** is an area of land measuring 4840 square yards or 4047 square metres. ❑ *The property is set in two acres of land.*

◆◇◇
N-COUNT

**acre|age** /eɪkərɪdʒ/ **(acreages)** **Acreage** is a large area of farm land. [FORMAL] ❑ *He has sown coffee on part of his acreage... Enormous acreages of soya beans are grown in the United States.*

N-VAR

**ac|rid** /ækrɪd/ An **acrid** smell or taste is strong and sharp, and usually unpleasant. ❑ *The room filled with the acrid smell of tobacco.*

ADJ: usu ADJ n = bitter

**ac|ri|mo|ni|ous** /ækrɪmoʊniəs/ **Acrimonious** words or quarrels are bitter and angry. [FORMAL] ❑ *There followed an acrimonious debate.* ♦ **ac|ri|mo|ni|ous|ly** *Our relationship ended acrimoniously.*

ADJ: usu ADJ n = bitter
ADV: ADV with v

**ac|ri|mo|ny** /ækrɪməni, AM -moʊni/ **Acrimony** is bitter and angry words or quarrels. [FORMAL] ❑ *The council's first meeting ended in acrimony.*

N-UNCOUNT

**ac|ro|bat** /ækrəbæt/ **(acrobats)** An **acrobat** is an entertainer who performs difficult physical acts such as jumping and balancing, especially in a circus.

N-COUNT

**ac|ro|bat|ic** /ækrəbætɪk/ An **acrobatic** movement or display involves difficult physical acts such as jumping and balancing, especially in a circus.

ADJ: usu ADJ n

**ac|ro|bat|ics** /ækrəbætɪks/ **Acrobatics** are acrobatic movements.

N-PLURAL

**ac|ro|nym** /ækrənɪm/ **(acronyms)** An **acronym** is a word composed of the first letters of the words in a phrase, especially when this is used as a name. An example of an acronym is NATO which is made up of the first letters of the 'North Atlantic Treaty Organization'.

N-COUNT

**across** /əkrɒs, AM əkrɔːs/ ◆◆◆

> In addition to the uses shown below, **across** is used in phrasal verbs such as 'come across', 'get across', and 'put across'.

[1] If someone or something goes **across** a place or a boundary, they go from one side of it to the other. ❑ *She walked across the floor and lay down on the bed... He watched Karl run across the street to Tommy. ...an expedition across Africa.* ♦ **Across** is also an adverb. ❑ *Richard stood up and walked across to the window.* [2] If something is situated or stretched **across** something else, it is situated or stretched from one side of it to the other. ❑ *...the floating bridge across Lake Washington in Seattle... He scrawled his name across the bill.* ♦ **Across** is also an adverb. ❑ *Trim toenails straight across using nail clippers.* [3] If something is lying **across** an object or place, it is resting on it and partly covering it. ❑ *She found her clothes lying across the chair... The wind pushed his hair across his face.* [4] Something that is **across** something such as a street, river, or area is on the other side of it. ❑ *Anyone from the houses across the road could see him... When I saw you across the room I knew I'd met you before.* ♦ **Across** is also an adverb. ❑ *They parked across from the Castro Theatre.* [5] If you look **across** at a place, person, or thing, you look towards them. ❑ *He glanced across at his sleeping wife. ...breathtaking views across to the hills.* [6] You use **across** to say that a particular expression is shown on someone's face. ❑ *An enormous grin spread across his face.* [7] If someone hits you **across** the face or head, they hit you on that part. ❑ *Graham hit him across the face with the gun.* [8] When something happens **across** a place or organization, it happens equally everywhere within it. ❑ *The film 'Hook' opens across America on December 11.* [9] When something happens **across** a political, religious, or social barrier, it involves people in different groups. ❑ *...parties competing across the political spectrum.* **across the board** → see **board**. [10] **Across** is used in measurements to

PREP
ADV: ADV after v
PREP
ADV: ADV after v
PREP = over
PREP
ADV: ADV after v
ADV: ADV after v, oft ADV prep
PREP = over
PREP
PREP
PREP
ADV:

show the width of something. ❑ *This hand-decorated plate measures 30cm across.* — amount ADV

**acryl|ic** /ækrɪlɪk/ — N-UNCOUNT: usu N n — **Acrylic** material is artificial and is manufactured by a chemical process.

**act** /ækt/ **(acts, acting, acted)** ◆◆◆

**1** VERB — When you **act**, you do something for a particular purpose. ❑ *The deaths occurred when police acted to stop widespread looting and vandalism... I do not doubt that the bank acted properly.* (V; V adv/prep)

**2** VERB — If you **act on** advice or information, you do what has been advised or suggested. ❑ *A patient will usually listen to the doctor's advice and act on it.* (V on/upon n)

**3** VERB = behave — If someone **acts** in a particular way, they behave in that way. ❑ *...a gang of youths who were acting suspiciously... He acted as if he hadn't heard any of it... Open wounds act like a magnet to flies.* (V adv; V as if; V like n)

**4** VERB — If someone or something **acts as** a particular thing, they have that role or function. ❑ *He acted both as the ship's surgeon and as chaplain for the men.* (V as/like n)

**5** VERB — If someone **acts** in a particular way, they pretend to be something that they are not. ❑ *Chris acted astonished as he examined the note... Kenworthy had tried not to act the policeman.* (V adj; V n)

**6** VERB — When professionals such as lawyers **act for** you, or **act on** your **behalf**, they are employed by you to deal with a particular matter. ❑ *...the law firm that acted for Diana during her marriage split... Because we travelled so much, Sam and I asked a broker to act on our behalf.* (V for n; V prep)

**7** VERB — If a force or substance **acts on** someone or something, it has a certain effect on them. ❑ *He's taking a dangerous drug: it acts very fast on the central nervous system.* (V on/upon n)

**8** VERB — If you **act**, or **act** a part in a play or film, you have a part in it. ❑ *She confessed to her parents her desire to act... She acted in her first film when she was 13 years old.* (V; V in n)

**9** N-COUNT: oft N of n — An **act** is a single thing that someone does. [FORMAL] ❑ *Language interpretation is the whole point of the act of reading.*

**10** N-SING = pretence — If you say that someone's behaviour is an **act**, you mean that it does not express their real feelings. ❑ *His anger was real. It wasn't an act.*

**11** N-COUNT — An **Act** is a law passed by the government. ❑ *...an Act of Parliament.*

**12** N-COUNT: oft N num — An **act** in a play, opera, or ballet is one of the main parts into which it is divided. ❑ *Act II contained one of the funniest scenes I have ever witnessed.*

**13** N-COUNT — An **act** in a show is a short performance which is one of several in the show. ❑ *This year numerous bands are playing, as well as comedy acts.*

**PHRASES**

**14** PHRASE: V inflects — If you **catch** someone **in the act**, you discover them doing something wrong or committing a crime. ❑ *The men were caught in the act of digging up buried explosives.*

**15** PHRASE: V inflects — If someone who has been behaving badly **cleans up** their **act**, they start to behave in a more acceptable or responsible way. [INFORMAL] ❑ *The nation's advertisers need to clean up their act.*

**16** PHRASE: V inflects — If you **get in on the act**, you take part in or take advantage of something that was started by someone else. [INFORMAL] ❑ *In the 1970s Kodak, anxious to get in on the act, launched its own instant camera.*

**17** PHRASE: v-link PHR -ing — You say that someone was **in the act of** doing something to indicate what they were doing when they were seen or interrupted. ❑ *Ken was in the act of paying his bill when Neil came up behind him.*

**18** PHRASE: V inflects — If you **get** your **act together**, you organize your life or your affairs so that you are able to achieve what you want or to deal with something effectively. [INFORMAL] ❑ *The Government should get its act together.*

**19** to **act** one's **age** → see **age**. to **act the fool** → see **fool**.

♦ **act out** PHRASAL VERB — If you **act out** an event which has happened, you copy the actions which took place and make them into a play. ❑ *I used to come home and act out the movie for the kids.* (V P n (not pron); Also V n P)

♦ **act up**

**1** PHRASAL VERB: usu cont = play up — If something **is acting up**, it is not working properly. [INFORMAL] ❑ *She was messing with the coffee pot, which was acting up again.* (V P)

**2** PHRASAL VERB: usu cont = play up — If a child **is acting up**, they are behaving badly. [INFORMAL]

**act|ing** /æktɪŋ/

**1** N-UNCOUNT — **Acting** is the activity or profession of performing in plays or films. ❑ *She pursued an acting career after four years of modelling.*

**2** ADJ: ADJ n — You use **acting** before the title of a job to indicate that someone is doing that job temporarily. ❑ *...the new acting President.*

**ac|tion** /ækʃən/ **(actions, actioning, actioned)** ◆◆◆

**1** N-UNCOUNT: usu with supp — **Action** is doing something for a particular purpose. ❑ *The government is taking emergency action to deal with a housing crisis.*

**2** N-COUNT — An **action** is something that you do on a particular occasion. ❑ *Jack was the sort of man who did not like his actions questioned.*

**3** N-COUNT = suit, case — To bring a legal **action** against someone means to bring a case against them in a court of law. [LEGAL] ❑ *Two leading law firms are to prepare legal actions against tobacco companies.*

**4** N-SING: the N — **The action** is all the important and exciting things that are happening in a situation. [INFORMAL] ❑ *Hollywood is where the action is now.*

**5** N-UNCOUNT: oft in N — The fighting which takes place in a war can be referred to as **action**. ❑ *Leaders in America have generally supported military action... 13 soldiers were killed and 10 wounded in action.*

**6** ADJ: ADJ n — An **action** movie is a film in which a lot of dangerous and exciting things happen. An **action** hero is the main character in one of these films.

**7** VERB: usu passive — If you **action** something that needs to be done, you deal with it. [BUSINESS] ❑ *Documents can be actioned, or filed immediately.* (be V-ed)

**PHRASES**

**8** PHRASE: v-link PHR, PHR after v — If someone or something is **out of action**, they are injured or damaged and cannot work or be used. ❑ *He's been out of action for 16 months with a serious knee injury.*

**9** PHRASE — If someone wants to have **a piece of the action** or **a slice of the action**, they want to take part in an exciting activity or situation, usually in order to make money or become more important.

**10** PHRASE: V inflects — If you **put** an idea or policy **into action**, you begin to use it or cause it to operate. ❑ *They have learned the lessons of business management theory, and put them into action.*

**ac|tion|able** /ækʃənəbəl/ ADJ: usu v-link ADJ — If something that you do or say to someone is **actionable**, it gives them a valid reason for bringing a legal case against you.

**ac|tion re|play** **(action replays)** N-COUNT — An **action replay** is a repeated showing, usually in slow motion, of an event that has just been on television. [BRIT]

> ✔ in AM, use **instant replay**

**ac|ti|vate** /æktɪveɪt/ **(activates, activating, activated)** VERB: usu passive — If a device or process **is activated**, something causes it to start working. ❑ *Video cameras with night vision can be activated by movement. ...a voice-activated computer.* (be V-ed; V-ed) ♦ **ac|ti|va|tion** N-UNCOUNT ❑ *A computer controls the activation of an air bag.*

**ac|tive** /æktɪv/ ◆◆◇

**1** ADJ — Someone who is **active** moves around a lot or does a lot of things. ❑ *Having an active youngster about the house can be quite wearing. ...a long and active life.*

**2** ADJ = lively — If you have an **active** mind or imagination, you are always thinking of new things. ❑ *...the tragedy of an active mind trapped by failing physical health.*

**3** ADJ: oft ADJ prep ≠ passive — If someone is **active** in an organization, cause, or campaign, they do things for it rather than just giving it their support. ❑ *...a chance for fathers to play a more active role in childcare.* ♦ **ac|tive|ly** ADV ❑ *They actively campaigned for the vote.*

**4** ADJ: ADJ n emphasis = positive — **Active** is used to emphasize that someone is taking action in order to achieve something, rather than just hoping for it or achieving it in an indirect way. ❑ *Companies need to take active steps to increase exports. ...active discouragement from teachers.* ♦ **ac|tive|ly** ADV: usu ADV with v ❑ *They have never been actively encouraged to take such risks.*

**5** ADJ: usu v-link ADJ, usu ADJ prep — If you say that a person or animal is **active** in a particular place or at a particular time, you mean that they are performing their usual activities or performing a particular activity. ❑ *Guerrilla groups are active in the province.*

**6** ADJ: usu ADJ n ≠ extinct — An **active** volcano has erupted recently or is expected to erupt quite soon. ❑ *...molten lava from an active volcano.*

**7** ADJ: usu ADJ n — An **active** substance has a chemical or biological effect on things. ❑ *The active ingredient in some* *of the mouthwashes was simply detergent.* 8 In grammar, **the active** or **the active voice** means the forms of a verb which are used when the subject refers to a person or thing that does something. For example, in 'I saw her yesterday', the verb is in the active. Compare **passive**. N-SING: *the* N

**ac|tive du|ty** Active duty means the same as **active service**. [mainly AM] N-UNCOUNT: oft *on* N

**ac|tive ser|vice** Someone who is **on active service** is taking part in a war as a member of the armed forces. [mainly BRIT] ❑ *In April 1944 he was killed on active service.* N-UNCOUNT: oft *on* N

**ac|tiv|ism** /æktɪvɪzəm/ **Activism** is the process of campaigning in public or working for an organization in order to bring about political or social change. N-UNCOUNT

**ac|tiv|ist** /æktɪvɪst/ **(activists)** An **activist** is a person who works to bring about political or social changes by campaigning in public or working for an organization. ❑ *The police say they suspect the attack was carried out by animal rights activists.* ◆◇◇ N-COUNT

**ac|tiv|ity** /æktɪvɪti/ **(activities)** 1 **Activity** is a situation in which a lot of things are happening or being done. ❑ *...an extraordinary level of activity in the government bonds market. ...the electrical activity of the brain.* ◆◆◇ N-UNCOUNT 2 An **activity** is something that you spend time doing. ❑ *You can take part in activities from canoeing to bird watching.* N-COUNT 3 The **activities** of a group are the things that they do in order to achieve their aims. ❑ *...a jail term for terrorist activities.* N-PLURAL: with supp

**act of God (acts of God)** An **act of God** is an event that is beyond human control, especially one in which something is damaged or someone is hurt. N-COUNT

**ac|tor** /æktəʳ/ **(actors)** An **actor** is someone whose job is acting in plays or films. 'Actor' in the singular usually refers to a man, but some women who act prefer to be called 'actors' rather than 'actresses'. ❑ *His father was an actor in the Cantonese Opera Company... You have to be a very good actor to play that part.* ◆◇◇ N-COUNT

**ac|tress** /æktrəs/ **(actresses)** An **actress** is a woman whose job is acting in plays or films. ❑ *She's a very great dramatic actress.* ◆◇◇ N-COUNT

**ac|tual** /æktʃuəl/ 1 You use **actual** to emphasize that you are referring to something real or genuine. ❑ *The segments are filmed using either local actors or the actual people involved... Officials admit the actual number of AIDS victims is much higher than statistics reflect.* ◆◇◇ ADJ: ADJ n [emphasis] = real 2 You use **actual** to contrast the important aspect of something with a less important aspect. ❑ *She had compiled pages of notes, but she had not yet gotten down to doing the actual writing.* ADJ: ADJ n [emphasis] 3 **in actual fact** → see **fact**.

**ac|tual bodi|ly harm** **Actual bodily harm** is a criminal offence in which someone gives another person a minor injury. N-UNCOUNT

**ac|tu|al|ity** /æktʃuælɪti/ **(actualities)** 1 You can use **in actuality** to emphasize that what you are saying is true, even when it conflicts or contrasts with what you have previously said. ❑ *In actuality, Teddie did not have a disorder but merely a difficult temperament.* PHRASE: PHR with cl [emphasis] = in reality, actually 2 **Actuality** is the state of really existing rather than being imagined. ❑ *It exists in dreams rather than actuality.* N-UNCOUNT = reality

**ac|tu|al|ly** /æktʃuəli/ 1 You use **actually** to indicate that a situation exists or happened, or to emphasize that it is true. ❑ *One afternoon, I grew bored and actually fell asleep for a few minutes... Interest is only payable on the amount actually borrowed.* ◆◆◆ ADV: ADV before v, ADV group [emphasis] 2 You use **actually** when you are correcting or contradicting someone. ❑ *No, I'm not a student. I'm a doctor, actually... 'So it's not a family show then?' — 'Well, actually, I think that's exactly what it is.'* ADV: ADV with cl [emphasis] 3 You can use **actually** when you are politely expressing an opinion that other people might not have expected from you. ❑ *'Do you think it's a good idea to socialize with one's patients?' — 'Actually, I do, I think it's a great idea.'* ADV: ADV with cl [politeness] 4 You use **actually** to introduce a new topic into a conversation. ❑ *Well actually, John, I rang you for some advice.* ADV: ADV with cl

**ac|tu|ari|al** /æktʃueəriəl/ **Actuarial** means relating to the work of an actuary. ❑ *The company's actuarial report is available on demand.* ADJ: ADJ n

**ac|tu|ary** /æktʃuəri, AM -tʃueri/ **(actuaries)** An **actuary** is a person who is employed by insurance companies to calculate how much they should charge their clients for insurance. N-COUNT

**ac|tu|ate** /æktʃueɪt/ **(actuates, actuating, actuated)** If a person **is actuated by** an emotion, that emotion makes them act in a certain way. If something **actuates** a device, the device starts working. ❑ *They were actuated by desire... The flow of current actuates the signal.* VERB = activate *be* V-ed V n

**acu|ity** /ækjuːɪti/ **Acuity** is sharpness of vision or hearing, or quickness of thought. [FORMAL] ❑ *We work on improving visual acuity.* N-UNCOUNT

**acu|men** /ækjʊmen, AM əkjuːmən/ **Acumen** is the ability to make good judgments and quick decisions. ❑ *His sharp business acumen meant he quickly rose to the top.* N-UNCOUNT: usu supp N

**acu|pres|sure** /ækjʊpreʃəʳ/ **Acupressure** is the treatment of pain by a type of massage in which pressure is put on certain areas of a person's body. N-UNCOUNT

**acu|punc|ture** /ækjʊpʌŋktʃəʳ/ **Acupuncture** is the treatment of a person's illness or pain by sticking small needles into their body at certain places. N-UNCOUNT

**acu|punc|tur|ist** /ækjʊpʌŋktʃərɪst/ **(acupuncturists)** An **acupuncturist** is a person who performs acupuncture. N-COUNT

**acute** /əkjuːt/ 1 You can use **acute** to indicate that an undesirable situation or feeling is very severe or intense. ❑ *The report has caused acute embarrassment to the government... The labour shortage is becoming acute.* ADJ = severe 2 An **acute** illness is one that becomes severe very quickly but does not last very long. Compare **chronic**. [MEDICAL] ❑ *...a patient with acute rheumatoid arthritis.* ADJ: ADJ n 3 If a person's or animal's sight, hearing, or sense of smell is **acute**, it is sensitive and powerful. ❑ *In the dark my sense of hearing becomes so acute.* ADJ = keen 4 An **acute** angle is less than 90°. Compare **obtuse** angle. ADJ 5 An **acute** accent is a symbol that is placed over vowels in some languages in order to indicate how that vowel is pronounced or over one letter in a word to indicate where it is stressed. You refer to a letter with this accent as, for example, e **acute**. For example, there is an acute accent over the letter 'e' in the French word 'café'. ADJ: ADJ n, n ADJ

**acute|ly** /əkjuːtli/ 1 If you feel or notice something **acutely**, you feel or notice it very strongly. ❑ *He was acutely aware of the odour of cooking oil.* ADV: ADV adj, ADV with v = keenly 2 If a feeling or quality is **acutely** unpleasant, it is extremely unpleasant. ❑ *It was an acutely uncomfortable journey back to London.* ADV: ADV adj, ADV with v = intensely

**ad** /æd/ **(ads)** An **ad** is an advertisement. [INFORMAL] ❑ *She replied to a lonely hearts ad.* ◆◇◇ N-COUNT

**AD** /eɪ diː/ You use **AD** in dates to indicate the number of years or centuries that have passed since the year in which Jesus Christ is believed to have been born. Compare **BC**. ❑ *The cathedral was destroyed by the Great Fire of 1136 AD... The Roman Empire was divided in the fourth century AD.*

**ad|age** /ædɪdʒ/ **(adages)** An **adage** is something which people often say and which expresses a general truth about some aspect of life. [OLD-FASHIONED] ❑ *...the old adage, 'Every baby brings its own love'.* N-COUNT = maxim, saying

**ada|gio** /ədɑːdʒioʊ, AM -dʒoʊ/ **(adagios)** 1 **Adagio** written above a piece of music means that it should be played slowly. ADV: ADV after v 2 An **adagio** is a piece of music that is played slowly. ❑ *...Samuel Barber's Adagio For Strings. ...the Adagio movement of his Sixth Symphony.* N-COUNT: usu sing

**ada|mant** /ædəmənt/ If someone is **adamant about** something, they are determined not to change their mind about it. ❑ *The prime minister* ADJ: usu v-link ADJ, oft ADJ that, ADJ *about* n/-ing *is adamant that he will not resign... Sue was adamant about that job in Australia.* ♦ **ada|mant|ly** *She was adamantly opposed to her husband travelling to Brussels.* ADV: usu ADV with v, also ADV adj

**Adam's ap|ple** /ædəmz æpəl/ **(Adam's apples)** Your **Adam's apple** is the lump that sticks out of the front of your neck below your throat. N-COUNT

**a|dapt** /ədæpt/ **(adapts, adapting, adapted)** [1] If you **adapt to** a new situation or **adapt yourself to** it, you change your ideas or behaviour in order to deal with it successfully. ❑ *The world will be different, and we will have to be prepared to adapt to the change... They have had to adapt themselves to a war economy.* VERB = adjust; V to n; V pron-refl to n, Also V [2] If you **adapt** something, you change it to make it suitable for a new purpose or situation. ❑ *Shelves were built to adapt the library for use as an office.* VERB = modify; V n; Also V n to n [3] If you **adapt** a book or play, you change it so that it can be made into a film or a television programme. ❑ *The scriptwriter helped him to adapt his novel for the screen... The film has been adapted from a play of the same title.* VERB; V n; V n [4] → See also **adapted**.

**adapt|able** /ədæptəbəl/ If you describe a person or animal as **adaptable**, you mean that they are able to change their ideas or behaviour in order to deal with new situations. ❑ *...a more adaptable and skilled workforce.* ADJ = flexible ♦ **adapt|abil|ity** /ədæptəbɪlɪti/ *The adaptability of wool is one of its great attractions.* N-UNCOUNT = flexibility

**ad|ap|ta|tion** /ædæpteɪʃən/ **(adaptations)** [1] An **adaptation** of a book or play is a film or a television programme that is based on it. ❑ *...Branagh's screen adaptation of Shakespeare's Henry the Fifth.* N-COUNT [2] **Adaptation** is the act of changing something or changing your behaviour to make it suitable for a new purpose or situation. ❑ *Most living creatures are capable of adaptation when compelled to do so.* N-UNCOUNT

**a|dapt|ed** /ədæptɪd/ If something is **adapted** to a particular situation or purpose, it is especially suitable for it. ❑ *The camel's feet, well adapted for dry sand, are useless on mud.* ADJ: v-link ADJ to/for n = suited

**adap|tion** /ədæpʃən/ **(adaptions)** **Adaption** means the same as **adaptation**. N-VAR

**adap|tive** /ədæptɪv/ **Adaptive** means having the ability or tendency to adapt to different situations. [FORMAL] ❑ *Societies need to develop highly adaptive behavioural rules for survival.* ADJ

**adap|tor** /ədæptəʳ/ **(adaptors)** also **adapter**. [1] An **adaptor** is a special device for connecting electrical equipment to a power supply, or for connecting different pieces of electrical or electronic equipment together. N-COUNT [2] The **adaptor** of a book or play is the person who rewrites it for a film or a television programme. N-COUNT

**add** /æd/ **(adds, adding, added)** ♦♦♦ [1] If you **add** one thing **to** another, you put it in or on the other thing, to increase, complete, or improve it. ❑ *Add the grated cheese to the sauce... Since 1908, chlorine has been added to drinking water... He wants to add a huge new sports complex to Binfield Manor.* VERB; V n to n; be V-ed to n; V n to n; Also V n [2] If you **add** numbers or amounts **together**, you calculate their total. ❑ *Banks add all the interest and other charges together... Two and three added together are five.* VERB ≠ subtract; V pl-n with together ♦ **Add up** means the same as **add**. ❑ *More than a quarter of seven year-olds cannot add up properly... We just added all the numbers up and divided one by the other... He said the numbers simply did not add up.* PHRASAL VERB; V P; V pl-n P; V P [3] If one thing **adds to** another, it makes the other thing greater in degree or amount. ❑ *This latest incident will add to the pressure on the government.* VERB; V to n [4] To **add** a particular quality **to** something means to cause it to have that quality. ❑ *The generous amount of garlic adds flavour... Pictures add interest to plain painted walls.* VERB; V n; V n to n [5] If you **add** something when you are speaking, you say something more. ❑ *'You can tell that he is extremely embarrassed,' Mr Brigden added... The President agreed, adding that he hoped for a peaceful solution.* VERB; V with quote; V that [6] **to add insult to injury** → see **insult**.

♦ **add in** If you **add in** something, you include it as a part of something else. ❑ *Once the vegetables start to cook add in a couple of tablespoons of water.* PHRASAL VERB; V P n (not pron)

♦ **add on** [1] If one thing **is added on** to another, it is attached to the other thing, or is made a part of it. ❑ *Holidaymakers can also add on a week in Majorca before or after the cruise... To the rear is a large dining room – added on early this century.* PHRASAL VERB: usu passive; V P n; V-ed P [2] If you **add on** an extra amount or item to a list or total, you include it. ❑ *Many loan application forms automatically add on insurance.* PHRASAL VERB; V P n (not pron); Also V n P

♦ **add up** [1] → see **add 2**. [2] If facts or events do not **add up**, they make you confused about a situation because they do not seem to be consistent. If something that someone has said or done **adds up**, it is reasonable and sensible. ❑ *Police said they arrested Olivia because her statements did not add up.* PHRASAL VERB: usu with neg; V P [3] If small amounts of something **add up**, they gradually increase. ❑ *Even small savings can add up.* PHRASAL VERB; V P

♦ **add up to** If amounts **add up to** a particular total, they result in that total when they are put together. ❑ *For a hit show, profits can add up to millions of dollars.* PHRASAL VERB = amount to; V P P n

**ADD** /eɪ diː diː/ **ADD** is an abbreviation for **attention deficit disorder**.

**add|ed** /ædɪd/ You use **added** to say that something has more of a particular thing or quality. ❑ *For added protection choose a lipstick with a sun screen.* ADJ: ADJ n = extra

**add|ed val|ue** In marketing, **added value** is something which makes a product more appealing to customers. [BUSINESS] N-UNCOUNT

**ad|den|dum** /ədendəm/ **(addenda** /ədendə/**)** An **addendum** is an additional section at the end of a book or document. N-COUNT = appendix

**add|er** /ædəʳ/ **(adders)** In Europe and Asia, an **adder** is a small poisonous snake that has a black pattern on its back. In North America, a number of different poisonous and non-poisonous snakes are called **adders**. N-COUNT = viper

**ad|dict** /ædɪkt/ **(addicts)** [1] An **addict** is someone who takes harmful drugs and cannot stop taking them. ❑ *He's only 24 years old and a drug addict.* N-COUNT: oft supp N [2] If you say that someone is an **addict**, you mean that they like a particular activity very much and spend as much time doing it as they can. ❑ *She is a TV addict and watches as much as she can.* N-COUNT: usu supp N

**ad|dict|ed** /ədɪktɪd/ [1] Someone who is **addicted to** a harmful drug cannot stop taking it. ❑ *Many of the women are addicted to heroin and cocaine.* ADJ: usu v-link ADJ, usu ADJ to n = hooked [2] If you say that someone is **addicted to** something, you mean that they like it very much and want to spend as much time doing it as possible. ❑ *She had become addicted to golf.* ADJ: usu v-link ADJ, usu ADJ to n

**ad|dic|tion** /ədɪkʃən/ **(addictions)** [1] **Addiction** is the condition of taking harmful drugs and being unable to stop taking them. ❑ *She helped him fight his drug addiction. ...long-term addiction to nicotine.* N-VAR: oft n N, N to n [2] An **addiction to** something is a very strong desire or need for it. ❑ *He needed money to feed his addiction to gambling.* N-VAR: oft N to n

**ad|dic|tive** /ədɪktɪv/ [1] If a drug is **addictive**, people who take it cannot stop taking it. ❑ *Cigarettes are highly addictive... Crack is the most addictive drug on the market.* ADJ [2] Something that is **addictive** is so enjoyable that it makes you want to do it or have it a lot. ❑ *Video movie-making can quickly become addictive.* ADJ

**ad|di|tion** /ədɪʃən/ **(additions)** ♦♦◇ [1] You use **in addition** when you want to mention another item connected with the subject you are discussing. ❑ *Part-time English classes are offered. In addition, students can take classes in word-processing and computing... There's a postage and packing fee in addition to the repair charge.* PHRASE: PHR with cl, oft PHR to n [2] An **addition to** something is a thing which is added to it. ❑ *This is a fine book; a worthy addition to the Cambridge Ency-* N-COUNT: usu with supp, oft N to n *clopedia series.* [3] **The addition of** something is the fact that it is added to something else. ❑ *It was completely refurbished in 1987, with the addition of a picnic site.* [4] **Addition** is the process of calculating the total of two or more numbers. ❑ *...simple addition and subtraction problems.* N-UNCOUNT: the N of n ≠ removal; N-UNCOUNT

**ad|di|tion|al** /ədɪʃənəl/ **Additional** things are extra things apart from the ones already present. ❑ *The US is sending additional troops to the region... The insurer will also have to pay the additional costs of the trial.* ◆◇◇ ADJ: usu ADJ n = supplementary, extra

**ad|di|tion|al|ly** /ədɪʃənəli/ [1] You use **additionally** to introduce something extra such as an extra fact or reason. [FORMAL] ❑ *You can pay bills over the Internet. Additionally, you can check your balance or order statements.* [2] **Additionally** is used to say that something happens to a greater extent than before. ❑ *The birds are additionally protected in the reserves at Birsay.* ADV: ADV with cl = further; ADV: ADV with v

**ad|di|tive** /ædɪtɪv/ **(additives)** An **additive** is a substance which is added in small amounts to foods or other things in order to improve them or to make them last longer. ❑ *Strict safety tests are carried out on food additives.* N-COUNT

**ad|dle** /ædəl/ **(addles, addling, addled)** If something **addles** someone's mind or brain, they become confused and unable to think properly. ❑ *I suppose the shock had addled his poor old brain.* VERB = befuddle; V n

**ad|dled** /ædəld/ If you describe someone as **addled**, you mean that they are confused or unable to think properly. ❑ *You're talking like an addled romantic.* ADJ: usu ADJ n = befuddled

**add-on** **(add-ons)** An **add-on** is an extra piece of equipment, especially computer equipment, that can be added to a larger one which you already own in order to improve its performance or its usefulness. ❑ *Speakers are sold as add-ons for personal stereos.* N-COUNT: oft N n

**ad|dress** /ədres, AM ædres/ **(addresses, addressing, addressed)** [1] Your **address** is the number of the house, flat, or apartment and the name of the street and the town where you live or work. ❑ *The address is 2025 M Street, Northwest, Washington, DC, 20036... We require details of your name and address.* [2] If a letter, envelope, or parcel **is addressed to** you, your name and address have been written on it. ❑ *Applications should be addressed to: The business affairs editor.* [3] The **address** of a website is its location on the Internet, for example http://www.cobuild.collins.co.uk. [COMPUTING] [4] If you **address** a group of people, you give a speech to them. ❑ *He is due to address a conference on human rights next week.* ♦ **Address** is also a noun. ❑ *The President gave an address to the American people.* [5] If you **address** someone or **address** a remark **to** them, you say something to them. [FORMAL] ❑ *The two foreign ministers did not address each other directly when they last met... He addressed his remarks to Eleanor, ignoring Maria.* [6] If you **address** a problem or task or if you **address yourself to** it, you try to understand it or deal with it. ❑ *Mr King sought to address those fears when he spoke at the meeting... Throughout the book we have addressed ourselves to the problem of ethics.* ◆◆◇ N-COUNT: usu poss N; VERB: usu passive be V-ed to n; N-COUNT; VERB V n; N-COUNT; VERB V n V n to n; VERB V n V pron-refl to n

**ad|dress book** **(address books)** [1] An **address book** is a book in which you write people's names and addresses. [2] An **address book** is a computer file which contains a list of e-mail addresses. [COMPUTING] N-COUNT; N-COUNT

**ad|dressee** /ædresiː/ **(addressees)** The **addressee** of a letter or parcel is the person or company that it is addressed to. [FORMAL] N-COUNT: usu the N in sing

**ad|duce** /ædjuːs, AM -duːs/ **(adduces, adducing, adduced)** If you **adduce** something such as a fact or reason, you mention it in order to support an argument. [FORMAL] ❑ *We can adduce evidence to support the claim.* VERB = cite; V n

**ad|enoids** /ædɪnɔɪdz/ **Adenoids** are soft lumps of flesh at the back and top of a person's throat that sometimes become swollen and have to be removed. N-PLURAL

**adept** /ædept/ Someone who is **adept at** something can do it skilfully. ❑ *He's usually very adept at keeping his private life out of the media.* ♦ **adept|ly** /ædeptli/ *Mrs Marcos' lawyer adeptly exploited the prosecution's weakness.* ADJ: usu v-link ADJ, usu ADJ at -ing/n; ADV: ADV with v

**ad|equa|cy** /ædɪkwəsi/ **Adequacy** is the quality of being good enough or great enough in amount to be acceptable. N-UNCOUNT: usu N of n ≠ inadequacy

**ad|equate** /ædɪkwət/ If something is **adequate**, there is enough of it or it is good enough to be used or accepted. ❑ *One in four people worldwide are without adequate homes... The old methods weren't adequate to meet current needs.* ♦ **ad|equate|ly** *Many students are not adequately prepared for higher education... I speak the language adequately.* ◆◇◇ ADJ: oft ADJ to-inf, ADJ for n ≠ inadequate; ADV: ADV with v

**ADHD** /eɪ diː eɪtʃ diː/ **ADHD** is an abbreviation for **attention deficit hyperactivity disorder**.

**ad|here** /ædhɪəʳ/ **(adheres, adhering, adhered)** [1] If you **adhere to** a rule or agreement, you act in the way that it says you should. ❑ *All members of the association adhere to a strict code of practice.* [2] If you **adhere to** an opinion or belief, you support or hold it. ❑ *He urged them to adhere to the values of Islam which defend the dignity of man.* [3] If something **adheres to** something else, it sticks firmly to it. ❑ *Small particles adhere to the seed... This sticky compound adheres well on this surface.* VERB V to n; VERB V to n; VERB V to n V adv/prep Also V

**ad|her|ence** /ædhɪərəns/ **Adherence** is the fact of adhering to a particular rule, agreement, or belief. ❑ *...strict adherence to the constitution.* N-UNCOUNT: usu N to n

**ad|her|ent** /ædhɪərənt/ **(adherents)** An **adherent** is someone who holds a particular belief or supports a particular person or group. ❑ *This idea is gaining adherents.* N-COUNT = follower, supporter

**ad|he|sion** /ædhiːʒən/ **Adhesion** is the ability of one thing to stick firmly to another. [FORMAL] ❑ *Better driving equipment will improve track adhesion in slippery conditions.* N-UNCOUNT

**ad|he|sive** /ædhiːsɪv/ **(adhesives)** [1] An **adhesive** is a substance such as glue, which is used to make things stick firmly together. ❑ *Glue the mirror in with a strong adhesive.* [2] An **adhesive** substance is able to stick firmly to something else. ❑ *...adhesive tape.* N-MASS; ADJ: usu ADJ n

**ad hoc** /æd hɒk/ An **ad hoc** activity or organization is done or formed only because a situation has made it necessary and is not planned in advance. ❑ *The Council meets on an ad hoc basis to discuss problems.* ADJ: usu ADJ n

**adieu** /ədjuː/ **(adieus) Adieu** means the same as **goodbye**. [LITERARY, OLD-FASHIONED] CONVENTION

**ad in|fi|ni|tum** /æd ɪnfɪnaɪtəm/ If something happens **ad infinitum**, it is repeated again and again in the same way. ❑ *This cycle repeats itself ad infinitum.* ADV: ADV after v

**adj.** **Adj.** is a written abbreviation for **adjective**.

**ad|ja|cent** /ədʒeɪsənt/ If one thing is **adjacent to** another, the two things are next to each other. ❑ *He sat in an adjacent room and waited. ...offices adjacent to the museum.* ADJ: oft ADJ to n

**ad|jec|ti|val** /ædʒɪktaɪvəl/ **Adjectival** means relating to adjectives or like an adjective. ❑ *...an adjectival phrase.* ADJ: usu ADJ n

**ad|jec|tive** /ædʒɪktɪv/ **(adjectives)** An **adjective** is a word such as 'big', 'dead', or 'financial' that describes a person or thing, or gives extra information about them. Adjectives usually come before nouns or after link verbs. N-COUNT

**ad|jec|tive group** **(adjective groups)** An **adjective group** or **adjectival group** is a group of words based on an adjective, such as 'very nice' or 'interested in football'. An adjective group can also consist simply of an adjective. N-COUNT

**ad|join** /ədʒɔɪn/ **(adjoins, adjoining, adjoined)** VERB If one room, place, or object **adjoins** another, they are next to each other. [FORMAL]

**ad|journ** /ədʒɜːʳn/ **(adjourns, adjourning, adjourned)** If a meeting or trial **is adjourned** or if it **adjourns**, it is stopped for a short time. VERB ❑ *The proceedings have now been adjourned until next week...* be V-ed *I am afraid the court may not adjourn until three or even later.* V

**ad|journ|ment** /ədʒɜːʳnmənt/ **(adjournments)** An **adjournment** is a temporary stopping of a trial, enquiry, or other meeting. N-COUNT = *suspension* ❑ *The court ordered a four month adjournment.*

**ad|judge** /ədʒʌdʒ/ **(adjudges, adjudging, adjudged)** If someone **is adjudged to** be something, they are judged or considered to be that thing. VERB: usu passive [FORMAL] ❑ *He was adjudged to be guilty...* be V-ed to-inf *He was adjudged the winner by 54 votes to 3.* be V-ed n

**ad|ju|di|cate** /ədʒuːdɪkeɪt/ **(adjudicates, adjudicating, adjudicated)** If you **adjudicate on** a dispute or problem, you make an official judgment or decision about it. VERB = *decide* [FORMAL] ❑ *...a commissioner to adjudicate on legal rights...* V prep *The international court of justice might be a suitable place to adjudicate claims.* V n, Also V ♦ **ad|ju|di|ca|tion** /ədʒuːdɪkeɪʃən/ **(adjudications)** N-VAR *...unbiased adjudication of cases of unfair dismissal.* ♦ **ad|ju|di|ca|tor** /ədʒuːdɪkeɪtəʳ/ **(adjudicators)** N-COUNT *...an independent adjudicator.*

**ad|junct** /ædʒʌŋkt/ **(adjuncts)** 1 Something that is an **adjunct to** something larger or more important is connected with it or helps to perform the same task. N-COUNT: oft N *to/of* n = *appendage* ❑ *Physical therapy is an important adjunct to drug treatments.* 2 In grammar, an **adjunct** is a word or group of words which indicates the circumstances of an action, event, or situation. An adjunct is usually a prepositional phrase or an adverb group. N-COUNT

**ad|just** /ədʒʌst/ **(adjusts, adjusting, adjusted)** ◆◇◇ 1 When you **adjust to** a new situation, you get used to it by changing your behaviour or your ideas. VERB ❑ *We have been preparing our fighters to adjust themselves to civil society...* V n *to* n *I felt I had adjusted to the idea of being a mother very well...* V *to* n *It has been hard to adjust but now I'm getting satisfaction from my work.* V ➔ See also **well-adjusted**. 2 If you **adjust** something, you change it so that it is more effective or appropriate. VERB ❑ *To attract investors, Panama has adjusted its tax and labour laws.* V n 3 If you **adjust** something such as your clothing or a machine, you correct or alter its position or setting. VERB ❑ *Liz adjusted her mirror and then edged the car out of its parking bay.* V n 4 If you **adjust** your vision or if your vision **adjusts**, the muscles of your eye or the pupils alter to cope with changes in light or distance. VERB ❑ *He stopped to try to adjust his vision to the faint starlight...* V n *We stood in the doorway until our eyes adjusted.* V

**ad|just|able** /ədʒʌstəbəl/ If something is **adjustable**, it can be changed to different positions or sizes. ADJ ≠ *fixed* ❑ *The bags have adjustable shoulder straps... The seats are fully adjustable.*

**ad|just|er** /ədʒʌstəʳ/ **(adjusters)** also **adjustor.** An **adjuster** is a device which allows you to alter a piece of equipment's position or setting. N-COUNT ❑ *...a seat belt adjuster.* ➔ See also **loss adjustor**.

**ad|just|ment** /ədʒʌstmənt/ **(adjustments)** 1 An **adjustment** is a small change that is made to something such as a machine or a way of doing something. N-COUNT: oft N *to/for/in* n ❑ *Compensation could be made by adjustments to taxation... Investment is up by 5.7% after adjustment for inflation.* 2 An **adjustment** is a change in a person's behaviour or thinking. N-COUNT: oft N *to* n ❑ *He will have to make major adjustments to his thinking if he is to survive in office.*

**ad|ju|tant** /ædʒʊtənt/ **(adjutants)** An **adjutant** is an officer in the army who deals with administrative work. N-COUNT

**ad-lib** **(ad-libs, ad-libbing, ad-libbed)** also **ad lib.** 1 If you **ad-lib** something in a play or a speech, you say something which has not been planned or written beforehand. VERB = *improvise* ❑ *He began comically ad-libbing a script...* V n *He's good at ad-libbing his way out of trouble...* V *way* prep *He is rather disjointed when he ad-libs.* V *...ad-libbed phrases.* V-ed 2 An **ad-lib** is something which is said without having been planned or written beforehand. N-COUNT = *improvisation* ❑ *Every time I fluffed a line Lenny got me out of trouble with a brilliant ad-lib.* ♦ **Ad lib** is also an adverb. ADV: ADV after v ❑ *I spoke from the pulpit ad lib.*

**ad|man** /ædmæn/ **(admen)** An **adman** is someone who works in advertising. N-COUNT [INFORMAL]

**ad|min** /ædmɪn/ **Admin** is the activity or process of organizing an institution or organization. N-UNCOUNT: oft N n = *administration* [INFORMAL] ❑ *I have two assistants who help with the admin.*

**ad|min|is|ter** /ədmɪnɪstəʳ/ **(administers, administering, administered)** 1 If someone **administers** something such as a country, the law, or a test, they take responsibility for organizing and supervising it. VERB ❑ *The plan calls for the UN to administer the country until elections can be held.* V n 2 If a doctor or a nurse **administers** a drug, they give it to a patient. VERB [FORMAL] ❑ *Paramedics are trained to administer certain drugs.* V n, Also V n *to* n

**ad|min|is|tra|tion** /ədmɪnɪstreɪʃən/ **(administrations)** ◆◆◇ 1 **Administration** is the range of activities connected with organizing and supervising the way that an organization or institution functions. N-UNCOUNT ❑ *Too much time is spent on administration. ...a master's degree in business administration.* 2 The **administration** of something is the process of organizing and supervising it. N-UNCOUNT ❑ *Standards in the administration of justice have degenerated.* 3 **The administration** of a company or institution is the group of people who organize and supervise it. N-SING: *the* N, usu n N ❑ *... a member of the college administration.* 4 You can refer to a country's government as **the administration**; used especially in the United States. N-COUNT: oft *the* n N

**ad|min|is|tra|tive** /ədmɪnɪstrətɪv, AM -streɪt-/ **Administrative** work involves organizing and supervising an organization or institution. ADJ: usu ADJ n ❑ *Other industries have had to sack managers to reduce administrative costs.*

**ad|min|is|tra|tor** /ədmɪnɪstreɪtəʳ/ **(administrators)** An **administrator** is a person whose job involves helping to organize and supervise the way that an organization or institution functions. N-COUNT

**ad|mi|rable** /ædmɪrəbəl/ An **admirable** quality or action is one that deserves to be praised and admired. ADJ ❑ *Beyton is an admirable character.* ♦ **ad|mi|rably** /ædmɪrəbli/ *Peter had dealt admirably with the sudden questions about Keith.* ADV: ADV with v, ADV adj/adv

**ad|mi|ral** /ædmərəl/ **(admirals)** An **admiral** is a very senior officer who commands a navy. N-COUNT; N-TITLE ❑ *...Admiral Hodges.*

**Ad|mi|ral|ty** /ædmərəlti/ In Britain, **the Admiralty** is the government department that is in charge of the navy. N-PROPER: *the* N

**ad|mi|ra|tion** /ædmɪreɪʃən/ **Admiration** is a feeling of great liking and respect for a person or thing. N-UNCOUNT: oft N *for/of* n, *in* N ❑ *I have always had the greatest admiration for him.*

**ad|mire** /ədmaɪəʳ/ **(admires, admiring, admired)** ◆◇◇ 1 If you **admire** someone or something, you like and respect them very much. VERB ❑ *He admired the way she had coped with life...* V n *All those who knew him will admire him for his work.* V n *for* n/-ing 2 If you **admire** someone or something, you look at them with pleasure. VERB ❑ *We took time to stop and admire the view.* V n 3 ➔ See also **admiring**.

**ad|mir|er** /ədmaɪərəʳ/ **(admirers)** If you are an **admirer** of someone, you like and respect them or their work very much. N-COUNT ❑ *He was an admirer of her grandfather's paintings.*

**ad|mir|ing** /ədmaɪərɪŋ/ An **admiring** expression shows that you like or respect someone or something. ADJ: usu ADJ n = *appreciative* ❑ *He cast her an admiring glance.*

**ad|mis|sible** /ədmɪsɪbəl/ If evidence is **admissible**, it is allowed in a court of law. ADJ: usu v-link ADJ ≠ *inadmissible* ❑ *Convic-*

*tions will rise steeply now photographic evidence is admissible.*

**ad|mis|sion** /ædmɪʃən/ **(admissions)** [1] **Admission** is permission given to a person to enter a place, or permission given to a country to enter an organization. **Admission** is also the act of entering a place. ❑ *Students apply for admission to a particular college. ...an increase in hospital admissions of children.* [2] **Admissions** to a place such as a school or university are the people who are allowed to enter or join it. ❑ *Each school sets its own admissions policy.* [3] **Admission** at a park, museum, or other place is the amount of money that you pay to enter it. ❑ *Gates open at 10.30am and admission is free.* ♦ **Admission** is also used before a noun. ❑ *The admission price is $8 for adults.* [4] An **admission** is a statement that something bad, unpleasant, or embarrassing is true. ❑ *By his own admission, he is not playing well.* N-VAR: oft N *to* n; N-PLURAL: oft N n; N-UNCOUNT; N-UNCOUNT: N n; N-VAR: oft N *of* n, N that

**ad|mit** /ædmɪt/ **(admits, admitting, admitted)** ◆◆◇ [1] If you **admit** that something bad, unpleasant, or embarrassing is true, you agree, often unwillingly, that it is true. ❑ *I am willing to admit that I do make mistakes... Up to two thirds of 14 to 16 year olds admit to buying drink illegally... I'd be ashamed to admit feeling jealous... None of these people will admit responsibility for their actions... 'Actually, most of my tennis is at club level,' he admitted.* [2] If someone **is admitted to** hospital, they are taken into hospital for treatment and kept there until they are well enough to go home. ❑ *She was admitted to hospital with a soaring temperature... He was admitted yesterday for treatment of blood clots in his lungs.* [3] If someone **is admitted to** an organization or group, they are allowed to join it. ❑ *He was admitted to the Academie Culinaire de France... The Parachute Regiment could be forced to admit women.* [4] To **admit** someone **to** a place means to allow them to enter it. ❑ *Embassy security personnel refused to admit him or his wife... Journalists are rarely admitted to the region.* VERB = confess ≠ deny; V that; V *to* -ing/n; V -ing; V n; V with quote; VERB: usu passive; *be* V-ed *to* n; *be* V-ed; VERB; *be* V-ed *to* n; V n; VERB; V n; V n *to* n

**ad|mit|tance** /ædmɪtəns/ **Admittance** is the act of entering a place or institution or the right to enter it. ❑ *We had not been able to gain admittance to the flat.* N-UNCOUNT: oft N *into/to* n = admission

**ad|mit|ted|ly** /ædmɪtɪdli/ You use **admittedly** when you are saying something which weakens the importance or force of your statement. ❑ *It's only a theory, admittedly, but the pieces fit together.* ADV: ADV with cl/group

**ad|mix|ture** /ædmɪkstʃəʳ/ **Admixture** means the same as **mixture**. [FORMAL] ❑ *...an admixture of fact and fantasy.* N-SING: usu N *of* n = mixture

**ad|mon|ish** /ædmɒnɪʃ/ **(admonishes, admonishing, admonished)** If you **admonish** someone, you tell them very seriously that they have done something wrong. [FORMAL] ❑ *They admonished me for taking risks with my health... She admonished him gently, 'You should rest, not talk so much.'* ♦ **ad|mon|ish|ment** **(admonishments)** *Sometimes he gave them a severe admonishment.* VERB = rebuke; V n *for* n/-ing; V n with quote; N-VAR

**ad|moni|tion** /ædmənɪʃən/ **(admonitions)** An **admonition** is a warning or criticism about someone's behaviour. [FORMAL] ❑ *She ignored the admonitions of her mother.* N-VAR = admonishment

**ad nau|seam** If someone does something **ad nauseam**, they do it repeatedly and over a long period of time so that it becomes annoying or boring. ❑ *We discussed it ad nauseam.* PHRASE: PHR after v = endlessly

**ado** /ədu:/ If you do something **without further ado** or **without more ado**, you do it at once and do not discuss or delay it any longer. [OLD-FASHIONED] ❑ *'And now, without further ado, let me introduce our benefactor.'* PHRASE: PHR with v

**ado|be** /ədoʊbi/ **Adobe** is a mixture of mud and straw that is dried into bricks in the sun and used for building, especially in hot countries. ❑ *...a few blocks of adobe houses.* N-UNCOUNT: usu N n

**ado|les|cence** /ædəlesəns/ **Adolescence** is the period of your life in which you develop from being a child into being an adult. ❑ *Some people become very self-conscious in adolescence.* N-UNCOUNT

**ado|les|cent** /ædəlesənt/ **(adolescents)** **Adolescent** is used to describe young people who are no longer children but who have not yet become adults. It also refers to their behaviour. ❑ *It is important that an adolescent boy should have an adult in whom he can confide. ...adolescent rebellion.* ♦ An **adolescent** is an adolescent boy or girl. ❑ *Young adolescents are happiest with small groups of close friends.* ADJ: usu ADJ n = teenage; N-COUNT = teenager

**adopt** /ədɒpt/ **(adopts, adopting, adopted)** ◆◆◇ [1] If you **adopt** a new attitude, plan, or way of behaving, you begin to have it. ❑ *Parliament adopted a resolution calling for the complete withdrawal of troops.* ♦ **adop|tion** /ədɒpʃən/ *...the adoption of Japanese management practices by British manufacturing.* [2] If you **adopt** someone else's child, you take it into your own family and make it legally your son or daughter. ❑ *There are hundreds of people desperate to adopt a child... The adopted child has the right to see his birth certificate.* ♦ **adopt|er** **(adopters)** *A social worker is appointed to interview the prospective adopters.* ♦ **adop|tion** **(adoptions)** *They gave their babies up for adoption.* VERB; V n; N-UNCOUNT; VERB; V n; V-ed; Also V; N-COUNT; N-VAR

**adop|tive** /ədɒptɪv/ [1] Someone's **adoptive** family is the family that adopted them. ❑ *He was brought up by adoptive parents in London.* [2] Someone's **adoptive** country or city is the one that they choose for their home, although they were not born there. ❑ *They threatened to expel him from his adoptive country.* ADJ: ADJ n; ADJ: ADJ n

**ador|able** /ədɔ:rəbəl/ If you say that someone or something is **adorable**, you are emphasizing that they are very attractive and you feel great affection for them. ❑ *We have three adorable children.* ADJ [emphasis]

**ado|ra|tion** /ædɔ:reɪʃən/ **Adoration** is a feeling of great admiration and love for someone or something. ❑ *He had been used to female adoration all his life.* N-UNCOUNT

**adore** /ədɔ:ʳ/ **(adores, adoring, adored)** [1] If you **adore** someone, you feel great love and admiration for them. ❑ *She adored her parents and would do anything to please them.* [2] If you **adore** something, you like it very much. [INFORMAL] ❑ *My mother adores bananas and eats two a day.* VERB: no cont; V n; VERB: no cont; V n

**ador|ing** /ədɔ:rɪŋ/ An **adoring** person is someone who loves and admires another person very much. ❑ *She can still pull in adoring audiences.* ♦ **ador|ing|ly** *...gazing adoringly at him.* ADJ; ADV

**adorn** /ədɔ:ʳn/ **(adorns, adorning, adorned)** If something **adorns** a place or an object, it makes it look more beautiful. ❑ *His watercolour designs adorn a wide range of books.* VERB = decorate; V n

**adorn|ment** /ədɔ:ʳnmənt/ **(adornments)** [1] An **adornment** is something that is used to make a person or thing more beautiful. ❑ *It was a building without any adornment or decoration.* [2] **Adornment** is the process of making something more beautiful by adding something to it. ❑ *Cosmetics are used for adornment.* N-VAR; N-UNCOUNT

**adrena|lin** /ədrenəlɪn/ also **adrenaline.** **Adrenalin** is a substance which your body produces when you are angry, scared, or excited. It makes your heart beat faster and gives you more energy. ❑ *Seeing the crowd really got my adrenalin pumping.* N-UNCOUNT

**adrift** /ədrɪft/ [1] If a boat is **adrift**, it is floating on the water and is not tied to anything or controlled by anyone. ❑ *They were spotted after three hours adrift in a dinghy.* [2] If someone is **adrift**, they feel alone with no clear idea of what they should do. ❑ *Amy had the growing sense that she was adrift and isolated.* [3] If something comes **adrift**, it is no longer attached to an object that it should be part of. [BRIT] ❑ *Three insulating panels had come adrift from the base of the vehicle.* ADJ: v-link ADJ, v n ADJ; ADJ: v-link ADJ, v n ADJ; ADJ: v-link ADJ, ADJ after v = loose

**adroit** /ədrɔɪt/ Someone who is **adroit** is quick and skilful in their thoughts, behaviour, or ADJ = adept actions. ❑ *She is a remarkably adroit and determined politician.*

**ADSL** /eɪ diː es el/ **ADSL** is a method of transmitting digital information at high speed over telephone lines. **ADSL** is an abbreviation for 'asynchronous digital subscriber line'. [COMPUTING] ❑ *ADSL is always on, which makes your PC much more vulnerable to hacking.*

**adu|la|tion** /ædʒʊleɪʃən/ **Adulation** is uncritical admiration and praise of someone or something. ❑ *The book was received with adulation by critics.* N-UNCOUNT = acclaim

**adu|la|tory** /ædʒʊleɪtəri, AM -tɔːri/ If someone makes an **adulatory** comment about someone, they praise them and show their admiration of them. ❑ *...adulatory reviews.* ADJ: usu ADJ n = laudatory

**adult** /ædʌlt, AM ədʌlt/ **(adults)** 1 An **adult** is a mature, fully developed person. An adult has reached the age when they are legally responsible for their actions. ❑ *Becoming a father signified that he was now an adult... Children under 14 must always be accompanied by an adult.* 2 An **adult** is a fully developed animal. ❑ *...a pair of adult birds.* 3 **Adult** means relating to the time when you are an adult, or typical of adult people. ❑ *I've lived most of my adult life in London.* 4 If you say that someone is **adult** about something, you think that they act in a mature, intelligent way, especially when faced with a difficult situation. ❑ *We were very adult about it. We discussed it rationally over a drink.* 5 You can describe things such as films or books as **adult** when they deal with sex in a very clear and open way. ❑ *...an adult movie.* ◆◆◇ N-COUNT ≠ minor; N-COUNT: oft N n ≠ juvenile; ADJ: ADJ n; ADJ: v-link ADJ [approval] = mature; ADJ

**adult edu|ca|tion** **Adult education** is education for adults in a variety of subjects, most of which are practical, not academic. Classes are often held in the evenings. ❑ *Most adult education centres offer computing courses.* N-UNCOUNT

**adul|ter|ate** /ədʌltəreɪt/ **(adulterates, adulterating, adulterated)** If something such as food or drink **is adulterated**, someone has made its quality worse by adding water or cheaper products to it. ❑ *The food had been adulterated to increase its weight.* ♦ **adul|tera|tion** /ədʌltəreɪʃən/ *...the adulteration of tobacco.* VERB: usu passive; *be* V-ed; N-UNCOUNT

**adul|ter|er** /ədʌltərər/ **(adulterers)** An **adulterer** is someone who commits adultery. N-COUNT

**adul|ter|ess** /ədʌltrɪs/ **(adulteresses)** An **adulteress** is a woman who commits adultery. [OLD-FASHIONED] N-COUNT

**adul|ter|ous** /ədʌltərəs/ An **adulterous** relationship is a sexual relationship between a married person and someone they are not married to. An **adulterous** person is someone who commits adultery. ADJ: usu ADJ n

**adul|tery** /ədʌltəri/ If a married person commits **adultery**, they have sex with someone that they are not married to. ❑ *She is going to divorce him on the grounds of adultery.* N-UNCOUNT

**adult|hood** /ædʌlthʊd, AM ədʌlt-/ **Adulthood** is the state of being an adult. ❑ *Few people nowadays are able to maintain friendships into adulthood.* N-UNCOUNT

**adv.** **Adv.** is a written abbreviation for **adverb**.

**ad|vance** /ædvɑːns, -væns/ **(advances, advancing, advanced)** 1 To **advance** means to move forward, often in order to attack someone. ❑ *Reports from Chad suggest that rebel forces are advancing on the capital... The water is advancing at a rate of 5cm a day. ...a picture of a man throwing himself before an advancing tank.* 2 To **advance** means to make progress, especially in your knowledge of something. ❑ *Medical technology has advanced considerably.* → See also **advanced**. 3 If you **advance** someone a sum of money, you lend it to them, or pay it to them earlier than arranged. ❑ *I advanced him some money, which he would repay on our way home... The bank advanced $1.2 billion to help the country with debt repayments.* 4 An **advance** is money which is lent or paid to someone before they would normally receive it. ❑ *She was paid a £100,000 advance for her next two novels.* 5 To **advance** an event, or the time or date of an event, means to bring it forward to an earlier time or date. ❑ *Too much protein in the diet may advance the ageing process.* 6 If you **advance** a cause, interest, or claim, you support it and help to make it successful. ❑ *When not producing art of his own, Oliver was busy advancing the work of others.* 7 When a theory or argument **is advanced**, it is put forward for discussion. ❑ *Many theories have been advanced as to why some women suffer from depression.* 8 An **advance** is a forward movement of people or vehicles, usually as part of a military operation. ❑ *...an advance on enemy positions.* 9 An **advance** in a particular subject or activity is progress in understanding it or in doing it well. ❑ *Air safety has not improved since the dramatic advances of the 1970s.* 10 If something is an **advance on** what was previously available or done, it is better in some way. ❑ *This could be an advance on the present situation.* 11 **Advance** booking, notice, or warning is done or given before an event happens. ❑ *They don't normally give any advance notice about which building they're going to inspect.* 12 An **advance** party or group is a small group of people who go on ahead of the main group. ❑ *The 20-strong advance party will be followed by another 600 soldiers as part of UN relief efforts.* ◆◆◇ VERB; V prep/adv; V; V-ing; VERB = progress; V; VERB = lend; V n n; V n; N-COUNT; VERB = bring forward ≠ put back; V n; VERB = further; V n; VERB: usu passive = put forward; *be* V-ed; N-VAR ≠ retreat; N-VAR = development; N-SING: usu *a* N *on* n; ADJ: ADJ n; ADJ: ADJ n = expeditionary

**PHRASES** 13 If one thing happens or is done **in advance of** another, it happens or is done before the other thing. ❑ *I had asked everyone to submit questions in advance of the meeting.* 14 If you do something **in advance**, you do it before a particular date or event. ❑ *The subject of the talk is announced a week in advance.* PREP-PHRASE = ahead; PHRASE: PHR after v

**ad|vanced** /ædvɑːnst, -vænst/ 1 An **advanced** system, method, or design is modern and has been developed from an earlier version of the same thing. ❑ *Without more training or advanced technical skills, they'll lose their jobs.* 2 A country that is **advanced** has reached a high level of industrial or technological development. ❑ *...a technologically advanced society.* 3 An **advanced** student has already learned the basic facts of a subject and is doing more difficult work. An **advanced** course of study is designed for such students. ❑ *The course is suitable for beginners and advanced students.* 4 Something that is at an **advanced** stage or level is at a late stage of development. ❑ *'Medicare' is available to victims of advanced kidney disease.* ◆◇◇ ADJ: usu ADJ n = up-to-date; ADJ; ADJ: usu ADJ n ≠ elementary; ADJ

**ad|vance|ment** /ædvɑːnsmənt, -væns-/ **(advancements)** 1 **Advancement** is progress in your job or in your social position. ❑ *He cared little for social advancement.* 2 The **advancement of** something is the process of helping it to progress or the result of its progress. ❑ *..her work for the advancement of the status of women.* N-UNCOUNT: oft adj N; N-VAR: oft N *of* n

**ad|van|tage** /ædvɑːntɪdʒ, -væn-/ **(advantages)** 1 An **advantage** is something that puts you in a better position than other people. ❑ *They are deliberately flouting the law in order to obtain an advantage over their competitors... A good crowd will be a definite advantage to me and the rest of the team.* 2 **Advantage** is the state of being in a better position than others who are competing against you. ❑ *Men have created a social and economic position of advantage for themselves over women.* 3 An **advantage** is a way in which one thing is better than another. ❑ *This custom-built kitchen has many advantages over a standard one.* ◆◆◇ N-COUNT ≠ disadvantage; N-UNCOUNT; N-COUNT: oft N *of* n ≠ disadvantage

**PHRASES** 4 If you **take advantage of** something, you make good use of it while you can. ❑ *I intend to take full advantage of this trip to buy the things we need.* 5 If someone **takes advantage of** you, they treat you unfairly for their own benefit, especially when you are trying to be kind or to help them. ❑ *She took advantage of him even after they were divorced.* 6 If you use or turn something **to** your **advantage**, you use it in order to PHRASE: V inflects, PHR n; PHRASE: V inflects, PHR n; PHRASE: PHR after v benefit from it, especially when it might be expected to harm or damage you. ❑ *The government have not been able to turn today's demonstration to their advantage.*

**ad|van|taged** /ædvɑːntɪdʒd, -væn-/ A person or place that is **advantaged** is in a better social or financial position than other people or places. ❑ *Some cities are always going to be more advantaged.*
ADJ = *privileged* ≠*disadvantaged*

**ad|van|ta|geous** /ædvənteɪdʒəs/ If something is **advantageous to** you, it is likely to benefit you. ❑ *Free exchange of goods was advantageous to all.*
ADJ: oft ADJ *to* n = *favourable* ≠*unfavourable*

**ad|vent** /ædvent/ **The advent of** an important event, invention, or situation is the fact of it starting or coming into existence. [FORMAL] ❑ *...the leap forward in communication made possible by the advent of the mobile phone.*
N-UNCOUNT: usu *the* N *of* n

**Ad|vent** In the Christian church, **Advent** is the period between Advent Sunday, the Sunday closest to the 30th of November, and Christmas Day.
N-UNCOUNT

**ad|ven|ture** /ædventʃəʳ/ **(adventures)** 1 If someone has an **adventure**, they become involved in an unusual, exciting, and rather dangerous journey or series of events. ❑ *I set off for a new adventure in the United States on the first day of the new year.* 2 **Adventure** is excitement and willingness to do new, unusual, or rather dangerous things. ❑ *Their cultural backgrounds gave them a spirit of adventure.*
1 N-COUNT 2 N-UNCOUNT

**ad|ven|ture play|ground** **(adventure playgrounds)** An **adventure playground** is an area of land for children to play in, usually in cities or in a park. It has wooden structures and equipment such as ropes, nets, and rubber tyres. [BRIT]
N-COUNT

**ad|ven|tur|er** /ædventʃərəʳ/ **(adventurers)** An **adventurer** is a person who enjoys going to new, unusual, and exciting places.
N-COUNT

**ad|ven|ture|some** /ædventʃəʳsəm/ **Adventuresome** means the same as **adventurous**. [AM] ❑ *Every day was exciting and adventuresome.*
ADJ

**ad|ven|tur|ism** /ædventʃərɪzəm/ **Adventurism** is a willingness to take risks, especially in order to obtain an unfair advantage in politics or business. ❑ *Lenin dismissed guerrilla warfare as 'adventurism.'*
N-UNCOUNT disapproval

**ad|ven|tur|ist** /ædventʃərɪst/ **(adventurists)** If you describe someone or something as **adventurist**, you disapprove of them because they are willing to take risks in order to gain an unfair advantage in business or politics. ❑ *...aggressive and adventurist foreign policy.* ♦ An **adventurist** is someone who behaves in an adventurist way. ❑ *...political adventurists.*
ADJ disapproval; N-COUNT

**ad|ven|tur|ous** /ædventʃərəs/ 1 Someone who is **adventurous** is willing to take risks and to try new methods. Something that is **adventurous** involves new things or ideas. ❑ *Warren was an adventurous businessman... The menu could have been more adventurous.* 2 Someone who is **adventurous** is eager to visit new places and have new experiences. ❑ *He had always wanted an adventurous life in the tropics.*
1 ADJ = *daring* 2 ADJ

**ad|verb** /ædvɜːʳb/ **(adverbs)** An **adverb** is a word such as 'slowly', 'now', 'very', 'politically', or 'fortunately' which adds information about the action, event, or situation mentioned in a clause.
N-COUNT

**ad|verb group** **(adverb groups)** An **adverb group** or **adverbial group** is a group of words based on an adverb, such as 'very slowly' or 'fortunately for us'. An adverb group can also consist simply of an adverb.
N-COUNT

**ad|ver|bial** /ædvɜːʳbiəl/ **Adverbial** means relating to adverbs or like an adverb. ❑ *...an adverbial expression.*
ADJ: usu ADJ n

**ad|ver|sar|ial** /ædvəʳseəriəl/ If you describe something as **adversarial**, you mean that it involves two or more people or organizations who are opposing each other. [FORMAL] ❑ *In our country there is an adversarial relationship between government and business.*
ADJ

**ad|ver|sary** /ædvəʳsəri, AM -seri/ **(adversaries)** Your **adversary** is someone you are competing with, or arguing or fighting against. ❑ *His political adversaries were creating a certain amount of trouble for him.*
N-COUNT: usu with supp = *opponent, enemy* ≠*ally*

**ad|verse** /ædvɜːʳs, AM ædvɜːrs/ **Adverse** decisions, conditions, or effects are unfavourable to you. ❑ *Despite the adverse conditions, the road was finished in just eight months.* ♦ **ad|verse|ly** *Price changes must not adversely affect the living standards of the people.*
ADJ: usu ADJ n ≠*favourable*; ADV: ADV with v

**ad|ver|sity** /ædvɜːʳsɪti/ **(adversities)** **Adversity** is a very difficult or unfavourable situation. ❑ *He showed courage in adversity.*
N-VAR: oft *in/of* N = *misfortune*

**ad|vert** /ædvɜːʳt/ **(adverts)** 1 An **advert** is an announcement in a newspaper, on television, or on a poster about something such as a product, event, or job. [BRIT] ❑ *I saw an advert for a job with a large engineering company.*
N-COUNT: oft N *for* n = *ad, advertisement*

☑ in AM, use **ad**

2 If you say that an example of something is **an advert for** that thing in general, you mean that it shows how good that thing is. [BRIT] ❑ *This courtroom battle has been a poor advert for English justice.* 3 You can use **the adverts** to refer to the interval in a commercial television programme, or between programmes, during which advertisements are shown. [BRIT, INFORMAL] ❑ *After the adverts, the presenter tried to pretend that everything was back to normal.*
2 N-COUNT: usu *a* N *for* n = *advertisement* 3 N-PLURAL: *the* N = *commercials*

☑ in AM, use **commercial break**

**ad|ver|tise** /ædvəʳtaɪz/ **(advertises, advertising, advertised)** ◆◇◇ 1 If you **advertise** something such as a product, an event, or a job, you tell people about it in newspapers, on television, or on posters in order to encourage them to buy the product, go to the event, or apply for the job. ❑ *The players can advertise baked beans, but not rugby boots... Religious groups are currently not allowed to advertise on television.* 2 If you **advertise for** someone to do something for you, for example to work for you or share your accommodation, you announce it in a newspaper, on television, or on a notice board. ❑ *We advertised for staff in a local newspaper.* 3 If you do not **advertise** the fact that something is the case, you try not to let other people know about it. ❑ *There is no need to advertise the fact that you are a single woman.* ➔ See also **advertising**.
1 VERB V n, V 2 VERB V *for* n 3 VERB: usu with brd-neg V n

**ad|ver|tise|ment** /ædvɜːʳtɪsmənt, AM ædvəʳtaɪz-/ **(advertisements)** 1 An **advertisement** is an announcement in a newspaper, on television, or on a poster about something such as a product, event, or job. [WRITTEN] ❑ *Miss Parrish recently placed an advertisement in the local newspaper.* 2 If you say that an example of something is **an advertisement for** that thing in general, you mean that it shows how good that thing is. [mainly BRIT] ❑ *The England team were a poor advertisement for European football tonight.*
1 N-COUNT: oft N *for* n = *advert, ad* 2 N-COUNT: usu *a* N *for* n

**ad|ver|tis|er** /ædvəʳtaɪzəʳ/ **(advertisers)** An **advertiser** is a person or company that pays for a product, event, or job to be advertised in a newspaper, on television, or on a poster.
N-COUNT

**ad|ver|tis|ing** /ædvəʳtaɪzɪŋ/ **Advertising** is the activity of creating advertisements and making sure people see them.
N-UNCOUNT

**ad|ver|tis|ing agen|cy** **(advertising agencies)** An **advertising agency** is a company whose business is to create advertisements for other companies or organizations. ❑ *Advertising agencies are losing their once-powerful grip on brand marketing.*
N-COUNT

**ad|ver|tis|ing cam|paign** **(advertising campaigns)** An **advertising campaign** is a planned series of advertisements. ❑ *The Govern-*
N-COUNT

*ment has launched an advertising campaign to encourage people to vote.*

**ad|ver|tori|al** /ædvɜːʳtɔːriəl/ **(advertorials)** [N-VAR] An **advertorial** is an advertisement that uses the style of newspaper or magazine articles or television documentary programmes, so that it appears to be giving facts and not trying to sell a product.

**ad|vice** /ædvaɪs/ ◆◆◇ 1 [N-UNCOUNT: oft N *on/about* n/wh/-ing] If you give someone **advice**, you tell them what you think they should do in a particular situation. ❑ *Don't be afraid to ask for advice about ordering the meal... Your community officer can give you advice on how to prevent crime in your area... Take my advice and stay away from him!... Most foreign nationals have now left the country on the advice of their governments.* 2 [PHRASE: V inflects] If you **take advice** or **take legal advice**, you ask a lawyer for his or her professional opinion on a situation. [FORMAL] ❑ *We are taking advice on legal steps to recover the money.*

**ad|vice col|umn** **(advice columns)** [N-COUNT] In a newspaper or magazine, the **advice column** contains letters from readers about their personal problems, and advice on what to do about them. [AM]

✔ in BRIT, use **agony column**

**ad|vice col|umn|ist** **(advice columnists)** [N-COUNT] An **advice columnist** is a person who writes a column in a newspaper or magazine in which they reply to readers who have written to them for advice on their personal problems. [AM]

✔ in BRIT, use **agony aunt**

**ad|vice line** **(advice lines)** [N-COUNT] An **advice line** is a service that you can telephone in order to get advice about something. ❑ *For help on crime prevention, call our 24-hour advice line.*

**ad|vis|able** /ædvaɪzəbᵊl/ [ADJ: v-link ADJ, oft *it* v-link ADJ to-inf = wise] If you tell someone that **it** is **advisable to** do something, you are suggesting that they should do it, because it is sensible or is likely to achieve the result they want. [FORMAL] ❑ *Because of the popularity of the region, it is advisable to book hotels or camp sites in advance.* ♦ **ad|vis|abil|ity** /ædvaɪzəbɪlɪti/ [N-UNCOUNT: *the* N *of* n] *I have doubts about the advisability of surgery in this case.*

**ad|vise** /ædvaɪz/ **(advises, advising, advised)** ◆◇◇ 1 [VERB] If you **advise** someone **to** do something, you tell them what you think they should do. ❑ *The minister advised him to leave as soon as possible...* [V n to-inf] *Herbert would surely advise her how to approach the bank...* [V n wh] *I would strongly advise against it...* [V *against* n] *Doctors advised that he should be transferred to a private room.* [V that] 2 [VERB] If an expert **advises** people **on** a particular subject, he or she gives them help and information on that subject. ❑ *...an officer who advises undergraduates on money matters...* [V n *on* n] *A family doctor will be able to advise on suitable birth control.* [V *on* n] 3 [VERB = inform, apprise] If you **advise** someone **of** a fact or situation, you tell them the fact or explain what the situation is. [V n *of* n] [FORMAL] ❑ *I think it best that I advise you of my decision to retire.* 4 → See also **ill-advised**, **well advised**.

**ad|vis|ed|ly** /ædvaɪzɪdli/ [ADV: ADV after v] If you say that you are using a word or expression **advisedly**, you mean that you have deliberately chosen to use it, even though it may sound unusual, wrong, or offensive, because it draws attention to what you are saying. ❑ *I say 'boys' advisedly because we are talking almost entirely about male behaviour... What a crazy scheme, and I use that term advisedly.*

**ad|vise|ment** /ædvaɪzmənt/ [PHRASE: V inflects] If someone in authority **takes** a matter **under advisement**, they decide that the matter needs to be considered more carefully, often by experts. [AM, FORMAL] ❑ *I will take the suggestion under advisement, and refer it to the board.*

**ad|vis|er** /ædvaɪzəʳ/ **(advisers)** also **advisor.** ◆◇◇ [N-COUNT: usu with supp, oft N *to* n] An **adviser** is an expert whose job is to give advice to another person or to a group of people. ❑ *In Washington, the President and his advisers spent the day in meetings. ...a careers adviser.*

**ad|vi|so|ry** /ædvaɪzəri/ **(advisories)** 1 [ADJ: usu ADJ n] An **advisory** group regularly gives suggestions and help to people or organizations, especially about a particular subject or area of activity. [FORMAL] ❑ *...members of the advisory committee on the safety of nuclear installations.* 2 [N-COUNT: usu supp N = warning] An **advisory** is an official announcement or report that warns people about bad weather, diseases, or other dangers or problems. [AM] ❑ *26 states have issued health advisories.*

**ad|vo|ca|cy** /ædvəkəsi/ 1 [N-SING: usu poss N *of* n = support] Someone's **advocacy of** a particular action or plan is their act of recommending it publicly. [FORMAL] ❑ *I support your advocacy of free trade.* 2 [N-UNCOUNT: usu N n = lobby] An **advocacy** group or organization is one that tries to influence the decisions of a government or other authority. [AM]

**ad|vo|cate** **(advocates, advocating, advocated)** ◆◇◇

✔ The verb is pronounced /ædvəkeɪt/. The noun is pronounced /ædvəkət/.

1 [VERB = recommend] If you **advocate** a particular action or plan, you recommend it publicly. [FORMAL] ❑ *Mr Williams is a conservative who advocates fewer government controls on business.* [V n] *...the tax policy advocated by the Opposition.* [V-ed] 2 [N-COUNT: oft N *of* n = proponent] An **advocate of** a particular action or plan is someone who recommends it publicly. [FORMAL] ❑ *He was a strong advocate of free market policies and a multi-party system.* 3 [N-COUNT = lawyer] An **advocate** is a lawyer who speaks in favour of someone or defends them in a court of law. [LEGAL] 4 [N-COUNT: with supp] An **advocate** for a particular group is a person who works for the interests of that group. [AM] ❑ *...advocates for the homeless.* → See also **devil's advocate**.

**aegis** /iːdʒɪs/ [PREP-PHRASE = under the auspices of] Something that is done **under the aegis of** a person or organization is done with their official support and backing. [FORMAL] ❑ *The space programme will continue under the aegis of the armed forces.*

**aeon** /iːɒn/ **(aeons)**

✔ in AM, use **eon**

[N-COUNT = age] An **aeon** is an extremely long period of time. ❑ *Aeons ago, there were deserts where there is now fertile land.*

**aer|ate** /eəreɪt/ **(aerates, aerating, aerated)** [VERB = oxygenate] To **aerate** a substance means to cause air or gas to pass through it. ❑ *Aerate the soil by spiking with a fork.* [V n]

**aer|ial** /eəriəl/ **(aerials)** 1 [ADJ: ADJ n] You talk about **aerial** attacks and **aerial** photographs to indicate that people or things on the ground are attacked or photographed by people in aeroplanes. ❑ *Weeks of aerial bombardment had destroyed factories and highways.* 2 [ADJ: ADJ n] You can use **aerial** to describe things that exist or happen above the ground or in the air. ❑ *The seagulls swirled in aerial combat over the barges.* 3 [N-COUNT] An **aerial** is a device or a piece of wire that receives television or radio signals and is usually attached to a radio, television, car, or building. [BRIT] → See pictures on pages 1705 and 1707. ❑ *...the radio aerials of taxis and cars.*

✔ in AM, use **antenna**

**aerie** /eri/ → see **eyrie**.

**aero-** /eərou-/ 1 [PREFIX] **aero-** is used at the beginning of words, especially nouns, that refer to things or activities connected with air or movement through the air. 2 [COMB in N-COUNT] **aero-** combines with nouns to form nouns relating to aeroplanes. ❑ *...the British aero-engine maker, Rolls-Royce.*

**aero|bat|ics** /eərəbætɪks/

✔ The form **aerobatic** is used as a modifier.

[N-PLURAL] **Aerobatics** are skilful displays of flying, usually to entertain people watching from the ground.

**aero|bic** /eəroubɪk/ [ADJ: usu ADJ n] **Aerobic** activity exercises and strengthens your heart and lungs. ❑ *Aerobic exercise gets the heart pumping and helps you to burn up the fat.*

**aero|bics** /eəroubɪks/ [N-UNCOUNT: oft N n] **Aerobics** is a form of exercise which increases the amount of oxygen in your blood, and strengthens your heart and lungs. The verb that follows **aerobics** may be either singular or plural. ❑ *I'd like to join an aerobics class to improve my fitness.*

**aero|drome** /eərədroʊm/ **(aerodromes)** An **aerodrome** is a place or area where small aircraft can land and take off. [BRIT] N-COUNT: oft in names = *airfield*

☑ in AM, use **airdrome**

**aero|dy|nam|ic** /eəroʊdaɪnæmɪk/ If something such as a car has an **aerodynamic** shape or design, it goes faster and uses less fuel than other cars because the air passes over it more easily. ❑ *The secret of the machine lies in the aerodynamic shape of the frame.* ♦ **aero|dy|nami|cal|ly** *Cars are becoming so aerodynamically efficient.* ADJ: usu ADJ n; ADV: ADV adj, ADV with v

**aero|dy|nam|ics** /eəroʊdaɪnæmɪks/

☑ The form **aerodynamic** is used as a modifier. In British English, **aerodynamics** is sometimes used as a plural noun, with a plural verb.

**Aerodynamics** is the study of the way in which objects move through the air. N-UNCOUNT

**aero|nau|ti|cal** /eərənɔːtɪkəl/ **Aeronautical** means involving or relating to the design and construction of aeroplanes. ❑ *...the biggest aeronautical research laboratory in Europe.* ADJ: ADJ n

**aero|naut|ics** /eərənɔːtɪks/ **Aeronautics** is the science of designing and building aeroplanes. N-UNCOUNT

**aero|plane** /eərəpleɪn/ **(aeroplanes)** An **aeroplane** is a vehicle with wings and one or more engines that enable it to fly through the air. [BRIT] N-COUNT = *plane, aircraft*

☑ in AM, use **airplane**

**aero|sol** /eərəsɒl, AM -sɔːl/ **(aerosols)** An **aerosol** is a small container in which a liquid such as paint or deodorant is kept under pressure. When you press a button, the liquid is forced out as a fine spray or foam. N-COUNT: oft N n

**aero|space** /eəroʊspeɪs/ **Aerospace** companies are involved in developing and making rockets, missiles, space vehicles, and related equipment. ❑ *...the US aerospace industry.* N-UNCOUNT: usu N n

**aes|thete** /iːsθiːt, AM es-/ **(aesthetes)**

☑ in AM, also use **esthete**

An **aesthete** is someone who loves and appreciates works of art and beautiful things. N-COUNT

**aes|thet|ic** /iːsθetɪk, AM es-/

☑ in AM, also use **esthetic**

**Aesthetic** is used to talk about beauty or art, and people's appreciation of beautiful things. ❑ *...products chosen for their aesthetic appeal as well as their durability and quality.* ♦ **The aesthetic** of a work of art is its aesthetic quality. ❑ *He responded very strongly to the aesthetic of this particular work.* ♦ **aes|theti|cal|ly** /iːsθetɪkli, AM es-/ *There is nothing aesthetically pleasing about this bridge.* ADJ; N-SING: the N; ADV: oft ADV with cl

**aes|thet|ics** /iːsθetɪks, AM es-/

☑ in AM, also use **esthetics**

**Aesthetics** is a branch of philosophy concerned with the study of the idea of beauty. N-UNCOUNT

**aeti|ol|ogy** /iːtiɒlədʒi/ → see **etiology**.

**afar** /əfɑːʳ/ **Afar** means a long way away. [LITERARY] ❑ *Seen from afar, its towering buildings beckon the visitor in.* ADV: usu *from* ADV, also ADV after v

**af|fable** /æfəbəl/ Someone who is **affable** is pleasant and friendly. ❑ *Mr Brooke is an extremely affable and approachable man.* ADJ = *amicable*

**af|fair** /əfeəʳ/ **(affairs)** ◆◆◇ [1] If an event or a series of events has been mentioned and you want to talk about it again, you can refer to it as **the affair**. ❑ *The government has mishandled the whole affair... The affair began when customs officials inspected a convoy of 60 tankers.* N-SING: *the* N = *business, matter* [2] You can refer to an important or interesting event or situation as **'the ... affair'**. [mainly JOURNALISM] ❑ *...the damage caused to the CIA and FBI in the aftermath of the Watergate affair.* N-SING: usu *the* n-proper N [3] You can describe the main quality of an event by saying that it is a particular kind of **affair**. ❑ *Michael said that his planned 10-day visit would be a purely private affair.* N-SING: usu supp N [4] You can describe an object as a particular kind of **affair** when you want to draw attention to a particular feature, or indicate that it is unusual. ❑ *All their beds were distinctive; Mac's was an iron affair with brass knobs.* N-SING: supp N [5] If two people who are not married to each other have an **affair**, they have a sexual relationship. ❑ *She was having an affair with someone at work.* → See also **love affair**. N-COUNT [6] You can use **affairs** to refer to all the important facts or activities that are connected with a particular subject. ❑ *He does not want to interfere in the internal affairs of another country.* → See also **current affairs**, **state of affairs**. N-PLURAL: usu supp N [7] Your **affairs** are all the matters connected with your life which you consider to be private and normally deal with yourself. ❑ *The unexpectedness of my father's death meant that his affairs were not entirely in order.* N-PLURAL: usu poss N [8] If you say that a decision or situation is someone's **affair**, you mean that it is their responsibility, and other people should not interfere. ❑ *If you wish to make a fool of yourself, that is your affair.* N-SING: poss N = *business*

**af|fect** /əfekt/ **(affects, affecting, affected)** ◆◆◇ [1] If something **affects** a person or thing, it influences them or causes them to change in some way. ❑ *Nicotine adversely affects the functioning of the heart and arteries. ...the worst-affected areas of Somalia.* VERB; V n; V-ed [2] If a disease **affects** someone, it causes them to become ill. ❑ *Arthritis is a crippling disease which affects people all over the world.* VERB = *afflict*; V n [3] If something or someone **affects** you, they make you feel a strong emotion, especially sadness or pity. ❑ *The divorce affected Jim deeply.* VERB; V n

**af|fec|ta|tion** /æfekteɪʃən/ **(affectations)** If you say that someone's attitude or behaviour is an **affectation**, you disapprove of the fact that it is not genuine or natural, but is intended to impress other people. ❑ *I wore sunglasses all the time and people thought it was an affectation.* N-VAR [disapproval]

**af|fect|ed** /əfektɪd/ If you describe someone's behaviour as **affected**, you disapprove of the fact that they behave in an unnatural way that is intended to impress other people. ❑ *She had an affected air and a disdainful look.* ADJ: usu ADJ n [disapproval] = *mannered* ≠ *natural*

**af|fect|ing** /əfektɪŋ/ If you describe something such as a story or a piece of music as **affecting**, you think it is good because it makes you feel a strong emotion, especially sadness or pity. [LITERARY] ❑ *...an affecting drama about a woman with a terminal illness.* ADJ [approval] = *moving, touching*

**af|fec|tion** /əfekʃən/ **(affections)** [1] If you regard someone or something with **affection**, you like them and are fond of them. ❑ *She thought of him with affection... She had developed quite an affection for the place.* N-UNCOUNT: oft N *for/of* n [2] Your **affections** are your feelings of love or fondness for someone. ❑ *The distant object of his affections is Caroline.* N-PLURAL: with poss

**af|fec|tion|ate** /əfekʃənət/ If you are **affectionate**, you show your love or fondness for another person in the way that you behave towards them. ❑ *They seemed devoted to each other and were openly affectionate.* ♦ **af|fec|tion|ate|ly** *He looked affectionately at his niece.* ADJ; ADV: ADV with v = *fondly*

**af|fi|da|vit** /æfɪdeɪvɪt/ **(affidavits)** An **affidavit** is a written statement which you swear is true and which may be used as evidence in a court of law. [LEGAL] N-COUNT

**af|fili|ate** **(affiliates, affiliating, affiliated)**

☑ The noun is pronounced /əfɪliət/. The verb is pronounced /əfɪlieɪt/.

[1] An **affiliate** is an organization which is officially connected with another, larger organization or is a member of it. [FORMAL] ❑ *The World Chess Federation has affiliates in around 120 countries.* N-COUNT: oft with poss [2] If an organization **affiliates to** or **with** another larger organization, it forms a close connection with the larger organization or becomes a member VERB

of it. [FORMAL] ❑ *All youth groups will have to affiliate to the National Youth Agency.* V to/with n

**af|fili|at|ed** /əfɪlieɪtɪd/ [1] If an organization is **affiliated with** another larger organization, it is officially connected with the larger organization or is a member of it. [FORMAL] ❑ *There are 73 unions affiliated to the Trades Union Congress.* [2] If a professional person, such as a lawyer or doctor, is **affiliated with** an organization, they are officially connected with that organization or do some official work for it. [FORMAL] ❑ *He will remain affiliated with the firm as a special associate director. ...our affiliated members.* ADJ: v-link ADJ to/with n, ADJ n; ADJ: v-link ADJ with/to n, ADJ n

**af|filia|tion** /əfɪlieɪʃᵊn/ **(affiliations)** [1] If one group has an **affiliation** with another group, it has a close or official connection with it. [FORMAL] ❑ *The group has no affiliation to any political party.* [2] If you have an **affiliation with** a group or another person, you have a close or official connection with them. [FORMAL] ❑ *...Johnson's affiliation with shoe company Nike... They asked what her political affiliations were.* N-VAR: oft N with/to n; N-VAR: oft N with/to n

**af|fin|ity** /əfɪnɪti/ **(affinities)** If you have an **affinity with** someone or something, you feel that you are similar to them or that you know and understand them very well. ❑ *He has a close affinity with the landscape he knew when he was growing up.* N-SING: also no det, with supp

**af|fin|ity card** **(affinity cards)** An **affinity card** is a type of credit card. The bank which issues the card gives a small amount of money to a charity or institution each time the customer spends a certain amount with their card. N-COUNT

**af|firm** /əfɜːʳm/ **(affirms, affirming, affirmed)** [1] If you **affirm** that something is true or that something exists, you state firmly and publicly that it is true or exists. [FORMAL] ❑ *The House of Lords affirmed that the terms of a contract cannot be rewritten retrospectively. ...a speech in which he affirmed a commitment to lower taxes... 'This place is a dump,' affirmed Miss T.* ♦ **af|fir|ma|tion** /æfəʳmeɪʃᵊn/ **(affirmations)** *The ministers issued an affirmation of their faith in the system.* [2] If an event **affirms** something, it shows that it is true or exists. [FORMAL] ❑ *Everything I had accomplished seemed to affirm that opinion.* ♦ **af|fir|ma|tion** *The high turnout was an affirmation of the importance that the voters attached to the election.* VERB = assert; V that; V n; V with quote; N-VAR; VERB = confirm; V n; N-UNCOUNT: also a N

**af|firma|tive** /əfɜːʳmətɪv/ [1] An **affirmative** word or gesture indicates that you agree with what someone has said or that the answer to a question is 'yes'. [FORMAL] ❑ *Haig was desperately eager for an affirmative answer.* ♦ **af|firma|tive|ly** *'Is that clear?' Bob nodded his head affirmatively.* [2] If you reply to a question **in the affirmative**, you say 'yes' or make a gesture that means 'yes'. [FORMAL] ❑ *He asked me if I was ready. I answered in the affirmative.* [3] In grammar, an **affirmative** clause is positive and does not contain a negative word. ADJ ≠ negative; ADV: ADV with v; PHRASE: PHR after v; ADJ ≠ negative

**af|firma|tive ac|tion** **Affirmative action** is the policy of giving jobs and other opportunities to members of groups such as racial minorities or women who might not otherwise have them. [AM] N-UNCOUNT

> in BRIT, use **positive discrimination**

**af|fix** **(affixes, affixing, affixed)**

> The verb is pronounced /əfɪks/. The noun is pronounced /æfɪks/.

[1] If you **affix** one thing **to** another, you stick it or attach it to the other thing. [FORMAL] ❑ *Complete the form and affix four tokens to its back... I covered the scroll in sealing wax, and affixed a red ribbon. ...special storage racks affixed to the sides of buses.* [2] An **affix** is a letter or group of letters, for example 'un-' or '-y', which is added to either the beginning or the end of a word to form a different word with a different meaning. For example, 'un-' is added to 'kind' to form 'unkind'. Compare **prefix** and **suffix**. VERB; V n to n; V n; V-ed; N-COUNT

**af|flict** /əflɪkt/ **(afflicts, afflicting, afflicted)** If you **are afflicted by** pain, illness, or disaster, it affects you badly and makes you suffer. [FORMAL] ❑ *Italy has been afflicted by political corruption for decades... There are two main problems which afflict people with hearing impairments.* VERB = affect; be V-ed by/with n; V n

**af|flic|tion** /əflɪkʃᵊn/ **(afflictions)** An **affliction** is something which causes physical or mental suffering. [FORMAL] ❑ *Hay fever is an affliction which arrives at an early age.* N-VAR

**af|flu|ence** /æfluəns/ **Affluence** is the state of having a lot of money or a high standard of living. [FORMAL] ❑ *The postwar era was one of new affluence for the working class.* N-UNCOUNT = prosperity

**af|flu|ent** /æfluənt/ If you are **affluent**, you have a lot of money. ❑ *Cigarette smoking used to be commoner among affluent people.* ♦ **The affluent** are people who are affluent. ❑ *The diet of the affluent has not changed much over the decades.* ADJ = prosperous, wealthy; N-PLURAL: the N

**af|ford** /əfɔːʳd/ **(affords, affording, afforded)** ◆◇◇ [1] If you **cannot afford** something, you do not have enough money to pay for it. ❑ *My parents can't even afford a new refrigerator... We couldn't afford to buy a new rug.* [2] If you say that you cannot **afford to** do something or allow it to happen, you mean that you must not do it or must prevent it from happening because it would be harmful or embarrassing to you. ❑ *We can't afford to wait... The country could not afford the luxury of an election.* [3] If someone or something **affords** you an opportunity or protection, they give it to you. [FORMAL] ❑ *This affords us the opportunity to ask questions about how the systems might change... It was a cold room, but it afforded a fine view of the Old City.* VERB; V n; V to-inf; VERB; V to-inf; V n; VERB; V n n; V n

**af|ford|able** /əfɔːʳdəbᵊl/ If something is **affordable**, most people have enough money to buy it. ❑ *...the availability of affordable housing.* ♦ **af|forda|bil|ity** /əfɔːʳdəbɪlɪti/ *...research into homelessness and housing affordability.* ADJ; N-UNCOUNT

**af|for|esta|tion** /æfɒrɪsteɪʃᵊn, AM -fɔːr-/ **Afforestation** is the process of planting large numbers of trees on land which has few or no trees on it. ❑ *Since the Sixties, afforestation has changed the Welsh countryside.* N-UNCOUNT

**af|fray** /əfreɪ/ An **affray** is a noisy and violent fight, especially in a public place. [FORMAL] N-SING: also no det

**af|front** /əfrʌnt/ **(affronts, affronting, affronted)** [1] If something **affronts** you, you feel insulted and hurt because of it. [FORMAL] ❑ *...an incident which particularly affronted Kasparov.* ♦ **af|front|ed** *He pretended to be affronted, but inwardly he was pleased.* [2] If something is an **affront to** you, it is an obvious insult to you. ❑ *It's an affront to human dignity to keep someone alive like this.* VERB; V n; ADJ: usu v-link ADJ; N-COUNT: usu sing, usu N to n = insult

**Af|ghan** /æfgæn/ **(Afghans)** **Afghan** means belonging or relating to Afghanistan, or to its people or language. ❑ *...the Afghan capital, Kabul.* ♦ An **Afghan** is a person who comes from Afghanistan. ADJ; N-COUNT

**afi|cio|na|do** /əfɪʃiənɑːdoʊ/ **(aficionados)** If someone is an **aficionado of** something, they like it and know a lot about it. ❑ *I happen to be an aficionado of the opera, and I love art museums. ...a jazz aficionado.* N-COUNT: usu with supp, oft N of n

**afield** /əfiːld/ [1] **Further afield** or **farther afield** means in places or areas other than the nearest or most obvious one. ❑ *They enjoy participating in a wide variety of activities, both locally and further afield.* [2] If someone comes **from far afield**, they come from a long way away. ❑ *Many of those arrested came from far afield.* PHRASE: oft from PHR; PHRASE: oft from PHR

**afire** /əfaɪəʳ/ If something is **afire** or is **set afire**, it is on fire or looks as if it is on fire. ADJ: v-link ADJ, v n ADJ

**aflame** /əfleɪm/ If something is on fire, you can say it is **aflame**. [LITERARY] ADJ: v-link ADJ, v n ADJ

**afloat** /əfloʊt/ [1] If someone or something is **afloat**, they remain partly above the surface of water and do not sink. ❑ *They talked modestly of their valiant efforts to keep the tanker afloat.* [2] If a ADV: usu ADV after v, also v-link ADV, n ADV; ADV:

person, business, or country stays **afloat** or is kept **afloat**, they have just enough money to pay their debts and continue operating. [BUSINESS] ❑ *They are borrowing just to stay afloat, not for investment.* [usu ADV after v, also v-link ADV, n ADV = solvent]

**afoot** /əfʊt/ If you say that a plan or scheme is **afoot**, it is already happening or being planned, but you do not know much about it. ❑ *Everybody knew that something awful was afoot.* [ADJ: v-link ADJ]

**afore|men|tioned** /əfɔːʳmenʃᵊnd/ If you refer to **the aforementioned** person or subject, you mean the person or subject that has already been mentioned. [FORMAL] ❑ *A declaration will be issued at the end of the aforementioned UN conference.* [ADJ: det ADJ, usu *the* ADJ n = aforesaid]

**afore|said** /əfɔːʳsed/ **Aforesaid** means the same as **aforementioned**. [FORMAL] ❑ *...the aforesaid organizations and institutions.* [ADJ: det ADJ, usu *the* ADJ n = aforementioned]

**afoul** /əfaʊl/ If you **run afoul of** someone or something, you do something which causes problems with them. [AM] ❑ *All of them had run afoul of the law at some time or other.* [PHRASE: V inflects, PHR n = fall foul of]

**afraid** /əfreɪd/ ◆◇◇ 1 If you are **afraid of** someone or **afraid to** do something, you are frightened because you think that something very unpleasant is going to happen to you. ❑ *She did not seem at all afraid... I was afraid of the other boys... I'm still afraid to sleep in my own bedroom.* [ADJ: v-link ADJ, oft ADJ *of* n, ADJ to-inf = frightened] 2 If you are **afraid for** someone else, you are worried that something horrible is going to happen to them. ❑ *She's afraid for her family in Somalia.* [ADJ: v-link ADJ, usu ADJ *for* n] 3 If you are **afraid** that something unpleasant will happen, you are worried that it may happen and you want to avoid it. ❑ *I was afraid that nobody would believe me... The Government is afraid of losing the election.* [ADJ: v-link ADJ, ADJ that, ADJ *of* -ing, ADJ to-inf] 4 If you want to apologize to someone or to disagree with them in a polite way, you can say **I'm afraid**. [SPOKEN] ❑ *We don't have anything like that, I'm afraid... I'm afraid I can't help you.* [PHRASE: PHR with cl, PHR that, politeness]

**afresh** /əfreʃ/ If you do something **afresh**, you do it again in a different way. ❑ *They believe that the only hope for the French left is to start afresh.* [ADV: ADV after v = anew]

**Af|ri|can** /æfrɪkən/ **(Africans)** 1 **African** means belonging or relating to the continent of Africa, or to its countries or people. ❑ *...the African continent. ...African countries.* [ADJ] 2 **African** means belonging or relating to black people who come from Africa. ❑ *...traditional African culture. ...dance music with African roots.* [ADJ] 3 **African** is used to describe someone, usually a black person, who comes from Africa. ❑ *...African women.* [ADJ] ♦ An **African** is someone who is African. ❑ *Fish is a staple in the diet of many Africans.* [N-COUNT]

**African-American** **(African-Americans)** **African-Americans** are black people living in the United States who are descended from families that originally came from Africa. ❑ *Today African-Americans are 12 percent of the population.* [N-COUNT] ♦ **African-American** is also an adjective. ❑ *...a group of African-American community leaders.* [ADJ]

**African-Caribbean** **(African-Caribbeans)** **African-Caribbean** refers to people from the Caribbean whose ancestors came from Africa. ❑ *...modern African-Caribbean culture.* [ADJ: usu ADJ n] ♦ An **African-Caribbean** is someone who is African-Caribbean. [N-COUNT]

**Af|ri|kaans** /æfrɪkɑːns/ **Afrikaans** is one of the official languages of South Africa. ❑ *...a radical Afrikaans newspaper.* [N-UNCOUNT: oft N n]

**Af|ri|kan|er** /æfrɪkɑːnəʳ/ **(Afrikaners)** **Afrikaner** means belonging or relating to the white people in South Africa whose ancestors were Dutch. [ADJ] ♦ An **Afrikaner** is someone who is Afrikaner. [N-COUNT]

**Afro** /æfroʊ/ **(Afros)** 1 **Afro** hair is very tightly curled and sticks out all around your head. [ADJ] 2 An **Afro** is an Afro hairstyle. [N-COUNT]

**Afro-** /æfroʊ-/ **Afro-** is used to form adjectives and nouns that describe something that is connected with Africa. ❑ *...very well known Afro-American family. ...an Afro-centric fashion show.* [COMB in ADJ and N-COUNT]

**Afro-Caribbean** **(Afro-Caribbeans)** **Afro-Caribbean** refers to people from the Caribbean whose ancestors came from Africa. ❑ *...Britain's Afro-Caribbean community.* [ADJ] ♦ An **Afro-Caribbean** is someone who is Afro-Caribbean. [N-COUNT]

**aft** /ɑːft, æft/ If you go **aft** in a boat or plane, you go to the back of it. If you are **aft**, you are in the back. [ADV: ADV after v, *be* ADV, oft ADV *of* n]

**af|ter** /ɑːftəʳ, æftəʳ/ ◆◆◆

> In addition to the uses shown below, **after** is used in phrasal verbs such as 'ask after', 'look after', and 'take after'.

1 If something happens **after** a particular date or event, it happens during the period of time that follows that date or event. ❑ *After 19 May, strikes were occurring on a daily basis... After breakfast Amy ordered a taxi... It wasn't until after Christmas that I met Paul.* [PREP ≠ before] ♦ **After** is also a conjunction. ❑ *After Don told me this, he spoke of his mother... Marina cared for him after he seriously injured his eye several years ago.* [CONJ] 2 If you do one thing **after** doing another, you do it during the period of time that follows the other thing. ❑ *After completing and signing it, please return the form to us in the envelope provided. ...women who have changed their mind after deciding not to have children.* [PREP: PREP -ing ≠ before] 3 You use **after** when you are talking about time. For example, if something is going to happen during **the day after** or **the weekend after** a particular time, it is going to happen during the following day or during the following weekend. ❑ *She's leaving the day after tomorrow.* [PREP: n PREP n] ♦ **After** is also an adverb. ❑ *Tomorrow. Or the day after.* [ADV: ADV after v] 4 If you go **after** someone, you follow or chase them. ❑ *He walked out, and Louise went after him. ...people who were after him for large amounts of money.* [PREP] 5 If you are **after** something, you are trying to get it. ❑ *They were after the money... I did eventually find what I was after.* [PREP] 6 If you call, shout, or stare **after** someone, you call, shout, or stare at them as they move away from you. ❑ *'Come back!' he called after me.* [PREP] 7 If you tell someone that one place is a particular distance **after** another, you mean that it is situated beyond the other place and further away from you. ❑ *A few kilometres after the village, turn right to Montelabate.* [PREP = past ≠ before] 8 If one thing is written **after** another thing on a page, it is written following it or underneath it. ❑ *I wrote my name after Penny's.* [PREP = following] 9 You use **after** in order to give the most important aspect of something when comparing it with another aspect. ❑ *After Germany, America is Britain's second-biggest customer.* [PREP] 10 To be named **after** someone means to be given the same name as them. [BRIT] ❑ *He persuaded Virginia to name the baby after him.* [PREP]

☑ in AM, use **for**

11 If you say **'after you'** to someone, you are being polite and allowing them to go in front of you or through a doorway before you do. [CONVENTION politeness] 12 **After** is used when telling the time. If it is, for example, **ten after six**, the time is ten minutes past six. [AM] [PREP ≠ before] 13 **after all** → see **all**.

PHRASES 14 If you do something to several things **one after the other** or **one after another**, you do it to one, then the next, and so on, with no break between your actions. ❑ *Sybil ate three biscuits, one after the other.* [PHRASE] 15 If something happens **day after day** or **year after year**, it happens every day or every year, for a long time. ❑ *...people who'd been coming here year after year.* [PHRASE]

**after-** /ɑːftəʳ-, æftəʳ-/ **After-** is added to nouns to form adjectives which indicate that something takes place or exists after an event or process. ❑ *...an after-dinner speech... After-tax profit fell by 28 percent.* [COMB in ADJ: ADJ n]

**after|care** /ɑːftəʳkeəʳ, æf-/

☑ in BRIT, also use **after-care**

**Aftercare** is the nursing and care of people who [N-UNCOUNT] have been treated in hospital, and who are now recovering. ❑ *As part of the treatment, he attended 15 weeks of after-care... Mr Lloyd specialised in after-care services.*

**after-effect** (**after-effects**)

✔ in AM, use **aftereffect**

The **after-effects** of an event, experience, or substance are the conditions which result from it. ❑ *...people still suffering from the after-effects of the world's worst nuclear accident.* N-COUNT: usu pl

**after|glow** /ɑːftəʳgloʊ, æf-/ [1] The **afterglow** is the glow that remains after a light has gone, for example after the sun has gone down. [LITERARY] ❑ *...the light of the sunset's afterglow.* N-UNCOUNT: oft with poss
[2] You can refer to the good feeling or effects that remain after an event as the **afterglow**. ❑ *...basking in the afterglow of their Champions League victory.* N-UNCOUNT: oft N *of* n

**after-hours** You use **after-hours** to describe activities which happen after the end of the usual time for them. ❑ *The school offers after-hours childcare.* ADJ: ADJ n

**after|life** /ɑːftəʳlaɪf, æf-/ (**afterlives**) also **after-life.** The **afterlife** is a life that some people believe begins when you die, for example a life in heaven or as another person or animal. N-COUNT: usu sing

**after|market** /ɑːftəʳmɑːʳkɪt, æf-/ [1] The **aftermarket** is all the related products that are sold after an item, especially a car, has been bought. [BUSINESS] N-SING [2] The **aftermarket** in shares and bonds is the buying and selling of them after they have been issued. [BUSINESS] N-SING

**after|math** /ɑːftəʳmɑːθ, æftəʳmæθ/ **The aftermath of** an important event, especially a harmful one, is the situation that results from it. ❑ *In the aftermath of the coup, the troops opened fire on the demonstrators.* N-SING: with supp, oft *the* N *of* n

**after|noon** /ɑːftəʳnuːn, æf-/ (**afternoons**) ◆◆◇ The **afternoon** is the part of each day which begins at lunchtime and ends at about six o'clock. ❑ *He's arriving in the afternoon... He had stayed in his room all afternoon. ...an afternoon news conference.* N-VAR

**after|noon tea** (**afternoon teas**) **Afternoon tea** is a small meal you can have in the afternoon. It includes a cup of tea and food such as sandwiches and cakes. [BRIT] N-VAR

**after-sales ser|vice** (**after-sales services**) A company's **after-sales service** is all the help and information that it provides to customers after they have bought a particular product. [BUSINESS] ❑ *...a local retailer who offers a good after-sales service... They are also attempting to keep the car buyer as a long-term customer by offering after-sales service.* N-VAR

**after-school** **After-school** activities are those that are organized for children in the afternoon or evening after they have finished school. ❑ *...an after-school childcare scheme.* ADJ: ADJ n

**after|shave** /ɑːftəʳʃeɪv, æf-/ (**aftershaves**) also **after-shave.** **Aftershave** is a liquid with a pleasant smell that men sometimes put on their faces after shaving. N-MASS

**after|shock** /ɑːftəʳʃɒk, æf-/ (**aftershocks**) [1] **Aftershocks** are smaller earthquakes which occur after a large earthquake. N-COUNT [2] People sometimes refer to the effects of an important event, especially a bad one, as the **aftershock**. [mainly JOURNALISM] ❑ *They were already under stress, thanks to the aftershock of last year's drought.* N-COUNT: usu with supp

**after|taste** /ɑːftəʳteɪst, æf-/ also **after-taste.** An **aftertaste** is a taste that remains in your mouth after you have finished eating or drinking something. N-SING: usu with supp

**after|thought** /ɑːftəʳθɔːt, æf-/ (**afterthoughts**) If you do or say something as **an afterthought**, you do or say it after something else as an addition, perhaps without careful thought. ❑ *Almost as an afterthought he added that he missed her.* N-COUNT: usu sing, usu *a* N

**after|wards** /ɑːftəʳwəʳdz, æf-/ ◆◇◇

✔ The form **afterward** is also used, mainly in American English.

If you do something or if something happens **afterwards**, you do it or it happens after a particular event or time that has already been mentioned. ❑ *Shortly afterwards, police arrested four suspects... James was taken to hospital but died soon afterwards.* ADV: ADV with cl

**after|word** /ɑːftəʳwɜːʳd/ An **afterword** is a short essay at the end of a book, usually written by the author. N-SING

**again** /əgen, əgeɪn/ ◆◆◆ [1] You use **again** to indicate that something happens a second time, or after it has already happened before. ❑ *He kissed her again... Again there was a short silence... I don't ever want to go through anything like that again.* ADV: ADV with v, ADV with cl
[2] You use **again** to indicate that something is now in a particular state or place that it used to be in. ❑ *He opened his attaché-case, removed a folder, then closed it again... I started to feel good about myself again.* ADV: ADV after v [3] You can use **again** when you want to point out that there is a similarity between the subject that you are talking about now and a previous subject. ❑ *Again the pregnancy was very similar to my previous two.* ADV: ADV cl [4] You can use **again** in expressions such as **but again**, **then again**, and **there again** when you want to introduce a remark which contrasts with or weakens something that you have just said. ❑ *It's easier to take a taxi. But then again you can't always get one.* ADV: ADV with cl [5] You can add **again** to the end of your question when you are asking someone to tell you something that you have forgotten or that they have already told you. [SPOKEN] ❑ *Sorry, what's your name again?* ADV: cl ADV
[6] You use **again** in expressions such as **half as much again** when you are indicating how much greater one amount is than another amount that you have just mentioned or are about to mention. ❑ *A similar wine from France would cost you half as much again.* ADV: amount ADV [7] You can use **again and again** or **time and again** to emphasize that something happens many times. ❑ *He would go over his work again and again until he had it right.* PHRASE: usu PHR after v [emphasis] = *repeatedly* [8] **now and again** → see **now**. **once again** → see **once**.

**against** /əgenst, əgeɪnst/ ◆◆◆

In addition to the uses shown below, **against** is used in phrasal verbs such as 'come up against', 'guard against', and 'hold against'.

[1] If one thing is leaning or pressing **against** another, it is touching it. ❑ *She leaned against him... On a table pushed against a wall there were bottles of beer and wine. ...the rain beating against the window panes.* PREP [2] If you are **against** something such as a plan, policy, or system, you think it is wrong, bad, or stupid. ❑ *Taxes are unpopular – it is understandable that voters are against them... Joan was very much against commencing drug treatment. ...a march to protest against job losses.* PREP ♦ **Against** is also an adverb. ❑ *The vote for the suspension of the party was 283 in favour with 29 against.* ADV: ADV after v [3] If you compete **against** someone in a game, you try to beat them. ❑ *The tour will include games against the Australian Barbarians.* PREP [4] If you take action **against** someone or something, you try to harm them. ❑ *Security forces are still using violence against opponents of the government.* PREP [5] If you take action **against** a possible future event, you try to prevent it. ❑ *...the fight against crime... I must warn you against raising your hopes.* PREP [6] If you do something **against** someone's wishes, advice, or orders, you do not do what they want you to do or tell you to do. ❑ *He discharged himself from hospital against the advice of doctors.* PREP [7] If you do something in order to protect yourself **against** something unpleasant or harmful, you do something which will make its effects on you less serious if it happens. ❑ *A business needs insurance against risks such as fire and* PREP

*flood.* [8] If you **have** something **against** someone or something, you dislike them. ❑ *Have you got something against women, Les?* [9] If something is **against** the law or **against** the rules, there is a law or a rule which says that you must not do it. ❑ *It is against the law to detain you against your will for any length of time.* [10] If you are moving **against** a current, tide, or wind, you are moving in the opposite direction to it. ❑ *...swimming upstream against the current.* [11] If something happens or is considered **against** a particular background of events, it is considered in relation to those events, because those events are relevant to it. ❑ *The profits rise was achieved against a backdrop of falling metal prices.* [12] If something is measured or valued **against** something else, it is measured or valued by comparing it with the other thing. ❑ *Our policy has to be judged against a clear test: will it improve the standard of education?... The US dollar is down against most foreign currencies today.* [13] If you discuss a particular set of facts or figures **as against** another set, you are comparing or contrasting the two sets of facts or figures. ❑ *Over 50% of divorced men regretted their divorce, as against 25% of women.* [14] The odds **against** something happening are the chances or odds that it will not happen. ❑ *The odds against him surviving are incredible.* ♦ **Against** is also an adverb. ❑ *What were the odds against?* [15] **up against** → see **up**. **against the clock** → see **clock**.

PHRASE: V inflects, PHR n; PREP; PREP ≠ with; PREP; PREP; PHRASE; PREP: n PREP; ADV: n ADV

**agape** /əgeɪp/ If you describe someone as having their mouth **agape**, their mouth is open very wide, often because they are very surprised by something. [WRITTEN] ❑ *She stood looking at Carmen with her mouth agape.* — ADJ: v-link ADJ

**ag|ate** /ægɪt/ **(agates) Agate** is a very hard stone which is used to make jewellery. — N-VAR

**age** /eɪdʒ/ **(ages, ageing, aging, aged)** ◆◆◆

> The spelling **aging** is also used, mainly in American English.

[1] Your **age** is the number of years that you have lived. ❑ *She has a nephew who is just ten years of age... At the age of sixteen he qualified for a place at the University of Hamburg... I admired him for being so confident at his age.* (N-VAR) [2] The **age** of a thing is the number of years since it was made. ❑ *Everything in the room looks in keeping with the age of the building.* (N-VAR) [3] **Age** is the state of being old or the process of becoming older. ❑ *Perhaps he has grown wiser with age... The fabric was showing signs of age.* (N-UNCOUNT) [4] When someone **ages**, or when something **ages** them, they seem much older and less strong or less alert. ❑ *He had always looked so young, but he seemed to have aged in the last few months... He was only in his mid-thirties, but already worry had aged him.* (VERB; V; V n) [5] An **age** is a period in history. ❑ *...the age of steam and steel. ...items of Bronze Age pottery.* (N-COUNT: usu with supp) [6] You can say **an age** or **ages** to mean a very long time. [INFORMAL] ❑ *He waited what seemed an age... The bus took absolutely ages to arrive.* (N-COUNT = forever) [7] → See also **aged**, **ageing**, **coming of age**, **dark age**, **golden age**, **Ice Age**, **Iron Age**, **middle age**, **Stone Age**.

PHRASES [8] If someone tells you to **act** your **age**, they are telling you to behave in a way that is suitable for someone your age, because they think you are behaving in a childish way. (PHRASE: V inflects [disapproval]) [9] If something **comes of age**, it reaches an important stage of development and is accepted by a large number of people. ❑ *Recycling is an issue that has come of age in Britain in the last decade.* (PHRASE: V inflects) [10] When someone **comes of age**, they become legally an adult. ❑ *The company was to be held in trust for Eddie until he came of age.* (PHRASE: V inflects) [11] Someone who is **under age** is not legally old enough to do something, for example to buy an alcoholic drink. ❑ *Because she was under age, her parents were still responsible for her. ...under age smoking.* (PHRASE: usu v-link PHR, PHR n)

**aged** ◆◇◇

> Pronounced /eɪdʒd/ for meaning 1, and /eɪdʒɪd/ for meanings 2 and 3.

[1] You use **aged** followed by a number to say how old someone is. ❑ *Alan has two children, aged eleven and nine.* (ADJ: usu n ADJ num) [2] **Aged** means very old. ❑ *She has an aged parent who's capable of being very difficult.* (ADJ: ADJ n) [3] You can refer to all people who are very old as **the aged**. ❑ *...people who work with the aged.* (N-PLURAL: the N) [4] → See also **middle-aged**.

**age group (age groups)** An **age group** is the people in a place or organization who were born during a particular period of time, for example all the people aged between 18 and 25. ❑ *...a style that would appeal to all age groups.* — N-COUNT

**age|ing** /eɪdʒɪŋ/ also **aging.** [1] Someone or something that is **ageing** is becoming older and less healthy or efficient. ❑ *John lives with his ageing mother... Ageing aircraft need more frequent safety inspections.* (ADJ: usu ADJ n) [2] **Ageing** is the process of becoming old or becoming worn out. (N-UNCOUNT)

**age|ism** /eɪdʒɪzəm/ **Ageism** is unacceptable behaviour that occurs as a result of the belief that older people are of less value than younger people. — N-UNCOUNT [disapproval]

**age|ist** /eɪdʒɪst/ **Ageist** behaviour is unacceptable behaviour based on the belief that older people are of less value than younger people. ❑ *...ageist bias from employers.* — ADJ [disapproval]

**age|less** /eɪdʒləs/ [1] If you describe someone as **ageless**, you mean that they never seem to look any older. [LITERARY] ❑ *She was rich, beautiful and seemingly ageless.* (ADJ) [2] If you describe something as **ageless**, you mean that it is impossible to tell how old it is, or that it seems to have existed for ever. [LITERARY] ❑ *...the ageless oceans.* (ADJ)

**age lim|it (age limits)** An **age limit** is the oldest or youngest age at which you are allowed under particular regulations to do something. ❑ *In some cases there is a minimum age limit.* — N-COUNT

**agen|cy** /eɪdʒənsi/ **(agencies)** ◆◆◇ [1] An **agency** is a business which provides a service on behalf of other businesses. [BUSINESS] ❑ *We had to hire maids through an agency.* → See also **advertising agency**, **employment agency**, **press agency**, **travel agency**. (N-COUNT: oft supp N) [2] An **agency** is a government organization responsible for a certain area of administration. ❑ *...the government agency which monitors health and safety at work in Britain.* (N-COUNT: oft supp N)

**agen|da** /ədʒendə/ **(agendas)** ◆◇◇ [1] You can refer to the political issues which are important at a particular time as an **agenda**. ❑ *Does television set the agenda on foreign policy?... The Danish president will put environmental issues high on the agenda.* → See also **hidden agenda**. (N-COUNT: with supp) [2] An **agenda** is a list of the items that have to be discussed at a meeting. ❑ *This is sure to be an item on the agenda next week.* (N-COUNT)

**agent** /eɪdʒənt/ **(agents)** ◆◆◇ [1] An **agent** is a person who looks after someone else's business affairs or does business on their behalf. [BUSINESS] ❑ *You are buying direct, rather than through an agent.* → See also **estate agent**, **press agent**, **travel agent**. (N-COUNT = rep, representative) [2] An **agent** in the arts world is a person who gets work for an actor or musician, or who sells the work of a writer to publishers. (N-COUNT) [3] An **agent** is a person who works for a country's secret service. ❑ *All these years he's been an agent for the East.* (N-COUNT) [4] A chemical that has a particular effect or is used for a particular purpose can be referred to as a particular kind of **agent**. ❑ *...the bleaching agent in white flour.* (N-COUNT: supp N)

**agent pro|vo|ca|teur** /æʒɒn prɒvɒkətɜːʳ/ **(agents provocateurs)** An **agent provocateur** is a person who is employed by the government or the police to encourage certain groups of people to break the law, so they can arrest them or make them lose public support. ❑ *Agents provocateurs may seek to discredit the opposition.* — N-COUNT

**age of con|sent** **The age of consent** is the age at which a person can legally agree to having a sexual relationship. ❑ *He was under the age of consent.* — N-SING: the N

**age-old** An **age-old** story, tradition, or problem has existed for many generations or centuries. [WRITTEN] ❑ *This age-old struggle for control had led to untold bloody wars.*
ADJ: usu ADJ n = ancient

**ag|glom|era|tion** /əglɒməreɪʃən/ **(agglomerations)** An **agglomeration of** things is a lot of different things gathered together, often in no particular order or arrangement. [FORMAL]
N-VAR: usu with supp = accumulation

**ag|gran|dize** /əgrændaɪz/ **(aggrandizes, aggrandizing, aggrandized)**

in BRIT, also use **aggrandise**

To **aggrandize** someone means to make them seem richer, more powerful, and more important than they really are. To **aggrandize** a building means to make it more impressive. ❑ *At the dinner table, my father would go on and on, showing off, aggrandising himself. ...plans to aggrandise the building.*
VERB [disapproval] V pron-refl V n

**ag|gran|dize|ment** /əgrændɪzmənt/

in BRIT, also use **aggrandisement**

If someone does something for **aggrandizement**, they do it in order to get power, wealth, and importance for themselves. [FORMAL] ❑ *It would be the first time in human history that economic necessity has prevailed over military aggrandizement.* → See also **self-aggrandizement**.
N-UNCOUNT: usu with supp [disapproval]

**ag|gra|vate** /ægrəveɪt/ **(aggravates, aggravating, aggravated)** [1] If someone or something **aggravates** a situation, they make it worse. ❑ *Stress and lack of sleep can aggravate the situation.*
VERB = exacerbate ≠ alleviate V n

[2] If someone or something **aggravates** you, they make you annoyed. [INFORMAL] ❑ *What aggravates you most about this country?*
VERB = annoy V n

♦ **ag|gra|vat|ing** *You don't realise how aggravating you can be.*
ADJ = annoying

♦ **ag|gra|va|tion** /ægrəveɪʃən/ **(aggravations)** *I just couldn't take the aggravation.*
N-VAR = annoyance

**ag|gra|vat|ed** /ægrəveɪtɪd/ **Aggravated** is used to describe a serious crime which involves violence. [LEGAL] ❑ *He was jailed for aggravated assault.*
ADJ: ADJ n

**ag|gre|gate** /ægrɪgət/ [1] An **aggregate** amount or score is made up of several smaller amounts or scores added together. ❑ *England have beaten the Welsh three times in succession with an aggregate score of 83-12.*
ADJ: ADJ n

♦ **Aggregate** is also a noun. ❑ *The highest aggregate came in the third round where Leeds and Middlesbrough drew 4-4.*
N-COUNT: usu sing

[2] An **aggregate** is a number of people or things that are being considered as a single thing. [FORMAL] ❑ *...society viewed as an aggregate of individuals.*
N-COUNT

**ag|gres|sion** /əgreʃən/ **(aggressions)** [1] **Aggression** is a quality of anger and determination that makes you ready to attack other people. ❑ *Aggression is by no means a male-only trait.*
N-UNCOUNT = belligerence ≠ gentleness

[2] **Aggression** is violent and attacking behaviour. ❑ *The raid was an unjustifiable act of aggression.*
N-VAR

**ag|gres|sive** /əgresɪv/ [1] An **aggressive** person or animal has a quality of anger and determination that makes them ready to attack other people. ❑ *Some children are much more aggressive than others... Aggressive behaviour is a sign of emotional distress.*
◆◇◇ ADJ = belligerent

♦ **ag|gres|sive|ly** *They'll react aggressively.*
ADV

♦ **ag|gres|sive|ness** *Her aggressiveness made it difficult for him to explain his own feelings.*
N-UNCOUNT = aggression

[2] People who are **aggressive** in their work or other activities behave in a forceful way because they are very eager to succeed. ❑ *He is respected as a very aggressive and competitive executive.*
ADJ

♦ **ag|gres|sive|ly** *...countries noted for aggressively pursuing energy efficiency.*
ADV: usu ADV with v

**ag|gres|sor** /əgresəʳ/ **(aggressors)** The **aggressor** in a fight or battle is the person, group, or country that starts it. ❑ *They have been the aggressors in this conflict.*
N-COUNT

**ag|grieved** /əgriːvd/ If you feel **aggrieved**, you feel upset and angry because of the way in which you have been treated. ❑ *I really feel aggrieved at this sort of thing.*
ADJ = resentful, bitter

**ag|gro** /ægroʊ/ [1] **Aggro** is the difficulties and problems that are involved in something. [BRIT, INFORMAL] ❑ *Simply phone the ticket hot-line and all that aggro will be a thing of the past.*
N-UNCOUNT = hassle

[2] **Aggro** is aggressive or violent behaviour. [BRIT, INFORMAL] ❑ *They could see there wasn't going to be any aggro and they left us to it.*
N-UNCOUNT

**aghast** /əgɑːst, əgæst/ If you are **aghast**, you are filled with horror and surprise. [FORMAL] ❑ *She watched aghast as his life flowed away.*
ADJ: ADJ after v, v-link ADJ, oft ADJ at n, ADJ n

**ag|ile** /ædʒaɪl, AM -dʒəl/ [1] Someone who is **agile** can move quickly and easily. ❑ *At 20 years old he was not as agile as he is now.*
ADJ = nimble

♦ **agil|ity** /ədʒɪlɪti/ *She blinked in surprise at his agility.*
N-UNCOUNT

[2] If you have an **agile** mind, you think quickly and intelligently. ❑ *She was quick-witted and had an extraordinarily agile mind.*
ADJ

♦ **agil|ity** *His intellect and mental agility have never been in doubt.*
N-UNCOUNT

**ag|ing** /eɪdʒɪŋ/ → see **age, ageing**.

**agi|tate** /ædʒɪteɪt/ **(agitates, agitating, agitated)** [1] If people **agitate for** something, they protest or take part in political activity in order to get it. ❑ *The women who worked in these mills had begun to agitate for better conditions.*
VERB V for n

[2] If you **agitate** something, you shake it so that it moves about. [FORMAL] ❑ *All you need to do is gently agitate the water with a finger or paintbrush.*
VERB V n

[3] If something **agitates** you, it worries you and makes you unable to think clearly or calmly. ❑ *The thought of them getting her possessions when she dies agitates her.*
VERB V n

[4] → See also **agitation**.

**agi|tat|ed** /ædʒɪteɪtɪd/ If someone is **agitated**, they are very worried or upset, and show this in their behaviour, movements, or voice. ❑ *Susan seemed agitated about something.*
ADJ = upset, distressed

**agi|ta|tion** /ædʒɪteɪʃən/ If someone is in a state of **agitation**, they are very worried or upset, and show this in their behaviour, movements, or voice. ❑ *Danny returned to Father's house in a state of intense agitation.* → See also **agitate**.
N-UNCOUNT = distress

**agi|ta|tor** /ædʒɪteɪtəʳ/ **(agitators)** If you describe someone involved in politics as an **agitator**, you disapprove of them because of the trouble they cause in organizing campaigns and protests. ❑ *...a famous actress who was accused of being a political agitator.*
N-COUNT: oft supp N [disapproval]

**agit|prop** /ædʒɪtprɒp/ also **agit-prop. Agitprop** is the use of artistic forms such as drama or posters to further political aims.
N-UNCOUNT

**aglow** /əgloʊ/ [1] If something is **aglow**, it is shining and bright with a soft, warm light. [LITERARY] ❑ *The night skies will be aglow with fireworks.*
ADJ: v-link ADJ, oft ADJ with n

[2] If someone is **aglow** or if their face is **aglow**, they look excited. [LITERARY] ❑ *'It was incredible,' Kurt says, suddenly aglow.*
ADJ: v-link ADJ, oft ADJ with n

**AGM** /eɪ dʒiː em/ **(AGMs)** also **agm.** The **AGM** of a company or organization is a meeting which it holds once a year in order to discuss the previous year's activities and accounts. **AGM** is an abbreviation for 'Annual General Meeting'. [BRIT, BUSINESS]
N-COUNT

**ag|nos|tic** /ægnɒstɪk/ **(agnostics)** [1] An **agnostic** believes that it is not possible to know whether God exists or not. Compare **atheist**.
N-COUNT

[2] **Agnostic** means relating to agnostics or to their beliefs. ❑ *You grew up in an agnostic household and have never been able to bring yourself to believe in God.*
ADJ

**ag|nos|ti|cism** /ægnɒstɪsɪzəm/ **Agnosticism** is the belief that it is not possible to say definitely whether or not there is a God. Compare **atheism**.
N-UNCOUNT

**ago** /əgoʊ/ You use **ago** when you are referring to past time. For example, if something happened one year **ago**, it is one year since it happened. If it happened a long time **ago**, it is a long time since it happened. ❑ *He was killed a few days ago in a skiing accident... The meeting is the first since the war began 14 years ago... Harry's daughter is dead. She died long ago.*
◆◆◆ ADV: ADV with v, n ADV, long ADV

**agog** /əgɒg/ If you are **agog**, you are excited about something, and eager to know more about it. ADJ: usu v-link ADJ, oft ADJ prep

**ago|nize** /ægənaɪz/ **(agonizes, agonizing, agonized)**

☑ in BRIT, also use **agonise**

If you **agonize over** something, you feel very anxious about it and spend a long time thinking about it. ❑ *Perhaps he was agonizing over the moral issues involved.* VERB; V over/about n

**ago|nized** /ægənaɪzd/

☑ in BRIT, also use **agonised**

**Agonized** describes something that you say or do when you are in great physical or mental pain. ❑ *...the agonised look on his face.* ADJ: usu ADJ n

**ago|niz|ing** /ægənaɪzɪŋ/

☑ in BRIT, also use **agonising**

1 Something that is **agonizing** causes you to feel great physical or mental pain. ❑ *He did not wish to die the agonizing death of his mother and brother.* ♦ **ago|niz|ing|ly** *Progress was agonizingly slow.* 2 **Agonizing** decisions and choices are very difficult to make. ❑ *He now faced an agonizing decision about his immediate future.* ADJ; ADV; ADJ

**ago|ny** /ægəni/ **Agony** is great physical or mental pain. ❑ *She called out in agony.* N-UNCOUNT: also N in pl; = torment

**ago|ny aunt (agony aunts)** An **agony aunt** is a person who writes a column in a newspaper or magazine in which they reply to readers who have written to them for advice on their personal problems. [BRIT] N-COUNT; = advice columnist

☑ in AM, use **advice columnist**

**ago|ny col|umn (agony columns)** In a British newspaper or magazine, the **agony column** contains letters from readers about their personal problems, and advice on what to do about them. [BRIT] N-COUNT; = advice column

☑ in AM, use **advice column**

**ago|ra|pho|bia** /ægərəfoʊbiə/ **Agoraphobia** is the fear of open or public places. N-UNCOUNT

**ago|ra|pho|bic** /ægərəfoʊbɪk/ **(agoraphobics)** Someone who is **agoraphobic** suffers from agoraphobia. ♦ An **agoraphobic** is someone who suffers from agoraphobia. ADJ: usu v-link ADJ; N-COUNT

**agrar|ian** /əgreəriən/ **Agrarian** means relating to the ownership and use of land, especially farmland, or relating to the part of a society or economy that is concerned with agriculture. ADJ: usu ADJ n

**agree** /əgriː/ **(agrees, agreeing, agreed)** 1 If people **agree with** each other about something, they have the same opinion about it or say that they have the same opinion. ❑ *If we agreed all the time it would be a bit boring, wouldn't it?... Both have agreed on the need for the money... So we both agree there's a problem?... I see your point but I'm not sure I agree with you... I agree with you that the open system is by far the best... 'It's appalling.' — 'It is. I agree.'... I agree that the demise of London zoo would be terrible... I agree with every word you've just said... 'Frankly I found it rather frightening.' 'A little startling,' Mark agreed.* 2 If you **agree to** do something, you say that you will do it. If you **agree to** a proposal, you accept it. ❑ *He agreed to pay me for the drawings... Donna agreed to both requests.* 3 If people **agree on** something, or in British English if they **agree** something, they all decide to accept or do something. ❑ *The warring sides have agreed on an unconditional ceasefire... We never agreed a date... The court had given the unions until September to agree terms with a buyer.* 4 If two people who are arguing about something **agree to disagree** or **agree to differ**, they decide to stop arguing because neither of them is going to change their opinion. ❑ *You and I are going to have to agree to disagree then.* 5 If you **agree with** an action or suggestion, you approve of it. ❑ *I don't agree with what they're doing.* 6 If one account of an event or one set of figures **agrees with** another, the two accounts or sets of figures are the same or are consistent with each other. ❑ *His second statement agrees with facts as stated by the other witnesses.* 7 If some food that you eat **does not agree with** you, it makes you feel ill. ❑ *I don't think the food here agrees with me.* 8 In grammar, if a word **agrees with** a noun or pronoun, it has a form that is appropriate to the number or gender of the noun or pronoun. For example, in 'He hates it', the singular verb agrees with the singular pronoun 'he'. 9 → See also **agreed**.

◆◆◆ V-RECIP; = concur; ≠ disagree; pl-n V; pl-n V; pl-n V that; V with n; V with n that; NON-RECIP: V; V that; V with n; V with quote; VERB; = consent; V to-inf; V to n; V-RECIP; pl-n V on/upon n; pl-n V n; V n with n; PHRASE: V inflects, pl-n PHR; VERB; ≠ disagree; V with n; V-RECIP; = tally; V with n; Also V; VERB: with neg; V with n; V-RECIP: V with n, pl-n V

**agree|able** /əgriːəbəl/ 1 If something is **agreeable**, it is pleasant and you enjoy it. ❑ *...workers in more agreeable and better paid occupations.* 2 If someone is **agreeable**, they are pleasant and try to please people. ❑ *...sharing a bottle of wine with an agreeable companion.* 3 If you are **agreeable to** something or if it is **agreeable to** you, you are willing to do it or to allow it to happen. [FORMAL] ❑ *If you are agreeable, my husband's office will make all the necessary arrangements. ...a solution that would be agreeable to all.* ADJ; = pleasant; ADJ; ADJ: v-link ADJ, oft ADJ to n

**agreed** /əgriːd/ 1 If people are **agreed on** something, they have reached a joint decision on it or have the same opinion about it. ❑ *Okay, so are we agreed on going north?... Everyone is agreed that something needs to be done about the situation.* 2 When you are discussing something, you can say **'Agreed?'** to check whether the other people agree with what you have just said. You can say **'Agreed'** if you agree with what someone has just said. [FORMAL, SPOKEN] ❑ *'That means we move out today. Agreed?' — 'Agreed.'* 3 → See also **agree**. ADJ: v-link ADJ, oft ADJ on n, ADJ that; CONVENTION [formulae] = o.k.

**agree|ment** /əgriːmənt/ **(agreements)** ◆◆◇ 1 An **agreement** is a formal decision about future action which is made by two or more countries, groups, or people. ❑ *It looks as though a compromise agreement has now been reached... The two countries signed an agreement to jointly launch satellites.* 2 **Agreement on** something is a joint decision that a particular course of action should be taken. ❑ *The two men had not reached agreement on any issues.* 3 **Agreement** with someone means having the same opinion as they have. ❑ *The judge kept nodding in agreement.* ● If you are **in agreement with** someone, you have the same opinion as they have. ❑ *Not all scholars are in agreement with her, however.* 4 **Agreement** to a course of action means allowing it to happen or giving it your approval. ❑ *The clinic doctor will then write to your GP to get his agreement.* ● If you are **in agreement with** a plan or proposal, you approve of it. ❑ *The president was in full agreement with the proposal.* 5 If there is **agreement** between two accounts of an event or two sets of figures, they are the same or are consistent with each other. ❑ *Many other surveys have produced results essentially in agreement with these figures.* 6 In grammar, **agreement** refers to the way that a word has a form appropriate to the number or gender of the noun or pronoun it relates to. N-COUNT: oft N to-inf, N prep; N-UNCOUNT: oft N on n; ≠ disagreement; N-UNCOUNT; ≠ disagreement; PHRASE: usu v-link PHR, v PHR, oft PHR with n; N-UNCOUNT; = consent; PHRASE: v-link PHR, usu PHR with n; N-UNCOUNT; = concurrence; N-UNCOUNT; = concord

**ag|ri|busi|ness** /ægribɪznɪs/ **(agribusinesses)** **Agribusiness** is the various businesses that produce, sell, and distribute farm products, especially on a large scale. [BUSINESS] N-UNCOUNT: also N in pl, oft N n

**ag|ri|cul|tur|al** /ægrɪkʌltʃərəl/ ◆◇◇ 1 **Agricultural** means involving or relating to agriculture. ❑ *...agricultural land. ...corn and other agricultural products.* 2 An **agricultural** place or society is one in which agriculture is important or highly developed. ❑ *...traditional agricultural societies.* ADJ: usu ADJ n; ADJ: usu ADJ n

**ag|ri|cul|tur|al|ist** /ægrɪkʌltʃərəlɪst/ **(agriculturalists)** An **agriculturalist** is someone who is an expert on agriculture and who advises farmers. N-COUNT

**ag|ri|cul|ture** /ægrɪkʌltʃəʳ/ ◆◇◇ **Agriculture** is farming and the methods that are used to raise and look after crops and animals. ❑ *The Ukraine is strong both in industry and agriculture.* N-UNCOUNT

**agro-** /ægrou-/ **Agro-** is used to form nouns and adjectives which refer to things relating to agriculture, or to agriculture combined with another activity. ❑ *...agro-chemical residues.* PREFIX

**agronomist** /əgrɒnəmɪst/ **(agronomists)** An **agronomist** is someone who studies the growing and harvesting of crops. N-COUNT

**aground** /əgraʊnd/ If a ship runs **aground**, it touches the ground in a shallow part of a river, lake, or the sea, and gets stuck. ADV: ADV after v

**ah** /ɑː/ **Ah** is used in writing to represent a noise that people make in conversation, for example to acknowledge or draw attention to something, or to express surprise or disappointment. ❑ *Ah, so many questions, so little time.* ◆◇◇ EXCLAM [feelings]

**aha** /ɑːhɑː/ **Aha** is used in writing to represent a noise that people make in conversation, for example to express satisfaction or surprise. ❑ *Aha! Here at last, the answer to my question.* EXCLAM [feelings]

**ahead**
① ADVERB USES
② PREPOSITION USES

**① ahead** /əhed/ ◆◆◇

> In addition to the uses shown below, **ahead** is used in phrasal verbs such as 'get ahead', 'go ahead', and 'press ahead'.

[1] Something that is **ahead** is in front of you. If you look **ahead**, you look directly in front of you. ❑ *Brett looked straight ahead... I peered ahead through the front screen... The road ahead was now blocked solid... Ahead, he saw the side railings of First Bridge over Crooked Brook.* ADV: ADV after v, n ADV, ADV with cl ≠ behind [2] You use **ahead** with verbs such as 'push', 'move', and 'forge' to indicate that a plan, scheme, or organization is making fast progress. ❑ *We are moving ahead with plans to send financial aid.* ADV: ADV after v = forward [3] If you are **ahead** in your work or achievements, you have made more progress than you expected to and are performing well. ❑ *First half profits have charged ahead from £127.6m to £134.2m... Children in small classes are several months ahead in reading.* ADV: *be* ADV, ADV after v, oft amount ADV [4] If a person or a team is **ahead** in a competition, they are winning. ❑ *Scotland were ahead in their European championship qualifier in Iceland... A goal would have put Dublin 6-1 ahead.* ADV: *be* ADV, ADV after v, oft amount ADV [5] **Ahead** also means in the future. ❑ *A much bigger battle is ahead for the president... Now I can remember without mourning, and begin to look ahead.* ADV: v-link ADV, ADV after v, n ADV [6] If you prepare or plan something **ahead**, you do it some time before a future event so that everything is ready for that event to take place. ❑ *The government wants figures that help it to plan ahead... Summer weddings need to be arranged months ahead.* ADV: ADV after v [7] If you go **ahead**, or if you go on **ahead**, you go in front of someone who is going to the same place so that you arrive there some time before they do. ❑ *I went ahead and waited with Sean.* ADV: ADV after v

**② ahead of** ◆◇◇

⇛ Please look at category 6 to see if the expression you are looking for is shown under another headword. [1] If someone is **ahead of** you, they are directly in front of you. If someone is moving **ahead of** you, they are in front of you and moving in the same direction. ❑ *I saw a man in a blue jacket thirty metres ahead of me... She walked ahead of Helene up the steps into the hotel.* PREP-PHRASE [2] If an event or period of time lies **ahead of** you, it is going to happen or take place soon or in the future. ❑ *I tried to think about all the problems that were ahead of me tomorrow... She spent all night thinking about the future that lay ahead of her... We have a very busy day ahead of us today.* PREP-PHRASE: PREP pron = before [3] In a competition, if a person or team does something **ahead of** someone else, they do it before the second person or team. ❑ *Millar finished 1 minute and 35 seconds ahead of Thierry Claveyrolat.* PREP-PHRASE: oft n PREP n [4] If something happens **ahead of** schedule or **ahead of** time, it happens earlier than was planned. ❑ *This dish may be prepared a day ahead of time and refrigerated.* PREP-PHRASE ≠ behind [5] If someone is **ahead of** someone else, they have made more progress and are more advanced in what they are doing. ❑ *Henry generally stayed ahead of the others in the academic subjects.* PREP-PHRASE [6] **one step ahead of** someone or something → see **step**. **ahead of** your **time** → see **time**.

**ahem** /əhem/ In writing, **ahem** is used to show that someone is being ironic. **Ahem** is also used to show that someone wants to get another person's attention. ❑ *It is not unknown for valuable display items to go, ahem, missing.* CONVENTION

**ahold** /əhould/ [1] If you **get ahold of** someone or something, you manage to contact, find, or get them. [AM, INFORMAL] ❑ *I tried again to get ahold of my cousin Joan.* PHRASE: V inflects, PHR n = get hold of [2] If you **get ahold of yourself**, you force yourself to become calm and sensible after a shock or in a difficult situation. [AM, INFORMAL] ❑ *I'm going to have to get ahold of myself.* PHRASE: V inflects, PHR pron-refl

**ahoy** /əhɔɪ/ **Ahoy** is something that people in boats shout in order to attract attention. ❑ *Ahoy there!... Ship ahoy!* EXCLAM

**AI** /eɪ aɪ/ **AI** is an abbreviation for **artificial intelligence**, or **artificial insemination**. N-UNCOUNT

**aid** /eɪd/ **(aids, aiding, aided)** [1] **Aid** is money, equipment, or services that are provided for people, countries, or organizations who need them but cannot provide them for themselves. ❑ *...regular flights carrying humanitarian aid to Cambodia... They have already pledged billions of dollars in aid. ...food aid convoys.* ◆◆◆ N-UNCOUNT: oft supp N, N *to* n [2] To **aid** a country, organization, or person means to provide them with money, equipment, or services that they need. ❑ *...US efforts to aid Kurdish refugees.* VERB V n ♦ **-aided** *...grant-aided factories. ...state-aided schools.* COMB in ADJ [3] To **aid** someone means to help or assist them. [WRITTEN] ❑ *...a software system to aid managers in advanced decision-making... The hunt for her killer will continue, with police aided by the army and air force.* VERB = help, assist V n V-ed ♦ **Aid** is also a noun. ❑ *He was forced to turn for aid to his former enemy.* N-UNCOUNT = assistance [4] If you perform a task **with the aid of** something, you need or use that thing to perform that task. ❑ *He succeeded with the aid of a completely new method he discovered.* N-UNCOUNT: usu *with/without the* N *n* = help [5] An **aid** is an object, device, or technique that makes something easier to do. ❑ *The book is an invaluable aid to teachers of literature.* N-COUNT: oft N *to* n [6] If something **aids** a process, it makes it easier or more likely to happen. ❑ *The export sector will aid the economic recovery... Calcium may aid in the prevention of colon cancer.* VERB V n V *in* n/-ing [7] → See also **Band-Aid**, **first aid**, **hearing aid**, **legal aid**.

**PHRASES** [8] An activity or event **in aid of** a particular cause or charity is intended to raise money for that cause or charity. [mainly BRIT] ❑ *...a charity performance in aid of Great Ormond Street Children's Hospital.* PHRASE: PHR n [9] If you **come** or **go to** someone's **aid**, you try to help them when they are in danger or difficulty. PHRASE: V inflects

**aide** /eɪd/ **(aides)** An **aide** is an assistant to someone who has an important job, especially in government or in the armed forces. ❑ *...a close aide to the Prime Minister.* N-COUNT

**aide-de-camp** /eɪd də kɒm/ **(aides-de-camp)** An **aide-de-camp** is an officer in the armed forces who helps an officer of higher rank. ❑ *...a colonel who had been aide-de-camp to the king.* N-COUNT

**aide-memoire** /eɪd memwɑːʳ/ **(aide-memoires)** also **aide-mémoire**. An **aide-memoire** is something such as a list that you use to remind you of something. N-COUNT

**AIDS** /eɪdz/ **AIDS** is a disease which destroys the natural system of protection that the body has against other diseases. **AIDS** is an abbreviation for 'acquired immune deficiency syndrome'. ◆◆◇ N-UNCOUNT

**ail** /eɪl/ **(ails, ailing, ailed)** If something **ails** a group or area of activity, it is a problem or source of trouble for that group or for people involved in VERB that activity. ❑ *A full-scale debate is under way on what ails the industry.* — V n

**ailer|on** /eɪlərɒn/ **(ailerons)** An **aileron** is a section on the back edge of the wing of an aircraft that can be raised or lowered in order to control the aircraft's movement. — N-COUNT

**ail|ing** /eɪlɪŋ/ [1] An **ailing** organization or society is in difficulty and is becoming weaker. ❑ *The rise in overseas sales is good news for the ailing American economy.* — ADJ: usu ADJ n
[2] If someone is **ailing**, they are ill and are not getting better. [OLD-FASHIONED] — ADJ

**ail|ment** /eɪlmənt/ **(ailments)** An **ailment** is an illness, especially one that is not very serious. ❑ *The pharmacist can treat common ailments.* — N-COUNT = affliction

**aim** /eɪm/ **(aims, aiming, aimed)** ◆◆◇ [1] If you **aim for** something or **aim to** do something, you plan or hope to achieve it. ❑ *He is aiming for the 100 metres world record. ...an appeal which aims to raise funds for children with special needs.* — VERB; V for/at n/-ing; V to-inf
[2] The **aim** of something that you do is the purpose for which you do it or the result that it is intended to achieve. ❑ *The aim of the festival is to increase awareness of Hindu culture and traditions. ...a research programme that has largely failed to achieve its principal aims.* — N-COUNT: oft with poss = objective
[3] If an action or plan **is aimed at** achieving something, it is intended or planned to achieve it. ❑ *The new measures are aimed at tightening existing sanctions. ...talks aimed at ending the war.* — V-PASSIVE; be V-ed at n/-ing; V-ed
[4] If you **aim to** do something, you decide or want to do it. [AM, INFORMAL] ❑ *Are you aiming to visit the gardens?* — VERB; V to-inf
[5] If your actions or remarks **are aimed at** a particular person or group, you intend that the person or group should notice them and be influenced by them. ❑ *His message was aimed at the undecided middle ground of Israeli politics... Advertising aimed at children should be curbed.* — VERB: usu passive; be V-ed at n; V-ed
[6] If you **aim** a weapon or object **at** something or someone, you point it towards them before firing or throwing it. ❑ *He was aiming the rifle at Wade. ...a missile aimed at the arms factory... I didn't know I was supposed to aim at the same spot all the time.* — VERB; V n at n; V-ed; V at n; Also V
[7] Your **aim** is your skill or action in pointing a weapon or other object at its target. ❑ *He stood with the gun in his right hand and his left hand steadying his aim.* — N-SING: oft poss N
[8] If you **aim** a kick or punch at someone, you try to kick or punch them. ❑ *They aimed kicks at his shins.* — VERB; V n prep/adv
**PHRASES** [9] When you **take aim**, you point a weapon or object at someone or something, before firing or throwing it. ❑ *She had spotted a man with a shotgun taking aim.* — PHRASE: V inflects
[10] If you **take aim at** someone or something, you criticize them strongly. [AM] ❑ *Republican strategists are taking particular aim at Democratic senators.* — PHRASE: V inflects, PHR n

**aim|less** /eɪmləs/ A person or activity that is **aimless** has no clear purpose or plan. ❑ *After several hours of aimless searching they were getting low on fuel.* — ADJ ≠ purposeful
♦ **aim|less|ly** *I wandered around aimlessly.* — ADV: ADV after v

**ain't** /eɪnt/ People sometimes use **ain't** instead of 'am not', 'aren't', 'isn't', 'haven't', and 'hasn't'. Some people consider this use to be incorrect. [DIALECT, SPOKEN] ❑ *Well, it's obvious, ain't it?*

**air** /eəʳ/ **(airs, airing, aired)** ◆◆◆ [1] **Air** is the mixture of gases which forms the earth's atmosphere and which we breathe. ❑ *Draughts help to circulate air... Keith opened the window and leaned out into the cold air. ...water and air pollutants.* — N-UNCOUNT
[2] **The air** is the space around things or above the ground. ❑ *Government troops broke up the protest by firing their guns in the air.* — N-SING: the N
[3] **Air** is used to refer to travel in aircraft. ❑ *Air travel will continue to grow at about 6% per year... Casualties had to be brought to hospital by air.* — N-UNCOUNT: usu N n, by N
[4] If you say that someone or something has a particular **air**, you mean that they give this general impression. ❑ *Jennifer regarded him with an air of amusement.* — N-SING: with supp, oft N of n
[5] If you say that someone is putting on **airs** or giving themselves **airs**, you are criticizing them for behaving as if they are better than other people. [INFORMAL] ❑ *We're poor and we never put on airs.* — N-PLURAL disapproval
[6] If a broadcasting company **airs** a television or radio programme, they show it on television or broadcast it on the radio. [mainly AM] ❑ *Tonight PBS will air a documentary called 'Democracy In Action'.* — VERB = broadcast; V n
♦ **air|ing** *...the airing of offensive material.* — N-SING
[7] If you **air** your opinions, you make them known to people. ❑ *The whole issue was thoroughly aired at the meeting.* — VERB = express; be V-ed
[8] If you **air** a room or building, you let fresh air into it. ❑ *One day a week her mother systematically cleaned and aired each room.* — VERB; V n
[9] If you **air** clothing or bedding, you put it somewhere warm to make sure that it is completely dry. — VERB
**PHRASES** [10] If you do something to **clear the air**, you do it in order to resolve any problems or disagreements that there might be. ❑ *...an inquiry just to clear the air and settle the facts of the case.* — PHRASE: V inflects
[11] If something is **in the air** it is felt to be present, but it is not talked about. ❑ *There was great excitement in the air.* — PHRASE
[12] If someone is **on the air**, they are broadcasting on radio or television. If a programme is **on the air**, it is being broadcast on radio or television. If it is **off the air**, it is not being broadcast. ❑ *She is going on the air as presenter of a new show... This message did not reach me until after the programme went off the air.* — PHRASE: v-link PHR, PHR after v
[13] If someone or something disappears **into thin air**, they disappear completely. If someone or something appears **out of thin air**, they appear suddenly and mysteriously. ❑ *He had materialized out of thin air; I had not seen or heard him coming.* — PHRASE: PHR after v
[14] If you say that a decision or a situation is **up in the air**, you mean that it has not yet been completely settled or planned. ❑ *He told reporters today that the president's trip to Moscow is up in the air.* — PHRASE: v-link PHR = undecided ≠ settled
[15] If you say that you are **walking on air** or **floating on air**, you mean that you feel extremely happy about something. ❑ *As soon as I know I'm in the team it's like I'm walking on air.* — PHRASE: V inflects

**air am|bu|lance (air ambulances)** An **air ambulance** is a helicopter or plane that is used for taking people to hospital. — N-COUNT: also by N

**air|bag** /eəʳbæg/ **(airbags)** also **air bag.** An **airbag** is a safety device in a car which automatically fills with air if the car crashes, and is designed to protect the people in the car when they are thrown forward in the crash. ➔ See picture on page 1708. — N-COUNT

**air base (air bases)** also **airbase.** An **air base** is a centre where military aircraft take off or land and are serviced, and where many of the centre's staff live. — N-COUNT

**air|bed** /eəʳbed/ **(airbeds)** also **air bed.** An **airbed** is a plastic or rubber mattress which can be folded or stored flat and which you fill with air before you use it. — N-COUNT

**air|borne** /eəʳbɔːʳn/ [1] If an aircraft is **airborne**, it is in the air and flying. ❑ *The pilot did manage to get airborne.* — ADJ: v-link ADJ
[2] **Airborne** troops use parachutes to get into enemy territory. ❑ *The allies landed thousands of airborne troops.* — ADJ: ADJ n
[3] **Airborne** means in the air or carried in the air. ❑ *Many people are allergic to airborne pollutants such as pollen.* — ADJ: usu ADJ n

**air brake (air brakes)** **Air brakes** are brakes which are used on heavy vehicles such as buses and trains and which are operated by means of compressed air. — N-COUNT

**air|brush** /eəʳbrʌʃ/ **(airbrushes, airbrushing, airbrushed)** [1] An **airbrush** is an artist's tool which sprays paint onto a surface. — N-COUNT
[2] To **airbrush** a photograph or other image means to change it using an airbrush, especially to make it more beautiful or perfect. ❑ *...bits of photos cut, pasted and airbrushed to create a convincing whole.* — VERB; V-ed; Also V n

**Air|bus** /eəʳbʌs/ **(Airbuses)** An **Airbus** is an aeroplane which is designed to carry a large number of passengers for fairly short distances. [TRADEMARK] — N-COUNT

**air-con** **Air-con** is the same as **air conditioning**. [INFORMAL] ❑ *The bus is a 45-seater with air-con and videos.* — N-UNCOUNT

**air con|di|tioned** If a room or vehicle is **air conditioned**, the air in it is kept cool and dry by means of a special machine. ❑ *...our new air conditioned trains.* ADJ

**air con|di|tion|er** **(air conditioners)** An **air conditioner** is a machine which keeps the air in a building cool and dry. N-COUNT

**air con|di|tion|ing** **Air conditioning** is a method of providing buildings and vehicles with cool dry air. N-UNCOUNT: oft N n

**air-cooled** An **air-cooled** engine is prevented from getting too hot when it is running by cool air that passes over it, rather than being cooled by a liquid. ❑ *The car was powered by a four cylinder air-cooled engine.* ADJ: usu ADJ n

**air|craft** /eəʳkrɑːft, -kræft/ **(aircraft)** An **aircraft** is a vehicle which can fly, for example an aeroplane or a helicopter. ❑ *The return flight of the aircraft was delayed... At least three military aircraft were destroyed.* ◆◆◇ N-COUNT

**air|craft car|ri|er** **(aircraft carriers)** An **aircraft carrier** is a warship with a long, flat deck where aircraft can take off and land. N-COUNT

**air|crew** /eəʳkruː/ **(aircrews)** also **air crew.** The **aircrew** on a plane are the pilot and other people who are responsible for flying it and for looking after any passengers who are on it. N-COUNT-COLL

**air|drome** /eəʳdroʊm/ **(airdromes)** An **airdrome** is a place or area where small aircraft can land and take off. [AM] N-COUNT = airfield

✔ in BRIT, use **aerodrome**

**air drop** **(air drops, air dropping, air dropped)** also **airdrop, air-drop.** 1 An **air drop** is a delivery of supplies by aircraft to an area that is hard to get to. The supplies are dropped from the aircraft on parachutes. N-COUNT 2 If a country or organization **air drops** supplies to a place, it drops supplies there from aircraft. VERB

**air|fare** /eəʳfeʳ/ **(airfares)** The **airfare** to a place is the amount it costs to fly there. N-COUNT

**air|field** /eəʳfiːld/ **(airfields)** An **airfield** is an area of ground where aircraft take off and land. It is smaller than an airport. N-COUNT

**air|flow** /eəʳfloʊ/ **(airflows)** The **airflow** around an object or vehicle is the way that the air flows around it. N-UNCOUNT

**air force** **(air forces)** An **air force** is the part of a country's armed forces that is concerned with fighting in the air. ❑ *...the United States Air Force.* ◆◇◇ N-COUNT

**air fresh|en|er** **(air fresheners)** An **air freshener** is a product people can buy which is meant to make rooms smell pleasant. N-VAR

**air|gun** /eəʳgʌn/ **(airguns)** also **air gun.** An **airgun** is a gun which is fired by means of air pressure. N-COUNT

**air|head** /eəʳhed/ **(airheads)** If you describe someone, especially a young woman, as an **airhead**, you are critical of them because you think they are not at all clever and are interested only in unimportant things. [INFORMAL] N-COUNT [disapproval]

**air host|ess** **(air hostesses)** An **air hostess** is a woman whose job is to look after the passengers in an aircraft. [BRIT, OLD-FASHIONED] N-COUNT = stewardess

✔ in AM, use **stewardess**

**air|ing cup|board** **(airing cupboards)** In British houses, an **airing cupboard** is a warm cupboard where you put clothes and other things that have been washed and partly dried, to make sure they are completely dry. N-COUNT

**air|less** /eəʳləs/ If a place is **airless**, there is no fresh air in it. ❑ *...a dark, airless room.* ADJ

**air|lift** /eəʳlɪft/ **(airlifts, airlifting, airlifted)** 1 An **airlift** is an operation to move people, troops, or goods by air, especially in a war or when land routes are closed. ❑ *President Garcia has ordered an airlift of food, medicines and blankets.* N-COUNT 2 If people, troops, or goods **are airlifted** somewhere, they are carried by air, especially in a war or when land routes are closed. ❑ *The injured were airlifted to hospital in Prestwick.* VERB: be V-ed to n

**air|line** /eəʳlaɪn/ **(airlines)** An **airline** is a company which provides regular services carrying people or goods in aeroplanes. ❑ *...the Dutch national airline KLM.* ◆◆◇ N-COUNT: oft in names

**air|lin|er** /eəʳlaɪnəʳ/ **(airliners)** An **airliner** is a large aeroplane that is used for carrying passengers. N-COUNT

**air|lock** /eəʳlɒk/ **(airlocks)** also **air lock.** 1 An **airlock** is a small room that is used to move between areas which do not have the same air pressure, for example in a spacecraft or submarine. N-COUNT 2 An **airlock** is a bubble of air in a pipe that prevents liquid from flowing through. N-COUNT

**air|mail** /eəʳmeɪl/ **Airmail** is the system of sending letters, parcels, and goods by air. ❑ *...an airmail letter... Goods are generally shipped by airmail.* N-UNCOUNT: oft N n, by N

**air|man** /eəʳmən/ **(airmen)** An **airman** is a man who flies aircraft, especially one who serves in his country's air force. N-COUNT: oft supp N

**air miles** **Air miles** are points that you collect when you buy certain goods or services and which you can use to pay for air travel. N-PLURAL

**air pis|tol** **(air pistols)** An **air pistol** is a small gun which is fired by means of air pressure. N-COUNT

**air|plane** /eəʳpleɪn/ **(airplanes)** An **airplane** is a vehicle with wings and one or more engines that enable it to fly through the air. [AM] N-COUNT

✔ in BRIT, use **aeroplane**

**air|play** /eəʳpleɪ/ The **airplay** which a piece of popular music receives is the number of times it is played on the radio. ❑ *Our first single got a lot of airplay.* N-UNCOUNT: oft supp N

**air|port** /eəʳpɔːʳt/ **(airports)** An **airport** is a place where aircraft land and take off, which has buildings and facilities for passengers. ❑ *...Heathrow Airport, the busiest international airport in the world.* ◆◆◇ N-COUNT: oft in names

**air|port nov|el** **(airport novels)** People sometimes refer to long novels such as thrillers and romances that are written in a popular style as **airport novels**. N-COUNT

**air|port tax** **(airport taxes)** **Airport tax** is a tax that airline passengers have to pay in order to use an airport. ❑ *Overnight return flights cost from £349 including airport taxes.* N-VAR

**air pow|er** also **airpower.** A nation's **air power** is the strength of its air force. ❑ *We will use air power to protect UN peacekeepers if necessary.* N-UNCOUNT

**air rage** **Air rage** is aggressive or violent behaviour by airline passengers. ❑ *Most air rage incidents involve heavy drinking.* N-UNCOUNT: oft N n

**air raid** **(air raids)** An **air raid** is an attack by military aircraft in which bombs are dropped. This expression is usually used by the country or group that is suffering the attack. ❑ *The war began with overnight air raids on Baghdad and Kuwait.* N-COUNT: oft N on n, N n

**air ri|fle** **(air rifles)** An **air rifle** is a rifle which is fired by means of air pressure. N-COUNT

**air|ship** /eəʳʃɪp/ **(airships)** An **airship** is an aircraft that consists of a large balloon which is filled with gas and is powered by an engine. It has a section underneath for passengers. N-COUNT

**air|show** /eəʳʃoʊ/ **(airshows)** also **air show.** An **airshow** is an event at which aeroplane pilots entertain the public by performing very skilful and complicated movements with the aircraft in the sky. N-COUNT

**air|space** /eəʳspeɪs/ also **air space.** A country's **airspace** is the part of the sky that is over that country and is considered to belong to it. ❑ *The plane left British airspace.* N-UNCOUNT: usu with supp

**air|speed** /eəʳspiːd/ **(airspeeds)** also **air speed.** An aircraft's **airspeed** is the speed at which it travels through the air. N-COUNT

**air strike** **(air strikes)** also **airstrike.** An **air strike** is an attack by military aircraft in which N-COUNT bombs are dropped. This expression is usually used by the country or group that is carrying out the attack. ❑ *A senior defence official said last night that they would continue the air strikes.*

**air|strip** /eəʳstrɪp/ **(airstrips)** An **airstrip** is a stretch of land which has been cleared so that aircraft can take off and land. ❑ *We landed on a grass airstrip, fifteen minutes after leaving Mahe.* N-COUNT

**air ter|mi|nal** **(air terminals)** An **air terminal** is a building in which passengers wait before they get on to an aeroplane. [mainly BRIT] N-COUNT

**air|tight** /eəʳtaɪt/ also **air-tight.** [1] If a container is **airtight**, its lid fits so tightly that no air can get in or out. ❑ *Store the cookies in an airtight tin.* ADJ [2] An **airtight** alibi, case, argument, or agreement is one that has been so carefully put together that nobody will be able to find a fault in it. [AM] ❑ *Mick had an airtight alibi.* ADJ

☑ in BRIT, use **watertight**

**air time** also **airtime.** The **airtime** that something gets is the amount of time taken up with broadcasts about it. ❑ *Even the best women's teams get little air time.* N-UNCOUNT

**air-to-air** **Air-to-air** combat is a battle between military aeroplanes where rockets or bullets are fired at one aeroplane from another. ❑ *...air-to-air missiles.* ADJ: ADJ n

**air traf|fic con|trol** [1] **Air traffic control** is the activity of organizing the routes that aircraft should follow, and telling pilots by radio which routes they should take. ❑ *...the nation's overburdened air-traffic-control system.* N-UNCOUNT: oft N n [2] **Air traffic control** is the group of people who organize the routes aircraft take. ❑ *They have to wait for clearance from air traffic control.* N-UNCOUNT-COLL

**air traf|fic con|trol|ler** **(air traffic controllers)** An **air traffic controller** is someone whose job is to organize the routes that aircraft should follow, and to tell pilots by radio which routes they should take. N-COUNT

**air|waves** /eəʳweɪvz/ also **air waves.** [1] **The airwaves** is used to refer to the activity of broadcasting on radio and television. For example, if someone says something over **the airwaves**, they say it on the radio or television. [JOURNALISM] ❑ *The election campaign has been fought not in street rallies but on the airwaves.* N-PLURAL: usu *the* N [2] **Airwaves** are the radio waves which are used in radio and television broadcasting. N-PLURAL

**air|way** /eəʳweɪ/ **(airways)** [1] A person's **airways** are the passages from their nose and mouth down to their lungs, through which air enters and leaves their body. ❑ *...an inflammation of the airways.* N-COUNT [2] **The airways** are all the routes that planes can travel along. ❑ *How does a private pilot get access to the airways?* N-PLURAL: usu *the* N [3] **Airways** means the same as **airwaves**. ❑ *The interview went out over the airways.* N-PLURAL: usu *the* N

**air|woman** /eəʳwʊmən/ **(airwomen)** An **airwoman** is a woman who flies aircraft, especially one who serves in her country's air force. N-COUNT

**air|worthy** /eəʳwɜːʳði/ If an aircraft is **airworthy**, it is safe to fly. ❑ *The mechanics work hard to keep the helicopters airworthy.* ADJ ♦ **air|worthiness** *All our aircraft have certificates of airworthiness.* N-UNCOUNT

**airy** /eəri/ **(airier, airiest)** [1] If a building or room is **airy**, it has a lot of fresh air inside, usually because it is large. ❑ *The bathroom has a light and airy feel.* ADJ ≠ *stuffy* [2] You can use **airy** to describe someone's behaviour when they are light-hearted and casual about things which some people take seriously. ❑ *Giving them an airy wave of his hand, the Commander sailed past.* ADJ: ADJ n = *casual*

**airy-fairy** If you describe someone's ideas as **airy-fairy**, you are critical of them because you think the ideas are vague, impractical, and unrealistic. [BRIT] ❑ *...their airy-fairy principles.* ADJ [disapproval]

**aisle** /aɪl/ **(aisles)** [1] An **aisle** is a long narrow gap that people can walk along between rows of seats in a public building such as a church or between rows of shelves in a supermarket. ❑ *...the frozen food aisle.* N-COUNT [2] **The aisle** is used in expressions such as **walking down the aisle** to refer to the activity of getting married. ❑ *He was in no hurry to walk down the aisle.* N-SING: *the* N

**ajar** /ədʒɑːʳ/ If a door is **ajar**, it is slightly open. ❑ *He left the door ajar in case I needed him.* ADJ: v-link ADJ

**aka** /eɪ keɪ eɪ/ also **a.k.a.** **aka** is an abbreviation for 'also known as'. **aka** is used especially when referring to someone's nickname or stage name. ❑ *...the writer Barbara Vine, aka Ruth Rendell.*

**akim|bo** /əkɪmboʊ/ If you stand **arms akimbo** or **with arms akimbo**, you stand with your hands on your hips and your elbows pointing outwards. [OLD-FASHIONED] PHRASE: usu PHR after v

**akin** /əkɪn/ If one thing is **akin to** another, it is similar to it in some way. [FORMAL] ❑ *Listening to his life story is akin to reading a good adventure novel.* ADJ: v-link ADJ *to* n

**à la** /ɑː lɑː/ If you do something **à la** a particular person, you do it in the same style or in the same way that they would do it. ❑ *...a crisp, tailored dress à la Audrey Hepburn.* PREP-PHRASE: PREP n-proper

**ala|bas|ter** /æləbɑːstəʳ, -bæs-/ **Alabaster** is a white stone that is used for making statues, vases, and ornaments. N-UNCOUNT: usu N n

**à la carte** /ɑː lɑː kɑːʳt/ An **à la carte** menu in a restaurant offers you a choice of individually priced dishes for each course. ❑ *You could choose as much or as little as you wanted from an à la carte menu.* ADJ: ADJ n ♦ **à la carte** is also an adverb. ❑ *A set meal is £26, or you can eat à la carte.* ADV: ADV after v

**alac|rity** /əlækrɪti/ If you do something **with alacrity**, you do it quickly and eagerly. [FORMAL] N-UNCOUNT: usu *with* N

**alarm** /əlɑːʳm/ **(alarms, alarming, alarmed)** ◆◇◇ [1] **Alarm** is a feeling of fear or anxiety that something unpleasant or dangerous might happen. ❑ *The latest news was greeted with alarm by MPs.* N-UNCOUNT: oft *with/in* N, N *over/about* n [2] If something **alarms** you, it makes you afraid or anxious that something unpleasant or dangerous might happen. ❑ *We could not see what had alarmed him.* VERB = *frighten* V n [3] An **alarm** is an automatic device that warns you of danger, for example by ringing a bell. ❑ *He heard the alarm go off.* N-COUNT [4] An **alarm** is the same as an **alarm clock**. N-COUNT [5] → See also **alarming, alarmed, burglar alarm, car alarm, false alarm, fire alarm, smoke alarm.**

PHRASES [6] If you say that something sets **alarm bells** ringing, you mean that it makes people feel worried or concerned about something. PHRASE: N inflects [7] If you **raise the alarm** or **sound the alarm**, you warn people of danger. ❑ *His family raised the alarm when he had not come home by 9pm.* PHRASE: V inflects

**alarm clock** **(alarm clocks)** An **alarm clock** is a clock that you can set to make a noise so that it wakes you up at a particular time. ❑ *I set my alarm clock for 4.30.* N-COUNT = *alarm*

**alarmed** /əlɑːʳmd/ If someone is **alarmed**, they feel afraid or anxious that something unpleasant or dangerous might happen. ❑ *They should not be too alarmed by the press reports.* ADJ: usu v-link ADJ, oft ADJ *by/at* n

**alarm|ing** /əlɑːʳmɪŋ/ Something that is **alarming** makes you feel afraid or anxious that something unpleasant or dangerous might happen. ❑ *The disease has spread at an alarming rate.* ADJ = *worrying* ♦ **alarm|ing|ly** *...the alarmingly high rate of heart disease.* ADV

**alarm|ist** /əlɑːʳmɪst/ **(alarmists)** Someone or something that is **alarmist** causes unnecessary fear or anxiety that something unpleasant or dangerous is going to happen. ❑ *Contrary to the more alarmist reports, he is not going to die.* ADJ

**alas** /əlæs/ You use **alas** to say that you think that the facts you are talking about are sad or unfortunate. [FORMAL] ❑ *Such scandals have not, alas, been absent... Alas, it's not that simple.* ADV: ADV with cl [feelings] = *sadly*

**Al|ba|nian** /ælbeɪniən/ **(Albanians)** [1] **Albanian** means belonging or relating to Albania, its ADJ people, language, or culture. ❑ *Her parents were Albanian. ...the Albanian coast.* [2] An **Albanian** is an Albanian citizen or a person of Albanian origin. N-COUNT [3] **Albanian** is the language spoken by people who live in Albania. N-UNCOUNT

**al|ba|tross** /ælbətrɒs, AM -trɔːs/ **(albatrosses)** [1] An **albatross** is a very large white seabird. N-COUNT [2] If you describe something or someone as an **albatross** around your neck, you mean that they cause you great problems from which you cannot escape, or they prevent you from doing what you want to do. ❑ *Privatization could become a political albatross for the ruling party.* N-COUNT: usu with supp disapproval

**al|be|it** /ɔːlbiːɪt/ You use **albeit** to introduce a fact or comment which reduces the force or significance of what you have just said. [FORMAL] ❑ *Charles's letter was indeed published, albeit in a somewhat abbreviated form.* ADV: ADV with cl/group = although

**al|bi|no** /ælbiːnoʊ, AM -baɪn-/ **(albinos)** An **albino** is a person or animal with very white skin, white hair, and pink eyes. N-COUNT ♦ **Albino** is also an adjective. ❑ *...an albino rabbit.* ADJ: ADJ n

**al|bum** /ælbəm/ **(albums)** [1] An **album** is a record with about 25 minutes of music on each side. You can also refer to a collection of songs that is available on a record, cassette, or CD as an **album**. ❑ *Chris likes music and has a large collection of albums and cassettes.* ◆◆◇ N-COUNT [2] An **album** is a book in which you keep things such as photographs or stamps that you have collected. ❑ *Theresa showed me her photo album.* N-COUNT: oft n N

**al|bu|min** /ælbjʊmɪn, AM ælbjuːmɪn/ **Albumin** is a protein that is found in blood plasma, egg white, and some other substances. N-UNCOUNT

**al|chemi|cal** /ælkemɪkᵊl/ **Alchemical** means relating to the science of alchemy. ❑ *...alchemical experiments.* ADJ: ADJ n

**al|che|mist** /ælkəmɪst/ **(alchemists)** An **alchemist** was a scientist in the Middle Ages who tried to discover how to change ordinary metals into gold. N-COUNT

**al|che|my** /ælkəmi/ **Alchemy** was a form of chemistry studied in the Middle Ages, which was concerned with trying to discover ways to change ordinary metals into gold. N-UNCOUNT

**al|co|hol** /ælkəhɒl, AM -hɔːl/ **(alcohols)** [1] Drinks that can make people drunk, such as beer, wine, and whisky, can be referred to as **alcohol**. ❑ *Do either of you smoke cigarettes or drink alcohol?* ◆◇◇ N-UNCOUNT [2] **Alcohol** is a colourless liquid that is found in drinks such as beer, wine, and whisky. It is also used in products such as perfumes and cleaning fluids. ❑ *...low-alcohol beer.* N-MASS

**al|co|hol|ic** /ælkəhɒlɪk, AM -hɔːl-/ **(alcoholics)** [1] An **alcoholic** is someone who cannot stop drinking large amounts of alcohol, even when this is making them ill. ❑ *He showed great courage by admitting that he is an alcoholic.* N-COUNT [2] **Alcoholic** drinks are drinks that contain alcohol. ❑ *...the serving of alcoholic drinks.* ADJ

**al|co|hol|ism** /ælkəhɒlɪzəm/ People who suffer from **alcoholism** cannot stop drinking large quantities of alcohol. ❑ *...the problems of alcoholism.* N-UNCOUNT

**al|cove** /ælkoʊv/ **(alcoves)** An **alcove** is a small area of a room which is formed by one part of a wall being built further back than the rest of the wall. ❑ *In the alcoves on either side of the fire were bookshelves.* N-COUNT = recess

**al den|te** /æl denteɪ/ If you cook pasta or a vegetable until it is **al dente**, you cook it just long enough so that it is neither hard nor soft but is firm and slightly chewy. ADJ: usu v-link ADJ

**al|der** /ɔːldəʳ/ **(alders)** An **alder** is a species of tree or shrub that grows especially in cool, damp places and loses its leaves in winter. N-VAR

**al|der|man** /ɔːldəʳmən/ **(aldermen)** [1] In some parts of the United States and Canada, an **alderman** is a member of the governing body of a city. N-COUNT; N-TITLE [2] Until 1974 in England and Wales, an **alderman** was a senior member of a local council who was elected by other councillors. N-COUNT; N-TITLE

**ale** /eɪl/ **(ales) Ale** is a kind of strong beer. ❑ *...our selection of ales and spirits.* → See also **ginger ale**, **real ale**. N-MASS

**alec** /ælɪk/ **(alecs)** → see **smart alec**.

**aleck** /ælɪk/ **(alecks)** → see **smart alec**.

**alert** /əlɜːʳt/ **(alerts, alerting, alerted)** [1] If you are **alert**, you are paying full attention to things around you and are able to deal with anything that might happen. ❑ *We all have to stay alert... He had been spotted by an alert neighbour.* ◆◇◇ ADJ = attentive ♦ **alert|ness** *The drug improved mental alertness.* N-UNCOUNT [2] If you are **alert to** something, you are fully aware of it. ❑ *The bank is already alert to the danger.* ADJ: v-link ADJ to n [3] An **alert** is a situation in which people prepare themselves for something dangerous that might happen soon. ❑ *Due to a security alert, this train will not be stopping at Oxford Circus.* N-COUNT [4] If you **alert** someone **to** a situation, especially a dangerous or unpleasant situation, you tell them about it. ❑ *He wanted to alert people to the activities of the group... I was hoping he'd alert the police.* VERB V n to n V n [5] → See also **red alert**.

PHRASES [6] If soldiers or police are **on alert**, they are ready to deal with anything that may happen. ❑ *Soldiers and police have been put on alert.* PHRASE: PHR after v, v-link PHR [7] If you are **on the alert for** something, you are ready to deal with it if it happens. ❑ *They want to be on the alert for similar buying opportunities.* PHRASE: PHR after v, v-link PHR

**A lev|el** /eɪ levᵊl/ **(A levels) A levels** are British educational qualifications which schoolchildren take when they are seventeen or eighteen years old. People usually need A levels if they want to go to university in Britain. ❑ *He left school with four A levels.* N-VAR

**al|fal|fa** /ælfælfə/ **Alfalfa** is a plant that is used for feeding farm animals. The shoots that develop from its seeds are sometimes eaten as a vegetable. N-UNCOUNT = lucerne

**al|fres|co** /ælfreskoʊ/ also **al fresco**. An **alfresco** activity, especially a meal, is one that takes place in the open air. ❑ *... an al fresco breakfast of fresh fruit.* ADJ: ADJ n = outdoor ♦ **Alfresco** is also an adverb. ❑ *He came across the man shaving alfresco.* ADV: ADV after v

**al|gae** /ældʒi, ælgaɪ/ **Algae** is a type of plant with no stems or leaves that grows in water or on damp surfaces. N-UNCOUNT-COLL

**al|gal** /ælgəl/ **Algal** means relating to algae. ❑ *Sewage nutrients do increase algal growth in the harbour.* ADJ: ADJ n

**al|ge|bra** /ældʒɪbrə/ **Algebra** is a type of mathematics in which letters are used to represent possible quantities. N-UNCOUNT

**al|ge|bra|ic** /ældʒɪbreɪɪk/ **Algebraic** equations, expressions, and principles are based on or use algebra. ADJ: ADJ n

**Al|ge|rian** /ældʒɪəriən/ **(Algerians)** [1] **Algerian** means belonging or relating to Algeria, or its people or culture. ❑ *...the Algerian desert. ...a young Algerian actor.* ◆◇◇ ADJ [2] An **Algerian** is an Algerian citizen or a person of Algerian origin. N-COUNT

**al|go|rithm** /ælgərɪðəm/ **(algorithms)** An **algorithm** is a series of mathematical steps, especially in a computer program, which will give you the answer to a particular kind of problem or question. N-COUNT

**alia** /eɪliə/ → see **inter alia**.

**ali|as** /eɪliəs/ **(aliases)** [1] An **alias** is a false name, especially one used by a criminal. ❑ *Using an alias, he had rented a house in Fleet, Hampshire.* N-COUNT [2] You use **alias** when you are mentioning another name that someone, especially a criminal or an actor, is known by. ❑ *...the defendant Pericles Pericleous, alias Peter Smith.* PREP: n-proper PREP n-proper

**ali|bi** /ælɪbaɪ/ **(alibis)** If you have an **alibi**, you can prove that you were somewhere else when a crime was committed. N-COUNT

**al|ien** /eɪliən/ **(aliens)** 1 **Alien** means belonging to a different country, race, or group, usually one you do not like or are frightened of. [FORMAL] ❑ *He said they were opposed to the presence of alien forces in the region.* (ADJ: usu ADJ n [disapproval] = foreign) 2 You use **alien** to describe something that seems strange and perhaps frightening, because it is not part of your normal experience. ❑ *His work offers an insight into an alien culture.* (ADJ: usu ADJ n = unfamiliar) 3 If something is **alien to** you or **to** your normal feelings or behaviour, it is not the way you would normally feel or behave. [FORMAL] ❑ *Such an attitude is alien to most businessmen.* (ADJ: v-link ADJ *to* n = foreign, unfamiliar) 4 An **alien** is someone who is not a legal citizen of the country in which they live. [FORMAL or LEGAL] (N-COUNT = foreigner) 5 In science fiction, an **alien** is a creature from outer space. (N-COUNT)

**al|ien|ate** /eɪliəneɪt/ **(alienates, alienating, alienated)** 1 If you **alienate** someone, you make them become unfriendly or unsympathetic towards you. ❑ *The government cannot afford to alienate either group.* (VERB; V n) 2 To **alienate** a person **from** someone or something that they are normally linked with means to cause them to be emotionally or intellectually separated from them. ❑ *His second wife, Alice, was determined to alienate him from his two boys.* (VERB; V n *from* n)

**alight** /əlaɪt/ **(alights, alighting, alighted)** 1 If something is **alight**, it is burning. ❑ *Several buildings were set alight.* (ADJ: v n ADJ, v-link ADJ = ablaze) 2 If someone's eyes are **alight** or if their face is **alight**, the expression in their eyes or on their face shows that they are feeling a strong emotion such as excitement or happiness. [LITERARY] ❑ *She paused and turned, her face alight with happiness.* (ADJ: v-link ADJ, oft ADJ *with* n) 3 If a bird or insect **alights** somewhere, it lands there. [LITERARY] ❑ *A thrush alighted on a branch of the pine tree.* (VERB; V prep/adv) 4 When you **alight** from a train, bus, or other vehicle, you get out of it after a journey. [FORMAL] (VERB = get off)

**align** /əlaɪn/ **(aligns, aligning, aligned)** 1 If you **align yourself with** a particular group, you support them because you have the same political aim. ❑ *There are signs that the prime minister is aligning himself with the liberals... He has attempted to align the Socialists with the environmental movement.* (VERB; V pron-refl prep; V n prep; Also V prep) 2 If you **align** something, you place it in a certain position in relation to something else, usually parallel to it. ❑ *A tripod will be useful to align and steady the camera.* (VERB; V n)

**align|ment** /əlaɪnmənt/ **(alignments)** 1 An **alignment** is support for a particular group, especially in politics, or for a side in a quarrel or struggle. ❑ *The church should have no political alignment.* (N-VAR = affiliation) 2 The **alignment** of something is its position in relation to something else or to its correct position. ❑ *...the alignment of mirrors in the telescope.* (N-UNCOUNT = position)

**alike** /əlaɪk/ 1 If two or more things are **alike**, they are similar in some way. ❑ *We looked very alike.* (ADJ: v-link ADJ ≠ different) 2 **Alike** means in a similar way. ❑ *...their assumption that all men and women think alike.* (ADV: ADV after v ≠ differently) 3 You use **alike** after mentioning two or more people, groups, or things in order to emphasize that you are referring to both or all of them. ❑ *The techniques are being applied almost everywhere by big and small firms alike.* (ADV: n *and* n ADV [emphasis] = equally) 4 → See also **look-alike**.

**ali|men|ta|ry ca|nal** /ælɪmentri kənæl/ **(alimentary canals)** The **alimentary canal** in a person or animal is the passage in their body through which food passes from their mouth to their anus. (N-COUNT)

**ali|mo|ny** /ælɪməni, AM -moʊni/ **Alimony** is money that a court of law orders someone to pay regularly to their former wife or husband after they have got divorced. Compare **palimony**. (N-UNCOUNT)

**alive** /əlaɪv/ ◆◇◇ 1 If people or animals are **alive**, they are not dead. ❑ *She does not know if he is alive or dead... They kept her alive on a life support machine.* (ADJ: v-link ADJ, *keep* n ADJ ≠ dead) 2 If you say that someone seems **alive**, you mean that they seem to be very lively and to enjoy everything that they do. ❑ *Our relationship made me feel more alive.* (ADJ: usu v-link ADJ) 3 If an activity, organization, or situation is **alive**, it continues to exist or function. ❑ *The big factories are trying to stay alive by cutting costs... Both communities have a tradition of keeping history alive.* (ADJ: v-link ADJ, *keep* n ADJ ≠ dead) 4 If a place is **alive with** something, there are a lot of people or things there and it seems busy or exciting. ❑ *The river was alive with birds.* (ADJ: v-link ADJ, usu ADJ *with* n)

**PHRASES** 5 If people, places, or events **come alive**, they start to be lively again after a quiet period. If someone or something **brings** them **alive**, they cause them to come alive. ❑ *The doctor's voice had come alive and his small eyes shone.* (PHRASE: V inflects) 6 If a story or description **comes alive**, it becomes interesting, lively, or realistic. If someone or something **brings** it **alive**, they make it seem more interesting, lively, or realistic. ❑ *She made history come alive with tales from her own memories.* (PHRASE: V inflects) 7 If you say that someone or something is **alive and kicking**, you are emphasizing not only that they continue to survive, but also that they are very active. ❑ *...worries that the secret police may still be alive and kicking.* (PHRASE: v-link PHR [emphasis]) 8 If you say that someone or something is **alive and well**, you are emphasizing that they continue to survive. ❑ *A man who went missing yesterday during a blizzard has been found alive and well.* (PHRASE: v-link PHR [emphasis])

**al|ka|li** /ælkəlaɪ/ **(alkalis)** An **alkali** is a substance with a pH value of more than 7. Alkalis form chemical salts when they are combined with acids. (N-MASS ≠ acid)

**al|ka|line** /ælkəlaɪn/ Something that is **alkaline** contains an alkali or has a pH value of more than 7. ❑ *Some soils are actually too alkaline for certain plant life.* (ADJ ≠ acidic) ♦ **al|ka|lin|ity** /ælkəlɪnɪti/ *A pH test measures the acidity or alkalinity of a substance.* (N-UNCOUNT ≠ acidity)

**all** /ɔːl/ ◆◆◆ 1 You use **all** to indicate that you are referring to the whole of a particular group or thing or to everyone or everything of a particular kind. ❑ *...the restaurant that Hugh and all his friends go to... He lost all his money at a blackjack table in Las Vegas.* (PREDET: PREDET det pl-n/n-uncount) ♦ **All** is also a determiner. ❑ *There is built-in storage space in all bedrooms... 85 percent of all American households owe money on mortgages... He was passionate about all literature.* (DET: DET pl-n/n-uncount) ♦ **All** is also a quantifier. ❑ *He was told to pack up all of his letters and personal belongings... He was talking to all of us.* (QUANT: QUANT *of* def-pl-n/def-n-uncount) ♦ **All** is also a pronoun. ❑ *We produce our own hair-care products, all based on herbal recipes... I'd spent all I had, every last penny.* (PRON) ♦ **All** is also an emphasizing pronoun. ❑ *Milk, oily fish and egg all contain vitamin D... We all admire professionalism and dedication.* (PRON: n PRON v) 2 You use **all** to refer to the whole of a particular period of time. ❑ *I had to cut grass all afternoon... She's been feeling bad all week.* (DET: DET sing-n) ♦ **All** is also a predeterminer. ❑ *She's worked all her life... He was looking at me all the time.* (PREDET: PREDET det sing-n) ♦ **All** is also a quantifier. ❑ *He spent all of that afternoon polishing the silver... Two-thirds of the women interviewed think about food a lot or all of the time.* (QUANT: QUANT *of* def-n) 3 You use **all** to refer to a situation or to life in general. ❑ *All is silent on the island now... As you'll have read in our news pages, all has not been well of late.* (PRON) 4 You use **all** to emphasize that something is completely true, or happens everywhere or always, or on every occasion. ❑ *He loves animals and he knows all about them... Parts for the aircraft will be made all round the world... I got scared and I ran and left her all alone... He was doing it all by himself.* (ADV: ADV prep/adv [emphasis]) 5 You use **all** at the beginning of a clause when you are emphasizing that something is the only thing that is important. ❑ *He said all that remained was to agree to a time and venue... All you ever want to do is go shopping!... All I could say was, 'I'm sorry'.* (PRON [emphasis]) 6 You use **all** in expressions such as **in all sincerity** and **in all probability** to emphasize that you are being sincere or that something is very likely. ❑ *In all fairness he had to admit that she was neither dishonest nor lazy.* (DET: *in* DET n-uncount [emphasis]) 7 You use **all** when you are talking about an equal score in a game. For example, if the score is three **all**, both players or teams have three points. (ADV: amount ADV) 8 **All** is used in structures such as (ADV:)

**all the more** or **all the better** to mean even more or even better than before. ❑ *The living room is decorated in pale colours that make it all the more airy.* [9] You use **all** in expressions such as **seen it all** and **done it all** to emphasize that someone has had a lot of experience of something. ❑ *...women who have it all: career, husband and children... Here's a man who has seen it all, tasted and heard it all.* — ADV *the* adv/adj-compar; PRON [emphasis]

**PHRASES** [10] You say **above all** to indicate that the thing you are mentioning is the most important point. ❑ *Above all, chairs should be comfortable.* — PHRASE: PHR with cl/group [emphasis]

[11] You use **after all** when introducing a statement which supports or helps explain something you have just said. ❑ *I thought you might know somebody. After all, you're the man with connections.* — PHRASE: PHR with cl

[12] You use **after all** when you are saying that something that you thought might not be the case is in fact the case. ❑ *I came out here on the chance of finding you at home after all.* — PHRASE

[13] You use **and all** when you want to emphasize that what you are talking about includes the thing mentioned, especially when this is surprising or unusual. ❑ *He dropped his sausage on the pavement and someone's dog ate it, mustard and all.* — PHRASE: n PHR [emphasis]

[14] You use **all in all** to introduce a summary or general statement. ❑ *We both thought that all in all it might not be a bad idea.* — PHRASE: PHR with cl

[15] You use **at all** at the end of a clause to give emphasis in negative statements, conditional clauses, and questions. ❑ *Robin never really liked him at all.* — PHRASE [emphasis]

[16] **All but** a particular person or thing means everyone or everything except that person or thing. ❑ *The general was an unattractive man to all but his most ardent admirers.* — PHRASE: PHR n

[17] You use **all but** to say that something is almost the case. ❑ *The concrete wall that used to divide this city has now all but gone.* — PHRASE: PHR -ed

[18] You use **for all** to indicate that the thing mentioned does not affect or contradict the truth of what you are saying. ❑ *For all its faults, the film instantly became a classic.* — PHRASE: PHR n = despite

[19] You use **for all** in phrases such as **for all I know**, and **for all he cares**, to emphasize that you do not know something or that someone does not care about something. ❑ *For all we know, he may even not be in this country... You can go right now for all I care.* — PHRASE: PHR with cl [emphasis]

[20] If you **give** your **all** or **put** your **all** into something, you make the maximum effort possible. ❑ *He puts his all into every game.* — PHRASE: V inflects

[21] **In all** means in total. ❑ *There was evidence that thirteen people in all had taken part in planning the murder.* — PHRASE: PHR with cl, amount PHR

[22] If something such as an activity is a particular price **all in**, that price includes everything that is offered. [mainly BRIT, INFORMAL] ❑ *Dinner is about £25 all in.* — PHRASE: amount PHR, PHR with cl

[23] You use **of all** to emphasize the words 'first' or 'last', or a superlative adjective or adverb. ❑ *First of all, answer these questions... Now she faces her toughest task of all.* — PHRASE: PHR with superl [emphasis]

[24] You use **of all** in expressions such as **of all people** or **of all things** when you want to emphasize someone or something surprising. ❑ *They met and fell in love in a supermarket, of all places.* — PHRASE: PHR n [emphasis]

[25] You use **all** in expressions like **of all the cheek** or **of all the luck** to emphasize how angry or surprised you are at what someone else has done or said. ❑ *Of all the lazy, indifferent, unbusinesslike attitudes to have!* — PHRASE [feelings]

[26] You use **all of** before a number to emphasize how small or large an amount is. ❑ *It took him all of 41 minutes to score his first goal.* — PHRASE: PHR amount [emphasis]

[27] You use **all that** in statements with negative meaning when you want to weaken the force of what you are saying. [SPOKEN] ❑ *He wasn't all that older than we were.* — PHRASE: PHR with brd-neg, PHR adj/adv [vagueness]

[28] You can say **that's all** at the end of a sentence when you are explaining something and want to emphasize that nothing more happens or is the case. ❑ *'Why do you want to know that?' he demanded. — 'Just curious, that's all.'* — PHRASE: cl PHR

[29] You use **all very well** to suggest that you do not really approve of something or you think that it is unreasonable. ❑ *It is all very well to urge people to give more to charity when they have less, but is it really fair?* — PHRASE: v-link PHR [disapproval]

**all-** /ɔːl-/ [1] **All-** is added to nouns or adjectives in order to form adjectives which describe something as consisting only of the thing mentioned or as having only the quality indicated. ❑ *...an all-star cast. ...all-cotton sheeting.* — COMB in ADJ: usu ADJ n

[2] **All-** is added to present participles or adjectives in order to form adjectives which describe something as including or affecting everything or everyone. ❑ *Nursing a demented person is an all-consuming task.* — COMB IN ADJ: usu ADJ n

[3] **All-** is added to nouns in order to form adjectives which describe something as being suitable for or including all types of a particular thing. ❑ *He wanted to form an all-party government of national unity.* — COMB in ADJ: usu ADJ n

**Allah** /æ̲lə, æ̲lɑː/ **Allah** is the name of God in Islam. — N-PROPER

**all-American** If you describe someone as an **all-American** boy or girl, you mean that they seem to have all the typical qualities that are valued by ordinary Americans, such as good looks and love of their country. — ADJ: ADJ n

**all-around** → see **all-round**.

**al|lay** /əle̲ɪ/ **(allays, allaying, allayed)** If you **allay** someone's fears or doubts, you stop them feeling afraid or doubtful. [FORMAL] ❑ *He did what he could to allay his wife's fears.* — VERB = calm; V n

**all clear** [1] **The all clear** is a signal that a dangerous situation, for example an air raid, has ended. ❑ *The all clear was sounded about 10 minutes after the alert was given.* ♦ **All clear** is also a convention. ❑ *'All clear,' Misha growled.* — N-SING: the N; CONVENTION

[2] If someone in authority gives you **the all clear**, they give you permission to continue with a plan or activity, usually after a problem has been sorted out. ❑ *I was given the all clear by the doctor to resume playing.* — N-SING: the N = go-ahead

**all-comers** also **all comers.** You use **all-comers** to refer to everyone who wants to take part in an activity, especially a competition. ❑ *This is her second season offering residential courses for all-comers.* — N-PLURAL

**al|le|ga|tion** /æ̲lɪge̲ɪʃᵊn/ **(allegations)** An **allegation** is a statement saying that someone has done something wrong. ❑ *The company has denied the allegations... Allegations of brutality and theft have been levelled at the army.* — ◆◇◇ N-COUNT = claim

**al|lege** /əle̲dʒ/ **(alleges, alleging, alleged)** If you **allege that** something bad is true, you say it but do not prove it. [FORMAL] ❑ *She alleged that there was rampant drug use among the male members of the group... The accused is alleged to have killed a man... It was alleged that the restaurant discriminated against black customers.* — VERB = claim; V that; *be* V-ed to-inf; *it be* V-ed that

**al|leged** /əle̲dʒd/ An **alleged** fact has been stated but has not been proved to be true. [FORMAL] ❑ *They have begun a hunger strike in protest at the alleged beating.* ♦ **al|leg|ed|ly** /əle̲dʒɪdli/ *His van allegedly struck the two as they were crossing a street.* — ◆◆◇ ADJ: ADJ n; ADV

**al|le|giance** /əli̲ːdʒᵊns/ **(allegiances)** Your **allegiance** is your support for and loyalty to a particular group, person, or belief. ❑ *My allegiance to Kendall and his company ran deep.* — N-VAR: oft N *to* n

**al|le|gori|cal** /æ̲lɪgɒ̲rɪkᵊl, AM -gɔ̲ːr-/ An **allegorical** story, poem, or painting uses allegory. ❑ *Every Russian knows the allegorical novel The Master And Margarita.* — ADJ

**al|le|go|ry** /æ̲lɪgəri, AM -gɔːri/ **(allegories)** [1] An **allegory** is a story, poem, or painting in which the characters and events are symbols of something else. Allegories are often moral, religious, or political. ❑ *The book is a kind of allegory of Latin American history.* — N-COUNT: oft N *of* n = parable

[2] **Allegory** is the use of characters and events in a story, poem, or painting to represent other things. ❑ *The poem's comic allegory was transparent.* — N-UNCOUNT

**al|le|gro** /əle̲groʊ/ **(allegros)** An **allegro** is a piece of classical music that should be played quickly and in a lively way. — N-COUNT: oft in names

**all-embracing** Something that is **all-embracing** includes or affects everyone or everything. ❑ *His hospitality was instantaneous and all-embracing.* ADJ = all-encompassing

**al\|ler\|gen** /ælərdʒen/ **(allergens)** An **allergen** is a substance that causes an allergic reaction in someone. [TECHNICAL] N-COUNT

**al\|ler\|gic** /əlɜːrdʒɪk/ [1] If you are **allergic to** something, you become ill or get a rash when you eat it, smell it, or touch it. ❑ *I'm allergic to cats.* ADJ: v-link ADJ to n [2] If you have an **allergic** reaction to something, you become ill or get a rash when you eat it, smell it, or touch it. ❑ *Soya milk can cause allergic reactions in some children.* ADJ: ADJ n

**al\|ler\|gist** /ælərdʒɪst/ **(allergists)** An **allergist** is a doctor who specializes in treating people with allergies. N-COUNT

**al\|ler\|gy** /ælərdʒi/ **(allergies)** If you have a particular **allergy**, you become ill or get a rash when you eat, smell, or touch something that does not normally make people ill. ❑ *Food allergies can result in an enormous variety of different symptoms.* N-VAR

**al\|le\|vi\|ate** /əliːvieɪt/ **(alleviates, alleviating, alleviated)** If you **alleviate** pain, suffering, or an unpleasant condition, you make it less intense or severe. [FORMAL] ❑ *Nowadays, a great deal can be done to alleviate back pain.* VERB = ease ≠ aggravate V n ♦ **al\|le\|via\|tion** /əliːvieɪʃən/ *Their energies were focussed on the alleviation of the refugees' misery.* N-UNCOUNT: usu N of n

**al\|ley** /æli/ **(alleys)** An **alley** is a narrow passage or street with buildings or walls on both sides. → See also **blind alley, bowling alley**. N-COUNT

**al\|ley cat (alley cats)** An **alley cat** is a cat that lives in the streets of a town, is rather fierce, and is usually not owned by anyone. N-COUNT

**alley\|way** /æliweɪ/ **(alleyways)** also **alley-way**. An **alleyway** is the same as an **alley**. N-COUNT

**al\|li\|ance** /əlaɪəns/ **(alliances)** ◆◇◇ [1] An **alliance** is a group of countries or political parties that are formally united and working together because they have similar aims. ❑ *The two parties were still too much apart to form an alliance.* N-COUNT = coalition [2] An **alliance** is a relationship in which two countries, political parties, or organizations work together for some purpose. ❑ *What will be the effect of the alliance between IBM and Apple?* N-COUNT: oft N with/between n, also in N with n = partnership

**al\|lied** /ælaɪd, AM əlaɪd/ ◆◇◇ [1] **Allied** forces or troops are armies from different countries who are fighting on the same side in a war. ❑ *...the approaching Allied forces.* ADJ: ADJ n [2] **Allied** countries, troops, or political parties are united by a political or military agreement. ❑ *...forces from three allied nations.* ADJ: ADJ n, v-link ADJ to n [3] If one thing or group is **allied to** another, it is related to it because the two things have particular qualities or characteristics in common. ❑ *...lectures on subjects allied to health, beauty and fitness.* ADJ: v-link ADJ to/with n, ADJ n = associated [4] Something that is **allied to** another thing occurs with the other thing. [FORMAL] ❑ *He possessed a raw energy allied to a feeling of something special. ...a disastrous rise in interest rates allied with a stock market slump.* ADJ: v-link ADJ to/with n = coupled

**al\|li\|ga\|tor** /ælɪgeɪtər/ **(alligators)** An **alligator** is a large reptile with short legs, a long tail and very powerful jaws. N-COUNT

**all-inclusive All-inclusive** is used to indicate that a price, especially the price of a holiday, includes all the charges and all the services offered. ❑ *An all-inclusive two-week holiday costs around £2880 per person.* ADJ: usu ADJ n

**al\|lit\|era\|tion** /əlɪtəreɪʃən/ **(alliterations) Alliteration** is the use in speech or writing of several words close together which all begin with the same letter or sound. [TECHNICAL] N-VAR

**al\|lit\|era\|tive** /əlɪtərətɪv, AM -təreɪtɪv/ **Alliterative** means relating to or connected with alliteration. [TECHNICAL] ❑ *Her campaign slogan, 'a president for the people', was pleasantly alliterative but empty.* ADJ

**al\|lo\|cate** /æləkeɪt/ **(allocates, allocating, allocated)** If one item or share of something **is allocated to** a particular person or **for** a particular purpose, it is given to that person or used for that purpose. ❑ *Tickets are limited and will be allocated to those who apply first... The 1985 federal budget allocated $7.3 billion for development programmes... Our plan is to allocate one member of staff to handle appointments.* VERB = assign, allot be V-ed to n V n for/to n V n to-inf

**al\|lo\|ca\|tion** /æləkeɪʃən/ **(allocations)** [1] An **allocation** is an amount of something, especially money, that is given to a particular person or used for a particular purpose. ❑ *The aid allocation for Pakistan was still under review.* N-COUNT [2] The **allocation** of something is the decision that it should be given to a particular person or used for a particular purpose. ❑ *Town planning and land allocation had to be coordinated.* N-UNCOUNT: usu with supp

**al\|lot** /əlɒt/ **(allots, allotting, allotted)** If something **is allotted to** someone, it is given to them as their share. ❑ *The seats are allotted to the candidates who have won the most votes... We were allotted half an hour to address the committee.* VERB: usu passive = assign, allocate be V-ed to n be V-ed n

**al\|lot\|ment** /əlɒtmənt/ **(allotments)** [1] In Britain, an **allotment** is a small area of land in a town which a person rents to grow plants and vegetables on. N-COUNT [2] An **allotment of** something is a share or amount of it that is given to someone. ❑ *His meager allotment of gas had to be saved for emergencies.* N-COUNT: oft N of n = allocation

**all-out** also **all out.** You use **all-out** to describe actions that are carried out in a very energetic and determined way, using all the resources available. ❑ *He launched an all-out attack on his critics.* ADJ: ADJ n ♦ **All out** is also an adverb. ❑ *We will be going all out to ensure it doesn't happen again.* ADV: ADV after v

**al\|low** /əlaʊ/ **(allows, allowing, allowed)** ◆◆◆ [1] If someone **is allowed to** do something, it is all right for them to do it and they will not get into trouble. ❑ *The children are not allowed to watch violent TV programmes... The Government will allow them to advertise on radio and television... They will be allowed home... Smoking will not be allowed.* VERB = permit, let ≠ forbid be V-ed to-inf V n to-inf be V-ed adv/prep be V-ed [2] If you **are allowed** something, you are given permission to have it or are given it. ❑ *Gifts like chocolates or flowers are allowed... He should be allowed the occasional treat.* VERB = permit ≠ forbid be V-ed be V-ed n [3] If you **allow** something **to** happen, you do not prevent it. ❑ *He won't allow himself to fail... If the soil is allowed to dry out the tree could die.* VERB = permit, let ≠ prevent V n to-inf V n to-inf [4] If one thing **allows** another thing **to** happen, the first thing creates the opportunity for the second thing to happen. ❑ *The compromise will allow him to continue his free market reforms. ...an attempt to allow the Moslem majority a greater share of power... She said this would allow more effective planning.* VERB = permit, let ≠ prevent V n n V n [5] If you **allow** a particular length of time or a particular amount of something **for** a particular purpose, you include it in your planning. ❑ *Please allow 28 days for delivery... Allow about 75ml (3fl oz) per six servings.* VERB V n for n V n [6] If you **allow that** something is true, you admit or agree that it is true. [FORMAL] ❑ *Warren also allows that capitalist development may, in its early stages, result in increased social inequality.* VERB = acknowledge V that [7] Some people use **Allow me to...** as a way of introducing something that they want to say or do. [FORMAL] ❑ *Allow me to introduce Dr Amberg.* PHRASE = permit me to

♦ **allow for** If you **allow for** certain problems or expenses, you include some extra time or money in your planning so that you can deal with them if they occur. ❑ *You have to allow for a certain amount of error.* PHRASAL VERB V P n

**al\|low\|able** /əlaʊəbəl/ [1] If people decide that something is **allowable**, they let it happen without trying to stop it. ❑ *Capital punishment is allowable only under exceptional circumstances.* ADJ = permissible [2] **Allowable** costs or expenses are amounts of money that you do not have to pay tax on. [BUSINESS] ADJ

**al\|low\|ance** /əlaʊəns/ **(allowances)** [1] An **allowance** is money that is given to someone, usually on a regular basis, in order to help them pay for the things that they need. ❑ *He lives on a* N-COUNT: usu with supp, oft N of amount *single parent's allowance of £70 a week.* 2 A child's **allowance** is money that is given to him or her every week or every month by his or her parents. [mainly AM] N-COUNT: usu poss N

in BRIT, use **pocket money**

3 Your tax **allowance** is the amount of money that you are allowed to earn before you have to start paying income tax. [BRIT] ❑ *...those earning less than the basic tax allowance.* N-COUNT: usu with supp

in AM, use **personal exemption**

4 A particular type of **allowance** is an amount of something that you are allowed in particular circumstances. ❑ *Most of our flights have a baggage allowance of 44lbs per passenger.* N-COUNT: with supp

PHRASES 5 If you **make allowances for** something, you take it into account in your decisions, plans, or actions. ❑ *We'll make allowances in the schedule for time off.* PHRASE: V and N inflect, oft PHR *for* n 6 If you **make allowances for** someone, you accept behaviour which you would not normally accept or deal with them less severely than you would normally, because of a problem that they have. ❑ *He's tired so I'll make allowances for him.* PHRASE: V inflects, oft PHR *for* n

**al|loy** /ælɔɪ/ **(alloys)** An **alloy** is a metal that is made by mixing two or more types of metal together. ❑ *Bronze is an alloy of copper and tin.* N-MASS

**all-powerful** An **all-powerful** person or organization has the power to do anything they want. ❑ *...the all-powerful labour unions.* ADJ

**all-purpose** You use **all-purpose** to refer to things that have lots of different uses or can be used in lots of different situations. ❑ *Use all-purpose flour if you cannot find pastry flour.* ADJ: ADJ n

**all right** ◆◆◇

in BRIT, also use **alright**

1 If you say that someone or something is **all right**, you mean that you find them satisfactory or acceptable. ❑ *Is it all right with you if we go now?... 'How was school?' — 'It was all right.'* ♦ **All right** is also used before a noun. [INFORMAL] ❑ *He's an all right kind of guy really.* ADJ: v-link ADJ = okay; ADJ: ADJ n 2 If you say that something happens or goes **all right**, you mean that it happens in a satisfactory or acceptable manner. ❑ *Things have thankfully worked out all right.* ADV: ADV after v = okay 3 If someone or something is **all right**, they are well or safe. ❑ *All she's worried about is whether he is all right... Are you feeling all right now?* ADJ: v-link ADJ = okay 4 You say **'all right'** when you are agreeing to something. ❑ *'I think you should go now.' — 'All right.'.* CONVENTION formulae = okay 5 You say **'all right?'** after you have given an instruction or explanation to someone when you are checking that they have understood what you have just said, or checking that they agree with or accept what you have just said. ❑ *Peter, you get half the fees. All right?* CONVENTION = okay 6 If someone in a position of authority says **'all right'**, and suggests talking about or doing something else, they are indicating that they want you to end one activity and start another. ❑ *All right, Bob. You can go now.* CONVENTION 7 You say **'all right'** during a discussion to show that you understand something that someone has just said, and to introduce a statement that relates to it. ❑ *'I'm a bit busy now.' — 'All right, why don't I come back later?'* CONVENTION = okay 8 You say **all right** before a statement or question to indicate that you are challenging or threatening someone. ❑ *All right, who are you and what are you doing in my office?* CONVENTION = okay

**all-round**

in AM, also use **all-around**

1 An **all-round** person is good at a lot of different skills, academic subjects, or sports. ❑ *He is a great all-round player.* ADJ: ADJ n 2 **All-round** means doing or relating to all aspects of a job or activity. ❑ *He demonstrated the all-round skills of a quarterback.* ADJ: ADJ n

**all-rounder** **(all-rounders)** Someone who is an **all-rounder** is good at a lot of different skills, academic subjects, or sports. [BRIT] ❑ *I class myself as an all-rounder.* N-COUNT

**all-seater** An **all-seater** stadium has enough seats for all the audience, rather than having some areas without seats where people stand. [BRIT] ADJ: usu ADJ n

**all-singing all-dancing** If you describe something new as **all-singing, all-dancing**, you mean that it is very modern and advanced, with a lot of additional features; used especially to show that you think a lot of these features are silly or unnecessary. [HUMOROUS] ❑ *...the executive's new all-singing, all-dancing website.* PHRASE: PHR n

**all|spice** /ɔːlspaɪs/ **Allspice** is a powder used as a spice in cooking, which is made from the berries of a tropical American tree. N-UNCOUNT = pimento

**all-star** An **all-star** cast, performance, or game is one which contains only famous or extremely good performers or players. ADJ: ADJ n

**all-time** You use **all-time** when you are comparing all the things of a particular type that there have ever been. For example, if you say that something is the **all-time** best, you mean that it is the best thing of its type that there has ever been. ❑ *The president's popularity nationally is at an all-time low... Duane Eddy is John Peel's all-time favourite artist.* ADJ: ADJ n

**al|lude** /əluːd/ **(alludes, alluding, alluded)** If you **allude to** something, you mention it in an indirect way. [FORMAL] ❑ *She also alluded to her rival's past marital troubles.* VERB = refer; V to n

**al|lure** /əljʊəʳ, AM əlʊr/ The **allure** of something or someone is the pleasing or exciting quality that they have. ❑ *It's a game that has really lost its allure.* N-UNCOUNT: usu with supp = attraction

**al|lur|ing** /əljʊərɪŋ, AM əlʊrɪŋ/ Someone or something that is **alluring** is very attractive. ❑ *...the most alluring city in South-East Asia.* ADJ = fascinating

**al|lu|sion** /əluːʒᵊn/ **(allusions)** An **allusion** is an indirect reference to someone or something. ❑ *The title is perhaps an allusion to AIDS.* N-VAR: oft N *to* n

**al|lu|sive** /əluːsɪv/ **Allusive** speech, writing, or art is full of indirect references to people or things. ❑ *His new play, Arcadia, is as intricate, elaborate and allusive as anything he has yet written.* ADJ

**al|lu|vial** /əluːviəl/ **Alluvial** soils are soils which consist of earth and sand left behind on land which has been flooded or where a river once flowed. [TECHNICAL] ADJ

**ally** **(allies, allying, allied)** ◆◆◇

The noun is pronounced /ælaɪ/. The verb is pronounced /əlaɪ/.

1 A country's **ally** is another country that has an agreement to support it, especially in war. ❑ *Washington would not take such a step without its allies' approval... The United States is a close ally of South Korea.* N-COUNT: with supp ≠ adversary 2 **The Allies** were the armed forces that fought against Germany and Japan in the Second World War. N-PLURAL: the N 3 If you describe someone as your **ally**, you mean that they help and support you, especially when other people are opposing you. ❑ *He is a close ally of the Prime Minister.* N-COUNT: with supp = supporter, friend ≠ enemy 4 If you **ally yourself with** someone or something, you give your support to them. ❑ *He will have no choice but to ally himself with the new movement.* VERB: V pron-refl with n 5 ➔ See also **allied**.

**alma ma|ter** /ælmə mɑːtəʳ, - meɪtəʳ/ **(alma maters)** 1 Your **alma mater** is the school or university which you went to. [FORMAL] N-COUNT: usu sing, usu with poss 2 A school or college's **alma mater** is its official song. [AM] N-SING

**al|ma|nac** /ɔːlmənæk/ **(almanacs)** also **almanack.** 1 An **almanac** is a book published every year which contains information about the movements of the planets, the changes of the moon and the tides, and the dates of important anniversaries. N-COUNT: oft in names 2 An **almanac** is a book published every year which contains information about events connected with a particular subject or activity, and facts and statistics about that activity. N-COUNT: oft in names

**al|ma|nack** /ɔːlmənæk/ **(almanacks)** → see **almanac.**

**al|mighty** /ɔːlmaɪti/ [1] **The Almighty** is another name for God. You can also refer to **Almighty God**. ❑ *Adam sought guidance from the Almighty.* [2] People sometimes say **God Almighty** or **Christ Almighty** to express their surprise, anger, or horror. These expressions could cause offence. [3] **Almighty** means very serious or great in extent. [INFORMAL] ❑ *We had an almighty row.* N-PROPER EXCLAM feelings ADJ: ADJ n emphasis

**al|mond** /ɑːmənd/ **(almonds)** [1] **Almonds** are pale oval nuts. They are often used in cooking. ❑ *...sponge cake flavoured with almonds.* → See also **sugared almond**. [2] An **almond** or an **almond tree**, is a tree on which almonds grow. ❑ *On the left was a plantation of almond trees.* N-VAR N-VAR

**al|most** /ɔːlmoʊst/ You use **almost** to indicate that something is not completely the case but is nearly the case. ❑ *The couple had been dating for almost three years... Storms have been hitting almost all of Britain recently... The effect is almost impossible to describe... The arrested man will almost certainly be kept at this police station... He contracted Spanish flu, which almost killed him.* ◆◆◆ ADV: ADV group, ADV before v = nearly

**alms** /ɑːmz/ **Alms** are gifts of money, clothes, or food to poor people. [OLD-FASHIONED] N-PLURAL

**alms|house** /ɑːmzhaʊs/ **(almshouses)** also **alms-house. Almshouses** are houses in Britain which were built and run by charities to provide accommodation for poor or old people who could not afford to pay rent. N-COUNT

**aloe vera** /æloʊ vɪərə/ **Aloe vera** is a substance that contains vitamins and minerals and is often used in cosmetics. **Aloe vera** is also the name of the plant from which this substance is extracted. N-UNCOUNT: oft N n

**aloft** /əlɒft, AM əlɔːft/ Something that is **aloft** is in the air or off the ground. [LITERARY] ❑ *He held the trophy proudly aloft.* ADV: ADV after v, be ADV

**alone** /əloʊn/ [1] When you are **alone**, you are not with any other people. ❑ *There is nothing so fearful as to be alone in a combat situation... He was all alone in the middle of the hall.* ♦ **Alone** is also an adverb. ❑ *She has lived alone in this house for almost five years now.* [2] If one person is **alone with** another person, or if two or more people are **alone**, they are together, without anyone else present. ❑ *I couldn't imagine why he would want to be alone with me... My brother and I were alone with Vincent.* [3] If you say that you are **alone** or feel **alone**, you mean that nobody who is with you, or nobody at all, cares about you. ❑ *Never in her life had she felt so alone, so abandoned.* [4] You say that one person or thing **alone** does something when you are emphasizing that only one person or thing is involved. ❑ *You alone should determine what is right for you... They were convicted on forensic evidence alone.* [5] If you say that one person or thing **alone** is responsible for part of an amount, you are emphasizing the size of that part and the size of the total amount. ❑ *The BBC alone is sending 300 technicians, directors and commentators.* [6] If someone is **alone in** doing something, they are the only person doing it, and so are different from other people. ❑ *Am I alone in thinking that this scandal should finish his career?* ♦ **Alone** is also an adverb. ❑ *I alone was sane, I thought, in a crazy world.* [7] When someone does something **alone**, they do it without help from other people. ❑ *Bringing up a child alone should give you a sense of achievement.* [8] If you **go it alone**, you do something without any help from other people. [INFORMAL] ❑ *I missed the stimulation of working with others when I tried to go it alone.* [9] to **leave** someone or something **alone** → see **leave. let alone** → see **let.** ◆◆◇ ADJ: v-link ADJ ADV: ADV after v ADJ: v-link ADJ, oft ADJ with n ADJ: v-link ADJ ADV: n ADV emphasis ADV: n ADV emphasis ADJ: v-link ADJ, oft ADJ in -ing/n = unique ADV: ADV prep, n ADV ADV: ADV after v PHRASE: V inflects

**along** /əlɒŋ, AM əlɔːŋ/ ◆◆◆

> In addition to the uses shown below, **along** is used in phrasal verbs such as 'go along with', 'play along', and 'string along'.

[1] If you move or look **along** something such as a road, you move or look towards one end of it. ❑ *Newman walked along the street alone... The young man led Mark Ryle along a corridor... I looked along the length of the building.* [2] If something is situated **along** a road, river, or corridor, it is situated in it or beside it. ❑ *...enormous traffic jams all along the roads. ...houses built on piles along the river.* [3] When someone or something moves **along**, they keep moving in a particular direction. ❑ *She skipped and danced along... The wide road was blocked solid with traffic that moved along sluggishly.* [4] If you say that something is going **along** in a particular way, you mean that it is progressing in that way. ❑ *...the negotiations which have been dragging along interminably... My life is going along nicely.* [5] If you take someone or something **along** when you go somewhere, you take them with you. ❑ *This is open to women of all ages, so bring along your friends and colleagues.* [6] If someone or something is coming **along** or is sent **along**, they are coming or being sent to a particular place. ❑ *She invited everyone she knew to come along.* PREP PREP ADV: ADV after v ADV: ADV after v ADV: ADV after v ADV: ADV after v

PHRASES [7] You use **along with** to mention someone or something else that is also involved in an action or situation. ❑ *The baby's mother escaped from the fire along with two other children.* [8] If something has been true or been present **all along**, it has been true or been present throughout a period of time. ❑ *I've been fooling myself all along.* [9] **along the way** → see **way.** PREP-PHRASE PHRASE: PHR with cl, PHR after v

**along|side** /əlɒŋsaɪd, AM -lɔːŋ-/ [1] If one thing is **alongside** another thing, the first thing is next to the second. ❑ *He crossed the street and walked alongside Central Park... Much of the industry was located alongside rivers.* ♦ **Alongside** is also an adverb. ❑ *He waited several minutes for a car to pull up alongside.* [2] If you work **alongside** other people, you all work together in the same place. ❑ *He had worked alongside Frank and Mark and they had become friends.* [3] If one thing exists or develops **alongside** another, the two things exist or develop together at the same time. ❑ *Her self-confidence will develop alongside her technique.* ◆◇◇ PREP ADV: ADV after v PREP PREP = together with

**aloof** /əluːf/ [1] Someone who is **aloof** is not very friendly and does not like to spend time with other people. ❑ *He seemed aloof and detached.* [2] If someone stays **aloof from** something, they do not become involved with it. [FORMAL] ❑ *The Government is keeping aloof from the controversy.* ADJ: usu v-link ADJ disapproval = distant ADJ: v-link ADJ from n

**aloud** /əlaʊd/ [1] When you say something, read, or laugh **aloud**, you speak or laugh so that other people can hear you. ❑ *When we were children, our father read aloud to us... 'You fool,' he said aloud.* [2] If you **think aloud**, you express your thoughts as they occur to you, rather than thinking first and then speaking. ADV: ADV after v ≠ silently PHRASE: V inflects

**al|paca** /ælpækə/ **(alpacas)** [1] **Alpaca** is a type of soft wool. ❑ *...a light-grey alpaca suit.* [2] **Alpacas** are South American animals similar to llamas. Their hair is the source of alpaca wool. N-UNCOUNT: oft N n N-COUNT

**al|pha|bet** /ælfəbet/ **(alphabets)** An **alphabet** is a set of letters usually presented in a fixed order which is used for writing the words of a particular language or group of languages. ❑ *The modern Russian alphabet has 31 letters... By two and a half he knew the alphabet.* N-COUNT

**al|pha|beti|cal** /ælfəbetɪkᵊl/ **Alphabetical** means arranged according to the normal order of the letters in the alphabet. ❑ *Their herbs and spices are arranged in alphabetical order.* ♦ **al|pha|beti|cal|ly** /ælfəbetɪkli/ *The catalog is organized alphabetically by label name.* ADJ: ADJ n ADV

**al|pine** /ælpaɪn/ **(alpines)** [1] **Alpine** means existing in or relating to mountains, especially the ones in Switzerland. ❑ *...grassy, alpine meadows.* [2] **Alpines** are small flowering plants that grow high up on mountains and are sometimes grown ADJ: usu ADJ n N-COUNT in gardens. There are many different types of alpines.

**al|ready** /ɔːlredi/ ◆◆◆ 1 You use **already** to show that something has happened, or that something had happened before the moment you are referring to. Speakers of British English use **already** with a verb in a perfect tense, putting it after 'have', 'has', or 'had', or at the end of a clause. Some speakers of American English use **already** with the simple past tense of the verb instead of a perfect tense. ❑ *They had already voted for him at the first ballot... I already told you not to come over... They've spent nearly a billion dollars on it already.* ADV: ADV before v, cl ADV

2 You use **already** to show that a situation exists at this present moment or that it exists at an earlier time than expected. You use **already** after the verb 'be' or an auxiliary verb, or before a verb if there is no auxiliary. When you want add emphasis, you can put **already** at the beginning of a sentence. ❑ *The authorities believe those security measures are already paying off... He was already rich... Get 10% off our already low prices!... Already, he has a luxurious villa in Formello.* ADV: ADV before v, ADV with group

**al|right** /ɔːlraɪt/ → see **all right**.

**Al|sa|tian** /ælseɪʃᵊn/ **(Alsatians)** An **Alsatian** is a large, usually fierce dog that is often used to guard buildings or by the police to help them find criminals. [BRIT] N-COUNT = German shepherd

☑ in AM, use **German shepherd**

**also** /ɔːlsoʊ/ ◆◆◆ 1 You can use **also** to give more information about a person or thing, or to add another relevant fact. ❑ *It is the work of Ivor Roberts-Jones, who also produced the statue of Churchill in Parliament Square... He is an asthmatic who was also anaemic... She has a reputation for brilliance. Also, she is gorgeous.* ADV: ADV before v, ADV with cl/group

2 You can use **also** to indicate that something you have just said about one person or thing is true of another person or thing. ❑ *His father, also a top-ranking officer, had perished during the war... We have been working very hard, and our families have also worked hard... Not only cancer, but also heart and lung disease are influenced by smoking.* ADV: ADV before v, ADV with group

**also-ran** **(also-rans)** If you describe someone as an **also-ran**, you mean that they have been or are likely to be unsuccessful in a contest. N-COUNT

**al|tar** /ɔːltəʳ/ **(altars)** An **altar** is a holy table in a church or temple. N-COUNT

**al|tar boy** **(altar boys)** In the Roman Catholic church, an **altar boy** is a boy who helps the priest during Mass. N-COUNT

**altar|piece** /ɔːltəʳpiːs/ **(altarpieces)** An **altarpiece** is a work of art behind the altar in a church. N-COUNT

**al|ter** /ɔːltəʳ/ ◆◇◇ **(alters, altering, altered)** If something **alters** or if you **alter** it, it changes. ❑ *Little had altered in the village... They have never altered their programmes by a single day.* VERB = change V V n

**al|tera|tion** /ɔːltəreɪʃᵊn/ **(alterations)** 1 An **alteration** is a change in or to something. ❑ *Making some simple alterations to your diet will make you feel fitter.* N-COUNT: usu N *to/in/of* n = change

2 The **alteration** of something is the process of changing it. ❑ *Her jacket was at the boutique waiting for alteration.* N-UNCOUNT

**al|ter|ca|tion** /ɔːltəʳkeɪʃᵊn/ **(altercations)** An **altercation** is a noisy argument or disagreement. [FORMAL] ❑ *I had a slight altercation with some people who objected to our filming.* N-COUNT: oft N *with/between* n = dispute

**al|ter ego** **(alter egos)** 1 Your **alter ego** is the other side of your personality from the one which people normally see. N-COUNT: usu with supp

2 You can describe the character that an actor usually plays on television or in films as his or her **alter ego**. ❑ *Barry Humphries's alter ego Dame Edna has taken the US by storm.* N-COUNT: usu with supp

**al|ter|nate** **(alternates, alternating, alternated)**

☑ The verb is pronounced /ɔːltəʳneɪt/. The adjective and noun are pronounced /ɔːltɜːʳnət/.

1 When you **alternate** two things, you keep using one then the other. When one thing **alternates with** another, the first regularly occurs after the other. ❑ *Her aggressive moods alternated with gentle or more co-operative states... The three acts will alternate as headliners throughout the tour... Now you just alternate layers of that mixture and eggplant... The band alternated romantic love songs with bouncy dance numbers.* V-RECIP V *between/with* n pl-n V V pl-n V n *with* n

♦ **al|ter|na|tion** /ɔːltəʳneɪʃᵊn/ **(alternations)** *The alternation of sun and snow continued for the rest of our holiday.* N-VAR

2 **Alternate** actions, events, or processes regularly occur after each other. ❑ *They were streaked with alternate bands of colour.* ADJ: ADJ n

♦ **al|ter|nate|ly** *He could alternately bully and charm people.* ADV: ADV with v, ADV adj

3 If something happens on **alternate** days, it happens on one day, then happens on every second day after that. In the same way, something can happen in **alternate** weeks, years, or other periods of time. ❑ *Lesley had agreed to Jim going skiing in alternate years.* ADJ: ADJ n

4 You use **alternate** to describe a plan, idea, or system which is different from the one already in operation and can be used instead of it. ❑ *His group was forced to turn back and take an alternate route.* ADJ: ADJ n = alternative

5 An **alternate** is a person or thing that replaces another, and can act or be used instead of them. [AM] ❑ *In most jurisdictions, twelve jurors and two alternates are chosen.* N-COUNT = substitute

6 **Alternate** is sometimes used, especially in American English, instead of **alternative** in meanings 3, 4, and 5. ❑ *...an alternate lifestyle.* ADJ: ADJ n

**al|ter|nat|ing cur|rent** **(alternating currents)** An **alternating current** is an electric current that continually changes direction as it flows. The abbreviation **AC** is also used. N-VAR

**al|ter|na|tive** /ɔːltɜːʳnətɪv/ **(alternatives)** ◆◆◇

☑ The form **alternate** is sometimes used, especially in American English, instead of **alternative** in meanings 3, 4, and 5.

1 If one thing is an **alternative to** another, the first can be found, used, or done instead of the second. ❑ *New ways to treat arthritis may provide an alternative to painkillers.* N-COUNT: oft N *to* n

2 An **alternative** plan or offer is different from the one that you already have, and can be done or used instead. ❑ *There were alternative methods of travel available.* ADJ: ADJ n = other, alternate

3 **Alternative** is used to describe something that is different from the usual things of its kind, or the usual ways of doing something, in modern Western society. For example, an **alternative** lifestyle does not follow conventional ways of living and working. ❑ *...unconventional parents who embraced the alternative lifestyle of the Sixties.* ADJ: ADJ n ≠ conventional

4 **Alternative** medicine uses traditional ways of curing people, such as medicines made from plants, massage, and acupuncture. ❑ *...alternative health care.* ADJ: ADJ n

5 **Alternative** energy uses natural sources of energy such as the sun, wind, or water for power and fuel, rather than oil, coal, or nuclear power. ADJ: ADJ n

**al|ter|na|tive|ly** /ɔːltɜːʳnətɪvli/ You use **alternatively** to introduce a suggestion or to mention something different to what has just been stated. ❑ *Allow about eight hours for the drive from Calais. Alternatively, you can fly to Brive.* ADV: ADV with cl

**al|ter|na|tor** /ɔːltəʳneɪtəʳ/ **(alternators)** An **alternator** is a device, used especially in a car, that creates an electrical current that changes direction as it flows. N-COUNT

**al|though** /ɔːlðoʊ/ ◆◆◆ 1 You use **although** to introduce a subordinate clause which contains a statement which contrasts with the statement in the main clause. ❑ *Although he is known to only a few, his reputation among them is very great... Although the shooting has stopped for now, the destruction left behind is enormous.* CONJ

2 You use **although** to introduce a subordinate clause which contains a statement which makes the main clause of the sentence seem surprising or unexpected. ❑ *Although I was only six, I can remember seeing it on TV.* CONJ = though

3 You use **although** to introduce a subordinate CONJ

clause which gives some information that is relevant to the main clause but modifies the strength of that statement. ❑ *He was in love with her, although he did not put that name to it.* = though [4] You use **although** when admitting a fact about something which you regard as less important than a contrasting fact. ❑ *Although they're expensive, they last forever and never go out of style.* CONJ

**al|time|ter** /æltɪmiːtəʳ, AM æltɪmɪtəʳ/ **(altimeters)** An **altimeter** is an instrument in an aircraft that shows the height of the aircraft above the ground. N-COUNT

**al|ti|tude** /æltɪtjuːd, AM -tuːd/ **(altitudes)** If something is at a particular **altitude**, it is at that height above sea level. ❑ *The aircraft had reached its cruising altitude of about 39,000 feet.* N-VAR: oft N *of* n

**alto** /æltoʊ/ **(altos)** [1] An **alto** is a woman who has a low singing voice. N-COUNT: oft N n [2] An **alto** or **male alto** is a man who has the highest male singing voice. N-COUNT [3] An **alto** musical instrument has a range of notes of medium pitch. ADJ: ADJ n

**al|to|geth|er** /ɔːltəgeðəʳ/ ◆◇◇ [1] You use **altogether** to emphasize that something has stopped, been done, or finished completely. ❑ *When Artie stopped calling altogether, Julie found a new man... His tour may have to be cancelled altogether.* ADV: ADV after v [emphasis] [2] You use **altogether** in front of an adjective or adverb to emphasize a quality that someone or something has. ❑ *The choice of language is altogether different... Today's celebrations have been altogether more sedate.* ADV: ADV adj/adv [emphasis] [3] You use **altogether** to modify a negative statement and make it less forceful. ❑ *We were not altogether sure that the comet would miss the Earth.* ADV: with neg, ADV group [4] You can use **altogether** to introduce a summary of what you have been saying. ❑ *Altogether, it was a delightful town garden, peaceful and secluded.* ADV: ADV with cl [5] If several amounts add up to a particular amount **altogether**, that amount is their total. ❑ *Britain has a dozen warships in the area, with a total of five thousand military personnel altogether.* ADV: ADV with amount

**al|tru|ism** /æltruɪzəm/ **Altruism** is unselfish concern for other people's happiness and welfare. N-UNCOUNT

**al|tru|is|tic** /æltruɪstɪk/ If your behaviour or motives are **altruistic**, you show concern for the happiness and welfare of other people rather than for yourself. ADJ = selfless ≠ selfish

**alu|min|ium** /æluːmɪniəm/ **Aluminium** is a lightweight metal used, for example, for making cooking equipment and aircraft parts. [BRIT] ❑ *...aluminium cans.* N-UNCOUNT

☑ in AM, use **aluminum**

**alu|mi|num** /əluːmɪnəm/ → see **aluminium**.

**alum|nus** /əlʌmnəs/ **(alumni** /əlʌmnaɪ/**)** The **alumni** of a school, college, or university are the people who used to be students there. [AM] N-COUNT

**al|ways** /ɔːlweɪz/ ◆◆◆ [1] If you **always** do something, you do it whenever a particular situation occurs. If you **always** did something, you did it whenever a particular situation occurred. ❑ *Whenever I get into a relationship, I always fall madly in love... She's always late for everything... We've always done it this way... Always lock your garage.* ADV: ADV before v ≠ never [2] If something is **always** the case, was **always** the case, or will **always** be the case, it is, was, or will be the case all the time, continuously. ❑ *We will always remember his generous hospitality... He was always cheerful.* ADV: ADV before v, ADV group ≠ never [3] If you say that something is **always** happening, especially something which annoys you, you mean that it happens repeatedly. ❑ *She was always moving things around.* ADV: ADV before v-cont = forever [4] You use **always** in expressions such as **can always** or **could always** when you are making suggestions or suggesting an alternative approach or method. ❑ *If you can't find any decent apples, you can always try growing them yourself.* ADV: *can/could* ADV inf [5] You can say that someone **always** was, for example, awkward or lucky to indicate that you are not surprised about what they are doing or have just done. ❑ *She's going to be fine. She always was pretty strong.* ADV: ADV before v

**Alzheimer's dis|ease** /æltshaɪməʳz dɪziːz/ or **Alzheimer's Alzheimer's disease** is a condition in which a person's brain gradually stops working properly. N-UNCOUNT

**am** /əm, STRONG æm/ **Am** is the first person singular of the present tense of **be**. **Am** is often shortened to **'m** in spoken English. The negative forms are 'I am not' and 'I'm not'. In questions and tags in spoken English, these are usually changed to 'aren't I'.

**AM** /eɪ em/ **(AMs)** An **AM** is a member of the Welsh Assembly. **AM** is an abbreviation for 'assembly member'. N-COUNT

**Am.** **Am.** is a written abbreviation for **American**.

**a.m.** /eɪ em/ also **am. a.m.** is used after a number to show that you are referring to a particular time between midnight and noon. Compare **p.m.** ❑ *The program starts at 9 a.m.*

**amalgam** /əmælgəm/ **(amalgams)** Something that is an **amalgam of** two or more things is a mixture of them. N-COUNT: oft N *of* pl-n = mixture

**amal|gam|ate** /əmælgəmeɪt/ **(amalgamates, amalgamating, amalgamated)** When two or more things, especially organizations, **amalgamate** or **are amalgamated**, they become one large thing. ❑ *The firm has amalgamated with an American company... The chemical companies had amalgamated into a vast conglomerate... The Visitors' Centre amalgamates the traditions of the Old World with the technology of the New.* V-RECIP = merge; V *with/into* n; pl-n V; V n *with/into* n ♦ **amal|gama|tion** /əmælgəmeɪʃən/ **(amalgamations)** *Athletics South Africa was formed by an amalgamation of two organisations.* N-VAR: oft N *of* n = merger

**amass** /əmæs/ **(amasses, amassing, amassed)** If you **amass** something such as money or information, you gradually get a lot of it. ❑ *How had he amassed his fortune?* VERB = accrue, accumulate; V n

**ama|teur** /æmətəʳ, AM -tʃɜːr/ **(amateurs)** ◆◇◇ [1] An **amateur** is someone who does something as a hobby and not as a job. ❑ *Jerry is an amateur who dances because he feels like it.* N-COUNT: oft N n ≠ professional [2] **Amateur** sports or activities are done by people as a hobby and not as a job. ❑ *...the local amateur dramatics society.* ADJ: ADJ n

**ama|teur|ish** /æmətərɪʃ, AM -tʃɜːrɪʃ/ If you describe something as **amateurish**, you think that it is not skilfully made or done. ❑ *The paintings looked amateurish.* ADJ [disapproval]

**ama|teur|ism** /æmətərɪzəm, AM -tʃɜːr-/ **Amateurism** is the belief that people should take part in sports and other activities as a hobby, for pleasure, rather than as a job, for money. ❑ *He is a staunch supporter of amateurism.* N-UNCOUNT ≠ professionalism

**amaze** /əmeɪz/ **(amazes, amazing, amazed)** If something **amazes** you, it surprises you very much. ❑ *He amazed us by his knowledge of Welsh history... The Riverside Restaurant promises a variety of food that never ceases to amaze!* VERB = astonish; V n; V ♦ **amazed** *He said most of the cast was amazed by the play's success.* ADJ: usu v-link ADJ

**amaze|ment** /əmeɪzmənt/ **Amazement** is the feeling you have when something surprises you very much. ❑ *I stared at her in amazement.* N-UNCOUNT: oft *in* N = astonishment

**amaz|ing** /əmeɪzɪŋ/ ◆◇◇ You say that something is **amazing** when it is very surprising and makes you feel pleasure, approval, or wonder. ❑ *It's amazing what we can remember with a little prompting.* ADJ: oft *it* v-link ADJ wh/that = astonishing ♦ **amaz|ing|ly** *She was an amazingly good cook.* ADV

**Ama|zon** /æməzən/ **(Amazons)** [1] In Greek mythology, the **Amazons** were a tribe of women who were very good at fighting. N-COUNT: usu pl [2] People sometimes refer to a tall, strong woman as an **Amazon**. N-COUNT

**Ama|zo|nian** /æməzoʊniən/ [1] **Amazonian** means related to the area around the river Amazon. ❑ *...the Amazonian rainforest.* ADJ: usu ADJ n [2] People sometimes describe a tall, strong woman as **Ama-**

**zonian**. ❑ *...an Amazonian blonde.* [3] **Amazonian** means belonging to or connected with the Amazons in Greek mythology. ❑ *...Amazonian queens.* ADJ: usu ADJ n / ADJ: usu ADJ n

**am|bas|sa|dor** /æmbæsədəʳ/ **(ambassadors)** ◆◇◇ N-COUNT: oft adj N, N *to* n An **ambassador** is an important official who lives in a foreign country and represents his or her own country's interests there. ❑ *...the German ambassador to Poland.*

**am|bas|sa|dor|ial** /æmbæsədɔːriəl/ ADJ: ADJ n **Ambassadorial** means belonging or relating to an ambassador. ❑ *...an ambassadorial post.*

**am|ber** /æmbəʳ/ [1] N-UNCOUNT: usu N n **Amber** is a hard yellowish-brown substance used for making jewellery. ❑ *...an amber choker with matching earrings.* [2] COLOUR: usu COLOUR n **Amber** is used to describe things that are yellowish-brown in colour. [3] COLOUR An **amber** traffic light is orange. ❑ *Cars did not stop when the lights were on amber.*

**am|bi|ance** /æmbiəns/ → see **ambience**.

**am|bi|dex|trous** /æmbidekstrəs/ ADJ: usu v-link ADJ Someone who is **ambidextrous** can use both their right hand and their left hand equally skilfully.

**am|bi|ence** /æmbiəns/ also **ambiance**. N-SING: also no det, oft N *of* n = atmosphere The **ambience of** a place is the character and atmosphere that it seems to have. [LITERARY] ❑ *The overall ambience of the room is cosy.*

**am|bi|ent** /æmbiənt/ [1] ADJ: ADJ n The **ambient** temperature is the temperature of the air above the ground in a particular place. [TECHNICAL] [2] ADJ: usu ADJ n **Ambient** sound or light is the sound or light which is all around you. [TECHNICAL] ❑ *...ambient sounds of children in the background.*

**am|bi|gu|ity** /æmbɪgjuːɪti/ **(ambiguities)** N-VAR If you say that there is **ambiguity** in something, you mean that it is unclear or confusing, or it can be understood in more than one way. ❑ *There is considerable ambiguity about what this part of the agreement actually means.*

**am|bigu|ous** /æmbɪgjuəs/ [1] ADJ = vague ≠ clear If you describe something as **ambiguous**, you mean that it is unclear or confusing because it can be understood in more than one way. ❑ *This agreement is very ambiguous and open to various interpretations.* ♦ **am|bigu|ous|ly** ADV: usu ADV with v, also ADV adj *Zaire's national conference on democracy ended ambiguously.* [2] ADJ If you describe something as **ambiguous**, you mean that it contains several different ideas or attitudes that do not fit well together. ❑ *Students have ambiguous feelings about their role in the world.*

**am|bit** /æmbɪt/ N-SING: usu with poss = scope The **ambit** of something is its range or extent. [FORMAL] ❑ *Her case falls within the ambit of moral law.*

**am|bi|tion** /æmbɪʃən/ **(ambitions)** ◆◇◇ [1] N-COUNT: oft N to-inf = goal If you have an **ambition to** do or achieve something, you want very much to do it or achieve it. ❑ *His ambition is to sail round the world.* [2] N-UNCOUNT **Ambition** is the desire to be successful, rich, or powerful. ❑ *Even when I was young I never had any ambition.*

**am|bi|tious** /æmbɪʃəs/ [1] ADJ Someone who is **ambitious** has a strong desire to be successful, rich, or powerful. ❑ *Chris is so ambitious, so determined to do it all.* [2] ADJ An **ambitious** idea or plan is on a large scale and needs a lot of work to be carried out successfully. ❑ *The ambitious project was completed in only nine months.*

**am|biva|lent** /æmbɪvələnt/ ADJ = unsure If you say that someone is **ambivalent about** something, they seem to be uncertain whether they really want it, or whether they really approve of it. ❑ *She remained ambivalent about her marriage.* ♦ **am|biva|lence** /æmbɪvələns/ **(ambivalences)** N-VAR: usu with supp, oft N *about/towards* n *I've never lied about my feelings, including my ambivalence about getting married again.*

**am|ble** /æmbəl/ **(ambles, ambling, ambled)** VERB = stroll When you **amble**, you walk slowly and in a relaxed manner. ❑ *Slowly they ambled back to the car.* V adv/prep

**am|bro|sia** /æmbroʊziə, AM -ʒiə/ N-UNCOUNT In Greek mythology, **ambrosia** is the food of the gods.

**am|bu|lance** /æmbjʊləns/ **(ambulances)** N-COUNT: also *by* N An **ambulance** is a vehicle for taking people to and from hospital.

**am|bu|lance|man** /æmbjʊlənsmæn/ **(ambulancemen)** N-COUNT An **ambulanceman** is a man who drives an ambulance or takes care of people in an ambulance on the way to hospital. [BRIT]

☑ in AM, use **ambulance driver**

**am|bush** /æmbʊʃ/ **(ambushes, ambushing, ambushed)** [1] VERB If a group of people **ambush** their enemies, they attack them after hiding and waiting for them. ❑ *The Guatemalan army says rebels ambushed and killed 10 patrolmen.* V n [2] N-VAR An **ambush** is an attack on someone by people who have been hiding and waiting for them. ❑ *A policeman has been shot dead in an ambush.* [3] PHRASE: PHR after v If someone is lying **in ambush**, they are hiding and waiting for someone, usually to attack them. ❑ *The gunmen, lying in ambush, opened fire, killing the driver.*

**ame|lio|rate** /əmiːliəreɪt/ **(ameliorates, ameliorating, ameliorated)** VERB = alleviate ≠ exacerbate If someone or something **ameliorates** a situation, they make it better or easier in some way. [FORMAL]

**amen** /ɑːmen, eɪ-/ CONVENTION **Amen** is said by Christians at the end of a prayer.

**ame|nable** /əmiːnəbəl/ ADJ: usu v-link ADJ, oft ADJ *to* n/-ing = agreeable If you are **amenable to** something, you are willing to do it or accept it. ❑ *The Jordanian leader seemed amenable to attending a conference.*

**amend** /əmend/ **(amends, amending, amended)** [1] VERB = revise If you **amend** something that has been written such as a law, or something that is said, you change it in order to improve it or make it more accurate. ❑ *The president agreed to amend the constitution and allow multi-party elections.* V n *...the amended version of the Act.* V-ed [2] PHRASE: V inflects, oft PHR *for* n/-ing If you **make amends** when you have harmed someone, you show that you are sorry by doing something to please them. ❑ *He wanted to make amends for causing their marriage to fail.*

**amend|ment** /əmendmənt/ **(amendments)** ◆◇◇ [1] N-VAR An **amendment** is a section that is added to a law or rule in order to change it. ❑ *...an amendment to the defense bill.* [2] N-COUNT = alteration An **amendment** is a change that is made to a piece of writing.

**amen|ity** /əmiːnɪti, AM -men-/ **(amenities)** N-COUNT: usu pl = facility **Amenities** are things such as shopping centres or sports facilities that are provided for people's convenience, enjoyment, or comfort. ❑ *The hotel amenities include health clubs, conference facilities, and banqueting rooms.*

**Am|er|asian** /æmereɪʒən/ **(Amerasians)** N-COUNT People who have one American parent and one Asian parent are sometimes referred to as **Amerasians**. ❑ *...discrimination against Amerasians in Vietnam.* ♦ **Amerasian** is also an adjective. ADJ ❑ *...an Amerasian boy.*

**Ameri|can** /əmerɪkən/ **(Americans)** ADJ An **American** person or thing belongs to or comes from the United States of America. ❑ *...the American Ambassador at the United Nations. ...the influence of American television and movies.* → See also **Latin American**. ♦ N-COUNT An **American** is someone who is American. ❑ *The 1990 Nobel Prize for medicine was won by two Americans.*

**Ameri|ca|na** /əmerɪkɑːnə/ N-UNCOUNT Objects that come from or relate to America are referred to as **Americana**, especially when they are in a collection. ❑ *...1950s Americana.*

**Ameri|can foot|ball** **(American footballs)**

☑ in AM, use **football**

[1] N-UNCOUNT **American football** is a game similar to rugby that is played by two teams of eleven players using an oval-shaped ball. Players try to score points by carrying the ball to their opponents' end of the field, or by kicking it over a bar fixed between two posts. [BRIT] [2] N-COUNT An **American football** is an oval-shaped ball used for playing American football. [BRIT]

**Ameri|can In|dian** (**American Indians**) American Indian people or things belong to or come from one of the native peoples of America. [mainly BRIT] ♦ An **American Indian** is someone who is American Indian. ADJ: usu ADJ n; N-COUNT

☑ in AM, use **Indian, Native American**

**Ameri|can|ism** /əmerɪkənɪzəm/ (**Americanisms**) An **Americanism** is an expression that is typical of people living in the United States of America. N-COUNT

**Ameri|cani|za|tion** /əmerɪkənaɪzeɪʃən/

☑ in BRIT, also use **Americanisation**

**Americanization** is the process by which people or countries become more and more similar to Americans and the United States. ❑ *...the Americanization of French culture.* N-UNCOUNT

**Ameri|can|ized** /əmerɪkənaɪzd/

☑ in BRIT, also use **Americanised**

If someone is **Americanized**, they do things in a way that is typical of the United States. ❑ *He is getting much too Americanized.* ADJ

**Am|er|in|dian** /æmərɪndiən/ (**Amerindians**) **Amerindian** means the same as **American Indian**.

**am|ethyst** /æməθɪst/ (**amethysts**) [1] **Amethysts** are clear purple stones, sometimes used to make jewellery. ❑ *The necklace consisted of amethysts set in gold. ...rows of amethyst beads.* N-VAR [2] **Amethyst** is used to describe things that are pale purple in colour. ❑ *...as the colours changed from green to amethyst. ...amethyst glass.* COLOUR

**ami|abil|ity** /eɪmiəbɪlɪti/ **Amiability** is the quality of being friendly and pleasant. [WRITTEN] ❑ *I found his amiability charming.* N-UNCOUNT = friendliness

**ami|able** /eɪmiəbəl/ Someone who is **amiable** is friendly and pleasant to be with. [WRITTEN] ADJ = friendly ♦ **ami|ably** ❑ *We chatted amiably about our old friends.* ADV: ADV with v

**ami|cable** /æmɪkəbəl/ When people have an **amicable** relationship, they are pleasant to each other and solve their problems without quarrelling. ❑ *The meeting ended on reasonably amicable terms.* ADJ = friendly ≠ hostile ♦ **ami|cably** /æmɪkəbli/ *He hoped the dispute could be settled amicably.* ADV: ADV with v

**amid** /əmɪd/ ◆◇◇

☑ The form **amidst** is also used, but is more literary.

[1] If something happens **amid** noises or events of some kind, it happens while the other things are happening. ❑ *A senior leader cancelled a trip to Britain yesterday amid growing signs of a possible political crisis.* PREP [2] If something is **amid** other things, it is surrounded by them. [LITERARY] PREP

**amid|ships** /əmɪdʃɪps/ **Amidships** means halfway along the length of a ship. ❑ *The ferry hit us amidships.* ADV: ADV after v

**amidst** /əmɪdst/ **Amidst** means the same as **amid**. [LITERARY] PREP = amid

**ami|no acid** /əmiːnoʊ æsɪd/ (**amino acids**) **Amino acids** are substances containing nitrogen and hydrogen and which are found in proteins. Amino acids occur naturally in the body. N-COUNT: usu pl

**amiss** /əmɪs/ [1] If you say that something is **amiss**, you mean there is something wrong. ❑ *Their instincts warned them something was amiss... Something is radically amiss in our health care system.* ADJ: v-link ADJ = wrong [2] If you say that something **would not go amiss** or **would not come amiss**, you mean that it would be pleasant and useful. [BRIT] ❑ *A bit of charm and humour would not go amiss.* PHRASE: V inflects

**am|ity** /æmɪti/ **Amity** is peaceful, friendly relations between people or countries. [FORMAL] ❑ *He wished to live in amity with his neighbour.* N-UNCOUNT = peace ≠ enmity

**ammo** /æmoʊ/ **Ammo** is ammunition for guns and other weapons. [INFORMAL] N-UNCOUNT

**am|mo|nia** /əmoʊniə/ **Ammonia** is a colourless liquid or gas with a strong, sharp smell. It is used in making household cleaning substances. N-UNCOUNT

**am|mu|ni|tion** /æmjʊnɪʃən/ [1] **Ammunition** is bullets and rockets that are made to be fired from guns. ❑ *He had only seven rounds of ammunition for the revolver.* N-UNCOUNT [2] You can describe information that you can use against someone in an argument or discussion as **ammunition**. ❑ *The improved trade figures have given the government fresh ammunition.* N-UNCOUNT

**am|ne|sia** /æmniːziə, -ʒə/ If someone is suffering from **amnesia**, they have lost their memory. N-UNCOUNT

**am|ne|si|ac** /æmniːziæk/ (**amnesiacs**) Someone who is **amnesiac** has lost their memory. ❑ *She was taken to hospital, apparently amnesiac and shocked.* ADJ ♦ An **amnesiac** is someone who is amnesiac. ❑ *Even profound amnesiacs can usually recall how to perform daily activities.* N-COUNT

**am|nes|ty** /æmnɪsti/ (**amnesties**) [1] An **amnesty** is an official pardon granted to a group of prisoners by the state. ❑ *Activists who were involved in crimes of violence will not automatically be granted amnesty.* N-VAR = pardon [2] An **amnesty** is a period of time during which people can admit to a crime or give up weapons without being punished. ❑ *The government has announced an immediate amnesty for rebel fighters.* N-COUNT

**am|nio|cen|tesis** /æmnioʊsentiːsɪs/ If a pregnant woman has an **amniocentesis**, fluid is removed from her womb in order to check that her unborn baby is not affected by certain genetic disorders. N-UNCOUNT

**amoe|ba** /əmiːbə/ (**amoebae** /əmiːbi/ or **amoebas**) An **amoeba** is the smallest kind of living creature. Amoebae consist of only one cell, and are found in water or soil. N-COUNT

**amok** /əmʌk, əmɒk/ If a person or animal **runs amok**, they behave in a violent and uncontrolled way. ❑ *A soldier was arrested after running amok with a vehicle through Berlin.* PHRASE: V inflects

**among** /əmʌŋ/ ◆◆◆

☑ The form **amongst** is also used, but is more literary.

[1] Someone or something that is situated or moving **among** a group of things or people is surrounded by them. ❑ *They walked among the crowds in Red Square. ...a little house among the trees.* PREP [2] If you are **among** people of a particular kind, you are with them and having contact with them. ❑ *Things weren't so bad, after all. I was among friends again... I was brought up among people who read and wrote a lot.* PREP [3] If someone or something is **among** a group, they are a member of that group and share its characteristics. ❑ *A fifteen year old girl was among the injured... Also among the speakers was the new American ambassador to Moscow.* PREP [4] If you want to focus on something that is happening within a particular group of people, you can say that it is happening **among** that group. ❑ *Unemployment is quite high, especially among young people.* PREP [5] If something happens **among** a group of people, it happens within the whole of that group or between the members of that group. ❑ *I am sick of all the quarrelling among politicians who should be concentrating on vital issues.* PREP [6] If something such as a feeling, opinion, or situation exists **among** a group of people, most of them have it or experience it. ❑ *The biggest fear among parents thinking of using the Internet is that their children will be exposed to pornography.* PREP [7] If something applies to a particular person or thing **among others**, it also applies to other people or things. ❑ *...a news conference attended among others by our foreign affairs correspondent.* PREP [8] If something is shared **among** a number of people, some of it is given to all of them. ❑ *Most of the furniture was left to the neighbours or distributed among friends.* PREP [9] If people talk, fight, or agree **among themselves**, they do it to- PREP: PREP pron-refl

gether, without involving anyone else. ❑ *European farm ministers disagree among themselves.*

**amongst** /əmʌŋst/ **Amongst** means the same as **among**. [LITERARY] PREP

**amor|al** /eɪmɒrəl, AM -mɔːr-/ If you describe someone as **amoral**, you do not like the way they behave because they do not seem to care whether what they do is right or wrong. ❑ *I strongly disagree with this amoral approach to politics.* ADJ [disapproval] ≠ *moral*

**amo|rous** /æmərəs/ If you describe someone's feelings or actions as **amorous**, you mean that they involve sexual desire. ADJ: usu ADJ n

**amor|phous** /əmɔːʳfəs/ Something that is **amorphous** has no clear shape or structure. [FORMAL] ❑ *A dark, strangely amorphous shadow filled the room. ...the amorphous mass of the unemployed.* ADJ: usu ADJ n = *shapeless*

**amor|tize** /əmɔːʳtaɪz, AM æmər-/ **(amortizes, amortizing, amortized)**

✔ in BRIT, also use **amortise**

In finance, if you **amortize** a debt, you pay it back in regular payments. [BUSINESS] ❑ *Business expenses had to be amortized over a 60 month period.* VERB = *pay off* be V-ed

**amount** /əmaʊnt/ **(amounts, amounting, amounted)** ◆◆◇ [1] The **amount of** something is how much there is, or how much you have, need, or get. ❑ *He needs that amount of money to survive... I still do a certain amount of work for them... Postal money orders are available in amounts up to $700.* N-VAR: usu N *of* n
[2] If something **amounts to** a particular total, all the parts of it add up to that total. ❑ *Consumer spending on sports-related items amounted to £9.75 billion.* VERB V *to* amount

♦ **amount to** If you say that one thing **amounts to** something else, you consider the first thing to be the same as the second thing. ❑ *The confessions were obtained by what amounts to torture.* PHRASAL VERB V P n

**amour** /æmʊəʳ/ **(amours)** An **amour** is a love affair, especially one which is kept secret. [LITERARY or OLD-FASHIONED] N-COUNT

**amp** /æmp/ **(amps)** [1] An **amp** is the same as an **ampere**. ❑ *Use a 3 amp fuse for equipment up to 720 watts.* [2] An **amp** is the same as an **amplifier**. [INFORMAL] N-COUNT N-COUNT

**ampere** /æmpeəʳ, AM -pɪəʳ/ **(amperes)**

✔ in BRIT, also use **ampère**

An **ampere** is a unit which is used for measuring electric current. The abbreviation **amp** is also used. N-COUNT

**am|pheta|mine** /æmfetəmiːn/ **(amphetamines) Amphetamine** is a drug which increases people's energy, makes them excited, and reduces their desire for food. N-MASS = *speed*

**am|phib|ian** /æmfɪbiən/ **(amphibians)**
[1] **Amphibians** are animals such as frogs and toads that can live both on land and in water. N-COUNT
[2] An **amphibian** is a vehicle which is able to move on both land and water, or an aeroplane which can land on both land and water. N-COUNT

**am|phibi|ous** /æmfɪbiəs/ [1] In an **amphibious** military operation, army and navy forces attack a place from the sea. ❑ *A third brigade is at sea, ready for an amphibious assault.* ADJ: ADJ n [2] An **amphibious** vehicle is able to move on both land and water. ADJ: ADJ n [3] **Amphibious** animals are animals such as frogs and toads that can live both on land and in water. ADJ

**am|phi|thea|tre** /æmfiθɪətəʳ/ **(amphitheatres)**

✔ in AM, use **amphitheater**

An **amphitheatre** is a large open area surrounded by rows of seats sloping upwards. Amphitheatres were built mainly in Greek and Roman times for the performance of plays. N-COUNT

**am|ple** /æmpᵊl/ **(ampler, amplest)** If there is an **ample** amount of something, there is enough of it and usually some extra. ❑ *There'll be ample opportunity to relax, swim and soak up some sun.* ADJ: usu ADJ n

♦ **am|ply** *They have been amply rewarded with huge salaries.* ADV: usu ADV with v, also ADV adj

**am|pli|fi|er** /æmplɪfaɪəʳ/ **(amplifiers)** An **amplifier** is an electronic device in a radio or stereo system which causes sounds or signals to get louder. N-COUNT

**am|pli|fy** /æmplɪfaɪ/ **(amplifies, amplifying, amplified)** [1] If you **amplify** a sound, you make it louder, usually by using electronic equipment. ❑ *This landscape seemed to trap and amplify sounds... The music was amplified with microphones... 'This is the police,' came the amplified voice from the helicopter.* ♦ **am|pli|fi|ca|tion** /æmplɪfɪkeɪʃᵊn/ *...a voice that needed no amplification.* [2] To **amplify** something means to increase its strength or intensity. ❑ *The mist had been replaced by a kind of haze that seemed to amplify the heat.* VERB V n V n V-ed N-UNCOUNT VERB V n

**am|pli|tude** /æmplɪtjuːd, AM -tuːd/ **(amplitudes)** In physics, the **amplitude** of a sound wave or electrical signal is its strength. [TECHNICAL] N-VAR

**am|poule** /æmpuːl/ **(ampoules)**

✔ in AM, use **ampule**

An **ampoule** is a small container, usually made of glass, that contains a drug which will be injected into someone. The abbreviation **amp** is also used. N-COUNT = *phial*

**am|pu|tate** /æmpjʊteɪt/ **(amputates, amputating, amputated)** To **amputate** someone's arm or leg means to cut all or part of it off in an operation because it is diseased or badly damaged. ❑ *To save his life, doctors amputated his legs... He had to have one leg amputated above the knee.* ♦ **am|pu|ta|tion** /æmpjʊteɪʃᵊn/ **(amputations)** *He lived only hours after the amputation.* VERB V n *have* n V-ed N-VAR

**am|pu|tee** /æmpjʊtiː/ **(amputees)** An **amputee** is someone who has had all or part of an arm or a leg amputated. N-COUNT

**amu|let** /æmjʊlət/ **(amulets)** An **amulet** is a small object that you wear or carry because you think it will bring you good luck and protect you from evil or injury. N-COUNT = *charm, talisman*

**amuse** /əmjuːz/ **(amuses, amusing, amused)**
[1] If something **amuses** you, it makes you want to laugh or smile. ❑ *The thought seemed to amuse him... Their antics never fail to amuse.* [2] If you **amuse yourself**, you do something in order to pass the time and not become bored. ❑ *I need distractions. I need to amuse myself so I won't keep thinking about things... Put a selection of baby toys in his cot to amuse him if he wakes early.* [3] → See also **amused, amusing**. VERB V n V VERB = *entertain* V pron-refl V n

**amused** /əmjuːzd/ [1] If you are **amused by** something, it makes you want to laugh or smile. ❑ *Sara was not at all amused by Franklin's teasing.* [2] If you **keep** someone **amused**, you find things to do which stop them getting bored. ❑ *Having pictures to colour will keep children amused for hours.* ADJ: usu v-link ADJ, oft ADJ *by/at* n, ADJ to-inf PHRASE: V inflects = *keep someone entertained*

**amuse|ment** /əmjuːzmənt/ **(amusements)**
[1] **Amusement** is the feeling that you have when you think that something is funny or amusing. ❑ *He stopped and watched with amusement to see the child so absorbed... Steamers tooted at us as sailors on deck waved in amusement.* N-UNCOUNT
[2] **Amusement** is the pleasure that you get from being entertained or from doing something interesting. ❑ *I stumbled sideways before landing flat on my back, much to the amusement of the rest of the lads.* [3] **Amusements** are ways of passing the time pleasantly. ❑ *People had very few amusements to choose from. There was no radio, or television.* N-UNCOUNT N-COUNT: usu pl = *pastime*
[4] **Amusements** are games, rides, and other things that you can enjoy, for example at a fairground or at the seaside. N-PLURAL

**amuse|ment ar|cade (amusement arcades)** An **amusement arcade** is a place where you can play games on machines which work when you put money in them. N-COUNT

**amuse|ment park** **(amusement parks)** An **amusement park** is the same as a **funfair**. [mainly AM] — N-COUNT

**amus|ing** /əmjuːzɪŋ/ Someone or something that is **amusing** makes you laugh or smile. ❑ *He had a terrific sense of humour and could be very amusing.* — ADJ = *entertaining*
♦ **amus|ing|ly** *The article must be amusingly written.* — ADV: ADV with v, ADV adj

**an** /ən, STRONG æn/ **An** is used instead of 'a', the indefinite article, in front of words that begin with vowel sounds. ➔ See also **a**. — DET

**-an** /-ən/ **(-ans)** [1] **-an** is added to the names of some places in order to form adjectives or nouns that refer to people or things which come from that place. ❑ *The Australian foreign minister... Mitch was a San Franciscan by birth.* — SUFFIX
[2] **-an** is added to the names of famous people to form adjectives or nouns that refer to people or things which are connected with or typical of that person's work or the time at which they lived. ❑ *...a great Shakespearean actor. ...an exhibition of fine Victorian furniture.* — SUFFIX

**ana|bol|ic ster|oid** /ænəbɒlɪk stɛrɔɪd, stɪər-/ **(anabolic steroids)** **Anabolic steroids** are drugs which people, especially athletes, take to make their muscles bigger and to give them more strength. — N-COUNT

**anach|ro|nism** /ənækrənɪzəm/ **(anachronisms)** [1] You say that something is an **anachronism** when you think that it is out of date or old-fashioned. ❑ *The President tended to regard the Church as an anachronism.* — N-COUNT
[2] An **anachronism** is something in a book, play, or film that is wrong because it did not exist at the time the book, play, or film is set. ❑ *The last paragraph contains an anachronism. The Holy Office no longer existed at that time.* — N-COUNT

**anach|ro|nis|tic** /ənækrənɪstɪk/ You say that something is **anachronistic** when you think that it is out of date or old-fashioned. ❑ *Many of its practices seem anachronistic.* — ADJ

**anaemia** /əniːmiə/ **(anaemias)**

> ✔ in AM, use **anemia**

**Anaemia** is a medical condition in which there are too few red cells in your blood, causing you to feel tired and look pale. — N-UNCOUNT: also N in pl

**anaemic** /əniːmɪk/

> ✔ in AM, use **anemic**

[1] Someone who is **anaemic** suffers from anaemia. — ADJ: usu v-link ADJ
[2] If you describe something as **anaemic**, you mean that it is not as strong or effective as you think it should be. ❑ *We will see some economic recovery, but it will be very anaemic.* — ADJ = *weak*

**an|aero|bic** /æneəroʊbɪk/ [1] **Anaerobic** creatures or processes do not need oxygen in order to function or survive. — ADJ
[2] **Anaerobic** exercise is exercise such as weight training that improves your strength but does not raise your heart rate. — ADJ

**an|aes|the|sia** /ænɪsθiːziə, -ʒə/ also **anesthesia**. **Anaesthesia** is the use of anaesthetics in medicine and surgery. — N-UNCOUNT

**an|aes|thet|ic** /ænɪsθetɪk/ **(anaesthetics)** **anesthetic. Anaesthetic** is a substance that doctors use to stop you feeling pain during an operation, either in the whole of your body when you are unconscious, or in a part of your body when you are awake. ❑ *The operation is carried out under a general anaesthetic.* — N-MASS: oft *under* N

**anaes|the|tist** /əniːsθətɪst/ **(anaesthetists)** An **anaesthetist** is a doctor who specializes in giving anaesthetics to patients. [BRIT] — N-COUNT

> ✔ in AM, use **anesthesiologist**

**anaes|the|tize** /əniːsθətaɪz/ **(anaesthetizes, anaesthetizing, anaesthetized)**

> ✔ The spellings **anesthetize** in American English, and **anaesthetise** in British English are also used.

[1] When a doctor or other trained person **anaesthetizes** a patient, they make the patient unconscious or unable to feel pain by giving them an anaesthetic. — VERB
[2] If something such as a drug **anaesthetizes** part or all of your body, it makes you unable to feel anything in that part of your body. — VERB = *numb*

**ana|gram** /ænəgræm/ **(anagrams)** An **anagram** is a word or phrase formed by changing the order of the letters in another word or phrase. For example, 'triangle' is an anagram of 'integral'. — N-COUNT

**anal** /eɪnəl/ **Anal** means relating to the anus of a person or animal. — ADJ: usu ADJ n

**an|alge|sic** /ænəldʒiːzɪk/ An **analgesic** drug reduces the effect of pain. [FORMAL] — ADJ: usu ADJ n = *painkilling*

**analo|gous** /ənæləgəs/ If one thing is **analogous to** another, the two things are similar in some way. [FORMAL] ❑ *Marine construction technology like this is very complex, somewhat analogous to trying to build a bridge under water.* — ADJ: usu v-link ADJ *to* n = *similar*

**ana|logue** /ænəlɒg, AM -lɔːg/ **(analogues)**

> ✔ The spelling **analog** is used in American English, and also in British English for meaning 2.

[1] If one thing is an **analogue of** another, it is similar in some way. [FORMAL] ❑ *No model can ever be a perfect analogue of nature itself.* — N-COUNT: oft N *of* n
[2] **Analogue** technology involves measuring, storing, or recording an infinitely variable amount of information by using physical quantities such as voltage. — ADJ: usu ADJ n
[3] An **analogue** watch or clock shows what it is measuring with a pointer on a dial rather than with a number display. Compare **digital**. — ADJ: usu ADJ n

**anal|ogy** /ənælədʒi/ **(analogies)** If you make or draw an **analogy between** two things, you show that they are similar in some way. ❑ *It is probably easier to make an analogy between the courses of the planets, and two trains travelling in the same direction.* — N-COUNT: oft N *between/with* n

**ana|lyse** /ænəlaɪz/ **(analyses, analysing, analysed)**

> ✔ in AM, use **analyze**

[1] If you **analyse** something, you consider it carefully or use statistical methods in order to fully understand it. ❑ *McCarthy was asked to analyse the data from the first phase of trials of the vaccine... This book teaches you how to analyse what is causing the stress in your life.* — VERB; V n; V wh
[2] If you **analyse** something, you examine it using scientific methods in order to find out what it consists of. ❑ *We haven't had time to analyse those samples yet... They had their tablets analysed to find out whether they were getting the real drug or not.* — VERB; V n; *have* n V-ed

**ana|lys|er** /ænəlaɪzər/ **(analysers)**

> ✔ in AM, use **analyzer**

[1] An **analyser** is a piece of equipment which is used to analyse the substances that are present in something such as a gas. ❑ *...an oxygen analyser.* — N-COUNT: usu n N
[2] An **analyser** is someone who analyses information. — N-COUNT = *analyst*

**analy|sis** /ənælɪsɪs/ **(analyses** /ənælɪsiːz/**)** ◆◇◇
[1] **Analysis** is the process of considering something carefully or using statistical methods in order to understand it or explain it. ❑ *We did an analysis of the way that government money has been spent in the past.* — N-VAR
[2] **Analysis** is the scientific process of examining something in order to find out what it consists of. ❑ *They collect blood samples for analysis at a national laboratory.* — N-VAR
[3] An **analysis** is an explanation or description that results from considering something carefully. ❑ *...coming up after the newscast, an analysis of President Bush's domestic policy.* — N-COUNT
[4] You use the expression **in the final analysis** or **in the last analysis** to indicate that the statement you are making is the most important or basic aspect of an issue. ❑ *I'm on the* — PHRASE: PHR with cl = *in the end*

*right track and I think in the final analysis people will understand that... Violence in the last analysis produces more violence.*

**ana|lyst** /ænəlɪst/ **(analysts)** 1 An **analyst** is a person whose job is to analyse a subject and give opinions about it. ❑ *...a political analyst.* ◆◆◇ N-COUNT
2 An **analyst** is someone, usually a doctor, who examines and treats people who are emotionally disturbed. N-COUNT = *psychoanalyst*

**ana|lyt|ic** /ænəlɪtɪk/ **Analytic** means the same as **analytical**. [mainly AM] ADJ

**ana|lyti|cal** /ænəlɪtɪkᵊl/ 1 An **analytical** way of doing something involves the use of logical reasoning. ❑ *I have an analytical approach to every survey.* ♦ **ana|lyti|cal|ly** /ænəlɪtɪkli/ *A teacher can encourage children to think analytically.* ADJ; ADV: ADV with v, ADV adj
2 **Analytical** research involves using chemical analysis. ❑ *All raw materials are subjected to our latest analytical techniques.* ADJ: ADJ n

**ana|lyze** /ænəlaɪz/ → see **analyse**.

**an|ar|chic** /ænɑːʳkɪk/ If you describe someone or something as **anarchic**, you disapprove of them because they do not recognize or obey any rules or laws. ❑ *...anarchic attitudes and complete disrespect for authority.* ADJ: usu ADJ n [disapproval]

**an|ar|chism** /ænəʳkɪzəm/ **Anarchism** is the belief that the laws and power of governments should be replaced by people working together freely. N-UNCOUNT

**an|ar|chist** /ænəʳkɪst/ **(anarchists)** 1 An **anarchist** is a person who believes in anarchism. ❑ *...a well-known anarchist poet.* N-COUNT: oft N n
2 If someone has **anarchist** beliefs or views, they believe in anarchism. ❑ *He was apparently quite converted from his anarchist views.* ADJ: ADJ n
3 If you say that someone is an **anarchist**, you disapprove of them because they seem to pay no attention to the rules or laws that everyone else obeys. ❑ *He was a social anarchist.* N-COUNT [disapproval]

**an|ar|chis|tic** /ænəʳkɪstɪk/ 1 An **anarchistic** person believes in anarchism. **Anarchistic** activity or literature promotes anarchism. ❑ *...an anarchistic revolutionary movement.* ADJ: usu ADJ n
2 If you describe someone as **anarchistic**, you disapprove of them because they pay no attention to the rules or laws that everyone else obeys. ❑ *The Hell's Angels were once the most notorious and anarchistic of motorbike gangs.* ADJ: usu ADJ n [disapproval]

**anarcho-** /ænɑːʳkoʊ-/ **Anarcho-** combines with nouns and adjectives to form words indicating that something is both anarchistic and the other thing that is mentioned. ❑ *In France there was a long tradition of anarcho-syndicalism.* COMB in ADJ and N

**an|ar|chy** /ænəʳki/ If you describe a situation as **anarchy**, you mean that nobody seems to be paying any attention to rules or laws. ❑ *Civil war and famine sent the nation plunging into anarchy.* N-UNCOUNT [disapproval] = *chaos*

**anath|ema** /ənæθəmə/ If something is **anathema to** you, you strongly dislike it. ❑ *Violence was anathema to them.* N-UNCOUNT: usu N *to* n

**ana|tomi|cal** /ænətɒmɪkᵊl/ **Anatomical** means relating to the structure of the bodies of people and animals. ❑ *...minute anatomical differences between insects.* ♦ **ana|tomi|cal|ly** /ænətɒmɪkli/ *I need my pictures to be anatomically correct.* ADJ: usu ADJ n; ADV

**anato|mist** /ənætəmɪst/ **(anatomists)** An **anatomist** is an expert in anatomy. N-COUNT

**anato|mize** /ənætəmaɪz/ **(anatomizes, anatomizing, anatomized)**

✔ in BRIT, also use **anatomise**

If you **anatomise** a subject or an issue, you examine it in great detail. [FORMAL] ❑ *The magazine is devoted to anatomizing the inadequacies of liberalism.* VERB; V n

**anato|my** /ənætəmi/ **(anatomies)** 1 **Anatomy** is the study of the structure of the bodies of people or animals. N-UNCOUNT
2 You can refer to your body as your **anatomy**. [HUMOROUS] N-COUNT: usu poss N
3 An animal's **anatomy** is the structure of its body. N-COUNT: oft with poss

**an|ces|tor** /ænsestəʳ/ **(ancestors)** 1 Your **ancestors** are the people from whom you are descended. ❑ *...our daily lives, so different from those of our ancestors... He could trace his ancestors back seven hundred years.* N-COUNT: usu pl, with poss ≠ *descendant*
2 An **ancestor of** something modern is an earlier thing from which it developed. ❑ *The direct ancestor of the modern cat was the Kaffir cat of ancient Egypt.* N-COUNT: usu N *of* n ≠ *descendant*

**an|ces|tral** /ænsestrəl/ You use **ancestral** to refer to a person's family in former times, especially when the family is important and has property or land which they have had for a long time. ❑ *...the family's ancestral home in southern Germany.* ADJ: usu ADJ n

**an|ces|try** /ænsestri/ **(ancestries)** Your **ancestry** is the fact that you are descended from certain people. ❑ *...a family who could trace their ancestry back to the sixteenth century.* N-COUNT: usu with supp

**an|chor** /æŋkəʳ/ **(anchors, anchoring, anchored)** 1 An **anchor** is a heavy hooked object that is dropped from a boat into the water at the end of a chain in order to make the boat stay in one place. N-COUNT
2 When a boat **anchors** or when you **anchor** it, its anchor is dropped into the water in order to make it stay in one place. ❑ *We could anchor off the pier... They anchored the boat.* VERB; V; V n
3 If you **anchor** an object somewhere, you fix it to something to prevent it moving from that place. ❑ *The roots anchor the plant in the earth... The child seat belt was not properly anchored to the car.* VERB = *tether*; V n prep; V-ed
4 The person who **anchors** a television or radio programme, especially a news programme, is the person who presents it and acts as a link between interviews and reports which come from other places or studios. [mainly AM] ❑ *Viewers saw him anchoring a five-minute summary of regional news. ...a series of cassettes on the Vietnam War, anchored by Mr. Cronkite.* VERB; V n; V-ed
5 The **anchor** on a television or radio programme, especially a news programme, is the person who presents it. [mainly AM] ❑ *He worked in the news division of ABC – he was the anchor of its 15-minute evening newscast.* N-COUNT
6 If a boat is **at anchor**, it is floating in a particular place and is prevented from moving by its anchor. PHRASE

**an|chor|age** /æŋkərɪdʒ/ **(anchorages)** An **anchorage** is a place where a boat can anchor safely. ❑ *The nearest safe anchorage was in Halifax, Nova Scotia... The vessel yesterday reached anchorage off Dubai.* N-VAR

**anchor|man** /æŋkəʳmæn/ **(anchormen)** also **anchor man.** The **anchorman** on a television or radio programme, especially a news programme, is the person who presents it. N-COUNT

**anchor|woman** /æŋkəʳwʊmən/ **(anchorwomen)** The **anchorwoman** on a television or radio programme, especially a news programme, is the woman who presents it. N-COUNT

**an|cho|vy** /æntʃəvi, AM -tʃoʊvi/ **(anchovies)** **Anchovies** are small fish that live in the sea. They are often eaten salted. N-VAR: oft N n

**an|cien re|gime** /ɑːnsjɒn reɪʒiːm/ 1 **The ancien regime** was the political and social system in France before the revolution of 1789. N-SING: usu *the* N
2 If a country has had the same political system for a long time and you disapprove of it, you can refer to it as **the ancien regime**. N-SING: usu *the* N [disapproval]

**an|cient** /eɪnʃənt/ 1 **Ancient** means belonging to the distant past, especially to the period in history before the end of the Roman Empire. ❑ *They believed ancient Greece and Rome were vital sources of learning.* ♦ **an|cient|ly** *Salisbury Plain was known anciently as Ellendune.* ◆◇◇ ADJ: ADJ n; ADV
2 **Ancient** means very old, or having existed for a long time. ❑ *...ancient Jewish tradition.* ADJ: usu ADJ n

**an|cient his|to|ry** **Ancient history** is the history of ancient civilizations, especially Greece and Rome. N-UNCOUNT

**an|cil|lary** /ænsɪləri, AM ænsəleri/ **(ancillaries)** 1 The **ancillary** workers in an institution are the people such as cleaners and cooks whose work supports the main work of the institution. ❑ *...an-* ADJ: ADJ n = *auxiliary*

*cillary staff. ...ancillary services like cleaning.* ♦ **Ancillary** is also a noun. ❑ *...ancillaries who look after the children in the playground.* [2] **Ancillary** means additional to something else. [FORMAL]
N-COUNT
ADJ: usu ADJ n

**and** /ənd, STRONG ænd/ ◆◆◆ [1] You use **and** to link two or more words, groups, or clauses. ❑ *When he returned, she and Simon had already gone... Between 1914 and 1920 large parts of Albania were occupied by the Italians... I'm going to write good jokes and become a good comedian... I'm 53 and I'm very happy.* [2] You use **and** to link two words or phrases that are the same in order to emphasize the degree of something, or to suggest that something continues or increases over a period of time. ❑ *Learning becomes more and more difficult as we get older... We talked for hours and hours... He lay down on the floor and cried and cried.* [3] You use **and** to link two statements about events when one of the events follows the other. ❑ *I waved goodbye and went down the stone harbour steps.* [4] You use **and** to link two statements when the second statement continues the point that has been made in the first statement. ❑ *You could only really tell the effects of the disease in the long term, and five years wasn't long enough.* [5] You use **and** to link two clauses when the second clause is a result of the first clause. ❑ *All through yesterday crowds have been arriving and by midnight thousands of people packed the square.* [6] You use **and** to interrupt yourself in order to make a comment on what you are saying. ❑ *As Downing claims, and as we noted above, reading is best established when the child has an intimate knowledge of the language.* [7] You use **and** at the beginning of a sentence to introduce something else that you want to add to what you have just said. Some people think that starting a sentence with **and** is ungrammatical, but it is now quite common in both spoken and written English. ❑ *Commuter airlines fly to out-of-the-way places. And business travelers are the ones who go to those locations.* [8] You use **and** to introduce a question which follows logically from what someone has just said. ❑ *'He used to be so handsome.' — 'And now?'.* [9] **And** is used by broadcasters and people making announcements to change a topic or to start talking about a topic they have just mentioned. ❑ *And now the drought in Sudan.* [10] You use **and** to indicate that two numbers are to be added together. ❑ *What does two and two make?* [11] **And** is used before a fraction that comes after a whole number. ❑ *McCain spent five and a half years in a prisoner of war camp in Vietnam. ...fourteen and a quarter per cent.* [12] You use **and** in numbers larger than one hundred, after the words 'hundred' or 'thousand' and before other numbers. ❑ *...three thousand and twenty-six pounds.*
CONJ; CONJ [emphasis]; CONJ = then; CONJ; CONJ; CONJ; CONJ; CONJ; CONJ; CONJ = plus; CONJ; CONJ

**an|dan|te** /ændænti/ **(andantes)** [1] **Andante** written above a piece of music means that it should be played fairly slowly. [2] An **andante** is a piece of music that is played fairly slowly. ❑ *...the lovely central Andante. ...the violas' Andante theme.*
ADV: ADV after v; N-COUNT: usu sing

**an|drogy|nous** /ændrɒdʒɪnəs/ [1] In biology, an **androgynous** person, animal, or plant has both male and female sexual characteristics. [TECHNICAL] [2] If you describe someone as **androgynous**, you mean that they are not distinctly masculine or feminine in appearance or in behaviour.
ADJ: usu ADJ n; ADJ: usu ADJ n

**an|drogy|ny** /ændrɒdʒɪni/ **Androgyny** is the state of being neither distinctly masculine nor distinctly feminine.
N-UNCOUNT

**an|droid** /ændrɔɪd/ **(androids)** In science fiction books and films, an **android** is a robot that looks like a human being.
N-COUNT

**an|ec|do|tal** /ænɪkdoutᵊl/ **Anecdotal** evidence is based on individual accounts, rather than on reliable research or statistics, and so may not be valid. ❑ *Anecdotal evidence suggests that sales in Europe have slipped.*
ADJ

**an|ec|dote** /ænɪkdout/ **(anecdotes)** An **anecdote** is a short, amusing account of something that has happened.
N-VAR: oft N *about* n

**anemia** /əniːmiə/ → see **anaemia**.

**anemic** /əniːmɪk/ → see **anaemic**.

**anemo|ne** /ənemənі/ **(anemones)** An **anemone** is a garden plant with red, purple, or white flowers.
N-COUNT

**an|es|the|sia** /ænɪsθiːziə, -ʒə/ → see **anaesthesia**.

**an|es|thesi|olo|gist** /ænɪsθiːziɒlədʒɪst/ **(anesthesiologists)** An **anesthesiologist** is a doctor who specializes in giving anaesthetics to patients. [AM]
N-COUNT

☑ in BRIT, use **anaesthetist**

**an|es|thet|ic** /ænɪsθetɪk/ → see **anaesthetic**.

**anes|the|tist** /əniːsθətɪst/ **(anesthetists)** An **anesthetist** is a nurse or other person who gives an anaesthetic to a patient. [AM]
N-COUNT

**anes|the|tize** /əniːsθətaɪz/ → see **anaesthetize**.

**anew** /ənjuː, AM ənuː/ If you do something **anew**, you do it again, often in a different way from before. [WRITTEN] ❑ *She's ready to start anew... He began his work anew.*
ADV: ADV after v = afresh

**an|gel** /eɪndʒᵊl/ **(angels)** [1] **Angels** are spiritual beings that some people believe are God's servants in heaven. [2] You can call someone you like very much an **angel** in order to show affection, especially when they have been kind to you or done you a favour. [3] If you describe someone as an **angel**, you mean that they seem to be very kind and good.
N-COUNT; N-COUNT [feelings]; N-COUNT [approval]

**an|gel|ic** /ændʒelɪk/ [1] You can describe someone as **angelic** if they are, or seem to be, very good, kind, and gentle. ❑ *...an angelic face... He looked angelic.* [2] **Angelic** means like angels or relating to angels. ❑ *...angelic choirs.*
ADJ: usu ADJ n [approval]; ADJ: ADJ n

**an|gel|ica** /ændʒelɪkə/ **Angelica** is the candied stems of the angelica plant which can be used in making cakes or sweets.
N-UNCOUNT

**an|ger** /æŋgəʳ/ **(angers, angering, angered)** ◆◇◇ [1] **Anger** is the strong emotion that you feel when you think that someone has behaved in an unfair, cruel, or unacceptable way. ❑ *He cried with anger and frustration... Ellen felt both despair and anger at her mother.* [2] If something **angers** you, it makes you feel angry. ❑ *The decision to allow more offshore oil drilling angered some Californians.*
N-UNCOUNT: oft N *at* n/-ing = rage, fury; VERB = enrage, infuriate V n

**an|gi|na** /ændʒaɪnə/ **Angina** is severe pain in the chest and left arm, caused by heart disease.
N-UNCOUNT

**an|gle** /æŋgᵊl/ **(angles, angling, angled)** ◆◇◇ [1] An **angle** is the difference in direction between two lines or surfaces. Angles are measured in degrees. ❑ *The boat is now leaning at a 30 degree angle.* → See also **right angle**. [2] An **angle** is the shape that is created where two lines or surfaces join together. ❑ *...the angle of the blade.* [3] An **angle** is the direction from which you look at something. ❑ *Thanks to the angle at which he stood, he could just see the sunset.* [4] You can refer to a way of presenting something or thinking about it as a particular **angle**. ❑ *He was considering the idea from all angles.* [5] If someone **is angling for** something, they are trying to get it without asking for it directly. ❑ *It sounds as if he's just angling for sympathy.* [6] If something **is at an angle**, it is leaning in a particular direction so that it is not straight, horizontal, or vertical. ❑ *An iron bar stuck out at an angle.*
N-COUNT; N-COUNT: usu *the* N *of* n; N-COUNT; N-COUNT: supp N; VERB: usu cont V *for* n; PHRASE: PHR after v, v-link PHR

**an|gler** /æŋgləʳ/ **(anglers)** An **angler** is someone who fishes with a fishing rod as a hobby.
N-COUNT

**An|gli|can** /æŋglɪkən/ **(Anglicans)** [1] **Anglican** means belonging or relating to the Church of England, or to the churches related to it. ❑ *...the Anglican Church. ...an Anglican priest.* [2] An **Anglican** is a Christian who is a member of the Church of England, or of one of the churches related to it.
ADJ: usu ADJ n; N-COUNT

**An|gli|can|ism** /æŋglɪkənɪzəm/ **Anglicanism** is the beliefs and practices of the Church of England, and of the churches related to it. N-UNCOUNT

**an|gli|cize** /æŋglɪsaɪz/ **(anglicizes, anglicizing, anglicized)**

✓ in BRIT, also use **anglicise**

If you **anglicize** something, you change it so that it resembles or becomes part of the English language or English culture. ❑ *He had anglicized his surname.* VERB V n ♦ **an|gli|cized** *...an Anglicised version of the Welsh name 'Llywelyn'.* ADJ

**an|gling** /æŋglɪŋ/ **Angling** is the activity or sport of fishing with a fishing rod. N-UNCOUNT

**Anglo-** /æŋgloʊ-/ [1] **Anglo-** combines with adjectives indicating nationality to form adjectives which describe something connected with relations between Britain and another country. ❑ *...the Anglo-Irish Agreement.* COMB in ADJ: ADJ n [2] **Anglo-** combines with adjectives indicating nationality to form adjectives which describe a person who has one British parent and one non-British parent. ❑ *He was born of Anglo-American parentage.* COMB in ADJ: ADJ n

**Anglo-Asian** **(Anglo-Asians)** An **Anglo-Asian** person is someone of Indian, Pakistani, or Bangladeshi origin who has grown up in Britain. ❑ *...the Anglo-Asian community.* ADJ: usu ADJ n = British Asian ♦ An **Anglo-Asian** is someone who is Anglo-Asian. N-COUNT = British Asian

**Anglo-Catholic** **(Anglo-Catholics)** [1] The **Anglo-Catholic** part of the Church of England, or of the churches related to it, is the part whose beliefs and practices are similar to those of the Catholic Church. ❑ *...a parish in the Anglo-Catholic tradition.* ADJ: ADJ n [2] An **Anglo-Catholic** is a Christian who belongs to the Anglo-Catholic section of the Church of England, or to the churches related to it. N-COUNT

**Anglo-Indian** **(Anglo-Indians)** [1] An **Anglo-Indian** person is someone whose family is partly British and partly Indian. ❑ *...Anglo-Indian writer Amitav Ghosh.* ADJ: usu ADJ n [2] An **Anglo-Indian** is someone who is Anglo-Indian. N-COUNT

**An|glo|phile** /æŋgloʊfaɪl/ **(Anglophiles)** If you describe a non-British person as **Anglophile**, you mean that they admire Britain and British culture. ❑ *...a Shakespeare sonnet taught to him by his Anglophile uncle.* ADJ ♦ **Anglophile** is also a noun. ❑ *He became a fanatical Anglophile.* N-COUNT

**An|glo|phone** /æŋgləfoʊn/ **(Anglophones)** [1] **Anglophone** communities are English-speaking communities in areas where more than one language is commonly spoken. ❑ *...anglophone Canadians. ...anglophone Africa.* ADJ: ADJ n [2] **Anglophones** are people whose native language is English or who speak English because they live in a country where English is one of the official languages. N-COUNT: usu pl

**Anglo-Saxon** **(Anglo-Saxons)** [1] The **Anglo-Saxon** period is the period of English history from the fifth century A.D. to the Norman Conquest in 1066. ❑ *...the grave of an early Anglo-Saxon king.* ADJ: usu ADJ n ♦ An **Anglo-Saxon** was someone who was Anglo-Saxon. ❑ *...the mighty sea power of the Anglo-Saxons.* N-COUNT [2] **Anglo-Saxon** people are members of or are descended from the English race. ❑ *...white Anglo-Saxon Protestant men.* ADJ ♦ **Anglo-Saxon** is also a noun. ❑ *The difference is, you are Anglo-Saxons, we are Latins.* N-COUNT [3] **Anglo-Saxon** attitudes or ideas have been strongly influenced by English culture. ❑ *Debilly had no Anglo-Saxon shyness about discussing money.* ADJ: usu ADJ n [4] **Anglo-Saxon** is the language that was spoken in England between the fifth century A.D. and the Norman Conquest in 1066. N-UNCOUNT

**An|go|lan** /æŋgoʊlᵊn/ **(Angolans)** [1] **Angolan** means belonging or relating to Angola or its people. ❑ *...the Angolan government.* ADJ: usu ADJ n [2] An **Angolan** is someone who comes from Angola. N-COUNT

**an|go|ra** /æŋgɔːrə/ [1] An **angora** goat or rabbit is a particular breed that has long silky hair. ADJ: ADJ n [2] **Angora** cloth or clothing is made from the hair of the angora goat or rabbit. ❑ *...an angora sweater.* N-UNCOUNT: usu N n

**an|gry** /æŋgri/ **(angrier, angriest)** When you are **angry**, you feel strong dislike or impatience about something. ❑ *She had been very angry at the person who stole her new bike... Are you angry with me for some reason?... I was angry about the rumours... He's angry that people have called him a racist... An angry mob gathered outside the courthouse.* ◆◇◇ ADJ: usu v-link ADJ, oft ADJ *at/with/about* n ♦ **an|gri|ly** /æŋgrɪli/ *Officials reacted angrily to those charges.* ADV: ADV with v

**angst** /æŋst/ **Angst** is a feeling of anxiety and worry. [JOURNALISM] N-UNCOUNT

**an|guish** /æŋgwɪʃ/ **Anguish** is great mental suffering or physical pain. [WRITTEN] ❑ *Mark looked at him in anguish.* N-UNCOUNT

**an|guished** /æŋgwɪʃt/ **Anguished** means showing or feeling great mental suffering or physical pain. [WRITTEN] ❑ *She let out an anguished cry.* ADJ: usu ADJ n

**an|gu|lar** /æŋgjʊləʳ/ **Angular** things have shapes that seem to contain a lot of straight lines and sharp points. ❑ *He had an angular face with prominent cheekbones.* ADJ: usu ADJ n

**ani|mal** /ænɪmᵊl/ **(animals)** [1] An **animal** is a living creature such as a dog, lion, or rabbit, rather than a bird, fish, insect, or human being. ❑ *He was attacked by wild animals... He had a real knowledge of animals, birds and flowers.* ◆◆◇ N-COUNT [2] Any living creature other than a human being can be referred to as an **animal**. ❑ *Language is something which fundamentally distinguishes humans from animals. ...a habitat for plants and animals.* N-COUNT [3] Any living creature, including a human being, can be referred to as an **animal**. ❑ *Watch any young human being, or any other young animal.* N-COUNT [4] **Animal** products come from animals rather than from plants. ❑ *The illegal trade in animal products continues to flourish.* ADJ

**ani|mal rights** People who are concerned with **animal rights** believe very strongly that animals should not be exploited or harmed by humans. N-UNCOUNT: oft N n

**ani|mal test|ing** **Animal testing** involves doing scientific tests on animals when developing new products or drugs. N-UNCOUNT

**ani|mate** **(animates, animating, animated)**

✓ The adjective is pronounced /ænɪmət/. The verb is pronounced /ænɪmeɪt/.

[1] Something that is **animate** has life, in contrast to things like stones and machines which do not. ❑ *...all aspects of the material world, animate and inanimate.* ADJ = living [2] To **animate** something means to make it lively or more cheerful. ❑ *The girls watched, little teasing smiles animating their faces.* VERB = enliven V n

**ani|mat|ed** /ænɪmeɪtɪd/ [1] Someone who is **animated** or who is having an **animated** conversation is lively and is showing their feelings. ❑ *She was seen in animated conversation with the singer Yuri Marusin.* ADJ ♦ **ani|mat|ed|ly** *Sammy was standing close to Ned, talking animatedly with him.* ADV: ADV with v [2] An **animated** film is one in which puppets or drawings appear to move. ADJ: ADJ n

**ani|ma|tion** /ænɪmeɪʃᵊn/ **(animations)** [1] **Animation** is the process of making films in which drawings or puppets appear to move. ❑ *...computer animation.* N-UNCOUNT [2] An **animation** is a film in which drawings or puppets appear to move. N-COUNT = cartoon [3] Someone with **animation** shows liveliness in the way that they speak, look, or behave. ❑ *They both spoke with animation.* N-UNCOUNT [4] → See also **suspended animation**.

**ani|ma|tor** /ænɪmeɪtəʳ/ **(animators)** An **animator** is a person who makes films by means of animation. N-COUNT

**ani|mos|ity** /ænɪmɒsɪti/ **(animosities)** **Animosity** is a strong feeling of dislike and anger. **Animosities** are feelings of this kind. ❑ *There's a long history of animosity between the two nations.* N-UNCOUNT: also N in pl = hostility

**ani|mus** /ænɪməs/ If a person has an **animus** against someone, they have a strong feeling of dislike for them, even when there is no good reason for it. [FORMAL] ❑ *Your animus towards him suggests that you are the wrong man for the job.* N-UNCOUNT: usu N prep = animosity

**an|ise** /ænɪs/ **Anise** is a plant with seeds that have a strong smell and taste. It is often made into an alcoholic drink. N-UNCOUNT

**ani|seed** /ænɪsiːd/ **Aniseed** is a substance made from the seeds of the anise plant. It is used as a flavouring in sweets, drinks, and medicine. N-UNCOUNT

**an|kle** /æŋkəl/ **(ankles)** Your **ankle** is the joint where your foot joins your leg. ❑ *John twisted his ankle badly.* N-COUNT: usu poss N

**an|nals** /ænəlz/ If something is **in the annals of** a nation or field of activity, it is recorded as part of its history. ❑ *He has become a legend in the annals of military history.* N-PLURAL: usu *in the* N *of* n

**an|nex** /æneks/ **(annexes, annexing, annexed)** If a country **annexes** another country or an area of land, it seizes it and takes control of it. ❑ *Rome annexed the Nabatean kingdom in 106 AD... Hitler was determined to annex Austria to Germany.* VERB V n V n *to* n
♦ **an|nexa|tion** /ænekseɪʃən/ **(annexations)** *...Indonesia's annexation of East Timor.* N-COUNT: usu sing

**an|nexe** /æneks/ **(annexes)** also **annex.** [1] An **annexe** is a building which is joined to or is next to a larger main building. ❑ *...setting up a museum in an annexe to the theatre.* [2] An **annexe to** a document is a section added to it at the end. ❑ *The Annex lists and discusses eight titles.* N-COUNT N-COUNT

**an|ni|hi|late** /ənaɪɪleɪt/ **(annihilates, annihilating, annihilated)** [1] To **annihilate** something means to destroy it completely. ❑ *The Army was annihilated.* ♦ **an|ni|hi|la|tion** /ənaɪɪleɪʃən/ *...the threat of nuclear war and annihilation of the human race.* [2] If you **annihilate** someone in a contest or argument, you totally defeat them. ❑ *The Dutch annihilated the Olympic champions 5-0.* VERB V n N-UNCOUNT: oft N *of* n VERB V n

**an|ni|ver|sa|ry** /ænɪvɜːʳsəri/ **(anniversaries)** An **anniversary** is a date which is remembered or celebrated because a special event happened on that date in a previous year. ❑ *...the one hundredth anniversary of the birth of Ho Chi Minh.* ◆◇◇ N-COUNT: usu ord N, *the* N *of* n

**an|no|tate** /ænoʊteɪt/ **(annotates, annotating, annotated)** If you **annotate** written work or a diagram, you add notes to it, especially in order to explain it. ❑ *Historians annotate, check and interpret the diary selections. ...an annotated bibliography.* VERB V n V-ed

**an|no|ta|tion** /ænoʊteɪʃən/ **(annotations)** [1] **Annotation** is the activity of annotating something. ❑ *She retained a number of copies for further annotation.* [2] An **annotation** is a note that is added to a text or diagram, often in order to explain it. ❑ *He supplied annotations to nearly 15,000 musical works.* N-UNCOUNT N-COUNT: usu pl = footnote

**an|nounce** /ənaʊns/ **(announces, announcing, announced)** [1] If you **announce** something, you tell people about it publicly or officially. ❑ *He will announce tonight that he is resigning from office... She was planning to announce her engagement to Peter... It was announced that the groups have agreed to a cease-fire.* [2] If you **announce** a piece of news or an intention, especially something that people may not like, you say it loudly and clearly, so that everyone you are with can hear it. ❑ *Peter announced that he had no intention of wasting his time at any university... 'I'm having a bath and going to bed,' she announced, and left the room.* [3] If an airport or railway employee **announces** something, they tell the public about it by means of a loudspeaker system. ❑ *Station staff announced the arrival of the train over the tannoy... They announced his plane was delayed.* ◆◆◆ VERB V that V n *it be* V-ed that VERB = declare V that V with quote VERB V n V that

**an|nounce|ment** /ənaʊnsmənt/ **(announcements)** [1] An **announcement** is a statement made to the public or to the media which gives information about something that has happened or that will happen. ❑ *Sir Robert made his announcement after talks with the President.* [2] The **announcement of** something that has happened is the act of telling people about it. ❑ *...the announcement of their engagement.* [3] An **announcement** in a public place, such as a newspaper or the window of a shop, is a short piece of writing telling people about something or asking for something. ❑ *He will place an announcement in the personal column of The Daily Telegraph.* ◆◇◇ N-COUNT: oft supp N, N that = declaration N-SING: usu N *of* n N-COUNT

**an|nounc|er** /ənaʊnsəʳ/ **(announcers)** [1] An **announcer** is someone who introduces programmes on radio or television or who reads the text of a radio or television advertisement. ❑ *The radio announcer said it was nine o'clock.* [2] The **announcer** at a railway station or airport is the person who makes the announcements. ❑ *The announcer apologised for the delay.* N-COUNT N-COUNT

**an|noy** /ənɔɪ/ **(annoys, annoying, annoyed)** If someone or something **annoys** you, it makes you fairly angry and impatient. ❑ *Try making a note of the things which annoy you... It annoyed me that I didn't have time to do more reading... It just annoyed me to hear him going on.* → See also **annoyed, annoying.** VERB = irritate V n *it* V n that *it* V n to-inf

**an|noy|ance** /ənɔɪəns/ **(annoyances)** [1] **Annoyance** is the feeling that you get when someone makes you feel fairly angry or impatient. ❑ *To her annoyance the stranger did not go away.* [2] An **annoyance** is something that makes you feel angry or impatient. ❑ *Inconsiderate neighbours can be more than an annoyance.* N-UNCOUNT: oft with poss = irritation N-COUNT: usu sing

**an|noyed** /ənɔɪd/ If you are **annoyed**, you are fairly angry about something. ❑ *She is hurt and annoyed that the authorities have banned her from working with children.* → See also **annoy.** ADJ: usu v-link ADJ, oft ADJ prep, ADJ that = angry

**an|noy|ing** /ənɔɪɪŋ/ Someone or something that is **annoying** makes you feel fairly angry and impatient. ❑ *You must have found my attitude annoying... The annoying thing about the scheme is that it's confusing.* ♦ **an|noy|ing|ly** *Alex looked annoyingly cheerful.* → See also **annoy.** ADJ = irritating ADV: usu ADV adj

**an|nual** /ænjuəl/ **(annuals)** [1] **Annual** events happen once every year. ❑ *...the annual conference of Britain's trade union movement... In its annual report, UNICEF says at least 40,000 children die every day.* ♦ **an|nual|ly** *Companies report to their shareholders annually.* [2] **Annual** quantities or rates relate to a period of one year. ❑ *The electronic and printing unit has annual sales of about $80 million.* ♦ **an|nual|ly** *El Salvador produces 100,000 tons of refined copper annually.* [3] An **annual** is a book or magazine that is published once a year. [4] An **annual** is a plant that grows and dies within one year. ◆◆◇ ADJ: ADJ n = yearly ADV: ADV with v ADJ: ADJ n = yearly ADV: ADV with v N-COUNT N-COUNT

**an|nu|ity** /ənjuːɪti, AM ənuːɪti/ **(annuities)** An **annuity** is an investment or insurance policy that pays someone a fixed sum of money each year. [BUSINESS] N-COUNT

**an|nul** /ənʌl/ **(annuls, annulling, annulled)** If an election or a contract **is annulled**, it is declared invalid, so that legally it is considered never to have existed. ❑ *The marriage was annulled last month.* VERB: usu passive *be* V-ed

**an|nul|ment** /ənʌlmənt/ **(annulments)** The **annulment** of a contract or marriage is an official declaration that it is invalid, so that legally it is considered never to have existed. ❑ *...the annulment of the elections.* N-VAR

**an|num** /ænəm/ → see **per annum.**

**An|nun|cia|tion** /ənʌnsieɪʃən/ In Christianity, **the Annunciation** was the announcement by the Archangel Gabriel to the Virgin Mary that she was going to give birth to the son of God. N-PROPER: *the* N

**an|ode** /ænoʊd/ **(anodes)** In electronics, an **anode** is the positive electrode in a cell such as a battery. Compare **cathode.** [TECHNICAL] N-COUNT

**ano|dyne** /ænədaɪn/ If you describe something as **anodyne**, you are criticizing it because it ADJ [disapproval] = bland has no strong characteristics and is not likely to excite, interest, or upset anyone. [FORMAL] ❑ *Their quarterly meetings were anodyne affairs.*

**anoint** /ənɔɪnt/ **(anoints, anointing, anointed)** 1 To **anoint** someone means to put oil or water on a part of their body, usually for religious reasons. ❑ *He anointed my forehead... The Pope has anointed him as Archbishop. ...the anointed king.* VERB V n V n as n V-ed
2 If a person in a position of authority **anoints** someone, they choose them to do a particular important job. [JOURNALISM] ❑ *The populist party anointed him as its candidate... Mr. Olsen has always avoided anointing any successor.* VERB V n as n V n

**anoma|lous** /ənɒmələs/ Something that is **anomalous** is different from what is usual or expected. [FORMAL] ❑ *For years this anomalous behaviour has baffled scientists.* ADJ = unusual

**anoma|ly** /ənɒməli/ **(anomalies)** If something is an **anomaly**, it is different from what is usual or expected. [FORMAL] ❑ *The British public's wariness of opera is an anomaly in Europe.* N-COUNT = oddity

**anon** /ənɒn/ **Anon** means quite soon. [LITERARY] ❑ *You shall see him anon.* ADV: ADV after v

**anon.** **Anon.** is often written after poems or other writing to indicate that the author is not known. **Anon.** is an abbreviation for 'anonymous'.

**anony|mous** /ənɒnɪməs/ 1 If you remain **anonymous** when you do something, you do not let people know that you were the person who did it. ❑ *You can remain anonymous if you wish... An anonymous benefactor stepped in to provide the prize money. ...anonymous phone calls.* ADJ
♦ **ano|nym|ity** /ænɒnɪmɪti/ *Both mother and daughter, who have requested anonymity, are doing fine.* N-UNCOUNT ♦ **anony|mous|ly** *The latest photographs were sent anonymously to the magazine's Paris headquarters.* ADV
2 Something that is **anonymous** does not reveal who you are. ❑ *Of course, that would have to be by anonymous vote.* ADJ: usu ADJ n ♦ **ano|nym|ity** *He claims many more people would support him in the anonymity of a voting booth.* N-UNCOUNT: with supp
3 If you describe a place as **anonymous**, you dislike it because it has no unusual or interesting features and seems unwelcoming. ❑ *It's nice to stay in a home rather than in an anonymous holiday villa.* ADJ disapproval ♦ **ano|nym|ity** *...the anonymity of the rented room.* N-UNCOUNT

**ano|rak** /ænəræk/ **(anoraks)** An **anorak** is a warm waterproof jacket, usually with a hood. N-COUNT

**ano|rexia** /ænəreksiə/ **Anorexia** or **anorexia nervosa** is an illness in which a person has an overwhelming fear of becoming fat, and so refuses to eat enough and becomes thinner and thinner. N-UNCOUNT

**ano|rex|ic** /ænəreksɪk/ **(anorexics)** If someone is **anorexic**, they are suffering from anorexia and so are very thin. ADJ ♦ An **anorexic** is someone who is anorexic. N-COUNT

**an|oth|er** /ənʌðəʳ/ ♦♦♦ 1 **Another** thing or person means an additional thing or person of the same type as one that already exists. ❑ *Mrs. Madrigal buttered another piece of toast... We're going to have another baby.* DET: DET sing-n ♦ **Another** is also a pronoun. ❑ *The demand generated by one factory required the construction of another.* PRON
2 You use **another** when you want to emphasize that an additional thing or person is different to one that already exists. ❑ *I think he's just going to deal with this problem another day... The counsellor referred her to another therapist.* DET: DET sing-n ♦ **Another** is also a pronoun. ❑ *He didn't really believe that any human being could read another's mind.* PRON
3 You use **another** at the beginning of a statement to link it to a previous statement. ❑ *Another change that Sue made was to install central heating.* DET: DET sing-n
4 You use **another** before a word referring to a distance, length of time, or other amount, to indicate an additional amount. ❑ *Continue down the same road for another 2 kilometres until you reach the church of Santa Maria... He believes prices will not rise by more than another 4 per cent.* DET: DET amount
5 You use **one another** to indicate that each member of a group does something to or for the other members. ❑ *...women learning to help themselves and one another.* PRON: v PRON, prep PRON

PHRASES 6 If you talk about **one** thing **after another**, you are referring to a series of repeated or continuous events. ❑ *They kept going, destroying one store after another.* PHRASE: PHR after v
7 You use **or another** in expressions such as **one kind or another** when you do not want to be precise about which of several alternatives or possibilities you are referring to. ❑ *...family members and visiting artists of one kind or another crowding the huge kitchen.* PHRASE: usu n PHR

**an|swer** /ɑːnsəʳ, æn-/ ♦♦♦ **(answers, answering, answered)** 1 When you **answer** someone who has asked you something, you say something back to them. ❑ *Just answer the question... He paused before answering... 'When?' asked Alba, 'Tonight', answered Tom... Williams answered that he had no specific proposals yet.* VERB V n V V with quote V that
2 An **answer** is something that you say when you answer someone. ❑ *Without waiting for an answer, he turned and went in through the door... I don't quite know what to say in answer to your question.* N-COUNT: also in N to n = reply, response
3 If you say that someone will not **take no for an answer**, you mean that they go on trying to make you agree to something even after you have refused. ❑ *He would never take no for an answer.* PHRASE: with brd-neg
4 If you **answer** a letter or advertisement, you write to the person who wrote it. ❑ *She answered an advert for a job as a cook.* VERB V n Also V
5 An **answer** is a letter that you write to someone who has written to you. ❑ *I wrote to him but I never had an answer back... She wrote to Roosevelt's secretary in answer to his letter of the day before.* N-COUNT: also in N to n = reply, response
6 When you **answer** the telephone, you pick it up when it rings. When you **answer** the door, you open it when you hear a knock or the bell. ❑ *She answered her phone on the first ring... A middle-aged woman answered the door.* VERB V n Also V ♦ **Answer** is also a noun. ❑ *I knocked at the front door and there was no answer.* N-COUNT: usu sing
7 An **answer to** a problem is a solution to it. ❑ *There are no easy answers to the problems facing the economy... Prison is not the answer for most young offenders.* N-COUNT: oft N to n
8 Someone's **answer to** a question in a test or quiz is what they write or say in an attempt to give the facts that are asked for. The **answer** to a question is the fact that was asked for. ❑ *Simply marking an answer wrong will not help the pupil to get future examples correct.* N-COUNT: oft N to n
9 When you **answer** a question in a test or quiz, you write or say something in an attempt to give the facts that are asked for. ❑ *To obtain her degree, she answered 81 questions over 10 papers.* VERB V n
10 Your **answer to** something that someone has said or done is what you say or do in response to it or in defence of yourself. ❑ *In answer to speculation that she wouldn't finish the race, she boldly declared her intention of winning it.* N-COUNT: also in N to n = reply, response
11 If you **answer** something that someone has said or done, you respond to it. ❑ *He answered her smile with one of his own... That statement seemed designed to answer criticism of allied bombing missions.* VERB = counter V n with n V n Also V n by -ing
12 If something **answers** a need or purpose, it satisfies it, because it has the right qualities. ❑ *We provide specially designed shopping trolleys to answer the needs of parents with young children.* VERB = satisfy V n
13 If someone or something **answers** a particular description or **answers to** it, they have the characteristics described. ❑ *Two men answering the description of the suspects tried to enter Switzerland... The Japanese never built any aircraft remotely answering to this description.* VERB = fit V n V to n

♦ **answer back** If someone, especially a child, **answers back**, they speak rudely to you when you speak to them. ❑ *She was punished by teachers for answering back... I always answered him back when I thought he was wrong.* PHRASAL VERB V P V n P

♦ **answer for** 1 If you have to **answer for** something bad or wrong you have done, you are punished for it. ❑ *He must be made to answer for his terrible crimes.* PHRASAL VERB V P n
2 If you say that someone **has a lot to answer for**, you are saying that their ac- PHRASE: have inflects

tions have led to problems which you think they are responsible for.

**an|swer|able** /ɑːnsərəbᵊl, æn-/ [1] If you are **answerable to** someone, you have to report to them and explain your actions. ❑ *Councils should be answerable to the people who elect them.* ADJ: v-link ADJ *to* n

[2] If you are **answerable for** your actions or **for** someone else's actions, you are considered to be responsible for them and if necessary must accept punishment for them. ❑ *He must be made answerable for these terrible crimes.* ADJ: v-link ADJ, usu ADJ *for* n = accountable

**an|swer|ing ma|chine** **(answering machines)** An **answering machine** is the same as an **answerphone**. N-COUNT

**an|swer|phone** /ɑːnsəʳfoʊn, æn-/ **(answerphones)** An **answerphone** is a device which you connect to your telephone and which records telephone calls while you are out. [mainly BRIT] N-COUNT = answering machine

**ant** /ænt/ **(ants)** **Ants** are small crawling insects that live in large groups. N-COUNT

**ant|acid** /æntæsɪd/ **(antacids)** **Antacid** is a substance that reduces the level of acid in the stomach. N-MASS

**an|tago|nise** /æntægənaɪz/ ➔ see **antagonize**.

**an|tago|nism** /æntægənɪzəm/ **(antagonisms)** **Antagonism** between people is hatred or dislike between them. **Antagonisms** are instances of this. ❑ *There is still much antagonism between trades unions and the oil companies... Old antagonisms resurfaced.* N-UNCOUNT: also N in pl = hostility

**an|tago|nist** /æntægənɪst/ **(antagonists)** Your **antagonist** is your opponent or enemy. ❑ *Spassky had never previously lost to his antagonist.* N-COUNT

**an|tago|nis|tic** /æntægənɪstɪk/ If a person is **antagonistic to** someone or something, they show hatred or dislike towards them. ❑ *Nearly all the women I interviewed were aggressively antagonistic to the idea.* ADJ: usu v-link ADJ, oft ADJ *to/towards* n

**an|tago|nize** /æntægənaɪz/ **(antagonizes, antagonizing, antagonized)**

✔ in BRIT, also use **antagonise**

If you **antagonize** someone, you make them feel angry or hostile towards you. ❑ *He didn't want to antagonize her.* VERB V n

**Ant|arc|tic** /æntɑːʳktɪk/ **The Antarctic** is the area around the South Pole. N-PROPER: *the* N

**ante** /ænti/ If you **up the ante** or **raise the ante**, you increase your demands when you are in dispute or fighting for something. [JOURNALISM] PHRASE: V inflects

**ant|eater** /æntiːtəʳ/ **(anteaters)** also **ant-eater.** An **anteater** is an animal with a long nose that eats termites or ants. Anteaters live in warm countries. N-COUNT

**ante|ced|ent** /æntɪsiːdᵊnt/ **(antecedents)** An **antecedent** of something happened or existed before it and was similar to it in some way. [FORMAL] ❑ *We shall first look briefly at the historical antecedents of this theory.* N-COUNT: usu with supp = precursor

**ante|cham|ber** /æntitʃeɪmbəʳ/ **(antechambers)** also **ante-chamber.** An **antechamber** is a small room leading into a larger room. N-COUNT = anteroom

**ante|di|lu|vian** /æntidɪluːviən/ **Antediluvian** things are old or old-fashioned. [HUMOROUS] ❑ *...antediluvian attitudes to women.* ADJ

**ante|lope** /æntɪloʊp/ **(antelopes** or **antelope)** An **antelope** is an animal like a deer, with long legs and horns, that lives in Africa or Asia. Antelopes are graceful and can run fast. There are many different types of antelope. N-COUNT

**ante|na|tal** /æntineɪtᵊl/ also **ante-natal.** **Antenatal** means relating to the medical care of women when they are expecting a baby. ❑ *...antenatal classes. ...antenatal care.* ADJ: ADJ n ≠ postnatal

**an|ten|na** /æntenə/ **(antennae** /ænteniː/ or **antennas)**

✔ **antennas** is the usual plural form for meaning 2.

[1] The **antennae** of something such as an insect or crustacean are the two long, thin parts attached to its head that it uses to feel things with. [2] An **antenna** is a device that sends and receives television or radio signals. ➔ See pictures on pages 1705 and 1707. N-COUNT: usu pl; N-COUNT = aerial

**ante-post** In gambling, **ante-post** bets are placed before the day of a particular race or competition. [BRIT] ❑ *...the ante-post favourite for the Epsom Classic, Celtic Swing.* ADJ: usu ADJ n

**ante|ri|or** /æntɪəriəʳ/ **Anterior** describes a part of the body that is situated at or towards the front of another part. [MEDICAL] ❑ *...the left anterior descending artery.* ADJ: usu ADJ n ≠ posterior

**ante|room** /æntiruːm/ **(anterooms)** also **ante-room.** An **anteroom** is a small room leading into a larger room. ❑ *He had been patiently waiting in the anteroom for an hour.* N-COUNT = antechamber

**an|them** /ænθəm/ **(anthems)** An **anthem** is a song which is used to represent a particular nation, society, or group and which is sung on special occasions. ❑ *The band played the Czech anthem.* ➔ See also **national anthem**. N-COUNT

**ant|hill** /ænthɪl/ **(anthills)** also **ant-hill.** An **anthill** is a pile of earth formed by ants when they are making a nest. N-COUNT

**an|thol|ogy** /ænθɒlədʒi/ **(anthologies)** An **anthology** is a collection of writings by different writers published together in one book. ❑ *...an anthology of poetry.* N-COUNT

**an|thra|cite** /ænθrəsaɪt/ **Anthracite** is a type of very hard coal which burns slowly, producing a lot of heat and very little smoke. N-UNCOUNT

**an|thrax** /ænθræks/ **Anthrax** is a disease of cattle and sheep, in which they get painful sores and a fever. Anthrax can be used in biological weapons. N-UNCOUNT

**an|thro|pol|ogy** /ænθrəpɒlədʒi/ **Anthropology** is the scientific study of people, society, and culture. N-UNCOUNT ♦ **an|thro|polo|gist** /ænθrəpɒlədʒɪst/ **(anthropologists)** ❑ *...an anthropologist who had been in China for three years.* N-COUNT

**an|thro|po|mor|phic** /ænθrəpəmɔːʳfɪk/ **Anthropomorphic** means relating to the idea that an animal, a god, or an object has feelings or characteristics like those of a human being. ❑ *...the anthropomorphic attitude to animals.* ADJ

**an|thro|po|mor|phism** /ænθrəpəmɔːʳfɪzəm/ **Anthropomorphism** is the idea that an animal, a god, or an object has feelings or characteristics like those of a human being. N-UNCOUNT

**anti** /ænti/ **(antis)** [1] You can refer to people who are opposed to a particular activity or idea as **antis**. [INFORMAL] ❑ *Despite what the antis would tell you, hunting is for people from all walks of life.* N-COUNT: usu pl, oft *the* N

[2] If someone is opposed to something you can say that they are **anti** it. [INFORMAL, SPOKEN] ❑ *That's why you're so anti other people smoking.* ADJ: v-link ADJ = against ≠ for

**anti-** /ænti-/ [1] **Anti-** is used to form adjectives and nouns that describe someone or something that is opposed to a particular system, practice, or group of people. ❑ *...anti-government demonstrations. ...anti-racist campaigners. ...anti-Fascists.* PREFIX

[2] **Anti-** is used to form adjectives and nouns that describe things that are intended to destroy something harmful or to prevent something from happening. ❑ *...anti-aircraft guns. ...anti-discrimination legislation. ...anti-inflammatory drugs.* PREFIX

**anti-abortionist** **(anti-abortionists)** An **anti-abortionist** is someone who wants to limit or prevent the legal availability of abortions. N-COUNT

**anti|bi|ot|ic** /æntibaɪɒtɪk/ **(antibiotics)** **Antibiotics** are medical drugs used to kill bacteria and treat infections. ❑ *...a course of antibiotics.* N-COUNT: usu pl

**anti|body** /æntibɒdi/ **(antibodies)** **Antibodies** are substances which a person's or an animal's body produces in their blood in order to destroy substances which carry disease. N-COUNT: usu pl

**an|tici|pate** /æntɪsɪpeɪt/ **(anticipates, anticipating, anticipated)** 1 If you **anticipate** an event, you realize in advance that it may happen and you are prepared for it. ❑ *At the time we couldn't have anticipated the result of our campaigning... It is anticipated that the equivalent of 192 full-time jobs will be lost... Officials anticipate that rivalry between leaders of the various drug factions could erupt into full scale war.* VERB = expect; V n; it be V-ed that; V that
2 If you **anticipate** a question, request, or need, you do what is necessary or required before the question, request, or need occurs. ❑ *What Jeff did was to anticipate my next question.* VERB; V n
3 If you **anticipate** something, you do it, think it, or say it before someone else does. ❑ *In the 50s, Rauschenberg anticipated the conceptual art movement of the 80s.* VERB; V n

**an|tici|pat|ed** /æntɪsɪpeɪtɪd/ If an event, especially a cultural event, is eagerly **anticipated**, people expect that it will be very good, exciting, or interesting. ❑ *...the most eagerly anticipated rock event of the year. ...one of the conference's most keenly anticipated debates.* ADJ = awaited

**an|tici|pa|tion** /æntɪsɪpeɪʃᵊn/ 1 **Anticipation** is a feeling of excitement about something pleasant or exciting that you know is going to happen. ❑ *There's been an atmosphere of anticipation around here for a few days now.* N-UNCOUNT
2 If something is done **in anticipation of** an event, it is done because people believe that event is going to happen. ❑ *Troops in the Philippines have been put on full alert in anticipation of trouble during a planned general strike.* PHRASE: PHR n

**an|tici|pa|tory** /æntɪsɪpeɪtəri, AM -pətɔːri/ An **anticipatory** feeling or action is one that you have or do because you are expecting something to happen soon. [FORMAL] ❑ *...an anticipatory smile.* ADJ: usu ADJ n

**anti|cli|max** /æntiklaɪmæks/ **(anticlimaxes)** You can describe something as an **anticlimax** if it disappoints you because it happens after something that was very exciting, or because it is not as exciting as you expected. ❑ *Barry's speech followed Dirk Bogarde's appearance, and was an inevitable anticlimax.* N-VAR = disappointment

**anti|clock|wise** /æntiklɒkwaɪz/ also **anti-clockwise.** If something is moving **anticlockwise**, it is moving in the opposite direction to the direction in which the hands of a clock move. [BRIT] ❑ *The cutters are opened by turning the knob anticlockwise.* ♦ **Anticlockwise** is also an adjective. ❑ *...an anticlockwise route around the coast.* ADV: ADV after v ≠ clockwise; ADJ: ADJ n

✔ in AM, use **counterclockwise**

**an|tics** /æntɪks/ **Antics** are funny, silly, or unusual ways of behaving. ❑ *Elizabeth tolerated Sarah's antics.* N-PLURAL

**anti|cy|clone** /æntisaɪkloʊn/ **(anticyclones)** An **anticyclone** is an area of high atmospheric pressure which causes settled weather conditions and, in summer, clear skies and high temperatures. N-COUNT

**anti-depressant** **(anti-depressants)** also **antidepressant.** An **anti-depressant** is a drug which is used to treat people who are suffering from depression. N-COUNT

**anti|dote** /æntidoʊt/ **(antidotes)** 1 An **antidote** is a chemical substance that stops or controls the effect of a poison. ❑ *When he returned, he noticed their sickness and prepared an antidote.* N-COUNT
2 Something that is an **antidote to** a difficult or unpleasant situation helps you to overcome the situation. ❑ *Massage is a wonderful antidote to stress.* N-COUNT: usu N to n = cure, remedy

**anti|freeze** /æntifriːz/ **Antifreeze** is a liquid which is added to water to stop it freezing. It is used in car radiators in cold weather. N-UNCOUNT: also a N

**anti|gen** /æntɪdʒən/ **(antigens)** An **antigen** is a substance that helps the production of antibodies. N-COUNT

**anti-hero** **(anti-heroes)** also **antihero.** An **anti-hero** is the main character in a novel, play, or film who is not morally good and does not behave like a typical hero. N-COUNT ≠ hero

**anti|his|ta|mine** /æntihɪstəmɪn/ **(antihistamines)** also **anti-histamine.** An **antihistamine** is a drug that is used to treat allergies. N-COUNT

**anti|mat|ter** /æntimætəʳ/ In science, **antimatter** is a form of matter whose particles have characteristics and properties opposite to those of ordinary matter. [TECHNICAL] N-UNCOUNT

**anti|oxi|dant** /æntiɒksɪdənt/ **(antioxidants)** also **anti-oxidant.** An **antioxidant** is a substance which slows down the damage that can be caused to other substances by the effects of oxygen. Foods which contain antioxidants are thought to be very good for you. N-COUNT

**anti|pas|to** /æntipæstoʊ/ **(antipasti)** **Antipasto** is the sort of food that is often served at the beginning of an Italian meal, for example cold meats and vegetables in olive oil. N-VAR

**an|tipa|thy** /æntɪpəθi/ **Antipathy** is a strong feeling of dislike or hostility towards someone or something. [FORMAL] ❑ *She'd often spoken of her antipathy towards London.* N-UNCOUNT: usu N prep

**An|tipo|dean** /æntɪpədiːən/ also **antipodean.** **Antipodean** describes people or things that come from or relate to Australia and New Zealand. [BRIT] ❑ *This New Zealand winery produces some of the best antipodean wines.* ADJ: usu ADJ n

**An|tipo|des** /æntɪpədiːz/ People sometimes refer to Australia and New Zealand as **the Antipodes**. [BRIT] N-PROPER: the N

**anti|quar|ian** /æntɪkweəriən/ **(antiquarians)** 1 **Antiquarian** means concerned with old and rare objects. ❑ *...an antiquarian bookseller. ...antiquarian and second-hand books.* ADJ: ADJ n
2 An **antiquarian** is the same as an **antiquary**. N-COUNT

**anti|quary** /æntɪkwəri, AM -kweri/ **(antiquaries)** An **antiquary** is a person who studies the past, or who collects or buys and sells old and valuable objects. N-COUNT = antiquarian

**anti|quat|ed** /æntɪkweɪtɪd/ If you describe something as **antiquated**, you are criticizing it because it is very old or old-fashioned. ❑ *Many factories are so antiquated they are not worth saving.* ADJ [disapproval]

**an|tique** /æntiːk/ **(antiques)** An **antique** is an old object such as a piece of china or furniture which is valuable because of its beauty or rarity. ❑ *...a genuine antique. ...antique silver jewellery.* ◆◇◇ N-COUNT: oft N n

**an|tiqued** /æntiːkt/ An **antiqued** object is modern but has been made to look like an antique. ❑ *Both rooms have antiqued pine furniture.* ADJ

**an|tiq|uity** /æntɪkwɪti/ **(antiquities)** 1 **Antiquity** is the distant past, especially the time of the ancient Egyptians, Greeks, and Romans. ❑ *...famous monuments of classical antiquity.* N-UNCOUNT
2 **Antiquities** are things such as buildings, statues, or coins that were made in ancient times and have survived to the present day. ❑ *...collectors of Roman antiquities.* N-COUNT: usu pl
3 The **antiquity** of something is its great age. ❑ *...a town of great antiquity.* N-UNCOUNT: with supp

**anti-Semite** /ænti siːmaɪt, AM - sem-/ **(anti-Semites)** An **anti-Semite** is someone who strongly dislikes and is prejudiced against Jewish people. N-COUNT

**anti-Semitic** also **antisemitic.** Someone or something that is **anti-Semitic** is hostile to or prejudiced against Jewish people. ADJ

**anti-Semitism** /ænti semɪtɪzəm/ **Anti-Semitism** is hostility to and prejudice against Jewish people. N-UNCOUNT

**anti|sep|tic** /æntiseptɪk/ **(antiseptics)** 1 **Antiseptic** is a substance that kills germs and harmful bacteria. ❑ *She bathed the cut with antiseptic.* N-MASS = disinfectant
2 Something that is **antiseptic** kills germs and harmful bacteria. ❑ *These vegetables and herbs have strong antiseptic qualities.* ADJ

**anti-social** also **antisocial.** 1 Someone who is **anti-social** is unwilling to meet and be friendly with other people. ❑ *...teenagers who will become aggressive and anti-social.* ADJ
2 **Anti-social** ADJ

behaviour is annoying or upsetting to other people.

**an|tith|esis** /æntɪθəsɪs/ **(antitheses** /æntɪθəsiːz/**)** **The antithesis of** something is its exact opposite. [FORMAL] ❑ *The little black dress is the anithesis of fussy dressing.*

N-COUNT: usu *the* N *of* n = opposite

**anti|theti|cal** /æntɪθe̱tɪkəl/ Something that is **antithetical to** something else is the opposite of it and is unable to exist with it. [WRITTEN] ❑ *Their priorities are antithetical to those of environmentalists.*

ADJ: usu v-link ADJ *to* n

**anti|trust** /æntitrʌst/ In the United States, **antitrust** laws are intended to stop large firms taking over their competitors, fixing prices with their competitors, or interfering with free competition in any way.

ADJ: ADJ n

**ant|ler** /æntləʳ/ **(antlers)** A male deer's **antlers** are the branched horns on its head.

N-COUNT

**an|to|nym** /æntənɪm/ **(antonyms)** The **antonym** of a word is a word which means the opposite. [FORMAL]

N-COUNT ≠ synonym

**antsy** /æntsi/ If someone is **antsy**, they are nervous or impatient. [AM, INFORMAL] ❑ *This is the end of a tour so I'm a little antsy, I guess.*

ADJ: usu v-link ADJ

**anus** /e̱ɪnəs/ **(anuses)** A person's **anus** is the hole from which faeces leaves their body.

N-COUNT

**an|vil** /ænvɪl/ **(anvils)** An **anvil** is a heavy iron block on which hot metals are beaten into shape.

N-COUNT

**anxi|ety** /æŋza̱ɪɪti/ **(anxieties)** **Anxiety** is a feeling of nervousness or worry. ❑ *Her voice was full of anxiety... Many editorials express their anxieties about the economic chaos in the country.*

◆◇◇ N-UNCOUNT: also N in pl

**anx|ious** /æŋkʃəs/ 1 If you are **anxious to** do something or **anxious that** something should happen, you very much want to do it or very much want it to happen. ❑ *Both the Americans and the Russians are anxious to avoid conflict in South Asia... He is anxious that there should be no delay... Those anxious for reform say that the present system is too narrow.* 2 If you are **anxious**, you are nervous or worried about something. ❑ *The foreign minister admitted he was still anxious about the situation in the country... A friend of mine is a very anxious person.* ♦ **anx|ious|ly** *They are waiting anxiously to see who will succeed him.* 3 An **anxious** time or situation is one during which you feel nervous and worried. ❑ *The Prime Minister faces anxious hours before the votes are counted tomorrow night.*

◆◇◇ ADJ: v-link ADJ, ADJ to-inf, ADJ that, ADJ prep = eager, keen
ADJ = nervous
ADV: ADV with v
ADJ: ADJ n = uneasy

**any** /e̱ni/ 1 You use **any** in statements with negative meaning to indicate that no thing or person of a particular type exists, is present, or is involved in a situation. ❑ *I never make any big decisions... We are doing this all without any support from the hospital... Earlier reports were unable to confirm that there were any survivors.* ♦ **Any** is also a quantifier. ❑ *You don't know any of my friends.* ♦ **Any** is also a pronoun. ❑ *The children needed new school clothes and Kim couldn't afford any.* 2 You use **any** in questions and conditional clauses to ask whether there is some of a particular thing or some of a particular group of people, or to suggest that there might be. ❑ *Do you speak any foreign languages?... Have you got any cheese I can have with this bread?* ♦ **Any** is also a quantifier. ❑ *Have you ever used a homeopathic remedy for any of the following reasons?* ♦ **Any** is also a pronoun. ❑ *The plants are inspected for insects and if I find any, they are squashed.* 3 You use **any** in positive statements when you are referring to someone or something of a particular kind that might exist, occur, or be involved in a situation, when their exact identity or nature is not important. ❑ *Any actor will tell you that it is easier to perform than to be themselves... I'm prepared to take any advice.* ♦ **Any** is also a quantifier. ❑ *It had been the biggest mistake any of them could remember.* ♦ **Any** is also a pronoun. ❑ *Clean the mussels and discard any that do not close.* 4 You can also use **any** to emphasize a comparative adjective or adverb in a negative statement. ❑ *I can't see things getting any easier for graduates.*

◆◆◆ DET: DET pl-n/n-uncount
QUANT: QUANT *of* def-n-uncount/def-pl-n
PRON: PRON after v
DET: DET pl-n/n-uncount
QUANT: QUANT *of* def-n-uncount/def-pl-n
PRON: PRON after v
DET
QUANT: QUANT *of* def-n-uncount/def-pl-n
PRON
ADV: ADV compar [emphasis]

PHRASES 5 If you say that someone or something is **not just any** person or thing, you mean that they are special in some way. ❑ *It's fashionable for young people to wear trainers, but not just any trainers.* 6 If something does not happen or is not true **any more** or **any longer**, it has stopped happening or is no longer true. ❑ *I don't want to see her any more... I couldn't keep the tears hidden any longer.* 7 **in any case** → see **case**. **by any chance** → see **chance**. **in any event** → see **event**. **not by any means** → see **means**. **any old** → see **old**. **at any rate** → see **rate**.

PHRASE: PHR n
PHRASE: PHR after v

**any|body** /e̱nibɒdi/ **Anybody** means the same as **anyone**.

◆◇◇ PRON

**any|how** /e̱nihaʊ/ 1 **Anyhow** means the same as **anyway**. 2 If you do something **anyhow**, you do it in a careless or untidy way. ❑ *...her long legs which she displayed all anyhow getting in and out of her car.*

ADV
ADV: ADV after v

**any|more** /e̱nimɔːʳ/

> ✓ In British English, the spelling **anymore** is sometimes considered incorrect, and **any more** is used instead.

If something does not happen or is not true **anymore**, it has stopped happening or is no longer true. ❑ *I don't ride my motorbike much anymore... I couldn't trust him anymore.*

ADV: ADV after v

**any|one** /e̱niwʌn/ or **anybody** 1 You use **anyone** or **anybody** in statements with negative meaning to indicate in a general way that nobody is present or involved in an action. ❑ *I won't tell anyone I saw you here... You needn't talk to anyone if you don't want to... He was far too scared to tell anybody.* 2 You use **anyone** or **anybody** in questions and conditional clauses to ask or talk about whether someone is present or doing something. ❑ *Why would anyone want that job?... If anyone deserves to be happy, you do.* 3 You use **anyone** or **anybody** before words which indicate the kind of person you are talking about. ❑ *It's not a job for anyone who is slow with numbers... Anybody interested in pop culture at all should buy 'Pure Cult'.* 4 You use **anyone** or **anybody** to refer to a person when you are emphasizing that it could be any person out of a very large number of people. ❑ *Anyone could be doing what I'm doing.* 5 You use **anyone who is anyone** and **anybody who is anybody** to refer to people who are important or influential.

◆◆◇ PRON
PRON
PRON: PRON cl/group
PRON [emphasis]
PHRASE

**any|place** /e̱nipleɪs/ **Anyplace** means the same as **anywhere**. [AM, INFORMAL]

ADV: ADV after v

**any|thing** /e̱nɪθɪŋ/ 1 You use **anything** in statements with negative meaning to indicate in a general way that nothing is present or that an action or event does not or cannot happen. ❑ *We can't do anything... She couldn't see or hear anything at all... By the time I get home, I'm too tired to do anything active.* 2 You use **anything** in questions and conditional clauses to ask or talk about whether something is present or happening. ❑ *What happened, is anything wrong?... Did you find anything?... Is there anything you can do to help?* 3 You can use **anything** before words which indicate the kind of thing you are talking about. ❑ *More than anything else, he wanted to become a teacher... Anything that's cheap this year will be even cheaper next year.* 4 You use **anything** to emphasize a possible thing, event, or situation, when you are saying that it could be any one of a very large number of things. ❑ *He is young, fresh, and ready for anything... At that point, anything could happen.* 5 You use **anything** in expressions such as **anything near**, **anything close to** and **anything like** to emphasize a statement that you are making. ❑ *Doctors have decided the only way he can live anything near a normal life is to give him an operation.* 6 When you do not want to be exact, you use **anything** to talk about a particular range

◆◆◆ PRON: v PRON, oft PRON adj
PRON: oft PRON adj
PRON: PRON cl/group
PRON [emphasis]
PRON: PRON prep [emphasis]
PRON: PRON *from* n *to* n,

of things or quantities. ❑ *Factory farming has turned the cow into a milk machine, producing anything from 25 to 40 litres of milk per day.* PRON *between n and n*

PHRASES 7 You use **anything but** in expressions such as **anything but quiet** and **anything but attractive** to emphasize that something is not the case. ❑ *There's no evidence that he told anyone to say anything but the truth.* PHRASE: v-link PHR, usu PHR adj/n [emphasis] 8 You can say that you **would not** do something **for anything** to emphasize that you definitely would not want to do or be a particular thing. [INFORMAL, SPOKEN] ❑ *I wouldn't want to move for anything in the world.* PHRASE [emphasis] 9 You use **if anything**, especially after a negative statement, to introduce a statement that adds to what you have just said. ❑ *I never had to clean up after him. If anything, he did most of the cleaning.* PHRASE: PHR with cl 10 You can add **or anything** to the end of a clause or sentence in order to refer vaguely to other things that are or may be similar to what has just been mentioned. [INFORMAL, SPOKEN] ❑ *Listen, if you talk to him or anything make sure you let us know, will you.* PHRASE [vagueness]

**any|time** /enitaɪm/ You use **anytime** to mean a point in time which is not fixed or set. ❑ *The college admits students anytime during the year... He can call me anytime.* ADV: ADV with v, oft ADV prep/cl

**any|way** /eniweɪ/ or **anyhow** ◆◆◇ 1 You use **anyway** or **anyhow** to indicate that a statement explains or supports a previous point. ❑ *I'm certain David's told you his business troubles. Anyway, it's no secret that he owes money... Mother certainly won't let him stay with her and anyhow he wouldn't.* ADV: ADV with cl = besides 2 You use **anyway** or **anyhow** to suggest that a statement is true or relevant in spite of other things that have been said. ❑ *I don't know why I settled on Aberdeen, but anyway I did... I wasn't qualified to apply for the job really but I got it anyhow.* ADV: ADV with cl 3 You use **anyway** or **anyhow** to correct or modify a statement, for example to limit it to what you definitely know to be true. ❑ *Mary Ann doesn't want to have children. Not right now, anyway.* ADV: cl/group ADV 4 You use **anyway** or **anyhow** to indicate that you are asking what the real situation is or what the real reason for something is. ❑ *What do you want from me, anyway?... Where the hell was Bud, anyhow?* ADV: cl ADV 5 You use **anyway** or **anyhow** to indicate that you are missing out some details in a story and are passing on to the next main point or event. ❑ *I was told to go to Reading for this interview. It was a very amusing affair. Anyhow, I got the job.* ADV: ADV with cl = well 6 You use **anyway** or **anyhow** to change the topic or return to a previous topic. ❑ *'I've got a terrible cold.' — 'Have you? Oh dear. Anyway, so you're not going to go away this weekend?'* ADV: ADV cl = well 7 You use **anyway** or **anyhow** to indicate that you want to end the conversation. ❑ *'Anyway, I'd better let you have your dinner. Give our love to Francis. Bye.'* ADV: ADV cl = well

**any|ways** /eniweɪz/ **Anyways** is a non-standard form of **anyway**. [AM, SPOKEN] ADV

**any|where** /eniʰweəʳ/ ◆◇◇ 1 You use **anywhere** in statements with negative meaning to indicate that a place does not exist. ❑ *I haven't got anywhere to live... There had never been such a beautiful woman anywhere in the world.* ADV: ADV after v, be ADV, oft ADV cl/group 2 You use **anywhere** in questions and conditional clauses to ask or talk about a place without saying exactly where you mean. ❑ *Did you try to get help from anywhere?... If she wanted to go anywhere at all she had to wait for her father to drive her.* ADV: ADV after v, be ADV, from ADV, oft ADV cl/group 3 You use **anywhere** before words that indicate the kind of place you are talking about. ❑ *He'll meet you anywhere you want... Let us know if you come across anywhere that has something special to offer.* ADV: ADV cl/group = anyplace 4 You use **anywhere** to refer to a place when you are emphasizing that it could be any of a large number of places. ❑ *Rachel would have known Julia Stone anywhere. ...jokes that are so funny they always work anywhere.* ADV: ADV after v, be ADV [emphasis] 5 When you do not want to be exact, you use **anywhere** to refer to a particular range of things. ❑ *His shoes cost anywhere from $200 up... My visits lasted anywhere from three weeks to two months.* ADV: ADV from/to n, ADV between pl-n, ADV up 6 You use **anywhere** in expressions such as **anywhere near** and **anywhere close to** to emphasize a statement that you are making. ❑ *There weren't anywhere near enough empty boxes.* ADV: ADV adj/adv [emphasis] 7 If you say that someone or something **is not getting anywhere** or **is not going anywhere**, you mean that they are not making progress or achieving a satisfactory result. ❑ *The conversation did not seem to be getting anywhere.* PHRASE: V inflects

**AOB** /eɪ oʊ biː/ **AOB** is a heading on an agenda for a meeting, to show that any topics not listed separately can be discussed at this point, usually the end. **AOB** is an abbreviation for 'any other business'.

**aor|ta** /eɪɔːʳtə/ **(aortas)** The **aorta** is the main artery through which blood leaves your heart before it flows through the rest of your body. N-COUNT

**apace** /əpeɪs/ If something develops or continues **apace**, it is developing or continuing quickly. [FORMAL] ADV: ADV after v = speedily, swiftly

**apart**
① POSITIONS AND STATES
② INDICATING EXCEPTIONS AND FOCUSING

① **apart** /əpɑːʳt/ ◆◆◇

In addition to the uses shown below, **apart** is used in phrasal verbs such as 'grow apart' and 'take apart'.

1 When people or things are **apart**, they are some distance from each other. ❑ *He was standing a bit apart from the rest of us, watching us... Ray and sister Renee lived just 25 miles apart from each other. ...regions that were too far apart to have any way of knowing about each other.* ADV: ADV after v, oft ADV from n 2 If two people or things move **apart** or are pulled **apart**, they move away from each other. ❑ *John and Isabelle moved apart, back into the sun... He tried in vain to keep the two dogs apart before the neighbour intervened.* ADV: ADV after v 3 If two people are **apart**, they are no longer living together or spending time together, either permanently or just for a short time. ❑ *It was the first time Jane and I had been apart for more than a few days... Mum and Dad live apart.* ADV: be ADV, ADV after v 4 If you take something **apart**, you separate it into the pieces that it is made of. If it comes or falls **apart**, its parts separate from each other. ❑ *When the clock stopped he took it apart to find out what was wrong... Many school buildings are unsafe, and some are falling apart.* ADV: ADV after v 5 If something such as an organization or relationship falls **apart**, or if something tears it **apart**, it can no longer continue because it has serious difficulties. ❑ *Any manager knows that his company will start falling apart if his attention wanders.* ADV: ADV after v 6 If something sets someone or something **apart**, it makes them different from other people or things. ❑ *What really sets Mr Thaksin apart is that he comes from northern Thailand.* ADV: ADV after v, n ADV 7 If people or groups are a long way **apart** on a particular topic or issue, they have completely different views and disagree about it. ❑ *Their concept of a performance and our concept were miles apart.* ADJ: v-link amount ADJ, oft ADJ on n 8 If you can't **tell** two people or things **apart**, they look exactly the same to you. ❑ *I can still only tell Mark and Dave apart by the colour of their shoes!* PHRASE: V inflects, usu with brd-neg

② **apart** /əpɑːʳt/ ◆◇◇ 1 You use **apart from** when you are making an exception to a general statement. ❑ *She was the only British competitor apart from Richard Meade.* PREP-PHRASE 2 You use **apart** when you are making an exception to a general statement. ❑ *This was, New York apart, the first American city I had ever been in where people actually lived downtown.* ADV: n ADV = excepted 3 You use **apart from** to indicate that you are aware of one aspect of a situation, but that you are going to focus on another aspect. ❑ *Illiteracy threatens Britain's industrial performance. But, quite apart from that, the individual who can't read or write is unlikely to get a job.* PREP-PHRASE

**apart|heid** /əpɑːʳthaɪt/ **Apartheid** was a political system in South Africa in which people were divided into racial groups and kept apart by law. ❑ *He praised her role in the struggle against apartheid. ...the anti-apartheid movement.* N-UNCOUNT

**apart|ment** /əpɑːʳtmənt/ **(apartments)** An **apartment** is a set of rooms for living in, usually on one floor of a large building. [mainly AM] → See picture on page 1706. ❑ *...bleak cities of concrete apartment blocks.* ◆◇◇ N-COUNT

☑ in BRIT, use **flat**

**apart|ment build|ing** **(apartment buildings)** or **apartment house** An **apartment building** or **apartment house** is a tall building which contains different apartments on different floors. [AM] → See picture on page 1706. N-COUNT

☑ in BRIT, use **block of flats**

**apa|thet|ic** /æpəθetɪk/ If you describe someone as **apathetic**, you are criticizing them because they do not seem to be interested in or enthusiastic about doing anything. ❑ *Even the most apathetic students are beginning to sit up and listen.* ADJ [disapproval]

**apa|thy** /æpəθi/ You can use **apathy** to talk about someone's state of mind if you are criticizing them because they do not seem to be interested in or enthusiastic about anything. N-UNCOUNT [disapproval]

**ape** /eɪp/ **(apes, aping, aped)** [1] **Apes** are chimpanzees, gorillas, and other animals in the same family. N-COUNT [2] If you **ape** someone's speech or behaviour, you imitate it. ❑ *Modelling yourself on someone is not the same as aping all they say or do.* VERB = copy, imitate V n

**ape|ri|tif** /æperɪtiːf/ **(aperitifs)** An **aperitif** is an alcoholic drink that you have before a meal. N-COUNT

**ap|er|ture** /æpəʳtʃəʳ/ **(apertures)** [1] An **aperture** is a narrow hole or gap. [FORMAL] ❑ *Through the aperture he could see daylight.* N-COUNT [2] In photography, the **aperture** of a camera is the size of the hole through which light passes to reach the film. N-COUNT

**apex** /eɪpeks/ **(apexes)** [1] **The apex of** an organization or system is the highest and most important position in it. ❑ *At the apex of the party was its central committee.* N-SING: usu the N of n = top [2] **The apex of** something is its pointed top or end. ❑ *...the apex of the pyramid.* N-COUNT: usu sing, oft the N of n

**Apex** also **APEX.** An **Apex** or an **Apex ticket** is a ticket for a journey by air or rail which costs less than the standard ticket, but which you have to book a specified period in advance. ❑ *The Apex fare is £195 return.* N-SING: usu N n

**apha|sia** /əfeɪziə, -ʒə/ **Aphasia** is a mental condition in which people are often unable to remember simple words or communicate. [MEDICAL] N-UNCOUNT

**aphid** /eɪfɪd/ **(aphids)** **Aphids** are very small insects which live on plants and suck their juices. N-COUNT: usu pl

**apho|rism** /æfərɪzəm/ **(aphorisms)** An **aphorism** is a short witty sentence which expresses a general truth or comment. [FORMAL] N-COUNT = witticism

**aph|ro|disi|ac** /æfrədɪziæk/ **(aphrodisiacs)** An **aphrodisiac** is a food, drink, or drug which is said to make people want to have sex. ❑ *Asparagus is reputed to be an aphrodisiac.* N-COUNT

**apiece** /əpiːs/ [1] If people have a particular number of things **apiece**, they have that number each. ❑ *He and I had two fish apiece.* ADV: amount ADV = each [2] If a number of similar things are for sale at a certain price **apiece**, that is the price for each one of them. ❑ *Entire roast chickens were sixty cents apiece.* ADV: amount ADV = each

**aplen|ty** /əplenti/ If you have something **aplenty**, you have a lot of it. [LITERARY] ❑ *There were problems aplenty at work.* ADV: n ADV

**aplomb** /əplɒm/ If you do something **with aplomb**, you do it with confidence in a relaxed way. [FORMAL] N-UNCOUNT: usu with N = poise

**apoca|lypse** /əpɒkəlɪps/ **The apocalypse** is the total destruction and end of the world. N-SING: usu the N

**apoca|lyp|tic** /əpɒkəlɪptɪk/ [1] **Apocalyptic** means relating to the total destruction of something, especially of the world. ❑ *...the reformer's apocalyptic warnings that the nation was running out of natural resources.* ADJ: usu ADJ n [2] **Apocalyptic** means relating to or involving predictions about future disasters and the destruction of the world. ❑ *...a gloomy and apocalyptic vision of a world hastening towards ruin.* ADJ: usu ADJ n

**apoc|ry|phal** /əpɒkrɪfəl/ An **apocryphal** story is one which is probably not true or did not happen, but which may give a true picture of someone or something. ADJ

**apo|gee** /æpədʒiː/ The **apogee** of something such as a culture or a business is its highest or its greatest point. [FORMAL] N-SING: with supp = peak

**apo|liti|cal** /eɪpəlɪtɪkəl/ [1] Someone who is **apolitical** is not interested in politics. ❑ *As a musician, you cannot be apolitical.* ADJ ≠ political [2] If you describe an organization or an activity as **apolitical**, you mean that it is not linked to a particular political party. ❑ *...the normally apolitical European Commission.* ADJ

**apolo|get|ic** /əpɒlədʒetɪk/ If you are **apologetic**, you show or say that you are sorry for causing trouble for someone, for hurting them, or for disappointing them. ❑ *The hospital staff were very apologetic but that couldn't really compensate... 'I don't follow football,' she said with an apologetic smile.* ADJ

♦ **apolo|geti|cal|ly** /əpɒlədʒetɪkli/ *'It's of no great literary merit,' he said, almost apologetically.* ADV: ADV with v

**apo|lo|gia** /æpəloʊdʒiə/ **(apologias)** An **apologia** is a statement in which you defend something that you strongly believe in, for example a way of life, a person's behaviour, or a philosophy. [FORMAL] ❑ *The left have seen the work as an apologia for privilege and property.* N-COUNT: usu sing

**apolo|gise** /əpɒlədʒaɪz/ → see **apologize**.

**apolo|gist** /əpɒlədʒɪst/ **(apologists)** An **apologist** is a person who writes or speaks in defence of a belief, a cause, or a person's life. [FORMAL] ❑ *'I am no apologist for Hitler,' observed Pyat.* N-COUNT

**apolo|gize** /əpɒlədʒaɪz/ **(apologizes, apologizing, apologized)**

☑ in BRIT, also use **apologise**

When you **apologize to** someone, you say that you are sorry that you have hurt them or caused trouble for them. You can say **'I apologize'** as a formal way of saying sorry. ❑ *I apologize for being late... Costello later apologized, saying he'd been annoyed by the man... He apologized to the people who had been affected.* VERB V for n/-ing V V to n Also V with quote

**apol|ogy** /əpɒlədʒi/ **(apologies)** [1] An **apology** is something that you say or write in order to tell someone that you are sorry that you have hurt them or caused trouble for them. ❑ *We received a letter of apology... He made a public apology for the team's performance.* N-VAR [2] If you offer or make your **apologies**, you apologize. [FORMAL] ❑ *When Mary finally appeared, she made her apologies to Mrs Madrigal.* N-PLURAL: usu poss N [3] If you say that you **make no apologies for** what you have done, you are emphasizing that you feel that you have done nothing wrong. ❑ *Union officials made no apologies for the threatened chaos.* PHRASE: V inflects

**apo|plec|tic** /æpəplektɪk/ If someone is **apoplectic**, they are extremely angry about something. [FORMAL] ADJ = furious, incensed

**apo|plexy** /æpəpleksi/ [1] **Apoplexy** is a stroke. [OLD-FASHIONED] N-UNCOUNT [2] **Apoplexy** is extreme anger. [FORMAL] ❑ *He has already caused apoplexy with his books on class and on war.* N-UNCOUNT

**apos|ta|sy** /əpɒstəsi/ If someone is accused of **apostasy**, they are accused of abandoning their religious faith, political loyalties, or principles. [FORMAL] ❑ *...a charge of apostasy.* N-UNCOUNT

**apos|tate** /əpɒsteɪt/ **(apostates)** An **apostate** is someone who has abandoned their religious faith, political loyalties, or principles. [FORMAL] N-COUNT = renegade, defector

**apos|tle** /əpɒsəl/ **(apostles)** [1] The **apostles** were the followers of Jesus Christ who went from place to place telling people about him and trying N-COUNT = disciple to persuade them to become Christians. [2] An **apostle of** a particular philosophy, policy, or cause is someone who strongly believes in it and works hard to promote it. ❑ *Her mother was a dedicated apostle of healthy eating.* [N-COUNT: usu N *of* n = *proponent*]

**Ap|os|tol|ic** /æpɒstɒlɪk/ [1] **Apostolic** means belonging or relating to a Christian religious leader, especially the Pope. ❑ *He was appointed Apostolic Administrator of Minsk by Pope John Paul II.* [ADJ] [2] **Apostolic** means belonging or relating to the early followers of Christ and to their teaching. ❑ *He saw his vocation as one of prayer and apostolic work.* [ADJ]

**apos|tro|phe** /əpɒstrəfi/ **(apostrophes)** An **apostrophe** is the mark ʼ when it is written to indicate that one or more letters have been left out of a word, as in 'isn't' and 'we'll'. It is also added to nouns to form possessives, as in 'Mike's car'. [N-COUNT]

**apoth|ecary** /əpɒθɪkri, AM -keri/ **(apothecaries)** An **apothecary** was a person who prepared medicines for people. [OLD-FASHIONED] [N-COUNT]

**apoth|eo|sis** /əpɒθioʊsɪs/ [1] If something is **the apotheosis of** something else, it is an ideal or typical example of it. [FORMAL] ❑ *The Oriental in Bangkok is the apotheosis of the grand hotel.* [N-SING: oft N *of* n = *epitome*] [2] If you describe an event or a time as someone's **apotheosis**, you mean that it was the high point in their career or their life. [FORMAL] ❑ *That night was Richard's apotheosis.* [N-SING: with poss]

**ap|pal** /əpɔːl/ **(appals, appalling, appalled)**

✔ in AM, use **appall**

If something **appals** you, it disgusts you because it seems so bad or unpleasant. ❑ *His ignorance appals me.* [VERB = *horrify* V n]

**ap|palled** /əpɔːld/ If you are **appalled** by something, you are shocked or disgusted because it is so bad or unpleasant. ❑ *We are all, of course, appalled that such items are still on sale in the shops.* [ADJ: usu v-link ADJ, usu ADJ *by/at* n]

**ap|pal|ling** /əpɔːlɪŋ/ [1] Something that is **appalling** is so bad or unpleasant that it shocks you. ❑ *They have been living under the most appalling conditions for two months.* [ADJ = *dreadful*] ♦ **ap|pal|ling|ly** *He says that he understands why they behaved so appallingly.* [ADV] [2] You can use **appalling** to emphasize that something is very great or severe. ❑ *I developed an appalling headache.* [ADJ emphasis] ♦ **ap|pal|ling|ly** *It's been an appallingly busy morning.* [ADV] [3] → See also **appal**.

**ap|pa|rat|chik** /æpərætʃɪk/ **(apparatchiks)** An **apparatchik** is someone who works for a government or a political party and who always obeys orders. [FORMAL] [N-COUNT disapproval]

**ap|pa|rat|us** /æpəreɪtəs, -ræt-/ **(apparatuses)** [1] The **apparatus** of an organization or system is its structure and method of operation. ❑ *For many years, the country had been buried under the apparatus of the regime.* [N-VAR: with supp] [2] **Apparatus** is the equipment, such as tools and machines, which is used to do a particular job or activity. ❑ *One of the boys had to be rescued by firemen wearing breathing apparatus.* [N-VAR: oft supp N]

**ap|par|el** /əpærəl/ **Apparel** means clothes, especially formal clothes worn on an important occasion. [mainly AM, FORMAL] ❑ *Women's apparel is offered in petite, regular, and tall models.* [N-UNCOUNT = *clothing*]

**ap|par|ent** /əpærənt/ [1] An **apparent** situation, quality, or feeling seems to exist, although you cannot be certain that it does exist. ❑ *I was a bit depressed by our apparent lack of progress.* [◆◇◇ ADJ: ADJ n] [2] If something is **apparent** to you, it is clear and obvious to you. ❑ *It has been apparent that in other areas standards have held up well.* [ADJ: v-link ADJ, oft *it* v-link ADJ that] [3] If you say that something happens **for no apparent reason**, you cannot understand why it happens. ❑ *The person may become dizzy for no apparent reason.* [PHRASE]

**ap|par|ent|ly** /əpærəntli/ [1] You use **apparently** to indicate that the information you are giving is something that you have heard, but you are not certain that it is true. ❑ *Oil prices fell this week to their lowest level in fourteen months, apparently because of over-production.* [◆◆◇ ADV: ADV with cl/group, ADV before v] [2] You use **apparently** to refer to something that seems to be true, although you are not sure whether it is or not. ❑ *The recent deterioration has been caused by an apparently endless recession.* [vagueness ADV: ADV with cl/group, ADV before v]

**ap|pa|ri|tion** /æpərɪʃən/ **(apparitions)** An **apparition** is someone you see or think you see but who is not really there as a physical being. [FORMAL] [N-COUNT]

**ap|peal** /əpiːl/ **(appeals, appealing, appealed)** ◆◆◇ [1] If you **appeal to** someone **to** do something, you make a serious and urgent request to them. ❑ *The Prime Minister appealed to young people to use their vote... He will appeal to the state for an extension of unemployment benefits... The United Nations has appealed for help from the international community.* [VERB V *to/for* n to-inf, V *to* n *for* n, V *for* n] [2] An **appeal** is a serious and urgent request. ❑ *Romania's government issued a last-minute appeal to him to call off his trip.* [N-COUNT: oft N *for/to* n, N to-inf] [3] An **appeal** is an attempt to raise money for a charity or for a good cause. ❑ *...an appeal to save a library containing priceless manuscripts.* [N-COUNT: oft N to-inf, N *for* n] [4] If you **appeal to** someone in authority against a decision, you formally ask them to change it. In British English, you **appeal against** something. In American English, you **appeal** something. ❑ *He said they would appeal against the decision... We intend to appeal the verdict... Maguire has appealed to the Supreme Court to stop her extradition.* [VERB V *against* n, V n, V *to* n to-inf] [5] An **appeal** is a formal request for a decision to be changed. ❑ *Heath's appeal against the sentence was later successful... The jury agreed with her, but she lost the case on appeal.* → See also **Court of Appeal**. [N-VAR] [6] If something **appeals to** you, you find it attractive or interesting. ❑ *On the other hand, the idea appealed to him.* [VERB V *to* n] [7] The **appeal** of something is a quality that it has which people find attractive or interesting. ❑ *Its new title was meant to give the party greater public appeal.* → See also **sex appeal**. [N-UNCOUNT: with supp = *attraction*] [8] → See also **appealing**.

**ap|peal court** **(appeal courts)** An **appeal court** is the same as a **Court of Appeal**. [N-COUNT]

**ap|peal|ing** /əpiːlɪŋ/ [1] Someone or something that is **appealing** is pleasing and attractive. ❑ *There was a sense of humour to what he did that I found very appealing.* [ADJ = *attractive*] [2] An **appealing** expression or tone of voice indicates to someone that you want help, advice, or approval. ❑ *She gave him a soft appealing look that would have melted solid ice.* [ADJ] [3] → See also **appeal**.

**ap|peal tri|bu|nal** **(appeal tribunals)** An **appeal tribunal** is a special court or committee that is formed to reconsider a decision made by another court or committee. [N-COUNT]

**ap|pear** /əpɪəʳ/ **(appears, appearing, appeared)** ◆◆◆ [1] If you say that something **appears to** be the way you describe it, you are reporting what you believe or what you have been told, though you cannot be sure it is true. ❑ *There appears to be increasing support for the leadership to take a more aggressive stance... The aircraft appears to have crashed near Katmandu... It appears that some missiles have been moved... It appears unlikely that the UN would consider making such a move... The presidency is beginning to appear a political irrelevance... He appeared willing to reach an agreement.* [V-LINK: no cont vagueness = *seem*; *there* V to-inf, V to-inf, *it* V that, *it* V adj that/to-inf, V n, V adj] [2] If someone or something **appears** to have a particular quality or characteristic, they give the impression of having that quality or characteristic. ❑ *She did her best to appear more self-assured than she felt... He is anxious to appear a gentleman... Under stress these people will appear to be superficial, over-eager and manipulative.* [V-LINK: no cont = *seem*; V adj, V n, V to-inf] [3] When someone or something **appears**, they move into a position where you can see them. ❑ *A woman appeared at the far end of the street.* [VERB V] [4] When something new **appears**, it begins to exist or reaches a stage of development where its existence can be noticed. ❑ *...small white flowers which appear in early summer... Slogans have appeared on walls around the city.* [VERB V, V] [5] When some- [VERB] thing such as a book **appears**, it is published or becomes available for people to buy. ❑ *...a poem which appeared in his last collection of verse.* V

6 When someone **appears in** something such as a play, a show, or a television programme, they take part in it. ❑ *Jill Bennett became John Osborne's fourth wife, and appeared in several of his plays... Student leaders appeared on television to ask for calm.* VERB V in n V on/at n

7 When someone **appears before** a court of law or **before** an official committee, they go there in order to answer charges or to give information as a witness. ❑ *Two other executives appeared at Worthing Magistrates' Court charged with tax fraud... The American will appear before members of the disciplinary committee at Portman Square.* VERB V in/at n V before n

**ap|pear|ance** /əpɪərəns/ **(appearances)** ◆◆◇ 1 When someone makes an **appearance** at a public event or in a broadcast, they take part in it. ❑ *It was the president's second public appearance to date... Keegan made 68 appearances in two seasons for Southampton, scoring 37 times.* N-COUNT: usu with supp, oft supp N 2 Someone's or something's **appearance** is the way that they look. ❑ *She used to be so fussy about her appearance.* N-SING: with supp 3 The **appearance of** someone or something in a place is their arrival there, especially when it is unexpected. ❑ *The sudden appearance of a few bags of rice could start a riot.* N-SING: with supp, oft N of n 4 The **appearance of** something new is its coming into existence or use. ❑ *Fears are growing of a cholera outbreak following the appearance of a number of cases in the city.* N-SING: with supp, oft N of n 5 If something has the **appearance of** a quality, it seems to have that quality. ❑ *We tried to meet both children's needs without the appearance of favoritism or unfairness.* N-SING: with supp

PHRASES 6 If something is true **to all appearances**, **from all appearances**, or **by all appearances**, it seems from what you observe or know about it that it is true. ❑ *He was a small and to all appearances an unassuming man.* PHRASE: PHR with cl/group 7 If you **keep up appearances**, you try to behave and dress in a way that people expect of you, even if you can no longer afford it. ❑ *His parents' obsession with keeping up appearances haunted his childhood.* PHRASE: V inflects 8 If you **put in an appearance** at an event, you go to it for a short time although you may not really want to, but do not stay. PHRASE: V inflects = show your face

**ap|pear|ance mon|ey** **Appearance money** is money paid to a famous person such as a sports star or film star for taking part in a public event. N-UNCOUNT

**ap|pease** /əpiːz/ **(appeases, appeasing, appeased)** If you try to **appease** someone, you try to stop them from being angry by giving them what they want. ❑ *Gandhi was accused by some of trying to appease both factions of the electorate.* VERB disapproval = placate V n

**ap|pease|ment** /əpiːzmənt/ **Appeasement** means giving people what they want to prevent them from harming you or being angry with you. [FORMAL] N-UNCOUNT disapproval

**ap|pel|lant** /əpelənt/ **(appellants)** An **appellant** is someone who is appealing against a court's decision after they have been judged guilty of a crime. [LEGAL] ❑ *The Court of Appeal upheld the appellants' convictions.* N-COUNT

**ap|pel|late court** /əpelɪt kɔːʳt/ **(appellate courts)** In the United States, an **appellate court** is a special court where people who have been convicted of a crime can appeal against their conviction. [AM] N-COUNT

✔ in BRIT, use **Court of Appeal**

**ap|pel|la|tion** /æpəleɪʃᵊn/ **(appellations)** An **appellation** is a name or title that a person, place, or thing is given. [FORMAL] ❑ *He earned the appellation 'rebel priest.'* N-COUNT = epithet

**ap|pend** /əpend/ **(appends, appending, appended)** When you **append** something **to** something else, especially a piece of writing, you attach it or add it to the end of it. [FORMAL] ❑ *Violet appended a note at the end of the letter... It was a relief that his real name hadn't been appended to the manuscript.* VERB V n be V-ed to n

**ap|pend|age** /əpendɪdʒ/ **(appendages)** An **appendage** is something that is joined to or connected with something larger or more important. [FORMAL] ❑ *...the growing demand in Wales for recognition that it was not just an appendage to England.* N-COUNT: oft N of/to n

**ap|pen|di|ces** /əpendɪsiːz/ **Appendices** is a plural form of **appendix**. [mainly BRIT]

**ap|pen|di|ci|tis** /əpendɪsaɪtɪs/ **Appendicitis** is an illness in which a person's appendix is infected and painful. N-UNCOUNT

**ap|pen|dix** /əpendɪks/ **(appendixes)**

✔ In British English, the plural form **appendices** /əpendɪsiːz/ is usually used for meaning 2.

1 Your **appendix** is a small closed tube inside your body which is attached to your digestive system. ❑ *...a burst appendix.* N-COUNT 2 An **appendix to** a book is extra information that is placed after the end of the main text. N-COUNT

**ap|pe|tite** /æpɪtaɪt/ **(appetites)** 1 Your **appetite** is your desire to eat. ❑ *He has a healthy appetite... Symptoms are a slight fever, headache and loss of appetite.* N-VAR 2 Someone's **appetite for** something is their strong desire for it. ❑ *...Americans' growing appetite for scandal.* N-COUNT: oft N for n

**ap|pe|tiz|er** /æpɪtaɪzəʳ/ **(appetizers)**

✔ in BRIT, also use **appetiser**

An **appetizer** is the first course of a meal. It consists of a small amount of food. N-COUNT

**ap|pe|tiz|ing** /æpɪtaɪzɪŋ/

✔ in BRIT, also use **appetising**

**Appetizing** food looks and smells good, so that you want to eat it. ❑ *...the appetising smell of freshly baked bread.* ADJ

**ap|plaud** /əplɔːd/ **(applauds, applauding, applauded)** 1 When a group of people **applaud**, they clap their hands in order to show approval, for example when they have enjoyed a play or concert. ❑ *The audience laughed and applauded... Every person stood to applaud his unforgettable act of courage.* VERB V V n 2 When an attitude or action **is applauded**, people praise it. ❑ *He should be applauded for his courage... This last move can only be applauded... She applauds the fact that they are promoting new ideas.* VERB be V-ed for n be V-ed V n

**ap|plause** /əplɔːz/ **Applause** is the noise made by a group of people clapping their hands to show approval. ❑ *They greeted him with thunderous applause. ...a round of applause.* N-UNCOUNT

**ap|ple** /æpᵊl/ **(apples)** ◆◇◇ 1 An **apple** is a round fruit with smooth green, yellow, or red skin and firm white flesh. ➔ See picture on page 1711. ❑ *I want an apple. ...his ongoing search for the finest varieties of apple. ...a large garden with apple trees in it.* ➔ See also **Adam's apple**, **Big Apple**, **crab apple**. N-VAR 2 If you say that someone is **the apple of** your **eye**, you mean that they are very important to you and you are extremely fond of them. ❑ *Penny's only son was the apple of her eye.* PHRASE: usu v-link PHR

**apple|cart** /æpᵊlkɑːʳt/ If you **upset the applecart**, you do something which causes a plan, system, or arrangement to go wrong. ❑ *They may also be friends of the chairman, so they are reluctant to upset the applecart.* PHRASE: V inflects

**ap|ple pie** **(apple pies)** 1 An **apple pie** is a kind of pie made with apples. N-COUNT

PHRASES 2 If a room or a desk is **in apple pie order**, it is neat and tidy, and everything is where it should be. ❑ *They found everything in apple-pie order.* PHRASE: v-link PHR 3 If you say that something is **as American as apple pie**, you mean that it is typically American. ❑ *Jeans are as American as apple pie.* PHRASE: v-link PHR

**ap|ple sauce** also **applesauce**. **Apple sauce** is a type of sauce made from puréed cooked apples. N-UNCOUNT

**ap|plet** /æplɪt/ **(applets)** An **applet** is a computer program which is contained within a page on the World Wide Web, and which transfers itself to your computer and runs automatically while you are looking at that Web page. [COMPUTING] N-COUNT

**ap|pli|ance** /əplaɪəns/ **(appliances)** [1] An **appliance** is a device or machine in your home that you use to do a job such as cleaning or cooking. Appliances are often electrical. [FORMAL] ❑ *He could also learn to use the vacuum cleaner, the washing machine and other household appliances.* N-COUNT [2] The **appliance** of a skill or of knowledge is its use for a particular purpose. ❑ *These advances were the result of the intellectual appliance of science.* N-SING: usu N *of* n

**ap|pli|cable** /æplɪkəbᵊl, əplɪkə-/ Something that is **applicable to** a particular situation is relevant to it or can be applied to it. ❑ *Appraisal has traditionally been seen as most applicable to those in management and supervisory positions.* ADJ: usu v-link ADJ, oft ADJ *to* n = *relevant*

**ap|pli|cant** /æplɪkənt/ **(applicants)** An **applicant for** something such as a job or a place at a college is someone who makes a formal written request to be given it. N-COUNT

**ap|pli|ca|tion** /æplɪkeɪʃᵊn/ **(applications)** ◆◇◇ [1] An **application for** something such as a job or membership of an organization is a formal written request for it. ❑ *His application for membership of the organisation was rejected... Tickets are available on application.* N-COUNT: usu with supp, oft N *for* n, N to-inf, also *on/upon* N [2] The **application of** a rule or piece of knowledge is the use of it in a particular situation. ❑ *Students learned the practical application of the theory they had learned in the classroom.* N-VAR: oft N *of/to* n [3] In computing, an **application** is a piece of software designed to carry out a particular task. N-COUNT [4] **Application** is hard work and concentration on what you are doing over a period of time. ❑ *...his immense talent, boundless energy and unremitting application.* N-UNCOUNT = *diligence* [5] The **application of** something to a surface is the act or process of putting it on or rubbing it into the surface. ❑ *With repeated applications of weedkiller, the weeds were overcome.* N-VAR: oft N *of* n

**ap|pli|ca|tor** /æplɪkeɪtəʳ/ **(applicators)** An **applicator** is a device that you use to put something somewhere when you do not want to touch it or do it with your hands. N-COUNT

**ap|plied** /əplaɪd/ An **applied** subject of study has a practical use, rather than being concerned only with theory. ❑ *...Applied Physics. ...plans to put more money into applied research.* ADJ: ADJ n ≠ *pure*

**ap|pli|que** /əpliːkeɪ, AM æplɪkeɪ/ also **appliqué.** **Applique** is the craft of sewing fabric shapes onto larger pieces of cloth. You can also use applique to refer to things you make using this craft. N-UNCOUNT

**ap|pli|qued** /əpliːkeɪd, AM æplɪkeɪd/ also **appliquéd.** **Appliqued** shapes or fabric are formed from pieces of fabric which are stitched on to clothes or larger pieces of cloth. ❑ *...a magnificent appliqued bedspread.* ADJ

**ap|ply** /əplaɪ/ **(applies, applying, applied)** ◆◆◇ [1] If you **apply for** something such as a job or membership of an organization, you write a letter or fill in a form in order to ask formally for it. ❑ *I am continuing to apply for jobs... They may apply to join the organization.* VERB V *for* n V to-inf [2] If you **apply yourself to** something or **apply** your mind **to** something, you concentrate hard on doing it or on thinking about it. ❑ *Faulks has applied himself to this task with considerable energy... In spare moments he applied his mind to how rockets could be used to make money.* VERB V pron-refl *to* n/-ing V n *to* n/wh Also V pron-refl [3] If something such as a rule or a remark **applies to** a person or in a situation, it is relevant to the person or the situation. ❑ *The convention does not apply to us... The rule applies where a person owns stock in a corporation.* VERB: no cont V *to* n V [4] If you **apply** something such as a rule, system, or skill, you use it in a situation or activity. ❑ *The Government appears to be applying the same principle... His project is concerned with applying the technology to practical business problems.* VERB V n V n *to* n [5] A name that **is applied to** someone or something is used to refer to them. ❑ *Connell said a new medical term should be applied to Berg's actions. He calls it 'medicide'.* VERB *be* V-ed *to* n [6] If you **apply** something **to** a surface, you put it on or rub it into the surface. ❑ *The right thing would be to apply direct pressure to the wound... Applying the dye can be messy, particularly on long hair.* VERB V n *to* n V n [7] → See also **applied**.

**ap|point** /əpɔɪnt/ **(appoints, appointing, appointed)** ◆◇◇ If you **appoint** someone **to** a job or official position, you formally choose them for it. ❑ *It made sense to appoint a banker to this job... The commission appointed a special investigator to conduct its own inquiry... The Prime Minister has appointed a civilian as defence minister... She was appointed a US delegate to the United Nations.* → See also **appointed**. VERB = *assign* V n *to* n V n to-inf V n *as* n *be* V-ed n Also V n n, V n

**ap|point|ed** /əpɔɪntɪd/ If something happens at the **appointed** time, it happens at the time that was decided in advance. [FORMAL] ADJ: ADJ n

**-appointed** /-əpɔɪntɪd/ **-appointed** combines with adverbs to form adjectives such as **well-appointed** that describe a building or room that is equipped or furnished in the way that is mentioned. [WRITTEN] ❑ *Sloan looked round the well-appointed kitchen.* → See also **self-appointed**. COMB in ADJ

**ap|poin|tee** /əpɔɪntiː/ **(appointees)** An **appointee** is someone who has been chosen for a particular job or position of responsibility. [FORMAL] ❑ *...Becket, a recent appointee to the Supreme Court.* N-COUNT

**ap|point|ment** /əpɔɪntmənt/ **(appointments)** ◆◇◇ [1] The **appointment** of a person **to** a particular job is the choice of that person to do it. ❑ *...his appointment as foreign minister in 1985.* N-VAR: usu with poss, oft N *to/as* n [2] An **appointment** is a job or position of responsibility. ❑ *Mr Fay is to take up an appointment as a researcher with the Royal Society.* N-COUNT = *post* [3] If you have an **appointment with** someone, you have arranged to see them at a particular time, usually in connection with their work or for a serious purpose. ❑ *She has an appointment with her accountant. ...a dental appointment.* N-COUNT: oft N *with* n, N to-inf [4] If something can be done **by appointment**, people can arrange in advance to do it at a particular time. ❑ *Viewing is by appointment only.* PHRASE

**ap|por|tion** /əpɔːʳʃᵊn/ **(apportions, apportioning, apportioned)** When you **apportion** something such as blame, you decide how much of it different people deserve or should be given. [FORMAL] ❑ *The experts are even-handed in apportioning blame among EU governments.* VERB V n prep

**ap|po|site** /æpəzɪt/ Something that is **apposite** is suitable for or appropriate to what is happening or being discussed. [FORMAL] ❑ *Recent events have made his central theme even more apposite.* ADJ = *relevant, apt*

**ap|po|si|tion** /æpəzɪʃᵊn/ If two noun groups referring to the same person or thing are **in apposition**, one is placed immediately after the other, with no conjunction joining them, as in 'Her father, Nigel, left home three months ago.' N-UNCOUNT: usu *in* N

**ap|prais|al** /əpreɪzᵊl/ **(appraisals)** [1] If you make an **appraisal of** something, you consider it carefully and form an opinion about it. ❑ *What is needed in such cases is a calm appraisal of the situation.* N-VAR: oft N *of* n = *evaluation* [2] **Appraisal** is the official or formal assessment of the strengths and weaknesses of someone or something. Appraisal often involves observation or some kind of testing. ❑ *Staff problems should be addressed through training and appraisals.* N-VAR: oft N *of* n = *evaluation*

**ap|praise** /əpreɪz/ **(appraises, appraising, appraised)** If you **appraise** something or someone, you consider them carefully and form an opinion about them. [FORMAL] ❑ *This prompted many employers to appraise their selection and recruitment policies.* VERB = *evaluate* V n

**ap|prais|er** /əpreɪzəʳ/ **(appraisers)** An **appraiser** is someone whose job is to estimate the cost or value of something such as property. [AM] N-COUNT

✔ in BRIT, use **valuer**

**ap|pre|ci|able** /əpriːʃəbəl/ An **appreciable** amount or effect is large enough to be important or clearly noticed. [FORMAL] ADJ: usu ADJ n = significant

**ap|pre|ci|ate** /əpriːʃieɪt/ **(appreciates, appreciating, appreciated)** ◆◇◇ 1 If you **appreciate** something, for example a piece of music or good food, you like it because you recognize its good qualities. ❑ *In time you'll appreciate the beauty and subtlety of this language.* VERB V n 2 If you **appreciate** a situation or problem, you understand it and know what it involves. ❑ *She never really appreciated the depth and bitterness of the Irish conflict... He appreciates that co-operation with the media is part of his professional duties.* VERB V n V that 3 If you **appreciate** something that someone has done for you or is going to do for you, you are grateful for it. ❑ *Peter stood by me when I most needed it. I'll always appreciate that... I'd appreciate it if you wouldn't mention it.* VERB V n V *it* if 4 If something that you own **appreciates** over a period of time, its value increases. ❑ *They don't have any confidence that houses will appreciate in value.* VERB ≠ depreciate V

**ap|pre|cia|tion** /əpriːʃieɪʃən/ **(appreciations)** 1 **Appreciation of** something is the recognition and enjoyment of its good qualities. ❑ *...an investigation into children's understanding and appreciation of art... Brian whistled in appreciation.* N-SING: also no det, oft N *of* n 2 Your **appreciation for** something that someone does for you is your gratitude for it. ❑ *He expressed his appreciation for what he called Saudi Arabia's moderate and realistic oil policies. ...the gifts presented to them in appreciation of their work.* N-SING: also no det, oft with poss, N *for* n = gratitude 3 An **appreciation of** a situation or problem is an understanding of what it involves. ❑ *They have a stronger appreciation of the importance of economic incentives.* N-SING: also no det, with supp, oft N *of* n = grasp 4 **Appreciation** in the value of something is an increase in its value over a period of time. ❑ *You have to take capital appreciation of the property into account.* N-UNCOUNT ≠ depreciation

**ap|pre|cia|tive** /əpriːʃətɪv/ 1 An **appreciative** reaction or comment shows the enjoyment that you are getting from something. ❑ *There is a murmur of appreciative laughter.* ADJ 2 If you are **appreciative of** something, you are grateful for it. ❑ *We have been very appreciative of their support.* ADJ: oft ADJ *of* n

**ap|pre|hend** /æprɪhend/ **(apprehends, apprehending, apprehended)** If the police **apprehend** someone, they catch them and arrest them. [FORMAL] ❑ *Police have not apprehended her killer.* VERB = catch V n

**ap|pre|hen|sion** /æprɪhenʃən/ **(apprehensions)** 1 **Apprehension** is a feeling of fear that something bad may happen. [FORMAL] ❑ *It reflects real anger and apprehension about the future... I tensed every muscle in my body in apprehension.* N-VAR = worry 2 The **apprehension of** someone who is thought to be a criminal is their capture or arrest by the police. [FORMAL] ❑ *...information leading to the apprehension of the alleged killer.* N-UNCOUNT: oft N *of* n

**ap|pre|hen|sive** /æprɪhensɪv/ Someone who is **apprehensive** is afraid that something bad may happen. ❑ *People are still terribly apprehensive about the future.* ADJ: usu v-link ADJ, oft ADJ *about* n/-ing

**ap|pren|tice** /əprentɪs/ **(apprentices, apprenticing, apprenticed)** 1 An **apprentice** is a young person who works for someone in order to learn their skill. ❑ *He left school at 15 and trained as an apprentice carpenter.* N-COUNT: oft N n 2 If a young person **is apprenticed to** someone, they go to work for them in order to learn their skill. ❑ *I was apprenticed to a builder when I was fourteen.* VERB: usu passive *be* V-ed *to* n

**ap|pren|tice|ship** /əprentɪsʃɪp/ **(apprenticeships)** Someone who has an **apprenticeship** works for a fixed period of time for a person who has a particular skill in order to learn the skill. **Apprenticeship** is the system of learning a skill like this. N-VAR

**ap|prise** /əpraɪz/ **(apprises, apprising, apprised)** When you **are apprised of** something, someone tells you about it. [FORMAL] ❑ *Have customers been fully apprised of the advantages?... We must apprise them of the dangers that may be involved.* VERB = notify *be* V-ed *of* n V n *of* n

**ap|proach** /əprəʊtʃ/ **(approaches, approaching, approached)** ◆◆◇ 1 When you **approach** something, you get closer to it. ❑ *He didn't approach the front door at once... When I approached, they grew silent... We turned to see the approaching car slow down.* VERB V n V V-ing ♦ **Approach** is also a noun. ❑ *At their approach the little boy ran away and hid. ...the approach of a low-flying helicopter.* N-COUNT: usu sing, with supp 2 An **approach to** a place is a road, path, or other route that leads to it. ❑ *The path serves as an approach to the boat house.* N-COUNT: usu N *to* n 3 If you **approach** someone **about** something, you speak to them about it for the first time, often making an offer or request. ❑ *When Chappel approached me about the job, my first reaction was of disbelief... He approached me to create and design the restaurant... Anna approached several builders and was fortunate to come across Eddie.* VERB: no cont V n prep V n to-inf V n ♦ **Approach** is also a noun. ❑ *There had already been approaches from buyers interested in the whole of the group.* N-COUNT: oft N *from/to* n 4 When you **approach** a task, problem, or situation in a particular way, you deal with it or think about it in that way. ❑ *The Bank has approached the issue in a practical way... Employers are interested in how you approach problems.* VERB = tackle, address V n prep/adv V n 5 Your **approach to** a task, problem, or situation is the way you deal with it or think about it. ❑ *We will be exploring different approaches to gathering information.* N-COUNT: usu with supp, oft N *to* -ing/n 6 As a future time or event **approaches**, it gradually gets nearer as time passes. ❑ *As autumn approached, the plants and colours in the garden changed. ...the approaching crisis.* VERB V V-ing ♦ **Approach** is also a noun. ❑ *...the festive spirit that permeated the house with the approach of Christmas.* N-SING: usu N *of* n 7 As you **approach** a future time or event, time passes so that you get gradually nearer to it. ❑ *We approach the end of the year with the economy slowing and little sign of cheer.* VERB V n 8 If something **approaches** a particular level or state, it almost reaches that level or state. ❑ *Oil prices have approached their highest level for almost ten years.* VERB V n

**ap|proach|able** /əprəʊtʃəbəl/ If you describe someone as **approachable**, you think that they are friendly and easy to talk to. ADJ [approval] ≠ aloof

**ap|pro|ba|tion** /æprəbeɪʃən/ **Approbation** is approval of something or agreement to it. [FORMAL] N-UNCOUNT = approval

**ap|pro|pri|ate** **(appropriates, appropriating, appropriated)** ◆◇◇

> The adjective is pronounced /əprəʊpriət/. The verb is pronounced /əprəʊprieɪt/.

1 Something that is **appropriate** is suitable or acceptable for a particular situation. ❑ *Dress neatly and attractively in an outfit appropriate to the job... The teacher can then take appropriate action.* ADJ: oft *it* v-link ADJ that/to-inf, ADJ *for/to* n ≠ inappropriate ♦ **ap|pro|pri|ate|ly** *It's entitled, appropriately enough, 'Art for the Nation'.* ADV 2 If someone **appropriates** something which does not belong to them, they take it, usually without the right to do so. [FORMAL] ❑ *Several other newspapers have appropriated the idea.* VERB = purloin V n

**ap|pro|pria|tion** /əprəʊprieɪʃən/ **(appropriations)** 1 An **appropriation** is an amount of money that a government or organization reserves for a particular purpose. [FORMAL] ❑ *The government raised defence appropriations by 12 per cent.* N-COUNT: usu with supp = allocation 2 **Appropriation of** something that belongs to someone else is the act of taking it, usually without having the right to do so. [FORMAL] ❑ *Other charges include fraud and illegal appropriation of land.* N-UNCOUNT: also *a* N, usu N *of* n

**ap|prov|al** /əpruːvəl/ **(approvals)** ◆◇◇ 1 If you win someone's **approval for** something that you ask for or suggest, they agree to it. ❑ *The chairman has also given his approval for an investigation into the case... The proposed modifications met with widespread approval.* N-UNCOUNT: usu with supp, oft with poss, N *for* n = sanction 2 **Approval** is a formal or official statement that something is acceptable. ❑ *The testing and approval of new drugs will be speeded up.* N-VAR 3 If someone or something has your **approval**, N-UNCOUNT:

you like and admire them. ❑ *His son had an obsessive drive to gain his father's approval.* — usu with poss

**ap|prove** /əpruːv/ **(approves, approving, approved)** ◆◆◇ [1] If you **approve of** an action, event, or suggestion, you like it or are pleased about it. ❑ *Not everyone approves of the festival.* [2] If you **approve of** someone or something, you like and admire them. ❑ *You've never approved of Henry, have you?* [3] If someone in a position of authority **approves** a plan or idea, they formally agree to it and say that it can happen. ❑ *The Russian Parliament has approved a program of radical economic reforms.* [4] → See also **approved**, **approving**.
— VERB: oft with brd-neg; V *of* n; VERB: oft with brd-neg; V *of* n; VERB = *sanction*; V n

**ap|proved** /əpruːvd/ An **approved** method or course of action is officially accepted as appropriate in a particular situation. ❑ *The approved method of cleaning is industrial sand-blasting.* — ADJ: usu ADJ n

**ap|proved school (approved schools)** In Britain in the past, an **approved school** was a boarding school where young people could be sent to stay if they had been found guilty of a crime. — N-COUNT

**ap|prov|ing** /əpruːvɪŋ/ An **approving** reaction or remark shows support for something, or satisfaction with it. ❑ *His mother leaned forward and gave him an approving look.* — ADJ: usu ADJ n ≠ *disapproving*

**approx.** **Approx.** is a written abbreviation for **approximately**. ❑ *Group Size: Approx. 12 to 16.*

**ap|proxi|mate (approximates, approximating, approximated)**

> ✓ The adjective is pronounced /əprɒksɪmət/. The verb is pronounced /əprɒksɪmeɪt/.

[1] An **approximate** number, time, or position is close to the correct number, time, or position, but is not exact. ❑ *The approximate cost varies from around £150 to £250... The times are approximate only.* ♦ **ap|proxi|mate|ly** *Approximately $150 million is to be spent on improvements.* [2] An idea or description that is **approximate** is not intended to be precise or accurate, but to give some indication of what something is like. ❑ *They did not have even an approximate idea what the Germans really wanted.* [3] If something **approximates to** something else, it is similar to it but is not exactly the same. ❑ *Something approximating to a fair outcome will be ensured... By about 6 weeks of age, most babies begin to show something approximating a day/night sleeping pattern.*
— ADJ ≠ *exact*; ADV: ADV num; ADJ; VERB; V *to* n; V n

**ap|proxi|ma|tion** /əprɒksɪmeɪʃ°n/ **(approximations)** [1] An **approximation** is a fact, object, or description which is similar to something else, but which is not exactly the same. ❑ *That is a fair approximation of the way in which the next boss is being chosen.* [2] An **approximation** is a number, calculation, or position that is close to a correct number, time, or position, but is not exact. ❑ *Clearly that's an approximation, but my guess is there'll be a reasonable balance.*
— N-COUNT: oft N *of/to* n; N-COUNT = *estimate*

**appt** **Appt** is a written abbreviation for **appointment**.

**Apr.** **Apr.** is a written abbreviation for **April**.

**apres-ski** /æpreɪ skiː/ also **après-ski**. **Apres-ski** is evening entertainment and social activities in places where people go skiing. — N-UNCOUNT: oft N n

**apri|cot** /eɪprɪkɒt/ **(apricots)** [1] An **apricot** is a small, soft, round fruit with yellowish-orange flesh and a stone inside. ❑ *...12 oz apricots, halved and stoned. ...apricot tart.* [2] **Apricot** is used to describe things that are yellowish-orange in colour. ❑ *The bridesmaids wore apricot and white organza.*
— N-VAR; COLOUR

**April** /eɪprɪl/ **(Aprils)** **April** is the fourth month of the year in the Western calendar. ❑ *The changes will be introduced in April... They were married on 7 April 1927 at Paddington Register Office.* — N-VAR

**April Fool (April Fools)** An **April Fool** is a trick that is played on April Fool's Day. — N-COUNT

**April Fool's Day** **April Fool's Day** is the 1st of April, the day on which people traditionally play tricks on each other. — N-UNCOUNT

**a prio|ri** /eɪ praɪɔːraɪ/ An **a priori** argument, reason, or probability is based on an assumed principle or fact, rather than on actual observed facts. ♦ **A priori** is also an adverb. ❑ *One assumes, a priori, that a parent would be better at dealing with problems.*
— ADJ: usu ADJ n; ADV: usu ADV *with* cl, also ADV after v

**apron** /eɪprən/ **(aprons)** An **apron** is a piece of clothing that you put on over the front of your normal clothes and tie round your waist, especially when you are cooking, in order to prevent your clothes from getting dirty. — N-COUNT

**ap|ro|pos** /æprəpoʊ/ [1] Something which is **apropos**, or **apropos of**, a subject or event, is connected with it or relevant to it. [FORMAL] ❑ *All my suggestions apropos the script were accepted.* [2] **Apropos** or **apropos of** is used to introduce something that you are going to say which is related to the subject you have just been talking about. [FORMAL] ❑ *Apropos Dudley Moore living in California he said, 'He loves the space, Californians have a lot of space.'*
— PREP = *with reference to*; PREP

**apt** /æpt/ [1] An **apt** remark, description, or choice is especially suitable. ❑ *The words of this report are as apt today as in 1929. ...an apt description of the situation.* ♦ **apt|ly** *...the beach in the aptly named town of Oceanside.* [2] If someone is **apt to** do something, they often do it and so it is likely that they will do it again. ❑ *She was apt to raise her voice and wave her hands about.*
— ADJ; ADV; ADJ: v-link ADJ to-inf = *liable*

**ap|ti|tude** /æptɪtjuːd, AM -tuːd/ **(aptitudes)** Someone's **aptitude for** a particular kind of work or activity is their ability to learn it quickly and to do it well. ❑ *An aptitude for computing is beneficial for students taking this degree.* — N-VAR: usu N *for* n/-ing

**ap|ti|tude test (aptitude tests)** An **aptitude test** is a test that is specially designed to find out how easily and how well you can do something. — N-COUNT

**aqua** /ækwə/ **Aqua** is the same as the colour **aquamarine**. ❑ *...floor-length curtains in restful aqua and lavender colours.* — COLOUR

**aqua|marine** /ækwəməriːn/ **(aquamarines)** [1] **Aquamarines** are clear, greenish-blue stones, sometimes used to make jewellery. ❑ *A necklace set with aquamarines. ...a large aquamarine ring.* [2] **Aquamarine** is used to describe things that are greenish-blue in colour. ❑ *...warm aquamarine seas and white beaches.*
— N-VAR; COLOUR

**aquar|ium** /əkweəriəm/ **(aquariums** or **aquaria** /əkweəriə/**)** [1] An **aquarium** is a building, often in a zoo, where fish and underwater animals are kept. [2] An **aquarium** is a glass tank filled with water, in which people keep fish.
— N-COUNT; N-COUNT

**Aquar|ius** /əkweəriəs/ [1] **Aquarius** is one of the twelve signs of the zodiac. Its symbol is a person pouring water. People who are born approximately between 20th January and 18th February come under this sign. [2] **An Aquarius** is a person whose sign of the zodiac is Aquarius.
— N-UNCOUNT; N-SING: *a* N

**aquat|ic** /əkwætɪk/ [1] An **aquatic** animal or plant lives or grows on or in water. ❑ *...aquatic birds.* [2] **Aquatic** means relating to water. ❑ *...aquatic consultant Ben Tucker. ...our aquatic resources.*
— ADJ: usu ADJ n; ADJ

**aque|duct** /ækwɪdʌkt/ **(aqueducts)** [1] An **aqueduct** is a long bridge with many arches, which carries a water supply or a canal over a valley. ❑ *...an old Roman aqueduct.* [2] An **aqueduct** is a large pipe or canal which carries a water supply to a city or a farming area. ❑ *...a nationwide system of aqueducts to carry water to the arid parts of this country.*
— N-COUNT; N-COUNT

**aque|ous** /eɪkwiəs/ In chemistry, an **aqueous** solution or cream has water as its base. [TECHNICAL] ❑ *...an aqueous solution containing various sodium salts.* — ADJ: ADJ n = *water-based*

**aqui|fer** /ækwɪfəʳ/ **(aquifers)** In geology, an **aquifer** is an area of rock underneath the sur- — N-COUNT face of the earth which absorbs and holds water. [TECHNICAL]

**aqui|line** /ækwɪlaɪn/ ADJ: usu ADJ n If someone has an **aquiline** nose or profile, their nose is large, thin, and usually curved. [FORMAL] ❑ *He had a thin aquiline nose and deep-set brown eyes.*

**Arab** /ærəb/ **(Arabs)** [1] N-COUNT **Arabs** are people who speak Arabic and who come from the Middle East and parts of North Africa. [2] ADJ: usu ADJ n **Arab** means belonging or relating to Arabs or to their countries or customs. ❑ *On the surface, it appears little has changed in the Arab world.*

**ara|besque** /ærəbesk/ **(arabesques)** N-COUNT An **arabesque** is a position in ballet dancing. The dancer stands on one leg with their other leg lifted and stretched out backwards, and their arms stretched out in front of them.

**Ara|bian** /əreɪbiən/ ADJ **Arabian** means belonging or relating to Arabia, especially to Saudi Arabia. ❑ *...the Arabian Peninsula.*

**Ara|bic** /ærəbɪk/ [1] N-UNCOUNT **Arabic** is a language that is spoken in the Middle East and in parts of North Africa. [2] ADJ Something that is **Arabic** belongs or relates to the language, writing, or culture of the Arabs. ❑ *...a large tapestry with swirling Arabic script. ...the development of modern Arabic literature. ...Arabic music.* [3] ADJ: ADJ n An **Arabic** numeral is one of the written figures such as 1, 2, 3, or 4.

**Ar|ab|ist** /ærəbɪst/ **(Arabists)** N-COUNT An **Arabist** is a person who supports Arab interests or knows a lot about the Arabic language.

**ar|able** /ærəbᵊl/ ADJ: usu ADJ n **Arable** farming involves growing crops such as wheat and barley rather than keeping animals or growing fruit and vegetables. **Arable** land is land that is used for arable farming.

**ar|bi|ter** /ɑːʳbɪtəʳ/ **(arbiters)** [1] N-COUNT = adjudicator An **arbiter** is a person or institution that judges and settles a quarrel between two other people or groups. [FORMAL] ❑ *He was the ultimate arbiter on both theological and political matters.* [2] N-COUNT: usu N *of* n An **arbiter of** taste or style is someone who has a lot of influence in deciding what is fashionable or socially desirable. [FORMAL]

**ar|bi|trage** /ɑːʳbɪtrɑːʒ/ N-UNCOUNT: oft N n In finance, **arbitrage** is the activity of buying shares or currency in one financial market and selling it at a profit in another. [BUSINESS]

**ar|bi|tra|ger** /ɑːʳbɪtrɑːʒɜːʳ/ **(arbitragers)** also **arbitrageur.** N-COUNT In finance, an **arbitrager** is someone who buys currencies, securities, or commodities on one country's market in order to make money by immediately selling them at a profit on another country's market. [BUSINESS]

**ar|bi|trary** /ɑːʳbɪtri, AM -treri/ ADJ [disapproval] If you describe an action, rule, or decision as **arbitrary**, you think that it is not based on any principle, plan, or system. It often seems unfair because of this. ❑ *Arbitrary arrests and detention without trial were common.* ♦ **ar|bi|trari|ly** /ɑːʳbɪtreərɪli/ ADV: ADV with v *The victims were not chosen arbitrarily.*

**ar|bi|trate** /ɑːʳbɪtreɪt/ **(arbitrates, arbitrating, arbitrated)** VERB When someone in authority **arbitrates between** two people or groups who are in dispute, they consider all the facts and make an official decision about who is right. ❑ V *between* pl-n *He arbitrates between investors and members of the association...* V *The tribunal had been set up to arbitrate in the dispute.* ♦ **ar|bi|tra|tor** /ɑːʳbɪtreɪtəʳ/ **(arbitrators)** N-COUNT *He served as an arbitrator in a series of commercial disputes in India.*

**ar|bi|tra|tion** /ɑːʳbɪtreɪʃᵊn/ N-UNCOUNT: oft N n **Arbitration** is the judging of a dispute between people or groups by someone who is not involved. ❑ *The matter is likely to go to arbitration.*

**ar|bor|eal** /ɑːʳbɔːriəl/ [1] ADJ: usu ADJ n **Arboreal** animals live in trees. [TECHNICAL] ❑ *...arboreal marsupials which resemble monkeys.* [2] ADJ: usu ADJ n **Arboreal** means relating to trees. [FORMAL] ❑ *...the arboreal splendor of the valley.*

**ar|bo|retum** /ɑːʳbəriːtəm/ **(arboreta** /ɑːʳbəriːtə/ or **arboretums)** N-COUNT An **arboretum** is a specially designed garden of different types of trees.

**ar|bour** /ɑːʳbəʳ/ **(arbours)**

☑ in AM, use **arbor**

N-COUNT = bower An **arbour** is a shelter in a garden which is formed by leaves and stems of plants growing close together over a light framework.

**arc** /ɑːʳk/ **(arcs)** [1] N-COUNT An **arc** is a smoothly curving line or movement. ❑ *The Aleutian chain is a long arc of islands in the North Pacific.* [2] N-COUNT In geometry, an **arc** is a part of the line that forms the outside of a circle. [TECHNICAL]

**ar|cade** /ɑːʳkeɪd/ **(arcades)** N-COUNT An **arcade** is a covered passage where there are shops or market stalls. ❑ *...a shopping arcade.*

**ar|cade game** **(arcade games)** N-COUNT An **arcade game** is a computer game of the type that is often played in amusement arcades.

**ar|cane** /ɑːʳkeɪn/ ADJ Something that is **arcane** is secret or mysterious. [FORMAL] ❑ *Until a few months ago few people outside the arcane world of contemporary music had heard of Gorecki.*

**arch** /ɑːʳtʃ/ **(arches, arching, arched)** [1] N-COUNT An **arch** is a structure that is curved at the top and is supported on either side by a pillar, post, or wall. [2] N-COUNT An **arch** is a curved line or movement. [3] N-COUNT The **arch** of your foot is the curved section at the bottom in the middle. [4] VERB If you **arch** a part of your body such as your back or if it **arches**, you bend it so that it forms a curve. ❑ V n *Don't arch your back, keep your spine straight.* Also V [5] VERB = raise If you **arch** your eyebrows or if they **arch**, you move them upwards as a way of showing surprise or disapproval. [LITERARY] ❑ V n *'Oh really?' he said, arching an eyebrow.* Also V [6] → See also **arched**.

**arch-** /ɑːʳtʃ-/ COMB in N-COUNT **Arch-** combines with nouns referring to people to form new nouns that refer to people who are extreme examples of something. For example, your **arch-rival** is the rival you most want to beat. ❑ *Neither he nor his arch-rival, Giuseppe De Rita, won. ...his arch-enemy.*

**ar|chae|ol|ogy** /ɑːʳkiɒlədʒi/ also **archeology.** N-UNCOUNT **Archaeology** is the study of the societies and peoples of the past by examining the remains of their buildings, tools, and other objects. ♦ **ar|chaeo|logi|cal** /ɑːʳkiəlɒdʒɪkᵊl/ ADJ: ADJ n ❑ *...one of the region's most important archaeological sites.* ♦ **ar|chae|olo|gist** /ɑːʳkiɒlədʒɪst/ **(archaeologists)** N-COUNT *The archaeologists found a house built around 300 BC, with a basement and attic.*

**ar|cha|ic** /ɑːʳkeɪɪk/ ADJ: usu ADJ n = antiquated **Archaic** means extremely old or extremely old-fashioned. ❑ *...archaic laws that are very seldom used.*

**arch|angel** /ɑːʳkeɪndʒᵊl/ **(archangels)** N-COUNT In the Jewish, Christian, and Muslim religions, an **archangel** is an angel of the highest rank.

**arch|bishop** /ɑːʳtʃbɪʃəp/ **(archbishops)** N-COUNT; N-TITLE In the Roman Catholic, Orthodox, and Anglican Churches, an **archbishop** is a bishop of the highest rank, who is in charge of all the bishops and priests in a particular country or region. ❑ *...the Archbishop of Canterbury. ...Archbishop Desmond Tutu.*

**arch|deacon** /ɑːʳtʃdiːkən/ **(archdeacons)** N-COUNT; N-TITLE An **archdeacon** is a high-ranking clergyman who works as an assistant to a bishop, especially in the Anglican church.

**arch|dio|cese** /ɑːʳtʃdaɪəsɪs/ **(archdioceses** /ɑːʳtʃdaɪəsiːz/) N-COUNT An **archdiocese** is the area over which an archbishop has control.

**arched** /ɑːʳtʃt/ [1] ADJ: usu ADJ n An **arched** roof, window, or doorway is curved at the top. [2] ADJ: usu ADJ n An **arched** bridge has arches as part of its structure. ❑ *...a fortified arched bridge spanning the River Severn.*

**ar|che|ol|ogy** /ɑːʳkiɒlədʒi/ → see **archaeology**.

**arch|er** /ɑːʳtʃəʳ/ **(archers)** N-COUNT An **archer** is someone who shoots arrows using a bow.

**ar|chery** /ɑːʳtʃəri/ **Archery** is a sport in which people shoot arrows at a target using a bow. N-UNCOUNT

**ar|che|typ|al** /ɑːʳkɪtaɪpᵊl/ Someone or something that is **archetypal** has all the most important characteristics of a particular kind of person or thing and is a perfect example of it. [FORMAL] ❑ *Cricket is the archetypal English game.* ADJ: usu ADJ n

**ar|che|type** /ɑːʳkɪtaɪp/ **(archetypes)** An **archetype** is something that is considered to be a perfect or typical example of a particular kind of person or thing, because it has all their most important characteristics. [FORMAL] ❑ *He came to this country 20 years ago and is the archetype of the successful Asian businessman.* N-COUNT = epitome

**ar|che|typi|cal** /ɑːʳkɪtɪpɪkᵊl/ **Archetypical** means the same as **archetypal**. ❑ *...an archetypical BBC voice.* ADJ: usu ADJ n

**archi|pela|go** /ɑːʳkɪpeləgoʊ/ **(archipelagos** or **archipelagoes)** An **archipelago** is a group of islands, especially small islands. N-COUNT

**archi|tect** /ɑːʳkɪtekt/ **(architects)** 1 An **architect** is a person who designs buildings. N-COUNT 2 You can use **architect** to refer to a person who plans large projects such as landscaping or railways. ❑ *...Paul Andreu, chief architect of French railways.* N-COUNT: with supp, oft N of n 3 The **architect of** an idea, event, or institution is the person who invented it or made it happen. [FORMAL] ❑ *...Russia's chief architect of economic reform.* N-COUNT: oft N of n

**archi|tec|tur|al** /ɑːʳkɪtektʃərəl/ **Architectural** means relating to the design and construction of buildings. ❑ *...Tibet's architectural heritage. ...the unique architectural style of towns like Lamu.* ADJ: usu ADJ n ♦ **archi|tec|tur|al|ly** *The old city centre is architecturally rich.* ADV: ADV adj, ADV with cl

**archi|tec|ture** /ɑːʳkɪtektʃəʳ/ **(architectures)** 1 **Architecture** is the art of planning, designing, and constructing buildings. ❑ *He studied classical architecture and design in Rome.* N-UNCOUNT 2 The **architecture** of a building is the style in which it is designed and constructed. ❑ *...a fine example of Moroccan architecture.* N-UNCOUNT: with supp 3 The **architecture of** something is its structure. [FORMAL] ❑ *...the crumbling intellectual architecture of modern society.* N-UNCOUNT: also N in pl, N of n

**ar|chiv|al** /ɑːʳkaɪvᵊl/ **Archival** means belonging or relating to archives. ❑ *...his extensive use of archival material.* ADJ: usu ADJ n

**ar|chive** /ɑːʳkaɪv/ **(archives)** 1 The **archive** or **archives** are a collection of documents and records that contain historical information. You can also use **archives** to refer to the place where archives are stored. ❑ *...the archives of the Imperial War Museum.* N-COUNT: usu pl 2 **Archive** material is information that comes from archives. ❑ *...pieces of archive film.* ADJ: ADJ n

**archi|vist** /ɑːʳkɪvɪst/ **(archivists)** An **archivist** is a person whose job is to collect, sort, and care for historical documents and records. N-COUNT

**arch|way** /ɑːʳtʃweɪ/ **(archways)** An **archway** is a passage or entrance that has a curved roof. ❑ *Access was via a narrow archway.* N-COUNT

**arc light** **(arc lights)** **Arc lights** are a type of very bright electric light. ❑ *...the brilliant glare of the arc lights.* N-COUNT: usu pl

**arc|tic** /ɑːʳktɪk/ 1 **The Arctic** is the area of the world around the North Pole. It is extremely cold and there is very little light in winter and very little darkness in summer. ❑ *...winter in the Arctic. ...Arctic ice.* N-PROPER: the N ≠ Antarctic 2 If you describe a place or the weather as **arctic**, you are emphasizing that it is extremely cold. [INFORMAL] ❑ *The bathroom, with its ancient facilities, is positively arctic.* ADJ emphasis = freezing

**Arc|tic Circle** **The Arctic Circle** is an imaginary line drawn around the northern part of the world at approximately 66° North. N-PROPER: the N

**ar|dent** /ɑːʳdᵊnt/ **Ardent** is used to describe someone who has extremely strong feelings about something or someone. ❑ *He's been one of the most ardent supporters of the administration's policy.* ADJ: usu ADJ n = fervent, passionate

**ar|dor** /ɑːʳdəʳ/ → see **ardour**.

**ar|dour** /ɑːʳdəʳ/

✔ in AM, use **ardor**

**Ardour** is a strong, intense feeling of love or enthusiasm for someone or something. [LITERARY] ❑ *...songs of genuine passion and ardour.* N-UNCOUNT = passion, fervour

**ar|du|ous** /ɑːʳdʒuəs/ Something that is **arduous** is difficult and tiring, and involves a lot of effort. ❑ *The task was more arduous than he had calculated.* ADJ

**are** /əʳ, STRONG ɑːʳ/ **Are** is the plural and the second person singular of the present tense of the verb **be**. **Are** is often shortened to **-'re** after pronouns in spoken English.

**area** /eəriə/ **(areas)** ◆◆◆ 1 An **area** is a particular part of a town, a country, a region, or the world. ❑ *...the large number of community groups in the area... 60 years ago half the French population still lived in rural areas.* N-COUNT 2 Your **area** is the part of a town, country, or region where you live. An organization's **area** is the part of a town, country, or region that it is responsible for. ❑ *Local authorities have been responsible for the running of schools in their areas... If there is an election in your area, you should go and vote.* N-COUNT: poss N 3 A particular **area** is a piece of land or part of a building that is used for a particular activity. ❑ *...a picnic area. ...the main check-in area located in Terminal 1.* N-COUNT: supp N 4 An **area** is a particular place on a surface or object, for example on your body. ❑ *You will notice that your baby has two soft areas on the top of his head.* N-COUNT: with supp 5 The **area** of a surface such as a piece of land is the amount of flat space or ground that it covers, measured in square units. ❑ *The islands cover a total area of 625.6 square kilometers.* N-VAR 6 You can use **area** to refer to a particular subject or topic, or to a particular part of a larger, more general situation or activity. ❑ *...the politically sensitive area of old age pensions.* N-COUNT: usu with supp 7 On a football pitch, **the area** is the same as the **penalty area**. [INFORMAL] N-COUNT: usu sing, the N = box 8 → See also **catchment area**, **disaster area**, **grey area**, **penalty area**.

**area code** **(area codes)** The **area code** for a particular city or region is the series of numbers that you have to dial before someone's personal number if you are making a telephone call to that place from a different area. [mainly AM] N-COUNT

✔ in BRIT, use **dialling code**

**arena** /əriːnə/ **(arenas)** 1 An **arena** is a place where sports, entertainments, and other public events take place. It has seats around it where people sit and watch. ❑ *...the largest indoor sports arena in the world.* N-COUNT = stadium 2 You can refer to a field of activity, especially one where there is a lot of conflict or action, as an **arena** of a particular kind. ❑ *He made it clear he had no intention of withdrawing from the political arena.* N-COUNT: usu with supp

**aren't** /ɑːʳnt, AM also ɑːrənt/ ◆◆◇ 1 **Aren't** is the usual spoken form of 'are not'. 2 **Aren't** is the form of 'am not' that is used in questions or tags in spoken English.

**Ar|gen|tine** /ɑːʳdʒəntaɪn/ **(Argentines)** **Argentine** means the same as **Argentinian**. ❑ *...Argentine agricultural products.* ADJ ♦ An **Argentine** is the same as an **Argentinian**. N-COUNT

**Ar|gen|tin|ian** /ɑːʳdʒəntɪniən/ **(Argentinians)** **Argentinian** means belonging or relating to Argentina or its people. ❑ *...the Argentinian capital, Buenos Aires.* ADJ = Argentine ♦ An **Argentinian** is someone who comes from Argentina. N-COUNT = Argentine

**ar|gon** /ɑːʳgɒn/ **Argon** is an inert gas which exists in very small amounts in the atmosphere. It is used in electric lights. N-UNCOUNT

**ar|got** /ɑːʳgoʊ/ **(argots)** An **argot** is a special language used by a particular group of people, which other people find difficult to understand. [FORMAL] ❑ *...the argot of teenagers. ...footballing argot.* N-VAR: usu with supp

**ar|gu|able** /ɑːʳgjuəbᵊl/ 1 If you say that **it is arguable that** something is true, you believe ADJ: oft it v-link ADJ that

that it can be supported by evidence and that many people would agree with it. [FORMAL] ❑ *It is arguable that this was not as grave a handicap as it might appear.* [2] An idea, point, or comment that is **arguable** is not obviously true or correct and should be questioned. [FORMAL] ❑ *It is arguable whether he ever had much control over the real economic power.* ADJ: usu v-link ADJ, oft *it* v-link ADJ whether = debatable

**ar|gu|ably** /ɑːʳgjuəbli/ You can use **arguably** when you are stating your opinion or belief, as a way of giving more authority to it. ❑ *They are arguably the most important band since The Rolling Stones.* ADV: ADV with cl/group, ADV before v

**ar|gue** /ɑːʳgjuː/ **(argues, arguing, argued)** ◆◆◇ [1] If one person **argues with** another, they speak angrily to each other about something that they disagree about. You can also say that two people **argue**. ❑ *We are concerned about players' behaviour, especially arguing with referees... They were still arguing; I could hear them down the road.* V-RECIP V with n pl-n V Also V about/over n [2] If you tell someone not to **argue with** you, you want them to do or believe what you say without protest or disagreement. ❑ *Don't argue with me... The children go to bed at 10.30. No one dares argue.* VERB: usu imper with neg V with n V [3] If you **argue with** someone **about** something, you discuss it with them, with each of you giving your different opinions. ❑ *He was arguing with the King about the need to maintain the cavalry at full strength... They are arguing over foreign policy... The two of them sitting in their office were arguing this point.* V-RECIP V with n about/over n pl-n V about/over n pl-n V n [4] If you **argue that** something is true, you state it and give the reasons why you think it is true. ❑ *His lawyers are arguing that he is unfit to stand trial... It could be argued that the British are not aggressive enough.* VERB V that it be V-ed that [5] If you **argue for** something, you say why you agree with it, in order to persuade people that it is right. If you **argue against** something, you say why you disagree with it, in order to persuade people that it is wrong. ❑ *The report argues against tax increases... I argued the case for an independent central bank.* VERB V for/against n V n [6] If you **argue**, you support your opinions with evidence in an ordered or logical way. ❑ *He argued persuasively, and was full of confidence.* VERB V adv/prep Also V [7] If you say that no-one can **argue with** a particular fact or opinion, you are emphasizing that it is obviously true and so everyone must accept it. [SPOKEN] ❑ *We produced the best soccer of the tournament. Nobody would argue with that.* VERB: with brd-neg [emphasis] V with n Also V that [8] to **argue the toss** → see **toss**.

**ar|gu|ment** /ɑːʳgjʊmənt/ **(arguments)** ◆◆◇ [1] An **argument** is a statement or set of statements that you use in order to try to convince people that your opinion about something is correct. ❑ *There's a strong argument for lowering the price... The doctors have set out their arguments against the proposals.* N-VAR: oft N for/against n/-ing, N that [2] An **argument** is a discussion or debate in which a number of people put forward different or opposing opinions. ❑ *The incident has triggered fresh arguments about the role of the extreme right in France.* N-VAR: oft N about/over n = debate [3] An **argument** is a conversation in which people disagree with each other angrily or noisily. ❑ *Anny described how she got into an argument with one of the marchers. ...a heated argument.* N-COUNT: oft N with n, N between pl-n [4] If you accept something without **argument**, you do not question it or disagree with it. ❑ *He complied without argument.* N-UNCOUNT: with brd-neg = question [5] → See also **counter-argument**.

**ar|gu|men|ta|tion** /ɑːʳgjʊmenteɪʃən/ **Argumentation** is the process of arguing in an organized or logical way, for example in philosophy. [FORMAL] N-UNCOUNT = argument, debate

**ar|gu|men|ta|tive** /ɑːʳgjʊmentətɪv/ Someone who is **argumentative** is always ready to disagree or start quarrelling with other people. ❑ *You're in an argumentative mood today!* ADJ [disapproval] = quarrelsome

**aria** /ɑːriə/ **(arias)** An **aria** is a song for one of the leading singers in an opera or choral work. N-COUNT

**arid** /ærɪd/ [1] **Arid** land is so dry that very few plants can grow on it. ❑ *...new strains of crops that can withstand arid conditions.* ADJ: usu ADJ n [2] If you describe something such as a period of your life or an academic subject as **arid**, you mean that it has so little interest, excitement, or purpose that it makes you feel bored or unhappy. ❑ *She had given him the only joy his arid life had ever known.* ADJ: usu ADJ n

**Aries** /eəriːz/ [1] **Aries** is one of the twelve signs of the zodiac. Its symbol is a ram. People who are born approximately between 21st March and 19th April come under this sign. N-UNCOUNT [2] An **Aries** is a person whose sign of the zodiac is Aries. N-SING: a N

**arise** /əraɪz/ **(arises, arising, arose, arisen** /ərɪzən/**)** ◆◇◇ [1] If a situation or problem **arises**, it begins to exist or people start to become aware of it. ❑ *The birds also attack crops when the opportunity arises.* VERB = occur V [2] If something **arises from** a particular situation, or **arises out of** it, it is created or caused by the situation. ❑ *...an overwhelming sense of guilt arising from my actions.* VERB V from/out of n [3] If something such as a new species, organization, or system **arises**, it begins to exist and develop. ❑ *Heavy Metal music really arose in the late 60s.* VERB V [4] When you **arise**, you get out of bed in the morning. [FORMAL] ❑ *He arose at 6:30 a.m. as usual.* VERB V [5] When you **arise from** a sitting or kneeling position, you stand up. [FORMAL] ❑ *When I arose from the chair, my father and Eleanor were in deep conversation... Arise, Sir William.* VERB V from n V

**ar|is|toc|ra|cy** /ærɪstɒkrəsi/ **(aristocracies)** **The aristocracy** is a class of people in some countries who have a high social rank and special titles. ❑ *...a member of the aristocracy.* N-COUNT-COLL = nobility

**aris|to|crat** /ærɪstəkræt, ərɪst-/ **(aristocrats)** An **aristocrat** is someone whose family has a high social rank, especially someone who has a title. N-COUNT

**aris|to|crat|ic** /ərɪstəkrætɪk/ **Aristocratic** means belonging to or typical of the aristocracy. ❑ *...a wealthy, aristocratic family.* ADJ: usu ADJ n

**arith|me|tic**

✔ The noun is pronounced /ərɪθmɪtɪk/. The adjective is pronounced /ærɪθmetɪk/.

[1] **Arithmetic** is the part of mathematics that is concerned with the addition, subtraction, multiplication, and division of numbers. ❑ *...an arithmetic test.* N-UNCOUNT [2] You can use **arithmetic** to refer to the process of doing a particular sum or calculation. ❑ *4,000 women put in ten rupees each, which if my arithmetic is right adds up to 40,000 rupees.* N-UNCOUNT: oft poss N [3] If you refer to **the arithmetic** of a situation, you are concerned with those aspects of it that can be expressed in numbers, and how they affect the situation. ❑ *The budgetary arithmetic suggests that government borrowing is set to surge.* N-UNCOUNT: usu the N [4] **Arithmetic** means relating to or consisting of calculations involving numbers. ❑ *...a processor which performs simple arithmetic operations such as adding or multiplying numbers.* ADJ: ADJ n

**arith|meti|cal** /ærɪθmetɪkəl/ **Arithmetical** calculations, processes, or skills involve the addition, subtraction, multiplication, or division of numbers. ADJ: usu ADJ n

**ark** /ɑːʳk/ In the Bible, **the ark** was a large boat which Noah built in order to save his family and two of every kind of animal from the Flood. N-SING: usu the N

**arm**
① PART OF YOUR BODY OR OF SOMETHING ELSE
② WEAPONS

**①arm** /ɑːʳm/ **(arms)** ◆◆◆ [1] Your **arms** are the two long parts of your body that are attached to your shoulders and that have your hands at the end. ❑ *She stretched her arms out... He had a large parcel under his left arm.* N-COUNT [2] The **arm** of a piece of clothing is the part of it that covers your arm. N-COUNT = sleeve [3] The **arm** of a chair is the part on which you rest your arm when you are sitting down. N-COUNT [4] An **arm of** an object is a long thin part of it that sticks out from the main part. ❑ *...the lever arm of the machine. ...the arms of the doctor's spectacles.* N-COUNT: usu N of n

5 An **arm of** land or water is a long thin area of it that is joined to a broader area. ❑ *At the end of the other arm of Cardigan Bay is Bardsey Island.* N-COUNT: usu N *of* n

6 An **arm of** an organization is a section of it that operates in a particular country or that deals with a particular activity. ❑ *Millicom Holdings is the British arm of an American company.* N-COUNT: usu sing, usu N *of* n = wing

**PHRASES** 7 If two people are walking **arm in arm**, they are walking together with their arms linked. ❑ *He walked from the court arm in arm with his wife.* PHRASE: usu v PHR, oft PHR *with* n

8 If you say that something costs **an arm and a leg**, you mean that it is very expensive. [INFORMAL] ❑ *A week at a health farm can cost an arm and a leg.* PHRASE: PHR after v

9 If you hold something **at arm's length**, you hold it away from your body with your arm straight. ❑ *He struck a match, and held it at arm's length.* PHRASE: usu PHR after v

10 If you **keep** someone **at arm's length**, you avoid becoming too friendly or involved with them. ❑ *She had always kept his family at arm's length.* PHRASE: V inflects

11 If you welcome some action or change **with open arms**, you are very pleased about it. If you welcome a person **with open arms**, you are very pleased about their arrival. ❑ *They would no doubt welcome the action with open arms.* PHRASE: PHR after v [approval]

12 If you **twist** someone's **arm**, you persuade them to do something. [INFORMAL] ❑ *She had twisted his arm to get him to invite her.* PHRASE: V and N inflect

② **arm** /ɑːʳm/ **(arms, arming, armed)** ◆◆◆ 1 **Arms** are weapons, especially bombs and guns. [FORMAL] ❑ *The IRA had extensive supplies of arms. ...arms control.* N-PLURAL: oft N n

2 If you **arm** someone **with** a weapon, you provide them with a weapon. ❑ *She'd been so terrified that she had armed herself with a loaded rifle... Arming the police doesn't deter crime.* VERB V n *with* n V n

3 If you **arm** someone **with** something that will be useful in a particular situation, you provide them with it. ❑ *She thought that if she armed herself with all the knowledge she could gather she could handle anything.* VERB V n *with* n

4 The **arms** of a city or of a noble family are its coat of arms. **Arms** is often used in the names of British pubs. ❑ *...china painted with the arms of Philippe V. ...his local pub, the Abercorn Arms.* N-PLURAL

5 → See also **armed**, **-armed**, **coat of arms**, **comrade-in-arms**, **small arms**.

**PHRASES** 6 A person's right to **bear arms** is their right to own and use guns, as a means of defence. PHRASE: V inflects

7 If soldiers **lay down** their **arms**, they stop fighting and give up their weapons. [OLD-FASHIONED] PHRASE: V inflects

8 If one group or country **takes up arms against** another, they prepare to attack and fight them. ❑ *They threatened to take up arms against the government if their demands were not met.* PHRASE: V inflects, oft PHR *against* n

9 If people are **up in arms about** something, they are very angry about it and are protesting strongly against it. ❑ *Environmental groups are up in arms about plans to sink an oil well here.* PHRASE: usu v-link PHR

**ar|ma|da** /ɑːʳmɑːdə/ **(armadas)** An **armada** is a large group of warships. N-COUNT: oft N *of* n

**ar|ma|dil|lo** /ɑːʳmədɪloʊ/ **(armadillos)** An **armadillo** is a small animal whose body is covered with large bony scales and which rolls itself into a ball when it is attacked. Armadillos are mainly found in South and Central America. N-COUNT

**Ar|ma|ged|don** /ɑːʳməgedᵊn/ **Armageddon** is a terrible battle or war that some people think will lead to the total destruction of the world or the human race. N-UNCOUNT

**Ar|ma|gnac** /ɑːʳmənjæk/ **(Armagnacs)** **Armagnac** is a type of brandy made in south-west France. N-MASS

**ar|ma|ments** /ɑːʳməmənts/ **Armaments** are weapons and military equipment belonging to an army or country. ❑ *...global efforts to reduce nuclear and other armaments.* N-PLURAL = arms

**arm|band** /ɑːʳmbænd/ **(armbands)** 1 An **armband** is a band of fabric that you wear round your upper arm in order to show that you have an official position or belong to a particular group. Some people also wear a black armband to show that a friend or relation has died. N-COUNT

2 **Armbands** are plastic rings filled with air that people who are learning to swim wear on their upper arms to help them float. [mainly BRIT] N-COUNT: usu pl

**arm|chair** /ɑːʳmtʃeəʳ/ **(armchairs)** 1 An **armchair** is a big comfortable chair which has a support on each side for your arms. N-COUNT

2 An **armchair** critic, fan, or traveller knows about a particular subject from reading or hearing about it rather than from practical experience. ADJ: ADJ n

**armed** /ɑːʳmd/ ◆◆◇ 1 Someone who is **armed** is carrying a weapon, usually a gun. ❑ *City police said the man was armed with a revolver. ...a barbed-wire fence patrolled by armed guards... The rebels are well organised, disciplined and very well armed.* ADJ

2 An **armed** attack or conflict involves people fighting with guns or carrying weapons. ❑ *They had been found guilty of armed robbery.* ADJ: ADJ n ≠unarmed

3 → See also **arm**, **-armed**.

**-armed** /-ɑːʳmd/ 1 **-armed** is used with adjectives to indicate what kind of arms someone has. ❑ *...plump-armed women in cotton dresses.* COMB in ADJ

2 **-armed** is used with adjectives such as 'nuclear' and nouns such as 'missile' to form adjectives that indicate what kind of weapons an army or person has. ❑ *...nuclear-armed navy vessels.* COMB in ADJ

3 → See also **armed**.

**armed forces** ◆◇◇ The **armed forces** or the **armed services** of a country are its military forces, usually the army, navy, marines, and air force. N-PLURAL

**arm|ful** /ɑːʳmfʊl/ **(armfuls)** An **armful of** something is the amount of it that you can carry fairly easily. ❑ *He hurried out with an armful of brochures.* N-COUNT: usu N *of* n = armload

**arm|hole** /ɑːʳmhoʊl/ **(armholes)** The **armholes** of something such as a shirt or dress are the openings through which you put your arms, or the places where the sleeves are attached. N-COUNT

**ar|mi|stice** /ɑːʳmɪstɪs/ An **armistice** is an agreement between countries who are at war with one another to stop fighting and to discuss ways of making peace. ❑ *Finally, the Bolsheviks signed an armistice with Germany.* N-SING

**arm|load** /ɑːʳmloʊd/ **(armloads)** An **armload of** something is the same as an **armful** of something. ❑ *...an armload of books.* N-COUNT: usu N *of* n = armful

**ar|mor** /ɑːʳməʳ/ → see **armour**.

**ar|mored** /ɑːʳməʳd/ → see **armoured**.

**ar|mor|er** /ɑːʳmərəʳ/ **(armorers)** → see **armourer**.

**ar|mory** /ɑːʳməri/ **(armories)** → see **armoury**.

**ar|mour** /ɑːʳməʳ/

✔ in AM, use **armor**

1 In former times, **armour** was special metal clothing that soldiers wore for protection in battle. ❑ *...knights in armour.* N-UNCOUNT

2 **Armour** consists of tanks and other military vehicles used in battle. [MILITARY] ❑ *...the biggest movement of heavy British armour since the Second World War.* N-UNCOUNT

3 **Armour** is a hard, usually metal, covering that protects a vehicle against attack. ❑ *...a formidable warhead that can penetrate the armour of most tanks.* N-UNCOUNT

4 → See also **body armour**. **knight in shining armour** → see **knight**.

**ar|moured** /ɑːʳməʳd/

✔ in AM, use **armored**

1 **Armoured** vehicles are fitted with a hard metal covering in order to protect them from gunfire and other missiles. ADJ: usu ADJ n

2 **Armoured** troops are troops in armoured vehicles. ADJ: usu ADJ n

**ar|mour|er** /ɑːʳmərəʳ/ **(armourers)**

✔ in AM, use **armorer**

An **armourer** is someone who makes or supplies weapons. N-COUNT

**armour-plated**

✔ in AM, use **armor-plated**

An **armour-plated** vehicle or building has a hard metal covering in order to protect it from gunfire ADJ: usu ADJ n and other missiles. ❑ *He has taken to travelling in an armour-plated car.*

**armour-plating**

☑ in AM, use **armor-plating**

The **armour-plating** on a vehicle or building is the hard metal covering which is intended to protect it from gunfire and other missiles. N-UNCOUNT

**ar|moury** /ɑːʳməri/ **(armouries)**

☑ in AM, use **armory**

[1] A country's **armoury** is all the weapons and military equipment that it has. ❑ *Nuclear weapons will play a less prominent part in NATO's armoury in the future.* N-COUNT: usu supp N [2] An **armoury** is a place where weapons, bombs, and other military equipment are stored. N-COUNT = arsenal [3] In the United States, an **armoury** is a building used by the National Guard or Army Reserve for meetings and training. N-COUNT [4] An **armoury** is a factory where weapons are made. [AM] N-COUNT [5] You can refer to a large number of things which someone has available for a particular purpose as their **armoury**. [BRIT] ❑ *The strongest weapon in the government's armoury is the price cuts announced on Saturday.* N-COUNT: usu sing, with supp = arsenal

**arm|pit** /ɑːʳmpɪt/ **(armpits)** Your **armpits** are the areas of your body under your arms where your arms join your shoulders. N-COUNT

**arm|rest** /ɑːʳmrest/ **(armrests)** also **arm rest.** The **armrests** on a chair are the two pieces on either side that support your arms when you are sitting down. N-COUNT

**arms race** An **arms race** is a situation in which two countries or groups of countries are continually trying to get more and better weapons than each other. N-SING

**army** /ɑːʳmi/ **(armies)** ◆◆◆ [1] An **army** is a large organized group of people who are armed and trained to fight on land in a war. Most armies are organized and controlled by governments. ❑ *After returning from France, he joined the army... The army is about to launch a major offensive.* N-COUNT-COLL [2] An **army of** people, animals, or things is a large number of them, especially when they are regarded as a force of some kind. ❑ *...data collected by an army of volunteers. ...armies of shoppers looking for bargains.* N-COUNT-COLL: N *of* n

**A-road** **(A-roads)** In some countries, an **A-road** is a major road. A-roads are narrower than motorways but are wider and straighter than B-roads. N-COUNT

**aro|ma** /əroʊmə/ **(aromas)** An **aroma** is a strong, pleasant smell. ❑ *...the wonderful aroma of freshly baked bread.* N-COUNT: usu with supp

**aroma|thera|pist** /əroʊməθerəpɪst/ **(aromatherapists)** An **aromatherapist** is a person who is qualified to practise aromatherapy. N-COUNT

**aroma|thera|py** /əroʊməθerəpi/ **Aromatherapy** is a type of treatment which involves massaging the body with special fragrant oils. N-UNCOUNT

**aro|mat|ic** /ærəmætɪk/ An **aromatic** plant or food has a strong, pleasant smell of herbs or spices. ❑ *...an evergreen shrub with deep green, aromatic leaves.* ADJ = fragrant

**arose** /əroʊz/ **Arose** is the past tense of **arise**.

**around** /əraʊnd/ ◆◆◆

> **Around** is an adverb and a preposition. In British English, the word 'round' is often used instead. **Around** is often used with verbs of movement, such as 'walk' and 'drive', and also in phrasal verbs such as 'get around' and 'hand around'.

[1] To be positioned **around** a place or object means to surround it or be on all sides of it. To move **around** a place means to go along its edge, back to your starting point. ❑ *She looked at the papers around her. ...a prosperous suburb built around a new mosque.* PREP ♦ **Around** is also an adverb. ❑ *...a village with a rocky river, a ruined castle and hills all around... The Memorial seems almost ugly, dominating the landscape for miles around.* ADV: n ADV [2] If you move **around** a corner or obstacle, you move to the other side of it. If you look **around** a corner or obstacle, you look to see what is on the other side. ❑ *The photographer stopped clicking and hurried around the corner... I peered around the edge of the shed – there was no sign of anyone else.* PREP [3] If you turn **around**, you turn so that you are facing in the opposite direction. ❑ *I turned around and wrote the title on the blackboard... He straightened up slowly and spun around on the stool to face us.* ADV: ADV after v [4] If you move **around** a place, you travel through it, going to most of its parts. If you look **around** a place, you look at every part of it. ❑ *I've been walking around Moscow and the town is terribly quiet... He glanced discreetly around the room at the other people.* PREP ♦ **Around** is also an adverb. ❑ *He backed away from the edge, looking all around at the flat horizon.* ADV: ADV after v [5] If someone moves **around** a place, they move through various parts of that place without having any particular destination. ❑ *They milled around the ballroom with video cameras.* PREP ♦ **Around** is also an adverb. ❑ *My mornings are spent rushing around after him.* ADV: ADV after v [6] If you go **around** to someone's house, you visit them. ❑ *She helped me unpack my things and then we went around to see the other girls.* ADV: ADV after v [7] You use **around** in expressions such as **sit around** and **hang around** when you are saying that someone is spending time in a place and not doing anything very important. ❑ *After breakfast the next morning they sat around for an hour discussing political affairs.* ADV: ADV after v ♦ **Around** is also a preposition. ❑ *He used to skip lessons and hang around the harbor with some other boys.* PREP [8] If you move things **around**, you move them so that they are in different places. ❑ *She moved things around so the table was beneath the windows.* ADV: ADV after v [9] If a wheel or object turns **around**, it turns. ❑ *The boat started to spin around in the water.* ADV: ADV after v [10] You use **around** to say that something happens in different parts of a place or area. ❑ *Elephants were often to be found in swamp in eastern Kenya around the Tana River. ...pests and diseases around the garden.* PREP ♦ **Around** is also an adverb. ❑ *Giovanni has the best Parma ham for miles around.* ADV: ADV after v, n ADV [11] If someone or something is **around**, they exist or are present in a place. ❑ *The blackbird had a quick, wary look in case the cat was anywhere around... Just having lots of people around that you can talk to is important.* ADV [12] The people **around** you are the people who you come into contact with, especially your friends and relatives, and the people you work with. ❑ *We change our behaviour by observing the behaviour of those around us... Those around her would forgive her for weeping.* PREP [13] If something such as a film, a discussion, or a plan is based **around** something, that thing is its main theme. ❑ *...the gentle comedy based around the Larkin family... The discussion centered around four subjects.* PREP [14] You use **around** in expressions such as **this time around** or **to come around** when you are describing something that has happened before or things that happen regularly. ❑ *Senator Bentsen has declined to get involved this time around... When July Fourth comes around, the residents of Columbia City throw a noisy party.* ADV: n ADV, ADV after v [15] When you are giving measurements, you can use **around** to talk about the distance along the edge of something round. ❑ *She was 40 inches around the hips.* PREP [16] **Around** means approximately. ❑ *My salary was around £19,000 plus a car and expenses.* ADV = about ♦ **Around** is also a preposition. ❑ *He expects the elections to be held around November.* PREP

**PHRASES** [17] **Around about** means approximately. [SPOKEN] ❑ *There is a Green party but it only scored around about 10 percent in the vote.* PREP-PHRASE [18] You say **all around** to indicate that something affects all parts of a situation or all members of a group. ❑ *He compared the achievements of the British and the French during 1916 and concluded that the latter were better all around.* PHRASE: cl PHR [19] If someone **has been** PHRASE

**around**, they have had a lot of experience of different people and situations. [INFORMAL] 20 **the other way around** → see **way**.

**around-the-clock** → see **clock**.

**arous|al** /əraʊzəl/ 1 **Arousal** is the state of being sexually excited. ❑ *...sexual arousal... Use this technique to control your level of arousal.* 2 **Arousal** is a state in which you feel excited or very alert, for example as a result of fear, stress, or anger. ❑ *Thinking angry thoughts can provoke strong physiological arousal.* N-UNCOUNT N-UNCOUNT

**arouse** /əraʊz/ **(arouses, arousing, aroused)** 1 If something **arouses** a particular reaction or attitude in people, it causes them to have that reaction or attitude. ❑ *We left in the daytime so as not to arouse suspicion.* 2 If something **arouses** a particular feeling or instinct that exists in someone, it causes them to experience that feeling or instinct strongly. ❑ *There is nothing like a long walk to arouse the appetite.* 3 If you **are aroused** by something, it makes you feel sexually excited. ❑ *Some men are aroused when their partner says erotic words to them.* ♦ **aroused** *Some men feel that they get most sexually aroused in the morning.* ♦ **arous|ing** *Being stroked by a partner is usually more arousing than stroking yourself.* VERB V n VERB V n VERB: usu passive *be* V-ed ADJ: usu v-link ADJ ADJ

**arr.** 1 **Arr.** is a written abbreviation for **arrives**. It is used on timetables to indicate what time a bus, train, or plane will reach a place. ❑ *...dep. Victoria 1927, arr. Ramsgate 2110.* 2 **Arr.** is a written abbreviation for **arranged**. It is used to show that a piece of music written by one person has been rewritten in a different way or for different instruments by another person. ❑ *'A Good New Year', sung by Kenneth McKellar, (Trad., Arr. Knight).*

**ar|raign** /əreɪn/ **(arraigns, arraigning, arraigned)** If someone **is arraigned** on a particular charge, they are brought before a court of law to answer that charge. [LEGAL] ❑ *He was arraigned for criminally abetting a traitor.* VERB: usu passive *be* V-ed *for* n/-ing

**ar|raign|ment** /əreɪnmənt/ **(arraignments)** **Arraignment** is when someone is brought before a court of law to answer a particular charge. [LEGAL] ❑ *They are scheduled for arraignment October 5th... Crowds appeared at the arraignments, clashing with security forces.* N-VAR

**ar|range** /əreɪndʒ/ **(arranges, arranging, arranged)** ◆◇◇ 1 If you **arrange** an event or meeting, you make plans for it to happen. ❑ *She arranged an appointment for Friday afternoon at four-fifteen.* 2 If you **arrange** with someone **to** do something, you make plans with them to do it. ❑ *I've arranged to see him on Friday morning... It was arranged that the party would gather for lunch in the Royal Garden Hotel... He had arranged for the boxes to be stored until they could be collected.* 3 If you **arrange** something **for** someone, you make it possible for them to have it or to do it. ❑ *I will arrange for someone to take you round... The hotel manager will arrange for a baby-sitter... I've arranged your hotels for you.* 4 If you **arrange** things somewhere, you place them in a particular position, usually in order to make them look attractive or tidy. ❑ *When she has a little spare time she enjoys arranging dried flowers.* 5 If a piece of music **is arranged by** someone, it is changed or adapted so that it is suitable for particular instruments or voices, or for a particular performance. VERB V n VERB V to-inf *it be* V-ed that V *for* n to-inf VERB V *for* n to-inf V *for* n V n VERB V n VERB: usu passive

**ar|ranged** /əreɪndʒd/ If you say how things are **arranged**, you are talking about their position in relation to each other or to something else. ❑ *The house itself is three stories high and arranged around a courtyard.* ADJ

**ar|ranged mar|riage** **(arranged marriages)** In an **arranged marriage**, the parents choose the person who their son or daughter will marry. N-COUNT

**ar|range|ment** /əreɪndʒmənt/ **(arrangements)** ◆◇◇ 1 **Arrangements** are plans and preparations which you make so that something will happen or be possible. ❑ *The staff is working frantically on final arrangements for the summit... She telephoned Ellen, but made no arrangements to see her. ...travel arrangements.* 2 An **arrangement** is an agreement that you make with someone to do something. ❑ *The caves can be visited only by prior arrangement... Her class teacher made a special arrangement to discuss her progress at school once a month.* 3 An **arrangement** of things, for example flowers or furniture, is a group of them displayed in a particular way. ❑ *The house was always decorated with imaginative flower arrangements.* 4 If someone makes an **arrangement** of a piece of music, they change it so that it is suitable for particular voices or instruments, or for a particular performance. ❑ *...an arrangement of a well-known piece by Mozart.* N-COUNT: usu pl, oft N *for* n, N to-inf N-COUNT: also *by* N N-COUNT: with supp N-COUNT: usu with supp

**ar|rang|er** /əreɪndʒə^r/ **(arrangers)** 1 An **arranger** is a musician who arranges music by other composers, either for particular instruments or voices, or for a particular performance. 2 An **arranger** is a person who arranges things for other people. ❑ *...a loan arranger.* N-COUNT N-COUNT

**ar|rant** /ærənt/ **Arrant** is used to emphasize that something or someone is very bad in some way. ❑ *That's arrant nonsense. ...an arrant coward.* ADJ: ADJ n [emphasis] = unmitigated

**ar|ray** /əreɪ/ **(arrays)** 1 An **array of** different things or people is a large number or wide range of them. ❑ *As the deadline approached she experienced a bewildering array of emotions.* 2 An **array of** objects is a collection of them that is displayed or arranged in a particular way. ❑ *We visited the local markets and saw wonderful arrays of fruit and vegetables.* N-COUNT-COLL: usu sing, N *of* n N-COUNT: usu sing, N *of* n

**ar|rayed** /əreɪd/ 1 If things are **arrayed** in a particular way, they are arranged or displayed in that way. [FORMAL] ❑ *Cartons of Chinese food were arrayed on a large oak table.* 2 If something such as a military force is **arrayed against** someone, it is ready and able to be used against them. [FORMAL] ADJ: v-link ADJ, usu ADJ prep/adv ADJ: v-link ADJ *against* n

**ar|rears** /ərɪə^rz/ 1 **Arrears** are amounts of money that you owe, especially regular payments that you should have made earlier. ❑ *They have promised to pay the arrears over the next five years.* N-PLURAL

**PHRASES** 2 If someone is **in arrears with** their payments, or has got **into arrears**, they have not paid the regular amounts of money that they should have paid. ❑ *...the 300,000 households who are more than six months in arrears with their mortgages.* 3 If sums of money such as wages or taxes are paid **in arrears**, they are paid at the end of the period of time to which they relate, for example after a job has been done and the wages have been earned. ❑ *Unemployment benefit is paid fortnightly in arrears.* PHRASE: v-link PHR, PHR after v, oft amount PHR, PHR *with/on* n PHRASE: PHR after v

**ar|rest** /ərest/ **(arrests, arresting, arrested)** ◆◆◇ 1 If the police **arrest** you, they take charge of you and take you to a police station, because they believe you may have committed a crime. ❑ *Police arrested five young men in connection with one of the attacks... The police say seven people were arrested for minor offences.* ♦ **Arrest** is also a noun. ❑ *Police chased the fleeing terrorists and later made two arrests... Murder squad detectives approached the man and placed him under arrest.* 2 If something or someone **arrests** a process, they stop it continuing. [FORMAL] ❑ *The sufferer may have to make major changes in his or her life to arrest the disease.* 3 If something interesting or surprising **arrests** your attention, you suddenly notice it and then continue to look at it or consider it carefully. [FORMAL] ❑ *The work of an architect of genius always arrests the attention no matter how little remains.* 4 → See also **house arrest**. VERB V n *be* V-ed *for* n N-VAR: oft *under* N VERB V n VERB V n

**ar|rest|able** /ərestəbəl/ An **arrestable** offence is an offence that you can be arrested for. ❑ *Possession of cannabis will no longer be an arrestable offence.* ADJ: usu ADJ n

**ar|ri|val** /əraɪvəl/ **(arrivals)** 1 When a person or vehicle arrives at a place, you can refer to their **arrival**. ❑ *...the day after his arrival in England... He* ◆◇◇ N-VAR: oft with poss, *on* N *was dead on arrival at the nearby hospital. ...the airport arrivals hall.* ≠ departure [2] When someone starts a new job, you can refer to their **arrival** in that job. ❑ *...the power vacuum created by the arrival of a new president.* N-VAR: oft with poss ≠ departure [3] When something is brought to you or becomes available, you can refer to its **arrival**. ❑ *I was flicking idly through a newspaper while awaiting the arrival of orange juice and coffee.* N-SING: usu with poss [4] When a particular time comes or a particular event happens, you can refer to its **arrival**. ❑ *He celebrated the arrival of the New Year with a party for his friends.* N-SING: usu N *of* n = coming [5] You can refer to someone who has just arrived at a place as a new **arrival**. ❑ *A high proportion of the new arrivals are skilled professionals.* N-COUNT: usu adj N = newcomer

**ar|rive** /əraɪv/ **(arrives, arriving, arrived)** ◆◆◇ [1] When a person or vehicle **arrives** at a place, they come to it at the end of a journey. ❑ *Fresh groups of guests arrived... The Princess Royal arrived at Gatwick this morning from Jamaica.* VERB ≠ depart V V prep/adv [2] When you **arrive** at a place, you come to it for the first time in order to stay, live, or work there. ❑ *...in the old days before the European settlers arrived in the country.* VERB V prep/adv [3] When something such as letter or meal **arrives**, it is brought or delivered to you. ❑ *Breakfast arrived while he was in the bathroom.* VERB V [4] When something such as a new product or invention **arrives**, it becomes available. ❑ *Several long-awaited videos will finally arrive in the shops this month.* VERB = appear V [5] When a particular moment or event **arrives**, it happens, especially after you have been waiting for it or expecting it. ❑ *The time has arrived when I need to give up smoking. ...the belief that the army would be much further forward before winter arrived.* VERB V V [6] When you **arrive at** something such as a decision, you decide something after thinking about it or discussing it. ❑ *...if the jury cannot arrive at a unanimous decision.* VERB V *at* n

**ar|ri|viste** /æriviːst/ **(arrivistes)** You describe someone as an **arriviste** when you are criticizing them because they are trying very hard to belong to an influential or important social group which you feel they have no right to belong to. [FORMAL] ❑ *...political arrivistes.* N-COUNT disapproval

**ar|ro|gant** /ærəgənt/ Someone who is **arrogant** behaves in a proud, unpleasant way towards other people because they believe that they are more important than others. ❑ *He was so arrogant... That sounds arrogant, doesn't it?* ADJ disapproval
♦ **ar|ro|gance** *At times the arrogance of those in power is quite blatant.* N-UNCOUNT

**ar|ro|gate** /ærəgeɪt/ **(arrogates, arrogating, arrogated)** If someone **arrogates to** themselves something such as a responsibility or privilege, they claim or take it even though they have no right to do so. [FORMAL] ❑ *The assembly arrogated to itself the right to make changes... He arrogated the privilege to himself alone.* VERB disapproval V *to* pron-refl n V n *to* pron-refl

**ar|row** /æroʊ/ **(arrows)** [1] An **arrow** is a long thin weapon which is sharp and pointed at one end and which often has feathers at the other end. An arrow is shot from a bow. ❑ *Warriors armed with bows and arrows and spears have invaded their villages.* N-COUNT [2] An **arrow** is a written or printed sign that consists of a straight line with another line bent at a sharp angle at one end. This is a printed arrow: →. The arrow points in a particular direction to indicate where something is. ❑ *A series of arrows points the way to the modest grave of Andrei Sakharov.* N-COUNT

**arrow|head** /æroʊhed/ **(arrowheads)** also **arrow-head.** An **arrowhead** is the sharp, pointed part of an arrow. N-COUNT

**arrow|root** /æroʊruːt/ **Arrowroot** is a substance obtained from a West Indian plant. It is used in cooking, for example for thickening sauces or in making biscuits. N-UNCOUNT

**arse** /ɑːʳs/ **(arses)** [1] Your **arse** is your bottom. [BRIT, INFORMAL, RUDE] N-COUNT

✔ in AM, use **ass**

[2] **a pain in the arse** → see **pain**.

**arse|hole** /ɑːʳshoʊl/ **(arseholes)** If one person calls another person an **arsehole**, they think that person is extremely stupid or has behaved in a stupid way. [BRIT, RUDE] N-COUNT disapproval

✔ in AM, use **asshole**

**ar|senal** /ɑːʳsənəl/ **(arsenals)** [1] An **arsenal** is a large collection of weapons and military equipment held by a country, group, or person. ❑ *Russia and the other republics are committed to destroying most of their nuclear arsenals.* N-COUNT: usu with supp [2] An **arsenal** is a building where weapons and military equipment are stored. N-COUNT = armoury [3] You can use **arsenal** to refer to a large number of tools, methods, or resources that someone has available to help them achieve what they want they want to do. ❑ *Managers use a full arsenal of motivational techniques to get employees to take risks.* N-COUNT: usu sing, with supp

**ar|senic** /ɑːʳsənɪk/ **Arsenic** is a very strong poison which can kill people. N-UNCOUNT

**ar|son** /ɑːʳsən/ **Arson** is the crime of deliberately setting fire to a building or vehicle. ❑ *...a terrible wave of rioting, theft and arson.* N-UNCOUNT

**ar|son|ist** /ɑːʳsənɪst/ **(arsonists)** An **arsonist** is a person who deliberately sets fire to a building or vehicle. N-COUNT

**art** /ɑːʳt/ **(arts)** ◆◆◆ [1] **Art** consists of paintings, sculpture, and other pictures or objects which are created for people to look at and admire or think deeply about. ❑ *...the first exhibition of such art in the West. ...contemporary and modern American art. ...Whitechapel Art Gallery.* N-UNCOUNT [2] **Art** is the activity or educational subject that consists of creating paintings, sculptures, and other pictures or objects for people to look at and admire or think deeply about. ❑ *...a painter, content to be left alone with her all-absorbing art. ...Farnham College of Art and Design. ...art lessons.* N-UNCOUNT [3] **The arts** are activities such as music, painting, literature, cinema, and dance, which people can take part in for enjoyment, or to create works which express serious meanings or ideas of beauty. ❑ *Catherine the Great was a patron of the arts and sciences. ...the art of cinema.* N-VAR: usu *the* N in pl [4] At a university or college, **arts** are subjects such as history, literature, or languages in contrast to scientific subjects. ❑ *...arts and social science graduates. ...the Faculty of Arts.* N-PLURAL: oft N n [5] **Arts** or **art** is used in the names of theatres or cinemas which show plays or films that are intended to make the audience think deeply about the content, and not simply to entertain them. ❑ *...the Cambridge Arts Cinema.* ADJ: ADJ n [6] If you describe an activity as an **art**, you mean that it requires skill and that people learn to do it by instinct or experience, rather than by learning facts or rules. ❑ *Fishing is an art.* N-COUNT [7] **Art** is an old-fashioned form of the second person singular of the present tense of the verb **be**. [8] → See also **Bachelor of Arts**, **fine art**, **martial art**, **Master of Arts**, **state-of-the-art**, **work of art**.

**Art Deco** /ɑːʳt dekoʊ/ also **art deco.** **Art Deco** is a style of decoration and architecture that was common in the 1920s and 30s. It uses simple, bold designs on materials such as plastic and glass. ❑ *...art deco lamps.* N-UNCOUNT: oft N n

**ar|te|fact** /ɑːʳtɪfækt/ **(artefacts)** also **artifact.** An **artefact** is an ornament, tool, or other object that is made by a human being, especially one that is historically or culturally interesting. N-COUNT

**ar|te|rial** /ɑːʳtɪəriəl/ [1] **Arterial** means involving or relating to your arteries and the movement of blood through your body. ❑ *...people with arterial disease.* ADJ: ADJ n [2] An **arterial** road or railway is a main road or railway within a complex road or railway system. ADJ: ADJ n

**ar|te|rio|sclero|sis** /ɑːʳtɪərioʊskleroʊsɪs/ **Arteriosclerosis** is a medical condition in which the walls of your arteries become hard and thick, so your blood cannot flow through them properly. [MEDICAL] N-UNCOUNT

**ar|tery** /ɑːʳtəri/ **(arteries)** [1] **Arteries** are the tubes in your body that carry blood from your heart to the rest of your body. Compare **vein**. ❑ *...patients suffering from blocked arteries.* N-COUNT [2] You can refer to an important main route within a complex road, railway, or river system as an **artery**. ❑ *Clarence Street was one of the north-bound arteries of the central business district.* N-COUNT

**art form** **(art forms)** If you describe an activity as an **art form**, you mean that it is concerned with creating objects, works, or performances that are beautiful or have a serious meaning. ❑ *...Indian dance and related art forms.* N-COUNT

**art|ful** /ɑːʳtfʊl/ [1] If you describe someone as **artful**, you mean that they are clever and skilful at achieving what they want, especially by deceiving people. ❑ *Some politicians have realised that there are more artful ways of subduing people than shooting or jailing them.* ADJ: usu ADJ n = crafty [2] If you use **artful** to describe the way someone has done or arranged something, you approve of it because it is clever or elegant. [FORMAL] ❑ *There is also an artful contrast of shapes.* ADJ: usu ADJ n [approval]

**art-house** also **arthouse.** An **art-house** film is a film that is intended to be a serious artistic work rather than a piece of popular entertainment. ADJ: ADJ n

**ar|thrit|ic** /ɑːʳθrɪtɪk/ [1] **Arthritic** is used to describe the condition, the pain, or the symptoms of arthritis. ❑ *I developed serious arthritic symptoms and chronic sinusitis.* ADJ: ADJ n [2] An **arthritic** person is suffering from arthritis, and cannot move very easily. **Arthritic** joints or hands are affected by arthritis. ❑ *...an elderly lady who suffered with arthritic hands.* ADJ

**ar|thri|tis** /ɑːʳθraɪtɪs/ **Arthritis** is a medical condition in which the joints in someone's body are swollen and painful. ❑ *I have a touch of arthritis in the wrist.* ➔ See also **rheumatoid arthritis.** N-UNCOUNT

**ar|ti|choke** /ɑːʳtɪtʃoʊk/ **(artichokes)** [1] **Artichokes** or **globe artichokes** are round green vegetables that have fleshy leaves arranged like the petals of a flower. [2] ➔ See also **Jerusalem artichoke.** N-VAR

**ar|ti|cle** /ɑːʳtɪkəl/ **(articles)** ◆◆◇ [1] An **article** is a piece of writing that is published in a newspaper or magazine. ❑ *...a newspaper article... According to an article in The Economist the drug could have side effects.* N-COUNT: oft N prep [2] You can refer to objects as **articles** of some kind. ❑ *...articles of clothing. ...household articles.* N-COUNT: oft N *of* n [3] If you describe something as **the genuine article**, you are emphasizing that it is genuine, and often that it is very good. ❑ *The vodka was the genuine article.* PHRASE: v-link PHR, PHR after v [emphasis] [4] An **article of** a formal agreement or document is a section of it which deals with a particular point. ❑ *...Article 50 of the UN charter.* N-COUNT: oft N *of* n, N num [5] Someone who is in **articles** is being trained as a lawyer or accountant by a firm with whom they have a written agreement. [BRIT] N-PLURAL: usu prep N [6] In grammar, an **article** is a kind of determiner. In English, 'a' and 'an' are called **the indefinite article**, and 'the' is called **the definite article**. N-COUNT

**ar|ti|cled** /ɑːʳtɪkəld/ In Britain, someone who is **articled to** a firm of lawyers or accountants is employed by the firm and is training to become qualified. ❑ *He was initially articled to a solicitor. ...an articled clerk.* ADJ: v-link ADJ *to* n, ADJ n

**ar|ti|cle of faith** **(articles of faith)** If something is an **article of faith** for a person or group, they believe in it totally. ❑ *For Republicans it is almost an article of faith that this tax should be cut.* N-COUNT

**ar|ticu|late** **(articulates, articulating, articulated)**

> ✔ The adjective is pronounced /ɑːʳtɪkjʊlət/. The verb is pronounced /ɑːʳtɪkjʊleɪt/.

[1] If you describe someone as **articulate**, you mean that they are able to express their thoughts and ideas easily and well. ❑ *She is an articulate young woman.* ADJ [approval] [2] When you **articulate** your ideas or feelings, you express them clearly in words. [FORMAL] ❑ *The president has been accused of failing to articulate an overall vision in foreign affairs.* VERB V n/wh [3] If you **articulate** something, you say it very clearly, so that each word or syllable can be heard. ❑ *He articulated each syllable carefully.* VERB V n

**ar|ticu|lat|ed** /ɑːʳtɪkjʊleɪtɪd/ An **articulated** vehicle, especially a lorry, is made in two or more sections which are joined together by metal bars, so that the vehicle can turn more easily. [BRIT] ADJ: usu ADJ n

> ✔ in AM, usually use **rig, trailer truck**

**ar|ticu|la|tion** /ɑːʳtɪkjʊleɪʃən/ [1] **Articulation** is the action of producing a sound or word clearly, in speech or music. [FORMAL] N-UNCOUNT [2] The **articulation of** an idea or feeling is the expression of it, especially in words. [FORMAL] ❑ *This was seen as a way of restricting women's articulation of grievances.* N-UNCOUNT: usu N *of* n

**ar|ti|fact** /ɑːʳtɪfækt/ ➔ see **artefact.**

**ar|ti|fice** /ɑːʳtɪfɪs/ **(artifices)** **Artifice** is the clever use of tricks and devices. [FORMAL] ❑ *Weegee's photographs are full of artfulness, and artifice.* N-VAR

**ar|ti|fi|cial** /ɑːʳtɪfɪʃəl/ [1] **Artificial** objects, materials, or processes do not occur naturally and are created by human beings, for example using science or technology. ❑ *...a wholefood diet free from artificial additives... The city is dotted with small lakes, natural and artificial.* ADJ = synthetic ≠ natural ♦ **ar|ti|fi|cial|ly** *...drugs which artificially reduce the patient's heart rate.* ADV: usu ADV with v, also ADV adj [2] An **artificial** state or situation exists only because someone has created it, and therefore often seems unnatural or unnecessary. ❑ *Removed from the artificial atmosphere of the fashion show, high-fashion clothes often look cheap and silly.* ADJ: usu ADJ n ♦ **ar|ti|fi|cial|ly** *...state subsidies that have kept retail prices artificially low.* ADV: ADV adj, ADV with v [3] If you describe someone or their behaviour as **artificial**, you disapprove of them because they pretend to have attitudes and feelings which they do not really have. ❑ *The voice was patronizing and affected, the accent artificial.* ADJ [disapproval]

**ar|ti|fi|cial in|semi|na|tion** **Artificial insemination** is a medical technique for making a woman pregnant by injecting previously stored sperm into her womb. Female animals can also be made pregnant by artificial insemination. The abbreviation **AI** is also used. N-UNCOUNT

**ar|ti|fi|cial in|tel|li|gence** **Artificial intelligence** is a type of computer technology which is concerned with making machines work in an intelligent way, similar to the way that the human mind works. The abbreviation **AI** is also used. N-UNCOUNT

**ar|ti|fi|cial res|pi|ra|tion** **Artificial respiration** is the forcing of air into the lungs of someone who has stopped breathing, usually by blowing through their mouth or nose, in order to keep them alive and to help them to start breathing again. ❑ *She was given artificial respiration and cardiac massage.* N-UNCOUNT

**ar|til|lery** /ɑːʳtɪləri/ [1] **Artillery** consists of large, powerful guns which are transported on wheels and used by an army. ❑ *Using tanks and heavy artillery, they seized the town. ...the sound of artillery fire.* N-UNCOUNT: oft N n [2] **The artillery** is the section of an army which is trained to use large, powerful guns. N-SING-COLL: *the* N

**ar|ti|san** /ɑːʳtɪzæn, AM -zən/ **(artisans)** An **artisan** is someone whose job requires skill with their hands. N-COUNT = craftsman

**art|ist** /ɑːʳtɪst/ **(artists)** ◆◆◇ [1] An **artist** is someone who draws or paints pictures or creates sculptures as a job or a hobby. ❑ *Each poster is signed by the artist... I'm not a good artist.* N-COUNT [2] An **artist** is a person who creates novels, poems, films, or other things which can be considered as works of art. ❑ *His books are enormously easy to read, yet he is a serious artist.* N-COUNT [3] An **artist** is a performer such as a musician, actor, or dancer. ❑ *...a popular artist who has sold millions of records.* N-COUNT [4] If you say that someone is an **artist** at a particular activity, you mean N-COUNT: usu with supp they are very skilled at it. ❑ *He is an exceptional footballer — an artist.*

**ar|tiste** /ɑːˈtiːst/ **(artistes)** An **artiste** is a professional entertainer, for example a singer or a dancer. [mainly BRIT] ❑ *...a cabaret artiste.* N-COUNT: oft supp N

**ar|tis|tic** /ɑːˈtɪstɪk/ 1 Someone who is **artistic** is good at drawing or painting, or arranging things in a beautiful way. ❑ *They encourage boys to be sensitive and artistic... Mary's got it all so nice – you remember how artistic she always was with colors.* ADJ 2 **Artistic** means relating to art or artists. ❑ *...the campaign for artistic freedom. ...their 1,300 year old artistic traditions.* ADJ: usu ADJ n ♦ **ar|tis|ti|cal|ly** /ɑːˈtɪstɪkli/ *...artistically gifted children... Artistically, the photographs are stunning.* ADV: usu ADV adj/-ed, ADV with cl 3 An **artistic** design or arrangement is beautiful. ❑ *...an artistic arrangement of stone paving.* ADJ ♦ **ar|tis|ti|cal|ly** *...artistically carved garden ornaments.* ADV: ADV after v, ADV -ed

**art|ist|ry** /ɑːˈtɪstri/ **Artistry** is the creative skill of an artist, writer, actor, or musician. ❑ *...portrait sculptors of considerable skill and artistry.* N-UNCOUNT: oft with poss

**art|less** /ɑːˈtləs/ Someone who is **artless** is simple and honest, and does not think of deceiving other people. ❑ *She was curiously artless. ...Hemingway's artless air and charming smile.* ADJ

**Art Nou|veau** /ɑːˈt nuːvoʊ/ also **art nouveau. Art Nouveau** is a style of decoration and architecture that was common in the 1890s. It is characterized by flowing lines and patterns of flowers and leaves. ❑ *We lunched at the stunning art nouveau Café American.* N-UNCOUNT: oft N n

**artsy** /ɑːˈtsi/ **Artsy** means the same as **arty**. [INFORMAL] ADJ

**artsy-fartsy** → see **arty-farty**.

**art|work** /ɑːˈtwɜːˈk/ **(artworks)** 1 **Artwork** is drawings and photographs that are prepared in order to be included in something such as a book or advertisement. ❑ *The artwork for the LP was done by Bill Hofstadter.* N-UNCOUNT 2 **Artworks** are paintings or sculptures which are of high quality. ❑ *The museum contains 6,000 contemporary and modern artworks. ...a magnificent collection of priceless artwork.* N-VAR = work of art

**arty** /ɑːˈti/ Someone who is **arty** seems very interested in drama, film, music, poetry, or painting. People often describe someone as arty when they want to suggest that the person is pretentious. [INFORMAL] ❑ *Didn't you find her a little bit too arty? ...an arty French film.* ADJ = artsy

**arty-farty** or **artsy-fartsy** If you describe someone as **arty-farty**, you are criticizing them for being interested in artistic ideas or activities that most people do not think are interesting or worthwhile. [BRIT, INFORMAL] ❑ *...an artsy-fartsy pretentious film.* ADJ disapproval = pretentious

**as**

① CONJUNCTION AND PREPOSITION USES

② USED WITH OTHER PREPOSITIONS AND CONJUNCTIONS

① **as** /əz, STRONG æz/ ◆◆◆

⇒ Please look at category 12 to see if the expression you are looking for is shown under another headword. 1 If something happens **as** something else happens, it happens at the same time. ❑ *Another policeman has been injured as fighting continued this morning... All the jury's eyes were on him as he continued... The play started as I got there.* CONJ 2 You use the structure **as...as** when you are comparing things. ❑ *I never went through a final exam that was as difficult as that one... There was no obvious reason why this could not be as good a film as the original.* PHRASE ♦ **As** is also a conjunction. ❑ *Being a mother isn't as bad as I thought at first!... I don't think he was ever as fit as he should have been.* PHRASE 3 You use **as...as** to emphasize amounts of something. ❑ *You can look forward to a significant cash return by saving from as little as £10 a month... She gets as many as eight thousand letters a month.* PHRASE emphasis 4 You use **as** when you are indicating what someone or something is or is thought to be, or what function they have. ❑ *He has worked as a diplomat in the US, Sudan and Saudi Arabia... The news apparently came as a complete surprise... I had natural ability as a footballer.* PREP 5 If you do something **as** a child or **as** a teenager, for example, you do it when you are a child or a teenager. ❑ *She loved singing as a child and started vocal training at 12.* PREP 6 You use **as** to say how something happens or is done, or to indicate that something happens or is done in the same way as something else. ❑ *I'll behave toward them as I would like to be treated... Today, as usual, he was wearing a three-piece suit... The book was banned in the US, as were two subsequent books.* CONJ 7 You use **as** in expressions like **as a result** and **as a consequence** to indicate how two situations or events are related to each other. ❑ *As a result of the growing fears about home security, more people are arranging for someone to stay in their home when they're away.* PREP 8 You use **as** to introduce short clauses which comment on the truth of what you are saying. ❑ *As you can see, we're still working... We were sitting, as I remember, in a riverside restaurant.* CONJ 9 You can use **as** to mean 'because' when you are explaining the reason for something. ❑ *Enjoy the first hour of the day. This is important as it sets the mood for the rest of the day.* CONJ = since

PHRASES 10 You say **as it were** in order to make what you are saying sound less definite. ❑ *I'd understood the words, but I didn't, as it were, understand the question.* PHRASE: PHR with cl vagueness 11 You use expressions such as **as it is**, **as it turns out**, and **as things stand** when you are making a contrast between a possible situation and what actually happened or is the case. ❑ *I want to work at home on a Tuesday but as it turns out sometimes it's a Wednesday or a Thursday.* PHRASE 12 **as against** → see **against**. **as ever** → see **ever**. **as a matter of fact** → see **fact**. **as follows** → see **follow**. **as long as** → see **long**. **as opposed to** → see **opposed**. **as regards** → see **regard**. **as soon as** → see **soon**. **as such** → see **such**. **as well** → see **well**. **as well as** → see **well**. **as yet** → see **yet**.

② **as** /əz, STRONG æz/ 1 You use **as for** and **as to** at the beginning of a sentence in order to introduce a slightly different subject that is still connected to the previous one. ❑ *I feel that there's a lot of pressure put on policemen. And as for putting guns in their hands, I don't think that's a very good idea at all.* ◆◆◆ PREP-PHRASE: PREP n/-ing 2 You use **as to** to indicate what something refers to. ❑ *They should make decisions as to whether the student needs more help.* PREP-PHRASE: PREP wh 3 If you say that something will happen **as of**, or in British English **as from**, a particular date or time, you mean that it will happen from that time on. ❑ *The border, effectively closed since 1981, will be opened as of January the 1st... She is to retire as from 1 October.* PREP-PHRASE 4 You use **as if** and **as though** when you are giving a possible explanation for something or saying that something appears to be the case when it is not. ❑ *Anne shrugged, as if she didn't know.* PHRASE

**asap** /eɪ es eɪ piː/ **asap** is an abbreviation for 'as soon as possible'. ❑ *The colonel ordered, 'I want two good engines down here asap.'* ADV: ADV after v

**as|bes|tos** /æsbestɒs/ **Asbestos** is a grey material which does not burn and which has been used as a protection against fire or heat. N-UNCOUNT: oft N n

**as|cend** /əsend/ **(ascends, ascending, ascended)** 1 If you **ascend** a hill or staircase, you go up it. [WRITTEN] ❑ *Mrs Clayton had to hold Lizzie's hand as they ascended the steps... Then we ascend steeply through forests of rhododendron.* VERB ≠ descend V n V prep/adv Also V 2 If a staircase or path **ascends**, it leads up to a higher position. [WRITTEN] VERB ≠ descend 3 If something **ascends**, it moves up, usually vertically or into the air. [WRITTEN] ❑ *Keep the drill steady while it ascends and descends.* VERB ≠ descend V 4 If someone **ascends to** an important position, they achieve it or are appointed to it. When someone VERB

**ascends** a throne, they become king, queen, or pope. [FORMAL] 5 → See also **ascending**.

**as|cend|ancy** /əse̲ndənsi/ also **ascendency.** If one group has **ascendancy** over another group, it has more power or influence than the other group. [FORMAL] ❑ *Although geographically linked, the two provinces have long fought for political ascendancy.* N-UNCOUNT = dominance

**as|cend|ant** /əse̲ndənt/ If someone or something is **in the ascendant**, they have or are getting more power, influence, or popularity than other people or things. [FORMAL] ❑ *Radical reformers are once more in the ascendant.* PHRASE: v-link PHR

**as|cend|ency** /əse̲ndənsi/ → see **ascendancy**.

**as|cend|ing** /əse̲ndɪŋ/ If a group of things is arranged in **ascending** order, each thing is bigger, greater, or more important than the thing before it. ❑ *Now draw or trace ten dinosaurs in ascending order of size.* → See also **ascend**. ADJ: ADJ n

**as|cen|sion** /əse̲nʃən/ 1 In some religions, when someone goes to heaven, you can refer to their **ascension to** heaven. ❑ *...the two-day holiday marking the Prophet's ascension to heaven.* N-SING: with poss
2 The **ascension** of a person **to** a high rank or important position is the act of reaching this position. [WRITTEN] ❑ *...50 years after his ascension to the Cambodian throne.* N-SING: with poss, usu N *to* n

**as|cent** /əse̲nt/ **(ascents)** 1 An **ascent** is an upward journey, especially when you are walking or climbing. ❑ *In 1955 he led the first ascent of Kangchenjunga, the world's third highest mountain.* N-COUNT: oft N *of* n ≠ descent
2 An **ascent** is an upward slope or path, especially when you are walking or climbing. ❑ *It was a tough course over a long, gradual ascent before the big climb of Bluebell Hill.* N-COUNT ≠ descent
3 An **ascent** is an upward, vertical movement. ❑ *Burke pushed the button and the elevator began its slow ascent.* N-COUNT: usu sing, oft poss N ≠ descent
4 The **ascent** of a person **to** a more important or successful position is the process of reaching this position. [WRITTEN] N-SING: usu with supp = rise
5 In some religions, when someone goes to heaven, you can refer to their **ascent to** heaven. N-SING: N prep

**as|cer|tain** /æ̲sərte̲ɪn/ **(ascertains, ascertaining, ascertained)** If you **ascertain** the truth about something, you find out what it is, especially by making a deliberate effort to do so. [FORMAL] VERB = establish
❑ *Through doing this, the teacher will be able to ascertain the extent to which the child understands what he is reading... Once they had ascertained that he was not a spy, they agreed to release him... Take time to ascertain what services your bank is providing, and at what cost.* V n; V that; V wh

**as|cet|ic** /əse̲tɪk/ **(ascetics)** An **ascetic** person has a way of life that is simple and strict, usually because of their religious beliefs. ADJ: usu ADJ n
♦ An **ascetic** is someone who is ascetic. N-COUNT

**as|ceti|cism** /əse̲tɪsɪzəm/ **Asceticism** is a simple, strict way of life with no luxuries or physical pleasures. N-UNCOUNT

**ascor|bic acid** /æskɔ̲ːrbɪk æ̲sɪd/ **Ascorbic acid** is another name for vitamin C. [TECHNICAL] N-UNCOUNT

**as|cribe** /əskra̲ɪb/ **(ascribes, ascribing, ascribed)** 1 If you **ascribe** an event or condition **to** a particular cause, you say or consider that it was caused by that thing. [FORMAL] ❑ *An autopsy eventually ascribed the baby's death to sudden infant death syndrome.* VERB = attribute; V n *to* n
2 If you **ascribe** a quality **to** someone, you consider that they possess it. [FORMAL] ❑ *We do not ascribe a superior wisdom to government or the state.* VERB = attribute; V n *to* n
3 If you **ascribe** something such as a quotation or a work of art **to** someone, you say that they said it or created it. [FORMAL] ❑ *He mistakenly ascribes the expression 'survival of the fittest' to Charles Darwin.* VERB = attribute; V n *to* n

**asexu|al** /eɪse̲kʃuəl/ 1 Something that is **asexual** involves no sexual activity. ❑ *Their relationship was totally asexual. ...asexual reproduction.* ADJ
♦ **asexu|al|ly** *Many fungi can reproduce asexually.* ADV: ADV with v, also ADV adj
2 **Asexual** creatures and plants have no sexual organs. ❑ *...asexual parasites.* ADJ
3 Someone who is **asexual** is not sexually attracted to other people. ❑ *It is another unfortunate myth of our culture that older people are asexual.* ADJ

**ash** /æ̲ʃ/ **(ashes)** 1 **Ash** is the grey or black powdery substance that is left after something is burnt. You can also refer to this substance as **ashes**. ❑ *A cloud of volcanic ash is spreading across wide areas of the Philippines... He brushed the cigarette ash from his sleeve.* N-UNCOUNT: also N in pl
2 A dead person's **ashes** are their remains after their body has been cremated. N-PLURAL: usu poss N
3 An **ash** is a tree that has smooth grey bark and loses its leaves in winter. N-VAR
♦ **Ash** is the wood from this tree. ❑ *The rafters are made from ash.* N-UNCOUNT

**ashamed** /əʃe̲ɪmd/ 1 If someone is **ashamed**, they feel embarrassed or guilty because of something they do or they have done, or because of their appearance. ❑ *I felt incredibly ashamed of myself for getting so angry... She was ashamed that she looked so shabby.* ADJ: v-link ADJ, usu ADJ *of*/*about* n, ADJ that ≠ proud
2 If you are **ashamed of** someone, you feel embarrassed to be connected with them, often because of their appearance or because you disapprove of something they have done. ❑ *I've never told this to anyone, but it's true, I was terribly ashamed of my mum.* ADJ: v-link ADJ *of* n ≠ proud
3 If someone is **ashamed to** do something, they do not want to do it because they feel embarrassed about it. ❑ *Women are often ashamed to admit they are being abused.* ADJ: v-link ADJ to-inf ≠ proud

**ash|en** /æ̲ʃən/ Someone who is **ashen** looks very pale, especially because they are ill, shocked, or frightened. ADJ = pallid

**ashen-faced** Someone who is **ashen-faced** looks very pale, especially because they are ill, shocked, or frightened. ❑ *The survivors were ashen-faced and visibly shaken.* ADJ

**ashore** /əʃɔ̲ːr/ Someone or something that comes **ashore** comes from the sea onto the shore. ❑ *Oil has come ashore on a ten mile stretch to the east of Plymouth.* ADV: ADV after v, *be* ADV

**ash|tray** /æ̲ʃtreɪ/ **(ashtrays)** An **ashtray** is a small dish in which smokers can put the ash from their cigarettes and cigars. N-COUNT

**Ash Wednes|day** **Ash Wednesday** is the first day of Lent. N-UNCOUNT

**Asian** /e̲ɪʒən/ **(Asians)** Someone or something that is **Asian** comes from or is associated with Asia. British people use this term especially to refer to India, Pakistan, and Bangladesh. Americans use this term especially to refer to China, Korea, Thailand, Japan, or Vietnam. ❑ *...Asian music. ...the Asian community in San Francisco.* ADJ
♦ An **Asian** is a person who comes from or is associated with a country or region in Asia. ❑ *Many of the shops were run by Asians.* N-COUNT

**Asi|at|ic** /e̲ɪʒiæ̲tɪk/ **Asiatic** means belonging or relating to Asia or its people. [OLD-FASHIONED] ADJ: ADJ n = Asian

**A-side** **(A-sides)** The **A-side** of a record that has been released as a single is the main song on it. You can also refer to the side of the record that contains this song as **the A-side**. Compare **B-side**. N-COUNT

**aside**
① ADVERB AND NOUN USES
② PREPOSITION USES

**①aside** /əsa̲ɪd/ **(asides)** ◆◇◇

In addition to the uses shown below, **aside** is used in phrasal verbs such as 'cast aside', 'stand aside', and 'step aside'.

1 If you move something **aside**, you move it to one side of you. ❑ *Sarah closed the book and laid it aside.* ADV: ADV after v
2 If you take or draw someone **aside**, you take them a little way away from a group of people in order to talk to them in private. ❑ *Will put his arm around her shoulders and drew her aside.* ADV: ADV after v
3 If you move **aside**, you get out of someone's way. ❑ *She had been standing in the doorway, but* ADV: ADV after v

now she stepped aside to let them pass. [4] If you set something such as time, money, or space **aside** for a particular purpose, you save it and do not use it for anything else. ❑ *She wants to put her pocket-money aside for holidays. ...the ground set aside for the new cathedral.* [5] If you brush or sweep **aside** a feeling or suggestion, you reject it. ❑ *Talk to a friend who will really listen and not brush aside your feelings... The Prime Minister swept aside concern about the rising cost of mortgages.* [6] You use **aside** to indicate that you have finished talking about something, or that you are leaving it out of your discussion, and that you are about to talk about something else. ❑ *Leaving aside the tiny minority who are clinically depressed, most people who have bad moods also have very good moods... Emotional arguments aside, here are the facts.* [7] An **aside** is a comment that a character in a play makes to the audience, which the other characters are supposed not to be able to hear. ❑ *Exasperated with her children, she rolls her eyes and mutters an aside to the camera, 'No wonder I drink!'* [8] An **aside** is something that you say that is not directly connected with what you are talking about. ❑ *The pace of the book is leisurely, with enjoyable literary and historical asides.*

ADV: ADV after v · ADV: ADV after v · ADV: ADV after v, n ADV = apart · N-COUNT · N-COUNT = digression

②**aside from** **Aside from** means the same as **apart from**. This form is more usual in American English. PREP-PHRASE = apart from

**asi|nine** /æsɪnaɪn/ If you describe something or someone as **asinine**, you mean that they are very foolish. [FORMAL] ❑ *...an asinine discussion.* ADJ [disapproval] = idiotic

**ask** /ɑːsk, æsk/ **(asks, asking, asked)** [1] If you **ask** someone something, you say something to them in the form of a question because you want to know the answer. ❑ *'How is Frank?' he asked... I asked him his name... I wasn't the only one asking questions... She asked me if I'd enjoyed my dinner... If Daniel asks what happened in court we will tell him... You will have to ask David about that... 'I'm afraid to ask what it cost.' — 'Then don't ask.'* [2] If you **ask** someone **to** do something, you tell them that you want them to do it. ❑ *We had to ask him to leave.* [3] If you **ask to** do something, you tell someone that you want to do it. ❑ *I asked to see the Director.* [4] If you **ask for** something, you say that you would like it. ❑ *I decided to go to the next house and ask for food.* [5] If you **ask for** someone, you say that you would like to speak to them. ❑ *There's a man at the gate asking for you.* [6] If you **ask** someone's permission, opinion, or forgiveness, you try to obtain it by putting a request to them. ❑ *Please ask permission from whoever pays the phone bill before making your call.* [7] If you **ask** someone **to** an event or place, you invite them to go there. ❑ *Couldn't you ask Jon to the party?... She asked me back to her house.* [8] If someone **is asking** a particular price **for** something, they are selling it for that price. ❑ *Mr Pantelaras was asking £6,000 for his collection.* [9] You reply **'don't ask me'** when you do not know the answer to a question, usually when you are annoyed or surprised that you have been asked. ❑ *'She's got other things on her mind, wouldn't you think?' 'Don't ask me,' murmured Chris. 'I've never met her.'*

◆◆◆ VERB · V with quote · V n n · V n · V n wh · V wh · V n about n · V · VERB · V n to-inf · VERB · V to-inf · VERB · V for n · VERB · V for n · VERB · V n · VERB · V n to/for n · V n adv · VERB · V n for n · CONVENTION [feelings]

PHRASES [10] You can say **'may I ask'** as a formal way of asking a question, which shows you are annoyed or suspicious about something. ❑ *May I ask where you're going, sir?* [11] You can say **'if you ask me'** to emphasize that you are stating your personal opinion. ❑ *He was nuts, if you ask me.* [12] If you say that someone **is asking for trouble** or **is asking for it**, you mean that they are behaving in a way that makes it very likely that they will get into trouble. ❑ *To go ahead with the match after such clear advice had been asking for trouble.*

PHRASE [feelings] · PHRASE: PHR with cl [emphasis] · PHRASE: V inflects

◆ **ask after** If someone **asks after** you, they ask someone how you are. ❑ *I had a letter from Jane. She asks after you.* PHRASAL VERB = inquire after · V P n

◆ **ask around**

✔ in BRIT, also use **ask round**

If you **ask around** or **ask round**, you ask several people a question. ❑ *Ask around to see what others living in your area think about their doctors.* PHRASAL VERB · V P

**askance** /əskæns/ [1] If you **look askance at** someone or something, you have a doubtful or suspicious attitude towards them. ❑ *They have always looked askance at the western notion of democracy.* [2] If you **look askance at** someone, you look at them in a doubtful or suspicious way. PHRASE: V inflects, usu PHR at n · PHRASE: V inflects, usu PHR at n

**askew** /əskjuː/ Something that is **askew** is not straight or not level with what it should be level with. ❑ *There were no shutters at the windows, and some of the doors hung askew.* ADJ: v-link ADJ

**ask|ing price** **(asking prices)** The **asking price** of something is the price which the person selling it says that they want for it, although they may accept less. ❑ *Offers 15% below the asking price are unlikely to be accepted.* N-COUNT: usu sing

**asleep** /əsliːp/ [1] Someone who is **asleep** is sleeping. ❑ *My four year-old daughter was asleep on the sofa.* ADJ: v-link ADJ ≠ awake

PHRASES [2] When you **fall asleep**, you start sleeping. ❑ *Sam snuggled down in his pillow and fell asleep.* [3] Someone who is **fast asleep** or **sound asleep** is sleeping deeply. PHRASE: V inflects · PHRASE: v-link PHR

**as|para|gus** /əspærəgəs/ **Asparagus** is a vegetable that is long and green and has small shoots at one end. It is cooked and served whole. N-UNCOUNT

**as|pect** /æspekt/ **(aspects)** [1] An **aspect** of something is one of the parts of its character or nature. ❑ *Climate and weather affect every aspect of our lives... He was interested in all aspects of the work here.* [2] The **aspect** of a building or window is the direction in which it faces. [FORMAL] ❑ *The house had a south-west aspect.* [3] In grammar, **aspect** is the way that a verb group shows whether an activity is continuing, is repeated, or is completed. For example, in 'They were laughing', the verb is in the progressive aspect and shows that the action was continuing. Compare **tense**.

◆◆◇ N-COUNT: usu with supp · N-COUNT: usu sing, usu with supp · N-UNCOUNT

**as|pen** /æspən/ **(aspens)** An **aspen** is a tall tree with leaves that move a lot in the wind. N-VAR

**as|per|ity** /æsperɪti/ If you say something **with asperity**, you say it impatiently and severely. [FORMAL] ❑ *'I told you Preskel had no idea,' remarked Kemp with some asperity.* N-UNCOUNT: oft with N = sharpness

**as|per|sions** /əspɜːʳʃənz, AM -ʒənz/ If you **cast aspersions on** someone or something, you suggest that they are not very good in some way. [FORMAL] PHRASE: V inflects, usu PHR on n

**as|phalt** /æsfælt, -fɔːlt/ **Asphalt** is a black substance used to make the surfaces of things such as roads and playgrounds. N-UNCOUNT: oft N n = tarmac

**as|phyxia** /æsfɪksiə/ **Asphyxia** is death or loss of consciousness caused by being unable to breathe properly. [MEDICAL] ❑ *Death was due to asphyxia through smoke inhalation.* N-UNCOUNT = suffocation

**as|phyxi|ate** /æsfɪksieɪt/ **(asphyxiates, asphyxiating, asphyxiated)** If someone **is asphyxiated**, they die or lose consciousness because they are unable to breathe properly. ❑ *Three people were asphyxiated in the crush for last week's train.* VERB: usu passive = suffocate · be V-ed

◆ **as|phyxia|tion** /æsfɪksieɪʃən/ *A post mortem examination found that she died from asphyxiation.* N-UNCOUNT

**as|pic** /æspɪk/ **Aspic** is a clear shiny jelly made from meat juices. It is used in making cold savoury meat dishes. ❑ *...cold chicken in aspic.* N-UNCOUNT

**as|pir|ant** /əspaɪrənt, æspɪrənt/ **(aspirants)** [1] Someone who is an **aspirant to** political power or to an important job has a strong desire to achieve it. [FORMAL] ❑ *...the young aspirant to power.* [2] **Aspirant** means the same as **aspiring**. [FORMAL] ❑ *...aspirant politicians.* N-COUNT · ADJ: ADJ n = would-be

**as|pi|ra|tion** /æspɪreɪʃən/ **(aspirations)** Someone's **aspirations** are their desire to achieve things. ❑ *...the needs and aspirations of our pupils. ...the republic's aspiration to statehood.* N-VAR: usu with supp

**as|pi|ra|tion|al** /æspɪreɪʃənəl/ [1] If you describe someone as **aspirational**, you mean that they have strong hopes of moving to a higher social status. [JOURNALISM] ❑ *...the typical tensions of an aspirational household.* [2] If you describe a product as **aspirational**, you mean that it is bought or enjoyed by people who have strong hopes of moving to a higher social class. [JOURNALISM] ❑ *Fine music, particularly opera, has become aspirational, like fine wine or foreign travel.* ADJ ADJ

**as|pire** /əspaɪəʳ/ **(aspires, aspiring, aspired)** If you **aspire to** something such as an important job, you have a strong desire to achieve it. ❑ *...people who aspire to public office... They aspired to be gentlemen, though they fell far short of the ideal.* → See also **aspiring**. VERB V *to* n/-ing V to-inf

**as|pi|rin** /æspɪrɪn/ **(aspirins** or **aspirin)** **Aspirin** is a mild drug which reduces pain and fever. N-VAR

**as|pir|ing** /əspaɪərɪŋ/ If you use **aspiring** to describe someone who is starting a particular career, you mean that they are trying to become successful in it. ❑ *Many aspiring young artists are advised to learn by copying the masters.* → See also **aspire**. ADJ: ADJ n

**ass** /æs/ **(asses)** [1] An **ass** is an animal which is related to a horse but which is smaller and has long ears. [2] If you describe someone as an **ass**, you think that they are silly or do silly things. [INFORMAL] ❑ *He was generally disliked and regarded as a pompous ass.* [3] Your **ass** is your bottom. [AM, INFORMAL, RUDE] N-COUNT N-COUNT disapproval N-COUNT

✔ in BRIT, use **arse**, **bum**

[4] Saying that someone can **kiss** your **ass** is a very rude way of expressing anger or disagreement. [AM, INFORMAL, RUDE] [5] **a pain in the ass** → see **pain**. PHRASE: V inflects feelings

**as|sail** /əseɪl/ **(assails, assailing, assailed)** [1] If someone **assails** you, they criticize you strongly. [WRITTEN] ❑ *The opposition's newspapers assail the government each day.* [2] If someone **assails** you, they attack you violently. [WRITTEN] ❑ *Her husband was assailed by a young man with a knife in a Glasgow park.* [3] If you **are assailed by** something unpleasant such as fears or problems, you are greatly troubled by a large number of them. [WRITTEN] ❑ *She is assailed by self-doubt and emotional insecurity.* VERB = attack V n VERB = attack V n VERB: usu passive = beset *be* V-ed

**as|sail|ant** /əseɪlənt/ **(assailants)** Someone's **assailant** is a person who has physically attacked them. [FORMAL] ❑ *Other party-goers rescued the injured man from his assailant.* N-COUNT: usu poss N = attacker

**as|sas|sin** /əsæsɪn/ **(assassins)** An **assassin** is a person who assassinates someone. ❑ *He saw the shooting and memorised the number of the assassin's car.* N-COUNT

**as|sas|si|nate** /əsæsɪneɪt/ **(assassinates, assassinating, assassinated)** When someone important **is assassinated**, they are murdered as a political act. ❑ *Would the USA be radically different today if Kennedy had not been assassinated?... The plot to assassinate Martin Luther King had started long before he was actually killed.* ♦ **as|sas|si|na|tion** /əsæsɪneɪʃən/ **(assassinations)** *She would like an investigation into the assassination of her husband... He lives in constant fear of assassination.* VERB *be* V-ed V n N-VAR: oft N *of* n, N n

**as|sault** /əsɔːlt/ **(assaults, assaulting, assaulted)** [1] An **assault** by an army is a strong attack made on an area held by the enemy. ❑ *The rebels are poised for a new assault on the government garrisons.* [2] **Assault** weapons such as rifles are intended for soldiers to use in battle rather than for purposes such as hunting. [3] An **assault on** a person is a physical attack on them. ❑ *The attack is one of a series of savage sexual assaults on women in the university area... At the police station, I was charged with assault.* [4] To **assault** someone means to physically attack them. ❑ *The gang assaulted him with iron bars... She may have been sexually assaulted by her killer.* [5] An **assault on** someone's beliefs is a strong criticism of them. ❑ *He leveled a verbal assault against his Democratic opponents.* ◆◇◇ N-COUNT: oft N *on/upon/against* n = attack ADJ: ADJ n N-VAR: oft N *on/upon* n VERB = attack V n V n N-COUNT: oft N *on/upon/against* n

**as|sault and bat|tery** **Assault and battery** is the crime of attacking someone and causing them physical harm. [LEGAL] N-UNCOUNT

**as|sault course** **(assault courses)** An **assault course** is an area of land covered with obstacles such as walls which people, especially soldiers, use to improve their skills and strength. [BRIT] N-COUNT

✔ in AM, use **obstacle course**

**as|say** /æseɪ/ **(assays)** An **assay** is a test of a substance to find out what chemicals it contains. It is usually carried out to find out how pure a substance is. [TECHNICAL] N-COUNT

**as|sem|blage** /əsemblɪdʒ/ **(assemblages)** An **assemblage of** people or things is a collection of them. [FORMAL] ❑ *He had an assemblage of old junk cars filling the backyard.* N-COUNT: oft N *of* n

**as|sem|ble** /əsembəl/ **(assembles, assembling, assembled)** [1] When people **assemble** or when someone **assembles** them, they come together in a group, usually for a particular purpose such as a meeting. ❑ *There wasn't even a convenient place for students to assemble between classes... Thousands of people, mainly Zulus, assembled in a stadium in Thokoza... He has assembled a team of experts to handle queries.* [2] To **assemble** something means to collect it together or to fit the different parts of it together. ❑ *Greenpeace managed to assemble enough boats to waylay the ship at sea.* VERB = gather V V *in/at* n V n VERB V n

**as|sem|bler** /əsembləʳ/ **(assemblers)** An **assembler** is a person, a machine, or a company which assembles the individual parts of a vehicle or a piece of equipment such as a computer. N-COUNT

**as|sem|bly** /əsembli/ **(assemblies)** [1] An **assembly** is a large group of people who meet regularly to make decisions or laws for a particular region or country. ❑ *...the campaign for the first free election to the National Assembly. ...an assembly of party members from the Russian republic.* [2] An **assembly** is a group of people gathered together for a particular purpose. ❑ *He waited until complete quiet settled on the assembly.* [3] When you refer to rights of **assembly** or restrictions on **assembly**, you are referring to the legal right that people have to gather together. [FORMAL] [4] In a school, **assembly** is a gathering of all the teachers and pupils at the beginning of every school day. ❑ *By 9, the juniors are in the hall for assembly. ...a long room with a stage at one end for assemblies.* [5] The **assembly** of a machine, device, or object is the process of fitting its different parts together. ❑ *For the rest of the day, he worked on the assembly of an explosive device.* ◆◇◇ N-COUNT: usu sing N-COUNT = gathering N-UNCOUNT: usu prep N N-VAR N-UNCOUNT

**as|sem|bly line** **(assembly lines)** An **assembly line** is an arrangement of workers and machines in a factory, where each worker deals with only one part of a product. The product passes from one worker to another until it is finished. N-COUNT

**as|sembly|man** /əsemblimən/ **(assemblymen)** In the United States, an **assemblyman** is an elected member of an assembly of people who make decisions and laws. N-COUNT; N-TITLE

**as|sem|bly plant** **(assembly plants)** An **assembly plant** is a factory where large items such as cars are put together, usually using parts which have been made in other factories. N-COUNT

**assembly|woman** /əsembliwʊmən/ **(assemblywomen)** In the United States, an **assemblywoman** is a female elected member of an assembly of people who make decisions and laws. N-COUNT; N-TITLE

**as|sent** /əsent/ **(assents, assenting, assented)** [1] If someone gives their **assent to** something that has been suggested, they formally agree to it. ❑ *He gave his assent to the proposed legislation.* [2] If you **assent to** something, you agree to it or agree with it. ❑ *I assented to the request of the American publishers to write this book.* N-UNCOUNT: oft with poss, N *to/for* n = agreement, consent VERB V *to* n

**as|sert** /əsɜːʳt/ **(asserts, asserting, asserted)**
1 If someone **asserts** a fact or belief, they state it firmly. [FORMAL] ❑ *Mr. Helm plans to assert that the bill violates the First Amendment... The defendants, who continue to assert their innocence, are expected to appeal... Altman asserted, 'We were making a political statement about western civilisation and greed.'* VERB = declare V that V n V with quote
♦ **as|ser|tion** /əsɜːʳʃᵊn/ **(assertions)** *There is no concrete evidence to support assertions that the recession is truly over.* N-VAR
2 If you **assert** your authority, you make it clear by your behaviour that you have authority. ❑ *After the war, the army made an attempt to assert its authority in the south of the country.* VERB = establish V n
♦ **as|ser|tion** *The decision is seen as an assertion of his authority within the company.* N-UNCOUNT: usu N *of* n
3 If you **assert** your right or claim to something, you insist that you have the right to it. ❑ *The republics began asserting their right to govern themselves.* VERB V n
♦ **as|ser|tion** *These institutions have made the assertion of ethnic identity possible.* N-UNCOUNT: usu N *of* n
4 If you **assert yourself**, you speak and act in a forceful way, so that people take notice of you. ❑ *He's speaking up and asserting himself confidently.* VERB V pron-refl

**as|ser|tive** /əsɜːʳtɪv/ Someone who is **assertive** states their needs and opinions clearly, so that people take notice. ❑ *Women have become more assertive in the past decade. ...an assertive style of management.* ADJ ≠ submissive
♦ **as|ser|tive|ly** *'You don't need to do that,' said Pearl assertively.* ADV: usu ADV with v
♦ **as|ser|tive|ness** *...an assertiveness training class.* N-UNCOUNT

**as|sess** /əses/ **(assesses, assessing, assessed)** ♦◇◇
1 When you **assess** a person, thing, or situation, you consider them in order to make a judgment about them. ❑ *Our correspondent has been assessing the impact of the sanctions... It would be a matter of assessing whether she was well enough to travel.* VERB = evaluate V n V wh
2 When you **assess** the amount of money that something is worth or should be paid, you calculate or estimate it. ❑ *Ask them to send you information on how to assess the value of your belongings.* VERB V n

**as|sess|ment** /əsesmənt/ **(assessments)** ♦◇◇
1 An **assessment** is a consideration of someone or something and a judgment about them. ❑ *There is little assessment of the damage to the natural environment.* N-VAR = evaluation
2 An **assessment** of the amount of money that something is worth or that should be paid is a calculation or estimate of the amount. ❑ *Price Waterhouse have traced the losses to lenders' inflated assessments of mortgaged property.* N-VAR = appraisal

**as|ses|sor** /əsesəʳ/ **(assessors)** 1 An **assessor** is a person who is employed to calculate the value of something, or the amount of money that should be paid, for example in tax. [BUSINESS] N-COUNT = appraiser
2 An **assessor** is a person who is an expert in a subject, especially someone asked to advise a court of law on that subject. N-COUNT
3 An **assessor** is a person who judges the performance of someone else, for example in an exam, at an interview or at a sporting event. N-COUNT

**as|set** /æset/ **(assets)** ♦♦◇ 1 Something or someone that is an **asset** is considered useful or helps a person or organization to be successful. ❑ *Her leadership qualities were the greatest asset of the Conservative Party.* N-COUNT
2 The **assets** of a company or a person are all the things that they own. [BUSINESS] ❑ *By the end of 1989 the group had assets of 3.5 billion francs.* N-PLURAL

**asset-stripping** If a person or company is involved in **asset-stripping**, they buy companies cheaply, sell off their assets to make a profit, and then close the companies down. [BUSINESS] N-UNCOUNT [disapproval]

**ass|hole** /æshoʊl/ **(assholes)** If one person calls another person an **asshole**, they think that person is extremely stupid or has behaved in a stupid way. [AM, RUDE] N-COUNT [disapproval]

✔ in BRIT, use **arsehole**

**as|sidu|ous** /əsɪdʒuəs/ Someone who is **assiduous** works hard or does things very thoroughly. ❑ *Podulski had been assiduous in learning his adopted language.* ADJ = diligent

**as|sign** /əsaɪn/ **(assigns, assigning, assigned)**
1 If you **assign** a piece of work **to** someone, you give them the work to do. ❑ *When I taught, I would assign a topic to children which they would write about... Later in the year, she'll assign them research papers... When teachers assign homework, students usually feel an obligation to do it.* VERB V n *to* n V n n V n
2 If you **assign** something **to** someone, you say that it is for their use. ❑ *The selling broker is then required to assign a portion of the commission to the buyer broker... He assigned her all his land in Ireland.* VERB = allocate V n *to* n V n n
3 If someone **is assigned to** a particular place, group, or person, they are sent there, usually in order to work at that place or for that person. ❑ *I was assigned to Troop A of the 10th Cavalry... Did you choose Russia or were you simply assigned there?... Each of us was assigned a minder, someone who looked after us.* VERB: usu passive *be* V-ed *to* n *be* V-ed adv *be* V-ed n
4 If you **assign** a particular function or value **to** someone or something, you say they have it. ❑ *Under Mr. Harel's system, each business must assign a value to each job... Assign the letters of the alphabet their numerical values – A equals 1, B equals 2, etc.* VERB V n *to* n V n n

**as|sig|na|tion** /æsɪgneɪʃᵊn/ **(assignations)** An **assignation** is a secret meeting with someone, especially with a lover. [FORMAL] ❑ *She had an assignation with her boyfriend.* N-COUNT: oft N *with* n

**as|sign|ment** /əsaɪnmənt/ **(assignments)**
1 An **assignment** is a task or piece of work that you are given to do, especially as part of your job or studies. ❑ *The assessment for the course involves written assignments and practical tests.* N-COUNT
2 You can refer to someone being given a particular task or job as their **assignment to** the task or job. ❑ *An Australian division scheduled for assignment to Greece was ordered to remain in Egypt.* N-UNCOUNT: oft N *to* n

**as|simi|late** /əsɪmɪleɪt/ **(assimilates, assimilating, assimilated)** 1 When people such as immigrants **assimilate into** a community or when that community **assimilates** them, they become an accepted part of it. ❑ *There is every sign that new Asian-Americans are just as willing to assimilate... His family tried to assimilate into the white and Hispanic communities... The Vietnamese are trying to assimilate themselves and become Americans.* VERB = integrate V V *into/with* n V pron-refl
♦ **as|simi|la|tion** /əsɪmɪleɪʃᵊn/ *They promote social integration and assimilation of minority ethnic groups into the culture.* N-UNCOUNT: usu N *of* n = integration
2 If you **assimilate** new ideas, techniques, or information, you learn them or adopt them. ❑ *I was speechless, still trying to assimilate the enormity of what he'd told me.* VERB = absorb V n
♦ **as|simi|la|tion** *This technique brings life to instruction and eases assimilation of knowledge.* N-UNCOUNT: usu N *of* n

**as|sist** /əsɪst/ **(assists, assisting, assisted)** ♦◇◇
1 If you **assist** someone, you help them to do a job or task by doing part of the work for them. ❑ *The family decided to assist me with my chores... Dr Amid was assisted by a young Asian nurse.* VERB = help V n *with* n *be* V-ed
2 If you **assist** someone, you give them information, advice, or money. ❑ *The public is urgently requested to assist police in tracing this man... Foreign Office officials assisted with transport and finance problems... The Authority will provide a welfare worker to assist you.* VERB = help V n *in* -ing V *with* n V n
3 If something **assists in** doing a task, it makes the task easier to do. ❑ *...a chemical that assists in the manufacture of proteins... Here are some good sources of information to assist you in making the best selection.* Also V n to-inf VERB V *in/with* n/-ing V n *in/with* n/-ing

**as|sis|tance** /əsɪstəns/ ♦◇◇ 1 If you give someone **assistance**, you help them do a job or task by doing part of the work for them. ❑ *Since 1976 he has been operating the shop with the assistance of volunteers... She can still come downstairs with assistance but she's very weak.* N-UNCOUNT: oft with poss = help, aid
2 If you give someone **assistance**, you give them information or advice. ❑ *Any assistance you could give the police will be greatly appreciated.* N-UNCOUNT = help, aid
3 If someone gives a person or country **assistance**, they help them by giving them money. ❑ *...a viable programme of eco-* N-UNCOUNT: oft supp N = help, aid

*nomic assistance.* [4] If something is done **with the assistance of** a particular thing, that thing is helpful or necessary for doing it. ❑ *The translations were carried out with the assistance of a medical dictionary.* N-UNCOUNT = help, aid

PHRASES [5] Someone or something that **is of assistance** to you is helpful or useful to you. ❑ *Can I be of any assistance?* PHRASE: V inflects, usu modal PHR [6] If you **come to** someone's **assistance**, you take action to help them. ❑ *They are appealing to the world community to come to Jordan's assistance.* PHRASE: V inflects

**as|sis|tant** /əsɪstənt/ **(assistants)** ◆◇◇ [1] **Assistant** is used in front of titles or jobs to indicate a slightly lower rank. For example, an assistant director is one rank lower than a director in an organization. ❑ *...the Assistant Secretary of Defense.* ADJ: ADJ n = deputy [2] Someone's **assistant** is a person who helps them in their work. ❑ *Kalan called his assistant, Hashim, to take over while he went out.* N-COUNT [3] An **assistant** is a person who works in a shop selling things to customers. ❑ *The assistant took the book and checked the price on the back cover.* N-COUNT = shop assistant

**as|sis|tant ref|eree (assistant referees)** An **assistant referee** is the same as a **linesman**. N-COUNT

**Assoc.** **Assoc.** is a written abbreviation for **association**, **associated**, or **associate**.

**as|so|ci|ate (associates, associating, associated)** ◆◇◇

> ✔ The verb is pronounced /əsoʊsieɪt/. The noun and adjective are pronounced /əsoʊsiət/.

[1] If you **associate** someone or something **with** another thing, the two are connected in your mind. ❑ *Through science we've got the idea of associating progress with the future.* VERB V n *with* n [2] If you **are associated with** a particular organization, cause, or point of view, or if you **associate yourself with** it, you support it publicly. ❑ *I haven't been associated with the project over the last year... The press feels the need to associate itself with the green movement.* VERB = affiliate *be* V-ed *with* n V pron-refl *with* n [3] If you say that someone **is associating with** another person or group of people, you mean they are spending a lot of time in the company of people you do not approve of. ❑ *What would they think if they knew that they were associating with a murderer?* VERB V *with* n [4] Your **associates** are the people you are closely connected with, especially at work. ❑ *...the restaurant owner's business associates.* N-COUNT: oft n N = colleague [5] **Associate** is used before a rank or title to indicate a slightly different or lower rank or title. ❑ *Mr Lin is associate director of the Institute.* ADJ: ADJ n

**as|so|ci|at|ed** /əsoʊsieɪtɪd/ ◆◇◇ [1] If one thing is **associated with** another, the two things are connected with each other. ❑ *These symptoms are particularly associated with migraine headaches.* ADJ: usu v-link ADJ *with* n [2] **Associated** is used in the name of a company that is made up of a number of smaller companies which have joined together. ❑ *...the Associated Press.* ADJ: ADJ n

**as|so|cia|tion** /əsoʊsieɪʃən/ **(associations)** ◆◆◇ [1] An **association** is an official group of people who have the same job, aim, or interest. ❑ *...the British Olympic Association... Research associations are often linked to a particular industry.* ➔ See also **housing association**. N-COUNT: oft in names [2] Your **association with** a person or a thing such as an organization is the connection that you have with them. ❑ *...the company's six-year association with retailer J.C. Penney Co.* N-COUNT: usu N *with* n = affiliation [3] If something has particular **associations** for you, it is connected in your mind with a particular memory, idea, or feeling. ❑ *He has a shelf full of things, each of which has associations for him.* N-COUNT: usu pl [4] If you do something **in association with** someone else, you do it together. PHRASE: PHR n

**as|so|cia|tive** /əsoʊʃətɪv, AM -ʃieɪtɪv/ **Associative** thoughts are things that you think of because you see, hear, or think of something that reminds you of those things or which you associate with those things. ❑ *The associative guilt was ingrained in his soul.* ADJ: usu ADJ n

**as|sort|ed** /əsɔːʳtɪd/ A group of **assorted** things is a group of similar things that are of different sizes or colours or have different qualities. ❑ *...swimsuits, sizes 12-18, in assorted colours.* ADJ: usu ADJ n = various

**as|sort|ment** /əsɔːʳtmənt/ **(assortments)** An **assortment** is a group of similar things that are of different sizes or colours or have different qualities. ❑ *...an assortment of cheese.* N-COUNT: oft N *of* n

**asst.** **Asst.** is an abbreviation for **assistant**.

**as|suage** /əsweɪdʒ/ **(assuages, assuaging, assuaged)** [1] If you **assuage** an unpleasant feeling that someone has, you make them feel it less strongly. [LITERARY] ❑ *To assuage his wife's grief, he took her on a tour of Europe.* VERB V n [2] If you **assuage** a need or desire for something, you satisfy it. [LITERARY] ❑ *The meat they'd managed to procure assuaged their hunger.* VERB V n

**as|sume** /əsjuːm, AM əsuːm/ **(assumes, assuming, assumed)** ◆◆◇ [1] If you **assume that** something is true, you imagine that it is true, sometimes wrongly. ❑ *It is a misconception to assume that the two continents are similar... If mistakes occurred, they were assumed to be the fault of the commander on the spot... 'Today?' — 'I'd assume so, yeah.'* VERB = presume V that *be* V-ed to-inf V *so* [2] If someone **assumes** power or responsibility, they take power or responsibility. ❑ *Mr Cross will assume the role of Chief Executive with a team of four directors.* VERB V n [3] If something **assumes** a particular quality, it begins to have that quality. ❑ *In his dreams, the mountains assumed enormous importance.* VERB = take on V n [4] You can use **let us assume** or **let's assume** when you are considering a possible situation or event, so that you can think about the consequences. ❑ *Let us assume those clubs actually win something. Then players will receive large bonuses... Let's assume for a moment that I am a litigant in your court.* ➔ See also **assuming**. PHRASE: PHR that

**as|sumed name (assumed names)** If you do something **under** an **assumed name**, you do it using a name that is not your real name. N-COUNT: usu *under* N = pseudonym

**as|sum|ing** /əsjuːmɪŋ, AM -suːm-/ You use **assuming** or **assuming that** when you are considering a possible situation or event, so that you can think about the consequences. ❑ *'Assuming you're right,' he said, 'there's not much I can do about it, is there?'.* CONJ

**as|sump|tion** /əsʌmpʃən/ **(assumptions)** ◆◇◇ [1] If you make an **assumption that** something is true or will happen, you accept that it is true or will happen, often without any real proof. ❑ *Dr Subroto questioned the scientific assumption on which the global warming theory is based.* N-COUNT: usu with supp, oft N that, adj N, N *of* n, *on* N [2] Someone's **assumption of** power or responsibility is their taking of it. ❑ *The government have retained the support which greeted their assumption of power last March.* N-UNCOUNT: N *of* n

**as|sur|ance** /əʃʊərəns/ **(assurances)** [1] If you give someone an **assurance that** something is true or will happen, you say that it is definitely true or will definitely happen, in order to make them feel less worried. ❑ *He would like an assurance that other forces will not move into the territory that his forces vacate... He will have been pleased by Marshal Yazov's assurance of the armed forces' loyalty.* N-VAR: oft N that, N *of* n = guarantee [2] If you do something **with assurance**, you do it with a feeling of confidence and certainty. ❑ *Masur led the orchestra with assurance... The EU is now acquiring greater assurance and authority.* N-UNCOUNT [3] **Assurance** is insurance that provides cover in the event of death. [BRIT] ❑ *...endowment assurance.* ➔ See also **life assurance**. N-UNCOUNT

**as|sure** /əʃʊəʳ/ **(assures, assuring, assured)** [1] If you **assure** someone **that** something is true or will happen, you tell them that it is definitely true or will definitely happen, often in order to make them less worried. ❑ *He hastened to assure me that there was nothing traumatic to report... 'Are you sure the raft is safe?' she asked anxiously. 'Couldn't be safer,' Max assured her confidently... Government officials recently assured Hindus of protection.* VERB = reassure V n that V n with quote V n *of* n

→ See also **assured**. [2] To **assure** someone **of** something means to make certain that they will get it. ❑ *Last night's resounding victory over Birmingham City has virtually assured them of promotion... Ways must be found to assure our children a decent start in life.* [3] You use phrases such as **I can assure you** or **let me assure you** to emphasize the truth of what you are saying. ❑ *I can assure you that the animals are well cared for.*
VERB = guarantee; V n *of* n; V n n; PHRASE: PHR that, PHR with cl [emphasis]

**as|sured** /əʃʊəʳd/ [1] Someone who is **assured** is very confident and relaxed. ❑ *He was infinitely more assured than in his more recent parliamentary appearances.* ♦ **as|sur|ed|ness** *This a lyrical work written with the authority and assuredness of an experienced writer.* [2] If something is **assured**, it is certain to happen. ❑ *Our victory is assured; nothing can stop us.* [3] If you are **assured of** something, you are certain to get it or achieve it. ❑ *Laura Davies is assured of a place in Europe's team.* [4] If you say that someone **can rest assured that** something is the case, you mean that it is definitely the case, so they do not need to worry about it. ❑ *Their parents can rest assured that their children's safety will be of paramount importance.*
◆◇◇ ADJ; N-UNCOUNT = assurance; ADJ: v-link ADJ ≠ uncertain; ADJ: v-link ADJ *of* n; PHRASE: PHR that, PHR with cl [emphasis]

**as|sur|ed|ly** /əʃʊəridli/ If something is **assuredly** true, it is definitely true. ❑ *He is, assuredly, not alone in believing they will win... The government most assuredly does believe in organic farming.*
ADV: ADV with cl/group, ADV before v = definitely

**as|ter|isk** /æstərɪsk/ **(asterisks)** An **asterisk** is the sign *. It is used especially to indicate that there is further information about something in another part of the text.
N-COUNT

**astern** /əstɜːʳn/ Something that is **astern** is at the back of a ship or behind the back part. [TECHNICAL]
ADV: *be* ADV

**as|ter|oid** /æstərɔɪd/ **(asteroids)** An **asteroid** is one of the very small planets that move around the sun between Mars and Jupiter.
N-COUNT

**asth|ma** /æsmə, AM æz-/ **Asthma** is a lung condition which causes difficulty in breathing.
N-UNCOUNT

**asth|mat|ic** /æsmætɪk, AM æz-/ **(asthmatics)** [1] People who suffer from asthma are sometimes referred to as **asthmatics**. ❑ *I have been an asthmatic from childhood and was never able to play any sports.* ♦ **Asthmatic** is also an adjective. ❑ *One child in ten is asthmatic.* [2] **Asthmatic** means relating to asthma. ❑ *...asthmatic breathing.*
N-COUNT; ADJ; ADJ: ADJ n

**astig|ma|tism** /əstɪgmətɪzəm/ If someone has **astigmatism**, the front of their eye has a slightly irregular shape, so they cannot see properly.
N-UNCOUNT

**aston|ish** /əstɒnɪʃ/ **(astonishes, astonishing, astonished)** If something or someone **astonishes** you, they surprise you very much. ❑ *Her dedication constantly astonishes me.*
VERB = amaze; V n

**aston|ished** /əstɒnɪʃt/ If you are **astonished** by something, you are very surprised about it. ❑ *They were astonished to find the driver was a six-year-old boy.*
ADJ: oft ADJ *by/at* n, ADJ to-inf, ADJ that

**aston|ish|ing** /əstɒnɪʃɪŋ/ Something that is **astonishing** is very surprising. ❑ *...an astonishing display of physical strength.* ♦ **aston|ish|ing|ly** *Isabella was an astonishingly beautiful young woman.*
ADJ = amazing; ADV: ADV adj/adv, ADV with cl

**aston|ish|ment** /əstɒnɪʃmənt/ **Astonishment** is a feeling of great surprise. ❑ *I spotted a shooting star which, to my astonishment, was bright green in colour... 'What?' Meg asked in astonishment.*
N-UNCOUNT = amazement

**astound** /əstaʊnd/ **(astounds, astounding, astounded)** If something **astounds** you, you are very surprised by it. ❑ *He used to astound his friends with feats of physical endurance.*
VERB = astonish; V n

**astound|ed** /əstaʊndɪd/ If you are **astounded by** something, you are very shocked or surprised that it could exist or happen. ❑ *I was astounded by its beauty... I am astounded at the comments made by the Chief Superintendent.*
ADJ: oft ADJ *by/at* n, ADJ to-inf, ADJ that = astonished

**astound|ing** /əstaʊndɪŋ/ If something is **astounding**, you are shocked or amazed that it could exist or happen. ❑ *The results are quite astounding.* ♦ **astound|ing|ly** *...astoundingly blue eyes.*
ADJ = amazing, astonishing; ADV: ADV adj/adv, ADV with cl

**as|tra|khan** /æstrəkæn/ **Astrakhan** is black or grey curly fur from the skins of lambs. It is used for making coats and hats. ❑ *...a coat with an astrakhan collar.*
N-UNCOUNT: usu N n

**as|tral** /æstrəl/ **Astral** means relating to the stars. [FORMAL]
ADJ

**astray** /əstreɪ/ [1] If you **are led astray** by someone or something, you behave badly or foolishly because of them. ❑ *The judge thought he'd been led astray by older children.* [2] If someone or something **leads** you **astray**, they make you believe something which is not true, causing you to make a wrong decision. ❑ *We drove east to Rostock, where my map led me astray.* [3] If something **goes astray**, it gets lost while it is being taken or sent somewhere. ❑ *Many items of mail being sent to her have gone astray.*
PHRASE: V inflects; PHRASE: V inflects = mislead; PHRASE: V inflects

**astride** /əstraɪd/ If you sit or stand **astride** something, you sit or stand with one leg on each side of it. ❑ *...three youths who stood astride their bicycles and stared.*
ADV: ADV after v, *be* ADV

**as|trin|gent** /əstrɪndʒənt/ **(astringents)** An **astringent** is a liquid that you put on your skin to make it less oily or to make cuts stop bleeding. ♦ **Astringent** is also an adjective. ❑ *...an astringent lotion.*
N-COUNT; ADJ: ADJ n

**astro-** /æstroʊ-/ **Astro-** is used to form words which refer to things relating to the stars or to outer space. ❑ *...astro-navigation.*
PREFIX

**as|trolo|ger** /əstrɒlədʒəʳ/ **(astrologers)** An **astrologer** is a person who uses astrology to try to tell you things about your character and your future.
N-COUNT

**as|trol|ogy** /əstrɒlədʒi/ **Astrology** is the study of the movements of the planets, sun, moon, and stars in the belief that these movements can have an influence on people's lives. ♦ **as|tro|logi|cal** /æstrəlɒdʒɪkəl/ ❑ *He has had a keen and lifelong interest in astrological research.*
N-UNCOUNT; ADJ: ADJ n

**as|tro|naut** /æstrənɔːt/ **(astronauts)** An **astronaut** is a person who is trained for travelling in a spacecraft.
N-COUNT

**as|trono|mer** /əstrɒnəməʳ/ **(astronomers)** An **astronomer** is a scientist who studies the stars, planets, and other natural objects in space.
N-COUNT

**as|tro|nomi|cal** /æstrənɒmɪkəl/ [1] If you describe an amount, especially the cost of something as **astronomical**, you are emphasizing that it is very large indeed. ❑ *Houses in the village are selling for astronomical prices.* ♦ **as|tro|nomi|cal|ly** /æstrənɒmɪkli/ *He was astronomically wealthy... House prices had risen astronomically.* [2] **Astronomical** means relating to astronomy. ❑ *...the British Astronomical Association.*
ADJ [emphasis]; ADV: ADV adj, ADV after v; ADJ: usu ADJ n

**as|trono|my** /əstrɒnəmi/ **Astronomy** is the scientific study of the stars, planets, and other natural objects in space.
N-UNCOUNT

**as|tro|physi|cist** /æstroʊfɪzɪsɪst/ **(astrophysicists)** An **astrophysicist** is someone who studies astrophysics.
N-COUNT

**as|tro|phys|ics** /æstroʊfɪzɪks/ **Astrophysics** is the study of the physical and chemical structure of the stars, planets, and other natural objects in space.
N-UNCOUNT

**as|tute** /əstjuːt, AM əstuːt/ If you describe someone as **astute**, you think they show an understanding of behaviour and situations, and are skilful at using this knowledge to their own advantage. ❑ *She was politically astute... He made a series of astute business decisions.* ♦ **as|tute|ly** *Oxford, as Evelyn Waugh astutely observed, is a city best seen in early summer.*
ADJ = shrewd; ADV: ADV with v = shrewdly

**asun|der** /əsʌndəʳ/ If something tears or is torn **asunder**, it is violently separated into two or more parts or pieces. [LITERARY]
ADV: ADV after v

**asy|lum** /əsaɪləm/ **(asylums)** [1] If a government gives a person from another country **asy-**
N-UNCOUNT = sanctuary

**lum**, they allow them to stay, usually because they are unable to return home safely for political reasons. ❑ *He applied for asylum in 1987 after fleeing the police back home.* [2] An **asylum** is a psychiatric hospital. [OLD-FASHIONED] N-COUNT

**asy|lum seek|er** **(asylum seekers)** An **asylum seeker** is a person who is trying to get asylum in a foreign country. ❑ *Fewer than 7% of asylum seekers are accepted as political refugees.* N-COUNT

**asym|met|ric** /eɪsɪmetrɪk/ **Asymmetric** means the same as **asymmetrical**. ADJ ≠ *symmetric*

**asym|met|ri|cal** /eɪsɪmetrɪkᵊl/ Something that is **asymmetrical** has two sides or halves that are different in shape, size, or style. ❑ *...asymmetrical shapes.* ADJ ≠ *symmetrical*

**asym|me|try** /eɪsɪmətri/ **(asymmetries)** **Asymmetry** is the appearance that something has when its two sides or halves are different in shape, size, or style. ❑ *...the asymmetry of Van de Velde's designs of this period.* N-VAR ≠ *symmetry*

**asymp|to|mat|ic** /eɪsɪmptəmætɪk/ If someone with a disease is **asymptomatic**, it means that they do not show any symptoms of the disease. [MEDICAL] ❑ *I have patients who are HIV-positive and asymptomatic.* ADJ

**at** /ət, STRONG æt/ ◆◆◆

> In addition to the uses shown below, **at** is used after some verbs, nouns, and adjectives to introduce extra information. **At** is also used in phrasal verbs such as 'keep on at' and 'play at'.

[1] You use **at** to indicate the place or event where something happens or is situated. ❑ *We had dinner at a restaurant in Attleborough... I didn't like being alone at home... Hamstrings are supporting muscles at the back of the thigh... The announcement was made at a news conference in Peking.* PREP

[2] If someone is **at** school or college, or **at** a particular school or college, they go there regularly to study. ❑ *He was shy and nervous as a boy, and unhappy at school... I majored in psychology at Hunter College.* PREP

[3] If you are **at** something such as a table, a door, or someone's side, you are next to it or them. ❑ *Graham was already at the door... At his side was a beautiful young woman... He gave the girl at the desk the message.* PREP

[4] When you are describing where someone or something is, you can say that they are **at** a certain distance. You can also say that one thing is **at** an angle in relation to another thing. ❑ *The two journalists followed at a discreet distance... The tree was leaning at a low angle from the ground.* PREP

[5] If something happens **at** a particular time, that is the time when it happens or begins to happen. ❑ *The funeral will be carried out this afternoon at 3.00... He only sees her at Christmas and Easter.* PREP

[6] If you do something **at** a particular age, you do it when you are that age. ❑ *Blake emigrated to Australia with his family at 13... Mary Martin has died at her home in California at the age of seventy-six.* PREP

[7] You use **at** to express a rate, frequency, level, or price. ❑ *I drove back down the highway at normal speed... Check the oil at regular intervals, and have the car serviced regularly... The submarine lies at a depth of 6,000 feet in the Barents Sea.* PREP

[8] You use **at** before a number or amount to indicate a measurement. ❑ *...as unemployment stays pegged at three million.* PREP: PREP amount

[9] If you look **at** someone or something, you look towards them. If you direct an object or a comment **at** someone, you direct it towards them. ❑ *He looked at Michael and laughed... The crowds became violent and threw petrol bombs at the police.* PREP

[10] You can use **at** after verbs such as 'smile' or 'wave' and before nouns referring to people to indicate that you have put on an expression or made a gesture which someone is meant to see or understand. ❑ *She opened the door and stood there, frowning at me... We waved at the staff to try to get the bill.* PREP: v PREP n

[11] If you point or gesture **at** something, you move your arm or head in its direction so that it will be noticed by someone you are with. ❑ *He pointed at the empty bottle and the waitress quickly replaced it... He gestured at the shelves. 'I've bought many books from him.'* PREP: v PREP n

[12] If you are working **at** something, you are dealing with it. If you are aiming **at** something, you are trying to achieve it. ❑ *She has worked hard at her marriage. ...a $1.04m grant aimed at improving student performance on placement examinations.* PREP

[13] If something is done **at** someone's invitation or request, it is done as a result of it. ❑ *She left the light on in the bathroom at his request.* PREP: PREP n with poss

[14] You use **at** to say that someone or something is in a particular state or condition. ❑ *I am afraid we are not at liberty to disclose that information... Their countries had been at war for nearly six weeks.* PREP: v-link PREP n

[15] You use **at** before a possessive pronoun and a superlative adjective to say that someone or something has more of a particular quality than at any other time. ❑ *He was at his happiest whilst playing cricket.* PREP: PREP poss adj-superl

[16] You use **at** to say how something is being done. ❑ *Three people were killed by shots fired at random from a minibus... Mr Martin was taken out of his car at gunpoint.* PREP

[17] You use **at** to show that someone is doing something repeatedly. ❑ *She lowered the handkerchief which she had kept dabbing at her eyes... Miss Melville took a cookie and nibbled at it.* PREP: v PREP n

[18] You use **at** to indicate an activity or task when saying how well someone does it. ❑ *I'm good at my work... Robin is an expert at cheesemaking.* PREP: adj PREP n, n PREP n, v PREP n

[19] You use **at** to indicate what someone is reacting to. ❑ *Eleanor was annoyed at having had to wait so long for him... The British team did not disguise their delight at their success.* PREP: adj PREP n, n PREP n, v PREP n

[20] **at all** → see **all**.

**ata|vis|tic** /ætəvɪstɪk/ **Atavistic** feelings or behaviour seem to be very primitive, like the feelings or behaviour of our earliest ancestors. [FORMAL] ❑ *...an atavistic fear of snakes.* ADJ: usu ADJ n = *primordial*

**ate** /et, eɪt/ **Ate** is the past tense of **eat**.

**at|el|ier** /ətelieɪ, AM ætᵊljeɪ/ **(ateliers)** An **atelier** is an artist's studio or workshop. N-COUNT

**athe|ism** /eɪθiɪzəm/ **Atheism** is the belief that there is no God. Compare **agnosticism**. N-UNCOUNT

**athe|ist** /eɪθiɪst/ **(atheists)** An **atheist** is a person who believes that there is no God. Compare **agnostic**. N-COUNT

**athe|is|tic** /eɪθiɪstɪk/ **Atheistic** means connected with or holding the belief that there is no God. ❑ *...atheistic philosophers.* ADJ

**ath|lete** /æθliːt/ **(athletes)** [1] An **athlete** is a person who does a sport, especially athletics, or track and field events. ❑ *Daley Thompson was a great athlete.* ◆◇◇ N-COUNT

[2] You can refer to someone who is fit and athletic as an **athlete**. ❑ *I was no athlete.* N-COUNT

**ath|lete's foot** **Athlete's foot** is a fungal infection in which the skin between the toes becomes cracked or peels off. N-UNCOUNT

**ath|let|ic** /æθletɪk/ [1] **Athletic** means relating to athletes and athletics. ❑ *They have been given college scholarships purely on athletic ability.* ADJ: ADJ n

[2] An **athletic** person is fit, and able to perform energetic movements easily. ❑ *Xandra is an athletic 36-year-old with a 21-year-old's body.* ADJ

**ath|leti|cism** /æθletɪsɪzəm/ **Athleticism** is someone's fitness and ability to perform well at sports or other physical activities. N-UNCOUNT

**ath|let|ics** /æθletɪks/ [1] **Athletics** refers to track and field sports such as running, the high jump, and the javelin. [mainly BRIT] ❑ *As the modern Olympics grew in stature, so too did athletics.* N-UNCOUNT

> ✔ in AM, use **track and field**

[2] **Athletics** refers to any kind of physical sports, exercise, or games. [AM] ❑ *...students who play intercollegiate athletics.* N-UNCOUNT

**-ation** /-eɪʃᵊn/ **(-ations)** **-ation** and **-ion** are added to some verbs in order to form nouns. Nouns formed in this way often refer to a state or process; for example, starvation is the process of SUFFIX starving, and victimization is the process of being victimized.

**atishoo** /ətɪʃuː/ **Atishoo** is used, especially in writing, to represent the sound that you make when you sneeze.

**at|las** /ætləs/ **(atlases)** An **atlas** is a book of maps. N-COUNT

**ATM** /eɪ tiː em/ **(ATMs)** An **ATM** is a machine built into the wall of a bank or other building, which allows people to take out money from their bank account by using a special card. **ATM** is an abbreviation for 'automated teller machine'. [mainly AM] N-COUNT

in BRIT, use **cash dispenser**

**at|mos|phere** /ætməsfɪəʳ/ **(atmospheres)** ◆◇◇
1 A planet's **atmosphere** is the layer of air or other gases around it. ❑ *...dangerous levels of pollution in the Earth's atmosphere.* N-COUNT: usu sing
2 The **atmosphere** of a place is the air that you breathe there. ❑ *These gases pollute the atmosphere of towns and cities.* N-COUNT: usu sing
3 The **atmosphere** of a place is the general impression that you get of it. ❑ *There's still an atmosphere of great hostility and tension in the city.* N-SING: usu with supp
4 If a place or an event has **atmosphere**, it is interesting. ❑ *The old harbour is still full of atmosphere and well worth visiting.* N-UNCOUNT = ambience

**at|mos|pher|ic** /ætməsferɪk/ 1 **Atmospheric** is used to describe something which relates to the earth's atmosphere. ❑ *...atmospheric gases. ...atmospheric pressure.* ADJ: usu ADJ n
2 If you describe a place or a piece of music as **atmospheric**, you like it because it has a particular quality which is interesting or exciting and makes you feel a particular emotion. ADJ: usu ADJ n approval

**at|mos|pher|ics** /ætməsferɪks/ **Atmospherics** are elements in something such as a piece of music or a book which create a certain atmosphere. ❑ *...Dickensian atmospherics.* N-PLURAL

**at|oll** /ætɒl, AM -tɔːl/ **(atolls)** An **atoll** is a ring of coral rock, or a group of coral islands surrounding a lagoon. N-COUNT

**atom** /ætəm/ **(atoms)** An **atom** is the smallest amount of a substance that can take part in a chemical reaction. N-COUNT

**atom|ic** /ətɒmɪk/ 1 **Atomic** means relating to power that is produced from the energy released by splitting atoms. ❑ *...atomic energy. ...atomic weapons.* ADJ: usu ADJ n = nuclear
2 **Atomic** means relating to the atoms of substances. ADJ: ADJ n

**atom|ic bomb** **(atomic bombs)**

The form **atom bomb** is also used, mainly in British English.

An **atomic bomb** or an **atom bomb** is a bomb that causes an explosion by a sudden release of energy that results from splitting atoms. N-COUNT

**aton|al** /eɪtoʊnᵊl/ **Atonal** music is music that is not written or played in any key or system of scales. ADJ: usu ADJ n

**atone** /ətoʊn/ **(atones, atoning, atoned)** If you **atone for** something that you have done, you do something to show that you are sorry you did it. [FORMAL] ❑ *He felt he had atoned for what he had done to his son.* VERB = repent; V for n

**atone|ment** /ətoʊnmənt/ If you do something as an **atonement for** doing something wrong, you do it to show that you are sorry. [FORMAL] ❑ *He's living in a monastery in a gesture of atonement for human rights abuses committed under his leadership.* N-UNCOUNT: oft N for n = repentance

**atop** /ətɒp/ If something is **atop** something else, it is on top of it. [AM; also BRIT, LITERARY] ❑ *Under the newspaper, atop a sheet of paper, lay an envelope.* PREP = on top of

**A to Z** /eɪ tə zed, AM - ziː/ **(A to Zs)** 1 An **A to Z** is a book of maps showing all the streets and roads in a particular city and its surrounding towns. [BRIT, TRADEMARK] N-COUNT
2 An **A to Z of** a particular subject is a book or programme which gives information on all aspects of it, arranging it in alphabetical order. ❑ *An A to Z of careers gives helpful information about courses.* N-SING: usu N of n

**atrium** /eɪtriəm/ **(atriums)** An **atrium** is a part of a building such as a hotel or shopping centre, which extends up through several floors of the building and often has a glass roof. N-COUNT

**atro|cious** /ətroʊʃəs/ 1 If you describe something as **atrocious**, you are emphasizing that its quality is very bad. ❑ *The food here is atrocious.* ♦ **atro|cious|ly** *He had written the note from memory, word perfect, and spelled atrociously.* ADJ emphasis = appalling, abominable; ADV: ADV adj/-ed, ADV after v
2 If you describe someone's behaviour or their actions as **atrocious**, you mean that it is unacceptable because it is extremely violent or cruel. ❑ *The judge said he had committed atrocious crimes against women.* ADJ = appalling
3 If you say that weather conditions are **atrocious**, you mean they are very bad, for example that it is extremely cold, wet, or windy. ADJ = appalling

**atroc|ity** /ətrɒsɪti/ **(atrocities)** An **atrocity** is a very cruel, shocking action. ❑ *The killing was cold-blooded, and those who committed this atrocity should be tried and punished.* N-VAR

**at|ro|phy** /ætrəfi/ **(atrophies, atrophying, atrophied)** If a muscle or other part of the body **atrophies**, it decreases in size or strength, often as a result of an illness. [FORMAL] VERB = wither, shrivel

**at|tach** /ətætʃ/ **(attaches, attaching, attached)** ◆◇◇
1 If you **attach** something to an object, you join it or fasten it to the object. ❑ *The gadget can be attached to any vertical surface... The astronauts will attach a motor that will boost the satellite into its proper orbit... For further information, please contact us on the attached form.* VERB; V n to n; V n; V-ed
2 If someone **attaches himself** or **herself** to you, they join you and stay with you, often without being invited to do so. ❑ *Natasha attached herself to the film crew filming at her orphanage.* VERB; V pron-refl to n
3 If people **attach** a quality **to** someone or something, or if it **attaches to** them, people consider that they have that quality. ❑ *The authorities attached much significance to his visit. ...the magic that still attaches to the word 'spy'. ...the stigma attached to mental illness.* VERB; V n to n; V to n; V-ed
4 If you **attach** conditions **to** something such as an agreement, you state that specific things must be done before the agreement is valid. ❑ *Activists are pressing the banks to attach political conditions to the signing of any new agreement.* VERB; V n to n
5 In computing, if you **attach** a file **to** a message that you send to someone, you send it with the message but separate from it. ❑ *It is possible to attach executable program files to e-mail.* VERB; V n to n
6 → See also **attached**. **no strings attached** → see **string**.

**at|ta|ché** /ətæʃeɪ, AM ætæʃeɪ/ **(attachés)** An **attaché** is a member of staff in an embassy, usually with a special responsibility for something. N-COUNT: usu supp N

**at|ta|ché case** **(attaché cases)** An **attaché case** is a flat case for holding documents. N-COUNT

**at|tached** /ətætʃt/ 1 If you are **attached to** someone or something, you like them very much. ❑ *She is very attached to her family and friends.* ADJ: v-link ADJ to n
2 If someone is **attached to** an organization or group of people, they are working with them, often only for a short time. ❑ *Ford was attached to the battalion's first line of transport.* ADJ: v-link ADJ to n
3 If one organization or institution is **attached to** a larger organization, it is part of that organization and is controlled and run by it. ❑ *At one time the schools were mainly attached to the church.* ADJ: v-link ADJ to n = affiliated

**at|tach|ment** /ətætʃmənt/ **(attachments)**
1 If you have an **attachment to** someone or something, you are fond of them or loyal to them. ❑ *As a teenager she formed a strong attachment to one of her teachers.* N-VAR: oft N to n
2 An **attachment** is a device that can be fixed onto a machine in order to enable it to do different jobs. ❑ *Some models come with attachments for dusting.* N-COUNT
3 An **attachment** is an extra document that is added to another document. ❑ *Justice Fitzgerald included a 120-* N-COUNT

*page discussion paper as an attachment to the annual report.* [4] In computing, an **attachment** is a file which is attached separately to a message that you send to someone. ❑ *When you send an e-mail you can also send a sound or graphic file as an attachment.* N-COUNT

**at|tack** /ətæk/ **(attacks, attacking, attacked)** ◆◆◆
[1] To **attack** a person or place means to try to hurt or damage them using physical violence. VERB ❑ *He bundled the old lady into her hallway and brutally attacked her...* V n *While Haig and Foch argued, the Germans attacked.* V ♦ **Attack** is also a noun. N-VAR: usu with supp ❑ *...a campaign of air attacks on strategic targets... Refugees had come under attack from federal troops.* [2] If you **attack** a person, belief, idea, or act, you criticize them strongly. VERB ❑ *He publicly attacked the people who've been calling for secret ballot nominations...* V n *A newspaper ran an editorial attacking him for being a showman.* V n for -ing ♦ **Attack** is also a noun. N-VAR: usu with supp ❑ *The role of the state as a prime mover in planning social change has been under attack... The committee yesterday launched a scathing attack on British business for failing to invest.* [3] If something such as a disease, a chemical, or an insect **attacks** something, it harms or spoils it. VERB ❑ *The virus seems to have attacked his throat...* V n *Several key crops failed when they were attacked by pests.* V n ♦ **Attack** is also a noun. N-UNCOUNT: also N in pl ❑ *The virus can actually destroy those white blood cells, leaving the body wide open to attack from other infections.* [4] If you **attack** a job or a problem, you start to deal with it in an energetic way. VERB ❑ *Any attempt to attack the budget problem is going to have to in some way deal with those issues.* V n [5] In games such as football, when one team **attacks** the opponent's goal, they try to score a goal. VERB ❑ *Now the US is controlling the ball and attacking the opponent's goal...* V n *The goal was just reward for Villa's decision to attack constantly in the second half.* V ♦ **Attack** is also a noun. N-COUNT ❑ *Lee was at the hub of some incisive attacks in the second half.*
[6] An **attack of** an illness is a short period in which you suffer badly from it. N-COUNT: with supp ❑ *It had brought on an attack of asthma.* [7] → See also **counterattack**, **heart attack**.

**at|tack|er** /ətækəʳ/ **(attackers)** You can refer to a person who attacks someone as their **attacker**. N-COUNT ❑ *There were signs that she struggled with her attacker before she was repeatedly stabbed.*

**at|tain** /əteɪn/ **(attains, attaining, attained)**
[1] If you **attain** something, you gain it or achieve it, often after a lot of effort. [FORMAL] VERB ❑ *Jim is halfway to attaining his pilot's licence.* V n [2] If you **attain** a particular state or condition, you may reach it as a result of natural development or work hard to attain this state. VERB ❑ *...attaining a state of calmness and confidence.* V n Also V to n

**at|tain|able** /əteɪnəbᵊl/ Something that is **attainable** can be achieved. ADJ = achievable ❑ *It is unrealistic to believe perfection is an attainable goal.*

**at|tain|ment** /əteɪnmənt/ **(attainments)**
[1] The **attainment of** an aim is the achieving of it. [FORMAL] N-UNCOUNT = achievement ❑ *...the attainment of independence.*
[2] An **attainment** is a skill you have learned or something you have achieved. [FORMAL] N-COUNT ❑ *...their educational attainments.*

**at|tempt** /ətempt/ **(attempts, attempting, attempted)** ◆◆◆ [1] If you **attempt to** do something, especially something difficult, you try to do it. VERB ❑ *The only time that we attempted to do something like that was in the city of Philadelphia...* V to-inf *Before I could attempt a reply he added over his shoulder: 'Wait there.'* V n [2] If you make an **attempt to** do something, you try to do it, often without success. N-COUNT: usu with supp, oft N to-inf ❑ *...a deliberate attempt to destabilise the defence... It was one of his rare attempts at humour.* [3] An **attempt on** someone's life is an attempt to kill them. N-COUNT: N on n ❑ *...an attempt on the life of the former Iranian Prime Minister.*

**at|tempt|ed** /əteṃptɪd/ An **attempted** crime or unlawful action is an unsuccessful effort to commit the crime or action. ADJ: ADJ n ❑ *...a case of attempted murder.*

**at|tend** /ətend/ **(attends, attending, attended)** ◆◆◇
[1] If you **attend** a meeting or other event, you are present at it. VERB ❑ *The meeting will be attended by finance ministers from many countries...* V n *We want the maximum number of people to attend to help us cover our costs.* V [2] If you **attend** an institution such as a school, college, or church, you go there regularly. VERB ❑ *They attended college together at the University of Pennsylvania.* V n [3] If you **attend to** something, you deal with it. If you **attend to** someone who is hurt or injured, you care for them. VERB ❑ *The staff will helpfully attend to your needs... The main thing is to attend to the injured.* V to n

**at|tend|ance** /ətendəns/ **(attendances)**
[1] Someone's **attendance** at an event or an institution is the fact that they are present at the event or go regularly to the institution. N-UNCOUNT: usu with supp ❑ *Her attendance at school was sporadic.* [2] The **attendance** at an event is the number of people who are present at it. N-VAR: usu with supp ❑ *Average weekly cinema attendance in February was 2.41 million... This year attendances were 28% lower than forecast.* [3] If someone is **in attendance** at a place or an event, they are there. PHRASE

**at|tend|ant** /ətendənt/ **(attendants)** [1] An **attendant** is someone whose job is to serve or help people in a place such as a petrol station, a car park, or a cloakroom. N-COUNT: usu n N ❑ *Tony Williams was working as a car-park attendant in Los Angeles.* [2] You use **attendant** to describe something that results from a thing already mentioned or that is connected with it. ADJ: ADJ n, v-link ADJ on/upon n = resulting ❑ *Mr Branson's victory, and all the attendant publicity, were well deserved. ...the risks attendant on the exploration of the unknown.*

**at|tend|ee** /ətendiː/ **(attendees)** The **attendees** at something such as a meeting or a conference are the people who are attending it. [mainly AM] N-COUNT

**at|tend|er** /ətendəʳ/ **(attenders)** The **attenders** at a particular place or event are the people who go there. N-COUNT: usu adj N, oft N at/in/of n ❑ *He was a regular attender at the opera.*

**at|ten|tion** /ətenʃᵊn/ **(attentions)** [1] If you give someone or something your **attention**, you look at it, listen to it, or think about it carefully. ◆◆◇ N-UNCOUNT: also N in pl, usu with poss ❑ *You have my undivided attention... Later he turned his attention to the desperate state of housing in the province. ...young children with short attention spans.*
[2] **Attention** is great interest that is shown in someone or something, particularly by the general public. N-UNCOUNT ❑ *Volume Two, sub-titled 'The Lawyers', will also attract considerable attention... The conference may help to focus attention on the economy.* [3] If someone or something is getting **attention**, they are being dealt with or cared for. N-UNCOUNT ❑ *Each year more than two million household injuries need medical attention.* [4] You can refer to someone's efforts to help you, or the interest they show in you, as their **attentions**, especially if you dislike or disapprove of them. N-PLURAL: usu the N of n ❑ *The only way to escape the unwanted attentions of the local men was not to go out.* [5] If you **bring** something **to** someone's **attention** or **draw** their **attention to** it, you tell them about it or make them notice it. N-UNCOUNT: usu with poss ❑ *If we don't keep bringing this to the attention of the people, nothing will be done.*

**PHRASES** [6] If someone or something **attracts** your **attention** or **catches** your **attention**, you suddenly notice them. PHRASE: V inflects ❑ *He sat at one of the round tables and tried to attract her attention.* [7] If you **pay attention to** someone, you watch them, listen to them, or take notice of them. If you **pay no attention to** someone, you behave as if you are not aware of them or as if they are not important. PHRASE: V inflects ❑ *More than ever before, the food industry is paying attention to young consumers... Other people walk along the beach at night, so I didn't pay any attention at first.* [8] When people **stand to attention** or **stand at attention**, they stand straight with their feet together and their arms at their sides. PHRASE: V inflects ❑ *Soldiers in full combat gear stood at attention.*

**at|ten|tion def|i|cit dis|or|der** **Attention deficit disorder** is a condition where people, especially children, are unable to concentrate on anything for very long and so find it difficult to learn and often behave in inappropriate ways. The abbreviation **ADD** is often used. N-UNCOUNT

**at|ten|tion def|i|cit hyper|ac|tiv|ity dis|or|der** **Attention deficit hyperactivity disorder** is a condition where people, especially children, are extremely active and unable to concentrate on anything for very long, with the result that they find it difficult to learn and often behave in inappropriate ways. The abbreviation **ADHD** is often used. N-UNCOUNT

**attention-grabbing** An **attention-grabbing** remark or activity is one that is intended to make people notice it. ❑ *...an attention-grabbing marketing campaign.* ADJ: usu ADJ n

**at|ten|tive** /ətentɪv/ [1] If you are **attentive**, you are paying close attention to what is being said or done. ❑ *He wishes the government would be more attentive to detail in their response.* ADJ ♦ **at|ten|tive|ly** *He questioned Chrissie, and listened attentively to what she told him.* ADV: usu ADV after v [2] Someone who is **attentive** is helpful and polite. ❑ *At society parties he is attentive to his wife.* ADJ: oft ADJ *to* n

**at|tenu|ate** /ətenjueɪt/ **(attenuates, attenuating, attenuated)** To **attenuate** something means to reduce it or weaken it. [FORMAL] ❑ *You could never eliminate risk, but training could attenuate it.* VERB V n

**at|tenu|at|ed** /ətenjueɪtɪd/ An **attenuated** object is unusually long and thin. [FORMAL] ❑ *...round arches and attenuated columns.* ADJ

**at|test** /ətest/ **(attests, attesting, attested)** To **attest** something or **attest to** something means to say, show, or prove that it is true. [FORMAL] ❑ *Police records attest to his long history of violence... I can personally attest that the cold and flu season is here.* VERB V *to* n V that

**at|tic** /ætɪk/ **(attics)** An **attic** is a room at the top of a house just below the roof. N-COUNT

**at|tire** /ətaɪəʳ/ Your **attire** is the clothes you are wearing. [FORMAL] ❑ *...seven women dressed in their finest attire.* N-UNCOUNT: usu supp N, with poss

**at|tired** /ətaɪəʳd/ If you describe how someone is **attired**, you are describing how they are dressed. [FORMAL] ❑ *He was faultlessly attired in black coat and striped trousers.* ADJ: v-link ADJ *in* n, adv ADJ

**at|ti|tude** /ætɪtjuːd, AM -tuːd/ **(attitudes)** ◆◆◇ [1] Your **attitude to** something is the way that you think and feel about it, especially when this shows in the way you behave. ❑ *...the general change in attitude towards handicapped people... His attitude made me angry.* N-VAR: usu with supp, oft N *to/towards* n [2] If you refer to someone as a person **with attitude**, you mean that they have a striking and individual style of behaviour, especially a forceful or aggressive one. [JOURNALISM] N-UNCOUNT

**at|ti|tu|di|nal** /ætɪtjuːdɪnᵊl, AM -tuːd-/ **Attitudinal** means related to people's attitudes and the way they look at their life. [FORMAL] ❑ *Does such an attitudinal change reflect real experiences in daily life?* ADJ: usu ADJ n

**at|tor|ney** /ətɜːʳni/ **(attorneys)** In the United States, an **attorney** or **attorney at law** is a lawyer. ❑ *...a prosecuting attorney.* → See also **District Attorney**. ◆◇◇ N-COUNT

**At|tor|ney Gen|er|al** **(Attorneys General)** A country's **Attorney General** is its chief law officer, who advises its government or ruler. N-COUNT

**at|tract** /ətrækt/ **(attracts, attracting, attracted)** ◆◆◇ [1] If something **attracts** people or animals, it has features that cause them to come to it. ❑ *The Cardiff Bay project is attracting many visitors... Warm weather has attracted the flat fish close to shore.* VERB V n V n adv/prep [2] If someone or something **attracts** you, they have particular qualities which cause you to like or admire them. If a particular quality **attracts** you **to** a person or thing, it is the reason why you like them. ❑ *He wasn't sure he'd got it right, although the theory attracted him by its logic... More people would be attracted to cycling if conditions were right.* VERB V n V n *to* n [3] If you **are attracted to** someone, you are interested in them sexually. ❑ *In spite of her hostility, she was attracted to him.* VERB *be* V-ed *to* n ♦ **at|tract|ed** *He was nice looking, but I wasn't deeply attracted to him.* ADJ: v-link ADJ, usu ADJ *to* n [4] If something **attracts** support, publicity, or money, it receives support, publicity, or money. ❑ *President Mwinyi said his country would also like to attract investment from private companies.* VERB V n [5] If one object **attracts** another object, it causes the second object to move towards it. ❑ *Anything with strong gravity attracts other things to it.* VERB V n *to* n Also V n [6] **to attract** someone's **attention** → see **attention**.

**at|trac|tion** /ətrækʃᵊn/ **(attractions)** [1] **Attraction** is a feeling of liking someone, and often of being sexually interested in them. ❑ *His love for her was not just physical attraction.* N-UNCOUNT [2] An **attraction** is a feature which makes something interesting or desirable. ❑ *...the attractions of living on the waterfront.* N-COUNT [3] An **attraction** is something that people can go to for interest or enjoyment, for example a famous building. ❑ *The walled city is an important tourist attraction.* N-COUNT

**at|trac|tive** /ətræktɪv/ ◆◇◇ [1] A person who is **attractive** is pleasant to look at. ❑ *She's a very attractive woman... He was always immensely attractive to women.* ADJ ≠ unattractive ♦ **at|trac|tive|ness** *Most of us would maintain that physical attractiveness does not play a major part in how we react to the people we meet.* N-UNCOUNT [2] Something that is **attractive** has a pleasant appearance or sound. ❑ *The creamy white flowers are attractive in the spring.* ADJ ≠ unattractive ♦ **at|trac|tive|ly** *It's an attractively illustrated, detailed guide that's very practical.* ADV: usu ADV -ed/adj [3] You can describe something as **attractive** when it seems worth having or doing. ❑ *Smoking is still attractive to many young people who see it as glamorous.* ADJ = appealing ≠ unattractive ♦ **at|trac|tive|ly** *The services are attractively priced and are tailored to suit individual requirements.* ADV: ADV -ed/adj

**at|trib|ut|able** /ətrɪbjʊtəbᵊl/ If something **is attributable to** an event, situation, or person, it is likely that it was caused by that event, situation or person. ❑ *10,000 deaths a year from chronic lung disease are attributable to smoking.* ADJ: v-link ADJ *to* n

**at|trib|ute** **(attributes, attributing, attributed)**

> ✔ The verb is pronounced /ətrɪbjuːt/. The noun is pronounced /ætrɪbjuːt/.

[1] If you **attribute** something **to** an event or situation, you think that it was caused by that event or situation. ❑ *Women tend to attribute their success to external causes such as luck.* VERB = ascribe V n *to* n [2] If you **attribute** a particular quality or feature **to** someone or something, you think that they have got it. ❑ *People were beginning to attribute superhuman qualities to him.* VERB = ascribe V n *to* n [3] If a piece of writing, a work of art, or a remark **is attributed to** someone, people say that they wrote it, created it, or said it. ❑ *This, and the remaining frescoes, are not attributed to Giotto.* VERB: usu passive *be* V-ed *to* n [4] An **attribute** is a quality or feature that someone or something has. ❑ *Cruelty is a normal attribute of human behaviour.* N-COUNT: usu with supp = characteristic

**at|tri|tion** /ətrɪʃᵊn/ **Attrition** is a process in which you steadily reduce the strength of an enemy by continually attacking them. [FORMAL] ❑ *The rebels have declared a cease-fire in their war of attrition against the government.* N-UNCOUNT

**at|tuned** /ətjuːnd, AM ətuːnd/ [1] If you are **attuned to** something, you can understand and appreciate it. ❑ *He seemed unusually attuned to people's feelings.* ADJ: v-link ADJ *to* n [2] If your ears are **attuned to** a sound, you can hear it and recognize it quickly. ❑ *Their ears were still attuned to the sounds of the London suburb.* ADJ: v-link ADJ *to* n

**atypi|cal** /eɪtɪpɪkᵊl/ Someone or something that is **atypical** is not typical of its kind. ❑ *The economy of the province was atypical because it was particularly small.* ADJ ≠ typical

**auber|gine** /oʊbəʳʒiːn/ **(aubergines)** An **aubergine** is a vegetable with a smooth, dark N-VAR purple skin. [BRIT]

☑ in AM, use **eggplant**

**auburn** /ɔːbəʳn/ **Auburn** hair is reddish brown. COLOUR

**auc|tion** /ɔːkʃᵊn/ **(auctions, auctioning, auctioned)** ◆◇◇ 1 An **auction** is a public sale where goods are sold to the person who offers the highest price. ❑ *Lord Salisbury bought the picture at auction in London some years ago.* N-VAR: oft *for/at* N, N n 2 If something **is auctioned**, it is sold in an auction. VERB

♦ **auction off** If you **auction off** something, you sell it to the person who offers the most money for it, often at an auction. ❑ *Her dresses will be auctioned off for charity... They take drug dealers' boats, cars and houses and auction them off.* PHRASAL VERB V P n (not pron) V n P

**auc|tion|eer** /ɔːkʃənɪəʳ/ **(auctioneers)** An **auctioneer** is a person in charge of an auction. N-COUNT

**auda|cious** /ɔːdeɪʃəs/ Someone who is **audacious** takes risks in order to achieve something. ❑ *...an audacious plan to win the presidency.* ADJ: usu ADJ n = daring

**audac|ity** /ɔːdæsɪti/ **Audacity** is audacious behaviour. ❑ *I was shocked at the audacity and brazenness of the gangsters.* N-UNCOUNT

**audible** /ɔːdɪbᵊl/ A sound that is **audible** is loud enough to be heard. ❑ *The Colonel's voice was barely audible.* ♦ **audibly** /ɔːdɪbli/ *Hugh sighed audibly.* ADJ ADV

**audi|ence** /ɔːdiəns/ **(audiences)** ◆◆◇ 1 The **audience** at a play, concert, film, or public meeting is the group of people watching or listening to it. ❑ *He was speaking to an audience of students at the Institute for International Affairs.* N-COUNT-COLL 2 The **audience** for a television or radio programme consists of all the people who watch or listen to it. ❑ *The concert will be relayed to a worldwide television audience estimated at one thousand million.* ➔ See also **studio audience**. N-COUNT-COLL: usu with supp 3 The **audience** of a writer or artist is the people who read their books or look at their work. ❑ *Say's writings reached a wide audience during his lifetime.* N-COUNT-COLL: usu sing 4 If you have an **audience with** someone important, you have a formal meeting with them. ❑ *The Prime Minister will seek an audience with the Queen later this morning.* N-COUNT: usu sing, oft N *with* n

**audio** /ɔːdioʊ/ **Audio** equipment is used for recording and reproducing sound. ❑ *She uses her vocal training to record audio tapes of books for blind people.* ADJ: ADJ n

**audio|tape** /ɔːdioʊteɪp/ **(audiotapes, audiotaping, audiotaped)** 1 **Audiotape** is magnetic tape which is used to record sound. N-UNCOUNT 2 An **audiotape** is a recording of speech, music, or other sounds on magnetic tape. [AM] N-COUNT

☑ in BRIT, usually use **cassette**

3 If you **audiotape** speech, music, or other sounds, you record them on magnetic tape. [AM] ❑ *We always audiotape these interviews.* VERB V n

☑ in BRIT, usually use **tape**

**audio-visual** also **audiovisual**. **Audiovisual** equipment and materials involve both recorded sound and pictures. ADJ: ADJ n

**audit** /ɔːdɪt/ **(audits, auditing, audited)** When an accountant **audits** an organization's accounts, he or she examines the accounts officially in order to make sure that they have been done correctly. ❑ *Each year they audit our accounts and certify them as being true and fair.* ♦ **Audit** is also a noun. ❑ *The bank first learned of the problem when it carried out an internal audit.* VERB V n N-COUNT

**audi|tion** /ɔːdɪʃᵊn/ **(auditions, auditioning, auditioned)** 1 An **audition** is a short performance given by an actor, dancer, or musician so that a director or conductor can decide if they are good enough to be in a play, film, or orchestra. N-COUNT: oft N *for* n 2 If you **audition** or if someone **auditions** you, you do an audition. ❑ *They're auditioning for new members of the cast for 'Miss Saigon' today... I heard your record and I want you to come and audition.* VERB V *for* n V Also V n, V n *for* n

**audi|tor** /ɔːdɪtəʳ/ **(auditors)** An **auditor** is an accountant who officially examines the accounts of organizations. N-COUNT

**audi|to|rium** /ɔːdɪtɔːriəm/ **(auditoriums** or **auditoria** /ɔːdɪtɔːriə/**)** 1 An **auditorium** is the part of a theatre or concert hall where the audience sits. N-COUNT 2 An **auditorium** is a large room, hall, or building which is used for events such as meetings and concerts. [AM] N-COUNT

**audi|tory** /ɔːdɪtri, AM -tɔːri/ **Auditory** means related to hearing. [TECHNICAL] ❑ *...the limits of the human auditory range.* ADJ: usu ADJ n

**au fait** /oʊ feɪ, AM ɔː -/ If you are **au fait with** something, you are familiar with it and know about it. ❑ *...children who are so much more au fait with today's technology.* ADJ: v-link ADJ *with* n

**Aug.** **Aug.** is a written abbreviation for **August**.

**aug|ment** /ɔːgment/ **(augments, augmenting, augmented)** To **augment** something means to make it larger, stronger, or more effective by adding something to it. [FORMAL] ❑ *While searching for a way to augment the family income, she began making dolls.* ♦ **aug|men|ta|tion** /ɔːgmenteɪʃᵊn/ *The augmentation of the army began along traditional lines.* VERB = supplement V n N-UNCOUNT: oft N *of* n

**augur** /ɔːgəʳ/ **(augurs, auguring, augured)** If something **augurs** well or badly **for** a person or a future situation, it is a sign that things will go well or badly. [FORMAL] ❑ *The renewed violence this week hardly augurs well for smooth or peaceful change.* VERB = bode V adv *for* n

**augu|ry** /ɔːgjʊri/ **(auguries)** An **augury** is a sign of what will happen in the future. [LITERARY] ❑ *The auguries of death are fast gathering round his head.* N-COUNT = omen

**august** /ɔːgʌst/ Someone or something that is **august** is dignified and impressive. [FORMAL] ❑ *...the august surroundings of the Liberal Club.* ADJ: usu ADJ n = imposing

**August** /ɔːgəst/ **(Augusts)** **August** is the eighth month of the year in the Western calendar. ❑ *The world premiere took place in August 1956... The trial will resume on August the twenty-second... This August has been the wettest for four years.* N-VAR

**auk** /ɔːk/ **(auks)** An **auk** is a seabird with a heavy body and short tail. N-COUNT

**Auld Lang Syne** /oʊld læŋ zaɪn/ **Auld Lang Syne** is a Scottish song about friendship that is traditionally sung as clocks strike midnight on New Year's Eve. N-PROPER

**aunt** /ɑːnt, ænt/ **(aunts)** Someone's **aunt** is the sister of their mother or father, or the wife of their uncle. ❑ *She wrote to her aunt in America... It was a present from Aunt Vera.* ➔ See also **agony aunt**. ◆◆◇ N-FAMILY; N-TITLE

**auntie** /ɑːnti, ænti/ **(aunties)** also **aunty**. Someone's **auntie** is their aunt. [INFORMAL] ❑ *His uncle is dead, but his auntie still lives here. ...my Auntie Elsie.* N-FAMILY; N-TITLE

**au pair** /oʊ peəʳ, AM ɔː -/ **(au pairs)** An **au pair** is a young person from a foreign country who lives with a family in order to learn the language and who helps to look after the children. N-COUNT

**aura** /ɔːrə/ **(auras)** An **aura** is a quality or feeling that seems to surround a person or place or to come from them. ❑ *She had an aura of authority.* N-COUNT: usu N *of* n = air

**aural** /ɔːrəl, aʊrəl/ **Aural** means related to the sense of hearing. Compare **acoustic**. ❑ *He became famous as an inventor of astonishing visual and aural effects.* ADJ: usu ADJ n

**aus|pices** /ɔːspɪsɪz/ If something is done **under the auspices of** a particular person or organization, or **under** someone's **auspices**, it is done with their support and approval. [FORMAL] PHRASE: PHR n

**aus|pi|cious** /ɔːspɪʃəs/ Something that is **auspicious** indicates that success is likely. [FORMAL] ❑ *His career as a playwright had an auspicious start.* ADJ ≠ inauspicious

**Aussie** /ɒzi, AM ɔːˈ-/ **(Aussies)** **Aussie** means Australian. [INFORMAL] ❑ *...Aussie comedy actor Paul Hogan.* ♦ An **Aussie** is a person from Australia. [INFORMAL] ADJ: ADJ n · N-COUNT

**aus|tere** /ɔːstɪəʳ/ 1 If you describe something as **austere**, you approve of its plain and simple appearance. ❑ *The church was austere and simple.* 2 If you describe someone as **austere**, you disapprove of them because they are strict and serious. ❑ *I found her a rather austere, distant, somewhat cold person.* 3 An **austere** way of life is one that is simple and without luxuries. ❑ *The life of the troops was still comparatively austere.* 4 An **austere** economic policy is one which reduces people's living standards sharply. ❑ *...a set of very austere economic measures to control inflation.* ADJ [approval] · ADJ [disapproval] · ADJ = spartan · ADJ

**aus|ter|ity** /ɔːsterɪti/ **(austerities)** 1 **Austerity** is a situation in which people's living standards are reduced because of economic difficulties. ❑ *...the years of austerity which followed the war.* 2 If you refer to something as showing **austerity**, you like its plain and simple appearance. [FORMAL] ❑ *...many abandoned buildings, some of which have a compact classical austerity and dignity.* N-UNCOUNT: also N in pl, oft N n · N-UNCOUNT [approval]

**Aus|tral|asian** /ɒstrəleɪʒᵊn, AM ɔːs-/ **Australasian** means belonging or relating to Australasia or to its people. ADJ: ADJ n

**Aus|tral|ian** /ɒstreɪliən/ **(Australians)** 1 Something that is **Australian** belongs or relates to Australia, or to its people or culture. ❑ *She went solo backpacking for eight months in the Australian outback.* 2 An **Australian** is someone who comes from Australia. ADJ · N-COUNT

**Aus|trian** /ɒstriən, AM ɔːs-/ **(Austrians)** 1 Something that is **Austrian** belongs or relates to Austria, or to its people or culture. ❑ *...the Austrian government.* 2 An **Austrian** is someone who comes from Austria. ADJ · N-COUNT

**Austro-** /ɒstroʊ, AM ɔːstroʊ/ **Austro-** combines with adjectives indicating nationality to form adjectives which describe something connected with Austria and another country. ❑ *...the Austro-Hungarian Empire.* COMB in ADJ

**auteur** /ɔːtɜːʳ/ **(auteurs)** You can refer to a film director as an **auteur** when they have a very strong artistic influence on the films they make. N-COUNT

**authen|tic** /ɔːθentɪk/ 1 An **authentic** person, object, or emotion is genuine. ❑ *...authentic Italian food... They have to look authentic.* ♦ **au|then|tic|ity** /ɔːθentɪsɪti/ *There are factors, however, that have cast doubt on the statue's authenticity.* 2 If you describe something as **authentic**, you mean that it is such a good imitation that it is almost the same as or as good as the original. ❑ *...patterns for making authentic frontier-style clothing.* 3 An **authentic** piece of information or account of something is reliable and accurate. ❑ *I had obtained the authentic details about the birth of the organization.* ADJ: usu ADJ n = real ≠ fake · N-UNCOUNT: usu with poss · ADJ: usu ADJ n [approval] · ADJ: usu ADJ n

**authen|ti|cate** /ɔːθentɪkeɪt/ **(authenticates, authenticating, authenticated)** If you **authenticate** something, you state officially that it is genuine after examining it. ❑ *He says he'll have no problem authenticating the stamp.* VERB · V n

**author** /ɔːθəʳ/ **(authors)** ♦♦◇ 1 The **author of** a piece of writing is the person who wrote it. ❑ *...Jill Phillips, author of the book 'Give Your Child Music'.* 2 An **author** is a person whose job is writing books. ❑ *Haruki Murakami is Japan's best-selling author.* 3 The **author of** a plan or proposal is the person who thinks of it and works out the details. ❑ *The authors of the plan believe they can reach this point within about two years.* 4 → See also **co-author**. N-COUNT: oft N *of* n · N-COUNT · N-COUNT: N *of* n

**author|ess** /ɔːθəres/ **(authoresses)** An **authoress** is a female author. Many female writers object to this word, and prefer to be called authors. N-COUNT

**autho|rial** /ɔːθɔːriəl/ **Authorial** means relating to the author of something such as a book or play. ❑ *There are times when the book suffers from excessive authorial control.* ADJ: ADJ n

**author|ing** /ɔːθərɪŋ/ **Authoring** is the creation of documents, especially for the Internet. [COMPUTING] ❑ *...software authoring tools.* N-UNCOUNT: oft N n

**author|ise** /ɔːθəraɪz/ → see **authorize**.

**authori|tar|ian** /ɔːθɒrɪteəriən, AM -θɔːr-/ **(authoritarians)** If you describe a person or an organization as **authoritarian**, you are critical of them controlling everything rather than letting people decide things for themselves. ❑ *Senior officers could be considering a coup to restore authoritarian rule.* ♦ An **authoritarian** is someone who is authoritarian. ❑ *Don became the overly strict authoritarian he felt his brother needed.* ADJ: usu ADJ n [disapproval] = dictatorial · N-COUNT

**authori|tari|an|ism** /ɔːθɒrɪteəriənɪzəm, AM -θɔːr-/ **Authoritarianism** is the state of being authoritarian or the belief that people with power, especially the State, have the right to control other people's actions. [FORMAL] N-UNCOUNT

**authori|ta|tive** /ɔːθɒrɪtətɪv, AM əθɔːrɪteɪtɪv/ 1 Someone or something that is **authoritative** gives an impression of power and importance and is likely to be obeyed. ❑ *He has a commanding presence and deep, authoritative voice.* 2 Someone or something that is **authoritative** has a lot of knowledge of a particular subject. ❑ *The first authoritative study of polio was published in 1840.* ADJ · ADJ

**author|ity** /ɔːθɒrɪti, AM -tɔːr-/ **(authorities)** ♦♦♦ 1 **The authorities** are the people who have the power to make decisions and to make sure that laws are obeyed. ❑ *This provided a pretext for the authorities to cancel the elections.* 2 An **authority** is an official organization or government department that has the power to make decisions. ❑ *...the Health Education Authority... Any alterations had to meet the approval of the local planning authority.* → See also **local authority**. 3 **Authority** is the right to command and control other people. ❑ *The judge had no authority to order a second trial.* 4 If someone has **authority**, they have a quality which makes other people take notice of what they say. ❑ *He had no natural authority and no capacity for imposing his will on others.* 5 **Authority** is official permission to do something. ❑ *The prison governor has refused to let him go, saying he must first be given authority from his own superiors.* 6 Someone who is an **authority on** a particular subject knows a lot about it. ❑ *He's universally recognized as an authority on Russian affairs.* 7 If you say you **have it on good authority that** something is true, you mean that you believe it is true because you trust the person who told you about it. ❑ *I have it on good authority that there's no way this light can cause skin cancer.* N-PLURAL: oft *the* N · N-COUNT: usu with supp, oft in names · N-UNCOUNT · N-UNCOUNT · N-UNCOUNT = authorization · N-COUNT: N *on* n = expert · PHRASE: V inflects, PHR that

**author|ize** /ɔːθəraɪz/ **(authorizes, authorizing, authorized)**

✓ in BRIT, also use **authorise**

If someone in a position of authority **authorizes** something, they give their official permission for it to happen. ❑ *It would certainly be within his power to authorize a police raid like that.* ♦ **authori|za|tion** /ɔːθəraɪzeɪʃᵊn/ **(authorizations)** *The United Nations will approve his request for authorization to use military force to deliver aid.* VERB = sanction · V n · N-VAR

**author|ship** /ɔːθəʳʃɪp/ The **authorship** of a piece of writing is the identity of the person who wrote it. N-UNCOUNT

**autism** /ɔːtɪzəm/ **Autism** is a mental disorder that affects children, particularly their ability to relate to other people. N-UNCOUNT

**autis|tic** /ɔːtɪstɪk/ An **autistic** person suffers from autism. ADJ

**auto** /ɔːtoʊ/ **(autos)** An **auto** is a car. [AM] ❑ *...the auto industry.* ♦◇◇ N-COUNT: oft N n

**auto|bahn** /ɔːtoʊbɑːn/ **(autobahns)** An **autobahn** is a German motorway. N-COUNT

**auto|bio|graphi|cal** /ɔːtoʊbaɪəgræfɪkᵊl/ An **autobiographical** piece of writing relates to ADJ events in the life of the person who has written it. ❑ *...a highly autobiographical novel of a woman's search for identity.*

**auto|bi|og|ra|phy** /ɔːtəbaɪɒgrəfi/ **(autobiographies)** Your **autobiography** is an account of your life, which you write yourself. ❑ *He published his autobiography last autumn.* [N-COUNT: usu with poss]

**autoc|ra|cy** /ɔːtɒkrəsi/ **(autocracies)**
1 **Autocracy** is government or control by one person who has complete power. ❑ *Many poor countries are abandoning autocracy.* [N-UNCOUNT] 2 An **autocracy** is a country or organization that is ruled by one person who has complete power. ❑ *She ceded all power to her son-in-law who now runs the country as an autocracy.* [N-COUNT]

**auto|crat** /ɔːtəkræt/ **(autocrats)** An **autocrat** is a person in authority who has complete power. [N-COUNT]

**auto|crat|ic** /ɔːtəkrætɪk/ An **autocratic** person or organization has complete power and makes decisions without asking anyone else's advice. ❑ *The people have grown intolerant in recent weeks of the King's autocratic ways.* [ADJ: usu ADJ n]

**Auto|cue** /ɔːtoʊkjuː/ **(Autocues)** An **Autocue** is a device used by people speaking on television or at a public event, which displays words for them to read. [BRIT, TRADEMARK] [N-COUNT]

☑ in AM, use **Teleprompter**

**auto|graph** /ɔːtəgrɑːf, -græf/ **(autographs, autographing, autographed)** 1 An **autograph** is the signature of someone famous which is specially written for a fan to keep. ❑ *He went backstage and asked for her autograph.* [N-COUNT: oft with poss] 2 If someone famous **autographs** something, they put their signature on it. ❑ *I autographed a copy of one of my books.* [VERB] [V n] *...an autographed photo of Clark Gable.* [V-ed]

**auto-immune** also **autoimmune. Auto-immune** describes medical conditions in which normal cells are attacked by the body's immune system. ❑ *...auto-immune diseases such as rheumatoid arthritis.* [ADJ: usu ADJ n]

**auto|mate** /ɔːtəmeɪt/ **(automates, automating, automated)** To **automate** a factory, office, or industrial process means to put in machines which can do the work instead of people. ❑ *He wanted to use computers to automate the process.* [VERB] [V n] ♦ **auto|ma|tion** /ɔːtəmeɪʃən/ *In the last ten years automation has reduced the work force here by half.* [N-UNCOUNT]

**auto|mat|ed** /ɔːtəmeɪtɪd/ An **automated** factory, office, or industrial process uses machines to do the work instead of people. [ADJ: usu ADJ n]

**auto|mat|ic** /ɔːtəmætɪk/ **(automatics)** 1 An **automatic** machine or device is one which has controls that enable it to perform a task without needing to be constantly operated by a person. **Automatic** methods and processes involve the use of such machines. ❑ *Modern trains have automatic doors.* [◆◇◇ ADJ] 2 An **automatic** is a gun that keeps firing shots until you stop pulling the trigger. ❑ *He drew his automatic and began running in the direction of the sounds.* [N-COUNT] 3 An **automatic** is a car in which the gears change automatically as the car's speed increases or decreases. [N-COUNT] 4 An **automatic** action is one that you do without thinking about it. ❑ *All of the automatic body functions, even breathing, are affected.* [ADJ] ♦ **auto|mati|cal|ly** /ɔːtəmætɪkli/ *Strangely enough, you will automatically wake up after this length of time.* [ADV: usu ADV with v] 5 If something such as an action or a punishment is **automatic**, it happens without people needing to think about it because it is the result of a fixed rule or method. ❑ *Those drivers should face an automatic charge of manslaughter.* [ADJ: usu ADJ n] ♦ **auto|mati|cal|ly** *As an account customer, you are automatically entitled to a variety of benefits.* [ADV: usu ADV with v, also ADV n/adj]

**auto|mat|ic pi|lot** or **autopilot** 1 If you are **on automatic pilot** or **on autopilot**, you are acting without thinking about what you are doing, usually because you have done it many times before. [PHRASE: v-link PHR, PHR after v] 2 An **automatic pilot** or an **autopilot** is a device in an aircraft that automatically keeps it on a particular course. [N-SING]

**auto|mat|ic trans|mis|sion** A car that is fitted with **automatic transmission** has a gear system in which the gears change automatically. [N-UNCOUNT]

**automa|ton** /ɔːtɒmətən/ **(automatons** or **automata** /ɔːtɒmətə/**)** 1 If you say that someone is an **automaton**, you are critical of them because they behave as if they are so tired or bored that they do things without thinking. [N-COUNT] [disapproval] 2 An **automaton** is a small, mechanical figure that can move automatically. [N-COUNT]

**auto|mo|bile** /ɔːtəməbiːl, AM -moʊbiːl/ **(automobiles)** An **automobile** is a car. [mainly AM] [N-COUNT]

**auto|mo|tive** /ɔːtəmoʊtɪv/ **Automotive** is used to refer to things relating to cars. ❑ *...a chain of stores selling automotive parts.* [ADJ: ADJ n]

**autono|mous** /ɔːtɒnəməs/ 1 An **autonomous** country, organization, or group governs or controls itself rather than being controlled by anyone else. ❑ *They proudly declared themselves part of a new autonomous province.* [ADJ: usu ADJ n = independent] 2 An **autonomous** person makes their own decisions rather than being influenced by someone else. ❑ *He treated us as autonomous individuals who had to learn to make up our own minds about important issues.* [ADJ: usu ADJ n = independent]

**autono|my** /ɔːtɒnəmi/ 1 **Autonomy** is the control or government of a country, organization, or group by itself rather than by others. ❑ *Activists stepped up their demands for local autonomy last month.* [N-UNCOUNT = independence] 2 **Autonomy** is the ability to make your own decisions about what to do rather than being influenced by someone else or told what to do. [FORMAL] ❑ *Each of the area managers enjoys considerable autonomy in the running of his own area.* [N-UNCOUNT = independence]

**auto|pi|lot** /ɔːtoʊpaɪlət/ **(autopilots)** → see **automatic pilot**.

**autop|sy** /ɔːtɒpsi/ **(autopsies)** An **autopsy** is an examination of a dead body by a doctor who cuts it open in order to try to discover the cause of death. [N-COUNT = post-mortem]

**autumn** /ɔːtəm/ **(autumns) Autumn** is the season between summer and winter when the weather becomes cooler and the leaves fall off the trees. [BRIT] [◆◇◇ N-VAR]

☑ in AM, usually use **fall**

**autum|nal** /ɔːtʌmnəl/ 1 **Autumnal** means having features that are characteristic of autumn. [LITERARY] ❑ *...the autumnal colours of the trees.* [ADJ] 2 **Autumnal** means happening in autumn. ❑ *...the autumnal equinox.* [ADJ]

**aux|ilia|ry** /ɔːgzɪljəri, AM -ləri/ **(auxiliaries)**
1 An **auxiliary** is a person who is employed to assist other people in their work. Auxiliaries are often medical workers or members of the armed forces. ❑ *Nursing auxiliaries provide basic care, but are not qualified nurses.* [N-COUNT = ancillary] 2 **Auxiliary** staff and troops assist other staff and troops. ❑ *The government's first concern was to augment the army and auxiliary forces.* [ADJ: ADJ n] 3 **Auxiliary** equipment is extra equipment that is available for use when necessary. ❑ *...an auxiliary motor. ...auxiliary fuel tanks.* [ADJ: ADJ n]
4 In grammar, an **auxiliary** or **auxiliary verb** is a verb which is used with a main verb, for example to form different tenses or to make the verb passive. In English, the basic auxiliary verbs are 'be', 'have', and 'do'. Modal verbs such as 'can' and 'will' are also sometimes called auxiliaries. [N-COUNT]

**avail** /əveɪl/ **(avails, availing, availed)** 1 If you do something **to no avail** or **to little avail**, what you do fails to achieve what you want. [WRITTEN] ❑ *His efforts were to no avail.* [PHRASE: PHR after v, v-link PHR] 2 If you **avail yourself of** an offer or an opportunity, you accept the offer or make use of the opportunity. [FORMAL] ❑ *Guests should feel at liberty to avail themselves of your facilities.* [VERB] [V pron-refl of n]

**avail|able** /əveɪləbəl/ 1 If something you want or need is **available**, you can find it or ob- [◆◆◆ ADJ]

tain it. ❑ *Since 1978, the amount of money available to buy books has fallen by 17%... There are three small boats available for hire.* ♦ **avail|abil|ity** /əveɪləbɪlɪti/ *...the easy availability of guns.* N-UNCOUNT: usu *the* N *of* n
[2] Someone who is **available** is not busy and is therefore free to talk to you or to do a particular task. ❑ *Mr Leach is on holiday and was not available for comment.* ADJ: v-link ADJ

**ava|lanche** /ævəlɑːntʃ, -læntʃ/ **(avalanches)** [1] An **avalanche** is a large mass of snow that falls down the side of a mountain. N-COUNT [2] You can refer to a very large quantity of things that all arrive or happen at the same time as an **avalanche of** them. ❑ *The newcomer was greeted with an avalanche of publicity.* N-SING: usu N *of* n

**avant-garde** /ævɒŋ gɑːʳd/ **Avant-garde** art, music, theatre, and literature is very modern and experimental. ❑ *...avant-garde concert music.* ADJ: usu ADJ n ♦ **Avant-garde** is also a noun. ❑ *He was an enthusiast for the avant-garde.* N-SING: *the* N

**ava|rice** /ævərɪs/ **Avarice** is extremely strong desire for money and possessions. [LITERARY] ❑ *He paid a month's rent in advance, just enough to satisfy the landlord's avarice.* N-UNCOUNT

**ava|ri|cious** /ævərɪʃəs/ An **avaricious** person is very greedy for money or possessions. ❑ *He sacrificed his own career so that his avaricious brother could succeed.* ADJ: usu ADJ n [disapproval]

**Ave.** **Ave.** is a written abbreviation for **avenue**. ❑ *...90 Dayton Ave.* N-IN-NAMES

**avenge** /əvendʒ/ **(avenges, avenging, avenged)** If you **avenge** a wrong or harmful act, you hurt or punish the person who is responsible for it. ❑ *He has devoted the past five years to avenging his daughter's death...* V n *She had decided to avenge herself and all the other women he had abused.* V pron-refl VERB

**av|enue** /ævɪnjuː, AM -nuː/ **(avenues)** [1] **Avenue** is sometimes used in the names of streets. The written abbreviation **Ave.** is also used. ❑ *...the most expensive stores on Park Avenue.* N-IN-NAMES [2] An **avenue** is a wide, straight road, especially one with trees on either side. N-COUNT [3] An **avenue** is a way of getting something done. ❑ *Talbot was presented with 80 potential avenues of investigation.* N-COUNT: with supp, oft N *of* n = channel

**aver** /əvɜːʳ/ **(avers, averring, averred)** If you **aver that** something is the case, you say very firmly that it is true. [FORMAL] ❑ *He avers that chaos will erupt if he loses...* V that *'Entertaining is something that everyone in the country can enjoy,' she averred.* V with quote. Also V. VERB = declare

**av|er|age** /ævərɪdʒ/ **(averages, averaging, averaged)** ◆◆◇ [1] An **average** is the result that you get when you add two or more numbers together and divide the total by the number of numbers you added together. ❑ *Take the average of those ratios and multiply by a hundred.* N-COUNT = mean ♦ **Average** is also an adjective. ❑ *The average price of goods rose by just 2.2%.* ADJ: ADJ n = mean [2] You use **average** to refer to a number or size that varies but is always approximately the same. ❑ *It takes an average of ten weeks for a house sale to be completed.* N-SING: *a* N *of* amount [3] An **average** person or thing is typical or normal. ❑ *The average adult man burns 1,500 to 2,000 calories per day.* ADJ: ADJ n [4] An amount or quality that is **the average** is the normal amount or quality for a particular group of things or people. ❑ *Most areas suffered more rain than usual, with Northern Ireland getting double the average for the month.* N-SING: *the* N = norm ♦ **Average** is also an adjective. ❑ *£2.20 for a beer is average. ...a woman of average height.* ADJ [5] Something that is **average** is neither very good nor very bad, usually when you had hoped it would be better. ❑ *I was only average academically.* ADJ [6] To **average** a particular amount means to do, get, or produce that amount as an average over a period of time. ❑ *We averaged 42 miles per hour.* VERB; V n

PHRASES [7] You say **on average** or **on an average** to indicate that a number is the average of several numbers. ❑ *American shares rose, on average, by 38%.* PHRASE: PHR with cl [8] If you say that something is true **on average**, you mean that it is generally true. ❑ *On average, American firms remain the most productive in the world.* PHRASE: PHR with cl [9] **law of averages** → see **law**.

♦ **average out** If a set of numbers **average out to** a particular figure or if you **average** them **out to** that figure, their average is calculated to be that figure. ❑ *There are six glasses of wine in one bottle, which averages out to 50p a glass...* V P *to/at* n *Averaging it out between us there's less than £10 a month each to live on.* V n P. Also V P n (not pron) PHRASAL VERB

**averse** /əvɜːʳs/ If you say that you are not **averse to** something, you mean that you quite like it or quite want to do it. [FORMAL] ❑ *He's not averse to publicity, of the right kind.* ADJ: usu with neg, v-link ADJ *to* n

**aver|sion** /əvɜːʳʃᵊn, AM -ʒᵊn/ **(aversions)** If you have an **aversion to** someone or something, you dislike them very much. ❑ *Many people have a natural and emotional aversion to insects.* N-VAR: usu N *to/for* n/-ing

**avert** /əvɜːʳt/ **(averts, averting, averted)** [1] If you **avert** something unpleasant, you prevent it from happening. ❑ *Talks with the teachers' union over the weekend have averted a strike.* VERB; V n [2] If you **avert** your eyes or gaze **from** someone or something, you look away from them. VERB

**aviary** /eɪvjəri/ **(aviaries)** An **aviary** is a large cage or covered area in which birds are kept. N-COUNT

**avia|tion** /eɪvieɪʃᵊn/ **Aviation** is the operation and production of aircraft. N-UNCOUNT

**avia|tor** /eɪvieɪtəʳ/ **(aviators)** An **aviator** is a pilot of a plane, especially in the early days of flying. [OLD-FASHIONED] N-COUNT

**avid** /ævɪd/ [1] You use **avid** to describe someone who is very enthusiastic about something that they do. ❑ *He misses not having enough books because he's an avid reader.* ADJ: usu ADJ n ♦ **av|id|ly** *Thank you for a most entertaining magazine, which I read avidly each month.* ADV: ADV with v [2] If you say that someone is **avid for** something, you mean that they are very eager to get it. ❑ *He was intensely eager, indeed avid, for wealth.* ADJ: v-link ADJ, usu ADJ *for* n ♦ **av|id|ly** *Western suppliers too are competing avidly for business abroad.* ADV: ADV with v

**avi|on|ics** /eɪviɒnɪks/ **Avionics** is the science of electronics used in aviation. [TECHNICAL] N-UNCOUNT

**avo|ca|do** /ævəkɑːdoʊ/ **(avocados)**

☑ in BRIT, also use **avocado pear**

**Avocados** are pear-shaped vegetables, with hard skins and large stones, which are usually eaten raw. N-VAR

**avo|ca|tion** /ævoʊkeɪʃᵊn/ **(avocations)** Your **avocation** is a job or activity that you do because you are interested in it, rather than to earn your living. [FORMAL] ❑ *He was a printer by trade and naturalist by avocation.* N-VAR

**avoid** /əvɔɪd/ **(avoids, avoiding, avoided)** ◆◆◇ [1] If you **avoid** something unpleasant that might happen, you take action in order to prevent it from happening. ❑ *The pilots had to take emergency action to avoid a disaster...* V n *Women have to dress modestly, to avoid being harassed by the locals.* V -ing VERB [2] If you **avoid** doing something, you choose not to do it, or you put yourself in a situation where you do not have to do it. ❑ *By borrowing from dozens of banks, he managed to avoid giving any of them an overall picture of what he was up to...* V -ing *He was always careful to avoid embarrassment.* V n VERB [3] If you **avoid** a person or thing, you keep away from them. When talking to someone, if you **avoid** the subject, you keep the conversation away from a particular topic. ❑ *She eventually had to lock herself in the toilets to avoid him.* V n VERB [4] If a person or vehicle **avoids** someone or something, they change the direction they are moving in, so that they do not hit them. ❑ *The driver had ample time to brake or swerve and avoid the woman.* V n VERB

**avoid|able** /əvɔɪdəbᵊl/ Something that is **avoidable** can be prevented from happening. ❑ *The tragedy was entirely avoidable.* ADJ

**avoid|ance** /əvɔɪdəns/ **Avoidance of** someone or something is the act of avoiding them. ❑ *...the avoidance of stress.*
N-UNCOUNT: usu N *of* n

**avow** /əvaʊ/ **(avows, avowing, avowed)** If you **avow** something, you admit it or declare it. [FORMAL] ❑ *...a public statement avowing neutrality.*
VERB; V n

**avowed** /əvaʊd/ 1 If you are an **avowed** supporter or opponent of something, you have declared that you support it or oppose it. [FORMAL] ❑ *She is an avowed vegetarian.*
ADJ: ADJ n
2 An **avowed** belief or aim is one that you have declared formally or publicly. [FORMAL] ❑ *...the council's avowed intention to stamp on racism.*
ADJ: ADJ n

**avun|cu|lar** /əvʌŋkjʊləʳ/ An **avuncular** man or a man with **avuncular** behaviour is friendly and helpful towards someone younger. [FORMAL] ❑ *He began to talk in his most gentle and avuncular manner.*
ADJ: usu ADJ n

**await** /əweɪt/ **(awaits, awaiting, awaited)** ◆◇◇ 1 If you **await** someone or something, you wait for them. [FORMAL] ❑ *He's awaiting trial, which is expected to begin early next year.*
VERB; V n
2 Something that **awaits** you is going to happen or come to you in the future. [FORMAL] ❑ *A nasty surprise awaited them in Rosemary Lane.*
VERB; V n

**awake** /əweɪk/ **(awakes, awaking, awoke, awoken)** 1 Someone who is **awake** is not sleeping. ❑ *I don't stay awake at night worrying about that... Nightmares kept me awake all night.*
ADJ: v-link ADJ, ADJ after v
2 Someone who is **wide awake** is fully awake and unable to sleep. ❑ *I could not relax and still felt wide awake.*
PHRASE: usu v-link PHR
3 When you **awake** or when something **awakes** you, you wake up. [LITERARY] ❑ *At midnight he awoke and listened to the radio for a few minutes... The sound of many voices awoke her with a start.*
VERB = wake up; V; V n

**awak|en** /əweɪkən/ **(awakens, awakening, awakened)** 1 To **awaken** a feeling in a person means to cause them to start having this feeling. [LITERARY] ❑ *The aim of the cruise was to awaken an interest in and an understanding of foreign cultures.*
VERB; V n
2 When you **awaken**, or when something or someone **awakens** you, you wake up. [LITERARY] ❑ *Unfortunately, Grandma always seems to awaken at awkward moments... He was snoring when Desmond awakened him.*
VERB = wake up; V; V n

**awak|en|ing** /əweɪkənɪŋ/ **(awakenings)** 1 The **awakening** of a feeling or realization is the start of it. ❑ *...the awakening of national consciousness in people.*
N-COUNT: usu sing, with supp
2 If you have a **rude awakening**, you are suddenly made aware of an unpleasant fact.
PHRASE

**award** /əwɔːʳd/ **(awards, awarding, awarded)** ◆◆◇ 1 An **award** is a prize or certificate that a person is given for doing something well. ❑ *She presented a bravery award to schoolgirl Caroline Tucker.*
N-COUNT: oft supp N, N *for* n
2 In law, an **award** is a sum of money that a court decides should be given to someone. ❑ *...workmen's compensation awards.*
N-COUNT
3 A pay **award** is an increase in pay for a particular group of workers. ❑ *...this year's average pay award for teachers of just under 8%.*
N-COUNT
4 If someone **is awarded** something such as a prize or an examination mark, it is given to them. ❑ *She was awarded the prize for both films... For his dedication the Mayor awarded him a medal of merit.*
VERB; *be* V-ed n; V n n
5 To **award** something **to** someone means to decide that it will be given to that person. ❑ *We have awarded the contract to a British shipyard... A High Court judge had awarded him £6 million damages.*
VERB; V n *to* n; V n n

**award-winning** An **award-winning** person or thing has won an award, especially an important or valuable one. ❑ *...an award-winning photo-journalist. ...his award-winning film.*
ADJ: ADJ n

**aware** /əweəʳ/ ◆◆◇ 1 If you are **aware of** something, you know about it. ❑ *Smokers are well aware of the dangers to their own health... He should have been aware of what his junior officers were doing... He must have been aware that my parents' marriage was breaking up.* ♦ **aware|ness** *The 1980s brought an awareness of green issues.*
ADJ: v-link ADJ, ADJ *of* n, ADJ that ≠ unaware; N-UNCOUNT
2 If you are **aware of** something, you realize that it is present or is happening because you hear it, see it, smell it, or feel it. ❑ *She was acutely aware of the noise of the city... Jane was suddenly aware that she was digging her nails into her thigh.*
ADJ: v-link ADJ, ADJ *of* n, ADJ that = conscious ≠ unaware
3 Someone who is **aware** notices what is happening around them or happening in the place where they live. ❑ *They are politically very aware.* ♦ **aware|ness** *He introduced radio to the school to increase the children's awareness.*
ADJ: v-link ADJ; N-UNCOUNT

**awash** /əwɒʃ/ 1 If the ground or a floor is **awash**, it is covered in water, often because of heavy rain or as the result of an accident. ❑ *The bathroom floor was awash.*
ADJ: v-link ADJ
2 If a place is **awash with** something, it contains a large amount of it. ❑ *This, after all, is a company which is awash with cash.*
ADJ: v-link ADJ, usu ADJ *with* n

**away** /əweɪ/ ◆◆◆

> **Away** is often used with verbs of movement, such as 'go' and 'drive', and also in phrasal verbs such as 'do away with' and 'fade away'.

1 If someone or something moves or is moved **away from** a place, they move or are moved so that they are no longer there. If you are **away from** a place, you are not in the place where people expect you to be. ❑ *An injured policeman was led away by colleagues... He walked away from his car... She drove away before either of them could speak again... Jason was away on a business trip.*
ADV: ADV after v, *be* ADV, oft ADV prep
2 If you look or turn **away from** something, you move your head so that you are no longer looking at it. ❑ *She quickly looked away and stared down at her hands... As he stands up, he turns his face away from her so that she won't see his tears.*
ADV: ADV after v, oft ADV prep
3 If you put or tidy something **away**, you put it where it should be. If you hide someone or something **away**, you put them in a place where nobody can see them or find them. ❑ *I put my journal away and prepared for bed... All her letters were carefully filed away in folders... I have $100m hidden away where no one will ever find it.*
ADV: ADV after v
4 If something is **away from** a person or place, it is at a distance from that person or place. ❑ *The two women were sitting as far away from each other as possible. ...a country estate thirty miles away from town.*
PREP-PHRASE
5 You use **away** to talk about future events. For example, if an event is a week **away**, it will happen after a week. ❑ *...the Washington summit, now only just over two weeks away.*
ADV: *be* amount ADV
6 When a sports team plays **away**, it plays on its opponents' ground. ❑ *...a sensational 4-3 victory for the team playing away.* ♦ **Away** is also an adjective. ❑ *Charlton are about to play an important away match.*
ADV: ADV after v; ADJ: ADJ n
7 You can use **away** to say that something slowly disappears, becomes less significant, or changes so that it is no longer the same. ❑ *So much snow has already melted away... His voice died away in a whisper.*
ADV: ADV after v
8 You use **away** to show that there has been a change or development from one state or situation to another. ❑ *There's been a dramatic shift away from traditional careers towards business and commerce.*
ADV: ADV after v, n ADV, oft ADV prep
9 You can use **away** to emphasize a continuous or repeated action. ❑ *He would often be working away on his word processor late into the night.*
ADV: ADV after v [emphasis]
10 You use **away** to show that something is removed. ❑ *The waitress whipped the plate away and put down my bill.*
ADV: ADV after v
11 **far and away** → see **far**. **right away** → see **right**.

**awe** /ɔː/ **(awes, awed)** 1 **Awe** is the feeling of respect and amazement that you have when you are faced with something wonderful and often rather frightening. ❑ *She gazed in awe at the great stones.*
N-UNCOUNT
2 If you **are awed by** someone or something, they make you feel respectful and amazed, though often rather frightened. ❑ *I am still awed by David's courage... The crowd listened in awed silence.*
VERB: usu passive, no cont; *be* V-ed; V-ed
3 If you **are in awe of** someone or if you **stand in awe of** them, you have a lot of respect for them and are slightly afraid of them.
PHRASE: V inflects

**awe-inspiring** If you describe someone or something as **awe-inspiring**, you are emphasizing that you think that they are remarkable and amazing, although sometimes rather frightening. ❑ *The higher we climbed, the more awe-inspiring the scenery became.*
ADJ
emphasis

**awe|some** /ɔːsəm/ An **awesome** person or thing is very impressive and often frightening. ❑ *...the awesome responsibility of sending men into combat.*
ADJ: usu ADJ n

**awe|struck** /ɔːstrʌk/ also **awe-struck.** If someone is **awestruck**, they are very impressed and amazed by something. [WRITTEN] ❑ *I stood and gazed at him, awestruck that anyone could be so beautiful.*
ADJ

**aw|ful** /ɔːfʊl/ 1 If you say that someone or something is **awful**, you dislike that person or thing or you think that they are not very good. ❑ *We met and I thought he was awful. ...an awful smell of paint... Even if the weather's awful there's lots to do... Jeans look awful on me.* ♦ **aw|ful|ness** *The programme's awfulness has ensured it is talked about.*
◆◇◇
ADJ
= dreadful
≠ wonderful
N-UNCOUNT

2 If you say that something is **awful**, you mean that it is extremely unpleasant, shocking, or bad. ❑ *Her injuries were massive. It was awful... Some of their offences are so awful they would chill the blood.*
ADJ
= horrific

3 If you look or feel **awful**, you look or feel ill. ❑ *I hardly slept at all and felt pretty awful.*
ADJ: v-link ADJ
= terrible

4 You can use **awful** with noun groups that refer to an amount in order to emphasize how large that amount is. ❑ *I've got an awful lot of work to do.* ♦ **aw|ful|ly** *Would you mind awfully waiting a bit, I'll be back right away.*
ADJ: ADJ n
emphasis
= tremendous
ADV: usu ADV adj/adv

5 You can use **awful** with adjectives that describe a quality in order to emphasize that particular quality. [AM, INFORMAL] ❑ *Gosh, you're awful pretty.*
ADV: ADV adj
emphasis
= very

**awhile** /əʰwaɪl/ **Awhile** means for a short time. It is more commonly spelled 'a while', which is considered more correct, especially in British English. ❑ *He worked awhile as a pharmacist in Cincinnati.*
ADV: usu ADV after v

**awk|ward** /ɔːkwəʳd/ 1 An **awkward** situation is embarrassing and difficult to deal with. ❑ *I was the first to ask him awkward questions but there'll be harder ones to come... There was an awkward moment as couples decided whether to stand next to their partners.* ♦ **awk|ward|ly** *There was an awkwardly long silence.*
ADJ
= tricky
ADV: ADV adj/-ed

2 Something that is **awkward to** use or carry is difficult to use or carry because of its design. A job that is **awkward** is difficult to do. ❑ *It was small but heavy enough to make it awkward to carry... Full-size tripods can be awkward, especially if you're shooting a low-level subject.* ♦ **awk|ward|ly** *The autoexposure button is awkwardly placed under the lens release button.*
ADJ: usu v-link ADJ, oft ADJ to-inf
= tricky
ADV: ADV -ed

3 An **awkward** movement or position is uncomfortable or clumsy. ❑ *Amy made an awkward gesture with her hands.* ♦ **awk|ward|ly** *He fell awkwardly and went down in agony clutching his right knee.*
ADJ
ADV: ADV with v

4 Someone who feels **awkward** behaves in a shy or embarrassed way. ❑ *Women frequently say that they feel awkward taking the initiative in sex.* ♦ **awk|ward|ly** *'This is Malcolm,' the girl said awkwardly, to fill the silence.*
ADJ
= uncomfortable
ADV: ADV with v

5 If you say that someone is **awkward**, you are critical of them because you find them unreasonable and difficult to live with or deal with. ❑ *She's got to an age where she is being awkward.*
ADJ
disapproval

**awn|ing** /ɔːnɪŋ/ **(awnings)** An **awning** is a piece of material attached to a caravan or building which provides shelter from the rain or sun.
N-COUNT
= canopy

**awoke** /əwoʊk/ **Awoke** is the past tense of **awake**.

**awok|en** /əwoʊkən/ **Awoken** is the past participle of **awake**.

**AWOL** /eɪwɒl/ 1 If someone in the Armed Forces goes **AWOL**, they leave their post without the permission of a superior officer. **AWOL** is an abbreviation for 'absent without leave'.
ADJ: usu v-link ADJ

2 If you say that someone has gone **AWOL**, you mean that they have disappeared without telling anyone where they were going. [INFORMAL]
ADJ: usu v-link ADJ

**awry** /əraɪ/ If something goes **awry**, it does not happen in the way it was planned. ❑ *She was in a fury over a plan that had gone awry.*
ADJ: v-link ADJ

**axe** /æks/ **(axes, axing, axed)**

| ✓ in AM, use **ax** |
|---|

1 An **axe** is a tool used for cutting wood. It consists of a heavy metal blade which is sharp at one edge and attached by its other edge to the end of a long handle. → See picture on page 1709.
N-COUNT

2 If someone's job or something such as a public service or a television programme **is axed**, it is ended suddenly and without discussion. ❑ *Community projects are being axed by hard-pressed social services departments.*
VERB: usu passive
= cut
be V-ed

3 If a person or institution is facing **the axe**, that person is likely to lose their job or that institution is likely to be closed, usually in order to save money. [JOURNALISM]
N-SING: the N

4 If someone **has an axe to grind**, they are doing something for selfish reasons. [INFORMAL] ❑ *He seems like a decent bloke and I've got no axe to grind with him.*
PHRASE: V inflects
disapproval

**axes**

| ✓ Pronounced /æksɪz/ for meaning 1, and /æksiːz/ for meaning 2. |
|---|

1 **Axes** is the plural of **axe**. 2 **Axes** is the plural of **axis**.

**axi|om** /æksiəm/ **(axioms)** An **axiom** is a statement or idea which people accept as being true. [FORMAL] ❑ *...the long-held axiom that education leads to higher income.*
N-COUNT: oft N that
= principle

**axio|mat|ic** /æksiəmætɪk/ If something is **axiomatic**, it seems to be obviously true. [FORMAL]
ADJ: oft it v-link ADJ that

**axis** /æksɪs/ **(axes)** 1 An **axis** is an imaginary line through the middle of something.
N-COUNT

2 An **axis** of a graph is one of the two lines on which the scales of measurement are marked.
N-COUNT

**axle** /æksəl/ **(axles)** An **axle** is a rod connecting a pair of wheels on a car or other vehicle.
N-COUNT

**aya|tol|lah** /aɪətɒlə/ **(ayatollahs)** An **ayatollah** is a type of Muslim religious leader.
N-COUNT; N-TITLE

**aye** /aɪ/ **(ayes)** also **ay.** 1 **Aye** means yes; used in some dialects of British English. ❑ *'Do you remember your first day at school?' — 'Oh aye. Yeah.'*
CONVENTION

2 If you vote **aye**, you vote in favour of something.
ADV

3 **The ayes** are the people who vote in favour of something.
N-PLURAL: the N

**azalea** /əzeɪliə/ **(azaleas)** An **azalea** is a woody plant with shiny, dark-green leaves which produces many brightly-coloured flowers in the spring.
N-COUNT

**az|ure** /æʒuəʳ/ **Azure** is used to describe things that are bright blue. [LITERARY] ❑ *...an azure sky.*
COLOUR: usu COLOUR n

# B b

**B, b** /biː/ **(B's, b's)** 1 **B** is the second letter of the English alphabet. 2 If you get a **B** as a mark for a piece of work or in an exam, your work is good. N-VAR N-VAR

**B2B** /biː tə biː/ **B2B** is the selling of goods and services by one company to another using the Internet. **B2B** is an abbreviation for 'business to business'. [BUSINESS] ❑ *American analysts have been somewhat cautious in estimating the size of the B2B market.* N-UNCOUNT: oft N n

**B2C** /biː tə siː/ **B2C** is the selling of goods and services by businesses to consumers using the Internet. **B2C** is an abbreviation for 'business to consumer'. [BUSINESS] ❑ *19 per cent of B2C companies are now worth little more than the cash on their balance sheets.* N-UNCOUNT: oft N n

**B4** **B4** is the written abbreviation for 'before', mainly used in text messages and e-mails.

**BA** /biː eɪ/ **(BAs)** also **B.A.** 1 A **BA** is a first degree in an arts or social science subject. **BA** is an abbreviation for 'Bachelor of Arts'. ❑ *I did a BA in film making.* 2 **BA** is written after someone's name to indicate that they have a BA. ❑ *...Helen Rich, BA (Hons).* N-COUNT

**bab|ble** /bæbᵊl/ **(babbles, babbling, babbled)** 1 If someone **babbles**, they talk in a confused or excited way. ❑ *Momma babbled on and on about how he was ruining me... They all babbled simultaneously... 'Er, hello, viewers,' he babbled.* 2 You can refer to people's voices as a **babble of** sound when they are excited and confused, preventing you from understanding what they are saying. ❑ *Kemp knocked loudly so as to be heard above the high babble of voices.* VERB V *on/away* V V with quote N-SING: usu N *of* n

**babe** /beɪb/ **(babes)** 1 Some people use **babe** as an affectionate way of addressing someone they love. [AM, INFORMAL] ❑ *I'm sorry, babe. I didn't mean it.* 2 Some men refer to an attractive young woman as a **babe**. This use could cause offence. [INFORMAL] 3 A **babe** is the same as a baby. [OLD-FASHIONED] ❑ *...newborn babes.* N-VOC [feelings] = honey N-COUNT N-COUNT

**ba|bel** /beɪbᵊl/ If there is a **babel** of voices, you hear a lot of people talking at the same time, so that you cannot understand what they are saying. ❑ *...a confused babel of sound.* N-SING = babble, hubbub

**ba|boon** /bæbuːn/ **(baboons)** A **baboon** is a large monkey that lives in Africa. N-COUNT

**baby** /beɪbi/ **(babies)** 1 A **baby** is a very young child, especially one that cannot yet walk or talk. ❑ *My wife has just had a baby... Claire had to dress her baby sister.* 2 A **baby** animal is a very young animal. ❑ *...a baby elephant. ...baby birds.* 3 **Baby** vegetables are vegetables picked when they are very small. ❑ *Serve with baby new potatoes.* 4 Some people use **baby** as an affectionate way of addressing someone, especially a young woman, or referring to them. [INFORMAL] ❑ *You have to wake up now, baby.* ◆◆◇ N-COUNT N-COUNT: usu N n ADJ: ADJ n N-VOC; N-COUNT: usu sing = love

**baby boom** **(baby booms)** A **baby boom** is a period of time when a lot of babies are born in a particular place. [INFORMAL] ❑ *I'm a product of the postwar baby boom.* N-COUNT: usu sing

**baby boom|er** /beɪbi buːməʳ/ **(baby boomers)** also **baby-boomer.** A **baby boomer** is someone who was born during a baby boom, especially during the years after the end of the Second World War. [mainly JOURNALISM, INFORMAL] N-COUNT: oft N n

**baby bug|gy** **(baby buggies)** 1 A **baby buggy** is a small folding seat with wheels, which a young child can sit in and which can be pushed around. [BRIT] N-COUNT = stroller, pushchair

☑ in AM, use **stroller**

2 A **baby buggy** is another word for a **baby carriage**. [AM] N-COUNT

**baby car|riage** **(baby carriages)** A **baby carriage** is a small vehicle in which a baby can lie as it is pushed along. [AM] N-COUNT

☑ in BRIT, use **pram**

**ba|by|hood** /beɪbihʊd/ Your **babyhood** is the period of your life when you were a baby. N-UNCOUNT

**ba|by|ish** /beɪbiɪʃ/ **Babyish** actions, feelings, or looks are like a baby's, or are immature. ❑ *...a fat, babyish face... I'm ashamed of the babyish nonsense I write.* ADJ: usu ADJ n

**baby|sit** /beɪbisɪt/ **(babysits, babysitting, babysat)** If you **babysit for** someone or **babysit** their children, you look after their children while they are out. ❑ *I promised to babysit for Mrs Plunkett... You can take it in turns to babysit... She had been babysitting him and his four-year-old sister.* ♦ **baby|sitter** **(babysitters)** *It can be difficult to find a good babysitter.* ♦ **baby|sitting** *Would you like me to do any babysitting?* VERB V *for* n V V n N-COUNT N-UNCOUNT

**baby talk** also **baby-talk. Baby talk** is the language used by babies when they are just learning to speak, or the way in which some adults speak when they are talking to babies. ❑ *Maria was talking baby talk to the little one.* N-UNCOUNT

**bac|ca|lau|re|ate** /bækəlɔːriət/ **(baccalaureates)** 1 The **baccalaureate** is an examination taken by students at the age of eighteen in France and some other countries. 2 In the United States, a **baccalaureate** service or address is a service that is held or a talk that is given during the ceremony when students receive their degrees. N-SING N-COUNT: usu N n

**bach|elor** /bætʃələʳ/ **(bachelors)** A **bachelor** is a man who has never married. N-COUNT

**Bach|elor of Arts** **(Bachelors of Arts)** A **Bachelor of Arts** is a first degree in an arts or social science subject. In British English, it can also mean a person with that degree. The abbreviation **BA** or **B.A.** is also used. N-COUNT

**Bach|elor of Sci|ence** **(Bachelors of Science)** A **Bachelor of Science** is a first degree in a science subject. In British English, it can also mean a person with that degree. The abbreviation **BSc** or **B.Sc.** is also used. N-COUNT

**bach|elor's de|gree** **(bachelor's degrees)** A **bachelor's degree** is a first degree awarded by universities. → See also **BA**, **BSc**. N-COUNT

**ba|cil|lus** /bəsɪləs/ **(bacilli)** A **bacillus** is any bacterium that has a long, thin shape. N-COUNT

**back**

1. ADVERB USES
2. OPPOSITE OF FRONT; NOUN AND ADJECTIVE USES
3. VERB USES

## ① **back** /bæk/ ◆◆◆

> In addition to the uses shown below, **back** is also used in phrasal verbs such as 'date back' and 'fall back on'.

⇛ Please look at category 17 to see if the expression you are looking for is shown under another headword. 1 If you move **back**, you move in the opposite direction to the one in which you are facing or in which you were moving before. ❑ *The photographers drew back to let us view the body... She stepped back from the door expectantly... He pushed her away and she fell back on the wooden bench.* [ADV: ADV after v, oft ADV prep] 2 If you go **back** somewhere, you return to where you were before. ❑ *I went back to bed... I'm due back in London by late afternoon... Smith changed his mind and moved back home... I'll be back as soon as I can... He made a round-trip to the terminal and back.* [ADV: ADV after v, be ADV, oft ADV prep/adv] 3 If someone or something is **back** in a particular state, they were in that state before and are now in it again. ❑ *The rail company said it expected services to get slowly back to normal... Denise hopes to be back at work by the time her daughter is one.* [ADV: ADV after v, be ADV, oft ADV prep] 4 If you give or put something **back**, you return it to the person who had it or to the place where it was before you took it. If you get or take something **back**, you then have it again after not having it for a while. ❑ *She handed the knife back... Put it back in the freezer... You'll get your money back.* [ADV: ADV after v, oft ADV prep] 5 If you put a clock or watch **back**, you change the time shown on it so that it shows an earlier time, for example when the time changes to winter time or standard time. [ADV: ADV after v] 6 If you write or call **back**, you write to or telephone someone after they have written to or telephoned you. If you look **back** at someone, you look at them after they have started looking at you. ❑ *They wrote back to me and they told me that I didn't have to do it... If the phone rings say you'll call back after dinner... Lee looked at Theodora. She stared back.* [ADV: ADV after v, oft ADV prep] 7 You can say that you go or come **back to** a particular point in a conversation to show that you are mentioning or discussing it again. ❑ *Can I come back to the question of policing once again?... Going back to the school, how many staff are there?* [ADV: ADV after v, ADV to n] 8 If something is or comes **back**, it is fashionable again after it has been unfashionable for some time. ❑ *Short skirts are back... Consensus politics could easily come back into fashion.* [ADV: ADV after v, be ADV, oft ADV prep] 9 If someone or something is kept or situated **back from** a place, they are at a distance away from it. ❑ *Keep back from the edge of the platform... I'm a few miles back from the border... He started for Dot's bedroom and Myrtle held him back.* [ADV: ADV after v, be ADV, oft ADV from n] 10 If something is held or tied **back**, it is held or tied so that it does not hang loosely over something. ❑ *The curtains were held back by tassels.* [ADV: ADV after v] 11 If you lie or sit **back**, you move your body backwards into a relaxed sloping or flat position, with your head and body resting on something. ❑ *She lay back and stared at the ceiling... She leaned back in her chair and smiled.* [ADV: ADV after v ≠ forward] 12 If you look or shout **back** at someone or something, you turn to look or shout at them when they are behind you. ❑ *Nick looked back over his shoulder and then stopped, frowning... He called back to her.* [ADV: ADV after v, oft ADV prep] 13 You use **back** in expressions like **back in London** or **back at the house** when you are giving an account, to show that you are going to start talking about what happened or was happening in the place you mention. ❑ *Meanwhile, back in London, Palace Pictures was collapsing... Later, back at home, the telephone rang.* [ADV: ADV with v, ADV prep] 14 If you talk about something that happened **back** in the past or several years **back**, you are emphasizing that it happened quite a long time ago. ❑ *The story starts back in 1950, when I was five... He contributed £50m to the project a few years back.* [ADV: ADV with v, ADV prep, n ADV] [emphasis] 15 If you think **back to** something that happened in the past, you remember it or try to remember it. ❑ *I thought back to the time in 1975 when my son was desperately ill.* [ADV: ADV after v, ADV to n] 16 If someone moves **back and forth**, they repeatedly move in one direction and then in the opposite direction. ❑ *He paced back and forth.* [PHRASE: PHR after v] 17 to **cast** your **mind back** → see **mind**.

## ② **back** /bæk/ **(backs)** ◆◆◆

⇛ Please look at category 17 to see if the expression you are looking for is shown under another headword. 1 A person's or animal's **back** is the part of their body between their head and their legs that is on the opposite side to their chest and stomach. ❑ *She turned her back to the audience... Three of the victims were shot in the back.* [N-COUNT: oft poss N] 2 The **back of** something is the side or part of it that is towards the rear or farthest from the front. The back of something is normally not used or seen as much as the front. ❑ *...a room at the back of the shop... She raised her hands to the back of her neck... Smooth the mixture with the back of a soup spoon.* [N-COUNT: usu sing, oft the N of n ≠ front] 3 **Back** is used to refer to the side or part of something that is towards the rear or farthest from the front. ❑ *He opened the back door... Ann could remember sitting in the back seat of their car. ...the path leading to the back garden.* [ADJ: ADJ n ≠ front] 4 The **back** of a chair or sofa is the part that you lean against when you sit on it. ❑ *There was a neatly folded pink sweater on the back of the chair.* [N-COUNT: usu sing, with supp] 5 The **back** of something such as a piece of paper or an envelope is the side which is less important. ❑ *Send your answers on the back of a postcard.* [N-COUNT: the N, usu sing ≠ front] 6 The **back** of a book is the part nearest the end, where you can find the index or the notes, for example. ❑ *...the index at the back of the book.* [N-COUNT: the N, usu sing ≠ front] 7 You can use **back** in expressions such as **round the back** and **out the back** to refer generally to the area behind a house or other building. [BRIT, SPOKEN] ❑ *He had chickens and things round the back.* [N-SING: prep the N] 8 You use **back** in expressions such as **out back** to refer to the area behind a house or other building. You also use **in back** to refer to the rear part of something, especially a car or building. [AM] ❑ *Dan informed her that he would be out back on the patio cleaning his shoes... Catlett got behind the wheel and I sat in back.* [N-UNCOUNT: prep N, oft N of n] 9 In team games such as football and hockey, a **back** is a player who is concerned mainly with preventing the other team from scoring goals, rather than scoring goals for their own team. [N-COUNT = defender ≠ forward] 10 In American football, a **back** is a player who stands behind the front line, runs with the ball and attacks rather than defends. [N-COUNT]

**PHRASES** 11 If you say that something was done **behind** someone's **back**, you disapprove of it because it was done without them knowing about it, in an unfair or dishonest way. ❑ *You eat her food, enjoy her hospitality and then criticize her behind her back.* [PHRASE: PHR after v] [disapproval] 12 If you **break the back of** a task or problem, you do the most difficult part of what is necessary to complete the task or solve the problem. ❑ *It seems at least that we've broken the back of inflation in this country.* [PHRASE: V inflects, PHR n] 13 If you are wearing something **back to front**, you are wearing it with the back of it at the front of your body. If you do something **back to front**, you do it the wrong way around, starting with the part that should come last. [mainly BRIT] ❑ *He wears his baseball cap back to front... The picture was printed back to front.* [PHRASE: PHR after v = backwards]

> ✔ in AM, use **backward**

14 If you say that one thing happens **on the back of** another thing, you mean that it happens after that other thing and in addition to it. ❑ *The cuts, if approved, come on the back of a difficult eight years that have seen three London fire stations closed.* [PHRASE] 15 If someone is **on the back foot**, or if something **puts** them **on the back foot**, they feel threatened and act defensively. ❑ *From now on Labour will be on the back foot on the subject of welfare. ...another scheme designed purely to put the Scots Nationalists on the back foot.* [PHRASE] 16 If someone or something **puts** your **back up** or **gets** your **back up**, they annoy you. [INFORMAL] ❑ *Some food label-* [PHRASE: V inflects = irritate]

*ling practices really get my back up.* 17 to **take a back seat** → see **seat**.

③**back** /bæ̱k/ **(backs, backing, backed)** ◆◆◆ 1 VERB If a building **backs onto** something, the back of it faces in the direction of that thing or touches the edge of that thing. ❑ *We live in a ground floor flat which backs onto a busy street... His garden backs onto a school.* V onto n, V onto n 2 VERB = reverse When you **back** a car or other vehicle somewhere or when it **backs** somewhere, it moves backwards. ❑ *He backed his car out of the drive... I heard the engines revving as the lorries backed and turned.* V n prep/adv, V, Also V n 3 VERB = support If you **back** a person or a course of action, you support them, for example by voting for them or giving them money. ❑ *There is a new witness to back his claim that he is a victim of mistaken identity.* V n ♦ **-backed** COMB in ADJ ...*government-backed loans to Egypt.* 4 VERB If you **back** a particular person, team, or horse in a competition, you predict that they will win, and usually you bet money that they will win. ❑ *Roland Nilsson last night backed Sheffield Wednesday to win the UEFA Cup... It is upsetting to discover that you have backed a loser.* V n to-inf, V n 5 VERB: usu passive If a singer **is backed by** a band or by other singers, they provide the musical background for the singer. ❑ *She was backed by acoustic guitar, bass and congas.* be V-ed by n 6 → See also **backing**.

♦ **back away** 1 PHRASAL VERB = retreat If you **back away from** a commitment that you made or something that you were involved with in the past, you try to show that you are no longer committed to it or involved with it. ❑ *The company backed away from plans to cut their pay by 15%... Until yesterday, Britain had backed away because it didn't like the cost.* V P from n, V P 2 PHRASAL VERB If you **back away**, you walk backwards away from someone or something, often because you are frightened of them. ❑ *James got to his feet and started to come over, but the girls hastily backed away.* V P, Also V P from n

♦ **back down** PHRASAL VERB If you **back down**, you withdraw a claim, demand, or commitment that you made earlier, because other people are strongly opposed to it. ❑ *It's too late to back down now... He had to back down on plans to backdate the tax changes.* V P, V P on/over n

♦ **back off** 1 PHRASAL VERB If you **back off**, you move away in order to avoid problems or a fight. ❑ *They backed off in horror.* V P 2 PHRASAL VERB If you **back off from** a claim, demand, or commitment that you made earlier, or if you **back off** it, you withdraw it. ❑ *A spokesman says the president has backed off from his threat to boycott the conference... The union has publicly backed off that demand.* V P from n, V P n

♦ **back out** PHRASAL VERB = pull out If you **back out**, you decide not to do something that you previously agreed to do. ❑ *Madonna backed out of the project after much wrangling... Wells was supposed to put up half the money, but later backed out.* V P of n, V P

♦ **back up** 1 PHRASAL VERB = support If someone or something **backs up** a statement, they supply evidence to suggest that it is true. ❑ *Radio signals received from the galaxy's centre back up the black hole theory.* V P n, Also V n P 2 PHRASAL VERB If you **back up** a computer file, you make a copy of it which you can use if the original file is damaged or lost. [COMPUTING] ❑ *Make a point of backing up your files at regular intervals... I get so annoyed when I lose work because I've forgotten to back it up.* V P n (not pron), V n P 3 PHRASAL VERB If an idea or intention **is backed up** by action, action is taken to support or confirm it. ❑ *The Secretary General says the declaration must now be backed up by concrete and effective actions... It is time the Government backed up its advert campaigns with tougher measures.* be V-ed P, V P n (not pron), Also V n P 4 PHRASAL VERB = support If you **back** someone **up**, you show your support for them. ❑ *His employers, Norfolk social services, backed him up.* V n P, Also V P n 5 PHRASAL VERB If you **back** someone **up**, you help them by confirming that what they are saying is true. ❑ *The girl denied being there, and the man backed her up.* V n P, Also V P n 6 PHRASAL VERB = reverse If you **back up**, the car or other vehicle that you are driving moves back a short distance. ❑ *Back up, Hans... A police van drove through the protesters and backed up to the front door of the house.* V P, V P to n 7 PHRASAL VERB If vehicles **back up**, they form a line of traffic which has to wait before it can move on. ❑ *Traffic into London on the M11 was backed up for several miles.* V-ed P, Also V P, V P n (not pron) 8 PHRASAL VERB If you **back up**, you move backwards a short distance. ❑ *I backed up carefully until I felt the wall against my back... She backed up a few steps.* V P, V P amount 9 → See also **backup**.

**back|ache** /bæ̱keɪk/ **(backaches)** N-VAR **Backache** is a dull pain in your back.

**back|bench** /bæ̱kbentʃ/ ADJ: ADJ n A **backbench** MP is a Member of Parliament who is not a minister and who does not hold an official position in his or her political party. [BRIT, AUSTRALIAN] ❑ *...the Conservative backbench MP Sir Teddy Taylor.*

**back|bencher** /bæ̱kbe̱ntʃəʳ/ **(backbenchers)** N-COUNT A **backbencher** is a Member of Parliament who is not a minister and who does not hold an official position in their political party. [BRIT] ❑ *...a senior Conservative backbencher.*

**back|benches** /bæ̱kbe̱ntʃɪz/ N-PLURAL: usu *the* N **The backbenches** are the seats in the British House of Commons where backbenchers sit. The Members of Parliament who sit on the backbenches are also referred to as the **backbenches**. [BRIT] ❑ *This issue is creating unrest on the backbenches.*

**back|bit|ing** /bæ̱kbaɪtɪŋ/ N-UNCOUNT disapproval If you accuse someone of **backbiting**, you mean that they say unpleasant or unkind things about someone who is not present, especially in order to stop them doing well at work.

**back|bone** /bæ̱kboʊn/ **(backbones)** 1 N-COUNT = spine Your **backbone** is the column of small linked bones down the middle of your back. 2 N-SING: usu with poss The **backbone** of an organization or system is the part of it that gives it its main strength. ❑ *The small business people of Britain are the economic backbone of the nation.*

**back-breaking** also **backbreaking**. ADJ: usu ADJ n **Back-breaking** work involves a lot of hard physical effort.

**back burn|er** also **backburner**. N-SING: usu *the* N If you put an issue **on the back burner**, you leave it in order to deal with it later because you now consider it to have become less urgent or important. ❑ *Many speculated that the US would put the peace process on the back burner.*

**back cata|logue** **(back catalogues)** N-COUNT: oft poss N A musical performer's **back catalogue** is the music which they recorded and released in the past rather than their latest recordings.

**back|cloth** /bæ̱kklɒθ, AM -klɔːθ/ **(backcloths)** 1 N-COUNT = backdrop A **backcloth** is a large piece of cloth, often with scenery or buildings painted on it, that is hung at the back of a stage while a play is being performed. [BRIT]

✔ in AM, use **backdrop**

2 N-SING: with supp, oft N *of* n = background The **backcloth to** an event is the general situation in which it happens. [BRIT, JOURNALISM or LITERARY] ❑ *I'm not impressed by the promise of tax cuts against the backcloth of a public-spending deficit.*

**back co̱py** **(back copies)** N-COUNT A **back copy** of a magazine or newspaper is the same as a **back issue**.

**back coun|try** also **backcountry**. N-SING: *the* N **The back country** is an area that is a long way from any city and has very few people living in it. [AM] ❑ *They have moved deep into the back country.*

**back|date** /bæ̱kde̱ɪt/ **(backdates, backdating, backdated)** also **back-date**. VERB If a document or an arrangement **is backdated**, it is valid from a date before the date when it is completed or signed. ❑ *The contract that was signed on Thursday morning was backdated to March 11... Anyone who has overpaid tax will be able to backdate their claim to last April.* be V-ed to n, V n to n, Also V n

**back|door** /bæ̱kdɔːʳ/ also **back door**. 1 ADJ: ADJ n disapproval = underhand You can use **backdoor** to describe an action or process if you disapprove of it because you think it has been done in a secret, indirect, or dishonest way. ❑ *He did the backdoor deals that allowed the government to get its budget through Parliament on time... He brushed aside talk of greedy MPs voting themselves a backdoor pay rise.* [2] If you say that someone is doing something through or by **the backdoor**, you disapprove of them because they are doing it in a secret, indirect, or dishonest way. ❑ *Dentists claim the Government is privatising dentistry through the back door.* N-SING: *the* N, usu prep N [disapproval]

**back|drop** /bækdrɒp/ **(backdrops)** [1] A **backdrop** is a large piece of cloth, often with scenery painted on it, that is hung at the back of a stage while a play is being performed. N-COUNT = backcloth [2] The **backdrop** to an object or a scene is what you see behind it. ❑ *Leeds Castle will provide a dramatic backdrop to a fireworks display next Saturday.* N-COUNT: usu N prep = background [3] The **backdrop** to an event is the general situation in which it happens. ❑ *The election will take place against a backdrop of increasing instability.* N-COUNT: usu N prep = background

**back|er** /bækəʳ/ **(backers)** A **backer** is someone who helps or supports a project, organization, or person, often by giving or lending money. ❑ *I was looking for a backer to assist me in the attempted buy-out.* N-COUNT

**back|fire** /bækfaɪəʳ, AM -faɪr/ **(backfires, backfiring, backfired)** [1] If a plan or project **backfires**, it has the opposite result to the one that was intended. ❑ *The President's tactics could backfire... It all backfired on me!* VERB V V *on/against* n [2] When a motor vehicle or its engine **backfires**, it produces an explosion in the exhaust pipe. ❑ *The car backfired.* VERB V

**back|gam|mon** /bækgæmən/ **Backgammon** is a game for two people, played on a board marked with long triangles. Each player has 15 wooden or plastic discs. The players throw dice and move the discs around the board. N-UNCOUNT

**back|ground** /bækgraʊnd/ **(backgrounds)** ◆◇◇ [1] Your **background** is the kind of family you come from and the kind of education you have had. It can also refer to such things as your social and racial origins, your financial status, or the type of work experience that you have. ❑ *She came from a working-class background... His background was in engineering.* N-COUNT: usu sing, usu with supp [2] The **background** to an event or situation consists of the facts that explain what caused it. ❑ *The meeting takes place against a background of continuing political violence. ...background information.* N-COUNT: usu sing, with supp, oft *against* N [3] **The background** is sounds, such as music, which you can hear but which you are not listening to with your full attention. ❑ *I kept hearing the sound of applause in the background... The background music was provided by an accordion player.* N-SING: *the* N ≠ foreground [4] You can use **background** to refer to the things in a picture or scene that are less noticeable or important than the main things or people in it. ❑ *...roses patterned on a blue background.* N-COUNT: usu sing ≠ foreground ● Someone who stays **in the background** avoids being noticed, although the things that they do are important or influential. ❑ *Rosemary likes to stay in the background.* PHRASE

**back|hand** /bækhænd/ **(backhands)** A **backhand** is a shot in tennis or squash, which you make with your arm across your body. ❑ *She practised her backhand.* N-VAR

**back|hand|ed** /bækhændɪd, AM -hændɪd/ also **back-handed.** [1] A **backhanded** compliment is a remark which seems to be an insult but could also be understood as a compliment. A **backhanded** compliment is also a remark which seems to be a compliment but could also be understood as an insult. ❑ *Saying she's improved comes over as a backhanded compliment.* ADJ: ADJ n [2] If you say that someone is doing something in a **backhanded** way, they are doing it indirectly. ❑ *In a backhanded way, I think a lot of my energy and strength comes from my campaigning.* ADJ: ADJ n [disapproval]

**back|hand|er** /bækhændəʳ/ **(backhanders)** also **back-hander.** A **backhander** is an amount of money that is illegally paid to someone in a position of authority in order to encourage them to do something. [BRIT, INFORMAL] N-COUNT = bribe

**back|ing** /bækɪŋ/ **(backings)** ◆◇◇ [1] If someone has the **backing of** an organization or an important person, they receive support or money from that organization or person in order to do something. ❑ *He said the president had the full backing of his government to negotiate a deal... Mr Bach set up his own consulting business with the backing of his old boss.* N-UNCOUNT: usu N *of/for* n = support [2] A **backing** is a layer of something such as cloth that is put onto the back of something in order to strengthen or protect it. N-VAR [3] The **backing** of a popular song is the music which is sung or played to accompany the main tune. ❑ *Sharon also sang backing vocals for Barry Manilow.* N-COUNT: oft N n

**back is|sue** **(back issues)** A **back issue** of a magazine or newspaper is one that was published some time ago and is not the most recent. N-COUNT = back number

**back|lash** /bæklæʃ/ A **backlash against** a tendency or recent development in society or politics, is a sudden, strong reaction against it. ❑ *...the male backlash against feminism. ...a right-wing backlash.* N-SING: usu with supp = reaction

**back|less** /bækləs/ A **backless** dress leaves most of a woman's back uncovered down to her waist. ADJ: usu ADJ n

**back|log** /bæklɒg, AM -lɔːg/ **(backlogs)** A **backlog** is a number of things which have not yet been done but which need to be done. ❑ *There is a backlog of repairs and maintenance in schools.* N-COUNT

**back num|ber** **(back numbers)** A **back number** of a magazine or newspaper is the same as a **back issue**. N-COUNT

**back|pack** /bækpæk/ **(backpacks)** A **backpack** is a bag with straps that go over your shoulders, so that you can carry things on your back when you are walking or climbing. N-COUNT = rucksack

**back|pack|er** /bækpækəʳ/ **(backpackers)** A **backpacker** is a person who goes travelling with a backpack. N-COUNT

**back|pack|ing** /bækpækɪŋ/ If you go **backpacking**, you go travelling with a backpack. N-UNCOUNT

**back pas|sage** **(back passages)** People sometimes refer to their rectum as their **back passage**. [BRIT, INFORMAL] N-COUNT

**back pay** **Back pay** is money which an employer owes an employee for work that he or she did in the past. [BUSINESS] ❑ *He will receive $6,000 in back pay.* N-UNCOUNT

**back-pedal** **(back-pedals, back-pedalling, back-pedalled)** also **backpedal.**

> ✔ The forms **back-pedaling** and **back-pedaled** are used in American English.

[1] If you **back-pedal**, you express a different or less forceful opinion about something from the one you have previously expressed. ❑ *Allen back-pedalled, saying that he had had no intention of offending them... He appeared to back-pedal on that statement.* VERB = backtrack V V *on* n [2] If you say that someone **back-pedals**, you disapprove of their behaviour because they are not doing what they promised. ❑ *She's backpedaled twice already... The cabinet may backpedal on these commitments.* VERB [disapproval] V V *on/from* n ♦ **back-pedalling** *...Britain's back-pedalling on reforms.* N-UNCOUNT

**back|rest** /bækrest/ **(backrests)** The **backrest** of a seat or chair is the part which you rest your back on. N-COUNT

**back road** **(back roads)** A **back road** is a small country road with very little traffic. N-COUNT

**back|room** /bækrʊm/ **(back rooms)** also **back-room, back room.** [1] A **backroom** is a room that is situated at the back of a building, especially a private room. ❑ *...the backroom of the officers' club.* N-COUNT [2] You can use **backroom** to refer to people in an organization who do important work but are not seen or known about by the public. You can also use **backroom** to refer to a place where such people work. ❑ *Public scrutiny* N-COUNT *had brought civil servants out from the backroom and into the spotlight. ...Mr Smith's backroom staff.* [3] If you refer to a deal made by someone such as a politician as a **backroom** deal, you disapprove of it because it has been made in a secret, dishonest way. ❑ *They have been calling the Presidency decision a backroom deal.* ADJ: ADJ n [disapproval]

**back|room boy** **(backroom boys)** also **backroom-boy.** You can refer to a man as a **backroom boy** when he does important work in an organization and has good ideas but is not seen or known about by the public. [BRIT] N-COUNT

**back-seat driv|er** **(back-seat drivers)** also **backseat driver.** [1] If you refer to a passenger in a car as a **back-seat driver**, they annoy you because they constantly give you advice. N-COUNT [disapproval] [2] If you refer to someone, especially a politician, as a **back-seat driver**, you disapprove of them because they try to influence a situation that does not concern them. ❑ *They accused the former prime minister of being a backseat driver.* N-COUNT [disapproval]

**back|side** /bæksaɪd/ **(backsides)** Your **backside** is the part of your body that you sit on. [INFORMAL] N-COUNT = bottom

**back-slapping** also **backslapping.** **Back-slapping** is noisy, cheerful behaviour which people use in order to show affection or appreciation to each other. N-UNCOUNT ♦ **Back-slapping** is also an adjective. ❑ *Scott breaks away from his back-slapping admirers.* ADJ: ADJ n

**back|slid|ing** /bækslaɪdɪŋ/ If you accuse someone of **backsliding**, you disapprove of them because they have failed to do something they promised or agreed to do, or have started again doing something undesirable that they had previously stopped doing. ❑ *...the government's backsliding on free market reforms... This may help to maintain the gains you've made and to prevent backsliding.* N-UNCOUNT [disapproval]

**back|stage** /bæksteɪdʒ/ In a theatre, **backstage** refers to the areas behind the stage. ❑ *He went backstage and asked for her autograph.* ADV: ADV after v ♦ **Backstage** is also an adjective. ❑ *...a backstage pass.* ADJ: ADJ n

**back street** **(back streets)** also **back-street, backstreet.** [1] A **back street** in a town or city is a small, narrow street with very little traffic. ❑ *The small church of San Michel is tucked away in a narrow back street of Port-au-Prince. ...backstreet garages.* N-COUNT [2] The **back streets** of a town or city are the areas of small, old, poor streets rather than the richer or newer areas. ❑ *...the back streets of Berlin.* N-PLURAL [3] **Back street** activities are carried out unofficially, secretly, and often illegally. ❑ *...back street abortions.* ADJ: ADJ n

**back|stroke** /bækstroʊk/ [1] **Backstroke** is a swimming stroke that you do lying on your back. N-UNCOUNT: also *the* N [2] **The backstroke** is a swimming race in which the competitors swim backstroke. ❑ *...the 100 metres backstroke.* N-SING: *the* N

**back|track** /bæktræk/ **(backtracks, backtracking, backtracked)** also **back-track.** [1] If you **backtrack on** a statement or decision you have made, you do or say something that shows that you no longer agree with it or support it. ❑ *The committee backtracked by scrapping the controversial bonus system... The finance minister backtracked on his decision.* VERB = back-pedal; V; V *on/from* n ♦ **back|track|ing** *He promised there would be no backtracking on policies.* N-UNCOUNT [2] If you **backtrack**, you go back along a path or route you have just used. ❑ *Leonard jumped in his car and started backtracking... We had to backtrack to the corner and cross the street.* VERB; V; V prep [3] If you **backtrack** in an account or explanation, you talk about things which happened before the ones you were previously talking about. ❑ *Can we just backtrack a little bit and look at your primary and secondary education?* VERB; V

**back|up** /bækʌp/ **(backups)** also **back-up.** [1] **Backup** consists of extra equipment, resources, or people that you can get help or support from if necessary. ❑ *There is no emergency back-up immediately available... Alternative treatments can provide a useful back-up to conventional treatment.* N-VAR [2] If you have something such as a second piece of equipment or set of plans as **backup**, you have arranged for them to be available for use in case the first one does not work. ❑ *Every part of the system has a backup... Computer users should make regular back-up copies of their work.* N-VAR

**back|ward** /bækwəʳd/

> In American English, **backward** is usually used as an adverb instead of **backwards**. **Backward** is also sometimes used in this way in formal British English. See **backwards** for these uses.

[1] A **backward** movement or look is in the direction that your back is facing. Some people use **backwards** for this meaning. ❑ *He unlocked the door of apartment two and disappeared inside after a backward glance at Larry... He did a backward flip.* ADJ: ADJ n ≠ forward [2] If someone takes a **backward** step, they do something that does not change or improve their situation, but causes them to go back a stage. ❑ *At a certain age, it's not viable for men to take a backward step into unskilled work.* ADJ: ADJ n ≠ forward [3] A **backward** country or society does not have modern industries and machines. ❑ *We need to accelerate the pace of change in our backward country.* ADJ ≠ developed ♦ **back|ward|ness** *I was astonished at the backwardness of our country at the time.* N-UNCOUNT [4] A **backward** child has difficulty in learning. ❑ *I was slow to walk and talk and my parents thought I was backward.* ADJ ♦ **back|ward|ness** *...her backwardness in practical and physical activities.* N-UNCOUNT

**backward-looking** also **backward looking.** If you describe someone or something as **backward-looking**, you disapprove of their attitudes, ideas, or actions because they are based on old-fashioned opinions or methods. ❑ *...a stagnant, backward-looking culture.* ADJ [disapproval] = regressive, reactionary ≠ forward-looking

**back|wards** /bækwəʳdz/

✔ in AM, use **backward**

[1] If you move or look **backwards**, you move or look in the direction that your back is facing. ❑ *The diver flipped over backwards into the water... He took two steps backward... Bess glanced backwards... Keeping your back straight, swing one leg backwards.* ADV: ADV after v ♦ **Backwards** is also an adjective. ❑ *Without so much as a backwards glance, he steered her towards the car.* ADJ: ADJ n [2] If you do something **backwards**, you do it in the opposite way to the usual way. ❑ *He works backwards, building a house from the top downwards.* ADV: ADV after v [3] You use **backwards** to indicate that something changes or develops in a way that is not an improvement, but is a return to old ideas or methods. ❑ *Greater government intervention in businesses would represent a step backwards. ...the blaming that keeps us looking backward.* ADV: ADV after v, n ADV [4] → See also **backward**. [5] If someone or something moves **backwards and forwards**, they move repeatedly first in one direction and then in the opposite direction. ❑ *Draw the floss backwards and forwards between the teeth. ...people travelling backwards and forwards to and from London.* PHRASE: PHR after v [6] to **bend over backwards** → see **bend**.

**back|wash** /bækwɒʃ/ The **backwash** of an event or situation is an unpleasant situation that exists after it and as a result of it. ❑ *...the backwash of the events of 1989.* N-SING = repercussions

**back|water** /bækwɔːtəʳ/ **(backwaters)** [1] A **backwater** is a place that is isolated. ❑ *...a quiet rural backwater.* N-COUNT: usu with supp [2] If you refer to a place or institution as a **backwater**, you think it is not developing properly because it is isolated from ideas and events in other places and institutions. ❑ *Britain could become a political backwater with no serious influence in the world.* N-COUNT: usu with supp [disapproval]

**back|woods** /bækwʊdz/ If you refer to an area as **the backwoods**, you mean that it is a N-PLURAL long way from large towns and is isolated from modern life. ❑ *...the backwoods of Louisiana.*

**back|woods|man** /bækwʊdzmən/ **(backwoodsmen)** N-COUNT **Backwoodsmen** are people, especially politicians, who like the old ways of doing things, or who are involved in an organization at a local level. [mainly BRIT] ❑ *...Republican Party backwoodsmen in the United States.*

**back|yard** /bækjɑːʳd/ **(backyards)** also **back yard.** 1 N-COUNT A **backyard** is an area of land at the back of a house. 2 N-COUNT: with poss If you refer to a country's own **backyard**, you are referring to its own territory or to somewhere that is very close and where that country wants to influence events. ❑ *Economics will not stop Europe's politicians complaining when jobs are lost in their own backyard.*

**ba|con** /beɪkən/ N-UNCOUNT **Bacon** is salted or smoked meat which comes from the back or sides of a pig.

**bac|te|ria** /bæktɪəriə/ N-PLURAL **Bacteria** are very small organisms. Some bacteria can cause disease. ❑ *Chlorine is added to kill bacteria.*

**bac|te|rial** /bæktɪəriəl/ ADJ: ADJ n **Bacterial** is used to describe things that relate to or are caused by bacteria. ❑ *Cholera is a bacterial infection.*

**bac|te|ri|ol|ogy** /bæktɪəriɒlədʒi/ N-UNCOUNT **Bacteriology** is the science and the study of bacteria. ♦ **bac|te|rio|logi|cal** /bæktɪəriəlɒdʒɪkəl/ ADJ: ADJ n ❑ *...the national bacteriological laboratory.*

**bac|te|rium** /bæktɪəriəm/ **Bacterium** is the singular of **bacteria**.

**bad** /bæd/ **(worse, worst)** ♦♦♦ 1 ADJ ≠ good Something that is **bad** is unpleasant, harmful, or undesirable. ❑ *The bad weather conditions prevented the plane from landing... We have been going through a bad time... I've had a bad day at work... Divorce is bad for children... Analysts fear the situation is even worse than the leadership admits.* 2 ADJ You use **bad** to indicate that something unpleasant or undesirable is severe or great in degree. ❑ *He had a bad accident two years ago and had to give up farming... This was a bad case of dangerous driving... The pain is often so bad she wants to scream... The floods are described as the worst in nearly fifty years.* 3 ADJ: usu ADJ n = poor ≠ good A **bad** idea, decision, or method is not sensible or not correct. ❑ *Economist Jeffrey Faux says a tax cut is a bad idea... Of course politicians will sometimes make bad decisions... That's not a bad way to proceed, just somewhat different... The worst thing you can do is underestimate an opponent.* 4 ADJ: usu ADJ n ≠ good If you describe a piece of news, an action, or a sign as **bad**, you mean that it is unlikely to result in benefit or success. ❑ *The closure of the project is bad news for her staff... It was a bad start in my relationship with Warr... The report couldn't have come at a worse time for the European Commission.* 5 ADJ = poor ≠ good Something that is **bad** is of an unacceptably low standard, quality, or amount. ❑ *Many old people in Britain are living in bad housing... The state schools' main problem is that teachers' pay is so bad... It was absolutely the worst food I have ever had.* 6 ADJ: v-link ADJ *at* -ing/n, ADJ n = poor ≠ good Someone who is **bad at** doing something is not skilful or successful at it. ❑ *He had increased Britain's reputation for being bad at languages... He was a bad driver... Rose was a poor cook and a worse mother.* 7 ADJ: v-link ADJ, oft *it* v-link ADJ that ≠ good If you say that it is **bad** that something happens, you mean that it is unacceptable, unfortunate, or wrong. ❑ *Not being able to hear doesn't seem as bad as not being able to see... You need at least ten pounds if you go to the cinema nowadays – it's really bad.* 8 ADJ: with neg You can say that something is **not bad** to mean that it is quite good or acceptable, especially when you are rather surprised about this. ❑ *'How much is he paying you?' — 'Oh, five thousand.' — 'Not bad.'... 'How are you, mate?' — 'Not bad, mate, how's yourself?'... He's not a bad chap – quite human for an accountant... That's not a bad idea.* 9 ADJ = wicked ≠ good A **bad** person has morally unacceptable attitudes and behaviour. ❑ *I was selling drugs, but I didn't think I was a bad person... He does not think that his beliefs make him any worse than any other man.* ♦ **bad|ness** N-UNCOUNT *They only recognise badness when they perceive it in others.* 10 ADJ = naughty A **bad** child disobeys rules and instructions or does not behave in a polite and correct way. ❑ *You are a bad boy for repeating what I told you... Many parents find it hard to discourage bad behaviour.* 11 ADJ: usu ADJ n If you are in a **bad** mood, you are angry and behave unpleasantly to people. ❑ *She is in a bit of a bad mood because she's just given up smoking.* 12 ADJ: *feel* ADJ, oft ADJ *about* n, ADJ that ≠ good If you **feel bad about** something, you feel rather sorry or guilty about it. ❑ *You don't have to feel bad about relaxing... I feel bad that he's doing most of the work... Are you trying to make me feel bad?* 13 ADJ: usu ADJ n If you have a **bad** back, heart, leg, or eye, it is injured, diseased, or weak. ❑ *Alastair has a bad back so we have a hard bed.* 14 ADJ: usu *go* ADJ, also ADJ n Food that has **gone bad** is not suitable to eat because it has started to decay. ❑ *They bought so much beef that some went bad.* 15 ADJ: usu ADJ n **Bad** language is language that contains offensive words such as swear words. ❑ *I don't like to hear bad language in the street... I said a bad word.* 16 → See also **worse, worst**. 17 PHRASE: oft *it* v-link PHR that [feelings] = a pity, a shame If you say that it is **too bad** that something is the case, you mean you are sorry or sad that it is the case. ❑ *It is too bad that Eleanor had to leave so soon... Too bad he used his intelligence for criminal purposes.* 18 CONVENTION [feelings] = hard luck If you say **'too bad'**, you are indicating that nothing can be done to change the situation, and that you do not feel sorry or sympathetic about this. ❑ *Too bad if you missed the bus.* 19 to **make the best of a bad job** → see **best**. **bad blood** → see **blood**. **bad luck** → see **luck**. to **get a bad press** → see **press**. to **go from bad to worse** → see **worse**.

**bad cheque** **(bad cheques)**

☑ in AM, use **bad check**

N-COUNT A **bad cheque** is a bank cheque that will not be paid because there is a mistake on it, or because there is not enough money in the account of the person who wrote the cheque.

**bad debt** **(bad debts)** N-COUNT A **bad debt** is a sum of money that has been lent but is not likely to be repaid. ❑ *The bank set aside £1.1 billion to cover bad debts from business failures.*

**bad|dy** /bædi/ **(baddies)** also **baddie.** N-COUNT: usu pl = bad guy ≠ goody A **baddy** is a person in a story or film who is considered to be evil or wicked, or who is fighting on the wrong side. You can also refer to the **baddies** in a situation in real life. [BRIT, INFORMAL] ❑ *...a baddie who's trying to take over the world.*

☑ in AM, usually use **bad guy**

**bade** /bæd, beɪd/ **Bade** is a past tense of **bid**.

**badge** /bædʒ/ **(badges)** N-COUNT A **badge** is a piece of metal or cloth which you wear to show that you belong to an organization or support a cause. American English usually uses **button** to refer to a small round metal badge.

**badg|er** /bædʒəʳ/ **(badgers, badgering, badgered)** 1 N-COUNT A **badger** is a wild animal which has a white head with two wide black stripes on it. Badgers live underground and usually come up to feed at night. 2 VERB If you **badger** someone, you repeatedly tell them to do something or repeatedly ask them questions. ❑ V n *She badgered her doctor time and again, pleading with him to do something...* V n to-inf *They kept phoning and writing, badgering me to go back...* V n *into* n/ing *Richard's mother badgered him into taking a Spanish wife.*

**bad guy** **(bad guys)** N-COUNT: usu pl = baddy ≠ good guy A **bad guy** is a person in a story or film who is considered to be evil or wicked, or who is fighting on the wrong side. You can also refer to the **bad guys** in a situation in real life. [INFORMAL] ❑ *In the end the 'bad guys' are caught and sent to jail.*

**bad hair day** **(bad hair days)** N-COUNT: usu sing People sometimes say they are having a **bad hair day** when they do not feel very happy or relaxed, especially because their hair does not look good. [INFORMAL] ❑ *All this fuss is because Carol is having a bad hair day.*

**badi|nage** /bædɪnɑːʒ, -nɑːʒ/ **Badinage** is humorous or light-hearted conversation that often involves teasing someone. [LITERARY] ❑ *...light-hearted badinage.* N-UNCOUNT = banter

**bad|ly** /bædli/ **(worse, worst)** ◆◇◇ 1 If something is done **badly** or goes **badly**, it is not very successful or effective. ❑ *I was angry because I played so badly... The whole project was badly managed... The coalition did worse than expected, getting just 11.6 per cent of the vote.* ADV: ADV with v ≠ well 2 If someone or something is **badly** hurt or **badly** affected, they are severely hurt or affected. ❑ *The bomb destroyed a police station and badly damaged a church... One man was killed and another badly injured... It was a gamble that went badly wrong.* ADV: ADV with v, ADV adj = seriously 3 If you want or need something **badly**, you want or need it very much. ❑ *Why do you want to go so badly?... Planes landed at Bagram airport today carrying badly needed food and medicine.* ADV: ADV with v = much 4 If someone behaves **badly** or treats other people **badly**, they act in an unkind, unpleasant, or unacceptable way. ❑ *They have both behaved very badly and I am very hurt... I would like to know why we pensioners are being so badly treated.* ADV: ADV with v ≠ well 5 If something reflects **badly** on someone or makes others think **badly** of them, it harms their reputation. ❑ *Teachers know that low exam results will reflect badly on them... Despite his illegal act, few people think badly of him.* ADV: ADV after v ≠ well 6 If a person or their job is **badly** paid, they are not paid very much for what they do. ❑ *You may have to work part-time, in a badly paid job with unsociable hours... This is the most dangerous professional sport there is, and the worst paid.* ADV: usu ADV -ed, also ADV after v = poorly ≠ well 7 → See also **worse**, **worst**.

**bad|ly off** **(worse off, worst off)**

✔ in AM, also use **bad off**

1 If you are **badly off**, you are in a bad situation. ❑ *The average working week in Japan is 42.3 hours, compared with 41.6 in the UK, so they are not too badly off.* ADJ: usu v-link ADJ 2 If you are **badly off**, you do not have much money. ❑ *It is outrageous that people doing well-paid jobs should moan about how badly off they are.* ADJ: usu v-link ADJ

**bad|min|ton** /bædmɪntən/ **Badminton** is a game played by two or four players on a rectangular court with a high net across the middle. The players try to score points by hitting a small object called a shuttlecock across the net using a racket. N-UNCOUNT

**bad-mouth** /bædmaʊð/ **(bad-mouths, bad-mouthing, bad-mouthed)** If someone **bad-mouths** you, they say unpleasant things about you, especially when you are not there to defend yourself. ❑ *Both men continually bad-mouthed each other.* VERB V n

**bad-tempered** Someone who is **bad-tempered** is not very cheerful and gets angry easily. ❑ *When his headaches developed Nick became bad-tempered and even violent.* ADJ = irritable

**baf|fle** /bæfəl/ **(baffles, baffling, baffled)** If something **baffles** you, you cannot understand it or explain it. ❑ *An apple tree producing square fruit is baffling experts.* VERB = puzzle V n ♦ **baf|fling** *I was constantly ill, with a baffling array of symptoms.* ADJ ♦ **baf|fled** *Police are baffled by the murder.* ADJ: usu v-link ADJ

**baf|fle|ment** /bæfəlmənt/ **Bafflement** is the state of being baffled. ❑ *The general response was one of understandable bafflement.* N-UNCOUNT = puzzlement

**bag** /bæg/ **(bags)** ◆◆◇ 1 A **bag** is a container made of thin paper or plastic, for example one that is used in shops to put things in that a customer has bought. N-COUNT ♦ A **bag** of things is the amount of things contained in a bag. N-COUNT: usu N *of* n 2 A **bag** is a strong container with one or two handles, used to carry things in. ❑ *She left the hotel carrying a shopping bag.* N-COUNT ♦ A **bag** of things is the amount of things contained in a bag. N-COUNT: usu N *of* n 3 A **bag** is the same as a **handbag**. N-COUNT 4 If you have **bags** under your eyes, you have folds of skin there, usually because you have not had enough sleep. N-PLURAL 5 If you say there is **bags of** something, you mean that there is a large amount of it. If you say that there are **bags of** things, you mean that there are a large number of them. [BRIT, INFORMAL] ❑ *...a hotel with bags of character.* QUANT: QUANT *of* pl-n/n-uncount [emphasis] = heaps of 6 → See also **bum bag**, **carrier bag**, **mixed bag**, **shoulder-bag**, **sleeping bag**, **tea bag**. 7 If you say that something is **in the bag**, you mean that you are certain that you will get it or achieve it. [INFORMAL] ❑ *'I'll get the Republican nomination,' he assured me. 'It's in the bag.'* PHRASE: usu v-link PHR 8 to **let the cat out of the bag** → see **cat**.

**ba|gel** /beɪgəl/ **(bagels)** A **bagel** is a ring-shaped bread roll. N-COUNT

**bag|gage** /bægɪdʒ/ 1 Your **baggage** consists of the bags that you take with you when you travel. ❑ *The passengers went through immigration control and collected their baggage. ...excess baggage.* N-UNCOUNT = luggage 2 You can use **baggage** to refer to someone's emotional problems, fixed ideas, or prejudices. ❑ *How much emotional baggage is he bringing with him into the relationship?* N-UNCOUNT: usu with supp

**bag|gage car** **(baggage cars)** A **baggage car** is a railway carriage, often without windows, which is used to carry luggage, goods, or mail. [AM] N-COUNT

✔ in BRIT, use **van**

**bag|gy** /bægi/ **(baggier, baggiest)** If a piece of clothing is **baggy**, it hangs loosely on your body. ❑ *...a baggy jumper.* ADJ ≠ tight

**bag lady** **(bag ladies)** A **bag lady** is a homeless woman who carries her possessions in shopping bags. N-COUNT

**bag|pipes** /bægpaɪps/

✔ The form **bagpipe** is used as a modifier.

**Bagpipes** are a musical instrument that is traditionally played in Scotland. You play the bagpipes by blowing air through a pipe into a bag, and then squeezing the bag to force the air out through other pipes. N-COUNT: usu pl, oft *the* N

**ba|guette** /bæget/ **(baguettes)** A **baguette** is a type of long, thin, white bread which is traditionally made in France. N-COUNT

**bah** /bɑː, bæ/ **'Bah'** is used in writing to represent a noise that people make in order to express contempt, disappointment, or annoyance. [OLD-FASHIONED] EXCLAM

**Ba|ha|mian** /bəheɪmiən/ **(Bahamians)** 1 **Bahamian** means belonging or relating to the Bahamas or to its people or culture. ADJ 2 **Bahamians** are people who come from the Bahamas. N-COUNT

**bail** /beɪl/ **(bails, bailing, bailed)**

✔ The spelling **bale** is also used for meaning 4, and for meanings 1 and 3 of the phrasal verb.

1 **Bail** is a sum of money that an arrested person or someone else puts forward as a guarantee that the arrested person will attend their trial in a law court. If the arrested person does not attend it, the money will be lost. ❑ *He was freed on bail pending an appeal... The high court set bail at $8,000.* N-UNCOUNT: oft *on* N 2 **Bail** is permission for an arrested person to be released after bail has been paid. ❑ *He was yesterday given bail by South Yorkshire magistrates.* N-UNCOUNT 3 If someone **is bailed**, they are released while they are waiting for their trial, after paying an amount of money to the court. ❑ *He was bailed for probation reports... He was bailed to appear before local magistrates on 5 November.* VERB: usu passive *be* V-ed *be* V-ed to-inf 4 If you **bail**, you use a container to remove water from a boat or from a place which is flooded. ❑ *We kept her afloat for a couple of hours by bailing frantically.* VERB V Also V n ♦ **Bail out** means the same as **bail**. ❑ *A crew was sent down the shaft to close it off and bail out all the water... The flood waters have receded since then, but residents are still bailing out.* PHRASAL VERB V P n (not pron) V P 5 If a prisoner **jumps bail**, he or she does not come back for his or her trial after being released on bail. ❑ *He had jumped bail last year while being tried on drug charges.* PHRASE: V inflects

♦ **bail out** 1 If you **bail** someone **out**, you help them out of a difficult situation, often by PHRASAL VERB

giving them money. ❑ *They will discuss how to bail the economy out of its slump.* [2] If you **bail** someone **out**, you pay bail on their behalf. ❑ *He has been jailed eight times. Each time, friends bailed him out.* [3] If a pilot **bails out of** an aircraft that is crashing, he or she jumps from it, using a parachute to land safely. ❑ *Reid was forced to bail out of the crippled aircraft... The pilot bailed out safely.* [4] → see **bail 4**.
V n P *of* n; Also V n P; PHRASAL VERB; V n P; Also V P n (not pron); PHRASAL VERB; V P *of* n; V P

**bail|iff** /beɪlɪf/ **(bailiffs)** [1] A **bailiff** is a law officer who makes sure that the decisions of a court are obeyed. Bailiffs can take a person's furniture or possessions away if the person owes money. [BRIT] [2] A **bailiff** is an official in a court of law who deals with tasks such as keeping control in court. [AM] [3] A **bailiff** is a person who is employed to look after land or property for the owner. [BRIT]
N-COUNT; N-COUNT; N-COUNT

**bairn** /beəʳn/ **(bairns)** A **bairn** is a child. [SCOTTISH] ❑ *He's a lovely bairn.*
N-COUNT

**bait** /beɪt/ **(baits, baiting, baited)** [1] **Bait** is food which you put on a hook or in a trap in order to catch fish or animals. [2] If you **bait** a hook or trap, you put bait on it or in it. ❑ *He baited his hook with pie... The boys dug pits and baited them so that they could spear their prey.* [3] To use something as **bait** means to use it to trick or persuade someone to do something. ❑ *Service stations use petrol as a bait to lure motorists into the restaurants and other facilities... Television programmes are essentially bait to attract an audience for advertisements.* [4] If you **bait** someone, you deliberately try to make them angry by teasing them. ❑ *He delighted in baiting his mother.* [5] If you **take the bait**, you react to something that someone has said or done exactly as they intended you to do. The expression **rise to the bait** is also used, mainly in British English. ❑ *When she attempts to make you feel guilty, don't take the bait.*
N-VAR; VERB; V n *with* n; V n; N-UNCOUNT: also *a* N; VERB = needle; V n; PHRASE: V inflects

**-baiting** /-beɪtɪŋ/ [1] You use **-baiting** after nouns to refer to the activity of attacking a particular group of people or laughing at their beliefs. [2] Badger-**baiting**, bear-**baiting**, and bull-**baiting** involve making these animals fight dogs, while making sure that the animals are unable to defend themselves properly.
COMB in N-UNCOUNT; COMB in N-UNCOUNT

**baize** /beɪz/ **Baize** is a thick woollen material which is used for covering tables on which games such as cards and snooker are played.
N-UNCOUNT

**bake** /beɪk/ **(bakes, baking, baked)** [1] If you **bake**, you spend some time preparing and mixing together ingredients to make bread, cakes, pies, or other food which is cooked in the oven. ❑ *How did you learn to bake cakes?... I love to bake.* ♦ **bak|ing** *On a Thursday she used to do all the baking.* [2] When a cake or bread **bakes** or when you **bake** it, it cooks in the oven without any extra liquid or fat. ❑ *Bake the cake for 35 to 50 minutes... The batter rises as it bakes. ...freshly baked bread.* [3] If places or people become extremely hot because the sun is shining very strongly, you can say that they **bake**. ❑ *If you closed the windows you baked... Britain bakes in a Mediterranean heatwave.* [4] A vegetable or fish **bake** is a dish that is made by chopping up and mixing together a number of ingredients and cooking them in the oven so that they form a fairly dry solid mass. [BRIT] ❑ *...an aubergine bake.* [5] → See also **baking**.
◆◇◇; VERB: no passive; V n; V; N-UNCOUNT: also *the* N; VERB; V n; V; V-ed; VERB; V; V; N-COUNT: usu n N

**baked beans** **Baked beans** are dried beans cooked in tomato sauce in Britain or cooked with salt pork in North America. Baked beans are usually sold in cans.
N-PLURAL

**Ba|ke|lite** /beɪkəlaɪt/ **Bakelite** is a type of hard plastic that was used in the past for making things such as telephones and radios. [TRADEMARK]
N-UNCOUNT

**bak|er** /beɪkəʳ/ **(bakers)** [1] A **baker** is a person whose job is to bake and sell bread, pastries, and cakes. [2] A **baker** or a **baker's** is a shop where bread and cakes are sold. ❑ *They're freshly baked. I fetched them from the baker's this morning.*
N-COUNT; N-COUNT

**bak|ery** /beɪkəri/ **(bakeries)** A **bakery** is a building where bread, pastries, and cakes are baked, or the shop where they are sold.
N-COUNT

**bake|ware** /beɪkweəʳ/ Tins, trays, and dishes that are used for baking can be referred to as **bakeware**.
N-UNCOUNT

**bak|ing** /beɪkɪŋ/ You can use **baking** to describe weather or a place that is very hot indeed. ❑ *...a baking July day... The coffins stood in the baking heat surrounded by mourners. ...the baking Jordanian desert.* ♦ **Baking** is also an adverb. ❑ *...the baking hot summer of 1969.* → See also **bake**.
ADJ: usu ADJ n; ADV: ADV adj

**bak|ing pow|der** **(baking powders)** **Baking powder** is an ingredient used in cake making. It causes cakes to rise when they are in the oven.
N-MASS

**bak|ing sheet** **(baking sheets)** A **baking sheet** is a flat piece of metal on which you bake foods such as biscuits or pies in an oven.
N-COUNT

**bak|ing soda** **Baking soda** is the same as **bicarbonate of soda**.
N-UNCOUNT

**bak|ing tray** **(baking trays)** A **baking tray** is the same as a **baking sheet**. [BRIT]
N-COUNT

**bala|cla|va** /bæləklɑːvə/ **(balaclavas)** A **balaclava** is a tight woollen hood that covers every part of your head except your face.
N-COUNT

**bal|ance** /bæləns/ **(balances, balancing, balanced)** [1] If you **balance** something somewhere, or if it **balances** there, it remains steady and does not fall. ❑ *I balanced on the ledge... He balanced a football on his head.* [2] **Balance** is the ability to remain steady when you are standing up. ❑ *The medicines you are currently taking could be affecting your balance.* [3] If you **balance** one thing **with** something different, each of the things has the same strength or importance. ❑ *Balance spicy dishes with mild ones... The state has got to find some way to balance these two needs... Supply and demand on the currency market will generally balance.* ♦ **bal|anced** *This book is a well balanced biography.* [4] A **balance** is a situation in which all the different parts are equal in strength or importance. ❑ *Their marriage is a delicate balance between traditional and contemporary values. ...the ecological balance of the forest.* [5] If you say that **the balance** tips in your favour, you start winning or succeeding, especially in a conflict or contest. ❑ *...a powerful new gun which could tip the balance of the war in their favour.* [6] If you **balance** one thing **against** another, you consider its importance in relation to the other one. ❑ *She carefully tried to balance religious sensitivities against democratic freedom.* [7] If someone **balances** their budget or if a government **balances** the economy of a country, they make sure that the amount of money that is spent is not greater than the amount that is received. ❑ *He balanced his budgets by rigid control over public expenditure.* [8] If you **balance** your books or make them **balance**, you prove by calculation that the amount of money you have received is equal to the amount that you have spent. ❑ *...teaching them to balance the books... To make the books balance, spending must fall and taxes must rise.* [9] The **balance** in your bank account is the amount of money you have in it. ❑ *I'd like to check the balance in my account please.* [10] **The balance** of an amount of money is what remains to be paid for something or what remains when part of the amount has been spent. ❑ *They were due to pay the balance on delivery.* [11] → See also **bank balance**.
◆◆◇; VERB; V prep/adv; V n prep/adv; N-UNCOUNT; V-RECIP; V n *with* n; V pl-n; pl-n V; ADJ: usu adv ADJ; N-SING: with supp, oft N *between* pl-n; N-SING: *the* N; VERB; V n *against* n; VERB; V n; VERB; V n; V; N-COUNT: usu with supp; N-SING: *the* N = remainder

**PHRASES** [12] If something hangs **in the balance**, it is uncertain whether it will happen or continue. ❑ *The fate of a project which could revolutionise the use of computers in hospitals hangs in the balance.* [13] If you **keep** your **balance**, for example when standing in a moving vehicle, you remain steady and do not fall over. If you **lose** your **balance**, you become unsteady and fall over. [14] If you are **off balance**, you are in an unsteady position and about to fall. ❑ *A gust of wind knocked him off balance and he fell face down in the mud.* [15] If you are thrown **off balance** by something, you are
PHRASE: PHR after v, v-link PHR; PHRASE: V inflects; PHRASE: PHR after v, v-link PHR; PHRASE: PHR after v

surprised or confused by it. ❑ *She was trying to behave as if his visit hadn't thrown her off balance.* 16 You can say **on balance** to indicate that you are stating an opinion after considering all the relevant facts or arguments. ❑ *On balance he agreed with Christine.* PHRASE: PHR with cl

♦ **balance out** If two or more opposite things **balance out** or if you **balance** them **out**, they become equal in amount, value, or effect. ❑ *Outgoings and revenues balanced out... The strenuous exercise undergone could balance out the increased calories.* PHRASAL VERB; V P; V P n (not pron); Also V n P

**bal|anced** /bælənst/ 1 A **balanced** report, book, or other document takes into account all the different opinions on something and presents information in a fair and reasonable way. ❑ *...a fair, balanced, comprehensive report.* 2 Something that is **balanced** is pleasing or useful because its different parts or elements are in the correct proportions. ❑ *...a balanced diet.* 3 Someone who is **balanced** remains calm and thinks clearly, even in a difficult situation. ❑ *I have to prove myself as a respectable, balanced, person.* 4 → See also **balance**. ADJ [approval]; ADJ [approval]; ADJ [approval]

**bal|ance of pay|ments** **(balances of payments)** A country's **balance of payments** is the difference, over a period of time, between the payments it makes to other countries for imports and the payments it receives from other countries for exports. [BUSINESS] ❑ *Britain's balance of payments deficit has improved slightly.* N-COUNT: usu sing

**bal|ance of pow|er** The **balance of power** is the way in which power is distributed between rival groups or countries. ❑ *...changes in the balance of power between the United States and Europe.* N-SING

**bal|ance of trade** **(balances of trade)** A country's **balance of trade** is the difference in value, over a period of time, between the goods it imports and the goods it exports. [BUSINESS] ❑ *The deficit in Britain's balance of trade in March rose to more than 2100 million pounds.* N-COUNT: usu sing

**bal|ance sheet** **(balance sheets)** A **balance sheet** is a written statement of the amount of money and property that a company or person has, including amounts of money that are owed or are owing. **Balance sheet** is also used to refer to the general financial state of a company. [BUSINESS] ❑ *Rolls-Royce needed a strong balance sheet.* N-COUNT

**bal|anc|ing act** **(balancing acts)** If you perform a **balancing act**, you try to deal successfully with two or more people, groups, or situations that are in opposition to each other. ❑ *...a delicate balancing act between a career, a home, and motherhood.* N-COUNT: usu sing = juggling act

**bal|co|ny** /bælkəni/ **(balconies)** 1 A **balcony** is a platform on the outside of a building, above ground level, with a wall or railing around it. 2 **The balcony** in a theatre or cinema is an area of seats above the main seating area. N-COUNT; N-SING = circle

**bald** /bɔːld/ **(balder, baldest)** 1 Someone who is **bald** has little or no hair on the top of their head. ❑ *The man's bald head was beaded with sweat.* ♦ **bald|ness** *He wears a cap to cover a spot of baldness.* 2 If a tyre is **bald**, its surface has worn down and it is no longer safe to use. 3 A **bald** statement is in plain language and contains no extra explanation or information. ❑ *The announcement came in a bald statement from the official news agency... The bald truth is he's just not happy.* ♦ **bald|ly** *'The leaders are outdated,' he stated baldly. 'They don't relate to young people.'* ADJ; N-UNCOUNT; ADJ; ADJ: ADJ n = blunt; ADV: ADV with v = bluntly

**bald eagle** **(bald eagles)** A **bald eagle** is a large eagle with a white head that lives in North America. It is the national bird of the United States of America. N-COUNT

**bal|der|dash** /bɔːldəʳdæʃ/ If you say that something that has been said or written is **balderdash**, you think it is completely untrue or very stupid. [OLD-FASHIONED] N-UNCOUNT [disapproval]

**bald|ing** /bɔːldɪŋ/ Someone who is **balding** is beginning to lose the hair on the top of their head. ❑ *He wore a straw hat to keep his balding head from getting sunburned.* ADJ

**baldy** /bɔːldi/ **(baldies)** People sometimes refer to a bald person as a **baldy**, especially if they are talking about them or to them in a friendly or humorous way. [INFORMAL] ❑ *The actor Patrick Stewart is a long-time baldy and proud of it... Get lost, baldy.* N-COUNT; also N-VOC

**bale** /beɪl/ **(bales, baling, baled)** 1 A **bale** is a large quantity of something such as hay, cloth, or paper, tied together tightly. ❑ *...bales of hay.* 2 If something such as hay, cloth, or paper **is baled**, it is tied together tightly. ❑ *Once hay has been cut and baled it has to go through some chemical processes.* 3 → See also **bail**. N-COUNT: usu pl, usu with supp; VERB; be V-ed; Also V n

**bale|ful** /beɪlfʊl/ **Baleful** means harmful, or expressing harmful intentions. [LITERARY] ❑ *...a baleful look.* ♦ **bale|ful|ly** *He watched her balefully.* ADJ: usu ADJ n; ADV: ADV with v

**balk** /bɔːlk, AM bɔːk/ **(balks, balking, balked)** also **baulk.** If you **balk at** something, you definitely do not want to do it or to let it happen. ❑ *Even biology undergraduates may balk at animal experiments... Last October the bank balked, alarmed that a $24m profit had turned into a $20m deficit.* VERB; V at n; V

**Bal|kani|za|tion** /bɔːlkənaɪzeɪʃᵊn/

> ✔ The spellings **balkanization**, and in British English **balkanisation** are also used.

If you disapprove of the division of a country into separate independent states, you can refer to the **Balkanization** of the country. ❑ *We can't accept the fragmentation or balkanization of the country.* N-UNCOUNT [disapproval]

**ball** /bɔːl/ **(balls, balling, balled)** 1 A **ball** is a round object that is used in games such as tennis, baseball, football, basketball, and cricket. ❑ *...a golf ball. ...a tennis ball.* 2 A **ball** is something or an amount of something that has a round shape. ❑ *Thomas screwed the letter up into a ball... They heard a loud explosion and saw a ball of fire go up.* 3 When you **ball** something or when it **balls**, it becomes round. ❑ *He picked up the sheets of paper, and balled them tightly in his fists... His hands balled into fists.* 4 **The ball of** your foot or **the ball of** your thumb is the rounded part where your toes join your foot or where your thumb joins your hand. 5 A **ball** is a large formal social event at which people dance. 6 A man's **balls** are his testicles. [INFORMAL, RUDE] 7 → See also **balls**. ◆◆◇ N-COUNT; N-COUNT: oft N of n; VERB; V n adv/prep; V adv/prep; N-COUNT: usu the N of n; N-COUNT; N-COUNT: usu pl

**PHRASES** 8 If you say that **the ball is in** someone's **court**, you mean that it is his or her responsibility to take the next action or decision in a situation. ❑ *The ball's now in your court – you have to decide what you're going to do.* 9 If you **get the ball rolling**, **set the ball rolling**, or **start the ball rolling**, you start something happening. ❑ *He will go to the Middle East next week to get the ball rolling again on peace talks.* 10 If someone is **on the ball**, they are very alert and aware of what is happening. ❑ *She really is on the ball; she's bought houses at auctions so she knows what she's doing.* 11 If someone refuses to **play ball**, they are unwilling to do what someone wants them to do. [INFORMAL] ❑ *The association has threatened to withdraw its support if the banks and building societies refuse to play ball.* PHRASE: V inflects; PHRASE: V inflects; PHRASE: v-link PHR; PHRASE: V inflects

**bal|lad** /bæləd/ **(ballads)** 1 A **ballad** is a long song or poem which tells a story in simple language. 2 A **ballad** is a slow, romantic, popular song. N-COUNT; N-COUNT

**bal|last** /bæləst/ **Ballast** is any substance that is used in ships or hot-air balloons to make them heavier and more stable. Ballast usually consists of water, sand, or iron. N-UNCOUNT

**ball bear|ing** **(ball bearings)** also **ball-bearing.** **Ball bearings** are small metal balls placed between the moving parts of a machine to make the parts move smoothly. N-COUNT

**ball boy** **(ball boys)** In a tennis match, the **ball boys** pick up any balls that go into the net or off the court and throw them back to the players. In N-COUNT a baseball game, the **ball boys** are in charge of collecting the balls that are hit out of the field.

**bal|le|ri|na** /bæləriːnə/ **(ballerinas)** A **ballerina** is a woman ballet dancer. N-COUNT

**bal|let** /bæleɪ, AM bæleɪ/ **(ballets)** [1] **Ballet** is a type of very skilled and artistic dancing with carefully planned movements. ❑ *I trained as a ballet dancer... She is also keen on the ballet.* N-UNCOUNT: also *the* N, oft N n [2] A **ballet** is an artistic work that is performed by ballet dancers. ❑ *The performance will include the premiere of three new ballets.* N-COUNT

**bal|let|ic** /bæletɪk/ If you describe someone's movements as **balletic**, you mean that they have some of the graceful qualities of ballet. ❑ *The subject seems to dance with balletic grace.* ADJ: usu ADJ n

**ball game (ball games)** also **ballgame.** [1] **Ball games** are games that are played with a ball such as tennis, baseball, and football. N-COUNT: usu pl [2] A **ball game** is a baseball match. [AM] ❑ *I'd still like to go to a ball game.* N-COUNT [3] You can use **ball game** to describe any situation or activity, especially one that involves competition. [JOURNALISM, SPOKEN] ❑ *Two of his biggest competitors are out of the ball game.* N-SING ● If you say that a situation is a **new ball game**, you mean that it is completely different from, or much more difficult than, the previous situation or any situation that you have experienced before. ❑ *He finds himself faced with a whole new ball game.* PHRASE

**ball girl (ball girls)** In a tennis match, the **ball girls** pick up any balls that go into the net or off the court and throw them back to the players. In a baseball game, the **ball girls** are in charge of collecting the balls that are hit out of the field. N-COUNT

**ball|gown** /bɔːlgaʊn/ **(ballgowns)** A **ballgown** is a long dress that women wear to formal dances. N-COUNT

**bal|lis|tic** /bəlɪstɪk/ [1] **Ballistic** means relating to ballistics. ❑ *...ballistic missiles... Ballistic tests have matched the weapons with bullets taken from the bodies of victims.* ADJ: ADJ n

PHRASES [2] If someone **goes ballistic**, they suddenly become very angry. [INFORMAL] ❑ *The singer went ballistic after one member of his band failed to show for a sound check.* PHRASE: V inflects [3] If something **goes ballistic**, it suddenly becomes very much greater or more powerful, often in a surprising or unwanted way. [INFORMAL] ❑ *August registrations have gone ballistic, accounting now for a quarter of the annual total.* PHRASE: V inflects = mushroom

**bal|lis|tics** /bəlɪstɪks/ **Ballistics** is the study of the movement of objects that are shot or thrown through the air, such as bullets fired from a gun. N-UNCOUNT

**bal|loon** /bəluːn/ **(balloons, ballooning, ballooned)** [1] A **balloon** is a small, thin, rubber bag that you blow air into so that it becomes larger and rounder or longer. Balloons are used as toys or decorations. N-COUNT [2] A **balloon** is a large, strong bag filled with gas or hot air, which can carry passengers in a container that hangs underneath it. ❑ *They are to attempt to be the first to circle the Earth non-stop by balloon.* N-COUNT: also *by* N [3] When something **balloons**, it increases rapidly in amount. ❑ *In London, the use of the Tube has ballooned... The budget deficit has ballooned to $25 billion.* VERB = soar, rocket V V *to* n

**bal|loon|ing** /bəluːnɪŋ/ **Ballooning** is the sport or activity of flying a hot-air balloon. N-UNCOUNT

**bal|loon|ist** /bəluːnɪst/ **(balloonists)** A **balloonist** is a person who flies a hot-air balloon. N-COUNT

**bal|lot** /bælət/ **(ballots, balloting, balloted)** ◆◇◇ [1] A **ballot** is a secret vote in which people select a candidate in an election, or express their opinion about something. ❑ *The result of the ballot will not be known for two weeks... Fifty of its members will be elected by direct ballot.* N-COUNT: also *by* N [2] A **ballot** is a piece of paper on which you indicate your choice or opinion in a secret vote. ❑ *Election boards will count the ballots by hand.* N-COUNT [3] If you **ballot** a group of people, you find out what they think about a subject by organizing a secret vote. ❑ *The union said they will ballot members on whether to strike.* VERB = poll V n ♦ **bal|lot|ing** *International observers say the balloting was fair.* N-UNCOUNT

**bal|lot box (ballot boxes)** [1] A **ballot box** is the box into which ballot papers are put after people have voted. N-COUNT [2] You can refer to the system of democratic elections as **the ballot box**. ❑ *Martinez expressed confidence of victory at the ballot box.* N-SING: *the* N

**bal|lot pa|per (ballot papers)** A **ballot paper** is a piece of paper on which you indicate your choice or opinion in an election or ballot. N-COUNT: usu pl

**bal|lot rig|ging** also **ballot-rigging. Ballot rigging** is the act of illegally changing the result of an election by producing a false record of the number of votes. ❑ *The poll was widely discredited after allegations of ballot rigging.* N-UNCOUNT

**ball|park** /bɔːlpɑːʳk/ **(ballparks)** also **ball park.** [1] A **ballpark** is a park or stadium where baseball is played. N-COUNT [2] A **ballpark** figure or **ballpark** estimate is an approximate figure or estimate. ❑ *I can't give you anything more than just sort of a ballpark figure... Ballpark estimates indicate a price tag of $90 million a month.* ADJ: ADJ n [3] If something such as an amount or claim is **in the ballpark**, it is approximately right, but not exact. [INFORMAL] ❑ *If you compare it to some of the other surveys that have been recently conducted, then it is in the general ballpark.* N-SING: *the* N [4] If you say that someone or something is **in the ballpark**, you mean that they are able to take part in a particular area of activity, especially because they are considered as good as others taking part. ❑ *This puts them in the ballpark and makes them a major player.* N-SING: *the* N

**ball|player** /bɔːlpleɪəʳ/ **(ballplayers)** also **ball player.** A **ballplayer** is a baseball player. [AM] N-COUNT

**ball|point** /bɔːlpɔɪnt/ **(ballpoints)** A **ballpoint** or a **ballpoint pen** is a pen with a very small metal ball at the end which transfers the ink from the pen onto a surface. N-COUNT = Biro

**ball|room** /bɔːlruːm/ **(ballrooms)** A **ballroom** is a very large room that is used for dancing. N-COUNT

**ball|room danc|ing Ballroom dancing** is a type of dancing in which a man and a woman dance together using fixed sequences of steps and movements. N-UNCOUNT

**balls** /bɔːlz/ **(ballses, ballsing, ballsed)** [1] If you say that someone has **balls**, you mean that they have courage. [INFORMAL, RUDE] ❑ *I never had the balls to do anything like this.* N-UNCOUNT: oft *the* N to-inf = guts [2] You can say '**balls**' or say that what someone says is **balls** when you think that it is stupid or wrong. [BRIT, INFORMAL, VERY RUDE] ❑ *What complete and utter balls!* EXCLAM; N-UNCOUNT [feelings]

♦ **balls up** If you **balls up** a task or activity, you do it very badly, making a lot of mistakes. [BRIT, INFORMAL, RUDE] ❑ *You have single-handedly ballsed up the best opportunity we've had!... I have no intention of letting you balls it up.* PHRASAL VERB = cock up V P n (not pron) V n P Also V P

**balls-up (balls-ups)** If you make a **balls-up** of something, you do it very badly and make a lot of mistakes. [BRIT, INFORMAL, RUDE] ❑ *He's made a real balls-up of this.* N-COUNT = cock-up

**ballsy** /bɔːlzi/ **(ballsier, ballsiest)** You can describe a person or their behaviour as **ballsy** if you admire them because you think they are energetic and brave. [INFORMAL] ❑ *...the most ballsy woman I know. ...ballsy, gutsy live rap music.* ADJ: oft ADJ n [approval]

**bal|ly|hoo** /bælihuː, AM -huː/ **(ballyhooing, ballyhooed)** [1] You can use **ballyhoo** to refer to great excitement or anger about something, especially when you disapprove of it because you think it is unnecessary or exaggerated. ❑ *They announced, amid much ballyhoo, that they had made a breakthrough.* N-UNCOUNT: also *a* N [disapproval] = to-do [2] If you say that something **is ballyhooed**, you mean that there is a lot of excitement about it and people are claiming that it is very good. You use this word especially when you think the thing is not as exciting or good as peo- VERB: usu passive [disapproval]

ple say. ❑ *The power of red wine to counteract high cholesterol has been ballyhooed in the press. ...the much-ballyhooed new Star Wars movie.* be V-ed V-ed

**balm** /bɑːm/ **(balms)** 1 **Balm** is a sweet-smelling oil that is obtained from some tropical trees and used to make creams that heal wounds or reduce pain. N-MASS 2 If you refer to something as **balm**, you mean that it makes you feel better. ❑ *The place is balm to the soul.* N-UNCOUNT: also a N [approval]

**balmy** /bɑːmi/ **Balmy** weather is fairly warm and pleasant. ❑ *...a balmy summer's evening.* ADJ: usu ADJ n

**ba|lo|ney** /bəloʊni/ If you say that an idea or statement is **baloney**, you disapprove of it and think that it is foolish or wrong. [mainly AM, INFORMAL] ❑ *That's a load of baloney.* N-UNCOUNT [disapproval] = rubbish, garbage

**bal|sa** /bɔːlsə/ **Balsa** or **balsa wood** is a very light wood from a South American tree. N-UNCOUNT

**bal|sam** /bɔːlsəm/ **Balsam** is a sweet-smelling oil that is obtained from certain trees or bushes and used to make medicines and perfumes. N-UNCOUNT

**bal|sam|ic vin|egar** /bɔːlsæmɪk vɪnɪgəʳ/ **Balsamic vinegar** is a type of vinegar which tastes sweet and is made from grape juice. N-UNCOUNT

**bal|ti** /bɔːlti/ **(baltis)** A **balti** is a vegetable or meat dish of Indian origin which is cooked and served in a bowl-shaped pan. N-VAR

**bal|us|trade** /bæləstreɪd, AM -streɪd/ **(balustrades)** A **balustrade** is a railing or wall on a balcony or staircase. N-COUNT

**bam|boo** /bæmbuː/ **(bamboos) Bamboo** is a tall tropical plant with hard, hollow stems. The young shoots of the plant can be eaten and the stems are used to make furniture. ❑ *...huts with walls of bamboo. ...bamboo shoots.* N-VAR

**bam|boo|zle** /bæmbuːzᵊl/ **(bamboozles, bamboozling, bamboozled)** To **bamboozle** someone means to confuse them greatly and often trick them. ❑ *He bamboozled Mercer into defeat... He was bamboozled by con men.* VERB = dupe V n into n be V-ed

**ban** /bæn/ **(bans, banning, banned)** 1 To **ban** something means to state officially that it must not be done, shown, or used. ❑ *Canada will ban smoking in all offices later this year. ...a banned substance.* ◆◆◇ VERB = prohibit V n V-ed ♦ **ban|ning (bannings)** *No reason was given for the banning of the magazine... Opposition groups see the bannings as the latest stage of a government clampdown.* N-VAR 2 A **ban** is an official ruling that something must not be done, shown, or used. ❑ *The General also lifted a ban on political parties.* N-COUNT: oft N on n 3 If you **are banned from** doing something, you are officially prevented from doing it. ❑ *He was banned from driving for three years.* VERB = bar be V-ed from n

**ba|nal** /bənɑːl, -næl/ If you describe something as **banal**, you do not like it because you think that it is so ordinary that it is not at all effective or interesting. ❑ *Bland, banal music tinkled discreetly from hidden loudspeakers.* ADJ [disapproval] ♦ You can refer to banal things as **the banal**. ❑ *The allegations ranged from the banal to the bizarre.* N-SING: the N ♦ **ba|nal|ity** /bənælɪti/ **(banalities)** *...the banality of life... Neil's ability to utter banalities never ceased to amaze me.* N-VAR

**ba|na|na** /bənɑːnə, -næn-/ **(bananas)** 1 **Bananas** are long curved fruit with yellow skins. ➔ See picture on page 1711. ❑ *...a bunch of bananas.* N-VAR 2 If someone is behaving in a silly or crazy way, or if they become extremely angry, you can say that they are going **bananas**. [INFORMAL] ❑ *Adamson's going to go bananas on this one.* ADJ: v-link ADJ

**ba|na|na peel (banana peels)** A **banana peel** is the same as a **banana skin**. [AM] N-COUNT

**ba|na|na re|pub|lic (banana republics)** Small, poor countries that are politically unstable are sometimes referred to as **banana republics**. [OFFENSIVE] N-COUNT

**ba|na|na skin (banana skins)** 1 The thick yellow or green covering of a banana is called a **banana skin**. [BRIT] N-COUNT

✔ in AM, use **banana peel**

2 If an important or famous person slips on a **banana skin**, they say or do something that makes them look stupid and causes them problems. [mainly BRIT, JOURNALISM] ❑ *...waiting for the government to slip on this week's banana skin.* N-COUNT

✔ in AM, use **banana peel**

**ba|na|na split (banana splits)** A **banana split** is a kind of dessert. It consists of a banana cut in half along its length, with ice cream, nuts, and sauce on top. N-COUNT

**band** /bænd/ **(bands, banding, banded)** 1 A **band** is a small group of musicians who play popular music such as jazz, rock, or pop. ❑ *He was a drummer in a rock band... Local bands provide music for dancing.* ➔ See also **one-man band**. ◆◆◇ N-COUNT-COLL 2 A **band** is a group of musicians who play brass and percussion instruments. ❑ *Bands played German marches.* ➔ See also **brass band**. N-COUNT-COLL 3 A **band of** people is a group of people who have joined together because they share an interest or belief. ❑ *Bands of government soldiers, rebels and just plain criminals have been roaming some neighborhoods. ...a small but growing band of Japanese companies taking their first steps into American publishing.* N-COUNT-COLL: with supp 4 A **band** is a flat, narrow strip of cloth which you wear round your head or wrists, or which forms part of a piece of clothing. ❑ *Almost all hospitals use a wrist-band of some kind with your name and details on it.* ➔ See also **armband**, **hatband**, **waistband**. N-COUNT 5 A **band** is a strip of something such as colour, light, land, or cloth which contrasts with the areas on either side of it. ❑ *...bands of natural vegetation between strips of crops... A band of light glowed in the space between floor and door.* N-COUNT: with supp 6 A **band** is a strip or loop of metal or other strong material which strengthens something, or which holds several things together. ❑ *Surgeons placed a metal band around the knee cap to help it knit back together. ...a strong band of flat muscle tissue.* ➔ See also **elastic band**, **rubber band**. N-COUNT 7 A **band** is a range of numbers or values within a system of measurement. ❑ *...a new tax band of 20p in the pound on the first £2,000 of taxable income.* ➔ See also **waveband**. N-COUNT: usu with supp 8 ➔ See also **wedding band**.

♦ **band together** If people **band together**, they meet and act as a group in order to try and achieve something. ❑ *Women banded together to protect each other.* PHRASAL VERB V P

**band|age** /bændɪdʒ/ **(bandages, bandaging, bandaged)** 1 A **bandage** is a long strip of cloth which is wrapped around a wounded part of someone's body to protect or support it. ❑ *We put some ointment and a bandage on his knee... His chest was swathed in bandages.* N-COUNT 2 If you **bandage** a wound or part of someone's body, you tie a bandage around it. ❑ *Apply a dressing to the wound and bandage it. ...a bandaged hand.* VERB V n V-ed ♦ **Bandage up** means the same as **bandage**. ❑ *I bandaged the leg up and gave her aspirin for the pain.* PHRASAL VERB V n P Also V P n

**Band-Aid (Band-Aids)** also **band-aid.** 1 A **Band-Aid** is a small piece of sticky tape that you use to cover small cuts or wounds on your body. [mainly AM, TRADEMARK] N-VAR

✔ in BRIT, use **plaster**

2 If you refer to a **Band-Aid** solution to a problem, you mean that you disapprove of it because you think that it will only be effective for a short period. ❑ *We need long-term solutions, not short-term Band-Aid ones.* ADJ: ADJ n [disapproval] = cosmetic

**ban|dan|na** /bændænə/ **(bandannas)** also **bandana.** A **bandanna** is a brightly-coloured piece of cloth which is worn around a person's neck or head. N-COUNT

**B&B** /biː ən biː/ **(B&Bs)** also **b&b.** 1 **B&B** is the same as **bed and breakfast**. ❑ *...three nights b&b.* N-UNCOUNT 2 A **B&B** is the same as a **bed and breakfast**. ❑ *There are B&Bs all over the islands.* N-COUNT

**band|ed** /bændɪd/ If something is **banded**, it has one or more bands on it, often of a different ADJ: oft ADJ in/with n colour which contrasts with the main colour. ❑ *...a stark tower, banded in dark and light stone.*

**-banded** /-bændɪd/ **-banded** combines with colours to indicate that something has bands of a particular colour. ❑ *Tables are set with white china and gold-banded silver cutlery.* COMB in ADJ = -striped

**ban|dit** /bændɪt/ **(bandits)** Robbers are sometimes called **bandits**, especially if they are found in areas where the law has broken down. ❑ *This is real bandit country.* N-COUNT = outlaw

**ban|dit|ry** /bændɪtri/ **Banditry** is used to refer to acts of robbery and violence in areas where the rule of law has broken down. N-UNCOUNT

**band|leader** /bændliːdəʳ/ **(bandleaders)** A **bandleader** is the person who conducts a band, especially a jazz band. N-COUNT

**band|saw** /bændsɔː/ **(bandsaws)** A **bandsaw** is an electric saw that consists of a metal band that turns round and is used for cutting wood, metal, and other materials. N-COUNT

**bands|man** /bændzmən/ **(bandsmen) Bandsmen** are musicians in a band, especially a military or brass band. N-COUNT: usu pl

**band|stand** /bændstænd/ **(bandstands)** 1 A **bandstand** is a platform with a roof where a military band or a brass band can play in the open air. N-COUNT: usu sing 2 A **bandstand** is a platform inside a hall or large room where the band that is playing at a dance or other occasion stands. [mainly AM] N-COUNT: usu sing

**band|wagon** /bændwægən/ **(bandwagons)** 1 You can refer to an activity or movement that has suddenly become fashionable or popular as a **bandwagon**. ❑ *So what is really happening as the information bandwagon starts to roll? ...the environmental bandwagon.* N-COUNT: usu sing 2 If someone, especially a politician, jumps or climbs **on the bandwagon**, they become involved in an activity or movement because it is fashionable or likely to succeed and not because they are really interested in it. ❑ *Many farms are jumping on the bandwagon and advertising organically grown food.* N-COUNT: usu sing [disapproval]

**band|width** /bændwɪdθ/ **(bandwidths)** A **bandwidth** is the range of frequencies used for a particular telecommunications signal, radio transmission, or computer network. N-VAR

**ban|dy** /bændi/ **(bandies, bandying, bandied)** If you **bandy** words **with** someone, you argue with them. ❑ *Brand shook his head. He was tired of bandying words with the man... The prosecution and defense were bandying accusations back and forth.* VERB V n *with* n V n adv

♦ **bandy about** or **bandy around** If someone's name or something such as an idea **is bandied about** or **is bandied around**, that person or that thing is discussed by many people in a casual way. ❑ *Young players now hear various sums bandied around about how much players are getting.* PHRASAL VERB: usu passive [disapproval] *be* V-ed P

**bane** /beɪn/ **The bane of** someone or **the bane of** someone's life is something that frequently makes them feel unhappy or annoyed. ❑ *Spots can be the bane of a teenager's life.* N-SING: usu *the* N *of* n

**bang** /bæŋ/ **(bangs, banging, banged)** 1 A **bang** is a sudden loud noise such as the noise of an explosion. ❑ *I heard four or five loud bangs... She slammed the door with a bang.* N-COUNT; SOUND 2 If something **bangs**, it makes a sudden loud noise, once or several times. ❑ *The engine spat and banged.* VERB V 3 If you **bang** a door or if it **bangs**, it closes suddenly with a loud noise. ❑ *...the sound of doors banging... All up and down the street the windows bang shut... The wind banged a door somewhere.* VERB = slam V V adj V n 4 If you **bang on** something or if you **bang** it, you hit it hard, making a loud noise. ❑ *We could bang on the desks and shout till they let us out... There is no point in shouting or banging the table.* VERB V *on* n V n 5 If you **bang** something on something or if you **bang** it down, you quickly and violently put it on a surface, because you are angry. ❑ *She banged his dinner on the table... He banged down the telephone.* VERB V n prep V n with adv 6 If you **bang** a part of your body, you accidentally knock it against something and hurt yourself. ❑ *She'd fainted and banged her head... He hurried into the hall, banging his shin against a chair in the darkness.* VERB V n V n *against/on* n ♦ **Bang** is also a noun. ❑ *...a nasty bang on the head.* N-COUNT 7 If you **bang into** something or someone, you bump or knock them hard, usually because you are not looking where you are going. ❑ *Various men kept banging into me in the narrow corridor.* VERB = bump V *into* n 8 **Bangs** are hair which is cut so that it hangs over your forehead. [AM] N-PLURAL

in BRIT, use **fringe**

9 You can use **bang** to emphasize expressions that indicate an exact position or an exact time. ❑ *...bang in the middle of the track... For once you leave bang on time for work.* ADV: ADV prep [emphasis] = right 10 → See also **big bang theory**.

**PHRASES** 11 If you say **bang goes** something, you mean that it is now obvious that it cannot succeed or be achieved. ❑ *There will be more work to do, not less. Bang goes the fantasy of retirement at 35.* PHRASE: V inflects, PHR n 12 If something begins or ends **with a bang**, it begins or ends with a lot of energy, enthusiasm, or success. ❑ *Her career began with a bang in 1986.* PHRASE: PHR after v 13 to **bang** your **head against a brick wall** → see **brick**.

**bang|er** /bæŋəʳ/ **(bangers)** 1 **Bangers** are sausages. [BRIT, INFORMAL] N-COUNT 2 You can describe a car as a **banger** if it is old and in very bad condition. [BRIT, INFORMAL] ❑ *...this clapped-out old banger.* N-COUNT: usu adj N 3 **Bangers** are fireworks that make a lot of noise. [BRIT] N-COUNT

**Bang|la|deshi** /bæŋglədeʃi/ **(Bangladeshis)** 1 **Bangladeshi** means belonging to or relating to Bangladesh, or to its people or culture. ADJ: usu ADJ n 2 The **Bangladeshis** are the people who come from Bangladesh. N-COUNT

**ban|gle** /bæŋgəl/ **(bangles)** A **bangle** is a decorated metal or wooden ring that you can wear round your wrist or ankle. N-COUNT

**bang-on** also **bang on.** If someone is **bang-on** with something, they are exactly right in their opinions or actions. [BRIT, INFORMAL] ❑ *If we are not bang-on with our preparations then we could have problems.* ADJ: v-link ADJ

**ban|ish** /bænɪʃ/ **(banishes, banishing, banished)** 1 If someone or something **is banished from** a place or area of activity, they are sent away from it and prevented from entering it. ❑ *I was banished to the small bedroom upstairs... They tried to banish him from politics.* VERB = expel *be* V-ed *from/to* n V n *from/to* n 2 If you **banish** something unpleasant, you get rid of it. ❑ *...a public investment programme intended to banish the recession.* VERB V n 3 If you **banish** the thought of something, you stop thinking about it. ❑ *He has now banished all thoughts of retirement... The past few days had been banished from his mind.* VERB V n *be* V-ed *from/to* n

**ban|ish|ment** /bænɪʃmənt/ **Banishment** is the act of banishing someone or the state of being banished. ❑ *...banishment to 'Devil's Island'.* N-UNCOUNT: usu N prep

**ban|is|ter** /bænɪstəʳ/ **(banisters)** also **bannister.** A **banister** is a rail supported by posts and fixed along the side of a staircase. The plural **banisters** can be used to refer to one of these rails. ❑ *I still remember sliding down the banisters.* N-COUNT

**ban|jo** /bændʒoʊ/ **(banjos)** A **banjo** is a musical instrument that looks like a guitar with a circular body, a long neck, and four or more strings. N-VAR: oft *the* N

**bank**

① FINANCE AND STORAGE
② AREAS AND MASSES
③ OTHER VERB USES

① **bank** /bæŋk/ **(banks, banking, banked)** ♦♦♦ 1 A **bank** is an institution where people or businesses can keep their money. ❑ *Which bank offers you the service that best suits your financial needs?... I had £10,000 in the bank.* N-COUNT 2 A **bank** is a building where a bank offers its services. N-COUNT 3 If you **bank** money, you pay it into a bank. ❑ *Once you have registered your particulars with an agency and it has banked your cheque, the process begins.* VERB V n 4 If you VERB

**bank with** a particular bank, you have an account with that bank. ❑ *My husband has banked with the Co-op since before the war.* [5] You use **bank** to refer to a store of something. For example, a blood **bank** is a store of blood that is kept ready for use. ❑ *...Britain's National Police Computer, one of the largest data banks in the world.* V with n; N-COUNT: with supp, usu n N

② **bank** /bæŋk/ **(banks)** [1] The **banks of** a river, canal, or lake are the raised areas of ground along its edge. ❑ *...30 miles of new developments along both banks of the Thames. ...an old warehouse on the banks of a canal.* [2] A **bank** of ground is a raised area of it with a flat top and one or two sloping sides. ❑ *...resting indolently upon a grassy bank.* [3] A **bank of** something is a long high mass of it. ❑ *On their journey south they hit a bank of fog off the north-east coast of Scotland.* [4] A **bank of** things, especially machines, switches, or dials, is a row of them, or a series of rows. ❑ *The typical laborer now sits in front of a bank of dials.* [5] → See also **banked**. N-COUNT: usu N of n = side; N-COUNT; N-COUNT: N of n; N-COUNT

③ **bank** /bæŋk/ **(banks, banking, banked)** When an aircraft **banks**, one of its wings rises higher than the other, usually when it is changing direction. ❑ *A plane took off and banked above the highway in front of him.* VERB; V

♦ **bank on** If you **bank on** something happening, you expect it to happen and rely on it happening. ❑ *'He's not still there, I suppose?' — 'I wouldn't bank on that,' she said.* PHRASAL VERB = count on; V P n

**bank|able** /bæŋkəbᵊl/ In the entertainment industry, someone or something that is described as **bankable** is very popular and therefore likely to be very profitable. ❑ *This movie made him the most bankable star in Hollywood.* ADJ: usu ADJ n

**bank ac|count** **(bank accounts)** A **bank account** is an arrangement with a bank which allows you to keep your money in the bank and to take some out when you need it. N-COUNT

**bank bal|ance** **(bank balances)** Your **bank balance** is the amount of money that you have in your bank account at a particular time. N-COUNT

**bank card** **(bank cards)** also **bankcard.** [1] A **bank card** is a plastic card which your bank gives you so you can get money from your bank account using a cash machine. It is also called an **ATM** card in American English. In Britain, you also use bank cards to prove who you are when you pay for something by cheque. [2] A **bank card** is a credit card that is supplied by a bank. [AM] N-COUNT; N-COUNT

**bank draft** **(bank drafts)** A **bank draft** is a cheque which you can buy from a bank in order to pay someone who is not willing to accept a personal cheque. ❑ *Payments should be made by credit card or bank draft in U.S. dollars.* N-COUNT

**banked** /bæŋkt/ [1] A **banked** stretch of road is higher on one side than the other. ❑ *He struggled to hold the bike down on the banked corners.* [2] If a place is **banked with** something, it is piled high with that thing. If something is **banked up**, it is piled high. ❑ *Flowerbeds and tubs are banked with summer bedding plants... The snow was banked up along the roadside.* ADJ: usu ADJ n; ADJ: v-link ADJ = piled

**bank|er** /bæŋkəʳ/ **(bankers)** A **banker** is someone who works in banking at a senior level. ❑ *...an investment banker. ...a merchant banker.* ◆◇◇ N-COUNT

**bank|er's draft** **(banker's drafts)** A **banker's draft** is the same as a **bank draft**. ❑ *You pay for the car by banker's draft in the local currency.* N-COUNT

**bank holi|day** **(bank holidays)** A **bank holiday** is a public holiday. [BRIT] N-COUNT

☑ in AM, usually use **national holiday**

**bank|ing** /bæŋkɪŋ/ **Banking** is the business activity of banks and similar institutions. ◆◇◇ N-UNCOUNT

**bank man|ag|er** **(bank managers)** A **bank manager** is someone who is in charge of a bank, or a particular branch of a bank, and who is involved in making decisions about whether or not to lend money to businesses and individuals. [BUSINESS] ❑ *This may have influenced your bank manager's decision not to give you a loan.* N-COUNT

**bank|note** /bæŋknoʊt/ **(banknotes)** also **bank note. Banknotes** are pieces of paper money. N-COUNT

**bank rate** **(bank rates)** The **bank rate** is the rate of interest at which a bank lends money, especially the minimum rate of interest that banks are allowed to charge, which is decided from time to time by the country's central bank. ❑ *...a sterling crisis that forced the bank rate up.* N-COUNT

**bank|roll** /bæŋkroʊl/ **(bankrolls, bankrolling, bankrolled)** [1] To **bankroll** a person, organization, or project means to provide the financial resources that they need. [mainly AM, INFORMAL] ❑ *The company has bankrolled a couple of local movies.* [2] A **bankroll** is the financial resources used to back a person, project, or institution. [AM] ❑ *We have a guaranteed minimum bankroll of £1.7m over the five albums.* VERB = finance; V n; N-SING

**bank|rupt** /bæŋkrʌpt/ **(bankrupts, bankrupting, bankrupted)** [1] People or organizations that go **bankrupt** do not have enough money to pay their debts. [BUSINESS] ❑ *If the firm cannot sell its products, it will go bankrupt... He was declared bankrupt after failing to pay a £114m loan guarantee.* [2] To **bankrupt** a person or organization means to make them go bankrupt. [BUSINESS] ❑ *The move to the market nearly bankrupted the firm and its director.* [3] A **bankrupt** is a person who has been declared bankrupt by a court of law. [BUSINESS] [4] If you say that something is **bankrupt**, you are emphasizing that it lacks any value or worth. ❑ *He thinks that European civilisation is morally bankrupt.* ADJ = insolvent; VERB; V n; N-COUNT; ADJ emphasis

**bank|rupt|cy** /bæŋkrʌptsi/ **(bankruptcies)** [1] **Bankruptcy** is the state of being bankrupt. [BUSINESS] ❑ *Many established firms were facing bankruptcy.* [2] A **bankruptcy** is an instance of an organization or person going bankrupt. [BUSINESS] ❑ *The number of corporate bankruptcies climbed in August.* [3] If you refer to something's **bankruptcy**, you are emphasizing that it is completely lacking in value or worth. ❑ *The massacre laid bare the moral bankruptcy of the regime.* N-UNCOUNT = insolvency; N-COUNT = insolvency; N-UNCOUNT: usu supp N emphasis

**bank state|ment** **(bank statements)** A **bank statement** is a printed document showing all the money paid into and taken out of a bank account. Bank statements are usually sent by a bank to a customer at regular intervals. N-COUNT

**banned sub|stance** **(banned substances)** In sport, **banned substances** are drugs that competitors are not allowed to take because they could artificially improve their performance. N-COUNT

**ban|ner** /bænəʳ/ **(banners)** [1] A **banner** is a long strip of cloth with something written on it. Banners are usually attached to two poles and carried during a protest or rally. ❑ *...a large crowd of students carrying banners denouncing the government.* [2] If someone does something **under the banner of** a particular cause, idea, or belief, they do it saying that they support that cause, idea, or belief. ❑ *Russia was the first country to forge a new economic system under the banner of Marxism.* N-COUNT; PHRASE: PHR n

**ban|ner head|line** **(banner headlines)** A **banner headline** is a large headline in a newspaper that stretches across the front page. ❑ *Today's front page of The Sun carries a banner headline 'The adulterer, the bungler and the joker.'* N-COUNT

**bannister** /bænɪstəʳ/ → see **banister**.

**banns** /bænz/ When a minister or priest reads or publishes **the banns**, he or she makes a public announcement in church that two people are going to be married. N-PLURAL: the N

**ban|quet** /bæŋkwɪt/ **(banquets)** A **banquet** is a grand formal dinner. ❑ *Last night he attended a state banquet at Buckingham Palace.* N-COUNT

**ban|quet|ing** /bæŋkwɪtɪŋ/ A **banqueting** hall or room is a large room where banquets are held. ADJ: ADJ n

**ban|quette** /bæŋket/ **(banquettes)** A **banquette** is a long, low, cushioned seat. Banquettes are usually long enough for more than one person to sit on at a time. N-COUNT

**ban|shee** /bænʃiː/ **(banshees)** In Irish folk stories, a **banshee** is a female spirit who warns you by her long, sad cry that someone in your family is going to die. N-COUNT

**ban|tam** /bæntəm/ **(bantams)** A **bantam** is a breed of small chicken. N-COUNT

**bantam|weight** /bæntəmweɪt/ **(bantamweights)** A **bantamweight** is a boxer who weighs between 51 and 53.5 kilograms, or a wrestler who weighs between 52 and 57 kilograms. A bantamweight is heavier than a flyweight but lighter than a featherweight. ❑ *...the European bantamweight title-holder.* N-COUNT: usu sing, oft N n

**ban|ter** /bæntəʳ/ **(banters, bantering, bantered)** 1 **Banter** is teasing or joking talk that is amusing and friendly. ❑ *She heard Tom exchanging good-natured banter with Jane.* N-UNCOUNT 2 If you **banter with** someone, you tease them or joke with them in an amusing, friendly way. ❑ *The soldiers bantered with him as though he was a kid brother... We bantered a bit while I tried to get the car started.* V-RECIP V with n pl-n V

**Ban|tu** /bæntuː, -tuː/ 1 **Bantu** means belonging or relating to a group of peoples in central and southern Africa. ADJ: ADJ n 2 **Bantu** languages belong to a group of languages spoken in central and southern Africa. ADJ: ADJ n

**bap** /bæp/ **(baps)** In some dialects of British English, a **bap** is a soft flat bread roll. N-COUNT

**bap|tise** /bæptaɪz/ → see **baptize**.

**bap|tism** /bæptɪzəm/ **(baptisms)** A **baptism** is a Christian ceremony in which a person is baptized. Compare **christening**. N-VAR

**bap|tis|mal** /bæptɪzməl/ **Baptismal** means relating to or connected with baptism. [FORMAL] ❑ *...the baptismal ceremony.* ADJ: ADJ n

**bap|tism of fire** **(baptisms of fire)** If someone who has just begun a new job has a **baptism of fire**, they immediately have to cope with very many severe difficulties and obstacles. ❑ *It was Mark's first introduction to royal duties and he came through his baptism of fire unscathed.* N-COUNT: usu sing

**Bap|tist** /bæptɪst/ **(Baptists)** 1 A **Baptist** is a Christian who believes that people should not be baptized until they are old enough to understand the meaning of baptism. N-COUNT 2 **Baptist** means belonging or relating to Baptists. ❑ *...a Baptist church.* ADJ: usu ADJ n

**bap|tize** /bæptaɪz/ **(baptizes, baptizing, baptized)**

☑ in BRIT, also use **baptise**

When someone **is baptized**, water is put on their heads or they are covered with water as a sign that their sins have been forgiven and that they have become a member of the Christian Church. Compare **christen**. ❑ *At this time she decided to become a Christian and was baptised.* VERB: usu passive be V-ed

**bar** /bɑːʳ/ **(bars, barring, barred)** ◆◆◇ 1 A **bar** is a place where you can buy and drink alcoholic drinks. [mainly AM] ❑ *...Devil's Herd, the city's most popular country-western bar.* N-COUNT 2 A **bar** is a room in a pub or hotel where alcoholic drinks are served. [BRIT] ❑ *I'll see you in the bar later... On the ship there are video lounges, a bar and a small duty-free shop.* N-COUNT 3 A **bar** is a counter on which alcoholic drinks are served. ❑ *Michael was standing alone by the bar when Brian rejoined him... He leaned forward across the bar.* → See also **coffee bar**, **public bar**, **singles bar**, **snack bar**, **wine bar**. N-COUNT 4 A **bar** is a long, straight, stiff piece of metal. ❑ *...a brick building with bars across the ground floor windows. ...a crowd throwing stones and iron bars.* N-COUNT 5 If you say that someone is **behind bars**, you mean that they are in prison. ❑ *Fisher was behind bars last night, charged with attempted murder... Nearly 5,000 people a year are put behind bars over motoring penalties.* PHRASE: PHR after v, v-link PHR 6 A **bar of** something is a piece of it which is roughly rectangular. ❑ *What is your favourite chocolate bar? ...a bar of soap.* N-COUNT: with supp 7 If you **bar** a door, you place something in front of it or a piece of wood or metal across it in order to prevent it from being opened. ❑ *For added safety, bar the door to the kitchen.* ♦ **barred** *The windows were closed and shuttered, the door was barred.* VERB V n ADJ: usu v-link ADJ 8 If you **bar** someone's way, you prevent them from going somewhere or entering a place, by blocking their path. ❑ *He stepped in front of her, barring her way.* VERB = block V n 9 If someone **is barred from** a place or **from** doing something, they are officially forbidden to go there or to do it. ❑ *Amnesty workers have been barred from Sri Lanka since 1982... Many jobs were barred to them.* VERB: usu passive = ban be V-ed from n be V-ed to n 10 If something is a **bar to** doing a particular thing, it prevents someone from doing it. ❑ *One of the fundamental bars to communication is the lack of a universally spoken, common language.* N-COUNT: usu N to n/-ing 11 If you say that there are **no holds barred** when people are fighting or competing for something, you mean that they are no longer following any rules in their efforts to win. ❑ *It is a war with no holds barred and we must prepare to resist.* PHRASE 12 You can use **bar** when you mean 'except'. For example, all the work **bar** the washing means all the work except the washing. ❑ *Bar a plateau in 1989, there has been a rise in inflation ever since the mid-1980's... The aim of the service was to offer everything the independent investor wanted, bar advice.* → See also **barring**. PREP = save ● You use **bar none** to add emphasis to a statement that someone or something is the best of their kind. ❑ *He is simply the best goalscorer we have ever had, bar none.* PHRASE emphasis = without exception 13 **The Bar** is used to refer to the profession of a barrister in England, or of any kind of lawyer in the United States. ❑ *Robert was planning to read for the Bar.* N-PROPER: the N 14 In music, a **bar** is one of the several short parts of the same length into which a piece of music is divided. [mainly BRIT] N-COUNT

☑ in AM, use **measure**

**barb** /bɑːʳb/ **(barbs)** 1 A **barb** is a sharp curved point near the end of an arrow or fish-hook which makes it difficult to pull out. N-COUNT 2 A **barb** is an unkind remark meant as a criticism of someone or something. ❑ *The barb stung her exactly the way he hoped it would.* N-COUNT = gibe

**Bar|ba|dian** /bɑːʳbeɪdiən/ **(Barbadians)** 1 **Barbadian** means belonging or relating to Barbados or its people. ADJ 2 A **Barbadian** is someone who comes from Barbados. N-COUNT

**bar|bar|ian** /bɑːʳbeəriən/ **(barbarians)** 1 In former times, **barbarians** were people from other countries who were thought to be uncivilized and violent. ❑ *The Roman Empire was overrun by Nordic barbarians.* N-COUNT 2 If you describe someone as a **barbarian**, you disapprove of them because they behave in a way that is cruel or uncivilized. ❑ *Our maths teacher was a bully and a complete barbarian... We need to fight this barbarian attitude to science.* N-COUNT disapproval

**bar|bar|ic** /bɑːʳbærɪk/ If you describe someone's behaviour as **barbaric**, you strongly disapprove of it because you think that it is extremely cruel or uncivilized. ❑ *This barbaric treatment of animals has no place in any decent society. ...a particularly barbaric act of violence.* ADJ disapproval

**bar|ba|rism** /bɑːʳbərɪzəm/ If you refer to someone's behaviour as **barbarism**, you strongly disapprove of it because you think that it is extremely cruel or uncivilized. ❑ *We do not ask for the death penalty: barbarism must not be met with barbarism.* N-UNCOUNT disapproval

**bar|bar|ity** /bɑːʳbærɪti/ **(barbarities)** If you refer to someone's behaviour as **barbarity**, you strongly disapprove of it because you think that it is extremely cruel. ❑ *...the barbarity of war.* N-VAR disapproval = savagery

**bar|ba|rous** /bɑːʳbərəs/ 1 If you describe something as **barbarous**, you strongly disapprove of it because you think that it is rough and uncivilized. ❑ *He thought the poetry of Whitman barbarous.* ADJ disapproval 2 If you describe something as **barba-** ADJ

**rous**, you strongly disapprove of it because you think that it is extremely cruel. ❑ *...a barbarous attack.* — disapproval = *barbaric*

**bar|becue** /bɑːʳbɪkjuː/ **(barbecues, barbecuing, barbecued)**

☑ in AM, also use **barbeque, Bar-B-Q**

1 A **barbecue** is a piece of equipment which you use for cooking on in the open air. — N-COUNT
2 If someone has a **barbecue**, they cook food on a barbecue in the open air. — N-COUNT
3 If you **barbecue** food, especially meat, you cook it on a barbecue. ❑ *Tuna can be grilled, fried or barbecued... Here's a way of barbecuing corn-on-the-cob that I learned in the States. ...barbecued chicken.* — VERB; be V-ed; V n; V-ed; Also V

**barbed** /bɑːʳbd/ A **barbed** remark or joke seems polite or humorous, but contains a cleverly hidden criticism. ❑ *...barbed comments.* — ADJ: usu ADJ n = *snide*

**barbed wire** **Barbed wire** is strong wire with sharp points sticking out of it, and is used to make fences. ❑ *The factory was surrounded by barbed wire. ...a barbed-wire fence.* — N-UNCOUNT: oft N n

**bar|ber** /bɑːʳbəʳ/ **(barbers)** 1 A **barber** is a man whose job is cutting men's hair. ❑ *...a barber's shop in south London.* — N-COUNT
2 A **barber's** is a shop where a barber works. [BRIT] ❑ *My Mum took me to the barber's.* — N-SING

☑ in AM, use **barber shop**

**barber|shop** /bɑːʳbəʳʃɒp/ **(barbershops)**
1 **Barbershop** is a style of singing where a small group of people, usually men, sing in close harmony and without any musical instruments accompanying them. ❑ *...a barbershop quartet.* — N-UNCOUNT: oft N n
2 → see **barber shop**.

**bar|ber shop (barber shops)**

☑ in AM, also use **barbershop**

A **barber shop** is a shop where a barber works. — N-COUNT

**bar|bie** /bɑːʳbi/ **(barbies)** A **barbie** is a **barbecue**. [BRIT, AUSTRALIAN, INFORMAL] — N-COUNT

**bar|bi|tu|rate** /bɑːʳbɪtʃʊrɪt/ **(barbiturates)** A **barbiturate** is a drug which people take to make them calm or to help them to sleep. ❑ *She was addicted to barbiturates.* — N-COUNT

**Bar-B-Q** /bɑːʳbɪkjuː/ → see **barbecue**.

**bar chart (bar charts)** A **bar chart** is a graph which uses parallel rectangular shapes to represent changes in the size, value, or rate of something or to compare the amount of something relating to a number of different countries or groups. [mainly BRIT] — N-COUNT

☑ in AM, use **bar graph**

**bar code (bar codes)** also **barcode.** A **bar code** is an arrangement of numbers and parallel lines that is printed on products to be sold in shops. The bar code can be read by computers. — N-COUNT

**bard** /bɑːʳd/ **(bards)** A **bard** is a poet. [LITERARY or OLD-FASHIONED] — N-COUNT

**Bard** People sometimes refer to William Shakespeare as **the Bard**. ❑ *...a new production of the Bard's early tragedy, Richard III.* — N-PROPER: the N

**bare** /beəʳ/ **(barer, barest, bares, baring, bared)** ◆◇◇
1 If a part of your body is **bare**, it is not covered by any clothing. ❑ *She was wearing only a thin robe over a flimsy nightdress, and her feet were bare... She had bare arms and a bare neck.* — ADJ
2 A **bare** surface is not covered or decorated with anything. ❑ *They would have liked bare wooden floors throughout the house.* — ADJ: usu ADJ n
3 If a tree or a branch is **bare**, it has no leaves on it. ❑ *...an old, twisted tree, its bark shaggy, many of its limbs brittle and bare.* — ADJ
4 If a room, cupboard, or shelf is **bare**, it is empty. ❑ *His fridge was bare apart from three very withered tomatoes... He led me through to a bare, draughty interviewing room.* — ADJ
5 An area of ground that is **bare** has no plants growing on it. ❑ *That's probably the most bare, bleak, barren and inhospitable island I've ever seen.* — ADJ
6 If someone gives you the **bare** facts or the **barest** details of something, they tell you only the most basic and important things. ❑ *Newspaper reporters were given nothing but the bare facts by the Superintendent in charge of the investigation.* — ADJ: det ADJ = *plain*
7 If you talk about the **bare** minimum or the **bare** essentials, you mean the very least that is necessary. ❑ *The army would try to hold the western desert with a bare minimum of forces... These are the bare essentials you'll need to dress your baby during the first few months.* — ADJ: det ADJ = *absolute*
8 **Bare** is used in front of an amount to emphasize how small it is. ❑ *Sales are growing for premium wines, but at a bare 2 percent a year.* — ADJ: a ADJ amount; emphasis = *mere*
9 If you **bare** something, you uncover it and show it. [WRITTEN] ❑ *Walsh bared his teeth in a grin.* — VERB; V n
10 **bare bones** → see **bone**.

PHRASES 11 If someone does something **with** their **bare hands**, they do it without using any weapons or tools. ❑ *Police believe the killer punched her to death with his bare hands... Rescuers were using their bare hands to reach the trapped miners.* — PHRASE: PHR after v
12 If you **lay** something **bare**, you uncover it completely so that it can then be seen. ❑ *The clearing out of disused workshops laid bare thousands of Italianate glazed tiles.* — PHRASE: V inflects = *expose*
13 If you **lay bare** something or someone, you reveal or expose them. ❑ *No one wants to expose themselves, lay their feelings bare.* — PHRASE: V inflects

**bare|back** /beəʳbæk/ If you ride **bareback**, you ride a horse without a saddle. ❑ *I rode bareback to the paddock.* — ADV: ADV after v ♦ **Bareback** is also an adjective. ❑ *She dreamed of being a bareback rider in a circus.* — ADJ: ADJ n

**bare-faced** also **barefaced.** You use **bare-faced** to describe someone's behaviour when you want to emphasize that they do not care that they are behaving wrongly. ❑ *What bare-faced cheek! ...crooked politicians who tell bare-faced lies.* — ADJ: ADJ n; emphasis = *brazen, shameless*

**bare|foot** /beəʳfʊt/ also **barefooted.** Someone who is **barefoot** or **barefooted** is not wearing anything on their feet. ❑ *I wore a white dress and was barefoot... Alan came running barefoot through the house.* — ADJ: v-link ADJ, ADJ after v, ADJ n

**bare|headed** /beəʳhedɪd/ Someone who is **bareheaded** is not wearing a hat or any other covering on their head. ❑ *He was bareheaded in the rain... I rode bareheaded.* — ADJ: usu v-link ADJ, ADJ after v

**bare|ly** /beəʳli/ ◆◇◇ 1 You use **barely** to say that something is only just true or only just the case. ❑ *Anastasia could barely remember the ride to the hospital... It was 90 degrees and the air conditioning barely cooled the room... His voice was barely audible.* — ADV: ADV before v, ADV group, oft ADV amount = *scarcely*
2 If you say that one thing had **barely** happened when something else happened, you mean that the first event was followed immediately by the second. ❑ *The Boeing 767 had barely taxied to a halt before its doors were flung open.* — ADV: ADV before v

**barf** /bɑːʳf/ **(barfs, barfing, barfed)** If someone **barfs**, they vomit. [mainly AM, INFORMAL] — VERB

**bar|fly** /bɑːʳflaɪ/ **(barflies)** A **barfly** is a person who spends a lot of time drinking in bars [AM, INFORMAL] — N-COUNT

**bar|gain** /bɑːʳgɪn/ **(bargains, bargaining, bargained)** ◆◇◇ 1 Something that is a **bargain** is good value for money, usually because it has been sold at a lower price than normal. ❑ *At this price the wine is a bargain.* — N-COUNT
2 A **bargain** is an agreement, especially a formal business agreement, in which two people or groups agree what each of them will do, pay, or receive. ❑ *I'll make a bargain with you. I'll play hostess if you'll include Matthew in your guest-list... The treaty was based on a bargain between the French and German governments.* — N-COUNT = *deal*
3 When people **bargain with** each other, they discuss what each of them will do, pay, or receive. ❑ *They prefer to bargain with individual clients, for cash... Shop in small local markets and don't be afraid to bargain.* — VERB = *negotiate*; V with n; V
♦ **bar|gain|er (bargainers)** *A union bargainer said that those jobs have been saved.* — N-COUNT ♦ **bar|gain|ing** *The government has called for sensible pay bargaining.* — N-UNCOUNT: oft supp N

PHRASES 4 If people **drive a hard bargain**, they argue with determination in order to achieve a deal which is favourable to themselves. ❑ *...a law* — PHRASE: V, ADJ, and N inflect *firm with a reputation for driving a hard bargain.* [5] You use **into the bargain** when mentioning an additional quantity, feature, fact, or action, to emphasize the fact that it is also involved. You can also say **in the bargain** in American English. ❑ *This machine is designed to save you effort, and keep your work surfaces tidy into the bargain... She is rich. Now you say she is a beauty into the bargain.* PHRASE: cl PHR [emphasis]

[6] If you **keep** your **side of the bargain**, you do what you have promised or arranged to do. ❑ *Dealing with this dictator wasn't an option. He wouldn't have kept his side of the bargain.* PHRASE: V inflects

♦ **bargain for** or **bargain on** If you have not **bargained for** or **bargained on** something that happens, you did not expect it to happen and so feel surprised or worried by it. ❑ *The effects of this policy were more than the government had bargained for.* PHRASAL VERB: usu with brd-neg; V P n

**bar|gain base|ment** also **bargain-basement.** If you refer to something as a **bargain basement** thing, you mean that it is cheap and not very good quality. ❑ *...a bargain-basement rock musical.* ADJ: ADJ n

**bar|gain hunt|er** **(bargain hunters)** also **bargain-hunter.** A **bargain hunter** is someone who is looking for goods that are value for money, usually because they are on sale at a lower price than normal. N-COUNT

**bar|gain|ing chip** **(bargaining chips)** In negotiations with other people, a **bargaining chip** is something that you are prepared to give up in order to obtain what you want. ❑ *Rubio suggests that oil be used as a bargaining chip in any trade talks.* N-COUNT = bargaining counter

**bar|gain|ing coun|ter** **(bargaining counters)** A **bargaining counter** is the same as a **bargaining chip.** [BRIT] N-COUNT

**barge** /bɑːʳdʒ/ **(barges, barging, barged)** [1] A **barge** is a long, narrow boat with a flat bottom. Barges are used for carrying heavy loads, especially on canals. ❑ *Carrying goods by train costs nearly three times more than carrying them by barge.* N-COUNT: also by N [2] If you **barge into** a place or **barge through** it, you rush or push into it in a rough and rude way. [INFORMAL] ❑ *Students tried to barge into the secretariat buildings.* VERB; V into/through n [3] If you **barge into** someone or **barge past** them, you bump against them roughly and rudely. [INFORMAL] ❑ *He barged past her and sprang at Gillian, knocking her to the floor.* VERB; V into/past n

♦ **barge in** If you **barge in** or **barge in on** someone, you rudely interrupt what they are doing or saying. [INFORMAL] ❑ *I'm sorry to barge in like this, but I have a problem I hope you can solve.* PHRASAL VERB; V P; Also V P on n

**barge pole** also **bargepole.** If you say that you **wouldn't touch** something **with a barge pole**, you mean that you would not want to have anything to do with it, either because you do not trust it, or because you do not like it. [BRIT, INFORMAL] PHRASE: V inflects

> in AM, use **wouldn't touch** something **with a ten-foot pole**

**bar graph** **(bar graphs)** A **bar graph** is the same as a **bar chart.** [AM] N-COUNT

**bari|tone** /bærɪtoʊn/ **(baritones)** In music, a **baritone** is a man with a fairly deep singing voice that is lower than that of a tenor but higher than that of a bass. N-COUNT

**bar|ium** /beəriəm/ **Barium** is a soft, silvery-white metal. N-UNCOUNT

**bark** /bɑːʳk/ **(barks, barking, barked)** [1] When a dog **barks**, it makes a short, loud noise, once or several times. ❑ *Don't let the dogs bark... A small dog barked at a seagull he was chasing.* ♦ **Bark** is also a noun. ❑ *The Doberman let out a string of roaring barks.* VERB; V; V at n; N-COUNT [2] If you **bark at** someone, you shout at them aggressively in a loud, rough voice. ❑ *I didn't mean to bark at you... A policeman held his gun in both hands and barked an order.* VERB; V at n; V n [3] **Bark** is the tough material that covers the outside of a tree. N-UNCOUNT [4] If you say that someone's **bark is worse than** their **bite**, you mean that they seem much more unpleasant or hostile than they really are. [INFORMAL] ❑ *She can be a bit tetchy but her bark is worse than her bite.* PHRASE: V inflects [5] to **be barking up the wrong tree** → see **tree**.

**bar|keep|er** /bɑːʳkiːpəʳ/ **(barkeepers)** A **barkeeper** is someone who serves drinks behind a bar. [AM] N-COUNT

**bark|ing mad** If you say that someone is **barking mad**, you mean that they are insane or are acting very strangely. [BRIT, INFORMAL] ❑ *The builder looked at me as though I was barking mad.* ADJ: v-link ADJ [disapproval] = bonkers

**bar|ley** /bɑːʳli/ **Barley** is a grain that is used to make food, beer, and whisky. ❑ *...fields of ripening wheat and barley.* N-UNCOUNT

**bar|ley sug|ar** **Barley sugar** is a sweet made from boiled sugar. N-UNCOUNT

**bar|ley wa|ter** **Barley water** is a drink made from barley. It is sometimes flavoured with orange or lemon. N-UNCOUNT

**bar|maid** /bɑːʳmeɪd/ **(barmaids)** A **barmaid** is a woman who serves drinks behind a bar. [mainly BRIT] N-COUNT

> in AM, use **bartender**

**bar|man** /bɑːʳmən/ **(barmen)** A **barman** is a man who serves drinks behind a bar. [mainly BRIT] N-COUNT

> in AM, use **bartender**

**bar mitz|vah** /bɑːʳ mɪtsvə/ **(bar mitzvahs)** A **bar mitzvah** is a ceremony that takes place on the thirteenth birthday of a Jewish boy, after which he is regarded as an adult. N-COUNT

**bar|my** /bɑːʳmi/ **(barmier, barmiest)** If you say that someone or something is **barmy**, you mean that they are slightly crazy or very foolish. [BRIT, INFORMAL] ❑ *...a barmy idea.* ADJ [disapproval] = crazy

**barn** /bɑːʳn/ **(barns)** A **barn** is a building on a farm in which crops or animal food can be kept. N-COUNT

**bar|na|cle** /bɑːʳnɪkəl/ **(barnacles)** **Barnacles** are small shellfish that fix themselves tightly to rocks and the bottoms of boats. N-COUNT

**barn dance** **(barn dances)** A **barn dance** is a social event people go to for country dancing. N-COUNT

**barn|storm** /bɑːʳnstɔːʳm/ **(barnstorms, barnstorming, barnstormed)** When people such as politicians or performers **barnstorm**, they travel around the country making speeches or giving shows. [AM] ❑ *He barnstormed across the nation, rallying the people to the cause... The president travels thousands of miles as he barnstorms the country. ...his barnstorming campaign for the governorship of Louisiana.* VERB; V prep/adv; V n; V-ing; Also V

**barn|storm|ing** /bɑːʳnstɔːʳmɪŋ/ A **barnstorming** performance is full of energy and very exciting to watch. [BRIT] ❑ *...a barnstorming performance by rock legends The Who.* ADJ: ADJ n [approval]

**barn|yard** /bɑːʳnjɑːʳd/ **(barnyards)** On a farm, **the barnyard** is the area in front of or next to a barn. N-COUNT: usu sing, oft the N

**ba|rom|eter** /bərɒmɪtəʳ/ **(barometers)** [1] A **barometer** is an instrument that measures air pressure and shows when the weather is changing. N-COUNT [2] If something is a **barometer of** a particular situation, it indicates how things are changing or how things are likely to develop. ❑ *In past presidential elections, Missouri has been a barometer of the rest of the country.* N-COUNT: with supp, oft N of n

**bar|on** /bærən/ **(barons)** [1] A **baron** is a man who is a member of the lowest rank of the nobility. [BRIT] ❑ *...their stepfather, Baron Michael Distemple.* N-COUNT; N-TITLE [2] You can use **baron** to refer to someone who controls a large amount of a particular industry or activity and who is therefore extremely powerful. ❑ *...the battle against the drug barons. ...the British press barons.* N-COUNT: with supp, usu n N

**bar|on|ess** /bærənes/ **(baronesses)** A **baroness** is a woman who is a member of the lowest N-COUNT; N-TITLE rank of the nobility, or who is the wife of a baron. [BRIT] ❑ *...Baroness Blatch.*

**bar|on|et** /bærənɪt/ **(baronets)** A **baronet** is a man who has been made a knight. When a baronet dies, the title is passed on to his son. [BRIT] N-COUNT

**ba|ro|nial** /bərouniəl/ 1 If you describe a house or room as **baronial**, you mean that it is large, impressive, and old-fashioned in appearance, and looks as if it belongs to someone from the upper classes. ❑ *...baronial manor houses.* ADJ: usu ADJ n
2 **Baronial** means relating to a baron or barons. ❑ *...the baronial feuding of the Middle Ages.* ADJ: ADJ n

**baro|ny** /bærəni/ **(baronies)** A **barony** is the rank or position of a baron. N-COUNT

**ba|roque** /bərɒk, AM -rouk/ 1 **Baroque** architecture and art is an elaborate style of architecture and art that was popular in Europe in the seventeenth and early eighteenth centuries. ❑ *The baroque church of San Leonardo is worth a quick look. ...a collection of treasures dating from the Middle Ages to the Baroque period.* ADJ: ADJ n ♦ The baroque style and period in art and architecture are sometimes referred to as **the baroque**. ❑ *...the seventeenth-century taste for the baroque.* N-SING: the N 2 **Baroque** music is a style of European music that was written in the 18th century. ADJ: ADJ n

**bar|rack** /bærək/ **(barracks, barracking, barracked)** 1 A **barracks** is a building or group of buildings where soldiers or other members of the armed forces live and work. 'Barracks' is the singular and plural form. ❑ *...an army barracks in the north of the city.* N-COUNT: oft in names 2 If people in an audience **barrack** public speakers or performers, they interrupt them, for example by making rude remarks. [BRIT] ❑ *Fans gained more enjoyment barracking him than cheering on the team.* VERB = heckle V n ♦ **bar|rack|ing** *He was affected badly by the barracking that he got from the crowd.* N-UNCOUNT = heckling

**bar|ra|cu|da** /bærəkjuːdə, AM -kuː-/ **(barracudas** or **barracuda)** A **barracuda** is a large tropical sea fish that eats other fish. N-COUNT

**bar|rage** /bærɑːʒ, AM bərɑːʒ/ **(barrages, barraging, barraged)**

> ✔ Pronounced /bɑːrɪdʒ/ for meaning 4 in American English.

1 A **barrage** is continuous firing on an area with large guns and tanks. ❑ *The two fighters were driven off by a barrage of anti-aircraft fire.* N-COUNT = bombardment 2 A **barrage of** something such as criticism or complaints is a large number of them directed at someone, often in an aggressive way. ❑ *He was faced with a barrage of angry questions from the floor.* N-COUNT: usu sing, oft N of n
3 If you **are barraged** by people or things, you have to deal with a great number of people or things you would rather avoid. ❑ *Doctors are complaining about being barraged by drug-company salesmen... Hughes was barraged with phone calls from friends who were furious at the indiscreet disclosures.* VERB: usu passive be V-ed by n be V-ed with n
4 A **barrage** is a structure that is built across a river to control the level of the water. ❑ *...a hydro-electric tidal barrage.* N-COUNT

**bar|rage bal|loon** **(barrage balloons)** **Barrage balloons** are large balloons which are fixed to the ground by strong steel cables. They are used in wartime, when the cables are intended to destroy low-flying enemy aircraft. N-COUNT

**bar|rel** /bærəl/ **(barrels, barrelling, barrelled)** ◆◇◇

> ✔ in AM, use **barreling, barreled**

1 A **barrel** is a large, round container for liquids or food. ❑ *The wine is aged for almost a year in oak barrels.* N-COUNT 2 In the oil industry, a **barrel** is a unit of measurement equal to 159 litres. ❑ *In 1989, Kuwait was exporting 1.5 million barrels of oil a day... Oil prices were closing at $19.76 a barrel.* N-COUNT: oft N of n 3 The **barrel** of a gun is the tube through which the bullet moves when the gun is fired. ❑ *He pushed the barrel of the gun into the other man's open mouth.* N-COUNT: oft N of n, n N 4 If a vehicle or person **is barreling** in a particular direction, they are moving very quickly in that direction. [mainly AM] ❑ *The car was barreling down the street at a crazy speed.* VERB = career V prep/adv 5 ➔ See also **pork barrel**.
PHRASES 6 If you say, for example, that someone moves or buys something **lock, stock, and barrel**, you are emphasizing that they move or buy every part or item of it. ❑ *They dug up their New Jersey garden and moved it lock, stock, and barrel back home.* PHRASE: PHR after v [emphasis] 7 If you say that someone is **scraping the barrel**, or **scraping the bottom of the barrel**, you disapprove of the fact that they are using or doing something of extremely poor quality. [INFORMAL] PHRASE: V inflects [disapproval]

**-barrelled** /-bærəld/

> ✔ in AM, use **-barreled**

**-barrelled** combines with adjectives to form adjectives that describe a gun which has a barrel or barrels of the specified type. ❑ *...a short-barreled rifle. ...a double-barrelled shotgun.* ➔ See also **double-barrelled**. COMB in ADJ

**bar|rel or|gan** **(barrel organs)** A **barrel organ** is a large machine that plays music when you turn the handle on the side. Barrel organs used to be played in the street to entertain people. N-COUNT

**bar|ren** /bærən/ 1 A **barren** landscape is dry and bare, and has very few plants and no trees. ❑ *...the Tibetan landscape of high barren mountains.* ADJ ≠ fertile 2 **Barren** land consists of soil that is so poor that plants cannot grow in it. ❑ *He also wants to use the water to irrigate barren desert land.* ADJ = infertile 3 If you describe something such as an activity or a period of your life as **barren**, you mean that you achieve no success during it or that it has no useful results. [WRITTEN] ❑ *...politics that are banal and barren of purpose. ...the player, who ended a 14-month barren spell by winning the Tokyo event in October.* ADJ: oft ADJ of n 4 If you describe a room or a place as **barren**, you do not like it because it has almost no furniture or other objects in it. [WRITTEN] ❑ *The room was austere, nearly barren of furniture or decoration.* ADJ: oft ADJ of n [disapproval] 5 A **barren** woman or female animal is unable to have babies. [OLD-FASHIONED] ❑ *He prayed that his barren wife would one day have a child.* ADJ = infertile

**bar|ri|cade** /bærɪkeɪd, AM -keɪd/ **(barricades, barricading, barricaded)** 1 A **barricade** is a line of vehicles or other objects placed across a road or open space to stop people getting past, for example during street fighting or as a protest. ❑ *Large areas of the city have been closed off by barricades set up by the demonstrators.* N-COUNT = blockade 2 If you **barricade** something such as a road or an entrance, you place a barricade or barrier across it, usually to stop someone getting in. ❑ *The rioters barricaded streets with piles of blazing tyres... The doors had been barricaded.* VERB V n V n 3 If you **barricade** yourself inside a room or building, you place barriers across the door or entrance so that other people cannot get in. ❑ *The students have barricaded themselves into their dormitory building... About forty prisoners are still barricaded inside the wrecked buildings.* VERB V pron-refl prep/adv V-ed

**bar|ri|er** /bæriəʳ/ **(barriers)** ◆◇◇ 1 A **barrier** is something such as a rule, law, or policy that makes it difficult or impossible for something to happen or be achieved. ❑ *Duties and taxes are the most obvious barrier to free trade.* N-COUNT: oft N to/against/between n = obstacle 2 A **barrier** is a problem that prevents two people or groups from agreeing, communicating, or working with each other. ❑ *There is no reason why love shouldn't cross the age barrier... When you get involved in sports and athletes, a lot of the racial barriers are broken down.* N-COUNT: oft supp N, N between pl-n
3 A **barrier** is something such as a fence or wall that is put in place to prevent people from moving easily from one area to another. ❑ *The demonstrators broke through heavy police barriers... As each woman reached the barrier one of the men glanced at her papers.* N-COUNT 4 A **barrier** is an object or layer that physically prevents something from moving from one place to another. ❑ *...a severe storm, which destroyed a natural barrier between the house and the lake... The packaging must provide an effective barrier to prevent contamination of the product.* N-COUNT: usu with supp 5 You can N-SING:

refer to a particular number or amount as a **barrier** when you think it is significant, because it is difficult or unusual to go above it. ❑ *They are fearful that unemployment will soon break the barrier of three million.* [6] → See also **crash barrier, sound barrier**. *the N, with supp*

**bar|ri|er meth|od (barrier methods) Barrier methods** of contraception involve the use of condoms, diaphragms, or other devices that physically prevent the sperm from reaching the egg. N-COUNT: usu pl

**bar|ring** /bɑːrɪŋ/ You use **barring** to indicate that the person, thing, or event that you are mentioning is an exception to your statement. ❑ *Barring accidents, I believe they will succeed.* PREP

**bar|rio** /bɑːrioʊ/ **(barrios)** [1] A **barrio** is a mainly Spanish-speaking area in an American city. [AM] ❑ *...the barrios of Santa Cruz.* N-COUNT [2] A **barrio** is an urban district in a Spanish-speaking country. [mainly AM] ❑ *...the barrios of Mexico City.* N-COUNT

**bar|ris|ter** /bærɪstəʳ/ **(barristers)** In England and Wales, a **barrister** is a lawyer who represents clients in the higher courts of law. Compare **solicitor**. N-COUNT

**bar|room** /bɑːʳruːm/ **(barrooms)** also **bar-room.** A **barroom** is a room or building in which alcoholic drinks are served over a counter. [AM] N-COUNT

☑ in BRIT, usually use **bar, pub**

**bar|row** /bæroʊ/ **(barrows)** [1] A **barrow** is the same as a **wheelbarrow**. N-COUNT [2] A **barrow** is a cart from which fruit or other goods are sold in the street. [BRIT] N-COUNT

☑ in AM, use **pushcart**

[3] A **barrow** is a large structure made of earth that people used to build over graves in ancient times. N-COUNT

**bar|row boy (barrow boys)** A **barrow boy** is a man or boy who sells fruit or other goods from a barrow in the street. [BRIT] N-COUNT

**bar|tender** /bɑːʳtendəʳ/ **(bartenders)** A **bartender** is a person who serves drinks behind a bar. [AM] N-COUNT

☑ in BRIT, use **barman, barmaid**

**bar|ter** /bɑːʳtəʳ/ **(barters, bartering, bartered)** If you **barter** goods, you exchange them for other goods, rather than selling them for money. ❑ *They have been bartering wheat for cotton and timber... The market-place and street were crowded with those who'd come to barter... Traders came to barter horses.* VERB = trade; V n *for* n; V; V n
♦ **Barter** is also a noun. ❑ *Overall, barter is a very inefficient means of organizing transactions. ...a barter economy.* N-UNCOUNT: oft N n

**ba|sal** /beɪsəl/ **Basal** means relating to or forming the base of something. [TECHNICAL] ❑ *...the basal layer of the skin.* ADJ: ADJ n

**bas|alt** /bæsɔːlt, AM bəsɔːlt/ **(basalts) Basalt** is a type of black rock that is produced by volcanoes. N-MASS

**base** /beɪs/ **(bases, basing, based, baser, basest)** [1] The **base** of something is its lowest edge or part. ❑ *There was a cycle path running along this side of the wall, right at its base... Line the base and sides of a 20cm deep round cake tin with paper.* ◆◆◆ N-COUNT: usu *the* N *of* n = bottom ≠ top
[2] The **base** of something is the lowest part of it, where it is attached to something else. ❑ *The surgeon placed catheters through the veins and arteries near the base of the head.* N-COUNT: usu *the* N *of* n
[3] The **base** of an object such as a box or vase is the lower surface of it that touches the surface it rests on. ❑ *Remove from the heat and plunge the base of the pan into a bowl of very cold water.* N-COUNT: usu with poss = bottom, underneath
[4] The **base** of an object that has several sections and that rests on a surface is the lower section of it. ❑ *The mattress is best on a solid bed base... The clock stands on an oval marble base, enclosed by a glass dome.* N-COUNT: usu with supp, oft n N
[5] A **base** is a layer of something which will have another layer added to it. ❑ *Spoon the mixture on to the biscuit base and cook in a pre-heated oven... On many modern wooden boats, epoxy coatings will have been used as a base for varnishing.* N-COUNT: usu with supp
[6] A position or thing that is a **base** for something is one from which that thing can be developed or achieved. ❑ *The family base was crucial to my development.* N-COUNT: usu sing, with supp = basis, foundation
[7] If you **base** one thing **on** another thing, the first thing develops from the second thing. ❑ *He based his conclusions on the evidence given by the captured prisoners.* VERB; V n *on/upon* n
♦ **based** *Three of the new products are based on traditional herbal medicines.* ADJ: v-link ADJ *on/upon* n
[8] A company's client **base** or customer **base** is the group of regular clients or customers that the company gets most of its income from. [BUSINESS] ❑ *The company has been expanding its customer base using trade magazine advertising.* N-COUNT
[9] A military **base** is a place which part of the armed forces works from. ❑ *Gunfire was heard at an army base close to the airport. ...a massive air base in eastern Saudi Arabia.* N-COUNT: usu supp N
[10] Your **base** is the main place where you work, stay, or live. ❑ *For most of the spring and early summer her base was her home in Scotland.* N-COUNT: usu poss N
[11] If a place is a **base** for a certain activity, the activity can be carried out at that place or from that place. ❑ *The two hotel-restaurants are attractive bases from which to explore southeast Tuscany.* N-COUNT: usu sing, usu N prep
[12] The **base** of a substance such as paint or food is the main ingredient of it, to which other substances can be added. ❑ *Drain off any excess marinade and use it as a base for a pouring sauce... Oils may be mixed with a base oil and massaged into the skin.* N-COUNT
[13] A **base** is a system of counting and expressing numbers. The decimal system uses base 10, and the binary system uses base 2. N-COUNT: also N num
[14] A **base** in baseball, softball, or rounders is one of the places at each corner of the square on the pitch. N-COUNT

**base|ball** /beɪsbɔːl/ **(baseballs)** [1] In America, **baseball** is a game played by two teams of nine players. Each player from one team hits a ball with a bat and then tries to run around three bases and get to the home base before the other team can get the ball back. ◆◇◇ N-UNCOUNT [2] A **baseball** is a small hard ball which is used in the game of baseball. N-COUNT

**base|board** /beɪsbɔːd/ **(baseboards)** A **baseboard** is a narrow length of wood which goes along the bottom of a wall in a room and makes a border between the walls and the floor. [AM] N-COUNT

☑ in BRIT, use **skirting board**

**based** /beɪst/ If you are **based** in a particular place, that is the place where you live or do most of your work. See also **base**. ❑ *Both firms are based in Kent... Based on the edge of Lake Matt, Sunbeam Yachts started boatbuilding in 1870.* ◆◆◆ ADJ: v-link ADJ = located

**-based** /-beɪst/ [1] **-based** combines with nouns referring to places to mean something positioned or existing mainly in the place mentioned, or operating or organized from that place. ❑ *...a Washington-based organization. ...land-based missiles.* COMB: COMB in ADJ
[2] **-based** combines with nouns to mean that the thing mentioned is a central part or feature. ❑ *...computer-based jobs. ...oil-based sauces.* COMB: COMB in ADJ
[3] **-based** combines with adverbs to mean having a particular kind of basis. ❑ *There are growing signs of more broadly-based popular unrest.* COMB: COMB in ADJ

**base|less** /beɪsləs/ If you describe an accusation, rumour, or report as **baseless**, you mean that it is not true and is not based on facts. ❑ *The charges against her are baseless. ...baseless allegations of drug taking.* ADJ = unfounded

**base|line** /beɪslaɪn/ **(baselines)** also **base-line.** [1] The **baseline** of a tennis, badminton, or basketball court is one of the lines at each end of the court that mark the limits of play. ❑ *Martinez, when she served, usually stayed on the baseline.* N-COUNT: usu sing [2] In baseball, the **baseline** is the line that a player must not cross when running between bases. N-COUNT: usu sing [3] A **baseline** is a value or starting point on a scale with which other values can be N-COUNT: usu sing, oft N *for* n/-ing compared. ❑ *You'll need such information to use as a baseline for measuring progress.*

**base|ment** /beɪsmənt/ **(basements)** The **basement** of a building is a floor built partly or completely below ground level. ❑ *They bought an old schoolhouse to live in and built a workshop in the basement.* N-COUNT

**base met|al** **(base metals)** A **base metal** is a metal such as copper, zinc, tin, or lead that is not a precious metal. N-VAR ≠ precious metal

**base rate** **(base rates)** In Britain, the **base rate** is the rate of interest that banks use as a basis when they are calculating the rates that they charge on loans. [BUSINESS] ❑ *Bank base rates of 7 per cent are too high.* N-COUNT

**bases**

> Pronounced /beɪsɪz/ for meaning 1. Pronounced /beɪsiːz/ and hyphenated ba|ses for meaning 2.

1 **Bases** is the plural of **base**. 2 **Bases** is the plural of **basis**.

**bash** /bæʃ/ **(bashes, bashing, bashed)** 1 A **bash** is a party or celebration, especially a large one held by an official organization or attended by famous people. [INFORMAL] ❑ *He threw one of the biggest showbiz bashes of the year as a 36th birthday party for Jerry Hall.* N-COUNT 2 If someone **bashes** you, they attack you by hitting or punching you hard. [INFORMAL] ❑ *If someone tried to bash my best mate they would have to bash me as well... I bashed him on the head and dumped him in the water... Two women were hurt and the chef was bashed over the head with a bottle.* VERB V n V n prep/adv *be/get* V-ed prep/adv 3 If you **bash** something, you hit it hard in a rough or careless way. [INFORMAL] ❑ *Too many golfers try to bash the ball out of sand. That spells disaster... A stand-in drummer bashes on a single snare and a pair of cymbals.* VERB V n prep/adv V prep/adv Also V n 4 If you get a **bash on** a part of your body, someone or something hits you hard, or you bump into something. [INFORMAL] N-COUNT: usu N *on* n = knock 5 To **bash** someone means to criticize them severely, usually in a public way. [JOURNALISM] ❑ *The President could continue to bash Democrats as being soft on crime.* VERB V n 6 → See also **-bashing**.

**-basher** /-bæʃəʳ/ **(-bashers)** **-basher** combines with nouns to form nouns referring to someone who is physically violent towards a particular type of person, or who is unfairly critical of a particular type of person. ❑ *...gay-bashers who go around looking for homosexuals to beat up.* COMB in N-COUNT [disapproval]

**bash|ful** /bæʃfʊl/ Someone who is **bashful** is shy and easily embarrassed. ❑ *He seemed bashful and awkward. ...a bashful young lady.* ADJ = shy ♦ **bash|ful|ly** /bæʃfʊli/ *'No,' Wang Fu said bashfully.* ADV: ADV with v ♦ **bash|ful|ness** *I was overcome with bashfulness when I met her.* N-UNCOUNT

**-bashing** /-bæʃɪŋ/ 1 **-bashing** combines with nouns to form nouns or adjectives that refer to strong, public, and often unfair criticism of the people or group mentioned. [JOURNALISM] ❑ *Tory-bashing or Labour-bashing will not be enough to shift bored, suspicious voters.* COMB in N-UNCOUNT, ADJ [disapproval] 2 **-bashing** combines with nouns to form nouns or adjectives that refer to the activity of violently attacking the people mentioned just because they belong to a particular group or community. ❑ *...an outburst of violent gay-bashing in New York and other cities.* COMB in N-UNCOUNT, ADJ [disapproval] 3 → See also **bash**.

**ba|sic** /beɪsɪk/ ◆◆◇ 1 You use **basic** to describe things, activities, and principles that are very important or necessary, and on which others depend. ❑ *One of the most basic requirements for any form of angling is a sharp hook. ...the basic skills of reading, writing and communicating. ...the basic laws of physics... Access to justice is a basic right.* ADJ: usu ADJ n = fundamental 2 **Basic** goods and services are very simple ones which every human being needs. You can also refer to people's **basic** needs for such goods and services. ❑ *...shortages of even the most basic foodstuffs... Hospitals lack even basic drugs for surgical operations. ...the basic needs of food and water.* ADJ: usu ADJ n 3 If one thing is **basic to** another, it is absolutely necessary to it, and the second thing cannot exist, succeed, or be imagined without it. ❑ *...an oily liquid, basic to the manufacture of a host of other chemical substances... There are certain ethical principles that are basic to all the great religions.* ADJ: v-link ADJ *to* n = central 4 You can use **basic** to emphasize that you are referring to what you consider to be the most important aspect of a situation, and that you are not concerned with less important details. ❑ *There are three basic types of tea... The basic design changed little from that patented by Edison more than 100 years ago... The basic point is that sanctions cannot be counted on to produce a sure result.* ADJ: ADJ n [emphasis] = fundamental 5 You can use **basic** to describe something that is very simple in style and has only the most necessary features, without any luxuries. ❑ *We provide 2-person tents and basic cooking and camping equipment. ...the extremely basic hotel room.* ADJ 6 **Basic** is used to describe a price or someone's income when this does not include any additional amounts. ❑ *...an increase of more than twenty per cent on the basic pay of a typical coalface worker... The basic price for a 10-minute call is only £2.49.* ADJ: ADJ n 7 The **basic** rate of income tax is the lowest or most common rate, which applies to people who earn average incomes. ❑ *All this is to be done without big rises in the basic level of taxation. ...a basic-rate taxpayer.* ADJ: ADJ n

**ba|si|cal|ly** /beɪsɪkli/ ◆◇◇ 1 You use **basically** for emphasis when you are stating an opinion, or when you are making an important statement about something. ❑ *This gun is designed for one purpose – it's basically to kill people... Basically I think he would be someone who complemented me in terms of character.* ADV: ADV with cl/group [emphasis] 2 You use **basically** to show that you are describing a situation in a simple, general way, and that you are not concerned with less important details. ❑ *Basically you've got two choices... It's basically a vegan diet.* ADV: ADV with cl/group, ADV before v

**ba|sics** /beɪsɪks/ 1 **The basics** of something are its simplest, most important elements, ideas, or principles, in contrast to more complicated or detailed ones. ❑ *They will concentrate on teaching the basics of reading, writing and arithmetic... A strong community cannot be built until the basics are in place... Let's get down to basics and stop horsing around.* N-PLURAL: usu *the* N, oft N *of* n = fundamentals 2 **Basics** are things such as simple food, clothes, or equipment that people need in order to live or to deal with a particular situation. ❑ *...supplies of basics such as bread and milk. ...items that are the basics of a stylish wardrobe.* N-PLURAL 3 If you talk about getting **back to basics**, you are suggesting that people have become too concerned with complicated details or new theories, and that they should concentrate on simple, important ideas or activities. ❑ *...a new 'back-to-basics' drive to raise standards of literacy in Britain's schools.* PHRASE: usu PHR after v, PHR n

**ba|sic train|ing** **Basic training** is the training that someone receives when they first join the armed forces. [AM] N-UNCOUNT

**bas|il** /bæzəl, AM beɪzəl/ **Basil** is a strong-smelling and strong-tasting herb that is used in cooking, especially with tomatoes. N-UNCOUNT

**ba|sili|ca** /bəzɪlɪkə/ **(basilicas)** A **basilica** is a church which is rectangular in shape and has a rounded end. N-COUNT

**ba|sin** /beɪsən/ **(basins)** 1 A **basin** is a large or deep bowl that you use for holding liquids, or for mixing or storing food. ❑ *Place the eggs and sugar in a large basin. ...a pudding basin.* N-COUNT ♦ A **basin of** something such as water is an amount of it that is contained in a basin. ❑ *We were given a basin of water to wash our hands in.* N-COUNT: N *of* n 2 A **basin** is the same as a **washbasin**. ❑ *...a cast-iron bath with a matching basin and wc.* N-COUNT 3 The **basin** of a large river is the area of land around it from which streams run down into it. ❑ *...the Amazon basin.* N-COUNT: with supp, oft in names 4 In geography, a **basin** is a particular region of the world where the earth's surface is lower than in other places. [TECHNICAL] ❑ *...countries around the* N-COUNT: with supp, oft in names

*Pacific Basin.* 5 A **basin** is a partially enclosed area of deep water where boats or ships are kept. N-COUNT: usu n N

**ba|sis** /beɪsɪs/ **(bases** /beɪsiːz/**)** 1 If something is done **on** a particular **basis**, it is done according to that method, system, or principle. ❑ *We're going to be meeting there on a regular basis... They want all groups to be treated on an equal basis... I've always worked on the basis that if I don't know anything technical I shan't be any worse off.* ◆◆◇ N-SING: with supp, usu *on* N 2 If you say that you are acting **on** the **basis of** something, you are giving that as the reason for your action. ❑ *McGregor must remain confined, on the basis of the medical reports we have received.* N-SING: *on* N, oft N *of* n, N that 3 The **basis** of something is its starting point or an important part of it from which it can be further developed. ❑ *Both factions have broadly agreed that the UN plan is a possible basis for negotiation. ...the subatomic particles that form the basis of nearly all matter on earth.* N-COUNT: usu sing, usu N *for/of* n = *foundation* 4 The **basis** for something is a fact or argument that you can use to prove or justify it. ❑ *...Japan's attempt to secure the legal basis to send troops overseas... This is a common fallacy which has no basis in fact.* N-COUNT: usu sing

**ba|sis point (basis points)** In finance, a **basis point** is one hundredth of a per cent (.01%). [BUSINESS] N-COUNT: usu pl

**bask** /bɑːsk, bæsk/ **(basks, basking, basked)** 1 If you **bask in** the sunshine, you lie somewhere sunny and enjoy the heat. ❑ *All through the hot, still days of their holiday Amy basked in the sun... Crocodiles bask on the small sandy beaches.* VERB V *in* n V 2 If you **bask in** someone's approval, favour, or admiration, you greatly enjoy their positive reaction towards you. ❑ *He has spent a month basking in the adulation of the fans back in Jamaica.* VERB V *in* n

**bas|ket** /bɑːskɪt, bæs-/ **(baskets)** 1 A **basket** is a stiff container that is used for carrying or storing objects. Baskets are made from thin strips of materials such as straw, plastic, or wire woven together. ❑ *...big wicker picnic baskets filled with sandwiches. ...a laundry basket.* N-COUNT ♦ A **basket of** things is a number of things contained in a basket. ❑ *...a small basket of fruit and snacks.* N-COUNT: N *of* n 2 In economics, a **basket of** currencies or goods is the average or total value of a number of different currencies or goods. [BUSINESS] ❑ *The pound's value against a basket of currencies hit a new low of 76.9.* N-COUNT: usu sing, N *of* n 3 In basketball, the **basket** is a net hanging from a ring through which players try to throw the ball in order to score points. N-COUNT 4 → See also **bread basket**, **hanging basket**, **wastepaper basket**. to **put all** your **eggs in one basket** → see **egg**.

**basket|ball** /bɑːskɪtbɔːl, bæs-/ **(basketballs)** 1 **Basketball** is a game in which two teams of five players each try to score goals by throwing a large ball through a circular net fixed to a metal ring at each end of the court. N-UNCOUNT 2 A **basketball** is a large ball which is used in the game of basketball. N-COUNT

**bas|ket case (basket cases)** 1 If someone describes a country or organization as a **basket case**, they mean that its economy or finances are in a seriously bad state. [INFORMAL] ❑ *The country is an economic basket case with chronic unemployment and rampant crime.* N-COUNT 2 If you describe someone as a **basket case**, you think that they are insane. [INFORMAL] ❑ *You're going to think I'm a basket case when I tell you this.* N-COUNT [disapproval] = *nutcase*

**bas-relief** /bɑːrɪliːf, bæs-/ **(bas-reliefs)** 1 **Bas-relief** is a technique of sculpture in which shapes are carved so that they stand out from the background. ❑ *...a classic white bas-relief design.* N-UNCOUNT 2 A **bas-relief** is a sculpture carved on a surface so that it stands out from the background. ❑ *...columns decorated with bas-reliefs.* N-COUNT

**bass (basses)** ◆◇◇

> Pronounced /beɪs/ for meanings 1 to 4, and /bæs/ for meaning 5. The plural of the noun in meaning 5 is **bass**.

1 A **bass** is a man with a very deep singing voice. ❑ *...the great Russian bass Chaliapin.* N-COUNT 2 A **bass** drum, guitar, or other musical instrument is one that produces a very deep sound. ❑ *...bass guitarist Dee Murray.* ADJ: ADJ n 3 In popular music, a **bass** is a bass guitar or a **double bass**. ❑ *...Dave Ranson on bass and Kenneth Blevins on drums.* N-VAR 4 On a stereo system or radio, the **bass** is the ability to reproduce the lower musical notes. The **bass** is also the knob which controls this. N-UNCOUNT 5 **Bass** are edible fish that are found in rivers and the sea. There are several types of bass. ❑ *They unloaded their catch of cod and bass.* N-VAR ♦ **Bass** is a piece of this fish eaten as food. ❑ *...a large fresh fillet of sea bass.* N-UNCOUNT: oft n N

**bas|set hound** /bæsɪt haʊnd/ **(basset hounds)** A **basset hound** is a dog with short strong legs, a long body, and long ears. It is kept as a pet or used for hunting. N-COUNT = *basset*

**bass|ist** /beɪsɪst/ **(bassists)** A **bassist** is someone who plays the bass guitar or the double bass. N-COUNT

**bas|soon** /bəsuːn/ **(bassoons)** A **bassoon** is a large musical instrument that is shaped like a tube and played by blowing into a curved metal pipe. N-VAR: oft *the* N

**bas|soon|ist** /bəsuːnɪst/ **(bassoonists)** A **bassoonist** is someone who plays the bassoon. N-COUNT

**bas|tard** /bɑːstərd, bæs-/ **(bastards)** 1 **Bastard** is an insulting word which some people use about a person, especially a man, who has behaved very badly. [INFORMAL, ⚠ VERY RUDE] N-COUNT [disapproval] 2 A **bastard** is a person whose parents were not married to each other at the time that he or she was born. This use could cause offence. [OLD-FASHIONED] N-COUNT: oft N n

**bas|tard|ized** /bɑːstərdaɪzd, bæs-/

> in BRIT, also use **bastardised**

If you refer to something as a **bastardized** form of something else, you mean that the first thing is similar to or copied from the second thing, but is of much poorer quality. [FORMAL] ADJ: usu ADJ n [disapproval]

**baste** /beɪst/ **(bastes, basting, basted)** If you **baste** meat, you pour hot fat and the juices from the meat itself over it while it is cooking. ❑ *Pam was in the middle of basting the turkey... Bake for 15-20 minutes, basting occasionally.* VERB V n V

**bas|ti|on** /bæstiən, AM -tʃən/ **(bastions)** If a system or organization is described as a **bastion of** a particular way of life, it is seen as being important and effective in defending that way of life. **Bastion** can be used both when you think that this way of life should be ended and when you think it should be defended. [FORMAL] ❑ *...a town which had been a bastion of white prejudice... The army is still one of the last male bastions.* N-COUNT: with supp, usu N *of* n = *stronghold*

**bat** /bæt/ **(bats, batting, batted)** 1 A **bat** is a specially shaped piece of wood that is used for hitting the ball in baseball, softball, cricket, rounders, or table tennis. ❑ *...a baseball bat.* ◆◇◇ N-COUNT 2 When you **bat**, you have a turn at hitting the ball with a bat in baseball, softball, cricket, or rounders. ❑ *Australia, put in to bat, made a cautious start.* VERB V ♦ **bat|ting** *...his batting average... He's likely to open the batting.* N-UNCOUNT 3 A **bat** is a small flying animal that looks like a mouse with wings made of skin. Bats are active at night. N-COUNT 4 → See also **old bat**.

PHRASES 5 When something surprising or shocking happens, if someone **doesn't bat an eyelid** in British English, or **doesn't bat an eye** in American English, they remain calm and do not show any reaction. PHRASE: V inflects 6 If someone does something **off** their **own bat**, they do it without anyone else suggesting it. [BRIT] ❑ *Whatever she did she did off her own bat. Whatever she did was nothing to do with me.* PHRASE: PHR after v 7 If something happens **right off the bat**, it happens immediately. [AM] ❑ *He learned right off the bat that you can't count on anything in this business.* PHRASE: usu PHR after v

**batch** /bætʃ/ **(batches)** A **batch of** things or people is a group of things or people of the same kind, especially a group that is dealt with at the same time or is sent to a particular place at the N-COUNT: oft N *of* n same time. ❑ *...the current batch of trainee priests... She brought a large batch of newspaper cuttings.*

**bat|ed** /beɪtɪd/ If you wait for something **with bated breath**, you wait anxiously to find out what will happen. [FORMAL] ❑ *We listened with bated breath to Grandma's stories of her travels.* PHRASE: usu PHR after v

**bath** /bɑːθ, bæθ/ **(baths, bathing, bathed)** ◆◇◇

> ✔ When the form **baths** is the plural of the noun it is pronounced /bɑːðz/ or /bæθs/ in British English, and /bæðz/ in American English. When it is used in the present tense of the verb, it is pronounced /bɑːθs/ or /bæθs/.

1 A **bath** is a container, usually a long rectangular one, which you fill with water and sit in while you wash your body. [BRIT] ❑ *In those days, only quite wealthy families had baths of their own.* N-COUNT

> ✔ in AM, use **bathtub**

2 When you have or take a **bath**, or when you are in the **bath**, you sit or lie in a bath filled with water in order to wash your body. ❑ *...if you have a bath every morning... Take a shower instead of a bath.* N-COUNT

3 If you **bath** someone, especially a child, you wash them in a bath. [BRIT] ❑ *Don't feel you have to bath your child every day.* ♦ **Bath** is also a noun. ❑ *The midwife gave him a warm bath.* VERB = bathe V n N-COUNT

> ✔ in AM, use **bathe**

4 When you **bath**, you have a bath. [BRIT] ❑ *The three children all bath in the same bath water.* VERB = bathe V prep/adv

> ✔ in AM, use **bathe**

5 A **bath** or a **baths** is a public building containing a swimming pool, and sometimes other facilities that people can use to have a wash or a bath. N-COUNT 6 A **bath** is a container filled with a particular liquid, such as a dye or an acid, in which particular objects are placed, usually as part of a manufacturing or chemical process. ❑ *...a developing photograph placed in a bath of fixer.* N-COUNT: usu with supp 7 → See also **bloodbath**, **bubble bath**, **swimming bath**, **Turkish bath**.

**bathe** /beɪð/ **(bathes, bathing, bathed)** 1 If you **bathe** in a sea, river, or lake, you swim, play, or wash yourself in it. Birds and animals can also **bathe**. [mainly BRIT, FORMAL] ❑ *The police have warned the city's inhabitants not to bathe in the polluted river.* ♦ **Bathe** is also a noun. ❑ *Fifty soldiers were taking an early morning bathe in a nearby lake.* ♦ **bath|ing** *Nude bathing is not allowed.* VERB V prep/adv Also V N-SING: usu *a* N N-UNCOUNT 2 When you **bathe**, you have a bath. [AM; also BRIT, FORMAL] ❑ *At least 60% of us now bathe or shower once a day.* VERB = bath V 3 If you **bathe** someone, especially a child, you wash them in a bath. [AM; also BRIT, FORMAL] ❑ *Back home, Shirley plays with, feeds and bathes the baby.* VERB = bath V n 4 If you **bathe** a part of your body or a wound, you wash it gently or soak it in a liquid. ❑ *Bathe the infected area in a salt solution.* VERB V n 5 If a place **is bathed in** light, it is covered with light, especially a gentle, pleasant light. ❑ *The arena was bathed in warm sunshine... The lamp behind him seems to bathe him in warmth.* VERB *be* V-ed *in* n V n *in* n Also V n 6 → See also **sunbathe**.

**bathed** /beɪðd/ 1 If someone is **bathed in** sweat, they are sweating a great deal. ❑ *Chantal was writhing in pain and bathed in perspiration.* ADJ: v-link ADJ *in* n 2 If someone is **bathed in** a particular emotion such as love, they feel it constantly in a pleasant way. [LITERARY] ❑ *...a physical sensation of being bathed in love.* ADJ: v-link ADJ *in* n

**bath|er** /beɪðəʳ/ **(bathers)** A **bather** is a person who is swimming in the sea, or in a river or lake. [mainly BRIT, FORMAL] N-COUNT = swimmer

**bath|house** /bɑːθhaʊs/ **(bathhouses)** also **bath house.** A **bathhouse** is a public or private building containing baths and often other facilities such as a sauna. N-COUNT

**bath|ing cos|tume** /beɪðɪŋ kɒstjuːm, AM -tuːm/ **(bathing costumes)** A **bathing costume** is a piece of clothing that is worn for swimming, especially by women and girls. [BRIT, OLD-FASHIONED] N-COUNT = swimsuit

**bath|ing suit** /beɪðɪŋ suːt/ **(bathing suits)** A **bathing suit** is a piece of clothing which people wear when they go swimming. N-COUNT = swimsuit

**bath|ing trunks** /beɪðɪŋ trʌŋks/ **Bathing trunks** are shorts that a man wears when he goes swimming. N-PLURAL = swimming trunks

**bath|mat** /bɑːθmæt, bæθ-/ **(bathmats)** also **bath mat.** A **bathmat** is a mat which you stand on while you dry yourself after getting out of the bath. N-COUNT

**ba|thos** /beɪθɒs/ In literary criticism, **bathos** is a sudden change in speech or writing from a serious or important subject to a ridiculous or very ordinary one. [TECHNICAL] N-UNCOUNT

**bath|robe** /bɑːθroʊb/ **(bathrobes)** 1 A **bathrobe** is a loose piece of clothing made of the same material as towels. You wear it before or after you have a bath or a swim. N-COUNT 2 A **bathrobe** is a **dressing gown**. N-COUNT

**bath|room** /bɑːθruːm, bæθ-/ **(bathrooms)** ◆◇◇ 1 A **bathroom** is a room in a house that contains a bath or shower, a washbasin, and sometimes a toilet. → See picture on page 1706. N-COUNT 2 A **bathroom** is a room in a house or public building that contains a toilet. [AM] ❑ *She had gone in to use the bathroom.* N-SING: usu *the* N = rest room

> ✔ in BRIT, usually use **toilet**

3 People say that they **are going to the bathroom** when they want to say that they are going to use the toilet. PHRASE: V inflects politeness

**bath tow|el** **(bath towels)** A **bath towel** is a very large towel used for drying your body after you have had a bath. N-COUNT

**bath|tub** /bɑːθtʌb, bæθ-/ **(bathtubs)** A **bathtub** is a long, usually rectangular container which you fill with water and sit in to wash your body. [AM] N-COUNT

> ✔ in BRIT, use **bath**

**bath wa|ter** also **bathwater.** Your **bath water** is the water in which you sit or lie when you have a bath. to **throw the baby out with the bath water** → see **baby**. N-UNCOUNT

**ba|tik** /bətiːk, bætɪk/ **(batiks)** 1 **Batik** is a process for printing designs on cloth. Wax is put on those areas of the cloth that you do not want to be coloured by dye. ❑ *...batik bedspreads.* N-UNCOUNT 2 A **batik** is a cloth which has been printed with a batik design. ❑ *...batik from Bali.* N-VAR

**bat|man** /bætmæn/ **(batmen)** In the British armed forces, an officer's **batman** is his personal servant. N-COUNT: usu sing, oft poss N

**ba|ton** /bætɒn, AM bətɑːn/ **(batons)** 1 A **baton** is a short heavy stick which is sometimes used as a weapon by the police. [BRIT] N-COUNT

> ✔ in AM, use **billy**, **billy club**

2 A **baton** is a light, thin stick used by a conductor to conduct an orchestra or a choir. N-COUNT 3 In athletics or track events, a **baton** is a short stick that is passed from one runner to another in a relay race. N-COUNT 4 A **baton** is a long stick with a knob on one end that is sometimes carried by a person marching in a parade. The baton is spun round, thrown into the air and caught. N-COUNT 5 If someone **passes the baton to** another person, they pass responsibility for something to that person. If someone **picks up the baton**, they take over responsibility for something. ❑ *Does this mean that the baton of leadership is going to be passed to other nations?* PHRASE: V inflects

**ba|ton charge** **(baton charges, baton charging, baton charged)** also **baton-charge.** A **baton charge** is an attacking forward movement made by a large group of policemen carrying batons. [BRIT] ♦ **Baton-charge** is also a verb. [JOURNALISM] ❑ *Police in riot gear baton-charged the crowd.* N-COUNT VERB V n

**bats|man** /bætsmən/ **(batsmen)** The **batsman** in a game of cricket is the player who is batting. ❑ *The batsman rose on his toes and played the* N-COUNT *rising ball down into the ground... He was the greatest batsman of his generation.*

**bat|tal|ion** /bətæljən/ **(battalions)** [1] A **battalion** is a large group of soldiers that consists of three or more companies. ❑ *Anthony was ordered to return to his battalion... He joined the second battalion of the Grenadier Guards.* — N-COUNT
[2] A **battalion of** people is a large group of them, especially a well-organized, efficient group that has a particular task to do. ❑ *There were battalions of highly paid publicists to see that such news didn't make the press.* — N-COUNT: N *of* n = horde

**bat|ten** /bætᵊn/ **(battens, battening, battened)**
[1] A **batten** is a long strip of wood that is fixed to something to strengthen it or to hold it firm. ❑ *...a batten to support the base timbers.* — N-COUNT
[2] If something **is battened** in place, it is made secure by having battens fixed across it or being closed firmly. ❑ *The roof was never securely battened down.* — VERB: usu passive; *be* V-ed adv/prep
[3] to **batten down the hatches** → see **hatch**.

**bat|ter** /bætəʳ/ **(batters, battering, battered)**
[1] If someone **is battered**, they are regularly hit and badly hurt by a member of their family or by their partner. ❑ *...evidence that the child was being battered. ...boys who witness fathers battering their mothers. ...battered wives.* — VERB: *be* V-ed; V n; V-ed
♦ **bat|ter|ing** *Leaving the relationship does not mean that the battering will stop.* — N-UNCOUNT
[2] To **batter** someone means to hit them many times, using fists or a heavy object. ❑ *He battered her around the head... He was battered unconscious.* — VERB: V n prep/adv; *be* V-ed adj
♦ **bat|tered** *Her battered body was discovered in a field.* — Also V n; ADJ
[3] If a place **is battered by** wind, rain, or storms, it is seriously damaged or affected by very bad weather. ❑ *The country has been battered by winds of between fifty and seventy miles an hour. ...a storm that's been battering the Northeast coastline.* — VERB: usu passive = pound; *be* V-ed; V n
[4] If you **batter** something, you hit it many times, using your fists or a heavy object. ❑ *They were battering the door, they were breaking in... Batter the steaks flat.* — VERB: V n; V n adj
[5] **Batter** is a mixture of flour, eggs, and milk that is used in cooking. ❑ *...pancake batter. ...fish in batter.* — N-VAR
[6] In sports such as baseball and softball, a **batter** is a person who hits the ball with a wooden bat. ❑ *...batters and pitchers.* — N-COUNT
[7] → See also **battered**, **battering**.

**bat|tered** /bætəʳd/ Something that is **battered** is old and in poor condition because it has been used a lot. ❑ *He drove up in a battered old car. ...a battered leather suitcase.* — ADJ

**bat|ter|ing** /bætərɪŋ/ **(batterings)** If something takes a **battering**, it suffers very badly as a result of a particular event or action. ❑ *Sterling took a battering yesterday as worries grew about the state of Britain's economy.* — N-COUNT = beating

**bat|ter|ing ram** **(battering rams)** also **battering-ram.** A **battering ram** is a long heavy piece of wood that is used to knock down the locked doors of buildings. ❑ *They got a battering ram to smash down the door.* — N-COUNT

**bat|tery** /bætəri/ **(batteries)** [1] **Batteries** are small devices that provide the power for electrical items such as radios and children's toys. ❑ *The shavers come complete with batteries. ...a battery-operated cassette player. ...rechargeable batteries.* — N-COUNT
[2] A car **battery** is a rectangular box containing acid that is found in a car engine. It provides the electricity needed to start the car. ❑ *...a car with a flat battery.* — N-COUNT
[3] A **battery of** equipment such as guns, lights, or computers is a large set of it kept together in one place. ❑ *They stopped beside a battery of abandoned guns. ...batteries of spotlights set up on rooftops.* — N-COUNT: usu N *of* n
[4] A **battery of** people or things is a very large number of them. ❑ *...a battery of journalists and television cameras.* — N-COUNT: N *of* n
[5] A **battery of** tests is a set of tests that is used to assess a number of different aspects of something, such as your health. ❑ *We give a battery of tests to each patient.* — N-COUNT: usu sing, usu N *of* n
[6] **Battery** farming is a system of breeding chickens and hens in which large numbers of them are kept in small cages, and used for their meat and eggs. [BRIT] ❑ *...battery hens being raised in dark, cramped conditions.* — ADJ: ADJ n
[7] → See also **assault and battery**. to **recharge** your **batteries** → see **recharge**.

**bat|tle** /bætᵊl/ **(battles, battling, battled)** ◆◆◇ [1] A **battle** is a violent fight between groups of people, especially one between military forces during a war. ❑ *...the victory of King William III at the Battle of the Boyne. ...after a gun battle between police and drug traffickers. ...men who die in battle.* — N-VAR
[2] A **battle** is a conflict in which different people or groups compete in order to achieve success or control. ❑ *...a renewed political battle over Britain's attitude to Europe. ...the eternal battle between good and evil in the world. ...a macho battle for supremacy.* — N-COUNT: usu with supp, oft N prep = struggle
[3] You can use **battle** to refer to someone's efforts to achieve something in spite of very difficult circumstances. ❑ *...the battle against crime... She has fought a constant battle with her weight... Greg lost his brave battle against cancer two years ago.* — N-COUNT: usu sing, oft N *against* n = fight
[4] To **battle with** an opposing group means to take part in a fight or contest against them. In American English, you can also say that one group or person **is battling** another. ❑ *Thousands of people battled with police and several were reportedly wounded... The sides must battle again for a quarter-final place on December 16... They're also battling the government to win compensation.* — V-RECIP: V *with/against* n; pl-n V; V n to-inf
[5] To **battle** means to try hard to do something in spite of very difficult circumstances. In British English, you **battle against** something or **with** something. In American English, you **battle** something. ❑ *Doctors battled throughout the night to save her life. ...a lone yachtsman returning from his months of battling with the elements... In Wyoming, firefighters are still battling the two blazes.* — VERB = fight: V to-inf; V *with/against* n; V n
♦ **bat|tler** **(battlers)** *If anyone can do it, he can. He's a battler and has a strong character.* — N-COUNT
[6] → See also **pitched battle**, **running battle**.

**PHRASES** [7] If one person or group **does battle with** another, they take part in a battle or contest against them. You can also say that two people or groups **do battle**. ❑ *...the notorious Montonero guerrilla group who did battle with the army during the dirty war.* — PHRASE: V inflects, PHR *with/against* n, pl-n PHR
[8] If you say that something is **half the battle**, you mean that it is the most important step towards achieving something. ❑ *Choosing the right type of paint for the job is half the battle.* — PHRASE: usu v-link PHR
[9] If you **are fighting a losing battle**, you are trying to achieve something but are not going to be successful. ❑ *The crew fought a losing battle to try to restart the engines. ...on a day when the sun is fighting a losing battle against the lowering clouds.* — PHRASE: V inflects, oft PHR *with/against* n, PHR to-inf
[10] If one group or person **battles it out with** another, they take part in a fight or contest against each other until one of them wins or a definite result is reached. You can also say that two groups or two people **battle it out**. ❑ *In the Cup Final, Leeds battled it out with the old enemy, Manchester United.* — PHRASE: V inflects, PHR *with* n, pl-n PHR
[11] If you say that someone **has lost the battle, but won the war**, you mean that although they have been defeated in a small conflict they have won a larger, more important one of which it was a part. If you say that someone **has won the battle but lost the war**, you mean that they have won the small conflict but lost the larger one. ❑ *The strikers may have won the battle, but they lost the war.* — PHRASE: Vs and *battle* inflect

**bat|tle-axe** **(battle-axes)**

> ✓ The spellings **battleaxe**, and in American English **battle-ax** are also used.

[1] If you call a middle-aged or older woman a **battle-axe**, you mean she is very difficult and unpleasant because of her fierce and determined attitude. [INFORMAL] — N-COUNT; disapproval = dragon
[2] A **battle-axe** is a large axe that was used as a weapon. — N-COUNT

**bat|tle cruis|er** **(battle cruisers)** also **battlecruiser.** A **battle cruiser** is a large fast warship that is lighter than a battleship and moves more easily. — N-COUNT

**bat|tle cry** **(battle cries)** also **battle-cry.** 1 A **battle cry** is a phrase that is used to encourage people to support a particular cause or campaign. ❑ *Their battle-cry will be: 'Sign this petition before they sign away your country.'* (N-COUNT = rallying cry) 2 A **battle cry** is a shout that soldiers give as they go into battle. (N-COUNT)

**battle|field** /bætəlfiːld/ **(battlefields)** 1 A **battlefield** is a place where a battle is fought. ❑ *...the battlefields of the Somme.* (N-COUNT = battleground) 2 You can refer to an issue or field of activity over which people disagree or compete as a **battlefield**. ❑ *...the domestic battlefield of family life.* (N-COUNT = battleground)

**battle|ground** /bætəlgraʊnd/ **(battlegrounds)** 1 A **battleground** is the same as a **battlefield**. (N-COUNT) 2 You can refer to an issue or field of activity over which people disagree or compete as a **battleground**. ❑ *...the battleground of education... Children's literature is an ideological battleground.* (N-COUNT = battlefield)

**bat|tle|ments** /bætəlmənts/ The **battlements** of a castle or fortress consist of a wall built round the top, with gaps through which guns or arrows can be fired. (N-PLURAL)

**battle|ship** /bætəlʃɪp/ **(battleships)** A **battleship** is a very large, heavily armed warship. (N-COUNT)

**bat|ty** /bæti/ **(battier, battiest)** If you say that someone is **batty**, you mean that they are rather eccentric or slightly crazy. [BRIT, INFORMAL] ❑ *Laura's going a bit batty. ...their batty uncle.* (ADJ disapproval = barmy)

**bau|ble** /bɔːbəl/ **(baubles)** A **bauble** is a small, cheap ornament or piece of jewellery. ❑ *...Christmas trees decorated with coloured baubles.* (N-COUNT = trinket)

**baulk** /bɔːlk, AM bɔːk/ ➔ see **balk**.

**baux|ite** /bɔːksaɪt/ **Bauxite** is a clay-like substance from which aluminium is obtained. (N-UNCOUNT)

**bawdy** /bɔːdi/ **(bawdier, bawdiest)** A **bawdy** story or joke contains humorous references to sex. [OLD-FASHIONED] (ADJ = lewd)

**bawl** /bɔːl/ **(bawls, bawling, bawled)** 1 If you **bawl**, you shout in a very loud voice, for example because you are angry or you want people to hear you. ❑ *When I came back to the hotel Laura and Peter were shouting and bawling at each other... Then a voice bawled: 'Lay off! I'll kill you, you little rascal!'... He tried to direct the video like a fashion show, bawling instructions to the girls.* (VERB = yell; V at n; V with quote; V n) ♦ **Bawl out** means the same as **bawl**. ❑ *Someone in the audience bawled out 'Not him again!'* (PHRASAL VERB; V P with quote; Also V P n, V n P) 2 If you say that a child **is bawling**, you are annoyed because it is crying loudly. ❑ *One of the toddlers was bawling, and the other had a runny nose. ...a bawling baby.* (VERB; V; V-ing)

**bay** /beɪ/ **(bays, baying, bayed)** ◆◇◇ 1 A **bay** is a part of a coast where the land curves inwards. ❑ *...a short ferry ride across the bay. ...the Bay of Bengal. ...the San Francisco Bay area.* (N-COUNT: oft in names) 2 A **bay** is a partly enclosed area, inside or outside a building, that is used for a particular purpose. ❑ *The animals are herded into a bay, then butchered... The car reversed into the loading bay.* (N-COUNT: oft supp N) 3 A **bay** is an area of a room which extends beyond the main walls of a house, especially an area with a large window at the front of a house. (N-COUNT) 4 A **bay** horse is reddish-brown in colour. (ADJ) 5 If a number of people **are baying for** something, they are demanding something angrily, usually that someone should be punished. ❑ *The referee ignored voices baying for a penalty. ...the baying crowd.* (VERB: usu cont = clamour; V for n; V-ing) 6 If a dog or wolf **bays**, it makes loud, long cries. ❑ *A dog suddenly howled, baying at the moon.* (VERB; V at n; Also V) 7 ➔ See also **sick bay**. 8 If you **keep** something or someone **at bay**, or **hold** them **at bay**, you prevent them from reaching, attacking, or affecting you. ❑ *Eating oranges keeps colds at bay... Prisoners armed with baseball bats used the hostages to hold police at bay.* (PHRASE: V inflects)

**bay leaf** **(bay leaves)** A **bay leaf** is a leaf of an evergreen tree that can be dried and used as a herb in cooking. (N-COUNT)

**bayo|net** /beɪənət/ **(bayonets, bayoneting, bayoneted)** 1 A **bayonet** is a long, sharp blade that can be fixed to the end of a rifle and used as a weapon. (N-COUNT) 2 To **bayonet** someone means to push a bayonet into them. ❑ *The soldiers were ordered to bayonet every man they could find.* (VERB; V n)

**bayou** /baɪuː/ **(bayous)** A **bayou** is a slow-moving, marshy area of water in the southern United States, especially Louisiana. (N-COUNT)

**bay win|dow** **(bay windows)** A **bay window** is a window that sticks out from the outside wall of a house. ➔ See picture on page 1705. (N-COUNT)

**ba|zaar** /bəzɑːʳ/ **(bazaars)** 1 In areas such as the Middle East and India, a **bazaar** is a place where there are many small shops and stalls. ❑ *Kamal was a vendor in Egypt's open-air bazaar.* (N-COUNT) 2 A **bazaar** is a sale to raise money for charity. ❑ *...a church bazaar.* (N-COUNT = fete)

**ba|zoo|ka** /bəzuːkə/ **(bazookas)** A **bazooka** is a long, tube-shaped gun that is held on the shoulder and fires rockets. (N-COUNT)

**BBC** /biː biː siː/ **The BBC** is a British organization which broadcasts programmes on radio and television. **BBC** is an abbreviation for 'British Broadcasting Corporation'. ❑ *The show was broadcast live by the BBC. ...the BBC correspondent in Tunis.* (N-PROPER: the N)

**BBQ** **BBQ** is the written abbreviation for **barbecue**.

**BC** /biː siː/ You use **BC** in dates to indicate a number of years or centuries before the year in which Jesus Christ is believed to have been born. Compare **AD**. ❑ *The brooch dates back to the fourth century BC.*

**be**
① AUXILIARY VERB USES
② OTHER VERB USES

① **be** /bi, STRONG biː/ **(am, are, is, being, was, were, been)** ◆◆◆

> In spoken English, forms of **be** are often shortened, for example 'I am' is shortened to 'I'm' and 'was not' is shortened to 'wasn't'.

1 You use **be** with a present participle to form the continuous tenses of verbs. ❑ *This is happening in every school throughout the country... She didn't always think carefully about what she was doing.* (AUX; AUX -ing; AUX -ing) **be going to** ➔ see **going**. 2 You use **be** with a past participle to form the passive voice. ❑ *Forensic experts were called in... Her husband was killed in a car crash... The cost of electricity from coal-fired stations is expected to fall... Similar action is being taken by the US government.* (AUX; AUX -ed; AUX -ed; AUX -ed; AUX -ed) 3 You use **be** with an infinitive to indicate that something is planned to happen, that it will definitely happen, or that it must happen. ❑ *The talks are to begin tomorrow... It was to be Johnson's first meeting with the board in nearly a month... You are to answer to Brian, to take your orders from him.* (AUX; AUX to-inf; AUX to-inf; AUX to-inf) **be about to** ➔ see **about**. 4 You use **be** with an infinitive to say or ask what should happen or be done in a particular situation, how it should happen, or who should do it. ❑ *What am I to do without him?... Who is to say which of them had more power?* (AUX; AUX to-inf; AUX to-inf) 5 You use **was** and **were** with an infinitive to talk about something that happened later than the time you are discussing, and was not planned or certain at that time. ❑ *Then he received a phone call that was to change his life... A few hours later he was to prove it.* (AUX; AUX to-inf; AUX to-inf) 6 You can say that something is **to be** seen, heard, or found in a particular place to mean that people can see it, hear it, or find it in that place. ❑ *Little traffic was to be seen on the streets... They are to be found all over the world.* (AUX; AUX -ed; AUX -ed)

② **be** /bi, STRONG biː/ **(am, are, is, being, was, were, been)** ◆◆◆

> In spoken English, forms of **be** are often shortened, for example 'I am' is shortened to 'I'm' and 'was not' is shortened to 'wasn't'.

1 You use **be** to introduce more information about the subject, such as its identity, nature, qualities, or position. ❑ *She's my mother... He is a very attractive man... My grandfather was a butcher... The fact that you were willing to pay in the end is all that matters... The sky was black... It is 1,267 feet high... Cheney was in Madrid... His house is next door... 'Is it safe?' — 'Well of course it is.'... He's still alive isn't he?* V-LINK; V n; V n; V n; V n; V adj, V adj; V prep, V adv; V, V
2 You use **be**, with 'it' as the subject, in clauses where you are describing something or giving your judgment of a situation. ❑ *It was too chilly for swimming... Sometimes it is necessary to say no... It is likely that investors will face losses... It's nice having friends to chat to... It's a good thing I brought lots of handkerchiefs... It's no good just having meetings... It's a good idea to avoid refined food... It's up to us to prove it.* V-LINK; it V adj; it V adj to-inf; it V adj that; it V adj -ing; it V n that; it V n -ing; it V n to-inf; it V prep to-inf
3 You use **be** with the impersonal pronoun 'there' in expressions like **there is** and **there are** to say that something exists or happens. ❑ *Clearly there is a problem here... There are very few cars on this street... There was nothing new in the letter.* V-LINK; there V n; there V n; there V n
4 You use **be** as a link between a subject and a clause and in certain other clause structures, as shown below. ❑ *It was me she didn't like, not what I represented... What the media should not do is to exploit people's natural fears... Our greatest problem is convincing them... The question was whether protection could be improved... All she knew was that I'd had a broken marriage... Local residents said it was as if there had been a nuclear explosion.* V-LINK; V n; V to-inf; V -ing; V wh; V that; V as if
5 You use **be** in expressions like **the thing is** and **the point is** to introduce a clause in which you make a statement or give your opinion. [SPOKEN] ❑ *The fact is, the players gave everything they had... The plan is good; the problem is it doesn't go far enough.* V-LINK; V cl; V cl
6 You use **be** in expressions like **to be fair**, **to be honest**, or **to be serious** to introduce an additional statement or opinion, and to indicate that you are trying to be fair, honest, or serious. ❑ *She's always noticed. But then, to be honest, Ghislaine likes being noticed... It enabled students to devote more time to their studies, or to be more accurate, more time to relaxation.* V-LINK; V adj; V adj
7 The form **'be'** is used occasionally instead of the normal forms of the present tense, especially after 'whether'. [FORMAL] ❑ *The chemical agent, whether it be mustard gas or nerve gas, can be absorbed by the skin.* V-LINK; be n
8 If something **is**, it exists. [mainly FORMAL or LITERARY] VERB
9 To **be yourself** means to behave in the way that is right and natural for you and your personality. ❑ *She'd learnt to be herself and to stand up for her convictions.* V-LINK; V pron-refl

**PHRASES** 10 If you talk about what would happen **if it wasn't for** someone or something, you mean that they are the only thing that is preventing it from happening. ❑ *I could happily move back into a flat if it wasn't for the fact that I'd miss my garden... If it hadn't been for her your father would be alive today.* PHRASE: V inflects, PHR n
11 You say **'Be that as it may'** when you want to move onto another subject or go further with the discussion, without deciding whether what has just been said is right or wrong. ❑ *'Is he still just as fat?' — 'I wouldn't know,' continued her mother, ignoring the interruption, 'and be that as it may, he has made a fortune.'* PHRASE [vagueness]

**be-** /bɪ-/ **Be-** can be added to a noun followed by an '-ed' suffix to form an adjective that indicates that a person is covered with or wearing the thing named. ❑ *...besuited men and bejewelled ladies. ...a bespectacled librarian.* PREFIX

**beach** /biːtʃ/ **(beaches, beaching, beached)** ◆◇◇
1 A **beach** is an area of sand or stones beside the sea. ❑ *...a beautiful sandy beach... I just want to lie on the beach in the sun.* N-COUNT = seashore
2 If something such as a boat **beaches**, or if it **is beached**, it is pulled or forced out of the water and onto land. ❑ *We beached the canoe, running it right up the bank... The boat beached on a mud flat.* VERB; V n; V

**beach ball (beach balls)** A **beach ball** is a large, light ball filled with air, which people play with, especially on the beach. N-COUNT

**beach bum (beach bums)** If you refer to someone as a **beach bum**, you mean that they spend a lot of time enjoying themselves on the beach or in the sea. N-COUNT

**beach|comber** /biːtʃkoʊməʳ/ **(beachcombers)** also **beach-comber.** A **beachcomber** is someone who spends their time wandering along beaches looking for things they can use. N-COUNT

**beach|front** /biːtʃfrʌnt/ A **beachfront** house, café, shop, or hotel is situated on or by a beach. ADJ: ADJ n

**beach|head** /biːtʃhed/ **(beachheads)** also **beach-head.** A **beachhead** is an area of land next to the sea or a river where an attacking force has taken control and can prepare to advance further inland. N-COUNT

**bea|con** /biːkən/ **(beacons)** 1 A **beacon** is a light or a fire, usually on a hill or tower, which acts as a signal or a warning. N-COUNT
2 If someone acts as a **beacon to** other people, they inspire or encourage them. ❑ *Our Parliament has been a beacon of hope to the peoples of Europe... General Rudnicki was a moral beacon for many exiled Poles.* N-COUNT: usu N to/of/for n

**bead** /biːd/ **(beads)** 1 **Beads** are small pieces of coloured glass, wood, or plastic with a hole through the middle. Beads are often put together on a piece of string or wire to make jewellery. ❑ *...a string of beads.* N-COUNT: usu pl
2 A **bead of** liquid or moisture is a small drop of it. ❑ *...beads of blood... He wiped away the beads of sweat on his forehead.* N-COUNT: usu N of n

**bead|ed** /biːdɪd/ 1 A **beaded** dress, cushion, or other object is decorated with beads. ADJ: usu ADJ n
2 If something is **beaded with** a liquid, it is covered in small drops of that liquid. ❑ *The man's bald head was beaded with sweat.* ADJ: v-link ADJ with n

**bead|ing** /biːdɪŋ/ 1 **Beading** is a narrow strip of wood that is used for decorating or edging furniture and doors. N-UNCOUNT
2 **Beading** is an arrangement of beads used for decorating clothes. ❑ *...a black velvet bodice with jet black beading.* N-UNCOUNT

**beady** /biːdi/ 1 **Beady** eyes are small, round, and bright. ADJ: usu ADJ n
2 If someone keeps a **beady** eye on a person or organization, they watch them carefully and suspiciously. ❑ *The chairman keeps a beady eye on things.* ADJ: ADJ n

**bea|gle** /biːgᵊl/ **(beagles)** A **beagle** is a short-haired black and brown dog with long ears and short legs. It is kept as a pet or sometimes used for hunting. N-COUNT

**beak** /biːk/ **(beaks)** A bird's **beak** is the hard curved or pointed part of its mouth. ❑ *...a black bird with a yellow beak.* N-COUNT = bill

**beak|er** /biːkəʳ/ **(beakers)** 1 A **beaker** is a plastic cup used for drinking, usually one with no handle. [BRIT] N-COUNT
2 A **beaker** is a large cup or glass. [AM] N-COUNT
3 A **beaker** is a glass or plastic jar which is used in chemistry. N-COUNT

**be-all and end-all** If something is **the be-all and end-all** to you, it is the only important thing in your life, or the only important feature of a particular activity. ❑ *For some people, competing is the be-all and end-all of their running.* PHRASE: v-link PHR, usu PHR of n

**beam** /biːm/ **(beams, beaming, beamed)** 1 If you say that someone **is beaming**, you mean that they have a big smile on their face because they are happy, pleased, or proud about something. [WRITTEN] ❑ *Frances beamed at her friend with undisguised admiration... 'Welcome back,' she beamed. ...the beaming face of a 41-year-old man on the brink of achieving his dreams.* VERB; V at/with n; V with quote; V-ing
2 A **beam** is a line of energy, radiation, or particles sent in a particular direction. ❑ *...high-energy laser beams. ...a beam of neutrons.* N-COUNT: usu n N, N of n
3 If something **beams** radio signals or television pictures or they **are beamed** somewhere, they are sent there by means of electronic equipment. ❑ *The interview was beamed live across America... The live satellite broadcast was beamed into homes across America. ...a ship which is due to begin* VERB; be V-ed prep/adv; V prep/adv; V n prep/adv

*beaming radio broadcasts to China.* 4 A **beam of** light is a line of light that shines from an object such as a lamp. *N-COUNT: usu N of n, n N* 5 If something such as the sun or a lamp **beams** down, it sends light to a place and shines on it. *VERB* ❑ *A sharp white spot-light beamed down on a small stage... All you see of the outside world is the sunlight beaming through the cracks in the roof.* *V adv/prep* *V adv/prep* 6 A **beam** is a long thick bar of wood, metal, or concrete, especially one used to support the roof of a building. *N-COUNT* ❑ *The ceilings are supported by oak beams.* 7 → See also **off-beam**.

**bean** /biːn/ **(beans)** ◆◇◇ 1 Beans such as green **beans**, French **beans**, or broad **beans** are the seeds of a climbing plant or the long thin cases which contain those seeds. *N-COUNT: usu pl, usu adj N* 2 Beans such as soya **beans** and kidney **beans** are the dried seeds of a bean plant. *N-COUNT: usu pl, usu n N* 3 Beans such as coffee **beans** or cocoa **beans** are the seeds of plants that are used to produce coffee, cocoa, and chocolate. *N-COUNT: usu pl, usu n N*
PHRASES 4 If someone is **full of beans**, they are very lively and have a lot of energy and enthusiasm. *PHRASE: v-link PHR* ❑ *Jem was full of beans after a long sleep.* 5 If you **spill the beans**, you tell someone something that people have been trying to keep secret. *PHRASE: V inflects*

**bean bag** **(bean bags)** also **beanbag.** A **bean bag** is a large round cushion filled with tiny pieces of plastic or rubber. It takes the shape of your body when you sit on it. *N-COUNT*

**bean coun|ter** **(bean counters)** also **bean-counter.** You can describe people such as accountants and business managers as **bean counters** if you disapprove of them because you think they are only interested in money. *N-COUNT* *disapproval* ❑ *...bean counters who tend to focus on controlling expenses.*

**bean curd** **Bean curd** is a soft white or brown food made from soya beans. *N-UNCOUNT = tofu*

**bean|feast** /biːnfiːst/ **(beanfeasts)** A **beanfeast** is a party or social event. [BRIT, INFORMAL] *N-COUNT*

**bean|pole** /biːnpoʊl/ **(beanpoles)** If you call someone a **beanpole**, you are criticizing them because you think that they are extremely tall and thin. [INFORMAL] *N-COUNT* *disapproval*

**bean sprout** **(bean sprouts)** also **beansprout. Bean sprouts** are small, long, thin shoots grown from beans. They are frequently used in Chinese cookery. *N-COUNT*

**bear**
① VERB USES
② NOUN USES

① **bear** /beəʳ/ **(bears, bearing, bore, borne)** ◆◆◇
⇒ Please look at category 18 to see if the expression you are looking for is shown under another headword. 1 If you **bear** something somewhere, you carry it there or take it there. [LITERARY] *VERB = carry* ❑ *They bore the oblong hardwood box into the kitchen and put it on the table.* *V n adv/prep* ♦ **-bearing** *...food-bearing lorries.* *COMB in ADJ* 2 If you **bear** something such as a weapon, you hold it or carry it with you. [FORMAL] *VERB* ❑ *...the constitutional right to bear arms.* *V n* ♦ **-bearing** *...rifle-bearing soldiers. ...hundreds of flag-bearing marchers.* *COMB in ADJ* 3 If one thing **bears** the weight of something else, it supports the weight of that thing. *VERB = support* ❑ *The ice was not thick enough to bear the weight of marching men.* *V n* ♦ **-bearing** *...the load-bearing joints of the body.* *COMB in ADJ* 4 If something **bears** a particular mark or characteristic, it has that mark or characteristic. *VERB* ❑ *The houses bear the marks of bullet holes. ...note paper bearing the Presidential seal... The room bore all the signs of a violent struggle.* *V n* *V n* *V n* 5 If you **bear** an unpleasant experience, you accept it because you are unable to do anything about it. *VERB = endure* ❑ *They will have to bear the misery of living in constant fear of war.* *V n* 6 If you can't **bear** someone or something, you dislike them very much. *VERB: with neg* ❑ *I can't bear people who make judgements and label me... He can't bear to talk about it, even to me.* *V n/-ing* *V to-inf* 7 If someone **bears** the cost of something, they pay for it. *VERB* ❑ *Patients should not have to bear the costs of their own treatment.* *V n* 8 If you **bear** the responsibility for something, you accept responsibility for it. *VERB = accept* ❑ *If a woman makes a decision to have a child alone, she should bear that responsibility alone.* *V n* 9 If one thing **bears** no resemblance or no relationship to another thing, they are not at all similar. *VERB: usu with brd-neg = have* ❑ *Their daily menus bore no resemblance whatsoever to what they were actually fed... For many software packages, the price bears little relation to cost.* *V n* *V n* 10 When a plant or tree **bears** flowers, fruit, or leaves, it produces them. *VERB = produce* ❑ *As the plants grow and start to bear fruit they will need a lot of water.* *V n* ♦ **-bearing** *...a strong, fruit-bearing apple tree.* *COMB in ADJ* 11 If something such as a bank account or an investment **bears** interest, interest is paid on it. [BUSINESS] *VERB* ❑ *The eight-year bond will bear annual interest of 10.5%.* *V n* ♦ **-bearing** *...interest-bearing current accounts.* *COMB in ADJ* 12 When a woman **bears** a child, she gives birth to him or her. [OLD-FASHIONED] *VERB* ❑ *Emma bore a son called Karl... She bore him a daughter, Suzanna.* *V n* *V n n* 13 If you **bear yourself** in a particular way, you move or behave in that way. [LITERARY] *VERB = carry* ❑ *There was elegance and simple dignity in the way he bore himself.* *V pron-refl adv/prep* 14 If you **bear** left or **bear** right when you are driving or walking along, you turn and continue in that direction. *VERB = veer* ❑ *Go left onto the A107 and bear left into Seven Sisters Road.* *V adv* 15 → See also **bore, borne**.
PHRASES 16 If you **bring** something **to bear on** a situation, you use it to deal with that situation. *PHRASE: V inflects* ❑ *British scientists have brought computer science to bear on this problem.* 17 If you **bring** pressure or influence **to bear on** someone, you use it to try and persuade them to do something. *PHRASE: V inflects* ❑ *His companions brought pressure to bear on him, urging him to stop wasting money.* 18 to **bear the brunt of** → see **brunt**. to **bear fruit** → see **fruit**. to **grin and bear it** → see **grin**. to **bear in mind** → see **mind**. to **bear witness to** → see **witness**.

♦ **bear down** 1 If someone or something **bears down on** you, they move quickly towards you in a threatening way. *PHRASAL VERB = advance* ❑ *A group of half a dozen men entered the pub and bore down on the bar.* *V P on n Also V P* 2 To **bear down on** something means to push or press downwards with steady pressure. *PHRASAL VERB* ❑ *The roof support structure had collapsed and the entire weight was bearing down on the ceiling.* *V P on n Also V P*

♦ **bear out** If someone or something **bears** a person **out** or **bears out** what that person is saying, they support what that person is saying. *PHRASAL VERB = confirm ≠ refute* ❑ *Recent studies have borne out claims that certain perfumes can bring about profound psychological changes.* *V P n (not pron) Also V n P*

♦ **bear with** If you ask someone to **bear with** you, you are asking them to be patient. *PHRASAL VERB* ❑ *If you'll bear with me, Frank, just let me try to explain.* *V P n*

② **bear** /beəʳ/ **(bears)** 1 A **bear** is a large, strong wild animal with thick fur and sharp claws. *N-COUNT* → See also **polar bear, teddy bear**. 2 On the stock market, **bears** are people who sell shares in expectation of a drop in price, in order to make a profit by buying them back again after a short time. Compare **bull**. [BUSINESS] *N-COUNT: usu pl*

**bear|able** /beərəbəl/ If something is **bearable**, you feel that you can accept it or deal with it. *ADJ: usu v-link ADJ = tolerable* ❑ *A cool breeze made the heat pleasantly bearable.*

**beard** /bɪəʳd/ **(beards)** A man's **beard** is the hair that grows on his chin and cheeks. *N-COUNT* ❑ *He's decided to grow a beard.*

**beard|ed** /bɪəʳdɪd/ A **bearded** man has a beard. *ADJ: usu ADJ n* ❑ *...a bearded 40-year-old sociology professor.*

**bear|er** /beərəʳ/ **(bearers)** 1 The **bearer of** something such as a message is the person who brings it to you. *N-COUNT: usu N of n* ❑ *I hate to be the bearer of bad news.* 2 A **bearer** of a particular thing is a person who carries it, especially in a ceremony. [FORMAL] *N-COUNT: usu n N* ❑ *...Britain's flag bearer at the Olympic Games opening ceremony.* 3 The **bearer of** something such as a document, a right, or an official position is the person who possesses it or holds it. [FORMAL] *N-COUNT: oft N of n, n N = holder* ❑ *...the traditional bourgeois notion of the citizen as a* *bearer of rights... Spanish identity documents state the bearer's profession.* 4 → See also **pallbearer**, **standard bearer**.

**bear hug** **(bear hugs)** A **bear hug** is a rather rough, tight, affectionate hug. N-COUNT

**bear|ing** /beərɪŋ/ **(bearings)** ◆◇◇ 1 If something **has a bearing on** a situation or event, it is relevant to it. PHRASE: V inflects = influence ❑ *Experts generally agree that diet has an important bearing on your general health... My father's achievements really don't have any bearing on what I do.* 2 Someone's **bearing** is the way in which they move or stand. N-SING: usu poss N [LITERARY] ❑ *She later wrote warmly of his bearing and behaviour.* 3 If you take a **bearing** with a compass, you use it to work out the direction in which a particular place lies or in which something is moving. N-COUNT = reading 4 If you **get** your **bearings** or **find** your **bearings**, you find out where you are or what you should do next. PHRASE: V inflects If you **lose** your **bearings**, you do not know where you are or what you should do next. ❑ *A sightseeing tour of the city is included to help you get your bearings.* 5 **Bearings** are small metal balls that are placed between moving parts of a machine in order to make them move smoothly and easily over each other. N-COUNT: usu pl ❑ *An oil seal was replaced, along with both front wheel bearings.* → See also **ball bearing**.

**-bearing** /-beərɪŋ/ **-bearing** combines with nouns to form adjectives which describe things that hold the specified substance inside them. COMB in ADJ ❑ *...oil-bearing rocks. ...malaria-bearing mosquitos.*

**bear|ish** /beərɪʃ/ On the stock market, if there is a **bearish** mood, prices are expected to fall. ADJ Compare **bullish**. [BUSINESS] ❑ *Dealers said investors remain bearish.*

**bear mar|ket** **(bear markets)** A **bear market** is a situation on the stock market when people are selling a lot of shares because they expect that the shares will decrease in value and that they will be able to make a profit by buying them again after a short time. N-COUNT ≠ bull market Compare **bull market**. [BUSINESS]

**bear|skin** /beəʳskɪn/ **(bearskins)** 1 A **bearskin** is a tall fur hat that is worn by some British soldiers on ceremonial occasions. N-COUNT 2 A **bearskin** is the skin and fur of a bear. N-COUNT

**beast** /biːst/ **(beasts)** You can refer to an animal as a **beast**, especially if it is a large, dangerous, or unusual one. N-COUNT [LITERARY] ❑ *...the threats our ancestors faced from wild beasts.*

**beast|ly** /biːstli/ 1 If you describe something as **beastly**, you mean that it is very unpleasant. ADJ = horrible, horrid [INFORMAL, OLD-FASHIONED] 2 If you describe someone as **beastly**, you mean that they are behaving unkindly. ADJ = horrible, horrid [INFORMAL, OLD-FASHIONED]

**beast of bur|den** **(beasts of burden)** A **beast of burden** is an animal such as an ox or a donkey that is used for carrying or pulling things. N-COUNT

**beat** /biːt/ **(beats, beating, beaten)** ◆◆◆

> The form **beat** is used in the present tense and is the past tense.

1 If you **beat** someone or something, you hit them very hard. VERB ❑ *My wife tried to stop them and they beat her...* V n *They were beaten to death with baseball bats.* V n to n 2 To **beat on**, **at**, or **against** something means to hit it hard, usually several times or continuously for a period of time. VERB = pound ❑ *There was dead silence but for a fly beating against the glass...* V against n *Nina managed to free herself and began beating at the flames with a pillow...* V at n *The rain was beating on the windowpanes.* V on n Also V n ♦ **Beat** is also a noun. N-SING ❑ *...the rhythmic beat of the surf.* ♦ **beat|ing** N-SING *...the silence broken only by the beating of the rain.* 3 When your heart or pulse **beats**, it continually makes regular rhythmic movements. VERB ❑ *I felt my heart beating faster.* V ♦ **Beat** is also a noun. N-COUNT: usu with supp ❑ *He could hear the beat of his heart... Most people's pulse rate is more than 70 beats per minute.* ♦ **beat|ing** N-SING *I could hear the beating of my heart.* 4 If you **beat** a drum or similar instrument, you hit it in order to make a sound. VERB You can also say that a drum **beats**. ❑ *When you beat the drum, you feel good.* V n *...drums beating and pipes playing.* V ♦ **Beat** is also a noun. N-SING ❑ *...the rhythmical beat of the drum.* 5 The **beat** of a piece of music is the main rhythm that it has. N-COUNT: usu sing, the N ❑ *...the thumping beat of rock music.* 6 In music, a **beat** is a unit of measurement. N-COUNT: usu pl The number of beats in a bar of a piece of music is indicated by two numbers at the beginning of the piece. ❑ *It's got four beats to a bar.* → See also **upbeat**, **downbeat**. 7 If you **beat** eggs, cream, or butter, you mix them thoroughly using a fork or beater. VERB ❑ *Beat the eggs and sugar until they start to thicken.* V n 8 When a bird or insect **beats** its wings or when its wings **beat**, its wings move up and down. VERB ❑ *Beating their wings they flew off...* V n *Its wings beat slowly.* V 9 If you **beat** someone in a competition or election, you defeat them. VERB ❑ *In yesterday's games, Switzerland beat the United States two-one...* V n *She was easily beaten into third place.* V n into n 10 If someone **beats** a record or achievement, they do better than it. VERB ❑ *He was as eager as his Captain to beat the record.* V n 11 If you **beat** something that you are fighting against, for example an organization, a problem, or a disease, you defeat it. VERB = conquer ❑ *It became clear that the Union was not going to beat the government.* V n 12 If an attack or an attempt **is beaten off** or **is beaten back**, it is stopped, often temporarily. VERB: usu passive ❑ *The rescuers were beaten back by strong winds and currents...* be V-ed adv *South Africa's ruling National Party has beaten off a right-wing challenge.* V adv n 13 If you say that one thing **beats** another, you mean that it is better than it. VERB: no cont [INFORMAL] ❑ *Being boss of a software firm beats selling insurance.* V n 14 If you say you can't **beat** a particular thing you mean that it is the best thing of its kind. VERB: no cont ❑ *You can't beat soap and water for cleansing.* V n 15 To **beat** a time limit or an event means to achieve something before that time or event. VERB ❑ *They were trying to beat the midnight deadline.* V n 16 A police officer's or journalist's **beat** is the area for which he or she is responsible. N-COUNT 17 You use **beat** in expressions such as 'It beats me' or 'What beats me is' to indicate that you cannot understand or explain something. VERB [INFORMAL, SPOKEN] ❑ *'What am I doing wrong, anyway?' — 'Beats me, Lewis.'* 18 → See also **beaten**, **beaten-up**, **beating**, **beat-up**.

**PHRASES** 19 If you intend to do something but someone **beats** you **to it**, they do it before you do. PHRASE: V inflects ❑ *Don't be too long about it or you'll find someone has beaten you to it.* 20 A police officer **on the beat** is on duty, walking around the area for which he or she is responsible. PHRASE: usu n PHR, v-link PHR ❑ *The officer on the beat picks up information; hears cries for help; makes people feel safe.* 21 If you **beat time to** a piece of music, you move your hand or foot up and down in time with the music. PHRASE: V inflects = keep time A conductor **beats time** to show the choir or orchestra how fast they should sing or play the music. ❑ *He beats time with hands and feet.* 22 to **beat** someone **black and blue** → see **black**. to **beat about the bush** → see **bush**. to **beat or knock the living daylights out of** someone → see **daylights**. to **beat the drum for** someone or something → see **drum**. to **beat** someone **at their own game** → see **game**. to **beat a retreat** → see **retreat**. to **beat, kick or knock the shit out of** someone → see **shit**.

♦ **beat down** 1 When the sun **beats down**, it is very hot and bright. PHRASAL VERB 2 When the rain **beats down**, it rains very hard. PHRASAL VERB = pour down ❑ *Even in the winter with the rain beating down, it's nice and cosy in there.* V P 3 If you **beat down** a person who is selling you something, you force them to accept a lower price for it than they wanted to get. PHRASAL VERB = knock down ❑ *A fair employer, when arranging for the pay of a carpenter, does not try to beat him down...* V n P *Beat down the seller to the price that suits you.* V P n (not pron)

♦ **beat out** 1 If you **beat out** sounds on a drum or similar instrument, you make the sounds by hitting the instrument. PHRASAL VERB = tap out ❑ *Drums and cymbals beat out a solemn rhythm.* V P n (not pron) 2 If you **beat out** a fire, you cause it to go out by hitting it, usually PHRASAL VERB with an object such as a blanket. ❑ *His brother beat out the flames with a blanket... She managed to beat the fire out.* V P n (not pron) V n P [3] If you **beat out** someone in a competition, you defeat them. [mainly AM] ❑ *Indianapolis beat out nearly 100 other cities as the site for a huge United Airlines maintenance center... If we are certain a rival will beat us out, we are wide open to jealousy.* PHRASAL VERB V P n (not pron) V n P

♦ **beat out of** If someone **beats** another person **out of** something, they get that thing by deceiving the other person or behaving dishonestly. ❑ *If he could beat his uncle out of a dollar he'd do it.* PHRASAL VERB V n P P n

♦ **beat up** [1] If someone **beats** a person **up**, they hit or kick the person many times. ❑ *Then they actually beat her up as well... The government supporters are beating up anyone they suspect of favouring the demonstrators.* PHRASAL VERB V n P V P n (not pron) [2] If you **beat yourself up** about something, you worry about it a lot or blame yourself for it. [INFORMAL] ❑ *Tell them you don't want to do it any more. Don't beat yourself up about it... I don't beat myself up. I don't deal with things I can't handle.* PHRASAL VERB V pron-refl P prep V pron-refl P ♦ **beating-up** (**beatings-up**) *There had been no violence, no beatings-up until then.* N-COUNT

♦ **beat up on** [1] If someone **beats up on** a person or **beats on** them, they hit or kick the person many times. [AM] ❑ *He beat up on my brother's kid one time.* PHRASAL VERB V P P n Also V P n [2] If someone **beats up on** another person, they threaten them or treat them unkindly. [AM, INFORMAL] ❑ *She had to beat up on every customer just to get the bills paid.* PHRASAL VERB V P P n

**beat|able** /biːtəbᵊl/ Someone who is **beatable** can be beaten. ❑ *All teams are beatable, but it's going to be very, very difficult.* ADJ: v-link ADJ

**beat|en** /biːtᵊn/ [1] **Beaten** earth has been pressed down, often by people's feet, until it is hard. ❑ *Before you is a well-worn path of beaten earth.* ◆◇◇ ADJ: ADJ n = trampled [2] A place that is **off the beaten track** is in an area where not many people live or go. ❑ *Tiny secluded beaches can be found off the beaten track.* PHRASE

**beaten-up** A **beaten-up** car or other object is old and in bad condition. ❑ *Her sandals were old and somewhat beaten-up, but very comfortable.* ADJ: ADJ n = battered

**beat|er** /biːtəʳ/ (**beaters**) [1] A **beater** is a tool or part of a machine which is used for beating things like eggs and cream. ❑ *Whisk the batter with a wire whisk or hand beater until it is smooth and light.* N-COUNT: oft n N = whisk [2] → See also **world beater**.

**bea|tif|ic** /biːətɪfɪk/ A **beatific** expression shows or expresses great happiness and calmness. [LITERARY] ❑ *...a beatific smile.* ADJ: usu ADJ n = blissful

**be|ati|fy** /biætɪfaɪ/ (**beatifies, beatifying, beatified**) When the Catholic church **beatifies** someone who is dead, it declares officially that they were a holy person, usually as the first step towards making them a saint. ❑ *In May, Pope John Paul is to beatify Gianna Beretta.* VERB V n ♦ **be|ati|fi|ca|tion** /biætɪfɪkeɪʃᵊn/ *Thousands attended the beatification of Juan Diego.* N-UNCOUNT

**beat|ing** /biːtɪŋ/ (**beatings**) [1] If someone is given a **beating**, they are hit hard many times, especially with something such as a stick. ❑ *...the savage beating of a black motorist by white police officers... The team secured pictures of prisoners showing signs of severe beatings.* ◆◇◇ N-COUNT [2] If something such as a business, a political party, or a team takes **a beating**, it is defeated by a large amount in a competition or election. ❑ *Our firm has taken a terrible beating in recent years.* N-SING: a N [3] If you say that something will **take some beating**, you mean that it is very good and it is unlikely that anything better will be done or made. [INFORMAL] ❑ *For sheer scale and grandeur, Leeds Castle in Kent takes some beating.* PHRASE: V inflects

**beat|nik** /biːtnɪk/ (**beatniks**) **Beatniks** were young people in the late 1950's who rejected traditional ways of living, dressing, and behaving. People sometimes use the word beatnik to refer to anyone who lives in an unconventional way. ❑ *...a beatnik art student.* N-COUNT

**beat-up** A **beat-up** car or other object is old and in bad condition. [INFORMAL] ❑ *...a beat-up old Fiat 131.* ADJ: ADJ n = battered

**beau** /boʊ/ (**beaux** or **beaus**) A woman's **beau** is her boyfriend or lover. [OLD-FASHIONED] N-COUNT: oft poss N = suitor

**beaut** /bjuːt/ (**beauts**) You describe someone or something as a **beaut** when you think they are very good. [mainly AM or AUSTRALIAN, INFORMAL] N-COUNT

**beau|te|ous** /bjuːtiəs/ **Beauteous** means the same as beautiful. [LITERARY] ADJ

**beau|ti|cian** /bjuːtɪʃᵊn/ (**beauticians**) A **beautician** is a person whose job is giving people beauty treatments such as doing their nails, treating their skin, and putting on their make-up. N-COUNT

**beau|ti|ful** /bjuːtɪfʊl/ [1] A **beautiful** person is very attractive to look at. ❑ *She was a very beautiful woman... To me he is the most beautiful child in the world.* ◆◆◇ ADJ ≠ ugly [2] If you describe something as **beautiful**, you mean that it is very attractive or pleasing. ❑ *New England is beautiful... It was a beautiful morning.* ADJ ♦ **beau|ti|ful|ly** /bjuːtɪfli/ *The children behaved beautifully. ...a beautifully clear, sunny day.* ADV: usu ADV after v [3] You can describe something that someone does as **beautiful** when they do it very skilfully. ❑ *That's a beautiful shot!* ♦ **beau|ti|ful|ly** *Arsenal played beautifully.* ADJ ADV: ADV after v, ADV -ed

**beau|ti|fy** /bjuːtɪfaɪ/ (**beautifies, beautifying, beautified**) If you **beautify** something, you make it look more beautiful. [FORMAL] ❑ *Claire worked to beautify the garden.* VERB = smarten V n

**beau|ty** /bjuːti/ (**beauties**) [1] **Beauty** is the state or quality of being beautiful. ❑ *...an area of outstanding natural beauty... Everyone admired her elegance and her beauty.* ◆◇◇ N-UNCOUNT [2] A **beauty** is a beautiful woman. [JOURNALISM] ❑ *She is known as a great beauty.* N-COUNT [3] You can say that something is a **beauty** when you think it is very good. [INFORMAL] ❑ *The pass was a real beauty, but the shot was poor.* N-COUNT [4] The **beauties** of something are its attractive qualities or features. [LITERARY] ❑ *He was beginning to enjoy the beauties of nature.* N-COUNT: usu pl, with supp [5] **Beauty** is used to describe people, products, and activities that are concerned with making women look beautiful. ❑ *Additional beauty treatments can be booked in advance.* ADJ: ADJ n [6] If you say that a particular feature is **the beauty of** something, you mean that this feature is what makes the thing so good. ❑ *There would be no effect on animals – that's the beauty of such water-based materials.* N-COUNT: usu the N of n = advantage

**beau|ty con|test** (**beauty contests**) A **beauty contest** is a competition in which young women are judged to decide which one is the most beautiful. N-COUNT

**beau|ty pag|eant** (**beauty pageants**) A **beauty pageant** is the same as a **beauty contest**. [AM] N-COUNT

**beau|ty par|lour** (**beauty parlours**)

☑ in AM, use **beauty parlor**

A **beauty parlour** is a place where women can go to have beauty treatments, for example to have their hair, nails or make-up done. N-COUNT = beauty salon

**beau|ty queen** (**beauty queens**) A **beauty queen** is a woman who has won a beauty contest. N-COUNT

**beau|ty sa|lon** (**beauty salons**) A **beauty salon** is the same as a **beauty parlour**. N-COUNT

**beau|ty shop** (**beauty shops**) A **beauty shop** is the same as a **beauty parlour**. [AM] N-COUNT

**beau|ty spot** (**beauty spots**) [1] A **beauty spot** is a place in the country that is popular because of its beautiful scenery. ❑ *The Valley of Vinales is a lush and fertile valley and one of Cuba's finest beauty spots.* N-COUNT [2] A **beauty spot** is a small, dark spot on the skin which is supposed to add to a woman's beauty. N-COUNT

**bea|ver** /biːvəʳ/ (**beavers, beavering, beavered**) [1] A **beaver** is a furry animal with a big flat tail and large teeth. Beavers use their teeth to cut N-COUNT wood and build dams in rivers. [2] **Beaver** is the fur of a beaver. ❑ *...a coat with a huge beaver collar.* N-UNCOUNT

♦ **beaver away** If you **are beavering away at** something, you are working very hard at it. ❑ *They had a team of architects beavering away at a scheme for the rehabilitation of District 6... They are beavering away to get everything ready for us.* PHRASAL VERB V P *at/on* n V P

**be|bop** /biːbɒp/ **Bebop** is a form of jazz music with complex harmonies and rhythms. The abbreviation **bop** is also used. N-UNCOUNT

**be|calmed** /bɪkɑːmd/ [1] If a sailing ship is **becalmed**, it is unable to move because there is no wind. ❑ *We were becalmed off Dungeness for several hours.* [2] If something such as the economy, a company, or a series of talks is **becalmed**, it is not progressing at all, although it should be. [LITERARY] ❑ *...the becalmed peace talks.* ADJ: usu v-link ADJ; ADJ = stagnant

**be|came** /bɪkeɪm/ **Became** is the past tense of **become**.

**be|cause** /bɪkɒz, AM bɪkɔːz/ [1] You use **because** when stating the reason for something. ❑ *He is called Mitch, because his name is Mitchell... Because it is an area of outstanding natural beauty, you can't build on it... 'Why didn't you tell me, Archie?' — 'Because you might have casually mentioned it to somebody else.'* [2] You use **because** when stating the explanation for a statement you have just made. ❑ *Maybe they just didn't want to ask too many questions, because they rented us a room without even asking to see our papers... The President has played a shrewd diplomatic game because from the outset he called for direct talks with the United States.* ♦♦♦ CONJ; CONJ

**PHRASES** [3] If an event or situation occurs **because of** something, that thing is the reason or cause. ❑ *Many families break up because of a lack of money... Because of the law in Ireland, we had to work out a way of getting her over to Britain.* [4] You use **just because** when you want to say that a particular situation should not necessarily make you come to a particular conclusion. [INFORMAL, SPOKEN] ❑ *Just because something has always been done a certain way does not make it right.* PREP-PHRASE; PHRASE

**beck** /bek/ If one person is **at** another's **beck and call**, they have to be constantly available and ready to do whatever is asked, and this often seems unfair or undesirable. PHRASE: v-link PHR

**beck|on** /bekən/ **(beckons, beckoning, beckoned)** [1] If you **beckon to** someone, you signal to them to come to you. ❑ *He beckoned to us... I beckoned her over... Hughes beckoned him to sit down on a sofa.* [2] If something **beckons**, it is so attractive to someone that they feel they must become involved in it. ❑ *All the attractions of the peninsula beckon... The bright lights of Hollywood beckon many.* [3] If something **beckons for** someone, it is very likely to happen to them. ❑ *The big time beckons for him... Old age beckons.* VERB V *to* n V n adv/prep V n to-inf Also V; VERB V V n Also V *to* n; VERB V *for* n V

**be|come** /bɪkʌm/ **(becomes, becoming, became)** ♦♦♦

> ✔ The form **become** is used in the present tense and is the past participle.

[1] If someone or something **becomes** a particular thing, they start to change and develop into that thing, or start to develop the characteristics mentioned. ❑ *I first became interested in Islam while I was doing my nursing training... As she reached the age of thirty she became convinced she would remain single all her life... After leaving school, he became a professional footballer.* [2] If something **becomes** someone, it makes them look attractive or it seems right for them. ❑ *Don't be crude tonight, Bernard, it doesn't become you.* [3] If you wonder **what** has **become of** someone or something, you wonder where they are and what has happened to them. ❑ *She thought constantly about her family; she might never know what had become of them.* V-LINK V adj V -ed V n; VERB: no passive, no cont = suit V n; PHRASE: V inflects

**be|com|ing** /bɪkʌmɪŋ/ [1] A piece of clothing, a colour, or a hairstyle that is **becoming** makes the person who is wearing it look attractive. [OLD-FASHIONED] ❑ *Softer fabrics are much more becoming than stiffer ones.* ♦ **be|com|ing|ly** *Her dress was of blue silk, quite light, and becomingly open at the neck.* [2] Behaviour that is **becoming** is appropriate and proper in the circumstances. ❑ *This behaviour is not any more becoming among our politicians than it is among our voters.* ADJ: usu v-link ADJ = fetching; ADV; ADJ: usu v-link ADJ = appropriate

**bed** /bed/ **(beds)** [1] A **bed** is a piece of furniture that you lie on when you sleep. ❑ *She went into her bedroom and lay down on the bed... We finally went to bed at about 4am... By the time we got back from dinner, Nona was already in bed... When she had gone Sam and Robina put the children to bed.* [2] If a place such as a hospital or a hotel has a particular number of **beds**, it is able to hold that number of patients or guests. [3] A **bed** in a garden or park is an area of ground that has been specially prepared so that plants can be grown in it. ❑ *...beds of strawberries and rhubarb.* [4] A **bed** of shellfish or plants is an area in the sea or in a lake where a particular type of shellfish or plant is found in large quantities. ❑ *The whole lake was rimmed with thick beds of reeds.* [5] The sea **bed** or a river **bed** is the ground at the bottom of the sea or of a river. ❑ *For three weeks a big operation went on to recover the wreckage from the sea bed.* [6] A **bed** of rock is a layer of rock that is found within a larger area of rock. ❑ *Between the white limestone and the greyish pink limestone is a thin bed of clay.* [7] If a recipe or a menu says that something is served on a **bed of** a food such as rice or vegetables, it means it is served on a layer of that food. ❑ *Heat the curry thoroughly and serve it on a bed of rice.* [8] → See also **-bedded, bedding.** ♦♦◇ N-COUNT: also prep N; N-COUNT; N-COUNT: usu n N, N *of* n; N-COUNT: usu with supp; N-COUNT: usu sing, usu with supp; N-COUNT: usu with supp; N-COUNT: usu sing, N *of* n

**PHRASES** [9] To **go to bed with** someone means to have sex with them. [10] If you say that someone **has made** their **bed** and must **lie in it**, you mean that since they have chosen to do a particular thing, they must now accept the unpleasant results of their action. [11] When you **make** the **bed**, you neatly arrange the sheets and covers of a bed so that it is ready to sleep in. [12] **bed of roses** → see **rose**. PHRASE: V inflects PHRASE; PHRASE: V and N inflect

**BEd** /biː ed/ **(BEds)**

> ✔ in AM, use **B.Ed.**

A **BEd** is a degree which usually takes four years to complete and which qualifies someone to teach in a school. **BEd** is an abbreviation for 'Bachelor of Education.' Compare **PGCE**. N-COUNT

**bed and break|fast** **(bed and breakfasts)** also **bed-and-breakfast.** [1] **Bed and breakfast** is a system of accommodation in a hotel or guest house, in which you pay for a room for the night and for breakfast the following morning. The abbreviation **B&B** is also used. [mainly BRIT] ❑ *Bed and breakfast costs from £30 per person per night.* [2] A **bed and breakfast** is a guest house that provides bed and breakfast accommodation. The abbreviation **B&B** is also used. [mainly BRIT] ❑ *Accommodation can be arranged at local bed and breakfasts.* N-UNCOUNT; N-COUNT

**be|daz|zled** /bɪdæzəld/ If you are **bedazzled by** someone or something, you are so amazed and impressed by them that you feel confused. ❑ *Many people are bedazzled by fame.* ADJ: oft ADJ *by* n

**bed|bug** /bedbʌg/ **(bedbugs)** A **bedbug** is a small insect with a round body and no wings which lives in dirty houses and feeds by biting people and sucking their blood when they are in bed. N-COUNT

**bed|chamber** /bedtʃeɪmbəʳ/ **(bedchambers)** also **bed-chamber.** A **bedchamber** is a **bedroom**. [FORMAL] N-COUNT

**bed|clothes** /bedkloʊðz/ **Bedclothes** are the sheets and covers which you put over yourself when you get into bed. N-PLURAL

**-bedded** /-bedɪd/ **-bedded** combines with numbers to form adjectives which indicate how many beds a room contains. **-bedded** combines with words such as 'twin' or 'double' to form ad- COMB in ADJ: usu ADJ n jectives which indicate what kind of beds a room contains. ❑ ...*a four-bedded room.* ...*twin-bedded cabins.*

**bed|ding** /bedɪŋ/ **Bedding** is sheets, blankets, and covers that are used on beds. N-UNCOUNT

**bed|ding plant** **(bedding plants)** A **bedding plant** is a plant which lasts for one year. It is put in a flower bed before it flowers, and is then removed when it has finished flowering. N-COUNT

**be|deck** /bɪdek/ **(bedecks, bedecking, bedecked)** If flags or other ornaments **bedeck** a place, a lot of them have been hung up to decorate it. [LITERARY] ❑ ...*flags bedecking the balcony.* VERB V n

**be|decked** /bɪdekt/ If a place is **bedecked with** flags or other ornaments, these things have been hung up to decorate it. [LITERARY] ❑ *The palace was bedecked with flags.* ♦ **Bedecked** is also a combining form. ❑ ...*a flower-bedecked stage.* ADJ: v-link ADJ *with/in* n, adv ADJ; COMB in ADJ

**be|dev|il** /bɪdevəl/ **(bedevils, bedevilling, bedevilled)**

☑ in AM, use **bedeviling, bedeviled**

If you **are bedevilled by** something unpleasant, it causes you a lot of problems over a period of time. [FORMAL] ❑ *His career was bedevilled by injury.* ...*a problem that has bedevilled service industries for decades.* VERB = beset; *be* V-ed; V n

**bed|fellow** /bedfeloʊ/ **(bedfellows)** You refer to two things or people as **bedfellows** when they have become associated or related in some way. ❑ *Sex and death are strange bedfellows.* N-COUNT: usu pl

**bed|head** /bedhed/ **(bedheads)** also **bedhead.** A **bedhead** is a board which is fixed to the end of a bed behind your head. [BRIT] N-COUNT

☑ in AM, use **headboard**

**bed|lam** /bedləm/ **Bedlam** means a great deal of noise and disorder. People often say 'It was bedlam' to mean 'There was bedlam'. ❑ *The crowd went absolutely mad. It was bedlam.* N-UNCOUNT = chaos

**bed lin|en** also **bed-linen.** **Bed linen** is sheets and pillowcases. ❑ ...*crisp white cotton bed linen.* N-UNCOUNT

**Bedou|in** /beduɪn/ **(Bedouins** or **Bedouin)** [1] A **Bedouin** is a member of a particular Arab tribe. [2] **Bedouin** means relating to the Bedouin people. ❑ ...*Bedouin carpets.* N-COUNT; ADJ

**bed|pan** /bedpæn/ **(bedpans)** also **bed-pan.** A **bedpan** is a shallow bowl shaped like a toilet seat, which is used instead of a toilet by people who are too ill to get out of bed. N-COUNT

**bed|post** /bedpoʊst/ **(bedposts)** also **bedpost.** A **bedpost** is one of the four vertical supports at the corners of a bed with an old-fashioned wooden or iron frame. N-COUNT

**be|drag|gled** /bɪdrægəld/ Someone or something that is **bedraggled** looks untidy because they have got wet or dirty. ❑ *He looked weary and bedraggled.* ...*a bedraggled group of journalists.* ADJ = scruffy

**bed|rid|den** /bedrɪdən/ Someone who is **bedridden** is so ill or disabled that they cannot get out of bed. ❑ *He had to spend two years bedridden with an injury.* ...*bedridden patients.* ADJ

**bed|rock** /bedrɒk/ [1] The **bedrock** of something is the principles, ideas, or facts on which it is based. ❑ *Mutual trust is the bedrock of a relationship.* ...*the bedrock principles of British democratic socialism.* [2] **Bedrock** is the solid rock in the ground which supports all the soil above it. N-SING = foundation; N-UNCOUNT

**bed|roll** /bedroʊl/ **(bedrolls)** also **bed-roll.** A **bedroll** is a rolled-up sleeping bag or other form of bedding, which you can carry with you. N-COUNT

**bed|room** /bedru:m/ **(bedrooms)** A **bedroom** is a room used for sleeping in. ➔ See picture on page 1706. ❑ ...*the spare bedroom.* ...*a two-bedroom apartment.* ◆◇◇ N-COUNT

**-bedroomed** /-bedru:md/ **-bedroomed** combines with numbers to form adjectives which indicate how many bedrooms a particular house or flat has. ❑ ...*a two-bedroomed flat.* COMB in ADJ

**bed|side** /bedsaɪd/ [1] Your **bedside** is the area beside your bed. ❑ *She put a cup of tea down on the bedside table... He drew a chair up to the bedside and sat down.* [2] If you talk about being at someone's **bedside**, you are talking about being near them when they are ill in bed. ❑ *She kept vigil at the bedside of her critically ill son.* N-SING: usu N n; N-SING: usu with poss

**bed|side man|ner** A doctor's **bedside manner** is the way in which they talk to their patients. N-SING

**bed|sit** /bedsɪt/ **(bedsits)** A **bedsit** is a room you rent which you use for both living in and sleeping in. [BRIT] ❑ *He was living alone in a dingy bedsit in London.* N-COUNT = bedsitter

**bed|sitter** /bedsɪtəʳ/ **(bedsitters)** also **bedsitter.** A **bedsitter** is the same as a **bedsit**. [BRIT] N-COUNT

**bed|sores** /bedsɔ:ʳz/ **Bedsores** are sore places on a person's skin, caused by having to lie in bed for a long time without changing position. N-PLURAL

**bed|spread** /bedspred/ **(bedspreads)** A **bedspread** is a decorative cover which is put over a bed, on top of the sheets and blankets. N-COUNT = coverlet

**bed|stead** /bedsted/ **(bedsteads)** A **bedstead** is the metal or wooden frame of an old-fashioned bed. N-COUNT

**bed|time** /bedtaɪm/ Your **bedtime** is the time when you usually go to bed. ❑ *It was eight-thirty, Trevor's bedtime.* ...*bedtime stories.* N-UNCOUNT

**bed|wet|ting** /bedwetɪŋ/ also **bedwetting.** **Bedwetting** means urinating in bed, usually by small children. N-UNCOUNT

**bee** /bi:/ **(bees)** [1] A **bee** is an insect with a yellow-and-black striped body that makes a buzzing noise as it flies. Bees make honey, and can sting. [2] If you **have a bee in** your **bonnet about** something, you are so enthusiastic or worried about it that you keep mentioning it or thinking about it. ❑ *He's got a bee in his bonnet about factory farming.* [3] A **bee** is a social event where people get together for a competition or to do something such as sew. [AM] ❑ *That year I won first prize in the spelling bee.* N-COUNT; PHRASE: V and *bee* inflect, oft PHR *about* n; N-COUNT: usu n N

**Beeb** /bi:b/ The **BBC** is sometimes called the **Beeb**. [BRIT, INFORMAL] ❑ *He joined the Beeb at 19.* N-PROPER: *the* N

**beech** /bi:tʃ/ **(beeches)** A **beech** or a **beech tree** is a tree with a smooth grey trunk. ❑ ...*the branch of a huge beech.* ♦ **Beech** is the wood of this tree. ❑ *The worktop is made of solid beech.* N-VAR; N-UNCOUNT

**beef** /bi:f/ **(beefs, beefing, beefed)** **Beef** is the meat of a cow, bull, or ox. ❑ ...*roast beef.* ...*beef stew.* ➔ See also **corned beef**. N-UNCOUNT

♦ **beef up** If you **beef up** something, you increase, strengthen, or improve it. ❑ *Both sides are still beefing up their military strength.* ...*a beefed up police presence.* PHRASAL VERB V P n (not pron) V-ed P Also V n P

**beef|bur|ger** /bi:fbɜ:ʳgəʳ/ **(beefburgers)** also **beef burger.** A **beefburger** is the same as a **hamburger**. [BRIT] ❑ ... *beefburgers and chips.* N-COUNT

**beef|cake** /bi:fkeɪk/ **(beefcakes)** Attractive men with large muscles can be referred to as **beefcake**. [INFORMAL] ❑ ...*beefcake photos.* N-VAR: oft N n = hunk

**Beef|eater** /bi:fi:tə/ **(Beefeaters)** **Beefeaters** are guards at the Tower of London. They wear a uniform made in the style of the sixteenth century. [BRIT] N-COUNT

**beef|steak** /bi:fsteɪk/ **(beefsteaks)** also **beef steak.** **Beefsteak** is **steak**. N-VAR

**beefy** /bi:fi/ **(beefier, beefiest)** Someone, especially a man, who is **beefy** has a big body and large muscles. ❑ ...*a beefy red-faced Englishman.* ADJ: usu ADJ n = brawny

**bee|hive** /bi:haɪv/ **(beehives)** A **beehive** is a structure in which bees are kept, which is designed so that the beekeeper can collect the honey that they produce. N-COUNT

**bee|keeper** /bi:ki:pəʳ/ **(beekeepers)** A **beekeeper** is a person who owns and takes care of bees. N-COUNT

**bee|keeping** /bi:ki:pɪŋ/ **Beekeeping** is the practice of owning and taking care of bees. N-UNCOUNT

**bee|line** /bi:laɪn/ also **bee-line.** If you **make a beeline for** a place, you go to it as quickly and directly as possible. [INFORMAL] ❑ *She made a beeline for the car.* PHRASE: V inflects, PHR n

**been** /bɪn, bi:n/ 1 **Been** is the past participle of **be**. 2 If you have **been** to a place, you have gone to it or visited it. ❑ *He's already been to Tunisia, and is to go on to Morocco and Mauritania... I've been there before.* VERB V prep/adv V prep/adv

**beep** /bi:p/ **(beeps, beeping, beeped)** 1 A **beep** is a short, loud sound like that made by a car horn or a telephone answering machine. N-COUNT; SOUND 2 If something such as a horn **beeps**, or you **beep** it, it makes a short, harsh sound. ❑ *A cellular telephone beeped... He beeped the horn.* VERB V V n

**beep|er** /bi:pəʳ/ **(beepers)** A **beeper** is a portable device that makes a beeping noise, usually to tell you to phone someone or to remind you to do something. ❑ *His beeper sounded and he picked up the telephone.* N-COUNT

**beer** /bɪəʳ/ **(beers) Beer** is a bitter alcoholic drink made from grain. ❑ *He sat in the kitchen drinking beer... We have quite a good range of beers.* ♦◇◇ N-MASS ♦ A glass of beer can be referred to as a **beer**. ❑ *Would you like a beer?* N-COUNT

**beer bel|ly** **(beer bellies)** If a man has a **beer belly**, he has a fat stomach because of drinking too much beer. ❑ *He was short and fat, with a large beer belly.* N-COUNT = paunch

**beer gut** **(beer guts)** also **beer-gut.** A **beer gut** is the same as a **beer belly**. N-COUNT

**beer|mat** /bɪəʳmæt/ **(beermats)** also **beer mat.** A **beermat** is a cardboard mat for resting your glass of beer on in a bar or pub. N-COUNT

**beery** /bɪəri/ If a person, especially a man, is described as **beery**, they have drunk a lot of beer. ❑ *...jolly, beery farmers. ...beery roars of applause.* ADJ: usu ADJ n

**bees|wax** /bi:zwæks/ **Beeswax** is wax that is made by bees and used especially for making candles and furniture polish. N-UNCOUNT

**beet** /bi:t/ **(beets)** 1 **Beet** is a crop with a thick round root. It is often used to feed animals, especially cows. ❑ *...fields of sweet corn and beet.* → See also **sugar beet**. N-UNCOUNT 2 **Beets** are dark red roots that are eaten as a vegetable. They are often preserved in vinegar. [AM] N-VAR: usu pl

✓ in BRIT, use **beetroot**

**bee|tle** /bi:təl/ **(beetles)** A **beetle** is an insect with a hard covering to its body. N-COUNT

**beet|root** /bi:tru:t/ **(beetroots) Beetroot** is a dark red root that is eaten as a vegetable. It is often preserved in vinegar. [BRIT] N-VAR

✓ in AM, use **beet**

**be|fall** /bɪfɔ:l/ **(befalls, befalling, befell, befallen)** If something bad or unlucky **befalls** you, it happens to you. [LITERARY] ❑ *...the disaster that befell the island of Flores.* VERB V n

**be|fit** /bɪfɪt/ **(befits, befitting, befitted)** If something **befits** a person or thing, it is suitable or appropriate for them. [FORMAL] ❑ *They offered him a post befitting his seniority and experience.* VERB = become V n

**be|fore** /bɪfɔ:ʳ/ ♦♦♦

> In addition to the uses shown below, **before** is used in the phrasal verbs 'go before' and 'lay before'.

1 If something happens **before** a particular date, time, or event, it happens earlier than that date, time, or event. ❑ *Annie was born a few weeks before Christmas... Before World War II, women were not recruited as intelligence officers... My husband rarely comes to bed before 2 or 3am.* PREP ≠ after ♦ **Before** is also a conjunction. ❑ *Stock prices climbed close to the peak they'd registered before the stock market crashed.* CONJ 2 If you do one thing **before** doing something else, you do it earlier than the other thing. ❑ *He spent his early life in Sri Lanka before moving to England... Before leaving, he went into his office to fill in the daily time sheet.* PREP: PREP -ing ≠ after ♦ **Before** is also a conjunction. ❑ *He took a cold shower and then towelled off before he put on fresh clothes.* CONJ 3 You use **before** when you are talking about time. For example, if something happened the day **before** a particular date or event, it happened during the previous day. ❑ *The war had ended only a month or so before.* ADV: n ADV ♦ **Before** is also a preposition. ❑ *It's interesting that he sent me the book twenty days before the deadline for my book.* PREP: n PREP n ♦ **Before** is also a conjunction. ❑ *Kelman had a book published in the US more than a decade before a British publisher would touch him.* CONJ 4 If you do something **before** someone else can do something, you do it when they have not yet done it. ❑ *Before Gallacher could catch up with the ball, Nadlovu had beaten him to it.* CONJ 5 If someone has done something **before**, they have done it on a previous occasion. If someone has not done something **before**, they have never done it. ❑ *I had met Professor Lown before... She had never been to Italy before.* ADV: ADV after v 6 If there is a period of time or if several things are done **before** something happens, it takes that amount of time or effort for this thing to happen. ❑ *It was some time before the door opened in response to his ring.* CONJ = until 7 If a particular situation has to happen **before** something else happens, this situation must happen or exist in order for the other thing to happen. ❑ *There was additional work to be done before all the troops would be ready.* CONJ 8 If someone is **before** something, they are in front of it. [FORMAL] ❑ *They drove through a tall iron gate and stopped before a large white villa.* PREP 9 If you tell someone that one place is a certain distance **before** another, you mean that they will come to the first place first. ❑ *The turn is about two kilometres before the roundabout.* PREP 10 If you appear or come **before** an official person or group, you go there and answer questions. ❑ *The Governor will appear before the committee next Tuesday.* PREP 11 If something happens **before** a particular person or group, it is seen by or happens while this person or this group is present. ❑ *The game followed a colourful opening ceremony before a crowd of seventy-four thousand.* PREP 12 If you have something such as a journey, a task, or a stage of your life **before** you, you must do it or live through it in the future. ❑ *Everyone in the room knew it was the single hardest task before them.* PREP: PREP pron = ahead of 13 When you want to say that one person or thing is more important than another, you can say that they come **before** the other person or thing. ❑ *Her husband, her children, and the Church came before her needs.* PREP: v PREP n 14 **before long** → see **long**.

**before|hand** /bɪfɔ:ʳhænd/ If you do something **beforehand**, you do it earlier than a particular event. ❑ *How could she tell beforehand that I was going to go out?* ADV: usu ADV after v, also ADV with cl

**be|friend** /bɪfrend/ **(befriends, befriending, befriended)** If you **befriend** someone, especially someone who is lonely or far from home, you make friends with them. ❑ *The film's about an elderly woman and a young nurse who befriends her.* VERB V n

**be|fud|dle** /bɪfʌdəl/ **(befuddles, befuddling, befuddled)** If something **befuddles** you, it confuses your mind or thoughts. ❑ *...problems that are befuddling them.* VERB = confuse V n ♦ **be|fud|dled** *...his befuddled manner. ...befuddled with drink.* ADJ

**beg** /beg/ **(begs, begging, begged)** 1 If you **beg** someone **to** do something, you ask them very anxiously or eagerly to do it. ❑ *I begged him to come back to England with me... I begged to be allowed to leave... We are not going to beg for help any more... They dropped to their knees and begged forgiveness.* VERB V n to-inf V to-inf-passive V for n V n 2 If someone who is poor **is begging**, they are asking people to give them food or money. ❑ *I was surrounded by people begging for food... There are thousands like him in Los Angeles, begging on the streets and sleeping rough... She was living alone, begging food from neighbors.* VERB: oft cont V for n V V n

**PHRASES** 3 You say 'I **beg to differ**' when you are politely emphasizing that you disagree with someone. *(PHRASE: V inflects; politeness)* 4 If you say that something **is going begging**, you mean that it is available but no one is using it or accepting it. ❑ *There is other housing going begging in town.* *(PHRASE: V inflects)* 5 If you say that something **begs** a particular **question**, you mean that it makes people want to ask that question; some people consider that this use is incorrect. ❑ *Hopewell's success begs the question: why aren't more companies doing the same?* *(PHRASE: V and N inflect)* 6 If you say that something **begs** a particular **question**, you mean that it assumes that the question has already been answered and so does not deal with it. [WRITTEN] ❑ *The research begs a number of questions.* *(PHRASE: V and N inflect)* 7 **I beg your pardon** → see **pardon**.

**be|gan** /bɪgæn/ **Began** is the past tense of **begin**.

**be|get** /bɪget/ **(begets, begetting, begot, begotten)** 1 To **beget** something means to cause it to happen or be created. [FORMAL] ❑ *Poverty begets debt.* *(VERB; V n)* 2 When a man **begets** a child, he becomes the father of that child. [OLD-FASHIONED] *(VERB = father)*

**be|get|ter** /bɪgetəʳ/ **(begetters)** The **begetter** of something has caused this thing to come into existence. [FORMAL] ❑ *Elvis Presley was the true begetter of modern youth culture.* *(N-COUNT: with poss)*

**beg|gar** /begəʳ/ **(beggars, beggaring, beggared)** 1 A **beggar** is someone who lives by asking people for money or food. *(N-COUNT)* 2 If something **beggars** a person, country, or organization, it makes them very poor. ❑ *He warned that lifting copyright restrictions could beggar the industry.* *(VERB; V n)* 3 If something **beggars belief**, it is impossible to believe it. If something **beggars description**, it is impossible to describe it. ❑ *The statistics beggar belief... His courage beggars description.* *(PHRASE: V inflects)*

**beg|ging bowl (begging bowls)** If a country or organization approaches other countries or organizations with a **begging bowl**, it asks them for money. [mainly BRIT] ❑ *He said earlier that he is not holding out a begging bowl.* *(N-COUNT)*

**beg|ging let|ter (begging letters)** A **begging letter** is a letter from a person or organization in which they ask you to send some money for a particular purpose. [mainly BRIT] ❑ *I wrote hundreds of begging letters to charities and businesses.* *(N-COUNT; disapproval)*

**be|gin** /bɪgɪn/ **(begins, beginning, began, begun)** ◆◆◆ 1 To **begin to** do something means to start doing it. ❑ *He stood up and began to move around the room... The weight loss began to look more serious... Snow began falling again.* *(VERB = start ≠ stop; V to-inf; V to-inf; V -ing)* 2 When something **begins** or when you **begin** it, it takes place from a particular time onwards. ❑ *The problems began last November... He has just begun his fourth year in hiding... The US is prepared to begin talks immediately.* *(VERB = start ≠ end; V; V n; V n)* 3 If you **begin with** something, or **begin by** doing something, this is the first thing you do. ❑ *Could I begin with a few formalities? ...a businessman who began by selling golf shirts from the boot of his car... He began his career as a sound editor.* *(VERB = start ≠ end; V with n; V by -ing; V n prep)* 4 You use **begin** to mention the first thing that someone says. ❑ *'Professor Theron,' he began, 'I'm very pleased to see you'... He didn't know how to begin.* *(VERB: no cont ≠ conclude; V with quote; V)* 5 If one thing **began as** another, it first existed in the form of the second thing. ❑ *What began as a local festival has blossomed into an international event.* *(VERB: no cont = start; V as n)* 6 If you say that a thing or place **begins** somewhere, you are talking about one of its limits or edges. ❑ *The fate line begins close to the wrist.* *(VERB: no cont ≠ end; V prep/adv)* 7 If a word **begins with** a particular letter, that is the first letter of that word. ❑ *The first word begins with an F.* *(VERB: no cont = start ≠ end; V with n)* 8 If you say that you cannot **begin to** imagine, understand, or explain something, you are emphasizing that it is almost impossible to explain, understand, or imagine. ❑ *You can't begin to imagine how much that saddens me.* *(VERB: no cont, with brd-neg; emphasis; V to-inf)*

**PHRASES** 9 You use **to begin with** when you are talking about the first stage of a situation, event, or process. ❑ *It was great to begin with but now it's difficult.* *(PHRASE: PHR with cl)* 10 You use **to begin with** to introduce the first of several things that you want to say. ❑ *'What do scientists you've spoken with think about that?' — 'Well, to begin with, they doubt it's going to work.'* *(PHRASE: PHR with cl = firstly)* 11 **to begin life** → see **life**.

**be|gin|ner** /bɪgɪnəʳ/ **(beginners)** A **beginner** is someone who has just started learning to do something and cannot do it very well yet. ❑ *The course is suitable for beginners and advanced students.* *(N-COUNT)*

**be|gin|ning** /bɪgɪnɪŋ/ **(beginnings)** ◆◇◇ 1 The **beginning of** an event or process is the first part of it. ❑ *This was also the beginning of her recording career... Think of this as a new beginning.* *(N-COUNT: usu sing = start ≠ end)* 2 The **beginnings of** something are the signs or events which form the first part of it. ❑ *The discussions were the beginnings of a dialogue with Moscow.* *(N-PLURAL: usu the N, oft N of n)* 3 **The beginning of** a period of time is the time at which it starts. ❑ *The wedding will be at the beginning of March.* *(N-SING: the N ≠ end)* 4 The **beginning of** a piece of written material is the first words or sentences of it. ❑ *...the question which was raised at the beginning of this chapter.* *(N-COUNT: usu sing, oft N of n ≠ end)* 5 If you talk about the **beginnings** of a person, company, or group, you are referring to their backgrounds or origins. ❑ *His views come from his own humble beginnings.* *(N-PLURAL: usu with supp)*

**be|gonia** /bɪgoʊniə/ **(begonias)** A **begonia** is a garden plant which has large brightly coloured leaves. *(N-COUNT)*

**be|got** /bɪgɒt/ **Begot** is the past tense of **beget**.

**be|got|ten** /bɪgɒtᵊn/ **Begotten** is the past participle of **beget**.

**be|grudge** /bɪgrʌdʒ/ **(begrudges, begrudging, begrudged)** 1 If you do not **begrudge** someone something, you do not feel angry, upset, or jealous that they have got it. ❑ *I certainly don't begrudge him the Nobel Prize.* *(VERB: usu with brd-neg; V n n)* 2 If you do not **begrudge** something such as time or money, you do not mind giving it up. ❑ *I do not begrudge the money I have lost.* *(VERB: usu with brd-neg; V n; Also V -ing)*

**be|grudg|ing|ly** /bɪgrʌdʒɪŋli/ If you do something **begrudgingly**, you do it unwillingly. ❑ *He agreed to her suggestion begrudgingly.* *(ADV: ADV with v = grudgingly)*

**be|guile** /bɪgaɪl/ **(beguiles, beguiling, beguiled)** 1 If something **beguiles** you, you are charmed and attracted by it. ❑ *I was beguiled by the romance and exotic atmosphere of the souks in Marrakech.* *(VERB; V n)* 2 If someone **beguiles** you **into** doing something, they trick you into doing it. ❑ *He used his newspapers to beguile the readers into buying shares in his company.* *(VERB; V n into -ing)*

**be|guil|ing** /bɪgaɪlɪŋ/ Something that is **beguiling** is charming and attractive. [WRITTEN] ❑ *Mombasa is a town with a beguiling Arabic flavour.* *(ADJ)* ♦ **be|guil|ing|ly** *He was beguilingly boyish and attractive.* *(ADV: ADV adj, ADV with v)*

**be|gun** /bɪgʌn/ **Begun** is the past participle of **begin**.

**be|half** /bɪhɑːf, -hæf/ ◆◇◇ 1 If you do something **on** someone's **behalf**, you do it for that person as their representative. The form **in** someone's **behalf** is also used, mainly in American English. ❑ *She made an emotional public appeal on her son's behalf... Secret Service officer Robin Thompson spoke on behalf of his colleagues.* *(PHRASE: PHR after v)* 2 If you feel, for example, embarrassed or angry **on** someone's **behalf**, you feel embarrassed or angry for them. ❑ *'What do you mean?' I asked, offended on Liddie's behalf.* *(PHRASE)*

**be|have** /bɪheɪv/ **(behaves, behaving, behaved)** ◆◇◇ 1 The way that you **behave** is the way that you do and say things, and the things that you do and say. ❑ *I couldn't believe these people were behaving in this way... He'd behaved badly.* *(VERB = act; V prep/adv; V prep/adv)* 2 If you **behave** or **behave yourself**, you act in the way that people think is correct and proper. ❑ *You have to behave... They were expected to behave themselves.* *(VERB; V; V pron-refl)* 3 In science, the way that something **behaves** is the things that it does. ❑ *Under certain* *(VERB; V prep/adv)* *conditions, electrons can behave like waves rather than particles.*

**-behaved** /-bɪheɪvd/ **-behaved** combines with adverbs such as 'well' or 'badly' to form adjectives that describe people's or animals' behaviour. ❑ *The children are well-behaved and keen to learn.* COMB in ADJ

**be|hav|iour** /bɪheɪvjəʳ/ **(behaviours)** ◆◆◇

✔ in AM, use **behavior**

1 People's or animals' **behaviour** is the way that they behave. You can refer to a typical and repeated way of behaving as a **behaviour**. ❑ *Make sure that good behaviour is rewarded. ...human sexual behaviour... These eating patterns are a learned behavior.* N-VAR: with supp = *conduct* 2 In science, the **behaviour** of something is the way that it behaves. ❑ *It will be many years before anyone can predict a hurricane's behavior with much accuracy.* N-UNCOUNT: also N in pl, with poss 3 If someone is **on** their **best behaviour**, they are trying very hard to behave well. PHRASE: v-link PHR

**be|hav|iour|al** /bɪheɪvjərəl/

✔ in AM, use **behavioral**

**Behavioural** means relating to the behaviour of a person or animal, or to the study of their behaviour. ❑ *...emotional and behavioural problems.* ADJ: ADJ n

**be|hav|iour|ism** /bɪheɪvjərɪzəm/

✔ in AM, use **behaviorism**

**Behaviourism** is the belief held by some psychologists that the only valid method of studying the psychology of people or animals is to observe how they behave. N-UNCOUNT ♦ **be|hav|iour|ist (behaviourists)** ❑ *Animal behaviourists have been studying these monkeys for decades.* N-COUNT

**be|head** /bɪhed/ **(beheads, beheading, beheaded)** If someone **is beheaded**, their head is cut off, usually because they have been found guilty of a crime. ❑ *Charles I was beheaded by the Cromwellians.* VERB: usu passive = *decapitate* be V-ed

**be|held** /bɪheld/ **Beheld** is the past tense of **behold**.

**be|he|moth** /bɪhiːmɒθ, AM -məθ/ **(behemoths)** If you refer to something as a **behemoth**, you mean that it is extremely large, and often that it is is unpleasant, inefficient, or difficult to manage. [JOURNALISM or LITERARY] ❑ *The city is a sprawling behemoth with no heart. ...his behemoth 1,047 page book.* N-COUNT disapproval = *monster*

**be|hest** /bɪhest/ **(behests)** If something is done **at** someone's **behest**, it is done because they have ordered or requested it. [FORMAL] ❑ *In 1970, at his new wife's behest, they moved to Southampton.* PHRASE: PHR after v

**behind**
① PREPOSITION AND ADVERB USES
② NOUN USE

**① be|hind** /bɪhaɪnd/ ◆◆◆

In addition to the uses shown below, **behind** is also used in a few phrasal verbs, such as 'fall behind' and 'lie behind'.

⇛ Please look at category 14 to see if the expression you are looking for is shown under another headword. 1 If something is **behind** a thing or person, it is on the other side of them from you, or nearer their back rather than their front. ❑ *I put one of the cushions behind his head... They were parked behind the truck.* PREP ♦ **Behind** is also an adverb. ❑ *Rising into the hills behind are 800 acres of parkland... She was attacked from behind.* ADV: usu n ADV, from ADV PREP 2 If you are walking or travelling **behind** someone or something, you are following them. ❑ *Keith wandered along behind him... Myra and Sam and the children were driving behind them.* PREP ♦ **Behind** is also an adverb. ❑ *The troopers followed behind, every muscle tensed for the sudden gunfire.* ADV: ADV after v 3 If someone is **behind** a desk, counter, or bar, they are on the other side of it from where you are. ❑ *The colonel was sitting behind a cheap wooden desk... He could just about see the little man behind the counter.* PREP 4 When you shut a door or gate **behind** you, you shut it after you have gone through it. ❑ *I walked out and closed the door behind me... He slammed the gate shut behind him.* PREP: PREP pron 5 The people, reason, or events **behind** a situation are the causes of it or are responsible for it. ❑ *It is still not clear who was behind the killing... He is embarrassed about the motives behind his decision.* PREP 6 If something or someone is **behind** you, they support you and help you. ❑ *He had the state's judicial power behind him.* PREP: PREP pron 7 If you refer to what is **behind** someone's outside appearance, you are referring to a characteristic which you cannot immediately see or is not obvious, but which you think is there. ❑ *What lay behind his anger was really the hurt he felt at Grace's refusal.* PREP 8 If you are **behind** someone, you are less successful than them, or have done less or advanced less. ❑ *Food production has already fallen behind the population growth.* PREP ≠ *ahead of* ♦ **Behind** is also an adverb. ❑ *The rapid development of technology means that she is now far behind, and will need retraining.* ADV: be ADV, ADV after v 9 If an experience is **behind** you, it happened in your past and will not happen again, or no longer affects you. ❑ *Maureen put the nightmare behind her.* PREP: PREP pron 10 If you have a particular achievement **behind** you, you have managed to reach this achievement, and other people consider it to be important or valuable. ❑ *He has 20 years of loyal service to Barclays Bank behind him.* PREP: have/with n PREP pron 11 If something is **behind** schedule, it is not as far advanced as people had planned. If someone is **behind** schedule, they are not progressing as quickly at something as they had planned. ❑ *The work is 22 weeks behind schedule.* PREP: oft n PREP n ≠ *ahead of* 12 If you stay **behind**, you remain in a place after other people have gone. ❑ *About 1,200 personnel will remain behind to take care of the air base.* ADV: ADV after v 13 If you leave something or someone **behind**, you do not take them with you when you go. ❑ *The rebels fled into the mountains, leaving behind their weapons and supplies.* ADV: ADV after v 14 to **do** something **behind** someone's **back** → see **back**. **behind bars** → see **bar**. **behind the scenes** → see **scene**. **behind the times** → see **time**.

**② be|hind** /bɪhaɪnd/ **(behinds)** Your **behind** is the part of your body that you sit on. N-COUNT = *bottom*

**behind-the-scenes** → see **scene**.

**be|hold** /bɪhoʊld/ **(beholds, beholding, beheld)** 1 If you **behold** someone or something, you see them. [LITERARY] ❑ *She looked into his eyes and beheld madness.* VERB V n 2 **lo and behold** → see **lo**.

**be|hold|en** /bɪhoʊldᵊn/ If you are **beholden to** someone, you are in debt to them in some way or you feel that you have a duty to them because they have helped you. ❑ *We feel really beholden to them for what they've done.* ADJ: v-link ADJ to n

**be|hold|er** /bɪhoʊldəʳ/ **(beholders)** 1 If you say that something such as beauty or art is **in the eye of the beholder**, you mean that it is a matter of personal opinion. ❑ *Beauty is in the eye of the beholder.* PHRASE: v-link PHR 2 **The beholder** of something is the person who is looking at it. [OLD-FASHIONED] N-COUNT: usu the N in sing

**be|hove** /bɪhoʊv/ **(behoves, behoved)**

✔ in AM, use **behoove**

If **it behoves** you **to** do something, it is right, necessary, or useful for you to do it. [FORMAL] ❑ *It behoves us to think of these dangers.* VERB it V n to-inf

**beige** /beɪʒ/ Something that is **beige** is pale brown in colour. ❑ *...a pair of beige shorts. ...muted shades of white and beige.* COLOUR

**be|ing** /biːɪŋ/ **(beings)** ◆◇◇ 1 **Being** is the present participle of **be**. 2 **Being** is used in non-finite clauses where you are giving the reason for something. ❑ *It being a Sunday, the old men had the day off... Of course, being young, I did not worry.* V-LINK V n V adj Also V prep 3 You can refer to any real or imaginary creature as a **being**. ❑ *...beings from outer space.* → See also **human being**. N-COUNT 4 **Being** is existence. Something that is **in being** or comes **into being** ex- N-UNCOUNT = *existence* ists. ❑ *Abraham Maslow described psychology as 'the science of being.'... The Kingdom of Italy formally came into being on 17 March 1861.* [5] You can use **being as** to introduce a reason for what you are saying. [mainly BRIT, INFORMAL, SPOKEN] ❑ *I used to go everywhere with my mother being as I was the youngest.* [6] → See also **well-being**. **other things being equal** → see **equal**. **for the time being** → see **time**. PHRASE

**be|jew|elled** /bɪdʒuːəld/

☑ in AM, use **bejeweled**

A **bejewelled** person or object is wearing a lot of jewellery or is decorated with jewels. ❑ *...bejewelled women. ...a bejewelled golden tiara.* ADJ: usu ADJ n

**be|la|bour** /bɪleɪbəʳ/ **(belabours, belabouring, belaboured)**

☑ in AM, use **belabor**

[1] If you **belabour** someone or something, you hit them hard and repeatedly. [OLD-FASHIONED] VERB = pummel
[2] If you say that someone **belabours** the point, you mean that they keep on talking about it, perhaps in an annoying or boring way. ❑ *I won't belabour the point, for this is a familiar story.* VERB = labour V n

**be|lat|ed** /bɪleɪtɪd/ A **belated** action happens later than it should have done. [FORMAL] ❑ *...the government's belated attempts to alleviate the plight of the poor. ...a belated birthday present.* ADJ
♦ **be|lat|ed|ly** *The leaders realized belatedly that the coup would be disastrous for everyone.* ADV: ADV with v

**belch** /beltʃ/ **(belches, belching, belched)** [1] If someone **belches**, they make a sudden noise in their throat because air has risen up from their stomach. ❑ *Garland covered his mouth with his hand and belched discreetly.* ♦ **Belch** is also a noun. ❑ *He drank and stifled a belch.* [2] If a machine or chimney **belches** something such as smoke or fire or if smoke or fire **belches** from it, large amounts of smoke or fire come from it. ❑ *Tired old trucks were struggling up the road below us, belching black smoke... Suddenly, clouds of steam started to belch from the engine.* ♦ **Belch out** means the same as **belch**. ❑ *The power-generation plant belched out five tonnes of ash an hour. ...the vast quantities of smoke belching out from the volcano.* VERB V N-COUNT VERB = emit V n V from/out of n PHRASAL VERB V P n (not pron) V P
♦ **belch out** → see **belch 2**.

**be|lea|guered** /bɪliːgəʳd/ [1] A **beleaguered** person, organization, or project is experiencing a lot of difficulties, opposition, or criticism. [FORMAL] ❑ *There have been seven coup attempts against the beleaguered government.* [2] A **beleaguered** place or army is surrounded by its enemies. [FORMAL] ❑ *The rebels continue their push towards the beleaguered capital.* ADJ: usu ADJ n ADJ = besieged

**bel|fry** /belfri/ **(belfries)** The **belfry** of a church is the top part of its tower, where the bells are. N-COUNT

**Bel|gian** /beldʒən/ **(Belgians)** **Belgian** means belonging or relating to Belgium or to its people. ADJ
♦ A **Belgian** is a person who comes from Belgium. N-COUNT

**be|lie** /bɪlaɪ/ **(belies, belying, belied)** [1] If one thing **belies** another, it hides the true situation and so creates a false idea or image of someone or something. ❑ *Her looks belie her 50 years.* [2] If one thing **belies** another, it proves that the other thing is not true or genuine. ❑ *The facts of the situation belie his testimony.* VERB V n VERB = disprove V n

**be|lief** /bɪliːf/ **(beliefs)** [1] **Belief** is a feeling of certainty that something exists, is true, or is good. ❑ *One billion people throughout the world are Muslims, united by belief in one god. ...a belief in personal liberty.* [2] Your religious or political **beliefs** are your views on religious or political matters. ❑ *He refuses to compete on Sundays because of his religious beliefs.* [3] If it is your **belief** that something is the case, it is your strong opinion that it is the case. ❑ *It is our belief that improvements in health care will lead to a stronger, more prosperous economy.* ◆◇◇ N-UNCOUNT: usu N in n N-PLURAL: usu supp N N-SING: usu N that

PHRASES [4] You use **beyond belief** to emphasize that something is true to a very great degree or that it happened to a very great degree. ❑ *We are devastated, shocked beyond belief.* [5] You use **contrary to popular belief** to introduce a statement that is the opposite to what is thought to be true by most ordinary people. ❑ *Contrary to popular belief, there is no evidence that what you look like makes much difference to your life.* [6] If you do one thing **in the belief that** another thing is true or will happen, you do it because you think, usually wrongly, that it is true or will happen. ❑ *Civilians had broken into the building, apparently in the belief that it contained food.* PHRASE: adj PHR, PHR after v [emphasis] PHRASE: PHR with cl PHRASE: PHR after v, PHR cl

**be|lief sys|tem** **(belief systems)** The **belief system** of a person or society is the set of beliefs that they have about what is right and wrong and what is true and false. ❑ *...the belief systems of various ethnic groups.* N-COUNT: oft with poss

**be|liev|able** /bɪliːvəbəl/ Something that is **believable** makes you think that it could be true or real. ❑ *This book is full of believable, interesting characters.* ADJ = credible ≠ unbelievable

**be|lieve** /bɪliːv/ **(believes, believing, believed)** [1] If you **believe** that something is true, you think that it is true, but you are not sure. [FORMAL] ❑ *Experts believe that the coming drought will be extensive... I believe you have something of mine... The main problem, I believe, lies elsewhere... We believe them to be hidden here in this apartment... 'You've never heard of him?' — 'I don't believe so.'* ◆◆◆ VERB = think V that V that V that V n to-inf V so/not Also V n adj
[2] If you **believe** someone or if you **believe** what they say or write, you accept that they are telling the truth. ❑ *He did not sound as if he believed her... Don't believe what you read in the papers.* VERB V n V n
[3] If you **believe in** fairies, ghosts, or miracles, you are sure that they exist or happen. If you **believe in** a god, you are sure of the existence of that god. ❑ *I don't believe in ghosts... Do you believe in magic?* VERB V in n Also V
[4] If you **believe in** a way of life or an idea, you are in favour of it because you think it is good or right. ❑ *He believed in marital fidelity.* VERB V in n
[5] If you **believe in** someone or what they are doing, you have confidence in them and think that they will be successful. ❑ *If you believe in yourself you can succeed.* VERB V in n
[6] **Believe** is used in expressions such as **I can't believe how** or **it's hard to believe that** in order to express surprise, for example because something bad has happened or something very difficult has been achieved. ❑ *Many officers I spoke to found it hard to believe what was happening.* VERB: with brd-neg [feelings] V wh Also V that

PHRASES [7] You can use **believe it or not** to emphasize that what you have just said is surprising. ❑ *That's normal, believe it or not.* [8] If you say **would you believe it**, you are emphasizing your surprise about something. ❑ *And would you believe it, he's younger than me!* [9] You can use **believe you me** to emphasize that what you are saying is true. ❑ *It's absolutely amazing, believe you me.* PHRASE: PHR with cl [emphasis] PHRASE: PHR with cl [emphasis] PHRASE: PHR with cl [emphasis]

**be|liev|er** /bɪliːvəʳ/ **(believers)** [1] If you are a great **believer in** something, you think that it is good, right, or useful. ❑ *Mum was a great believer in herbal medicines.* [2] A **believer** is someone who is sure that God exists or that their religion is true. ❑ *I made no secret of the fact that I was not a believer.* N-COUNT: N in n, usu adj N N-COUNT

**be|lit|tle** /bɪlɪtəl/ **(belittles, belittling, belittled)** If you **belittle** someone or something, you say or imply that they are unimportant or not very good. ❑ *We must not belittle her outstanding achievement.* VERB = downplay V n

**bell** /bel/ **(bells)** [1] A **bell** is a device that makes a ringing sound and is used to give a signal or to attract people's attention. ❑ *I've been ringing the door bell, there's no answer.* [2] A **bell** is a hollow metal object shaped like a cup which has a piece hanging inside it that hits the sides and makes a sound. ❑ *My brother, Neville, was born on a Sunday, when all the church bells were ringing.* ◆◇◇ N-COUNT N-COUNT

PHRASES [3] If something is **as clear as a bell**, it is very clear indeed. ❑ *There are 80 of these pictures and they're all as clear as a bell.* [4] If you say that PHRASE: usu v-link PHR PHRASE:

something **rings a bell**, you mean that it reminds you of something, but you cannot remember exactly what it is. [INFORMAL] ❑ *The description of one of the lads is definitely familiar. It rings a bell.* V inflects

**bell-bottoms**

✓ The form **bell-bottom** is used as a modifier.

**Bell-bottoms** are trousers that are very wide at the bottom of the leg, near your feet. ❑ *Flares, loons and bell-bottoms are back. ...bell-bottom trousers.* N-PLURAL: oft N n

**bell|boy** /belbɔɪ/ **(bellboys)** A **bellboy** is a man or boy who works in a hotel, carrying bags or bringing things to the guests' rooms. N-COUNT = bellhop

**belle** /bel/ **(belles)** A **belle** is a beautiful woman, especially the most beautiful woman at a party or in a group. [OLD-FASHIONED] N-COUNT = beauty

**bel|li|cose** /belɪkous, -kouz/ You use **bellicose** to refer to aggressive actions or behaviour that are likely to start an argument or a fight. [LITERARY] ❑ *He expressed alarm about the government's increasingly bellicose statements.* ADJ = belligerent

**-bellied** /-belid/ **-bellied** can be added to an adjective to describe someone or something that has a stomach of a particular kind. ❑ *The fat-bellied officer stood near the door. ...the yellow-bellied sea-snake.* → See also **pot-bellied**. COMB in ADJ

**bel|lig|er|ent** /bɪlɪdʒərənt/ A **belligerent** person is hostile and aggressive. ❑ *He was almost back to his belligerent mood of twelve months ago.* ADJ = aggressive ♦ **bel|lig|er|ent|ly** *'Why not?' he asked belligerently.* ADV ♦ **bel|lig|er|ence** *He could be accused of passion, but never belligerence.* N-UNCOUNT = aggression

**bel|low** /belou/ **(bellows, bellowing, bellowed)** 1 If someone **bellows**, they shout angrily in a loud, deep voice. ❑ *'I didn't ask to be born!' she bellowed... She prayed she wouldn't come in and find them there, bellowing at each other... He bellowed information into the mouthpiece of his portable telephone.* ♦ **Bellow** is also a noun. ❑ *I was distraught and let out a bellow of tearful rage.* 2 When a large animal such as a bull or an elephant **bellows**, it makes a loud and deep noise. ❑ *A heifer bellowed in her stall.* 3 A **bellows** is or **bellows** are a device used for blowing air into a fire in order to make it burn more fiercely. VERB; V with quote; V at n; V n prep; Also V; N-COUNT; VERB; V; N-COUNT: also *a pair of* N

**bell pep|per** **(bell peppers)** A **bell pepper** is a hollow green, red, or yellow vegetable with seeds. [mainly AM] → See picture on page 1712. N-COUNT

✓ in BRIT, usually use **pepper**

**bell ring|er** **(bell ringers)** also **bell-ringer.** A **bell ringer** is someone who rings church bells or hand bells, especially as a hobby. N-COUNT

**bell|wether** /belweðəʳ/ **(bellwethers)** If you describe something as a **bellwether**, you mean that it is an indication of the way a situation is changing. [mainly AM, JOURNALISM] ❑ *For decades the company was the bellwether of the British economy... IBM is considered the bellwether stock on Wall Street.* N-COUNT: usu sing, oft N n

**bel|ly** /beli/ **(bellies)** 1 The **belly** of a person or animal is their stomach or abdomen. In British English, this is an informal or literary use. ❑ *She laid her hands on her swollen belly... You'll eat so much your belly'll be like a barrel.* → See also **beer belly**, **pot belly**. 2 If a company **goes belly up**, it does not have enough money to pay its debts. [INFORMAL] ❑ *I really can't afford to see this company go belly up.* N-COUNT: with poss = stomach, tummy; PHRASE: V inflects = go bust

**belly|ache** /belieɪk/ **(bellyaches, bellyaching, bellyached)** also **belly-ache.** 1 **Bellyache** is a pain inside your abdomen, especially in your stomach. [INFORMAL] 2 If you say that someone **is bellyaching**, you mean they complain loudly and frequently about something and you think this is unreasonable or unjustified. [INFORMAL] ❑ *...belly-aching about recession.* N-VAR = stomach-ache; VERB: usu cont = complain; V about n; Also V

**bel|ly but|ton** **(belly buttons)** Your **belly button** is the small round thing in the centre of your stomach. [INFORMAL] N-COUNT = navel

**bel|ly danc|er** **(belly dancers)** also **belly-dancer.** A **belly dancer** is a woman who performs a Middle Eastern dance in which she moves her hips and abdomen about. N-COUNT

**bel|ly laugh** **(belly laughs)** also **belly-laugh.** A **belly laugh** is a very loud, deep laugh. ❑ *Each gag was rewarded with a generous belly-laugh.* N-COUNT

**be|long** /bɪlɒŋ, AM -lɔːŋ/ **(belongs, belonging, belonged)** ◆◇◇ 1 If something **belongs to** you, you own it. ❑ *The house had belonged to her family for three or four generations.* 2 You say that something **belongs to** a particular person when you are guessing, discovering, or explaining that it was produced by or is part of that person. ❑ *The handwriting belongs to a male.* 3 If someone **belongs to** a particular group, they are a member of that group. ❑ *I used to belong to a youth club.* 4 If something or someone **belongs in** or **to** a particular category, type, or group, they are of that category, type, or group. ❑ *The judges could not decide which category it belonged in.* 5 If something **belongs to** a particular time, it comes from that time. ❑ *The pictures belong to an era when there was a preoccupation with high society.* 6 If you say that something **belongs to** someone, you mean that person has the right to it. ❑ *...but the last word belonged to Rosanne.* 7 If you say that a time **belongs to** a particular system or way of doing something, you mean that that time is or will be characterized by it. ❑ *The future belongs to democracy.* 8 If a baby or child **belongs to** a particular adult, that adult is his or her parent or the person who is looking after him or her. ❑ *He deduced that the two children belonged to the couple.* 9 When lovers say that they **belong together**, they are expressing their closeness or commitment to each other. ❑ *I really think that we belong together... He belongs with me.* 10 If a person or thing **belongs** in a particular place or situation, that is where they should be. ❑ *You don't belong here... I'm so glad to see you back where you belong... They need to feel they belong.* ♦ **be|long|ing** *...a man utterly without a sense of belonging.* VERB: no cont; V to n; VERB: no cont; V to n; VERB: no cont; V to n; VERB: no cont; V in/to n; VERB: no cont; V to n; VERB: no cont; V to n; VERB: no cont; V to n; VERB: no cont; V to n; V-RECIP: no cont; V together; V with n; VERB: no cont; V adv/prep; V adv/prep; V; N-UNCOUNT

**be|long|ings** /bɪlɒŋɪŋz, AM -lɔːŋ-/ Your **belongings** are the things that you own, especially things that are small enough to be carried. ❑ *I collected my belongings and left.* N-PLURAL: usu poss N

**be|lov|ed** /bɪlʌvɪd/

✓ When the adjective is not followed by a noun it is pronounced /bɪlʌvd/ and is hyphenated be|loved.

1 A **beloved** person, thing, or place is one that you feel great affection for. ❑ *He lost his beloved wife last year.* 2 Your **beloved** is the person that you love. [OLD-FASHIONED] ❑ *He takes his beloved into his arms.* ADJ: usu ADJ n; N-SING: usu poss N

**be|low** /bɪlou/ 1 If something is **below** something else, it is in a lower position. ❑ *He appeared from the apartment directly below Leonard's... The path runs below a long brick wall... The sun had already sunk below the horizon.* ♦ **Below** is also an adverb. ❑ *...a view to the street below... Spread out below was a great crowd.* 2 If something is **below ground** or **below the ground**, it is in the ground. ❑ *They have designed a system which pumps up water from 70m below ground.* 3 You use **below** in a piece of writing to refer to something that is mentioned later. ❑ *Please write to me at the address below.* 4 If something is **below** a particular amount, rate, or level, it is less than that amount, rate, or level. ❑ *Night temperatures can drop below 15 degrees Celsius... Rainfall has been below average.* ♦ **Below** is also an adverb. ❑ *...temperatures at zero or below.* 5 If someone is **below** you in an organization, they are lower in rank. ❑ *Such people often experience less stress than those in the ranks immediately below them.* 6 **below par** → see **par**. ◆◆◇ PREP ≠ above; ADV: n ADV, ADV after v; PHRASE; ADV: n ADV, ADV after v; PREP ≠ above; ADV; PREP ≠ above

**be|low stairs** also **below-stairs.** People sometimes use **below stairs** to refer to the serv- ADV: n ADV, ADV after v ants in a rich household and the things that are connected with them. ❑ *...a glimpse of life below stairs at Buckingham Palace.* ♦ **Below-stairs** is also an adjective. [ADJ: usu ADJ n] ❑ *...the below-stairs world of a 1920s country house.*

**below-the-belt** → see **belt**.

**below-the-line promotion** **(below-the-line promotions)** **Below-the-line promotion** is the use of promotional methods that can be controlled by the company selling the goods or service, such as in-store offers and direct selling. Compare **above-the-line promotion**. [BUSINESS] [N-VAR] ❑ *The advertising campaign will be supported by a PR and below-the-line promotion.*

**belt** /belt/ **(belts, belting, belted)** ◆◇◇ 1 A **belt** is a strip of leather or cloth that you fasten round your waist. [N-COUNT] ❑ *He wore a belt with a large brass buckle.* → See also **safety belt**, **seat belt**. 2 A **belt** in a machine is a circular strip of rubber that is used to drive moving parts or to move objects along. [N-COUNT] ❑ *The turning disc is connected by a drive belt to an electric motor.* → See also **conveyor belt**, **fan belt**. 3 A **belt** of land or sea is a long, narrow area of it that has some special feature. [N-COUNT: with supp = strip] ❑ *Miners in Zambia's northern copper belt have gone on strike.* → See also **Bible Belt**, **commuter belt**, **green belt**. 4 If someone **belts** you, they hit you very hard. [INFORMAL] [VERB = thump] ❑ *'Is it right she belted old George in the gut?' she asked.* [V n] ♦ **Belt** is also a noun. [N-COUNT] ❑ *Father would give you a belt over the head with the scrubbing brush.* 5 If you **belt** somewhere, you move or travel there very fast. [INFORMAL] [VERB = dash] ❑ *We belted down Iveagh Parade to where the motor was.* [V prep/adv] 6 → See also **belted**.

PHRASES 7 Something that is **below the belt** is cruel and unfair. [PHRASE] ❑ *Do you think it's a bit below the belt what they're doing? ...this kind of below-the-belt discrimination.* 8 If you have to **tighten** your **belt**, you have to spend less money and manage without things because you have less money than you used to have. [PHRASE: V inflects] ❑ *Clearly, if you are spending more than your income, you'll need to tighten your belt.* 9 If you have something **under** your **belt**, you have already achieved it or done it. [PHRASE: have/with n PHR] ❑ *Clare is now a full-time author with six books, including four novels, under her belt.*

♦ **belt out** If you **belt out** a song, you sing or play it very loudly. [INFORMAL] [PHRASAL VERB] ❑ *He held a three-hour family Karaoke session in his hotel, belting out Sinatra and Beatles hits.* [V P n] [Also V n P]

**belted** /beltɪd/ If someone's jacket or coat, for example, is **belted**, it has a belt fastened round it. [ADJ] ❑ *She wore a brown suede jacket, belted at the waist.*

**belt-tightening** If you need to do some **belt-tightening**, you must spend less money and manage without things because you have less money than you used to have. [N-UNCOUNT] ❑ *This will cause further belt-tightening in the public services.*

**beltway** /beltweɪ/ **(beltways)** A **beltway** is a road that goes around a city or town, to keep traffic away from the centre. [AM] [N-COUNT]

✔ in BRIT, use **ring road**

**bemoan** /bɪmoʊn/ **(bemoans, bemoaning, bemoaned)** If you **bemoan** something, you express sorrow or dissatisfaction about it. [FORMAL] [VERB = lament] ❑ *Universities and other research establishments bemoan their lack of funds.* [V n]

**bemuse** /bɪmjuːz/ **(bemuses, bemusing, bemused)** If something **bemuses** you, it puzzles or confuses you. [VERB = bewilder] ❑ *The sheer quantity of detail would bemuse even the most clear-headed author.* [V n]

**bemused** /bɪmjuːzd/ If you are **bemused**, you are puzzled or confused. [ADJ = bewildered] ❑ *He was rather bemused by children... Mr. Sebastian was looking at the boys with a bemused expression.* ♦ **bemusedly** [ADV: ADV after v] *He was staring bemusedly at the picture of himself.*

**bemusement** /bɪmjuːzmənt/ **Bemusement** is the feeling that you have when you are puzzled or confused by something. [N-UNCOUNT] ❑ *A look of bemusement spread across their faces.*

**bench** /bentʃ/ **(benches)** 1 A **bench** is a long seat of wood or metal that two or more people can sit on. [N-COUNT] ❑ *He sat down on a park bench.* 2 A **bench** is a long, narrow table in a factory or laboratory. [N-COUNT] ❑ *...the laboratory bench.* 3 In parliament, different groups sit on different **benches**. For example, the government sits on the government **benches**. [BRIT] [N-PLURAL] ❑ *...the opposition benches.* → See also **backbench**, **backbencher**, **backbenches**, **front bench**. 4 In a court of law, **the bench** is the judge or magistrates. [N-SING-COLL: the N] ❑ *The chairman of the bench adjourned the case until October 27.*

**benchmark** /bentʃmɑːʳk/ **(benchmarks)** also **bench mark**. A **benchmark** is something whose quality or quantity is known and which can therefore be used as a standard with which other things can be compared. [N-COUNT: usu sing, oft N *for* n = yardstick] ❑ *The truck industry is a benchmark for the economy.*

**benchmarking** /bentʃmɑːʳkɪŋ/ In business, **benchmarking** is a process in which a company compares its products and methods with those of the most successful companies in its field, in order to try to improve its own performance. [BUSINESS] [N-UNCOUNT]

**bend** /bend/ **(bends, bending, bent)** ◆◇◇ 1 When you **bend**, you move the top part of your body downwards and forwards. Plants and trees also **bend**. [VERB] ❑ *I bent over and kissed her cheek... She bent and picked up a plastic bucket... She was bent over the sink washing the dishes.* [V adv/prep] [V] [V-ed] 2 When you **bend** your head, you move your head forwards and downwards. [VERB] ❑ *Rick appeared, bending his head a little to clear the top of the door.* [V n] 3 When you **bend** a part of your body such as your arm or leg, or when it **bends**, you change its position so that it is no longer straight. [VERB] ❑ *These cruel devices are designed to stop prisoners bending their legs... As you walk faster, you will find the arms bend naturally.* [V n] [V] ♦ **bent** [ADJ] *Keep your knees slightly bent.* 4 If you **bend** something that is flat or straight, you use force to make it curved or to put an angle in it. [VERB ≠ straighten] ❑ *Bend the bar into a horseshoe... She'd cut a jagged hole in the tin, bending a knife in the process.* [V n prep] [V n] ♦ **bent** [ADJ] *...a length of bent wire.* 5 When a road, beam of light, or other long thin thing **bends**, or when something **bends** it, it changes direction to form a curve or angle. [VERB] ❑ *The road bent slightly to the right... Glass bends light of different colours by different amounts.* [V] [V n] 6 A **bend** in a road, pipe, or other long thin object is a curve or angle in it. [N-COUNT] ❑ *The crash occurred on a sharp bend.* 7 If someone **bends to** your wishes, they believe or do something different, usually when they do not want to. [VERB] ❑ *Congress has to bend to his will... Do you think she's likely to bend on her attitude to Europe?* [V *to* n] [V] 8 If you **bend** rules or laws, you interpret them in a way that allows you to do something they would not normally allow you to do. [VERB] ❑ *A minority of officers were prepared to bend the rules.* [V n] 9 If you **bend** the truth or **bend** the facts, you say something that is not exactly true. [VERB] ❑ *Sometimes we bend the truth a little in order to spare them the pain of the real facts.* [V n] 10 → See also **bent**, **hairpin bend**.

PHRASES 11 If you say that someone **is bending over backwards to** be helpful or kind, you are emphasizing that they are trying very hard to be helpful or kind. [PHRASE: V inflects, usu PHR to-inf] [emphasis] ❑ *People are bending over backwards to please customers.* 12 If you say that someone or something **drives you round the bend**, you mean that you dislike them and they annoy or upset you very much. [BRIT, INFORMAL] [PHRASE: V inflects] [feelings] ❑ *And can you make that tea before your fidgeting drives me completely round the bend.*

**bended** /bendɪd/ If you ask someone for something **on bended knee**, you ask them very seriously for it. [FORMAL] [PHRASE: usu PHR after v] ❑ *We beg the Government on bended knees not to cut this budget.*

**bend|er** /bendəʳ/ **(benders)** If someone goes **on** a **bender**, they drink a very large amount of alcohol. [INFORMAL] N-COUNT: usu sing, usu *on* N

**bendy** /bendi/ **(bendier, bendiest)** A **bendy** object bends easily into a curved or angled shape. ❑ *...a bendy toy whose limbs bend in every direction.* ADJ: usu ADJ n = flexible

**be|neath** /bɪniːθ/ ◆◇◇ 1 Something that is **beneath** another thing is under the other thing. ❑ *She could see his muscles beneath his T-shirt... She found pleasure in sitting beneath the trees. ...the frozen grass crunching beneath his feet.* ♦ **Beneath** is also an adverb. ❑ *On a shelf beneath he spotted a photo album.* PREP = under ≠ above ADV: n ADV, ADV after v = below 2 If you talk about what is **beneath** the surface of something, you are talking about the aspects of it which are hidden or not obvious. ❑ *...emotional strains beneath the surface... Beneath the festive mood there is an underlying apprehension.* PREP = under 3 If you say that someone or something is **beneath** you, you feel that they are not good enough for you or not suitable for you. ❑ *They decided she was marrying beneath her... Many find themselves having to take jobs far beneath them.* PREP

**Ben|edic|tine** /benɪdɪktin, -tiːn/ **(Benedictines)** A **Benedictine** is a monk or nun who is a member of a Christian religious community that follows the rule of St. Benedict. ❑ *...the famous Benedictine abbey of St Mary.* N-COUNT: oft N n

**ben|edic|tion** /benɪdɪkʃᵊn/ **(benedictions)** 1 A **benediction** is a kind of Christian prayer. [FORMAL] ❑ *The minister pronounced the benediction... The Pope's hands were raised in benediction.* N-VAR = blessing 2 You can refer to something that makes people feel protected and at peace as a **benediction**. ❑ *She could only raise her hand in a gesture of benediction.* N-VAR

**ben|efac|tor** /benɪfæktəʳ/ **(benefactors)** A **benefactor** is a person who helps a person or organization by giving them money. ❑ *In his old age he became a benefactor of the arts.* N-COUNT: oft N *of* n = patron, sponsor

**be|nefi|cent** /bɪnefɪsᵊnt/ A **beneficent** person or thing helps people or results in something good. [FORMAL] ❑ *...optimism about the beneficent effects of new technology.* ADJ: usu ADJ n

**ben|efi|cial** /benɪfɪʃᵊl/ Something that is **beneficial** helps people or improves their lives. ❑ *...vitamins which are beneficial to our health... Using computers has a beneficial effect on children's learning.* ADJ: oft ADJ *to* n

**bene|fi|ciary** /benɪfɪʃəri, AM -ʃieri/ **(beneficiaries)** 1 Someone who is a **beneficiary of** something is helped by it. ❑ *The main beneficiaries of pension equality so far have been men.* N-COUNT: oft N *of* n = recipient 2 The **beneficiaries** of a will are legally entitled to receive money or property from someone when that person dies. N-COUNT

**ben|efit** /benɪfɪt/ ◆◆◇ **(benefits, benefiting** or **benefitting, benefited** or **benefitted)** 1 The **benefit of** something is the help that you get from it or the advantage that results from it. ❑ *Each family farms individually and reaps the benefit of its labor... I'm a great believer in the benefits of this form of therapy... For maximum benefit, use your treatment every day.* N-VAR: oft N *of* n = profit, advantage 2 If something is **to** your **benefit** or is **of benefit to** you, it helps you or improves your life. ❑ *This could now work to Albania's benefit... I hope what I have written will be of benefit to someone else who may feel the same way.* N-UNCOUNT: oft with poss, *of* N *to* n = advantage 3 If you **benefit from** something or if it **benefits** you, it helps you or improves your life. ❑ *Both sides have benefited from the talks. ...a variety of government programs benefiting children.* VERB = profit V *from* n V n Also V 4 If you have the **benefit of** some information, knowledge, or equipment, you are able to use it so that you can achieve something. ❑ *Steve didn't have the benefit of a formal college education.* N-UNCOUNT: N *of* n = advantage 5 **Benefit** is money that is given by the government to people who are poor, ill, or unemployed. ❑ *...the removal of benefit from school-leavers.* N-VAR: oft *on* N 6 A **benefit**, or a **benefit** concert or dinner, is an event that is held in order to raise money for a particular charity or person. ❑ *I am organising a benefit gig in Bristol to raise these funds.* N-COUNT: oft N n 7 → See also **fringe benefit, unemployment benefit**.

PHRASES 8 If you give someone **the benefit of the doubt**, you treat them as if they are telling the truth or as if they have behaved properly, even though you are not sure that this is the case. ❑ *At first I gave him the benefit of the doubt.* PHRASE: usu PHR after v 9 If you say that someone is doing something **for the benefit of** a particular person, you mean that they are doing it for that person. ❑ *You need people working for the benefit of the community.* PHRASE: PHR after v

**Bene|lux** /benɪlʌks/ The **Benelux** countries are Belgium, the Netherlands, and Luxembourg. ADJ: ADJ n

**be|nevo|lent** /bɪnevələnt/ 1 If you describe a person in authority as **benevolent**, you mean that they are kind and fair. ❑ *The company has proved to be a most benevolent employer.* ADJ ♦ **be|nevo|lent|ly** *Thorne nodded his understanding, smiling benevolently.* ADV: ADV with v ♦ **be|nevo|lence** *A bit of benevolence from people in power is not what we need.* N-UNCOUNT 2 **Benevolent** is used in the names of some organizations that give money and help to people who need it. [BRIT] ❑ *...the Army Benevolent Fund.* ADJ: ADJ n

**Ben|ga|li** /beŋgɔːli/ **(Bengalis)** 1 **Bengali** means belonging or relating to Bengal, or to its people or language. ❑ *She married a Bengali doctor.* ADJ ♦ A **Bengali** is a person who comes from Bangladesh or West Bengal. N-COUNT 2 **Bengali** is the language that is spoken by people who live in Bangladesh and by many people in West Bengal. N-UNCOUNT

**be|night|ed** /bɪnaɪtɪd/ If you describe people or the place where they live as **benighted**, you think they are unfortunate or do not know anything. [LITERARY] ❑ *Famine hit that benighted country once more.* ADJ: ADJ n disapproval

**be|nign** /bɪnaɪn/ 1 You use **benign** to describe someone who is kind, gentle, and harmless. ❑ *They are normally a more benign audience.* ADJ: usu ADJ n = charitable ♦ **be|nign|ly** *I just smiled benignly and stood back.* ADV 2 A **benign** substance or process does not have any harmful effects. ❑ *We're taking relatively benign medicines and we're turning them into poisons.* ADJ: usu ADJ n 3 A **benign** tumour will not cause death or serious harm. [MEDICAL] ❑ *It wasn't cancer, only a benign tumour.* ADJ: usu ADJ n ≠ malignant 4 **Benign** conditions are pleasant or make it easy for something to happen. ❑ *They enjoyed an especially benign climate.* ADJ: usu ADJ n

**bent** /bent/ 1 **Bent** is the past tense and past participle of **bend**. 2 If an object is **bent**, it is damaged and no longer has its correct shape. ❑ *The trees were all bent and twisted from the wind.* ADJ 3 If a person is **bent**, their body has become curved because of old age or disease. [WRITTEN] ❑ *...a bent, frail, old man.* ADJ 4 If someone is **bent on** doing something, especially something harmful, they are determined to do it. ❑ *He's bent on suicide.* ADJ: v-link ADJ *on/upon* n/-ing disapproval 5 If you have a **bent for** something, you have a natural ability to do it or a natural interest in it. ❑ *His bent for natural history directed him towards his first job.* N-SING: with supp, oft N *for* n = flair 6 If someone is **of** a particular **bent**, they hold a particular set of beliefs. ❑ *...economists of a socialist bent.* N-SING: adj N = persuasion 7 If you say that someone in a position of responsibility is **bent**, you mean that they are dishonest or do illegal things. [BRIT, INFORMAL] ❑ *...this bent accountant.* ADJ 8 If someone is **bent double**, the top part of their body is leaning forward towards their legs, usually because they are in great pain or because they are laughing a lot. In American English, you can also say that someone is **bent over double**. ❑ *He left the courtroom on the first day bent double with stomach pain.* PHRASE: oft PHR *with/in* n

**ben|zene** /benziːn/ **Benzene** is a clear, colourless liquid which is used to make plastics. N-UNCOUNT

**be|queath** /bɪkwiːð/ **(bequeaths, bequeathing, bequeathed)** 1 If you **bequeath** your money or property **to** someone, you legally state that they should have it when you die. [FORMAL] ❑ *He bequeathed all his silver to his children.* VERB = leave V n *to* n 2 If you **bequeath** an idea or system, you leave it for other people to use or develop. [FORMAL] ❑ *He bequeaths* VERB V n n *his successor an economy that is doing quite well... It is true that colonialism did not bequeath much to Africa.* V n to n Also V n

**be|quest** /bɪkwest/ **(bequests)** A **bequest** is money or property which you legally leave to someone when you die. ❑ *The church here was left a bequest to hire doctors who would work amongst the poor.* N-COUNT

**be|rate** /bɪreɪt/ **(berates, berating, berated)** If you **berate** someone, you speak to them angrily about something they have done wrong. [FORMAL] ❑ *Marion berated Joe for the noise he made.* VERB = chide, rebuke V n for n Also V n

**Ber|ber** /bɜːʳbəʳ/ **(Berbers) Berber** means belonging or relating to a particular Muslim people in North Africa, or to their language or customs. ADJ ♦ A **Berber** is a person from the Berber community. N-COUNT

**be|reaved** /bɪriːvd/ A **bereaved** person is one who has a relative or close friend who has recently died. ❑ *Mr Dinkins visited the bereaved family to offer comfort.* ADJ: usu ADJ n ♦ **The bereaved** are people who are bereaved. ❑ *He wanted to show his sympathy for the bereaved.* N-PLURAL: the N

**be|reave|ment** /bɪriːvmənt/ **(bereavements) Bereavement** is the sorrow you feel or the state you are in when a relative or close friend dies. ❑ *...those who have suffered a bereavement.* N-VAR = loss

**be|reft** /bɪreft/ If a person or thing is **bereft of** something, they no longer have it. [FORMAL] ❑ *The place seemed to be utterly bereft of human life.* ADJ: usu v-link ADJ, usu ADJ of n = devoid

**be|ret** /bereɪ, AM bəreɪ/ **(berets)** A **beret** is a circular, flat hat that is made of soft material and has no brim. N-COUNT

**berk** /bɜːʳk/ **(berks)** If you call someone a **berk**, you think they are stupid or irritating. [BRIT, INFORMAL, OFFENSIVE] N-COUNT disapproval

**ber|ry** /beri/ **(berries) Berries** are small, round fruit that grow on a bush or a tree. Some berries are edible, for example blackberries and raspberries. N-COUNT

**ber|serk** /bəʳzɜːʳk, -sɜːʳk/ 1 **Berserk** means crazy and out of control. ❑ *He tossed back his head in a howl of berserk laughter.* ADJ = mad 2 If someone or something **goes berserk**, they lose control of themselves and become very angry or violent. ❑ *When I saw him I went berserk.* PHRASE: V inflects = go mad

**berth** /bɜːʳθ/ **(berths, berthing, berthed)** 1 If you **give** someone or something **a wide berth**, you avoid them because you think they are unpleasant, or dangerous, or simply because you do not like them. ❑ *She gives showbiz parties a wide berth.* PHRASE: V inflects 2 A **berth** is a bed on a boat, train, or caravan. ❑ *Goldring booked a berth on the first boat he could.* N-COUNT 3 A **berth** is a space in a harbour where a ship stays for a period of time. N-COUNT = mooring 4 When a ship **berths**, it sails into harbour and stops at the quay. ❑ *As the ship berthed in New York, McClintock was with the first immigration officers aboard.* VERB V ♦ **berthed** *There the Gripsholm was berthed next to another ship.* ADJ: usu v-link ADJ, usu ADJ prep

**be|seech** /bɪsiːtʃ/ **(beseeches, beseeching, beseeched)** If you **beseech** someone **to** do something, you ask them very eagerly and anxiously. [LITERARY] ❑ *She beseeched him to cut his drinking and his smoking... 'Please stay and read to me, mummy' he beseeched.* VERB = beg V n to-inf V with quote Also V n, V n for n

**be|seech|ing** /bɪsiːtʃɪŋ/ A **beseeching** expression, gesture, or tone of voice suggests that the person who has or makes it very much wants someone to do something. [WRITTEN] ❑ *She looked up at him with beseeching eyes.* ADJ = imploring ♦ **be|seech|ing|ly** *Hugh looked at his father beseechingly.* ADV: ADV after v

**be|set** /bɪset/ **(besets, besetting)**

> ✔ The form **beset** is used in the present tense and is the past tense and past participle.

If someone or something **is beset by** problems or fears, they have many problems or fears which affect them severely. ❑ *The country is beset by severe economic problems. ...the problems now besetting the country.* VERB be V-ed by/with n V n

**be|side** /bɪsaɪd/ ◆◇◇ 1 Something that is **beside** something else is at the side of it or next to it. ❑ *On the table beside an empty plate was a pile of books... I moved from behind my desk to sit beside her.* PREP → See also **besides**. 2 If you are **beside yourself with** anger or excitement, you are extremely angry or excited. ❑ *Cathy was beside herself with excitement.* PHRASE: v-link PHR, oft PHR with n **beside the point** → see **point**.

**be|sides** /bɪsaɪdz/ ◆◇◇ 1 **Besides** something or **beside** something means in addition to it. ❑ *I think she has many good qualities besides being very beautiful... There was only one person besides Ford who knew Julia Jameson.* PREP: oft PREP -ing ♦ **Besides** is also an adverb. ❑ *You get to sample lots of baked things and take home masses of cookies besides.* ADV: cl ADV 2 **Besides** is used to emphasize an additional point that you are making, especially one that you consider to be important. ❑ *The house was too expensive and too big. Besides, I'd grown fond of our little rented house.* ADV: ADV with cl, not last in cl

**be|siege** /bɪsiːdʒ/ **(besieges, besieging, besieged)** 1 If you **are besieged by** people, many people want something from you and continually bother you. ❑ *She was besieged by the press and the public.* VERB: usu passive be V-ed 2 If soldiers **besiege** a place, they surround it and wait for the people in it to stop fighting or resisting. ❑ *The main part of the army moved to Sevastopol to besiege the town... The Afghan air force was using helicopters to supply the besieged town.* VERB V n V-ed

**be|smirch** /bɪsmɜːʳtʃ/ **(besmirches, besmirching, besmirched)** If you **besmirch** someone or their reputation, you say that they are a bad person or that they have done something wrong, usually when this is not true. [LITERARY] ❑ *He has accused local people of trying to besmirch his reputation.* VERB = sully V n

**be|sot|ted** /bɪsɒtɪd/ If you are **besotted with** someone or something, you like them so much that you seem foolish or silly. ❑ *He became so besotted with her that even his children were forgotten.* ADJ: usu v-link ADJ, oft ADJ with n = infatuated

**be|speak** /bɪspiːk/ **(bespeaks, bespeaking, bespoke, bespoken)** If someone's action or behaviour **bespeaks** a particular quality, feeling, or experience, it shows that quality, feeling, or experience. [LITERARY, OLD-FASHIONED] VERB = indicate

**be|spec|ta|cled** /bɪspektəkəld/ Someone who is **bespectacled** is wearing glasses. [WRITTEN] ❑ *Mr Merrick was a slim, quiet, bespectacled man.* ADJ: usu ADJ n

**be|spoke** /bɪspoʊk/ 1 A **bespoke** craftsman such as a tailor makes and sells things that are specially made for the customer who ordered them. [BRIT, FORMAL] ❑ *...suits made by a bespoke tailor.* ADJ: ADJ n 2 **Bespoke** things such as clothes have been specially made for the customer who ordered them. [BRIT, FORMAL] ❑ *In the basement fifteen employees are busy making bespoke coats.* ADJ: ADJ n

**best** /best/ ◆◆◆ 1 **Best** is the superlative of **good**. ❑ *If you want further information the best thing to do is have a word with the driver as you get on the bus... It's not the best place to live if you wish to develop your knowledge and love of mountains.* 2 **Best** is the superlative of **well**. ❑ *James Fox is best known as the author of White Mischief.* 3 **The best** is used to refer to things of the highest quality or standard. ❑ *We offer only the best to our clients... He'll have the best of care.* N-SING: the N ≠ worst 4 Someone's **best** is the greatest effort or highest achievement or standard that they are capable of. ❑ *Miss Blockey was at her best when she played the piano... One needs to be a first-class driver to get the best out of that sort of machinery.* N-SING: oft poss N 5 If you say that something is **the best** that can be done or hoped for, you think it is the most pleasant, successful, or useful thing that can be done or hoped for. ❑ *A draw seems the best they can hope for... The best we can do is try to stay cool and muddle through.* N-SING: the N 6 If you like something **best** or like it **the best**, you prefer it. ❑ *The thing I liked best about the show was the music... Mother liked it best when Daniel got money... What was the role you loved the best?* ADV: ADV after v, oft the ADV = most 7 **Best** is used to form the superlative of compound adjectives beginning with 'good' and 'well'. For example, the superlative of 'well-known' is 'best-known'. [8] → See also **second best**, **Sunday best**.

**PHRASES** [9] You can say '**All the best**' when you are saying goodbye to someone, or at the end of a letter. ❑ *Wish him all the best, and tell him we miss him.* CONVENTION [formulae] [10] You use **best of all** to indicate that what you are about to mention is the thing that you prefer or that has most advantages out of all the things you have mentioned. ❑ *It was comfortable and cheap: best of all, most of the rent was being paid by two American friends.* PHRASE: PHR with cl/group [11] If someone does something **as best** they **can**, they do it as well as they can, although it is very difficult. ❑ *The older people were left to carry on as best they could.* PHRASE: V inflects, PHR after v [12] You use **at best** to indicate that even if you describe something as favourably as possible or if it performs as well as it possibly can, it is still not very good. ❑ *This policy, they say, is at best confused and at worst non-existent.* PHRASE: PHR with cl/group [13] If you **do** your **best** or **try** your **best to** do something, you try as hard as you can to do it, or do it as well as you can. ❑ *I'll do my best to find out... It wasn't her fault, she was trying her best to help.* PHRASE: V inflects, oft PHR to-inf [14] If you say that something is **for the best**, you mean it is the most desirable or helpful thing that could have happened or could be done, considering all the circumstances. ❑ *Whatever the circumstances, parents are supposed to know what to do for the best.* PHRASE: PHR after v, v-link PHR [15] If two people are **the best of friends**, they are close friends, especially when they have had a disagreement or fight in the past. ❑ *Magda is now married to George Callerby and we are the best of friends.* PHRASE: usu v-link PHR [16] If you say that a particular person **knows best**, you mean that they have a lot of experience and should therefore be trusted to make decisions for other people. ❑ *He was convinced that doctors and dentists knew best.* PHRASE: V inflects [17] If you **make the best of** something, you accept an unsatisfactory situation cheerfully and try to manage as well as you can. In British English, you can also say that you **make the best of a bad job**. ❑ *She instilled in the children the virtues of good hard work, and making the best of what you have.* PHRASE: V inflects [18] **to the best of** your **ability** → see **ability**. **to hope for the best** → see **hope**. **to the best of** your **knowledge** → see **knowledge**. **best of luck** → see **luck**. **the best part** → see **part**. **at the best of times** → see **time**. **the best of both worlds** → see **world**.

**bes|tial** /bestiəl, AM -stʃəl/ If you describe behaviour or a situation as **bestial**, you mean that it is very unpleasant or disgusting. ❑ *...the bestial conditions into which the city has sunk.* ADJ = brutish

**bes|ti|al|ity** /bestiælɪti, AM -tʃæl-/ [1] **Bestiality** is disgusting behaviour. [FORMAL] ❑ *It is shocking that humans can behave with such bestiality towards others.* N-UNCOUNT [2] **Bestiality** is sexual activity in which a person has sex with an animal. N-UNCOUNT

**best man** The **best man** at a wedding is the man who assists the bridegroom. N-SING

**be|stow** /bɪstoʊ/ **(bestows, bestowing, bestowed)** To **bestow** something **on** someone means to give or present it to them. [FORMAL] ❑ *The Queen has bestowed a knighthood on him.* VERB = confer V n *on/upon* n

**be|stride** /bɪstraɪd/ **(bestrides, bestriding, bestrode, bestridden)** To **bestride** something means to be the most powerful and important person or thing in it. [LITERARY] ❑ *America's media companies bestride the globe.* VERB V n

**best sell|er (best sellers)** also **bestseller.** A **best seller** is a book of which a great number of copies has been sold. N-COUNT = blockbuster

**best-selling** also **bestselling.** [1] A **best-selling** product such as a book is very popular and a large quantity of it has been sold. ADJ: ADJ n [2] A **best-selling** author is an author who has sold a very large number of copies of his or her book. ADJ: ADJ n

**bet** /bet/ **(bets, betting)** ◆◇◇

> ✔ The form **bet** is used in the present tense and is the past tense and past participle.

[1] If you **bet on** the result of a horse race, football game, or other event, you give someone a sum of money which they give you back with extra money if the result is what you predicted, or which they keep if it is not. ❑ *Jockeys are forbidden to bet on the outcome of races... I bet £10 on a horse called Premonition... He bet them 500 pounds they would lose.* VERB V *on* n V amount *on* n V n amount that ♦ **Bet** is also a noun. ❑ *Do you always have a bet on the Grand National?* N-COUNT ♦ **bet|ting** *...his thousand-pound fine for illegal betting. ...betting shops.* N-UNCOUNT [2] A **bet** is a sum of money which you give to someone when you bet. ❑ *You can put a bet on almost anything these days.* N-COUNT [3] If someone **is betting** that something will happen, they are hoping or expecting that it will happen. [JOURNALISM] ❑ *The party is betting that the presidential race will turn into a battle for younger voters... People were betting on a further easing of credit conditions.* VERB: only cont V that V *on* n [4] → See also **betting**.

**PHRASES** [5] You use expressions such as '**I bet**', '**I'll bet**', and '**you can bet**' to indicate that you are sure something is true. [INFORMAL] ❑ *I bet you were good at games when you were at school... I'll bet they'll taste out of this world.* PHRASE [6] If you tell someone that something is a **good bet**, you are suggesting that it is the thing or course of action that they should choose. [INFORMAL] ❑ *Your best bet is to choose a guest house.* PHRASE [7] If you say that it is **a good bet** or **a safe bet** that something is true or will happen, you are saying that it is extremely likely to be true or to happen. [INFORMAL] ❑ *It is a safe bet that the current owners will not sell.* PHRASE: usu *it* v-link PHR that [8] If you **hedge** your **bets**, you follow two courses of action to avoid making a decision between two things because you cannot decide which one is right. ❑ *NASA is hedging its bets and adopting both strategies.* PHRASE: V inflects = *play safe* [9] You use **I bet** or **I'll bet** in reply to a statement to show that you agree with it or that you expected it to be true, usually when you are annoyed or amused by it. [INFORMAL, SPOKEN] ❑ *'I'd like to ask you something,' I said. 'I bet you would,' she grinned.* PHRASE: oft PHR that [feelings] [10] You can use **my bet is** or **it's my bet** to give your personal opinion about something, when you are fairly sure that you are right. [INFORMAL] ❑ *My bet is that next year will be different... It's my bet that he's the guy behind this killing.* PHRASE [11] If you say **don't bet on** something or **I wouldn't bet on** something, you mean that you do not think that something is true or will happen. [INFORMAL, SPOKEN] ❑ *'We'll never get a table in there' — 'Don't bet on it.'* PHRASE [12] If you reply '**Do you want to bet?**' or '**Want a bet?**' to someone, you mean you are certain that what they have said is wrong. [INFORMAL, SPOKEN] ❑ *'Money can't buy happiness' — 'Want to bet?'* CONVENTION [13] You use '**You bet**' or '**you bet your life**' to say yes in an emphatic way or to emphasize a reply or statement. [INFORMAL, SPOKEN] ❑ *'It's settled, then?' — 'You bet.'... 'Are you afraid of snakes?' — 'You bet your life I'm afraid of snakes.'* PHRASE [emphasis]

**beta block|er** /biːtə blɒkəʳ, AM beɪtə -/ **(beta blockers)** A **beta blocker** is a drug which is used to treat people who have high blood pressure or heart problems. N-COUNT

**bete noire** /bet nwɑːʳ/ also **bête noire.** If you refer to someone or something as your **bete noire**, you mean that you have a particular dislike for them or that they annoy you a great deal. ❑ *Our real bete noire is the car boot sale.* N-SING: oft with poss = bugbear

**be|tide** /bɪtaɪd/ If you say **woe betide** anyone who does a particular thing, you mean that something unpleasant will happen to them if they do it. [FORMAL] ❑ *Woe betide anyone who got in his way.* PHRASE: PHR n

**be|to|ken** /bɪtoʊkən/ **(betokens, betokening, betokened)** If something **betokens** something VERB else, it is a sign of this thing. [FORMAL] ❑ *The president alone betokened the national identity.* [= indicate, signal] [V n]

**be|tray** /bɪtreɪ/ **(betrays, betraying, betrayed)** 1 If you **betray** someone who loves or trusts you, your actions hurt and disappoint them. [VERB] ❑ *When I tell someone I will not betray his confidence I keep my word... The President betrayed them when he went back on his promise not to raise taxes.* [V n] ♦ **be|tray|er (betrayers)** *She was her friend and now calls her a betrayer.* [N-COUNT] 2 If someone **betrays** their country or their friends, they give information to an enemy, putting their country's security or their friends' safety at risk. [VERB] ❑ *They offered me money if I would betray my associates... The group were informers, and they betrayed the plan to the Germans.* [V n] [V n to n] ♦ **be|tray|er** *'Traitor!' she screamed. 'Betrayer of England!'* [N-COUNT] 3 If you **betray** an ideal or your principles, you say or do something which goes against those beliefs. [VERB] ❑ *We betray the ideals of our country when we support capital punishment.* [V n] ♦ **be|tray|er** *Babearth regarded the middle classes as the betrayers of the Revolution.* [N-COUNT] 4 If you **betray** a feeling or quality, you show it without intending to. [VERB] [≠ conceal] ❑ *She studied his face, but it betrayed nothing.* [V n]

**be|tray|al** /bɪtreɪəl/ **(betrayals)** A **betrayal** is an action which betrays someone or something, or the fact of being betrayed. [N-VAR: oft N of n] ❑ *She felt that what she had done was a betrayal of Patrick.*

**be|troth|al** /bɪtroʊðəl/ **(betrothals)** A **betrothal** is an agreement to be married. [OLD-FASHIONED] [N-VAR]

**be|trothed** /bɪtroʊðd/ If you are **betrothed to** someone, you have agreed to marry them. [OLD-FASHIONED] [ADJ: usu v-link ADJ, oft ADJ to n] ♦ Your **betrothed** is the person you are betrothed to. [N-SING: usu poss N]

**bet|ter** /betəʳ/ **(betters, bettering, bettered)** ♦♦♦ 1 **Better** is the comparative of **good**. 2 **Better** is the comparative of **well**. 3 If you like one thing **better than** another, you like it more. [ADV: ADV after v] ❑ *I like your interpretation better than the one I was taught... They liked it better when it rained.* 4 If you are **better** after an illness or injury, you have recovered from it. If you feel **better**, you no longer feel so ill. [ADJ: v-link ADJ] ❑ *He is much better now, he's fine... The doctors were saying there wasn't much hope of me getting better.* 5 You use **had better** or **'d better** when you are advising, warning, or threatening someone, or expressing an opinion about what should happen. [PHRASE] ❑ *It's half past two. I think we had better go home... You'd better run if you're going to get your ticket.* ♦ In spoken English, people sometimes use **better** without 'had' or 'be' before it. It has the same meaning. ❑ *Better not say too much aloud.* 6 If you say that you expect or deserve **better**, you mean that you expect or deserve a higher standard of achievement, behaviour, or treatment from people than they have shown you. [PRON] ❑ *Our long-suffering mining communities deserve better than this.* 7 If someone **betters** a high achievement or standard, they achieve something higher. [VERB] ❑ *He recorded a time of 4 minutes 23, bettering the old record of 4-24.* [V n] 8 If you **better** your situation, you improve your social status or the quality of your life. If you **better yourself**, you improve your social status. [VERB] ❑ *He had dedicated his life to bettering the lot of the oppressed people of South Africa... Our parents chose to come here with the hope of bettering themselves.* [V n] [V pron-refl] 9 **Better** is used to form the comparative of compound adjectives beginning with 'good' and 'well.' For example, the comparative of 'well-off' is 'better-off.'

**PHRASES** 10 You can say that someone **is better** doing one thing than another, or **it is better** doing one thing than another, to advise someone about what they should do. [PHRASE: V inflects, PHR -ing, PHR -ed] ❑ *Wouldn't it be better putting a time-limit on the task?... Subjects like this are better left alone.* 11 If something changes **for the better**, it improves. [PHRASE: PHR after v] ❑ *He dreams of changing the world for the better.* 12 If a feeling such as jealousy, curiosity, or anger **gets the better of** you, it becomes too strong for you to hide or control. [PHRASE: V inflects, PHR n] ❑ *She didn't allow her emotions to get the better of her.* 13 If you **get the better of** someone, you defeat them in a contest, fight, or argument. [PHRASE: V inflects, PHR n] ❑ *He is used to tough defenders, and he usually gets the better of them.* 14 If someone **knows better than to** do something, they are old enough or experienced enough to know it is the wrong thing to do. [PHRASE: V inflects, oft PHR than to-inf] ❑ *She knew better than to argue with Adeline.* 15 If you **know better than** someone, you have more information, knowledge, or experience than them. [PHRASE: V inflects, oft PHR than n] ❑ *He thought he knew better than I did, though he was much less experienced.* 16 If you say that someone would **be better off** doing something, you are advising them to do it or expressing the opinion that it would benefit them to do it. [PHRASE: PHR -ing/prep/adv] ❑ *If you've got bags you're better off taking a taxi.* 17 If you **go one better**, you do something better than it has been done before or obtain something better than someone else has. [PHRASE: V inflects, oft PHR than n] ❑ *Now General Electric have gone one better than nature and made a diamond purer than the best quality natural diamonds.* 18 You say **'That's better'** in order to express your approval of what someone has said or done, or to praise or encourage them. [CONVENTION] ❑ *'I came to ask your advice – no, to ask for your help.' — 'That's better. And how can I help you?'* 19 You can say **'so much the better'** or **'all the better'** to indicate that it is desirable that a particular thing is used, done, or available. [PHRASE] ❑ *Use strong white flour, and if you can get hold of durum wheat flour, then so much the better.* 20 You can use expressions like **'The** bigger **the better'** or **'The** sooner **the better'** to say that you would prefer it if something is big or happens soon. [PHRASE] ❑ *The Irish love a party, the bigger the better.* 21 If you intend to do something and then **think better of it**, you decide not to do it because you realize it would not be sensible. [PHRASE: V inflects] ❑ *Alberg opened his mouth, as if to protest. But he thought better of it.* 22 If you say that something has happened or been done **for better or worse**, you mean that you are not sure whether the consequences will be good or bad, but they will have to be accepted because the action cannot be changed. [PHRASE: PHR after v, PHR with cl] ❑ *I married you for better or worse, knowing all about these problems.* 23 **against** your **better judgment** → see **judgment**. **to be better than nothing** → see **nothing**. **the better part** → see **part**.

**bet|ter|ment** /betəʳmənt/ The **betterment of** something is the act or process of improving its standard or status. [FORMAL] [N-UNCOUNT: oft N of n = improvement] ❑ *His research is for the betterment of mankind.*

**bet|ting** /betɪŋ/ If you say **the betting is** that something will happen or is true, you are suggesting that it is very likely to happen or to be true. [PHRASE: PHR that] ❑ *The betting is that the experience will make Japan more competitive still.*

**bet|ting shop (betting shops)** A **betting shop** is a place where people can go to bet on something such as a horse race. [BRIT] [N-COUNT = bookie's]

**be|tween** /bɪtwiːn/ ♦♦♦

> In addition to the uses shown below, **between** is used in a few phrasal verbs, such as 'come between'.

1 If something is **between** two things or is **in between** them, it has one of the things on one side of it and the other thing on the other side. [PREP: usu PREP pl-n] ❑ *She left the table to stand between the two men... Charlie crossed between the traffic to the far side of the street.* 2 If people or things travel **between** two places, they travel regularly from one place to the other and back again. [PREP: PREP pl-n] ❑ *I spent a lot of time in the early Eighties travelling between London and Bradford.* 3 A relationship, discussion, or difference **between** two people, groups, or things is one that involves them both or relates to them both. [PREP: PREP pl-n] ❑ *I think the relationship between patients and doctors has got a lot less personal... There has always been a difference between community radio and commercial radio.*

4 If something stands **between** you and what you want, it prevents you from having it. ❑ *His sense of duty often stood between him and the enjoyment of life.* 5 If something is **between** two amounts or ages, it is greater or older than the first one and smaller or younger than the second one. ❑ *Amsterdam is fun – a third of its population is aged between 18 and 30.* 6 If something happens **between** or **in between** two times or events, it happens after the first time or event and before the second one. ❑ *The canal was built between 1793 and 1797.* ♦ **Between** is also an adverb. ❑ *...a journey by jetfoil, coach and two aircraft, with a four-hour wait in Bangkok in between.* 7 If you must choose **between** two or more things, you must choose just one of them. ❑ *Students will be able to choose between English, French and Russian as their first foreign language.* 8 If people or places have a particular amount of something **between** them, this is the total amount that they have. ❑ *The three sites employ 12,500 people between them.* 9 When something is divided or shared **between** people, they each have a share of it. ❑ *There is only one bathroom shared between eight bedrooms.* 10 When you introduce a statement by saying '**between you and me**' or '**between ourselves**', you are indicating that you do not want anyone else to know what you are saying. ❑ *Between you and me, though, it's been awful for business... Between ourselves, I know he wants to marry her.*
PREP: PREP n *and* n / PREP: PREP num *and* num / PREP: PREP pl-n, PREP num *and* num / ADV: ADV with cl/group / PREP: PREP pl-n / PREP: PREP pron / PREP: PREP pl-n = amongst / PHRASE: PHR with cl

**bev|elled** /bevəld/
✔ in AM, use **beveled**
If a piece of wood, metal, or glass has **bevelled** edges, its edges are cut sloping. ❑ *...a huge mirror with deep bevelled edges.*
ADJ: usu ADJ n

**bev|er|age** /bevərɪdʒ/ **(beverages)** **Beverages** are drinks. [FORMAL] ❑ *Alcoholic beverages are served in the hotel lounge. ...foods and beverages.*
N-COUNT: usu pl, oft adj N = drink

**bev|vy** /bevi/ **(bevvies)** If you have a few **bevvies**, you have a few alcoholic drinks. [BRIT, INFORMAL] ❑ *It was just one of those things that happens after a few bevvies.*
N-COUNT: usu pl

**bevy** /bevi/ **(bevies)** A **bevy of** people is a group of people all together in one place. ❑ *...a bevy of bright young officers.*
N-COUNT: usu sing, N *of* n = group

**be|wail** /bɪweɪl/ **(bewails, bewailing, bewailed)** If you **bewail** something, you express great sorrow about it. [JOURNALISM, LITERARY] ❑ *...songs that bewail his dissatisfaction in love.*
VERB / V n

**be|ware** /bɪweəʳ/ If you tell someone to **beware of** a person or thing, you are warning them that the person or thing may harm them or be dangerous. ❑ *Beware of being too impatient with others... Beware, this recipe is not for slimmers.*
VERB: only imper and inf / V *of* n/-ing / V

**be|wil|der** /bɪwɪldəʳ/ **(bewilders, bewildering, bewildered)** If something **bewilders** you, it is so confusing or difficult that you cannot understand it. ❑ *The silence from Alex had hurt and bewildered her.*
VERB = perplex / V n

**be|wil|dered** /bɪwɪldəʳd/ If you are **bewildered**, you are very confused and cannot understand something or decide what you should do. ❑ *Some shoppers looked bewildered by the sheer variety of goods on offer.*
ADJ

**be|wil|der|ing** /bɪwɪldərɪŋ/ A **bewildering** thing or situation is very confusing and difficult to understand or to make a decision about. ❑ *A glance along his bookshelves reveals a bewildering array of interests... The choice of excursions was bewildering.* ♦ **be|wil|der|ing|ly** *The cast of characters in the scandal is bewilderingly large.*
ADJ / ADV: usu ADV adj/adv

**be|wil|der|ment** /bɪwɪldəʳmənt/ **Bewilderment** is the feeling of being bewildered. ❑ *He shook his head in bewilderment.*
N-UNCOUNT: oft *in* N

**be|witch** /bɪwɪtʃ/ **(bewitches, bewitching, bewitched)** If someone or something **bewitches** you, you are so attracted to them that you cannot think about anything else. ❑ *She was not moving, as if someone had bewitched her.* ♦ **be|witch|ing** *Frank was a quiet young man with bewitching brown eyes.*
VERB / V n / ADJ

**be|yond** /bɪjɒnd/ ◆◆◇ 1 If something is **beyond** a place or barrier, it is on the other side of it. ❑ *They heard footsteps in the main room, beyond a door.* ♦ **Beyond** is also an adverb. ❑ *The house had a fabulous view out to the Strait of Georgia and the Rockies beyond.* 2 If something happens **beyond** a particular time or date, it continues after that time or date has passed. ❑ *Few jockeys continue race-riding beyond the age of 40.* ♦ **Beyond** is also an adverb. ❑ *The financing of home ownership will continue through the 1990s and beyond.* 3 If something extends **beyond** a particular thing, it affects or includes other things. ❑ *His interests extended beyond the fine arts to international politics and philosophy.* 4 You use **beyond** to introduce an exception to what you are saying. ❑ *I knew nothing beyond a few random facts.* 5 If something goes **beyond** a particular point or stage, it progresses or increases so that it passes that point or stage. ❑ *Their five-year relationship was strained beyond breaking point... It seems to me he's beyond caring about what anybody does.* 6 If something is, for example, **beyond** understanding or **beyond** belief, it is so extreme in some way that it cannot be understood or believed. ❑ *What Jock had done was beyond my comprehension... Sweden is lovely in summer – cold beyond belief in winter.* 7 If you say that something is **beyond** someone, you mean that they cannot deal with it. ❑ *The situation was beyond her control.* 8 **beyond the pale** → see **pale**. **beyond** someone's **means** → see **means**. **beyond** your **wildest dreams** → see **dream**. **beyond a joke** → see **joke**.
PREP / ADV: n ADV, *and* ADV / PREP = past / ADV: *and* ADV / PREP / PREP / PREP: oft PREP -ing / PREP / PREP

**bha|ji** /bɑːdʒi/ **(bhajis)** A **bhaji** is a small piece of food of Indian origin, made of vegetables fried in batter with spices. ❑ *...an onion bhaji.*
N-COUNT

**bhan|gra** /bæŋgrə/ also **Bhangra**. **Bhangra** is a form of dance music that comes from India and uses traditional Indian instruments.
N-UNCOUNT

**bi** /baɪ/ **Bi** means the same as **bisexual**. [INFORMAL]
ADJ

**bi-** /baɪ-/ 1 **Bi-** is used at the beginning of nouns and adjectives that have 'two' as part of their meaning. ❑ *...a bi-cultural society.* 2 **Bi-** is used to form adjectives and adverbs indicating that something happens twice in a period of time or happens once in two periods of time that follow each other. ❑ *Students meet biweekly to discuss their experiences. ...a bimonthly magazine.*
PREFIX / PREFIX

**bi|an|nual** /baɪænjuəl/ A **biannual** event happens twice a year. ❑ *You will need to have a routine biannual examination.* ♦ **bi|an|nu|al|ly** *Only since 1962 has the show been held biannually.*
ADJ: usu ADJ n / ADV: ADV after v

**bias** /baɪəs/ **(biases, biasing, biased)** 1 **Bias** is a tendency to prefer one person or thing to another, and to favour that person or thing. ❑ *Bias against women permeates every level of the judicial system... There were fierce attacks on the BBC for alleged political bias.* 2 **Bias** is a concern with or interest in one thing more than others. ❑ *The Department has a strong bias towards neuroscience.* 3 To **bias** someone means to influence them in favour of a particular choice. ❑ *We mustn't allow it to bias our teaching.*
N-VAR: usu with supp = prejudice / N-VAR: with supp / VERB / V n

**bi|ased** /baɪəst/ 1 If someone is **biased**, they prefer one group of people to another, and behave unfairly as a result. You can also say that a process or system is **biased**. ❑ *He seemed a bit biased against women in my opinion... The judge was biased.* 2 If something is **biased towards** one thing, it is more concerned with it than with other things. ❑ *University funding was tremendously biased towards scientists.*
ADJ: usu v-link ADJ, oft ADJ *against/in favour of* n = prejudiced / ADJ: v-link ADJ *towards* n

**bib** /bɪb/ **(bibs)** A **bib** is a piece of cloth or plastic which is worn by very young children to protect their clothes while they are eating.
N-COUNT

**Bi|ble** /baɪbəl/ **(Bibles)** 1 **The Bible** is the holy book on which the Jewish and Christian religions are based. 2 A **Bible** is a copy of the Bible. ◆◇◇ N-PROPER: *the* N; N-COUNT

**Bi|ble Belt** also **bible belt.** Parts of the southern United States are referred to as **the Bible Belt** because Protestants with strong beliefs have a lot of influence there. N-PROPER: *the* N

**bib|li|cal** /bɪblɪkəl/ **Biblical** means contained in or relating to the Bible. ❑ *The community's links with Syria date back to biblical times.* ADJ: usu ADJ n

**bib|li|og|ra|phy** /bɪbliɒgrəfi/ **(bibliographies)** 1 A **bibliography** is a list of books on a particular subject. ❑ *At the end of this chapter there is a select bibliography of useful books.* 2 A **bibliography** is a list of the books and articles that are referred to in a particular book. N-COUNT; N-COUNT

**bi|carb** /baɪkɑːʳb/ **Bicarb** is an abbreviation for **bicarbonate of soda**. [INFORMAL] N-UNCOUNT

**bi|car|bo|nate of soda** /baɪkɑːʳbəneɪt əv soʊdə/ **Bicarbonate of soda** is a white powder which is used in baking to make cakes rise, and also as a medicine for your stomach. N-UNCOUNT

**bi|cen|tenary** /baɪsentiːnəri, AM -ten-/ **(bicentenaries)** A **bicentenary** is a year in which you celebrate something important that happened exactly two hundred years earlier. [BRIT] N-COUNT

✓ in AM, use **bicentennial**

**bi|cen|ten|nial** /baɪsenteniəl/ **(bicentennials)** 1 A **bicentennial** is the same as a **bicentenary**. [mainly AM] 2 **Bicentennial** celebrations are held to celebrate a bicentenary. N-COUNT; ADJ: ADJ n

**bi|ceps** /baɪseps/ **(biceps)** Your **biceps** are the large muscles at the front of the upper part of your arms. N-COUNT: usu pl

**bick|er** /bɪkəʳ/ **(bickers, bickering, bickered)** When people **bicker**, they argue or quarrel about unimportant things. ❑ *I went into medicine to care for patients, not to waste time bickering over budgets. ...as states bicker over territory... He is still bickering with the control tower over admissible approach routes.* ♦ **bick|er|ing** *The election will end months of political bickering.* V-RECIP = squabble; V over/about n (non recip); pl-n V over/about n; V with n; N-UNCOUNT

**bi|cy|cle** /baɪsɪkəl/ **(bicycles)** A **bicycle** is a vehicle with two wheels which you ride by sitting on it and pushing two pedals with your feet. You steer it by turning a bar that is connected to the front wheel. N-COUNT = bike

**bi|cy|clist** /baɪsɪklɪst/ **(bicyclists)** A **bicyclist** is someone who enjoys cycling. [OLD-FASHIONED] N-COUNT = cyclist

**bid**
① ATTEMPTING OR OFFERING
② SAYING SOMETHING

① **bid** /bɪd/ **(bids, bidding)** ◆◆◇

✓ The form **bid** is used in the present tense and is the past tense and past participle.

1 A **bid for** something or a **bid to** do something is an attempt to obtain it or do it. [JOURNALISM] ❑ *...Sydney's successful bid for the 2000 Olympic Games... The Government has already closed down two newspapers in a bid to silence its critics.* 2 A **bid** is an offer to pay a particular amount of money for something that is being sold. ❑ *Hanson made an agreed takeover bid of £351 million.* 3 If you **bid for** something or **bid to** do something, you try to obtain it or do it. ❑ *Singapore Airlines is rumoured to be bidding for a management contract to run both airports... I don't think she is bidding to be Prime Minister again.* 4 If you **bid for** something that is being sold, you offer to pay a particular amount of money for it. ❑ *She decided to bid for a Georgian dressing table... The bank announced its intention to bid... He certainly wasn't going to bid $18 billion for this company.* ♦ **bid|ding** *The bidding starts at £2 million.* N-COUNT: N for n, N to-inf = attempt; N-COUNT; VERB: V for n, V to-inf; VERB: V for n, V, V n; N-UNCOUNT

② **bid** /bɪd/ **(bids, bidding, bade, bidden)**

✓ American English sometimes uses the form **bid** for the past tense.

1 If you **bid** someone farewell, you say goodbye to them. If you **bid** them goodnight, you say goodnight to them. [FORMAL] ❑ *She bade farewell to her son... I bade her goodnight.* 2 ➔ See also **bidding**. VERB = wish; V n to n; V n n

**bid|den** /bɪdən/ **Bidden** is a past participle of **bid**.

**bid|der** /bɪdəʳ/ **(bidders)** 1 A **bidder** is someone who offers to pay a certain amount of money for something that is being sold. If you sell something to the highest **bidder**, you sell it to the person who offers the most money for it. ❑ *The sale will be made to the highest bidder subject to a reserve price being attained.* 2 A **bidder for** something is someone who is trying to obtain it or do it. ❑ *...bidders for two licences to develop cellular telephone systems in Greece.* N-COUNT: usu supp N; N-COUNT: usu with supp, oft N for n

**bid|ding** /bɪdɪŋ/ 1 If you do something **at** someone's **bidding**, you do it because they have asked you to do it. [FORMAL] ❑ *At his bidding, the delegates rose and sang the national anthem.* 2 If you say that someone **does** another person's **bidding**, you disapprove of the fact that they do exactly what the other person asks them to do, even when they do not want to. [FORMAL] ❑ *She is very clever at getting men to do her bidding!* 3 ➔ See also **bid**. PHRASE; PHRASE: V inflects [disapproval] = obey

**bid|dy** /bɪdi/ **(biddies)** If someone describes an old woman as an old **biddy**, they are saying in an unkind way that they think she is silly or unpleasant. [INFORMAL] ❑ *We're not just a lot of old biddies going on about jam.* N-COUNT [disapproval]

**bide** /baɪd/ **(bides, biding, bided)** If you **bide** your **time**, you wait for a good opportunity before doing something. ❑ *He was content to bide his time patiently, waiting for the opportunity to approach her.* PHRASE: V inflects

**bi|det** /biːdeɪ, AM biːdeɪ/ **(bidets)** A **bidet** is a low fixed container in a bathroom which you can use to wash your bottom. N-COUNT

**bid price** **(bid prices)** The **bid price** of a particular stock or share is the price that investors are willing to pay for it. [BUSINESS] ❑ *Speculation centred on a likely bid price of 380p a share.* N-COUNT

**bi|en|nial** /baɪeniəl/ **(biennials)** A **biennial** event happens or is done once every two years. ❑ *...the biennial Commonwealth conference.* ADJ: ADJ n

**biff** /bɪf/ **(biffs, biffing, biffed)** If you **biff** someone, you hit them with your fist. [INFORMAL, OLD-FASHIONED] VERB

**bi|fo|cals** /baɪfoʊkəlz/

✓ The form **bifocal** is used as a modifier.

**Bifocals** are glasses with lenses made in two halves. The top part is for looking at things some distance away, and the bottom part is for reading and looking at things that are close. ❑ *Mrs Bierce wears thick bifocal lenses.* N-PLURAL

**bi|fur|cate** /baɪfɜːkeɪt/ **(bifurcates, bifurcating, bifurcated)** If something such as a line or path **bifurcates** or **is bifurcated**, it divides into two parts which go in different directions. ❑ *The blood supply bifurcates between eight and thirty times before reaching each particular location in the body.* ♦ **bi|fur|ca|tion** /baɪfɜːkeɪʃən/ **(bifurcations)** *...the bifurcation between high art and popular culture.* VERB: V, Also V n; N-VAR

**big** /bɪg/ **(bigger, biggest)** 1 A **big** person or thing is large in physical size. ❑ *Australia's a big country... Her husband was a big man... The car was too big to fit into our garage.* 2 Something that is **big** consists of many people or things. ❑ *The crowd included a big contingent from Ipswich. ...the big backlog of applications.* 3 If you describe something such as a problem, increase, or change as a **big** one, you mean it is great in degree, extent, or importance. ❑ *Her problem was just too big for her to tackle on her own... There could soon be a big increase in unemployment.* 4 A **big** organization employs many people and has many customers. ❑ *Exchange is largely controlled by big banks.* ◆◆◆ ADJ = large ≠ small; ADJ = large ≠ small; ADJ = serious ≠ small; ADJ = large ≠ small

...*one of the biggest companies in Italy.* 5 [ADJ: ADJ n, v-link ADJ *in* n] If you say that someone is **big in** a particular organization, activity, or place, you mean that they have a lot of influence or authority in it. [INFORMAL] ❑ *Their father was very big in the army... I'm sure all the big names will come to the club.* 6 [ADJ: ADJ n] [emphasis] If you call someone a **big** bully or a **big** coward, you are emphasizing your disapproval of them. [INFORMAL] 7 [ADJ: ADJ n] Children often refer to their older brother or sister as their **big** brother or sister. 8 [ADJ: ADJ n = capital] Capital letters are sometimes referred to as **big** letters. [INFORMAL] ❑ ...*a big letter J.* 9 [ADJ: usu ADJ n] **Big** words are long or rare words which have meanings that are difficult to understand. [INFORMAL] ❑ *They use a lot of big words.*

**PHRASES** 10 [PHRASE: V inflects] If you **make it big**, you become successful or famous. [INFORMAL] ❑ *We're not just looking at making it big in the UK, we want to be big internationally.* 11 [PHRASE: V inflects] If you **think big**, you make plans on a large scale, often using a lot of time, effort, or money. ❑ *Maybe we're not thinking big enough.* 12 [PHRASE: PHR after v] If something is happening **in a big way**, it is happening on a large scale. [INFORMAL] ❑ *I think boxing will take off in a big way here.*

**bigamist** /bɪgəmɪst/ **(bigamists)** [N-COUNT] A **bigamist** is a person who commits the crime of marrying someone when they are already legally married to someone else.

**bigamous** /bɪgəməs/ [ADJ] A **bigamous** marriage is one in which one of the partners is already legally married to someone else.

**bigamy** /bɪgəmi/ [N-UNCOUNT] **Bigamy** is the crime of marrying a person when you are already legally married to someone else.

**Big Apple** [N-PROPER: *the* N] People sometimes refer to the city of New York as **the Big Apple**. [INFORMAL] ❑ *The main attractions of the Big Apple are well documented.*

**big band** **(big bands)** [N-COUNT] A **big band** is a large group of musicians who play jazz or dance music. Big bands were especially popular from the 1930s to the 1950s.

**big bang theory** [N-SING: *the* N] In astronomy **the big bang theory** is a theory that suggests that the universe was created as a result of an extremely large explosion.

**Big Brother** [N-UNCOUNT] [disapproval] People sometimes use **Big Brother** to refer to a person, government, or organization when they think it has complete control over people and is always checking what they do. ❑ *It's an attempt to control what reaches the public. Big Brother is watching.*

**big business** 1 [N-UNCOUNT] **Big business** is business which involves very large companies and very large sums of money. ❑ *Big business will never let petty nationalism get in the way of a good deal.* 2 [N-UNCOUNT] Something that is **big business** is something which people spend a lot of money on, and which has become an important commercial activity. ❑ *Sport has become big business.*

**big cat** **(big cats)** [N-COUNT] **Big cats** are lions, tigers, and other large wild animals in the cat family.

**big city** [N-SING: *the* N] **The big city** is used to refer to a large city which seems attractive to someone because they think there are many exciting things to do there, and many opportunities to earn a lot of money. ❑ ...*a country girl who dreams of the big city and bright lights.*

**big deal** 1 [N-SING] If you say that something is a **big deal**, you mean that it is important or significant in some way. [INFORMAL] ❑ *I felt the pressure on me, winning was such a big deal for the whole family... It's no big deal.* 2 [PHRASE: V inflects, PHR *out of/of/about* n] If someone **makes a big deal out of** something, they make a fuss about it or treat it as if it were very important. [INFORMAL] ❑ *The Joneses make a big deal out of being 'different'.* 3 [CONVENTION] [feelings] You can say '**big deal**' to someone to show that you are not impressed by something that they consider important or impressive. [INFORMAL] ❑ *'You'll miss The Brady Bunch.'— 'Big deal.'*

**big dipper** **(big dippers)** [N-COUNT = roller coaster] A **big dipper** is a fairground ride that carries people up and down steep slopes on a narrow railway at high speed. [BRIT]

**big fish** **(big fish)** 1 [N-COUNT ≠ small fry] If you describe someone as a **big fish**, you believe that they are powerful or important in some way. [INFORMAL] ❑ *The four men arrested were described as really big fish by the U.S. Drug Enforcement Agency.* 2 [PHRASE: v-link PHR] If you say that someone is a **big fish in a small pond**, you mean that they are powerful or important but only within a small group of people. [INFORMAL] ❑ *In South Africa, Jani was a big fish in a small pond.*

**big game** [N-UNCOUNT] Large wild animals such as lions and elephants that are hunted for sport are often referred to as **big game**.

**biggie** /bɪgi/ **(biggies)** [N-COUNT] People sometimes refer to something or someone successful, well-known, or big as a **biggie**. [INFORMAL] ❑ ...*Hollywood box-office biggies.*

**biggish** /bɪgɪʃ/ [ADJ] Something that is **biggish** is fairly big. [INFORMAL] ❑ ...*a biggish room.*

**big gun** **(big guns)** [N-COUNT] If you refer to someone as a **big gun**, you mean that they have a lot of power or influence. [INFORMAL] ❑ ...*the legal big guns who will prepare his defence.*

**big head** **(big heads)** [N-COUNT] [disapproval] [= know-all] If you describe someone as a **big head**, you disapprove of them because they think they are very clever and know everything. [INFORMAL]

**big-headed** [ADJ] [disapproval] [= conceited] If you describe someone as **big-headed**, you disapprove of them because they think they are very clever and know everything. ❑ ...*an arrogant, big-headed man.*

**big-hearted** [ADJ: usu ADJ n ≠ mean-spirited] If you describe someone as **big-hearted**, you think they are kind and generous to other people, and always willing to help them. [WRITTEN] ❑ ...*a big-hearted Irishman.*

**big hitter** **(big hitters)** also **big-hitter.** 1 [N-COUNT] A **big hitter** is a sportsperson such as a golfer or tennis player who hits the ball with a lot of force. ❑ *The Uruguayan-born big-hitter smashed 28 aces.* 2 [N-COUNT] A **big hitter** is a powerful or influential person, especially in business or politics. [INFORMAL] ❑ ...*if Tony Blair fails to persuade a Cabinet big hitter to take on the job.*

**big money** [N-UNCOUNT] **Big money** is an amount of money that seems very large to you, especially money which you get easily. ❑ *They began to make big money during the war.*

**big mouth** **(big mouths)** [N-COUNT] [disapproval] If you say that someone is a **big mouth** or that they have a **big mouth**, you mean that they tell other people things that should have been kept secret. [INFORMAL] ❑ *Why don't you shut your big mouth?*

**big name** **(big names)** [N-COUNT] A **big name** is a person who is successful and famous because of their work. ❑ ...*all the big names in rock and pop.*

**big noise** **(big noises)** [N-COUNT = big shot] Someone who is a **big noise** has an important position in a group or organization. [BRIT, INFORMAL]

**bigot** /bɪgət/ **(bigots)** [N-COUNT] [disapproval] If you describe someone as a **bigot**, you mean that they are bigoted.

**bigoted** /bɪgətɪd/ [ADJ] [disapproval] Someone who is **bigoted** has strong, unreasonable prejudices or opinions and will not change them, even when they are proved to be wrong. ❑ *He was bigoted and racist.*

**bigotry** /bɪgətri/ [N-UNCOUNT] **Bigotry** is the possession or expression of strong, unreasonable prejudices or opinions. ❑ *He deplored religious bigotry.*

**big screen** [N-SING: *the* N ≠ small screen] When people talk about **the big screen**, they are referring to films that are made for cinema rather than for television. ❑ *She returns to the big screen to play Candy's overbearing mother, Rose.*

**big shot** **(big shots)** [N-COUNT] A **big shot** is an important and powerful person in a group or organization. [INFORMAL] ❑ *He's a big shot in Chilean politics.*

**big-ticket** [ADJ: ADJ n] If you describe something as a **big-ticket** item, you mean that it costs a lot of money. [mainly AM] ❑ *Supercomputers are big-ticket items.*

**big time** also **big-time**. [1] You can use **big time** to refer to the highest level of an activity or sport where you can achieve the greatest amount of success or importance. If you describe a person as **big time**, you mean they are successful and important. [INFORMAL] ❑ *He took a long time to settle in to big-time football. ...a big-time investment banker.* ADJ: usu ADJ n
[2] If someone hits **the big time**, they become famous or successful in a particular area of activity. [INFORMAL] ❑ *He hit the big time with films such as Ghost and Dirty Dancing.* N-SING: the N
[3] You can use **big time** if you want to emphasize the importance or extent of something that has happened. [AM, INFORMAL] ❑ *They screwed things up big time... America lost big-time.* ADV: ADV after v [emphasis]

**big toe** (**big toes**) Your **big toe** is the largest toe on your foot. N-COUNT

**big top** The large round tent that a circus uses for its performances is called the **big top**. N-SING

**big wheel** (**big wheels**) A **big wheel** is a very large upright wheel with carriages around the edge of it which people can ride in. Big wheels are often found at theme parks or fun fairs. [BRIT] N-COUNT

☑ in AM, use **ferris wheel**

**big|wig** /bɪgwɪg/ (**bigwigs**) If you refer to an important person as a **bigwig**, you are being rather disrespectful. [INFORMAL] N-COUNT [disapproval]

**bi|jou** /biːʒuː/ Small houses are sometimes described as **bijou** houses in order to make them sound attractive or fashionable. ❑ *...a bijou Mayfair flat.* ADJ: ADJ n

**bike** /baɪk/ (**bikes, biking, biked**) [1] A **bike** is a bicycle or a motorcycle. [INFORMAL] ◆◇◇ N-COUNT
[2] To **bike** somewhere means to go there on a bicycle. [INFORMAL] ❑ *I biked home from the beach.* VERB = cycle V adv/prep

**bike lane** (**bike lanes**) A **bike lane** is a part of the road which is intended to be used only by people riding bicycles. N-COUNT

**bik|er** /baɪkəʳ/ (**bikers**) [1] **Bikers** are people who ride around on motorbikes, usually in groups. N-COUNT
[2] People who ride bicycles are called **bikers**. [AM] N-COUNT

☑ in BRIT, use **cyclist**

**bike|way** /baɪkweɪ/ (**bikeways**) A **bikeway** is a road, route, or path intended for use by cyclists. [AUSTRALIAN] N-COUNT = cycleway

**bi|ki|ni** /bɪkiːni/ (**bikinis**) A **bikini** is a two-piece swimming costume worn by women. N-COUNT

**bi|ki|ni line** A woman's **bikini line** is the edges of the area where her pubic hair grows. N-SING

**bi|lat|er|al** /baɪlætərəl/ **Bilateral** negotiations, meetings, or agreements, involve only the two groups or countries that are directly concerned. [FORMAL] ❑ *...bilateral talks between Britain and America.* ADJ: ADJ n ♦ **bi|lat|er|al|ly** *Disputes and differences between the two neighbours would be solved bilaterally.* ADV: usu ADV after v, ADV adj

**bil|berry** /bɪlbəri/ (**bilberries**) A **bilberry** is a small, round, dark-blue fruit that grows on bushes in northern Europe. N-COUNT

**bile** /baɪl/ [1] **Bile** is a liquid produced by your liver which helps you to digest fat. N-UNCOUNT
[2] **Bile** is the bad-smelling liquid that comes out of your mouth when you vomit with no food in your stomach. N-UNCOUNT
[3] **Bile** is anger or bitterness towards someone or something. [LITERARY] ❑ *He aims his bile at religion, drugs, and politics.* N-UNCOUNT

**bilge** /bɪldʒ/ (**bilges**) The **bilge** or the **bilges** are the flat bottom part of a ship or boat. N-COUNT

**bi|lin|gual** /baɪlɪŋgwəl/ [1] **Bilingual** means involving or using two languages. ❑ *...bilingual education. ...the Collins bilingual dictionaries.* ADJ: ADJ n
[2] Someone who is **bilingual** can speak two languages equally well, usually because they learned both languages as a child. ❑ *He is bilingual in an Asian language and English.* ADJ: v-link ADJ

**bi|lin|gual|ism** /baɪlɪŋgwəlɪzəm/ **Bilingualism** is the ability to speak two languages equally well. N-UNCOUNT

**bili|ous** /bɪliəs/ [1] If someone describes the appearance of something as **bilious**, they mean that they think it looks unpleasant and rather disgusting. [WRITTEN] ❑ *...a bilious shade of green.* ADJ: usu ADJ n [disapproval]
[2] If you feel **bilious**, you feel sick and have a headache. ❑ *She is suffering a bilious attack.* ADJ
[3] **Bilious** is sometimes used to describe the feelings or behaviour of someone who is extremely angry or bad-tempered. [WRITTEN] ❑ *His speech was a bilious, rancorous attack on young people.* ADJ: usu ADJ n

**bilk** /bɪlk/ (**bilks, bilking, bilked**) To **bilk** someone **out of** something, especially money, means to cheat them out of it. [AM, INFORMAL] ❑ *They are charged with bilking investors out of millions of dollars.* VERB = cheat V n *out of* n Also V n

**bill** /bɪl/ (**bills, billing, billed**) [1] A **bill** is a written statement of money that you owe for goods or services. ❑ *They couldn't afford to pay the bills... He paid his bill for the newspapers promptly. ...phone bills.* ◆◆◇ N-COUNT
[2] If you **bill** someone **for** goods or services you have provided them with, you give or send them a bill stating how much money they owe you for these goods or services. ❑ *Are you going to bill me for this?* VERB: no cont V n *for* n Also V n
[3] **The bill** in a restaurant is a piece of paper on which the price of the meal you have just eaten is written and which you are given before you pay. [BRIT] N-SING: the N

☑ in AM, use **check**

[4] A **bill** is a piece of paper money. [AM] ❑ *...a large quantity of US dollar bills.* N-COUNT: usu supp N

☑ in BRIT, use **note**

[5] In government, a **bill** is a formal statement of a proposed new law that is discussed and then voted on. ❑ *This is the toughest crime bill that Congress has passed in a decade... The bill was approved by a large majority.* N-COUNT: usu sing, usu with supp
[6] The **bill** of a show or concert is a list of the entertainers who will take part in it. N-SING
[7] If someone **is billed to** appear in a particular show, it has been advertised that they are going to be in it. ❑ *She was billed to play the Red Queen in Snow White.* VERB: usu passive *be* V-ed to-inf ♦ **bill|ing** *...their quarrels over star billing.* N-UNCOUNT
[8] If you **bill** a person or event **as** a particular thing, you advertise them in a way that makes people think they have particular qualities or abilities. ❑ *They bill it as Britain's most exciting museum.* VERB V n *as* n
[9] A bird's **bill** is its beak. N-COUNT
[10] → See also **Private Member's Bill**.

PHRASES [11] If you say that someone or something **fits the bill** or **fills the bill**, you mean that they are suitable for a particular job or purpose. ❑ *If you fit the bill, send a CV to Rebecca Rees.* PHRASE: V inflects
[12] If you have to **foot the bill for** something, you have to pay for it. ❑ *Who is footing the bill for her extravagant holiday?* PHRASE: V inflects

**bill|board** /bɪlbɔːʳd/ (**billboards**) A **billboard** is a very large board on which posters are displayed. N-COUNT = hoarding

**-billed** /-bɪld/ **-billed** combines with adjectives to indicate that a bird has a beak of a particular kind or appearance. ❑ *...yellow-billed ducks.* COMB in ADJ

**bil|let** /bɪlɪt/ (**billets, billeting, billeted**) [1] If members of the armed forces **are billeted** in a particular place, that place is provided for them to stay in for a period of time. ❑ *The soldiers were billeted in private homes.* VERB: usu passive *be* V-ed adv/prep
[2] A **billet** is a house where a member of the armed forces has been billeted. N-COUNT

**bill|fold** /bɪlfoʊld/ (**billfolds**) A **billfold** is a small flat folded case, usually made of leather or plastic, where you can keep banknotes and credit cards. [AM] N-COUNT

☑ in BRIT, use **wallet**

**bil|liards** /bɪliəʳdz/

☑ The form **billiard** is used as a modifier.

[1] **Billiards** is a game played on a large table, in N-UNCOUNT

which you use a long stick called a cue to hit balls against each other or into pockets around the sides of the table. [BRIT]

☑ in AM, use **pocket billiards, pool**

2 **Billiards** is a game played on a large table, in which you use a long stick called a cue to hit balls against each other or against the walls around the sides of the table. [AM] N-UNCOUNT

**bil|lion** /bɪljən/ **(billions)** ◆◆◆

☑ The plural form is **billion** after a number, or after a word or expression referring to a number, such as 'several' or 'a few'.

1 A **billion** is a thousand million. ❑ *...3 billion dollars... This year, almost a billion birds will be processed in the region.* NUM 2 If you talk about **billions of** people or things, you mean that there is a very large number of them but you do not know or do not want to say exactly how many. ❑ *Biological systems have been doing this for billions of years... He urged US executives to invest billions of dollars in his country.* QUANT-PLURAL: QUANT *of* pl-n ♦ You can also use **billions** as a pronoun. ❑ *He thought that it must be worth billions.* PRON

**bil|lion|aire** /bɪljəneəʳ/ **(billionaires)** A **billionaire** is an extremely rich person who has money or property worth at least a thousand million pounds or dollars. N-COUNT

**bil|lionth** /bɪljənθ/ **(billionths)** 1 The **billionth** item in a series is the one you count as number one billion. ❑ *Disney will claim its one billionth visitor before the end of the century.* ORD 2 A **billionth** is one of a billion equal parts of something. ❑ *...a billionth of a second.* FRACTION

**bill of fare** **(bills of fare)** The **bill of fare** at a restaurant is a list of the food for a meal from which you may choose what you want to eat. [OLD-FASHIONED] N-COUNT = menu

**Bill of Rights** A **Bill of Rights** is a written list of citizens' rights which is usually part of the constitution of a country. N-SING

**bil|low** /bɪloʊ/ **(billows, billowing, billowed)** 1 When something made of cloth **billows**, it swells out and moves slowly in the wind. ❑ *The curtains billowed in the breeze... Her pink dress billowed out around her.* VERB V V *out* 2 When smoke or cloud **billows**, it moves slowly upwards or across the sky. ❑ *Steam billowed out from under the bonnet. ...billowing clouds of cigarette smoke.* VERB V prep/adv V-ing 3 A **billow of** smoke or dust is a large mass of it rising slowly into the air. ❑ *...smoke stacks belching billows of almost solid black smoke.* N-COUNT: usu N *of* n = cloud

**bil|ly** /bɪli/ **(billies)** A **billy** or **billy club** is a short heavy stick which is sometimes used as a weapon by the police. [AM] N-COUNT = baton

☑ in BRIT, use **baton**

**bil|ly goat** /bɪli goʊt/ **(billy goats)** A **billy goat** is a male goat. N-COUNT

**bim|bo** /bɪmboʊ/ **(bimbos)** If someone calls a young woman a **bimbo**, they think that although she is pretty she is rather stupid. [INFORMAL] N-COUNT disapproval

**bi|month|ly** /baɪmʌnθli/

☑ in BRIT, also use **bi-monthly**

A **bimonthly** event or publication happens or appears every two months. ❑ *...bimonthly newsletters.* ADJ: usu ADJ n

**bin** /bɪn/ **(bins, binning, binned)** 1 A **bin** is a container that you put rubbish in. [mainly BRIT] ❑ *He screwed the paper small and chucked it in the bin.* N-COUNT

☑ in AM, usually use **garbage can, trash can**

2 A **bin** is a container that you keep or store things in. ❑ *...a bread bin. ...big steel storage bins.* N-COUNT: oft n N 3 If you **bin** something, you throw it away. [BRIT, INFORMAL] ❑ *He decided to bin his paintings.* VERB V n

**bi|na|ry** /baɪnəri/ 1 The **binary** system expresses numbers using only the two digits 0 and 1. It is used especially in computing. ADJ: usu ADJ n 2 **Binary** is the binary system of expressing numbers. ❑ *The machine does the calculations in binary.* N-UNCOUNT 3 **Binary** describes something that has two different parts. [FORMAL] ❑ *...a binary star.* ADJ: ADJ n

**bi|na|ry code** **(binary codes)** **Binary code** is a computer code that uses the binary number system. [COMPUTING] ❑ *The instructions are translated into binary code, a form that computers can easily handle.* N-VAR

**bind** /baɪnd/ **(binds, binding, bound)** 1 If something **binds** people **together**, it makes them feel as if they are all part of the same group or have something in common. ❑ *It is the memory and threat of persecution that binds them together. ...the social and political ties that bind the USA to Britain. ...a group of people bound together by shared language, culture, and beliefs.* VERB V pl-n *together* V n prep/adv V-ed Also V n 2 If you **are bound** by something such as a rule, agreement, or restriction, you are forced or required to act in a certain way. ❑ *The Luxembourg-based satellite service is not bound by the same strict rules as the BBC... The authorities will be legally bound to arrest any suspects... The treaty binds them to respect their neighbour's independence.* VERB *be* V-ed *by* n *be* V-ed to-inf V n to-inf ♦ **bound** *Few of them feel bound by any enduring loyalties.* ADJ: v-link ADJ *by* n 3 If you **bind** something or someone, you tie rope, string, tape, or other material around them so that they are held firmly. ❑ *Bind the ends of the cord together with thread. ...the red tape which was used to bind the files.* VERB V n adv/prep V n 4 When a book **is bound**, the pages are joined together and the cover is put on. ❑ *Each volume is bound in bright-coloured cloth... Their business came from a few big publishers, all of whose books they bound. ...four immaculately bound hardbacks.* VERB *be* V-ed *in* n V n V-ed ♦ **-bound** *...leather-bound stamp albums.* COMB in ADJ 5 → See also **binding, bound, double bind.**

♦ **bind over** If someone **is bound over** by a court or a judge, they are given an order and must do as the order says for a particular period of time. [LEGAL] ❑ *On many occasions demonstrators were bound over to keep the peace... They put us in a cell, and the next day some bumbling judge bound us over... This imposes a duty on courts to bind over parents when they have no control over their children.* PHRASAL VERB *be* V-ed P to-inf V n P V P n Also V P n to-inf

**bind|er** /baɪndəʳ/ **(binders)** A **binder** is a hard cover with metal rings inside, which is used to hold loose pieces of paper. N-COUNT

**bind|ing** /baɪndɪŋ/ **(bindings)** 1 A **binding** promise, agreement, or decision must be obeyed or carried out. ❑ *...proposals for a legally binding commitment on nations to stabilise emissions of carbon dioxide... The panel's decisions are secret and not binding on the government.* ADJ: oft ADJ *on* n 2 The **binding** of a book is its cover. ❑ *Its books are noted for the quality of their paper and bindings.* N-VAR: oft with poss 3 **Binding** is a strip of material that you put round the edge of a piece of cloth or other object in order to protect or decorate it. ❑ *...the Regency mahogany dining table with satinwood binding.* N-VAR 4 **Binding** is a piece of rope, cloth, tape, or other material that you wrap around something so that it can be gripped firmly or held in place. N-VAR 5 → See also **bind.**

**bind|weed** /baɪndwiːd/ **Bindweed** is a wild plant that winds itself around other plants and makes it difficult for them to grow. N-UNCOUNT

**binge** /bɪndʒ/ **(binges, bingeing, binged)** 1 If you go on a **binge**, you do too much of something, such as drinking alcohol, eating, or spending money. [INFORMAL] ❑ *She went on occasional drinking binges.* N-COUNT 2 If you **binge**, you do too much of something, such as drinking alcohol, eating, or spending money. [INFORMAL] ❑ *I haven't binged since 1986... I binged on pizzas or milkshakes.* VERB V V *on* n

**bin|go** /bɪŋgoʊ/ 1 **Bingo** is a game in which each player has a card with numbers on. Someone calls out numbers and if you are the first person to have all your numbers called out, you win the game. N-UNCOUNT 2 You can say **'bingo!'** when something pleasant happens, especially in a surprising, unexpected, or sudden way. ❑ *I was in a market in Tangier and bingo! I found this.* EXCLAM

**bin|lin|er** **(bin liners)** A **bin liner** is a plastic bag that you put inside a waste bin or dustbin. [BRIT] N-COUNT

in AM, use **garbage bag, trash bag**

**bin|ocu|lars** /bɪnɒkjʊləʳz/ **Binoculars** consist of two small telescopes joined together side by side, which you look through in order to look at things that are a long way away. N-PLURAL: also *a pair of* N

**bio-** /baɪoʊ-, baɪɒ-/ **Bio-** is used at the beginning of nouns and adjectives that refer to life or to the study of living things. ❑ *...bio-engineering.* PREFIX

**bio|chemi|cal** /baɪoʊkemɪkəl/ **Biochemical** changes, reactions, and mechanisms relate to the chemical processes that happen in living things. ADJ: ADJ n

**bio|chem|ist** /baɪoʊkemɪst/ **(biochemists)** A **biochemist** is a scientist or student who studies biochemistry. N-COUNT

**bio|chem|is|try** /baɪoʊkemɪstri/ 1 **Biochemistry** is the study of the chemical processes that happen in living things. N-UNCOUNT 2 The **biochemistry** of a living thing is the chemical processes that happen in it or are involved in it. N-UNCOUNT

**bio|degrad|able** /baɪoʊdɪgreɪdəbəl/ Something that is **biodegradable** breaks down or decays naturally without any special scientific treatment, and can therefore be thrown away without causing pollution. ❑ *...a natural and totally biodegradable plastic.* ADJ

**bio|di|ver|sity** /baɪoʊdaɪvɜːʳsɪti/ **Biodiversity** is the existence of a wide variety of plant and animal species living in their natural environment. N-UNCOUNT

**bio|en|gi|neer|ing** /baɪoʊendʒɪnɪərɪŋ/ 1 People sometimes use **bioengineering** to talk about genetic engineering. N-UNCOUNT 2 **Bioengineering** is the use of engineering techniques to solve medical problems, for example to design and make artificial arms and legs. N-UNCOUNT

**bi|og|raph|er** /baɪɒgrəfəʳ/ **(biographers)** Someone's **biographer** is a person who writes an account of their life. N-COUNT: oft with poss

**bio|graphi|cal** /baɪəgræfɪkəl/ **Biographical** facts, notes, or details are concerned with the events in someone's life. ❑ *The book contains few biographical details.* ADJ: usu ADJ n

**bi|og|ra|phy** /baɪɒgrəfi/ **(biographies)** 1 A **biography** of someone is an account of their life, written by someone else. N-COUNT: oft with poss 2 **Biography** is the branch of literature which deals with accounts of people's lives. ❑ *...a volume of biography.* N-UNCOUNT

**biol.** **Biol.** is a written abbreviation for **biology** or **biological**.

**bio|logi|cal** /baɪəlɒdʒɪkəl/ 1 **Biological** is used to describe processes and states that occur in the bodies and cells of living things. ❑ *The living organisms somehow concentrated the minerals by biological processes... This is a natural biological response.* ADJ: usu ADJ n ♦ **bio|logi|cal|ly** /baɪəlɒdʒɪkli/ *Much of our behaviour is biologically determined.* ADV: ADV with cl/group, ADV with v 2 **Biological** is used to describe activities concerned with the study of living things. ❑ *...the university's school of biological sciences.* ADJ: ADJ n 3 **Biological** weapons and **biological** warfare involve the use of bacteria or other living organisms in order to attack human beings, animals, or plants. ❑ *Such a war could result in the use of chemical and biological weapons.* ADJ: usu ADJ n 4 **Biological** pest control is the use of bacteria or other living organisms in order to destroy other organisms which are harmful to plants or crops. ❑ *...Jim Litsinger, a consultant on biological control of agricultural pests.* ADJ: ADJ n 5 A child's **biological** parents are the man and woman who caused him or her to be born, rather than other adults who look after him or her. ❑ *...foster parents for young teenagers whose biological parents have rejected them.* ADJ: ADJ n = natural

**bio|logi|cal clock** **(biological clocks)** Your **biological clock** is your body's way of registering time. It does not rely on events such as day or night, but on factors such as your habits, your age, and chemical changes taking place in your body. ❑ *For women, the 'biological clock' governs the time for having children.* N-COUNT: oft poss N

**bio|logi|cal di|ver|sity** **Biological diversity** is the same as **biodiversity**. N-UNCOUNT

**bi|ol|ogy** /baɪɒlədʒi/ 1 **Biology** is the science which is concerned with the study of living things. N-UNCOUNT ♦ **bi|olo|gist** /baɪɒlədʒɪst/ **(biologists)** ❑ *...biologists studying the fruit fly.* N-COUNT 2 The **biology** of a living thing is the way in which its body or cells behave. ❑ *The biology of these diseases is terribly complicated. ...human biology.* N-UNCOUNT: the N of n, supp N 3 → See also **molecular biology**.

**bio|medi|cal** /baɪoʊmedɪkəl/ **Biomedical** research examines the effects of drugs and medical techniques on the biological systems of living creatures. ❑ *Biomedical research will enable many individuals infected with HIV to live longer, more comfortable lives.* ADJ: ADJ n

**bi|on|ic** /baɪɒnɪk/ In science fiction books or films, a **bionic** person is someone who has special powers, such as being exceptionally strong or having exceptionally good sight, because parts of their body have been replaced by electronic machinery. ❑ *...the Bionic Woman.* ADJ: usu ADJ n

**bio|pic** /baɪoʊpɪk/ **(biopics)** A **biopic** is a film that tells the story of someone's life. N-COUNT

**bi|op|sy** /baɪɒpsi/ **(biopsies)** A **biopsy** is the removal and examination of fluids or tissue from a patient's body in order to discover why they are ill. N-VAR

**bio|sphere** /baɪəsfɪəʳ/ **The biosphere** is the part of the earth's surface and atmosphere where there are living things. [TECHNICAL] N-SING: usu *the* N

**bio|tech** /baɪoʊtek/ **Biotech** means the same as **biotechnology**. ❑ *...the biotech industry.* N-UNCOUNT: usu N n

**bio|tech|no|logi|cal** /baɪoʊteknəlɒdʒɪkəl/ **Biotechnological** means relating to biotechnology. [TECHNICAL] ❑ *...modern biotechnological methods of genetic manipulation.* ADJ: ADJ n

**bio|tech|nol|ogy** /baɪoʊteknɒlədʒi/ **Biotechnology** is the use of living parts such as cells or bacteria in industry and technology. [TECHNICAL] N-UNCOUNT ♦ **bio|tech|nolo|gist** /baɪoʊteknɒlədʒɪst/ **(biotechnologists)** ❑ *...biotechnologists turning proteins into pharmaceuticals.* N-COUNT

**bio|ter|ror|ism** /baɪoʊterərɪzəm/ also **bio-terrorism**. **Bioterrorism** is terrorism that involves the use of biological weapons. ❑ *...the threat of bioterrorism.* N-UNCOUNT ♦ **bio|ter|ror|ist** /baɪoʊterərɪst/ **(bioterrorists)** *...the war against bioterrorists. ...a bioterrorist attack.* N-COUNT: oft N n

**bi|par|ti|san** /baɪpɑːʳtɪzæn, AM baɪpɑːrtɪzən/ **Bipartisan** means concerning or involving two different political parties or groups. ❑ *...a bipartisan approach to educational reform.* ADJ: usu ADJ n

**bi|ped** /baɪped/ **(bipeds)** A **biped** is a creature with two legs. [TECHNICAL] N-COUNT

**bi|plane** /baɪpleɪn/ **(biplanes)** A **biplane** is an old-fashioned type of aeroplane with two pairs of wings, one above the other. N-COUNT

**bi|po|lar** /baɪpoʊləʳ/ **Bipolar** systems or situations are dominated by two strong and opposing opinions or elements. [FORMAL] ❑ *...the bipolar world of the Cold War years.* ADJ: usu ADJ n

**birch** /bɜːʳtʃ/ **(birches)** A **birch** is a type of tall tree with thin branches. N-VAR

**bird** /bɜːʳd/ **(birds)** ◆◆◇ 1 A **bird** is a creature with feathers and wings. Female birds lay eggs. Most birds can fly. N-COUNT 2 Some men refer to young women as **birds**. This use could cause offence. [BRIT, INFORMAL] N-COUNT 3 → See also **early bird, game bird**.

PHRASES 4 If you refer to two people as **birds of a feather**, you mean that they have the same interests or are very similar. PHRASE: v-link PHR 5 **A bird in the hand** is something that you already have and do not PHRASE want to risk losing by trying to get something else. [6] If you say that a **little bird** told you about something, you mean that someone has told you about it, but you do not want to say who it was. PHRASE [7] If you say that doing something will **kill two birds with one stone**, you mean that it will enable you to achieve two things that you want to achieve, rather than just one. PHRASE: V inflects

**bird|cage** /bɜːʳdkeɪdʒ/ **(birdcages)** also **bird cage.** A **birdcage** is a cage in which birds are kept. N-COUNT

**birdie** /bɜːʳdi/ **(birdies, birdying, birdied)** [1] In golf, if you get a **birdie**, you get the golf ball into a hole in one stroke fewer than the number of strokes which has been set as the standard for a good player. N-COUNT [2] If a golfer **birdies** a hole, he or she gets a birdie at that hole. ❑ *He birdied five of the first seven holes.* VERB V n

**bird|life** /bɜːʳdlaɪf/ also **bird life.** The **birdlife** in a place is all the birds that live there. N-UNCOUNT

**bird|like** /bɜːʳdlaɪk/ also **bird-like.** If someone has a **birdlike** manner, they move or look like a bird. ❑ *...the birdlike way she darted about.* ADJ

**bird of para|dise** **(birds of paradise)** A **bird of paradise** is a songbird which is found mainly in New Guinea. The male birds have very brightly coloured feathers. N-COUNT

**bird of pas|sage** **(birds of passage)** If you refer to someone as a **bird of passage**, you mean that they are staying in a place for a short time before going to another place. ❑ *Most of these emigrants were birds of passage who returned to Spain after a relatively short stay.* N-COUNT

**bird of prey** **(birds of prey)** A **bird of prey** is a bird such as an eagle or a hawk that kills and eats other birds and animals. N-COUNT

**bird's eye view** **(bird's eye views)** You say that you have a **bird's eye view of** a place when you are looking down at it from a great height, so that you can see a long way but everything looks very small. N-COUNT: usu sing

**bird|song** /bɜːʳdsɒŋ, AM -sɔːŋ/ **(birdsongs)** also **bird song. Birdsong** is the sound of a bird or birds calling in a way which sounds musical. ❑ *The air is filled with birdsong.* N-UNCOUNT: also N in pl

**bird ta|ble** **(bird tables)** A **bird table** is a small wooden platform on a pole which some people put in their garden in order to put food for the birds on it. N-COUNT

**bird-watcher** **(bird-watchers)** also **birdwatcher.** A **bird-watcher** is a person whose hobby is watching and studying wild birds in their natural surroundings. N-COUNT

**bird-watching** also **birdwatching. Bird-watching** is the activity of watching and studying wild birds in their natural surroundings. N-UNCOUNT

**Biro** /baɪroʊ/ **(Biros)** A **Biro** is a pen with a small metal ball at its tip which transfers the ink onto the paper. [BRIT, TRADEMARK] N-COUNT

**birth** /bɜːʳθ/ **(births)** [1] When a baby is born, you refer to this event as his or her **birth**. ❑ *It was the birth of his grandchildren which gave him greatest pleasure... She weighed 5lb 7oz at birth. ...premature births.* ◆◇◇ N-VAR [2] You can refer to the beginning or origin of something as its **birth**. ❑ *...the birth of popular democracy.* N-UNCOUNT: with poss [3] Some people talk about a person's **birth** when they are referring to the social position of the person's family. ❑ *...men of low birth... His birth, background and career show that you can make it in this country on merit alone.* N-UNCOUNT: usu supp N [4] → See also **date of birth**, **home birth**.

PHRASES [5] If, for example, you are French **by birth**, you are French because your parents are French, or because you were born in France. ❑ *Sadrudin was an Iranian by birth.* PHRASE: adj/n PHR [6] When a woman **gives birth**, she produces a baby from her body. ❑ *She's just given birth to a baby girl.* PHRASE: V inflects [7] To **give birth to** something such as an idea means to cause it to start to exist. ❑ *In 1980, strikes at the Lenin shipyards gave birth to the Solidarity trade union.* PHRASE: V inflects [8] The country, town, or village **of** your **birth** is the place where you were born. PHRASE: n PHR

**birth cer|tifi|cate** **(birth certificates)** Your **birth certificate** is an official document which gives details of your birth, such as the date and place of your birth, and the names of your parents. N-COUNT

**birth con|trol** **Birth control** means planning whether to have children, and using contraception to prevent having them when they are not wanted. N-UNCOUNT

**birth|date** /bɜːʳθdeɪt/ **(birthdates)** Your **birthdate** is the same as your **date of birth**. N-COUNT

**birth|day** /bɜːʳθdeɪ, -di/ **(birthdays)** Your **birthday** is the anniversary of the date on which you were born. ◆◇◇ N-COUNT

**birth|day suit** **(birthday suits)** If you are in your **birthday suit**, you are not wearing any clothes. [INFORMAL, HUMOROUS or OLD-FASHIONED] N-COUNT: poss N

**birth|ing** /bɜːʳθɪŋ/ **Birthing** means relating to or used during the process of giving birth. ❑ *The hospital has pioneered the use of birthing pools.* ADJ: ADJ n

**birth|mark** /bɜːʳθmɑːʳk/ **(birthmarks)** A **birthmark** is a mark on someone's skin that has been there since they were born. N-COUNT

**birth|place** /bɜːʳθpleɪs/ **(birthplaces)** [1] Your **birthplace** is the place where you were born. [WRITTEN] N-COUNT [2] The **birthplace of** something is the place where it began. ❑ *...Athens, the birthplace of the ancient Olympics.* N-COUNT: usu N *of* n

**birth rate** **(birth rates)** also **birth-rate.** The **birth rate** in a place is the number of babies born there for every 1000 people during a particular period of time. ❑ *The UK has the highest birth rate among 15 to 19-year-olds in Western Europe. ...a falling birth-rate.* N-COUNT

**birth|right** /bɜːʳθraɪt/ **(birthrights)** Something that is your **birthright** is something that you feel you have a basic right to have, simply because you are a human being. ❑ *Freedom is the natural birthright of every human.* N-COUNT: usu sing

**bis|cuit** /bɪskɪt/ **(biscuits)** [1] A **biscuit** is a small flat cake that is crisp and usually sweet. [BRIT] N-COUNT

☑ in AM, use **cookie**

[2] A **biscuit** is a small round dry cake that is made with baking powder, baking soda, or yeast. [AM] N-COUNT [3] If someone has done something very stupid, rude, or selfish, you can say that they **take the biscuit** or that what they have done **takes the biscuit**, to emphasize your surprise at their behaviour. [BRIT] PHRASE: V inflects emphasis

☑ in AM, use **take the cake**

**bi|sect** /baɪsekt/ **(bisects, bisecting, bisected)** If something long and thin **bisects** an area or line, it divides the area or line in half. ❑ *The main street bisects the town from end to end.* VERB V n

**bi|sex|ual** /baɪsekʃuəl/ **(bisexuals)** Someone who is **bisexual** is sexually attracted to both men and women. ♦ **Bisexual** is also a noun. ❑ *He was an active bisexual.* ♦ **bi|sexu|al|ity** /baɪsekʃuælɪti/ *Lillian opened up to Frank about her bisexuality.* ADJ N-COUNT N-UNCOUNT

**bish|op** /bɪʃəp/ **(bishops)** [1] A **bishop** is a clergyman of high rank in the Roman Catholic, Anglican, and Orthodox churches. N-COUNT; N-TITLE; N-VOC [2] In chess a **bishop** is a piece that can be moved diagonally across the board on squares that are the same colour. N-COUNT

**bish|op|ric** /bɪʃəprɪk/ **(bishoprics)** A **bishopric** is the area for which a bishop is responsible, or the rank or office of being a bishop. N-COUNT

**bi|son** /baɪsᵊn/ **(bison)** A **bison** is a large hairy animal with a large head that is a member of the cattle family. They used to be very common in North America and Europe. [mainly BRIT] N-COUNT = *buffalo*

☑ in AM, usually use **buffalo**

**bis|tro** /biːstroʊ/ **(bistros)** A **bistro** is a small, informal restaurant or a bar where food is served. N-COUNT

**bit** /bɪt/ **(bits)** 1 **A bit of** something is a small amount of it. ❑ *All it required was a bit of work... I got paid a little bit of money.* ◆◆◆ QUANT: QUANT *of* n-uncount 2 **A bit** means to a small extent or degree. It is sometimes used to make a statement less extreme. ❑ *This girl was a bit strange... She looks a bit like his cousin Maureen... That sounds a bit technical... Isn't that a bit harsh?* PHRASE: PHR adj/adv/prep [vagueness] = slightly 3 You can use **a bit of** to make a statement less forceful. For example, the statement 'It's a bit of a nuisance' is less forceful than 'It's a nuisance'. ❑ *It's all a bit of a mess... This comes as a bit of a disappointment.* PHRASE: PHR n [vagueness] 4 **Quite a bit** means quite a lot. ❑ *They're worth quite a bit of money... Things have changed quite a bit... He's quite a bit older than me.* PHRASE: PHR *of* n, PHR after v, PHR compar 5 You use **a bit** before 'more' or 'less' to mean a small amount more or a small amount less. ❑ *I still think I have a bit more to offer... Maybe we'll hear a little bit less noise.* PHRASE: PHR *more/less* 6 If you do something **a bit**, you do it for a short time. In British English, you can also say that you do something **for a bit**. ❑ *Let's wait a bit... I hope there will be time to talk a bit... That should keep you busy for a bit.* PHRASE: PHR with v 7 **A bit of** something is a small part or section of it. [mainly BRIT] ❑ *That's the bit of the meeting that I missed... Now comes the really important bit... The best bit was walking along the glacier.* N-COUNT: with supp, oft N *of* n = part 8 A **bit** of something is a small piece of it. [mainly BRIT] ❑ *Only a bit of string looped round a nail in the doorpost held it shut. ...crumpled bits of paper.* N-COUNT: usu N *of* n = piece 9 You can use **bit** to refer to a particular item or to one of a group or set of things. For example, a **bit of** information is an item of information. ❑ *There was one bit of vital evidence which helped win the case... Not one single bit of work has been started towards the repair of this road.* N-COUNT: usu N *of* n 10 In computing, a **bit** is the smallest unit of information that is held in a computer's memory. It is either 1 or 0. Several bits form a byte. N-COUNT 11 A **bit** is $12\frac{1}{2}$ cents; mainly used in expressions such as two **bits**, which means 25 cents, or **four bits**, which means 50 cents. [AM] N-COUNT 12 **Bit** is the past tense of **bite**.

**PHRASES** 13 If something happens **bit by bit**, it happens in stages. ❑ *Bit by bit I began to understand what they were trying to do.* PHRASE: PHR with v 14 If someone **is champing at the bit** or **is chomping at the bit**, they are very impatient to do something, but they are prevented from doing it, usually by circumstances that they have no control over. ❑ *I expect you're champing at the bit, so we'll get things going as soon as we can.* PHRASE: V inflects 15 If you **do** your **bit**, you do something that, to a small or limited extent, helps to achieve something. ❑ *Marcie always tried to do her bit.* PHRASE: V inflects 16 You say that one thing is **every bit as** good, interesting, or important **as** another to emphasize that the first thing is just as good, interesting, or important as the second. ❑ *My dinner jacket is every bit as good as his.* PHRASE: PHR adj/adv [emphasis] 17 If you say that something is **a bit much**, you are annoyed because you think someone has behaved in an unreasonable way. [mainly BRIT, INFORMAL] ❑ *It's a bit much expecting me to dump your boyfriend for you.* PHRASE: v-link PHR [feelings] 18 You use **not a bit** when you want to make a strong negative statement. [mainly BRIT] ❑ *I'm really not a bit surprised... 'Are you disappointed?' — 'Not a bit.'* PHRASE [emphasis] 19 You say **not a bit of it** to emphasize that something that you might expect to be the case is not the case. [BRIT] ❑ *Did he give up? Not a bit of it!* PHRASE [emphasis] 20 You can use **bits and pieces** or **bits and bobs** to refer to a collection of different things. [INFORMAL] PHRASE 21 If you **get the bit between** your **teeth**, or **take the bit between** your **teeth**, you become very enthusiastic about a job you have to do. PHRASE: V inflects 22 If something is smashed or blown **to bits**, it is broken into a number of pieces. If something falls **to bits**, it comes apart so that it is in a number of pieces. ❑ *She found a pretty yellow jug smashed to bits.* PHRASE: PHR after v 23 **thrilled to bits** → see **thrilled**.

**bitch** /bɪtʃ/ **(bitches, bitching, bitched)** 1 If someone calls a woman a **bitch**, they are saying in a very rude way that they think she behaves in a very unpleasant way. [INFORMAL, ⚠ VERY RUDE] → See also **son of a bitch**. N-COUNT [disapproval] 2 If you say that someone **is bitching about** something, you mean that you disapprove of the fact that they are complaining about it in an unpleasant way. [INFORMAL] ❑ *They're forever bitching about everybody else.* VERB: oft cont [disapproval] V *about* n Also V 3 A **bitch** is a female dog. N-COUNT

**bitchy** /bɪtʃi/ If someone is being **bitchy** or is making **bitchy** remarks, they are saying unkind things about someone. [INFORMAL] ❑ *I'm sorry. I know I was bitchy on the phone.* ♦ **bitchi|ness** *There's a lot of bitchiness.* ADJ [disapproval] = catty N-UNCOUNT

**bite** /baɪt/ **(bites, biting, bit, bitten)** 1 If you **bite** something, you use your teeth to cut into it, for example in order to eat it or break it. If an animal or person **bites** you, they use their teeth to hurt or injure you. ❑ *Both sisters bit their nails as children... He bit into his sandwich... He had bitten the cigarette in two... Llamas won't bite or kick.* ◆◆◆ VERB V n V *into* n V n adv/prep V 2 A **bite** of something, especially food, is the action of biting it. ❑ *He took another bite of apple... You cannot eat a bun in one bite.* ♦ A **bite** is also the amount of food you take into your mouth when you bite it. ❑ *Look forward to eating the food and enjoy every bite.* N-COUNT: oft N *of* n N-COUNT 3 If you have **a bite** to eat, you have a small meal or a snack. [INFORMAL] ❑ *It was time to go home for a little rest and a bite to eat.* N-SING: *a* N, usu N to-inf 4 If a snake or a small insect **bites** you, it makes a mark or hole in your skin, and often causes the surrounding area of your skin to become painful or itchy. ❑ *We were all badly bitten by mosquitoes.* VERB V n Also V 5 A **bite** is an injury or a mark on your body where an animal, snake, or small insect has bitten you. ❑ *Any dog bite, no matter how small, needs immediate medical attention.* N-COUNT: oft n N 6 When an action or policy begins to **bite**, it begins to have a serious or harmful effect. ❑ *As the sanctions begin to bite there will be more political difficulties ahead... The recession started biting deeply into British industry.* VERB V V prep/adv 7 If an object **bites** into a surface, it presses hard against it or cuts into it. ❑ *There may even be some wire or nylon biting into the flesh.* VERB V prep/adv Also V, V n 8 If you say that a food or drink has **bite**, you like it because it has a strong or sharp taste. ❑ *...the addition of tartaric acid to give the wine some bite.* N-UNCOUNT [approval] 9 If the air or the wind has **a bite**, it feels very cold. ❑ *There was a bite in the air, a smell perhaps of snow.* N-SING: *a* N 10 If a fish **bites** when you are fishing, it takes the hook or bait at the end of your fishing line in its mouth. ❑ *After half an hour, the fish stopped biting and we moved on.* ♦ **Bite** is also a noun. ❑ *If I don't get a bite in a few minutes I lift the rod and twitch the bait.* VERB V N-COUNT 11 → See also **love bite**, **nail-biting**.

**PHRASES** 12 If someone **bites the hand that feeds** them, they behave badly or in an ungrateful way towards someone who they depend on. ❑ *She may be cynical about the film industry, but ultimately she has no intention of biting the hand that feeds her.* PHRASE: Vs inflect 13 If you **bite** your **lip** or your **tongue**, you stop yourself from saying something that you want to say, because it would be the wrong thing to say in the circumstances. ❑ *I must learn to bite my lip... He bit his tongue as he found himself on the point of saying 'follow that car'.* PHRASE: V and N inflect 14 If something **takes a bite out of** a sum of money, part of the money is spent or taken away in order to pay for it. ❑ *Local taxes are going to be taking a bigger bite out of people's income than they ever have before.* PHRASE: V inflects, PHR n 15 someone's **bark is worse than** their **bite** → see **bark**. to **bite the bullet** → see **bullet**. to **bite off more than** one **can chew** → see **chew**. to **bite the dust** → see **dust**.

**bite-sized** also **bite-size**. 1 **Bite-sized** pieces of food are small enough to fit easily in your mouth. ❑ *...bite-sized pieces of cheese.* ADJ: usu ADJ n 2 If you describe something as **bite-sized**, you like it because it is small enough to be considered or dealt with easily. ❑ *...bite-size newspaper items.* ADJ: usu ADJ n [approval]

**bit|ing** /baɪtɪŋ/ [1] **Biting** wind or cold is extremely cold. ❑ *...a raw, biting northerly wind... Antarctic air brought biting cold to southern Chile on Thursday.* [2] **Biting** criticism or wit is very harsh or unkind, and is often caused by such feelings as anger or dislike. ❑ *...a furore caused by the author's biting satire on the Church.* — ADJ: usu ADJ n = piercing; ADJ: usu ADJ n

**bit|map** /bɪtmæp/ **(bitmaps, bitmapping, bitmapped)** A **bitmap** is a type of graphics file on a computer. [COMPUTING] ❑ *...bitmap graphics for representing complex images such as photographs.* ♦ **Bitmap** is also a verb. ❑ *Bitmapped maps require huge storage space.* — N-COUNT; VERB V-ed

**bit part (bit parts)** also **bit-part.** A **bit part** is a small and unimportant role for an actor in a film or play. — N-COUNT

**bit|ten** /bɪtᵊn/ **Bitten** is the past participle of **bite**.

**bit|ter** /bɪtəʳ/ **(bitterest, bitters)** [1] In a **bitter** argument or conflict, people argue very angrily or fight very fiercely. ❑ *...the scene of bitter fighting during the Second World War. ...a bitter attack on the Government's failure to support manufacturing.* ♦ **bit|ter|ly** *Any such thing would be bitterly opposed by most of the world's democracies. ...a bitterly fought football match.* ♦ **bit|ter|ness** *The rift within the organization reflects the growing bitterness of the dispute.* [2] If someone is **bitter** after a disappointing experience or after being treated unfairly, they continue to feel angry about it. ❑ *She is said to be very bitter about the way she was sacked... His long life was marked by bitter personal and political memories.* ♦ **bit|ter|ly** *'And he sure didn't help us,' Grant said bitterly. ...the party bureaucrats who bitterly resented their loss of power.* ♦ **bit|ter|ness** *I still feel bitterness and anger towards the person who knocked me down.* [3] A **bitter** experience makes you feel very disappointed. You can also use **bitter** to emphasize feelings of disappointment. ❑ *I think the decision was a bitter blow from which he never quite recovered... The statement was greeted with bitter disappointment by many of the other delegates.* ♦ **bit|ter|ly** *I was bitterly disappointed to have lost yet another race so near the finish.* [4] **Bitter** weather, or a **bitter** wind, is extremely cold. ❑ *Outside, a bitter east wind was accompanied by flurries of snow.* ♦ **bit|ter|ly** *It's been bitterly cold here in Moscow.* [5] A **bitter** taste is sharp, not sweet, and often slightly unpleasant. ❑ *The leaves taste rather bitter.* [6] **Bitter** is a kind of beer that is light brown in colour. [BRIT] ❑ *...a pint of bitter.* [7] If you say that you will continue doing something **to the bitter end**, especially something difficult or unpleasant, you are emphasizing that you will continue doing it until it is completely finished. ❑ *The guerrillas would fight to the bitter end, he said, in order to achieve their main goal.* [8] **a bitter pill** → see **pill**. — ◆◇◇ ADJ; ADV: usu ADV with v, also ADV adj; N-UNCOUNT; ADJ; ADV: usu ADV with v, also ADV adj; N-UNCOUNT; ADJ: usu ADJ n; ADV: ADV adj, ADV with v; ADJ; ADV: ADV adj; ADJ ≠ sweet; N-MASS; PHRASE: PHR after v [emphasis]

**bit|ter|ly** /bɪtəʳli/ You use **bitterly** when you are describing an attitude which involves strong, unpleasant emotions such as anger or dislike. ❑ *We are bitterly upset at what has happened.* — ADV: ADV adj

**bitter|sweet** /bɪtəʳswiːt/ also **bitter-sweet.** [1] If you describe an experience as **bittersweet**, you mean that it has some happy aspects and some sad ones. ❑ *...bittersweet memories of his first appearance for the team.* [2] A **bittersweet** taste seems bitter and sweet at the same time. ❑ *...a wine with a bitter-sweet flavour.* — ADJ; ADJ

**bit|ty** /bɪti/ [1] If you say that something is **bitty**, you mean that it seems to be formed from a lot of different parts which you think do not fit together or go together well. [BRIT, INFORMAL] ❑ *The programme was bitty and pointless.* [2] If you describe someone or something as a little **bitty** person or thing, you are emphasizing that they are very small. [AM, INFORMAL] ❑ *She's just a little bitty wisp of a girl.* — ADJ; ADJ: ADJ n [emphasis]

**bi|tu|men** /bɪtʃʊmɪn, AM bɪtuːmən/ **Bitumen** is a black sticky substance which is obtained from tar or petrol and is used in making roads. — N-UNCOUNT

**bivou|ac** /bɪvuæk/ **(bivouacs, bivouacking, bivouacked)** [1] A **bivouac** is a temporary camp made by soldiers or mountain climbers. [2] If you **bivouac** in a particular place, you stop and stay in a bivouac there. ❑ *We bivouacked on the outskirts of the city.* — N-COUNT; VERB V prep/adv Also V

**bi|week|ly** /baɪwiːkli/ A **biweekly** event or publication happens or appears once every two weeks. [AM] ❑ *He used to see them at the biweekly meetings. ...Beverage Digest, the industry's biweekly newsletter.* ♦ **Biweekly** is also an adverb. ❑ *The group meets on a regular basis, usually weekly or biweekly.* — ADJ: ADJ n; ADV: ADV with v

✔ in BRIT, use **fortnightly**

**biz** /bɪz/ [1] **Biz** is sometimes used to refer to the entertainment business, especially pop music or films. [JOURNALISM, INFORMAL] ❑ *...a girl in the music biz.* [2] → See also **showbiz**. — N-SING: oft n N

**bi|zarre** /bɪzɑːʳ/ Something that is **bizarre** is very odd and strange. ❑ *The game was also notable for the bizarre behaviour of the team's manager.* ♦ **bi|zarre|ly** *She dressed bizarrely.* — ADJ = weird; ADV

**blab** /blæb/ **(blabs, blabbing, blabbed)** If someone **blabs about** something secret, they tell people about it. [INFORMAL] ❑ *Her mistake was to blab about their affair... No blabbing to your mates!... She'll blab it all over the school.* — VERB V about n; V to n; V n prep; Also V

**black** /blæk/ **(blacker, blackest, blacks, blacking, blacked)** [1] Something that is **black** is of the darkest colour that there is, the colour of the sky at night when there is no light at all. ❑ *She was wearing a black coat with a white collar... He had thick black hair... I wear a lot of black... He was dressed all in black.* [2] A **black** person belongs to a race of people with dark skins, especially a race from Africa. ❑ *He worked for the rights of black people. ...the traditions of the black community.* [3] Black people are sometimes referred to as **blacks**. This use could cause offence. ❑ *There are about thirty-one million blacks in the US.* [4] **Black** coffee or tea has no milk or cream added to it. ❑ *A cup of black tea or black coffee contains no calories... I drink coffee black.* [5] If you describe a situation as **black**, you are emphasizing that it is very bad indeed. ❑ *It was, he said later, one of the blackest days of his political career... The future for the industry looks even blacker.* [6] If someone is in a **black** mood, they feel very miserable and depressed. ❑ *Her mood was blacker than ever.* [7] **Black** humour involves jokes about sad or difficult situations. ❑ *'So you can all go over there and get shot,' he said, with the sort of black humour common among British troops here... It's a black comedy of racial prejudice, mistaken identity and thwarted expectations.* [8] People who believe in **black** magic believe that it is possible to communicate with evil spirits. ❑ *He was also alleged to have conducted black magic ceremonies... The King was unjustly accused of practising the black arts.* — ◆◆◆ COLOUR; ADJ; N-COUNT: usu pl; ADJ: ADJ n, v n ADJ; ADJ [emphasis]; ADJ; ADJ: usu ADJ n; ADJ: ADJ n

PHRASES [9] If you say that someone is **black and blue**, you mean that they are badly bruised. ❑ *Whenever she refused, he'd beat her black and blue... Bud's nose was still black and blue.* [10] If a person or an organization is **in the black**, they do not owe anyone any money. ❑ *Until his finances are in the black I don't want to get married.* [11] If someone gives you a **black look**, they look at you in a way that shows that they are very angry about something. ❑ *Passing my stall, she cast black looks at the amount of stuff still unsold.* — PHRASE: usu PHR after v, v-link PHR; PHRASE: v-link PHR, PHR after v ≠ in the red; PHRASE: N inflects, usu PHR after v

♦ **black out** [1] If you **black out**, you lose consciousness for a short time. ❑ *Samadov said that he felt so ill that he blacked out.* [2] If a place **is blacked out**, it is in darkness, usually because it has no electricity supply. ❑ *Large parts of the capital were blacked out after electricity pylons were blown up.* [3] If a film or a piece of writing **is blacked out**, it is prevented from being broadcast or published, usually because it contains information which is secret or offensive. ❑ *TV pictures of the demonstration were blacked out.* [4] If you **black** — PHRASAL VERB = pass out V P; PHRASAL VERB be V-ed P; PHRASAL VERB: usu passive = censor be V-ed P; PHRASAL VERB out a piece of writing, you colour over it in black so that it cannot be seen. ❑ *U.S. government specialists went through each page, blacking out any information a foreign intelligence expert could use.* = censor V P n Also V n P [5] If you **black out** the memory of something, you try not to remember it because it upsets you. ❑ *I tried not to think about it. I blacked it out.* ➔ See also **blackout**. PHRASAL VERB = blot out V n P Also V P n (not pron)

**Black Af|ri|ca** Black Africa is the part of Africa to the south of the Sahara Desert. N-PROPER

**black and white** also **black-and-white.** [1] In a **black and white** photograph or film, everything is shown in black, white, and grey. ❑ *...old black and white film footage... The pictures were in black and white.* COLOUR [2] A **black and white** television set shows only black-and-white pictures. ADJ: usu ADJ n [3] A **black and white** issue or situation is one which involves issues which seem simple and therefore easy to make decisions about. ❑ *But this isn't a simple black and white affair, Marianne... She saw things in black and white.* ADJ = clear-cut [4] You say that something is **in black and white** when it has been written or printed, and not just said. ❑ *He'd seen the proof in black and white.* PHRASE: PHR after v, v-link PHR

**black|ball** /blækbɔːl/ **(blackballs, blackballing, blackballed)** If the members of a club **blackball** someone, they vote against that person being allowed to join their club. ❑ *Members can blackball candidates in secret ballots.* VERB V n

**black belt** **(black belts)** [1] A **black belt** is worn by someone who has reached a very high standard in a sport such as judo or karate. ❑ *He holds a black belt in karate.* N-COUNT [2] You can refer to someone who has a black belt in judo or karate as a **black belt**. ❑ *Murray is a judo black belt.* N-COUNT

**black|berry** /blækbəri, AM -beri/ **(blackberries)** A **blackberry** is a small, soft black or dark purple fruit. N-COUNT

**black|bird** /blækbɜːʳd/ **(blackbirds)** [1] A **blackbird** is a common European bird. The male has black feathers and a yellow beak, and the female has brown feathers. N-COUNT [2] A **blackbird** is a common North American bird. The male has black feathers and often a red patch on its wings. N-COUNT

**black|board** /blækbɔːʳd/ **(blackboards)** A **blackboard** is a dark-coloured board that you can write on with chalk. Blackboards are often used by teachers in the classroom. [BRIT] N-COUNT: usu *the* N in sing

✔ in AM, use **chalkboard**

**black box** **(black boxes)** [1] A **black box** is an electronic device in an aircraft which records information about its flights. Black boxes are often used to provide evidence about accidents. N-COUNT [2] You can refer to a system or device as a **black box** when you know that it produces a particular result but you have no understanding of how it works. ❑ *They were part of the black box associated with high-flyer management development.* N-COUNT: usu sing

**black|cur|rant** /blækkʌrənt, AM -kɜːrənt/ **(blackcurrants)** In Europe, **blackcurrants** are a type of very small, dark purple fruits that grow in bunches on bushes. [BRIT] ❑ *...a carton of blackcurrant drink.* N-COUNT

**black econo|my** The **black economy** consists of the buying, selling, and producing of goods or services that goes on without the government being informed, so that people can avoid paying tax on them. [BRIT] ❑ *...an attempt to clamp down on the black economy.* N-SING

**black|en** /blækən/ **(blackens, blackening, blackened)** [1] To **blacken** something means to make it black or very dark in colour. Something that **blackens** becomes black or very dark in colour. ❑ *The married women of Shitamachi maintained the custom of blackening their teeth... You need to grill the tomatoes until the skins blacken.* VERB V n V [2] If someone **blackens** your character, they make other people believe that you are a bad person. ❑ *They're trying to blacken our name.* VERB V n

**black eye** **(black eyes)** If someone has a **black eye**, they have a dark-coloured bruise around their eye. ❑ *He punched her in the face at least once giving her a black eye.* N-COUNT: usu sing

**black|head** /blækhed/ **(blackheads)** **Blackheads** are small, dark spots on someone's skin caused by blocked pores. N-COUNT: usu pl

**black hole** **(black holes)** **Black holes** are areas in space, where gravity is so strong that nothing, not even light, can escape from them. Black holes are thought to be formed by collapsed stars. N-COUNT

**black ice** **Black ice** is a thin, transparent layer of ice on a road or path that is very difficult to see. N-UNCOUNT

**black|ish** /blækɪʃ/ Something that is **blackish** is very dark in colour. ❑ *The water was blackish... Katy has long blackish hair.* COLOUR

**black|list** /blæklɪst/ **(blacklists, blacklisting, blacklisted)** [1] If someone is on a **blacklist**, they are seen by a government or other organization as being one of a number of people who cannot be trusted or who have done something wrong. ❑ *A government official disclosed that they were on a secret blacklist.* N-COUNT [2] If someone **is blacklisted** by a government or organization, they are put on a blacklist. ❑ *He has been blacklisted since being convicted of possessing marijuana in 1969. ...the full list of blacklisted airports.* VERB: usu passive *be* V-ed V-ed ♦ **black|list|ing** *...a victim of Hollywood's notorious blacklisting.* N-UNCOUNT

**black|mail** /blækmeɪl/ **(blackmails, blackmailing, blackmailed)** [1] **Blackmail** is the action of threatening to reveal a secret about someone, unless they do something you tell them to do, such as giving you money. ❑ *It looks like the pictures were being used for blackmail.* N-UNCOUNT [2] If you describe an action as emotional or moral **blackmail**, you disapprove of it because someone is using a person's emotions or moral values to persuade them to do something against their will. ❑ *The tactics employed can range from overt bullying to subtle emotional blackmail.* N-UNCOUNT [disapproval] [3] If one person **blackmails** another person, they use blackmail against them. ❑ *The government insisted that it would not be blackmailed by violence... I thought he was trying to blackmail me into saying whatever he wanted.* VERB V n V n *into* -ing/n ♦ **black|mail|er** **(blackmailers)** *The nasty thing about a blackmailer is that his starting point is usually the truth.* N-COUNT

**black mark** **(black marks)** A **black mark against** someone is something bad that they have done or a bad quality that they have which affects the way people think about them. ❑ *There was one black mark against him.* N-COUNT

**black mar|ket** **(black markets)** If something is bought or sold **on the black market**, it is bought or sold illegally. ❑ *There is a plentiful supply of arms on the black market.* N-COUNT

**black mar|ket|eer** **(black marketeers)** A **black marketeer** is someone who sells goods on the black market. [JOURNALISM] N-COUNT

**black|ness** /blæknəs/ **Blackness** is the state of being very dark. [LITERARY] ❑ *The twilight had turned to a deep blackness.* N-UNCOUNT

**black|out** /blækaʊt/ **(blackouts)** also **black-out.** [1] A **blackout** is a period of time during a war in which towns and buildings are made dark so that they cannot be seen by enemy planes. ❑ *...blackout curtains.* N-COUNT: usu sing [2] If a **blackout** is imposed on a particular piece of news, journalists are prevented from broadcasting or publishing it. ❑ *...a media blackout imposed by the Imperial Palace... Journalists said there was a virtual news blackout about the rally.* N-COUNT: usu sing, usu n N [3] If there is a power **blackout**, the electricity supply to a place is temporarily cut off. ❑ *There was an electricity black-out in a large area in the north of the country.* N-COUNT: usu sing, usu n N = power cut [4] If you have a **blackout**, you temporarily lose consciousness. ❑ *I suffered a black-out which lasted for several minutes.* N-COUNT

**black pep|per** **Black pepper** is pepper which is dark in colour and has been made from N-UNCOUNT the dried berries of the pepper plant, including their black outer cases.

**black pud|ding** **(black puddings)** **Black pudding** is a thick sausage which has a black skin and is made from pork fat and pig's blood. [mainly BRIT] [N-VAR]

**black sheep** If you describe someone as **the black sheep of** their family or of a group that they are a member of, you mean that they are considered bad or worthless by other people in that family or group. [N-COUNT: usu sing, oft *the* N *of* n] [disapproval]

**black|smith** /blæksmɪθ/ **(blacksmiths)** A **blacksmith** is a person whose job is making things by hand out of metal that has been heated to a high temperature. [N-COUNT]

**black spot** **(black spots)** also **blackspot.** 1 If you describe a place, time, or part of a situation as a **black spot**, you mean that it is particularly bad or likely to cause problems. [BRIT] ❑ *There are recognised black spots in marriages which can lead to trouble.* [N-COUNT] 2 A **black spot** is a place on a road where accidents often happen. [BRIT] ❑ *The accident happened on a notorious black spot on the A43.* [N-COUNT]

**black tie** also **black-tie.** 1 A **black tie** event is a formal social event such as a party at which people wear formal clothes called evening dress. ❑ *...a black-tie dinner for former students.* [ADJ: usu ADJ n] 2 If a man is dressed in **black tie**, he is wearing formal evening dress, which includes a dinner jacket or tuxedo and a bow tie. ❑ *Most of the guests will be wearing black tie.* [N-UNCOUNT]

**black|top** /blæktɒp/ **Blacktop** is a hard black substance which is used as a surface for roads. [AM] ❑ *...waves of heat rising from the blacktop.* [N-UNCOUNT]

✔ in BRIT, use **tarmac**

**blad|der** /blædəʳ/ **(bladders)** Your **bladder** is the part of your body where urine is stored until it leaves your body. → See also **gall bladder**. [N-COUNT]

**blade** /bleɪd/ **(blades)** 1 The **blade** of a knife, axe, or saw is the edge, which is used for cutting. → See picture on page 1709. ❑ *Many of these tools have sharp blades, so be careful.* [N-COUNT] 2 The **blades** of a propeller are the long, flat parts that turn round. [N-COUNT: usu pl] 3 The **blade** of an oar is the thin flat part that you put into the water. [N-COUNT] 4 A **blade** of grass is a single piece of grass. [N-COUNT] 5 → See also **razor blade**, **shoulder blade**. **rotor blade** → see **rotor**.

**blag** /blæg/ **(blags, blagging, blagged)** To **blag** something such as a concert ticket means to persuade someone to give it to you free. [BRIT, INFORMAL] ❑ *She'd heard he was a musician and blagged a tape off a friend of his.* [VERB] [V n] [Also V *way* prep/adv]

**blah** /blɑː/ You use **blah, blah, blah** to refer to something that is said or written without giving the actual words, because you think that they are boring or unimportant. [INFORMAL] ❑ *...the different challenges of their career, their need to change, to evolve, blah blah blah.* [CONVENTION]

**blame** /bleɪm/ **(blames, blaming, blamed)** ◆◆◇ 1 If you **blame** a person or thing **for** something bad, you believe or say that they are responsible for it or that they caused it. ❑ *The commission is expected to blame the army for many of the atrocities... Ms Carey appeared to blame her breakdown on EMI's punishing work schedule... If it wasn't Sam's fault, why was I blaming him?* [VERB] [V n *for* n] [V n *on* n] [V n] ♦ **Blame** is also a noun. ❑ *Nothing could relieve my terrible sense of blame.* [N-UNCOUNT] 2 The **blame for** something bad that has happened is the responsibility for causing it or letting it happen. ❑ *Some of the blame for the miscarriage of justice must be borne by the solicitors... The president put the blame squarely on his opponent.* [N-UNCOUNT: oft N *for* n/-ing] 3 If you say that you do not **blame** someone **for** doing something, you mean that you consider it was a reasonable thing to do in the circumstances. ❑ *I do not blame them for trying to make some money... He slammed the door and stormed off. I could hardly blame him.* [VERB: usu with brd-neg] [V n *for* -ing] [V n]

PHRASES 4 If someone is **to blame for** something bad that has happened, they are responsible for causing it. ❑ *If their forces were not involved, then who is to blame?... The policy is partly to blame for causing the worst unemployment in Europe.* [PHRASE: v-link PHR] 5 If you say that someone **has only** themselves **to blame** or **has no-one but** themselves **to blame**, you mean that they are responsible for something bad that has happened to them and that you have no sympathy for them. ❑ *My life is ruined and I suppose I only have myself to blame.* [PHRASE: V inflects]

**blame|less** /bleɪmləs/ Someone who is **blameless** has not done anything wrong. ❑ *He feels he is blameless... The US itself, of course, is not entirely blameless in trading matters.* [ADJ]

**blanch** /blɑːntʃ, blæntʃ/ **(blanches, blanching, blanched)** 1 If you **blanch**, you suddenly become very pale. ❑ *His face blanched as he looked at Sharpe's blood-drenched uniform... She felt herself blanch at the unpleasant memories.* [VERB] [V] [V *at* n] 2 If you say that someone **blanches at** something, you mean that they find it unpleasant and do not want to be involved with it. ❑ *Everything he had said had been a mistake. He blanched at his miscalculations.* [VERB] [V *at* n] 3 If you **blanch** vegetables, fruit, or nuts, you put them into boiling water for a short time, usually in order to remove their skins, or to prepare them for freezing. ❑ *Skin the peaches by blanching them.* [VERB] [V n]

**blanc|mange** /bləmɒndʒ/ **(blancmanges)** **Blancmange** is a cold dessert that is made from milk, sugar, cornflour or corn starch, and flavouring and looks rather like jelly. [N-VAR]

**bland** /blænd/ **(blander, blandest)** 1 If you describe someone or something as **bland**, you mean that they are rather dull and unexciting. ❑ *Serle has a blander personality than Howard. ...a bland, 12-storey office block.* [ADJ] ♦ **bland|ness** *...the blandness of television.* [N-UNCOUNT] 2 Food that is **bland** has very little flavour. ❑ *It tasted bland and insipid, like warmed cardboard.* [ADJ]

**blan|dish|ments** /blændɪʃmənts/ **Blandishments** are pleasant things that someone says to another person in order to persuade them to do something. [FORMAL] ❑ *At first Lewis resisted their blandishments.* [N-PLURAL: oft with poss = *flattery*]

**bland|ly** /blændli/ If you do something **blandly**, you do it in a calm and quiet way. ❑ *'It's not important,' he said blandly... The nurse smiled blandly.* [ADV: ADV with v]

**blank** /blæŋk/ **(blanks, blanking, blanked)** 1 Something that is **blank** has nothing on it. ❑ *We could put some of the pictures over on that blank wall over there... He tore a blank page from his notebook. ...blank cassettes.* [ADJ] 2 A **blank** is a space which is left in a piece of writing or on a printed form for you to fill in particular information. ❑ *Put a word in each blank to complete the sentence.* [N-COUNT] 3 If you look **blank**, your face shows no feeling, understanding, or interest. ❑ *Abbot looked blank. 'I don't quite follow, sir.'... His daughter gave him a blank look.* [ADJ] ♦ **blank|ly** *She stared at him blankly.* [ADV: ADV with v] ♦ **blank|ness** *His eyes have the blankness of someone half-asleep.* [N-UNCOUNT] 4 If your mind or memory is **a blank**, you cannot think of anything or remember anything. ❑ *I'm sorry, but my mind is a blank... I came round in hospital and did not know where I was. Everything was a complete blank.* [N-SING: *a* N] 5 **Blanks** are gun cartridges which contain explosive but do not contain a bullet, so that they cause no harm when the gun is fired. ❑ *...a starter pistol which only fires blanks.* [N-COUNT: usu pl] 6 → See also **point-blank**.

PHRASES 7 If you **draw a blank** when you are looking for someone or something, you do not succeed in finding them. [INFORMAL] ❑ *They drew a blank in their search for the driver.* [PHRASE: V inflects] 8 If your mind **goes blank**, you are suddenly unable to think of anything appropriate to say, for example in reply to a question. ❑ *My mind went totally blank.* [PHRASE: V inflects]

♦ **blank out** If you **blank out** a particular feeling or thought, you do not allow yourself to experience that feeling or to have that thought. [PHRASAL VERB = *block out*]

❑ *I learned to blank those feelings out... I was trying to blank out previous situations from my mind.* V n P / V P n (not pron)

**blank cheque** (**blank cheques**)

✔ in AM, use **blank check**

1 If someone is given a **blank cheque**, they are given the authority to spend as much money as they need or want. [JOURNALISM] ❑ *We are not prepared to write a blank cheque for companies that have run into trouble.* N-COUNT 2 If someone is given a **blank cheque**, they are given the authority to do what they think is best in a particular situation. [JOURNALISM] ❑ *He was, in a sense, given a blank cheque to negotiate the new South Africa.* N-COUNT = carte blanche

**blan|ket** /blæŋkɪt/ (**blankets, blanketing, blanketed**) 1 A **blanket** is a large square or rectangular piece of thick cloth, especially one which you put on a bed to keep you warm. N-COUNT 2 A **blanket of** something such as snow is a continuous layer of it which hides what is below or beyond it. ❑ *The mud disappeared under a blanket of snow... Cold damp air brought in the new year under a blanket of fog.* N-COUNT: usu sing, N *of* n 3 If something such as snow **blankets** an area, it covers it. ❑ *More than a foot of snow blanketed parts of Michigan.* VERB V n 4 You use **blanket** to describe something when you want to emphasize that it affects or refers to every person or thing in a group, without any exceptions. ❑ *There's already a blanket ban on foreign unskilled labour in Japan.* ADJ: usu ADJ n [emphasis] = comprehensive 5 → See also **electric blanket**, **security blanket**, **wet blanket**.

**blank verse** **Blank verse** is poetry that does not rhyme. In English literature it usually consists of lines with five stressed syllables. N-UNCOUNT

**blare** /bleəʳ/ (**blares, blaring, blared**) If something such as a siren or radio **blares** or if you **blare** it, it makes a loud, unpleasant noise. ❑ *The fire engines were just pulling up, sirens blaring... I blared my horn.* VERB V / V n ♦ **Blare** is also a noun. ❑ *...the blare of a radio through a thin wall.* N-SING: N *of* n ♦ **Blare out** means the same as **blare**. ❑ *Music blares out from every cafe. ...giant loudspeakers which blare out patriotic music and the speeches of their leader.* PHRASAL VERB V P / V P n (not pron) / Also V n P

**blar|ney** /blɑːʳni/ **Blarney** is things someone says that are flattering and amusing but probably untrue, and which you think they are only saying in order to please you or to persuade you to do something. N-UNCOUNT [disapproval]

**bla|sé** /blɑːzeɪ, AM blɑːzeɪ/ also **blase.** If you describe someone as **blasé**, you mean that they are not easily impressed, excited, or worried by things, usually because they have seen or experienced them before. ❑ *Far too many people are blasé about their driving skills. ...his seemingly blasé attitude.* ADJ: oft ADJ *about* n [disapproval]

**blas|pheme** /blæsfiːm/ (**blasphemes, blaspheming, blasphemed**) If someone **blasphemes**, they say rude or disrespectful things about God or religion, or they use God's name as a swear word. ❑ *'Don't blaspheme,' my mother said... The spiritual leader charged that the book blasphemed against Islam.* VERB V / V *against* n ♦ **blas|phem|er** (**blasphemers**) *Such a figure is liable to be attacked as a blasphemer.* N-COUNT

**blas|phe|mous** /blæsfəməs/ You can describe someone who shows disrespect for God or a religion as **blasphemous**. You can also describe what they are saying or doing as **blasphemous**. ❑ *She was accused of being blasphemous... Critics attacked the film as blasphemous.* ADJ

**blas|phe|my** /blæsfəmi/ (**blasphemies**) You can describe something that shows disrespect for God or a religion as **blasphemy**. ❑ *He was found guilty of blasphemy and sentenced to three years in jail.* N-VAR

**blast** /blɑːst, blæst/ (**blasts, blasting, blasted**) ♦◇◇ 1 A **blast** is a big explosion, especially one caused by a bomb. ❑ *250 people were killed in the blast.* N-COUNT 2 If something **is blasted** into a particular place or state, an explosion causes it to be in that place or state. If a hole **is blasted** in something, it is created by an explosion. ❑ *His left arm was blasted off by some kind of a bomb... The explosion which followed blasted out the external supporting wall of her flat.* VERB *be* V-ed prep/adv / V n with adv / Also V n adj, V n prep 3 If workers **are blasting** rock, they are using explosives to make holes in it or destroy it, for example so that a road or tunnel can be built. ❑ *Their work was taken up with boring and blasting rock with gelignite... They're using dynamite to blast away rocks to put a road in.* VERB V n / V n with adv / Also V ♦ **blast|ing** *Three miles away there was a salvo of blasting in the quarry.* N-UNCOUNT 4 To **blast** someone means to shoot them with a gun. [JOURNALISM] ❑ *...a son who blasted his father to death after a life-time of bullying... Alan Barnett, 28, was blasted with a sawn-off shotgun in Oldham on Thursday.* VERB V n *to* n / *be* V-ed *with* ♦ **Blast** is also a noun. ❑ *...the man who killed Nigel Davies with a shotgun blast.* N-COUNT 5 If someone **blasts** their way somewhere, they get there by shooting at people or causing an explosion. ❑ *The police were reported to have blasted their way into the house using explosives... One armoured column attempted to blast a path through a barricade of buses and trucks.* VERB V *way* prep/adv / V n prep/adv 6 If something **blasts** water or air somewhere, it sends out a sudden, powerful stream of it. ❑ *A blizzard was blasting great drifts of snow across the lake.* VERB V n prep/adv ♦ **Blast** is also a noun. ❑ *Blasts of cold air swept down from the mountains.* N-COUNT: usu N *of* n 7 If you **blast** something such as a car horn, or if it **blasts**, it makes a sudden, loud sound. If something **blasts** music, or music **blasts**, the music is very loud. ❑ *...drivers who do not blast their horns... The sound of western music blasted as she entered.* VERB V n / V ♦ **Blast** is also a noun. ❑ *The buzzer suddenly responded in a long blast of sound.* N-COUNT: usu N *of* n 8 If something such as a radio or a heater is on **full blast**, or on **at full blast**, it is producing as much sound or power as it is able to. ❑ *In many of those homes the television is on full blast 24 hours a day.* PHRASE: PHR after v, v-link PHR

♦ **blast away** 1 If a gun, or a person firing a gun, **blasts away**, the gun is fired continuously for a period of time. ❑ *Suddenly all the men pull out pistols and begin blasting away.* PHRASAL VERB V P 2 If something such as a radio or a pop group **is blasting away**, it is producing a loud noise. ❑ *Clock-radios blast away until you get up.* PHRASAL VERB = blare out V P

♦ **blast off** When a space rocket **blasts off**, it leaves the ground at the start of its journey. → See also **blast-off**. PHRASAL VERB

♦ **blast out** If music or noise **is blasting out**, loud music or noise is being produced. ❑ *...loudspeakers blasting out essential tourist facts in every language known to man... Pop music can be heard 10 miles away blasting out from the huge tented shanty-town.* PHRASAL VERB = blare out V P n (not pron) / V P

**blast|ed** /blɑːstɪd, blæstɪd/ 1 Some people use **blasted** to express anger or annoyance at something or someone. [INFORMAL, OLD-FASHIONED] ADJ: ADJ n [feelings] 2 A **blasted** landscape has very few plants or trees, and makes you feel sad or depressed when you look at it. [LITERARY] ❑ *...the blasted landscape where the battle was fought.* ADJ: usu ADJ n = bleak

**blast fur|nace** (**blast furnaces**) A **blast furnace** is a large structure in which iron ore is heated under pressure so that it melts and the pure iron metal separates out and can be collected. N-COUNT

**blast-off** **Blast-off** is the moment when a rocket leaves the ground and rises into the air to begin a journey into space. ❑ *The original planned launch was called off four minutes before blast-off.* N-UNCOUNT

**bla|tant** /bleɪtᵊnt/ You use **blatant** to describe something bad that is done in an open or very obvious way. ❑ *Outsiders will continue to suffer the most blatant discrimination. ...a blatant attempt to spread the blame for the fiasco... The elitism was blatant.* ADJ [emphasis] ♦ **bla|tant|ly** *...a blatantly sexist question... They said the song blatantly encouraged the killing of policemen.* ADV: ADV adj, ADV with v

**bla|tant|ly** /bleɪtᵊntli/ **Blatantly** is used to add emphasis when you are describing states or situations which you think are bad. ❑ *It became blatantly obvious to me that the band wasn't going to last... For years, blatantly false assertions have gone unchallenged.* ADV: usu ADV adj, also ADV with v, ADV with cl [emphasis]

**blath|er** /blæðəʳ/ **(blathers, blathering, blathered)** If someone **is blathering on about** something, they are talking for a long time about something that you consider boring or unimportant. ❑ *The old men blather on and on... Stop blathering... He kept on blathering about police incompetence.* ♦ **Blather** is also a noun. ❑ *All this is blather.*
VERB · V on · V · V about n · N-UNCOUNT

**blaze** /bleɪz/ **(blazes, blazing, blazed)** 1 When a fire **blazes**, it burns strongly and brightly. ❑ *Three people died as wreckage blazed, and rescuers fought to release trapped drivers. ...a blazing fire.* 2 A **blaze** is a large fire which is difficult to control and which destroys a lot of things. [JOURNALISM] ❑ *Two firemen were hurt in a blaze which swept through a tower block last night.* 3 If something **blazes with** light or colour, it is extremely bright. [LITERARY] ❑ *The gardens blazed with colour.* ♦ **Blaze** is also a noun. ❑ *I wanted the front garden to be a blaze of colour.* 4 **A blaze of** publicity or attention is a great amount of it. ❑ *He was arrested in a blaze of publicity. ...the sporting career that began in a blaze of glory.* 5 If guns **blaze**, or **blaze away**, they fire continuously, making a lot of noise. ❑ *Guns were blazing, flares going up and the sky was lit up all around... She took the gun and blazed away with calm and deadly accuracy.* 6 **with all guns blazing** → see **gun**. 7 If someone **blazes a trail**, they discover or develop something new. ❑ *These surgeons have blazed the trail in the treatment of bomb victims.*
VERB · V · V-ing · N-COUNT: usu sing · VERB · V with n · N-COUNT: usu a N of n · N-SING: a N of n · VERB · V · V away · PHRASE: V inflects = lead the way

**blaz|er** /bleɪzəʳ/ **(blazers)** A **blazer** is a kind of jacket which is often worn by members of a particular group, especially schoolchildren and members of a sports team.
N-COUNT

**blaz|ing** /bleɪzɪŋ/ **Blazing** sun or **blazing hot** weather is very hot. ❑ *Quite a few people were eating outside in the blazing sun.*
ADJ: ADJ n

**bldg** **(bldgs)**

> in AM, use **bldg.**

**Bldg** is a written abbreviation for **building**, and is used especially in the names of buildings. ❑ *...Old National Bank Bldg.*

**bleach** /bliːtʃ/ **(bleaches, bleaching, bleached)** 1 If you **bleach** something, you use a chemical to make it white or pale in colour. ❑ *These products don't bleach the hair. ...bleached pine tables. ...a bleaching agent.* 2 If the sun **bleaches** something, or something **bleaches**, its colour gets paler until it is almost white. ❑ *The tree's roots are stripped and hung to season and bleach... The sun will bleach the hairs on your face.* 3 **Bleach** is a chemical that is used to make cloth white, or to clean things thoroughly and kill germs.
VERB · V n · V-ed · V-ing · VERB · V · V n · N-MASS

**bleach|ers** /bliːtʃəʳz/ **The bleachers** are a part of an outdoor sports stadium, or the seats in that area, which are usually uncovered and are the least expensive place where people can sit. [AM]
N-PLURAL: usu the N

**bleak** /bliːk/ **(bleaker, bleakest)** 1 If a situation is **bleak**, it is bad, and seems unlikely to improve. ❑ *The immediate outlook remains bleak... Many predicted a bleak future.* ♦ **bleak|ness** *The continued bleakness of the American job market was blamed.* 2 If you describe a place as **bleak**, you mean that it looks cold, empty, and unattractive. ❑ *The island's pretty bleak. ...bleak inner-city streets.* 3 When the weather is **bleak**, it is cold, dull, and unpleasant. ❑ *The weather can be quite bleak on the coast.* 4 If someone looks or sounds **bleak**, they look or sound depressed, as if they have no hope or energy. ❑ *Alberg gave him a bleak stare.* ♦ **bleak|ly** *'There is nothing left,' she says bleakly.*
ADJ = gloomy ≠ bright · N-UNCOUNT: usu with supp, oft N of n · ADJ · ADJ · ADJ · ADV: usu ADV with v, also ADV adj

**bleary** /blɪəri/ If your eyes are **bleary**, they look dull or tired, as if you have not had enough sleep or have drunk too much alcohol. ❑ *I arrived bleary-eyed and rumpled... He stared at Leo with great bleary eyes.*
ADJ

**bleat** /bliːt/ **(bleats, bleating, bleated)** 1 When a sheep or goat **bleats**, it makes the sound that sheep and goats typically make. ❑ *From the slope below, the wild goats bleated faintly. ...a small flock of bleating ewes and lambs.* ♦ **Bleat** is also a noun. ❑ *...the faint bleat of a distressed animal.* 2 If you say that someone **bleats about** something, you mean that they complain about it in a way which makes them sound weak and irritating. ❑ *They are always bleating about 'unfair' foreign competition... Don't come bleating to me every time something goes wrong.*
VERB · V · V-ing · N-COUNT · VERB disapproval = whinge, whine · V about n · V prep/adv · Also V that

**bled** /bled/ **Bled** is the past tense and past participle of **bleed**.

**bleed** /bliːd/ **(bleeds, bleeding, bled)** 1 When you **bleed**, you lose blood from your body as a result of injury or illness. ❑ *His head had struck the sink and was bleeding... She's going to bleed to death!* ♦ **bleed|ing** *This results in internal bleeding.* 2 If the colour of one substance **bleeds into** the colour of another substance that it is touching, it goes into the other thing so that its colour changes in an undesirable way. ❑ *The colouring pigments from the skins are not allowed to bleed into the grape juice.* 3 If someone **is being bled**, money or other resources are gradually being taken away from them. ❑ *We have been gradually bled for twelve years... They mean to bleed the British to the utmost.* 4 → See also **nosebleed**.
VERB · V · V to n · N-UNCOUNT · VERB · V prep · VERB disapproval · be V-ed · V n

**bleed|ing** /bliːdɪŋ/ **Bleeding** is used by some people to emphasize what they are saying, especially when they feel strongly about something or dislike something. [BRIT, INFORMAL, RUDE]
ADJ: ADJ n · emphasis

**bleed|ing edge**

> The spelling **bleeding-edge** is used for meaning 2.

1 If you are **at the bleeding edge of** a particular field of activity, you are involved in its most advanced or most exciting developments. ❑ *McNally has spent 17 years at the bleeding edge of computing.* 2 **Bleeding-edge** equipment or technology is the most advanced that there is in a particular field. ❑ *...an RAF facility with bleeding-edge electronics and communications systems.*
N-SING · ADJ

**bleed|ing heart** **(bleeding hearts)** also **bleeding-heart**. If you describe someone as a **bleeding heart**, you are criticizing them for being sympathetic towards people who are poor and suffering, without doing anything practical to help. ❑ *I'm not a bleeding heart liberal.*
N-COUNT: oft N n · disapproval

**bleep** /bliːp/ **(bleeps, bleeping, bleeped)** 1 A **bleep** is a short, high-pitched sound, usually one of a series, that is made by an electrical device. [mainly BRIT] 2 If something electronic **bleeps**, it makes a short, high-pitched sound. [mainly BRIT] ❑ *When we turned the boat about, the signal began to bleep again constantly.*
N-COUNT = beep · VERB = beep · V

**bleep|er** /bliːpəʳ/ **(bleepers)** A **bleeper** is the same as a **beeper**. [BRIT, INFORMAL]
N-COUNT

**blem|ish** /blemɪʃ/ **(blemishes, blemishing, blemished)** 1 A **blemish** is a small mark on something that spoils its appearance. ❑ *Every piece is closely scrutinised, and if there is the slightest blemish on it, it is rejected.* 2 A **blemish on** something is a small fault in it. ❑ *This is the one blemish on an otherwise resounding success.* 3 If something **blemishes** someone's character or reputation, it spoils it or makes it seem less good than it was in the past. ❑ *He wasn't about to blemish that pristine record.*
N-COUNT · N-COUNT: oft N on n = imperfection · VERB = tarnish · V n

**blem|ished** /blemɪʃt/ You use **blemished** to describe something such as someone's skin or a piece of fruit when its appearance is spoiled by small marks. ❑ *...a skin tonic for oily, blemished complexions.*
ADJ: usu ADJ n

**blend** /blend/ **(blends, blending, blended)** 1 If you **blend** substances together or if they **blend**, you mix them together so that they become one substance. ❑ *Blend the butter with the sugar and beat until light and creamy... Blend the ingredients until you have a smooth cream... Put the soap and water in a pan and leave to stand until they have blended.*
V-RECIP · V n with n · V pl-n · pl-n V · Also V

2 A **blend of** things is a mixture or combination of them that is useful or pleasant. ❑ *The public areas offer a subtle blend of traditional charm with modern amenities.* 3 When colours, sounds, or styles **blend**, they come together or are combined in a pleasing way. ❑ *You could paint the walls and ceilings the same colour so they blend together. ...the picture, furniture and porcelain collections that blend so well with the house itself.* 4 If you **blend** ideas, policies, or styles, you use them together in order to achieve something. ❑ *His 'cosmic vision' is to blend Christianity with 'the wisdom of all world religions'. ...a band that blended jazz and classical music.* N-COUNT: usu sing, usu N *of* n; V-RECIP; pl-n V; V *with* n; VERB; V n *with* n; V n

♦ **blend in** or **blend into** 1 If something **blends into** the background, it is so similar to the background that it is difficult to see or hear it separately. ❑ *The toad had changed its colour to blend in with its new environment. ...a continuous pale neutral grey, almost blending into the sky.* 2 If someone **blends into** a particular group or situation, they seem to belong there, because their appearance or behaviour is similar to that of the other people involved. ❑ *It must have reinforced my determination to blend into my surroundings... She felt she would blend in nicely... He blended in with the crowd at the art sale.* PHRASAL VERB; V P *with* n; V P n; PHRASAL VERB; V P n; V P; V P *with* n

**blend|er** /blendəʳ/ **(blenders)** A **blender** is an electrical kitchen appliance used for mixing liquids and soft foods together or turning fruit or vegetables into liquid. N-COUNT

**bless** /bles/ **(blesses, blessing, blessed)**
1 When someone such as a priest **blesses** people or things, he asks for God's favour and protection for them. ❑ *...asking for all present to bless this couple and their loving commitment to one another.* VERB; V n
2 **Bless** is used in expressions such as '**God bless**' or '**bless you**' to express affection, thanks, or good wishes. [INFORMAL, SPOKEN] ❑ *'Bless you, Eva,' he whispered... God bless and thank you all so much.* 3 You can say '**bless you**' to someone who has just sneezed. [SPOKEN] 4 ➔ See also **blessed, blessing**. CONVENTION [feelings]; CONVENTION [formulae]

**bless|ed**

> ✓ Pronounced /blest/ for meaning 1, and /blesɪd/ for meaning 2.

1 If someone is **blessed with** a particular good quality or skill, they have that good quality or skill. ❑ *Both are blessed with uncommon ability to fix things.* 2 You use **blessed** to describe something that you think is wonderful, and that you are grateful for or relieved about. ❑ *Rainy weather brings blessed relief to hay fever victims.* ♦ **bless|ed|ly** *Most British election campaigns are blessedly brief.* 3 ➔ See also **bless**. ADJ: v-link ADJ *with* n; ADJ: ADJ n [approval]; ADV: usu ADV adj, also ADV with cl

**bless|ing** /blesɪŋ/ **(blessings)** 1 A **blessing** is something good that you are grateful for. ❑ *Rivers are a blessing for an agricultural country. ...the blessings of prosperity.* 2 If something is done with someone's **blessing**, it is done with their approval and support. ❑ *With the blessing of the White House, a group of Democrats in Congress is meeting to find additional budget cuts... In April Thai and Indonesian leaders gave their formal blessing to the idea.* N-COUNT; N-COUNT: usu sing, with poss = approval
3 A **blessing** is a prayer asking God to look kindly upon the people who are present or the event that is taking place. 4 ➔ See also **bless**. N-COUNT

**PHRASES** 5 If you tell someone to **count** their **blessings**, you are saying that they should think about how lucky they are instead of complaining. ❑ *Some would argue this was no burden in fact, and that she should count her blessings.* 6 If you say that something is **a blessing in disguise**, you mean that it causes problems and difficulties at first but later you realize that it was the best thing that could have happened. ❑ *The failure to conclude the trade talks last December could prove a blessing in disguise.* 7 If you say that a situation is **a mixed blessing**, you mean that it has disadvantages as well as advantages. ❑ *For ordinary Italians, Sunday's news probably amounts to a mixed blessing.* PHRASE: V inflects; PHRASE: usu v-link PHR; PHRASE: usu v-link PHR

**blew** /bluː/ **Blew** is the past tense of **blow**.

**blight** /blaɪt/ **(blights, blighting, blighted)**
1 You can refer to something as a **blight** when it causes great difficulties, and damages or spoils other things. ❑ *This discriminatory policy has really been a blight on America... Manchester still suffers from urban blight and unacceptable poverty.* 2 If something **blights** your life or your hopes, it damages and spoils them. If something **blights** an area, it spoils it and makes it unattractive. ❑ *An embarrassing blunder nearly blighted his career before it got off the ground. ...a strategy to redevelop blighted inner-city areas.* 3 **Blight** is a disease which makes plants dry up and die. N-VAR: usu with supp; VERB; V n; V-ed; N-UNCOUNT: also N in pl

**blight|er** /blaɪtəʳ/ **(blighters)** 1 You can refer to someone you do not like as a **blighter**. [BRIT, INFORMAL] ❑ *He was a nasty little blighter.* 2 You can use **blighter** as an informal way of referring to someone. [BRIT] ❑ *Lucky blighter, thought King.* N-COUNT [disapproval]; N-COUNT = fellow

**Blighty** /blaɪti/ **Blighty** is a way of referring to England. [BRIT, HUMOROUS, OLD-FASHIONED] ❑ *See you back in Blighty!* N-PROPER

**bli|mey** /blaɪmi/ You say **blimey** when you are surprised by something or feel strongly about it. [BRIT, INFORMAL] ❑ *'We walked all the way to Moseley.' — 'Blimey!'* EXCLAM [feelings]

**blimp** /blɪmp/ **(blimps)** A **blimp** is the same as an **airship**. N-COUNT

**blind** /blaɪnd/ **(blinds, blinding, blinded)** ◆◇◇
1 Someone who is **blind** is unable to see because their eyes are damaged. ❑ *I started helping him run the business when he went blind.* ♦ **The blind** are people who are blind. ❑ *He was a teacher of the blind.* ♦ **blind|ness** *Early diagnosis and treatment can usually prevent blindness.* 2 If something **blinds** you, it makes you unable to see, either for a short time or permanently. ❑ *The sun hit the windscreen, momentarily blinding him.* 3 If you are **blind with** something such as tears or a bright light, you are unable to see for a short time because of the tears or light. ❑ *Her mother groped for the back of the chair, her eyes blind with tears.* ♦ **blind|ly** *Lettie groped blindly for the glass.* ADJ; N-PLURAL: *the* N; N-UNCOUNT; VERB; V n; ADJ: v-link ADJ, usu ADJ *with* n; ADV
4 If you say that someone is **blind to** a fact or a situation, you mean that they ignore it or are unaware of it, although you think that they should take notice of it or be aware of it. ❑ *All the time I was blind to your suffering.* ♦ **blind|ness** *...blindness in government policy to the very existence of the unemployed.* 5 If something **blinds** you **to** the real situation, it prevents you from realizing that it exists or from understanding it properly. ❑ *He never allowed his love of Australia to blind him to his countrymen's faults.* 6 You can describe someone's beliefs or actions as **blind** when you think that they seem to take no notice of important facts or behave in an unreasonable way. ❑ *...her blind faith in the wisdom of the Church... Lesley yelled at him with blind, hating rage.* 7 A **blind** corner is one that you cannot see round because something is blocking your view. ❑ *He tried to overtake three cars on a blind corner and crashed head-on into a lorry.* 8 A **blind** is a roll of cloth or paper which you can pull down over a window as a covering. ➔ See also **Venetian blind**. 9 ➔ See also **blinding, blindly, colour-blind**. 10 If you say that someone **is turning a blind eye to** something bad or illegal that is happening, you mean that you think they are pretending not to notice that it is happening so that they will not have to do anything about it. ❑ *Teachers are turning a blind eye to pupils smoking at school, a report reveals today.* ADJ: v-link ADJ *to* n [disapproval]; N-UNCOUNT; VERB; V n *to* n; ADJ: usu ADJ n [disapproval]; ADJ: ADJ n; N-COUNT; PHRASE: V inflects [disapproval]

**blind al|ley** **(blind alleys)** If you describe a situation as a **blind alley**, you mean that progress is not possible or that the situation can have no useful results. ❑ *The Internet has proved a blind alley for many firms.* N-COUNT = dead end

**blind date** **(blind dates)** A **blind date** is an arrangement made for you to spend a romantic evening with someone you have never met before. N-COUNT

**blind|er** /blaɪndəʳ/ **(blinders) Blinders** are the same as **blinkers**. [AM] N-PLURAL

**blind|fold** /blaɪndfoʊld/ **(blindfolds, blindfolding, blindfolded)** [1] A **blindfold** is a strip of cloth that is tied over someone's eyes so that they cannot see. N-COUNT [2] If you **blindfold** someone, you tie a blindfold over their eyes. ❑ *His abductors blindfolded him and drove him to a flat in southern Beirut... The report says prisoners were often kept blindfolded.* VERB V n V-ed [3] If someone does something **blindfold**, they do it while wearing a blindfold. ❑ *The Australian chess grandmaster Ian Rogers took on six opponents blindfold and beat five.* ADJ: ADJ after v [4] If you say that you **can** do something **blindfold**, you are emphasizing that you can do it easily, for example because you have done it many times before. ❑ *He read the letter again although already he could have recited its contents blindfold.* PHRASE emphasis

**blind|ing** /blaɪndɪŋ/ [1] A **blinding** light is extremely bright. ❑ *The doctor worked busily beneath the blinding lights of the delivery room.* ADJ: usu ADJ n = dazzling [2] You use **blinding** to emphasize that something is very obvious. ❑ *The miseries I went through made me suddenly realise with a blinding flash what life was all about.* ADJ: ADJ n emphasis ♦ **blind|ing|ly** *It is so blindingly obvious that defence must be the responsibility of the state.* ADV: ADV adj/adv [3] **Blinding** pain is very strong pain. ❑ *There was a pain then, a quick, blinding agony that jumped along Danlo's spine.* ADJ: usu ADJ n

**blind|ly** /blaɪndli/ If you say that someone does something **blindly**, you mean that they do it without having enough information, or without thinking about it. ❑ *Don't just blindly follow what the banker says... Without adequate information, many students choose a college almost blindly.* ➔ See also **blind**. ADV: usu ADV with v, also ADV adj, ADV with cl disapproval

**blind spot** **(blind spots)** [1] If you say that someone has a **blind spot** about something, you mean that they seem to be unable to understand it or to see how important it is. ❑ *The prime minister has a blind spot on ethical issues... When I was single I never worried about money – it was a bit of a blind spot.* N-COUNT [2] A **blind spot** is an area in your range of vision that you cannot see properly but which you really should be able to see. For example, when you are driving a car, the area just behind your shoulders is often a blind spot. N-COUNT

**blind trust** **(blind trusts)** A **blind trust** is a financial arrangement in which someone's investments are managed without the person knowing where the money is invested. **Blind trusts** are used especially by people such as members of parliament, so that they cannot be accused of using their position to make money unfairly. [BUSINESS] ❑ *His shares were placed in a blind trust when he became a government minister.* N-COUNT

**blink** /blɪŋk/ **(blinks, blinking, blinked)** [1] When you **blink** or when you **blink** your eyes, you shut your eyes and very quickly open them again. ❑ *Kathryn blinked and forced a smile... She was blinking her eyes rapidly... He blinked at her.* VERB V V n V at n ♦ **Blink** is also a noun. ❑ *He kept giving quick blinks.* N-COUNT [2] When a light **blinks**, it flashes on and off. ❑ *Green and yellow lights blinked on the surface of the harbour... A warning light blinked on.* VERB V V on/out/off [3] If a machine goes **on the blink**, it stops working properly. [INFORMAL] ❑ *...an old TV that's on the blink.* PHRASE: usu v-link PHR

**blink|ered** /blɪŋkəʳd/ A **blinkered** view, attitude, or approach is narrow and does not take into account other people's opinions. A **blinkered** person has this kind of attitude. [BRIT] ❑ *They've got a very blinkered view of life... Haig was limited by his blinkered approach to strategy and tactics.* ADJ disapproval = narrow-minded

**blink|ers** /blɪŋkəʳz/ **Blinkers** are two pieces of leather which are placed at the side of a horse's eyes so that it can only see straight ahead. [mainly BRIT] N-PLURAL

✔ in AM, use **blinders**

**blip** /blɪp/ **(blips)** [1] A **blip** is a small spot of light, sometimes occurring with a short, high-pitched sound, which flashes on and off regularly on a piece of equipment such as a radar screen. N-COUNT [2] A **blip** in a straight line, such as the line on a graph, is a point at which the line suddenly makes a sharp change of direction before returning to its original direction. N-COUNT [3] A **blip** in a situation is a sudden but temporary change or interruption in it. ❑ *Interest rates generally have been declining since last spring, despite a few upward blips in recent weeks.* N-COUNT

**bliss** /blɪs/ **Bliss** is a state of complete happiness. ❑ *It was a scene of such domestic bliss.* N-UNCOUNT

**bliss|ful** /blɪsfʊl/ [1] A **blissful** situation or period of time is one in which you are extremely happy. ❑ *We spent a blissful week together... There's just nothing more blissful than lying by that pool.* ADJ ♦ **bliss|ful|ly** /blɪsfʊli/ *We're blissfully happy... The summer passed blissfully.* ADV: ADV adj, ADV after v [2] If someone is in **blissful** ignorance of something unpleasant or serious, they are totally unaware of it. ❑ *Many country parishes were still living in blissful ignorance of the post-war crime wave.* ADJ: ADJ n ♦ **bliss|ful|ly** *At first, he was blissfully unaware of the conspiracy against him.* ADV: usu ADV adj, also ADV before v

**blis|ter** /blɪstəʳ/ **(blisters, blistering, blistered)** [1] A **blister** is a painful swelling on the surface of your skin. Blisters contain a clear liquid and are usually caused by heat or by something repeatedly rubbing your skin. N-COUNT [2] When your skin **blisters** or when something **blisters** it, blisters appear on it. ❑ *The affected skin turns red and may blister... The sap of this plant blisters the skin. ...pausing to bathe their blistered feet.* VERB V V n V-ed

**blis|ter|ing** /blɪstərɪŋ/ [1] **Blistering** heat is very great heat. ❑ *...a blistering summer day.* ADJ: usu ADJ n [2] A **blistering** remark expresses great anger or dislike. ❑ *The president responded to this with a blistering attack on his critics.* ADJ: usu ADJ n [3] **Blistering** is used to describe actions in sport to emphasize that they are done with great speed or force. [JOURNALISM] ❑ *Sharon Wild set a blistering pace to take the lead.* ADJ: ADJ n emphasis

**blithe** /blaɪð/ You use **blithe** to indicate that something is done casually, without serious or careful thought. ❑ *It does so with blithe disregard for best scientific practice.* ADJ: usu ADJ n disapproval ♦ **blithe|ly** *Your editorial blithely ignores the hard facts.* ADV: ADV with v, ADV adj

**blitz** /blɪts/ **(blitzes, blitzing, blitzed)** [1] If a city or building **is blitzed** during a war, it is attacked by bombs dropped by enemy aircraft. ❑ *In the autumn of 1940 London was blitzed by an average of two hundred aircraft a night... They blitzed the capital with tanks, artillery, anti-aircraft weapons and machine guns.* VERB be V-ed V n [2] The heavy bombing of British cities by German aircraft in 1940 and 1941 is referred to as **the Blitz**. N-PROPER: the N [3] If you have a **blitz on** something, you make a big effort to deal with it or to improve it. [INFORMAL] ❑ *Regional accents are still acceptable but there is to be a blitz on incorrect grammar.* N-COUNT: with supp, oft N on n [4] An advertising or publicity **blitz** is a major effort to make the public aware of something. ❑ *On December 8 the media blitz began in earnest.* N-COUNT: with supp

**blitz|krieg** /blɪtskriːg/ **(blitzkriegs)** [1] A **blitzkrieg** is a fast and intense military attack that takes the enemy by surprise and is intended to achieve a very quick victory. N-COUNT [2] Journalists sometimes refer to a rapid and powerful attack or campaign in, for example, sport, politics, or advertising as a **blitzkrieg**. [INFORMAL] ❑ *...a blitzkrieg of media hype.* N-COUNT

**bliz|zard** /blɪzəʳd/ **(blizzards)** A **blizzard** is a very bad snowstorm with strong winds. N-COUNT

**bloat|ed** /bloʊtɪd/ [1] If someone's body or a part of their body is **bloated**, it is much larger than normal, usually because it has a lot of liquid or gas inside it. ❑ *...the bloated body of a dead bullock... His face was bloated.* ADJ = swollen [2] If you feel **bloated** after eating a large meal, you feel very full and uncomfortable. ❑ *Diners do not want to leave the table feeling bloated.* ADJ: v-link ADJ [3] If you describe an organiza- ADJ:

tion as **bloated**, you mean that it is larger and less efficient than it should be. ❑ *...its massive state apparatus and bloated bureaucracy.* usu ADJ n

**bloat|ing** /bloutɪŋ/ **Bloating** is the swelling of a body or part of a body, usually because it has a lot of gas or liquid in it. ❑ *...abdominal bloating and pain.* N-UNCOUNT = swelling

**blob** /blɒb/ **(blobs)** [1] A **blob of** thick or sticky liquid is a small, often round, amount of it. [INFORMAL] ❑ *...a blob of chocolate mousse.* N-COUNT: usu with supp [2] You can use **blob** to refer to something that you cannot see very clearly, for example because it is in the distance. [INFORMAL] ❑ *You could just see vague blobs of faces.* N-COUNT

**bloc** /blɒk/ **(blocs)** A **bloc** is a group of countries which have similar political aims and interests and that act together over some issues. ❑ *...the former Soviet bloc. ...the world's largest trading bloc.* ➔ See also **en bloc**. N-COUNT

**block** /blɒk/ **(blocks, blocking, blocked)** ◆◆◇ [1] A **block** of flats or offices is a large building containing them. ➔ See picture on page 1706. ❑ *...blocks of council flats. ...a white-painted apartment block.* N-COUNT: usu with supp, oft N *of* n [2] A **block** in a town is an area of land with streets on all its sides. ❑ *She walked four blocks down High Street... He walked around the block three times.* N-COUNT [3] A **block of** a substance is a large rectangular piece of it. ❑ *...a block of ice.* N-COUNT: usu N *of* n [4] To **block** a road, channel, or pipe means to put an object across it or in it so that nothing can pass through it or along it. ❑ *Some students today blocked a highway in the center of the city... He can clear blocked drains.* VERB V n V-ed [5] If something **blocks** your view, it prevents you from seeing something because it is between you and that thing. ❑ *...a row of spruce trees that blocked his view of the long north slope of the mountain.* VERB = obstruct V n [6] If you **block** someone's way, you prevent them from going somewhere or entering a place by standing in front of them. ❑ *I started to move round him, but he blocked my way.* VERB V n [7] If you **block** something that is being arranged, you prevent it from being done. ❑ *For years the country has tried to block imports of various cheap foreign products.* VERB V n [8] A **block of** something such as tickets or shares is a large quantity of them, especially when they are all sold at the same time and are in a particular sequence or order. ❑ *Those booking a block of seats get them at reduced rates.* N-COUNT: usu N *of* n [9] If you have a **mental block** or a **block**, you are temporarily unable to do something that you can normally do which involves using, thinking about, or remembering something. N-COUNT: usu supp N [10] ➔ See also **breeze-block**, **building block**, **roadblock**, **starting block**, **stumbling block**, **tower block**. **a chip off the old block** ➔ see **chip**.

♦ **block in** If you **are blocked in**, someone has parked their car in such a way that you cannot drive yours away. ❑ *Our cars get blocked in and we can't leave for ages... Oh, is that your car outside? I may have blocked you in.* PHRASAL VERB *get* V-ed P V n P Also V P n (not pron)

♦ **block off** When you **block off** a door, window, or passage, you put something across it so that nothing can pass through it. ❑ *They had blocked off the fireplaces to stop draughts.* PHRASAL VERB V P n (not pron) Also V n P

♦ **block out** [1] If someone **blocks out** a thought, they try not to think about it. ❑ *She accuses me of having blocked out the past... I had to block the thought out of my mind.* PHRASAL VERB V P n (not pron) V n P *of* n [2] Something that **blocks out** light prevents it from reaching a place. ❑ *Thick chipboard across the window frames blocked out the daylight... Those clouds would have cast shadows that would have blocked some sunlight out.* PHRASAL VERB V P n (not pron) V n P

**block|ade** /blɒkeɪd/ **(blockades, blockading, blockaded)** [1] A **blockade** of a place is an action that is taken to prevent goods or people from entering or leaving it. ❑ *Striking lorry drivers agreed to lift their blockades of main roads. ...the economic blockade of Lithuania.* N-COUNT: oft N *of* n [2] If a group of people **blockade** a place, they stop goods or people from reaching that place. If they **blockade** a road or a port, they stop people using that road or port. ❑ *Truck drivers have blockaded roads to show their anger over new driving regulations.* VERB V n Also V-ed

**block|age** /blɒkɪdʒ/ **(blockages)** A **blockage** in a pipe, tube, or tunnel is an object which blocks it, or the state of being blocked. ❑ *...a total blockage in one of the coronary arteries.* N-COUNT: oft N *in/of* n

**block|bust|er** /blɒkbʌstəʳ/ **(blockbusters)** A **blockbuster** is a film or book that is very popular and successful, usually because it is very exciting. [INFORMAL] N-COUNT

**block|bust|ing** /blɒkbʌstɪŋ/ A **blockbusting** film or book is one that is very successful, usually because it is very exciting. [JOURNALISM, INFORMAL] ❑ *...the blockbusting sci-fi movie 'Suburban Commando'.* ADJ: ADJ n

**block capi|tals** **Block capitals** are simple capital letters that are not decorated in any way. N-PLURAL: usu *in* N

**block let|ters** **Block letters** are the same as **block capitals**. N-PLURAL: usu *in* N

**block vote** **(block votes)** A **block vote** is a large number of votes that are all cast in the same way by one person on behalf of a group of people. N-COUNT

**bloke** /blouk/ **(blokes)** A **bloke** is a man. [BRIT, INFORMAL] ❑ *He is a really nice bloke.* N-COUNT

**blonde** /blɒnd/ **(blondes, blonder, blondest)**

> ✓ The form **blonde** is usually used to refer to women, and **blond** to refer to men.

[1] A woman who has **blonde** hair has pale-coloured hair. Blonde hair can be very light brown or light yellow. The form **blond** is used when describing men. ❑ *There were two little girls, one Asian and one with blonde hair... The baby had blond curls.* COLOUR [2] Someone who is **blonde** has blonde hair. ❑ *He was blonder than his brother. ...the striking blond actor.* ADJ [3] A **blonde** is a woman who has blonde hair. N-COUNT

**blonde bomb|shell** **(blonde bombshells)** Journalists sometimes use **blonde bombshell** to refer to a woman with blonde hair who is very attractive. [JOURNALISM, INFORMAL] N-COUNT

**blood** /blʌd/ ◆◆◇ [1] **Blood** is the red liquid that flows inside your body, which you can see if you cut yourself. N-UNCOUNT [2] You can use **blood** to refer to the race or social class of someone's parents or ancestors. ❑ *There was Greek blood in his veins.* N-UNCOUNT: usu supp N

PHRASES [3] If you say that there is **bad blood between** people, you mean that they have argued about something and dislike each other. ❑ *There is, it seems, some bad blood between Mills and the Baldwins.* PHRASE: oft PHR *between* pl-n [4] If you say that something **makes** your **blood boil**, you are emphasizing that it makes you very angry. ❑ *It makes my blood boil to think two thugs decided to pick on an innocent young girl.* PHRASE: V inflects [emphasis] [5] If something violent and cruel is done **in cold blood**, it is done deliberately and in an unemotional way. ❑ *The crime had been committed in cold blood.* ➔ See also **cold-blooded**. PHRASE: PHR after v [disapproval] [6] If you say that something **makes** your **blood run cold** or **makes** your **blood freeze**, you mean that it makes you feel very frightened. ❑ *The rage in his eyes made her blood run cold... He could hear a sudden roaring. His blood froze.* PHRASE: V inflects [emphasis] [7] If you say that someone has a person's **blood on** their **hands**, you mean that they are responsible for that person's death. ❑ *He has my son's blood on his hands. I hope it haunts him for the rest of his days.* PHRASE [8] If a quality or talent is **in** your **blood**, it is part of your nature, and other members of your family have it too. ❑ *Diplomacy was in his blood: his ancestors had been feudal lords... He has adventure in his blood.* PHRASE: oft v-link PHR [9] You can use the expressions **new blood**, **fresh blood**, or **young blood** to refer to people who are brought into an organization to improve it by thinking of new ideas or new ways of doing things. ❑ *...a major reshuffle of the cabinet to bring in new blood.* PHRASE [10] If you say that someone **sweats blood** trying to do something, you are emphasizing that they try very hard to do it. ❑ *I had to sweat blood for an M.A.* PHRASE: V inflects [emphasis]

11 flesh and blood → see **flesh**. own flesh and blood → see **flesh**.

**blood and thun|der** also **blood-and-thunder.** A **blood and thunder** performer or performance is very loud and emotional. ❑ *He was a blood-and-thunder preacher.* ADJ: ADJ n

**blood bank** (**blood banks**) A **blood bank** is a place where blood which has been taken from blood donors is stored until it is needed for people in hospital. N-COUNT

**blood|bath** /blʌdbɑːθ, -bæθ/ (**bloodbaths**) also **blood bath.** If you describe an event as a **bloodbath**, you are emphasizing that a lot of people were killed very violently. ❑ *The war degenerated into a bloodbath of tribal killings.* N-COUNT [emphasis]

**blood broth|er** (**blood brothers**) also **blood-brother.** A man's **blood brother** is a man he has sworn to treat as a brother, often in a ceremony which involves mixing a small amount of their blood. N-COUNT

**blood count** (**blood counts**) Your **blood count** is the number of red and white cells in your blood. A **blood count** can also refer to a medical examination which determines the number of red and white cells in your blood. ❑ *Her blood count was normal... We do a blood count to ensure that all is well.* N-COUNT

**blood-curdling** also **bloodcurdling.** A **blood-curdling** sound or story is very frightening and horrible. ❑ *...blood-curdling tales.* ADJ: usu ADJ n

**blood do|nor** (**blood donors**) A **blood donor** is someone who gives some of their blood so that it can be used in operations. N-COUNT

**blood feud** (**blood feuds**) A **blood feud** is a long-lasting, bitter disagreement between two or more groups of people, particularly family groups. Blood feuds often involve members of each group murdering or fighting with members of the other. N-COUNT = vendetta

**blood group** (**blood groups**) Someone's **blood group** is the type of blood that they have in their body. There are four main types: A, B, AB, and O. N-COUNT: oft poss N = blood type

**blood heat** **Blood heat** is a temperature of 37°C, which is about the same as the normal temperature of the human body. N-UNCOUNT

**blood|hound** /blʌdhaʊnd/ (**bloodhounds**) A **bloodhound** is a large dog with a very good sense of smell. Bloodhounds are often used to find people or other animals by following their scent. N-COUNT

**blood|less** /blʌdləs/ 1 A **bloodless** coup or victory is one in which nobody is killed. ❑ *Reports from the area indicate that it was a bloodless coup... The campaign would be short and relatively bloodless.* ♦ **blood|less|ly** *This war had to be fought fast and relatively bloodlessly.* 2 If you describe someone's face or skin as **bloodless**, you mean that it is very pale. ❑ *...her face grey and bloodless.* ADJ; ADV: ADV with v; ADJ = ashen

**blood-letting** 1 **Blood-letting** is violence or killing between groups of people, especially between rival armies. ❑ *Once again there's been ferocious blood-letting in the township.* 2 Journalists sometimes refer to a bitter quarrel between two groups of people from within the same organization as **blood-letting**. ❑ *Hopefully a satisfactory solution can be reached without much blood letting.* N-UNCOUNT; N-UNCOUNT

**blood|line** /blʌdlaɪn/ (**bloodlines**) A person's **bloodline** is their ancestors over many generations, and the characteristics they are believed to have inherited from these ancestors. N-COUNT: usu with supp

**blood lust** also **blood-lust.** If you say that someone is driven by a **blood lust**, you mean that they are acting in an extremely violent way because their emotions have been aroused by the events around them. ❑ *The mobs became driven by a crazed blood-lust to take the city.* N-UNCOUNT: also a N

**blood mon|ey** 1 If someone makes a payment of **blood money** to the family of someone who has been killed, they pay that person's family a sum of money as compensation. ❑ *Defence lawyers have still not agreed to terms for payment of blood money to the victims' families.* 2 **Blood money** is money that is paid to someone for murdering someone. N-UNCOUNT; N-UNCOUNT

**blood poi|son|ing** **Blood poisoning** is a serious illness resulting from an infection in your blood. N-UNCOUNT

**blood pres|sure** Your **blood pressure** is the amount of force with which your blood flows around your body. ❑ *Your doctor will monitor your blood pressure... Prime Minister Pavlov had been taken ill with high blood pressure.* N-UNCOUNT

**blood pud|ding** (**blood puddings**) **Blood pudding** is another word for **black pudding**. N-VAR

**blood-red** also **blood red.** Something that is **blood-red** is bright red in colour. ❑ *...blood-red cherries.* COLOUR

**blood re|la|tion** (**blood relations**) also **blood relative.** A **blood relation** or **blood relative** is someone who is related to you by birth rather than by marriage. N-COUNT

**blood|shed** /blʌdʃed/ **Bloodshed** is violence in which people are killed or wounded. ❑ *The government must increase the pace of reforms to avoid further bloodshed.* N-UNCOUNT

**blood|shot** /blʌdʃɒt/ If your eyes are **bloodshot**, the parts that are usually white are red or pink. Your eyes can be bloodshot for a variety of reasons, for example because you are tired or you have drunk too much alcohol. ❑ *John's eyes were bloodshot and puffy.* ADJ

**blood sport** (**blood sports**) also **bloodsport. Blood sports** are sports such as hunting in which animals are killed. N-COUNT

**blood|stain** /blʌdsteɪn/ (**bloodstains**) A **bloodstain** is a mark on a surface caused by blood. N-COUNT

**blood|stained** /blʌdsteɪnd/ Someone or something that is **bloodstained** is covered with blood. ❑ *The killer must have been heavily bloodstained. ...bloodstained clothing.* ADJ

**blood|stock** /blʌdstɒk/ Horses that are bred for racing are referred to as **bloodstock**. N-UNCOUNT: usu N n

**blood|stream** /blʌdstriːm/ (**bloodstreams**) Your **bloodstream** is the blood that flows around your body. ❑ *The disease releases toxins into the bloodstream.* N-COUNT: usu sing, the N, poss N

**blood|sucker** /blʌdsʌkəʳ/ (**bloodsuckers**) 1 A **bloodsucker** is any creature that sucks blood from a wound that it has made in an animal or person. 2 If you call someone a **bloodsucker**, you disapprove of them because you think they do not do anything worthwhile but live off the efforts of other people. ❑ *At last he was free from the financial bloodsuckers.* N-COUNT; N-COUNT [disapproval]

**blood test** (**blood tests**) A **blood test** is a medical examination of a small amount of your blood. N-COUNT

**blood|thirsty** /blʌdθɜːʳsti/ **Bloodthirsty** people are eager to use violence or display a strong interest in violent things. You can also use **bloodthirsty** to refer to very violent situations. ❑ *They were savage and bloodthirsty. ...some of the most tragic scenes witnessed even in this bloodthirsty war.* ADJ

**blood trans|fu|sion** (**blood transfusions**) A **blood transfusion** is a process in which blood is injected into the body of a person who is badly injured or ill. N-VAR = transfusion

**blood type** (**blood types**) Someone's **blood type** is the same as their **blood group**. N-COUNT

**blood ves|sel** (**blood vessels**) **Blood vessels** are the narrow tubes through which your blood flows. N-COUNT: usu pl

**bloody** /blʌdi/ (**bloodier, bloodiest, bloodies, bloodying, bloodied**) ◆◇◇ 1 **Bloody** is used by some people to emphasize what they are saying, especially when they are angry. [BRIT, RUDE] ADJ: usu ADJ n [emphasis] 2 If you describe a situation or event as **bloody**, you mean ADJ: usu ADJ n that it is very violent and a lot of people are killed. ❑ *Forty-three demonstrators were killed in bloody clashes... They came to power in 1975 after a bloody civil war.* ♦ **bloodi|ly** *Rebellions in the area were bloodily repressed by pro-government forces.* [ADV: ADV with v] 3 You can describe someone or something as **bloody** if they are covered in a lot of blood. ❑ *He was arrested last October still carrying a bloody knife... Yulka's fingers were bloody and cracked.* [ADJ: usu ADJ n] ♦ **bloodi|ly** *The soldier reeled bloodily away.* [ADV: ADV with v] 4 If you have **bloodied** part of your body, there is blood on it, usually because you have had an accident or you have been attacked. ❑ *One of our children fell and bloodied his knee... She stared at her own bloodied hands, unable to think or move.* [VERB] [V n] [V-ed]

**Bloody Mary** /blʌdi meəri/ **(Bloody Marys)** also **bloody mary**. A **Bloody Mary** is a drink made from vodka and tomato juice. [N-COUNT]

**bloody-minded** If you say that someone is being **bloody-minded**, you are showing that you disapprove of their behaviour because you think they are being deliberately difficult instead of being helpful. [BRIT, INFORMAL] ❑ *He had a reputation for being bloody-minded and difficult.* [ADJ] [disapproval] ♦ **bloody-mindedness** *This is sheer bloody-mindedness. ...a rare mixture of courage and bloody-mindedness.* [N-UNCOUNT]

**bloom** /bluːm/ **(blooms, blooming, bloomed)** 1 A **bloom** is the flower on a plant. [LITERARY or TECHNICAL] ❑ *...the sweet fragrance of the white blooms... Harry carefully picked the bloom.* [N-COUNT = flower] 2 A plant or tree that is **in bloom** has flowers on it. ❑ *...a pink climbing rose in full bloom. ...the sweet smell of the blackberry in bloom.* [PHRASE] 3 When a plant or tree **blooms**, it produces flowers. When a flower **blooms**, it opens. ❑ *This plant blooms between May and June.* [VERB] [V] ♦ **-blooming** *...the scent of night-blooming flowers.* [COMB in ADJ] 4 If someone or something **blooms**, they develop good, attractive, or successful qualities. ❑ *Not many economies bloomed in 1990, least of all gold exporters like Australia... She bloomed into an utterly beautiful creature.* [VERB = blossom] [V] [V into n] 5 If something such as someone's skin has a **bloom**, it has a fresh and healthy appearance. ❑ *The skin loses its youthful bloom.* [N-UNCOUNT: also a N = glow] 6 → See also **blooming**.

**bloom|ers** /bluːməʳz/ **Bloomers** are an old-fashioned kind of women's underwear which consists of wide, loose trousers gathered at the knees. [N-PLURAL: also a pair of N]

**bloom|ing** /bluːmɪŋ/ Someone who is **blooming** looks attractively healthy and full of energy. ❑ *If they were blooming with confidence they wouldn't need me... She's in blooming health.* [ADJ]

**bloop|er** /bluːpəʳ/ **(bloopers)** A **blooper** is a silly mistake. [mainly AM, INFORMAL] ❑ *...the overwhelming appeal of television bloopers.* [N-COUNT]

**blos|som** /blɒsəm/ **(blossoms, blossoming, blossomed)** 1 **Blossom** is the flowers that appear on a tree before the fruit. ❑ *The cherry blossom came out early in Washington this year. ...the blossoms of plants, shrubs and trees.* [N-VAR: oft supp N] 2 If someone or something **blossoms**, they develop good, attractive, or successful qualities. ❑ *Why do some people take longer than others to blossom?... What began as a local festival has blossomed into an international event. ...the blossoming relationship between Israel and Eastern Europe.* [VERB = bloom] [V] [V into n] [V-ing] ♦ **blos|som|ing** *...the blossoming of British art, pop and fashion.* [N-UNCOUNT: N of n] 3 When a tree **blossoms**, it produces blossom. ❑ *Rain begins to fall and peach trees blossom.* [VERB] [V]

**blot** /blɒt/ **(blots, blotting, blotted)** 1 If something is a **blot on** a person's or thing's reputation, it spoils their reputation. ❑ *...a blot on the reputation of the architectural profession... This drugs scandal is another blot on the Olympics.* [N-COUNT: N on n] 2 A **blot** is a drop of liquid that has fallen on to a surface and has dried. ❑ *...an ink blot.* [N-COUNT] 3 If you **blot** a surface, you remove liquid from it by pressing a piece of soft paper or cloth onto it. ❑ *Before applying make-up, blot the face with a tissue to remove any excess oils.* [VERB] [V n] [Also V n adj] 4 If you describe something such as a building as **a blot on the landscape**, you mean that you think it is very ugly and spoils an otherwise attractive place. ❑ *The developers insist the £80m village will not leave a blot on the landscape.* [PHRASE: blot inflects]

♦ **blot out** 1 If one thing **blots out** another thing, it is in front of the other thing and prevents it from being seen. ❑ *About the time the three climbers were halfway down, clouds blotted out the sun. ...with mist blotting everything out except the endless black of the spruce on either side.* [PHRASAL VERB] [V P n (not pron)] [V n P] 2 If you try to **blot out** a memory, you try to forget it. If one thought or memory **blots out** other thoughts or memories, it becomes the only one that you can think about. ❑ *Are you saying that she's trying to blot out all memory of the incident?... The boy has gaps in his mind about it. He is blotting certain things out... She has suffered an extremely unhappy childhood, but simply blotted it out of her memory.* [PHRASAL VERB = block out] [V P n (not pron)] [V n P] [V n P of n]

**blotch** /blɒtʃ/ **(blotches)** A **blotch** is a small unpleasant-looking area of colour, for example on someone's skin. [N-COUNT = mark]

**blotched** /blɒtʃt/ Something that is **blotched** has blotches on it. ❑ *Her face is blotched and swollen. ...a dozen cargo planes blotched with camouflage colors.* [ADJ: oft ADJ with n = marked]

**blotchy** /blɒtʃi/ Something that is **blotchy** has blotches on it. ❑ *My skin goes red and blotchy. ...blotchy marks on the leaves.* [ADJ]

**blot|ter** /blɒtəʳ/ **(blotters)** A **blotter** is a large sheet of blotting paper kept in a special holder on a desk. [N-COUNT]

**blot|ting pa|per** **Blotting paper** is thick soft paper that you use for soaking up and drying ink on a piece of paper. [N-UNCOUNT]

**blouse** /blaʊz, AM blaʊs/ **(blouses)** A **blouse** is a kind of shirt worn by a girl or woman. [N-COUNT]

**blow**
① VERB USES
② NOUN USES

① **blow** /bloʊ/ **(blows, blowing, blew, blown)** ◆◆◇
⇒ Please look at category 12 to see if the expression you are looking for is shown under another headword. 1 When a wind or breeze **blows**, the air moves. ❑ *We woke to find a gale blowing outside.* [VERB] [V] 2 If the wind **blows** something somewhere or if it **blows** there, the wind moves it there. ❑ *Strong winds blew away most of the dust... Her cap fell off in the street and blew away... The bushes and trees were blowing in the wind.* [VERB] [V n with adv] [V adv/prep] [V] [Also V n prep] 3 If you **blow**, you send out a stream of air from your mouth. ❑ *Danny rubbed his arms and blew on his fingers to warm them... Take a deep breath and blow.* [VERB] [V prep/adv] [V] 4 If you **blow** something somewhere, you move it by sending out a stream of air from your mouth. ❑ *He picked up his mug and blew off the steam.* [VERB] [V n with adv] [Also V n prep] 5 If you **blow** bubbles or smoke rings, you make them by blowing air out of your mouth through liquid or smoke. ❑ *He blew a ring of blue smoke.* [VERB] [V n] 6 When a whistle or horn **blows** or someone **blows** it, they make a sound by blowing into it. ❑ *The whistle blew and the train slid forward... A guard was blowing his whistle.* [VERB] [V] [V n] 7 When you **blow** your nose, you force air out of it through your nostrils in order to clear it. ❑ *He took out a handkerchief and blew his nose.* [VERB] [V n] 8 To **blow** something **out**, **off**, or **away** means to remove or destroy it violently with an explosion. ❑ *The can exploded, wrecking the kitchen and bathroom and blowing out windows... Rival gunmen blew the city to bits.* [VERB] [V n with adv] [V n prep] 9 If you say that something **blows** an event, situation, or argument into a particular extreme state, especially an uncertain or unpleasant state, you mean that it causes it to be in that state. ❑ *Someone took an inappropriate use of words on my part and tried to blow it into a major controversy.* [VERB] [V n prep] 10 If you **blow** a large amount of money, you spend it quickly on luxuries. [INFORMAL] ❑ *My brother lent me some money and I went and blew the lot.* [VERB] [V n] 11 If you **blow** a chance or attempt to do something, you make a mistake which wastes the chance or causes the attempt to

fail. [INFORMAL] ❑ *He has almost certainly blown his chance of touring India this winter. ...the high-risk world of real estate, where one careless word could blow a whole deal... Oh you fool! You've blown it!* (V n; V n; V it) 12 ➔ See also **full-blown**, **overblown**. to **blow away the cobwebs** ➔ see **cobweb**. to **blow** someone's **cover** ➔ see **cover**. to **blow hot and cold** ➔ see **hot**. to **blow a kiss** ➔ see **kiss**. to **blow** your **top** ➔ see **top**. to **blow the whistle** ➔ see **whistle**.

♦ **blow out** 1 If you **blow out** a flame or a candle, you blow at it so that it stops burning. ❑ *I blew out the candle.* (PHRASAL VERB; V P n (not pron); Also V n P) 2 ➔ See also **blowout**.

♦ **blow over** If something such as trouble or an argument **blows over**, it ends without any serious consequences. ❑ *Wait, and it'll all blow over.* (PHRASAL VERB; V P)

♦ **blow up** 1 If someone **blows** something **up** or if it **blows up**, it is destroyed by an explosion. ❑ *He was jailed for 45 years for trying to blow up a plane... Their boat blew up as they slept.* (PHRASAL VERB; V P n; V P; Also V n P) 2 If you **blow up** something such as a balloon or a tyre, you fill it with air. ❑ *Other than blowing up a tyre I hadn't done any car maintenance.* (PHRASAL VERB; V P n; Also V n P) 3 If a wind or a storm **blows up**, the weather becomes very windy or stormy. ❑ *A storm blew up over the mountains.* (PHRASAL VERB; V P) 4 If you **blow up at** someone, you lose your temper and shout at them. [INFORMAL] ❑ *I'm sorry I blew up at you... When Myra told Karp she'd expose his past, he blew up.* (PHRASAL VERB; = explode; V P at n; V P) 5 If someone **blows** an incident **up** or if it **blows up**, it is made to seem more serious or important than it really is. ❑ *Newspapers blew up the story... The media may be blowing it up out of proportion... The scandal blew up into a major political furore.* (PHRASAL VERB; V P n, V n P; V P prep/adv; Also V P) 6 If a photographic image **is blown up**, a large copy is made of it. ❑ *The image is blown up on a large screen. ...two blown up photos of Paddy.* (PHRASAL VERB; be V-ed P; V-ed P; Also V P n, V n P) 7 ➔ See also **blow-up**.

② **blow** /bləʊ/ **(blows)** 1 If someone receives a **blow**, they are hit with a fist or weapon. ❑ *He went off to hospital after a blow to the face.* (◆◇◇ N-COUNT: oft N to/on n) 2 If something that happens is a **blow to** someone or something, it is very upsetting, disappointing, or damaging to them. ❑ *That ruling comes as a blow to environmentalists... His death dealt a severe blow to the army's morale.* (N-COUNT: oft N to n) 3 If two people or groups **come to blows**, they start fighting. ❑ *The representatives almost came to blows at a meeting.* (PHRASE: V inflects)

**blow-by-blow** A **blow-by-blow** account of an event describes every stage of it in great detail. [INFORMAL] ❑ *She wanted a blow-by-blow account of what happened.* (ADJ: usu ADJ n)

**blow-dry** **(blow-dries, blow-drying, blow-dried)** If you **blow-dry** your hair, you dry it with a hairdryer, often to give it a particular style. ❑ *I find it hard to blow-dry my hair... He has blow-dried blonde hair.* (VERB; V n; V-ed) ♦ **Blow-dry** is also a noun. ❑ *The price of a cut and blow-dry varies widely.* (N-SING)

**blow|er** /bləʊəʳ/ **The blower** is the telephone. [BRIT, INFORMAL, OLD-FASHIONED] (N-SING: the N)

**blow|lamp** /bləʊlæmp/ **(blowlamps)** also **blow lamp**. A **blowlamp** is a device which produces a hot flame, and is used to heat metal or remove old paint. [BRIT] (N-COUNT; = blowtorch)

☑ in AM, use **blowtorch**

**blown** /bləʊn/ **Blown** is the past participle of **blow**.

**blow|out** /bləʊaʊt/ **(blowouts)** also **blow-out**. 1 A **blowout** is a large meal, often a celebration with family or friends, at which people may eat too much. [INFORMAL] ❑ *Once in a while we had a major blowout.* (N-COUNT) 2 If you have a **blowout** while you are driving a car, one of the tyres suddenly bursts. ❑ *A lorry travelling south had a blow-out and crashed.* (N-COUNT; = puncture) 3 A **blowout in** an amount or a price is a sudden increase in it. [AUSTRALIAN, JOURNALISM] ❑ *...a blowout in surgery costs.* (N-COUNT: oft N in n)

**blow|torch** /bləʊtɔːʳtʃ/ **(blowtorches)** A **blowtorch** is the same as a **blowlamp**. (N-COUNT)

**blow-up** **(blow-ups)** also **blowup**. 1 A **blow-up** is a photograph or picture that has been made bigger. [INFORMAL] ❑ *...yellowing blow-ups of James Dean.* (N-COUNT) 2 A **blow-up** is a sudden fierce argument. [INFORMAL] ❑ *He and Cohen appeared headed for a major blowup.* (N-COUNT: oft N with)

**blub** /blʌb/ **(blubs, blubbing, blubbed)** If someone **blubs**, they cry because they are unhappy or frightened. [BRIT, INFORMAL] ❑ *Don't blub.* (VERB; = cry, blubber; V)

**blub|ber** /blʌbəʳ/ **(blubbers, blubbering, blubbered)** 1 **Blubber** is the fat of whales, seals, and similar sea animals. ❑ *The baby whale develops a thick layer of blubber to protect it from the cold sea.* (N-UNCOUNT) 2 If someone **blubbers**, they cry noisily and in an unattractive way. [INFORMAL] ❑ *She started to blubber like a child.* (VERB; V)

**bludg|eon** /blʌdʒᵊn/ **(bludgeons, bludgeoning, bludgeoned)** 1 To **bludgeon** someone means to hit them several times with a heavy object. ❑ *He broke into the old man's house and bludgeoned him with a hammer... A wealthy businessman has been found bludgeoned to death.* (VERB; V n; V-ed to n) 2 If someone **bludgeons** you **into** doing something, they make you do it by behaving aggressively. ❑ *Their approach simply bludgeons you into submission.* (VERB; = bulldoze; V n into n/-ing)

**blue** /bluː/ **(bluer, bluest, blues)** 1 Something that is **blue** is the colour of the sky on a sunny day. ❑ *There were swallows in the cloudless blue sky... She fixed her pale blue eyes on her father's. ...colourful blues and reds.* (◆◆◆ COLOUR) 2 **The blues** is a type of music which was developed by African American musicians in the southern United States. It is characterized by a slow tempo and a strong rhythm. (N-PLURAL: the N) 3 If you have got **the blues**, you feel sad and depressed. [INFORMAL] ❑ *Interfering in-laws are the prime sources of the blues.* (N-PLURAL: the N) 4 If you are feeling **blue**, you are feeling sad or depressed, often when there is no particular reason. [INFORMAL] ❑ *There's no earthly reason for me to feel so blue.* (ADJ: v-link ADJ; = down) 5 **Blue** films, stories, or jokes are about sex. ❑ *...a secret stash of porn mags and blue movies.* (ADJ: ADJ n) 6 If something happens **out of the blue**, it happens unexpectedly. ❑ *One of them wrote to us out of the blue several years later.* (PHRASE) 7 **blue moon** ➔ see **moon**.

**blue baby** **(blue babies)** A **blue baby** is a baby whose skin is slightly blue because it has been born with something wrong with its heart. (N-COUNT)

**blue|bell** /bluːbel/ **(bluebells)** **Bluebells** are plants that have blue bell-shaped flowers on thin upright stems. Bluebells flower in the spring. (N-COUNT)

**blue|berry** /bluːbəri, AM -beri/ **(blueberries)** A **blueberry** is a small dark blue fruit that is found in North America. Blueberries are usually cooked before they are eaten. (N-COUNT)

**blue-black** Something that is **blue-black** is bluish black in colour. ❑ *...blue-black feathers.* (COLOUR)

**blue-blooded** A **blue-blooded** person is from a royal or noble family. ❑ *...blue-blooded aristocrats.* (ADJ)

**blue book** **(blue books)** also **Blue Book**. A **blue book** is an official government report or register of statistics. [BRIT] (N-COUNT)

**blue|bottle** /bluːbɒtᵊl/ **(bluebottles)** A **bluebottle** is a large fly with a shiny dark-blue body. (N-COUNT)

**blue chip** **(blue chips)** **Blue chip** stocks and shares are an investment which are considered fairly safe to invest in while also being profitable. [BUSINESS] ❑ *Blue chip issues were sharply higher, but the rest of the market actually declined slightly by the end of the day.* (N-COUNT: oft N n)

**blue-collar** **Blue-collar** workers work in industry, doing physical work, rather than in offices. (ADJ: ADJ n; ≠ white-collar)

**blue-eyed boy** **(blue-eyed boys)** Someone's **blue-eyed boy** is a young man who they like better than anyone else and who therefore receives better treatment than other people. [BRIT] ❑ *He was the media's blue-eyed boy.* (N-COUNT: oft poss N; disapproval; = darling, favourite)

☑ in AM, use **fair-haired boy**

**blue|grass** /bluːgrɑːs, -græs/ **Bluegrass** is a style of fast folk music that began in the Southern United States. N-UNCOUNT

**blue|ish** /bluːɪʃ/ → see **bluish**.

**blue jeans** **Blue jeans** are the same as **jeans**. ❑ *...faded blue jeans.* N-PLURAL: also *a pair of* N

**blue|print** /bluːprɪnt/ **(blueprints)** [1] A **blueprint for** something is a plan or set of proposals that shows how it is expected to work. ❑ *The country's president will offer delegates his blueprint for the country's future. ...the blueprint of a new plan of economic reform.* [2] A **blueprint** of an architect's building plans or a designer's pattern is a photographic print consisting of white lines on a blue background. Blueprints contain all of the information that is needed to build or make something. ❑ *...a blueprint of the whole place, complete with heating ducts and wiring... The documents contain a blueprint for a nuclear device.* [3] A genetic **blueprint** is a pattern which is contained within all living cells. This pattern decides how the organism develops and what it looks like. ❑ *The offspring contain a mixture of the genetic blueprint of each parent.* N-COUNT: usu N *for* n; N-COUNT: usu with supp = *design*; N-COUNT: usu with supp

**blue rib|and** /bluː rɪbənd/ **(blue ribands)** also **blue ribband.** If someone or something wins the **blue riband** in a competition, they win first prize. The prize is sometimes in the shape of a blue ribbon. [BRIT] ❑ *Olga did not win the all-round championship, the blue riband event.* N-COUNT

☑ in AM, use **blue ribbon**

**blue rib|bon** **(blue ribbons)** A **blue ribbon** is the same as a **blue riband**. [AM] N-COUNT

**blue|stocking** /bluːstɒkɪŋ/ **(bluestockings)** also **blue-stocking.** A **bluestocking** is an intellectual woman. [OLD-FASHIONED] N-COUNT disapproval

**bluesy** /bluːzi/ If you describe a song or the way it is performed as **bluesy**, you mean that it is performed in a way that is characteristic of the blues. ❑ *...bluesy sax-and-strings theme music.* ADJ: usu ADJ n

**blue tit** **(blue tits)** A **blue tit** is a small European bird with a blue head, wings, and tail, and a yellow front. N-COUNT

**bluff** /blʌf/ **(bluffs, bluffing, bluffed)** [1] A **bluff** is an attempt to make someone believe that you will do something when you do not really intend to do it. ❑ *It is essential to build up the military option and show that this is not a bluff... What we're at here is a game of bluff.* → See also **double bluff**. [2] If you **call** someone's **bluff**, you tell them to do what they have been threatening to do, because you are sure that they will not really do it. ❑ *The Socialists have decided to call the opposition's bluff.* [3] If you **bluff**, you make someone believe that you will do something when you do not really intend to do it, or that you know something when you do not really know it. ❑ *Either side, or both, could be bluffing... In each case the hijackers bluffed the crew using fake grenades.* N-VAR; PHRASE: V inflects; VERB; V; V n

**blu|ish** /bluːɪʃ/ also **blueish.** Something that is **bluish** is slightly blue in colour. ❑ *...bluish-grey eyes.* COLOUR

**blun|der** /blʌndəʳ/ **(blunders, blundering, blundered)** [1] A **blunder** is a stupid or careless mistake. ❑ *I think he made a tactical blunder by announcing it so far ahead of time.* [2] If you **blunder**, you make a stupid or careless mistake. ❑ *No doubt I had blundered again.* [3] If you **blunder into** a dangerous or difficult situation, you get involved in it by mistake. ❑ *People wanted to know how they had blundered into war, and how to avoid it in future.* [4] If you **blunder** somewhere, you move there in a clumsy and careless way. ❑ *He had blundered into the table, upsetting the flowers.* N-COUNT; VERB; V; VERB; V *into* n; VERB; V prep/adv

**blunt** /blʌnt/ **(blunter, bluntest, blunts, blunting, blunted)** [1] If you are **blunt**, you say exactly what you think without trying to be polite. ❑ *She is blunt about her personal life... She told the industry in blunt terms that such discrimination is totally unacceptable.* ♦ **blunt|ly** *'I don't believe you!' Jeanne said bluntly... To put it bluntly, he became a pain.* ♦ **blunt|ness** *His bluntness got him into trouble.* [2] A **blunt** object has a rounded or flat end rather than a sharp one. ❑ *One of them had been struck 13 times over the head with a blunt object.* [3] A **blunt** knife or blade is no longer sharp and does not cut well. [4] If something **blunts** an emotion, a feeling or a need, it weakens it. ❑ *The constant repetition of violence has blunted the human response to it.* ADJ; ADV: ADV with v; N-UNCOUNT: oft poss N; ADJ: ADJ n ≠*pointed*; ADJ ≠*sharp*; VERB; V n

**blur** /blɜːʳ/ **(blurs, blurring, blurred)** [1] A **blur** is a shape or area which you cannot see clearly because it has no distinct outline or because it is moving very fast. ❑ *Out of the corner of my eye I saw a blur of movement on the other side of the glass... Her face is a blur.* [2] When a thing **blurs** or when something **blurs** it, you cannot see it clearly because its edges are no longer distinct. ❑ *This creates a spectrum of colours at the edges of objects which blurs the image... If you move your eyes and your head, the picture will blur.* ♦ **blurred** *...blurred black and white photographs.* [3] If something **blurs** an idea or a distinction between things, that idea or distinction no longer seems clear. ❑ *...her belief that scientists are trying to blur the distinction between 'how' and 'why' questions.* ♦ **blurred** *The line between fact and fiction is becoming blurred.* [4] If your vision **blurs**, or if something **blurs** it, you cannot see things clearly. ❑ *Her eyes, behind her glasses, began to blur... Sweat ran from his forehead into his eyes, blurring his vision.* ♦ **blurred** *...visual disturbances like eye-strain and blurred vision.* N-COUNT: oft N *of* n; VERB; V n; V; ADJ; VERB = *obscure*; V n; ADJ; VERB; V; V n; ADJ

**blurb** /blɜːʳb/ **(blurbs)** **The blurb** about a new book, film, or exhibition is information about it that is written in order to attract people's interest. [INFORMAL] N-COUNT: usu sing, oft *the* N

**blur|ry** /blɜːri/ A **blurry** shape is one that has an unclear outline. ❑ *...a blurry picture of a man.* ADJ = *blurred*

**blurt** /blɜːʳt/ **(blurts, blurting, blurted)** If someone **blurts** something, they say it suddenly, after trying hard to keep quiet or to keep it secret. ❑ *'I was looking for Sally', he blurted, and his eyes filled with tears.* VERB; V with quote; Also V that

♦ **blurt out** If someone **blurts** something **out**, they blurt it. [INFORMAL] ❑ *'You're mad,' the driver blurted out... Over the food, Richard blurted out what was on his mind.* PHRASAL VERB; V P with quote; V P n; Also V n P

**blush** /blʌʃ/ **(blushes, blushing, blushed)** When you **blush**, your face becomes redder than usual because you are ashamed or embarrassed. ❑ *'Hello, Maria,' he said, and she blushed again... I blushed scarlet at my stupidity.* ♦ **Blush** is also a noun. ❑ *'The most important thing is to be honest,' she says, without the trace of a blush.* VERB; V; V colour; N-COUNT

**blush|er** /blʌʃəʳ/ **(blushers)** **Blusher** is a coloured substance that women put on their cheeks. N-MASS

**blus|ter** /blʌstəʳ/ **(blusters, blustering, blustered)** If you say that someone **is blustering**, you mean that they are speaking aggressively but without authority, often because they are angry or offended. ❑ *'That's lunacy,' he blustered... He was still blustering, but there was panic in his eyes.* ♦ **Bluster** is also a noun. ❑ *...the bluster of the Conservatives' campaign.* VERB; V with quote; V; N-UNCOUNT

**blus|tery** /blʌstəri/ **Blustery** weather is rough, windy, and often rainy, with the wind often changing in strength or direction. ❑ *It's a cold night here, with intermittent rain showers and a blustery wind. ...a cool, blustery day.* ADJ

**Blvd**

☑ in AM, use **Blvd.**

**Blvd** is a written abbreviation for **boulevard**. It is used especially in addresses and on maps or signs. ❑ *...1515 Wilson Blvd., Arlington, VA 22209.*

**B-movie** **(B-movies)** A **B-movie** is a film which is produced quickly and cheaply and is often considered to have little artistic value. ❑ *...some old Hollywood B-movie.* N-COUNT

**bn.** **bn.** is a written abbreviation for **billion**. ❑ *...total value, dollars bn 15.6.*

**B.O.** /biː oʊ/ **B.O.** is an unpleasant smell caused by sweat on a person's body. **B.O.** is an abbreviation for 'body odour'. [BRIT] N-UNCOUNT

**boa** /boʊə/ **(boas)** 1 A **boa** or a **feather boa** is a long soft scarf made of feathers or of short pieces of very light fabric. ❑ *She wore a large pink boa around her neck.* N-COUNT 2 A **boa** is the same as a **boa constrictor**. N-COUNT

**boa con|stric|tor** **(boa constrictors)** A **boa constrictor** is a large snake that kills animals by wrapping itself round their bodies and squeezing them to death. Boa constrictors are found mainly in South and Central America and the West Indies. N-COUNT

**boar** /bɔːʳ/ **(boars)**

> ✔ The plural **boar** can also be used for meaning 1.

1 A **boar** or a **wild boar** is a wild pig. ❑ *Wild boar are numerous in the valleys.* N-COUNT 2 A **boar** is a male pig. N-COUNT

**board** /bɔːʳd/ **(boards, boarding, boarded)** ◆◆◇ 1 A **board** is a flat, thin, rectangular piece of wood or plastic which is used for a particular purpose. ❑ *...a chopping board.* N-COUNT: usu n N 2 A **board** is a square piece of wood or stiff cardboard that you use for playing games such as chess. ❑ *...a draughts board.* N-COUNT 3 You can refer to a blackboard or a noticeboard as a **board**. ❑ *He wrote a few more notes on the board.* N-COUNT 4 **Boards** are long flat pieces of wood which are used, for example, to make floors or walls. ❑ *The floor was draughty bare boards.* N-COUNT 5 **The board** of a company or organization is the group of people who control it and direct it. [BUSINESS] ❑ *Arthur wants to put his recommendation before the board at a meeting tomorrow. ...the agenda for the September 12 board meeting.* ➔ See also **board of directors**. N-COUNT: oft *the* N in sing = management 6 **Board** is used in the names of various organizations which are involved in dealing with a particular kind of activity. ❑ *The Scottish Tourist Board said 33,000 Japanese visited Scotland last year. ...the US National Transportation Safety Board.* N-COUNT: usu *the* n N 7 When you **board** a train, ship, or aircraft, you get on it in order to travel somewhere. [FORMAL] ❑ *I boarded the plane bound for England.* VERB = get on V n Also V 8 **Board** is the food which is provided when you stay somewhere, for example in a hotel. ❑ *Free room and board are provided for all hotel staff.* N-UNCOUNT 9 ➔ See also **bulletin board**.

**PHRASES** 10 An arrangement or deal that is **above board** is legal and is being carried out honestly and openly. ❑ *All I knew about were Antony's own financial dealings, which were always above board.* PHRASE: usu v-link PHR 11 If a policy or a situation applies **across the board**, it affects everything or everyone in a particular group. ❑ *There are hefty charges across the board for one-way rental... The President promised across-the-board tax cuts if re-elected.* PHRASE: usu PHR after v, PHR n 12 If something **goes by the board**, it is rejected or ignored, or is no longer possible. ❑ *It's a case of not what you know but who you know in this world today and qualifications quite go by the board.* PHRASE: V inflects 13 When you are **on board** a train, ship, or aircraft, you are on it or in it. ❑ *They arrived at Gatwick airport on board a plane chartered by the Italian government. ...a naval task force with two thousand marines on board.* PHRASE: PHR after v, v-link PHR, oft PHR n 14 If someone **sweeps the board** in a competition or election, they win nearly everything that it is possible to win. ❑ *Spain swept the board in boys' team competitions.* PHRASE: V inflects 15 If you **take on board** an idea or a problem, you begin to accept it or understand it. ❑ *I hope that they will take on board some of what you have said.* PHRASE: V inflects

♦ **board up** If you **board up** a door or window, you fix pieces of wood over it so that it is covered up. ❑ *Shopkeepers have boarded up their windows.* ♦ **board|ed up** *Half the shops are boarded up on the estate's small shopping street.* PHRASAL VERB V P n Also V n P ADJ

**board and lodg|ing** If you are provided with **board and lodging**, you are provided with food and a place to sleep, especially as part of the conditions of a job. ❑ *You get a big salary incentive and free board and lodging too.* N-UNCOUNT

**board|er** /bɔːʳdəʳ/ **(boarders)** A **boarder** is a pupil who lives at school during the term. [BRIT] ❑ *Sue was a boarder at Benenden.* N-COUNT

**board game** **(board games)** also **board-game**. A **board game** is a game such as chess or backgammon, which people play by moving small objects around on a board. ❑ *...a new board game played with dice.* N-COUNT

**board|ing** /bɔːʳdɪŋ/ 1 **Boarding** is an arrangement by which children live at school during the school term. ❑ *...the master in charge of boarding... Annual boarding fees are £10,350.* N-UNCOUNT 2 **Boarding** is long, flat pieces of wood which can be used to make walls, doors, and fences. ❑ *...the white-painted boarding in the sitting room.* N-UNCOUNT

**board|ing card** **(boarding cards)** A **boarding card** is a card which a passenger must have when boarding a plane or a boat. N-COUNT

**board|ing house** **(boarding houses)**

> ✔ The spellings **boardinghouse** in American English, and **boarding-house** in British English are also used.

A **boarding house** is a house which people pay to stay in for a short time. N-COUNT = guest house

**board|ing school** **(boarding schools)** also **boarding-school**. A **boarding school** is a school which some or all of the pupils live in during the school term. Compare **day school**. N-VAR

**board of di|rec|tors** **(boards of directors)** A company's **board of directors** is the group of people elected by its shareholders to manage the company. [BUSINESS] ❑ *The Board of Directors has approved the decision unanimously.* N-COUNT

**board|room** /bɔːʳdruːm/ **(boardrooms)** also **board room**. The **boardroom** is a room where the board of a company meets. [BUSINESS] ❑ *Everyone had already assembled in the boardroom for the 9:00 a.m. session.* N-COUNT

**board|walk** /bɔːʳdwɔːk/ **(boardwalks)** A **boardwalk** is a path made of wooden boards, especially one along a beach. [AM] N-COUNT

**boast** /boʊst/ **(boasts, boasting, boasted)** 1 If someone **boasts** about something that they have done or that they own, they talk about it very proudly, in a way that other people may find irritating or offensive. ❑ *Witnesses said Furci boasted that he took part in killing them... Carol boasted about her costume... He's boasted of being involved in the arms theft... We remember our mother's stern instructions not to boast.* VERB disapproval V that V *about* n V *of* -ing V Also V with quote ♦ **Boast** is also a noun. ❑ *It is the charity's proud boast that it has never yet turned anyone away.* N-COUNT: oft N that, N prep 2 If someone or something can **boast** a particular achievement or possession, they have achieved or possess that thing. ❑ *The houses will boast the latest energy-saving technology.* VERB V n

**boast|ful** /boʊstfʊl/ If someone is **boastful**, they talk too proudly about something that they have done or that they own. ❑ *I'm not being boastful. ...boastful predictions.* ADJ disapproval

**boat** /boʊt/ **(boats)** ◆◆◇ 1 A **boat** is something in which people can travel across water. ❑ *One of the best ways to see the area is in a small boat... The island may be reached by boat from the mainland.* N-COUNT: also *by* N 2 You can refer to a passenger ship as a **boat**. ❑ *When the boat reached Cape Town, we said a temporary goodbye.* N-COUNT 3 ➔ See also **gravy boat, rowing boat**.

**PHRASES** 4 If you say that someone has **missed the boat**, you mean that they have missed an opportunity and may not get another. PHRASE: V inflects 5 If you **push the boat out**, you spend a lot of money on something, especially in order to celebrate. [BRIT] ❑ *I earn enough to push the boat out now and again.* PHRASE: V inflects 6 If you say that someone **is rocking the boat**, you mean that they are upsetting a calm situation and causing trouble. ❑ *I said I didn't want* PHRASE: V inflects *to rock the boat in any way.* [7] If two or more people are **in the same boat**, they are in the same unpleasant situation. PHRASE: usu v-link PHR

**boat|builder** /boʊtbɪldəʳ/ **(boatbuilders)** also **boat builder.** A **boatbuilder** is a person or company that makes boats. N-COUNT

**boat|building** /boʊtbɪldɪŋ/ also **boat-building. Boatbuilding** is the craft or industry of making boats. ❑ *Sunbeam Yachts started boatbuilding in 1870.* N-UNCOUNT

**boat|er** /boʊtəʳ/ **(boaters)** A **boater** or a **straw boater** is a hard straw hat with a flat top and brim which is often worn for certain social occasions in the summer. N-COUNT

**boat|house** /boʊthaʊs/ **(boathouses)** also **boat house.** A **boathouse** is a building at the edge of a lake, in which boats are kept. N-COUNT

**boat|ing** /boʊtɪŋ/ **Boating** is travelling on a lake or river in a small boat for pleasure. ❑ *You can go boating or play tennis. ...a boating accident.* N-UNCOUNT: oft N n

**boat|load** /boʊtloʊd/ **(boatloads)** also **boat load.** A **boatload of** people or things is a lot of people or things that are, or were, in a boat. ❑ *...a boatload of rice.* N-COUNT: oft N *of* n

**boat|man** /boʊtmən/ **(boatmen)** A **boatman** is a man who is paid by people to take them across an area of water in a small boat, or a man who hires boats out to them for a short time. N-COUNT

**boat peo|ple** **Boat people** are people who escape from their country in small boats to travel to another country in the hope that they will be able to live there.. ❑ *...Vietnamese boat people.* N-PLURAL

**boat train** **(boat trains)** A **boat train** is a train that takes you to or from a port. N-COUNT

**boat|yard** /boʊtjɑːʳd/ **(boatyards)** A **boatyard** is a place where boats are built and repaired or kept. N-COUNT

**bob** /bɒb/ **(bobs, bobbing, bobbed)** [1] If something **bobs**, it moves up and down, like something does when it is floating on water. ❑ *Huge balloons bobbed about in the sky above.* [2] If you **bob** somewhere, you move there quickly so that you disappear from view or come into view. ❑ *She handed over a form, then bobbed down again behind a typewriter.* [3] When you **bob** your head, you move it quickly up and down once, for example when you greet someone. ❑ *A hostess stood at the top of the steps and bobbed her head at each passenger.* ♦ **Bob** is also a noun. ❑ *The young man smiled with a bob of his head.* [4] A **bob** is a fairly short hair style for women in which the hair is the same length all the way round, except for the front. [5] **Bits and bobs** are small objects or parts of something. [mainly BRIT, INFORMAL] ❑ *The microscope contains a few hundred dollars-worth of electronic bits and bobs.* VERB; V prep/adv; VERB; V adv/prep; VERB = nod; V n; N-COUNT = nod; N-COUNT; PHRASE

**bobbed** /bɒbd/ If a woman's hair is **bobbed**, it is cut in a bob. ADJ

**bob|bin** /bɒbɪn/ **(bobbins)** A **bobbin** is a small round object on which thread or wool is wound to hold it, for example on a sewing machine. N-COUNT

**bob|ble** /bɒbᵊl/ **(bobbles)** A **bobble** is a small ball of material, usually made of wool, which is used for decorating clothes. [BRIT] ❑ *...the bobble on his nightcap.* N-COUNT

✔ in AM, usually use **tassel**

**bob|ble hat** **(bobble hats)** A **bobble hat** is a woollen hat with a bobble on it. [BRIT] N-COUNT

**bob|by** /bɒbi/ **(bobbies)** A **bobby** is a British policeman, usually of the lowest rank. [BRIT, INFORMAL, OLD-FASHIONED] ❑ *These days, the bobby on the beat is a rare sight.* N-COUNT = cop

**bob|by pin** **(bobby pins)** A **bobby pin** is a small piece of metal or plastic bent back on itself, which someone uses to hold their hair in position. [AM] N-COUNT

✔ in BRIT, use **hairgrip**

**bob|cat** /bɒbkæt/ **(bobcats)** A **bobcat** is an animal in the cat family which has reddish-brown fur with dark spots or stripes and a short tail. Bobcats live in North America. ❑ *Bobcats roam wild in the mountains.* N-COUNT

**bob|sled** /bɒbsled/ **(bobsleds)** A **bobsled** is the same as a **bobsleigh**. [mainly AM] N-COUNT

**bob|sleigh** /bɒbsleɪ/ **(bobsleighs)** A **bobsleigh** is a vehicle with long thin strips of metal fixed to the bottom, which is used for racing downhill on ice. [BRIT] N-COUNT

✔ in AM, use **bobsled**

**bod** /bɒd/ **(bods)** A **bod** is a person. [BRIT, INFORMAL] ❑ *He was definitely a bit of an odd bod.* N-COUNT: usu supp N = chap

**bode** /boʊd/ **(bodes, boding, boded)** If something **bodes** ill, it makes you think that something bad will happen in the future. If something **bodes** well, it makes you think that something good will happen. [FORMAL] ❑ *She says the way the bill was passed bodes ill for democracy... Grace had dried her eyes. That boded well.* VERB; V adv *for* n; V adv

**bodge** /bɒdʒ/ **(bodges, bodging, bodged)** If you **bodge** something, you make it or mend it in a way that is not as good as it should be. [BRIT, INFORMAL] ❑ *I thought he had bodged the repair.* VERB = botch; V n

**bod|ice** /bɒdɪs/ **(bodices)** The **bodice** of a dress is the part above the waist. ❑ *...dress with a fitted bodice and circle skirt.* N-COUNT

**bod|ice rip|per** **(bodice rippers)** You can refer to a film or novel which is set in the past and which includes a lot of sex scenes as a **bodice ripper**, especially if you do not think it is very good and is just intended to entertain people. N-COUNT disapproval

**bodice-ripping** A **bodice-ripping** film or novel is one which is set in the past and which includes a lot of sex scenes. You use this word especially if you do not think it is very good and is just intended to entertain people. ❑ *...bodice-ripping yarns on TV.* ADJ: ADJ n disapproval

**bodi|ly** /bɒdɪli/ [1] Your **bodily** needs and functions are the needs and functions of your body. ❑ *There's more to eating than just bodily needs.* ➔ See also **grievous bodily harm**. [2] You use **bodily** to indicate that an action involves the whole of someone's body. ❑ *I was hurled bodily to the deck.* ADJ: ADJ n; ADV: ADV with v

**bodi|ly func|tion** **(bodily functions)** A person's **bodily functions** are the normal physical processes that regularly occur in their body, particularly the ability to urinate and defecate. ❑ *The child was not able to speak, walk properly or control bodily functions.* N-COUNT

**body** /bɒdi/ **(bodies)** [1] Your **body** is all your physical parts, including your head, arms, and legs. ❑ *The largest organ in the body is the liver.* [2] You can also refer to the main part of your body, except for your arms, head, and legs, as your **body**. ❑ *Lying flat on the floor, twist your body on to one hip and cross your upper leg over your body.* [3] You can refer to a person's dead body as a **body**. ❑ *Officials said they had found no traces of violence on the body of the politician.* [4] A **body** is an organized group of people who deal with something officially. ❑ *...the Chairman of the policemen's representative body, the Police Federation. ...the main trade union body, COSATU, Congress of South African Trade Unions.* [5] A **body of** people is a group of people who are together or who are connected in some way. ❑ *...that large body of people which teaches other people how to teach.* [6] **The body of** something such as a building or a document is the main part of it or the largest part of it. ❑ *The main body of the church had been turned into a massive television studio.* [7] The **body** of a car or aeroplane is the main part of it, not including its engine, wheels, or wings. ❑ *The only shade was under the body of the plane.* [8] A **body of** water is a large area of water, such as a lake or a sea. ❑ *It is* ◆◆◆ N-COUNT; N-COUNT = torso, trunk; N-COUNT = corpse; N-COUNT: usu with supp = organization; N-COUNT: N *of* n = group; N-SING: *the* N *of* n = bulk; N-COUNT: usu with supp = shell; N-COUNT: N *of* n

probably the most polluted body of water in the world. [9] A **body of** information is a large amount of it. ❑ *An increasing body of evidence suggests that all of us have cancer cells in our bodies at times during our lives.* N-COUNT: N *of* n = quantity [10] If you say that an alcoholic drink has **body**, you mean that it has a full and strong flavour. ❑ *...a dry wine with good body.* N-UNCOUNT [11] → See also **foreign body**, **heavenly body**.

**body ar|mour**

✔ in AM, use **body armor**

**Body armour** is special protective clothing which people such as soldiers and police officers sometimes wear when they are in danger of being attacked with guns or other weapons. N-UNCOUNT

**body bag** **(body bags)** A **body bag** is a specially designed large plastic bag which is used to carry a dead body away, for example when someone has been killed in a battle or an accident. ❑ *...the prospect of young soldiers coming home in body bags.* N-COUNT

**body blow** **(body blows)** also **body-blow.** A **body blow** is something that causes great disappointment and difficulty to someone who is trying to achieve something. ❑ *His resignation was a body blow to the team.* N-COUNT = setback

**body|builder** /bɒdibɪldəʳ/ **(bodybuilders)** also **body builder.** A **bodybuilder** is a person who does special exercises regularly in order to make his or her muscles grow bigger. N-COUNT

**body|building** /bɒdibɪldɪŋ/ also **body building. Bodybuilding** is the activity of doing special exercises regularly in order to make your muscles grow bigger. N-UNCOUNT

**body clock** **(body clocks)** Your **body clock** is the internal biological mechanism which causes your body to automatically behave in particular ways at particular times of the day. ❑ *Jet lag is caused because the body clock does not readjust immediately to the time change.* N-COUNT: usu sing

**body|guard** /bɒdigɑːʳd/ **(bodyguards)** A **bodyguard** is a person or a group of people employed to protect someone. ❑ *Three of his bodyguards were injured in the attack... The King had brought his own bodyguard of twenty armed men.* N-COUNT

**body lan|guage** also **body-language.** Your **body language** is the way in which you show your feelings or thoughts to other people by means of the position or movements of your body, rather than with words. N-UNCOUNT

**body odour**

✔ in AM, use **body odor**

**Body odour** is an unpleasant smell caused by sweat on a person's body. N-UNCOUNT = B.O.

**body poli|tic** **The body politic** is all the people of a nation when they are considered as a complete political group. [FORMAL] ❑ *...the king was the head of the body politic.* N-SING: usu *the* N

**body search** **(body searches, body searching, body searched)** also **body-search.** If a person **is body searched**, someone such as a police officer searches them while they remain clothed. Compare **strip-search**. ❑ *Foreign journalists were body-searched by airport police.* VERB *be* V-ed Also V n ♦ **Body search** is also a noun. ❑ *Fans may undergo body searches by security guards.* N-COUNT

**body stock|ing** **(body stockings)** A **body stocking** is a piece of clothing that covers the whole of someone's body and fits tightly. Body stockings are often worn by dancers. N-COUNT

**body|suit** /bɒdisuːt/ **(bodysuits)** A **bodysuit** is a piece of women's clothing that fits tightly over the top part of the body and fastens between the legs. N-COUNT = body

**body|work** /bɒdiwɜːʳk/ The **bodywork** of a motor vehicle is the outside part of it. ❑ *A second hand car dealer will always look at the bodywork rather than the engine.* N-UNCOUNT

**Boer** /bo͟ʊəʳ, bɔ͟ːʳ/ **(Boers)** The **Boers** are the descendants of the Dutch people who went to live in South Africa. N-COUNT

**bof|fin** /bɒfɪn/ **(boffins)** [1] A **boffin** is a scientist, especially one who is doing research. [BRIT, INFORMAL] ❑ *The boffins of Imperial College in London think they may have found a solution.* N-COUNT = egghead [2] Very clever people are sometimes called **boffins**. [BRIT, INFORMAL] ❑ *A computer boffin is set to make £5million from his revolutionary photo technology.* N-COUNT

**bog** /bɒg/ **(bogs, bogging, bogged)** A **bog** is an area of land which is very wet and muddy. N-COUNT

♦ **bog down** If a plan or process **bogs down** or if something **bogs** it **down**, it is delayed and no progress is made. ❑ *We intended from the very beginning to bog the prosecution down over who did this... The talks have bogged down over the issue of military reform.* → See also **bogged down**. PHRASAL VERB V n P, V P

**bo|gey** /bo͟ʊgi/ **(bogeys)**

✔ The spelling **bogy** and the plural form **bogies** are also used.

A **bogey** is something or someone that people are worried about, perhaps without much cause or reason. ❑ *Age is another bogey for actresses.* N-COUNT: usu with supp ♦ **Bogey** is also an adjective. ❑ *Did people still tell their kids imbecilic scare stories about bogey policewomen?* ADJ: ADJ n

**bogey|man** /bo͟ʊgimæn/ **(bogeymen)**

✔ The spellings **bogey man**, and in American English **boogeyman** are also used.

[1] A **bogeyman** is someone whose ideas or actions are disapproved of by some people, and who is described by them as evil or unpleasant in order to make other people afraid. [mainly BRIT] ❑ *The media depict him as a left-wing bogeyman.* N-COUNT: usu with supp [disapproval] = monster [2] A **bogeyman** is an imaginary evil spirit. Some parents tell their children that the bogeyman will catch them if they behave badly. N-COUNT: oft *the* N

**bogged down** If you get **bogged down in** something, it prevents you from making progress or getting something done. ❑ *But why get bogged down in legal details?... Sometimes this fact is obscured because churches get so bogged down by unimportant rules.* ADJ: v-link ADJ, usu ADJ *in* n

**bog|gle** /bɒgəl/ **(boggles, boggling, boggled)** If you say that the mind **boggles at** something or that something **boggles** the mind, you mean that it is so strange or amazing that it is difficult to imagine or understand. ❑ *The mind boggles at the possibilities that could be in store for us... The good grace with which they face the latest privations makes the mind boggle... The management group's decision still boggled his mind.* → See also **mind-boggling**. VERB V *at* n, V, V n

**bog|gy** /bɒgi/ **Boggy** land is very wet and muddy land. ADJ

**bog-standard** If you describe something as **bog-standard** you mean that is an ordinary example of its kind, with no exciting or interesting features. [BRIT, INFORMAL] ❑ *'The Bodyguard' is a fairly bog-standard thriller.* ADJ: usu ADJ n [disapproval] = common or garden

**bo|gus** /bo͟ʊgəs/ If you describe something as **bogus**, you mean that it is not genuine. ❑ *...their bogus insurance claim... He said these figures were bogus and totally inaccurate.* ADJ = phoney

**bogy** /bo͟ʊgi/ **(bogies)** → see **bogey**.

**bo|he|mian** /boʊhi͟ːmiən/ **(bohemians)** You can use **bohemian** to describe artistic people who live in an unconventional way. ❑ *...a bohemian writer. ...the bohemian lifestyle of the French capital.* ADJ: usu ADJ n ♦ A **bohemian** is someone who lives in a bohemian way. ❑ *I am a bohemian. I have no roots.* N-COUNT

**Bo|he|mian** /bəhi͟ːmiən/ **Bohemian** means belonging or relating to Bohemia or its people. ADJ

**boil** /bɔ͟ɪl/ **(boils, boiling, boiled)** ◆◇◇ [1] When a hot liquid **boils** or when you **boil** it, bubbles appear in it and it starts to change into steam or vapour. ❑ *I stood in the kitchen, waiting for the water to boil... Boil the water in the saucepan and add the sage. ...a saucepan of boiling water.* VERB V, V n, V-ing [2] When you **boil** a kettle or pan, or put it on to **boil**, you heat the VERB water inside it until it boils. ❑ *He had nothing to do but boil the kettle and make the tea... Marianne put the kettle on to boil.* V n / V [3] When a kettle or pan **is boiling**, the water inside it has reached boiling point. ❑ *Is the kettle boiling?* VERB: only cont [4] When you **boil** food, or when it **boils**, it is cooked in boiling water. ❑ *Boil the chick peas, add garlic and lemon juice... I'd peel potatoes and put them on to boil. ...boiled eggs and toast.* V / VERB / V n / V / V-ed [5] If you **are boiling with** anger, you are very angry. ❑ *I used to be all sweetness and light on the outside, but inside I would be boiling with rage.* VERB: usu cont / V with n [6] A **boil** is a red, painful swelling on your skin, which contains a thick yellow liquid called pus. N-COUNT = cyst [7] → See also **boiling**. [8] When you **bring** a liquid **to the boil**, you heat it until it boils. When it **comes to the boil**, it begins to boil. ❑ *Put water, butter and lard into a saucepan and bring slowly to the boil.* PHRASE: V inflects [9] to **make** someone's **blood boil** → see **blood**.

♦ **boil down** When you **boil down** a liquid or food, or when it **boils down**, it is boiled until there is less of it because some of the water in it has changed into steam or vapour. ❑ *He boils down red wine and uses what's left.* PHRASAL VERB = reduce / V P n (not pron)

♦ **boil down to** If you say that a situation or problem **boils down to** a particular thing or can **be boiled down to** a particular thing, you mean that this is the most important or the most basic aspect of it. ❑ *What they want boils down to just one thing. It is land.* PHRASAL VERB = amount to / V P P n

♦ **boil over** [1] When a liquid that is being heated **boils over**, it rises and flows over the edge of the container. ❑ *Heat the liquid in a large, wide container rather than a high narrow one, or it can boil over.* PHRASAL VERB / V P [2] When someone's feelings **boil over**, they lose their temper or become violent. ❑ *Sometimes frustration and anger can boil over into direct and violent action.* PHRASAL VERB = erupt / V P

**boiled sweet** (**boiled sweets**) **Boiled sweets** are hard sweets that are made from boiled sugar. [BRIT] N-COUNT

✔ in AM, use **hard candy**

**boil|er** /bɔɪləʳ/ (**boilers**) A **boiler** is a device which burns gas, oil, electricity, or coal in order to provide hot water, especially for the central heating in a building. N-COUNT

**boil|er suit** (**boiler suits**) A **boiler suit** consists of a single piece of clothing that combines trousers and a jacket. You wear it over your clothes in order to protect them from dirt while you are working. [BRIT] N-COUNT = overalls

✔ in AM, use **overalls**

**boil|ing** /bɔɪlɪŋ/ [1] Something that is **boiling** or **boiling hot** is very hot. ❑ *'It's boiling in here,' complained Miriam... Often the food may be bubbling and boiling hot on the top, but the inside may still be cold.* ADJ = baking [2] If you say that you are **boiling** or **boiling hot**, you mean that you feel very hot, usually unpleasantly hot. ❑ *When everybody else is boiling hot, I'm freezing!* ADJ: v-link ADJ = sweltering

**boil|ing point** also **boiling-point**. [1] The **boiling point** of a liquid is the temperature at which it starts to change into steam or vapour. For example, the boiling point of water is 100° centigrade. ❑ *The boiling point of water is 373 K... Heat the cream to boiling point and pour three quarters of it over the chocolate.* N-UNCOUNT [2] If a situation reaches **boiling point**, the people involved have become so angry that they can no longer remain calm and in control of themselves. ❑ *The situation is rapidly reaching boiling point, and the army has been put on stand-by.* N-UNCOUNT

**bois|ter|ous** /bɔɪstərəs/ Someone who is **boisterous** is noisy, lively, and full of energy. ❑ *...a boisterous but good-natured crowd... Most of the children were noisy and boisterous.* ADJ ♦ **bois|ter|ous|ly** *Her friends laughed boisterously, too.* ADV: ADV with v, ADV adj

**bold** /bəʊld/ (**bolder, boldest**) [1] Someone who is **bold** is not afraid to do things which involve risk or danger. ❑ *Amrita becomes a bold, daring rebel... In 1960 this was a bold move... Poland was already making bold economic reforms.* ADJ = brave ≠ cautious ♦ **bold|ly** *You can and must act boldly and confidently.* ADV: ADV with v ♦ **bold|ness** *Don't forget the boldness of his economic programme.* N-UNCOUNT [2] Someone who is **bold** is not shy or embarrassed in the company of other people. ❑ *I don't feel I'm being bold, because it's always been natural for me to just speak out about whatever disturbs me.* ADJ: usu v-link ADJ = brave ≠ timid ♦ **bold|ly** *'You should do it,' the girl said, boldly.* ADV [3] A **bold** colour or pattern is very bright and noticeable. ❑ *...bold flowers in various shades of red, blue or white. ...bold, dramatic colours.* ADJ ♦ **bold|ly** *The design is pretty startling and very boldly coloured.* ADV [4] **Bold** lines or designs are drawn in a clear, strong way. ❑ *Each picture is shown in colour on one page and as a bold outline on the opposite page.* ADJ = vivid [5] **Bold** is print which is thicker and looks blacker than ordinary printed letters. [TECHNICAL] N-UNCOUNT: usu N n

**bo|lero** (**boleros**)

✔ Pronounced /bɒlərəʊ, AM bəleroʊ/ for meaning 1, and /bəleərəʊ/ for meaning 2.

[1] A **bolero** is a very short jacket, sometimes without sleeves. Boleros are worn mainly by women. N-COUNT [2] The **bolero** is a traditional Spanish dance. ❑ *They danced a romantic bolero together.* N-COUNT

**Bo|liv|ian** /bəlɪviən/ (**Bolivians**) **Bolivian** means belonging or relating to Bolivia or its people. ADJ ♦ A **Bolivian** is a person who comes from Bolivia. N-COUNT

**bol|lard** /bɒlɑːʳd/ (**bollards**) [1] **Bollards** are short thick concrete posts that are used to prevent cars from going on to someone's land or on to part of a road. [BRIT] N-COUNT [2] **Bollards** are strong wooden or metal posts on the side of a river or harbour. Boats are tied to them. N-COUNT

**bol|locks** /bɒləks/ [1] **Bollocks** is used by some people to express disagreement, dislike, or annoyance. [BRIT, INFORMAL, RUDE] EXCLAM; N-UNCOUNT [feelings] [2] A man's **bollocks** are his testicles. [BRIT, INFORMAL, RUDE] N-PLURAL

**Bol|she|vik** /bɒlʃɪvɪk/ (**Bolsheviks**) [1] **Bolshevik** is used to describe the political system and ideas that Lenin and his supporters introduced in Russia after the Russian Revolution of 1917. ❑ *Seventy-four years after the Bolshevik Revolution, the Soviet era ended. ...anti-Bolshevik forces.* ADJ [2] A **Bolshevik** was a person who supported Lenin and his political ideas. N-COUNT

**Bol|she|vism** /bɒlʃɪvɪzəm/ **Bolshevism** is the political system and ideas that Lenin and his supporters introduced in Russia after the Russian Revolution of 1917. N-UNCOUNT

**bol|shy** /bɒlʃi/ also **bolshie**. If you say that someone is **bolshy**, you mean that they easily get angry and often do not do what other people want them to do. [BRIT, INFORMAL] ❑ *Carol is bolshy at not getting promotion.* ADJ [disapproval] = stroppy

**bol|ster** /bəʊlstəʳ/ (**bolsters, bolstering, bolstered**) [1] If you **bolster** something such as someone's confidence or courage, you increase it. ❑ *Hopes of an early cut in interest rates bolstered confidence.* VERB = boost / V n [2] If someone tries to **bolster** their position in a situation, they try to strengthen it. ❑ *Britain is free to adopt policies to bolster its economy.* VERB = boost / V n ♦ **Bolster up** means the same as **bolster**. ❑ *...an aid programme to bolster up their troubled economy.* PHRASAL VERB / V P n / Also V n P [3] A **bolster** is a firm pillow shaped like a long tube which is sometimes put across a bed under the ordinary pillows. N-COUNT

♦ **bolster up** → see **bolster 2**.

**bolt** /bəʊlt/ (**bolts, bolting, bolted**) [1] A **bolt** is a long metal object which screws into a nut and is used to fasten things together. → See picture on page 1709. N-COUNT [2] When you **bolt** one thing to another, you fasten them firmly together, using a bolt. ❑ *There's no need to bolt it to seat belt anchorage points... Bolt the components together. ...a wooden* VERB / V n to n / V n with together/on *bench which was bolted to the floor.* [3] A **bolt** on a door or window is a metal bar that you can slide across in order to fasten the door or window. [V-ed] [N-COUNT] ❑ *I heard the sound of a bolt being slowly and reluctantly slid open.* [4] When you **bolt** a door or window, you slide the bolt across to fasten it. [VERB] [V n] ❑ *He reminded her that he would have to lock and bolt the kitchen door after her. ...the heavy bolted doors .* [V-ed] [5] If a person or animal **bolts**, they suddenly start to run very fast, often because something has frightened them. [VERB] [V] ❑ *The pig rose squealing and bolted... I made some excuse and bolted for the exit.* [V prep/adv] [6] If you **bolt** your food, you eat it so quickly that you hardly chew it or taste it. [VERB] [V n] ❑ *Being under stress can cause you to miss meals, or bolt your food.* ♦ **Bolt down** means the same as **bolt**. [PHRASAL VERB] [V P n] [Also V n P] ❑ *Back then I could bolt down three or four burgers and a pile of French fries.* [7] A **bolt of** lightning is a flash of lightning that is seen as a white line in the sky. [N-COUNT: N *of* n] ❑ *Suddenly a bolt of lightning crackled through the sky.* [8] If someone is sitting or standing **bolt upright**, they are sitting or standing very straight. [PHRASE: usu v PHR] ❑ *When I pushed his door open, Trevor was sitting bolt upright in bed.* [9] **nuts and bolts** → see **nut**.

♦ **bolt down** → see **bolt 6**.

**bolt-hole** **(bolt-holes)** also **bolthole.** If you say that someone has a **bolt-hole** to go to, you mean that there is somewhere that they can go when they want to get away from people that they know. [N-COUNT] [= *refuge*] [BRIT] ❑ *The hotel is an ideal bolt-hole for Londoners.*

**bomb** /bɒm/ **(bombs, bombing, bombed)** ◆◆◇ [1] A **bomb** is a device which explodes and damages or destroys a large area. [N-COUNT] ❑ *Bombs went off at two London train stations... It's not known who planted the bomb... Most of the bombs fell in the south... There were two bomb explosions in the city overnight.* [2] Nuclear weapons are sometimes referred to as **the bomb**. [N-SING: *the* N] ❑ *They are generally thought to have the bomb.* [3] When people **bomb** a place, they attack it with bombs. [VERB] [V n] ❑ *Airforce jets bombed the airport.* ♦ **bomb|ing** **(bombings)** [N-VAR] *Aerial bombing of rebel positions is continuing... There has been a series of car bombings.* [4] → See also **petrol bomb**, **pipe bomb**.

♦ **bomb out** If a building or area **is bombed out**, it is destroyed by bombs. If people **are bombed out**, their houses are destroyed by bombs. [PHRASAL VERB] [*be* V-ed P] ❑ *London had been bombed out.* → See also **bombed-out**.

**bom|bard** /bɒmbɑːʳd/ **(bombards, bombarding, bombarded)** [1] If you **bombard** someone **with** something, you make them face a great deal of it. For example, if you **bombard** them **with** questions or criticism, you keep asking them a lot of questions or you keep criticizing them. [VERB] [V n *with* n] ❑ *He bombarded Catherine with questions to which he should have known the answers... I've been bombarded by the press and television since I came back from Norway.* [*be* V-ed *by* n] [2] When soldiers **bombard** a place, they attack it with continuous heavy gunfire or bombs. [VERB] [V n] ❑ *Rebel artillery units have regularly bombarded the airport.*

**bom|bard|ment** /bɒmbɑːʳdmənt/ **(bombardments)** [1] A **bombardment** is a strong and continuous attack of gunfire or bombing. [N-VAR: usu with supp] [= *attack*] ❑ *The city has been flattened by heavy artillery bombardments... The capital is still under constant bombardment by the rebel forces.* [2] A **bombardment of** ideas, demands, questions, or criticisms is an aggressive and exhausting stream of them. [N-VAR: oft N *of* n] [= *onslaught*] ❑ *...the constant bombardment of images urging that work was important.*

**bom|bast** /bɒmbæst/ **Bombast** is trying to impress people by saying things that sound impressive but have little meaning. [N-UNCOUNT] [disapproval] [= *pomposity*] ❑ *There was no bombast or conceit in his speech.*

**bom|bas|tic** /bɒmbæstɪk/ If you describe someone as **bombastic**, you are criticizing them for trying to impress other people by saying things that sound impressive but have little meaning. [ADJ] [disapproval] [= *pompous*] ❑ *He was vain and bombastic. ...the bombastic style adopted by his predecessor.*

**bomb dis|pos|al** **Bomb disposal** is the job of dealing with bombs which have not exploded, by taking out the fuse or by blowing them up in a controlled explosion. [N-UNCOUNT: usu N n] ❑ *...an Army bomb disposal squad.*

**bombed-out** A **bombed-out** building has been damaged or destroyed by a bomb. [ADJ: ADJ n] ❑ *...a bombed-out hospital.*

**bomb|er** /bɒməʳ/ **(bombers)** [1] A **bomber** is a military aircraft which drops bombs. [N-COUNT] ❑ *...a high speed bomber with twin engines.* [2] **Bombers** are people who cause bombs to explode in public places. [N-COUNT] ❑ *Detectives hunting the London bombers will be keen to interview him.*

**bomb|er jack|et** **(bomber jackets)** A **bomber jacket** is a short jacket which is gathered into a band at the waist or hips. [N-COUNT] ❑ *...a black leather bomber jacket.*

**bomb|shell** /bɒmʃel/ **(bombshells)** A **bombshell** is a sudden piece of bad or unexpected news. [N-COUNT] ❑ *His resignation after thirteen years is a political bombshell.* ● If someone **drops a bombshell**, they give you a sudden piece of bad or unexpected news. [PHRASE: V and N inflect] ❑ *He dropped the bombshell. He told me he was dying.* → See also **blonde bombshell**.

**bomb site** **(bomb sites)** also **bombsite.** A **bomb site** is an empty area where a bomb has destroyed all the buildings. [N-COUNT] ❑ *In London, where I grew up, we were surrounded by bomb sites.*

**bona fide** /boʊnə faɪdi/ If something or someone is **bona fide**, they are genuine or real. [ADJ: usu ADJ n] [= *genuine*] [≠ *bogus*] [FORMAL] ❑ *We are happy to donate to bona fide charitable causes.*

**bona fi|des** /boʊnə faɪdiz/ Someone's **bona fides** are their good or sincere intentions. [N-PLURAL: usu with poss] [LEGAL or FORMAL] ❑ *Mr Perks questioned them at length to establish their bona fides.*

**bo|nan|za** /bənænzə/ **(bonanzas)** You can refer to a sudden great increase in wealth, success, or luck as a **bonanza**. [N-COUNT] [= *windfall*] ❑ *The expected sales bonanza hadn't materialised.*

**bonce** /bɒns/ **(bonces)** Your **bonce** is your head. [N-COUNT: oft poss N] [BRIT, INFORMAL]

**bond** /bɒnd/ **(bonds, bonding, bonded)** ◆◆◇ [1] A **bond between** people is a strong feeling of friendship, love, or shared beliefs and experiences that unites them. [N-COUNT: oft N *between* pl-n] ❑ *The experience created a very special bond between us. ...the bond that linked them.* [2] When people **bond with** each other, they form a relationship based on love or shared beliefs and experiences. You can also say that people **bond** or that something **bonds** them. [V-RECIP] ❑ *Belinda was having difficulty bonding with the baby... They all bonded while writing graffiti together... What had bonded them instantly and so completely was their similar background... The players are bonded by a spirit that is rarely seen in an English team.* [V *with* n] [pl-n V] [V pl-n] [V-ed] [Also V n *with* n] ♦ **bond|ing** *They expect bonding to occur naturally.* [N-UNCOUNT] [3] A **bond between** people or groups is a close connection that they have with each other, for example because they have a special agreement. [N-COUNT: with supp] [= *link*] ❑ *...the strong bond between church and nation... There are tangible signs that the republic's successfully breaking its bonds with Moscow.* [4] A **bond** between two things is the way in which they stick to one another or are joined in some way. [N-COUNT] ❑ *The superglue may not create a bond with some plastics.* [5] When one thing **bonds with** another, it sticks to it or becomes joined to it in some way. You can also say that two things **bond together**, or that something **bonds** them **together**. [V-RECIP] ❑ *Diamond does not bond well with other materials... In graphite sheets, carbon atoms bond together in rings... Strips of wood are bonded together and moulded by machine.* [V *with* n] [pl-n V *together*] [*be* V-ed *together*] [6] When a government or company issues a **bond**, it borrows money from investors. The certificate which is issued to investors who lend [N-COUNT] money is also called a **bond**. [BUSINESS] ❑ *Most of it will be financed by government bonds. ...the recent sharp decline in bond prices.* → See also **junk bond**, **premium bond**.

**bond|age** /bɒndɪdʒ/ 1 **Bondage** is the condition of being someone's property and having to work for them. ❑ *Masters sometimes allowed their slaves to buy their way out of bondage.* N-UNCOUNT *= slavery*
2 **Bondage** is the condition of not being free because you are strongly influenced by something or someone. [FORMAL] ❑ *All people, she said, lived their lives in bondage to hunger, pain and lust.* N-UNCOUNT: oft N *to* n
3 **Bondage** is the practice of being tied up or tying your partner up in order to gain sexual pleasure. N-UNCOUNT

**bond|ed** /bɒndɪd/ A **bonded** company has entered into a legal agreement which offers its customers some protection if the company does not fulfil its contract with them. [BUSINESS] ❑ *The company is a fully bonded member of the Association of British Travel Agents.* ADJ

**bond|holder** /bɒndhoʊldəʳ/ **(bondholders)** also **bond holder.** A **bondholder** is a person who owns one or more investment bonds. [BUSINESS] N-COUNT

**bone** /boʊn/ **(bones, boning, boned)** ◆◇◇ 1 Your **bones** are the hard parts inside your body which together form your skeleton. ❑ *Many passengers suffered broken bones... Stephen fractured a thigh bone... The body is made up primarily of bone, muscle, and fat... She scooped the chicken bones back into the stewpot.* N-VAR 2 If you **bone** a piece of meat or fish, you remove the bones from it before cooking it. ❑ *Make sure that you do not pierce the skin when boning the chicken thighs.* VERB V n 3 A **bone** tool or ornament is made of bone. ❑ *...a small, expensive pocketknife with a bone handle.* ADJ: usu ADJ n 4 → See also **marrow bone**, **T-bone steak**.
PHRASES 5 The **bare bones of** something are its most basic parts or details. ❑ *There are not even the bare bones of a garden here – I've got nothing.* PHRASE 6 If something is too **close to the bone**, it makes you feel uncomfortable because it is very close to the truth or to the real nature of something. PHRASE: usu v-link PHR 7 If you **make no bones about** something, you talk openly about it, rather than trying to keep it a secret. ❑ *Some of them make no bones about their political views.* PHRASE: V inflects, usu PHR *about* n 8 If you **make no bones about** doing something that is unpleasant or difficult or that might upset someone else, you do it without hesitating. ❑ *Stafford-Clark made no bones about reapplying for the job when Daldry was standing for it.* PHRASE: V inflects, usu PHR *about* -ing
9 If something such as costs are cut **to the bone**, they are reduced to the minimum possible. ❑ *It has survived by cutting its costs to the bone... Profit margins have been slashed to the bone in an attempt to keep turnover moving.* PHRASE: PHR after v 10 You use **to the bone** to indicate that you are very deeply affected by something. For example, if you feel chilled **to the bone**, your whole body feels extremely cold, often because you have had a shock. ❑ *What I saw chilled me to the bone.* PHRASE: PHR after v

**bone chi|na** **Bone china** is a kind of thin china that contains powdered bone. N-UNCOUNT

**-boned** /-boʊnd/ **-boned** combines with adjectives such as 'big' and 'fine' to form adjectives which describe a person as having a particular type of bone structure or build. ❑ *He was about seven years old, small and fine-boned like his mother.* COMB in ADJ

**bone dry** also **bone-dry.** If you say that something is **bone dry**, you are emphasizing that it is very dry indeed. ❑ *Now the river bed is bone dry.* ADJ [emphasis]

**bone mar|row** **Bone marrow** is the soft fatty substance inside human or animal bones. ❑ *There are 2,000 children worldwide who need a bone marrow transplant.* N-UNCOUNT *= marrow*

**bone meal** also **bonemeal. Bone meal** is a substance made from animal bones which is used as a fertilizer. N-UNCOUNT

**bone of con|ten|tion** **(bones of contention)** If a particular matter or issue is a **bone of contention**, it is the subject of a disagreement or argument. ❑ *The main bone of contention is the temperature level of the air-conditioners.* N-COUNT

**bon|fire** /bɒnfaɪəʳ/ **(bonfires)** A **bonfire** is a fire that is made outdoors, usually to burn rubbish. Bonfires are also sometimes lit as part of a celebration. ❑ *With bonfires outlawed in urban areas, gardeners must cart their refuse to a dump.* N-COUNT

**Bon|fire Night** also **bonfire night. Bonfire Night** is the popular name for **Guy Fawkes Night**. N-UNCOUNT

**bong** /bɒŋ/ **(bongs)** A **bong** is a long, deep sound such as the sound made by a big bell. N-COUNT; SOUND

**bon|go** /bɒŋgoʊ/ **(bongos)** A **bongo** is a small drum that you play with your hands. N-COUNT

**bon|ho|mie** /bɒnəmi/ **Bonhomie** is happy, good-natured friendliness. [FORMAL] ❑ *He was full of bonhomie.* N-UNCOUNT

**bonk** /bɒŋk/ **(bonks, bonking, bonked)** If two people **bonk**, they have sexual intercourse. [BRIT, INFORMAL] V-RECIP

**bonk|ers** /bɒŋkəʳz/ If you say that someone is **bonkers**, you mean that they are silly or act in a crazy way. [BRIT, INFORMAL] ❑ *The man must be bonkers to take such a risk... I nearly went bonkers with frustration.* ADJ: v-link ADJ [disapproval] *= barmy, crazy*

**bon mot** /bɒn moʊ/ **(bons mots** or **bon mots)** A **bon mot** is a clever, witty remark. [WRITTEN] ❑ *...a cheeky bon mot.* N-COUNT *= witticism*

**bon|net** /bɒnɪt/ **(bonnets)** 1 The **bonnet** of a car is the metal cover over the engine at the front. [BRIT] → See picture on page 1707. ❑ *When I eventually stopped and lifted the bonnet, the noise seemed to be coming from the alternator.* N-COUNT

☑ in AM, use **hood**

2 A **bonnet** is a hat with ribbons that are tied under the chin. Bonnets are now worn by babies. In the past, they were also worn by women. N-COUNT

**bon|ny** /bɒni/ **(bonnier, bonniest)** Someone or something that is **bonny** is attractive and nice to look at. [mainly SCOTTISH or NORTHERN ENGLISH] ❑ *Jemima was a bonny Highland lassie of 15.* ADJ *= lovely*

**bon|sai** /bɒnsaɪ/ **(bonsai)** 1 A **bonsai** is a tree or shrub that has been kept very small by growing it in a little pot and cutting it in a special way. ❑ *...a beautiful Japanese bonsai tree.* N-COUNT: oft N n
2 **Bonsai** is the art of growing very small shrubs and trees. N-UNCOUNT

**bo|nus** /boʊnəs/ **(bonuses)** 1 A **bonus** is an extra amount of money that is added to someone's pay, usually because they have worked very hard. ❑ *Workers in big firms receive a substantial part of their pay in the form of bonuses and overtime. ...a £15 bonus. ...a special bonus payment.* N-COUNT 2 A **bonus** is something good that you get in addition to something else, and which you would not usually expect. ❑ *We felt we might finish third. Any better would be a bonus... It's made from natural ingredients, but with the added bonus of containing 30 per cent less fat than ordinary cheese.* N-COUNT *= plus* 3 A **bonus** is a sum of money that an insurance company pays to its policyholders, for example a percentage of the company's profits. ❑ *These returns will not be enough to meet the payment of annual bonuses to policyholders.* N-COUNT

**bon voy|age** /bɒn vɔɪɑːʒ/ You say '**bon voyage**' to someone who is going on a journey, as a way of saying goodbye and wishing them good luck. ❑ *Goodbye! Bon voyage!* CONVENTION [formulae]

**bony** /boʊni/ 1 Someone who has a **bony** face or **bony** hands, for example, has a very thin face or very thin hands, with very little flesh covering their bones. ❑ *...an old man with a bony face and white hair... He poked a long bony finger in Billy's chest.* ADJ: usu ADJ n 2 The **bony** parts of a person's or animal's body are the parts made of bone. ❑ *...the bony ridge of the eye socket.* ADJ: usu ADJ n

**boo** /buː/ **(boos, booing, booed)** 1 If you **boo** a speaker or performer, you shout 'boo' or make other loud sounds to indicate that you do not like them, their opinions, or their performance. ❑ *People were booing and throwing things at them... Demonstrators booed and jeered him... He was booed off the stage.* ♦ **Boo** is also a noun. ❑ *She was greeted with boos and hisses.* ♦ **boo|ing** *The fans are entitled to their opinion but booing doesn't help anyone.* VERB; V; V n; be V-ed; N-COUNT: usu pl; N-UNCOUNT
2 You say '**Boo!**' loudly and suddenly when you want to surprise someone who does not know that you are there. 3 → See also **peekaboo**. EXCLAM

**boob** /buːb/ **(boobs, boobing, boobed)** 1 A woman's **boobs** are her breasts. [INFORMAL, RUDE] N-COUNT: usu pl = breast
2 If you **boob**, you make a mistake. [BRIT, INFORMAL] ❑ *Is their timing right, or have they boobed again?* ♦ **Boob** is also a noun. ❑ *The government once again has made a big boob.* VERB; V; N-COUNT = blunder

**boob tube** **(boob tubes)** 1 **The boob tube** is the television. [mainly AM, INFORMAL] ❑ *...hours spent in front of the boob tube.* N-SING: the N

in BRIT, use **idiot box**

2 A **boob tube** is a piece of women's clothing made of stretchy material that covers only her chest. [BRIT, INFORMAL] N-COUNT

in AM, use **tube top**

**boo|by prize** /buːbi praɪz/ **(booby prizes)** The **booby prize** is a prize given as a joke to the person who comes last in a competition. N-COUNT

**booby-trap** /buːbi træp/ **(booby-traps, booby-trapping, booby-trapped)** also **booby trap**. 1 A **booby-trap** is something such as a bomb which is hidden or disguised and which causes death or injury when it is touched. ❑ *Police were checking the area for booby traps.* N-COUNT: oft N n
2 If something **is booby-trapped**, a booby-trap is placed in it or on it. ❑ *...fears that the area may have been booby trapped... His booby-trapped car exploded.* VERB: usu passive; be V-ed; V-ed

**boogey|man** /buːgimæn/ **(boogeymen)** → see **bogeyman**.

**boo|gie** /buːgi/ **(boogies, boogying** or **boogieing, boogied)** When you **boogie**, you dance to fast pop music. [INFORMAL, OLD-FASHIONED] ❑ *At night, a good place to boogie through till sunrise is the Pink Panther Bar.* VERB; V

**book** /bʊk/ **(books, booking, booked)** ♦♦♦ 1 A **book** is a number of pieces of paper, usually with words printed on them, which are fastened together and fixed inside a cover of stronger paper or cardboard. Books contain information, stories, or poetry, for example. ❑ *His eighth book came out earlier this year and was an instant best-seller. ...the author of a book on politics. ...reference books.* N-COUNT
2 A **book of** something such as stamps, matches, or tickets is a small number of them fastened together between thin cardboard covers. ❑ *Can I have a book of first class stamps please?* N-COUNT: usu N of n
3 When you **book** something such as a hotel room or a ticket, you arrange to have it or use it at a particular time. ❑ *British officials have booked hotel rooms for the women and children... Laurie revealed she had booked herself a flight home last night. ...three-star restaurants that are normally booked for months in advance.* VERB = reserve; V n; V n n; V-ed
4 A company's or organization's **books** are its records of money that has been spent and earned or of the names of people who belong to it. [BUSINESS] ❑ *For the most part he left the books to his managers and accountants... Around 12 per cent of the people on our books are in the computing industry.* N-PLURAL
5 When a referee **books** a football player who has seriously broken the rules of the game, he or she officially writes down the player's name. ❑ *League referee Keith Cooper booked him in the first half for a tussle with the goalie.* VERB; V n
6 When a police officer **books** someone, he or she officially records their name and the offence that they may be charged with. ❑ *They took him to the station and booked him for assault with a deadly weapon.* VERB = charge; V n
7 In a very long written work such as the Bible, a **book** is one of the sections into which it is divided. N-COUNT
8 → See also **booking, cheque book, phone book**.
PHRASES 9 If you **bring** someone **to book**, you punish them for an offence or make them explain their behaviour officially. ❑ *Police should be asked to investigate so that the guilty can be brought to book soon.* PHRASE: V inflects
10 If you say that someone or something is **a closed book**, you mean that you do not know anything about them. ❑ *Frank Spriggs was a very able man but something of a closed book... Economics was a closed book to him.* PHRASE: v-link PHR
11 If a hotel, restaurant, theatre, or transport service is **fully booked**, or **booked solid**, it is booked up. ❑ *The car ferries from the mainland are often fully booked by February.* PHRASE: v-link PHR
12 **In my book** means 'in my opinion' or 'according to my beliefs'. ❑ *The greatest manager there has ever been, or ever will be in my book, is retiring.* PHRASE: PHR with cl = to my mind
13 to **cook the books** → see **cook**. to **take a leaf from** someone's **book** → see **leaf**.
♦ **book in** or **book into** When you **book into** a hotel or when you **book in**, you officially state that you have arrived to stay there, usually by signing your name in a register. [BRIT] ❑ *He was happy to book into the Royal Pavilion Hotel... Today Mahoney booked himself into one of the best hotels in Sydney.* PHRASAL VERB = check in, check into ≠ check out, check out of; V P n; V n P n; Also V p, V n P

in AM, use **check in, check into**

**book|able** /bʊkəbᵊl/ 1 If something such as a theatre seat or plane ticket is **bookable**, it can be booked in advance. [mainly BRIT] ❑ *Tours leave from Palma and are bookable at some hotels or any travel agency.* ADJ: usu v-link ADJ
2 In sports such as football, a **bookable** offence is an action for which a player can be officially warned by the referee. ❑ *Both men were dismissed for a second bookable offence.* ADJ

**book|binder** /bʊkbaɪndəʳ/ **(bookbinders)** also **book-binder**. A **bookbinder** is a person whose job is fastening books together and putting covers on them. N-COUNT

**book|bind|ing** /bʊkbaɪndɪŋ/ also **book-binding**. **Bookbinding** is the work of fastening books together and putting covers on them. N-UNCOUNT

**book|case** /bʊkkeɪs/ **(bookcases)** A **bookcase** is a piece of furniture with shelves that you keep books on. N-COUNT

**book club** **(book clubs)** A **book club** is an organization that offers books at reduced prices to its members. N-COUNT

**booked up** 1 If a hotel, restaurant, theatre, or transport service is **booked up**, it has no rooms, tables, or tickets left for a time or date. [mainly BRIT] ❑ *St Just seemed pretty booked up, but we managed to find a room at the George.* ADJ: v-link ADJ = full
2 If someone is **booked up**, they have made so many arrangements that they have no more time to do things. [mainly BRIT] ❑ *Mr Wilson's diary is booked up for months ahead.* ADJ: v-link ADJ

**book|end** /bʊkend/ **(bookends)** also **book-end**. **Bookends** are a pair of supports used to hold a row of books in an upright position by placing one at each end of the row. N-COUNT: usu pl

**bookie** /bʊki/ **(bookies)** A **bookie** is the same as a **bookmaker**. [INFORMAL] N-COUNT

**book|ing** /bʊkɪŋ/ **(bookings)** A **booking** is the arrangement that you make when you book something such as a hotel room, a table at a restaurant, a theatre seat, or a place on public transport. ❑ *I suggest you tell him there was a mistake over his late booking.* N-COUNT: usu with supp = reservation

**book|ing clerk** **(booking clerks)** A **booking clerk** is a person who sells tickets, especially in a railway station. [BRIT] ❑ *...a railway booking clerk.* N-COUNT

**book|ing of|fice** **(booking offices)** A **booking office** is a room where tickets are sold and booked, especially in a theatre or station. [BRIT] N-COUNT = ticket office

in AM, use **ticket office**

**book|ish** /bʊkɪʃ/ Someone who is **bookish** spends a lot of time reading serious books. ADJ disapproval = studious

**book|keeper** /bʊkiːpəʳ/ **(bookkeepers)** also **book-keeper.** A **bookkeeper** is a person whose job is to keep an accurate record of the money that is spent and received by a business or other organization. [BUSINESS] N-COUNT

**book|keeping** /bʊkiːpɪŋ/ also **book-keeping. Bookkeeping** is the job or activity of keeping an accurate record of the money that is spent and received by a business or other organization. [BUSINESS] N-UNCOUNT

**book|let** /bʊklət/ **(booklets)** A **booklet** is a small book that has a paper cover and that gives you information about something. N-COUNT = *pamphlet*

**book|maker** /bʊkmeɪkəʳ/ **(bookmakers)** A **bookmaker** is a person whose job is to take your money when you bet and to pay you money if you win. N-COUNT

**book|making** /bʊkmeɪkɪŋ/ **Bookmaking** is the activity of taking people's money when they bet and paying them money if they win. ❑ *...an Internet bookmaking business.* N-UNCOUNT: oft N n

**book|mark** /bʊkmɑːʳk/ **(bookmarks)** 1 A **bookmark** is a narrow piece of card or leather that you put between the pages of a book so that you can find a particular page easily. N-COUNT 2 In computing, a **bookmark** is the address of an Internet site that you put into a list on your computer so that you can return to it easily. [COMPUTING] ❑ *This makes it extremely simple to save what you find with an electronic bookmark so you can return to it later.* N-COUNT

**book|plate** /bʊkpleɪt/ **(bookplates)** A **bookplate** is a piece of decorated paper which is stuck in the front of a book and on which the owner's name is printed or written. N-COUNT

**book|sell|er** /bʊkseləʳ/ **(booksellers)** A **bookseller** is a person who sells books. N-COUNT

**book|shelf** /bʊkʃelf/ **(bookshelves)** A **bookshelf** is a shelf on which you keep books. N-COUNT

**book|shop** /bʊkʃɒp/ **(bookshops)** A **bookshop** is a shop where books are sold. [BRIT] N-COUNT

☑ in AM, use **bookstore**

**book|stall** /bʊkstɔːl/ **(bookstalls)** 1 A **bookstall** is a long table from which books and magazines are sold, for example at a conference or in a street market. N-COUNT 2 A **bookstall** is a small shop with an open front where books and magazines are sold. Bookstalls are usually found in railway stations and airports. [BRIT] N-COUNT = *kiosk*

☑ in AM, usually use **newsstand**

**book|store** /bʊkstɔːʳ/ **(bookstores)** A **bookstore** is a shop where books are sold. [mainly AM] N-COUNT

☑ in BRIT, usually use **bookshop**

**book value** **(book values)** In business, the **book value** of an asset is the value it is given in the account books of the company that owns it. [BUSINESS] ❑ *The insured value of the airplane was greater than its book value.* N-COUNT

**book|worm** /bʊkwɜːʳm/ **(bookworms)** If you describe someone as a **bookworm**, you mean they are very fond of reading. [INFORMAL] N-COUNT

**boom** /buːm/ **(booms, booming, boomed)** ◆◇◇ 1 If there is a **boom** in the economy, there is an increase in economic activity, for example in the amount of things that are being bought and sold. ❑ *An economic boom followed, especially in housing and construction... The 1980s were indeed boom years. ...the cycle of boom and bust which has damaged us for 40 years.* N-COUNT: usu sing ≠ *slump* 2 A **boom in** something is an increase in its amount, frequency, or success. ❑ *The boom in the sport's popularity has meant more calls for stricter safety regulations... Public transport has not been able to cope adequately with the travel boom.* N-COUNT: usu sing, with supp, oft N *in* n ≠ *slump* 3 If the economy or a business **is booming**, the amount of things being bought or sold is increasing. ❑ *By 1988 the economy was booming... It has a booming tourist industry.* VERB V, V-ing 4 On a boat, **the boom** is the long pole which is attached to the bottom of the sail and to the mast and which you move when you want to alter the direction in which you are sailing. N-COUNT: usu sing, *the* N 5 When something such as someone's voice, a cannon, or a big drum **booms**, it makes a loud, deep sound that lasts for several seconds. ❑ *'Ladies,' boomed Helena, without a microphone, 'we all know why we're here tonight.'... Thunder boomed like battlefield cannons over Crooked Mountain.* VERB V with quote V prep/adv Also V ♦ **Boom out** means the same as **boom.** ❑ *Music boomed out from loudspeakers... A megaphone boomed out, 'This is the police.'... He turned his sightless eyes their way and boomed out a greeting.* PHRASAL VERB V P prep/adv V P with quote V P n Also V P ♦ **Boom** is also a noun. ❑ *The stillness of night was broken by the boom of a cannon.* N-COUNT; SOUND 6 → See also **baby boom**.

♦ **boom out** → see **boom 5**.

**boom box** **(boom boxes)** A **boom box** is a large portable machine for playing music, especially one that is played loudly in public by young people. [mainly AM, INFORMAL] N-COUNT

☑ in BRIT, use **ghetto-blaster**

**boom-bust cy|cle** **(boom-bust cycles)** A **boom-bust cycle** is a series of events in which a rapid increase in business activity in the economy is followed by a rapid decrease in business activity, and this process is repeated again and again. [BUSINESS] ❑ *We must avoid the damaging boom-bust cycles which characterised the 1980s.* N-COUNT

**boom|er|ang** /buːməræŋ/ **(boomerangs, boomeranging, boomeranged)** 1 A **boomerang** is a curved piece of wood which comes back to you if you throw it in the correct way. Boomerangs were first used by the people who were living in Australia when Europeans arrived there. N-COUNT 2 If a plan **boomerangs**, its result is not the one that was intended and is harmful to the person who made the plan. ❑ *The trick boomeranged, though... He risks defeat in the referendum which he called, but which threatens to boomerang against him.* VERB = *backfire* V V *on/against* n

**boom town** **(boom towns)** A **boom town** is a town which has rapidly become very rich and full of people, usually because industry or business has developed there. ❑ *Brisbane has become the boom town for Australian film and television.* N-COUNT

**boon** /buːn/ **(boons)** You can describe something as a **boon** when it makes life better or easier for someone. ❑ *This battery booster is a boon for photographers.* N-COUNT: usu *a* N *to/for* n

**boon|dog|gle** /buːndɒgl/ **(boondoggles)** People sometimes refer to an official organization or activity as a **boondoggle** when they think it wastes a lot of time and money and does not achieve much. [AM, INFORMAL] ❑ *The new runway is a billion-dollar boondoggle.* N-COUNT disapproval

**boor** /bʊəʳ/ **(boors)** If you refer to someone as a **boor**, you think their behaviour and attitudes are rough, uneducated, and rude. N-COUNT disapproval = *oaf*

**boor|ish** /bʊərɪʃ/ **Boorish** behaviour is rough, uneducated, and rude. ❑ *...their boorish rejection of the ageing movie star.* ADJ = *oafish*

**boost** /buːst/ **(boosts, boosting, boosted)** ◆◇◇ 1 If one thing **boosts** another, it causes it to increase, improve, or be more successful. ❑ *It wants the government to take action to boost the economy... The move is designed to boost sales during the peak booking months of January and February.* VERB V n V n ♦ **Boost** is also a noun. ❑ *It would get the economy going and give us the boost that we need.* N-COUNT: usu sing 2 If something **boosts** your confidence or morale, it improves it. ❑ *We need a big win to boost our confidence.* VERB = *bolster* V n ♦ **Boost** is also a noun. ❑ *It did give me a boost to win such a big event.* N-COUNT: usu sing

**boost|er** /buːstəʳ/ **(boosters)** 1 A **booster** is something that increases a positive or desirable quality. ❑ *It was amazing what a morale booster her visits proved... Praise is a great confidence booster.* N-COUNT: usu n N 2 A **booster** is an extra engine in a machine such as a space rocket, which provides an extra amount of power at certain times. ❑ *Ground controllers will then fire the booster, sending the satellite* N-COUNT *into its proper orbit.* 3 A **booster** is a small injection of a drug that you have some time after a larger injection, in order to make sure that the first injection will remain effective. N-COUNT 4 A **booster** is someone who supports a sports team, organization, person, or place very enthusiastically. [AM] ❑ *A former associate of Mr. Pierce's was among the project's boosters.* N-COUNT: oft supp N, N n = supporter

**boost|er seat** **(booster seats)** also **booster cushion.** A **booster seat** or a **booster cushion** is a special seat which allows a small child to sit in a higher position, for example at a table or in a car. N-COUNT

**boot** /buːt/ **(boots, booting, booted)** ◆◇◇ 1 **Boots** are shoes that cover your whole foot and the lower part of your leg. ❑ *He sat in a kitchen chair, reached down and pulled off his boots... He was wearing riding pants, high boots, and spurs.* ➔ See also **wellington.** N-COUNT 2 **Boots** are strong, heavy shoes which cover your ankle and which have thick soles. You wear them to protect your feet, for example when you are walking or taking part in sport. ❑ *The soldiers' boots resounded in the street.* N-COUNT 3 If you **boot** something such as a ball, you kick it hard. [INFORMAL] ❑ *He booted the ball 40 yards back up field.* VERB V n adv/prep 4 The **boot** of a car is a covered space at the back or front, in which you carry things such as luggage and shopping. [BRIT] ➔ See picture on page 1707. ❑ *He opened the boot to put my bags in.* N-COUNT

✔ in AM, use **trunk**

**PHRASES** 5 If you **get the boot** or **are given the boot**, you are told that you are not wanted any more, either in your job or by someone you are having a relationship with. [INFORMAL] ❑ *She was a disruptive influence, and after a year or two she got the boot.* PHRASE: V inflects 6 If someone **puts the boot in**, they attack another person by saying something cruel, often when the person is already feeling weak or upset. [BRIT, INFORMAL] PHRASE: V inflects 7 You can say **to boot** to emphasize that you have added something else to something or to a list of things that you have just said. [FORMAL] ❑ *He is making money and receiving free advertising to boot!* PHRASE: cl/group PHR [emphasis] = into the bargain

♦ **boot out** If someone **boots** you **out of** a job, organization, or place, you are forced to leave it. [INFORMAL] ❑ *Schools are booting out record numbers of unruly pupils.* PHRASAL VERB = kick out V P n (not pron) Also V n P

♦ **boot up** When you **boot up** a computer, you make it ready to use by putting in the instructions which it needs in order to start working. [COMPUTING] ❑ *I can boot up from a floppy disk, but that's all... Go over to your PC and boot it up.* PHRASAL VERB V P from/with n V n P

**boot camp** **(boot camps)** In the United States, a **boot camp** is a camp where people who have just joined the army, navy, or marines are trained. [AM] N-VAR

**bootee** /buːtiː/ **(bootees** or **booties)** 1 **Bootees** are short woollen socks that babies wear instead of shoes. N-COUNT: usu pl 2 **Bootees** are short boots which come to just above the ankle. They are worn especially by women and girls. N-COUNT

**booth** /buːð/ **(booths)** 1 A **booth** is a small area separated from a larger public area by screens or thin walls where, for example, people can make a telephone call or vote in private. ❑ *I called her from a public phone booth near the entrance to the bar.* N-COUNT: usu n N = cubicle 2 A **booth** in a restaurant or café consists of a table with long fixed seats on two or sometimes three sides of it. ❑ *They sat in a corner booth, away from other diners.* N-COUNT

**boot|lace** /buːtleɪs/ **(bootlaces)** A **bootlace** is a long thin cord which is used to fasten a boot. N-COUNT: usu pl

**boot|leg** /buːtleg/ **(bootlegs, bootlegging, bootlegged)** 1 **Bootleg** is used to describe something that is made secretly and sold illegally. ❑ *...a bootleg recording of the band's 1977 tour of Scandinavia. ...bootleg liquor.* ADJ: ADJ n = illegal ≠ legal 2 To **bootleg** something such as a recording means to make and sell it illegally. ❑ *He has sued a fan for bootlegging his concerts... Avid Bob Dylan fans treasure bootlegged recordings.* VERB V n V-ed ♦ **Bootleg** is also a noun. ❑ *The record was a bootleg.* N-COUNT ♦ **boot|leg|ger** **(bootleggers)** *Bootleggers sold 75 million dollars-worth of copies.* N-COUNT

**boot|straps** /buːtstræps/ If you have **pulled yourself up by** your **bootstraps**, you have achieved success by your own efforts, starting from very difficult circumstances and without help from anyone. PHRASE: V inflects

**boo|ty** /buːti/ **Booty** is a collection of valuable things stolen from a place, especially by soldiers after a battle. ❑ *Troops destroyed the capital and confiscated many works of art as war booty.* N-UNCOUNT = spoils

**booze** /buːz/ **(boozes, boozing, boozed)** 1 **Booze** is alcoholic drink. [INFORMAL] ❑ *...booze and cigarettes. ...empty bottles of booze.* N-UNCOUNT: also the N 2 If people **booze**, they drink alcohol. [INFORMAL] ❑ *...a load of drunken businessmen who had been boozing all afternoon.* VERB V ♦ **booz|ing** *She had to contend with the boozing and girl-chasing of her husband.* N-UNCOUNT

**boozed** /buːzd/ If someone is **boozed** or **boozed up**, they are drunk. [INFORMAL] ❑ *He's half asleep and a bit boozed.* ADJ: usu v-link ADJ

**booz|er** /buːzəʳ/ **(boozers)** 1 A **boozer** is a **pub**. [BRIT, INFORMAL] ❑ *They're in the boozer most nights.* N-COUNT 2 A **boozer** is a person who drinks a lot of alcohol. [INFORMAL] ❑ *I thought he was a bit of a boozer.* N-COUNT

**booze-up** **(booze-ups)** In Britain, a **booze-up** is a party or other social gathering where people drink a lot of alcohol. [INFORMAL] ❑ *...a booze-up at the rugby club.* N-COUNT

**boozy** /buːzi/ A **boozy** person is someone who drinks a lot of alcohol. [INFORMAL] ❑ *...a cheerful, boozy chain-smoker.* ADJ: usu ADJ n

**bop** /bɒp/ **(bops, bopping, bopped)** 1 A **bop** is a dance. [BRIT, INFORMAL] ❑ *People just want a good tune and a good bop.* N-COUNT = dance 2 If you **bop**, you dance. [BRIT, INFORMAL] ❑ *He was bopping around, snapping his fingers... Guests bopped and jigged the night away to the disco beat.* VERB = dance V adv/prep V 3 ➔ See also **bebop**.

**bop|per** /bɒpəʳ/ ➔ see **teenybopper**.

**bo|rax** /bɔːræks/ **Borax** is a white powder used, for example, in the making of glass and as a cleaning chemical. N-UNCOUNT

**bor|del|lo** /bɔːʳdeloʊ/ **(bordellos)** A **bordello** is a **brothel**. [LITERARY] N-COUNT

**bor|der** /bɔːʳdəʳ/ **(borders, bordering, bordered)** ◆◆◇ 1 The **border** between two countries or regions is the dividing line between them. Sometimes **the border** also refers to the land close to this line. ❑ *They fled across the border. ...the isolated jungle area near the Panamanian border... Clifford is enjoying life north of the border. ...the Mexican border town of Tijuana.* N-COUNT = frontier 2 A country that **borders** another country, a sea, or a river is next to it. ❑ *...the European and Arab countries bordering the Mediterranean.* VERB V n ♦ **Border on** means the same as **border**. ❑ *Both republics border on the Black Sea.* PHRASAL VERB V P n 3 A **border** is a strip or band around the edge of something. ❑ *...pillowcases trimmed with a hand-crocheted border.* N-COUNT 4 In a garden, a **border** is a long strip of ground along the edge planted with flowers. ❑ *...a lawn flanked by wide herbaceous borders. ...border plants.* N-COUNT 5 If something **is bordered** by another thing, the other thing forms a line along the edge of it. ❑ *...the mile of white sand beach bordered by palm trees and tropical flowers... Caesar marched north into the forests that border the Danube River.* VERB = flank V-ed V n

♦ **border on** If you talk about a characteristic or situation **bordering on** something, usually something that you consider bad, you mean that it is almost that thing. ❑ *The atmosphere borders on the surreal.* ➔ See also **border 2**. PHRASAL VERB = verge on V P n

**border|land** /bɔːʳdəʳlænd/ **(borderlands)** 1 The **borderland between** two things is an area which contains features from both of these things so that it is not possible to say that it belongs to one or the other. ❑ *...on the borderland be-* N-SING: usu with supp tween sleep and waking.* [2] The area of land close to the border between two countries or major areas can be called the **borderlands**. ❑ *...Lebanon's southern borderlands.* N-COUNT: usu pl

**border|line** /bɔːʳdəʳlaɪn/ **(borderlines)** [1] The **borderline between** two different or opposite things is the division between them. ❑ *...a task which involves exploring the borderline between painting and photography.* N-COUNT: usu N *between/of* n [2] Something that is **borderline** is only just acceptable as a member of a class or group. ❑ *Some were obviously unsuitable and could be ruled out at once. Others were borderline cases.* ADJ

**bore** /bɔːʳ/ **(bores, boring, bored)** ◆◇◇ [1] If someone or something **bores** you, you find them dull and uninteresting. ❑ *Dickie bored him all through the meal with stories of the Navy... Life in the country bores me.* VERB V n *with* n V n [2] If someone or something **bores** you **to tears**, **bores** you **to death**, or **bores** you **stiff**, they bore you very much indeed. [INFORMAL] ❑ *...a handsome engineer who bored me to tears with his tales of motorway maintenance.* PHRASE: V inflects [emphasis] [3] You describe someone as a **bore** when you think that they talk in a very uninteresting way. ❑ *There is every reason why I shouldn't enjoy his company – he's a bore and a fool.* N-COUNT [4] You can describe a situation as **a bore** when you find it annoying. ❑ *It's a bore to be sick, and the novelty of lying in bed all day wears off quickly.* N-SING: *a* N = *drag* [5] If you **bore** a hole in something, you make a deep round hole in it using a special tool. ❑ *Get the special drill bit to bore the correct-size hole for the job.* VERB V n [6] **Bore** is the past tense of **bear**. [7] → See also **bored**, **boring**.

**-bore** /-bɔːʳ/ **-bore** combines with numbers to form adjectives which indicate the size of the barrel of a gun. ❑ *He had a 12-bore shotgun.* COMB in ADJ: ADJ n

**bored** /bɔːʳd/ If you are **bored**, you feel tired and impatient because you have lost interest in something or because you have nothing to do. ❑ *I am getting very bored with this entire business.* ADJ: usu v-link ADJ, oft ADJ *with* n/-ing

**bore|dom** /bɔːʳdəm/ **Boredom** is the state of being bored. ❑ *He had given up attending lectures out of sheer boredom... They often find they begin to chat to relieve the boredom of the flight.* N-UNCOUNT

**bore|hole** /bɔːʳhoʊl/ **(boreholes)** A **borehole** is a deep round hole made by a special tool or machine, especially one that is made in the ground when searching for oil or water. N-COUNT

**bor|ing** /bɔːrɪŋ/ Someone or something **boring** is so dull and uninteresting that they make people tired and impatient. ❑ *Not only are mothers not paid but also most of their boring or difficult work is unnoticed. ...boring television programmes.* ADJ = *dull, tedious* ≠ *interesting* ♦ **bor|ing|ly** *The meal itself was not so good – everything was boringly brown including the vegetables.* ADV: usu ADV adj

**born** /bɔːʳn/ ◆◆◇ [1] When a baby **is born**, it comes out of its mother's body at the beginning of its life. In formal English, if you say that someone **is born of** someone or **to** someone, you mean that person is their parent. ❑ *My mother was 40 when I was born... He was born of German parents and lived most of his life abroad... Willie Smith was the second son born to Jean and Stephen.* V-PASSIVE *be* V-ed *be* V-ed *of/to* n V-ed *of/to* n [2] If someone **is born with** a particular disease, problem, or characteristic, they have it from the time they are born. ❑ *He was born with only one lung... Some people are born brainy... I think he was born to be editor of a tabloid newspaper... We are all born leaders; we just need the right circumstances in which to flourish.* V-PASSIVE: no cont *be* V-ed *with* n *be* V-ed adj *be* V-ed to-inf *be* V-ed n [3] You can use **be born** in front of a particular name to show that a person was given this name at birth, although they may be better known by another name. [FORMAL] ❑ *She was born Jenny Harvey on June 11, 1946.* V-PASSIVE: no cont *be* V-ed n [4] You use **born** to describe someone who has a natural ability to do a particular activity or job. For example, if you are a **born** cook, you have a natural ability to cook well. ❑ *Jack was a born teacher.* ADJ: ADJ n [5] When an idea or organization **is born**, it comes into existence. If something **is born of** a particular emotion or activity, it exists as a result of that emotion or activity. [FORMAL] ❑ *Congress passed the National Security Act, and the CIA was born... Energy conservation as a philosophy was born out of the 1973 oil crisis.* V-PASSIVE *be* V-ed *be* V-ed *out of/of* n [6] → See also **-born**, **first born**, **newborn**. [7] to **be born and bred** → see **breed**. to **be born with a silver spoon in** your **mouth** → see **spoon**.

**-born** /-bɔːʳn/ **-born** combines with adjectives that relate to countries or with the names of towns and areas to form adjectives that indicate where someone was born. [JOURNALISM] ❑ *The German-born photographer was admired by writers such as Oscar Wilde.* COMB in ADJ: usu ADJ n

**born-again** [1] A **born-again** Christian is a person who has become an evangelical Christian as a result of a religious experience. ADJ [2] You can use **born-again** to describe someone who has adopted a new set of beliefs or a new way of life and is very enthusiastic about it. ❑ *As a 'born-again' cyclist I had decided that this season I would ride in a few races.* ADJ

**borne** /bɔːʳn/ **Borne** is the past participle of **bear**.

**-borne** /-bɔːʳn/ **-borne** combines with nouns to form adjectives that describe the method or means by which something is carried or moved. ❑ *...water-borne diseases. ...a mosquito-borne infection. ...rocket-borne weapons.* COMB in ADJ: usu ADJ n

**bor|ough** /bʌrə, AM bɜːroʊ/ **(boroughs)** A **borough** is a town, or a district within a large town, which has its own council. ❑ *...the New York City borough of Brooklyn.* N-COUNT: oft *the* N *of* n, N n

**bor|row** /bɒroʊ/ **(borrows, borrowing, borrowed)** ◆◇◇ [1] If you **borrow** something that belongs to someone else, you take it or use it for a period of time, usually with their permission. ❑ *Can I borrow a pen please?... He wouldn't let me borrow his clothes.* VERB ≠ *lend* V n V n [2] If you **borrow** money **from** someone or **from** a bank, they give it to you and you agree to pay it back at some time in the future. ❑ *Morgan borrowed £5,000 from his father to form the company 20 years ago... It's so expensive to borrow from finance companies... He borrowed heavily to get the money together.* VERB V n *from* n V *from* n V Also V n [3] If you **borrow** a book **from** a library, you take it away for a fixed period of time. ❑ *I couldn't afford to buy any, so I borrowed them from the library.* VERB V n *from* n [4] If you **borrow** something such as a word or an idea from another language or from another person's work, you use it in your own language or work. ❑ *I borrowed his words for my book's title... Their engineers are happier borrowing other people's ideas than developing their own.* VERB V n V n [5] Someone who **is living on borrowed time** or who **is on borrowed time** has continued to live or to do something for longer than was expected, and is likely to die or be stopped from doing it soon. ❑ *Perhaps that illness, diagnosed as fatal, gave him a sense of living on borrowed time.* PHRASE: V inflects

**bor|row|er** /bɒroʊəʳ/ **(borrowers)** A **borrower** is a person or organization that borrows money. N-COUNT ≠ *lender*

**bor|row|ing** /bɒroʊɪŋ/ **(borrowings)** **Borrowing** is the activity of borrowing money. ❑ *We have allowed spending and borrowing to rise in this recession.* N-UNCOUNT: also N in pl

**bor|stal** /bɔːʳstəl/ **(borstals)** In Britain in the past, a **borstal** was a kind of prison for young criminals, who were not old enough to be sent to ordinary prisons. N-VAR = *reform school*

**bos|om** /bʊzəm/ **(bosoms)** [1] A woman's breasts are sometimes referred to as her **bosom** or her **bosoms**. [OLD-FASHIONED] ❑ *...a large young mother with a baby resting against her ample bosom.* N-COUNT = *bust* [2] A **bosom** friend is a friend who you know very well and like very much indeed. ❑ *They were bosom friends... Sakota was her cousin and bosom pal.* ADJ: ADJ n

**boss** /bɒs/ **(bosses, bossing, bossed)** ◆◆◇ [1] Your **boss** is the person in charge of the organization or department where you work. ❑ *He cannot stand his boss... Occasionally I have to go and ask the boss* N-COUNT: usu with supp, oft poss N for a rise. 2 If you are **the boss** in a group or relationship, you are the person who makes all the decisions. [INFORMAL] ❑ *He thinks he's the boss.* N-COUNT: usu *the* N in sing

3 If you say that someone **bosses** you, you mean that they keep telling you what to do in a way that is irritating. ❑ *We cannot boss them into doing more... 'You are not to boss me!' she shouted.* VERB = order around; V n prep/adv; V n

♦ **Boss around**, or in British English **boss about**, means the same as **boss**. ❑ *He started bossing people around and I didn't like what was happening.* PHRASAL VERB V n P; Also V P n (not pron) 4 If you **are** your **own boss**, you work for yourself or make your own decisions and do not have anyone telling you what to do. ❑ *I'm very much my own boss and no one interferes with what I do.* PHRASE: V inflects

♦ **boss around** or **boss about** → see **boss 3**.

**bossy** /bɒsi/ If you describe someone as **bossy**, you mean that they enjoy telling people what to do. ❑ *She remembers being a rather bossy little girl.* ♦ **bossi|ness** *They resent what they see as bossiness.* ADJ [disapproval]; N-UNCOUNT

**bo|sun** /boʊsᵊn/ **(bosuns)** The **bosun** on a ship is the officer whose job it is to look after the ship and its equipment. N-COUNT: oft *the* N

**bot** /bɒt/ **(bots)** A **bot** is a computer program that carries out tasks for other programs or users, especially on the Internet. [COMPUTING] N-COUNT

**bo|tan|ic** /bətænɪk/ **Botanic** means the same as **botanical**. ADJ: ADJ n

**bo|tani|cal** /bətænɪkᵊl/ **(botanicals)** 1 **Botanical** books, research, and activities relate to the scientific study of plants. ❑ *The area is of great botanical interest. ...botanical gardens.* ADJ: ADJ n 2 **Botanicals** are drugs which are made from plants. ❑ *The most effective new botanicals are extracts from cola nut and marine algae.* N-COUNT

**bota|nist** /bɒtənɪst/ **(botanists)** A **botanist** is a scientist who studies plants. N-COUNT

**bota|ny** /bɒtəni/ **Botany** is the scientific study of plants. N-UNCOUNT

**botch** /bɒtʃ/ **(botches, botching, botched)** 1 If you **botch** something that you are doing, you do it badly or clumsily. [INFORMAL] ❑ *It is a silly idea and he has botched it. ...a botched job.* VERB = bungle; V n; V-ed ♦ **Botch up** means the same as **botch**. ❑ *I hate having builders botch up repairs on my house... Hemingway complained that Nichols had 'botched everything up'.* PHRASAL VERB = mess up; V P n (not pron); V n P

2 If you **make a botch of** something that you are doing, you botch it. [INFORMAL] ❑ *I rather made a botch of that whole thing.* N-COUNT: usu sing = mess

**botch-up** **(botch-ups)** A **botch-up** is the same as a **botch**. [INFORMAL] ❑ *They were victims of a computer botch-up.* N-COUNT: usu sing

**both** /boʊθ/ ◆◆◆ 1 You use **both** when you are referring to two people or things and saying that something is true about each of them. ❑ *She cried out in fear and flung both arms up to protect her face... Put both vegetables into a bowl and crush with a potato masher.* DET: DET pl-n ♦ **Both** is also a quantifier. ❑ *Both of these women have strong memories of the Vietnam War... We're going to Andreas's Boutique to pick out something original for both of us.* QUANT: QUANT *of* pl-n ♦ **Both** is also a pronoun. ❑ *Miss Brown and her friend, both from Stoke, were arrested on the 8th of June... Will there be public-works programmes, or community service, or both?* PRON ♦ **Both** is also an emphasizing pronoun. ❑ *He visited the Institute of Neurology in Havana where they both worked... 'Well, I'll leave you both, then,' said Gregory.* PRON: n PRON ♦ **Both** is also a predeterminer. ❑ *Both the band's writers are fascinating lyricists... Both the horses were out, tacked up and ready to ride.* PREDET: PREDET det pl-n [emphasis] 2 You use the structure **both...and** when you are giving two facts or alternatives and emphasizing that each of them is true or possible. ❑ *Now women work both before and after having their children... Any such action would have to be approved by both American and Saudi leaders.* CONJ

**both|er** /bɒðəʳ/ **(bothers, bothering, bothered)** ◆◇◇ 1 If you do not **bother to** do something or if you do not **bother with** it, you do not do it, consider it, or use it because you think it is unnecessary or because you are too lazy. ❑ *Lots of people don't bother to go through a marriage ceremony these days... Most of the papers didn't even bother reporting it... Nothing I do makes any difference anyway, so why bother? ...and he does not bother with a helmet either.* VERB: with brd-neg; V to-inf; V -ing; V; V *with/about* n

2 **Bother** means trouble or difficulty. You can also use **bother** to refer to an activity which causes this, especially when you would prefer not to do it or get involved with it. ❑ *I usually buy sliced bread – it's less bother... Most men hate the bother of shaving.* N-UNCOUNT: also *a* N = trouble 3 If something **bothers** you, or if you **bother** about it, it worries, annoys, or upsets you. ❑ *Is something bothering you?... That kind of jealousy doesn't bother me... It bothered me that boys weren't interested in me... Never bother about people's opinions.* VERB: V n; *it* V n that/wh; V *about* n; Also *it* V n to-inf ♦ **both|ered** *I was bothered about the blister on my hand... I'm not bothered if he has another child.* ADJ: v-link ADJ, oft ADJ *about* n 4 If someone **bothers** you, they talk to you when you want to be left alone or interrupt you when you are busy. ❑ *We are playing a trick on a man who keeps bothering me... I don't know why he bothers me with this kind of rubbish.* VERB: V n; V n *with/about* n 5 If you say that you **can't be bothered to** do something, you mean that you are not going to do it because you think it is unnecessary or because you are too lazy. ❑ *I just can't be bothered to look after the house.* PHRASE: V inflects, usu PHR to-inf 6 **hot and bothered** → see **hot**.

**both|er|some** /bɒðəʳsəm/ Someone or something that is **bothersome** is annoying or irritating. [OLD-FASHIONED] ADJ = troublesome

**Bo|tox** /boʊtɒks/ **Botox** is a substance that is injected into the face in order to make the skin look smoother. [TRADEMARK] ❑ *...Botox injections.* N-UNCOUNT: oft N n

**bot|tle** /bɒtᵊl/ **(bottles, bottling, bottled)** ◆◆◇ 1 A **bottle** is a glass or plastic container in which drinks and other liquids are kept. Bottles are usually round with straight sides and a narrow top. ❑ *There were two empty beer bottles on the table... He was pulling the cork from a bottle of wine. ...Victorian scent bottles.* N-COUNT ♦ A **bottle of** something is an amount of it contained in a bottle. ❑ *He had drunk half a bottle of whisky.* N-COUNT: usu N *of* n 2 To **bottle** a drink or other liquid means to put it into bottles after it has been made. ❑ *This is a large truck which has equipment to automatically bottle the wine. ...bottled water.* VERB: V n; V-ed 3 A **bottle** is a drinking container used by babies. It has a special rubber part at the top through which they can suck their drink. N-COUNT: usu with supp 4 → See also **bottled**, **feeding bottle**, **hot-water bottle**, **water bottle**.

♦ **bottle up** If you **bottle up** strong feelings, you do not express them or show them, especially when this makes you tense or angry. ❑ *Tension in the home increases if you bottle things up... Be assertive rather than bottle up your anger.* PHRASAL VERB [disapproval] V n P; V P n (not pron)

**bot|tle bank** **(bottle banks)** A **bottle bank** is a large container into which people can put empty bottles so that the glass can be used again. [BRIT] N-COUNT

**bot|tled** /bɒtᵊld/ **Bottled** gas is kept under pressure in special metal cylinders which can be moved from one place to another. → See also **bottle**. ADJ: usu ADJ n

**bottle-feed** **(bottle-feeds, bottle-feeding, bottle-fed)** If you **bottle-feed** a baby, you give it milk or a liquid like milk in a bottle rather than the baby sucking milk from its mother's breasts. ❑ *New fathers love bottle feeding their babies. ...a bottle-fed baby.* VERB ≠ breast feed; V n; V-ed

**bottle-green** also **bottle green.** Something that is **bottle-green** is dark green in colour. COLOUR

**bottle|neck** /bɒtᵊlnek/ **(bottlenecks)** 1 A **bottleneck** is a place where a road becomes narrow or where it meets another road so that the traffic slows down or stops, often causing traffic jams. N-COUNT 2 A **bottleneck** is a situation that stops a N-COUNT process or activity from progressing. ❑ *He pushed everyone full speed ahead until production hit a bottleneck.*

**bottle-opener** **(bottle-openers)** A **bottle-opener** is a metal device for removing caps or tops from bottles. N-COUNT

**bot|tler** /bɒtələʳ/ **(bottlers)** A **bottler** is a person or company that puts drinks into bottles. N-COUNT

**bot|tom** /bɒtəm/ **(bottoms, bottoming, bottomed)** ◆◆◇ [1] **The bottom of** something is the lowest or deepest part of it. ❑ *He sat at the bottom of the stairs... Answers can be found at the bottom of page 8. ...the bottom of the sea.* N-COUNT: usu *the* N in sing, oft N *of* n ≠top [2] The **bottom** thing or layer in a series of things or layers is the lowest one. ❑ *There's an extra duvet in the bottom drawer of the cupboard.* ADJ: ADJ n ≠top [3] **The bottom of** an object is the flat surface at its lowest point. You can also refer to the inside or outside of this surface as the **bottom**. ❑ *Spread the onion slices on the bottom of the dish. ...the bottom of their shoes. ...a suitcase with a false bottom.* N-COUNT: usu *the* N in sing, usu with supp = base [4] If you say that **the bottom** has dropped or fallen out of a market or industry, you mean that people have stopped buying the products it sells. [BUSINESS, JOURNALISM] ❑ *The bottom had fallen out of the city's property market.* N-SING: *the* N [5] **The bottom of** a street or garden is the end farthest away from you or from your house. [BRIT] ❑ *...the Cathedral at the bottom of the street.* N-SING: *the* N, usu N *of* n = end

✔ in AM, usually use **end**

[6] **The bottom of** a table is the end farthest away from where you are sitting. **The bottom of** a bed is the end where you usually rest your feet. [BRIT] ❑ *Malone sat down on the bottom of the bed.* N-SING: *the* N, usu N *of* n = end

✔ in AM, usually use **end**

[7] **The bottom of** an organization or career structure is the lowest level in it, where new employees often start. ❑ *He had worked in the theatre for many years, starting at the bottom. ...a contract researcher at the bottom of the pay scale.* N-SING: *the* N, oft N *of* n ≠top [8] If someone is **bottom** or at **the bottom** in a survey, test, or league their performance is worse than that of all the other people involved. ❑ *He was always bottom of the class... The team is close to bottom of the League.* N-SING: *the* N, also no det ≠top [9] Your **bottom** is the part of your body that you sit on. ❑ *If there was one thing she could change about her body it would be her bottom.* N-COUNT: oft poss N [10] The lower part of a bikini, tracksuit, or pair of pyjamas can be referred to as the **bottoms** or the **bottom**. ❑ *She wore blue tracksuit bottoms. ...a skimpy bikini bottom.* N-COUNT: usu pl, oft n N ≠top [11] → See also **-bottomed**, **rock bottom**.

**PHRASES** [12] You use **at bottom** to emphasize that you are stating what you think is the real nature of something or the real truth about a situation. ❑ *The two systems are, at bottom, conceptual models... At bottom, such an attitude is born not of concern for your welfare, but out of fear of losing you.* PHRASE: PHR with cl [emphasis] [13] If something is **at the bottom of** a problem or unpleasant situation, it is the real cause of it. ❑ *Often I find that anger and resentment are at the bottom of the problem.* PHRASE: PHR n [14] You can say that you mean something **from the bottom of** your **heart** to emphasize that you mean it very sincerely. ❑ *I'm happy, and I mean that from the bottom of my heart... I want to thank everyone from the bottom of my heart.* PHRASE: *heart* inflects, PHR after v, PHR with cl [emphasis] [15] If you want to **get to the bottom of** a problem, you want to solve it by finding out its real cause. ❑ *I have to get to the bottom of this mess.* PHRASE: V inflects, PHR n [16] to **scrape the bottom of the barrel** → see **barrel**.

♦ **bottom out** If a trend such as a fall in prices **bottoms out**, it stops getting worse or decreasing, and remains at a particular level or amount. [JOURNALISM] ❑ *He expects the recession to bottom out.* PHRASAL VERB = level out; V P

**-bottomed** /-bɒtəmd/ **-bottomed** can be added to adjectives or nouns to form adjectives that indicate what kind of bottom an object or person has. ❑ *...a glass-bottomed boat.* COMB in ADJ

**bot|tom|less** /bɒtəmləs/ [1] If you describe a supply of something as **bottomless**, you mean that it seems so large that it will never run out. ❑ *Princess Anne does not have a bottomless purse.* ADJ [2] If you describe something as **bottomless**, you mean that it is so deep that it seems to have no bottom. ❑ *His eyes were like bottomless brown pools.* ADJ [3] If you describe something as a **bottomless pit**, you mean that it seems as if you can take things from it and it will never be empty or put things in it and it will never be full. ❑ *A gold mine is not a bottomless pit, the gold runs out... The problem is we don't have a bottomless pit of resources.* PHRASE

**bottom line** **(bottom lines)** [1] **The bottom line** in a decision or situation is the most important factor that you have to consider. ❑ *The bottom line is that it's not profitable.* N-COUNT: usu sing, usu *the* N [2] The **bottom line** in a business deal is the least a person is willing to accept. ❑ *She says £95,000 is her bottom line.* N-COUNT: usu sing, usu poss N [3] The **bottom line** is the total amount of money that a company has made or lost over a particular period of time. [BUSINESS] ❑ *...to force chief executives to look beyond the next quarter's bottom line.* N-COUNT: oft poss N

**botu|lism** /bɒtʃʊlɪzəm/ **Botulism** is a serious form of food poisoning. [MEDICAL] N-UNCOUNT

**bou|doir** /buːdwɑːʳ/ **(boudoirs)** A **boudoir** is a woman's bedroom or private sitting room. [OLD-FASHIONED] N-COUNT

**bouf|fant** /buːfɒn, AM buːfɑːnt/ A **bouffant** hairstyle is one in which your hair is high and full. ❑ *...blonde bouffant hairdos.* ADJ: usu ADJ n

**bou|gain|vil|lea** /buːgənvɪliə/ **(bougainvilleas)**

✔ in BRIT, also use **bougainvillaea**

**Bougainvillea** is a climbing plant that has thin, red or purple flowers and grows mainly in hot countries. N-VAR

**bough** /baʊ/ **(boughs)** A **bough** is a large branch of a tree. [LITERARY] ❑ *I rested my fishing rod against a pine bough.* N-COUNT

**bought** /bɔːt/ **Bought** is the past tense and past participle of **buy**.

**bouil|la|baisse** /buːjəbes/ **Bouillabaisse** is a rich stew or soup of fish and vegetables. N-UNCOUNT: also *a* N

**bouil|lon** /buːjɒn, AM bʊljɑːn/ **(bouillons)** **Bouillon** is a liquid made by boiling meat and bones or vegetables in water and used to make soups and sauces. N-VAR = stock

**boul|der** /boʊldəʳ/ **(boulders)** A **boulder** is a large rounded rock. N-COUNT

**boules** /buːl/ **Boules** is a game in which a small ball is thrown and then the players try to throw other balls as close to the first ball as possible. N-UNCOUNT

**boule|vard** /buːləvɑːʳd, AM bʊl-/ **(boulevards)** A **boulevard** is a wide street in a city, usually with trees along each side. ❑ *...Lenton Boulevard.* N-COUNT: oft in names = avenue

**bounce** /baʊns/ **(bounces, bouncing, bounced)** [1] When an object such as a ball **bounces** or when you **bounce** it, it moves upwards from a surface or away from it immediately after hitting it. ❑ *I bounced a ball against the house... My father would burst into the kitchen bouncing a football. ...a falling pebble, bouncing down the eroded cliff... They watched the dodgem cars bang and bounce.* VERB; V n prep; V n; V prep/adv; V; Also V n with adv ♦ **Bounce** is also a noun. ❑ *The wheelchair tennis player is allowed two bounces of the ball.* N-COUNT [2] If sound or light **bounces off** a surface or **is bounced off** it, it reaches the surface and is reflected back. ❑ *Your arms and legs need protection from light bouncing off glass... They work by bouncing microwaves off solid objects.* VERB; V *off* n; V n *off* n [3] If something **bounces** or if something **bounces** it, it swings or moves up and down. ❑ *Her long black hair bounced as she walked... Then I noticed the car was bouncing up and down as if someone were jumping on it... The wind was bouncing the branches of the big oak trees.* VERB = bob; V; V adv; V n [4] If you **bounce** on a soft surface, you jump up and VERB down on it repeatedly. ❑ *She lets us do anything, even bounce on our beds.* [5] If someone **bounces** somewhere, they move there in an energetic way, because they are feeling happy. ❑ *Moira bounced into the office.* [6] If you **bounce** your ideas **off** someone, you tell them to that person, in order to find out what they think about them. ❑ *It was good to bounce ideas off another mind... Let's bounce a few ideas around.* [7] If a cheque **bounces** or if a bank **bounces** it, the bank refuses to accept it and pay out the money, because the person who wrote it does not have enough money in their account. ❑ *Our only complaint would be if the cheque bounced... His bank wrongly bounced cheques worth £75,000.* [8] If an e-mail or other electronic message **bounces**, it is returned to the person who sent it because the address was wrong or because of a problem with one of the computers involved in sending it. [COMPUTING]

V prep/adv Also V VERB V prep/adv VERB V n *off* n V n *around* VERB V V n VERB

♦ **bounce back** If you **bounce back** after a bad experience, you return very quickly to your previous level of success, enthusiasm, or activity. ❑ *We lost two or three early games in the World Cup, but we bounced back... He is young enough to bounce back from this disappointment.*

PHRASAL VERB = recover V P V P prep/adv

**bounc|er** /baʊnsəʳ/ **(bouncers)** A **bouncer** is a man who stands at the door of a club, prevents unwanted people from coming in, and makes people leave if they cause trouble.

N-COUNT

**bounc|ing** /baʊnsɪŋ/ If you say that someone is **bouncing with** health, you mean that they are very healthy. You can also refer to a **bouncing** baby. ❑ *They are bouncing with health in the good weather... Derek is now the proud father of a bouncing baby girl.* → See also **bounce**.

ADJ: v-link ADJ *with* n, ADJ n

**bouncy** /baʊnsi/ [1] Someone or something that is **bouncy** is very lively. ❑ *She was bouncy and full of energy.* [2] A **bouncy** thing can bounce very well or makes other things bounce well. ❑ *...a children's paradise filled with bouncy toys. ...a bouncy chair.*

ADJ ADJ: usu ADJ n

**bouncy cas|tle** **(bouncy castles)** A **bouncy castle** is a large object filled with air, often in the shape of a castle, which children play on at a fairground or other outdoor event.

N-COUNT

**bound**
① BE BOUND
② OTHER USES

① **bound** /baʊnd/ [1] **Bound** is the past tense and past participle of **bind**. [2] If you say that something **is bound to** happen, you mean that you are sure it will happen, because it is a natural consequence of something that is already known or exists. ❑ *There are bound to be price increases next year... If you are topless in a public place, this sort of thing is bound to happen.* [3] If you say that something **is bound to** happen or be true, you feel confident and certain of it, although you have no definite knowledge or evidence. [SPOKEN] ❑ *I'll show it to Benjamin. He's bound to know... We'll have more than one child, and one of them's bound to be a boy.* [4] If one person, thing, or situation is **bound to** another, they are closely associated with each other, and it is difficult for them to be separated or to escape from each other. ❑ *We are as tightly bound to the people we dislike as to the people we love.* [5] If a vehicle or person is **bound for** a particular place, they are travelling towards it. ❑ *The ship was bound for Italy. ...a Russian plane bound for Berlin.* ♦ **Bound** is also a combining form. ❑ *...a Texas-bound oil freighter. ...homeward-bound commuters.*

◆◇◇ PHRASE PHRASE ADJ: v-link ADJ *to* n ADJ: v-link ADJ *for* n COMB in ADJ

**PHRASES** [6] If something is **bound up in** a particular form or place, it is fixed in that form or contained in that place. ❑ *The manager of a company does not like having a large chunk of his wealth bound up in its shares.* [7] If one thing is **bound up with** or **in** another, they are closely connected with each other, and it is difficult to consider the two things separately. ❑ *My fate was bound up with hers... Their interests were completely bound up in their careers.* [8] → See also **bind over**.

PHRASE: PHR n = tied up in PHRASE: PHR n, usu v-link PHR = tied up with

② **bound** /baʊnd/ **(bounds, bounding, bounded)** [1] **Bounds** are limits which normally restrict what can happen or what people can do. ❑ *Changes in temperature occur slowly and are constrained within relatively tight bounds. ...a forceful personality willing to go beyond the bounds of convention. ...the bounds of good taste.* [2] If an area of land **is bounded by** something, that thing is situated around its edge. ❑ *Kirgizia is bounded by Uzbekistan, Kazakhstan and Tajikistan. ...the trees that bounded the car park. ...the park, bounded by two busy main roads and a huge housing estate.* [3] If someone's life or situation **is bounded by** certain things, those are its most important aspects and it is limited or restricted by them. ❑ *Our lives are bounded by work, family and television.* [4] If a person or animal **bounds** in a particular direction, they move quickly with large steps or jumps. ❑ *He bounded up the steps and pushed the bell of the door.* [5] A **bound** is a long or high jump. [LITERARY] ❑ *With one bound Jack was free.* [6] If the quantity or performance of something **bounds** ahead, it increases or improves quickly and suddenly. ❑ *The shares bounded ahead a further 11p to 311p.*

◆◇◇ N-PLURAL: usu *within/beyond* N VERB *be* V-ed *by* n V n V-ed V-PASSIVE *be* V-ed *by* n VERB = leap V prep/adv N-COUNT: usu sing VERB V adv

**PHRASES** [7] If you say that a feeling or quality **knows no bounds**, you are emphasizing that it is very strong or intense. ❑ *The passion of Argentinian football fans knows no bounds.* [8] If a place is **out of bounds**, people are not allowed to go there. ❑ *For the last few days the area has been out of bounds to foreign journalists.* [9] If something is **out of bounds**, people are not allowed to do it, use it, see it, or know about it. ❑ *American parents may soon be able to rule violent TV programmes out of bounds.* [10] **leaps and bounds** → see **leap**.

PHRASE: V inflects [emphasis] PHRASE: v-link PHR, PHR after v, oft PHR *to* n PHRASE: v-link PHR, PHR after v

**-bound** /-baʊnd/ [1] **-bound** combines with nouns to form adjectives which describe a person who finds it impossible or very difficult to leave the specified place. ❑ *Andrew has been left wheelchair-bound after the accident... I'm pretty desk-bound, which is very frustrating.* [2] **-bound** combines with nouns to form adjectives which describe a place that is greatly affected by the specified type of weather. ❑ *Three people were hurt in a 12-car pile up on a fog-bound motorway yesterday.* [3] **-bound** combines with nouns to form adjectives which describe something or someone that is prevented from working properly or is badly affected by the specified situation. [WRITTEN] ❑ *...the somewhat tradition-bound officers of the navy.* [4] → See also **duty-bound**, **muscle-bound**.

COMB in ADJ COMB in ADJ COMB in ADJ

**bounda|ry** /baʊndəri/ **(boundaries)** [1] The **boundary of** an area of land is an imaginary line that separates it from other areas. ❑ *...the Bow Brook which forms the western boundary of the wood... Drug traffickers operate across national boundaries.* [2] The **boundaries of** something such as a subject or activity are the limits that people think that it has. ❑ *The boundaries between history and storytelling are always being blurred and muddled. ...extending the boundaries of press freedom.*

N-COUNT: oft N *of/between* n = border, frontier N-COUNT: usu pl, oft N *of/between* n

**bound|er** /baʊndəʳ/ **(bounders)** If you call a man a **bounder**, you mean he behaves in an unkind, deceitful, or selfish way. [BRIT, OLD-FASHIONED]

N-COUNT = cad

**bound|less** /baʊndləs/ If you describe something as **boundless**, you mean that there seems to be no end or limit to it. ❑ *His reforming zeal was boundless.*

ADJ = infinite, limitless

**boun|ti|ful** /baʊntɪfʊl/ [1] A **bountiful** supply or amount of something pleasant is a large one. ❑ *State aid is less bountiful than it was before. ...a bountiful harvest of fruits and vegetables.* [2] A **bountiful** area or period of time produces or provides large amounts of something, especially food. ❑ *The land is bountiful and no one starves.*

ADJ = plentiful ADJ = rich

**boun|ty** /baʊnti/ **(bounties)** [1] You can refer to something that is provided in large amounts as **bounty**. [LITERARY] ❑ *...autumn's bounty of fruits,*

N-VAR: with supp

*seeds and berries.* 2 A **bounty** is money that is offered as a reward for doing something, especially for finding or killing a particular person. ❑ *They paid bounties for people to give up their weapons.* N-COUNT

**boun|ty hunt|er** **(bounty hunters)** A **bounty hunter** is someone who tries to find or kill someone in order to get the reward that has been offered. N-COUNT

**bou|quet** /boʊkeɪ, buː-/ **(bouquets)** 1 A **bouquet** is a bunch of flowers which is attractively arranged. ❑ *The woman carried a bouquet of dried violets.* N-COUNT: oft N *of* n 2 The **bouquet** of something, especially wine, is the pleasant smell that it has. ❑ *...a Sicilian wine with a light red colour and a bouquet of cloves.* N-VAR = *fragrance*

**bou|quet gar|ni** /boʊkeɪ gɑːʳniː, buː-/ A **bouquet garni** is a bunch of herbs that are tied together and used in cooking to add flavour to the food. N-SING: also no det

**bour|bon** /bɜːʳbən/ **(bourbons)** **Bourbon** is a type of whisky that is made mainly in America. ❑ *I poured a little more bourbon into my glass.* N-MASS ♦ A **bourbon** is a small glass of bourbon. N-COUNT

**bour|geois** /bʊəʳʒwɑː/ 1 If you describe people, their way of life, or their attitudes as **bourgeois**, you disapprove of them because you consider them typical of conventional middle-class people. ❑ *He's accusing them of having a bourgeois and limited vision.* ADJ [disapproval] 2 → See also **petit bourgeois**.

**bour|geoi|sie** /bʊəʳʒwɑːziː/ In Marxist theory, **the bourgeoisie** are the middle-class people who own most of the wealth in a capitalist system. [TECHNICAL] ❑ *...the suppression of the proletariat by the bourgeoisie.* → See also **petit bourgeoisie**. N-SING-COLL: *the* N

**bourse** /bʊəʳs/ **(bourses)** A country's or region's **bourse** is its stock exchange. N-COUNT: also in names

**bout** /baʊt/ **(bouts)** 1 If you have a **bout of** an illness or of an unpleasant feeling, you have it for a short period. ❑ *He was recovering from a severe bout of flu... I was suffering with a bout of nerves.* N-COUNT: usu N *of* n 2 A **bout of** something that is unpleasant is a short time during which it occurs a great deal. ❑ *The latest bout of violence has claimed twenty four lives... A half-hour daily walk can be more beneficial than one hard bout of exercise a week.* N-COUNT: usu N *of* n = *spell* 3 A **bout** is a boxing or wrestling match. ❑ *This will be his eighth title bout in 19 months.* N-COUNT

**bou|tique** /buːtiːk/ **(boutiques)** A **boutique** is a small shop that sells fashionable clothes, shoes, or jewellery. N-COUNT

**bo|vine** /boʊvaɪn/ 1 **Bovine** means relating to cattle. [TECHNICAL] ADJ: usu ADJ n 2 If you describe someone's behaviour or appearance as **bovine**, you think that they are stupid or slow. ❑ *I'm depressed by the bovine enthusiasm of the crowd's response.* ADJ: usu ADJ n [disapproval]

**bow**
① BENDING OR SUBMITTING
② PART OF A SHIP
③ OBJECTS

① **bow** /baʊ/ **(bows, bowing, bowed)** 1 When you **bow to** someone, you briefly bend your body towards them as a formal way of greeting them or showing respect. ❑ *They bowed low to Louis and hastened out of his way... He bowed slightly before taking her bag.* VERB V *to* n V ♦ **Bow** is also a noun. ❑ *I gave a theatrical bow and waved.* N-COUNT: usu sing 2 If you **bow** your head, you bend it downwards so that you are looking towards the ground, for example because you want to show respect or because you are thinking deeply about something. ❑ *The Colonel bowed his head and whispered a prayer of thanksgiving... She stood still, head bowed, hands clasped in front of her.* VERB = *lower* V n V-ed 3 If you **bow to** pressure or to someone's wishes, you agree to do what they want you to do. ❑ *Some shops are bowing to consumer pressure and stocking organically grown vegetables.* VERB = *yield* V *to* n 4 If you **are bowed** by something, you are made unhappy and anxious by it, and lose hope. ❑ *...their determination not to be bowed in the face of the allied attacks.* V-PASSIVE *be* V-ed ♦ To **be bowed down** means the same as to **be bowed**. ❑ *I am bowed down by my sins.* PHRASAL VERB *be* V-ed P

♦ **bow down** 1 If you refuse to **bow down to** another person, you refuse to show them respect or to behave in a way which you think would make you seem weaker or less important than them. ❑ *We should not have to bow down to anyone.* PHRASAL VERB: oft with brd-neg = *kow-tow* V P *to* n 2 → See also **bow 4**.

♦ **bow out** If you **bow out** of something, you stop taking part in it. [WRITTEN] ❑ *He had bowed out gracefully when his successor had been appointed.* PHRASAL VERB = *step down* V P Also V P *of* n

② **bow** /baʊ/ **(bows)** The front part of a ship is called **the bow** or **the bows**. The plural **bows** can be used to refer either to one or to more than one of these parts. ❑ *The waves were about five feet now, and the bow of the boat was leaping up and down.* N-COUNT

③ **bow** /boʊ/ **(bows)** 1 A **bow** is a knot with two loops and two loose ends that is used in tying shoelaces and ribbons. ❑ *Add a length of ribbon tied in a bow.* N-COUNT 2 A **bow** is a weapon for shooting arrows which consists of a long piece of curved wood with a string attached to both its ends. ❑ *Some of the raiders were armed with bows and arrows.* N-COUNT 3 The **bow** of a violin or other stringed instrument is a long thin piece of wood with fibres stretched along it, which you move across the strings of the instrument in order to play it. N-COUNT

**bowd|ler|ize** /baʊdləraɪz, AM boʊd-/ **(bowdlerizes, bowdlerizing, bowdlerized)**

✔ in BRIT, also use **bowdlerise**

To **bowdlerize** a book or film means to take parts of it out before publishing it or showing it. ❑ *I'm bowdlerizing it – just slightly changing one or two words so listeners won't be upset. ...a bowdlerised version of the song.* VERB [disapproval] V n V-ed

**bowed**

✔ Pronounced /boʊd/ for meaning 1, and /baʊd/ for meaning 2.

1 Something that is **bowed** is curved. ❑ *...an old lady with bowed legs.* ADJ ≠ *straight* 2 If a person's body is **bowed**, it is bent forward. ❑ *He walked aimlessly along street after street, head down and shoulders bowed.* ADJ ≠ *erect* 3 → See also **bow**.

**bow|el** /baʊəl/ **(bowels)** 1 Your **bowels** are the tubes in your body through which digested food passes from your stomach to your anus. N-COUNT 2 You can refer in a polite way to someone getting rid of the waste from their body by saying that they move, open, or empty their **bowels**. N-PLURAL 3 You can refer to the parts deep inside something such as the earth, a building, or a machine as **the bowels of** that thing. [HUMOROUS or LITERARY] ❑ *...deep in the bowels of the earth... Lyn went off into the dark bowels of the building.* N-PLURAL: *the* N *of* n = *recesses*

**bow|er** /baʊəʳ/ **(bowers)** A **bower** is a shady, leafy shelter in a garden or wood. [LITERARY] N-COUNT

**bowl** /boʊl/ **(bowls, bowling, bowled)** 1 A **bowl** is a round container with a wide uncovered top. Some kinds of bowl are used, for example, for serving or eating food from, or in cooking, while other larger kinds are used for washing or cleaning. ❑ *Put all the ingredients into a large bowl.* ◆◇◇ N-COUNT 2 The contents of a bowl can be referred to as a **bowl of** something. ❑ *...a bowl of soup.* N-COUNT: usu N *of* n 3 You can refer to the hollow rounded part of an object as its **bowl**. ❑ *He smacked the bowl of his pipe into his hand. ...the toilet bowl.* N-COUNT: usu with supp 4 **Bowls** is a game in which players try to roll large wooden balls as near as possible to a small wooden ball. Bowls is usually played outdoors on grass. [BRIT] N-UNCOUNT

✔ in AM, use **lawn bowling**

5 A set of **bowls** is a set of round wooden balls that you play bowls with. N-COUNT: usu pl 6 In a sport such as cricket, when a bowler **bowls** a ball, he or she sends it down the pitch towards a batsman. ❑ *I* VERB V n

*can't see the point of bowling a ball like that... He bowled so well that we won two matches.* [7] If you **bowl along** in a car or on a boat, you move along very quickly, especially when you are enjoying yourself. ❑ *Veronica looked at him, smiling, as they bowled along.* [8] A large stadium where sports or concerts take place is sometimes called a **Bowl**. ❑ *...the Crystal Palace Bowl. ...the Rose Bowl.* [9] → See also **bowling, begging bowl, fruit bowl, mixing bowl, punch bowl, salad bowl, sugar bowl.** V / VERB / V prep/adv / N-IN-NAMES: *the* n N

♦ **bowl over** [1] To **bowl** someone **over** means to push into them and make them fall to the ground. ❑ *The only physical risk I ran was being bowled over by one of the many joggers... Some people had to cling to trees as the flash flood bowled them over.* [2] If you **are bowled over by** something, you are very impressed or surprised by it. ❑ *Like any tourist, I was bowled over by India. ...a man who bowled her over with his humour and charm.* PHRASAL VERB = knock over / *be* V-ed P / V n P (not pron) / Also V P n / PHRASAL VERB / *be* V-ed P / V n P / Also V P n (not pron)

**bow|ler** /bo͟ʊləʳ/ **(bowlers)** The **bowler** in a sport such as cricket is the player who is bowling the ball. ❑ *He's a rather good fast bowler.* N-COUNT

**bow|ler hat (bowler hats)** A **bowler hat** is a round, hard, black hat with a narrow brim which is worn by men, especially British businessmen. Bowler hats are no longer very common. [mainly BRIT] N-COUNT = bowler

☑ in AM, use **derby**

**bowl|ful** /bo͟ʊlfʊl/ **(bowlfuls)** The contents of a bowl can be referred to as a **bowlful of** something. ❑ *They ate a large bowlful of cereal... I had a mixed salad – a huge bowlful for £3.20.* N-COUNT: usu N *of* n

**bowl|ing** /bo͟ʊlɪŋ/ [1] **Bowling** is a game in which you roll a heavy ball down a narrow track towards a group of wooden objects and try to knock down as many of them as possible. ❑ *I go bowling for relaxation.* [2] In a sport such as cricket, **bowling** is the action or activity of bowling the ball towards the batsman. N-UNCOUNT / N-UNCOUNT

**bowl|ing al|ley (bowling alleys)** A **bowling alley** is a building which contains several tracks for bowling. N-COUNT

**bowl|ing green (bowling greens)** A **bowling green** is an area of very smooth, short grass on which the game of bowls or lawn bowling is played. N-COUNT

**bow tie** /bo͟ʊ ta͟ɪ/ **(bow ties)** also **bow-tie**. A **bow tie** is a tie in the form of a bow. Bow ties are worn by men, especially for formal occasions. N-COUNT

**box** /bɒ̱ks/ **(boxes, boxing, boxed)** [1] A **box** is a square or rectangular container with hard or stiff sides. Boxes often have lids. ❑ *He reached into the cardboard box beside him... They sat on wooden boxes. ...the box of tissues on her desk.* ♦ A **box of** something is an amount of it contained in a box. ❑ *She ate two boxes of liqueurs.* [2] A **box** is a square or rectangle that is printed or drawn on a piece of paper, a road, or on some other surface. [3] In football, **the box** is the penalty area of the field. ❑ *He scored from the penalty spot after being brought down in the box.* [4] A **box** is a small separate area in a theatre or at a sports ground or stadium, where a small number of people can sit to watch the performance or game. [5] Television is sometimes referred to as **the box**. [BRIT, INFORMAL] ❑ *Do you watch it live at all or do you watch it on the box?* [6] **Box** is used before a number as a postal address by organizations that receive a lot of mail. ❑ *...Country Crafts, Box 111, Landisville.* [7] **Box** is a small evergreen tree with dark leaves which is often used to form hedges. ❑ *...box hedges.* [8] To **box** means to fight someone according to the rules of boxing. ❑ *At school I boxed and played rugby... The two fighters had previously boxed a 12-round match.* [9] → See also **boxed, boxing, black box, chocolate-box, lunch box, phone box, post office box, postbox, sentry box, signal box, telephone box.** ◆◆◇ N-COUNT / N-COUNT: usu N *of* n / N-COUNT: usu with supp / N-SING: *the* N / N-COUNT / N-SING: *the* N = telly / N-COUNT: with supp, usu N num / N-UNCOUNT: oft N n / VERB / V / V n / Also V *as* n

♦ **box in** [1] If you **are boxed in**, you are unable to move from a particular place because you are surrounded by other people or cars. ❑ *Armstrong was boxed in with 300 metres to go... The black cabs cut in front of them, trying to box them in.* [2] If something **boxes** you **in**, it puts you in a situation where you have very little choice about what you can do. ❑ *Part of winning a mandate is having clear goals and not boxing yourself in... We are not trying to box anybody in, we are trying to find a satisfactory way forward.* ♦ **boxed in** *The Chancellor is boxed in by inflation targets and sterling.* PHRASAL VERB = hem in / V-ed P / V n P / PHRASAL VERB / V n P / V P n (not pron) / ADJ: usu v-link ADJ

**box|car** /bɒ̱kskɑːʳ/ **(boxcars)** A **boxcar** is a railway carriage, often without windows, which is used to carry luggage, goods, or mail. [AM] N-COUNT

☑ in BRIT, use **van**

**boxed** /bɒ̱kst/ A **boxed** set or collection of things is sold in a box. ❑ *... a boxed set of six cups and saucers... This boxed collection captures 64 of the greatest modern love songs.* → See also **box**. ADJ: usu ADJ n

**box|er** /bɒ̱ksəʳ/ **(boxers)** A **boxer** is someone who takes part in the sport of boxing. N-COUNT

**box|er shorts Boxer shorts** are loose-fitting men's underpants that are shaped like the shorts worn by boxers. N-PLURAL: also *a pair of* N

**box|ing** /bɒ̱ksɪŋ/ **Boxing** is a sport in which two people wearing large padded gloves fight according to special rules. N-UNCOUNT

**Box|ing Day Boxing Day** is the 26th of December, the day after Christmas Day. [BRIT] N-UNCOUNT

**box|ing glove (boxing gloves) Boxing gloves** are big padded gloves worn for boxing. N-COUNT

**box|ing ring (boxing rings)** A **boxing ring** is a raised square platform with ropes around it in which boxers fight. N-COUNT

**box lunch (box lunches)** A **box lunch** is food, for example sandwiches, which you take to work, to school, or on a trip and eat as your lunch. [AM] N-COUNT

☑ in BRIT, use **packed lunch**

**box num|ber (box numbers)** A **box number** is a number used as an address, for example one given by a newspaper for replies to a private advertisement, or one used by an organization for the letters sent to it. N-COUNT

**box of|fice (box offices)** also **box-office.** [1] The **box office** in a theatre, cinema, or concert hall is the place where the tickets are sold. [2] When people talk about **the box office**, they are referring to the degree of success of a film or play in terms of the number of people who go to watch it or the amount of money it makes. ❑ *The film has taken £180 million at the box office... The film was a huge box-office success.* N-COUNT / N-SING: usu *the* N, N n

**box|wood** /bɒ̱kswʊd/ **Boxwood** is a type of wood which is obtained from a box tree. N-UNCOUNT

**boxy** /bɒ̱ksi/ Something that is **boxy** is similar to a square in shape and usually plain. ❑ *...short boxy jackets.* ADJ: usu ADJ n

**boy** /bɔ͟ɪ/ **(boys)** [1] A **boy** is a child who will grow up to be a man. ❑ *I knew him when he was a little boy... He was still just a boy.* [2] You can refer to a young man as a **boy**, especially when talking about relationships between boys and girls. ❑ *...the age when girls get interested in boys.* [3] Someone's **boy** is their son. [INFORMAL] ❑ *Eric was my cousin Edward's boy... I have two boys.* [4] You can refer to a man as a **boy**, especially when you are talking about him in an affectionate way. [INFORMAL] ❑ *...the local boy who made President... 'Come on boys', he shouted to the sailors.* [5] → See also **backroom boy, blue-eyed boy, bully-boy, head boy, messenger boy, office boy, old boy, stable boy, Teddy boy.** [6] Some people say **'boy'** or **'oh boy'** in order to express feelings of excitement or admiration. [mainly AM, INFORMAL] ❑ *Oh Boy! Just think what I could tell him.* ◆◆◆ N-COUNT / N-COUNT / N-COUNT: usu poss N / N-COUNT: with supp [feelings] = lad / EXCLAM [feelings]

**boy band (boy bands)** A **boy band** is a band consisting of young men who sing pop music and N-COUNT dance. Boy bands are especially popular with teenage girls.

**boy|cott** /bɔɪkɒt/ **(boycotts, boycotting, boycotted)** If a country, group, or person **boycotts** a country, organization, or activity, they refuse to be involved with it in any way because they disapprove of it. ❑ *The main opposition parties are boycotting the elections.* ♦ **Boycott** is also a noun. ❑ *Opposition leaders had called for a boycott of the vote.* VERB; V n; N-COUNT: oft N *of/against/on* n

**boy|friend** /bɔɪfrend/ **(boyfriends)** Someone's **boyfriend** is a man or boy with whom they are having a romantic or sexual relationship. ❑ *I don't know if she's got a boyfriend or not.* ◆◇◇ N-COUNT: oft poss N

**boy|hood** /bɔɪhʊd/ **Boyhood** is the period of a male person's life during which he is a boy. ❑ *He has been a Derby County supporter since boyhood.* N-UNCOUNT

**boy|ish** /bɔɪɪʃ/ 1 If you describe a man as **boyish**, you mean that he is like a boy in his appearance or behaviour, and you find this characteristic quite attractive. ❑ *She was relieved to see his face light up with a boyish grin... He loves to learn, and has a boyish enthusiasm for life.* ♦ **boy|ish|ly** *John grinned boyishly.* 2 If you describe a girl or woman as **boyish**, you mean that she looks like a boy, for example because she has short hair or small breasts. ❑ *...her tall, boyish figure.* ADJ: usu ADJ n [approval]; ADV; ADJ

**boy rac|er** **(boy racers)** British journalists sometimes refer to young men who drive very fast, especially in expensive and powerful cars, as **boy racers**. ❑ *Bad driving is not just the preserve of boy racers.* N-COUNT [disapproval]

**Boy Scout** **(Boy Scouts)** also **boy scout**. 1 **The Boy Scouts** is an organization for boys which teaches them discipline and practical skills. ❑ *He's in the Boy Scouts.* 2 A **Boy Scout** is a boy who is a member of the Boy Scouts. N-PROPER-COLL: the N = Scouts; N-COUNT = Scout

**bozo** /boʊzoʊ/ **(bozos)** If you say that someone is a **bozo**, you mean that you think they are stupid. [INFORMAL] ❑ *He makes 'em look like bozos.* N-COUNT [disapproval] = idiot

**bps** /biː piː es/ **bps** is a measurement of the speed at which computer data is transferred, for example by a modem. **bps** is an abbreviation for 'bits per second'. [COMPUTING] ❑ *A minimum 28,800 bps modem is probably the slowest you'll want to put up with.*

**Br.** **Br.** is a written abbreviation for **British**.

**bra** /brɑː/ **(bras)** A **bra** is a piece of underwear that women wear to support their breasts.

**brace** /breɪs/ **(braces, bracing, braced)** 1 If you **brace yourself for** something unpleasant or difficult, you prepare yourself for it. ❑ *He braced himself for the icy plunge into the black water... She braced herself, as if to meet a blow.* 2 If you **brace yourself against** something or **brace** part of your body **against** it, you press against something in order to steady your body or to avoid falling. ❑ *Elaine braced herself against the dresser and looked in the mirror... He braced his back against the wall.* 3 If you **brace** your shoulders or knees, you keep them stiffly in a particular position. ❑ *He braced his shoulders as the snow slashed across his face.* 4 To **brace** something means to strengthen or support it with something else. ❑ *Overhead, the lights showed the old timbers, used to brace the roof.* 5 You can refer to two things of the same kind as a **brace of** that thing. The plural form is also **brace**. ❑ *...a brace of bottles of Mercier Rose champagne. ...a few brace of grouse.* 6 A **brace** is a device attached to a part of a person's body, for example to a weak leg, in order to strengthen or support it. ❑ *She wears a neck brace.* 7 A **brace** is a metal device that can be fastened to a child's teeth in order to help them grow straight. 8 **Braces** are a pair of straps that pass over your shoulders and fasten to your trousers at the front and back in order to stop them from falling down. [BRIT] VERB; V pron-refl *for* n; V pron-refl; VERB; V pron-refl *against* n; V n *against* n; VERB; V n; VERB; V n; N-COUNT: usu N *of* n; N-COUNT: oft n N = support; N-COUNT; N-PLURAL

☑ in AM, use **suspenders**

9 **Braces** or **curly braces** are a pair of written marks that you place around words, numbers, or parts of a computer code, for example to indicate that they are connected in some way or are separate from other parts of the writing or code. [AM] N-COUNT

☑ in BRIT, usually use **curly brackets**

**brace|let** /breɪslɪt/ **(bracelets)** A **bracelet** is a chain or band, usually made of metal, which you wear around your wrist as jewellery. N-COUNT

**brac|ing** /breɪsɪŋ/ If you describe something, especially a place, climate, or activity as **bracing**, you mean that it makes you feel fresh and full of energy. ❑ *...a bracing walk.* ADJ = invigorating

**brack|en** /brækən/ **Bracken** is a large plant with leaves that are divided into many thin sections. It grows on hills and in woods. N-UNCOUNT

**brack|et** /brækɪt/ **(brackets, bracketing, bracketed)** 1 If you say that someone or something is in a particular **bracket**, you mean that they come within a particular range, for example a range of incomes, ages, or prices. ❑ *...a 33% top tax rate on everyone in these high-income brackets... Do you fall outside that age bracket?* 2 **Brackets** are pieces of metal, wood, or plastic that are fastened to a wall in order to support something such as a shelf. ❑ *Fix the beam with the brackets and screws. ...adjustable wall brackets.* 3 If two or more people or things **are bracketed together**, they are considered to be similar or related in some way. ❑ *The Magi, Bramins, and Druids were bracketed together as men of wisdom... Austrian wine styles are often bracketed with those of northern Germany.* 4 **Brackets** are a pair of written marks that you place round a word, expression, or sentence in order to indicate that you are giving extra information. In British English, curved marks like these are also called **brackets**, but in American English, they are called **parentheses**. ❑ *The prices in brackets are special rates for the under 18s.* 5 **Brackets** are pair of marks that are placed around a series of symbols in a mathematical expression to indicate that those symbols function as one item within the expression. N-COUNT: usu n N; N-COUNT; VERB = categorize; pl-n *be* V-ed *together*; *be* V-ed *with* n; N-COUNT: usu pl, oft *in* N = parenthesis; N-COUNT: usu pl

**brack|ish** /brækɪʃ/ **Brackish** water is slightly salty and unpleasant. ❑ *...shallow pools of brackish water.* ADJ: usu ADJ n

**brag** /bræg/ **(brags, bragging, bragged)** If you **brag**, you say in a very proud way that you have something or have done something. ❑ *He's always bragging about his prowess as a cricketer... He'll probably go around bragging to his friends... The chairman never tires of bragging that he and Mr. McCormack are old friends.* VERB [disapproval] = boast; V *about* n; V *to* n; V that; Also V with quote, V

**Brah|min** /brɑːmɪn/ **(Brahmins)** also **Brahman**. A **Brahmin** is a Hindu of the highest social rank. N-COUNT

**braid** /breɪd/ **(braids, braiding, braided)** 1 **Braid** is a narrow piece of decorated cloth or twisted threads, which is used to decorate clothes or curtains. ❑ *...a plum-coloured uniform with lots of gold braid.* 2 If you **braid** hair or a group of threads, you twist three or more lengths of the hair or threads over and under each other to make one thick length. [AM] ❑ *She had almost finished braiding Louisa's hair... He pictured her with long black braided hair.* N-UNCOUNT; VERB; V n; V-ed

☑ in BRIT, use **plait**

3 A **braid** is a length of hair which has been divided into three or more lengths and then braided. [AM] N-COUNT

☑ in BRIT, use **plait**

**braid|ed** /breɪdɪd/ A piece of clothing that is **braided** is decorated with braid. ADJ

**Braille** /breɪl/ **Braille** is a system of printing for blind people. The letters are printed as groups of raised dots that you can feel with your fingers. N-UNCOUNT

**brain** /breɪn/ **(brains)** ◆◆◇ 1 N-COUNT Your **brain** is the organ inside your head that controls your body's activities and enables you to think and to feel things such as heat and pain. ❑ *Her father died of a brain tumour.* 2 N-COUNT: usu poss N = mind, intellect Your **brain** is your mind and the way that you think. ❑ *Once you stop using your brain you soon go stale... Stretch your brain with this puzzle.* 3 N-COUNT If someone has **brains** or a good **brain**, they have the ability to learn and understand things quickly, to solve problems, and to make good decisions. ❑ *I had a good brain and the teachers liked me.* 4 N-COUNT: usu pl, the N behind/of n If someone is **the brains** behind an idea or an organization, he or she had that idea or makes the important decisions about how that organization is managed. [INFORMAL] ❑ *Mr White was the brains behind the scheme... Some investigators regarded her as the brains of the gang.* 5 PHRASE: V inflects If you **pick** someone's **brains**, you ask them to help you with a problem because they know more about the subject than you. [INFORMAL] ❑ *Why should a successful company allow another firm to pick its brains?* 6 to **rack** your **brains** → see **rack**.

**brain|child** /breɪntʃaɪld/ also **brain-child**. N-SING: with poss Someone's **brainchild** is an idea or invention that they have thought up or created. ❑ *The record was the brainchild of rock star Bob Geldof.*

**brain dam|age** N-UNCOUNT If someone suffers **brain damage**, their brain is damaged by an illness or injury so that they cannot function normally. ❑ *He suffered severe brain damage after a motorbike accident.*

**brain-damaged** ADJ Someone who is **brain-damaged** has suffered brain damage. ❑ *The accident left the boy severely brain-damaged and almost totally reliant on others.*

**brain-dead** also **brain dead, braindead.** 1 ADJ If someone is declared **brain-dead**, they have suffered brain death. 2 ADJ disapproval If you say that someone is **brain-dead**, you are saying in a cruel way that you think they are very stupid.

**brain death** N-UNCOUNT **Brain death** occurs when someone's brain stops functioning, even though their heart may be kept beating using a machine.

**brain drain** N-SING When people talk about a **brain drain**, they are referring to the movement of a large number of scientists or academics away from their own country to other countries where the conditions and salaries are better.

**-brained** /-breɪnd/ COMB in ADJ disapproval You can combine **-brained** with nouns to form adjectives which describe the quality of someone's mind when you consider that person to be rather stupid. ❑ *...a scatter-brained professor.* → See also **hare-brained**.

**brain|less** /breɪnləs/ ADJ disapproval = stupid If you describe someone or something as **brainless**, you mean that you think they are stupid. ❑ *I got treated as if I was a bit brainless.*

**brain|power** /breɪnpaʊəʳ/ 1 N-UNCOUNT **Brainpower** is intelligence or the ability to think. [JOURNALISM] ❑ *She admired Robert's brainpower.* 2 N-UNCOUNT You can refer to the intelligent people in an organization or country as its **brainpower**. [JOURNALISM] ❑ *A country's principal resource is its brainpower.*

**brain|storm** /breɪnstɔːʳm/ **(brainstorms, brainstorming, brainstormed)** 1 N-COUNT If you have a **brainstorm**, you suddenly become unable to think clearly. [BRIT] ❑ *I can have a brainstorm and be very extravagant.* 2 N-COUNT = brainwave If you have a **brainstorm**, you suddenly have a clever idea. [AM] ❑ *'Look,' she said, getting a brainstorm, 'Why don't you invite them here?'*

✔ in BRIT, usually use **brainwave**

3 VERB If a group of people **brainstorm**, they have a meeting in which they all put forward as many ideas and suggestions as they can think of. ❑ V *The women meet twice a month to brainstorm and set business goals for each other...* V n *We can brainstorm a list of the most influential individuals in the company.*

♦ **brain|storming** N-UNCOUNT *Hundreds of ideas had been tried and discarded during two years of brainstorming.*

**brain teas|er** **(brain teasers)** also **brain-teaser.** N-COUNT = puzzle A **brain teaser** is a question, problem, or puzzle that is difficult to answer or solve, but is not serious or important.

**brain|wash** /breɪnwɒʃ/ **(brainwashes, brainwashing, brainwashed)** VERB If you **brainwash** someone, you force them to believe something by continually telling them that it is true, and preventing them from thinking about it properly. ❑ V n into -ing *They brainwash people into giving up all their money...* be V-ed to-inf *We were brainwashed to believe we were all equal.* Also V n

**brain|wave** /breɪnweɪv/ **(brainwaves)** 1 N-COUNT If you have a **brainwave**, you suddenly have a clever idea. [BRIT] ❑ *In 1980 she had a brainwave that changed her life.*

✔ in AM, usually use **brainstorm**

2 N-PLURAL **Brainwaves** are electrical signals produced by the brain which can be recorded and measured. ❑ *His brainwaves were constantly monitored.*

**brainy** /breɪni/ **(brainier, brainiest)** ADJ = smart Someone who is **brainy** is clever and good at learning. [INFORMAL] ❑ *I don't class myself as being very intelligent or brainy.*

**braise** /breɪz/ **(braises, braising, braised)** VERB When you **braise** meat or a vegetable, you fry it quickly and then cook it slowly in a covered dish with a small amount of liquid. ❑ V n *I braised some beans to accompany a shoulder of lamb.* V-ed *...braised cabbage.*

**brake** /breɪk/ **(brakes, braking, braked)** 1 N-COUNT **Brakes** are devices in a vehicle that make it go slower or stop. → See picture on page 1708. ❑ *The brakes began locking... A seagull swooped down in front of her car, causing her to slam on the brakes.* 2 VERB When a vehicle or its driver **brakes**, or when a driver **brakes** a vehicle, the driver makes it slow down or stop by using the brakes. ❑ V *She braked sharply to avoid another car...* V n *He lit a cigarette and braked the car slightly...* V to n *She braked to a halt and switched off.* Also V n to n 3 N-COUNT You can use **brake** in a number of expressions to indicate that something has slowed down or stopped. ❑ *Illness had put a brake on his progress.*

**bram|ble** /bræmbəl/ **(brambles)** N-COUNT: usu pl **Brambles** are wild prickly bushes that produce blackberries. ❑ *I became caught in the brambles.*

**bran** /bræn/ N-UNCOUNT **Bran** is the outer skin of grain that is left when the grain has been used to make flour. ❑ *...oat bran.*

**branch** /brɑːntʃ, bræntʃ/ **(branches, branching, branched)** ◆◇◇ 1 N-COUNT The **branches** of a tree are the parts that grow out from its trunk and have leaves, flowers, or fruit growing on them. 2 N-COUNT: oft N of n A **branch of** a business or other organization is one of the offices, shops, or groups which belong to it and which are located in different places. ❑ *The local branch of Bank of America is handling the accounts... National is Britain's leading autocare service with over 400 branches nationwide.* 3 N-COUNT: with supp, oft N of n, adj N A **branch of** an organization such as the government or the police force is a department that has a particular function. ❑ *Senate employees could take their employment grievances to another branch of government... He had a fascination for submarines and joined this branch of the service. ...the Metropolitan Police Special Branch.* 4 N-COUNT: N of n A **branch of** a subject is a part or type of it. ❑ *Oncology is the branch of medicine dealing with tumors.* 5 N-COUNT: usu N of n A **branch of** your family is a group of its members who are descended from one particular person. ❑ *This is one of the branches of the Roosevelt family.*

♦ **branch off** PHRASAL VERB A road or path that **branches off** from another one starts from it and goes in a slightly different direction. If you **branch off** somewhere, you change the direction in which you are going. ❑ V P prep/adv *After a few miles, a small road branched off to the right.* Also V P, V P n

♦ **branch out** PHRASAL VERB If a person or an organization **branches out**, they do something that is different from their normal activities or work. ❑ V P prep/adv *I con-*

*tinued studying moths, and branched out to other insects.* Also V P

**branch line (branch lines)** A **branch line** is a railway line that goes to small towns rather than one that goes between large cities. N-COUNT

**brand** /brænd/ **(brands, branding, branded)** ♦◇◇
1 A **brand** of a product is the version of it that is made by one particular manufacturer. ❑ *Winston is a brand of cigarette... I bought one of the leading brands. ...a supermarket's own brand.* N-COUNT: oft N *of* n, adj N = make
2 A **brand of** something such as a way of thinking or behaving is a particular kind of it. ❑ *The British brand of socialism was more interested in reform than revolution.* N-COUNT: N *of* n = strain
3 If someone **is branded** as something bad, people think they are that thing. ❑ *I was instantly branded as a rebel... The company has been branded racist by some of its own staff... The US administration recently branded him a war criminal.* VERB = label *be* V-ed *as* n *be* V-ed adj V n n Also V n *as* n, V n adj
4 When you **brand** an animal, you put a permanent mark on its skin in order to show who it belongs to, usually by burning a mark onto its skin. ❑ *The owner couldn't be bothered to brand the cattle.* VERB V n
♦ **Brand** is also a noun. ❑ *A brand was a mark of ownership burned into the hide of an animal with a hot iron.* N-COUNT
5 A **brand** is a permanent mark on the skin of an animal, which shows who it belongs to. N-COUNT

**brand|ed** /brændɪd/ A **branded** product is one which is made by a well-known manufacturer and has the manufacturer's label on it. [BRIT, BUSINESS] ❑ *Supermarket lines are often cheaper than branded goods.* ADJ: ADJ n

☑ in AM, use **brand-name product**

**brand im|age (brand images)** The **brand image** of a particular brand of product is the image or impression that people have of it, usually created by advertising. [BUSINESS] ❑ *Few products have brand images anywhere near as strong as Levi's.* N-COUNT

**brand|ing** /brændɪŋ/ The **branding** of a product is the presentation of it to the public in a way that makes it easy for people to recognize or identify. [BUSINESS] ❑ *Local companies find the sites and build the theme parks, while we will look after the branding.* N-UNCOUNT

**bran|dish** /brændɪʃ/ **(brandishes, brandishing, brandished)** If you **brandish** something, especially a weapon, you hold it in a threatening way. ❑ *He appeared in the lounge brandishing a knife.* VERB V n

**brand lead|er (brand leaders)** The **brand leader** of a particular product is the brand of it that most people choose to buy. [BUSINESS] ❑ *In office supplies, we're the brand leader.* N-COUNT

**brand name (brand names)** The **brand name** of a product is the name the manufacturer gives it and under which it is sold. [BUSINESS] ❑ *When it comes to soft drinks Coca-Cola is the biggest selling brand name in Britain.* N-COUNT

**brand-new** A **brand-new** object is completely new. ❑ *Yesterday he went off to buy himself a brand-new car.* ADJ

**bran|dy** /brændi/ **(brandies)** 1 **Brandy** is a strong alcoholic drink. It is often drunk after a meal. N-MASS
2 A **brandy** is a glass of brandy. ❑ *After a couple of brandies Michael started telling me his life story.* N-COUNT

**bran|dy snap (brandy snaps)** **Brandy snaps** are very thin crisp biscuits in the shape of hollow cylinders. They are flavoured with ginger and are often filled with cream. N-COUNT

**brash** /bræʃ/ **(brasher, brashest)** If you describe someone or their behaviour as **brash**, you disapprove of them because you think that they are too confident and aggressive. ❑ *On stage she seems hard, brash and uncompromising.* ADJ [disapproval]
♦ **brash|ly** *I brashly announced to the group that NATO needed to be turned around.* ADV: ADV with v, ADV adj
♦ **brash|ness** *He was a typical showman with a brashness bordering on arrogance.* N-UNCOUNT

**brass** /brɑːs, bræs/ 1 **Brass** is a yellow-coloured metal made from copper and zinc. It is used especially for making ornaments and musical instruments. ❑ *The instrument is beautifully made in brass.* N-UNCOUNT
2 **The brass** is the section of an orchestra which consists of brass wind instruments such as trumpets and horns. N-SING
3 If you **get down to brass tacks**, you discuss the basic, most important facts of a situation. ❑ *Angola's ruling party was due to get down to brass tacks today with a debate on the party's record.* PHRASE: V inflects

**brass band (brass bands)** A **brass band** is a band that is made up of brass and percussion instruments. N-COUNT

**bras|se|rie** /bræsəri, AM -riː/ **(brasseries)** A **brasserie** is a small and usually cheap restaurant or bar. N-COUNT

**bras|si|ca** /bræsɪkə/ **(brassicas)** **Brassicas** are vegetables such as cabbages, broccoli and turnips. N-COUNT: oft N n

**bras|siere** /bræziəʳ, AM brəzɪr/ **(brassieres)** A **brassiere** is the same as a **bra**. [OLD-FASHIONED] N-COUNT

**brass rub|bing (brass rubbings)** A **brass rubbing** is a picture made by placing a piece of paper over a brass plate that has writing or a picture on it, and rubbing it with a wax crayon. N-COUNT

**brassy** /brɑːsi, bræsi/ **(brassier, brassiest)**
1 **Brassy** music is bold, harsh, and loud. ❑ *Musicians blast their brassy jazz from street corners.* ADJ
2 If you describe a woman's appearance or her behaviour as **brassy**, you think that she does not have good taste, and that she dresses or behaves in a way that is too loud or vulgar. ❑ *...Alec and his brassy blonde wife.* ADJ [disapproval]
3 Something that is **brassy** has a yellow metallic colour and sometimes looks cheap. ❑ *A woman with big brassy ear-rings.* ADJ

**brat** /bræt/ **(brats)** If you call someone, especially a child, a **brat**, you mean that he or she behaves badly or annoys you. [INFORMAL] ❑ *He's a spoilt brat.* N-COUNT [disapproval]

**brat pack (brat packs)** A **brat pack** is a group of young people, especially actors or writers, who are popular or successful at the moment. [JOURNALISM] ❑ *...the Hollywood Brat Pack.* N-COUNT

**bra|va|do** /brəvɑːdoʊ/ **Bravado** is an appearance of courage or confidence that someone shows in order to impress other people. ❑ *'You won't get away with this,' he said with unexpected bravado.* N-UNCOUNT

**brave** /breɪv/ **(braver, bravest, braves, braving, braved)** ♦◇◇
1 Someone who is **brave** is willing to do things which are dangerous, and does not show fear in difficult or dangerous situations. ❑ *He was not brave enough to report the loss of the documents. ...those brave people who dared to challenge the Stalinist regimes.* ADJ = courageous ≠ cowardly
♦ **brave|ly** *Mr Kim bravely stood up to authority.* ADV
2 If you **brave** unpleasant or dangerous conditions, you deliberately expose yourself to them, usually in order to achieve something. [WRITTEN] ❑ *Thousands have braved icy rain to demonstrate their support.* VERB V n
3 If someone **is putting on a brave face** or **is putting a brave face on** a difficult situation, they are pretending that they are happy or satisfied when they are not. ❑ *He felt disappointed but he tried to put on a brave face.* PHRASE: V inflects

**brave new world** If someone refers to a **brave new world**, they are talking about a situation or system that has recently been created and that people think will be successful and fair. ❑ *...the brave new world of internet banking.* N-SING: usu N *of* n

**brav|ery** /breɪvəri/ **Bravery** is brave behaviour or the quality of being brave. ❑ *He deserves the highest praise for his bravery.* N-UNCOUNT = courage ≠ cowardice

**bra|vo** /brɑːvoʊ/ Some people say '**bravo**' to express appreciation when someone has done something well. [OLD-FASHIONED] ❑ *'Bravo, Rena! You're right,' the students said.* EXCLAM = well done

**bra|vu|ra** /brəvjʊərə, AM -vʊrə/ 1 If you say that someone is doing something with **bravura**, you mean that they are using unnecessary extra actions that emphasize their skill or importance. [LITERARY] ❑ *The film is directed with a technical bravura and visual splendour.* N-UNCOUNT
2 A **bravura** perfor- ADJ:

mance or piece of work is done with bravura. [LITERARY] ❑ *...a bravura performance from Durham's scorer, Brian Hunt.* usu ADJ n

**brawl** /brɔːl/ **(brawls, brawling, brawled)** 1 A **brawl** is a rough or violent fight. ❑ *He had been in a drunken street brawl.* N-COUNT 2 If someone **brawls**, they fight in a very rough or violent way. ❑ *He was suspended for a year from University after brawling with police over a speeding ticket... Two gangs of youths brawled on the dance floor of the ferry.* V-RECIP V with n pl-n V ♦ **brawl|ing** *The brawling between the England fans and locals last night went on for several hours.* N-UNCOUNT

**brawn** /brɔːn/ **Brawn** is physical strength. ❑ *He's got plenty of brains as well as brawn.* N-UNCOUNT = muscle

**brawny** /brɔːni/ Someone who is **brawny** is strong and has big muscles. ❑ *...a brawny young man.* ADJ = strapping

**bray** /breɪ/ **(brays, braying, brayed)** When a donkey **brays**, it makes a loud harsh sound. ❑ *The donkey brayed and tried to bolt.* VERB V

**bra|zen** /breɪzᵊn/ If you describe a person or their behaviour as **brazen**, you mean that they are very bold and do not care what other people think about them or their behaviour. ❑ *They're quite brazen about their bisexuality, it doesn't worry them.* ADJ ♦ **bra|zen|ly** *He was brazenly running a $400,000-a-month drug operation from the prison.* ADV: ADV with v, also ADV adj

♦ **brazen out** If you have done something wrong and you **brazen** it **out**, you behave confidently in order not to appear ashamed, even though you probably do feel ashamed. ❑ *If you are caught simply argue that 'everyone does it' and brazen it out... The president brazened out his misdeeds... Stung by recent publicity, the Home Office now seems to be trying to brazen this issue out.* PHRASAL VERB V it P V P n (not pron) V n P

**bra|zi|er** /breɪziəʳ, AM -ʒər/ **(braziers)** 1 A **brazier** is a large metal container in which coal or charcoal is burned to keep people warm when they are outside in cold weather, for example because of their work. N-COUNT 2 A **brazier** is a grill that you use for cooking, usually with charcoal. [AM] N-COUNT

**Bra|zil|ian** /brəzɪliən/ **(Brazilians) Brazilian** means belonging or relating to Brazil, or to its people or culture. ADJ ♦ A **Brazilian** is a person who comes from Brazil. N-COUNT

**breach** /briːtʃ/ **(breaches, breaching, breached)** 1 If you **breach** an agreement, a law, or a promise, you break it. ❑ *The newspaper breached the code of conduct on privacy.* VERB = violate V n 2 A **breach of** an agreement, a law, or a promise is an act of breaking it. ❑ *The congressman was accused of a breach of secrecy rules. ...a $1 billion breach of contract suit.* N-VAR = violation 3 A **breach in** a relationship is a serious disagreement which often results in the relationship ending. [FORMAL] ❑ *Their actions threatened a serious breach in relations between the two countries. ...the breach between Tito and Stalin.* N-COUNT: usu N in/between n = rift, rupture 4 If someone or something **breaches** a barrier, they make an opening in it, usually leaving it weakened or destroyed. [FORMAL] ❑ *Fire may have breached the cargo tanks and set the oil ablaze.* VERB = rupture V n 5 If you **breach** someone's security or their defences, you manage to get through and attack an area that is heavily guarded and protected. ❑ *The bomber had breached security by hurling his dynamite from a roof overlooking the building.* VERB V n ♦ **Breach** is also a noun. ❑ *...widespread breaches of security at Ministry of Defence bases.* N-COUNT 6 If you **step into the breach**, you do a job or task which someone else was supposed to do or has done in the past, because they are suddenly unable to do it. ❑ *I was persuaded to step into the breach temporarily when they became too ill to continue.* PHRASE: V inflects

**breach of the peace** **(breaches of the peace)** A **breach of the peace** is noisy or violent behaviour in a public place which is illegal because it disturbs other people. [LEGAL] ❑ *He admitted causing a breach of the peace... Four men were found guilty of breach of the peace.* N-VAR

**bread** /bred/ **(breads, breading, breaded)** ♦◇◇ 1 **Bread** is a very common food made from flour, water, and yeast. ❑ *...a loaf of bread... There is more fibre in wholemeal bread than in white bread.* N-MASS 2 If food such as fish or meat **is breaded**, it is covered in tiny pieces of dry bread called breadcrumbs. It can then be fried or grilled. ❑ *It is important that food be breaded just minutes before frying.* VERB: usu passive be V-ed ♦ **bread|ed** *...breaded fish.* ADJ

**bread and but|ter** also **bread-and-butter.** 1 Something that is the **bread and butter** of a person or organization is the activity or work that provides the main part of their income. ❑ *The mobile phone business was actually his bread and butter.* N-UNCOUNT: usu with poss 2 **Bread and butter** issues or matters are ones which are important to most people, because they affect them personally. ❑ *The opposition gained support by concentrating on bread-and-butter matters.* ADJ: ADJ n

**bread bas|ket** **(bread baskets)** also **bread-basket.** If an area or region is described as the **bread basket** of a country, it provides a lot of the food for that country because crops grow very easily there. It therefore produces wealth for the country. ❑ *The north-west became the country's bread-basket.* N-COUNT: usu with poss

**bread bin** **(bread bins)** A **bread bin** is a wooden, metal, or plastic container for storing bread. [BRIT] N-COUNT

☑ in AM, use **breadbox**

**bread|board** /bredbɔːʳd/ **(breadboards)** also **bread board.** A **breadboard** is a flat piece of wood used for cutting bread on. N-COUNT

**bread|box** /bredbɒks/ **(breadboxes)** also **bread box.** A **breadbox** is the same as a **bread bin.** [AM] N-COUNT

**bread|crumb** /bredkrʌm/ **(breadcrumbs)** **Breadcrumbs** are tiny pieces of dry bread. They are used in cooking. N-COUNT: usu pl

**bread|fruit** /bredfruːt/ **(breadfruit)** **Breadfruit** are large round fruit that grow on trees in the Pacific Islands and in tropical parts of America and that, when baked, look and feel like bread. N-VAR

**bread|line** /bredlaɪn/ Someone who is **on the breadline** is very poor indeed. ❑ *We lived on the breadline to get our son through college... They're not exactly on the breadline.* N-SING: usu on the N

**breadth** /bretθ, AM bredθ/ 1 The **breadth of** something is the distance between its two sides. ❑ *The breadth of the whole camp was 400 paces.* N-UNCOUNT: oft N of n = width 2 The **breadth of** something is its quality of consisting of or involving many different things. ❑ *Older people have a tremendous breadth of experience... His breadth of knowledge filled me with admiration.* N-UNCOUNT: oft N of n = range 3 If you say that someone does something or something happens throughout or across **the length and breadth of** a place, you are emphasizing that it happens everywhere in that place. ❑ *The group built their reputation by playing across the length and breadth of North America... She has travelled the length and breadth of Britain.* PHRASE: PHR n [emphasis] 4 → See also **hair's breadth**.

**bread|winner** /bredwɪnəʳ/ **(breadwinners)** also **bread-winner.** The **breadwinner** in a family is the person in it who earns the money that the family needs for essential things. ❑ *I've always paid the bills and been the breadwinner.* N-COUNT

**break** /breɪk/ **(breaks, breaking, broke, broken)** ♦♦♦ 1 When an object **breaks** or when you **break** it, it suddenly separates into two or more pieces, often because it has been hit or dropped. ❑ *He fell through the window, breaking the glass... The plate broke... Break the cauliflower into florets... The plane broke into three pieces. ...bombed-out buildings, surrounded by broken glass and rubble... The only sound was the crackle of breaking ice.* VERB V n V V n into pl-n V into pl-n V-ed V-ing 2 If you **break** a part of your body such as your leg, your arm, or your nose, or if a bone **breaks**, you are injured because a bone cracks or splits. ❑ *She broke a leg in a skiing accident... Old bones break easi-* VERB V n V

ly... Several people were treated for broken bones.* V-ed
♦ **Break** is also a noun. ❑ *It has caused a bad break to Gabriella's leg.* N-COUNT
3 If a surface, cover, or seal **breaks** or if something **breaks** it, a hole or tear is made in it, so that a substance can pass through. VERB ❑ *Once you've broken the seal of a bottle there's no way you can put it back together again... The bandage must be put on when the blister breaks... Do not use the cream on broken skin.* V n V V-ed
4 When a tool or piece of machinery **breaks** or when you **break** it, it is damaged and no longer works. VERB ❑ *When the clutch broke, the car was locked into second gear... The lead biker broke his bike chain.* V V n Also V-ed
5 If you **break** a rule, promise, or agreement, you do something that you should not do according to that rule, promise, or agreement. VERB ❑ *We didn't know we were breaking the law. ...broken promises.* V n V-ed
6 If you **break** free or loose, you free yourself from something or escape from it. VERB ❑ *She broke free by thrusting her elbow into his chest.* V adj
7 If someone **breaks** something, especially a difficult or unpleasant situation that has existed for some time, they end it or change it. VERB ❑ *New proposals have been put forward to break the deadlock among rival factions... The country is heading towards elections which may break the party's long hold on power.* V n V n ♦ **Break** is also a noun. ❑ *Nothing that might lead to a break in the deadlock has been discussed yet.* N-COUNT: usu sing
8 If someone or something **breaks** a silence, they say something or make a noise after a long period of silence. VERB ❑ *Hugh broke the silence. 'Is she always late?' he asked.* V n
9 If there is a **break in** the cloud or weather, it changes and there is a short period of sunshine or fine weather. N-COUNT ❑ *A sudden break in the cloud allowed rescuers to spot Michael Benson.*
10 If you **break with** a group of people or a traditional way of doing things, or you **break** your connection with them, you stop being involved with that group or stop doing things in that way. VERB ❑ *In 1959, Akihito broke with imperial tradition by marrying a commoner... They were determined to break from precedent... They have yet to break the link with the trade unions.* V *with* n V *from* n V n *with* n Also V n ♦ **Break** is also a noun. ❑ *Making a completely clean break with the past, the couple got rid of all their old furniture.* N-COUNT: usu sing
11 If you **break** a habit or if someone **breaks** you **of** it, you no longer have that habit. VERB ❑ *If you continue to smoke, keep trying to break the habit... The professor hoped to break the students of the habit of looking for easy answers.* V n V n *of* n
12 To **break** someone means to destroy their determination and courage, their success, or their career. VERB = destroy ❑ *He never let his jailers break him... Ken's wife, Vicki, said: 'He's a broken man.'* V n V-ed
13 If someone **breaks for** a short period of time, they rest or change from what they are doing for a short period. VERB ❑ *They broke for lunch.* V
14 A **break** is a short period of time when you have a rest or a change from what you are doing, especially if you are working or if you are in a boring or unpleasant situation. N-COUNT: oft N *from/in* n ❑ *They may be able to help with childcare so that you can have a break... I thought a 15 min break from his work would do him good... She rang Moira during a coffee break.* ➔ See also **lunch break**, **tea break**.
15 A **break** is a short holiday. N-COUNT ❑ *They are currently taking a short break in Spain.*
16 If you **break** your journey somewhere, you stop there for a short time so that you can have a rest. VERB ❑ *Because of the heat we broke our journey at a small country hotel.* V n
17 To **break** the force of something such as a blow or fall means to weaken its effect, for example by getting in the way of it. VERB ❑ *He sustained serious neck injuries after he broke someone's fall.* V n
18 When a piece of news **breaks**, people hear about it from the newspapers, television, or radio. VERB ❑ *The news broke that the Prime Minister had resigned... He resigned from his post as Bishop when the scandal broke.* V V
19 When you **break** a piece of bad news to someone, you tell it to them, usually in a kind way. VERB ❑ *Then Louise broke the news that she was leaving me... I worried for ages and decided that I had better break it to her.* V n V n *to* n
20 A **break** is a lucky opportunity that someone gets to achieve something. [INFORMAL] N-COUNT ❑ *He went into TV and got his first break playing opposite Sid James in the series 'Citizen James'.*
21 If you **break** a record, you beat the previous record for a particular achievement. VERB ❑ *Jurassic Park had broken all box office records.* V n ➔ See also **record-breaking**.
22 When day or dawn **breaks**, it starts to grow light after the night has ended. VERB ❑ *They continued the search as dawn broke.* V ➔ See also **daybreak**.
23 When a wave **breaks**, it passes its highest point and turns downwards, for example when it reaches the shore. VERB ❑ *Danny listened to the waves breaking against the shore.* V
24 If you **break** a secret code, you work out how to understand it. VERB = crack ❑ *It was feared they could break the Allies' codes.* V n
25 If someone's voice **breaks** when they are speaking, it changes its sound, for example because they are sad or afraid. VERB ❑ *Godfrey's voice broke, and halted.* V
26 When a boy's voice **breaks**, it becomes deeper and sounds more like a man's voice. VERB ❑ *He sings with the strained discomfort of someone whose voice hasn't quite broken.* V
27 If the weather **breaks** or a storm **breaks**, it suddenly becomes rainy or stormy after a period of sunshine. VERB ❑ *I've been waiting for the weather to break.* V
28 In tennis, if you **break** your opponent's serve, you win a game in which your opponent is serving. VERB ❑ *He broke McEnroe's serve.* V n ♦ **Break** is also a noun. ❑ *A single break of serve settled the first two sets.* N-COUNT
29 ➔ See also **broke**, **broken**, **heartbreak**, **heartbreaking**, **heartbroken**, **outbreak**.

PHRASES 30 **The break of day** or **the break of dawn** is the time when it begins to grow light after the night. [LITERARY] PHRASE: prep PHR ❑ *'I,' he finished poetically, 'will watch over you to the break of day.'*
31 You can say '**give me a break**' to show that you are annoyed by what someone has said or done. [INFORMAL] CONVENTION feelings ❑ *'I'm a real intellectual-type guy, Tracy,' James joked. 'Oh, give me a break,' Tracy moaned.*
32 If you **make a break** or **make a break for it**, you run to escape from something. PHRASE: V inflects ❑ *The moment had come to make a break or die.*
33 to **break cover** ➔ see **cover**. to **break even** ➔ see **even**. to **break new ground** ➔ see **ground**. to **break** someone's **heart** ➔ see **heart**. **all hell breaks loose** ➔ see **hell**. to **break the ice** ➔ see **ice**. to **break ranks** ➔ see **rank**. to **break wind** ➔ see **wind**.

♦ **break away** 1 If you **break away from** someone who is trying to hold you or catch you, you free yourself and run away. PHRASAL VERB = cut loose ❑ *I broke away from him and rushed out into the hall... Willie Hamilton broke away early in the race.* V P *from* n V P
2 If you **break away from** something or someone that restricts you or controls you, you succeed in freeing yourself from them. PHRASAL VERB ❑ *Aboriginal art has finally gained recognition and broken away from being labelled as 'primitive' or 'exotic'.* V P *from* n/-ing

♦ **break down** 1 If a machine or a vehicle **breaks down**, it stops working. PHRASAL VERB ❑ *Their car broke down.* V P
2 If a discussion, relationship, or system **breaks down**, it fails because of a problem or disagreement. PHRASAL VERB ❑ *Talks with business leaders broke down last night... Paola's marriage broke down.* V P V P
3 To **break down** something such as an idea or statement means to separate it into smaller parts in order to make it easier to understand or deal with. PHRASAL VERB ❑ *The report breaks down the results region by region... These rules tell us how a sentence is broken down into phrases.* V P n *be* V-ed P *into* n, Also V n P *into* n
4 When a substance **breaks down** or when something **breaks** it **down**, a biological or chemical process causes it to separate into the substances which make it up. PHRASAL VERB ❑ *Over time, the protein in the eggshell breaks down into its constituent amino acids... The oil is attacked by naturally occurring microbes which break it down.* V P V n P Also V P n
5 If someone **breaks down**, they lose control of themselves and start crying. PHRASAL VERB ❑ *Because he was being so kind and concerned, I broke down and cried.* V P
6 If you **break down** a door or barrier, you hit it so hard that it falls to the ground. PHRASAL VERB ❑ *An unruly mob broke down police barricades and stormed the court-* V P n (not pron)

room... Firemen were called after his father failed to break the door down. *(V n P)* [7] To **break down** barriers or prejudices that separate people or restrict their freedom means to change people's attitudes so that the barriers or prejudices no longer exist. *(PHRASAL VERB, approval)* ❑ *His early experience enabled him to break down barriers between Scottish Catholics and Protestants.* *(V P n (not pron), Also V n P)* [8] → See also **breakdown**, **broken-down**.

♦ **break in** [1] If someone, usually a thief, **breaks in**, they get into a building by force. *(PHRASAL VERB)* ❑ *Masked robbers broke in and made off with $8,000.* *(V P)* → See also **break-in**. [2] If you **break in** on someone's conversation or activity, you interrupt them. *(PHRASAL VERB = butt in)* ❑ *O'Leary broke in on his thoughts...* *(V P on n)* *Mrs Southern listened keenly, occasionally breaking in with pertinent questions...* *(V P)* *'She told you to stay here,' Mike broke in.* *(V P with quote)* [3] If you **break** someone **in**, you get them used to a new job or situation. *(PHRASAL VERB)* ❑ *The band are breaking in a new backing vocalist.* *(V P n, Also V n P)* [4] If you **break in** something new, you gradually use or wear it for longer and longer periods until it is ready to be used or worn all the time. *(PHRASAL VERB)* ❑ *When breaking in an engine, you probably should refrain from high speed for the first thousand miles.* *(V P n (not pron), Also V n P)*

♦ **break into** [1] If someone **breaks into** a building, they get into it by force. *(PHRASAL VERB)* ❑ *There was no one nearby who might see him trying to break into the house.* *(V P n)* [2] If someone **breaks into** something they suddenly start doing it. For example if someone **breaks into** a run they suddenly start running, and if they **break into** song they suddenly start singing. *(PHRASAL VERB)* ❑ *The moment she was out of sight she broke into a run...* *(V P n)* *Then, breaking into a smile, he said, 'I brought you something.'* *(V P n)* [3] If you **break into** a profession or area of business, especially one that is difficult to succeed in, you manage to have some success in it. *(PHRASAL VERB)* ❑ *She finally broke into films after an acclaimed stage career.* *(V P n)*

♦ **break off** [1] If part of something **breaks off** or if you **break** it **off**, it comes off or is removed by force. *(PHRASAL VERB)* ❑ *The two wings of the aircraft broke off on impact...* *(V P)* *Grace broke off a large piece of the clay...* *(V P n)* *They've torn down wooden fences and broken branches off trees.* *(V n P n, Also V n P)* [2] If you **break off** when you are doing or saying something, you suddenly stop doing it or saying it. *(PHRASAL VERB)* ❑ *Llewelyn broke off in mid-sentence...* *(V P)* *The commander of the German task force radioed that he was breaking off the action.* *(V P n (not pron), Also V n P)* [3] If someone **breaks off** a relationship, they end it. *(PHRASAL VERB)* ❑ *The two West African states had broken off relations two years ago...* *(pl-n V P n (not pron))* *He doesn't seem to have the courage to break it off with her.* *(V it P with n (non-recip))*

♦ **break out** [1] If something such as war, fighting, or disease **breaks out**, it begins suddenly. *(PHRASAL VERB)* ❑ *He was 29 when war broke out...* *(V P)* *I was in a nightclub in Brixton and a fight broke out.* *(V P)* [2] If a prisoner **breaks out of** a prison, they escape from it. *(PHRASAL VERB)* ❑ *The two men broke out of their cells and cut through a perimeter fence.* *(V P of n, Also V P)* → See also **breakout**. [3] If you **break out of** a dull situation or routine, you manage to change it or escape from it. *(PHRASAL VERB)* ❑ *It's taken a long time to break out of my own conventional training...* *(V P of n)* *If her marriage becomes too restrictive, she will break out and seek new horizons.* *(V P)* [4] If you **break out in** a rash or a sweat, a rash or sweat appears on your skin. *(PHRASAL VERB)* ❑ *A person who is allergic to cashews may break out in a rash when he consumes these nuts...* *(V P in n)* *A line of sweat broke out on her forehead and she thought she might faint.* *(V P)*

♦ **break through** [1] If you **break through** a barrier, you succeed in forcing your way through it. *(PHRASAL VERB)* ❑ *Protesters tried to break through a police cordon...* *(V P n)* *About fifteen inmates broke through onto the roof.* *(V P)* [2] If you **break through**, you achieve success even though there are difficulties and obstacles. *(PHRASAL VERB)* ❑ *There is still scope for new writers to break through...* *(V P)* *I broke through the poverty barrier and it was education that did it.* *(V P n)* [3] → See also **breakthrough**.

♦ **break up** [1] When something **breaks up** or when you **break** it **up**, it separates or is divided into several smaller parts. *(PHRASAL VERB)* ❑ *There was a danger of the ship breaking up completely...* *(V P)* *Break up the chocolate and melt it...* *(V P n (not pron))* *He broke the bread up into chunks and gave Meer a big one...* *(V n P into n)* *Tanks are strongly built. It is a complicated and difficult process to break them up.* *(V n P)* [2] If you **break up with** your boyfriend, girlfriend, husband, or wife, your relationship with that person ends. *(PHRASAL VERB = split up)* ❑ *My girlfriend had broken up with me...* *(V P with n)* *He felt appalled by the whole idea of marriage so we broke up.* *(pl-n V P)* [3] If a marriage **breaks up** or if someone **breaks** it **up**, the marriage ends and the partners separate. *(PHRASAL VERB)* ❑ *MPs say they work too hard and that is why so many of their marriages break up...* *(V P)* *Fred has given me no good reason for wanting to break up our marriage.* *(V P n (not pron))* [4] When a meeting or gathering **breaks up** or when someone **breaks** it **up**, it is brought to an end and the people involved in it leave. *(PHRASAL VERB = disperse)* ❑ *A neighbour asked for the music to be turned down and the party broke up...* *(V P)* *Police used tear gas to break up a demonstration...* *(V P n (not pron))* *He charged into the crowd. 'Break it up,' he shouted.* *(V n P)* [5] When a school or the pupils in it **break up**, the school term ends and the pupils start their holidays. [BRIT] *(PHRASAL VERB ≠ go back)* ❑ *It's the last week before they break up, and they're doing all kinds of Christmas things.* *(V P)* [6] If you say that someone **is breaking up** when you are speaking to them on a mobile telephone, you mean that you can only hear parts of what they are saying because the signal is interrupted. *(PHRASAL VERB)* ❑ *The line's gone; I think you're breaking up.* *(V P)* [7] → See also **break-up**.

**break|able** /breɪkəbəl/ **(breakables)** **Breakable** objects are easy to break by accident. *(ADJ: usu ADJ n)* ❑ *Put away any valuable or breakable objects.* ♦ **Breakables** are breakable objects. *(N-PLURAL)* ❑ *Keep breakables out of reach of very young children.*

**break|age** /breɪkɪdʒ/ **(breakages)** [1] **Breakage** is the act of breaking something. *(N-VAR)* ❑ *Brushing wet hair can cause stretching and breakage... Check that your insurance policy covers breakages and damage during removals.* [2] A **breakage** is something that has been broken. *(N-COUNT: usu pl)* ❑ *Check that everything is in good repair before moving in, as you have to replace breakages.*

**break|away** /breɪkəweɪ/ A **breakaway** group is a group of people who have separated from a larger group, for example because of a disagreement. *(ADJ: ADJ n = splinter)* ❑ *Sixteen members of Parliament have formed a breakaway group.*

**break|down** /breɪkdaʊn/ **(breakdowns)** [1] The **breakdown of** something such as a relationship, plan, or discussion is its failure or ending. *(N-COUNT: usu sing, oft N of/in n = collapse)* ❑ *...the breakdown of talks between the US and EU officials. ...the irretrievable breakdown of a marriage.* [2] If you have a **breakdown**, you become very depressed, so that you are unable to cope with your life. *(N-COUNT: usu sing, oft adj N)* ❑ *My personal life was terrible. My mother had died, and a couple of years later I had a breakdown.* → See also **nervous breakdown**. [3] If a car or a piece of machinery has a **breakdown**, it stops working. *(N-COUNT)* ❑ *Her old car was unreliable, so the trip was plagued by breakdowns.* [4] A **breakdown of** something is a list of its separate parts. *(N-COUNT: usu N of n = analysis)* ❑ *The organisers were given a breakdown of the costs.*

**break|er** /breɪkər/ **(breakers)** **Breakers** are big sea waves, especially at the point when they just reach the shore. *(N-COUNT)* → See also **ice-breaker**, **lawbreaker**, **record-breaker**, **strike-breaker**.

**break-even point** When a company reaches **break-even point**, the money it makes from the sale of goods or services is just enough to cover the cost of supplying those goods or services, but not enough to make a profit. [BUSINESS] *(N-SING)* ❑ *'Terminator 2' finally made $200 million, which was considered to be the break-even point for the picture.*

**break|fast** /brekfəst/ **(breakfasts, breakfasting, breakfasted)** ◆◇◇ [1] **Breakfast** is the first meal of the day. It is usually eaten in the early part of the morning. *(N-VAR)* ❑ *What's for breakfast? ...breakfast cereal.* → See also **bed and breakfast**, **continental breakfast**, **English breakfast**. [2] When you *(VERB)*

**breakfast**, you have breakfast. [FORMAL] ❑ *All the ladies breakfasted in their rooms.* V adv/prep

**break|fast ta|ble** **(breakfast tables)** You refer to a table as **the breakfast table** when it is being used for breakfast. ❑ *...reading the morning papers at the breakfast table.* N-COUNT: usu sing, *the* N

**break|fast tele|vi|sion** **Breakfast television** refers to television programmes which are broadcast in the morning at the time when most people are having breakfast. [BRIT] N-UNCOUNT

**break|fast time** also **breakfast-time. Breakfast time** is the period of the morning when most people have their breakfast. ❑ *By breakfast-time he was already at his desk.* N-UNCOUNT: oft prep N

**break-in** **(break-ins)** If there has been a **break-in**, someone has got into a building by force. ❑ *The break-in had occurred just before midnight.* N-COUNT = *burglary*

**break|ing point** If something or someone has reached **breaking point**, they have so many problems or difficulties that they can no longer cope with them, and may soon collapse or be unable to continue. ❑ *The report on the riot exposed a prison system stretched to breaking point.* N-UNCOUNT: also *the/a* N

**break|neck** /breɪknek/ If you say that something happens or travels at **breakneck** speed, you mean that it happens or travels very fast. ❑ *Jack drove to Mayfair at breakneck speed.* ADJ: ADJ n

**break|out** /breɪkaʊt/ **(breakouts)** also **break-out.** If there has been a **break-out**, someone has escaped from prison. ❑ *High Point prison had the highest number of breakouts of any jail in Britain.* N-COUNT = *escape*

**break|through** /breɪkθruː/ **(breakthroughs)** A **breakthrough** is an important development or achievement. ❑ *The company looks poised to make a significant breakthrough in China.* N-COUNT: oft N *in* n

**break-up** **(break-ups)** also **breakup.** 1 The **break-up of** a marriage, relationship, or association is the act of it finishing or coming to an end because the people involved decide that it is not working successfully. ❑ *...the acrimonious break-up of the meeting's first session. ...a marital break-up.* N-COUNT: usu N *of* n, n N = *collapse* 2 The **break-up of** an organization or a country is the act of it separating or dividing into several parts. ❑ *...the break-up of British Rail for privatisation... At no time did a majority of Czechoslavakia's citizens support the country's break-up.* N-COUNT: usu N *of* n

**break|water** /breɪkwɔːtəʳ/ **(breakwaters)** A **breakwater** is a wooden or stone wall that extends from the shore into the sea and is built in order to protect a harbour or beach from the force of the waves. N-COUNT

**breast** /brest/ **(breasts)** ◆◇◇ 1 A woman's **breasts** are the two soft, round parts on her chest that can produce milk to feed a baby. ❑ *She wears a low-cut dress which reveals her breasts... As my newborn cuddled at my breast, her tiny fingers stroked my skin.* N-COUNT: oft poss N ♦ **-breasted** *She was slim and muscular and full-breasted.* COMB in ADJ 2 A person's **breast** is the upper part of his or her chest. [LITERARY] ❑ *He struck his breast in a dramatic gesture.* N-COUNT: poss N 3 A bird's **breast** is the front part of its body. ❑ *The cock's breast is tinged with chestnut.* N-COUNT ♦ **-breasted** *...flocks of red-breasted parrots.* COMB in ADJ 4 The **breast** of a shirt, jacket, or coat is the part which covers the top part of the chest. ❑ *He reached into his breast pocket for his cigar case.* N-SING: *the* N 5 You can refer to piece of meat that is cut from the front of a bird or lamb as **breast**. ❑ *...a chicken breast with vegetables. ...breast of lamb.* N-VAR 6 → See also **double-breasted**, **single-breasted**.

**breast|bone** /brestboʊn/ **(breastbones)** also **breast bone.** Your **breastbone** is the long, flat bone which goes from your throat to the bottom of your ribs and to which your ribs are attached. N-COUNT = *sternum*

**breast-feed** **(breast-feeds, breast-feeding, breast-fed)** also **breastfeed, breast feed.** When a woman **breast-feeds** her baby, she feeds it with milk from her breasts, rather than from a bottle. ❑ *Not all women have the choice whether or not to breast feed their babies... Leading scientists claim breast-fed babies are intellectually brighter.* VERB = *suckle* V n V-ed Also V ♦ **breast-feeding** *There are many advantages to breast feeding.* N-UNCOUNT

**breast milk** also **breast-milk. Breast milk** is the white liquid produced by women to breast-feed their babies. N-UNCOUNT

**breast|plate** /brestpleɪt/ **(breastplates)** A **breastplate** is a piece of armour that covers and protects the chest. N-COUNT

**breast pock|et** **(breast pockets)** The **breast pocket** of a man's coat or jacket is a pocket, usually on the inside, next to his chest. ❑ *I kept the list in my breast pocket.* N-COUNT: with poss

**breast|stroke** /breststroʊk/ **Breaststroke** is a swimming stroke which you do lying on your front, moving your arms and legs horizontally in a circular motion. N-UNCOUNT: also *the* N

**breath** /breθ/ **(breaths)** ◆◇◇ 1 Your **breath** is the air that you let out through your mouth when you breathe. If someone has **bad breath**, their breath smells unpleasant. ❑ *I could smell the whisky on his breath... Smoking causes bad breath.* N-VAR: oft poss N 2 When you take a **breath**, you breathe in once. ❑ *He took a deep breath, and began to climb the stairs... Gasping for breath, she leaned against the door... He spoke for one and a half hours and barely paused for breath.* N-VAR

PHRASES 3 If you go outside **for a breath of fresh air** or **for a breath of air**, you go outside because it is unpleasantly warm indoors. PHRASE: *breath* inflects 4 If you describe something new or different as **a breath of fresh air**, you mean that it makes a situation or subject more interesting or exciting. ❑ *Her brisk treatment of an almost taboo subject was a breath of fresh air.* PHRASE: usu v-link PHR [approval] 5 When you **get** your **breath back** after doing something energetic, you start breathing normally again. [BRIT] ❑ *I reached out a hand to steady myself against the house while I got my breath back.* PHRASE: V inflects 6 When you **catch** your **breath** while you are doing something energetic, you stop for a short time so that you can start breathing normally again. ❑ *He had stopped to catch his breath and make sure of his directions.* PHRASE: V and N inflect 7 If something makes you **catch** your **breath**, it makes you take a short breath of air, usually because it shocks you. ❑ *Kenny caught his breath as Nikko nearly dropped the bottle.* PHRASE: V inflects = *gasp* 8 If you **hold** your **breath**, you make yourself stop breathing for a few moments, for example because you are under water. ❑ *I held my breath and sank under the water.* PHRASE: V and N inflect 9 If you say that someone **is holding** their **breath**, you mean that they are waiting anxiously or excitedly for something to happen. [WRITTEN] ❑ *The whole world holds its breath for this speech.* PHRASE: V and N inflect, oft PHR *for* n 10 If you are **out of breath**, you are breathing very quickly and with difficulty because you have been doing something energetic. ❑ *There she was, slightly out of breath from running.* PHRASE: v-link PHR 11 You can use **in the same breath** or **in the next breath** to indicate that someone says two very different or contradictory things, especially when you are criticizing them. ❑ *He hailed this week's arms agreement but in the same breath expressed suspicion about the motivations of the United States.* PHRASE: PHR cl [disapproval] 12 If you are **short of breath**, you find it difficult to breathe properly, for example because you are ill. You can also say that someone suffers from **shortness of breath**. ❑ *She felt short of breath and flushed... Any exercise that causes undue shortness of breath should be stopped.* PHRASE: usu v-link PHR 13 If you say that something **takes** your **breath away**, you are emphasizing that it is extremely beautiful or surprising. ❑ *I heard this song on the radio and it just took my breath away.* PHRASE: V inflects [emphasis] = *astound* 14 If you say something **under** your **breath**, you say it in a very quiet voice, often because you do not want other people to hear what you are saying. ❑ *Walsh muttered something under his breath.* PHRASE: PHR after v 15 **with bated breath** → see **bated**.

**breath|able** /briːðəbᵊl/ A **breathable** fabric allows air to pass through it easily, so that clothing made from it does not become too warm or uncomfortable.
ADJ

**breatha|lyze** /breθəlaɪz/ **(breathalyzes, breathalyzing, breathalyzed)**

✔ in BRIT, also use **breathalyse**

If the driver of a car **is breathalyzed** by the police, they ask him or her to breathe into a special bag or device in order to test whether he or she has drunk too much alcohol. [mainly BRIT] ❑ *She was breathalysed and found to be over the limit.*
VERB: usu passive
*be* V-ed

**Breatha|lyz|er** /breθəlaɪzəʳ/ **(Breathalyzers)**

✔ in BRIT, also use **Breathalyser**

A **Breathalyzer** is a bag or electronic device that the police use to test whether a driver has drunk too much alcohol. [TRADEMARK]
N-COUNT

**breathe** /briːð/ **(breathes, breathing, breathed)** [1] When people or animals **breathe**, they take air into their lungs and let it out again. When they **breathe** smoke or a particular kind of air, they take it into their lungs and let it out again as they breathe. ❑ *He stood there breathing deeply and evenly... No American should have to drive out of town to breathe clean air... A thirteen year old girl is being treated after breathing in smoke.* ♦ **breath|ing** *Her breathing became slow and heavy... He heard only deep breathing.* [2] If someone **breathes** something, they say it very quietly. [LITERARY] ❑ *'You don't understand,' he breathed.* [3] If you do not **breathe** a word about something, you say nothing about it, because it is a secret. ❑ *He never breathed a word about our conversation.* [4] If someone **breathes** life, confidence, or excitement **into** something, they improve it by adding this quality. [WRITTEN] ❑ *It is the readers who breathe life into a newspaper with their letters.* [5] to **be breathing down** someone's **neck** → see **neck**. to breathe a **sigh of relief** → see **sigh**.
◆◇◇ VERB; V; V n; V n with *in/out*; N-UNCOUNT: usu with supp; VERB; V with quote; Also V n; VERB: with brd-neg, no cont; V n; VERB = instil; V n *into* n

♦ **breathe in** When you **breathe in**, you take some air into your lungs. ❑ *She breathed in deeply.*
PHRASAL VERB; V P

♦ **breathe out** When you **breathe out**, you send air out of your lungs through your nose or mouth. ❑ *Breathe out and ease your knees in toward your chest.*
PHRASAL VERB; V P

**breath|er** /briːðəʳ/ **(breathers)** If you take a **breather**, you stop what you are doing for a short time and have a rest. [INFORMAL] ❑ *Relax and take a breather whenever you feel that you need one.*
N-COUNT: usu sing

**breath|ing space** **(breathing spaces)** A **breathing space** is a short period of time between two activities in which you can recover from the first activity and prepare for the second one. ❑ *Firms need a breathing space if they are to recover.*
N-VAR = respite

**breath|less** /breθləs/ [1] If you are **breathless**, you have difficulty in breathing properly, for example because you have been running or because you are afraid or excited. ❑ *I was a little breathless and my heartbeat was bumpy and fast.* ♦ **breath|less|ly** *'I'll go in,' he said breathlessly.* ♦ **breath|less|ness** *Asthma causes wheezing and breathlessness.* [2] You use **breathless** for emphasis when you are describing feelings of excitement or exciting situations. ❑ *Technology has advanced at a breathless pace. ...the breathless excitement of early 1988, when hundreds and thousands of citizens gathered nightly for political meetings.* ♦ **breath|less|ly** *Nancy waited breathlessly for him to go on.*
ADJ: usu v-link ADJ; ADV: ADV with v, also ADV adj; N-UNCOUNT; ADJ: ADJ n [emphasis]; ADV: usu ADV with v, also ADV adj

**breath|taking** /breθteɪkɪŋ/ also **breath-taking**. If you say that something is **breathtaking**, you are emphasizing that it is extremely beautiful or amazing. ❑ *The house has breathtaking views from every room... Some of their football was breathtaking.* ♦ **breath|taking|ly** *...the most breathtakingly beautiful scenery in Germany.*
ADJ [emphasis]; ADV: usu ADV adj, also ADV after v

**breath test** **(breath tests)** A **breath test** is a test carried out by police in which a driver blows into a piece of equipment to show how much alcohol he or she has drunk. ❑ *Police will conduct random breath tests.*
N-COUNT

**breathy** /breθi/ If someone has a **breathy** voice, you can hear their breath when they speak or sing. ❑ *Her voice was suddenly breathy.*
ADJ

**bred** /bred/ [1] **Bred** is the past tense and past participle of **breed**. [2] → See also **ill-bred**, **pure-bred**, **well-bred**.

**breech** /briːtʃ/ **(breeches** /briːtʃɪz/**)** The **breech** of a gun is the part of the barrel at the back into which you load the bullets.
N-COUNT

**breeches** /brɪtʃɪz/ **Breeches** are trousers which reach as far as your knees. [OLD-FASHIONED] ❑ *...riding breeches.*
N-PLURAL: also *a pair of* N

**breed** /briːd/ **(breeds, breeding, bred)** [1] A **breed** of a pet animal or farm animal is a particular type of it. For example, terriers are a breed of dog. ❑ *...rare breeds of cattle... Certain breeds are more dangerous than others.* [2] If you **breed** animals or plants, you keep them for the purpose of producing more animals or plants with particular qualities, in a controlled way. ❑ *He lived alone, breeding horses and dogs... These dogs are bred to fight.* → See also **cross-breed**. ♦ **breed|ing** *There is potential for selective breeding for better yields.* [3] When animals **breed**, they have babies. ❑ *Frogs will usually breed in any convenient pond... The area now attracts over 60 species of breeding birds.* ♦ **breed|ing** *During the breeding season the birds come ashore.* [4] If you say that something **breeds** bad feeling or bad behaviour, you mean that it causes bad feeling or bad behaviour to develop. ❑ *If they are unemployed it's bound to breed resentment... Violence breeds violence.* [5] You can refer to someone or something as one of a particular **breed of** person or thing when you want to talk about what they are like. ❑ *Sue is one of the new breed of British women squash players who are making a real impact... The new breed of walking holidays puts the emphasis on enjoyment, not endurance.* [6] → See also **breeding**, **ill-bred**, **pure-bred**, **well-bred**. [7] Someone who was **born and bred** in a place was born there and grew up there. ❑ *I was born and bred in the highlands.* [8] **familiarity breeds contempt** → see **familiarity**.
◆◇◇ N-COUNT; VERB; V n; *be* V-ed to-inf; N-UNCOUNT; VERB; V; V-ing; N-UNCOUNT: oft N n; VERB = create; V n; N-COUNT: usu sing, with supp = strain; PHRASE

**breed|er** /briːdəʳ/ **(breeders)** **Breeders** are people who breed animals or plants. ❑ *Her father was a well-known racehorse breeder.* → See also **fast-breeder reactor**.
N-COUNT: usu with supp

**breed|ing** /briːdɪŋ/ If someone says that a person has **breeding**, they mean that they think the person is from a good social background and has good manners. ❑ *It's a sign of good breeding to know the names of all your staff.* → See also **breed**.
N-UNCOUNT

**breed|ing ground** **(breeding grounds)** [1] If you refer to a situation or place as a **breeding ground for** something bad such as crime, you mean that this thing can easily develop in that situation or place. ❑ *Flaws in the system have created a breeding ground for financial scandals.* [2] The **breeding ground for** a particular type of creature is the place where this creature breeds easily. ❑ *Warm milk is the ideal breeding ground for bacteria.*
N-COUNT: usu sing, with supp, usu N *for* n; N-COUNT: with supp

**breeze** /briːz/ **(breezes, breezing, breezed)** [1] A **breeze** is a gentle wind. ❑ *...a cool summer breeze.* [2] If you **breeze into** a place or a position, you enter it in a very casual or relaxed manner. ❑ *Lopez breezed into the quarter-finals of the tournament... 'Are you all right?' Francine asked as she breezed in with the mail.* [3] If you **breeze through** something such as a game or test, you cope with it easily. ❑ *John seems to breeze effortlessly through his many commitments at work.*
N-COUNT; VERB; V prep/adv; V prep/adv; VERB; V *through* n; Also V *through*

**breeze-block** **(breeze-blocks)** also **breeze block**. A **breeze-block** is a large, grey brick made from ashes and cement. [BRIT]
N-COUNT

✔ in AM, use **cinder block**

**breezy** /bri:zi/ 1 If you describe someone as **breezy**, you mean that they behave in a casual, cheerful, and confident manner. ❑ *...his bright and breezy personality... Mona tried to sound breezy.* ♦ **breezi|ly** /bri:zɪli/ *'Hi,' he said breezily.* 2 When the weather is **breezy**, there is a fairly strong but pleasant wind blowing. ❑ *The day was breezy and warm.* ADJ ADV ADJ

**breth|ren** /breðrɪn/ You can refer to the members of a particular organization or group, especially a religious group, as **brethren**. [OLD-FASHIONED] ❑ *Sri Lankans share a common ancestry with their Indian brethren.* N-PLURAL: oft with poss

**brev|ity** /brevɪti/ The **brevity of** something is the fact that it is short or lasts for only a short time. [FORMAL] ❑ *The bonus of this homely soup is the brevity of its cooking time.* N-UNCOUNT: oft N *of* n

**brew** /bru:/ **(brews, brewing, brewed)** 1 If you **brew** tea or coffee, you make it by pouring hot water over tea leaves or ground coffee. ❑ *I'll get Venner to brew some tea.* 2 A **brew** is a particular kind of tea or coffee. It can also be a particular pot of tea or coffee. ❑ *...a mild herbal brew.* 3 If a person or company **brews** beer, they make it. ❑ *I brew my own beer.* ♦ **brew|ing** *...the brewing of home-made alcohol.* 4 If a storm **is brewing**, large clouds are beginning to form and the sky is becoming dark because there is going to be a storm. ❑ *We'd seen the storm brewing when we were out in the boat.* 5 If an unpleasant or difficult situation **is brewing**, it is starting to develop. ❑ *At home a crisis was brewing... There's trouble brewing.* 6 A **brew of** several things is a mixture of those things. ❑ *Most cities generate a complex brew of pollutants. ...a potent brew of smooth salesmanship and amateur psychiatry.* VERB V n N-COUNT: usu with supp VERB V n N-UNCOUNT VERB: usu cont V VERB: usu cont V V N-COUNT: usu sing, N *of* n

**brew|er** /bru:əʳ/ **(brewers) Brewers** are people or companies who make beer. N-COUNT

**brew|ery** /bru:əri/ **(breweries)** A **brewery** is a place where beer is made. N-COUNT

**bri|ar** /braɪəʳ/ **(briars)** A **briar** is a wild rose with long, prickly stems. N-COUNT

**bribe** /braɪb/ **(bribes, bribing, bribed)** 1 A **bribe** is a sum of money or something valuable that one person offers or gives to another in order to persuade him or her to do something. ❑ *He was being investigated for receiving bribes.* 2 If one person **bribes** another, they give them a bribe. ❑ *He was accused of bribing a senior bank official... The government bribed the workers to be quiet.* N-COUNT VERB V n V n to-inf

**brib|ery** /braɪbəri/ **Bribery** is the act of offering someone money or something valuable in order to persuade them to do something for you. ❑ *He was jailed on charges of bribery.* N-UNCOUNT

**bric-a-brac** /brɪkəbræk/ **Bric-a-brac** is a number of small ornamental objects of no great value. N-UNCOUNT = *knick-knacks*

**brick** /brɪk/ **(bricks)** 1 **Bricks** are rectangular blocks of baked clay used for building walls, which are usually red or brown. **Brick** is the material made up of these blocks. → See picture on page 1705. ❑ *She built bookshelves out of bricks and planks. ...a tiny garden surrounded by high brick walls.* N-VAR

**PHRASES** 2 If you **are banging** your **head against a brick wall**, what you are saying or doing is not having any effect although you keep saying or doing it. [INFORMAL] ❑ *I wanted to sort out this problem with him, but it was like banging my head against a brick wall.* 3 If you **hit a brick wall** or **come up against a brick wall**, you are unable to continue or make progress because something stops you. [INFORMAL] ❑ *After that my career just seemed to hit a brick wall.* 4 You can use **bricks and mortar** to refer to houses and other buildings, especially when they are considered as an investment. ❑ *As an investment, bricks and mortar are not what they were.* 5 to **come down on** somebody **like a ton of bricks** → see **ton**. PHRASE: V inflects, usu cont PHRASE: V inflects PHRASE

**brick|bat** /brɪkbæt/ **(brickbats) Brickbats** are very critical or insulting remarks which are made in public about someone or something. N-COUNT: usu pl

**brickie** /brɪki/ **(brickies)** A **brickie** is the same as a **bricklayer**. [BRIT, INFORMAL] N-COUNT = *bricklayer*

**brick|layer** /brɪkleɪəʳ/ **(bricklayers)** A **bricklayer** is a person whose job is to build walls using bricks. N-COUNT

**brick|work** /brɪkwɜːʳk/ You can refer to the bricks in the walls of a building as the **brickwork**. ❑ *There were cracks in the brickwork.* N-UNCOUNT = *masonry*

**brid|al** /braɪdᵊl/ **Bridal** is used to describe something that belongs or relates to a bride, or to both a bride and her bridegroom. ❑ *She wore a floor length bridal gown. ...the bridal party.* ADJ: ADJ n = *wedding*

**bride** /braɪd/ **(brides)** A **bride** is a woman who is getting married or who has just got married. N-COUNT

**bride|groom** /braɪdgru:m/ **(bridegrooms)** A **bridegroom** is a man who is getting married. N-COUNT = *groom*

**brides|maid** /braɪdzmeɪd/ **(bridesmaids)** A **bridesmaid** is a woman or a girl who helps and accompanies a bride on her wedding day. N-COUNT

**bride-to-be** **(brides-to-be)** A **bride-to-be** is a woman who is soon going to be married. N-COUNT

**bridge** /brɪdʒ/ **(bridges, bridging, bridged)** ◆◆◇ 1 A **bridge** is a structure that is built over a railway, river, or road so that people or vehicles can cross from one side to the other. ❑ *He walked back over the railway bridge. ...the Golden Gate Bridge.* 2 A **bridge** between two places is a piece of land that joins or connects them. ❑ *...a land bridge linking Serbian territories.* 3 To **bridge** the gap between two people or things means to reduce it or get rid of it. ❑ *It is unlikely that the two sides will be able to bridge their differences.* 4 Something that **bridges** the gap between two very different things has some of the qualities of each of these things. ❑ *...the singer who bridged the gap between pop music and opera.* 5 If something or someone acts as a **bridge** between two people, groups, or things, they connect them. ❑ *We hope this book will act as a bridge between doctor and patient... They saw themselves as a bridge to peace.* 6 **The bridge** is the place on a ship from which it is steered. 7 The **bridge** of your nose is the thin top part of it, between your eyes. ❑ *On the bridge of his hooked nose was a pair of gold rimless spectacles.* 8 The **bridge** of a pair of glasses is the part that rests on your nose. 9 The **bridge** of a violin, guitar, or other stringed instrument is the small piece of wood under the strings that holds them up. 10 **Bridge** is a card game for four players in which the players begin by declaring how many tricks they expect to win. 11 → See also **suspension bridge**. **water under the bridge** → see **water**. N-COUNT N-COUNT: usu with supp VERB = *overcome* V n VERB V n N-COUNT: usu N prep N-COUNT: usu sing N-COUNT: usu sing, usu N *of* n N-COUNT: usu sing N-COUNT: usu sing N-UNCOUNT

**bridge|head** /brɪdʒhed/ **(bridgeheads)** A **bridgehead** is a good position which an army has taken in the enemy's territory and from which it can advance or attack. ❑ *A bridgehead was established.* N-COUNT

**bridg|ing loan** **(bridging loans)** A **bridging loan** is money that a bank lends you for a short time, for example so that you can buy a new house before you have sold the one you already own. [BRIT] N-COUNT

**bri|dle** /braɪdᵊl/ **(bridles, bridling, bridled)** 1 A **bridle** is a set of straps that is put around a horse's head and mouth so that the person riding or driving the horse can control it. 2 If you **bridle**, you show that you are angry or offended by moving your head and body upwards in a proud way. [LITERARY] ❑ *She bridled, then simply shook her head... Alex bridled at the shortness of Pamela's tone.* N-COUNT VERB = *bristle* V V *at* n

**bri|dle path** **(bridle paths)** also **bridlepath**. A **bridle path** is a path intended for people riding horses. N-COUNT = *bridleway*

**bridle|way** /braɪdᵊlweɪ/ **(bridleways)** A **bridleway** is the same as a **bridle path**. [BRIT] N-COUNT

**Brie** /briː/ also **brie.** **Brie** is a type of cheese that comes from France. It is soft and creamy with a white skin. N-UNCOUNT

**brief** /briːf/ **(briefer, briefest, briefs, briefing, briefed)** ◆◆◇ 1 Something that is **brief** lasts for only a short time. ❑ *She once made a brief appearance on television... This time their visit is brief.* ADJ = fleeting ≠ lengthy 2 A **brief** speech or piece of writing does not contain too many words or details. ❑ *In a brief statement, he concentrated entirely on international affairs... Write a very brief description of a typical problem.* ADJ = short 3 If you are **brief**, you say what you want to say in as few words as possible. ❑ *Now please be brief – my time is valuable.* ADJ: v-link ADJ = succinct 4 You can describe a period of time as **brief** if you want to emphasize that it is very short. ❑ *For a few brief minutes we forgot the anxiety and anguish.* ADJ: usu ADJ n [emphasis] ≠ long 5 Men's or women's underpants can be referred to as **briefs**. ❑ *A bra and a pair of briefs lay on the floor.* N-PLURAL: also *a pair of* N 6 If someone **briefs** you, especially about a piece of work or a serious matter, they give you information that you need before you do it or consider it. ❑ *A Defense Department spokesman briefed reporters... The Prime Minister has been briefed by her parliamentary aides.* VERB = fill in V n V n 7 If someone gives you a **brief**, they officially give you responsibility for dealing with a particular thing. [mainly BRIT, FORMAL] ❑ *...customs officials with a brief to stop foreign porn coming into Britain.* N-COUNT: oft N to-inf = responsibility 8 → See also **briefer**, **briefing**. 9 You can say **in brief** to indicate that you are about to say something in as few words as possible or to give a summary of what you have just said. ❑ *In brief, take no risks.* PHRASE: PHR with cl

♦ **brief against** If someone, especially a politician, **briefs against** another person, he or she tries to harm the other person's reputation by saying something unfavourable about them. [BRIT] ❑ *Ministerial colleagues were briefing against him.* PHRASAL VERB V P n

**brief|case** /briːfkeɪs/ **(briefcases)** A **briefcase** is a case used for carrying documents in. N-COUNT

**brief|er** /briːfəʳ/ **(briefers)** A **briefer** is an official who has the job of giving information about something, for example a war. ❑ *Military briefers say no planes were shot down today.* N-COUNT: usu supp N

**brief|ing** /briːfɪŋ/ **(briefings)** A **briefing** is a meeting at which information or instructions are given to people, especially before they do something. ❑ *They're holding a press briefing tomorrow... Security staff did not then receive any briefing before they started each shift.* → See also **brief**. N-VAR

**brief|ly** /briːfli/ 1 Something that happens or is done **briefly** happens or is done for a very short period of time. ❑ *He smiled briefly... Guerillas captured and briefly held an important provincial capital.* ADV: ADV with v 2 If you say or write something **briefly**, you use very few words or give very few details. ❑ *There are four basic alternatives; they are described briefly below.* ADV: ADV with v 3 You can say **briefly** to indicate that you are about to say something in as few words as possible. ❑ *Briefly, no less than nine of our agents have passed information to us.* ADV: ADV with cl

**brig** /brɪg/ **(brigs)** 1 A **brig** is a type of ship with two masts and square sails. N-COUNT 2 A **brig** is a prison on a ship, especially a warship. [AM] N-COUNT

**Brig.** **Brig.** is a written abbreviation for **brigadier**. [BRIT] ❑ *...Brig. Douglas Erskin Crum.*

**bri|gade** /brɪgeɪd/ **(brigades)** A **brigade** is one of the groups which an army is divided into. ❑ *...the men of the Seventh Armoured Brigade.* → See also **fire brigade**. N-COUNT-COLL

**briga|dier** /brɪgədɪəʳ/ **(brigadiers)** A **brigadier** is a senior officer in the British armed forces who is in charge of a brigade and has the rank above colonel and below major general. N-COUNT; N-TITLE

**briga|dier gen|er|al** **(brigadier generals)** also **brigadier-general.** In the United States, a **brigadier general** is a senior officer in the armed forces who is often in charge of a brigade and has a rank above colonel and below major general. ❑ *...Brigadier General Gary Whipple of the Louisiana National Guard.* N-COUNT; N-TITLE

**brig|and** /brɪgənd/ **(brigands)** A **brigand** is someone who attacks people and robs them, especially in mountains or forests. [LITERARY] ❑ *...a notorious brigand who hijacked trains.* N-COUNT = bandit

**bright** /braɪt/ **(brighter, brightest)** ◆◆◇ 1 A **bright** colour is strong and noticeable, and not dark. ❑ *...a bright red dress. ...the bright uniforms of the guards parading at Buckingham Palace.* ADJ: usu ADJ n, ADJ colour ♦ **bright|ly** *...a display of brightly coloured flowers.* ADV ♦ **bright|ness** *You'll be impressed with the brightness and the beauty of the colors.* N-UNCOUNT: oft *the* N *of* n 2 A **bright** light, object, or place is shining strongly or is full of light. ❑ *...a bright October day... She leaned forward, her eyes bright with excitement.* ADJ ≠ dull ♦ **bright|ly** *...a warm, brightly lit room... The sun shone brightly.* ADV: ADV with v ♦ **bright|ness** *An astronomer can determine the brightness of each star.* N-UNCOUNT: oft *the* N *of* n 3 If you describe someone as **bright**, you mean that they are quick at learning things. ❑ *I was convinced that he was brighter than average.* ADJ: usu v-link ADJ = clever 4 A **bright** idea is clever and original. ❑ *Ford had the bright idea of paying workers enough to buy cars.* ADJ: usu ADJ n = clever 5 If someone looks or sounds **bright**, they look or sound cheerful and lively. ❑ *The boy was so bright and animated... 'May I help you?' said a bright American voice over the telephone.* ADJ = cheerful, lively ♦ **bright|ly** *He smiled brightly as Ben approached.* ADV: ADV with v 6 If the future is **bright**, it is likely to be pleasant or successful. ❑ *Both had successful careers and the future looked bright... There are much brighter prospects for a comprehensive settlement than before.* ADJ = promising ≠ bleak 7 If you **look on the bright side**, you try to be cheerful about a bad situation by thinking of some advantages that could result from it, or thinking that it is not as bad as it could have been. PHRASE: V inflects

**bright|en** /braɪtᵊn/ **(brightens, brightening, brightened)** 1 If someone **brightens** or their face **brightens**, they suddenly look happier. ❑ *Seeing him, she seemed to brighten a little.* VERB V ♦ **Brighten up** means the same as **brighten**. ❑ *He brightened up a bit.* PHRASAL VERB V P 2 If your eyes **brighten**, you suddenly look interested or excited. ❑ *His eyes brightened and he laughed... Her tearful eyes brightened with interest.* VERB V V *with* n 3 If someone or something **brightens** a place, they make it more colourful and attractive. ❑ *Tubs planted with wallflowers brightened the area outside the door.* VERB V n ♦ **Brighten up** means the same as **brighten**. ❑ *David spotted the pink silk lampshade in a shop and thought it would brighten up the room.* PHRASAL VERB V P n (not pron) Also V n P 4 If someone or something **brightens** a situation or the situation **brightens**, it becomes more pleasant, enjoyable, or favourable. ❑ *That does not do much to brighten the prospects of kids in the city... It is undeniable that the economic picture is brightening.* VERB = improve V n V ♦ **Brighten up** means the same as **brighten**. ❑ *His cheerful face brightens up the dullest of days.* PHRASAL VERB V P n Also V P 5 When a light **brightens** a place or when a place **brightens**, it becomes brighter or lighter. ❑ *The sky above the ridge of mountains brightened... The late afternoon sun brightened the interior of the church.* VERB V V n 6 If the weather **brightens**, it becomes less cloudy or rainy, and the sun starts to shine. ❑ *By early afternoon the weather had brightened.* VERB V ♦ **Brighten up** means the same as **brighten**. ❑ *Hopefully it will brighten up, or we'll be coming back early.* PHRASAL VERB *it* V P

**bright lights** If someone talks about **the bright lights**, they are referring to life in a big city where you can do a lot of enjoyable and exciting things and be successful. ❑ *The bright lights of Hollywood beckon many.* N-PLURAL: *the* N

**bright spark** **(bright sparks)** If you say that some **bright spark** had a particular idea or did something, you mean that their idea or action was clever, or that it seemed clever but was silly in some way. [BRIT, INFORMAL] ❑ *'Why not give out one of the cybercafe's e-mail addresses?' suggested one bright spark... Some bright spark turned the heating off last night!* N-COUNT

**brill** /brɪl/ If you say that something is **brill**, you are very pleased about it or think that it is very good. [BRIT, INFORMAL] ❑ *What a brill idea!* ADJ = wonderful, great

**bril|liant** /brɪliənt/ ◆◇◇ 1 A **brilliant** person, idea, or performance is extremely clever or skilful. ❑ *She had a brilliant mind... It was his brilliant performance in 'My Left Foot' that established his reputation.* ADJ: usu ADJ n ♦ **bril|liant|ly** *It is a very high quality production, brilliantly written and acted.* ADV ♦ **bril|liance** *He was a deeply serious musician who had shown his brilliance very early.* N-UNCOUNT: oft with poss 2 You can say that something is **brilliant** when you are very pleased about it or think that it is very good. [mainly BRIT, INFORMAL, SPOKEN] ❑ *If you get a chance to see the show, do go – it's brilliant... My sister's given me this brilliant book.* ADJ = great ≠ awful ♦ **bril|liant|ly** *It's extremely hard working together but on the whole it works brilliantly and we're still good friends.* ADV: ADV with v, ADV adj/adv 3 A **brilliant** career or success is very successful. ❑ *He served four years in prison, emerging to find his brilliant career in ruins... The raid was a brilliant success.* ADJ: usu ADJ n ♦ **bril|liant|ly** *The strategy worked brilliantly.* ADV 4 A **brilliant** colour is extremely bright. ❑ *...a brilliant white open-necked shirt.* ADJ: ADJ n ♦ **bril|liant|ly** *Many of the patterns show brilliantly coloured flowers.* ADV: ADV adj/-ed ♦ **bril|liance** *...an iridescent blue butterfly in all its brilliance.* N-UNCOUNT 5 You describe light, or something that reflects light, as **brilliant** when it shines very brightly. ❑ *The event was held in brilliant sunshine.* ADJ ♦ **bril|liant|ly** *It's a brilliantly sunny morning.* ADV ♦ **bril|liance** *His eyes became accustomed to the dark after the brilliance of the sun outside.* N-UNCOUNT

**brim** /brɪm/ **(brims, brimming, brimmed)** 1 The **brim** of a hat is the wide part that sticks outwards at the bottom. ❑ *Rain dripped from the brim of his baseball cap. ...a flat black hat with a wide brim.* N-COUNT: oft N of n, adj N ♦ **-brimmed** *...a floppy-brimmed hat.* COMB in ADJ: usu ADJ n 2 If someone or something **is brimming with** a particular quality, they are full of that quality. ❑ *England are brimming with confidence after two straight wins in the tournament.* VERB: usu cont, V with n ♦ **Brim over** means the same as **brim**. ❑ *Her heart brimmed over with love and adoration for Charles.* PHRASAL VERB, V P with n 3 When your eyes **are brimming with** tears, they are full of fluid because you are upset, although you are not actually crying. ❑ *Michael looked at him imploringly, eyes brimming with tears.* Also V P, VERB, V with n ♦ **Brim over** means the same as **brim**. ❑ *When she saw me, her eyes brimmed over with tears and she could not speak.* PHRASAL VERB, V P with n 4 If something **brims with** particular things, it is packed full of them. ❑ *The flowerbeds brim with a mixture of lilies and roses.* Also V P, VERB, V with n 5 If something, especially a container, **is filled to the brim** or **full to the brim with** something, it is filled right up to the top. ❑ *Richard filled her glass right up to the brim.* PHRASE: V inflects

♦ **brim over** → see **brim 2, 3**.

**brim|ful** /brɪmfʊl/ Someone who is **brimful of** an emotion or quality feels or seems full of it. An object or place that is **brimful of** something is full of it. ❑ *She was brimful of energy and enthusiasm... The United States is brimful with highly paid doctors.* ADJ: v-link ADJ of/with n = full

**brim|stone** /brɪmstoʊn/ 1 **Brimstone** is the same as **sulphur**. [OLD-FASHIONED] N-UNCOUNT 2 When people talk about **fire and brimstone**, they are referring to hell and how they think people are punished there after death. [LITERARY] PHRASE

**brine** /braɪn/ **(brines) Brine** is salty water, especially salty water that is used for preserving food. ❑ *Soak the walnuts in brine for four or five days.* N-MASS

**bring** /brɪŋ/ **(brings, bringing, brought)** ◆◆◆ 1 If you **bring** someone or something with you when you come to a place, they come with you or you have them with you. ❑ *Remember to bring an apron or an old shirt to protect your clothes... Come to my party and bring a girl with you... Someone went upstairs and brought down a huge kettle... My father brought home a book for me.* VERB: V n, V n, V n with adv, V n for n, with adv 2 If you **bring** something somewhere, you move it there. ❑ *Reaching into her pocket, she brought out a cigarette... Her mother brought her hands up to her face.* VERB: V n with adv, V n with adv, Also V n prep 3 If you **bring** something that someone wants or needs, you get it for them or carry it to them. ❑ *He poured a brandy for Dena and brought it to her... The stewardess kindly brought me a blanket.* VERB: V n to/for n, V n n, Also V n 4 To **bring** something or someone to a place or position means to cause them to come to the place or move into that position. ❑ *I told you about what brought me here... Edna Leitch survived a gas blast which brought her home crashing down on top of her.* VERB: V n prep/adv, V n -ing 5 If you **bring** something new **to** a place or group of people, you introduce it to that place or cause those people to hear or know about it. ❑ *...the drive to bring art to the public.* VERB: V n to n 6 To **bring** someone or something into a particular state or condition means to cause them to be in that state or condition. ❑ *He brought the car to a stop in front of the square... His work as a historian brought him into conflict with the political establishment... They have brought down income taxes.* VERB: V n prep, V n prep, V n with adv 7 If something **brings** a particular feeling, situation, or quality, it makes people experience it or have it. ❑ *He called on the United States to play a more effective role in bringing peace to the region... Banks have brought trouble on themselves by lending rashly... He brought to the job not just considerable experience but passionate enthusiasm... Her three children brought her joy.* VERB: V n to/on/from n, V n to/on/from n, V to n n, V n n 8 If a period of time **brings** a particular thing, it happens during that time. ❑ *For Sandro, the new year brought disaster... We don't know what the future will bring.* VERB: V n, V n 9 If you **bring** a legal action **against** someone or **bring** them **to** trial, you officially accuse them of doing something illegal. ❑ *He campaigned relentlessly to bring charges of corruption against former members of the government... The ship's captain and crew may be brought to trial and even sent to prison.* VERB: V n against n, be V-ed to n 10 If a television or radio programme **is brought to** you **by** an organization, they make it, broadcast it, or pay for it to be made or broadcast. [mainly BRIT] ❑ *You're listening to Science in Action, brought to you by the BBC World Service... We'll be bringing you all the details of the day's events.* VERB: be V-ed to n by n, V n n

✓ in AM, usually use **sponsor**

11 When you are talking, you can say that something **brings** you **to** a particular point in order to indicate that you have now reached that point and are going to talk about a new subject. ❑ *And that brings us to the end of this special report from Germany.* VERB: V n to n 12 If you cannot **bring yourself to** do something, you cannot do it because you find it too upsetting, embarrassing, or disgusting. ❑ *It is all very tragic and I am afraid I just cannot bring myself to talk about it at the moment.* VERB: with brd-neg, V pron-refl to-inf 13 to **bring** something **alive** → see **alive**. to **bring** something **to bear** → see **bear**. to **bring the house down** → see **house**. to **bring up the rear** → see **rear**.

♦ **bring about** To **bring** something **about** means to cause it to happen. ❑ *The only way they can bring about political change is by putting pressure on the country.* PHRASAL VERB = cause, V P n (not pron), Also V n P

♦ **bring along** If you **bring** someone or something **along**, you bring them with you when you come to a place. ❑ *They brought along Laura Jane in a pram... Dad brought a notebook along to the beach, in case he was seized by sudden inspiration.* PHRASAL VERB, V P n (not pron), V n P

♦ **bring back** 1 Something that **brings back** a memory makes you think about it. ❑ *Your article brought back sad memories for me... Talking about it brought it all back.* PHRASAL VERB, V P n (not pron), V n P 2 When people **bring back** a practice or fashion that existed at an earlier time, they introduce it again. ❑ *The House of Commons is to debate once again whether to bring back the death penalty.* PHRASAL VERB = revive, V P n (not pron), Also V n P

♦ **bring down** 1 When people or events **bring down** a government or ruler, they cause the government or ruler to lose power. ❑ *They were threatening to bring down the government by withdrawing from the ruling coalition... His challenge to Mrs Thatcher brought her down.* PHRASAL VERB = topple, V P n (not pron), V n P 2 If someone or something **brings down** a person or aeroplane, they cause them to fall, usually by shooting them. PHRASAL VERB

❑ *Military historians may never know what brought down the jet.* V P n (not pron) Also V n P

♦ **bring forward** [1] If you **bring forward** a meeting or event, you arrange for it to take place at an earlier date or time than had been planned. ❑ *He had to bring forward an 11 o'clock meeting so that he could get to the funeral on time.* PHRASAL VERB = put forward ≠ put back V P n (not pron) Also V n P [2] If you **bring forward** an argument or proposal, you state it so that people can consider it. ❑ *The Government will bring forward several proposals for legislation.* PHRASAL VERB = put forward V P n Also V n P

♦ **bring in** [1] When a government or organization **brings in** a new law or system, they introduce it. ❑ *The government brought in a controversial law under which it could take any land it wanted.* PHRASAL VERB = introduce V P n (not pron) Also V n P [2] Someone or something that **brings in** money makes it or earns it. ❑ *I have three part-time jobs, which bring in about £14,000 a year.* PHRASAL VERB V P n Also V n P [3] If you **bring in** someone from outside a team or organization, you invite them to do a job or join in an activity or discussion. ❑ *The firm decided to bring in a new management team.* PHRASAL VERB = call in V P n (not pron) Also V n P

♦ **bring off** If you **bring off** something difficult, you do it successfully. ❑ *They were about to bring off an even bigger coup... He thought his book would change society. But he didn't bring it off.* PHRASAL VERB = pull off V P n (not pron) V n P

♦ **bring on** If something **brings on** an illness, pain, or feeling, especially one that you often suffer from, it causes you to have it. ❑ *Severe shock can bring on an attack of acne... Bob died of a heart attack, brought on by his lifestyle.* PHRASAL VERB V P n (not pron) V-ed P Also V n P

♦ **bring out** [1] When a person or company **brings out** a new product, especially a new book or CD, they produce it and put it on sale. ❑ *A journalist all his life, he's now brought out a book.* PHRASAL VERB V P n (not pron) Also V n P [2] Something that **brings out** a particular kind of behaviour or feeling in you causes you to show it, especially when it is something you do not normally show. ❑ *He is totally dedicated and brings out the best in his pupils.* PHRASAL VERB V P n (not pron) Also V n P

♦ **bring up** [1] When someone **brings up** a child, they look after it until it is an adult. If someone **has been brought up** in a certain place or with certain attitudes, they grew up in that place or were taught those attitudes when they were growing up. ❑ *She brought up four children... His grandmother and his father brought him up... We'd been brought up to think that borrowing money was bad... I was brought up a Methodist.* PHRASAL VERB = raise V P n V n P *be* V-ed P to-inf *be* V-ed P n [2] If you **bring up** a particular subject, you introduce it into a discussion or conversation. ❑ *He brought up a subject rarely raised during the course of this campaign... Why are you bringing it up now?* PHRASAL VERB = raise V P n (not pron) V n P [3] If someone **brings up** food or wind, food or air is forced up from their stomach through their mouth. ❑ *It's hard for the baby to bring up wind.* PHRASAL VERB V P n

**bring-and-buy sale** **(bring-and-buy sales)** A **bring-and-buy sale** is an informal sale to raise money for a charity or other organization. People who come to the sale bring things to be sold and buy things that other people have brought. [BRIT] N-COUNT

**bring|er** /brɪŋəʳ/ **(bringers)** A **bringer of** something is someone who brings or provides it. [LITERARY] ❑ *He was the bringer of good news.* N-COUNT: with supp, usu N *of* n

**brink** /brɪŋk/ If you are **on the brink of** something, usually something important, terrible, or exciting, you are just about to do it or experience it. ❑ *Their economy is teetering on the brink of collapse... Failure to communicate had brought the two nations to the brink of war.* N-SING: usu *on/to/from the* N *of* n = verge

**brink|man|ship** /brɪŋkmənʃɪp/ **Brinkmanship** is a method of behaviour, especially in politics, in which you deliberately get into dangerous situations which could result in disaster but which could also bring success. [JOURNALISM] ❑ *There is a lot of political brinkmanship involved in this latest development.* N-UNCOUNT

**bri|oche** /briɒʃ/ **(brioches)** **Brioche** is a kind of sweet bread. ❑ *I'll have coffee and a brioche.* N-VAR

**brisk** /brɪsk/ **(brisker, briskest)** [1] A **brisk** activity or action is done quickly and in an energetic way. ❑ *Taking a brisk walk can often induce a feeling of well-being... The horse broke into a brisk trot.* ADJ: usu ADJ n ♦ **brisk|ly** *Eve walked briskly down the corridor to her son's room.* ADV: ADV with v ♦ **brisk|ness** *With determined briskness, Amy stood up and put their cups back on the tray.* N-UNCOUNT [2] If trade or business is **brisk**, things are being sold very quickly and a lot of money is being made. [BUSINESS] ❑ *Vendors were doing a brisk trade in souvenirs.* ADJ = good ♦ **brisk|ly** *A trader said gold sold briskly on the local market.* ADV: ADV after v [3] If the weather is **brisk**, it is cold and fresh. ❑ *The breeze was cool, brisk and invigorating.* ADJ = bracing [4] Someone who is **brisk** behaves in a busy, confident way which shows that they want to get things done quickly. ❑ *The Chief summoned me downstairs. He was brisk and businesslike.* ADJ = business-like ♦ **brisk|ly** *'Anyhow,' she added briskly, 'it's none of my business.'* ADV: ADV with v

**bris|ket** /brɪskɪt/ **Brisket** is a cut of beef that comes from the breast of the cow. N-UNCOUNT

**bris|tle** /brɪsᵊl/ **(bristles)** [1] **Bristles** are the short hairs that grow on a man's chin after he has shaved. The hairs on the top of a man's head can also be called **bristles** when they are cut very short. ❑ *...two days' growth of bristles.* N-COUNT: usu pl = stubble [2] The **bristles** of a brush are the thick hairs or hair-like pieces of plastic which are attached to it. ➔ See picture on page 1709. ❑ *As soon as the bristles on your toothbrush begin to wear, throw it out.* N-COUNT [3] **Bristles** are thick, strong animal hairs that feel hard and rough. ❑ *It has a short stumpy tail covered with bristles.* N-COUNT

**bris|tling** /brɪslɪŋ/ [1] **Bristling** means thick, hairy, and rough. It is used to describe things such as moustaches, beards, or eyebrows. ❑ *...a bristling white moustache.* ADJ: ADJ n [2] If you describe someone's attitude as **bristling**, you are emphasizing that it is full of energy and enthusiasm. ❑ *...bristling, exuberant, rock'n'roll.* ADJ: ADJ n [emphasis]

**bris|tly** /brɪsli/ [1] **Bristly** hair is thick and rough. ❑ *His bristly red hair was standing on end.* ADJ: usu ADJ n = stubbly [2] If a man's chin is **bristly**, it is covered with bristles because he has not shaved recently. ❑ *...the giant's bristly cheek.* ADJ

**Brit** /brɪt/ **(Brits)** British people are sometimes referred to as **Brits**. [INFORMAL] ❑ *Holiday mad Brits are packing their buckets and spades and heading for the sun.* N-COUNT

**Brit|ish** /brɪtɪʃ/ [1] **British** means belonging or relating to the United Kingdom, or to its people or culture. ADJ [2] **The British** are the people of Great Britain. N-PLURAL

**Brit|ish Asian** **(British Asians)** A **British Asian** person is someone of Indian, Pakistani, or Bangladeshi origin who has grown up in Britain. ADJ: usu ADJ n = Anglo-Asian ♦ A **British Asian** is someone who is British Asian. N-COUNT = Anglo-Asian

**Brit|ish|er** /brɪtɪʃə/ **(Britishers)** In American English or old-fashioned British English, British people are sometimes informally referred to as **Britishers**. N-COUNT

**Brit|ish Sum|mer Time** **British Summer Time** is a period in the spring and summer during which the clocks are put forward, so that people can have an extra hour of daylight in the evening. [BRIT] ❑ *When we put the clocks forward in March we go into British Summer Time.* N-UNCOUNT

✔ in AM, use **daylight saving time**

**Brit|on** /brɪtᵊn/ **(Britons)** A **Briton** is a British citizen, or a person of British origin. [FORMAL] ❑ *The role is played by seventeen-year-old Briton Jane March.* N-COUNT

**Brit|pop** /brɪtpɒp/ **Britpop** is a type of pop music made by British bands. It was especially popular in the mid-1990s. ❑ *...Oasis and other Britpop bands.* N-UNCOUNT

**brit|tle** /brɪtᵊl/ [1] An object or substance that is **brittle** is hard but easily broken. ❑ *Pine is brittle and breaks. ...the dry, brittle ends of the hair.* ADJ [2] If ADJ you describe a situation, relationship, or someone's mood as **brittle**, you mean that it is unstable, and may easily change. ❑ *These incidents suggest the peace in Northern Ireland is still brittle.* = *fragile*

**broach** /broʊtʃ/ **(broaches, broaching, broached)** When you **broach** a subject, especially a sensitive one, you mention it in order to start a discussion on it. ❑ *Eventually I broached the subject of her early life.* VERB; V n

**broad** /brɔːd/ **(broader, broadest)** ◆◆◇ 1 Something that is **broad** is wide. ❑ *His shoulders were broad and his waist narrow... The hills rise green and sheer above the broad river. ...a broad expanse of green lawn.* ADJ ≠ narrow 2 A **broad** smile is one in which your mouth is stretched very wide because you are very pleased or amused. ❑ *He greeted them with a wave and a broad smile.* ADJ: usu ADJ n ♦ **broad|ly** *Charles grinned broadly.* ADV 3 You use **broad** to describe something that includes a large number of different things or people. ❑ *A broad range of issues was discussed. ...a broad coalition of workers, peasants, students and middle class professionals.* ADJ: usu ADJ n = wide ≠ narrow ♦ **broad|ly** *This gives children a more broadly based education.* ADV: ADV with v 4 You use **broad** to describe a word or meaning which covers or refers to a wide range of different things. ❑ *The term Wissenschaft has a much broader meaning than the English word 'science'. ...restructuring in the broad sense of the word.* ADJ: usu ADJ n = general ≠ narrow ♦ **broad|ly** *We define education very broadly and students can study any aspect of its consequences for society.* ADV: ADV with v 5 You use **broad** to describe a feeling or opinion that is shared by many people, or by people of many different kinds. ❑ *The agreement won broad support in the US Congress. ...a film with broad appeal.* ADJ: ADJ n = wide-spread ≠ limited ♦ **broad|ly** *The new law has been broadly welcomed by road safety organisations.* ADV: ADV with v 6 A **broad** description or idea is general rather than detailed. ❑ *These documents provided a broad outline of the Society's development... In broad terms, this means that the closer you live to a school, the more likely it is that your child will get a place there.* ADJ: usu ADJ n = general ♦ **broad|ly** *There are, broadly speaking, three ways in which this is done... Broadly, it makes connections between ideas about healing and how they link to plants.* ADV: ADV with v, ADV with cl/group 7 A **broad** hint is a very obvious hint. ❑ *They've been giving broad hints about what to expect.* ADJ: ADJ n ≠ subtle ♦ **broad|ly** *He hinted broadly that he would like to come.* ADV 8 A **broad** accent is strong and noticeable. ❑ *...a Briton who spoke in a broad Yorkshire accent.* ADJ 9 → See also **broadly**. **in broad daylight** → see **daylight**.

**B-road** **(B-roads)** also **B road.** A **B-road** is a minor road. [BRIT] N-COUNT

**broad|band** /brɔːdbænd/ **Broadband** is a method of sending many electronic messages at the same time, using a wide range of frequencies. [COMPUTING] ❑ *The two companies said they planned to develop new broadband services for customers in the UK.* N-UNCOUNT: oft N n

**broad bean** **(broad beans)** **Broad beans** are flat round beans that are light green in colour and are eaten as a vegetable. [mainly BRIT] N-COUNT: usu pl

✔ in AM, use **fava beans**

**broad-brush** also **broad brush.** A **broad-brush** approach, strategy, or solution deals with a problem in a general way rather than concentrating on details. ❑ *He's giving a broad brush approach to the subject.* ADJ: usu ADJ n

**broad|cast** /brɔːdkɑːst, -kæst/ **(broadcasts, broadcasting)** ◆◇◇

✔ The form **broadcast** is used in the present tense and is the past tense and past participle of the verb.

1 A **broadcast** is a programme, performance, or speech on the radio or on television. ❑ *In a broadcast on state radio the government also announced that it was willing to resume peace negotiations.* N-COUNT = programme 2 To **broadcast** a programme means to send it out by radio waves, so that it can be heard on the radio or seen on television. ❑ *The concert will be broadcast live on television and radio... CNN also broadcasts in Europe.* VERB = transmit; be V-ed adv/prep; V; Also V n

**broad|cast|er** /brɔːdkɑːstəʳ, -kæst-/ **(broadcasters)** A **broadcaster** is someone who gives talks or takes part in interviews and discussions on radio or television programmes. N-COUNT

**broad|cast|ing** /brɔːdkɑːstɪŋ, -kæst-/ **Broadcasting** is the making and sending out of television and radio programmes. ❑ *If this happens it will change the face of religious broadcasting. ...the state broadcasting organisation.* ◆◇◇ N-UNCOUNT

**broad|en** /brɔːdᵊn/ **(broadens, broadening, broadened)** 1 When something **broadens**, it becomes wider. ❑ *The trails broadened into roads... The smile broadened to a grin.* VERB = widen; V into/to n 2 When you **broaden** something such as your experience or popularity or when it **broadens**, the number of things or people that it includes becomes greater. ❑ *We must broaden our appeal... The political spectrum has broadened.* VERB; V n; V

**broad|ly** /brɔːdli/ You can use **broadly** to indicate that something is generally true. ❑ *The President broadly got what he wanted out of his meeting... The idea that software is capable of any task is broadly true in theory.* → See also **broad**. ADV: ADV with cl = largely

**broad|ly based**

✔ in BRIT, also use **broadly-based**

Something that is **broadly based** involves many different kinds of things or people. ❑ *... a broadly-based political movement for democracy.* ADJ: usu ADJ n

**broad-minded** also **broadminded.** If you describe someone as **broad-minded**, you approve of them because they are willing to accept types of behaviour which other people consider immoral. ❑ *...a fair and broad-minded man.* ADJ [approval] ≠ narrow-minded

**broad|sheet** /brɔːdʃiːt/ **(broadsheets)** A **broadsheet** is a newspaper that is printed on large sheets of paper. Broadsheets are generally considered to be more serious than other newspapers. Compare **tabloid**. N-COUNT

**broad|side** /brɔːdsaɪd/ **(broadsides)** 1 A **broadside** is a strong written or spoken attack on a person or institution. ❑ *The Social Democratic leader launched a broadside against both monetary and political union.* N-COUNT: oft N against n 2 If a ship is **broadside to** something, it has its longest side facing in the direction of that thing. [TECHNICAL] ❑ *The ship was moored broadside to the pier.* ADV: ADV after v, be ADV, oft ADV on, ADV to n

**bro|cade** /brəkeɪd/ **(brocades)** **Brocade** is a thick, expensive material, often made of silk, with a raised pattern on it. ❑ *...a brocade waistcoat.* N-MASS

**broc|co|li** /brɒkəli/ **Broccoli** is a vegetable with green stalks and green or purple tops. → See picture on page 1712. N-UNCOUNT

**bro|chure** /broʊʃəʳ, AM broʊʃʊr/ **(brochures)** A **brochure** is a magazine or thin book with pictures that gives you information about a product or service. ❑ *...travel brochures.* N-COUNT

**brogue** /broʊg/ **(brogues)** 1 If someone has a **brogue**, they speak English with a strong accent, especially Irish or Scots. ❑ *Gill speaks in a quiet Irish brogue.* N-SING 2 **Brogues** are thick leather shoes which have an elaborate pattern punched into the leather. N-COUNT: usu pl

**broil** /brɔɪl/ **(broils, broiling, broiled)** When you **broil** food, you cook it using very strong heat directly above or below it. [AM] ❑ *I'll broil the lobster. ...broiled chicken.* VERB; V n; V-ed

✔ in BRIT, use **grill**

**broil|er** /brɔɪləʳ/ **(broilers)** A **broiler** is a part of a stove which produces strong heat and cooks food placed underneath it. [AM] N-COUNT

✔ in BRIT, use **grill**

**broil|ing** /brɔɪlɪŋ/ If the weather is **broiling**, it is very hot. [AM, INFORMAL] ❑ *...the broiling midday sun.* ADJ = sweltering ≠ freezing

**broke** /broʊk/ 1 **Broke** is the past tense of **break**. 2 If you are **broke**, you have no money. ADJ:

[INFORMAL] ❑ *What do you mean, I've got enough money? I'm as broke as you are.* v-link ADJ

**PHRASES** 3 If a company or person **goes broke**, they lose money and are unable to continue in business or to pay their debts. [INFORMAL, BUSINESS] ❑ *Balton went broke twice in his career.* PHRASE: V inflects 4 If you **go for broke**, you take the most extreme or risky of the possible courses of action in order to try and achieve success. [INFORMAL] ❑ *It was a sharp disagreement about whether to go for broke or whether to compromise.* PHRASE: V inflects ≠play safe

**bro|ken** /broʊkən/ 1 **Broken** is the past participle of **break**. 2 A **broken** line is not continuous but has gaps or spaces in it. ❑ *A broken blue line means the course of a waterless valley.* ADJ: ADJ n = dotted 3 You can use **broken** to describe a marriage that has ended in divorce, or a home in which the parents of the family are divorced, when you think this is a sad or bad thing. ❑ *She spoke for the first time about the traumas of a broken marriage... Children from broken homes are more likely to leave home before the age of 18.* ADJ: ADJ n [disapproval] 4 If someone talks in **broken** English, for example, or in **broken** French, they speak slowly and make a lot of mistakes because they do not know the language very well. ❑ *Eric could only respond in broken English.* ADJ: ADJ n ≠fluent, perfect

**broken-down** A **broken-down** vehicle or machine no longer works because it has something wrong with it. ❑ *...a broken-down car.* ADJ: usu ADJ n

**broken-hearted** Someone who is **broken-hearted** is very sad and upset because they have had a serious disappointment. ADJ

**bro|ker** /broʊkəʳ/ (**brokers, brokering, brokered**) ◆◇◇ 1 A **broker** is a person whose job is to buy and sell shares, foreign money, or goods for other people. [BUSINESS] N-COUNT 2 If a country or government **brokers** an agreement, a ceasefire, or a round of talks, they try to negotiate or arrange it. ❑ *The United Nations brokered a peace in Mogadishu at the end of March.* VERB = negotiate; V n

**bro|ker|age** /broʊkərɪdʒ/ (**brokerages**) A **brokerage** or a **brokerage** firm is a company of brokers. [BUSINESS] ❑ *...Japan's four biggest brokerages.* N-COUNT: usu N n

**brol|ly** /brɒli/ (**brollies**) A **brolly** is the same as an **umbrella**. [BRIT, INFORMAL] N-COUNT

**bro|mide** /broʊmaɪd/ (**bromides**) 1 **Bromide** is a drug which used to be given to people to calm their nerves when they were worried or upset. ❑ *...a dose of bromide.* N-MASS 2 A **bromide** is a comment which is intended to calm someone down when they are angry, but which has been expressed so often that it has become boring and meaningless. [FORMAL] ❑ *The meeting produced the usual bromides about macroeconomic policy, third-world debt and the environment.* N-COUNT = platitude

**bron|chial** /brɒŋkiəl/ **Bronchial** means affecting or concerned with the bronchial tubes. [MEDICAL] ❑ *She suffers from bronchial asthma.* ADJ: ADJ n

**bron|chial tube** (**bronchial tubes**) Your **bronchial tubes** are the two tubes which connect your windpipe to your lungs. [MEDICAL] N-COUNT: usu pl

**bron|chi|tis** /brɒŋkaɪtɪs/ **Bronchitis** is an illness like a very bad cough, in which your bronchial tubes become sore and infected. ❑ *He was in bed with bronchitis.* N-UNCOUNT

**bron|co** /brɒŋkoʊ/ (**broncos**) In the western United States, especially in the 19th century, a wild horse was sometimes referred to as a **bronco**. ❑ *...two cowboys riding bucking broncos.* N-COUNT

**bronze** /brɒnz/ 1 **Bronze** is a yellowish-brown metal which is a mixture of copper and tin. ❑ *...a bronze statue of Giorgi Dimitrov.* N-UNCOUNT 2 A **bronze** is a **bronze medal**. N-COUNT 3 Something that is **bronze** is yellowish-brown in colour. ❑ *...huge bronze chrysanthemums.* COLOUR

**Bronze Age** The **Bronze Age** was a period of time which began when people started making things from bronze about 4,000–6,000 years ago. N-PROPER: the N

**bronzed** /brɒnzd/ Someone who is **bronzed** is attractively brown because they have been in the sun. ❑ *He's bronzed from a short holiday in California.* ADJ = tanned

**bronze med|al** (**bronze medals**) A **bronze medal** is a medal made of bronze or bronze-coloured metal that is given as a prize to the person who comes third in a competition, especially a sports contest. N-COUNT

**brooch** /broʊtʃ/ (**brooches**) A **brooch** is a small piece of jewellery which has a pin at the back so it can be fastened on a dress, blouse, or coat. N-COUNT

**brood** /bruːd/ (**broods, brooding, brooded**) 1 A **brood** is a group of baby birds that were born at the same time to the same mother. N-COUNT: usu with supp 2 You can refer to someone's young children as their **brood** when you want to emphasize that there are a lot of them. ❑ *...a large brood of children.* N-COUNT: usu sing [emphasis] 3 If someone **broods** over something, they think about it a lot, seriously and often unhappily. ❑ *She constantly broods about her family... I continued to brood. Would he always be like this?* VERB; V over/on/about n; V

**brood|ing** /bruːdɪŋ/ 1 **Brooding** is used to describe an atmosphere or feeling that makes you feel anxious or slightly afraid. [LITERARY] ❑ *The same heavy, brooding silence descended on them.* ADJ: usu ADJ n 2 If someone's expression or appearance is **brooding**, they look as if they are thinking deeply and seriously about something, especially something that is making them unhappy. [LITERARY] ❑ *She kissed him and gazed into his dark, brooding eyes.* ADJ: usu ADJ n

**broody** /bruːdi/ 1 You say that someone is **broody** when they are thinking a lot about something in an unhappy way. ❑ *He became very withdrawn and broody.* ADJ 2 A **broody** hen is ready to lay or sit on eggs. ADJ 3 If you describe a young woman as **broody**, you mean that she wants to have a baby and she keeps thinking about it. [BRIT, INFORMAL] ADJ: usu v-link ADJ

**brook** /brʊk/ (**brooks, brooking, brooked**) 1 A **brook** is a small stream. N-COUNT 2 If someone in a position of authority will **brook no** interference or opposition, they will not accept any interference or opposition from others. ❑ *From childhood on, she'd had a plan of action, one that would brook no interference.* VERB = tolerate, allow; V n

**broom** /bruːm/ (**brooms**) 1 A **broom** is a kind of brush with a long handle. You use a broom for sweeping the floor. N-COUNT 2 **Broom** is a wild bush with a lot of tiny yellow flowers. N-UNCOUNT

**broom|stick** /bruːmstɪk/ (**broomsticks**) 1 A **broomstick** is an old-fashioned broom which has a bunch of small sticks at the end. N-COUNT 2 A **broomstick** is the handle of a broom. N-COUNT

**Bros.** **Bros.** is an abbreviation for **brothers**. It is usually used as part of the name of a company. [BUSINESS] ❑ *...Lazard Bros. of New York.*

**broth** /brɒθ, AM brɔːθ/ (**broths**) **Broth** is a kind of soup. It usually has vegetables or rice in it. N-VAR

**broth|el** /brɒθəl/ (**brothels**) A **brothel** is a building where men can go to pay to have sex with prostitutes. N-COUNT

**broth|er** /brʌðəʳ/ (**brothers**) ◆◆◆

> The old-fashioned form **brethren** is still sometimes used as the plural for meanings 2 and 3.

1 Your **brother** is a boy or a man who has the same parents as you. ❑ *Oh, so you're Peter's younger brother... Have you got any brothers and sisters?* → See also **half-brother**, **stepbrother**. N-COUNT: oft poss N 2 You can describe a man as your **brother** if he belongs to the same race, religion, country, profession, or trade union as you, or if he has similar ideas to you. ❑ *He told reporters he'd come to be with his Latvian brothers.* N-COUNT: usu poss N 3 **Brother** is a title given to a man who belongs to a religious community such as a monastery. ❑ *...Brother Otto. ...the Christian Brothers* N-TITLE; N-COUNT; N-VOC

*community which owns the castle.* [4] **Brothers** is used in the names of some companies and shops. ❑ *...the film company Warner Brothers.* N-IN-NAMES

**brother|hood** /brʌðəʳhʊd/ **(brotherhoods)** [1] **Brotherhood** is the affection and loyalty that you feel for people who you have something in common with. ❑ *People threw flowers into the river between the two countries as a symbolic act of brotherhood.* N-UNCOUNT [2] A **brotherhood** is an organization whose members all have the same political aims and beliefs or the same job or profession. ❑ *...a secret international brotherhood.* N-COUNT: usu with supp

**brother-in-law** **(brothers-in-law)** Someone's **brother-in-law** is the brother of their husband or wife, or the man who is married to their sister. N-COUNT: usu poss N

**broth|er|ly** /brʌðəʳli/ A man's **brotherly** feelings are feelings of love and loyalty which you expect a brother to show. ❑ *...family loyalty and brotherly love... He gave her a brief, brotherly kiss.* ADJ: usu ADJ n

**brought** /brɔːt/ **Brought** is the past tense and past participle of **bring**.

**brou|ha|ha** /bruːhɑːhɑː/ A **brouhaha** is an excited and critical fuss or reaction to something. [mainly JOURNALISM] ❑ *...the recent brouhaha over a congressional pay raise.* N-SING: also no det [disapproval]

**brow** /braʊ/ **(brows)** [1] Your **brow** is your forehead. ❑ *He wiped his brow with the back of his hand.* N-COUNT: usu poss N = forehead • to **knit** your **brow** → see **knit**. [2] Your **brows** are your eyebrows. ❑ *He had thick brown hair and shaggy brows.* N-COUNT: usu pl [3] The **brow of** a hill is the top part of it. ❑ *He was on the look-out just below the brow of the hill.* N-COUNT: usu N *of* n

**brow|beat** /braʊbiːt/ **(browbeats, browbeating, browbeaten)**

> The form **browbeat** is used in the present tense and is also the past tense.

If someone tries to **browbeat** you, they try to force you to do what they want. ❑ *...attempts to deceive, con, or browbeat the voters... When I backed out of the 100 metres, an older kid tried to browbeat me into it.* VERB; V n; V n *into* n ♦ **brow|beat|en** *...the browbeaten employees.* ADJ

**brown** /braʊn/ **(browner, brownest, browns, browning, browned)** ◆◆◆ [1] Something that is **brown** is the colour of earth or of wood. ❑ *...her deep brown eyes... The stairs are decorated in golds and earthy browns.* COLOUR [2] You can describe a white-skinned person as **brown** when they have been sitting in the sun until their skin has become darker than usual. ❑ *I don't want to be really really brown, just have a nice light golden colour.* ADJ: usu v-link ADJ = tanned [3] A **brown** person is someone who belongs to a race of people who have brown-coloured skins. ❑ *...a slim brown man with a speckled turban.* ADJ: usu ADJ n [4] **Brown** is used to describe grains that have not had their outer layers removed, and foods made from these grains. ❑ *...brown bread. ...spicy tomato sauce served over a bed of brown rice.* ADJ: usu ADJ n ≠ white [5] When food **browns** or when you **brown** food, you cook it, usually for a short time on a high flame. ❑ *Cook for ten minutes until the sugar browns... He browned the chicken in a frying pan.* VERB; V; V n

**browned off** If you say that you are **browned off**, you mean that you are annoyed and depressed. [mainly BRIT, INFORMAL] ❑ *Sorry, I'm just thoroughly browned off.* ADJ: usu v-link ADJ = fed up

**brown|field** /braʊnfiːld/ **Brownfield** land is land in a town or city where houses or factories have been built in the past, but which is not being used at the present time. ❑ *By 2005 he wants half of all new houses to be built on previously developed land: so-called brownfield sites.* ADJ: ADJ n

**brown goods** **Brown goods** are electrical appliances such as televisions and audio equipment. Compare **white goods**. ❑ *Revenue from brown goods, including televisions and hi-fis, rose nearly 12 per cent.* N-PLURAL

**brownie** /braʊni/ **(brownies)**

> The spelling **Brownie** is also used for meaning 2.

[1] **Brownies** are small flat biscuits or cakes. They are usually chocolate flavoured and have nuts in them. ❑ *...chocolate brownies. ...a tray of brownies.* N-COUNT: oft n N [2] **The Brownies** is a junior version of the Girl Guides in Britain for girls between the ages of seven and ten, or of the Girl Scouts in the United States for girls between the ages of six and eight. N-PROPER-COLL: *the* N ♦ A **Brownie** is a girl who is a member of the Brownies. N-COUNT

**brownie point** **(brownie points)** If someone does something to score **brownie points**, they do it because they think they will be praised for it. ❑ *They're just trying to score brownie points with politicians.* N-COUNT: usu pl [disapproval]

**brown|ish** /braʊnɪʃ/ Something that is **brownish** is slightly brown in colour. COLOUR

**brown-nosing** If you accuse someone of **brown-nosing**, you are saying in a rather offensive way that they are agreeing with someone important in order to get their support. ❑ *Brown-nosing the power brokers won't save you.* N-UNCOUNT [disapproval]

**brown|stone** /braʊnstoʊn/ **(brownstones)** In the United States, a **brownstone** is a type of house which was built during the 19th century. Brownstones have a front that is made from a reddish-brown stone. N-COUNT

**browse** /braʊz/ **(browses, browsing, browsed)** [1] If you **browse** in a shop, you look at things in a fairly casual way, in the hope that you might find something you like. ❑ *I stopped in several bookstores to browse... I'm just browsing around.* VERB; V; V prep/adv ♦ **Browse** is also a noun. ❑ *...a browse around the shops.* N-COUNT: usu sing [2] If you **browse through** a book or magazine, you look through it in a fairly casual way. ❑ *...sitting on the sofa browsing through the TV pages of the paper.* VERB; V prep [3] If you **browse** on a computer, you search for information in computer files or on the Internet, especially on the World Wide Web. [COMPUTING] ❑ *Try browsing around in the network bulletin boards.* VERB; V adv/prep [4] When animals **browse**, they feed on plants. ❑ *...the three red deer stags browsing 50 yards from my lodge on the fringes of the forest.* VERB; V; Also V *on* n, V n

**brows|er** /braʊzəʳ/ **(browsers)** [1] A **browser** is a piece of computer software that you use to search for information on the Internet, especially on the World Wide Web. [COMPUTING] N-COUNT [2] A **browser** is someone who browses in a shop. ❑ *...a casual browser.* N-COUNT

**bruise** /bruːz/ **(bruises, bruising, bruised)** [1] A **bruise** is an injury which appears as a purple mark on your body, although the skin is not broken. ❑ *How did you get that bruise on your cheek?... She was treated for cuts and bruises.* N-COUNT [2] If you **bruise** a part of your body, a bruise appears on it, for example because something hits you. If you **bruise** easily, bruises appear when something hits you only slightly. ❑ *I had only bruised my knee... Some people bruise more easily than others.* VERB; V n; V adv ♦ **bruised** *I escaped with severely bruised legs.* ADJ [3] If a fruit, vegetable, or plant **bruises** or **is bruised**, it is damaged by being handled roughly, making a mark on the skin. ❑ *Cut them off the plants, being careful not to bruise them. ...bruised tomatoes and cucumbers... Be sure to store them carefully as they bruise easily.* VERB; V n; V-ed; V adv; Also V ♦ **Bruise** is also a noun. ❑ *...bruises on the fruit's skin.* N-COUNT [4] If you **are bruised** by an unpleasant experience, it makes you feel unhappy or upset. ❑ *The government will be bruised by yesterday's events.* VERB: usu passive *be* V-ed ♦ **bruis|ing** *...the bruising experience of near-bankruptcy.* ADJ: usu ADJ n

**bruis|er** /bruːzəʳ/ **(bruisers)** A **bruiser** is someone who is tough, strong, and aggressive, and enjoys a fight or argument. [INFORMAL] ❑ *He has a reputation as a political bruiser.* N-COUNT [disapproval]

**bruis|ing** /bruːzɪŋ/ [1] If someone has **bruising** on their body, they have bruises on it. [FOR- N-UNCOUNT = bruises

MAL] ❑ *She had quite severe bruising and a cut lip.* [2] In a **bruising** battle or encounter, people fight or compete with each other in a very aggressive or determined way. [JOURNALISM] ❑ *The administration hopes to avoid another bruising battle over civil rights.* ADJ: usu ADJ n

**Brum|mie** /brʌmi/ **(Brummies) Brummie** means belonging to or coming from Birmingham in England. [INFORMAL] ♦ A **Brummie** is someone who comes from Birmingham. ADJ: usu ADJ n; N-COUNT

**brunch** /brʌntʃ/ **(brunches) Brunch** is a meal that is eaten in the late morning. It is a combination of breakfast and lunch. N-VAR

**bru|nette** /bruːnet/ **(brunettes)** A **brunette** is a white-skinned woman or girl with dark brown hair. N-COUNT

**brunt** /brʌnt/ To **bear the brunt** or **take the brunt of** something unpleasant means to suffer the main part or force of it. ❑ *Young people are bearing the brunt of unemployment... A child's head tends to take the brunt of any fall.* PHRASE: V inflects, usu PHR *of* n

**bru|schet|ta** /bruːʃetə/ **(bruschettas) Bruschetta** is a slice of toasted bread which is brushed with olive oil and usually covered with chopped tomatoes. N-VAR

**brush** /brʌʃ/ **(brushes, brushing, brushed)** ♦◇◇ [1] A **brush** is an object which has a large number of bristles or hairs fixed to it. You use brushes for painting, for cleaning things, and for tidying your hair. ❑ *We gave him paint and brushes... Stains are removed with buckets of soapy water and scrubbing brushes. ...a hair brush.* N-COUNT [2] If you **brush** something or **brush** something such as dirt off it, you clean it or tidy it using a brush. ❑ *Have you brushed your teeth?... She brushed the powder out of her hair... Using a small brush, he brushed away the fine sawdust.* VERB: V n; V n prep; V n with adv ♦ **Brush** is also a noun. ❑ *I gave it a quick brush with my hairbrush.* N-SING: *a* N [3] If you **brush** something **with** a liquid, you apply a layer of that liquid using a brush. ❑ *Take a sheet of filo pastry and brush it with melted butter.* VERB: V n *with* n [4] If you **brush** something somewhere, you remove it with quick light movements of your hands. ❑ *He brushed his hair back with both hands... He brushed the snow off the windshield.* VERB: V n with adv; V n prep [5] If one thing **brushes against** another or if you **brush** one thing **against** another, the first thing touches the second thing lightly while passing it. ❑ *Something brushed against her leg... I felt her dark brown hair brushing the back of my shoulder... She knelt and brushed her lips softly across Michael's cheek.* VERB: V prep; V n; V n prep [6] If you **brush past** someone or **brush by** them, you almost touch them as you go past them. [WRITTEN] ❑ *My father would burst into the kitchen, brushing past my mother.* VERB: V prep/adv [7] If you have a **brush with** someone, you have an argument or disagreement with them. You use **brush** when you want to make an argument or disagreement sound less serious than it really is. ❑ *My first brush with a headmaster came six years ago... It is his third brush with the law in less than a year.* N-COUNT: usu N *with* n [vagueness] [8] If you have a **brush with** a particular situation, usually an unpleasant one, you almost experience it. ❑ *...the trauma of a brush with death... The corporation is fighting to survive its second brush with bankruptcy.* N-COUNT: N *with* n = encounter [9] **Brush** is an area of rough open land covered with small bushes and trees. You also use **brush** to refer to the bushes and trees on this land. ❑ *...the brush fire that destroyed nearly 500 acres. ...a meadow of low brush and grass.* N-UNCOUNT = bush [10] → See also **broad-brush, nail brush**. [11] **tarred with the same brush** → see **tar**.

♦ **brush aside** or **brush away** If you **brush aside** or **brush away** an idea, remark, or feeling, you refuse to consider it because you think it is not important or useful, even though it may be. ❑ *Perhaps you shouldn't brush the idea aside too hastily... He brushed away my views on politics.* PHRASAL VERB = dismiss; V n P; V P n

♦ **brush up** or **brush up on** If you **brush up** something or **brush up on** it, you practise it or improve your knowledge of it. ❑ *I had hoped to brush up my Spanish... Eleanor spent much of the summer brushing up on her driving.* PHRASAL VERB; V P n (not pron); V P P n

**brushed** /brʌʃt/ **Brushed** cotton, nylon, or other fabric feels soft and furry. ADJ: ADJ n

**brush-off** If someone gives you **the brush-off** when you speak to them, they refuse to talk to you or be nice to you. [INFORMAL] ❑ *I wanted to keep in touch, but when I called him he gave me the brush-off.* N-SING

**brush|stroke** /brʌʃstroʊk/ **(brushstrokes) Brushstrokes** are the marks made on a surface by a painter's brush. ❑ *He paints with harsh, slashing brushstrokes.* N-COUNT

**brush|wood** /brʌʃwʊd/ **Brushwood** consists of small pieces of wood that have broken off trees and bushes. N-UNCOUNT

**brush|work** /brʌʃwɜːʳk/ An artist's **brushwork** is their way of using their brush to put paint on a canvas and the effect that this has in the picture. ❑ *... the texture of the artist's brushwork.* N-UNCOUNT

**brusque** /brʌsk/ If you describe a person or their behaviour as **brusque**, you mean that they deal with things, or say things, quickly and shortly, so that they seem to be rude. ❑ *The doctors are brusque and busy... They received a characteristically brusque reply from him.* ADJ = abrupt ♦ **brusque|ly** *'It's only a sprain,' Paula said brusquely.* ADV: ADV with v

**brus|sels sprout** /brʌsəlz spraʊt/ **(brussels sprouts)** also **Brussels sprout. Brussels sprouts** are vegetables that look like tiny cabbages. → See picture on page 1712. N-COUNT: usu pl = sprout

**bru|tal** /bruːtᵊl/ [1] A **brutal** act or person is cruel and violent. ❑ *He was the victim of a very brutal murder. ...the brutal suppression of anti-government protests... Jensen is a dangerous man, and can be very brutal and reckless.* ADJ = vicious, savage ♦ **bru|tal|ly** *Her real parents had been brutally murdered.* ADV: usu ADV with v [2] If someone expresses something unpleasant with **brutal** honesty or frankness, they express it in a clear and accurate way, without attempting to disguise its unpleasantness. ❑ *It was refreshing to talk about themselves and their feelings with brutal honesty... He took an anguished breath. He had to be brutal and say it.* ADJ ♦ **bru|tal|ly** *The talks had been brutally frank.* ADV [3] **Brutal** is used to describe things that have an unpleasant effect on people, especially when there is no attempt by anyone to reduce their effect. ❑ *The dip in prices this summer will be brutal... The 20th century brought brutal change to some countries.* ADJ ♦ **bru|tal|ly** *The early-morning New York air can be brutally cold.* ADV: usu ADV with v, also ADV adj

**bru|tal|ise** /bruːtəlaɪz/ → see **brutalize**.

**bru|tal|ity** /bruːtælɪti/ **(brutalities) Brutality** is cruel and violent treatment or behaviour. A **brutality** is an instance of cruel and violent treatment or behaviour. ❑ *...police brutality. ...the atrocities and brutalities committed by a former regime.* N-VAR

**bru|tal|ize** /bruːtəlaɪz/ **(brutalizes, brutalizing, brutalized)**

✓ in BRIT, also use **brutalise**

[1] If an unpleasant experience **brutalizes** someone, it makes them cruel or violent. ❑ *Here's a man who has brutalized his own people... He was brutalized by the experience of being in prison.* VERB: V n; V-ed [2] If one person **brutalizes** another, they treat them in a cruel or violent way. ❑ *... a 15th century explorer who brutalized people and enslaved them.* VERB: V n

**brute** /bruːt/ **(brutes)** [1] If you call someone, usually a man, a **brute**, you mean that they are rough, violent, and insensitive. ❑ *...a drunken brute.* N-COUNT [disapproval] [2] When you refer to **brute** strength or force, you are contrasting it with gentler methods or qualities. ❑ *He used brute force to take control... Boxing is a test of skill and technique, rather than brute strength.* ADJ: ADJ n

**brut|ish** /bruːtɪʃ/ If you describe a person or their behaviour as **brutish**, you think that they are brutal and uncivilised. ❑ *The man was brutish and coarse. ...brutish bullying.* ADJ [disapproval]

**BS** /biː es/ 1 **BS** is an abbreviation for 'British Standard', which is a standard that something sold in Britain must reach in a test to prove that it is satisfactory or safe. Each standard has a number for reference. ❑ *Does your electric blanket conform to BS 3456?* 2 A **BS** is the same as a **BSc.** [AM]

**BSc** /biː es siː/ **(BScs)** also **B.Sc.** 1 A **BSc** is a first degree in a science subject. **BSc** is an abbreviation for 'Bachelor of Science'. ❑ *He completed his BSc in chemistry in 1934.* 2 **BSc** is written after someone's name to indicate that they have a BSc. ❑ *...J. Hodgkison BSc.* N-COUNT

**BSE** /biː es iː/ **BSE** is a disease which affects the nervous system of cattle and kills them. **BSE** is an abbreviation for 'bovine spongiform encephalopathy'. N-UNCOUNT

**B-side (B-sides)** The **B-side** of a pop record has the less important or less popular song on it. Compare **A-side.** ❑ *...a compilation of the band's A and B-sides.* N-COUNT

**BTW** BTW is the written abbreviation for 'by the way', often used in e-mail.

**bub|ble** /bʌbᵊl/ **(bubbles, bubbling, bubbled)** 1 **Bubbles** are small balls of air or gas in a liquid. ❑ *Ink particles attach themselves to air bubbles and rise to the surface. ...a bubble of gas trapped under the surface.* N-COUNT 2 A **bubble** is a hollow ball of soapy liquid that is floating in the air or standing on a surface. ❑ *With soap and water, bubbles and boats, children love bathtime.* N-COUNT 3 A **bubble** is a situation in which large numbers of people want to buy shares in a company that is new or not yet financially successful, and pay more than the shares are worth. When it becomes clear that the shares are worth less than people paid for them, you can say that the **bubble** has burst. [BUSINESS] ❑ *Everyone is hoping that these hi-tech companies will turn out to be the Microsofts of the future. At the moment they look more like the focus of a speculative bubble... When the development bubble burst, federal regulators started probing the balance sheets of the biggest banks.* N-COUNT 4 In a cartoon, a speech **bubble** is the shape which surrounds the words which a character is thinking or saying. N-COUNT 5 When a liquid **bubbles**, bubbles move in it, for example because it is boiling or moving quickly. ❑ *Heat the seasoned stock until it is bubbling... The fermenting wine has bubbled up and over the top.* VERB V V adv/prep 6 A feeling, influence, or activity that **is bubbling** away continues to occur. ❑ *...political tensions that have been bubbling away for years.* VERB: usu cont V adv/prep 7 Someone who **is bubbling with** a good feeling is so full of it that they keep expressing the way they feel to everyone around them. ❑ *She came to the phone bubbling with excitement.* VERB: usu cont V with n ♦ **Bubble over** means the same as **bubble.** ❑ *He was quite tireless, bubbling over with vitality.* PHRASAL VERB V P with n ♦ **Bubble** is also a noun. ❑ *As she spoke she felt a bubble of optimism rising inside her.* N-COUNT: usu N of n

♦ **bubble over** → see **bubble 6.**

**bub|ble and squeak** **Bubble and squeak** is a dish made from a mixture of cold cooked cabbage, potato, and sometimes meat. It can be grilled or fried. N-UNCOUNT

**bub|ble bath (bubble baths)** 1 **Bubble bath** is a liquid that smells nice and makes a lot of bubbles when you add it to your bath water. N-UNCOUNT 2 When you have a **bubble bath**, you lie in a bath of water with bubble bath in it. ❑ *...a long, relaxing bubble bath.* N-COUNT

**bub|ble gum** also **bubblegum. Bubble gum** is a sweet substance similar to chewing gum. You can blow it out of your mouth so it makes the shape of a bubble. ❑ *I got bubblegum on the seat of Nanna's car.* N-UNCOUNT

**bub|bly** /bʌbli/ 1 Someone who is **bubbly** is very lively and cheerful and talks a lot. ❑ *...a bubbly girl who loves to laugh... She had a bright and bubbly personality.* ADJ [approval] = bouncy 2 Champagne is sometimes called **bubbly.** [INFORMAL] ❑ *Guests were presented with glasses of bubbly on arrival.* N-UNCOUNT 3 If something is **bubbly**, it has a lot of bubbles in it. ❑ *Melt the butter over a medium-low heat. When it is melted and bubbly, put in the flour.* ADJ

**bu|bon|ic plague** /bjuːbɒnɪk pleɪg, AM buː-/ **Bubonic plague** is a serious infectious disease spread by rats. It killed many people during the Middle Ages. N-UNCOUNT = plague

**buc|ca|neer** /bʌkənɪəʳ/ **(buccaneers)** 1 A **buccaneer** was a **pirate**, especially one who attacked and stole from Spanish ships in the 17th and 18th centuries. N-COUNT 2 If you describe someone as a **buccaneer**, you mean that they are clever and successful, especially in business, but you do not completely trust them. [BRIT] N-COUNT

**buc|ca|neer|ing** /bʌkənɪərɪŋ/ If you describe someone as **buccaneering**, you mean that they enjoy being involved in risky or even dishonest activities, especially in order to make money. [BRIT] ❑ *...a buccaneering British businessman.* ADJ: ADJ n

**buck** /bʌk/ **(bucks, bucking, bucked)** 1 A **buck** is a US or Australian dollar. [INFORMAL] ❑ *That would probably cost you about fifty bucks... Why can't you spend a few bucks on a coat?* N-COUNT = dollar 2 A **buck** is the male of various animals, including the deer, antelope, rabbit and kangaroo. N-COUNT 3 If someone has **buck** teeth, their upper front teeth stick forward out of their mouth. ADJ: ADJ n 4 If a horse **bucks**, it kicks both of its back legs wildly into the air, or jumps into the air wildly with all four feet off the ground. ❑ *The stallion bucked as he fought against the reins holding him tightly in.* VERB V 5 If you **buck** the trend, you obtain different results from others in the same area. If you **buck** the system, you get what you want by breaking or ignoring the rules. ❑ *While other newspapers are losing circulation, we are bucking the trend... He wants to be the tough rebel who bucks the system.* VERB V n V n

**PHRASES** 6 If you get more **bang for the buck**, you spend your money wisely and get more for your money than if you were to spend it in a different way. [mainly AM, INFORMAL] ❑ *I think it's very important for those governments to do whatever they can to get a bigger bang for the buck.* PHRASE: usu v compar PHR = value for money 7 When someone makes **a fast buck** or makes **a quick buck**, they earn a lot of money quickly and easily, often by doing something which is considered to be dishonest. [INFORMAL] ❑ *His life isn't ruled by looking for a fast buck... They were just in it to make a quick buck.* PHRASE: usu v PHR 8 If you are trying to **make a buck**, you are trying to earn some money. [INFORMAL] ❑ *The owners don't want to overlook any opportunity to make a buck.* PHRASE: V inflects 9 If you **pass the buck**, you refuse to accept responsibility for something, and say that someone else is responsible. [INFORMAL] ❑ *David says the responsibility is Mr Smith's and it's no good trying to pass the buck.* PHRASE: V inflects 10 If you say '**The buck stops here**' or '**The buck stops with** me', you mean that you have to take responsibility for something and will not try to pass the responsibility on to someone else. [INFORMAL] ❑ *The buck stops with him. He is ultimately responsible for every aspect of the broadcast.* PHRASE: V inflects

♦ **buck for** If you **are bucking for** something, you are working very hard to get it. [AM] ❑ *She is bucking for a promotion.* PHRASAL VERB V P n

♦ **buck up** 1 If you **buck** someone **up** or **buck up** their spirits, you say or do something to make them more cheerful. [BRIT, INFORMAL] ❑ *Anything anybody said to him to try and buck him up wouldn't sink in... The aim, it seemed, was to buck up their spirits in the face of the recession.* PHRASAL VERB = cheer up V n P V P n (not pron) 2 If you tell someone to **buck up** or to **buck up** their ideas, you are telling them to start behaving in a more positive and efficient manner. [INFORMAL] ❑ *People are saying if we don't buck up we'll be in trouble... Buck up your ideas or you'll get more of the same treatment.* PHRASAL VERB = pull one's socks up V P V P n (not pron)

**buck|et** /bʌkɪt/ **(buckets)** A **bucket** is a round metal or plastic container with a handle attached to its sides. Buckets are often used for holding and carrying water. ❑ *We drew water in a bucket from* N-COUNT *the well outside the door.* ♦ A **bucket of** water is the amount of water contained in a bucket. ❑ *She threw a bucket of water over them.* N-COUNT: usu N *of* n

**buck|et|ful** /bʌkɪtfʊl/ **(bucketfuls)** 1 A **bucketful of** something is the amount contained in a bucket. N-COUNT: usu N *of* n = *bucket* 2 If someone produces or gets something **by the bucketful**, they produce or get something in large quantities. [INFORMAL] ❑ *Over the years they have sold records by the bucketful.* PHRASE: PHR after v

**buck|et seat** **(bucket seats)** A **bucket seat** is a seat for one person in a car or aeroplane which has rounded sides that partly enclose and support the body. N-COUNT

**buck|le** /bʌkᵊl/ **(buckles, buckling, buckled)** 1 A **buckle** is a piece of metal or plastic attached to one end of a belt or strap, which is used to fasten it. ❑ *He wore a belt with a large brass buckle.* N-COUNT 2 When you **buckle** a belt or strap, you fasten it. ❑ *A door slammed in the house and a man came out buckling his belt.* VERB V n 3 If an object **buckles** or if something **buckles** it, it becomes bent as a result of very great heat or force. ❑ *The door was beginning to buckle from the intense heat... A freak wave had buckled the deck.* VERB V V n 4 If your legs or knees **buckle**, they bend because they have become very weak or tired. ❑ *Mcanally's knees buckled and he crumpled down onto the floor.* VERB V

**buck|led** /bʌkᵊld/ **Buckled** shoes have buckles on them, either to fasten them or as decoration. ADJ: ADJ n

**Buck's Fizz** also **Bucks Fizz. Buck's Fizz** is a drink made by mixing champagne or another fizzy white wine with orange juice. [BRIT] N-UNCOUNT

**buck|shot** /bʌkʃɒt/ **Buckshot** consists of pieces of lead fired from a gun when hunting animals. N-UNCOUNT

**buck|skin** /bʌkskɪn/ **Buckskin** is soft, strong leather made from the skin of a deer or a goat. N-UNCOUNT

**buck|wheat** /bʌkʰwiːt/ **Buckwheat** is a type of small black grain used for feeding animals and making flour. **Buckwheat** also refers to the flour itself. N-UNCOUNT

**bu|col|ic** /bjuːkɒlɪk/ **Bucolic** means relating to the countryside. [LITERARY] ❑ *...the bucolic surroundings of Chantilly.* ADJ: usu ADJ n = *rustic*

**bud** /bʌd/ **(buds, budding, budded)** 1 A **bud** is a small pointed lump that appears on a tree or plant and develops into a leaf or flower. ❑ *Rosanna's favourite time is early summer, just before the buds open.* N-COUNT 2 When a tree or plant **is budding**, buds are appearing on it or are beginning to open. ❑ *The leaves were budding on the trees below.* VERB: usu cont V 3 → See also **budding**, **cotton bud**, **taste bud**.

PHRASES 4 When a tree or plant is **in bud** or has come **into bud**, it has buds on it. ❑ *The flowers are bronzy in bud and bright yellow when open. ...almond trees that should come into bud soon.* PHRASE 5 If you **nip** something such as bad behaviour **in the bud**, you stop it before it can develop very far. [INFORMAL] ❑ *It is important to recognize jealousy and to nip it in the bud before it gets out of hand.* PHRASE: V inflects

**Buddha** /bʊdə/ **(Buddhas)** 1 **Buddha** is the title given to Gautama Siddhartha, the religious teacher and founder of Buddhism. N-PROPER: oft *the* N 2 A **Buddha** is a statue or picture of the Buddha. N-COUNT

**Bud|dhism** /bʊdɪzəm/ **Buddhism** is a religion which teaches that the way to end suffering is by overcoming your desires. N-UNCOUNT

**Bud|dhist** /bʊdɪst/ **(Buddhists)** 1 A **Buddhist** is a person whose religion is Buddhism. N-COUNT 2 **Buddhist** means relating or referring to Buddhism. ❑ *...Buddhist monks. ...Buddhist philosophy.* ADJ: usu ADJ n

**bud|ding** /bʌdɪŋ/ 1 If you describe someone as, for example, a **budding** businessman or a **budding** artist, you mean that they are starting to succeed or become interested in business or art. ❑ *The forum is now open to all budding entrepreneurs... Budding linguists can tune in to the activity cassettes in French, German, Spanish and Italian.* ADJ: ADJ n 2 You use **budding** to describe a situation that is just beginning. ❑ *Our budding romance was over. ...Russia's budding democracy.* ADJ: ADJ n

**bud|dy** /bʌdi/ **(buddies)** A **buddy** is a close friend, usually a male friend of a man. [mainly AM] ❑ *We became great buddies.* N-COUNT = *pal*

**budge** /bʌdʒ/ **(budges, budging, budged)** 1 If someone will not **budge** on a matter, or if nothing **budges** them, they refuse to change their mind or to come to an agreement. ❑ *The Americans are adamant that they will not budge on this point... No amount of prodding will budge him.* VERB: with brd-neg V V n 2 If someone or something will not **budge**, they will not move. If you cannot **budge** them, you cannot make them move. ❑ *Her mother refused to budge from London... I got a grip on the boat and pulled but I couldn't budge it.* VERB: with brd-neg V V n

**budg|eri|gar** /bʌdʒərigɑːʳ/ **(budgerigars)** **Budgerigars** are small, brightly-coloured birds from Australia that people often keep as pets. N-COUNT

**budg|et** /bʌdʒɪt/ **(budgets, budgeting, budgeted)** ◆◆◇ 1 Your **budget** is the amount of money that you have available to spend. The **budget** for something is the amount of money that a person, organization, or country has available to spend on it. ❑ *She will design a fantastic new kitchen for you – and all within your budget... Someone had furnished the place on a tight budget... This year's budget for AIDS prevention probably won't be much higher.* N-COUNT: with supp 2 The **budget** of an organization or country is its financial situation, considered as the difference between the money it receives and the money it spends. [BUSINESS] ❑ *The hospital obviously needs to balance the budget each year. ...his readiness to raise taxes as part of an effort to cut the budget deficit.* N-COUNT 3 In Britain, the **Budget** is the financial plan in which the government states how much money it intends to raise through taxes and how it intends to spend it. The **Budget** is also the speech in which this plan is announced. ❑ *...other indirect tax changes announced in the Budget.* N-PROPER 4 If you **budget** certain amounts of money for particular things, you decide that you can afford to spend those amounts on those things. ❑ *The company has budgeted $10 million for advertising... The movie is only budgeted at $10 million... I'm learning how to budget.* ♦ **budg|et|ing** *We have continued to exercise caution in our budgeting for the current year.* VERB V amount *for* n *be* V-ed *at* amount V N-UNCOUNT 5 **Budget** is used in advertising to suggest that something is being sold cheaply. ❑ *Cheap flights are available from budget travel agents from £240.* ADJ: ADJ n = *economy*

♦ **budget for** If you **budget for** something, you take account of it when you are deciding how much you can afford to spend on different things. ❑ *The authorities had budgeted for some non-payment.* PHRASAL VERB = *allow for* V P n

**-budget** /-bʌdʒɪt/ **-budget** combines with adjectives such as 'low' and 'big' to form adjectives which indicate how much money is spent on something, especially the making of a film. ❑ *They were small, low-budget films, shot on location. ...a big-budget adventure movie starring Mel Gibson.* COMB in ADJ

**budg|et|ary** /bʌdʒɪtəri, AM -teri/ A **budgetary** matter or policy is concerned with the amount of money that is available to a country or organization, and how it is to be spent. [FORMAL] ❑ *There are huge budgetary pressures on all governments in Europe to reduce their armed forces.* ADJ: ADJ n

**budgie** /bʌdʒi/ **(budgies)** A **budgie** is the same as a **budgerigar**. [INFORMAL] N-COUNT

**buff** /bʌf/ **(buffs, buffing, buffed)** 1 Something that is **buff** is pale brown in colour. ❑ *He took a largish buff envelope from his pocket.* COLOUR 2 You use **buff** to describe someone who knows a lot about a particular subject. For example, if you describe someone as a film **buff**, you mean that they know a lot about films. [INFORMAL] ❑ *Judge Lanier is a real film buff.* N-COUNT: supp N = *enthusiast* 3 If you **buff** the surface of something, for example your car or your shoes, you rub it with a piece of soft material in order to make it VERB = *polish*

shine. ❑ *He was already buffing the car's hubs.* V n
♦ **buff|ing** *Regular buffing helps prevent nails from splitting.* N-UNCOUNT

**buf|fa|lo** /bʌfəloʊ/ **(buffaloes** or **buffalo)** A **buffalo** is a wild animal like a large cow with horns that curve upwards. Buffalo are usually found in southern and eastern Africa. N-COUNT

**buff|er** /bʌfəʳ/ **(buffers, buffering, buffered)**
1 A **buffer** is something that prevents something else from being harmed or that prevents two things from harming each other. ❑ *Keep savings as a buffer against unexpected cash needs... The Prison Service acts as a buffer between the minister and his critics.* N-COUNT: oft N *against/between* n, N n 2 If something **is buffered**, it is protected from harm. ❑ *The company is buffered by long-term contracts with growers.* VERB *be* V-ed 3 The **buffers** on a train or at the end of a railway line are two metal discs on springs that reduce the shock when a train hits them. [mainly BRIT] Also V n N-COUNT: usu pl 4 A **buffer** is an area in a computer's memory where information can be stored for a short time. [COMPUTING] N-COUNT

**buff|er state (buffer states)** A **buffer state** is a peaceful country situated between two or more larger hostile countries. ❑ *Turkey and Greece were buffer states against the former Soviet Union.* N-COUNT

**buff|er zone (buffer zones)** A **buffer zone** is an area created to separate opposing forces or groups which belongs to neither of them. N-COUNT

**buf|fet (buffets, buffeting, buffeted)**

> ✔ Pronounced /bʌfeɪ, AM bʊfeɪ/ for meanings 1 to 3, and /bʌfɪt/ for meanings 4 and 5.

1 A **buffet** is a meal of cold food that is displayed on a long table at a party or public occasion. Guests usually serve themselves from the table. ❑ *...a buffet lunch.* N-COUNT: oft N n 2 A **buffet** is a café, usually in a hotel or station. ❑ *We sat in the station buffet sipping tea.* N-COUNT: oft n N 3 On a train, the **buffet** or the **buffet car** is the carriage or car where meals and snacks are sold. [BRIT] N-COUNT: usu sing

> ✔ in AM, use **dining car**

4 If something **is buffeted** by strong winds or by stormy seas, it is repeatedly struck or blown around by them. ❑ *Their plane had been severely buffeted by storms... Storms swept the country, closing roads, buffeting ferries and killing as many as 30 people.* VERB *be* V-ed V n ♦ **buf|fet|ing (buffetings)** *...the buffetings of the winds.* N-COUNT 5 If an economy or government **is buffeted by** difficult or unpleasant situations, it experiences many of them. ❑ *The whole of Africa had been buffeted by social and political upheavals.* VERB *be* V-ed

**buf|foon** /bʌfuːn/ **(buffoons)** If you call someone a **buffoon**, you mean that they often do foolish things. [OLD-FASHIONED] N-COUNT [disapproval] = clown

**buf|foon|ery** /bʌfuːnəri/ **Buffoonery** is foolish behaviour that makes you laugh. [OLD-FASHIONED] N-UNCOUNT

**bug** /bʌg/ **(bugs, bugging, bugged)** 1 A **bug** is an insect or similar small creature. [INFORMAL] ❑ *We noticed tiny bugs that were all over the walls.* N-COUNT: usu pl 2 A **bug** is an illness which is caused by small organisms such as bacteria. [INFORMAL] ❑ *I think I've got a bit of a stomach bug. ...the killer brain bug meningitis.* N-COUNT 3 If there is a **bug** in a computer program, there is a mistake in it. [COMPUTING] ❑ *There is a bug in the software.* N-COUNT 4 A **bug** is a tiny hidden microphone which transmits what people are saying. ❑ *There was a bug on the phone.* N-COUNT 5 If someone **bugs** a place, they hide tiny microphones in it which transmit what people are saying. ❑ *He heard that they were planning to bug his office.* VERB V n ♦ **bug|ging** *...an electronic bugging device.* N-UNCOUNT 6 You can say that someone has been bitten by a particular **bug** when they suddenly become very enthusiastic about something. [INFORMAL] ❑ *I've definitely been bitten by the gardening bug... Roundhay Park in Leeds was the place I first got the fishing bug.* N-SING: oft n N 7 If someone or something **bugs** you, they worry or annoy you. [INFORMAL] ❑ *I only did it to bug my parents.* VERB V n

**bug|bear** /bʌgbeəʳ/ **(bugbears)** Something or someone that is your **bugbear** worries or upsets you. ❑ *Money is my biggest bugbear.* N-COUNT

**bug-eyed** A **bug-eyed** person or animal has eyes that stick out. [INFORMAL] ❑ *...bug-eyed monsters... We were bug-eyed in wonderment.* ADJ

**bug|ger** /bʌgəʳ/ **(buggers, buggering, buggered)** 1 Some people use **bugger** to describe a person who has done something annoying or stupid. [mainly BRIT, INFORMAL, RUDE] N-COUNT: oft adj N [disapproval] 2 Some people say that a job or task is **a bugger** when it is difficult to do. [BRIT, INFORMAL, RUDE] N-SING: *a* N 3 Some people use **bugger** in expressions such as **bugger him** or **bugger the cost** in order to emphasize that they do not care about the person or thing that the word or phrase refers to. [BRIT, INFORMAL, RUDE] VERB: only imper, V n [feelings] = sod 4 To **bugger** someone means to have anal intercourse with them. VERB 5 Some people say **bugger it** or **bugger** when they are angry that something has gone wrong. [BRIT, INFORMAL, RUDE] EXCLAM [feelings]
♦ **bugger about** or **bugger around** If someone **buggers about** or **buggers around**, they waste time doing unnecessary things. [BRIT, INFORMAL, RUDE] PHRASAL VERB: V P [disapproval]
♦ **bugger off** If someone **buggers off**, they go away quickly and suddenly. People often say **bugger off** as a rude way of telling someone to go away. [BRIT, INFORMAL, RUDE] PHRASAL VERB: V P = sod off
♦ **bugger up** If someone **buggers** something **up**, they ruin it or spoil it. [BRIT, INFORMAL, RUDE] PHRASAL VERB: V n P [disapproval]

**bug|ger all** also **bugger-all. Bugger all** is a rude way of saying 'nothing'. [BRIT, INFORMAL, RUDE] PRON

**bug|gered** /bʌgəʳd/ 1 If someone says that they will be **buggered** if they will do something, they mean that they do not want to do it and they will definitely not do it. [BRIT, INFORMAL, RUDE] ADJ: v-link ADJ [emphasis] 2 If someone says that they are **buggered**, they mean that they are very tired. [BRIT, INFORMAL, RUDE] ADJ: v-link ADJ 3 If someone says that something is **buggered**, they mean that it is completely ruined or broken. [BRIT, INFORMAL, RUDE] ADJ: usu v-link ADJ

**bug|gery** /bʌgəri/ **Buggery** is anal intercourse. N-UNCOUNT

**bug|gy** /bʌgi/ **(buggies)** 1 A **buggy** is the same as a **baby buggy**. N-COUNT 2 A **buggy** is a small lightweight carriage pulled by one horse. N-COUNT

**bu|gle** /bjuːgəl/ **(bugles)** A **bugle** is a simple brass musical instrument that looks like a small trumpet. Bugles are often used in the army to announce when activities such as meals are about to begin. N-COUNT

**bu|gler** /bjuːgləʳ/ **(buglers)** A **bugler** is someone who plays the bugle. N-COUNT

**build** /bɪld/ **(builds, building, built)** ♦♦♦ 1 If you **build** something, you make it by joining things together. ❑ *Developers are now proposing to build a hotel on the site... The house was built in the early 19th century.* VERB = construct V n V n ♦ **build|ing** *In Japan, the building of Kansai airport continues.* N-UNCOUNT ♦ **built** *Even newly built houses can need repairs... It's a product built for safety. ...structures that are built to last.* ADJ: adv ADJ, ADJ *for* n, ADJ to-inf 2 If you **build** something **into** a wall or object, you make it in such a way that it is in the wall or object, or is part of it. ❑ *If the TV was built into the ceiling, you could lie there while watching your favourite programme.* VERB *be* V-ed *into* n 3 If people **build** an organization, a society, or a relationship, they gradually form it. ❑ *He and a partner set up on their own and built a successful fashion company... Their purpose is to build a fair society and a strong economy... I wanted to build a relationship with my team.* VERB V n V n V n ♦ **build|ing** *...the building of the great civilisations of the ancient world.* N-UNCOUNT: usu *the* N *of* n 4 If you **build** an organization, system, or product **on** something, you base it on it. ❑ *We will then have a firmer foundation of fact on which to build theories.* VERB V n prep 5 If you **build** something **into** a policy, system, or product, you make it part of it. ❑ *We have to build computers into the school curriculum...* VERB = incorporate V n into n

*How much delay should we build into the plan?* 6 To **build** someone's confidence or trust means to increase it gradually. If someone's confidence or trust **builds**, it increases gradually. ❑ *Diplomats hope the meetings will build mutual trust... Usually when we're six months or so into a recovery, confidence begins to build.* ♦ **Build up** means the same as **build**. ❑ *The delegations had begun to build up some trust in one another... We will start to see the confidence in the housing market building up again.* 7 If you **build on** the success of something, you take advantage of this success in order to make further progress. ❑ *The new regime has no successful economic reforms on which to build.* 8 If pressure, speed, sound, or excitement **builds**, it gradually becomes greater. ❑ *Pressure built yesterday for postponement of the ceremony... The last chords of the suite build to a crescendo.* ♦ **Build up** means the same as **build**. ❑ *We can build up the speed gradually and safely... Economists warn that enormous pressures could build up, forcing people to emigrate westwards.* 9 Someone's **build** is the shape that their bones and muscles give to their body. ❑ *He's described as around thirty years old, six feet tall and of medium build.* 10 → See also **building**, **built**.

VERB; V n; V; PHRASAL VERB; V P n (not pron); V P; Also V P *to* n; VERB; V *on/upon* n; VERB; V; V *to/into* n; PHRASAL VERB; V P n (not pron); V P; Also V P *to* n; N-VAR

♦ **build up** 1 If you **build up** something or if it **builds up**, it gradually becomes bigger, for example because more is added to it. ❑ *The regime built up the largest army in Africa... Slowly a thick layer of fat builds up on the pan's surface.* 2 If you **build** someone **up**, you help them to feel stronger or more confident, especially when they have had a bad experience or have been ill. ❑ *Build her up with kindness and a sympathetic ear.* 3 If you **build** someone or something **up**, you make them seem important or exciting, for example by talking about them a lot. ❑ *The media will report on it and the tabloids will build it up... Historians built him up as the champion of parliament.* 4 → See also **build 6, 8**, **build-up**, **built-up**.

PHRASAL VERB; V P n; V P; Also V n P, V P *to* n; PHRASAL VERB; V n P; PHRASAL VERB; V n P; V n P *as* n/-ing

♦ **build up to** If you **build up to** something you want to do or say, you try to prepare people for it by starting to do it or introducing the subject gradually. ❑ *Other actions we need to take may be more difficult, and we may have to build up to them gradually.*

PHRASAL VERB; V P P n

**build|er** /bɪldəʳ/ **(builders)** A **builder** is a person whose job is to build or repair houses and other buildings. ❑ *The builders have finished the roof.*

N-COUNT

**build|ing** /bɪldɪŋ/ **(buildings)** A **building** is a structure that has a roof and walls, for example a house or a factory. ❑ *...the upper floor of the building... Crowds gathered around the Parliament building.*

◆◆◆ N-COUNT

**build|ing block** **(building blocks)** If you describe something as a **building block** of something, you mean it is one of the separate parts that combine to make that thing. ❑ *...molecules that are the building blocks of all life on earth.*

N-COUNT: usu with supp

**build|ing site** **(building sites)** A **building site** is an area of land on which a building or a group of buildings is in the process of being built or altered.

N-COUNT = construction site

**build|ing so|ci|ety** **(building societies)** In Britain, a **building society** is a business which will lend you money when you want to buy a house. You can also invest money in a building society, where it will earn interest. Compare **savings and loan** association.

N-COUNT

**build-up** **(build-ups)** also **buildup**, **build up**. 1 A **build-up** is a gradual increase in something. ❑ *There has been a build-up of troops on both sides of the border... The disease can also cause a build up of pressure in the inner ear leading to severe earache.* 2 The **build-up** to an event is the way that journalists, advertisers, or other people talk about it a lot in the period of time immediately before it, and try to make it seem important and exciting. ❑ *The exams came, almost an anti-climax after the build-up that the students had given them.*

N-COUNT: usu sing, oft N *of* n; N-COUNT: usu sing, oft N *to* n

**built** /bɪlt/ 1 **Built** is the past tense and past participle of **build**. 2 If you say that someone is **built** in a particular way, you are describing the kind of body they have. ❑ *...a strong, powerfully-built man of 60... He was a huge man, built like an oak tree.* → See also **well-built**.

ADJ: adv ADJ, ADJ *like* n, ADJ *for* n/-ing

**built-in** **Built-in** devices or features are included in something as a part of it, rather than being separate. ❑ *...modern cameras with built-in flash units... We're going to have built-in cupboards in the bedrooms.*

ADJ: ADJ n = fitted

**built-up** A **built-up** area is an area such as a town or city which has a lot of buildings in it. ❑ *A speed limit of 30 mph was introduced in built-up areas.*

ADJ: usu ADJ n

**bulb** /bʌlb/ **(bulbs)** 1 A **bulb** is the glass part of an electric lamp, which gives out light when electricity passes through it. ❑ *The stairwell was lit by a single bulb.* 2 A **bulb** is a root shaped like an onion that grows into a flower or plant. ❑ *...tulip bulbs.*

N-COUNT = light bulb; N-COUNT

**bulb|ous** /bʌlbəs/ Something that is **bulbous** is round and fat in a rather ugly way. ❑ *...his bulbous purple nose.*

ADJ: usu ADJ n

**Bul|gar|ian** /bʌlgeəriən/ **(Bulgarians)** 1 **Bulgarian** means belonging or relating to Bulgaria, or to its people, language, or culture. 2 A **Bulgarian** is a Bulgarian citizen, or a person of Bulgarian origin. 3 **Bulgarian** is the main language spoken by people who live in Bulgaria.

ADJ; N-COUNT; N-UNCOUNT

**bulge** /bʌldʒ/ **(bulges, bulging, bulged)** 1 If something such as a person's stomach **bulges**, it sticks out. ❑ *Jiro waddled closer, his belly bulging and distended... He bulges out of his black T-shirt... He is 6ft 3ins with bulging muscles.* 2 If someone's eyes or veins **are bulging**, they seem to stick out a lot, often because the person is making a strong physical effort or is experiencing a strong emotion. ❑ *He shouted at his brother, his neck veins bulging. ...bulging eyes.* 3 If you say that something **is bulging with** things, you are emphasizing that it is full of them. ❑ *They returned home with the car bulging with boxes. ...a bulging briefcase.* 4 **Bulges** are lumps that stick out from a surface which is otherwise flat or smooth. ❑ *Why won't those bulges on your hips and thighs go?* 5 If there is a **bulge in** something, there is a sudden large increase in it. ❑ *...a bulge in aircraft sales.*

VERB; V; V adv/prep; V-ing; VERB = protrude; V; V-ing; VERB: oft cont; V *with* n; V-ing; Also V; N-COUNT; N-COUNT: usu sing, with supp, oft N *in/of* n

**bu|limia** /buːlɪmiə/ **Bulimia** or **bulimia nervosa** is an illness in which a person has a very great fear of becoming fat, and so they make themselves vomit after eating.

N-UNCOUNT

**bu|limic** /buːlɪmɪk/ **(bulimics)** If someone is **bulimic**, they are suffering from bulimia. ❑ *...bulimic patients... I was anorexic and bulimic.* ♦ A **bulimic** is someone who is bulimic. ❑ *...a former bulimic.*

ADJ; N-COUNT

**bulk** /bʌlk/ 1 You can refer to something's **bulk** when you want to emphasize that it is very large. [WRITTEN] ❑ *...the shadowy bulk of an ancient barn.* 2 You can refer to a large person's body or to their weight or size as their **bulk**. ❑ *Bannol lowered his bulk carefully into the chair... Despite his bulk he moved lightly on his feet.* 3 The **bulk of** something is most of it. ❑ *The bulk of the text is essentially a review of these original documents... The vast bulk of imports and exports are carried by sea.* ♦ **Bulk** is also a pronoun. ❑ *They come from all over the world, though the bulk is from the Indian subcontinent.* 4 If you buy or sell something **in bulk**, you buy or sell it in large quantities. ❑ *Buying in bulk is more economical than shopping for small quantities. ...bulk purchasing.*

N-SING: with supp [emphasis]; N-SING: usu poss N; QUANT: QUANT *of* def-n = majority; PRON; N-UNCOUNT: *in* N, N n

**bulk|head** /bʌlkhed/ **(bulkheads)** A **bulkhead** is a wall which divides the inside of a ship or aeroplane into separate sections. [TECHNICAL]

N-COUNT = partition

**bulky** /bʌlki/ **(bulkier, bulkiest)** Something that is **bulky** is large and heavy. Bulky things are often difficult to move or deal with. ❑ *...bulky items like lawn mowers.*

ADJ

**bull** /bʊl/ **(bulls)** 1 A **bull** is a male animal of the cow family. N-COUNT 2 Some other male animals, including elephants and whales, are called **bulls**. N-COUNT ❑ *...a massive bull elephant with huge tusks.* 3 On the stock market, **bulls** are people who buy shares in expectation of a price rise, in order to make a profit by selling the shares again after a short time. Compare **bear**. [BUSINESS] N-COUNT 4 If you say that something is **bull** or a load of **bull**, you mean that it is complete nonsense or absolutely untrue. [INFORMAL] N-UNCOUNT ❑ *I think it's a load of bull.* 5 → See also **cock-and-bull story, pit bull terrier**. 6 If you **take the bull by the horns**, you do something that you feel you ought to do even though it is difficult, dangerous, or unpleasant. PHRASE: V inflects ❑ *Now is the time for the Chancellor to take the bull by the horns and announce a two per cent cut in interest rates.* 7 **like a red rag to a bull** → see **rag**.

**bull bar** **(bull bars)** On some motor vehicles, **bull bars** are metal bars fixed to the front that are designed to protect it if it crashes. N-COUNT: usu pl

**bull|dog** /bʊldɒg, AM -dɔːg/ **(bulldogs)** A **bulldog** is a small dog with a large square head and short hair. N-COUNT

**bull|dog clip** **(bulldog clips)** A **bulldog clip** is a metal clip with a spring lever that opens and closes two flat pieces of metal. It is used for holding papers together. [BRIT] N-COUNT

**bull|doze** /bʊldoʊz/ **(bulldozes, bulldozing, bulldozed)** 1 If people **bulldoze** something such as a building, they knock it down using a bulldozer. VERB ❑ *She defeated developers who wanted to bulldoze her home to build a supermarket.* V n 2 If people **bulldoze** earth, stone, or other heavy material, they move it using a bulldozer. VERB ❑ *Last week, the department's road builders began to bulldoze a water meadow on Twyford Down.* V n 3 If someone **bulldozes** a plan **through** or **bulldozes** another person **into** doing something, they get what they want in an unpleasantly forceful way. VERB disapproval ❑ *The party in power planned to bulldoze through a full socialist programme...* V n with *through* *The coalition bulldozed the resolution through the plenary session...* V n *through* n *My parents tried to bulldoze me into going to college.* V n *into* n/-ing

**bull|doz|er** /bʊldoʊzəʳ/ **(bulldozers)** A **bulldozer** is a large vehicle with a broad metal blade at the front, which is used for knocking down buildings or moving large amounts of earth. N-COUNT

**bul|let** /bʊlɪt/ **(bullets)** 1 A **bullet** is a small piece of metal with a pointed or rounded end, which is fired out of a gun. N-COUNT → See also **plastic bullet, rubber bullet**. 2 If someone **bites the bullet**, they accept that they have to do something unpleasant but necessary. [JOURNALISM] PHRASE: V inflects ❑ *Tour operators may be forced to bite the bullet and cut prices.*

**bul|letin** /bʊlɪtɪn/ **(bulletins)** 1 A **bulletin** is a short news report on the radio or television. N-COUNT ❑ *...the early morning news bulletin.* 2 A **bulletin** is a short official announcement made publicly to inform people about an important matter. N-COUNT ❑ *At 3.30 p.m. a bulletin was released announcing that the president was out of immediate danger.* 3 A **bulletin** is a regular newspaper or leaflet that is produced by an organization or group such as a school or church. N-COUNT

**bul|letin board** **(bulletin boards)** 1 A **bulletin board** is a board which is usually attached to a wall in order to display notices giving information about something. [mainly AM] N-COUNT

✔ in BRIT, use **noticeboard**

2 In computing, a **bulletin board** is a system that enables users to send and receive messages of general interest. [COMPUTING] N-COUNT ❑ *The Internet is the largest computer bulletin board in the world.*

**bul|let point** **(bullet points)** A **bullet point** is one of a series of important items for discussion or action in a document, usually marked by a square or round symbol. N-COUNT ❑ *Use bold type for headings and bullet points for noteworthy achievements.*

**bullet-proof** also **bulletproof.** Something that is **bullet-proof** is made of a strong material that bullets cannot pass through. ADJ ❑ *...bullet-proof glass. ...a bullet-proof vest.*

**bull|fight** /bʊlfaɪt/ **(bullfights)** A **bullfight** is a public entertainment in which people fight and kill bulls. Bullfights take place in Spain, Portugal, and Latin America. N-COUNT

**bull|fighter** /bʊlfaɪtəʳ/ **(bullfighters)** A **bullfighter** is the person who tries to injure or kill the bull in a bullfight. N-COUNT = matador

**bull|fighting** /bʊlfaɪtɪŋ/ **Bullfighting** is the public entertainment in which people try to kill bulls in bullfights. N-UNCOUNT

**bull|finch** /bʊlfɪntʃ/ **(bullfinches)** A **bullfinch** is a type of small European bird. The male has a black head and a pinkish-red breast. N-COUNT

**bull|frog** /bʊlfrɒg, AM -frɔːg/ **(bullfrogs)** A **bullfrog** is a type of large frog which makes a very loud noise. N-COUNT

**bull|horn** /bʊlhɔːʳn/ **(bullhorns)** A **bullhorn** is a device for making your voice sound louder in the open air. [AM] N-COUNT

✔ in BRIT, use **loudhailer, megaphone**

**bul|lion** /bʊliən/ **Bullion** is gold or silver, usually in the form of bars. N-UNCOUNT

**bull|ish** /bʊlɪʃ/ 1 On the stock market, if there is a **bullish** mood, prices are expected to rise. Compare **bearish**. [BUSINESS] ADJ ❑ *The market opened in a bullish mood.* 2 If someone is **bullish about** something, they are cheerful and optimistic about it. ADJ: oft ADJ *about/on* n = optimistic ❑ *Faldo was bullish about his chances of winning a third British Open.*

**bull mar|ket** **(bull markets)** A **bull market** is a situation on the stock market when people are buying a lot of shares because they expect that the shares will increase in value and that they will be able to make a profit by selling them again after a short time. Compare **bear market**. [BUSINESS] N-COUNT

**bull|ock** /bʊlək/ **(bullocks)** A **bullock** is a young bull that has been castrated. N-COUNT

**bull|ring** /bʊlrɪŋ/ **(bullrings)** A **bullring** is a circular area of ground surrounded by rows of seats where bullfights take place. N-COUNT

**bull's-eye** **(bull's-eyes)** 1 **The bull's-eye** is the small circular area at the centre of a target. N-COUNT: usu *the* N in sing ❑ *Five of his bullets had hit the bull's-eye.* 2 In shooting or the game of darts, a **bull's-eye** is a shot or throw of a dart that hits the bull's-eye. N-COUNT 3 If something that you do or say hits **the bull's eye**, it has exactly the effect that you intended it to have. [INFORMAL] N-COUNT

**bull|shit** /bʊlʃɪt/ **(bullshits, bullshitting, bullshitted)** 1 If you say that something is **bullshit**, you are saying that it is nonsense or completely untrue. [INFORMAL, RUDE] N-UNCOUNT disapproval = crap ❑ *All the rest I said, all that was bullshit.* 2 If you say that someone **is bullshitting** you, you mean that what they are telling you is nonsense or completely untrue. [INFORMAL, RUDE] VERB ❑ *Don't bullshit me, Brian!...* V n *He's basically bullshitting.* V

**bull ter|ri|er** **(bull terriers)** A **bull terrier** is a breed of strong dog with a short, whitish coat and a thick neck. N-COUNT → See also **pit bull terrier**.

**bull|whip** /bʊlʰwɪp/ **(bullwhips)** A **bullwhip** is a very long, heavy whip. N-COUNT

**bul|ly** /bʊli/ **(bullies, bullying, bullied)** 1 A **bully** is someone who uses their strength or power to hurt or frighten other people. N-COUNT ❑ *I fell victim to the office bully.* 2 If someone **bullies** you, they use their strength or power to hurt or frighten you. VERB ❑ *I wasn't going to let him bully me.* V n ♦ **bul|ly|ing** N-UNCOUNT *...schoolchildren who were victims of bullying.* 3 If someone **bullies** you **into** something, they make you do it by using force or threats. VERB ❑ *We think an attempt to bully them into submission would be counterproductive...* V n *into* n/-ing *She used to* *bully me into doing my schoolwork... The government says it will not be bullied by the press.* V n *into* n/ing; *be* V-ed

**bully-boy** **(bully-boys)** also **bully boy.** 1 If you describe a man as a **bully-boy**, you disapprove of him because he is rough and aggressive. ❑ *...bully-boys and murderers.* N-COUNT disapproval 2 If you say that someone uses **bully-boy** tactics, you disapprove of them because they use rough and aggressive methods. [JOURNALISM] ❑ *Some people accuse the tax inspectors of bully-boy tactics.* ADJ: ADJ n disapproval

**bul|wark** /bʊlwəʳk/ **(bulwarks)** A **bulwark against** something protects you against it. A **bulwark of** something protects it. ❑ *The abbeys were founded in the 12th century by King David as a bulwark against the English.* N-COUNT: oft N *against/of* n

**bum** /bʌm/ **(bums, bumming, bummed)** 1 Someone's **bum** is the part of their body which they sit on. [BRIT, INFORMAL] N-COUNT: poss N = bottom 2 A **bum** is a person who has no permanent home or job and who gets money by working occasionally or by asking people for money. [AM, INFORMAL] N-COUNT 3 If someone refers to another person as a **bum**, they think that person is worthless or irresponsible. [INFORMAL] ❑ *You're all a bunch of bums.* N-COUNT disapproval 4 Some people use **bum** to describe a situation that they find unpleasant or annoying. [INFORMAL] ❑ *He knows you're getting a bum deal.* ADJ: ADJ n 5 If you **bum** something off someone, you ask them for it and they give it to you. [INFORMAL] ❑ *Mind if I bum a cigarette?* VERB V n 6 If you **bum around**, you go from place to place without any particular destination, either for enjoyment or because you have nothing else to do. [INFORMAL] ❑ *I think they're just bumming around at the moment, not doing a lot... She went off to bum round the world with a boyfriend.* VERB V *around*; V *round* n 7 → See also **beach bum**.

**bum bag** **(bum bags)** A **bum bag** consists of a small bag attached to a belt which you wear round your waist. You use it to carry things such as money and keys. [BRIT] N-COUNT

☑ in AM, use **fanny pack**

**bum|ble** /bʌmbᵊl/ **(bumbles, bumbling, bumbled)**

♦ **bumble around**

☑ in BRIT, also use **bumble about**

When someone **bumbles around** or **bumbles about**, they behave in a confused, disorganized way, making mistakes and usually not achieving anything. ❑ *Most of us are novices on the computer – just bumbling about on them.* PHRASAL VERB V P

**bumble|bee** /bʌmbᵊlbiː/ **(bumblebees)** also **bumble bee.** A **bumblebee** is a large hairy bee. N-COUNT

**bum|bling** /bʌmblɪŋ/ If you describe a person or their behaviour as **bumbling**, you mean that they behave in a confused, disorganized way, making mistakes and usually not achieving anything. ❑ *...a clumsy, bumbling, inarticulate figure.* ADJ: ADJ n

**bumf** /bʌmf/ also **bumph. Bumf** consists of documents containing information which you may not need or find interesting. [BRIT, INFORMAL] ❑ *These days, we are bombarded with endless junk mail, fliers, and general bumf.* N-UNCOUNT

**bum|mer** /bʌməʳ/ **(bummers)** If you say that something is **a bummer**, you mean that it is unpleasant or annoying. [INFORMAL] ❑ *I had a bummer of a day... What a bummer!* N-COUNT: usu sing

**bump** /bʌmp/ **(bumps, bumping, bumped)** 1 If you **bump** into something or someone, you accidentally hit them while you are moving. ❑ *They stopped walking and he almost bumped into them... He bumped his head on the low beams of the house.* VERB V *into/against* n; V n ♦ **Bump** is also a noun. ❑ *Small children often cry after a minor bump.* N-COUNT 2 A **bump** is the action or the dull sound of two heavy objects hitting each other. ❑ *I felt a little bump and I knew instantly what had happened... The child took five steps, and then sat down with a bump.* N-COUNT 3 A **bump** is a minor injury or swelling that you get if you bump into something or if something hits you. ❑ *She fell against our coffee table and got a large bump on her forehead.* N-COUNT = lump 4 If you have a **bump** while you are driving a car, you have a minor accident in which you hit something. [INFORMAL] N-COUNT = accident, crash 5 A **bump** on a road is a raised, uneven part. ❑ *The truck hit a bump and bounced.* N-COUNT 6 If a vehicle **bumps over** a surface, it travels in a rough, bouncing way because the surface is very uneven. ❑ *We left the road, and again bumped over the mountainside.* VERB V prep/adv Also V *way* adv/prep 7 → See also **goose bumps.** 8 If someone **comes down to earth with a bump**, they suddenly start recognizing unpleasant facts after a period of time when they have not been doing this. ❑ *Company bosses have come back down to earth with a bump after a period of post-election euphoria.* PHRASE: PHR after v emphasis

♦ **bump into** If you **bump into** someone you know, you meet them unexpectedly. [INFORMAL] ❑ *I happened to bump into Mervyn Johns in the hallway.* PHRASAL VERB = run into V P n

♦ **bump off** To **bump** someone **off** means to kill them. [often HUMOROUS, INFORMAL] ❑ *They will probably bump you off anyway! ...the hit man he's hired to bump off his wife.* PHRASAL VERB V n P; V P n (not pron)

**bump|er** /bʌmpəʳ/ **(bumpers)** 1 **Bumpers** are bars at the front and back of a vehicle which protect it if it bumps into something. → See picture on page 1707. N-COUNT 2 A **bumper** crop or harvest is one that is larger than usual. ❑ *...a bumper crop of rice... In the state of Iowa, it's been a bumper year for corn.* ADJ: ADJ n 3 If you say that something is **bumper** size, you mean that it is very large. ❑ *...bumper profits. ...a bumper pack of matches.* ADJ: ADJ n

**bump|er car** **(bumper cars)** A **bumper car** is a small electric car with a wide rubber bumper all round. People drive bumper cars around a special enclosure at a fairground. N-COUNT

**bump|er stick|er** **(bumper stickers)** A **bumper sticker** is a small piece of paper or plastic with words or pictures on it, designed for sticking onto the back of your car. It usually has a political, religious, or humorous message. ❑ *...a bumper sticker that said, 'Happiness Is Being a Grandmother'.* N-COUNT

**bumph** /bʌmf/ → see **bumf**.

**bump|kin** /bʌmpkɪn/ **(bumpkins)** If you refer to someone as a **bumpkin**, you think they are uneducated and stupid because they come from the countryside. ❑ *...unsophisticated country bumpkins.* N-COUNT disapproval = yokel

**bump|tious** /bʌmpʃəs/ If you say that someone is **bumptious**, you are criticizing them because they are very pleased with themselves and their opinions. ❑ *...a bumptious bureaucrat.* ADJ disapproval

**bumpy** /bʌmpi/ **(bumpier, bumpiest)** 1 A **bumpy** road or path has a lot of bumps on it. ❑ *...bumpy cobbled streets.* ADJ ≠ smooth 2 A **bumpy** journey is uncomfortable and rough, usually because you are travelling over an uneven surface. ❑ *...a hot and bumpy ride across the desert.* ADJ

**bun** /bʌn/ **(buns)** 1 **Buns** are small bread rolls. They are sometimes sweet and may contain dried fruit or spices. ❑ *...a currant bun.* N-COUNT: oft n N 2 **Buns** are small sweet cakes. They often have icing on the top. [BRIT] N-COUNT 3 If a woman has her hair in a **bun**, she has fastened it tightly on top of her head or at the back of her head in the shape of a ball. N-COUNT

**bunch** /bʌntʃ/ **(bunches, bunching, bunched)** ◆◇◇ 1 A **bunch of** people is a group of people who share one or more characteristics or who are doing something together. [INFORMAL] ❑ *My neighbours are a bunch of busybodies... We were a pretty inexperienced bunch of people really... The players were a great bunch.* N-COUNT: usu sing, oft N *of* n, adj N = lot 2 A **bunch of** flowers is a number of flowers with their stalks held or tied together. ❑ *He had left a huge bunch of flowers in her hotel room.* N-COUNT: usu sing, usu N *of* n 3 A **bunch of** bananas or grapes is a group of them growing on the same stem. ❑ *Lili* N-COUNT: usu sing, usu N *of* n *had fallen asleep clutching a fat bunch of grapes.* 4 A **bunch of** keys is a set of keys kept together on a metal ring. ❑ *George took out a bunch of keys and went to work on the complicated lock.* 5 A **bunch of** things is a number of things, especially a large number. [AM, INFORMAL] ❑ *We did a bunch of songs together.* ♦ **Bunch** is also a pronoun. ❑ *I'd like to adopt a multi-racial child. In fact, I'd love a whole bunch.* 6 If a girl has her hair **in bunches**, it is parted down the middle and tied on each side of her head. [BRIT] 7 If clothing **bunches around** a part of your body, it forms a set of creases around it. ❑ *She clutches the sides of her skirt until it bunches around her waist.*

N-COUNT: usu sing, usu N of n · QUANT: QUANT of pl-n · PRON · N-PLURAL: usu in N · VERB · V around n

♦ **bunch up** or **bunch together** If people or things **bunch up** or **bunch together** or if you **bunch** them **up** or **bunch** them **together**, they move close to each other so that they form a small tight group. ❑ *They were bunching up, almost treading upon each other's heels... People were bunched up at all the exits... If they need to bunch aircraft more closely together to bring in one that is short of fuel, they will do so.*

PHRASAL VERB · V P · V-ed P · V n P

**bun|dle** /bʌndəl/ **(bundles, bundling, bundled)** 1 A **bundle of** things is a number of them that are tied together or wrapped in a cloth or bag so that they can be carried or stored. ❑ *He gathered the bundles of clothing into his arms... I have about 20 year's magazines tied up in bundles.* 2 If you describe someone as, for example, a **bundle of** fun, you are emphasizing that they are full of fun. If you describe someone as a **bundle of** nerves, you are emphasizing that they are very nervous. ❑ *I remember Mickey as a bundle of fun, great to have around... Life at high school wasn't a bundle of laughs, either.* 3 If you refer to a **bundle of** things, you are emphasizing that there is a wide range of them. ❑ *The profession offers a bundle of benefits, not least of which is extensive training.* 4 If someone **is bundled** somewhere, someone pushes them there in a rough and hurried way. ❑ *He was bundled into a car and driven 50 miles to a police station.* 5 To **bundle** software means to sell it together with a computer, or with other hardware or software, as part of a set. [COMPUTING] ❑ *It's cheaper to buy software bundled with a PC than separately.*

N-COUNT: oft N of n · N-SING: a N of n, emphasis · N-COUNT: N of n, emphasis = package · VERB · be V-ed prep/adv Also V n prep/adv · VERB · V-ed

**bung** /bʌŋ/ **(bungs, bunging, bunged)** 1 A **bung** is a round piece of wood, cork, or rubber which you use to close the hole in a container such as a barrel or flask. 2 If you **bung** something somewhere, you put it there in a quick and careless way. [BRIT, INFORMAL] ❑ *Pour a whole lot of cold water over the rice, and bung it in the oven.* 3 If something is **bunged up**, it is blocked. [BRIT, INFORMAL] ❑ *The sink's bunged up again... My nose is all bunged up.*

N-COUNT = stopper · VERB = stick · V n prep/adv · ADJ: usu v-link ADJ

**bun|ga|low** /bʌŋgəloʊ/ **(bungalows)** A **bungalow** is a house which has only one level, and no stairs. ➔ See picture on page 1706.

N-COUNT

**bungee jump|ing** /bʌndʒi dʒʌmpɪŋ/ If someone goes **bungee jumping**, they jump from a high place such as a bridge or cliff with a long piece of strong elastic cord tied around their ankle connecting them to the bridge or cliff.

N-UNCOUNT

**bun|gle** /bʌŋgəl/ **(bungles, bungling, bungled)** If you **bungle** something, you fail to do it properly, because you make mistakes or are clumsy. ❑ *Two prisoners bungled an escape bid after running either side of a lamp-post while handcuffed. ...the FBI's bungled attempt to end the 51 day siege.* ♦ **Bungle** is also a noun. ❑ *...an appalling administrative bungle.* ♦ **bun|gling** *...a bungling burglar.*

VERB = botch · V n · V-ed · N-COUNT · ADJ

**bun|gler** /bʌŋglər/ **(bunglers)** A **bungler** is a person who often fails to do things properly because they make mistakes or are clumsy.

N-COUNT

**bun|ion** /bʌnjən/ **(bunions)** A **bunion** is a large painful lump on the first joint of a person's big toe.

N-COUNT

**bunk** /bʌŋk/ **(bunks)** 1 A **bunk** is a bed that is fixed to a wall, especially in a ship or caravan. ❑ *He left his bunk and went up on deck again.* 2 If you describe something as **bunk**, you think that it is foolish or untrue. [INFORMAL] ❑ *...Henry Ford's opinion that 'history is bunk'.*

N-COUNT · N-UNCOUNT disapproval = nonsense

**bunk bed** **(bunk beds)** **Bunk beds** are two beds fixed one above the other in a frame.

N-COUNT

**bun|ker** /bʌŋkər/ **(bunkers)** 1 A **bunker** is a place, usually underground, that has been built with strong walls to protect it against heavy gunfire and bombing. ❑ *...an extensive network of fortified underground bunkers.* 2 A **bunker** is a container for coal or other fuel. 3 On a golf course, a **bunker** is a large area filled with sand, which is deliberately put there as an obstacle that golfers must try to avoid.

N-COUNT · N-COUNT · N-COUNT

**bun|kum** /bʌŋkəm/ If you say that something that has been said or written is **bunkum**, you mean that you think it is completely untrue or very stupid. [INFORMAL, OLD-FASHIONED]

N-UNCOUNT disapproval = balderdash

**bun|ny** /bʌni/ **(bunnies)** A **bunny** or a **bunny rabbit** is a child's word for a rabbit. [INFORMAL]

N-COUNT

**bunt|ing** /bʌntɪŋ/ **Bunting** consists of rows of small coloured flags that are used to decorate streets and buildings on special occasions. ❑ *Red, white and blue bunting hung in the city's renovated train station.*

N-UNCOUNT

**buoy** /bɔɪ, AM buːi/ **(buoys, buoying, buoyed)** 1 A **buoy** is a floating object that is used to show ships and boats where they can go and to warn them of danger. 2 If someone in a difficult situation **is buoyed** by something, it makes them feel more cheerful and optimistic. ❑ *In May they danced in the streets, buoyed by their victory... German domestic consumption buoyed the German economy.* ♦ **Buoy up** means the same as **buoy**. ❑ *They are buoyed up by a sense of hope.*

N-COUNT · VERB · be V-ed by n · V n · PHRASAL VERB be V-ed P Also V n P

**buoy|an|cy** /bɔɪənsi/ 1 **Buoyancy** is the ability that something has to float on a liquid or in the air. ❑ *Air can be pumped into the diving suit to increase buoyancy.* 2 **Buoyancy** is a feeling of cheerfulness. ❑ *...a mood of buoyancy and optimism.* 3 There is economic **buoyancy** when the economy is growing. ❑ *The likelihood is that the slump will be followed by a period of buoyancy.*

N-UNCOUNT · N-UNCOUNT · N-UNCOUNT

**buoy|ant** /bɔɪənt/ 1 If you are in a **buoyant** mood, you feel cheerful and behave in a lively way. ❑ *You will feel more buoyant and optimistic about the future than you have for a long time.* 2 A **buoyant** economy is a successful one in which there is a lot of trade and economic activity. ❑ *We have a buoyant economy and unemployment is considerably lower than the regional average... Analysts expect the share price to remain buoyant.* 3 A **buoyant** object floats on a liquid. ❑ *This was such a small and buoyant boat.*

ADJ = cheerful · ADJ · ADJ

**bur|ble** /bɜːrbəl/ **(burbles, burbling, burbled)** 1 If something **burbles**, it makes a low continuous bubbling sound. ❑ *The water burbled over gravel... The river gurgled and burbled.* 2 If you say that someone **is burbling**, you mean that they are talking in a confused way. ❑ *He burbled something incomprehensible... Key burbled about the wonderful people who contribute to tourism... He burbles on about freedom.*

VERB · V prep · V · VERB · V n · V about n · V on about n

**bur|den** /bɜːrdən/ **(burdens, burdening, burdened)** ◆◇◇ 1 If you describe a problem or a responsibility as a **burden**, you mean that it causes someone a lot of difficulty, worry, or hard work. ❑ *The developing countries bear the burden of an enormous external debt... Her death will be an impossible burden on Paul... The financial burden will be more evenly shared.* 2 A **burden** is a heavy load that is difficult to carry. [FORMAL] 3 If someone **burdens** you **with** something that is likely to worry you, for example a problem or a difficult decision, they tell you about it. ❑ *We decided not to burden him with the news.* 4 ➔ See also **beast of burden**.

N-COUNT: usu with supp, oft N of/on n · N-COUNT · VERB · V n with n Also V n

**bur|dened** /bɜːrdənd/ 1 If you are **burdened** with something, it causes you a lot of

ADJ: v-link ADJ with/by n

worry or hard work. ❑ *Nicaragua was burdened with a foreign debt of $11 billion... They may be burdened by guilt and regret.* [2] If you describe someone as **burdened** with a heavy load, you are emphasizing that it is very heavy and that they are holding it or carrying it with difficulty. ❑ *Anna and Rosemary arrived burdened by bags and food baskets.* ADJ: v-link ADJ *with/by* n [emphasis]

**bur|den|some** /bɜːʳdənsəm/ If you describe something as **burdensome**, you mean it is worrying or hard to deal with. [WRITTEN] ❑ *...a burdensome debt... The load was too burdensome.* ADJ = onerous

**bu|reau** /bjʊ̲ərou/

> The usual plural in British English is **bureaux**. The usual plural in American English is **bureaus**.

[1] A **bureau** is an office, organization, or government department that collects and distributes information. ❑ *...the Federal Bureau of Investigation. ...the Citizens' Advice Bureau.* N-COUNT; N-IN-NAMES [2] A **bureau** is an office of a company or organization which has its main office in another town or country. [mainly AM, BUSINESS] ❑ *...the Wall Street Journal's Washington bureau.* N-COUNT = office [3] A **bureau** is a writing desk with shelves and drawers and a lid that opens to form the writing surface. [BRIT] N-COUNT [4] A **bureau** is a chest of drawers. [AM] N-COUNT

**bu|reau|cra|cy** /bjʊrɒ̲krəsi/ **(bureaucracies)** [1] A **bureaucracy** is an administrative system operated by a large number of officials. ❑ *State bureaucracies can tend to stifle enterprise and initiative.* N-COUNT: usu pl [2] **Bureaucracy** refers to all the rules and procedures followed by government departments and similar organizations, especially when you think that these are complicated and cause long delays. ❑ *People usually complain about having to deal with too much bureaucracy.* N-UNCOUNT [disapproval]

**bu|reau|crat** /bjʊ̲ərəkræt/ **(bureaucrats) Bureaucrats** are officials who work in a large administrative system. You can refer to officials as bureaucrats especially if you disapprove of them because they seem to follow rules and procedures too strictly. ❑ *The economy is still controlled by bureaucrats.* N-COUNT: usu pl [disapproval]

**bu|reau|crat|ic** /bjʊ̲ərəkræ̲tɪk/ **Bureaucratic** means involving complicated rules and procedures which can cause long delays. ❑ *Diplomats believe that bureaucratic delays are inevitable... The department has become a bureaucratic nightmare.* ADJ: usu ADJ n

**bu|reaux** /bjʊ̲ərouz/ **Bureaux** is a plural form of **bureau**.

**bur|geon** /bɜːʳdʒən/ **(burgeons, burgeoning, burgeoned)** If something **burgeons**, it grows or develops rapidly. [LITERARY] ❑ *My confidence began to burgeon later in life. ...Japan's burgeoning satellite-TV industry.* VERB V V-ing

**burg|er** /bɜːʳgəʳ/ **(burgers)** A **burger** is a flat round mass of minced meat or vegetables, which is fried and often eaten in a bread roll. ❑ *...burger and chips. ...vegetable burgers.* N-COUNT

**burgh|er** /bɜːʳgəʳ/ **(burghers)** The **burghers** of a town or city are the people who live there, especially the richer or more respectable people. [OLD-FASHIONED] N-COUNT: usu pl

**bur|glar** /bɜːʳgləʳ/ **(burglars)** A **burglar** is a thief who enters a house or other building by force. ❑ *Burglars broke into their home.* N-COUNT

**bur|glar alarm (burglar alarms)** A **burglar alarm** is an electric device that makes a bell ring loudly if someone tries to enter a building by force. N-COUNT

**bur|glar|ize** /bɜːʳgləraɪz/ **(burglarizes, burglarizing, burglarized)** If a building **is burglarized**, a thief enters it by force and steals things. [AM] ❑ *Her home was burglarized.* VERB: usu passive *be* V-ed

> in BRIT, use **burgle**

**bur|gla|ry** /bɜːʳgləri/ **(burglaries)** If someone commits a **burglary**, they enter a building by force and steal things. **Burglary** is the act of doing this. ❑ *An 11-year-old boy committed a burglary... He's been arrested for burglary.* N-VAR

**bur|gle** /bɜːʳgəl/ **(burgles, burgling, burgled)** If a building **is burgled**, a thief enters it by force and steals things. [BRIT] ❑ *I found that my flat had been burgled... Two teenagers burgled the home of Mr Jones's mother.* VERB *be* V-ed V n

> in AM, use **burglarize**

**bur|gun|dy** /bɜːʳgəndi/ **(burgundies)** [1] **Burgundy** is used to describe things that are purplish-red in colour. ❑ *He was wearing a burgundy polyester jacket. ...burgundy-coloured armchairs.* COLOUR [2] **Burgundy** is a type of wine. It can be white or red in colour and comes from the region of France called Burgundy. ❑ *...a bottle of white burgundy.* N-MASS

**bur|ial** /be̲riəl/ **(burials)** A **burial** is the act or ceremony of putting a dead body into a grave in the ground. ❑ *The priest prepared the body for burial... He can have a decent burial.* N-VAR

**bur|ial ground (burial grounds)** A **burial ground** is a place where bodies are buried, especially an ancient place. ❑ *...an ancient burial ground.* N-COUNT = graveyard

**bur|lap** /bɜːʳlæp/ **Burlap** is a thick, rough fabric that is used for making sacks. [AM] ❑ *...a burlap sack.* N-UNCOUNT

> in BRIT, use **hessian**

**bur|lesque** /bɜːrle̲sk/ **(burlesques)** A **burlesque** is a performance or a piece of writing that makes fun of something by copying it in an exaggerated way. You can also use **burlesque** to refer to a situation in real life that is like this. ❑ *The book read like a black comic burlesque. ...a trio of burlesque Moscow stereotypes.* N-VAR

**bur|ly** /bɜːʳli/ **(burlier, burliest)** A **burly** man has a broad body and strong muscles. ❑ *He was a big, burly man.* ADJ: usu ADJ n

**Bur|mese** /bɜːʳmiːz/ **(Burmese)** [1] **Burmese** means belonging or relating to Burma, or to its people, language, or culture. Burma is now known as Myanmar. ADJ [2] A **Burmese** is a Burmese citizen or a person of Burmese origin. N-COUNT [3] **Burmese** is the main language spoken by the people who live in Burma, now known as Myanmar. N-UNCOUNT

**burn** /bɜːʳn/ **(burns, burning, burned, burnt)** ◆◆◇

> The past tense and past participle is **burned** in American English, and **burned** or **burnt** in British English.

[1] If there is a fire or a flame somewhere, you say that there is a fire or flame **burning** there. ❑ *Fires were burning out of control in the center of the city... There was a fire burning in the large fireplace.* VERB V V [2] If something **is burning**, it is on fire. ❑ *When I arrived one of the vehicles was still burning... That boy was rescued from a burning house.* ♦ **burn|ing** *When we arrived in our village there was a terrible smell of burning.* VERB V V-ing N-UNCOUNT [3] If you **burn** something, you destroy or damage it with fire. ❑ *Protesters set cars on fire and burned a building... Coal fell out of the fire, and burned the carpet.* ♦ **burn|ing** *The French government has criticized the burning of a US flag outside the American Embassy.* VERB V n V n N-UNCOUNT [4] If you **burn** a fuel or if it **burns**, it is used to produce heat, light, or energy. ❑ *The power stations burn coal from the Ruhr region... Manufacturers are working with new fuels to find one that burns more cleanly than petrol.* VERB V n V [5] If you **burn** something that you are cooking or if it **burns**, you spoil it by using too much heat or cooking it for too long. ❑ *I burnt the toast... Watch them carefully as they finish cooking because they can burn easily.* ♦ **burnt** *...the smell of burnt toast.* VERB V n V ADJ [6] If you **burn** part of your body, **burn yourself**, or **are burnt**, you are injured by fire or by something very hot. ❑ *Take care not to burn your fingers... If you are badly burnt, seek medical attention.* ♦ **Burn** is also a noun. ❑ *She suffered appalling burns to her back.* VERB V n, be V-ed Also V pron-refl N-COUNT [7] If someone **is burnt** or **burnt** to death, they are killed by fire. ❑ *Women were burned as witches in the middle ages... At least 80 people were* VERB: usu passive *be* V-ed *as* n *be* V-ed *to* n

*burnt to death when their bus caught fire.* 8 If a light **is burning**, it is shining. [LITERARY] ❑ *The building was darkened except for a single light burning in a third-story window.* 9 If your face **is burning**, it is red because you are embarrassed or upset. ❑ *Liz's face was burning.* 10 If you **are burning with** an emotion or **are burning to** do something, you feel that emotion or the desire to do that thing very strongly. ❑ *The young boy was burning with a fierce ambition... Dan burned to know what the reason could be.* 11 If you **burn** or get **burned** in the sun, the sun makes your skin become red and sore. ❑ *Build up your tan slowly and don't allow your skin to burn... Summer sun can burn fair skin in minutes.* 12 If a part of your body **burns** or if something **burns** it, it has a painful, hot or stinging feeling. ❑ *My eyes burn from staring at the needle... His face was burning with cold. ...delicious Indian recipes which won't burn your throat.* 13 To **burn** a CD-ROM means to write or copy data onto it. [COMPUTING, INFORMAL] ❑ *You can use this software to burn custom compilations of your favorite tunes.* 14 → See also **burning**. to **burn the candle at both ends** → see **candle**. to **get** your **fingers burned** → see **finger**. to **burn** something **to the ground** → see **ground**. to **burn the midnight oil** → see **midnight**. to **have money to burn** → see **money**.

VERB · V · VERB: usu cont · V · VERB · V with n · V to-inf · VERB · V · V n · VERB · V · V with n · V n · VERB · V n

♦ **burn down** If a building **burns down** or if someone **burns** it **down**, it is completely destroyed by fire. ❑ *Six months after Bud died, the house burned down... Anarchists burnt down a restaurant.*

PHRASAL VERB · V P · V P n (not pron) Also V n P

♦ **burn off** If someone **burns off** energy, they use it. ❑ *This will improve your performance and help you burn off calories.*

PHRASAL VERB · V P n (not pron) Also V n P

♦ **burn out** 1 If a fire **burns itself out**, it stops burning because there is nothing left to burn. ❑ *Fire officials let the fire burn itself out.* 2 → See also **burnout**, **burnt-out**.

PHRASAL VERB · V pron-refl P

♦ **burn up** 1 If something **burns up** or if fire **burns** it **up**, it is completely destroyed by fire or strong heat. ❑ *The satellite re-entered the atmosphere and burned up... Fires have burned up 180,000 acres of timber.* 2 If something **burns up** fuel or energy, it uses it. ❑ *Brisk walking burns up more calories than slow jogging.*

PHRASAL VERB · V P · V P n Also V n P · PHRASAL VERB · V P n (not pron) Also V n P

**burned-out** → see **burnt-out**.

**burn|er** /bɜːʳnəʳ/ **(burners)** A **burner** is a device which produces heat or a flame, especially as part of a cooker, stove, or heater. ❑ *He put the frying pan on the gas burner.* → See also **back burner**, **front burner**.

N-COUNT

**burn|ing** /bɜːʳnɪŋ/ 1 You use **burning** to describe something that is extremely hot. ❑ *...the burning desert of Central Asia.* ♦ **Burning** is also an adverb. ❑ *He touched the boy's forehead. It was burning hot.* 2 If you have a **burning** interest in something or a **burning** desire to do something, you are extremely interested in it or want to do it very much. ❑ *I had a burning ambition to become a journalist... She had a burning desire to wreak revenge.* 3 A **burning** issue or question is a very important or urgent one that people feel very strongly about. ❑ *The burning question in this year's debate over the federal budget is: whose taxes should be raised?*

ADJ · ADV: ADV adj = scorching · ADJ: ADJ n = passionate · ADJ: ADJ n

**bur|nish** /bɜːʳnɪʃ/ **(burnishes, burnishing, burnished)** To **burnish** the image of someone or something means to improve their image. [WRITTEN] ❑ *The European Parliament badly needs a president who can burnish its image.*

VERB = improve · V n

**bur|nished** /bɜːʳnɪʃt/ You can describe something as **burnished** when it is bright or smooth. [LITERARY] ❑ *The clouds glowed like burnished gold.*

ADJ: usu ADJ n = polished

**burn|out** /bɜːʳnaʊt/ also **burn-out**. If someone suffers **burnout**, they exhaust themselves at an early stage in their life or career because they have achieved too much too quickly. [INFORMAL]

N-UNCOUNT

**burnt** /bɜːʳnt/ **Burnt** is a past tense and past participle of **burn**.

**burnt-out** also **burned-out**. 1 **Burnt-out** vehicles or buildings have been so badly damaged by fire that they can no longer be used. ❑ *...a burnt-out car.* 2 If someone is **burnt-out**, they exhaust themselves at an early stage in their life or career because they have achieved too much too quickly. [INFORMAL] ❑ *But everyone I know who kept it up at that intensity is burnt out.*

ADJ: usu ADJ n · ADJ

**burp** /bɜːʳp/ **(burps, burping, burped)** When someone **burps**, they make a noise because air from their stomach has been forced up through their throat. ❑ *Charlie burped loudly.* ♦ **Burp** is also a noun. ❑ *There followed a barely audible burp.*

VERB = belch · V · N-COUNT

**burr** /bɜːʳ/ **(burrs)**

> The spelling **bur** is also used for meaning 1.

1 A **burr** is the part of some plants which contains seeds and which has little hooks on the outside so that it sticks to clothes or fur. 2 If someone has a **burr**, they speak English with a regional accent in which 'r' sounds are pronounced more strongly than in the standard British way of speaking. ❑ *...a warm West Country burr.*

N-COUNT · N-COUNT: usu sing

**bur|row** /bʌroʊ, AM bɜː-/ **(burrows, burrowing, burrowed)** 1 A **burrow** is a tunnel or hole in the ground that is dug by an animal such as a rabbit. 2 If an animal **burrows** into the ground or into a surface, it moves through it by making a tunnel or hole. ❑ *The larvae burrow into cracks in the floor.* 3 If you **burrow** in a container or pile of things, you search there for something using your hands. ❑ *He burrowed into the pile of charts feverishly.* 4 If you **burrow** into something, you move underneath it or press against it, usually in order to feel warmer or safer. ❑ *She turned her face away from him, burrowing into her heap of covers.*

N-COUNT · VERB = tunnel · V prep/adv · VERB · V prep/adv · VERB · V prep/adv

**bur|sar** /bɜːʳsəʳ/ **(bursars)** The **bursar** of a school or college is the person who is in charge of its finance or general administration.

N-COUNT = treasurer

**bur|sa|ry** /bɜːʳsəri/ **(bursaries)** A **bursary** is a sum of money which is given to someone to allow them to study in a college or university. [mainly BRIT]

N-COUNT = scholarship

**burst** /bɜːʳst/ **(bursts, bursting)** ◆◇◇

> The form **burst** is used in the present tense and is the past tense and past participle.

1 If something **bursts** or if you **burst** it, it suddenly breaks open or splits open and the air or other substance inside it comes out. ❑ *The driver lost control when a tyre burst... It is not a good idea to burst a blister. ...a flood caused by a burst pipe.* 2 If a dam **bursts**, or if something **bursts** it, it breaks apart because the force of the river is too great. ❑ *A dam burst and flooded their villages.* 3 If a river **bursts** its banks, the water rises and goes on to the land. ❑ *Monsoons caused the river to burst its banks.* 4 When a door or lid **bursts** open, it opens very suddenly and violently because someone pushes it or there is great pressure behind it. ❑ *The door burst open and an angry young nurse appeared.* 5 To **burst into** or **out** of a place means to enter or leave it suddenly with a lot of energy or force. ❑ *Gunmen burst into his home and opened fire.* 6 If you say that something **bursts** onto the scene, you mean that it suddenly starts or becomes active, usually after developing quietly for some time. [JOURNALISM] ❑ *He burst onto the fashion scene in the early 1980s.* 7 A **burst of** something is a sudden short period of it. ❑ *...a burst of machine-gun fire... The current flows in little bursts.*

VERB · V · V n · V-ed · VERB · V, Also V n · VERB · V n · VERB = fly · V open/apart · VERB = rush · V prep/adv · VERB · V onto/upon n · N-COUNT: usu N of n

♦ **burst into** 1 If you **burst into** tears, laughter, or song, you suddenly begin to cry, laugh, or sing. ❑ *She burst into tears and ran from the kitchen. ...books that cause adults to burst into helpless laughter.* 2 If you say that something **bursts into** a particular situation or state, you mean that it suddenly changes into that situation or state. ❑ *This weekend's fighting is threatening to*

PHRASAL VERB · V P n · V P n · PHRASAL VERB · V P n

*burst into full-scale war.* 3 to **burst into flames** → see **flame**.

♦ **burst out** If someone **bursts out** laughing, crying, or making another noise, they suddenly start making that noise. You can also say that a noise **bursts out**. ❑ *The class burst out laughing... Then the applause burst out... Everyone burst out into conversation.*
PHRASAL VERB
V P -ing
V P
V P *into/in* n

**burst|ing** /bɜːʳstɪŋ/ 1 If a place is **bursting with** people or things, it is full of them. ❑ *The place appears to be bursting with women directors. ...a terraced vegetable garden, bursting with produce.*
ADJ: v-link ADJ, usu ADJ *with* n

2 If you say that someone is **bursting with** a feeling or quality, you mean that they have a great deal of it. ❑ *I was bursting with curiosity. ...a character bursting with energy and vivacity.*
ADJ: v-link ADJ *with* n

3 If you are **bursting to** do something, you are very eager to do it. [INFORMAL] ❑ *She was bursting to tell everyone.* 4 → See also **burst**.
ADJ: v-link ADJ to-inf

**bury** /beri/ **(buries, burying, buried)** 1 To **bury** something means to put it into a hole in the ground and cover it up with earth. ❑ *They make the charcoal by burying wood in the ground and then slowly burning it. ...squirrels who bury nuts and seeds. ...buried treasure.*
◆◇◇
VERB
V n prep/adv
V n
V-ed

2 To **bury** a dead person means to put their body into a grave and cover it with earth. ❑ *...soldiers who helped to bury the dead in large communal graves... I was horrified that people would think I was dead and bury me alive... More than 9,000 men lie buried here.*
VERB
V n
V n adj
V-ed

3 If someone says they **have buried** one of their relatives, they mean that one of their relatives has died. ❑ *He had buried his wife some two years before he retired.*
VERB
V n

4 If you **bury** something under a large quantity of things, you put it there, often in order to hide it. ❑ *I was looking for my handbag, which was buried under a pile of old newspapers.*
VERB
V n prep/adv

5 If something **buries** a place or person, it falls on top of them so that it completely covers them and often harms them in some way. ❑ *Latest reports say that mud slides buried entire villages... He was buried under the debris for several hours.*
VERB
V n
V-ed

6 If you **bury** your head or face in something, you press your head or face against it, often because you are unhappy. ❑ *She buried her face in the pillows.*
VERB = hide
V n prep/adv

7 If something **buries itself** somewhere, or if you **bury** it there, it is pushed very deeply in there. ❑ *The missile buried itself deep in the grassy hillside... He stood on the sidewalk with his hands buried in the pockets of his dark overcoat.*
VERB
V pron-refl prep/adv
V-ed
Also V n prep/adv

8 to **bury the hatchet** → see **hatchet**.

**bus** /bʌs/ **(buses, busses, bussing, bussed)** ◆◇◇

> ✔ The plural form of the noun is **buses**. The third person singular of the verb is **busses**. American English uses the spellings **buses, busing, bused** for the verb.

1 A **bus** is a large motor vehicle which carries passengers from one place to another. Buses drive along particular routes, and you have to pay to travel in them. ❑ *He missed his last bus home... They had to travel everywhere by bus.*
N-COUNT: also *by* N

2 When someone is **bussed** to a particular place or when they **bus** there, they travel there on a bus. ❑ *On May Day hundreds of thousands used to be bussed in to parade through East Berlin... To get our Colombian visas we bussed back to Medellin... Essential services were provided by Serbian workers bussed in from outside the province.*
VERB
*be* V-ed adv/prep
V adv/prep
V-ed
Also V n adv/prep

3 In some parts of the United States, when children are **bused** to school, they are transported by bus to a school in a different area so that children of different races can be educated together. ❑ *Many schools were in danger of closing because the children were bused out to other neighborhoods.* ♦ **bus|ing** *The courts ordered busing to desegregate the schools.*
VERB: usu passive
*be* V-ed adv/prep
N-UNCOUNT

**bus boy** **(bus boys)** A **bus boy** is someone whose job is to set or clear tables in a restaurant. [AM]
N-COUNT

**bush** /bʊʃ/ **(bushes)** 1 A **bush** is a large plant which is smaller than a tree and has a lot of branches. ❑ *Trees and bushes grew down to the water's edge.*
N-COUNT = shrub

2 The wild, uncultivated parts of some hot countries are referred to as **the bush**. ❑ *They walked through the dense Mozambican bush for thirty six hours.*
N-SING: usu *the* N, oft N n

3 If you tell someone not to **beat about the bush**, you mean that you want them to tell you something immediately and quickly, rather than in a complicated, indirect way. ❑ *Stop beating about the bush. What's he done?*
PHRASE: V inflects, usu with brd-neg

**bushed** /bʊʃt/ If you say that you are **bushed**, you mean that you are extremely tired. [INFORMAL] ❑ *I'm bushed. I'm going to bed.*
ADJ: v-link ADJ = beat

**bush|el** /bʊʃᵊl/ **(bushels)** A **bushel** is a unit of volume that is used for measuring agricultural produce such as corn or beans. A bushel is equivalent in volume to eight gallons.
N-COUNT

**Bush|man** /bʊʃmæn/ **(Bushmen)** A **Bushman** is an aboriginal person from the southwestern part of Africa, especially the Kalahari desert region.
N-COUNT

**bushy** /bʊʃi/ **(bushier, bushiest)** 1 **Bushy** hair or fur is very thick. ❑ *...bushy eyebrows. ...a bushy tail.*
ADJ: usu ADJ n

2 A **bushy** plant has a lot of leaves very close together. ❑ *...strong, sturdy, bushy plants.*
ADJ

**busi|ly** /bɪzɪli/ If you do something **busily**, you do it in a very active way. ❑ *The two saleswomen were busily trying to keep up with the demand.*
ADV: ADV with v

**busi|ness** /bɪznɪs/ **(businesses)** 1 **Business** is work relating to the production, buying, and selling of goods or services. ❑ *...young people seeking a career in business... Jennifer has an impressive academic and business background. ...Harvard Business School.*
◆◆◆
N-UNCOUNT

2 **Business** is used when talking about how many products or services a company is able to sell. If **business** is good, a lot of products or services are being sold and if **business** is bad, few of them are being sold. ❑ *They worried that German companies would lose business... Business is booming.*
N-UNCOUNT

3 A **business** is an organization which produces and sells goods or which provides a service. ❑ *The company was a family business... The majority of small businesses go broke within the first twenty-four months... He was short of cash after the collapse of his business.*
N-COUNT = company, firm

4 **Business** is work or some other activity that you do as part of your job and not for pleasure. ❑ *I'm here on business... You can't mix business with pleasure. ...business trips.*
N-UNCOUNT: oft *on* N

5 You can use **business** to refer to a particular area of work or activity in which the aim is to make a profit. ❑ *May I ask you what business you're in? ...the music business.*
N-SING: oft supp N

6 You can use **business** to refer to something that you are doing or concerning yourself with. ❑ *...recording Ben as he goes about his business... There was nothing left for the teams to do but get on with the business of racing.*
N-SING: with supp

7 You can use **business** to refer to important matters that you have to deal with. ❑ *The most important business was left to the last... I've got some unfinished business to attend to.*
N-UNCOUNT

8 If you say that something is your **business**, you mean that it concerns you personally and that other people have no right to ask questions about it or disagree with it. ❑ *My sex life is my business... If she doesn't want the police involved, that's her business... It's not our business.*
N-UNCOUNT: with poss = affair, concern

9 You can use **business** to refer in a general way to an event, situation, or activity. For example, you can say something is 'a wretched business' or you can refer to 'this assassination business'. ❑ *We have sorted out this wretched business at last... This whole business is very puzzling.*
N-SING: supp N = affair

10 You can use **business** when describing a task that is unpleasant in some way. For example, if you say that doing something is a costly **business**, you mean that it costs a lot. [INFORMAL] ❑ *Coastal defence is a costly business... Parenting can be a stressful business.*
N-SING: supp N = affair

11 → See also **big business**, **show business**.

**PHRASES** 12 If two people or companies **do business with** each other, one sells goods or services to the other. ❑ *I was fascinated by the different people who did business with me.*
PHRASE: V inflects, PHR *with* n, pl-n PHR

13 If you say that someone **has no business to** be in a place or **to**
PHRASE: V inflects, PHR to-inf,

do something, you mean that they have no right to be there or to do it. ❑ *Really I had no business to be there at all.* [14] A company that is **in business** is operating and trading. ❑ *You can't stay in business without cash.* [15] If you say you **are in business**, you mean you have everything you need to start something immediately. [INFORMAL, SPOKEN] ❑ *All you need is a microphone, and you're in business.* [16] If you say that someone **means business**, you mean they are serious and determined about what they are doing. [INFORMAL] ❑ *Now people are starting to realise that he means business.* [17] If you say to someone '**mind your own business**' or '**it's none of your business**', you are rudely telling them not to ask about something that does not concern them. [INFORMAL] ❑ *I asked Laura what was wrong and she told me to mind my own business.* [18] If a shop or company goes **out of business** or is put **out of business**, it has to stop trading because it is not making enough money. ❑ *Thousands of firms could go out of business.* [19] In a difficult situation, if you say it is **business as usual**, you mean that people will continue doing what they normally do. ❑ *The Queen was determined to show it was business as usual.* PHR -ing / PHRASE: v-link PHR / PHRASE: V inflects, v-link PHR / PHRASE: V inflects / PHRASE / PHRASE: PHR after v / PHRASE: usu v-link PHR

**busi|ness an|gel** **(business angels)** A **business angel** is a person who gives financial support to a commercial venture and receives a share of any profits from it, but who does not expect to be involved in its management. N-COUNT

**busi|ness card** **(business cards)** A person's **business card** or their **card** is a small card which they give to other people, and which has their name and details of their job and company printed on it. N-COUNT: oft poss N

**busi|ness class** Business class seating on an aeroplane costs less than first class but more than economy class. ❑ *You can pay to be upgraded to a business class seat.* ♦ **Business class** is also an adverb. ❑ *They flew business class.* ♦ **Business class** is the business class seating on an aeroplane. ❑ *The Australian team will be seated in business class.* ADJ: ADJ n / ADV: ADV after v / N-UNCOUNT

**busi|ness end** The **business end of** a tool or weapon is the end of it which does the work or causes damage rather than the end that you hold. [INFORMAL] ❑ *...the business end of a vacuum cleaner.* N-SING: usu N *of* n

**busi|ness hours** **Business hours** are the hours of the day in which a shop or a company is open for business. ❑ *All showrooms are staffed during business hours.* N-PLURAL

**business|like** /bɪznəslaɪk/ If you describe someone as **businesslike**, you mean that they deal with things in an efficient way without wasting time. ❑ *Mr. Penn sounds quite businesslike... This activity was carried on in a businesslike manner.* ADJ = *efficient*

**business|man** /bɪznɪsmæn/ **(businessmen)** A **businessman** is a man who works in business. ◆◇◇ N-COUNT

**busi|ness per|son** **(business people)** **Business people** are people who work in business. ❑ *...a self-employed business person.* N-COUNT

**busi|ness plan** **(business plans)** A **business plan** is a detailed plan for setting up or developing a business, especially one that is written in order to borrow money. ❑ *She learned how to write a business plan for the catering business she wanted to launch.* N-COUNT

**busi|ness school** **(business schools)** A **business school** is a school or college which teaches business subjects such as economics and management. N-COUNT

**business|woman** /bɪznɪswʊmən/ **(businesswomen)** A **businesswoman** is a woman who works in business. N-COUNT

**busk** /bʌsk/ **(busks, busking, busked)** People who **busk** play music or sing for money in the streets or other public places. [BRIT] ❑ *They spent their free time in Glasgow busking in Argyle Street.* ♦ **busk|ing** *Passers-by in the area have been treated to some high-quality busking.* VERB / V / N-UNCOUNT

**busk|er** /bʌskə^r/ **(buskers)** A **busker** is a person who sings or plays music for money in streets and other public places. [BRIT] N-COUNT

**bus lane** **(bus lanes)** A **bus lane** is a part of the road which is intended to be used only by buses. N-COUNT

**bus|load** /bʌsloʊd/ **(busloads)** A **busload of** people is a large number of passengers on a bus. ❑ *...a busload of Japanese tourists.* N-COUNT: usu N *of* n

**bus|man's holi|day** /bʌsmənz hɒlɪdeɪ/ If you have a holiday, but spend it doing something similar to your usual work, you can refer to it as a **busman's holiday**. N-SING

**bus shel|ter** **(bus shelters)** A **bus shelter** is a bus stop that has a roof and at least one open side. N-COUNT

**bus stop** **(bus stops)** A **bus stop** is a place on a road where buses stop to let passengers on and off. N-COUNT

**bust** /bʌst/ **(busts, busting, busted)**

> ✔ The form **bust** is used as the present tense of the verb, and can also be used as the past tense and past participle.

[1] If you **bust** something, you break it or damage it so badly that it cannot be used. [INFORMAL] ❑ *They will have to bust the door to get him out.* [2] If someone **is busted**, the police arrest them. [INFORMAL] ❑ *They were busted for possession of cannabis.* [3] If police **bust** a place, they go to it in order to arrest people who are doing something illegal. [INFORMAL] ❑ *...police success in busting UK-based drug factories.* ♦ **Bust** is also a noun. ❑ *Six tons of cocaine were seized last week in Panama's biggest drug bust.* [4] A company or fund that is **bust** has no money left and has been forced to close down. [INFORMAL, BUSINESS] ❑ *It is taxpayers who will pay most of the bill for bailing out bust banks.* [5] If a company **goes bust**, it loses so much money that it is forced to close down. [INFORMAL, BUSINESS] ❑ *...a Swiss company which went bust last May.* [6] A **bust** is a statue of the head and shoulders of a person. ❑ *...a bronze bust of the Queen.* [7] You can use **bust** to refer to a woman's breasts, especially when you are describing their size. ❑ *Good posture also helps your bust look bigger.* VERB / V n / VERB: usu passive *be* V-ed / VERB / V n / N-COUNT / ADJ / PHRASE: V inflects / N-COUNT: oft N *of* n / N-COUNT

**-buster** /-bʌstə^r/ **(-busters)** [1] **-buster** combines with nouns to form new nouns which refer to someone who breaks a particular law. ❑ *The Security Council will consider taking future actions against sanction-busters. ...copyright-busters.* [2] **-buster** combines with nouns to form new nouns which refer to someone or something that fights or overcomes the specified crime or undesirable activity. ❑ *Hoover was building his reputation as a crime-buster. ...fraud-busters.* COMB in N-COUNT = *-breaker* / COMB in N-COUNT

**bust|ier** /bʌstiə^r/ **(bustiers)** A **bustier** is a type of close-fitting strapless top worn by women. N-COUNT

**bus|tle** /bʌsᵊl/ **(bustles, bustling, bustled)** [1] If someone **bustles** somewhere, they move there in a hurried way, often because they are very busy. ❑ *She bustled about, turning on lights, moving pillows around on the sofa.* [2] A place that **is bustling with** people or activity is full of people who are very busy or lively. ❑ *The sidewalks are bustling with people... The main attraction was the bustling market.* [3] **Bustle** is busy, noisy activity. ❑ *...the hustle and bustle of modern life.* VERB / V prep/adv / VERB / V *with* n / V-ing / N-UNCOUNT: oft N *of* n

**bust-up** **(bust-ups)** [1] A **bust-up** is a serious quarrel, often resulting in the end of a relationship. [INFORMAL] ❑ *She had had this bust-up with her family.* [2] A **bust-up** is a fight. [BRIT, INFORMAL] ❑ *...a bust-up which she says left her seriously hurt.* N-COUNT = *row* / N-COUNT

**busty** /bʌsti/ If you describe a woman as **busty**, you mean that she has large breasts. [INFORMAL] ADJ

**busy** /bɪzi/ **(busier, busiest, busies, busying, busied)** [1] When you are **busy**, you are working hard or concentrating on a task, so that you are not free to do anything else. ❑ *What is it? I'm busy... They are busy preparing for a hectic day's activ-* ◆◇◇ ADJ *ity on Saturday... Rachel said she would be too busy to come... Phil Martin is an exceptionally busy man.* [2] ADJ: usu ADJ n = hectic ≠ quiet A **busy** time is a period of time during which you have a lot of things to do. ❑ *It'll have to wait. This is our busiest time... Even with her busy schedule she finds time to watch TV... I had a busy day and was rather tired.* [3] ADJ: v-link ADJ, oft ADJ -ing = preoccupied If you say that someone is **busy** thinking or worrying about something, you mean that it is taking all their attention, often to such an extent that they are unable to think about anything else. ❑ *Companies are so busy analysing the financial implications that they overlook the effect on workers... Most people are too busy with their own troubles to give much help.* [4] VERB If you **busy yourself** with something, you occupy yourself by dealing with it. ❑ *He busied himself with the camera...* V pron-refl *with* n *She busied herself getting towels ready...* V pron-refl -ing *For a while Kathryn busied herself in the kitchen.* V pron-refl [5] ADJ A **busy** place is full of people who are doing things or moving about. ❑ *The Strand is one of London's busiest and most affluent streets... The ward was busy and Amy hardly had time to talk.* [6] ADJ: usu v-link ADJ = engaged When a telephone line is **busy**, you cannot make your call because the line is already being used by someone else. [mainly AM] ❑ *I tried to reach him, but the line was busy.* [7] → See also **busily**.

**busy|body** /bɪzibɒdi/ **(busybodies)** N-COUNT [disapproval] If you refer to someone as a **busybody**, you are criticizing the way they interfere in other people's affairs. [INFORMAL] ❑ *This government is full of interfering busybodies.*

**but** /bət, STRONG bʌt/ ◆◆◆ [1] CONJ You use **but** to introduce something which contrasts with what you have just said, or to introduce something which adds to what you have just said. ❑ *'You said you'd stay till tomorrow.' — 'I know, Bel, but I think I would rather go back.'... Place the saucepan over moderate heat until the cider is very hot but not boiling... He not only wants to be taken seriously as a musician, but as a poet too.* [2] CONJ You use **but** when you are about to add something further in a discussion or to change the subject. ❑ *They need to recruit more people into the prison service. But another point I'd like to make is that many prisons were built in the nineteenth century.* [3] CONJ You use **but** after you have made an excuse or apologized for what you are just about to say. ❑ *Please excuse me, but there is something I must say... I'm sorry, but it's nothing to do with you... Forgive my asking, but you're not very happy, are you?* [4] CONJ [feelings] You use **but** to introduce a reply to someone when you want to indicate surprise, disbelief, refusal, or protest. ❑ *'I don't think I should stay in this house.' — 'But why?'... 'Somebody wants you on the telephone' — 'But no one knows I'm here!'* [5] PREP: n PREP n **But** is used to mean 'except'. ❑ *Europe will be represented in all but two of the seven races... He didn't speak anything but Greek... The crew of the ship gave them nothing but bread to eat.* [6] ADV: ADV n, ADV num **But** is used to mean 'only'. [FORMAL] ❑ *This is but one of the methods used to try and get alcoholics to give up drink. ...Napoleon and Marie Antoinette, to name but two who had stayed in the great state rooms.* [7] N-PLURAL You use **buts** in expressions like '**no buts**' and '**ifs and buts**' to refer to reasons someone gives for not doing something, especially when you do not think that they are good reasons. ❑ *'B-b-b-b-but' I stuttered. — 'Never mind the buts,' she ranted... He committed a crime, no ifs or buts about it.*

**PHRASES** [8] PHRASE: PHR inf [emphasis] You use **cannot but**, **could not but**, and **cannot help but** when you want to emphasize that you believe something must be true and that there is no possibility of anything else being the case. [FORMAL] ❑ *The pistol was positioned where I couldn't help but see it... She could not but congratulate him.* [9] PHRASE: PHR n/-ing You use **but for** to introduce the only factor that causes a particular thing not to happen or not to be completely true. ❑ *...the small square below, empty but for a delivery van and a clump of palm trees.* [10] PHRASE: PHR cl You use **but then** or **but then again** before a remark which slightly contradicts what you have just said. ❑ *My husband spends hours in the bathroom, but then again so do I.* [11] PHRASE: PHR cl You use **but then** before a remark which suggests that what you have just said should not be regarded as surprising. ❑ *He was a fine young man, but then so had his father been... Sonia might not speak the English language well, but then who did?* [12] **all but** → see **all**. **anything but** → see **anything**.

**bu|tane** /bjuːteɪn/ N-UNCOUNT **Butane** is a gas that is obtained from petroleum and is used as a fuel.

**butch** /bʊtʃ/ [1] ADJ If you describe a woman as **butch**, you mean that she behaves or dresses in a masculine way. This use could cause offence. [INFORMAL] [2] ADJ = macho If you describe a man as **butch**, you mean that he behaves in an extremely masculine way. [INFORMAL]

**butch|er** /bʊtʃəʳ/ **(butchers, butchering, butchered)** [1] N-COUNT A **butcher** is a shopkeeper who cuts up and sells meat. Some butchers also kill animals for meat and make foods such as sausages and meat pies. [2] N-COUNT: oft *the* N A **butcher** or a **butcher's** is a shop where meat is sold. [3] VERB: *be* V-ed To **butcher** an animal means to kill it and cut it up for meat. ❑ *Pigs were butchered, hams were hung to dry from the ceiling.* [4] N-COUNT [disapproval] You can refer to someone as a **butcher** when they have killed a lot of people in a very cruel way, and you want to express your horror and disgust. ❑ *Klaus Barbie was known in France as the Butcher of Lyon.* [5] VERB [disapproval] = slaughter You can say that someone **has butchered** people when they have killed a lot of people in a very cruel way, and you want to express your horror and disgust. ❑ *Guards butchered 1,350 prisoners.* V n

**butch|ery** /bʊtʃəri/ [1] N-UNCOUNT [disapproval] You can refer to the cruel killing of a lot of people as **butchery** when you want to express your horror and disgust at this. ❑ *In her view, war is simply a legalised form of butchery.* [2] N-UNCOUNT **Butchery** is the work of cutting up meat and preparing it for sale. ❑ *...a carcass hung up for butchery.*

**but|ler** /bʌtləʳ/ **(butlers)** N-COUNT A **butler** is the most important male servant in a wealthy house.

**butt** /bʌt/ **(butts, butting, butted)** [1] N-COUNT Someone's **butt** is their bottom. [AM, INFORMAL] ❑ *Frieda grinned, pinching him on the butt.* [2] N-COUNT: oft n N, N *of* n The **butt** or the **butt end of** a weapon or tool is the thick end of its handle. ❑ *Troops used tear gas and rifle butts to break up the protests.* [3] N-COUNT: oft n N, N *of* n The **butt of** a cigarette or cigar is the small part of it that is left when someone has finished smoking it. [4] N-COUNT: usu with supp A **butt** is a large barrel used for collecting or storing liquid. [5] N-SING: usu *the* N *of* n = target If someone or something is **the butt of** jokes or criticism, people often make fun of them or criticize them. ❑ *He is still the butt of cruel jokes about his humble origins.* [6] VERB If a person or animal **butts** you, they hit you with the top of their head. ❑ *Lawrence kept on butting me but the referee did not warn him.* V n Also V n prep [7] → See also **head-butt**, **water butt**.

♦ **butt in** PHRASAL VERB [disapproval] = interrupt If you say that someone **is butting in**, you are criticizing the fact that they are joining in a conversation or activity without being asked to. ❑ *Sorry, I don't mean to butt in...* V P *'I should think not,' Sarah butted in.* V P with quote Also V P *on* n

**but|ter** /bʌtəʳ/ **(butters, buttering, buttered)** ◆◇◇ [1] N-MASS **Butter** is a soft yellow substance made from cream. You spread it on bread or use it in cooking. ❑ *...bread and butter... Pour the melted butter into a large mixing bowl.* [2] VERB If you **butter** something such as bread or toast, you spread butter on it. ❑ *She spread pieces of bread on the counter and began buttering them.* V n *...buttered scones.* V-ed [3] → See also **bread and butter**, **peanut butter**.

♦ **butter up** PHRASAL VERB If someone **butters** you **up**, they try to please you because they want you to help or support them. [BRIT, INFORMAL] ❑ *The bank has to butter up investors because it is in a fiercely competitive market...* V P n (not pron) *I tried buttering her up. 'I've always admired people with these sorts of talents.'* V n P

**but|ter bean** **(butter beans)** **Butter beans** are the yellowish flat round seeds of a kind of bean plant. They are eaten as a vegetable, and in Britain they are usually sold dried rather than fresh. [N-COUNT: usu pl]

**butter|cup** /bʌtəʳkʌp/ **(buttercups)** A **buttercup** is a small plant with bright yellow flowers. [N-COUNT]

**butter|fly** /bʌtəʳflaɪ/ **(butterflies)** 1 A **butterfly** is an insect with large colourful wings and a thin body. [N-COUNT] 2 **Butterfly** is a swimming stroke which you do lying on your front, kicking your legs and bringing your arms over your head together. [N-UNCOUNT: also the N] 3 If you have **butterflies in** your **stomach** or have **butterflies**, you are very nervous or excited about something. [INFORMAL] ❑ *An exam, or even an exciting social event may produce butterflies in the stomach.* [PHRASE]

**butter|milk** /bʌtəʳmɪlk/ **Buttermilk** is the liquid that remains when fat has been removed from cream when butter is being made. You can drink buttermilk or use it in cooking. [N-UNCOUNT]

**butter|scotch** /bʌtəʳskɒtʃ/ 1 **Butterscotch** is a hard yellowish-brown sweet made from butter and sugar boiled together. [N-UNCOUNT] 2 A **butterscotch** flavoured or coloured thing has the flavour or colour of butterscotch. ❑ *...butterscotch sauce.* [N-UNCOUNT: usu N n]

**but|tery** /bʌtəri/ **Buttery** food contains butter or is covered with butter. ❑ *...buttery new potatoes. ...the buttery taste of the pastry.* [ADJ: usu ADJ n]

**but|tock** /bʌtək/ **(buttocks)** Your **buttocks** are the two rounded fleshy parts of your body that you sit on. [N-COUNT]

**but|ton** /bʌtᵊn/ **(buttons, buttoning, buttoned)** [◆◇◇] 1 **Buttons** are small hard objects sewn on to shirts, coats, or other pieces of clothing. You fasten the clothing by pushing the buttons through holes called buttonholes. ❑ *...a coat with brass buttons.* [N-COUNT] 2 If you **button** a shirt, coat, or other piece of clothing, you fasten it by pushing its buttons through the buttonholes. ❑ *Ferguson stood up and buttoned his coat.* [VERB; V n] ♦ **Button up** means the same as **button**. ❑ *I buttoned up my coat; it was chilly... The young man slipped on the shirt and buttoned it up... It was freezing out there even in his buttoned-up overcoat.* [PHRASAL VERB; V P n (not pron); V n P; V-ed P] 3 A **button** is a small object on a machine or electrical device that you press in order to operate it. ❑ *He reached for the remote control and pressed the 'play' button.* [N-COUNT] 4 A **button** is a small piece of metal or plastic which you wear in order to show that you support a particular movement, organization, or person. You fasten a button to your clothes with a pin. [AM] [N-COUNT]

✓ in BRIT, use **badge**

♦ **button up** → see **button 2**.

**button-down** A **button-down** shirt or a shirt with a **button-down** collar has a button under each end of the collar which you can fasten. [ADJ: ADJ n]

**but|toned up** also **buttoned-up**. If you say that someone is **buttoned up**, you mean that they do not usually talk about their thoughts and feelings. [INFORMAL] ❑ *...the buttoned-up wife of an English clergyman.* [ADJ = reserved]

**button|hole** /bʌtᵊnhoʊl/ **(buttonholes, buttonholing, buttonholed)** 1 A **buttonhole** is a hole that you push a button through in order to fasten a shirt, coat, or other piece of clothing. [N-COUNT] 2 A **buttonhole** is a flower that you wear on your coat or dress. [BRIT] [N-COUNT] 3 If you **buttonhole** someone, you stop them and make them listen to you. ❑ *Several people buttonholed television reporters to explain to them their reasons for not voting.* [VERB; V n]

**but|ton mush|room** **(button mushrooms)** **Button mushrooms** are small mushrooms used in cooking. [N-COUNT: usu pl]

**but|tress** /bʌtrəs/ **(buttresses)** **Buttresses** are supports, usually made of stone or brick, that support a wall. [N-COUNT]

**but|ty** /bʌti/ **(butties)** A **butty** is a sandwich. [BRIT, INFORMAL] [N-COUNT = sarnie]

**bux|om** /bʌksəm/ If you describe a woman as **buxom**, you mean that she looks healthy and attractive and has a rounded body and big breasts. ❑ *Melissa was a tall, buxom blonde.* [ADJ: usu ADJ n]

**buy** /baɪ/ **(buys, buying, bought)** [◆◆◆] 1 If you **buy** something, you obtain it by paying money for it. ❑ *He could not afford to buy a house... Lizzie bought herself a mountain bike... I'd like to buy him lunch.* [VERB; V n; V pron-refl n; V n n] 2 If you talk about the quantity or standard of goods an amount of money **buys**, you are referring to the price of the goods or the value of the money. ❑ *About £35,000 buys a habitable house... If the pound's value is high, British investors will spend their money abroad because the pound will buy them more.* [VERB; V n; V n n] 3 If you **buy** something like time, freedom, or victory, you obtain it but only by offering or giving up something in return. ❑ *It was a risky operation, but might buy more time... For them, affluence was bought at the price of less freedom in their work environment.* [VERB; V n; V n] 4 If you say that a person can **be bought**, you are criticizing the fact that they will give their help or loyalty to someone in return for money. ❑ *Once he shows he can be bought, they settle down to a regular payment.* [VERB: usu passive; disapproval; = bribe; be V-ed] 5 If you **buy** an idea or a theory, you believe and accept it. [INFORMAL] ❑ *I'm not buying any of that nonsense.* [VERB; V n] ♦ **Buy into** means the same as **buy**. ❑ *I bought into the popular myth that when I got the new car or the next house, I'd finally be happy.* [PHRASAL VERB; V P n] 6 If something is a good **buy**, it is of good quality and not very expensive. ❑ *This was still a good buy even at the higher price.* [N-COUNT: supp N = bargain]

♦ **buy into** If you **buy into** a company or an organization, you buy part of it, often in order to gain some control of it. [BUSINESS] ❑ *Other companies could buy into the firm.* → See also **buy 5**. [PHRASAL VERB; V P n]

♦ **buy off** If you say that a person or organization **buys off** another person or group, you are criticizing the fact that they are giving them something such as money so that they will not complain or cause trouble. ❑ *...policies designed to buy off the working-class vote... In buying your children all these things, you are in a sense buying them off.* [PHRASAL VERB; disapproval; V P n (not pron); V n P]

♦ **buy out** If you **buy** someone **out**, you buy their share of something such as a company or piece of property that you previously owned together. ❑ *The bank had to pay to buy out most of the 200 former partners... He bought his brother out for $17 million.* → See also **buyout**. [PHRASAL VERB; V P n (not pron); V n P]

♦ **buy up** If you **buy up** land, property, or a commodity, you buy large amounts of it, or all that is available. ❑ *The mention of price rises sent citizens out to their shops to buy up as much as they could... The tickets will be on sale from somewhere else because the agencies have bought them up.* [PHRASAL VERB; V P n (not pron); V n P]

**buy-back** **(buy-backs)** A **buy-back** is a situation in which a company buys shares back from its investors. [BUSINESS] ❑ *...a share buy-back scheme... The company announced an extensive stock buy-back program.* [N-COUNT]

**buy|er** /baɪəʳ/ **(buyers)** [◆◇◇] 1 A **buyer** is a person who is buying something or who intends to buy it. ❑ *Car buyers are more interested in safety and reliability than speed.* [N-COUNT ≠ seller] 2 A **buyer** is a person who works for a large store deciding what goods will be bought from manufacturers to be sold in the store. [N-COUNT]

**buy|er's mar|ket** When there is a **buyer's market** for a particular product, there are more of the products for sale than there are people who want to buy them, so buyers have a lot of choice and can make prices come down. [BUSINESS] [N-SING]

**buy|out** /baɪaʊt/ **(buyouts)** A **buyout** is the buying of a company, especially by its managers or employees. [BUSINESS] ❑ *It is thought that a management buyout is one option.* → See also **MBO**. [N-COUNT: oft supp N]

**buzz** /bʌz/ **(buzzes, buzzing, buzzed)** 1 If something **buzzes** or **buzzes** somewhere, it [VERB] makes a long continuous sound, like the noise a bee makes when it is flying. ❑ *The intercom buzzed* V *and he pressed down the appropriate switch... Attack* V prep/adv *helicopters buzzed across the city.* ♦ **Buzz** is also a noun. ❑ *...the irritating buzz of an insect.* N-COUNT; SOUND ♦ **buzz|ing** *He switched off the transformer and the buzzing stopped.* N-UNCOUNT [2] If people **are buzzing around**, they are moving around quickly and busily. [WRITTEN] ❑ *A few tourists were buzzing about.* VERB = race V adv/prep [3] If questions or ideas **are buzzing around** your head, or if your head **is buzzing with** questions or ideas, you are thinking about a lot of things, often in a confused way. ❑ *Many more questions were buzzing around in my head... Top style consultants will leave you buzzing with new ideas.* VERB V *around in* n V *with* n Also V [4] If a place **is buzzing with** activity or conversation, there is a lot of activity or conversation there, especially because something important or exciting is about to happen. ❑ *The rehearsal studio is buzzing with lunchtime activity. ...Hong Kong's buzzing, pulsating atmosphere.* VERB: usu cont V *with* n V-ing Also V, V prep [5] You can use **buzz** to refer to a long continuous sound, usually caused by lots of people talking at once. ❑ *A buzz of excitement filled the courtroom as the defendant was led in. ...the excited buzz of conversation.* N-SING: usu N *of* n [6] If something gives you a **buzz**, it makes you feel very happy or excited for a short time. [INFORMAL] ❑ *Performing still gives him a buzz... He got a buzz from creating confrontations.* N-SING [7] You can use **buzz** to refer to a word, idea, or activity which has recently become extremely popular. ❑ *...the latest buzz phrase in garden design circles... Sex education in schools was the buzz topic.* ADJ: ADJ n [8] If an aircraft **buzzes** a place, it flies low over it, usually in a threatening way. ❑ *American fighter planes buzzed the city.* VERB V n

**buz|zard** /bʌzəʳd/ **(buzzards)** A **buzzard** is a large bird of prey. N-COUNT

**buzz|er** /bʌzəʳ/ **(buzzers)** A **buzzer** is an electrical device that is used to make a buzzing sound for example, to attract someone's attention. N-COUNT

**buzz|saw** /bʌzsɔː/ **(buzzsaws)** A **buzzsaw** is an electric saw consisting of a round metal disk with a sharp serrated edge. It is powered by an electric motor and is used for cutting wood and other materials. [AM] N-COUNT

✓ in BRIT, use **circular saw**

**buzz|word** /bʌzwɜːʳd/ **(buzzwords)** also **buzz word.** A **buzzword** is a word or expression that has become fashionable in a particular field and is being used a lot by the media. ❑ *Biodiversity was the buzzword of the Rio Earth Summit.* N-COUNT

**buzzy** /bʌzi/ **(buzzier, buzziest)** If a place, event, or atmosphere is **buzzy**, it is lively, interesting, and modern. [INFORMAL] ❑ *The cafe has an intimate but buzzy atmosphere.* ADJ

**by** ♦♦♦

✓ The preposition is pronounced /baɪ/. The adverb is pronounced /baɪ/.

> In addition to the uses shown below, **by** is used in phrasal verbs such as 'abide by', 'put by', and 'stand by'.

[1] If something is done **by** a person or thing, that person or thing does it. ❑ *The feast was served by his mother and sisters... I was amazed by their discourtesy and lack of professionalism... The town has been under attack by rebel groups for a week now.* PREP [2] If you say that something such as a book, a piece of music, or a painting is **by** a particular person, you mean that this person wrote it or created it. ❑ *...a painting by Van Gogh... 'Jacob's Ladder', the newest film by Adrian Lyne, is a post-Vietnam horror story.* PREP [3] If you do something **by** a particular means, you do it using that thing. ❑ *We'll be travelling by car. ...dinners by candlelight.* PREP [4] If you achieve one thing **by** doing another thing, your action enables you to achieve the first thing. ❑ *Make the sauce by boiling the cream and stock together in a pan... The all-female yacht crew made history by becoming the first to sail round the world... By using the air ambulance to transport patients between hospitals, they can save up to £15,000 per patient.* PREP: PREP -ing [5] You use **by** in phrases such as 'by chance' or 'by accident' to indicate whether or not an event was planned. ❑ *I met him by chance out walking yesterday... He opened Ingrid's letter by mistake... Whether by design or accident his timing was perfect.* PREP [6] If someone is a particular type of person **by** nature, **by** profession, or **by** birth, they are that type of person because of their nature, their profession, or the family they were born into. ❑ *I am certainly lucky to have a kind wife who is loving by nature... She's a nurse by profession and now runs a counselling service for women... Her parents were in fact American by birth.* PREP: adj/n PREP n [7] If something must be done **by** law, it happens according to the law. If something is the case **by** particular standards, it is the case according to the standards. ❑ *Pharmacists are required by law to give the medicine prescribed by the doctor. ...evening wear that was discreet by his standards.* PREP [8] If you say what someone means **by** a particular word or expression, you are saying what they intend the word or expression to refer to. ❑ *Stella knew what he meant by 'start again'... 'You're unbelievably lucky' — 'What do you mean by that?'* PREP [9] If you hold someone or something **by** a particular part of them, you hold that part. ❑ *He caught her by the shoulder and turned her around... She was led by the arm to a small room at the far end of the corridor... He picked up the photocopy by one corner and put it in his wallet.* PREP [10] Someone or something that is **by** something else is beside it and close to it. ❑ *Judith was sitting in a rocking-chair by the window... Felicity Maxwell stood by the bar and ordered a glass of wine... Emma was by the door.* ♦ **By** is also an adverb. ❑ *Large numbers of security police stood by.* PREP ADV: ADV after v [11] If a person or vehicle goes **by** you, they move past you without stopping. ❑ *A few cars passed close by me... He kept walking and passed by me on his side of the street.* ♦ **By** is also an adverb. ❑ *The bomb went off as a police patrol went by.* PREP: v PREP n ADV: ADV after v [12] If you stop **by** a place, you visit it for a short time. ❑ *We had made arrangements to stop by her house in Pacific Grove.* ♦ **By** is also an adverb. ❑ *I'll stop by after dinner and we'll have that talk.* PREP ADV: ADV after v [13] If something happens **by** a particular time, it happens at or before that time. ❑ *By eight o'clock he had arrived at my hotel... We all knew by then that the affair was practically over.* PREP [14] If you do something **by** day, you do it during the day. If you do it **by** night, you do it during the night. ❑ *By day a woman could safely walk the streets, but at night the pavements became dangerous... She had no wish to hurry alone through the streets of London by night.* PREP [15] In arithmetic, you use **by** before the second number in a multiplication or division sum. ❑ *...an apparent annual rate of 22.8 per cent (1.9 multiplied by 12)... 230cm divided by 22cm is 10.45cm.* PREP: PREP num [16] You use **by** to talk about measurements of area. For example, if a room is twenty feet **by** fourteen feet, it measures twenty feet in one direction and fourteen feet in the other direction. ❑ *Three prisoners were sharing one small cell 3 metres by 2 metres.* PREP: PREP num [17] If something increases or decreases **by** a particular amount, that amount is gained or lost. ❑ *Violent crime has increased by 10 percent since last year... Their pay has been cut by one-third.* PREP: PREP amount [18] Things that are made or sold **by** the million or **by** the dozen are made or sold in those quantities. ❑ *Parcels arrived by the dozen from America... Liberty fabrics, both for furnishing and for dress-making, are sold by the metre.* PREP: PREP *the* n [19] You use **by** in expressions such as 'minute by minute' and 'drop by drop' to talk about things that happen gradually, not all at once. ❑ *His father began to lose his memory bit by bit, becoming increasingly forgetful.* PREP: n PREP n

PHRASES [20] If you are **by yourself**, you are alone. ❑ *...a dark-haired man sitting by himself in a corner.* PHRASE: PHR after v = alone [21] If you do something **by yourself**, you PHRASE: PHR after v succeed in doing it without anyone helping you. ❑ *I didn't know if I could raise a child by myself.*

**bye** /baɪ/ **Bye** and **bye-bye** are informal ways of saying goodbye. ◆◇◇ CONVENTION

**bye-law** → see **bylaw.**

**by-election** **(by-elections)** A **by-election** is an election that is held to choose a new member of parliament when a member has resigned or died. [BRIT] N-COUNT

**Bye|lo|rus|sian** /bieloʊrʌʃᵊn/ **(Byelorussians)** [1] **Byelorussian** means belonging or relating to Byelorussia or to its people or culture. ADJ [2] A **Byelorussian** is a Byelorussian citizen, or a person of Byelorussian origin. N-COUNT

**by|gone** /baɪgɒn, AM -gɔːn/ **(bygones)** [1] **Bygone** means happening or existing a very long time ago. ❑ *The book recalls other memories of a bygone age. ...bygone generations.* ADJ: ADJ n = past [2] If two people **let bygones be bygones**, they decide to forget about unpleasant things that have happened between them in the past. PHRASE

**by|law** /baɪlɔː/ **(bylaws)** also **bye-law, by-law.** [1] A **bylaw** is a law which is made by a local authority and which applies only in their area. [BRIT] ❑ *The by-law makes it illegal to drink in certain areas.* N-COUNT [2] A **bylaw** is a rule which controls the way an organization is run. [AM] ❑ *Under the company's bylaws, he can continue as chairman until the age of 70.* N-COUNT

**by|line** /baɪlaɪn/ **(bylines)** also **by-line.** A **byline** is a line at the top of an article in a newspaper or magazine giving the author's name. N-COUNT

**by|pass** /baɪpɑːs, -pæs/ **(bypasses, bypassing, bypassed)** [1] If you **bypass** someone or something that you would normally have to get involved with, you ignore them, often because you want to achieve something more quickly. ❑ *A growing number of employers are trying to bypass the unions altogether... Regulators worry that controls could easily be bypassed.* VERB = sidestep V n V n [2] A **bypass** is a surgical operation performed on or near the heart, in which the flow of blood is redirected so that it does not flow through a part of the heart which is diseased or blocked. ❑ *...heart bypass surgery.* N-COUNT: oft N n [3] If a surgeon **bypasses** a diseased artery or other part of the body, he or she performs an operation so that blood or other bodily fluids do not flow through it. ❑ *Small veins are removed from the leg and used to bypass the blocked up stretch of coronary arteries.* VERB V n [4] A **bypass** is a main road which takes traffic around the edge of a town rather than through its centre. ❑ *A new bypass around the city is being built. ...the Hereford bypass.* N-COUNT: oft in names after n [5] If a road **bypasses** a place, it goes around it rather than through it. ❑ *...money for new roads to bypass cities.* VERB V n [6] If you **bypass** a place when you are travelling, you avoid going through it. ❑ *The rebel forces simply bypassed Zwedru on their way further south.* VERB V n

**by-product** **(by-products)** also **byproduct.** [1] A **by-product** is something which is produced during the manufacture or processing of another product. ❑ *The raw material for the tyre is a by-product of petrol refining.* N-COUNT: oft N of n [2] Something that is a **by-product of** an event or situation happens as a result of it, although it is usually not expected or planned. ❑ *A by-product of their meeting was the release of these fourteen men.* N-COUNT: oft N of n = side-effect

**byre** /baɪəʳ/ **(byres)** A **byre** is a cowshed. [BRIT, LITERARY or OLD-FASHIONED] N-COUNT

**by|stander** /baɪstændəʳ/ **(bystanders)** A **bystander** is a person who is present when something happens and who sees it but does not take part in it. ❑ *It looks like an innocent bystander was killed instead of you.* N-COUNT

**byte** /baɪt/ **(bytes)** In computing, a **byte** is a unit of storage approximately equivalent to one printed character. ❑ *...two million bytes of data.* N-COUNT

**by|way** /baɪweɪ/ **(byways)** [1] A **byway** is a small road which is not used by many cars or people. ❑ *...the highways and byways of America.* N-COUNT: usu pl [2] The **byways of** a subject are the less important or less well known areas of it. ❑ *My research focuses on the byways of children's literature.* N-COUNT: usu pl, usu N of n

**by|word** /baɪwɜːʳd/ **(bywords)** [1] Someone or something that is a **byword for** a particular quality is well known for having that quality. ❑ *...the Rolls-Royce brand name, a byword for quality.* N-COUNT: N for n [2] A **byword** is a word or phrase which people often use. ❑ *Loyalty and support became the bywords of the day.* N-COUNT

**byz|an|tine** /bɪzæntaɪn, AM bɪzəntiːn/ also **Byzantine.** [1] **Byzantine** means related to or connected with the Byzantine Empire. ❑ *...Byzantine civilisation... There are also several well-preserved Byzantine frescoes.* ADJ: ADJ n [2] If you describe a system or process as **byzantine**, you are criticizing it because it seems complicated or secretive. ADJ: usu ADJ n [disapproval]

# C c

**C, c** /siː/ **(C's, c's)** 1 **C** is the third letter of the English alphabet. N-VAR 2 In music, **C** is the first note in the scale of C major. N-VAR 3 If you get a **C** as a mark for a piece of work or in an exam, your work is average. N-VAR 4 **c.** is written in front of a date or number to indicate that it is approximate. **c.** is an abbreviation for 'circa'. ❑ *...the museum's recreation of a New York dining-room (c. 1825-35).* 5 **C** or **c** is used as an abbreviation for words beginning with c, such as 'copyright' or 'Celsius'. ❑ *Heat the oven to 180°C.* 6 ➔ See also **C-in-C**, **c/o**.

**cab** /kæb/ **(cabs)** 1 A **cab** is a taxi. N-COUNT 2 The **cab** of a truck or train is the front part in which the driver sits. N-COUNT ❑ *A Luton van has additional load space over the driver's cab.*

**ca|bal** /kəbæl/ **(cabals)** If you refer to a group of politicians or other people as a **cabal**, you are criticizing them because they meet and decide things secretly. N-COUNT: usu with supp [disapproval] ❑ *Harding had been chosen by a cabal of fellow senators at an early morning meeting. ...a secret government cabal.*

**caba|ret** /kæbəreɪ, AM -reɪ/ **(cabarets)** 1 **Cabaret** is live entertainment consisting of dancing, singing, or comedy acts that are performed in the evening in restaurants or nightclubs. N-UNCOUNT: oft N n ❑ *Helen made a successful career in cabaret.* 2 A **cabaret** is a show that is performed in a restaurant or nightclub, and that consists of dancing, singing, or comedy acts. N-COUNT ❑ *Peter and I also did a cabaret at the Corn Exchange.*

**cab|bage** /kæbɪdʒ/ **(cabbages)** A **cabbage** is a round vegetable with white, green or purple leaves that is usually eaten cooked. N-VAR ➔ See picture on page 1712.

**cab|bie** /kæbi/ **(cabbies)** also **cabby.** A **cabbie** is a person who drives a taxi. [INFORMAL] N-COUNT = cab driver

**ca|ber** /keɪbəʳ/ **(cabers)** A **caber** is a long, heavy, wooden pole. It is thrown into the air as a test of strength in the traditional Scottish sport called 'tossing the caber'. N-COUNT

**cab|in** /kæbɪn/ **(cabins)** 1 A **cabin** is a small room in a ship or boat. N-COUNT ❑ *He showed her to a small cabin.* 2 A **cabin** is one of the areas inside a plane. N-COUNT ❑ *He sat quietly in the First Class cabin, looking tired.* 3 A **cabin** is a small wooden house, especially one in an area of forests or mountains. N-COUNT ❑ *...a log cabin.*

**cab|in crew** **(cabin crews)** The **cabin crew** on an aircraft are the people whose job is to look after the passengers. N-COUNT-COLL

**cab|in cruis|er** **(cabin cruisers)** A **cabin cruiser** is a motor boat which has a cabin for people to live or sleep in. N-COUNT

**cabi|net** /kæbɪnɪt/ **(cabinets)** ◆◆◇ 1 A **cabinet** is a cupboard used for storing things such as medicine or alcoholic drinks or for displaying decorative things in. N-COUNT: usu n N ❑ *He looked at the display cabinet with its gleaming sets of glasses.* ➔ See also **filing cabinet**. 2 The **Cabinet** is a group of the most senior ministers in a government, who meet regularly to discuss policies. N-COUNT: oft N n ❑ *The announcement came after a three-hour Cabinet meeting in Downing Street. ...a former Cabinet Minister.*

**cabi|net mak|er** **(cabinet makers)** also **cabinetmaker.** A **cabinet maker** is a person who makes high-quality wooden furniture. N-COUNT

**ca|ble** /keɪbəl/ **(cables, cabling, cabled)** ◆◇◇ 1 A **cable** is a thick wire, or a group of wires inside a rubber or plastic covering, which is used to carry electricity or electronic signals. N-VAR ❑ *...overhead power cables. ...strings of coloured lights with weatherproof cable.* 2 A **cable** is a kind of very strong, thick rope, made of wires twisted together. N-VAR ❑ *...the heavy anchor cable... Steel cable will be used to replace worn ropes.* 3 **Cable** is used to refer to television systems in which the signals are sent along underground wires rather than by radio waves. N-UNCOUNT: oft N n ❑ *They ran commercials on cable systems across the country... The channel is only available on cable.* 4 A **cable** is the same as a **telegram**. N-COUNT ❑ *She sent a cable to her mother.* 5 If a country, a city, or someone's home **is cabled**, cables and other equipment are put in place so that the people there can receive cable television. VERB: usu passive ❑ *In France, 27 major cities are soon to be cabled... In the UK, 254,000 homes are cabled.* be V-ed, V-ed 6 ➔ See also **cabling**.

**ca|ble car** **(cable cars)** A **cable car** is a vehicle for taking people up mountains or steep hills. It is pulled by a moving cable. N-COUNT

**ca|ble tele|vi|sion** **Cable television** is a television system in which signals are sent along wires rather than by radio waves. N-UNCOUNT

**ca|bling** /keɪblɪŋ/ **Cabling** is used to refer to electrical or electronic cables, or to the process of putting them in a place. N-UNCOUNT ❑ *...modern offices equipped with computer cabling.* ➔ See also **cable**.

**cache** /kæʃ/ **(caches)** 1 A **cache** is a quantity of things such as weapons that have been hidden. N-COUNT: with supp = store ❑ *A huge arms cache was discovered by police. ...a cache of weapons and explosives.* 2 A **cache** or **cache memory** is an area of computer memory that is used for temporary storage of data and can be accessed more quickly than the main memory. N-COUNT [COMPUTING] ❑ *In your Web browser's cache are the most recent Web files that you have downloaded.*

**ca|chet** /kæʃeɪ, AM kæʃeɪ/ If someone or something has a certain **cachet**, they have a quality which makes people admire them or approve of them. N-SING: with supp [approval] [WRITTEN] ❑ *A Mercedes carries a certain cachet.*

**cack-handed** /kæk hændɪd/ If you describe someone as **cack-handed**, you mean that they handle things in an awkward or clumsy way. ADJ [disapproval] = clumsy [BRIT, INFORMAL] ❑ *...the cack-handed way they handled the incident.*

**cack|le** /kækəl/ **(cackles, cackling, cackled)** If someone **cackles**, they laugh in a loud unpleasant way, often at something bad that happens to someone else. VERB ❑ *The old lady cackled, pleased to have produced so dramatic a reaction.* V ♦ **Cackle** is also a noun. N-COUNT ❑ *He let out a brief cackle.*

**ca|copho|nous** /kəkɒfənəs/ If you describe a mixture of sounds as **cacophonous**, you mean that they are loud and unpleasant. ADJ: usu ADJ n ≠ harmonious ❑ *...the cacophonous beat of pop music.*

**ca|copho|ny** /kəkɒfəni/ **(cacophonies)** You can describe a loud, unpleasant mixture of sounds as a **cacophony**. N-COUNT: usu sing, usu N *of* n ❑ *All around was bubbling a cacophony of voices.*

**cac|tus** /kæktəs/ **(cactuses** or **cacti** /kæktaɪ/**)** A **cactus** is a thick fleshy plant that grows in N-COUNT many hot, dry parts of the world. Cacti have no leaves and many of them are covered in prickles.

**cad** /kæd/ **(cads)** If you say that a man is a **cad**, you mean that he treats other people, especially women, badly or unfairly. [OLD-FASHIONED] ❑ *He's a scoundrel! A cad!* N-COUNT

**CAD** /kæd/ **CAD** refers to the use of computer software in the design of things such as cars, buildings, and machines. **CAD** is an abbreviation for 'computer aided design'. [COMPUTING] ❑ *...CAD software.* N-UNCOUNT

**ca|dav|er** /kədævəʳ/ **(cadavers)** A **cadaver** is a dead body. [FORMAL] N-COUNT = corpse

**ca|dav|er|ous** /kədævərəs/ If you describe someone as **cadaverous**, you mean they are extremely thin and pale. [WRITTEN] ❑ *...a tall man with a long, cadaverous face.* ADJ: usu ADJ n

**cad|die** /kædi/ **(caddies, caddying, caddied)** also **caddy.** 1 In golf, a **caddie** is a person who carries golf clubs and other equipment for a player. N-COUNT 2 If you **caddie for** a golfer, you act as their caddie. ❑ *Lil caddied for her son.* VERB V for n Also V

**ca|dence** /keɪdᵊns/ **(cadences)** 1 The **cadence** of someone's voice is the way their voice gets higher and lower as they speak. [FORMAL] ❑ *He recognized the Polish cadences in her voice.* N-COUNT = intonation 2 A **cadence** is the phrase that ends a section of music or a complete piece of music. N-COUNT

**ca|den|za** /kədenzə/ **(cadenzas)** In classical music, a **cadenza** is a long and difficult solo passage in a piece for soloist and orchestra. N-COUNT

**ca|det** /kədet/ **(cadets)** A **cadet** is a young man or woman who is being trained in the armed services or the police. ❑ *...army cadets. ...the Cadet Corps.* N-COUNT

**cadge** /kædʒ/ **(cadges, cadging, cadged)** If someone **cadges** food, money, or help from you, they ask you for it and succeed in getting it. [mainly BRIT, INFORMAL] ❑ *Can I cadge a cigarette?... He could cadge a ride from somebody.* VERB = scrounge V n V n from/off n

**cad|mium** /kædmiəm/ **Cadmium** is a soft bluish-white metal that is used in the production of nuclear energy. N-UNCOUNT

**ca|dre** /kɑːdəʳ, AM -dreɪ/ **(cadres)** A **cadre** is a small group of people who have been specially chosen, trained, and organized for a particular purpose. ❑ *...an elite cadre of international managers.* N-COUNT: usu with supp

**Cae|sar|ean** /sɪzeəriən/ **(Caesareans)** A **Caesarean** or a **Caesarean section** is an operation in which a baby is lifted out of a woman's womb through an opening cut in her abdomen. ❑ *My youngest daughter was born by Caesarean.* N-COUNT: also by N

**Caesar sal|ad** /siːzəʳ sæləd/ **(Caesar salads)** also **caesar salad. Caesar salad** is a type of salad containing lettuce, eggs, cheese, and small pieces of fried bread, served with a dressing of oil, vinegar, and herbs. N-VAR

**café** /kæfeɪ, AM kæfeɪ/ **(cafés)** also **cafe.** 1 A **café** is a place where you can buy drinks, simple meals, and snacks, but, in Britain, not usually alcoholic drinks. N-COUNT 2 A street **café** or a pavement **café** is a café which has tables and chairs on the pavement outside it where people can eat and drink. ❑ *...an Italian street café. ...sidewalk cafés and boutiques.* N-COUNT: n N

**café bar** **(café bars)** A **café bar** is a café where you can also buy alcoholic drinks. N-COUNT

**caf|eteria** /kæfɪtɪəriə/ **(cafeterias)** A **cafeteria** is a restaurant where you choose your food from a counter and take it to your table after paying for it. Cafeterias are usually found in public buildings such as hospitals, colleges, and stores. N-COUNT = canteen

**caf|eti|ère** /kæfətjeəʳ/ **(cafetières)** A **cafetière** is a type of coffee pot that has a disk with small holes in it attached to the lid. You push the lid down to separate the liquid from the ground coffee when it is ready to drink. N-COUNT

**caff** /kæf/ **(caffs)** A **caff** is a café which serves simple British food such as fried eggs, bacon, and sausages. [BRIT, INFORMAL] ❑ *...a transport caff.* N-COUNT

**caf|feine** /kæfiːn, AM kæfiːn/ **Caffeine** is a chemical substance found in coffee, tea, and cocoa, which affects your brain and body and makes you more active. N-UNCOUNT

**caf|tan** /kæftæn/ **(caftans)** also **kaftan.** A **caftan** is a long loose garment with long sleeves. Caftans are worn by men in Arab countries, and by women in America and Europe. N-COUNT

**cage** /keɪdʒ/ **(cages)** 1 A **cage** is a structure of wire or metal bars in which birds or animals are kept. ❑ *I hate to see birds in cages.* → See also **rib cage.** N-COUNT 2 If someone **rattles** your **cage**, they do something which is intended to make you feel nervous. ❑ *If he's trying to rattle your cage, it's working.* PHRASE: V and N inflect

**caged** /keɪdʒd/ A **caged** bird or animal is inside a cage. ❑ *Mark was still pacing like a caged animal.* ADJ

**cag|ey** /keɪdʒi/ If you say that someone is being **cagey** about something, you mean that you think they are deliberately not giving you much information or expressing an opinion about it. ❑ *He is cagey about what he was paid for the business.* ADJ = guarded

**ca|hoots** /kəhuːts/ If you say that one person is **in cahoots with** another, you do not trust the first person because you think that they are planning something secretly with the other. ❑ *In his view they were all in cahoots with the police.* PHRASE: usu v-link PHR, oft PHR with n [disapproval]

**cairn** /keəʳn/ **(cairns)** A **cairn** is a pile of stones which marks a boundary, a route across rough ground, or the top of a mountain. A cairn is sometimes also built in memory of someone. N-COUNT

**ca|jole** /kədʒoul/ **(cajoles, cajoling, cajoled)** If you **cajole** someone **into** doing something, you get them to do it after persuading them for some time. ❑ *It was he who had cajoled Garland into doing the film... He cajoled Mr Dobson to stand for mayor.* VERB V n into -ing V n to-inf Also V n, V

**Ca|jun** /keɪdʒən/ **(Cajuns)** 1 **Cajun** means belonging or relating to a group of people who live mainly in Louisiana in the United States, and are descended from French people. Cajun is also used to refer to the language and culture of these people. ❑ *They played some Cajun music. ...Cajun food.* ADJ: usu ADJ n 2 A **Cajun** is a person of Cajun origin. N-COUNT 3 **Cajun** is a dialect of French spoken by Cajun people. ❑ *...the first book ever written in Cajun.* N-UNCOUNT

**cake** /keɪk/ **(cakes)** 1 A **cake** is a sweet food made by baking a mixture of flour, eggs, sugar, and fat in an oven. Cakes may be large and cut into slices or small and intended for one person only. ❑ *...a piece of cake... Would you like some chocolate cake? ...little cakes with white icing.* ◆◇◇ N-VAR 2 Food that is formed into flat round shapes before it is cooked can be referred to as **cakes**. ❑ *...fish cakes. ...home-made potato cakes.* N-COUNT: usu supp N 3 A **cake of** soap is a small block of it. ❑ *...a small cake of lime-scented soap.* N-COUNT: usu N of n

**PHRASES** 4 If you think that someone wants the benefits of doing two things when it is only reasonable to expect the benefits of doing one, you can say that they want to **have** their **cake and eat it**. ❑ *What he wants is a switch to a market economy in a way which does not reduce people's standard of living. To many this sounds like wanting to have his cake and eat it.* PHRASE: Vs inflect [disapproval] 5 If you think something is very easy to do, you can say it is **a piece of cake**. People often say this to stop someone feeling worried about doing something they have to do. [INFORMAL] ❑ *Just another surveillance job, old chap. Piece of cake to somebody like you.* PHRASE: usu v-link PHR 6 If someone has done something very stupid, rude, or selfish, you can say that they **take the cake** or that what they have done **takes the cake**, to emphasize your surprise at their behaviour. [AM] PHRASE: V inflects [emphasis] = take the biscuit

✔ in BRIT, use **take the biscuit**

[7] **the icing on the cake** → see **icing**.

**caked** /keɪkt/ If something is **caked with** mud, blood, or dirt, it is covered with a thick dry layer of it. ❑ *Her shoes were caked with mud.* ♦ **Caked** is also a combining form. ❑ *...herds of mud-caked cattle and sheep.* ADJ: usu v-link ADJ *with/in* n = encrusted; COMB in ADJ: usu ADJ n = encrusted

**cake mix (cake mixes) Cake mix** is a powder that you mix with eggs and water or milk to make a cake. You bake the mixture in the oven. N-VAR

**cake pan (cake pans)** A **cake pan** is a metal container that you bake a cake in. [AM] N-COUNT

☑ in BRIT, usually use **cake tin**

**cake tin (cake tins)** A **cake tin** is a metal container that you bake a cake in. [BRIT] N-COUNT

☑ in AM, usually use **cake pan**

**cal** /kæl/ **(cals) Cals** are units of measurement for the energy value of food. **Cal** is an abbreviation for 'calorie'. ❑ *...325 cals per serving.* N-COUNT: usu pl, num N

**cala|mine** /kæləmaɪn/ **Calamine** is a liquid that you can put on your skin when it is sore or itchy. ❑ *...calamine lotion.* N-UNCOUNT: oft N n

**ca|lami|tous** /kəlæmɪtəs/ If you describe an event or situation as **calamitous**, you mean it is very unfortunate or serious. [FORMAL] ❑ *...the calamitous state of the country.* ADJ = disastrous

**ca|lam|ity** /kəlæmɪti/ **(calamities)** A **calamity** is an event that causes a great deal of damage, destruction, or personal distress. [FORMAL] ❑ *He described drugs as the greatest calamity of the age... It could only end in calamity.* N-VAR = disaster

**cal|ci|fied** /kælsɪfaɪd/ Body tissue that is **calcified** has become hard because of the presence of substances called calcium salts. ❑ *...calcified tissue.* ADJ

**cal|cium** /kælsiəm/ **Calcium** is a soft white element which is found in bones and teeth, and also in limestone, chalk, and marble. N-UNCOUNT

**cal|cu|lable** /kælkjʊləbᵊl/ **Calculable** amounts or consequences can be calculated. ADJ

**cal|cu|late** /kælkjʊleɪt/ **(calculates, calculating, calculated)** [1] If you **calculate** a number or amount, you discover it from information that you already have, by using arithmetic, mathematics, or a special machine. ❑ *From this you can calculate the total mass in the Galaxy... We calculate that the average size farm in Lancaster County is 65 acres.* VERB = work out; V n; V that

[2] If you **calculate** the effects of something, especially a possible course of action, you think about them in order to form an opinion or decide what to do. ❑ *I believe I am capable of calculating the political consequences accurately... The President is calculating that this will somehow relieve the international pressure on him.* VERB; V n; V that

**cal|cu|lat|ed** /kælkjʊleɪtɪd/ [1] If something is **calculated to** have a particular effect, it is specially done or arranged in order to have that effect. ❑ *Their movements through the region were calculated to terrify landowners into abandoning their holdings.* ADJ: v-link ADJ to-inf [2] If you say that something is not **calculated to** have a particular effect, you mean that it is unlikely to have that effect. ❑ *Such a statement was hardly calculated to deter future immigrants.* ADJ: with brd-neg, v-link ADJ to-inf = likely [3] You can describe a clever or dishonest action as **calculated** when it is very carefully planned or arranged. ❑ *Irene's cleaning the floor had been a calculated attempt to cover up her crime.* ADJ: usu ADJ n [4] If you take a **calculated** risk, you do something which you think might be successful, although you have fully considered the possible bad consequences of your action. ADJ: ADJ n

**cal|cu|lat|ing** /kælkjʊleɪtɪŋ/ If you describe someone as **calculating**, you disapprove of the fact that they deliberately plan to get what they want, often by hurting or harming other people. ❑ *Northbridge is a cool, calculating and clever criminal who could strike again.* ADJ [disapproval]

**cal|cu|la|tion** /kælkjʊleɪʃᵊn/ **(calculations)** [1] A **calculation** is something that you think about and work out mathematically. **Calculation** is the process of working something out mathematically. ❑ *Leonard made a rapid calculation: he'd never make it in time. ...the calculation of their assets.* N-VAR: oft N *of* n

[2] A **calculation** is something that you think carefully about and arrive at a conclusion on after having considered all the relevant factors. ❑ *For the President, the calculations are equally difficult. If the peacekeeping operation goes wrong he risks appearing weak.* N-VAR

**cal|cu|la|tor** /kælkjʊleɪtəʳ/ **(calculators)** A **calculator** is a small electronic device that you use for making mathematical calculations. ❑ *...a pocket calculator.* N-COUNT

**cal|cu|lus** /kælkjʊləs/ **Calculus** is a branch of advanced mathematics which deals with variable quantities. N-UNCOUNT

**cal|en|dar** /kælɪndəʳ/ **(calendars)** [1] A **calendar** is a chart or device which displays the date and the day of the week, and often the whole of a particular year divided up into months, weeks, and days. ❑ *There was a calendar on the wall above, with large squares around the dates.* N-COUNT [2] A **calendar** is a particular system for dividing time into periods such as years, months, and weeks, often starting from a particular point in history. ❑ *The Christian calendar was originally based on the Julian calendar of the Romans.* N-COUNT: usu supp N [3] You can use **calendar** to refer to a series or list of events and activities which take place on particular dates, and which are important for a particular organization, community, or person. ❑ *It is one of the British sporting calendar's most prestigious events.* N-COUNT: usu sing, usu with poss = diary

**cal|en|dar month (calendar months)** [1] A **calendar month** is one of the twelve months of the year. ❑ *Winners will be selected at the end of each calendar month.* N-COUNT [2] A **calendar month** is the period from a particular date in one month to the same date in the next month, for example from April 4th to May 4th. N-COUNT

**cal|en|dar year (calendar years)** A **calendar year** is a period of twelve months from January 1 to December 31. **Calendar year** is often used in business to compare with the **financial year**. N-COUNT

**calf** /kɑːf, AM kæf/ **(calves** /kɑːvz, AM kævz/ **)** [1] A **calf** is a young cow. N-COUNT [2] Some other young animals, including elephants and whales, are called **calves**. N-COUNT [3] Your **calf** is the thick part at the back of your leg, between your ankle and your knee. ❑ *...a calf injury.* N-COUNT

**calf-length Calf-length** skirts, dresses, and coats come to halfway between your knees and ankles. ❑ *...a black, calf-length coat.* ADJ: ADJ n

**calf|skin** /kɑːfskɪn, AM kæf-/ **Calfskin** shoes and clothing are made from the skin of a calf. ❑ *...calfskin boots.* N-UNCOUNT: oft N n

**cali|ber** /kælɪbəʳ/ → see **calibre**.

**cali|brate** /kælɪbreɪt/ **(calibrates, calibrating, calibrated)** [1] If you **calibrate** an instrument or tool, you mark or adjust it so that you can use it to measure something accurately. [TECHNICAL] ❑ *...instructions on how to calibrate a thermometer.* VERB; V n [2] If you **calibrate** something, you measure it accurately. [WRITTEN] ❑ *...a way of calibrating the shift of opinion within the Labour Party.* VERB; V n ♦ **cali|bra|tion (calibrations)** *...the precise calibration of the achievement level of those observed.* N-VAR

**cali|bre** /kælɪbəʳ/ **(calibres)**

☑ in AM, use **caliber**

[1] The **calibre of** a person is the quality or standard of their ability or intelligence, especially when this is high. ❑ *I was impressed by the high calibre of the researchers and analysts.* N-UNCOUNT: with supp, usu adj N, N *of* n [2] The **calibre of** something is its quality, especially when it is good. ❑ *The calibre of teaching at this school was very high.* N-UNCOUNT: with supp, oft N *of* n [3] The **calibre** of a gun is the width of the inside of its barrel. [TECHNICAL] ❑ *...a .22 calibre rifle.* N-COUNT: usu with supp, oft num N, adj N

**cali|co** /kælɪkoʊ/ **(calicoes) Calico** is plain white fabric made from cotton. N-MASS

**cali|per** /kælɪpəʳ/ **(calipers)** also **calliper.** 1 **Calipers** are an instrument consisting of two long, thin pieces of metal joined together at one end, and are used to measure the size of things. [N-COUNT: usu pl, also *a pair of* N] 2 **Calipers** are devices consisting of metal rods held together by straps, which are used to support a person's legs when they cannot walk properly. [N-COUNT: usu pl]

**ca|liph** /keɪlɪf/ **(caliphs)** also **calif.** A **Caliph** was a Muslim ruler. ❑ *...the caliph of Baghdad.* [N-COUNT; N-TITLE]

**cal|is|then|ics** /kælɪsθenɪks/ also **callis-thenics. Calisthenics** are simple exercises that you can do to keep fit and healthy. [N-PLURAL]

**call** /kɔːl/ **(calls, calling, called)** ◆◆◆ 1 If you **call** someone or something **by** a particular name or title, you give them that name or title. [VERB] ❑ *'Doctor...' — 'Will you please call me Sarah?'... Everybody called each other by their surnames.* [V n n] [V n *by* n] ♦ **called** *There are two men called Buckley at the Home Office. ...a device called an optical amplifier.* [ADJ: v-link ADJ] 2 If you **call** someone or something a particular thing, you suggest they are that thing or describe them as that thing. [VERB] ❑ *The speech was interrupted by members of the Conservative Party, who called him a traitor... She calls me lazy and selfish... He called it particularly cynical to begin releasing the hostages on Christmas Day... Anyone can call themselves a psychotherapist.* [V n n] [V n adj] [V *it* adj to-inf] [V pron-refl n] 3 If you **call** something, you say it in a loud voice, because you are trying to attract someone's attention. [VERB] ❑ *He could hear the others downstairs in different parts of the house calling his name... 'Boys!' she called again.* [V n] [V with quote] ♦ **Call out** means the same as **call**. [PHRASAL VERB] ❑ *The butcher's son called out a greeting... The train stopped and a porter called out, 'Middlesbrough!'* [V P n (not pron)] [V P with quote] 4 If you **call** someone, you telephone them. [VERB = phone] ❑ *Would you call me as soon as you find out?... A friend of mine gave me this number to call... 'May I speak with Mr Coyne, please?' — 'May I ask who's calling?'* [V n] [V n] [V] 5 If you **call** someone such as a doctor or the police, you ask them to come to you, usually by telephoning them. [VERB] ❑ *He screamed for his wife to call an ambulance... One night he was called to see a woman with tuberculosis.* [V n] [*be* V-ed to-inf] 6 If you **call** someone, you ask them to come to you by shouting to them. [VERB] ❑ *She called her young son: 'Here, Stephen, come and look at this!'... He called me over the Tannoy.* [V n] [V n prep] 7 When you make a telephone **call**, you telephone someone. [N-COUNT] ❑ *I made a phone call to the United States to talk to a friend... I've had hundreds of calls from other victims.* 8 If someone in authority **calls** something such as a meeting, rehearsal, or election, they arrange for it to take place at a particular time. [VERB] ❑ *The Committee decided to call a meeting of the All India Congress... The RSC was calling a press conference to announce the theatre's closure.* [V n] [V n] 9 If someone **is called** before a court or committee, they are ordered to appear there, usually to give evidence. [VERB: usu passive = summon] ❑ *The child waited two hours before she was called to give evidence... I was called as an expert witness.* [*be* V-ed to-inf] [*be* V-ed prep] 10 If you **call** somewhere, you make a short visit there. [VERB] ❑ *A market researcher called at the house where he was living... Andrew now came almost weekly to call.* [V prep/adv] [V] ♦ **Call** is also a noun. [N-COUNT] ❑ *He decided to pay a call on Tommy Cummings.* 11 When a train, bus, or ship **calls** somewhere, it stops there for a short time to allow people to get on or off. [VERB] ❑ *The steamer calls at several ports along the way.* [V prep/adv] 12 To **call** a game or sporting event means to cancel it, for example because of rain or bad light. [AM] [VERB = call off] ❑ *We called the next game.* [V n] 13 If there is a **call for** something, someone demands that it should happen. [N-COUNT: usu N *for* n, N to-inf] ❑ *There have been calls for a new kind of security arrangement... Almost all workers heeded a call by the trade unions to stay at home for the duration of the strike.* 14 If there is little or no **call for** something, very few people want it to be done or provided. [N-UNCOUNT: with brd-neg, N *for* n = demand] ❑ *'Have you got just plain chocolate?' — 'No, I'm afraid there's not much call for that.'* 15 The **call of** something such as a place is the way it attracts or interests you strongly. [N-SING: with poss = pull, lure] 16 The **call** of a particular bird or animal is the characteristic sound that it makes. [N-COUNT] ❑ *...a wide range of animal noises and bird calls.* 17 → See also **calling, so-called.**

**PHRASES** 18 If you say that **there is no call for** someone to behave in a particular way, you are criticizing their behaviour, usually because you think it is rude. [PHRASE: PHR n to-inf, PHR n] [disapproval] [= there is no need for] ❑ *There was no call for him to single you out from all the others.* 19 If someone is **on call**, they are ready to go to work at any time if they are needed, especially if there is an emergency. [PHRASE: PHR after v, v-link PHR] ❑ *In theory I'm on call day and night. ...a doctor on call.* 20 If you **call in sick**, you telephone the place where you work to tell them you will not be coming to work because you are ill. [PHRASE: V inflects] ❑ *'Shouldn't you be at work today?' — 'I called in sick.'* 21 to **call** someone's **bluff** → see **bluff**. to **call it a day** → see **day**. to **call a halt** → see **halt**. to **call** something **to mind** → see **mind**. **call of nature** → see **nature**. to **call** something your **own** → see **own**. to **call** something **into question** → see **question**. to **call it quits** → see **quit**. to **call a spade a spade** → see **spade**. to **call the tune** → see **tune**. **too close to call** → see **close**.

♦ **call back** If you **call** someone **back**, you telephone them again or in return for a telephone call that they have made to you. [PHRASAL VERB = ring back] ❑ *If we're not around she'll take a message and we'll call you back.* [V n P]

♦ **call for** 1 If you **call for** someone, you go to the building where they are, so that you can both go somewhere. [PHRASAL VERB] ❑ *I shall be calling for you at seven o'clock.* [V P n] 2 If you **call for** something, you demand that it should happen. [PHRASAL VERB] ❑ *They angrily called for Robinson's resignation.* [V P n] 3 If something **calls for** a particular action or quality, it needs it or makes it necessary. [PHRASAL VERB = demand, require] ❑ *It's a situation that calls for a blend of delicacy and force.* [V P n]

♦ **call in** 1 If you **call** someone **in**, you ask them to come and help you or do something for you. [PHRASAL VERB] ❑ *Call in an architect or surveyor to oversee the work.* [V P n (not pron)] 2 If you **call in** somewhere, you make a short visit there. [PHRASAL VERB = drop in] ❑ *He just calls in occasionally... I got into the habit of calling in on Gloria on my way home.* [V P] [V P *on* n]

♦ **call off** If you **call off** an event that has been planned, you cancel it. [PHRASAL VERB] ❑ *He has called off the trip... The union threatened a strike but called it off at the last minute.* [V P n (not pron)] [V n P]

♦ **call on** or **call upon** 1 If you **call on** someone **to** do something or **call upon** them **to** do it, you say publicly that you want them to do it. [PHRASAL VERB] ❑ *One of Kenya's leading churchmen has called on the government to resign.* [V P n to-inf] 2 If you **call on** someone or **call upon** someone, you pay them a short visit. [PHRASAL VERB] ❑ *Sofia was intending to call on Miss Kitts.* [V P n]

♦ **call out** If you **call** someone **out**, you order or request that they come to help, especially in an emergency. [PHRASAL VERB] ❑ *Colombia has called out the army and imposed emergency measures... I called the doctor out... The fire brigade should always be called out to a house fire.* [V P n (not pron)] [V n P] [*be* V-ed P *to* n] → See also **call 3**.

♦ **call up** 1 If you **call** someone **up**, you telephone them. [mainly AM] [PHRASAL VERB] ❑ *When I'm in Pittsburgh, I call him up... He called up the museum... Sometimes I'd even call up at 4 a.m.* [V n P] [V P n (not pron)] [V P] 2 If someone **is called up**, they are ordered to join the army, navy, or air force. [PHRASAL VERB = draft] ❑ *Youngsters coming up to university were being called up... The United States has called up some 150,000 military reservists.* [*be* V-ed P] [V P n (not pron)] [Also V n P] 3 If someone **is called up**, they are chosen to play in a sports team. [PHRASAL VERB] ❑ *He is likely to be called up for Thursday's match against Italy.* [*be* V-ed P] → See also **call-up**.

♦ **call upon** → see **call on**.

**call box** **(call boxes)** also **call-box.** 1 A **call box** is the same as a **telephone box**. [BRIT] [N-COUNT] 2 A **call box** is a telephone in a box or case, often on a pole, that is at the side of a road and that you can use in emergencies. [mainly AM] [N-COUNT]

**call cen|tre** **(call centres)**

✓ in AM, use **call center**

A **call centre** is an office where people work answering or making telephone calls for a particular company. [N-COUNT]

**call|er** /kɔːləʳ/ **(callers)** 1 A **caller** is a person who is making a telephone call. ❑ *An anonymous caller told police what had happened.* N-COUNT 2 A **caller** is a person who comes to see you for a short visit. ❑ *She ushered her callers into a cluttered living-room.* N-COUNT = *visitor*

**call girl (call girls)** A **call girl** is a prostitute who makes appointments by telephone. N-COUNT

**cal|lig|ra|pher** /kəlɪgrəfəʳ/ **(calligraphers)** A **calligrapher** is a person skilled in the art of calligraphy. ❑ *She is a skilled calligrapher.* N-COUNT

**cal|lig|ra|phy** /kəlɪgrəfi/ **Calligraphy** is the art of producing beautiful handwriting using a brush or a special pen. N-UNCOUNT

**call-in (call-ins)** A **call-in** is a programme on radio or television in which people telephone with questions or opinions and their calls are broadcast. [AM] ❑ *...a call-in show on Los Angeles radio station KABC.* N-COUNT

in BRIT, use **phone-in**

**call|ing** /kɔːlɪŋ/ **(callings)** A **calling** is a profession or career which someone is strongly attracted to, especially one which involves helping other people. ❑ *He was a consultant physician, a serious man dedicated to his calling.* N-COUNT: usu sing = *vocation*

**call|ing card (calling cards)** A **calling card** is a small card with personal information about you on it, such as your name and address, which you can give to people when you go to visit them. [mainly AM] N-COUNT = *card*

**cal|li|per** /kælɪpəʳ/ → see **caliper**.

**cal|lis|then|ics** /kælɪsθenɪks/ → see **calisthenics**.

**cal|lous** /kæləs/ A **callous** person or action is very cruel and shows no concern for other people or their feelings. ❑ *...his callous disregard for human life.* ADJ ♦ **cal|lous|ness** *...the callousness of Raymond's murder.* N-UNCOUNT ♦ **cal|lous|ly** *He is accused of consistently and callously ill-treating his wife.* ADV: ADV with v

**cal|loused** /kæləst/ also **callused.** A foot or hand that is **calloused** is covered in calluses. ❑ *...blunt, calloused fingers.* ADJ

**cal|low** /kæloʊ/ A **callow** young person has very little experience or knowledge of the way they should behave as an adult. ❑ *...a callow youth.* ADJ: usu ADJ n

**call sign (call signs)** A **call sign** is the letters and numbers which identify a person, vehicle, or organization that is broadcasting on the radio or sending messages by radio. N-COUNT

**call-up (call-ups)** 1 If a person gets their **call-up** papers, they receive an official order to join the armed forces. ADJ: ADJ n = *draft* 2 A **call-up** is an occasion on which people are ordered to report for service in the armed forces. ❑ *The call-up of National Guard and reserve units begun in late August.* N-COUNT

**cal|lus** /kæləs/ **(calluses)** A **callus** is an unwanted area of thick skin, usually on the palms of your hands or the soles of your feet, which has been caused by something rubbing against it. N-COUNT

**call wait|ing** **Call waiting** is a telephone service that sends you a signal if another call arrives while you are already on the phone. N-UNCOUNT: oft N n

**calm** /kɑːm/ **(calmer, calmest, calms, calming, calmed)** ◆◇◇ 1 A **calm** person does not show or feel any worry, anger, or excitement. ❑ *She is usually a calm and diplomatic woman... Try to keep calm and just tell me what happened... She sighed, then continued in a soft, calm voice.* ADJ ♦ **Calm** is also a noun. ❑ *He felt a sudden sense of calm, of contentment.* N-UNCOUNT: also *a* N ♦ **calm|ly** *Alan looked at him and said calmly, 'I don't believe you.'* ADV: usu ADV with v 2 If you **calm** someone, you do something to make them feel less angry, worried, or excited. ❑ *She was breathing quickly and tried to calm herself... Some people say smoking calms your nerves.* VERB V n V n ♦ **calm|ing** *...a fresh, cool fragrance which produces a very calming effect on the mind.* ADJ 3 **Calm** is used to refer to a quiet, still, or peaceful atmosphere in a place. ❑ *...the rural calm of Grand Rapids, Michigan.* N-UNCOUNT = *peace* 4 If someone says that a place is **calm**, they mean that it is free from fighting or public disorder, when trouble has recently occurred there or had been expected. [JOURNALISM] ❑ *The city of Sarajevo appears relatively calm today.* ADJ: usu v-link ADJ = *peaceful* ♦ **Calm** is also a noun. ❑ *Community and church leaders have appealed for calm and no retaliation.* N-UNCOUNT: also *a* N 5 To **calm** a situation means to reduce the amount of trouble, violence, or panic there is. ❑ *Mr Beazer tried to calm the protests by promising to keep the company's base in Pittsburgh.* VERB V n 6 If the sea or a lake is **calm**, the water is not moving very much and there are no big waves. ❑ *...as we slid into the calm waters of Cowes Harbour.* ADJ = *still* ≠ *rough* 7 **Calm** weather is pleasant weather with little or no wind. ❑ *Tuesday was a fine, clear and calm day.* ADJ 8 In sailing, a flat **calm** or a dead **calm** is a condition of the sea or the weather in which there is very little wind or movement of the water. [TECHNICAL] N-COUNT: usu supp N 9 When the sea **calms**, it becomes still because the wind stops blowing strongly. When the wind **calms**, it stops blowing strongly. ❑ *Dawn came, the sea calmed but the cold was as bitter as ever.* VERB V 10 You can use **the calm before the storm** to refer to a quiet period in which there is little or no activity, before a period in which there is a lot of trouble or intense activity. PHRASE

♦ **calm down** 1 If you **calm down**, or if someone **calms** you **down**, you become less angry, upset, or excited. ❑ *Calm down for a minute and listen to me... Do not have a drink or take drugs to calm yourself down.* PHRASAL VERB V P V n P Also V P n 2 If things **calm down**, or someone or something **calms** things **down**, the amount of activity, trouble, or panic is reduced. ❑ *We will go back to normal when things calm down... Neil Howorth, director of the academy, tried to calm things down.* PHRASAL VERB = *settle down* V P V n P

**calm|ly** /kɑːmli/ You can use **calmly** to emphasize that someone is behaving in a very controlled or ordinary way in a frightening or unusual situation. [WRITTEN] ❑ *The gunmen calmly walked away and escaped in a waiting car.* → See also **calm**. ADV: ADV with v [emphasis]

**Cal|or Gas** /kæləʳ gæs/ **Calor gas** is gas in liquid form which is sold in special containers so that people can use it in places which are not connected to the gas supply, such as tents or caravans. [TRADEMARK] N-UNCOUNT

**ca|lor|ic** /kəlɔːrɪk/ **Caloric** means relating to calories. ❑ *...a daily caloric intake of from 400 to 1200 calories.* ADJ: ADJ n

**calo|rie** /kæləri/ **(calories)** **Calories** are units used to measure the energy value of food. People who are on diets try to eat food that does not contain many calories. ❑ *A glass of wine does have quite a lot of calories. ...calorie controlled diets.* → See also **-calorie**. N-COUNT

**-calorie** /-kæləri/ **-calorie** is used after adjectives such as low or high to indicate that food contains a small or a large number of calories. ❑ *...low-calorie margarine. ...reduced-calorie mayonnaise.* COMB in ADJ: usu ADJ n

**calo|rif|ic** /kælərɪfɪk/ The **calorific** value of something, or its **calorific** content, is the number of calories it contains. [TECHNICAL] ❑ *...food with a high calorific value.* ADJ: usu ADJ n

**cal|um|ny** /kæləmni/ **(calumnies)** **Calumny** or a **calumny** is an untrue statement made about someone in order to reduce other people's respect and admiration for them. [FORMAL] ❑ *He was the victim of calumny.* N-VAR = *slander*

**calve** /kɑːv, AM kæv/ **(calves, calving, calved)** 1 When a cow **calves**, it gives birth to a calf. ❑ *When his cows calve each year he keeps one or two calves for his family.* VERB V 2 Some other female animals, including elephants and whales, are said to **calve** when they give birth to their young. ❑ *The whales migrate some 6,000 miles to breed and calve in the warm lagoons.* VERB V 3 **Calves** is the plural of **calf**.

**Cal|vin|ist** /kælvɪnɪst/ **(Calvinists)** 1 **Calvinist** means belonging or relating to a strict Protestant church started by John Calvin. ❑ *...the Cal-* ADJ: ADJ n *vinist work ethic.* 2 A **Calvinist** is a member of the Calvinist church. N-COUNT

**ca|lyp|so** /kəlɪpsoʊ/ **(calypsos)** A **calypso** is a song about a current subject, sung in a style which originally comes from the West Indies. N-COUNT

**ca|ma|ra|derie** /kæmərɑːdəri, AM kɑːm-/ **Camaraderie** is a feeling of trust and friendship among a group of people who have usually known each other for a long time or gone through some kind of experience together. ❑ *...the loyalty and camaraderie of the wartime Army.* N-UNCOUNT

**cam|ber** /kæmbəʳ/ **(cambers)** A **camber** is a gradual downward slope from the centre of a road to each side of it. N-COUNT

**cam|cord|er** /kæmkɔːʳdəʳ/ **(camcorders)** A **camcorder** is a portable video camera which records both pictures and sound. N-COUNT

**came** /keɪm/ **Came** is the past tense of **come**.

**cam|el** /kæməl/ **(camels)** A **camel** is a large animal that lives in deserts and is used for carrying goods and people. Camels have long necks and one or two lumps on their backs called humps. **the straw that broke the camel's back** → see **straw**. N-COUNT

**camel-hair**

> ✔ The spellings **camel hair**, and in American English **camel's hair** are also used.

A **camel-hair** coat is made of a kind of soft, thick woollen cloth, usually creamy brown in colour. ADJ: ADJ n

**ca|mel|lia** /kəmiːliə/ **(camellias)** A **camellia** is a large bush that has shiny leaves and large white, pink, or red flowers similar to a rose. N-COUNT

**Cam|em|bert** /kæmɒmbeəʳ/ **(Camemberts)** N-VAR **Camembert** is a type of cheese that comes from Northern France. It is soft and creamy with a white skin.

**cameo** /kæmioʊ/ **(cameos)** 1 A **cameo** is a short description or piece of acting which expresses cleverly and neatly the nature of a situation, event, or person's character. ❑ *He played a cameo role, that of a young Aids patient in hospital.* N-COUNT
2 A **cameo** is a piece of jewellery, usually oval in shape, consisting of a raised stone figure or design fixed on to a flat stone of another colour. ❑ *...a cameo brooch.* N-COUNT

**cam|era** /kæmrə/ **(cameras)** 1 A **camera** is a piece of equipment that is used for taking photographs, making films, or producing television pictures. ❑ *Her gran lent her a camera for a school trip to Venice and Egypt. ...a video camera... They were caught speeding by hidden cameras.* ◆◆◇ N-COUNT

PHRASES 2 If someone or something is **on camera**, they are being filmed. ❑ *Just about anything could happen and we'll be there to catch it on camera when it does.* PHRASE: usu PHR after v, v-link PHR
3 If you do something or if something happens **off camera**, you do it or it happens when not being filmed. ❑ *They were anything but friendly off-camera, refusing even to take the same lift. ...off-camera interviews.* PHRASE: usu PHR after v, PHR n
4 If a trial is held **in camera**, the public and the press are not allowed to attend. [FORMAL] ❑ *This morning's appeal was held in camera.* PHRASE: PHR after v

**camera|man** /kæmrəmæn/ **(cameramen)** A **cameraman** is a person who operates a camera for television or film making. N-COUNT

**camera-shy** Someone who is **camera-shy** is nervous and uncomfortable about being filmed or about having their photograph taken. ADJ

**camera|work** /kæmrəwɜːʳk/ The **camerawork** in a film is the way it has been filmed, especially if the style is interesting or unusual in some way. ❑ *The director employs sensuous, atmospheric camerawork and deft dramatic touches.* N-UNCOUNT

**cami|sole** /kæmɪsoʊl/ **(camisoles)** A **camisole** is a short piece of clothing that women wear on the top half of their bodies underneath a shirt or blouse, for example. ❑ *...silk camisoles.* N-COUNT

**camo|mile** /kæməmaɪl/ also **chamomile.** **Camomile** is a scented plant with flowers like small daisies. The flowers can be used to make herbal tea. N-UNCOUNT

**camou|flage** /kæməflɑːʒ/ **(camouflages, camouflaging, camouflaged)** 1 **Camouflage** consists of things such as leaves, branches, or brown and green paint, which are used to make it difficult for an enemy to see military forces and equipment. ❑ *They were dressed in camouflage and carried automatic rifles. ...a camouflage jacket.* N-UNCOUNT: also a N, oft N n
2 If military buildings or vehicles **are camouflaged**, things such as leaves, branches, or brown and green paint are used to make it difficult for an enemy to see them. ❑ *You won't see them from the air. They'd be very well camouflaged.* VERB: usu passive; be V-ed
3 If you **camouflage** something such as a feeling or a situation, you hide it or make it appear to be something different. ❑ *I think that there has been an attempt to camouflage what really happened.* ♦ **Camouflage** is also a noun. ❑ *The constant partygoing of her later years was a desperate camouflage for her grief.* VERB = conceal; V n; N-UNCOUNT: also a N
4 **Camouflage** is the way in which some animals are coloured and shaped so that they cannot easily be seen in their natural surroundings. N-UNCOUNT: also a N

**camp** /kæmp/ **(camps, camping, camped)** ◆◆◇
1 A **camp** is a collection of huts and other buildings that is provided for a particular group of people, such as refugees, prisoners, or soldiers, as a place to live or stay. ❑ *...a refugee camp... 2,500 foreign prisoners-of-war, including Americans, had been held in camps near Tambov.* N-COUNT: oft n N
2 A **camp** is an outdoor area with buildings, tents, or caravans where people stay on holiday. N-VAR
3 A **camp** is a collection of tents or caravans where people are living or staying, usually temporarily while they are travelling. ❑ *...gypsy camps... We'll make camp on that hill ahead.* N-VAR
4 If you **camp** somewhere, you stay or live there for a short time in a tent or caravan, or in the open air. ❑ *We camped near the beach.* ♦ **Camp out** means the same as **camp**. ❑ *For six months they camped out in a caravan in a meadow at the back of the house.* ♦ **camp|ing** *They went camping in the wilds. ...a camping trip.* VERB; V; PHRASAL VERB V P; N-UNCOUNT
5 You can refer to a group of people who all support a particular person, policy, or idea as a particular **camp**. ❑ *The press release provoked furious protests from the Gore camp and other top Democrats.* N-COUNT: usu supp N
6 If you describe someone's behaviour, performance, or style of dress as **camp**, you mean that it is exaggerated and amusing, often in a way that is thought to be typical of some male homosexuals. [INFORMAL] ❑ *James Barron turns in a delightfully camp performance.* ♦ **Camp** is also a noun. ❑ *The video was seven minutes of high camp and melodrama.* ADJ; N-UNCOUNT
7 → See also **camped**, **aide-de-camp**, **concentration camp**, **holiday camp**, **labour camp**, **prison camp**, **training camp**.
8 If a performer **camps it up**, they deliberately perform in an exaggerated and often amusing way. [INFORMAL] PHRASE: V inflects

♦ **camp out** If you say that people **camp out** somewhere in the open air, you are emphasizing that they stay there for a long time, because they are waiting for something to happen. ❑ *...reporters who had camped out in anticipation of her arrival.* → see **camp 4**. PHRASAL VERB emphasis; V P

**cam|paign** /kæmpeɪn/ **(campaigns, campaigning, campaigned)** ◆◆◆
1 A **campaign** is a planned set of activities that people carry out over a period of time in order to achieve something such as social or political change. ❑ *During his election campaign he promised to put the economy back on its feet. ...the campaign against public smoking.* N-COUNT: oft N to-inf, N for/against n
2 If someone **campaigns for** something, they carry out a planned set of activities over a period of time in order to achieve their aim. ❑ *We are campaigning for law reform... They have been campaigning to improve the legal status of women.* VERB; V for/against n; V to-inf
3 In a war, a **campaign** is a series of planned movements carried out by armed forces. ❑ *The allies are* N-COUNT: oft n N = operation

*intensifying their air campaign.* [4] → See also **advertising campaign**.

**cam|paign|er** /kæmpeɪnəʳ/ **(campaigners)** A **campaigner** is a person who campaigns for social or political change. ❑ *...anti-hunting campaigners.* N-COUNT: oft supp N, N *for/against* n

**camp bed** **(camp beds)** A **camp bed** is a small bed that you can fold up. [BRIT] N-COUNT

✔ in AM, use **cot**

**camped** /kæmpt/ If people are **camped** or **camped out** somewhere in the open air, they are living, staying, or waiting there, often in tents. ❑ *Most of the refugees are camped high in the mountains.* ADJ: v-link ADJ, usu ADJ prep/adv

**camp|er** /kæmpəʳ/ **(campers)** [1] A **camper** is someone who is camping somewhere. N-COUNT [2] A **camper** is the same as a **camper van**. N-COUNT

**camp|er van** **(camper vans)** A **camper van** is a van which is equipped with beds and cooking equipment so that you can live, cook, and sleep in it. N-COUNT

**camp|fire** /kæmpfaɪəʳ/ **(campfires)** also **camp fire.** A **campfire** is a fire that you light out of doors when you are camping. N-COUNT

**camp fol|low|er** **(camp followers)** also **camp-follower.** [1] If you describe someone as a **camp follower**, you mean that they do not officially belong to a particular group or movement but support it for their own advantage. ❑ *...the Tory leader's friends and camp followers.* N-COUNT [disapproval] [2] **Camp followers** are people who travel with an army or other group, especially members of soldiers' families, or people who supply goods and services to the army. N-COUNT

**camp|ground** /kæmpgraʊnd/ **(campgrounds)** A **campground** is the same as a **campsite**. [mainly AM] N-COUNT

**cam|phor** /kæmfəʳ/ **Camphor** is a strong-smelling white substance used in various medicines, in mothballs, and in making plastics. N-UNCOUNT

**camp|ing site** **(camping sites)** A **camping site** is the same as a **campsite**. N-COUNT

**camp|site** /kæmpsaɪt/ **(campsites)** A **campsite** is a place where people who are on holiday can stay in tents. N-COUNT

**cam|pus** /kæmpəs/ **(campuses)** A **campus** is an area of land that contains the main buildings of a university or college. ❑ *Private automobiles are not allowed on campus.* N-COUNT: also prep N

**campy** /kæmpi/ **Campy** means the same as **camp**. ❑ *...a campy spy spoof.* ADJ = camp

**cam|shaft** /kæmʃɑːft, -ʃæft/ **(camshafts)** A **camshaft** is a rod in an engine and works to change circular motion into motion up and down or from side to side. N-COUNT

**can**
① MODAL USES
② CONTAINER

① **can** /kən, STRONG kæn/ ◆◆◆

✔ **Can** is a modal verb. It is used with the base form of a verb. The form **cannot** is used in negative statements. The usual spoken form of **cannot** is **can't**, pronounced /kɑːnt, AM kænt/.

[1] You use **can** when you are mentioning a quality or fact about something which people may make use of if they want to. ❑ *Pork is also the most versatile of meats. It can be roasted whole or in pieces... A central reservation number operated by the resort can direct you to accommodations that best suit your needs... A selected list of some of those stocking a comprehensive range can be found in Chapter 8.* MODAL
[2] You use **can** to indicate that someone has the ability or opportunity to do something. ❑ *Don't worry yourself about me, I can take care of myself... I can't give you details because I don't actually have any details... See if you can find Karlov and tell him we are ready for dinner... 'You're needed here, Livy' — 'But what can I do?'... Customers can choose from sixty hit titles before buying.* MODAL
[3] You use **cannot** to indicate that someone is not able to do something because circumstances make it impossible for them to do it. ❑ *We cannot buy food, clothes and pay for rent and utilities on $20 a week... She cannot sleep and the pain is often so bad she wants to scream.* MODAL
[4] You use **can** to indicate that something is true sometimes or is true in some circumstances. ❑ *...long-term therapy that can last five years or more... Exercising alone can be boring... Coral can be yellow, blue, or green.* MODAL
[5] You use **cannot** and **can't** to state that you are certain that something is not the case or will not happen. ❑ *From her knowledge of Douglas's habits, she feels sure that the attacker can't have been Douglas... Things can't be that bad... You can't be serious, Mrs Lorimer?* MODAL
[6] You use **can** to indicate that someone is allowed to do something. You use **cannot** or **can't** to indicate that someone is not allowed to do something. ❑ *You must buy the credit life insurance before you can buy the disability insurance... Here, can I really have your jeans when you grow out of them?... We can't answer any questions, I'm afraid.* MODAL
[7] You use **cannot** or **can't** when you think it is very important that something should not happen or that someone should not do something. ❑ *It is an intolerable situation and it can't be allowed to go on... The Commission can't demand from Sweden more than it demands from its own members.* MODAL [emphasis] = mustn't
[8] You use **can**, usually in questions, in order to make suggestions or to offer to do something. ❑ *This old lady was struggling out of the train and I said, 'Oh, can I help you?'... Hello John. What can we do for you?... You can always try the beer you know – it's usually all right in this bar.* MODAL
[9] You use **can** in questions in order to make polite requests. You use **can't** in questions in order to request strongly that someone does something. ❑ *Can I have a look at that?... Can you please help?... Can you fill in some of the details of your career?... Why can't you leave me alone?* MODAL [politeness]
[10] You use **can** as a polite way of interrupting someone or of introducing what you are going to say next. [FORMAL, SPOKEN] ❑ *Can I interrupt you just for a minute?... But if I can interrupt, Joe, I don't think anybody here is personally blaming you.* MODAL = may
[11] You use **can** with verbs such as 'imagine', 'think', and 'believe' in order to emphasize how you feel about a particular situation. [INFORMAL or SPOKEN] ❑ *You can imagine he was terribly upset... You can't think how glad I was to see them all go.* MODAL [emphasis]
[12] You use **can** in questions with 'how' to indicate that you feel strongly about something. [SPOKEN] ❑ *How can you complain about higher taxes?... How can you say such a thing?... How can you expect me to believe your promises?* MODAL [emphasis]

② **can** /kæn/ **(cans, canning, canned)** [1] A **can** is a metal container in which something such as food, drink, or paint is put. The container is usually sealed to keep the contents fresh. ❑ *...empty beer cans. ...cans of paint and brushes.* N-COUNT = tin [2] When food or drink **is canned**, it is put into a metal container and sealed so that it will remain fresh. ❑ *...fruits and vegetables that will be canned, skinned, diced or otherwise processed... It was always roast lamb and canned peas for Sunday lunch.* VERB: usu passive = tin; *be* V-ed; V-ed [3] **The can** is the toilet. [AM, INFORMAL] N-SING: *the* N [4] If you **are canned**, you are dismissed from your job. [AM, INFORMAL] ❑ *The extremists prevailed, and the security minister was canned.* VERB; *be* V-ed [5] → See also **canned**.

**Ca|na|dian** /kəneɪdiən/ **(Canadians)** [1] **Canadian** means belonging or relating to Canada, or to its people or culture. ADJ [2] A **Canadian** is a Canadian citizen, or a person of Canadian origin. N-COUNT

**ca|nal** /kənæl/ **(canals)** [1] A **canal** is a long, narrow stretch of water that has been made for boats to travel along or to bring water to a particular area. ❑ *...the Grand Union Canal. ...Venetian canals and bridges.* N-COUNT [2] A **canal** is a narrow tube inside your body for carrying food, air, or other N-COUNT: usu supp N substances. ❑ *...delaying the food's progress through the alimentary canal.*

**ca|nal boat** **(canal boats)** A **canal boat** is a long, narrow boat used for travelling on canals. N-COUNT

**cana|pé** /kænəpeɪ/ **(canapés)** **Canapés** are small pieces of biscuit or toast with food such as meat, cheese, or pâté on top. They are often served with drinks at parties. N-COUNT: usu pl

**ca|nard** /kænɑːʳd, AM kənɑːrd/ **(canards)** A **canard** is an idea or a piece of information that is false, especially one that is spread deliberately in order to harm someone or their work. ❑ *The charge that Harding was a political stooge may be a canard.* N-COUNT

**ca|nary** /kəneəri/ **(canaries)** **Canaries** are small yellow birds which sing beautifully and are often kept as pets. N-COUNT

**ca|nary yel|low** Something that is **canary yellow** is a light yellow in colour. ❑ *...a canary yellow dress.* COLOUR

**can-can** **The can-can** is a dance in which women kick their legs in the air to fast music. ❑ *...can-can dancers from the Moulin Rouge.* N-SING: oft *the* N

**can|cel** /kænsᵊl/ **(cancels, cancelling, cancelled)** ◆◇◇

✔ in AM, use **canceling, canceled**

1 If you **cancel** something that has been arranged, you stop it from happening. If you **cancel** an order for goods or services, you tell the person or organization supplying them that you no longer wish to receive them. ❑ *The Russian foreign minister yesterday cancelled his visit to Washington... Many trains have been cancelled and a limited service is operating on other lines... There is normally no refund should a client choose to cancel.* VERB V n V n V
♦ **can|cel|la|tion** /kænsəleɪʃᵊn/ **(cancellations)** *Outbursts of violence forced the cancellation of Haiti's first free elections in 1987. ...passengers who suffer delays and cancellations on planes, trains, ferries and buses.* N-VAR: oft N *of* n
2 If someone in authority **cancels** a document, an insurance policy, or a debt, they officially declare that it is no longer valid or no longer legally exists. ❑ *He intends to try to leave the country, in spite of a government order cancelling his passport... She learned her insurance had been canceled by Pacific Mutual Insurance Company.* VERB V n V n
♦ **can|cel|la|tion** *...a march by groups calling for cancellation of Third World debt.* N-UNCOUNT: with supp
3 To **cancel** a stamp or a cheque means to mark it to show that it has already been used and cannot be used again. ❑ *The new device can also cancel the check after the transaction is complete. ...cancelled stamps.* VERB V n V-ed

♦ **cancel out** If one thing **cancels out** another thing, the two things have opposite effects, so that when they are combined no real effect is produced. ❑ *He wonders if the different influences might not cancel each other out... The goal was cancelled out just before half-time by Craig McLurg.* PHRASAL VERB V n P V n P Also V P n (not pron)

**can|cer** /kænsəʳ/ **(cancers)** **Cancer** is a serious disease in which cells in a person's body increase rapidly in an uncontrolled way, producing abnormal growths. ❑ *Her mother died of breast cancer... Ninety per cent of lung cancers are caused by smoking.* ◆◆◇ N-VAR: oft n N

**Can|cer** **(Cancers)** 1 **Cancer** is one of the twelve signs of the zodiac. Its symbol is a crab. People who are born approximately between the 21st of June and the 22nd of July come under this sign. N-UNCOUNT 2 A **Cancer** is a person whose sign of the zodiac is Cancer. N-COUNT

**can|cer|ous** /kænsərəs/ **Cancerous** cells or growths are cells or growths that are the result of cancer. ❑ *...production of cancerous cells... Nine out of ten lumps are not cancerous.* ADJ

**can|de|la|bra** /kændəlɑːbrə/ **(candelabras)** A **candelabra** is an ornamental holder for two or more candles. N-COUNT

**can|de|la|brum** /kændəlɑːbrəm/ **(candelabra)** A **candelabrum** is the same as a **candelabra**. N-COUNT

**can|did** /kændɪd/ 1 When you are **candid** about something or with someone, you speak honestly. ❑ *I haven't been completely candid with him. ...a candid interview.* ADJ: oft ADJ *about* n, ADJ *with* n = frank 2 A **candid** photograph of someone is one that was taken when the person did not know they were being photographed. ADJ: ADJ n

**can|di|da|cy** /kændɪdəsi/ **(candidacies)** Someone's **candidacy** is their position of being a candidate in an election. ❑ *Today he is formally announcing his candidacy for President.* N-VAR: oft with poss

**can|di|date** /kændɪdeɪt/ **(candidates)** 1 A **candidate** is someone who is being considered for a position, for example someone who is running in an election or applying for a job. ❑ *The Democratic candidate is still leading in the polls... We all spoke to them and John emerged as the best candidate.* ◆◆◇ N-COUNT: oft N *for* n 2 A **candidate** is someone who is taking an examination. [BRIT] N-COUNT 3 A **candidate** is someone who is studying for a degree at a college. [AM] N-COUNT
4 A **candidate** is a person or thing that is regarded as being suitable for a particular purpose or as being likely to do or be a particular thing. ❑ *Those who are overweight or indulge in high-salt diets are candidates for hypertension.* N-COUNT: usu N *for* n

**can|di|da|ture** /kændɪdətʃəʳ/ **(candidatures)** **Candidature** means the same as **candidacy**. [BRIT, FORMAL] N-VAR: usu poss N

**can|died** /kændid/ Food such as **candied** fruit has been covered with sugar or has been cooked in sugar syrup. ❑ *...candied orange peel.* ADJ: usu ADJ n

**can|dle** /kændᵊl/ **(candles)** 1 A **candle** is a stick of hard wax with a piece of string called a wick through the middle. You light the wick in order to give a steady flame that provides light. ❑ *The bedroom was lit by a single candle.* N-COUNT 2 If you **burn the candle at both ends**, you try to do too many things in too short a period of time so that you have to stay up very late at night and get up very early in the morning to get them done. PHRASE: V inflects

**candle|light** /kændᵊllaɪt/ **Candlelight** is the light that a candle produces. ❑ *They dined by candlelight.* N-UNCOUNT

**candle|lit** /kændᵊllɪt/ A **candlelit** room or table is lit by the light of candles. ❑ *...a candlelit dinner for two.* ADJ: usu ADJ n

**candle|stick** /kændᵊlstɪk/ **(candlesticks)** A **candlestick** is a narrow object with a hole at the top which holds a candle. N-COUNT

**can-do** If you say that someone has a **can-do** attitude, you approve of them because they are confident and willing to deal with problems or new tasks, rather than complaining or giving up. [INFORMAL] ❑ *He is known for his optimistic can-do attitude.* ADJ: ADJ n [approval] = positive ≠ negative

**can|dour** /kændəʳ/

✔ in AM, use **candor**

**Candour** is the quality of speaking honestly and openly about things. ❑ *...a brash, forceful man, noted both for his candour and his quick temper.* N-UNCOUNT = frankness

**can|dy** /kændi/ **(candies)** **Candy** is sweet foods such as toffees or chocolate. [AM] ❑ *...a piece of candy. ...a large box of candies.* N-VAR

✔ in BRIT, usually use **sweets**

**can|dy bar** **(candy bars)** A **candy bar** is a long, thin, sweet food, usually covered in chocolate. [AM] N-COUNT

**candy|floss** /kændiflɒs, AM -flɔːs/ also **candy-floss**. 1 **Candyfloss** is a large pink or white mass of sugar threads that is eaten from a stick. It is sold at fairs or other outdoor events. [BRIT] N-UNCOUNT

✔ in AM, use **cotton candy**

2 If you think something such as a CD or film has no real value, you can say that it is **candy-** N-UNCOUNT: oft N n [disapproval]

**floss.** [BRIT] ❑ *She took to writing candyfloss romances.*

**cane** /keɪn/ **(canes)** 1 **Cane** is used to refer to the long, hollow, hard stems of plants such as bamboo. Strips of cane are often used to make furniture, and some types of cane can be crushed and processed to make sugar. ❑ *...cane furniture. ...cane sugar... Bamboo produces an annual crop of cane... Dig out and burn infected canes.* N-VAR: oft N n 2 A **cane** is a long thin stick with a curved or round top which you can use to support yourself when you are walking, or which in the past was fashionable to carry with you. N-COUNT 3 A **cane** is a long, thin, flexible stick which in the past was used to hit people, especially children at school, as a punishment. ❑ *Until the 1980s some criminals were still flogged with a rattan cane as a punishment.* N-COUNT ♦ **The cane** is used to refer to the punishment of being hit with a cane. N-SING: the N 4 → See also **sugar cane**.

**ca|nine** /keɪnaɪn/ **Canine** means relating to dogs. ❑ *...research into canine diseases.* ADJ: ADJ n

**can|is|ter** /kænɪstəʳ/ **(canisters)** 1 A **canister** is a strong metal container. It is used to hold gases or chemical substances. ❑ *Riot police hurled tear gas canisters and smoke bombs into the crowd. ...canisters of commercial fuel.* N-COUNT: usu n N 2 A **canister** is a metal, plastic, or china container with a lid. It is used for storing food such as sugar and flour. N-COUNT 3 A **canister** is a flat round container. It is usually made of metal and is used to store photographic film. N-COUNT: usu with supp

**can|ker** /kæŋkəʳ/ **(cankers)** 1 A **canker** is something evil that spreads and affects things or people. [FORMAL] ❑ *...the canker of jealousy.* N-COUNT 2 **Canker** is a disease which affects the wood of shrubs and trees, making the outer layer come away to expose the inside of the stem. ❑ *In gardens, cankers are most prominent on apples and pear trees.* N-VAR

**can|na|bis** /kænəbɪs/ **Cannabis** is the hemp plant when it is used as a drug. N-UNCOUNT

**canned** /kænd/ **Canned** music, laughter, or applause on a television or radio programme has been recorded beforehand and is added to the programme to make it sound as if there is a live audience. → See also **can**. ADJ: usu ADJ n

**can|nel|lo|ni** /kænəloʊni/ **Cannelloni** is large tube-shaped pieces of pasta that contain a filling of meat, cheese, or vegetables. N-UNCOUNT

**can|nery** /kænəri/ **(canneries)** A **cannery** is a factory where food is canned. N-COUNT

**can|ni|bal** /kænɪbᵊl/ **(cannibals)** **Cannibals** are people who eat the flesh of other human beings. ❑ *...a tropical island inhabited by cannibals.* N-COUNT

**can|ni|bal|ism** /kænɪbəlɪzəm/ If a group of people practise **cannibalism**, they eat the flesh of other people. N-UNCOUNT

**can|ni|bal|is|tic** /kænɪbəlɪstɪk/ **Cannibalistic** people and practices are connected with cannibalism. ❑ *...lurid cannibalistic feasts.* ADJ: usu ADJ n

**can|ni|bal|ize** /kænɪbəlaɪz/ **(cannibalizes, cannibalizing, cannibalized)**

✓ in BRIT, also use **cannibalise**

1 If you **cannibalize** something, you take it to pieces and use it to make something else. ❑ *They cannibalized damaged planes for the parts.* VERB V n 2 If one of a company's products **cannibalizes** the company's sales, people buy it instead of any of the company's other products. [BUSINESS] ❑ *A website need not cannibalise existing sales.* VERB V n

**can|non** /kænən/ **(cannons)** 1 A **cannon** is a large gun, usually on wheels, which used to be used in battles. N-COUNT 2 A **cannon** is a heavy automatic gun, especially one that is fired from an aircraft. N-COUNT 3 If someone is a **loose cannon**, they do whatever they want and nobody can predict what they are going to do. ❑ *Max is a loose cannon politically.* PHRASE: usu v-link PHR → See also **water cannon**.

**can|non|ade** /kænəneɪd/ **(cannonades)** A **cannonade** is an intense continuous attack of gunfire. ❑ *...the distant thunder of a cannonade.* N-COUNT = barrage

**cannon|ball** /kænənbɔːl/ **(cannonballs)** also **cannon ball.** A **cannonball** is a heavy metal ball that is fired from a cannon. N-COUNT

**can|non fod|der** also **cannon-fodder.** If someone in authority regards people they are in charge of as **cannon fodder**, they do not care if these people are harmed or lost in the course of their work. ❑ *The conscripts were treated as cannon fodder.* N-UNCOUNT

**can|not** /kænɒt, kənɒt/ **Cannot** is the negative form of **can**.

**can|ny** /kæni/ **(cannier, canniest)** A **canny** person is clever and able to think quickly. You can also describe a person's behaviour as **canny**. ❑ *He was far too canny to risk giving himself away.* ADJ: usu ADJ n = shrewd

**ca|noe** /kənuː/ **(canoes)** A **canoe** is a small, narrow boat that you move through the water using a stick with a wide end called a paddle. N-COUNT

**ca|noe|ing** /kənuːɪŋ/ **Canoeing** is the sport of using and racing a canoe. ❑ *They went canoeing in the wilds of Canada.* N-UNCOUNT

**ca|noe|ist** /kənuːɪst/ **(canoeists)** A **canoeist** is someone who is skilled at racing and performing tests of skill in a canoe. N-COUNT

**can|on** /kænən/ **(canons)** A **canon** is a member of the clergy who is on the staff of a cathedral. N-COUNT

**ca|noni|cal** /kənɒnɪkᵊl/ If something has **canonical** status, it is accepted as having all the qualities that a thing of its kind should have. ❑ *...Ballard's status as a canonical writer.* ADJ: ADJ n

**can|on|ize** /kænənaɪz/ **(canonizes, canonizing, canonized)**

✓ in BRIT, also use **canonise**

If a dead person **is canonized**, it is officially announced by the Catholic Church that he or she is a saint. ❑ *Joan of Arc was finally canonized in 1920.* VERB: usu passive be V-ed

**can|on law** **Canon law** is the law of the Christian church. It has authority only for that church and its members. ❑ *The Church's canon law forbids remarriage of divorced persons.* N-UNCOUNT

**ca|noo|dle** /kənuːdᵊl/ **(canoodles, canoodling, canoodled)** If two people **are canoodling**, they are kissing and holding each other a lot. [mainly OLD-FASHIONED] ❑ *He was seen canoodling with his new girlfriend.* V-RECIP V with n Also pl-n V

**can open|er** **(can openers)** A **can opener** is the same as a **tin opener**. → See picture on page 1710. N-COUNT

**cano|pied** /kænəpid/ A **canopied** building or piece of furniture is covered with a roof or a piece of material supported by poles. ❑ *...a canopied Elizabethan bed.* ADJ: usu ADJ n

**cano|py** /kænəpi/ **(canopies)** 1 A **canopy** is a decorated cover, often made of cloth, which is placed above something such as a bed or a seat. N-COUNT 2 A **canopy** is a layer of something that spreads out and covers an area, for example the branches and leaves that spread out at the top of trees in a forest. ❑ *The trees formed such a dense canopy that all beneath was a deep carpet of pine-needles.* N-COUNT: usu sing

**cant** /kænt/ If you refer to moral or religious statements as **cant**, you are criticizing them because you think the person making them does not really believe what they are saying. ❑ *...politicians holding forth with their usual hypocritical cant.* N-UNCOUNT [disapproval]

**can't** /kɑːnt, AM kænt/ **Can't** is the usual spoken form of 'cannot'.

**can|ta|loupe** /kæntəluːp, AM -loʊp/ **(cantaloupes)** also **cantaloup.** A **cantaloupe** is a type of **melon**. N-COUNT

**can|tan|ker|ous** /kæntæŋkərəs/ Someone who is **cantankerous** is always finding things to argue or complain about. [WRITTEN] ❑ *...a cantankerous old man.* ADJ: usu ADJ n

**can|ta|ta** /kæntɑːtə/ **(cantatas)** A **cantata** is a fairly short musical work for singers and instruments. N-COUNT

**can|teen** /kæntiːn/ **(canteens)** 1 A **canteen** is a place in a factory, shop, or college where meals are served to the people who work or study there. ❑ *...a school canteen. ...canteen food.* N-COUNT = cafeteria 2 A **canteen** is a small plastic bottle for carrying water and other drinks. Canteens are used by soldiers. ❑ *...a full canteen of water.* N-COUNT 3 A **canteen of** cutlery is a set of knives, forks, and spoons in a specially designed box. N-COUNT: usu N *of* n

**can|ter** /kæntəʳ/ **(canters, cantering, cantered)** When a horse **canters**, it moves at a speed that is slower than a gallop but faster than a trot. ❑ *The competitors cantered into the arena to conclude the closing ceremony.* VERB V prep/adv ♦ **Canter** is also a noun. ❑ *Carnac set off at a canter.* N-COUNT: usu sing

**can|ti|lever** /kæntɪliːvəʳ/ **(cantilevers)** A **cantilever** is a long piece of metal or wood used in a structure such as a bridge. One end is fastened to something and the other end is used to support part of the structure. ❑ *...the old steel cantilever bridge.* N-COUNT

**can|ti|levered** /kæntɪliːvəʳd/ A **cantilevered** structure is constructed using cantilevers. ❑ *...a cantilevered balcony.* ADJ: usu ADJ n

**can|ton** /kæntɒn/ **(cantons)** A **canton** is a political or administrative region in some countries, for example Switzerland. ❑ *...the Swiss canton of Berne.* N-COUNT

**Can|ton|ese** /kæntəniːz/ **(Cantonese)** 1 **Cantonese** means belonging or relating to the Chinese provinces of Canton and Kwangtung. ADJ 2 The **Cantonese** are the people who live in or come from the Chinese provinces of Canton and Kwangtung. N-COUNT: usu pl 3 **Cantonese** is the language spoken in the Chinese provinces of Guango, Kwansai, and Hong Kong, as well as in other parts of the world. N-UNCOUNT

**can|ton|ment** /kæntuːnmənt, AM -toʊn-/ **(cantonments)** A **cantonment** is a group of buildings or a camp where soldiers live. N-COUNT

**can|vas** /kænvəs/ **(canvases)** 1 **Canvas** is a strong, heavy cloth that is used for making things such as tents, sails, and bags. ❑ *...a canvas bag.* N-UNCOUNT 2 A **canvas** is a piece of canvas or similar material on which an oil painting can be done. N-VAR 3 A **canvas** is a painting that has been done on canvas. ❑ *The show includes canvases by masters like Carpaccio, Canaletto and Guardi.* N-COUNT = painting

**can|vass** /kænvəs/ **(canvasses, canvassing, canvassed)** 1 If you **canvass for** a particular person or political party, you go around an area trying to persuade people to vote for that person or party. ❑ *I'm canvassing for the Conservative Party.* VERB V *for* n ♦ **can|vass|er (canvassers)** *...a Conservative canvasser.* N-COUNT 2 If you **canvass** public opinion, you find out how people feel about a particular subject. ❑ *Members of Parliament are spending the weekend canvassing opinion in their constituencies.* VERB V n

**can|yon** /kænjən/ **(canyons)** A **canyon** is a long, narrow valley with very steep sides. ❑ *...the Grand Canyon.* N-COUNT; N-IN-NAMES

**cap** /kæp/ **(caps, capping, capped)** ◆◇◇ 1 A **cap** is a soft, flat hat with a curved part at the front which is called a peak. Caps are usually worn by men and boys. ❑ *...a dark blue baseball cap.* N-COUNT: oft supp N 2 A **cap** is a special hat which is worn as part of a uniform. ❑ *...a frontier guard in olive-grey uniform and a peaked cap.* N-COUNT: oft supp N 3 If a sports player **is capped**, they are chosen to represent their country in a team game such as football, rugby, or cricket. [BRIT] ❑ *Rees, 32, has been capped for England 23 times. ...England's most capped rugby union player.* VERB: usu passive *be* V-ed V-ed 4 If a sports player represents their country in a team game such as football, rugby, or cricket, you can say that they have been awarded a **cap**. [BRIT] ❑ *Mark Davis will win his first cap for Wales in Sunday's Test match against Australia.* N-COUNT 5 If the government **caps** an organization, council, or budget, it limits the amount of money that the organization or council is allowed to spend, or limits the size of the budget. ❑ *The Secretary of State for Environment has the power to cap councils which spend excessively.* VERB V n 6 The **cap** of a bottle is its lid. ❑ *She unscrewed the cap of her water bottle and gave him a drink.* N-COUNT 7 A **cap** is a circular rubber device that a woman places inside her vagina to prevent herself from becoming pregnant. [BRIT] N-COUNT 8 If someone says that a good or bad event **caps** a series of events, they mean it is the final event in the series, and the other events were also good or bad. [JOURNALISM] ❑ *The unrest capped a weekend of right-wing attacks on foreigners.* VERB V n 9 If someone's teeth **are capped**, covers are fixed over them so that they look better. ❑ *He suddenly smiled, revealing teeth that had recently been capped... I had my teeth capped.* VERB: usu passive *be* V-ed *have* n V-ed 10 → See also **ice cap**.

**ca|pa|bil|ity** /keɪpəbɪlɪti/ **(capabilities)** 1 If you have the **capability** or the **capabilities** to do something, you have the ability or the qualities that are necessary to do it. ❑ *People experience differences in physical and mental capability depending on the time of day... The standards set four years ago in Seoul will be far below the athletes' capabilities now.* N-VAR: with supp, oft adj N, N to-inf = ability 2 A country's military **capability** is its ability to fight in a war. ❑ *Their military capability has been reduced because their air force has proved not to be effective.* N-VAR: with supp, usu adj N, N to-inf

**ca|pable** /keɪpəbᵊl/ ◆◇◇ 1 If a person or thing is **capable of** doing something, they have the ability to do it. ❑ *He appeared hardly capable of conducting a coherent conversation... The kitchen is capable of catering for several hundred people.* ADJ: v-link ADJ *of* -ing/n ≠ incapable 2 Someone who is **capable** has the skill or qualities necessary to do a particular thing well, or is able to do most things well. ❑ *She's a very capable speaker... Her husband was such a fine, capable man.* ADJ = competent, able ♦ **ca|pably** /keɪpəbli/ *Happily it was all dealt with very capably by the police and security people.* ADV: ADV with v

**ca|pa|cious** /kəpeɪʃəs/ Something that is **capacious** has a lot of space to put things in. [FORMAL] ❑ *...her capacious handbag.* ADJ: usu ADJ n

**ca|paci|tor** /kəpæsɪtəʳ/ **(capacitors)** A **capacitor** is a device for accumulating electric charge. N-COUNT

**ca|pac|ity** /kəpæsɪti/ **(capacities)** ◆◇◇ 1 Your **capacity for** something is your ability to do it, or the amount of it that you are able to do. ❑ *Our capacity for giving care, love and attention is limited... Her mental capacity and temperament are as remarkable as his. ...people's creative capacities.* N-VAR: oft with poss, N *for* n/-ing, N to-inf 2 The **capacity** of something such as a factory, industry, or region is the quantity of things that it can produce or deliver with the equipment or resources that are available. ❑ *Bread factories are working at full capacity... The region is valued for its coal and vast electricity-generating capacity.* N-UNCOUNT 3 The **capacity** of a piece of equipment is its size or power, often measured in particular units. ❑ *...an aircraft with a bomb-carrying capacity of 454 kg.* N-COUNT 4 The **capacity** of a container is its volume, or the amount of liquid it can hold, measured in units such as litres or gallons. ❑ *...the fuel tanks, which had a capacity of 140 litres... Grease 6 ramekin dishes of 150 ml (5-6 fl oz) capacity.* N-VAR 5 The **capacity** of a building, place, or vehicle is the number of people or things that it can hold. If a place is filled **to capacity**, it is as full as it can possibly be. ❑ *Each stadium had a seating capacity of about 50,000... Toronto hospital maternity wards were filled to capacity.* N-SING: also no det, oft *to* N 6 A **capacity** crowd or audience completely fills a theatre, sports stadium, or other place. ❑ *A capacity crowd of 76,000 people was at Wembley football stadium for the event.* ADJ: ADJ n 7 If you do something **in** a particular **capacity**, you do it as part of a particular job or duty, or because you are representing a particular organization or person. [WRITTEN] ❑ *Ms Halliwell visited the Philippines in her capacity as a Special Repre-* N-COUNT: with supp, *in* N, oft poss N *as* n *sentative of Unicef... This article is written in a personal capacity.*

**cape** /keɪp/ **(capes)** 1 A **cape** is a large piece of land that sticks out into the sea from the coast. ❑ *In 1978, Naomi James became the first woman to sail solo around the world via Cape Horn.* 2 A **cape** is a short cloak. ❑ *...a woollen cape.* N-COUNT; N-IN-NAMES / N-COUNT

**ca|per** /keɪpəʳ/ **(capers, capering, capered)** 1 **Capers** are the small green buds of caper plants. They are usually sold preserved in vinegar. N-COUNT: usu pl 2 If you **caper about**, you run and jump around because you are happy or excited. ❑ *They were capering about, shouting and laughing.* VERB V adv/prep

**ca|pil|lary** /kəpɪləri, AM kæpəleri/ **(capillaries)** **Capillaries** are tiny blood vessels in your body. N-COUNT

**capi|tal** /kæpɪtᵊl/ **(capitals)** 1 **Capital** is a large sum of money which you use to start a business, or which you invest in order to make more money. [BUSINESS] ❑ *Companies are having difficulty in raising capital... A large amount of capital is invested in all these branches.* ◆◆◆ N-UNCOUNT 2 You can use **capital** to refer to buildings or machinery which are necessary to produce goods or to make companies more efficient, but which do not make money directly. [BUSINESS] ❑ *...capital equipment that could have served to increase production. ...capital investment.* N-UNCOUNT: usu N n 3 **Capital** is the part of an amount of money borrowed or invested which does not include interest. [BUSINESS] ❑ *With a conventional repayment mortgage, the repayments consist of both capital and interest.* N-UNCOUNT 4 The **capital** of a country is the city or town where its government or parliament meets. ❑ *...Kathmandu, the capital of Nepal.* N-COUNT: usu *the* N in sing, oft N *of* n 5 If a place is **the capital of** a particular industry or activity, it is the place that is most famous for it, because it happens in that place more than anywhere else. ❑ *Colmar has long been considered the capital of the wine trade. ...New York, the fashion capital of the world.* N-COUNT: usu *the* N in sing, with supp 6 **Capitals** or **capital letters** are written or printed letters in the form which is used at the beginning of sentences or names. 'T', 'B', and 'F' are capitals. ❑ *The name and address are written in capitals.* N-COUNT 7 A **capital** offence is one that is so serious that the person who commits it can be punished by death. ❑ *Espionage is a capital offence in this country. ...Americans wrongly convicted of capital crimes.* ADJ: ADJ n 8 → See also **working capital**. 9 If you say that someone **is making capital out of** a situation, you disapprove of the way they are gaining an advantage for themselves through other people's efforts or bad luck. [FORMAL] ❑ *He rebuked the President for trying to make political capital out of the hostage situation.* PHRASE: V inflects, PHR n [disapproval]

**capi|tal ac|count** **(capital accounts)** 1 A country's **capital account** is the part of its balance of payments that is concerned with the movement of capital. N-COUNT 2 A **capital account** is a financial statement showing the capital value of a company on a particular date. [BUSINESS] N-COUNT

**capi|tal gains** **Capital gains** are the profits that you make when you buy something and then sell it again at a higher price. [BUSINESS] ❑ *He called for the reform of capital gains tax.* N-PLURAL

**capi|tal goods** **Capital goods** are used to make other products. Compare **consumer goods**. [BUSINESS] N-PLURAL

**capi|tal in|flow** **(capital inflows)** In economics, **capital inflow** is the amount of capital coming into a country, for example in the form of foreign investment. [BUSINESS] ❑ *...a large drop in the capital inflow into America.* N-VAR

**capital-intensive** **Capital-intensive** industries and businesses need the investment of large sums of money. Compare **labour-intensive**. [BUSINESS] ADJ

**capi|tal|ise** /kæpɪtəlaɪz/ → see **capitalize**.

**capi|tal|ism** /kæpɪtəlɪzəm/ **Capitalism** is an economic and political system in which property, business, and industry are owned by private individuals and not by the state. ❑ *...the return of capitalism to Hungary.* N-UNCOUNT

**capi|tal|ist** /kæpɪtəlɪst/ **(capitalists)** 1 A **capitalist** country or system supports or is based on the principles of capitalism. ❑ *I'm a strong believer in the capitalist system. ...capitalist economic theory.* ADJ 2 A **capitalist** is someone who believes in and supports the principles of capitalism. ❑ *...relations between capitalists and workers.* N-COUNT 3 A **capitalist** is someone who owns a business which they run in order to make a profit for themselves. ❑ *They argue that only private capitalists can remake Poland's economy.* N-COUNT = entrepreneur

**capi|tal|ist|ic** /kæpɪtəlɪstɪk/ **Capitalistic** means supporting or based on the principles of capitalism. ❑ *...the forces of capitalistic greed. ...capitalistic economic growth.* ADJ: ADJ n

**capi|tal|ize** /kæpɪtəlaɪz/ **(capitalizes, capitalizing, capitalized)**

in BRIT, also use **capitalise**

1 If you **capitalize on** a situation, you use it to gain some advantage for yourself. ❑ *The rebels seem to be trying to capitalize on the public's discontent with the government.* VERB V *on/upon* n 2 In business, if you **capitalize** something that belongs to you, you sell it in order to make money. [BUSINESS] ❑ *Our intention is to capitalize the company by any means we can... The company will be capitalized at £2 million.* VERB V n *be* V-ed *at* amount ♦ **capi|tali|za|tion** /kæpɪtəlaɪzeɪʃᵊn/ ...*a massive capitalization programme.* N-UNCOUNT

**capi|tal let|ter** **(capital letters)** **Capital letters** are the same as **capitals**. N-COUNT

**capi|tal pun|ish|ment** **Capital punishment** is punishment which involves the legal killing of a person who has committed a serious crime such as murder. ❑ *Most democracies have abolished capital punishment.* N-UNCOUNT

**ca|pitu|late** /kəpɪtʃʊleɪt/ **(capitulates, capitulating, capitulated)** If you **capitulate**, you stop resisting and do what someone else wants you to do. ❑ *The club eventually capitulated and now grants equal rights to women... In less than two hours Cohen capitulated to virtually every demand.* VERB = submit, yield V V *to* n

**ca|pon** /keɪpən/ **(capons)** A **capon** is a male chicken that has had its sex organs removed and has been specially fattened up to be eaten. N-COUNT

**cap|puc|ci|no** /kæpətʃiːnoʊ/ **(cappuccinos)** **Cappuccino** is coffee which is made using milk and has froth and sometimes powdered chocolate on top. ♦ A **cappuccino** is a cup of cappuccino. N-UNCOUNT / N-COUNT

**ca|price** /kæpriːs/ **(caprices)** A **caprice** is an unexpected action or decision which has no strong reason or purpose. [FORMAL] ❑ *I lived in terror of her sudden caprices and moods.* N-VAR = whim, impulse

**ca|pri|cious** /kæprɪʃəs/ Someone who is **capricious** often changes their mind unexpectedly. ❑ *The Union accused Walesa of being capricious and undemocratic.* ADJ = fickle

**Cap|ri|corn** /kæprɪkɔːʳn/ **(Capricorns)** 1 **Capricorn** is one of the twelve signs of the zodiac. Its symbol is a goat. People who are born approximately between the 22nd of December and the 19th of January come under this sign. N-UNCOUNT 2 A **Capricorn** is a person whose sign of the zodiac is Capricorn. N-COUNT

**cap|si|cum** /kæpsɪkəm/ **(capsicums)** **Capsicums** are **peppers**. N-VAR

**cap|size** /kæpsaɪz, AM kæpsaɪz/ **(capsizes, capsizing, capsized)** If you **capsize** a boat or if it **capsizes**, it turns upside down in the water. ❑ *The sea got very rough and the boat capsized... I didn't count on his capsizing the raft.* VERB = overturn V V n

**cap|stan** /kæpstən/ **(capstans)** A **capstan** is a machine consisting of a drum that turns round and pulls in a heavy rope or something attached to a rope, for example an anchor. N-COUNT

**cap|sule** /kæpsjuːl, AM kæpsᵊl/ **(capsules)** 1 A **capsule** is a very small tube containing powdered or liquid medicine, which you swallow. N-COUNT

❑ *...cod liver oil capsules.* [2] A **capsule** is a small container with a drug or other substance inside it, which is used for medical or scientific purposes. ❑ *They first implanted capsules into the animals' brains.* N-COUNT [3] A space **capsule** is the part of a spacecraft in which people travel, and which often separates from the main rocket. ❑ *A Russian space capsule is currently orbiting the Earth.* N-COUNT

**Capt.** **Capt.** is a written abbreviation for **captain**. ❑ *Capt. Hunt asked which engine was on fire.* N-TITLE

**cap|tain** /kæptɪn/ **(captains, captaining, captained)** ◆◆◇ [1] In the army, navy, and some other armed forces, a **captain** is an officer of middle rank. ❑ *...a captain in the British army... Are all your weapons in place, Captain?* N-TITLE; N-COUNT; N-VOC [2] The **captain of** a sports team is the player in charge of it. ❑ *...Bob Willis, the former England cricket captain.* N-COUNT: oft N *of* n, n N = skipper [3] The **captain** of a ship is the sailor in charge of it. ❑ *...the captain of the aircraft carrier Saratoga.* N-COUNT: oft N *of* n = skipper [4] The **captain** of an aeroplane is the pilot in charge of it. N-COUNT; N-TITLE [5] In the United States and some other countries, a **captain** is a police officer or fireman of fairly senior rank. N-COUNT; N-TITLE [6] If you **captain** a team or a ship, you are the captain of it. ❑ *...Murdo McLeod, who captained Hibernian's League-Cup-winning team in 1991.* VERB = skipper V n

**cap|tain|cy** /kæptɪnsi/ The **captaincy** of a team is the position of being captain. ❑ *His captaincy of the team was ended by mild eye trouble.* N-UNCOUNT: oft *the* N, poss N

**cap|tain of in|dus|try** **(captains of industry)** You can refer to the owners or senior managers of industrial companies as **captains of industry**. N-COUNT

**cap|tion** /kæpʃᵊn/ **(captions)** ◆◆◇ A **caption** is the words printed underneath a picture or cartoon which explain what it is about. ❑ *On the back of the photo is written the simple caption, 'Mrs. Monroe'.* N-COUNT

**cap|ti|vate** /kæptɪveɪt/ **(captivates, captivating, captivated)** If you **are captivated** by someone or something, you find them fascinating and attractive. ❑ *I was captivated by her brilliant mind... For 40 years she has captivated the world with her radiant looks.* VERB *be* V-ed V n

**cap|ti|vat|ing** /kæptɪveɪtɪŋ/ Someone or something that is **captivating** fascinates or attracts you. ❑ *...her captivating smile and alluring looks.* ADJ = fascinating

**cap|tive** /kæptɪv/ **(captives)** [1] A **captive** person or animal is being kept imprisoned or enclosed. [LITERARY] ❑ *Her heart had begun to pound inside her chest like a captive animal.* ADJ ♦ A **captive** is someone who is captive. ❑ *He described the difficulties of surviving for four months as a captive.* N-COUNT = prisoner [2] A **captive** audience is a group of people who are not free to leave a certain place and so have to watch or listen. A **captive** market is a group of people who cannot choose whether or where to buy things. ❑ *We all performed action songs, sketches and dances before a captive audience of parents and patrons... Airlines consider business travellers a captive market.* ADJ: ADJ n [3] If you **take** someone **captive** or **hold** someone **captive**, you take or keep them as a prisoner. ❑ *Richard was finally released on February 4, one year after he'd been taken captive.* PHRASE: V inflects

**cap|tive breed|ing** **Captive breeding** is the breeding of wild animals in places such as zoos, especially animals which have become rare in the wild. N-UNCOUNT

**cap|tiv|ity** /kæptɪvɪti/ **Captivity** is the state of being kept imprisoned or enclosed. ❑ *The great majority of barn owls are reared in captivity... An American missionary was released today after more than two months of captivity.* N-UNCOUNT: oft *in/of* N

**cap|tor** /kæptəʳ/ **(captors)** You can refer to the person who has captured a person or animal as their **captor**. ❑ *They did not know what their captors planned for them.* N-COUNT: usu poss N

**cap|ture** /kæptʃəʳ/ **(captures, capturing, captured)** ◆◇◇ [1] If you **capture** someone or something, you catch them, especially in a war. ❑ *The guerrillas shot down one aeroplane and captured the pilot... The Russians now appear ready to capture more territory from the Chechens. ...the murders of fifteen thousand captured Polish soldiers.* VERB V n V n *from* n V-ed ♦ **Capture** is also a noun. ❑ *...the final battles which led to the army's capture of the town... The shooting happened while the man was trying to evade capture by the security forces.* N-UNCOUNT: oft with poss [2] If something or someone **captures** a particular quality, feeling, or atmosphere, they represent or express it successfully. ❑ *Their mood was captured by one who said, 'Students here don't know or care about campus issues.'* VERB: no cont = encapsulate V n [3] If something **captures** your attention or imagination, you begin to be interested or excited by it. If someone or something **captures** your heart, you begin to love them or like them very much. ❑ *...the great names of the Tory party who usually capture the historian's attention. ...one man's undying love for the woman who captured his heart.* VERB V n V n [4] If an event **is captured** in a photograph or on film, it is photographed or filmed. ❑ *The incident was captured on videotape... The images were captured by TV crews filming outside the base. ...photographers who captured the traumatic scene.* VERB *be* V-ed *on/in* n *be* V-ed V n [5] If you **capture** something that you are trying to obtain in competition with other people, you succeed in obtaining it. ❑ *In 1987, McDonald's captured 19 percent of all fast-food sales.* VERB = win, secure V n

**car** /kɑːʳ/ **(cars)** ◆◆◆ [1] A **car** is a motor vehicle with room for a small number of passengers. ❑ *He had left his tickets in his car... They arrived by car.* N-COUNT: also *by* N [2] A **car** is one of the separate sections of a train. [AM] N-COUNT

> ✔ in BRIT, usually use **carriage**

[3] Railway carriages are called **cars** when they are used for a particular purpose. [BRIT] ❑ *He made his way into the dining car for breakfast.* N-COUNT: usu supp N [4] → See also **cable car**.

**ca|rafe** /kəræf/ **(carafes)** A **carafe** is a glass container in which you serve water or wine. ❑ *He ordered a carafe of wine.* N-COUNT: oft N *of* n

**car alarm** **(car alarms)** A **car alarm** is a device in a car which makes a loud noise if anyone tries to break into the vehicle. ❑ *He returned to the airport to find his car alarm going off.* N-COUNT

**cara|mel** /kærəmel/ **(caramels)** [1] A **caramel** is a chewy sweet food made from sugar, butter, and milk. N-VAR [2] **Caramel** is burnt sugar used for colouring and flavouring food. N-UNCOUNT: also *a* N

**cara|mel|ize** /kærəməlaɪz/ **(caramelizes, caramelizing, caramelized)**

> ✔ in BRIT, also use **caramelise**

[1] If sugar **caramelizes**, it turns to caramel as a result of being heated. ❑ *Cook until the sugar starts to caramelize.* VERB V [2] If you **caramelize** something such as fruit, you cook it with sugar so that it is coated with caramel. ❑ *Start by caramelizing some onions. ...caramelised apples and pears.* VERB V n V-ed

**cara|pace** /kærəpeɪs/ **(carapaces)** [1] A **carapace** is the protective shell on the back of some animals such as tortoises or crabs. [FORMAL] N-COUNT [2] You can refer to an attitude that someone has in order to protect themselves as their **carapace**. [LITERARY] ❑ *The arrogance became his protective carapace.* N-COUNT: usu with supp

**car|at** /kærət/ **(carats)** [1] A **carat** is a unit for measuring the weight of diamonds and other precious stones. It is equal to 0.2 grams. ❑ *The gemstone is 28.6 millimetres high and weighs 139.43 carats. ...a huge eight-carat diamond.* N-COUNT: usu num N [2] **Carat** is used after a number to indicate how pure gold is. The purest gold is 24-carat gold. ❑ *...a 14-carat gold fountain pen.* COMB in ADJ

**cara|van** /kærəvæn/ **(caravans)** [1] A **caravan** is a vehicle without an engine that can be pulled by a car or van. It contains beds and cooking equipment so that people can live or spend their holidays in it. [mainly BRIT] N-COUNT

> ✔ in AM, usually use **trailer**

[2] A **caravan** is a group of people and animals or vehicles who travel together. N-COUNT

**cara|van|ning** /kærəvænɪŋ/ **Caravanning** is the activity of having a holiday in a caravan. [BRIT] ❑ *He was on a caravanning holiday.* N-UNCOUNT

**cara|van site** **(caravan sites)** A **caravan site** is an area of land where people can stay in a caravan on holiday, or where people live in caravans. [BRIT] N-COUNT

✔ in AM, use **trailer park**

**cara|way** /kærəweɪ/ **Caraway** is a plant with strong-tasting seeds that are used in cooking. Caraway seeds are often used to flavour bread and cakes. N-UNCOUNT: oft N n

**car|bine** /kɑːʳbaɪn, AM -biːn/ **(carbines)** A **carbine** is a light automatic rifle. N-COUNT

**car|bo|hy|drate** /kɑːʳboʊhaɪdreɪt/ **(carbohydrates)** **Carbohydrates** are substances, found in certain kinds of food, that provide you with energy. Foods such as sugar and bread that contain these substances can also be referred to as **carbohydrates**. ❑ *...carbohydrates such as bread, pasta or chips.* N-VAR: usu pl

**car|bol|ic acid** /kɑːʳbɒlɪk æsɪd/ **Carbolic acid** or **carbolic** is a liquid that is used as a disinfectant and antiseptic. ❑ *Carbolic acid is usually used for cleaning... She smelled strongly of carbolic soap.* N-UNCOUNT

**car bomb** **(car bombs)** A **car bomb** is a bomb which is inside a car, van, or truck. N-COUNT

**car|bon** /kɑːʳbən/ **Carbon** is a chemical element that diamonds and coal are made up of. ◆◇◇ N-UNCOUNT

**car|bon|ate** /kɑːʳbəneɪt/ **(carbonates)** **Carbonate** is used in the names of some substances that are formed from carbonic acid, which is a compound of carbon dioxide and water. ❑ *...1,500 milligrams of calcium carbonate. ...carbonate of ammonia solution.* N-VAR: oft N n, N *of* n

**car|bon|at|ed** /kɑːʳbəneɪtɪd/ **Carbonated** drinks are drinks that contain small bubbles of carbon dioxide. ❑ *...colas and other carbonated soft drinks.* ADJ: usu ADJ n = *fizzy*

**car|bon copy** **(carbon copies)** [1] If you say that one person or thing is a **carbon copy of** another, you mean that they look or behave exactly like them. ❑ *She's a carbon copy of her mother.* N-COUNT: usu N *of* n
[2] A **carbon copy** is a copy of a piece of writing that is made using carbon paper. N-COUNT

**car|bon cred|it** **(carbon credits)** **Carbon credits** are an allowance that certain companies have, permitting them to burn a certain amount of fossil fuels. ❑ *By investing in efficient plant it could generate lots of valuable carbon credits to sell to wealthier, more wasteful nations.* N-COUNT: usu pl

**car|bon da|ting** **Carbon dating** is a system of calculating the age of a very old object by measuring the amount of radioactive carbon it contains. N-UNCOUNT

**car|bon di|ox|ide** **Carbon dioxide** is a gas. It is produced by animals and people breathing out, and by chemical reactions. N-UNCOUNT

**car|bon mon|ox|ide** **Carbon monoxide** is a poisonous gas that is produced especially by the engines of vehicles. N-UNCOUNT

**car|bon pa|per** **Carbon paper** is thin paper with a dark substance on one side. You use it to make copies of letters, bills, and other papers. ❑ *The drawing is transferred onto the wood by means of carbon paper.* N-UNCOUNT

**car|bon tax** **(carbon taxes)** A **carbon tax** is a tax on the burning of fuels such as coal, gas, and oil. Its aim is to reduce the amount of carbon dioxide released into the atmosphere. N-COUNT

**car boot sale** **(car boot sales)** A **car boot sale** is a sale where people sell things they own and do not want from a little stall or from the back of their car. [BRIT] N-COUNT

✔ in AM, use **garage sale**

**car|bun|cle** /kɑːʳbʌŋkəl/ **(carbuncles)** A **carbuncle** is a large swelling under the skin. N-COUNT = *boil*

**car|bu|ret|tor** /kɑːʳbəretəʳ, AM -reɪtəʳ/ **(carburettors)**

✔ in AM, use **carburetor**

A **carburettor** is the part of an engine, usually in a car, in which air and petrol are mixed together to form a vapour which can be burned. N-COUNT

**car|cass** /kɑːʳkəs/ **(carcasses)**

✔ in BRIT, also use **carcase**

A **carcass** is the body of a dead animal. ❑ *A cluster of vultures crouched on the carcass of a dead buffalo.* N-COUNT

**car|cino|gen** /kɑːʳsɪnədʒən, kɑːʳsɪnədʒen/ **(carcinogens)** A **carcinogen** is a substance which can cause cancer. [MEDICAL] N-COUNT

**car|cino|gen|ic** /kɑːʳsɪnədʒenɪk/ A substance that is **carcinogenic** is likely to cause cancer. [MEDICAL] ADJ

**car|ci|no|ma** /kɑːʳsɪnoʊmə/ **(carcinomas)**
[1] **Carcinoma** is a type of cancer. [MEDICAL] N-UNCOUNT
[2] **Carcinomas** are malignant tumours. [MEDICAL] N-COUNT

**card** /kɑːʳd/ **(cards)** [1] A **card** is a piece of stiff paper or thin cardboard on which something is written or printed. ❑ *Check the numbers below against the numbers on your card.* ◆◆◇ N-COUNT
[2] A **card** is a piece of cardboard or plastic, or a small document, which shows information about you and which you carry with you, for example to prove your identity. ❑ *They check my bag and press card. ...her membership card... The authorities have begun to issue ration cards.* N-COUNT: with supp, usu n N
[3] A **card** is a rectangular piece of plastic, issued by a bank, company, or shop, which you can use to buy things or obtain money. ❑ *He paid the whole bill with an American Express card... Holidaymakers should beware of using plastic cards in foreign cash dispensers.* N-COUNT: oft n-proper N
[4] A **card** is a folded piece of stiff paper with a picture and sometimes a message printed on it, which you send to someone on a special occasion. ❑ *She sends me a card on my birthday. ...millions of get-well cards.* N-COUNT: oft supp N
[5] A **card** is the same as a **postcard**. ❑ *Send your details on a card to the following address.* N-COUNT
[6] A **card** is a piece of thin cardboard carried by someone such as a business person in order to give to other people. A card shows the name, address, telephone number, and other details of the person who carries it. [BUSINESS] ❑ *Here's my card. You may need me.* N-COUNT: oft poss N = *business card*
[7] **Cards** are thin pieces of cardboard with numbers or pictures printed on them which are used to play various games. ❑ *...a pack of cards.* N-COUNT: usu pl = *playing card*
[8] If you are playing **cards**, you are playing a game using cards. ❑ *They enjoy themselves drinking wine, smoking and playing cards.* N-UNCOUNT
[9] You can use **card** to refer to something that gives you an advantage in a particular situation. If you play a particular **card**, you use that advantage. ❑ *It was his strongest card in their relationship – that she wanted him more than he wanted her... This permitted Western manufacturers to play their strong cards: capital and technology.* N-COUNT
[10] **Card** is strong, stiff paper or thin cardboard. ❑ *She put the pieces of card in her pocket.* N-UNCOUNT
[11] → See also **bank card**, **business card**, **calling card**, **cash card**, **cheque card**, **Christmas card**, **credit card**, **gold card**, **identity card**, **index card**, **payment card**, **place card**, **playing card**, **report card**, **smart card**, **wild card**.

PHRASES [12] If you say that something is **on the cards** in British English, or **in the cards** in American English, you mean that it is very likely to happen. ❑ *Last summer she began telling friends that a New Year marriage was on the cards.* PHRASE: usu v-link PHR = *likely* ≠ *unlikely*
[13] If you say that someone will achieve success if they **play** their **cards right**, you mean that they will achieve success if they act skilfully and use the advantages that they have. ❑ *He could even be the next manager of the England team if he plays his cards right.* PHRASE: V inflects
[14] If you **put** or **lay** your **cards on the table**, you deal with a situation by speaking openly about your feelings, ideas, or plans. ❑ *Put* PHRASE: V inflects

your cards on the table and be very clear about your complaints.

**car|da|mom** /kɑːʳdəməm/ **(cardamoms)** also **cardamon.** **Cardamom** is a spice. It comes from the seeds of a plant grown in Asia. N-VAR

**card|board** /kɑːʳdbɔːʳd/ **Cardboard** is thick, stiff paper that is used, for example, to make boxes and models. ❑ *...a cardboard box. ...a life-size cardboard cut-out of a police officer.* N-UNCOUNT: oft N n

**card-carrying** 1 A **card-carrying** member of a particular group or political party is an official member of that group or party, rather than someone who supports it. ❑ *I've been a card-carrying member of the Labour party for five years.* ADJ: ADJ n 2 If you describe someone as, for example, a **card-carrying** feminist, you are emphasizing the fact that they believe strongly in and try to carry out the ideas of feminism. ADJ: ADJ n [emphasis]

**card game** **(card games)** A **card game** is a game that is played using a set of playing cards. N-COUNT

**card|holder** /kɑːʳdhoʊldəʳ/ **(cardholders)** A **cardholder** is someone who has a bank card or credit card. ❑ *The average cardholder today carries three to four bank cards.* N-COUNT

**car|di|ac** /kɑːʳdiæk/ **Cardiac** means relating to the heart. [MEDICAL] ❑ *The king was suffering from cardiac weakness.* ADJ: ADJ n

**car|di|ac ar|rest** **(cardiac arrests)** A **cardiac arrest** is a heart attack. [MEDICAL] N-VAR = heart attack

**cardie** /kɑːʳdi/ **(cardies)** A **cardie** is the same as a **cardigan**. [BRIT, INFORMAL] N-COUNT

**car|di|gan** /kɑːʳdɪgən/ **(cardigans)** A **cardigan** is a knitted woollen sweater that you can fasten at the front with buttons or a zip. N-COUNT

**car|di|nal** /kɑːʳdnəl/ **(cardinals)** 1 A **cardinal** is a high-ranking priest in the Catholic church. ❑ *In 1448, Nicholas was appointed a cardinal... They were encouraged by a promise from Cardinal Winning.* N-COUNT; N-TITLE 2 A **cardinal** rule or quality is the one that is considered to be the most important. [FORMAL] ❑ *As a salesman, your cardinal rule is to do everything you can to satisfy a customer.* ADJ: ADJ n = chief, principal 3 A **cardinal** is a common North American bird. The male has bright red feathers. N-COUNT

**car|di|nal num|ber** **(cardinal numbers)** A **cardinal number** is a number such as 1, 3, or 10 that tells you how many things there are in a group but not what order they are in. Compare **ordinal number**. N-COUNT

**car|di|nal point** **(cardinal points)** The **cardinal points** are the four main points of the compass, north, south, east, and west. N-COUNT

**car|di|nal sin** **(cardinal sins)** If you describe an action as a **cardinal sin**, you are indicating that some people strongly disapprove of it. ❑ *I committed the physician's cardinal sin: I got involved with my patients.* N-COUNT

**card in|dex** **(card indexes)** A **card index** is a number of cards with information written on them which are arranged in a particular order, usually alphabetical, so that you can find the information you want easily. N-COUNT

**car|di|olo|gist** /kɑːʳdiɒlədʒɪst/ **(cardiologists)** A **cardiologist** is a doctor who specializes in the heart and its diseases. N-COUNT

**car|di|ol|ogy** /kɑːʳdiɒlədʒi/ **Cardiology** is the study of the heart and its diseases. N-UNCOUNT

**car|dio|vas|cu|lar** /kɑːʳdioʊvæskjʊləʳ/ **Cardiovascular** means relating to the heart and blood vessels. [MEDICAL] ❑ *Smoking places you at serious risk of cardiovascular and respiratory disease.* ADJ: ADJ n

**card ta|ble** **(card tables)** also **card-table.** A **card table** is a small light table which can be folded up and which is sometimes used for playing games of cards on. N-COUNT

**care** /keəʳ/ **(cares, caring, cared)** ◆◆◆ 1 If you **care about** something, you feel that it is important and are concerned about it. ❑ *...a company that cares about the environment. ...young men who did not care whether they lived or died... Does anybody know we're here, does anybody care?* VERB: no cont V about n V wh V 2 If you **care for** someone, you feel a lot of affection for them. ❑ *He wanted me to know that he still cared for me. ...people who are your friends, who care about you.* ♦ **car|ing** *...the 'feminine' traits of caring and compassion.* VERB: no cont [approval] V for/about n Also V N-UNCOUNT 3 If you **care for** someone or something, you look after them and keep them in a good state or condition. ❑ *They hired a nurse to care for her. ...these distinctive cars, lovingly cared for by private owners. ...well-cared-for homes.* ♦ **Care** is also a noun. ❑ *Most of the staff specialise in the care of children. ...sensitive teeth which need special care... She denied the murder of four children who were in her care.* VERB V for n V for n V-ed N-UNCOUNT: usu with supp 4 Children who are **in care** are looked after by the state because their parents are dead or unable to look after them properly. [BRIT] ❑ *...a home for children in care... She was taken into care as a baby.* N-UNCOUNT: oft *in* N 5 If you say that you do not **care for** something or someone, you mean that you do not like them. [OLD-FASHIONED] ❑ *She had met both sons and did not care for either.* VERB: no cont, with brd-neg V for n 6 If you say that someone does something when they **care to** do it, you mean that they do it, although they should do it more willingly or more often. ❑ *The woman tells anyone who cares to listen that she's going through hell... Experts reveal only as much as they care to.* VERB: no cont = choose V to-inf V to-inf 7 You can ask someone if they would **care for** something or if they would **care to** do something as a polite way of asking if they would like to have or do something. ❑ *Would you care for some orange juice?... He said he was off to the beach and would we care to join him.* VERB: no cont [politeness] = like V for n V to-inf 8 If you do something **with care**, you give careful attention to it because you do not want to make any mistakes or cause any damage. ❑ *Condoms are an effective method of birth control if used with care... We'd taken enormous care in choosing the location.* N-UNCOUNT: oft *with* N 9 Your **cares** are your worries, anxieties, or fears. ❑ *Lean back in a hot bath and forget all the cares of the day... Johnson seemed without a care in the world.* N-COUNT = worry 10 → See also **caring**, **aftercare**, **day care**, **intensive care**.

**PHRASES** 11 You can use **for all** I **care** to emphasize that it does not matter at all to you what someone does. ❑ *You can go right now for all I care.* PHRASE: V inflects, PHR with cl [emphasis] 12 If you say that you **couldn't care less about** someone or something, you are emphasizing that you are not interested in them or worried about them. In American English, you can also say that you **could care less**, with the same meaning. ❑ *I couldn't care less about the bloody woman... I used to be proud working for them; now I could care less. I'm just out here for the money.* PHRASE: V inflects, oft PHR *about* n [emphasis] 13 If someone sends you a letter or parcel **care of** a particular person or place, they send it to that person or place, and it is then passed on to you. In American English, you can also say **in care of**. ❑ *Please write to me care of the publishers.* PHRASE: PHR n 14 If you **take care of** someone or something, you look after them and prevent them from being harmed or damaged. ❑ *There was no one else to take care of their children... You have to learn to take care of your possessions.* PHRASE: V inflects, PHR n = look after 15 You can say **'Take care'** when saying goodbye to someone. CONVENTION [formulae] 16 If you **take care to** do something, you make sure that you do it. ❑ *Foley followed Albert through the gate, taking care to close the latch.* PHRASE: V inflects, usu PHR to-inf 17 To **take care of** a problem, task, or situation means to deal with it. ❑ *They leave it to the system to try and take care of the problem... 'Do you need clean sheets?' — 'No. Mrs. May took care of that.'* PHRASE: V inflects, PHR n = deal with 18 You can say **'Who cares?'** to emphasize that something does not matter to you at all. ❑ *Who cares about some stupid vacation?... 'But we might ruin the stove.' — 'Who cares?'* PHRASE: oft PHR *about* n [emphasis]

**ca|reen** /kəriːn/ **(careens, careening, careened)** To **careen** somewhere means to rush forward in an uncontrollable way. [mainly AM] ❑ *He stood to one side as they careened past him.* VERB = career, hurtle V prep/adv

**ca|reer** /kərɪə^r/ **(careers, careering, careered)** ◆◆◇
1 N-COUNT A **career** is the job or profession that someone does for a long period of their life. ❑ *She is now concentrating on a career as a fashion designer. ...a career in journalism. ...a political career.*
2 N-COUNT Your **career** is the part of your life that you spend working. ❑ *During his career, he wrote more than fifty plays... She began her career as a teacher.*
3 ADJ: ADJ n **Careers** advice or guidance in British English, or **career** advice or guidance in American English, consists of information about different jobs and help with deciding what kind of job you want to do. ❑ *Get hold of the company list from your careers advisory service.*
4 VERB: oft cont = hurtle If a person or vehicle **careers** somewhere, they move fast and in an uncontrolled way. ❑ *His car careered into a river... He went careering off down the track.* V prep/adv, V prep/adv

**ca|reer break** **(career breaks)** N-COUNT If someone takes a **career break**, they stop working in their particular profession for a period of time, with the intention of returning to it later. [BUSINESS] ❑ *Many women still take career breaks to bring up children.*

**ca|reer|ist** /kərɪərɪst/ ADJ: usu ADJ n **Careerist** people are ambitious and think that their career is more important than anything else. ❑ *...careerist politicians.*

**ca|reer wom|an** **(career women)** N-COUNT A **career woman** is a woman with a career who is interested in working and progressing in her job, rather than staying at home looking after the house and children.

**care|free** /keə^rfriː/ ADJ: usu ADJ n A **carefree** person or period of time doesn't have or involve any problems, worries, or responsibilities. ❑ *Chantal remembered carefree past summers at the beach.*

**care|ful** /keə^rfʊl/ ◆◆◇
1 ADJ: usu v-link ADJ, oft ADJ *about/with/of* n, ADJ to-inf ≠ careless If you are **careful**, you give serious attention to what you are doing, in order to avoid harm, damage, or mistakes. If you are **careful to** do something, you make sure that you do it. ❑ *Careful on those stairs!... We had to be very careful not to be seen... Pupils will need careful guidance on their choice of options.* ♦ **care|ful|ly** ADV: ADV with v ≠ carelessly *Have a nice time, dear, and drive carefully... He had chosen his words carefully in declaring that the murderers were madmen.*
2 ADJ: usu ADJ n = painstaking **Careful** work, thought, or examination is thorough and shows a concern for details. ❑ *He has decided to prosecute her after careful consideration of all the relevant facts... What we now know about the disease was learned by careful study of diseased organs.* ♦ **care|ful|ly** ADV: ADV with v *He explained very carefully what he was doing.*
3 ADJ: v-link ADJ *about/of* -ing If you tell someone to be **careful about** doing something, you think that what they intend to do is probably wrong, and that they should think seriously before they do it. ❑ *I think you should be careful about talking of the rebels as heroes.* ♦ **care|ful|ly** ADV: ADV after v *He should think carefully about actions like this which play into the hands of his opponents.*
4 ADJ: usu v-link ADJ *with* n = prudent If you are **careful with** something such as money or resources, you use or spend only what is necessary. ❑ *It would force industries to be more careful with natural resources.*

**care|giv|er** /keə^rgɪvə^r/ **(caregivers)** also **care giver.** N-COUNT A **caregiver** is someone who is responsible for looking after another person, for example, a person who is disabled, ill, or very young. [mainly AM] ❑ *It is nearly always women who are the primary care givers.*

**care home** **(care homes)** N-COUNT: usu with supp A **care home** is a large house or institution where people with particular problems or special needs are looked after. ❑ *...a residential care home for the elderly.*

**care|less** /keə^rləs/
1 ADJ: oft ADJ *with* n ≠ careful If you are **careless**, you do not pay enough attention to what you are doing, and so you make mistakes, or cause harm or damage. ❑ *I'm sorry. How careless of me... Some mothers were a bit careless with money... Mr Clarke had pleaded guilty to causing death by careless driving.* ♦ **care|less|ly** ADV: ADV with v *She was fined £100 for driving carelessly.* ♦ **care|less|ness** N-UNCOUNT *The defence conceded stupid goals through sheer carelessness.*
2 ADJ: oft ADJ *of/about* n If you say that someone is **careless of** something such as their health or appearance, you mean that they do not seem to be concerned about it, or do nothing to keep it in a good condition. ❑ *He had shown himself careless of personal safety where the life of his colleagues might be at risk... That shows a fairly careless attitude to clothes, doesn't it?*

**care|less|ly** /keə^rləsli/ ADV: ADV with v = casually If someone does something **carelessly**, they do it without much thought or effort. [WRITTEN] ❑ *He carelessly left the garage door unlocked... 'Oh,' he said carelessly. 'I'm in no hurry to get back.'* ➔ See also **careless**.

**car|er** /keərə^r/ **(carers)** N-COUNT A **carer** is someone who is responsible for looking after another person, for example, a person who is disabled, ill, or very young. [BRIT] ❑ *Women are more likely than men to be carers of elderly dependent relatives.*
✓ in AM, use **caregiver**, **caretaker**

**ca|ress** /kəres/ **(caresses, caressing, caressed)** VERB = stroke If you **caress** someone, you stroke them gently and affectionately. [WRITTEN] ❑ *He was gently caressing her golden hair.* V n ♦ **Caress** is also a noun. N-COUNT ❑ *Margaret took me to one side, holding my arm in a gentle caress.*

**care|taker** /keə^rteɪkə^r/ **(caretakers)**
1 N-COUNT A **caretaker** is a person whose job it is to look after a large building such as a school or a block of flats or apartments, and deal with small repairs to it. [BRIT]
✓ in AM, use **janitor**
2 N-COUNT A **caretaker** is a person whose job it is to take care of a house or property when the owner is not there.
3 ADJ: ADJ n = acting A **caretaker** government or leader is in charge temporarily until a new government or leader is appointed. ❑ *The military intends to hand over power to a caretaker government and hold elections within six months.*
4 N-COUNT A **caretaker** is someone who is responsible for looking after another person, for example, a person who is disabled, ill, or very young. [mainly AM]
✓ in BRIT, use **carer**

**care work|er** **(care workers)** N-COUNT A **care worker** is someone whose job involves helping people who have particular problems or special needs, for example in a care home. ➔ See also **health care worker**.

**care|worn** /keə^rwɔː^rn/ ADJ A person who looks **careworn** looks worried, tired, and unhappy. ❑ *Her face was careworn with anxiety.*

**car|go** /kɑː^rgoʊ/ **(cargoes)** N-VAR: oft N *of* n = consignment The **cargo** of a ship or plane is the goods that it is carrying. ❑ *The boat calls at the main port to load its regular cargo of bananas. ...cargo planes.*

**Car|ib|bean** /kærəbiːən, AM kərɪbiən/ **(Caribbeans)**
1 N-PROPER: the N **The Caribbean** is the sea which is between the West Indies, Central America and the north coast of South America.
2 ADJ **Caribbean** means belonging or relating to the Caribbean Sea and its islands, or to its people. ♦ A **Caribbean** is a person from a Caribbean island. N-COUNT ➔ See also **Afro-Caribbean**.

**cari|bou** /kærɪbuː/ **(caribou)** N-COUNT A **caribou** is a large north American deer.

**cari|ca|ture** /kærɪkətʃʊə^r, AM -tʃər/ **(caricatures, caricaturing, caricatured)**
1 N-COUNT: oft N *of* n A **caricature of** someone is a drawing or description of them that exaggerates their appearance or behaviour in a humorous or critical way. ❑ *The poster showed a caricature of Hitler with a devil's horns and tail.*
2 VERB If you **caricature** someone, you draw or describe them in an exaggerated way in order to be humorous or critical. ❑ *Her political career has been caricatured in headlines... He was caricatured as a turnip.* V n, be V-ed *as* n
3 N-COUNT: usu N *of* n [disapproval] If you describe something as a **caricature of** an event or situation, you mean that it is a very exaggerated account of it. ❑ *Hall is angry at what he sees as a caricature of the training offered to modern-day social workers.*

**cari|ca|tur|ist** /kærɪkətʃʊərɪst/ **(caricaturists)** N-COUNT A **caricaturist** is a person who shows other people in an exaggerated way in order to be humorous or critical, especially in drawings or cartoons.

**car|ies** /keəriz/ **Caries** is decay in teeth. N-UNCOUNT [TECHNICAL] ❑ *...dental caries.*

**car|ing** /keərɪŋ/ ◆◇◇ 1 If someone is **caring**, they are affectionate, helpful, and sympathetic. ADJ ❑ *He is a lovely boy, very gentle and caring. ...a loving, caring husband.* 2 The **caring** professions are those such as nursing and social work that are involved with looking after people who are ill or who need help in coping with their lives. ADJ: ADJ n [BRIT] ❑ *The course is also suitable for those in the caring professions. ...the caring services.* 3 ➔ See also **care**.

**car-jacker** **(car-jackers)** A **car-jacker** is someone who attacks and steals from people who are driving their own cars. N-COUNT

**car|jack|ing** /kɑːʳdʒækɪŋ/ **(carjackings)** A **carjacking** is an attack on a person who is driving their own car during which things may be stolen or they may be harmed physically. N-VAR

**car|load** /kɑːʳloʊd/ **(carloads)** A **carload of** people or things is as many people or things as a car can carry. N-COUNT: usu N *of* n ❑ *Wherever he goes, a carload of soldiers goes with him.*

**car|mine** /kɑːʳmaɪn, -mɪn/ **Carmine** is a deep bright red colour. COLOUR [LITERARY] ❑ *...a tulip with carmine petals.*

**car|nage** /kɑːʳnɪdʒ/ **Carnage** is the violent killing of large numbers of people, especially in a war. N-UNCOUNT = *slaughter* [LITERARY] ❑ *...his strategy for stopping the carnage in Kosovo.*

**car|nal** /kɑːʳnəl/ **Carnal** feelings and desires are sexual and physical, without any spiritual element. ADJ: usu ADJ n = *sexual* [FORMAL] ❑ *Their ruling passion is that of carnal love.*

**car|na|tion** /kɑːʳneɪʃən/ **(carnations)** A **carnation** is a plant with white, pink, or red flowers. N-COUNT

**car|ni|val** /kɑːʳnɪvəl/ **(carnivals)** 1 A **carnival** is a public festival during which people play music and sometimes dance in the streets. N-COUNT 2 A **carnival** is a travelling show which is held in a park or field and at which there are machines to ride on, entertainments, and games. N-COUNT [AM]

✔ in BRIT, use **funfair**

**car|ni|vore** /kɑːʳnɪvɔːʳ/ **(carnivores)** 1 A **carnivore** is an animal that eats meat. N-COUNT [TECHNICAL] 2 If you describe someone as a **carnivore**, you are saying, especially in a humorous way, that they eat meat. N-COUNT = *meat-eater* ≠ *vegetarian* ❑ *This is a vegetarian dish that carnivores love.*

**car|nivo|rous** /kɑːʳnɪvərəs/ 1 **Carnivorous** animals eat meat. ADJ [TECHNICAL] ❑ *Snakes are carnivorous.* 2 **Carnivorous** can be used, especially humorously, to describe someone who eats meat. ADJ = *meat-eating*

**car|ob** /kærəb/ **(carobs)** 1 A **carob** or **carob tree** is a Mediterranean tree that stays green all year round. It has dark brown fruit that tastes similar to chocolate. N-COUNT 2 The dark brown fruit of the carob tree can be referred to as **carob**. It is often made into powder and used instead of chocolate. N-UNCOUNT: oft N n ❑ *If you do yearn for chocolate, try a carob bar instead.*

**car|ol** /kærəl/ **(carols) Carols** are Christian religious songs that are sung at Christmas. N-COUNT ❑ *...carol singers at the door.*

**ca|rot|id ar|tery** /kərɒtɪd ɑːʳtəri/ **(carotid arteries)** A **carotid artery** is one of the two arteries in the neck that supply the head with blood. N-COUNT [MEDICAL]

**ca|rouse** /kəraʊz/ **(carouses, carousing, caroused)** If you say that people **are carousing**, you mean that they are behaving very noisily and drinking a lot of alcohol as they enjoy themselves. VERB ❑ *They told him to stay home with his wife instead of going out and carousing with friends.* V

**carou|sel** /kærəsel/ **(carousels)** 1 At an airport, a **carousel** is a moving surface from which passengers can collect their luggage. N-COUNT 2 A **carousel** is a large circular machine with seats, often in the shape of animals or cars. People can sit on it and go round and round for fun. N-COUNT = *merry-go-round, roundabout*

**carp** /kɑːʳp/ **(carps, carping, carped)**

✔ **carp** can also be used as the plural form for meaning 1.

1 A **carp** is a kind of fish that lives in lakes and rivers. N-VAR 2 If you say that someone **is carping**, you mean that they keep criticizing or complaining about someone or something, especially in a way you think is unnecessary or annoying. VERB [disapproval] ❑ *He cannot understand why she's constantly carping at him.* V *at/about* n ♦ **carp|ing** *She was in no mood to put up with Blanche's carping.* N-UNCOUNT

**car park** **(car parks)** also **carpark.** A **car park** is an area or building where people can leave their cars. N-COUNT [BRIT]

✔ in AM, use **parking lot**

**car|pen|ter** /kɑːʳpɪntəʳ/ **(carpenters)** A **carpenter** is a person whose job is making and repairing wooden things. N-COUNT

**car|pen|try** /kɑːʳpɪntri/ **Carpentry** is the activity of making and repairing wooden things. N-UNCOUNT

**car|pet** /kɑːʳpɪt/ **(carpets, carpeting, carpeted)** 1 A **carpet** is a thick covering of soft material which is laid over a floor or a staircase. N-VAR ❑ *They put down wooden boards, and laid new carpets on top. ...the stain on our living-room carpet.* 2 If a floor or a room **is carpeted**, a carpet is laid on the floor. VERB: usu passive ❑ *The room had been carpeted and the windows glazed with coloured glass...* *be* V-ed *The main gaming room was thickly carpeted.* V-ed 3 A **carpet of** something such as leaves or plants is a layer of them which covers the ground. N-COUNT: usu sing, usu N *of* n = *layer* [LITERARY] ❑ *The carpet of leaves in my yard became more and more noticeable.* 4 If the ground **is carpeted with** something such as leaves or plants, it is completely covered by them. VERB: usu passive = *cover* [LITERARY] ❑ *The ground was thickly carpeted with pine needles.* *be* V-ed *with* n 5 ➔ See also **carpeting, red carpet.** to **sweep** something **under the carpet** ➔ see **sweep**.

**carpet|bag|ger** /kɑːʳpɪtbægəʳ/ **(carpetbaggers)** If you call someone a **carpetbagger**, you disapprove of them because they are trying to become a politician in an area which is not their home, simply because they think they are more likely to succeed there. N-COUNT [disapproval] [AM]

**car|pet bomb|ing** **Carpet bombing** is heavy bombing from aircraft, with the intention of hitting as many places as possible in a particular area. N-UNCOUNT

**car|pet|ing** /kɑːʳpɪtɪŋ/ You use **carpeting** to refer to a carpet, or to the type of material that is used to make carpets. N-UNCOUNT ❑ *...a bedroom with wall-to-wall carpeting... Carpeting is a reasonably cheap floor-covering.* ➔ See also **carpet**.

**car|pet slip|per** **(carpet slippers) Carpet slippers** are soft, comfortable slippers. N-COUNT

**car pool** /kɑːʳpuːl/ **(car pools, car pooling, car pooled)** also **carpool, car-pool.** 1 A **car pool** is an arrangement where a group of people take turns driving each other to work, or driving each other's children to school. In American English, **car pool** is sometimes used to refer simply to people travelling together in a car. N-COUNT: also N n ❑ *...the carpool lanes in LA.* 2 If a group of people **carpool**, they take turns driving each other to work, or driving each other's children to school. VERB [mainly AM or AUSTRALIAN] ❑ *The government says fewer Americans are carpooling to work.* V 3 A **car pool** is a number of cars that are owned by a company or organization for the use of its employees or members. N-COUNT [BUSINESS]

**car port** **(car ports)** also **carport.** A **car port** is a shelter for cars which is attached to a house and consists of a flat roof supported on pillars. N-COUNT

**car|riage** /kærɪdʒ/ **(carriages)** 1 A **carriage** is an old-fashioned vehicle, usually for a small number of passengers, which is pulled by horses. ❑ *The President-elect followed in an open carriage drawn by six beautiful gray horses.* 2 A **carriage** is one of the separate, long sections of a train that carries passengers. [BRIT] N-COUNT: also *by* N; N-COUNT = coach

in AM, usually use **car**

3 A **carriage** is the same as a **baby carriage**. [AM] 4 **Carriage** is the cost or action of transporting or delivering goods. [BRIT, FORMAL] ❑ *It costs £10.86 for one litre including carriage.* N-COUNT; N-UNCOUNT

in AM, usually use **delivery charge**

5 Your **carriage** is the way you hold your body and head when you are walking, standing, or sitting. [LITERARY] ❑ *Her legs were long and fine, her hips slender, her carriage erect.* N-UNCOUNT: usu with poss = bearing

**carriage|way** /kærɪdʒweɪ/ **(carriageways)** A **carriageway** is one side of a road on which traffic travelling in opposite directions is separated by a barrier. [BRIT] N-COUNT

**car|ri|er** /kæriəʳ/ **(carriers)** 1 A **carrier** is a vehicle that is used for carrying people, especially soldiers, or things. ❑ *There were armoured personnel carriers and tanks on the streets.* → See also **aircraft carrier**. 2 A **carrier** is a passenger airline. ❑ *Switzerland's national carrier, Swissair, has been having a hard time recently.* 3 A **carrier** is a person or an animal that is infected with a disease and so can make other people or animals ill. ❑ *...an AIDS carrier. ...carriers of disease such as mosquitoes and worms.* ◆◇◇ N-COUNT; N-COUNT; N-COUNT: usu n N, N *of* n

**car|ri|er bag** **(carrier bags)** A **carrier bag** is a bag made of plastic or paper which has handles and which you carry shopping in. [BRIT] N-COUNT

in AM, usually use **shopping bag**

**car|ri|on** /kæriən/ **Carrion** is the decaying flesh of dead animals. N-UNCOUNT

**car|rot** /kærət/ **(carrots)** 1 **Carrots** are long, thin, orange-coloured vegetables. They grow under the ground, and have green shoots above the ground. → See picture on page 1712. 2 Something that is offered to people in order to persuade them to do something can be referred to as a **carrot**. Something that is meant to persuade people not to do something can be referred to in the same sentence as a 'stick'. ❑ *They will be set targets, with a carrot of extra cash if they achieve them... Why the new emphasis on sticks instead of diplomatic carrots?* → See also **carrot and stick**. N-VAR; N-COUNT = incentive

**car|rot and stick** also **carrot-and-stick**. If an organization has a **carrot and stick** approach or policy, they offer people things in order to persuade them to do something and punish them if they refuse to do it. ❑ *The government is proclaiming a carrot-and-stick approach to the problem.* ADJ: ADJ n

**car|ry** /kæri/ **(carries, carrying, carried)** 1 If you **carry** something, you take it with you, holding it so that it does not touch the ground. ❑ *He was carrying a briefcase... He carried the plate through to the dining room... If your job involves a lot of paperwork, you're going to need something to carry it all in.* 2 If you **carry** something, you have it with you wherever you go. ❑ *You have to carry a bleeper so that they can call you in at any time.* 3 If something **carries** a person or thing somewhere, it takes them there. ❑ *Flowers are designed to attract insects which then carry the pollen from plant to plant... The ship could carry seventy passengers.* 4 If a person or animal **is carrying** a disease, they are infected with it and can pass it on to other people or animals. ❑ *Frogs eat pests which destroy crops and carry diseases.* 5 If an action or situation has a particular quality or consequence, you can say that it **carries** it. ❑ *Check that any medication you're taking carries no risk for your developing baby.* 6 If a quality or advantage **carries** someone into a particular position or through a difficult situation, it helps them to achieve that position or deal with that situation. ❑ *He had the ruthless streak necessary to carry him into the Cabinet.* 7 If you **carry** an idea or a method to a particular extent, you use or develop it to that extent. ❑ *It's not such a new idea, but I carried it to extremes... We could carry that one step further by taking the same genes and putting them into another crop.* 8 If a newspaper or poster **carries** a picture or a piece of writing, it contains it or displays it. ❑ *Several papers carry the photograph of Mr Anderson.* 9 In a debate, if a proposal or motion **is carried**, a majority of people vote in favour of it. ❑ *A motion backing its economic policy was carried by 322 votes to 296.* 10 If a crime **carries** a particular punishment, a person who is found guilty of that crime will receive that punishment. ❑ *It was a crime of espionage and carried the death penalty.* 11 If a sound **carries**, it can be heard a long way away. ❑ *Even in this stillness Leaphorn doubted if the sound would carry far.* 12 If a candidate or party **carries** a state or area, they win the election in that state or area. [AM] ❑ *George W. Bush carried the state with 56 percent of the vote.* ◆◆◆ VERB; V n; V n prep/adv; V n prep/adv; VERB; V n; VERB = transport; V n adv/prep; V n; VERB; V n; VERB: no passive, no cont; V n; VERB; V n prep/adv; VERB = take; V n prep/adv; V n prep/adv; VERB; V n; VERB: usu passive; *be* V-ed; VERB: no cont; V n; VERB; V adv; Also V; VERB: no passive; V n

in BRIT, usually use **take**

13 If you **carry yourself** in a particular way, you walk and move in that way. ❑ *They carried themselves with great pride and dignity.* 14 If a woman **is carrying** a child, she is pregnant. [OLD-FASHIONED] 15 If you **get carried away** or **are carried away**, you are so eager or excited about something that you do something hasty or foolish. ❑ *I got completely carried away and almost cried.* 16 to **carry the can** → see **can**. to **carry conviction** → see **conviction**. to **carry the day** → see **day**. to **carry weight** → see **weight**. VERB; V pron-refl prep/adv; VERB: usu cont; PHRASE: V inflects

♦ **carry off** 1 If you **carry** something **off**, you do it successfully. ❑ *He's got the experience and the authority to carry it off.* 2 If you **carry off** a prize or a trophy, you win it. ❑ *It carried off the Evening Standard drama award for best play.* PHRASAL VERB; V n P; Also V P n; PHRASAL VERB; V P n (not pron); Also V n P

♦ **carry on** 1 If you **carry on** doing something, you continue to do it. ❑ *The assistant carried on talking... Her bravery has given him the will to carry on with his life and his work... His eldest son Joseph carried on his father's traditions... 'Do you mind if I just start with the few formal questions please?' — 'Carry on.'* 2 If you **carry on** an activity, you do it or take part in it for a period of time. ❑ *The consulate will carry on a political dialogue with Indonesia.* 3 If you say that someone **is carrying on**, you are irritated with them because they are talking very excitedly and saying a lot of unnecessary things. [INFORMAL] ❑ *She was screaming and carrying on... He was carrying on about some stupid television series.* PHRASAL VERB = continue; V P -ing; V P *with* n; V P n (not pron); V P; PHRASAL VERB = conduct; V P n (not pron); PHRASAL VERB disapproval = make a fuss; V P; V P *about* n

♦ **carry out** If you **carry out** a threat, task, or instruction, you do it or act according to it. ❑ *Police say they believe the attacks were carried out by nationalists... Commitments have been made with very little intention of carrying them out.* PHRASAL VERB; V P n (not pron); V n P

♦ **carry over** If something **carries over** or **is carried over** from one situation **to** another, it continues to exist or apply in the new situation. ❑ *Priestley's rational outlook in science carried over to religion... Springs and wells were decorated, a custom which was carried over into Christian times in Europe.* PHRASAL VERB; V P *into/to* n; *be* V-ed P *into/to* n

♦ **carry through** If you **carry** something **through**, you do it or complete it, often in spite of difficulties. ❑ *We don't have the confidence that the UN will carry through a sustained program... The state announced a clear-cut policy and set out to carry it through.* PHRASAL VERB; V P n (not pron); V n P

**carry|all** /kæriɔːl/ **(carryalls)** A **carryall** is a large bag made of nylon, canvas, or leather, which you use to carry your clothes and other possessions, for example when you are travelling. [mainly AM] N-COUNT

in BRIT, usually use **holdall**

**carry|cot** /kæ̲rikɒt/ **(carrycots)** A **carrycot** is a small bed for babies which has handles so it can be carried. [BRIT] N-COUNT

**cart** /kɑ̲ːʳt/ **(carts, carting, carted)** 1 A **cart** is an old-fashioned wooden vehicle that is used for transporting goods or people. Some carts are pulled by animals. ❑ *...a country where horse-drawn carts far outnumber cars.* N-COUNT = wagon 2 If you **cart** things or people somewhere, you carry them or transport them there, often with difficulty. [INFORMAL] ❑ *After both their parents died, one of their father's relatives carted off the entire contents of the house.* VERB V n with adv 3 A **cart** is a small vehicle with a motor. [AM] ❑ *He drove up in a golf cart to watch them.* N-COUNT 4 A **cart** or a **shopping cart** is a large metal basket on wheels which is provided by shops such as supermarkets for customers to use while they are in the shop. [AM] N-COUNT

✔ in BRIT, use **trolley**

**carte blanche** /kɑ̲ːʳt blɒnʃ/ If someone gives you **carte blanche**, they give you the authority to do whatever you think is right. ❑ *They gave him carte blanche to make decisions.* N-UNCOUNT: oft N to-inf

**car|tel** /kɑːʳte̲l/ **(cartels)** A **cartel** is an association of similar companies or businesses that have grouped together in order to prevent competition and to control prices. [BUSINESS] ❑ *...a drug cartel.* N-COUNT

**cart|horse** /kɑ̲ːʳthɔːʳs/ **(carthorses)** also **cart-horse.** A **carthorse** is a large, powerful horse that is used to pull carts or farm machinery. ❑ *Where we use tractors, obviously they used carthorses in those days.* N-COUNT

**car|ti|lage** /kɑ̲ːʳtɪlɪdʒ/ **(cartilages) Cartilage** is a strong, flexible substance in your body, especially around your joints and in your nose. ❑ *...a serious knee cartilage injury.* N-VAR

**car|tog|ra|pher** /kɑːʳtɒ̲grəfəʳ/ **(cartographers)** A **cartographer** is a person whose job is drawing maps. N-COUNT

**car|tog|ra|phy** /kɑːʳtɒ̲grəfi/ **Cartography** is the art or activity of drawing maps and geographical charts. N-UNCOUNT

**car|ton** /kɑ̲ːʳtᵊn/ **(cartons)** 1 A **carton** is a plastic or cardboard container in which food or drink is sold. ❑ *...a two-pint carton of milk.* N-COUNT: oft N *of* n 2 A **carton** is a large, strong cardboard box in which goods are stored and transported. [AM] N-COUNT

**car|toon** /kɑːʳtu̲ːn/ **(cartoons)** 1 A **cartoon** is a humorous drawing or series of drawings in a newspaper or magazine. ❑ *...one of Britain's best-loved cartoon characters, Rupert the Bear.* ➔ See also **strip cartoon**. N-COUNT 2 A **cartoon** is a film in which all the characters and scenes are drawn rather than being real people or objects. ❑ *...the Saturday morning cartoons.* N-COUNT

**car|toon|ist** /kɑːʳtu̲ːnɪst/ **(cartoonists)** A **cartoonist** is a person whose job is to draw cartoons for newspapers and magazines. N-COUNT

**car|toon strip** **(cartoon strips)** A **cartoon strip** is a series of drawings that tells a story. [mainly BRIT] N-COUNT = strip cartoon

**car|tridge** /kɑ̲ːʳtrɪdʒ/ **(cartridges)** 1 A **cartridge** is a metal or cardboard tube containing a bullet and an explosive substance. Cartridges are used in guns. N-COUNT 2 A **cartridge** is part of a machine or device that can be easily removed and replaced when it is worn out or empty. N-COUNT

**cart|wheel** /kɑ̲ːʳthwiːl/ **(cartwheels)** If you do a **cartwheel**, you do a fast, circular movement with your body. You fall sideways, put your hands on the ground, swing your legs over, and return to a standing position. N-COUNT

**carve** /kɑ̲ːʳv/ **(carves, carving, carved)** 1 If you **carve** an object, you make it by cutting it out of a substance such as wood or stone. If you **carve** something such as wood or stone into an object, you make the object by cutting it out. ❑ *One of the prisoners has carved a beautiful wooden chess set... He carves his figures from white pine... I picked up a piece of wood and started carving. ...carved stone figures.* ➔ See also **carving**. VERB = sculpt V n V n prep V V-ed 2 If you **carve** writing or a design **on** an object, you cut it into the surface of the object. ❑ *He carved his name on his desk... The ornately carved doors were made in the seventeenth century.* VERB V n *in/on* n V-ed 3 If you **carve** a piece of cooked meat, you cut slices from it so that you can eat it. ❑ *Andrew began to carve the chicken... Carve the beef into slices.* VERB V n V n *into* n

♦ **carve up** If you say that someone **carves** something **up**, you disapprove of the way they have divided it into small parts. ❑ *He has set about carving up the company which Hammer created from almost nothing... They have begun carving the country up like a pie.* PHRASAL VERB disapproval V P n (not pron) V n P

**carv|er** /kɑ̲ːʳvəʳ/ **(carvers)** A **carver** is a person who carves wood or stone, as a job or as a hobby. ❑ *The ivory industry employed about a thousand carvers.* N-COUNT: oft n N

**carv|ing** /kɑ̲ːʳvɪŋ/ **(carvings)** 1 A **carving** is an object or a design that has been cut out of a material such as stone or wood. ❑ *...a wood carving of a human hand.* N-COUNT: oft n N 2 **Carving** is the art of carving objects, or of carving designs or writing on objects. N-UNCOUNT: usu n N

**carv|ing knife** **(carving knives)** A **carving knife** is a long sharp knife that is used to cut cooked meat. N-COUNT

**cas|cade** /kæske̲ɪd/ **(cascades, cascading, cascaded)** 1 If you refer to a **cascade of** something, you mean that there is a large amount of it. [LITERARY] ❑ *The women have lustrous cascades of black hair.* N-COUNT: usu N *of* n 2 If water **cascades** somewhere, it pours or flows downwards very fast and in large quantities. ❑ *She hung on as the freezing, rushing water cascaded past her.* VERB V adv/prep

**case**

① INSTANCES AND OTHER ABSTRACT MEANINGS
② CONTAINERS
③ GRAMMAR TERM

① **case** /ke̲ɪs/ **(cases)** ♦♦♦ 1 A particular **case** is a particular situation or incident, especially one that you are using as an individual example or instance of something. ❑ *Surgical training takes at least nine years, or 11 in the case of obstetrics... One of the effects of dyslexia, in my case at least, is that you pay tremendous attention to detail... The Honduran press published reports of eighteen cases of alleged baby snatching.* N-COUNT: oft *in* N, N *of* n 2 A **case** is a person or their particular problem that a doctor, social worker, or other professional is dealing with. ❑ *...the case of a 57-year-old man who had suffered a stroke... Some cases of arthritis respond to a gluten-free diet... Child protection workers were meeting to discuss her case.* N-COUNT 3 If you say that someone is a sad **case** or a hopeless **case**, you mean that they are in a sad situation or a hopeless situation. ❑ *I knew I was going to make it – that I wasn't a hopeless case.* ➔ See also **basket case, nutcase**. N-COUNT: adj N 4 A **case** is a crime or mystery that the police are investigating. ❑ *Mr. Hitchens said you have solved some very unusual cases.* N-COUNT 5 The **case for** or **against** a plan or idea consists of the facts and reasons used to support it or oppose it. ❑ *He sat there while I made the case for his dismissal... Both these facts strengthen the case against hanging... She argued her case.* N-COUNT: usu sing, oft N *for/against* n 6 In law, a **case** is a trial or other legal inquiry. ❑ *It can be difficult for public figures to win a libel case... The case was brought by his family, who say their reputation has been damaged by allegations about him.* ➔ See also **test case**. N-COUNT

**PHRASES** 7 You say **in any case** when you are adding something which is more important than what you have just said, but which supports or corrects it. ❑ *The concert was booked out, and in any case, most of the people gathered in the square could not afford the price of a ticket.* PHRASE: PHR with cl emphasis = anyway, besides 8 You say **in any case** after talking about things that you are not PHRASE: PHR with cl emphasis sure about, to emphasize that your next statement is the most important thing or the thing that you are sure about. ❑ *Either he escaped, or he came to grief. In any case, he was never seen again.* = at any rate

PHRASE [9] If you do something **in case** or **just in case** a particular thing happens, you do it because that thing might happen. ❑ *In case anyone was following me, I made an elaborate detour.*

PREP-PHRASE: PHR n [10] If you do something or have something **in case of** a particular thing, you do it or have it because that thing might happen or be true. ❑ *Many shops along the route have been boarded up in case of trouble.*

PHRASE: PHR with cl [feelings] [11] You use **in case** in expressions like 'in case you didn't know' or 'in case you've forgotten' when you are telling someone in a rather irritated way something that you think is either obvious or none of their business. ❑ *She's nervous about something, in case you didn't notice.*

PHRASE: PHR with cl [12] You say **in that case** or **in which case** to indicate that what you are going to say is true if the possible situation that has just been mentioned actually exists. ❑ *Members are concerned that a merger might mean higher costs, in which case they would oppose it.*

PHRASE: PHR with cl [13] You can say that you are doing something **just in case** to refer vaguely to the possibility that a thing might happen or be true, without saying exactly what it is. ❑ *I guess we've already talked about this but I'll ask you again just in case.*

PHRASE [14] You say **as the case may be** or **whatever the case may be** to indicate that the statement you are making applies equally to the two or more alternatives that you have mentioned. ❑ *They know how everything works – or doesn't work, as the case may be.*

PHRASE [15] If you say that a task or situation is **a case of** a particular thing, you mean that it consists of that thing or can be described as that thing. ❑ *It's not a case of whether anyone would notice or not.*

PHRASE [16] If you say that something is **a case in point**, you mean that it is a good example of something you have just mentioned. ❑ *In many cases religious persecution is the cause of people fleeing their country. A case in point is colonial India.*

PHRASE: V inflects [17] If you say that something **is the case**, you mean that it is true or correct. ❑ *You'll probably notice her having difficulty swallowing. If this is the case, give her plenty of liquids... Consumers had hoped the higher prices would mean more goods in stores. But that was not the case.*

PHRASE [18] If you say that someone is **on the case**, you mean that they are aware of a particular problem and are trying to resolve it. ❑ *The CompuServe management is on the case now, and it looks as if things will return to normal soon.*

**② case** /keɪs/ **(cases)** N-COUNT: oft n N [1] A **case** is a container that is specially designed to hold or protect something. ❑ *...a black case for his spectacles.* ➔ See also **attaché case**, **bookcase**, **briefcase**, **packing case**, **pillowcase**, **showcase**. N-COUNT [2] A **case** is a suitcase. N-COUNT: oft N of n [3] A **case of** wine or other alcoholic drink is a box containing a number of bottles, usually twelve, which is sold as a single unit.

**③ case** /keɪs/ **(cases)** N-COUNT [1] In the grammar of many languages, the **case** of a group such as a noun group or adjective group is the form it has which shows its relationship to other groups in the sentence. ➔ see **accusative**, **nominative**. [2] ➔ See also **lower case**, **upper case**.

**case|book** /keɪsbʊk/ **(casebooks)** N-COUNT A **casebook** is a written record of the cases dealt with by someone such as a doctor, social worker, or police officer.

**case his|to|ry** **(case histories)** N-COUNT A person's **case history** is the record of past events or problems that have affected them, especially their medical history. ❑ *I took her to a homoeopath, who started by taking a very long and detailed case history.*

**case law** N-UNCOUNT **Case law** is law that has been established by following decisions made by judges in earlier cases. [LEGAL]

**case|load** /keɪsloʊd/ **(caseloads)** N-COUNT: oft with poss The **caseload** of someone such as a doctor, social worker, or lawyer is the number of cases that they have to deal with. ❑ *Social workers say the average caseload is 32 families per employee.*

**case|ment** /keɪsmənt/ **(casements)** N-COUNT A **casement** or a **casement window** is a window that opens by means of hinges, usually at the side. [WRITTEN]

**case-sensitive** ADJ In computing, if a written word such as a password is **case-sensitive**, it must be written in a particular form, for example using all capital letters or all small letters, in order for the computer to recognize it. [COMPUTING]

**case study** **(case studies)** N-COUNT A **case study** is a written account that gives detailed information about a person, group, or thing and their development over a period of time. ❑ *...a large case study of malaria in West African children.*

**case|work** /keɪswɜːʳk/ N-UNCOUNT **Casework** is social work that involves actually dealing or working with the people who need help.

**case|worker** /keɪswɜːʳkəʳ/ **(caseworkers)** N-COUNT A **caseworker** is someone who does casework.

**cash** /kæʃ/ **(cashes, cashing, cashed)** ◆◆◇ N-UNCOUNT [1] **Cash** is money in the form of notes and coins rather than cheques. ❑ *...two thousand pounds in cash.* ➔ See also **hard cash**, **petty cash**. N-UNCOUNT = money [2] **Cash** means the same as money, especially money which is immediately available. [INFORMAL] ❑ *...a state-owned financial-services group with plenty of cash.* VERB [3] If you **cash** a cheque, you exchange it at a bank for the amount of money that it is worth. V n ❑ *There are similar charges if you want to cash a cheque at a branch other than your own.*

♦ **cash in** PHRASAL VERB [disapproval] [1] If you say that someone **cashes in on** a situation, you are criticizing them for using it to gain an advantage, often in an unfair or dishonest way. V P *on* n ❑ *Residents said local gang leaders had cashed in on the violence to seize valuable land.* PHRASAL VERB [2] If you **cash in** something such as an insurance policy, you exchange it for money. V P n (not pron) Also V n P ❑ *Avoid cashing in a policy early as you could lose out heavily... He did not cash in his shares.*

**cash-and-carry** **(cash-and-carries)** N-COUNT A **cash-and-carry** is a large shop where you can buy goods in larger quantities and at lower prices than in ordinary shops. Cash-and-carries are mainly used by people in business to buy goods for their shops or companies.

**cash card** **(cash cards)** also **cashcard.** N-COUNT A **cash card** is a card that banks give to their customers so that they can get money out of a cash dispenser. [BRIT]

**cash cow** **(cash cows)** N-COUNT In business, a **cash cow** is a product or investment that steadily continues to be profitable. [BUSINESS]

**cash crop** **(cash crops)** N-COUNT A **cash crop** is a crop that is grown in order to be sold. ❑ *Cranberries have become a major cash crop.*

**cash desk** **(cash desks)** N-COUNT A **cash desk** is a place in a large shop where you pay for the things you want to buy. [BRIT]

☑ in AM, use **cashier's desk**

**cash dis|pens|er** **(cash dispensers)** N-COUNT = cashpoint A **cash dispenser** is a machine built into the wall of a bank or other building, which allows people to take out money from their bank account using a special card. [BRIT]

☑ in AM, use **ATM**

**cash|ew** /kæʃuː, kæʃuː/ **(cashews)** N-COUNT A **cashew** or a **cashew nut** is a curved nut that you can eat.

**cash flow** also **cashflow.** N-UNCOUNT The **cash flow** of a firm or business is the movement of money into and out of it. [BUSINESS] ❑ *A French-based pharmaceuticals company ran into cash-flow problems and faced liquidation.*

**cash|ier** /kæʃɪəʳ/ **(cashiers)** N-COUNT A **cashier** is a person who customers pay money to or get money from in places such as shops or banks.

**cash|ier's check** **(cashier's checks)** A **cashier's check** is one which a cashier signs and which is drawn on a bank's own funds. [AM] N-COUNT

**cash|ier's desk** **(cashier's desks)** A **cashier's desk** is the same as a **cash desk**. [AM] N-COUNT

**cash|mere** /kæʃmɪəʳ, AM kæʒmɪr/ **Cashmere** is a kind of very fine, soft wool. ❑ *...a big soft cashmere sweater.* N-UNCOUNT: oft N n

**cash|point** /kæʃpɔɪnt/ **(cashpoints)** A **cashpoint** is the same as a **cash dispenser**. [BRIT] N-COUNT

✓ in AM, use **ATM**

**cash reg|is|ter** **(cash registers)** A **cash register** is a machine in a shop, pub, or restaurant that is used to add up and record how much money people pay, and in which the money is kept. N-COUNT = till

**cash-starved** A **cash-starved** company or organization does not have enough money to operate properly, usually because another organization, such as the government, is not giving them the money that they need. [BUSINESS, JOURNALISM] ❑ *We are heading for a crisis, with cash-starved councils forced to cut back on vital community services.* ADJ: usu ADJ n

**cash-strapped** If a person or organization is **cash-strapped**, they do not have enough money to buy or pay for the things they want or need. [JOURNALISM] ❑ *Union leaders say the wage package is the best they believe the cash-strapped government will offer.* ADJ: usu ADJ n

**cas|ing** /keɪsɪŋ/ **(casings)** A **casing** is a substance or object that covers something and protects it. ❑ *...the outer casings of missiles.* N-COUNT: oft supp N

**ca|si|no** /kəsiːnoʊ/ **(casinos)** A **casino** is a building or room where people play gambling games such as roulette. N-COUNT

**cask** /kɑːsk, kæsk/ **(casks)** A **cask** is a wooden barrel that is used for storing things, especially alcoholic drink. ❑ *...casks of sherry.* N-COUNT = barrel

**cas|ket** /kɑːskɪt, kæsk-/ **(caskets)** [1] A **casket** is a small box in which you keep valuable things. [LITERARY] N-COUNT [2] A **casket** is a **coffin**. [mainly AM] N-COUNT

**cas|sa|va** /kəsɑːvə/ [1] **Cassava** is a South American plant with thick roots. It is grown for food. N-UNCOUNT = manioc [2] **Cassava** is a substance that comes from the root of the cassava plant and is used to make flour. N-UNCOUNT

**cas|se|role** /kæsəroʊl/ **(casseroles)** [1] A **casserole** is a dish made of meat and vegetables that have been cooked slowly in a liquid. ❑ *...a huge beef casserole, full of herbs, vegetables and wine.* N-COUNT: oft n N [2] A **casserole** or a **casserole dish** is a large heavy container with a lid. You cook casseroles and other dishes in it. ❑ *...a flameproof casserole.* N-COUNT

**cas|sette** /kəset/ **(cassettes)** [1] A **cassette** is a small, flat, rectangular plastic case containing magnetic tape which is used for recording and playing back sound or film. ❑ *His two albums released on cassette have sold more than 10 million copies.* N-COUNT: also on N = tape [2] A **cassette** is the container or case for the film that you load into a camera. N-COUNT

**cas|sette play|er** **(cassette players)** A **cassette player** is a machine that is used for playing cassettes and sometimes also recording them. N-COUNT

**cas|sette re|cord|er** **(cassette recorders)** A **cassette recorder** is a machine that is used for recording and listening to cassettes. N-COUNT = tape recorder

**cas|sock** /kæsək/ **(cassocks)** A **cassock** is a long piece of clothing, often black, that is worn by members of the clergy in some churches. N-COUNT

**cast** /kɑːst, kæst/ **(casts, casting)** ◆◆◇

✓ The form **cast** is used in the present tense and is the past tense and past participle.

[1] The **cast** of a play or film is all the people who act in it. ❑ *The show is very amusing and the cast are very good.* N-COUNT-COLL [2] To **cast** an actor **in** a play or film means to choose them to act a particular role in it. ❑ *The world premiere of Harold Pinter's new play casts Ian Holm in the lead role... He was cast as a college professor... He had no trouble casting the movie.* VERB V n in/as n V n in/as n V n ♦ **cast|ing** *...the casting director of Ealing film studios.* N-UNCOUNT: oft N of n, N n [3] To **cast** someone **in** a particular way or **as** a particular thing means to describe them in that way or suggest they are that thing. ❑ *Democrats have been worried about being cast as the party of the poor... Holland would never dare cast himself as a virtuoso pianist.* VERB V n as/in n V pron-refl as/in n [4] If you **cast** your eyes or **cast** a look in a particular direction, you look quickly in that direction. [WRITTEN] ❑ *He cast a stern glance at the two men... I cast my eyes down briefly... The maid, casting black looks, hurried out.* VERB V n prep/adv V n prep/adv V n [5] If something **casts** a light or shadow somewhere, it causes it to appear there. [WRITTEN] ❑ *The moon cast a bright light over the yard... They flew in over the beach, casting a huge shadow.* VERB V n prep V n [6] To **cast** doubt **on** something means to cause people to be unsure about it. ❑ *Last night a top criminal psychologist cast doubt on the theory.* VERB V n on n [7] When you **cast** your vote in an election, you vote. ❑ *About ninety-five per cent of those who cast their votes approve the new constitution... Gaviria had been widely expected to obtain well over half the votes cast.* VERB V n V-ed [8] To **cast** something or someone somewhere means to throw them there. [LITERARY] ❑ *Any true lover casting a pin into the fountain and gazing into it will see his or her future partner... John had Maude and her son cast into a dungeon.* VERB V n prep have n V-ed prep [9] To **cast** an object means to make it by pouring a liquid such as hot metal into a specially shaped container and leaving it there until it becomes hard. ❑ *...sculptures cast in bronze.* VERB V-ed in n [10] A **cast** is a model that has been made by pouring a liquid such as plaster or hot metal onto something or into something, so that when it hardens it has the same shape as that thing. ❑ *An orthodontist took a cast of the inside of Billy's mouth.* N-COUNT: oft N of n [11] A **cast** is the same as a **plaster cast**. N-COUNT [12] → See also **casting**. [13] to **cast aspersions** → see **aspersions**. **the die is cast** → see **die**. to **cast** your **mind back** → see **mind**. to **cast** your **net wider** → see **net**.

♦ **cast around for**

✓ in BRIT, also use **cast about for**

If you **cast around for** something or **cast about for** it, you try to find it or think of it. ❑ *She had been casting around for a good excuse to go to New York.* PHRASAL VERB V P P n

♦ **cast aside** If you **cast aside** someone or something, you get rid of them because they are no longer necessary or useful to you. ❑ *Sweden needs to cast aside outdated policies and thinking.* PHRASAL VERB V P n (not pron)

♦ **cast off** [1] If you **cast off** something, you get rid of it because it is no longer necessary or useful to you, or because it is harmful to you. [LITERARY] ❑ *The essay exhorts women to cast off their servitude to husbands and priests.* PHRASAL VERB V P n (not pron) [2] If you are on a boat and you **cast off**, you untie the rope that is keeping the boat in a fixed position. ❑ *He cast off, heading out to the bay.* PHRASAL VERB V P

**cas|ta|nets** /kæstənets/ **Castanets** are a Spanish musical instrument consisting of two small round pieces of wood or plastic held together by a cord. You hold the castanets in your hand and knock the pieces together with your fingers. N-PLURAL: also a pair of N

**cast|away** /kɑːstəweɪ, kæst-/ **(castaways)** A **castaway** is a person who has managed to swim or float to a lonely island or shore after their boat has sunk. N-COUNT

**caste** /kɑːst, kæst/ **(castes)** [1] A **caste** is one of the traditional social classes into which people are divided in a Hindu society. ❑ *Most of the upper castes worship the Goddess Kali.* N-COUNT [2] **Caste** is the system of dividing people in a society into different social classes. ❑ *The caste system shapes nearly every facet of Indian life.* N-UNCOUNT

**cas|tel|lat|ed** /kæstəleɪtɪd/ A **castellated** wall or building looks like a castle. [TECHNICAL] ❑ *...a 19th-century castellated mansion.* ADJ: usu ADJ n

**cast|er** /kɑːstəʳ, kæstəʳ/ → see **castor**.

**cast|er sug|ar** also **castor sugar.** **Caster sugar** is white sugar that has been ground into fine grains. It is used in cooking. [BRIT] N-UNCOUNT

☑ in AM, use **superfine sugar**

**cas|ti|gate** /kæstɪgeɪt/ **(castigates, castigating, castigated)** If you **castigate** someone or something, you speak to them angrily or criticize them severely. [FORMAL] ❑ *Marx never lost an opportunity to castigate colonialism... She castigated him for having no intellectual interests.* VERB; V n; V n *for* n/-ing ♦ **cas|ti|ga|tion** /kæstɪgeɪʃ<sup></sup>ən/ *...Bradley's public castigation of the police chief.* N-UNCOUNT

**cast|ing** /kɑːstɪŋ, kæst-/ **(castings)** A **casting** is an object or piece of machinery which has been made by pouring a liquid such as hot metal into a container, so that when it hardens it has the required shape. → See also **cast**. N-COUNT = cast

**cast|ing vote** **(casting votes)** When a committee has given an equal number of votes for and against a proposal, the chairperson can give a **casting vote**. This vote decides whether or not the proposal will be passed. ❑ *The vote was tied and a local union leader used his casting vote in favour of the return to work.* N-COUNT: usu sing

**cast iron** 1 **Cast iron** is iron which contains a small amount of carbon. It is hard and cannot be bent so it has to be made into objects by casting. ❑ *Made from cast iron, it is finished in graphite enamel. ...the cast-iron chair legs.* N-UNCOUNT 2 A **cast-iron** guarantee or alibi is one that is absolutely certain to be effective and will not fail you. ❑ *They would have to offer cast-iron guarantees to invest in long-term projects.* ADJ: usu ADJ n

**cas|tle** /kɑːsəl, kæsəl/ **(castles)** 1 A **castle** is a large building with thick, high walls. Castles were built by important people, such as kings, in former times, especially for protection during wars and battles. → See also **sand castle**. ◆◇◇ N-COUNT 2 In chess, a **castle** is a piece that can be moved forwards, backwards, or sideways. N-COUNT = rook

**cast-off** **(cast-offs)** also **castoff.** **Cast-off** things, especially clothes, are ones which someone no longer uses because they are old or unfashionable, and which they give to someone else or throw away. ❑ *Alexandra looked plump and awkward in her cast-off clothing.* ADJ: ADJ n ♦ **Cast-off** is also a noun. ❑ *I never had anything new to wear as a child, only a cousin's cast-offs.* N-COUNT: usu pl

**cas|tor** /kɑːstəʳ, kæst-/ **(castors)** also **caster.** **Castors** are small wheels fitted to a piece of furniture so that it can be moved more easily. N-COUNT

**cas|tor oil** **Castor oil** is a thick yellow oil that is obtained from the seeds of the castor oil plant. It has a very unpleasant taste and in former times was used as a medicine. N-UNCOUNT

**cas|tor sug|ar** → see **caster sugar**.

**cas|trate** /kæstreɪt, AM kæstreɪt/ **(castrates, castrating, castrated)** To **castrate** a male animal or a man means to remove his testicles. ❑ *In the ancient world, it was probably rare to castrate a dog or cat. ...a castrated male horse.* VERB; V n; V-ed ♦ **cas|tra|tion** /kæstreɪʃən/ **(castrations)** *...the castration of male farm animals.* N-VAR

**cas|ual** /kæʒuəl/ 1 If you are **casual**, you are, or you pretend to be, relaxed and not very concerned about what is happening or what you are doing. ❑ *It's difficult for me to be casual about anything... He's an easy-going, friendly young man with a casual sort of attitude towards money.* ADJ ♦ **casu|al|ly** *'No need to hurry,' Ben said casually.* ADV: ADV with v 2 A **casual** event or situation happens by chance or without planning. ❑ *What you mean as a casual remark could be misinterpreted... Even a casual observer could hardly have failed to notice the heightening of an already tense atmosphere.* ADJ: ADJ n 3 **Casual** clothes are ones that you normally wear at home or on holiday, and not on formal occasions. ❑ *I also bought some casual clothes for the weekend.* ADJ: ADJ n ≠ formal ♦ **casu|al|ly** *The couple were both smartly but casually dressed.* ADV: ADV -ed, ADV after v 4 **Casual** work is done for short periods and not on a permanent or regular basis. ❑ *...establishments which employ people on a casual basis, such as pubs and restaurants... It became increasingly expensive to hire casual workers.* ADJ: ADJ n = temporary ≠ permanent

**casu|al|ize** /kæʒuəlaɪz/ **(casualizes, casualizing, casualized)**

☑ in BRIT, also use **casualise**

If a business **casualizes** its employees or **casualizes** their labour, it replaces employees with permanent contracts and full rights with employees with temporary contracts and few rights. [BUSINESS] ❑ *...a casualised workforce.* VERB; V-ed; Also V n ♦ **casu|ali|za|tion** /kæʒuəlaɪzeɪʃən/ *...the casualisation of employment.* N-UNCOUNT: oft N *of* n

**casu|al|ty** /kæʒuəlti/ **(casualties)** 1 A **casualty** is a person who is injured or killed in a war or in an accident. ❑ *Troops fired on demonstrators near the Royal Palace causing many casualties.* ◆◇◇ N-COUNT 2 A **casualty of** a particular event or situation is a person or a thing that has suffered badly as a result of that event or situation. ❑ *Fiat has been one of the greatest casualties of the recession.* N-COUNT: usu N *of* n = victim 3 **Casualty** is the part of a hospital where people who have severe injuries or sudden illnesses are taken for emergency treatment. [BRIT] ❑ *I was taken to casualty at St Thomas's Hospital.* N-UNCOUNT

☑ in AM, use **emergency room**

**casu|ist|ry** /kæzjuɪstri, AM kæʒu-/ **Casuistry** is the use of clever arguments to persuade or trick people. [FORMAL] N-UNCOUNT disapproval

**cat** /kæt/ **(cats)** 1 A **cat** is a furry animal that has a long tail and sharp claws. Cats are often kept as pets. ◆◇◇ N-COUNT 2 **Cats** are lions, tigers, and other wild animals in the same family. N-COUNT 3 → See also **Cheshire cat**, **fat cat**, **wildcat**.

PHRASES 4 If you **let the cat out of the bag**, you tell people about something that was being kept secret. You often do this by mistake. PHRASE: V inflects 5 In a fight or contest, if one person plays **cat and mouse**, or a **game of cat and mouse**, with the other, the first person tries to confuse or deceive the second in order to defeat them. ❑ *After three hours of playing cat and mouse, they threatened to open fire on our vessel, so we stopped.* PHRASE: usu v PHR, PHR n 6 If you **put the cat among the pigeons** or **set the cat among the pigeons**, you cause fierce argument or discussion by doing or saying something. [BRIT] ❑ *The bank is poised to put the cat among the pigeons this morning by slashing the cost of borrowing.* PHRASE: V inflects 7 If you say **'There's no room to swing a cat'** or **'You can't swing a cat'**, you mean that the place you are talking about is very small or crowded. ❑ *It was described as a large, luxury mobile home, but there was barely room to swing a cat.* PHRASE: with brd-neg, usu v-link PHR

**cata|clysm** /kætəklɪzəm/ **(cataclysms)** A **cataclysm** is an event that causes great change or harm. [FORMAL] N-COUNT

**cata|clys|mic** /kætəklɪzmɪk/ A **cataclysmic** event is one that changes a situation or society very greatly, especially in an unpleasant way. [FORMAL] ❑ *Few had expected that change to be as cataclysmic as it turned out to be.* ADJ

**cata|comb** /kætəkuːm, AM -koʊm/ **(catacombs)** **Catacombs** are ancient underground passages and rooms, especially under a city, where people used to be buried. N-COUNT: usu pl

**Cata|lan** /kætəlæn/ 1 Something that is **Catalan** belongs or relates to Catalonia, its people, or its language. Catalonia is a region of Spain. ADJ: usu ADJ n 2 **Catalan** is one of the languages spoken in Catalonia. N-UNCOUNT

**cata|logue** /kætəlɒg/ **(catalogues, cataloguing, catalogued)**

☑ in AM, usually use **catalog**

1 A **catalogue** is a list of things such as the goods you can buy from a particular company, the objects in a museum, or the books in a library. ❑ *...the world's biggest seed catalogue.* N-COUNT = list 2 To **catalogue** things means to make a list of them. ❑ *The* VERB = list; V n

*Royal Greenwich Observatory was founded to observe and catalogue the stars.* [3] A **catalogue of** similar things, especially bad things, is a number of them considered or discussed one after another. ❑ *...the latest tragedy in a catalogue of disasters.* N-COUNT: N *of* n

**cata|lyse** /kætəlaɪz/ **(catalyses, catalysing, catalysed)**

☑ in AM, use **catalyze**

[1] If something **catalyses** a thing or a situation, it makes it active. [FORMAL] ❑ *Any unexpected circumstance that arises may catalyze a sudden escalation of violence.* VERB V n [2] In chemistry, if something **catalyses** a reaction or event, it causes it to happen. [TECHNICAL] ❑ *The wires do not have a large enough surface to catalyse a big explosion.* VERB V n

**ca|taly|sis** /kətælɪsɪs/ **Catalysis** is the speeding up of a chemical reaction by adding a catalyst to it. [TECHNICAL] N-UNCOUNT

**cata|lyst** /kætəlɪst/ **(catalysts)** [1] You can describe a person or thing that causes a change or event to happen as a **catalyst**. ❑ *I very much hope that this case will prove to be a catalyst for change... He said he saw the bank's role as a catalyst to encourage foreign direct investment.* N-COUNT: oft N *for* n [2] In chemistry, a **catalyst** is a substance that causes a chemical reaction to take place more quickly. N-COUNT

**cata|lyt|ic** /kætəlɪtɪk/ [1] In chemistry, a **catalytic** substance or a substance with **catalytic** properties is a substance which increases the speed of a chemical reaction. ❑ *...carbon molecules with unusual chemical and catalytic properties.* ADJ: ADJ n [2] If you describe a person or thing as having a **catalytic** effect, you mean that they cause things to happen or they increase the speed at which things happen. [FORMAL] ❑ *Governments do, however, have a vital catalytic role in orchestrating rescue operations.* ADJ: usu ADJ n

**cata|lyt|ic con|vert|er** **(catalytic converters)** A **catalytic converter** is a device which is fitted to a car's exhaust to reduce the pollution coming from it. N-COUNT

**cata|ma|ran** /kætəməræn/ **(catamarans)** A **catamaran** is a sailing boat with two parallel hulls that are held in place by a single deck. N-COUNT

**cata|pult** /kætəpʌlt/ **(catapults, catapulting, catapulted)** [1] A **catapult** is a device for shooting small stones. It is made of a Y-shaped stick with a piece of elastic tied between the two top parts. [BRIT] N-COUNT

☑ in AM, use **slingshot**

[2] If someone or something **catapults** or **is catapulted** through the air, they are thrown very suddenly, quickly, and violently through it. ❑ *We've all seen enough dummies catapulting through windscreens in TV warnings to know the dangers of not wearing seat belts... He was catapulted into the side of the van.* VERB V prep *be* V-ed prep/adv [3] If something **catapults** you into a particular state or situation, or if you **catapult** there, you are suddenly and unexpectedly caused to be in that state or situation. ❑ *Suddenly she was catapulted into his jet-set lifestyle... Affleck catapulted to fame after picking up an Oscar.* VERB *be* V-ed prep/adv V *to* n

**cata|ract** /kætərækt/ **(cataracts)** **Cataracts** are layers over a person's eyes that prevent them from seeing properly. Cataracts usually develop because of old age or illness. ❑ *Age is not a factor in cataract surgery.* N-COUNT: usu pl, N n

**ca|tarrh** /kətɑːʳ/ **Catarrh** is a medical condition in which a lot of mucus is produced in your nose and throat. You may get catarrh when you have a cold. N-UNCOUNT

**ca|tas|tro|phe** /kətæstrəfi/ **(catastrophes)** A **catastrophe** is an unexpected event that causes great suffering or damage. ❑ *From all points of view, war would be a catastrophe.* N-COUNT = disaster

**cata|stroph|ic** /kætəstrɒfɪk/ [1] Something that is **catastrophic** involves or causes a sudden terrible disaster. ❑ *A tidal wave caused by the earthquake hit the coast causing catastrophic damage... The water shortage in this country is potentially catastrophic.* ADJ = disastrous ♦ **cata|strophi|cal|ly** /kætəstrɒfɪkli/ *The faulty left-hand engine failed catastrophically as the aircraft approached the airport.* ADV: usu ADV after v, also ADV adj/-ed/adv [2] If you describe something as **catastrophic**, you mean that it is very bad or unsuccessful. ❑ *...another catastrophic attempt to arrest control from a rival Christian militia... His mother's untimely death had a catastrophic effect on him.* ADJ = disastrous ♦ **cata|strophi|cal|ly** *By the time we had to sell, prices had fallen catastrophically.* ADV: usu ADV after v

**cata|ton|ic** /kætətɒnɪk/ If you describe someone as being in a **catatonic** state, you mean that they are not moving or responding at all, usually as a result of illness, shock, or drugs. [MEDICAL or LITERARY] ❑ *...and the traumatised heroine sinks into a catatonic trance.* ADJ

**cat|bird seat** /kætbɜːʳd siːt/ If you say that someone is **in the catbird seat**, you think that their situation is very good. [AM, INFORMAL] ❑ *If he had not been hurt, his team would be sitting in the catbird seat.* PHRASE: v-link PHR

**cat bur|glar** **(cat burglars)** A **cat burglar** is a thief who steals from houses or other buildings by climbing up walls and entering through windows or through the roof. N-COUNT

**cat|call** /kætkɔːl/ **(catcalls)** **Catcalls** are loud noises that people make to show that they disapprove of something they are watching or listening to. ❑ *The crowd responded with boos and catcalls.* N-COUNT: usu pl = jeer ≠ cheer

**catch** /kætʃ/ **(catches, catching, caught)** ◆◆◇ [1] If you **catch** a person or animal, you capture them after chasing them, or by using a trap, net, or other device. ❑ *Police say they are confident of catching the gunman... Where did you catch the fish?... I wondered if it was an animal caught in a trap.* VERB = capture V n V n V-ed [2] If you **catch** an object that is moving through the air, you seize it with your hands. ❑ *I jumped up to catch a ball and fell over.* VERB V n ♦ **Catch** is also a noun. ❑ *He missed the catch and the match was lost.* N-COUNT [3] If you **catch** a part of someone's body, you take or seize it with your hand, often in order to stop them going somewhere. ❑ *Liz caught his arm... He knelt beside her and caught her hand in both of his... Garrido caught her by the wrist.* VERB = seize V n V n prep V n prep [4] If one thing **catches** another, it hits it accidentally or manages to hit it. ❑ *The stinging slap almost caught his face... I may have caught him with my elbow but it was just an accident... He caught her on the side of her head with his other fist.* VERB V n V n *with* n V n *on* n [5] If something **catches on** or **in** an object or if an object **catches** something, it accidentally becomes attached to the object or stuck in it. ❑ *Her ankle caught on a root, and she almost lost her balance... A man caught his foot in the lawnmower.* VERB V prep V n prep [6] When you **catch** a bus, train, or plane, you get on it in order to travel somewhere. ❑ *We were in plenty of time for Anthony to catch the ferry... He caught a taxi to Harrods.* VERB = get V n V n prep [7] If you **catch** someone doing something wrong, you see or find them doing it. ❑ *He caught a youth breaking into a car... Three years ago my wife and I divorced. I caught her with her boss.* VERB V n -ing V n prep [8] If you **catch yourself** doing something, especially something surprising, you suddenly become aware that you are doing it. ❑ *I caught myself feeling almost sorry for poor Mr Laurence.* VERB = find V pron-refl -ing [9] If you **catch** something or **catch** a glimpse of it, you notice it or manage to see it briefly. ❑ *As she turned back she caught the puzzled look on her mother's face... He caught a glimpse of the man's face in a shop window.* VERB V n V n [10] If you **catch** something that someone has said, you manage to hear it. ❑ *I do not believe I caught your name... The men out in the corridor were trying to catch what they said.* VERB V n V wh [11] If you **catch** a TV or radio programme or an event, you manage to see or listen to it. ❑ *Bill turns on the radio to catch the local news.* VERB V n [12] If you **catch** someone, you manage to contact or meet them to talk to them, especially when they are just about to go somewhere else. ❑ *I dialled Elizabeth's number thinking I might catch her before she left for work... Hello, Dolph. Glad I caught you.* VERB V n V n [13] If something or someone **catches** VERB

you by surprise or at a bad time, you were not expecting them or do not feel able to deal with them. ❑ *She looked as if the photographer had caught her by surprise... I'm sorry but I just cannot say anything. You've caught me at a bad time... The sheer number of spectators has caught everyone unprepared.* V n prep V n prep V n adj
14 If something **catches** your attention or your eye, you notice it or become interested in it. ❑ *My shoes caught his attention... A quick movement across the aisle caught his eye.* VERB V n V n
15 If you **are caught** in a storm or other unpleasant situation, it happens when you cannot avoid its effects. ❑ *When he was fishing off the island he was caught in a storm and almost drowned... Visitors to the area were caught between police and the rioters.* V-PASSIVE *be/get* V-ed prep *be/get* V-ed prep
16 If you **are caught between** two alternatives or two people, you do not know which one to choose or follow. ❑ *The Jordanian leader is caught between both sides in the dispute... She was caught between envy and admiration.* V-PASSIVE *be* V-ed *between* pl-n *be* V-ed *between* pl-n
17 If you **catch** a cold or a disease, you become ill with it. ❑ *The more stress you are under, the more likely you are to catch a cold.* VERB V n
18 To **catch** liquids or small pieces that fall from somewhere means to collect them in a container. ❑ *...a specially designed breadboard with a tray to catch the crumbs.* VERB = *collect* V n
19 If something **catches** the light or if the light **catches** it, it reflects the light and looks bright or shiny. ❑ *They saw the ship's guns, catching the light of the moon... Often a fox goes across the road in front of me and I just catch it in the headlights.* VERB V n V n *in* n
20 A **catch** on a window, door, or container is a device that fastens it. ❑ *She fiddled with the catch of her bag.* N-COUNT
21 A **catch** is a hidden problem or difficulty in a plan or an offer that seems surprisingly good. ❑ *The catch is that you work for your supper, and the food and accommodation can be very basic.* N-COUNT: usu sing = *snag*
22 When people have been fishing, their **catch** is the total number of fish that they have caught. ❑ *The catch included one fish over 18 pounds.* N-COUNT
23 **Catch** is a game in which children throw a ball to each other. N-UNCOUNT
24 **Catch** is a game in which one child chases other children and tries to touch or catch one of them. N-UNCOUNT = *tag*
25 → See also **catching**.
26 You can say things such as '**You wouldn't catch me doing that**' to emphasize that you would never do a particular thing. [INFORMAL] ❑ *You wouldn't catch me in there, I can tell you.* PHRASE: PHR -ing, PHR prep/adv [emphasis]
27 to **catch** your **breath** → see **breath**. to **catch fire** → see **fire**. to **catch hold of** something → see **hold**. to **be caught short** → see **short**. to **catch sight of** something → see **sight**.

♦ **catch on** 1 If you **catch on to** something, you understand it, or realize that it is happening. ❑ *He got what he could out of me before I caught on to the kind of person he'd turned into... Wait a minute! I'm beginning to catch on.* PHRASAL VERB V P *to* n V P
2 If something **catches on**, it becomes popular. ❑ *The idea has been around for ages without catching on.* PHRASAL VERB V P

♦ **catch out** To **catch** someone **out** means to cause them to make a mistake that reveals that they are lying about something, do not know something, or cannot do something. [mainly BRIT] ❑ *Detectives followed him for months hoping to catch him out in some deception... The government has been caught out by the speed of events.* PHRASAL VERB V n P prep V n P prep Also V n P, V P n

♦ **catch up** 1 If you **catch up with** someone who is in front of you, you reach them by walking faster than they are walking. ❑ *I stopped and waited for her to catch up... We caught up with the nuns.* PHRASAL VERB V P V P *with* n
2 To **catch up with** someone means to reach the same standard, stage, or level that they have reached. ❑ *Most late developers will catch up with their friends... John began the season better than me but I have fought to catch up... During the evenings, the school is used by kids who want to catch up on English and mathematics.* PHRASAL VERB V P *with* n V P V P *on/in* n
3 If you **catch up on** an activity that you have not had much time to do recently, you spend time doing it. ❑ *I was catching up on a bit of reading.* PHRASAL VERB V P *on/with* n
4 If you **catch up** on friends who you have not seen for some time or on their lives, you talk to them and find out what has happened in their lives since you last talked together. ❑ *The ladies spent some time catching up on each other's health and families... She plans to return to Dublin to catch up with the relatives she has not seen since she married.* PHRASAL VERB V P *on* n V P *with* n
5 If you **are caught up in** something, you are involved in it, usually unwillingly. ❑ *The people themselves weren't part of the conflict; they were just caught up in it.* PHRASAL VERB *be* V-ed P *in* n

♦ **catch up with** 1 When people **catch up with** someone who has done something wrong, they succeed in finding them in order to arrest or punish them. ❑ *The law caught up with him yesterday.* PHRASAL VERB V P P n
2 If something **catches up with** you, you are forced to deal with something unpleasant that happened or that you did in the past, which you have been able to avoid until now. ❑ *Although he subsequently became a successful businessman, his criminal past caught up with him.* PHRASAL VERB V P P n

**Catch-22** /kætʃ twenti tuː/ also **Catch 22.** If you describe a situation as a **Catch-22**, you mean it is an impossible situation because you cannot do one thing until you do another thing, but you cannot do the second thing until you do the first thing. ❑ *It's a Catch 22 situation here. Nobody wants to support you until you're successful, but without the support how can you ever be successful?* N-SING: oft N n

**catch-all** (**catch-alls**)

[AM] in AM, also use **catchall**

A **catch-all** is a term or category which includes many different things. ❑ *Globalisation is a catch-all to describe increased international trade... Indigestion is a catch-all term for any kind of stomach distress.* N-COUNT

**catch|er** /kætʃəʳ/ (**catchers**) In baseball, the **catcher** is the player who stands behind the batter. The catcher has a special glove for catching the ball. N-COUNT

**catch|ing** /kætʃɪŋ/ If an illness or a disease is **catching**, it is easily passed on or given to someone else. [INFORMAL] ❑ *There are those who think eczema is catching.* ADJ: v-link ADJ = *infectious*

**catch|ment** /kætʃmənt/ (**catchments**) In geography, **catchment** is the process of collecting water, in particular the process of water flowing from the ground and collecting in a river. **Catchment** is also the water that is collected in this way. [TECHNICAL] N-COUNT

**catch|ment area** (**catchment areas**) 1 The **catchment area of** a school, hospital, or other service is the area that it serves. [BRIT] ❑ *...the catchment areas of the district general hospitals.* N-COUNT: oft N *of* n
2 In geography, the **catchment area** of a river is the area of land from which water flows into the river. [TECHNICAL] N-COUNT

**catch-phrase** (**catch-phrases**) also **catch phrase.** A **catch-phrase** is a sentence or phrase which becomes popular or well-known, often because it is frequently used by a famous person. N-COUNT

**catchy** /kætʃi/ (**catchier, catchiest**) If you describe a tune, name, or advertisement as **catchy**, you mean that it is attractive and easy to remember. ❑ *The songs were both catchy and original... The initiative has been given the supposedly catchy title of the 'Citizen's Charter'.* ADJ

**cat|echism** /kætɪkɪzəm/ (**catechisms**) In a Catholic, Episcopal, or Orthodox Church, the **catechism** is a series of questions and answers about religious beliefs, which has to be learned by people before they can become full members of that Church. N-COUNT: usu sing

**cat|egor|ic** /kætɪgɒrɪk, AM -gɔːr-/ **Categoric** means the same as **categorical**. ADJ

**cat|egori|cal** /kætɪgɒrɪkəl, AM -gɔːr-/ If you are **categorical** about something, you state your views very definitely and firmly. ❑ *...his categorical denial of the charges of sexual harassment.* ADJ = *unequivocal*
♦ **cat|egori|cal|ly** /kætɪgɒrɪkli, AM -gɔːr-/ *They totally and categorically deny the charges... He stated* ADV: ADV with v

*categorically that this would be his last season in Formula One.* = unequivocally

**cat|ego|rize** /kætɪgəraɪz/ **(categorizes, categorizing, categorized)**

in BRIT, also use **categorise**

If you **categorize** people or things, you divide them into sets or you say which set they belong to. ❑ *Lindsay, like his films, is hard to categorise... Make a list of your child's toys and then categorise them as sociable or antisocial. ...new ways of categorizing information.* ♦ **cat|ego|ri|za|tion** /kætɪgəraɪzeɪʃən/ **(categorizations)** *...the categorisation of new types of missiles.* VERB = classify V n V n as n V-ing N-VAR = classification

**cat|ego|ry** /kætɪgri, AM -gɔːri/ **(categories)** If people or things are divided into **categories**, they are divided into groups in such a way that the members of each group are similar to each other in some way. ❑ *This book clearly falls into the category of fictionalised autobiography... The tables were organised into six different categories.* ◆◇◇ N-COUNT = class

**ca|ter** /keɪtəʳ/ **(caters, catering, catered)** 1 In British English, to **cater for** a group of people means to provide all the things that they need or want. In American English, you say you **cater to** a person or group of people. ❑ *Minorca is the sort of place that caters for families... We cater to an exclusive clientele.* 2 In British English, to **cater for** something means to take it into account. In American English, you say you **cater to** something. ❑ *...shops that cater for the needs of men... Exercise classes cater to all levels of fitness.* 3 If a person or company **caters for** an occasion such as a wedding or a party, they provide food and drink for all the people there. ❑ *Nunsmere Hall can cater for receptions of up to 300 people... Does he cater parties too?* → See also **catering**, **self-catering**. VERB V for n V to n VERB V for n V to n VERB V for n V n

**ca|ter|er** /keɪtərəʳ/ **(caterers)** **Caterers** are people or companies that provide food and drink for a place such as an office or for special occasions such as weddings and parties. ❑ *...food brought in from outside caterers.* N-COUNT

**ca|ter|ing** /keɪtərɪŋ/ **Catering** is the activity of providing food and drink for a large number of people, for example at weddings and parties. ❑ *He recently did the catering for a presidential reception.* N-UNCOUNT: also *the* N, oft N n

**cat|er|pil|lar** /kætəʳpɪləʳ/ **(caterpillars)** A **caterpillar** is a small, worm-like animal that feeds on plants and eventually develops into a butterfly or moth. N-COUNT

**cat|er|waul** /kætəʳwɔːl/ **(caterwauls, caterwauling, caterwauled)** If a person or animal **caterwauls**, they make a loud, high, unpleasant noise like the noise that cats make when they fight. ❑ *...shrieking and caterwauling in mock distress.* ♦ **Caterwaul** is also a noun. ❑ *...blood-curdling caterwauls.* ♦ **cat|er|waul|ing** *...high-pitched moaning and caterwauling.* VERB = wail V N-COUNT N-UNCOUNT = wailing

**cat|fight** /kætfaɪt/ **(catfights)** A **catfight** is an angry fight or quarrel, especially between women. [mainly JOURNALISM] ❑ *A catfight has erupted over who will get top billing.* N-COUNT

**cat|fish** /kætfɪʃ/ **(catfish)** **Catfish** are a type of fish that have long thin spines around their mouths. N-VAR

**ca|thar|sis** /kəθɑːʳsɪs/ **Catharsis** is getting rid of unhappy memories or strong emotions such as anger or sadness by expressing them in some way. ❑ *He wrote out his rage and bewilderment, which gradually became a form of catharsis leading to understanding.* N-UNCOUNT

**ca|thar|tic** /kəθɑːʳtɪk/ Something that is **cathartic** has the effect of catharsis. [FORMAL] ❑ *His laughter was cathartic, an animal yelp that brought tears to his eyes.* ADJ

**ca|thedral** /kəθiːdrəl/ **(cathedrals)** A **cathedral** is a very large and important church which has a bishop in charge of it. ❑ *...St. Paul's Cathedral. ...the cathedral city of Canterbury.* N-COUNT

**Cath|er|ine wheel** /kæθərɪn hwiːl/ **(Catherine wheels)** also **catherine wheel.** A **Catherine wheel** is a firework in the shape of a circle which spins round and round. N-COUNT

**cath|eter** /kæθɪtəʳ/ **(catheters)** A **catheter** is a tube which is used to introduce liquids into a human body or to withdraw liquids from it. [MEDICAL] N-COUNT

**cath|ode** /kæθoʊd/ **(cathodes)** A **cathode** is the negative electrode in a cell such as a battery. Compare **anode**. N-COUNT

**cathode-ray tube** **(cathode-ray tubes)** A **cathode-ray tube** is a device in televisions and computer terminals which sends an image onto the screen. [TECHNICAL] N-COUNT

**Catho|lic** /kæθlɪk/ **(Catholics)** 1 The **Catholic** Church is the branch of the Christian Church that accepts the Pope as its leader and is based in the Vatican in Rome. ❑ *...the Catholic Church. ...Catholic priests. ...the Catholic faith.* → See also **Anglo-Catholic**. 2 A **Catholic** is a member of the Catholic Church. ❑ *At least nine out of ten Mexicans are baptised Catholics.* 3 If you describe a collection of things or people as **catholic**, you are emphasizing that they are very varied. ❑ *He was a man of catholic tastes, a lover of grand opera, history and the fine arts.* ◆◇◇ ADJ: usu ADJ n N-COUNT ADJ = wide

**Ca|tholi|cism** /kəθɒlɪsɪzəm/ **Catholicism** is the traditions, the behaviour, and the set of Christian beliefs that are held by Catholics. ❑ *...her conversion to Catholicism.* N-UNCOUNT

**cat|kin** /kætkɪn/ **(catkins)** A **catkin** is a long, thin, soft flower that hangs on some trees, for example birch trees and hazel trees. N-COUNT

**cat|nap** /kætnæp/ **(catnaps)** also **cat-nap.** A **catnap** is a short sleep, usually one which you have during the day. [INFORMAL] N-COUNT = doze, nap

**cat|suit** /kætsuːt/ **(catsuits)** A **catsuit** is a piece of women's clothing that is made in one piece and fits tightly over the body and legs. [BRIT] N-COUNT

**cat|sup** /kætsəp/ → see **ketchup**.

**cat|tery** /kætəri/ **(catteries)** A **cattery** is a place where you can leave your cat to be looked after when you go on holiday. [BRIT] N-COUNT

**cat|tle** /kætəl/ **Cattle** are cows and bulls. ❑ *...the finest herd of beef cattle for two hundred miles.* N-PLURAL

**cat|tle grid** **(cattle grids)** A **cattle grid** is a set of metal bars in the surface of a road which prevents cattle and sheep from walking along the road, but allows people and vehicles to pass. [BRIT] N-COUNT

in AM, use **cattle guard**

**cat|tle guard** **(cattle guards)** A **cattle guard** is the same as a **cattle grid**. [AM] N-COUNT

**cattle|man** /kætəlmæn/ **(cattlemen)** A **cattleman** is a man who looks after or owns cattle, especially in North America or Australia. N-COUNT = rancher

**cat|tle mar|ket** **(cattle markets)** 1 A **cattle market** is a market where cattle are bought and sold. 2 If you refer to an event such as a disco or a beauty contest as a **cattle market**, you disapprove of it because women are considered there only in terms of their sexual attractiveness. N-COUNT N-COUNT disapproval

**cat|tle prod** **(cattle prods)** A **cattle prod** is an object shaped like a long stick. Farmers make cattle move in a particular direction by pushing the cattle prod against the bodies of the animals. ❑ *...an electric cattle prod.* N-COUNT

**cat|ty** /kæti/ **(cattier, cattiest)** If someone, especially a woman or girl, is being **catty**, they are being unpleasant and unkind. [INFORMAL] ❑ *...catty remarks.* ADJ = bitchy

**cat|walk** /kætwɔːk/ **(catwalks)** 1 At a fashion show, the **catwalk** is a narrow platform that models walk along to display clothes. 2 A **catwalk** is a narrow bridge high in the air, for example between two parts of a tall building, on the outside of a large structure, or over a stage. N-COUNT: usu sing N-COUNT

**Cau|ca|sian** /kɔːkeɪʒən/ **(Caucasians)** [1] A **Caucasian** person is a white person. [FORMAL] ❑ *...a 25-year-old Caucasian male.* ♦ A **Caucasian** is someone who is Caucasian. ❑ *Ann Hamilton was a Caucasian from New England.* [2] Anthropologists use **Caucasian** to refer to someone from a racial grouping coming from Europe, North Africa, and western Asia. [TECHNICAL] ❑ *...blue eyes and Caucasian features.* ♦ A **Caucasian** is someone who is Caucasian.
ADJ = white; N-COUNT; ADJ: usu ADJ n; N-COUNT

**cau|cus** /kɔːkəs/ **(caucuses)** A **caucus** is a group of people within an organization who share similar aims and interests or who have a lot of influence. [FORMAL] ❑ *...the Black Caucus of minority congressmen.*
N-COUNT

**caught** /kɔːt/ **Caught** is the past tense and past participle of **catch**.

**caul|dron** /kɔːldrən/ **(cauldrons)** A **cauldron** is a very large, round metal pot used for cooking over a fire. In stories and fairy tales, a **cauldron** is used by witches for their spells.
N-COUNT

**cau|li|flow|er** /kɒliflaʊəʳ, AM kɔː-/ **(cauliflowers)** **Cauliflower** is a large round vegetable that has a hard white centre surrounded by green leaves. → See picture on page 1712.
N-VAR

**caus|al** /kɔːzəl/ If there is a **causal** relationship between two things, one thing is responsible for causing the other thing. [FORMAL] ❑ *Rawlins stresses that it is impossible to prove a causal link between the drug and the deaths.*
ADJ: usu ADJ n

**cau|sal|ity** /kɔːzælɪti/ **Causality** is the relationship of cause and effect. [FORMAL] ❑ *...the chain of causality that produces an earthquake.*
N-UNCOUNT

**cau|sa|tion** /kɔːzeɪʃən/ [1] The **causation** of something, usually something bad, is the factors that have caused it. [FORMAL] ❑ *The gene is only part of the causation of illness.* [2] **Causation** is a study of the factors involved in causing something. [FORMAL]
N-UNCOUNT; N-UNCOUNT

**causa|tive** /kɔːzətɪv/ **Causative** factors are ones which are responsible for causing something. [FORMAL] ❑ *Both nicotine and carbon monoxide inhaled with cigarette smoking have been incriminated as causative factors.*
ADJ: ADJ n

**cause** /kɔːz/ **(causes, causing, caused)** ◆◆◆ [1] The **cause of** an event, usually a bad event, is the thing that makes it happen. ❑ *Smoking is the biggest preventable cause of death and disease... The causes are a complex blend of local and national tensions.* [2] To **cause** something, usually something bad, means to make it happen. ❑ *Attempts to limit family size among some minorities are likely to cause problems... This was a genuine mistake, but it did cause me some worry. ...a protein that gets into animal cells and attacks other proteins, causing disease to spread. ...the damage to Romanian democracy caused by events of the past few days.* [3] If you have **cause for** a particular feeling or action, you have good reasons for feeling it or doing it. ❑ *Only a few people can find any cause for celebration... Both had much cause to be grateful for the secretiveness of government in Britain.* [4] A **cause** is an aim or principle which a group of people supports or is fighting for. ❑ *Refusing to have one leader has not helped the cause.* → See also **lost cause**.
N-COUNT: oft N *of* n ≠ effect; VERB V n; V n n; V n to-inf; V-ed; N-UNCOUNT: N *for* n, N to-inf = reason; N-COUNT

PHRASES [5] You use **cause and effect** to talk about the way in which one thing is caused by another. ❑ *...fundamental laws of biological cause and effect.* [6] If you say that something is **in a good cause** or **for a good cause**, you mean that it is worth doing or giving to because it will help other people, for example by raising money for charity. ❑ *The Raleigh International Bike Ride is open to anyone who wants to raise money for a good cause.*
PHRASE; PHRASE

**'cause** /kəz/ also **cause**. **'Cause** is an informal way of saying **because**. ❑ *30 families are suffering 'cause they're out of work.*
CONJ

**cause cé|lè|bre** /koʊz seɪlebrə/ **(causes célèbres)** also **cause celebre**. A **cause célèbre** is an issue, person, or criminal trial that has attracted a lot of public attention and discussion. [FORMAL] ❑ *The Kravchenko trial became a cause celebre in Paris and internationally.*
N-COUNT

**cause|way** /kɔːzweɪ/ **(causeways)** A **causeway** is a raised path or road that crosses water or wet land.
N-COUNT

**caus|tic** /kɔːstɪk/ [1] **Caustic** chemical substances are very powerful and can dissolve other substances. ❑ *...caustic cleaning agents... Remember that this is caustic; use gloves or a spoon.* [2] A **caustic** remark is extremely critical, cruel, or bitter. [FORMAL] ❑ *His abrasive wit and caustic comments were an interviewer's nightmare.*
ADJ = corrosive; ADJ = bitter, acid

**caus|tic so|da** **Caustic soda** is a powerful chemical substance used to make strong soaps and clean drains.
N-UNCOUNT

**cau|ter|ize** /kɔːtəraɪz/ **(cauterizes, cauterizing, cauterized)**

in BRIT, also use **cauterise**

If a doctor **cauterizes** a wound, he or she burns it with heat or with a chemical in order to close it up and prevent it from becoming infected. ❑ *He cauterized the wound with a piece of red-hot iron.*
V n

**cau|tion** /kɔːʃən/ **(cautions, cautioning, cautioned)** [1] **Caution** is great care which you take in order to avoid possible danger. ❑ *Extreme caution should be exercised when buying part-worn tyres... The Chancellor is a man of caution.* [2] If someone **cautions** you, they warn you about problems or danger. ❑ *Tony cautioned against misrepresenting the situation... The statement clearly was intended to caution Seoul against attempting to block the council's action again... He cautioned that opposition attacks on the ruling party would not further political co-operation.* ♦ **Caution** is also a noun. ❑ *There was a note of caution for the Treasury in the figures.* [3] If someone who has broken the law **is cautioned** by the police, they are warned that if they break the law again official action will be taken against them. [BRIT] ❑ *The two men were cautioned but police say they will not be charged.* ♦ **Caution** is also a noun. ❑ *In November 1987 Paula escaped with a caution. In October 1988 she was fined.* [4] If someone who has been arrested **is cautioned**, the police warn them that anything they say may be used as evidence in a trial. [BRIT] ❑ *Nobody was cautioned after arrest.* [5] If you **throw caution to the wind**, you behave in a way that is not considered sensible or careful. ❑ *I threw caution to the wind and rode as fast as I could.* [6] to **err on the side of** caution → see **err**.
N-UNCOUNT; VERB = warn; V *against* n/-ing; V n *against/about* n/-ing; V that; N-UNCOUNT = warning; VERB: usu passive; *be* V-ed; N-COUNT; VERB: usu passive; *be* V-ed; PHRASE: V inflects

**cau|tion|ary** /kɔːʃənri, AM -neri/ A **cautionary** story or a **cautionary** note to a story is one that is intended to give a warning to people. ❑ *An editorial in The Times sounds a cautionary note.*
ADJ: usu ADJ n

**cau|tious** /kɔːʃəs/ ◆◇◇ [1] Someone who is **cautious** acts very carefully in order to avoid possible danger. ❑ *The scientists are cautious about using enzyme therapy on humans... He is a very cautious man.* ♦ **cau|tious|ly** *David moved cautiously forward and looked over the edge... Cautiously, he moved himself into an upright position.* [2] If you describe someone's attitude or reaction as **cautious**, you mean that it is limited or careful. ❑ *He has been seen as a champion of a more cautious approach to economic reform.* ♦ **cau|tious|ly** *I am cautiously optimistic that a new government will be concerned and aware about the environment... Rebel sources have so far reacted cautiously to the threat.*
ADJ: oft ADJ *about* n/-ing = careful ≠ rash; ADV: usu ADV with v, also ADV adj; ADJ = circumspect ≠ rash; ADV: usu ADV adj, also ADV with v ≠ rashly

**cav|al|cade** /kævəlkeɪd/ **(cavalcades)** A **cavalcade** is a procession of people on horses or in cars or carriages. ❑ *...a cavalcade of limousines and police motorcycles.*
N-COUNT: oft N *of* n

**cava|lier** /kævəlɪəʳ/ If you describe a person or their behaviour as **cavalier**, you are criticizing them because you think that they do not consider other people's feelings or take account of the seriousness of a situation. ❑ *The Editor takes a cavalier attitude to the concept of fact checking.*
ADJ disapproval

**cav|al|ry** /kævəlri/ 1 The **cavalry** is the part of an army that uses armoured vehicles for fighting. ❑ *...the US Army's 1st Cavalry Division.* N-SING 2 The **cavalry** is the group of soldiers in an army who ride horses. ❑ *...a young cavalry officer.* N-SING

**cav|al|ry|man** /kævəlrimæn/ **(cavalrymen)** A **cavalryman** is a soldier who is in the cavalry, especially one who rides a horse. N-COUNT

**cave** /keɪv/ **(caves, caving, caved)** A **cave** is a large hole in the side of a cliff or hill, or one that is under the ground. ❑ *...a cave more than 1,000 feet deep.* ◆◇◇ N-COUNT

♦ **cave in** 1 If something such as a roof or a ceiling **caves in**, it collapses inwards. ❑ *Part of the roof has caved in.* PHRASAL VERB = collapse V P 2 If you **cave in**, you suddenly stop arguing or resisting, especially when people put pressure on you to stop. ❑ *After a ruinous strike, the union caved in... The Prime Minister has caved in to backbench pressure... He's caved in on capital punishment.* PHRASAL VERB = give in V P V P to n V P on n

**ca|veat** /kæviæt, AM keɪv-/ **(caveats)** A **caveat** is a warning of a specific limitation of something such as information or an agreement. [FORMAL] ❑ *There was one caveat: he was not to enter into a merger or otherwise weaken the Roche family's control of the firm.* N-COUNT: oft N that

**ca|veat emp|tor** /kæviæt emptɔːʳ, AM keɪv-/ **Caveat emptor** means 'let the buyer beware', and is a warning to someone buying something that it is their responsibility to identify and accept any faults in it. [FORMAL, WRITTEN] CONVENTION

**cave-in** **(cave-ins)** A **cave-in** is the sudden collapse of the roof of a cave or mine. N-COUNT

**cave|man** /keɪvmæn/ **(cavemen)** **Cavemen** were people in prehistoric times who lived mainly in caves. N-COUNT

**cav|er** /keɪvəʳ/ **(cavers)** A **caver** is someone who goes into underground caves as a sport. N-COUNT

**cav|ern** /kævəʳn/ **(caverns)** A **cavern** is a large deep cave. N-COUNT

**cav|ern|ous** /kævəʳnəs/ A **cavernous** room or building is very large inside, and so it reminds you of a cave. ❑ *The work space is a bare and cavernous warehouse.* ADJ

**cavi|ar** /kæviɑːʳ/ **(caviars)** also **caviare.** **Caviar** is the salted eggs of a fish called a sturgeon. N-MASS

**cav|il** /kævəl/ **(cavils, cavilling, cavilled)**

✔ in AM, use **caviling, caviled**

If you say that someone **cavils at** something, you mean that they make criticisms of it that you think are unimportant or unnecessary. [FORMAL] ❑ *Let us not cavil too much... I don't think this is the time to cavil at the wording of the report.* ♦ **Cavil** is also a noun. ❑ *These cavils aside, most of the essays are very good indeed.* VERB: no passive [disapproval] = quibble V V at n N-COUNT

**cav|ity** /kævɪti/ **(cavities)** 1 A **cavity** is a space or hole in something such as a solid object or a person's body. [FORMAL] N-COUNT 2 In dentistry, a **cavity** is a hole in a tooth, caused by decay. [TECHNICAL] N-COUNT

**cav|ity wall** **(cavity walls)** A **cavity wall** is a wall that consists of two separate walls with a space between them. Cavity walls help to keep out noise and cold. [mainly BRIT] ❑ *...cavity wall insulation.* N-COUNT: oft N n

**ca|vort** /kəvɔːʳt/ **(cavorts, cavorting, cavorted)** 1 When people **cavort**, they leap about in a noisy and excited way. ❑ *You can enjoy a quick snack while your children cavort in the sand.* VERB = romp V 2 **Cavort** is sometimes used by journalists to suggest that people were behaving in a playfully sexual way. ❑ *It was claimed she cavorted with a police sergeant in a Jacuzzi but she denies this.* VERB = romp V with n

**caw** /kɔː/ **(caws, cawing, cawed)** When a bird such as a crow or a rook **caws**, it makes a loud harsh sound. ❑ *Outside, a raven cawed.* VERB V

**cay|enne pep|per** /kaɪen pepəʳ/ **Cayenne pepper** or **cayenne** is a red powder with a hot taste which is made from dried peppers and is used to flavour food. ❑ *Season with salt, pepper and a pinch of cayenne.* N-UNCOUNT

**CB** /siː biː/ **CB**, an abbreviation for 'Citizens' Band', is a range of radio frequencies which the general public is allowed to use to send messages to each other. It is used especially by truck drivers and other drivers who use radio sets in their vehicles. N-UNCOUNT

**cc** /siː siː/ 1 You use **cc** when referring to the volume or capacity of something such as the size of a car engine. **cc** is an abbreviation for 'cubic centimetres'. ❑ *...1,500 cc sports cars.* 2 **cc** is used at the end of a business letter to indicate that a copy is being sent to another person. [BUSINESS] ❑ *...cc J. Chater, S. Cooper.*

**CCTV** /siː siː tiː viː/ **CCTV** is an abbreviation for 'closed-circuit television'. ❑ *...a CCTV camera... The girls were filmed on CCTV.* N-UNCOUNT

**CD** /siː diː/ **(CDs)** **CDs** are small plastic discs on which sound, especially music, is recorded. **CDs** can also be used to store information which can be read by a computer. **CD** is an abbreviation for 'compact disc'. ❑ *The Beatles' Red and Blue compilations are issued on CD for the first time next month.* ◆◇◇ N-COUNT

**CD burn|er** **(CD burners)** A **CD burner** is the same as a **CD writer**. [COMPUTING] N-COUNT

**CD play|er** **(CD players)** A **CD player** is a machine on which you can play CDs. ◆◇◇ N-COUNT

**Cdr**

✔ in AM, also use **CDR**

**Cdr** is the written abbreviation for **Commander** when it is used as a title. ❑ *...Cdr A.C. Moore.* N-TITLE

**CD-R** **(CD-Rs)** /siː diː ɑːʳ/ A **CD-R** is a CD which is capable of recording sound and images, for example from another CD or from the Internet. **CD-R** is an abbreviation for 'compact disc recordable'. N-COUNT

**CD-ROM** /siː diː rɒm/ **(CD-ROMs)** A **CD-ROM** is a CD on which a very large amount of information can be stored and then read using a computer. **CD-ROM** is an abbreviation for 'compact disc read-only memory'. [COMPUTING] ❑ *The collected Austen novels on CD-ROM will cost £35.* ◆◇◇ N-COUNT

**CD-ROM drive** /siː diː rɒm draɪv/ **(CD-ROM drives)** A **CD-ROM drive** is the device that you use with a computer to play CD-ROMs. [COMPUTING] N-COUNT

**CD-RW** **(CR-RWs)** /siː diː ɑːʳ dʌbəljuː/ A **CD-RW** is a CD which is capable of recording sound and images, for example from another CD or from the Internet. **CD-R** is an abbreviation for 'compact disc rewritable'. N-COUNT

**CD writ|er** **(CD writers)** A **CD writer** is a piece of computer equipment that you use for copying data from a computer onto a CD. [COMPUTING] N-COUNT

**cease** /siːs/ **(ceases, ceasing, ceased)** 1 If something **ceases**, it stops happening or existing. [FORMAL] ❑ *At one o'clock the rain had ceased.* ◆◇◇ VERB V 2 If you **cease to** do something, you stop doing it. [FORMAL] ❑ *He never ceases to amaze me... A small number of firms have ceased trading.* VERB V to-inf V -ing 3 If you **cease** something, you stop it happening or working. [FORMAL] ❑ *The Tundra Times, a weekly newspaper in Alaska, ceased publication this week.* VERB = stop V n

**cease|fire** /siːsfaɪəʳ/ **(ceasefires)** also **cease-fire.** A **ceasefire** is an arrangement in which countries or groups of people that are fighting each other agree to stop fighting. ❑ *They have agreed to a ceasefire after three years of conflict.* ◆◇◇ N-COUNT = truce

**cease|less** /siːsləs/ If something, often something unpleasant, is **ceaseless**, it continues for a long time without stopping or changing. [FORMAL] ❑ *There is a ceaseless struggle from noon to night.* ♦ **cease|less|ly** *The characters complain ceaselessly about food queues, prices and corruption.* ADJ = endless ADV: usu ADV with v

**ce|dar** /siːdəʳ/ **(cedars)** A **cedar** is a large evergreen tree with wide branches and small thin N-COUNT leaves called needles. ♦ **Cedar** is the wood of this tree. ❑ *The yacht is built of cedar strip planking.* N-UNCOUNT: oft N n

**cede** /siːd/ **(cedes, ceding, ceded)** If someone in a position of authority **cedes** land or power **to** someone else, they let them have the land or power, often as a result of military or political pressure. [FORMAL] ❑ *Only a short campaign took place in Puerto Rico, but after the war Spain ceded the island to America... The General had promised to cede power by January.* VERB; V n to n; V n

**ce|dil|la** /sɪdɪlə/ **(cedillas)** A **cedilla** is a symbol that is written under the letter 'c' in French, Portuguese, and some other languages to show that you pronounce it like a letter 's' rather than like a letter 'k'. It is written ç. N-COUNT

**cei|lidh** /keɪli/ **(ceilidhs)** A **ceilidh** is an informal entertainment, especially in Scotland or Ireland, at which there is folk music, singing, and dancing. N-COUNT

**ceil|ing** /siːlɪŋ/ **(ceilings)** 1 A **ceiling** is the horizontal surface that forms the top part or roof inside a room. ❑ *The rooms were spacious, with tall windows and high ceilings... The study was lined from floor to ceiling on every wall with bookcases.* N-COUNT 2 A **ceiling on** something such as prices or wages is an official upper limit that cannot be broken. ❑ *...an informal agreement to put a ceiling on salaries... The agreement sets the ceiling of twenty-two-point-five million barrels a day on OPEC production.* N-COUNT: oft N of n = limit

**ce|leb** /sɪleb/ **(celebs)** A **celeb** is the same as a **celebrity**. [mainly JOURNALISM, INFORMAL] N-COUNT

**cel|ebrant** /selɪbrənt/ **(celebrants)** A **celebrant** is a person who performs or takes part in a religious ceremony. [FORMAL] N-COUNT

**cel|ebrate** /selɪbreɪt/ **(celebrates, celebrating, celebrated)** ◆◇◇ 1 If you **celebrate**, you do something enjoyable because of a special occasion or to mark someone's success. ❑ *I was in a mood to celebrate... Tom celebrated his 24th birthday two days ago.* VERB; V; V n 2 If an organization or country **is celebrating** an anniversary, it has existed for that length of time and is doing something special because of it. ❑ *The Society is celebrating its tenth anniversary this year.* VERB; V n 3 When priests **celebrate** Holy Communion or Mass, they officially perform the actions and ceremonies that are involved. ❑ *Pope John Paul celebrated mass today in a city in central Poland.* VERB; V n

**cel|ebrat|ed** /selɪbreɪtɪd/ A **celebrated** person or thing is famous and much admired. ❑ *He was soon one of the most celebrated young painters in England.* ADJ: usu ADJ n = renowned

**cel|ebra|tion** /selɪbreɪʃᵊn/ **(celebrations)** ◆◇◇ 1 A **celebration** is a special enjoyable event that people organize because something pleasant has happened or because it is someone's birthday or anniversary. ❑ *I can tell you, there was a celebration in our house that night. ...his eightieth birthday celebrations.* N-COUNT 2 The **celebration of** something is praise and appreciation which is given to it. ❑ *This was not a memorial service but a celebration of his life.* N-SING: usu N of n

**cel|ebra|tory** /seləbreɪtəri, AM selɪbrətɔːri/ A **celebratory** meal, drink, or other activity takes place to celebrate something such as a birthday, anniversary, or victory. ❑ *That night she, Nicholson and the crew had a celebratory dinner.* ADJ: usu ADJ n

**ce|leb|rity** /sɪlebrɪti/ **(celebrities)** 1 A **celebrity** is someone who is famous, especially in areas of entertainment such as films, music, writing, or sport. ❑ *In 1944, at the age of 30, Hersey suddenly became a celebrity. ...a host of celebrities.* N-COUNT = star 2 If a person or thing achieves **celebrity**, they become famous, especially in areas of entertainment such as films, music, writing, or sport. ❑ *Joanna has finally made it to the first rank of celebrity after 25 years as an actress.* N-UNCOUNT

**cel|ery** /seləri/ **Celery** is a vegetable with long pale green stalks. It is eaten raw in salads. ➔ See picture on page 1712. ❑ *...a stick of celery.* N-UNCOUNT

**ce|les|tial** /sɪlestiəl/ **Celestial** is used to describe things relating to heaven or to the sky. [LITERARY] ❑ *Gravity governs the motions of celestial bodies.* ADJ

**celi|ba|cy** /selɪbəsi/ **Celibacy** is the state of being celibate. N-UNCOUNT

**celi|bate** /selɪbət/ **(celibates)** 1 Someone who is **celibate** does not marry or have sex, because of their religious beliefs. ❑ *The Pope bluntly told the world's priests yesterday to stay celibate.* ADJ ♦ A **celibate** is someone who is celibate. N-COUNT 2 Someone who is **celibate** does not have sex during a particular period of their life. ❑ *I was celibate for two years.* ADJ: usu v-link ADJ

**cell** /sel/ **(cells)** ◆◆◇ 1 A **cell** is the smallest part of an animal or plant that is able to function independently. Every animal or plant is made up of millions of cells. ❑ *Those cells divide and give many other different types of cells. ...blood cells... Soap destroys the cell walls of bacteria.* N-COUNT 2 A **cell** is a small room in which a prisoner is locked. A **cell** is also a small room in which a monk or nun lives. N-COUNT 3 You can refer to a small group of people within a larger organization as a **cell**. N-COUNT: usu n N

**cel|lar** /seləʳ/ **(cellars)** 1 A **cellar** is a room underneath a building, which is often used for storing things in. ❑ *The box of papers had been stored in a cellar at the family home.* N-COUNT 2 A person's or restaurant's **cellar** is the collection of different wines that they have. ❑ *...the restaurant's extensive wine cellar.* N-COUNT: usu sing

**cel|list** /tʃelɪst/ **(cellists)** A **cellist** is someone who plays the cello. N-COUNT

**cell|mate** /selmeɪt/ **(cellmates)** also **cell-mate.** In a prison, someone's **cellmate** is the person they share their cell with. N-COUNT: usu with poss

**cel|lo** /tʃeloʊ/ **(cellos)** A **cello** is a musical instrument with four strings that looks like a large violin. You play the cello with a bow while sitting down and holding it upright between your legs. N-VAR: oft the N

**cel|lo|phane** /seləfeɪn/ **Cellophane** is a thin, transparent material that is used to wrap things. [TRADEMARK] ❑ *She tore off the cellophane, pulled out a cigarette, and lit it. ...a cellophane wrapper.* N-UNCOUNT

**cell|phone** /selfoʊn/ **(cellphones)** also **cell-phone.** A **cellphone** is the same as a **cellular phone**. [mainly AM] N-COUNT = mobile phone

**cel|lu|lar** /seljʊləʳ/ **Cellular** means relating to the cells of animals or plants. ❑ *Many toxic effects can be studied at the cellular level.* ADJ: usu ADJ n

**cel|lu|lar phone** **(cellular phones)** A **cellular phone** or **cellular telephone** is a type of telephone which does not need wires to connect it to a telephone system. [mainly AM] N-COUNT = cellphone, mobile phone

✔ in BRIT, use **mobile phone**

**cel|lu|lite** /seljʊlaɪt/ **Cellulite** is lumpy fat which people may get under their skin, especially on their thighs. N-UNCOUNT

**cel|lu|loid** /seljʊlɔɪd/ You can use **celluloid** to refer to films and the cinema. ❑ *King's works seem to lack something on celluloid.* N-UNCOUNT: oft N n

**cel|lu|lose** /seljʊloʊs/ **Cellulose** is a substance that exists in the cell walls of plants and is used to make paper, plastic, and various fabrics and fibres. N-UNCOUNT

**Celsius** /selsiəs/ **Celsius** is a scale for measuring temperature, in which water freezes at 0 degrees and boils at 100 degrees. It is represented by the symbol °C. ❑ *Highest temperatures 11° Celsius, that's 52° Fahrenheit.* ADJ: n/num ADJ = centigrade ♦ **Celsius** is also a noun. ❑ *The thermometer shows the temperature in Celsius and Fahrenheit.* N-UNCOUNT

**Celt** /kelt, selt/ **(Celts)** If you describe someone as a **Celt**, you mean that they are part of the racial group which comes from Scotland, Wales, Ireland, and some other areas such as Brittany. N-COUNT

**Celt|ic** /keltɪk, sel-/ If you describe something as **Celtic**, you mean that it is connected with the ADJ: usu ADJ n people and the culture of Scotland, Wales, Ireland, and some other areas such as Brittany. ❑ *...important figures in Celtic tradition.*

**ce|ment** /sɪme̱nt/ **(cements, cementing, cemented)** 1 **Cement** is a grey powder which is mixed with sand and water in order to make concrete. ❑ *...a mixture of wet sand and cement.* N-UNCOUNT
2 **Cement** is the same as **concrete**. ❑ *...the hard cold cement floor.* N-UNCOUNT
3 Glue that is made for sticking particular substances together is sometimes called **cement**. ❑ *Stick the pieces on with tile cement.* N-UNCOUNT: usu n N
4 Something that **cements** a relationship or agreement makes it stronger. ❑ *Nothing cements a friendship between countries so much as trade.* VERB V n
5 If things **are cemented** together, they are stuck or fastened together. ❑ *Most artificial joints are cemented into place.* VERB: usu passive *be* V-ed prep/adv

**ce|me̱nt mix|er** **(cement mixers)** A **cement mixer** is a machine with a large revolving container into which builders put cement, sand, and water in order to make concrete. N-COUNT

**cem|etery** /se̱mətri, AM -teri/ **(cemeteries)** A **cemetery** is a place where dead people's bodies or their ashes are buried. N-COUNT = graveyard

**ceno|taph** /se̱nətɑːf, -tæf/ **(cenotaphs)** A **cenotaph** is a structure that is built in honour of soldiers who died in a war. N-COUNT

**cen|sor** /se̱nsəʳ/ **(censors, censoring, censored)** 1 If someone in authority **censors** letters or the media, they officially examine them and cut out any information that is regarded as secret. ❑ *The military-backed government has heavily censored the news.* VERB V n
2 A **censor** is a person who has been officially appointed to examine letters or the media and to cut out any parts that are regarded as secret. ❑ *The report was cleared by the American military censors.* N-COUNT
3 If someone in authority **censors** a book, play, or film, they officially examine it and cut out any parts that are considered to be immoral or inappropriate. ❑ *ITV companies tend to censor bad language in feature films.* VERB V n
4 A **censor** is a person who has been officially appointed to examine plays, films, and books and to cut out any parts that are considered to be immoral. ❑ *...the British Board of Film Censors.* N-COUNT

**cen|so̱ri|ous** /sensɔ̱ːriəs/ If you describe someone as **censorious**, you do not like the way they strongly disapprove of and criticize someone else's behaviour. [FORMAL] ❑ *Despite strong principles he was never censorious.* ADJ [disapproval] = critical

**cen|sor|ship** /se̱nsəʳʃɪp/ **Censorship** is the censoring of books, plays, films, or reports, especially by government officials, because they are considered immoral or secret in some way. ❑ *The government today announced that press censorship was being lifted.* N-UNCOUNT

**cen|sure** /se̱nʃəʳ/ **(censures, censuring, censured)** If you **censure** someone **for** something that they have done, you tell them that you strongly disapprove of it. [FORMAL] ❑ *The ethics committee may take a decision to admonish him or to censure him... I would not presume to censure Osborne for hating his mother.* ♦ **Censure** is also a noun. ❑ *It is a controversial policy which has attracted international censure.* VERB = criticize V n V n *for* -ing/n N-UNCOUNT

**cen|sus** /se̱nsəs/ **(censuses)** A **census** is an official survey of the population of a country that is carried out in order to find out how many people live there and to obtain details of such things as people's ages and jobs. N-COUNT

**cent** /se̱nt/ **(cents)** A **cent** is a small unit of money worth one hundredth of some currencies, for example the dollar and the euro. ❑ *A cup of rice which cost thirty cents a few weeks ago is now being sold for up to one dollar... We haven't got a cent.* N-COUNT: usu num N
→ See also **per cent**.

**cen|taur** /se̱ntɔːʳ/ **(centaurs)** In classical mythology, a **centaur** is a creature with the head, arms, and body of a man, and the body and legs of a horse. N-COUNT

**cen|te|nar|ian** /se̱ntɪne̱əriən/ **(centenarians)** A **centenarian** is someone who is a hundred years old or older. ❑ *Japan has more than 4,000 centenarians.* N-COUNT

**cen|te|nary** /sentiːnəri, AM -te̱n-/ **(centenaries)** The **centenary of** an event such as someone's birth is the 100th anniversary of that event. [mainly BRIT] ❑ *...the centenary of the death of the Dutch painter, Vincent Van Gogh.* N-COUNT: oft N *of* n

in AM, use **centennial**

**cen|ten|nial** /sente̱niəl/ A **centennial** is the same as a **centenary**. [mainly AM; also BRIT, FORMAL] ❑ *The centennial Olympics will be in Atlanta, Georgia.* N-SING: oft N n

**cen|ter** /se̱ntəʳ/ → see **centre**.

**cen|ti|grade** /se̱ntɪgreɪd/ **Centigrade** is a scale for measuring temperature, in which water freezes at 0 degrees and boils at 100 degrees. It is represented by the symbol °C. ❑ *...daytime temperatures of up to forty degrees centigrade.* ♦ **Centigrade** is also a noun. ❑ *The number at the bottom is the recommended water temperature in Centigrade.* ADJ: usu n/num ADJ = Celsius N-UNCOUNT

**cen|ti|li|tre** /se̱ntɪliːtəʳ/ **(centilitres)**

in AM, use **centiliter**

A **centilitre** is a unit of volume in the metric system equal to ten millilitres or one-hundredth of a litre. N-COUNT

**cen|ti|me|tre** /se̱ntɪmiːtəʳ/ **(centimetres)**

in AM, use **centimeter**

A **centimetre** is a unit of length in the metric system equal to ten millimetres or one-hundredth of a metre. ❑ *...a tiny fossil plant, only a few centimetres high.* N-COUNT

**cen|ti|pede** /se̱ntɪpiːd/ **(centipedes)** A **centipede** is a long, thin creature with a lot of legs. N-COUNT

**cen|tral** /se̱ntrəl/ 1 Something that is **central** is in the middle of a place or area. ❑ *...Central America's Caribbean coast. ...a rich woman living in central London.* ♦ **cen|tral|ly** *The main cabin has its full-sized double bed centrally placed with plenty of room around it.* ♦♦♦ ADJ ADV: ADV -ed, ADV after v
2 A place that is **central** is easy to reach because it is in the centre of a city, town, or particular area. ❑ *...a central location in the capital.* ♦ **cen|tral|ly** *...this centrally located hotel, situated on the banks of the Marne Canal.* ADJ ADV: ADV -ed, ADV after v
3 A **central** group or organization makes all the important decisions that are followed throughout a larger organization or a country. ❑ *There is a lack of trust towards the central government in Rome. ...the central committee of the Cuban communist party.* ♦ **cen|tral|ly** *This is a centrally planned economy.* ADJ: ADJ n ADV: ADV -ed, ADV after v
4 The **central** person or thing in a particular situation is the most important one. ❑ *Black dance music has been central to mainstream pop since the early '60s. ...a central part of their culture.* ♦ **cen|tral|ity** *The centrality of the German economy to the welfare of Europe must be recognised.* ♦ **cen|tral|ly** *In her memoirs Naomi is quick to acknowledge that her grandmother was centrally important in her venture as a writer.* ADJ: oft ADJ *to* n N-UNCOUNT: usu N *of* n ADV: ADV with cl/group, ADV after v

**ce̱n|tral hea̱t|ing** **Central heating** is a heating system for buildings. Air or water is heated in one place and travels round a building through pipes and radiators. N-UNCOUNT

**cen|tral|ise** /se̱ntrəlaɪz/ → see **centralize**.

**cen|tral|ism** /se̱ntrəlɪzəm/ **Centralism** is a way of governing a country, or organizing something such as industry, education, or politics, which involves having one central group of people who give instructions to everyone else. N-UNCOUNT

**cen|tral|ist** /se̱ntrəlɪst/ **(centralists)** **Centralist** organizations govern a country or organize things using one central group of people who control and instruct everyone else. ❑ *...a strong centralist state.* ♦ A **centralist** is someone with centralist views. ADJ: usu ADJ n N-COUNT

**cen|tral|ize** /se̱ntrəlaɪz/ **(centralizes, centralizing, centralized)**

in BRIT, also use **centralise**

To **centralize** a country, state, or organization means to create a system in which one central group of people gives instructions to regional groups. ❑ *In the mass production era multinational firms tended to centralize their operations... The economy of the times made it difficult to support centralized rule.* ♦ **cen|trali|za|tion** /sentrəlaɪzeɪʃᵊn/ *Nowhere in Britain has bureaucratic centralization proceeded with more pace than in Scotland.* VERB; V n; V-ed; N-UNCOUNT

**cen|tral|ly heat|ed** A **centrally heated** building or room has central heating. ❑ *Centrally heated offices tend to be stuffy.* ADJ: usu ADJ n

**cen|tral nerv|ous sys|tem** (**central nervous systems**) Your **central nervous system** is the part of your nervous system that consists of the brain and spinal cord. N-COUNT

**cen|tral res|er|va|tion** (**central reservations**) The **central reservation** is the strip of ground, often covered with grass, that separates the two sides of a major road. [BRIT] N-COUNT

> in AM, use **median**, **median strip**

**cen|tre** /sentəʳ/ (**centres, centring, centred**) ♦♦♦

> in AM, use **center**

[1] A **centre** is a building where people have meetings, take part in a particular activity, or get help of some kind. ❑ *We went to a party at the leisure centre. ...the National Exhibition Centre.* N-COUNT: usu with supp, oft in names after n [2] If an area or town is a **centre** for an industry or activity, that industry or activity is very important there. ❑ *London is also the major international insurance centre.* N-COUNT: with supp [3] The **centre** of something is the middle of it. ❑ *A large wooden table dominates the centre of the room... Bake until light golden and crisp around the edges and slightly soft in the centre.* N-COUNT: usu sing [4] The **centre** of a town or city is the part where there are the most shops and businesses and where a lot of people come from other areas to work or shop. ❑ *...the city centre.* N-COUNT: usu sing [5] If something or someone is at the **centre of** a situation, they are the most important thing or person involved. ❑ *...the man at the centre of the controversy... At the centre of the inquiry has been concern for the pensioners involved.* N-COUNT: usu sing, usu N *of* n [6] If someone or something is the **centre of** attention or interest, people are giving them a lot of attention. ❑ *The rest of the cast was used to her being the centre of attention... The centre of attraction was Pierre Auguste Renoir's oil painting.* N-COUNT: usu sing, N *of* n = focus [7] In politics, **the centre** refers to groups and their beliefs, when they are considered to be neither left-wing nor right-wing. ❑ *The Democrats have become a party of the centre. ...the centre parties.* N-SING: *the* N, oft N n [8] If something **centres** or **is centred on** a particular thing or person, that thing or person is the main subject of attention. ❑ *...a plan which centred on academic achievement and motivation... When working with patients, my efforts are centred on helping them to overcome illness.* ♦ **-centred** *...a child-centred approach to teaching.* VERB; V *on/around* n; *be* V-ed *on/around* n; COMB in ADJ [9] If an industry or event **is centred** in a place, or if it **centres** there, it takes place to the greatest extent there. ❑ *The fighting has been centred around the town of Vucovar... The disturbances have centred round the two main university areas... Between 100 and 150 travellers' vehicles were scattered around the county, with the largest gathering centred on Ampfield.* VERB; *be* V-ed prep; V prep; V-ed [10] → See also **community centre**, **detention centre**, **garden centre**, **health centre**, **job centre**, **left-of-centre**, **nerve centre**, **reception centre**, **remand centre**, **right-of-centre**, **shopping centre**.

**cen|tred** /sentəʳd/

> in AM, use **centered**

If an industry or event is **centred** in a place, it takes place to the greatest extent there. ❑ *The tremor was centred in the Gulf of Sirte.* ADJ: v-link ADJ prep

**-centred** /-sentəʳd/

> in AM, use **-centered**

**-centred** can be added to adjectives and nouns to indicate what kind of a centre something has. ❑ *...lemon-centered white chocolates.* → See also **centre**, **self-centred**. COMB in ADJ

**centre|fold** /sentəʳfoʊld/ (**centrefolds**)

> in AM, use **centerfold**

A **centrefold** is a picture that covers the two central pages of a magazine, especially a photograph of a naked or partly naked woman. N-COUNT

**centre-forward** (**centre-forwards**) A **centre-forward** in a team sport such as football or hockey is the player or position in the middle of the front row of attacking players. N-COUNT

**cen|tre of grav|ity** (**centres of gravity**) The **centre of gravity** of an object is a point in it. If this point is above the base of the object, it stays stable, rather than falling over. N-COUNT

**centre|piece** /sentəʳpiːs/ (**centrepieces**)

> in AM, use **centerpiece**

[1] The **centrepiece of** something is the best or most interesting part of it. ❑ *The centrepiece of the plan is the idea of regular referendums, initiated by voters.* N-COUNT: usu N *of* n [2] A **centrepiece** is an ornament which you put in the middle of something, especially a dinner table. N-COUNT

**cen|tre stage**

> The spellings **centre-stage** in British English, and **center stage** in American English are also used.

If something or someone takes **centre stage**, they become very important or noticeable. ❑ *Nuclear proliferation has returned to centre stage in international affairs.* N-UNCOUNT: also *the* N

**cen|trifu|gal force** /sentrɪfjʊgᵊl fɔːʳs/ In physics, **centrifugal force** is the force that makes objects move outwards when they are spinning around something or travelling in a curve. ❑ *The juice is extracted by centrifugal force.* N-UNCOUNT

**cen|tri|fuge** /sentrɪfjuːdʒ/ (**centrifuges**) A **centrifuge** is a machine that spins mixtures of different substances around very quickly so that they separate by centrifugal force. N-COUNT

**cen|trist** /sentrɪst/ (**centrists**) **Centrist** policies and parties are moderate rather than extreme. ❑ *He had left the movement because it had abandoned its centrist policies.* ♦ A **centrist** is someone with centrist views. ADJ: usu ADJ n; N-COUNT

**cen|tu|ri|on** /sentjʊəriən, AM -tʊr-/ (**centurions**) A **centurion** was an officer in the Roman army. N-COUNT

**cen|tu|ry** /sentʃəri/ (**centuries**) ♦♦♦ [1] A **century** is a period of a hundred years that is used when stating a date. For example, the 19th century was the period from 1801 to 1900. ❑ *...celebrated figures of the late eighteenth century. ...a 17th-century merchant's house.* N-COUNT: usu ord N [2] A **century** is any period of a hundred years. ❑ *The drought there is the worst in a century.* N-COUNT [3] In cricket, a **century** is a score of one hundred runs or more by one batsman. N-COUNT

**CEO** /siː iː oʊ/ (**CEOs**) **CEO** is an abbreviation for **chief executive officer**. N-COUNT

**ce|ram|ic** /sɪræmɪk/ (**ceramics**) [1] **Ceramic** is clay that has been heated to a very high temperature so that it becomes hard. ❑ *...ceramic tiles. ...items made from hand-painted ceramic.* N-MASS: usu N n [2] **Ceramics** are ceramic ornaments or objects. ❑ *...a collection of Chinese ceramics.* N-COUNT: usu pl [3] **Ceramics** is the art of making artistic objects out of clay. N-UNCOUNT

**ce|real** /sɪəriəl/ (**cereals**) [1] **Cereal** or **breakfast cereal** is a food made from grain. It is mixed with milk and eaten for breakfast. ❑ *I have a bowl of cereal every morning.* N-MASS [2] **Cereals** are plants such as wheat, corn, or rice that produce grain. ❑ *...the rich cereal-growing districts of the Paris Basin.* N-COUNT

**cere|bral** /serɪbrəl, AM səriːbrəl/ [1] If you describe someone or something as **cerebral**, you mean that they are intellectual rather than emotional. [FORMAL] ❑ *Washington struck me as a precarious place from which to publish such a cerebral news-* ADJ = intellectual paper. [2] **Cerebral** means relating to the brain. [MEDICAL] ❑ *...a cerebral haemorrhage.* ADJ: ADJ n

**cere|bral pal|sy** **Cerebral palsy** is a condition caused by damage to a baby's brain before or during its birth, which makes its limbs and muscles permanently weak. N-UNCOUNT

**cer|emo|nial** /serɪmoʊniəl/ [1] Something that is **ceremonial** relates to a ceremony or is used in a ceremony. ❑ *He represented the nation on ceremonial occasions... Feathers of various kinds are used by Native Americans for ceremonial purposes.* ADJ: ADJ n
[2] A position, function, or event that is **ceremonial** is considered to be representative of an institution, but has very little authority or influence. ❑ *Up to now the post of president has been largely ceremonial.* ADJ

**cer|emo|ni|ous|ly** /serɪmoʊniəsli/ If someone does something **ceremoniously**, they do it in an extremely formal way. [WRITTEN] ❑ *They ceremoniously cut a piece of ribbon, declaring the exhibition open... He thanked her ceremoniously.* ADV: ADV with v

**cer|emo|ny** /serɪməni, AM -moʊni/ **(ceremonies)** ◆◇◇ [1] A **ceremony** is a formal event such as a wedding. ❑ *...his grandmother's funeral, a private ceremony attended only by the family... Today's award ceremony took place at the British Embassy in Tokyo.* N-COUNT
[2] **Ceremony** consists of the special things that are said and done on very formal occasions. ❑ *The Republic was proclaimed in public with great ceremony.* N-UNCOUNT: usu *with* N
[3] If you do something **without ceremony**, you do it quickly and in a casual way. ❑ *'Is Hilton here?' she asked without ceremony.* [4] → See also **master of ceremonies**. N-UNCOUNT: *without* N

**ce|rise** /səriːs/ Something that is **cerise** is a bright pinkish red. COLOUR

**cert** /sɜːʳt/ **(certs)** If you say that someone or something is a **cert**, you mean that you are certain they will succeed. [BRIT, INFORMAL] ❑ *There's no such things as a cert in horse racing... Anthony was a dead cert for promotion.* N-COUNT

**cert.** **(certs)** **Cert.** is a written abbreviation for **certificate**.

| **certain** |
|---|
| ① BEING SURE |
| ② REFERRING AND INDICATING AMOUNT |

**① cer|tain** /sɜːʳtᵊn/ [1] If you are **certain** about something, you firmly believe it is true and have no doubt about it. If you are not **certain** about something, you do not have definite knowledge about it. ❑ *She's absolutely certain she's going to make it in the world... We are not certain whether the appendix had already burst or not... It wasn't a balloon – I'm certain of that.* ◆◇◇ ADJ: v-link ADJ, oft ADJ that/wh, ADJ *of/about* n = sure
[2] If you say that something is **certain to** happen, you mean that it will definitely happen. ❑ *However, the scheme is certain to meet opposition from fishermen's leaders... Brazil need to beat Uruguay to be certain of a place in the finals... The Prime Minister is heading for certain defeat if he forces a vote... Victory looked certain.* ADJ: oft ADJ to-inf, *it* v-link ADJ that/wh, ADJ *of* n/-ing
[3] If you say that something is **certain**, you firmly believe that it is true, or have definite knowledge about it. ❑ *One thing is certain, both have the utmost respect for each other... It is certain that Rodney arrived the previous day.* ADJ: v-link ADJ, oft *it* v-link ADJ that/wh
PHRASES [4] If you know something **for certain**, you have no doubt at all about it. ❑ *Hill had to find out for certain.* PHRASE: PHR with cl (not first in cl)
[5] If you **make certain that** something is the way you want or expect it to be, you take action to ensure that it is. ❑ *Firstly, they must make certain that their pension needs are adequately catered for.* PHRASE: V inflects = make sure

**② cer|tain** /sɜːʳtᵊn/ [1] You use **certain** to indicate that you are referring to one particular thing, person, or group, although you are not saying exactly which it is. ❑ *There will be certain people who'll say 'I told you so!'... Leaflets have been air dropped telling people to leave certain areas.* ◆◆◇ ADJ: det ADJ, ADJ n
[2] When you refer to **certain of** a group of people or things, you are referring to some particular members of that group. [FORMAL] ❑ *They'll have to give up completely on certain of their studies.* QUANT: QUANT *of* def-pl-n = some
[3] You can use **a certain** before the name of a person in order to indicate that you do not know the person or anything else about them. ❑ *She managed to arrange for them to be hidden in the house of a certain Father Boduen.* ADJ: *a* ADJ n-proper
[4] You use **a certain** to indicate that something such as a quality or condition exists, and often to suggest that it is not great in amount or degree. ❑ *That was the very reason why he felt a certain bitterness.* ADJ: *a* ADJ sing-n/n-uncount

**cer|tain|ly** /sɜːʳtᵊnli/ [1] You use **certainly** to emphasize what you are saying when you are making a statement. ❑ *The bombs are almost certainly part of a much bigger conspiracy... Today's inflation figure is certainly too high... Certainly, pets can help children develop friendship skills.* ◆◆◇ ADV: ADV with cl/group [emphasis] = undoubtedly
[2] You use **certainly** when you are agreeing with what someone has said. ❑ *'In any case you remained friends.' — 'Certainly.'... 'You keep out of their way don't you?' — 'I certainly do.'* ADV: ADV as reply
[3] You say **certainly not** when you want to say 'no' in a strong way. ❑ *'Perhaps it would be better if I withdrew altogether.' — 'Certainly not!'* ADV as reply [emphasis]

**cer|tain|ty** /sɜːʳtᵊnti/ **(certainties)** [1] **Certainty** is the state of being definite or of having no doubts at all about something. ❑ *I have told them with absolute certainty there'll be no change of policy... There is too little certainty about the present state of the German economy.* N-UNCOUNT: oft *with* N, N that
[2] **Certainty** is the fact that something is certain to happen. ❑ *A general election became a certainty three weeks ago. ...the certainty of more violence and bloodshed.* N-UNCOUNT: also *a* N = inevitability
[3] **Certainties** are things that nobody has any doubts about. ❑ *There are no certainties in modern Europe.* N-COUNT: usu pl

**cer|ti|fi|able** /sɜːʳtɪfaɪəbᵊl/ If you describe someone as **certifiable**, you think that their behaviour is extremely unreasonable or foolish. [mainly BRIT, INFORMAL] ❑ *...if he can convince the committee that he is not certifiable.* ADJ [disapproval] = crazy

**cer|tifi|cate** /səʳtɪfɪkət/ **(certificates)** [1] A **certificate** is an official document stating that particular facts are true. ❑ *...birth certificates. ...share certificates.* N-COUNT: usu with supp
[2] A **certificate** is an official document that you receive when you have completed a course of study or training. The qualification that you receive is sometimes also called a **certificate**. ❑ *To the right of the fireplace are various framed certificates. ...the Post-Graduate Certificate of Education.* N-COUNT: with supp

**cer|tifi|cat|ed** /səʳtɪfɪkeɪtɪd/ A **certificated** person has been awarded a certificate to prove that they have achieved a certain level or standard. [mainly BRIT] ❑ *...a genuine certificated physician.* ADJ: usu ADJ n = certified

**cer|ti|fy** /sɜːʳtɪfaɪ/ **(certifies, certifying, certified)** [1] If someone in an official position **certifies** something, they officially state that it is true. ❑ *...if the president certified that the project would receive at least $650m from overseas sources... The National Election Council is supposed to certify the results of the election... It has been certified as genuine... Mrs Simpson was certified dead later that day.* VERB; V that; V n; *be* V-ed *as* adj; *be* V-ed adj
♦ **cer|ti|fi|ca|tion** /səʳtɪfɪkeɪʃᵊn/ **(certifications)** *An employer can demand written certification that the relative is really ill.* N-VAR
[2] If someone **is certified as** a particular kind of worker, they are given a certificate stating that they have successfully completed a course of training in their profession. ❑ *They wanted to get certified as divers. ...a certified accountant.* ♦ **cer|ti|fi|ca|tion** *Pupils would be offered on-the-job training leading to the certification of their skill in a particular field.* VERB: usu passive; *get* V-ed *as* n; V-ed; N-UNCOUNT: oft N *of* n

**cer|ti|tude** /sɜːʳtɪtjuːd, AM -tuːd/ **(certitudes)** **Certitude** is the same as **certainty**. [FORMAL] ❑ *We have this definite certitude that Cicippio will be freed.* N-UNCOUNT: also N in pl, oft N that

**cer|vi|cal** /sɜːʳvɪkᵊl, səʳvaɪkᵊl/ [1] **Cervical** means relating to the cervix. [MEDICAL] ❑ *...the number of women dying from cervical cancer.* ADJ: ADJ n

2 **Cervical** means relating to the neck. [MEDICAL] ❑ *...the discs in the upper cervical spine.* ADJ: ADJ n

**cer|vix** /sɜːʳvɪks/ **(cervixes** or **cervices** /səʳvaɪsiːz/**)** The **cervix** is the entrance to the womb. [MEDICAL] N-COUNT

**ces|sa|tion** /seseɪʃᵊn/ The **cessation of** something is the stopping of it. [FORMAL] ❑ *He would not agree to a cessation of hostilities.* N-UNCOUNT: also *a* N, usu with supp, oft N *of* n

**cess|pit** /sespɪt/ **(cesspits)** A **cesspit** is a hole or tank in the ground into which waste water and sewage flow. N-COUNT = *cesspool*

**cess|pool** /sespuːl/ **(cesspools)** A **cesspool** is the same as a **cesspit**. N-COUNT

**ce|ta|cean** /sɪteɪʃᵊn/ **(cetaceans)** **Cetaceans** are animals such as whales, dolphins, and porpoises. N-COUNT: usu pl

**cet|era** → see **etcetera**.

**cf.** **cf.** is used in writing to introduce something that should be considered in connection with the subject you are discussing. ❑ *For the more salient remarks on the matter, cf. Isis Unveiled, Vol. I.* = *compare*

**CFC** /siː ef siː/ **(CFCs)** **CFCs** are gases that are used in things such as aerosols and refrigerators and can cause damage to the ozone layer. **CFC** is an abbreviation for 'chlorofluorocarbon'. N-COUNT

**CFS** /siː ef es/ **CFS** is an abbreviation for **chronic fatigue syndrome**. N-UNCOUNT = *ME*

**ch.** **(chs)** **Ch.** is a written abbreviation for **chapter**. N-VAR num

**cha-cha** /tʃɑː tʃɑː/ **(cha-chas)** A **cha-cha** is a Latin American dance with small fast steps. N-COUNT: oft *the* N

**chafe** /tʃeɪf/ **(chafes, chafing, chafed)** 1 If your skin **chafes** or **is chafed** by something, it becomes sore as a result of something rubbing against it. ❑ *My shorts were chafing my thighs... His wrists began to chafe against the cloth strips binding them... The messenger bent and scratched at his knee where the strapping chafed.* 2 If you **chafe at** something such as a restriction, you feel annoyed about it. [FORMAL] ❑ *He had chafed at having to take orders from another... He was chafing under the company's new ownership.* VERB; V n; V *against* n; V; VERB: no passive; V *at/under/against* n/-ing

**chaff** /tʃɑːf, tʃæf/ 1 **Chaff** is the outer part of grain such as wheat. It is removed before the grain is used as food. 2 If you **separate the wheat from the chaff** or **sort the wheat from the chaff**, you decide which people or things in a group are good or important and which are not. ❑ *It isn't always easy to separate the wheat from the chaff.* N-UNCOUNT; PHRASE: V inflects

**chaf|finch** /tʃæfɪntʃ/ **(chaffinches)** A **chaffinch** is a small European bird. Male chaffinches have reddish-brown fronts and grey heads. N-COUNT

**cha|grin** /ʃægrɪn, AM ʃəgrɪn/ **Chagrin** is a feeling of disappointment, upset, or annoyance, perhaps because of your own failure. [FORMAL, WRITTEN] ❑ *One of the first things we did when we moved in, to the chagrin of the architect, was to replace the leaded windows.* N-UNCOUNT: usu with poss

**cha|grined** /ʃægrɪnd, AM ʃəgrɪnd/ If you are **chagrined by** something, it disappoints, upsets, or annoys you, perhaps because of your own failure. [WRITTEN] ❑ *The chair of the committee did not appear chagrined by the compromises and delays.* ADJ: usu v-link ADJ

**chain** /tʃeɪn/ **(chains, chaining, chained)** ◆◇◇ 1 A **chain** consists of metal rings connected together in a line. → See picture on page 1708. ❑ *His open shirt revealed a fat gold chain... The dogs were leaping and growling at the full stretch of their chains.* 2 If prisoners are **in chains**, they have thick rings of metal round their wrists or ankles to prevent them from escaping. ❑ *He'd spent four and a half years in windowless cells, much of the time in chains.* 3 If a person or thing **is chained to** something, they are fastened to it with a chain. ❑ *The dog was chained to the leg of the one solid garden seat... She chained her bike to the railings... We were sitting together in our cell, chained to the wall.* ♦ **Chain up** means the same as **chain**. ❑ *I'll lock the doors and chain you up... All the rowing boats were chained up.* 4 A **chain of** things is a group of them existing or arranged in a line. ❑ *...a chain of islands known as the Windward Islands... Students tried to form a human chain around the parliament.* 5 A **chain of** shops, hotels, or other businesses is a number of them owned by the same person or company. ❑ *...a large supermarket chain. ...Italy's leading chain of cinemas.* 6 A **chain of** events is a series of them happening one after another. ❑ *...the bizarre chain of events that led to his departure in January 1938.* 7 → See also **food chain**. N-COUNT; N-PLURAL: *in* N; VERB; *be* V-ed *to* n; V n *to* n; V-ed; PHRASAL VERB; V n P; V-ed P; N-COUNT: N *of* n; N-COUNT: with supp; N-SING: N *of* n = *series*

♦ **chain up** → see **chain 3**.

**chained** /tʃeɪnd/ If you say that someone is **chained to** a person or a situation, you are emphasizing that there are reasons why they cannot leave that person or situation, even though you think they might like to. ❑ *At work, he was chained to a system of boring meetings.* ADJ: v-link ADJ *to* n

**chain gang** **(chain gangs)** In the United States, a **chain gang** is a group of prisoners who are chained together to do work outside their prison. Chain gangs existed especially in former times. N-COUNT

**chain let|ter** **(chain letters)** A **chain letter** is a letter, often with a promise of money, that is sent to several people who send copies on to several more people. Chain letters are illegal in some countries. N-COUNT

**chain mail** **Chain mail** is a kind of armour made from small metal rings joined together so that they look like cloth. N-UNCOUNT

**chain re|ac|tion** **(chain reactions)** 1 A **chain reaction** is a series of chemical changes, each of which causes the next. 2 A **chain reaction** is a series of events, each of which causes the next. ❑ *The powder immediately ignited and set off a chain reaction of explosions.* N-COUNT; N-COUNT

**chain saw** **(chain saws)** also **chainsaw.** A **chain saw** is a big saw with teeth fixed in a chain that is driven round by a motor. N-COUNT

**chain-smoke** **(chain-smokes, chain-smoking, chain-smoked)** Someone who **chain-smokes** smokes cigarettes or cigars continuously. ❑ *Melissa had chain-smoked all evening while she waited for a phone call from Tom.* VERB; V; Also V n

**chain-smoker** **(chain-smokers)** also **chain smoker.** A **chain-smoker** is a person who chain-smokes. N-COUNT

**chain store** **(chain stores)** also **chain-store.** A **chain store** is one of several similar shops that are owned by the same person or company, especially one that sells a variety of things. N-COUNT

**chair** /tʃeəʳ/ **(chairs, chairing, chaired)** ◆◆◇ 1 A **chair** is a piece of furniture for one person to sit on. Chairs have a back and four legs. ❑ *He rose from his chair and walked to the window.* 2 At a university, a **chair** is the post of professor. ❑ *He has been appointed to the chair of sociology at Southampton University.* 3 The person who is the **chair of** a committee or meeting is the person in charge of it. ❑ *She is the chair of the Defense Advisory Committee on Women in the Military.* 4 If you **chair** a meeting or a committee, you are the person in charge of it. ❑ *He was about to chair a meeting in Venice of EU foreign ministers.* 5 **The chair** is the same as the **electric chair**. [AM] N-COUNT; N-COUNT: usu sing, oft N *of/in* n; N-COUNT: usu sing, oft N *of* n = *chairperson*; VERB; V n; N-SING: *the* N

**chair lift** **(chair lifts)** also **chairlift.** A **chair lift** is a line of chairs that hang from a moving cable and carry people up and down a mountain or ski slope. N-COUNT

**chair|man** /tʃeəʳmən/ **(chairmen)** ◆◆◇ 1 The **chairman** of a committee, organization, or company is the head of it. ❑ *Glyn Ford is chairman of the Committee which produced the report... I had done business with the company's chairman.* 2 The **chairman** of a meeting or debate is the person in charge, who decides when each person is allowed to speak. ❑ *The chairman declared the meeting open... I hear you, Mr. Chairman.* N-COUNT: oft with poss; N-COUNT; N-VOC: *Mr/Madam* N

**chair|man|ship** /tʃeəʳmənʃɪp/ **(chairmanships)** The **chairmanship** of a committee or organization is the fact of being its chairperson. Someone's **chairmanship** can also mean the period during which they are chairperson. ❑ *The Government has set up a committee under the chairmanship of Professor Roy Goode.* N-VAR: usu with supp

**chair|person** /tʃeəʳpɜːʳsən/ **(chairpersons)** The **chairperson** of a meeting, committee, or organization is the person in charge of it. ❑ *She's the chairperson of the safety committee.* N-COUNT

**chair|woman** /tʃeəʳwʊmən/ **(chairwomen)** The **chairwoman** of a meeting, committee, or organization is the woman in charge of it. ❑ *Primakov was in Japan meeting with the chairwoman of the Socialist Party there.* N-COUNT

**chaise longue** /ʃeɪz lɒŋ/ **(chaises longues)**

> ✓ The singular and the plural are both pronounced in the same way.

A **chaise longue** is a kind of sofa with only one arm and usually a back along half its length. N-COUNT

**chaise lounge** /ʃeɪz laʊndʒ/ **(chaise lounges)** A **chaise lounge** is the same as a **chaise longue**. [AM] N-COUNT

**cha|let** /ʃæleɪ, AM ʃæleɪ/ **(chalets)** A **chalet** is a small wooden house, especially in a mountain area or a holiday camp. N-COUNT

**chal|ice** /tʃælɪs/ **(chalices)** 1 A **chalice** is a large gold or silver cup with a stem. Chalices are used to hold wine in the Christian service of Holy Communion. N-COUNT 2 If you refer to a job or an opportunity as a **poisoned chalice**, you mean that it seems to be very attractive but you believe it will lead to failure. ❑ *He does not regard his new job as a poisoned chalice.* PHRASE: usu v-link PHR, PHR after v

**chalk** /tʃɔːk/ **(chalks, chalking, chalked)** 1 **Chalk** is a type of soft white rock. You can use small pieces of it for writing or drawing with. ❑ *...the highest chalk cliffs in Britain... Her skin was chalk white and dry-looking.* N-UNCOUNT: oft N n 2 **Chalk** is small sticks of chalk, or a substance similar to chalk, used for writing or drawing with. ❑ *...somebody writing with a piece of chalk. ...drawing a small picture with coloured chalks.* N-UNCOUNT: also N in pl 3 If you **chalk** something, you draw or write it using a piece of chalk. ❑ *He chalked the message on the blackboard... There was a blackboard with seven names chalked on it.* VERB V n V-ed 4 If you say that two people or things are like **chalk and cheese**, you are emphasizing that they are completely different from each other. [BRIT] ❑ *The two places, he insists, are as different as chalk and cheese... We are very aware of our differences, we accept that we are chalk and cheese.* PHRASE [emphasis]

♦ **chalk up** If you **chalk up** a success, a victory, or a number of points in a game, you achieve it. ❑ *Andy Wilkinson chalked up his first win of the season.* PHRASAL VERB = notch up V P n (not pron)

**chalk|board** /tʃɔːkbɔːʳd/ **(chalkboards)** A **chalkboard** is a dark-coloured board that you can write on with chalk. Chalkboards are often used by teachers in the classroom. [mainly AM] N-COUNT

> ✓ in BRIT, use **blackboard**

**chalky** /tʃɔːki/ 1 Something that is **chalky** contains chalk or is covered with chalk. ❑ *The chalky soil around Saumur produces the famous Anjou wines.* ADJ 2 Something that is **chalky** is a pale dull colour or has a powdery texture. ❑ *Her face became a chalky white.* ADJ

**chal|lenge** /tʃælɪndʒ/ **(challenges, challenging, challenged)** ◆◆◇ 1 A **challenge** is something new and difficult which requires great effort and determination. ❑ *I like a big challenge and they don't come much bigger than this... The new government's first challenge is the economy.* N-VAR 2 If someone **rises to the challenge**, they act in response to a difficult situation which is new to them and are successful. ❑ *The new Germany must rise to the challenge of its enhanced responsibilities.* PHRASE: V inflects 3 A **challenge to** something is a questioning of its truth or value. A **challenge to** someone is a questioning of their authority. ❑ *The demonstrators have now made a direct challenge to the authority of the government.* N-VAR: oft N to n 4 If you **challenge** ideas or people, you question their truth, value, or authority. ❑ *Democratic leaders have challenged the president to sign the bill... The move was immediately challenged by two of the republics... I challenged him on the hypocrisy of his political attitudes.* VERB V n to-inf be V-ed V n on/about n 5 If you **challenge** someone, you invite them to fight or compete with you in some way. ❑ *A mum slashed a neighbour's car tyre and challenged her to a fight after their daughters fell out... He left a note at the scene of the crime, challenging detectives to catch him... We challenged a team who called themselves 'College Athletes'.* VERB V n to n V n to-inf V n

♦ **Challenge** is also a noun. ❑ *A third presidential candidate emerged to mount a serious challenge and throw the campaign wide open.* N-COUNT 6 → See also **challenged**, **challenging**.

**chal|lenged** /tʃælɪndʒd/ If you say that someone is **challenged** in a particular way, you mean that they have a disability in that area. **Challenged** is often combined with inappropriate words for humorous effect. ❑ *...terms like 'vertically-challenged' – meaning short... She ran off with an intellectually challenged ski instructor.* ADJ: adv ADJ

**chal|leng|er** /tʃælɪndʒəʳ/ **(challengers)** A **challenger** is someone who competes with you for a position or title that you already have, for example being a sports champion or a political leader. ❑ *Draskovic has emerged as by far the strongest challenger to the leader of the Serbian government.* N-COUNT: oft N to/for n

**chal|leng|ing** /tʃælɪndʒɪŋ/ 1 A **challenging** task or job requires great effort and determination. ❑ *Mike found a challenging job as a computer programmer... I'm ready to do all those things which are more challenging.* ADJ = demanding 2 If you do something in a **challenging** way, you seem to be inviting people to argue with you or compete against you in some way. ❑ *Mona gave him a challenging look.* ADJ: usu ADJ n = defiant

**cham|ber** /tʃeɪmbəʳ/ **(chambers)** ◆◇◇ 1 A **chamber** is a large room, especially one that is used for formal meetings. ❑ *We are going to make sure we are in the council chamber every time he speaks.* N-COUNT: usu supp N 2 You can refer to a country's parliament or to one section of it as a **chamber**. ❑ *More than 80 parties are contesting seats in the two-chamber parliament... Signor Amato's government has only a 16-seat majority in the Chamber of Deputies.* N-COUNT = house 3 A **chamber** is a room designed and equipped for a particular purpose. ❑ *For many, the dentist's surgery remains a torture chamber.* → See also **gas chamber**. N-COUNT: with supp

**cham|ber|lain** /tʃeɪmbəʳlɪn/ **(chamberlains)** A **chamberlain** is the person who is in charge of the household affairs of a king, queen, or person of high social rank. N-COUNT

**chamber|maid** /tʃeɪmbəʳmeɪd/ **(chambermaids)** A **chambermaid** is a woman who cleans and tidies the bedrooms in a hotel. N-COUNT

**cham|ber mu|sic** **Chamber music** is classical music written for a small number of instruments. N-UNCOUNT

**cham|ber of com|merce** **(chambers of commerce)** A **chamber of commerce** is an organization of businessmen that promotes local commercial interests. [BUSINESS] N-COUNT

**cham|ber or|ches|tra** **(chamber orchestras)** A **chamber orchestra** is a small orchestra which plays classical music. N-COUNT

**cham|ber pot** **(chamber pots)** A **chamber pot** is a round container shaped like a very large cup. Chamber pots used to be kept in bedrooms so that people could urinate in them instead of having to leave their room during the night. N-COUNT

**cha|me|le|on** /kəmiːliən/ **(chameleons)** A **chameleon** is a kind of lizard whose skin changes colour to match the colour of its surroundings. N-COUNT

**cham|ois** /ʃæmi/ **(chamois)**

✔ **Pronounced** /ʃæmwɑː/ for meaning 1 in British English.

1 **Chamois** are small animals rather like goats that live in the mountains of Europe and South West Asia. N-COUNT 2 A **chamois** or a **chamois leather** is a soft leather cloth used for cleaning and polishing. N-COUNT

**chamo|mile** /kæməmaɪl/ → see **camomile**.

**champ** /tʃæmp/ **(champs)** A **champ** is the same as a **champion**. [INFORMAL] ❑ *...the reigning European heavyweight champ.* N-COUNT: oft n N

**cham|pagne** /ʃæmpeɪn/ **(champagnes)** **Champagne** is an expensive French white wine with bubbles in. It is often drunk to celebrate something. N-MASS

**cham|pers** /ʃæmpəʳz/ **Champers** is champagne. [BRIT, INFORMAL] N-UNCOUNT = bubbly

**cham|pi|on** /tʃæmpiən/ **(champions, championing, championed)** ◆◆◇ 1 A **champion** is someone who has won the first prize in a competition, contest, or fight. ❑ *...a former Olympic champion... Kasparov became world champion. ...a champion boxer and skier.* N-COUNT: usu with supp 2 If you are a **champion of** a person, a cause, or a principle, you support or defend them. ❑ *He was once known as a champion of social reform.* N-COUNT: with supp, usu N of n 3 If you **champion** a person, a cause, or a principle, you support or defend them. ❑ *He passionately championed the poor... The amendments had been championed by pro-democracy activists.* VERB V n V n

**cham|pi|on|ship** /tʃæmpiənʃɪp/ **(championships)** ◆◆◇ 1 A **championship** is a competition to find the best player or team in a particular sport. ❑ *...the world chess championship.* N-COUNT: usu supp N 2 **The championship** refers to the title or status of being a sports champion. ❑ *This season I expect us to retain the championship and win the European Cup.* N-SING: the N

**chance** /tʃɑːns, tʃæns/ **(chances, chancing, chanced)** ◆◆◆ 1 If there is a **chance of** something happening, it is possible that it will happen. ❑ *Do you think they have a chance of beating Australia?... This partnership has a good chance of success... The specialist who carried out the brain scan thought Tim's chances of survival were still slim... There was really very little chance that Ben would ever have led a normal life.* N-VAR: oft N of -ing/n, N that 2 If you have a **chance to** do something, you have the opportunity to do it. ❑ *The electoral council announced that all eligible people would get a chance to vote... I felt I had to give him a chance.* N-COUNT: usu N to-inf, N for n to-inf 3 A **chance** meeting or event is one that is not planned or expected. ❑ *...a chance meeting.* ADJ: ADJ n ♦ **Chance** is also a noun. ❑ *...a victim of chance and circumstance.* N-UNCOUNT 4 If you **chance to** do something or **chance on** something, you do it or find it although you had not planned or tried to. [FORMAL] ❑ *It was just then that I chanced to look round.* *...Christopher Columbus, who chanced upon the Dominican Republic nearly 500 years ago.* VERB V to-inf V upon/on/across n 5 If you **chance** something, you do it even though there is a risk that you may not succeed or that something bad may happen. ❑ *Andy knew the risks. I cannot believe he would have chanced it... He decided no assassin would chance a shot from amongst that crowd.* VERB = risk V it V n 6 → See also **off-chance**.

PHRASES 7 Something that happens **by chance** was not planned by anyone. ❑ *He had met Mr Maude by chance.* PHRASE: PHR after v, PHR with cl 8 You can use **by any chance** when you are asking questions in order to find out whether something that you think might be true is actually true. ❑ *Are they by any chance related?* PHRASE: PHR with cl (not first in cl) = perhaps 9 If you say that someone **stands a chance of** achieving something, you mean that they are likely to achieve it. If you say that someone doesn't **stand a chance of** achieving something, you mean that they cannot possibly achieve it. ❑ *Being very good at science subjects, I stood a good chance of gaining high grades... Neither is seen as standing any chance of snatching the leadership from him.* PHRASE: V inflects, usu PHR of -ing 10 When you **take a chance**, you try to do something although there is a large risk of danger or failure. ❑ *You take a chance on the weather if you holiday in the UK... They were taking no chances.* PHRASE: V and N inflect

**chan|cel** /tʃɑːnsəl, tʃænsəl/ **(chancels)** The **chancel** is the part of a church containing the altar, where the clergy and the choir usually sit. N-COUNT

**chan|cel|lery** /tʃɑːnsələri, tʃæns-/ **(chancelleries)** 1 A **chancellery** is the building where a chancellor has his offices. N-COUNT 2 **The chancellery** is the officials who work in a chancellor's office. ❑ *He is a former head of the chancellery.* N-SING: usu the N

**Chan|cel|lor** /tʃɑːnsləʳ, tʃæns-/ **(Chancellors)** ◆◆◇ 1 **Chancellor** is the title of the head of government in Germany and Austria. ❑ *...Chancellor Gerhard Schröder of Germany. ...as the Chancellor arrived.* N-TITLE; N-COUNT: usu the N 2 In Britain, the **Chancellor** is the Chancellor of the Exchequer. N-COUNT: usu the N 3 The **Chancellor** of a British university is the official head of the university. The Chancellor does not take part in running the university. N-COUNT: usu the N 4 The head of some American universities is called **the Chancellor**. N-COUNT: usu the N 5 → See also **vice-chancellor**.

**Chan|cel|lor of the Ex|cheq|uer** **(Chancellors of the Exchequer)** The **Chancellor of the Exchequer** is the minister in the British government who makes decisions about finance and taxes. N-COUNT

**chan|cel|lor|ship** /tʃɑːnsləʳʃɪp, tʃæns-/ **The chancellorship** is the position of chancellor. Someone's **chancellorship** is the period of time when they are chancellor. ❑ *Austria prospered under Kreisky's chancellorship.* N-SING: usu the N

**chan|cer** /tʃɑːnsə, tʃænsə/ **(chancers)** You can refer to someone as a **chancer** if you think they use opportunities for their own advantage and often pretend to have skills they do not have. [INFORMAL] ❑ *...a corrupt, opportunistic chancer.* N-COUNT

**Chan|cery** /tʃɑːnsəri, tʃæns-/ In Britain, **the Chancery** or **Chancery Division** is the Lord Chancellor's court, which is a division of the High Court of Justice. N-SING: also in N

**chancy** /tʃɑːnsi, tʃænsi/ Something that is **chancy** involves a lot of risk or uncertainty. [INFORMAL] ❑ *Investment is becoming a chancy business.* ADJ = risky

**chan|de|lier** /ʃændəlɪəʳ/ **(chandeliers)** A **chandelier** is a large, decorative frame which holds light bulbs or candles and hangs from the ceiling. N-COUNT

**change** /tʃeɪndʒ/ **(changes, changing, changed)** ◆◆◆ 1 If there is a **change in** something, it becomes different. ❑ *The ambassador appealed for a change in US policy... What is needed is a change of attitude on the part of architects... There are going to have to be some drastic changes... In Zaire political change is on its way... 1998 was an important year for everyone: a time of change.* → See also **sea change**. N-VAR: usu with supp 2 If you say that something is a **change** or **makes a change**, you mean that it is enjoyable because it is different from what you are used to. ❑ *It is a complex system, but it certainly makes a change... Do you feel like you could do with a change?* N-SING approval 3 If you **change from** one thing **to** another, you stop using or doing the first one and start using or doing the second. ❑ *His doctor increased the dosage but did not change to a different medication... He changed from voting against to abstaining.* VERB V to n V from -ing/n to 4 When something **changes** or when you **change** it, it becomes different. ❑ *We are trying to detect and understand how the climates change... In the union office, the mood gradually changed from resignation to rage... She has now changed into a happy, self-confident woman... They should change the law to make it illegal to own replica weapons... Trees are changing colour earlier than last year... He is a changed man since you left... A changing world has put pressures on the corporation.* VERB = alter V V from n to n V into n V n V n V-ed V-ing 5 To **change** something means to replace it with something new or different. ❑ *I paid £80 to have my car radio fixed and I bet all they did was change a fuse... If you want to change your doctor there are two ways of doing it.* VERB V n V n ♦ **Change** is also a noun. ❑ *A change of* N-COUNT:

*leadership alone will not be enough.* [6] When you **change** your clothes or **change**, you take some or all of your clothes off and put on different ones. ❑ *Ben had merely changed his shirt... They had allowed her to shower and change... I changed into a tracksuit... I've got to get changed first. I've got to put my uniform on.* [7] A **change of** clothes is an extra set of clothes that you take with you when you go to stay somewhere or to take part in an activity. ❑ *He stuffed a bag with a few changes of clothing.* [8] When you **change** a bed or **change** the sheets, you take off the dirty sheets and put on clean ones. ❑ *After changing the bed, I would fall asleep quickly... I changed the sheets on your bed today.* [9] When you **change** a baby or **change** its nappy or diaper, you take off the dirty one and put on a clean one. ❑ *She criticizes me for the way I feed or change him... He needs his nappy changed.* [10] When you **change** buses, trains, or planes or **change**, you get off one bus, train, or plane and get on to another in order to continue your journey. ❑ *At Glasgow I changed trains for Greenock... We were turned off the train at Hanover, where we had to change.* [11] When you **change** gear or **change** into another gear, you move the gear lever on a car, bicycle, or other vehicle in order to use a different gear. [BRIT] ❑ *The driver tried to change gear, then swerved... He looked up into the mirror as he changed through his gears.*

oft a N of n / VERB / V n / V / V into/out of n / get V-ed / N-COUNT: N of n / VERB / V n / V n / VERB / V n / V-ed / VERB / V n / V / VERB / V n / V prep

✓ in AM, use **shift**

[12] Your **change** is the money that you receive when you pay for something with more money than it costs because you do not have exactly the right amount of money. ❑ *'There's your change.' — 'Thanks very much.'... They told the shopkeeper to keep the change.* [13] **Change** is coins, rather than paper money. ❑ *Thieves ransacked the office, taking a sack of loose change... The man in the store won't give him change for the phone unless he buys something.* → See also **small change**. [14] If you have **change for** larger notes, bills, or coins, you have the same value in smaller notes, bills, or coins, which you can give to someone in exchange. ❑ *The courier had change for a £10 note.* ● If you **make change**, you give someone smaller notes, bills, or coins, in exchange for the same value of larger ones. [AM] [15] When you **change** money, you exchange it for the same amount of money in a different currency, or in smaller notes, bills, or coins. ❑ *You can expect to pay the bank a fee of around 1% to 2% every time you change money... If you travel frequently, find an agency that will change one foreign currency directly into another.* [16] If you say that you are doing something or something is happening **for a change**, you mean that you do not usually do it or it does not usually happen, and you are happy to be doing it or that it is happening. ❑ *Now let me ask you a question, for a change... Liz settled back in her seat, comfortably relaxed, enjoying being driven for a change.* [17] to change **for the better** → see **better**. to **change hands** → see **hand**. **a change of heart** → see **heart**. to **change** your **mind** → see **mind**. to **change places** → see **place**. to **ring the changes** → see **ring**. to **change the subject** → see **subject**. to **change tack** → see **tack**. to **change** your **tune** → see **tune**. to change **for the worse** → see **worse**.

N-UNCOUNT / N-UNCOUNT / N-UNCOUNT: usu N for n / PHRASE / VERB / V n / V n into n / PHRASE: PHR with cl

♦ **change down** When you **change down**, you move the gear lever in the vehicle you are driving in order to use a lower gear. [BRIT] ❑ *Changing down, he turned into the drive... I braked at the second corner and changed down to third.*

PHRASAL VERB / V P / V P to n

✓ in AM, use **shift down**

♦ **change over** If you **change over from** one thing **to** another, you stop doing one thing and start doing the other. ❑ *We are gradually changing over to a completely metric system... The two men swapped places, always extinguishing the light when they changed over.* → See also **changeover**.

PHRASAL VERB / V P from/to n / V P

♦ **change up** When you **change up**, you move the gear lever in the vehicle you are driving in order to use a higher gear. [BRIT] ❑ *I accelerated and changed up.*

PHRASAL VERB / V P

✓ in AM, use **shift up**

**change|able** /tʃeɪndʒəbᵊl/ Someone or something that is **changeable** is likely to change many times. ❑ *The forecast is for changeable weather.*

ADJ = unsettled

**change|ling** /tʃeɪndʒlɪŋ/ **(changelings)** A **changeling** is a child who was put in the place of another child when they were both babies. In stories changelings were often taken or left by fairies. [LITERARY]

N-COUNT

**change man|age|ment** **Change management** is a style of management that aims to encourage organizations and individuals to deal effectively with the changes taking place in their work. [BUSINESS] ❑ *She is hoping to go into change management or IT management when she graduates.*

N-UNCOUNT

**change of life** **The change of life** is the **menopause**.

N-SING: the N

**change|over** /tʃeɪndʒoʊvəʳ/ **(changeovers)** A **changeover** is a change from one activity or system to another. ❑ *He again called for a faster changeover to a market economy... Right now we are in the changeover period between autumn and winter.*

N-COUNT

**change purse** **(change purses)** A **change purse** is a very small bag that people, especially women, keep their money in. [AM]

N-COUNT

✓ in BRIT, use **purse**

**chang|ing room** **(changing rooms)** A **changing room** is a room where you can change your clothes and usually have a shower, for example at a sports centre.

N-COUNT

**chan|nel** /tʃænᵊl/ **(channels, channelling, channelled)** ◆◆◇

✓ in AM, use **channeling, channeled**

[1] A **channel** is a television station. ❑ *...the only serious current affairs programme on either channel. ...the presenter of Channel 4 News.* [2] A **channel** is a band of radio waves on which radio messages can be sent and received. [3] If you do something through a particular **channel**, or particular **channels**, that is the system or organization that you use to achieve your aims or to communicate. ❑ *The Americans recognise that the UN can be the channel for greater diplomatic activity... Moscow and the Baltic republics are re-opening channels of communication.* [4] If you **channel** money or resources into something, you arrange for them to be used for that thing, rather than for a wider range of things. ❑ *Jacques Delors wants a system set up to channel funds to the poor countries.* [5] If you **channel** your energies or emotions **into** something, you concentrate on or do that one thing, rather than a range of things. ❑ *Stephen is channelling his energies into a novel called Blue.* [6] A **channel** is a passage along which water flows. ❑ *Keep the drainage channel clear.* [7] A **channel** is a route used by boats. [8] **The Channel** or **the English Channel** is the narrow area of water between England and France.

N-COUNT; N-IN-NAMES = station / N-COUNT / N-COUNT: with supp, oft adj N, N for/of n / VERB / V n prep / VERB / V n into n / N-COUNT / N-COUNT / N-PROPER: the N

**channel-hopping** **Channel-hopping** means switching quickly between different television channels because you are looking for something interesting to watch. [BRIT]

N-UNCOUNT

✓ in AM, use **channel-surfing**

**channel-surfing** **Channel-surfing** is the same as **channel-hopping**. [mainly AM]

N-UNCOUNT

**chant** /tʃɑːnt, tʃænt/ **(chants, chanting, chanted)** [1] A **chant** is a word or group of words that is repeated over and over again. ❑ *He was greeted by the chant of 'Judas! Judas!'.* [2] A **chant** is a religious song or prayer that is sung on only a few notes. ❑ *...a Buddhist chant.* [3] If you **chant** something or if you **chant**, you repeat the same words over and over again. ❑ *Demonstrators chant-*

N-COUNT: oft N of n / N-COUNT: usu adj N / VERB / V n

*ed slogans... The crowd chanted 'We are with you.'... Several thousand people chanted and demonstrated outside the building.* [V with quote] [V] [Also V that] ♦ **chant|ing** *A lot of the chanting was in support of the deputy Prime Minister.* [N-UNCOUNT] 4 If you **chant** or if you **chant** something, you sing a religious song or prayer. ❑ *Muslims chanted and prayed... Mr Sharma lit incense and chanted Sanskrit mantras.* [VERB] [V] [V n] ♦ **chant|ing** *The chanting inside the temple stopped.* [N-UNCOUNT]

**Cha|nu|kah** /hɑːnəkə/ **Chanukah** is the same as **Hanukkah**. [N-UNCOUNT]

**cha|os** /keɪɒs/ **Chaos** is a state of complete disorder and confusion. ❑ *The world's first transatlantic balloon race ended in chaos last night.* [◆◇◇] [N-UNCOUNT]

**cha|ot|ic** /keɪɒtɪk/ Something that is **chaotic** is in a state of complete disorder and confusion. ❑ *Mullins began to rummage among the chaotic mess of papers on his desk.* [ADJ]

**chap** /tʃæp/ **(chaps)** 1 A **chap** is a man or boy. [mainly BRIT, INFORMAL] ❑ *She thought he was a very nice chap.* [N-COUNT] [= bloke, guy] 2 → See also **chapped**.

**chap.** **(chaps)** **Chap.** is a written abbreviation for **chapter**. ❑ *Today the best tests are performed in the hospital (see chap. 17).* [N-VAR num]

**chap|el** /tʃæpᵊl/ **(chapels)** 1 A **chapel** is a part of a church which has its own altar and which is used for private prayer. ❑ *...the chapel of the Virgin Mary.* [N-COUNT: oft *the* N *of* n] 2 A **chapel** is a small church attached to a hospital, school, or prison. ❑ *We married in the chapel of Charing Cross Hospital in London.* [N-COUNT] 3 A **chapel** is a building used for worship by members of some Christian churches. **Chapel** refers to the religious services that take place there. ❑ *...a Methodist chapel... On Sundays, the family went three times to chapel.* [N-VAR]

**chap|er|one** /ʃæpəroʊn/ **(chaperones, chaperoning, chaperoned)** also **chaperon.** 1 A **chaperone** is someone who accompanies another person somewhere in order to make sure that they do not come to any harm. [N-COUNT] 2 If you **are chaperoned by** someone, they act as your chaperone. ❑ *We were chaperoned by our aunt.* [VERB: usu passive] [*be* V-ed]

**chap|lain** /tʃæplɪn/ **(chaplains)** A **chaplain** is a member of the Christian clergy who does religious work in a place such as a hospital, school, prison, or in the armed forces. ❑ *He joined the 40th Division as an army chaplain.* [N-COUNT: oft n N]

**chap|lain|cy** /tʃæplɪnsi/ **(chaplaincies)** 1 A **chaplaincy** is the building or office in which a chaplain works. [N-COUNT] 2 A **chaplaincy** is the position or work of a chaplain. ❑ *...the chaplaincy of the Royal Hospital.* [N-COUNT]

**chapped** /tʃæpt/ If your skin is **chapped**, it is dry, cracked, and sore. ❑ *...chapped hands... Her skin felt chapped.* [ADJ]

**chap|py** /tʃæpi/ **(chappies)** A **chappy** is the same as a **chap**. [BRIT, INFORMAL] ❑ *His cheeky chappy image is reinforced by the spiky hair and the wide grin.* [N-COUNT]

**chap|ter** /tʃæptəʳ/ **(chapters)** 1 A **chapter** is one of the parts that a book is divided into. Each chapter has a number, and sometimes a title. ❑ *Chromium supplements were used successfully in the treatment of diabetes (see Chapter 4)... I took the title of this chapter from one of my favorite books.* [◆◆◇] [N-COUNT: also N num] 2 A **chapter in** someone's life or **in** history is a period of time during which a major event or series of related events takes place. [WRITTEN] ❑ *This had been a particularly difficult chapter in Lebanon's recent history. ...one of the most dramatic chapters of recent British politics.* [N-COUNT: supp N, oft N *in* n, adj N]

**chap|ter house** **(chapter houses)** 1 A **chapter house** is the building or set of rooms in the grounds of a cathedral where the members of the clergy hold their meetings. [N-COUNT] 2 In a university or college, a **chapter house** is the place where a fraternity or sorority lives or meets. [AM] [N-COUNT]

**char** /tʃɑːʳ/ **(chars, charring, charred)** 1 If food **chars** or if you **char** it, it burns slightly and turns black as it is cooking. ❑ *Toast hazelnuts on a baking sheet until the skins char... Halve the peppers and char the skins under a hot grill.* [VERB] [V] [V n] ♦ **char|ring** *The chops should be cooked over moderate heat to prevent excessive charring.* [N-UNCOUNT] 2 → See also **charred**.

**chara|banc** /ʃærəbæŋ/ **(charabancs)** A **charabanc** is a large old-fashioned coach with several rows of seats. Charabancs were used especially for taking people on trips or on holiday. [BRIT] [N-COUNT]

**char|ac|ter** /kærɪktəʳ/ **(characters)** 1 The **character** of a person or place consists of all the qualities they have that make them distinct from other people or places. ❑ *Perhaps there is a negative side to his character that you haven't seen yet... The character of this country has been formed by immigration.* [◆◆◇] [N-COUNT: usu with supp] [= nature] 2 If something has a particular **character**, it has a particular quality. ❑ *The financial concessions granted to British Aerospace were, he said, of a precarious character... The state farms were semi-military in character.* [N-SING: usu supp N, also *in* N] [= nature] 3 You can use **character** to refer to the qualities that people from a particular place are believed to have. ❑ *Individuality is a valued and inherent part of the British character.* [N-SING: supp N] 4 You use **character** to say what kind of person someone is. For example, if you say that someone is a strange **character**, you mean they are strange. ❑ *It's that kind of courage and determination that makes him such a remarkable character... What a sad character that Nigel is.* [N-COUNT: usu adj N] 5 Your **character** is your personality, especially how reliable and honest you are. If someone is **of** good **character**, they are reliable and honest. If they are **of** bad **character**, they are unreliable and dishonest. ❑ *He's begun a series of personal attacks on my character... Mr Bartman was a man of good character.* [N-VAR: usu supp N] 6 If you say that someone has **character**, you mean that they have the ability to deal effectively with difficult, unpleasant, or dangerous situations. ❑ *She showed real character in her attempts to win over the crowd... I didn't know Ron had that much strength of character.* [N-UNCOUNT] [approval] 7 If you say that a place has **character**, you mean that it has an interesting or unusual quality which makes you notice it and like it. ❑ *An ugly shopping centre stands across from one of the few buildings with character.* [N-UNCOUNT] [approval] 8 The **characters** in a film, book, or play are the people that it is about. ❑ *The film is autobiographical and the central character is played by Collard himself... He's made the characters believable.* [N-COUNT] 9 If you say that someone is a **character**, you mean that they are interesting, unusual, or amusing. [INFORMAL] ❑ *He'll be sadly missed. He was a real character.* [N-COUNT] 10 A **character** is a letter, number, or other symbol that is written or printed. [N-COUNT] 11 If someone's actions are **in character**, they are doing what you would expect them to do, knowing what kind of person they are. If their actions are **out of character**, they are not doing what you would expect them to do. ❑ *It was entirely in character for Rachel to put her baby first... What else could make him behave so out of character?* [PHRASE: usu v-link PHR]

**char|ac|ter ac|tor** **(character actors)** A **character actor** is an actor who specializes in playing unusual or eccentric people. [N-COUNT]

**char|ac|ter as|sas|si|na|tion** **(character assassinations)** A **character assassination** is a deliberate attempt to destroy someone's reputation, especially by criticizing them in an unfair and dishonest way when they are not present. ❑ *A full-scale character assassination of the dead woman got underway in the tabloid press.* [N-VAR]

**char|ac|ter|ful** /kærɪktəʳfʊl/ If you describe something as **characterful**, you mean that it is pleasant and interesting. [JOURNALISM] ❑ *...small characterful hotels serving local cuisine.* [ADJ: usu ADJ n] [≠ characterless]

**char|ac|ter|is|tic** /kærɪktərɪstɪk/ **(characteristics)** 1 The **characteristics** of a person or thing are the qualities or features that belong to them and make them recognizable. ❑ *Genes determine the characteristics of every living thing. ...their physical characteristics.* [◆◇◇] [N-COUNT: usu pl, usu with supp] [= feature, trait] 2 A quality or feature that [ADJ:]

is **characteristic of** someone or something is one which is often seen in them and seems typical of them. ❑ *Windmills are a characteristic feature of the Mallorcan landscape... Nehru responded with characteristic generosity.* ♦ **char|ac|ter|is|ti|cal|ly** /kærɪktərɪstɪkli/ *He replied in characteristically robust style.* oft ADJ *of* n = typical ≠uncharacteristic ADV: usu ADV adj, also ADV with v, ADV with cl

**char|ac|teri|za|tion** /kærɪktəraɪzeɪʃən/ **(characterizations)**

in BRIT, also use **characterisation**

**Characterization** is the way an author or an actor describes or shows what a character is like. ❑ *...Chaucer's characterization of Criseyde.* → See also **characterize.** N-VAR

**char|ac|ter|ize** /kærɪktəraɪz/ **(characterizes, characterizing, characterized)**

in BRIT, also use **characterise**

1 If something **is characterized by** a particular feature or quality, that feature or quality is an obvious part of it. [FORMAL] ❑ *This election campaign has been characterized by violence... A bold use of colour characterizes the bedroom.* 2 If you **characterize** someone or something **as** a particular thing, you describe them as that thing. [FORMAL] ❑ *Both companies have characterized the relationship as friendly.* VERB be V-ed *by* n V n VERB = describe V n *as* adj/n

**char|ac|ter|less** /kærɪktərləs/ If you describe something as **characterless**, you mean that it is dull and uninteresting. ❑ *The town is boring and characterless. ...a bland and characterless meal.* ADJ ≠characterful

**char|ac|ter rec|og|ni|tion** **Character recognition** is a process which allows computers to recognize written or printed characters such as numbers or letters and to change them into a form that the computer can use. [COMPUTING] N-UNCOUNT

**cha|rade** /ʃərɑːd, AM -reɪd/ **(charades)** 1 If you describe someone's actions as a **charade**, you mean that their actions are so obviously false that they do not convince anyone. ❑ *I wondered why he had gone through the elaborate charade... The UN at the moment is still trying to maintain the charade of neutrality.* 2 **Charades** is a game for teams of players in which one team acts a word or phrase, syllable by syllable, until other players guess the whole word or phrase. N-COUNT: usu sing [disapproval] N-UNCOUNT

**char|coal** /tʃɑːrkoʊl/ **Charcoal** is a black substance obtained by burning wood without much air. It can be burned as a fuel, and small sticks of it are used for drawing with. N-UNCOUNT

**chard** /tʃɑːrd/ **Chard** is a plant with a round root, large leaves, and a thick stalk. N-UNCOUNT

**charge** /tʃɑːrdʒ/ **(charges, charging, charged)** ♦♦♦

1 If you **charge** someone an amount of money, you ask them to pay that amount for something that you have sold to them or done for them. ❑ *Even local nurseries charge £100 a week... The hospitals charge the patients for every aspirin... Some banks charge if you access your account to determine your balance. ...the architect who charged us a fee of seven hundred and fifty pounds.* 2 To **charge** something **to** a person or organization means to tell the people providing it to send the bill to that person or organization. To **charge** something **to** someone's account means to add it to their account so they can pay for it later. ❑ *Go out and buy a pair of glasses, and charge it to us... All transactions have been charged to your account.* 3 A **charge** is an amount of money that you have to pay for a service. ❑ *We can arrange this for a small charge... Customers who arrange overdrafts will face a monthly charge of £5.* 4 A **charge** is a formal accusation that someone has committed a crime. ❑ *He may still face criminal charges... They appeared at court yesterday to deny charges of murder.* 5 When the police **charge** someone, they formally accuse them of having done something illegal. ❑ *They have the evidence to charge him... Police have charged Mr Bell with murder.* 6 If you **charge** someone **with** doing something wrong or unpleasant, you publicly say that they have done it. [WRITTEN] ❑ *He charged the minister with lying about the economy.* 7 If you take **charge of** someone or something, you make yourself responsible for them and take control over them. If someone or something is **in** your **charge**, you are responsible for them. ❑ *A few years ago Bacryl took charge of the company... I have been given charge of this class... They would never forget their time in his charge.* 8 If you are **in charge** in a particular situation, you are the most senior person and have control over something or someone. ❑ *Who's in charge here? ...the Swiss governess in charge of the smaller children.* 9 If you describe someone as your **charge**, they have been given to you to be looked after and you are responsible for them. ❑ *The coach tried to get his charges motivated.* 10 If you **charge** towards someone or something, you move quickly and aggressively towards them. ❑ *He charged through the door to my mother's office... He ordered us to charge. ...a charging bull.* ♦ **Charge** is also a noun. ❑ *...a bayonet charge.* 11 To **charge** a battery means to pass an electrical current through it in order to make it more powerful or to make it last longer. ❑ *Alex had forgotten to charge the battery.* ♦ **Charge up** means the same as **charge.** ❑ *There was nothing in the brochure about having to drive the car every day to charge up the battery.* 12 An electrical **charge** is an amount of electricity that is held in or carried by something. [TECHNICAL] 13 → See also **charged, baton charge, cover charge, depth charge, service charge.** 14 If something is **free of charge**, it does not cost anything. ❑ *The leaflet is available free of charge from post offices.* VERB V n V n *for* n V V n n VERB = bill V n *to* n V n *to* n N-COUNT N-COUNT VERB V n V n *with* n VERB = accuse V n *with* -ing/n N-UNCOUNT: usu N *of* n PHRASE: v-link PHR, oft PHR *of* n N-COUNT: usu pl, poss N VERB V prep/adv V V-ing N-COUNT VERB V n PHRASAL VERB V P n (not pron) N-COUNT: usu sing PHRASE = free

♦ **charge up** → see **charge 11.**

**charge|able** /tʃɑːrdʒəbəl/ 1 If something is **chargeable**, you have to pay a sum of money for it. [FORMAL] ❑ *The day of departure is not chargeable if rooms are vacated by 12.00 noon.* 2 If something is **chargeable**, you have to pay tax on it. [FORMAL] ❑ *...the taxpayer's chargeable gain.* ADJ: usu v-link ADJ ADJ

**charge card** **(charge cards)** also **chargecard.** 1 A **charge card** is a plastic card that you use to buy goods on credit from a particular store or group of stores. Compare **credit card.** [BRIT] 2 A **charge card** is the same as a **credit card.** [AM] N-COUNT N-COUNT

**charged** /tʃɑːrdʒd/ 1 If a situation is **charged**, it is filled with emotion and therefore very tense or exciting. ❑ *There was a highly charged atmosphere... A wedding is an emotionally charged situation.* 2 **Charged** particles carry an electrical charge. ❑ *...negatively charged ions.* ADJ: usu adv ADJ ADJ: oft adv ADJ

**char|gé d'af|faires** /ʃɑːrʒeɪ dæfeər/ **(chargés d'affaires)** 1 A **chargé d'affaires** is a person appointed to act as head of a diplomatic mission in a foreign country while the ambassador is away. 2 A **chargé d'affaires** is the head of a minor diplomatic mission in a foreign country. N-COUNT N-COUNT

**charge nurse** **(charge nurses)** A **charge nurse** is a nurse who is in charge of a hospital ward. [BRIT] N-COUNT

**charg|er** /tʃɑːrdʒər/ **(chargers)** 1 A **charger** is a device used for charging or recharging batteries. ❑ *He forgot the charger for his mobile phone.* 2 A **charger** was a strong horse that a knight in the Middle Ages used to ride in battle. N-COUNT N-COUNT

**char-grilled** also **chargrilled.** **Chargrilled** meat or fish has been cooked so that it burns slightly and turns black. [BRIT] ADJ: usu ADJ n

in AM, usually use **charbroiled**

**chari|ot** /tʃæriət/ **(chariots)** In ancient times, **chariots** were fast-moving vehicles with two wheels that were pulled by horses. N-COUNT

**cha|ris|ma** /kərɪzmə/ You say that someone has **charisma** when they can attract, influence, and inspire people by their personal qualities. N-UNCOUNT

❑ *He has neither the policies nor the personal charisma to inspire people.*

**char|is|mat|ic** /kærɪzmætɪk/ A **charismatic** person attracts, influences, and inspires people by their personal qualities. ❑ *...her striking looks and charismatic personality.* ADJ: usu ADJ n

**chari|table** /tʃærɪtəbᵊl/ [1] A **charitable** organization or activity helps and supports people who are ill, disabled, or very poor. ❑ *...charitable work for the handicapped.* ADJ: ADJ n [2] Someone who is **charitable** to people is kind or understanding towards them. ❑ *They were rather less than charitable towards the referee.* ADJ: usu v-link ADJ

**char|ity** /tʃærɪti/ **(charities)** ◆◇◇ [1] A **charity** is an organization which raises money in order to help people who are ill, disabled, or very poor. ❑ *The National Trust is a registered charity. ...an Aids charity.* N-COUNT: oft supp N [2] If you give money **to charity**, you give it to one or more charitable organizations. If you do something **for charity**, you do it in order to raise money for one or more charitable organizations. ❑ *He made substantial donations to charity... Gooch will be raising money for charity. ...a charity event.* N-UNCOUNT [3] People who live on **charity** live on money or goods which other people give them because they are poor. ❑ *My mum was very proud. She wouldn't accept charity... Her husband is unemployed and the family depends on charity.* N-UNCOUNT [4] **Charity** is kindness and understanding towards other people. [FORMAL] N-UNCOUNT

**char|ity shop** **(charity shops)** A **charity shop** is a shop that sells used goods cheaply and gives its profits to a charity. [BRIT] N-COUNT

☑ in AM, use **thrift shop**

**char|la|tan** /ʃɑːʳlətᵊn/ **(charlatans)** You describe someone as a **charlatan** when they pretend to have skills or knowledge that they do not really possess. [FORMAL] ❑ *He was exposed as a charlatan.* N-COUNT [disapproval]

**Charles|ton** /tʃɑːʳlstən/ **The Charleston** is a lively dance that was popular in the 1920s. N-SING: usu *the* N

**charm** /tʃɑːʳm/ **(charms, charming, charmed)** [1] **Charm** is the quality of being pleasant or attractive. ❑ *'Snow White and the Seven Dwarfs', the 1937 Disney classic, has lost none of its original charm... The house had its charms, not the least of which was the furniture that came with it.* N-VAR [2] Someone who has **charm** behaves in a friendly, pleasant way that makes people like them. ❑ *He was a man of great charm and distinction.* N-UNCOUNT [3] If you **charm** someone, you please them, especially by using your charm. ❑ *He even charmed Mrs Prichard, carrying her shopping and flirting with her, though she's 83.* VERB V n [4] A **charm** is a small ornament that is fixed to a bracelet or necklace. N-COUNT [5] A **charm** is an act, saying, or object that is believed to have magic powers. ❑ *...a good luck charm.* N-COUNT [6] If you say that something **worked like a charm**, you mean that it was very effective or successful. ❑ *Economically, the policy worked like a charm.* PHRASE: V inflects

**charmed** /tʃɑːʳmd/ A **charmed** place, time, or situation is one that is very beautiful or pleasant, and seems slightly separate from the real world or real life. [WRITTEN] ❑ *...the charmed atmosphere of Oxford in the late Twenties.* ADJ: ADJ n

**charmed cir|cle** If you refer to a group of people as a **charmed circle**, you mean that they seem to have special power or influence, and do not allow anyone else to join their group. [LITERARY] ❑ *...the immense role played by this very small charmed circle of critics.* N-SING

**charm|er** /tʃɑːʳməʳ/ **(charmers)** If you refer to someone, especially a man, as a **charmer**, you think that they behave in a very charming but rather insincere way. ❑ *He comes across as an intelligent, sophisticated, charmer.* → See also **snake charmer**. N-COUNT [disapproval]

**charm|ing** /tʃɑːʳmɪŋ/ [1] If you say that something is **charming**, you mean that it is very pleasant or attractive. ❑ *...a charming little fishing village. ...the charming custom of wearing a rose on that day.* ADJ ♦ **charm|ing|ly** *There's something charmingly old-fashioned about his brand of entertainment.* ADV: ADV adj, ADV after v [2] If you describe someone as **charming**, you mean they behave in a friendly, pleasant way that makes people like them. ❑ *...a charming young man... He can be charming to his friends.* ADJ ♦ **charm|ing|ly** *Calder smiled charmingly and put out his hand. 'A pleasure, Mrs Talbot.'* ADV: ADV after v

**charm|less** /tʃɑːʳmləs/ If you say that something or someone is **charmless**, you mean that they are unattractive or uninteresting. [WRITTEN] ❑ *...flat, charmless countryside.* ADJ ≠ *charming*

**charm of|fen|sive** If you say that someone has launched a **charm offensive**, you disapprove of the fact that they are being very friendly to their opponents or people who are causing problems for them. [JOURNALISM] ❑ *He launched what was called a charm offensive against MPs who might not support the Government.* N-SING [disapproval]

**char|nel house** /tʃɑːʳnᵊl haʊs/ **(charnel houses)** A **charnel house** is a place where the bodies and bones of dead people are stored. N-COUNT

**charred** /tʃɑːʳd/ **Charred** plants, buildings, or vehicles have been badly burnt and have become black because of fire. ❑ *...the charred remains of a tank.* ADJ: usu ADJ n = *burnt*

**chart** /tʃɑːʳt/ **(charts, charting, charted)** ◆◇◇ [1] A **chart** is a diagram, picture, or graph which is intended to make information easier to understand. ❑ *Male unemployment was 14.2%, compared with 5.8% for women (see chart on next page)... The chart below shows our top 10 choices.* → See also **bar chart**, **flow chart**, **pie chart**. N-COUNT = *diagram* [2] A **chart** is a map of the sea or stars. ❑ *...charts of Greek waters.* N-COUNT [3] If you **chart** an area of land, sea, or sky, or a feature in that area, you make a map of the area or show the feature in it. ❑ *Ptolemy charted more than 1000 stars in 48 constellations... These seas have been well charted.* VERB = *map* V n V n [4] **The charts** are the official lists that show which CDs have sold the most copies each week. ❑ *This album confirmed The Orb's status as national stars, going straight to Number One in the charts... They topped both the US singles and album charts at the same time.* N-COUNT: usu pl = *hit parade* [5] If you **chart** the development or progress of something, you observe it and record or show it. You can also say that a report or graph **charts** the development or progress of something. ❑ *Bulletin boards charted each executive's progress.* VERB = *record* V n

**char|ter** /tʃɑːʳtəʳ/ **(charters, chartering, chartered)** ◆◇◇ [1] A **charter** is a formal document describing the rights, aims, or principles of an organization or group of people. ❑ *...Article 50 of the United Nations Charter.* N-COUNT: with supp [2] A **charter** plane or boat is one which is hired for use by a particular person or group and which is not part of a regular service. ❑ *...the last charter plane carrying out foreign nationals. ...frequent charter flights to Spain.* ADJ: ADJ n [3] If a person or organization **charters** a plane, boat, or other vehicle, they hire it for their own use. ❑ *He chartered a jet to fly her home from California to Switzerland... Yesterday, a cargo ship chartered by the UN arrived in the capital carrying 1,550 tons of rice.* VERB V n V-ed [4] If you describe a decision or policy as **a charter for** someone or something you disapprove of, you mean that it is likely to help or encourage them. ❑ *They described the Home Office scheme as a 'charter for cheats'.* PHRASE

**char|tered** /tʃɑːʳtəʳd/ **Chartered** is used to indicate that someone, such as an accountant or a surveyor, has formally qualified in their profession. [BRIT] ADJ: ADJ n

☑ in AM, usually use **certified**

**char|ter mem|ber** **(charter members)** A **charter member of** a club, group, or organization is one of the first members, often one who was involved in setting it up. [AM] N-COUNT: usu N *of* n

☑ in BRIT, use **founder member**

**char|woman** /tʃɑːʳwʊmən/ **(charwomen)** A **charwoman** is a woman who is employed to clean houses or offices. [BRIT, OLD-FASHIONED] N-COUNT = cleaner

**chary** /tʃeəri/ If you are **chary of** doing something, you are fairly cautious about doing it. ❑ *I am rather chary of making too many idiotic mistakes.* ADJ: v-link ADJ, usu ADJ of/about -ing/n

**chase** /tʃeɪs/ **(chases, chasing, chased)** 1 If you **chase** someone, or **chase after** them, you run after them or follow them quickly in order to catch or reach them. ❑ *She chased the thief for 100 yards... He said nothing to waiting journalists, who chased after him as he left.* ♦ **Chase** is also a noun. ❑ *He was reluctant to give up the chase... Police said he was arrested without a struggle after a car chase through the streets of Biarritz.* ◆◇◇ VERB = pursue V n V after n N-COUNT = pursuit 2 If you **are chasing** something you want, such as work or money, you are trying hard to get it. ❑ *In Wales, 14 people are chasing every job. ...publishers and booksellers chasing after profits from high-volume sales.* ♦ **Chase** is also a noun. ❑ *They took an invincible lead in the chase for the championship.* VERB V n V after n N-SING: N for n 3 If someone **chases** someone that they are attracted to, or **chases after** them, they try hard to persuade them to have a sexual relationship with them. ❑ *I'm not very good at flirting or chasing women... 'I was always chasing after unsuitable men,' she says.* ♦ **Chase** is also a noun. ❑ *The chase is always much more exciting than the conquest anyway.* VERB V n V after n N-SING: the N 4 If someone **chases** you from a place, they force you to leave by using threats or violence. ❑ *Many of the local farmers will then chase you off their land quite aggressively... Angry demonstrators chased him away.* VERB V n from/out of/off n V n away/off/out 5 If someone **cuts to the chase**, they start talking about or dealing with what is important, instead of less important things. ❑ *Hi everyone, we all know why we are here today, so let's cut to the chase.* PHRASE: V inflects 6 To **chase** someone **from** a job or a position or **from** power means to force them to leave it. ❑ *His single-minded pursuit of European union helped chase Mrs Thatcher from power.* VERB V n from/out of n 7 If you **chase** somewhere, you run or rush there. ❑ *They chased down the stairs into the narrow, dirty street.* VERB = race, dash V prep/adv 8 → See also **wild goose chase**.

**PHRASES** 9 If you **give chase**, you run after someone or follow them quickly in order to catch them. ❑ *Other officers gave chase but the killers escaped.* PHRASE: V inflects 10 If you talk about **the thrill of the chase**, you are referring to the excitement that people feel when they are trying hard to get something. ❑ *People who adore the thrill of the chase know that prizes, like diamonds, are worth striving for.* PHRASE

♦ **chase away** If someone or something **chases away** worries, fears, or other bad feelings, they cause those feelings to change and become happier. [WRITTEN] ❑ *Ellery's return will help to chase away some of the gloom.* PHRASAL VERB = get rid of V P n (not pron)

♦ **chase down** 1 If you **chase** someone **down**, you run after them or follow them quickly and catch them. [mainly AM] ❑ *Ness chased the thief down and held him until police arrived... For thousands of years chasing down game was the main activity in which humans were involved.* PHRASAL VERB V n P V P n (not pron) 2 If you **chase** someone or something **down**, you manage to find them after searching for them. ❑ *That's when I chased her down to be the singer in my band... Bank officials argued that it is not their job to chase down every asset of every bank debtor.* PHRASAL VERB = track down V n P V P n (not pron)

♦ **chase up** 1 If you **chase up** something that is needed or needs dealing with, you find it or find out what is being done about it. ❑ *When I didn't hear from the suppliers or receive a refund, I chased the matter up... The authority can chase up the source of the pollution and demand that the owner clean it up.* PHRASAL VERB V n P V P n (not pron) 2 If you **chase** someone **up**, you look for them and find them because you want them to do something or give you something. ❑ *...the story of a man who comes to Hollywood to chase up a client who has defaulted on a debt.* PHRASAL VERB = track down V P n (not pron) Also V n P

**chas|er** /tʃeɪsəʳ/ **(chasers)** A **chaser** is an alcoholic drink that you have after you have drunk a stronger or weaker alcoholic drink. ❑ *...whiskey with beer chasers.* N-COUNT: oft n N

**chasm** /kæzəm/ **(chasms)** 1 A **chasm** is a very deep crack in rock, earth, or ice. 2 If you say that there is a **chasm** between two things or between two groups of people, you mean that there is a very large difference between them. ❑ *...the chasm that divides the worlds of university and industry. ...the chasm between rich and poor in America.* N-COUNT N-COUNT: usu with supp, oft N between pl-n = gulf, gap

**chas|sis** /ʃæsi/

> ✔ **chassis** /ʃæsiz/ can also be used as the plural form.

A **chassis** is the framework that a vehicle is built on. → See picture on page 1707. N-COUNT

**chaste** /tʃeɪst/ If you describe a person or their behaviour as **chaste**, you mean that they do not have sex with anyone, or they only have sex with their husband or wife. [OLD-FASHIONED] ❑ *He remained chaste.* ADJ

**chas|ten** /tʃeɪsᵊn/ **(chastens, chastening, chastened)** If you **are chastened by** something, it makes you regret that you have behaved badly or stupidly. [FORMAL] ❑ *He has clearly not been chastened by his thirteen days in detention... A chastened Agassi flew home for a period of deep contemplation.* VERB: usu passive be V-ed by n V-ed Also be V-ed into n/-ing
♦ **chas|tened** *The President now seems a more chastened and less confident politician than when he set out a week ago.* ADJ

**chas|ten|ing** /tʃeɪsənɪŋ/ A **chastening** experience makes you regret that you have behaved badly or stupidly. ❑ *From this chastening experience he learnt some useful lessons.* ADJ

**chas|tise** /tʃæstaɪz/ **(chastises, chastising, chastised)** If you **chastise** someone, you speak to them angrily or punish them for something wrong that they have done. [FORMAL] ❑ *Thomas Rane chastised Peters for his cruelty... The Securities Commission chastised the firm but imposed no fine... I just don't want you to chastise yourself.* VERB = reprimand V n V n V pron-refl

**chas|tise|ment** /tʃæstaɪzmənt/ **Chastisement** is the same as punishment. [OLD-FASHIONED] N-UNCOUNT: also a N

**chas|tity** /tʃæstɪti/ **Chastity** is the state of not having sex with anyone, or of only having sex with your husband or wife. [OLD-FASHIONED] ❑ *He took a vow of chastity and celibacy.* N-UNCOUNT

**chat** /tʃæt/ **(chats, chatting, chatted)** When people **chat**, they talk to each other in an informal and friendly way. ❑ *The women were chatting... I was chatting to him the other day... We chatted about old times.* ♦ **Chat** is also a noun. ❑ *I had a chat with John.* ◆◇◇ V-RECIP pl-n V V to/with n V about n N-COUNT

♦ **chat up** If you **chat** someone **up**, usually someone you do not know very well, you talk to them in a friendly way because you are sexually attracted to them. [BRIT, INFORMAL] ❑ *He'd spent most of that evening chatting up one of my friends... She was chatting one of the guys up.* PHRASAL VERB V P n (not pron) V n P

**châ|teau** /ʃætoʊ/ **(châteaux** /ʃætoʊz/**)** also **chateau.** A **château** is a large country house or castle in France. N-COUNT

**chat|elaine** /ʃætəleɪn/ **(chatelaines)** A **chatelaine** is the female owner, or the wife of the owner, of a castle or large country house. N-COUNT

**chat|line** /tʃætlaɪn/ **(chatlines)** also **chat line.** People phone in to **chatlines** to have conversations with other people who have also phoned in. [BRIT] ❑ *She started using chat lines basically for someone to talk to.* N-COUNT

**chat room** **(chat rooms)** A **chat room** is a site on the Internet where people can exchange messages about a particular subject. [COMPUTING] N-COUNT

**chat show** **(chat shows)** A **chat show** is a television or radio show in which people talk in a friendly, informal way about different topics. [BRIT] N-COUNT

> ✔ in AM, use **talk show**

**chat|tel** /tʃætᵊl/ **(chattels) Chattels** are things that belong to you. [OLD-FASHIONED] ❑ *They were slaves, to be bought and sold as chattels.* N-VAR

**chat|ter** /tʃætəʳ/ **(chatters, chattering, chattered)** [1] If you **chatter**, you talk quickly and continuously, usually about things which are not important. ❑ *Everyone's chattering away in different languages... Erica was friendly and chattered about Andrew's children... He listened to chattering maids as they passed by.* ♦ **Chatter** is also a noun. ❑ *...idle chatter... Lila kept up a steady stream of chatter.* [2] If your teeth **chatter**, they keep knocking together because you are very cold or very nervous. ❑ *She was so cold her teeth chattered.* [3] When birds or animals **chatter**, they make high-pitched noises. [LITERARY] ❑ *Birds were chattering somewhere.* ♦ **Chatter** is also a noun. ❑ *...almond trees vibrating with the chatter of crickets.*
VERB; V adv/prep; V *about* n; V-ing; N-UNCOUNT; VERB; V; VERB; V; N-UNCOUNT: usu *the* N *of* n

**chatter|box** /tʃætəʳbɒks/ **(chatterboxes)** A **chatterbox** is someone who talks a lot. [INFORMAL] N-COUNT

**chat|ter|ing clas|ses** **The chattering classes** are people such as journalists, broadcasters, or public figures who comment on events but have little or no influence over them. [BRIT, JOURNALISM] ❑ *Radical feminism is currently the fashionable topic among the chattering classes.* N-PLURAL: usu *the* N [disapproval]

**chat|ty** /tʃæti/ [1] Someone who is **chatty** talks a lot in a friendly, informal way. ❑ *She's quite a chatty person.* [2] A **chatty** style of writing or talking is friendly and informal. ❑ *He wrote a chatty letter to his wife.* ADJ = talkative; ADJ

**chat-up line** **(chat-up lines)** A **chat-up line** is a remark that someone makes in order to start a conversation with someone they do not know but find sexually attractive. [BRIT] N-COUNT

✔ in AM, use **line**

**chauf|feur** /ʃoʊfəʳ, ʃoʊfɜːʳ/ **(chauffeurs, chauffeuring, chauffeured)** [1] The **chauffeur** of a rich or important person is the man or woman who is employed to look after their car and drive them around in it. [2] If you **chauffeur** someone somewhere, you drive them there in a car, usually as part of your job. ❑ *It was certainly useful to have her there to chauffeur him around... Caroline had a chauffeured car waiting to take her to London.*
N-COUNT; VERB; V n adv/prep; V-ed; Also V n

**chau|vin|ism** /ʃoʊvɪnɪzəm/ **Chauvinism** is a strong, unreasonable belief that your own country is more important and morally better than other people's. ❑ *It may also appeal to the latent chauvinism of many ordinary people.* ➔ See also **male chauvinism**. ♦ **chau|vin|ist** **(chauvinists)** *Antwerpers are so convinced that their city is best that other Belgians think them chauvinists.* ➔ See also **male chauvinist**.
N-UNCOUNT [disapproval]; N-COUNT

**chau|vin|is|tic** /ʃoʊvɪnɪstɪk/ [1] If you describe someone as **chauvinistic**, you believe that they think their own country is more important and morally better than any other. ❑ *...national narrow-mindedness and chauvinistic arrogance.* [2] If you describe a man or his behaviour as **chauvinistic**, you disapprove of him for believing that men are naturally better and more important than women. ❑ *My ex-boyfriend Anthony was very chauvinistic.*
ADJ: usu ADJ n [disapproval]; ADJ [disapproval]

**cheap** /tʃiːp/ **(cheaper, cheapest)** ◆◆◇ [1] Goods or services that are **cheap** cost less money than usual or than you expected. ❑ *Smoke detectors are cheap and easy to put up... Running costs are coming down because of cheaper fuel... They served breakfast all day and sold it cheap.* ♦ **cheap|ly** *It will produce electricity more cheaply than a nuclear plant.* ♦ **cheap|ness** *The cheapness and simplicity of the design makes it ideal for our task.* [2] If you describe goods as **cheap**, you mean they cost less money than similar products but their quality is poor. ❑ *Don't resort to cheap copies; save up for the real thing. ...a tight suit made of some cheap material.* [3] If you describe someone's remarks or actions as **cheap**, you mean that they are unkindly or insincerely using a situation to benefit themselves or to harm someone else. ❑ *These tests will inevitably be used by politicians to make cheap political points.* [4] If you describe someone as **cheap**, you are criticizing them for being unwilling to spend money. [AM] ❑ *Oh, please, Dad, just this once don't be cheap.* [5] If someone does or buys something **on the cheap**, they spend less money than they should because they are more concerned with what it costs than with its quality. [INFORMAL] ❑ *Most modern housing estates are terrible and inevitably done on the cheap.*
ADJ: v-link ADJ, ADJ n, v n ADJ ≠ expensive, dear; ADV: ADV after v; N-UNCOUNT; ADJ: ADJ n = shoddy; ADJ: ADJ n [disapproval]; ADJ: usu v-link ADJ [disapproval] = mean; PHRASE: PHR after v [disapproval]

**cheap|en** /tʃiːpən/ **(cheapens, cheapening, cheapened)** If something **cheapens** a person or thing, it lowers their reputation or position. ❑ *When America boycotted the Moscow Olympics it cheapened the medals won... Love is a word cheapened by overuse.* VERB; V n; V n

**cheapo** /tʃiːpoʊ/ **Cheapo** things are very inexpensive and probably of poor quality. [INFORMAL] ❑ *...cheapo deals on wobbly airlines.* ADJ: ADJ n

**cheap shot** **(cheap shots)** A **cheap shot** is a comment someone makes which you think is unfair or unkind. N-COUNT [disapproval]

**cheap|skate** /tʃiːpskeɪt/ **(cheapskates)** If you say that someone is a **cheapskate**, you think that they are mean and do not like spending money. ❑ *Tell your husband not to be a cheapskate.* N-COUNT [disapproval] = skinflint

**cheat** /tʃiːt/ **(cheats, cheating, cheated)** [1] When someone **cheats**, they do not obey a set of rules which they should be obeying, for example in a game or exam. ❑ *Students may be tempted to cheat in order to get into top schools.* ♦ **cheat|ing** *In an election in 1988, he was accused of cheating by his opponent.* [2] Someone who is a **cheat** does not obey a set of rules which they should be obeying. ❑ *Cheats will be disqualified.* [3] If someone **cheats** you **out of** something, they get it from you by behaving dishonestly. ❑ *The company engaged in a deliberate effort to cheat them out of their pensions... Many brokers were charged with cheating customers in commodity trades.* [4] If you say that someone **cheats death**, you mean they only just avoid being killed. [JOURNALISM] ❑ *He cheated death when he was rescued from the roof of his blazing cottage.*
VERB; V; N-UNCOUNT; N-COUNT; VERB; V n *out of/of* n; V n; PHRASE: V inflects

♦ **cheat on** [1] If someone **cheats on** their husband, wife, or partner, they have a sexual relationship with another person. [INFORMAL] ❑ *I'd found Philippe was cheating on me and I was angry and hurt.* [2] If someone **cheats on** something such as an agreement or their taxes, they do not do what they should do under a set of rules. [mainly AM] ❑ *Their job is to check that none of the signatory countries is cheating on the agreement.*
PHRASAL VERB; V P n; PHRASAL VERB; V P n

**cheat|er** /tʃiːtəʳ/ **(cheaters)** A **cheater** is someone who cheats. [mainly AM] N-COUNT

**check** /tʃek/ **(checks, checking, checked)** ◆◆◇ [1] If you **check** something such as a piece of information or a document, you make sure that it is correct or satisfactory. ❑ *Check the accuracy of everything in your CV... I think there is an age limit, but I'd have to check... She hadn't checked whether she had a clean ironed shirt... He checked that he had his room key... I shall need to check with the duty officer.* ➔ See also **cross-check**. ♦ **Check** is also a noun. ❑ *He is being constantly monitored with regular checks on his blood pressure. ...a security check.* [2] If you **check on** someone or something, you make sure they are in a safe or satisfactory condition. ❑ *He decided to check on things at the warehouse.* [3] If you **check** something that is written on a piece of paper, you put a mark, like a V with the right side extended, next to it to show that something is correct or has been selected or dealt with. [AM] ❑ *Frequently, men who check answer (b) have not actually had the experience of being repeatedly rejected by women.*
VERB; V n; V; V wh; V that; V *with* n; N-COUNT: usu with supp; VERB; V *on* n; VERB; V n

✔ in BRIT, usually use **tick**

[4] To **check** something, usually something bad, VERB

means to stop it from spreading or continuing. = curb ❑ *Sex education is also expected to help check the* V n *spread of AIDS.* 5 If you **check yourself** or if VERB something **checks** you, you suddenly stop what you are doing or saying. ❑ *He was about to lose his* V pron-refl *temper but checked himself in time... I held up one fin-* V n *ger to check him.* 6 When you **check** your lug- VERB gage at an airport, you give it to an official so that it can be taken on to your plane. ❑ *We arrived at* V n *the airport, checked our baggage and wandered around the gift shops.* ♦ To **check in** your luggage PHRASAL VERB means the same as to **check** it. ❑ *They checked in* V P n (not pron) Also V n P *their luggage and found seats in the departure lounge.* 7 The **check** in a restaurant is a piece of paper N-COUNT = bill on which the price of your meal is written and which you are given before you pay. [mainly AM]

✔ in BRIT, use **bill**

8 In a game of chess, you say **check** when you CONVENTION are attacking your opponent's king. 9 A pattern N-COUNT: oft N n of squares, usually of two colours, can be referred to as **checks** or a **check**. ❑ *Styles include stripes and checks. ...a red and white check dress.* 10 If PHRASE: V inflects something or someone **is held in check** or **is kept in check**, they are controlled and prevented from becoming too great or powerful. ❑ *Life on Earth will become unsustainable unless population growth is held in check.* 11 A **check** is the same as a **cheque**. [AM] 12 → See also **double-check**, **rain check**, **spot check**.

♦ **check in** 1 When you **check in** or **check** PHRASAL VERB = register ≠ check out **into** a hotel or clinic, or if someone **checks** you **in**, you arrive and go through the necessary procedures before you stay there. ❑ *I'll ring the hotel.* V P *I'll tell them we'll check in tomorrow... He has checked* V P n *into an alcohol treatment centre... Check us in at the* V n P *hotel and wait for my call.* 2 When you **check in** PHRASAL VERB at an airport, you arrive and show your ticket before going on a flight. ❑ *He had checked in at* V P *Amsterdam's Schiphol airport for a flight to Manchester.* → See also **check-in**, **check 6**.

♦ **check off** When you **check** things **off**, you PHRASAL VERB = tick off check or count them while referring to a list of them, to make sure you have considered all of them. ❑ *Once you've checked off the items you* V P n (not pron) *ordered, put this record in your file... I haven't* V n P *checked them off but I would say that's about the number.*

♦ **check out** 1 When you **check out of** a PHRASAL VERB ≠ check in hotel or clinic where you have been staying, or if someone **checks** you **out**, you pay the bill and leave. ❑ *They packed and checked out of the hotel... I* V P *of* n *was disappointed to miss Bryan, who had just checked* V P *out... I'd like to check him out of here the day after to-* V n P *of* n *morrow.* 2 If you **check out** something or some- PHRASAL VERB = investigate one, you find out information about them to make sure that everything is correct or satisfactory. ❑ *Maybe we ought to go down to the library and* V n P *check it out... The police had to check out the call.* V P n (not pron) 3 If something **checks out**, it is correct or satis- PHRASAL VERB factory. ❑ *She was in San Diego the weekend Jensen* V *got killed. It checked out.* 4 → See also **checkout**.

♦ **check up** 1 If you **check up on** some- PHRASAL VERB thing, you find out information about it. ❑ *It is* V P *on* n *certainly worth checking up on your benefit entitlements... The Government employs tax inspectors to* V P *check up and make sure people pay all their tax.* → See also **check-up**. 2 If you **check up on** some- PHRASAL VERB one, you obtain information about them, usually secretly. ❑ *I'm sure he knew I was checking up on* V P *on* n *him.*

**check|book** /tʃekbʊk/ → see **cheque book**.

**checked** /tʃekt/ Something that is **checked** ADJ = check has a pattern of small squares, usually of two colours. ❑ *He was wearing blue jeans and checked shirt.*

**check|er** /tʃekəʳ/ **(checkers)** 1 **Checkers** is a N-UNCOUNT game for two people, played with 24 round pieces on a board. [AM]

✔ in BRIT, use **draughts**

2 A **checker** is a person or machine that has the N-COUNT job of checking something. ❑ *Modern word processors usually have spelling checkers and even grammar checkers.*

**checker|board** /tʃekəʳbɔːʳd/ **(checkerboards)**

✔ in BRIT, also use **chequerboard**

1 A **checkerboard** is a square board with 64 N-COUNT black and white squares that is used for playing checkers or chess. [AM]

✔ in BRIT, use **draughts board**, **chessboard**

2 A **checkerboard** pattern is made up of equal- ADJ: ADJ n sized squares of two different colours, usually black and white.

**check|ered** /tʃekəʳd/ → see **chequered**.

**check-in** **(check-ins)** At an airport, a **check-in** N-COUNT is the counter or desk where you check in.

**check|ing ac|count** **(checking accounts)** A **checking account** is a personal bank ac- N-COUNT count which you can take money out of at any time using your cheque book or cash card. [AM]

✔ in BRIT, usually use **current account**

**check|list** /tʃeklɪst/ **(checklists)** A **checklist** N-COUNT: usu with supp, oft N *of* n = list is a list of all the things that you need to do, information that you want to find out, or things that you need to take somewhere, which you make in order to ensure that you do not forget anything. ❑ *Make a checklist of the tools and materials you will need.*

**check mark** **(check marks)** A **check mark** is N-COUNT a written mark like a V with the right side extended. It is used to show that something is correct or has been selected or dealt with. [AM]

✔ in BRIT, use **tick**

**check|mate** /tʃekmeɪt/ In chess, **check-** N-UNCOUNT = mate **mate** is a situation in which you cannot stop your king being captured and so you lose the game.

**check|out** /tʃekaʊt/ **(checkouts)** also **check-out**. In a supermarket, a **checkout** is a N-COUNT counter where you pay for things you are buying. ❑ *...queuing at the checkout in Sainsbury's.*

**check|point** /tʃekpɔɪnt/ **(checkpoints)** A N-COUNT **checkpoint** is a place where traffic is stopped so that it can be checked.

**check-up** **(check-ups)** also **checkup**. A N-COUNT **check-up** is a medical examination by your doctor or dentist to make sure that there is nothing wrong with your health. ❑ *The disease was detected during a routine check-up.*

**ched|dar** /tʃedəʳ/ **(cheddars)** **Cheddar** is a N-MASS type of hard yellow cheese, originally made in Britain.

**cheek** /tʃiːk/ **(cheeks)** 1 Your **cheeks** are the N-COUNT sides of your face below your eyes. ❑ *Tears were running down her cheeks... She kissed him lightly on both cheeks.* ♦ **-cheeked** *...rosy-cheeked, smiling* COMB in ADJ *children.* 2 You say that someone has a **cheek** N-SING: also no det, oft *the* N to-inf when you are annoyed or shocked at something unreasonable that they have done. [INFORMAL] ❑ *I'm amazed they had the cheek to ask in the first place... I still think it's a bit of a cheek sending a voucher rather than a refund... The cheek of it, lying to me like that!* 3 If you **turn the other cheek** PHRASE: V inflects when someone harms or insults you, you do not harm or insult them in return. 4 **cheek by jowl** → see **jowl**.

**cheek|bone** /tʃiːkboʊn/ **(cheekbones)** Your N-COUNT: usu pl **cheekbones** are the two bones in your face just below your eyes. ❑ *She was very beautiful, with high cheekbones.*

**cheeky** /tʃiːki/ **(cheekier, cheekiest)** If you de- ADJ scribe a person or their behaviour as **cheeky**, you think that they are slightly rude or disrespectful but in a charming or amusing way. [mainly BRIT]

❑ *The boy was cheeky and casual... Martin gave her a cheeky grin.* ♦ **cheeki|ly** /tʃiːkɪli/ *He strolled cheekily past the commissionaires for a free wash in the gentlemen's cloakroom.*
ADV: usu ADV with v, also ADV with cl

**cheer** /tʃɪəʳ/ **(cheers, cheering, cheered)** ◆◇◇
1 When people **cheer**, they shout loudly to show their approval or to encourage someone who is doing something such as taking part in a game. ❑ *The crowd cheered as Premier Wayne Goss unveiled a lifesize statue of poet Banjo Paterson... Swiss fans cheered Jakob Hlasek during yesterday's match with Courier. ...the Irish Americans who came to the park to cheer for their boys... Cheering crowds lined the route.* ♦ **Cheer** is also a noun. ❑ *The colonel was rewarded with a resounding cheer from the men.*
VERB ≠ boo, jeer; V; V n; V for n; V-ing; N-COUNT
2 If you **are cheered by** something, it makes you happier or less worried. ❑ *Stephen noticed that the people around him looked cheered by his presence... The weather was perfect for a picnic, he told himself, but the thought did nothing to cheer him.* ♦ **cheer|ing** *...very cheering news for all of us.*
VERB = hearten ≠ sadden; be V-ed; V n; ADJ = heartening
3 People sometimes say '**Cheers**' to each other just before they drink an alcoholic drink. [mainly BRIT]
CONVENTION formulae
4 Some people say '**Cheers**' as a way of saying 'thank you' or 'goodbye'. [BRIT, INFORMAL]
CONVENTION formulae

♦ **cheer on** When you **cheer** someone **on**, you shout loudly in order to encourage them, for example when they are taking part in a game. ❑ *A thousand supporters packed into the stadium to cheer them on... Most will probably be cheering on their favourite players.*
PHRASAL VERB; V n P; V P n (not pron)

♦ **cheer up** When you **cheer up** or when something **cheers** you **up**, you stop feeling depressed and become more cheerful. ❑ *I think he misses her terribly. You might cheer him up... I wrote that song just to cheer myself up... Cheer up, better times may be ahead.*
PHRASAL VERB; V n P; V pron-refl P; V P; Also V P n (not pron)

**cheer|ful** /tʃɪəʳfʊl/ 1 Someone who is **cheerful** is happy and shows this in their behaviour. ❑ *They are both very cheerful in spite of their colds... Jack sounded quite cheerful about the idea.* ♦ **cheer|ful|ly** *'We've come with good news,' Pat said cheerfully... She greeted him cheerfully.* ♦ **cheer|ful|ness** *I remember this extraordinary man with particular affection for his unfailing cheerfulness.*
ADJ = cheery; ADV: ADV with v; N-UNCOUNT: oft adj N
2 Something that is **cheerful** is pleasant and makes you feel happy. ❑ *The nursery is bright and cheerful, with plenty of toys.*
ADJ

**cheerio** /tʃɪərioʊ/ People sometimes say '**Cheerio**' as a way of saying goodbye. [BRIT, INFORMAL]
CONVENTION formulae = bye

**cheer|leader** /tʃɪəʳliːdəʳ/ **(cheerleaders)** A **cheerleader** is one of the people who leads the crowd in cheering at a large public event, especially a sports event.
N-COUNT

**cheer|less** /tʃɪəʳləs/ **Cheerless** places or weather are dull and depressing. ❑ *The kitchen was dank and cheerless. ...a bleak, cheerless day.*
ADJ = gloomy

**cheery** /tʃɪəri/ **(cheerier, cheeriest)** If you describe a person or their behaviour as **cheery**, you mean that they are cheerful and happy. ❑ *She was cheery and talked to them about their problems.* ♦ **cheeri|ly** *'Come on in,' she said cheerily.*
ADJ = cheerful; ADV

**cheese** /tʃiːz/ **(cheeses)** ◆◇◇ 1 **Cheese** is a solid food made from milk. It is usually white or yellow. ❑ *...bread and cheese. ...cheese sauce... He cut the mould off a piece of cheese. ...delicious French cheeses.* → See also **cottage cheese, cream cheese, goat cheese, macaroni cheese.**
N-MASS
2 **as different as chalk and cheese** → see **chalk**.

**cheese|board** /tʃiːzbɔːʳd/ **(cheeseboards)** also **cheese board.** A **cheeseboard** is a board from which cheese is served at a meal.
N-COUNT: usu sing

**cheese|burg|er** /tʃiːzbɜːʳgəʳ/ **(cheeseburgers)** A **cheeseburger** is a flat round piece of cooked meat called a burger with a slice of cheese on top, served in a bread roll.
N-COUNT

**cheese|cake** /tʃiːzkeɪk/ **(cheesecakes)** **Cheesecake** is a dessert that consists of a base made from broken biscuits covered with a soft sweet mixture containing cream cheese.
N-VAR

**cheese|cloth** /tʃiːzklɒθ, AM -klɔːθ/ **Cheesecloth** is cotton cloth that is very thin and light. There are tiny holes between the threads of the cloth. ❑ *...cheesecloth shirts.*
N-UNCOUNT

**cheesed off** /tʃiːzd ɒf/ If you are **cheesed off**, you are annoyed, bored, or disappointed. [BRIT, INFORMAL] ❑ *Jean was thoroughly cheesed off by the whole affair.*
ADJ: v-link ADJ

**cheesy** /tʃiːzi/ **(cheesier, cheesiest)**
1 **Cheesy** food is food that tastes or smells of cheese. ❑ *...cheesy biscuits.*
ADJ: usu ADJ n
2 If you describe something as **cheesy**, you mean that it is cheap, unpleasant, or insincere. [INFORMAL] ❑ *...a cheesy Baghdad hotel... Politicians persist in imagining that 'the people' warm to their cheesy slogans.*
ADJ disapproval

**chee|tah** /tʃiːtə/ **(cheetahs)** A **cheetah** is a wild animal that looks like a large cat with black spots on its body. Cheetahs can run very fast.
N-COUNT

**chef** /ʃef/ **(chefs)** A **chef** is a cook in a restaurant or hotel.
N-COUNT

**chemi|cal** /kemɪkəl/ **(chemicals)** ◆◆◇
1 **Chemical** means involving or resulting from a reaction between two or more substances, or relating to the substances that something consists of. ❑ *...chemical reactions that cause ozone destruction. ...the chemical composition of the ocean. ...chemical weapons.* ♦ **chemi|cal|ly** /kemɪkli/ *...chemically treated foods... The medicine chemically affects your physiology.*
ADJ: ADJ n; ADV: ADV with v, ADV adj
2 **Chemicals** are substances that are used in a chemical process or made by a chemical process. ❑ *The whole food chain is affected by the over-use of chemicals in agriculture. ...the chemical industry.*
N-COUNT: usu pl

**chemi|cal en|gi|neer** **(chemical engineers)** A **chemical engineer** is a person who designs and constructs the machines needed for industrial chemical processes.
N-COUNT

**chemi|cal en|gi|neer|ing** **Chemical engineering** is the designing and constructing of machines that are needed for industrial chemical processes.
N-UNCOUNT

**che|mise** /ʃəmiːz/ **(chemises)** A **chemise** is a long, loose piece of underwear worn by women in former times.
N-COUNT

**chem|ist** /kemɪst/ **(chemists)** 1 A **chemist** or a **chemist's** is a shop where drugs and medicines are sold or given out, and where you can buy cosmetics and some household goods. [BRIT] ❑ *There are many creams available from the chemist which should clear the infection.*
N-COUNT: oft the N = pharmacy
2 A **chemist** is someone who works in a chemist's shop and is qualified to prepare and sell medicines. [BRIT]
N-COUNT = pharmacist

☑ in AM, use **druggist, pharmacist**

3 A **chemist** is a person who does research connected with chemistry or who studies chemistry. ❑ *She worked as a research chemist.*
N-COUNT

**chem|is|try** /kemɪstri/ 1 **Chemistry** is the scientific study of the structure of substances and of the way that they react with other substances.
N-UNCOUNT
2 The **chemistry** of an organism or a material is the chemical substances that make it up and the chemical reactions that go on inside it. ❑ *We have literally altered the chemistry of our planet's atmosphere... If the supply of vitamins and minerals in the diet is inadequate, this will result in changes in body chemistry.*
N-UNCOUNT: usu with supp
3 If you say that there is **chemistry** between two people, you mean that is obvious they are attracted to each other or like each other very much. ❑ *...the extraordinary chemistry between Ingrid and Bogart.*
N-UNCOUNT

**chemo|thera|py** /kiːmoʊθerəpi/ **Chemotherapy** is the treatment of disease using chemicals. It is often used in treating cancer.
N-UNCOUNT

**che|nille** /ʃəniːl/ **Chenille** is cloth or clothing made from a type of thick furry thread.
N-UNCOUNT

**cheque** /tʃek/ **(cheques)**

☑ in AM, use **check**

A **cheque** is a printed form on which you write an amount of money and who it is to be paid to. Your bank then pays the money to that person from your account. ❑ *He wrote them a cheque for £10,000... I'd like to pay by cheque.* → See also **blank cheque, traveller's cheque.** N-COUNT: also *by* N

**cheque book** **(cheque books)**

> The spellings **chequebook**, and in American English **checkbook**, are also used.

A **cheque book** is a book of cheques which your bank gives you so that you can pay for things by cheque. N-COUNT

**cheque|book jour|nal|ism** also **cheque-book journalism.**

> in AM, use **checkbook journalism**

**Chequebook journalism** is the practice of paying people large sums of money for information about crimes or famous people in order to get material for newspaper articles. N-UNCOUNT [disapproval]

**cheque card** **(cheque cards)** In Britain, a **cheque card** or a **cheque guarantee card** is a small plastic card given to you by your bank and which you have to show when you are paying for something by cheque or when you are cashing a cheque at another bank. N-COUNT

**chequer|board** /tʃekəʳbɔːʳd/ → see **checkerboard.**

**cheq|uered** /tʃekəʳd/

> in AM, use **checkered**

1 If a person or organization has had a **chequered** career or history, they have had a varied past with both good and bad periods. ❑ *He had a chequered political career spanning nearly forty years... Alan had led a very chequered past and had been to prison lots of times.* ADJ: usu ADJ n 2 Something that is **chequered** has a pattern with squares of two or more different colours. ❑ *...red chequered tablecloths.* ADJ: ADJ n = checked

**cher|ish** /tʃerɪʃ/ **(cherishes, cherishing, cherished)** 1 If you **cherish** something such as a hope or a pleasant memory, you keep it in your mind for a long period of time. ❑ *The president will cherish the memory of this visit to Ohio.* VERB = treasure, V n ♦ **cher|ished** *...the cherished dream of a world without wars.* ADJ: ADJ n 2 If you **cherish** someone or something, you take good care of them because you love them. ❑ *The previous owners had cherished the house.* VERB, V n ♦ **cher|ished** *He described the picture as his most cherished possession.* ADJ: ADJ n 3 If you **cherish** a right, a privilege, or a principle, you regard it as important and try hard to keep it. ❑ *These people cherish their independence and sovereignty.* VERB, V n ♦ **cher|ished** *Freud called into question some deeply cherished beliefs.* ADJ: ADJ n

**che|root** /ʃəruːt/ **(cheroots)** A **cheroot** is a cigar with both ends cut flat. N-COUNT

**cher|ry** /tʃeri/ **(cherries)** 1 **Cherries** are small, round fruit with red skins. → See picture on page 1711. N-COUNT 2 A **cherry** or a **cherry tree** is a tree that cherries grow on. N-COUNT

**cherry-pick** /tʃeripɪk/ **(cherry-picks, cherry-picking, cherry-picked)** If someone **cherry-picks** people or things, they choose the best ones from a group of them, often in a way that other people consider unfair. ❑ *The club is in debt while others are queuing to cherry-pick their best players.* VERB, V n

**cher|ub** /tʃerəb/ **(cherubs)** A **cherub** is a kind of angel that is represented in art as a naked child with wings. N-COUNT

**che|ru|bic** /tʃəruːbɪk/ If someone looks **cherubic**, they look sweet and innocent like a cherub. [LITERARY] ❑ *...her beaming, cherubic face.* ADJ

**cher|vil** /tʃɜːʳvɪl/ **Chervil** is a herb that tastes like aniseed. N-UNCOUNT

**Chesh|ire cat** /tʃeʃəʳ kæt/ If someone is grinning **like a Cheshire cat** or **like the Cheshire cat**, they are smiling very widely. ❑ *He had a grin on his face like a Cheshire Cat. ...a Cheshire Cat smile.* PHRASE

**chess** /tʃes/ **Chess** is a game for two people, played on a chessboard. Each player has 16 pieces, including a king. Your aim is to move your pieces so that your opponent's king cannot escape being taken. ❑ *...the world chess championships.* N-UNCOUNT

**chess|board** /tʃesbɔːʳd/ **(chessboards)** A **chessboard** is a square board with 64 black and white squares that is used for playing chess. N-COUNT

**chest** /tʃest/ **(chests)** 1 Your **chest** is the top part of the front of your body where your ribs, lungs, and heart are. ❑ *He crossed his arms over his chest... He was shot in the chest... He complained of chest pain.* ◆◇◇ N-COUNT: oft poss N 2 A **chest** is a large, heavy box used for storing things. ❑ *At the very bottom of the chest were his carving tools. ...a treasure chest. ...a medicine chest.* N-COUNT = trunk 3 If you **get** something **off** your **chest**, you talk about something that has been worrying you. ❑ *I feel it's done me good to get it off my chest.* PHRASE: V inflects ≠ bottle up

**chest|nut** /tʃesnʌt/ **(chestnuts)** 1 A **chestnut** or **chestnut tree** is a tall tree with broad leaves. → See also **horse chestnut.** N-COUNT 2 **Chestnuts** are the reddish-brown nuts that grow on chestnut trees. You can eat chestnuts. N-COUNT 3 Something that is **chestnut** is dark reddish-brown in colour. ❑ *...a woman with chestnut hair. ...a chestnut mare.* COLOUR

**chest of drawers** **(chests of drawers)** A **chest of drawers** is a low, flat piece of furniture with drawers in which you keep clothes and other things. N-COUNT

**chesty** /tʃesti/ If you have a **chesty** cough, you have a lot of mucus in your lungs. [BRIT] ADJ: ADJ n

**chev|ron** /ʃevrɒn/ **(chevrons)** A **chevron** is a V shape. ❑ *The chevron or arrow road sign indicates a sharp bend to the left or right.* N-COUNT

**chew** /tʃuː/ **(chews, chewing, chewed)** 1 When you **chew** food, you use your teeth to break it up in your mouth so that it becomes easier to swallow. ❑ *Be certain to eat slowly and chew your food extremely well... Daniel leaned back on the sofa, still chewing on his apple. ...the sound of his mother chewing and swallowing.* VERB, V n, V *at/on* n, V 2 If you **chew** gum or tobacco, you keep biting it and moving it around your mouth to taste the flavour of it. You do not swallow it. ❑ *One girl was chewing gum.* VERB, V n 3 If you **chew** your lips or your fingernails, you keep biting them because you are nervous. ❑ *He chewed his lower lip nervously.* VERB, V n 4 If a person or animal **chews** an object, they bite it with their teeth. ❑ *They pause and chew their pencils... One owner left his pet under the stairs where the animal chewed through electric cables.* VERB = bite, V n, V prep 5 If you say that someone **has bitten off more than** they **can chew**, you mean that they are trying to do something which is too difficult for them. ❑ *Micky is used to handling dodgy deals but this time fears he may have bitten off more than he can chew.* PHRASE: *bite* inflects 6 to **chew the cud** → see **cud.**

♦ **chew up** 1 If you **chew** food **up**, you chew it until it is completely crushed or soft. ❑ *I took one of the pills and chewed it up.* PHRASAL VERB, V n P, Also V P n 2 If something **is chewed up**, it has been destroyed or damaged in some way. [INFORMAL] ❑ *Every spring the ozone is chewed up, and the hole appears. ...rebels who are now chewing up Government-held territory... This town is notorious for chewing people up and spitting them out.* PHRASAL VERB, *be* V-ed P, V P n (not pron), V n P

**chew|ing gum** **Chewing gum** is a kind of sweet that you can chew for a long time. You do not swallow it. ❑ *...a stick of chewing gum.* N-UNCOUNT = gum

**chewy** /tʃuːi/ **(chewier, chewiest)** If food is **chewy**, it needs to be chewed a lot before it becomes soft enough to swallow. ❑ *The meat was too chewy. ...chewy chocolate cookies.* ADJ

**chia|ro|scu|ro** /kiærəskʊəroʊ/ **Chiaroscuro** is the use of light and shade in a picture, or the effect produced by light and shade in a place. ❑ *...the natural chiaroscuro of the place.* N-UNCOUNT

**chic** /ʃiːk/ [1] Something or someone that is **chic** is fashionable and sophisticated. ❑ *Her gown was very French and very chic.* ADJ = stylish [2] **Chic** is used to refer to a particular style or to the quality of being chic. ❑ *...French designer chic.* N-UNCOUNT

**chi|can|ery** /ʃɪkeɪnəri/ **(chicaneries)** **Chicanery** is using cleverness to cheat people. [FORMAL] N-UNCOUNT: also N in pl = trickery

**chi|ca|no** /tʃɪkeɪnoʊ/ **(chicanos)** A **chicano** is an American citizen, whose family originally came from Mexico. [AM] ❑ *...views expressed by one young Chicano interviewed by Phinney.* N-COUNT

**chick** /tʃɪk/ **(chicks)** A **chick** is a baby bird. N-COUNT

**chick|en** /tʃɪkɪn/ **(chickens, chickening, chickened)** ◆◇◇ [1] **Chickens** are birds which are kept on a farm for their eggs and for their meat. ❑ *Lionel built a coop so that they could raise chickens and have a supply of fresh eggs. ...free-range chickens.* N-COUNT = hen ♦ **Chicken** is the flesh of this bird eaten as food. ❑ *...roast chicken with wild mushrooms. ...chicken soup.* N-UNCOUNT [2] If someone calls you a **chicken**, they mean that you are afraid to do something. [INFORMAL] ❑ *I'm scared of the dark. I'm a big chicken.* N-COUNT disapproval = coward ♦ **Chicken** is also an adjective. ❑ *Why are you so chicken, Gregory?* ADJ: v-link ADJ

PHRASES [3] If you say that someone **is counting** their **chickens**, you mean that they are assuming that they will be successful or get something, when this is not certain. ❑ *I don't want to count my chickens before they are hatched.* PHRASE: V inflects [4] If you describe a situation as a **chicken and egg** situation, you mean that it is impossible to decide which of two things caused the other one. ❑ *It's a chicken and egg situation. Does the deficiency lead to the eczema or has the eczema led to certain deficiencies?* PHRASE: PHR n [5] **chickens come home to roost** → see **roost**.

♦ **chicken out** If someone **chickens out of** something they were intending to do, they decide not to do it because they are afraid. [INFORMAL] ❑ *His mother complains that he makes excuses to chicken out of family occasions such as weddings... I had never ridden on a motor-cycle before. But it was too late to chicken out.* PHRASAL VERB V P *of* n V P

**chick|en feed** also **chickenfeed.** If you think that an amount of money is so small it is hardly worth having or considering, you can say that it is **chicken feed**. ❑ *I was making a million a year, but that's chicken feed in the pop business.* N-UNCOUNT = peanuts

**chicken|pox** /tʃɪkɪnpɒks/ also **chicken pox. Chickenpox** is a disease which gives you a high temperature and red spots that itch. N-UNCOUNT

**chick|en wire** **Chicken wire** is a type of thin wire netting. N-UNCOUNT

**chick flick** **(chick flicks)** A **chick flick** is a romantic film that is not very serious and is intended to appeal to women. [INFORMAL] N-COUNT

**chick lit** **Chick lit** is modern fiction about the lives and romantic problems of young women, usually written by young women. [INFORMAL] N-UNCOUNT

**chick|pea** /tʃɪkpiː/ **(chickpeas)** also **chick pea. Chickpeas** are hard round seeds that look like pale brown peas. They can be cooked and eaten. N-COUNT: usu pl

**chick|weed** /tʃɪkwiːd/ **Chickweed** is a plant with small leaves and white flowers which grows close to the ground. N-UNCOUNT

**chico|ry** /tʃɪkəri/ **Chicory** is a plant with crunchy bitter tasting leaves. It is eaten in salads, and its roots are sometimes used instead of coffee. N-UNCOUNT

**chide** /tʃaɪd/ **(chides, chiding, chided)** If you **chide** someone, you speak to them angrily because they have done something wicked or foolish. [OLD-FASHIONED] ❑ *Cross chided himself for worrying... He gently chided the two women.* VERB = scold V n *for/about* -ing/n V n

**chief** /tʃiːf/ **(chiefs)** ◆◆◆ [1] The **chief** of an organization is the person who is in charge of it. ❑ *...a commission appointed by the police chief. ...Putin's chief of security.* N-COUNT: with supp [2] The **chief** of a tribe is its leader. ❑ *...Sitting Bull, chief of the Sioux tribes of the Great Plains.* N-COUNT; N-TITLE [3] **Chief** is used in the job titles of the most senior worker or workers of a particular kind in an organization. ❑ *...the chief test pilot.* ADJ: ADJ n = head [4] The **chief** cause, part, or member of something is the most important one. ❑ *Financial stress is well established as a chief reason for divorce... The job went to one of his chief rivals.* ADJ: ADJ n = main, principal

**Chief Con|sta|ble** **(Chief Constables)** A **Chief Constable** is the officer who is in charge of the police force in a particular county or area in Britain. N-COUNT; N-TITLE

**chief ex|ecu|tive of|fic|er** **(chief executive officers)** The **chief executive officer** of a company is the person who has overall responsibility for the management of that company. The abbreviation **CEO** is often used. [BUSINESS] N-COUNT

**Chief Jus|tice** **(Chief Justices)** A **Chief Justice** is the most important judge of a court of law, especially a supreme court. N-COUNT; N-TITLE

**chief|ly** /tʃiːfli/ You use **chiefly** to indicate that a particular reason, emotion, method, or feature is the main or most important one. ❑ *He joined the consular service, chiefly because this was one of the few job vacancies.* ADV: ADV with cl/group, ADV with v = mainly, primarily

**Chief of Staff** **(Chiefs of Staff)** The **Chiefs of Staff** are the highest-ranking officers of each service of the armed forces. N-COUNT

**chief|tain** /tʃiːftən/ **(chieftains)** A **chieftain** is the leader of a tribe. ❑ *...the legendary British chieftain, King Arthur.* N-COUNT

**chif|fon** /ʃɪfɒn, AM ʃɪfɑːn/ **(chiffons)** **Chiffon** is a kind of very thin silk or nylon cloth that you can see through. ❑ *...floaty chiffon skirts.* N-MASS

**chi|gnon** /ʃiːnjɒn, AM ʃiːnjɑːn/ **(chignons)** A **chignon** is a knot of hair worn at the back of a woman's head. N-COUNT = bun

**Chi|hua|hua** /tʃɪwɑːwɑː/ **(Chihuahuas)** also **chihuahua.** A **Chihuahua** is a very small dog with short hair. N-COUNT

**chil|blain** /tʃɪlbleɪn/ **(chilblains)** **Chilblains** are painful red swellings which people sometimes get on their fingers or toes in cold weather. N-COUNT: usu pl

**child** /tʃaɪld/ **(children)** ◆◆◆ [1] A **child** is a human being who is not yet an adult. ❑ *When I was a child I lived in a country village... He's just a child. ...a child of six... It was only suitable for children.* N-COUNT [2] Someone's **children** are their sons and daughters of any age. ❑ *How are the children?... The young couple decided to have a child.* N-COUNT

**child|bearing** /tʃaɪldbeərɪŋ/ [1] **Childbearing** is the process of giving birth to babies. N-UNCOUNT [2] A woman of **childbearing** age is of an age when women are normally able to give birth to children. ADJ: ADJ n

**child ben|efit** In Britain, **child benefit** is an amount of money paid weekly by the state to families for each of their children. N-UNCOUNT

**child|birth** /tʃaɪldbɜːʳθ/ **Childbirth** is the act of giving birth to a child. ❑ *She died in childbirth.* N-UNCOUNT = labour

**child|care** /tʃaɪldkeəʳ/ **Childcare** refers to looking after children, and to the facilities which help parents to do so. ❑ *Both partners shared childcare.* N-UNCOUNT

**child|hood** /tʃaɪldhʊd/ **(childhoods)** ◆◇◇ A person's **childhood** is the period of their life when they are a child. ❑ *She had a happy childhood. ...childhood illnesses.* N-VAR: oft poss N, N n

**child|ish** /tʃaɪldɪʃ/ [1] **Childish** means relating to or typical of a child. ❑ *...childish enthusiasm.* ADJ: usu ADJ n [2] If you describe someone, especially an adult, as **childish**, you disapprove of them because they behave in an immature way. ❑ *...Penny's selfish and childish behaviour... Don't be so childish.* ADJ disapproval = immature

**child|less** /tʃaɪldləs/ Someone who is **childless** has no children. ❑ *...childless couples.* ADJ

**child|like** /tʃaɪldlaɪk/ You describe someone as **childlike** when they seem like a child in their character, appearance, or behaviour. ❑ *His most enduring quality is his childlike innocence.* ADJ

**child|minder** /tʃaɪldmaɪndəʳ/ **(childminders)** N-COUNT A **childminder** is someone whose job it is to look after children when the children's parents are away or are at work. Childminders usually work in their own homes. [BRIT]

**child|minding** /tʃaɪldmaɪndɪŋ/ also **child-minding. Childminding** is looking after children when it is done by someone such as a childminder. [BRIT] N-UNCOUNT

**child prodi|gy** **(child prodigies)** A **child prodigy** is a child with a very great talent. ❑ *She was a child prodigy, giving concerts before she was a teenager.* N-COUNT

**child|proof** /tʃaɪldpruːf/ also **child proof.** Something that is **childproof** is designed in a way which ensures that children cannot harm it or be harmed by it. ❑ *The rear doors include childproof locks.* ADJ

**chil|dren** /tʃɪldrən/ **Children** is the plural of **child**.

**chili** /tʃɪli/ **(chilies** or **chilis)** ➔ see **chilli**.

**chill** /tʃɪl/ **(chills, chilling, chilled)** 1 When you **chill** something or when it **chills**, you lower its temperature so that it becomes colder but does not freeze. ❑ *Chill the fruit salad until serving time... These doughs can be rolled out while you wait for the pastry to chill. ...a glass of chilled champagne.* VERB ≠ warm up; V n; V; V-ed 2 When cold weather or something cold **chills** a person or a place, it makes that person or that place feel very cold. ❑ *An exposed garden may be chilled by cold winds... Wade placed his chilled hands on the radiator and warmed them... The boulder sheltered them from the chilling wind.* VERB; V n; V-ed; V-ing 3 If something sends a **chill** through you, it gives you a sudden feeling of fear or anxiety. ❑ *The violence used against the students sent a chill through Indonesia... He smiled, an odd, dreamy smile that sent chills up my back.* N-COUNT = shiver 4 A **chill** is a mild illness which can give you a slight fever and headache. ❑ *He caught a chill while performing at a rain-soaked open-air venue.* N-COUNT 5 **Chill** weather is cold and unpleasant. ❑ *...chill winds, rain and choppy seas.* ♦ **Chill** is also a noun. ❑ *...the cold chill of the night.* ADJ: ADJ n; N-SING

♦ **chill out** To **chill out** means to relax after you have done something tiring or stressful. [INFORMAL] ❑ *After raves, we used to chill out in each others' bedrooms.* PHRASAL VERB = relax; V P

**chill|er** /tʃɪləʳ/ **(chillers)** A **chiller** is a very frightening film or novel. N-COUNT

**chil|li** /tʃɪli/ **(chillies** or **chillis)** also **chili. Chillies** are small red or green peppers. They have a very hot taste and are used in cooking. N-VAR

**chil|li con car|ne** /tʃɪli kɒn kɑːʳni/ **Chilli con carne** is a dish made from minced meat, vegetables, and powdered or fresh chillies. N-UNCOUNT

**chill|ing** /tʃɪlɪŋ/ If you describe something as **chilling**, you mean it is frightening. ❑ *He described in chilling detail how he attacked her during one of their frequent rows.* ♦ **chill|ing|ly** *...since the murder of a London teenager in chillingly similar circumstances in February.* ADJ: usu ADJ n; ADV: usu ADV adj

**chil|li pow|der** also **chili powder. Chilli powder** is a very hot-tasting powder made mainly from dried chillies. It is used in cooking. N-UNCOUNT

**chill-out** **Chill-out** places or things are intended to help you relax. [BRIT, INFORMAL] ❑ *...some summer chill-out music.* ADJ: ADJ n

**chil|ly** /tʃɪli/ **(chillier, chilliest)** 1 Something that is **chilly** is unpleasantly cold. ❑ *It was a chilly afternoon... The rooms had grown chilly.* 2 If you feel **chilly**, you feel rather cold. ❑ *I'm a bit chilly.* 3 You say that relations between people are **chilly** or that a person's response is **chilly** when they are not friendly, welcoming, or enthusiastic. ❑ *I was slightly afraid of their chilly distant politeness.* ADJ: oft it v-link ADJ; ADJ: v-link ADJ; ADJ

**chime** /tʃaɪm/ **(chimes, chiming, chimed)** 1 When a bell or a clock **chimes**, it makes ringing sounds. ❑ *He heard the front doorbell chime. ...as the Guildhall clock chimed three o'clock. ...a mahogany chiming clock.* VERB; V; V n; V-ing 2 A **chime** is a ringing sound made by a bell, especially when it is part of a clock. ❑ *The ceremony started as the chimes of midnight struck.* N-COUNT 3 **Chimes** are a set of small objects which make a ringing sound when they are blown by the wind. ❑ *...the haunting sound of the wind chimes.* N-PLURAL: usu supp N

♦ **chime in** If you **chime in**, you say something just after someone else has spoken. ❑ *'Why?' Pete asked impatiently. — 'Yes, why?' Bob chimed in. 'It seems like a good idea to me.'... At this, some of the others chime in with memories of prewar deprivations.* PHRASAL VERB; V P with quote; V P with n; Also V P

♦ **chime in with** or **chime with** If one thing **chimes in with** another thing or **chimes with** it, the two things are similar or consistent with each other. ❑ *He has managed to find a response to each new political development that chimes in with most Germans' instinct... The president's remarks do not entirely chime with those coming from American and British politicians.* PHRASAL VERB; V P P n; V P n

**chi|mera** /kaɪmɪərə/ **(chimeras)** 1 A **chimera** is an unrealistic idea that you have about something or a hope that you have that is unlikely to be fulfilled. [FORMAL] ❑ *Religious unity remained as much a chimera as ever.* N-COUNT 2 In Greek mythology, a **chimera** is a creature with the head of a lion, the body of a goat, and the tail of a snake. N-COUNT

**chim|ney** /tʃɪmni/ **(chimneys)** A **chimney** is a pipe through which smoke goes up into the air, usually through the roof of a building. ➔ See picture on page 1705. ❑ *This gas fire doesn't need a chimney.* N-COUNT

**chim|ney breast** **(chimney breasts)** also **chimney-breast.** A **chimney breast** is the part of a wall in a room which is built out round a chimney. [BRIT] N-COUNT

**chimney|piece** /tʃɪmnipiːs/ **(chimneypieces)** also **chimney-piece.** A **chimneypiece** is the same as a **mantlepiece**. [BRIT] N-COUNT

**chim|ney pot** **(chimney pots)** also **chimney-pot.** A **chimney pot** is a short pipe which is fixed on top of a chimney. ➔ See picture on page 1705. N-COUNT

**chim|ney stack** **(chimney stacks)** also **chimney-stack.** A **chimney stack** is the brick or stone part of a chimney that is above the roof of a building. [BRIT] ➔ See picture on page 1705. N-COUNT

**chim|ney sweep** **(chimney sweeps)** also **chimney-sweep.** A **chimney sweep** is a person whose job is to clean the soot out of chimneys. N-COUNT

**chimp** /tʃɪmp/ **(chimps)** A **chimp** is the same as a **chimpanzee**. [INFORMAL] N-COUNT

**chim|pan|zee** /tʃɪmpænziː/ **(chimpanzees)** A **chimpanzee** is a kind of small African ape. N-COUNT

**chin** /tʃɪn/ **(chins)** Your **chin** is the part of your face that is below your mouth and above your neck. ❑ *...a double chin... He rubbed the gray stubble on his chin.* N-COUNT

**chi|na** /tʃaɪnə/ 1 **China** is a hard white substance made from clay. It is used to make things such as cups, bowls, plates, and ornaments. ❑ *...a small boat made of china. ...china cups.* ➔ See also **bone china**. N-UNCOUNT: oft N n 2 Cups, bowls, plates, and ornaments made of china are referred to as **china**. ❑ *Judy collects blue and white china.* N-UNCOUNT

**Chi|na tea** **China tea** is tea made from large dark green or reddish-brown tea leaves. It is usually drunk without milk or sugar. N-UNCOUNT

**China|town** /tʃaɪnətaʊn/ **Chinatown** is the name given to the area in a city where there are many Chinese shops and restaurants, and which is a social centre for the Chinese community in the city. N-UNCOUNT

**Chi|nese** /tʃaɪniːz/ **(Chinese)** 1 Something that is **Chinese** relates or belongs to China or its languages or people. ♦ The **Chinese** are the people who come from China. 2 The languages that ADJ; N-COUNT: usu pl; N-UNCOUNT are spoken in China, especially Mandarin, are often referred to as **Chinese**.

**chink** /tʃɪŋk/ **(chinks)** 1 A **chink** in a surface is a very narrow crack or opening in it. ❑ *...a chink in the wall... He peered through a chink in the curtains.* N-COUNT: usu N *in* n

2 A **chink of** light is a small patch of light that shines through a small opening in something. ❑ *I noticed a chink of light at the end of the corridor.* N-COUNT: N *of* n

**chi|nos** /tʃiːnoʊz/ **Chinos** are casual, loose trousers made from cotton. N-PLURAL: also *a pair of* N

**chintz** /tʃɪnts/ **(chintzes)** **Chintz** is a cotton fabric decorated with flowery patterns. ❑ *...chintz curtains.* N-MASS

**chintzy** /tʃɪntsi/ 1 Something that is **chintzy** is decorated or covered with chintz. [BRIT] ❑ *...chintzy armchairs.* ADJ 2 If you describe something as **chintzy**, you mean that it is showy and looks cheap. [mainly AM] ❑ *...a chintzy table lamp.* ADJ disapproval

3 You can describe someone as **chintzy** if they are mean and seem to spend very little money compared with other people. [AM, INFORMAL] ❑ *...disadvantages such as depending on chintzy and humiliating public dole for income.* ADJ disapproval

**chip** /tʃɪp/ **(chips, chipping, chipped)** 1 **Chips** are long, thin pieces of potato fried in oil or fat and eaten hot, usually with a meal. [BRIT] ❑ *I had fish and chips in a cafe.* ◆◇◇ N-COUNT: usu pl

☑ in AM, use **French fries**

2 **Chips** or **potato chips** are very thin slices of fried potato that are eaten cold as a snack. [AM] ❑ *...a package of onion-flavored potato chips.* N-COUNT: usu pl

☑ in BRIT, use **crisps**

3 A silicon **chip** is a very small piece of silicon with electronic circuits on it which is part of a computer or other piece of machinery. N-COUNT 4 A **chip** is a small piece of something or a small piece which has been broken off something. ❑ *It contains real chocolate chips... Teichler's eyes gleamed like chips of blue glass.* N-COUNT: oft supp N 5 A **chip** in something such as a piece of china or furniture is where a small piece has been broken off it. ❑ *The washbasin had a small chip.* N-COUNT 6 If you **chip** something or if it **chips**, a small piece is broken off it. ❑ *The blow chipped the woman's tooth... Steel baths are lighter but chip easily.* VERB V n V ♦ **chipped** *They drank out of chipped mugs.* ADJ 7 **Chips** are plastic counters used in gambling to represent money. ❑ *He put the pile of chips in the center of the table and drew a card.* N-COUNT: usu pl 8 In discussions between people or governments, a **chip** or a **bargaining chip** is something of value which one side holds, which can be exchanged for something they want from the other side. ❑ *The information could be used as a bargaining chip to extract some parallel information from Britain.* N-COUNT 9 ➔ See also **blue chip**.

**PHRASES** 10 If you describe someone as **a chip off the old block**, you mean that they are just like one of their parents in character or behaviour. ❑ *Her fifth child was born, a son who Sally at first thought was another chip off the old block.* PHRASE: usu v-link PHR 11 If you say that something happens **when the chips are down**, you mean it happens when a situation gets very difficult. [INFORMAL] ❑ *When the chips are down, she's very tough.* PHRASE 12 If you say that someone has **a chip on** their **shoulder**, you think that they feel inferior or that they believe they have been treated unfairly. [INFORMAL] ❑ *He had this chip on his shoulder about my mum and dad thinking that they're better than him.* PHRASE: Ns inflect, usu *have/with* PHR

♦ **chip away at** 1 If you **chip away at** something such as an idea, a feeling, or a system, you gradually make it weaker or less likely to succeed by repeated efforts. ❑ *Instead of an outright coup attempt, the rebels want to chip away at her authority.* PHRASAL VERB = erode V P P n 2 If you **chip away at** a debt or an amount of money, you gradually reduce it. ❑ *The group had hoped to chip away at its debts by selling assets.* PHRASAL VERB V P P n

♦ **chip in** 1 When a number of people **chip in**, each person gives some money so that they can pay for something together. [INFORMAL] ❑ *They chip in for the petrol and food... The brothers chip in a certain amount of money each month to hire a home health aide.* PHRASAL VERB = contribute V P V P n Also V P with n 2 If someone **chips in** during a conversation, they interrupt it in order to say something. [INFORMAL] ❑ *'That's true,' chipped in Quaver... He chipped in before Clements could answer.* PHRASAL VERB V P with quote V P

**chip|board** /tʃɪpbɔːʳd/ **Chipboard** is a hard material made out of very small pieces of wood which have been pressed together. It is often used for making doors and furniture. N-UNCOUNT

**chip|munk** /tʃɪpmʌŋk/ **(chipmunks)** A **chipmunk** is a small animal with a large furry tail and a striped back. N-COUNT

**Chippendale** /tʃɪpəndeɪl/ **Chippendale** is a style of furniture from the eighteenth century. ❑ *...a pair of Chippendale chairs.* ADJ: ADJ n

**chip|per** /tʃɪpəʳ/ **Chipper** means cheerful and lively. [OLD-FASHIONED] ADJ

**chip|pings** /tʃɪpɪŋz/ Wood **chippings** or stone **chippings** are small pieces of wood or stone which are used, for example, to cover surfaces such as paths or roads. N-PLURAL: usu n N

**chip|py** /tʃɪpi/ **(chippies)** also **chippie.** A **chippy** is the same as a **chip shop**. [BRIT, INFORMAL] ❑ *I go to the chippy at least once a week.* N-COUNT

**chip shop** **(chip shops)** A **chip shop** is a shop which sells hot food such as fish and chips, fried chicken, sausages, and meat pies. The food is cooked in the shop and people take it away to eat at home or in the street. [BRIT] N-COUNT = fish and chip shop

**chi|ropo|dist** /kɪrɒpədɪst/ **(chiropodists)** A **chiropodist** is a person whose job is to treat and care for people's feet. N-COUNT = podiatrist

**chi|ropo|dy** /kɪrɒpədi/ **Chiropody** is the professional treatment and care of people's feet. N-UNCOUNT = podiatry

**chi|ro|prac|tic** /kaɪərəpræktɪk/ **Chiropractic** is the treatment of injuries by pressing and moving people's joints, especially the spine. N-UNCOUNT

**chi|ro|prac|tor** /kaɪərəpræktəʳ/ **(chiropractors)** A **chiropractor** is a person who treats injuries by chiropractic. N-COUNT

**chirp** /tʃɜːʳp/ **(chirps, chirping, chirped)** When a bird or an insect such as a cricket or grasshopper **chirps**, it makes short high-pitched sounds. ❑ *The crickets chirped faster and louder.* VERB = chirrup V ♦ **Chirp** is also a noun. ❑ *The chirps of the small garden birds sounded distant.* N-COUNT ♦ **chirp|ing** *...the chirping of birds.* N-UNCOUNT

**chirpy** /tʃɜːʳpi/ **(chirpier, chirpiest)** If you describe a person or their behaviour as **chirpy**, you mean they are very cheerful and lively. [INFORMAL] ❑ *Hutson is a small, chirpy bloke... She sounded quite chirpy, all she needs is rest.* ADJ = cheerful

**chir|rup** /tʃɪrəp, AM tʃɜːrəp/ **(chirrups, chirruping, chirruped)** If a person or bird **chirrups**, they make short high-pitched sounds. ❑ *'My gosh,' she chirruped... I woke up to the sound of larks chirruping.* VERB = chirp V with quote V Also V n

**chis|el** /tʃɪzəl/ **(chisels, chiselling, chiselled)**

☑ in AM, use **chiseling, chiseled**

1 A **chisel** is a tool that has a long metal blade with a sharp edge at the end. It is used for cutting and shaping wood and stone. ➔ See picture on page 1709. N-COUNT 2 If you **chisel** wood or stone, you cut and shape it using a chisel. ❑ *They sit and chisel the stone to size.* VERB V n

**chis|elled** /tʃɪzəld/

☑ in AM, use **chiseled**

If you say that someone, usually a man, has **chiselled** features, you mean that their face has a strong, clear bone structure. ❑ *Women find his chiselled features irresistible. ...a chiselled jaw.* ADJ: usu ADJ n

**chit** /tʃɪt/ **(chits)** A **chit** is a short official note, such as a receipt, an order, or a memo, usually signed by someone in authority. [BRIT; also AM, MILITARY] ❑ *Schrader initialled the chit for the barman.* N-COUNT

**chit-chat** also **chitchat.** **Chit-chat** is informal talk about things that are not very important. ❑ *Not being a mother, I found the chit-chat exceedingly dull.* N-UNCOUNT

**chiv|al|ric** /ʃɪvælrɪk/ **Chivalric** means relating to or connected with the system of chivalry that was believed in and followed by medieval knights. ❑ *...chivalric ideals.* ADJ: ADJ n

**chiv|al|rous** /ʃɪvəlrəs/ A **chivalrous** man is polite, kind, and unselfish, especially towards women. ❑ *He was handsome, upright and chivalrous.* ADJ approval

**chiv|al|ry** /ʃɪvəlri/ 1 **Chivalry** is polite, kind, and unselfish behaviour, especially by men towards women. ❑ *Marie seemed to revel in his old-fashioned chivalry.* N-UNCOUNT = gallantry 2 In the Middle Ages, **chivalry** was the set of rules and way of behaving which knights were expected to follow. ❑ *...the age of chivalry.* N-UNCOUNT

**chives** /tʃaɪvz/ **Chives** are the long thin hollow green leaves of a herb with purple flowers. Chives are cut into small pieces and added to food to give it a flavour similar to onions. N-PLURAL

**chiv|vy** /tʃɪvi/ **(chivvies, chivvying, chivvied)** If you **chivvy** someone, you keep telling them to do something that they do not want to do. [BRIT] ❑ *Jovial ladies chivvy you into ordering more than you can eat!... He chivvies the troops along with a few well-directed words.* VERB V n *into* -ing/n V n with adv

**chlo|ride** /klɔːraɪd/ **(chlorides)** **Chloride** is a chemical compound of chlorine and another substance. ❑ *The scientific name for common salt is sodium chloride.* N-MASS: oft n N

**chlo|rin|at|ed** /klɔːrɪneɪtɪd/ **Chlorinated** water, for example drinking water or water in a swimming pool, has been cleaned by adding chlorine to it. ❑ *...swimming in chlorinated pools.* ADJ: usu ADJ n

**chlo|rine** /klɔːriːn/ **Chlorine** is a strong-smelling gas that is used to clean water and to make cleaning products. N-UNCOUNT

**chloro|fluoro|car|bon** /klɔːroʊflʊəroʊkaːʳbən/ **(chlorofluorocarbons)** **Chlorofluorocarbons** are the same as **CFCs**. N-COUNT

**chlo|ro|form** /klɒrəfɔːʳm, AM klɔːr-/ **Chloroform** is a colourless liquid with a strong sweet smell, which makes you unconscious if you breathe its vapour. N-UNCOUNT

**chlo|ro|phyll** /klɒrəfɪl, AM klɔːr-/ **Chlorophyll** is a green substance in plants which enables them to use the energy from sunlight in order to grow. N-UNCOUNT

**choc-ice** /tʃɒk aɪs, AM tʃɔːk -/ **(choc-ices)** also **choc ice.** A **choc-ice** is a small block of ice cream covered in chocolate. [BRIT] N-COUNT

**chock-a-block** /tʃɒk ə blɒk/ A place that is **chock-a-block** is very full of people, things, or vehicles. [INFORMAL] ❑ *The small roads are chock-a-block with traffic.* ADJ: v-link ADJ, oft ADJ *with* n = packed

**chock-full** /tʃɒk fʊl/ Something that is **chock-full** is completely full. [INFORMAL] ❑ *The 32-page catalog is chock-full of things that add fun to festive occasions.* ADJ: v-link ADJ, usu ADJ *of* n

**cho|co|hol|ic** /tʃɒkəhɒlɪk, AM tʃɔːkəhɔːlɪk/ **(chocoholics)** A **chocoholic** is someone who eats a great deal of chocolate and finds it hard to stop themselves eating it. [INFORMAL] ❑ *The Confectionery Warehouse is a chocoholic's dream.* N-COUNT

**choco|late** /tʃɒklɪt, AM tʃɔːk-/ **(chocolates)** ◆◇◇ 1 **Chocolate** is a sweet hard food made from cocoa beans. It is usually brown in colour and is eaten as a sweet. ❑ *...a bar of chocolate... Do you want some chocolate? ...rich chocolate cake.* → See also **milk chocolate**, **plain chocolate**. N-MASS 2 **Chocolate** or **hot chocolate** is a drink made from a powder containing chocolate. It is usually made with hot milk. ❑ *...a small cafeteria where the visitors can buy tea, coffee and chocolate... I sipped the hot chocolate she had made.* N-UNCOUNT ♦ A cup of chocolate can be referred to as a **chocolate** or a **hot chocolate**. ❑ *I'll have a hot chocolate please.* N-COUNT 3 **Chocolates** are small sweets or nuts covered with a layer of chocolate. They are usually sold in a box. ❑ *...a box of chocolates... Here, have a chocolate.* N-COUNT 4 **Chocolate** is used to describe things that are dark brown in colour. ❑ *The curtains and the coverlet of the bed were chocolate velvet... She placed the chocolate-colored coat beside the case.* COLOUR

**chocolate-box** also **chocolate box.** **Chocolate-box** places or images are very pretty but in a boring or conventional way. [BRIT] ❑ *...a village of chocolate-box timbered houses.* ADJ: ADJ n

**choice** /tʃɔɪs/ **(choices, choicer, choicest)** ◆◆◇ 1 If there is a **choice of** things, there are several of them and you can choose the one you want. ❑ *It's available in a choice of colours... At lunchtime, there's a choice between the buffet or the set menu... Club Sportif offer a wide choice of holidays.* N-COUNT = selection 2 Your **choice** is someone or something that you choose from a range of things. ❑ *Although he was only grumbling, his choice of words made Rodney angry.* N-COUNT: usu poss N 3 **Choice** means of very high quality. [FORMAL] ❑ *...Fortnum and Mason's choicest chocolates.* ADJ: ADJ n = select

PHRASES 4 If you **have no choice but** to do something or **have little choice but** to do it, you cannot avoid doing it. ❑ *They had little choice but to agree to what he suggested.* PHRASE: V inflects 5 The thing or person **of** your **choice** is the one that you choose. ❑ *...tickets to see the football team of your choice... In many societies children still marry someone of their parents' choice.* PHRASE: n PHR 6 The item **of choice** is the one that most people prefer. ❑ *The drug is set to become the treatment of choice for asthma worldwide.* PHRASE: PHR after n

**choir** /kwaɪəʳ/ **(choirs)** A **choir** is a group of people who sing together, for example in a church or school. ❑ *He has been singing in his church choir since he was six.* N-COUNT

**choir|boy** /kwaɪəʳbɔɪ/ **(choirboys)** A **choirboy** is a boy who sings in a church choir. N-COUNT

**choir|master** /kwaɪəʳmaːstəʳ, -mæst-/ **(choirmasters)** A **choirmaster** is a person whose job is to train a choir. N-COUNT

**choke** /tʃoʊk/ **(chokes, choking, choked)** 1 When you **choke** or when something **chokes** you, you cannot breathe properly or get enough air into your lungs. ❑ *The coffee was almost too hot to swallow and made him choke for a moment... A small child could choke on the doll's hair... Dense smoke swirled and billowed, its rank fumes choking her... The girl choked to death after breathing in smoke... Within minutes the hall was full of choking smoke.* VERB V V *on* n V n V *to* n V-ing 2 To **choke** someone means to squeeze their neck until they are dead. ❑ *The men pushed him into the entrance of a nearby building where they choked him with his tie.* VERB = strangle V n 3 If a place **is choked with** things or people, it is full of them and they prevent movement in it. ❑ *The village's roads are choked with traffic... His pond has been choked by the fast-growing weed.* VERB: usu passive be V-ed *with* n be V-ed *by* n 4 The **choke** in a car, truck, or other vehicle is a device that reduces the amount of air going into the engine and makes it easier to start. N-COUNT: usu sing, usu *the* N

♦ **choke back** If you **choke back** tears or a strong emotion, you force yourself not to show your emotion. ❑ *Choking back tears, he said Mary died in his arms.* PHRASAL VERB = suppress V P n (not pron)

♦ **choke off** To **choke off** financial growth means to restrict or control the rate at which a country's economy can grow. ❑ *They warned the Chancellor that raising taxes in the Budget could choke off the recovery.* PHRASAL VERB V P n (not pron)

**choked** /tʃoʊkt/ If you say something in a **choked** voice or if your voice is **choked with** emotion, your voice does not have its full sound, because you are upset or frightened. ❑ *'Why did Ben do that?' she asked, in a choked voice... One young conscript rose with a message of thanks, his voice choked with emotion.* ADJ: ADJ n, v-link ADJ *with* n

**chok|er** /tʃoʊkəʳ/ **(chokers)** A **choker** is a necklace or band of material that fits very closely round a woman's neck. ❑ *...a pearl choker.* N-COUNT

**chol|era** /kɒlərə/ **Cholera** is a serious disease that often kills people. It is caused by drinking infected water or by eating infected food. ❑ *...a cholera epidemic.* N-UNCOUNT

**chol|er|ic** /kɒlərɪk/ A **choleric** person gets angry very easily. You can also use **choleric** to describe a person who is very angry. [FORMAL] ❑ *...his choleric disposition... He was affable at one moment, choleric the next.* ADJ

**cho|les|ter|ol** /kəlestərɒl, AM -rɔːl/ **Cholesterol** is a substance that exists in the fat, tissues, and blood of all animals. Too much cholesterol in a person's blood can cause heart disease. ❑ *...a dangerously high cholesterol level.* N-UNCOUNT

**chomp** /tʃɒmp/ **(chomps, chomping, chomped)** If a person or animal **chomps** their **way through** food or **chomps on** food, they chew it noisily. [INFORMAL] ❑ *On the diet I would chomp my way through breakfast, even though I'm never hungry in the morning... I lost a tooth while chomping on a French baguette!* to **chomp at the bit** → see **bit**. VERB = munch; V *way through* n; V prep/adv; Also V n

**choose** /tʃuːz/ **(chooses, choosing, chose, chosen)** ◆◆◇ 1 If you **choose** someone or something **from** several people or things that are available, you decide which person or thing you want to have. ❑ *They will be able to choose their own leaders in democratic elections... This week he has chosen Peter Mandelson to replace Mo Mowlam... There are several patchwork cushions to choose from... Houston was chosen as the site for the convention... He did well in his chosen profession.* VERB = select; V n; V n to-inf; V *from/between* n; *be* V-ed *as* n; V-ed 2 If you **choose to** do something, you do it because you want to or because you feel that it is right. ❑ *They knew that discrimination was going on, but chose to ignore it... You can just take out the interest each year, if you choose.* VERB; V to-inf; V

PHRASES 3 If there is **little to choose between** people or things or **nothing to choose between** them, it is difficult to decide which is better or more suitable. [mainly BRIT] ❑ *There is very little to choose between the world's top tennis players.* PHRASE: v-link PHR 4 The **chosen few** are a small group who are treated better than other people. You sometimes use this expression when you think this is unfair. ❑ *Learning should no longer be an elitist pastime for the chosen few.* PHRASE = elite 5 to **pick and choose** → see **pick**.

**choosy** /tʃuːzi/ Someone who is **choosy** is difficult to please because they will only accept something if it is exactly what they want or if it is of very high quality. [mainly INFORMAL] ❑ *Skiers should be particularly choosy about the insurance policy they buy.* ADJ: usu v-link ADJ, oft ADJ *about* n/wh = selective

**chop** /tʃɒp/ **(chops, chopping, chopped)** ◆◇◇ 1 If you **chop** something, you cut it into pieces with strong downward movements of a knife or an axe. ❑ *Chop the butter into small pieces... Visitors were set to work chopping wood. ...chopped tomatoes.* VERB; V n *into* n; V n; V-ed 2 A **chop** is a small piece of meat cut from the ribs of a sheep or pig. ❑ *...grilled lamb chops.* N-COUNT: usu n N

PHRASES 3 When people **chop and change**, they keep changing their minds about what to do or how to act. [BRIT, INFORMAL] ❑ *Don't ask me why they have chopped and changed so much.* PHRASE: Vs inflect 4 If something is **for the chop** or is going to **get the chop**, it is going to be stopped or closed. If someone is **for the chop**, they are going to lose their job or position. [BRIT, INFORMAL] ❑ *He won't say which programmes are for the chop.* PHRASE

♦ **chop down** If you **chop down** a tree, you cut through its trunk with an axe so that it falls to the ground. ❑ *Sometimes they have to chop down a tree for firewood.* PHRASAL VERB = cut down; V P n (not pron); Also V n P

♦ **chop off** To **chop off** something such as a part of someone's body means to cut it off. ❑ *She chopped off her golden, waist-length hair... They dragged him to the village square and chopped his head off.* PHRASAL VERB = cut off; V P n (not pron); V n P

♦ **chop up** If you **chop** something **up**, you chop it into small pieces. ❑ *Chop up three firm tomatoes. ...chopped up banana.* PHRASAL VERB = cut up; V P n; V-ed P

**chop|per** /tʃɒpəʳ/ **(choppers)** A **chopper** is a helicopter. [INFORMAL] ❑ *Overhead, the chopper roared and the big blades churned the air.* N-COUNT

**chop|ping board** **(chopping boards)** A **chopping board** is a wooden or plastic board that you chop meat and vegetables on. [BRIT] N-COUNT

✓ in AM, usually use **cutting board**

**chop|py** /tʃɒpi/ **(choppier, choppiest)** When water is **choppy**, there are a lot of small waves on it because there is a wind blowing. ❑ *A gale was blowing and the sea was choppy.* ADJ = rough

**chop|stick** /tʃɒpstɪk/ **(chopsticks)** **Chopsticks** are a pair of thin sticks which people in China and the Far East use to eat their food. N-COUNT: usu pl

**chop suey** /tʃɒp suːi/ **Chop suey** is a Chinese-style dish that consists of meat and vegetables that have been stewed together. N-UNCOUNT

**cho|ral** /kɔːrəl/ **Choral** music is sung by a choir. ❑ *His collection of choral music from around the world is called 'Voices'.* ADJ: usu ADJ n

**cho|rale** /kɔːrɑːl, -ræl/ **(chorales)** 1 A **chorale** is a piece of music sung as part of a church service. ❑ *...a Bach chorale.* N-COUNT 2 A **chorale** is a group of people who sing together. [AM] N-COUNT

**chord** /kɔːʳd/ **(chords)** 1 A **chord** is a number of musical notes played or sung at the same time with a pleasing effect. ❑ *...the opening chords of 'Stairway to Heaven'.* → See also **vocal cords**. N-COUNT 2 If something **strikes a chord with** you, it makes you feel sympathy or enthusiasm. ❑ *Mr Jenkins' arguments for stability struck a chord with Europe's two most powerful politicians.* PHRASE: V inflects

**chore** /tʃɔːʳ/ **(chores)** 1 A **chore** is a task that you must do but that you find unpleasant or boring. ❑ *She sees exercise primarily as an unavoidable chore.* N-COUNT: usu sing 2 **Chores** are tasks such as cleaning, washing, and ironing that have to be done regularly at home. ❑ *My husband and I both go out to work so we share the household chores.* N-COUNT: usu pl

**cho|reo|graph** /kɒriəgrɑːf, AM kɔːriəgræf/ **(choreographs, choreographing, choreographed)** When someone **choreographs** a ballet or other dance, they invent the steps and movements and tell the dancers how to perform them. ❑ *Achim had choreographed the dance in Act II himself... She has danced, choreographed, lectured and taught all over the world.* VERB; V n; V

**cho|reo|graphed** /kɒriəgrɑːft, AM kɔːriəgræft/ You describe an activity involving several people as **choreographed** when it is arranged but is intended to appear natural. ❑ *...a carefully choreographed White House meeting between the two presidents.* ADJ

**cho|reog|ra|pher** /kɒriɒgrəfəʳ, AM kɔː-/ **(choreographers)** A **choreographer** is someone who invents the movements for a ballet or other dance and tells the dancers how to perform them. N-COUNT

**cho|reo|graph|ic** /kɒriəgræfɪk, AM kɔː-/ **Choreographic** means relating to or connected with choreography. ❑ *...his choreographic work for The Birmingham Royal Ballet.* ADJ: usu ADJ n

**cho|reog|ra|phy** /kɒriɒgrəfi, AM kɔː-/ **Choreography** is the inventing of steps and movements for ballets and other dances. N-UNCOUNT

**chor|is|ter** /kɒrɪstəʳ, AM kɔː-/ **(choristers)** A **chorister** is a singer in a church choir. N-COUNT

**chor|tle** /tʃɔːʳtəl/ **(chortles, chortling, chortled)** To **chortle** means to laugh in a way that shows you are very pleased. [WRITTEN] ❑ *There was silence for a moment, then Larry began chortling like an idiot.* VERB; V ♦ **Chortle** is also a noun. ❑ *He gave a chortle.* N-COUNT

**cho|rus** /kɔːrəs/ **(choruses, chorusing, chorused)** 1 A **chorus** is a part of a song which is repeated after each verse. ❑ *Caroline sang two verses and the chorus of her song... Everyone joined in the chorus.* N-COUNT = refrain 2 A **chorus** is a large group of people N-COUNT who sing together. ❑ *The chorus was singing 'The Ode to Joy'.* [3] A **chorus** is a piece of music written to be sung by a large group of people. ❑ *...the Hallelujah Chorus.* [4] A **chorus** is a group of singers or dancers who perform together in a show, in contrast to the soloists. ❑ *Students played the lesser parts and sang in the chorus.* [5] When there is a **chorus of** criticism, disapproval, or praise, that attitude is expressed by a lot of people at the same time. ❑ *The government is defending its economic policies against a growing chorus of criticism.* [6] When people **chorus** something, they say it or sing it together. [WRITTEN] ❑ *'Hi,' they chorused.* [7] → See also **dawn chorus**. = choir N-COUNT N-COUNT N-COUNT: usu sing, oft N *of* n VERB V with quote

**cho|rus girl** **(chorus girls)** also **chorus-girl.** A **chorus girl** is a young woman who sings or dances as part of a group in a show or film. N-COUNT

**chose** /tʃoʊz/ **Chose** is the past tense of **choose**.

**cho|sen** /tʃoʊzᵊn/ **Chosen** is the past participle of **choose**.

**chow** /tʃaʊ/ **(chows)** [1] Food can be referred to as **chow**. [AM, INFORMAL] ❑ *Help yourself to some chow.* [2] A **chow** is a kind of dog that has a thick coat and a curled tail. Chows originally came from China. N-UNCOUNT N-COUNT

**chow|der** /tʃaʊdəʳ/ **(chowders)** **Chowder** is a thick soup containing pieces of fish. N-MASS: usu n N

**chow mein** /tʃaʊ meɪn, - miːn/ **Chow mein** is a Chinese-style dish that consists of fried noodles, cooked meat, and vegetables. ❑ *...chicken chow mein.* N-UNCOUNT

**Christ** /kraɪst/ **Christ** is one of the names of Jesus, whom Christians believe to be the son of God and whose teachings are the basis of Christianity. ❑ *...the teachings of Christ.* N-PROPER

**chris|ten** /krɪsᵊn/ **(christens, christening, christened)** [1] When a baby **is christened**, he or she is given a name during the Christian ceremony of baptism. Compare **baptize**. ❑ *She was born in March and christened in June... She was christened Susan.* [2] You say that you **christen** a person, place, or object a particular name if you choose a name for them and start calling them by that name. [INFORMAL] ❑ *The pair were christened 'The Women in Black' after they both wore black dresses at a party.* [3] You say that you **christen** something new when you use it for the first time, especially if you do something special to mark the occasion. [INFORMAL] ❑ *To christen the new hall, a number of great orchestras have been invited to play.* VERB: usu passive *be* V-ed *be* V-ed n-proper VERB V n n VERB V n

**Chris|ten|dom** /krɪsᵊndəm/ All the Christian people and countries in the world can be referred to as **Christendom**. [OLD-FASHIONED] N-PROPER

**chris|ten|ing** /krɪsᵊnɪŋ/ **(christenings)** A **christening** is a Christian ceremony in which a baby is made a member of the Christian church and is officially given his or her name. Compare **baptism**. ❑ *...my granddaughter's christening. ...a christening robe.* N-COUNT

**Christian** /krɪstʃən/ **(Christians)** [1] A **Christian** is someone who follows the teachings of Jesus Christ. ❑ *He was a devout Christian.* [2] **Christian** means relating to Christianity or Christians. ❑ *...the Christian Church. ...the Christian faith... Most of my friends are Christian.* ◆◆◇ N-COUNT ADJ: usu ADJ n

**Chris|ti|an|ity** /krɪstiænɪti/ **Christianity** is a religion that is based on the teachings of Jesus Christ and the belief that he was the son of God. ❑ *He converted to Christianity that day.* N-UNCOUNT

**Christian name** **(Christian names)** Some people refer to their first names as their **Christian names**. ❑ *Despite my attempts to get him to call me by my Christian name he insisted on addressing me as 'Mr Kennedy'.* N-COUNT

**Christian Sci|ence** **Christian Science** is a type of Christianity which emphasizes the use of prayer to cure illness. ❑ *...members of the Christian Science Church.* N-UNCOUNT: oft N n

**Christ|mas** /krɪsməs/ **(Christmases)** [1] **Christmas** is a Christian festival when the birth of Jesus Christ is celebrated. Christmas is celebrated on the 25th of December. ❑ *The day after Christmas is generally a busy one for retailers... Merry Christmas, Mom.* [2] **Christmas** is the period of several days around and including Christmas Day. ❑ *He'll be in the hospital over Christmas, so we'll be spending our Christmas Day there.* N-VAR: oft N n N-VAR: oft N n

**Christ|mas cake** **(Christmas cakes)** A **Christmas cake** is a special cake that is eaten at Christmas in Britain and some other countries. N-VAR

**Christ|mas card** **(Christmas cards)** **Christmas cards** are cards with greetings, which people send to their friends and family at Christmas. N-COUNT

**Christ|mas Day** **Christmas Day** is the 25th of December, when Christmas is celebrated. N-UNCOUNT

**Christ|mas Eve** **Christmas Eve** is the 24th of December, the day before Christmas Day. N-UNCOUNT

**Christ|mas pud|ding** **(Christmas puddings)** **Christmas pudding** is a special pudding that is eaten at Christmas. [mainly BRIT] N-VAR = plum pudding

**Christ|mas stock|ing** **(Christmas stockings)** A **Christmas stocking** is a long sock which children hang up on Christmas Eve. During the night, parents fill the stocking with small presents. N-COUNT = stocking

**Christ|massy** /krɪsməsi/

✔ in AM, also use **Christmasy**

Something that is **Christmassy** is typical of or suitable for Christmas. [INFORMAL] ❑ *Choose Christmassy colours such as red and green.* ADJ

**Christ|mas tree** **(Christmas trees)** A **Christmas tree** is a fir tree, or an artificial tree that looks like a fir tree, which people put in their houses at Christmas and decorate with coloured lights and ornaments. N-COUNT

**chro|mat|ic** /krəmætɪk/ [1] In music, **chromatic** means related to the scale that consists only of semitones. ❑ *...the notes of the chromatic scale.* [2] **Chromatic** means related to colours. ADJ ADJ: usu ADJ n

**chrome** /kroʊm/ **Chrome** is metal plated with chromium. ❑ *...old-fashioned chrome taps.* N-UNCOUNT: oft N n

**chro|mium** /kroʊmiəm/ **Chromium** is a hard, shiny metallic element, used to make steel alloys and to coat other metals. ❑ *...chromium-plated fire accessories.* N-UNCOUNT

**chro|mo|so|mal** /kroʊməsoʊmᵊl/ **Chromosomal** means relating to or connected with chromosomes. ❑ *...chromosomal abnormalities.* ADJ: ADJ n

**chro|mo|some** /kroʊməsoʊm/ **(chromosomes)** A **chromosome** is a part of a cell in an animal or plant. It contains genes which determine what characteristics the animal or plant will have. ❑ *Each cell of our bodies contains 46 chromosomes.* N-COUNT

**chron|ic** /krɒnɪk/ [1] A **chronic** illness or disability lasts for a very long time. Compare **acute**. ❑ *...chronic back pain.* ♦ **chroni|cal|ly** /krɒnɪkli/ *Most of them were chronically ill.* [2] You can describe someone's bad habits or behaviour as **chronic** when they have behaved like that for a long time and do not seem to be able to stop themselves. ❑ *...a chronic worrier.* [3] A **chronic** situation or problem is very severe and unpleasant. ❑ *One cause of the artist's suicide seems to have been chronic poverty.* ♦ **chroni|cal|ly** *Research and technology are said to be chronically underfunded.* ADJ: usu ADJ n ADV: ADV adj/-ed ADJ: ADJ n ADJ: usu ADJ n = severe ADV: ADV adj/-ed

**chron|ic fa|tigue syn|drome** **Chronic fatigue syndrome** is an illness that is thought to be caused by a virus, and which affects people for a long period of time. Its symptoms include tiredness and aching muscles. The abbreviation **CFS** is often used. N-UNCOUNT = ME

**chroni|cle** /krɒnɪkᵊl/ **(chronicles, chronicling, chronicled)** [1] To **chronicle** a series of events means to write about them or show them in broadcasts in the order in which they happened. ❑ *The series chronicles the everyday adventures of two* VERB = recount V n *eternal bachelors.* ♦ **chroni|cler** **(chroniclers)** *...the chronicler of the English civil war.* [N-COUNT] [2] A **chronicle** is an account or record of a series of events. ❑ *...this vast chronicle of Napoleonic times.* [N-COUNT: usu N *of* n] [3] **Chronicle** is sometimes used as part of the name of a newspaper. ❑ *...the San Francisco Chronicle.* [N-IN-NAMES]

**chrono|logi|cal** /krɒnəlɒdʒɪkᵊl/ [1] If things are described or shown in **chronological** order, they are described or shown in the order in which they happened. ❑ *I have arranged these stories in chronological order.* [ADJ: usu ADJ n] ♦ **chrono|logi|cal|ly** *The portrait exhibition is organised chronologically.* [ADV: ADV after v, ADV -ed/adj] [2] If you refer to someone's **chronological** age, you are referring to the number of years they have lived, in contrast to their mental age or the stage they have reached in their physical or emotional development. [FORMAL] [ADJ: ADJ n]

**chro|nol|ogy** /krənɒlədʒi/ **(chronologies)** [1] The **chronology of** a series of past events is the times at which they happened in the order in which they happened. ❑ *She gave him a factual account of the chronology of her brief liaison.* [N-UNCOUNT: oft N *of* n] [2] A **chronology** is an account or record of the times and the order in which a series of past events took place. ❑ *The second part of Duffy's book is a detailed chronology of the Reformation.* [N-COUNT: oft N *of* n = account]

**chro|nom|eter** /krɒnɒmɪtəʳ/ **(chronometers)** A **chronometer** is an extremely accurate clock that is used especially by sailors at sea. [N-COUNT]

**chrysa|lis** /krɪsəlɪs/ **(chrysalises)** [1] A **chrysalis** is a butterfly or moth in the stage between being a larva and an adult. [N-COUNT] [2] A **chrysalis** is the hard, protective covering that a chrysalis has. ❑ *...a butterfly emerging from its chrysalis.* [N-COUNT]

**chry|san|themum** /krɪzænθəməm/ **(chrysanthemums)** A **chrysanthemum** is a large garden flower with many long, thin petals. [N-COUNT]

**chub|by** /tʃʌbi/ **(chubbier, chubbiest)** A **chubby** person is rather fat. ❑ *Do you think I'm too chubby? ...his chubby hands.* [ADJ ≠ skinny]

**chuck** /tʃʌk/ **(chucks, chucking, chucked)** [1] When you **chuck** something somewhere, you throw it there in a casual or careless way. [INFORMAL] [VERB = throw] ❑ *I took a great dislike to the clock, so I chucked it in the dustbin.* [V n prep/adv] [2] If you **chuck** your job or some other activity, you stop doing it. [INFORMAL] [VERB] ❑ *Last summer, he chucked his 10-year career as a London stockbroker and headed for the mountains.* [V n] ♦ In British English **chuck in** and **chuck up** mean the same as **chuck**. [PHRASAL VERB] ❑ *Almost half the British public think about chucking in their jobs and doing their own thing at least once a month.* [V P n (not pron) Also V n P] [3] If your girlfriend or boyfriend **chucks** you, they end the relationship. [INFORMAL] [VERB] ❑ *There wasn't a great fuss when I chucked her.* [V n] [4] A **chuck** is a device for holding a tool in a machine such as a drill. ➔ See picture on page 1709. [N-COUNT]

♦ **chuck away** If you **chuck** something **away**, you throw it away or waste it. [INFORMAL] [PHRASAL VERB] ❑ *You cannot chuck money away on luxuries like that.* [V n P]

♦ **chuck in** ➔ see **chuck 2**.

♦ **chuck out** [1] If you **chuck** something **out**, you throw it away, because you do not need it or cannot use it. [INFORMAL] [PHRASAL VERB = throw away] ❑ *Many companies have struggled valiantly to use less energy and chuck out less rubbish.* [V P n (not pron) Also V n P] [2] If a person **is chucked out of** a job, a place, or their home, they are forced by other people to leave. [INFORMAL] [PHRASAL VERB] ❑ *Any head teacher who made errors like this would be chucked out...* [*be* V-ed P] *I was chucked out of my London flat in 1960...* [*be* V-ed P *of* n] *Her parents are going to chuck her out on the street.* [V n P]

♦ **chuck up** ➔ see **chuck 2**.

**chuck|le** /tʃʌkᵊl/ **(chuckles, chuckling, chuckled)** When you **chuckle**, you laugh quietly. [VERB] ❑ *The banker chuckled and said, 'Of course not.'...* [V] *He chuckled at her forthrightness.* [V *at/over* n] ♦ **Chuckle** is also a noun. [N-COUNT] ❑ *He gave a little chuckle.*

**chuffed** /tʃʌft/ If you are **chuffed about** something, you are very pleased about it. [BRIT, INFORMAL] [ADJ: v-link ADJ, oft ADJ *about/with* n, ADJ to-inf, ADJ that] ❑ *She had just moved into a new house and was pretty chuffed about that.*

**chug** /tʃʌg/ **(chugs, chugging, chugged)** When a vehicle **chugs** somewhere, it goes there slowly, noisily and with difficulty. [VERB] ❑ *The train chugs down the track.* [V prep/adv]

**chum** /tʃʌm/ **(chums)** Your **chum** is your friend. [INFORMAL, OLD-FASHIONED] [N-COUNT: usu with poss = pal] ❑ *...his old chum Anthony.*

**chum|my** /tʃʌmi/ **(chummier, chummiest)** If people or social events are **chummy**, they are pleasant and friendly. [INFORMAL, OLD-FASHIONED] [ADJ = friendly]

**chump** /tʃʌmp/ **(chumps)** If you call someone who you like a **chump**, you are telling them that they have done something rather stupid or foolish, or that they are always doing stupid things. [INFORMAL] [N-COUNT] [disapproval] [= idiot] ❑ *The guy's a chump. I could do a better job myself.*

**chunk** /tʃʌŋk/ **(chunks)** [1] **Chunks of** something are thick solid pieces of it. ❑ *...a chunk of meat... Cut the melon into chunks.* [N-COUNT: oft N *of* n = lump] [2] A **chunk of** something is a large amount or large part of it. [INFORMAL] [N-COUNT: usu N *of* n] ❑ *The company owns a chunk of farmland near Gatwick Airport.*

**chunky** /tʃʌŋki/ **(chunkier, chunkiest)** [1] A **chunky** person is broad and heavy. ❑ *The soprano was a chunky girl from California.* [ADJ: usu ADJ n] [2] A **chunky** object is large and thick. ❑ *...a chunky sweater. ...chunky jewellery.* [ADJ: usu ADJ n]

**church** /tʃɜːʳtʃ/ **(churches)** [1] A **church** is a building in which Christians worship. You usually refer to this place as **church** when you are talking about the time that people spend there. ❑ *...one of Britain's most historic churches. ...St Helen's Church... I didn't see you in church on Sunday.* [◆◆◇] [N-VAR] [2] A **Church** is one of the groups of people within the Christian religion, for example Catholics or Methodists, that have their own beliefs, clergy, and forms of worship. ❑ *...co-operation with the Catholic Church... Church leaders said he was welcome to return.* [N-COUNT: usu with supp, oft adj N, N *of* n]

**church|goer** /tʃɜːʳtʃgoʊəʳ/ **(churchgoers)** also **church-goer.** A **churchgoer** is a person who goes to church regularly. [N-COUNT]

**church|man** /tʃɜːʳtʃmən/ **(churchmen)** A **churchman** is the same as a clergyman. [FORMAL] [N-COUNT]

**Church of Eng|land** The **Church of England** is the main church in England. It has the Queen as its head and it does not recognize the authority of the Pope. [N-PROPER: *the* N]

**church school** **(church schools)** A **church school** is a school which has a special relationship with a particular branch of the Christian church, and where there is strong emphasis on worship and the teaching of religion. [N-COUNT]

**church|warden** /tʃɜːʳtʃwɔːʳdᵊn/ **(churchwardens)** In the Anglican Church, a **churchwarden** is the person who has been chosen by a congregation to help the vicar of a parish with administration and other duties. [N-COUNT]

**church|yard** /tʃɜːʳtʃjɑːʳd/ **(churchyards)** A **churchyard** is an area of land around a church where dead people are buried. [N-COUNT]

**churl|ish** /tʃɜːʳlɪʃ/ Someone who is **churlish** is unfriendly, bad-tempered, or impolite. ❑ *She would think him churlish if he refused... The room was so lovely it seemed churlish to argue.* [ADJ: oft *it* v-link ADJ to-inf] [disapproval]

**churn** /tʃɜːʳn/ **(churns, churning, churned)** [1] A **churn** is a container which is used for making butter. [N-COUNT: oft n N] [2] If something **churns** water, mud, or dust, it moves it about violently. [VERB] ❑ *Ferries churn the waters of Howe Sound from Langdale to Horseshoe Bay.* [V n] *...unsurfaced roads now churned into mud by the annual rains.* [V-ed] ♦ **Churn up** means the same as **churn**. [PHRASAL VERB] ❑ *The recent rain had churned up the waterfall into a muddy whirlpool...* [V P n (not pron)] *Occasionally they slap the water with their tails or churn it up in play.* [V n P] *...muddy, churned-up ground.* [V-ed P] [3] If you say that your stomach **is churning**, you mean that you feel sick. You can also say that something **churns** your stomach. ❑ *My stomach churned as I stood up.* [VERB = heave] [V, Also V n]

♦ **churn out** To **churn out** something means to produce large quantities of it very quickly. [INFORMAL] ❑ *He began to churn out literary compositions in English.* PHRASAL VERB V P n (not pron) Also V n P

♦ **churn up** → see **churn 2**.

**churn|ing** /tʃɜːʳnɪŋ/ **Churning** water is moving about violently. [LITERARY] ❑ *...anything to take our minds off that gap and the brown, churning water below.* ADJ: ADJ n = swirling

**chute** /ʃuːt/ **(chutes)** [1] A **chute** is a steep, narrow slope down which people or things can slide. ❑ *Passengers escaped from the plane's front four exits by sliding down emergency chutes.* N-COUNT: oft n N [2] A **chute** is a parachute. [INFORMAL] ❑ *You can release the chute with either hand, but it is easier to do it with the left.* N-COUNT

**chut|ney** /tʃʌtni/ **(chutneys)** **Chutney** is a cold sauce made from fruit, vinegar, sugar, and spices. It is sold in jars and you eat it with meat or cheese. ❑ *...mango chutney.* N-MASS

**chutz|pah** /hʊtspə/

✔ in AM, also use **chutzpa**

If you say that someone has **chutzpah**, you mean that you admire the fact that they are not afraid or embarrassed to do or say things that shock, surprise, or annoy other people. ❑ *Einstein had the chutzpah to discard common sense and long-established theory.* N-UNCOUNT [approval]

**CIA** /siː aɪ eɪ/ **The CIA** is the government organization in the United States that collects secret information about other countries. **CIA** is an abbreviation for 'Central Intelligence Agency'. N-PROPER: the N

**cia|bat|ta** /tʃəbætə/ **Ciabatta** or **ciabatta bread** is a type of white Italian bread that is made with olive oil. N-UNCOUNT

**ciao** /tʃaʊ/ Some people say '**Ciao**' as an informal way of saying goodbye to someone who they expect to see again soon. CONVENTION [formulae] = see you

**ci|ca|da** /sɪkɑːdə, AM -keɪdə/ **(cicadas)** A **cicada** is a large insect that lives in hot countries and makes a loud high-pitched noise. N-COUNT

**CID** /siː aɪ diː/ **The CID** is the branch of the police force in Britain concerned with finding out who has committed crimes. **CID** is an abbreviation for 'Criminal Investigation Department'. N-PROPER: oft the N

**ci|der** /saɪdəʳ/ **(ciders)** **Cider** is a drink made from apples which in Britain usually contains alcohol. In the United States, **cider** does not usually contain alcohol, and if it does contain alcohol, it is usually called **hard cider**. ♦ A glass of cider can be referred to as a **cider**. ❑ *He ordered a cider.* N-MASS N-COUNT

**ci|gar** /sɪgɑːʳ/ **(cigars)** **Cigars** are rolls of dried tobacco leaves which people smoke. ❑ *He was sitting alone smoking a big cigar.* N-COUNT

**ciga|rette** /sɪgəret/ **(cigarettes)** **Cigarettes** are small tubes of paper containing tobacco which people smoke. ❑ *He went out to buy a packet of cigarettes.* ◆◇◇ N-COUNT

**ciga|rette butt** **(cigarette butts)**

✔ in BRIT, also use **cigarette end**

A **cigarette butt** or a **cigarette end** is the part of a cigarette that you throw away when you have finished smoking it. N-COUNT = butt, stub

**ciga|rette hold|er** **(cigarette holders)** also **cigarette-holder**. A **cigarette holder** is a narrow tube that you can put a cigarette into in order to hold it while you smoke it. N-COUNT

**ciga|rette light|er** **(cigarette lighters)** A **cigarette lighter** is a device which produces a small flame when you press a switch and which you use to light a cigarette or cigar. N-COUNT = lighter

**cig|gy** /sɪgi/ **(ciggies)** also **ciggie**. A **ciggy** is a cigarette. [BRIT, INFORMAL] N-COUNT

**C-in-C** A **C-in-C** is the same as a **commander-in-chief**. N-SING

**cinch** /sɪntʃ/ If you say that something is a **cinch**, you mean that you think it is very easy to do. [INFORMAL] ❑ *It sounds difficult, but compared to full-time work it was a cinch.* N-SING: a N = doddle

**cin|der block** /sɪndəʳ blɒk/ **(cinder blocks)** also **cinderblock**. A **cinder block** is a large grey brick made from coal cinders and cement which is used for building. [AM] N-COUNT: oft N n

✔ in BRIT, use **breeze-block**

**Cinderella** /sɪndərelə/ **(Cinderellas)** If you describe a person or organization as a **Cinderella**, you mean that they receive very little attention and that they deserve to receive more. ❑ *It is a Cinderella of charities, and needs more help.* N-COUNT: usu sing, oft N n

**cin|ders** /sɪndəʳz/ **Cinders** are the black pieces that are left after something such as wood or coal has burned away. ❑ *The wind sent sparks and cinders flying.* N-PLURAL = embers

**cine** /sɪni/ **Cine** is used to refer to things that are used in or connected with the making or showing of films. ❑ *...a cine camera. ...a cine projector.* ADJ: ADJ n

**cin|ema** /sɪnɪmɑː/ **(cinemas)** [1] A **cinema** is a place where people go to watch films for entertainment. [mainly BRIT] ❑ *The country has relatively few cinemas.* ◆◇◇ N-COUNT

✔ in AM, usually use **movie theater**, **movie house**

[2] You can talk about **the cinema** when you are talking about seeing a film in a cinema. [mainly BRIT] ❑ *I can't remember the last time we went to the cinema.* N-SING: the N

✔ in AM, usually use **the movies**

[3] **Cinema** is the business and art of making films. ❑ *Contemporary African cinema has much to offer in its vitality and freshness.* N-UNCOUNT = film

**cin|emat|ic** /sɪnɪmætɪk/ **Cinematic** means relating to films made for the cinema. ❑ *...a genuine cinematic masterpiece.* ADJ: usu ADJ n

**cin|ema|tog|ra|pher** /sɪnɪmətɒgrəfəʳ/ **(cinematographers)** A **cinematographer** is a person who decides what filming techniques should be used during the shooting of a film. N-COUNT

**cin|ema|tog|ra|phy** /sɪnɪmətɒgrəfi/ **Cinematography** is the technique of making films for the cinema. ❑ *...an admirer of Arthur Jafa's breathtaking cinematography.* N-UNCOUNT

**cin|na|mon** /sɪnəmən/ **Cinnamon** is a sweet spice used for flavouring food. N-UNCOUNT

**ci|pher** /saɪfəʳ/ **(ciphers)** also **cypher**. A **cipher** is a secret system of writing that you use to send messages. ❑ *...converting their messages into ciphers.* N-COUNT = code

**cir|ca** /sɜːʳkə/ **Circa** is used in front of a particular year to say that this is the approximate date when something happened or was made. [FORMAL] ❑ *The story tells of a runaway slave girl in Louisiana, circa 1850.* PREP = around

**cir|cle** /sɜːʳkᵊl/ **(circles, circling, circled)** [1] A **circle** is a shape consisting of a curved line completely surrounding an area. Every part of the line is the same distance from the centre of the area. ❑ *The flag was red, with a large white circle in the center... I wrote down the number 46 and drew a circle around it.* ◆◆◇ N-COUNT = ring [2] A **circle of** something is a round flat piece or area of it. ❑ *Cut out 4 circles of pastry. ...a circle of yellow light.* N-COUNT: usu N of n = ring [3] A **circle of** objects or people is a group of them arranged in the shape of a circle. ❑ *The monument consists of a circle of gigantic stones... We stood in a circle holding hands.* N-COUNT: oft N of n = ring [4] If something **circles** an object or a place, or **circles around** it, it forms a circle around it. ❑ *This is the ring road that circles the city. ...the long curving driveway that circled around the vast clipped lawn.* VERB = encircle V n V around/round n [5] If an aircraft or a bird **circles** or **circles** something, it moves round in a circle in the air. ❑ *The plane circled, awaiting permission to land... There were two helicopters circling around. ...like a hawk circling prey.* VERB V V adv/prep V n [6] To **circle around** someone or something, or to **circle** them, means to move around them. VERB

❑ *Emily kept circling around her mother... The silent wolves would track and circle them before attacking.* V around/round n V n [7] If you **circle** something on a piece of paper, you draw a circle around it. ❑ *Circle the correct answers on the coupon below.* VERB = ring V n [8] You can refer to a group of people as a **circle** when they meet each other regularly because they are friends or because they belong to the same profession or share the same interests. ❑ *He has a small circle of friends... Alton has made himself fiercely unpopular in certain circles.* N-COUNT: with supp [9] In a theatre or cinema, **the circle** is an area of seats on the upper floor. N-SING: the N [10] → See also **Arctic Circle, dress circle, inner circle, vicious circle, virtuous circle.** [11] If you say that you **have come full circle** or **have turned full circle**, you mean that after a long series of events or changes the same situation that you started with still exists. ❑ *We've come full circle and dark-blue jeans are once again the height of style.* PHRASE: V inflects

**cir|cuit** /sɜːʳkɪt/ **(circuits)** ◆◇◇ [1] An electrical **circuit** is a complete route which an electric current can flow around. ❑ *Any attempts to cut through the cabling will break the electrical circuit.* → See also **closed-circuit, short-circuit.** N-COUNT [2] A **circuit** is a series of places that are visited regularly by a person or group, especially as a part of their job. ❑ *It's a common problem, the one I'm asked about most when I'm on the lecture circuit.* N-COUNT: usu supp N [3] A racing **circuit** is a track on which cars, motorbikes, or cycles race. [mainly BRIT] N-COUNT [4] A **circuit of** a place or area is a journey all the way round it. [FORMAL] ❑ *She made a slow circuit of the room.* N-COUNT: usu N of n

**cir|cuit board** **(circuit boards)** A **circuit board** is the same as a **printed circuit board**. N-COUNT

**cir|cuit break|er** **(circuit breakers)** also **circuit-breaker.** A **circuit breaker** is a device which can stop the flow of electricity around a circuit by switching itself off if anything goes wrong. ❑ *There is an internal circuit breaker to protect the instrument from overload.* N-COUNT

**cir|cui|tous** /səʳkjuːɪtəs/ A **circuitous** route is long and complicated rather than simple and direct. [FORMAL] ❑ *The cabdriver took them on a circuitous route to the police station.* ADJ: usu ADJ n = roundabout

**cir|cuit|ry** /sɜːʳkɪtri/ **Circuitry** is a system of electric circuits. ❑ *The computer's entire circuitry was on a single board.* N-UNCOUNT

**cir|cuit train|ing** **Circuit training** is a type of physical training in which you do a series of different exercises, each for a few minutes. N-UNCOUNT

**cir|cu|lar** /sɜːʳkjʊləʳ/ **(circulars)** [1] Something that is **circular** is shaped like a circle. ❑ *...a circular hole twelve feet wide and two feet deep... Place your hands on your shoulders and move your elbows up, back, and down, in a circular motion.* → See also **semi-circular.** ADJ: usu ADJ n [2] A **circular** journey or route is one in which you go to a place and return by a different route. ❑ *Both sides of the river can be explored on this circular walk.* ADJ: usu ADJ n [3] A **circular** argument or theory is not valid because it uses a statement to prove something which is then used to prove the statement. ADJ [4] A **circular** is an official letter or advertisement that is sent to a large number of people at the same time. ❑ *The proposal has been widely publicised in BBC-TV press information circulars sent to 1,800 newspapers.* N-COUNT

**cir|cu|lar saw** **(circular saws)** A **circular saw** is a round metal disk with a sharp edge which is used for cutting wood and other materials. [BRIT] N-COUNT

✔ in AM, use **buzzsaw**

**cir|cu|late** /sɜːʳkjʊleɪt/ **(circulates, circulating, circulated)** [1] If a piece of writing **circulates** or **is circulated**, copies of it are passed round among a group of people. ❑ *The document was previously circulated in New York at the United Nations... Public employees, teachers and liberals are circulating a petition for his recall... This year anonymous leaflets have been circulating in Peking.* VERB be V-ed V n V ♦ **cir|cu|la|tion** /sɜːʳkjʊleɪʃᵊn/ *...an inquiry into the circulation of 'unacceptable literature'.* N-UNCOUNT: usu the N of n [2] If something such as a rumour **circulates** or **is circulated**, the people in a place tell it to each other. ❑ *Rumours were already beginning to circulate that the project might have to be abandoned... I deeply resented those sort of rumours being circulated at a time of deeply personal grief.* VERB = spread V be V-ed Also V n [3] When something **circulates**, it moves easily and freely within a closed place or system. ❑ *...a virus which circulates via the bloodstream and causes ill health in a variety of organs... Cooking odors can circulate throughout the entire house.* VERB V V Also V prep ♦ **cir|cu|la|tion** *The north pole is warmer than the south and the circulation of air around it is less well contained. ...the principle of free circulation of goods.* N-UNCOUNT [4] If you **circulate** at a party, you move among the guests and talk to different people. ❑ *Let me get you something to drink, then I must circulate.* VERB V

**cir|cu|la|tion** /sɜːʳkjʊleɪʃᵊn/ **(circulations)** [1] The **circulation** of a newspaper or magazine is the number of copies that are sold each time it is produced. ❑ *The Daily News once had the highest circulation of any daily in the country... The paper has proved unable to maintain its circulation figures.* N-COUNT: with supp [2] Your **circulation** is the movement of blood through your body. ❑ *Anyone with heart, lung or circulation problems should seek medical advice before flying. ...cold spots in the fingers caused by poor circulation.* N-UNCOUNT [3] → See also **circulate.** [4] If something such as money is **in circulation**, it is being used by the public. If something is **out of circulation** or has been **withdrawn from circulation**, it is no longer available for use by the public. ❑ *...a society like America, with perhaps 180 million guns in circulation. ...the decision to take 50 and 100 ruble bills out of circulation.* PHRASE

**cir|cu|la|tory** /sɜːʳkjʊleɪtəri, AM -lətɔːri/ **Circulatory** means relating to the circulation of blood in the body. [MEDICAL] ❑ *...the human circulatory system.* ADJ: ADJ n

**cir|cum|cise** /sɜːʳkəmsaɪz/ **(circumcises, circumcising, circumcised)** [1] If a boy or man **is circumcised**, the loose skin at the end of his penis is cut off. ❑ *He had been circumcised within eight days of birth as required by Jewish law.* VERB: usu passive be V-ed ♦ **cir|cum|ci|sion** /sɜːʳkəmsɪʒᵊn/ *Jews and Moslems practise circumcision for religious reasons.* N-UNCOUNT: also a N [2] In some cultures, if a girl or woman **is circumcised**, her clitoris is cut or cut off. ❑ *An estimated number of 90 to 100 million women around the world living today have been circumcised.* VERB: usu passive be V-ed ♦ **cir|cum|ci|sion** *...a campaigner against female circumcision.* N-UNCOUNT

**cir|cum|fer|ence** /səʳkʌmfrəns/ [1] The **circumference** of a circle, place, or round object is the distance around its edge. ❑ *...a scientist calculating the earth's circumference... The island is 3.5 km in circumference.* N-UNCOUNT [2] The **circumference** of a circle, place, or round object is its edge. ❑ *Cut the salmon into long strips and wrap it round the circumference of the bread.* N-UNCOUNT

**cir|cum|flex** /sɜːʳkəmfleks/ **(circumflexes)** A **circumflex** or a **circumflex accent** is a symbol written over a vowel in French and other languages, usually to indicate that it should be pronounced longer than usual. It is used for example in the word 'rôle'. N-COUNT

**cir|cum|lo|cu|tion** /sɜːʳkəmloʊkjuːʃᵊn/ **(circumlocutions)** A **circumlocution** is a way of saying or writing something using more words than are necessary instead of being clear and direct. [FORMAL] N-VAR

**cir|cum|navi|gate** /sɜːʳkəmnævɪgeɪt/ **(circumnavigates, circumnavigating, circumnavigated)** If someone **circumnavigates** the world or an island, they sail all the way around it. [FORMAL] ❑ *For this year at least, our race to circumnavigate the globe in less than 80 days is over.* VERB V n

**cir|cum|scribe** /sɜːʳkəmskraɪb/ **(circumscribes, circumscribing, circumscribed)** If someone's power or freedom **is circumscribed**, it is limited or restricted. [FORMAL] ❑ *The army evidently fears that, under him, its activities would be se-* VERB = limit be V-ed *verely circumscribed... There are laws circumscribing the right of individual citizens to cause bodily harm to others.* V n

**cir|cum|spect** /sɜːʳkəmspekt/ If you are **circumspect**, you are cautious in what you do and say and do not take risks. [FORMAL] ❑ *The banks should have been more circumspect in their dealings.* ♦ **cir|cum|spect|ly** *I would suggest that for the time being you behave as circumspectly as possible in political matters.* ADJ = cautious, careful ≠ reckless; ADV: ADV after v = cautiously ≠ recklessly

**cir|cum|spec|tion** /sɜːʳkəmspekʃᵊn/ **Circumspection** is cautious behaviour and a refusal to take risks. [FORMAL] ❑ *This is a region to be treated with circumspection.* N-UNCOUNT: oft with N = caution, care

**cir|cum|stance** /sɜːʳkəmstæns/ **(circumstances)** ◆◇◇ [1] The **circumstances** of a particular situation are the conditions which affect what happens. ❑ *Recent opinion polls show that 60 percent favor abortion under certain circumstances... I wish we could have met under happier circumstances.* N-COUNT: usu pl, with supp [2] The **circumstances** of an event are the way it happened or the causes of it. ❑ *I'm making inquiries about the circumstances of Mary Dean's murder... Hundreds of people had died there in terrible circumstances during and after the revolution.* N-PLURAL: with supp, oft the N of n [3] Your **circumstances** are the conditions of your life, especially the amount of money that you have. ❑ *...help and support for the single mother, whatever her circumstances... I wouldn't have expected to find you in such comfortable circumstances.* N-PLURAL: usu with poss = situation [4] Events and situations which cannot be controlled are sometimes referred to as **circumstance**. ❑ *There are those, you know, who, by circumstance, end up homeless... You might say that we've been victims of circumstance.* N-UNCOUNT

**PHRASES** [5] You can emphasize that something must not or will not happen by saying that it must not or will not happen **under any circumstances**. ❑ *She made it clear that under no circumstances would she cancel the trip.* PHRASE: PHR with cl [emphasis] [6] You can use **in the circumstances** or **under the circumstances** before or after a statement to indicate that you have considered the conditions affecting the situation before making the statement. ❑ *Under the circumstances, a crash was unavoidable.* PHRASE: PHR with cl

**cir|cum|stan|tial** /sɜːʳkəmstænʃᵊl/ **Circumstantial** evidence is evidence that makes it seem likely that something happened, but does not prove it. [FORMAL] ❑ *Fast work by the police had started producing circumstantial evidence.* ADJ: usu ADJ n

**cir|cum|vent** /sɜːʳkəmvent/ **(circumvents, circumventing, circumvented)** If someone **circumvents** a rule or restriction, they avoid having to obey the rule or restriction, in a clever and perhaps dishonest way. [FORMAL] ❑ *Military planners tried to circumvent the treaty.* VERB = get round; V n

**cir|cus** /sɜːʳkəs/ **(circuses)** [1] A **circus** is a group that consists of clowns, acrobats, and animals which travels around to different places and performs shows. ❑ *My real ambition was to work in a circus. ...circus performers.* ♦ **The circus** is the show performed by these people. ❑ *My dad took me to the circus.* N-COUNT; N-SING: the N [2] If you describe a group of people or an event as a **circus**, you disapprove of them because they attract a lot of attention but do not achieve anything useful. ❑ *It could well turn into some kind of a media circus.* N-SING [disapproval]

**cir|rho|sis** /sɪroʊsɪs/ **Cirrhosis** or **cirrhosis of the liver** is a disease which destroys a person's liver and which can kill them. It is often caused by drinking too much alcohol. N-UNCOUNT

**cis|sy** /sɪsi/ → see **sissy**.

**cis|tern** /sɪstəʳn/ **(cisterns)** [1] A **cistern** is a container which stores the water supply for a building, or that holds the water for flushing a toilet. [mainly BRIT] N-COUNT = tank

✔ in AM, usually use **tank**

[2] A **cistern** is a container for storing rain water. [mainly AM] N-COUNT

✔ in BRIT, usually use **water butt**

**cita|del** /sɪtədᵊl/ **(citadels)** [1] In the past, a **citadel** was a strong building in or near a city, where people could shelter for safety. ❑ *The citadel at Besançon towered above the river.* N-COUNT = fortress [2] If you describe a system or organization as a **citadel of** a particular way of life, usually one you disapprove of, you mean that it is powerful and effective in defending that way of life. [FORMAL] ❑ *The business is no longer regarded as a citadel of commerce.* N-COUNT: usu N of n [disapproval] = bastion, stronghold

**ci|ta|tion** /saɪteɪʃᵊn/ **(citations)** [1] A **citation** is an official document or speech which praises a person for something brave or special that they have done. ❑ *His citation says he showed outstanding and exemplary courage.* N-COUNT [2] A **citation** from a book or other piece of writing is a passage or phrase from it. [FORMAL] N-COUNT = quotation [3] A **citation** is the same as a **summons**. [AM] ❑ *The court could issue a citation and fine Ms. Robbins.* N-COUNT

**cite** /saɪt/ **(cites, citing, cited)** ◆◇◇ [1] If you **cite** something, you quote it or mention it, especially as an example or proof of what you are saying. [FORMAL] ❑ *She cites a favourite poem by George Herbert... I am merely citing his reaction as typical of British industry... Spain was cited as the most popular holiday destination.* VERB; V n; V n as adj/n; V n as adj/n [2] To **cite** a person means to officially name them in a legal case. To **cite** a reason or cause means to state it as the official reason for your case. ❑ *They cited Alex's refusal to return to the marital home... Three admirals and a top Navy civilian will be cited for failing to act on reports of sexual assaults.* VERB; V n; be V-ed for -ing [3] If someone **is cited**, they are officially ordered to appear before a court. [AM, LEGAL] ❑ *The judge ruled a mistrial and cited the prosecutors for outrageous misconduct.* VERB; V n

✔ in BRIT, use **be summonsed**

**citi|zen** /sɪtɪzᵊn/ **(citizens)** ◆◆◇ [1] Someone who is a **citizen** of a particular country is legally accepted as belonging to that country. ❑ *...American citizens... The life of ordinary citizens began to change.* N-COUNT: usu with supp [2] The **citizens of** a town or city are the people who live there. ❑ *...the citizens of Buenos Aires.* N-COUNT: usu N of n [3] → See also **senior citizen**.

**citi|zen|ry** /sɪtɪzᵊnri/ The people living in a country, state, or city can be referred to as the **citizenry**. [AM; also BRIT, FORMAL] ❑ *He used the medium of radio when he wanted to enlist public support or reassure the citizenry.* N-SING-COLL

**Citi|zens' Band** **Citizens' Band** is a range of radio frequencies which the general public is allowed to use to send messages to each other. It is used especially by truck drivers and other drivers who use radio sets in their vehicles. The abbreviation **CB** is often used. ❑ *...citizens' band radios.* N-PROPER: oft N n

**citi|zen|ship** /sɪtɪzᵊnʃɪp/ [1] If you have **citizenship** of a country, you are legally accepted as belonging to it. ❑ *After 15 years in the USA, he has finally decided to apply for American citizenship.* N-UNCOUNT: oft adj N [2] **Citizenship** is the fact of belonging to a community because you live in it, and the duties and responsibilities that this brings. ❑ *Their German peers had a more developed sense of citizenship.* N-UNCOUNT

**cit|ric acid** /sɪtrɪk æsɪd/ **Citric acid** is a weak acid found in many kinds of fruit, especially citrus fruit such as oranges and lemons. N-UNCOUNT

**cit|rus** /sɪtrəs/ A **citrus** fruit is a juicy fruit with a sharp taste such as an orange, lemon, or grapefruit. ❑ *...citrus groves.* ADJ: ADJ n

**city** /sɪti/ **(cities)** A **city** is a large town. ❑ *...the city of Bologna. ...a busy city centre.* ◆◆◆ N-COUNT

**City** **The City** is the part of London where many important financial institutions have their main offices. People often refer to these financial institutions as **the City**. ❑ *...a foreign bank in the City... The City fears that profits could fall.* N-PROPER: the N

**city cen|tre** **(city centres)** The **city centre** is the busiest part of a city, where most of the shops and businesses are. [mainly BRIT] ❑ *There is high demand for city centre offices.* N-COUNT: oft the N

**city fa|thers** also **City Fathers.** You can refer to the members of a city council or city's government as the **city fathers.** ❑ *The city fathers have just given final approval to a new stadium.* N-PLURAL

**city hall** **(city halls)** also **City Hall.** The **city hall** is the building which a city council uses as its main offices. ❑ *They massed in front of the city hall. ...at Sheffield City Hall.* N-COUNT; N-PROPER

**city slick|er** **(city slickers)** If you refer to someone as a **city slicker**, you mean that they live and work in a city and are used to city life. [INFORMAL] ❑ *...the city slickers in the capital.* N-COUNT

**civ|ic** /sɪvɪk/ 1 You use **civic** to describe people or things that have an official status in a town or city. ❑ *...the businessmen and civic leaders of Manchester.* ADJ: ADJ n = municipal 2 You use **civic** to describe the duties or feelings that people have because they belong to a particular community. ❑ *...a sense of civic pride.* ADJ: ADJ n

**civ|ics** /sɪvɪks/ **Civics** is the study of the rights and duties of the citizens of a society. [mainly AM] ❑ *...my high-school civics class.* N-UNCOUNT: oft N n

**civ|il** /sɪvᵊl/ ◆◆◇ 1 You use **civil** to describe events that happen within a country and that involve the different groups of people in it. ❑ *...civil unrest.* ADJ: ADJ n 2 You use **civil** to describe people or things in a country that are not connected with its armed forces. ❑ *...the US civil aviation industry.* ADJ: usu ADJ n ≠ military 3 You use **civil** to describe things that are connected with the state rather than with a religion. ❑ *They were married on August 9 in a civil ceremony in Venice. ...Jewish civil and religious law.* ADJ: ADJ n ≠ religious 4 You use **civil** to describe the rights that people have within a society. ❑ *...a United Nations covenant on civil and political rights.* ADJ: ADJ n 5 Someone who is **civil** is polite in a formal way, but not particularly friendly. [FORMAL] ❑ *As visitors, the least we can do is be civil to the people in their own land.* ADJ = polite ♦ **civ|il|ly** *The man nodded civilly to Sharpe, then consulted a notebook.* ADV ♦ **ci|vil|ity** /sɪvɪlɪti/ *...civility to underlings.* N-UNCOUNT

**civ|il de|fence**

> in AM, use **civil defense**

**Civil defence** is the organization and training of the ordinary people in a country so that they can help the armed forces, medical services, or police force, for example if the country is attacked by an enemy. ❑ *...a civil defence exercise.* N-UNCOUNT: oft N n

**civ|il dis|obedi|ence** **Civil disobedience** is the refusal by ordinary people in a country to obey laws or pay taxes, usually as a protest. ❑ *The opposition threatened a campaign of civil disobedience.* N-UNCOUNT

**civ|il en|gi|neer** **(civil engineers)** A **civil engineer** is a person who plans, designs, and constructs roads, bridges, harbours, and public buildings. N-COUNT

**civ|il en|gi|neer|ing** **Civil engineering** is the planning, design, and building of roads, bridges, harbours, and public buildings. ❑ *The Channel Tunnel project is the biggest civil engineering project in Europe.* N-UNCOUNT

**ci|vil|ian** /sɪvɪliən/ **(civilians)** ◆◇◇ 1 In a military situation, a **civilian** is anyone who is not a member of the armed forces. ❑ *The safety of civilians caught up in the fighting must be guaranteed.* N-COUNT 2 In a military situation, **civilian** is used to describe people or things that are not military. ❑ *...the country's civilian population. ...civilian casualties. ...a soldier in civilian clothes.* ADJ: usu ADJ n ≠ military

**civi|li|sa|tion** /sɪvɪlaɪzeɪʃᵊn/ → see **civilization**.

**civi|lise** /sɪvɪlaɪz/ → see **civilize**.

**civi|lised** /sɪvɪlaɪzd/ → see **civilized**.

**ci|vil|ity** /sɪvɪlɪti/ → see **civil**.

**civi|li|za|tion** /sɪvɪlaɪzeɪʃᵊn/ **(civilizations)**

> in BRIT, also use **civilisation**

1 A **civilization** is a human society with its own social organization and culture. ❑ *The ancient civilizations of Central and Latin America were founded upon corn.* N-VAR 2 **Civilization** is the state of having an advanced level of social organization and a comfortable way of life. ❑ *...our advanced state of civilisation.* N-UNCOUNT

**civi|lize** /sɪvɪlaɪz/ **(civilizes, civilizing, civilized)**

> in BRIT, also use **civilise**

To **civilize** a person or society means to educate them and improve their way of life. ❑ *...a comedy about a man who tries to civilise a woman – but she ends up civilising him... It exerts a civilizing influence on mankind.* VERB V n V-ing

**civi|lized** /sɪvɪlaɪzd/

> in BRIT, also use **civilised**

1 If you describe a society as **civilized**, you mean that it is advanced and has sensible laws and customs. ❑ *I believed that in civilized countries, torture had ended long ago.* ADJ [approval] 2 If you describe a person or their behaviour as **civilized**, you mean that they are polite and reasonable. ❑ *I wrote to my ex-wife. She was very civilised about it.* ADJ

**civ|il law** **Civil law** is the part of a country's set of laws which is concerned with the private affairs of citizens, for example marriage and property ownership, rather than with crime. N-UNCOUNT: oft *the* N ≠ criminal law

**civ|il lib|er|ties**

> The form **civil liberty** is used as a modifier.

A person's **civil liberties** are the rights they have to say, think, and do what they want as long as they respect other people's rights. ❑ *...his commitment to human rights and civil liberties. ...civil liberty campaigners.* N-PLURAL = human rights

**Civ|il List** **The Civil List** is money paid by the state every year to members of the British Royal Family to cover their living expenses. N-PROPER: *the* N

**civ|il rights** **Civil rights** are the rights that people have in a society to equal treatment and equal opportunities, whatever their race, sex, or religion. ❑ *...the civil rights movement. ...violations of civil rights.* N-PLURAL: oft N n

**civ|il serv|ant** **(civil servants)** A **civil servant** is a person who works in the Civil Service in Britain and some other countries, or for the local, state, or federal government in the United States. N-COUNT

**Civ|il Ser|vice** also **civil service.** The **Civil Service** of a country consists of its government departments and all the people who work in them. In many countries, the departments concerned with military and legal affairs are not part of the Civil Service. ❑ *...a job in the Civil Service.* N-SING: usu *the* N

**civ|il war** **(civil wars)** ◆◇◇ A **civil war** is a war which is fought between different groups of people who live in the same country. ❑ *...the Spanish Civil War.* N-COUNT

**civ|vies** /sɪviz/ People in the armed forces use **civvies** to refer to ordinary clothes that are not part of a uniform. [INFORMAL] ❑ *They might have been soldiers in civvies.* N-PLURAL: oft *in* N

**civ|vy street** /sɪvi striːt/ People in the armed forces use **civvy street** to refer to life and work which is not connected with the armed forces. [BRIT, INFORMAL] N-UNCOUNT: usu prep N

**CJD** /siː dʒeɪ diː/ **CJD** is an incurable brain disease that affects human beings and is believed to be caused by eating beef from cows with BSE. **CJD** is an abbreviation for 'Creutzfeld Jacob disease'. N-UNCOUNT

**cl** **cl** is a written abbreviation for **centilitre**. ❑ *...two 75cl bottles of quality wine.*

**clack** /klæk/ **(clacks, clacking, clacked)** If things **clack** or if you **clack** them, they make a short loud noise, especially when they hit each other. ❑ *The windshield wipers clacked back and forth... I clacked one ski against the other and almost tripped.* VERB V V n ♦ **Clack** is also a noun. ❑ *...listening to the clack of her shoes on the stairs... Her bracelets were going clack-clack-clack, she was shaking so hard.* N-SING: SOUND

**clad** /klæd/ 1 If you are **clad in** particular clothes, you are wearing them. [LITERARY] ❑ *...the figure of a woman, clad in black. ...posters of scantily-* ADJ: v-link ADJ *in* n, adv ADJ *clad women.* ♦ **Clad** is also a combining form. COMB in ADJ ❑ *...the leather-clad biker.* [2] A building, part of a building, or mountain that is **clad with** something is covered by that thing. [LITERARY] ❑ *The walls and floors are clad with ceramic tiles.* ♦ **Clad** is also a combining form. ❑ *...the distant shapes of snow-clad mountains.* ADJ: v-link ADJ *in/with* n COMB in ADJ

**clad|ding** /klædɪŋ/ [1] **Cladding** is a covering of tiles, wooden boards, or other material that is fixed to the outside of a building to protect it against bad weather or to make it look more attractive. ❑ *...stone cladding.* [2] **Cladding** is a layer of metal which is put round fuel rods in a nuclear reactor. N-UNCOUNT: oft n N = *facing* N-UNCOUNT

**claim** /kleɪm/ **(claims, claiming, claimed)** ♦♦♦ [1] If you say that someone **claims that** something is true, you mean they say that it is true but you are not sure whether or not they are telling the truth. ❑ *He claimed that it was all a conspiracy against him... A man claiming to be a journalist threatened to reveal details about her private life... 'I had never received one single complaint against me,' claimed the humiliated doctor... He claims a 70 to 80 per cent success rate.* VERB = *maintain* V that V to-inf V with quote V n [2] A **claim** is something which someone says which they cannot prove and which may be false. ❑ *He repeated his claim that the people of Trinidad and Tobago backed his action... He rejected claims that he had affairs with six women.* N-COUNT: usu with supp, oft N that [3] If you say that someone **claims** responsibility or credit for something, you mean they say that they are responsible for it, but you are not sure whether or not they are telling the truth. ❑ *An underground organisation has claimed responsibility for the bomb explosion.* VERB V n [4] If you **claim** something, you try to get it because you think you have a right to it. ❑ *Now they are returning to claim what was theirs.* VERB V n [5] A **claim** is a demand for something that you think you have a right to. ❑ *Rival claims to Macedonian territory caused conflict in the Balkans.* N-COUNT: oft N *to* n [6] If someone **claims** a record, title, or prize, they gain or win it. [JOURNALISM] ❑ *Zhuang claimed the record in 54.64 seconds.* VERB V n [7] If you have a **claim on** someone or their attention, you have the right to demand things from them or to demand their attention. ❑ *She'd no claims on him now... He was surrounded by people, all with claims on his attention.* N-COUNT: N *on* n [8] If something or someone **claims** your attention, they need you to spend your time and effort on them. ❑ *There is already a long list of people claiming her attention.* VERB V n [9] If you **claim** money from the government, an insurance company, or another organization, you officially apply to them for it, because you think you are entitled to it according to their rules. ❑ *Some 25 per cent of the people who are entitled to claim State benefits do not do so... John had taken out redundancy insurance but when he tried to claim, he was refused payment... They intend to claim for damages against the three doctors.* ♦ **Claim** is also a noun. ❑ *...the office which has been dealing with their claim for benefit... Last time we made a claim on our insurance they paid up really quickly.* VERB V n V V *for* n N-COUNT: oft N *for* n [10] If you **claim** money or other benefits from your employers, you demand them because you think you deserve or need them. ❑ *The union claimed a pay rise worth four times the rate of inflation.* ♦ **Claim** is also a noun. ❑ *They are making substantial claims for improved working conditions... Electricity workers have voted for industrial action in pursuit of a pay claim.* VERB V n N-COUNT: oft N *for* n [11] If you say that a war, disease, or accident **claims** someone's life, you mean that they are killed in it or by it. [FORMAL] ❑ *Heart disease is the biggest killer, claiming 180,000 lives a year.* VERB V n [12] → See also **no claims**.

PHRASES [13] Someone's **claim to fame** is something quite important or interesting that they have done or that is connected with them. ❑ *Barbara Follett's greatest claim to fame is that she taught Labour MPs how to look good on television.* PHRASE: *claim* inflects, oft poss PHR [14] If you **lay claim to** something you do not have, you say that it belongs to you. [FORMAL] ❑ *Five Asian countries lay claim to the islands.* PHRASE: V inflects, PHR n [15] to **stake a claim** → see **stake**.

**claim|ant** /kleɪmənt/ **(claimants)** [1] A **claimant** is someone who is receiving money from the state because they are unemployed or they are unable to work because they are ill. [BRIT] ❑ *...benefit claimants.* N-COUNT [2] A **claimant** is someone who asks to be given something which they think they are entitled to. ❑ *The compensation will be split between 140 claimants.* N-COUNT

**claims ad|just|er** **(claims adjusters)** also **claims adjustor.** A **claims adjuster** is someone who is employed by an insurance company to decide how much money a person making a claim should receive. [AM, BUSINESS] N-COUNT = *insurance adjuster*

✔ in BRIT, use **loss adjuster**

**clair|voy|ant** /kleəʳvɔɪənt/ **(clairvoyants)** [1] Someone who is believed to be **clairvoyant** is believed to know about future events or to be able to communicate with dead people. ❑ *...clairvoyant powers.* ADJ [2] A **clairvoyant** is someone who claims to be clairvoyant. N-COUNT

**clam** /klæm/ **(clams, clamming, clammed)** **Clams** are a kind of shellfish which can be eaten. N-COUNT
♦ **clam up** If someone **clams up**, they stop talking, often because they are shy or to avoid giving away secrets. [INFORMAL] ❑ *As soon as I told her my name, she clammed up.* PHRASAL VERB V P

**clam|ber** /klæmbəʳ/ **(clambers, clambering, clambered)** If you **clamber** somewhere, you climb there with difficulty, usually using your hands as well as your feet. ❑ *They clambered up the stone walls of a steeply terraced olive grove.* VERB = *scramble* V prep/adv

**clam|my** /klæmi/ Something that is **clammy** is unpleasantly damp or sticky. ❑ *My shirt was clammy with sweat.* ADJ

**clam|or|ous** /klæmərəs/ If you describe people or their voices as **clamorous**, you mean they are talking loudly or shouting. [LITERARY] ❑ *...the crowded, clamorous streets.* ADJ: usu ADJ n

**clam|our** /klæməʳ/ **(clamours, clamouring, clamoured)**

✔ in AM, use **clamor**

[1] If people **are clamouring for** something, they are demanding it in a noisy or angry way. [JOURNALISM] ❑ *...competing parties clamouring for the attention of the voter... At breakfast next morning my two grandsons were clamouring to go swimming.* ♦ **Clamour** is also a noun. ❑ *...the clamour for his resignation.* VERB V *for* n V to-inf N-SING: oft N *for* n [2] **Clamour** is used to describe the loud noise of a large group of people talking or shouting together. ❑ *She could hear a clamour in the road outside.* N-SING

**clamp** /klæmp/ **(clamps, clamping, clamped)** [1] A **clamp** is a device that holds two things firmly together. N-COUNT [2] When you **clamp** one thing **to** another, you fasten the two things together with a clamp. ❑ *Somebody forgot to bring along the U-bolts to clamp the microphones to the pole.* VERB V n *to* n [3] To **clamp** something in a particular place means to put it or hold it there firmly and tightly. ❑ *Simon finished dialing and clamped the phone to his ear... He clamped his lips together... You beg him to try just one spoonful, and he clamps his mouth shut... Peter jumped to his feet with his hand clamped to his neck.* VERB V n prep V n *together* V n adj V-ed [4] A **clamp** is a large metal device which is fitted to the wheel of an illegally parked car or other vehicle in order to prevent it from being driven away. The driver has to pay to have the clamp removed. [BRIT] N-COUNT

✔ in AM, use **Denver boot**

[5] To **clamp** a car means to fit a clamp to one of its wheels so that it cannot be driven away. [BRIT] ❑ *Courts in Scotland have ruled it illegal to clamp a car parked on private ground and then to demand a fine.* VERB V n

✔ in AM, use **boot**

♦ **clamp|ing** *The AA called for laws to regulate clamping firms.* N-UNCOUNT

♦ **clamp down** To **clamp down on** people or activities means to take strong official action to stop or control them. [JOURNALISM] ❑ *If the government clamps down on the protestors, that will only serve to strengthen them in the long run... Banking regulators failed to clamp down until earlier this month.* PHRASAL VERB = crack down; V P on n; V P

**clamp|down** /klæmpdaʊn/ **(clampdowns)** also **clamp-down.** A **clampdown** is a sudden restriction on a particular activity by a government or other authority. [JOURNALISM] ❑ *...a clampdown on the employment of illegal immigrants.* N-COUNT: oft N on n

**clan** /klæn/ **(clans)** [1] A **clan** is a group which consists of families that are related to each other. ❑ *...rival clans.* N-COUNT [2] You can refer to a group of people with the same interests as a **clan**. [INFORMAL] ❑ *...a powerful clan of industrialists from Monterrey.* N-COUNT

**clan|des|tine** /klændestɪn/ Something that is **clandestine** is hidden or kept secret, often because it is illegal. [FORMAL] ❑ *...their clandestine meetings.* ADJ: usu ADJ n = secret

**clang** /klæŋ/ **(clangs, clanging, clanged)** When a large metal object **clangs**, it makes a loud noise. ❑ *The door clanged shut behind them.* ♦ **Clang** is also a noun. ❑ *He pulled the gates to with a clang.* VERB; V; N-VAR

**clang|er** /klæŋəʳ/ **(clangers)** You can refer to something stupid or embarrassing that someone does or says as a **clanger**. [BRIT, INFORMAL] N-COUNT ● If you say that you have **dropped a clanger**, you mean that you have done or said something stupid or embarrassing. [BRIT, INFORMAL] PHRASE: V and N inflect

**clank** /klæŋk/ **(clanks, clanking, clanked)** When large metal objects **clank**, they make a noise because they are hitting together or hitting against something hard. ❑ *A pan rattled and clanked... 'Here we are now,' Beth said, as the train clanked into a tiny station. ...the clanking noise of the ferry.* VERB; V; V prep; V-ing

**clan|nish** /klænɪʃ/ If you describe a group of people as **clannish**, you mean that they often spend time together and may seem unfriendly to other people who are not in the group. [INFORMAL] ❑ *They were a clannish lot, not given to welcoming strangers.* ADJ = cliquey

**clans|man** /klænzmən/ **(clansmen) Clansmen** are people who are members of the same **clan**. N-COUNT: usu pl

**clap** /klæp/ **(claps, clapping, clapped)** [1] When you **clap**, you hit your hands together to show appreciation or attract attention. ❑ *The men danced and the women clapped... Midge clapped her hands, calling them back to order... Londoners came out on to the pavement to wave and clap the marchers.* ♦ **Clap** is also a noun. ❑ *Let's give the children a big clap.* VERB; V; V n; V n; N-SING: a N [2] If you **clap** your hand or an object onto something, you put it there quickly and firmly. ❑ *I clapped a hand over her mouth.* VERB; V n prep [3] A **clap of thunder** is a sudden and loud noise of thunder. N-COUNT: N of n [4] to **clap eyes on** someone → see **eye**.

**clap|board** /klæpbɔːʳd, klæbəʳd/ **(clapboards)** [1] A **clapboard** building has walls which are covered with long narrow pieces of wood, usually painted white. ADJ: ADJ n [2] A **clapboard** is the same as a **clapperboard**. [AM] N-COUNT

**clapped-out** also **clapped out.** If you describe a person or a machine as **clapped-out**, you mean that they are old and no longer able to work properly. [BRIT, INFORMAL] ❑ *...his clapped-out old car. ...clapped out comedians.* ADJ: usu ADJ n [disapproval]

**clapper|board** /klæpəʳbɔːʳd/ **(clapperboards)** also **clapper-board.** A **clapperboard** consists of two pieces of wood that are connected by a hinge and hit together before each scene when making a film, to make it easier to match the sound and pictures of different scenes. [BRIT] N-COUNT

☑ in AM, use **clapboard**

**clap|trap** /klæptræp/ If you describe something that someone says as **claptrap**, you mean that it is stupid or foolish although it may sound important. [INFORMAL] ❑ *This is the claptrap that politicians have peddled many times before.* N-UNCOUNT [disapproval] = drivel

**clar|et** /klærət/ **(clarets)** [1] **Claret** is a type of French red wine. N-MASS [2] Something that is **claret** is purplish-red in colour. [LITERARY] COLOUR

**clari|fied** /klærɪfaɪd/ **Clarified** butter has been made clear by being heated. ADJ

**clari|fy** /klærɪfaɪ/ **(clarifies, clarifying, clarified)** To **clarify** something means to make it easier to understand, usually by explaining it in more detail. [FORMAL] ❑ *A bank spokesman was unable to clarify the situation.* VERB; V n ♦ **clari|fi|ca|tion** /klærɪfɪkeɪʃᵊn/ **(clarifications)** *The union has written to Zurich asking for clarification of the situation.* N-VAR

**clari|net** /klærɪnet/ **(clarinets)** A **clarinet** is a musical instrument in the shape of a pipe. You play the clarinet by blowing into it and covering and uncovering the holes with your fingers. N-VAR: oft the N

**clari|net|tist** /klærɪnetɪst/ **(clarinettists)** also **clarinetist.** A **clarinettist** is someone who plays the clarinet. N-COUNT

**clari|on call** **(clarion calls)** A **clarion call** is a strong and emotional appeal to people to do something. [LITERARY] ❑ *Paine's words are a clarion call for democracy.* N-COUNT

**clar|ity** /klærɪti/ [1] The **clarity** of something such as a book or argument is its quality of being well explained and easy to understand. ❑ *...the ease and clarity with which the author explains difficult technical and scientific subjects.* N-UNCOUNT = lucidity [2] **Clarity** is the ability to think clearly. ❑ *In business circles he is noted for his flair and clarity of vision.* N-UNCOUNT: oft N of n [3] **Clarity** is the quality of being clear in outline or sound. ❑ *This remarkable technology provides far greater clarity than conventional x-rays.* N-UNCOUNT = precision

**clash** /klæʃ/ **(clashes, clashing, clashed)** ◆◇◇ [1] When people **clash**, they fight, argue, or disagree with each other. [JOURNALISM] ❑ *A group of 400 demonstrators clashed with police... Behind the scenes, Parsons clashed with almost everyone on the show... The United States and Israel clashed over demands for a UN investigation into the killings.* ♦ **Clash** is also a noun. ❑ *There have been a number of clashes between police in riot gear and demonstrators.* V-RECIP; V with n; V with n; pl-n V; N-COUNT: oft N between/with n [2] Beliefs, ideas, or qualities that **clash with** each other are very different from each other and therefore are opposed. ❑ *Don't make any policy decisions which clash with official company thinking... Here, morality and good sentiments clash headlong.* ♦ **Clash** is also a noun. ❑ *Inside government, there was a clash of views.* V-RECIP; V with n; pl-n V; N-COUNT: N of n [3] If one event **clashes with** another, the two events happen at the same time so that you cannot attend both of them. ❑ *The detective changed his holiday dates when his flight was brought forward and it now clashed with the trial.* VERB; V with n [4] If one colour or style **clashes with** another, the colours or styles look ugly together. You can also say that two colours or styles **clash**. ❑ *The red door clashed with the soft, natural tones of the stone walls... So what if the colours clashed?* V-RECIP; V with n; pl-n V

**clasp** /klɑːsp, klæsp/ **(clasps, clasping, clasped)** [1] If you **clasp** someone or something, you hold them tightly in your hands or arms. ❑ *She clasped the children to her... He paced the corridor, hands clasped behind his back.* VERB; V n; V-ed [2] A **clasp** is a small device that fastens something. ❑ *...the clasp of her handbag.* N-COUNT: usu with supp

**class** /klɑːs, klæs/ **(classes, classing, classed)** ◆◆◆ [1] A **class** is a group of pupils or students who are taught together. ❑ *He had to spend about six months in a class with younger students... Reducing class sizes should be a top priority.* N-COUNT [2] A **class** is a course of teaching in a particular subject. ❑ *He acquired a law degree by taking classes at night... I go to dance classes here in New York.* N-COUNT: oft n N = lesson [3] If you do something **in class**, you do it during a lesson in school. ❑ *There is lots of reading in class.* N-UNCOUNT: in N [4] The students in a school or university who finish their course in a particular year are often referred to as the **class of** N-SING: N of date that year. ❑ *These two members of Yale's Class of '57 never miss a reunion.* 5 **Class** refers to the division of people in a society into groups according to their social status. ❑ *...the relationship between social classes. ...the characteristics of the British class structure.* ➔ See also **chattering classes, middle class, upper class, working class.** 6 A **class of** things is a group of them with similar characteristics. ❑ *...the division of the stars into six classes of brightness.* 7 If someone or something **is classed as** a particular thing, they are regarded as belonging to that group of things. ❑ *Since the birds interbreed they cannot be classed as different species... I class myself as an ordinary working person... I would class my garden as medium in size... Malaysia wants to send back refugees classed as economic migrants.* 8 If you say that someone or something has **class**, you mean that they are elegant and sophisticated. [INFORMAL] ❑ *He's got the same style off the pitch as he has on it – sheer class.* 9 ➔ See also **business class, first-class, second-class, third-class, top-class, world-class.** 10 If someone is **in a class of** their **own**, they have more of a particular skill or quality than anyone else. If something is **in a class of its own**, it is better than any other similar thing. ❑ *As a player, he was in a class of his own.*

N-VAR; N-COUNT: usu N *of* n; VERB; *be* V-ed *as* n/adj; V pron-refl *as* n; V n *as* adj/n; V-ed; N-UNCOUNT [approval]; PHRASE: usu v-link PHR

**class ac|tion (class actions)** A **class action** is a legal case brought by a group of people rather than an individual. N-COUNT: usu sing

**class-conscious** Someone who is **class-conscious** is very aware of the differences between the various classes of people in society, and often has a strong feeling of belonging to a particular class. ❑ *Nineteenth-century Britain was a class-conscious society.* ♦ **class-consciousness** *There was very little snobbery or class-consciousness in the wartime navy.* ADJ; N-UNCOUNT

**clas|sic** /klæsɪk/ **(classics)** 1 A **classic** example of a thing or situation has all the features which you expect such a thing or situation to have. ❑ *The debate in the mainstream press has been a classic example of British hypocrisy... His first two goals were classic cases of being in the right place at the right time.* ♦ **Classic** is also a noun. ❑ *It was a classic of interrogation: first the bully, then the kind one who offers sympathy.* 2 A **classic** film, piece of writing, or piece of music is of very high quality and has become a standard against which similar things are judged. ❑ *...the classic children's film Huckleberry Finn. ...a classic study of the American penal system.* ♦ **Classic** is also a noun. ❑ *The record won a gold award and remains one of the classics of modern popular music. ...a film classic.* 3 A **classic** is a book which is well-known and considered to be of a high literary standard. You can refer to such books generally as **the classics**. ❑ *As I grow older, I like to reread the classics regularly.* 4 **Classic** style is simple and traditional and is not affected by changes in fashion. ❑ *Wear classic clothes which feel good and look good... These are classic designs which will fit in well anywhere.* 5 **Classics** is the study of the ancient Greek and Roman civilizations, especially their languages, literature, and philosophy. ❑ *...a Classics degree.*

◆◆◇ ADJ: usu ADJ n = typical; N-COUNT: oft N *of* n; ADJ: ADJ n; N-COUNT: usu with supp; N-COUNT; ADJ: usu ADJ n; N-UNCOUNT

**clas|si|cal** /klæsɪkᵊl/ 1 You use **classical** to describe something that is traditional in form, style, or content. ❑ *Fokine did not change the steps of classical ballet; instead he found new ways of using them. ...the scientific attitude of Smith and earlier classical economists.* 2 **Classical** music is music that is considered to be serious and of lasting value. 3 **Classical** is used to describe things which relate to the ancient Greek or Roman civilizations. ❑ *...the healers of ancient Egypt and classical Greece.*

◆◇◇ ADJ: usu ADJ n ≠ modern; ADJ: usu ADJ n; ADJ: usu ADJ n

**clas|si|cal|ly** /klæsɪkli/ 1 Someone who has been **classically** trained in something such as art, music, or ballet has learned the traditional skills and methods of that subject. ❑ *Peter is a classically trained pianist.* 2 **Classically** is used to indicate that something is based on or reminds people of the culture of ancient Greece and Rome. ❑ *...the classically inspired church of S. Francesco.*

ADV: ADV -ed; ADV: ADV adj/-ed

**clas|si|cism** /klæsɪsɪzəm/ **Classicism** is a style of art practised especially in the 18th century in Europe. It has simple regular forms and the artist does not attempt to express strong emotions. N-UNCOUNT

**clas|si|cist** /klæsɪsɪst/ **(classicists)** 1 A **classicist** is someone who studies the ancient Greek and Roman civilizations, especially their languages, literature, and philosophy. 2 In the arts, especially in architecture, a **classicist** is someone who follows the principles of classicism in their work. N-COUNT; N-COUNT

**clas|si|fi|ca|tion** /klæsɪfɪkeɪʃᵊn/ **(classifications)** A **classification** is a division or category in a system which divides things into groups or types. ❑ *Its tariffs cater for four basic classifications of customer.* ➔ See also **classify**. N-COUNT

**clas|si|fied** /klæsɪfaɪd/ **Classified** information or documents are officially secret. ❑ *He has a security clearance that allows him access to classified information.* ADJ

**clas|si|fied ad (classified ads) Classified ads** or **classified advertisements** are small advertisements in a newspaper or magazine. They are usually from a person or small company. N-COUNT

**clas|si|fieds** /klæsɪfaɪdz/ **The classifieds** are the same as **classified ads**. N-PLURAL: usu *the* N

**clas|si|fy** /klæsɪfaɪ/ **(classifies, classifying, classified)** To **classify** things means to divide them into groups or types so that things with similar characteristics are in the same group. ❑ *It is necessary initially to classify the headaches into certain types... The coroner immediately classified his death as a suicide.* ♦ **clas|si|fi|ca|tion** /klæsɪfɪkeɪʃᵊn/ **(classifications)** *...the British Board of Film Classification.* VERB = categorize; V n; V n *as* n; N-VAR

**class|less** /klɑːsləs, klæs-/ When politicians talk about a **classless** society, they mean a society in which people are not affected by social status. ❑ *...the new Prime Minister's vision of a classless society.* ADJ: usu ADJ n [approval]

**class|mate** /klɑːsmeɪt, klæs-/ **(classmates)** Your **classmates** are students who are in the same class as you at school or college. N-COUNT: oft poss N

**class|room** /klɑːsruːm, klæs-/ **(classrooms)** A **classroom** is a room in a school where lessons take place. N-COUNT

**classy** /klɑːsi, klæsi/ **(classier, classiest)** If you describe someone or something as **classy**, you mean they are stylish and sophisticated. [INFORMAL] ❑ *The German star put in a classy performance.* ADJ

**clat|ter** /klætəʳ/ **(clatters, clattering, clattered)** 1 If you say that people or things **clatter** somewhere, you mean that they move there noisily. ❑ *He turned and clattered down the stairs.* 2 If something hard **clatters**, it makes repeated short noises as it hits against another hard thing. [LITERARY] ❑ *She set her cup down, and it clattered against the saucer.* ♦ **Clatter** is also a noun. ❑ *From somewhere distant he heard the clatter of a typewriter.* VERB; V prep/adv; VERB; V prep; N-SING: usu with supp

**clause** /klɔːz/ **(clauses)** 1 A **clause** is a section of a legal document. ❑ *He has a clause in his contract which entitles him to a percentage of the profits. ...a complaint alleging a breach of clause 4 of the code.* 2 In grammar, a **clause** is a group of words containing a verb. Sentences contain one or more clauses. There are finite clauses and non-finite clauses. ➔ See also **main clause, relative clause, subordinate clause**. N-COUNT: oft N num; N-COUNT

**claus|tro|pho|bia** /klɔːstrəfoʊbiə/ Someone who suffers from **claustrophobia** feels very uncomfortable or anxious when they are in small or enclosed places. N-UNCOUNT

**claus|tro|pho|bic** /klɔːstrəfoʊbɪk/ 1 You describe a place or situation as **claustrophobic** when it makes you feel uncomfortable and unhappy because you are enclosed or restricted. ❑ *They lived in an unhealthily claustrophobic atmosphere... The house felt too claustrophobic.* 2 If you ADJ; ADJ:

feel **claustrophobic**, you feel very uncomfortable or anxious when you are in a small, crowded, or enclosed place. ❑ *The churning, pressing crowds made her feel claustrophobic.* — usu v-link ADJ

**clavi|chord** /klævɪkɔːʳd/ **(clavichords)** A **clavichord** is a musical instrument rather like a small piano. When you press the keys, small pieces of metal come up and hit the strings. Clavichords were especially popular during the eighteenth century. — N-VAR: oft *the* N

**clavi|cle** /klævɪkᵊl/ **(clavicles)** Your **clavicles** are your collar bones. [MEDICAL] — N-COUNT

**claw** /klɔː/ **(claws, clawing, clawed)** 1 The **claws** of a bird or animal are the thin, hard, curved nails at the end of its feet. ❑ *The cat tried to cling to the edge by its claws.* — N-COUNT: usu pl 2 The **claws** of a lobster, crab, or scorpion are the two pointed parts at the end of its legs which are used for holding things. — N-COUNT: usu pl 3 If an animal **claws at** something, it scratches or damages it with its claws. ❑ *The wolf clawed at the tree and howled the whole night.* — VERB; V *at* n 4 To **claw at** something mean to try very hard to get hold of it. ❑ *His fingers clawed at Blake's wrist.* — VERB; V *at* n 5 If you **claw** your **way** somewhere, you move there with great difficulty, trying desperately to find things to hold on to. ❑ *Some did manage to claw their way up iron ladders to the safety of the upper deck.* — VERB; V *way* prep/adv

♦ **claw back** 1 If someone **claws back** some of the money or power they had lost, they get some of it back again. [BRIT] ❑ *They will eventually be able to claw back all or most of the debt.* — PHRASAL VERB; V P n (not pron) 2 If a government **claws back** money, it finds a way of taking money back from people that it gave money to in another way. [BRIT] ❑ *The Chancellor will try to claw back £3.5 billion in next year's Budget.* — PHRASAL VERB; V P n (not pron); Also V n P

**clay** /kleɪ/ **(clays)** 1 **Clay** is a kind of earth that is soft when it is wet and hard when it is dry. Clay is shaped and baked to make things such as pots and bricks. ❑ *...the heavy clay soils of Cambridgeshire... As the wheel turned, the potter shaped and squeezed the lump of clay into a graceful shape. ...a little clay pot.* — N-MASS: oft N n 2 In tennis, matches played on **clay** are played on courts whose surface is covered with finely crushed stones or brick. ❑ *He was a clay-court specialist who won Wimbledon five times.* — N-UNCOUNT: oft *on* N, N n

**clay pi|geon (clay pigeons) Clay pigeons** are discs of baked clay which are thrown into the air by a machine as targets for gun shooting practice. ❑ *...hunting and clay-pigeon shooting.* — N-COUNT: usu N n

**clean** /kliːn/ **(cleaner, cleanest, cleans, cleaning, cleaned)** ◆◆◇ 1 Something that is **clean** is free from dirt or unwanted marks. ❑ *He wore his cleanest slacks, a clean shirt and a navy blazer... Disease has not been a problem because clean water is available... The metro is efficient and spotlessly clean.* — ADJ ≠dirty 2 You say that people or animals are **clean** when they keep themselves or their surroundings clean. — ADJ ≠dirty 3 A **clean** fuel or chemical process does not create many harmful or polluting substances. ❑ *Fans of electric cars say they are clean, quiet and economical.* — ADJ ≠dirty ♦ **clean|ly** *Manufacturers are working with new fuels to find one that burns more cleanly than petrol.* — ADV: ADV after v 4 If you **clean** something or **clean** dirt off it, you make it free from dirt and unwanted marks, for example by washing or wiping it. If something **cleans** easily, it is easy to clean. ❑ *Her father cleaned his glasses with a paper napkin... It took half an hour to clean the orange powder off the bath... Wood flooring not only cleans easily, but it's environmentally friendly into the bargain.* — VERB; V n; V n prep/adv; V adv ♦ **Clean** is also a noun. ❑ *Give the cooker a good clean.* — N-SING 5 If you **clean** a room or house, you make the inside of it and the furniture in it free from dirt and dust. ❑ *With them also lived Mary Burinda, who cooked and cleaned... She got up early and cleaned the flat.* — VERB; V; V n ♦ **clean|ing** *I do the cleaning myself.* — N-UNCOUNT 6 If you describe something such as a book, joke, or lifestyle as **clean**, you think that they are not sexually immoral or offensive. ❑ *They're trying to show clean, wholesome, decent movies... Flirting is good clean fun.* — ADJ [approval] ≠dirty

7 If someone has a **clean** reputation or record, they have never done anything illegal or wrong. ❑ *Accusations of tax evasion have tarnished his clean image... You can hire these from most car hire firms, provided you have a clean driving licence.* — ADJ 8 A **clean** game or fight is carried out fairly, according to the rules. ❑ *He called for a clean fight in the election and an end to 'negative campaigning'.* — ADJ: usu ADJ n = fair ≠dirty ♦ **clean|ly** *The game had been cleanly fought from the start.* — ADV: ADV after v, ADV -ed 9 A **clean** sheet of paper has no writing or drawing on it. ❑ *Take a clean sheet of paper and down the left-hand side make a list.* — ADJ: usu ADJ n = blank 10 If you make a **clean** break or start, you end a situation completely and start again in a different way. ❑ *She wanted to make a clean break from her mother and father.* — ADJ: ADJ n 11 **Clean** is used to emphasize that something was done completely. [INFORMAL] ❑ *It burned clean through the seat of my overalls... I clean forgot everything I had prepared.* — ADV: usu ADV prep/adv, also ADV before v [emphasis] 12 You can describe an action as **clean** to indicate that it is carried out simply and quickly without mistakes. ❑ *They were more concerned about the dogs' welfare than a clean getaway.* — ADJ: usu ADJ n ≠messy ♦ **clean|ly** *I struck the ball cleanly and my shot was on target.* — ADV: ADV after v, ADV -ed 13 If you **come clean about** something that you have been keeping secret, you admit it or tell people about it. [INFORMAL] ❑ *It would be better if you come clean about it and let her know what kind of man she is seeing.* — PHRASE: V inflects, oft PHR *about/on* n 14 to **clean up** your **act** → see **act**. to **keep** your **nose clean** → see **nose**. **a clean slate** → see **slate**. to **wipe the slate clean** → see **slate**. **a clean sweep** → see **sweep**. **clean as a whistle** → see **whistle**.

♦ **clean out** 1 If you **clean out** something such as a cupboard, room, or container, you take everything out of it and clean the inside of it thoroughly. ❑ *Mr. Wall asked if I would help him clean out the bins... If you are using the same pan, clean it out.* — PHRASAL VERB; V P n (not pron); V n P 2 If someone **cleans** you **out**, they take all the money and valuables you have. If they **clean out** a place, they take everything of value that is in it. [INFORMAL] ❑ *I'm sure the burglars waited until my insurance claim was through and came back to clean me out again... When they first captured the port, they virtually cleaned out its warehouses.* — PHRASAL VERB; V n P; V P n (not pron)

♦ **clean up** 1 If you **clean up** a mess or **clean up** a place where there is a mess, you make things tidy and free of dirt again. ❑ *Police in the city have been cleaning up the debris left by a day of violent confrontation... Nina and Mary were in the kitchen, cleaning up after dinner.* — PHRASAL VERB; V P n (not pron); V P 2 To **clean up** something such as the environment or an industrial process means to make it free from substances or processes that cause pollution. ❑ *Under pressure from the public, many regional governments cleaned up their beaches.* — PHRASAL VERB; V P n (not pron) 3 If the police or authorities **clean up** a place or area of activity, they make it free from crime, corruption, and other unacceptable forms of behaviour. ❑ *After years of neglect and decline the city was cleaning itself up... Since then, the authorities have tried to clean up the sport.* — PHRASAL VERB; V n P; V P n (not pron) 4 If you go and **clean up**, you make yourself clean and tidy, especially after doing something that has made you dirty. ❑ *Johnny, go inside and get cleaned up... I cleaned myself up a bit, and got the baby ready.* — PHRASAL VERB; V P; V pron-refl P 5 If someone **cleans up**, they make a large profit or get a lot of money. [INFORMAL] ❑ *It has cleaned up at the box office.* — PHRASAL VERB; V P

♦ **clean up after** If you **clean up after** someone, you clean or tidy a place that they have made dirty or untidy. ❑ *At the end, he nursed Lilly and cleaned up after her without minding.* — PHRASAL VERB; V P P n

**clean-cut** Someone, especially a boy or man, who is **clean-cut** has a neat, tidy appearance. ❑ *...his clean-cut good looks.* — ADJ

**clean|er** /kliːnəʳ/ **(cleaners)** 1 A **cleaner** is someone who is employed to clean the rooms and furniture inside a building. — N-COUNT 2 A **cleaner** is someone whose job is to clean a particular type of thing. ❑ *He was a window cleaner.* — N-COUNT: n N 3 A **cleaner** is a substance used for cleaning things. ❑ *...oven* — N-MASS: usu n N *cleaner. ...abrasive cleaners.* 4 A **cleaner** is a device used for cleaning things. ❑ *...an air cleaner.* [N-COUNT: usu n N] → See also **pipe cleaner**, **vacuum cleaner**. 5 A **cleaner** or a **cleaner's** is a shop where things such as clothes are dry-cleaned. [N-COUNT: oft *the* N]

**clean|ing lady** **(cleaning ladies)** A **cleaning lady** is a woman who is employed to clean the rooms and furniture inside a building. [N-COUNT = *cleaner*]

**clean|ing wom|an** **(cleaning women)** A **cleaning woman** is the same as a **cleaning lady**. [N-COUNT]

**clean|li|ness** /klenlɪnəs/ **Cleanliness** is the degree to which people keep themselves and their surroundings clean. ❑ *Many of Britain's beaches fail to meet minimum standards of cleanliness. ...the importance of personal cleanliness.* [N-UNCOUNT]

**cleanse** /klenz/ **(cleanses, cleansing, cleansed)** 1 To **cleanse** a place, person, or organization **of** something dirty, unpleasant, or evil means to make them free from it. ❑ *Straight after your last cigarette your body will begin to cleanse itself of tobacco toxins... Confession cleanses the soul.* [VERB] [V n *of* n] [V n] 2 If you **cleanse** your skin or a wound, you clean it. ❑ *Catherine demonstrated the proper way to cleanse the face. ...cleansing lotions.* [VERB] [V n] [V-ing]

**cleans|er** /klenzəʳ/ **(cleansers)** 1 A **cleanser** is a liquid or cream that you use for cleaning your skin. [N-MASS] 2 A **cleanser** is a liquid or powder that you use in cleaning kitchens and bathrooms. [mainly AM] [N-MASS]

**clean-shaven** If a man is **clean-shaven**, he does not have a beard or a moustache. [ADJ]

**clean-up** **(clean-ups)**

✔ in AM, use **cleanup**

A **clean-up** is the removing of dirt, pollution, crime, or corruption from somewhere. ❑ *...the need for a clean-up of Italian institutions... The Governor has now called in the National Guard to assist the cleanup operation.* [N-COUNT]

**clear** /klɪəʳ/ **(clearer, clearest, clears, clearing, cleared)** ◆◆◆ 1 Something that is **clear** is easy to understand, see, or hear. ❑ *The book is clear, readable and adequately illustrated... The space telescope has taken the clearest pictures ever of Pluto... He repeated his answer, this time in a clear, firm tone of voice.* [ADJ ≠ *unclear*] ♦ **clear|ly** *Whales journey up the coast of Africa, clearly visible from the beach... It was important for children to learn to express themselves clearly.* [ADV: usu ADV -ed/adj, also ADV after v] 2 Something that is **clear** is obvious and impossible to be mistaken about. ❑ *It was a clear case of homicide... The clear message of the scientific reports is that there should be a drastic cut in car use... A spokesman said the British government's position is perfectly clear... It's not clear whether the incident was an accident or deliberate.* [ADJ: oft *it* v-link ADJ that/wh ≠ *unclear*] ♦ **clear|ly** *Clearly, the police cannot break the law in order to enforce it.* [ADV: ADV with cl/group = *obviously*] 3 If you are **clear about** something, you understand it completely. ❑ *It is important to be clear about what Chomsky is doing here... People use scientific terms with no clear idea of their meaning.* [ADJ: usu v-link ADJ *about/on* n/wh] 4 If your mind or your way of thinking is **clear**, you are able to think sensibly and reasonably, and you are not affected by confusion or by a drug such as alcohol. ❑ *She needed a clear head to carry out her instructions.* [ADJ] ♦ **clear|ly** *The only time I can think clearly is when I'm alone.* [ADV: ADV after v] 5 To **clear** your mind or your head means to free it from confused thoughts or from the effects of a drug such as alcohol. ❑ *He walked up Fifth Avenue to clear his head... Our therapists will show you how to clear your mind of worries.* [VERB] [V n] [V n *of* n] 6 A **clear** substance is one which you can see through and which has no colour, like clean water. ❑ *...a clear glass panel... The water is clear and plenty of fish are visible.* [ADJ: usu ADJ n = *transparent*] 7 If a surface, place, or view is **clear**, it is free of unwanted objects or obstacles. ❑ *The runway is clear – go ahead and land... Caroline prefers her worktops to be clear of clutter... The windows will allow a clear view of the beach.* [ADJ: usu v-link ADJ] 8 When you **clear** an area or place or **clear** something **from** it, you remove things from it that you do not want to be there. ❑ *To clear the land and harvest the bananas they decided they needed a male workforce... Workers could not clear the tunnels of smoke... Firemen were still clearing rubble from apartments damaged at the scene of the attack.* [VERB] [V n] [V n *of* n] [V n *from/off* n] 9 If something or someone **clears** the way or the path **for** something to happen, they make it possible. ❑ *The Prime Minister resigned today, clearing the way for the formation of a new government.* [VERB] [V n *for* n] 10 If it is a **clear** day or if the sky is **clear**, there is no mist, rain, or cloud. ❑ *On a clear day you can see the French coast... The winter sky was clear.* [ADJ] 11 When fog or mist **clears**, it gradually disappears. ❑ *The early morning mist had cleared.* [VERB] [V] 12 **Clear** eyes look healthy, attractive, and shining. ❑ *...clear blue eyes... Her eyes were clear and steady.* [ADJ] 13 If your skin is **clear**, it is healthy and free from spots. [ADJ] 14 If you say that your conscience is **clear**, you mean you do not think you have done anything wrong. ❑ *Mr Garcia said his conscience was clear over the jail incidents.* [ADJ] 15 If something or someone is **clear of** something else, it is not touching it or is a safe distance away from it. ❑ *As soon as he was clear of the terminal building he looked round.* [ADJ: v-link ADJ *of* n, v n ADJ] 16 If an animal or person **clears** an object or **clears** a certain height, they jump over the object, or over something that height, without touching it. ❑ *Sotomayor, the Cuban holder of the world high jump record, cleared 2.36 metres.* [VERB] [V n] 17 When a bank **clears** a cheque or when a cheque **clears**, the bank agrees to pay the sum of money mentioned on it. ❑ *Polish banks can still take two or three weeks to clear a cheque... Allow time for the cheque to clear.* [VERB] [V n] [V] 18 If a course of action **is cleared**, people in authority give permission for it to happen. ❑ *Linda Gradstein has this report from Jerusalem, which was cleared by an Israeli censor... Within an hour, the helicopter was cleared for take-off.* [VERB: usu passive] [*be* V-ed] [*be* V-ed *for* n] 19 If someone **is cleared**, they are proved to be not guilty of a crime or mistake. ❑ *She was cleared of murder and jailed for just five years for manslaughter... In a final effort to clear her name, Eunice has written a book.* [VERB] [*be* V-ed *of* n/-ing] [V n] 20 → See also **clearing**, **crystal clear**. 21 You can say **'Is that clear?'** or **'Do I make myself clear?'** after you have told someone your wishes or instructions, to make sure that they have understood you, and to emphasize your authority. ❑ *We're only going for half an hour, and you're not going to buy anything. Is that clear?* [CONVENTION]

**PHRASES** 22 If someone is **in the clear**, they are not in danger, or are not blamed or suspected of anything. ❑ *The Audit Commission said that the ministry was in the clear.* [PHRASE: v-link PHR, PHR after v] 23 If you **make** something **clear**, you say something in a way that makes it impossible for there to be any doubt about your meaning, wishes, or intentions. ❑ *Mr O'Friel made it clear that further insults of this kind would not be tolerated... The far-right has now made its intentions clear.* [PHRASE: V inflects, oft PHR that] 24 If something or someone is a certain amount **clear of** a competitor, they are that amount ahead of them in a competition or race. [BRIT] ❑ *Keegan's team are now seven points clear of West Ham... He crossed the line three seconds clear of Tom Snape.* [PREP-PHRASE: amount PREP n] 25 If you **steer clear** or **stay clear of** someone or something, you avoid them. ❑ *The rabbis try to steer clear of political questions.* [PHRASE: V inflects, oft PHR *of* n] 26 to **clear the air** → see **air**. **the coast is clear** → see **coast**. to **clear the decks** → see **deck**. **loud and clear** → see **loud**. to **clear** your **throat** → see **throat**.

♦ **clear away** When you **clear** things **away** or **clear away**, you put away the things that you have been using, especially for eating or cooking. ❑ *The waitress had cleared away the plates and brought coffee... Tania cooked, served, and cleared away.* [PHRASAL VERB] [V P n (not pron)] [V P] [Also V n P]

♦ **clear off** If you tell someone to **clear off**, you are telling them rather rudely to go away. [INFORMAL] ❑ *The boys told me to clear off.* [PHRASAL VERB] [disapproval] [V P]

♦ **clear out** 1 If you tell someone to **clear out of** a place or to **clear out**, you are telling them rather rudely to leave the place. [INFORMAL] ❑ *She turned to the others in the room. 'The rest of you clear out of here.'... 'Clear out!' he bawled. 'Private property!'* 2 If you **clear out** a container, room, or house, you tidy it and throw away the things in it that you no longer want. ❑ *I took the precaution of clearing out my desk before I left.* ➔ See also **clear-out**.
PHRASAL VERB [disapproval] = get out; V P *of* n; V P; PHRASAL VERB; V P n (not pron); Also V n P

♦ **clear up** 1 When you **clear up** or **clear** a place **up**, you tidy things and put them away. ❑ *After breakfast they played outside in the garden while I cleared up... I cleared up my messy bedroom.* 2 To **clear up** a problem, misunderstanding, or mystery means to settle it or find a satisfactory explanation for it. ❑ *During dinner the confusion was cleared up: they had mistaken me for Kenny.* ➔ See also **clear-up**. 3 To **clear up** a medical problem, infection, or disease means to cure it or get rid of it. If a medical problem **clears up**, it goes away. ❑ *Antibiotics should be used to clear up the infection... Acne often clears up after the first three months of pregnancy.* 4 When the weather **clears up**, it stops raining or being cloudy. ❑ *It all depends on the weather clearing up.*
PHRASAL VERB; V P; V P n (not pron); Also V n P; PHRASAL VERB = sort out; V P n; Also V n P; PHRASAL VERB; V P n (not pron); V P; Also V n P; PHRASAL VERB; V P

**clear|ance** /klɪərəns/ **(clearances)** 1 **Clearance** is the removal of old buildings, trees, or other things that are not wanted from an area. ❑ *...a slum clearance operation in Nairobi... The UN pledged to help supervise the clearance of mines.* 2 If you get **clearance to** do or have something, you get official approval or permission to do or have it. ❑ *Thai Airways said the plane had been given clearance to land.* 3 The **clearance** of a bridge is the distance between the lowest point of the bridge and the road or the water under the bridge. ❑ *The lowest fixed bridge has 12.8m clearance.*
N-VAR; N-VAR = authorization; N-VAR

**clear|ance sale** **(clearance sales)** A **clearance sale** is a sale in which the goods in a shop are sold at reduced prices, because the shopkeeper wants to get rid of them quickly or because the shop is closing down.
N-COUNT

**clear-cut** Something that is **clear-cut** is easy to recognize and quite distinct. ❑ *This was a clear-cut case of the original land owner being in the right... The issue is not so clear cut.*
ADJ

**clear-headed** If you describe someone as **clear-headed**, you mean that they are sensible and think clearly, especially in difficult situations. ❑ *...his clear-headed grasp of the laws of economics.*
ADJ [approval]

**clear|ing** /klɪərɪŋ/ **(clearings)** A **clearing** is a small area in a forest where there are no trees or bushes. ❑ *A helicopter landed in a clearing in the dense jungle.*
N-COUNT

**clear|ing bank** **(clearing banks)** The **clearing banks** are the main banks in Britain. Clearing banks use the central clearing house in London to deal with other banks. [BUSINESS]
N-COUNT

**clear|ing house** **(clearing houses)** also **clearing-house.** 1 If an organization acts as a **clearing house**, it collects, sorts, and distributes specialized information. ❑ *The centre will act as a clearing house for research projects for former nuclear scientists.* 2 A **clearing house** is a central bank which deals with all the business between the banks that use its services. [BUSINESS]
N-COUNT; N-COUNT

**clear-out** **(clear-outs)** When you have a **clear-out**, you collect together all the things that you do not want and throw them away. [BRIT, INFORMAL]
N-COUNT: usu sing

**clear-sighted** If you describe someone as **clear-sighted**, you admire them because they are able to understand situations well and to make sensible judgments and decisions about them. ❑ *Try to keep a clear-sighted view of your objective.*
ADJ [approval]

**clear-up** The **clear-up** rate for a crime or in an area is the percentage of criminals caught by the police, compared to the total number of crimes reported. [BRIT] ❑ *The clear-up rate for murders remains high.*
ADJ: ADJ n

**cleat** /kliːt/ **(cleats)** A **cleat** is a kind of hook with two ends which is used to hold ropes, especially on sailing boats.
N-COUNT

**cleav|age** /kliːvɪdʒ/ **(cleavages)** A woman's **cleavage** is the space between her breasts, especially the top part which you see if she is wearing a dress with a low neck.
N-COUNT

**cleave** /kliːv/ **(cleaves, cleaving)**

> ✔ The past tense can be either **cleaved** or **clove**; the past participle can be **cleaved**, **cloven**, or **cleft** for meaning 1, and is **cleaved** for meaning 2.

1 To **cleave** something means to split or divide it into two separate parts, often violently. [LITERARY] ❑ *They just cleave the stone along the cracks.* 2 If someone **cleaves to** something or **to** someone else, they begin or continue to have strong feelings of loyalty towards them. [FORMAL] ❑ *She has cleaved to these principles all her life.*
VERB = split; V n; VERB; V *to* n

**cleav|er** /kliːvəʳ/ **(cleavers)** A **cleaver** is a knife with a large square blade, used for chopping meat or vegetables. ❑ *...a meat cleaver.*
N-COUNT

**clef** /klef/ **(clefs)** A **clef** is a symbol at the beginning of a line of music that indicates the pitch of the written notes.
N-COUNT

**cleft** /kleft/ **(clefts)** 1 A **cleft** in a rock or in the ground is a narrow opening in it. ❑ *...a narrow cleft in the rocks too small for humans to enter.* 2 A **cleft** in someone's chin is a line down the middle of it. 3 If someone has a **cleft** chin, they have a cleft in their chin.
N-COUNT = fissure; N-COUNT; ADJ: ADJ n

**cleft pal|ate** **(cleft palates)** If someone has a **cleft palate**, they were born with a narrow opening along the roof of their mouth which makes it difficult for them to speak properly.
N-VAR

**clema|tis** /klemətɪs/ **(clematises** or **clematis)** A **clematis** is a type of flowering shrub which can be grown to climb up walls or fences. There are many different varieties of clematis.
N-VAR

**clem|en|cy** /klemənsi/ If someone is granted **clemency**, they are punished less severely than they could be. [FORMAL] ❑ *Seventeen prisoners held on death row are to be executed after their pleas for clemency were turned down.*
N-UNCOUNT

**clem|ent** /klemənt/ **Clement** weather is pleasantly mild and dry. [FORMAL]
ADJ: usu ADJ n ≠ inclement

**clem|en|tine** /kleməntaɪn/ **(clementines)** A **clementine** is a fruit that looks like a small orange.
N-COUNT

**clench** /klentʃ/ **(clenches, clenching, clenched)** 1 When you **clench** your fist or your fist **clenches**, you curl your fingers up tightly, usually because you are very angry. ❑ *Alex clenched her fists and gritted her teeth... She pulled at his sleeve and he turned on her, fists clenching again before he saw who it was. ...angry protestors with clenched fists.* 2 When you **clench** your teeth or they **clench**, you squeeze your teeth together firmly, usually because you are angry or upset. ❑ *Patsy had to clench her jaw to suppress her anger... Slowly, he released his breath through clenched teeth.* 3 If you **clench** something in your hand or in your teeth, you hold it tightly with your hand or your teeth. ❑ *I clenched the arms of my chair.*
VERB; V n; V; V-ed; VERB = grit; V n; V-ed; Also V; VERB = grip; V n

**cler|gy** /klɜːʳdʒi/ The **clergy** are the official leaders of the religious activities of a particular group of believers. ❑ *These proposals met opposition from the clergy.*
N-PLURAL: oft *the* N

**clergy|man** /klɜːʳdʒimən/ **(clergymen)** A **clergyman** is a male member of the clergy.
N-COUNT

**cler|ic** /klerɪk/ **(clerics)** A **cleric** is a member of the clergy. ❑ *His grandfather was a Muslim cleric.*
N-COUNT

**cleri|cal** /klerɪkəl/ 1 **Clerical** jobs, skills, and workers are concerned with work that is done in an office. ❑ *...a strike by clerical staff in all government departments... The hospital blamed the mix-up*
ADJ: ADJ n = administrative

on a clerical error. 2 **Clerical** means relating to the clergy. ❑ *...Iran's clerical leadership.* ADJ: ADJ n

**clerk** /klɑːʳk, AM klɜːrk/ **(clerks, clerking, clerked)** 1 A **clerk** is a person who works in an office, bank, or law court and whose job is to look after the records or accounts. ❑ *She was offered a job as an accounts clerk with a travel firm.* N-COUNT 2 In a hotel, office, or hospital, a **clerk** is the person whose job is to answer the telephone and deal with people when they arrive. [mainly AM] ❑ *...a hotel clerk.* N-COUNT 3 A **clerk** is someone who works in a store. [AM] N-COUNT = sales clerk 4 To **clerk** means to work as a clerk. [mainly AM] ❑ *Gene clerked at the auction.* VERB V

**clev|er** /klevəʳ/ **(cleverer, cleverest)** ◆◇◇ 1 Someone who is **clever** is intelligent and able to understand things easily or plan things well. ❑ *He's a very clever man... My sister was always a lot cleverer than I was.* ADJ ♦ **clev|er|ly** *She would cleverly pick up on what I said.* ADV ♦ **clev|er|ness** *Her cleverness seems to get in the way of her emotions.* N-UNCOUNT 2 A **clever** idea, book, or invention is extremely effective and shows the skill of the people involved. ❑ *...a clever and gripping novel. ...this clever new gadget.* ADJ: usu ADJ n = ingenious ♦ **clev|er|ly** *...a cleverly designed swimsuit.* ADV: ADV -ed

**cli|ché** /kliːʃeɪ, AM kliːʃeɪ/ **(clichés)**

✓ in BRIT, also use **cliche**

A **cliché** is an idea or phrase which has been used so much that it is no longer interesting or effective or no longer has much meaning. ❑ *I've learned that the cliche about life not being fair is true.* N-COUNT [disapproval]

**cli|chéd** /kliːʃeɪd, AM kliːʃeɪd/

✓ in BRIT, also use **cliched**

If you describe something as **clichéd**, you mean that it has been said, done, or used many times before, and is boring or untrue. ❑ *The dialogue and acting in Indecent Proposal are tired, cliched and corny.* ADJ [disapproval]

**click** /klɪk/ **(clicks, clicking, clicked)** 1 If something **clicks** or if you **click** it, it makes a short, sharp sound. ❑ *The applause rose to a crescendo and cameras clicked... He clicked off the radio... Blake clicked his fingers at a passing waiter, who hurried across to them.* VERB V V n with off/on V n ♦ **Click** is also a noun. ❑ *The telephone rang three times before I heard a click and then her recorded voice.* N-COUNT 2 If you **click on** an area of a computer screen, you point the cursor at that area and press one of the buttons on the mouse in order to make something happen. [COMPUTING] ❑ *I clicked on a link and recent reviews of the production came up.* VERB: no passive V on n Also V, V n ♦ **Click** is also a noun. ❑ *You can check your email with a click of your mouse.* N-COUNT: usu sing 3 When you suddenly understand something, you can say that it **clicks**. [INFORMAL] ❑ *When I saw the television report, it all clicked... It suddenly clicked that this was fantastic fun.* VERB V it V that 4 to **click into place** → see **place**.

**click|able** /klɪkəbᵊl/ A **clickable** image on a computer screen is one that you can point the cursor at and click on, in order to make something happen. [COMPUTING] ❑ *...a Web site with clickable maps showing hotel locations.* ADJ

**cli|ent** /klaɪənt/ **(clients)** A **client** of a professional person or organization is a person or company that receives a service from them in return for payment. [BUSINESS] ❑ *...a solicitor and his client... The company required clients to pay substantial fees in advance.* ◆◇◇ N-COUNT

**cli|ent base (client bases)** A business's **client base** is the same as its **customer base**. [BUSINESS] ❑ *Enviros Consulting has a client base of more than 2,000 organisations worldwide.* N-COUNT

**cli|en|tele** /kliːɒntel, klaɪən-/ The **clientele** of a place or organization are its customers or clients. ❑ *This pub had a mixed clientele.* N-SING-COLL

**cli|ent state (client states)** A **client state** is a country which is controlled or influenced by another larger and more powerful state, or which depends on this state for support and protection. ❑ *...France and its African client states.* N-COUNT

**cliff** /klɪf/ **(cliffs)** A **cliff** is a high area of land with a very steep side, especially one next to the sea. ❑ *The car rolled over the edge of a cliff.* N-COUNT

**cliff|hanger** /klɪfhæŋəʳ/ **(cliffhangers)** also **cliff-hanger.** A **cliffhanger** is a situation or part of a play or film that is very exciting or frightening because you are left for a long time not knowing what will happen next. ❑ *The election is likely to be a cliff-hanger. ...cliffhanger endings to keep you in suspense.* N-COUNT

**cliff|top** /klɪftɒp/ **(clifftops)** A **clifftop** is the area of land around the top of a cliff. ❑ *...a house on the clifftop. ...25 acres of spectacular clifftop scenery.* N-COUNT

**cli|mac|tic** /klaɪmæktɪk/ A **climactic** moment in a story or a series of events is one in which a very exciting or important event occurs. [FORMAL] ❑ *...the film's climactic scene.* ADJ: ADJ n

**cli|mate** /klaɪmət/ **(climates)** 1 The **climate** of a place is the general weather conditions that are typical of it. ❑ *...the hot and humid climate of Cyprus.* ◆◇◇ N-VAR 2 You can use **climate** to refer to the general atmosphere or situation somewhere. ❑ *The economic climate remains uncertain. ...the existing climate of violence and intimidation.* N-COUNT: usu with supp

**cli|mat|ic** /klaɪmætɪk/ **Climatic** conditions, changes, and effects relate to the general weather conditions of a place. ❑ *...the threat of rising sea levels and climatic change from overheating of the atmosphere.* ADJ: ADJ n

**cli|ma|tolo|gist** /klaɪmətɒlədʒɪst/ **(climatologists)** A **climatologist** is someone who studies climates. N-COUNT

**cli|max** /klaɪmæks/ **(climaxes, climaxing, climaxed)** 1 The **climax of** something is the most exciting or important moment in it, usually near the end. ❑ *For Pritchard, reaching an Olympics was the climax of her career... It was the climax to 24 hours of growing anxiety... The last golf tournament of the European season is building up to a dramatic climax.* N-COUNT: oft N of/to n 2 The event that **climaxes** a sequence of events is an exciting or important event that comes at the end. You can also say that a sequence of events **climaxes with** a particular event. [JOURNALISM] ❑ *The demonstration climaxed two weeks of strikes... They've just finished a sell-out UK tour that climaxed with a three-night stint at Brixton Academy.* VERB V n V with n 3 A **climax** is an **orgasm**. N-VAR 4 When someone **climaxes**, they have an orgasm. ❑ *Often, a man can enjoy making love but may not be sufficiently aroused to climax.* VERB V

**climb** /klaɪm/ **(climbs, climbing, climbed)** ◆◇◇ 1 If you **climb** something such as a tree, mountain, or ladder, or **climb up** it, you move towards the top of it. If you **climb down** it, you move towards the bottom of it. ❑ *He picked up his suitcase and climbed the stairs... I told her about him climbing up the drainpipe... Kelly climbed down the ladder into the water... Children love to climb.* VERB V n V up n V down n V ♦ **Climb** is also a noun. ❑ *...an hour's leisurely climb through olive groves and vineyards.* N-COUNT: oft N prep 2 If you **climb** somewhere, you move there carefully, for example because you are moving into a small space or trying to avoid falling. ❑ *The girls hurried outside, climbed into the car, and drove off... He must have climbed out of his cot.* VERB V prep/adv V prep/adv 3 When something such as an aeroplane **climbs**, it moves upwards to a higher position. When the sun **climbs**, it moves higher in the sky. ❑ *The plane took off for LA, lost an engine as it climbed, and crashed just off the runway.* VERB = rise V Also V prep 4 When something **climbs**, it increases in value or amount. ❑ *The nation's unemployment rate has been climbing steadily since last June... Prices have climbed by 21% since the beginning of the year... The FA Cup Final's audience climbed to 12.3 million... Jaguar shares climbed 43 pence to 510 pence.* VERB V V by amount V to/from amount V amount 5 → See also **climbing**. **a mountain to climb** → see **mountain**.

♦ **climb down** If you **climb down** in an argument or dispute, you admit that you are wrong, PHRASAL VERB = back down or change your intentions or demands. ❑ *If Lafontaine is forced to climb down, he may wish to reconsider his position... He has climbed down on pledges to reduce capital gains tax.* V P; V P on/over n

**climb-down** **(climb-downs)** also **climbdown.** A **climb-down** in an argument or dispute is the act of admitting that you are wrong or of changing your intentions or demands. ❑ *In an embarrassing climb-down, the Home Secretary lifted the deportation threat.* N-COUNT

**climb|er** /klaɪməʳ/ **(climbers)** 1 A **climber** is someone who climbs rocks or mountains as a sport or a hobby. N-COUNT 2 A **climber** is a plant that grows upwards by attaching itself to other plants or objects. N-COUNT

**climb|ing** /klaɪmɪŋ/ **Climbing** is the activity of climbing rocks or mountains. → See also **climb**, **rock climbing**, **social climbing**. N-UNCOUNT

**climb|ing frame** **(climbing frames)** A **climbing frame** is a structure that has been made for children to climb and play on. It consists of metal or wooden bars joined together. [BRIT] N-COUNT

☑ in AM, use **jungle gym**

**clime** /klaɪm/ **(climes)** You use **clime** in expressions such as **warmer climes** and **foreign climes** to refer to a place that has a particular kind of climate. [LITERARY] ❑ *He left Britain for the sunnier climes of Southern France.* N-COUNT: usu pl, usu adj N

**clinch** /klɪntʃ/ **(clinches, clinching, clinched)** 1 If you **clinch** something you are trying to achieve, such as a business deal or victory in a contest, you succeed in obtaining it. ❑ *Hibernian clinched the First Division title when they beat Hamilton 2-0... This has fuelled speculation that he is about to clinch a deal with an American engine manufacturer.* VERB = secure; V n; V n with n 2 The thing that **clinches** an uncertain matter settles it or provides a definite answer. ❑ *Evidently this information clinched the matter... That was the clue which clinched it for us.* VERB; V n; V it

**clinch|er** /klɪntʃəʳ/ **(clinchers)** A **clincher** is a fact or argument that finally proves something, settles a dispute, or helps someone achieve a victory. [INFORMAL] ❑ *DNA fingerprinting has proved the clincher in this investigation... The clincher was City's second goal, scored minutes from the end.* N-COUNT

**cling** /klɪŋ/ **(clings, clinging, clung)** 1 If you **cling to** someone or something, you hold onto them tightly. ❑ *Another man was rescued as he clung to the riverbank... They hugged each other, clinging together under the lights.* VERB; V to/onto n; V together 2 If someone **clings to** a position or a possession they have, they do everything they can to keep it even though this may be very difficult. ❑ *He appears determined to cling to power... Another minister clung on with a majority of only 18... Japan's productivity has overtaken America in some industries, but elsewhere the United States has clung on to its lead.* VERB; V to/onto n; V on; V on to n

**cling|film** /klɪŋfɪlm/ also **cling film.** **Clingfilm** is a thin, clear, stretchy plastic that you use to cover food in order to keep it fresh. [BRIT] N-UNCOUNT

☑ in AM, use **plastic wrap**, **Saran wrap**

**clingy** /klɪŋi/ 1 If you describe someone as **clingy**, you mean that they become very attached to people and depend on them too much. ❑ *A very clingy child can drive a parent to distraction.* ADJ disapproval = clinging 2 **Clingy** clothes fit tightly round your body. ❑ *...long clingy skirts.* ADJ = clinging

**clin|ic** /klɪnɪk/ **(clinics)** A **clinic** is a building where people go to receive medical advice or treatment. ❑ *...a family planning clinic.* ◆◇◇ N-COUNT

**clini|cal** /klɪnɪkəl/ 1 **Clinical** means involving or relating to the direct medical treatment or testing of patients. [MEDICAL] ❑ *The first clinical trials were expected to begin next year. ...a clinical psychologist.* ADJ: ADJ n ♦ **clini|cal|ly** /klɪnɪkli/ *It has been clinically proved that it is better to stretch the tight muscles first.* ADV: usu ADV adj/-ed 2 You use **clinical** to describe thought or behaviour which is very logical and does not involve any emotion. ❑ *All this questioning is so analytical and clinical – it kills romance.* ADJ disapproval = impersonal

**clini|cal tri|al** **(clinical trials)** When a new type of drug or medical treatment undergoes **clinical trials**, it is tested directly on patients to see if it is effective. ❑ *Two rival laser surgery systems are undergoing clinical trials in the US.* N-COUNT

**cli|ni|cian** /klɪnɪʃən/ **(clinicians)** A **clinician** is a doctor who specializes in clinical work. N-COUNT

**clink** /klɪŋk/ **(clinks, clinking, clinked)** If objects made of glass, pottery, or metal **clink** or if you **clink** them, they touch each other and make a short, light sound. ❑ *She clinked her glass against his... They clinked glasses... The empty whisky bottle clinked against the seat... Their glasses clinked, their eyes met.* V-RECIP; V n against/with n; V pl-n; V against n; pl-n V ♦ **Clink** is also a noun. ❑ *...the clink of a spoon in a cup.* N-COUNT; SOUND

**clip** /klɪp/ **(clips, clipping, clipped)** 1 A **clip** is a small device, usually made of metal or plastic, that is specially shaped for holding things together. ❑ *She took the clip out of her hair.* N-COUNT 2 When you **clip** things together or when things **clip** together, you fasten them together using a clip or clips. ❑ *He clipped his safety belt to a fitting on the deck... He clipped his cufflinks neatly in place. ...an electronic pen which clips to the casing... His flashlight was still clipped to his belt.* VERB; V n to/on n; V n prep/adv; V to n; V-ed 3 A **clip** from a film or a radio or television programme is a short piece of it that is broadcast separately. ❑ *...a clip from the movie 'Shane'.* N-COUNT: oft n N, N from/of n 4 If you **clip** something, you cut small pieces from it, especially in order to shape it. ❑ *I saw an old man out clipping his hedge.* VERB; V n 5 If you **clip** something out of a newspaper or magazine, you cut it out. ❑ *Kids in his neighborhood clipped his picture from the newspaper and carried it around.* VERB; V n from/out of n 6 If something **clips** something else, it hits it accidentally at an angle before moving off in a different direction. ❑ *The lorry clipped the rear of a tanker and then crashed into a second truck.* VERB; V n 7 → See also **clipping**, **clipped**, **bulldog clip**, **paper clip**.

**clip|board** /klɪpbɔːʳd/ **(clipboards)** 1 A **clipboard** is a board with a clip at the top. It is used to hold together pieces of paper that you need to carry around, and provides a firm base for writing. N-COUNT 2 In computing, a **clipboard** is a file where you can temporarily store text or images from one document until you are ready to use them again. [COMPUTING] N-COUNT

**clip-on** A **clip-on** object is designed to be fastened to something by means of a clip. ❑ *...a clip-on tie. ...a clip-on light.* ADJ: ADJ n

**clipped** /klɪpt/ 1 **Clipped** means neatly cut. ❑ *...a quiet street of clipped hedges and flowering gardens.* ADJ: usu ADJ n 2 If you say that someone has a **clipped** way of speaking, you mean they speak with quick, short sounds, and usually that they sound upper-class. ❑ *The Chief Constable's clipped tones crackled over the telephone line.* ADJ

**clip|per** /klɪpəʳ/ **(clippers)** **Clippers** are a tool used for cutting small amounts from something, especially from someone's hair or nails. N-PLURAL: also a pair of N

**clip|ping** /klɪpɪŋ/ **(clippings)** 1 A **clipping** is an article, picture, or advertisement that has been cut from a newspaper or magazine. ❑ *...bulletin boards crowded with newspaper clippings.* N-COUNT: oft n N = cutting 2 **Clippings** are small pieces of something that have been cut from something larger. ❑ *Having mown the lawn, there are all those grass clippings to get rid of. ...nail clippings.* N-COUNT: usu pl, oft n N

**clique** /kliːk/ **(cliques)** If you describe a group of people as a **clique**, you mean that they spend a lot of time together and seem unfriendly towards people who are not in the group. N-COUNT disapproval

**cli|quey** /kliːki/

☑ in AM, usually use **cliquish**

If you describe a group of people or their behaviour as **cliquey**, you mean they spend their time only with other members of the group and seem unfriendly towards people who are not in the group. ❑ *...cliquey gossip.* ADJ disapproval

**clito|ral** /klɪtərəl/ **Clitoral** means concerned with or relating to the clitoris. ❑ *...clitoral stimulation.* ADJ: ADJ n

**clito|ris** /klɪtərɪs/ **(clitorises)** The **clitoris** is a part at the front of a woman's sexual organs where she can feel sexual pleasure. N-COUNT

**Cllr. Cllr.** is a written abbreviation for **Councillor.** [BRIT] ❑ *...Cllr. Ned Dewitt.* N-TITLE

**cloak** /kloʊk/ **(cloaks, cloaking, cloaked)** 1 A **cloak** is a long, loose, sleeveless piece of clothing which people used to wear over their other clothes when they went out. N-COUNT 2 A **cloak of** something such as mist or snow completely covers and hides something. ❑ *Today most of England will be under a cloak of thick mist.* N-SING: N of n = blanket 3 If you refer to something as a **cloak**, you mean that it is intended to hide the truth about something. ❑ *Preparations for the wedding were made under a cloak of secrecy.* N-SING: N of/for n 4 To **cloak** something means to cover it or hide it. [WRITTEN] ❑ *...the decision to cloak major tourist attractions in unsightly hoardings... The beautiful sweeping coastline was cloaked in mist.* VERB V n in n V-ed

**cloak-and-dagger** also **cloak and dagger.** A **cloak-and-dagger** activity is one which involves mystery and secrecy. ❑ *She was released from prison in a cloak and dagger operation yesterday.* ADJ: usu ADJ n

**cloak|room** /kloʊkruːm/ **(cloakrooms)** 1 In a public building, the **cloakroom** is the place where people can leave their coats, umbrellas, and so on. ❑ *...a cloakroom attendant.* N-COUNT 2 A **cloakroom** is a room containing toilets in a public building or a room containing a toilet on the ground floor of someone's house. [BRIT] N-COUNT

**clob|ber** /klɒbəʳ/ **(clobbers, clobbering, clobbered)** 1 You can refer to someone's possessions, especially their clothes, as their **clobber.** [BRIT, INFORMAL] N-UNCOUNT 2 If you **clobber** someone, you hit them. [INFORMAL] ❑ *Hillary clobbered him with a vase.* VERB V n

**cloche** /klɒʃ/ **(cloches)** A **cloche** is a long, low cover made of glass or clear plastic that is put over young plants to protect them from the cold. N-COUNT

**clock** /klɒk/ **(clocks, clocking, clocked)** ◆◇◇ 1 A **clock** is an instrument, for example in a room or on the outside of a building, that shows what time of day it is. ❑ *He was conscious of a clock ticking... He also repairs clocks and watches. ...a digital clock.* N-COUNT 2 A time **clock** in a factory or office is a device that is used to record the hours that people work. Each worker puts a special card into the device when they arrive and leave, and the times are recorded on the card. ❑ *Government workers were made to punch time clocks morning, noon and night.* N-COUNT: oft n N 3 In a car, **the clock** is the instrument that shows the speed of the car or the distance it has travelled. [mainly BRIT] ❑ *The car had 160,000 miles on the clock.* N-COUNT: usu sing, the N 4 To **clock** a particular time or speed in a race means to reach that time or speed. ❑ *Elliott clocked the fastest time this year for the 800 metres.* VERB V n 5 If something or someone **is clocked at** a particular time or speed, their time or speed is measured at that level. ❑ *He has been clocked at 11 seconds for 100 metres.* VERB: usu passive be V-ed at amount 6 → See also **alarm clock, biological clock, body clock, cuckoo clock, grandfather clock, o'clock.**

**PHRASES** 7 If you are doing something **against the clock**, you are doing it in a great hurry, because there is very little time. ❑ *The emergency services were working against the clock as the tide began to rise... It's now become a race against the clock.* PHRASE: PHR after v, n PHR 8 If something is done **round the clock** or **around the clock**, it is done all day and all night without stopping. ❑ *Rescue services have been working round the clock to free stranded motorists.* PHRASE: PHR with v, PHR n 9 If you want to **turn the clock back** or **put the clock back**, you want to return to a situation that used to exist, usually because the present situation is unpleasant. ❑ *In some ways we wish we could turn the clock back... We cannot put back the clock.* PHRASE: V inflects

♦ **clock in** When you **clock in** at work, you arrive there or put a special card into a device to show what time you arrived. ❑ *I have to clock in by eight.* PHRASAL VERB ≠clock off V P

♦ **clock off** When you **clock off** at work, you leave work or put a special card into a device to show what time you left. ❑ *The Night Duty Officer was ready to clock off... They clocked off duty and left at ten to three.* PHRASAL VERB ≠clock in V P V P n

♦ **clock on** When workers **clock on** at a factory or office, they put a special card into a device to show what time they arrived. ❑ *They arrived to clock on and found the factory gates locked.* PHRASAL VERB = clock in V P

♦ **clock out Clock out** means the same as **clock off.** ❑ *She had clocked out of her bank at 5.02pm using her plastic card.* PHRASAL VERB V P of n Also V P

♦ **clock up** If you **clock up** a large number or total of things, you reach that number or total. ❑ *In two years, he clocked up over 100 victories.* PHRASAL VERB = notch up V P n (not pron)

**clock tow|er (clock towers)** A **clock tower** is a tall, narrow building with a clock at the top. N-COUNT

**clock|wise** /klɒkwaɪz/ When something is moving **clockwise**, it is moving in a circle in the same direction as the hands on a clock. ❑ *He told the children to start moving clockwise around the room.* ♦ **Clockwise** is also an adjective. ❑ *Gently swing your right arm in a clockwise direction.* ADV: ADV after v ≠anti-clockwise, counterclockwise ADJ: ADJ n

**clock|work** /klɒkwɜːʳk/ 1 A **clockwork** toy or device has machinery inside it which makes it move or operate when it is wound up with a key. ❑ *...a clockwork train-set.* ADJ: ADJ n 2 If you say that something happens **like clockwork**, you mean that it happens without any problems or delays, or happens regularly. ❑ *The Queen's holiday is arranged to go like clockwork, everything preplanned to the minute.* PHRASE: PHR after v

**clod** /klɒd/ **(clods)** A **clod of** earth is a large lump of earth. N-COUNT: oft N of n

**clog** /klɒg/ **(clogs, clogging, clogged)** 1 When something **clogs** a hole or place, it blocks it so that nothing can pass through. ❑ *Dirt clogs the pores, causing spots... The traffic clogged the Thames bridges.* VERB = block V n V n 2 **Clogs** are heavy leather or wooden shoes with thick wooden soles. N-COUNT: usu pl

♦ **clog up** When something **clogs up** a place, or when it **clogs up**, it becomes blocked so that little or nothing can pass through. ❑ *22,000 tourists were clogging up the pavements... The result is that the lungs clog up with a thick mucus.* PHRASAL VERB V P n (not pron) V P

**clois|ter** /klɔɪstəʳ/ **(cloisters)** A **cloister** is a covered area round a square in a monastery or a cathedral. N-COUNT

**clois|tered** /klɔɪstəʳd/ If you have a **cloistered** way of life, you live quietly and are not involved in the normal busy life of the world around you. ❑ *...the cloistered world of royalty.* ADJ: usu ADJ n = sheltered

**clone** /kloʊn/ **(clones, cloning, cloned)** 1 If someone or something is a **clone** of another person or thing, they are so similar to this person or thing that they seem to be exactly the same as them. ❑ *Designers are mistaken if they believe we all want to be supermodel clones.* N-COUNT: usu with supp 2 A **clone** is an animal or plant that has been produced artificially, for example in a laboratory, from the cells of another animal or plant. A clone is exactly the same as the original animal or plant. N-COUNT 3 To **clone** an animal or plant means to produce it as a clone. ❑ *The idea of cloning extinct life forms still belongs to science fiction.* VERB V n

**close**

① SHUTTING OR COMPLETING
② NEARNESS; ADJECTIVE USES
③ NEARNESS; VERB USES
④ USED AS A ROAD NAME

① **close** /kloʊz/ **(closes, closing, closed)** ◆◆◆
⇒ Please look at category 12 to see if the expression you are looking for is shown under another headword. 1 When you **close** something such as a door or lid or when it **closes**, it moves so that a hole, gap, or opening is covered. ❑ *If you are cold, close the window... Zacharias heard the door* VERB = shut ≠open V n V

*close... Keep the curtains closed.* [2] When you **close** something such as an open book or umbrella, you move the different parts of it together. ❑ *Slowly he closed the book.* (V-ed; VERB; V n)

[3] If you **close** something such as a computer file or window, you give the computer an instruction to remove it from the screen. [COMPUTING] ❑ *To close your document, press CTRL+W on your keyboard.* (VERB; V n)

[4] When you **close** your eyes or your eyes **close**, your eyelids move downwards, so that you can no longer see. ❑ *Bess closed her eyes and fell asleep... When we sneeze, our eyes close.* (VERB; V n; V)

[5] When a place **closes** or **is closed**, work or activity stops there for a short period. ❑ *Shops close only on Christmas Day and New Year's Day... It was Saturday; they could close the office early... Government troops closed the airport... The restaurant was closed for the night.* (VERB = shut ≠open; V; V n; V n; V-ed)

[6] If a place such as a factory, shop, or school **closes**, or if it **is closed**, all work or activity stops there permanently. ❑ *Many enterprises will be forced to close... If they do close the local college I'll have to go to Worcester.* ♦ **Close down** means the same as **close**. ❑ *Minford closed down the business and went into politics... Many of the smaller stores have closed down.* ♦ **clos|ing** *...since the closing of the steelworks in nearby Duquesne in 1984.* (VERB; V; V n; PHRASAL VERB; V P n; Also V n P; V P; N-SING = closure)

[7] To **close** a road or border means to block it in order to prevent people from using it. ❑ *They were cut off from the West in 1948 when their government closed that border crossing.* (VERB; V n)

[8] To **close** a conversation, event, or matter means to bring it to an end or to complete it. ❑ *Judge Isabel Oliva said last night: 'I have closed the case. There was no foul play.'... The Prime Minister is said to now consider the matter closed. ...the closing ceremony of the National Political Conference.* (VERB; V n; V-ed; V-ing)

[9] If you **close** a bank account, you take all your money out of it and inform the bank that you will no longer be using the account. ❑ *He had closed his account with the bank five years earlier.* (VERB ≠open; V n)

[10] On the stock market or the currency markets, if a share price or a currency **closes** at a particular value, that is its value at the end of the day's business. [BUSINESS] ❑ *Dawson shares closed at 219p, up 5p... The US dollar closed higher in Tokyo today.* (VERB ≠open; V prep/adv; V adj-compar)

[11] **The close of** a period of time or an activity is the end of it. To bring or draw something **to a close** means to end it. ❑ *By the close of business last night, most of the big firms were hailing yesterday's actions as a success... Brian's retirement brings to a close a glorious chapter in British football history.* (N-SING: oft *the* N *of* n, *to a* N = end)

[12] → See also **closed**, **closing**. to **close the door on** something → see **door**. to **close** your **eyes to** something → see **eye**. to **close ranks** → see **rank**.

♦ **close down** → see **close 6**.

♦ **close off** To **close** something **off** means to separate it from other things or people so that they cannot go there. ❑ *Police closed off about 12 blocks of a major San Francisco thoroughfare for today's march.* (PHRASAL VERB = seal off; V P n (not pron))

♦ **close up** [1] If someone **closes up** a building, they shut it completely and securely, often because they are going away. ❑ *Just close up the shop... The summer house had been closed up all year.* (PHRASAL VERB = shut up, lock up; V P n (not pron); V-ed)

[2] If an opening, gap, or something hollow **closes up**, or if you **close** it **up**, it becomes closed or covered. ❑ *Don't use cold water as it shocks the blood vessels into closing up.* (PHRASAL VERB; V P; Also V n P)

② **close** /klous/ **(closer, closest)** ♦♦♦

⇛ Please look at category 18 to see if the expression you are looking for is shown under another headword. [1] If one thing or person is **close to** another, there is only a very small distance between them. ❑ *Her lips were close to his head and her breath tickled his ear... The man moved closer, lowering his voice... The tables were pushed close together so diners could talk across the aisles.* ♦ **close|ly** *Wherever they went they were closely followed by security men.* (ADJ: v-link ADJ, ADJ after v, oft ADJ prep/adv = near; ADV: ADV after v, ADV -ed)

[2] You say that people are **close to** each other when they like each other very much and know each other very well. ❑ *She and Linda became very close... As a little girl, Karan was closest to her sister Gail... I shared a house with a close friend from school.* ♦ **close|ness** *I asked whether her closeness to her mother ever posed any problems.* (ADJ: oft ADJ *to* n; N-UNCOUNT)

[3] Your **close** relatives are the members of your family who are most directly related to you, for example your parents and your brothers or sisters. ❑ *...large changes such as the birth of a child or death of a close relative.* (ADJ: ADJ n ≠distant)

[4] A **close** ally or partner of someone knows them well and is very involved in their work. ❑ *He was once regarded as one of Mr Brown's closest political advisers... A senior source close to Mr Blair told us: 'Our position has not changed.'* (ADJ: usu ADJ n, also v-link ADJ *to* n)

[5] **Close** contact or co-operation involves seeing or communicating with someone often. ❑ *Both nations are seeking closer links with the West... He lived alone, keeping close contact with his three grown-up sons.* ♦ **close|ly** *We work closely with the careers officers in schools.* (ADJ: ADJ n; ADV: ADV after v)

[6] If there is a **close** connection or resemblance between two things, they are strongly connected or are very similar. ❑ *There is a close connection between pain and tension... Clare's close resemblance to his elder sister invoked a deep dislike in him.* ♦ **close|ly** *...a pattern closely resembling a cross. ...fruits closely related to the orange.* (ADJ: usu ADJ n = strong; ADV: ADV before v, ADV -ed)

[7] **Close** inspection or observation of something is careful and thorough. ❑ *He discovered, on closer inspection, that the rocks contained gold... Let's have a closer look.* ♦ **close|ly** *If you look closely at many of the problems in society, you'll see evidence of racial discrimination.* (ADJ = thorough; ADV: ADV with v)

[8] A **close** competition or election is won or seems likely to be won by only a small amount. ❑ *It is still a close contest between two leading opposition parties... It's going to be very close.* ♦ **close|ly** *This will be a closely fought race.* (ADJ; ADV: usu ADV -ed)

[9] If you are **close to** something or if it is **close**, it is likely to happen or come soon. If you are **close to** doing something, you are likely to do it soon. ❑ *She sounded close to tears... A senior White House official said the agreement is close... He's close to signing a contract.* (ADJ: v-link ADJ, usu ADJ *to* n/-ing = near)

[10] If something is **close** or comes **close to** something else, it almost is, does, or experiences that thing. ❑ *An airliner came close to disaster while approaching Heathrow Airport.* (ADJ: v-link ADJ, usu ADJ *to* n = near)

[11] If the atmosphere somewhere is **close**, it is unpleasantly warm with not enough air. (ADJ)

**PHRASES** [12] Something that is **close by** or **close at hand** is near to you. ❑ *Did a new hairdressing shop open close by?... His wife remains behind in Germany, but Jason, his 18-year-old son, is closer at hand.* (PHRASE: usu v-link PHR, PHR after v = nearby)

[13] If you describe an event as a **close shave**, a **close thing**, or a **close call**, you mean that an accident or a disaster very nearly happened. ❑ *You had a close shave, but you knew when you accepted this job that there would be risks.* (PHRASE)

[14] If you **keep a close eye on** someone or something or **keep a close watch on** them, you observe them carefully to make sure they are progressing as you want them to. ❑ *The President's foreign policy team are keeping a close eye on events.* (PHRASE: V inflects, usu PHR *on* n)

[15] **Close to** a particular amount or distance means slightly less than that amount or distance. In British English, you can also say **close on** a particular amount or distance. ❑ *Sisulu spent close to 30 years in prison... Catering may now account for close on a quarter of pub turnover.* (PREP-PHRASE: PREP amount = almost, nearly)

[16] If you look at something **close up** or **close to**, you look at it when you are very near to it. ❑ *They always look smaller close up.* → See also **close-up**. (PHRASE: usu PHR after v, v-link PHR)

[17] If something such as a competition or an election is **too close to call**, it is not possible to predict who will win because it seems likely to be won by only a very small margin. [JOURNALISM] ❑ *In the Senate, the count is too close to call at this point.* (PHRASE: PHR with cl)

[18] **at close quarters** → see **quarter**. **at close range** → see **range**.

③ **close** /klouz/ **(closes, closing, closed)** If you **are closing on** someone or something that you are following, you are getting nearer and nearer to them. ❑ *I was within 15 seconds of the guy in second place and closing on him.* (♦◇◇; VERB; V *on* n)

♦ **close in** [1] If a group of people **close in on** a person or place, they come nearer and near- (PHRASAL VERB = move in) er to them and gradually surround them. ❑ *Hitler himself committed suicide as Soviet forces were closing in on Berlin... As Parretti walked across the tarmac, fraud officers closed in.* V P *on* n / V P 2 When winter or darkness **closes in**, it arrives. ❑ *The dark nights and cold weather are closing in.* PHRASAL VERB = descend V P

④**Close** /kloʊs/ **(Closes) Close** is used in the names of some streets in Britain. ❑ *...116 Dendridge Close.* N-IN-NAMES: n N

**close-cropped** /kloʊs krɒpt/ **Close-cropped** hair or grass is cut very short. ADJ: usu ADJ n

**closed** /kloʊzd/ 1 A **closed** group of people does not welcome new people or ideas from outside. ❑ *It was to be a closed circle of no more than twelve women... It is a closed society in the sense that they've not been exposed to many things.* ADJ: usu ADJ n ≠ open 2 → See also **close**. **a closed book** → see **book**. **behind closed doors** → see **door**.

**closed-circuit** also **closed circuit**. A **closed-circuit** television or video system is one that operates within a limited area such as a building. ❑ *There's a closed-circuit television camera in the reception area.* ADJ: ADJ n

**closed shop** **(closed shops)** If a factory, shop, or other business is a **closed shop**, the employees must be members of a particular trade union. [BUSINESS] ❑ *...the trade union which they are required to join under the closed shop agreement.* N-COUNT

**close-fitting** /kloʊs fɪtɪŋ/ **Close-fitting** clothes fit tightly and show the shape of your body. ADJ: usu ADJ n

**close-knit** /kloʊs nɪt/ A **close-knit** group of people are closely linked, do things together, and take an interest in each other. ❑ *Events over the last year have created a close-knit community.* ADJ: usu ADJ n

**close-run** /kloʊs rʌn/ If you describe something such as a race or contest as a **close-run** thing, you mean that it was only won by a very small amount. ❑ *In such a close-run race as this election, the campaign becomes all important.* ADJ: ADJ n

**close sea|son** /kloʊs siːzən/

☑ in AM, use **closed season**

In football and some other sports, the **close season** is the period of the year when the sport is not played professionally. [BRIT] ❑ *Football clubs have been busy in the close season transfer market.* N-SING

**clos|et** /klɒzɪt/ **(closets)** 1 A **closet** is a piece of furniture with doors at the front and shelves inside, which is used for storing things. [AM] N-COUNT

☑ in BRIT, use **cupboard**

2 A **closet** is a very small room for storing things, especially one without windows. [AM; also BRIT, OLD-FASHIONED] N-COUNT 3 **Closet** is used to describe a person who has beliefs, habits, or feelings which they keep secret, often because they are embarrassed about them. **Closet** is also used of their beliefs, habits, or feelings. ❑ *He is a closet Fascist.* ADJ: ADJ n 4 → See also **closeted**. **a skeleton in the closet** → see **skeleton**.

**clos|et|ed** /klɒzɪtɪd/ If you are **closeted with** someone, you are talking privately to them. [FORMAL or LITERARY] ❑ *Charles and I were closeted in his study for the briefing session.* ADJ: v-link ADJ, usu ADJ *with*/*in* n

**close-up** /kloʊs ʌp/ **(close-ups)** A **close-up** is a photograph or a picture in a film that shows a lot of detail because it is taken very near to the subject. ❑ *...a close-up of Harvey's face.* N-COUNT ● If you see something **in close-up**, you see it in great detail in a photograph or piece of film which has been taken very near to the subject. ❑ *Hughes stared up at him in close-up from the photograph.* PHRASE

**clos|ing** /kloʊzɪŋ/ The **closing** part of an activity or period of time is the final part of it. ❑ *He entered RAF service in the closing stages of the war.* → See also **close**. ADJ: ADJ n

**clos|ing price** **(closing prices)** On the stock exchange, the **closing price** of a share is its price at the end of a day's business. [BUSINESS] ❑ *The price is slightly above yesterday's closing price.* N-COUNT

**clos|ing time** **(closing times) Closing time** is the time when something such as a shop, library, or pub closes and people have to leave. ❑ *We were in the pub until closing time.* N-VAR

**clo|sure** /kloʊʒəʳ/ **(closures)** 1 The **closure** of a place such as a business or factory is the permanent ending of the work or activity there. ❑ *...the closure of the Ravenscraig steelworks... Almost three in four clinics say they face closure by the end of the year.* N-VAR 2 The **closure** of a road or border is the blocking of it in order to prevent people from using it. N-COUNT: usu with supp 3 If someone achieves **closure**, they succeed in accepting something bad that has happened to them. [mainly AM] ❑ *I asked McKeown if the reunion was meant to achieve closure.* N-UNCOUNT

**clot** /klɒt/ **(clots, clotting, clotted)** 1 A **clot** is a sticky lump that forms when blood dries up or becomes thick. ❑ *He needed emergency surgery to remove a blood clot from his brain.* N-COUNT 2 When blood **clots**, it becomes thick and forms a lump. ❑ *The patient's blood refused to clot... Aspirin apparently thins the blood and inhibits clotting.* VERB V V-ing

**cloth** /klɒθ, AM klɔːθ/ **(cloths)** 1 **Cloth** is fabric which is made by weaving or knitting a substance such as cotton, wool, silk, or nylon. Cloth is used especially for making clothes. ❑ *She began cleaning the wound with a piece of cloth.* N-MASS = fabric, material 2 A **cloth** is a piece of cloth which you use for a particular purpose, such as cleaning something or covering something. ❑ *Clean the surface with a damp cloth. ...a tray covered with a cloth.* N-COUNT 3 **The cloth** is sometimes used to refer to Christian priests and ministers. ❑ *...a man of the cloth.* N-SING: *the* N

**cloth cap** **(cloth caps)** A **cloth cap** is a soft flat cap with a stiff, curved part at the front called a peak. Cloth caps are usually worn by men. N-COUNT

**clothe** /kloʊð/ **(clothes, clothing, clothed)** To **clothe** someone means to provide them with clothes to wear. ❑ *She was on her own with two kids to feed and clothe.* → See also **clothed**, **clothes**, **clothing**. VERB V n

**clothed** /kloʊðd/ If you are **clothed in** a certain way, you are dressed in that way. ❑ *He lay down on the bed fully clothed. ...women clothed in black.* ADJ: adv ADJ, v-link ADJ *in* n = dressed

**clothes** /kloʊðz/ **Clothes** are the things that people wear, such as shirts, coats, trousers, and dresses. ❑ *Moira walked upstairs to change her clothes... He dressed quickly in casual clothes.* → See also **plain-clothes**. ◆◆◇ N-PLURAL

**clothes horse** **(clothes horses)** 1 A **clothes horse** is a folding frame used inside someone's house to hang washing on while it dries. N-COUNT 2 If you describe someone, especially a woman, as a **clothes horse**, you mean that they are fashionable and think a lot about their clothes, but have little intelligence or no other abilities. N-COUNT disapproval

**clothes|line** /kloʊðzlaɪn/ **(clotheslines)** also **clothes line**. A **clothesline** is a thin rope on which you hang washing so that it can dry. N-COUNT = washing line

**clothes peg** **(clothes pegs)** A **clothes peg** is a small device which you use to fasten clothes to a washing line. [BRIT] N-COUNT

☑ in AM, use **clothespin**

**clothes|pin** /kloʊðzpɪn/ **(clothespins)** A **clothespin** is the same as a **clothes peg**. [AM] N-COUNT

**cloth|ing** /kloʊðɪŋ/ **Clothing** is the things that people wear. ❑ *Some locals offered food and clothing to the refugees... What is your favourite item of clothing?... Wear protective clothing.* ◆◇◇ N-UNCOUNT

**clot|ted cream** **Clotted cream** is very thick cream made by heating milk gently and taking the cream off the top. It is made mainly in the south west of England. N-UNCOUNT

**cloud** /klaʊd/ **(clouds, clouding, clouded)** 1 A **cloud** is a mass of water vapour that floats in the sky. Clouds are usually white or grey in colour. ❑ *...the varied shapes of the clouds... The sky was almost entirely obscured by cloud. ...the risks involved in* ◆◇◇ N-VAR

*flying through cloud.* 2 A **cloud of** something such as smoke or dust is a mass of it floating in the air. ❑ *The hens darted away on all sides, raising a cloud of dust.* 3 If you say that something **clouds** your view of a situation, you mean that it makes you unable to understand the situation or judge it properly. ❑ *Perhaps anger had clouded his vision, perhaps his judgment had been faulty... In his latter years religious mania clouded his mind.* 4 If you say that something **clouds** a situation, you mean that it makes it unpleasant. ❑ *The atmosphere has already been clouded by the BJP's anger at the media.* 5 If glass **clouds** or if moisture **clouds** it, tiny drops of water cover the glass, making it difficult to see through. ❑ *The mirror clouded beside her cheek... I run the water very hot, clouding the mirror.* 6 If you say that someone is **on cloud nine**, you are emphasizing that they are very happy. [INFORMAL] ❑ *When Michael was born I was on cloud nine.* 7 **every cloud has a silver lining** → see **silver lining**.
N-COUNT: usu N *of* n; VERB; V n; V n; VERB; V n; VERB = *mist*; V; V n; PHRASE: usu v-link PHR; emphasis

♦ **cloud over** If the sky **clouds over**, it becomes covered with clouds. ❑ *After a fine day, the sky had clouded over and suddenly rain lashed against the windows.* → See also **cloud 5**. PHRASAL VERB; V P

**cloud|burst** /klaʊdbɜːʳst/ **(cloudbursts)** A **cloudburst** is a sudden, very heavy fall of rain. N-COUNT

**cloud-cuckoo-land** If you say that someone is living in **cloud-cuckoo-land**, you are criticizing them because they think there are no problems and that things will happen exactly as they want them to, when this is obviously not the case. [mainly BRIT] ❑ *I was living in cloud-cuckoo-land about my salary expectations.* N-UNCOUNT: also *a* N; disapproval

**cloud|less** /klaʊdləs/ If the sky is **cloudless**, there are no clouds in it. ADJ ≠ *cloudy*

**cloudy** /klaʊdi/ **(cloudier, cloudiest)** 1 If it is **cloudy**, there are a lot of clouds in the sky. ❑ *...a windy, cloudy day.* 2 A **cloudy** liquid is less clear than it should be. ADJ; ADJ

**clout** /klaʊt/ **(clouts, clouting, clouted)** 1 If you **clout** someone, you hit them. [INFORMAL] ❑ *Rachel clouted him... The officer clouted her on the head.* ♦ **Clout** is also a noun. ❑ *I was half tempted to give one of them a clout myself.* 2 A person or institution that has **clout** has influence and power. [INFORMAL] ❑ *Mr Sutherland may have the clout needed to push the two trading giants into a deal.* VERB; V n; V n *on* n; N-COUNT; N-UNCOUNT = *influence*

**clove** /kloʊv/ **(cloves)** 1 **Cloves** are small dried flower buds which are used as a spice. ❑ *...chicken soup with cloves.* 2 A **clove of** garlic is one of the sections of a garlic bulb. N-VAR; N-COUNT: usu N *of* n

**clo|ven hoof** /kloʊvᵊn huːf/ **(cloven hooves** or **cloven hoofs)** Animals that have **cloven hooves** have feet that are divided into two parts. Cows, sheep, and goats have cloven hooves. N-COUNT

**clo|ver** /kloʊvəʳ/ **(clovers)** **Clover** is a small plant with pink or white ball-shaped flowers. ❑ *...a four leaf clover.* N-VAR

**clown** /klaʊn/ **(clowns, clowning, clowned)** 1 A **clown** is a performer in a circus who wears funny clothes and bright make-up, and does silly things in order to make people laugh. 2 If you **clown**, you do silly things in order to make people laugh. ❑ *Bruno clowned and won affection everywhere.* ♦ **Clown around** and **clown about** mean the same as **clown**. ❑ *Bev made her laugh, the way she was always clowning around.* ♦ **clown|ing** *She senses that behind the clowning there is a terrible sense of anguish.* 3 If you say that someone is a **clown**, you mean that they say funny things or do silly things to amuse people. ❑ *He was laughing, the clown of the twosome.* 4 If you describe someone as a **clown**, you disapprove of them and have no respect for them. [INFORMAL] ❑ *I still think I could do a better job than those clowns in Washington.* N-COUNT; VERB = *mess around*; V; PHRASAL VERB; V P; N-UNCOUNT; N-COUNT = *joker*; N-COUNT; disapproval = *idiot, fool*

**clown|ish** /klaʊnɪʃ/ If you describe a person's appearance or behaviour as **clownish**, you mean that they look or behave rather like a clown, and often that they appear rather foolish. ❑ *He had a clownish sense of humour.* ADJ

**cloy|ing** /klɔɪɪŋ/ You use **cloying** to describe something that you find unpleasant because it is much too sweet, or too sentimental. ❑ *Her cheap, cloying scent enveloped him.* ADJ

**cloze** /kloʊz/ **(clozes)** In language teaching, a **cloze** test is a test in which words are removed from a text and replaced with spaces. The task of the learner is to fill each space with the missing word or a suitable word. [TECHNICAL] N-COUNT: usu N n = *gap-fill*

**club** /klʌb/ **(clubs, clubbing, clubbed)** 1 A **club** is an organization of people interested in a particular activity or subject who usually meet on a regular basis. ❑ *...the Chorlton Conservative Club. ...a youth club... He was club secretary.* 2 A **club** is a place where the members of a club meet. ❑ *I stopped in at the club for a drink.* 3 A **club** is a team which competes in sporting competitions. ❑ *...Liverpool football club.* 4 A **club** is the same as a **nightclub**. ❑ *It's a big dance hit in the clubs. ...the London club scene.* 5 A **club** is a long, thin, metal stick with a piece of wood or metal at one end that you use to hit the ball in golf. ❑ *...a six-iron club.* 6 A **club** is a thick heavy stick that can be used as a weapon. ❑ *Men armed with knives and clubs attacked his home.* 7 To **club** a person or animal means to hit them hard with a thick heavy stick or a similar weapon. ❑ *Two thugs clubbed him with baseball bats... Clubbing baby seals to death for their pelts is wrong.* 8 **Clubs** is one of the four suits in a pack of playing cards. Each card in the suit is marked with one or more black symbols: ♣. ❑ *...the ace of clubs.* ♦ A **club** is a playing card of this suit. ❑ *The next player discarded a club.* ◆◆◆ N-COUNT; N-COUNT: oft poss N; N-COUNT; N-COUNT; N-COUNT = *golf club*; N-COUNT; VERB; V n; V n *to* n; N-UNCOUNT-COLL; N-COUNT

♦ **club together** If people **club together** to do something, they all give money towards the cost of it. [BRIT] ❑ *For my thirtieth birthday, my friends clubbed together and bought me a watch.* PHRASAL VERB; V P

**club|bable** /klʌbəbᵊl/ A **clubbable** person is friendly and likes being with other people, which makes them good members of social clubs. ❑ *He is a clubbable chap.* ADJ

**club|ber** /klʌbəʳ/ **(clubbers)** A **clubber** is someone who regularly goes to nightclubs. N-COUNT

**club|bing** /klʌbɪŋ/ **Clubbing** is the activity of going to night clubs. N-UNCOUNT

**club|by** /klʌbi/ If you describe an institution or a group of people as **clubby**, you mean that all the people in it are friendly with each other and do not welcome other people in. [INFORMAL] ❑ *Politics is clubby, careerist, and cynical.* ADJ = *cliquey*

**club foot** **(club feet)**

✓ in AM, usually use **clubfoot**

If someone has a **club foot**, they are born with a badly twisted foot. N-COUNT

**club|house** /klʌbhaʊs/ **(clubhouses)** also **club-house**. A **clubhouse** is a place where the members of a club, especially a sports club, meet. N-COUNT

**club|land** /klʌblænd/ 1 A city's **clubland** is the area that contains all the best nightclubs. [BRIT] ❑ *...London's clubland.* 2 **Clubland** refers to the most popular nightclubs and the people that go to them. [BRIT] ❑ *...a contemporary clubland sound.* N-UNCOUNT; N-UNCOUNT: oft N n

**club soda** **Club soda** is fizzy water used for mixing with alcoholic drinks and fruit juice. [mainly AM] N-UNCOUNT = *soda water*

**cluck** /klʌk/ **(clucks, clucking, clucked)** When a hen **clucks**, it makes short, low noises. ❑ *Chickens clucked in the garden.* VERB; V

**clue** /kluː/ **(clues)** 1 A **clue to** a problem or mystery is something that helps you to find the answer to it. ❑ *Geneticists in Canada have discovered a clue to the puzzle of why our cells get old and die.* 2 A **clue** is an object or piece of information that helps someone solve a crime. ❑ *The vital clue to the killer's identity was his nickname, Peanuts.* 3 A **clue** in a crossword or game is information which is N-COUNT: oft N *to* n; N-COUNT: oft N *to* n; N-COUNT given to help you to find the answer to a question. [4] If you **haven't a clue** about something, you do not know anything about it or you have no idea what to do about it. [INFORMAL] ❑ *I haven't a clue what I'll give Carl for his birthday next year.* PHRASE: usu PHR wh

**clued-up** also **clued up.** If you say that someone is **clued-up on** a particular subject, you are showing your approval of the fact that they have a great deal of detailed knowledge and information about it. [BRIT, INFORMAL] ❑ *I've always found him clued-up on whatever he was talking about.* ADJ: usu v-link ADJ, oft ADJ *on* n/wh [approval]

**clue|less** /kluːləs/ If you describe someone as **clueless**, you are showing your disapproval of the fact that they do not know anything about a particular subject or that they are incapable of doing a particular thing properly. [INFORMAL] ❑ *I came into adult life clueless about a lot of things that most people take for granted.* ADJ: oft ADJ *about* n [disapproval]

**clump** /klʌmp/ **(clumps, clumping, clumped)** [1] A **clump of** things such as trees or plants is a small group of them growing together. ❑ *...a clump of trees bordering a side road.* N-COUNT: oft N *of* n, *in* N in pl = cluster [2] A **clump** of things such as wires or hair is a group of them collected together in one place. ❑ *I was combing my hair and it was just falling out in clumps.* N-COUNT: oft N *of* n, *in* N in pl [3] If things **clump together**, they gather together and form small groups or lumps. ❑ *Brown rice takes longer to cook but it doesn't clump together as easily as white rice.* VERB V *together*

**clumpy** /klʌmpi/ **(clumpier, clumpiest)** **Clumpy** means big and clumsy. ❑ *...clumpy shoes.* ADJ

**clum|sy** /klʌmzi/ **(clumsier, clumsiest)** [1] A **clumsy** person moves or handles things in a careless, awkward way, often so that things are knocked over or broken. ❑ *Unfortunately, I was still very clumsy behind the wheel of the jeep.* ADJ = awkward ♦ **clum|si|ly** /klʌmzɪli/ *The rooks flew clumsily towards their nests.* ADV: ADV with v ♦ **clum|si|ness** *Ben's biggest problem is clumsiness.* N-UNCOUNT [2] A **clumsy** action or statement is not skilful or is likely to upset people. ❑ *The action seemed a clumsy attempt to topple the Janata Dal government... He denied the announcement was clumsy and insensitive.* ADJ ♦ **clum|si|ly** *If the matter were handled clumsily, it could cost Miriam her life.* ADV: usu ADV with v ♦ **clum|si|ness** *I was ashamed at my clumsiness and insensitivity.* N-UNCOUNT

**clung** /klʌŋ/ **Clung** is the past tense and past participle of **cling**.

**clunk** /klʌŋk/ **(clunks)** A **clunk** is a sound made by a heavy object hitting something hard. ❑ *Something fell to the floor with a clunk.* N-COUNT: usu sing; SOUND

**clunk|er** /klʌŋkəʳ/ **(clunkers)** If you describe a machine, especially a car, as a **clunker**, you mean that it is very old and almost falling apart. [AM] N-COUNT = banger

**clunky** /klʌŋki/ If you describe something as **clunky**, you mean that it is solid, heavy, and rather awkward. ❑ *...a clunky piece of architecture.* ADJ: usu ADJ n

**clus|ter** /klʌstəʳ/ **(clusters, clustering, clustered)** [1] A **cluster of** people or things is a small group of them close together. ❑ *There's no town here, just a cluster of shops, cabins and motels at the side of the highway.* N-COUNT: oft N *of* n [2] If people **cluster together**, they gather together in a small group. ❑ *The passengers clustered together in small groups... The children clustered around me.* → See also **clustered**. VERB V *together* V *around/round* n

**clus|ter bomb** **(cluster bombs)** A **cluster bomb** is a type of bomb which is dropped from an aircraft. It contains a large number of smaller bombs that spread out before they hit the ground. N-COUNT

**clus|tered** /klʌstəʳd/ If people or things are **clustered** somewhere, there is a group of them close together there. ❑ *Officials were clustered at every open office door, talking excitedly.* ADJ: v-link ADJ prep/adv

**clutch** /klʌtʃ/ **(clutches, clutching, clutched)** [1] If you **clutch at** something or **clutch** something, you hold it tightly, usually because you are afraid or anxious. ❑ *I staggered and had to clutch at a chair for support... She was clutching a photograph.* VERB = grasp, grip V *at* n V n [2] If someone is in another person's **clutches**, that person has captured them or has power over them. ❑ *Stojanovic escaped their clutches by jumping from a moving vehicle.* N-PLURAL: usu with poss = grasp [3] In a vehicle, the **clutch** is the pedal that you press before you change gear. → See picture on page 1708. ❑ *Laura let out the clutch and pulled slowly away down the drive.* N-COUNT [4] **to clutch at straws** → see **straw**.

**clut|ter** /klʌtəʳ/ **(clutters, cluttering, cluttered)** [1] **Clutter** is a lot of things in an untidy state, especially things that are not useful or necessary. ❑ *Caroline prefers her worktops to be clear of clutter.* N-UNCOUNT [2] If things or people **clutter** a place, they fill it in an untidy way. ❑ *Empty soft-drink cans clutter the desks... The roads were cluttered with cars and vans.* VERB V n *be* V-ed *with* n ♦ **Clutter up** means the same as **clutter**. ❑ *The vehicles cluttered up the car park... This room is so impressive it would be a shame to clutter it up.* PHRASAL VERB V P n V n P Also V n P *with* n

**cm** **cm** is the written abbreviation for **centimetre** or **centimetres**. ❑ *His height had increased by 2.5 cm.*

**Cmdr** **Cmdr** is a written abbreviation for **Commander**. ❑ *...Cmdr Richard Mason.*

**c/o** You write **c/o** before an address on an envelope when you are sending it to someone who is staying or working at that address, often for only a short time. **c/o** is an abbreviation for 'care of'. ❑ *...Mr A D Bright, c/o Sherman Ltd, 62 Burton Road, Bristol 8.*

**co-** /koʊ-/ [1] **co-** is used to form verbs or nouns that refer to people sharing things or doing things together. ❑ *...commercial co-operation between the two countries... He co-produced the album with Bowie.* PREFIX [2] **co-** is used to form nouns that refer to people who share a job or task with someone else. ❑ *His co-workers hated him... He is now co-partner in a new property company.* PREFIX

**Co.** ◆◆◇ [1] **Co.** is used as an abbreviation for **company** when it is part of the name of an organization. [BUSINESS] ❑ *...the Blue Star Amusement Co.* [2] **Co.** is used as a written abbreviation for **county** before the names of some counties, especially in Ireland. ❑ *...Co. Waterford.* [3] You use **and co.** after someone's name to mean the group of people associated with that person. [INFORMAL] ❑ *Wayne Hussey and co. will be playing two live sets each evening.* PHRASE: n-proper PHR

**C.O.** /siː oʊ/ **(C.O.s)** A soldier's **C.O.** is his or her **commanding officer**. N-COUNT

**coach** /koʊtʃ/ **(coaches, coaching, coached)** ◆◆◇ [1] A **coach** is someone who trains a person or team of people in a particular sport. ❑ *Tony Woodcock has joined German amateur team SC Brueck as coach.* N-COUNT = trainer [2] When someone **coaches** a person or a team, they help them to become better at a particular sport. ❑ *Beckenbauer coached the West Germans to success in the World Cup final in Italy... I had coached the Alliance team for some time.* VERB = train V n *to* n V n [3] A **coach** is a person who is in charge of a sports team. [mainly AM] N-COUNT

> in BRIT, usually use **manager**

[4] In baseball, a **coach** is a member of a team who stands near the first or third base, and gives signals to other members of the team who are on bases and are trying to score. [AM] N-COUNT [5] A **coach** is someone who gives people special teaching in a particular subject, especially in order to prepare them for an examination. ❑ *What you need is a drama coach.* N-COUNT: oft n N = tutor [6] If you **coach** someone, you give them special teaching in a particular subject, especially in order to prepare them for an examination. ❑ *He gently coached me in French.* VERB V n [7] A **coach** is a large, comfortable bus that carries passengers on long journeys. [BRIT] ❑ *As we headed back to Calais, the coach was badly delayed by roadworks... I hate travelling by coach.* N-COUNT: also *by* N

> in AM, use **bus**

[8] A **coach** is one of the separate sections of a train that carries passengers. [BRIT] ❑ *The train was an elaborate affair of sixteen coaches.* N-COUNT

> in AM, use **car**

9 A **coach** is an enclosed vehicle with four wheels which is pulled by horses, and in which people used to travel. Coaches are still used for ceremonial events in some countries, such as Britain. N-COUNT

**coach|load** /koʊtʃloʊd/ **(coachloads)** also **coach-load.** A **coachload of** people is a group of people who are travelling somewhere together in a coach. [BRIT] ❑ *Dorset is as yet unspoilt by coachloads of tourists.* N-COUNT: usu N *of* n

**coach|man** /koʊtʃmən/ **(coachmen)** A **coachman** was a man who drove a coach that was pulled by horses. [OLD-FASHIONED] N-COUNT

**coach sta|tion** **(coach stations)** A **coach station** is an area or a building which coaches leave from or arrive at on regular journeys. [BRIT] N-COUNT

✔ in AM, use **bus station**

**co|agu|late** /koʊæɡjʊleɪt/ **(coagulates, coagulating, coagulated)** When a liquid **coagulates**, it becomes very thick. ❑ *The blood coagulates to stop wounds bleeding.* VERB = congeal V ♦ **co|agu|la|tion** /koʊæɡjʊleɪʃən/ *Blood becomes stickier to help coagulation in case of a cut.* N-UNCOUNT

**coal** /koʊl/ **(coals)** ◆◇◇ 1 **Coal** is a hard black substance that is extracted from the ground and burned as fuel. ❑ *Gas-fired electricity is cheaper than coal.* N-UNCOUNT 2 **Coals** are burning pieces of coal. ❑ *It is important to get the coals white-hot before you start cooking.* N-PLURAL

**coa|lesce** /koʊəles/ **(coalesces, coalescing, coalesced)** If two or more things **coalesce**, they come together and form a larger group or system. [FORMAL] ❑ *Cities, if unrestricted, tend to coalesce into bigger and bigger conurbations... His sporting and political interests coalesced admirably in his writing about climbing.* VERB = merge V prep V

**coal|face** /koʊlfeɪs/ **(coalfaces)** In a coal mine, the **coalface** is the part where the coal is being cut out of the rock. N-COUNT

**coal|field** /koʊlfiːld/ **(coalfields)** A **coalfield** is a region where there is coal under the ground. ❑ *The park lies on top of a coalfield.* N-COUNT

**coa|li|tion** /koʊəlɪʃən/ **(coalitions)** ◆◇◇ 1 A **coalition** is a government consisting of people from two or more political parties. ❑ *Since June the country has had a coalition government.* N-COUNT: oft N n 2 A **coalition** is a group consisting of people from different political or social groups who are co-operating to achieve a particular aim. ❑ *He had been opposed by a coalition of about 50 civil rights, women's and Latino organizations.* N-COUNT: oft N *of* n = alliance

**coal mine** **(coal mines)** also **coalmine.** A **coal mine** is a place where coal is dug out of the ground. N-COUNT

**coal min|er** **(coal miners)** also **coalminer.** A **coal miner** is a person whose job is mining coal. N-COUNT

**coal scut|tle** **(coal scuttles)** A **coal scuttle** is a container for keeping coal in. [mainly BRIT] N-COUNT

**coal tar** also **coal-tar. Coal tar** is a thick black liquid made from coal which is used for making drugs and chemical products. ❑ *...coal tar dyes.* N-UNCOUNT

**coarse** /kɔːʳs/ **(coarser, coarsest)** 1 **Coarse** things have a rough texture because they consist of thick threads or large pieces. ❑ *...a jacket made of very coarse cloth. ...a beach of coarse black sand.* ADJ = rough ≠ fine ♦ **coarse|ly** *...coarsely ground black pepper.* ADV 2 If you describe someone as **coarse**, you mean that he or she talks and behaves in a rude and offensive way. ❑ *The soldiers did not bother to moderate their coarse humour in her presence.* ADJ disapproval = vulgar, crude ♦ **coarse|ly** *The women laughed coarsely at some vulgar joke.* ADV: ADV with v

**coars|en** /kɔːʳsən/ **(coarsens, coarsening, coarsened)** 1 If something **coarsens** or **is coarsened**, it becomes thicker or rougher in texture. ❑ *Skin thickens, dries and coarsens after sun exposure.* VERB V *...his gnarled, coarsened features.* V-ed 2 If someone's behaviour or speech **coarsens** or if they **coarsen** it, they become less polite or they begin to speak in a less pleasant way. ❑ *Her voice has deepened and coarsened with the years... He had coarsened his voice to an approximation of Cockney.* VERB V V n

**coast** /koʊst/ **(coasts, coasting, coasted)** ◆◆◇ 1 The **coast** is an area of land that is next to the sea. ❑ *Camp sites are usually situated along the coast, close to beaches. ...the west coast of Scotland.* N-COUNT: oft adj N, N *of* n 2 If a vehicle **coasts** somewhere, it continues to move there with the motor switched off, or without being pushed or pedalled. ❑ *I switched off the engine and coasted round the corner.* VERB V prep/adv 3 If you say that **the coast is clear**, you mean that there is nobody around to see you or catch you. ❑ *You can come out now,' he called. 'The coast is clear. She's gone.'* PHRASE: V inflects

**coast|al** /koʊstəl/ **Coastal** is used to refer to things that are in the sea or on the land near a coast. ❑ *Local radio stations serving coastal areas often broadcast forecasts for yachtsmen... The fish are on sale from our own coastal waters.* ADJ: ADJ n

**coast|er** /koʊstəʳ/ **(coasters)** 1 A **coaster** is a small mat that you put underneath a glass or cup to protect the surface of a table. N-COUNT 2 A **coaster** is a ship that sails along the coast taking goods to ports. [BRIT] N-COUNT 3 → See also **roller-coaster**.

**coast|guard** /koʊstɡɑːʳd/ **(coastguards)**

✔ in AM, usually use **Coast Guard**

1 A **coastguard** is an official who watches the sea near a coast in order to get help for sailors when they need it and to stop illegal activities. [mainly BRIT] N-COUNT ♦ **The coastguard** is the organization to which coastguards belong. [BRIT] ❑ *The survivors were lifted off by two helicopters, one from the Coastguard and one from the RAF.* N-SING: the N 2 The **Coast Guard** is a part of a country's military forces and is responsible for protecting the coast, carrying out rescues, and doing police work along the coast. [AM] ❑ *The US Coast Guard says it rescued more than 100 Haitian refugees.* N-COUNT ♦ A **Coast Guard** is a member of the coastguard. [AM] ❑ *The boat was intercepted by US Coast Guards.* N-COUNT

**coast|line** /koʊstlaɪn/ **(coastlines)** A country's **coastline** is the outline of its coast. ❑ *Thousands of volunteers gave up part of their weekend to clean up the California coastline.* N-VAR: oft supp N

**coat** /koʊt/ **(coats, coating, coated)** ◆◇◇ 1 A **coat** is a piece of clothing with long sleeves which you wear over your other clothes when you go outside. ❑ *He turned off the television, put on his coat and walked out.* N-COUNT 2 An animal's **coat** is the fur or hair on its body. ❑ *Vitamin B6 is great for improving the condition of dogs' and horses' coats.* N-COUNT: usu with poss 3 If you **coat** something **with** a substance or **in** a substance, you cover it with a thin layer of the substance. ❑ *Coat the fish with seasoned flour.* VERB V n *with/in* n ♦ **coat|ed** *TV pictures showed a dying bird coated with oil... Dip the pieces so they are completely coated.* ADJ: v-link ADJ, ADJ *with/in* n, adv ADJ 4 A **coat of** paint or varnish is a thin layer of it on a surface. ❑ *The front door needs a new coat of paint.* N-COUNT: oft N *of* n

**-coated** /koʊtɪd/ 1 **-coated** combines with colour adjectives such as 'white' and 'red', or words for types of coat like 'fur', to form adjectives that describe someone as wearing a certain sort of coat. ❑ *At the top of the stairs stood the white-coated doctors.* COMB in ADJ: ADJ n 2 **-coated** combines with names of substances such as 'sugar' and 'plastic' to form adjectives that describe something as being covered with a thin layer of that substance. ❑ *...chocolate-coated sweets. ...plastic-coated wire.* COMB in ADJ

**coat hang|er** **(coat hangers)** also **coathanger.** A **coat hanger** is a curved piece of wood, metal, or plastic that you hang a piece of clothing on. N-COUNT

**coat|ing** /koʊtɪŋ/ **(coatings)** A **coating of** a substance is a thin layer of it spread over a surface. ❑ *Under the coating of dust and cobwebs, he discovered a fine French Louis XVI clock.* N-COUNT: usu with supp

**coat of arms** **(coats of arms)** The **coat of arms** of a family, town, or organization is a special design in the form of a shield that they use as a symbol of their identity. [mainly BRIT] N-COUNT: usu with supp = crest

**coat-tails** also **coattails.** 1 **Coat-tails** are the two long pieces at the back of a **tailcoat.** N-PLURAL: oft poss N 2 If you do something **on the coat-tails of** someone else, you are able to do it because of the other person's success, and not because of your own efforts. ❑ *They accused him of riding on the coat-tails of the president.* PHRASE: usu PHR after v

**co-author** **(co-authors, co-authoring, co-authored)** also **coauthor.** 1 The **co-authors of** a book, play, or report are the people who have written it together. ❑ *He is co-author, with Andrew Blowers, of 'The International Politics of Nuclear Waste'.* N-COUNT: oft N *of* n 2 If two or more people **co-author** a book, play, or report, they write it together. ❑ *He's co-authored a book on Policy for Tourism... Karen Matthews co-authored the study with Lewis Kullers.* VERB V n V n *with* n

**coax** /kouks/ **(coaxes, coaxing, coaxed)** 1 If you **coax** someone **into** doing something, you gently try to persuade them to do it. ❑ *After lunch, she watched, listened and coaxed Bobby into talking about himself... The government coaxed them to give up their strike by promising them temporary residence permits.* VERB V n prep V n to-inf 2 If you **coax** something such as information out of someone, you gently persuade them to give it to you. ❑ *The WPC talked yesterday of her role in trying to coax vital information from the young victim.* VERB V n *out of/from* n

**cob** /kɒb/ **(cobs)** 1 A **cob** is a round loaf of bread. [BRIT] N-COUNT 2 A **cob** is a type of short strong horse. N-COUNT 3 → See also **corn on the cob.**

**co|balt** /koubɔːlt/ 1 **Cobalt** is a hard silvery-white metal which is used to harden steel and for producing a blue dye. ❑ *...a country rich in copper, cobalt and diamonds.* N-UNCOUNT 2 **Cobalt** or **cobalt blue** is a deep blue colour. ❑ *...a woman in a soft cobalt blue dress.* COLOUR

**cob|ble** /kɒbᵊl/ **(cobbles, cobbling, cobbled)** **Cobbles** are the same as **cobblestones.** ❑ *They found Trish sitting on the cobbles of the stable yard.* N-COUNT: usu pl

♦ **cobble together** If you say that someone has **cobbled** something **together**, you mean that they have made or produced it roughly or quickly. ❑ *The group had cobbled together a few decent songs... You can cobble it together from any old combination of garments.* PHRASAL VERB [disapproval] V P n (not pron) V n P

**cob|bled** /kɒbᵊld/ A **cobbled** street has a surface made of cobblestones. ❑ *Cottrell strode out across the cobbled courtyard.* ADJ: usu ADJ n

**cob|bler** /kɒbləʳ/ **(cobblers)** 1 A **cobbler** is a person whose job is to make or mend shoes. [OLD-FASHIONED] N-COUNT 2 If you describe something that someone has just said as **cobblers**, you mean that you think it is nonsense. [BRIT, INFORMAL] ❑ *These guys talk an awful load of old cobblers.* N-UNCOUNT = *codswallop*

**cobble|stone** /kɒbᵊlstoun/ **(cobblestones)** **Cobblestones** are stones with a rounded upper surface which used to be used for making streets. ❑ *...the narrow, cobblestone streets of the Left Bank.* N-COUNT: usu pl

**co|bra** /koubrə/ **(cobras)** A **cobra** is a kind of poisonous snake that can make the skin on the back of its neck into a hood. N-COUNT

**cob|web** /kɒbweb/ **(cobwebs)** 1 A **cobweb** is the net which a spider makes for catching insects. N-COUNT 2 If something **blows** or **clears away the cobwebs**, it makes you feel more mentally alert and lively when you had previously been feeling tired. ❑ *...a walk on the South Downs to blow away the cobwebs.* PHRASE: V inflects

**cob|webbed** /kɒbwebd/ A **cobwebbed** surface is covered with cobwebs. ❑ *...cobwebbed racks of wine bottles.* ADJ: usu ADJ n

**co|caine** /koukeɪn/ **Cocaine** is a powerful drug which some people take for pleasure, but which they can become addicted to. N-UNCOUNT

**coc|cyx** /kɒksɪks/ **(coccyxes)**

> ✔ The plural **coccyges** is used in American English.

The **coccyx** is the small triangular bone at the lower end of the spine in human beings and some apes. N-COUNT

**cochi|neal** /kɒtʃɪniːl/ **Cochineal** is a red substance that is used for colouring food. N-UNCOUNT

**coch|lea** /kɒkliə/ **(cochleae)** The **cochlea** is the spiral-shaped part of the inner ear. N-COUNT

**cock** /kɒk/ **(cocks, cocking, cocked)** 1 A **cock** is an adult male chicken. [mainly BRIT] ❑ *The cock was announcing the start of a new day.* N-COUNT

> ✔ in AM, use **rooster**

2 You refer to a male bird, especially a male game bird, as a **cock** when you want to distinguish it from a female bird. [mainly BRIT] ❑ *...a cock pheasant.* N-COUNT: oft N n 3 A man's **cock** is his penis. [INFORMAL, ⚠ VERY RUDE] N-COUNT 4 → See also **stopcock.** 5 to **cock a snook at** someone → see **snook.**

♦ **cock up** If you **cock** something **up**, you ruin it by doing something wrong. [BRIT, INFORMAL, RUDE] ❑ *'Seems like I've cocked it up,' Egan said... They've cocked up the address.* → See also **cock-up.** PHRASAL VERB V n P V P n (not pron)

**cock-a-hoop** If you are **cock-a-hoop**, you are extremely pleased about something that you have done. [INFORMAL, OLD-FASHIONED] ADJ: usu v-link ADJ

**cock-and-bull sto|ry** **(cock-and-bull stories)** If you describe something that someone tells you as a **cock-and-bull story**, you mean that you do not believe it is true. [INFORMAL] N-COUNT

**cocka|tiel** /kɒkətiːəl/ **(cockatiels)** A **cockatiel** is a bird similar to a cockatoo that is often kept as a pet. N-COUNT

**cocka|too** /kɒkətuː, AM -tuː/ **(cockatoos)** A **cockatoo** is a kind of parrot from Australia or New Guinea which has a bunch of feathers called a crest on its head. N-COUNT

**cocked hat** **(cocked hats)** 1 A **cocked hat** is a hat with three corners that used to be worn with some uniforms. N-COUNT 2 If you say that one thing **knocks** another thing **into a cocked hat**, you mean that it is much better or much more significant than the other thing. ❑ *This design knocks everything else into a cocked hat.* PHRASE: V inflects

**cock|er|el** /kɒkərəl/ **(cockerels)** A **cockerel** is a young male chicken. [mainly BRIT] N-COUNT

**cock|er span|iel** /kɒkəʳ spænjəl/ **(cocker spaniels)** A **cocker spaniel** is a breed of small dog with silky hair and long ears. N-COUNT

**cock|eyed** /kɒkaɪd, AM -aɪd/ also **cock-eyed.** 1 If you say that an idea or scheme is **cockeyed**, you mean that you think it is very unlikely to succeed. ❑ *She has some cockeyed delusions about becoming a pop star.* ADJ 2 If something is **cockeyed**, it looks wrong because it is not in a level or straight position. ❑ *...dusty photographs hanging at cockeyed angles on the walls.* ADJ

**cock|le** /kɒkᵊl/ **(cockles)** **Cockles** are small edible shellfish. N-COUNT: usu pl

**cock|ney** /kɒkni/ **(cockneys)** 1 A **cockney** is a person who was born in the East End of London. ❑ *...a Cockney cab driver.* N-COUNT: oft N n 2 **Cockney** is the dialect and accent of the East End of London. ❑ *The man spoke with a Cockney accent.* N-UNCOUNT

**cock|pit** /kɒkpɪt/ **(cockpits)** In an aeroplane or racing car, the **cockpit** is the part where the pilot or driver sits. N-COUNT

**cock|roach** /kɒkroutʃ/ **(cockroaches)** A **cockroach** is a large brown insect that is sometimes found in warm places or where food is kept. N-COUNT

**cock|sure** /kɒkʃʊəʳ/ Someone who is **cocksure** is so confident and sure of their abilities that they annoy other people. [OLD-FASHIONED] ADJ [disapproval] = *cocky*

**cock|tail** /kɒkteɪl/ **(cocktails)** 1 A **cocktail** is an alcoholic drink which contains several ingredients. ❑ *On arrival, guests are offered wine or a champagne cocktail.* N-COUNT 2 A **cocktail** is a mixture of a number of different things, especially ones that do not go together well. ❑ *The court was told she had taken a cocktail of drugs and alcohol.* N-COUNT: oft N *of* n 3 → See also **fruit cocktail, prawn cocktail, Molotov cocktail.**

**cock|tail dress** **(cocktail dresses)** A **cocktail dress** is a dress that is suitable for formal social occasions. N-COUNT

**cock|tail lounge** **(cocktail lounges)** A **cocktail lounge** is a room in a hotel, restaurant, or club where you can buy alcoholic drinks. ❑ *Let's meet in the cocktail lounge at the Hilton.* N-COUNT

**cock|tail par|ty** **(cocktail parties)** A **cocktail party** is a party, usually held in the early evening, where cocktails or other alcoholic drinks are served. People often dress quite formally for them. N-COUNT

**cock-up** **(cock-ups)** If you make a **cock-up** of something, you ruin it by doing something wrong. [BRIT, INFORMAL, RUDE] ❑ *He was in danger of making a real cock-up of this.* N-COUNT

**cocky** /kɒki/ **(cockier, cockiest)** Someone who is **cocky** is so confident and sure of their abilities that they annoy other people. [INFORMAL] ❑ *He was a little bit cocky when he was about 11 because he was winning everything.* ADJ disapproval = cocksure

**co|coa** /koʊkoʊ/ [1] **Cocoa** is a brown powder made from the seeds of a tropical tree. It is used in making chocolate. ❑ *The Ivory Coast became the world's leading cocoa producer. ...cocoa beans.* N-UNCOUNT [2] **Cocoa** is a hot drink made from cocoa powder and milk or water. N-UNCOUNT

**coco|nut** /koʊkənʌt/ **(coconuts)** [1] A **coconut** is a very large nut with a hairy shell, which has white flesh and milky juice inside it. ❑ *...the smell of roasted meats mingled with spices, coconut oil and ripe tropical fruits.* N-COUNT [2] **Coconut** is the white flesh of a coconut. ❑ *...desiccated coconut.* N-UNCOUNT

**coco|nut milk** **Coconut milk** is the milky juice inside coconuts. N-UNCOUNT

**coco|nut palm** **(coconut palms)** A **coconut palm** is a tall tree on which coconuts grow. N-COUNT

**co|coon** /kəkuːn/ **(cocoons, cocooning, cocooned)** [1] A **cocoon** is a covering of silky threads that the larvae of moths and other insects make for themselves before they grow into adults. N-COUNT [2] If you are in a **cocoon of** something, you are wrapped up in it or surrounded by it. ❑ *He stood there in a cocoon of golden light.* N-COUNT: usu N *of* n [3] If you are living in a **cocoon**, you are in an environment in which you feel protected and safe, and sometimes isolated from everyday life. ❑ *You cannot live in a cocoon and overlook these facts.* N-COUNT: usu N *of* n [4] If something **cocoons** you **from** something, it protects you or isolates you from it. ❑ *There is nowhere to hide when things go wrong, no organisation to cocoon you from blame... The playwright cocooned himself in a world of pretence.* VERB V n *from/in* n V pron-refl *in* n

**co|cooned** /kəkuːnd/ [1] If someone is **cocooned in** blankets or clothes, they are completely wrapped in them. ❑ *She is comfortably cocooned in pillows. ...my snugly cocooned baby sleeping in his pram.* ADJ: usu v-link ADJ, oft ADJ *in* n [2] If you say that someone is **cocooned**, you mean that they are isolated and protected from everyday life and problems. ❑ *She was cocooned in a private world of privilege... They were cocooned from the experience of poverty.* ADJ: oft ADJ *in/from* n = cloistered

**cod** /kɒd/ **(cods** or **cod)** [1] **Cod** are a type of large edible fish. ♦ **Cod** is this fish eaten as food. ❑ *A Catalan speciality is to serve salt cod cold.* N-VAR N-UNCOUNT [2] You use **cod** to describe something which is not genuine and which is intended to deceive or amuse people by looking or sounding like the real thing. [BRIT] ❑ *...a cod documentary on what animals think of living in a zoo.* ADJ: ADJ n = mock

**coda** /koʊdə/ **(codas)** [1] A **coda** is a separate passage at the end of something such as a book or a speech that finishes it off. N-COUNT [2] In music, a **coda** is the final part of a fairly long piece of music which is added in order to finish it off in a pleasing way. N-COUNT

**cod|dle** /kɒdᵊl/ **(coddles, coddling, coddled)** To **coddle** someone means to treat them too kindly or protect them too much. ❑ *She coddled her youngest son madly.* VERB disapproval V n

**code** /koʊd/ **(codes, coding, coded)** ◆◇◇ [1] A **code** is a set of rules about how people should behave or about how something must be done. ❑ *...Article 159 of the Turkish penal code. ...local building codes.* N-COUNT: oft n N, N *of* n [2] A **code** is a system of replacing the words in a message with other words or symbols, so that nobody can understand it unless they know the system. ❑ *They used elaborate secret codes, as when the names of trees stood for letters... If you can't remember your number, write it in code in a diary.* N-COUNT: also *in* N [3] A **code** is a group of numbers or letters which is used to identify something, such as a postal address or part of a telephone system. ❑ *Callers dialing the wrong area code will not get through.* N-COUNT [4] A **code** is any system of signs or symbols that has a meaning. ❑ *It will need different microchips to reconvert the digital code back into normal TV signals.* N-COUNT [5] The genetic **code** of a person, animal or plant is the information contained in DNA which determines the structure and function of cells, and the inherited characteristics of all living things. ❑ *Scientists provided the key to understanding the genetic code that determines every bodily feature.* N-COUNT: with supp [6] To **code** something means to give it a code or to mark it with its code. ❑ *He devised a way of coding every statement uniquely.* VERB V n [7] Computer **code** is a system or language for expressing information and instructions in a form which can be understood by a computer. [COMPUTING] N-UNCOUNT [8] → See also **bar code**, **Highway Code**, **machine code**, **morse code**, **postcode**, **zip code**.

**cod|ed** /koʊdɪd/ [1] **Coded** messages have words or symbols which represent other words, so that the message is secret unless you know the system behind the code. ❑ *In a coded telephone warning, Scotland Yard were told four bombs had been planted in the area.* ADJ: usu ADJ n [2] If someone is using **coded** language, they are expressing their opinion in an indirect way, usually because that opinion is likely to offend people. ❑ *It's widely assumed that his lyrics were coded references to homosexuality.* ADJ: usu ADJ n [3] **Coded** electronic signals use a binary system of digits which can be decoded by an appropriate machine. [TECHNICAL] ❑ *The coded signal is received by satellite dish aerials.* ADJ: ADJ n

**co|deine** /koʊdiːn/ **Codeine** is a drug which is used to relieve pain, especially headaches, and the symptoms of a cold. N-UNCOUNT

**code name** **(code names, code naming, code named)** also **codename, code-name.** [1] A **code name** is a name used for someone or something in order to keep their identity secret. ❑ *One of their informers was working under the code name Czerny.* N-COUNT: usu N n [2] If a military or police operation **is code-named** something, it is given a name which only the people involved in it know. ❑ *The operation was code-named Moonlight Sonata. ...a military contingent, code-named Sparrowhawk.* VERB: usu passive *be* V-ed n V-ed

**code of con|duct** **(codes of conduct)** The **code of conduct** for a group or organization is an agreement on rules of behaviour for the members of that group or organization. ❑ *Doctors in Britain say a new code of conduct is urgently needed to protect the doctor-patient relationship.* N-COUNT

**code of prac|tice** **(codes of practice)** A **code of practice** is a set of written rules which explains how people working in a particular profession should behave. ❑ *The auctioneers are violating a code of practice by dealing in stolen goods.* N-COUNT

**co-dependent** **(co-dependents)** A **co-dependent** person is in an unsatisfactory relationship with someone who is ill or an addict, but does not want the relationship to end. [TECHNICAL] ❑ *Guys can be co-dependent, too.* ♦ **Co-dependent** is also a noun. ❑ *The program is geared around the problems of being a co-dependent.* ♦ **co-dependency** *...the dangers of co-dependency.* ADJ N-COUNT N-UNCOUNT

**code word** **(code words)** also **codeword, code-word.** A **code word** is a word or phrase that has a special meaning, different from its nor- N-COUNT mal meaning, for the people who have agreed to use it in this way. ❑ *...magnum, the code word for launching a radar attack.*

**co|dex** /koʊdeks/ **(codices)** A **codex** is an ancient type of book which was written by hand, not printed. N-COUNT

**codg|er** /kɒdʒəʳ/ **(codgers)** **Old codger** is a disrespectful way of referring to an old man. N-COUNT: usu adj N [disapproval]

**co|di|ces** /koʊdɪsiːz/ **Codices** is the plural of **codex**.

**codi|cil** /koʊdɪsɪl, AM kɑːd-/ **(codicils)** A **codicil** is an instruction that is added to a will after the main part of it has been written. [LEGAL] N-COUNT

**codi|fy** /koʊdɪfaɪ, AM kɑːd-/ **(codifies, codifying, codified)** If you **codify** a set of rules, you define them or present them in a clear and ordered way. ❑ *The latest draft of the agreement codifies the panel's decision.* ♦ **codi|fi|ca|tion** /koʊdɪfɪkeɪʃən, AM kɑːd-/ *The codification of the laws began in the 1840s.* VERB; V n; N-UNCOUNT: usu N of n

**cod|ing** /koʊdɪŋ/ **Coding** is a method of making something easy to recognize or distinct, for example by colouring it. ❑ *...a colour coding that will ensure easy reference for potential users.* N-UNCOUNT: usu adj N

**cod-liver oil** also **cod liver oil. Cod liver oil** is a thick yellow oil which is given as a medicine, especially to children, because it is full of vitamins A and D. N-UNCOUNT

**cod|piece** /kɒdpiːs/ **(codpieces)** A **codpiece** was a piece of material worn by men in the 15th and 16th centuries to cover their genitals. N-COUNT

**cods|wallop** /kɒdzwɒləp/ If you describe something that someone has just said as **codswallop**, you mean that you think it is nonsense. [BRIT, INFORMAL] ❑ *This is a load of codswallop.* N-UNCOUNT [disapproval] = cobblers

**co-ed (co-eds)**

✔ in AM, usually use **coed**

[1] A **co-ed** school or college is the same as a co-educational school or college. ❑ *He was educated at a co-ed comprehensive school.* ADJ = mixed ≠ single-sex [2] A **co-ed** is a female student at a co-educational college or university. [AM, INFORMAL] ❑ *...two University of Florida coeds.* N-COUNT [3] A **co-ed** sports facility or sporting activity is one that both males and females use or take part in at the same time. [AM] ❑ *You have a choice of co-ed or single-sex swimming exercise classes.* ADJ: ADJ n ≠ single-sex

✔ in BRIT, usually use **mixed**

**co-educational** also **coeducational.** A **co-educational** school, college, or university is attended by both boys and girls. ❑ *The college has been co-educational since 1971.* ADJ

**co|ef|fi|cient** /koʊɪfɪʃənt/ **(coefficients)** A **coefficient** is a number that expresses a measurement of a particular quality of a substance or object under specified conditions. [TECHNICAL] ❑ *...production coefficients.* N-COUNT: usu with supp

**co|erce** /koʊɜːʳs/ **(coerces, coercing, coerced)** If you **coerce** someone **into** doing something, you make them do it, although they do not want to. [FORMAL] ❑ *Potter had argued that the government coerced him into pleading guilty.* VERB = pressurize; V n into -ing/n

**co|er|cion** /koʊɜːʳʃən/ **Coercion** is the act or process of persuading someone forcefully to do something that they do not want to do. ❑ *It was vital that the elections should be free of coercion or intimidation.* N-UNCOUNT

**co|er|cive** /koʊɜːʳsɪv/ **Coercive** measures are intended to force people to do something that they do not want to do. ❑ *The eighteenth-century Admiralty had few coercive powers over its officers.* ADJ: usu ADJ n

**co|ex|ist** /koʊɪgzɪst/ **(coexists, coexisting, coexisted)** also **co-exist.** If one thing **coexists with** another, they exist together at the same time or in the same place. You can also say that two things **coexist**. ❑ *Pockets of affluence coexist with poverty... Bankers and clockmakers have coexisted in the City for hundreds of years.* V-RECIP; V with n; pl-n V

**co|ex|ist|ence** /koʊɪgzɪstəns/ also **co-existence.** The **coexistence of** one thing **with** another is the fact that they exist together at the same time or in the same place. ❑ *He also believed in coexistence with the West.* N-UNCOUNT: oft N of/ with/ between n

**C of E** **C of E** is an abbreviation for **Church of England**. ❑ *Mrs Steele was head of Didcot's C of E primary school.*

**cof|fee** /kɒfi, AM kɔːfi/ **(coffees)** [1] **Coffee** is a hot drink made with water and ground or powdered coffee beans. ❑ *Would you like some coffee?* ♦ A **coffee** is a cup of coffee. ❑ *I made a coffee.* [2] **Coffee** is the roasted beans or powder from which the drink is made. ❑ *Brazil harvested 28m bags of coffee in 1991, the biggest crop for four years. ...superior quality coffee.* ◆◇◇ N-UNCOUNT; N-COUNT; N-MASS

**cof|fee bar** **(coffee bars)** A **coffee bar** is a small café where non-alcoholic drinks and snacks are sold. N-COUNT

**cof|fee bean** **(coffee beans)** **Coffee beans** are small dark brown beans that are roasted and ground to make coffee. They are the seeds of the coffee plant. N-COUNT: usu pl

**cof|fee break** **(coffee breaks)** A **coffee break** is a short period of time, usually in the morning or afternoon, when you stop working and have a cup of coffee. ❑ *It looks like she'll be too busy to stop for a coffee break.* N-COUNT

**cof|fee cup** **(coffee cups)** also **coffee-cup.** A **coffee cup** is a cup in which coffee is served. Coffee cups are usually smaller than tea cups. N-COUNT

**cof|fee grind|er** **(coffee grinders)** A **coffee grinder** is a machine for grinding coffee beans. N-COUNT

**cof|fee house** **(coffee houses)** also **coffee-house.** A **coffee house** is a kind of bar where people sit to drink coffee and talk. Coffee houses were especially popular in Britain in the 18th century. N-COUNT

**cof|fee morn|ing** **(coffee mornings)** A **coffee morning** is a social event at which coffee and tea are served. It takes place in the morning, and is usually intended to raise money for charity. [BRIT] N-COUNT

**cof|fee pot** **(coffee pots)** also **coffeepot.** A **coffee pot** is a tall narrow pot with a spout and a lid, in which coffee is made or served. N-COUNT

**cof|fee shop** **(coffee shops)** also **coffee-shop.** A **coffee shop** is a kind of restaurant that sells coffee, tea, cakes, and sometimes sandwiches and light meals. N-COUNT

**cof|fee ta|ble** **(coffee tables)** also **coffee-table.** A **coffee table** is a small low table in a living room. N-COUNT

**coffee-table book** **(coffee-table books)** A **coffee-table book** is a large expensive book with a lot of pictures, which is designed to be looked at rather than to be read properly, and is usually placed where people can see it easily. N-COUNT

**cof|fer** /kɒfəʳ/ **(coffers)** [1] A **coffer** is a large strong chest used for storing valuable objects such as money or gold and silver. [OLD-FASHIONED] N-COUNT [2] The **coffers of** an organization consist of the money that it has to spend, imagined as being collected together in one place. ❑ *The proceeds from the lottery go towards sports and recreation, as well as swelling the coffers of the government.* N-PLURAL: with supp, oft N of n, n N

**cof|fin** /kɒfɪn, AM kɔːfɪn/ **(coffins)** [1] A **coffin** is a box in which a dead body is buried or cremated. N-COUNT [2] If you say that one thing is **a nail in the coffin of** another thing, you mean that it will help bring about its end or failure. ❑ *A fine would be the final nail in the coffin of the airline.* PHRASE: oft PHR of n

**cog** /kɒg/ **(cogs)** [1] A **cog** is a wheel with square or triangular teeth around the edge, which is used in a machine to turn another wheel or part. N-COUNT [2] If you describe someone as **a cog in a machine** or **wheel**, you mean that they are a small part of a large organization or group. ❑ *Mr Lake was an important cog in the Republican campaign machine.* PHRASE: v-link PHR

**co|gent** /koʊdʒᵊnt/ A **cogent** reason, argument, or example is strong and convincing. [FORMAL] ❑ *There were perfectly cogent reasons why Julian Cavendish should be told of the Major's impending return.* ♦ **co|gen|cy** *The film makes its points with cogency and force.* ADJ = convincing; N-UNCOUNT

**cogi|tate** /kɒdʒɪteɪt/ **(cogitates, cogitating, cogitated)** If you **are cogitating**, you are thinking deeply about something. [FORMAL] ❑ *He sat silently cogitating. ...to cogitate on the meaning of life.* ♦ **cogi|ta|tion** /kɒdʒɪteɪʃᵊn/ *After much cogitation, we decided to move to the Isle of Wight.* VERB; V; V on/about n; N-UNCOUNT

**cog|nac** /kɒnjæk, AM koʊn-/ **(cognacs)** also **Cognac. Cognac** is a type of brandy made in the south west of France. ❑ *...a bottle of Cognac. ...one of the world's finest cognacs.* ♦ A **cognac** is a glass of cognac. ❑ *Phillips ordered a cognac.* N-MASS; N-COUNT

**cog|nate** /kɒgneɪt/ **Cognate** things are related to each other. [FORMAL] ❑ *...cognate words.* ADJ: oft ADJ with n

**cog|ni|sance** /kɒgnɪzᵊns/ → see **cognizance**.

**cog|ni|sant** /kɒgnɪzᵊnt/ → see **cognizant**.

**cog|ni|tion** /kɒgnɪʃᵊn/ **Cognition** is the mental process involved in knowing, learning, and understanding things. [FORMAL] ❑ *...processes of perception and cognition.* N-UNCOUNT

**cog|ni|tive** /kɒgnɪtɪv/ **Cognitive** means relating to the mental process involved in knowing, learning, and understanding things. [TECHNICAL or FORMAL] ❑ *As children grow older, their cognitive processes become sharper.* ADJ: ADJ n

**cog|ni|zance** /kɒgnɪzᵊns/

✔ in BRIT, also use **cognisance**

[1] If you **take cognizance of** something, you take notice of it or acknowledge it. [FORMAL] ❑ *The government failed to take cognisance of their protest.* PHRASE: V inflects = acknowledge

[2] **Cognizance** is knowledge or understanding. [FORMAL] ❑ *...the teacher's developing cognizance of the child's intellectual activity.* N-UNCOUNT: oft N of n

**cog|ni|zant** /kɒgnɪzᵊnt/

✔ in BRIT, also use **cognisant**

If someone is **cognizant of** something, they are aware of it or understand it. [FORMAL] ❑ *We are cognizant of the problem.* ADJ: v-link ADJ, usu ADJ of n = conscious

**co|gno|scen|ti** /kɒnjəʃenti/ The **cognoscenti** are the people who know a lot about a particular subject. [FORMAL] ❑ *She has an international reputation among film cognoscenti.* N-PLURAL: oft n N = connoisseurs

**co|hab|it** /koʊhæbɪt/ **(cohabits, cohabiting, cohabited)** If two people **are cohabiting**, they are living together and have a sexual relationship, but are not married. [FORMAL] ❑ *In Italy people hardly ever cohabit... The dentist left his wife of 15 years and openly cohabited with his receptionist... Any solicitor will tell you, if you're cohabiting and the man leaves you, you haven't got a leg to stand on.* ♦ **co|habi|ta|tion** /koʊhæbɪteɪʃᵊn/ *The decline in marriage has been offset by a rise in cohabitation.* V-RECIP; pl-n V; V with n; V (non-recip); N-UNCOUNT

**co|here** /koʊhɪəʳ/ **(coheres, cohering, cohered)** If the different elements of a piece of writing, a piece of music, or a set of ideas **cohere**, they fit together well so that they form a united whole. ❑ *The various elements of the novel fail to cohere... This coheres with Peel's championing of alternative music... The empire could not cohere as a legitimate whole.* V-RECIP = hang together; pl-n V; V with n; V (non-recip)

**co|her|ence** /koʊhɪərəns/ **Coherence** is a state or situation in which all the parts or ideas fit together well so that they form a united whole. ❑ *The anthology has a surprising sense of coherence.* N-UNCOUNT

**co|her|ent** /koʊhɪərənt/ [1] If something is **coherent**, it is well planned, so that it is clear and sensible and all its parts go well with each other. ❑ *He has failed to work out a coherent strategy for modernising the service... The President's policy is perfectly coherent.* ♦ **co|her|ence** *The campaign was widely criticised for making tactical mistakes and for a lack of coherence.* ADJ ≠ muddled; N-UNCOUNT

[2] If someone is **coherent**, they express their thoughts in a clear and calm way, so that other people can understand what they are saying. ❑ *He's so calm when he answers questions in interviews. I wish I could be that coherent.* ♦ **co|her|ence** *She lost consciousness and when she came round she still lacked coherence and focus.* ADJ: v-link ADJ ≠ incoherent; N-UNCOUNT

**co|he|sion** /koʊhiːʒᵊn/ If there is **cohesion** within a society, organization, or group, the different members fit together well and form a united whole. ❑ *By 1990, it was clear that the cohesion of the armed forces was rapidly breaking down.* N-UNCOUNT

**co|he|sive** /koʊhiːsɪv/ Something that is **cohesive** consists of parts that fit together well and form a united whole. ❑ *Huston had assembled a remarkably cohesive and sympathetic cast.* ADJ

**co|hort** /koʊhɔːʳt/ **(cohorts)** A person's **cohorts** are their friends, supporters, or associates. ❑ *Drake and his cohorts were not pleased with my appointment.* N-COUNT: usu poss N [disapproval]

**coiffed** /kwɑːft/ If someone has neatly **coiffed** hair, their hair is very carefully arranged. [FORMAL] ❑ *Her hair was perfectly coiffed.* ADJ: usu adv ADJ

**coif|fure** /kwɑːfjʊəʳ/ **(coiffures)** A person's **coiffure** is their hairstyle. [FORMAL] ❑ *...her immaculate golden coiffure.* N-COUNT

**coif|fured** /kwɑːfjʊəʳd/ **Coiffured** means the same as **coiffed**. [FORMAL] ADJ: usu adv ADJ

**coil** /kɔɪl/ **(coils, coiling, coiled)** [1] A **coil of** rope or wire is a length of it that has been wound into a series of loops. ❑ *Tod shook his head angrily and slung the coil of rope over his shoulder... The steel arrives at the factory in coils.* N-COUNT: oft N of n

[2] A **coil** is one loop in a series of loops. ❑ *Pythons kill by tightening their coils so that their victim cannot breathe.* N-COUNT

[3] A **coil** is a thick spiral of wire through which an electrical current passes. N-COUNT

[4] The **coil** is a contraceptive device used by women. It is fitted inside a woman's womb, usually for several months or years. N-COUNT: usu the N in sing

[5] If you **coil** something, you wind it into a series of loops or into the shape of a ring. If it **coils around** something, it forms loops or a ring. ❑ *He turned off the water and began to coil the hose... A huge rattlesnake lay coiled on the blanket.* ♦ **Coil up** means the same as **coil**. ❑ *Once we have the wire, we can coil it up into the shape of a spring... Her hair was coiled up on top of her head.* VERB; V n; V-ed; PHRASAL VERB; V n P; V-ed P; Also V P n (not pron)

**coiled** /kɔɪld/ **Coiled** means in the form of a series of loops. ❑ *...a heavy coiled spring. ...special coiled kettle flexes.* ADJ: ADJ n

**coin** /kɔɪn/ **(coins, coining, coined)** [1] A **coin** is a small piece of metal which is used as money. ❑ *...50 pence coins. ...Frederick's gold coin collection.* N-COUNT

[2] If you **coin** a word or a phrase, you are the first person to say it. ❑ *Jaron Lanier coined the term 'virtual reality' and pioneered its early development.* VERB; V n

**PHRASES** [3] You say **'to coin a phrase'** to show that you realize you are making a pun or using a cliché. ❑ *Fifty local musicians have, to coin a phrase, banded together to form the Jazz Umbrella.* PHRASE

[4] You use **the other side of the coin** to mention a different aspect of a situation. ❑ *These findings are a reminder that low pay is the other side of the coin of falling unemployment.* PHRASE: PHR with cl

**coin|age** /kɔɪnɪdʒ/ [1] **Coinage** is the coins which are used in a country. ❑ *...the world's finest collection of medieval European coinage.* N-UNCOUNT

[2] **Coinage** is the system of money used in a country. ❑ *It took four years for Britain just to decimalise its own coinage.* N-UNCOUNT

**co|in|cide** /koʊɪnsaɪd/ **(coincides, coinciding, coincided)** [1] If one event **coincides with** another, they happen at the same time. ❑ *The exhibition coincides with the 50th anniversary of his death... The beginning of the solar and lunar years coincided every 13 years.* V-RECIP; V with n; pl-n V

[2] If the ideas or interests of two or more people **coincide**, they are the same. ❑ *The kids' views on life don't always coincide, but they're not afraid of voicing their opinions... He gave great encouragement to his students, especially if their passions happened to coincide with his own.* V-RECIP; pl-n V; V with n

**co|in|ci|dence** /koʊɪnsɪdəns/ **(coincidences)** N-VAR A **coincidence** is when two or more similar or related events occur at the same time by chance and without any planning. ❑ *Mr. Berry said the timing was a coincidence and that his decision was unrelated to Mr. Roman's departure... The premises of Chabert and Sons were situated by the river and, by coincidence, not too far away from where Eric Talbot had met his death.*

**co|in|ci|dent** /koʊɪnsɪdənt/ 1 **Coincident** events happen at the same time. [FORMAL] ❑ *...coincident birth times... Coincident with the talks, the bank was permitted to open a New York branch.* ADJ: oft v-link ADJ *with* n 2 **Coincident** opinions, ideas, or policies are the same or are very similar to each other. [FORMAL] ❑ *Their aims are coincident with ours... Coincident interests with the corporate rich and political directorate are pointed out.* ADJ: oft v-link ADJ *with* n

**co|in|ci|dent|al** /koʊɪnsɪdentᵊl/ Something that is **coincidental** is the result of a coincidence and has not been deliberately arranged. ❑ *Any resemblance to actual persons, places or events is purely coincidental.* ADJ: usu v-link ADJ, oft *it* v-link ADJ that

**co|in|ci|dent|al|ly** /koʊɪnsɪdentli/ You use **coincidentally** when you want to draw attention to a coincidence. ❑ *Coincidentally, I had once found myself in a similar situation.* ADV: usu ADV with cl/group, also ADV before v

**coir** /kɔɪəʳ/ **Coir** is a rough material made from coconut shells which is used to make ropes and mats. N-UNCOUNT

**coi|tal** /koʊɪtᵊl/ **Coital** means connected with or relating to sexual intercourse. [TECHNICAL] ❑ *...coital techniques.* ADJ: ADJ n

**coi|tus** /koʊɪtəs/ **Coitus** is sexual intercourse. [TECHNICAL] N-UNCOUNT

**coke** /koʊk/ 1 **Coke** is a solid black substance that is produced from coal and is burned as a fuel. ❑ *...a coke-burning stove.* N-UNCOUNT 2 **Coke** is the same as **cocaine**. [INFORMAL] N-UNCOUNT

**col.** **(cols) col.** is a written abbreviation for **column** and **colour**.

**Col.** **Col.** is a written abbreviation for **Colonel** when it is being used as a title in front of someone's name. ❑ *...Col. Frank Weldon.* N-TITLE

**cola** /koʊlə/ **(colas) Cola** is a sweet brown non-alcoholic fizzy drink. ❑ *...a can of cola.* N-MASS

**co|la|da** /kɒlɑːdə/ **(coladas)** → see **pina colada**.

**col|an|der** /kɒləndə, kʌl-/ **(colanders)** A **colander** is a container in the shape of a bowl with holes in it which you wash or drain food in. N-COUNT

**cold** /koʊld/ **(colder, coldest, colds)** ◆◆◇

1 Something that is **cold** has a very low temperature or a lower temperature than is normal or acceptable. ❑ *Rinse the vegetables under cold running water... He likes his tea neither too hot nor too cold... Your dinner's getting cold.* ◆ **cold|ness** *She complained about the coldness of his hands.* ADJ ≠hot, warm; N-UNCOUNT: usu with supp

2 If it is **cold**, or if a place is **cold**, the temperature of the air is very low. ❑ *It was bitterly cold... The house is cold because I can't afford to turn the heat on... This is the coldest winter I can remember.* ◆ **cold|ness** *Within quarter of an hour the coldness of the night had gone.* ADJ: oft *it* v-link ADJ; ADJ ≠hot, warm; N-UNCOUNT: usu with supp

3 Cold weather or low temperatures can be referred to as **the cold**. ❑ *He must have come inside to get out of the cold... His feet were blue with cold.* N-UNCOUNT: also *the* N ≠heat

4 If you are **cold**, your body is at an unpleasantly low temperature. ❑ *I was freezing cold... I'm hungry, I'm cold and I've nowhere to sleep.* ADJ: usu v-link ADJ

5 **Cold** food, such as salad or meat that has been cooked and cooled, is not intended to be eaten hot. ❑ *A wide variety of hot and cold snacks will be available. ...cold meats.* ADJ: usu ADJ n ≠hot

6 **Cold** colours or **cold** light give an impression of coldness. ❑ *Generally, warm colours advance in painting and cold colours recede. ...the cold blue light from a streetlamp.* ADJ ≠warm

7 A **cold** person does not show much emotion, especially affection, and therefore seems unfriendly and unsympathetic. If someone's voice is **cold**, they speak in an unfriendly unsympathetic way. ❑ *What a cold, unfeeling woman she was... 'Send her away,' Eve said in a cold, hard voice.* ◆ **cold|ly** *'I'll see you in the morning,' Hugh said to her coldly.* ◆ **cold|ness** *His coldness angered her.* ADJ disapproval ≠warm; ADV; N-UNCOUNT

8 A **cold** trail or scent is one which is old and therefore difficult to follow. ❑ *He could follow a cold trail over hard ground and even over stones.* ADJ ≠fresh

9 If you have a **cold**, you have a mild, very common illness which makes you sneeze a lot and gives you a sore throat or a cough. N-COUNT

10 → See also **common cold**.

**PHRASES** 11 If you **catch cold**, or **catch a cold**, you become ill with a cold. ❑ *Let's dry our hair so we don't catch cold.* PHRASE: V inflects 12 If something **leaves** you **cold**, it fails to excite or interest you. ❑ *Lawrence is one of those writers who either excite you enormously or leave you cold.* PHRASE: V inflects 13 If someone is **out cold**, they are unconscious or sleeping very heavily. ❑ *She was out cold but still breathing.* PHRASE: v-link PHR 14 **in cold blood** → see **blood**. to **get cold feet** → see **foot**. to **blow hot and cold** → see **hot**. to **pour cold water on** something → see **water**.

**cold-blooded** 1 Someone who is **cold-blooded** does not show any pity or emotion. ❑ *...a cold-blooded murderer... This was a brutal and cold-blooded killing.* ADJ disapproval 2 **Cold-blooded** animals have a body temperature that changes according to the surrounding temperature. Reptiles, for example, are cold-blooded. ADJ ≠warm-blooded

**cold call** **(cold calls, cold calling, cold called)**

1 If someone makes a **cold call**, they telephone or visit someone they have never contacted, without making an appointment, in order to try and sell something. ❑ *She had worked as a call centre operator making cold calls for time-share holidays.* N-COUNT

2 To **cold call** means to make a cold call. ❑ *You should refuse to meet anyone who cold calls with an offer of financial advice.* ◆ **cold calling** *We will adhere to strict sales ethics, with none of the cold calling that has given the industry such a bad name.* VERB V, Also V n; N-UNCOUNT

**cold com|fort** If you say that a slightly encouraging fact or event is **cold comfort to** someone, you mean that it gives them little or no comfort because their situation is so difficult or unpleasant. ❑ *These figures may look good on paper but are cold comfort to the islanders themselves.* N-UNCOUNT: oft N *to/for* n

**cold cuts** **Cold cuts** are thin slices of cooked meat which are served cold. [AM] N-PLURAL

**cold fish** If you say that someone is a **cold fish**, you think that they are unfriendly and unemotional. N-SING disapproval

**cold frame** **(cold frames)** A **cold frame** is a wooden frame with a glass top in which you grow small plants to protect them from cold weather. N-COUNT

**cold-hearted** A **cold-hearted** person does not feel any affection or sympathy towards other people. ❑ *...a cold-hearted killer.* ADJ: usu ADJ n disapproval ≠warm-hearted

**cold shoul|der** **(cold-shoulders, cold-shouldering, cold-shouldered)**

✔ The form **cold-shoulder** is used for the verb.

1 If one person gives another **the cold shoulder**, they behave towards them in an unfriendly way, to show them that they do not care about them or that they want them to go away. ❑ *But when Gough looked to Haig for support, he was given the cold shoulder.* N-SING: usu *the* N

2 If one person **cold-shoulders** another, they give them the cold-shoulder. ❑ *Even her own party considered her shrewish and nagging, and cold-shouldered her in the corridors.* VERB V n

**cold snap** **(cold snaps)** A **cold snap** is a short period of cold and icy weather. N-COUNT: usu sing

**cold sore** **(cold sores)** **Cold sores** are small sore spots that sometimes appear on or near someone's lips and nose when they have a cold. [mainly BRIT] N-COUNT

✔ in AM, usually use **fever blister**

**cold stor|age** If something such as food is put in **cold storage**, it is kept in an artificially N-UNCOUNT cooled place in order to preserve it. ❑ *The strawberries are kept in cold storage to prevent them spoiling during transportation.*

**cold store (cold stores)** A **cold store** is a building or room which is artificially cooled so that food can be preserved in it. [BRIT] N-COUNT

**cold sweat (cold sweats)** If you are **in a cold sweat**, you are sweating and feel cold, usually because you are very afraid or nervous. ❑ *He awoke from his sleep in a cold sweat.* N-COUNT: usu sing, usu *in/into* N

**cold tur|key** **Cold turkey** is the unpleasant physical reaction that people experience when they suddenly stop taking a drug that they have become addicted to. [INFORMAL] ❑ *The quickest way to get her off the drug was to let her go cold turkey.* N-UNCOUNT

**Cold War** also **cold war. The Cold War** was the period of hostility and tension between the Soviet bloc and the Western powers that followed the Second World War. ❑ *...the first major crisis of the post-Cold War era.* N-PROPER: *the* N

**cole|slaw** /koʊlslɔː/ **Coleslaw** is a salad of chopped raw cabbage, carrots, onions, and sometimes other vegetables, usually with mayonnaise. N-UNCOUNT

**col|ic** /kɒlɪk/ **Colic** is an illness in which you get severe pains in your stomach and bowels. Babies especially suffer from colic. N-UNCOUNT

**col|icky** /kɒlɪki/ If someone, especially a baby, is **colicky**, they are suffering from colic. ADJ

**co|li|tis** /kəlaɪtɪs/ **Colitis** is an illness in which your colon becomes inflamed. [TECHNICAL] N-UNCOUNT

**col|labo|rate** /kəlæbəreɪt/ **(collaborates, collaborating, collaborated)** 1 When one person or group **collaborates with** another, they work together, especially on a book or on some research. ❑ *He collaborated with his son Michael on the English translation of a text on food production... The government is urging Japan's firms to collaborate with foreigners. ...a place where professionals and amateurs collaborated in the making of music... The two men met and agreed to collaborate.* 2 If someone **collaborates with** an enemy that is occupying their country during a war, they help them. ❑ *He was accused of having collaborated with the secret police.* V-RECIP; V *with* n *on/in* n/-ing; V *with* n; pl-n V *on/in* n/-ing; pl-n V; VERB [disapproval]; V *with* n; Also V

**col|labo|ra|tion** /kəlæbəreɪʃən/ **(collaborations)** 1 **Collaboration** is the act of working together to produce a piece of work, especially a book or some research. ❑ *Close collaboration between the Bank and the Fund is not merely desirable, it is essential. ...scientific collaborations... Drummond was working on a book in collaboration with Zodiac Mindwarp.* 2 A **collaboration** is a piece of work that has been produced as the result of people or groups working together. ❑ *He was also a writer of beautiful stories, some of which are collaborations with his fiancee.* 3 **Collaboration** is the act of helping an enemy who is occupying your country during a war. ❑ *She faced charges of collaboration.* N-VAR: oft N *with* n, N *between* pl-n, *in* N; N-COUNT: usu N *between* pl-n, N *with* n; N-UNCOUNT: usu with supp, oft N *with* n [disapproval]

**col|labo|ra|tion|ist** /kəlæbəreɪʃənɪst/ A **collaborationist** government or individual is one that helps or gives support to the enemy during the war. ❑ *Quinn headed the collaborationist government throughout the war.* ADJ: usu ADJ n [disapproval]

**col|labo|ra|tive** /kəlæbərətɪv, AM -reɪt-/ A **collaborative** piece of work is done by two or more people or groups working together. [FORMAL] ❑ *...a collaborative research project... 'The First Day' is their first collaborative album.* ADJ: ADJ n

**col|labo|ra|tor** /kəlæbəreɪtəʳ/ **(collaborators)** 1 A **collaborator** is someone that you work with to produce a piece of work, especially a book or some research. ❑ *The Irvine group and their collaborators are testing whether lasers do the job better.* 2 A **collaborator** is someone who helps an enemy who is occupying their country during a war. ❑ *Two alleged collaborators were shot dead by masked activists.* N-COUNT: oft poss N; N-COUNT [disapproval]

**col|lage** /kɒlɑːʒ, AM kəlɑːʒ/ **(collages)** 1 A **collage** is a picture that has been made by sticking pieces of coloured paper and cloth onto paper. 2 **Collage** is the method of making pictures by sticking pieces of coloured paper and cloth onto paper. N-COUNT; N-UNCOUNT

**col|la|gen** /kɒlədʒən/ **Collagen** is a protein that is found in the bodies of people and animals. It is often used as an ingredient in cosmetics or is injected into the face in cosmetic surgery, in order to make the skin look younger. ❑ *The collagen that is included in face creams comes from animal skin. ...collagen injections.* N-UNCOUNT

**col|lapse** /kəlæps/ **(collapses, collapsing, collapsed)** ◆◆◇ 1 If a building or other structure **collapses**, it falls down very suddenly. ❑ *A section of the Bay Bridge had collapsed... Most of the deaths were caused by landslides and collapsing buildings.* ♦ **Collapse** is also a noun. ❑ *Governor Deukmejian called for an inquiry into the freeway's collapse.* 2 If something, for example a system or institution, **collapses**, it fails or comes to an end completely and suddenly. ❑ *His business empire collapsed under a massive burden of debt... The rural people have been impoverished by a collapsing economy.* ♦ **Collapse** is also a noun. ❑ *The coup's collapse has speeded up the drive to independence... Their economy is teetering on the brink of collapse.* 3 If you **collapse**, you suddenly faint or fall down because you are very ill or weak. ❑ *He collapsed following a vigorous exercise session at his home.* ♦ **Collapse** is also a noun. ❑ *A few days after his collapse he was sitting up in bed.* 4 If you **collapse** onto something, you sit or lie down suddenly because you are very tired. ❑ *She arrived home exhausted and barely capable of showering before collapsing on her bed.* VERB; V; V-ing; N-UNCOUNT; VERB; V; V-ing; N-UNCOUNT; VERB; V; N-UNCOUNT; VERB; V prep; Also V

**col|laps|ible** /kəlæpsɪbəl/ A **collapsible** object is designed to be folded flat when it is not being used. ❑ *...a collapsible chair.* ADJ: usu ADJ n = folding

**col|lar** /kɒləʳ/ **(collars, collaring, collared)** 1 The **collar** of a shirt or coat is the part which fits round the neck and is usually folded over. ❑ *His tie was pulled loose and his collar hung open. ...a coat with a huge fake fur collar.* ➔ See also **blue-collar, dog-collar, white-collar.** 2 A **collar** is a band of leather or plastic which is put round the neck of a dog or cat. 3 If you **collar** someone who has done something wrong or who is running away, you catch them and hold them so that they cannot escape. [INFORMAL] ❑ *As Kerr fled towards the exit, Boycott collared him at the ticket barrier.* N-COUNT; N-COUNT; VERB = grab; V n

**collar|bone** /kɒləʳboʊn/ **(collarbones)**

✔ in BRIT, also use **collar bone**

Your **collarbones** are the two long bones which run from throat to your shoulders. ❑ *Harold had a broken collarbone.* N-COUNT

**col|lar|less** /kɒləʳləs/ A **collarless** shirt or jacket has no collar. ADJ: ADJ n

**col|late** /kəleɪt/ **(collates, collating, collated)** When you **collate** pieces of information, you gather them all together and examine them. ❑ *Roberts has spent much of his working life collating the data on which the study was based.* ♦ **col|la|tion** /kəleɪʃən/ *Many countries have no laws governing the collation of personal information.* VERB; V n; N-UNCOUNT: oft N *of* n

**col|lat|er|al** /kəlætərəl/ **Collateral** is money or property which is used as a guarantee that someone will repay a loan. [FORMAL] ❑ *Most people here cannot borrow from banks because they lack collateral.* N-UNCOUNT: oft *as* N = security

**col|lat|er|al dam|age** **Collateral damage** is accidental injury to non-military people or damage to non-military buildings which occurs during a military operation. ❑ *To minimize collateral damage maximum precision in bombing was required.* N-UNCOUNT

**col|league** /kɒliːg/ **(colleagues)** ◆◆◇ Your **colleagues** are the people you work with, especially in a professional job. ❑ *A colleague urged him to see a psychiatrist, but Faulkner refused.* N-COUNT: oft with poss

**col|lect** /kəlekt/ **(collects, collecting, collected)** ◆◆◇ 1 If you **collect** a number of things, you bring them together from several places or from VERB = gather several people. ❑ *Two young girls were collecting firewood on the beach... 1.5 million signatures have been collected this week alone.* [2] If you **collect** things, such as stamps or books, as a hobby, you get a large number of them over a period of time because they interest you. ❑ *One of Tony's hobbies was collecting rare birds.* ♦ **col|lect|ing** *...hobbies like stamp collecting, reading and fishing.* [3] When you **collect** someone or something, you go and get them from the place where they are waiting for you or have been left for you. [BRIT] ❑ *David always collects Alistair from school on Wednesdays... After collecting the cash, the kidnapper made his escape down the disused railway line.* V n / V n / VERB / V n / N-UNCOUNT: with supp, oft n N / VERB = pick up / V n from n / V n

✓ in AM, usually use **pick up**

[4] If a substance **collects** somewhere, or if something **collects** it, it keeps arriving over a period of time and is held in that place or thing. ❑ *Methane gas does collect in the mines around here. ...water tanks which collect rainwater from the house roof.* [5] If something **collects** light, energy, or heat, it attracts it. ❑ *Like a telescope it has a curved mirror to collect the sunlight.* [6] If you **collect for** a charity or **for** a present for someone, you ask people to give you money for it. ❑ *Are you collecting for charity?... They collected donations for a fund to help military families.* [7] If you **collect yourself** or **collect** your thoughts, you make an effort to calm yourself or prepare yourself mentally. ❑ *She paused for a moment to collect herself... He was grateful for a chance to relax and collect his thoughts.* [8] A **collect call** is a telephone call that is paid for by the person receiving it, not the person making it. [AM] ❑ *She received a collect phone call from Alaska.* ● If you **call collect** when you make a telephone call, the person who you are phoning pays the cost of the call and not you. [AM] ❑ *Should you lose your ticket call collect on STA's helpline.* VERB / V prep/adv / V n / Also V / VERB / V n / VERB / V for n / V n for n / Also V n / VERB = compose / V pron-refl / V n / ADJ: ADJ n / PHRASE: V inflects

✓ in BRIT, usually use **reverse the charges**

**col|lect|able** /kəle̱ktəbᵊl/ also **collectible.** A **collectable** object is one which is valued very highly by collectors because it is rare or beautiful. ❑ *Many of these cushions have survived and are very collectible.* ADJ

**col|lect|ed** /kəle̱ktɪd/ [1] An author's **collected** works or letters are all their works or letters published in one book or in a set of books. ❑ *...the collected works of Rudyard Kipling.* [2] If you say that someone is **collected**, you mean that they are very calm and self-controlled, especially when they are in a difficult or serious situation. ❑ *Police say she was cool and collected during her interrogation.* [3] → See also **collect**. ADJ: ADJ n = complete / ADJ: usu v-link ADJ

**col|lect|ible** /kəle̱ktɪbᵊl/ → see **collectable**.

**col|lect|ing** /kəle̱ktɪŋ/ A **collecting** tin or box is one that is used to collect money for charity. [BRIT] ADJ: ADJ n

✓ in AM, use **collection box**

→ See also **collect**.

**col|lec|tion** /kəle̱kʃᵊn/ **(collections)** [1] A **collection** of things is a group of similar things that you have deliberately acquired, usually over a period of time. ❑ *The Art Gallery of Ontario has the world's largest collection of sculptures by Henry Moore... He made the mistake of leaving his valuable record collection with a former girlfriend.* [2] A **collection of** stories, poems, or articles is a number of them published in one book. ❑ *The Brookings Institution has assembled a collection of essays from foreign affairs experts.* [3] A **collection of** things is a group of things. ❑ *Wye Lea is a collection of farm buildings that have been converted into an attractive complex.* [4] A fashion designer's new **collection** consists of the new clothes they have designed for the next season. [5] **Collection** is the act of collecting something from a place or from people. ❑ *Money can be sent to any one of 22,000 agents worldwide for collection. ...computer systems to speed up collection of information.* [6] If you organize a **collection** for charity, you collect money from people to give to charity. ❑ *I asked my headmaster if he could arrange a collection for a refugee charity.* [7] A **collection** is money that is given by people in church during some Christian services. ◆◆◇ N-COUNT: oft N of n / N-COUNT: oft N of n / N-COUNT: usu N of n / N-COUNT / N-UNCOUNT / N-COUNT / N-COUNT

**col|lec|tion box (collection boxes)** A **collection box** is a box or tin that is used to collect money for charity. [AM] N-COUNT

**col|lec|tive** /kəle̱ktɪv/ **(collectives)** [1] **Collective** actions, situations, or feelings involve or are shared by every member of a group of people. ❑ *It was a collective decision... The country's politicians are already heaving a collective sigh of relief.* ♦ **col|lec|tive|ly** *The Cabinet is collectively responsible for policy.* [2] A **collective** amount of something is the total obtained by adding together the amounts that each person or thing in a group has. ❑ *Their collective volume wasn't very large.* ♦ **col|lec|tive|ly** *In 1968 the states collectively spent $2 billion on it.* [3] The **collective** term for two or more types of thing is a general word or expression which refers to all of them. ❑ *Social science is a collective name, covering a series of individual sciences.* ♦ **col|lec|tive|ly** *...other sorts of cells (known collectively as white corpuscles).* [4] A **collective** is a business or farm which is run, and often owned, by a group of people who take an equal share of any profits. [BUSINESS] ❑ *He will see that he is participating in all the decisions of the collective.* ◆◇◇ ADJ: ADJ n = joint / ADV: oft ADV with cl / ADJ: ADJ n = combined / ADV: ADV with v / ADJ: ADJ n / ADV: ADV with v / N-COUNT = co-operative

**col|lec|tive bar|gain|ing** When a trade union engages in **collective bargaining**, it has talks with an employer about its members' pay and working conditions. [BUSINESS] N-UNCOUNT

**col|lec|tive noun (collective nouns)** A **collective noun** is a noun such as 'family' or 'team' that refers to a group of people or things. N-COUNT

**col|lec|tive un|con|scious** In psychology, **the collective unconscious** consists of the basic ideas and images that all people are believed to share because they have inherited them. N-SING: usu *the* N

**col|lec|ti|vise** /kəle̱ktɪvaɪz/ → see **collectivize.**

**col|lec|tiv|ism** /kəle̱ktɪvɪzəm/ **Collectivism** is the political belief that a country's industries and services should be owned and controlled by the state or by all the people in a country. Socialism and communism are both forms of collectivism. N-UNCOUNT

**col|lec|tiv|ist** /kəle̱ktɪvɪst/ **Collectivist** means relating to collectivism. ❑ *...collectivist ideals.* ADJ: usu ADJ n

**col|lec|ti|vize** /kəle̱ktɪvaɪz/ **(collectivizes, collectivizing, collectivized)**

✓ in BRIT, also use **collectivise**

If farms or factories **are collectivized**, they are brought under state ownership and control, usually by combining a number of small farms or factories into one large one. ❑ *Most large businesses were collectivized at the start of the war... He forced the country to collectivize agriculture. ...large collectivised farms.* ♦ **col|lec|tivi|za|tion** /kəle̱ktɪvaɪze̱ɪʃᵊn/ *...the collectivisation of agriculture.* VERB / *be* V-ed / V n / V-ed / N-UNCOUNT: oft N of n

**col|lec|tor** /kəle̱ktəʳ/ **(collectors)** [1] A **collector** is a person who collects things of a particular type as a hobby. ❑ *...a stamp-collector. ...a respected collector of Indian art.* [2] You can use **collector** to refer to someone whose job is to take something such as money, tickets, or rubbish from people. For example, a rent **collector** collects rent from people. ❑ *He earned his living as a tax collector. ...a garbage collector.* N-COUNT: oft n N, N of n / N-COUNT: with supp, usu n N

**col|lec|tor's item (collector's items)** A **collector's item** is an object which is highly valued by collectors because it is rare or beautiful. N-COUNT

**col|lege** /kɒ̱lɪdʒ/ **(colleges)** [1] A **college** is an institution where students study after they have left school. ❑ *Their daughter Joanna is doing business studies at a local college... He is now a profes-* ◆◆◇ N-VAR; N-IN-NAMES *sor of economics at Western New England College in Springfield, Massachusetts.* [2] A **college** is one of the institutions which some British universities are divided into. ❑ *He was educated at Balliol College, Oxford.* N-COUNT: oft in names after n [3] At some universities in the United States, **colleges** are divisions which offer degrees in particular subjects. ❑ *...a professor at the University of Florida College of Law.* N-COUNT; N-IN-NAMES [4] **College** is used in Britain in the names of some secondary schools which charge fees. ❑ *In 1854, Cheltenham Ladies' College became the first girls' public school.* N-IN-NAMES

**col|legi|ate** /kəliːdʒiət/ **Collegiate** means belonging or relating to a college or to college students. [mainly AM] ❑ *The 1933 national collegiate football championship was won by Michigan. ...collegiate life.* ADJ: ADJ n = college

**col|lide** /kəlaɪd/ **(collides, colliding, collided)** [1] If two or more moving people or objects **collide**, they crash into one another. If a moving person or object **collides with** a person or object that is not moving, they crash into them. ❑ *Two trains collided head-on in north-eastern Germany early this morning... Racing up the stairs, he almost collided with Daisy... He collided with a pine tree near the North Gate.* V-RECIP; pl-n V; V with n; V with n (non-recip) [2] If the aims, opinions, or interests of one person or group **collide with** those of another person or group, they are very different from each other and are therefore opposed. ❑ *The aims of the negotiators in New York again seem likely to collide with the aims of the warriors in the field... What happens when the two interests collide will make a fascinating spectacle.* V-RECIP = clash; V with n; pl-n V

**col|lie** /kɒli/ **(collies)** A **collie** or a **collie dog** is a dog with long hair and a long, narrow nose. N-COUNT

**col|liery** /kɒljəri/ **(collieries)** A **colliery** is a coal mine and all the buildings and equipment which are connected with it. [BRIT] N-COUNT = pit

**col|li|sion** /kəlɪʒən/ **(collisions)** [1] A **collision** occurs when a moving object crashes into something. ❑ *They were on their way to the Shropshire Union Canal when their van was involved in a collision with a car... I saw a head-on collision between two aeroplanes.* N-VAR: oft N with/between n = crash [2] A **collision of** cultures or ideas occurs when two very different cultures or people meet and conflict. ❑ *The play represents the collision of three generations.* N-COUNT: oft N of/between/with n = clash

**col|li|sion course** [1] If two or more people or things are **on a collision course**, there is likely to be a sudden and violent disagreement between them. ❑ *The two communities are now on a collision course... Britain's universities are set on a collision course with the government.* N-SING: usu on a N, oft N with n [2] If two or more people or things are **on a collision course**, they are likely to meet and crash into each other violently. ❑ *There is an asteroid on a collision course with the Earth.* N-SING: usu on a N, oft N with n

**col|lo|cate** **(collocates, collocating, collocated)**

> ✔ The noun is pronounced /kɒləkət/. The verb is pronounced /kɒləkeɪt/.

[1] In linguistics, a **collocate** of a particular word is another word which often occurs with that word. [TECHNICAL] N-COUNT [2] In linguistics, if one word **collocates with** another, they often occur together. [TECHNICAL] ❑ *'Detached' collocates with 'house'.* V-RECIP; V with n; Also pl-n V

**col|lo|ca|tion** /kɒləkeɪʃən/ **(collocations)** In linguistics, **collocation** is the way that some words occur regularly whenever another word is used. [TECHNICAL] ❑ *...the basic notion of collocation.* N-VAR

**col|lo|quial** /kəloʊkwiəl/ **Colloquial** words and phrases are informal and are used mainly in conversation. ❑ *...a colloquial expression.* ADJ
♦ **col|lo|qui|al|ly** *The people who write parking tickets in New York are known colloquially as 'brownies'.* ADV: ADV with v

**col|lo|qui|al|ism** /kəloʊkwiəlɪzəm/ **(colloquialisms)** A **colloquialism** is a colloquial word or phrase. N-COUNT

**col|lude** /kəluːd/ **(colludes, colluding, colluded)** If one person **colludes with** another, they co-operate with them secretly or illegally. ❑ *Several local officials are in jail on charges of colluding with the Mafia... My mother colluded in the myth of him as the swanky businessman... The store's 'no refunds' policy makes it harder for dishonest cashiers and customers to collude.* V-RECIP; disapproval; V with n; V in n/-ing; pl-n V

**col|lu|sion** /kəluːʒən/ **Collusion** is secret or illegal co-operation, especially between countries or organizations. [FORMAL] ❑ *He found no evidence of collusion between record companies and retailers.* N-UNCOUNT: usu N between pl-n, N with n, in N; disapproval

**col|lu|sive** /kəluːsɪv/ **Collusive** behaviour involves secret or illegal co-operation, especially between countries or organizations. [FORMAL] ❑ *...collusive business practices.* ADJ: usu ADJ n; disapproval

**co|logne** /kəloʊn/ **(colognes)** **Cologne** is a kind of weak perfume. N-MASS = eau de cologne

**Co|lom|bian** /kəlʌmbiən/ **(Colombians)** [1] **Colombian** means belonging or relating to Colombia or its people or culture. ADJ [2] A **Colombian** is a Colombian citizen, or a person of Colombian origin. N-COUNT

**co|lon** /koʊlən/ **(colons)** [1] A **colon** is the punctuation mark : which you can use in several ways. For example, you can put it before a list of things or before reported speech. N-COUNT [2] Your **colon** is the part of your intestine above your rectum. ❑ *...cancer of the colon.* N-COUNT

**colo|nel** /kɜːʳnəl/ **(colonels)** A **colonel** is a senior officer in an army, air force, or the marines. ❑ *This particular place was run by an ex-Army colonel. ...Colonel Edward Staley.* ◆◇◇ N-COUNT; N-TITLE; N-VOC

**co|lo|nial** /kəloʊniəl/ [1] **Colonial** means relating to countries that are colonies, or to colonialism. ❑ *...the 31st anniversary of Jamaica's independence from British colonial rule. ...the colonial civil service.* ADJ: ADJ n [2] A **Colonial** building or piece of furniture was built or made in a style that was popular in America in the 17th and 18th centuries. [mainly AM] ❑ *...the white colonial houses on the north side of the campus.* ADJ: usu ADJ n

**co|lo|ni|al|ism** /kəloʊniəlɪzəm/ **Colonialism** is the practice by which a powerful country directly controls less powerful countries and uses their resources to increase its own power and wealth. ❑ *...the bitter oppression of slavery and colonialism... It is interesting to reflect why European colonialism ended.* N-UNCOUNT

**co|lo|ni|al|ist** /kəloʊniəlɪst/ **(colonialists)** [1] **Colonialist** means relating to colonialism. ❑ *...the European colonialist powers.* ADJ [2] A **colonialist** is a person who believes in colonialism or helps their country to get colonies. ❑ *...rulers who were imposed on the people by the colonialists.* N-COUNT

**colo|nist** /kɒlənɪst/ **(colonists)** **Colonists** are the people who start a colony or the people who are among the first to live in a particular colony. ❑ *...the early American colonists.* N-COUNT

**colo|nize** /kɒlənaɪz/ **(colonizes, colonizing, colonized)**

> ✔ in BRIT, also use **colonise**

[1] If people **colonize** a foreign country, they go to live there and take control of it. ❑ *The first British attempt to colonize Ireland was in the twelfth century... For more than 400 years, we were a colonized people.* VERB; V n; V-ed [2] When large numbers of animals **colonize** a place, they go to live there and make it their home. ❑ *Toads are colonising the whole place.* VERB; V n [3] When an area **is colonized by** a type of plant, the plant grows there in large amounts. ❑ *The area was then colonized by scrub.* VERB: usu passive be V-ed by n

**col|on|nade** /kɒləneɪd/ **(colonnades)** A **colonnade** is a row of evenly spaced columns. ❑ *...a colonnade with stone pillars.* N-COUNT

**col|on|nad|ed** /kɒləneɪdɪd/ A **colonnaded** building has evenly spaced columns. ADJ: ADJ n

**colo|ny** /kɒləni/ **(colonies)** [1] A **colony** is a country which is controlled by a more powerful country. ❑ *In France's former North African colonies, anti-French feeling is growing.* N-COUNT: usu supp N [2] You can refer to a N-COUNT:

place where a particular group of people lives as a particular kind of **colony**. ❑ *...a penal colony. ...industrial colonies.* 3 A **colony of** birds, insects, or animals is a group of them that live together. ❑ *The Shetlands are famed for their colonies of sea birds.* — usu with supp; N-COUNT: oft N *of* n

**col|or** /kʌləʳ/ → see **colour**.

**col|ora|tion** /kʌləreɪʃᵊn/ The **coloration** of an animal or a plant is the colours and patterns on it. ❑ *...plants with yellow or red coloration.* — N-UNCOUNT

**colo|ra|tu|ra** /kɒlərətʊərə, AM kʌl-/ **(coloraturas)** 1 **Coloratura** is very complicated and difficult music for a solo singer, especially in opera. [TECHNICAL] 2 A **coloratura** is a singer, usually a woman, who is skilled at singing coloratura. [TECHNICAL] — N-UNCOUNT; N-COUNT: oft N n

**col|ori|za|tion** /kʌləraɪzeɪʃᵊn/ **Colorization** is a technique used to add colour to old black and white films. ❑ *...the colorization of old film classics.* — N-UNCOUNT

**col|or|ized** /kʌləraɪzd/ A **colorized** film is an old black and white film which has had colour added to it using a special technique. ❑ *The film is available in a colorized version.* — ADJ: usu ADJ n

**co|los|sal** /kəlɒsᵊl/ If you describe something as **colossal**, you are emphasizing that it is very large. ❑ *There has been a colossal waste of public money... The task they face is colossal.* ♦ **co|los|sal|ly** *Their policies have been colossally destructive.* — ADJ [emphasis] = enormous, immense; ADV: ADV adj

**co|los|sus** /kəlɒsəs/ **(colossi** /kəlɒsaɪ/**)** 1 If you describe someone or something as a **colossus**, you think that they are extremely important and great in ability or size. [JOURNALISM] ❑ *...saxophone colossus Sonny Rollins... He became a colossus of the labour movement.* 2 A **colossus** is an extremely large statue. — N-COUNT: usu sing, oft N *of* n [emphasis] = giant; N-COUNT

**co|los|to|my** /kəlɒstəmi/ **(colostomies)** A **colostomy** is a surgical operation in which a permanent opening from the colon is made. [MEDICAL] — N-COUNT

**col|our** /kʌləʳ/ **(colours, colouring, coloured)** ♦♦♦

☑ in AM, use **color**

1 The **colour** of something is the appearance that it has as a result of the way in which it reflects light. Red, blue, and green are colours. ❑ *'What colour is the car?' — 'Red.'... Her silk dress was sky-blue, the colour of her eyes... Judi's favourite colour is pink... The badges come in twenty different colours and shapes.* — N-COUNT: usu with supp
2 A **colour** is a substance you use to give something a particular colour. Dyes and make-up are sometimes referred to as **colours**. ❑ *...The Body Shop Herbal Hair Colour... It is better to avoid all food colours. ...the latest lip and eye colours.* — N-VAR
3 If you **colour** something, you use something such as dyes or paint to change its colour. ❑ *Many women begin colouring their hair in their mid-30s... We'd been making cakes and colouring the posters... The petals can be cooked with rice to colour it yellow.* ♦ **col|our|ing** *They could not afford to spoil those maps by careless colouring.* — VERB; V n; V n; V n colour; N-UNCOUNT
4 If someone **colours**, their face becomes redder than it normally is, usually because they are embarrassed. ❑ *Andrew couldn't help noticing that she coloured slightly.* — VERB = blush; V
5 Someone's **colour** is the colour of their skin. People often use **colour** in this way to refer to a person's race. ❑ *I don't care what colour she is... He acknowledged that Mr Taylor's colour and ethnic origins were utterly irrelevant in the circumstances.* — N-COUNT: usu sing, oft poss N [politeness]
6 A **colour** television, photograph, or picture is one that shows things in all their colours, and not just in black, white, and grey. ❑ *In Japan 99 per cent of all households now have a colour television set.* — ADJ: usu ADJ n
7 **Colour** is a quality that makes something especially interesting or exciting. ❑ *She had resumed the travel necessary to add depth and colour to her novels.* → See also **local colour**. — N-UNCOUNT
8 If something **colours** your opinion, it affects the way that you think about something. ❑ *The attitude of the parents toward the usefulness of what is learned must colour the way children approach school.* — VERB = affect; V n
9 A country's national **colours** are the colours of its national flag. ❑ *The Opera House is decorated with the Hungarian national colours: green, red and white.* — N-PLURAL
10 People sometimes refer to the flag of a particular part of an army, navy, or air force, or the flag of a particular country as its **colours**. ❑ *Troops raised the country's colors in a special ceremony. ...the battalion's colours.* — N-PLURAL: poss N
11 A sports team's **colours** are the colours of the clothes they wear when they play. ❑ *I was wearing the team's colours.* — N-PLURAL
12 → See also **coloured**, **colouring**.

PHRASES 13 If you pass a test **with flying colours**, you have done very well in the test. ❑ *So far McAllister seemed to have passed all the tests with flying colors.* — PHRASE: PHR after v
14 If a film or television programme is **in colour**, it has been made so that you see the picture in all its colours, and not just in black, white, or grey. ❑ *Was he going to show the film? Was it in colour?* — PHRASE: v-link PHR, PHR after v
15 People **of colour** are people who belong to a race with dark skins. ❑ *Black communities spoke up to defend the rights of all people of color.* — PHRASE: n PHR [politeness]
16 If you see someone **in their true colours** or if they **show** their **true colours**, you realize what they are really like. ❑ *The children are seeing him in his true colours for the first time now... Here, the organization has had time to show its true colours, to show its inefficiency and its bungling.* — PHRASE: PHR after v

♦ **colour in** If you **colour in** a drawing, you give it different colours using crayons or paints. ❑ *Draw simple shapes for your child to colour in.* — PHRASAL VERB; V P n (not pron) Also V n P

**col|our|ant** /kʌlərənt/ **(colourants)**

☑ in AM, use **colorant**

A **colourant** is a substance that is used to give something a particular colour. ❑ *...a new range of hair colourants.* — N-COUNT

**colour-blind**

☑ in AM, use **color-blind**

1 Someone who is **colour-blind** cannot see the difference between colours, especially between red and green. ❑ *Sixteen times as many men are colour-blind as women.* ♦ **colour-blindness** *What exactly is colour-blindness and how do you find out if you have it?* 2 A **colour-blind** system or organization does not treat people differently according to their race or nationality. ❑ *...the introduction of more colour-blind anti-poverty programmes.* — ADJ: usu v-link ADJ; N-UNCOUNT; ADJ

**colour-coded**

☑ in AM, use **color-coded**

Things that are **colour-coded** use colours to represent different features or functions. ❑ *The contents are emptied into color-coded buckets.* — ADJ

**col|oured** /kʌləʳd/ ♦◇◇

☑ in AM, use **colored**

1 Something that is **coloured** a particular colour is that colour. ❑ *The illustration shows a cluster of five roses coloured apricot orange. ...a cheap gold-coloured bracelet.* — ADJ
2 Something that is **coloured** is a particular colour or combination of colours, rather than being just white, black, or the colour that it is naturally. ❑ *You can often choose between plain white or coloured and patterned scarves. ...brightly coloured silks laid out on market stalls.* — ADJ
3 A **coloured** person belongs to a race of people with dark skins. [OFFENSIVE, OLD-FASHIONED] — ADJ: usu ADJ n

**col|our|fast** /kʌləʳfɑːst, -fæst/

☑ in AM, use **colorfast**

A fabric that is **colourfast** has a colour that will not get paler when the fabric is washed or worn. — ADJ

**col|our|ful** /kʌləʳfʊl/

☑ in AM, use **colorful**

1 Something that is **colourful** has bright colours or a lot of different colours. ❑ *The flowers were colourful and the scenery magnificent... People wore colorful clothes and seemed to be having a good time.* ♦ **col|our|ful|ly** *...the sight of dozens of colourfully dressed people.* 2 A **colourful** story is full of exciting details. ❑ *The story she told was certainly col-* — ADJ; ADV; ADJ

*ourful, and extended over her life in England, Germany and Spain. ...the country's colourful and often violent history.* 3 A **colourful** character is a person who behaves in an interesting and amusing way. ❑ *Casey Stengel was probably the most colorful character in baseball.* 4 If someone has had a **colourful** past or a **colourful** career, they have been involved in exciting but often slightly shocking things. ❑ *More details surfaced of her colourful past as the story developed.* 5 **Colourful** language is rude or offensive language.

ADJ: usu ADJ n
ADJ: usu ADJ n
ADJ: usu ADJ n [politeness = bad]

**col|our|ing** /kʌlərɪŋ/

✓ in AM, use **coloring**

1 The **colouring** of something is the colour or colours that it is. ❑ *Other countries vary the coloring of their bank notes as well as their size. ...the scenery was losing its bright colouring.* 2 Someone's **colouring** is the colour of their hair, skin, and eyes. ❑ *None of them had their father's dark colouring... Choose shades which tone in with your natural colouring.* 3 **Colouring** is a substance that is used to give colour to food. ❑ *A few drops of green food colouring were added.* 4 → See also **colour**.

N-UNCOUNT: usu with poss
N-UNCOUNT: usu with poss
N-UNCOUNT

**col|our|ing book** **(colouring books)**

✓ in AM, use **coloring book**

A **colouring book** is a book of simple drawings which children can colour in.

N-COUNT

**col|our|ist** /kʌlərɪst/ **(colourists)**

✓ in AM, use **colorist**

1 A **colourist** is someone such as an artist or a fashion designer who uses colours in an interesting and original way. 2 A **colourist** is a hairdresser who specializes in colouring people's hair.

N-COUNT
N-COUNT

**col|our|less** /kʌləʳləs/

✓ in AM, use **colorless**

1 Something that is **colourless** has no colour at all. ❑ *...a colourless, almost odourless liquid with a sharp, sweetish taste.* 2 If someone's face is **colourless**, it is very pale, usually because they are frightened, shocked, or ill. ❑ *Her face was colourless, and she was shaking... His complexion was colorless and he hadn't shaved.* 3 **Colourless** people or places are dull and uninteresting. ❑ *We hurried through the colourless little town set on the fast-flowing Nyakchu.*

ADJ
ADJ: usu v-link ADJ
ADJ: usu ADJ n

**col|our scheme** **(colour schemes)**

✓ in AM, use **color scheme**

In a room or house, the **colour scheme** is the way in which colours have been used to decorate it. ❑ *...a stylish colour scheme of olive green and mustard.*

N-COUNT

**col|our sup|plement** **(colour supplements)** A **colour supplement** is a colour magazine which is one of the sections of a newspaper, especially at weekends. [BRIT]

N-COUNT

✓ in AM, use **supplement**

**colt** /koʊlt/ **(colts)** A **colt** is a young male horse.

N-COUNT

**colt|ish** /koʊltɪʃ/ A young person or animal that is **coltish** is full of energy but clumsy or awkward, because they lack physical skill or control. ❑ *...coltish teenagers.*

ADJ

**col|umn** /kɒləm/ **(columns)** 1 A **column** is a tall, often decorated cylinder of stone which is built to honour someone or forms part of a building. ❑ *...a London landmark, Nelson's Column in Trafalgar Square.* 2 A **column** is something that has a tall narrow shape. ❑ *The explosion sent a column of smoke thousands of feet into the air.* 3 A **column** is a group of people or animals which moves in a long line. ❑ *There were reports of columns of military vehicles appearing on the streets.* 4 On a printed page such as a page of a dictionary, newspaper, or printed chart, a **column** is one of two or more vertical sections which are read downwards. ❑ *We had stupidly been looking at the wrong column of figures.* 5 In a newspaper or magazine, a **column** is a section that is always written by the same person or is always about the same topic. ❑ *She also writes a regular column for the Times Educational Supplement.* 6 → See also **agony column**, **gossip column**, **personal column**, **spinal column**, **steering column**.

◆◇◇
N-COUNT = pillar
N-COUNT: usu N of n
N-COUNT: usu N of n
N-COUNT
N-COUNT: usu supp N

**col|umn|ist** /kɒləmɪst/ **(columnists)** A **columnist** is a journalist who regularly writes a particular kind of article in a newspaper or magazine. ❑ *Clarence Page is a columnist for the Chicago Tribune.*

N-COUNT: oft N for n

**coma** /koʊmə/ **(comas)** Someone who is **in a coma** is in a state of deep unconsciousness. ❑ *She was in a coma for seven weeks.*

N-COUNT: usu in/into N

**co|ma|tose** /koʊmətoʊs/ 1 A person who is **comatose** is in a coma. [MEDICAL] ❑ *The right side of my brain had been so severely bruised that I was comatose for a month.* 2 A person who is **comatose** is in a deep sleep, usually because they are tired or have drunk too much alcohol. [INFORMAL] ❑ *Grandpa lies comatose on the sofa.*

ADJ
ADJ: oft ADJ after v

**comb** /koʊm/ **(combs, combing, combed)** 1 A **comb** is a flat piece of plastic or metal with narrow pointed teeth along one side, which you use to tidy your hair. 2 When you **comb** your hair, you tidy it using a comb. ❑ *Salvatore combed his hair carefully... Her reddish hair was cut short and neatly combed.* 3 If you **comb** a place, you search everywhere in it in order to find someone or something. ❑ *Officers combed the woods for the murder weapon... They fanned out and carefully combed the temple grounds.* 4 If you **comb through** information, you look at it very carefully in order to find something. ❑ *Eight policemen then spent two years combing through the evidence.* 5 → See also **fine-tooth comb**.

N-COUNT
VERB
V n
V-ed
VERB
V n for n
V n
VERB
V through n

**com|bat** **(combats, combating** or **combatting, combated** or **combatted)**

◆◇◇

✓ The noun is pronounced /kɒmbæt/. The verb is pronounced /kəmbæt/.

1 **Combat** is fighting that takes place in a war. ❑ *Over 16 million men had died in combat... Yesterday saw hand-to-hand combat in the city. ...combat aircraft.* 2 A **combat** is a battle, or a fight between two people. ❑ *It was the end of a long combat.* 3 If people in authority **combat** something, they try to stop it happening. ❑ *Congress has criticised new government measures to combat crime.*

N-UNCOUNT
N-COUNT
VERB
V n

**com|bat|ant** /kɒmbətᵊnt, AM kəmbæt-/ **(combatants)** A **combatant** is a person, group, or country that takes part in the fighting in a war. ❑ *I have never suggested that UN forces could physically separate the combatants in the region... They come from the combatant nations.*

N-COUNT: usu pl

**com|bat|ive** /kɒmbətɪv, AM kəmbætɪv/ A person who is **combative** is aggressive and eager to fight or argue. ❑ *He conducted the meeting in his usual combative style, refusing to admit any mistakes.*
♦ **com|bat|ive|ness** *They quickly developed a reputation for combativeness.*

ADJ
N-UNCOUNT

**com|bat trou|sers** **Combat trousers** are large, loose trousers with lots of pockets. ❑ *He was wearing black combat trousers and a hooded fleece.*

N-PLURAL: also a pair of N

**com|bi|na|tion** /kɒmbɪneɪʃᵊn/ **(combinations)** A **combination of** things is a mixture of them. ❑ *...a fantastic combination of colours. ...the combination of science and art.*

◆◇◇
N-COUNT: usu N of n

**com|bi|na|tion lock** **(combination locks)** A **combination lock** is a lock which can only be opened by turning a dial or a number of dials according to a particular series of letters or numbers. ❑ *...a briefcase with combination locks.*

N-COUNT

**com|bine** **(combines, combining, combined)**

◆◇◇

✓ The verb is pronounced /kəmbaɪn/. The noun is pronounced /kɒmbaɪn/.

1 If you **combine** two or more things or if they **combine**, they exist together. ❑ *The Church has something to say on how to combine freedom with responsibility... Relief workers say it's worse than ever as*

V-RECIP
V n with n
pl-n V

*disease and starvation combine to kill thousands... A stagnant economy combined with a surge in the number of teenagers is likely to have contributed to rising crime levels in the US.* V-ed Also V *with* n, V pl-n

2 If you **combine** two or more things or if they **combine**, they join together to make a single thing. ❑ *David Jacobs was given the job of combining the data from these 19 studies into one giant study... Combine the flour with 3 tablespoons water to make a paste... Carbon, hydrogen and oxygen combine chemically to form carbohydrates and fats... Combined with other compounds, they created a massive dynamite-type bomb.* V-RECIP V pl-n V n *with* n pl-n V V-ed Also V *with* n

3 If someone or something **combines** two qualities or features, they have both those qualities or features at the same time. ❑ *Their system seems to combine the two ideals of strong government and proportional representation. ...a clever, far-sighted lawyer who combines legal expertise with social concern... Her tale has a consciously youthful tone and storyline, combined with a sly humour.* VERB V pl-n V n *with* n V-ed

4 If someone **combines** two activities, they do them both at the same time. ❑ *It is possible to combine a career with being a mother... He will combine the two jobs over the next three years.* VERB V n *with* n/-ing V pl-n

5 If two or more groups or organizations **combine** or if someone **combines** them, they join to form a single group or organization. ❑ *...an announcement by Steetley and Tarmac of a joint venture that would combine their operations... Different states or groups can combine to enlarge their markets.* V-RECIP = *amalgamate* V pl-n pl-n V

6 A **combine** is a group of people or organizations that are working or acting together. ❑ *...Veba, an energy-and-chemicals combine that is Germany's fourth-biggest company.* N-COUNT

**com|bined** /kəmbaɪnd/ 1 A **combined** effort or attack is made by two or more groups of people at the same time. ❑ *These refugees are looked after by the combined efforts of the host countries and non-governmental organisations.* ADJ: ADJ n = *joint*

2 The **combined** size or quantity of two or more things is the total of their sizes or quantities added together. ❑ *Such a merger would be the largest in US banking history, giving the two banks combined assets of some $146 billion* ADJ: ADJ n = *total*

**com|bine har|vest|er** **(combine harvesters)** A **combine harvester** is a large machine which is used on farms to cut, sort, and clean grain. N-COUNT

**com|bin|ing form** **(combining forms)** A **combining form** is a word that is used, or used with a particular meaning, only when joined to another word. For example, '-legged' as in 'four-legged' and '-fold' as in 'fivefold' are combining forms. N-COUNT

**com|bo** /kɒmboʊ/ **(combos)** A **combo** is a small group of musicians who play jazz, dance, or popular music. [INFORMAL] ❑ *...a new-wave rock combo.* N-COUNT = *band*

**com|bus|tible** /kəmbʌstɪbəl/ A **combustible** material or gas catches fire and burns easily. [FORMAL] ❑ *The ability of coal to release a combustible gas has long been known.* ADJ: usu ADJ n = *inflammable*

**com|bus|tion** /kəmbʌstʃən/ **Combustion** is the act of burning something or the process of burning. [TECHNICAL] ❑ *The energy is released by combustion on the application of a match.* → See also **internal combustion engine**. N-UNCOUNT: oft N n

**come** /kʌm/ **(comes, coming, came)** ◆◆◆

> The form **come** is used in the present tense and is the past participle.

> **Come** is used in a large number of expressions which are explained under other words in this dictionary. For example, the expression 'to come to terms with something' is explained at 'term'.

1 When a person or thing **comes** to a particular place, especially to a place where you are, they move there. ❑ *Two police officers came into the hall... Come here, Tom... You'll have to come with us... We heard the train coming... Can I come too?... The impact blew out some of the windows and the sea came rushing in.* VERB V prep/adv V V V -ing prep/adv

2 When someone **comes to** do something, they move to the place where someone else is in order to do it, and they do it. In British English, someone can also **come and** do something and in American English, someone can **come** do something. However, you always say that someone **came and** did something. ❑ *Eleanor had come to visit her... Come and meet Roger... I want you to come visit me.* VERB V to-inf V *and* v V inf

3 When you **come to** a place, you reach it. ❑ *He came to a door that led into a passageway.* VERB V *to* n

4 If something **comes up to** a particular point or **down to** it, it is tall enough, deep enough, or long enough to reach that point. ❑ *The water came up to my chest... I wore a large shirt of Jamie's which came down over my hips.* VERB V *up/down* prep

5 If something **comes apart** or **comes to pieces**, it breaks into pieces. If something **comes off** or **comes away**, it becomes detached from something else. ❑ *The pistol came to pieces, easily and quickly... The door knobs came off in our hands.* VERB V adv/prep V adv/prep

6 You use **come** in expressions such as **come to an end** or **come into operation** to indicate that someone or something enters or reaches a particular state or situation. ❑ *The Communists came to power in 1944... I came into contact with very bright Harvard and Yale students... Their worst fears may be coming true.* V-LINK V *to* n V *into* n V adj

7 If someone **comes to** do something, they do it at the end of a long process or period of time. ❑ *She said it so many times that she came to believe it.* VERB V to-inf

8 You can ask how something **came to** happen when you want to know what caused it to happen or made it possible. ❑ *How did you come to meet him?* VERB V to-inf

9 When a particular event or time **comes**, it arrives or happens. ❑ *The announcement came after a meeting at the Home Office... The time has come for us to move on... There will come a time when the crisis will occur.* ♦ **com|ing** *Most of my patients welcome the coming of summer.* VERB V prep/adv V *there* V n N-SING: usu *the* N *of* n

10 You can use **come** before a date, time, or event to mean when that date, time, or event arrives. For example, you can say **come the spring** to mean 'when the spring arrives'. ❑ *Come the election on the 20th of May, we will have to decide.* PREP

11 If a thought, idea, or memory **comes to** you, you suddenly think of it or remember it. ❑ *He was about to shut the door when an idea came to him... Then it came to me that perhaps he did understand.* VERB = *occur* V *to* n *it* V *to* n that

12 If money or property is going to **come to** you, you are going to inherit or receive it. ❑ *He did have pension money coming to him when the factory shut down.* VERB V *to* n

13 If a case **comes before** a court or tribunal or **comes to** court, it is presented there so that the court or tribunal can examine it. ❑ *The membership application came before the Council of Ministers in September... President Cristiani expected the case to come to court within ninety days.* VERB V *before* n V *to* n

14 If something **comes to** a particular number or amount, it adds up to it. ❑ *Lunch came to $80.* VERB V *to* amount

15 If someone or something **comes from** a particular place or thing, that place or thing is their origin, source, or starting point. ❑ *Nearly half the students come from abroad... Chocolate comes from the cacao tree... The term 'claret', used to describe Bordeaux wines, may come from the French word 'clairet'.* VERB V *from* n V *from* n V *from* n

16 Something that **comes from** something else or **comes of** it is the result of it. ❑ *There is a feeling of power that comes from driving fast... He asked to be transferred there some years ago, but nothing came of it.* VERB V *from* n/-ing V *of* n/-ing

17 If someone or something **comes** first, next, or last, they are first, next, or last in a series, list, or competition. ❑ *The two countries have been unable to agree which step should come next... The horse had already won at Lincolnshire and come second at Lowesby.* VERB V ord V ord

18 If a type of thing **comes in** a particular range of colours, forms, styles, or sizes, it can have any of those colours, forms, styles, or sizes. ❑ *Bikes come in all shapes and sizes... The wallpaper comes in black and white only.* VERB V *in* n V *in* n

19 You use **come** in expressions such as **it came as a surprise** when indicating a person's reaction to something that happens. ❑ *Ma-* VERB

*jor's reply came as a complete surprise to the House of Commons... The arrest has come as a terrible shock.* [V as n to n]
20 The next subject in a discussion that you **come to** is the one that you talk about next. ❑ *Finally in the programme, we come to the news that the American composer and conductor, Leonard Bernstein, has died... That is another matter altogether. And we shall come to that next.* [V as n] [VERB] [V to n] [V to n]
21 To **come** means to have an orgasm. [INFORMAL] [VERB: V]
22 → See also **coming, comings and goings.**

**PHRASES**
23 If you say that someone is, for example, **as** good **as they come**, or **as** stupid **as they come**, you are emphasizing that they are extremely good or extremely stupid. ❑ *The new finance minister was educated at Oxford and is as traditional as they come.* [PHRASE] [emphasis]
24 You can use the expression **when it comes down to it** or **when you come down to it** for emphasis, when you are giving a general statement or conclusion. ❑ *When you come down to it, however, the basic problems of life have not changed.* [PHRASE: PHR with cl] [emphasis]
25 If you say that someone **has it coming to** them, you mean that they deserve everything bad that is going to happen to them, because they have done something wrong or are a bad person. If you say that someone **got what was coming to** them, you mean that they deserved the punishment or bad experience that they have had. [INFORMAL] ❑ *He was pleased that Brady was dead because he probably had it coming to him.* [PHRASE: V inflects]
26 You use the expression **come to think of it** to indicate that you have suddenly realized something, often something obvious. ❑ *You know, when you come to think of it, this is very odd.* [PHRASE: PHR with cl]
27 When you refer to a time or an event **to come** or one that is still **to come**, you are referring to a future time or event. ❑ *I hope in years to come he will reflect on his decision... The worst of the storm is yet to come.* [PHRASE: usu n PHR, also v-link PHR]
28 You can use the expression **when it comes to** or **when it comes down to** in order to introduce a new topic or a new aspect of a topic that you are talking about. ❑ *Most of us know we should cut down on fat. But knowing such things isn't much help when it comes to shopping and eating... However, when it comes down to somebody that they know, they have a different feeling.* [PHRASE: PHR n/-ing]
29 You can use expressions like **I know where you're coming from** or **you can see where she's coming from** to say that you understand someone's attitude or point of view. ❑ *To understand why they are doing it, it is necessary to know where they are coming from.* [PHRASE: V inflects]

♦ **come about** When you say how or when something **came about**, you say how or when it happened. ❑ *Any possible solution to the Irish question can only come about through dialogue... That came about when we went to Glastonbury last year... Thus it came about that, after many years as an interior designer and antiques dealer, he combined both businesses.* [PHRASAL VERB] [V P *through* n] [V P] [*it* V P that]

♦ **come across** 1 If you **come across** something or someone, you find them or meet them by chance. ❑ *I came across a group of children playing.* [PHRASAL VERB = encounter] [V P n]
2 If someone or what they are saying **comes across** in a particular way, they make that impression on people who meet them or are listening to them. ❑ *When sober he can come across as an extremely pleasant and charming young man... He came across very, very well.* [PHRASAL VERB = come over] [V P *as* n] [V P adv]

♦ **come along** 1 You tell someone to **come along** to encourage them in a friendly way to do something, especially to attend something. ❑ *There's a big press launch today and you're most welcome to come along.* [PHRASAL VERB = come on] [V P]
2 You say **'come along'** to someone to encourage them to hurry up, usually when you are rather annoyed with them. ❑ *Come along, Osmond. No sense in your standing around.* [CONVENTION = come on]
3 When something or someone **comes along**, they occur or arrive by chance. ❑ *I waited a long time until a script came along that I thought was genuinely funny... It was lucky you came along.* [PHRASAL VERB] [V P] [V P]
4 If something **is coming along**, it is developing or making progress. ❑ *Pentagon spokesman Williams says those talks are coming along quite well... How's Ferguson coming along?* [PHRASAL VERB] [V P adv] [V P]

♦ **come around**

> in BRIT, also use **come round**

1 If someone **comes around** or **comes round to** your house, they call there to see you. ❑ *Beryl came round this morning to apologize... Quite a lot of people came round to the house.* [PHRASAL VERB = come over] [V P] [V P *to* n]
2 If you **come around** or **come round to** an idea, you eventually change your mind and accept it or agree with it. ❑ *It looks like they're coming around to our way of thinking... She will eventually come round.* [PHRASAL VERB] [V P *to* n] [V P]
3 When something **comes around** or **comes round**, it happens as a regular or predictable event. ❑ *I hope still to be in the side when the World Cup comes around next year.* [PHRASAL VERB] [V P]
4 When someone who is unconscious **comes around** or **comes round**, they recover consciousness. ❑ *When I came round I was on the kitchen floor.* [PHRASAL VERB = come to] [V P]

♦ **come at** If a person or animal **comes at** you, they move towards you in a threatening way and try to attack you. ❑ *He maintained that he was protecting himself from Mr Cox, who came at him with an axe.* [PHRASAL VERB] [V P n *with* n] [Also V P n]

♦ **come back** 1 If something that you had forgotten **comes back to** you, you remember it. ❑ *He was also an MP – I'll think of his name in a moment when it comes back to me... When I thought about it, it all came back.* [PHRASAL VERB] [V P *to* n] [V P]
2 When something **comes back**, it becomes fashionable again. ❑ *I'm glad hats are coming back.* [PHRASAL VERB] [V P]
3 → See also **comeback.**

♦ **come back to** If you **come back to** a topic or point, you talk about it again later. ❑ *'What does that mean please?' — 'I'm coming back to that. Just write it down for the minute.'* [PHRASAL VERB] [V P P n]

♦ **come between** If someone or something **comes between** two people, or **comes between** a person and a thing, they make the relationship or connection between them less close or happy. ❑ *It's difficult to imagine anything coming between them.* [PHRASAL VERB: no passive] [V P pl-n]

♦ **come by** To **come by** something means to obtain it or find it. ❑ *How did you come by that cheque?* [PHRASAL VERB] [V P n]

♦ **come down** 1 If the cost, level, or amount of something **comes down**, it becomes less than it was before. ❑ *Interest rates should come down... If you buy three bottles, the bottle price comes down to £2.42... The price of petrol is coming down by four pence a gallon.* [PHRASAL VERB ≠ go up] [V P] [V P *to/from* n] [V P *by* n]
2 If something **comes down**, it falls to the ground. ❑ *The cold rain came down.* [PHRASAL VERB] [V P]

♦ **come down on** 1 If you **come down on** one side of an argument, you declare that you support that side. ❑ *He clearly and decisively came down on the side of President Rafsanjani.* [PHRASAL VERB] [V P P n]
2 If you **come down on** someone, you criticize them severely or treat them strictly. ❑ *If Douglas came down hard enough on him, Dale would rebel.* [PHRASAL VERB] [V P P n]

♦ **come down to** If a problem, decision, or question **comes down to** a particular thing, that thing is the most important factor involved. ❑ *Walter Crowley says the problem comes down to money... I think that it comes down to the fact that people do feel very dependent on their automobile... What it comes down to is, there are bad people out there, and somebody has to deal with them.* [PHRASAL VERB] [V P P n] [*it* V P P n] [*it* V P P n]

♦ **come down with** If you **come down with** an illness, you get it. ❑ *Thomas came down with chickenpox at the weekend.* [PHRASAL VERB] [V P P n]

♦ **come for** If people such as soldiers or police **come for** you, they come to find you, usually in order to harm you or take you away, for example to prison. ❑ *Lotte was getting ready to fight if they came for her.* [PHRASAL VERB] [V P n]

♦ **come forward** If someone **comes forward**, they offer to do something or to give some information in response to a request for help. ❑ *A* [PHRASAL VERB] [V P] *vital witness came forward to say that she saw Tanner wearing the boots.*

♦ **come in** [1] If information, a report, or a telephone call **comes in**, it is received. ❑ *Reports are now coming in of trouble at yet another jail.* [2] If you have some money **coming in**, you receive it regularly as your income. ❑ *She had no money coming in and no funds.* [3] If someone **comes in on** a discussion, arrangement, or task, they join it. ❑ *Can I come in here too, on both points?... He had a designer come in and redesign the uniforms.* [4] When a new idea, fashion, or product **comes in**, it becomes popular or available. ❑ *It was just when geography was really beginning to change and lots of new ideas were coming in.* [5] If you ask where something or someone **comes in**, you are asking what their role is in a particular matter. ❑ *Rose asked, 'But where do we come in, Henry?'* [6] When the tide **comes in**, the water in the sea gradually moves so that it covers more of the land.

PHRASAL VERB; V P; PHRASAL VERB: usu cont; V P; PHRASAL VERB; V P *on* n; V P; PHRASAL VERB; V P; PHRASAL VERB; V P; PHRASAL VERB: V P; ≠ go out

♦ **come in for** If someone or something **comes in for** criticism or blame, they receive it. ❑ *The plans have already come in for fierce criticism in many quarters of the country.*

PHRASAL VERB; V P P n

♦ **come into** [1] If someone **comes into** some money, some property, or a title, they inherit it. ❑ *My father has just come into a fortune in diamonds.* [2] If someone or something **comes into** a situation, they have a role in it. ❑ *We don't really know where Hortense comes into all this.*

PHRASAL VERB: no passive = inherit; V P n; PHRASAL VERB: no passive; V P n

♦ **come off** [1] If something **comes off**, it is successful or effective. ❑ *It was a good try but it didn't quite come off.* [2] If someone **comes off** worst in a contest or conflict, they are in the worst position after it. If they **come off** best, they are in the best position. ❑ *Some Democrats still have bitter memories of how, against all odds, they came off worst during the inquiry.* [3] If you **come off** a drug or medicine, you stop taking it. ❑ *...people trying to come off tranquillizers.* [4] You say **'come off it'** to someone to show them that you think what they are saying is untrue or wrong. [INFORMAL, SPOKEN]

PHRASAL VERB; V P; PHRASAL VERB; V P adv; PHRASAL VERB: no passive; V P n; CONVENTION

♦ **come on** [1] You say **'Come on'** to someone to encourage them to do something they do not much want to do. [SPOKEN] ❑ *Come on Doreen, let's dance.* [2] You say **'Come on'** to someone to encourage them to hurry up. [SPOKEN] [3] If you have an illness or a headache **coming on**, you can feel it starting. ❑ *Tiredness and fever are much more likely to be a sign of flu coming on.* [4] If something or someone **is coming on** well, they are developing well or making good progress. ❑ *Lee is coming on very well now and it's a matter of deciding how to fit him into the team.* [5] When something such as a machine or system **comes on**, it starts working or functioning. ❑ *The central heating was coming on and the ancient wooden boards creaked.* [6] If a new season or type of weather **is coming on**, it is starting to arrive. ❑ *Winter was coming on again... I had two miles to go and it was just coming on to rain.*

CONVENTION = come along; CONVENTION = come along; PHRASAL VERB: usu cont; V P; PHRASAL VERB: usu cont = come along; V P adv; PHRASAL VERB ≠ go off; V P; PHRASAL VERB: usu cont; V P; *it* V P to-inf

♦ **come on to** [1] When you **come on to** a particular topic, you start discussing it. ❑ *We're now looking at a smaller system but I'll come on to that later.* [2] If someone **comes on to** you, they show that they are interested in starting a sexual relationship with you. [INFORMAL] ❑ *I don't think that a woman, by using make-up, is trying to come on to a man.*

PHRASAL VERB; V P P n; PHRASAL VERB; V P P n

♦ **come out** [1] When a new product such as a book or CD **comes out**, it becomes available to the public. ❑ *The book comes out this week.* [2] If a fact **comes out**, it becomes known to people. ❑ *The truth is beginning to come out about what happened... It will come out that she has covertly donated considerable sums to the IRA.* [3] When a gay person **comes out**, they let people know that they are gay. ❑ *...the few gay men there who dare to come out... I came out as a lesbian when I was still in my teens.* [4] To **come out** in a particular way means to be in the position or state described at the end of a process or event. ❑ *In this grim little episode of recent American history, few people come out well... So what makes a good marriage? Faithfulness comes out top of the list... Julian ought to have resigned, then he'd have come out of it with some credit.* [5] If you **come out for** something, you declare that you support it. If you **come out against** something, you declare that you do not support it. ❑ *Its members had come out virtually unanimously against the tests.* [6] When a group of workers **comes out** on strike, they go on strike. [BRIT] ❑ *On September 18 the dockers again came out on strike.*

PHRASAL VERB; V P; PHRASAL VERB; V P; *it* V P that; PHRASAL VERB; V P; V P *as* n/adj; PHRASAL VERB; V P adv/prep; V P adj; V P *of* n adv/prep; PHRASAL VERB; V P prep/adv; PHRASAL VERB; V P prep

☑ in AM, use **go out on strike**

[7] If a photograph does not **come out**, it does not appear or is unclear when it is developed and printed. ❑ *None of her snaps came out.* [8] When the sun, moon, or stars **come out**, they appear in the sky. ❑ *Oh, look. The sun's come out.*

PHRASAL VERB; V P; PHRASAL VERB ≠ go in; V P

♦ **come out in** If you **come out in** spots, you become covered with them. [BRIT] ❑ *When I changed to a new soap I came out in a terrible rash.*

PHRASAL VERB: no passive = break out in; V P P n

☑ in AM, use **break out**

♦ **come out with** If you **come out with** a remark, especially a surprising one, you make it. ❑ *Everyone who heard it just burst out laughing when he came out with it.*

PHRASAL VERB: no passive; V P n

♦ **come over** [1] If a feeling or desire, especially a strange or surprising one, **comes over** you, it affects you strongly. ❑ *As I entered the corridor which led to my room that eerie feeling came over me... I'm sorry, I don't know what came over me.* [2] If someone **comes over all** dizzy or shy, for example, they suddenly start feeling or acting in that way. ❑ *When Connie pours her troubles out to him, Joe comes over all sensitive.* [3] If someone or what they are saying **comes over** in a particular way, they make that impression on people who meet them or are listening to them. ❑ *You come over as a capable and amusing companion.*

PHRASAL VERB: no passive; V P n; V P n; PHRASAL VERB; V P adj; PHRASAL VERB = come across; V P *as* n

♦ **come round** → see **come around**.

♦ **come through** [1] To **come through** a dangerous or difficult situation means to survive it and recover from it. ❑ *The city had faced racial crisis and come through it.* [2] If a feeling or message **comes through**, it is clearly shown in what is said or done. ❑ *I hope my love for the material came through, because it is a great script.* [3] If something **comes through**, it arrives, especially after some procedure has been carried out. ❑ *The news came through at about five o'clock on election day.* [4] If you **come through** with what is expected or needed from you, you succeed in doing or providing it. ❑ *He puts his administration at risk if he doesn't come through on these promises for reform... We found that we were totally helpless, and our women came through for us.*

PHRASAL VERB: no passive; V P n; PHRASAL VERB = come across; V P; PHRASAL VERB; V P; PHRASAL VERB; V P *on/with* n; V P *for* n

♦ **come to** When someone who is unconscious **comes to**, they recover consciousness. ❑ *When he came to and raised his head he saw Barney.*

PHRASAL VERB = come around; V P

♦ **come under** [1] If you **come under** attack or pressure, for example, people attack you or put pressure on you. ❑ *His relationship with the KGB came under scrutiny.* [2] If something **comes under** a particular authority, it is managed or controlled by that authority. ❑ *They were neglected before because they did not come under the Ministry of Defence.* [3] If something **comes under** a particular heading, it is in the category mentioned. ❑ *There was more news about Britain, but it came under the heading of human interest.*

PHRASAL VERB: no passive; V P n; PHRASAL VERB: no passive; V P n; PHRASAL VERB: no passive; V P n

♦ **come up** [1] If someone **comes up** or **comes up to** you, they approach you until they are standing close to you. ❑ *Her cat came up and rubbed itself against their legs... He came up to me and said: 'Come on, John.'* [2] If something **comes up** in a conversation or meeting, it is mentioned or discussed. ❑ *The subject came up at a news conference in Peking today.* [3] If something **is coming up**, it is about to happen or take place. ❑ *We do*

PHRASAL VERB; V P; V P *to* n; PHRASAL VERB = crop up; V P; PHRASAL VERB; V P

have elections coming up. [4] If something **comes up**, it happens unexpectedly. ❑ *I was delayed – something came up at home.* [5] If a job **comes up** or if something **comes up for** sale, it becomes available. ❑ *A research fellowship came up at Girton and I applied for it and got it... The house came up for sale and the couple realised they could just about afford it.* [6] When the sun or moon **comes up**, it rises. ❑ *It will be so great watching the sun come up.* [7] In law, when a case **comes up**, it is heard in a court of law. ❑ *He is one of the reservists who will plead not guilty when their cases come up.* — PHRASAL VERB; V P; PHRASAL VERB; V P; V P for n; PHRASAL VERB ≠go down; V P; PHRASAL VERB; V P

♦ **come up against** If you **come up against** a problem or difficulty, you are faced with it and have to deal with it. ❑ *We came up against a great deal of resistance in dealing with the case.* — PHRASAL VERB; V P P n

♦ **come up for** When someone or something **comes up for** consideration or action of some kind, the time arrives when they have to be considered or dealt with. ❑ *The TV rights contract came up for renegotiation in 1988.* — PHRASAL VERB; V P P n

♦ **come upon** [1] If you **come upon** someone or something, you meet them or find them by chance. ❑ *I came upon an irresistible item at a yard sale.* [2] If an attitude or feeling **comes upon** you, it begins to affect you. [LITERARY] ❑ *A sense of impending doom came upon all of us.* — PHRASAL VERB = come across; V P n; PHRASAL VERB; V P n

♦ **come up to** To **be coming up to** a time or state means to be getting near to it. ❑ *It's just coming up to ten minutes past eleven now.* — PHRASAL VERB: usu cont = approach; V P P n

♦ **come up with** [1] If you **come up with** a plan or idea, you think of it and suggest it. ❑ *Several of the members have come up with suggestions of their own.* [2] If you **come up with** a sum of money, you manage to produce it when it is needed. ❑ *If Warren can come up with the $15 million, we'll go to London.* — PHRASAL VERB; V P P n; PHRASAL VERB; V P P n

**come|back** **(comebacks)** [1] If someone such as an entertainer or sports personality makes a **comeback**, they return to their profession or sport after a period away. ❑ *Sixties singing star Petula Clark is making a comeback.* [2] If something makes a **comeback**, it becomes fashionable again. ❑ *Tight fitting T-shirts are making a comeback.* [3] If you have no **comeback** when someone has done something wrong to you, there is nothing you can do to have them punished or held responsible. — N-COUNT; N-COUNT; N-UNCOUNT: with brd-neg = redress

**co|median** /kəmiːdiən/ **(comedians)** A **comedian** is an entertainer whose job is to make people laugh, by telling jokes or funny stories. — N-COUNT = comic

**co|medic** /kəmiːdɪk/ **Comedic** means relating to comedy. [FORMAL] ❑ *...a festival of comedic talent from around the world.* — ADJ: usu ADJ n ≠tragic

**co|medi|enne** /kəmiːdien/ **(comediennes)** A **comedienne** is a female entertainer whose job is to make people laugh, by telling jokes or funny stories. — N-COUNT = comic

**come|down** /kʌmdaʊn/

☑ in BRIT, also use **come-down**

If you say that something is **a comedown**, you think that it is not as good as something else that you have just done or had. ❑ *The prospect of relegation is a comedown for a club that finished second two seasons ago.* — N-SING: a N

**com|edy** /kɒmədi/ **(comedies)** [1] **Comedy** consists of types of entertainment, such as plays and films, or particular scenes in them, that are intended to make people laugh. ❑ *Actor Dom Deluise talks about his career in comedy. ...a TV comedy series.* [2] A **comedy** is a play, film, or television programme that is intended to make people laugh. [3] The **comedy** of a situation involves those aspects of it that make you laugh. ❑ *Jackie sees the comedy in her millionaire husband's thrifty habits.* [4] ➔ See also **situation comedy**. — ◆◇◇ N-UNCOUNT; N-COUNT ≠tragedy; N-UNCOUNT = humour

**come|ly** /kʌmli/ **(comelier, comeliest)** A **comely** woman is attractive. [OLD-FASHIONED] — ADJ: usu ADJ n

**come-on** **(come-ons)** A **come-on** is a gesture or remark which someone, especially a woman, makes in order to encourage another person to make sexual advances to them. [INFORMAL] ❑ *He ignores come-ons from the many women who seem to find him attractive.* — N-COUNT

**com|er** /kʌməʳ/ **(comers)** You can use **comers** to refer to people who arrive at a particular place. ❑ *I arrived at the church at two-thirty p.m. to find some early comers outside the main door... The first comer was the Sultan himself.* ➔ See also **all-comers**, **latecomer**, **newcomer**. — N-COUNT: usu pl, supp N

**com|et** /kɒmɪt/ **(comets)** A **comet** is a bright object with a long tail that travels around the sun. ❑ *Halley's Comet is going to come back in 2061.* — N-COUNT

**come|up|pance** /kʌmʌpəns/ also **come-uppance.** If you say that someone has got their **comeuppance**, you approve of the fact that they have been punished or have suffered for something wrong that they have done. [INFORMAL] ❑ *The central character is a bad man who shoots people and gets his comeuppance.* — N-SING: usu poss N [approval] = just deserts

**com|fort** /kʌmfəʳt/ **(comforts, comforting, comforted)** [1] If you are doing something **in comfort**, you are physically relaxed and contented, and are not feeling any pain or other unpleasant sensations. ❑ *This will enable the audience to sit in comfort while watching the shows... The shoe has padding around the collar, heel and tongue for added comfort.* [2] **Comfort** is a style of life in which you have enough money to have everything you need. ❑ *Surely there is some way of ordering our busy lives so that we can live in comfort and find spiritual harmony too.* [3] **Comfort** is what you feel when worries or unhappiness stop. ❑ *He welcomed the truce, but pointed out it was of little comfort to families spending Christmas without a loved one... He will be able to take some comfort from inflation figures due on Friday... He found comfort in Eva's blind faith in him.* ➔ See also **cold comfort**. [4] If you refer to a person, thing, or idea as a **comfort**, you mean that it helps you to stop worrying or makes you feel less unhappy. ❑ *It's a comfort talking to you... Being able to afford a drink would be a comfort in these tough times.* [5] If you **comfort** someone, you make them feel less worried, unhappy, or upset, for example by saying kind things to them. ❑ *Ned put his arm around her, trying to comfort her.* [6] **Comforts** are things which make your life easier and more pleasant, such as electrical devices you have in your home. ❑ *She enjoys the material comforts married life has brought her... Electricity provides us with warmth and light and all our modern home comforts.* ➔ See also **creature comforts**. [7] If you say that something is, for example, **too close for comfort**, you mean you are worried because it is closer than you would like it to be. ❑ *The bombs fell in the sea, many too close for comfort... Although crimes against visitors were falling, the levels of crime were still too high for comfort.* — ◆◇◇ N-UNCOUNT: oft in/for N ≠discomfort; N-UNCOUNT: oft in N; N-UNCOUNT; N-COUNT: usu sing, oft N to n, it v-link N to-inf/-ing; VERB = console; V n; N-COUNT: usu pl; PHRASE: PHR after v, v-link PHR

**com|fort|able** /kʌmftəbᵊl/ [1] If a piece of furniture or an item of clothing is **comfortable**, it makes you feel physically relaxed when you use it, for example because it is soft. ❑ *...a comfortable fireside chair... Trainers are so comfortable to wear.* [2] If a building or room is **comfortable**, it makes you feel physically relaxed when you spend time in it, for example because it is warm and has nice furniture. ❑ *A home should be comfortable and friendly. ...somewhere warm and comfortable.* ♦ **com|fort|ably** /kʌmftəbli/ *...the comfortably furnished living room.* [3] If you are **comfortable**, you are physically relaxed because of the place or position you are sitting or lying in. ❑ *Lie down on your bed and make yourself comfortable... She tried to maneuver her body into a more comfortable position.* ♦ **com|fort|ably** *Are you sitting comfortably?... He would be tucked comfortably into bed.* [4] If you say that someone is **comfortable**, you mean that they have enough money to be able to live without financial problems. ❑ *'Is he rich?' — 'He's com-* — ◆◇◇ ADJ ≠uncomfortable; ADJ; ADV: usu ADV -ed; ADJ ≠uncomfortable; ADV: ADV with v; ADJ *fortable.'... She came from a stable, comfortable, middle-class family.* ♦ **com|fort|ably** *Cayton describes himself as comfortably well-off.* [5] In a race, competition, or election, if you have a **comfortable** lead, you are likely to win it easily. If you gain a **comfortable** victory or majority, you win easily. ❑ *By half distance we held a comfortable two-lap lead... He appeared to be heading for a comfortable victory.* ♦ **com|fort|ably** *...the Los Angeles Raiders, who comfortably beat the Bears earlier in the season.* [6] If you feel **comfortable with** a particular situation or person, you feel confident and relaxed with them. ❑ *Nervous politicians might well feel more comfortable with a step-by-step approach... He liked me and I felt comfortable with him... I'll talk to them, but I won't feel comfortable about it.* ♦ **com|fort|ably** *They talked comfortably of their plans.* [7] When a sick or injured person is said to be **comfortable**, they are in a stable physical condition. ❑ *He was described as comfortable in hospital last night.* [8] A **comfortable** life, job, or situation does not cause you any problems or worries. ❑ *...a comfortable teaching job at a university... Kohl's retirement looks far from comfortable.*

ADV | ADJ: ADJ n | ADV: ADV with v = easily | ADJ: v-link ADJ, oft ADJ prep | ADV: ADV after v | ADJ | ADJ

**com|fort|ably** /kʌmfəʳtəbli/ If you do something **comfortably**, you do it easily. ❑ *Only take upon yourself those things that you know you can manage comfortably... Three of the six have comfortably exceeded their normal life expectancy.* ➔ See also **comfortable**. ADV: ADV with v

**com|fort|ably off** If someone is **comfortably off**, they have enough money to be able to live without financial problems. ❑ *He had no plans to retire even though he is now very comfortably off.* ADJ: usu v-link ADJ

**com|fort|er** /kʌmfəʳtəʳ/ **(comforters)** [1] A **comforter** is a person or thing that comforts you. ❑ *He became Vivien Leigh's devoted friend and comforter.* [2] A **comforter** is a large cover filled with feathers or similar material which you put over yourself in bed instead of a sheet and blankets. [AM] N-COUNT | N-COUNT

✓ in BRIT, use **duvet**, **quilt**

**com|fort|ing** /kʌmfəʳtɪŋ/ If you say that something is **comforting**, you mean it makes you feel less worried or unhappy. ❑ *My mother had just died and I found the book very comforting... In the midst of his feelings of impotence, a comforting thought arrived.* ♦ **com|fort|ing|ly** *'Everything's under control here,' her mother said comfortingly. 'You've nothing to worry about.'* ADJ | ADV: usu ADV with v, ADV adj, also ADV with cl

**com|frey** /kʌmfri/ **Comfrey** is a herb that is used to make drinks and medicines. N-UNCOUNT

**com|fy** /kʌmfi/ **(comfier, comfiest)** A **comfy** item of clothing, piece of furniture, room, or position is a comfortable one. [INFORMAL] ❑ *Loose-fitting shirts are comfy. ...a comfy chair.* ADJ

**com|ic** /kɒmɪk/ **(comics)** [1] If you describe something as **comic**, you mean that it makes you laugh, and is often intended to make you laugh. ❑ *The novel is comic and tragic... Most of these trips had exciting or comic moments.* [2] **Comic** is used to describe comedy as a form of entertainment, and the actors and entertainers who perform it. ❑ *Grodin is a fine comic actor. ...a comic opera.* [3] A **comic** is an entertainer who tells jokes in order to make people laugh. [4] A **comic** is a magazine that contains stories told in pictures. [mainly BRIT] ❑ *Joe loved to read 'Superman' comics.* ADJ | ADJ: ADJ n | N-COUNT = comedian | N-COUNT = comic book

✓ in AM, usually use **comic book**

**comi|cal** /kɒmɪkəl/ If you describe something as **comical**, you mean that it makes you want to laugh because it seems funny or silly. ❑ *Her expression is almost comical... Events took a comical turn.* ♦ **comi|cal|ly** /kɒmɪkli/ *She raised her eyebrows comically.* ADJ = funny | ADV: ADV with v, ADV adj

**com|ic book** **(comic books)** A **comic book** is a magazine that contains stories told in pictures. [mainly AM] N-COUNT = comic

✓ in BRIT, usually use **comic**

**com|ic strip** **(comic strips)** A **comic strip** is a series of drawings that tell a story, especially in a newspaper or magazine. N-COUNT

**com|ing** /kʌmɪŋ/ A **coming** event or time is an event or time that will happen soon. ❑ *This obviously depends on the weather in the coming months.* ◆◆◆ ADJ: ADJ n

**com|ing of age** [1] When something reaches an important stage of development and is accepted by a large number of people, you can refer to this as its **coming of age**. ❑ *...postwar Germany's final coming-of-age as an independent sovereign state.* [2] Someone's **coming of age** is the time when they become legally an adult. ❑ *...traditional coming-of-age ceremonies.* N-SING: with supp | N-SING: with poss

**com|ings and go|ings** **Comings and goings** refers to the way people keep arriving at and leaving a particular place. ❑ *They noted the comings and goings of the journalists.* N-PLURAL: with poss

**com|ma** /kɒmə/ **(commas)** A **comma** is the punctuation mark , which is used to separate parts of a sentence or items in a list. N-COUNT

**com|mand** /kəmɑːnd, -mænd/ **(commands, commanding, commanded)** [1] If someone in authority **commands** you to do something, they tell you that you must do it. [mainly WRITTEN] ❑ *He commanded his troops to attack... 'Get in your car and follow me,' he commanded... He commanded that roads be built to link castles across the land... 'Don't panic,' I commanded myself.* ♦ **Command** is also a noun. ❑ *The tanker failed to respond to a command to stop. ...the note of command in his voice.* [2] If you **command** something such as respect or obedience, you obtain it because you are popular, famous, or important. ❑ *...an excellent physician who commanded the respect of all his colleagues.* [3] If an army or country **commands** a place, they have total control over it. ❑ *Yemen commands the strait at the southern end of the Red Sea.* ♦ **Command** is also a noun. ❑ *...the struggle for command of the air.* [4] An officer who **commands** part of an army, navy, or air force is responsible for controlling and organizing it. ❑ *...the French general who commands the UN troops in the region... He didn't just command. He personally fought in several heavy battles.* ♦ **Command** is also a noun. ❑ *In 1942 he took command of 108 Squadron.* [5] In the armed forces, a **command** is a group of officers who are responsible for organizing and controlling part of an army, navy, or air force. ❑ *He had authorisation from the military command to retaliate.* [6] In computing, a **command** is an instruction that you give to a computer. [7] If someone has **command** of a situation, they have control of it because they have, or seem to have, power or authority. ❑ *Mr Baker would take command of the campaign... In times of currency crisis interest rates can raised as a sign that a government is in command.* [8] Your **command of** something, such as a foreign language, is your knowledge of it and your ability to use this knowledge. ❑ *His command of English was excellent.* [9] ➔ See also **high command**, **second-in-command**. [10] If you have a particular skill or particular resources **at** your **command**, you have them and can use them fully. [FORMAL] ❑ *The country should have the right to defend itself with all legal means at its command.*

◆◇◇ | VERB = instruct, order | V n to-inf | V with quote | V that | V n with quote | N-VAR | VERB: no cont | V n | VERB = rule | V n | N-UNCOUNT: usu N *of* n | VERB | V n | V | N-UNCOUNT = charge | N-COUNT-COLL: usu supp N | N-COUNT | N-UNCOUNT | N-UNCOUNT: N *of* n | PHRASE

**com|man|dant** /kɒməndænt/ **(commandants)** A **commandant** is an army officer in charge of a particular place or group of people. N-COUNT; N-TITLE

**com|mand econo|my** **(command economies)** In a **command economy**, business activities and the use of resources are decided by the government, and not by market forces. [BUSINESS] ❑ *...the Czech Republic's transition from a command economy to a market system.* N-COUNT

**com|man|deer** /kɒməndɪəʳ/ **(commandeers, commandeering, commandeered)** [1] If the armed forces **commandeer** a vehicle or building owned by someone else, they officially take charge of it so that they can use it. ❑ *The soldiers commandeered vehicles in the capital and occupied the televi-* VERB = requisition | V n

sion station... *They drove in convoy round the city in commandeered cars.* [2] To **commandeer** something owned by someone else means to take charge of it so that you can use it. ❑ *The hijacker commandeered the plane on a domestic flight.*
V-ed; VERB; disapproval; = appropriate; V n

**com|mand|er** /kəmɑːndəʳ, -mænd-/ **(commanders)** ◆◇◇ [1] A **commander** is an officer in charge of a military operation or organization. ❑ *The commander and some of the men had been released. ...Commander Bob Marks.* [2] A **commander** is an officer in the Royal Navy or the U.S. Navy.
N-COUNT; N-TITLE; N-VOC; N-COUNT; N-TITLE; N-VOC

**commander-in-chief** **(commanders-in-chief)** A **commander-in-chief** is an officer in charge of all the forces in a particular area. ❑ *He was to be the commander-in-chief of the armed forces.*
N-COUNT; N-TITLE

**com|mand|ing** /kəmɑːndɪŋ, -mænd-/ [1] If you are in a **commanding** position or situation, you are in a strong or powerful position or situation. ❑ *Right now you're in a more commanding position than you have been for ages... The French vessel has a commanding lead.* [2] If you describe someone as **commanding**, you mean that they are powerful and confident. ❑ *Lovett was a tall, commanding man with a waxed gray mustache... The voice at the other end of the line was serious and commanding.* [3] → See also **command**.
ADJ: usu ADJ n; ADJ; approval; = authoritative

**com|mand|ing of|fic|er** **(commanding officers)** A **commanding officer** is an officer who is in charge of a military unit. ❑ *He got permission from his commanding officer to join me.*
N-COUNT

**com|mand|ment** /kəmɑːndmənt, -mænd-/ **(commandments)** **The Ten Commandments** are the ten rules of behaviour which, according to the Old Testament of the Bible, people should obey.
N-COUNT

**com|man|do** /kəmɑːndoʊ, -mænd-/ **(commandos** or **commandoes)** [1] A **commando** is a group of soldiers who have been specially trained to carry out surprise attacks. ❑ *...a small commando of marines... The hostages were freed in the commando raid.* [2] A **commando** is a soldier who is a member of a commando.
N-COUNT: oft N n; N-COUNT

**com|mand per|for|mance** **(command performances)** A **command performance** is a special performance of a play or show which is given for a head of state.
N-COUNT

**com|mand post** **(command posts)** A **command post** is a place from which a commander in the army controls and organizes his forces.
N-COUNT

**com|memo|rate** /kəmeməreɪt/ **(commemorates, commemorating, commemorated)** To **commemorate** an important event or person means to remember them by means of a special action, ceremony, or specially created object. ❑ *One room contained a gallery of paintings commemorating great moments in baseball history.* ♦ **com|memo|ra|tion** /kəmemәreɪʃən/ **(commemorations)** *...the 50th Anniversary Commemoration of the Warsaw Ghetto Uprising.*
VERB; = celebrate; V n; N-VAR: usu with supp

**com|memo|ra|tive** /kəmemərətɪv/ A **commemorative** object or event is intended to make people remember a particular event or person. ❑ *The Queen unveiled a commemorative plaque.*
ADJ: ADJ n

**com|mence** /kəmens/ **(commences, commencing, commenced)** When something **commences** or you **commence** it, it begins. [FORMAL] ❑ *The academic year commences at the beginning of October... They commenced a systematic search... The hunter knelt beside the animal carcass and commenced to skin it.*
VERB; = begin; V; V n/-ing; V to-inf

**com|mence|ment** /kəmensmənt/ **(commencements)** [1] The **commencement** of something is its beginning. [FORMAL] ❑ *All applicants should be at least 16 years of age at the commencement of this course.* [2] **Commencement** is a ceremony at a university, college, or high school at which students formally receive their degrees or diplomas. [AM]
N-UNCOUNT: usu *the* N *of* n; N-VAR: usu N n

✔ in BRIT, use **graduation**

**com|mend** /kəmend/ **(commends, commending, commended)** [1] If you **commend** someone or something, you praise them formally. [FORMAL] ❑ *I commended her for that action... I commend Ms. Orth on writing such an informative article... The book was widely commended for its candour... The reports commend her bravery... His actions were commended by the Jury.* ♦ **com|men|da|tion** /kɒmendeɪʃən/ **(commendations)** *The Company received a commendation from the Royal Society of Arts.* [2] If someone **commends** a person or thing **to** you, they tell you that you will find them good or useful. [FORMAL] ❑ *I can commend it to him as a realistic course of action.*
VERB; V n *for/on* n/-ing; V n; N-COUNT; VERB; = recommend; V n *to* n

**com|mend|able** /kəmendəbəl/ If you describe someone's behaviour as **commendable**, you approve of it or are praising it. [FORMAL] ❑ *Mr Sparrow has acted with commendable speed.*
ADJ; approval; = admirable

**com|men|su|rate** /kəmensərət/ If the level of one thing is **commensurate with** another, the first level is in proportion to the second. [FORMAL] ❑ *Employees are paid salaries commensurate with those of teachers.*
ADJ: v-link ADJ *with/to* n, ADJ n

**com|ment** /kɒment/ **(comments, commenting, commented)** ◆◆◇ [1] If you **comment on** something, you give your opinion about it or you give an explanation for it. ❑ *Stratford police refuse to comment on whether anyone has been arrested... You really can't comment till you know the facts... 'I'm always happy with new developments,' he commented... Stuart commented that this was very true.* [2] A **comment** is something that you say which expresses your opinion of something or which gives an explanation of it. ❑ *He made his comments at a news conference in Amsterdam... There's been no comment so far from police about the allegations... Lady Thatcher, who is abroad, was not available for comment.* [3] If an event or situation is a **comment on** something, it reveals something about that thing, usually something bad. ❑ *He argues that family problems are typically a comment on some unresolved issues in the family.* [4] People say **'no comment'** as a way of refusing to answer a question, usually when it is asked by a journalist. ❑ *No comment. I don't know anything.*
VERB; V *on* n/wh; V; V with quote; V that; N-VAR; N-SING: usu *a* N *on* n = reflection; CONVENTION

**com|men|tary** /kɒməntri, AM -teri/ **(commentaries)** [1] A **commentary** is a description of an event that is broadcast on radio or television while the event is taking place. ❑ *He gave the listening crowd a running commentary... That programme will include live commentary on the England-Ireland game.* [2] A **commentary** is an article or book which explains or discusses something. ❑ *Mr Rich will be writing a twice-weekly commentary on American society and culture.* [3] **Commentary** is discussion or criticism of something. ❑ *The show mixed comedy with social commentary.*
N-VAR; N-COUNT; N-UNCOUNT: also *a* N, with supp = comment

**com|men|tate** /kɒmənteɪt/ **(commentates, commentating, commentated)** To **commentate** means to give a radio or television commentary on an event. ❑ *They are in Sweden to commentate on the European Championships... He commentates for the BBC.*
VERB; V *on* n; V

**com|men|ta|tor** /kɒmənteɪtəʳ/ **(commentators)** ◆◇◇ [1] A **commentator** is a broadcaster who gives a radio or television commentary on an event. ❑ *...a sports commentator.* [2] A **commentator** is someone who often writes or broadcasts about a particular subject. ❑ *...a political commentator... A. M. Babu is a commentator on African affairs.*
N-COUNT: usu with supp; N-COUNT: usu with supp

**com|merce** /kɒmɜːʳs/ ◆◇◇ **Commerce** is the activities and procedures involved in buying and selling things. ❑ *They have made their fortunes from industry and commerce.* → See also **chamber of commerce**.
N-UNCOUNT

**com|mer|cial** /kəmɜːʳʃəl/ **(commercials)** ◆◆◇ [1] **Commercial** means involving or relating to the buying and selling of goods. ❑ *Docklands in its heyday was a major centre of industrial and commercial activity... Attacks were reported on police, vehicles and commercial premises.* [2] **Commercial** organi-
ADJ: usu ADJ n; ADJ

zations and activities are concerned with making money or profits, rather than, for example, with scientific research or providing a public service. ❑ *British Rail has indeed become more commercial over the past decade... Conservationists in Chile are concerned over the effect of commercial exploitation of forests... Whether the project will be a commercial success is still uncertain.* ♦ **com|mer|cial|ly** *British Aerospace reckon that the plane will be commercially viable if 400 can be sold... Insulin is produced commercially from animals.* ADV: usu ADV adj, ADV with v, also ADV with cl [3] A **commercial** product is made to be sold to the public. ❑ *They are the leading manufacturer in both defence and commercial products.* ADJ: ADJ n ♦ **com|mer|cial|ly** *It was the first commercially available machine to employ artificial intelligence.* ADV: usu ADV adj, also ADV with v [4] A **commercial** vehicle is a vehicle used for carrying goods, or passengers who pay. ADJ: usu ADJ n [5] **Commercial** television and radio are paid for by the broadcasting of advertisements, rather than by the government. ❑ *...Classic FM, the first national commercial radio station.* ADJ: usu ADJ n ≠ *public service* [6] **Commercial** is used to describe something such as a film or a type of music that it is intended to be popular with the public, and is not very original or of high quality. ❑ *There's a feeling among a lot of people that music has become too commercial.* ADJ [7] A **commercial** is an advertisement that is broadcast on television or radio. N-COUNT

**com|mer|cial bank** **(commercial banks)** A **commercial bank** is a bank which makes short-term loans using money from current or checking accounts. [BUSINESS] N-COUNT

**com|mer|cial break** **(commercial breaks)** A **commercial break** is the interval during a commercial television programme, or between programmes, during which advertisements are shown. N-COUNT

**com|mer|cial|ism** /kəmɜːʳʃəlɪzəm/ **Commercialism** is the practice of making a lot of money from things without caring about their quality. ❑ *Koons has engrossed himself in a world of commercialism that most modern artists disdain.* N-UNCOUNT [disapproval]

**com|mer|cial|ize** /kəmɜːʳʃəlaɪz/ **(commercializes, commercializing, commercialized)**

✓ in BRIT, also use **commercialise**

If something **is commercialized**, it is used or changed in such a way that it makes money or profits, often in a way that people disapprove of. ❑ *It seems such a pity that a distinguished and honored name should be commercialized in such a manner... Federal agencies should commercialize research.* VERB [disapproval] *be* V-ed, V n ♦ **com|mer|cial|ized** *Rock'n'roll has become so commercialized and safe since punk.* ADJ ♦ **com|mer|ciali|za|tion** /kəmɜːʳʃəlaɪzeɪʃən/ *...the commercialization of Christmas.* N-UNCOUNT: oft N *of* n

**com|mie** /kɒmi/ **(commies)** A **commie** is the same as a **communist**. [INFORMAL] N-COUNT [disapproval]

**com|mis|er|ate** /kəmɪzəreɪt/ **(commiserates, commiserating, commiserated)** If you **commiserate with** someone, you show them pity or sympathy when something unpleasant has happened to them. ❑ *When I lost, he commiserated with me.* VERB, V *with* n

**com|mis|sari|at** /kɒmɪseəriət/ **(commissariats)** A **commissariat** is a military department that is in charge of food supplies. N-COUNT

**com|mis|sary** /kɒmɪsəri, AM -seri/ **(commissaries)** A **commissary** is a shop that provides food and equipment in a place such as a military camp or a prison. [AM] N-COUNT

**com|mis|sion** /kəmɪʃən/ **(commissions, commissioning, commissioned)** ♦♦◇ [1] If you **commission** something or **commission** someone **to** do something, you formally arrange for someone to do a piece of work for you. ❑ *The Ministry of Agriculture commissioned a study into low-input farming... You can commission them to paint something especially for you. ...specially commissioned reports.* VERB, V n, V n to-inf, V-ed ♦ **Commission** is also a noun. ❑ *He approached John Wexley with a commission to write the screenplay of the film.* N-VAR [2] A **commission** is a piece of work that someone is asked to do and is paid for. ❑ *Just a few days ago, I finished a commission.* N-COUNT [3] **Commission** is a sum of money paid to a salesperson for every sale that he or she makes. If a salesperson is paid **on commission**, the amount they receive depends on the amount they sell. ❑ *The salesmen work on commission only... He also got a commission for bringing in new clients.* N-VAR: oft *on* N [4] If a bank or other company charges **commission**, they charge a fee for providing a service, for example for exchanging money or issuing an insurance policy. [BUSINESS] ❑ *Sellers pay a fixed commission fee.* N-UNCOUNT [5] A **commission** is a group of people who have been appointed to find out about something or to control something. ❑ *The authorities have been asked to set up a commission to investigate the murders. ...the Press Complaints Commission.* N-COUNT-COLL [6] If a member of the armed forces receives a **commission**, he or she becomes an officer. ❑ *He accepted a commission as a naval officer.* N-COUNT [7] If something, for example a ship or a piece of equipment, is **out of commission**, it is broken and cannot be used until it is repaired. ❑ *The operator expects the ship to be out of commission until the end of September.* PHRASE: v-link PHR, PHR after v [8] → See also **High Commission**.

**com|mis|sion|er** /kəmɪʃənəʳ/ **(commissioners)** also **Commissioner.** ♦◇◇ A **commissioner** is an important official in a government department or other organization. ❑ *...the European Commissioner for External Affairs. ...police commissioner.* N-COUNT: usu with supp → See also **High Commissioner**.

**com|mit** /kəmɪt/ **(commits, committing, committed)** ♦♦◇ [1] If someone **commits** a crime or a sin, they do something illegal or bad. ❑ *I have never committed any crime... This is a man who has committed murder.* VERB, V n, V n [2] If someone **commits suicide**, they deliberately kill themselves. ❑ *There are unconfirmed reports he tried to commit suicide.* VERB, V n [3] If you **commit** money or resources **to** something, you decide to use them for a particular purpose. ❑ *They called on Western nations to commit more money to the poorest nations... He should not commit American troops without the full consent of Congress.* VERB, V n *to/for* n/-ing, V n [4] If you **commit yourself to** something, you say that you will definitely do it. If you **commit yourself to** someone, you decide that you want to have a long-term relationship with them. ❑ *I would advise people to think very carefully about committing themselves to working Sundays... I'd like a friendship that might lead to something deeper, but I wouldn't want to commit myself too soon... You don't have to commit to anything over the phone.* VERB, V pron-refl *to* -ing/n, V pron-refl, V *to* n, Also V n *to* n ♦ **com|mit|ted** *He said that the government remained committed to peace. ...a committed socialist.* ADJ: oft ADJ *to* n/-ing [5] If you do not want to **commit yourself on** something, you do not want to say what you really think about it or what you are going to do. ❑ *It isn't their diplomatic style to commit themselves on such a delicate issue... She didn't want to commit herself one way or the other.* VERB: with brd-neg, V pron-refl *on* n, V pron-refl [6] If someone **is committed to** a hospital, prison, or other institution, they are officially sent there for a period of time. ❑ *Arthur's drinking caused him to be committed to a psychiatric hospital.* VERB: usu passive, *be* V-ed *to* n, Also *be* V-ed [7] In the British legal system, if someone **is committed for trial**, they are sent by magistrates to stand trial in a crown court. ❑ *He is expected to be committed for trial at Liverpool Crown Court.* VERB: usu passive, *be* V-ed *for* n [8] If you **commit** something **to** paper or **to** writing, you record it by writing it down. If you **commit** something **to** memory, you learn it so that you will remember it. ❑ *She had not committed anything to paper about it... I'll repeat that so you can commit it to memory.* VERB, V n *to* n, V n *to* n

**com|mit|ment** /kəmɪtmənt/ **(commitments)** ♦♦◇ [1] **Commitment** is a strong belief in an idea or system. ❑ *...commitment to the ideals of Bolshevism.* N-UNCOUNT: oft N *to* n [2] A **commitment** is something which regularly takes up some of your time because of an agreement you have made or because of responsibilities that you have. ❑ *Work commitments* N-COUNT

forced her to uproot herself and her son from Reykjavik. [3] If you make a **commitment to** do something, you promise that you will do it. [FORMAL] ❑ *We made a commitment to keep working together... They made a commitment to peace.* N-COUNT: usu N to-inf, N *to* n
[4] **Commitment** is the process of officially sending someone to a prison or to hospital. [AM] N-VAR

✔ in BRIT, use **committal**

**com|mit|tal** /kəmɪtəl/ **(committals) Committal** is the process of officially sending someone to a prison or to hospital. [BRIT] ❑ *...his committal to prison. ...committal proceedings.* N-VAR

✔ in AM, use **commitment**

**com|mit|tee** /kəmɪti/ **(committees)** A **committee** is a group of people who meet to make decisions or plans for a larger group or organization that they represent. ❑ *...a committee of ministers. ...an elected Management Committee who serve the Association on a voluntary basis.* ◆◆◆ N-COUNT-COLL: usu with supp

**com|mode** /kəmoʊd/ **(commodes)** [1] A **commode** is a movable piece of furniture shaped like a chair, which has a large pot below or inside it. It is used as a toilet, especially by people who are too ill to be able to walk easily. [mainly BRIT] N-COUNT
[2] A **commode** is a toilet. [AM] N-COUNT

**com|mo|di|ous** /kəmoʊdiəs/ A **commodious** room or house is large and has a lot of space. [WRITTEN] ADJ: usu ADJ n

**com|mod|ity** /kəmɒdɪti/ **(commodities)** A **commodity** is something that is sold for money. [BUSINESS] ❑ *The government increased prices on several basic commodities like bread and meat.* N-COUNT

**com|mo|dore** /kɒmədɔːr/ **(commodores)** A **commodore** is an officer of senior rank in the navy, especially the British Royal Navy. N-COUNT; N-TITLE

**com|mon** /kɒmən/ **(commoner, commonest, commons)** [1] If something is **common**, it is found in large numbers or it happens often. ❑ *His name was Hansen, a common name in Norway... Oil pollution is the commonest cause of death for seabirds... It was common practice for prisoners to carve objects from animal bones to pass the time.* ◆◆◆ ADJ ≠ uncommon, rare
♦ **com|mon|ly** *Parsley is probably the most commonly used of all herbs.* ADV: ADV with v
[2] If something is **common to** two or more people or groups, it is done, possessed, or used by them all. ❑ *Moldavians and Romanians share a common language... Such behaviour is common to all young people.* ADJ: oft ADJ *to* n
[3] When there are more animals or plants of a particular species than there are of related species, then the first species is called **common**. ❑ *...the common house fly.* ADJ: ADJ n
[4] **Common** is used to indicate that someone or something is of the ordinary kind and not special in any way. ❑ *Common salt is made up of 40% sodium and 60% chloride.* ADJ: ADJ n
[5] **Common** decency or **common** courtesy is the decency or courtesy which most people have. You usually talk about this when someone has not shown these characteristics in their behaviour to show your disapproval of them. ❑ *He didn't have the common courtesy to ask permission.* ADJ: oft with brd-neg, ADJ n [disapproval]
[6] You can use **common** to describe knowledge, an opinion, or a feeling that is shared by people in general. ❑ *It is common knowledge that swimming is one of the best forms of exercise.* ADJ: ADJ n
♦ **com|mon|ly** *A little adolescent rebellion is commonly believed to be healthy.* ADV: ADV -ed
[7] If you describe someone or their behaviour as **common**, you mean that they show a lack of taste, education, and good manners. ❑ *She might be a little common at times, but she was certainly not boring.* ADJ [disapproval] ≠ refined
[8] A **common** is an area of grassy land, usually in or near a village or small town, where the public is allowed to go. ❑ *We are warning women not to go out on to the common alone. ...Wimbledon Common.* N-COUNT; N-IN-NAMES
[9] **The Commons** is the same as the **House of Commons**. The members of the House of Commons can also be referred to as **the Commons**. ❑ *The Prime Minister is to make a statement in the Commons this afternoon... The Commons has spent over three months on the bill.* N-PROPER-COLL
[10] → See also **lowest common denominator**.
PHRASES [11] If two or more things have something **in common**, they have the same characteristic or feature. ❑ *The oboe and the clarinet have got certain features in common... In common with most Italian lakes, access to the shores of Orta is restricted.* PHRASE: oft PHR *with* n
[12] If two or more people have something **in common**, they share the same interests or experiences. ❑ *He had very little in common with his sister.* PHRASE: usu *have* n PHR, oft PHR *with* n
[13] **common ground** → see **ground**. **the common touch** → see **touch**.

**com|mon|al|ity** /kɒmənælɪti/ **(commonalities) Commonality** is used to refer to a feature or purpose that is shared by two or more people or things. [FORMAL] ❑ *We don't have the same commonality of interest... There are an amazing number of commonalities between systems.* N-VAR: oft N *of* n

**com|mon cold (common colds) The common cold** is a mild illness. If you have it, your nose is blocked or runny and you have a sore throat or a cough. N-COUNT: usu sing, *the* N

**com|mon cur|ren|cy** If you say that an idea or belief has become **common currency**, you mean it is widely used and accepted. ❑ *The story that she was trapped in a loveless marriage became common currency.* N-UNCOUNT

**com|mon de|nomi|na|tor (common denominators)** [1] In mathematics, a **common denominator** is a number which can be divided exactly by all the denominators in a group of fractions. N-COUNT
[2] A **common denominator** is a characteristic or attitude that is shared by all members of a group of people. ❑ *I think the only common denominator of success is hard work.* N-COUNT
[3] → See also **lowest common denominator**.

**com|mon|er** /kɒmənər/ **(commoners)** In countries which have a nobility, **commoners** are the people who are not members of the nobility. ❑ *It's only the second time a potential heir to the throne has married a commoner.* N-COUNT

**com|mon land (common lands) Common land** is land which everyone is allowed to use. N-UNCOUNT: also N in pl

**com|mon law** also **common-law**. [1] **Common law** is the system of law which is based on judges' decisions and on custom rather than on written laws. ❑ *Canadian libel law is based on English common law.* N-UNCOUNT
[2] A **common law** relationship is regarded as a marriage because it has lasted a long time, although no official marriage contract has been signed. ❑ *...his common law wife.* ADJ: ADJ n

**com|mon mar|ket (common markets)** [1] A **common market** is an organization of countries who have agreed to trade freely with each other and make common decisions about industry and agriculture. [BUSINESS] ❑ *...the Central American Common Market.* N-COUNT
[2] **The Common Market** is the former name of the **European Union**. Some people still refer to the European Union as the **Common Market**. N-PROPER: *the* N

**com|mon noun (common nouns)** A **common noun** is a noun such as 'tree', 'water', or 'beauty' that is not the name of one particular person or thing. Compare **proper noun**. N-COUNT

**common-or-garden** also **common or garden**. You can use **common-or-garden** to describe something you think is ordinary and not special in any way. [mainly BRIT] ❑ *It's not just a common-or-garden phone!* ADJ: ADJ n

✔ in AM, use **garden-variety**

**common|place** /kɒmənpleɪs/ **(commonplaces)** [1] If something is **commonplace**, it happens often or is often found, and is therefore not surprising. ❑ *Foreign vacations have become commonplace.* ADJ: usu v-link ADJ
[2] A **commonplace** is a remark or opinion that is often expressed and is therefore not original or interesting. ❑ *It is a commonplace to say that Northern Ireland is a backwater in the modern Europe.* N-COUNT: usu sing

**com|mon room** **(common rooms)** also **common-room.** A **common room** is a room in a university or school where people can sit, talk, and relax. [mainly BRIT] N-COUNT

**com|mon sense** also **commonsense.** Your **common sense** is your natural ability to make good judgments and to behave in a practical and sensible way. ❑ *Use your common sense. ...a common-sense approach.* N-UNCOUNT

**com|mon stock** **Common stock** refers to the shares in a company that are owned by people who have a right to vote at the company's meetings and to receive part of the company's profits after the holders of preferred stock have been paid. [AM, BUSINESS] ❑ *The company priced its offering of 2.7 million shares of common stock at 20 cents a share.* ➔ See also **preferred stock**. N-UNCOUNT

☑ in BRIT use **ordinary shares**

**common|wealth** /kɒmənwelθ/ [1] **The Commonwealth** is an organization consisting of the United Kingdom and most of the countries that were previously under its rule. N-PROPER: the N [2] **Commonwealth** is used in the official names of some countries, groups of countries, or parts of countries. ❑ *...the Commonwealth of Australia. ...the Commonwealth of Independent States, which replaced the Soviet Union.* N-IN-NAMES: the N of n

**com|mo|tion** /kəmoʊʃən/ **(commotions)** A **commotion** is a lot of noise, confusion, and excitement. ❑ *He heard a commotion outside.* N-VAR

**comms** /kɒmz/ **Comms** is an abbreviation for **communications**. [INFORMAL] ❑ *...comms software.* N-PLURAL

**com|mu|nal** /kɒmjʊnəl, AM kəmjuːnəl/ [1] **Communal** means relating to particular groups in a country or society. ❑ *Communal violence broke out in different parts of the country. ...inter-communal relations.* ADJ: ADJ n [2] You use **communal** to describe something that is shared by a group of people. ❑ *The inmates ate in a communal dining room. ...communal ownership.* ADJ: usu ADJ n ♦ **com|mu|nal|ly** *Meals are taken communally in the dining room.* ADV: usu ADV after v

**com|mune** **(communes, communing, communed)**

☑ The noun is pronounced /kɒmjuːn/. The verb is pronounced /kəmjuːn/.

[1] A **commune** is a group of people who live together and share everything. ❑ *Mack lived in a commune.* N-COUNT [2] In France and some other countries, a **commune** is a town, village, or area which has its own council. N-COUNT [3] If you say that someone **is communing with** an animal or spirit, or **with** nature, you mean that they appear to be communicating with it. [LITERARY] ❑ *She would happily trot behind him as he set off to commune with nature.* VERB V with n

**com|mu|ni|cable** /kəmjuːnɪkəbəl/ A **communicable** disease is one that can be passed on to other people. [MEDICAL] ADJ: usu ADJ n = infectious, contagious

**com|mu|ni|cant** /kəmjuːnɪkənt/ **(communicants)** A **communicant** is a person in the Christian church who receives communion. [FORMAL] N-COUNT

**com|mu|ni|cate** /kəmjuːnɪkeɪt/ **(communicates, communicating, communicated)** ◆◇◇ [1] If you **communicate with** someone, you share or exchange information with them, for example by speaking, writing, or using equipment. You can also say that two people **communicate**. ❑ *My natural mother has never communicated with me... Officials of the CIA depend heavily on electronic mail to communicate with each other... They communicated in sign language.* V-RECIP; V with n; pl-n V with pron-recip; pl-n V ♦ **com|mu|ni|ca|tion** *Lithuania hasn't had any direct communication with Moscow. ...use of the radio telephone for communication between controllers and pilots.* N-UNCOUNT: oft N with/between n [2] If you **communicate** information, a feeling, or an idea **to** someone, you let them know about it. ❑ *They successfully communicate their knowledge to others... People must communicate their feelings.* VERB; V n to n; V n [3] If one person **communicates with** another, they successfully make each other aware of their feelings and ideas. You can also say that two people **communicate**. ❑ *He was never good at communicating with the players... Family therapy showed us how to communicate with each other. ...considerate individuals who can communicate and work in a team.* V-RECIP; V with n; pl-n V with pron-recip; pl-n V ♦ **com|mu|ni|ca|tion** *There was a tremendous lack of communication between us. ...communication skills.* N-UNCOUNT: oft N with/between n ♦ **com|mu|ni|ca|tor** **(communicators)** *She's a good communicator.* N-COUNT

**com|mu|ni|ca|tion** /kəmjuːnɪkeɪʃən/ **(communications)** ◆◇◇ [1] **Communications** are the systems and processes that are used to communicate or broadcast information, especially by means of electricity or radio waves. ❑ *...a communications satellite. ...communications equipment.* N-PLURAL: oft N n [2] A **communication** is a message. [FORMAL] ❑ *The ambassador has brought with him a communication from the President.* N-COUNT [3] ➔ See also **communicate**.

**com|mu|ni|ca|tive** /kəmjuːnɪkətɪv/ [1] Someone who is **communicative** talks to people, for example about their feelings, and tells people things. ❑ *She has become a lot more tolerant and communicative.* ADJ = open [2] **Communicative** means relating to the ability to communicate. ❑ *We have a very communicative approach to teaching languages.* ADJ: usu ADJ n

**com|mun|ion** /kəmjuːnjən/ **(communions)** [1] **Communion** with nature or with a person is the feeling that you are sharing thoughts or feelings with them. ❑ *...communion with nature.* N-UNCOUNT: also a N, oft N with n [2] **Communion** is the Christian ceremony in which people eat bread and drink wine in memory of Christ's death. ❑ *Most villagers took communion only at Easter.* N-UNCOUNT: also N in pl

**com|mu|ni|qué** /kəmjuːnɪkeɪ, AM -keɪ/ **(communiqués)** A **communiqué** is an official statement or announcement. [FORMAL] ❑ *The communiqué said military targets had been hit.* N-COUNT

**com|mun|ism** /kɒmjʊnɪzəm/ also **Communism.** **Communism** is the political belief that all people are equal and that workers should control the means of producing things. ❑ *...the ultimate triumph of communism in the world.* N-UNCOUNT ≠ capitalism

**com|mun|ist** /kɒmjʊnɪst/ **(communists)** ◆◆◇ [1] A **communist** is someone who believes in communism. N-COUNT [2] **Communist** means relating to communism. ❑ *...the Communist Party.* ADJ: usu ADJ n

**com|mu|nity** /kəmjuːnɪti/ **(communities)** ◆◆◆ [1] **The community** is all the people who live in a particular area or place. ❑ *He's well liked by people in the community... The growth of such vigilante gangs has worried community leaders, police and politicians.* N-SING-COLL: usu the N [2] A particular **community** is a group of people who are similar in some way. ❑ *The police haven't really done anything for the black community in particular. ...the business community.* N-COUNT-COLL: usu supp N [3] **Community** is friendship between different people or groups, and a sense of having something in common. ❑ *Two of our greatest strengths are diversity and community.* N-UNCOUNT

**com|mu|nity cen|tre** **(community centres)**

☑ in AM, use **community center**

A **community centre** is a place that is specially provided for the people, groups, and organizations in a particular area, where they can go in order to meet one another and do things. N-COUNT

**com|mu|nity col|lege** **(community colleges)** A **community college** is a local college where students from the surrounding area can take courses in practical or academic subjects. [AM] N-COUNT

**com|mu|nity po|lic|ing** **Community policing** is a system in which policemen work only in one particular area of the community, so that everyone knows them. N-UNCOUNT

**com|mu|nity ser|vice** **Community service** is unpaid work that criminals sometimes do as a punishment instead of being sent to prison. ❑ *He was sentenced to 140 hours community service.* N-UNCOUNT

**com|mute** /kəmjuːt/ **(commutes, commuting, commuted)** [1] If you **commute**, you travel a long distance every day between your home and your place of work. ❑ *Mike commutes to London every day... McLaren began commuting between Paris and London... He's going to commute.* ♦ **com|mut|er (commuters)** *The number of commuters to London has dropped by 100,000. ...a commuter train.* [2] A **commute** is the journey that you make when you commute. [mainly AM] ❑ *The average Los Angeles commute is over 60 miles a day.* [3] If a death sentence or prison sentence **is commuted to** a less serious punishment, it is changed to that punishment. ❑ *His death sentence was commuted to life imprisonment... Prison sentences have been commuted.*
VERB; V to/from n; V between n and n, V; N-COUNT; N-COUNT; VERB: usu passive; be V-ed to n; be V-ed

**com|mut|er belt (commuter belts)** A **commuter belt** is the area surrounding a large city, where many people who work in the city live. ❑ *...people who live in the commuter belt around the capital.*
N-COUNT

**com|pact (compacts, compacting, compacted)**

> The adjective and verb are pronounced /kəmpækt/. The noun is pronounced /kɒmpækt/.

[1] **Compact** things are small or take up very little space. You use this word when you think this is a good quality. ❑ *...my compact office in Washington. ...the new, more compact Czech government.* ♦ **com|pact|ness** *The very compactness of the cottage made it all the more snug and appealing.* [2] A **compact** person is small but strong. ❑ *He was compact, probably no taller than me.* [3] A **compact** cassette, camera, or car is a small type of cassette, camera, or car. [4] To **compact** something means to press it so that it becomes more solid. [FORMAL] ❑ *The Smith boy was compacting the trash... The soil settles and is compacted by the winter rain.*
ADJ: usu ADJ n [approval]; N-UNCOUNT; ADJ; ADJ: ADJ n; VERB = compress; V n; V n

**com|pact disc (compact discs)**

> in AM, also use **compact disk**

**Compact discs** are small shiny discs that contain music or computer information. The abbreviation **CD** is also used.
N-COUNT: also on N

**com|pan|ion** /kəmpænjən/ **(companions)** A **companion** is someone who you spend time with or who you are travelling with. ❑ *Fred had been her constant companion for the last six years of her life... I asked my travelling companion what he thought of the situation in Algeria.*
N-COUNT

**com|pan|ion|able** /kəmpænjənəbᵊl/ If you describe a person as **companionable**, you mean they are friendly and pleasant to be with. [WRITTEN] ♦ **com|pan|ion|ably** /kəmpænjənəbli/ ❑ *They walked companionably back to the house.*
ADJ [approval] = affable; ADV: ADV with v

**com|pan|ion|ship** /kəmpænjənʃɪp/ **Companionship** is having someone you know and like with you, rather than being on your own. ❑ *I depended on his companionship and on his judgment.*
N-UNCOUNT = company

**com|pan|ion|way** /kəmpænjənweɪ/ **(companionways)** A **companionway** is a staircase or ladder that leads from one deck to another on a ship.
N-COUNT

**com|pa|ny** /kʌmpəni/ **(companies)** [1] A **company** is a business organization that makes money by selling goods or services. ❑ *Sheila found some work as a secretary in an insurance company. ...the Ford Motor Company.* [2] A **company** is a group of opera singers, dancers, or actors who work together. ❑ *...the Phoenix Dance Company.* [3] A **company** is a group of soldiers that is usually part of a battalion or regiment, and that is divided into two or more platoons. ❑ *The division will consist of two tank companies and one infantry company.* [4] **Company** is having another person or other people with you, usually when this is pleasant or stops you feeling lonely. ❑ *'I won't stay long.' — 'No, please. I need the company'... Ross had always enjoyed the company of women... I'm not in the mood for company.* [5] → See also **joint-stock company, public company.**
◆◆◆ N-COUNT-COLL; N-IN-NAMES = firm; N-COUNT-COLL; N-IN-NAMES; N-COUNT; N-IN-NAMES; N-UNCOUNT

PHRASES [6] If you say that someone **is in good company**, you mean that they should not be ashamed of a mistake or opinion, because some important or respected people have made the same mistake or have the same opinion. ❑ *Mr Koo is in good company. The prime minister made a similar slip a couple of years back.* [7] If you **have company**, you have a visitor or friend with you. ❑ *He didn't say he had had company.* [8] When you are **in company**, you are with a person or group of people. ❑ *When they were in company she always seemed to dominate the conversation.* [9] If you feel, believe, or know something **in company with** someone else, you both feel, believe, or know it. [FORMAL] ❑ *Saudi Arabia, in company with some other Gulf oil states, is concerned to avoid any repetition of the two oil price shocks of the 1970s.* [10] If you **keep** someone **company**, you spend time with them and stop them feeling lonely or bored. ❑ *Why don't you stay here and keep Emma company?* [11] If you **keep company with** a person or **with** a particular kind of person, you spend a lot of time with them. ❑ *He keeps company with all sorts of lazy characters.* [12] If two or more people **part company**, they go in different directions after going in the same direction together. [WRITTEN] ❑ *The three of them parted company at the bus stop.* [13] If you **part company with** someone, you end your association with them, often because of a disagreement. [FORMAL] ❑ *The tennis star has parted company with his Austrian trainer... We have agreed to part company after differences of opinion.*
PHRASE: V inflects; PHRASE: V inflects; PHRASE: v-link PHR, PHR after v ≠ alone; PREP-PHRASE: PHR n; PHRASE: V inflects; PHRASE: V inflects; PHRASE: V inflects, pl-n PHR, PHR with n; PHRASE: V inflects, PHR with n, pl-n PHR

**com|pa|ny car (company cars)** A **company car** is a car which an employer gives to an employee to use as their own, usually as a benefit of having a particular job, or because their job involves a lot of travelling. [BUSINESS]
N-COUNT

**com|pa|ny sec|re|tary (company secretaries)** A **company secretary** is a person whose job within a company is to keep the legal affairs, accounts, and administration in order. [BRIT, BUSINESS]
N-COUNT

**com|pa|rable** /kɒmpərəbᵊl/ [1] Something that is **comparable** to something else is roughly similar, for example in amount or importance. ❑ *...paying the same wages to men and women for work of comparable value... Farmers were meant to get an income comparable to that of townspeople... The risk it poses is comparable with smoking just one cigarette every year.* [2] If two or more things are **comparable**, they are of the same kind or are in the same situation, and so they can reasonably be compared. ❑ *In other comparable countries real wages increased much more rapidly... By contrast, the comparable figure for the Netherlands is 16 per cent.*
ADJ: oft ADJ to/with n = similar; ADJ = equivalent

**com|para|tive** /kəmpærətɪv/ **(comparatives)** [1] You use **comparative** to show that you are judging something against a previous or different situation. For example, **comparative** calm is a situation which is calmer than before or calmer than the situation in other places. ❑ *...those who manage to reach the comparative safety of Fendel... The task was accomplished with comparative ease.* ♦ **com|para|tive|ly** *...a comparatively small nation. ...children who find it comparatively easy to make and keep friends.* [2] A **comparative** study is a study that involves the comparison of two or more things of the same kind. ❑ *...a comparative study of the dietary practices of people from various regions of India. ...a professor of English and comparative literature.* [3] In grammar, the **comparative** form of an adjective or adverb shows that something has more of a quality than something else has. For example, 'bigger' is the comparative form of 'big', and 'more quickly' is the comparative form of 'quickly'. Compare **superlative.** ♦ **Comparative** is also a noun. ❑ *The comparative of 'pretty' is 'prettier'.*
ADJ: ADJ n = relative; ADV: ADV adj/adv; ADJ: ADJ n; ADJ: ADJ n; N-COUNT: oft the N

**com|pare** /kəmpeəʳ/ **(compares, comparing, compared)** ◆◇◇ VERB 1 When you **compare** things, you consider them and discover the differences or similarities between them. ❑ *Compare the two illustrations in Fig 60... Was it fair to compare independent schools with state schools?... Note how smooth the skin of the upper arm is, then compare it to the skin on the elbow.* [V pl-n; V n with n; V n to n] to **compare notes** → see **note**. 2 If you **compare** one person or thing **to** another, you say that they are like the other person or thing. ❑ *Some commentators compared his work to that of James Joyce... I can only compare the experience to falling in love.* [VERB = liken; V n to/with n/-ing] 3 If one thing **compares** favourably **with** another, it is better than the other thing. If it **compares** unfavourably, it is worse than the other thing. ❑ *Our road safety record compares favourably with that of other European countries... How do the two techniques compare in terms of application?* [V-RECIP; V adv with n; pl-n V adv] 4 If you say that something does not **compare with** something else, you mean that it is much worse. ❑ *The flowers here do not compare with those at home.* [VERB: usu with neg; V with n] 5 → See also **compared**.

**com|pared** /kəmpeəʳd/ ◆◆◇ PREP-PHRASE 1 If you say, for example, that one thing is large or small **compared with** another or **compared to** another, you mean that it is larger or smaller than the other thing. ❑ *The room was light and lofty compared with our Tudor ones... Columbia was a young city compared to venerable Charleston.* 2 You talk about one situation or thing **compared with** another or **compared to** another when contrasting the two situations or things. ❑ *In 1800 Ireland's population was nine million, compared to Britain's 16 million.* [PREP-PHRASE]

**com|pari|son** /kəmpærɪsən/ **(comparisons)** ◆◇◇ 1 When you make a **comparison**, you consider two or more things and discover the differences between them. ❑ *...a comparison of the British and German economies... Its recommendations are based on detailed comparisons between the public and private sectors... There are no previous statistics for comparison.* [N-VAR: oft N of/between pl-n] 2 When you make a **comparison**, you say that one thing is like another in some way. ❑ *It is demonstrably an unfair comparison... The comparison of her life to a sea voyage simplifies her experience.* [N-COUNT]

**PHRASES** 3 If you say, for example, that something is large or small **in comparison with**, **in comparison to**, or **by comparison with** something else, you mean that it is larger or smaller than the other thing. ❑ *The amount of carbon dioxide released by human activities such as burning coal and oil is small in comparison... Those places are modern by comparison with Tresillian.* [PHRASE: oft PHR with/to n] 4 If you say **there is no comparison between** one thing and another, you mean that you think the first thing is much better than the second, or very different from it. ❑ *There is no comparison between the knowledge and skill of such a player and the ordinary casual participant.* [PHRASE: oft PHR between pl-n; emphasis]

**com|part|ment** /kəmpɑːʳtmənt/ **(compartments)** 1 A **compartment** is one of the separate spaces into which a railway carriage is divided. ❑ *On the way home we shared our first class compartment with a group of businessmen.* [N-COUNT] 2 A **compartment** is one of the separate parts of an object that is used for keeping things in. ❑ *...the secret compartment of my jewel box.* [N-COUNT] → See also **glove compartment**.

**com|part|men|tal|ize** /kɒmpɑːʳtmentəlaɪz/ **(compartmentalizes, compartmentalizing, compartmentalized)**

☑ in BRIT, also use **compartmentalise**

To **compartmentalize** something means to divide it into separate sections. ❑ *Traditionally men have compartmentalized their lives, never letting their personal lives encroach upon their professional lives.* [VERB; V-ed; Also V n into n] ♦ **com|part|men|tal|ized** *...the compartmentalised world of Japanese finance.* [ADJ]

**com|pass** /kʌmpəs/ **(compasses)** 1 A **compass** is an instrument that you use for finding directions. It has a dial and a magnetic needle that always points to the north. ❑ *We had to rely on a compass and a lot of luck to get here.* [N-COUNT] 2 **Compasses** are a hinged V-shaped instrument that you use for drawing circles. [N-PLURAL: also *a pair of* N]

**com|pas|sion** /kəmpæʃən/ **Compassion** is a feeling of pity, sympathy, and understanding for someone who is suffering. ❑ *Elderly people need time and compassion from their physicians.* [N-UNCOUNT]

**com|pas|sion|ate** /kəmpæʃənət/ If you describe someone or something as **compassionate**, you mean that they feel or show pity, sympathy, and understanding for people who are suffering. ❑ *My father was a deeply compassionate man... She has a wise, compassionate face.* [ADJ: usu ADJ n; approval]

**com|pas|sion|ate leave** **Compassionate leave** is time away from your work that your employer allows you for personal reasons, especially when a member of your family dies or is seriously ill. [N-UNCOUNT]

**com|pass point** **(compass points)** A **compass point** is one of the 32 marks on the dial of a compass that show direction, for example north, south, east, and west. [N-COUNT]

**com|pat|ible** /kəmpætɪbəl/ 1 If things, for example systems, ideas, and beliefs, are **compatible**, they work well together or can exist together successfully. ❑ *Free enterprise, he argued, was compatible with Russian values and traditions... Marriage and the life I live just don't seem compatible.* [ADJ: oft ADJ with n; ≠ incompatible] ♦ **com|pat|ibil|ity** /kəmpætɪbɪlɪti/ *National courts can freeze any law while its compatibility with European legislation is being tested.* [N-UNCOUNT: oft N with/of/between n] 2 If you say that you are **compatible** with someone, you mean that you have a good relationship with them because you have similar opinions and interests. ❑ *Mildred and I are very compatible. She's interested in the things that interest me.* [ADJ: oft ADJ with n; ≠ incompatible] ♦ **com|pat|ibil|ity** *As a result of their compatibility, Haig and Fraser were able to bring about wide-ranging reforms.* [N-UNCOUNT] 3 If one make of computer or computer equipment is **compatible with** another make, especially IBM, they can be used together and can use the same software. [COMPUTING] [ADJ: oft ADJ with n]

**com|pat|ri|ot** /kəmpætriət, AM -peɪt-/ **(compatriots)** Your **compatriots** are people from your own country. ❑ *Chris Robertson of Australia beat his compatriot Chris Dittmar in the final.* [N-COUNT: usu poss N = countryman]

**com|pel** /kəmpel/ **(compels, compelling, compelled)** 1 If a situation, a rule, or a person **compels** you **to** do something, they force you to do it. ❑ *...the introduction of legislation to compel cyclists to wear a helmet... Local housing authorities have been compelled by the housing crisis to make offers of substandard accommodation.* [VERB; V n to-inf; V n to-inf] 2 If you **feel compelled to** do something, you feel that you must do it, because it is the right thing to do. ❑ *I felt morally compelled to help.* [PHRASE: V inflects, PHR to-inf]

**com|pel|ling** /kəmpelɪŋ/ 1 A **compelling** argument or reason is one that convinces you that something is true or that something should be done. ❑ *Factual and forensic evidence makes a suicide verdict the most compelling answer to the mystery of his death.* [ADJ: usu ADJ n] 2 If you describe something such as a film or book, or someone's appearance, as **compelling**, you mean you want to keep looking at it or reading it because you find it so interesting. ❑ *...a frighteningly violent yet compelling film.* [ADJ]

**com|pen|dium** /kəmpendiəm/ **(compendiums)** A **compendium** is a short but detailed collection of information, usually in a book. ❑ *The Roman Catholic Church has issued a compendium of its teachings.* [N-COUNT]

**com|pen|sate** /kɒmpənseɪt/ **(compensates, compensating, compensated)** 1 To **compensate** someone **for** money or things that they have lost means to pay them money or give them something to replace that money or those things. ❑ *To* [VERB; V n for n] *ease financial difficulties, farmers could be compensated for their loss of subsidies.* (Also V n) 2 If you **compensate for** a lack of something or **for** something you have done wrong, you do something to make the situation better. (VERB) ❑ *The company agreed to keep up high levels of output in order to compensate for supplies lost...* (V *for* n) *She would then feel guilt for her anger and compensate by doing even more for the children.* (V) 3 Something that **compensates for** something else balances it or reduces its effects. (VERB) ❑ *MPs say it is crucial that a system is found to compensate for inflation.* (V *for* n) 4 If you try to **compensate for** something that is wrong or missing in your life, you try to do something that removes or reduces the harmful effects. (VERB) ❑ *No supportive words could ever compensate for the pain of being separated from her children for 10 years.* (V *for* n)

**com|pen|sa|tion** /kɒmpənseɪʃən/ **(compensations)** ◆◇◇ 1 **Compensation** is money that someone who has experienced loss or suffering claims from the person or organization responsible, or from the state. (N-UNCOUNT) ❑ *He received one year's salary as compensation for loss of office... The Court ordered Dr Williams to pay £300 compensation and £100 costs after admitting assault.* 2 If something is some **compensation for** something bad that has happened, it makes you feel better. (N-VAR: oft N *for* n/-ing) ❑ *Helen gained some compensation for her earlier defeat by winning the final open class... Despite a reduction in earnings there are compensations in moving to the north-east where the quality of life is excellent.*

**com|pen|sa|tory** /kɒmpənseɪtəri, AM kəmpensətɔːri/ 1 **Compensatory** payments involve money paid as compensation. [FORMAL] (ADJ: usu ADJ n) ❑ *The jury awarded $11.2 million in compensatory damages.* 2 **Compensatory** measures are designed to help people who have special problems or disabilities. [FORMAL] (ADJ: usu ADJ n) ❑ *Money should be spent on compensatory programmes for deprived pre-school and infant-school children.*

**com|pere** /kɒmpeər/ **(comperes, compering, compered)** 1 A **compere** is the person who introduces the people taking part in a radio or television show or a live show. [BRIT] (N-COUNT = host)

✔ in AM, use **emcee**

2 The person who **comperes** a show introduces the people who take part in it. [BRIT] (VERB = host) ❑ *Sarita Sagharwal compered the programme...* (V n) *They asked Paul to compere.* (V)

✔ in AM, use **emcee**

**com|pete** /kəmpiːt/ **(competes, competing, competed)** ◆◇◇ 1 When one firm or country **competes with** another, it tries to get people to buy its own goods in preference to those of the other firm or country. You can also say that two firms or countries **compete**. (V-RECIP) ❑ *The banks have long competed with American Express's charge cards and various store cards...* (V *with* n) *The stores will inevitably end up competing with each other in their push for increased market shares...* (pl-n V *with* pron-recip) *Banks and building societies are competing fiercely for business...* (pl-n V *for* n) *The American economy, and its ability to compete abroad, was slowing down according to the report.* (V (non-recip) Also pl-n V) 2 If you **compete with** someone **for** something, you try to get it for yourself and stop the other person getting it. You can also say that two people **compete for** something. (V-RECIP) ❑ *Kangaroos compete with sheep and cattle for sparse supplies of food and water...* (V *with* n *for* n) *Schools should not compete with each other or attempt to poach pupils...* (pl-n V *with* pron-recip) *More than 2300 candidates from 93 political parties are competing for 486 seats.* (pl-n V *for* n) 3 If you **compete** in a contest or a game, you take part in it. (VERB) ❑ *He will be competing in the London-Calais-London race...* (V prep) *It is essential for all players who wish to compete that they earn computer ranking points.* (V) 4 → See also **competing**.

**com|pe|tence** /kɒmpɪtəns/ **Competence** is the ability to do something well or effectively. (N-UNCOUNT) ❑ *His competence as an economist had been reinforced by his successful fight against inflation.*

**com|pe|ten|cy** /kɒmpɪtənsi/ **Competency** means the same as **competence**. (N-UNCOUNT) ❑ *...managerial competency.*

**com|pe|tent** /kɒmpɪtənt/ 1 Someone who is **competent** is efficient and effective. (ADJ) ❑ *He was a loyal, distinguished and very competent civil servant. ...a competent performance.* ♦ **com|pe|tent|ly** (ADV: ADV with v, ADV adj) *The government performed competently in the face of multiple challenges.* 2 If you are **competent to** do something, you have the skills, abilities, or experience necessary to do it well. (ADJ: oft ADJ to-inf = qualified) ❑ *Most adults do not feel competent to deal with a medical emergency involving a child.*

**com|pet|ing** /kəmpiːtɪŋ/ **Competing** ideas, requirements, or interests cannot all be right or satisfied at the same time. (ADJ: ADJ n = conflicting) ❑ *They talked about the competing theories of the origin of life. ...the competing demands of work and family.* → See also **compete**.

**com|pe|ti|tion** /kɒmpɪtɪʃən/ **(competitions)** ◆◆◇ 1 **Competition** is a situation in which two or more people or groups are trying to get something which not everyone can have. (N-UNCOUNT: usu with supp, oft adj N, N prep) ❑ *There's been some fierce competition for the title... It was in these studios that young painters found the support and stimulating competition of peers.* 2 **The competition** is the person or people you are competing with. (N-SING: usu *the* N) ❑ *I have to change my approach, the competition is too good now.* 3 **Competition** is an activity involving two or more firms, in which each firm tries to get people to buy its own goods in preference to the other firms' goods. (N-UNCOUNT: usu with supp, oft adj N, N prep) ❑ *The deal would have reduced competition in the commuter-aircraft market... Clothing stores also face heavy competition from factory outlets.* 4 The **competition** is the goods that a rival organization is selling. (N-UNCOUNT) ❑ *The American aerospace industry has been challenged by some stiff competition.* 5 A **competition** is an event in which many people take part in order to find out who is best at a particular activity. (N-VAR) ❑ *...a surfing competition... He will be banned from international competition for four years.*

**com|peti|tive** /kəmpetɪtɪv/ ◆◇◇ 1 **Competitive** is used to describe situations or activities in which people or firms compete with each other. (ADJ) ❑ *Only by keeping down costs will America maintain its competitive advantage over other countries... Japan is a highly competitive market system... Universities are very competitive for the best students.* ♦ **com|peti|tive|ly** (ADV: ADV after v) *He's now back up on the slopes again, skiing competitively in events for the disabled.* 2 A **competitive** person is eager to be more successful than other people. (ADJ) ❑ *He has always been ambitious and fiercely competitive... I'm a very competitive person and I was determined not be beaten.* ♦ **com|peti|tive|ly** (ADV: ADV after v) *They worked hard together, competitively and under pressure.* ♦ **com|peti|tive|ness** (N-UNCOUNT) *I can't stand the pace, I suppose, and the competitiveness, and the unfriendliness.* 3 Goods or services that are at a **competitive** price or rate are likely to be bought, because they are less expensive than other goods of the same kind. (ADJ) ❑ *Only those homes offered for sale at competitive prices will secure interest from serious purchasers.* ♦ **com|peti|tive|ly** (ADV: ADV -ed, ADV after v) *...a number of early Martin and Gibson guitars, which were competitively priced.* ♦ **com|peti|tive|ness** (N-UNCOUNT) *It is only on the world market that we can prove the competitiveness and quality of our goods.*

**com|peti|tor** /kəmpetɪtər/ **(competitors)** ◆◇◇ 1 A company's **competitors** are companies who are trying to sell similar goods or services to the same people. (N-COUNT: oft poss N = rival) ❑ *The bank isn't performing as well as some of its competitors.* 2 A **competitor** is a person who takes part in a competition or contest. (N-COUNT) ❑ *Herbert Blocker of Germany, one of the oldest competitors, won the individual silver medal.*

**com|pi|la|tion** /kɒmpɪleɪʃən/ **(compilations)** A **compilation** is a book, CD, or programme that contains many different items that have been gathered together, usually ones which have already appeared in other places. (N-COUNT = collection) ❑ *His latest album* *release is a compilation of his jazz works over the past decade.* → See also **compile**.

**com|pile** /kəmpaɪl/ **(compiles, compiling, compiled)** When you **compile** something such as a report, book, or programme, you produce it by collecting and putting together many pieces of information. ❑ *The book took 10 years to compile... A report compiled by the Fed's Philadelphia branch described the economy as weak.* VERB V n V-ed

**com|pil|er** /kəmpaɪləʳ/ **(compilers)** 1 A **compiler** is someone who compiles books, reports, or lists of information. 2 A **compiler** is a computer program which converts language that people can use into a code that the computer can understand. [COMPUTING] N-COUNT: oft N *of* n; N-COUNT

**com|pla|cen|cy** /kəmpleɪsᵊnsi/ **Complacency** is being complacent about a situation. ❑ *...a worrying level of complacency about the risks of infection from AIDS... She warned that there was no room for complacency on inflation.* N-UNCOUNT [disapproval]

**com|pla|cent** /kəmpleɪsᵊnt/ A **complacent** person is very pleased with themselves or feels that they do not need to do anything about a situation, even though the situation may be uncertain or dangerous. ❑ *We cannot afford to be complacent about our health. ...the Chancellor's complacent attitude towards the far-right's activities.* ADJ [disapproval]

**com|plain** /kəmpleɪn/ **(complains, complaining, complained)** ◆◆◇ 1 If you **complain about** a situation, you say that you are not satisfied with it. ❑ *Miners have complained bitterly that the government did not fulfill their promises... The American couple complained about the high cost of visiting Europe... They are liable to face more mistreatment if they complain to the police... People should complain when they consider an advert offensive... 'I do everything you ask of me,' he complained.* VERB V that V *about/of* n V *to* n V V with quote 2 If you **complain of** pain or illness, you say that you are feeling pain or feeling ill. ❑ *He complained of a headache.* VERB V *of* n

**com|plain|ant** /kəmpleɪnənt/ **(complainants)** A **complainant** is a person who starts a court case in a court of law. [LEGAL] N-COUNT ≠ respondent

**com|plain|er** /kəmpleɪnəʳ/ **(complainers)** A **complainer** is someone who complains a lot about their problems or about things they do not like. ❑ *He was a terrible complainer – always moaning about something.* N-COUNT [disapproval] = moaner

**com|plaint** /kəmpleɪnt/ **(complaints)** ◆◇◇ 1 A **complaint** is a statement in which you express your dissatisfaction with a particular situation. ❑ *There's been a record number of complaints about the standard of service on Britain's railways... People have been reluctant to make formal complaints to the police.* N-VAR: oft N *about* n 2 A **complaint** is a reason for complaining. ❑ *My main complaint is that we can't go out on the racecourse anymore.* N-COUNT 3 You can refer to an illness as a **complaint**, especially if it is not very serious. ❑ *Eczema is a common skin complaint which often runs in families.* N-COUNT = ailment

**com|plai|sant** /kəmpleɪzᵊnt/ If you are **complaisant**, you are willing to accept what other people are doing without complaining. [OLD-FASHIONED] ADJ

**com|ple|ment** **(complements, complementing, complemented)**

> ✔ The verb is pronounced /kɒmplɪment/. The noun is pronounced /kɒmplɪmənt/.

1 If one thing **complements** another, it goes well with the other thing and makes its good qualities more noticeable. ❑ *Nutmeg, parsley and cider all complement the flavour of these beans well.* VERB = set off V n 2 If people or things **complement** each other, they are different or do something different, which makes them a good combination. ❑ *There will be a written examination to complement the practical test... We complement one another perfectly.* VERB V n V n 3 Something that is a **complement to** something else complements it. ❑ *The green wallpaper is the perfect complement to the old pine of the dresser.* N-COUNT: usu sing, oft N *to* n 4 The **complement of** things or people that something has is the number of things or people that it normally has, which enable it to function properly. [FORMAL] ❑ *Each ship had a complement of around a dozen officers and 250 men.* N-COUNT: usu sing, oft N *of* n 5 In grammar, the **complement** of a link verb is an adjective group or noun group which comes after the verb and describes or identifies the subject. For example, in the sentence 'They felt very tired', 'very tired' is the complement. In 'They were students', 'students' is the complement. N-COUNT

**com|ple|men|tary** /kɒmplɪmentri/ 1 **Complementary** things are different from each other but make a good combination. [FORMAL] ❑ *To improve the quality of life through work, two complementary strategies are necessary... He has done experiments complementary to those of Eigen.* ADJ: usu ADJ n, also v-link ADJ *to* n ♦ **com|ple|men|ta|rity** /kɒmplɪmentærɪti/ *...the complementarity between public and private authorities.* N-UNCOUNT 2 **Complementary** medicine refers to ways of treating patients which are different from the ones used by most Western doctors, for example acupuncture and homoeopathy. ❑ *...combining orthodox treatment with a wide range of complementary therapies.* ADJ: ADJ n = alternative ≠ orthodox, conventional

**com|ple|men|ta|tion** /kɒmplɪmenteɪʃᵊn/ In linguistics, a **complementation** pattern of a verb, noun, or adjective is the patterns that typically follow it. [TECHNICAL] N-UNCOUNT: usu N n

**com|plete** /kəmpliːt/ **(completes, completing, completed)** ◆◆◆ 1 You use **complete** to emphasize that something is as great in extent, degree, or amount as it possibly can be. ❑ *The rebels had taken complete control... It shows a complete lack of understanding by management... The resignation came as a complete surprise... He was the complete opposite of Raymond.* ADJ: usu ADJ n [emphasis] = total, absolute ≠ partial ♦ **com|plete|ly** *Dozens of flats had been completely destroyed. ...something completely different.* ADV: ADV with v, ADV adj/adv 2 You can use **complete** to emphasize that you are referring to the whole of something and not just part of it. ❑ *A complete tenement block was burnt to the ground... The job sheets eventually filled a complete book.* ADJ: ADJ n [emphasis] = entire, whole 3 If something is **complete**, it contains all the parts that it should contain. ❑ *The list may not be complete. ...a complete dinner service.* ADJ ♦ **com|plete|ness** *...the accuracy and completeness of the information obtained.* N-UNCOUNT 4 To **complete** a set or group means to provide the last item that is needed to make it a full set or group. ❑ *...the stickers needed to complete the collection.* VERB: no cont V n 5 The **complete** works of a writer are all their books or poems published together in one book or as a set of books. ❑ *...the Complete Works of William Shakespeare.* ADJ: ADJ n 6 If one thing comes **complete with** another, it has that thing as an extra or additional part. ❑ *The diary comes complete with a gold-coloured ballpoint pen.* PREP-PHRASE: PREP n 7 If something is **complete**, it has been finished. ❑ *The work of restoring the farmhouse is complete... It'll be two years before the process is complete.* ADJ: v-link ADJ ≠ incomplete 8 If you **complete** something, you finish doing, making, or producing it. ❑ *Peter Mayle has just completed his first novel. ...the rush to get the stadiums completed on time.* VERB V n get n V-ed ♦ **com|ple|tion** /kəmpliːʃᵊn/ **(completions)** *The project is nearing completion... House completions for the year should be up from 1,841 to 2,200.* N-VAR 9 If you **complete** something, you do all of it. ❑ *She completed her degree in two years... This book took years to complete.* VERB: no cont = finish V n V n 10 If you **complete** a form or questionnaire, you write the answers or information asked for in it. ❑ *Simply complete the coupon below... Use the enclosed envelope to return your completed survey.* VERB = fill in V n V-ed

**com|plex** /kɒmpleks/ **(complexes)** ◆◆◇

> ✔ The adjective is pronounced /kəmpleks/ in American English.

1 Something that is **complex** has many different parts, and is therefore often difficult to understand. ❑ *...in-depth coverage of today's complex issues. ...a complex system of voting. ...her complex personality. ...complex machines.* ADJ = complicated ≠ simple 2 In grammar, a ADJ: ADJ n

**complex** sentence contains one or more subordinate clauses as well as a main clause. Compare **compound**. 3 N-COUNT: usu with supp A **complex** is a group of buildings designed for a particular purpose, or one large building divided into several smaller areas. ❑ *...plans for constructing a new stadium and leisure complex. ...a complex of offices and flats.* 4 N-COUNT If someone has a **complex** about something, they have a mental or emotional problem relating to it, often because of an unpleasant experience in the past. ❑ *I have never had a complex about my height. ...a deranged attacker, driven by a persecution complex.*
→ See also **guilt complex**, **inferiority complex**.

**com|plex|ion** /kəmplekʃᵊn/ **(complexions)** 1 N-COUNT: oft adj N When you refer to someone's **complexion**, you are referring to the natural colour or condition of the skin on their face. ❑ *She had short brown hair and a pale complexion.* 2 N-COUNT: with supp The **complexion** of something is its general nature or character. [FORMAL] ❑ *But surely this puts a different complexion on things.*

**com|plex|ities** /kəmpleksɪtiz/ N-PLURAL: usu with supp The **complexities** of something are the many complicated factors involved in it. ❑ *The issue is surrounded by legal complexities.*

**com|plex|ity** /kəmpleksɪti/ N-UNCOUNT: usu with supp ≠ simplicity **Complexity** is the state of having many different parts connected or related to each other in a complicated way. ❑ *...a diplomatic tangle of great complexity. ...the increasing complexity of modern weapon systems.*

**com|pli|ance** /kəmplaɪəns/ N-UNCOUNT: oft N *with* n **Compliance with** something, for example a law, treaty, or agreement means doing what you are required or expected to do. [FORMAL] ❑ *The company says it is in full compliance with US labor laws.*

**com|pli|ant** /kəmplaɪənt/ ADJ = pliant, pliable If you say that someone is **compliant**, you mean they willingly do what they are asked to do. [FORMAL] ❑ *...a docile and compliant workforce.*

**com|pli|cate** /kɒmplɪkeɪt/ **(complicates, complicating, complicated)** VERB To **complicate** something means to make it more difficult to understand or deal with. ❑ V n *The day's events, he said, would only complicate the task of the peacekeeping forces...* V n *To complicate matters further, everybody's vitamin requirements vary.*

**com|pli|cat|ed** /kɒmplɪkeɪtɪd/ ◆◇◇ ADJ = complex ≠ uncomplicated, simple If you say that something is **complicated**, you mean it has so many parts or aspects that it is difficult to understand or deal with. ❑ *The situation in Lebanon is very complicated. ...a very complicated voting system.*

**com|pli|ca|tion** /kɒmplɪkeɪʃᵊn/ **(complications)** 1 N-COUNT A **complication** is a problem or difficulty that makes a situation harder to deal with. ❑ *The age difference was a complication to the relationship... An added complication is the growing concern for the environment.* 2 N-COUNT A **complication** is a medical problem that occurs as a result of another illness or disease. ❑ *Blindness is a common complication of diabetes... He died of complications from a heart attack.*

**com|plic|it** /kəmplɪsɪt/ ADJ: usu ADJ *in* n If someone is **complicit in** a crime or unfair activity, they are involved in it. [JOURNALISM] ❑ *He did not witness her execution, yet he and the others are complicit in her death.*

**com|plic|ity** /kəmplɪsɪti/ N-UNCOUNT: oft N *in* n = collusion **Complicity** is involvement with other people in an illegal activity or plan. [FORMAL] ❑ *Recently a number of policemen were sentenced to death for their complicity in the murder... He is accused of complicity with the leader of the coup, former Colonel Gregorio Honasan.*

**com|pli|ment** **(compliments, complimenting, complimented)**

> ✓ The verb is pronounced /kɒmplɪment/. The noun is pronounced /kɒmplɪmənt/.

1 N-COUNT A **compliment** is a polite remark that you say to someone to show that you like their appearance, appreciate their qualities, or approve of what they have done. ❑ *You can do no harm by paying a woman compliments... 'Well done, Cassandra,' Crook said. She blushed, but accepted the compliment with good grace.* 2 VERB If you **compliment** someone, you pay them a compliment. ❑ V n *on* n *They complimented me on the way I looked each time they saw me.* 3 N-PLURAL: usu poss N, oft N *to* n [politeness] You can refer to your **compliments** when you want to express thanks, good wishes, or respect to someone in a formal way. ❑ *My compliments to the chef.*

**PHRASES** 4 PHRASE: V inflects If you say that someone **returns the compliment**, you mean that they do the same thing to someone else as that person has done to them. ❑ *The actors have entertained us so splendidly during this weekend, I think it's time we returned the compliment.* 5 PHRASE: PHR after v [politeness] If you say that you are giving someone something **with** your **compliments**, you are saying in a polite and fairly formal way that you are giving it to them, especially as a gift or a favour. ❑ *Please give this to your boss with my compliments.*

**com|pli|men|tary** /kɒmplɪmentəri/ 1 ADJ: usu v-link ADJ = flattering If you are **complimentary** about something, you express admiration for it. ❑ *The staff have been very complimentary, and so have the customers... We often get complimentary remarks regarding the cleanliness of our patio.* 2 ADJ: usu ADJ n A **complimentary** seat, ticket, or book is given to you free. ❑ *He had complimentary tickets to take his wife to see the movie.*

**com|ply** /kəmplaɪ/ **(complies, complying, complied)** VERB If someone or something **complies with** an order or set of rules, they are in accordance with what is required or expected. ❑ V *with* n *The commander said that the army would comply with the ceasefire...* V *There are calls for his resignation, but there is no sign yet that he will comply.*

**com|po|nent** /kəmpoʊnənt/ **(components)** ◆◇◇ 1 N-COUNT The **components** of something are the parts that it is made of. ❑ *Enriched uranium is a key component of a nuclear weapon... The management plan has four main components... They were automotive component suppliers to motor manufacturers.* 2 ADJ: ADJ n The **component** parts of something are the parts that make it up. ❑ *Gorbachev failed to keep the component parts of the Soviet Union together... Polish workers will now be making component parts for Boeing 757s.*

**com|port** /kəmpɔːʳt/ **(comports, comporting, comported)** VERB If you **comport yourself** in a particular way, you behave in that way. [FORMAL] ❑ V pron-refl prep/adv *He comports himself with modesty.*

**com|pose** /kəmpoʊz/ **(composes, composing, composed)** 1 VERB = make up The things that something **is composed of** are its parts or members. The separate things that **compose** something are the parts or members that form it. ❑ *be* V-ed *of* n *The force would be composed of troops from NATO countries...* V n *Protein molecules compose all the complex working parts of living cells...* V-ed *They agreed to form a council composed of leaders of the rival factions.* 2 VERB When someone **composes** a piece of music, they write it. ❑ V n *Vivaldi composed a large number of very fine concertos...* V *Cale also uses electronic keyboards to compose.* 3 VERB If you **compose** something such as a letter, poem, or speech, you write it, often using a lot of concentration or skill. [FORMAL] ❑ V n *He started at once to compose a reply to Anna...* V-ed *The document composed in Philadelphia transformed the confederation of sovereign states into a national government.* 4 VERB If you **compose yourself** or if you **compose** your features, you succeed in becoming calm after you have been angry, excited, or upset. ❑ V pron-refl *She quickly composed herself as the car started off...* V n *Then he composed his features, took Godwin's hand awkwardly and began to usher him from the office.*

**com|posed** /kəmpoʊzd/ ADJ: usu v-link ADJ If someone is **composed**, they are calm and able to control their feelings. ❑ *Laura was very calm and composed.*

**com|pos|er** /kəmpoʊzəʳ/ **(composers)** N-COUNT A **composer** is a person who writes music, especially classical music.

**com|po|site** /kɒmpəzɪt, AM kəmpɑːzɪt/ **(composites)** A **composite** object or item is made up of several different things, parts, or substances. ❑ *Galton devised a method of creating composite pictures in which the features of different faces were superimposed over one another.* ♦ **Composite** is also a noun. ❑ *Spain is a composite of diverse traditions and people.* ADJ: usu ADJ n; N-COUNT: usu sing, oft N *of* n

**com|po|si|tion** /kɒmpəzɪʃən/ **(compositions)** 1 When you talk about the **composition** of something, you are referring to the way in which its various parts are put together and arranged. ❑ *Television has transformed the size and social composition of the audience at great sporting occasions... Forests vary greatly in composition from one part of the country to another.* N-UNCOUNT: usu with supp, oft N *of* n = make-up 2 The **compositions** of a composer, painter, or other artist are the works of art that they have produced. ❑ *Mozart's compositions are undoubtedly amongst the world's greatest.* N-COUNT 3 A **composition** is a piece of written work that children write at school. N-COUNT = essay 4 **Composition** is the technique or skill involved in creating a work of art. ❑ *He taught the piano, organ and composition.* N-UNCOUNT

**com|po|si|tion|al** /kɒmpəzɪʃənəl/ **Compositional** refers to the way composers and artists use their skills or techniques in their work. [TECHNICAL] ❑ *...Mozart's compositional style.* ADJ: ADJ n

**com|posi|tor** /kəmpɒzɪtəʳ/ **(compositors)** A **compositor** is a person who arranges the text and pictures of a book, magazine, or newspaper before it is printed. N-COUNT

**com|post** /kɒmpɒst, AM -poʊst/ **(composts, composting, composted)** 1 **Compost** is a mixture of decayed plants and vegetable waste which is added to the soil to help plants grow. ❑ *...a small compost heap.* N-UNCOUNT 2 **Compost** is specially treated soil that you buy and use to grow seeds and plants in pots. N-MASS 3 To **compost** things such as unwanted bits of plants means to make them into compost. ❑ *Cut down and compost spent cucumbers, tomatoes and other crops.* VERB V n

**com|po|sure** /kəmpoʊʒəʳ/ **Composure** is the appearance or feeling of calm and the ability to control your feelings. [FORMAL] ❑ *For once Dimbleby lost his composure. It was all he could do to stop tears of mirth falling down his cheeks.* N-UNCOUNT

**com|pote** /kɒmpoʊt/ **(compotes) Compote** is fruit stewed with sugar or in syrup. N-VAR

**com|pound (compounds, compounding, compounded)**

> ✓ The noun is pronounced /kɒmpaʊnd/. The verb is pronounced /kəmpaʊnd/.

1 A **compound** is an enclosed area of land that is used for a particular purpose. ❑ *Police fired on them as they fled into the embassy compound. ...a military compound.* N-COUNT = enclosure 2 In chemistry, a **compound** is a substance that consists of two or more elements. ❑ *Organic compounds contain carbon in their molecules.* N-COUNT 3 If something is a **compound of** different things, it consists of those things. [FORMAL] ❑ *Honey is basically a compound of water, two types of sugar, vitamins and enzymes.* N-COUNT: usu sing, usu N *of* n = mixture 4 **Compound** is used to indicate that something consists of two or more parts or things. ❑ *...a tall shrub with shiny compound leaves. ...the compound microscope.* ADJ: ADJ n = composite ≠ simple 5 In grammar, a **compound** noun, adjective, or verb is one that is made up of two or more words, for example 'fire engine', 'bottle-green', and 'force-feed'. ADJ: ADJ n 6 In grammar, a **compound** sentence is one that is made up of two or more main clauses. Compare **complex**. ADJ: ADJ n 7 To **compound** a problem, difficulty, or mistake means to make it worse by adding to it. [FORMAL] ❑ *Additional bloodshed and loss of life will only compound the tragedy... The problem is compounded by the medical system here.* VERB = add to V n V n

**com|pound|ed** /kɒmpaʊndɪd/ If something is **compounded of** different things, it is a mixture of those things. [FORMAL] ❑ *...an emotion oddly compounded of pleasure and bitterness.* ADJ: v-link ADJ *of* n

**com|pound frac|ture (compound fractures)** A **compound fracture** is a fracture in which the broken bone sticks through the skin. N-COUNT

**com|pound in|ter|est Compound interest** is interest that is calculated both on an original sum of money and on interest which has previously been added to the sum. Compare **simple interest**. [BUSINESS] N-UNCOUNT

**com|pre|hend** /kɒmprɪhend/ **(comprehends, comprehending, comprehended)** If you cannot **comprehend** something, you cannot understand it. [FORMAL] ❑ *I just cannot comprehend your attitude... Whenever she failed to comprehend she invariably laughed.* VERB: with brd-neg = understand V n V

**com|pre|hen|sible** /kɒmprɪhensɪbəl/ Something that is **comprehensible** can be understood. [FORMAL] ❑ *He spoke abruptly, in barely comprehensible Arabic.* ADJ ≠ incomprehensible

**com|pre|hen|sion** /kɒmprɪhenʃən/ **(comprehensions)** 1 **Comprehension** is the ability to understand something. [FORMAL] ❑ *This was utterly beyond her comprehension.* N-UNCOUNT = understanding 2 **Comprehension** is full knowledge and understanding of the meaning of something. [FORMAL] ❑ *They turned to one another with the same expression of dawning comprehension, surprise, and relief.* N-UNCOUNT 3 When pupils do **comprehension**, they do an exercise to find out how well they understand a piece of spoken or written language. N-VAR

**com|pre|hen|sive** /kɒmprɪhensɪv/ **(comprehensives)** ◆◇◇ 1 Something that is **comprehensive** includes everything that is needed or relevant. ❑ *The Rough Guide to Nepal is a comprehensive guide to the region.* ADJ = complete ≠ partial 2 In Britain, a **comprehensive** is a state school in which children of all abilities are taught together. ❑ *...Birmingham's inner-city comprehensives... She taught French at Cheam Comprehensive in South London.* N-COUNT; N-IN-NAMES ♦ **Comprehensive** is also an adjective. ❑ *He left comprehensive school at the age of 16.* ADJ: ADJ n

**com|pre|hen|sive|ly** /kɒmprɪhensɪvli/ Something that is done **comprehensively** is done thoroughly. ❑ *England were comprehensively beaten by South Africa.* ADV: usu ADV with v

**com|press (compresses, compressing, compressed)**

> ✓ The verb is pronounced /kəmpres/. The noun is pronounced /kɒmpres/.

1 When you **compress** something or when it **compresses**, it is pressed or squeezed so that it takes up less space. ❑ *Poor posture, sitting or walking slouched over, compresses the body's organs... Air will compress but the brake fluid won't.* VERB V n V ♦ **com|pres|sion** /kəmpreʃən/ *The compression of the wood is easily achieved.* N-UNCOUNT 2 If you **compress** something such as a piece of writing or a description, you make it shorter. ❑ *All those three books are compacted and compressed into one book.* VERB = condense V n 3 If an event **is compressed into** a short space of time, it is given less time to happen than normal or previously. ❑ *The four debates will be compressed into an unprecedentedly short eight-day period... Some courses such as engineering had to be compressed.* VERB: usu passive be V-ed *into* n be V-ed 4 A **compress** is a pad of wet or dry cloth pressed on part of a patient's body to reduce fever. ❑ *Sore throats may be relieved by cold compresses.* N-COUNT

**com|pressed** /kəmprest/ **Compressed** air or gas is squeezed into a small space or container and is therefore at a higher pressure than normal. It is used especially as a source of power for machines. ADJ: usu ADJ n

**com|pres|sor** /kəmpresəʳ/ **(compressors)** A **compressor** is a machine or part of a machine that squeezes gas or air and makes it take up less space. N-COUNT

**com|prise** /kəmpraɪz/ **(comprises, comprising, comprised)** 1 If you say that something **comprises** or **is comprised of** a number of things or people, you mean it has them as its parts or members. [FORMAL] ❑ *The special cabinet* VERB V n *committee comprises Mr Brown, Mr Mandelson, and Mr Straw... The task force is comprised of congressional leaders, cabinet heads and administration officials... A crowd comprised of the wives and children of scientists staged a demonstration.* (be V-ed of n; V-ed) [2] The things or people that **comprise** something are the parts or members that form it. [FORMAL] ❑ *Women comprise 44% of hospital medical staff.* (VERB = form, make up; V n)

**com|pro|mise** /kɒmprəmaɪz/ **(compromises, compromising, compromised)** ◆◇◇ [1] A **compromise** is a situation in which people accept something slightly different from what they really want, because of circumstances or because they are considering the wishes of other people. ❑ *Encourage your child to reach a compromise between what he wants and what you want... The government's policy of compromise is not universally popular.* (N-VAR) [2] If you **compromise with** someone, you reach an agreement with them in which you both give up something that you originally wanted. You can also say that two people or groups **compromise**. ❑ *The government has compromised with its critics over monetary policies... 'Nine,' said I. 'Nine thirty,' tried he. We compromised on 9.15... Israel had originally wanted $1 billion in aid, but compromised on the $650 million.* (V-RECIP; V with n over n; pl-n V on n; V on n (non-recip)) [3] If someone **compromises** themselves or **compromises** their beliefs, they do something which damages their reputation for honesty, loyalty, or high moral principles. ❑ *...members of the government who have compromised themselves by co-operating with the emergency committee... He would rather shoot himself than compromise his principles.* (VERB [disapproval]; V pron-refl; V n)

**com|pro|mis|ing** /kɒmprəmaɪzɪŋ/ If you describe information or a situation as **compromising**, you mean that it reveals an embarrassing or guilty secret about someone. ❑ *How had this compromising picture come into the possession of the press?* (ADJ: usu ADJ n)

**comp|trol|ler** /kəntroʊləʳ/ **(comptrollers)** A **comptroller** is someone who is in charge of the accounts of a business or a government department; used mainly in official titles. [BUSINESS] ❑ *...Robert Clarke, US Comptroller of the Currency.* (N-COUNT: oft N of n)

**com|pul|sion** /kəmpʌlʃᵊn/ **(compulsions)** [1] A **compulsion** is a strong desire to do something, which you find difficult to control. ❑ *He felt a sudden compulsion to drop the bucket and run.* (N-COUNT: oft N to-inf = urge) [2] If someone uses **compulsion** in order to get you to do something, they force you to do it, for example by threatening to punish you if you do not do it. ❑ *Many universities argued that students learned more when they were in classes out of choice rather than compulsion.* (N-UNCOUNT = coercion)

**com|pul|sive** /kəmpʌlsɪv/ [1] You use **compulsive** to describe people or their behaviour when they cannot stop doing something wrong, harmful, or unnecessary. ❑ *...a compulsive liar... He was a compulsive gambler and often heavily in debt.* (ADJ: ADJ n) ♦ **com|pul|sive|ly** *John is compulsively neat and clean, he's terrified of germs.* (ADV: ADV with v, ADV adj ADJ) [2] If a book or television programme is **compulsive**, it is so interesting that you do not want to stop reading or watching it. ❑ *The BBC series Hot Chefs is compulsive viewing.* ♦ **com|pul|sive|ly** *...a series of compulsively readable novels.* (ADV: ADV adj)

**com|pul|so|ry** /kəmpʌlsəri/ If something is **compulsory**, you must do it or accept it, because it is the law or because someone in a position of authority says you must. ❑ *In East Germany learning Russian was compulsory... Many young men are trying to get away from compulsory military conscription.* (ADJ = mandatory) ♦ **com|pul|so|ri|ly** /kəmpʌlsərɪli/ *Five of the company's senior managers have been made compulsorily redundant.* (ADV: ADV with v, ADV adj)

**com|punc|tion** /kəmpʌŋkʃᵊn/ If you say that someone **has no compunction about** doing something, you mean that they do it without feeling ashamed or guilty. ❑ *He has no compunction about relating how he killed his father.* (N-UNCOUNT [disapproval])

**com|pu|ta|tion** /kɒmpjʊteɪʃᵊn/ **(computations) Computation** is mathematical calculation. ❑ *The discrepancies resulted from different methods of computation... He took a few notes and made computations.* (N-VAR = calculation)

**com|pu|ta|tion|al** /kɒmpjʊteɪʃənᵊl/ **Computational** means using computers. ❑ *...the limits of the computational methods available 50 years ago.* (ADJ: usu ADJ n)

**com|pute** /kəmpjuːt/ **(computes, computing, computed)** To **compute** a quantity or number means to calculate it. ❑ *I tried to compute the cash value of the ponies and horse boxes.* (VERB = calculate; V n)

**com|put|er** /kəmpjuːtəʳ/ **(computers)** ◆◆◇ A **computer** is an electronic machine that can store and deal with large amounts of information. ❑ *The data are then fed into a computer... The car was designed by computer.* → See also **personal computer**. (N-COUNT: also by/on N)

**com|put|er|ate** /kəmpjuːtərət/ If someone is **computerate**, they have enough skill and knowledge to be able to use a computer. (ADJ = computer-literate)

**com|put|er game (computer games)** A **computer game** is a game that you play on a computer or on a small portable piece of electronic equipment. (N-COUNT)

**com|put|er|ize** /kəmpjuːtəraɪz/ **(computerizes, computerizing, computerized)**

☑ in BRIT, also use **computerise**

To **computerize** a system, process, or type of work means to arrange for a lot of the work to be done by computer. ❑ *I'm trying to make a spreadsheet up to computerize everything that's done by hand at the moment... Many hospitals say they simply can't afford to computerize.* (VERB; V n; V) ♦ **com|put|eri|za|tion** /kəmpjuːtəraɪzeɪʃᵊn/ *...the benefits of computerization.* (N-UNCOUNT)

**com|put|er|ized** /kəmpjuːtəraɪzd/

☑ in BRIT, also use **computerised**

[1] A **computerized** system, process, or business is one in which the work is done by computer. ❑ *The National Cancer Institute now has a computerized system that can quickly provide information. ...the most highly computerized businesses.* (ADJ: usu ADJ n) [2] **Computerized** information is stored on a computer. ❑ *Computerized data bases are proliferating fast... The public registry in Panama City keeps computerized records of all companies.* (ADJ: usu ADJ n)

**computer-literate** If someone is **computer-literate**, they have enough skill and knowledge to be able to use a computer. ❑ *We look for applicants who are numerate, computer-literate and energetic self-starters.* (ADJ = computerate)

**com|pu|ting** /kəmpjuːtɪŋ/ [1] **Computing** is the activity of using a computer and writing programs for it. ❑ *Courses range from cookery to computing.* (N-UNCOUNT) [2] **Computing** means relating to computers and their use. ❑ *Many graduates are employed in the electronics and computing industries.* (ADJ: ADJ n)

**com|rade** /kɒmreɪd, AM -ræd/ **(comrades)** Your **comrades** are your friends, especially friends that you share a difficult or dangerous situation with. [LITERARY] ❑ *Unlike so many of his comrades he survived the war.* (N-COUNT: usu poss N)

**comrade-in-arms (comrades-in-arms)** also **comrade in arms**. A **comrade-in-arms** is someone who has worked for the same cause or purpose as you and has shared the same difficulties and dangers. ❑ *...Deng Xiaoping, Mao's longtime comrade-in-arms.* (N-COUNT: oft poss N)

**com|rade|ly** /kɒmreɪdli, AM -ræd-/ If you do something in a **comradely** way, you are being pleasant and friendly to other people. [FORMAL] ❑ *They worked in comradely silence.* (ADJ: usu ADJ n = friendly)

**com|rade|ship** /kɒmreɪdʃɪp, AM -ræd-/ **Comradeship** is friendship between a number of people who are doing the same work or who share the same difficulties or dangers. ❑ *...the comradeship of his fellow soldiers.* (N-UNCOUNT)

**con** /kɒn/ **(cons, conning, conned)** 1 If someone **cons** you, they persuade you to do something or believe something by telling you things that are not true. [INFORMAL] ❑ *He claimed that the businessman had conned him of £10,000... White conned his way into a job as a warehouseman with Dutch airline, KLM... The British motorist has been conned by the government.* (VERB = cheat, trick; V n of/out of/into n/-ing; V way into n; be V-ed; Also V n) 2 A **con** is a trick in which someone deceives you by telling you something that is not true. [INFORMAL] ❑ *Slimming snacks that offer miraculous weight loss are a con.* (N-COUNT) 3 A **con** is the same as a **convict**. [INFORMAL] (N-COUNT) 4 → See also **mod cons. pros and cons** → see **pro**.

**Con** 1 **Con** is the written abbreviation for **constable**, when it is part of a policeman's title. [BRIT] ❑ *...Det Con Terence Woodwiss.* (N-TITLE) 2 **Con** is the written abbreviation for **Conservative**. [BRIT] ❑ *...Philip Goodhart MP for Beckenham (Con).*

**con art|ist** **(con artists)** A **con artist** is someone who tricks other people into giving them their money or property. (N-COUNT = con man)

**conc.** **Conc.** is the written abbreviation for **concessionary**. [BRIT] ❑ *The guided tours cost £4 (conc £3.50).*

**con|cat|ena|tion** /kɒnkætəneɪʃən/ A **concatenation of** things or events is their occurrence one after another, because they are linked. [FORMAL] ❑ *...the Internet, the world's biggest concatenation of computing power.* (N-UNCOUNT: usu N of n)

**con|cave** /kɒnkeɪv, kɒnkeɪv/ A surface that is **concave** curves inwards in the middle. ❑ *...a concave stomach.* (ADJ ≠ convex)

**con|ceal** /kənsiːl/ **(conceals, concealing, concealed)** 1 If you **conceal** something, you cover it or hide it carefully. ❑ *Frances decided to conceal the machine behind a hinged panel... Five people were arrested for carrying concealed weapons.* (VERB; V n; V-ed) 2 If you **conceal** a piece of information or a feeling, you do not let other people know about it. ❑ *Robert could not conceal his relief... She knew at once that he was concealing something from her.* (VERB ≠ reveal; V n; V n from n) 3 If something **conceals** something else, it covers it and prevents it from being seen. ❑ *...a pair of carved Indian doors which conceal a built-in cupboard.* (VERB; V n)

**con|ceal|ment** /kənsiːlmənt/ 1 **Concealment** is the state of being hidden or the act of hiding something. ❑ *...the concealment of weapons.* (N-UNCOUNT) 2 The **concealment of** information or a feeling involves keeping it secret. ❑ *His concealment of his true motives was masterly... I think there was deliberate concealment of relevant documents.* (N-UNCOUNT: oft N of n)

**con|cede** /kənsiːd/ **(concedes, conceding, conceded)** ◆◇◇ 1 If you **concede** something, you admit, often unwillingly, that it is true or correct. ❑ *Bess finally conceded that Nancy was right... 'Well,' he conceded, 'I do sometimes mumble a bit.'... Mr. Chapman conceded the need for Nomura's U.S. unit to improve its trading skills.* (VERB; V that; V with quote; V n) 2 If you **concede** something **to** someone, you allow them to have it as a right or privilege. ❑ *The government conceded the right to establish independent trade unions... Facing total defeat in Vietnam, the French subsequently conceded full independence to Laos.* (VERB = cede; V n; V n to n) 3 If you **concede** something, you give it to the person who has been trying to get it from you. ❑ *A strike by some ten thousand bank employees has ended after the government conceded some of their demands.* (VERB; V n) 4 In sport, if you **concede** goals or points, you are unable to prevent your opponent from scoring them. [BRIT] ❑ *They conceded four goals to Leeds United... Luton conceded a free kick on the edge of the penalty area.* (VERB; V n to n; V n)

✔ in AM, use **give up**

5 If you **concede** a game, contest, or argument, you end it by admitting that you can no longer win. ❑ *Reiner, 56, has all but conceded the race to his rival... Alain Prost finished third and virtually conceded the world championship.* (VERB; V n to n; V n) 6 If you **concede** defeat, you accept that you have lost a struggle. ❑ *Airtours conceded defeat in its attempt to take control of holiday industry rival Owners Abroad... He happily conceded the election.* (VERB = accept; V n; V n)

**con|ceit** /kənsiːt/ **(conceits)** **Conceit** is very great pride in your abilities or achievements that other people feel is too great. ❑ *Pamela knew she was a good student, and that was not just a conceit.* (N-UNCOUNT: also a N; disapproval; = arrogance)

**con|ceit|ed** /kənsiːtɪd/ If you say that someone is **conceited**, you are showing your disapproval of the fact that they are far too proud of their abilities or achievements. ❑ *I thought him conceited and arrogant.* (ADJ; disapproval; = arrogant)

**con|ceiv|able** /kənsiːvəbəl/ If something is **conceivable**, you can imagine it or believe it. ❑ *It is just conceivable that a single survivor might be found.* (ADJ: oft it v-link ADJ that; ≠ inconceivable)

**con|ceive** /kənsiːv/ **(conceives, conceiving, conceived)** 1 If you cannot **conceive of** something, you cannot imagine it or believe it. ❑ *I just can't even conceive of that quantity of money... He was immensely ambitious but unable to conceive of winning power for himself.* (VERB: usu with brd-neg; V of n/-ing; V of n/-ing; Also V that) 2 If you **conceive** something **as** a particular thing, you consider it to be that thing. ❑ *The ancients conceived the earth as afloat in water... We conceive of the family as being in a constant state of change... Elvis conceived of himself as a ballad singer.* (VERB; V n as n/-ing; V of n as n/-ing) 3 If you **conceive** a plan or idea, you think of it and work out how it can be done. ❑ *She had conceived the idea of a series of novels... He conceived of the first truly portable computer in 1968.* (VERB; V n; V of n) 4 When a woman **conceives**, she becomes pregnant. ❑ *Women, he says, should give up alcohol before they plan to conceive... A mother who already has non-identical twins is more likely to conceive another set of twins.* (VERB; V; V n)

**con|cen|trate** /kɒnsəntreɪt/ **(concentrates, concentrating, concentrated)** ◆◇◇ 1 If you **concentrate on** something, or **concentrate** your mind **on** it, you give all your attention to it. ❑ *It was up to him to concentrate on his studies and make something of himself... At work you need to be able to concentrate... This helps you to be aware of time and concentrates your mind on the immediate task.* (VERB; V on n/-ing; V; V n on n) 2 If something **is concentrated in** an area, it is all there rather than being spread around. ❑ *Most development has been concentrated in and around cities.* (VERB: usu passive; be V-ed in n; Also be V-ed adv) 3 **Concentrate** is a liquid or substance from which water has been removed in order to make it stronger, or to make it easier to store. ❑ *...orange juice made from concentrate.* (N-MASS) 4 If you say that an unpleasant fact or situation **concentrates** someone's **mind**, you mean that it makes them think clearly, because they are aware of the serious consequences if they do not. ❑ *A term in prison will concentrate his mind wonderfully.* (PHRASE: V and N inflect)

**con|cen|trat|ed** /kɒnsəntreɪtɪd/ 1 A **concentrated** liquid has been increased in strength by having water removed from it. ❑ *Sweeten dishes sparingly with honey, or concentrated apple or pear juice.* (ADJ) 2 A **concentrated** activity is directed with great intensity in one place. ❑ *...a more concentrated effort to reach out to troubled kids.* (ADJ: usu ADJ n = concerted ≠ half-hearted)

**con|cen|tra|tion** /kɒnsəntreɪʃən/ **(concentrations)** ◆◇◇ 1 **Concentration** on something involves giving all your attention to it. ❑ *Neal kept interrupting, breaking my concentration... We lacked concentration and it cost us the goal and the game.* (N-UNCOUNT) 2 A **concentration of** something is a large amount of it or large numbers of it in a small area. ❑ *The area has one of the world's greatest concentrations of wildlife... There's been too much concentration of power in the hands of central authorities.* (N-VAR: usu N of n) 3 The **concentration of** a substance is the proportion of essential ingredients or substances in it. ❑ *pH is a measure of the concentration of free hydrogen atoms in a solution.* (N-VAR: with supp, oft N of n, n N)

**con|cen|tra|tion camp** **(concentration camps)** A **concentration camp** is a prison in which large numbers of ordinary people are kept in very bad conditions, usually during a war. (N-COUNT)

**con|cen|tric** /kənsentrɪk/ [ADJ: ADJ n] **Concentric** circles or rings have the same centre. ❑ *On a blackboard, he drew five concentric circles.*

**con|cept** /kɒnsept/ **(concepts)** [◆◇◇ N-COUNT: oft N *of* n = notion] A **concept** is an idea or abstract principle. ❑ *She added that the concept of arranged marriages is misunderstood in the west.*

**con|cep|tion** /kənsepʃᵊn/ **(conceptions)** 1 [N-VAR: usu N *of* n = notion] A **conception of** something is an idea that you have of it in your mind. ❑ *My conception of a garden was based on gardens I had visited in England... I see him as someone with not the slightest conception of teamwork.* 2 [N-VAR] **Conception** is the process in which the egg in a woman is fertilized and she becomes pregnant. ❑ *Six weeks after conception your baby is the size of your little fingernail.*

**con|cep|tual** /kənseptʃuəl/ [ADJ: ADJ n] **Conceptual** means related to ideas and concepts formed in the mind. ❑ *...replacing old laws with new within the same conceptual framework.* ♦ **con|cep|tu|al|ly** [ADV: usu ADV with v, ADV adj, also ADV with cl] *The monograph is conceptually confused, unclear in its structure and weak in its methodology.*

**con|cep|tu|al|ize** /kənseptʃuəlaɪz/ **(conceptualizes, conceptualizing, conceptualized)**

in BRIT, also use **conceptualise**

[VERB] If you **conceptualize** something, you form an idea of it in your mind. ❑ [V n] *How we conceptualize things has a lot to do with what we feel...* [V n *as* n] *Tiffany conceptualized herself as a mother, whose primary task was to feed her baby.*

**con|cern** /kənsɜːʳn/ **(concerns, concerning, concerned)** [◆◆◆] 1 [N-UNCOUNT: oft N prep, N that] **Concern** is worry about a situation. ❑ *The group has expressed concern about reports of political violence in Africa... The move follows growing public concern over the spread of the disease... There is no cause for concern.* 2 [VERB: no cont] If something **concerns** you, it worries you. ❑ [V n] *The growing number of people seeking refuge in Thailand is beginning to concern Western aid agencies...* [*it* V n that] *It concerned her that Bess was developing a crush on Max.* ♦ **con|cerned** [ADJ: usu v-link ADJ, oft ADJ *about/for* n, ADJ that] *Academics and employers are deeply concerned that students are not sufficiently prepared mathematically for university courses. ...a phone call from a concerned neighbor.* 3 [N-COUNT: usu with poss = worry] A **concern** is a fact or situation that worries you. ❑ *His concern was that people would know that he was responsible... Unemployment was the electorate's main concern.* 4 [N-VAR: oft N *with* n] Someone's **concern with** something is their feeling that it is important. ❑ *...a story that illustrates how dangerous excessive concern with safety can be.* 5 [N-COUNT: usu with poss] Someone's **concerns** are the things that they consider to be important. ❑ *Feminism must address issues beyond the concerns of middle-class whites.* 6 [N-VAR: oft poss N] **Concern for** someone is a feeling that you want them to be happy, safe, and well. If you do something out of **concern for** someone, you do it because you want them to be happy, safe, and well. ❑ *Without her care and concern, he had no chance at all... He had only gone along out of concern for his two grandsons.* 7 [VERB] If you **concern yourself with** something, you give it attention because you think that it is important. ❑ [V pron-refl *with* n] *I didn't concern myself with politics.* ♦ **con|cerned** [ADJ: v-link ADJ *with* n] *The agency is more concerned with making arty ads than understanding its clients' businesses.* 8 [VERB: no cont] If something such as a book or a piece of information **concerns** a particular subject, it is about that subject. ❑ [V n] *The bulk of the book concerns Sandy's two middle-aged children...* [V pron-refl *with* n] *Chapter 2 concerns itself with the methodological difficulties.* ♦ **con|cerned** [ADJ: v-link ADJ *with* n] *Randolph's work was exclusively concerned with the effects of pollution on health.* 9 [VERB: no cont] If a situation, event, or activity **concerns** you, it affects or involves you. ❑ [V n] *It was just a little unfinished business from my past, and it doesn't concern you at all.* ♦ **con|cerned** [ADJ: n ADJ, v-link ADJ *in/with* n] *It's a very stressful situation for everyone concerned... I believe he was concerned in all those matters you mention.* 10 [N-SING: with poss = affair, business] If a situation or problem is your **concern**, it is something that you have a duty or responsibility to be involved with. ❑ *The technical aspects were the concern of the Army... I would be glad to get rid of them myself. But that is not our concern.* 11 [N-COUNT: oft supp N] You can refer to a company or business as a **concern**, usually when you are describing what type of company or business it is. [FORMAL, BUSINESS] ❑ *If not a large concern, Queensbury Nursery was at least a successful one.*

**PHRASES** 12 [PHRASE: PHR with cl] You can say **'as far as I'm concerned'** to indicate that you are giving your own opinion. ❑ *As far as I'm concerned the officials incited the fight.* 13 [PHRASE: PHR with cl] You can say **as far as** something **is concerned** to indicate the subject that you are talking about. ❑ *As far as starting a family is concerned, the trend is for women having their children later in life.* 14 [PHRASE: N inflects, oft *as* PHR, v-link PHR] If a company is a **going concern**, it is actually doing business, rather than having stopped trading or not yet having started trading. [BUSINESS] ❑ *The receivers will always prefer to sell a business as a going concern.* 15 [PHRASE: oft PHR *to* n] If something is **of concern to** someone, they find it worrying and unsatisfactory. ❑ *Any injury to a child is a cause of great concern to us... The survey's findings are a matter of great concern.* 16 [PHRASE: oft PHR *to* n] If something is **of concern to** you, it is important to you. ❑ *How they are paid should be of little concern to the bank as long as they are paid.*

**con|cerned** /kənsɜːʳnd/ [◆◇◇] 1 → see **concern**. 2 [ADJ: v-link ADJ to-inf] If you are **concerned to** do something, you want to do it because you think it is important. ❑ *We were very concerned to keep the staff informed about what we were doing.*

**con|cern|ing** /kənsɜːʳnɪŋ/ [PREP: oft n PREP n = about] You use **concerning** to indicate what a question or piece of information is about. [FORMAL] ❑ *...various questions concerning pollution and the environment.*

**con|cert** /kɒnsəʳt/ **(concerts)** [◆◇◇] 1 [N-COUNT] A **concert** is a performance of music. ❑ *...a short concert of piano music... I've been to plenty of live rock concerts. ...a new concert hall.* 2 [PHRASE: PHR after v] If a musician or group of musicians appears **in concert**, they are giving a live performance. ❑ *I want people to remember Elvis in concert.*

**con|cert|ed** /kənsɜːʳtɪd/ 1 [ADJ: ADJ n] A **concerted** action is done by several people or groups working together. ❑ *Martin Parry, author of the report, says it's time for concerted action by world leaders.* 2 [ADJ: ADJ n = concentrated] If you make a **concerted** effort to do something, you try very hard to do it. ❑ *He made a concerted effort to win me away from my steady, sweet but boring boyfriend.*

**con|cert|go|er** /kɒnsəʳtgoʊəʳ/ **(concertgoers)** also **concert-goer.** [N-COUNT] A **concertgoer** is someone who goes to concerts regularly.

**con|cer|ti|na** /kɒnsəʳtiːnə/ **(concertinas)** [N-VAR: oft *the* N] A **concertina** is a musical instrument consisting of two end pieces with stiff paper or cloth that folds up between them. You play the concertina by pressing the buttons on the end pieces while moving them together and apart.

**concert|master** /kɒnsəʳtmɑːstəʳ, -mæst-/ **(concertmasters)** [N-COUNT] The **concertmaster** of an orchestra is the most senior violin player, who acts as a deputy to the conductor. [AM, AUSTRALIAN]

in BRIT, use **leader**

**con|cer|to** /kəntʃeəʳtoʊ/ **(concertos)** [N-COUNT: usu with supp] A **concerto** is a piece of music written for one or more solo instruments and an orchestra. ❑ *...Tchaikovsky's First Piano Concerto. ...a wonderful concerto for two violins and string orchestra.*

**con|ces|sion** /kənseʃᵊn/ **(concessions)** [◆◇◇] 1 [N-COUNT: oft N *to/from* n] If you make a **concession to** someone, you agree to let them do or have something, especially in order to end an argument or conflict. ❑ *The King made major concessions to end the confrontation with his people.* 2 [N-COUNT] A **concession** is a special right or privilege that is given to someone. ❑ *...tax concessions for mothers who stay at home with their children.* 3 [N-COUNT] A **concession** is a special price which is lower than the usual price and which is often given to old people, students, and the unemployed. [BRIT]

❑ *Open daily; admission £1.10 with concessions for children and OAPs.*

✓ in AM, use **reduction**

4 A **concession** is an arrangement where someone is given the right to sell a product or to run a business, especially in a building belonging to another business. [mainly AM, BUSINESS] N-COUNT

✓ in BRIT, usually use **franchise**

**con|ces|sion|aire** /kənseʃəneəʳ/ **(concessionaires)** A **concessionaire** is a person or company that has the right to sell a product or to run a business, especially in a building belonging to another business. [AM, BUSINESS] N-COUNT

✓ in BRIT, use **franchisee**

**con|ces|sion|ary** /kənseʃənri/ A **concessionary** price is a special price which is lower than the normal one and which is often given to old people, students, and the unemployed. [BRIT] ❑ *There are concessionary rates for students.* ADJ: ADJ n

✓ in AM, use **reduced**

**con|ces|sion|er** /kənseʃənəʳ/ **(concessioners)** A **concessioner** is the same as a **concessionaire**. [AM, BUSINESS] N-COUNT

✓ in BRIT, use **franchisee**

**con|ces|sive clause** /kənsesɪv klɔːz/ **(concessive clauses)** A **concessive clause** is a subordinate clause which refers to a situation that contrasts with the one described in the main clause. For example, in the sentence 'Although he was tired, he couldn't get to sleep', the first clause is a concessive clause. [TECHNICAL] N-COUNT

**conch** /kɒntʃ, kɒŋk/ **(conches)** A **conch** is a shellfish with a large shell rather like a snail's. A **conch** or a **conch shell** is the shell of this creature. N-COUNT

**con|ci|erge** /kɒnsieəʳʒ/ **(concierges)** A **concierge** is a person, especially in France, who looks after a block of flats and checks people entering and leaving the building. N-COUNT

**con|cili|ate** /kənsɪlieɪt/ **(conciliates, conciliating, conciliated)** If you **conciliate** someone, you try to end a disagreement with them. [FORMAL] ❑ *His duty was to conciliate the people, not to provoke them... The President has a strong political urge to conciliate... He spoke in a low, nervous, conciliating voice.* VERB V n V V-ing

**con|cili|ation** /kənsɪlieɪʃən/ **Conciliation** is willingness to end a disagreement or the process of ending a disagreement. ❑ *The experience has left him sceptical about efforts at conciliation.* N-UNCOUNT

**con|cilia|tory** /kənsɪliətri, AM -tɔːri/ When you are **conciliatory** in your actions or behaviour, you show that you are willing to end a disagreement with someone. ❑ *The President's speech was hailed as a conciliatory gesture toward business.* ADJ

**con|cise** /kənsaɪs/ 1 Something that is **concise** says everything that is necessary without using any unnecessary words. ❑ *Burton's text is concise and informative.* ♦ **con|cise|ly** *He'd delivered his report clearly and concisely.* 2 A **concise** edition of a book, especially a dictionary, is shorter than the original edition. ❑ *...Sotheby's Concise Encyclopedia of Porcelain.* ADJ = succinct; ADV: ADV with v; ADJ: ADJ n

**con|clave** /kɒŋkleɪv/ **(conclaves)** A **conclave** is a meeting at which the discussions are kept secret. The meeting which is held to elect a new Pope is called a conclave. N-COUNT

**con|clude** /kənkluːd/ **(concludes, concluding, concluded)** ◆◇◇ 1 If you **conclude that** something is true, you decide that it is true using the facts you know as a basis. ❑ *Larry had concluded that he had no choice but to accept Paul's words as the truth... So what can we conclude from this debate?... 'The situation in the inner cities is bad and getting worse,' she concluded.* 2 When you **conclude**, you say the last thing that you are going to say. [FORMAL] ❑ *'It's a waste of time,' he concluded... I would like to conclude by saying that I do enjoy your magazine.* ♦ **con|clud|ing** *On the radio I caught Mr Hague's concluding remarks at the Blackpool conference.* 3 When something **concludes**, or when you **conclude** it, you end it. [FORMAL] ❑ *The evening concluded with dinner and speeches... The Group of Seven major industrial countries concluded its annual summit meeting today.* 4 If one person or group **concludes** an agreement, such as a treaty or business deal, **with** another, they arrange it. You can also say that two people or groups **conclude** an agreement. [FORMAL] ❑ *Mexico and the Philippines have both concluded agreements with their commercial bank creditors... If the clubs cannot conclude a deal, an independent tribunal will decide.* VERB V that V n from n V with quote; VERB ≠ begin V with quote V; ADJ: ADJ n; VERB = end ≠ begin V adv/prep V n; V-RECIP V n with n pl-n V n

**con|clu|sion** /kənkluːʒən/ **(conclusions)** ◆◇◇ 1 When you come to a **conclusion**, you decide that something is true after you have thought about it carefully and have considered all the relevant facts. ❑ *Over the years I've come to the conclusion that she's a very great musician... I have tried to give some idea of how I feel – other people will no doubt draw their own conclusions.* 2 The **conclusion** of something is its ending. ❑ *At the conclusion of the programme, I asked the children if they had any questions they wanted to ask me.* 3 The **conclusion** of a treaty or a business deal is the act of arranging it or agreeing it. ❑ *...the expected conclusion of a free-trade agreement between Mexico and the United States.* N-COUNT: oft N that; N-SING: also no det, usu with supp = end; N-SING: usu with supp

**PHRASES** 4 You can refer to something that seems certain to happen as **a foregone conclusion**. ❑ *It was a foregone conclusion that I would end up in the same business as him.* 5 You say **'in conclusion'** to indicate that what you are about to say is the last thing that you want to say. ❑ *In conclusion, walking is a cheap, safe, enjoyable and readily available form of exercise.* 6 If you say that someone **jumps to a conclusion**, you are critical of them because they decide too quickly that something is true, when they do not know all the facts. ❑ *I didn't want her to jump to the conclusion that the divorce was in any way her fault.* PHRASE: oft *it* v-link PHR that = certainty; PHRASE: PHR with cl; PHRASE: V and N inflect, oft PHR that [disapproval]

**con|clu|sive** /kənkluːsɪv/ **Conclusive** evidence shows that something is certainly true. ❑ *Her attorneys claim there is no conclusive evidence that any murders took place... Research on the matter is far from conclusive.* ♦ **con|clu|sive|ly** *A new study proved conclusively that smokers die younger than non-smokers.* ADJ; ADV: ADV with v

**con|coct** /kənkɒkt/ **(concocts, concocting, concocted)** 1 If you **concoct** an excuse or explanation, you invent one that is not true. ❑ *Mr Ferguson said the prisoner concocted the story to get a lighter sentence.* 2 If you **concoct** something, especially something unusual, you make it by mixing several things together. ❑ *Eugene was concocting Rossini Cocktails from champagne and pureed raspberries.* VERB V n; VERB V n

**con|coc|tion** /kənkɒkʃən/ **(concoctions)** A **concoction** is something that has been made out of several things mixed together. ❑ *...a concoction of honey, yogurt, oats, and apples.* N-COUNT: oft N *of* n

**con|comi|tant** /kənkɒmɪtənt/ **(concomitants)** 1 **Concomitant** is used to describe something that happens at the same time as another thing and is connected with it. [FORMAL] ❑ *Cultures that were better at trading saw a concomitant increase in their wealth... This approach was concomitant with the move away from relying solely on official records.* 2 A **concomitant of** something is another thing that happens at the same time and is connected with it. [FORMAL] ❑ *The right to deliberately alter quotations is not a concomitant of a free press.* ADJ: ADJ n, v-link ADJ *with* n; N-COUNT: oft N *of* n

**con|cord** /kɒŋkɔːʳd/ 1 **Concord** is a state of peaceful agreement. [FORMAL] ❑ *They expressed the hope that he would pursue a neutral and balanced policy for the sake of national concord.* 2 In grammar, **concord** refers to the way that a word has a form appropriate to the number or gender of the noun or pronoun it relates to. For example, in 'He N-UNCOUNT = harmony ≠ discord; N-UNCOUNT = agreement hates it', there is concord between the singular form of the verb and the singular pronoun 'he'.

**con|cord|ance** /kənkɔːʳdəns/ **(concordances)** 1 If there is **concordance between** two things, they are similar to each other or consistent with each other. [FORMAL] ❑ *...a partial concordance between theoretical expectations and empirical evidence.* 2 A **concordance** is a list of the words in a text or group of texts, with information about where in the text each word occurs and how often it occurs. The sentences each word occurs in are often given. N-VAR N-COUNT

**con|course** /kɒŋkɔːʳs/ **(concourses)** A **concourse** is a wide hall in a public building, for example a hotel, airport, or station. N-COUNT

**con|crete** /kɒŋkriːt/ **(concretes, concreting, concreted)** ◆◇◇ 1 **Concrete** is a substance used for building which is made by mixing together cement, sand, small stones, and water. ❑ *The posts have to be set in concrete... They had lain on sleeping bags on the concrete floor.* 2 When you **concrete** something such as a path, you cover it with concrete. ❑ *He merely cleared and concreted the floors.* 3 You use **concrete** to indicate that something is definite and specific. ❑ *He had no concrete evidence... I must have something to tell him. Something concrete.* ♦ **con|crete|ly** *...by way of making their point more concretely.* 4 A **concrete** object is a real, physical object. ❑ *...using concrete objects to teach addition and subtraction.* 5 A **concrete** noun is a noun that refers to a physical object rather than to a quality or idea. 6 If a plan or idea is **set in concrete** or **embedded in concrete**, it is fixed and cannot be changed. ❑ *As Mr Blunkett emphasised, nothing is yet set in concrete.* N-UNCOUNT: oft N n; VERB; V n; ADJ: usu ADJ n; ADV: oft ADV with cl; ADJ: usu ADJ n; ADJ: ADJ n ≠ abstract; PHRASE: v-link PHR

**con|crete jun|gle** **(concrete jungles)** If you refer to a city or area as a **concrete jungle**, you mean that it has a lot of modern buildings and you think it is ugly or unpleasant to live in. N-COUNT [disapproval]

**con|cu|bine** /kɒŋkjʊbaɪn/ **(concubines)** In former times, a **concubine** was a woman who lived with and had a sexual relationship with a man of higher social rank without being married to him. N-COUNT

**con|cur** /kənkɜːʳ/ **(concurs, concurring, concurred)** If one person **concurs with** another person, the two people agree. You can also say that two people **concur**. [FORMAL] ❑ *Local feeling does not necessarily concur with the press... Daniels and Franklin concurred in an investigator's suggestion that the police be commended... Butler and Stone concur that the war threw people's lives into a moral relief... Four other judges concurred... After looking at the jug, Faulkner concurred that it was late Roman, third or fourth century.* V-RECIP = agree; V with n; V in n; pl-n V that; pl-n V; NON-RECIP: V that

**con|cur|rence** /kənkʌrəns, AM -kɜːr-/ **(concurrences)** 1 Someone's **concurrence** is their agreement to something. [FORMAL] ❑ *Any change ought not to be made without the general concurrence of all concerned.* 2 If there is a **concurrence of** two or more things, they happen at the same time. ❑ *The concurrence of their disappearances had to be more than coincidental.* N-VAR: oft with poss = agreement; N-VAR

**con|cur|rent** /kənkʌrənt, AM -kɜːr-/ **Concurrent** events or situations happen at the same time. ❑ *Galerie St. Etienne is holding three concurrent exhibitions... Concurrent with her acting career, Bron has managed to write two books of her own.* ♦ **con|cur|rent|ly** *He was jailed for 33 months to run concurrently with a sentence he is already serving for burglary.* ADJ: usu ADJ n, also v-link ADJ with n, v-link ADJ; ADV: ADV with v

**con|cussed** /kənkʌst/ If someone is **concussed**, they lose consciousness or feel sick or confused because they have been hit hard on the head. ❑ *My left arm is badly bruised and I was slightly concussed.* ADJ: usu v-link ADJ

**con|cus|sion** /kənkʌʃən/ **(concussions)** If you suffer **concussion** after a blow to your head, you lose consciousness or feel sick or confused. ❑ *Nicky was rushed to hospital with concussion... She fell off a horse and suffered a concussion.* N-VAR

**con|demn** /kəndem/ **(condemns, condemning, condemned)** ◆◇◇ 1 If you **condemn** something, you say that it is very bad and unacceptable. ❑ *Political leaders united yesterday to condemn the latest wave of violence... Graham was right to condemn his players for lack of ability, attitude and application. ...a document that condemns sexism as a moral and social evil.* 2 If someone **is condemned to** a punishment, they are given this punishment. ❑ *He was condemned to life imprisonment. ...appeals by prisoners condemned to death.* 3 If circumstances **condemn** you **to** an unpleasant situation, they make it certain that you will suffer in that way. ❑ *Their lack of qualifications condemned them to a lifetime of boring, usually poorly-paid work.* 4 If authorities **condemn** a building, they officially decide that it is not safe and must be pulled down or repaired. ❑ *State officials said the court's ruling clears the way for proceedings to condemn buildings in the area.* 5 → See also **condemned**. VERB = denounce ≠ condone; V n; V n for n; V n as n; VERB: usu passive = sentence; be V-ed to n; V-ed; VERB = doom; V n to n/-ing; VERB; V n

**con|dem|na|tion** /kɒndemneɪʃən/ **(condemnations)** **Condemnation** is the act of saying that something or someone is very bad and unacceptable. ❑ *There was widespread condemnation of Saturday's killings... The raids have drawn a strong condemnation from the United Nations Security Council.* N-VAR: with supp, usu N of n

**con|dem|na|tory** /kɒndemneɪtəri, AM kəndemnətɔːri/ **Condemnatory** means expressing strong disapproval. [FORMAL] ❑ *He was justified in some of his condemnatory outbursts.* ADJ

**con|demned** /kəndemd/ 1 A **condemned** man or woman is going to be executed. ❑ *...prison officers who had sat with the condemned man during his last days.* 2 A **condemned** building is in such a bad condition that it is not safe to live in, and so its owners are officially ordered to pull it down or repair it. ❑ *They took over a condemned 1960s tower block last year for one night.* ADJ; ADJ

**con|demned cell** **(condemned cells)** A **condemned cell** is a prison cell for someone who is going to be executed. [BRIT] N-COUNT

**con|den|sa|tion** /kɒndenseɪʃən/ **Condensation** consists of small drops of water which form when warm water vapour or steam touches a cold surface such as a window. ❑ *He used his sleeve to wipe the condensation off the glass.* N-UNCOUNT

**con|dense** /kəndens/ **(condenses, condensing, condensed)** 1 If you **condense** something, especially a piece of writing or speech, you make it shorter, usually by including only the most important parts. ❑ *We have learnt how to condense serious messages into short, self-contained sentences.* 2 When a gas or vapour **condenses**, or **is condensed**, it changes into a liquid. ❑ *Water vapour condenses to form clouds... The compressed gas is cooled and condenses into a liquid.* VERB; V n into n; Also V n; VERB; V; V into/out of n; Also V n

**con|densed** /kəndenst/ 1 A **condensed** book, explanation, or piece of information has been made shorter, usually by including only the most important parts. ❑ *The Council was merely given a condensed version of what had already been disclosed in Washington.* 2 **Condensed** liquids have been made thicker by removing some of the water in them. ❑ *...condensed mushroom soup.* ADJ: usu ADJ n; ADJ: usu ADJ n = concentrated

**con|densed milk** **Condensed milk** is very thick sweetened milk that is sold in cans. N-UNCOUNT

**con|den|ser** /kəndensəʳ/ **(condensers)** 1 A **condenser** is a device that cools gases into liquids. 2 A **condenser** is a device for accumulating electric charge. N-COUNT; N-COUNT = capacitor

**con|de|scend** /kɒndɪsend/ **(condescends, condescending, condescended)** 1 If someone **condescends to** do something, they agree to do it, but in a way which shows that they think they are better than other people and should not have to do it. ❑ *When he condescended to speak, he contradicted himself three or four times in the space of* VERB [disapproval]; V to-inf half an hour. [2] If you say that someone **condescends to** other people, you are showing your disapproval of the fact that they behave in a way which shows that they think they are superior to other people. ❑ *Don't condescend to me.* — VERB [disapproval] V to n, Also V

**con|de|scend|ing** /kɒndɪseṉdɪŋ/ If you say that someone is **condescending**, you are showing your disapproval of the fact that they talk or behave in a way which shows that they think they are superior to other people. ❑ *I'm fed up with your money and your whole condescending attitude.* — ADJ [disapproval]

**con|de|scen|sion** /kɒndɪseṉʃᵊn/ **Condescension** is condescending behaviour. ❑ *There was a tinge of condescension in her greeting.* — N-UNCOUNT [disapproval]

**con|di|ment** /kɒndɪmənt/ **(condiments)** A **condiment** is a substance such as salt, pepper, or mustard that you add to food when you eat it in order to improve the flavour. — N-COUNT

**con|di|tion** /kəndɪʃᵊn/ **(conditions, conditioning, conditioned)** ◆◆◆ [1] If you talk about the **condition** of a person or thing, you are talking about the state that they are in, especially how good or bad their physical state is. ❑ *He remains in a critical condition in a California hospital... The two-bedroom chalet is in good condition... You can't drive in that condition.* — N-SING: also no det, with supp [2] The **conditions** under which something is done or happens are all the factors or circumstances which directly affect it. ❑ *This change has been timed under laboratory conditions... The mild winter has created the ideal conditions for an ant population explosion.* — N-PLURAL: usu with supp [3] The **conditions** in which people live or work are the factors which affect their comfort, safety, or health. ❑ *People are living in appalling conditions... He could not work in these conditions any longer.* — N-PLURAL: usu with supp [4] A **condition** is something which must happen or be done in order for something else to be possible, especially when this is written into a contract or law. ❑ *...economic targets set as a condition for loan payments. ...terms and conditions of employment... Egypt had agreed to a summit subject to certain conditions.* — N-COUNT: with supp = requirement [5] If someone has a particular **condition**, they have an illness or other medical problem. ❑ *Doctors suspect he may have a heart condition.* — N-COUNT: usu with supp = complaint, disorder [6] If someone **is conditioned** by their experiences or environment, they are influenced by them over a period of time so that they do certain things or think in a particular way. ❑ *We are all conditioned by early impressions and experiences... You have been conditioned to believe that it is weak to be scared... I just feel women are conditioned into doing housework. ...a conditioned response.* — VERB: usu passive; be V-ed; be V-ed to-inf; be V-ed into -ing/n; V-ed ♦ **con|di|tion|ing** *Because of social conditioning, men don't expect themselves to be managed by women.* — N-UNCOUNT [7] To **condition** your hair or skin means to put something on it which will keep it in good condition. ❑ *...a protein which is excellent for conditioning dry and damaged hair.* — VERB V n

**PHRASES** [8] If you say that someone is **in no condition to** do something, you mean that they are too ill, upset, or drunk to do it. ❑ *She was clearly in no condition to see anyone.* — PHRASE: v-link PHR, usu PHR to-inf = unfit [9] When you agree to do something **on condition that** something else happens, you mean that you will only do it if this other thing also happens. ❑ *He spoke to reporters on condition that he was not identified.* — PHRASE [10] If someone is **out of condition**, they are unhealthy and unfit, because they do not do enough exercise. ❑ *He was too out of condition to clamber over the top.* — PHRASE: usu v-link PHR = unfit [11] **in mint condition** → see **mint**.

**con|di|tion|al** /kəndɪʃᵊnᵊl/ [1] If a situation or agreement is **conditional on** something, it will only happen or continue if this thing happens. ❑ *Their support is conditional on his proposals meeting their approval. ...a conditional offer.* — ADJ: oft ADJ on n/-ing ♦ **con|di|tion|al|ly** /kəndɪʃᵊnəli/ *Mr Smith has conditionally agreed to buy a shareholding in the club.* — ADV: ADV with v [2] In grammar, a **conditional** clause is a subordinate clause which refers to a situation which may exist or whose possible consequences you are considering. Most conditional clauses begin with 'if' or 'unless', for example 'If that happens, we'll be in big trouble' and 'You don't have to come unless you want to'. — ADJ: ADJ n

**con|di|tion|al dis|charge (conditional discharges)** If someone who is convicted of an offence is given a **conditional discharge** by a court, they are not punished unless they later commit a further offence. [BRIT, LEGAL] — N-COUNT: usu sing

**con|di|tion|er** /kəndɪʃənəʳ/ **(conditioners)** [1] A **conditioner** is a substance which you can put on your hair after you have washed it to make it softer. — N-MASS [2] A **conditioner** is a thick liquid which you can use when you wash clothes in order to make them feel softer. — N-MASS: oft n N [3] → See also **air-conditioner**.

**con|do** /kɒndoʊ/ **(condos) Condo** means the same as **condominium**. [AM, INFORMAL] — N-COUNT

**con|do|lence** /kəndoʊləns/ **(condolences)** [1] A message of **condolence** is a message in which you express your sympathy for someone because one of their friends or relatives has died recently. ❑ *Neil sent him a letter of condolence.* — N-UNCOUNT [2] When you offer or express your **condolences** to someone, you express your sympathy for them because one of their friends or relatives has died recently. ❑ *He expressed his condolences to the families of the people who died in the incident.* — N-PLURAL

**con|dom** /kɒndɒm/ **(condoms)** A **condom** is a covering made of thin rubber which a man can wear on his penis as a contraceptive or as protection against disease during sexual intercourse. — N-COUNT

**con|do|min|ium** /kɒndəmɪniəm/ **(condominiums)** [1] A **condominium** is an apartment building in which each apartment is owned by the person who lives there. [AM] — N-COUNT [2] A **condominium** is one of the privately owned apartments in a condominium. [AM] — N-COUNT

**con|done** /kəndoʊn/ **(condones, condoning, condoned)** If someone **condones** behaviour that is morally wrong, they accept it and allow it to happen. ❑ *I have never encouraged nor condoned violence.* — VERB: oft with brd-neg ≠ condemn; V n

**con|dor** /kɒndɔːʳ/ **(condors)** A **condor** is a large South American bird that eats the meat of dead animals. — N-COUNT

**con|du|cive** /kəndjuːsɪv, AM -duːsɪv/ If one thing is **conducive to** another thing, it makes the other thing likely to happen. ❑ *Sometimes the home environment just isn't conducive to reading.* — ADJ: usu v-link ADJ, usu ADJ to n/-ing

**con|duct (conducts, conducting, conducted)** ◆◆◇

> ✓ The verb is pronounced /kəndʌkt/. The noun is pronounced /kɒndʌkt/.

[1] When you **conduct** an activity or task, you organize it and carry it out. ❑ *I decided to conduct an experiment... He said they were conducting a campaign against democrats across the country.* — VERB = carry out; V n; V n [2] The **conduct of** a task or activity is the way in which it is organized and carried out. ❑ *Also up for discussion will be the conduct of free and fair elections.* — N-SING: with supp [3] If you **conduct** yourself in a particular way, you behave in that way. ❑ *The way he conducts himself reflects on the party and will increase criticisms against him... Most people believe they conduct their private and public lives in accordance with Christian morality.* — VERB; V pron-refl prep/adv; V n [4] Someone's **conduct** is the way they behave in particular situations. ❑ *He has trouble understanding that other people judge him by his conduct.* — N-UNCOUNT: with supp = behaviour [5] When someone **conducts** an orchestra or choir, they stand in front of it and direct its performance. ❑ *Dennis had recently begun a successful career conducting opera in Europe... Solti will continue to conduct here and abroad.* — VERB; V n; V [6] If something **conducts** heat or electricity, it allows heat or electricity to pass through it or along it. ❑ *Water conducts heat faster than air.* — VERB: no cont; V n

**con|duct|ed tour (conducted tours)** A **conducted tour** is a visit to a building, town, or area during which someone goes with you and explains everything to you. — N-COUNT = guided tour

**con|duc|tion** /kəndʌkʃən/ **Conduction** is the process by which heat or electricity passes through or along something. [TECHNICAL] ❑ *Temperature becomes uniform by heat conduction until finally a permanent state is reached.* — N-UNCOUNT: usu with supp

**con|duc|tive** /kəndʌktɪv/ A **conductive** substance is able to conduct things such as heat and electricity. [TECHNICAL] ❑ *Salt water is much more conductive than fresh water is.* — ADJ
♦ **con|duc|tiv|ity** /kɒndʌktɪvɪti/ *...a device which monitors electrical conductivity.* — N-UNCOUNT

**con|duc|tor** /kəndʌktəʳ/ **(conductors)** 1 A **conductor** is a person who stands in front of an orchestra or choir and directs its performance. — N-COUNT
2 On a bus, the **conductor** is the person whose job is to sell tickets to the passengers. — N-COUNT
3 On a train, a **conductor** is a person whose job is to travel on the train in order to help passengers and check tickets. [AM] — N-COUNT

☑ in BRIT, use **guard**

4 A **conductor** is a substance that heat or electricity can pass through or along. ➔ See also **lightning conductor, semiconductor**. — N-COUNT

**con|duit** /kɒndjuɪt, AM -duɪt/ **(conduits)** 1 A **conduit** is a small tunnel, pipe, or channel through which water or electrical wires go. — N-COUNT
2 A **conduit** is a person or country that links two or more other people or countries. ❑ *Pakistan became a conduit for drugs produced in Afghanistan.* — N-COUNT: oft N *for/to* n

**cone** /koʊn/ **(cones)** 1 A **cone** is a shape with a circular base and smooth curved sides ending in a point at the top. — N-COUNT
2 A **cone** is the fruit of a tree such as a pine or fir. ❑ *...a bowl of fir cones.* — N-COUNT
3 A **cone** is a thin, cone-shaped biscuit that is used for holding ice cream. You can also refer to an ice cream that you eat in this way as a **cone**. ❑ *She stopped by the ice-cream shop and had a chocolate cone.* — N-COUNT
4 ➔ See also **pine cone, traffic cone**.

**con|fec|tion** /kənfekʃən/ **(confections)** You can refer to a sweet food that someone has made as a **confection**. [WRITTEN] ❑ *...a confection made with honey and nuts.* — N-COUNT

**con|fec|tion|er** /kənfekʃənəʳ/ **(confectioners)** A **confectioner** is a person whose job is making or selling sweets and chocolates. — N-COUNT

**con|fec|tion|ers' sug|ar** **Confectioners' sugar** is very fine white sugar that is used for making icing and candy. [AM] — N-UNCOUNT

☑ in BRIT, use **icing sugar**

**con|fec|tion|ery** /kənfekʃənri, AM -neri/ **Confectionery** is sweets and chocolates. [WRITTEN] ❑ *...hand-made confectionery.* — N-UNCOUNT = sweets

**con|fed|era|cy** /kənfedərəsi/ **(confederacies)** A **confederacy** is a union of states or people who are trying to achieve the same thing. ❑ *They've entered this new confederacy because the central government's been unable to control the collapsing economy.* — N-COUNT

**con|fed|er|ate** /kənfedərət/ **(confederates)** Someone's **confederates** are the people they are working with in a secret activity. — N-COUNT = accomplice

**con|fed|era|tion** /kənfedəreɪʃən/ **(confederations)** A **confederation** is an organization or group consisting of smaller groups or states, especially one that exists for business or political purposes. ❑ *...the Confederation of Indian Industry. ...plans to partition the republic into a confederation of mini-states.* — N-COUNT; N-IN-NAMES

**con|fer** /kənfɜːʳ/ **(confers, conferring, conferred)** 1 When you **confer with** someone, you discuss something with them in order to make a decision. You can also say that two people **confer**. ❑ *He conferred with Hill and the others in his office... His doctors conferred by telephone and agreed that he must get away from his family for a time.* — V-RECIP; V *with* n; pl-n V
2 To **confer** something such as power or an honour **on** someone means to give it to them. [FORMAL] ❑ *The constitution also confers large powers on Brazil's 25 constituent states... Never imagine that rank confers genuine authority.* — VERB; V n *on* n; V n

**con|fer|ence** /kɒnfrəns/ **(conferences)** ♦♦♦ 1 A **conference** is a meeting, often lasting a few days, which is organized on a particular subject or to bring together people who have a common interest. ❑ *The President summoned all the state governors to a conference on education. ...the Conservative Party conference... Last weekend the Roman Catholic Church in Scotland held a conference, attended by 450 delegates.* — N-COUNT
2 A **conference** is a meeting at which formal discussions take place. ❑ *They sat down at the dinner table, as they always did, before the meal, for a conference... Her employer was in conference with two lawyers and did not want to be interrupted.* — N-COUNT: also *in* N
3 ➔ See also **press conference**.

**con|fer|ence call** **(conference calls)** A **conference call** is a phone call in which more than two people take part. [BUSINESS] ❑ *There are daily conference calls with Washington.* — N-COUNT

**con|fess** /kənfes/ **(confesses, confessing, confessed)** 1 If someone **confesses** to doing something wrong, they admit that they did it. ❑ *He had confessed to seventeen murders... I had expected her to confess that she only wrote these books for the money... Most rape victims confess a feeling of helplessness... Ray changed his mind, claiming that he had been forced into confessing... 'I played a very bad match,' he confessed.* — VERB = admit ≠ deny; V *to* n/-ing; V that; V n; V; V with quote
2 If someone **confesses** or **confesses** their sins, they tell God or a priest about their sins so that they can be forgiven. ❑ *You just go to the church and confess your sins... Once we have confessed our failures and mistakes to God, we should stop feeling guilty.* — VERB; V n; V n *to* n
3 You use expressions like **'I confess'**, **'I must confess'**, or **'I have to confess'** to apologize slightly for admitting something you are ashamed of or that you think might offend or annoy someone. ❑ *I confess it's got me baffled... I must confess I'm not a great enthusiast for long political programmes.* — PHRASE: PHR with cl [politeness] = admit

**con|fessed** /kənfest/ You use **confessed** to describe someone who openly admits that they have a particular fault or have done something wrong. ❑ *She is is a confessed monarchist.* — ADJ: ADJ n = self-confessed

**con|fes|sion** /kənfeʃən/ **(confessions)** 1 A **confession** is a signed statement by someone in which they admit that they have committed a particular crime. ❑ *They forced him to sign a confession.* — N-COUNT
2 **Confession** is the act of admitting that you have done something that you are ashamed of or embarrassed about. ❑ *The diaries are a mixture of confession and observation... I have a confession to make.* — N-VAR
3 If you make a **confession of** your beliefs or feelings, you publicly tell people that this is what you believe or feel. ❑ *...Tatyana's confession of love.* — N-VAR: usu N *of* n = declaration
4 In the Catholic church and in some other churches, if you go to **confession**, you privately tell a priest about your sins and ask for forgiveness. ❑ *He never went to Father Porter for confession again.* — N-VAR

**con|fes|sion|al** /kənfeʃənəl/ **(confessionals)** 1 A **confessional** is the small room in a church where Christians, especially Roman Catholics, go to confess their sins. — N-COUNT
2 A **confessional** speech or writing contains confessions. ❑ *The convictions rest solely on disputed witness and confessional statements.* — ADJ

**con|fes|sor** /kənfesəʳ/ **(confessors)** 1 A **confessor** is a priest who hears a person's confession. — N-COUNT
2 If you describe someone as your **confessor**, you mean that they are the person you can talk to about your secrets or problems. ❑ *He was their adviser, confidant and father confessor.* — N-COUNT

**con|fet|ti** /kənfeti/ **Confetti** is small pieces of coloured paper that people throw over the bride and bridegroom at a wedding. — N-UNCOUNT

**con|fi|dant** /kɒnfɪdænt, -dænt/ **(confidants)** Someone's **confidant** is a man who they are able to discuss their private problems with. ❑ *...a close confidant of the president.* — N-COUNT: usu with poss

**con|fi|dante** /kɒnfɪdænt, -dænt/ **(confidantes)** Someone's **confidante** is a woman who they are able to discuss their private problems with. ❑ *You are her closest friend and confidante.* N-COUNT: usu with poss

**con|fide** /kənfaɪd/ **(confides, confiding, confided)** If you **confide in** someone, you tell them a secret. ❑ *I knew she had some fundamental problems in her marriage because she had confided in me a year earlier... He confided to me that he felt like he was being punished... On New Year's Eve he confided that he had suffered rather troubling chest pains... I confided my worries to Michael.* VERB V *in* n V *to* n that V that V n *to* n Also V with quote

**con|fi|dence** /kɒnfɪdəns/ [1] If you have **confidence in** someone, you feel that you can trust them. ❑ *I have every confidence in you... This has contributed to the lack of confidence in the police... His record on ceasefires inspires no confidence.* ◆◆◇ N-UNCOUNT: usu N *in* n = faith [2] If you have **confidence**, you feel sure about your abilities, qualities, or ideas. ❑ *The band is on excellent form and brimming with confidence... I always thought the worst of myself and had no confidence whatsoever.* N-UNCOUNT [3] If you can say something **with confidence**, you feel certain it is correct. ❑ *I can say with confidence that such rumors were totally groundless.* N-UNCOUNT: usu *with* N [4] If you tell someone something **in confidence**, you tell them a secret. ❑ *We told you all these things in confidence... Even telling Lois seemed a betrayal of confidence.* N-UNCOUNT: usu *in* N ● If you **take** someone **into** your **confidence**, you tell them a secret. ❑ *If your daughter takes you into her confidence, don't rush off to tell your husband.* PHRASE: V inflects [5] → See also **vote of no confidence**.

**con|fi|dence game** **(confidence games)** A **confidence game** is the same as a **confidence trick**. [mainly AM] N-COUNT

**con|fi|dence man** **(confidence men)** A **confidence man** is a man who persuades people to give him their money or property by lying to them. [mainly AM] N-COUNT = con man

**con|fi|dence trick** **(confidence tricks)** A **confidence trick** is a trick in which someone deceives you by telling you something that is not true, often to trick you out of money. [mainly BRIT] N-COUNT

✔ in AM, usually use **confidence game**

**con|fi|dent** /kɒnfɪdənt/ [1] If you are **confident** about something, you are certain that it will happen in the way you want it to. ❑ *I am confident that everything will come out right in time... Mr Ryan is confident of success... Management is confident about the way business is progressing.* ◆◇◇ ADJ: usu v-link ADJ, oft ADJ that, ADJ prep ≠ sceptical ♦ **con|fi|dent|ly** *I can confidently promise that this year is going to be very different.* ADV: ADV with v [2] If a person or their manner is **confident**, they feel sure about their own abilities, qualities, or ideas. ❑ *In time he became more confident and relaxed.* ADJ = self-assured ♦ **con|fi|dent|ly** *She walked confidently across the hall.* ADV: usu ADV with v [3] If you are **confident that** something is true, you are sure that it is true. A **confident** statement is one that the speaker is sure is true. ❑ *She is confident that everybody is on her side... 'Bet you I can', comes the confident reply.* ADJ: oft ADJ that ♦ **con|fi|dent|ly** *I can confidently say that none of them were or are racist.* ADV: ADV with v

**con|fi|den|tial** /kɒnfɪdenʃəl/ [1] Information that is **confidential** is meant to be kept secret or private. ❑ *She accused them of leaking confidential information about her private life... We'll take good care and keep what you've told us strictly confidential, Mr. Lane.* ADJ ♦ **con|fi|den|tial|ly** *People can phone in the knowledge that any information they give will be treated confidentially.* ADV: ADV with v ♦ **con|fi|den|ti|al|ity** /kɒnfɪdenʃiælɪti/ *...the confidentiality of the client-solicitor relationship.* N-UNCOUNT [2] If you talk to someone in a **confidential** way, you talk to them quietly because what you are saying is secret or private. ❑ *'Look,' he said in a confidential tone, 'I want you to know that me and Joey are cops.'... His face suddenly turned solemn, his voice confidential.* ADJ: usu ADJ n ♦ **con|fi|den|tial|ly** *Nash hadn't raised his voice, still spoke rather softly, confidentially.* ADV: ADV after v

**con|fi|den|tial|ly** /kɒnfɪdenʃəli/ **Confidentially** is used to say that what you are telling someone is a secret and should not be discussed with anyone else. ❑ *Confidentially, I am not sure that it wasn't above their heads.* → See also **confidential**. ADV: ADV with cl

**con|figu|ra|tion** /kənfɪgureɪʃən, AM -fɪgjə-/ **(configurations)** [1] A **configuration** is an arrangement of a group of things. [FORMAL] ❑ *...Stonehenge, in south-western England, an ancient configuration of giant stones.* N-COUNT [2] The **configuration** of a computer system is way in which all its parts, such as the hardware and software, are connected together in order for the computer to work. [COMPUTING] N-UNCOUNT

**con|fig|ure** /kənfɪgəʳ, AM -gjər/ **(configures, configuring, configured)** If you **configure** a piece of computer equipment, you set it up so that it is ready for use. [COMPUTING] ❑ *How easy was it to configure the software?* VERB V n

**con|fine** **(confines, confining, confined)**

✔ The verb is pronounced /kənfaɪn/. The noun **confines** is pronounced /kɒnfaɪnz/.

[1] To **confine** something **to** a particular place or group means to prevent it from spreading beyond that place or group. ❑ *Health officials have successfully confined the epidemic to the Tabatinga area... The US will soon be taking steps to confine the conflict.* VERB = restrict V n *to* n V n [2] If you **confine yourself** or your activities **to** something, you do only that thing and are involved with nothing else. ❑ *He did not confine himself to the one language... His genius was not confined to the decoration of buildings.* VERB = limit, restrict V pron-refl *to* n V-ed [3] If someone **is confined to** a mental institution, prison, or other place, they are sent there and are not allowed to leave for a period of time. ❑ *The woman will be confined to a mental institution.* VERB: usu passive be V-ed *to* n [4] Something that is within the **confines of** an area or place is within the boundaries enclosing it. [FORMAL] ❑ *The movie is set entirely within the confines of the abandoned factory.* N-PLURAL: usu prep *the* N of n [5] The **confines of** a situation, system, or activity are the limits or restrictions it involves. ❑ *...away from the confines of the British class system... I can't stand the confines of this marriage.* N-PLURAL: usu *the* N *of* n = constraints

**con|fined** /kənfaɪnd/ [1] If something is **confined to** a particular place, it exists only in that place. If it is **confined to** a particular group, only members of that group have it. ❑ *The problem is not confined to Germany... These dangers are not confined to smokers.* ADJ: v-link ADJ *to* n = restricted [2] A **confined** space or area is small and enclosed by walls. ❑ *His long legs bent up in the confined space.* ADJ: usu ADJ n [3] If someone is **confined to** a wheelchair, bed, or house, they have to stay there, because they are disabled or ill. ❑ *He had been confined to a wheelchair since childhood.* ADJ: v-link ADJ *to* n

**con|fine|ment** /kənfaɪnmənt/ **Confinement** is the state of being forced to stay in a prison or another place which you cannot leave. ❑ *She had been held in solitary confinement for four months.* N-UNCOUNT

**con|firm** /kənfɜːʳm/ **(confirms, confirming, confirmed)** [1] If something **confirms** what you believe, suspect, or fear, it shows that it is definitely true. ❑ *X-rays have confirmed that he has not broken any bones... These new statistics confirm our worst fears about the depth of the recession.* ◆◆◇ VERB: no cont V that V n ♦ **con|fir|ma|tion** /kɒnfəʳmeɪʃən/ *They took her resignation from Bendix as confirmation of their suspicions.* N-UNCOUNT [2] If you **confirm** something that has been stated or suggested, you say that it is true because you know about it. ❑ *The spokesman confirmed that the area was now in rebel hands... He confirmed what had long been feared.* VERB V that V n ♦ **con|fir|ma|tion** *She glanced over at James for confirmation.* N-UNCOUNT [3] If you **confirm** an arrangement or appointment, you say that it is definite, usually in a letter or on the telephone. ❑ *You make the reservation, and I'll confirm it in writing.* VERB V n ♦ **con|fir|ma|tion** *Travel arrangements are subject* N-UNCOUNT *to confirmation by State Tourist Organisations.* 4 If someone **is confirmed**, they are formally accepted as a member of a Christian church during a ceremony in which they say they believe what the church teaches. ❑ *He was confirmed as a member of the Church of England.* ♦ **con|fir|ma|tion** **(confirmations)** *...when I was being prepared for Confirmation... Flu prevented her from attending her daughter's confirmation.* 5 If something **confirms** you **in** your decision, belief, or opinion, it makes you think that you are definitely right. ❑ *It has confirmed me in my decision not to become a nun.* 6 If someone **confirms** their position, role, or power, they do something to make their power, position, or role stronger or more definite. ❑ *Williams has confirmed his position as the world's number one snooker player.* 7 If something **confirms** you **as** something, it shows that you definitely deserve a name, role, or position. ❑ *His new role could confirm him as one of our leading actors.*

VERB: usu passive · be V-ed · N-VAR · VERB: no cont · V n *in* n · VERB · V n · VERB · V n *as* n

**con|firmed** /kənfɜːʳmd/ You use **confirmed** to describe someone who has a particular habit or belief that they are very unlikely to change. ❑ *I'm a confirmed bachelor.*

ADJ: ADJ n

**con|fis|cate** /kɒnfɪskeɪt/ **(confiscates, confiscating, confiscated)** If you **confiscate** something **from** someone, you take it away from them, usually as a punishment. ❑ *There is concern that police use the law to confiscate assets from people who have committed minor offences... They confiscated weapons, ammunition and propaganda material.* ♦ **con|fis|ca|tion** /kɒnfɪskeɪʃᵊn/ **(confiscations)** *The new laws allow the confiscation of assets purchased with proceeds of the drugs trade.*

VERB = seize · V n *from* n · V n · N-VAR: oft N *of* n = seizure

**con|fit** /kɒnfiː/ **(confits)** **Confit** is meat such as goose or duck which has been cooked and preserved in its own fat. ❑ *...confit of duck.*

N-MASS

**con|fla|gra|tion** /kɒnfləgreɪʃᵊn/ **(conflagrations)** A **conflagration** is a fire that burns over a large area and destroys property. [FORMAL]

N-COUNT = blaze

**con|flate** /kənfleɪt/ **(conflates, conflating, conflated)** If you **conflate** two or more descriptions or ideas, or if they **conflate**, you combine them in order to produce a single one. [FORMAL] ❑ *Her letters conflate past and present... Unfortunately the public conflated fiction with reality and made her into a saint... The two meanings conflated.*

V-RECIP · V pl-n · V n *with* n · pl-n V

**con|flict** **(conflicts, conflicting, conflicted)** ◆◆◇

> The noun is pronounced /kɒnflɪkt/. The verb is pronounced /kənflɪkt/.

1 **Conflict** is serious disagreement and argument about something important. If two people or groups are **in conflict**, they have had a serious disagreement or argument and have not yet reached agreement. ❑ *Try to keep any conflict between you and your ex-partner to a minimum... Employees already are in conflict with management over job cuts.* 2 **Conflict** is a state of mind in which you find it impossible to make a decision. ❑ *...the anguish of his own inner conflict.* 3 **Conflict** is fighting between countries or groups of people. [JOURNALISM or WRITTEN] ❑ *...talks aimed at ending four decades of conflict.* 4 A **conflict** is a serious difference between two or more beliefs, ideas, or interests. If two beliefs, ideas, or interests are **in conflict**, they are very different. ❑ *There is a conflict between what they are doing and what you want... Do you feel any conflict of loyalties?... The two objectives are in conflict.* 5 If ideas, beliefs, or accounts **conflict**, they are very different from each other and it seems impossible for them to exist together or to each be true. ❑ *Personal ethics and professional ethics sometimes conflict... He held firm opinions which usually conflicted with my own. ...three powers with conflicting interests.*

N-UNCOUNT: oft *in/into* N · N-UNCOUNT = turmoil · N-VAR · N-VAR: oft N *between* pl-n · V-RECIP = clash · pl-n V · V *with* n · V-ing

**con|flu|ence** /kɒnfluəns/ The **confluence** of two rivers is the place where they join and become one larger river. ❑ *The 160-metre falls mark the dramatic confluence of the rivers Nera and Velino.*

N-SING: oft N *of* n

**con|form** /kənfɔːʳm/ **(conforms, conforming, conformed)** 1 If something **conforms to** something such as a law or someone's wishes, it is of the required type or quality. ❑ *The Night Rider lamp has been designed to conform to new British Standard safety requirements.* 2 If you **conform**, you behave in the way that you are expected or supposed to behave. ❑ *Many children who can't or don't conform are often bullied... He did not feel obliged to conform to the rules that applied to ordinary men.* 3 If someone or something **conforms to** a pattern or type, they are very similar to it. ❑ *I am well aware that we all conform to one stereotype or another.*

VERB · V *to/with* n · VERB ≠ rebel · V · V *to/with* n · VERB · V *to* n

**con|form|ist** /kənfɔːʳmɪst/ **(conformists)** Someone who is **conformist** behaves or thinks like everyone else rather than doing things that are original. ❑ *He may have to become more conformist if he is to prosper again.* ♦ A **conformist** is someone who is conformist.

ADJ · N-COUNT

**con|form|ity** /kənfɔːʳmɪti/ 1 If something happens **in conformity with** something such as a law or someone's wishes, it happens as the law says it should, or as the person wants it to. ❑ *The prime minister is, in conformity with the constitution, chosen by the president.* 2 **Conformity** means behaving in the same way as most other people. ❑ *Excessive conformity is usually caused by fear of disapproval.*

N-UNCOUNT: oft *in* N *with* n · N-UNCOUNT

**con|found** /kənfaʊnd/ **(confounds, confounding, confounded)** If someone or something **confounds** you, they make you feel surprised or confused, often by showing you that your opinions or expectations of them were wrong. ❑ *The choice of Governor may confound us all.*

VERB · V n

**con|front** /kənfrʌnt/ **(confronts, confronting, confronted)** ◆◇◇ 1 If you **are confronted with** a problem, task, or difficulty, you have to deal with it. ❑ *She was confronted with severe money problems... Ministers underestimated the magnitude of the task confronting them.* 2 If you **confront** a difficult situation or issue, you accept the fact that it exists and try to deal with it. ❑ *We are learning how to confront death... NATO countries have been forced to confront fundamental moral questions.* 3 If you **are confronted** by something that you find threatening or difficult to deal with, it is there in front of you. ❑ *I was confronted with an array of knobs, levers, and switches.* 4 If you **confront** someone, you stand or sit in front of them, especially when you are going to fight, argue, or compete with them. ❑ *She pushed her way through the mob and confronted him face to face... The candidates confronted each other during a televised debate.* 5 If you **confront** someone **with** something, you present facts or evidence to them in order to accuse them of something. ❑ *She had decided to confront Kathryn with what she had learnt... I could not bring myself to confront him about it... His confronting me forced me to search for the answers.*

VERB = face · be V-ed *with/by* n · V n · VERB = face · V n · V n · VERB: usu passive = face · be V-ed *with/by* n · VERB · V n · V n · VERB · V n *with* n · V n *about* n · V n

**con|fron|ta|tion** /kɒnfrʌnteɪʃᵊn/ **(confrontations)** ◆◇◇ A **confrontation** is a dispute, fight, or battle between two groups of people. ❑ *The commission remains so weak that it will continue to avoid confrontation with governments.*

N-VAR: oft N *with/between* n

**con|fron|ta|tion|al** /kɒnfrʌnteɪʃənᵊl/ If you describe the way that someone behaves as **confrontational**, you are showing your disapproval of the fact that they are aggressive and likely to cause an argument or dispute. ❑ *The committee's confrontational style of campaigning has made it unpopular.*

ADJ [disapproval]

**con|fuse** /kənfjuːz/ **(confuses, confusing, confused)** 1 If you **confuse** two things, you get them mixed up, so that you think one of them is the other one. ❑ *Great care is taken to avoid confusing the two types of projects... I can't see how anyone could confuse you with another!* ♦ **con|fu|sion** /kənfjuːʒᵊn/ *Use different colours of felt pen on your sketch to avoid confusion.* 2 To **confuse** someone means to make it difficult for them to know ex-

VERB · V pl-n · V n *with* n · N-UNCOUNT · VERB

actly what is happening or what to do. ❑ *German politics surprised and confused him.* [3] To **confuse** a situation means to make it complicated or difficult to understand. ❑ *To further confuse the issue, there is an enormous variation in the amount of sleep people feel happy with.* — V n; VERB; V n

**con|fused** /kənfjuːzd/ [1] If you are **confused**, you do not know exactly what is happening or what to do. ❑ *A survey showed people were confused about what they should eat to stay healthy... Things were happening too quickly and Brian was confused.* [2] Something that is **confused** does not have any order or pattern and is difficult to understand. ❑ *The situation remains confused as both sides claim success.* — ADJ: oft ADJ *about/by* n = bewildered; ADJ

**con|fus|ing** /kənfjuːzɪŋ/ Something that is **confusing** makes it difficult for people to know exactly what is happening or what to do. ❑ *The statement is highly confusing.* — ADJ ≠ clear

**con|fu|sion** /kənfjuːʒən/ **(confusions)** [1] If there is **confusion** about something, it is not clear what the true situation is, especially because people believe different things. ❑ *There's still confusion about the number of casualties... Omissions in my recent article must have caused confusion.* [2] **Confusion** is a situation in which everything is in disorder, especially because there are lots of things happening at the same time. ❑ *There was confusion when a man fired shots.* [3] → See also **confuse**. — N-VAR; N-UNCOUNT

**con|ga** /kɒŋgə/ **(congas)** If a group of people dance a **conga**, they dance in a long winding line, with each person holding on to the back of the person in front. — N-COUNT

**con|geal** /kəndʒiːl/ **(congeals, congealing, congealed)** When a liquid **congeals**, it becomes very thick and sticky and almost solid. ❑ *The blood had started to congeal. ...spilled wine mingled with congealed soup.* — VERB; V; V-ed

**con|gen|ial** /kəndʒiːniəl/ A **congenial** person, place, or environment is pleasant. [FORMAL] ❑ *He is back in more congenial company.* — ADJ: usu ADJ n = agreeable

**con|geni|tal** /kəndʒenɪtəl/ [1] A **congenital** disease or medical condition is one that a person has had from birth, but is not inherited. [MEDICAL] ❑ *When John was 17, he died of congenital heart disease.* ♦ **con|geni|tal|ly** *...congenitally deaf patients.* [2] A **congenital** characteristic or feature in a person is so strong that you cannot imagine it ever changing, although there may seem to be no reason for it. ❑ *He was a congenital liar and usually in debt.* ♦ **con|geni|tal|ly** *I admit to being congenitally lazy.* — ADJ: usu ADJ n; ADV: ADV adj/-ed; ADJ: usu ADJ n = incorrigible; ADV

**con|ger** /kɒŋgəʳ/ **(congers)** A **conger** or a **conger eel** is a large fish that looks like a snake. — N-VAR

**con|gest|ed** /kəndʒestɪd/ [1] A **congested** road or area is extremely crowded and blocked with traffic or people. ❑ *He first promised two weeks ago to clear Britain's congested roads... Some areas are congested with both cars and people.* [2] If a part of the body is **congested**, it is blocked. [FORMAL] ❑ *The arteries in his neck had become fatally congested.* — ADJ; ADJ = blocked

**con|ges|tion** /kəndʒestʃən/ [1] If there is **congestion** in a place, the place is extremely crowded and blocked with traffic or people. ❑ *The problems of traffic congestion will not disappear in a hurry.* [2] **Congestion** in a part of the body is a medical condition in which the part becomes blocked. [FORMAL] ❑ *...nasal congestion.* — N-UNCOUNT: usu with supp, oft adj N; N-UNCOUNT: usu with supp, oft adj N

**con|ges|tion charge** **(congestion charges)** **Congestion charges** refer to money motorists must pay in order to drive in some city centres. Congestion charges are intended to reduce traffic within those areas. ♦ **con|ges|tion charg|ing** ❑ *...the decision on whether to introduce congestion charging on urban roads.* — N-COUNT; N-UNCOUNT

**con|ges|tive** /kəndʒestɪv/ A **congestive** disease is a medical condition where a part of the body becomes blocked. [MEDICAL] ❑ *...congestive heart failure.* — ADJ: ADJ n

**con|glom|er|ate** /kənglɒmərət/ **(conglomerates)** A **conglomerate** is a large business firm consisting of several different companies. [BUSINESS] ❑ *Fiat is Italy's largest industrial conglomerate.* — N-COUNT: oft adj N

**con|glom|era|tion** /kənglɒməreɪʃən/ **(conglomerations)** A **conglomeration of** things is a group of many different things, gathered together. [FORMAL] ❑ *...a conglomeration of peoples speaking different languages.* — N-COUNT: usu N *of* n

**con|gratu|late** /kəngrætʃʊleɪt/ **(congratulates, congratulating, congratulated)** [1] If you **congratulate** someone, you say something to show you are pleased that something nice has happened to them. ❑ *She congratulated him on the birth of his son... I was absolutely astonished by the reaction to our engagement. Everyone started congratulating us.* ♦ **con|gratu|la|tion** /kəngrætʃʊleɪʃən/ *We have received many letters of congratulation.* [2] If you **congratulate** someone, you praise them for something good that they have done. ❑ *I really must congratulate the organisers for a well run and enjoyable event... We specifically wanted to congratulate certain players.* [3] If you **congratulate yourself**, you are pleased about something that you have done or that has happened to you. ❑ *Waterstone has every reason to congratulate himself.* — VERB; V n *on/for* n/-ing; V n; N-UNCOUNT; VERB; V n *for/on* n/-ing; V n; VERB; V pron-refl

**con|gratu|la|tions** /kəngrætʃʊleɪʃənz/ [1] You say '**Congratulations**' to someone in order to congratulate them on something nice that has happened to them or something good that they have done. ❑ *Congratulations, you have a healthy baby boy... Congratulations to everybody who sent in their ideas.* [2] If you offer someone your **congratulations**, you congratulate them on something nice that has happened to them or on something good that they have done. ❑ *The club also offers its congratulations to D. Brown on his appointment as president.* — CONVENTION [formulae]; N-PLURAL

**con|gratu|la|tory** /kəngrætʃʊleɪtəri, AM -lətɔːri/ A **congratulatory** message expresses congratulations. ❑ *He sent Kim a congratulatory letter.* — ADJ

**con|gre|gant** /kɒŋgrɪgənt/ **(congregants)** **Congregants** are members of a congregation. [mainly AM] — N-COUNT

**con|gre|gate** /kɒŋgrɪgeɪt/ **(congregates, congregating, congregated)** When people **congregate**, they gather together and form a group. ❑ *Visitors congregated on Sunday afternoons to view public exhibitions.* — VERB; V

**con|gre|ga|tion** /kɒŋgrɪgeɪʃən/ **(congregations)** The people who are attending a church service or who regularly attend a church service are referred to as the **congregation**. ❑ *Most members of the congregation begin arriving a few minutes before services.* — N-COUNT-COLL

**con|gress** /kɒŋgres/ **(congresses)** A **congress** is a large meeting that is held to discuss ideas and policies. ❑ *A lot has changed after the party congress.* — N-COUNT-COLL: usu with supp

**Con|gress** **Congress** is the elected group of politicians that is responsible for making the law in the United States. It consists of two parts: the House of Representatives and the Senate. ❑ *We want to cooperate with both the administration and Congress.* — ◆◆◇ N-PROPER-COLL

**con|gres|sion|al** /kəngreʃənəl/ also **Congressional.** A **congressional** policy, action, or person relates to the United States Congress. ❑ *The president explained his plans to congressional leaders.* — ◆◇◇ ADJ: ADJ n

**Congress|man** /kɒŋgrɪsmən/ **(Congressmen)** also **congressman.** A **Congressman** is a male member of the US Congress, especially of the House of Representatives. — N-COUNT; N-TITLE

**Congress|person** /kɒŋgrɪspɜːʳsən/ **(Congresspeople)** also **congressperson.** A — N-COUNT

**Congressperson** is a member of the US Congress, especially of the House of Representatives.

**Congress|woman** /kɒŋgrɪswʊmən/ **(Congresswomen)** also **congresswoman.** A **Congresswoman** is a female member of the US Congress, especially of the House of Representatives. ❑ *The meeting was organised by Congresswoman Maxine Waters.*
N-COUNT; N-TITLE

**con|gru|ence** /kɒŋgruəns/ **Congruence** is when two things are similar or fit together well. [FORMAL] ❑ *...a necessary congruence between political, cultural and economic forces.*
N-UNCOUNT: also *a* N, usu N *between* pl-n

**con|gru|ent** /kɒŋgruənt/ If one thing is **congruent with** another thing, they are similar or fit together well. [FORMAL] ❑ *They want to work in an organisation whose values are congruent with their own.*
ADJ: usu v-link ADJ, usu ADJ *with* n

**coni|cal** /kɒnɪkᵊl/ A **conical** object is shaped like a cone. ❑ *We were soon aware of a great conical shape to the north-east.*
ADJ: usu ADJ n

**co|ni|fer** /kɒnɪfəʳ/ **(conifers) Conifers** are a group of trees and shrubs, for example pine trees and fir trees, that grow in cooler areas of the world. They have fruit called cones, and very thin leaves called needles which they do not normally lose in winter.
N-COUNT

**co|nif|er|ous** /kənɪfərəs, AM koʊ-/ A **coniferous** forest or wood is made up of conifers.
ADJ: usu ADJ n

**con|jec|tur|al** /kəndʒektʃərəl/ A statement that is **conjectural** is based on information that is not certain or complete. [FORMAL] ❑ *There is something undeniably conjectural about such claims.*
ADJ

**con|jec|ture** /kəndʒektʃəʳ/ **(conjectures, conjecturing, conjectured)** 1 A **conjecture** is a conclusion that is based on information that is not certain or complete. [FORMAL] ❑ *That was a conjecture, not a fact... There are several conjectures... The attitudes of others were matters of conjecture although there were plenty of rumours about how individuals had behaved.* 2 When you **conjecture**, you form an opinion or reach a conclusion on the basis of information that is not certain or complete. [FORMAL] ❑ *He conjectured that some individuals may be able to detect major calamities... This may be true or partly true; we are all conjecturing here.*
N-VAR = surmise; VERB = surmise; V that; V

**con|join** /kəndʒɔɪn/ **(conjoins, conjoining, conjoined)** If two or more things **conjoin** or if you **conjoin** them, they are united and joined together. [FORMAL] ❑ *The wisdom of the retired generals and backbench MPs conjoins... America's rise in rates was conjoined with higher rates elsewhere. ...if we conjoin the two responses.*
V-RECIP; pl-n V; *be* V-ed *with* n; V pl-n; Also V n *with* n, V *with* n

**con|joined twin** /kəndʒɔɪnd twɪn/ **(conjoined twins) Conjoined twins** are twins who are born with their bodies joined.
N-COUNT

**con|ju|gal** /kɒndʒʊgᵊl/ **Conjugal** means relating to marriage and the relationship between a husband and wife, especially their sexual relationship. [FORMAL] ❑ *...a man deprived of his conjugal rights.*
ADJ: ADJ n

**con|ju|gate** /kɒndʒʊgeɪt/ **(conjugates, conjugating, conjugated)** When pupils or teachers **conjugate** a verb, they give its different forms in a particular order. ❑ *...a child who can read at one and is conjugating Latin verbs at four.*
VERB; V n

**con|junc|tion** /kəndʒʌŋkʃᵊn/ **(conjunctions)** 1 A **conjunction of** two or more things is the occurrence of them at the same time or place. [FORMAL] ❑ *...the conjunction of two events. ...a conjunction of religious and social factors.* 2 In grammar, a **conjunction** is a word or group of words that joins together words, groups, or clauses. In English, there are co-ordinating conjunctions such as 'and' and 'but', and subordinating conjunctions such as 'although', 'because', and 'when'. 3 If one thing is done or used **in conjunction with** another, the two things are done or used together. [FORMAL] ❑ *The army should have operated in conjunction with the fleet to raid the enemy's coast.*
N-COUNT: usu N *of* n; N-COUNT; PHRASE: usu PHR *with* n = together

**con|junc|ti|vi|tis** /kəndʒʌŋktɪvaɪtɪs/ **Conjunctivitis** is an eye infection which causes the thin skin that covers the eye to become red. [MEDICAL]
N-UNCOUNT

**con|jure** /kʌndʒəʳ, AM kɑːn-/ **(conjures, conjuring, conjured)** If you **conjure** something out of nothing, you make it appear as if by magic. ❑ *Thirteen years ago she found herself having to conjure a career from thin air... They managed to conjure a victory.* ♦ **Conjure up** means the same as **conjure.** ❑ *Every day a different chef will be conjuring up delicious dishes in the restaurant.*
VERB; V n *from/out of* n; V n; PHRASAL VERB; V P n (not pron); Also V n P

♦ **conjure up** 1 If you **conjure up** a memory, picture, or idea, you create it in your mind. ❑ *When we think of adventurers, many of us conjure up images of larger-than-life characters trekking to the North Pole.* 2 If something such as a word or sound **conjures up** particular images or ideas, it makes you think of them. ❑ *Jimmy Buffett's music conjures up a warm night in the tropics... What does the word 'feminist' conjure up for you?* 3 → see **conjure**.
PHRASAL VERB; V P n (not pron); Also V n P; PHRASAL VERB = evoke; V P n (not pron); V P n (not pron)

**con|jur|er** /kʌndʒərəʳ, AM kɑːn-/ **(conjurers)** also **conjuror.** A **conjurer** is a person who entertains people by doing magic tricks.
N-COUNT = magician

**con|jur|ing trick (conjuring tricks)** A **conjuring trick** is a trick in which something is made to appear or disappear as if by magic.
N-COUNT

**con|jur|or** /kʌndʒərəʳ, AM kɑːn-/ → see **conjurer**.

**conk** /kɒŋk/ **(conks, conking, conked)**

♦ **conk out** If something such as a machine or a vehicle **conks out**, it stops working or breaks down. [INFORMAL] ❑ *The dynamo conked out so we've got no electricity.*
PHRASAL VERB; V P

**conk|er** /kɒŋkəʳ/ **(conkers)** 1 **Conkers** are round brown nuts which come from horse chestnut trees. [BRIT] 2 **Conkers** is a children's game in which you tie a conker to a piece of string and try to break your opponent's conker by hitting it as hard as you can with your own. [BRIT]
N-COUNT; N-UNCOUNT

**con man (con men)** also **conman.** A **con man** is a man who persuades people to give him their money or property by lying to them. ❑ *A few years ago she was the victim of a con man.*
N-COUNT

**con|nect** /kənekt/ **(connects, connecting, connected)** 1 If something or someone **connects** one thing **to** another, or if one thing **connects to** another, the two things are joined together. ❑ *You can connect the machine to your hi-fi... The traditional method is to enter the exchanges at night and connect the wires... Two cables connect to each corner of the plate. ...a television camera connected to the radio telescope.* 2 If a piece of equipment or a place **is connected to** a source of power or water, it is joined to that source so that it has power or water. ❑ *These appliances should not be connected to power supplies... Ischia was now connected to the mainland water supply.* ♦ **Connect up** means the same as **connect.** ❑ *The shower is easy to install – it needs only to be connected up to the hot and cold water supply... They turned the barricade into a potential death trap by connecting it up to the mains.* 3 If a telephone operator **connects** you, he or she enables you to speak to another person by telephone. ❑ *To call the police, an ambulance or the fire brigade dial 999 and the operator will connect you... He asked to be connected to the central switchboard.* 4 If two things or places **connect** or if something **connects** them, they are joined and people or things can pass between them. ❑ *...the long hallway that connects the rooms... The fallopian tubes connect the ovaries with the uterus... His workshop connected with a small building in the garden... The two rooms have connecting doors.* 5 If one train or plane, for example, **connects with** another, it arrives at a time which allows passengers to change to the other one in order to continue their journey. ❑ *...a train connecting with a ferry to Ireland... My connecting plane didn't depart for another*
V-RECIP = attach ≠ disconnect; V n *to* n; V pl-n; V *to* n; V-ed; Also pl-n V; VERB; *be* V-ed *to* n; V-ed; Also V n *to* n; PHRASAL VERB; *be* V-ed P *to* n; V n P *to* n; Also V P n *to* n; VERB = put through; V n; *be* V-ed *to* n; Also V n *to* n; V-RECIP; V pl-n; V n *with* n; V *with* n; V-ing; Also pl-n V; V-RECIP = link up; V *with/to* n; V-ing

*six hours.* [6] If you **connect to** a particular plane or train, or if another plane or train **connects** you **to** it, you change to that plane or train from another one in order to continue your journey. ❑ *...business travellers wanting to connect to a long-haul flight... That will connect you with time to spare for the seven o'clock Concorde.* (Also pl-n V; VERB; V to n; V n; Also V n to n) [7] If you **connect** a person or thing **with** something, you realize that there is a link or relationship between them. ❑ *I hoped he would not connect me with that now-embarrassing review I'd written seven years earlier... I wouldn't have connected the two things.* (VERB = associate; V n with/to n; V pl-n) [8] Something that **connects** a person or thing **with** something else shows or provides a link or relationship between them. ❑ *A search of Brady's house revealed nothing that could connect him with the robberies... What connects them?* (VERB = link; V n with/to n; V pl-n)

♦ **connect up** → see **connect 2**.

**con|nect|ed** /kənektɪd/ If one thing is **connected with** another, there is a link or relationship between them. ❑ *Have you ever had any skin problems connected with exposure to the sun?... The dispute is not directly connected to the negotiations.* → See also **connect**, **well-connected**. (ADJ: usu v-link ADJ, oft ADJ with/to n)

**con|nec|tion** /kənekʃən/ **(connections)** ◆◇◇

in BRIT, also use **connexion**

[1] A **connection** is a relationship between two things, people, or groups. ❑ *There was no evidence of a connection between BSE and the brain diseases recently confirmed in cats... The police say he had no connection with the security forces.* (N-VAR: usu N prep = association, link) [2] A **connection** is a joint where two wires or pipes are joined together. ❑ *Check all radiators for small leaks, especially round pipework connections.* (N-COUNT) [3] If a place has good road, rail, or air **connections**, many places can be directly reached from there by car, train, or plane. ❑ *Fukuoka has excellent air and rail connections to the rest of the country.* (N-COUNT: usu n N) [4] If you get a **connection** at a station or airport, you catch a train, bus, or plane, after getting off another train, bus, or plane, in order to continue your journey. ❑ *My flight was late and I missed the connection.* (N-COUNT: usu sing) [5] Your **connections** are the people who you know or are related to, especially when they are in a position to help you. ❑ *She used her connections to full advantage.* (N-PLURAL) [6] If you write or talk to someone **in connection with** something, you write or talk to them about that thing. [FORMAL] ❑ *13 men have been questioned in connection with the murder.* (PREP-PHRASE)

**con|nec|tive** /kənektɪv/ **(connectives)** A **connective** is the same as a **conjunction**. (N-COUNT)

**con|nec|tive tis|sue** **Connective tissue** is the substance in the bodies of animals and people which fills in the spaces between organs and connects muscles and bones. [TECHNICAL] (N-UNCOUNT)

**con|nec|tiv|ity** /kɒnektɪvəti/ **Connectivity** is the ability of a computing device to connect to other computers or to the Internet. [COMPUTING] ❑ *...a DVD video and CD player with Internet connectivity.* (N-UNCOUNT)

**con|nect|or** /kənektəʳ/ **(connectors)** A **connector** is a device that joins two pieces of equipment, wire, or piping together. (N-COUNT)

**con|nex|ion** /kənekʃən/ → see **connection**.

**con|niv|ance** /kənaɪvəns/ **Connivance** is a willingness to allow or assist something to happen even though you know it is wrong. ❑ *The deficit had grown with the connivance of the banks... The goods were exported with official connivance.* (N-UNCOUNT: usu with supp, oft with the N of n; disapproval)

**con|nive** /kənaɪv/ **(connives, conniving, connived)** If one person **connives with** another **to** do something, they secretly try to achieve something which will benefit both of them. ❑ *He accused ministers of conniving with foreign companies to tear up employment rights... Senior politicians connived to ensure that he was not released. ...local authorities suspected of conniving with the Mafia.* (V-RECIP; disapproval; V with n to-inf; pl-n V to-inf; V with n)

**con|niv|ing** /kənaɪvɪŋ/ If you describe someone as **conniving**, you mean you dislike them because they make secret plans in order to get things for themselves or harm other people. ❑ *Edith was seen as a conniving, greedy woman.* (ADJ: usu ADJ n; disapproval = scheming)

**con|nois|seur** /kɒnəsɜːʳ/ **(connoisseurs)** A **connoisseur** is someone who knows a lot about the arts, food, drink, or some other subject. ❑ *Sarah tells me you're something of an art connoisseur. ...connoisseurs of good food.* (N-COUNT: oft n N, N of n)

**con|no|ta|tion** /kɒnəteɪʃən/ **(connotations)** The **connotations** of a particular word or name are the ideas or qualities which it makes you think of. ❑ *It's just one of those words that's got so many negative connotations... 'Urchin', with its connotation of mischievousness, may not be a particularly apt word.* (N-COUNT: usu with supp, oft N of n = association)

**con|note** /kənəʊt/ **(connotes, connoting, connoted)** If a word or name **connotes** something, it makes you think of a particular idea or quality. [FORMAL] ❑ *The term 'organization' often connotes a sense of neatness.* (VERB = suggest, imply; V n)

**con|quer** /kɒŋkəʳ/ **(conquers, conquering, conquered)** [1] If one country or group of people **conquers** another, they take complete control of their land. ❑ *During 1936, Mussolini conquered Abyssinia... Early in the eleventh century the whole of England was again conquered by the Vikings.* (VERB; V n; be V-ed) [2] If you **conquer** something such as a problem, you succeed in ending it or dealing with it successfully. ❑ *He has never conquered his addiction to smoking. ...the first man in history to conquer Everest.* (VERB; V n; V n)

**con|quer|or** /kɒŋkərəʳ/ **(conquerors)** The **conquerors** of a country or group of people are the people who have taken complete control of that country or group's land. ❑ *The people of an oppressed country obey their conquerors because they want to go on living.* (N-COUNT: usu pl)

**con|quest** /kɒŋkwest/ **(conquests)** [1] **Conquest** is the act of conquering a country or group of people. ❑ *He had led the conquest of southern Poland in 1939... After the Norman Conquest the forest became a royal hunting preserve.* (N-UNCOUNT: also N in pl, oft N of n) [2] **Conquests** are lands that have been conquered in war. ❑ *He had realized that Britain could not have peace unless she returned at least some of her former conquests.* (N-COUNT: usu pl) [3] If someone makes a **conquest**, they succeed in attracting and usually sleeping with another person. You usually use **conquest** when you want to indicate that this relationship is not important to the person concerned. ❑ *Despite his conquests, he remains lonely and isolated.* (N-COUNT: usu poss N) [4] You can refer to the person that someone has succeeded in attracting as their **conquest**. ❑ *Pushkin was a womaniser whose conquests included everyone from prostitutes to princesses.* (N-COUNT: oft poss N) [5] **The conquest of** something such as a problem is success in ending it or dealing with it. ❑ *The conquest of inflation has been the Government's overriding economic priority for nearly 15 years.* (N-SING: usu the N of n = defeat)

**con|quis|ta|dor** /kɒnkwɪstədɔːʳ/ **(conquistadors** or **conquistadores)** The **conquistadors** were the sixteenth century Spanish conquerors of Central and South America. (N-COUNT)

**con|science** /kɒnʃəns/ **(consciences)**

[1] Your **conscience** is the part of your mind that tells you whether what you are doing is right or wrong. If you have a **guilty conscience**, you feel guilty about something because you know it was wrong. If you have a **clear conscience**, you do not feel guilty because you know you have done nothing wrong. ❑ *I have battled with my conscience over whether I should actually send this letter... What if he got a guilty conscience and brought it back?... I could go away again with a clear conscience.* (N-COUNT: usu sing, with supp, oft poss N, adj N) [2] **Conscience** is doing what you believe is right even though it might be unpopular, difficult, or dangerous. ❑ *He refused for reasons of conscience to sign a new law legalising abortion. ...the law on freedom of conscience and religious organizations.* → See also **prisoner of conscience**. (N-UNCOUNT) [3] **Conscience** is a feeling of guilt because you know you have done something that is wrong. ❑ *I'm so glad he* (N-UNCOUNT)

*had a pang of conscience... They have shown a ruthless lack of conscience.*

**PHRASES** [4] If you say that you cannot do something **in all conscience, in good conscience,** or **in conscience**, you mean that you cannot do it because you think it is wrong. ❑ *She could not, in good conscience, back out on her deal with him.* [5] If you have something **on** your **conscience**, you feel guilty because you know you have done something wrong. ❑ *Now the murderer has two deaths on his conscience.*

PHRASE: PHR with cl, with brd-neg
PHRASE: PHR after v, v-link PHR

**con|sci|en|tious** /kɒnʃienʃəs/ Someone who is **conscientious** is very careful to do their work properly. ❑ *We are generally very conscientious about our work.* ♦ **con|sci|en|tious|ly** *He studied conscientiously and enthusiastically.*

ADJ
ADV: usu ADV with v

**con|sci|en|tious ob|ject|or (conscientious objectors)** A **conscientious objector** is a person who refuses to join the armed forces because they think that it is morally wrong to do so.

N-COUNT

**con|scious** /kɒnʃəs/ [1] If you are **conscious of** something, you notice it or realize that it is happening. ❑ *She was very conscious of Max studying her... Conscious that he was becoming light-headed again, he went over to the window.* [2] If you are **conscious of** something, you think about it a lot, especially because you are unhappy about it or because you think it is important. ❑ *I'm very conscious of my weight.* [3] A **conscious** decision or action is made or done deliberately with you giving your full attention to it. ❑ *I don't think we ever made a conscious decision to have a big family... Make a conscious effort to relax your muscles.* ♦ **con|scious|ly** *Sophie was not consciously seeking a replacement after her father died.* [4] Someone who is **conscious** is awake rather than asleep or unconscious. ❑ *She was fully conscious all the time and knew what was going on.* [5] **Conscious** memories or thoughts are ones that you are aware of. ❑ *He had no conscious memory of his four-week stay in hospital.* ♦ **con|scious|ly** *Most people cannot consciously remember much before the ages of 5 to 7 years.*

◆◇◇
ADJ: v-link ADJ *of* n/-ing, v-link ADJ that = *aware*
ADJ: v-link ADJ *of* n/-ing, v-link ADJ that = *aware*
ADJ: usu ADJ n = *deliberate*
ADV: ADV with v
ADJ: usu v-link ADJ ≠ *unconscious*
ADJ: ADJ n ≠ *unconscious*
ADV: ADV with v, ADV adj

**-conscious** /kɒnʃəs/ **-conscious** combines with words such as 'health', 'fashion', 'politically', and 'environmentally' to form adjectives which describe someone who believes that the aspect of life indicated is important. ❑ *We're all becoming increasingly health-conscious these days.*

COMB in ADJ

**con|scious|ness** /kɒnʃəsnəs/ **(consciousnesses)** [1] Your **consciousness** is your mind and your thoughts. ❑ *That idea has been creeping into our consciousness for some time.* [2] The **consciousness** of a group of people is their set of ideas, attitudes, and beliefs. ❑ *The Greens were the catalysts of a necessary change in the European consciousness.* [3] You use **consciousness** to refer to an interest in and knowledge of a particular subject or idea. ❑ *Her political consciousness sprang from her upbringing when her father's illness left the family short of money.* [4] **Consciousness** is the state of being awake rather than being asleep or unconscious. If someone **loses consciousness**, they become unconscious, and if they **regain consciousness**, they become conscious after being unconscious. ❑ *She banged her head and lost consciousness... He drifted in and out of consciousness.* [5] → See also **stream of consciousness**.

◆◇◇
N-COUNT: usu sing, usu poss N = *awareness*
N-UNCOUNT: with supp = *mentality*
N-UNCOUNT: supp N = *awareness*
N-UNCOUNT

**con|scious|ness rais|ing** **Consciousness raising** is the process of developing awareness of an unfair situation, with the aim of making people want to help in changing it. ❑ *...consciousness-raising groups.*

N-UNCOUNT: oft N n

**con|script (conscripts, conscripting, conscripted)**

> The noun is pronounced /kɒnskrɪpt/. The verb is pronounced /kənskrɪpt/.

[1] A **conscript** is a person who has been made to join the armed forces of a country. [2] If someone **is conscripted**, they are officially made to join the armed forces of a country. ❑ *He was conscripted into the German army... Peter was conscripted like every other young man.*

N-COUNT ≠ *volunteer*
VERB: usu passive = *draft*
*be* V-ed *into* n
*be* V-ed

**con|scrip|tion** /kənskrɪpʃən/ **Conscription** is officially making people in a particular country join the armed forces. ❑ *All adult males will be liable for conscription.*

N-UNCOUNT

**con|se|crate** /kɒnsɪkreɪt/ **(consecrates, consecrating, consecrated)** When a building, place, or object **is consecrated**, it is officially declared to be holy. When a person **is consecrated**, they are officially declared to be a bishop. ❑ *The church was consecrated in 1234... He defied Pope John Paul II by consecrating four bishops without his approval.*

VERB
*be* V-ed
V n

**con|secu|tive** /kənsekjʊtɪv/ **Consecutive** periods of time or events happen one after the other without interruption. ❑ *The Cup was won for the third consecutive year by the Toronto Maple Leafs.* ♦ **con|secu|tive|ly** *...a CD player which plays six CDs consecutively.*

ADJ: usu ADJ n = *successive*
ADV: ADV after v

**con|sen|sual** /kənsenʃuəl/ [1] A **consensual** approach, view, or decision is one that is based on general agreement among all the members of a group. ❑ *Consultation is traditional in the consensual Belgian system of labour relations.* [2] If sexual activity is **consensual**, both partners willingly take part in it. [LEGAL] ❑ *Consensual sexual contact between two males can be a criminal activity.*

ADJ: usu ADJ n
ADJ

**con|sen|sus** /kənsensəs/ A **consensus** is general agreement among a group of people. ❑ *The consensus amongst the world's scientists is that the world is likely to warm up over the next few decades... The question of when the troops should leave would be decided by consensus.*

N-SING: also no det

**con|sent** /kənsent/ **(consents, consenting, consented)** [1] If you give your **consent to** something, you give someone permission to do it. [FORMAL] ❑ *At approximately 11:30 p.m., Pollard finally gave his consent to the search... Can my child be medically examined without my consent?* [2] If you **consent to** something, you agree to do it or to allow it to be done. [FORMAL] ❑ *He finally consented to go... He asked Ginny if she would consent to a small celebration after the christening... I was a little surprised when she consented.* [3] → See also **age of consent**.

N-UNCOUNT: usu with poss
VERB = *agree*
V to-inf
V *to* n/-ing
V

**con|sent|ing** /kənsentɪŋ/ A **consenting** adult is a person who is considered to be old enough to make their own decisions about who they have sex with. ❑ *What consenting adults do in private is their own business.*

ADJ: ADJ n

**con|se|quence** /kɒnsɪkwens/ **(consequences)** [1] The **consequences of** something are the results or effects of it. ❑ *Her lawyer said she understood the consequences of her actions and was prepared to go to jail... An economic crisis may have tremendous consequences for our global security.*

**PHRASES** [2] If one thing happens and then another thing happens **in consequence** or **as a consequence**, the second thing happens as a result of the first. ❑ *His death was totally unexpected and, in consequence, no plans had been made for his replacement. ...people who are suffering and dying as a consequence of cigarette smoking.* [3] Something or someone **of consequence** is important or valuable. If something or someone is **of** no **consequence**, or **of** little **consequence**, they are not important or valuable. [FORMAL] ❑ *As an overseer, he suddenly found himself a person of consequence... Where he is from is of no consequence to me.* [4] If you tell someone that they must **take the consequences** or **face the consequences**, you warn them that something unpleasant will happen to them if they do not stop behaving in a particular way. ❑ *These pilots must now face the consequences of their actions and be brought to trial... If climate changes continue, we will suffer the consequences.*

◆◇◇
N-COUNT: usu with supp, oft N *of* n
PHRASE: PHR with cl/group
PHRASE: oft with brd-neg, n PHR, v-link PHR = *importance*
PHRASE: V inflects

**con|se|quent** /kɒnsɪkwənt/ **Consequent** means happening as a direct result of an event or

ADJ: usu ADJ n,

situation. [FORMAL] ❑ *The warming of the Earth and the consequent climatic changes affect us all.* — also n ADJ upon/on n

**con|se|quen|tial** /kɒnsɪkwenʃəl/ [1] **Consequential** means the same as **consequent**. [FORMAL] ❑ *The actual estimate for extra staff and consequential costs such as accommodation was an annual £9.18m.* — ADJ: ADJ n = consequent [2] Something that is **consequential** is important or significant. [FORMAL] ❑ *From a medical standpoint a week is usually not a consequential delay.* — ADJ = significant ≠ inconsequential

**con|se|quent|ly** /kɒnsɪkwentli/ **Consequently** means as a result. [FORMAL] ❑ *Grandfather Dingsdale had sustained a broken back while working in the mines. Consequently, he spent the rest of his life in a wheelchair.* — ADV: ADV with cl

**con|serv|an|cy** /kənsɜːʳvənsi/ **Conservancy** is used in the names of organizations that work to preserve and protect the environment. ❑ *...the Nature Conservancy Council.* — N-UNCOUNT: usu N n = conservation

**con|ser|va|tion** /kɒnsəʳveɪʃən/ [1] **Conservation** is saving and protecting the environment. ❑ *...a four-nation regional meeting on elephant conservation. ...tree-planting and other conservation projects.* — N-UNCOUNT: usu with supp [2] **Conservation** is saving and protecting historical objects or works of art such as paintings, sculptures, or buildings. ❑ *Then he began his most famous work, the conservation and rebinding of the Book of Kells.* — N-UNCOUNT [3] The **conservation** of a supply of something is the careful use of it so that it lasts for a long time. ❑ *...projects aimed at promoting energy conservation.* — N-UNCOUNT: usu with supp

**con|ser|va|tion area** **(conservation areas)** [1] In Britain, a **conservation area** is an area where birds and animals are protected. ❑ *...wildlife conservation areas.* — N-COUNT [2] In Britain, a **conservation area** is an area where old buildings are protected and new building is controlled. — N-COUNT

**con|ser|va|tion|ist** /kɒnsəʳveɪʃənɪst/ **(conservationists)** A **conservationist** is a someone who cares greatly about the conservation of the environment and who works to protect it. — N-COUNT = environmentalist

**con|serva|tism** /kənsɜːʳvətɪzəm/

> The spelling **Conservatism** is also used for meaning 1.

[1] **Conservatism** is a political philosophy which believes that if changes need to be made to society, they should be made gradually. You can also refer to the political beliefs of a conservative party in a particular country as **Conservatism**. ❑ *...the philosophy of modern Conservatism.* — N-UNCOUNT [2] **Conservatism** is unwillingness to accept changes and new ideas. ❑ *The conservatism of the literary establishment in this country is astounding.* — N-UNCOUNT

**con|serva|tive** /kənsɜːʳvətɪv/ **(conservatives)** ◆◆◇

> The spelling **Conservative** is also used for meaning 1.

[1] A **Conservative** politician or voter is a member of or votes for the Conservative Party in Britain. ❑ *Most Conservative MPs appear happy with the government's reassurances. ...disenchanted Conservative voters.* — ADJ = Tory ♦ **Conservative** is also a noun. ❑ *In 1951 the Conservatives were returned to power.* — N-COUNT [2] Someone who is **conservative** has right-wing views. ❑ *...counties whose citizens invariably support the most conservative candidate in any election.* — ADJ = right-wing ♦ **Conservative** is also a noun. ❑ *The new judge is 50-year-old David Suitor who's regarded as a conservative.* — N-COUNT [3] Someone who is **conservative** or has **conservative** ideas is unwilling to accept changes and new ideas. ❑ *It is essentially a narrow and conservative approach to child care.* — ADJ [4] If someone dresses in a **conservative** way, their clothes are conventional in style. ❑ *The girl was well dressed, as usual, though in a more conservative style.* — ADJ ♦ **con|ser|va|tive|ly** *She was always very conservatively dressed when we went out.* — ADV: ADV with v [5] A **conservative** estimate or guess is one in which you are cautious and estimate or guess a low amount which is probably less that the real amount. ❑ *A conservative estimate of the bill, so far, is about £22,000... This guess is probably on the conservative side.* — ADJ: usu ADJ n ♦ **con|ser|va|tive|ly** *The bequest is conservatively estimated at £30 million.* — ADV: ADV with v

**Con|serva|tive Par|ty** **The Conservative Party** is the main right of centre party in Britain. — N-PROPER: usu *the* N

**con|serva|toire** /kənsɜːʳvətwɑːʳ/ **(conservatoires)** A **conservatoire** is an institution where musicians are trained. ❑ *...the Paris Conservatoire.* — N-COUNT: oft in names

**con|ser|va|tor** /kənsɜːʳvətəʳ/ **(conservators)** A **conservator** is someone whose job is to clean and repair historical objects or works of art. — N-COUNT

**con|serva|tory** /kənsɜːʳvətri, AM -tɔːri/ **(conservatories)** [1] A **conservatory** is a room with glass walls and a glass roof, which is attached to a house. People often grow plants in a conservatory. — N-COUNT [2] A **conservatory** is an institution where musicians are trained. ❑ *...the New England Conservatory of Music.* — N-COUNT; N-IN-NAMES

**con|serve** **(conserves, conserving, conserved)**

> The verb is pronounced /kənsɜːʳv/. The noun is pronounced /kɒnsɜːʳv/.

[1] If you **conserve** a supply of something, you use it carefully so that it lasts for a long time. ❑ *The republic's factories have closed for the weekend to conserve energy.* — VERB = save; V n [2] To **conserve** something means to protect it from harm, loss, or change. ❑ *...a big increase in US aid to help developing countries conserve their forests.* — VERB = preserve; V n [3] **Conserve** is jam containing a large proportion of fruit, usually in whole pieces. — N-MASS

**con|sid|er** /kənsɪdəʳ/ **(considers, considering, considered)** ◆◆◆ [1] If you **consider** a person or thing **to** be something, you have the opinion that this is what they are. ❑ *We don't consider our customers to be mere consumers; we consider them to be our friends... I had always considered myself a strong, competent woman... I consider activities such as jogging and weightlifting as unnatural... Barbara considers that pet shops which sell customers these birds are very unfair.* — VERB; V n to-inf; V n n/adj; V n *as* adj/n; V that [2] If you **consider** something, you think about it carefully. ❑ *The government is being asked to consider a plan to fix the date of the Easter break... Consider how much you can afford to pay for a course, and what is your upper limit.* — VERB; V n; V wh [3] If you **are considering** doing something, you intend to do it, but have not yet made a final decision whether to do it. ❑ *I had seriously considered telling the story from the point of view of the wives... They are considering the launch of their own political party.* — VERB; V -ing; V n [4] → See also **considered**, **considering**.

**con|sid|er|able** /kənsɪdərəbəl/ **Considerable** means great in amount or degree. [FORMAL] ❑ *To be without Pearce would be a considerable blow... Doing it properly makes considerable demands on our time... Vets' fees can be considerable, even for routine visits.* — ◆◆◇ ADJ: usu ADJ n = substantial ♦ **con|sid|er|ably** *Children vary considerably in the rate at which they learn these lessons... Their dinner parties had become considerably less formal.* — ADV: ADV with v, ADV compar = significantly

**con|sid|er|ate** /kənsɪdərət/ Someone who is **considerate** pays attention to the needs, wishes, or feelings of other people. ❑ *I think he's the most charming, most considerate man I've ever known... I've always understood one should try and be considerate of other people.* — ADJ: oft ADJ *of* n [approval] ≠ inconsiderate

**con|sid|era|tion** /kənsɪdəreɪʃən/ **(considerations)** ◆◇◇ [1] **Consideration** is careful thought about something. ❑ *He said there should be careful consideration of the future role of the BBC.* — N-UNCOUNT [2] If something is **under consideration**, it is being discussed. ❑ *Several proposals are under consideration by the state assembly.* — N-UNCOUNT: *under* N [3] If you show **consideration**, you pay attention to the needs, wishes, or feelings of other people. ❑ *Show consideration for other rail travellers... Really, her tone said, some people have absolutely no consideration.* — N-UNCOUNT: oft N *for* n [4] A **consideration** is something that should be thought about, especially when you are planning or deciding — N-COUNT: usu supp N = factor

something. ❑ *A major consideration when choosing a dog is the size of your house and garden.* 5 If you **take** something **into consideration**, you think about it because it is relevant to what you are doing. ❑ *Safe driving is good driving because it takes into consideration the lives of other people.*
PHRASE: V inflects

**con|sid|ered** /kənsɪdəʳd/ A **considered** opinion or act is the result of careful thought. ❑ *We would hope to be able to give a considered response to the unions' proposals by the end of the year.* → See also **consider**.
ADJ: ADJ n

**con|sid|er|ing** /kənsɪdərɪŋ/ ◆◇◇ 1 You use **considering** to indicate that you are thinking about a particular fact when making a judgment or giving an opinion. ❑ *The former hostage is in remarkably good shape considering his ordeal.* 2 You use **considering that** to indicate that you are thinking about a particular fact when making a judgment or giving an opinion. ❑ *Considering that you are no longer involved with this man, your response is a little extreme.* 3 When you are giving an opinion or making a judgment, you can use **considering** to suggest that you have thought about all the circumstances, and often that something has succeeded in spite of these circumstances. [SPOKEN] ❑ *I think you're pretty safe, considering.*
PREP / CONJ / ADV: cl ADV

**con|sign** /kənsaɪn/ (**consigns, consigning, consigned**) To **consign** something or someone **to** a place where they will be forgotten about, or **to** an unpleasant situation or place, means to put them there. [FORMAL] ❑ *For decades, many of Malevich's works were consigned to the basements of Soviet museums.*
VERB / V n *to* n

**con|sign|ment** /kənsaɪnmənt/ (**consignments**) A **consignment of** goods is a load that is being delivered to a place or person. ❑ *The first consignment of food has already left Bologna.*
N-COUNT: oft N *of* n = batch

**con|sist** /kənsɪst/ (**consists, consisting, consisted**) ◆◇◇ 1 Something that **consists of** particular things or people is formed from them. ❑ *Breakfast consisted of porridge served with butter.* 2 Something that **consists in** something else has that thing as its main or only part. ❑ *His work as a consultant consisted in advising foreign companies on the siting of new factories.*
VERB / V *of* n/-ing / VERB / V *in* n/-ing

**con|sist|en|cy** /kənsɪstənsi/ 1 **Consistency** is the quality or condition of being consistent. ❑ *He scores goals with remarkable consistency... There's always a lack of consistency in matters of foreign policy.* 2 The **consistency** of a substance is how thick or smooth it is. ❑ *Dilute the paint with water until it is the consistency of milk.*
N-UNCOUNT / N-UNCOUNT: usu with supp

**con|sist|ent** /kənsɪstənt/ ◆◇◇ 1 Someone who is **consistent** always behaves in the same way, has the same attitudes towards people or things, or achieves the same level of success in something. ❑ *Becker has never been the most consistent of players anyway. ...his consistent support of free trade.* ♦ **con|sist|ent|ly** *It's something I have consistently denied... Jones and Armstrong maintain a consistently high standard.* 2 If one fact or idea is **consistent with** another, they do not contradict each other. ❑ *This result is consistent with the findings of Garnett & Tobin.* 3 An argument or set of ideas that is **consistent** is one in which no part contradicts or conflicts with any other part. ❑ *These are clear consistent policies which we are putting into place.*
ADJ / ADV: ADV with v, ADV adj/adv / ADJ: v-link ADJ, usu ADJ *with* n / ADJ = coherent

**con|so|la|tion prize** (**consolation prizes**) 1 A **consolation prize** is a small prize which is given to a person who fails to win a competition. 2 A **consolation prize** is something that is arranged for or is given to a person to make them feel happier when they have failed to achieve something better. ❑ *Her appointment was seen as a consolation prize after she lost the election.*
N-COUNT / N-COUNT

**con|sole** (**consoles, consoling, consoled**)

> ✔ The verb is pronounced /kənsoʊl/. The noun is pronounced /kɒnsoʊl/.

1 If you **console** someone who is unhappy about something, you try to make them feel more cheerful. ❑ *'Never mind, Ned,' he consoled me... Often they cry, and I have to play the role of a mother, consoling them... I can console myself with the fact that I'm not alone... He consoled himself that Emmanuel looked like a nice boy, who could be a good playmate for his daughter.* ♦ **con|so|la|tion** /kɒnsəleɪʃən/ (**consolations**) *The only consolation for the Scottish theatre community is that they look likely to get another chance... He knew then he was right, but it was no consolation.* 2 A **console** is a panel with a number of switches or knobs that is used to operate a machine.
VERB = comfort / V with quote / V n / V pron-refl *with/for* n / V pron-refl that / N-VAR = comfort / N-COUNT

**con|soli|date** /kənsɒlɪdeɪt/ (**consolidates, consolidating, consolidated**) 1 If you **consolidate** something that you have, for example power or success, you strengthen it so that it becomes more effective or secure. ❑ *Brydon's team-mate Martin Williamson consolidated his lead in the National League when he won the latest round.* 2 To **consolidate** a number of small groups or firms means to make them into one large organization. ❑ *Judge Charles Schwartz is giving the state 60 days to disband and consolidate Louisiana's four higher education boards.*
VERB / V n / VERB / V n

**con|som|mé** /kɒnsɒmeɪ, AM kɒnsəmeɪ/ (**consommés**) **Consommé** is a thin, clear soup, usually made from meat juices. ❑ *...chicken consommé.*
N-MASS: oft n N

**con|so|nant** /kɒnsənənt/ (**consonants**) A **consonant** is a sound such as 'p', 'f', 'n', or 't' which you pronounce by stopping the air flowing freely through your mouth. Compare **vowel**.
N-COUNT

**con|sort** (**consorts, consorting, consorted**)

> ✔ The verb is pronounced /kənsɔːʳt/. The noun is pronounced /kɒnsɔːʳt/.

1 If you say that someone **consorts with** a particular person or group, you mean that they spend a lot of time with them, and usually that you do not think this is a good thing. [FORMAL] ❑ *He regularly consorted with known drug-dealers.* 2 The ruling monarch's wife or husband is called their **consort**. ❑ *At tea-time, Victoria sang duets with her Consort, Prince Albert... She was surely the most distinguished queen consort we have had.*
VERB disapproval = associate / V *with* n / N-COUNT; N-TITLE: oft n N

**con|sor|tium** /kənsɔːʳtiəm/ (**consortia** /kənsɔːʳtiə/ or **consortiums**) A **consortium** is a group of people or firms who have agreed to co-operate with each other. ❑ *The consortium includes some of the biggest building contractors in Britain.*
N-COUNT-COLL

**con|spicu|ous** /kənspɪkjuəs/ 1 If someone or something is **conspicuous**, people can see or notice them very easily. ❑ *The most conspicuous way in which the old politics is changing is in the growing use of referendums... You may feel tearful in situations where you feel conspicuous.* ♦ **con|spicu|ous|ly** *Johnston's name was conspicuously absent from the list.* 2 If you say that someone or something is **conspicuous by** their **absence**, you are drawing attention to the fact that they are not in a place or situation where you think they should be. ❑ *He played no part in the game and was conspicuous by his absence in the post-match celebrations.*
ADJ / ADV: ADV with v, ADV adj / PHRASE

**con|spicu|ous con|sump|tion** **Conspicuous consumption** means spending your money in such a way that other people can see how wealthy you are. ❑ *It was an age of conspicuous consumption – those who had money liked to display it.*
N-UNCOUNT

**con|spira|cy** /kənspɪrəsi/ (**conspiracies**) 1 **Conspiracy** is the secret planning by a group of people to do something illegal. ❑ *Seven men, all from Bristol, admitted conspiracy to commit arson... He believes there probably was a conspiracy to kill President Kennedy in 1963.* 2 A **conspiracy** is an agreement between a group of people which other people think is wrong or is likely to be harmful. ❑ *There was no evidence to link the brigade to any conspiracy against Mr Bush.*
N-VAR: oft N to-inf / N-COUNT: oft N to-inf

**con|spir|a|cy theo|ry** **(conspiracy theories)** N-COUNT A **conspiracy theory** is a belief that a group of people are secretly trying to harm someone or achieve something. You usually use this term to suggest that you think this is unlikely. ❑ *Did you ever swallow the conspiracy theory about Kennedy?*

**con|spira|tor** /kənspɪrətəʳ/ **(conspirators)** N-COUNT A **conspirator** is a person who joins a conspiracy.

**con|spira|to|rial** /kənspɪrətɔːriəl/ ADJ: usu ADJ n If someone does something such as speak or smile in a **conspiratorial** way, they do it in a way that suggests they are sharing a secret with someone. ❑ *His voice had sunk to a conspiratorial whisper.*

**con|spire** /kənspaɪəʳ/ **(conspires, conspiring, conspired)** 1 V-RECIP = plot If two or more people or groups **conspire to** do something illegal or harmful, they make a secret agreement to do it. ❑ *They'd conspired to overthrow the government.* pl-n V to-inf *...a defendant convicted of conspiring with his brother to commit robberies...* V with n to-inf *I had a persecution complex and thought people were conspiring against me.* pl-n V against n Also V with n 2 VERB = combine If events **conspire to** produce a particular result, they seem to work together to cause this result. ❑ *History and geography have conspired to bring Greece to a moment of decision...* V to-inf *But fateful forces beyond the band's control were to conspire against them.* V against n

**con|sta|ble** /kʌnstəbᵊl, kɒn-/ **(constables)** 1 N-COUNT; N-TITLE; N-VOC In Britain and some other countries, a **constable** is a police officer of the lowest rank. ❑ *He was a constable at Sutton police station. ...Constable Stuart Clark... Thanks for your help, Constable.* → See also **Chief Constable**. 2 N-COUNT; N-TITLE In the United States, a **constable** is an official who helps keep the peace in a town. They are lower in rank than a sheriff.

**con|stabu|lary** /kənstæbjʊləri, AM -leri/ **(constabularies)** 1 N-COUNT In Britain and some other countries, a **constabulary** is the police force of a particular area. ❑ *...the Chief Constable of the Nottinghamshire Constabulary.* 2 N-COUNT In the United States, a **constabulary** is the constables in a particular area, or the area that they are responsible for.

**con|stan|cy** /kɒnstənsi/ 1 N-UNCOUNT **Constancy** is the quality of staying the same even though other things change. ❑ *We live in a world without constancy.* 2 N-UNCOUNT [approval] = fidelity **Constancy** is the quality of being faithful and loyal to a particular person or belief. ❑ *...those who have proved their constancy in love.*

**con|stant** /kɒnstənt/ **(constants)** ◆◆◇ 1 ADJ: usu ADJ n = continual You use **constant** to describe something that happens all the time or is always there. ❑ *Inflation is a constant threat... He has been her constant companion for the last four months.* ♦ **con|stant|ly** ADV: usu ADV with v, also ADV adv/adj *The direction of the wind is constantly changing.* 2 ADJ = stable If an amount or level is **constant**, it stays the same over a particular period of time. ❑ *The average speed of the winds remained constant.* 3 N-COUNT ≠ variable A **constant** is a thing or value that always stays the same. ❑ *In the world of fashion it sometimes seems that the only constant is ceaseless change.*

**con|stel|la|tion** /kɒnstəleɪʃᵊn/ **(constellations)** N-COUNT A **constellation** is a group of stars which form a pattern and have a name. ❑ *...a planet orbiting a star in the constellation of Cepheus.*

**con|ster|na|tion** /kɒnstəʳneɪʃᵊn/ N-UNCOUNT = dismay **Consternation** is a feeling of anxiety or fear. [FORMAL] ❑ *His decision caused consternation in the art photography community.*

**con|sti|pat|ed** /kɒnstɪpeɪtɪd/ ADJ: usu v-link ADJ Someone who is **constipated** has difficulty in getting rid of solid waste from their body.

**con|sti|pa|tion** /kɒnstɪpeɪʃᵊn/ N-UNCOUNT **Constipation** is a medical condition which causes people to have difficulty getting rid of solid waste from their body.

**con|stitu|en|cy** /kənstɪtʃuənsi/ **(constituencies)** 1 N-COUNT A **constituency** is an area for which someone is elected as the representative in a parliament or government. 2 N-COUNT: usu with supp A particular **constituency** is a section of society that may give political support to a particular party or politician. ❑ *In France, farmers are a powerful political constituency.*

**con|stitu|ent** /kənstɪtʃuənt/ **(constituents)** 1 N-COUNT A **constituent** is someone who lives in a particular constituency, especially someone who is able to vote in an election. 2 N-COUNT: usu N of n A **constituent of** a mixture, substance, or system is one of the things from which it is formed. ❑ *Caffeine is the active constituent of drinks such as tea and coffee.* 3 ADJ: ADJ n The **constituent** parts of something are the things from which it is formed. [FORMAL] ❑ *...a plan to split the company into its constituent parts and sell them separately.*

**con|stitu|ent as|sem|bly** **(constituent assemblies)** N-COUNT A **constituent assembly** is a body of representatives that is elected to create or change their country's constitution.

**con|sti|tute** /kɒnstɪtjuːt, AM -tuːt/ **(constitutes, constituting, constituted)** 1 V-LINK: no cont If something **constitutes** a particular thing, it can be regarded as being that thing. ❑ *Testing patients without their consent would constitute a professional and legal offence.* V n 2 V-LINK: no cont = comprise If a number of things or people **constitute** something, they are the parts or members that form it. ❑ *Volunteers constitute more than 95% of The Center's work force.* V n 3 VERB: usu passive = set up When something such as a committee or government **is constituted**, it is formally established and given authority to operate. [FORMAL] ❑ *On 6 July a People's Revolutionary Government was constituted...* be V-ed *The accused will appear before a specially constituted military tribunal.* V-ed

**con|sti|tu|tion** /kɒnstɪtjuːʃᵊn, AM -tuː-/ **(constitutions)** ◆◇◇ 1 N-COUNT The **constitution** of a country or organization is the system of laws which formally states people's rights and duties. ❑ *The club's constitution prevented women from becoming full members.* 2 N-COUNT: usu sing Your **constitution** is your health. ❑ *He must have an extremely strong constitution.*

**con|sti|tu|tion|al** /kɒnstɪtjuːʃənᵊl, AM -tuː-/ ◆◇◇ ADJ: usu ADJ n **Constitutional** means relating to the constitution of a particular country or organization. ❑ *Political leaders are making no progress in their efforts to resolve the country's constitutional crisis.*

**con|sti|tu|tion|al|ity** /kɒnstɪtjuːʃənælɪti, AM -tuː-/ N-UNCOUNT: usu the N of n In a particular political system, **the constitutionality of** a law or action is the fact that it is allowed by the constitution. [FORMAL] ❑ *They plan to challenge the constitutionality of the law.*

**con|strain** /kənstreɪn/ **(constrains, constraining, constrained)** 1 VERB To **constrain** someone or something means to limit their development or force them to behave in a particular way. [FORMAL] ❑ *Women are too often constrained by family commitments and by low expectations.* be V-ed 2 PHRASE: V inflects, PHR to-inf If you **feel constrained to** do something, you feel that you must do it, even though you would prefer not to. ❑ *For some reason he felt constrained to lower his voice.*

**con|straint** /kənstreɪnt/ **(constraints)** 1 N-COUNT: oft adj N, N on n A **constraint** is something that limits or controls what you can do. ❑ *Their decision to abandon the trip was made because of financial constraints.* 2 N-UNCOUNT = restraint **Constraint** is control over the way you behave which prevents you from doing what you want to do.

**con|strict** /kənstrɪkt/ **(constricts, constricting, constricted)** 1 VERB If a part of your body, especially your throat, **is constricted** or if it **constricts**, something causes it to become narrower. ❑ *Severe migraine can be treated with a drug which constricts the blood vessels...* V n *My throat constricted, so that I had to concentrate on breathing.* V 2 VERB = limit If something **constricts** you, it limits your actions so that you cannot do what you want to do. ❑ *She objects to the tests the Government's advisers have devised because they constrict her teaching style.* V n

**con|stric|tion** /kənstrɪkʃᵊn/ **(constrictions)** N-COUNT: usu pl = restriction **Constrictions** are rules or factors which limit what you can do and prevent you from doing what you want to do. ❑ *I hated the constrictions of school.* → See also **constrict**.

**con|struct** /kənstrʌkt/ **(constructs, constructing, constructed)** [1] *VERB = build* If you **construct** something such as a building, road, or machine, you build it or make it. ❑ *V n* *The French constructed a series of fortresses from Dunkirk on the Channel coast to Douai... The boxes should be constructed from rough-sawn timber...* *be V-ed from/of/out of n* *They thought he had escaped through a specially constructed tunnel.* *V-ed* [2] *VERB = create* If you **construct** something such as an idea, a piece of writing, or a system, you create it by putting different parts together. ❑ *V n* *He eventually constructed a business empire which ran to Thailand and Singapore... The novel is constructed from a series of on-the-spot reports.* *be V-ed from/out of n* *...using carefully constructed tests.* *V-ed*

**con|struc|tion** /kənstrʌkʃᵊn/ **(constructions)** ◆◇◇ [1] *N-UNCOUNT ≠ demolition* **Construction** is the building of things such as houses, factories, roads, and bridges. ❑ *He'd already started construction on a hunting lodge. ...the only nuclear power station under construction in Britain. ...the downturn in the construction industry.* [2] *N-UNCOUNT: with supp* The **construction** of something such as a vehicle or machine is the making of it. ❑ *...companies who have long experience in the construction of those types of equipment... With the exception of teak, this is the finest wood for boat construction.* [3] *N-UNCOUNT: with poss = creation* The **construction** of something such as a system is the creation of it. ❑ *...the construction of a just system of criminal justice.* [4] *N-COUNT: usu supp N = structure* You can refer to an object that has been built or made as a **construction**. ❑ *The British pavilion is an impressive steel and glass construction the size of Westminster Abbey.* [5] *N-UNCOUNT: usu with supp* You use **construction** to refer to the structure of something and the way it has been built or made. ❑ *The Shakers believed that furniture should be plain, simple, useful, practical and of sound construction... The chairs were light in construction yet extremely strong.* [6] *N-COUNT = structure* A grammatical **construction** is a particular arrangement of words in a sentence, clause, or phrase. ❑ *Avoid complex verbal constructions.*

**con|struc|tive** /kənstrʌktɪv/ *ADJ = positive ≠ negative* A **constructive** discussion, comment, or approach is useful and helpful rather than negative and unhelpful. ❑ *She welcomes constructive criticism... After their meeting, both men described the talks as frank, friendly and constructive.*

**con|struc|tive dis|mis|sal** *N-UNCOUNT* If an employee claims **constructive dismissal**, they begin a legal action against their employer in which they claim that they were forced to leave their job because of the behaviour of their employer. [BUSINESS] ❑ *The woman claims she was the victim of constructive dismissal after being demoted.*

**con|struc|tor** /kənstrʌktəʳ/ **(constructors)** *N-COUNT* A racing car **constructor** or aircraft **constructor** is a company that builds cars or aircraft.

**con|strue** /kənstruː/ **(construes, construing, construed)** *VERB* If something **is construed** in a particular way, its nature or meaning is interpreted in that way. [FORMAL] ❑ *What may seem helpful behaviour to you can be construed as interference by others...* *be V-ed as n* *He may construe the approach as a hostile act...* *V n as n* *We are taught to construe these terms in a particular way.* *V n prep/adv*

**con|sul** /kɒnsᵊl/ **(consuls)** *N-COUNT: oft supp N; N-TITLE* A **consul** is an official who is sent by his or her government to live in a foreign city in order to look after all the people there that belong to his or her own country.

**con|su|lar** /kɒnsjʊləʳ, AM -sə-/ *ADJ: ADJ n* **Consular** means involving or relating to a consul or the work of a consul. ❑ *If you need to return to the UK quickly, British Consular officials may be able to arrange it.*

**con|su|late** /kɒnsjʊlət, AM -sə-/ **(consulates)** *N-COUNT: oft supp N* A **consulate** is the place where a consul works. ❑ *They managed to make contact with the British consulate in Lyons.*

**con|sult** /kənsʌlt/ **(consults, consulting, consulted)** ◆◇◇ [1] *VERB* If you **consult** an expert or someone senior to you or **consult with** them, you ask them for their opinion and advice about what you should do or their permission to do something. ❑ *V n prep* *Consult your doctor about how much exercise you should attempt...* *wh/wh-to-inf* *He needed to consult with an attorney...* *V with n* *If you are in any doubt, consult a financial adviser.* *V n* [2] *V-RECIP* If a person or group of people **consults with** other people or **consults** them, they talk and exchange ideas and opinions about what they might decide to do. ❑ *After consulting with her daughter and manager she decided to take on the part, on her terms...* *V with n* *The two countries will have to consult their allies...* *V n* *The umpires consulted quickly.* *pl-n V* [3] *VERB* If you **consult** a book or a map, you look in it or look at it in order to find some information. ❑ *Consult the chart on page 44 for the correct cooking times.* *V n*

**con|sul|tan|cy** /kənsʌltənsi/ **(consultancies)** [1] *N-COUNT* A **consultancy** is a company that gives expert advice on a particular subject. ❑ *A survey of 57 hospitals by Newchurch, a consultancy, reveals striking improvements.* [2] *N-UNCOUNT: oft N n* **Consultancy** is expert advice on a particular subject which a person or group is paid to provide to a company or organization. ❑ *The project provides both consultancy and training.*

**con|sult|ant** /kənsʌltənt/ **(consultants)** ◆◇◇ [1] *N-COUNT: oft N n* A **consultant** is an experienced doctor with a high position, who specializes in one area of medicine. [mainly BRIT] ❑ *Shirley's brother is now a consultant heart surgeon in Sweden.*

☑ in AM, usually use **specialist**

[2] *N-COUNT: oft N to n, supp N* A **consultant** is a person who gives expert advice to a person or organization on a particular subject. ❑ *...a team of management consultants sent in to reorganise the department.*

**con|sul|ta|tion** /kɒnsəlteɪʃᵊn/ **(consultations)** [1] *N-VAR* A **consultation** is a meeting which is held to discuss something. **Consultation** is discussion about something. ❑ *Next week he'll be in Florida for consultations with President Mitterrand... The plans were drawn up in consultation with the World Health Organisation.* [2] *N-VAR* A **consultation with** a doctor or other expert is a meeting with them to discuss a particular problem and get their advice. **Consultation** is the process of getting advice from a doctor or other expert. [mainly BRIT] ❑ *A personal diet plan is devised after a consultation with a nutritionist.* [3] *N-COUNT* A **consultation** is a meeting where several doctors discuss a patient and his or her condition and treatment. [AM] [4] *N-UNCOUNT* **Consultation** of a book or other source of information is looking at it in order to find out certain facts. ❑ *With such excellent studies available for consultation, it should be easy to avoid the pitfalls.*

**con|sul|ta|tive** /kənsʌltətɪv/ *ADJ: usu ADJ n = advisory* A **consultative** committee or document gives advice or makes proposals about a particular problem or subject. ❑ *...the consultative committee on local government finance.*

**con|sult|ing room** **(consulting rooms)** *N-COUNT* A doctor's or therapist's **consulting room** is the room in which they see their patients. [BRIT]

☑ in AM, use **doctor's office**

**con|sum|able** /kənsjuːməbᵊl, AM -suː-/ **(consumables)** *ADJ: usu ADJ n* **Consumable** goods are items which are intended to be bought, used, and then replaced. ❑ *...demand for consumable articles.* ♦ **Consumable** is also a noun. *N-COUNT: usu pl* ❑ *Suppliers add computer consumables, office equipment and furniture to their product range.*

**con|sume** /kənsjuːm, AM -suːm/ **(consumes, consuming, consumed)** [1] *VERB* If you **consume** something, you eat or drink it. [FORMAL] ❑ *V n* *Many people experienced a drop in their cholesterol levels when they consumed oat bran.* [2] *VERB* To **consume** an amount of fuel, energy, or time means to use it up. ❑ *V n* *Some of the most efficient refrigerators consume 70 percent less electricity than traditional models.* [3] *VERB* If a feeling or idea **consumes** you, it affects you very strongly indeed. ❑ *The memories consumed him.* [4] → See also **consumed**, **consuming**. V n

**con|sumed** /kənsjuːmd, AM -suːmd/ If you are **consumed with** a feeling or idea, it affects you very strongly indeed. [LITERARY] ❑ *They are consumed with jealousy at her success.* ADJ: v-link ADJ *with/by* n = eaten up

**con|sum|er** /kənsjuːməʳ, AM -suː-/ **(consumers)** A **consumer** is a person who buys things or uses services. ❑ *...improving public services and consumer rights.* ◆◆◇ N-COUNT: oft N n

**con|sum|er cred|it** **Consumer credit** is money that is lent to people by organizations such as banks, building societies, and shops so that they can buy things. ❑ *New consumer credit fell to $3.7 billion in August.* N-UNCOUNT

**con|sum|er du|rable** **(consumer durables)** **Consumer durables** are goods which are expected to last a long time, and are bought infrequently. [BRIT] N-COUNT: usu pl

☑ in AM, use **durable goods**

**con|sum|er goods** **Consumer goods** are items bought by people for their own use, rather than by businesses. Compare **capital goods**. N-PLURAL

**con|sum|er|ism** /kənsjuːmərɪzəm, AM -suː-/ [1] **Consumerism** is the belief that it is good to buy and use a lot of goods. ❑ *They have clearly embraced Western consumerism.* [2] **Consumerism** is the protection of the rights and interests of consumers. N-UNCOUNT: oft supp N [disapproval] N-UNCOUNT

**con|sum|er|ist** /kənsjuːmərɪst, AM -suː-/ **Consumerist** economies are ones which encourage people to consume a lot of goods. [BUSINESS] ❑ *...our consumerist society.* ADJ: usu ADJ n [disapproval]

**con|sum|er so|ci|ety** **(consumer societies)** You can use **consumer society** to refer to a society where people think that spending money on goods and services is very important. N-COUNT: usu sing

**con|sum|ing** /kənsjuːmɪŋ, AM -suː-/ A **consuming** passion or interest is more important to you than anything else. ❑ *He has developed a consuming passion for chess.* → See also **consume**, **time-consuming**. ADJ: usu ADJ n

**con|sum|mate** /kɒnsəmeɪt/ **(consummates, consummating, consummated)** [1] You use **consummate** to describe someone who is extremely skilful. [FORMAL] ❑ *He acted the part with consummate skill... Those familiar with Sanders call him a consummate politician.* [2] If two people **consummate** a marriage or relationship, they make it complete by having sex. [FORMAL] ❑ *They consummated their passion only after many hesitations and delays.* ADJ: usu ADJ n; VERB; V n

**con|sump|tion** /kənsʌmpʃᵊn/ [1] The **consumption** of fuel or natural resources is the amount of them that is used or the act of using them. ❑ *The laws have led to a reduction in fuel consumption in the US. ...a tax on the consumption of non-renewable energy resources.* [2] The **consumption** of food or drink is the act of eating or drinking something, or the amount that is eaten or drunk. [FORMAL] ❑ *Most of the wine was unfit for human consumption... The average daily consumption of fruit and vegetables is around 200 grams.* [3] **Consumption** is the act of buying and using things. ❑ *Recycling the waste from our increased consumption is better than burning it.* [4] → See also **conspicuous consumption**. N-UNCOUNT: with supp; N-UNCOUNT: usu with supp; N-UNCOUNT

**con|sump|tive** /kənsʌmptɪv/ A **consumptive** person suffers from **tuberculosis**. [OLD-FASHIONED] ADJ: usu ADJ n

**cont.** **Cont.** is an abbreviation for 'continued', which is used at the bottom of a page to indicate that a letter or text continues on another page.

**con|tact** /kɒntækt/ **(contacts, contacting, contacted)** [1] **Contact** involves meeting or communicating with someone, especially regularly. ❑ *Opposition leaders are denying any contact with the government in Kabul... He forbade contacts between directors and executives outside his presence.* [2] If you are **in contact with** someone, you regularly meet them or communicate with them. ❑ *He was in direct contact with the kidnappers... We do keep in contact.* [3] If you **contact** someone, you telephone them, write to them, or go to see them in order to tell or ask them something. ❑ *Contact the Tourist Information Bureau for further details... When she first contacted me Frances was upset.* [4] If you come **into contact with** someone or something, you meet that person or thing in the course of your work or other activities. ❑ *The college has brought me into contact with western ideas.* [5] If you **make contact with** someone, you find out where they are and talk or write to them. ❑ *Then, after she had become famous, he tried to make contact with her.* [6] If you **lose contact with** someone who you have been friendly with, you no longer see them, speak to them, or write to them. ❑ *Though they all live nearby, I lost contact with them really quickly... Mother and son lost contact when Nicholas was in his early twenties.* [7] When people or things are in **contact**, they are touching each other. ❑ *They compared how these organisms behaved when left in contact with different materials... The cry occurs when air is brought into contact with the baby's larynx... There was no physical contact, nor did I want any.* [8] Radio **contact** is communication by means of radio. ❑ *...a technical problem reported by the pilot moments before he lost contact with the control tower.* [9] A **contact** is someone you know in an organization or profession who helps you or gives you information. ❑ *Their contact in the United States Embassy was called Phil.* [10] to **make eye contact** → see **eye**. ◆◆◇ N-COUNT: also N in pl, oft N *with/between* n; PHRASE: usu v-link PHR, oft PHR *with* n; VERB; V n; V n; N-UNCOUNT: *into* N *with* n; PHRASE: V inflects, PHR *with* n, pl-n V; PHRASE: V inflects, PHR *with* n, pl-n V; N-UNCOUNT: oft *in/into* N *with* n; N-UNCOUNT; N-COUNT

**con|tact lens** **(contact lenses)** **Contact lenses** are small plastic lenses that you put on the surface of your eyes to help you see better, instead of wearing glasses. N-COUNT: usu pl

**con|ta|gion** /kənteɪdʒᵊn/ **Contagion** is the spreading of a particular disease by someone touching another person who is already affected by the disease. ❑ *They have been reluctant to admit AIDS patients, in part because of unfounded fears of contagion.* N-UNCOUNT

**con|ta|gious** /kənteɪdʒəs/ [1] A disease that is **contagious** can be caught by touching people or things that are infected with it. Compare **infectious**. ❑ *...a highly contagious disease of the lungs.* [2] A feeling or attitude that is **contagious** spreads quickly among a group of people. ❑ *Antonio has a contagious enthusiasm for the beautiful aspect of food.* ADJ; ADJ: usu v-link ADJ = infectious

**con|tain** /kənteɪn/ **(contains, containing, contained)** [1] If something such as a box, bag, room, or place **contains** things, those things are inside it. ❑ *The bag contained a Christmas card... Factory shops contain a wide range of cheap furnishings... The 77,000-acre estate contains five of the highest peaks in Scotland.* [2] If a substance **contains** something, that thing is a part of it. ❑ *Many cars run on petrol which contains lead.* [3] If writing, speech, or film **contains** particular information, ideas, or images, it includes them. ❑ *This sheet contained a list of problems a patient might like to raise with the doctor... The two discs also contain two of Britten's lesser-known song-cycles.* [4] If a group or organization **contains** a certain number of people, those are the people that are in it. ❑ *The committee contains 11 Democrats and nine Republicans.* [5] If you **contain** something, you control it and prevent it from spreading or increasing. ❑ *More than a hundred firemen are still trying to contain the fire at the plant.* [6] If you cannot **contain** a feeling such as excitement or anger, or if you cannot **contain yourself**, you cannot prevent yourself from showing your feelings. ❑ *But he was bursting with curiosity, and one day he just couldn't contain himself. 'What are you going to do?' he asked... Evans could barely contain his delight: 'I'm so proud of her,' he said.* [7] → See also **self-contained**. ◆◆◇ VERB: no cont; V n; V n; V n; VERB: no cont; V n; VERB: no cont; V n; V n; VERB: no cont; V n; VERB; V n; VERB; V pron-refl; V n

**con|tain|er** /kənteɪnəʳ/ **(containers)** 1 A **container** is something such as a box or bottle that is used to hold or store things in. ❑ *...the plastic containers in which fish are stored and sold.* 2 A **container** is a very large metal or wooden box used for transporting goods so that they can be loaded easily onto ships and lorries.
N-COUNT: usu supp N
N-COUNT: usu N *of* n

**con|tain|er ship** **(container ships)** A **container ship** is a ship that is designed for carrying goods that are packed in large metal or wooden boxes.
N-COUNT

**con|tain|ment** /kənteɪnmənt/ 1 **Containment** is the action or policy of keeping another country's power or area of control within acceptable limits or boundaries. 2 The **containment of** something dangerous or unpleasant is the act or process of keeping it under control within a particular area or place. ❑ *Fire crews are hoping they can achieve full containment of the fire before the winds pick up.*
N-UNCOUNT
N-UNCOUNT: usu N *of* n = control

**con|tami|nant** /kəntæmɪnənt/ **(contaminants)** A **contaminant** is something that contaminates a substance such as water or food. [FORMAL] ❑ *Contaminants found in poultry will also be found in their eggs.*
N-COUNT: usu pl

**con|tami|nate** /kəntæmɪneɪt/ **(contaminates, contaminating, contaminated)** If something **is contaminated by** dirt, chemicals, or radiation, they make it dirty or harmful. ❑ *Have any fish been contaminated in the Arctic Ocean? ...vast tracts of empty land, much of it contaminated by years of army activity.* ♦ **con|tami|nat|ed** *Nuclear weapons plants across the country are heavily contaminated with toxic wastes... More than 100,000 people could fall ill after drinking contaminated water.* ♦ **con|tami|na|tion** /kəntæmɪneɪʃᵊn/ *The contamination of the sea around Capri may be just the beginning.*
VERB
*be* V-ed
V-ed
ADJ
N-UNCOUNT: usu with supp

**con|tem|plate** /kɒntəmpleɪt/ **(contemplates, contemplating, contemplated)** 1 If you **contemplate** an action, you think about whether to do it or not. ❑ *For a time he contemplated a career as an army medical doctor... She contemplates leaving for the sake of the kids.* 2 If you **contemplate** an idea or subject, you think about it carefully for a long time. ❑ *As he lay in his hospital bed that night, he cried as he contemplated his future.* ♦ **con|tem|pla|tion** /kɒntəmpleɪʃᵊn/ *It is a place of quiet contemplation.* 3 If you **contemplate** something or someone, you look at them for a long time. ❑ *He contemplated his hands, still frowning.* ♦ **con|tem|pla|tion** *He was lost in the contemplation of the landscape for a while.*
VERB = consider
V n/-ing
V n/-ing
VERB
V n
N-UNCOUNT
VERB
V n
N-UNCOUNT: oft N *of* n

**con|tem|pla|tive** /kəntemplətɪv/ Someone who is **contemplative** thinks deeply, or is thinking in a serious and calm way. ❑ *Martin is a quiet, contemplative sort of chap.*
ADJ

**con|tem|po|ra|neous** /kəntempəreɪniəs/ If two events or situations are **contemporaneous**, they happen or exist during the same period of time. [FORMAL] ❑ *...the contemporaneous development of a separate and quite recognisable Scottish school of art.*
ADJ

**con|tem|po|rary** /kəntempərəri, AM -pəreri/ **(contemporaries)** 1 **Contemporary** things are modern and relate to the present time. ❑ *She writes a lot of contemporary music for people like Whitney Houston... Only the names are ancient; the characters are modern and contemporary.* 2 **Contemporary** people or things were alive or happened at the same time as something else you are talking about. ❑ *...drawing upon official records and the reports of contemporary witnesses.* 3 Someone's **contemporary** is a person who is or was alive at the same time as them. ❑ *Like most of my contemporaries, I grew up in a vastly different world.*
◆◇◇
ADJ: usu ADJ n
ADJ: usu ADJ n
N-COUNT: usu pl, poss N

**con|tempt** /kəntempt/ 1 If you have **contempt for** someone or something, you have no respect for them or think that they are unimportant. ❑ *He has contempt for those beyond his immediate family circle... I hope voters will treat his advice with the contempt it deserves.* 2 If you **hold** someone or something **in contempt**, you feel contempt for them. ❑ *Small wonder that many voters hold their politicians in contempt.* **familiarity breeds contempt** → see **familiarity**.
N-UNCOUNT: oft N *for* n
PHRASE: V inflects

**con|tempt|ible** /kəntemptɪbᵊl/ If you feel that someone or something is **contemptible**, you feel strong dislike and disrespect for them. [FORMAL] ❑ *...this contemptible act of violence.*
ADJ = despicable

**con|tempt of court** **Contempt of court** is the criminal offence of disobeying an instruction from a judge or a court of law. [LEGAL] ❑ *He faced imprisonment for contempt of court.*
N-UNCOUNT = contempt

**con|temp|tu|ous** /kəntemptʃuəs/ If you are **contemptuous of** someone or something, you do not like or respect them at all. ❑ *He's openly contemptuous of all the major political parties... She gave a contemptuous little laugh.*
ADJ: usu v-link ADJ, oft ADJ *of* n

**con|tend** /kəntend/ **(contends, contending, contended)** 1 If you have to **contend with** a problem or difficulty, you have to deal with it or overcome it. ❑ *It is time, once again, to contend with racism... American businesses could soon have a new kind of lawsuit to contend with.* 2 If you **contend that** something is true, you state or argue that it is true. [FORMAL] ❑ *The government contends that he is fundamentalist.* 3 If you **contend with** someone **for** something such as power, you compete with them to try to get it. ❑ *...the two main groups contending for power. ...with 10 UK construction yards contending with rivals from Norway, Holland, Italy and Spain. ...a binding political settlement between the contending parties.*
VERB
V *with* n
V *with* n
VERB
V that
V-RECIP
pl-n V *for* n
V *with* n
V-ing

**con|tend|er** /kəntendəʳ/ **(contenders)** A **contender** is someone who takes part in a competition. [JOURNALISM] ❑ *Her trainer said yesterday that she would be a strong contender for a place in Britain's Olympic squad.*
N-COUNT: usu with supp, oft N *for/in* n

| content |
|---|
| ① NOUN USES |
| ② ADJECTIVE AND VERB USES |

① **con|tent** /kɒntent/ **(contents)** 1 The **contents** of a container such as a bottle, box, or room are the things that are inside it. ❑ *Empty the contents of the pan into the sieve... Sandon Hall and its contents will be auctioned by Sotheby's on October 6.* 2 If you refer to the **content** or **contents** of something such as a book, speech, or television programme, you are referring to the subject that it deals with, the story that it tells, or the ideas that it expresses. ❑ *She is reluctant to discuss the content of the play... The letter's contents were not disclosed.* 3 The **contents** of a book are its different chapters and sections, usually shown in a list at the beginning of the book. ❑ *There is no initial list of contents.* 4 The **content** of something such as an educational course or a programme of action is the elements that it consists of. ❑ *Previous students have had nothing but praise for the course content and staff.* 5 You can use **content** to refer to the amount or proportion of something that a substance contains. ❑ *Sunflower margarine has the same fat content as butter.*
◆◇◇
N-PLURAL: usu with supp, oft N *of* n
N-UNCOUNT: also N in pl, usu N *of* n
N-PLURAL
N-UNCOUNT: usu with supp, oft N *of* n
N-SING: n N

② **con|tent** /kəntent/ **(contents, contenting, contented)**
⇒ Please look at category 4 to see if the expression you are looking for is shown under another headword. 1 If you are **content with** something, you are willing to accept it, rather than wanting something more or something better. ❑ *I'm perfectly content with the way the campaign has gone... Not content with rescuing one theatre, Sally Green has taken on another.* 2 If you are **content**, you are fairly happy or satisfied. ❑ *He says his daughter is quite content.* 3 If you **content yourself with** something, you accept it and do not try to do or have other things. ❑ *He wisely contented himself with his family and his love of nature... Most manufac-*
ADJ: v-link ADJ, ADJ to-inf, ADJ *with* n/-ing
ADJ: v-link ADJ
VERB
V pron-refl *with* n
V pron-refl

*turers content themselves with updating existing models.* [4] **to your heart's content** → see **heart**. *with/by -ing*

**con|tent|ed** /kəntentɪd/ If you are **contented**, you are satisfied with your life or the situation you are in. ❑ *Whenever he returns to this place he is happy and contented... She was gazing at him with a soft, contented smile on her face.* ADJ

**con|ten|tion** /kəntenʃən/ **(contentions)** [1] Someone's **contention** is the idea or opinion that they are expressing in an argument or discussion. ❑ *This evidence supports their contention that the outbreak of violence was prearranged.* N-COUNT: usu poss N = claim [2] If something is a cause **of contention**, it is a cause of disagreement or argument. ❑ *A particular source of contention is plans to privatise state-run companies.* → See also **bone of contention**. N-UNCOUNT: usu n of N [3] If you are **in contention** in a contest, you have a chance of winning it. ❑ *He was in contention for a place in the European championship squad.* PHRASE: v-link PHR

**con|ten|tious** /kəntenʃəs/ A **contentious** issue causes a lot of disagreement or arguments. [FORMAL] ❑ *Sanctions are expected to be among the most contentious issues. ...a country where land prices are politically contentious.* ADJ = controversial

**con|tent|ment** /kəntentmənt/ **Contentment** is a feeling of quiet happiness and satisfaction. ❑ *I cannot describe the feeling of contentment that was with me at that time.* N-UNCOUNT ≠ discontent

**con|tent pro|vid|er** **(content providers)** A **content provider** is a company that supplies material such as text, music, or images for use on websites. [COMPUTING] ❑ *...content providers such as MSN and Freeserve.* N-COUNT

**con|test** **(contests, contesting, contested)** ◆◇◇

> The noun is pronounced /kɒntest/. The verb is pronounced /kəntest/.

[1] A **contest** is a competition or game in which people try to win. ❑ *Few contests in the recent history of British boxing have been as thrilling. ...a writing contest.* → See also **beauty contest**. N-COUNT [2] A **contest** is a struggle to win power or control. ❑ *The state election due in November will be the last such ballot before next year's presidential contest. ...a clear contest between church and state.* N-COUNT [3] If someone **contests** an election or competition, they take part in it and try to win it. [mainly BRIT] ❑ *He quickly won his party's nomination to contest the elections. ...a closely contested regional flower show.* VERB V n V-ed [4] If you **contest** a statement or decision, you object to it formally because you think it is wrong or unreasonable. ❑ *Your former employer has to reply within 14 days in order to contest the case... Gender discrimination is a hotly contested issue.* VERB = dispute V n V-ed

**con|test|ant** /kəntestənt/ **(contestants)** A **contestant** in a competition or quiz is a person who takes part in it. N-COUNT = competitor

**con|text** /kɒntekst/ **(contexts)** [1] The **context of** an idea or event is the general situation that relates to it, and which helps it to be understood. ❑ *We are doing this work in the context of reforms in the economic, social and cultural spheres. ...the historical context in which Chaucer wrote.* ◆◇◇ N-VAR: usu with supp, oft adj N, N of n [2] The **context** of a word, sentence, or text consists of the words, sentences, or text before and after it which help to make its meaning clear. ❑ *Without a context, I would have assumed it was written by a man.* N-VAR

**PHRASES** [3] If something is seen **in context** or if it is put **into context**, it is considered together with all the factors that relate to it. ❑ *Taxation is not popular in principle, merely acceptable in context... It is important that we put Jesus into the context of history.* PHRASE [4] If a statement or remark is quoted **out of context**, the circumstances in which it was said are not correctly reported, so that it seems to mean something different from the meaning that was intended. ❑ *Thomas says that he has been taken out of context on the issue.* PHRASE

**con|tex|tual** /kəntekstʃuəl/ A **contextual** issue or account relates to the context of something. [FORMAL] ❑ *The writer builds up a clever contextual picture of upper class life.* ADJ: usu ADJ n

**con|tigu|ous** /kəntɪgjuəs/ Things that are **contiguous** are next to each other or touch each other. [FORMAL] ❑ *Its vineyards are virtually contiguous with those of Ausone. ...two years of travel throughout the 48 contiguous states.* ADJ: oft ADJ to/with n = adjacent, adjoining

**con|ti|nent** /kɒntɪnənt/ **(continents)** [1] A **continent** is a very large area of land, such as Africa or Asia, that consists of several countries. ❑ *She loved the African continent... Dinosaurs evolved when most continents were joined in a single land mass.* ◆◇◇ N-COUNT [2] People sometimes use **the Continent** to refer to the continent of Europe except for Britain. [mainly BRIT] ❑ *Its shops are among the most stylish on the Continent.* N-PROPER: the N

**con|ti|nen|tal** /kɒntɪnentəl/ **(continentals)** [1] **Continental** means situated on or belonging to the continent of Europe except for Britain. [mainly BRIT] ❑ *He sees no signs of improvement in the UK and continental economy.* ADJ: ADJ n [2] A **continental** is someone who comes from the continent of Europe. [BRIT, INFORMAL] N-COUNT: usu pl [3] If you describe someone or something as **continental**, you think that they are typical of the continent of Europe. [BRIT, INFORMAL] ADJ: usu v-link ADJ [4] **Continental** is used to refer to something that belongs to or relates to a continent. ❑ *The most ancient parts of the continental crust are 4000 million years old.* ADJ: ADJ n [5] The **continental** United States consists of all the states which are situated on the continent of North America, as opposed to Hawaii and territories such as the Virgin Islands. [mainly AM] ❑ *Shipping is included on orders sent within the continental U.S.* ADJ: usu ADJ n [6] **Continental** means existing or happening in the American colonies during the American Revolution. [AM] ❑ *...George Washington, Commander of the Continental Army.* ADJ: usu ADJ n [7] **Continentals** were soldiers who fought in the Continental Army against the British in the American Revolution. [AM] N-COUNT

**con|ti|nen|tal break|fast** **(continental breakfasts)** A **continental breakfast** is breakfast that consists of food such as bread, butter, jam, and a hot drink. There is no cooked food. N-COUNT

**con|ti|nen|tal drift** **Continental drift** is the slow movement of the Earth's continents towards and away from each other. N-UNCOUNT

**con|ti|nen|tal shelf** The **continental shelf** is the area which forms the edge of a continent, ending in a steep slope to the depths of the ocean. ❑ *...the deep water off the Continental Shelf.* N-UNCOUNT

**con|tin|gen|cy** /kəntɪndʒənsi/ **(contingencies)** [1] A **contingency** is something that might happen in the future. [FORMAL] ❑ *I need to examine all possible contingencies.* N-VAR = possibility, eventuality [2] A **contingency** plan or measure is one that is intended to be used if a possible situation actually occurs. [FORMAL] ❑ *We have contingency plans.* ADJ: ADJ n

**con|tin|gent** /kəntɪndʒənt/ **(contingents)** [1] A **contingent of** police, soldiers, or military vehicles is a group of them. [FORMAL] ❑ *There were contingents from the navies of virtually all EU countries.* N-COUNT: usu with supp, oft N of n [2] A **contingent** is a group of people representing a country or organization at a meeting or other event. [FORMAL] ❑ *The strong British contingent suffered mixed fortunes.* N-COUNT: usu with supp, oft adj N [3] If something is **contingent on** something else, the first thing depends on the second in order to happen or exist. [FORMAL] ❑ *In effect, growth is contingent on improved incomes for the mass of the low-income population.* ADJ: usu ADJ on/upon n/-ing = dependent

**con|tin|ual** /kəntɪnjuəl/ [1] A **continual** process or situation happens or exists without stopping. ❑ *The school has been in continual use since 1883... Despite continual pain, he refused all drugs.* ♦ **con|tinu|al|ly** *She cried almost continually and threw temper tantrums.* ADJ: ADJ n = continuous ADV: usu ADV with v [2] **Continual** events happen again and again. ❑ *...the government's continual demands for cash to finance its chronic deficit... She suffered continual police harassment.* ADJ: ADJ n

♦ **con|tinu|al|ly** *Malcolm was continually changing his mind.* ADV: usu ADV with v

**con|tinu|ance** /kəntɪnjuəns/ The **continuance** of something is its continuation. [FORMAL] ❑ *...thus ensuring the continuance of the human species.* N-UNCOUNT: usu with poss = continuation

**con|tinu|ation** /kəntɪnjueɪʃən/ **(continuations)** [1] The **continuation of** something is the fact that it continues, rather than stopping. ❑ *It's the coalition forces who are to blame for the continuation of the war.* N-VAR: usu with poss [2] Something that is a **continuation of** something else is closely connected with it or forms part of it. ❑ *It would just be a continuation of previous visits he has made to Israel.* N-COUNT: usu sing, N *of* n

**con|tinue** /kəntɪnjuː/ **(continues, continuing, continued)** ♦♦♦ [1] If someone or something **continues to** do something, they keep doing it and do not stop. VERB ❑ *I hope they continue to fight for equal justice after I'm gone...* V to-inf *Interest rates continue to fall...* V to-inf *They are determined to continue working when they reach retirement age...* V -ing *There is no reason why you should not continue with any sport or activity you already enjoy.* V *with* n [2] If something **continues** or if you **continue** it, it does not stop happening. VERB ❑ *He insisted that the conflict would continue until conditions were met for a ceasefire...* V *Outside the building people continue their vigil, huddling around bonfires.* V n *...the continued existence of a species.* V-ed [3] If you **continue** with something, you start doing it again after a break or interruption. VERB = carry on ❑ *I went up to my room to continue with my packing...* V *with* n *She looked up for a moment, then continued drawing.* V -ing [4] If something **continues** or if you **continue** it, it starts again after a break or interruption. VERB ❑ *He denies 18 charges. The trial continues today...* V *Once, he did dive for cover but he soon reappeared and continued his activities.* V n [5] If you **continue**, you begin speaking again after a pause or interruption. VERB ❑ *'You have no right to intimidate this man,' Alison continued...* V with quote *Tony drank some coffee before he continued...* V *Please continue.* V [6] If you **continue as** something or **continue** in a particular state, you remain in a particular job or state. VERB ❑ *He had hoped to continue as a full-time career officer...* V *as* n *For ten days I continued in this state.* V prep [7] If you **continue** in a particular direction, you keep walking or travelling in that direction. VERB ❑ *He continued rapidly up the path, not pausing until he neared the Chapter House.* V prep/adv

**con|tinu|ing edu|ca|tion** **Continuing education** is education for adults in a variety of subjects, most of which are practical, not academic. N-UNCOUNT

**con|ti|nu|ity** /kɒntɪnjuːɪti, AM -nuː-/ **(continuities)** [1] **Continuity** is the fact that something continues to happen or exist, with no great changes or interruptions. N-VAR ❑ *An historical awareness also imparts a sense of continuity. ...a tank designed to ensure continuity of fuel supply during aerobatics.* [2] In film making, **continuity** is the way that things filmed at different times are made to look as if they were filmed at the same time or in the right sequence. N-UNCOUNT [TECHNICAL] ❑ *Walt and I referred to a video cassette of the original footage to check continuity and lighting.*

**con|ti|nu|ity an|nounc|er** **(continuity announcers)** A **continuity announcer** is someone who introduces the next programme on a radio or television station. N-COUNT

**con|tinu|ous** /kəntɪnjuəs/ [1] A **continuous** process or event continues for a period of time without stopping. ADJ: usu ADJ n = unbroken ❑ *Residents report that they heard continuous gunfire. ...all employees who had a record of five years' continuous employment with the firm.* ♦ **con|tinu|ous|ly** *The civil war has raged almost continuously since 1976... It is the oldest continuously inhabited city in America.* ADV: usu ADV with v [2] A **continuous** line or surface has no gaps or holes in it. ADJ: usu ADJ n ❑ *...a continuous line of boats.* [3] In English grammar, **continuous** verb groups are formed using the auxiliary 'be' and the present participle of a verb, as in 'I'm feeling a bit tired' and 'She had been watching them for some time'. Continuous verb groups are used especially when you are focusing on a particular moment. Compare **simple**. ADJ = progressive

**con|tinu|ous as|sess|ment** If pupils or students undergo **continuous assessment**, they get qualifications partly or entirely based on the work they do during the year, rather than on exam results. [BRIT] N-UNCOUNT

**con|tin|uum** /kəntɪnjuəm/ **(continua** /kəntɪnjuə/ or **continuums)** A **continuum** is a set of things on a scale, which have a particular characteristic to different degrees. [FORMAL] ❑ *These various complaints are part of a continuum of ill-health.* N-COUNT: usu sing

**con|tort** /kəntɔːʳt/ **(contorts, contorting, contorted)** If someone's face or body **contorts** or **is contorted**, it moves into an unnatural and unattractive shape or position. VERB ❑ *His face contorts as he screams out the lyrics...* V *The gentlest of her caresses would contort his already tense body...* V n *Brenner was breathing hard, his face contorted with pain.* V-ed

**con|tor|tion** /kəntɔːʳʃən/ **(contortions)** **Contortions** are movements of your body or face into unusual shapes or positions. N-COUNT ❑ *I had to admire the contortions of the gymnasts.*

**con|tor|tion|ist** /kəntɔːʳʃənɪst/ **(contortionists)** A **contortionist** is someone who twists their body into strange and unnatural shapes and positions in order to entertain other people, for example in a circus. N-COUNT

**con|tour** /kɒntʊəʳ/ **(contours)** [1] You can refer to the general shape or outline of an object as its **contours**. N-COUNT: usu pl, usu with supp, oft N *of* n [LITERARY] ❑ *...the texture and colour of the skin, the contours of the body.* [2] A **contour** on a map is a line joining points of equal height and indicating hills, valleys, and the steepness of slopes. N-COUNT ❑ *...a contour map showing two hills and this large mountain in the middle.*

**con|toured** /kɒntʊəʳd/ A **contoured** surface has curves and slopes on it, rather than being flat. ADJ: ADJ n ❑ *...the lush fairways and contoured greens of the course... Sophia settled into her comfortably contoured seat.*

**contra|band** /kɒntrəbænd/ **Contraband** refers to goods that are taken into or out of a country illegally. N-UNCOUNT: oft N n ❑ *Most of the city markets were flooded with contraband goods.*

**contra|cep|tion** /kɒntrəsepʃən/ **Contraception** refers to methods of preventing pregnancy. N-UNCOUNT = birth control ❑ *Use a reliable method of contraception.*

**contra|cep|tive** /kɒntrəseptɪv/ **(contraceptives)** [1] A **contraceptive** method or device is a method or a device which a woman uses to prevent herself from becoming pregnant. ADJ: ADJ n ❑ *It was at that time she started taking the contraceptive pill.* [2] A **contraceptive** is a device or drug that prevents a woman from becoming pregnant. N-COUNT ❑ *...oral contraceptives.*

**con|tract** **(contracts, contracting, contracted)** ♦♦◇

> ✓ The noun is pronounced /kɒntrækt/. The verb is pronounced /kəntrækt/.

[1] A **contract** is a legal agreement, usually between two companies or between an employer and employee, which involves doing work for a stated sum of money. N-COUNT ❑ *The company won a prestigious contract for work on Europe's tallest building... He was given a seven-year contract with an annual salary of $150,000.* [2] If you **contract with** someone **to** do something, you legally agree to do it for them or for them to do it for you. VERB [FORMAL] ❑ *You can contract with us to deliver your cargo...* V *with* n to-inf *The Boston Museum of Fine Arts has already contracted to lease part of its collection to a museum in Japan.* V to-inf [3] When something **contracts** or when something **contracts** it, it becomes smaller or shorter. VERB ❑ *Blood is only expelled from the heart when it contracts...* V *New research shows that an excess of meat and salt can contract muscles.* V n ♦ **con|trac|tion** /kəntrækʃən/ **(contractions)** N-VAR *...the contraction and expansion of blood vessels... Foods and fluids are mixed in the stom-*

*ach by its muscular contractions.* [4] [VERB] When something such as an economy or market **contracts**, it becomes smaller. ❑ [V] *The manufacturing economy contracted in October for the sixth consecutive month.* [5] [VERB: no cont] If you **contract** a serious illness, you become ill with it. [FORMAL] ❑ [V n] *He contracted AIDS from a blood transfusion...* [V-ed] *Ovarian cancer is the sixth most common cancer contracted by women.* [6] [VERB = enter into] If you **contract** a marriage, alliance, or other relationship with someone, you arrange to have that relationship with them. [FORMAL] ❑ [V n] *She contracted a formal marriage to a British ex-serviceman.* [7] [N-COUNT: usu N *on* n] If there is a **contract on** a person or on their life, someone has made an arrangement to have them killed. [INFORMAL] ❑ *The convictions resulted in the local crime bosses putting a contract on him.* [8] [PHRASE: oft PHR *to* n] If you are **under contract to** someone, you have signed a contract agreeing to work for them, and for no-one else, during a fixed period of time. ❑ *The director wanted Olivia de Havilland, then under contract to Warner Brothers.*

♦ **contract out** [PHRASAL VERB] [1] If a company **contracts out** work, they employ other companies to do it. [BUSINESS] ❑ [V P n *to* n] *Firms can contract out work to one another...* [V P n] *When Barclays Bank contracted out its cleaning, the new company was cheaper.* [V n P; Also V n P *to* n, V P] *...the trend of contracting services out rather than performing them in-house.* [2] [PHRASAL VERB] If a person or group **contracts out of** a system or scheme, they formally say that they do not want to take part in it. [BRIT] ❑ [V P *of* n] *Employees can contract out of their employer's occupational pension scheme.* [V P] *...a free deal which automatically converts into a pay as-you-go service unless you contract out.*

**con|trac|tion** /kəntrækʃən/ **(contractions)** [1] [N-COUNT] When a woman who is about to give birth has **contractions**, she experiences a very strong, painful tightening of the muscles of her womb. [2] [N-COUNT] A **contraction** is a shortened form of a word or words. ❑ *'It's' (with an apostrophe) should be used only as a contraction for 'it is'.* [3] → See also **contract**.

**con|trac|tor** /kɒntræktəʳ, kəntræk-/ **(contractors)** [N-COUNT: oft n N] A **contractor** is a person or company that does work for other people or organizations. [BUSINESS] ❑ *...a major US defense contractor.*

**con|trac|tual** /kəntræktʃuəl/ [ADJ: usu ADJ n] A **contractual** arrangement or relationship involves a legal agreement between people. [FORMAL] ❑ *The company has not fulfilled certain contractual obligations.* ♦ **con|trac|tu|al|ly** [ADV: usu ADV after v, ADV -ed/adj] *Rank was contractually obliged to hand him a cheque for $30 million.*

**contra|dict** /kɒntrədɪkt/ **(contradicts, contradicting, contradicted)** [1] [VERB] If you **contradict** someone, you say that what they have just said is wrong, or suggest that it is wrong by saying something different. ❑ [V n] *She dared not contradict him...* [V n] *His comments appeared to contradict remarks made earlier in the day by the chairman...* [V pron-refl] *He often talks in circles, frequently contradicting himself and often ends up saying nothing.* [2] [VERB] If one statement or piece of evidence **contradicts** another, the first one makes the second one appear to be wrong. ❑ [V n] *The result seems to contradict a major U.S. study reported last November.*

**contra|dic|tion** /kɒntrədɪkʃən/ **(contradictions)** [N-COUNT: oft N *between* pl-n, N *of* n] If you describe an aspect of a situation as a **contradiction**, you mean that it is completely different from other aspects, and so makes the situation confused or difficult to understand. ❑ *The performance seemed to me unpardonable, a contradiction of all that the Olympics is supposed to be... The militants see no contradiction in using violence to bring about a religious state.*

**contra|dic|tory** /kɒntrədɪktəri, AM -tɔːri/ [ADJ] If two or more facts, ideas, or statements are **contradictory**, they state or imply that opposite things are true. ❑ *Customs officials have made a series of contradictory statements about the equipment. ...advice that sometimes is contradictory and confusing.*

**contra|flow** /kɒntrəfloʊ/ **(contraflows)** [N-COUNT] A **contraflow** is a situation in which vehicles travelling on a main road in one direction have to use lanes that are normally used by traffic travelling in the opposite direction, because the road is being repaired. [BRIT] ❑ *...a contraflow between Junctions Eleven and Twelve of the M5.*

**contra|in|di|ca|tion** /kɒntrəɪndɪkeɪʃən/ **(contraindications)** also **contra-indication.** [N-COUNT: usu pl] **Contraindications** are specific medical reasons for not using a particular treatment for a medical condition in the usual way. [MEDICAL] ❑ *Contraindications for this drug include liver or kidney impairment.*

**con|tral|to** /kəntræltoʊ/ **(contraltos)** [N-COUNT: oft N n] A **contralto** is a woman with a low singing voice. ❑ *The score calls for a contralto... I had a very low contralto voice.*

**con|trap|tion** /kəntræpʃən/ **(contraptions)** [N-COUNT = gadget] You can refer to a device or machine as a **contraption**, especially when it looks strange or you do not know what it is used for. ❑ *...a strange contraption called the General Gordon Gas Bath.*

**con|trar|ian** /kəntreəriən/ **(contrarians)** [N-COUNT: oft N n] A **contrarian** is a person who deliberately behaves in a way that is different from the people around them. [FORMAL] ❑ *He is by nature a contrarian. ...the young contrarian intellectual.*

**con|tra|ry** /kɒntrəri, AM -treri/ [1] [ADJ: usu v-link ADJ *to* n] Ideas, attitudes, or reactions that are **contrary to** each other are completely different from each other. ❑ *This view is contrary to the aims of critical social research for a number of reasons... Several of those present, including Weinberger, had contrary information.*

PHRASES [2] [PREP-PHRASE emphasis] If you say that something is true **contrary to** other people's beliefs or opinions, you are emphasizing that it is true and that they are wrong. ❑ *Contrary to popular belief, moderate exercise actually decreases your appetite.* [3] [PHRASE: PHR with cl] You use **on the contrary** when you have just said or implied that something is not true and are going to say that the opposite is true. ❑ *It is not an idea around which the Community can unite. On the contrary, I see it as one that will divide us.* [4] [PHRASE emphasis] You can use **on the contrary** when you are disagreeing strongly with something that has just been said or implied, or are making a strong negative reply. ❑ *'People just don't do things like that.' — 'On the contrary, they do them all the time.'* [5] [PHRASE: PHR with cl emphasis = quite the opposite] You can use **quite the contrary** to emphasize a previous negative statement, or when you are making a strong negative reply. ❑ *I'm not a feminist, quite the contrary.* [6] [PHRASE: n PHR] When a particular idea is being considered, evidence or statements **to the contrary** suggest that this idea is not true or that the opposite is true. ❑ *That does not automatically mean, however, that the money supply has been curbed, and there is considerable evidence to the contrary.*

**con|trast** **(contrasts, contrasting, contrasted)** ◆◇◇

> ✔ The noun is pronounced /kɒntrɑːst, -træst/.
> The verb is pronounced /kəntrɑːst, -træst/.

[1] [N-VAR: oft N *between* pl-n] A **contrast** is a great difference between two or more things which is clear when you compare them. ❑ *...the contrast between town and country... The two visitors provided a startling contrast in appearance... Silk was used with wool for contrast.* [2] [PHRASE: PHR with cl] You say **by contrast** or **in contrast**, or **in contrast to** something, to show that you are mentioning a very different situation from the one you have just mentioned. ❑ *The private sector, by contrast, has plenty of money to spend... In contrast, the lives of girls in well-to-do families were often very sheltered... In contrast to similar services in France and Germany, Intercity rolling stock is very rarely idle.* [3] [PHRASE: v-link PHR, usu PHR *to* n] If one thing is **in contrast to** another, it is very different from it. ❑ *His public statements have always been in marked contrast to those of his son.* [4] [N-COUNT: oft N *to/with* n] If one thing is a **contrast to** another, it is very different from it. ❑ *The boy's room is a complete contrast to the guest room. ...a country of great contrasts.* [5] [VERB] If you **contrast** one thing **with** another, you point out or consider the differences between those things. ❑ [V n *with* n] *She contrasted the situation then with the*

*present crisis... In this section we contrast four possible broad approaches.* V pl-n **6** If one thing **contrasts with** another, it is very different from it. V-RECIP ❑ *Johnson's easy charm contrasted sharply with the prickliness of his boss...* V *with* n *Paint the wall in a contrasting colour.* V-ing Also pl-n V **7** **Contrast** is the degree of difference between the darker and lighter parts of a photograph, television picture, or painting. N-UNCOUNT

**contra|vene** /kɒntrəviːn/ **(contravenes, contravening, contravened)** To **contravene** a law or rule means to do something that is forbidden by the law or rule. VERB = break [FORMAL] ❑ *The Board has banned the film on the grounds that it contravenes criminal libel laws.* V n ♦ **contra|ven|tion** /kɒntrəvenʃən/ **(contraventions)** *The government has lent millions of pounds to debt-ridden banks in contravention of local banking laws.* N-VAR: oft *in* N *of* n

**con|tre|temps** /kɒntrətɒm/ **(contretemps)** A **contretemps** is a small disagreement that is rather embarrassing. N-COUNT: usu sing = dispute [LITERARY] ❑ *He was briefly arrested in Rome after a contretemps with Italian police.*

**con|trib|ute** /kəntrɪbjuːt/ **(contributes, contributing, contributed)** ◆◇◇ **1** If you **contribute to** something, you say or do things to help to make it successful. VERB ❑ *The three sons also contribute to the family business...* V *to* n *He believes he has something to contribute to a discussion concerning the uprising.* V n *to* n Also V **2** To **contribute** money or resources **to** something means to give money or resources to help pay for something or to help achieve a particular purpose. VERB = donate ❑ *The US is contributing $4 billion in loans, credits and grants...* V n *NATO officials agreed to contribute troops and equipment to such an operation if the UN Security Council asked for it.* V n *to/towards* n Also V ♦ **con|tribu|tor** /kəntrɪbjʊtəʳ/ **(contributors)** *...the largest net contributors to EU funds.* N-COUNT **3** If something **contributes to** an event or situation, it is one of the causes of it. VERB ❑ *The report says design faults in both the vessels contributed to the tragedy...* V *to* n *Stress, both human and mechanical, may also be a contributing factor.* V-ing **4** If you **contribute to** a magazine, newspaper, or book, you write things that are published in it. VERB ❑ *I was asked to contribute to a newspaper article making predictions for the new year...* V *to* n *Frank Deford is a contributing editor for Vanity Fair magazine.* V-ing ♦ **con|tribu|tor** **(contributors)** *Reporter Alan Nearn covers Central America and is a regular contributor to The New Yorker.* N-COUNT

**con|tri|bu|tion** /kɒntrɪbjuːʃən/ **(contributions)** ◆◇◇ **1** If you make a **contribution to** something, you do something to help make it successful or to produce it. N-COUNT: oft N *to* n ❑ *He was awarded a prize for his contribution to world peace.* **2** A **contribution** is a sum of money that you give in order to help pay for something. N-COUNT: oft N *of* n = donation ❑ *This list ranked companies that make charitable contributions of a half million dollars or more.* **3** A **contribution to** a magazine, newspaper, or book is something that you write to be published in it. N-COUNT

**con|tribu|tor** /kəntrɪbjʊtəʳ/ **(contributors)** You can use **contributor** to refer to one of the causes of an event or situation, especially if that event or situation is an unpleasant one. N-COUNT: oft N *to* n ❑ *Old buses are major contributors to pollution in British cities.* → See also **contribute**.

**con|tribu|tory** /kəntrɪbjʊtəri, AM -tɔːri/ A **contributory** factor of a problem or accident is one of the things which caused it to exist or happen. ADJ: usu ADJ n [FORMAL] ❑ *We now know that repressing anger is a contributory factor in many physical illnesses.*

**con|trite** /kəntraɪt, kɒntraɪt/ If you are **contrite**, you are very sorry because you have done something wrong. ADJ: usu v-link ADJ = apologetic [FORMAL]

**con|triv|ance** /kəntraɪvəns/ **(contrivances)** **1** If you describe something as a **contrivance**, you disapprove of it because it is unnecessary and artificial. N-VAR disapproval [FORMAL] ❑ *They wear simple clothes and shun modern contrivances... Music with a tendency towards contrivance and lack of substance.* **2** A **contrivance** is an unfair or dishonest scheme or trick to gain an advantage for yourself. N-COUNT = ploy ❑ *...some contrivance to raise prices.*

**con|trive** /kəntraɪv/ **(contrives, contriving, contrived)** **1** If you **contrive** an event or situation, you succeed in making it happen, often by tricking someone. VERB [FORMAL] ❑ *The oil companies were accused of contriving a shortage of gasoline to justify price increases.* V n **2** If you **contrive to** do something difficult, you succeed in doing it. VERB [FORMAL] ❑ *The orchestra contrived to produce some of its best playing for years.* V to-inf

**con|trived** /kəntraɪvd/ **1** If you say that something someone says or does is **contrived**, you think it is false and deliberate, rather than natural and not planned. ADJ disapproval = artificial ≠ spontaneous ❑ *There was nothing contrived or calculated about what he said... It mustn't sound like a contrived compliment.* **2** If you say that the plot of a play, film, or novel is **contrived**, you mean that it is unlikely and unconvincing. ADJ disapproval ❑ *The plot seems contrived.*

**con|trol** /kəntroʊl/ **(controls, controlling, controlled)** ◆◆◆ **1** **Control of** an organization, place, or system is the power to make all the important decisions about the way that it is run. N-UNCOUNT: oft N *of/over* n ❑ *The restructuring involves Mr Ronson giving up control of the company... The first aim of his government would be to establish control over the republic's territory.* ● If you are **in control of** something, you have the power to make all the important decisions about the way it is run. PHRASE: usu v-link PHR, usu PHR *of* n ❑ *Nobody knows who is in control of the club... In the West, people feel more in control of their own lives.* ● If something is **under** your **control**, you have the power to make all the important decisions about the way that it is run. PHRASE: PHR after v, v-link PHR ❑ *All the newspapers were taken under government control.* **2** If you have **control** of something or someone, you are able to make them do what you want them to do. N-UNCOUNT: oft N *of/over* n ❑ *He lost control of his car... Some teachers have more control over pupils than their parents have.* **3** If you show **control**, you prevent yourself behaving in an angry or emotional way. N-UNCOUNT ❑ *He had a terrible temper, and sometimes he would completely lose control... He was working hard to keep control of himself.*
**4** The people who **control** an organization or place have the power to take all the important decisions about the way that it is run. VERB ❑ *He now controls the largest retail development empire in southern California...* V n *Minebea ended up selling its controlling interest in both firms.* V-ing ♦ **-controlled** *AGA Gas is Swedish-controlled. ...the state-controlled media.* COMB in ADJ **5** To **control** a piece of equipment, process, or system means to make it work in the way that you want it to work. VERB ❑ *...a computerised system to control the gates.* V n *...the controlled production of energy from sugar by a cell.* V-ed ♦ **-controlled** *...computer-controlled traffic lights.* COMB in ADJ **6** When a government **controls** prices, wages, or the activity of a particular group, it uses its power to restrict them. VERB ❑ *The federal government tried to control rising health-care costs.* V n ♦ **Control** is also a noun. N-UNCOUNT: with supp ❑ *Control of inflation remains the government's absolute priority.* **7** If you **control yourself**, or if you **control** your feelings, voice, or expression, you make yourself behave calmly even though you are feeling angry, excited, or upset. VERB = restrain ❑ *Jo was advised to learn to control herself...* V pron-refl *I just couldn't control my temper.* V n ♦ **con|trolled** *Her manner was quiet and very controlled.* ADJ = restrained **8** To **control** something dangerous means to prevent it from becoming worse or from spreading. VERB ❑ *One of the biggest tasks will be to control the spread of malaria.* V n **9** A **control** is a device such as a switch or lever which you use in order to operate a machine or other piece of equipment. N-COUNT ❑ *I practised operating the controls. ...the control box.* ● If someone is **at the controls of** a machine or other piece of equipment, they are operating it. PHRASE ❑ *He died of a heart attack while at the controls of the plane.* **10** **Controls** are the methods that a government uses to restrict increases, for example in prices, wages, or weapons. N-VAR ❑ *Critics question whether price controls would do any good... They have very*

*strict gun control in Sweden.* [11] **Control** is used to refer to a place where your documents or luggage are officially checked when you enter a foreign country. ❑ *He went straight through Passport Control without incident.* N-VAR: n N [12] ➔ See also **air traffic control**, **birth control**, **quality control**, **remote control**, **stock control**.

PHRASES [13] If something is **out of control**, no-one has any power over it. ❑ *The fire is burning out of control.* PHRASE: usu v PHR, v-link PHR [14] If something harmful is **under control**, it is being dealt with successfully and is unlikely to cause any more harm. ❑ *If the current violence is to be brought under control, the government needs to act.* PHRASE: v-link PHR, PHR after v

**con|trol freak** **(control freaks)** If you say that someone is a **control freak**, you mean that they want to be in control of every situation they find themselves in. [INFORMAL] N-COUNT disapproval

**con|trol|lable** /kəntroʊləbəl/ If something is **controllable** you are able to control or influence it. ❑ *This makes the surfboards more controllable. ...controllable aspects of life.* ADJ

**con|trol|ler** /kəntroʊlər/ **(controllers)** [1] A **controller** is a person who has responsibility for a particular organization or for a particular part of an organization. [mainly BRIT] ❑ *...the job of controller of BBC 1. ...the financial controller of W H Smith.* N-COUNT: oft N *of* n ➔ See also **air traffic controller**. [2] A **controller** is the same as a **comptroller**. N-COUNT

**con|trol tow|er** **(control towers)** A **control tower** is a building at an airport from which instructions are given to aircraft when they are taking off or landing. You can also refer to the people who work in a control tower as the **control tower**. ❑ *The pilot told the control tower that he'd run into technical trouble.* N-COUNT

**con|tro|ver|sial** /kɒntrəvɜːrʃəl/ ◆◇◇ If you describe something or someone as **controversial**, you mean that they are the subject of intense public argument, disagreement, or disapproval. ❑ *Immigration is a controversial issue in many countries... The changes are bound to be controversial.* ADJ

♦ **con|tro|ver|sial|ly** *More controversially, he claims that these higher profits cover the cost of finding fresh talent.* ADV: usu ADV with cl, also ADV with v

**con|tro|ver|sy** /kɒntrəvɜːrsi, kəntrɒvərsi/ ◆◇◇ **(controversies)** **Controversy** is a lot of discussion and argument about something, often involving strong feelings of anger or disapproval. ❑ *The proposed cuts have caused considerable controversy.* N-VAR: oft N *over/about* n

**con|tu|sion** /kəntjuːʒən, AM -tuː-/ **(contusions)** A **contusion** is a **bruise**. [MEDICAL] N-COUNT

**co|nun|drum** /kənʌndrəm/ **(conundrums)** A **conundrum** is a problem or puzzle which is difficult or impossible to solve. [FORMAL] ❑ *...this theological conundrum of the existence of evil and suffering in a world created by a good God.* N-COUNT

**con|ur|ba|tion** /kɒnərbeɪʃən/ **(conurbations)** A **conurbation** consists of a large city together with the smaller towns around it. [mainly BRIT, FORMAL] ❑ *...London and all the other major conurbations.* N-COUNT

**con|va|lesce** /kɒnvəles/ **(convalesces, convalescing, convalesced)** If you **are convalescing**, you are resting and getting your health back after an illness or operation. [FORMAL] ❑ *After two weeks, I was allowed home, where I convalesced for three months. ...those convalescing from illness or surgery.* VERB = recuperate; V; V *from* n

**con|va|les|cence** /kɒnvəlesəns/ **Convalescence** is the period or process of becoming healthy and well again after an illness or operation. [FORMAL] N-UNCOUNT = recuperation

**con|va|les|cent** /kɒnvəlesənt/ **Convalescent** means relating to convalescence. [FORMAL] ❑ *...an officers' convalescent home.* ADJ: usu ADJ n

**con|vec|tion** /kənvekʃən/ **Convection** is the process by which heat travels through air, water, and other gases and liquids. [TECHNICAL] ❑ *...clouds which lift warm, moist air by convection high into the atmosphere.* N-UNCOUNT

**con|vec|tor heat|er** **(convector heaters)** A **convector heater** is a heater that heats a room by means of hot air. N-COUNT

**con|vene** /kənviːn/ **(convenes, convening, convened)** If someone **convenes** a meeting or conference, they arrange for it to take place. You can also say that people **convene** or that a meeting **convenes**. [FORMAL] ❑ *Last August he convened a meeting of his closest advisers at Camp David... Senior officials convened in October 1991 in London.* VERB; V n; V

**con|ven|er** /kənviːnər/ ➔ see **convenor**.

**con|veni|ence** /kənviːniəns/ **(conveniences)** [1] If something is done for your **convenience**, it is done in a way that is useful or suitable for you. ❑ *He was happy to make a detour for her convenience. ...the need to put the rights of citizens above the convenience of elected officials.* N-UNCOUNT: with poss ● If something is arranged to happen **at your convenience**, it happens at a time which is most suitable for you. [FORMAL] ❑ *Delivery times are arranged at your convenience.* PHRASE: PHR with v [2] If you describe something as a **convenience**, you mean that it is very useful. ❑ *Mail order is a convenience for buyers who are too busy to shop.* N-COUNT [3] **Conveniences** are pieces of equipment designed to make your life easier. ❑ *...an apartment with all the modern conveniences.* N-COUNT: usu pl [4] A public **convenience** is a building containing toilets which is provided in a public place for anyone to use. [BRIT, FORMAL] ❑ *...the cubicles of a public convenience.* N-COUNT: usu supp N [5] ➔ See also **convenient**.

**con|veni|ence food** **Convenience food** is frozen, dried, or canned food that can be heated and prepared very quickly and easily. ❑ *I rely too much on convenience food.* N-UNCOUNT

**con|veni|ence store** **(convenience stores)** A **convenience store** is a shop which sells mainly food and which is usually open until late at night. N-COUNT

**con|veni|ent** /kənviːniənt/ [1] If a way of doing something is **convenient**, it is easy, or very useful or suitable for a particular purpose. ❑ *...a flexible and convenient way of paying for business expenses... The family thought it was more convenient to eat in the kitchen.* ADJ: oft *it* v-link ADJ to-inf ≠ inconvenient ♦ **con|veni|ence** *They may use a credit card for convenience.* N-UNCOUNT ♦ **con|veni|ent|ly** *The body spray slips conveniently into your sports bag for freshening up after a game.* ADV: usu ADV with v, also ADV with cl [2] If you describe a place as **convenient**, you are pleased because it is near to where you are, or because you can reach another place from there quickly and easily. ❑ *The town is well placed for easy access to London and convenient for Heathrow Airport... Martin drove along until he found a convenient parking place.* ADJ: oft ADJ *for* n approval = handy ♦ **con|veni|ent|ly** *It was very conveniently situated just across the road from the City Reference Library.* ADV [3] A **convenient** time to do something, for example to meet someone, is a time when you are free to do it or would like to do it. ❑ *Would this evening be convenient for you?* ADJ ≠ inconvenient [4] If you describe someone's attitudes or actions as **convenient**, you think they are only adopting those attitudes or performing those actions in order to avoid something difficult or unpleasant. ❑ *We cannot make this minority a convenient excuse to turn our backs... It does seem a bit convenient, doesn't it?* ADJ disapproval ♦ **con|veni|ent|ly** *They've conveniently forgotten the risk of heart disease... Conveniently, he had developed amnesia about that part of his life.* ADV: usu ADV before v, also ADV with cl

**con|ven|or** /kənviːnər/ **(convenors)** also **convener**. [1] A **convenor** is a trade union official who organizes the union representatives at a particular factory. [BRIT] N-COUNT [2] A **convenor** is someone who convenes a meeting. N-COUNT

**con|vent** /kɒnvənt/ **(convents)** A **convent** is a building in which a community of nuns live. N-COUNT

**con|ven|tion** /kənvenʃən/ ◆◇◇ **(conventions)** [1] A **convention** is a way of behaving that is considered to be correct or polite by most people in a society. ❑ *It's just a social convention that men don't wear skirts... Despite her wish to defy convention,* N-VAR = custom *she had become pregnant and married at 21.* 2 In art, literature, or the theatre, a **convention** is a traditional method or style. ❑ *...the stylistic conventions of Egyptian art.* N-COUNT 3 A **convention** is an official agreement between countries or groups of people. ❑ *...the UN convention on climate change. ...the Geneva convention.* N-COUNT: oft n N 4 A **convention** is a large meeting of an organization or political group. ❑ *...the annual convention of the Society of Professional Journalists. ...the Republican convention.* N-COUNT = conference

**con|ven|tion|al** /kənvenʃənəl/ ◆◇◇ 1 Someone who is **conventional** has behaviour or opinions that are ordinary and normal. ❑ *...a respectable married woman with conventional opinions.* ADJ ≠ unconventional ♦ **con|ven|tion|al|ly** *People still wore their hair short and dressed conventionally.* ADV: usu ADV with v 2 A **conventional** method or product is one that is usually used or that has been in use for a long time. ❑ *...the risks and drawbacks of conventional family planning methods... These discs hold more than 400 times as much information as a conventional computer floppy disk.* ADJ: usu ADJ n = traditional ♦ **con|ven|tion|al|ly** *Organically grown produce does not differ greatly in appearance from conventionally grown crops.* ADV: ADV with v 3 **Conventional** weapons and wars do not involve nuclear explosives. ❑ *We must reduce the danger of war by controlling nuclear, chemical and conventional arms.* ADJ: usu ADJ n 4 **conventional wisdom** → see **wisdom**.

**con|ven|tion|eer** /kənvenʃənɪəʳ/ **(conventioneers)** **Conventioneers** are people who are attending a convention. [AM] N-COUNT: usu pl

**con|vent school** **(convent schools)** A **convent school** is a school where many of the teachers are nuns. N-COUNT

**con|verge** /kənvɜːʳdʒ/ **(converges, converging, converged)** 1 If people or vehicles **converge on** a place, they move towards it from different directions. ❑ *Competitors from more than a hundred countries have converged on Sheffield for the Games.* VERB V on n 2 If roads or lines **converge**, they meet or join at a particular place. [FORMAL] ❑ *As they flow south, the five rivers converge.* VERB ≠ diverge pl-n V 3 If different ideas or societies **converge**, they stop being different and become similar to each other. ❑ *Speeches delivered by Mr Dewar and Mr Wallace indicated their views were converging... The views of the richest householders converged with those of the poorest and created a new consensus.* V-RECIP ≠ diverge pl-n V V with n

**con|ver|gence** /kənvɜːʳdʒəns/ **(convergences)** The **convergence** of different ideas, groups, or societies is the process by which they stop being different and become more similar. [FORMAL] ❑ *...the need to move towards greater economic convergence.* N-VAR ≠ divergence

**con|ver|sant** /kənvɜːʳsənt/ If you are **conversant with** something, you are familiar with it and able to deal with it. [FORMAL] ❑ *Those in business are not, on the whole, conversant with basic scientific principles.* ADJ: v-link ADJ, usu ADJ with n

**con|ver|sa|tion** /kɒnvəʳseɪʃən/ **(conversations)** ◆◇◇ 1 If you have a **conversation with** someone, you talk with them, usually in an informal situation. ❑ *He's a talkative guy, and I struck up a conversation with him... I waited for her to finish a telephone conversation.* N-COUNT

PHRASES 2 If you say that people are **in conversation**, you mean that they are talking together. ❑ *When I arrived I found her in conversation with Mrs Williams.* PHRASE: v-link PHR 3 If you **make conversation**, you talk to someone in order to be polite and not because you really want to. ❑ *He had been trying to make conversation.* PHRASE: V inflects

**con|ver|sa|tion|al** /kɒnvəʳseɪʃənəl/ **Conversational** means relating to, or similar to, casual and informal talk. ❑ *His father wanted him to learn conversational German.* ADJ: usu ADJ n

**con|ver|sa|tion|al|ist** /kɒnvəʳseɪʃənəlɪst/ **(conversationalists)** A good **conversationalist** is someone who talks about interesting things when they have conversations. ❑ *Joan is a brilliant conversationalist.* N-COUNT: usu adj N

**con|verse** **(converses, conversing, conversed)**

> ✓ The verb is pronounced /kənvɜːʳs/. The noun is pronounced /kɒnvɜːʳs/.

1 If you **converse with** someone, you talk to them. You can also say that two people **converse**. [FORMAL] ❑ *Luke sat directly behind the pilot and conversed with him... They were conversing in German, their only common language.* V-RECIP V with n pl-n V 2 **The converse** of a statement is its opposite or reverse. [FORMAL] ❑ *What you do for a living is critical to where you settle and how you live - and the converse is also true.* N-SING: the N = opposite

**con|verse|ly** /kɒnvɜːʳsli, kənvɜːʳsli/ You say **conversely** to indicate that the situation you are about to describe is the opposite or reverse of the one you have just described. [FORMAL] ❑ *In real life, nobody was all bad, nor, conversely, all good.* ADV: ADV with cl

**con|ver|sion** /kənvɜːʳʃən/ **(conversions)** 1 **Conversion** is the act or process of changing something into a different state or form. ❑ *...the conversion of disused rail lines into cycle routes... A loft conversion can add considerably to the value of a house.* N-VAR: usu with supp 2 If someone changes their religion or beliefs, you can refer to their **conversion to** their new religion or beliefs. ❑ *...his conversion to Christianity... It's hard to trust the President's conversion.* N-VAR: usu with supp, oft with poss

**con|vert** **(converts, converting, converted)** ◆◇◇

> ✓ The verb is pronounced /kənvɜːʳt/. The noun is pronounced /kɒnvɜːʳt/.

1 If one thing **is converted** or **converts into** another, it is changed into a different form. ❑ *The signal will be converted into digital code. ...naturally occurring substances which the body can convert into vitamins. ...a table that converts into an ironing board.* VERB be V-ed into/to n V n into/to n V into/to n 2 If someone **converts** a room or building, they alter it in order to use it for a different purpose. ❑ *By converting the loft, they were able to have two extra bedrooms. ...the entrepreneur who wants to convert County Hall into an hotel... He is living in a converted barn.* VERB V n V n into n V-ed 3 If you **convert** a vehicle or piece of equipment, you change it so that it can use a different fuel. ❑ *Save money by converting your car to unleaded... The programme to convert every gas burner in Britain took 10 years.* VERB V n to/into n V n 4 If you **convert** a quantity **from** one system of measurement **to** another, you calculate what the quantity is in the second system. ❑ *Converting metric measurements to U.S. equivalents is easy.* VERB V n prep Also V n 5 If someone **converts** you, they persuade you to change your religious or political beliefs. You can also say that someone **converts to** a different religion. ❑ *If you try to convert him, you could find he just walks away... He was a major influence in converting Godwin to political radicalism... He converted to Catholicism in 1917.* VERB V n V n to n V to n 6 A **convert** is someone who has changed their religious or political beliefs. ❑ *She, too, was a convert to Roman Catholicism. ...a Muslim convert now known as Yusuf Islam.* N-COUNT: oft N to n 7 If someone **converts** you **to** something, they make you very enthusiastic about it. ❑ *He quickly converted me to the joys of cross-country skiing.* VERB V n to n Also V n 8 If you describe someone as a **convert to** something, you mean that they have recently become very enthusiastic about it. ❑ *...recent converts to vegetarianism.* N-COUNT: usu N to n 9 **to preach to the converted** → see **preach**.

**con|vert|er** /kənvɜːʳtəʳ/ **(converters)** A **converter** is a device that changes something into a different form. → See also **catalytic converter**. N-COUNT

**con|vert|ible** /kənvɜːʳtɪbəl/ **(convertibles)** 1 A **convertible** is a car with a soft roof that can be folded down or removed. ❑ *Her own car is a convertible Golf.* N-COUNT 2 In finance, **convertible** investments or money can be easily exchanged for other forms of investments or money. [BUSINESS] ❑ *...the introduction of a convertible currency.* ADJ ♦ **con|vert|ibil|ity** /kənvɜːʳtɪbɪlɪti/ *...the convertibility of the rouble. ...rapid export growth based on currency convertibility.* N-UNCOUNT

**con|vex** /kɒnveks/ **Convex** is used to describe something that curves outwards in the middle. ❑ *...the large convex mirror above the fireplace.* ADJ ≠ concave

**con|vey** /kənveɪ/ **(conveys, conveying, conveyed)** [1] To **convey** information or feelings means to cause them to be known or understood by someone. ❑ *In every one of her pictures she conveys a sense of immediacy... He also conveyed his views and the views of the bureaucracy.* VERB = communicate; V n; V n [2] To **convey** someone or something to a place means to carry or transport them there. [FORMAL] ❑ *The railway company extended a branch line to Brightlingsea to convey fish direct to Billingsgate.* VERB = transport; V n

**con|vey|ance** /kənveɪəns/ **(conveyances)** [1] A **conveyance** is a vehicle. [LITERARY] ❑ *Mahoney had never seen such a conveyance before.* N-COUNT = vehicle [2] The **conveyance** of something is the process of carrying or transporting it from one place to another. [FORMAL] ❑ *...the conveyance of bicycles on Regional Railways trains.* N-UNCOUNT: with supp = transport

**con|vey|anc|ing** /kənveɪənsɪŋ/ **Conveyancing** is the process of transferring the legal ownership of property. [mainly BRIT, LEGAL] N-UNCOUNT

**con|vey|or belt** /kənveɪəʳ belt/ **(conveyor belts)** [1] A **conveyor belt** or a **conveyor** is a continuously moving strip of rubber or metal which is used in factories for moving objects along so that they can be dealt with as quickly as possible. ❑ *The damp bricks went along a conveyor belt into another shed to dry.* N-COUNT [2] If you describe a situation as a **conveyor belt**, you dislike it because it produces things or people which are all the same or always deals with things or people in the same way. N-COUNT [disapproval]

**con|vict** **(convicts, convicting, convicted)** ◆◇◇

✓ The verb is pronounced /kənvɪkt/. The noun is pronounced /kɒnvɪkt/.

[1] If someone **is convicted of** a crime, they are found guilty of that crime in a law court. ❑ *In 1977 he was convicted of murder and sentenced to life imprisonment... There was insufficient evidence to convict him. ...a convicted drug dealer.* VERB; be V-ed of n/-ing; V n; V-ed [2] A **convict** is someone who is in prison. [JOURNALISM] N-COUNT = prisoner

**con|vic|tion** /kənvɪkʃᵊn/ **(convictions)** ◆◇◇ [1] A **conviction** is a strong belief or opinion. ❑ *It is our firm conviction that a step forward has been taken... Their religious convictions prevented them from taking up arms.* N-COUNT: usu N that = belief [2] If you have **conviction**, you have great confidence in your beliefs or opinions. ❑ *'We shall, sir,' said Thorne, with conviction.* N-UNCOUNT [3] If something **carries conviction**, it is likely to be true or likely to be believed. ❑ *Nor did his denial carry conviction.* PHRASE: V inflects [4] If someone has a **conviction**, they have been found guilty of a crime in a court of law. ❑ *He will appeal against his conviction.* N-COUNT

**con|vince** /kənvɪns/ **(convinces, convincing, convinced)** ◆◇◇ [1] If someone or something **convinces** you **of** something, they make you believe that it is true or that it exists. ❑ *Although I soon convinced him of my innocence, I think he still has serious doubts about my sanity... The waste disposal industry is finding it difficult to convince the public that its operations are safe.* VERB; V n of n; V n that [2] If someone or something **convinces** you **to** do something, they persuade you to do it. [mainly AM] ❑ *That weekend in Plattsburgh, he convinced her to go ahead and marry Bud.* VERB = persuade; V n to-inf

**con|vinced** /kənvɪnst/ If you are **convinced that** something is true, you feel sure that it is true. ❑ *He was convinced that I was part of the problem... He became convinced of the need for cheap editions of good quality writing.* ◆◇◇ ADJ: usu v-link ADJ, usu ADJ that, ADJ of n

**con|vinc|ing** /kənvɪnsɪŋ/ If you describe someone or something as **convincing**, you mean that they make you believe that a particular thing is true, correct, or genuine. ❑ *Scientists say there is no convincing evidence that power lines have anything to do with cancer... He sounded very convincing.* ADJ ≠ unconvincing ♦ **con|vinc|ing|ly** *He argued forcefully and convincingly that they were likely to bankrupt the budget.* ADV: usu ADV with v, also ADV adj

**con|viv|ial** /kənvɪviəl/ **Convivial** people or occasions are pleasant, friendly, and relaxed. [FORMAL] ❑ *...looking forward to a convivial evening... The atmosphere was quite convivial.* ADJ [approval]

**con|vo|ca|tion** /kɒnvəkeɪʃᵊn/ **(convocations)** A **convocation** is a meeting or ceremony attended by a large number of people. [FORMAL] ❑ *...a convocation of the American Youth Congress.* N-COUNT

**con|vo|lut|ed** /kɒnvəlu:tɪd/ If you describe a sentence, idea, or system as **convoluted**, you mean that it is complicated and difficult to understand. [FORMAL] ❑ *Despite its length and convoluted plot, 'Asta's Book' is a rich and rewarding read.* ADJ [disapproval] = complicated ≠ straightforward

**con|vo|lu|tion** /kɒnvəlu:ʃᵊn/ **(convolutions)** [1] **Convolutions** are curves on an object or design that has a lot of curves. [LITERARY] N-COUNT: usu pl [2] You can use **convolutions** to refer to a situation that is very complicated. [LITERARY] ❑ *...the thorny convolutions of love.* N-VAR: oft N of n

**con|voy** /kɒnvɔɪ/ **(convoys)** A **convoy** is a group of vehicles or ships travelling together. ❑ *...a U.N. convoy carrying food and medical supplies... They travel in convoy with armed guards.* N-COUNT: also in N

**con|vulse** /kənvʌls/ **(convulses, convulsing, convulsed)** If someone **convulses** or if they **are convulsed by** or **with** something, their body moves suddenly in an uncontrolled way. ❑ *Olivia's face convulsed in a series of twitches... He let out a cry that convulsed his bulky frame and jerked his arm... The opposing team were so convulsed with laughter that they almost forgot to hit the ball.* VERB; V; V n; be V-ed with n

**con|vul|sion** /kənvʌlʃᵊn/ **(convulsions)** [1] If someone has **convulsions**, they suffer uncontrollable movements of their muscles. N-COUNT [2] If there are **convulsions** in a country, system, or organization, there are major unexpected changes in it. ❑ *...the political convulsions that led to de Gaulle's return to power in May 1958.* N-COUNT

**con|vul|sive** /kənvʌlsɪv/ A **convulsive** movement or action is sudden and cannot be controlled. [FORMAL] ❑ *She thought she could never stop until convulsive sobs racked her even more.* ADJ: usu ADJ n

**coo** /ku:/ **(coos, cooing, cooed)** [1] When a dove or pigeon **coos**, it makes the soft sounds that doves and pigeons typically make. ❑ *Pigeons fluttered in and out, cooing gently.* VERB; V [2] When someone **coos**, they speak in a very soft, quiet voice which is intended to sound attractive. ❑ *She paused to coo at the baby... 'Isn't this marvelous?' she cooed.* VERB; V at/over n; V with quote

**cook** /kʊk/ **(cooks, cooking, cooked)** ◆◆◇ [1] When you **cook** a meal, you prepare food for eating by heating it. ❑ *I have to go and cook the dinner... Chefs at the St James Court restaurant have cooked for the Queen... We'll cook them a nice Italian meal.* VERB; V n; V; V n n ♦ **cook|ing** *Her hobbies include music, dancing, sport and cooking.* N-UNCOUNT [2] When you **cook** food, or when food **cooks**, it is heated until it is ready to be eaten. ❑ *...some basic instructions on how to cook a turkey... Let the vegetables cook gently for about 10 minutes... Drain the pasta as soon as it is cooked.* VERB; V n; V; V-ed [3] A **cook** is a person whose job is to prepare and cook food, especially in someone's home or in an institution. ❑ *They had a butler, a cook, and a maid.* N-COUNT = chef [4] If you say that someone is a good **cook**, you mean they are good at preparing and cooking food. N-COUNT: adj N [5] If you say that someone **has cooked the books**, you mean that they have changed figures or a written record in order to deceive people. [INFORMAL] PHRASE: V inflects [6] → See also **cooking**.

♦ **cook up** [1] If someone **cooks up** a dishonest scheme, they plan it. [INFORMAL] ❑ *He must have cooked up his scheme on the spur of the moment.* PHRASAL VERB; V P n (not pron); Also V n P [2] If someone **cooks up** an explanation or a story, they make it up. [INFORMAL] ❑ *She'll cook up a convincing explanation.* PHRASAL VERB; V P n (not pron); Also V n P

**cook|book** /kʊkbʊk/ **(cookbooks)** also **cook-book**. A **cookbook** is a book that contains recipes for preparing food. N-COUNT

**cook|er** /kʊkəʳ/ **(cookers)** A **cooker** is a large metal device for cooking food using gas or electricity. A cooker usually consists of a grill, an oven, and some gas or electric rings. [BRIT] ❑ *...a gas cooker.* ➔ See also **pressure cooker**. N-COUNT

✔ in AM, usually use **stove**

**cook|ery** /kʊkəri/ **Cookery** is the activity of preparing and cooking food. N-UNCOUNT

**cook|ery book** **(cookery books)** A **cookery book** is the same as a **cookbook**. [BRIT] N-COUNT

**cookie** /kʊki/ **(cookies)** [1] A **cookie** is a sweet biscuit. [mainly AM] [2] If you say that someone is a **tough cookie**, you mean that they have a strong and determined character. [INFORMAL] [3] A **cookie** is a piece of computer software which enables a website you have visited to recognize you if you visit it again. [COMPUTING] N-COUNT; PHRASE: N inflects; N-COUNT

**cook|ing** /kʊkɪŋ/ [1] **Cooking** is food which has been cooked. ❑ *The menu is based on classic French cooking.* [2] **Cooking** ingredients or equipment are used in cookery. ❑ *Finely slice the cooking apples. ...cooking pots.* [3] ➔ See also **cook**. ◆◇◇ N-UNCOUNT: usu supp N; ADJ: ADJ n

**cook|out** /kʊkaʊt/ **(cookouts)** A **cookout** is the same as a **barbecue**. [AM] N-COUNT

**cook|top** /kʊktɒp/ **(cooktops)** A **cooktop** is a surface on top of a cooker or set into a work surface, which can be heated in order to cook things on it. [mainly AM] N-COUNT

**cook|ware** /kʊkweəʳ/ **Cookware** is the range of pans and pots which are used in cooking. ❑ *...several lines of popular cookware and utensils.* N-UNCOUNT

**cool** /kuːl/ **(cooler, coolest, cools, cooling, cooled)** [1] Something that is **cool** has a temperature which is low but not very low. ❑ *I felt a current of cool air... The vaccines were kept cool in refrigerators.* [2] If it is **cool**, or if a place is **cool**, the temperature of the air is low but not very low. ❑ *Thank goodness it's cool in here... Store grains and cereals in a cool, dry place. ...a cool November evening.* ♦ **Cool** is also a noun. ❑ *She walked into the cool of the hallway.* [3] Clothing that is **cool** is made of thin material so that you do not become too hot in hot weather. ❑ *In warm weather, you should wear clothing that is cool and comfortable.* [4] **Cool** colours are light colours which give an impression of coolness. ❑ *Choose a cool colour such as cream.* [5] When something **cools** or when you **cool** it, it becomes lower in temperature. ❑ *Drain the meat and allow it to cool... Huge fans will have to cool the concrete floor to keep it below 150 degrees. ...a cooling breeze.* ♦ To **cool down** means the same as to **cool**. ❑ *Avoid putting your car away until the engine has cooled down... The other main way the body cools itself down is by panting.* [6] When a feeling or emotion **cools**, or when you **cool** it, it becomes less powerful. ❑ *Within a few minutes tempers had cooled... His weird behaviour had cooled her passion.* [7] If you say that a person or their behaviour is **cool**, you mean that they are calm and unemotional, especially in a difficult situation. ❑ *He was marvelously cool again, smiling as if nothing had happened.* ♦ **cool|ly** *Everyone must think this situation through calmly and coolly. ...coolly 'objective' professionals.* [8] If you say that a person or their behaviour is **cool**, you mean that they are unfriendly or not enthusiastic. ❑ *I didn't like him at all. I thought he was cool, aloof, and arrogant... The idea met with a cool response.* ♦ **cool|ly** *'It's your choice, Nina,' David said coolly.* [9] If you say that a person or their behaviour is **cool**, you mean that they are fashionable and attractive. [INFORMAL] ❑ *He was trying to be really cool and trendy.* [10] If you say that someone is **cool about** something, you mean that they accept it and are not angry or upset about it. [mainly AM, INFORMAL] ❑ *Bev was really cool about it all.* [11] If you say that something is **cool**, you think it is very good. [INFORMAL] ❑ *Kathleen gave me a really cool dress.* [12] You can use **cool** to emphasize that an amount or figure is very large, especially when it has been obtained easily. [INFORMAL] ❑ *Columbia recently re-signed the band for a cool $30 million.*

◆◆◇ ADJ ≠ warm; ADJ: oft *it* v-link ADJ ≠ warm; N-SING: *the* N, oft N *of* n; ADJ ≠ warm; ADJ: ADJ n ≠ warm; VERB V, V n, V-ing; PHRASAL VERB V P, V n P; VERB V, V n; ADJ approval = calm; ADV; ADJ; ADV: ADV with v, also ADV adj; ADJ approval; ADJ: v-link ADJ, oft ADJ *about* n approval; ADJ = neat; ADJ: ADJ n emphasis

PHRASES [13] If you **keep** your **cool** in a difficult situation, you manage to remain calm. If you **lose** your **cool**, you get angry or upset. [INFORMAL] ❑ *She kept her cool and managed to get herself out of the ordeal.* [14] If you **play it cool**, you deliberately behave in a calm, unemotional way because you do not want people to know you are enthusiastic or angry about something. [INFORMAL] ❑ *It's ridiculous to play it cool if someone you're mad about is mad about you too.* [15] **as cool as a cucumber** ➔ see **cucumber**. PHRASE: V inflects; PHRASE: V inflects

♦ **cool down** [1] ➔ see **cool 5**. [2] If someone **cools down** or if you **cool** them **down**, they become less angry than they were. ❑ *He has had time to cool down and look at what happened more objectively... First McNeil had to cool down the volatile Australian 20-year old.* PHRASAL VERB = calm down; V P; V P n (not pron)

♦ **cool off** If someone or something **cools off**, or if you **cool** them **off**, they become cooler after having been hot. ❑ *Maybe he's trying to cool off out there in the rain... She made a fanning motion, pretending to cool herself off... Cool off the carrots quickly.* PHRASAL VERB; V P; V n P; V P n (not pron)

**cool|ant** /kuːlənt/ **(coolants)** **Coolant** is a liquid used to keep a machine or engine cool while it is operating. N-MASS

**cool|er** /kuːləʳ/ **(coolers)** A **cooler** is a container for keeping things cool, especially drinks. ➔ See also **cool**. N-COUNT = cool box

**cool-headed** If you describe someone as **cool-headed**, you mean that they stay calm in difficult situations. ❑ *She has a reputation for being calm and cool-headed. ...a cool-headed, responsible statesman.* ADJ approval = calm

**cooling-off period** **(cooling-off periods)** A **cooling-off period** is an agreed period of time during which two sides with opposing views try to resolve a dispute before taking any serious action. ❑ *There should be a seven-day cooling-off period between a strike ballot and industrial action.* N-COUNT

**cool|ing tow|er** **(cooling towers)** A **cooling tower** is a very large, round, high building which is used to cool water from factories or power stations. ❑ *...landscapes dominated by cooling towers and factory chimneys.* N-COUNT

**coon** /kuːn/ **(coons)** [1] A **coon** is a **raccoon**. [AM, INFORMAL] [2] **Coon** is an extremely offensive word for a black person. [INFORMAL, ⚠ VERY OFFENSIVE] N-COUNT; N-COUNT

**coop** /kuːp/ **(coops)** A **coop** is a cage where you keep small animals or birds such as chickens and rabbits. N-COUNT

**co-op** **(co-ops)** A **co-op** is a co-operative. [INFORMAL] ❑ *The co-op sells the art work at exhibitions.* N-COUNT

**cooped up** /kuːpt ʌp/ If you say that someone is **cooped up**, you mean that they live or are kept in a place which is too small, or which does not allow them much freedom. ❑ *He is cooped up in a cramped cell with 10 other inmates.* ADJ: v-link ADJ

**coop|er** /kuːpəʳ/ **(coopers)** A **cooper** is a person who makes barrels. [OLD-FASHIONED] N-COUNT

**co-operate** **(co-operates, co-operating, co-operated)** also **cooperate**. [1] If you **co-operate with** someone, you work with them or help them for a particular purpose. You can also say that two people **co-operate**. ❑ *The UN had been co-operating with the State Department on a plan to find countries willing to take the refugees... The couple spoke about how they would co-operate in the raising of their child.* ♦ **co-operation** *A deal with Japan could indeed open the door to economic co-operation with East Asia.* [2] If you **co-operate**, you do what someone has asked or told you to do. ❑ *He agreed to co-operate with the police investigation... The plan failed because the soldiers refused to co-operate.* ♦ **co-operation** *The police underlined the importance of the public's co-operation in the hunt for the bombers.* ◆◇◇ V-RECIP; V with n; pl-n V; N-UNCOUNT; VERB; V with n; V; N-UNCOUNT = assistance

**co-operative** **(co-operatives)** also **cooperative.** 1 A **co-operative** is a business or organization run by the people who work for it, or owned by the people who use it. These people share its benefits and profits. [BUSINESS] ❑ *They decided a housing co-operative was the way to regenerate Ormiston Crescent... The restaurant is run as a cooperative.* 2 A **co-operative** activity is done by people working together. ❑ *He was transferred to FBI custody in a smooth co-operative effort between Egyptian and US authorities.* ♦ **co-operatively** *They agreed to work co-operatively to ease tensions wherever possible.* 3 If you say that someone is **co-operative**, you mean that they do what you ask them to without complaining or arguing. ❑ *I made every effort to be co-operative.*
N-COUNT = collective; ADJ: usu ADJ n; ADV: ADV after v; ADJ = obliging

**co-operative so|ci|ety** **(co-operative societies)** In Britain, a **co-operative society** is a commercial organization with several shops in a particular district. Customers can join this organization and get a share of its profits.
N-COUNT = co-op

**co-opt** **(co-opts, co-opting, co-opted)** 1 If you **co-opt** someone, you persuade them to help or support you. ❑ *Mr Wallace tries to co-opt rather than defeat his critics.* 2 If someone **is co-opted into** a group, they are asked by that group to become a member, rather than joining or being elected in the normal way. ❑ *He was co-opted into the Labour Government of 1964... He's been authorised to co-opt anyone he wants to join him.* 3 If a group or political party **co-opts** a slogan or policy, they take it, often from another group or political party, and use it themselves. ❑ *He co-opted many nationalist slogans and cultivated a populist image.*
VERB; V n; VERB; be V-ed into/onto n; V n; VERB; V n

**co-ordinate** **(co-ordinates, co-ordinating, coordinated)** also **coordinate.**

> The verb is pronounced /koʊɔːʳdɪneɪt/. The noun is pronounced /koʊɔːʳdɪnət/.

1 If you **co-ordinate** an activity, you organize the various people and things involved in it. ❑ *Government officials visited the earthquake zone on Thursday morning to co-ordinate the relief effort.* ♦ **co-ordinated** *...a rapid and well co-ordinated international rescue operation.* ♦ **co-ordinator** **(coordinators)** *...the party's campaign co-ordinator, Mr Peter Mandelson.* 2 If you **co-ordinate** clothes or furnishings that are used together, or if they **coordinate**, they are similar in some way and look nice together. ❑ *She'll show you how to co-ordinate pattern and colours... Tie it with fabric bows that coordinate with other furnishings... Colours and looks must fit the themes of the seasons so that the shops co-ordinate well. ...curtains and co-ordinating bed covers.* 3 **Co-ordinates** are pieces of clothing or soft furnishings which are similar and which are intended to be worn or used together. ❑ *...new lingerie co-ordinates.* 4 If you **co-ordinate** the different parts of your body, you make them work together efficiently to perform particular movements. ❑ *They spend several weeks each year undergoing intensive treatment which enables them to coordinate their limbs better.* 5 The **co-ordinates** of a point on a map or graph are the two sets of numbers or letters that you need in order to find that point. [TECHNICAL] ❑ *Can you give me your coordinates?*
VERB; V n; ADJ; N-COUNT: usu with supp; V-RECIP; V pl-n; V with n; pl-n V; V-ing; N-PLURAL; VERB; V n; N-COUNT: usu pl

**co-ordinating con|junc|tion** **(coordinating conjunctions)** A **co-ordinating conjunction** is a word such as 'and', 'or', or 'but' which joins two or more words, groups, or clauses of equal status, for example two main clauses. Compare **subordinating conjunction**. [TECHNICAL]
N-COUNT

**co-ordination** 1 **Co-ordination** means organizing the activities of two or more groups so that they work together efficiently and know what the others are doing. ❑ *...the lack of coordination between the civilian and military authorities.* ● If you do something **in co-ordination with** someone else, you both organize your activities so that you work together efficiently. ❑ *...operating either in coordination with federal troops or alone.* 2 **Co-ordination** is the ability to use the different parts of your body together efficiently. ❑ *To improve hand-eye co-ordination, practise throwing and catching balls.*
N-UNCOUNT: oft N between/of n; PREP-PHRASE; N-UNCOUNT

**coot** /kuːt/ **(coots)** A **coot** is a water bird with black feathers and a white patch on its forehead.
N-COUNT

**cop** /kɒp/ **(cops)** A **cop** is a policeman or policewoman. [INFORMAL] ❑ *Frank didn't like having the cops know where to find him.*
N-COUNT

**cope** /koʊp/ **(copes, coping, coped)** 1 If you **cope with** a problem or task, you deal with it successfully. ❑ *It was amazing how my mother coped with bringing up three children on less than three pounds a week... The problems were an annoyance, but we managed to cope.* 2 If you have to **cope with** an unpleasant situation, you have to accept it or bear it. ❑ *She has had to cope with losing all her previous status and money.* 3 If a machine or a system can **cope with** something, it is large enough or complex enough to deal with it satisfactorily. ❑ *New blades have been designed to cope with the effects of dead insects... The speed of economic change has been so great that the tax-collecting system has been unable to cope.*
◆◇◇ VERB = manage; V with n/-ing; V; VERB = contend; V with n/-ing; VERB; V with n; V

**copi|er** /kɒpiəʳ/ **(copiers)** 1 A **copier** is a machine which makes exact copies of writing or pictures on paper, usually by a photographic process. 2 A **copier** is someone who copies what someone else has done. ❑ *...their reputation as a copier of other countries' designs, patents, and inventions.*
N-COUNT = photocopier; N-COUNT

**co-pilot** **(co-pilots)** The **co-pilot** of an aircraft is a pilot who assists the chief pilot.
N-COUNT

**co|pi|ous** /koʊpiəs/ A **copious** amount of something is a large amount of it. ❑ *I went out for a meal last night and drank copious amounts of red wine... He attended his lectures and took copious notes.* ♦ **co|pi|ous|ly** *Some of the victims were bleeding copiously.*
ADJ: usu ADJ n = abundant; ADV: ADV after v, ADV -ed

**cop-out** **(cop-outs)** If you refer to something as a **cop-out**, you think that it is a way for someone to avoid doing something that they should do. [INFORMAL] ❑ *To decline to vote is a cop-out... The film's ending is an unsatisfactory cop-out.*
N-COUNT: usu sing [disapproval]

**cop|per** /kɒpəʳ/ **(coppers)** 1 **Copper** is reddish brown metal that is used to make things such as coins and electrical wires. ❑ *Chile is the world's largest producer of copper. ...a copper mine.* 2 **Copper** is sometimes used to describe things that are reddish-brown in colour. [LITERARY] ❑ *His hair has reverted back to its original copper hue.* 3 A **copper** is a policeman or a policewoman. [BRIT, INFORMAL] ❑ *...your friendly neighbourhood copper.*
N-UNCOUNT; ADJ: usu ADJ n; N-COUNT

**copper-bottomed** If you describe something as **copper-bottomed**, you believe that it is certain to be successful. [BRIT] ❑ *Their copperbottomed scheme went badly wrong.*
ADJ: usu ADJ n

**cop|pery** /kɒpəri/ A **coppery** colour is reddish-brown like copper. ❑ *...pale coppery leaves.*
ADJ: usu ADJ n

**cop|pice** /kɒpɪs/ **(coppices, coppicing, coppiced)** 1 A **coppice** is a small group of trees growing very close to each other. [BRIT] ❑ *...coppices of willow.*
N-COUNT = copse

> in AM, use **copse**

2 To **coppice** trees or bushes means to cut off parts of them, in order to make them look more attractive or to make it easier to obtain wood from them. [mainly BRIT, TECHNICAL] ❑ *It is best to coppice the trees in the winter before the sap rises. ...extensive oak woods with coppiced hazel and sweet chestnut. ...areas where coppicing of hawthorn and hazel occurs.*
VERB; V n; V-ed; V-ing

**cops-and-robbers** A **cops-and-robbers** film, television programme, or book is one whose story involves the police trying to catch criminals.
ADJ: ADJ n

**copse** /kɒps/ **(copses)** A **copse** is a small group of trees growing very close to each other. ❑ *...a little copse of fir trees.*
N-COUNT

**cop|ter** /kɒptəʳ/ **(copters)** A **copter** is a helicopter. [INFORMAL] N-COUNT

**Cop|tic** /kɒptɪk/ **Coptic** means belonging or relating to a part of the Christian Church which was started in Egypt. ❑ *The Coptic Church is among the oldest churches of Christianity.* ADJ: ADJ n

**copu|la** /kɒpjʊlə/ **(copulas)** A **copula** is the same as a **linking verb**. N-COUNT

**copu|late** /kɒpjʊleɪt/ **(copulates, copulating, copulated)** If one animal or person **copulates with** another, they have sex. You can also say that two animals or people copulate. [TECHNICAL] ❑ *During the time she is paired to a male, the female allows no other males to copulate with her... Whales take twenty-four hours to copulate.* ♦ **copu|la|tion** /kɒpjʊleɪʃ^ə^n/ **(copulations)** *...acts of copulation.* V-RECIP V with n pl-n V N-VAR

**copy** /kɒpi/ **(copies, copying, copied)** [1] If you make a **copy of** something, you produce something that looks like the original thing. ❑ *The reporter apparently obtained a copy of Steve's resignation letter.* [2] If you **copy** something, you produce something that looks like the original thing. ❑ *She never participated in obtaining or copying any classified documents for anyone. ...top designers, whose work has been widely copied... He copied the chart from a book.* [3] If you **copy** a piece of writing, you write it again exactly. ❑ *He would allow John slyly to copy his answers to impossibly difficult algebra questions... He copied the data into a notebook... We're copying from textbooks because we don't have enough to go round.* ♦ **Copy out** means the same as **copy**. ❑ *He wrote the title on the blackboard, then copied out the text sentence by sentence... 'Did he leave a phone number?' — 'Oh, yes.' She copied it out for him.* [4] If you **copy** a person or what they do, you try to do what they do or try to be like them, usually because you admire them or what they have done. ❑ *Children can be seen to copy the behaviour of others whom they admire or identify with. ...the coquettish gestures she had copied from actresses in soap operas.* ♦ **copy|ing** *Children learn by copying.* [5] A **copy of** a book, newspaper, or CD is one of many that are exactly the same. ❑ *I bought a copy of 'USA Today' from a street-corner machine... You can obtain a copy for $2 from New York Central Art Supply.* [6] In journalism, **copy** is written material that is ready to be printed or read in a broadcast. [TECHNICAL] ❑ *...his ability to write the most lyrical copy in the history of sports television. ...advertising copy.* [7] In journalism, **copy** is news or information that can be used in an article in a newspaper. [TECHNICAL] ❑ *...journalists looking for good copy.* [8] → See also **back copy**, **carbon copy**, **hard copy**. ◆◆◇ N-COUNT: usu N of n = duplicate VERB V n V n V n from n VERB V n V n into n V from n PHRASAL VERB V P n (not pron) V n P VERB = imitate V n V n from n N-UNCOUNT N-COUNT: oft N of n N-UNCOUNT N-UNCOUNT

**copy|book** /kɒpibʊk/ [1] A **copybook** action is done perfectly, according to established rules. [mainly BRIT] ❑ *Yuri gave a copybook display.* [2] If you **blot** your **copybook**, you spoil your good reputation by doing something wrong. [mainly BRIT] ❑ *Alec blotted his copybook – got sent home for bad behaviour.* ADJ: usu ADJ n PHRASE: V inflects

**copy|cat** /kɒpikæt/ **(copycats)** also **copy-cat.** [1] A **copycat** crime is committed by someone who is copying someone else. ❑ *...a series of copycat attacks by hooligan gangs.* [2] If you call someone a **copycat**, you are accusing them of copying your behaviour, dress, or ideas. [INFORMAL] ❑ *The Beatles have copycats all over the world.* ADJ: ADJ n N-COUNT [disapproval]

**copy|ist** /kɒpiɪst/ **(copyists)** A **copyist** copies other people's music or paintings or, in the past, made written copies of documents. ❑ *She copies the true artist's signature as part of a painting, as do most copyists.* N-COUNT

**copy|right** /kɒpiraɪt/ **(copyrights)** If someone has **copyright** on a piece of writing or music, it is illegal to reproduce or perform it without their permission. ❑ *To order a book one first had to get permission from the monastery that held the copyright... She threatened legal action against the Sun for breach of copyright.* N-VAR

**copy|right|ed** /kɒpiraɪtɪd/ **Copyrighted** material is protected by a copyright. ❑ *They used copyrighted music without permission.* ADJ

**copy|writer** /kɒpiraɪtəʳ/ **(copywriters)** A **copywriter** is a person whose job is to write the words for advertisements. N-COUNT

**co|quette** /kɒket, AM koʊ-/ **(coquettes)** A **coquette** is a woman who behaves in a coquettish way. N-COUNT = flirt

**co|quet|tish** /kɒketɪʃ, AM koʊ-/ If you describe a woman as **coquettish**, you mean she acts in a playful way that is intended to make men find her attractive. ❑ *...a coquettish glance.* ADJ = flirtatious

**cor** /kɔːʳ/ You can say **cor** when you are surprised or impressed. [BRIT, INFORMAL] EXCLAM [feelings]

**cora|cle** /kɒrək^ə^l, AM kɔː-/ **(coracles)** In former times, a **coracle** was a simple round rowing boat made of woven sticks covered with animal skins. N-COUNT

**cor|al** /kɒrəl, AM kɔː-/ **(corals)** [1] **Coral** is a hard substance formed from the bones of very small sea animals. It is often used to make jewellery. ❑ *The women have elaborate necklaces of turquoise and pink coral.* [2] **Corals** are very small sea animals. [3] Something that is **coral** is dark orangey-pink in colour. ❑ *...coral lipstick. ...the coral-colored flower buds.* N-VAR N-COUNT COLOUR

**cor|al reef (coral reefs)** A **coral reef** is a long narrow mass of coral and other substances, the top of which is usually just above or just below the surface of the sea. ❑ *An unspoilt coral reef encloses the bay.* N-COUNT

**cord** /kɔːʳd/ **(cords)** [1] **Cord** is strong, thick string. ❑ *The door had been tied shut with a length of nylon cord. ...gilded cords and tassels.* [2] **Cord** is wire covered in rubber or plastic which connects electrical equipment to an electricity supply. → See picture on page 1709. ❑ *...electrical cord... We used so many lights that we needed four extension cords.* [3] **Cords** are trousers made of **corduroy**. ❑ *He had bare feet, a T-shirt and cords on.* [4] **Cord** means made of **corduroy**. ❑ *...a pair of cord trousers.* [5] → See also **spinal cord**, **umbilical cord**, **vocal cords**. N-VAR N-VAR = cable, flex N-PLURAL: also a pair of N ADJ: ADJ n

**cor|dial** /kɔːʳdiəl, AM -dʒəl/ **(cordials)** [1] **Cordial** means friendly. [FORMAL] ❑ *He had never known him to be so chatty and cordial.* ♦ **cor|di|al|ly** *They all greeted me very cordially.* [2] **Cordial** is a sweet non-alcoholic drink made from fruit juice. [BRIT] ADJ ≠ hostile ADV: ADV with v N-MASS

**cord|ite** /kɔːʳdaɪt/ **Cordite** is an explosive substance used in guns and bombs. N-UNCOUNT

**cord|less** /kɔːʳdləs/ A **cordless** telephone or piece of electric equipment is operated by a battery fitted inside it and is not connected to the electricity mains. ❑ *The waitress approached Picone with a cordless phone.* ADJ: usu ADJ n

**cor|don** /kɔːʳd^ə^n/ **(cordons, cordoning, cordoned)** A **cordon** is a line or ring of police, soldiers, or vehicles preventing people from entering or leaving an area. ❑ *Police formed a cordon between the two crowds.* N-COUNT

♦ **cordon off** If police or soldiers **cordon off** an area, they prevent people from entering or leaving it, usually by forming a line or ring. ❑ *Police cordoned off part of the city centre... The police cordoned everything off.* PHRASAL VERB = close off V P n (not pron) V n P

**cor|don bleu** /kɔːʳdɒn blɜː/ **Cordon bleu** is used to describe cookery or cooks of the highest standard. ❑ *I took a cordon bleu cookery course.* ADJ: ADJ n

**cor|du|roy** /kɔːʳdərɔɪ/ **(corduroys)** [1] **Corduroy** is thick cotton cloth with parallel raised lines on the outside. ❑ *...a corduroy jacket.* [2] **Corduroys** are trousers made out of corduroy. N-UNCOUNT N-PLURAL

**core** /kɔːʳ/ **(cores, coring, cored)** [1] The **core** of a fruit is the central part of it. It contains seeds or pips. → See picture on page 1711. ❑ *Peel the pears and remove the cores.* [2] If you **core** a fruit, you remove its core. ❑ *...machines for peeling and coring apples.* [3] The **core** of an object, building, ◆◇◇ N-COUNT: oft n N VERB V n N-COUNT:

or city is the central part of it. ❑ *...the earth's core... The core of the city is a series of ancient squares.* usu with poss = centre
4 **The core of** something such as a problem or an issue is the part of it that has to be understood or accepted before the whole thing can be understood or dealt with. ❑ *...the ability to get straight to the core of a problem.* N-SING: the N, usu N *of* n = heart
5 A **core** team or a **core** group is a group of people who do the main part of a job or piece of work. Other people may also help, but only for limited periods of time. ❑ *We already have our core team in place... A core of about six staff would continue with the project.* N-SING: N n, N *of* n
6 In a school or college, **core** subjects are a group of subjects that have to be studied. ❑ *The core subjects are English, mathematics and science. ...a core of nine academic subjects.* N-SING: usu N n
7 The **core** businesses or the **core** activities of a company or organization are their most important ones. ❑ *The group plans to concentrate on six core businesses... However, the main core of the company performed outstandingly.* N-SING: usu N n
8 → See also **hard core**, **hard-core**, **soft-core**.
PHRASES 9 You can use **to the core** to describe someone who is a very strong supporter of someone or something and will never change their views. For example, you can say that someone is Republican **to the core**. ❑ *The villagers are royalist to the core.* PHRASE: adj/n PHR = through and through
10 If someone is shaken **to the core** or shocked **to the core**, they are extremely shaken or shocked. ❑ *Leonard was shaken to the core; he'd never seen or read anything like it.* PHRASE: usu -ed PHR

**co-religionist** **(co-religionists)**

✔ in AM, usually use **coreligionist**

A person's **co-religionists** are people who have the same religion. [FORMAL] ❑ *They will turn for help to their co-religionists in the Middle East.* N-COUNT: usu pl, oft poss N

**cor|gi** /kɔːʳgi/ **(corgis)** A **corgi** is a type of small dog with short legs and a pointed nose. N-COUNT

**co|ri|an|der** /kɒriændəʳ, AM kɔː-/ **Coriander** is a plant with seeds that are used as a spice and leaves that are used as a herb. N-UNCOUNT

**cork** /kɔːʳk/ **(corks)** 1 **Cork** is a soft, light substance which forms the bark of a type of Mediterranean tree. ❑ *...cork floors. ...cork-soled clogs.* N-UNCOUNT
2 A **cork** is a piece of cork or plastic that is pushed into the opening of a bottle to close it. N-COUNT

**cork|er** /kɔːʳkəʳ/ **(corkers)** If you say that someone or something is a **corker**, you mean that they are very good. [BRIT, INFORMAL, OLD-FASHIONED] N-COUNT

**cork|screw** /kɔːʳkskruː/ **(corkscrews)** A **corkscrew** is a device for pulling corks out of bottles. → See picture on page 1710. N-COUNT

**cor|mo|rant** /kɔːʳmərənt/ **(cormorants)** A **cormorant** is a type of dark-coloured bird with a long neck. Cormorants usually live near the sea and eat fish. N-COUNT

**corn** /kɔːʳn/ **(corns)** 1 **Corn** is used to refer to crops such as wheat and barley. It can also be used to refer to the seeds from these plants. [BRIT] ❑ *...fields of corn... He filled the barn to the roof with corn.* N-UNCOUNT

✔ in AM, use **grain**

2 **Corn** is the same as **maize**. ❑ *...rows of corn in an Iowa field.* N-UNCOUNT
3 **Corns** are small, painful areas of hard skin which can form on your foot, especially near your toes. N-COUNT: usu pl
4 → See also **popcorn**, **sweetcorn**.

**corn|bread** /kɔːʳnbred/ also **corn bread. Cornbread** is bread made from ground maize or corn. It is popular in the United States. N-UNCOUNT

**corn cob** **(corn cobs)** also **corncob. Corn cobs** are the long rounded parts of the maize or corn plant on which small yellow seeds grow, and which is eaten as a vegetable. N-COUNT: usu pl

**cor|nea** /kɔːʳniə/ **(corneas)** The **cornea** is the transparent skin covering the outside of your eye. N-COUNT

**cor|neal** /kɔːʳniəl/ **Corneal** means relating to the cornea. ❑ *...corneal scars.* ADJ: ADJ n

**corned beef** /kɔːʳnd biːf/ **Corned beef** is beef which has been cooked and preserved in salt water. N-UNCOUNT

**cor|ner** /kɔːʳnəʳ/ **(corners, cornering, cornered)** ◆◆◇ 1 A **corner** is a point or an area where two or more edges, sides, or surfaces of something join. ❑ *He saw the corner of a magazine sticking out from under the blanket... Write 'By Airmail' in the top left hand corner.* N-COUNT: usu with supp
2 The **corner** of a room, box, or similar space is the area inside it where its edges or walls meet. ❑ *...a card table in the corner of the living room... The ball hurtled into the far corner of the net... Finally I spotted it, in a dark corner over by the piano.* N-COUNT
3 The **corner of** your mouth or eye is the side of it. ❑ *Out of the corner of her eye she saw that a car had stopped.* N-COUNT: usu sing, oft N *of* n
4 The **corner** of a street is the place where one of its sides ends as it joins another street. ❑ *We can't have police officers on every corner... He waited until the man had turned a corner.* N-COUNT: usu with supp
5 A **corner** is a bend in a road. ❑ *...a sharp corner.* N-COUNT = bend
6 In football, hockey, and some other sports, a **corner** is a free shot or kick taken from the corner of the pitch. N-COUNT
7 If you **corner** a person or animal, you force them into a place they cannot escape from. ❑ *A police motor-cycle chased his car twelve miles, and cornered him near Rome... He was still sitting huddled like a cornered animal.* VERB V n V-ed
8 If you **corner** someone, you force them to speak to you when they have been trying to avoid you. ❑ *Golan managed to corner the young producer-director for an interview.* VERB V n
9 If a company or place **corners** an area of trade, they gain control over it so that no one else can have any success in that area. [BUSINESS] ❑ *This restaurant has cornered the Madrid market for specialist paellas.* VERB = monopolize V n
10 If a car, or the person driving it, **corners** in a particular way, the car goes round bends in roads in this way. ❑ *Peter drove jerkily, cornering too fast and fumbling the gears.* VERB V adv/prep
PHRASES 11 If you say that something is **around the corner**, you mean that it will happen very soon. In British English, you can also say that something is **round the corner**. ❑ *The Chancellor of the Exchequer says that economic recovery is just around the corner.* PHRASE: usu v-link PHR = imminent
12 If you say that something is **around the corner**, you mean that it is very near. In British English, you can also say that something is **round the corner**. ❑ *My new place is just around the corner.* PHRASE: v-link PHR, PHR after v
13 If you **cut corners**, you do something quickly by doing it in a less thorough way than you should. ❑ *Take your time, don't cut corners and follow instructions to the letter.* PHRASE: V inflects [disapproval]
14 You can use expressions such as **the four corners of the world** to refer to places that are a long way from each other. [WRITTEN] ❑ *They've combed the four corners of the world for the best accessories.* PHRASE: PHR n
15 If you are **in a corner** or **in a tight corner**, you are in a situation which is difficult to deal with and get out of. ❑ *The government is in a corner on interest rates... He appears to have backed himself into a tight corner.* PHRASE: N inflects, v-link PHR, PHR after v = in a tight spot

**cor|ner shop** **(corner shops)** also **corner-shop.** A **corner shop** is a small shop, usually on the corner of a street, that sells mainly food and household goods. [BRIT] N-COUNT

✔ in AM, use **corner store**

**corner|stone** /kɔːʳnəʳstoun/ **(cornerstones)** also **corner-stone.** The **cornerstone of** something is the basic part of it on which its existence, success, or truth depends. [FORMAL] ❑ *Research is the cornerstone of the profession.* N-COUNT: oft N *of* n = keystone

**cor|ner store** **(corner stores)** A **corner store** is the same as a **corner shop**. [AM] N-COUNT

**cor|net** /kɔːʳnɪt, AM kɔːʳnet/ **(cornets)** 1 A **cornet** is a musical instrument that looks like a small trumpet. N-VAR: oft *the* N
2 An ice cream **cornet** is a soft thin biscuit shaped like a cone with ice cream in it. [BRIT] N-COUNT = cone

**corn ex|change** **(corn exchanges)** also **Corn Exchange.** A **corn exchange** is a large build- N-COUNT ing where, in former times, grain was bought and sold. [BRIT]

**corn|field** /kɔːʳnfiːld/ **(cornfields)** also **corn field.** A **cornfield** is a field in which corn is being grown. N-COUNT

**corn|flake** /kɔːʳnfleɪk/ **(cornflakes)** **Cornflakes** are small flat pieces of maize that are eaten with milk as a breakfast cereal. They are popular in Britain and the United States. N-COUNT: usu pl

**corn|flour** /kɔːʳnflaʊəʳ/ also **corn flour.** **Cornflour** is a fine white powder made from maize and is used to make sauces thicker. [BRIT] N-UNCOUNT

in AM, use **cornstarch**

**corn|flower** /kɔːʳnflaʊəʳ/ **(cornflowers)** **Cornflowers** are small plants with flowers that are usually blue. ❑ *Her eyes were a bright, cornflower blue.* N-VAR

**cor|nice** /kɔːʳnɪs/ **(cornices)** A **cornice** is a strip of plaster, wood, or stone which goes along the top of a wall or building. N-COUNT

**Cor|nish** /kɔːʳnɪʃ/ 1 **Cornish** means belonging or relating to the English county of Cornwall. ❑ *...the rugged Cornish coast. ...Cornish fishermen.* ADJ 2 **The Cornish** are the people of Cornwall. N-PLURAL: the N

**Cor|nish pasty** **(Cornish pasties)** also **cornish pasty.** A **Cornish pasty** is a small pie with meat and vegetables inside. [BRIT] N-COUNT

**corn|meal** /kɔːʳnmiːl/ also **corn meal.** **Cornmeal** is a powder made from maize. It is used in cooking. N-UNCOUNT

**corn on the cob** **(corn on the cobs)** also **corn-on-the-cob.** **Corn on the cob** is the long rounded part of the maize or corn plant on which small yellow seeds grow, and which is eaten as a vegetable. N-VAR

**corn|starch** /kɔːʳnstɑːʳtʃ/ also **corn starch.** **Cornstarch** is the same as **cornflour**. [AM] N-UNCOUNT

**cor|nu|co|pia** /kɔːʳnjʊkoʊpiə/ A **cornucopia of** things is a large number of different things. [LITERARY] ❑ *...a table festooned with a cornucopia of fruit.* N-SING = abundance

**corny** /kɔːʳni/ **(cornier, corniest)** If you describe something as **corny**, you mean that it is obvious or sentimental and not at all original. ❑ *I know it sounds corny, but I'm really not motivated by money.* ADJ disapproval

**cor|ol|lary** /kərɒləri, AM kɔːrəleri/ **(corollaries)** A **corollary** of something is an idea, argument, or fact that results directly from it. [FORMAL] ❑ *The number of prisoners increased as a corollary of the government's determination to combat crime.* N-COUNT: oft with poss = consequence

**co|ro|na** /kəroʊnə/ The sun's **corona** is its outer atmosphere. [TECHNICAL] N-SING

**coro|nary** /kɒrənri, AM kɔːrəneri/ **(coronaries)** 1 **Coronary** means belonging or relating to the heart. [MEDICAL] ❑ *If all the coronary arteries are free of significant obstructions, all parts of the heart will receive equal amounts of oxygen.* ADJ: ADJ n 2 If someone has a **coronary**, they collapse because the flow of blood to their heart is blocked by a large lump of blood called a clot. N-COUNT = heart attack

**coro|nary throm|bo|sis** **(coronary thromboses)** A **coronary thrombosis** is the same as a **coronary**. [MEDICAL] N-VAR

**coro|na|tion** /kɒrəneɪʃən, AM kɔːr-/ **(coronations)** A **coronation** is the ceremony at which a king or queen is crowned. ❑ *...the coronation of Her Majesty Queen Elizabeth II.* N-COUNT

**coro|ner** /kɒrənəʳ, AM kɔːr-/ **(coroners)** A **coroner** is an official who is responsible for investigating the deaths of people who have died in a sudden, violent, or unusual way. ❑ *The coroner recorded a verdict of accidental death.* N-COUNT

**coro|net** /kɒrənət, AM kɔːrənet/ **(coronets)** A **coronet** is a small crown. N-COUNT

**Corp.** **Corp.** is a written abbreviation for **corporation**. [BUSINESS] ❑ *...Sony Corp. of Japan.* ◆◆◇

**cor|po|ra** /kɔːʳpərə/ **Corpora** is a plural of **corpus**.

**cor|po|ral** /kɔːʳprəl/ **(corporals)** A **corporal** is a non-commissioned officer in the army or United States Marines. ❑ *The corporal shouted an order at the men. ...Corporal Devereux.* N-COUNT; N-TITLE

**cor|po|ral pun|ish|ment** **Corporal punishment** is the punishment of people by hitting them. N-UNCOUNT

**cor|po|rate** /kɔːʳpərət/ **Corporate** means relating to business corporations or to a particular business corporation. [BUSINESS] ❑ *...the UK corporate sector. ...a corporate lawyer... This established a strong corporate image.* ◆◇◇ ADJ: ADJ n

**cor|po|rate hos|pi|tal|ity** **Corporate hospitality** is the entertainment that a company offers to its most valued clients, for example by inviting them to sporting events and providing them with food and drink. [BUSINESS] ❑ *...corporate hospitality at football grounds. ...executives in a corporate hospitality tent.* N-UNCOUNT

**cor|po|rate raid|er** **(corporate raiders)** A **corporate raider** is a person or organization that tries to take control of a company by buying a large number of its shares. [BUSINESS] N-COUNT

**cor|po|ra|tion** /kɔːʳpəreɪʃən/ **(corporations)** ◆◇◇ 1 A **corporation** is a large business or company. [BUSINESS] ❑ *...multi-national corporations. ...the Seiko Corporation.* N-COUNT; N-IN-NAMES 2 In some large British cities, the **corporation** is the local authority that is responsible for providing public services. ❑ *...the corporation's task of regenerating 900 acres of the inner city.* N-COUNT = local authority

**cor|po|ra|tion tax** **Corporation tax** is a tax that companies have to pay on the profits they make. [BUSINESS] N-UNCOUNT

**cor|po|rat|ism** /kɔːʳprətɪzəm/ **Corporatism** is the organization and control of a country by groups who share a common interest or profession. ❑ *'The age of corporatism must be put firmly behind us,' he proclaimed.* N-UNCOUNT disapproval

**cor|po|rat|ist** /kɔːʳprətɪst/ **(corporatists)** 1 You use **corporatist** to describe organizations, ideas, or systems which follow the principles of corporatism. ❑ *... a corporatist political system.* ADJ: usu ADJ n disapproval 2 A **corporatist** is someone who believes in the principles of corporatism. ❑ *The defeat of the corporatists is easy to understand.* N-COUNT disapproval

**cor|po|real** /kɔːʳpɔːriəl/ **Corporeal** means involving or relating to the physical world rather than the spiritual world. [FORMAL] ❑ *...man's corporeal existence.* ADJ: usu ADJ n = physical

**corps** /kɔːʳ/ **(corps)** 1 A **corps** is a part of the army which has special duties. ❑ *...the Army Medical Corps. ...the Russian Officer Corps.* N-COUNT; N-IN-NAMES 2 **The Corps** is the United States Marine Corps. [AM] ❑ *...seventy-five men, all combat veterans, all members of The Corps' most exclusive unit.* N-COUNT: the N 3 A **corps** is a small group of people who do a special job. ❑ *...the diplomatic corps. ...the foreign press corps.* N-COUNT: supp N

**corps de bal|let** /kɔːʳ də bæleɪ, AM - bæleɪ/ In ballet, the **corps de ballet** is the group of dancers who dance together, in contrast to the main dancers, who dance by themselves. N-SING

**corpse** /kɔːʳps/ **(corpses)** A **corpse** is a dead body, especially the body of a human being. N-COUNT = body

**cor|pu|lent** /kɔːʳpjʊlənt/ If you describe someone as **corpulent**, you mean they are fat. [LITERARY] ❑ *...a rather corpulent farmer.* ADJ

**cor|pus** /kɔːʳpəs/ **(corpora** /kɔːʳpərə/ or **corpuses)** A **corpus** is a large collection of written or spoken texts that is used for language research. [TECHNICAL] N-COUNT: usu with supp

**cor|pus|cle** /kɔːʳpʌsəl, AM -pəsəl/ **(corpuscles)** **Corpuscles** are red or white blood cells. ❑ *Deficiency of red corpuscles is caused by a lack of iron.* N-COUNT: usu pl

**cor|ral** /kərɑːl, AM -ræl/ **(corrals)** In North America, a **corral** is a space surrounded by a fence where cattle or horses are kept. N-COUNT

**cor|rect** /kərekt/ ◆◆◇ **(corrects, correcting, corrected)** 1 If something is **correct**, it is in accordance with the facts and has no mistakes. [FORMAL] ADJ = right ≠ incorrect ❑ *The correct answers can be found at the bottom of page 8... The following information was correct at time of going to press.* ♦ **cor|rect|ly** *Did I pronounce your name correctly?* ADV: ADV with v ♦ **cor|rect|ness** *Ask the investor to check the correctness of what he has written.* N-UNCOUNT = accuracy 2 If someone is **correct**, what they have said or thought is true. [FORMAL] ADJ: v-link ADJ = right ≠ wrong ❑ *You are absolutely correct. The leaves are from a bay tree... If Casey is correct, the total cost of the cleanup would come to $110 billion.* 3 The **correct** thing or method is the thing or method that is required or is most suitable in a particular situation. ADJ: ADJ n = right ❑ *The use of the correct materials was crucial. ...the correct way to produce a crop of tomato plants.* ♦ **cor|rect|ly** *If correctly executed, this shot will give them a better chance of getting the ball close to the hole.* ADV: ADV with v = properly 4 If you say that someone is **correct in** doing something, you approve of their action. ADJ: usu ADJ *in* -ing/n = right ❑ *You are perfectly correct in trying to steer your mother towards increased independence... I think the president was correct to reject the offer.* ♦ **cor|rect|ly** *When an accident happens, quite correctly questions are asked.* ADV: ADV with cl 5 If you **correct** a problem, mistake, or fault, you do something which puts it right. VERB = rectify ❑ *He has criticised the government for inefficiency and delays in correcting past mistakes.* V n ♦ **cor|rec|tion** /kərekʃᵊn/ **(corrections)** N-VAR *...legislation to require the correction of factual errors... We will then make the necessary corrections.* 6 If you **correct** someone, you say something which you think is more accurate or appropriate than what they have just said. VERB ❑ *'Actually, that isn't what happened,' George corrects me... I must correct him on a minor point.* V n with quote, V n 7 When someone **corrects** a piece of writing, they look at it and mark the mistakes in it. VERB ❑ *It took an extraordinary effort to focus on preparing his classes or correcting his students' work.* V n 8 If a person or their behaviour is **correct**, their behaviour is in accordance with social or other rules. ADJ = proper ❑ *I think English men are very polite and very correct.* ♦ **cor|rect|ly** *The High Court of Parliament began very correctly with a prayer for the Queen.* ADV: ADV with v ♦ **cor|rect|ness** *...his stiff-legged gait and formal correctness.* N-UNCOUNT

**cor|rec|tion** /kərekʃᵊn/ **(corrections)** 1 **Corrections** are marks or comments made on a piece of work, especially school work, which indicate where there are mistakes and what are the right answers. N-COUNT: usu pl 2 **Correction** is the punishment of criminals. [mainly AM] N-UNCOUNT: oft N n ❑ *...jails and other parts of the correction system.* 3 → See also **correct**.

**cor|rec|tion|al** /kərekʃənəl/ **Correctional** means related to prisons. [mainly AM] ADJ: ADJ n ❑ *He is currently being held in a metropolitan correctional center.*

**cor|rec|tive** /kərektɪv/ **(correctives)** 1 **Corrective** measures or techniques are intended to put right something that is wrong. ADJ: usu ADJ n = remedial ❑ *Scientific institutions have been reluctant to take corrective action... He has received extensive corrective surgery to his skull.* 2 If something is a **corrective to** a particular view or account, it gives a more accurate or fairer picture than there would have been without it. [FORMAL] N-COUNT: oft N *to* n ❑ *...a useful corrective to the mistaken view that all psychologists are behaviourists.*

**cor|re|late** /kɒrəleɪt, AM kɔːr-/ **(correlates, correlating, correlated)** 1 If one thing **correlates with** another, there is a close similarity or connection between them, often because one thing causes the other. You can also say that two things **correlate**. [FORMAL] V-RECIP ❑ *Obesity correlates with increased risk for hypertension and stroke... The political opinions of spouses correlate more closely than their heights... The loss of respect for British science is correlated to reduced funding... At the highest executive levels earnings and performance aren't always correlated.* V *with/to* n, pl-n V, *be* V-ed *with/to* n, *be* V-ed 2 If you **correlate** things, you work out the way in which they are connected or the way they influence each other. [FORMAL] VERB ❑ *Attempts to correlate specific language functions with particular parts of the brain have not advanced very far... Lieutenant Ryan closed his eyes, first mentally viewing the different crime scenes, then correlating the data.* V n *with* n, V n

**cor|re|la|tion** /kɒrəleɪʃᵊn, AM kɔːr-/ **(correlations)** A **correlation between** things is a connection or link between them. [FORMAL] N-COUNT: oft N *between* pl-n ❑ *...the correlation between smoking and disease.*

**cor|rela|tive** /kɒrelətɪv/ **(correlatives)** If one thing is a **correlative of** another, the first thing is caused by the second thing, or occurs together with it. [FORMAL] N-COUNT: oft N *of* n ❑ *Man has rights only in so far as they are a correlative of duty.*

**cor|re|spond** /kɒrɪspɒnd, AM kɔːr-/ **(corresponds, corresponding, corresponded)** 1 If one thing **corresponds to** another, there is a close similarity or connection between them. You can also say that two things **correspond**. V-RECIP ❑ *Racegoers will be given a number which will correspond to a horse running in a race... The two maps of London correspond closely... Her expression is concerned but her body-language does not correspond.* V *to/with* n, pl-n V, V (non-recip) ♦ **cor|re|spond|ing** *March and April sales this year were up 8 per cent on the corresponding period in 1992.* ADJ: ADJ n 2 If you **correspond with** someone, you write letters to them. You can also say that two people **correspond**. V-RECIP ❑ *She still corresponds with American friends she met in Majorca nine years ago... We corresponded regularly.* V *with* n, pl-n V

**cor|re|spond|ence** /kɒrɪspɒndəns, AM kɔːr-/ **(correspondences)** 1 **Correspondence** is the act of writing letters to someone. N-UNCOUNT: also *a* N, oft N *with* n ❑ *The judges' decision is final and no correspondence will be entered into... His interest in writing came from a long correspondence with a close college friend.* 2 Someone's **correspondence** is the letters that they receive or send. N-UNCOUNT ❑ *He always replied to his correspondence.* 3 If there is a **correspondence between** two things, there is a close similarity or connection between them. N-COUNT: oft N *between* pl-n ❑ *In African languages there is a close correspondence between sounds and letters.*

**cor|re|spond|ence course (correspondence courses)** A **correspondence course** is a course in which you study at home, receiving your work by post and sending it back by post. N-COUNT ❑ *I took a correspondence course in computing.*

**cor|re|spond|ent** /kɒrɪspɒndənt, AM kɔːr-/ ◆◆◇ **(correspondents)** A **correspondent** is a newspaper or television journalist, especially one who specializes in a particular type of news. N-COUNT = reporter ❑ *...our Diplomatic Correspondent Mark Brayne.*

**cor|re|spond|ing|ly** /kɒrɪspɒndɪŋli, AM kɔːr-/ You use **correspondingly** when describing a situation which is closely connected with one you have just mentioned or is similar to it. ADV: ADV with v, ADV adj/adv ❑ *As his political stature has shrunk, he has grown correspondingly more dependent on the army.*

**cor|ri|dor** /kɒrɪdɔːʳ, AM kɔːrɪdər/ **(corridors)** 1 A **corridor** is a long passage in a building or train, with doors and rooms on one or both sides. N-COUNT 2 A **corridor** is a strip of land that connects one country to another or gives it a route to the sea through another country. N-COUNT ❑ *East Prussia and the rest of Germany were separated, in 1919, by the Polish corridor.*

**cor|robo|rate** /kərɒbəreɪt/ **(corroborates, corroborating, corroborated)** To **corroborate** something that has been said or reported means to provide evidence or information that supports it. [FORMAL] VERB = confirm ❑ *I had access to a wide range of documents which corroborated the story.* V n ♦ **cor|robo|ra|tion** /kərɒbəreɪʃᵊn/ *He could not get a single witness to establish independent corroboration of his version of the accident.* N-UNCOUNT = confirmation

**cor|robo|ra|tive** /kərɒbərətɪv, AM -reɪtɪv/ **Corroborative** evidence or information supports an idea, account, or argument. [FORMAL] ADJ: ADJ n ❑ *...a written statement supported by other corroborative evidence.*

**cor|rode** /kəroʊd/ **(corrodes, corroding, corroded)** 1 If metal or stone **corrodes**, or **is cor-** VERB

**roded**, it is gradually destroyed by a chemical or by rust. ❑ *He has devised a process for making gold wires which neither corrode nor oxidise... Engineers found the structure had been corroded by moisture... Acid rain destroys trees and corrodes buildings.* ♦ **cor|rod|ed** *The investigators found that the underground pipes were badly corroded.* [2] To **corrode** something means to gradually make it worse or weaker. [LITERARY] ❑ *Suffering was easier to bear than the bitterness he felt corroding his spirit.* V / be V-ed / V n / ADJ / VERB / V n

**cor|ro|sion** /kərouʒᵊn/ **Corrosion** is the damage that is caused when something is corroded. ❑ *Zinc is used to protect other metals from corrosion.* N-UNCOUNT

**cor|ro|sive** /kərousɪv/ [1] A **corrosive** substance is able to destroy solid materials by a chemical reaction. ❑ *Sodium and sulphur are highly corrosive.* [2] If you say that something has a **corrosive** effect, you mean that it gradually causes serious harm. [FORMAL] ❑ *...the corrosive effects of inflation.* ADJ / ADJ = damaging

**cor|ru|gat|ed** /kɒrəgeɪtɪd, AM kɔːr-/ **Corrugated** metal or cardboard has been folded into a series of small parallel folds to make it stronger. ❑ *...a hut with a corrugated iron roof.* ADJ: usu ADJ n

**cor|rupt** /kərʌpt/ **(corrupts, corrupting, corrupted)** [1] Someone who is **corrupt** behaves in a way that is morally wrong, especially by doing dishonest or illegal things in return for money or power. ❑ *...to save the nation from corrupt politicians of both parties... He had accused three opposition members of corrupt practices.* ♦ **cor|rupt|ly** *...several government officials charged with acting corruptly.* [2] If someone **is corrupted by** something, it causes them to become dishonest and unjust and unable to be trusted. ❑ *It is sad to see a man so corrupted by the desire for money and power.* [3] To **corrupt** someone means to cause them to stop caring about moral standards. ❑ *...warning that television will corrupt us all... Cruelty depraves and corrupts.* [4] If something **is corrupted**, it becomes damaged or spoiled in some way. ❑ *Some of the finer type-faces are corrupted by cheap, popular computer printers. ...corrupted data.* ADJ ≠ scrupulous / ADV: ADV with v / VERB: usu passive / be V-ed / VERB / V n / V / VERB: usu passive be V-ed / V-ed

**cor|rup|tion** /kərʌpʃᵊn/ **Corruption** is dishonesty and illegal behaviour by people in positions of authority or power. ❑ *Distribution of food throughout the country is being hampered by inefficiency and corruption.* ◆◇◇ N-UNCOUNT

**cor|sage** /kɔːʳsɑːʒ/ **(corsages)** A **corsage** is a very small bunch of flowers that is fastened to a woman's dress below the shoulder. N-COUNT

**cor|set** /kɔːʳsɪt/ **(corsets)** A **corset** is a stiff piece of underwear worn by some women, especially in the past. It fits tightly around their hips and waist and makes them thinner around the waist when they wear it. N-COUNT

**cor|set|ed** /kɔːʳsɪtɪd/ A woman who is **corseted** is wearing a corset. ADJ

**cor|tege** /kɔːʳteɪʒ, AM -teʒ/ **(corteges)** also **cortège.** A **cortege** is a procession of people who are walking or riding in cars to a funeral. N-COUNT-COLL

**cor|tex** /kɔːʳteks/ **(cortices** /kɔːʳtɪsiːz/) **The cortex** of the brain or of another organ is its outer layer. [MEDICAL] ❑ *...the cerebral cortex.* N-COUNT: usu sing, oft the N

**cor|ti|sone** /kɔːʳtɪzoun/ **Cortisone** is a hormone used in the treatment of arthritis, allergies, and some skin diseases. N-UNCOUNT

**co|rus|cat|ing** /kɒrəskeɪtɪŋ, AM kɔːr-/ A **coruscating** speech or performance is lively, intelligent, and impressive. [LITERARY] ❑ *...coruscating humour.* ADJ: usu ADJ n [approval] = dazzling, brilliant

**cor|vette** /kɔːʳvet/ **(corvettes)** A **corvette** is a small fast warship that is used to protect other ships from attack. N-COUNT

**'cos** /kəz/ also **cos.** **'Cos** is an informal way of saying **because**. [BRIT, SPOKEN] ❑ *It was absolutely horrible going up the hills 'cos they were really, really steep.* ◆◆◇ CONJ

✔ in AM, use **'cause**

**cosh** /kɒʃ/ **(coshes, coshing, coshed)** [1] A **cosh** is a heavy piece of rubber or metal which is used as a weapon. [BRIT] [2] To **cosh** someone means to hit them hard on the head with a cosh or a similar weapon. [BRIT] ❑ *...robbers who punched Tom and coshed Helen.* N-COUNT / VERB / V n

**cos|met|ic** /kɒzmetɪk/ **(cosmetics)** [1] **Cosmetics** are substances such as lipstick or powder, which people put on their face to make themselves look more attractive. [2] If you describe measures or changes as **cosmetic**, you mean they improve the appearance of a situation or thing but do not change its basic nature, and you are usually implying that they are inadequate. ❑ *It is a cosmetic measure which will do nothing to help the situation long term.* N-COUNT: usu pl / ADJ [disapproval] = superficial

**cos|met|ic sur|gery** **Cosmetic surgery** is surgery done to make a person look more attractive. N-UNCOUNT

**cos|mic** /kɒzmɪk/ [1] **Cosmic** means occurring in, or coming from, the part of space that lies outside Earth and its atmosphere. ❑ *...cosmic radiation. ...cosmic debris.* [2] **Cosmic** means belonging or relating to the universe. ❑ *...the cosmic laws governing our world.* ADJ: usu ADJ n / ADJ: usu ADJ n

**cos|mic rays** **Cosmic rays** are rays that reach earth from outer space and consist of atomic nuclei. N-PLURAL

**cos|mol|ogy** /kɒzmɒlədʒi/ **(cosmologies)** [1] A **cosmology** is a theory about the origin and nature of the universe. ❑ *...the ideas implicit in Big Bang cosmology.* [2] **Cosmology** is the study of the origin and nature of the universe. ♦ **cos|molo|gist** **(cosmologists)** ❑ *...astronomers and cosmologists.* ♦ **cos|mo|logi|cal** /kɒzməlɒdʒɪkᵊl/ *...cosmological sciences.* N-VAR / N-UNCOUNT / N-COUNT / ADJ: ADJ n

**cos|mo|naut** /kɒzmənɔːt/ **(cosmonauts)** A **cosmonaut** is an **astronaut** from the former Soviet Union. N-COUNT

**cos|mo|poli|tan** /kɒzməpɒlɪtən/ [1] A **cosmopolitan** place or society is full of people from many different countries and cultures. ❑ *London has always been a cosmopolitan city.* [2] Someone who is **cosmopolitan** has had a lot of contact with people and things from many different countries and as a result is very open to different ideas and ways of doing things. ❑ *The family are rich, and extremely sophisticated and cosmopolitan.* ADJ [approval] ≠ parochial / ADJ [approval] ≠ parochial

**cos|mos** /kɒzmɒs, AM -məs/ **The cosmos** is the universe. [LITERARY] ❑ *...the natural laws of the cosmos.* N-SING: the N

**cos|set** /kɒsɪt/ **(cossets, cosseting** or **cossetting, cosseted** or **cossetted)** If someone **is cosseted**, everything possible is done for them and they are protected from anything unpleasant. ❑ *Our kind of travel is definitely not suitable for people who expect to be cosseted.* VERB: usu passive = pamper / be V-ed

**cost** /kɒst, AM kɔːst/ **(costs, costing)** ◆◆◆

✔ The form **cost** is used in the present tense, and is also the past tense and participle, except for meaning 4, where the form **costed** is used.

[1] The **cost of** something is the amount of money that is needed in order to buy, do, or make it. ❑ *The cost of a loaf of bread has increased five-fold... In 1989 the price of coffee fell so low that in many countries it did not even cover the cost of production... Badges are also available at a cost of £2.50.* [2] If something **costs** a particular amount of money, you can buy, do, or make it for that amount. ❑ *This course is limited to 12 people and costs £50... It's going to cost me over $100,000 to buy new trucks.* [3] Your **costs** are the total amount of money that you must spend on running your home or business. ❑ *Costs have been cut by 30 to 50 per cent.* [4] When something that you plan to do or make **is costed**, the amount of money you need is calculated in advance. ❑ *Everything that goes into making a programme, staff, rent, lighting, is now costed. ...seventy apartments, shops, offices, a restaurant and* N-COUNT: usu sing, oft N of n / VERB / V amount / V n amount / N-PLURAL / VERB: usu passive / be V-ed / V-ed

*hotel, costed at around 10 million pounds.* ♦ **Cost out** means the same as **cost**. ❑ *...training days for charity staff on how to draw up contracts and cost out proposals... It is always worth having a loft conversion costed out.* PHRASAL VERB V P n (not pron) *have* n V-ed P Also V n P

5 If someone is ordered by a court of law to pay **costs**, they have to pay a sum of money towards the expenses of a court case they are involved in. ❑ *He was jailed for 18 months and ordered to pay £550 costs.* N-PLURAL

6 If something is sold **at cost**, it is sold for the same price as it cost the seller to buy it. ❑ *...a store that provided cigarettes and candy bars at cost.* N-UNCOUNT: prep N = cost price

7 The **cost of** something is the loss, damage, or injury that is involved in trying to achieve it. ❑ *In March Mr Salinas shut down the city's oil refinery at a cost of $500 million and 5,000 jobs. ...being so afraid of something that you feel you have to avoid it whatever the cost to your lifestyle.* N-SING: oft N *of* n

8 If an event or mistake **costs** you something, you lose that thing as the result of it. ❑ *...a six-year-old boy whose life was saved by an operation that cost him his sight... The increase will hurt small business and cost many thousands of jobs.* VERB V n n V n

**PHRASES** 9 If you say that something must be avoided **at all costs**, you are emphasizing that it must not be allowed to happen under any circumstances. ❑ *They told Jacques Delors a disastrous world trade war must be avoided at all costs.* PHRASE: PHR after v [emphasis]

10 If you say that something must be done **at any cost**, you are emphasizing that it must be done, even if this requires a lot of effort or money. ❑ *This book is of such importance that it must be published at any cost.* PHRASE: PHR after v [emphasis]

11 If you say that something **costs money**, you mean that it has to be paid for, and perhaps cannot be afforded. ❑ *Well-designed clothes cost money.* PHRASE: V inflects

12 If you know something **to** your **cost**, you know it because of an unpleasant experience that you have had. ❑ *Kathryn knows to her cost the effect of having served a jail sentence.* PHRASE: PHR after v

13 to **cost** someone **dear** → see **dear**.

♦ **cost out** → see **cost** 4.

**cost ac|count|ing** **Cost accounting** is the recording and analysis of all the various costs of running a business. [BUSINESS] N-UNCOUNT

**co-star** **(co-stars, co-starring, co-starred)**

✔ in AM, also use **costar**

1 An actor's or actress's **co-stars** are the other actors or actresses who also have one of the main parts in a particular film. ❑ *During the filming, Curtis fell in love with his co-star, Christine Kaufmann.* N-COUNT: usu poss N

2 If an actor or actress **co-stars with** another actor or actress, the two of them have the main parts in a particular film. ❑ *This fall she co-stars in a film with the acclaimed British actor Kenneth Branagh... Wright and Penn met when they co-starred in the movie 'State Of Grace'... Cosby had originally selected her to co-star in his movie 'Leonard Part 6'.* V-RECIP V *with* n pl-n V *in* n V *in* n (non-recip)

3 If a film **co-stars** particular actors, they have the main parts in it. ❑ *Produced by Oliver Stone, 'Wild Palms' co-stars Dana Delaney, Jim Belushi and Angie Dickinson.* VERB V n

**cost-effective** Something that is **cost-effective** saves or makes a lot of money in comparison with the costs involved. ❑ *The bank must be run in a cost-effective way.* ♦ **cost-effectively** *The management tries to produce the magazine as cost-effectively as possible.* ♦ **cost-effectiveness** *A Home Office report has raised doubts about the cost-effectiveness of the proposals.* ADJ ADV: ADV after v N-UNCOUNT

**cost|ing** /kɒstɪŋ, AM kɔːst-/ **(costings)** A **costing** is an estimate of all the costs involved in a project or a business venture. [mainly BRIT, BUSINESS] ❑ *We'll put together a proposal, including detailed costings, free of charge.* N-VAR = estimate

✔ in AM, use **costs**

**cost|ly** /kɒstli, AM kɔːst-/ **(costlier, costliest)**

1 If you say that something is **costly**, you mean that it costs a lot of money, often more than you would want to pay. ❑ *Having professionally made curtains can be costly, so why not make your own?* ADJ = expensive ≠ inexpensive

2 If you describe someone's action or mistake as **costly**, you mean that it results in a serious disadvantage for them, for example the loss of a large amount of money or the loss of their reputation. ❑ *Psychometric tests can save organizations from grim and costly mistakes.* ADJ

**cost of liv|ing** The **cost of living** is the average amount of money that people in a particular place need in order to be able to afford basic food, housing, and clothing. ❑ *Companies are moving jobs to towns with a lower cost of living.* N-SING

**cost-plus** A **cost-plus** basis for a contract about work to be done is one in which the buyer agrees to pay the seller or contractor all the cost plus a profit. ❑ *All vessels were to be built on a cost-plus basis.* ADJ: ADJ n

**cost price** **(cost prices)** If something is sold **at cost price**, it is sold for the same price as it cost the seller to buy it. [BRIT] ❑ *...a factory shop where you can buy very fashionable shoes at cost price.* N-VAR: oft *at* N = cost

**cos|tume** /kɒstjuːm, AM -tuːm/ **(costumes)**

1 An actor's or performer's **costume** is the set of clothes they wear while they are performing. ❑ *Even from a distance the effect of his fox costume was stunning... The performers, in costume and make-up, were walking up and down backstage... In all, she has eight costume changes.* N-VAR

2 The clothes worn by people at a particular time in history, or in a particular country, are referred to as a particular type of **costume**. ❑ *...men and women in eighteenth-century costume.* N-UNCOUNT: supp N = dress

3 A **costume** play or drama is one which is set in the past and in which the actors wear the type of clothes that were worn in that period. ❑ *...a lavish costume drama set in Ireland and the US in the 1890s.* ADJ: ADJ n

**cos|tume jew|el|lery**

✔ in AM, use **costume jewelry**

**Costume jewellery** is jewellery made from cheap materials. N-UNCOUNT

**cos|tum|er** /kɒstjuːməʳ/ **(costumers)** A **costumer** is the same as a **costumier**. [AM] N-COUNT

**cos|tumi|er** /kɒstjuːmiəʳ, AM -tuː-/ **(costumiers)** A **costumier** is a person or company that makes or supplies costumes. [mainly BRIT] ❑ *...a theatrical costumier.* N-COUNT

✔ in AM, use **costumer**

**cosy** /koʊzi/ **(cosier, cosiest)**

✔ in AM, use **cozy**

1 A house or room that is **cosy** is comfortable and warm. ❑ *Downstairs there's a breakfast room and guests can relax in the cosy bar.* ♦ **co|si|ly** /koʊzɪli/ *We took time to relax in the cosily decorated drawing room.* ADJ = homely ADV

2 If you are **cosy**, you are comfortable and warm. ❑ *They like to make sure their guests are comfortable and cosy.* ♦ **co|si|ly** *He was settled cosily in the corner with an arm round Lynda.* ADJ: v-link ADJ ADV: ADV after v

3 You use **cosy** to describe activities that are pleasant and friendly, and involve people who know each other well. ❑ *...a cosy chat between friends.* ♦ **co|si|ly** *...chatting cosily with friends over coffee.* ADJ = intimate ADV: ADV with v

**cot** /kɒt/ **(cots)** 1 A **cot** is a bed for a baby, with bars or panels round it so that the baby cannot fall out. [BRIT] N-COUNT

✔ in AM, use **crib**

2 A **cot** is a narrow bed, usually made of canvas fitted over a frame which can be folded up. [AM] N-COUNT

✔ in BRIT, use **camp bed**

**cot death** **(cot deaths)** **Cot death** is the sudden death of a baby while it is asleep, although the baby had not previously been ill. [BRIT] N-VAR

✔ in AM, use **crib death**

**co|terie** /koʊtəri/ **(coteries)** A **coterie of** a particular kind is a small group of people who are close friends or have a common interest, and who do not want other people to join them. [FORMAL] ❑ *The songs he recorded were written by a small coterie of dedicated writers.* N-COUNT-COLL: usu with supp = circle, set

**cot|tage** /kɒtɪdʒ/ **(cottages)** A **cottage** is a small house, usually in the country. → See picture on page 1706. ❑ *They used to have a cottage in N.W. Scotland... My sister Yvonne also came to live at Ockenden Cottage with me.* ◆◇◇ N-COUNT; N-IN-NAMES

**cot|tage cheese** **Cottage cheese** is a soft, white, lumpy cheese made from sour milk. N-UNCOUNT

**cot|tage in|dus|try** **(cottage industries)** A **cottage industry** is a small business that is run from someone's home, especially one that involves a craft such as knitting or pottery. [BUSINESS] ❑ *Bookbinding is largely a cottage industry.* N-COUNT

**cot|tage loaf** **(cottage loaves)** A **cottage loaf** is a loaf of bread which has a smaller round part on top of a larger round part. [BRIT] N-COUNT

**cot|tage pie** **(cottage pies)** **Cottage pie** is a dish which consists of minced meat in gravy with mashed potato on top. [BRIT] N-VAR = *shepherd's pie*

**cot|tag|ing** /kɒtɪdʒɪŋ/ **Cottaging** is homosexual activity between men in public toilets. [BRIT, INFORMAL] N-UNCOUNT

**cot|ton** /kɒtᵊn/ **(cottons, cottoning, cottoned)** ◆◇◇
1 **Cotton** is a type of cloth made from soft fibres from a particular plant. ❑ *...a cotton shirt.* N-MASS: oft N n
2 **Cotton** is a plant which is grown in warm countries and which produces soft fibres used in making cotton cloth. ❑ *...a large cotton plantation in Tennessee.* N-UNCOUNT
3 **Cotton** is thread that is used for sewing, especially thread that is made from cotton. [mainly BRIT] ❑ *There's a needle and cotton there.* N-MASS

✔ in AM, use **thread**

4 **Cotton** or **absorbent cotton** is a soft mass of cotton, used especially for applying liquids or creams to your skin. [AM] N-UNCOUNT

✔ in BRIT, use **cotton wool**

♦ **cotton on** If you **cotton on to** something, you understand it or realize it, especially without people telling you about it. [BRIT, INFORMAL] ❑ *She had already cottoned on to the fact that the nanny was not all she appeared... It wasn't until he started laughing that they cottoned on!* PHRASAL VERB = *catch on* V P *to* n; V P

♦ **cotton to** If you **cotton to** someone or something, you start to like them. [AM, INFORMAL] ❑ *His style of humor was very human, and that's why people cotton to him... It seemed to me that I was being shut out of the dialogue and that's something I just don't cotton to.* PHRASAL VERB: no passive V P n; V P n

**cot|ton bud** **(cotton buds)** A **cotton bud** is a small stick with a ball of cotton wool at each end, which people use, for example, for applying make-up. [BRIT] N-COUNT

✔ in AM, use **Q-tip**

**cot|ton can|dy** **Cotton candy** is a large pink or white mass of sugar threads that is eaten from a stick. It is sold at fairs or other outdoor events. [AM] N-UNCOUNT

✔ in BRIT, use **candyfloss**

**cotton|wood** /kɒtᵊnwʊd/ **(cottonwoods)** A **cottonwood** or a **cottonwood tree** is a kind of tree that grows in North America and has seeds that are covered with hairs that look like cotton. N-COUNT

**cot|ton wool** **Cotton wool** is a soft mass of cotton, used especially for applying liquids or creams to your skin. [BRIT] N-UNCOUNT

✔ in AM, use **cotton**

**couch** /kaʊtʃ/ **(couches, couching, couched)**
1 A **couch** is a long, comfortable seat for two or three people. N-COUNT
2 A **couch** is a narrow bed which patients lie on while they are being examined or treated by a doctor. N-COUNT
3 If a statement **is couched in** a particular style of language, it is expressed in that style of language. [WRITTEN] ❑ *The new centre-right government's radical objectives are often couched in moderate terms.* VERB: usu passive = *phrase* be V-ed *in/as* n

**cou|chette** /kuːʃet/ **(couchettes)** A **couchette** is a bed on a train or a boat which is either folded against the wall or used as an ordinary seat during the day. [mainly BRIT] N-COUNT

**couch po|ta|to** **(couch potatoes)** A **couch potato** is someone who spends most of their time watching television and does not exercise or have any interesting hobbies. [INFORMAL] ❑ *...couch potatoes flicking through endless satellite TV channels.* N-COUNT disapproval

**cou|gar** /kuːgəʳ/ **(cougars)** A **cougar** is a wild member of the cat family. Cougars have brownish-grey fur and live in mountain regions of North and South America. [mainly AM] N-COUNT = *mountain lion, puma*

✔ in BRIT, use **puma**

**cough** /kɒf, AM kɔːf/ **(coughs, coughing, coughed)** ◆◇◇
1 When you **cough**, you force air out of your throat with a sudden, harsh noise. You often cough when you are ill, or when you are nervous or want to attract someone's attention. ❑ *Graham began to cough violently... He coughed. 'Excuse me, Mrs Allsworthy, could I have a word?'* VERB V V
♦ **Cough** is also a noun. ❑ *They were interrupted by an apologetic cough.* N-COUNT
♦ **cough|ing** *He was then overcome by a terrible fit of coughing.* N-UNCOUNT
2 A **cough** is an illness in which you cough often and your chest or throat hurts. ❑ *...if you have a persistent cough for over a month.* N-COUNT
3 If you **cough** blood or mucus, it comes up out of your throat or mouth when you cough. ❑ *I started coughing blood so they transferred me to a hospital.* VERB V n
♦ **Cough up** means the same as **cough**. ❑ *On the chilly seas, Keats became feverish, continually coughing up blood.* PHRASAL VERB V P n (not pron) Also V n P

♦ **cough up** If you **cough up** an amount of money, you pay or spend that amount, usually when you would prefer not to. [INFORMAL] ❑ *I'll have to cough up $10,000 a year for tuition... Will this be enough to persuade Congress to cough up?* → See also **cough 3**. PHRASAL VERB = *fork out* V P n *for* n; V P; Also V P n, V P *for* n

**cough medi|cine** **(cough medicines)** **Cough medicine** is liquid medicine that you take when you have a cough. N-MASS

**cough mix|ture** **(cough mixtures)** **Cough mixture** is the same as **cough medicine**. [BRIT] N-MASS

**could** /kəd, STRONG kʊd/ ◆◆◆

✔ **Could** is a modal verb. It is used with the base form of a verb. **Could** is sometimes considered to be the past form of **can**, but in this dictionary the two words are dealt with separately.

1 You use **could** to indicate that someone had the ability to do something. You use **could not** or **couldn't** to say that someone was unable to do something. ❑ *For my return journey, I felt I could afford the extra and travel first class... I could see that something was terribly wrong... When I left school at 16, I couldn't read or write... There was no way she could have coped with a baby around.* MODAL
2 You use **could** to indicate that something sometimes happened. ❑ *Though he had a temper and could be nasty, it never lasted... He could be very pleasant when he wanted to.* MODAL
3 You use **could have** to indicate that something was a possibility in the past, although it did not actually happen. ❑ *He could have made a fortune as a lawyer... He did not regret saying what he did but felt that he could have expressed it differently.* MODAL
4 You use **could** to indicate that something is possibly true, or that it may possibly happen. ❑ *Doctors told him the disease could have been caused by years of working in smokey clubs... An improvement in living standards could be years away.* MODAL = *might*
5 You use **could not** or **couldn't** to indicate that it is not possible that something is true. ❑ *Anne couldn't be expected to understand the situation... He couldn't have been more than fourteen years old.* MODAL
6 You use **could** to talk about a possibility, ability, or opportunity that depends on other conditions. ❑ *Their hope was that a new and better East Germany could be born... I knew that if I spoke to Myra, I could get her to call my father.* MODAL
7 You use **could** when you are saying that one thing or situation resembles another. ❑ *The charming characters she draws look like they could have* MODAL

*walked out of the 1920s.* 8 You use **could**, or **couldn't** in questions, when you are making offers and suggestions. ❑ *I could call the local doctor... You could look for a career abroad where environmental jobs are better paid and more secure... It would be a good idea if you could do this exercise twice or three times on separate days.* MODAL

9 You use **could** in questions when you are making a polite request or asking for permission to do something. Speakers sometimes use **couldn't** instead of 'could' to show that they realize that their request may be refused. ❑ *Could I stay tonight?... Could I speak to you in private a moment, John?... He asked if he could have a cup of coffee... Couldn't I watch you do it?* MODAL politeness

10 People sometimes use structures with **if I could** or **could I** as polite ways of interrupting someone or of introducing what they are going to say next. [FORMAL, SPOKEN] ❑ *Well, if I could just interject... Could I ask you if there have been any further problems?... First of all, could I begin with an apology for a mistake I made last week?* MODAL politeness = may

11 You use **could** to say emphatically that someone ought to do the thing mentioned, especially when you are annoyed because they have not done it. You use **why couldn't** in questions to express your surprise or annoyance that someone has not done something. ❑ *We've come to see you, so you could at least stand and greet us properly... Idiot! You could have told me!... He could have written... Why couldn't she have said something?* MODAL emphasis

12 You use **could** when you are expressing strong feelings about something by saying that you feel as if you want to do the thing mentioned, although you do not do it. ❑ *'Welcome back' was all they said. I could have kissed them!... She could have screamed with tension.* MODAL emphasis

13 You use **could** after 'if' when talking about something that you do not have the ability or opportunity to do, but which you are imagining in order to consider what the likely consequences might be. ❑ *If I could afford it I'd have four television sets... If only I could get some sleep, I would be able to cope.* MODAL

14 You use **could not** or **couldn't** with comparatives to emphasize that someone or something has as much as is possible of a particular quality. For example, if you say 'I couldn't be happier', you mean that you are extremely happy. ❑ *The rest of the players are a great bunch of lads and I couldn't be happier... The news couldn't have come at a better time.* MODAL emphasis

15 In speech, you use **how could** in questions to emphasize that you feel strongly about something bad that has happened. ❑ *How could you allow him to do something like that?... How could she do this to me?* MODAL emphasis

16 **could do with** → see **do**.

**couldn't** /kʊdənt/ **Couldn't** is the usual spoken form of 'could not'.

**could've** /kʊdəv/ **Could've** is the usual spoken form of 'could have', when 'have' is an auxiliary verb.

**coun|cil** /kaʊnsəl/ **(councils)** ◆◆◆ 1 A **council** is a group of people who are elected to govern a local area such as a city or, in Britain, a county. ❑ *...Cheshire County Council... The city council has voted almost unanimously in favour. ...David Ward, one of just two Liberal Democrats on the council.* N-COUNT-COLL; N-IN-NAMES = local authority

2 **Council** houses or flats are owned by the local council, and people pay rent to live in them. [BRIT] ❑ *There is a shortage of council housing.* ADJ: ADJ n

3 **Council** is used in the names of some organizations. ❑ *...the National Council for Civil Liberties. ...community health councils.* N-COUNT-COLL: usu in names

4 In some organizations, the **council** is the group of people that controls or governs it. ❑ *The permanent council of the Organization of American States meets today here in Washington.* N-COUNT-COLL: usu sing, usu with supp

5 A **council** is a specially organized, formal meeting that is attended by a particular group of people. ❑ *President Najibullah said he would call a grand council of all Afghans.* N-COUNT = conference

**coun|cil house** **(council houses)** In Britain, a **council house** is a house that is owned by a local council and that people can rent at a low cost. N-COUNT

**coun|cil|lor** /kaʊnsələʳ/ **(councillors)**

✔ in AM, use **councilor**

A **councillor** is a member of a local council. ❑ *...Councillor Michael Poulter.* N-COUNT; N-TITLE

**council|man** /kaʊnsəlmən/ **(councilmen)** A **councilman** is a man who is a member of a local council. [AM] ❑ *...a city councilman.* N-COUNT; N-TITLE

✔ in BRIT, use **councillor**

**coun|cil of war** **(councils of war)** A **council of war** is a meeting that is held in order to decide how a particular threat or emergency should be dealt with. [FORMAL] N-COUNT

**coun|cil tax** In Britain, **council tax** is a tax that you pay to your local authority in order to pay for local services such as schools, libraries, and rubbish collection. The amount of council tax that you pay depends on the value of the house or flat where you live. N-UNCOUNT: also *the* N

**coun|cil|woman** /kaʊnsəlwʊmən/ **(councilwomen)** A **councilwoman** is a woman who is a member of a local council. [AM] ❑ *...Councilwoman Johnson.* N-COUNT; N-TITLE

✔ in BRIT, use **councillor**

**coun|sel** /kaʊnsəl/ **(counsels, counselling, counselled)** ◆◇◇

✔ in AM, use **counseling**, **counseled**

1 **Counsel** is advice. [FORMAL] ❑ *He had always been able to count on her wise counsel... His parishioners sought his counsel and loved him.* N-UNCOUNT

2 If you **counsel** someone **to** take a course of action, or if you **counsel** a course of action, you advise that course of action. [FORMAL] ❑ *My advisers counselled me to do nothing... The prime minister was right to counsel caution about military intervention.* VERB V n to-inf V n

3 If you **counsel** people, you give them advice about their problems. ❑ *...a psychologist who counsels people with eating disorders... Crawford counsels her on all aspects of her career.* VERB V n V n *on* n

4 Someone's **counsel** is the lawyer who gives them advice on a legal case and speaks on their behalf in court. ❑ *Singleton's counsel said after the trial that he would appeal.* N-COUNT: oft supp N

**coun|sel|ling** /kaʊnsəlɪŋ/

✔ in AM, use **counseling**

**Counselling** is advice which a therapist or other expert gives to someone about a particular problem. N-UNCOUNT

**coun|sel|lor** /kaʊnsələʳ/ **(counsellors)**

✔ in AM, use **counselor**

A **counsellor** is a person whose job is to give advice to people who need it, especially advice on their personal problems. N-COUNT

**count** /kaʊnt/ **(counts, counting, counted)** ◆◆◇

1 When you **count**, you say all the numbers one after another up to a particular number. ❑ *He was counting slowly under his breath... Brian counted to twenty and lifted his binoculars.* VERB V V *to* num

2 If you **count** all the things in a group, you add them up in order to find how many there are. ❑ *I counted the money. It was more than five hundred pounds... I counted 34 wild goats grazing... With more than 90 percent of the votes counted, the Liberals should win nearly a third of the seats.* ♦ **Count up** means the same as **count**. ❑ *Couldn't we just count up our ballots and bring them to the courthouse?* ♦ **count|ing** *The counting of votes is proceeding smoothly.* VERB V n V num V-ed Also V PHRASAL VERB V P n (not pron) N-UNCOUNT: usu *the* N *of* n

3 A **count** is the action of counting a particular set of things, or the number that you get when you have counted them. ❑ *The final count in last month's referendum showed 56.7 per cent in favour.* N-COUNT: usu supp N

4 You use **count** when referring to the level or amount of something that someone or something has. ❑ *A glass or two of wine will not significantly add to the calorie count.* → See also **blood count**, **pollen count**. N-COUNT: n N

5 You use **count** in expressions such as **a count of three** or **a count of ten** when you are measuring a length of time by counting slowly up to a certain number. ❑ *Hold your breath for a count of* N-SING: N *of* num

*five, then slowly breathe out.* [6] If something or someone **counts for** something or **counts**, they are important or valuable. ❑ *Surely it doesn't matter where charities get their money from: what counts is what they do with it... When I first came to college I realised that brainpower didn't count for much.* VERB = matter; V; V for amount

[7] If something **counts** or **is counted as** a particular thing, it is regarded as being that thing, especially in particular circumstances or under particular rules. ❑ *No one agrees on what counts as a desert... Two of the trucks were stopped because they had tents in them, and under the commanders' definition of humanitarian aid, that didn't count... They can count it as a success.* VERB; V as n/-ing/adj; V; V n as n

[8] If you **count** something when you are making a calculation, you include it in that calculation. ❑ *It's under 7 percent only because statistics don't count the people who aren't qualified to be in the work force... The years before their arrival in prison are not counted as part of their sentence.* VERB = include; V n; be V-ed as n; Also V n as n

[9] You can use **count** to refer to one or more points that you are considering. For example, if someone is wrong **on two counts**, they are wrong in two ways. ❑ *'You drink Scotch,' she said. 'All Republicans drink Scotch.' — 'Wrong on both counts. I'm a Democrat, and I drink bourbon.'* N-COUNT: on supp N

[10] In law, a **count** is one of a number of charges brought against someone in court. ❑ *He was indicted by a grand jury on two counts of murder.* N-COUNT: usu N of n

PHRASES [11] If you **keep count of** a number of things, you note or keep a record of how many have occurred. If you **lose count of** a number of things, you cannot remember how many have occurred. ❑ *The authorities say they are not able to keep count of the bodies still being found as helicopters search the area... She'd lost count of the interviews she'd been called for.* PHRASE: V inflects, oft PHR of n

[12] If someone is **out for the count**, they are unconscious or very deeply asleep. [INFORMAL] PHRASE: v-link PHR

[13] If you say that someone should **stand up and be counted**, you mean that they should say publicly what they think, and not hide it or be ashamed of it. ❑ *Those involved and benefiting from the scandal must be prepared to stand up and be counted.* PHRASE

[14] to **count** your **blessings** → see **blessing**.

♦ **count against** If something **counts against** you, it may cause you to be rejected or punished, or cause people to have a lower opinion of you. ❑ *He is highly regarded, but his youth might count against him.* PHRASAL VERB; V P n

♦ **count in** If you tell someone to **count** you **in**, you mean that you want to be included in an activity. ❑ *She shrugged. 'You can count me in, I guess.'* PHRASAL VERB: usu imper ≠ count out; V n P

♦ **count on** or **count upon** [1] If you **count on** something or **count upon** it, you expect it to happen and include it in your plans. ❑ *The government thought it could count on the support of the trades unions.* PHRASAL VERB; V P n/-ing

[2] If you **count on** someone or **count upon** them, you rely on them to support you or help you. ❑ *Don't count on Lillian... I can always count on you to cheer me up.* PHRASAL VERB; V P n; V P n to-inf

♦ **count out** [1] If you **count out** a sum of money, you count the notes or coins as you put them in a pile one by one. ❑ *Mr. Rohmbauer counted out the money and put it in an envelope.* PHRASAL VERB; V P n (not pron) Also V n P

[2] If you tell someone to **count** you **out**, you mean that you do not want to be included in an activity. ❑ *If this is the standard to which I have to drop to gain membership, then count me out!* PHRASAL VERB: usu imper ≠ count in; V n P

♦ **count towards**

✔ in AM, usually use **count toward**

If something **counts towards** or **counts toward** an achievement or right, it is included as one of the things that give you the right to it. ❑ *In many courses, work from the second year onwards can count towards the final degree.* PHRASAL VERB; V P n

♦ **count up** → see **count** 2.

♦ **count upon** → see **count on**.

**Count** /kaʊnt/ **(Counts)** A **Count** is a European nobleman with the same rank as an English earl. ❑ *Her father was a Polish Count.* N-COUNT; N-TITLE; N-VOC

**count|able noun** /kaʊntəbᵊl naʊn/ **(countable nouns)** A **countable noun** is the same as a **count noun**. N-COUNT

**count|down** /kaʊntdaʊn/ **(countdowns)** [1] A **countdown** is the counting aloud of numbers in reverse order before something happens, especially before a spacecraft is launched. ❑ *The countdown has begun for the launch later today of the American space shuttle.* N-SING: also no det

[2] The **countdown** to an event is the period of time leading up to the event. ❑ *...the countdown to the next election.* N-COUNT

**coun|te|nance** /kaʊntɪnəns/ **(countenances, countenancing, countenanced)** [1] If someone will not **countenance** something, they do not agree with it and will not allow it to happen. [FORMAL] ❑ *Jake would not countenance Janis's marrying while still a student.* VERB: usu with brd-neg; V n

[2] Someone's **countenance** is their face. [LITERARY] N-COUNT

**coun|ter** /kaʊntəʳ/ **(counters, countering, countered)** ◆◇◇ [1] In a place such as a shop or café, a **counter** is a long narrow table or flat surface at which customers are served. ❑ *...those fellows we see working behind the counter at our local video rental store. ...the cosmetics counter.* N-COUNT

[2] If you do something to **counter** a particular action or process, you do something which has an opposite effect to it or makes it less effective. ❑ *The leadership discussed a plan of economic measures to counter the effects of such a blockade... Sears then countered by filing an antitrust lawsuit.* VERB; V n; V by -ing

[3] Something that is **a counter to** something else has an opposite effect to it or makes it less effective. ❑ *...NATO's traditional role as a counter to the military might of the Warsaw pact.* N-SING: a N to n

[4] If you **counter** something that someone has said, you say something which shows that you disagree with them or which proves that they are wrong. ❑ *Both of them had to counter fierce criticism... The union countered with letters rebutting the company's claims... The Prime Minister countered by stating that he had grave misgivings about the advice he had been given... 'But Peter, it's not that simple,' Goldstone countered in a firm voice.* VERB; V n; V with n; V by -ing; V with quote Also V that

[5] A **counter** is a mechanical or electronic device which keeps a count of something and displays the total. ❑ *...an answerphone with an LED display call counter.* N-COUNT: usu supp N

[6] A **counter** is a small, flat, round object used in board games. N-COUNT

[7] → See also **bargaining counter**, **bean counter**, **Geiger counter**, **rev counter**.

PHRASES [8] If a medicine can be bought **over the counter**, you do not need a prescription to buy it. ❑ *Are you taking any other medicines whether on prescription or bought over the counter? ...basic over-the-counter remedies.* PHRASE

[9] **Over-the-counter** shares are bought and sold directly rather than on a stock exchange. [BUSINESS] PHRASE: usu PHR n

[10] If one thing **runs counter to** another, or if one thing **is counter to** another, the first thing is the opposite of the second thing or conflicts with it. [FORMAL] ❑ *Much of the plan runs counter to European agriculture and environmental policy.* PHRASE: V inflects, PHR to n

[11] If someone buys or sells goods **under the counter**, they buy or sell them secretly and illegally. ❑ *The smugglers allegedly sold the gold under the counter, cheating the VAT man out of £5 million.* PHRASE: PHR after v

**counter-** /kaʊntəʳ-/ **Counter-** is used to form words which refer to actions or activities that are intended to prevent other actions or activities or that respond to them. ❑ *The army now appears to have launched a counter-offensive. ...the chief of counter-terrorist operations. ...a counter-demonstration by anti-war protesters.* PREFIX

**counter|act** /kaʊntərækt/ **(counteracts, counteracting, counteracted)** To **counteract** something means to reduce its effect by doing something that produces an opposite effect. ❑ *My husband has to take several pills to counteract high blood pressure.* VERB; V n

**counter-argument** **(counter-arguments)**

☑ in AM, usually use **counterargument**

A **counter-argument** is an argument that makes an opposing point to another argument. ❑ *...an attempt to develop a counter-argument to the labor theory.* N-COUNT

**counter-attack** **(counter-attacks, counter-attacking, counter-attacked)** also **counterattack.** If you **counter-attack**, you attack someone who has attacked you. ❑ *The security forces counter-attacked the following day and quelled the unrest.* ♦ **Counter-attack** is also a noun. ❑ *The army began its counter-attack this morning.* VERB = retaliate V; N-COUNT

**counter|bal|ance** /kaʊntəʳbæləns/ **(counterbalances, counterbalancing, counterbalanced)** also **counter-balance.** [1] To **counterbalance** something means to balance or correct it with something that has an equal but opposite effect. ❑ *Add honey to counterbalance the acidity.* [2] Something that is a **counterbalance to** something else counterbalances that thing. ❑ *...organisations set up as a counterbalance to groups allied to the ANC.* VERB = offset; V n; N-COUNT: oft N *to* n

**counter|blast** /kaʊntəʳblɑːst, -blæst/ **(counterblasts)** also **counter-blast.** A **counterblast** is a strong angry reply to something that has been said, written, or done. [JOURNALISM] ❑ *British experts delivered a strong counter-blast to the Professor's claims.* N-COUNT: oft N *to* n

**counter|clockwise** /kaʊntəʳklɒkwaɪz/ also **counter-clockwise.** If something is moving **counterclockwise**, it is moving in the opposite direction to the direction in which the hands of a clock move. [AM] ❑ *Rotate the head clockwise and counterclockwise.* ♦ **Counterclockwise** is also an adjective. ❑ *The dance moves in a counter-clockwise direction.* ADV: ADV after v ≠ clockwise; ADJ: ADJ n ≠ clockwise

☑ in BRIT, use **anticlockwise**

**counter-culture** **(counter-cultures)** also **counterculture.** **Counter-culture** is a set of values, ideas, and ways of behaving that are completely different from those of the rest of society. ❑ *...a history of British counter-culture.* N-VAR

**counter-espionage**

☑ in AM, use **counterespionage**

**Counter-espionage** is the same as **counter-intelligence**. N-UNCOUNT

**counter|feit** /kaʊntəʳfɪt/ **(counterfeits, counterfeiting, counterfeited)** [1] **Counterfeit** money, goods, or documents are not genuine, but have been made to look exactly like genuine ones in order to deceive people. ❑ *He admitted possessing and delivering counterfeit currency.* ♦ **Counterfeit** is also a noun. ❑ *Levi Strauss says counterfeits of the company's jeans are flooding Europe.* [2] If someone **counterfeits** something, they make a version of it that is not genuine but has been made to look genuine in order to deceive people. ❑ *...the coins Davies is alleged to have counterfeited.* ♦ **counter|feit|er** **(counterfeiters)** *...a gang of counterfeiters.* ADJ: usu ADJ n = fake; N-COUNT = fake; VERB; V n; N-COUNT: usu pl

**counter|foil** /kaʊntəʳfɔɪl/ **(counterfoils)** A **counterfoil** is the part of a cheque, ticket, or other document that you keep when you give the other part to someone else. N-COUNT

**counter-intelligence** also **counter intelligence, counterintelligence.** **Counter-intelligence** consists of actions that a country takes in order to find out whether another country is spying on it and to prevent it from doing so. ❑ *...the FBI's department of counter-intelligence. ...a counter-intelligence officer.* N-UNCOUNT: oft N n

**counter|mand** /kaʊntəʳmɑːnd, -mænd/ **(countermands, countermanding, countermanded)** If you **countermand** an order, you cancel it, usually by giving a different order. [FORMAL] ❑ *I can't countermand an order Winger's given.* VERB = override, overrule V n

**counter-measure** **(counter-measures)** also **countermeasure.** A **counter-measure** is an action that you take in order to weaken the effect of another action or a situation, or to make it harmless. ❑ *Because the threat never developed, we didn't need to take any real countermeasures.* N-COUNT

**counter|pane** /kaʊntəʳpeɪn/ **(counterpanes)** A **counterpane** is a decorative cover on a bed. [OLD-FASHIONED] N-COUNT

**counter|part** /kaʊntəʳpɑːʳt/ **(counterparts)** Someone's or something's **counterpart** is another person or thing that has a similar function or position in a different place. ❑ *The Foreign Secretary telephoned his Italian counterpart to protest.* ◆◇◇ N-COUNT: with supp, usu poss N

**counter|point** /kaʊntəʳpɔɪnt/ **(counterpoints)** Something that is a **counterpoint to** something else contrasts with it in a satisfying way. [JOURNALISM] ❑ *Paris is just a short train journey away, providing the perfect counterpoint to the peace and quiet of Reims.* N-COUNT: usu sing, oft N *to* n = complement

**counter-productive** also **counterproductive.** Something that is **counter-productive** achieves the opposite result from the one that you want to achieve. ❑ *In practice, however, such an attitude is counter-productive.* ADJ: usu v-link ADJ

**counter-revolution** **(counter-revolutions)**

☑ in AM, also use **counterrevolution**

[1] A **counter-revolution** is a revolution that is intended to reverse the effects of a previous revolution. ❑ *The consequences of the counter-revolution have been extremely bloody.* [2] You can refer to activities that are intended to reverse the effects of a previous revolution as **counter-revolution**. ❑ *Such actions would be regarded as counter-revolution.* N-COUNT; N-UNCOUNT

**counter-revolutionary** **(counter-revolutionaries)**

☑ in AM, also use **counterrevolutionary**

[1] **Counter-revolutionary** activities are activities intended to reverse the effects of a previous revolution. ❑ *...counter-revolutionary propaganda.* [2] A **counter-revolutionary** is a person who is trying to reverse the effects of a previous revolution. ADJ; N-COUNT

**counter|sign** /kaʊntəʳsaɪn/ **(countersigns, countersigning, countersigned)** If you **countersign** a document, you sign it after someone else has signed it. ❑ *The President has so far refused to countersign the Prime Minister's desperate decree.* VERB; V n

**counter|ten|or** /kaʊntəʳtenəʳ/ **(countertenors)** also **counter-tenor.** A **countertenor** is a man who sings with a high voice that is similar to a low female singing voice. N-COUNT = alto

**counter|top** /kaʊntəʳtɒp/ **(countertops)** A **countertop** is a flat surface in a kitchen which is easily cleaned and on which you can prepare food. [AM] N-COUNT

☑ in BRIT, use **worktop, work surface**

**counter|vail|ing** /kaʊntəʳveɪlɪŋ/ A **countervailing** force, power, or opinion is one which is of equal strength to another one but is its opposite or opposes it. [FORMAL] ❑ *Their strategy is expansionist and imperialist, and it is greatest in effect, of course, when there is no countervailing power.* ADJ: ADJ n

**counter|weight** /kaʊntəʳweɪt/ **(counterweights)** A **counterweight** is an action or proposal that is intended to balance or counter other actions or proposals. ❑ *His no-inflation bill serves as a useful counterweight to proposals less acceptable to the Committee.* N-COUNT: oft N n

**coun|tess** /kaʊntɪs/ **(countesses)** A **countess** is a woman who has the same rank as a count or earl, or who is married to a count or earl. ❑ *...the Countess of Lichfield.* N-COUNT; N-TITLE; N-VOC

**count|ing** /kaʊntɪŋ/ [1] **Not counting** a particular thing means not including that thing. **Counting** a particular thing means including that thing. ❑ *...an average operating profit of 15% to* PREP = including

*16% of sales, not counting administrative expenses.* [2] If you say **and counting** after a number or an amount of something, you mean that the number or amount is continuing to increase. ❑ *There is a 1,700-year-old tea tree still living in southern China which is more than 100 feet tall and counting.* PHRASE: amount PHR

**count|less** /kaʊntləs/ **Countless** means very many. ❑ *There are countless small ski areas dotted about the province.* ADJ: ADJ n = innumerable

**count noun** **(count nouns)** A **count noun** is a noun such as 'bird', 'chair', or 'year' which has a singular and a plural form and is always used after a determiner in the singular. N-COUNT = countable noun

**coun|tri|fied** /kʌntrɪfaɪd/ [1] You use **countrified** to describe something that seems or looks like something in the country, rather than in a town. ❑ *The house was so handsome, with a lovely countrified garden.* ADJ: usu ADJ n [2] **Countrified** is used to describe pop music that sounds similar to country music. [JOURNALISM] ❑ *The sound veers between jazz and countrified blues.* ADJ: usu ADJ n

**coun|try** /kʌntri/ **(countries)** ◆◆◆ [1] A **country** is one of the political units which the world is divided into, covering a particular area of land. ❑ *Indonesia is the fifth most populous country in the world. ...that disputed boundary between the two countries... Young people do move around the country quite a bit these days.* N-COUNT [2] The people who live in a particular country can be referred to as **the country**. ❑ *Seventy per cent of this country is opposed to blood sports.* N-SING: usu *the* N [3] **The country** consists of places such as farms, open fields, and villages which are away from towns and cities. ❑ *...a healthy life in the country... She was cycling along a country road near Compiegne.* N-SING: *the* N = countryside [4] A particular kind of **country** is an area of land which has particular characteristics or is connected with a particular well-known person. ❑ *Varese Ligure is a small town in mountainous country east of Genoa.* N-UNCOUNT: supp N [5] **Country** music is popular music from the southern United States. ❑ *...a famous country singer named Katie Cocker.* N-UNCOUNT: usu N n

**PHRASES** [6] If you travel **across country**, you travel through country areas, avoiding major roads and towns. ❑ *From here we walked across country to Covington.* PHRASE: v PHR [7] If you travel **across country**, you travel a long distance, from one part of a country to another. ❑ *We've just moved all the way across country to begin a new life.* PHRASE: v PHR [8] If a head of government or a government **goes to the country**, they hold a general election. [BRIT] ❑ *The Prime Minister does not have to go to the country for another year.* PHRASE: V inflects

**coun|try and west|ern** also **country-and-western**. **Country and western** is the same as country music. ❑ *...a successful country and western singer.* N-UNCOUNT: oft N n

**coun|try club** **(country clubs)** A **country club** is a club in the country where you can play sports and attend social events. N-COUNT

**coun|try cous|in** **(country cousins)** If you refer to someone as a **country cousin**, you think that they are unsophisticated because they come from the country. N-COUNT

**coun|try danc|ing** **Country dancing** is traditional dancing in which people dance in rows or circles. N-UNCOUNT

**coun|try house** **(country houses)** A **country house** is a large, often attractive, house in the country, usually one that is or was owned by a rich or noble family. [BRIT] N-COUNT

**country|man** /kʌntrimən/ **(countrymen)** [1] Your **countrymen** are people from your own country. ❑ *He lost last year's final to fellow countryman Michael Stich.* N-COUNT: usu poss N = compatriot [2] A **countryman** is a person who lives in the country rather than in a city or a town. ❑ *He had the red face of a countryman.* N-COUNT

**coun|try seat** **(country seats)** A **country seat** is a large house with land in the country which is owned by someone who also owns a house in a town. ❑ *His family have a country seat in Oxfordshire.* N-COUNT

**country|side** /kʌntrisaɪd/ ◆◇◇ **The countryside** is land which is away from towns and cities. ❑ *I've always loved the English countryside... We are surrounded by lots of beautiful countryside.* N-UNCOUNT: oft *the* N

**country|wide** /kʌntriwaɪd/ Something that happens or exists **countrywide** happens or exists throughout the whole of a particular country. ❑ *Armed robbery and abduction have been on the increase countrywide... They sent out questionnaires to 100 schools countrywide.* ADV: ADV after v, n ADV = nationwide ♦ **Countrywide** is also an adjective. ❑ *...a countrywide network of volunteers.* ADJ: ADJ n

**country|woman** /kʌntriwʊmən/ **(countrywomen)** [1] A **countrywoman** is a woman who lives in the country rather than in a city or a town. ❑ *She had the slow, soft voice of a countrywoman.* N-COUNT [2] Your **countrywomen** are women from your own country. ❑ *Britain's Martine Le Moignan defeated her countrywoman Suzanne Horner in four games.* N-COUNT: usu poss N = compatriot

**coun|ty** /kaʊnti/ **(counties)** ◆◆◇ A **county** is a region of Britain, Ireland, or the USA which has its own local government. ❑ *Over 50 events are planned throughout the county.* N-COUNT

**coun|ty coun|cil** **(county councils)** A **county council** is an organization which runs local government in a county in Britain. ❑ *...Devon County Council.* N-COUNT; N-IN-NAMES

**coun|ty court** **(county courts)** A **county court** is a local court which deals with private disputes between people, but does not deal with serious crimes. [BRIT] N-COUNT

**coun|ty seat** **(county seats)** A **county seat** is the same as a **county town**. [AM] N-COUNT

**coun|ty town** **(county towns)** A **county town** is the most important town in a county, where the local government is. [BRIT] ❑ *We met in Dorchester, Dorset's bustling county town.* N-COUNT

☑ in AM, use **county seat**

**coup** /kuː/ **(coups)** ◆◇◇ [1] When there is a **coup**, a group of people seize power in a country. ❑ *...a military coup... They were sentenced to death for their part in April's coup attempt.* N-COUNT = coup d'état [2] A **coup** is an achievement which is thought to be especially good because it was very difficult. ❑ *The sale is a big coup for the auction house.* N-COUNT

**coup de grace** /kuː də grɑːs/ A **coup de grace** is an action or event which finally destroys something, for example an institution, which has been gradually growing weaker. [FORMAL] ❑ *Irving Kristol delivered the coup de grace in a letter dated June 12: they had decided to reject the proposal.* N-SING = death blow

**coup d'état** /kuː deɪtɑː/ **(coups d'état)** When there is a **coup d'état**, a group of people seize power in a country. N-COUNT = coup

**coupe** /kuːp/ **(coupes)** A **coupe** is the same as a **coupé**. [AM] N-COUNT

**cou|pé** /kuːpeɪ/ **(coupés)** A **coupé** is a car with a fixed roof, a sloping back, two doors, and seats for four people. [BRIT] N-COUNT

☑ in AM, use **coupe**

**cou|ple** /kʌpᵊl/ **(couples, coupling, coupled)** ◆◆◇ [1] If you refer to **a couple of** people or things, you mean two or approximately two of them, although the exact number is not important or you are not sure of it. ❑ *Across the street from me there are a couple of police officers standing guard... I think the trouble will clear up in a couple of days. ...a small working-class town in Massachusetts, a couple of hundred miles from New York City.* QUANT: QUANT *of* pl-n ♦ **Couple** is also a determiner in spoken American English, and before 'more' and 'less'. ❑ *...a couple weeks before the election... I think I can play maybe for a couple more years.* DET ♦ **Couple** is also a pronoun. ❑ *I've got a couple that don't look too bad.* PRON [2] A **couple** is two people who are married, living together, or having a sexual relationship. ❑ *The couple have no children. ...after burglars ransacked an elderly couple's* N-COUNT-COLL home. [3] A **couple** is two people that you see together on a particular occasion or that have some association. ❑ *...as the four couples began the opening dance.* N-COUNT-COLL [4] If you say that one thing produces a particular effect when it **is coupled with** another, you mean that the two things combine to produce that effect. ❑ *...a problem that is coupled with lower demand for the machines themselves... Over-use of those drugs, coupled with poor diet, leads to physical degeneration.* VERB: usu passive = combine; be V-ed *with* n; V-ed [5] If one piece of equipment **is coupled to** another, it is joined to it so that the two pieces of equipment work together. ❑ *Its engine is coupled to a semiautomatic gearbox... The various systems are coupled together in complex arrays.* VERB: usu passive; be V-ed *to* n; be V-ed *together* [6] ➔ See also **coupling**.

**cou|plet** /kʌplɪt/ **(couplets)** A **couplet** is two lines of poetry which come next to each other, especially two lines that rhyme with each other and are the same length. ❑ *...rhyming couplets.* N-COUNT

**cou|pling** /kʌplɪŋ/ **(couplings)** [1] A **coupling** is a device which is used to join two vehicles or pieces of equipment together. ❑ *Before driving away, re-check the trailer coupling.* N-COUNT: oft supp N [2] An act of sexual intercourse is sometimes referred to as a **coupling**. [FORMAL] ❑ *...sexual couplings.* N-COUNT [3] ➔ See also **couple**.

**cou|pon** /kuːpɒn/ **(coupons)** [1] A **coupon** is a piece of printed paper which allows you to pay less money than usual for a product, or to get it free. ❑ *Bring the coupon below to any Tecno store and pay just £10.99. ...a 50p money-off coupon.* N-COUNT = voucher [2] A **coupon** is a small form, for example in a newspaper or magazine, which you send off to ask for information, to order something, or to enter a competition. ❑ *Send the coupon with a cheque for £18.50, made payable to 'Good Housekeeping'.* N-COUNT

**cour|age** /kʌrɪdʒ, AM kɜːr-/ ◆◇◇ [1] **Courage** is the quality shown by someone who decides to do something difficult or dangerous, even though they may be afraid. ❑ *General Lewis Mackenzie has impressed everyone with his authority and personal courage... They do not have the courage to apologise for their actions.* ➔ See also **Dutch courage**. N-UNCOUNT = bravery [2] If you have **the courage of** your **convictions**, you have the confidence to do what you believe is right, even though other people may not agree or approve. ❑ *Developers should have the courage of their convictions and stick to what they do best.* PHRASE: PHR after v to **pluck up the courage** ➔ see **pluck**.

**cou|ra|geous** /kəreɪdʒəs/ Someone who is **courageous** shows courage. ❑ *It was a very frightening experience and they were very courageous... It was a courageous decision, and one that everybody admired.* ADJ = brave

**cour|gette** /kʊəʳʒet/ **(courgettes)** **Courgettes** are long thin vegetables with dark green skin. ➔ See picture on page 1712. [BRIT] N-VAR

✔ in AM, use **zucchini**

**cou|ri|er** /kʊriəʳ/ **(couriers, couriering, couriered)** [1] A **courier** is a person who is paid to take letters and parcels direct from one place to another. ❑ *The cheques were delivered to the bank by a private courier firm.* N-COUNT [2] A **courier** is a person employed by a travel company to look after people who are on holiday. N-COUNT = rep [3] If you **courier** something somewhere, you send it there by courier. ❑ *I couriered it to Darren in New York.* VERB: V n *to* n; Also V n

**course** /kɔːʳs/ **(courses, coursing, coursed)** ◆◆◆ [1] **Course** is often used in the expression 'of course', or instead of 'of course' in informal spoken English. See **of course**. [2] The **course** of a vehicle, especially a ship or aircraft, is the route along which it is travelling. ❑ *Aircraft can avoid each other by going up and down, as well as by altering course to left or right... The tug was seaward of the Hakai Passage on a course that diverged from the Calvert Island coastline.* N-UNCOUNT: also *a* N [3] A **course of** action is an action or a series of actions that you can do in a particular situation. ❑ *My best course of action was to help Gill by being loyal, loving and endlessly sympathetic... Vietnam is trying to decide on its course for the future.* N-COUNT: usu sing [4] You can refer to the way that events develop as, for example, **the course of history** or **the course of events**. ❑ *...a series of decisive naval battles which altered the course of history.* N-SING: *the* N *of* n [5] A **course** is a series of lessons or lectures on a particular subject. ❑ *...a course in business administration... I'm shortly to begin a course on the modern novel.* ➔ See also **access course**, **correspondence course**, **refresher course**, **sandwich course**. N-COUNT: oft N *in/on* n [6] A **course of** medical treatment is a series of treatments that a doctor gives someone. ❑ *Treatment is supplemented with a course of antibiotics to kill the bacterium.* N-COUNT: N *of* n [7] A **course** is one part of a meal. ❑ *The lunch was excellent, especially the first course. ...a three-course dinner.* N-COUNT: usu supp N [8] In sport, a **course** is an area of land where races are held or golf is played, or the land over which a race takes place. ❑ *Only 12 seconds separated the first three riders on the Bickerstaffe course.* N-COUNT: usu with supp [9] The **course** of a river is the channel along which it flows. ❑ *Romantic chateaux and castles overlook the river's twisting course.* N-COUNT

**PHRASES** [10] If something happens **in the course of** a particular period of time, it happens during that period of time. ❑ *In the course of the 1930s steel production in Britain approximately doubled... We struck up a conversation, in the course of which it emerged that he was a sailing man.* PREP-PHRASE = during [11] If you do something **as a matter of course**, you do it as part of your normal work or way of life. ❑ *If police are carrying arms as a matter of course then doesn't it encourage criminals to carry them?* PHRASE: PHR after v [12] If a ship or aircraft is **on course**, it is travelling along the correct route. If it is **off course**, it is no longer travelling along the correct route. ❑ *The ill fated ship was sent off course into shallow waters and rammed by another vessel.* PHRASE: PHR after v, v-link PHR [13] If you are **on course for** something, you are likely to achieve it. ❑ *The company is on course for profits of £20m in the next financial year.* PREP-PHRASE: usu v-link PREP [14] If something **runs its course** or **takes its course**, it develops naturally and comes to a natural end. ❑ *They estimated that between 17,000 and 20,000 cows would die before the epidemic had run its course.* PHRASE: V inflects [15] If you **stay the course**, you finish something that you have started, even though it has become very difficult. ❑ *The oldest president in American history had stayed the course for two terms.* PHRASE: V inflects [16] If something changes or becomes true **in the course of time**, it changes or becomes true over a long period of time. ❑ *In the course of time, many of their myths become entangled.* PHRASE: PHR with cl [17] **in due course** ➔ see **due**.

**course book** **(course books)** also **coursebook.** A **course book** is a textbook that students and teachers use as the basis of a course. N-COUNT

**course work** also **coursework. Course work** is work that students do during a course, rather than in exams, especially work that counts towards a student's final grade. ❑ *Some 20 per cent of marks are awarded for coursework.* N-UNCOUNT

**cours|ing** /kɔːʳsɪŋ/ **Coursing** is a sport in which rabbits or hares are hunted with dogs. N-UNCOUNT

**court**
① NOUN USES
② VERB USES

① **court** /kɔːʳt/ **(courts)** ◆◆◆ [1] A **court** is a place where legal matters are decided by a judge and jury or by a magistrate. ❑ *At this rate, we could find ourselves in the divorce courts! ...a county court judge... He was deported on a court order following a conviction for armed robbery... The 28-year-old striker was in court last week for breaking a rival player's jaw.* N-COUNT: oft n N, N n, also *in/at* N [2] You can refer to the people in a court, especially the judge, jury, or magistrates, as a **court.** ❑ *A court at Tampa, Florida has convicted five officials on drugs charges.* N-COUNT [3] A **court** is an area in which you play a game such as tennis, basketball, badminton, or squash. ❑ *The hotel has several tennis and* N-COUNT: usu supp N, also *on/off* N squash courts... She watched a few of the games while waiting to go on court. [4] The **court** of a king or queen is the place where he or she lives and carries out ceremonial or administrative duties. ❑ *She came to visit England, where she was presented at the court of James I.* [5] → See also **Crown Court, High Court, kangaroo court.** N-COUNT: oft with poss, also *at* N

**PHRASES** [6] If you **go to court** or **take** someone **to court**, you take legal action against them. ❑ *They have received at least twenty thousand pounds each but had gone to court to demand more. ...members of trade associations who want to take bad debtors to court.* PHRASE: V inflects [7] If someone **holds court** in a place, they are surrounded by a lot of people who are paying them a lot of attention because they are interesting or famous. ❑ *...in the days when Marlene Dietrich and Ernest Hemingway held court in the famous El Floridita club.* PHRASE: V inflects [8] If a legal matter is decided or settled **out of court**, it is decided without legal action being taken in a court of law. ❑ *...a payment of two million pounds in an out of court settlement.* PHRASE: PHR after v, PHR n

② **court** /kɔːʳt/ **(courts, courting, courted)** [1] To **court** a particular person, group, or country means to try to please them or improve your relations with them, often so that they will do something that you want them to do. [JOURNALISM] ❑ *Both Democratic and Republican parties are courting former supporters of Ross Perot.* VERB V n [2] If you **court** something such as publicity or popularity, you try to attract it. ❑ *Having spent a lifetime avidly courting publicity, Paul has suddenly become secretive.* VERB V n [3] If you **court** something unpleasant such as disaster or unpopularity, you act in a way that makes it likely to happen. ❑ *If he thinks he can remain in power by force he is courting disaster.* VERB = *invite* V n

**cour|teous** /kɜːʳtiəs/ Someone who is **courteous** is polite and respectful to other people. ❑ *He was a kind and courteous man... My friend's reply was courteous but firm.* ♦ **cour|teous|ly** *Then he nodded courteously to me and walked off to perform his unpleasant duty.* ADJ = *polite* ADV: usu ADV with v, also ADV adj

**cour|tesan** /kɔːʳtɪzæn, AM -zən/ **(courtesans)** In former times, a **courtesan** was a woman who had sexual relationships with rich and powerful men for money. N-COUNT

**cour|tesy** /kɜːʳtɪsi/ **(courtesies)** [1] **Courtesy** is politeness, respect, and consideration for others. [FORMAL] ❑ *...a gentleman who behaves with the utmost courtesy towards ladies... He did not even have the courtesy to reply to my fax.* N-UNCOUNT = *politeness* [2] If you refer to **the courtesy of** doing something, you are referring to a polite action. [FORMAL] ❑ *By extending the courtesy of a phone call to my clients, I was building a personal relationship with them.* N-SING: usu *the* N *of* -ing/n [3] **Courtesies** are polite, conventional things that people say in formal situations. [FORMAL] N-COUNT: usu pl [4] **Courtesy** is used to describe services that are provided free of charge by an organization to its customers, or to the general public. ❑ *A courtesy shuttle bus operates between the hotel and the town. ...a courtesy phone.* ADJ: ADJ n [5] A **courtesy** call or a **courtesy** visit is a formal visit that you pay someone as a way of showing them politeness or respect. ❑ *The President paid a courtesy call on Emperor Akihito.* ADJ: ADJ n [6] A **courtesy** title is a title that someone is allowed to use, although it has no legal or official status. ❑ *Both were accorded the courtesy title of Lady.* N-UNCOUNT: N n, *by* N

**PHRASES** [7] If something is provided **courtesy of** someone or **by courtesy of** someone, they provide it. You often use this expression in order to thank them. ❑ *The waitress brings over some congratulatory glasses of champagne, courtesy of the restaurant.* PREP-PHRASE [8] If you say that one thing happens **courtesy of** another or **by courtesy of** another, you mean that the second thing causes or is responsible for the first thing. ❑ *The air was fresh, courtesy of three holes in the roof... As millions will have seen, by courtesy of the slow motion re-runs, the referee made a mistake.* PREP-PHRASE

**court|house** /kɔːʳthaʊs/ **(courthouses)** [1] A **courthouse** is a building in which a court of law meets. [AM] N-COUNT

✓ in BRIT, use **court**

[2] A **courthouse** is a building used by the government of a county. [AM] N-COUNT

**cour|ti|er** /kɔːʳtiəʳ/ **(courtiers)** **Courtiers** were noblemen and women who spent a lot of time at the court of a king or queen. N-COUNT

**court|ly** /kɔːʳtli/ You use **courtly** to describe someone whose behaviour is very polite, often in a rather old-fashioned way. [LITERARY] ❑ *The waiter made a courtly bow.* ADJ

**court mar|tial** **(court martials, court martialling, court martialled)** also **court-martial.**

✓ The spellings **court martialing** and **court martialed** are used in American English; **courts martial** is also used as a plural form for the noun.

[1] A **court martial** is a trial in a military court of a member of the armed forces who is charged with breaking a military law. ❑ *He is due to face a court-martial on drugs charges... He was arrested, tried by court martial and shot.* N-VAR [2] If a member of the armed forces **is court martialled**, he or she is tried in a military court. ❑ *I was court-martialled and sentenced to six months in a military prison.* VERB: usu passive *be* V-ed

**Court of Ap|peal** **(Courts of Appeal)**

✓ in AM, usually use **Court of Appeals**

A **Court of Appeal** is a court which deals with appeals against legal judgments. ❑ *The case is being referred to the Court of Appeal.* N-COUNT

**court of in|quiry** **(courts of inquiry)** A **court of inquiry** is a group of people who are officially appointed to investigate a serious accident or incident, or an official investigation into a serious accident or incident. [mainly BRIT] ❑ *The government has instituted a court of inquiry to look into the allegations.* N-COUNT

**court of law** **(courts of law)** When you refer to a **court of law**, you are referring to a legal court, especially when talking about the evidence that might be given in a trial. ❑ *We have a witness who would swear to it in a court of law.* N-COUNT

**court|room** /kɔːʳtruːm/ **(courtrooms)** A **courtroom** is a room in which a legal court meets. N-COUNT = *court*

**court|ship** /kɔːʳtʃɪp/ **(courtships)** [1] **Courtship** is the activity of courting or the time during which a man and a woman are courting. [OLD-FASHIONED] ❑ *After a short courtship, she accepted his marriage proposal.* N-VAR [2] The **courtship** of male and female animals is their behaviour before they have sex. ❑ *Courtship is somewhat vocal with a lot of displaying by the male.* N-UNCOUNT

**court shoe** **(court shoes)** **Court shoes** are women's shoes that do not cover the top part of the foot and are usually made of plain leather with no design. [BRIT] N-COUNT

✓ in AM, use **pumps**

**court|yard** /kɔːʳtjɑːʳd/ **(courtyards)** A **courtyard** is an open area of ground which is surrounded by buildings or walls. ❑ *They walked through the arch and into the cobbled courtyard.* N-COUNT

**cous|cous** /kuːskuːs/ **Couscous** is a type of food that is made from crushed steamed wheat, or a dish consisting of this food served with a spicy stew. It is traditionally eaten in North Africa. N-UNCOUNT

**cous|in** /kʌzᵊn/ **(cousins)** Your **cousin** is the child of your uncle or aunt. ❑ *My cousin Mark helped me... We are cousins.* → See also **country cousin, second cousin.** ◆◆◇ N-COUNT: oft with poss

**cou|ture** /kuːtjʊəʳ, AM -tʊr/ **Couture** is the designing and making of expensive fashionable clothes, or the clothes themselves. [FORMAL] ❑ *...Christian Lacroix's first Paris couture collection.* N-UNCOUNT: oft N n = *haute couture*

**cou|tu|ri|er** /kuːtʊərieɪ, AM kuːtʊrieɪ/ **(couturiers)** A **couturier** is a person who designs, makes, and sells expensive, fashionable clothes for women. N-COUNT = designer

**cove** /koʊv/ **(coves)** A **cove** is a part of a coast where the land curves inwards so that the sea is partly enclosed. ❑ *...a hillside overlooking Fairview Cove.* N-COUNT; N-IN-NAMES

**cov|en** /kʌvən/ **(covens)** A **coven** is a group of witches. N-COUNT-COLL

**cov|enant** /kʌvənənt/ **(covenants)** 1 A **covenant** is a formal written agreement between two or more people or groups of people which is recognized in law. ❑ *...the International Covenant on Civil and Political Rights.* N-COUNT 2 A **covenant** is a formal written promise to pay a sum of money each year for a fixed period, especially to a charity. [mainly BRIT] ❑ *If you make regular gifts through a covenant we can reclaim the income tax which you have already paid on this money.* N-COUNT: also by N

✔ in AM, usually use **pledge**

**Cov|en|try** /kɒvəntri, AM kʌvɪntri/ If people **send** you **to Coventry**, they avoid speaking to you whenever they meet you, as a way of punishing you for something that you have done. [BRIT] PHRASE: V inflects

**cov|er** /kʌvəʳ/ **(covers, covering, covered)** ◆◆◆
1 If you **cover** something, you place something else over it in order to protect it, hide it, or close it. ❑ *Cover the casserole with a tight-fitting lid... He whimpered and covered his face... Keep what's left in a covered container in the fridge.* VERB V n with n V n V-ed 2 If one thing **covers** another, it has been placed over it in order to protect it, hide it, or close it. ❑ *His finger went up to touch the black patch which covered his eye... His head was covered with a khaki turban.* VERB V n be V-ed with n 3 If one thing **covers** another, it forms a layer over its surface. ❑ *The clouds had spread and nearly covered the entire sky... The desk was completely covered with papers.* VERB V n be V-ed with/in n 4 To **cover** something **with** or **in** something else means to put a layer of the second thing over its surface. ❑ *The trees in your garden may have covered the ground with apples, pears or plums.* VERB V n with/in n 5 If you **cover** a particular distance, you travel that distance. ❑ *It would not be easy to cover ten miles on that amount of petrol.* VERB V n 6 To **cover** someone or something means to protect them from attack, for example by pointing a gun in the direction of people who may attack them, ready to fire the gun if necessary. ❑ *You go first. I'll cover you.* VERB V n 7 **Cover** is protection from enemy attack that is provided for troops or ships carrying out a particular operation, for example by aircraft. ❑ *They said they could not provide adequate air cover for ground operations.* N-UNCOUNT = protection 8 **Cover** is trees, rocks, or other places where you shelter from the weather or from an attack, or hide from someone. ❑ *Charles lit the fuses and they ran for cover.* N-UNCOUNT = shelter 9 An insurance policy that **covers** a person or thing guarantees that money will be paid by the insurance company in relation to that person or thing. ❑ *Their insurer paid the £900 bill, even though the policy did not strictly cover it... You should take out travel insurance covering you and your family against theft.* VERB V n V n against n 10 Insurance **cover** is a guarantee from an insurance company that money will be paid by them if it is needed. ❑ *Make sure that the firm's insurance cover is adequate.* N-UNCOUNT = protection 11 If a law **covers** a particular set of people, things, or situations, it applies to them. ❑ *The law covers four categories of experiments.* VERB V n 12 If you **cover** a particular topic, you discuss it in a lecture, course, or book. ❑ *The Oxford Chemistry Primers aim to cover important topics in organic chemistry.* VERB = deal with V n 13 If journalists, newspapers, or television companies **cover** an event, they report on it. ❑ *Robinson was sent to Italy to cover the 1990 World Cup.* VERB V n 14 If a sum of money **covers** something, it is enough to pay for it. ❑ *Send it to the address given with £1.50 to cover postage and administration.* VERB V n 15 A **cover** is something which is put over an object, usually in order to protect it. ❑ *...a family room with washable covers on the furniture. ...a duvet cover.* N-COUNT: oft n N 16 The **covers** on your bed are the things such as sheets and blankets that you have on top of you. N-PLURAL: usu the N = bedclothes 17 The **cover** of a book or a magazine is the outside part of it. ❑ *...a small spiral-bound booklet with a green cover... I used to read every issue from cover to cover.* N-COUNT 18 Something that is a **cover** for secret or illegal activities seems respectable or normal, and is intended to hide the activities. ❑ *They set up a spurious temple that was a cover for sexual debauchery... As a cover story he generally tells people he is a freelance photographer.* N-COUNT: usu sing = front 19 If you **cover for** someone who is doing something secret or illegal, you give false information or do not give all the information you have, in order to protect them. ❑ *Why would she cover for someone who was trying to kill her?* VERB V for n 20 If you **cover for** someone who is ill or away, you do their work for them while they are not there. ❑ *She did not have enough nurses to cover for those who went ill or took holiday.* VERB V for n 21 To **cover** a song originally performed by someone else means to record a new version of it. ❑ *He must make a decent living from other artists covering his songs.* VERB V n 22 A **cover** is the same as a **cover version**. ❑ *The single is a cover of an old Rolling Stones song.* N-COUNT: usu N of n 23 → See also **covered**, **covering**.

PHRASES 24 To **blow** someone's **cover** means to cause their true identity or the true nature of their work to be revealed. [INFORMAL] ❑ *The young man looked embarrassed, as if he were a spy whose cover had been blown.* PHRASE: V inflects 25 If you **break cover**, you leave a place where you have been hiding or sheltering from attack, usually in order to run to another place. ❑ *They began running again, broke cover and dashed towards the road.* PHRASE: V inflects 26 If you **take cover**, you shelter from gunfire, bombs, or the weather. ❑ *Shoppers took cover behind cars as police marksmen returned fire.* PHRASE: V inflects, oft PHR prep = shelter 27 If you are **under cover**, you are under something that protects you from gunfire, bombs, or the weather. ❑ *'Get under cover!' shouted Billy, and we darted once more for the tables.* PHRASE: PHR after v, v-link PHR 28 If you do something **under cover of** a particular situation, you are able to do it without being noticed because of that situation. ❑ *They move under cover of darkness.* PREP-PHRASE 29 If you **cover** your **back** or **cover** your **rear**, you do something in order to protect yourself, for example against criticism or against accusations of doing something wrong. ❑ *The canny Premier covered his back by pointing out that he was of Scottish stock.* PHRASE: V inflects

♦ **cover up** 1 If you **cover** something or someone **up**, you put something over them in order to protect or hide them. ❑ *He fell asleep in the front room so I covered him up with a duvet.* PHRASAL VERB V n P Also V P n (not pron) 2 If you **cover up** something that you do not want people to know about, you hide the truth about it. ❑ *He suspects there's a conspiracy to cover up the crime... They knew they had done something terribly wrong and lied to cover it up... How do we know you're not just covering up for your friend?* → See also **cover-up**. PHRASAL VERB V P n (not pron) V n P V P for n

**cov|er|age** /kʌvərɪdʒ/ The **coverage** of something in the news is the reporting of it. ❑ *Now a special TV network gives live coverage of most races.* ◆◇◇ N-UNCOUNT

**cov|er charge** **(cover charges)** A **cover charge** is a sum of money that you must pay in some restaurants and nightclubs in addition to the money that you pay there for your food and drink. N-COUNT: usu sing

**cov|ered** /kʌvəʳd/ A **covered** area is an area that has a roof. ❑ *There are 40 shops, cafes and restaurants in a covered mall.* ADJ: ADJ n

**cov|ered wag|on** **(covered wagons)** A **covered wagon** is a wagon that has an arched canvas roof and is pulled by horses. Covered wagons were used by the early American settlers as they travelled across the country. N-COUNT

**cov|er girl** **(cover girls)** A **cover girl** is an attractive woman whose photograph appears on the front of a magazine. N-COUNT

**cov|er|ing** /kʌvərɪŋ/ **(coverings)** A **covering** is a layer of something that protects or hides something else. ❑ *Leave a thin covering of fat... Sawdust was used as a hygienic floor covering.* N-COUNT

**cov|er|ing let|ter** **(covering letters)** A **covering letter** is a letter that you send with a parcel or with another letter in order to provide extra information. [BRIT] N-COUNT

in AM, use **cover letter**

**cov|er|let** /kʌvərlɪt/ **(coverlets)** A **coverlet** is the same as a **bedspread**. [OLD-FASHIONED] N-COUNT

**cov|er let|ter** **(cover letters)** A **cover letter** is the same as a **covering letter**. [AM] N-COUNT

**cov|er|mount** /kʌvərmaʊnt/ **(covermounts)** A **covermount** is a small gift attached to the front cover of a magazine. N-COUNT

**cover-mounted** also **covermounted.** **Cover-mounted** items such as cassettes, videos and CDs are attached to the front of a magazine as free gifts. ❑ *The first issue has a cover-mounted CD-ROM.* ADJ

**cov|ert** /kʌvərt, koʊvɜːrt/ **Covert** activities or situations are secret or hidden. [FORMAL] ❑ *They have been supplying covert military aid to the rebels.* ADJ: usu ADJ n ≠ overt
♦ **cov|ert|ly** *They covertly observed Lauren, who was sitting between Ned and Algie at a nearby table.* ADV: usu ADV with v ≠ overtly

**cover-up** **(cover-ups)**

in AM, also use **coverup**

A **cover-up** is an attempt to hide a crime or mistake. ❑ *General Schwarzkopf denied there'd been any cover-up.* N-COUNT

**cov|er ver|sion** **(cover versions)** A **cover version of** a song is a version of it recorded by a singer or band who did not originally perform the song. ❑ *...a new album of Cole Porter cover versions.* N-COUNT: oft N *of* n = cover

**cov|et** /kʌvɪt/ **(covets, coveting, coveted)** If you **covet** something, you strongly want to have it for yourself. [FORMAL] ❑ *She coveted his job so openly that conversations between them were tense.* VERB V n

**cov|et|ed** /kʌvɪtɪd/ You use **coveted** to describe something that very many people would like to have. ❑ *...one of sport's most coveted trophies. ...a supply of highly coveted hard currency.* ADJ: usu ADJ n

**cov|et|ous** /kʌvɪtəs/ A **covetous** person has a strong desire to possess something, especially something that belongs to another person. [FORMAL] ❑ *Even here a red Lamborghini Diablo sports car attracts covetous stares.* ADJ disapproval

**cov|ey** /kʌvi/ **(coveys)** A **covey of** grouse or partridges is a small group of them. N-COUNT: oft N *of* n

**cow** /kaʊ/ **(cows, cowing, cowed)** 1 A **cow** is a large female animal that is kept on farms for its milk. People sometimes refer to male and female animals of this species as **cows**. ❑ *Dad went out to milk the cows. ...a herd of cows.* → See also **cattle**. ◆◇◇ N-COUNT
2 Some female animals, including elephants and whales, are called **cows**. ❑ *...a cow elephant.* N-COUNT: oft N n
3 If someone describes a woman as a **cow**, they dislike her and think that she is unpleasant or stupid. [INFORMAL, OFFENSIVE] N-COUNT disapproval
4 If someone **is cowed**, they are made afraid, or made to behave in a particular way because they have been frightened or badly treated. [FORMAL] ❑ *The government, far from being cowed by these threats, has vowed to continue its policy. ...cowing them into submission.* VERB = intimidate; *be* V-ed; V n *into* n/-ing
♦ **cowed** *By this time she was so cowed by the beatings that she meekly obeyed.* ADJ: oft ADJ *by* n
5 → See also **mad cow disease, sacred cow**.

**cow|ard** /kaʊərd/ **(cowards)** If you call someone a **coward**, you disapprove of them because they are easily frightened and avoid dangerous or difficult situations. ❑ *She accused her husband of being a coward.* N-COUNT disapproval

**cow|ard|ice** /kaʊərdɪs/ **Cowardice** is cowardly behaviour. ❑ *He openly accused his opponents of cowardice.* N-UNCOUNT ≠ bravery, courage

**cow|ard|ly** /kaʊərdli/ If you describe someone as **cowardly**, you disapprove of them because they are easily frightened and avoid doing dangerous and difficult things. ❑ *I was too cowardly to complain. ...a cowardly act of violence.* ADJ disapproval ≠ brave, courageous

**cow|bell** /kaʊbel/ **(cowbells)** A **cowbell** is a small bell that is hung around a cow's neck so that the ringing sound makes it possible to find the cow. N-COUNT

**cow|boy** /kaʊbɔɪ/ **(cowboys)** 1 A **cowboy** is a male character in a western. ❑ *...cowboy films.* N-COUNT
2 A **cowboy** is a man employed to look after cattle in North America, especially in former times. N-COUNT
3 You can refer to someone who runs a business as a **cowboy** if they run it dishonestly or are not experienced, skilful, or careful in their work. [BRIT] ❑ *We don't want to look like a bunch of cowboys.* N-COUNT: oft N n disapproval

**cow|er** /kaʊər/ **(cowers, cowering, cowered)** If you **cower**, you bend forward and downwards because you are very frightened. ❑ *The hostages cowered in their seats.* VERB V

**cow|hide** /kaʊhaɪd/ **Cowhide** is leather made from the skin of a cow. ❑ *...cowhide boots.* N-UNCOUNT: oft N n

**cowl** /kaʊl/ **(cowls)** A **cowl** is a large loose hood covering a person's head, or their head and shoulders. Cowls are worn especially by monks. N-COUNT

**co-worker** **(co-workers)** Your **co-workers** are the people you work with, especially people on the same job or project as you. N-COUNT = colleague

**cow|pat** /kaʊpæt/ **(cowpats)** also **cow pat.** A **cowpat** is a pile of faeces from a cow. N-COUNT

**cow|shed** /kaʊʃed/ **(cowsheds)** A **cowshed** is a building where cows are kept or milked. N-COUNT

**cow|slip** /kaʊslɪp/ **(cowslips)** A **cowslip** is a small wild plant with yellow, sweet-smelling flowers. N-COUNT

**cox** /kɒks/ **(coxes)** In a rowing boat, the **cox** is the person who gives instructions to the rowers. N-COUNT

**cox|swain** /kɒksən/ **(coxswains)** The **coxswain** of a lifeboat or other small boat is the person who steers the boat. N-COUNT

**coy** /kɔɪ/ 1 A **coy** person is shy, or pretends to be shy, about love and sex. ❑ *She is modest without being coy.* ADJ
♦ **coy|ly** *She smiled coyly at Algie as he took her hand and raised it to his lips.* ADV: ADV with v
2 If someone is being **coy**, they are unwilling to talk about something that they feel guilty or embarrassed about. ❑ *Mr Alexander is not the slightest bit coy about his ambitions.* ADJ: usu v-link ADJ, oft ADJ *about* n = reticent
♦ **coy|ly** *The administration coyly refused to put a firm figure on the war's costs.* ADV: ADV with v

**coy|ote** /kaɪoʊti/ **(coyotes)** A **coyote** is a small wolf which lives in the plains of North America. N-COUNT

**coy|pu** /kɔɪpuː/ **(coypus)** A **coypu** is a large South American rodent which lives near water. N-COUNT

**cozy** /koʊzi/ → see **cosy**.

**Cpl.** **Cpl.** is the written abbreviation for **corporal** when it is used as a title. ❑ *...Cpl. G. Walker.* N-TITLE

**CPU** /siː piː juː/ **(CPUs)** In a computer, the **CPU** is the part that processes all the data and makes the computer work. **CPU** is an abbreviation for 'central processing unit'. [COMPUTING] N-COUNT

**crab** /kræb/ **(crabs)** A **crab** is a sea creature with a flat round body covered by a shell, and five pairs of legs with large claws on the front pair. Crabs usually move sideways. N-COUNT
♦ **Crab** is the flesh of this creature eaten as food. N-UNCOUNT

**crab ap|ple** **(crab apples)** A **crab apple** is a tree like an apple tree that produces small sour fruit. N-COUNT

**crab|by** /kræbi/ Someone who is **crabby** is bad-tempered and unpleasant to people. [INFORMAL] ADJ

**crab|meat** /kræbmiːt/ also **crab meat.** **Crabmeat** is the part of a crab that you eat. N-UNCOUNT

**crack**
① VERB USES
② NOUN AND ADJECTIVE USES

① **crack** /kræk/ **(cracks, cracking, cracked)** ◆◇◇
1 If something hard **cracks**, or if you **crack** it, it becomes slightly damaged, with lines appearing on its surface. ❑ *A gas main had cracked under my neighbour's garage and gas had seeped into our homes... Remove the dish from the oven, crack the salt crust and you will find the skin just peels off the fish.* VERB V V n
2 If something **cracks**, or if you **crack** it, it makes a sharp sound like the sound of a piece of wood breaking. ❑ *Thunder cracked in the sky... He cracked his fingers nervously.* VERB V V n
3 If you **crack** a hard part of your body, such as your knee or your head, you hurt it by accidentally hitting it hard against something. ❑ *He cracked his head on the pavement and was knocked cold.* VERB = bang, bash V n
4 When you **crack** something that has a shell, such as an egg or a nut, you break the shell in order to reach the inside part. ❑ *Crack the eggs into a bowl.* VERB = break V n
5 If you **crack** a problem or a code, you solve it, especially after a lot of thought. ❑ *He has finally cracked the system after years of painstaking research.* VERB V n
6 If someone **cracks**, they lose control of their emotions or actions because they are under a lot of pressure. [INFORMAL] ❑ *She's calm and strong, and she is just not going to crack.* VERB V
7 If your voice **cracks** when you are speaking or singing, it changes in pitch because you are feeling a strong emotion. ❑ *Her voice cracked and she began to cry.* VERB V
8 If you **crack** a joke, you tell it. ❑ *He cracked jokes and talked about beer and girls.* VERB V n
9 → See also **cracked**, **cracking**.
10 If you say that something is **not all it's cracked up to be**, you mean that it is not as good as other people have said it is. [INFORMAL] ❑ *Package holidays are not always all they're cracked up to be.* PHRASE: V inflects

♦ **crack down** If people in authority **crack down on** a group of people, they become stricter in making the group obey rules or laws. ❑ *The government has cracked down hard on those campaigning for greater democracy... There has been a lot of drinking. We are cracking down now. Anyone who gets caught is fired.* → See also **crackdown**. PHRASAL VERB = clamp down V P on n V P

♦ **crack up** 1 If someone **cracks up**, they are under such a lot of emotional strain that they become mentally ill. [INFORMAL] ❑ *She would have cracked up if she hadn't allowed herself some fun.* PHRASAL VERB V P
2 If you **crack up** or if someone or something **cracks** you **up**, you laugh a lot. [INFORMAL] ❑ *She told stories that cracked me up and I swore to write them down so you could enjoy them too... We all just cracked up laughing.* PHRASAL VERB V n P V P

② **crack** /kræk/ **(cracks)** 1 A **crack** is a very narrow gap between two things, or between two parts of a thing. ❑ *Kathryn had seen him through a crack in the curtains.* N-COUNT = chink
2 If you open something such as a door, window, or curtain **a crack**, you open it only a small amount. ❑ *He went to the door, opened it a crack, and listened.* N-SING
3 A **crack** is a line that appears on the surface of something when it is slightly damaged. ❑ *The plate had a crack in it... Hundreds of office buildings and homes developed large cracks in walls and ceilings.* N-COUNT
4 A **crack** is a sharp sound, like the sound of a piece of wood breaking. ❑ *Suddenly there was a loud crack and glass flew into the car... 'Crack!' – The first shot rang out, hitting Paolo.* N-COUNT; SOUND
5 If you have or take a **crack at** something, you make an attempt to do or achieve something. [INFORMAL] ❑ *I should love to have a crack at the Olympia title in my last year.* N-SING: N at n/-ing = go, shot
6 A **crack** is a slightly rude or cruel joke. ❑ *When Paul made the crack about the 'famous girl detective', I began to suspect that he had it in for you.* N-COUNT
7 **Crack** is a very pure form of the drug cocaine. → See also **crack cocaine**. N-UNCOUNT
8 A **crack** soldier or sportsman is highly trained and very skilful. ❑ *...a crack undercover police officer.* ADJ: ADJ n
9 → See also **craic**.
10 If you say that someone does something **at the crack of dawn**, you are emphasizing that they do it very early in the morning. ❑ *I often start work at the crack of dawn when there is a big order to get out.* PHRASE: PHR after v [emphasis]

**crack co|caine** also **crack-cocaine**. **Crack cocaine** is a form of the drug cocaine which has been purified and made into crystals. N-UNCOUNT = crack

**crack|down** /krækdaʊn/ **(crackdowns)** A **crackdown** is strong official action that is taken to punish people who break laws. ❑ *...anti-government unrest that ended with the violent army crackdown.* N-COUNT

**cracked** /krækt/ 1 An object that is **cracked** has lines on its surface because it is damaged. ❑ *The ceiling was grey and cracked. ...a cracked mirror.* ADJ
2 A **cracked** voice or a **cracked** musical note sounds rough and unsteady. ❑ *When he spoke, his voice was hoarse and cracked.* ADJ

**crack|er** /krækəʳ/ **(crackers)** 1 A **cracker** is a thin, crisp biscuit which is often eaten with cheese. N-COUNT
2 If you say that someone or something is a **cracker**, you like and admire them very much. [BRIT, INFORMAL] ❑ *She's a cracker... 'Dude' is a cracker of an album.* N-COUNT: oft N of n
3 A **cracker** is a hollow cardboard tube covered with coloured paper. Crackers make a loud noise when they are pulled apart and usually contain a small toy and a paper hat. In Britain they are used mainly at Christmas. ❑ *...a Christmas cracker.* N-COUNT

**crack|ing** /krækɪŋ/ 1 You use **cracking** to describe something you think is very good or exciting. [BRIT, INFORMAL] ❑ *It's a cracking novel.* ADJ: usu ADJ n = great, brilliant
2 If you tell someone to **get cracking**, you are telling them to start doing something immediately. [BRIT, INFORMAL] ❑ *Mark, you'd better get cracking, the sooner the better.* PHRASE: get inflects

**crack|le** /krækəl/ **(crackles, crackling, crackled)** If something **crackles**, it makes a rapid series of short, harsh noises. ❑ *The radio crackled again. ...a crackling fire.* ♦ **Crackle** is also a noun. ❑ *...the crackle of flames and gunfire.* VERB V V-ing N-COUNT

**crack|ly** /krækəli/ Something that is **crackly**, especially a recording or broadcast, has or makes a lot of short, harsh noises. ❑ *...a crackly phone line.* ADJ

**crack|pot** /krækpɒt/ **(crackpots)** If you describe someone or their ideas as **crackpot**, you disapprove of them because you think that their ideas are strange and crazy. [INFORMAL] ❑ *...crackpot schemes.* ♦ A **crackpot** is a crackpot person. ❑ *She was no more a crackpot than the rest of us.* ADJ: ADJ n [disapproval] N-COUNT = nutter

**cra|dle** /kreɪdəl/ **(cradles, cradling, cradled)**
1 A **cradle** is a baby's bed with high sides. Cradles often have curved bases so that they rock from side to side. N-COUNT = crib
2 The **cradle** is the part of a telephone on which the receiver rests while it is not being used. ❑ *I dropped the receiver back in the cradle.* N-COUNT
3 A **cradle** is a frame which supports or protects something. ❑ *He fixed the towing cradle round the hull.* N-COUNT
4 A place that is referred to as **the cradle of** something is the place where it began. ❑ *Mali is the cradle of some of Africa's richest civilizations.* N-COUNT: usu sing, the N of n
5 If you **cradle** someone or something **in** your arms or hands, you hold them carefully and gently. ❑ *I cradled her in my arms... He was sitting at the big table cradling a large bowl of milky coffee.* VERB V n in n V n
6 If something affects you **from the cradle to the grave**, it affects you throughout your life. ❑ *The bond of brotherhood was one to last from the cradle to the grave.* PHRASE: PHR after v

**craft** /krɑːft, kræft/ **(crafts, crafting, crafted)** ◆◇◇

✔ **craft** is both the singular and the plural form for meaning 1.

1 You can refer to a boat, a spacecraft, or an aircraft as a **craft**. ❑ *With great difficulty, the fisherman manoeuvred his small craft close to the reef.* → See also **landing craft**. N-COUNT
2 A **craft** is an activity such as weaving, carving, or pottery that involves making things skilfully with your hands. ❑ *All kinds of traditional craft industries are preserved here.* N-COUNT
3 You can use **craft** to refer to any activity or job N-COUNT

that involves doing something skilfully. ❑ *Maurice Murphy, one of the country's leading classical trumpeters, learnt his craft with the Black Dyke Mills band.* [4] If something **is crafted**, it is made skilfully. ❑ *The windows would probably have been crafted in the latter part of the Middle Ages... Many delegates were willing to craft a compromise... The author extracts the maximum from every carefully-crafted scene in this witty tale. ...original, hand-crafted bags at affordable prices.* VERB be V-ed V n V-ed V-ed

**craft fair** **(craft fairs)** A **craft fair** is an event at which people sell goods they have made. N-COUNT

**craftily** /krɑːftɪli, kræft-/ → see **crafty**.

**crafts|man** /krɑːftsmən, kræft-/ **(craftsmen)** A **craftsman** is a man who makes things skilfully with his hands. ❑ *The table in the kitchen was made by a local craftsman.* N-COUNT

**crafts|man|ship** /krɑːftsmənʃɪp, kræft-/ [1] **Craftsmanship** is the skill that someone uses when they make beautiful things with their hands. ❑ *It is easy to appreciate the craftsmanship of Armani.* [2] **Craftsmanship** is the quality that something has when it is beautiful and has been very carefully made. ❑ *His canoes are known for their style, fine detail and craftsmanship.* N-UNCOUNT N-UNCOUNT

**crafts|people** /krɑːftspiːpəl, kræft-/ **Craftspeople** are people who make things skilfully with their hands. ❑ *...highly skilled craftspeople.* N-PLURAL

**crafts|wom|an** /krɑːftswʊmən, kræfts-/ **(craftswomen)** A **craftswoman** is a woman who makes things skilfully with her hands. N-COUNT

**crafty** /krɑːfti, kræfti/ **(craftier, craftiest)** If you describe someone as **crafty**, you mean that they achieve what they want in a clever way, often by deceiving people. ❑ *...a crafty, lying character who enjoys plotting against others... A crafty look came to his eyes.* ADJ = cunning

**crag** /kræg/ **(crags)** A **crag** is a steep rocky cliff or part of a mountain. N-COUNT

**crag|gy** /krægi/ [1] A **craggy** cliff or mountain is steep and rocky. ❑ *...tiny villages on craggy cliffs.* [2] A **craggy** face has large features and deep lines. ❑ *He's a very small man with a lined, craggy face.* ADJ: usu ADJ n ADJ: usu ADJ n

**craic** /kræk/

✔ in BRIT, also use **crack**

If you are talking about something that you did and you say 'the **craic** was great', or 'it was a good **craic**', you mean that you had a really good time, especially because everyone was talking, joking, and laughing. [IRISH, INFORMAL] ❑ *They go to the pubs not for the drink alone, but for the crack.* N-SING

**cram** /kræm/ **(crams, cramming, crammed)** [1] If you **cram** things or people **into** a container or place, you put them into it, although there is hardly enough room for them. ❑ *While nobody was looking, she squashed her school hat and crammed it into a wastebasket... I crammed my bag full of swimsuits and T-shirts and caught the sleeper down to Beziers... She crammed her mouth with caviar.* [2] If people **cram into** a place or vehicle or **cram** a place or vehicle, so many of them enter it at one time that it is completely full. ❑ *We crammed into my car and set off... Friends and admirers crammed the chapel at the small Los Angeles cemetery where Monroe is buried.* [3] If you **are cramming for** an examination, you are learning as much as possible in a short time just before you take the examination. ❑ *She was cramming for her Economics exam.* VERB = stuff V n prep/adv V n *full of* n V n *with* n VERB = pack V prep V n VERB V *for* n

♦ **cram|ming** *It would take two or three months of cramming to prepare for Vermont's bar exam.* N-UNCOUNT

**crammed** /kræmd/ [1] If a place is **crammed with** things or people, it is full of them, so that there is hardly room for anything or anyone else. ❑ *The house is crammed with priceless furniture and works of art.* [2] If people or things are **crammed into** a place or vehicle, it is full of them. ADJ: usu v-link ADJ, usu ADJ *with/full of* n = bursting, packed ADJ: v-link ADJ prep/adv

❑ *Between two and three thousand refugees were crammed into the church buildings.* = packed

**cram|mer** /kræməʳ/ **(crammers)** A **crammer** is a school, teacher, or book which prepares students for an exam by teaching them a lot in a short time. [BRIT] N-COUNT

**cramp** /kræmp/ **(cramps, cramping, cramped)** [1] **Cramp** is a sudden strong pain caused by a muscle suddenly contracting. You sometimes get cramp in a muscle after you have been making a physical effort over a long period of time. ❑ *Hillsden was complaining of cramp in his calf muscles... She started getting stomach cramps this morning.* [2] If someone or something **cramps** your **style**, their presence or existence restricts your behaviour in some way. [INFORMAL] ❑ *Like more and more women, she believes marriage would cramp her style.* N-UNCOUNT: also N in pl PHRASE: V inflects

**cramped** /kræmpt/ A **cramped** room or building is not big enough for the people or things in it. ❑ *There are hundreds of families living in cramped conditions on the floor of the airport lounge.* ADJ = confined ≠ spacious, roomy

**cram|pon** /kræmpɒn/ **(crampons)** **Crampons** are metal plates with spikes underneath which mountain climbers fasten to the bottom of their boots, especially when there is snow or ice, in order to make climbing easier. N-COUNT: usu pl

**cran|berry** /krænbəri, AM -beri/ **(cranberries)** **Cranberries** are red berries with a sour taste. They are often used to make a sauce or jelly that you eat with meat. N-COUNT: usu pl, oft N n

**crane** /kreɪn/ **(cranes, craning, craned)** [1] A **crane** is a large machine that moves heavy things by lifting them in the air. ❑ *The little prefabricated hut was lifted away by a huge crane.* [2] A **crane** is a kind of large bird with a long neck and long legs. [3] If you **crane** your neck or head, you stretch your neck in a particular direction in order to see or hear something better. ❑ *She craned her neck to get a better view... Children craned to get close to him... She craned forward to look at me.* N-COUNT N-COUNT VERB V n V to-inf V adv/prep

**crane|fly** /kreɪnflaɪ/ **(craneflies)** also **crane fly.** A **cranefly** is a harmless flying insect with long legs. N-COUNT = daddy longlegs

**cra|nial** /kreɪniəl/ **Cranial** means relating to your cranium. [TECHNICAL] ❑ *...cranial bleeding.* ADJ: ADJ n

**cra|nium** /kreɪniəm/ **(craniums** or **crania** /kreɪniə/**)** Your **cranium** is the round part of your skull that contains your brain. [TECHNICAL] N-COUNT

**crank** /kræŋk/ **(cranks, cranking, cranked)** [1] If you call someone a **crank**, you think their ideas or behaviour are strange. [INFORMAL] ❑ *The Prime Minister called Councillor Marshall 'a crank'.* [2] A **crank** is a device that you turn in order to make something move. [3] If you **crank** an engine or machine, you make it move or function, especially by turning a handle. ❑ *The chauffeur got out to crank the motor.* N-COUNT disapproval N-COUNT VERB V n

♦ **crank up** [1] If you **crank up** a machine or a device, you make it function harder or at a greater level. [BRIT] ❑ *Just crank up your hearing aid a peg or two.* [2] If you **crank up** a machine or device, you start it. [AM] ❑ *...May's warm weather, which caused Americans to crank up their air conditioners.* [3] If you **crank up** the volume of something, you turn it up until it is very loud. ❑ *Someone cranked up the volume of the public address system... By about six, they're cranking the music up loud again.* [4] To **crank** something **up** means to increase it or make it more intense. [mainly BRIT] ❑ *The legal authorities cranked up the investigation.* PHRASAL VERB V P n Also V n P PHRASAL VERB = start up V P n Also V n P PHRASAL VERB = turn up V P n V n P adj Also V n P PHRASAL VERB V P n (not pron)

**crank|shaft** /kræŋkʃɑːft, -ʃæft/ **(crankshafts)** A **crankshaft** is the main shaft of an internal combustion engine. ❑ *The engine had a broken crankshaft.* N-COUNT

**cranky** /kræŋki/ [1] If you describe ideas or ways of behaving as **cranky**, you disapprove of them because you think they are strange. [INFORMAL] ❑ *Vegetarianism has shed its cranky image.* [2] **Cranky** means bad-tempered. [AM, INFORMAL] ADJ disapproval = eccentric ADJ

❑ *It was a long trek, and Jack and I both started to get cranky after about ten minutes.* = ratty

**cran|ny** /krǽni/ **(crannies)** **Crannies** are very narrow openings or spaces in something. ❑ *They fled like lizards into crannies in the rocks.* **every nook and cranny** → see **nook**. N-COUNT: usu pl = crevice

**crap** /krǽp/ **(craps, crapping, crapped)** [1] If you describe something as **crap**, you think that it is wrong or of very poor quality. [INFORMAL, RUDE] ♦ **Crap** is also a noun. ❑ *It is a tedious, humourless load of crap.* [2] **Crap** is sometimes used to refer to faeces. [INFORMAL, RUDE] [3] To **crap** means to get rid of faeces from your body. [INFORMAL, RUDE] [4] **Craps** or **crap** is a gambling game, played mainly in North America, in which you throw two dice and bet what the total will be. ❑ *I'll shoot some craps or play some blackjack.* ADJ disapproval; N-UNCOUNT = rubbish; N-UNCOUNT; VERB: V; N-UNCOUNT

**crap|py** /krǽpi/ **(crappier, crappiest)** If you describe something as **crappy**, you think it is of very poor quality. Many people consider this word offensive. [INFORMAL] ❑ *...reading a crappy detective novel.* ADJ: usu ADJ n disapproval

**crash** /krǽʃ/ **(crashes, crashing, crashed)** [1] A **crash** is an accident in which a moving vehicle hits something and is damaged or destroyed. ❑ *His elder son was killed in a car crash a few years ago. ...a plane crash.* [2] If a moving vehicle **crashes** or if the driver **crashes** it, it hits something and is damaged or destroyed. ❑ *The plane crashed mysteriously near the island of Ustica. ...when his car crashed into the rear of a van... Even his death, after crashing his motorcycle on a bridge in New Orleans, was spectacular... Her body was found near a crashed car.* [3] If something **crashes** somewhere, it moves and hits something else violently, making a loud noise. ❑ *The door swung inwards to crash against a chest of drawers behind it... I heard them coming, crashing through the undergrowth, before I saw them.* [4] A **crash** is a sudden, loud noise. ❑ *Two people in the flat recalled hearing a loud crash about 1.30 a.m.* [5] If a business or financial system **crashes**, it fails suddenly, often with serious effects. [BUSINESS] ❑ *When the market crashed, they assumed the deal would be cancelled.* ♦ **Crash** is also a noun. ❑ *He predicted correctly that there was going to be a stock market crash.* [6] If a computer or a computer program **crashes**, it fails suddenly. [COMPUTING] ❑ *...after the computer crashed for the second time in 10 days.* ◆◆◇ N-COUNT: oft n N = accident; VERB; V; V into n; V n; V-ed; VERB; V prep/adv; V prep/adv; N-COUNT; VERB; V; N-COUNT; VERB; V

♦ **crash out** If someone **crashes out** somewhere, they fall asleep where they are because they are very tired or drunk. [INFORMAL] ❑ *I just want to crash out on the sofa... The band are crashed out on the floor.* PHRASAL VERB = flake out; V P; V-ed P

**crash bar|ri|er** **(crash barriers)** A **crash barrier** is a strong low fence built along the side of a road or between the two halves of a motorway in order to prevent accidents. [BRIT] N-COUNT

☑ in AM, use **guardrail**

**crash course** **(crash courses)** A **crash course in** a particular subject is a short course in which you are taught basic facts or skills, for example before you start a new job. ❑ *I did a 15-week crash course in typing.* N-COUNT: usu with supp, oft N *in* n

**crash hel|met** **(crash helmets)** A **crash helmet** is a helmet that motorcyclists wear in order to protect their heads if they have an accident. N-COUNT

**crash-land** **(crash-lands, crash-landing, crash-landed)** also **crash land.** If a pilot **crash-lands** an aircraft, or if it **crash-lands**, it lands more quickly and less safely than usual, for example when there is something wrong with the aircraft, and it cannot land normally. ❑ *He arrives in his biplane and crash lands it in a tree... A light aircraft crash-landed on a putting green yesterday.* ♦ **crash-landing** **(crash-landings)** *His plane made a crash-landing during a sandstorm yesterday.* VERB; V n; V; N-COUNT

**crass** /krǽs/ **(crasser, crassest)** **Crass** behaviour is stupid and does not show consideration for other people. ❑ *The government has behaved with crass insensitivity.* ♦ **crass|ly** *...one of the most crassly stupid political acts of modern times... These teachings can be crassly misinterpreted.* ADJ; ADV: ADV adj, ADV with v

**crate** /kreɪt/ **(crates, crating, crated)** [1] A **crate** is a large box used for transporting or storing things. ❑ *...a pile of wooden crates... A crane was already unloading crates and pallets.* [2] If something **is crated**, it is packed in a crate so that it can be transported or stored somewhere safely. ❑ *The much repaired plane was crated for the return journey.* [3] A **crate** is a plastic or wire box divided into sections which is used for carrying bottles. ♦ A **crate of** something is the amount of it that is contained in a crate. ❑ *We've also got a bonus quiz with crates of beer as prizes!* N-COUNT; VERB: usu passive; be V-ed; N-COUNT; N-COUNT: usu N *of* n

**cra|ter** /kreɪtəʳ/ **(craters)** A **crater** is a very large hole in the ground, which has been caused by something hitting it or by an explosion. N-COUNT

**cra|tered** /kreɪtəʳd/ If the surface of something is **cratered**, it has many craters in it. ❑ *... the Moon's cratered surface.* ADJ: usu ADJ n

**cra|vat** /krəvǽt/ **(cravats)** A **cravat** is a piece of folded cloth which a man wears wrapped around his neck. N-COUNT

**crave** /kreɪv/ **(craves, craving, craved)** If you **crave** something, you want to have it very much. ❑ *There may be certain times of day when smokers crave their cigarette... You may be craving for some fresh air.* ♦ **crav|ing** **(cravings)** *...a craving for sugar. ...her craving to be loved.* VERB; V n; V *for* n; Also V to-inf; N-COUNT: usu with supp

**cra|ven** /kreɪvᵊn/ Someone who is **craven** is very cowardly. [WRITTEN] ❑ *They condemned the deal as a craven surrender.* ADJ disapproval ≠ courageous

**craw|fish** /krɔːfɪʃ/ **(crawfish)** A **crawfish** is a small shellfish with five pairs of legs which lives in rivers and streams. You can eat some types of crawfish. [AM] N-COUNT = crayfish

☑ in BRIT, use **crayfish**

**crawl** /krɔːl/ **(crawls, crawling, crawled)** [1] When you **crawl**, you move forward on your hands and knees. ❑ *Don't worry if your baby seems a little reluctant to crawl or walk... I began to crawl on my hands and knees towards the door... As he tried to crawl away, he was hit in the shoulder.* [2] When an insect **crawls** somewhere, it moves there quite slowly. ❑ *I watched the moth crawl up the outside of the lampshade.* [3] If someone or something **crawls** somewhere, they move or progress slowly or with great difficulty. ❑ *I crawled out of bed at nine-thirty... Hairpin turns force the car to crawl at 10 miles an hour in some places.* ♦ **Crawl** is also a noun. ❑ *The traffic on the approach road slowed to a crawl.* [4] If you say that a place **is crawling with** people or animals, you are emphasizing that it is full of them. [INFORMAL] ❑ *This place is crawling with police.* [5] **The crawl** is a kind of swimming stroke which you do lying on your front, swinging one arm over your head, and then the other arm. [6] If something **makes** your **skin crawl** or **makes** your **flesh crawl**, it makes you feel shocked or disgusted. ❑ *I hated this man, his very touch made my skin crawl.* [7] → See also **kerb-crawling, pub crawl**. VERB; V; V prep/adv; V prep/adv; VERB; V prep; VERB; V prep/adv; V; N-SING: *a* N; VERB: only cont emphasis V *with* n; N-SING: *the* N; PHRASE: V inflects

**crawl|er** /krɔːləʳ/ **(crawlers)** A **crawler** is a computer program that visits websites and collects information when you do an Internet search. [COMPUTING] N-COUNT

**cray|fish** /kreɪfɪʃ/ **(crayfish)** A **crayfish** is a small shellfish with five pairs of legs which lives in rivers and streams. You can eat some types of crayfish. N-COUNT = crawfish

**cray|on** /kreɪɒn/ **(crayons)** A **crayon** is a pencil containing coloured wax or clay, or a rod of coloured wax used for drawing. N-COUNT

**craze** /kreɪz/ **(crazes)** If there is a **craze** for something, it is very popular for a short time. ❑ *Walking is the latest fitness craze.* N-COUNT: usu with supp = fad

**crazed** /kreɪzd/ **Crazed** people are wild and uncontrolled, and perhaps insane. [WRITTEN] ❑ *A crazed gunman slaughtered five people last night.* ADJ: usu ADJ n = crazy

**-crazed** /-kreɪzd/ **-crazed** combines with nouns to form adjectives that describe people whose behaviour is wild and uncontrolled because of the thing the noun refers to. ❑ *...a drug-crazed killer.* COMB in ADJ

**cra|zi|ly** /kreɪzɪli/ If something moves **crazily**, it moves in a way or in a direction that you do not expect. [WRITTEN] ❑ *The ball bounced crazily over his shoulder into the net.* → See also **crazy**. ADV: ADV after v = wildly

**cra|zy** /kreɪzi/ **(crazier, craziest, crazies)** ◆◇◇ 1 If you describe someone or something as **crazy**, you think they are very foolish or strange. [INFORMAL] ❑ *People thought they were all crazy to try to make money from manufacturing... That's why he's got so caught up with this crazy idea about Mr. Trancas.* ADJ disapproval ♦ **cra|zi|ly** *The teenagers shook their long, black hair and gesticulated crazily.* ADV: ADV after v, ADV adj 2 Someone who is **crazy** is insane. [INFORMAL] ❑ *If I sat home and worried about all this stuff, I'd go crazy... He strides around the room beaming like a crazy man.* ADJ = mad ♦ **Crazy** is also a noun. ❑ *Outside, mumbling, was one of New York's ever-present crazies.* N-COUNT = loony 3 If you are **crazy about** something, you are very enthusiastic about it. If you are **not crazy about** something, you do not like it. [INFORMAL] ❑ *He's still crazy about both his work and his hobbies.* ADJ: v-link ADJ *about* n = mad ♦ **Crazy** is also a combining form. ❑ *Every football-crazy schoolboy in Europe dreams of one day being involved in the championships.* COMB in ADJ 4 If you are **crazy about** someone, you are deeply in love with them. [INFORMAL] ❑ *None of that matters, because we're crazy about each other.* ADJ: v-link ADJ *about* n 5 If something or someone makes you **crazy** or drives you **crazy**, they make you extremely annoyed or upset. [INFORMAL] ❑ *This sitting around is driving me crazy... When Jock woke up and found you gone he went crazy.* ADJ: v-link ADJ = mad 6 You use **like crazy** to emphasize that something happens to a great degree. [INFORMAL] ❑ *The stuff was selling like crazy.* PHRASE: PHR after v emphasis = like mad

**cra|zy pav|ing** **Crazy paving** is pieces of stone of different shapes fitted together to make a path or flat area. N-UNCOUNT

**creak** /kriːk/ **(creaks, creaking, creaked)** If something **creaks**, it makes a short, high-pitched sound when it moves. ❑ *The ancient bed-springs creaked... The door creaked open. ...the creaking stairs.* VERB V, V adj, V-ing ♦ **Creak** is also a noun. ❑ *The door was pulled open with a creak.* N-COUNT

**creaky** /kriːki/ 1 A **creaky** object creaks when it moves. ❑ *She pushed open a creaky door.* ADJ 2 If you describe something as **creaky**, you think it is bad in some way because it is old or old-fashioned. ❑ *...its creaky and corrupt political system.* ADJ

**cream** /kriːm/ **(creams, creaming, creamed)** ◆◆◇ 1 **Cream** is a thick yellowish-white liquid taken from milk. You can use it in cooking or put it on fruit or desserts. ❑ *...strawberries and cream.* → See also **clotted cream, double cream, single cream, sour cream, whipping cream**. N-UNCOUNT 2 **Cream** is used in the names of soups that contain cream or milk. ❑ *...cream of mushroom soup.* N-UNCOUNT: N *of* n 3 A **cream** is a substance that you rub into your skin, for example to keep it soft or to heal or protect it. ❑ *Gently apply the cream to the affected areas. ...sun protection creams.* → See also **face cream**. N-VAR 4 Something that is **cream** is yellowish-white in colour. ❑ *...cream silk stockings. ...a cream-coloured Persian cat.* COLOUR 5 **Cream** is used in expressions such as **the cream of society** and **the cream of British athletes** to refer to the best people or things of a particular kind. ❑ *The Ball was attended by the cream of Hollywood society.* N-SING-COLL: *the* N *of* n ● You can refer to the best people or things of a particular kind as **the cream of the crop**. PHRASE 6 → See also **ice cream, peaches and cream, salad cream, shaving cream**.

♦ **cream off** 1 To **cream off** part of a group of people means to take them away and treat them in a special way, because they are better than the others. ❑ *The private schools cream off many of the best pupils.* PHRASAL VERB disapproval V P n 2 If a person or organization **creams off** a large amount of money, they take it and use it for themselves. [INFORMAL] ❑ *This means smaller banks can cream off big profits during lending booms.* PHRASAL VERB disapproval V P n (not pron)

**cream cheese** **Cream cheese** is a very rich, soft white cheese. N-UNCOUNT

**cream crack|er** **(cream crackers)** **Cream crackers** are crisp dry biscuits which are eaten with cheese. [BRIT] N-COUNT = cracker

**cream|er** /kriːməʳ/ **(creamers)** **Creamer** is a white powder that is used in tea and coffee instead of milk. ❑ *...coffee whitened with a non-dairy creamer.* N-MASS

**cream|ery** /kriːməri/ **(creameries)** A **creamery** is a place where milk and cream are made into butter and cheese. N-COUNT = dairy

**cream of tar|tar** **Cream of tartar** is a white powder used in baking. N-UNCOUNT

**cream tea** **(cream teas)** In Britain, a **cream tea** is an afternoon meal that consists of tea to drink and small cakes called scones that are eaten with jam and cream. Cream teas are served in places such as tea shops. N-COUNT

**creamy** /kriːmi/ **(creamier, creamiest)** 1 Food or drink that is **creamy** contains a lot of cream or milk. ❑ *...rich, creamy coffee. ...a creamy chocolate and nut candy bar.* ADJ 2 Food that is **creamy** has a soft smooth texture and appearance. ❑ *...creamy mashed potato... Whisk the mixture until it is smooth and creamy.* ADJ

**crease** /kriːs/ **(creases, creasing, creased)** 1 **Creases** are lines that are made in cloth or paper when it is crushed or folded. ❑ *She stood up, frowning at the creases in her silk dress... Papa flattened the creases of the map with his broad hands.* N-COUNT: usu pl 2 If cloth or paper **creases** or if you **crease** it, lines form in it when it is crushed or folded. ❑ *Most outfits crease a bit when you are travelling... Liz sat down on the bed, lowering herself carefully so as not to crease her skirt.* VERB = crumple V, V n ♦ **creased** *His clothes were creased, as if he had slept in them.* ADJ 3 **Creases** in someone's skin are lines which form where their skin folds when they move. ❑ *When Crevecoeur smiled, the creases in his face deepened.* N-COUNT = wrinkle ♦ **creased** *...Jock's creased drunken face.* ADJ 4 In cricket, **the crease** is a line on the playing surface where the batsman stands. ❑ *Haynes was still at the crease, unbeaten on 84.* N-SING: *the* N, poss N

**cre|ate** /krieɪt/ **(creates, creating, created)** ◆◆◆ 1 To **create** something means to cause it to happen or exist. ❑ *We set business free to create more jobs in Britain... Criticizing will only destroy a relationship and create feelings of failure.* VERB = produce ≠destroy V n, V n ♦ **crea|tion** /krieɪʃᵊn/ *These businesses stimulate the creation of local jobs.* N-UNCOUNT: usu N *of* n 2 When someone **creates** a new product or process, they invent it or design it. ❑ *It is really great for a radio producer to create a show like this.* VERB V n

**crea|tion** /krieɪʃᵊn/ **(creations)** 1 In many religions, **creation** is the making of the universe, earth, and creatures by God. ❑ *For the first time since creation, the survival of the Earth is entirely in our hands.* N-UNCOUNT: also *the* N 2 People sometimes refer to the whole universe as **creation**. [LITERARY] N-UNCOUNT 3 You can refer to something that someone has made as a **creation**, especially if it shows skill, imagination, or artistic ability. ❑ *The bathroom is entirely my own creation.* N-COUNT: usu with supp 4 → See also **create**.

**crea|tion|ism** /krieɪʃᵊnɪzəm/ **Creationism** is the belief that the account of the creation of the universe in the Bible is true, and that the theory of evolution is incorrect. N-UNCOUNT

**crea|tion|ist** /krieɪʃᵊnɪst/ **(creationists)** A **creationist** is someone who believes that the story of the creation of the universe in the Bible is true, and who rejects the theory of evolution. N-COUNT ≠evolutionist

**crea|tive** /krieɪtɪv/ ◆◇◇ 1 A **creative** person has the ability to invent and develop original ADJ: usu ADJ n ideas, especially in the arts. ❑ *Like so many creative people he was never satisfied. ...her obvious creative talents.* ♦ **crea|tiv|ity** /kriːeɪtɪvɪti/ *American art reached a peak of creativity in the '50s and 60s.* N-UNCOUNT

[2] **Creative** activities involve the inventing and making of new kinds of things. ❑ *...creative writing... Cooking is creative.* ADJ: usu ADJ n

[3] If you use something in a **creative** way, you use it in a new way that produces interesting and unusual results. ❑ *...his creative use of words.* ♦ **crea|tive|ly** *Genet teaches you to think creatively.* ADJ: usu ADJ n; ADV

**crea|tive ac|count|ing** **Creative accounting** is when companies present or organize their accounts in such a way that they gain money for themselves or give a false impression of their profits. ❑ *Much of the apparent growth in profits that occurred in the 1980s was the result of creative accounting.* N-UNCOUNT [disapproval]

**crea|tor** /krieɪtəʳ/ **(creators)** [1] The **creator** of something is the person who made it or invented it. ❑ *...Ian Fleming, the creator of James Bond.* N-COUNT: usu with poss

[2] God is sometimes referred to as **the Creator**. ❑ *This was the first object placed in the heavens by the Creator.* N-PROPER: the N

**crea|ture** /kriːtʃəʳ/ **(creatures)** [1] You can refer to any living thing that is not a plant as a **creature**, especially when it is of an unknown or unfamiliar kind. People also refer to imaginary animals and beings as **creatures**. ❑ *Alaskan Eskimos believe that every living creature possesses a spirit... The garden is surrounded by a hedge in which many small creatures can live.* N-COUNT = being

[2] If you say that someone is a particular type of **creature**, you are focusing on a particular quality they have. ❑ *She's charming, a sweet creature... She was a creature of the emotions, rather than reason.* **a creature of habit** → see **habit**. N-COUNT: with supp

**crea|ture com|forts** **Creature comforts** are the things that you need to feel comfortable in a place, for example good food and modern equipment. ❑ *They appreciate all the creature comforts of home.* N-PLURAL

**crèche** /kreʃ/ **(crèches)** also **creche**. A **crèche** is a place where small children can be left to be looked after while their parents are doing something else. [BRIT] N-COUNT

☑ in AM, use **day nursery**

**cre|dence** /kriːdᵊns/ [1] If something lends or gives **credence to** a theory or story, it makes it easier to believe. [FORMAL] ❑ *Good studies are needed to lend credence to the notion that genuine progress can be made in this important field.* N-UNCOUNT = credibility

[2] If you give **credence to** a theory or story, you believe it. [FORMAL] ❑ *You're surely not giving any credence to this story of Hythe's?* N-UNCOUNT

**cre|den|tials** /krɪdenʃᵊlz/ [1] Someone's **credentials** are their previous achievements, training, and general background, which indicate that they are qualified to do something. ❑ *...her credentials as a Bach specialist... I can testify to the credentials of the clientele.* N-PLURAL: with supp

[2] Someone's **credentials** are a letter or certificate that proves their identity or qualifications. ❑ *Britain's new ambassador to Lebanon has presented his credentials to the President.* N-PLURAL: usu poss N

**cred|ibil|ity** /kredɪbɪlɪti/ If someone or something has **credibility**, people believe in them and trust them. ❑ *The police have lost their credibility.* N-UNCOUNT

**cred|ibil|ity gap** A **credibility gap** is the difference between what a person says or promises and what they actually think or do. ❑ *There is a credibility gap developing between employers and employees.* N-SING

**cred|ible** /kredɪbᵊl/ [1] **Credible** means able to be trusted or believed. ❑ *Baroness Thatcher's claims seem credible to many... But in order to maintain a credible threat of intervention, we have to maintain a credible alliance.* ADJ = plausible

[2] A **credible** candidate, policy, or system, for example, is one that appears to have a chance of being successful. ❑ *Mr Robertson would be a credible candidate.* ADJ

**cred|it** /kredɪt/ **(credits, crediting, credited)** ◆◆◇ [1] If you are allowed **credit**, you are allowed to pay for goods or services several weeks or months after you have received them. ❑ *The group can't get credit to buy farming machinery... You can ask a dealer for a discount whether you pay cash or buy on credit.* N-UNCOUNT: oft on N

[2] If someone or their bank account is **in credit**, their bank account has money in it. [mainly BRIT] ❑ *The idea that I could be charged when I'm in credit makes me very angry... Interest is payable on credit balances.* N-UNCOUNT: in N, N n

[3] When a sum of money **is credited to** an account, the bank adds that sum of money to the total in the account. ❑ *She noticed that only $80,000 had been credited to her account... Midland decided to change the way it credited payments to accounts... Interest is calculated daily and credited once a year, on 1 April.* VERB ≠ debit; be V-ed to n; V n to n; be V-ed; Also V n

[4] A **credit** is a sum of money which is added to an account. ❑ *The statement of total debits and credits is known as a balance.* N-COUNT ≠ debit

[5] A **credit** is an amount of money that is given to someone. ❑ *Senator Bill Bradley outlined his own tax cut, giving families $350 in tax credits per child.* N-COUNT = allowance

[6] If you get **the credit for** something good, people praise you because you are responsible for it, or are thought to be responsible for it. ❑ *It would be wrong for us to take all the credit... Some of the credit for her relaxed manner must go to Andy.* N-UNCOUNT: oft the N for n/-ing ≠ blame

[7] If people **credit** someone **with** an achievement or if it **is credited to** them, people say or believe that they were responsible for it. ❑ *The staff are crediting him with having saved Hythe's life... The screenplay for 'Gabriel Over the White House' is credited to Carey Wilson.* VERB; V n with -ing/n; be V-ed to n

[8] If you **credit** someone **with** a quality, you believe or say that they have it. ❑ *I wonder why you can't credit him with the same generosity of spirit.* VERB; V n with n

[9] If you say that someone is **a credit to** someone or something, you mean that their qualities or achievements will make people have a good opinion of the person or thing mentioned. ❑ *He is one of the greatest British players of recent times and is a credit to his profession.* N-SING: a N to n ≠ disgrace

[10] The list of people who helped to make a film, a CD, or a television programme is called **the credits**. N-COUNT: usu pl

[11] A **credit** is a successfully completed part of a higher education course. At some universities and colleges you need a certain number of credits to be awarded a degree. N-COUNT

PHRASES [12] If you say that something **does** someone **credit**, you mean that they should be praised or admired because of it. ❑ *You're a nice girl, Lettie, and your kind heart does you credit.* PHRASE: V inflects

[13] To **give** someone **credit for** a good quality means to believe that they have it. ❑ *Bratbakk had more ability than the media gave him credit for.* PHRASE: V inflects, PHR n

[14] You say **on the credit side** in order to introduce one or more good things about a situation or person, usually when you have already mentioned the bad things about them. ❑ *On the credit side, he's always been wonderful with his mother.* PHRASE: PHR with cl

[15] If something is **to** someone's **credit**, they deserve praise for it. ❑ *She had managed to pull herself together and, to her credit, continued to look upon life as a positive experience.* PHRASE: PHR with cl, it v-link PHR that

[16] If you already have one or more achievements **to** your **credit**, you have achieved them. ❑ *I have twenty novels and countless magazine stories to my credit.* PHRASE

**cred|it|able** /kredɪtəbᵊl/ [1] A **creditable** performance or achievement is of a reasonably high standard. ❑ *They turned out a quite creditable performance.* ADJ = respectable

[2] If you describe someone's actions or aims as **creditable**, you mean that they are morally good. ❑ *Not a very creditable attitude, I'm afraid.* ADJ

**cred|it card** **(credit cards)** A **credit card** is a plastic card that you use to buy goods on credit. Compare **charge card**. N-COUNT

**cred|it hour** **(credit hours)** A **credit hour** is a credit that a school or college awards to students N-COUNT who have completed a course of study. [AM] ❑ *Now he needs only two credit hours to graduate.*

**cred|it note** **(credit notes)** A **credit note** is a piece of paper that a shop gives you when you return goods that you have bought from it. It states that you are entitled to take goods of the same value without paying for them. [BRIT] N-COUNT

in AM, use **credit slip**

**cred|i|tor** /kredɪtəʳ/ **(creditors)** Your **creditors** are the people who you owe money to. ❑ *The company said it would pay in full all its creditors.* N-COUNT: usu pl ≠ debtor

**cred|it rat|ing** Your **credit rating** is a judgment of how likely you are to pay money back if you borrow it or buy things on credit. N-SING

**cred|it slip** **(credit slips)** A **credit slip** is the same as a **credit note**. [AM] N-COUNT

**cred|it trans|fer** **(credit transfers)** 1 A **credit transfer** is a direct payment of money from one bank account into another. [BRIT] N-COUNT: also by N

in AM, use **money transfer**

2 If a student has a **credit transfer** when they change from one school or college to another, their credits are transferred from their old school or college to their new one. [AM] N-COUNT

**credit|worthy** /kredɪtwɜːʳði/ also **credit-worthy.** A **creditworthy** person or organization is one who can safely be lent money or allowed to have goods on credit, for example because in the past they have always paid back what they owe. ❑ *Building societies make loans to creditworthy customers.* ♦ **credit|worthi|ness** *They now take extra steps to verify the creditworthiness of customers.* ADJ N-UNCOUNT

**cre|do** /kriːdoʊ, kreɪ-/ **(credos)** A **credo** is a set of beliefs, principles, or opinions that strongly influence the way a person lives or works. [FORMAL] ❑ *Lord Clarendon's liberal credo was one of the foundations of his political conduct.* N-COUNT = creed

**cre|du|lity** /krɪdjuːlɪti, AM -duː-/ **Credulity** is a willingness to believe that something is real or true. [WRITTEN] ❑ *The plot does stretch credulity.* N-UNCOUNT

**credu|lous** /kredʒʊləs/ If you describe someone as **credulous**, you have a low opinion of them because they are too ready to believe what people tell them and are easily deceived. ❑ *...quack doctors charming money out of the pockets of credulous health-hungry citizens.* ADJ disapproval = gullible

**creed** /kriːd/ **(creeds)** 1 A **creed** is a set of beliefs, principles, or opinions that strongly influence the way people live or work. [FORMAL] ❑ *...their devotion to their creed of self-help.* 2 A **creed** is a religion. [FORMAL] ❑ *The centre is open to all, no matter what race or creed.* N-COUNT = credo N-COUNT = faith

**creek** /kriːk/ **(creeks)** 1 A **creek** is a narrow place where the sea comes a long way into the land. [BRIT] 2 A **creek** is a small stream or river. [AM] ❑ *Follow Austin Creek for a few miles.* 3 If someone is **up the creek**, they are in a bad or difficult situation, or are wrong in some way. You can also say that someone is **up the creek without a paddle.** [INFORMAL] N-COUNT: oft in names N-COUNT: oft in names PHRASE: v-link PHR

**creep** /kriːp/ **(creeps, creeping, crept)**

1 When people or animals **creep** somewhere, they move quietly and slowly. ❑ *Back I go to the hotel and creep up to my room... The rabbit creeps away and hides in a hole.* 2 If something **creeps** somewhere, it moves very slowly. ❑ *Mist had crept in again from the sea.* 3 If something **creeps** in or **creeps** back, it begins to occur or becomes part of something without people realizing or without them wanting it. ❑ *Insecurity might creep in... An increasing ratio of mistakes, perhaps induced by tiredness, crept into her game. ...a proposal that crept through unnoticed at the National Council in December.* 4 If a rate or number **creeps up** to a higher level, it gradually reaches that level. ❑ *The inflation rate has been creeping up to 9.5 per cent... The average number of students in each class is creeping up from three to four.* 5 If you describe someone as a **creep**, you mean that you dislike them a great deal, especially because they are insincere and flatter people. [INFORMAL] 6 If someone or something **gives** you **the creeps**, they make you feel very nervous or frightened. [INFORMAL] ❑ *I always hated that statue. It gave me the creeps.* 7 to **make** someone's **flesh creep** → see **flesh**. VERB V adv/prep V adv/prep VERB V adv/prep VERB V in V into n V adv/prep VERB V up to n V up Also V adj-compar N-COUNT disapproval PHRASE: V inflects

♦ **creep up on** 1 If you **creep up on** someone, you move slowly closer to them without being seen by them. ❑ *They'll creep up on you while you're asleep.* 2 If a feeling or state **creeps up on** you, you hardly notice that it is beginning to affect you or happen to you. ❑ *The desire to be a mother may creep up on you unexpectedly.* PHRASAL VERB V P P n PHRASAL VERB V P P n

**creep|er** /kriːpəʳ/ **(creepers)** **Creepers** are plants with long stems that wind themselves around objects. N-COUNT

**creepy** /kriːpi/ **(creepier, creepiest)** If you say that something or someone is **creepy**, you mean they make you feel very nervous or frightened. [INFORMAL] ❑ *There were certain places that were really creepy at night.* ADJ

**creepy-crawly** /kriːpi krɔːli/ **(creepy-crawlies)** You can refer to insects as **creepy-crawlies** when they give you a feeling of fear or disgust. This word is mainly used by children. [mainly BRIT, INFORMAL] N-COUNT: usu pl disapproval

**cre|mate** /krɪmeɪt, AM kriːmeɪt/ **(cremates, cremating, cremated)** When someone **is cremated**, their dead body is burned, usually as part of a funeral service. ❑ *She wants Chris to be cremated.* ♦ **cre|ma|tion** /krɪmeɪʃᵊn/ **(cremations)** *At Miss Garbo's request there was a cremation after a private ceremony... Half of California's deceased opt for cremation.* VERB: usu passive be V-ed N-VAR

**crema|to|rium** /kremətɔːriəm/ **(crematoria** /kremətɔːriə/ or **crematoriums)** A **crematorium** is a building in which the bodies of dead people are burned. N-COUNT

**crema|tory** /kriːmətɔːri/ **(crematories)** A **crematory** is the same as a **crematorium**. [AM] N-COUNT

**crème de la crème** /krem də lɑː krem/ If you refer to someone or something as **the crème de la crème**, you mean they are the very best person or thing of their kind. [JOURNALISM] ❑ *...the crème de la crème of fashion designers.* N-SING: the N approval

**crème fraiche** /krem freʃ/ **Crème fraiche** is a type of thick, slightly sour cream. N-UNCOUNT

**cren|el|lat|ed** /krenəleɪtɪd/

in AM, also use **crenelated**

In a castle, a **crenellated** wall has gaps in the top or openings through which to fire at attackers. [TECHNICAL] ❑ *...crenellated turrets.* ADJ: usu ADJ n

**cre|ole** /kriːoʊl/ **(creoles)** also **Creole.** 1 A **creole** is a language that has developed from a mixture of different languages and has become the main language in a particular place. ❑ *She begins speaking in the Creole of Haiti. ...French Creole.* 2 A **Creole** is a person of mixed African and European race, who lives in the West Indies and speaks a creole language. 3 A **Creole** is a person descended from the Europeans who first settled in the West Indies or the southern United States of America. 4 **Creole** means belonging to or relating to the Creole community. ❑ *Coconut Rice Balls is a Creole dish.* N-VAR = patois N-COUNT N-COUNT ADJ: usu ADJ n

**creo|sote** /kriːəsoʊt/ **Creosote** is a thick dark liquid made from coal tar which is used to prevent wood from rotting. N-UNCOUNT

**crepe** /kreɪp/ **(crepes)** 1 **Crepe** is a thin fabric with an uneven surface and is made of cotton, silk, or wool. ❑ *Use a crepe bandage to support the affected area.* 2 A **crepe** is a thin **pancake**. ❑ *...chicken-filled crepes.* 3 **Crepe** is a type of rubber with a rough surface. ❑ *...a pair of crepe-soled ankle-boots.* N-UNCOUNT: oft N n N-COUNT N-UNCOUNT: oft N n

**crepe pa|per** **Crepe paper** is stretchy paper with an uneven surface. Coloured crepe paper is often used for making decorations. N-UNCOUNT

**crept** /krept/ **Crept** is the past tense and past participle of **creep**.

**cre|pus|cu|lar** /krɪpʌskjʊləʳ/ **Crepuscular** means relating to **twilight**. [LITERARY] ❑ *...peering through the crepuscular gloom.* ADJ: ADJ n

**cre|scen|do** /krɪʃendoʊ/ **(crescendos)** 1 A **crescendo** is a noise that gets louder and louder. Some people also use **crescendo** to refer to the point when a noise is at its loudest. ❑ *The applause rose to a crescendo and cameras clicked.* N-COUNT: usu sing, oft N *of* n 2 People sometimes describe an increase in the intensity of something, or its most intense point, as a **crescendo**. [JOURNALISM] ❑ *There was a crescendo of parliamentary and press criticism.* N-COUNT: usu sing 3 In music, a **crescendo** is a section of a piece of music in which the music gradually gets louder and louder. N-COUNT: usu sing

**cres|cent** /kresᵊnt, krez-/ **(crescents)** 1 A **crescent** is a curved shape that is wider in the middle than at its ends, like the shape of the moon during its first and last quarters. It is the most important symbol of the Islamic faith. ❑ *A glittering Islamic crescent tops the mosque. ...a narrow crescent of sand dunes. ...a crescent moon.* N-COUNT 2 **Crescent** is sometimes used as part of the name of a street or row of houses that is usually built in a curve. [mainly BRIT] ❑ *...44 Colville Crescent.* N-IN-NAMES

**cress** /kres/ 1 **Cress** is a plant with small green leaves that are used in salads or to decorate food. See also **mustard and cress**. N-UNCOUNT 2 **Watercress** is sometimes referred to as **cress**. N-UNCOUNT

**crest** /krest/ **(crests)** 1 The **crest of** a hill or a wave is the top of it. N-COUNT ● If you say that you are **on the crest of a wave**, you mean that you are feeling very happy and confident because things are going well for you. ❑ *The band are riding on the crest of a wave with the worldwide success of their number one selling single.* PHRASE: v-link PHR, PHR after v 2 A bird's **crest** is a group of upright feathers on the top of its head. ❑ *Both birds had a dark blue crest.* N-COUNT 3 A **crest** is a design that is the symbol of a noble family, a town, or an organization. ❑ *On the wall is the family crest.* N-COUNT

**crest|ed** /krestɪd/ 1 A **crested** bird is a bird that has a crest on its head. ❑ *...crested hawks.* ADJ: ADJ n 2 **Crested** objects have on them the crest of a noble family, a town, or an organization. ❑ *...crested writing paper.* ADJ: usu ADJ n

**crest|fallen** /krestfɔːlən/ If you look **crestfallen**, you look sad and disappointed about something. ADJ: usu v-link ADJ

**cret|in** /kretɪn, AM kriːtᵊn/ **(cretins)** If you call someone a **cretin**, you think they are very stupid. [OFFENSIVE] N-COUNT [disapproval] = moron

**cret|in|ous** /kretɪnəs, AM kriːtənəs/ If you describe someone as **cretinous**, you think they are very stupid. [OFFENSIVE] ADJ [disapproval] = moronic

**cre|vasse** /krɪvæs/ **(crevasses)** A **crevasse** is a large, deep crack in thick ice or rock. ❑ *He fell down a crevasse.* N-COUNT

**crev|ice** /krevɪs/ **(crevices)** A **crevice** is a narrow crack or gap, especially in a rock. ❑ *...a huge boulder with rare ferns growing in every crevice.* N-COUNT

**crew** /kruː/ **(crews, crewing, crewed)** 1 The **crew** of a ship, an aircraft, or a spacecraft is the people who work on and operate it. ❑ *The mission for the crew of the space shuttle Endeavour is essentially over... The surviving crew members were ferried ashore.* ◆◇◇ N-COUNT-COLL 2 A **crew** is a group of people with special technical skills who work together on a task or project. ❑ *...a two-man film crew making a documentary.* N-COUNT: usu with supp 3 If you **crew** a boat, you work on it as part of the crew. ❑ *She was already a keen and experienced sailor, having crewed in both Merlin and Grayling... There were to be five teams of three crewing the boat. ...a fully crewed yacht.* VERB V V n V-ed 4 You can use **crew** to refer to a group of people you disapprove of. [INFORMAL] ❑ *This crew of killers and life-wreckers are headed by the mad but cunning Nino Brown.* N-SING-COLL: oft N *of* n [disapproval]

**crew cut** **(crew cuts)** also **crewcut.** A **crew cut** is a man's hairstyle in which his hair is cut very short. N-COUNT

**crew|man** /kruːmæn/ **(crewmen)** A **crewman** is a member of a crew. N-COUNT

**crew neck** **(crew necks)**

☑ in AM, use **crewneck**

A **crew neck** or a **crew neck** sweater is a sweater with a round neck. N-COUNT

**crib** /krɪb/ **(cribs)** A **crib** is a bed for a small baby. [mainly AM] N-COUNT

☑ in BRIT, usually use **cot**

**crib death** **(crib deaths)** **Crib death** is the sudden death of a baby while it is asleep, although the baby had not previously been ill. [AM] N-VAR

☑ in BRIT, use **cot death**

**crick** /krɪk/ **(cricks)** If you have a **crick** in your neck or in your back, you have a pain there caused by muscles becoming stiff. N-COUNT

**crick|et** /krɪkɪt/ **(crickets)** 1 **Cricket** is an outdoor game played between two teams. Players try to score points, called runs, by hitting a ball with a wooden bat. ❑ *During the summer term we would play cricket at the village ground. ...the Yorkshire County Cricket Club.* ◆◇◇ N-UNCOUNT 2 A **cricket** is a small jumping insect that produces short, loud sounds by rubbing its wings together. N-COUNT

**crick|et|er** /krɪkɪtəʳ/ **(cricketers)** A **cricketer** is a person who plays cricket. N-COUNT

**crick|et|ing** /krɪkɪtɪŋ/ **Cricketing** means relating to or taking part in cricket. ❑ *...Australia's cricketing heroes. ...his cricketing career.* ADJ: ADJ n

**cri|er** /kraɪəʳ/ → see **town crier**.

**cri|key** /kraɪki/ Some people say **crikey** in order to express surprise, especially at something unpleasant. [INFORMAL] EXCLAM [feelings] = blimey

**crime** /kraɪm/ **(crimes)** 1 A **crime** is an illegal action or activity for which a person can be punished by law. ❑ *He and Lieutenant Cassidy were checking the scene of the crime... Mr Steele has committed no crime and poses no danger to the public... We need a positive programme of crime prevention.* ◆◆◇ N-VAR 2 If you say that doing something is a **crime**, you think it is very wrong or a serious mistake. ❑ *It would be a crime to travel all the way to Australia and not stop in Sydney.* N-COUNT: usu sing, oft *it* v-link N to-inf [disapproval] = sin

**crime scene** **(crime scenes)** A **crime scene** is a place that is being investigated by the police because a crime has taken place there. ❑ *Photographs of the crime scene began to arrive within twenty minutes.* N-COUNT

**crime wave** also **crimewave.** When more crimes than usual are committed in a particular place, you can refer to this as a **crime wave**. ❑ *The country is in the grip of a teenage crime wave.* N-SING

**crimi|nal** /krɪmɪnᵊl/ **(criminals)** 1 A **criminal** is a person who regularly commits crimes. ❑ *A group of gunmen attacked a prison and set free nine criminals in Moroto.* ◆◆◇ N-COUNT 2 **Criminal** means connected with crime. ❑ *Her husband faces various criminal charges.* ADJ: usu ADJ n 3 If you describe an action as **criminal**, you think it is very wrong or a serious mistake. ❑ *He said a full-scale dispute involving strikes would be criminal.* ADJ: usu v-link ADJ [disapproval]

**crimi|nal court** **(criminal courts)** A **criminal court** is a law court that deals with criminal offences. N-COUNT

**crimi|nal|ize** /krɪmɪnəlaɪz/ **(criminalizes, criminalizing, criminalized)**

☑ in BRIT, also use **criminalise**

If a government **criminalizes** an action or person, it officially declares that the action or the person's behaviour is illegal. ❑ *There is no move to criminalise alcohol.* VERB V n

**crimi|nol|ogy** /krɪmɪnɒlədʒi/ **Criminology** is the scientific study of crime and criminals. N-UNCOUNT

♦ **crimi|nolo|gist** /krɪmɪnɒlədʒɪst/ **(criminologists)** ❑ *...a criminologist at the University of Montreal.* N-COUNT

**crimp** /krɪmp/ **(crimps, crimping, crimped)** 1 If you **crimp** something such as a piece of fabric or pastry, you make small folds in it. ❑ *Crimp the edges to seal them tightly.* VERB V n 2 To **crimp** something means to restrict or reduce it. [AM] ❑ *The dollar's recent strength is crimping overseas sales and profits.* VERB V n

**Crimp|lene** /krɪmpliːn/ also **crimplene**. **Crimplene** is an artificial fabric used for making clothes which does not crease easily. [mainly BRIT, TRADEMARK] N-UNCOUNT: oft N n

**crim|son** /krɪmzᵊn/ **(crimsons)** Something that is **crimson** is deep red in colour. ❑ *...a mass of crimson flowers.* COLOUR

**cringe** /krɪndʒ/ **(cringes, cringing, cringed)** If you **cringe at** something, you feel embarrassed or disgusted, and perhaps show this feeling in your expression or by making a slight movement. ❑ *Molly had cringed when Ann started picking up the guitar... Chris had cringed at the thought of using her own family for publicity... I cringed in horror.* VERB = recoil V V *at* n V *in* n

**crin|kle** /krɪŋkᵊl/ **(crinkles, crinkling, crinkled)** 1 If something **crinkles** or if you **crinkle** it, it becomes slightly creased or folded. ❑ *He shrugged whimsically, his eyes crinkling behind his glasses... When she laughs, she crinkles her perfectly-formed nose.* VERB V V n 2 **Crinkles** are small creases or folds. N-COUNT

**crin|kly** /krɪŋkli/ A **crinkly** object has many small creases or folds in it or in its surface. ❑ *...her big crinkly face. ...crinkly paper.* ADJ: usu ADJ n

**crino|line** /krɪnəlɪn/ **(crinolines)** A **crinoline** was a round frame which women wore under their skirts in the 19th century. N-COUNT

**crip|ple** /krɪpᵊl/ **(cripples, crippling, crippled)** 1 A person with a physical disability or a serious permanent injury is sometimes referred to as a **cripple**. [OFFENSIVE] ❑ *She has gone from being a healthy, fit, and sporty young woman to being a cripple.* N-COUNT 2 If someone **is crippled** by an injury, it is so serious that they can never move their body properly again. ❑ *Mr Easton was seriously crippled in an accident and had to leave his job... He had been warned that another bad fall could cripple him for life... He heaved his crippled leg into an easier position.* VERB *be* V-ed V n V-ed 3 If something **cripples** a person, it causes them severe psychological or emotional problems. ❑ *Howard wanted to be a popular singer, but stage fright crippled him... I'm not perfect but I'm also not emotionally crippled or lonely.* VERB V n V-ed 4 To **cripple** a machine, organization, or system means to damage it severely or prevent it from working properly. ❑ *A total cut-off of supplies would cripple the country's economy... The pilot was able to maneuver the crippled aircraft out of the hostile area.* VERB V n V-ed

**crip|pling** /krɪplɪŋ/ 1 A **crippling** illness or disability is one that severely damages your health or your body. ❑ *Arthritis and rheumatism are prominent crippling diseases.* ADJ: ADJ n 2 If you say that an action, policy, or situation has a **crippling** effect on something, you mean it has a very serious, harmful effect. ❑ *The high cost of capital has a crippling effect on many small American high-tech firms.* ADJ: usu ADJ n

**cri|sis** /kraɪsɪs/ **(crises** /kraɪsiːz/**)** A **crisis** is a situation in which something or someone is affected by one or more very serious problems. ❑ *Natural disasters have obviously contributed to the continent's economic crisis... The Italian political system has been judged to be in terminal crisis for decades. ...children's illnesses or other family crises. ...someone to turn to in moments of crisis.* ◆◆◇ N-VAR: oft supp N

**cri|sis man|age|ment** People use **crisis management** to refer to a management style that concentrates on solving the immediate problems occurring in a business rather than looking for long-term solutions. [BUSINESS] ❑ *Today's NSC is overcome by day-to-day crisis management. ...a crisis-management team.* N-UNCOUNT

**crisp** /krɪsp/ **(crisper, crispest, crisps, crisping, crisped)** 1 Food that is **crisp** is pleasantly hard, or has a pleasantly hard surface. ❑ *Bake the potatoes for 15 minutes, till they're nice and crisp. ...crisp bacon. ...crisp lettuce.* ♦ **crisp|ness** *The pizza base should retain its crispness without becoming brittle.* ♦ **crisp|ly** *...crisply fried onion rings.* ADJ approval ≠ soggy N-UNCOUNT ADV 2 If food **crisps** or if you **crisp** it, it becomes pleasantly hard, for example because you have heated it at a high temperature. ❑ *Cook the bacon until it begins to crisp... Spread breadcrumbs on a dry baking sheet and crisp them in the oven.* VERB V V n 3 **Crisps** are very thin slices of fried potato that are eaten cold as a snack. [BRIT] ❑ *...a packet of crisps. ...cheese and onion potato crisps.* N-COUNT: usu pl

☑ in AM, use **chips** or **potato chips**

4 Weather that is pleasantly fresh, cold, and dry can be described as **crisp**. ❑ *...a crisp autumn day.* ADJ approval 5 **Crisp** cloth or paper is clean and has no creases in it. ❑ *I slipped between the crisp clean sheets. ...crisp banknotes.* ♦ **crisp|ly** *...his crisply pressed suit.* ADJ: usu ADJ n ADV

**crisp|bread** /krɪspbred/ **(crispbreads) Crispbreads** are thin dry biscuits made from wheat or rye. They are often eaten instead of bread by people who want to lose weight. N-VAR

**crispy** /krɪspi/ **(crispier, crispiest)** Food that is **crispy** is pleasantly hard, or has a pleasantly hard surface. ❑ *...crispy fried onions. ...crispy bread rolls.* ADJ approval = crisp

**criss-cross** /krɪs krɒs, AM - krɔːs/ **(criss-crosses, criss-crossing, criss-crossed)** also **criss-cross.** 1 If a person or thing **criss-crosses** an area, they travel from one side to the other and back again many times, following different routes. If a number of things **criss-cross** an area, they cross it, and cross over each other. ❑ *They criss-crossed the country by bus... Telephone wires criss-cross the street.* VERB V n V n 2 If two sets of lines or things **criss-cross**, they cross over each other. ❑ *Wires criss-cross between the tops of the poles, forming a grid... The roads here are quite a maze, criss-crossing one another in a fashion that at times defies logic.* V-RECIP pl-n V V pron-recip 3 A **criss-cross** pattern or design consists of lines crossing each other. ❑ *Slash the tops of the loaves with a sharp serrated knife in a criss-cross pattern.* ADJ: ADJ n

**cri|teri|on** /kraɪtɪəriən/ **(criteria** /kraɪtɪəriə/**)** A **criterion** is a factor on which you judge or decide something. ❑ *The most important criterion for entry is that applicants must design and make their own work.* N-COUNT: oft N *for* n/-ing

**crit|ic** /krɪtɪk/ **(critics)** 1 A **critic** is a person who writes about and expresses opinions about things such as books, films, music, or art. ❑ *The New York critics had praised her performance.* ◆◆◇ N-COUNT: oft n N = reviewer 2 Someone who is a **critic** of a person or system disapproves of them and criticizes them publicly. ❑ *Her critics accused her of caring only about success.* N-COUNT: usu with poss

**criti|cal** /krɪtɪkᵊl/ 1 A **critical** time, factor, or situation is extremely important. ❑ *The incident happened at a critical point in the campaign... He says setting priorities is of critical importance... How you finance a business is critical to the success of your venture.* ♦ **criti|cal|ly** /krɪtɪkli/ *Economic prosperity depends critically on an open world trading system... It was a critically important moment in his career.* ◆◆◇ ADJ = crucial ADV: ADV with v, ADV adj 2 A **critical** situation is very serious and dangerous. ❑ *The German authorities are considering an airlift if the situation becomes critical... Its day-to-day finances are in a critical state.* ♦ **criti|cal|ly** *Moscow is running critically low on food supplies.* ADJ ADV: usu ADV adj 3 If a person is **critical** or in a **critical** condition in hospital, they are seriously ill. ❑ *Ten of the injured are said to be in critical condition.* ♦ **criti|cal|ly** *She was critically ill.* ADJ ADV: usu ADV adj 4 To be **critical of** someone or something means to criticize them. ❑ *His report is highly critical of the trial judge... He has apologised for critical remarks he made about the referee.* ♦ **criti|cal|ly** *She spoke critically of Lara.* ADJ: oft ADJ *of* n ADV 5 A **critical** approach to something involves examining and judging it carefully. ❑ *We need to become critical text-readers. ...the critical* ADJ: ADJ n *analysis of political ideas.* ♦ **criti|cal|ly** *Wyman watched them critically.* ADV 6 If something or someone receives **critical** acclaim, critics say that they are very good. ❑ *The film met with considerable critical and public acclaim.* ADJ: ADJ n

**criti|cal mass** 1 In physics, the **critical mass** of a substance is the minimum amount of it that is needed for a nuclear chain reaction. [TECHNICAL] N-SING: also no det 2 A **critical mass** of something is an amount of it that makes it possible for something to happen or continue. ❑ *Only in this way can the critical mass of participation be reached.* N-SING: also no det

**criti|cise** /krɪtɪsaɪz/ → see **criticize**.

**criti|cism** /krɪtɪsɪzəm/ **(criticisms)** ◆◆◇ 1 **Criticism** is the action of expressing disapproval of something or someone. A **criticism** is a statement that expresses disapproval. ❑ *This policy had repeatedly come under strong criticism on Capitol Hill... The criticism that the English do not truly care about their children was often voiced.* N-VAR: oft N *of* n, N that ≠ praise 2 **Criticism** is a serious examination and judgment of something such as a book or play. ❑ *She has published more than 20 books including novels, poetry and literary criticism.* N-UNCOUNT

**criti|cize** /krɪtɪsaɪz/ **(criticizes, criticizing, criticized)** ◆◇◇

✔ in BRIT, also use **criticise**

If you **criticize** someone or something, you express your disapproval of them by saying what you think is wrong with them. ❑ *His mother had rarely criticized him or any of her children... The minister criticised the police for failing to come up with any leads.* VERB ≠ praise V n, V n *for* n/-ing

**cri|tique** /krɪtiːk/ **(critiques)** A **critique** is a written examination and judgment of a situation or of a person's work or ideas. [FORMAL] ❑ *She had brought a book, a feminist critique of Victorian lady novelists.* N-COUNT: oft N *of* n

**crit|ter** /krɪtəʳ/ **(critters)** A **critter** is a living creature. [AM, INFORMAL] ❑ *...little furry critters.* N-COUNT

**croak** /kroʊk/ **(croaks, croaking, croaked)** 1 When a frog or bird **croaks**, it makes a harsh, low sound. ❑ *Thousands of frogs croaked in the reeds by the riverbank.* VERB V ♦ **Croak** is also a noun. ❑ *...the guttural croak of the frogs.* N-COUNT 2 If someone **croaks** something, they say it in a low, rough voice. ❑ *Tiller moaned and managed to croak, 'Help me.'... She croaked something unintelligible.* VERB V with quote V n ♦ **Croak** is also a noun. ❑ *His voice was just a croak.* N-COUNT

**croaky** /kroʊki/ If someone's voice is **croaky**, it is low and rough. ADJ

**cro|chet** /kroʊʃeɪ, AM kroʊʃeɪ/ **(crochets, crocheting, crocheted)** 1 **Crochet** is a way of making cloth out of cotton or wool by using a needle with a small hook at the end. ❑ *...a black crochet waistcoat.* N-UNCOUNT 2 If you **crochet**, you make cloth by using a needle with a small hook at the end. ❑ *She offered to teach me to crochet... Ma and I crocheted new quilts. ...crocheted rugs.* VERB V V n V-ed

**crock** /krɒk/ **(crocks)** 1 A **crock** is a clay pot or jar. [OLD-FASHIONED] N-COUNT 2 If you describe someone as an old **crock**, you mean that they are old and weak. [BRIT, INFORMAL, OLD-FASHIONED] N-COUNT 3 If you describe what someone has said as **a crock**, you mean that you think it is foolish, wrong, or untrue. [mainly AM, INFORMAL] N-COUNT: usu sing disapproval 4 **a crock of gold** → see **gold**.

**crock|ery** /krɒkəri/ **Crockery** is the plates, cups, saucers, and dishes that you use at meals. [mainly BRIT] ❑ *We had no fridge, cooker, cutlery or crockery.* N-UNCOUNT

**croco|dile** /krɒkədaɪl/ **(crocodiles)** A **crocodile** is a large reptile with a long body and strong jaws. Crocodiles live in rivers and eat meat. N-COUNT

**croco|dile tears** If someone is crying **crocodile tears**, their tears and sadness are not genuine or sincere. ❑ *The sight of George shedding crocodile tears made me sick.* N-PLURAL

**cro|cus** /kroʊkəs/ **(crocuses)** **Crocuses** are small white, yellow, or purple flowers that are grown in parks and gardens in the early spring. N-COUNT

**croft** /krɒft, AM krɔːft/ **(crofts)** In Scotland, a **croft** is a small piece of land which is owned and farmed by one family and which provides them with food. ❑ *...a remote croft near Loch Nevis.* N-COUNT

**croft|er** /krɒftəʳ, AM krɔːft-/ **(crofters)** In Scotland, a **crofter** is a person who lives on a croft or small farm. N-COUNT

**croft|ing** /krɒftɪŋ, AM krɔːft-/ In Scotland, **crofting** is the activity of farming on small pieces of land. ❑ *...isolated crofting communities.* N-UNCOUNT: oft N n

**crois|sant** /kwæsɒn, AM kwɑːsɑːn/ **(croissants)** **Croissants** are small, sweet bread rolls in the shape of a crescent that are eaten for breakfast. ❑ *...coffee and croissants.* N-VAR

**crone** /kroʊn/ **(crones)** A **crone** is an ugly old woman. [LITERARY] N-COUNT

**cro|ny** /kroʊni/ **(cronies)** You can refer to friends that someone spends a lot of time with as their **cronies**, especially when you disapprove of them. [INFORMAL] ❑ *He returned from a lunchtime drinking session with his business cronies.* N-COUNT: usu poss N disapproval

**cro|ny|ism** /kroʊniɪzəm/ If you accuse someone in authority of **cronyism**, you mean that they use their power or authority to get jobs for their friends. [JOURNALISM] N-UNCOUNT disapproval

**crook** /krʊk/ **(crooks, crooking, crooked)** 1 A **crook** is a dishonest person or a criminal. [INFORMAL] ❑ *The man is a crook and a liar.* N-COUNT 2 **The crook of** your arm or leg is the soft inside part where you bend your elbow or knee. ❑ *She hid her face in the crook of her arm.* N-COUNT: usu sing, the N *of* n 3 If you **crook** your arm or finger, you bend it. ❑ *He crooked his finger: 'Come forward,' he said.* VERB V n 4 A **crook** is a long pole with a large hook at the end. A crook is carried by a bishop in religious ceremonies, or by a shepherd. ❑ *...a shepherd's crook.* N-COUNT 5 If someone says they will do something **by hook or by crook**, they are determined to do it, even if they have to make a great effort or use dishonest means. ❑ *They intend to get their way, by hook or by crook.* PHRASE: PHR with cl, PHR with v

**crook|ed** /krʊkɪd/ 1 If you describe something as **crooked**, especially something that is usually straight, you mean that it is bent or twisted. ❑ *...the crooked line of his broken nose. ...a crooked little tree.* ADJ ≠ straight 2 A **crooked** smile is uneven and bigger on one side than the other. ❑ *Polly gave her a crooked grin.* ADJ = lopsided ♦ **crook|ed|ly** *Nick was smiling crookedly at her.* ADV 3 If you describe a person or an activity as **crooked**, you mean that they are dishonest or criminal. [INFORMAL] ❑ *...a crooked cop.* ADJ = bent

**croon** /kruːn/ **(croons, crooning, crooned)** 1 If you **croon**, you sing or hum quietly and gently. ❑ *He would much rather have been crooning in a smoky bar... Later in the evening, Lewis began to croon another Springsteen song.* VERB V V n 2 If one person talks to another in a soft gentle voice, you can describe them as **crooning**, especially if you think they are being sentimental or insincere. ❑ *'Dear boy,' she crooned, hugging him heartily... The man was crooning soft words of encouragement to his wife.* VERB V with quote V n Also V

**croon|er** /kruːnəʳ/ **(crooners)** A **crooner** is a male singer who sings sentimental songs, especially the love songs of the 1930s and 1940s. N-COUNT

**crop** /krɒp/ **(crops, cropping, cropped)** ◆◇◇ 1 **Crops** are plants such as wheat and potatoes that are grown in large quantities for food. ❑ *Rice farmers here still plant and harvest their crops by hand... The main crop is wheat and this is grown even on the very steep slopes.* → See also **cash crop**. N-COUNT 2 The plants or fruits that are collected at harvest time are referred to as a **crop**. ❑ *Each year it produces a fine crop of fruit... The US government says that this year's corn crop should be about 8 percent more than last year.* N-COUNT: usu with supp = harvest 3 You can refer to a group of people or things that have appeared together as a **crop of** people or things. [INFORMAL] ❑ *The present crop of books and documentaries about Marilyn* N-SING: N *of* n = batch

*Monroe exploit the thirtieth anniversary of her death.* [4] VERB When a plant **crops**, it produces fruits or parts which people want. ❑ V *Although these vegetables adapt well to our temperate climate, they tend to crop poorly.* [5] VERB To **crop** someone's hair means to cut it short. ❑ V n *She cropped her hair and dyed it blonde.* ♦ ADJ **cropped** *She had cropped grey hair.* [6] N-COUNT: usu sing A **crop** is a short hairstyle. ❑ *She had her long hair cut into a boyish crop.* [7] VERB If you **crop** a photograph, you cut part of it off, in order to get rid of part of the picture or to be able to frame it. ❑ V n *I decided to crop the picture just above the water line...* be V-ed from n *Her husband was cropped from the photograph.* [8] **the cream of the crop** → see **cream**.

♦ **crop up** PHRASAL VERB = come up If something **crops up**, it appears or happens, usually unexpectedly. ❑ V P *His name has cropped up at every selection meeting this season.*

**cropped** /krɒpt/ ADJ: usu ADJ n **Cropped** items of clothing are shorter than normal. ❑ *Women athletes wear cropped tops and tight shorts.* → See also **crop**.

**crop|per** /krɒpəʳ/ PHRASE: V inflects If you say that someone **has come a cropper**, you mean that they have had an unexpected and embarrassing failure. [INFORMAL] ❑ *...internet businesses that came a cropper.*

**crop top** (**crop tops**) N-COUNT A **crop top** is a very short, usually tight, top worn by a girl or a woman.

**cro|quet** /kroʊkeɪ, AM kroʊkeɪ/ N-UNCOUNT **Croquet** is a game played on grass in which the players use long wooden sticks called mallets to hit balls through metal arches.

**cro|quette** /kroʊket/ (**croquettes**) N-COUNT **Croquettes** are small amounts of mashed potato or meat rolled in breadcrumbs and fried.

**cross**
① VERB AND NOUN USES
② ADJECTIVE USE

① **cross** /krɒs, AM krɔːs/ (**crosses, crossing, crossed**) ◆◆◇
⇛ Please look at category 16 to see if the expression you are looking for is shown under another headword. [1] VERB If you **cross** something such as a room, a road, or an area of land or water, you move or travel to the other side of it. If you **cross to** a place, you move or travel over a room, road, or area of land or water in order to reach that place. ❑ V n *She was partly to blame for failing to look as she crossed the road...* V n *Nine Albanians have crossed the border into Greece and asked for political asylum...* V to/into n *Egan crossed to the drinks cabinet and poured a Scotch.* [2] VERB A road, railway, or bridge that **crosses** an area of land or water passes over it. ❑ V n *The Defford to Eckington road crosses the river half a mile outside Eckington.* [3] V-RECIP Lines or roads that **cross** meet and go across each other. ❑ pl-n V *...the intersection where Main and Center streets cross...* V n *It is near where the pilgrimage route crosses the road to Quimper.* [4] VERB If someone or something **crosses** a limit or boundary, for example the limit of acceptable behaviour, they go beyond it. ❑ V n *I normally never write into magazines but Mr Stubbs has finally crossed the line.* [5] VERB If an expression **crosses** someone's face, it appears briefly on their face. [WRITTEN] ❑ V n *Berg tilts his head and a mischievous look crosses his face.* [6] N-COUNT A **cross** is a shape that consists of a vertical line or piece with a shorter horizontal line or piece across it. It is the most important Christian symbol. ❑ *Round her neck was a cross on a silver chain.* [7] VERB If Christians **cross themselves**, they make the sign of a cross by moving their hand across the top half of their body. ❑ V pron-refl *'Holy Mother of God!' Marco crossed himself.* [8] N-COUNT = burden If you describe something as a **cross** that someone has to bear, you mean it is a problem or disadvantage which they have to deal with or bear. ❑ *My wife is much cleverer than me; it is a cross I have to bear.* [9] N-COUNT A **cross** is a written mark in the shape of an X. You can use it, for example, to indicate that an answer to a question is wrong, to mark the position of something on a map, or to indicate your vote on a ballot paper. ❑ *Put a tick next to those activities you like and a cross next to those you dislike.* [10] VERB: usu passive If a cheque **is crossed**, two parallel lines are drawn across it or printed on it to indicate that it must be paid into a bank account and cannot be cashed. [BRIT] ❑ be V-ed *Cheques/postal orders should be crossed and made payable to Newmarket Promotions.* V-ed *...a crossed cheque.* [11] VERB If you **cross** your arms, legs, or fingers, you put one of them on top of the other. ❑ V n *Jill crossed her legs and rested her chin on one fist, as if lost in deep thought...* V-ed *He was sitting there in the living room with his legs crossed.* [12] VERB If you **cross** someone who is likely to get angry, you oppose them or refuse to do what they want. ❑ V n *If you ever cross him, forget it, you're finished.* [13] N-SING: a N between pl-n Something that is **a cross between** two things is neither one thing nor the other, but a mixture of both. ❑ *It was a lovely dog. It was a cross between a collie and a golden retriever.* [14] N-COUNT In some team sports such as football and hockey, a **cross** is the passing of the ball from the side of the field to a player in the centre, usually in front of the goal. ❑ *Le Tissier hit an accurate cross to Groves.* [15] ADJ: ADJ n A **cross** street is a road that crosses another more important road. [AM] ❑ *The Army boys had personnel carriers blockading the cross streets.* [16] → See also **crossing**. to **cross** your **fingers** → see **finger**. **cross** my **heart** → see **heart**. to **cross** your **mind** → see **mind**. people's **paths cross** → see **path**. to **cross the Rubicon** → see **Rubicon**. to **cross swords** → see **sword**.

♦ **cross off** PHRASAL VERB If you **cross off** words on a list, you decide that they no longer belong on the list, and often you draw a line through them to indicate this. ❑ V P n (not pron) *I checked the chart and found I had crossed off the wrong thing...* V n P *They have enough trouble finding nutritious food without crossing meat off their shopping lists.* Also V n P

♦ **cross out** PHRASAL VERB = delete If you **cross out** words on a page, you draw a line through them, because they are wrong or because you want to change them. ❑ V P n (not pron) *He crossed out 'fellow subjects', and instead inserted 'fellow citizens'.* Also V n P

② **cross** /krɒs, AM krɔːs/ (**crosser, crossest**) ADJ: usu v-link ADJ = annoyed Someone who is **cross** is rather angry or irritated. ❑ *I'm terribly cross with him... She was rather cross about having to trail across London.* ♦ ADV: ADV with v **cross|ly** *'No, no, no,' Morris said crossly.*

**cross|bar** /krɒsbɑːʳ, AM krɔːs-/ (**crossbars**) [1] N-COUNT A **crossbar** is a horizontal piece of wood attached to two upright pieces, for example a part of the goal in football. [2] N-COUNT The **crossbar** of a man's or boy's bicycle is the horizontal metal bar between the handlebars and the saddle. → See picture on page 1708.

**cross|bones** /krɒsboʊnz, AM krɔːs-/ → see **skull and crossbones**.

**cross-border** [1] ADJ: ADJ n = overseas ≠ domestic **Cross-border** trade occurs between companies in different countries. ❑ *Currency-conversion costs remain one of the biggest obstacles to cross-border trade.* [2] ADJ: ADJ n **Cross-border** attacks involve people crossing a border and going a short way into another country. ❑ *...a cross-border raid into Zambian territory.*

**cross|bow** /krɒsboʊ, AM krɔːs-/ (**crossbows**) N-COUNT A **crossbow** is a weapon consisting of a small, powerful bow that is fixed across a piece of wood, and aimed like a gun.

**cross-breed** (**cross-breeds, cross-breeding, cross-bred**) also **crossbreed**. [1] V-RECIP If one species of animal or plant **cross-breeds with** another, they reproduce, and new or different animals or plants are produced. You can also say that someone **cross-breeds** something such as an animal or plant. ❑ V with n *By cross-breeding with our native red deer, the skia deer have affected the gene pool...* V n with n *Unfortunately attempts to crossbreed it with other potatoes have been unsuccessful...* V pl-n *They created an elite herd by cross-breeding goats from around the globe.* V-ed *...a cross-bred labrador.* [2] N-COUNT A **cross-breed** is an animal that is the result of cross-breeding.

**cross-Channel** also **cross-channel.** ADJ: ADJ n **Cross-Channel** travel is travel across the English Channel, especially by boat. ❑ *...the cross-channel ferry... Dieppe has plenty to attract cross-Channel visitors.*

**cross-check** **(cross-checks, cross-checking, cross-checked)** If you **cross-check** information, VERB you check that it is correct using a different method or source from the one originally used to obtain it. ❑ *You have to scrupulously check and cross-check everything you hear... His version will later be cross-checked against that of the university... They want to ensure such claims are justified by cross-checking with other records.* V n; *be* V-ed *against* n; V *with* n; Also V, V n *with* n

**cross-country** [1] **Cross-country** is the sport of running, riding, or skiing across open countryside rather than along roads or around a running track. ❑ *She finished third in the world cross-country championships in Antwerp.* N-UNCOUNT: oft N n [2] A **cross-country** journey involves less important roads or railway lines, or takes you from one side of a country to the other. ❑ *...cross-country rail services.* ADJ: ADJ n ♦ **Cross-country** is also an adverb. ❑ *I drove cross-country in his van.* ADV: ADV after v

**cross-cultural** **Cross-cultural** means involving two or more different cultures. ❑ *Minority cultures within the United States often raised issues of cross-cultural conflict.* ADJ: ADJ n

**cross-current** **(cross-currents)**

✔ in AM, also use **crosscurrent**

[1] A **cross-current** is a current in a river or sea that flows across another current. ❑ *Cross-currents can sweep the strongest swimmer helplessly away.* N-COUNT: usu pl [2] You can refer to conflicting ideas or traditions as **cross-currents.** ❑ *...the cross-currents within the Conservative Party.* N-COUNT: usu pl, usu with supp

**cross-dress** **(cross-dresses, cross-dressing, cross-dressed)** If someone **cross-dresses**, they wear the clothes of the opposite sex, especially for sexual pleasure. ❑ *If they want to cross-dress that's fine.* VERB; V ♦ **cross-dresser** **(cross-dressers)** *The Society maintains that the majority of cross-dressers are heterosexual.* N-COUNT = transvestite ♦ **cross-dressing** *Cross-dressing is far more common than we realise.* N-UNCOUNT = transvestism

**cross-examine** **(cross-examines, cross-examining, cross-examined)** When a lawyer **cross-examines** someone during a trial or hearing, he or she questions them about the evidence that they have already given. ❑ *The accused's lawyers will get a chance to cross-examine him... You know you are liable to be cross-examined mercilessly about the assault.* VERB; V n; *be* V-ed *about* n ♦ **cross-examination** **(cross-examinations)** *...during the cross-examination of a witness in a murder case... Under cross-examination, he admitted the state troopers used more destructive ammunition than usual.* N-VAR

**cross-eyed** Someone who is **cross-eyed** has eyes that seem to look towards each other. ADJ

**cross|fire** /krɒsfaɪəʳ, AM krɔːs-/ also **cross-fire.** [1] **Crossfire** is gunfire, for example in a battle, that comes from two or more different directions and passes through the same area. N-UNCOUNT [2] If you are **caught in the crossfire**, you become involved in an unpleasant situation in which people are arguing with each other, although you do not want to be involved or say which person you agree with. ❑ *They say they are caught in the cross-fire between the education establishment and the government.* PHRASE: v-link PHR

**cross|ing** /krɒsɪŋ, AM krɔːs-/ **(crossings)** [1] A **crossing** is a journey by boat or ship to a place on the other side of a sea, river, or lake. ❑ *The vessel docked in Swansea after a ten-hour crossing.* N-COUNT [2] A **crossing** is a place where two roads, paths, or lines cross. N-COUNT [3] A **crossing** is the same as a **pedestrian crossing**. [BRIT] ❑ *A car hit her on a crossing.* N-COUNT

✔ in AM, use **crosswalk**

→ See also **pelican crossing**, **zebra crossing**.

[4] A **crossing** is the same as a **grade crossing** or a **level crossing**. N-COUNT

**cross-legged** If someone is sitting **cross-legged**, they are sitting on the floor with their legs bent so that their knees point outwards. ❑ *He sat cross-legged on the floor.* ADV: ADV after v

**cross|over** /krɒsoʊvəʳ, AM krɔːs-/ **(crossovers)** [1] A **crossover** of one style and another, especially in music or fashion, is a combination of the two different styles. ❑ *...the contemporary crossover of pop, jazz and funk.* N-VAR: oft N n [2] In music or fashion, if someone makes a **crossover from** one style **to** another, they become successful outside the style they were originally known for. ❑ *I told her the crossover from actress to singer is easier than singer to actress.* N-SING: usu N *from/to* n

**cross-purposes** also **cross purposes.** If people are **at cross-purposes**, they do not understand each other because they are working towards or talking about different things without realizing it. ❑ *The two friends find themselves at cross-purposes with the officials.* PHRASE: PHR after v, v-link PHR, oft PHR *with* n

**cross-question** **(cross-questions, cross-questioning, cross-questioned)** If you **cross-question** someone, you ask them a lot of questions about something. ❑ *The police came back and cross-questioned Des again.* VERB; V n

**cross-reference** **(cross-references, cross-referencing, cross-referenced)** [1] A **cross-reference** is a note in a book which tells you that there is relevant or more detailed information in another part of the book. N-COUNT [2] If something such as a book **is cross-referenced**, cross-references are put in it. ❑ *Nearly 2,300 plant lists have been checked and cross-referenced. ...an index of products and services which is cross-referenced to the supplying companies.* VERB: usu passive; *be* V-ed; V-ed

**cross|roads** /krɒsroʊdz, AM krɔːs-/ **(crossroads)** [1] A **crossroads** is a place where two roads meet and cross each other. ❑ *Turn right at the first crossroads.* N-COUNT [2] If you say that something is **at a crossroads**, you mean that it has reached a very important stage in its development where it could go one way or another. ❑ *The company was clearly at a crossroads.* N-SING: oft *at a* N

**cross-section** **(cross-sections)** also **cross section.** [1] If you refer to a **cross-section of** particular things or people, you mean a group of them that you think is typical or representative of all of them. ❑ *I was surprised at the cross-section of people there... It is good that there is a wide cross-section of sport on television.* N-COUNT: usu N *of* n [2] A **cross-section** of an object is what you would see if you could cut straight through the middle of it. ❑ *...a cross-section of an airplane... The hall is square in cross-section.* N-COUNT: also *in* N

**cross-stitch** also **cross stitch.** **Cross-stitch** is a type of decorative sewing where one stitch crosses another. N-UNCOUNT

**cross|walk** /krɒswɔːk, AM krɔːs-/ **(crosswalks)** A **crosswalk** is a place where pedestrians can cross a street and where drivers must stop to let them cross. [AM] N-COUNT

✔ in BRIT, usually use **pedestrian crossing**

**cross|wind** /krɒswɪnd, AM krɔːs-/ **(crosswinds)** also **cross-wind.** A **crosswind** is a strong wind that blows across the direction that vehicles, boats, or aircraft are travelling in, and that makes it difficult for them to keep moving steadily forward. N-COUNT

**cross|wise** /krɒswaɪz, AM krɔːs-/

✔ in AM, also use **crossways**

**Crosswise** means diagonally across something. ❑ *Rinse and slice the courgettes crosswise.* ADV: ADV after v = diagonally

**cross|word** /krɒswɜːʳd, AM krɔːs-/ **(crosswords)** A **crossword** or **crossword puzzle** is a word game in which you work out the answers and write them in the white squares of a pattern of small black and white squares. N-COUNT

**crotch** /krɒtʃ/ **(crotches)** [1] Your **crotch** is the part of your body between the tops of your legs. ❑ *Glover kicked him hard in the crotch.* [N-COUNT] [2] The **crotch** of something such as a pair of trousers is the part that covers the area between the tops of your legs. ❑ *They were too long in the crotch.* [N-COUNT]

**crotch|et** /krɒtʃɪt/ **(crotchets)** A **crotchet** is a musical note that has a time value equal to two quavers. [mainly BRIT] [N-COUNT]

✔ in AM, use **quarter note**

**crotch|ety** /krɒtʃɪti/ A **crotchety** person is bad-tempered and easily irritated. [INFORMAL] ❑ *...a crotchety old man.* [ADJ: usu ADJ n = grumpy]

**crouch** /kraʊtʃ/ **(crouches, crouching, crouched)** If you **are crouching**, your legs are bent under you so that you are close to the ground and leaning forward slightly. ❑ *We were crouching in the bushes... The man was crouched behind the Mercedes.* [VERB = squat; V prep/adv; V-ed] ♦ **Crouch** is also a noun. ❑ *They walked in a crouch, each bent over close to the ground.* [N-SING] ♦ **Crouch down** means the same as **crouch**. ❑ *He crouched down and reached under the mattress... He crouched down beside him.* [PHRASAL VERB; V P; V P prep/adv]

**croup** /kruːp/ **Croup** is a disease which children sometimes suffer from that makes it difficult for them to breathe and causes them to cough a lot. [N-UNCOUNT: also *the* N]

**crou|pi|er** /kruːpieɪ, AM -iər/ **(croupiers)** A **croupier** is the person in charge of a gambling table in a casino, who collects the bets and pays money to the people who have won. [N-COUNT]

**crou|ton** /kruːtɒn/ **(croutons)** **Croutons** are small pieces of toasted or fried bread that are added to soup just before you eat it. [N-COUNT: usu pl]

**crow** /kroʊ/ **(crows, crowing, crowed)** [1] A **crow** is a large black bird which makes a loud, harsh noise. [N-COUNT] [2] When a cock **crows**, it makes a loud sound, often early in the morning. ❑ *The cock crows and the dawn chorus begins.* [VERB; V] [3] If you say that someone **is crowing about** something they have achieved or are pleased about, you disapprove of them because they keep telling people proudly about it. [INFORMAL] ❑ *Edwards is already crowing about his assured victory... We've seen them all crowing that the movement is dead.* [VERB disapproval = boast; V *about/over* n; V that] [4] If you say that a place is a particular distance away **as the crow flies**, you mean that it is that distance away measured in a straight line. ❑ *I live at Mesa, Washington, about 10 miles as the crow flies from Hanford.* [PHRASE: oft amount PHR]

**crow|bar** /kroʊbɑːʳ/ **(crowbars)** A **crowbar** is a heavy iron bar which is used as a lever. [N-COUNT]

**crowd** /kraʊd/ **(crowds, crowding, crowded)** ◆◆◇ [1] A **crowd** is a large group of people who have gathered together, for example to watch or listen to something interesting, or to protest about something. ❑ *A huge crowd gathered in a square outside the Kremlin walls... The crowd were enormously enthusiastic... The explosions took place in shopping centres as crowds of people were shopping for Mothers' Day.* [N-COUNT-COLL: oft N *of* n = throng] [2] A particular **crowd** is a group of friends, or a set of people who share the same interests or job. [INFORMAL] ❑ *All the old crowd have come out for this occasion.* [N-COUNT: usu supp N] [3] When people **crowd around** someone or something, they gather closely together around them. ❑ *The hungry refugees crowded around the tractors... Police blocked off the road as hotel staff and guests crowded around.* [VERB = cluster; V *round/around* n; V *round/around*] [4] If people **crowd into** a place or **are crowded into** a place, large numbers of them enter it so that it becomes very full. ❑ *Hundreds of thousands of people have crowded into the center of the Lithuanian capital, Vilnius... One group of journalists were crowded into a minibus... 'Bravo, bravo,' chanted party workers crowded in the main hall.* [VERB = pack, cram; V *into* n; *be* V-ed *into* n; V-ed] [5] If a group of people **crowd** a place, there are so many of them there that it is full. ❑ *Thousands of demonstrators crowded the streets shouting slogans.* [VERB = pack; V n] [6] If people **crowd** you, they stand very closely around you trying to see or speak to you, so that you feel uncomfortable. ❑ *It had been a tense, restless day with people crowding her all the time.* [VERB; V n]

♦ **crowd in** If problems or thoughts **crowd in on** you, a lot of them happen to you or affect you at the same time, so that they occupy all your attention and make you feel unable to escape. ❑ *Everything is crowding in on me... She tried to sleep, but thoughts crowded in and images flashed into her mind.* [PHRASAL VERB; V P *on* n; V P]

♦ **crowd out** If one thing **crowds out** another, it is so successful or common that the other thing does not have the opportunity to be successful or exist. ❑ *In the 1980s American exports crowded out European films.* [PHRASAL VERB = squeeze out; V P n (not pron); Also V n P]

**crowd|ed** /kraʊdɪd/ [1] If a place is **crowded**, it is full of people. ❑ *He peered slowly around the small crowded room.* [ADJ: oft ADJ *with* n] [2] If a place is **crowded**, a lot of people live there. ❑ *...a crowded city of 2 million.* [ADJ] [3] If your timetable, your life, or your mind is **crowded**, it is full of events, activities, or thoughts. ❑ *Never before has a summit had such a crowded agenda.* [ADJ: oft ADJ *with* n = packed]

**crowd-pleaser** **(crowd-pleasers)** also **crowd pleaser.** If you describe a performer, politician, or sports player as a **crowd-pleaser**, you mean they always please their audience. You can also describe an action or event as a **crowd-pleaser**. ❑ *He gets spectacular goals and is a real crowd pleaser.* [N-COUNT]

**crowd-puller** **(crowd-pullers)** also **crowd puller.** If you describe a performer or event as a **crowd-puller**, you mean that they attract a large audience. ❑ *The exhibition is hardly a crowd-puller.* [N-COUNT]

**crown** /kraʊn/ **(crowns, crowning, crowned)** ◆◇◇ [1] A **crown** is a circular ornament, usually made of gold and jewels, which a king or queen wears on their head at official ceremonies. You can also use **crown** to refer to anything circular that is worn on someone's head. ❑ *...a crown of flowers.* [N-COUNT] [2] The government of a country that has a king or queen is sometimes referred to as **the Crown**. In British criminal cases the prosecutor is **the Crown**. ❑ *She says the sovereignty of the Crown must be preserved. ...a Minister of the Crown. ...chief witness for the Crown.* [N-PROPER: *the* N] [3] When a king or queen **is crowned**, a crown is placed on their head as part of a ceremony in which they are officially made king or queen. ❑ *Elizabeth was crowned in Westminster Abbey on 2 June 1953... Two days later, Juan Carlos was crowned king. ...the newly crowned King.* [VERB: usu passive; *be* V-ed; *be* V-ed n; V-ed] [4] Your **crown** is the top part of your head, at the back. ❑ *He laid his hand gently on the crown of her head.* [N-COUNT: usu sing, usu with supp] [5] A **crown** is an artificial top piece fixed over a broken or decayed tooth. [N-COUNT] [6] In sport, winning an important competition is sometimes referred to as a **crown**. ❑ *...his dream of a fourth Wimbledon crown.* [N-COUNT: oft n N] [7] An achievement or event that **crowns** something makes it perfect, successful, or complete. ❑ *The summit was crowned by the signing of the historic START treaty. ...the crowning achievement of his career.* [VERB; V n; V-ing]

**Crown Court** **(Crown Courts)** In England and Wales, a **Crown Court** is a court in which criminal cases are tried by a judge and jury rather than by a magistrate. ❑ *He appeared at Manchester Crown Court on Thursday on a drink-driving charge.* [N-COUNT: usu sing, oft in names]

**crown jew|el** **(crown jewels)** **The Crown Jewels** are the crown, sceptre, and other precious objects which are used on important official occasions by the King or Queen. [N-PLURAL: *the* N]

**Crown Prince** **(Crown Princes)** A **Crown Prince** is a prince who will be king of his country when the present king or queen dies. ❑ *...the crown prince's palace. ...Sultan Mahmood's son, Crown Prince Ibrahim Mahmood.* [N-COUNT: usu *the* N in sing; N-TITLE]

**Crown Prin|cess** **(Crown Princesses)** A **Crown Princess** is a princess who is the wife of a Crown Prince, or will be queen of her country when the present king or queen dies. ❑ *...his second wife, Crown Princess Catherine.* [N-COUNT: usu *the* N in sing; N-TITLE]

**crown pros|ecu|tor** **(crown prosecutors)** In Britain, a **crown prosecutor** is a lawyer who works for the state and who prosecutes people who are accused of crimes. N-COUNT: usu sing

**crow's feet** **Crow's feet** are **wrinkles** which some older people have at the outside corners of their eyes. N-PLURAL

**crow's nest** On a ship, the **crow's nest** is a small platform high up on the mast, where a person can go to look in all directions. N-SING

**cru|cial** /kruːʃᵊl/ ◆◇◇ If you describe something as **crucial**, you mean it is extremely important. ❑ *He had administrators under him but took the crucial decisions himself... Improved consumer confidence is crucial to an economic recovery.* ADJ: oft ADJ *to* n = critical ♦ **cru|cial|ly** *Chewing properly is crucially important... Crucially, though, it failed to secure the backing of the banks.* ADV

**cru|ci|ble** /kruːsɪbᵊl/ **(crucibles)** 1 A **crucible** is a pot in which metals or other substances can be melted or heated up to very high temperatures. N-COUNT 2 **Crucible** is used to refer to a situation in which something is tested or a conflict takes place, often one which produces something new. [LITERARY] ❑ *...a system in which ideas are tested in the crucible of party contention.* N-SING: oft N *of* n

**cru|ci|fix** /kruːsɪfɪks/ **(crucifixes)** A **crucifix** is a cross with a figure of Christ on it. N-COUNT

**cru|ci|fix|ion** /kruːsɪfɪkʃᵊn/ **(crucifixions)** 1 **Crucifixion** is a way of killing people which was common in the Roman Empire, in which they were tied or nailed to a cross and left to die. ❑ *...her historical novel about the crucifixion of Christians in Rome.* N-VAR 2 **The Crucifixion** is the crucifixion of Christ. ❑ *...the central message of the Crucifixion.* N-PROPER: the N

**cru|ci|form** /kruːsɪfɔːʳm/ A **cruciform** building or object is shaped like a cross. [FORMAL] ❑ *...a cruciform tower.* ADJ: usu ADJ n

**cru|ci|fy** /kruːsɪfaɪ/ **(crucifies, crucifying, crucified)** 1 If someone **is crucified**, they are killed by being tied or nailed to a cross and left to die. ❑ *...the day that Christ was crucified.* VERB: usu passive, *be* V-ed 2 To **crucify** someone means to criticize or punish them severely. [INFORMAL] ❑ *She'll crucify me if she finds you still here.* VERB, V n

**crude** /kruːd/ **(cruder, crudest, crudes)** 1 A **crude** method or measurement is not exact or detailed, but may be useful or correct in a rough, general way. ❑ *Standard measurements of blood pressure are an important but crude way of assessing the risk of heart disease or strokes.* ADJ = rough ♦ **crude|ly** *The donors can be split – a little crudely – into two groups.* ADV: usu ADV with v, also ADV adj 2 If you describe an object that someone has made as **crude**, you mean that it has been made in a very simple way or from very simple parts. ❑ *...crude wooden boxes.* ADJ ♦ **crude|ly** *...a crudely carved wooden form.* ADV: usu ADV -ed 3 If you describe someone as **crude**, you disapprove of them because they speak or behave in a rude, offensive, or unsophisticated way. ❑ *Nev! Must you be quite so crude? ...crude language.* ADJ [disapproval] = coarse ♦ **crude|ly** *He hated it when she spoke so crudely.* ADV: usu ADV with v 4 **Crude** substances are in a natural or unrefined state, and have not yet been used in manufacturing processes. ❑ *...8.5 million tonnes of crude steel.* ADJ: ADJ n = raw ≠ refined 5 **Crude** is the same as **crude oil**. N-MASS

**crude oil** **Crude oil** is oil in its natural state before it has been processed or refined. N-UNCOUNT

**crudi|tés** /kruːdɪteɪ, AM -teɪ/ **Crudités** are pieces of raw vegetable, often served before a meal. N-PLURAL

**cru|el** /kruːəl/ **(crueller, cruellest)**

☑ in AM, use **crueler**, **cruelest**

1 Someone who is **cruel** deliberately causes pain or distress to people or animals. ❑ *Children can be so cruel... Don't you think it's cruel to cage a creature up?* ADJ: oft *it* v-link ADJ to-inf ≠ kind ♦ **cru|el|ly** *Douglas was often cruelly tormented by jealous siblings.* ADV: ADV with v 2 A situation or event that is **cruel** is very harsh and causes people distress. ❑ *...struggling to survive in a cruel world with which they cannot cope.* ADJ ♦ **cru|el|ly** *His life has been cruelly shattered by an event not of his own making.* ADV: usu ADV with v

**cru|el|ty** /kruːəlti/ **(cruelties)** **Cruelty** is behaviour that deliberately causes pain or distress to people or animals. ❑ *Britain had laws against cruelty to animals but none to protect children... He had been unable to escape the cruelties of war.* N-VAR: usu with supp, oft N *to* n

**cru|et** /kruːɪt/ **(cruets)** 1 A **cruet** is a small container, or set of containers, for salt, pepper, or mustard which is used at meals. [BRIT] ❑ *...a cruet set.* N-COUNT 2 A **cruet** is a small glass bottle that contains oil or vinegar and is used at the table at meals. [AM] N-COUNT

**cruise** /kruːz/ ◆◇◇ **(cruises, cruising, cruised)** 1 A **cruise** is a holiday during which you travel on a ship or boat and visit a number of places. ❑ *He and his wife were planning to go on a world cruise.* N-COUNT 2 If you **cruise** a sea, river, or canal, you travel around it or along it on a cruise. ❑ *She wants to cruise the canals of France in a barge... During their summer holidays they cruised further afield to Normandy and Brittany.* VERB, V n, V prep/adv 3 If a car, ship, or aircraft **cruises** somewhere, it moves there at a steady comfortable speed. ❑ *A black and white police car cruised past.* VERB, V prep/adv 4 If a team or sports player **cruises to** victory, they win easily. [JOURNALISM] ❑ *Graf looked in awesome form as she cruised to an easy victory.* VERB, V *to* n

**cruise mis|sile** **(cruise missiles)** A **cruise missile** is a missile which carries a nuclear warhead and which is guided by a computer. N-COUNT

**cruis|er** /kruːzəʳ/ **(cruisers)** 1 A **cruiser** is a motor boat which has an area for people to live or sleep. ❑ *...a motor cruiser.* → See also **cabin cruiser**. N-COUNT: oft n N 2 A **cruiser** is a large fast warship. ❑ *Italy had lost three cruisers and two destroyers.* N-COUNT 3 A **cruiser** is a police car. [AM] N-COUNT

**cruiser|weight** /kruːzəʳweɪt/ **(cruiserweights)** A **cruiserweight** is another name for a **light heavyweight**. [mainly BRIT] N-COUNT

**crumb** /krʌm/ **(crumbs)** 1 **Crumbs** are tiny pieces that fall from bread, biscuits, or cake when you cut it or eat it. ❑ *I stood up, brushing crumbs from my trousers.* N-COUNT: usu pl 2 A **crumb of** something, for example information, is a very small amount of it. ❑ *At last Andrew gave them a crumb of information.* N-COUNT: usu N *of* n

**crum|ble** /krʌmbᵊl/ **(crumbles, crumbling, crumbled)** 1 If something **crumbles**, or if you **crumble** it, it breaks into a lot of small pieces. ❑ *Under the pressure, the flint crumbled into fragments... Roughly crumble the cheese into a bowl.* VERB, V, V n 2 If an old building or piece of land **is crumbling**, parts of it keep breaking off. ❑ *The high and low-rise apartment blocks built in the 1960s are crumbling... The cliffs were estimated to be crumbling into the sea at the rate of 10ft an hour.* VERB = disintegrate, V, V prep/adv ♦ **Crumble away** means the same as **crumble**. ❑ *Britain's coastline stretches 4000 kilometres and much of it is crumbling away.* PHRASAL VERB, V P 3 If something such as a system, relationship, or hope **crumbles**, it comes to an end. ❑ *Their economy crumbled under the weight of United Nations sanctions.* VERB, V ♦ **Crumble away** means the same as **crumble**. ❑ *Opposition more or less crumbled away.* PHRASAL VERB 4 If someone **crumbles**, they stop resisting or trying to win, or become unable to cope. ❑ *He is a skilled and ruthless leader who isn't likely to crumble under pressure.* VERB, V 5 A **crumble** is a baked pudding made from fruit covered with a mixture of flour, butter, and sugar. [BRIT] ❑ *...apple crumble.* N-VAR: usu n N

♦ **crumble away** → see **crumble 2, 3**.

**crum|bly** /krʌmbli/ **(crumblier, crumbliest)** Something that is **crumbly** is easily broken into a lot of little pieces. ❑ *...crumbly cheese.* ADJ

**crum|my** /krʌmi/ **(crummier, crummiest)** Something that is **crummy** is unpleasant, of very poor quality, or not good enough. [INFORMAL] ❑ *When I first came here, I had a crummy flat.* ADJ: usu ADJ n [disapproval]

**crum|pet** /krʌmpɪt/ **(crumpets)** 1 **Crumpets** are round, flat pieces of a substance like N-COUNT

bread or batter with small holes in them. You toast them and eat them with butter. [mainly BRIT]
2 Some men refer to attractive women as **crumpet**. This use could cause offence. [BRIT, INFORMAL] N-UNCOUNT

**crum|ple** /krʌmpᵊl/ **(crumples, crumpling, crumpled)** 1 If you **crumple** something such as paper or cloth, or if it **crumples**, it is squashed and becomes full of untidy creases and folds. ❑ *She crumpled the paper in her hand... The front and rear of the car will crumple during a collision.* ♦ **Crumple up** means the same as **crumple**. ❑ *She crumpled up her coffee cup... Nancy looked at the note angrily, then crumpled it up and threw it in a nearby wastepaper basket.* ♦ **crum|pled** *His uniform was crumpled, untidy, splashed with mud.* 2 If someone **crumples**, they collapse, for example when they have received a shock. [WRITTEN] ❑ *His body crumpled... He immediately crumpled to the floor... Chance McAllister lay crumpled on the floor.* VERB; V n; V; PHRASAL VERB; V P n (not pron); V n P; ADJ; VERB; V; V prep; V-ed

♦ **crumple up** → see **crumple 1**.

**crunch** /krʌntʃ/ **(crunches, crunching, crunched)** 1 If you **crunch** something hard, such as a sweet, you crush it noisily between your teeth. ❑ *She sucked an ice cube into her mouth, and crunched it loudly... Richard crunched into the apple.* 2 If something **crunches** or if you **crunch** it, it makes a breaking or crushing noise, for example when you step on it. ❑ *A piece of china crunched under my foot... He crunched the sheets of paper in his hands.* ♦ **Crunch** is also a noun. ❑ *She heard the crunch of tires on the gravel driveway.* 3 If you **crunch** across a surface made of very small stones, you move across it causing it to make a crunching noise. ❑ *I crunched across the gravel. ...wheels crunching over a stony surface.* 4 You can refer to an important time or event, for example when an important decision has to be made, as **the crunch**. ❑ *He can rely on my support when the crunch comes... The Prime Minister is expected to call a crunch meeting on Monday.* ● If you say that something will happen **if** or **when it comes to the crunch**, you mean that it will happen if or when the time comes when something has to be done. ❑ *If it comes to the crunch, I'll resign over this.* 5 To **crunch** numbers means to do a lot of calculations using a calculator or computer. ❑ *I pored over the books with great enthusiasm, often crunching the numbers until 1:00 a.m.* 6 A situation in which a business or economy has very little money can be referred to as a **crunch**. [BUSINESS] ❑ *...a financial crunch that could threaten the company's future.* VERB; V n; V *into/on* n; VERB = scrunch; V; V n; N-COUNT; SOUND; VERB; V prep/adv; V prep/adv; N-SING: usu *the* N, oft N n; PHRASE: V inflects; VERB; V n; N-COUNT: usu supp N = crisis

**crunchy** /krʌntʃi/ **(crunchier, crunchiest)** Food that is **crunchy** is pleasantly hard or crisp so that it makes a noise when you eat it. ❑ *...fresh, crunchy vegetables.* ADJ [approval] = crisp

**cru|sade** /kruːseɪd/ **(crusades, crusading, crusaded)** 1 A **crusade** is a long and determined attempt to achieve something for a cause that you feel strongly about. ❑ *Footballers launched an unprecedented crusade against racism on the terraces.* 2 If you **crusade** for a particular cause, you make a long and determined effort to achieve something for it. ❑ *...a newspaper that has crusaded against the country's cocaine traffickers. ...an adopted boy whose cause is taken up by a crusading lawyer.* 3 **The Crusades** were the wars that were fought by Christians in Palestine against the Muslims during the eleventh, twelfth, and thirteenth centuries. N-COUNT: oft N *against/for* n, N to-inf = campaign; VERB = campaign; V *against/for* n; V-ing; N-PROPER-PLURAL: *the* N

**cru|sad|er** /kruːseɪdəʳ/ **(crusaders)** 1 A **crusader for** a cause is someone who does a lot in support of it. ❑ *He has set himself up as a crusader for higher press and broadcasting standards.* 2 A **Crusader** was a knight who fought in the Crusades. N-COUNT: with supp; N-COUNT

**crush** /krʌʃ/ **(crushes, crushing, crushed)** 1 To **crush** something means to press it very hard so that its shape is destroyed or so that it breaks into pieces. ❑ *Andrew crushed his empty can... Peel and crush the garlic. ...crushed ice.* 2 To **crush** a protest or movement, or a group of opponents, means to defeat it completely, usually by force. ❑ *The military operation was the first step in a plan to crush the uprising.* ♦ **crush|ing** *...the violent crushing of anti-government demonstrations.* 3 If you **are crushed** by something, it upsets you a great deal. ❑ *Listen to criticism but don't be crushed by it.* 4 If you **are crushed** against someone or something, you are pushed or pressed against them. ❑ *We were at the front, crushed against the stage.* 5 A **crush** is a crowd of people close together, in which it is difficult to move. ❑ *Franklin and his thirteen-year-old son somehow got separated in the crush.* 6 If you have a **crush on** someone, you are in love with them but do not have a relationship with them. [INFORMAL] ❑ *She had a crush on you, you know.* VERB; V n; V n; V-ed; VERB; V n; N-UNCOUNT: usu N *of* n; VERB: usu passive *be* V-ed; VERB: usu passive *be* V-ed prep; N-COUNT: usu sing; N-COUNT: usu N *on* n

**crush|er** /krʌʃəʳ/ **(crushers)** A **crusher** is a piece of equipment used for crushing things. ❑ *...a garlic crusher.* N-COUNT: usu n N

**crush|ing** /krʌʃɪŋ/ A **crushing** defeat, burden, or disappointment is a very great or severe one. ❑ *His loss would be a crushing blow to Liverpool's title hopes.* ADJ: ADJ n [emphasis]

**crush|ing|ly** /krʌʃɪŋli/ You can use **crushingly** to emphasize the degree of a negative quality. ❑ *...a collection of crushingly bad jokes.* ADV: ADV adj [emphasis]

**crust** /krʌst/ **(crusts)** 1 The **crust** on a loaf of bread is the outside part. 2 A pie's **crust** is its cooked pastry. 3 A **crust** is a hard layer of something, especially on top of a softer or wetter substance. ❑ *As the water evaporates, a crust of salt is left on the surface of the soil.* 4 The earth's **crust** is its outer layer. ❑ *Earthquakes leave scars in the earth's crust.* 5 → See also **upper crust**. N-COUNT; N-COUNT; N-COUNT; N-COUNT: with supp

**crus|ta|cean** /krʌsteɪʃᵊn/ **(crustaceans)** A **crustacean** is an animal with a hard shell and several pairs of legs, which usually lives in water. Crabs, lobsters, and shrimps are crustaceans. N-COUNT

**crust|ed** /krʌstɪd/ If something is **crusted with** a substance, it is covered with a hard or thick layer of that substance. [LITERARY] ❑ *...flat grey stones crusted with lichen.* ♦ **Crusted** is also a combining form. ❑ *He sat down to remove his mud-crusted boots.* ADJ: oft ADJ *with* n = encrusted; COMB in ADJ

**crusty** /krʌsti/ **(crustier, crustiest)** **Crusty** bread has a hard, crisp outside. ❑ *...crusty French loaves.* ADJ: usu ADJ n

**crutch** /krʌtʃ/ **(crutches)** 1 A **crutch** is a stick whose top fits round or under the user's arm, which someone with an injured foot or leg uses to support their weight when walking. ❑ *I can walk without the aid of crutches... I was on crutches for a while.* 2 If you refer to someone or something as a **crutch**, you mean that they give you help or support. ❑ *He gave up the crutch of alcohol.* 3 Your **crutch** is the same as your **crotch**. [mainly BRIT] ❑ *He kicked him in the crutch.* N-COUNT: usu pl, oft *on* N; N-SING; N-COUNT

**crux** /krʌks/ **The crux of** a problem or argument is the most important or difficult part of it which affects everything else. ❑ *He said the crux of the matter was economic policy.* N-SING: *the* N, usu N *of* n

**cry** /kraɪ/ **(cries, crying, cried)** 1 When you **cry**, tears come from your eyes, usually because you are unhappy or hurt. ❑ *I hung up the phone and started to cry... Please don't cry... He cried with anger and frustration. ...a crying baby.* ♦ **Cry** is also a noun. ❑ *A nurse patted me on the shoulder and said, 'You have a good cry, dear.'* ♦ **cry|ing** *She had been unable to sleep for three days because of her 13-week-old son's crying.* 2 If you **cry** something, you shout it or say it loudly. ❑ *'Nancy Drew,' she cried, 'you're under arrest!'.* ♦ **Cry out** means the same as **cry**. ❑ *'You're wrong, quite wrong!' Henry cried out, suddenly excited... According to the legend, she cried out that no storm was going to stop her from finishing her ride.* 3 A **cry** is a loud, high sound that you make when you feel a strong emotion such as fear, pain, or pleasure. ❑ *A cry of horror broke from me... With a cry, she rushed forward.* 4 A **cry** is a shouted word or phrase, usually one that is intended to attract someone's attention. ❑ *Thou-* ◆◆◇ VERB; V; V *with* n; V-ing; N-SING; N-UNCOUNT: usu with poss; VERB; V with quote; PHRASAL VERB; V P with quote; V P that; N-COUNT: oft N *of* n; N-COUNT: oft N *of/for* n = shout

*sands of Ukrainians burst into cries of 'bravo' on the steps of the parliament... Passers-by heard his cries for help.* → See also **battle cry**, **rallying cry**. 5 You can refer to a public protest about something or an appeal for something as a **cry** of some kind. [JOURNALISM] ❑ *There have been cries of outrage about this expenditure.* 6 A bird's or animal's **cry** is the loud, high sound that it makes. ❑ *...the cry of a seagull.* 7 → See also **crying**. 8 Something that is **a far cry from** something else is very different from it. ❑ *Their lives are a far cry from his own poor childhood.* 9 You use the expression **for crying out loud** in order to show that you are annoyed or impatient, or to add force to a question or request. [INFORMAL, SPOKEN] ❑ *I mean, what's he ever done in his life, for crying out loud?* 10 to **cry** your **eyes out** → see **eye**. **a shoulder to cry on** → see **shoulder**.

N-COUNT: usu N *of/for* n; N-COUNT = *call*; PHRASE: v-link PHR, PHR n; EXCLAM: PHR with cl [feelings]

♦ **cry off** If you **cry off**, you tell someone that you cannot do something that you have agreed or arranged to do. ❑ *Barron invited her to the races and she agreed, but she caught flu and had to cry off at the last minute.* PHRASAL VERB; V P

♦ **cry out** If you **cry out**, you call out loudly because you are frightened, unhappy, or in pain. ❑ *He was crying out in pain on the ground when the ambulance arrived... Hart cried out as his head struck rock.* → See also **cry 2**. PHRASAL VERB; V P *in* n; V P

♦ **cry out for** If you say that something **cries out for** a particular thing or action, you mean that it needs that thing or action very much. ❑ *This is a disgraceful state of affairs and cries out for a thorough investigation.* PHRASAL VERB; V P P n

**cry|baby** /kraɪbeɪbi/ **(crybabies)** also **cry-baby, cry baby.** If someone calls a child a **crybaby**, they mean that the child cries a lot for no good reason. [INFORMAL] N-COUNT [disapproval]

**cry|ing** /kraɪɪŋ/ 1 If you say that there is **a crying need for** something, you mean that there is a very great need for it. ❑ *There is a crying need for more magistrates from the ethnic minority communities.* 2 You can say that something is **a crying shame** if you are annoyed and upset about it. ❑ *It's a crying shame that police have to put up with these mindless attacks.* 3 → See also **cry**.

PHRASE: v-link PHR, PHR n; PHRASE: v-link PHR, oft *it* v-link PHR that [feelings]

**cryo|gen|ics** /kraɪoʊdʒenɪks/

✓ The form **cryogenic** is used as a modifier.

**Cryogenics** is a branch of physics that studies what happens to things at extremely low temperatures. N-PLURAL

**crypt** /krɪpt/ **(crypts)** A **crypt** is an underground room underneath a church or cathedral. ❑ *...people buried in the crypt of an old London church.* N-COUNT

**cryp|tic** /krɪptɪk/ A **cryptic** remark or message contains a hidden meaning or is difficult to understand. ❑ *He has issued a short, cryptic statement denying the spying charges... My father's notes are more cryptic here.* ♦ **cryp|ti|cal|ly** *'Not necessarily,' she says cryptically.* ADJ; ADV: ADV with v

**crypto-** /krɪptoʊ-/ **Crypto-** is added to adjectives and nouns to form other adjectives and nouns which refer to people who have hidden beliefs and principles. COMB in ADJ and N

**crys|tal** /krɪstᵊl/ **(crystals)** 1 A **crystal** is a small piece of a substance that has formed naturally into a regular symmetrical shape. ❑ *...salt crystals. ...a single crystal of silicon.* → See also **liquid crystal**, **liquid crystal display**. 2 **Crystal** is a transparent rock that is used to make jewellery and ornaments. ❑ *...a strand of crystal beads.* 3 **Crystal** is a high quality glass, usually with patterns cut into its surface. ❑ *Some of the finest drinking glasses are made from lead crystal. ...crystal glasses.* 4 Glasses and other containers made of crystal are referred to as **crystal**. ❑ *Get out your best china and crystal.*

◆◇◇ N-COUNT: oft n N; N-VAR; N-UNCOUNT; N-UNCOUNT

**crys|tal ball** **(crystal balls)** If you say that someone, especially an expert, looks into a **crystal ball**, you mean that they are trying to predict the future. Crystal balls are traditionally used by fortune-tellers. ❑ *Local economists have looked into their crystal balls and seen something rather nasty.* N-COUNT

**crys|tal clear** 1 Water that is **crystal clear** is absolutely clear and transparent like glass. ❑ *The cliffs, lapped by a crystal-clear sea, remind her of Capri.* 2 If you say that a message or statement is **crystal clear**, you are emphasizing that it is very easy to understand. ❑ *The message is crystal clear – if you lose weight, you will have a happier, healthier, better life.*

ADJ; ADJ: usu v-link ADJ [emphasis]

**crys|tal|line** /krɪstᵊlaɪn/ 1 A **crystalline** substance is in the form of crystals or contains crystals. ❑ *Diamond is the crystalline form of the element carbon.* 2 **Crystalline** means clear or bright. [LITERARY] ❑ *...a huge plain dotted with crystalline lakes.*

ADJ: usu ADJ n; ADJ: usu ADJ n

**crys|tal|lize** /krɪstᵊlaɪz/ **(crystallizes, crystallizing, crystallized)**

✓ in BRIT, also use **crystallise**

1 If you **crystallize** an opinion or idea, or if it **crystallizes**, it becomes fixed and definite in someone's mind. ❑ *He has managed to crystallise the feelings of millions of ordinary Russians... Now my thoughts really began to crystallise.* 2 If a substance **crystallizes**, or something **crystallizes** it, it turns into crystals. ❑ *Don't stir or the sugar will crystallise. ...a 19th century technique that actually crystallizes the tin.*

VERB; V n; V; VERB; V; V n

**crys|tal|lized** /krɪstᵊlaɪzd/

✓ in BRIT, also use **crystallised**

**Crystallized** fruits and sweets are covered in sugar which has been melted and then allowed to go hard. ADJ: usu ADJ n

**CS gas** **CS gas** is a gas which causes you to cry and makes breathing painful. It is sometimes used by the police to control a crowd which is rioting. [BRIT] N-UNCOUNT = *tear gas*

**cub** /kʌb/ **(cubs)**

✓ The spelling **Cub** is also used for meanings 2 and 3.

1 A **cub** is a young wild animal such as a lion, wolf, or bear. ❑ *...three five-week-old lion cubs.* 2 **The Cubs** or **the Cub Scouts** is a version of the Scouts for boys between the ages of eight and ten. 3 A **cub** or a **cub scout** is a boy who is a member of the Cubs.

N-COUNT: oft n N; N-PROPER-COLL: *the* N; N-COUNT

**Cu|ban** /kjuːbən/ **(Cubans)** 1 **Cuban** means belonging or relating to Cuba, or to its people or culture. 2 A **Cuban** is a Cuban citizen, or a person of Cuban origin. ADJ; N-COUNT

**cubby-hole** /kʌbi hoʊl/ **(cubby-holes)** also **cubbyhole.** A **cubby-hole** is a very small room or space for storing things. ❑ *It's in the cubby-hole under the stairs.* N-COUNT

**cube** /kjuːb/ **(cubes, cubing, cubed)** 1 A **cube** is a solid object with six square surfaces which are all the same size. ❑ *...cold water with ice cubes in it... The cabinet comes with locks and key and is shaped like a cube.* 2 When you **cube** food, you cut it into cube-shaped pieces. ❑ *Remove the seeds and stones and cube the flesh... Serve with cubed bread.* 3 **The cube of** a number is another number that is produced by multiplying the first number by itself twice. For example, the cube of 2 is 8.

N-COUNT: usu with supp; VERB; V n; V-ed; N-COUNT: usu sing, usu *the* N *of* n

**cube root** **(cube roots)** **The cube root of** a number is another number that makes the first number when it is multiplied by itself twice. For example, the cube root of 8 is 2. N-COUNT: usu sing, *the* N *of* n

**cu|bic** /kjuːbɪk/ **Cubic** is used in front of units of length to form units of volume such as 'cubic metre' and 'cubic foot'. ❑ *...3 billion cubic metres of soil.* ADJ: ADJ n

**cu|bi|cle** /kjuːbɪkᵊl/ **(cubicles)** A **cubicle** is a very small enclosed area, for example one where you can have a shower or change your clothes. ❑ *...a separate shower cubicle.* N-COUNT

**Cub|ism** /kjuːbɪzəm/ **Cubism** is a style of art, begun in the early twentieth century, in which objects are represented as if they could be seen from several different positions at the same time, using many lines and geometric shapes. N-UNCOUNT

**Cub|ist** /kjuːbɪst/ **(Cubists)** 1 A **Cubist** is an artist who painted in the style of Cubism. N-COUNT 2 **Cubist** art is art in the style of Cubism. ❑ *...Picasso's seminal Cubist painting, 'The Poet'.* ADJ: ADJ n

**cub re|port|er** **(cub reporters)** A **cub reporter** is a young newspaper journalist who is still being trained. ❑ *He had been a cub reporter for the Kansas City Star.* N-COUNT

**cub scout** → see **cub**.

**cuck|old** /kʌkoʊld/ **(cuckolds, cuckolding, cuckolded)** 1 A **cuckold** is a man whose wife is having an affair with another man. [LITERARY] N-COUNT 2 If a married woman is having an affair, she and her lover **are cuckolding** her husband. [LITERARY] ❑ *His wife had cuckolded him.* VERB V n

**cuckoo** /kʊkuː/ **(cuckoos)** A **cuckoo** is a bird that has a call of two quick notes, and lays its eggs in other birds' nests. N-COUNT

**cuckoo clock** **(cuckoo clocks)** A **cuckoo clock** is a clock with a door from which a toy cuckoo comes out and makes noises like a cuckoo every hour or half hour. N-COUNT

**cu|cum|ber** /kjuːkʌmbəʳ/ **(cucumbers)** 1 A **cucumber** is a long thin vegetable with a hard green skin and wet transparent flesh. It is eaten raw in salads. → See picture on page 1712. N-VAR 2 If you say that someone is **as cool as a cucumber**, you are emphasizing that they are very calm and relaxed, especially when you would not expect them to be. ❑ *You can hardly be held responsible for Darrow waltzing in, cool as a cucumber, and demanding thousands of pounds.* PHRASE [emphasis]

**cud** /kʌd/ When animals such as cows or sheep **chew the cud**, they slowly chew their partly digested food over and over again in their mouth before finally swallowing it. PHRASE: V inflects = *ruminate*

**cud|dle** /kʌdəl/ **(cuddles, cuddling, cuddled)** If you **cuddle** someone, you put your arms round them and hold them close as a way of showing your affection. ❑ *He cuddled the newborn girl... They always used to kiss and cuddle in front of everyone.* V-RECIP = *hug* V n (non-recip) pl-n V ♦ **Cuddle** is also a noun. ❑ *Give her a cuddle.* N-COUNT

**cud|dly** /kʌdəli/ **(cuddlier, cuddliest)** 1 A **cuddly** person or animal makes you want to cuddle them. ❑ *He is a small, cuddly man with spectacles.* ADJ [approval] 2 **Cuddly** toys are soft toys that look like animals. ADJ: ADJ n

**cudg|el** /kʌdʒəl/ **(cudgels)** 1 A **cudgel** is a thick, short stick that is used as a weapon. N-COUNT 2 If you **take up the cudgels for** someone or something, you speak or fight in support of them. ❑ *The trade unions took up the cudgels for the 367 staff made redundant.* PHRASE: V inflects, oft PHR *for/against* n

**cue** /kjuː/ **(cues, cueing, cued)** 1 In the theatre or in a musical performance, a performer's **cue** is something another performer says or does that is a signal for them to begin speaking, playing, or doing something. ❑ *I had never known him miss a cue.* ◆◇◇ N-COUNT: oft with poss 2 If one performer **cues** another, they say or do something which is a signal for the second performer to begin speaking, playing, or doing something. ❑ *He read the scene, with Seaton cueing him.* VERB V n 3 If you say that something that happens is a **cue for** an action, you mean that people start doing that action when it happens. ❑ *That was the cue for several months of intense bargaining.* N-COUNT: oft N *for* n, N to-inf 4 A **cue** is a long, thin wooden stick that is used to hit the ball in games such as snooker, billiards, and pool. N-COUNT

PHRASES 5 If you say that something happened **on cue** or **as if on cue**, you mean that it happened just when it was expected to happen, or just at the right time. ❑ *Kevin arrived right on cue to care for Harry.* PHRASE 6 If you **take** your **cue from** someone or something, you do something similar in a particular situation. ❑ *Taking his cue from his companion, he apologized for his earlier display of temper.* PHRASE: V inflects, usu PHR *from* n

**cuff** /kʌf/ **(cuffs, cuffing, cuffed)** 1 The **cuffs** of a shirt or dress are the parts at the ends of the sleeves, which are thicker than the rest of the sleeve. ❑ *...a pale blue shirt with white collar and cuffs.* N-COUNT: usu pl 2 The **cuffs** on a pair of pants or trousers are the parts at the ends of the legs, which are folded up. [AM] ❑ *...the cuffs of his jeans.* N-COUNT: usu pl

✔ in BRIT, use **turn-up**

3 If the police **cuff** someone, they put handcuffs on them. [INFORMAL] ❑ *She hoped they wouldn't cuff her hands behind her back.* VERB V n 4 An **off-the-cuff** remark is made without being prepared or thought about in advance. ❑ *I didn't mean any offence. It was a flippant, off-the-cuff remark.* PHRASE: PHR n, PHR after v

**cuff|link** /kʌflɪŋk/ **(cufflinks)** **Cufflinks** are small decorative objects used for holding together shirt cuffs around the wrist. ❑ *...a pair of gold cufflinks.* N-COUNT: usu pl

**cui|sine** /kwɪziːn/ **(cuisines)** 1 The **cuisine** of a country or district is the style of cooking that is characteristic of that place. ❑ *The cuisine of Japan is low in fat. ...traditional French cuisine.* N-VAR: usu with supp = *cooking* 2 The skill or profession of cooking unusual or interesting food can be referred to as **cuisine**. ❑ *...residential courses in gourmet cuisine.* N-UNCOUNT

**cul-de-sac** /kʌl dɪ sæk, AM - sæk/ **(cul-de-sacs)** A **cul-de-sac** is a short road which is closed off at one end. [mainly BRIT] ❑ *...a four-bedroom detached house in a quiet cul-de-sac.* N-COUNT: usu sing = *close*

✔ in AM, usually use **dead end**

**culi|nary** /kʌlɪnəri, AM kjuːləneri/ **Culinary** means concerned with cooking. [FORMAL] ❑ *She was keen to acquire more advanced culinary skills.* ADJ: ADJ n

**cull** /kʌl/ **(culls, culling, culled)** 1 If items or ideas **are culled from** a particular source or number of sources, they are taken and gathered together. ❑ *All this, needless to say, had been culled second-hand from radio reports... Laura was passing around photographs she'd culled from the albums at home.* VERB be V-ed *from* n V n *from* n 2 To **cull** animals means to kill the weaker animals in a group in order to reduce their numbers. ❑ *The national parks department is planning to cull 2000 elephants.* VERB V n ♦ **Cull** is also a noun. ❑ *In the reserves of Zimbabwe and South Africa, annual culls are already routine.* N-COUNT ♦ **cull|ing** *The culling of seal cubs has led to an outcry from environmental groups.* N-UNCOUNT: usu with supp

**cul|mi|nate** /kʌlmɪneɪt/ **(culminates, culminating, culminated)** If you say that an activity, process, or series of events **culminates in** or **with** a particular event, you mean that event happens at the end of it. ❑ *They had an argument, which culminated in Tom getting drunk.* VERB = *conclude* V *in/with* n

**cul|mi|na|tion** /kʌlmɪneɪʃən/ Something, especially something important, that is **the culmination of** an activity, process, or series of events happens at the end of it. ❑ *Their arrest was the culmination of an operation in which 120 other people were detained.* N-SING: usu *the* N *of* n

**cu|lottes** /kjuːlɒts, AM kuː-/ **Culottes** are knee-length women's trousers that look like a skirt. N-PLURAL: also *a pair of* N

**cul|pable** /kʌlpəbəl/ If someone or their conduct is **culpable**, they are responsible for something wrong or bad that has happened. [FORMAL] ❑ *Their decision to do nothing makes them culpable. ...manslaughter resulting from culpable negligence.* ADJ ♦ **cul|pabil|ity** /kʌlpəbɪlɪti/ *He added there was clear culpability on the part of the government.* N-UNCOUNT

**cul|prit** /kʌlprɪt/ **(culprits)** 1 When you are talking about a crime or something wrong that has been done, you can refer to the person who did it as **the culprit**. ❑ *All the men were being deported even though the real culprits in the fight have not been identified.* N-COUNT: usu *the* N = *offender* 2 When you are talking about a problem or bad situation, you can refer to its cause as **the culprit**. ❑ *About 10% of Japanese* N-COUNT *teenagers are overweight. Nutritionists say the main culprit is increasing reliance on Western fast food.*

**cult** /kʌlt/ **(cults)** [1] A **cult** is a fairly small religious group, especially one which is considered strange. ❑ *The teenager may have been abducted by a religious cult.* N-COUNT: usu sing, oft N of n [2] **Cult** is used to describe things that are very popular or fashionable among a particular group of people. ❑ *Since her death, she has become a cult figure... The film is destined to become a cult classic.* ADJ: ADJ n [3] Someone or something that is a **cult** has become very popular or fashionable among a particular group of people. ❑ *Ludlam was responsible for making Ridiculous Theatre something of a cult.* N-SING [4] The **cult** of something is a situation in which people regard that thing as very important or special. ❑ *Meanwhile the personality cult around this campaigner grew.* N-COUNT: usu the N of n; disapproval

**cul|ti|vate** /kʌltɪveɪt/ **(cultivates, cultivating, cultivated)** [1] If you **cultivate** land or crops, you prepare land and grow crops on it. ❑ *She also cultivated a small garden of her own. ...the few patches of cultivated land.* VERB; V n; V-ed ♦ **cul|ti|va|tion** /kʌltɪveɪʃən/ *...the cultivation of fruits and vegetables... Farmers with many acres under cultivation profited.* N-UNCOUNT: usu with supp, prep N [2] If you **cultivate** an attitude, image, or skill, you try hard to develop it and make it stronger or better. ❑ *Cultivating a positive mental attitude towards yourself can reap tremendous benefits.* VERB; V n ♦ **cul|ti|va|tion** *...the cultivation of a positive approach to life and health.* N-UNCOUNT: usu N of n [3] If you **cultivate** someone or **cultivate** a friendship with them, you try hard to develop a friendship with them. ❑ *Howe carefully cultivated Daniel C. Roper, the Assistant Postmaster General... Estonia has done much to cultivate the friendship of western European countries.* VERB; V n; V n

**cul|ti|vat|ed** /kʌltɪveɪtɪd/ [1] If you describe someone as **cultivated**, you mean they are well educated and have good manners. [FORMAL] ❑ *His mother was an elegant, cultivated woman.* ADJ = refined [2] **Cultivated** plants have been developed for growing on farms or in gardens. ❑ *...a mixture of wild and cultivated varieties.* ADJ: ADJ n ≠ wild

**cul|ti|va|tor** /kʌltɪveɪtəʳ/ **(cultivators)** A **cultivator** is a tool or machine which is used to break up the earth or to remove weeds, for example in a garden or field. N-COUNT

**cul|tur|al** /kʌltʃərəl/ ◆◇◇ [1] **Cultural** means relating to a particular society and its ideas, customs, and art. ❑ *...a deep sense of personal honor which was part of his cultural heritage. ...the Rajiv Gandhi Foundation which promotes cultural and educational exchanges between Britain and India.* ADJ: usu ADJ n ♦ **cul|tur|al|ly** *...an informed guide to culturally and historically significant sites... Culturally, they have much in common with their neighbours just across the border.* ADV: ADV adj, ADV with cl [2] **Cultural** means involving or concerning the arts. ❑ *...the sponsorship of sports and cultural events by tobacco companies.* ADJ: ADJ n ♦ **cul|tur|al|ly** *...one of our better-governed, culturally active regional centres – Manchester or Birmingham, say.* ADV: ADV adj, ADV with cl

**cul|tur|al aware|ness** Someone's **cultural awareness** is their understanding of the differences between themselves and people from other countries or other backgrounds, especially differences in attitudes and values. ❑ *...programs to promote diversity and cultural awareness within the industry.* N-UNCOUNT

**cul|ture** /kʌltʃəʳ/ ◆◆◇ **(cultures, culturing, cultured)** [1] **Culture** consists of activities such as the arts and philosophy, which are considered to be important for the development of civilization and of people's minds. ❑ *...aspects of popular culture. ...France's Minister of Culture and Education.* N-UNCOUNT [2] A **culture** is a particular society or civilization, especially considered in relation to its beliefs, way of life, or art. ❑ *...people from different cultures... I was brought up in a culture that said you must put back into the society what you have taken out.* N-COUNT [3] The **culture** of a particular organization or group consists of the habits of the people in it and the way they generally behave. ❑ *But social workers say that this has created a culture of dependency, particularly in urban areas.* N-COUNT: usu with supp [4] In science, a **culture** is a group of bacteria or cells which are grown, usually in a laboratory as part of an experiment. [TECHNICAL] ❑ *...a culture of human cells.* N-COUNT [5] In science, to **culture** a group of bacteria or cells means to grow them, usually in a laboratory as part of an experiment. [TECHNICAL] ❑ *To confirm the diagnosis, the hospital laboratory must culture a colony of bacteria.* VERB; V n

**cul|tured** /kʌltʃəʳd/ If you describe someone as **cultured**, you mean that they have good manners, are well educated, and know a lot about the arts. ❑ *He is a cultured man with a wide circle of friends.* ADJ

**cul|tured pearl** **(cultured pearls)** A **cultured pearl** is a pearl that is created by putting sand or grit into an oyster. N-COUNT

**cul|ture shock** **Culture shock** is a feeling of anxiety, loneliness, and confusion that people sometimes experience when they first arrive in another country. ❑ *Callum, recently arrived in Glasgow, is jobless, homeless, friendless, and suffering from culture shock.* N-UNCOUNT: also a N

**cul|vert** /kʌlvəʳt/ **(culverts)** A **culvert** is a water pipe or sewer that crosses under a road or railway. N-COUNT

**-cum-** /-kʌm-/ **-cum-** is put between two nouns to form a noun referring to something or someone that is partly one thing and partly another. ❑ *...a dining-room-cum-study.* COMB in N-COUNT

**cum|ber|some** /kʌmbəʳsəm/ [1] Something that is **cumbersome** is large and heavy and therefore difficult to carry, wear, or handle. ❑ *Although the machine looks cumbersome, it is actually easy to use.* ADJ = unwieldy [2] A **cumbersome** system or process is very complicated and inefficient. ❑ *...an old and cumbersome computer system.* ADJ = clumsy

**cum|in** /kʌmɪn/ **Cumin** is a sweet-smelling spice, and is popular in Indian cooking. N-UNCOUNT

**cum|mer|bund** /kʌməʳbʌnd/ **(cummerbunds)** A **cummerbund** is a wide piece of cloth worn round the waist as part of a man's evening dress. N-COUNT

**cu|mu|la|tive** /kjuːmjʊlətɪv/ If a series of events have a **cumulative** effect, each event makes the effect greater. ❑ *It is simple pleasures, such as a walk on a sunny day, which have a cumulative effect on our mood.* ADJ ♦ **cu|mu|la|tive|ly** *His administration was plagued by one petty scandal after another, cumulatively very damaging.* ADV

**cu|mu|lus** /kjuːmjʊləs/ **(cumuli** /kjuːmjʊlaɪ/**)** **Cumulus** is a type of thick white cloud formed when hot air rises very quickly. ❑ *...huge cumulus clouds.* N-VAR

**cun|ni|lin|gus** /kʌnɪlɪŋgəs/ **Cunnilingus** is oral sex which involves someone using their mouth to stimulate a woman's genitals. N-UNCOUNT

**cun|ning** /kʌnɪŋ/ [1] Someone who is **cunning** has the ability to achieve things in a clever way, often by deceiving other people. ❑ *These disturbed kids can be cunning. ...Mr Blair's cunning plan.* ADJ = crafty ♦ **cun|ning|ly** *They were cunningly disguised in golf clothes.* ADV: usu ADV with v [2] **Cunning** is the ability to achieve things in a clever way, often by deceiving other people. ❑ *...one more example of the cunning of today's art thieves.* N-UNCOUNT

**cunt** /kʌnt/ **(cunts)** [1] **Cunt** is an offensive word that some people use to refer to a woman's vagina. [⚠ VERY RUDE] N-COUNT [2] If someone calls another person a **cunt**, they are expressing contempt for that person. [⚠ VERY RUDE] N-COUNT; disapproval

**cup** /kʌp/ ◆◆◆ **(cups, cupping, cupped)** [1] A **cup** is a small round container that you drink from. Cups usually have handles and are made from china or plastic. ❑ *...cups and saucers.* N-COUNT ♦ A **cup of** something is the amount of something contained in a cup. ❑ *Mix about four cups of white flour with a pinch of salt.* N-COUNT: usu N of n [2] Things, or parts of things, that are small, round, and hollow in shape can be referred N-COUNT: oft N of n to as **cups**. ❑ *...the brass cups of the small chandelier.* [3] A **cup** is a large metal cup with two handles that is given to the winner of a game or competition. N-COUNT = trophy [4] **Cup** is used in the names of some sports competitions in which the prize is a cup. N-COUNT: usu *the* n N ❑ *Sri Lanka's cricket team will play India in the final of the Asia Cup.* [5] If you **cup** your **hands**, you make them into a curved shape like a cup. VERB ❑ *He cupped his hands around his mouth and called out for Diane...* V n prep *David knelt, cupped his hands and splashed river water on to his face...* V n *She held it in her cupped hands for us to see.* V-ed [6] If you **cup** something in your hands, you make your hands into a curved dish-like shape and support it or hold it gently. VERB ❑ *He cupped her chin in the palm of his hand...* V n prep *He cradled the baby in his arms, his hands cupping her tiny skull.* V n [7] **not** your **cup of tea** → see **tea**.

**cup|board** /kʌbəʳd/ **(cupboards)** [1] A **cupboard** is a piece of furniture that has one or two doors, usually contains shelves, and is used to store things. In British English, **cupboard** refers to all kinds of furniture like this. In American English, **closet** is usually used instead to refer to larger pieces of furniture. N-COUNT ❑ *The kitchen cupboard was stocked with tins of soup and food.* [2] A **cupboard** is a very small room that is used to store things, especially one without windows. [BRIT] N-COUNT

☑ in AM, use **closet**

[3] **a skeleton in the cupboard** → see **skeleton**.

**cup|cake** /kʌpkeɪk/ **(cupcakes) Cupcakes** are small iced cakes for one person. N-COUNT

**cup|ful** /kʌpfʊl/ **(cupfuls)** A **cupful of** something is the amount of something a cup can contain. N-COUNT: usu N *of* n ❑ *...a cupful of warm milk.*

**cu|pid** /kjuːpɪd/ **(cupids)** also **Cupid. Cupid** is the Roman god of love. He is usually shown as a baby boy with wings and a bow and arrow. N-PROPER ● If you say that someone **is playing cupid**, you mean that they are trying to bring two people together to start a romantic relationship. PHRASE ❑ *...the aristocrat who played Cupid to the Duke and Duchess.*

**cu|po|la** /kjuːpələ/ **(cupolas)** A **cupola** is a roof or part of a roof that is shaped like a dome. [FORMAL] N-COUNT = dome

**cup|pa** /kʌpə/ **(cuppas)** A **cuppa** is a cup of tea. [BRIT, INFORMAL] N-COUNT ❑ *Have you time for a cuppa?*

**cup tie (cup ties)** also **cup-tie.** In sports, especially football, a **cup tie** is a match between two teams who are taking part in a competition in which the prize is a cup. [BRIT] N-COUNT

**cur** /kɜːʳ/ **(curs)** A **cur** is an unfriendly dog, especially a mongrel. [OLD-FASHIONED] N-COUNT

**cur|able** /kjʊərəbᵊl/ If a disease or illness is **curable**, it can be cured. ADJ ≠ incurable ❑ *Most skin cancers are completely curable if detected in the early stages.*

**cu|rate (curates, curating, curated)**

☑ The noun is pronounced /kjʊərət/. The verb is pronounced /kjʊreɪt/.

[1] A **curate** is a clergyman in the Anglican Church who helps the priest. N-COUNT [2] If an exhibition **is curated** by someone, they organize it. VERB: usu passive ❑ *The Hayward exhibition has been curated by the artist Bernard Luthi.* *be* V-ed

**cu|ra|tive** /kjʊərətɪv/ Something that has **curative** properties can cure people's illnesses. [FORMAL] ADJ = healing ❑ *Ancient civilizations believed in the curative powers of fresh air and sunlight.*

**cu|ra|tor** /kjʊreɪtəʳ/ **(curators)** A **curator** is someone who is in charge of the objects or works of art in a museum or art gallery. N-COUNT

**cu|ra|to|rial** /kjʊrətɔːriəl/ **Curatorial** means relating to curators and their work. [FORMAL] ADJ: ADJ n ❑ *...the museum's curatorial team.*

**curb** /kɜːʳb/ **(curbs, curbing, curbed)** [1] If you **curb** something, you control it and keep it within limits. VERB = check, restrain ❑ *...advertisements aimed at curbing the spread of Aids...* V n *Inflation needs to be curbed in Russia.* *be* V-ed ♦ **Curb** is also a noun. N-COUNT: oft N *on* n ❑ *He called for much stricter curbs on immigration.* [2] If you **curb** an emotion or your behaviour, you keep it under control. VERB = check, restrain ❑ *He curbed his temper.* V n [3] → see **kerb**.

**curd** /kɜːʳd/ **(curds)** The thick white substance which is formed when milk turns sour can be referred to as **curds**. N-VAR: usu pl

**cur|dle** /kɜːʳdᵊl/ **(curdles, curdling, curdled)** If milk or eggs **curdle** or if you **curdle** them, they separate into different bits. VERB ❑ *The sauce should not boil or the egg yolk will curdle...* V *The herb has been used for centuries to curdle milk.* V n

**cure** /kjʊəʳ/ **(cures, curing, cured)** ◆◇◇ [1] If doctors or medical treatments **cure** an illness or injury, they cause it to end or disappear. VERB ❑ *Her cancer can only be controlled, not cured.* V n [2] If doctors or medical treatments **cure** a person, they make the person well again after an illness or injury. VERB = heal ❑ *MDT is an effective treatment and could cure all the leprosy sufferers worldwide...* V n *Almost overnight I was cured...* V n *Now doctors believe they have cured him of the disease.* V n *of* n [3] A **cure for** an illness is a medicine or other treatment that cures the illness. N-COUNT: oft N *for* n ❑ *Atkinson has been told rest is the only cure for his ankle injury.* [4] If someone or something **cures** a problem, they bring it to an end. VERB ❑ *Private firms are willing to make large scale investments to help cure Russia's economic troubles.* V n [5] A **cure for** a problem is something that will bring it to an end. N-COUNT: usu with supp, oft N *for* n ❑ *The magic cure for inflation does not exist.* [6] If an action or event **cures** someone **of** a habit or an attitude, it makes them stop having it. VERB ❑ *The experience was a detestable ordeal, and it cured him of any ambitions to direct again...* V n *of* n *He went to a clinic to cure his drinking and overeating.* V n [7] When food, tobacco, or animal skin **is cured**, it is dried, smoked, or salted so that it will last for a long time. VERB: usu passive ❑ *Legs of pork were cured and smoked over the fire.* *be* V-ed *...sliced cured ham.* V-ed

**cure-all (cure-alls)** A **cure-all** is something that is believed, usually wrongly, to be able to solve all the problems someone or something has, or to cure a wide range of illnesses. N-COUNT: oft N *for* n = panacea ❑ *He said the introduction of market discipline to the economy was not a magic cure-all for its problems.*

**cur|few** /kɜːʳfjuː/ **(curfews)** A **curfew** is a law stating that people must stay inside their houses after a particular time at night, for example during a war. N-VAR ❑ *The village was placed under curfew... In Lucknow crowds of people defied the curfew to celebrate on the streets.*

**cu|rio** /kjʊəriou/ **(curios)** A **curio** is an object such as a small ornament which is unusual and fairly rare. N-COUNT ❑ *...Oriental curios. ...antique and curio shops.*

**cu|ri|os|ity** /kjʊəriɒsɪti/ **(curiosities)** [1] **Curiosity** is a desire to know about something. N-UNCOUNT ❑ *Ryle accepted more out of curiosity than anything else... To satisfy our own curiosity we traveled to Baltimore.* [2] A **curiosity** is something that is unusual, interesting, and fairly rare. N-COUNT ❑ *There is much to see in the way of castles, curiosities, and museums.*

**cu|ri|ous** /kjʊəriəs/ ◆◇◇ [1] If you are **curious about** something, you are interested in it and want to know more about it. ADJ: usu v-link ADJ, oft ADJ *about* n ❑ *Steve was intensely curious about the world I came from. ...a group of curious villagers.* ♦ **cu|ri|ous|ly** *The woman in the shop had looked at them curiously.* ADV: ADV after v [2] If you describe something as **curious**, you mean that it is unusual or difficult to understand. ADJ = odd, peculiar ❑ *The pageant promises to be a curious mixture of the ancient and modern... The naval high command's response to these developments is rather curious.* ♦ **cu|ri|ous|ly** *Harry was curiously silent through all this.* ADV: ADV adj, ADV with cl

**curl** /kɜːʳl/ **(curls, curling, curled)** [1] If you have **curls**, your hair is in the form of tight curves and spirals. N-COUNT ❑ *...the little girl with blonde curls.* [2] If your hair has **curl**, it is full of curls. N-UNCOUNT ❑ *Dry curly hair naturally for maximum curl and shine.* [3] If your hair **curls** or if you **curl** it, it is full of curls. VERB ❑ *She has hair that refuses to curl...* V *Maria had curled her hair for the event...* V n *Afro hair is short and tightly curled.* V-ed

4 A **curl of** something is a piece or quantity of it that is curved or spiral in shape. ❑ *A thin curl of smoke rose from a rusty stove. ...curls of lemon peel.* N-COUNT: usu with supp, oft N *of* n
5 If your toes, fingers, or other parts of your body **curl**, or if you **curl** them, they form a curved or round shape. ❑ *His fingers curled gently round her wrist... Raise one foot, curl the toes and point the foot downwards... She sat with her legs curled under her.* VERB = bend; V prep/adv; V n; V-ed
6 If something **curls** somewhere, or if you **curl** it there, it moves there in a spiral or curve. ❑ *Smoke was curling up the chimney... He curled the ball into the net.* VERB; V prep/adv; V n prep/adv
7 If a person or animal **curls into** a ball, they move into a position in which their body makes a rounded shape. ❑ *He wanted to curl into a tiny ball... The kitten was curled on a cushion on the sofa.* ♦ **Curl up** means the same as **curl**. ❑ *In colder weather, your cat will curl up into a tight, heat-conserving ball... She curled up next to him... He was asleep there, curled up in the fetal position.* VERB; V *into* n; V-ed; PHRASAL VERB; V P *into* n; V P; V-ed P
8 When a leaf, a piece of paper, or another flat object **curls**, its edges bend towards the centre. ❑ *The rose leaves have curled because of an attack by grubs.* ♦ **Curl up** means the same as **curl**. ❑ *The corners of the lino were curling up.* VERB; V; PHRASAL VERB; V P

♦ **curl up** → see **curl 7, 8**.

**curl|er** /kɜːʳləʳ/ **(curlers)** **Curlers** are small plastic or metal tubes that women roll their hair round in order to make it curly. ❑ *...a woman with her hair in curlers.* N-COUNT = roller

**cur|lew** /kɜːʳljuː/ **(curlews)** A **curlew** is a large brown bird with long legs and a long curved beak. Curlews live near water and have a very distinctive cry. N-COUNT

**cur|li|cue** /kɜːʳlɪkjuː/ **(curlicues)** **Curlicues** are decorative twists and curls, usually carved or made with a pen. [LITERARY] ❑ *...the gothic curlicues of cottages and churches.* N-COUNT: usu pl

**curly** /kɜːʳli/ **(curlier, curliest)** 1 **Curly** hair is full of curls. ❑ *I've got naturally curly hair... Her hair was dark and curly.* ADJ ≠ straight
2 **Curly** is sometimes used to describe things that are curved or spiral in shape. ❑ *...cauliflowers with extra long curly leaves. ...dragons with curly tails.* ADJ: usu ADJ n ≠ straight

**cur|mudg|eon** /kəʳmʌdʒən/ **(curmudgeons)** If you call someone a **curmudgeon**, you do not like them because they are mean or bad-tempered. [OLD-FASHIONED] ❑ *...such a terrible old curmudgeon.* N-COUNT [disapproval]

**cur|mudg|eon|ly** /kəʳmʌdʒənli/ If you describe someone as **curmudgeonly**, you do not like them because they are mean or bad-tempered. [OLD-FASHIONED] ADJ [disapproval]

**cur|rant** /kʌrənt, AM kɜːr-/ **(currants)** 1 **Currants** are small dried black grapes, used especially in cakes. N-COUNT
2 **Currants** are bushes which produce edible red, black, or white berries. The berries are also called **currants**. → See also **blackcurrant**, **redcurrant**. N-COUNT

**cur|ren|cy** /kʌrənsi, AM kɜːr-/ **(currencies)** ◆◇◇
1 The money used in a particular country is referred to as its **currency**. ❑ *Tourism is the country's top earner of foreign currency... More people favour a single European currency than oppose it.* N-VAR
2 If a custom, idea, or word has **currency**, it is used and accepted by a lot of people at a particular time. [FORMAL] ❑ *'Loop' is one of those computer words that has gained currency in society.* N-UNCOUNT = acceptance
3 → See also **common currency**.

**cur|rent** /kʌrənt, AM kɜːr-/ **(currents)** ◆◆◆ 1 A **current** is a steady and continuous flowing movement of some of the water in a river, lake, or sea. ❑ *Under normal conditions, the ocean currents of the tropical Pacific travel from east to west... The couple were swept away by the strong current.* N-COUNT
2 A **current** is a steady flowing movement of air. ❑ *I felt a current of cool air blowing in my face.* N-COUNT: usu with supp
3 An electric **current** is a flow of electricity through a wire or circuit. ❑ *A powerful electric current is passed through a piece of graphite.* N-COUNT
4 A particular **current** is a particular feeling, idea, or quality that exists within a group of people. ❑ *Each party represents a distinct current of thought.* N-COUNT: with supp, oft N *of* n
5 **Current** means happening, being used, or being done at the present time. ❑ *The current situation is very different to that in 1990... He plans to repeal a number of current policies.* ♦ **cur|rent|ly** *Twelve potential vaccines are currently being tested on human volunteers.* ADJ: usu ADJ n; ADV: ADV before v
6 Ideas and customs that are **current** are generally accepted and used by most people. ❑ *Current thinking suggests that toxins only have a small part to play in the build up of cellulite.* ADJ
7 → See also **alternating current**, **direct current**.

**cur|rent ac|count** **(current accounts)** 1 A **current account** is a personal bank account which you can take money out of at any time using your cheque book or cash card. [BRIT] ❑ *His current account was seriously overdrawn.* N-COUNT

✔ in AM, use **checking account**

2 A country's **current account** is the difference in value between its exports and imports over a particular period of time. [BUSINESS] ❑ *Portugal will probably have a small current-account surplus for 1992.* N-COUNT: usu sing, oft N n

**cur|rent af|fairs** If you refer to **current affairs**, you are referring to political events and problems in society which are discussed in newspapers, and on television and radio. ❑ *...the BBC's current affairs programme 'Panorama'.* N-PLURAL

**cur|rent as|sets** **(current assets)** **Current assets** are assets which a company does not use on a continuous basis, such as stocks and debts, but which can be converted into cash within one year. [BUSINESS] ❑ *The company lists its current assets at $56.9 million.* N-COUNT

**cur|ricu|lum** /kərɪkjʊləm/ **(curriculums** or **curricula** /kərɪkjʊlə/) 1 A **curriculum** is all the different courses of study that are taught in a school, college, or university. ❑ *Russian is the one compulsory foreign language on the school curriculum.* → See also **National Curriculum**. N-COUNT
2 A particular **curriculum** is one particular course of study that is taught in a school, college, or university. ❑ *...the history curriculum.* N-COUNT: usu n N = syllabus

**cur|ricu|lum vitae** /kərɪkjʊləm viːtaɪ, AM -ti/ A **curriculum vitae** is the same as a **CV**. [mainly BRIT] N-SING

✔ in AM, use **résumé**

**cur|ried** /kʌrid, AM kɜːrid/ **Curried** meat or vegetables have been flavoured with hot spices. ADJ: ADJ n

**cur|ry** /kʌri, AM kɜːri/ **(curries, currying, curried)** 1 **Curry** is a dish composed of meat and vegetables, or just vegetables, in a sauce containing hot spices. It is usually eaten with rice and is one of the main dishes of India. ❑ *...vegetable curry... I went for a curry last night.* N-VAR
2 If one person tries to **curry favour with** another, they do things in order to try to gain their support or cooperation. ❑ *Politicians are eager to promote their 'happy family' image to curry favour with voters.* PHRASE: V inflects, oft PHR *with* n

**cur|ry pow|der** **(curry powders)** **Curry powder** is a powder made from a mixture of spices. It is used in cooking, especially when making curry. N-MASS

**curse** /kɜːʳs/ **(curses, cursing, cursed)** 1 If you **curse**, you use rude or offensive language, usually because you are angry about something. [WRITTEN] ❑ *I cursed and hobbled to my feet.* ♦ **Curse** is also a noun. ❑ *He shot her an angry look and a curse.* VERB = swear; V; N-COUNT
2 If you **curse** someone, you say insulting things to them because you are angry with them. ❑ *Grandma protested, but he cursed her and rudely pushed her aside... He cursed himself for having been so careless.* VERB; V n; V pron-refl
3 If you **curse** something, you complain angrily about it, especially using rude language. ❑ *So we set off again, cursing the delay, towards the west.* VERB; V n
4 If you say that there is a **curse on** someone, you mean that there seems to be a supernatural power causing unpleasant things to happen to them. ❑ *Maybe there is a curse on my family.* N-COUNT: oft N *on/upon* n
5 You can refer to something that causes a great deal of N-COUNT: usu sing, oft N *of* n

trouble or harm as a **curse**. ❑ *Apathy is the long-standing curse of British local democracy.* = plague

**curs|ed** /kɜːʳst/ [1] If you are **cursed with** something, you are very unlucky in having it. ❑ *Bulman was cursed with a poor memory for names.* ADJ: v-link ADJ *with* n
[2] Someone or something that is **cursed** is suffering as the result of a curse. ❑ *The whole family seemed cursed.* ADJ: usu v-link ADJ

**cur|sor** /kɜːʳsəʳ/ **(cursors)** On a computer screen, the **cursor** is a small shape that indicates where anything that is typed by the user will appear. [COMPUTING] N-COUNT

**cur|sory** /kɜːʳsəri/ A **cursory** glance or examination is a brief one in which you do not pay much attention to detail. ❑ *Burke cast a cursory glance at the menu, then flapped it shut.* ADJ: ADJ n = perfunctory

**curt** /kɜːʳt/ If you describe someone as **curt**, you mean that they speak or reply in a brief and rather rude way. ❑ *Her tone of voice was curt... 'The matter is closed,' was the curt reply.* ADJ = abrupt, brusque ♦ **curt|ly** *'I'm leaving,' she said curtly.* ADV: ADV with v

**cur|tail** /kɜːʳteɪl/ **(curtails, curtailing, curtailed)** If you **curtail** something, you reduce or limit it. [FORMAL] ❑ *NATO plans to curtail the number of troops being sent to the region.* VERB = restrict V n

**cur|tail|ment** /kɜːʳteɪlmənt/ The **curtailment of** something is the act of reducing or limiting it. [FORMAL] ❑ *...the curtailment of presidential power.* N-SING: usu N *of* n

**cur|tain** /kɜːʳtᵊn/ **(curtains)** ◆◇◇ [1] **Curtains** are large pieces of material which you hang from the top of a window. [mainly BRIT] ❑ *Her bedroom curtains were drawn.* N-COUNT

> in AM, usually use **drapes**

[2] **Curtains** are pieces of very thin material which you hang in front of windows in order to prevent people from seeing in. [AM] N-COUNT

> in BRIT, use **net curtains**

[3] In a theatre, **the curtain** is the large piece of material that hangs in front of the stage until a performance begins. ❑ *The curtain rises toward the end of the Prelude.* N-SING: the N [4] You can refer to something as a **curtain** when it is thick and difficult to see through or get past. [LITERARY] ❑ *He saw something dark disappear behind the curtain of leaves.* N-SING: usu N *of* n → See also **Iron Curtain**. [5] If something **brings down the curtain on** an event or situation, it causes or marks the end of it. ❑ *Management changes are under way that will finally bring down the curtain on Lord Forte's extraordinary working life.* PHRASE: V inflects, PHR n

**cur|tain call** **(curtain calls)** also **curtain-call.** In a theatre, when actors or performers take a **curtain call**, they come forward to the front of the stage after a performance in order to receive the applause of the audience. ❑ *They took 23 curtain calls.* N-COUNT

**cur|tained** /kɜːʳtᵊnd/ A **curtained** window, door, or other opening has a curtain hanging across it. ❑ *...heavily curtained windows.* ADJ: usu ADJ n

**curtain-raiser** **(curtain-raisers)** A **curtain-raiser** is an event, especially a sporting event or a performance, that takes place before a more important one, or starts off a series of events. [JOURNALISM] ❑ *The three-race series will be a curtain-raiser to the Monaco Grand Prix in May.* N-COUNT: usu sing

**curt|sy** /kɜːʳtsi/ **(curtsies, curtsying, curtsied)** also **curtsey.** If a woman or a girl **curtsies**, she lowers her body briefly, bending her knees and sometimes holding her skirt with both hands, as a way of showing respect for an important person. ❑ *We were taught how to curtsy to the Queen... Ingrid shook the Duchess's hand and curtsied.* VERB V *to* n V ♦ **Curtsy** is also a noun. ❑ *She gave a curtsy.* N-COUNT

**cur|va|ceous** /kɜːʳveɪʃəs/ If someone describes a woman as **curvaceous**, they think she is attractive because of the curves of her body. ❑ *...a curvaceous blonde.* ADJ [approval] = curvy

**cur|va|ture** /kɜːʳvətʃəʳ/ The **curvature of** something is its curved shape, especially when this shape is part of the circumference of a circle. [TECHNICAL] ❑ *...the curvature of the earth.* N-UNCOUNT: oft N *of* n

**curve** /kɜːʳv/ **(curves, curving, curved)** [1] A **curve** is a smooth, gradually bending line, for example part of the edge of a circle. ❑ *...the curve of his lips. ...a curve in the road.* N-COUNT: usu with supp [2] If something **curves**, or if someone or something **curves** it, it has the shape of a curve. ❑ *Her spine curved... The track curved away below him. ...a knife with a slightly curving blade... A small, unobtrusive smile curved the cook's thin lips.* VERB V V adv/prep V-ing V n [3] If something **curves**, it moves in a curve, for example through the air. ❑ *The ball curved strangely in the air.* VERB V [4] You can refer to a change in something as a particular **curve**, especially when it is represented on a graph. ❑ *Each firm will face a downward-sloping demand curve.* N-COUNT: usu with supp → See also **learning curve**. [5] If someone **throws** you **a curve** or if they **throw** you **a curve ball**, they surprise you by doing something you do not expect. [mainly AM] ❑ *At the last minute, I threw them a curve ball by saying, 'We're going to bring spouses'.* PHRASE: V inflects

**curved** /kɜːʳvd/ A **curved** object has the shape of a curve or has a smoothly bending surface. ❑ *...a small, curved staircase. ...the curved lines of the chairs.* ADJ

**curvy** /kɜːʳvi/ If someone describes a woman as **curvy**, they think she is attractive because of the curves of her body. [INFORMAL] ADJ [approval] = curvaceous

**cush|ion** /kʊʃᵊn/ **(cushions, cushioning, cushioned)** [1] A **cushion** is a fabric case filled with soft material, which you put on a seat to make it more comfortable. ❑ *...a velvet cushion.* N-COUNT [2] A **cushion** is a soft pad or barrier, especially one that protects something. ❑ *The company provides a styrofoam cushion to protect the tablets during shipping.* N-COUNT [3] Something that **cushions** an object when it hits something protects it by reducing the force of the impact. ❑ *There is also a new steering wheel with an energy absorbing rim to cushion the driver's head in the worst impacts... The suspension is designed to cushion passengers from the effects of riding over rough roads.* VERB V n V n *from* n [4] To **cushion** the effect of something unpleasant means to reduce it. ❑ *They said Western aid was needed to cushion the blows of vital reform... The subsidies are designed to cushion farmers against unpredictable weather.* VERB V n V n *against* n [5] Something that is a **cushion against** something unpleasant reduces its effect. ❑ *Housing benefit provides a cushion against hardship.* N-COUNT: usu sing, usu with supp

**cush|ion|ing** /kʊʃənɪŋ/ **Cushioning** is something soft that protects an object when it hits something. ❑ *Running shoes have extra cushioning.* N-UNCOUNT

**cushy** /kʊʃi/ **(cushier, cushiest)** A **cushy** job or situation is pleasant because it does not involve much work or effort. [INFORMAL] ❑ *...a cushy job in the civil service.* ADJ: usu ADJ n

**cusp** /kʌsp/ If you say that someone or something is **on the cusp**, you mean they are between two states, or are about to be in a particular state. ❑ *I am sitting on the cusp of middle age.* PHRASE: PHR after v, v-link PHR

**cuss** /kʌs/ **(cusses, cussing, cussed)** If someone **cusses**, they swear at someone or use bad language. [INFORMAL, OLD-FASHIONED] ❑ *Tosh was known to be a man who would cuss and shout... He rails and cusses at those pop stars.* VERB = curse V V *at* n Also V n

**cus|tard** /kʌstəʳd/ **(custards)** **Custard** is a sweet yellow sauce made from milk and eggs or from milk and a powder. It is eaten with fruit and puddings. ❑ *...bananas and custard.* N-MASS

**cus|tard pie** **(custard pies)** **Custard pies** are artificial pies which people sometimes throw at each other as a joke. ❑ *...a custard pie fight.* N-COUNT

**cus|to|dial** /kʌstoʊdiəl/ [1] **Custodial** means relating to keeping people in prison. [mainly BRIT, FORMAL] ❑ *If he is caught again he will be given a custodial sentence.* ADJ: ADJ n [2] If a child's parents are divorced or separated, the **custodial** parent is the parent who has custody of the child. [LEGAL] ADJ: ADJ n

**cus|to|dian** /kʌstoʊdiən/ **(custodians)** The **custodian** of an official building, a companies' assets, or something else valuable is the person who is officially in charge of it. ❑ *...the custodian of the holy shrines in Mecca and Medina.* N-COUNT

**cus|to|dy** /kʌstədi/ [1] **Custody** is the legal right to keep and look after a child, especially the right given to a child's mother or father when they get divorced. ❑ *I'm going to go to court to get custody of the children... Child custody is normally granted to the mother.* N-UNCOUNT: oft N *of* n [2] Someone who is **in custody** or has been taken **into custody** has been arrested and is being kept in prison until they can be tried in a court. ❑ *Three people appeared in court and two of them were remanded in custody... She was taken into custody later that day.* PHRASE: PHR after v [3] If someone is being held in a particular type of **custody**, they are being kept in a place that is similar to a prison. ❑ *Barrett was taken into protective custody.* N-UNCOUNT: usu with supp

**cus|tom** /kʌstəm/ **(customs)** [1] A **custom** is an activity, a way of behaving, or an event which is usual or traditional in a particular society or in particular circumstances. ❑ *The custom of lighting the Olympic flame goes back centuries... Chung has tried to adapt to local customs.* N-VAR: usu with supp, oft N *of* -ing [2] If it is your **custom to** do something, you usually do it in particular circumstances. ❑ *It was his custom to approach every problem cautiously.* N-SING: oft with poss [3] If a shop has your **custom**, you regularly buy things there. [BRIT, FORMAL] ❑ *You have the right to withhold your custom if you so wish.* N-UNCOUNT: usu with poss [4] → See also **customs**.

**cus|tom|ary** /kʌstəmri, AM -meri/ [1] **Customary** is used to describe things that people usually do in a particular society or in particular circumstances. [FORMAL] ❑ *It is customary to offer a drink or a snack to guests.* ADJ: oft *it* v-link ADJ to-inf = usual [2] **Customary** is used to describe something that a particular person usually does or has. ❑ *Yvonne took her customary seat behind her desk.* ADJ: ADJ n = usual

**custom-built** If something **is custom-built**, it is built according to someone's special requirements. ❑ *The machine was custom-built by Steve Roberts. ...a custom-built kitchen.* V-PASSIVE = custom-made *be* V-ed; V-ed

**cus|tom|er** /kʌstəməʳ/ **(customers)** [1] A **customer** is someone who buys goods or services, especially from a shop. ❑ *Our customers have very tight budgets. ...the quality of customer service.* ◆◆◇ N-COUNT [2] You can use **customer** in expressions such as **a cool customer** or **a tough customer** to indicate what someone's behaviour or character is like. [INFORMAL] ❑ *...two pretty awkward customers.* N-COUNT: adj N

**cus|tom|er base** **(customer bases)** A business's **customer base** is all its regular customers, considered as a group. [BUSINESS] ❑ *...Halifax's customer base of 21 million people.* N-COUNT

**cus|tom|er re|la|tions** [1] **Customer relations** are the relationships that a business has with its customers and the way in which it treats them. [BUSINESS] ❑ *Good customer relations require courtesy, professionalism and effective response.* N-PLURAL [2] **Customer relations** is the department within a company that deals with complaints from customers. [BUSINESS] ❑ *...Tucson Electric's customer-relations department.* N-UNCOUNT

**cus|tom|er sat|is|fac|tion** When customers are pleased with the goods or services they have bought, you can refer to **customer satisfaction**. ❑ *I really believe that it is possible to both improve customer satisfaction and reduce costs... Customer satisfaction with their mobile service runs at more than 90 per cent.* N-UNCOUNT

**cus|tom|er ser|vice** **Customer service** refers to the way that companies behave towards their customers, for example how well they treat them. [BUSINESS] ❑ *...a mail-order business with a strong reputation for customer service... The firm has an excellent customer service department.* N-UNCOUNT

**cus|tom|ize** /kʌstəmaɪz/ **(customizes, customizing, customized)**

> in BRIT, also use **customise**

If you **customize** something, you change its appearance or features to suit your tastes or needs. ❑ *...a control that allows photographers to customise the camera's basic settings. ...customized software.* VERB V n; V-ed

**custom-made** If something **is custom-made**, it is made according to someone's special requirements. ❑ *Furniture can also be custom-made to suit your own requirements. ...a custom-made suit.* V-PASSIVE *be* V-ed; V-ed

**cus|toms** /kʌstəmz/ [1] **Customs** is the official organization responsible for collecting taxes on goods coming into a country and preventing illegal goods from being brought in. ❑ *...components similar to those seized by British customs. ...customs officers.* N-PROPER: oft N n [2] **Customs** is the place where people arriving from a foreign country have to declare goods that they bring with them. ❑ *He walked through customs.* N-UNCOUNT [3] **Customs** duties are taxes that people pay for importing and exporting goods. ADJ: ADJ n [4] → See also **custom**.

**Cus|toms and Ex|cise** **Customs and Excise** is a British government department which is responsible for collecting taxes on imported and exported goods. Compare **Customs Service**. N-PROPER

**Cus|toms Ser|vice** **The Customs Service** is a United States federal organization which is responsible for collecting taxes on imported and exported goods. Compare **Customs and Excise**. N-PROPER

**cut** /kʌt/ **(cuts, cutting)** ◆◆◆

> The form **cut** is used in the present tense and is the past tense and past participle.

[1] If you **cut** something, you use a knife or a similar tool to divide it into pieces, or to mark it or damage it. If you **cut** a shape or a hole in something, you make the shape or hole by using a knife or similar tool. ❑ *Mrs. Haines stood nearby, holding scissors to cut a ribbon... The thieves cut a hole in the fence... Mr. Long was now cutting himself a piece of the pink cake... You can hear the saw as it cuts through the bones. ...thinly cut cucumber sandwiches.* VERB V n; V n prep/adv; V n n; V *through* n; V-ed ♦ **Cut** is also a noun. ❑ *The operation involves making several cuts in the cornea.* N-COUNT [2] If you **cut yourself** or **cut** a part of your body, you accidentally injure yourself on a sharp object so that you bleed. ❑ *Johnson cut himself shaving... I started to cry because I cut my finger... Blood from his cut lip trickled over his chin.* VERB V pron-refl; V n; V-ed ♦ **Cut** is also a noun. ❑ *He had sustained a cut on his left eyebrow. ...cuts and bruises.* N-COUNT [3] If you **cut** something such as grass, your hair, or your fingernails, you shorten them using scissors or another tool. ❑ *The most recent tenants hadn't even cut the grass... You've had your hair cut, it looks great... She had dark red hair, cut short.* VERB V n; *have* n V-ed; V-ed ♦ **Cut** is also a noun. ❑ *Prices vary from salon to salon, starting at £17 for a cut and blow-dry.* N-SING [4] The way that clothes **are cut** is the way they are designed and made. ❑ *...badly cut blue suits.* VERB: usu passive V-ed [5] If you **cut across** or **through** a place, you go through it because it is the shortest route to another place. ❑ *He decided to cut across the Heath, through Greenwich Park.* VERB V *across/through* n → See also **short cut**. [6] If you **cut** something, you reduce it. ❑ *The first priority is to cut costs... The UN force is to be cut by 90%. ...a deal to cut 50 billion dollars from the federal deficit.* VERB = reduce V n; V n *by* amount; V amount *from/off* n ♦ **Cut** is also a noun. ❑ *The economy needs an immediate 2 per cent cut in interest rates. ...the government's plans for tax cuts.* N-COUNT: with supp, oft N *in* n [7] If you **cut** a text, broadcast, or performance, you shorten it. If you **cut** a part of a text, broadcast, or performance, you do not publish, broadcast, or perform that part. ❑ *The audience wants more music and less drama, so we've cut some scenes.* VERB V n ♦ **Cut** is also a noun. ❑ *It has been found necessary to make some cuts in the text.* N-COUNT [8] To **cut** a supply of something means to stop providing it or stop it being provided. ❑ *They used pressure tactics to force them to return, including cutting food and water supplies.* VERB V n ♦ **Cut** is also a noun. ❑ *The strike had already led to cuts in electricity and water supplies in many areas.* N-COUNT: with supp, usu N *in* n [9] If you **cut** a pack of playing cards, you divide it into VERB

two. ❑ *Place the cards face down on the table and cut them.* (V n) [10] (CONVENTION) When the director of a film says '**cut**', they want the actors and the camera crew to stop filming. [11] (VERB) When a singer or band **cuts** a CD, they make a recording of their music. ❑ *She eventually cut her own album.* (V n) [12] (VERB) When a child **cuts** a tooth, a new tooth starts to grow through the gum. ❑ *Many infants do not cut their first tooth until they are a year old.* (V n) [13] (VERB = skip) If a child **cuts** classes or **cuts** school, they do not go to classes or to school when they are supposed to. [mainly AM] ❑ *Cutting school more than once in three months is a sign of trouble.* (V n) [14] (VERB [feelings]) If you tell someone to **cut** something, you are telling them in an irritated way to stop it. [mainly AM, INFORMAL] ❑ *Why don't you just cut the crap and open the door.* (V n) [15] (N-COUNT: with supp) A **cut** of meat is a piece or type of meat which is cut in a particular way from the animal, or from a particular part of it. ❑ *Use a cheap cut such as spare rib chops.* [16] (N-SING: oft poss N = share) Someone's **cut** of the profits or winnings from something, especially ones that have been obtained dishonestly, is their share. [INFORMAL] ❑ *The lawyers, of course, take their cut of the little guy's winnings.* [17] (N-COUNT) A **cut** is a narrow valley which has been cut through a hill so that a road or railroad track can pass through. [AM]

✓ in BRIT, use **cutting**

[18] → See also **cutting**.

**PHRASES** [19] (PHRASE: v-link PHR n) If you say that someone or something is **a cut above** other people or things of the same kind, you mean they are better than them. [INFORMAL] ❑ *Joan Smith's detective stories are a cut above the rest.* [20] (PHRASE: v-link PHR, PHR n = clear-cut) If you say that a situation or solution is **cut and dried**, you mean that it is clear and definite. ❑ *Unfortunately, things cannot be as cut and dried as many people would like... We are aiming for guidelines, not cut-and-dried answers.* [21] (PHRASE: usu with broad neg) If you say that someone can't **cut it**, you mean that they do not have the qualities needed to do a task or cope with a situation. [INFORMAL] ❑ *He doesn't think English-born players can cut it abroad.* [22] (PHRASE) If you talk about **the cut and thrust of** an activity, you are talking about the aspects of it that make it exciting and challenging. ❑ *...cut-and-thrust debate between two declared adversaries.* [23] (PHRASE: V inflects) If you say that something **cuts both ways**, you mean that it can have two opposite effects, or can have both good and bad effects. ❑ *This publicity cuts both ways. It focuses on us as well as on them.* [24] to cut something **to the bone** → see **bone**. to **cut corners** → see **corner**. to **cut the mustard** → see **mustard**. to **cut** someone **to the quick** → see **quick**. to **cut a long story short** → see **story**. to **cut** your **teeth on** something → see **tooth**.

♦ **cut across** (PHRASAL VERB) If an issue or problem **cuts across** the division between two or more groups of people, it affects or matters to people in all the groups. ❑ *The problem cuts across all socioeconomic lines and affects all age groups.* (V P n)

♦ **cut back** (PHRASAL VERB) If you **cut back** something such as expenditure or **cut back on** it, you reduce it. ❑ *They will be concerned to cut back expenditure on unnecessary items...* (V P n (not pron)) *The Government has cut back on defence spending...* (V P *on* n) *We have been cutting back a bit: we did have thirteen horses, but now it's nine.* (V P) (Also V n P) → See also **cutback**.

♦ **cut down** [1] (PHRASAL VERB) If you **cut down on** something or **cut down** something, you use or do less of it. ❑ *He cut down on coffee and cigarettes, and ate a balanced diet...* (V P *on* n) *Car owners were asked to cut down travel...* (V P n) *If you spend more than your income, can you try to cut down?* (V P, Also V n P) [2] (PHRASAL VERB) If you **cut down** a tree, you cut through its trunk so that it falls to the ground. ❑ *A vandal with a chainsaw cut down a tree.* (V P n (not pron)) (Also V n P)

♦ **cut in** (PHRASAL VERB = break in) If you **cut in on** someone, you interrupt them when they are speaking. ❑ *Immediately, Daniel cut in on Joanne's attempts at reassurance...* (V P *on* n) *'Not true,' the Duchess cut in.* (V P with quote) (Also V P)

♦ **cut off** [1] (PHRASAL VERB) If you **cut** something **off**, you remove it with a knife or a similar tool. ❑ *Mrs Kreutz cut off a generous piece of the meat...* (V P n) *He cut me off a slice...* (V n P n) *He threatened to cut my hair off.* (V n P) [2] (PHRASAL VERB = isolate) To **cut** someone or something **off** means to separate them from things that they are normally connected with. ❑ *One of the goals of the campaign is to cut off the elite Republican Guard from its supplies...* (V P n (not pron) *from* n) *The storm has cut us off.* (V n P) ♦ **cut off** (ADJ) *Without a car we still felt very cut off.* [3] (PHRASAL VERB) To **cut off** a supply of something means to stop providing it or stop it being provided. ❑ *The rebels have cut off electricity from the capital...* (V P n (not pron)) *Why cut the money off?* (V n P) [4] (PHRASAL VERB = disconnect) If you get **cut off** when you are on the telephone, the line is suddenly disconnected and you can no longer speak to the other person. ❑ *When you do get through, you've got to say your piece quickly before you get cut off...* (*get/be* V-ed P) *I'm going to cut you off now because we've got lots of callers waiting.* (V n P) [5] (PHRASAL VERB) If you **cut** someone **off** when they are speaking, you interrupt them and stop them from speaking. ❑ *'But, sir, I'm under orders to – ' Clark cut him off. 'Don't argue with me.'* (V n P) (Also V P n (not pron)) [6] → See also **cut-off**. to **cut off** your **nose to spite** your **face** → see **spite**.

♦ **cut out** [1] (PHRASAL VERB) If you **cut** something **out**, you remove or separate it from what surrounds it using scissors or a knife. ❑ *Cut out the coupon and send those cheques off today...* (V P n (not pron)) *I cut it out and pinned it to my studio wall.* (V n P) [2] (PHRASAL VERB = cut, omit) If you **cut out** a part of a text, you do not print, publish, or broadcast that part, because to include it would make the text too long or unacceptable. ❑ *I listened to the programme and found they'd cut out all the interesting stuff...* (V P n (not pron)) *Her editors wanted her to cut out the poetry from her novel.* (V P n *from/of* n) [3] (PHRASAL VERB = eliminate) To **cut out** something unnecessary or unwanted means to remove it completely from a situation. For example, if you **cut out** a particular type of food, you stop eating it, usually because it is bad for you. ❑ *I've simply cut egg yolks out entirely...* (V n P) *A guilty plea cuts out the need for a long trial.* (V P n (not pron)) [4] (PHRASAL VERB [feelings]) If you tell someone to **cut** something **out**, you are telling them in an irritated way to stop it. [INFORMAL] ❑ *Do yourself a favour, and cut that behaviour out...* (V n P) *'Cut it out, Chip,' I said...* (V *it* P) *He had better cut out the nonsense.* (V P n) [5] (PHRASAL VERB = exclude ≠ include) If you **cut** someone **out of** an activity, you do not allow them to be involved in it. If you **cut** someone **out of** a will, you do not allow them to share in it. ❑ *Environmentalists say this would cut them out of the debate over what to do with public lands...* (V n P *of* n) *'Cut her out of your will,' urged his nephew...* (V n P *of* n) *He felt that he was being cut out.* (*be* V-ed P) [6] (PHRASAL VERB) If an object **cuts out** the light, it is between you and the light so that you are in the dark. ❑ *The curtains were half drawn to cut out the sunlight.* (V P n) (Also V n P) [7] (PHRASAL VERB) If an engine **cuts out**, it suddenly stops working. ❑ *The helicopter crash landed when one of its two engines cut out.* (V P) [8] → See also **cut out**, **cut-out**. to **have** your **work cut out** → see **work**.

♦ **cut up** [1] (PHRASAL VERB) If you **cut** something **up**, you cut it into several pieces. ❑ *He sits in his apartment cutting up magazines...* (V P n (not pron)) *Halve the tomatoes, then cut them up coarsely.* (V n P) → See also **cut up**. [2] (PHRASAL VERB) If one driver **cuts** another driver **up**, the first driver goes too close in front of the second one, for example after passing them. ❑ *They were crossing from lane to lane, cutting everyone up.* (V n P)

**cut and dried** → see **cut**.

**cut|away** /kʌtəweɪ/ (**cutaways**) also **cut-away.** [1] (N-COUNT) In a film or video, a **cutaway** or a **cutaway shot** is a picture that shows something different from the main thing that is being shown. ❑ *I asked the cameraman to give me some cutaways for the interviews.* [2] (N-COUNT) A **cutaway** or a **cutaway** coat or jacket is one which is cut diagonally from the front to the back, so that the back is longer. [AM]

✓ in BRIT, use **tailcoat**

[3] (ADJ: ADJ n) A **cutaway** picture shows what something such as a machine looks like inside.

**cut|back** /kʌtbæk/ **(cutbacks)** also **cut-back.** A **cutback** is a reduction that is made in something. ❑ *London Underground said it may have to axe 500 signalling jobs because of government cutbacks in its investment.* N-COUNT: oft N *in* n = cut

**cute** /kjuːt/ **(cuter, cutest)** 1 Something or someone that is **cute** is very pretty or attractive, or is intended to appear pretty or attractive. [INFORMAL] ❑ *Oh, look at that dog! He's so cute. ...a cute little baby.* 2 If you describe someone as **cute**, you think they are sexually attractive. [mainly AM, INFORMAL] ❑ *There was this girl, and I thought she was really cute.* 3 If you describe someone as **cute**, you mean that they deal with things cleverly. [AM] ❑ *That's a cute trick.* ADJ = sweet; ADJ; ADJ = clever

**cute|sy** /kjuːtsi/ If you describe someone or something as **cutesy**, you dislike them because you think they are unpleasantly pretty and sentimental. [INFORMAL] ❑ *...cutesy paintings of owls.* ADJ: usu ADJ n [disapproval]

**cut glass** also **cut-glass. Cut glass** is glass that has patterns cut into its surface. ❑ *...a cut-glass bowl.* N-UNCOUNT: oft N n

**cu|ti|cle** /kjuːtɪkəl/ **(cuticles)** Your **cuticles** are the skin at the base of each of your fingernails. N-COUNT

**cut|lass** /kʌtləs/ **(cutlasses)** A **cutlass** is a short sword that used to be used by sailors. N-COUNT

**cut|lery** /kʌtləri/ 1 **Cutlery** consists of the knives, forks, and spoons that you eat your food with. [BRIT] ❑ *She arranged plates and cutlery on a small table.* N-UNCOUNT

☑ in AM, use **silverware, flatware**

2 You can refer to knives and tools used for cutting as **cutlery**. [AM] N-UNCOUNT

**cut|let** /kʌtlət/ **(cutlets)** A **cutlet** is a small piece of meat which is usually fried or grilled. ❑ *...grilled lamb cutlets.* N-COUNT

**cut-off** **(cut-offs)** also **cutoff.** 1 A **cut-off** or a **cut-off** point is the level or limit at which you decide that something should stop happening. ❑ *The cut-off date for registering is yet to be announced... On young girls it can look really great, but there is a definite age cut-off on this.* 2 The **cut-off of** a supply or service is the complete stopping of the supply or service. ❑ *A total cut-off of supplies would cripple the country's economy.* N-COUNT: usu sing, oft N n; N-COUNT: usu sing

**cut out** If you are not **cut out for** a particular type of work, you do not have the qualities that are needed to be able to do it well. ❑ *I left medicine anyway. I wasn't really cut out for it.* ADJ: usu with brd-neg, v-link ADJ, ADJ *for* n, ADJ to-inf

**cut-out** **(cut-outs)** 1 A cardboard **cut-out** is a shape that has been cut from thick card. ❑ *You'd swear he was a cardboard cut-out except that he'd moved his rifle.* 2 A **cut-out** is a device that turns off a machine automatically in particular circumstances. ❑ *Use a kettle with an automatic cut-out so it doesn't boil for longer than necessary.* N-COUNT; N-COUNT: oft N n

**cut-price** **Cut-price** goods or services are cheaper than usual. [BRIT] ❑ *...a shop selling cut-price videos and CDs in Oxford Street. ...cut-price tickets.* ADJ: ADJ n

☑ in AM, use **cut-rate**

**cut-rate** **Cut-rate** goods or services are cheaper than usual. ❑ *...cut-rate auto insurance.* ADJ: ADJ n = cut-price

**cut|ter** /kʌtəʳ/ **(cutters)** 1 A **cutter** is a tool that you use for cutting through something. ❑ *...a pastry cutter. ...wire cutters.* 2 A **cutter** is a person who cuts or reduces something. ❑ *He has been using every opportunity to boost his credibility as a budget cutter.* N-COUNT: usu n N; N-COUNT: with supp

**cut-throat** If you describe a situation as **cut-throat**, you mean that the people or companies involved all want success and do not care if they harm each other in getting it. ❑ *...the cut-throat competition in personal computers.* ADJ: usu ADJ n [disapproval] = ruthless

**cut|ting** /kʌtɪŋ/ **(cuttings)** 1 A **cutting** is a piece of writing which has been cut from a newspaper or magazine. [BRIT] ❑ *Here are the press cuttings and reviews.* ◆◇◇ N-COUNT = clipping

☑ in AM, use **clipping**

2 A **cutting** from a plant is a part of the plant that you have cut off so that you can grow a new plant from it. ❑ *Take cuttings from it in July or August.* 3 A **cutting** is a narrow valley cut through a hill so that a railway line or road can pass through. [BRIT] N-COUNT; N-COUNT

☑ in AM, use **cut**

4 A **cutting** remark is unkind and likely to hurt someone's feelings. ❑ *People make cutting remarks to help themselves feel superior or powerful.* ADJ

**cut|ting board** **(cutting boards)** A **cutting board** is a wooden or plastic board that you chop meat and vegetables on. [AM] N-COUNT

☑ in BRIT, usually use **chopping board**

**cut|ting edge**

☑ The spelling **cutting-edge** is used for meaning 3.

1 If you are **at the cutting edge of** a particular field of activity, you are involved in its most important or most exciting developments. ❑ *This shipyard is at the cutting edge of world shipbuilding technology.* 2 If someone or something gives you a **cutting edge**, they give you an advantage over your competitors. ❑ *If Pearce had been fit, we would have won. We missed the cutting edge he would have given us.* 3 **Cutting-edge** techniques or equipment are the most advanced that there are in a particular field. ❑ *What we are planning is cutting-edge technology never seen in Australia before.* N-SING: usu *at/on the* N *of* n = forefront; N-SING; ADJ: usu ADJ n

**cut|ting room** **The cutting room** in a film production company is the place where the film is edited. ❑ *Her scene ended up on the cutting room floor.* N-SING: usu *the* N

**cuttle|fish** /kʌtəlfɪʃ/ **(cuttlefish)** A **cuttlefish** is a sea animal that has a soft body and a hard shell inside. N-COUNT

**cut up** If you are **cut up about** something that has happened, you are very unhappy because of it. [mainly BRIT, INFORMAL] ❑ *Terry was very cut up about Jim's death.* ADJ: v-link ADJ

**CV** /siː viː/ **(CVs)** Your **CV** is a brief written account of your personal details, your education, and the jobs you have had. You can send a CV when you are applying for a job. **CV** is an abbreviation for 'curriculum vitae'. [mainly BRIT] ❑ *Send them a copy of your CV.* ◆◇◇ N-COUNT

☑ in AM, use **résumé**

**cwt** **cwt** is a written abbreviation for **hundredweight**.

**-cy** /-si/ **(-cies)** 1 **-cy** replaces '-te', '-t', and '-tic' at the end of some adjectives to form nouns referring to the state or quality described by the adjective. ❑ *...the emotional intimacy of a family... They were sworn to secrecy.* 2 **-cy** is added to some nouns referring to people with a particular rank or post in order to form nouns that refer to this rank or post. ❑ *He is likely to retain the England captaincy. ...the university chaplaincy.* SUFFIX; SUFFIX

**CYA** **CYA** is the written abbreviation for 'see you', mainly used in text messages and e-mails. [COMPUTING]

**cya|nide** /saɪənaɪd/ **Cyanide** is a highly poisonous substance. N-UNCOUNT

**cy|ber|café** /saɪbəʳkæfeɪ/ **(cybercafés)** A **cybercafé** is a café where people can pay to use the Internet. N-COUNT

**cy|ber|net|ics** /saɪbəʳnetɪks/ **Cybernetics** is a branch of science which involves studying the way electronic machines and human brains work, and developing machines that do things or think rather like people. N-UNCOUNT

**cy|ber|punk** /saɪbəʳpʌŋk/ **Cyberpunk** is a type of science fiction. N-UNCOUNT

**cy|ber|sex** /saɪbəʳseks/ **Cybersex** involves using the Internet for sexual purposes, especially by exchanging sexual messages with another person. ❑ *A man was found guilty yesterday of stabbing* N-UNCOUNT *his wife after he became jealous of her cybersex relationship.*

**cy|ber|space** /saɪbəʳspeɪs/ [N-UNCOUNT] In computer technology, **cyberspace** refers to data banks and networks, considered as a place. [COMPUTING]

**cy|ber|squatting** /saɪbəʳskwɒtɪŋ/ [N-UNCOUNT] **Cybersquatting** involves buying an Internet domain name that might be wanted by another person, business, or organization with the intention of selling it to them and making a profit. [COMPUTING] ♦ **cy|ber|squatter (cybersquatters)** [N-COUNT] ❑ *The old official club website address has been taken over by cybersquatters.*

**cy|borg** /saɪbɔːʳg/ **(cyborgs)** [N-COUNT] In science fiction, a **cyborg** is a being that is part human and part machine, or a machine that looks like a human being.

**cyc|la|men** /sɪkləmən/ **(cyclamen)** [N-COUNT] A **cyclamen** is a plant with white, pink, or red flowers.

**cy|cle** /saɪkəl/ **(cycles, cycling, cycled)** ◆◇◇ 1 [VERB; V prep/adv; V; V n] If you **cycle**, you ride a bicycle. ❑ *He cycled to Ingwold... Britain could save £4.6 billion a year in road transport costs if more people cycled... Over 1000 riders cycled 100 miles around the Vale of York.* ♦ **cy|cling** [N-UNCOUNT] *The quiet country roads are ideal for cycling.* 2 [N-COUNT] A **cycle** is a bicycle. ❑ *...an eight-mile cycle ride.* 3 [N-COUNT] A **cycle** is a motorcycle. [AM] 4 [N-COUNT: usu with supp, oft N *of* n] A **cycle** is a series of events or processes that is repeated again and again, always in the same order. ❑ *...the life cycle of the plant.* 5 [N-COUNT: usu pl] A **cycle** is a single complete series of movements in an electrical, electronic, or mechanical process. ❑ *...10 cycles per second.*

**cy|cle path (cycle paths)** [N-COUNT] A **cycle path** is a special path on which people can travel by bicycle separately from motor vehicles.

**cy|cle|way** /saɪkəlweɪ/ **(cycleways)** [N-COUNT] A **cycleway** is a special road, route, or path intended for use by cyclists. [BRIT]

☑ in AM, use **bikeway**

**cy|clic** /sɪklɪk, saɪk-/ [ADJ] **Cyclic** means the same as **cyclical**.

**cy|cli|cal** /sɪklɪkəl, saɪk-/ [ADJ] A **cyclical** process is one in which a series of events happens again and again in the same order. ❑ *...the cyclical nature of the airline business.*

**cy|clist** /saɪklɪst/ **(cyclists)** [N-COUNT] A **cyclist** is someone who rides a bicycle, or is riding a bicycle.

**cy|clone** /saɪkloʊn/ **(cyclones)** [N-COUNT] A **cyclone** is a violent tropical storm in which the air goes round and round.

**cyg|net** /sɪgnɪt/ **(cygnets)** [N-COUNT] A **cygnet** is a young swan.

**cyl|in|der** /sɪlɪndəʳ/ **(cylinders)** 1 [N-COUNT] A **cylinder** is an object with flat circular ends and long straight sides. ❑ *...a cylinder of foam... It was recorded on a wax cylinder.* 2 [N-COUNT: usu with supp] A gas **cylinder** is a cylinder-shaped container in which gas is kept under pressure. ❑ *...oxygen cylinders.* 3 [N-COUNT] In an engine, a **cylinder** is a cylinder-shaped part in which a piston moves backwards and forwards. ❑ *...a 2.5 litre, four-cylinder engine.*

**cy|lin|dri|cal** /sɪlɪndrɪkəl/ [ADJ] Something that is **cylindrical** is in the shape of a cylinder. ❑ *...a cylindrical aluminium container... It is cylindrical in shape.*

**cym|bal** /sɪmbəl/ **(cymbals)** [N-COUNT] A **cymbal** is a flat circular brass object that is used as a musical instrument. You hit it with a stick or hit two cymbals together, making a loud noise.

**cyn|ic** /sɪnɪk/ **(cynics)** [N-COUNT] A **cynic** is someone who believes that people always act selfishly. ❑ *I have come to be very much of a cynic in these matters.*

**cyni|cal** /sɪnɪkəl/ 1 [ADJ; ≠ idealistic] If you describe someone as **cynical**, you mean they believe that people always act selfishly. ❑ *...his cynical view of the world.* ♦ **cyni|cal|ly** [ADV: ADV with v] *As one former customer said cynically, 'He's probably pocketed the difference!'* 2 [ADJ: usu v-link ADJ, usu ADJ *about* n] If you are **cynical about** something, you do not believe that it can be successful or that the people involved are honest. ❑ *It's hard not to be cynical about reform.*

**cyni|cal|ly** /sɪnɪkli/ [ADV: usu ADV before v] [disapproval] If you say that someone is **cynically** doing something, you mean they are doing it to benefit themselves and they do not care that they are deceiving, harming, or using people. ❑ *He accused the mainstream political parties of cynically exploiting this situation.* ➔ See also **cynical**.

**cyni|cism** /sɪnɪsɪzəm/ 1 [N-UNCOUNT; ≠ idealism] **Cynicism** is the belief that people always act selfishly. ❑ *I found Ben's cynicism wearing at times.* 2 [N-UNCOUNT] **Cynicism about** something is the belief that it cannot be successful or that the people involved are not honourable. ❑ *This talk betrays a certain cynicism about free trade.*

**cy|pher** /saɪfəʳ/ ➔ see **cipher**.

**cy|press** /saɪprəs/ **(cypresses)** [N-COUNT] A **cypress** is a type of **conifer**.

**Cyp|ri|ot** /sɪpriət/ **(Cypriots)** 1 [ADJ] **Cypriot** means belonging or relating to Cyprus, or to its people or culture. 2 [N-COUNT] A **Cypriot** is a Cypriot citizen, or a person of Cypriot origin.

**Cy|ril|lic** /sɪrɪlɪk/ also **cyrillic.** [ADJ: ADJ n] The **Cyrillic** alphabet is the alphabet that is used to write some Slavonic languages, such as Russian and Bulgarian.

**cyst** /sɪst/ **(cysts)** [N-COUNT] A **cyst** is a growth containing liquid that appears inside your body or under your skin. ❑ *He had a minor operation to remove a cyst.*

**cyst|ic fi|bro|sis** /sɪstɪk faɪbroʊsɪs/ [N-UNCOUNT] **Cystic fibrosis** is a serious disease of the glands which usually affects children and can make breathing difficult.

**cys|ti|tis** /sɪstaɪtɪs/ [N-UNCOUNT] **Cystitis** is a bladder infection. [MEDICAL] ❑ *...an attack of cystitis.*

**czar** /zɑːʳ/ ➔ see **tsar**.

**cza|ri|na** /zɑːriːnə/ ➔ see **tsarina**.

**czar|ist** /zɑːrɪst/ ➔ see **tsarist**.

**Czech** /tʃek/ **(Czechs)** 1 [ADJ] **Czech** means belonging or relating to the Czech Republic, or to its people, language, or culture. 2 [N-COUNT] A **Czech** is a Czech citizen, or a person of Czech origin. 3 [N-UNCOUNT] **Czech** is the language spoken in the Czech Republic.

**Czecho|slo|vak** /tʃekəsloʊvæk/ **(Czechoslovaks)** 1 [ADJ: usu ADJ n] **Czechoslovak** means belonging or relating to the former state of Czechoslovakia. 2 [N-COUNT] A **Czechoslovak** was a Czechoslovak citizen, or a person of Czechoslovak origin.

**Czecho|slo|va|kian** /tʃekəsləvækiən/ **(Czechoslovakians)** 1 [ADJ] **Czechoslovakian** means the same as **Czechoslovak**. 2 [N-COUNT] A **Czechoslovakian** was a Czechoslovak citizen, or a person of Czechoslovak origin.

# D d

**D, d** /diː/ **(D's, d's)** D is the fourth letter of the English alphabet. N-VAR

**-'d**

> Pronounced /-d/ after a vowel sound and /-əd/ after a consonant sound.

1 **-'d** is a spoken form of 'had', especially when 'had' is an auxiliary verb. It is added to the end of the pronoun which is the subject of the verb. For example, 'you had' can be shortened to 'you'd'. 2 **-'d** is a spoken form of 'would'. It is added to the end of the pronoun which is the subject of the verb. For example, 'I would' can be shortened to 'I'd'.

**d'** /d-/ → see **d'you**.

**D.A.** /diː eɪ/ **(D.A.s)** A **D.A.** is a **District Attorney**. [AM] N-COUNT

**dab** /dæb/ **(dabs, dabbing, dabbed)** 1 If you **dab** something, you touch it several times using quick, light movements. If you **dab** a substance onto a surface, you put it there using quick, light movements. ❑ *She arrived weeping, dabbing her eyes with a tissue... She dabbed iodine on the cuts on her forehead... He dabbed at his lips with the napkin.* VERB V n V n prep/adv V *at* n 2 A **dab of** something is a small amount of it that is put onto a surface. [INFORMAL] ❑ *...a dab of glue.* N-COUNT: N *of* n 3 A **dab** is a small flat fish with rough scales. N-VAR

**DAB** /dæb/ **DAB** is the transmission of digital stereo over conventional radio channels. **DAB** is an abbreviation for 'digital audio broadcasting'. ❑ *DAB is the radio system of the 21st Century.*

**dab|ble** /dæbᵊl/ **(dabbles, dabbling, dabbled)** If you **dabble in** something, you take part in it but not very seriously. ❑ *He dabbled in business... Magicians do not dabble, they work hard.* VERB V *in/with/at* n V

**dab hand** **(dab hands)** In British English, if you are a **dab hand at** something, you are very good at doing it. [INFORMAL] ❑ *She's a dab hand at DIY.* N-COUNT: usu N *at* n/-ing

**dace** /deɪs/ **(dace)** A **dace** is a type of fish that lives in rivers and lakes. N-VAR

**da|cha** /dætʃə, AM dɑːtʃə/ **(dachas)** A **dacha** is a country house in Russia. N-COUNT

**dachs|hund** /dækshʊnd, AM dɑːksʊnt/ **(dachshunds)** A **dachshund** is a small dog that has very short legs, a long body, and long ears. N-COUNT

**dad** /dæd/ **(dads)** Your **dad** is your father. [INFORMAL] ❑ *How do you feel, Dad?... He's living with his mum and dad.* ◆◇◇ N-FAMILY

**dad|dy** /dædi/ **(daddies)** Children often call their father **daddy**. [INFORMAL] ❑ *Look at me, Daddy!... She wanted her mummy and daddy.* N-FAMILY

**dad|dy longlegs** /dædi lɒŋlegz, AM - lɔːŋ-/ **(daddy longlegs)** A **daddy longlegs** is a flying insect with very long legs. N-COUNT = *cranefly*

**dado** /deɪdoʊ/ **(dados)** A **dado** is a strip of wood that can be fixed to the lower part of a wall. The wall is then often decorated differently above and below the **dado**. N-COUNT

**daf|fo|dil** /dæfədɪl/ **(daffodils)** A **daffodil** is a yellow spring flower with a central part shaped like a tube and a long stem. N-COUNT

**daffy** /dæfi/ If you describe a person or thing as **daffy**, you mean that they are strange or foolish, but in a rather attractive way. [INFORMAL] ❑ *Daisy called her daffy, but goodhearted. ...a daffy storyline.* ADJ approval

**daft** /dɑːft, dæft/ **(dafter, daftest)** If you describe a person or their behaviour as **daft**, you think that they are stupid, impractical, or rather strange. [BRIT, INFORMAL] ❑ *He's not so daft as to listen to rumours... Don't be daft!* ADJ = *silly*

**dag|ger** /dægəʳ/ **(daggers)** 1 A **dagger** is a weapon like a knife with two sharp edges. N-COUNT 2 If you say that two people are **at daggers drawn**, you mean that they are having an argument and are still very angry with each other. [BRIT] ❑ *She and her mother were at daggers drawn.* PHRASE

**dahl|ia** /deɪliə/ **(dahlias)** A **dahlia** is a garden flower with a lot of brightly coloured petals. N-COUNT

**dai|ly** /deɪli/ **(dailies)** 1 If something happens **daily**, it happens every day. ❑ *Cathay Pacific flies daily non-stop to Hong Kong from Heathrow... The Visitor Centre is open daily 8.30 a.m. – 4.30 p.m.* ◆◆◇ ADV: ADV after v ♦ **Daily** is also an adjective. ❑ *They held daily press briefings.* ADJ: ADJ n 2 **Daily** quantities or rates relate to a period of one day. ❑ *...a diet containing adequate daily amounts of fresh fruit... Our average daily turnover is about £300.* ADJ: ADJ n 3 A **daily** is a newspaper that is published every day of the week except Sunday. ❑ *Copies of the local daily had been scattered on a table.* N-COUNT ♦ **Daily** is also an adjective. ❑ *He studied the daily papers.* ADJ: ADJ n 4 Your **daily life** is the things that you do every day as part of your normal life. ❑ *...the failure of the government to improve most people's daily lives.* PHRASE: N inflects

**dain|ty** /deɪnti/ **(daintier, daintiest)** If you describe a movement, person, or object as **dainty**, you mean that they are small, delicate, and pretty. ❑ *...dainty pink flowers.* ADJ ♦ **dain|ti|ly** *She walked daintily down the steps.* ADV: ADV with v, ADV adj

**dai|qui|ri** /daɪkɪri, dæk-/ **(daiquiris)** A **daiquiri** is a drink made with rum, lime or lemon juice, sugar, and ice. N-COUNT

**dairy** /deəri/ **(dairies)** 1 A **dairy** is a shop or company that sells milk and food made from milk, such as butter, cream, and cheese. N-COUNT 2 **Dairy** is used to refer to foods such as butter and cheese that are made from milk. ❑ *...dairy produce. ...vitamins found in eggs, meat and dairy products.* ADJ: ADJ n 3 **Dairy** is used to refer to the use of cattle to produce milk rather than meat. ❑ *...a small vegetable and dairy farm. ...the feeding of dairy cows.* ADJ: ADJ n

**dais** /deɪɪs/ **(daises)** A **dais** is a raised platform in a hall. N-COUNT

**dai|sy** /deɪzi/ **(daisies)** A **daisy** is a small wild flower with a yellow centre and white petals. N-COUNT

**dai|sy chain** **(daisy chains)** also **daisy-chain.** A **daisy chain** is a string of daisies that have been joined together by their stems to make a necklace. [mainly BRIT] N-COUNT

**dal** /dɑːl/ **(dals)** also **dhal. Dal** is an Indian dish made from pulses such as chick peas or lentils. N-VAR

**dale** /deɪl/ **(dales)** A **dale** is a valley. [BRIT] N-COUNT

**dal|li|ance** /dæliəns/ **(dalliances)** 1 If two people have a brief romantic relationship, you can say that they have a **dalliance** with each other, especially if they do not take it seriously. [OLD-FASHIONED] N-VAR: oft N *with* n 2 Someone's **dalliance with** something is a brief involvement with it. [OLD- N-COUNT: oft poss N, N *with* n

FASHIONED] ❑ *...my brief dalliance with higher education.*

**dal|ly** /dæli/ **(dallies, dallying, dallied)** 1 If you **dally**, you act or move very slowly, wasting time. [OLD-FASHIONED] ❑ *The bureaucrats dallied too long... He did not dally over the choice of a suitable partner.* VERB; V; V over n/-ing; Also V with n 2 If someone **dallies with** you, they have a romantic, but not serious, relationship with you. [OLD-FASHIONED] ❑ *In the past he dallied with actresses and lady novelists.* VERB; V with n

**Dal|ma|tian** /dælmeɪʃᵊn/ **(Dalmatians)** N-COUNT A **Dalmatian** is a large dog with short, smooth, white hair and black or dark brown spots.

**dam** /dæm/ **(dams, damming, dammed)** 1 N-COUNT A **dam** is a wall that is built across a river in order to stop the water flowing and to make a lake. ❑ *...plans to build a dam on the Danube River.* 2 VERB To **dam** a river means to build a dam across it. ❑ *...plans to dam the nearby Delaware River.* V n

**dam|age** /dæmɪdʒ/ **(damages, damaging, damaged)** ◆◆◇ 1 VERB To **damage** an object means to break it, spoil it physically, or stop it from working properly. ❑ *He maliciously damaged a car with a baseball bat... The sun can damage your skin.* V n 2 VERB = harm To **damage** something means to cause it to become less good, pleasant, or successful. ❑ *Jackson doesn't want to damage his reputation as a political personality.* V n ♦ **dam|ag|ing** ADJ = harmful *Is the recycling process in itself damaging to the environment?* 3 N-UNCOUNT: oft N to n **Damage** is physical harm that is caused to an object. ❑ *The blast caused extensive damage to the house... Many professional boxers end their careers with brain damage.* 4 N-UNCOUNT: oft N to n **Damage** consists of the unpleasant effects that something has on a person, situation, or type of activity. ❑ *Incidents of this type cause irreparable damage to relations with the community.* 5 N-PLURAL If a court of law awards **damages** to someone, it orders money to be paid to them by a person who has damaged their reputation or property, or who has injured them. ❑ *He was vindicated in court and damages were awarded.*

**dam|age limi|ta|tion** N-UNCOUNT **Damage limitation** is action that is taken to make the bad results of something as small as possible, when it is impossible to avoid bad results completely. [BRIT] ❑ *The meeting was merely an exercise in damage limitation.*

☑ in AM, use **damage control**

**dam|ask** /dæməsk/ **(damasks)** N-MASS **Damask** is a type of heavy cloth with a pattern woven into it.

**dame** /deɪm/ **(dames)** 1 N-TITLE **Dame** is a title given to a woman as a special honour because of important service or work that she has done. [BRIT] ❑ *...Dame Judi Dench.* 2 N-COUNT A **dame** is a woman. This use could cause offence. [AM, INFORMAL, OLD-FASHIONED] ❑ *Who does that dame think she is?*

**dam|mit** /dæmɪt/ → see **damn**.

**damn** /dæm/ **(damns, damning, damned)** 1 EXCLAM [feelings] **Damn**, **damn it**, and **dammit** are used by some people to express anger or impatience. [INFORMAL, RUDE] ❑ *Don't be flippant, damn it! This is serious.* 2 ADJ: ADJ n [emphasis] **Damn** is used by some people to emphasize what they are saying. [INFORMAL, RUDE] ❑ *There's not a damn thing you can do about it now.* ♦ **Damn** is also an adverb. ADV: ADV adj/adv ❑ *As it turned out, I was damn right.* 3 VERB = slam If you say that a person or a news report **damns** something such as a policy or action, you mean that they are very critical of it. ❑ *...a sensational book in which she damns the ultra-right party.* V n 4 → See also **damned**, **damning**.

PHRASES 5 PHRASE: V inflects [emphasis] If you say that someone **does not give a damn** about something, you are emphasizing that they do not care about it at all. [INFORMAL, RUDE] 6 PHRASE: usu PHR n [emphasis] Some people say **as near as damn it** or **as near as dammit** to emphasize that what they have said is almost completely accurate, but not quite. [BRIT, INFORMAL, RUDE] ❑ *It's as near as damn it the same thing.*

**dam|nable** /dæmnəbᵊl/ ADJ: ADJ n [emphasis] You use **damnable** to emphasize that you dislike or disapprove of something a great deal. [OLD-FASHIONED, RUDE] ❑ *What a damnable climate we have!* ♦ **dam|nably** /dæmnəbli/ ADV: ADV adj *It was damnably unfair that he should suffer so much.*

**dam|na|tion** /dæmneɪʃᵊn/ N-UNCOUNT According to some religions, if someone suffers **damnation**, they have to stay in hell for ever after they have died because of their sins. ❑ *...a fear of eternal damnation.*

**damned** /dæmd/ 1 ADJ: ADJ n [emphasis] **Damned** is used by some people to emphasize what they are saying, especially when they are angry or frustrated. [INFORMAL, RUDE] ❑ *They're a damned nuisance.* ♦ **Damned** is also an adverb. ADV: ADV adj/adv ❑ *We are making a damned good profit, I tell you that.* 2 PHRASE: V inflects [emphasis] If someone says '**I'm damned if I'm** going to do it' or '**I'll be damned if I'll** do it', they are emphasizing that they do not intend to do something and think it is unreasonable for anyone to expect them to do it. [INFORMAL, RUDE]

**damned|est** /dæmdɪst/ PHRASE: V inflects, usu PHR to-inf If you say that you will **do** your **damnedest** to achieve something, you mean that you will try as hard as you can to do it, even though you think that it will take a lot of effort. [INFORMAL, RUDE] ❑ *I did my damnedest to persuade her.*

**damn fool** ADJ: ADJ n [emphasis] **Damn fool** means 'very stupid'. [AM, INFORMAL, OLD-FASHIONED, RUDE] ❑ *What a damn fool thing to do!*

**damn|ing** /dæmɪŋ/ ADJ If you describe evidence or a report as **damning**, you mean that it suggests very strongly that someone is guilty of a crime or has made a serious mistake. ❑ *...a damning report into his handling of the affair.*

**Damocles** /dæməkliːz/ PHRASE If you say that someone has the **Sword of Damocles** hanging over their head, you mean that they are in a situation in which something very bad could happen to them at any time. [LITERARY]

**damp** /dæmp/ **(damper, dampest, damps, damping, damped)** 1 ADJ = moist Something that is **damp** is slightly wet. ❑ *Her hair was still damp... She wiped the table with a damp cloth.* 2 N-UNCOUNT **Damp** is moisture that is found on the inside walls of a house or in the air. ❑ *There was damp everywhere and the entire building was in need of rewiring.* → See also **rising damp**. 3 VERB = dampen If you **damp** something, you make it slightly wet. ❑ *Hillsden damped a hand towel and laid it across her forehead.* V n

♦ **damp down** PHRASAL VERB To **damp down** something such as a strong emotion, an argument, or a crisis means to make it calmer or less intense. ❑ *His hand moved to his mouth as he tried to damp down the panic.* V P n (not pron)

**damp course** **(damp courses)** N-COUNT A **damp course** is a layer of waterproof material which is put into the bottom of the outside wall of a building to prevent moisture from rising. [BRIT]

**damp|en** /dæmpən/ **(dampens, dampening, dampened)** 1 VERB To **dampen** something such as someone's enthusiasm or excitement means to make it less lively or intense. ❑ *Nothing seems to dampen his perpetual enthusiasm.* V n ♦ PHRASAL VERB To **dampen** something **down** means the same as to **dampen** it. ❑ *Although unemployment rose last month, this is unlikely to dampen down wage demands... The economy overheated and the Government used to interest rates to dampen it down.* V P n (not pron); V n P 2 VERB If you **dampen** something, you make it slightly wet. ❑ *She took the time to dampen a washcloth and do her face.* V n

**damp|en|er** /dæmpnəʳ/ PHRASE: V inflects, PHR n To **put a dampener on** something means the same as to **put a damper on** it. ❑ *Boy, did this woman know how to put a dampener on your day.*

**damp|er** /dæmpəʳ/ **(dampers)** PHRASE: V inflects, PHR n To **put a damper on** something means to have an effect on it which stops it being as enjoyable or as successful as it should be. [INFORMAL] ❑ *The cold weather put a damper on our plans.*

**damp|ness** /dæmpnəs/ **Dampness** is moisture in the air, or on the surface of something. ❑ *The tins had to be kept away from dampness.* N-UNCOUNT = *moisture*

**damp-proof course** **(damp-proof courses)** A **damp-proof course** is the same as a **damp course**. N-COUNT

**dam|sel** /dæmzəl/ **(damsels)** A **damsel** is a young, unmarried woman. [LITERARY, OLD-FASHIONED] ❑ *He keeps coming to the aid of this damsel in distress.* N-COUNT = *maiden*

**dam|son** /dæmzən/ **(damsons)** A **damson** is a small, sour, purple plum. N-COUNT

**dance** /dɑːns, dæns/ **(dances, dancing, danced)** ◆◆◇ 1 When you **dance**, you move your body and feet in a way which follows a rhythm, usually in time to music. ❑ *Polly had never learned to dance... I like to dance to the music on the radio.* VERB V V *to* n 2 A **dance** is a particular series of graceful movements of your body and feet, which you usually do in time to music. ❑ *Sometimes the people doing this dance hold brightly colored scarves... She describes the tango as a very sexy dance.* N-COUNT 3 When you **dance with** someone, the two of you take part in a dance together, as partners. You can also say that two people **dance**. ❑ *It's a terrible thing when nobody wants to dance with you... Shall we dance?... He asked her to dance.* V-RECIP V *with* n pl-n V V (non-recip) ♦ **Dance** is also a noun. ❑ *Come and have a dance with me.* N-COUNT 4 A **dance** is a social event where people dance with each other. ❑ *...the school dance.* N-COUNT 5 **Dance** is the activity of performing dances, as a public entertainment or an art form. ❑ *She loves dance, drama and music. ...dance classes.* N-UNCOUNT 6 If you **dance** a particular kind of dance, you do it or perform it. ❑ *Then we put the music on, and we all danced the Charleston.* VERB V n 7 If you **dance** somewhere, you move there lightly and quickly, usually because you are happy or excited. [LITERARY] ❑ *He danced off down the road.* VERB V adv/prep 8 If you say that something **dances**, you mean that it moves about, or seems to move about, lightly and quickly. [LITERARY] ❑ *Light danced on the surface of the water.* VERB V adv/prep 9 to **dance to** someone's **tune** → see **tune**. to **make a song and dance about** → see **song and dance**.

**dance floor** **(dance floors)** also **dancefloor.** In a restaurant or night club, the **dance floor** is the area where people can dance. N-COUNT

**dance hall** **(dance halls)** **Dance halls** were large rooms or buildings where people used to pay to go and dance, usually in the evening. [OLD-FASHIONED] N-COUNT

**danc|er** /dɑːnsəʳ, dæns-/ **(dancers)** 1 A **dancer** is a person who earns money by dancing, or a person who is dancing. ❑ *His previous girlfriend was a dancer with the Royal Ballet.* N-COUNT 2 If you say that someone is a good **dancer** or a bad **dancer**, you are saying how well or badly they can dance. ❑ *He was the best dancer in LA.* N-COUNT: adj N

**dance stu|dio** **(dance studios)** A **dance studio** is a place where people pay to learn how to dance. N-COUNT

**danc|ing** /dɑːnsɪŋ, dæns-/ When people dance for enjoyment or to entertain others, you can refer to this activity as **dancing**. ❑ *All the schools have music and dancing as part of the curriculum... Let's go dancing tonight. ...dancing shoes.* ◆◇◇ N-UNCOUNT

**dan|de|lion** /dændɪlaɪən/ **(dandelions)** A **dandelion** is a wild plant which has yellow flowers with lots of thin petals. When the petals of each flower drop off, a fluffy white ball of seeds grows. N-COUNT

**dan|druff** /dændrʌf/ **Dandruff** is small white pieces of dead skin in someone's hair, or fallen from someone's hair. ❑ *He has very bad dandruff.* N-UNCOUNT

**dan|dy** /dændi/ **(dandies)** 1 A **dandy** is a man who thinks a great deal about his appearance and always dresses in smart clothes. N-COUNT 2 If you say that something is **dandy**, you mean it is good or just right. [AM, INFORMAL, OLD-FASHIONED] ADJ = *great*

**Dane** /deɪn/ **(Danes)** A **Dane** is a person who comes from Denmark. N-COUNT

**dan|ger** /deɪndʒəʳ/ **(dangers)** ◆◆◇ 1 **Danger** is the possibility that someone may be harmed or killed. ❑ *My friends endured tremendous danger in order to help me... His life could be in danger.* N-UNCOUNT ≠ *safety* 2 A **danger** is something or someone that can hurt or harm you. ❑ *...the dangers of smoking... Britain's roads are a danger to cyclists.* N-COUNT: usu N *of* -ing/n, N *to* n = *threat* 3 If there is a **danger that** something unpleasant will happen, it is possible that it will happen. ❑ *There is a real danger that some people will no longer be able to afford insurance... If there is a danger of famine, we should help.* N-SING: also no det, N that, N *of* n/-ing 4 If someone who has been seriously ill is **out of danger**, they are still ill, but they are not expected to die. PHRASE: v-link PHR

**dan|ger|ous** /deɪndʒərəs/ If something is **dangerous**, it is able or likely to hurt or harm you. ❑ *It's a dangerous stretch of road. ...dangerous drugs... It's dangerous to jump to early conclusions.* ◆◆◇ ADJ: oft *it* v-link ADJ to-inf = *unsafe* ♦ **dan|ger|ous|ly** *He is dangerously ill... The coach rocked dangerously.* ADV: usu ADV adj/adv/-ed, also ADV after v

**dan|gle** /dæŋgəl/ **(dangles, dangling, dangled)** 1 If something **dangles from** somewhere or if you **dangle** it somewhere, it hangs or swings loosely. ❑ *A gold bracelet dangled from his left wrist... He and I were sitting out on his jetty dangling our legs in the water.* VERB V prep/adv V n prep/adv 2 If you say that someone **is dangling** something attractive **before** you, you mean they are offering it to you in order to try to influence you in some way. ❑ *They've dangled rich rewards before me.* VERB V n *before/in front of* n

**Dan|ish** /deɪnɪʃ/ 1 **Danish** means belonging or relating to Denmark, its people, its language, or culture. ADJ: usu ADJ n 2 **Danish** is the language spoken in Denmark. N-UNCOUNT

**Dan|ish pas|try** **(Danish pastries)** **Danish pastries** are cakes made from sweet pastry. They are often filled with things such as apple or almond paste. N-COUNT

**dank** /dæŋk/ A **dank** place, especially an underground place such as a cave, is unpleasantly damp and cold. ❑ *The kitchen was dank and cheerless.* ADJ

**dap|per** /dæpəʳ/ A man who is **dapper** has a very neat and clean appearance, and is often also small and thin. ❑ *...a dapper little man.* ADJ

**dap|pled** /dæpəld/ You use **dappled** to describe something that has dark or light patches on it, or that is made up of patches of light and shade. ❑ *...a dappled horse... The path was dappled with sunlight.* ADJ: ADJ n, v-link ADJ *with/by/in* n

**dare** /deəʳ/ **(dares, daring, dared)** ◆◇◇

> **Dare** sometimes behaves like an ordinary verb, for example 'He dared to speak' and 'He doesn't dare to speak' and sometimes like a modal, for example 'He daren't speak'.

1 If you do not **dare to** do something, you do not have enough courage to do it, or you do not want to do it because you fear the consequences. If you **dare to** do something, you do something which requires a lot of courage. ❑ *Most people hate Harry but they don't dare to say so... We have had problems in our family that I didn't dare tell Uncle.* VERB: oft with brd-neg V to-inf V inf ♦ **Dare** is also a modal. ❑ *Dare she risk staying where she was?... The government dare not raise interest rates again... 'Are you coming with me?' — 'I can't, Alice. I daren't.'* MODAL 2 If you **dare** someone **to** do something, you challenge them to prove that they are not frightened of doing it. ❑ *Over coffee, she lit a cigarette, her eyes daring him to comment.* VERB V n to-inf 3 A **dare** is a challenge which one person gives to another to do something dangerous or frightening. ❑ *When found, the children said they'd run away for a dare.* N-COUNT: usu sing, usu *as/for/on a* N

PHRASES 4 If you say to someone '**don't you dare**' do something, you are telling them not to PHRASE: oft PHR inf [feelings]

do it and letting them know that you are angry. [SPOKEN] ❑ *Allen, don't you dare go anywhere else, you hear?* 5 You say '**how dare you**" when you are very shocked and angry about something that someone has done. [SPOKEN] ❑ *How dare you pick up the phone and listen in on my conversations!* PHRASE: usu PHR inf [feelings] 6 You use '**dare I say it**' when you know that what you are going to say will disappoint or annoy someone. ❑ *Politicians usually attract younger women, dare I say it, because of the status they have in society.* PHRASE: PHR with cl [politeness] 7 You can use '**I dare say**' or '**I daresay**' before or after a statement to indicate that you believe it is probably true. PHRASE: PHR that, cl PHR = I suppose

**dare|devil** /deə^rdevəl/ **(daredevils)** 1 **Daredevil** people enjoy doing physically dangerous things. ❑ *A daredevil parachutist jumped from the top of Tower Bridge today.* ♦ **Daredevil** is also a noun. ❑ *He was a daredevil when young.* ADJ: ADJ n; N-COUNT 2 You use **daredevil** to describe actions that are physically dangerous and require courage. ❑ *The show's full of daredevil feats.* ADJ: ADJ n

**daren't** /deə^rnt/ **Daren't** is the usual spoken form of 'dare not'.

**dare|say** /deə^rseɪ/ → see **dare**.

**dar|ing** /deərɪŋ/ 1 People who are **daring** are willing to do or say things which are new or which might shock or anger other people. ❑ *Bergit was probably more daring than I was... He realized this to be a very daring thing to ask.* ♦ **dar|ing|ly** *...a daringly low-cut dress.* ADJ = bold; ADV: ADV with v, ADV adj 2 A **daring** person is willing to do things that might be dangerous. ❑ *His daring rescue saved the lives of the youngsters.* ADJ: usu ADJ n = bold 3 **Daring** is the courage to do things which might be dangerous or which might shock or anger other people. ❑ *His daring may have cost him his life.* N-UNCOUNT = bravery, boldness ≠ cowardice

**dark** /dɑː^rk/ **(darker, darkest)** ◆◆◇ 1 When it is **dark**, there is not enough light to see properly, for example because it is night. ❑ *It was too dark inside to see much... People usually draw the curtains once it gets dark... She snapped off the light and made her way back through the dark kitchen.* ♦ **dark|ness** *The light went out, and the room was plunged into darkness.* ♦ **dark|ly** *...a darkly lit, seedy dance hall.* ADJ ≠ light; N-UNCOUNT; ADV: ADV -ed 2 **The dark** is the lack of light in a place. ❑ *I've always been afraid of the dark.* N-SING: the N ≠ light 3 If you describe something as **dark**, you mean that it is black in colour, or a shade that is close to black. ❑ *He wore a dark suit and carried a black attaché case.* ♦ **dark|ly** *Joanne's freckles stood out darkly against her pale skin.* ADJ ≠ light; ADV 4 When you use **dark** to describe a colour, you are referring to a shade of that colour which is close to black, or seems to have some black in it. ❑ *She was wearing a dark blue dress.* COMB in COLOUR ≠ light 5 If someone has **dark** hair, eyes, or skin, they have brown or black hair, eyes, or skin. ❑ *He had dark, curly hair.* ADJ 6 If you describe a white person as **dark**, you mean that they have brown or black hair, and often a brownish skin. ❑ *Carol is a tall, dark, Latin type of woman.* ADJ ≠ fair 7 A **dark** period of time is unpleasant or frightening. ❑ *This was the darkest period of the war.* ADJ: usu ADJ n = black 8 A **dark** place or area is mysterious and not fully known about. ❑ *...the dark recesses of the mind.* ADJ: ADJ n 9 **Dark** thoughts are sad, and show that you are expecting something unpleasant to happen. [LITERARY] ❑ *Troy's chatter kept me from thinking dark thoughts.* ADJ: usu ADJ n = gloomy 10 **Dark** looks or remarks make you think that the person giving them wants to harm you or that something horrible is going to happen. [LITERARY] ❑ *...dark threats.* ♦ **dark|ly** *'Something's wrong here,' she said darkly.* ADJ: usu ADJ n = sinister; ADV: ADV with v 11 If you describe something as **dark**, you mean that it is related to things that are serious or unpleasant, rather than light-hearted. ❑ *Their dark humor never failed to astound him.* ♦ **dark|ly** *The atmosphere after Wednesday's debut was as darkly comic as the film itself.* ADJ: usu ADJ n; ADV: ADV adj 12 → See also **pitch-dark**.

PHRASES 13 If you do something **after dark**, you do it when the sun has set and night has begun. ❑ *They avoid going out alone after dark.* PHRASE 14 If you do something **before dark**, you do it before the sun sets and night begins. ❑ *They'll be back well before dark.* PHRASE 15 If you are **in the dark about** something, you do not know anything about it. ❑ *The investigators admit that they are completely in the dark about the killing.* PHRASE: v-link PHR, PHR after v, oft PHR about n 16 If you describe something someone says or does as **a shot in the dark** or **a stab in the dark**, you mean they are guessing that what they say is correct or that what they do will be successful. ❑ *Every single one of those inspired guesses had been shots in the dark.* PHRASE: shot inflects

**dark age (dark ages)** also **Dark Age.** 1 If you refer to a period in the history of a society as a **dark age**, you think that it is characterized by a lack of knowledge and progress. [WRITTEN] ❑ *The Education Secretary accuses teachers of wanting to return to a dark age.* N-COUNT [disapproval] 2 **The Dark Ages** are the period of European history between about 500 A.D. and about 1000 A.D. N-PROPER: the N

**dark|en** /dɑː^rkən/ **(darkens, darkening, darkened)** 1 If something **darkens** or if a person or thing **darkens** it, it becomes darker. ❑ *The sky darkened abruptly... She had put on her make-up and darkened her eyelashes.* VERB ≠ lighten; V; V n 2 If someone's mood **darkens** or if something **darkens** their mood, they suddenly become rather unhappy. [LITERARY] ❑ *My sunny mood suddenly darkened... Nothing was going to darken his mood today.* VERB; V; V n 3 If someone's face **darkens**, they suddenly look angry. [LITERARY] ❑ *Rawley's face darkened again.* VERB; V

**dark|ened** /dɑː^rkənd/ A **darkened** building or room has no lights on inside it. ❑ *He drove past darkened houses.* ADJ: ADJ n

**dark glasses** **Dark glasses** are glasses which have dark-coloured lenses to protect your eyes in the sunshine. N-PLURAL: also a pair of N = sunglasses

**dark horse (dark horses)** If you describe someone as a **dark horse**, you mean that people know very little about them, although they may have recently had success or may be about to have success. N-COUNT

**dark mat|ter** **Dark matter** is material that is believed to form a large part of the universe, but which has never been seen. N-UNCOUNT

**dark|room** /dɑː^rkruːm/ **(darkrooms)** A **darkroom** is a room which can be sealed off from natural light and is lit only by red light. It is used for developing photographs. N-COUNT

**dar|ling** /dɑː^rlɪŋ/ **(darlings)** 1 You call someone **darling** if you love them or like them very much. ❑ *Thank you, darling.* N-VOC [feelings] 2 Some people use **darling** to describe someone or something that they love or like very much. [INFORMAL] ❑ *To have a darling baby boy was the greatest gift I could imagine.* ADJ: ADJ n 3 If you describe someone as a **darling**, you are fond of them and think that they are nice. [INFORMAL] ❑ *He's such a darling.* N-COUNT 4 The **darling of** a group of people is someone who is especially liked by that group. ❑ *Rajneesh was the darling of a prosperous family.* N-COUNT: with poss

**darn** /dɑː^rn/ **(darns, darning, darned)** 1 If you **darn** something knitted or made of cloth, you mend a hole in it by sewing stitches across the hole and then weaving stitches in and out of them. ❑ *Aunt Emilie darned old socks.* ♦ **darn|ing** *...chores such as sewing and darning.* VERB; V n; N-UNCOUNT 2 People sometimes use **darn** or **darned** to emphasize what they are saying, often when they are annoyed. [INFORMAL] ❑ *There's not a darn thing he can do about it.* ♦ **Darn** is also an adverb. ❑ *...the desire to be free to do just as we darn well please.* ADJ: ADJ n [emphasis] = damn, damned; ADV: ADV adj/adv 3 You can say **I'll be darned** to show that you are very surprised about something. [AM, INFORMAL] ❑ *'A talking pig!' he exclaimed. 'Well, I'll be darned.'* PHRASE [feelings]

**dart** /dɑː^rt/ **(darts, darting, darted)** 1 If a person or animal **darts** somewhere, they move there suddenly and quickly. [WRITTEN] ❑ *Ingrid darted across the deserted street.* VERB; V prep/adv 2 If you **dart** a look **at** someone or something, or if your eyes **dart to** them, you look at them very quickly. [LITERARY] ❑ *She darted a sly sideways glance at Bramwell... The* VERB; V n at n conductor's eyes darted to Wilfred, then fixed on Michael again. *(V prep/adv)* [3] A **dart** is a small, narrow object with a sharp point which can be thrown or shot. *(N-COUNT)* ❑ *Markov died after being struck by a poison dart.* [4] **Darts** is a game in which you throw darts at a round board which has numbers on it. *(N-UNCOUNT)*

**dart|board** /dɑːʳtbɔːʳd/ **(dartboards)** A **dartboard** is a circular board with numbers on it which is used as the target in a game of darts. *(N-COUNT)*

**dash** /dæʃ/ **(dashes, dashing, dashed)** [1] If you **dash** somewhere, you run or go there quickly and suddenly. *(VERB)* ❑ *Suddenly she dashed down to the cellar.* *(V adv/prep)* ♦ **Dash** is also a noun. *(N-SING)* ❑ *...a 160-mile dash to hospital.* [2] If you say that you have to **dash**, you mean that you are in a hurry and have to leave immediately. [INFORMAL] *(VERB: no cont = rush)* ❑ *Oh, Tim! I'm sorry but I have to dash.* *(V)* [3] A **dash of** something is a small quantity of it which you add when you are preparing food or mixing a drink. *(N-COUNT: usu N of n)* ❑ *Add a dash of balsamic vinegar.* [4] A **dash of** a quality is a small amount of it that is found in something and often makes it more interesting or distinctive. *(N-COUNT: usu N of n)* ❑ *...a story with a dash of mystery thrown in.* [5] If you **dash** something **against** a wall or other surface, you throw or push it violently, often so hard that it breaks. [LITERARY] *(VERB)* ❑ *She seized the doll and dashed it against the stone wall with tremendous force.* *(V n against n; Also V n prep)* [6] If an event or person **dashes** someone's hopes or expectations, it destroys them by making it impossible that the thing that is hoped for or expected will ever happen. [JOURNALISM, LITERARY] *(VERB)* ❑ *The announcement dashed hopes of an early end to the crisis... They had their championship hopes dashed by a 3-1 defeat.* *(V n; have n V-ed)* [7] A **dash** is a straight, horizontal line used in writing, for example to separate two main clauses whose meanings are closely connected. *(N-COUNT)* [8] The **dash** of a car is its **dashboard**. *(N-COUNT)* [9] If you **make a dash for** a place, you run there very quickly, for example to escape from someone or something. *(PHRASE: V inflects, PHR n)* ❑ *I made a dash for the front door but he got there before me.*

♦ **dash off** [1] If you **dash off to** a place, you go there very quickly. *(PHRASAL VERB)* ❑ *He dashed off to lunch at the Hard Rock Cafe.* *(V P to n)* [2] If you **dash off** a piece of writing, you write or compose it very quickly, without thinking about it very much. *(PHRASAL VERB)* ❑ *He dashed off a couple of novels.* *(V P n (not pron))*

**dash|board** /dæʃbɔːʳd/ **(dashboards)** The **dashboard** in a car is the panel facing the driver's seat where most of the instruments and switches are. *(N-COUNT)* → See picture on page 1708.

**dash|ing** /dæʃɪŋ/ A **dashing** person or thing is very stylish and attractive. [OLD-FASHIONED] *(ADJ: usu ADJ n)* ❑ *He was the very model of the dashing RAF pilot.*

**das|tard|ly** /dæstəʳdli/ [1] If you describe an action as **dastardly**, you mean it is wicked and intended to hurt someone. [OLD-FASHIONED] *(ADJ: ADJ n)* [2] If you describe a person as **dastardly**, you mean they are wicked. [OLD-FASHIONED] *(ADJ: ADJ n)*

**DAT** /dæt/ **DAT** is a type of magnetic tape used to make very high quality recordings of sound by recording it in digital form. **DAT** is an abbreviation for 'digital audio tape'. *(N-UNCOUNT)*

**da|ta** /deɪtə/ [1] You can refer to information as **data**, especially when it is in the form of facts or statistics that you can analyse. In American English, **data** is usually a plural noun. In technical or formal British English, **data** is sometimes a plural noun, but at other times, it is an uncount noun. *(◆◆◇ N-UNCOUNT; also N-PLURAL)* ❑ *The study was based on data from 2,100 women... To cope with these data, hospitals bought large mainframe computers.* [2] **Data** is information that can be stored and used by a computer program. [COMPUTING] *(N-UNCOUNT)* ❑ *You can compress huge amounts of data on to a CD-ROM.*

**da|ta bank** **(data banks)** also **databank.** A **data bank** is the same as a **database**. *(N-COUNT)*

**data|base** /deɪtəbeɪs/ **(databases)** also **data base.** A **database** is a collection of data that is stored in a computer and that can easily be used and added to. *(N-COUNT)* ❑ *They maintain a database of hotels that cater for businesswomen.*

**da|ta min|ing** **Data mining** involves collecting information from data stored in a database, for example in order to find out about people's shopping habits. [COMPUTING] *(N-UNCOUNT)* ❑ *Data mining is used to analyse individuals' buying habits.*

**da|ta pro|cess|ing** **Data processing** is the series of operations that are carried out on data, especially by computers, in order to present, interpret, or obtain information. *(N-UNCOUNT)* ❑ *Taylor's company makes data-processing systems.*

**date** /deɪt/ **(dates, dating, dated)** [1] A **date** is a specific time that can be named, for example a particular day or a particular year. *(◆◆◇ N-COUNT)* ❑ *What's the date today?... You will need to give the dates you wish to stay and the number of rooms you require.* [2] If you **date** something, you give or discover the date when it was made or when it began. *(VERB)* ❑ *I think we can date the decline of Western Civilization quite precisely... Archaeologists have dated the fort to the reign of Emperor Antoninus Pius.* *(V n; V n to n)* [3] When you **date** something such as a letter or a cheque, you write that day's date on it. *(VERB)* ❑ *Once the decision is reached, he can date and sign the sheet... The letter is dated 2 July 1993.* *(V n; V-ed)* [4] If you want to refer to an event without saying exactly when it will happen or when it happened, you can say that it will happen or happened **at** some **date** in the future or past. *(N-SING: with supp, at N)* ❑ *Retain copies of all correspondence, since you may need them at a later date.* [5] **To date** means up until the present time. *(PHRASE: PHR with cl)* ❑ *'Dottie' is by far his best novel to date.* [6] If something **dates**, it goes out of fashion and becomes unacceptable to modern tastes. *(VERB)* ❑ *A black coat always looks smart and will never date.* *(V)* [7] If your ideas, what you say, or the things that you like or can remember **date** you, they show that you are quite old or older than the people you are with. *(VERB)* ❑ *It's going to date me now. I attended that school from 1969 to 1972.* *(V n)* [8] A **date** is an appointment to meet someone or go out with them, especially someone with whom you are having, or may soon have, a romantic relationship. *(N-COUNT)* ❑ *I have a date with Bob.* [9] If you have a date with someone with whom you are having, or may soon have, a romantic relationship, you can refer to that person as your **date**. *(N-COUNT: usu poss N)* ❑ *He lied to Essie, saying his date was one of the girls in the show.* [10] If you **are dating** someone, you go out with them regularly because you are having, or may soon have, a romantic relationship with them. You can also say that two people **are dating**. *(V-RECIP)* ❑ *For a year I dated a woman who was a research assistant... They've been dating for three months.* *(V n; pl-n V)* [11] A **date** is a small, dark-brown, sticky fruit with a stone inside. Dates grow on palm trees in hot countries. *(N-COUNT)* [12] → See also **blind date**, **carbon dating**, **dated**, **out of date**, **up to date**.

♦ **date back** If something **dates back to** a particular time, it started or was made at that time. *(PHRASAL VERB)* ❑ *...a palace dating back to the 16th century... This tradition dates back over 200 years.* *(V P to n; V P amount)*

♦ **date from** If something **dates from** a particular time, it started or was made at that time. *(PHRASAL VERB)* ❑ *The present controversy dates from 1986.* *(V P n)*

**dat|ed** /deɪtɪd/ **Dated** things seem old-fashioned, although they may once have been fashionable or modern. *(ADJ)* ❑ *...people in dated dinner-jackets.*

**date of birth** **(dates of birth)** Your **date of birth** is the exact date on which you were born, including the year. *(N-COUNT: oft poss N)* ❑ *The registration form showed his date of birth as August 2, 1979.*

**date palm** **(date palms)** A **date palm** is a palm tree on which dates grow. *(N-COUNT)*

**date rape** **Date rape** is when a man **rapes** a woman after having spent the evening socially with her. *(N-UNCOUNT)*

**da|ting** /deɪtɪŋ/ **Dating** agencies or services are for people who are trying to find a girlfriend or boyfriend. ❑ *I joined a dating agency.* ADJ: ADJ n

**da|tive** /deɪtɪv/ In the grammar of some languages, for example Latin, **the dative**, or the **dative** case, is the case used for a noun when it is the indirect object of a verb, or when it comes after some prepositions. N-SING: the N

**da|tum** /deɪtəm, dɑːtəm/ → see **data**.

**daub** /dɔːb/ **(daubs, daubing, daubed)** When you **daub** a substance such as mud or paint on something, you spread it on that thing in a rough or careless way. ❑ *The make-up woman daubed mock blood on Jeremy... They sent death threats and daubed his home with slogans.* VERB; V n prep/adv; V n with n

**daugh|ter** /dɔːtəʳ/ **(daughters)** Someone's **daughter** is their female child. ❑ *...Flora and her daughter Catherine. ...the daughter of a university professor... I have two daughters.* ◆◆◆ N-COUNT: oft with poss

**daughter-in-law** **(daughters-in-law)** Someone's **daughter-in-law** is the wife of their son. N-COUNT: usu poss N

**daunt** /dɔːnt/ **(daunts, daunting, daunted)** If something **daunts** you, it makes you feel slightly afraid or worried about dealing with it. ❑ *...a gruelling journey that would have daunted a woman half her age.* ♦ **daunt|ed** *It is hard to pick up such a book and not to feel a little daunted.* VERB; V n; ADJ: v-link ADJ

**daunt|ing** /dɔːntɪŋ/ Something that is **daunting** makes you feel slightly afraid or worried about dealing with it. ❑ *They were faced with the daunting task of restoring the house.* ♦ **daunt|ing|ly** *She is dauntingly articulate.* ADJ = intimidating; ADV

**daunt|less** /dɔːntləs/ A **dauntless** person is brave and confident and not easily frightened. [LITERARY] ❑ *...their dauntless courage.* ADJ = resolute

**dau|phin** /dɔːfɪn, doʊfæn/ also **Dauphin.** In former times, the king and queen of France's oldest son was called **the dauphin**. N-SING: the N

**daw|dle** /dɔːdᵊl/ **(dawdles, dawdling, dawdled)** If you **dawdle**, you spend more time than is necessary going somewhere. ❑ *Eleanor will be back any moment, if she doesn't dawdle.* VERB; V

**dawn** /dɔːn/ **(dawns, dawning, dawned)** 1 **Dawn** is the time of day when light first appears in the sky, just before the sun rises. ❑ *Nancy woke at dawn.* N-VAR 2 **The dawn of** a period of time or a situation is the beginning of it. [LITERARY] ❑ *...the dawn of the radio age.* N-SING: usu the N of n 3 If something **is dawning**, it is beginning to develop or come into existence. [WRITTEN] ❑ *Throughout Europe a new railway age, that of the high-speed train, has dawned.* ♦ **dawn|ing** *...the dawning of the space age.* VERB; V; N-SING: oft the VERB 4 When you say that a particular day **dawned**, you mean it arrived or began, usually when it became light. [WRITTEN] ❑ *When the great day dawned, the first concern was the weather.* V 5 **at the crack of dawn** → see **crack**.

♦ **dawn on** or **dawn upon** If a fact or idea **dawns on** you, you realize it. ❑ *It gradually dawned on me that I still had talent and ought to run again... Then the chilling truth dawned on Captain Gary Snavely.* PHRASAL VERB = strike; it V P n that; V P n

**dawn cho|rus** **The dawn chorus** is the singing of birds at dawn. [BRIT] N-SING

**dawn raid** **(dawn raids)** 1 If police officers carry out a **dawn raid**, they go to someone's house very early in the morning to search it or arrest them. ❑ *Thousands of pounds worth of drugs were seized in dawn raids yesterday.* N-COUNT 2 If a person or company carries out a **dawn raid**, they try to buy a large number of a company's shares at the start of a day's trading, especially because they want to buy the whole company. [BUSINESS] ❑ *Southern acquired 11.2 per cent of Sweb in a dawn raid on Monday.* N-COUNT

**day** /deɪ/ **(days)** 1 A **day** is one of the seven twenty-four hour periods of time in a week. ◆◆◆ N-COUNT 2 **Day** is the time when it is light, or the time when you are up and doing things. ❑ *27 million working days are lost each year due to work accidents and sickness... He arranged for me to go down to London one day a week... The snack bar is open during the day.* N-VAR ≠ night 3 You can refer to a particular period in history as a particular **day** or as particular **days**. ❑ *He began to talk about the Ukraine of his uncle's day... She is doing just fine these days.* N-COUNT: with supp

**PHRASES** 4 If something happens **day after day**, it happens every day without stopping. ❑ *The newspaper job had me doing the same thing day after day.* PHRASE 5 **In this day and age** means in modern times. ❑ *Even in this day and age the old attitudes persist.* PHRASE 6 If you say that something **has seen better days**, you mean that it is old and in poor condition. ❑ *The tweed jacket she wore had seen better days.* PHRASE: V inflects 7 If you **call it a day**, you decide to stop what you are doing because you are tired of it or because it is not successful. ❑ *Faced with mounting debts, the decision to call it a day was inevitable.* PHRASE: V inflects 8 If someone **carries the day**, they are the winner in a contest such as a battle, debate, or sporting competition. [JOURNALISM] ❑ *For the time being, the liberals seem to have carried the day.* PHRASE: V inflects 9 If you say that something **has had** its **day**, you mean that the period during which it was most successful or popular has now passed. ❑ *Beat music may finally have had its day.* PHRASE: V inflects 10 If something **makes** your **day**, it makes you feel very happy. [INFORMAL] ❑ *Come on, Bill. Send Tom a card and make his day.* PHRASE: V inflects 11 **One day** or **some day** or **one of these days** means at some time in the future. ❑ *I too dreamed of living in London one day... I hope some day you will find the woman who will make you happy.* PHRASE: PHR with cl 12 If you say that something happened **the other day**, you mean that it happened a few days ago. ❑ *I phoned your office the other day.* PHRASE: PHR with cl 13 If someone or something **saves the day** in a situation which seems likely to fail, they manage to make it successful. ❑ *...this story about how he saved the day at his daughter's birthday party.* PHRASE: V inflects 14 If something happens **from day to day** or **day by day**, it happens each day. ❑ *Your needs can differ from day to day... I live for the moment, day by day, not for the past.* PHRASE 15 If it is a month or a year **to the day** since a particular thing happened, it is exactly a month or a year since it happened. ❑ *It was January 19, a year to the day since he had arrived in Singapore.* PHRASE: amount PHR 16 **To this day** means up until and including the present time. ❑ *To this day young Zulu boys practise fighting.* PHRASE: PHR with cl 17 If a particular person, group, or thing **wins the day**, they win a battle, struggle, or competition. If they **lose the day**, they are defeated. [mainly JOURNALISM] ❑ *His determination and refusal to back down had won the day.* PHRASE: V inflects 18 If you say that a task is **all in a day's work** for someone, you mean that they do not mind doing it although it may be difficult, because it is part of their job or because they often do it. ❑ *For war reporters, dodging snipers' bullets is all in a day's work.* PHRASE: usu v-link PHR, oft PHR for n 19 your **day in court** → see **court**. **it's early days** → see **early**. **at the end of the day** → see **end**. **late in the day** → see **late**. someone's **days are numbered** → see **number**. **the good old days** → see **old**.

**-day** /-deɪ/ You use **-day** with a number to indicate how long something lasts. ❑ *The Sudanese leader has left for a two-day visit to Zambia.* COMB in ADJ

**day|break** /deɪbreɪk/ **Daybreak** is the time in the morning when light first appears. ❑ *Pedro got up every morning before daybreak.* N-UNCOUNT = dawn

**day care** **Day care** is care that is provided during the day for people who cannot look after themselves, such as small children, old people, or people who are ill. Day care is provided by paid workers. ❑ *...a day-care centre for elderly people.* N-UNCOUNT: oft N n

**day|dream** /deɪdriːm/ **(daydreams, daydreaming, daydreamed)** also **day-dream.** 1 If you **daydream**, you think about pleasant things for a period of time, usually about things that you would like to happen. ❑ *Do you work hard for suc-* VERB; V about n *cess rather than daydream about it?... He daydreams of being a famous journalist... I am inclined to daydream.* V of n/-ing V [2] A **daydream** is a series of pleasant thoughts, usually about things that you would like to happen. ❑ *He escaped into daydreams of beautiful women.* N-COUNT

**Day-Glo** /deɪ gloʊ/ also **Dayglo. Day-Glo** colours are shades of orange, pink, green, and yellow which are so bright that they seem to glow. [TRADEMARK] N-UNCOUNT: usu N n

**day job** If someone tells you **not to give up the day job**, they are saying that they think you should continue doing what you are good at, rather than trying something new which they think you will fail at. [HUMOROUS] PHRASE: V inflects

**day|light** /deɪlaɪt/ [1] **Daylight** is the natural light that there is during the day, before it gets dark. ❑ *Lack of daylight can make people feel depressed.* N-UNCOUNT [2] **Daylight** is the time of day when it begins to get light. ❑ *Quinn returned shortly after daylight yesterday morning.* N-UNCOUNT [3] If you say that a crime is committed **in broad daylight**, you are expressing your surprise that it is done during the day when people can see it, rather than at night. ❑ *A girl was attacked on a train in broad daylight.* PHRASE: PHR after v emphasis

**day|light rob|bery** If someone charges you a great deal of money for something and you think this is unfair or unreasonable, you can refer to this as **daylight robbery**. [BRIT, INFORMAL] ❑ *They're just ripping the fans off; it's daylight robbery.* N-UNCOUNT disapproval

**day|lights** /deɪlaɪts/ [1] If you **knock the living daylights out of** someone, or **beat the living daylights out of** them, you hit them very hard many times. [INFORMAL] PHRASE: V inflects [2] If someone or something **scares the living daylights out of** you, they make you feel extremely scared. [INFORMAL] PHRASE: V inflects

**Day|light Sav|ing Time** also **daylight saving time. Daylight Saving Time** is a period of time in the summer when the clocks are set one hour forward, so that people can have extra light in the evening. [AM] N-UNCOUNT

✔ in BRIT, use **British Summer Time**

**day|long** /deɪlɒŋ, AM -lɔːŋ/ **Daylong** is used to describe an event or activity that lasts for the whole of one day. [mainly AM] ❑ *...a daylong meeting.* ADJ: ADJ n

**day nurse|ry (day nurseries)** A **day nursery** is a place where children who are too young to go to school can be left all day while their parents are at work. N-COUNT = crèche

**day off (days off)** A **day off** is a day when you do not go to work, even though it is usually a working day. ❑ *It was Mrs Dearden's day off, and Paul was on duty in her place.* N-COUNT

**day of reck|on|ing** If someone talks about the **day of reckoning**, they mean a day or time in the future when people will be forced to deal with an unpleasant situation which they have avoided until now. ❑ *The day of reckoning is coming for the water company directors.* N-SING: usu the N

**day one** If something happens **from day one** of a process, it happens right from the beginning. If it happens **on day one**, it happens right at the beginning. ❑ *This has been a bad inquiry from day one.* N-SING

**day re|lease** also **day-release. Day release** is a system in which workers spend one day each week at a college in order to study a subject connected with their work. [BRIT] N-UNCOUNT

**day re|turn (day returns)** A **day return** is a train or bus ticket which allows you to go somewhere and come back on the same day for a lower price than an ordinary return ticket. [BRIT] N-COUNT

✔ in AM, use **round trip ticket**

**day room (day rooms)** A **day room** is a room in a hospital where patients can sit and relax during the day. N-COUNT

**day school (day schools)** A **day school** is a school where the students go home every evening and do not live at the school. Compare **boarding school**. N-COUNT

**day|time** /deɪtaɪm/ [1] **The daytime** is the part of a day between the time when it gets light and the time when it gets dark. ❑ *In the daytime he stayed up in his room, sleeping, or listening to music... Please give a daytime telephone number.* N-SING: the N, also no det [2] **Daytime** television and radio is broadcast during the morning and afternoon on weekdays. ❑ *...ITV's new package of daytime programmes.* ADJ: ADJ n

**day-to-day Day-to-day** things or activities exist or happen every day as part of ordinary life. ❑ *I am a vegetarian and use a lot of lentils in my day-to-day cooking.* ADJ: ADJ n

**day trad|er (day traders)** On the stock market, **day traders** are traders who buy and sell particular securities on the same day. [BUSINESS] N-COUNT

**day trip (day trips)** also **day-trip.** A **day trip** is a journey to a place and back again on the same day, usually for pleasure. N-COUNT

**day-tripper (day-trippers)** also **day tripper.** A **day-tripper** is someone who goes on a day trip. [BRIT] N-COUNT

**daze** /deɪz/ If someone is **in a daze**, they are feeling confused and unable to think clearly, often because they have had a shock or surprise. ❑ *For 35 minutes I was walking around in a daze.* N-SING: oft in a N

**dazed** /deɪzd/ If someone is **dazed**, they are confused and unable to think clearly, often because of shock or a blow to the head. ❑ *At the end of the interview I was dazed and exhausted.* ADJ = confused

**daz|zle** /dæzəl/ **(dazzles, dazzling, dazzled)** [1] If someone or something **dazzles** you, you are extremely impressed by their skill, qualities, or beauty. ❑ *George dazzled her with his knowledge of the world... The movie's special effects fail to dazzle.* VERB V n with n V [2] The **dazzle of** something is a quality it has, such as beauty or skill, which is impressive and attractive. ❑ *The dazzle of stardom and status attracts them.* N-SING: with poss [3] If a bright light **dazzles** you, it makes you unable to see properly for a short time. ❑ *The sun, glinting from the pool, dazzled me.* VERB V n [4] The **dazzle** of a light is its brightness, which makes it impossible for you to see properly for a short time. ❑ *The sun's dazzle on the water hurts my eyes.* N-UNCOUNT: also a N [5] → See also **razzle-dazzle**.

**dazz|ling** /dæzlɪŋ/ [1] Something that is **dazzling** is very impressive or beautiful. ❑ *He gave Alberg a dazzling smile.* ♦ **dazz|ling|ly** *The view was dazzlingly beautiful.* ADJ = stunning ADV [2] A **dazzling** light is very bright and makes you unable to see properly for a short time. ❑ *He shielded his eyes against the dazzling declining sun.* ♦ **dazz|ling|ly** *The loading bay seemed dazzlingly bright.* ADJ ADV: ADV adj

**DC** /diː siː/ **DC** is used to refer to an electric current that always flows in the same direction. **DC** is an abbreviation for 'direct current'. N-UNCOUNT

**D-day** You can use **D-day** to refer to the day that is chosen for the beginning of an important activity. ❑ *D-day for my departure was set for 29th June.* N-UNCOUNT

**DDT** /diː diː tiː/ **DDT** is a poisonous substance which is used for killing insects. N-UNCOUNT

**de-** /diː-/ [1] **De-** is added to a verb in order to change the meaning of the verb to its opposite. ❑ *...becoming desensitized to the harmful consequences of violence. ...how to decontaminate industrial waste sites.* PREFIX [2] **De-** is added to a noun in order to make it a verb referring to the removal of the thing described by the noun. ❑ *I've defrosted the freezer... The fires are likely to permanently deforest the land.* PREFIX

**dea|con** /diːkən/ **(deacons)** A **deacon** is a member of the clergy, for example in the Church of England, who is lower in rank than a priest. N-COUNT

**de|ac|tiv|ate** /diæktɪveɪt/ **(deactivates, deactivating, deactivated)** If someone **deactivates** an explosive device or an alarm, they make it harm- VERB = disable less or impossible to operate. ❑ *Russia is deactivating some of its deadliest missiles.* V n

**dead** /ded/ ◆◆◇ [1] A person, animal, or plant that is **dead** is no longer living. ❑ *Her husband's been dead a year now... The group had shot dead another hostage. ...old newspapers and dead flowers.* ADJ ≠ alive ♦ **The dead** are people who are dead. ❑ *The dead included six people attending a religious ceremony.* N-PLURAL: the N [2] If you describe a place or a period of time as **dead**, you do not like it because there is very little activity taking place in it. ❑ *...some dead little town where the liveliest thing is the flies.* ADJ [disapproval] [3] Something that is **dead** is no longer being used or is finished. ❑ *The dead cigarette was still between his fingers.* ADJ [4] If you say that an idea, plan, or subject is **dead**, you mean that people are no longer interested in it or willing to develop it any further. ❑ *It's a dead issue, Baxter.* ADJ [5] A **dead** language is no longer spoken or written as a means of communication, although it may still be studied. ❑ *We used to grumble that we were wasting time learning a dead language.* ADJ: usu ADJ n [6] A telephone or piece of electrical equipment that is **dead** is no longer functioning, for example because it no longer has any electrical power. ❑ *On another occasion I answered the phone and the line went dead.* ADJ: usu v-link ADJ [7] In sport, when a ball is **dead**, it has gone outside the playing area, or a situation has occurred in which the game has to be temporarily stopped, and none of the players can score points or gain an advantage. [JOURNALISM] ADJ [8] **Dead** is used to mean 'complete' or 'absolute', especially before the words 'centre', 'silence', and 'stop'. ❑ *They hurried about in dead silence, with anxious faces... Lila's boat came to a dead stop.* ADJ: ADJ n [emphasis] [9] **Dead** means 'precisely' or 'exactly'. ❑ *Mars was visible, dead in the centre of the telescope... Their arrows are dead on target.* ADV: ADV prep/adv/adj [emphasis] [10] **Dead** is sometimes used to mean 'very'. [BRIT, INFORMAL, SPOKEN] ❑ *I am dead against the legalisation of drugs.* ADV: ADV adj/adv/prep [emphasis] [11] If you reply **'Over my dead body'** when a plan or action has been suggested, you are emphasizing that you dislike it, and will do everything you can to prevent it. [INFORMAL] ❑ *'Let's invite her to dinner.' — 'Over my dead body!'* CONVENTION [emphasis]

**PHRASES** [12] If you say that something such as an idea or situation is **dead and buried**, you are emphasizing that you think that it is completely finished or past, and cannot happen or exist again in the future. ❑ *I thought the whole business was dead and buried.* PHRASE: v-link PHR [emphasis] [13] If you say that a person or animal **dropped dead** or **dropped down dead**, you mean that they died very suddenly and unexpectedly. ❑ *He dropped dead on the quayside.* PHRASE: V inflects [14] If you say that you **feel dead** or **are half dead**, you mean that you feel very tired or ill and very weak. [INFORMAL] ❑ *You looked half dead after that journey.* PHRASE: v-link PHR [emphasis] [15] If something happens **in the dead of night**, **at dead of night**, or **in the dead of winter**, it happens in the middle part of the night or the winter, when it is darkest or coldest. [LITERARY] ❑ *We buried it in the garden at dead of night.* PHRASE [16] If you say that you wouldn't **be seen dead** or **be caught dead** in particular clothes, places, or situations, you are expressing strong dislike or disapproval of them. [INFORMAL] ❑ *I wouldn't be seen dead in a straw hat.* PHRASE: PHR prep, PHR -ing [emphasis] [17] To **stop dead** means to suddenly stop happening or moving. To **stop** someone or something **dead** means to cause them to suddenly stop happening or moving. ❑ *We all stopped dead and looked at it.* PHRASE: V inflects [18] If you say that someone or something is **dead in the water**, you are emphasizing that they have failed, and that there is little hope of them being successful in the future. ❑ *A 'no' vote would have left the treaty dead in the water.* PHRASE: v-link PHR [emphasis] [19] to **flog a dead horse** → see **flog**. **a dead loss** → see **loss**. **a dead ringer** → see **ringer**. to **stop dead in** your **tracks** → see **track**.

**dead|beat** /dedbiːt/ **(deadbeats)** If you refer to someone as a **deadbeat**, you are criticizing them because you think they are lazy and do not want to be part of ordinary society. [AM, INFORMAL] N-COUNT [disapproval]

**dead-beat** also **dead beat.** If you are **dead-beat**, you are very tired and have no energy left. [INFORMAL] ADJ: v-link ADJ = shattered

**dead duck** **(dead ducks)** If you describe someone or something as a **dead duck**, you are emphasizing that you think they have absolutely no chance of succeeding. [INFORMAL] N-COUNT [emphasis]

**dead|en** /dedᵊn/ **(deadens, deadening, deadened)** If something **deadens** a feeling or a sound, it makes it less strong or loud. ❑ *He needs morphine to deaden the pain in his chest.* VERB V n

**dead end** **(dead ends)** [1] If a street is a **dead end**, there is no way out at one end of it. N-COUNT [2] A **dead end** job or course of action is one that you think is bad because it does not lead to further developments or progress. ❑ *Waitressing was a dead-end job.* N-COUNT: oft N n

**dead|en|ing** /dedᵊnɪŋ/ A **deadening** situation destroys people's enthusiasm and imagination. ❑ *She was bored with the deadening routine of her life.* ADJ: usu ADJ n

**dead hand** You can refer to **the dead hand of** a particular thing when that thing has a bad or depressing influence on a particular situation. [mainly BRIT] ❑ *...the dead hand of bureaucracy.* N-SING: usu the N of n

**dead-head** **(dead-heads, dead-heading, dead-headed)** also **deadhead.** [1] To **dead-head** a plant which is flowering means to remove all the dead flowers from it. [BRIT] ❑ *Dead-head roses as the blooms fade.* VERB V n [2] If you say that someone is a **deadhead**, you mean that they are stupid or slow. [AM, INFORMAL] N-COUNT

**dead heat** **(dead heats)** If a race or contest is **a dead heat**, two or more competitors are joint winners, or are both winning at a particular moment in the race or contest. In American English, you can say that a race or contest is **in a dead heat**. ❑ *The race ended in a dead heat between two horses.* N-COUNT

**dead let|ter** **(dead letters)** If you say that a law or agreement is a **dead letter**, you mean that it still exists but people ignore it. ❑ *No one does anything about it and the law becomes a dead letter.* N-COUNT

**dead|line** /dedlaɪn/ ◆◇◇ **(deadlines)** A **deadline** is a time or date before which a particular task must be finished or a particular thing must be done. ❑ *We were not able to meet the deadline because of manufacturing delays... The deadline for submissions to the competition will be Easter 1994.* N-COUNT: oft N for n/-ing

**dead|lock** /dedlɒk/ **(deadlocks)** If a dispute or series of negotiations reaches **deadlock**, neither side is willing to give in at all and no agreement can be made. ❑ *They called for a compromise on all sides to break the deadlock in the world trade talks.* N-VAR

**dead|locked** /dedlɒkt/ If a dispute or series of negotiations is **deadlocked**, no agreement can be reached because neither side will give in at all. You can also say that the people involved are **deadlocked**. ❑ *The peace talks have been deadlocked over the issue of human rights since August.* ADJ: v-link ADJ, oft ADJ over n

**dead|ly** /dedli/ **(deadlier, deadliest)** [1] If something is **deadly**, it is likely or able to cause someone's death, or has already caused someone's death. ❑ *He was acquitted on charges of assault with a deadly weapon. ...a deadly disease currently affecting dolphins... Passive smoking can be deadly too.* ADJ = lethal, fatal [2] If you describe a person or their behaviour as **deadly**, you mean that they will do or say anything to get what they want, without caring about other people. ❑ *The Duchess levelled a deadly look at Nikko.* ADJ [disapproval] [3] You can use **deadly** to emphasize that something has a particular quality, especially an unpleasant or undesirable quality. ❑ *Broadcast news was accurate and reliable but deadly dull.* ADV: ADV adj [emphasis] = deathly [4] A **deadly** situation has unpleasant or dangerous consequences. ❑ *...the deadly combination of low expectations and low achievement.* ADJ: usu ADJ n [5] **Deadly** enemies ADJ or rivals fight or compete with each other in a very aggressive way. ❑ *The two became deadly enemies.*

**dead meat** If you say that someone is **dead meat**, you mean that they are in very serious trouble that may result in them being hurt or injured in some way. [INFORMAL, SPOKEN] N-UNCOUNT

**dead|pan** /dedpæn/ **Deadpan** humour is when you appear to be serious and are hiding the fact that you are joking or teasing someone. ❑ *...her natural capacity for irony and deadpan humour.* ADJ

**dead weight** (**dead weights**) 1 A **dead weight** is a load which is surprisingly heavy and difficult to lift. N-COUNT 2 You can refer to something that makes change or progress difficult as a **dead weight**. ❑ *...the dead weight of traditional policies.* N-COUNT: usu sing

**dead wood** People or things that have been used for a very long time and that are no longer considered to be useful can be referred to as **dead wood**. ❑ *...the idea that historical linguistics is so much dead wood.* N-UNCOUNT [disapproval]

**deaf** /def/ (**deafer, deafest**) 1 Someone who is **deaf** is unable to hear anything or is unable to hear very well. ❑ *She is now profoundly deaf.* ADJ ♦ **The deaf** are people who are deaf. ❑ *Many regular TV programs are captioned for the deaf.* N-PLURAL: the N ♦ **deaf|ness** *Because of her deafness she was hard to make conversation with.* N-UNCOUNT 2 If you say that someone is **deaf to** people's requests, arguments, or criticisms, you are criticizing them because they refuse to pay attention to them. ❑ *The provincial assembly were deaf to all pleas for financial help.* ADJ: v-link ADJ to n [disapproval] = impervious 3 to **fall on deaf ears** → see **ear**. to **turn a deaf ear** → see **ear**.

**deaf|en** /defən/ (**deafens, deafening, deafened**) 1 If a noise **deafens** you, it is so loud that you cannot hear anything else at the same time. ❑ *The noise of the typewriters deafened her.* VERB V n 2 If you **are deafened by** something, you are made deaf by it, or are unable to hear for some time. ❑ *He was deafened by the noise from the gun.* VERB: usu passive be V-ed 3 → See also **deafening**.

**deaf|en|ing** /defənɪŋ/ 1 A **deafening** noise is a very loud noise. ❑ *...the deafening roar of fighter jets taking off.* ADJ 2 If you say there was a **deafening silence**, you are emphasizing that there was no reaction or response to something that was said or done. ❑ *When we ask people for suggestions we get a deafening silence.* ADJ [emphasis]

**deaf-mute** (**deaf-mutes**) A **deaf-mute** is someone who cannot hear or speak. This word could cause offence. N-COUNT

| deal |
|---|
| ① QUANTIFIER USES |
| ② VERB AND NOUN USES |

①**deal** /diːl/ If you say that you need or have **a great deal of** or **a good deal of** a particular thing, you are emphasizing that you need or have a lot of it. ❑ *...a great deal of money... I am in a position to save you a good deal of time.* ◆◇◇ QUANT: QUANT of n-uncount/def-n [emphasis] ♦ **Deal** is also an adverb. ❑ *Their lives became a good deal more comfortable... He depended a great deal on his wife for support.* ADV: ADV compar, ADV after v ♦ **Deal** is also a pronoun. ❑ *Although he had never met Geoffrey Hardcastle, he knew a good deal about him.* PRON

②**deal** /diːl/ (**deals, dealing, dealt**) ◆◆◆
⇛ Please look at category 7 to see if the expression you are looking for is shown under another headword. 1 If you **make** a **deal**, **do** a **deal**, or **cut** a **deal**, you complete an agreement or an arrangement with someone, especially in business. [BUSINESS] ❑ *Japan will have to do a deal with America on rice imports... The two sides tried and failed to come to a deal... He was involved in shady business deals.* N-COUNT 2 If a person, company, or shop **deals in** a particular type of goods, their business involves buying or selling those goods. [BUSINESS] ❑ *They deal in antiques. ...the rights of our citizens to hold and to deal in foreign currency.* VERB V in n V in n 3 If someone **deals** illegal drugs, they sell them. ❑ *I certainly don't deal drugs.* VERB V n ♦ **deal|ing** *...his involvement in drug dealing and illegal money laundering.* N-UNCOUNT: oft n N 4 If someone has had a **bad deal**, they have been unfortunate or have been treated unfairly. ❑ *The people of Liverpool have had a bad deal for many, many years.* N-COUNT: adj N 5 If you **deal** playing cards, you give them out to the players in a game of cards. ❑ *The croupier dealt each player a card, face down... He once dealt cards in an illegal gambling joint.* VERB V n n V n ♦ **Deal out** means the same as **deal**. ❑ *Dalton dealt out five cards to each player.* PHRASAL VERB V P n (not pron) 6 If an event **deals a blow to** something or someone, it causes them great difficulties or makes failure more likely. [JOURNALISM] ❑ *The summer drought has dealt a heavy blow to the government's economic record.* PHRASE: V inflects 7 → See also **dealings**, **wheel and deal**. **a raw deal** → see **raw**.

♦ **deal out** If someone **deals out** a punishment or harmful action, they punish or harm someone. [WRITTEN] ❑ *...a failure to deal out effective punishment to aggressors.* PHRASAL VERB = mete out V P n (not pron) to n

♦ **deal with** 1 When you **deal with** something or someone that needs attention, you give your attention to them, and often solve a problem or make a decision concerning them. ❑ *...the way that building societies deal with complaints... The President said the agreement would allow other vital problems to be dealt with.* PHRASAL VERB = handle V P n V P n 2 If you **deal with** an unpleasant emotion or an emotionally difficult situation, you recognize it, and remain calm and in control of yourself in spite of it. ❑ *She saw a psychiatrist who used hypnotism to help her deal with her fear.* PHRASAL VERB V P n 3 If a book, speech, or film **deals with** a particular thing, it has that thing as its subject or is concerned with it. ❑ *...the parts of his book which deal with contemporary Paris.* PHRASAL VERB V P n 4 If you **deal with** a particular person or organization, you have business relations with them. ❑ *When I worked in Florida I dealt with British people all the time.* PHRASAL VERB V P n

**deal|er** /diːləʳ/ (**dealers**) 1 A **dealer** is a person whose business involves buying and selling things. ❑ *...an antique dealer. ...dealers in commodities and financial securities.* → See also **wheeler-dealer**. ◆◇◇ N-COUNT 2 A **dealer** is someone who buys and sells illegal drugs. ❑ *They aim to clear every dealer from the street.* N-COUNT

**deal|er|ship** /diːləʳʃɪp/ (**dealerships**) A **dealership** is a company that sells cars, usually for one car company. ❑ *...a car dealership.* N-COUNT

**deal|ing room** (**dealing rooms**) A **dealing room** is a place where shares, currencies, or commodities are bought and sold. [BUSINESS] N-COUNT

**deal|ings** /diːlɪŋz/ Someone's **dealings with** a person or organization are the relations that they have with them or the business that they do with them. ❑ *He has learnt little in his dealings with the international community.* N-PLURAL: usu with supp, oft N with n

**deal-maker** (**deal-makers**) also **dealmaker**. A **deal-maker** is someone in business or politics who makes deals. N-COUNT ♦ **deal-making** ❑ *...a chairman with a reputation for deal-making. ...Britain's deal-making culture.* N-UNCOUNT: oft N n

**dealt** /delt/ **Dealt** is the past tense and past participle of **deal**.

**dean** /diːn/ (**deans**) 1 A **dean** is an important official at a university or college. ❑ *She was Dean of the Science faculty at Sophia University.* N-COUNT 2 A **dean** is a priest who is the main administrator of a large church. ❑ *...Alan Webster, former Dean of St Paul's.* N-COUNT

**dear** /dɪəʳ/ (**dearer, dearest, dears**) 1 You use **dear** to describe someone or something that you feel affection for. ❑ *Mrs Cavendish is a dear friend of mine.* ◆◇◇ ADJ: ADJ n 2 If something is **dear to** you or **dear to** your **heart**, you care deeply about it. ❑ *This is a subject very dear to the hearts of academics up and down the country.* ADJ: v-link ADJ to n 3 You use **dear** in expressions such as **'my dear fellow'**, **'dear girl'**, or **'my dear Richard'** when you are addressing someone whom you know and are fond of. You can also ADJ: ADJ n [feelings] use expressions like this in a rude way to indicate that you think you are superior to the person you are addressing. [BRIT] ❑ *Of course, Toby, my dear fellow, of course.* 4 **Dear** is written at the beginning of a letter, followed by the name or title of the person you are writing to. ❑ *Dear Peter, I have been thinking about you so much during the past few days.* 5 In British English, you begin formal letters with '**Dear Sir**' or '**Dear Madam**'. In American English, you begin them with 'Sir' or 'Madam'. [WRITTEN] ❑ *'Dear sir,' she began.* 6 You can call someone **dear** as a sign of affection. ❑ *You're a lot like me, dear.* 7 You can use **dear** in expressions such as '**oh dear**', '**dear me**', and '**dear, dear**' when you are sad, disappointed, or surprised about something. ❑ *'Oh dear, oh dear.' McKinnon sighed. 'You, too.'* 8 If you say that something is **dear**, you mean that it costs a lot of money, usually more than you can afford or more than you think it should cost. [mainly BRIT, INFORMAL] ❑ *CDs here are much dearer than in the States.* 9 If something that someone does **costs** them **dear**, they suffer a lot as a result of it. ❑ *Such complacency is costing the company dear.*

ADJ: ADJ n / CONVENTION / N-VOC [feelings] / EXCLAM [feelings] / ADJ: usu v-link ADJ [disapproval] = expensive ≠ cheap / PHRASE: V inflects

**dear|est** /dɪərɪst/ 1 When you are writing to someone you are very fond of, you can use **dearest** at the beginning of the letter before the person's name or the word you are using to address them. ❑ *Dearest Maria, Aren't I terrible, not coming back like I promised?* 2 **nearest and dearest** → see **near**.

ADJ: ADJ n

**dearie** /dɪəri/ Some people use **dearie** as a friendly way of addressing someone, or as a way of showing that they think they are superior. [BRIT, INFORMAL]

N-VOC [feelings] = dear

**dear|ly** /dɪəʳli/ 1 If you love someone **dearly**, you love them very much. [FORMAL] ❑ *She loved her father dearly.* 2 If you would **dearly** like to do or have something, you would very much like to do it or have it. [FORMAL] ❑ *I would dearly love to marry.* 3 If you **pay dearly for** doing something or if it **costs** you **dearly**, you suffer a lot as a result. [FORMAL] ❑ *He drank too much and is paying dearly for it.*

ADV: ADV with v [emphasis] / ADV: ADV before v [emphasis] / PHRASE: V inflects

**dearth** /dɜːʳθ/ If there is **a dearth of** something, there is not enough of it. ❑ *...the dearth of good fiction by English authors.*

N-SING: usu N *of* n = lack

**death** /deθ/ **(deaths)** 1 **Death** is the permanent end of the life of a person or animal. ❑ *1.5 million people are in immediate danger of death from starvation. ...the thirtieth anniversary of her death... There had been a death in the family... He almost bled to death after a bullet severed an artery.* 2 A particular kind of **death** is a particular way of dying. ❑ *They made sure that he died a horrible death.* 3 **The death of** something is the permanent end of it. ❑ *It meant the death of everything he had ever been or ever hoped to be.*

◆◆◇ N-VAR ≠ birth, life / N-COUNT: with supp / N-SING: usu *the* N *of* n = end

PHRASES 4 If you say that someone is **at death's door**, you mean they are very ill indeed and likely to die. [INFORMAL] ❑ *He told his boss a tale about his mother being at death's door.* 5 If you say that you will **fight to the death** for something, you are emphasizing that you will do anything to achieve or protect it, even if you suffer as a consequence. ❑ *She'd have fought to the death for that child.* 6 If you refer to a fight or contest as **a fight to the death**, you are emphasizing that it will not stop until the death or total victory of one of the opponents. ❑ *He now faces a fight to the death to reach the quarter-finals.* 7 If you say that something is a matter **of life and death**, you are emphasizing that it is extremely important, often because someone may die or suffer great harm if people do not act immediately. ❑ *Well, never mind, John, it's not a matter of life and death.* 8 If someone **is put to death**, they are executed. [FORMAL] ❑ *Those put to death by firing squad included three generals.* 9 You use **to death** after a verb to indicate that a particular action or process results in someone's death. ❑ *He was stabbed to death. ...relief missions to try to keep the country's population from starving to death... He almost bled to death after the bullet severed an artery.* 10 You use **to death** after an adjective or a verb to emphasize the action, state, or feeling mentioned. For example, if you are **frightened to death** or **bored to death**, you are extremely frightened or bored. ❑ *He scares teams to death with his pace and power.*

PHRASE: v-link PHR / PHRASE: V inflects [emphasis] / PHRASE [emphasis] / PHRASE: n *of* PHR, PHR n [emphasis] / PHRASE: V inflects / PHRASE: PHR after v / PHRASE: adj PHR, PHR after v [emphasis]

**death|bed** /deθbed/ **(deathbeds)** If someone is **on** their **deathbed**, they are in a bed and about to die. ❑ *He promised his mother on her deathbed that he would never marry.*

N-COUNT: usu sing, usu with poss, oft *on* N

**death blow** also **death-blow.** If you say that an event or action deals **a death blow to** something such as a plan or hope, or is **a death blow to** something, you mean that it puts an end to it. [JOURNALISM] ❑ *The deportations would be a death blow to the peace process.*

N-SING: oft N *to* n

**death camp** **(death camps)** A **death camp** is a place where prisoners are kept, especially during a war, and where many of them die or are killed.

N-COUNT

**death cer|tifi|cate** **(death certificates)** A **death certificate** is an official certificate signed by a doctor which states the cause of a person's death.

N-COUNT

**death duties** **Death duties** were a tax which had to be paid on the money and property of someone who had died. This tax is now called **inheritance tax**. [BRIT]

N-PLURAL

**death knell** also **death-knell.** If you say that something sounds **the death knell for** a particular person or thing, you mean it will cause that person or thing to fail, end, or cease to exist. ❑ *The tax increase sounded the death knell for the business.*

N-SING: usu *the* N *for/of* n

**death|ly** /deθli/ 1 If you say that someone is **deathly** pale or **deathly** still, you are emphasizing that they are very pale or still, like a dead person. [LITERARY] ❑ *Bernadette turned deathly pale.* 2 If you say that there is a **deathly** silence or a **deathly** hush, you are emphasizing that it is very quiet. [LITERARY] ❑ *A deathly silence hung over the square.*

ADV: ADV adj [emphasis] / ADJ: ADJ n [emphasis]

**death mask** **(death masks)** also **death-mask.** A **death mask** is a model of someone's face, which is made from a mould that was taken of their face soon after they died.

N-COUNT

**death pen|al|ty** **The death penalty** is the punishment of death used in some countries for people who have committed very serious crimes. ❑ *If convicted for murder, both youngsters could face the death penalty.*

N-SING: usu *the* N

**death rate** **(death rates)** The **death rate** is the number of people per thousand who die in a particular area during a particular period of time. ❑ *By the turn of the century, Pittsburgh had the highest death rate in the United States.*

N-COUNT

**death rat|tle** also **death-rattle.** If you say that one thing is the **death rattle** of another, you mean that the first thing is a sign that very soon the second thing will come to an end. [JOURNALISM] ❑ *His rhetoric sounds like the death rattle of a fading leadership.*

N-SING

**death row** /deθ roʊ/ If someone is **on death row**, they are in the part of a prison which contains the cells for criminals who have been sentenced to death. [AM] ❑ *He has been on Death Row for 11 years.*

N-UNCOUNT: oft *on* N

**death sen|tence** **(death sentences)** A **death sentence** is a punishment of death given by a judge to someone who has been found guilty of a serious crime such as murder. ❑ *His original death sentence was commuted to life in prison.*

N-COUNT

**death squad** **(death squads)** **Death squads** are groups of people who operate illegally and carry out the killing of people such as their political opponents or criminals.

N-COUNT

**death taxes** **Death taxes** were a tax which had to be paid on the money and property of

N-PLURAL

someone who had died. This tax is now called **inheritance tax**. [AM]

**death throes** also **death-throes**. 1 The **death throes of** something are its final stages, just before it fails completely or ends. [LITERARY] N-PLURAL: usu with poss 2 If a person or animal is **in** their **death throes**, they are dying and making violent, uncontrolled movements, usually because they are suffering great pain. N-PLURAL: oft *in* poss N

**death toll** **(death tolls)** also **death-toll**. The **death toll** of an accident, disaster, or war is the number of people who die in it. N-COUNT

**death trap** **(death traps)** also **death-trap**. If you say that a place or vehicle is a **death trap**, you mean it is in such bad condition that it might cause someone's death. [INFORMAL] ❑ *Badly-built kit cars can be death traps.* N-COUNT

**death war|rant** **(death warrants)** also **death-warrant**. 1 A **death warrant** is an official document which orders that someone is to be executed as a punishment for a crime. N-COUNT 2 If you say that someone **is signing their own death warrant**, you mean that they are behaving in a way which will cause their ruin or death. ❑ *By accusing the King of murder, he signed his own death warrant.* PHRASE: V inflects

**death wish** also **death-wish**. A **death wish** is a conscious or unconscious desire to die or be killed. N-SING

**deb** /deb/ **(debs)** A **deb** is the same as a **debutante**. N-COUNT

**de|ba|cle** /deɪbɑːkəl, AM dɪb-/ **(debacles)**

✓ in BRIT, also use **débâcle**

A **debacle** is an event or attempt that is a complete failure. ❑ *After the debacle of the war the world was never the same again.* N-COUNT = fiasco

**de|bar** /dɪbɑːʳ, diː-/ **(debars, debarring, debarred)** If you **are debarred from** doing something, you are prevented from doing it by a law or regulation. [FORMAL] ❑ *If found guilty, she could be debarred from politics for seven years.* VERB: usu passive = ban *be* V-ed *from* n/-ing

**de|base** /dɪbeɪs/ **(debases, debasing, debased)** To **debase** something means to reduce its value or quality. [FORMAL] ❑ *Politicians have debased the meaning of the word 'freedom'.* VERB = degrade V n ♦ **de|based** ...*the debased standards of today's media.* ADJ

**de|base|ment** /dɪbeɪsmənt/ **Debasement** is the action of reducing the value or quality of something. [FORMAL] ❑ *...the debasement of popular culture.* N-UNCOUNT: oft N *of* n

**de|bat|able** /dɪbeɪtəbəl/ If you say that something is **debatable**, you mean that it is not certain. ❑ *Whether we can stay in this situation is debatable... It is debatable whether or not antibiotics would make any difference.* ADJ: usu v-link ADJ, oft *it* v-link ADJ wh

**de|bate** /dɪbeɪt/ **(debates, debating, debated)** ◆◆◇ 1 A **debate** is a discussion about a subject on which people have different views. ❑ *An intense debate is going on within the Israeli government... There has been a lot of debate among scholars about this.* N-VAR: oft N *on/over/about* n = discussion 2 A **debate** is a formal discussion, for example in a parliament or institution, in which people express different opinions about a particular subject and then vote on it. ❑ *There are expected to be some heated debates in parliament over the next few days.* N-COUNT: oft N *on/about* n ♦ **de|bat|ing** ...*debating skills.* N-UNCOUNT 3 If people **debate** a topic, they discuss it fairly formally, putting forward different views. You can also say that one person **debates** a topic **with** another person. ❑ *The United Nations Security Council will debate the issue today... Scholars have debated whether or not Yagenta became a convert... He likes to debate issues with his friends.* V-RECIP pl-n V n pl-n V wh V n *with* n 4 If you **debate** whether to do something or what to do, you think or talk about possible courses of action before deciding exactly what you are going to do. ❑ *Taggart debated whether to have yet another double vodka... I debated going back inside, but decided against it.* VERB V wh V -ing 5 If you say that a matter is **open to debate**, you mean that people have different opinions about it, or it has not yet been firmly decided. ❑ *Which of them has more musical talent is open to debate.* PHRASE: v-link PHR

**de|bat|er** /dɪbeɪtəʳ/ **(debaters)** A **debater** is someone who takes part in debates. ❑ *They are skilled debaters.* N-COUNT: oft adj N

**de|bauched** /dɪbɔːtʃt/ If you describe someone as **debauched**, you mean they behave in a way that you think is socially unacceptable, for example because they drink a lot of alcohol or have sex with a lot of people. [OLD-FASHIONED] ❑ *...a debt-ridden and debauched lifestyle.* ADJ [disapproval]

**de|bauch|ery** /dɪbɔːtʃəri/ You use **debauchery** to refer to the drinking of alcohol or to sexual activity if you disapprove of it or regard it as excessive. ❑ *...scenes of drunkenness and debauchery.* N-UNCOUNT [disapproval]

**de|ben|ture** /dɪbentʃəʳ/ **(debentures)** A **debenture** is a type of savings bond which offers a fixed rate of interest over a long period. Debentures are usually issued by a company or a government agency. [BUSINESS] N-COUNT

**de|bili|tate** /dɪbɪlɪteɪt/ **(debilitates, debilitating, debilitated)** 1 If you **are debilitated by** something such as an illness, it causes your body or mind to become gradually weaker. [FORMAL] ❑ *Stewart took over yesterday when Russell was debilitated by a stomach virus.* VERB: usu passive *be* V-ed *by* n ♦ **de|bili|tat|ing** ...*a debilitating illness.* ADJ ♦ **de|bili|tat|ed** *Occasionally a patient is so debilitated that he must be fed intravenously.* ADJ 2 To **debilitate** an organization, society, or government means to gradually make it weaker. [FORMAL] ❑ *...their efforts to debilitate the political will of the Western alliance.* VERB V n ♦ **de|bili|tat|ing** ...*years of debilitating economic crisis.* ADJ ♦ **de|bili|tat|ed** ...*the debilitated ruling party.* ADJ

**de|bil|ity** /dɪbɪlɪti/ **(debilities)** **Debility** is a weakness of a person's body or mind, especially one caused by an illness. [FORMAL] ❑ *...exhaustion or post-viral debility.* N-VAR = infirmity

**deb|it** /debɪt/ **(debits, debiting, debited)** 1 When your bank **debits** your account, money is taken from it and paid to someone else. ❑ *We will always confirm the revised amount to you in writing before debiting your account.* VERB V n 2 A **debit** is a record of the money taken from your bank account, for example when you write a cheque. ❑ *The total of debits must balance the total of credits.* N-COUNT 3 → See also **direct debit**.

**deb|it card** **(debit cards)** A **debit card** is a bank card that you can use to pay for things. When you use it the money is taken out of your bank account immediately. N-COUNT

**debo|nair** /debəneəʳ/ A man who is **debonair** is confident, charming, and well-dressed. ❑ *He was a handsome, debonair, death-defying racing-driver.* ADJ = suave

**de|brief** /diːbriːf/ **(debriefs, debriefing, debriefed)** When someone such as a soldier, diplomat, or astronaut **is debriefed**, they are asked to give a report on an operation or task that they have just completed. ❑ *The men have been debriefed by British and Saudi officials... He went to Rio after the CIA had debriefed him.* VERB *be* V-ed V n

**de|brief|ing** /diːbriːfɪŋ/ **(debriefings)** A **debriefing** is a meeting where someone such as a soldier, diplomat, or astronaut is asked to give a report on an operation or task that they have just completed. ❑ *A debriefing would follow this operation, to determine where it went wrong.* N-VAR

**de|bris** /deɪbri, AM deɪbriː/ **Debris** is pieces from something that has been destroyed or pieces of rubbish or unwanted material that are spread around. ❑ *A number of people were killed by flying debris.* N-UNCOUNT

**debt** /det/ **(debts)** ◆◆◇ 1 A **debt** is a sum of money that you owe someone. ❑ *Three years later, he is still paying off his debts. ...reducing the country's $18 billion foreign debt.* → See also **bad debt**. N-VAR

2 **Debt** is the state of owing money. ❑ *Stress is a main reason for debt.* ● If you are **in debt** or **get into debt**, you owe money. If you are **out of debt** or **get out of debt**, you succeed in paying all the money that you owe. ❑ *He was already deeply in debt through gambling losses... How can I accumulate enough cash to get out of debt?* 3 You use **debt** in expressions such as **I owe you a debt** or **I am in your debt** when you are expressing gratitude for something that someone has done for you. [FORMAL] ❑ *He was so good to me that I can never repay the debt I owe him.* — N-UNCOUNT; PHRASE; N-COUNT: usu sing, oft *in* poss N; feelings

**debt bur|den** **(debt burdens)** A **debt burden** is a large amount of money that one country or organization owes to another and which they find very difficult to repay. ❑ *...the massive debt burden of the Third World.* — N-COUNT

**debt|or** /detəʳ/ **(debtors)** A **debtor** is a country, organization, or person who owes money. ❑ *...the situation of debtor countries.* — N-COUNT: oft N n

**debt-ridden** **Debt-ridden** countries, companies, or people owe extremely large amounts of money. ❑ *...the debt-ridden economies of Latin America.* — ADJ: usu ADJ n

**de|bug** /diːbʌg/ **(debugs, debugging, debugged)** When someone **debugs** a computer program, they look for the faults in it and correct them so that it will run properly. [COMPUTING] ❑ *The production lines ground to a halt for hours while technicians tried to debug software.* — VERB; V n

**de|bunk** /diːbʌŋk/ **(debunks, debunking, debunked)** If you **debunk** a widely held belief, you show that it is false. If you **debunk** something that is widely admired, you show that it is not as good as people think it is. ❑ *Historian Michael Beschloss debunks a few myths.* — VERB; V n

**de|but** /deɪbjuː, AM deɪbjuː/ **(debuts)** The **debut** of a performer or sports player is their first public performance, appearance, or recording. ❑ *Dundee United's Dave Bowman makes his international debut. ...her debut album 'Sugar Time'.* — ◆◇◇ N-COUNT: oft with poss

**debu|tante** /debjʊtɑːnt/ **(debutantes)** A **debutante** is a young woman from the upper classes who has started going to social events with other young people. [OLD-FASHIONED] — N-COUNT

**Dec.** **Dec.** is a written abbreviation for **December**.

**dec|ade** /dekeɪd/ **(decades)** A **decade** is a period of ten years, especially one that begins with a year ending in 0, for example 1980 to 1989. ❑ *...the last decade of the nineteenth century.* — ◆◆◇ N-COUNT

**deca|dent** /dekədənt/ If you say that a person or society is **decadent**, you think that they have low moral standards and are interested mainly in pleasure. ❑ *...the excesses and stresses of their decadent rock 'n' roll lifestyles.* ♦ **deca|dence** *The empire had for years been falling into decadence.* — ADJ; disapproval; N-UNCOUNT

**de|caf** /diːkæf/ **(decafs)** also **decaff. Decaf** is decaffeinated coffee. [INFORMAL] — N-MASS

**de|caf|fein|at|ed** /diːkæfɪneɪtɪd/ **Decaffeinated** coffee has had most of the caffeine removed from it. — ADJ: usu ADJ n

**de|cal** /diːkæl/ **(decals)** **Decals** are pieces of paper with a design on one side. The design can be transferred onto a surface by heating it, soaking it in water, or pressing it hard. [AM] — N-COUNT

✔ in BRIT, use **transfer**

**de|camp** /dɪkæmp/ **(decamps, decamping, decamped)** If you **decamp**, you go away from somewhere secretly or suddenly. ❑ *We all decamped to the pub.* — VERB; V

**de|cant** /dɪkænt/ **(decants, decanting, decanted)** If you **decant** a liquid **into** another container, you put it into another container. [FORMAL] ❑ *She always used to decant the milk into a jug.* — VERB; V n *into* n

**de|cant|er** /dɪkæntəʳ/ **(decanters)** A **decanter** is a glass container that you use for serving wine, sherry, or port. — N-COUNT

**de|capi|tate** /dɪkæpɪteɪt/ **(decapitates, decapitating, decapitated)** If someone **is decapitated**, their head is cut off. [FORMAL] ❑ *A worker was decapitated when a lift plummeted down the shaft on top of him.* ♦ **de|capi|ta|tion** /dɪkæpɪteɪʃən/ **(decapitations)** *...executions by decapitation.* — VERB; *be* V-ed; N-VAR

**de|cath|lon** /dɪkæθlɒn/ **(decathlons)** The **decathlon** is a competition in which athletes compete in 10 different sporting events. — N-COUNT: oft *the* N

**de|cay** /dɪkeɪ/ **(decays, decaying, decayed)** 1 When something such as a dead body, a dead plant, or a tooth **decays**, it is gradually destroyed by a natural process. ❑ *The bodies buried in the fine ash slowly decayed... The ground was scattered with decaying leaves.* ♦ **Decay** is also a noun. ❑ *When not removed, plaque causes tooth decay and gum disease.* ♦ **de|cayed** *...decayed teeth.* 2 If something such as a society, system, or institution **decays**, it gradually becomes weaker or its condition gets worse. ❑ *Popular cinema seems to have decayed.* ♦ **Decay** is also a noun. ❑ *There are problems of urban decay and gang violence.* — VERB = rot; V; V-ing; N-UNCOUNT; ADJ; VERB; V; N-UNCOUNT

**de|ceased** /dɪsiːst/ **(deceased)** 1 **The deceased** is used to refer to a particular person or to particular people who have recently died. [LEGAL] ❑ *The identities of the deceased have now been determined.* 2 A **deceased** person is one who has recently died. [FORMAL] ❑ *...his recently deceased mother.* — N-COUNT: *the* N; ADJ

**de|ceit** /dɪsiːt/ **(deceits)** **Deceit** is behaviour that is deliberately intended to make people believe something which is not true. ❑ *They have been involved in a campaign of deceit.* — N-VAR = deception

**de|ceit|ful** /dɪsiːtfʊl/ If you say that someone is **deceitful**, you mean that they behave in a dishonest way by making other people believe something that is not true. ❑ *The ambassador called the report deceitful and misleading.* — ADJ

**de|ceive** /dɪsiːv/ **(deceives, deceiving, deceived)** 1 If you **deceive** someone, you make them believe something that is not true, usually in order to get some advantage for yourself. ❑ *He has deceived and disillusioned us all... If you can make the last 10 seconds exciting, you can deceive your audience into thinking it's been like that all along.* 2 If you **deceive yourself**, you do not admit to yourself something that you know is true. ❑ *Alcoholics are notorious for their ability to deceive themselves about the extent of their problem.* 3 If something **deceives** you, it gives you a wrong impression and makes you believe something that is not true. ❑ *His gentle, kindly appearance did not deceive me.* — VERB; V n; V n *into* -ing; VERB; V pron-refl; VERB = mislead; V n

**de|cel|er|ate** /diːseləreɪt/ **(decelerates, decelerating, decelerated)** 1 When a vehicle or machine **decelerates** or when someone in a vehicle **decelerates**, the speed of the vehicle or machine is reduced. ❑ *...the sensation of the train decelerating.* ♦ **de|cel|era|tion** /diːseləreɪʃən/ *The harder the brake pedal is pressed, the greater the car's deceleration.* 2 When the rate of something such as inflation or economic growth **decelerates**, it slows down. *Inflation has decelerated remarkably over the past two years.* ♦ **de|cel|era|tion** *...a significant deceleration in the annual rate of growth.* — VERB ≠ accelerate; V; N-UNCOUNT ≠ acceleration; VERB ≠ accelerate; V; N-UNCOUNT ≠ acceleration

**De|cem|ber** /dɪsembəʳ/ **(Decembers)** **December** is the twelfth and last month of the year in the Western calendar. ❑ *...a bright morning in mid-December... Her baby was born on 4th December.* — N-VAR

**de|cen|cy** /diːsənsi/ 1 **Decency** is the quality of following accepted moral standards. ❑ *His sense of decency forced him to resign.* 2 If you say that someone **did not have the decency to** do something, you are criticizing them because there was a particular action which they did not do but which you believe they ought to have done. ❑ *Nobody had the decency to inform me of what was planned.* — N-UNCOUNT; PHRASE: oft with brd-neg, V inflects, PHR to-inf; disapproval

**de|cent** /diːsənt/ 1 **Decent** is used to describe something which is considered to be of an acceptable standard or quality. ❑ *Nearby is a village* — ADJ: usu ADJ n = reasonable *with a decent pub.* ♦ **de|cent|ly** *The allies say they will treat their prisoners decently.* ADV: ADV with v, also ADV adj [2] **Decent** is used to describe something which is morally correct or acceptable. ❑ *But, after a decent interval, trade relations began to return to normal.* ♦ **de|cent|ly** *And can't you dress more decently – people will think you're a tramp.* ADJ: usu ADJ n; ADV: usu ADV with v, also ADV adj [3] **Decent** people are honest and behave in a way that most people approve of. ❑ *The majority of people around here are decent people.* ADJ: usu ADJ n

**de|cen|tral|ize** /diːsentrəlaɪz/ **(decentralizes, decentralizing, decentralized)**

✓ in BRIT, also use **decentralise**

To **decentralize** government or a large organization means to move some departments away from the main administrative area, or to give more power to local departments. VERB ❑ *They have decentralised the company and made it less bureaucratic.* V n *...the need to decentralize and devolve power to regional governments.* V ♦ **de|cen|trali|za|tion** /diːsentrəlaɪzeɪʃən/ *...increased decentralisation and greater powers for regional authorities.* N-UNCOUNT

**de|cep|tion** /dɪsepʃən/ **(deceptions)** **Deception** is the act of deceiving someone or the state of being deceived by someone. ❑ *He admitted conspiring to obtain property by deception.* N-VAR

**de|cep|tive** /dɪseptɪv/ If something is **deceptive**, it encourages you to believe something which is not true. ❑ *Appearances can be deceptive.* ADJ = *misleading* ♦ **de|cep|tive|ly** *The storyline is deceptively simple.* ADV

**deci|bel** /desɪbel/ **(decibels)** A **decibel** is a unit of measurement which is used to indicate how loud a sound is. ❑ *Continuous exposure to sound above 80 decibels could be harmful.* N-COUNT: oft num N

**de|cide** /dɪsaɪd/ **(decides, deciding, decided)** ♦♦♦ [1] If you **decide** to do something, you choose to do it, usually after you have thought carefully about the other possibilities. VERB ❑ *She decided to do a secretarial course...* V to-inf *He has decided that he doesn't want to embarrass the movement and will therefore step down...* V that *The house needed totally rebuilding, so we decided against buying it...* V *against/in favour of* n/-ing *I had a cold and couldn't decide whether to go to work or not...* V wh *Think about it very carefully before you decide.* V [2] If a person or group of people **decides** something, they choose what something should be like or how a particular problem should be solved. VERB ❑ *She was still young, he said, and that would be taken into account when deciding her sentence.* V n [3] If an event or fact **decides** something, it makes it certain that a particular choice will be made or that there will be a particular result. VERB ❑ *The goal that decided the match came just before the interval...* V n *The results will decide if he will win a place at a good university...* V wh *Luck is certainly one deciding factor.* V-ing [4] If you **decide** that something is true, you form that opinion about it after considering the facts. VERB ❑ *He decided Franklin must be suffering from a bad cold...* V that *I couldn't decide whether he was incredibly brave or just insane.* V wh [5] If something **decides** you to do something, it is the reason that causes you to choose to do it. VERB ❑ *The banning of his play decided him to write about censorship...* V n to-inf *I don't know what finally decided her, but she agreed.* V n Also V n that

♦ **decide on** If you **decide on** something or **decide upon** something, you choose it from two or more possibilities. PHRASAL VERB ❑ *After leaving university, Therese decided on a career in publishing.* V P n

**de|cid|ed** /dɪsaɪdɪd/ **Decided** means clear and definite. ❑ *Her ignorance of the area put her at a decided disadvantage.* ADJ: ADJ n = *definite*

**de|cid|ed|ly** /dɪsaɪdɪdli/ **Decidedly** means to a great extent and in a way that is very obvious. ❑ *Sometimes he is decidedly uncomfortable at what he sees on the screen.* ADV: ADV group

**de|cid|er** /dɪsaɪdəʳ/ **(deciders)** [1] In sport, a **decider** is one of the games in a series, which establishes which player or team wins the series. N-COUNT [BRIT, JOURNALISM] ❑ *He won the decider which completed England's 3-2 victory over Austria.* [2] In games such as football and hockey, **the decider** is the last goal to be scored in a match that is won by a difference of only one goal. N-COUNT [BRIT, JOURNALISM] ❑ *McGrath scored the decider in Villa's 2-1 home win over Forest.*

**de|cidu|ous** /dɪsɪdʒuəs/ A **deciduous** tree or bush is one that loses its leaves in the autumn every year. ADJ: usu ADJ n ≠*evergreen*

**deci|mal** /desɪməl/ **(decimals)** [1] A **decimal** system involves counting in units of ten. ADJ: ADJ n ❑ *...the decimal system of metric weights and measures.* [2] A **decimal** is a fraction that is written in the form of a dot followed by one or more numbers which represent tenths, hundredths, and so on: for example .5, .51, .517. N-COUNT ❑ *...simple math concepts, such as decimals and fractions.*

**deci|mal point** **(decimal points)** A **decimal point** is the dot in front of a decimal fraction. N-COUNT

**deci|mate** /desɪmeɪt/ **(decimates, decimating, decimated)** [1] To **decimate** something such as a group of people or animals means to destroy a very large number of them. VERB ❑ *The pollution could decimate the river's thriving population of kingfishers.* V n [2] To **decimate** a system or organization means to reduce its size and effectiveness greatly. VERB ❑ *...a recession which decimated the nation's manufacturing industry.* V n

**de|ci|pher** /dɪsaɪfəʳ/ **(deciphers, deciphering, deciphered)** If you **decipher** a piece of writing or a message, you work out what it says, even though it is very difficult to read or understand. VERB ❑ *I'm still no closer to deciphering the code.* V n

**de|ci|sion** /dɪsɪʒən/ **(decisions)** ♦♦♦ [1] When you make a **decision**, you choose what should be done or which is the best of various possible actions. N-COUNT: oft N to-inf, N *on* n/wh ❑ *A decision was taken to discipline Marshall... I don't want to make the wrong decision and regret it later.* [2] **Decision** is the act of deciding something or the need to decide something. N-UNCOUNT ❑ *The moment of decision cannot be delayed.* [3] **Decision** is the ability to decide quickly and definitely what to do. N-UNCOUNT = *decisiveness* ❑ *He is very much a man of decision and action.*

**decision-making** **Decision-making** is the process of reaching decisions, especially in a large organization or in government. N-UNCOUNT

**de|ci|sive** /dɪsaɪsɪv/ [1] If a fact, action, or event is **decisive**, it makes it certain that there will be a particular result. ADJ ❑ *...his decisive victory in the presidential elections.* ♦ **de|ci|sive|ly** *The plan was decisively rejected by Congress three weeks ago.* ADV: usu ADV with v [2] If someone is **decisive**, they have or show an ability to make quick decisions in a difficult or complicated situation. ADJ ❑ *He should give way to a younger, more decisive leader.* ♦ **de|ci|sive|ly** *'I'll call for you at half ten,' she said decisively.* ADV ♦ **de|ci|sive|ness** *His supporters admire his decisiveness.* N-UNCOUNT

**deck** /dek/ **(decks, decking, decked)** ♦◇◇ [1] A **deck** on a vehicle such as a bus or ship is a lower or upper area of it. N-COUNT: oft supp N ❑ *...a luxury liner with five passenger decks.* → See also **flight deck**. [2] The **deck** of a ship is the top part of it that forms a floor in the open air which you can walk on. N-COUNT: also *on* N ❑ *She stood on the deck and waved.* [3] A tape **deck** or record **deck** is a piece of equipment on which you play tapes or records. N-COUNT: oft n N ❑ *I stuck a tape in the deck.* [4] A **deck** of cards is a complete set of playing cards. N-COUNT [AM] ❑ *Matt picked up the cards and shuffled the deck.*

✓ in BRIT, usually use **pack**

[5] A **deck** is a flat wooden area next to a house, where people can sit and relax or eat. N-COUNT ❑ *A natural timber deck leads into the main room of the home.* [6] If something **is decked with** pretty things, it is decorated with them. VERB [WRITTEN] ❑ *Villagers decked the streets with bunting...* V n *with* n *The house was decked with flowers.* V-ed [7] If you **clear the decks**, you get ready to start something new by finishing any work that has to be done or getting rid of any problems that PHRASE: V inflects

are in the way. ❑ *Clear the decks before you think of taking on any more responsibilities.*

♦ **deck out** If a person or thing **is decked out with** or **in** something, they are decorated with it or wearing it, usually for a special occasion. ❑ *The cab was decked out with multi-coloured lights... She had decked him out from head to foot in expensive clothes.* PHRASAL VERB be V-ed P V n P Also V P n (not pron)

**deck|chair** /de̲ktʃeəʳ/ **(deckchairs)** also **deck chair.** A **deckchair** is a simple chair with a folding frame, and a piece of canvas as the seat and back. Deckchairs are usually used on the beach, on a ship, or in the garden. N-COUNT

**-decker** /-de̲kəʳ/ **-decker** is used after adjectives like 'double' and 'single' to indicate how many levels or layers something has. ❑ *...a red double-decker bus full of tourists. ...a triple-decker peanut butter and jelly sandwich.* COMB in ADJ: ADJ n

**deck|hand** /de̲khænd/ **(deckhands)** A **deckhand** is a person who does the cleaning and other work on the deck of a ship. N-COUNT

**deck shoe** **(deck shoes)** **Deck shoes** are flat casual shoes made of canvas or leather. N-COUNT

**de|claim** /dɪkle̲ɪm/ **(declaims, declaiming, declaimed)** If you **declaim**, you speak dramatically, as if you were acting in a theatre. [WRITTEN] ❑ *He raised his fist and declaimed: 'Liar and cheat!'... He used to declaim French verse to us.* VERB V with quote V n Also V, V that

**de|clama|tory** /dɪklæ̲mətri, AM -tɔːri/ A **declamatory** phrase, statement, or way of speaking is dramatic and confident. [FORMAL] ADJ

**dec|la|ra|tion** /de̲kləre̲ɪʃᵊn/ **(declarations)** ◆◇◇ [1] A **declaration** is an official announcement or statement. ❑ *They will sign the declaration tomorrow... The opening speeches sounded more like declarations of war than offerings of peace.* [2] A **declaration** is a firm, emphatic statement which shows that you have no doubts about what you are saying. ❑ *...declarations of undying love.* [3] A **declaration** is a written statement about something which you have signed and which can be used as evidence in a court of law. ❑ *On the customs declaration, the sender labeled the freight as agricultural machinery.* N-COUNT: oft N *of* n; N-COUNT; N-COUNT

**de|clare** /dɪkle̲əʳ/ **(declares, declaring, declared)** ◆◆◇ [1] If you **declare** that something is true, you say that it is true in a firm, deliberate way. You can also **declare** an attitude or intention. [WRITTEN] ❑ *Speaking outside Ten Downing Street, she declared that she would fight on... 'I'm absolutely thrilled to have done what I've done,' he declared... He declared his intention to become the best golfer in the world.* [2] If you **declare** something, you state officially and formally that it exists or is the case. ❑ *The government is ready to declare a permanent ceasefire... His lawyers are confident that the judges will declare Mr Stevens innocent... The U.N. has declared it to be a safe zone... You may have to declare that you have had an HIV test.* [3] If you **declare** goods that you have bought in another country or money that you have earned, you say how much you have bought or earned so that you can pay tax on it. ❑ *Your income must be declared on this form.* VERB = announce; V that; V with quote; V n; VERB; V n; V n adj; V n to-inf; V that; VERB; V n

**de|clas|si|fy** /diːklæ̲sɪfaɪ/ **(declassifies, declassifying, declassified)** If secret documents or records **are declassified**, it is officially stated that they are no longer secret. ❑ *These reports were only declassified last year.* VERB: usu passive be V-ed

**de|cline** /dɪkla̲ɪn/ **(declines, declining, declined)** ◆◆◇ [1] If something **declines**, it becomes less in quantity, importance, or strength. ❑ *The number of staff has declined from 217,000 to 114,000... Hourly output by workers declined 1.3% in the first quarter... Union membership and union power are declining fast. ...a declining birth rate.* [2] If you **decline** something or **decline to** do something, you politely refuse to accept it or do it. [FORMAL] ❑ *He declined their invitation... The band declined to comment on the story... He offered the boys some coffee. They declined politely.* [3] If there is a **decline in** something, it becomes less in quantity, importance, or quality. ❑ *There wasn't such a big decline in enrollments after all... The first signs of economic decline became visible.* VERB V from/to/by amount; V amount; V; V-ing; VERB V n; V to-inf; V; N-VAR: oft N with poss, N *in* n

**PHRASES** [4] If something is **in decline** or **on the decline**, it is gradually decreasing in importance, quality, or power. ❑ *Thankfully the smoking of cigarettes is on the decline.* [5] If something **goes** or **falls into decline**, it begins to gradually decrease in importance, quality, or power. ❑ *Libraries are an investment for the future and they should not be allowed to fall into decline.* PHRASE: v-link PHR; PHRASE

**de|code** /diːko̲ʊd/ **(decodes, decoding, decoded)** [1] If you **decode** a message that has been written or spoken in a code, you change it into ordinary language. ❑ *All he had to do was decode it and pass it over.* [2] A device that **decodes** a broadcast signal changes it into a form that can be displayed on a television screen. ❑ *About 60,000 subscribers have special adapters to receive and decode the signals.* VERB = decipher ≠ encode V n; VERB V n

**de|cod|er** /diːko̲ʊdəʳ/ **(decoders)** A **decoder** is a device used to decode messages or signals sent in code, for example the television signals from a satellite. N-COUNT

**de|colo|niza|tion** /diːkɒ̲lənaɪze̲ɪʃᵊn/

✔ in BRIT, also use **decolonisation**

**Decolonization** means giving political independence to a country that was previously a colony. N-UNCOUNT ≠ colonization

**de|com|mis|sion** /diːkəmɪ̲ʃᵊn/ **(decommissions, decommissioning, decommissioned)** When something such as a nuclear reactor or a large machine **is decommissioned**, it is taken to pieces because it is no longer going to be used. ❑ *HMS Warspite was decommissioned as part of defence cuts.* VERB be V-ed

**de|com|pose** /diːkəmpo̲ʊz/ **(decomposes, decomposing, decomposed)** When things such as dead plants or animals **decompose**, or when something **decomposes** them, they change chemically and begin to decay. ❑ *...a dead body found decomposing in a wood... The debris slowly decomposes into compost... The fertiliser releases nutrients gradually as bacteria decompose it.* VERB = rot, decay; V; V into n; V n

♦ **de|com|posed** *The body was too badly decomposed to be identified at once.* ADJ

**de|com|po|si|tion** /diːkɒmpəzɪ̲ʃᵊn/ **Decomposition** is the process of decay that takes place when a living thing changes chemically after dying. [FORMAL] N-UNCOUNT

**de|com|pres|sion** /diːkəmpre̲ʃᵊn/ [1] **Decompression** is the reduction of the force on something that is caused by the weight of the air. ❑ *Decompression blew out a window in the plane.* [2] **Decompression** is the process of bringing someone back to the normal pressure of the air after they have been deep underwater. ❑ *...a decompression chamber.* N-UNCOUNT; N-UNCOUNT: usu N n

**de|con|gest|ant** /diːkəndʒe̲stənt/ **(decongestants)** A **decongestant** is a medicine which helps someone who has a cold to breathe more easily. N-MASS

**de|con|struct** /diːkənstrʌ̲kt/ **(deconstructs, deconstructing, deconstructed)** In philosophy and literary criticism, to **deconstruct** an idea or text means to show the contradictions in its meaning, and to show how it does not fully explain what it claims to explain. [TECHNICAL] ❑ *She sets up a rigorous intellectual framework to deconstruct various categories of film.* VERB V n

♦ **de|con|struc|tion** /diːkənstrʌ̲kʃᵊn/ *...the deconstruction of the macho psyche.* N-UNCOUNT

**de|con|tami|nate** /diːkəntæ̲mɪneɪt/ **(decontaminates, decontaminating, decontaminated)** To **decontaminate** something means to remove all germs or dangerous substances from it. ❑ *...procedures for decontaminating pilots hit by chemical weapons.* VERB V n

♦ **de|con|tami|na|tion** /diːkəntæmɪ- N-UNCOUNT

neɪʃᵊn/ *The land will require public money for decontamination.*

**de|con|trol** /diːkəntroʊl/ **(decontrols, decontrolling, decontrolled)** When governments **decontrol** an activity, they remove controls from it so that companies or organizations have more freedom. [mainly AM] ❑ *The Russian government chose not to decontrol oil and gas prices last January.* ♦ **Decontrol** is also a noun. ❑ *...continuing decontrol of banking institutions.*
VERB = deregulate; V n; N-VAR: oft n N, N *of* n

**de|cor** /deɪkɔːʳ, AM deɪkɔːr/ The **decor** of a house or room is its style of furnishing and decoration. ❑ *The decor is simple – black lacquer panels on white walls.*
N-UNCOUNT

**deco|rate** /dekəreɪt/ **(decorates, decorating, decorated)** ◆◇◇ [1] If you **decorate** something, you make it more attractive by adding things to it. ❑ *He decorated his room with pictures of all his favorite sports figures... Use shells to decorate boxes, trays, mirrors or even pots.* [2] If you **decorate** a room or the inside of a building, you put new paint or wallpaper on the walls and ceiling, and paint the woodwork. ❑ *When they came to decorate the rear bedroom, it was Jemma who had the final say... The boys are planning to decorate when they get the time... I had the flat decorated quickly so that Philippa could move in.* ♦ **deco|rat|ing** *I did a lot of the decorating myself.* ♦ **deco|ra|tion** *The renovation process and decoration took four months.* [3] If someone **is decorated**, they are given a medal or other honour as an official reward for something that they have done. ❑ *He was decorated for bravery in battle.*
VERB; V n *with* n; V n; VERB; V n; V; *have* n V-ed; N-UNCOUNT; N-UNCOUNT; VERB: usu passive; *be* V-ed

**deco|ra|tion** /dekəreɪʃᵊn/ **(decorations)** [1] The **decoration** of a room is its furniture, wallpaper, and ornaments. ❑ *The decoration and furnishings had to be practical enough for a family home.* [2] **Decorations** are features that are added to something in order to make it look more attractive. ❑ *The only wall decorations are candles and a single mirror.* [3] **Decorations** are brightly coloured objects such as pieces of paper and balloons, which you put up in a room on special occasions to make it look more attractive. ❑ *Festive paper decorations had been hung from the ceiling.* [4] A **decoration** is an official title or honour which is given to someone, usually in the form of a medal, as a reward for military bravery or public service. ❑ *He was awarded several military decorations.* [5] → See also **decorate**.
N-UNCOUNT: oft with poss = decor; N-VAR; N-COUNT: usu pl; N-COUNT

**deco|ra|tive** /dekərətɪv/ Something that is **decorative** is intended to look pretty or attractive. ❑ *The curtains are for purely decorative purposes and do not open or close.*
ADJ

**deco|ra|tor** /dekəreɪtəʳ/ **(decorators)** [1] A **decorator** is a person whose job is to paint houses or put wallpaper up. [BRIT] [2] A **decorator** is a person who is employed to design and decorate the inside of people's houses. [AM]
N-COUNT; N-COUNT

✔ in BRIT, use **interior decorator**

**deco|rous** /dekərəs/ **Decorous** behaviour is very respectable, calm, and polite. [FORMAL] ♦ **deco|rous|ly** ❑ *He sipped his drink decorously.*
ADJ = seemly, proper; ADV

**de|co|rum** /dɪkɔːrəm/ **Decorum** is behaviour that people consider to be correct, polite, and respectable. [FORMAL] ❑ *I was treated with decorum and respect throughout the investigation.*
N-UNCOUNT = politeness

**de|cou|ple** /diːkʌpᵊl/ **(decouples, decoupling, decoupled)** If two countries, organizations, or ideas that were connected in some way **are decoupled**, the connection between them is ended. [FORMAL] ❑ *...a conception which decouples culture and politics... The issue threatened to decouple Europe from the United States.*
VERB; V pl-n; V n *from* n

**de|coy** /diːkɔɪ/ **(decoys)** If you refer to something or someone as a **decoy**, you mean that they are intended to attract people's attention and deceive them, for example by leading them into a trap or away from a particular place. ❑ *He was booked on a flight leaving that day, but that was just a decoy.*
N-COUNT

**de|crease** **(decreases, decreasing, decreased)**

✔ The verb is pronounced /dɪkriːs/. The noun is pronounced /diːkriːs/.

[1] When something **decreases** or when you **decrease** it, it becomes less in quantity, size, or intensity. ❑ *Population growth is decreasing by 1.4% each year... The number of independent firms decreased from 198 to 96... Raw-steel production by the nation's mills decreased 2.1% last week... Since 1945 air forces have decreased in size... Gradually decrease the amount of vitamin C you are taking... We've got stable labor, decreasing interest rates, low oil prices.* [2] A **decrease in** the quantity, size, or intensity of something is a reduction in it. ❑ *...a decrease in the number of young people out of work... Bank base rates have fallen from 10 per cent to 6 per cent – a decrease of 40 per cent.*
VERB; V *by* amount; V *from/to* amount; V amount; V *in* n; V n; V-ing; N-COUNT: oft N *in/of* n

**de|cree** /dɪkriː/ **(decrees, decreeing, decreed)** [1] A **decree** is an official order or decision, especially one made by the ruler of a country. ❑ *In July he issued a decree ordering all unofficial armed groups in the country to disband.* [2] If someone in authority **decrees** that something must happen, they decide or state this officially. ❑ *The UN Security Council has decreed that the election must be held by May... The king decreed a general amnesty.* [3] A **decree** is a judgment made by a law court. [mainly AM] ❑ *...court decrees.*
N-COUNT: also *by* N = order; VERB = order; V that; V n; N-COUNT

**de|cree ab|so|lute** **(decrees absolute)** A **decree absolute** is the final order made by a court in a divorce case which ends a marriage completely.
N-COUNT: usu sing

**de|cree nisi** /dɪkriː naɪsaɪ/ **(decrees nisi)** A **decree nisi** is an order made by a court which states that a divorce must take place at a certain time in the future unless a good reason is produced to prevent this.
N-COUNT: usu sing

**de|crep|it** /dɪkrepɪt/ Something that is **decrepit** is old and in bad condition. Someone who is **decrepit** is old and weak. ❑ *The film had been shot in a decrepit old police station.*
ADJ

**de|crepi|tude** /dɪkrepɪtjuːd, AM -tuːd/ **Decrepitude** is the state of being very old and in poor condition. [FORMAL] ❑ *The building had a general air of decrepitude and neglect.*
N-UNCOUNT

**de|crimi|nal|ize** /diːkrɪmɪnəlaɪz/ **(decriminalizes, decriminalizing, decriminalized)**

✔ in BRIT, also use **decriminalise**

When a criminal offence **is decriminalized**, the law changes so that it is no longer a criminal offence. ❑ *...the question of whether prostitution should be decriminalized.* ♦ **de|crimi|nali|za|tion** /diːkrɪmɪnəlaɪzeɪʃᵊn/ *...the decriminalisation of homosexuality in the Isle of Man.*
VERB; *be* V-ed; Also V n; N-UNCOUNT: oft N *of* n

**de|cry** /dɪkraɪ/ **(decries, decrying, decried)** If someone **decries** an idea or action, they criticize it strongly. [FORMAL] ❑ *He is impatient with those who decry the scheme... People decried the campaign as a waste of money.*
VERB = denounce; V n; V n *as* n

**dedi|cate** /dedɪkeɪt/ **(dedicates, dedicating, dedicated)** [1] If you say that someone **has dedicated** themselves **to** something, you approve of the fact that they have decided to give a lot of time and effort to it because they think that it is important. ❑ *Back on the island, he dedicated himself to politics... Bessie has dedicated her life to caring for others.* ♦ **dedi|cat|ed** *He's quite dedicated to his students.* ♦ **dedi|ca|tion** *We admire her dedication to the cause of humanity.* [2] If someone **dedicates** something such as a book, play, or piece of music **to** you, they mention your name, for example in the front of a book or when a piece of music is performed, as a way of showing affection or respect for you. ❑ *She dedicated her first album to Woody Allen.*
VERB [approval] = devote; V pron-refl *to* n/-ing; V n *to* n/-ing; ADJ: oft ADJ *to* n; N-UNCOUNT: oft N *to* n; VERB; V n *to* n

**dedi|cat|ed** /dedɪkeɪtɪd/ [1] You use **dedicated** to describe someone who enjoys a particu-
ADJ: usu ADJ n

lar activity very much and spends a lot of time doing it. ❑ *Her great-grandfather had clearly been a dedicated and stoical traveller.* [2] You use **dedicated** to describe something that is made, built, or designed for one particular purpose or thing. ❑ *Such areas should also be served by dedicated cycle routes. ...the world's first museum dedicated to ecology.* [3] → See also **dedicate**.
ADJ: oft ADJ *to* n

**dedi|ca|tion** /dedɪkeɪʃᵊn/ **(dedications)** A **dedication** is a message which is written at the beginning of a book, or a short announcement which is sometimes made before a play or piece of music is performed, as a sign of affection or respect for someone. → See also **dedicate**.
N-COUNT

**de|duce** /dɪdjuːs, AM -duːs/ **(deduces, deducing, deduced)** If you **deduce** something or **deduce** that something is true, you reach that conclusion because of other things that you know to be true. ❑ *Alison had cleverly deduced that I was the author of the letter... The date of the document can be deduced from references to the Civil War... She hoped he hadn't deduced the reason for her visit.*
VERB; V that; *be* V-ed *from* n; V n

**de|duct** /dɪdʌkt/ **(deducts, deducting, deducted)** When you **deduct** an amount from a total, you subtract it from the total. ❑ *The company deducted this payment from his compensation.*
VERB; V n *from* n; Also V n

**de|duc|tion** /dɪdʌkʃᵊn/ **(deductions)** [1] A **deduction** is a conclusion that you have reached about something because of other things that you know to be true. ❑ *It was a pretty astute deduction.*
N-COUNT: oft N *about* n

[2] **Deduction** is the process of reaching a conclusion about something because of other things that you know to be true. ❑ *...a case that tested his powers of deduction.*
N-UNCOUNT

[3] A **deduction** is an amount that has been subtracted from a total. ❑ *...your gross income (before tax and National Insurance deductions).*
N-COUNT

[4] **Deduction** is the act or process of subtracting an amount of money from a total amount. ❑ *After the deduction of tax at 20 per cent, the interest rate will be 6.2 per cent.*
N-UNCOUNT

**de|duc|tive** /dɪdʌktɪv/ **Deductive** reasoning involves drawing conclusions logically from other things that are already known. [FORMAL]
ADJ: usu ADJ n

**deed** /diːd/ **(deeds)** [1] A **deed** is something that is done, especially something that is very good or very bad. [LITERARY] ❑ *...the warm feeling one gets from doing a good deed.*
N-COUNT = act

[2] A **deed** is a document containing the terms of an agreement, especially an agreement concerning the ownership of land or a building. [LEGAL] ❑ *He asked if I had the deeds to his father's property.*
N-COUNT

**deed poll** In Britain, if you change your name **by deed poll**, you change it officially and legally.
PHRASE: PHR after v

**deem** /diːm/ **(deems, deeming, deemed)** If something **is deemed to** have a particular quality or **to** do a particular thing, it is considered to have that quality or do that thing. [FORMAL] ❑ *French and German were deemed essential... He says he would support the use of force if the UN deemed it necessary... I was deemed to be a competent shorthand typist.*
VERB = judge; *be* V-ed adj/n; V n adj/n; *be* V-ed to-inf

**deep** /diːp/ **(deeper, deepest)** ◆◆◇ [1] If something is **deep**, it extends a long way down from the ground or from the top surface of something. ❑ *The water is very deep and mysterious-looking... Den had dug a deep hole in the centre of the garden... Kelly swore quietly, looking at the deep cut on his left hand. ...a deep ravine.* ♦ **Deep** is also an adverb. ❑ *Deep in the earth's crust the rock may be subjected to temperatures high enough to melt it... Gingerly, she put her hand in deeper, to the bottom.* ♦ **deep|ly** *There isn't time to dig deeply and put in manure or compost.*
ADJ ≠ shallow; ADV: ADV prep/adv, ADV after v; ADV: ADV after v, ADV adj/-ed

[2] A **deep** container, such as a cupboard, extends or measures a long distance from front to back. ❑ *The wardrobe was very deep.*
ADJ

[3] You use **deep** to talk or ask about how much something measures from the surface to the bottom, or from front to back. ❑ *I found myself in water only three feet deep... The mud is ankle deep around Shush Square... How deep did the snow get?* ♦ **Deep** is also a combining form. ❑ *...an inch-deep stab wound.*
ADJ: amount ADJ, n ADJ, *how* ADJ, *as* ADJ *as*, ADJ-compar *than*; COMB in ADJ

[4] **Deep** in an area means a long way inside it. ❑ *They were now deep inside rebel territory.*
ADV: ADV prep/adv, ADV after v

[5] If you say that things or people are **two**, **three**, or **four deep**, you mean that there are two, three, or four rows or layers of them there. ❑ *A crowd three deep seemed paralysed by the images on these monitors.*
ADV: num ADV

[6] You use **deep** to emphasize the seriousness, strength, importance, or degree of something. ❑ *I had a deep admiration for Sartre... He wants to express his deep sympathy to the family.* ♦ **deep|ly** *Our meetings and conversations left me deeply depressed.*
ADJ: usu ADJ n [emphasis] = profound; ADV = profoundly

[7] If you experience or feel something **deep inside** you or **deep down**, you feel it very strongly even though you do not necessarily show it. ❑ *Deep down, she supported her husband's involvement in the organization.*
ADV: ADV prep/adv, ADV with cl

[8] If you are in a **deep** sleep, you are sleeping peacefully and it is difficult to wake you. ❑ *Una soon fell into a deep sleep.* ♦ **deep|ly** *She slept deeply but woke early.*
ADJ: ADJ n ≠ light; ADV: ADV after v

[9] If you are **deep in** thought or **deep in** conversation, you are concentrating very hard on what you are thinking or saying and are not aware of the things that are happening around you. ❑ *Abby had been so deep in thought that she had walked past her aunt's car without even seeing it.*
ADJ: v-link ADJ *in* n

[10] A **deep** breath or sigh uses or fills the whole of your lungs. ❑ *Cal took a long, deep breath, struggling to control his own emotions.* ♦ **deep|ly** *She sighed deeply and covered her face with her hands.*
ADJ: ADJ n; ADV: ADV after v

[11] You use **deep** to describe colours that are strong and fairly dark. ❑ *The sky was deep blue and starry.* ♦ **Deep** is also an adjective. [12] A **deep** ❑ *...deep colours.* sound is low in pitch. ❑ *His voice was deep and mellow... They heard a deep, distant roar.*
COMB in COLOUR; ADJ: usu ADJ n ≠ pale; ADJ ≠ high

[13] If you describe someone as **deep**, you mean that they are quiet and reserved in a way that makes you think that they have good qualities such as intelligence or determination. ❑ *James is a very deep individual.*
ADJ ≠ shallow

[14] If you describe something such as a problem or a piece of writing as **deep**, you mean that it is important, serious, or complicated. ❑ *They're written as adventure stories. They're not intended to be deep.*
ADJ

[15] If you are **deep in** debt, you have a lot of debts. ❑ *He is so deep in debt and desperate for money that he's apparently willing to say anything.* ♦ **deep|ly** *Because of her medical and her legal bills, she is now penniless and deeply in debt.*
ADV: ADV *in/into* n; ADV: ADV *in/into* n

**PHRASES** [16] If you know something **deep down** or **deep down inside**, you know that it is true, but you are not always conscious of it or willing to admit it to yourself. ❑ *We knew deep down that we could do it... Deep down, we had always detested each other.*
PHRASE: PHR after v, PHR with cl

[17] If you say that you **took a deep breath** before doing something dangerous or frightening, you mean that you tried to make yourself feel strong and confident. ❑ *I took a deep breath and went in.*
PHRASE: V inflects

[18] If you say that something **goes deep** or **runs deep**, you mean that it is very serious or strong and is hard to change. ❑ *His anger and anguish clearly went deep.*
PHRASE: V inflects

[19] **in at the deep end** → see **end**. **in deep water** → see **water**.

**deep|en** /diːpən/ **(deepens, deepening, deepened)** [1] If a situation or emotion **deepens** or if something **deepens** it, it becomes stronger and more intense. ❑ *If this is not stopped, the financial crisis will deepen... Surviving tough times can really deepen your relationship.*
VERB; V; V n

[2] If you **deepen** your knowledge or understanding of a subject, you learn more about it and become more interested in it. ❑ *He did not get a chance to deepen his knowledge of Poland.*
VERB = broaden; V n

[3] When a sound **deepens** or **is deepened**, it becomes lower in tone. ❑ *Her voice has deepened and coarsened with the years... The music room had been made to reflect and deepen sounds.*
VERB; V; V n

[4] When your breathing **deepens**, or you **deepen** it, you take more air into your lungs when you breathe. ❑ *He heard her breathing deepen... When you are ready to finish the exercise, gradually deepen your breathing.*
VERB; V; V n

[5] If people **deepen** something,
VERB

they increase its depth by digging out its lower surface. ❑ *...a major project to deepen the channel.* V n
[6] Something such as a river or a sea **deepens** where the bottom begins to slope downwards. ❑ *As we drew nearer to it the water gradually deepened.* VERB V

**deep freeze** **(deep freezes)** also **deep-freeze.** A **deep freeze** is the same as a **freezer**. N-COUNT

**deep-fry** **(deep-fries, deep-frying, deep-fried)** If you **deep-fry** food, you fry it in a large amount of fat or oil. ❑ *Heat the oil and deep-fry the fish fillets.* VERB V n

**deep-rooted** **Deep-rooted** means the same as **deep-seated**. ❑ *...long-term solutions to a deep-rooted problem.* ADJ: usu ADJ n

**deep-sea** **Deep-sea** activities take place in the areas of the sea that are a long way from the coast. ❑ *...deep-sea diving. ...a deep-sea fisherman.* ADJ: ADJ n

**deep-seated** A **deep-seated** problem, feeling, or belief is difficult to change because its causes have been there for a long time. ❑ *The country is still suffering from deep-seated economic problems.* ADJ: usu ADJ n

**deep-set** **Deep-set** eyes seem to be further back in the face than most people's eyes. [WRITTEN] ❑ *He had deep-set brown eyes.* ADJ: usu ADJ n

**deep-six** **(deep-sixes, deep-sixing, deep-sixed)** To **deep-six** something means to get rid of it or destroy it. [mainly AM, INFORMAL] ❑ *I'd simply like to deep-six this whole project.* VERB V n

**Deep South** **The Deep South** consists of the states that are furthest south in the United States. N-SING: *the* N

**deep vein throm|bo|sis** **(deep vein thromboses)** **Deep vein thrombosis** is a serious medical condition caused by blood clots in the legs moving up to the lungs. The abbreviation **DVT** is also used. [MEDICAL] ❑ *He could have died after developing deep vein thrombosis during a flight to Sydney.* N-VAR

**deer** /dɪəʳ/ **(deer)** A **deer** is a large wild animal that eats grass and leaves. A male deer usually has large, branching horns. N-COUNT

**deer|stalker** /dɪəʳstɔːkəʳ/ **(deerstalkers)** A **deerstalker** is an old-fashioned hat with parts at the sides which can be folded down to cover the ears. Deerstalkers are usually worn by men. N-COUNT

**de|face** /dɪfeɪs/ **(defaces, defacing, defaced)** If someone **defaces** something such as a wall or a notice, they spoil it by writing or drawing things on it. ❑ *It's illegal to deface banknotes.* VERB V n

**de fac|to** /deɪ fæktoʊ/ **De facto** is used to indicate that something is a particular thing, even though it was not planned or intended to be that thing. [FORMAL] ❑ *This might be interpreted as a de facto recognition of the republic's independence.* ♦ **De facto** is also an adverb. ❑ *They will be de facto in a state of war.* ADJ: ADJ n ≠ *de jure* ADV: ADV with cl

**defa|ma|tion** /defəmeɪʃᵊn/ **Defamation** is the damaging of someone's good reputation by saying something bad and untrue about them. [FORMAL] ❑ *He sued for defamation.* N-UNCOUNT

**de|fama|tory** /dɪfæmətri, AM -tɔːri/ Speech or writing that is **defamatory** is likely to damage someone's good reputation by saying something bad and untrue about them. [FORMAL] ❑ *The article was highly defamatory.* ADJ

**de|fame** /dɪfeɪm/ **(defames, defaming, defamed)** If someone **defames** another person or thing, they say bad and untrue things about them. [FORMAL] ❑ *Sgt Norwood complained that the article defamed him.* VERB V n

**de|fault** /dɪfɔːlt/ **(defaults, defaulting, defaulted)**

> ✔ Pronounced /diːfɔːlt/ for meaning 2.

[1] If a person, company, or country **defaults on** something that they have legally agreed to do, such as paying some money or doing a piece of work before a particular time, they fail to do it. [LEGAL] ❑ *The credit card business is down, and more borrowers are defaulting on loans.* ♦ **Default** is also a noun. ❑ *The corporation may be charged with default on its contract with the government.* VERB V *on* n N-UNCOUNT: oft N prep, *in* N
[2] A **default** situation is what exists or happens unless someone or something changes it. ❑ *...default passwords installed on commercial machines.* ADJ: ADJ n
[3] In computing, the **default** is a particular set of instructions which the computer always uses unless the person using the computer gives other instructions. [COMPUTING] ❑ *The default is usually the setting that most users would probably choose. ...default settings.* N-UNCOUNT
[4] If something happens **by default**, it happens only because something else which might have prevented it or changed it has not happened. [FORMAL] ❑ *I would rather pay the individuals than let the money go to the State by default.* PHRASE: PHR after v, PHR with cl

**de|fault|er** /dɪfɔːltəʳ/ **(defaulters)** A **defaulter** is someone who does not do something that they are legally supposed to do, such as make a payment at a particular time, or appear in a court of law. N-COUNT

**de|feat** /dɪfiːt/ **(defeats, defeating, defeated)** ◆◆◇
[1] If you **defeat** someone, you win a victory over them in a battle, game, or contest. ❑ *His guerrillas defeated the colonial army in 1954.* VERB = beat V n
[2] If a proposal or motion in a debate **is defeated**, more people vote against it than for it. ❑ *The proposal was defeated by just one vote.* VERB: usu passive *be* V-ed
[3] If a task or a problem **defeats** you, it is so difficult that you cannot do it or solve it. ❑ *There were times when the challenges of writing such a huge novel almost defeated her.* VERB V n
[4] To **defeat** an action or plan means to cause it to fail. ❑ *The navy played a limited but significant role in defeating the rebellion.* VERB = thwart V n
[5] **Defeat** is the experience of being beaten in a battle, game, or contest, or of failing to achieve what you wanted to. ❑ *The most important thing is not to admit defeat until you really have to... The vote is seen as a defeat for the anti-abortion lobby.* N-VAR

**de|feat|ism** /dɪfiːtɪzəm/ **Defeatism** is a way of thinking or talking which suggests that you expect to be unsuccessful. ❑ *...the mood of economic defeatism.* N-UNCOUNT

**de|feat|ist** /dɪfiːtɪst/ **(defeatists)** A **defeatist** is someone who thinks or talks in a way that suggests that they expect to be unsuccessful. ♦ **Defeatist** is also an adjective. ❑ *There is no point going out there with a defeatist attitude.* N-COUNT ADJ

**def|ecate** /defəkeɪt/ **(defecates, defecating, defecated)** When people and animals **defecate**, they get rid of waste matter from their body through their anus. [FORMAL] ♦ **def|eca|tion** /defəkeɪʃᵊn/ ❑ *The drug's side-effects can include involuntary defecation.* VERB N-UNCOUNT

**de|fect** **(defects, defecting, defected)**

> ✔ The noun is pronounced /diːfekt/. The verb is pronounced /dɪfekt/.

[1] A **defect** is a fault or imperfection in a person or thing. ❑ *He was born with a hearing defect. ...a defect in the aircraft caused the crash.* N-COUNT: usu with supp = imperfection
[2] If you **defect**, you leave your country, political party, or other group, and join an opposing country, party, or group. ❑ *He tried to defect to the West last year. ...a KGB officer who defected in 1963.* ♦ **de|fec|tion** /dɪfekʃᵊn/ **(defections)** *...the defection of at least sixteen Parliamentary deputies.* VERB V *to/from* n V N-VAR

**de|fec|tive** /dɪfektɪv/ If something is **defective**, there is something wrong with it and it does not work properly. ❑ *Retailers can return defective merchandise.* ADJ

**de|fec|tor** /dɪfektəʳ/ **(defectors)** A **defector** is someone who leaves their country, political party, or other group, and joins an opposing country, party, or group. N-COUNT: usu with supp

**de|fence** /dɪfens/ **(defences)** ◆◆◇

> ✔ The spelling **defense** is used in American English, and in meaning 8 is pronounced /diːfens/.

[1] **Defence** is action that is taken to protect N-UNCOUNT

someone or something against attack. ❑ *The land was flat, giving no scope for defence... By wielding a knife in defence you run the risk of having it used against you.* [2] **Defence** is the organization of a country's armies and weapons, and their use to protect the country or its interests. *N-UNCOUNT: oft N n* ❑ *Twenty eight percent of the federal budget is spent on defense. ...the French defence minister.* [3] The **defences** of a country or region are all its armed forces and weapons. *N-PLURAL* ❑ *...the need to maintain Britain's defences at a sufficiently high level.* [4] A **defence** is something that people or animals can use or do to protect themselves. *N-COUNT: oft N against n = protection* ❑ *The immune system is our main defence against disease.* [5] A **defence** is something that you say or write which supports ideas or actions that have been criticized or questioned. *N-COUNT: oft N of n, also in N = justification* ❑ *Chomsky's defence of his approach goes further.* [6] In a court of law, an accused person's **defence** is the process of presenting evidence in their favour. *N-COUNT: oft with poss* ❑ *He has insisted on conducting his own defence.* [7] **The defence** is the case that is presented by a lawyer in a trial for the person who has been accused of a crime. You can also refer to this person's lawyers as **the defence**. *N-SING: usu the N* ❑ *The defence was that the records of the interviews were fabricated by the police.* [8] In games such as football or hockey, the **defence** is the group of players in a team who try to stop the opposing players scoring a goal or a point. *N-SING-COLL: oft poss N, also in N ≠ attack* ❑ *Their defence, so strong last season, has now conceded 12 goals in six games... I still prefer to play in defence.* [9] If you come **to** someone's **defence**, you help them by doing or saying something to protect them. *PHRASE: PHR after v* ❑ *He realized none of his schoolmates would come to his defense.*

**de|fence|less** /dɪfensləs/
✔ in AM, use **defenseless**

If someone or something is **defenceless**, they are weak and unable to defend themselves properly. *ADJ = helpless* ❑ *...a savage attack on a defenceless young girl.*

**de|fence mecha|nism** (**defence mechanisms**) A **defence mechanism** is a way of behaving or thinking which is not conscious or deliberate and is an automatic reaction to unpleasant experiences or feelings such as anxiety and fear. *N-COUNT*

**de|fend** /dɪfend/ (**defends, defending, defended**) ◆◆◇ [1] If you **defend** someone or something, you take action in order to protect them. *VERB ≠ attack* *V n* ❑ *His courage in defending religious and civil rights inspired many outside the church.* [2] If you **defend** someone or something when they have been criticized, you argue in support of them. *VERB ≠ attack* *V n* ❑ *Matt defended all of Clarence's decisions, right or wrong.* [3] When a lawyer **defends** a person who has been accused of something, the lawyer argues on their behalf in a court of law that the charges are not true. *VERB* *V n* ❑ *...a lawyer who defended political prisoners during the military regime...* *V n against n* *He has hired a lawyer to defend him against the allegations...* *V* *Guy Powell, defending, told magistrates: 'It's a sad and disturbing case.'* [4] When a sports player plays in the tournament which they won the previous time it was held, you can say that they **are defending** their title. *VERB* [JOURNALISM] *V n* ❑ *Torrence expects to defend her title successfully in the next Olympics.*

**de|fend|ant** /dɪfendənt/ (**defendants**) A **defendant** is a person who has been accused of breaking the law and is being tried in court. *N-COUNT*

**de|fend|er** /dɪfendəʳ/ (**defenders**) [1] If someone is a **defender of** a particular thing or person that has been criticized, they argue or act in support of that thing or person. *N-COUNT: usu N of n* ❑ *...the most ardent defenders of conventional family values.* [2] A **defender** in a game such as football or hockey is a player whose main task is to try and stop the other side scoring. *N-COUNT*

**de|fense** /dɪfens/ → see **defence**.

**de|fen|sible** /dɪfensɪbᵊl/ An opinion, system, or action that is **defensible** is one that people can argue is right or good. *ADJ ≠ indefensible* ❑ *Her reasons for acting are morally defensible.*

**de|fen|sive** /dɪfensɪv/ [1] You use **defensive** to describe things that are intended to protect someone or something. *ADJ: usu ADJ n* ❑ *The Government hastily organized defensive measures against the raids.* [2] Someone who is **defensive** is behaving in a way that shows they feel unsure or threatened. *ADJ* ❑ *Like their children, parents are often defensive about their private lives.* ♦ **de|fen|sive|ly** *ADV* *'Oh, I know,' said Kate, defensively.* ♦ **de|fen|sive|ness** *N-UNCOUNT* *He felt a certain defensiveness about his position.* [3] If someone is **on the defensive**, they are trying to protect themselves or their interests because they feel unsure or threatened. *PHRASE: usu v-link PHR, PHR after v* ❑ *Accusations are likely to put the other person on the defensive.* [4] In sports, **defensive** play is play that is intended to prevent your opponent from scoring goals or points against you. *ADJ: usu ADJ n ≠ attacking* ❑ *I'd always played a defensive game, waiting for my opponent to make a mistake.* ♦ **de|fen|sive|ly** *ADV: ADV after v* *Mexico did not play defensively.*

**de|fer** /dɪfɜːʳ/ (**defers, deferring, deferred**) [1] If you **defer** an event or action, you arrange for it to happen at a later date, rather than immediately or at the previously planned time. *VERB = postpone, delay* *V n/-ing* ❑ *Customers often defer payment for as long as possible.* [2] If you **defer to** someone, you accept their opinion or do what they want you to do, even when you do not agree with it yourself, because you respect them or their authority. *VERB* *V to n* ❑ *Doctors are encouraged to defer to experts.*

**def|er|ence** /defrəns/ **Deference** is a polite and respectful attitude towards someone, especially because they have an important position. *N-UNCOUNT: oft N to n* ❑ *The old sense of deference and restraint in royal reporting has vanished.*

**def|er|en|tial** /defərenʃᵊl/ Someone who is **deferential** is polite and respectful towards someone else. *ADJ: oft ADJ to n* ❑ *They like five-star hotels and deferential treatment.* ♦ **def|er|en|tial|ly** *ADV: ADV with v* *The old man spoke deferentially.*

**de|fer|ment** /dɪfɜːʳmənt/ (**deferments**) **Deferment** means arranging for something to happen at a later date. *N-VAR* [FORMAL] ❑ *...the deferment of debt repayments.*

**de|fer|ral** /dɪfɜːrəl/ (**deferrals**) **Deferral** means the same as **deferment**. *N-VAR*

**de|fi|ance** /dɪfaɪəns/ [1] **Defiance** is behaviour or an attitude which shows that you are not willing to obey someone. *N-UNCOUNT: oft N of n* ❑ *...his courageous defiance of the government.* [2] If you do something **in defiance of** a person, rule, or law, you do it even though you know that you are not allowed to do it. *PHRASE: PHR n* ❑ *Thousands of people have taken to the streets in defiance of the curfew.*

**de|fi|ant** /dɪfaɪənt/ If you say that someone is **defiant**, you mean they show aggression or independence by refusing to obey someone. *ADJ* ❑ *The players are in defiant mood as they prepare for tomorrow's game.* ♦ **de|fi|ant|ly** *ADV: usu ADV with v* *They defiantly rejected any talk of a compromise.*

**de|fib|ril|la|tor** /diːfɪbrɪleɪtəʳ/ (**defibrillators**) A **defibrillator** is a machine that starts the heart beating normally again after a heart attack, by giving it an electric shock. *N-COUNT* [MEDICAL]

**de|fi|cien|cy** /dɪfɪʃᵊnsi/ (**deficiencies**) [1] **Deficiency in** something, especially something that your body needs, is not having enough of it. *N-VAR: with supp* ❑ *They did blood tests on him for signs of vitamin deficiency.* [2] A **deficiency** that someone or something has is a weakness or imperfection in them. *N-VAR: with supp = weakness* [FORMAL] ❑ *...a serious deficiency in our air defence.*

**de|fi|cient** /dɪfɪʃᵊnt/ [1] If someone or something is **deficient in** a particular thing, they do not have the full amount of it that they need in order to function normally or work properly. *ADJ: usu v-link ADJ, usu ADJ in n = lacking* [FORMAL] ❑ *...a diet deficient in vitamin B.* ♦ **Deficient** is also a combining form. *COMB in ADJ* ❑ *Vegetarians can become iron-deficient.* [2] Someone or something that is **deficient** is not good enough for a par- *ADJ = inadequate* ticular purpose. [FORMAL] ❑ *...deficient landing systems.*

**defi|cit** /dẹfəsɪt/ **(deficits)** A **deficit** is the amount by which something is less than what is required or expected, especially the amount by which the total money received is less than the total money spent. ❑ *They're ready to cut the federal budget deficit for the next fiscal year.* ● If an account or organization is **in deficit**, more money has been spent than has been received. ❑ *The current account of the balance of payments is in deficit.* ◆◆◇ N-COUNT: oft n N; PHRASE: usu v-link PHR

**de|file** /dɪfaɪl/ **(defiles, defiling, defiled)** [1] To **defile** something that people think is important or holy means to do something to it or say something about it which is offensive. [LITERARY] ❑ *He had defiled the sacred name of the Holy Prophet.* [2] A **defile** is a very narrow valley or passage, usually through mountains. [FORMAL] VERB; V n; N-COUNT = pass

**de|fin|able** /dɪfaɪnəbᵊl/ Something that is **definable** can be described or identified. ❑ *Many suffered from a definable alcohol, drug, or mental disorder. ...groups broadly definable as conservative.* ADJ

**de|fine** /dɪfaɪn/ **(defines, defining, defined)** [1] If you **define** something, you show, describe, or state clearly what it is and what its limits are, or what it is like. ❑ *We were unable to define what exactly was wrong with him... He was asked to define his concept of cool.* ♦ **de|fined** *...a party with a clearly defined programme and strict rules of membership.* [2] If you **define** a word or expression, you explain its meaning, for example in a dictionary. ❑ *Collins English Dictionary defines a workaholic as 'a person obsessively addicted to work'.* ◆◇◇ VERB; V wh; V n; ADJ: usu adv ADJ = delineated; VERB; V n as n

**de|fined** /dɪfaɪnd/ If something is clearly **defined** or strongly **defined**, its outline is clear or strong. ❑ *A clearly defined track now leads down to the valley.* ADJ: usu adv ADJ

**defi|nite** /dẹfɪnɪt/ [1] If something such as a decision or an arrangement is **definite**, it is firm and clear, and unlikely to be changed. ❑ *It's too soon to give a definite answer... Her Royal Highness has definite views about most things... She made no definite plans for her future.* [2] **Definite** evidence or information is true, rather than being someone's opinion or guess. ❑ *We didn't have any definite proof.* [3] You use **definite** to emphasize the strength of your opinion or belief. ❑ *There has already been a definite improvement... That's a very definite possibility.* [4] Someone who is **definite** behaves or talks in a firm, confident way. ❑ *Mary is very definite about this.* ADJ; ADJ: usu ADJ n; ADJ: ADJ n [emphasis] = real; ADJ

**defi|nite ar|ti|cle** **(definite articles)** The word 'the' is sometimes called **the definite article**. N-COUNT: usu *the* N

**defi|nite|ly** /dẹfɪnɪtli/ [1] You use **definitely** to emphasize that something is the case, or to emphasize the strength of your intention or opinion. ❑ *I'm definitely going to get in touch with these people... 'I think the earlier ones are a lot better.' — 'Mm, definitely.'* [2] If something has been **definitely** decided, the decision will not be changed. ❑ *He told them that no venue had yet been definitely decided.* ◆◇◇ ADV: ADV before v, ADV with cl/group [emphasis] = certainly; ADV: ADV before v

**defi|ni|tion** /dẹfɪnɪʃᵊn/ **(definitions)** [1] A **definition** is a statement giving the meaning of a word or expression, especially in a dictionary. ❑ *There is no general agreement on a standard definition of intelligence.* ● If you say that something has a particular quality **by definition**, you mean that it has this quality simply because of what it is. ❑ *Human perception is highly imperfect and by definition subjective.* [2] **Definition** is the quality of being clear and distinct. ❑ *The speakers criticised his new programme for lack of definition.* ◆◇◇ N-COUNT: oft N *of* n; PHRASE: PHR with cl; N-UNCOUNT

**de|fini|tive** /dɪfɪnɪtɪv/ [1] Something that is **definitive** provides a firm conclusion that cannot be questioned. ❑ *No one has come up with a definitive answer as to why this should be so.* ♦ **de|fini|tive|ly** *The Constitution did not definitively rule out divorce.* [2] A **definitive** book or performance is thought to be the best of its kind that has ever been done or that will ever be done. ❑ *His 'An Orkney Tapestry' is still the definitive book on the islands.* ADJ: usu ADJ n; ADV; ADJ: usu ADJ n

**de|flate** /dɪfleɪt/ **(deflates, deflating, deflated)** [1] If you **deflate** someone or something, you take away their confidence or make them seem less important. ❑ *Britain's other hopes of medals were deflated earlier in the day.* ♦ **de|flat|ed** *When she refused I felt deflated.* [2] When something such as a tyre or balloon **deflates**, or when you **deflate** it, all the air comes out of it. ❑ *When it returns to shore, the life-jacket will deflate and revert to a harness... We deflate the tyres to make it easier to cross the desert.* VERB; V n; ADJ; VERB ≠ inflate; V; V n

**de|fla|tion** /diːfleɪʃᵊn, dɪf-/ **Deflation** is a reduction in economic activity that leads to lower levels of industrial output, employment, investment, trade, profits, and prices. [BUSINESS] N-UNCOUNT ≠ inflation

**de|fla|tion|ary** /diːfleɪʃənri, AM -neri/ A **deflationary** economic policy or measure is one that is intended to or likely to cause deflation. [BUSINESS] ADJ: usu ADJ n ≠ inflationary

**de|flect** /dɪflẹkt/ **(deflects, deflecting, deflected)** [1] If you **deflect** something such as criticism or attention, you act in a way that prevents it from being directed towards you or affecting you. ❑ *Cage changed his name to deflect accusations of nepotism... It's a maneuver to deflect the attention of the people from what is really happening.* [2] To **deflect** someone **from** a course of action means to make them decide not to continue with it by putting pressure on them or by offering them something desirable. ❑ *The war did not deflect him from the path he had long ago taken... Never let a little problem deflect you.* [3] If you **deflect** something that is moving, you make it go in a slightly different direction, for example by hitting or blocking it. ❑ *My forearm deflected most of the first punch.* VERB; V n; V n from n; VERB; V n from n/-ing; V n; VERB; V n

**de|flec|tion** /dɪflẹkʃᵊn/ **(deflections)** [1] The **deflection** of something means making it change direction. [TECHNICAL] ❑ *...the deflection of light as it passes through the slits in the grating.* [2] In sport, the **deflection** of a ball, kick, or shot is when the ball hits an object and then travels in a different direction. N-VAR; N-COUNT

**de|flow|er** /diːflaʊəʳ/ **(deflowers, deflowering, deflowered)** When a woman **is deflowered**, she has sexual intercourse with a man for the first time. [LITERARY] ❑ *Nora was deflowered by a man who worked in a soda-water factory.* VERB; be V-ed; Also V n

**de|fo|li|ant** /diːfoʊliənt/ **(defoliants)** A **defoliant** is a chemical used on trees and plants to make all their leaves fall off. Defoliants are especially used in war to remove protection from an enemy. N-MASS

**de|fo|li|ate** /diːfoʊlieɪt/ **(defoliates, defoliating, defoliated)** To **defoliate** an area or the plants in it means to cause the leaves on the plants to fall off or be destroyed. This is done especially in war to remove protection from an enemy. ❑ *Dioxin was the ingredient in Agent Orange, used to defoliate Vietnam.* ♦ **de|fo|lia|tion** /diːfoʊlieɪʃᵊn/ *...preventing defoliation of trees by caterpillars.* VERB; V n; N-UNCOUNT

**de|for|est** /diːfɒrɪst, AM -fɔːr-/ **(deforests, deforesting, deforested)** If an area **is deforested**, all the trees there are cut down or destroyed. ❑ *400,000 square kilometres of the Amazon basin have already been deforested.* ♦ **de|for|esta|tion** /diːfɒrɪsteɪʃᵊn, AM -fɔːr-/ *...the ecological crisis of deforestation.* VERB: usu passive; be V-ed; N-UNCOUNT

**de|form** /dɪfɔːʳm/ **(deforms, deforming, deformed)** If something **deforms** a person's body or something else, it causes it to have an unnatural shape. In technical English, you can also say that the second thing **deforms**. ❑ *Bad rheumatoid arthritis deforms limbs. ...the ability of a metal to deform to a new shape without cracking.* ♦ **de|formed** *He was born with a deformed right leg.* ♦ **de|for|ma|tion** /diːfɔːʳmeɪʃᵊn/ **(deforma-** VERB; V n; V; ADJ; N-VAR

**tions)** *Changing stresses bring about more cracking and rock deformation.*

**de|form|ity** /dɪfɔːʳmɪti/ **(deformities)** 1 A **deformity** is a part of someone's body which is not the normal shape because of injury or illness, or because they were born this way. ❑ *...facial deformities in babies.* N-COUNT 2 **Deformity** is the condition of having a deformity. ❑ *The bones begin to grind against each other, leading to pain and deformity.* N-UNCOUNT

**de|fraud** /dɪfrɔːd/ **(defrauds, defrauding, defrauded)** If someone **defrauds** you, they take something away from you or stop you from getting what belongs to you by means of tricks and lies. ❑ *He pleaded guilty to charges of conspiracy to defraud the government. ...allegations that he defrauded taxpayers of thousands of dollars.* VERB; V n; V n *of/out of* n

**de|fray** /dɪfreɪ/ **(defrays, defraying, defrayed)** If you **defray** someone's costs or expenses, you give them money which represents the amount that they have spent, for example while they have been doing something for you or acting on your behalf. [FORMAL] ❑ *The government has committed billions toward defraying the costs of the war.* VERB; V n

**de|frock** /diːfrɒk/ **(defrocked)** If a priest **is defrocked**, he is forced to stop being a priest because of bad behaviour. ❑ *He was preaching heresy and had to be defrocked. ...a defrocked priest.* V-PASSIVE; *be* V-ed; V-ed

**de|frost** /diːfrɒst, AM -frɔːst/ **(defrosts, defrosting, defrosted)** 1 When you **defrost** frozen food or when it **defrosts**, you allow or cause it to become unfrozen so that you can eat it or cook it. ❑ *She has a microwave, but uses it mainly for defrosting bread... Once the turkey has defrosted, remove the giblets.* VERB ≠ freeze; V n; V 2 When you **defrost** a fridge or freezer, you switch it off or press a special switch so that the ice inside it can melt. You can also say that a fridge or freezer **is defrosting**. ❑ *Defrost the fridge regularly so that it works at maximum efficiency.* VERB; V n; Also V

**deft** /deft/ **(defter, deftest)** A **deft** action is skilful and often quick. [WRITTEN] ❑ *With a deft flick of his foot, Mr Worth tripped one of the raiders up.* ADJ ♦ **deft|ly** *One of the waiting servants deftly caught him as he fell.* ADV ♦ **deft|ness** *...Dr Holly's surgical deftness and experience.* N-UNCOUNT

**de|funct** /dɪfʌŋkt/ If something is **defunct**, it no longer exists or has stopped functioning or operating. ❑ *...the leader of the now defunct Social Democratic Party.* ADJ

**de|fuse** /diːfjuːz/ **(defuses, defusing, defused)** 1 If you **defuse** a dangerous or tense situation, you calm it. ❑ *The organization helped defuse potentially violent situations.* VERB; V n 2 If someone **defuses** a bomb, they remove the fuse so that it cannot explode. ❑ *Police have defused a bomb found in a building in London.* VERB; V n

**defy** /dɪfaɪ/ **(defies, defying, defied)** 1 If you **defy** someone or something that is trying to make you behave in a particular way, you refuse to obey them and behave in that way. ❑ *This was the first (and last) time that I dared to defy my mother.* VERB; V n 2 If you **defy** someone **to** do something, you challenge them to do it when you think that they will be unable to do it or too frightened to do it. ❑ *I defy you to come up with one major accomplishment of the current Prime Minister.* VERB = dare; V n to-inf 3 If something **defies** description or understanding, it is so strange, extreme, or surprising that it is almost impossible to understand or explain. ❑ *It's a devastating and barbaric act that defies all comprehension.* VERB: no passive, no cont; V n

**de|gen|era|cy** /dɪdʒenərəsi/ If you refer to the behaviour of a group of people as **degeneracy**, you mean that you think it is shocking, immoral, or disgusting. ❑ *...the moral degeneracy of society.* N-UNCOUNT [disapproval] = depravity

**de|gen|er|ate** **(degenerates, degenerating, degenerated)**

> ✔ The verb is pronounced /dɪdʒenəreɪt/. The adjective and noun are pronounced /dɪdʒenərət/.

1 If you say that someone or something **degenerates**, you mean that they become worse in some way, for example weaker, lower in quality, or more dangerous. ❑ *Inactivity can make your joints stiff, and the bones may begin to degenerate. ...a very serious humanitarian crisis which could degenerate into a catastrophe.* VERB = deteriorate; V; V *into* n ♦ **de|gen|era|tion** /dɪdʒenəreɪʃᵊn/ *...various forms of physical and mental degeneration.* N-UNCOUNT 2 If you describe a person or their behaviour as **degenerate**, you disapprove of them because you think they have low standards of behaviour or morality. ❑ *...a group of degenerate computer hackers.* ADJ [disapproval] 3 If you refer to someone as a **degenerate**, you disapprove of them because you think they have low standards of behaviour or morality. N-COUNT [disapproval]

**de|gen|era|tive** /dɪdʒenərətɪv/ A **degenerative** disease or condition is one that gets worse as time progresses. ❑ *...degenerative diseases of the brain, like Alzheimer's.* ADJ: usu ADJ n

**deg|ra|da|tion** /degrədeɪʃᵊn/ **(degradations)** 1 You use **degradation** to refer to a situation, condition, or experience which you consider shameful and disgusting, especially one which involves poverty or immorality. ❑ *They were sickened by the scenes of misery and degradation they found.* N-VAR [disapproval] 2 **Degradation** is the process of something becoming worse or weaker, or being made worse or weaker. ❑ *I feel this signals the degradation of American culture.* N-UNCOUNT: with supp 3 The **degradation** of land or of the environment is the process of its becoming damaged and poorer, for example because of the effects of pollution, industry, and modern agricultural methods. [TECHNICAL] N-UNCOUNT: usu with supp

**de|grade** /dɪgreɪd/ **(degrades, degrading, degraded)** 1 Something that **degrades** someone causes people to have less respect for them. ❑ *...the notion that pornography degrades women... When I asked him if he had ever been to a prostitute he said he wouldn't degrade himself like that.* VERB; V n; V pron-refl ♦ **de|grad|ing** *Mr Porter was subjected to a degrading strip-search.* ADJ 2 To **degrade** something means to cause it to get worse. [FORMAL] ❑ *...the ability to meet human needs indefinitely without degrading the environment.* VERB; V n 3 In science, if a substance **degrades** or if something **degrades** it, it changes chemically and decays or separates into different substances. [TECHNICAL] ❑ *This substance degrades rapidly in the soil. ...the ability of these enzymes to degrade cellulose.* VERB = break down; V; V n

**de|gree** /dɪgriː/ **(degrees)** 1 You use **degree** to indicate the extent to which something happens or is the case, or the amount which something is felt. ❑ *These man-made barriers will ensure a very high degree of protection... Politicians have used television with varying degrees of success.* ◆◆◇ N-COUNT: with supp, usu N *of* n ● If something has **a degree of** a particular quality, it has a small but significant amount of that quality. ❑ *Their wages do, however, allow them a degree of independence.* PHRASE: PHR n 2 A **degree** is a unit of measurement that is used to measure temperatures. It is often written as °, for example 23°. ❑ *It's over 80 degrees outside.* N-COUNT: usu num N 3 A **degree** is a unit of measurement that is used to measure angles, and also longitude and latitude. It is often written as °, for example 23°. ❑ *It was pointing outward at an angle of 45 degrees.* N-COUNT: usu num N 4 A **degree** at a university or college is a course of study that you take there, or the qualification that you get when you have passed the course. ❑ *He took a master's degree in economics at Yale University. ...the first year of a degree course.* N-COUNT: usu with supp 5 → See also **first-degree**, **second-degree**, **third-degree**.

PHRASES 6 If something happens **by degrees**, it happens slowly and gradually. ❑ *The crowd in Robinson's Coffee-House was thinning, but only by degrees.* PHRASE = gradually 7 You use expressions such as **to some degree**, **to a large degree**, or **to a certain degree** in order to indicate that something is partly true, but not entirely true. ❑ *These statements are,* PHRASE: PHR with cl [vagueness] *to some degree, all correct.* 8 You use expressions such as **to what degree** and **to the degree that** when you are discussing how true a statement is, or in what ways it is true. ❑ *To what degree would you say you had control over things that went on?* PHRASE [vagueness] *= to what extent, to the extent that*

**de|hu|man|ize** /diːhjuːmənaɪz/ **(dehumanizes, dehumanizing, dehumanized)**

✔ in BRIT, also use **dehumanise**

If you say that something **dehumanizes** people, you mean it takes away from them good human qualities such as kindness, generosity, and independence. ❑ *The years of civil war have dehumanized all of us.* VERB; V n

**de|hu|midi|fi|er** /diːhjuːmɪdɪfaɪəʳ/ **(dehumidifiers)** A **dehumidifier** is a machine that is used to reduce the amount of moisture in the air. N-COUNT

**de|hy|drate** /diːhaɪdreɪt, -haɪdreɪt/ **(dehydrates, dehydrating, dehydrated)** 1 When something such as food **is dehydrated**, all the water is removed from it, often in order to preserve it. ❑ *Normally specimens have to be dehydrated.* VERB: usu passive *= dry*; *be* V-ed ♦ **de|hy|drat|ed** *Dehydrated meals, soups and sauces contain a lot of salt.* ADJ 2 If you **dehydrate** or if something **dehydrates** you, you lose too much water from your body so that you feel weak or ill. ❑ *People can dehydrate in weather like this... Alcohol quickly dehydrates your body.* VERB; V; V n ♦ **de|hy|dra|tion** /diːhaɪdreɪʃᵊn/ *...a child who's got diarrhoea and is suffering from dehydration.* N-UNCOUNT

**dei|fi|ca|tion** /deɪɪfɪkeɪʃᵊn, AM diː-/ If you talk about the **deification** of someone or something, you mean that they are regarded with very great respect and are not criticized at all. [FORMAL] ❑ *...the deification of science in the 1940s.* N-UNCOUNT: usu with supp

**dei|fy** /deɪɪfaɪ, AM diː-/ **(deifies, deifying, deified)** If someone **is deified**, they are considered to be a god or are regarded with very great respect. [FORMAL] ❑ *Valentino was virtually deified by legions of female fans.* VERB: usu passive; *be* V-ed

**deign** /deɪn/ **(deigns, deigning, deigned)** If you say that someone **deigned** to do something, you are expressing your disapproval of the fact that they did it unwillingly, because they thought they were too important to do it. [FORMAL] ❑ *At last, Harper deigned to speak.* VERB [disapproval]; V to-inf

**de|ism** /deɪɪzəm, AM diː-/ **Deism** is the belief that there is a God who made the world but does not influence human lives. N-UNCOUNT

**de|ity** /deɪɪtɪ, AM diː-/ **(deities)** A **deity** is a god or goddess. [FORMAL] N-COUNT: usu with supp

**déjà vu** /deɪʒɑː vuː/ **Déjà vu** is the feeling that you have already experienced the things that are happening to you now. ❑ *The sense of déjà vu was overwhelming.* N-UNCOUNT

**de|ject|ed** /dɪdʒektɪd/ If you are **dejected**, you feel miserable or unhappy, especially because you have just been disappointed by something. ❑ *Everyone has days when they feel dejected or down.* ADJ *= despondent* ♦ **de|ject|ed|ly** *Passengers queued dejectedly for the increasingly dirty toilets.* ADV: ADV with v

**de|jec|tion** /dɪdʒekʃᵊn/ **Dejection** is a feeling of sadness that you get, for example, when you have just been disappointed by something. ❑ *There was a slight air of dejection about her.* N-UNCOUNT *= despondency*

**de jure** /deɪ dʒʊəreɪ, AM diː dʒʊri/ **De jure** is used to indicate that something legally exists or is a particular thing. [LEGAL] ❑ *...politicians and kings, de jure leaders of men.* ADJ: ADJ n *≠ de facto* ♦ **De jure** is also an adverb. ❑ *The Synod's declarations prevailed de jure but not de facto in the Roman Catholic Church down to the Reformation era.* ADV: ADV with cl *≠ de facto*

**de|lay** /dɪleɪ/ **(delays, delaying, delayed)** ◆◆◇ 1 If you **delay** doing something, you do not do it immediately or at the planned or expected time, but you leave it until later. ❑ *For sentimental reasons I wanted to delay my departure until June... So don't delay, write in now for your chance of a free gift.* VERB *= postpone*; V n/-ing; V 2 To **delay** someone or something means to make them late or to slow them down. ❑ *Can you delay him in some way?... The passengers were delayed for an hour.* VERB *= hold up*; V n; V n 3 If you **delay**, you deliberately take longer than necessary to do something. ❑ *If he delayed any longer, the sun would be up.* VERB; V 4 If there is a **delay**, something does not happen until later than planned or expected. ❑ *Although the tests have caused some delay, flights should be back to normal this morning.* N-VAR *= hold-up* 5 **Delay** is a failure to do something immediately or in the required or usual time. ❑ *We'll send you a quote without delay.* N-UNCOUNT

**de|layed ac|tion** A **delayed action** mechanism causes a delay on the device it is fitted to, so that it does not work as soon as you switch it on or operate it. ❑ *...a type of delayed action parachute.* ADJ: ADJ n

**de|lay|er|ing** /diːleɪərɪŋ/ **Delayering** is the process of simplifying the administrative structure of a large organization in order to make it more efficient. [BUSINESS] N-UNCOUNT

**de|lay|ing tac|tic** **(delaying tactics)** **Delaying tactics** are things that someone does in order to deliberately delay the start or progress of something. ❑ *Ministers are using delaying tactics to postpone the report yet again.* N-COUNT: usu pl

**de|lec|table** /dɪlektəbᵊl/ If you describe something, especially food or drink, as **delectable**, you mean that it is very pleasant. ❑ *...delectable wine.* ADJ *= delicious*

**de|lec|ta|tion** /diːlekteɪʃᵊn/ If you do something **for** someone's **delectation**, you do it to give them enjoyment or pleasure. [FORMAL] ❑ *She makes scones and cakes for the delectation of visitors.* PHRASE: PHR with poss

**del|egate** **(delegates, delegating, delegated)** ◆◇◇

✔ The noun is pronounced /delɪgət/. The verb is pronounced /delɪgeɪt/.

1 A **delegate** is a person who is chosen to vote or make decisions on behalf of a group of other people, especially at a conference or a meeting. N-COUNT *= representative* 2 If you **delegate** duties, responsibilities, or power **to** someone, you give them those duties, those responsibilities, or that power so that they can act on your behalf. ❑ *He plans to delegate more authority to his deputies... Many employers find it hard to delegate.* VERB; V n *to* n; V ♦ **del|ega|tion** *A key factor in running a business is the delegation of responsibility.* N-UNCOUNT: usu with supp 3 If you **are delegated to** do something, you are given the duty of acting on someone else's behalf by making decisions, voting, or doing some particular work. ❑ *Officials have now been delegated to start work on a draft settlement.* VERB: usu passive *= appoint*; *be* V-ed to-inf

**del|ega|tion** /delɪgeɪʃᵊn/ **(delegations)** A **delegation** is a group of people who have been sent somewhere to have talks with other people on behalf of a larger group of people. ❑ *He was sent to New York as part of the Dutch delegation to the United Nations.* → See also **delegate**. ◆◇◇ N-COUNT

**de|lete** /dɪliːt/ **(deletes, deleting, deleted)** If you **delete** something that has been written down or stored in a computer, you cross it out or remove it. ❑ *He also deleted files from the computer system.* VERB; V n ♦ **de|letion** /dɪliːʃᵊn/ **(deletions)** *This involved the deletion of a great deal of irrelevant material.* N-VAR

**del|eteri|ous** /delɪtɪəriəs/ Something that has a **deleterious** effect on something has a harmful effect on it. [FORMAL] ❑ *Petty crime is having a deleterious effect on community life.* ADJ *= detrimental*

**deli** /deli/ **(delis)** A **deli** is a shop or part of a shop that sells food such as cheese and cold meat. **Deli** is an abbreviation for 'delicatessen'. N-COUNT

**de|lib|er|ate** **(deliberates, deliberating, deliberated)** ◆◇◇

✔ The adjective is pronounced /dɪlɪbərət/. The verb is pronounced /dɪlɪbəreɪt/.

1 If you do something that is **deliberate**, you planned or decided to do it beforehand, and so it happens on purpose rather than by chance. ❑ *Witnesses say the firing was deliberate and sustained.* ADJ *= intentional*

♦ **de|lib|er|ate|ly** *It looks as if the blaze was started deliberately... Mr Christopher's answer was deliberately vague.* [2] If a movement or action is **deliberate**, it is done slowly and carefully. ❑ *...stepping with deliberate slowness up the steep paths.* ♦ **de|lib|er|ate|ly** *The Japanese have acted calmly and deliberately.* [3] If you **deliberate**, you think about something carefully, especially before making a very important decision. ❑ *She deliberated over the decision for a long time before she made up her mind... The Court of Criminal Appeals has been deliberating his case for almost two weeks.* — ADV: ADV with v, ADV adj; ADJ; ADV: ADV after v; VERB = ponder; V over/about n; V n

**de|lib|era|tion** /dɪlɪbəreɪʃən/ **(deliberations)** [1] **Deliberation** is the long and careful consideration of a subject. ❑ *After much deliberation, a decision was reached.* [2] **Deliberations** are formal discussions where an issue is considered carefully. ❑ *Their deliberations were rather inconclusive.* [3] If you say or do something with **deliberation**, you do it slowly and carefully. ❑ *Fred spoke with deliberation... My mother folded her coat across the back of the chair with careful deliberation.* — N-UNCOUNT; N-PLURAL; N-UNCOUNT: usu with N

**de|lib|era|tive** /dɪlɪbərətɪv/ A **deliberative** institution or procedure has the power or the right to make important decisions. [FORMAL] ❑ *...a deliberative chamber like the House of Commons.* — ADJ usu ADJ n: usu ADJ n

**deli|ca|cy** /delɪkəsi/ **(delicacies)** [1] **Delicacy** is the quality of being easy to break or harm, and refers especially to people or things that are attractive or graceful. ❑ *...the delicacy of a rose.* [2] If you say that a situation or problem is **of** some **delicacy**, you mean that it is difficult to handle and needs careful and sensitive treatment. ❑ *There is a matter of some delicacy which I would like to discuss.* [3] If someone handles a difficult situation **with delicacy**, they handle it very carefully, making sure that nobody is offended. ❑ *Both countries are behaving with rare delicacy.* [4] A **delicacy** is a rare or expensive food that is considered especially nice to eat. ❑ *Smoked salmon was considered an expensive delicacy.* — N-UNCOUNT; N-UNCOUNT: usu with supp; N-UNCOUNT: oft with N = sensitivity; N-COUNT

**deli|cate** /delɪkət/ [1] Something that is **delicate** is small and beautifully shaped. ❑ *He had delicate hands.* ♦ **deli|cate|ly** *She was a shy, delicately pretty girl with enormous blue eyes.* [2] Something that is **delicate** has a colour, taste, or smell which is pleasant and not strong or intense. ❑ *Young haricot beans have a tender texture and a delicate, subtle flavour.* ♦ **deli|cate|ly** *...a soup delicately flavoured with nutmeg.* [3] If something is **delicate**, it is easy to harm, damage, or break, and needs to be handled or treated carefully. ❑ *Although the coral looks hard, it is very delicate.* [4] Someone who is **delicate** is not healthy and strong, and becomes ill easily. ❑ *She was physically delicate and psychologically unstable.* [5] You use **delicate** to describe a situation, problem, matter, or discussion that needs to be dealt with carefully and sensitively in order to avoid upsetting things or offending people. ❑ *The European members are afraid of upsetting the delicate balance of political interests.* ♦ **deli|cate|ly** *...a delicately-worded memo.* [6] A **delicate** task, movement, action, or product needs or shows great skill and attention to detail. ❑ *...a long and delicate operation carried out at a hospital in Florence.* ♦ **deli|cate|ly** *...the delicately embroidered sheets.* — ADJ: usu ADJ n = dainty; ADV: ADV adj/-ed = daintily; ADJ = subtle; ADV: ADV -ed/adj; ADJ = fragile ≠ robust; ADJ: usu v-link ADJ = frail; ADJ; ADV: ADV with v; ADJ; ADV: ADV with v

**deli|ca|tes|sen** /delɪkətesən/ **(delicatessens)** A **delicatessen** is a shop that sells high quality foods such as cheeses and cold meats that have been imported from other countries. — N-COUNT

**de|li|cious** /dɪlɪʃəs/ [1] Food that is **delicious** has a very pleasant taste. ❑ *There's always a wide selection of delicious meals to choose from.* ♦ **de|li|cious|ly** *This yoghurt has a deliciously creamy flavour.* [2] If you describe something as **delicious**, you mean that it is very pleasant. ❑ *...that delicious feeling of surprise.* ♦ **de|li|cious|ly** *It leaves your hair smelling deliciously fresh and fragrant.* — ADJ = tasty; ADV: ADV adj/-ed; ADJ: usu ADJ n; ADV: ADV adj/-ed

**de|light** /dɪlaɪt/ **(delights, delighting, delighted)** ♦◇◇ [1] **Delight** is a feeling of very great pleasure. ❑ *Throughout the house, the views are a constant source of surprise and delight... Andrew roared with delight when he heard Rachel's nickname for the baby... To my great delight, it worked perfectly.* [2] If someone **takes delight** or **takes a delight in** something, they get a lot of pleasure from it. ❑ *Haig took obvious delight in proving his critics wrong.* [3] You can refer to someone or something that gives you great pleasure or enjoyment as a **delight**. ❑ *Sampling the local cuisine is one of the delights of a holiday abroad.* [4] If something **delights** you, it gives you a lot of pleasure. ❑ *She has created a style of music that has delighted audiences all over the world.* [5] If you **delight in** something, you get a lot of pleasure from it. ❑ *Generations of adults and children have delighted in the story... He delighted in sharing his love of birds with children.* — N-UNCOUNT; PHRASE: V inflects, usu PHR in -ing/n; N-COUNT: oft N of n/-ing, N to-inf [approval] = joy; VERB V n; VERB V in n/-ing; V in n/-ing

**de|light|ed** /dɪlaɪtɪd/ ♦◇◇ [1] If you are **delighted**, you are extremely pleased and excited about something. ❑ *I know Frank will be delighted to see you... He said that he was delighted with the public response.* ♦ **de|light|ed|ly** *'There!' Jackson exclaimed delightedly.* [2] If someone invites or asks you to do something, you can say that you would be **delighted** to do it, as a way of showing that you are very willing to do it. ❑ *'You must come to Tinsley's graduation party.' — 'I'd be delighted.'* — ADJ: usu v-link ADJ, oft ADJ to-inf, ADJ with n; ADV: ADV with v; ADJ: v-link ADJ, oft ADJ to-inf [feelings]

**de|light|ful** /dɪlaɪtfʊl/ If you describe something or someone as **delightful**, you mean they are very pleasant. ❑ *It was the most delightful garden I had ever seen.* ♦ **de|light|ful|ly** *...a delightfully refreshing cologne.* — ADJ = lovely; ADV: ADV adj/-ed

**de|lim|it** /dɪlɪmɪt/ **(delimits, delimiting, delimited)** If you **delimit** something, you fix or establish its limits. [FORMAL] ❑ *This is not meant to delimit what approaches social researchers can adopt.* — VERB V n

**de|lin|eate** /dɪlɪnieɪt/ **(delineates, delineating, delineated)** [1] If you **delineate** something such as an idea or situation, you describe it or define it, often in a lot of detail. [FORMAL] ❑ *Biography must to some extent delineate characters.* [2] If you **delineate** a border, you say exactly where it is going to be. [FORMAL] ❑ *...an agreement to delineate the border.* — VERB V n; VERB V n

**de|lin|quen|cy** /dɪlɪŋkwənsi/ **(delinquencies)** **Delinquency** is criminal behaviour, especially that of young people. ❑ *He had no history of delinquency.* → See also **juvenile delinquency**. — N-UNCOUNT: also N in pl

**de|lin|quent** /dɪlɪŋkwənt/ **(delinquents)** Someone, usually a young person, who is **delinquent** repeatedly commits minor crimes. ❑ *...remand homes for delinquent children.* ♦ **Delinquent** is also a noun. ❑ *...a nine-year-old delinquent.* → See also **juvenile delinquent**. — ADJ; N-COUNT

**de|liri|ous** /dɪlɪəriəs/ [1] Someone who is **delirious** is unable to think or speak in a sensible and reasonable way, usually because they are very ill and have a fever. ❑ *I was delirious and blacked out several times.* [2] Someone who is **delirious** is extremely excited and happy. ❑ *I was delirious with joy.* ♦ **de|liri|ous|ly** *Dora returned from her honeymoon deliriously happy.* — ADJ: usu v-link ADJ; ADJ: oft ADJ with n = ecstatic; ADV: usu ADV adj, also ADV after v

**de|lir|ium** /dɪlɪəriəm/ If someone is suffering from **delirium**, they are not able to think or speak in a sensible and reasonable way because they are very ill and have a fever. ❑ *In her delirium, she had fallen to the floor several times.* — N-UNCOUNT

**de|list** /diːlɪst/ **(delists, delisting, delisted)** If a company **delists** or if its shares **are delisted**, its shares are removed from the official list of shares that can be traded on the stock market. [BUSINESS] ❑ *The group asked the Stock Exchange to delist the shares of four of its companies... The shares dived and were delisted from the London market.* — VERB V n; be V-ed from n; Also V

**de|liv|er** /dɪlɪvəʳ/ **(delivers, delivering, delivered)** ♦♦◇ [1] If you **deliver** something somewhere, you take it there. ❑ *The Canadians plan to deliver* — VERB V n to n more food to southern Somalia... The spy returned to deliver a second batch of classified documents.* [V n] 2 If you **deliver** something that you have promised to do, make, or produce, you do, make, or produce it. ❑ *They have yet to show that they can really deliver working technologies... We don't promise what we can't deliver.* [VERB; V n; V] 3 If you **deliver** a person or thing into someone's care, you give them responsibility for that person or thing. [FORMAL] ❑ *Mrs Montgomery was delivered into Mr Hinchcliffe's care... David delivered Holly gratefully into the woman's outstretched arms.* [VERB = hand over; be V-ed into/to n; V n into/to n] 4 If you **deliver** a lecture or speech, you give it in public. [FORMAL] ❑ *The president will deliver a speech about schools.* [VERB; V n] 5 When someone **delivers** a baby, they help the woman who is giving birth to the baby. ❑ *Her husband had to deliver the baby himself.* [VERB; V n] 6 If someone **delivers** a blow to someone else, they hit them. [WRITTEN] ❑ *Those blows to the head could have been delivered by a woman.* [VERB; be V-ed; Also V n]

**de|liv|er|ance** /dɪlɪvərəns/ **Deliverance** is rescue from imprisonment, danger, or evil. [LITERARY] ❑ *The opening scene shows them celebrating their sudden deliverance from war.* [N-UNCOUNT: oft N from n]

**de|liv|ery** /dɪlɪvəri/ **(deliveries)** ◆◇◇ 1 **Delivery** or a **delivery** is the bringing of letters, parcels, or other goods to someone's house or to another place where they want them. ❑ *It is available at £108, including VAT and delivery. ...the delivery of goods and resources.* [N-VAR: oft N of n] 2 A **delivery** of something is the goods that are delivered. ❑ *I got a delivery of fresh eggs this morning.* [N-COUNT: usu with supp] 3 A **delivery** person or service delivers things to a place. ❑ *...a pizza delivery man.* [ADJ: ADJ n] 4 You talk about someone's **delivery** when you are referring to the way in which they give a speech or lecture. ❑ *His speeches were magnificently written but his delivery was hopeless.* [N-UNCOUNT: usu poss N] 5 **Delivery** is the process of giving birth to a baby. ❑ *In the end, it was an easy delivery: a fine baby boy.* [N-VAR = birth]

**de|liv|ery room** **(delivery rooms)** In a hospital, the **delivery room** is the room where women give birth to their babies. [N-COUNT]

**dell** /del/ **(dells)** A **dell** is a small valley which has trees growing in it. [LITERARY] [N-COUNT]

**del|phin|ium** /delfɪniəm/ **(delphiniums)** A **delphinium** is a garden plant which has a tall stem with blue flowers growing up it. [N-COUNT]

**del|ta** /deltə/ **(deltas)** A **delta** is an area of low, flat land shaped like a triangle, where a river splits and spreads out into several branches before entering the sea. ❑ *...the Mississippi delta.* [N-COUNT: oft n N]

**de|lude** /dɪluːd/ **(deludes, deluding, deluded)** 1 If you **delude yourself**, you let yourself believe that something is true, even though it is not true. ❑ *The President was deluding himself if he thought he was safe from such action... We delude ourselves that we are in control... I had deluded myself into believing that it would all come right in the end.* [VERB; V pron-refl; V pron-refl that; V pron-refl into -ing] 2 To **delude** someone **into** thinking something means to make them believe what is not true. ❑ *Television deludes you into thinking you have experienced reality, when you haven't... He had been unwittingly deluded by their mystical nonsense.* [VERB = deceive; V n into -ing; be V-ed]

**de|lud|ed** /dɪluːdɪd/ Someone who is **deluded** believes something that is not true. ❑ *...deluded fanatics.* [ADJ = misguided]

**del|uge** /delju:dʒ/ **(deluges, deluging, deluged)** 1 A **deluge of** things is a large number of them which arrive or happen at the same time. ❑ *A deluge of manuscripts began to arrive in the post... This has brought a deluge of criticism.* [N-COUNT: usu sing, usu N of n = flood] 2 If a place or person **is deluged with** things, a large number of them arrive or happen at the same time. ❑ *During 1933, Papen's office was deluged with complaints.* [VERB: usu passive; be V-ed with/by n] 3 A **deluge** is a sudden, very heavy fall of rain. ❑ *About a dozen homes were damaged in the deluge.* [N-COUNT = downpour]

**de|lu|sion** /dɪluːʒᵊn/ **(delusions)** 1 A **delusion** is a false idea. ❑ *I was under the delusion that he intended to marry me.* [N-COUNT: usu with supp] 2 **Delusion** is the state of believing things that are not true. ❑ *This was not optimism, it was delusion.* [N-UNCOUNT] 3 If someone has **delusions of grandeur**, they think and behave as if they are much more important or powerful than they really are. [PHRASE; disapproval]

**deluxe** /dɪ lʌks/

✔ in BRIT, also use **de luxe**

**Deluxe** goods or services are better in quality and more expensive than ordinary ones. ❑ *...a rare, highly prized deluxe wine.* [ADJ: ADJ n, n ADJ = luxury]

**delve** /delv/ **(delves, delving, delved)** 1 If you **delve into** something, you try to discover new information about it. ❑ *Tormented by her ignorance, Jenny delves into her mother's past... If you're interested in a subject, use the Internet to delve deeper.* [VERB = dig, probe; V into n; V adv] 2 If you **delve inside** something such as a cupboard or a bag, you search inside it. [WRITTEN] ❑ *She delved into her rucksack and pulled out a folder.* [VERB; V prep/adv]

**dema|gog|ic** /deməgɒdʒɪk/ If you say that someone such as a politician is **demagogic**, you are criticizing them because you think they try to win people's support by appealing to their emotions rather than using reasonable arguments. [FORMAL] [ADJ; disapproval]

**dema|gogue** /deməgɒg, AM -gɔːg/ **(demagogues)**

✔ in AM, also use **demagog**

If you say that someone such as a politician is a **demagogue** you are criticizing them because you think they try to win people's support by appealing to their emotions rather than using reasonable arguments. [N-COUNT: oft adj N; disapproval]

**dema|gogy** /deməgɒdʒi/ or **demagoguery** You can refer to a method of political rule as **demagogy** if you disapprove of it because you think it involves appealing to people's emotions rather than using reasonable arguments. [N-UNCOUNT; disapproval]

**de|mand** /dɪmɑːnd, -mænd/ **(demands, demanding, demanded)** ◆◆◆ 1 If you **demand** something such as information or action, you ask for it in a very forceful way. ❑ *Mr Byers last night demanded an immediate explanation from the Education Secretary... Russia demanded that Unita send a delegation to the peace talks... The hijackers are demanding to speak to representatives of both governments... 'What did you expect me to do about it?' she demanded.* [VERB; V n from n; V that; V to-inf; V with quote] 2 If one thing **demands** another, the first needs the second in order to happen or be dealt with successfully. ❑ *He said the task of reconstruction would demand much patience, hard work and sacrifice.* [VERB = require; V n] 3 A **demand** is a firm request for something. ❑ *There have been demands for services from tenants up there.* [N-COUNT: usu with supp] 4 If you refer to **demand**, or to the **demand for** something, you are referring to how many people want to have it, do it, or buy it. ❑ *Another flight would be arranged on Saturday if sufficient demand arose... Demand for coal is down and so are prices.* [N-UNCOUNT ≠ supply] 5 **The demands of** something or its **demands on** you are the things which it needs or the things which you have to do for it. ❑ *...the demands and challenges of a new job.* [N-PLURAL: usu N of n, N on n]

**PHRASES** 6 If someone or something is **in demand** or **in great demand**, they are very popular and a lot of people want them. ❑ *He was much in demand as a lecturer in the US.* [PHRASE: v-link PHR] 7 If someone or something **makes demands on** you, they require you to do things which need a lot of time, energy, or money. ❑ *I had no right to make demands on his time.* [PHRASE: V inflects, usu PHR on n] 8 If something is available or happens **on demand**, you can have it or it happens whenever you want it or ask for it. ❑ *...a national commitment to providing treatment on demand for drug abusers.* [PHRASE]

**de|mand|ing** /dɪmɑːndɪŋ, -mænd-/ 1 A **demanding** job or task requires a lot of your time, energy, or attention. ❑ *He found he could no longer cope with his demanding job.* [ADJ: usu ADJ n] 2 People who are **demanding** are not easily satisfied or pleased. ❑ *Ricky was a very demanding child.* [ADJ]

**de|mar|cate** /diːmɑːʳkeɪt, AM dɪmɑːrk-/ **(demarcates, demarcating, demarcated)** If you **demarcate** something, you establish its boundaries or limits. [FORMAL] ❑ *A special UN commission was formed to demarcate the border.*
VERB = *delineate* — V n

**de|mar|ca|tion** /diːmɑːʳkeɪʃᵊn/ **Demarcation** is the establishment of boundaries or limits separating two areas, groups, or things. [FORMAL] ❑ *Talks were continuing about the demarcation of the border between the two countries.*
N-UNCOUNT: oft N n

**de|mean** /dɪmiːn/ **(demeans, demeaning, demeaned)** 1 If you **demean yourself**, you do something which makes people have less respect for you. ❑ *I wasn't going to demean myself by acting like a suspicious wife.* 2 To **demean** someone or something means to make people have less respect for them. ❑ *Some groups say that pornography demeans women.*
VERB — V pron-refl — VERB = *degrade* — V n

**de|mean|ing** /dɪmiːnɪŋ/ Something that is **demeaning** makes people have less respect for the person who is treated in that way, or who does that thing. ❑ *...demeaning sexist comments.*
ADJ: oft ADJ *to* n = *degrading*

**de|mean|our** /dɪmiːnəʳ/

✔ in AM, use **demeanor**

Your **demeanour** is the way you behave, which gives people an impression of your character and feelings. [FORMAL] ❑ *...her calm and cheerful demeanour.*
N-UNCOUNT: usu poss N

**de|ment|ed** /dɪmentɪd/ 1 Someone who is **demented** has a severe mental illness, especially Alzheimer's disease. [MEDICAL or OLD-FASHIONED] 2 If you describe someone as **demented**, you think that their actions are strange, foolish, or uncontrolled. [INFORMAL] ❑ *Sid broke into demented laughter.*
ADJ — ADJ disapproval = *crazy*

**de|men|tia** /dɪmenʃə/ **(dementias) Dementia** is a serious illness of the mind. [MEDICAL]
N-VAR

**dem|erara sug|ar** /deməreərə ʃʊgəʳ/ **Demerara sugar** is a type of brown sugar. It is made from sugar cane that is grown in the West Indies. [BRIT]
N-UNCOUNT

**de|merge** /diːmɜːʳdʒ/ **(demerges, demerging, demerged)** If a large company **is demerged** or **demerges**, it is broken down into several smaller companies. [BRIT, BUSINESS] ❑ *His ultimate aim is to demerge the group... Many companies merge and few demerge.*
VERB ≠ *merge* — V n — V

**de|merg|er** /diːmɜːʳdʒəʳ/ **(demergers)** A **demerger** is the separation of a large company into several smaller companies. [BRIT, BUSINESS]
N-COUNT ≠ *merger*

**de|mer|it** /diːmerɪt/ **(demerits)** The **demerits of** something or someone are their faults or disadvantages. [FORMAL] ❑ *...articles debating the merits and demerits of the three candidates.*
N-COUNT: usu pl, usu with poss ≠ *merit*

**demi-** /demi-/ **Demi-** is used at the beginning of some words to refer to something equivalent to half of the object or amount indicated by the rest of the word.
PREFIX

**demi|god** /demigɒd/ **(demigods)** 1 In mythology, a **demigod** is a less important god, especially one who is half god and half human. 2 If you describe a famous or important person such as a politician, writer, or musician as a **demigod**, you mean that you disapprove of the way in which people admire them and treat them like a god.
N-COUNT — N-COUNT disapproval

**de|mili|ta|rize** /diːmɪlɪtəraɪz/ **(demilitarizes, demilitarizing, demilitarized)**

✔ in BRIT, also use **demilitarise**

To **demilitarize** an area means to ensure that all military forces are removed from it. ❑ *He said the UN had made remarkable progress in demilitarizing the region.* ♦ **de|mili|ta|ri|za|tion** /diːmɪlɪtəraɪzeɪʃᵊn/ *Demilitarization of the country was out of the question.*
VERB — V n — N-UNCOUNT

**de|mise** /dɪmaɪz/ The **demise** of something or someone is their end or death. [FORMAL] ❑ *...the demise of the reform movement.*
N-SING: usu with poss

**demo** /demoʊ/ **(demos)** 1 A **demo** is a **demonstration** by a group of people to show their opposition to something or their support for something. [BRIT, INFORMAL] ❑ *...an anti-racist demo.* 2 A **demo** is a CD or tape with a sample of someone's music recorded on it. [INFORMAL] ❑ *He listened to one of my demo tapes.*
N-COUNT — N-COUNT: oft N n

**de|mob** /diːmɒb/ Someone's **demob** is their release from the armed forces. [BRIT, INFORMAL] ❑ *I didn't get back to Brussels until after my demob.*
N-UNCOUNT

**de|mobbed** /diːmɒbd/ When soldiers **are demobbed**, they are released from the armed forces. [BRIT, INFORMAL] ❑ *I'm still in the air force, though I'll be demobbed in a couple of months. ...housing and retraining demobbed soldiers.*
V-PASSIVE — *be* V-ed — V-ed

**de|mo|bi|lize** /diːmoʊbɪlaɪz/ **(demobilizes, demobilizing, demobilized)**

✔ in BRIT, also use **demobilise**

If a country or armed force **demobilizes** its troops, or if its troops **demobilize**, its troops are released from service and allowed to go home. ❑ *Both sides have agreed to demobilize 70% of their armies... It is unlikely that the rebels will agree to demobilise.* ♦ **de|mo|bi|li|za|tion** /diːmoʊbɪlaɪzeɪʃᵊn/ *...the demobilisation of a 100,000 strong army.*
VERB — V n — V — N-UNCOUNT: usu with supp

**de|moc|ra|cy** /dɪmɒkrəsi/ **(democracies)** ◆◆◇ 1 **Democracy** is a system of government in which people choose their rulers by voting for them in elections. ❑ *...the spread of democracy in Eastern Europe. ...the pro-democracy movement.* 2 A **democracy** is a country in which the people choose their government by voting for it. ❑ *The new democracies face tough challenges.* 3 **Democracy** is a system of running organizations, businesses, and groups in which each member is entitled to vote and take part in decisions. ❑ *...the union's emphasis on industrial democracy.*
N-UNCOUNT — N-COUNT: usu supp N — N-UNCOUNT: usu supp N

**demo|crat** /deməkræt/ **(democrats)** ◆◆◇ 1 A **Democrat** is a member or supporter of a particular political party which has the word 'democrat' or 'democratic' in its title, for example the Democratic Party in the United States. ❑ *...a senior Christian Democrat... Congressman Tom Downey is a Democrat from New York.* 2 A **democrat** is a person who believes in the ideals of democracy, personal freedom, and equality. ❑ *This is the time for democrats and not dictators.*
N-COUNT: oft supp N — N-COUNT

**demo|crat|ic** /deməkrætɪk/ ◆◆◇ 1 A **democratic** country, government, or political system is governed by representatives who are elected by the people. ❑ *Bolivia returned to democratic rule in 1982, after a series of military governments.* ♦ **demo|crati|cal|ly** /deməkrætɪkli/ *That June, Yeltsin became Russia's first democratically elected President.* 2 Something that is **democratic** is based on the idea that everyone should have equal rights and should be involved in making important decisions. ❑ *Education is the basis of a democratic society.* ♦ **demo|crati|cal|ly** *This committee will enable decisions to be made democratically.* 3 **Democratic** is used in the titles of some political parties. ❑ *...the Social Democratic Party.*
ADJ: usu ADJ n — ADV: ADV adj, ADV with v — ADJ — ADV — ADJ: ADJ n

**de|moc|ra|tize** /dɪmɒkrətaɪz/ **(democratizes, democratizing, democratized)**

✔ in BRIT, also use **democratise**

If a country or a system **is democratized**, it is made democratic. [JOURNALISM] ❑ *...a further need to democratize the life of society as a whole.* ♦ **de|moc|ra|ti|za|tion** /dɪmɒkrətaɪzeɪʃᵊn/ *...the democratisation of Eastern Europe.*
VERB — V n — N-UNCOUNT: oft *the* N *of* n

**de|mo|graph|ic** /deməgræfɪk/ **(demographics)** 1 **Demographic** means relating to or concerning demography. 2 The **demographics** of a place or society are the statistics relating to the people who live there. ❑ *...the changing demographics of the United States.* 3 In business, a **demographic** is a group of people in a society, es-
ADJ: ADJ n — N-PLURAL: oft N *of* n — N-SING

pecially people in a particular age group. [BUSINESS] ❑ *Most of our listeners are in the 25-39 demographic.*

**de|mog|ra|phy** /dɪmɒgrəfi/ **Demography** is the study of the changes in numbers of births, deaths, marriages, and cases of disease in a community over a period of time. N-UNCOUNT
♦ **de|mog|ra|pher (demographers)** ❑ *...a political-ly astute economist and demographer.* N-COUNT

**de|mol|ish** /dɪmɒlɪʃ/ **(demolishes, demolishing, demolished)** 1 To **demolish** something such as a building means to destroy it completely. ❑ *A storm moved directly over the island, demolishing buildings and flooding streets.* VERB V n 2 If you **demolish** someone's ideas or arguments, you prove that they are completely wrong or unreasonable. ❑ *Our intention was to demolish the rumours that have surrounded him.* VERB V n

**demo|li|tion** /deməlɪʃᵊn/ **(demolitions)** The **demolition** of a building is the act of deliberately destroying it, often in order to build something else in its place. ❑ *The project required the total demolition of the old bridge.* N-VAR

**de|mon** /diːmən/ **(demons)** 1 A **demon** is an evil spirit. ❑ *...a woman possessed by demons.* N-COUNT 2 If you approve of someone because they are very skilled at what they do or because they do it energetically, you can say that they do it like a **demon**. ❑ *He played like a demon.* N-COUNT [approval]

**de|mon|ic** /dɪmɒnɪk/ **Demonic** means coming from or belonging to a demon or being like a demon. ❑ *...demonic forces. ...a demonic grin.* ADJ: usu ADJ n

**de|mon|ize** /diːmənaɪz/ **(demonizes, demonizing, demonized)**

✔ in BRIT, also use **demonise**

If people **demonize** someone, they convince themselves that that person is evil. ❑ *Each side began to demonize the other.* VERB V n

**de|mon|ol|ogy** /diːmənɒlədʒi/ **Demonology** is a set of beliefs which says that a particular situation or group of people is evil or unacceptable. ❑ *...the usual deranged Right-wing stereotype of fascist Left demonology.* N-UNCOUNT

**de|mon|strable** /dɪmɒnstrəbᵊl/ A **demonstrable** fact or quality can be shown to be true or to exist. [FORMAL] ❑ *The road safety programme is having a demonstrable effect on road users.* ADJ: usu ADJ n
♦ **de|mon|strably** /dɪmɒnstrəbli/ *...demonstrably false statements.* ADV

**dem|on|strate** /demənstreɪt/ **(demonstrates, demonstrating, demonstrated)** ♦◇◇ 1 To **demonstrate** a fact means to make it clear to people. ❑ *The study also demonstrated a direct link between obesity and mortality... You have to demonstrate that you are reliable... They are anxious to demonstrate to the voters that they have practical policies... He's demonstrated how a campaign based on domestic issues can move votes.* VERB = show, prove V n V that V *to* n that V wh 2 If you **demonstrate** a particular skill, quality, or feeling, you show by your actions that you have it. ❑ *Have they, for example, demonstrated a commitment to democracy?* VERB = show, display V n
3 When people **demonstrate**, they march or gather somewhere to show their opposition to something or their support for something. ❑ *30,000 angry farmers demonstrated against possible cuts in subsidies... In the cities vast crowds have been demonstrating for change... Thousands of people demonstrated outside the parliament building.* VERB = protest V *against* n V *for* n V 4 If you **demonstrate** something, you show people how it works or how to do it. ❑ *The BBC has just successfully demonstrated a new digital radio transmission system... A style consultant will demonstrate how to dress to impress.* VERB V n V how

**dem|on|stra|tion** /demənstreɪʃᵊn/ **(demonstrations)** ♦◇◇ 1 A **demonstration** is a march or gathering which people take part in to show their opposition to something or their support for something. ❑ *Riot police broke up a demonstration by students.* N-COUNT 2 A **demonstration** of something is a talk by someone who shows you how to do it or how it works. ❑ *...a cookery demonstration.* N-COUNT: usu with supp 3 A **demonstration of** a fact or situation is a clear proof of it. ❑ *This is a clear demonstration of how technology has changed.* N-COUNT: usu N *of* n 4 A **demonstration of** a quality or feeling is an expression of it. ❑ *There's been no public demonstration of opposition to the President.* N-COUNT: N *of* n = display

**de|mon|stra|tive** /dɪmɒnstrətɪv/ **(demonstratives)** 1 Someone who is **demonstrative** shows affection freely and openly. ❑ *We came from the English tradition of not being demonstrative.* ADJ ≠ reserved
♦ **de|mon|stra|tive|ly** *Some children respond more demonstratively than others.* ADV 2 In grammar, the words 'this', 'that', 'these', and 'those' are sometimes called **demonstratives**. N-COUNT

**de|mon|stra|tor** /demənstreɪtəʳ/ **(demonstrators)** ♦◇◇ 1 **Demonstrators** are people who are marching or gathering somewhere to show their opposition to something or their support for something. ❑ *I saw the police using tear gas to try and break up a crowd of demonstrators.* N-COUNT: usu pl 2 A **demonstrator** is a person who shows people how something works or how to do something. N-COUNT

**de|mor|al|ize** /dɪmɒrəlaɪz, AM -mɔːr-/ **(demoralizes, demoralizing, demoralized)**

✔ in BRIT, also use **demoralise**

If something **demoralizes** someone, it makes them lose so much confidence in what they are doing that they want to give up. ❑ *Clearly, one of the objectives is to demoralize the enemy troops in any way they can.* VERB V n
♦ **de|mor|al|ized** *The ship's crew were now exhausted and utterly demoralized.* ADJ

**de|mor|al|iz|ing** /dɪmɒrəlaɪzɪŋ, AM -mɔːr-/

✔ in BRIT, also use **demoralising**

If something is **demoralizing**, it makes you lose so much confidence in what you are doing that you want to give up. ❑ *Redundancy can be a demoralising prospect.* ADJ = disheartening

**de|mote** /dɪmoʊt/ **(demotes, demoting, demoted)** 1 If someone **demotes** you, they give you a lower rank or a less important position than you already have, often as a punishment. ❑ *It's very difficult to demote somebody who has been standing in during maternity leave.* VERB ≠ promote V n
♦ **de|mo|tion** /dɪmoʊʃᵊn/ **(demotions)** *He is seeking redress for what he alleges was an unfair demotion.* N-VAR ≠ promotion 2 If a team in a sports league **is demoted**, that team has to compete in the next competition in a lower division, because it was one of the least successful teams in the higher division. [BRIT] ❑ *The club was demoted at the end of last season.* VERB: usu passive ≠ promote *be* V-ed
♦ **de|mo|tion** *The team now almost certainly faces demotion.* N-VAR ≠ promotion

**de|mot|ic** /dɪmɒtɪk/ 1 **Demotic** language is the type of informal language used by ordinary people. [FORMAL] ❑ *...television's demotic style of language.* ADJ = colloquial 2 **Demotic** is used to describe something or someone that is typical of ordinary people. [FORMAL] ❑ *...demotic entertainments such as TV soap operas.* ADJ: usu ADJ n = popular

**de|mur** /dɪmɜːʳ/ **(demurs, demurring, demurred)** 1 If you **demur**, you say that you do not agree with something or will not do something that you have been asked to do. [FORMAL] ❑ *The doctor demurred, but Piercey was insistent.* VERB V 2 If you do something **without demur**, you do it immediately and without making any protest. [FORMAL] ❑ *When Scobie opened the door and stood aside for her to enter, she did so without demur.* PHRASE: PHR after v

**de|mure** /dɪmjʊəʳ/ 1 If you describe someone, usually a young woman, as **demure**, you mean they are quiet and rather shy, usually in a way that you like and find appealing, and behave very correctly. ❑ *She's very demure and sweet.* ADJ [approval]
♦ **de|mure|ly** *She smiled demurely.* ADV: usu ADV with v 2 **Demure** clothes do not reveal your body and they give the impression that you are shy and behave correctly. [WRITTEN] ❑ *...a demure high-necked white blouse.* ADJ: usu ADJ n
♦ **de|mure|ly** *She was demurely dressed in a black woollen suit.* ADV: ADV -ed, ADV after v

**de|mu|tu|alise** /diːmjuːtʃuəlaɪz/ **(demutualises, demutualising, demutualised)** If a building society or insurance company **demutualises**, it abandons its mutual status and becomes a limited company. [BRIT, BUSINESS] ❑ *97 per cent of the group's members support its plans to demutualise.* VERB V
♦ **de|mu|tu|ali|sa|tion** /diːmjuːtʃuəlaɪzeɪʃən/ *Policyholders voted for demutualisation.* N-UNCOUNT

**de|mys|ti|fy** /diːmɪstɪfaɪ/ **(demystifies, demystifying, demystified)** If you **demystify** something, you make it easier to understand by giving a clear explanation of it. ❑ *This book aims to demystify medical treatments.* VERB

**den** /den/ **(dens)** 1 A **den** is the home of certain types of wild animals such as lions or foxes. N-COUNT 2 Your **den** is a quiet room in your house where you can go to study, work, or carry on a hobby without being disturbed. [AM] N-COUNT 3 A **den** is a secret place where people meet, usually for a dishonest purpose. ❑ *I could provide you with the addresses of at least three illegal drinking dens.* N-COUNT: usu supp N 4 If you describe a place as a **den of** a particular type of bad or illegal behaviour, you mean that a lot of that type of behaviour goes on there. ❑ *...the one-bedroomed flat that was to become his den of savage debauchery.* N-COUNT: N *of* n

**de|na|tion|al|ize** /diːnæʃənəlaɪz/ **(denationalizes, denationalizing, denationalized)**

in BRIT, also use **denationalise**

To **denationalize** an industry or business means to transfer it into private ownership so that it is no longer owned and controlled by the state. [OLD-FASHIONED, BUSINESS] ❑ *The government started to denationalize many financial institutions.* VERB = privatize ≠ nationalize V n
♦ **de|na|tion|ali|za|tion** /diːnæʃənəlaɪzeɪʃən/ *...the denationalisation of industry.* N-UNCOUNT = privatization

**de|ni|al** /dɪnaɪəl/ **(denials)** 1 A **denial** of something is a statement that it is not true, does not exist, or did not happen. ❑ *Despite official denials, the rumours still persist... Denial of the Mafia's existence is nothing new.* N-VAR: oft N *of* n 2 The **denial of** something to someone is the act of refusing to let them have it. [FORMAL] ❑ *...the denial of visas to international relief workers.* N-UNCOUNT: usu N *of* n 3 In psychology, **denial** is when a person cannot or will not accept an unpleasant truth. ❑ *...an addict who is in denial about his addiction.* N-UNCOUNT

**den|ier** /deniəʳ/ **Denier** is used when indicating the thickness of stockings and tights. ❑ *...fifteen-denier stockings.* N-UNCOUNT: num N

**deni|grate** /denɪgreɪt/ **(denigrates, denigrating, denigrated)** If you **denigrate** someone or something, you criticize them unfairly or insult them. ❑ *The amendment prohibits obscene or indecent materials which denigrate the objects or beliefs of a particular religion.* VERB V n ♦ **deni|gra|tion** /denɪgreɪʃən/ *...the denigration of minorities in this country.* N-UNCOUNT: usu N *of* n

**den|im** /denɪm/ **Denim** is a thick cotton cloth, usually blue, which is used to make clothes. Jeans are made from denim. ❑ *...a light blue denim jacket.* N-UNCOUNT: oft N n

**den|ims** /denɪmz/ **Denims** are casual trousers made of denim. ❑ *She was dressed in blue denims.* N-PLURAL: also *a pair of* N = jeans

**deni|zen** /denɪzən/ **(denizens)** A **denizen of** a particular place is a person, animal, or plant that lives or grows in this place. [FORMAL] ❑ *Gannets are denizens of the open ocean.* N-COUNT: usu N *of* n

**de|nomi|na|tion** /dɪnɒmɪneɪʃən/ **(denominations)** 1 A particular **denomination** is a particular religious group which has slightly different beliefs from other groups within the same faith. ❑ *Acceptance of women preachers varies greatly from denomination to denomination.* N-COUNT 2 The **denomination** of a banknote or coin is its official value. ❑ *...a pile of bank notes, mostly in small denominations.* N-COUNT

**de|nomi|na|tion|al** /dɪnɒmɪneɪʃənəl/ **Denominational** means relating to or organized by a particular religious denomination. ❑ *...a multi-denominational group of religious leaders.* ADJ: ADJ n

**de|nomi|na|tor** /dɪnɒmɪneɪtəʳ/ **(denominators)** In mathematics, **the denominator** is the number which appears under the line in a fraction. → See also **common denominator, lowest common denominator.** N-COUNT

**de|note** /dɪnoʊt/ **(denotes, denoting, denoted)** 1 If one thing **denotes** another, it is a sign or indication of it. [FORMAL] ❑ *Red eyes denote strain and fatigue... There was a message waiting, denoting that someone had been here ahead of her.* VERB = indicate V n V that 2 What a symbol **denotes** is what it represents. [FORMAL] ❑ *In figure 24 'D' denotes quantity demanded and 'S' denotes quantity supplied.* VERB = represent V n

**de|noue|ment** /deɪnuːmɒn/ **(denouements)** also **dénouement.** In a book, play, or series of events, the **denouement** is the sequence of events at the end, when things come to a conclusion. ❑ *...an unexpected denouement.* N-COUNT: usu sing

**de|nounce** /dɪnaʊns/ **(denounces, denouncing, denounced)** 1 If you **denounce** a person or an action, you criticize them severely and publicly because you feel strongly that they are wrong or evil. ❑ *German leaders denounced the attacks and pleaded for tolerance... Some 25,000 demonstrators denounced him as a traitor.* VERB V n V n *as* n/adj 2 If you **denounce** someone who has broken a rule or law, you report them to the authorities. ❑ *...informers who might denounce you at any moment.* VERB V n Also V n *to* n

**dense** /dens/ **(denser, densest)** 1 Something that is **dense** contains a lot of things or people in a small area. ❑ *Where Bucharest now stands, there once was a large, dense forest... They thrust their way through the dense crowd.* ADJ ≠ sparse ♦ **dense|ly** *Java is a densely populated island.* ADV: usu ADV -ed ≠ sparsely 2 **Dense** fog or smoke is difficult to see through because it is very heavy and dark. ❑ *A dense column of smoke rose several miles into the air.* ADJ = thick 3 In science, a **dense** substance is very heavy in relation to its volume. [TECHNICAL] ❑ *...a small dense star.* ADJ 4 If you say that someone is **dense**, you mean that you think they are stupid and that they take a long time to understand simple things. [INFORMAL] ❑ *He's not a bad man, just a bit dense.* ADJ: v-link ADJ = thick

**den|sity** /densɪti/ **(densities)** 1 **Density** is the extent to which something is filled or covered with people or things. ❑ *...a law which restricts the density of housing... The region has a very high population density.* N-VAR: usu with supp, oft N *of* n 2 In science, the **density** of a substance or object is the relation of its mass or weight to its volume. [TECHNICAL] N-VAR: usu with supp, oft with poss

**dent** /dent/ **(dents, denting, dented)** 1 If you **dent** the surface of something, you make a hollow area in it by hitting or pressing it. ❑ *Its brass feet dented the carpet's thick pile.* VERB V n ♦ **dent|ed** *Watch out for bargains, but never buy dented cans.* ADJ 2 A **dent** is a hollow in the surface of something which has been caused by hitting or pressing it. ❑ *There was a dent in the car which hadn't been there before.* N-COUNT 3 If something **dents** your ideas or your pride, it makes you realize that your ideas are wrong, or that you are not as good or successful as you thought. ❑ *This has not dented the City's enthusiasm for the company.* VERB V n

**den|tal** /dentəl/ **Dental** is used to describe things that relate to teeth or to the care and treatment of teeth. ❑ *You can get free dental treatment. ...the dental profession.* ADJ: ADJ n

**den|tal floss** **Dental floss** is a type of thread that is used to clean the gaps between your teeth. → See also **floss.** N-UNCOUNT

**den|tist** /dentɪst/ **(dentists)** A **dentist** is a person who is qualified to examine and treat people's teeth. ❑ *Visit your dentist twice a year for a check-up.* N-COUNT ♦ **The dentist** or **the dentist's** is used to refer to the surgery or clinic where a dentist works. ❑ *It's worse than being at the dentist's.* N-SING: *the* N

**den|tis|try** /dentɪstri/ **Dentistry** is the work done by a dentist. N-UNCOUNT

**den|tures** /dentʃəʳz/

The form **denture** is used as a modifier.

**Dentures** are artificial teeth worn by people who no longer have all their own teeth. N-PLURAL = *false teeth*

**de|nude** /dɪnjuːd, AM -nuːd/ **(denudes, denuding, denuded)** [1] To **denude** an area means to destroy the plants in it. [FORMAL] ❑ *Mining would pollute the lake and denude the forest.* VERB V n [2] To **denude** someone or something **of** a particular thing means to take it away from them. [FORMAL] ❑ *The Embassy is now denuded of all foreign and local staff.* VERB = *divest* V n *of* n

**de|nun|cia|tion** /dɪnʌnsieɪʃən/ **(denunciations)** [1] **Denunciation of** someone or something is severe public criticism of them. ❑ *On September 24, he wrote a stinging denunciation of his critics.* N-VAR: oft N *of* n = *condemnation* [2] **Denunciation** is the act of reporting someone who has broken a rule or law to the authorities. ❑ *...the denunciation of Jews to the Nazis during the Second World War.* N-VAR

**Den|ver boot** /denvəʳ buːt/ **(Denver boots)** A **Denver boot** is a large metal device which is fitted to the wheel of an illegally parked car or other vehicle in order to prevent it from being driven away. The driver has to pay to have the device removed. [AM] N-COUNT

in BRIT, use **clamp**, **wheel clamp**

**deny** /dɪnaɪ/ **(denies, denying, denied)** ◆◆◇ [1] When you **deny** something, you state that it is not true. ❑ *She denied both accusations... The government has denied that there was a plot to assassinate the president... They all denied ever having seen her.* VERB ≠ *admit* V n V that V -ing [2] If you **deny** someone something that they need or want, you refuse to let them have it. ❑ *If he is unlucky, he may find that his ex-partner denies him access to his children... Don't deny yourself pleasure.* VERB = *refuse* V n n V pron-refl n

**de|odor|ant** /dioʊdərənt/ **(deodorants) Deodorant** is a substance that you can use on your body to hide or prevent the smell of sweat. N-MASS

**de|odor|ize** /dioʊdəraɪz/ **(deodorizes, deodorizing, deodorized)**

in BRIT, also use **deodorise**

If you **deodorize** something, you remove unpleasant smells from it. [FORMAL] ❑ *The machine uses minute quantities of ozone to sterilise and deodorise refrigerated food vehicles. ...a deodorising foot spray.* VERB V n V-ing

**de|part** /dɪpɑːʳt/ **(departs, departing, departed)** [1] When something or someone **departs from** a place, they leave it and start a journey to another place. ❑ *Our tour departs from Heathrow Airport on 31 March and returns 16 April... In the morning Mr McDonald departed for Sydney... The coach departs Potsdam in the morning.* VERB V *from* n V *for* n V n [2] If you **depart from** a traditional, accepted, or agreed way of doing something, you do it in a different or unexpected way. ❑ *Why is it in this country that we have departed from good educational sense?* VERB = *deviate* V *from* n [3] If someone **departs** from a job, they resign from it or leave it. In American English, you can say that someone **departs** a job. ❑ *Lipton is planning to depart from the company he founded. ...a number of staff departed during his reign as rector of the Royal College of Art... He departed baseball in the '60s.* VERB V *from* n V V n

**de|part|ed** /dɪpɑːʳtɪd/ **Departed** friends or relatives are people who have died. [FORMAL] ❑ *...departed friends.* ♦ **The departed** are people who have died. ❑ *We held services for the departed.* ADJ: usu ADJ n N-PLURAL: the N = *deceased*

**de|part|ment** /dɪpɑːʳtmənt/ **(departments)** ◆◆◆ [1] A **department** is one of the sections in an organization such as a government, business, or university. A department is also one of the sections in a large shop. ❑ *...the U.S. Department of Health, Education and Welfare... He moved to the sales department. ...the jewelry department.* N-COUNT: usu with supp [2] If you say that a task or area of knowledge **is not** your **department**, you mean that you are not responsible for it or do not know much about it. ❑ *'I'm afraid the name means nothing to me,' he said. 'That's not my department.'* PHRASE: V inflects

**de|part|men|tal** /diːpɑːʳtmentəl/ **Departmental** is used to describe the activities, responsibilities, or possessions of a department in a government, company, or other organization. ❑ *...the departmental budget.* ADJ: ADJ n

**de|part|ment store (department stores)** A **department store** is a large shop which sells many different kinds of goods. N-COUNT

**de|par|ture** /dɪpɑːʳtʃəʳ/ **(departures)** ◆◇◇ [1] **Departure** or a **departure** is the act of going away from somewhere. ❑ *...the President's departure for Helsinki... They hoped this would lead to the departure of all foreign forces from the country... The airline has more than 90 scheduled departures from here every day.* N-VAR: oft with poss ≠ *arrival* [2] The **departure** of a person **from** a job, or a member from an organization, is their act of leaving it or being forced to leave it. [FORMAL] ❑ *This would inevitably involve his departure from the post of Prime Minister.* N-VAR: with poss, oft N *from* n [3] If someone does something different or unusual, you can refer to their action as a **departure**. ❑ *Taylor announced another departure from practice in that England will train at Wembley.* N-COUNT: oft N *from* n = *deviation*

**de|par|ture lounge (departure lounges)** In an airport, the **departure lounge** is the place where passengers wait before they get onto their plane. N-COUNT

**de|par|ture tax (departure taxes) Departure tax** is a tax that airline passengers have to pay in order to use an airport. ❑ *Many countries charge departure tax in US dollars rather than local currency.* N-VAR = *airport tax*

**de|pend** /dɪpend/ **(depends, depending, depended)** ◆◆◇ [1] If you say that one thing **depends on** another, you mean that the first thing will be affected or determined by the second. ❑ *The cooking time needed depends on the size of the potato... How much it costs depends upon how much you buy.* VERB V *on/upon* n V *on/upon* wh [2] If you **depend on** someone or something, you need them in order to be able to survive physically, financially, or emotionally. ❑ *He depended on his writing for his income... Choosing the right account depends on working out your likely average balance.* VERB = *rely* V *on/upon* n/-ing V *on/upon* n/-ing [3] If you can **depend on** a person, organization, or law, you know that they will support you or help you when you need them. ❑ *'You can depend on me,' Cross assured him.* VERB = *rely* V *on/upon* n [4] You use **depend** in expressions such as **it depends** to indicate that you cannot give a clear answer to a question because the answer will be affected or determined by other factors. ❑ *'But how long can you stay in the house?' — 'I don't know. It depends.'... It all depends on your definition of punk, doesn't it?* VERB *it/that* V *it* V *on* n/wh [5] You use **depending on** when you are saying that something varies according to the circumstances mentioned. ❑ *I tend to have a different answer, depending on the family.* PREP-PHRASE: PREP n/wh

**de|pend|able** /dɪpendəbəl/ If you say that someone or something is **dependable**, you approve of them because you feel that you can be sure that they will always act consistently or sensibly, or do what you need them to do. ❑ *He was a good friend, a dependable companion.* ADJ approval = *reliable*

**de|pend|ant** /dɪpendənt/ **(dependants)** also **dependent.** Your **dependants** are the people you support financially, such as your children. [FORMAL] ❑ *The British Legion raises funds to help ex-service personnel and their dependants.* N-COUNT

**de|pend|ence** /dɪpendəns/ [1] Your **dependence on** something or someone is your need for them in order to succeed or be able to survive. ❑ *...the city's traditional dependence on tourism.* N-UNCOUNT: usu N *on* n = *reliance* [2] If you talk about drug **dependence** or alcohol **dependence**, you are referring to a situation where someone is addicted to drugs or is an alcoholic. N-UNCOUNT: usu n N = *addiction* [3] You talk about the **dependence** of one thing **on** another when the first thing will be affected or determined by the second. ❑ *...the dependence of circulation on production.* N-UNCOUNT: usu with supp

**de|pend|en|cy** /dɪpe̲ndənsi/ **(dependencies)** 1 A **dependency** is a country which is controlled by another country. N-COUNT 2 You talk about someone's **dependency** when they have a deep emotional, physical, or financial need for a particular person or thing, especially one that you consider excessive or undesirable. ❑ *We worried about his dependency on his mother.* N-UNCOUNT: oft N *on* n ≠ independence 3 If you talk about alcohol **dependency** or chemical **dependency**, you are referring to a situation where someone is an alcoholic or is addicted to drugs. [mainly AM] ❑ *In 1985, he began to show signs of alcohol and drug dependency.* N-VAR: usu n N = addiction

**de|pend|ent** /dɪpe̲ndənt/ 1 To be **dependent on** something or someone means to need them in order to succeed or be able to survive. ❑ *The local economy is overwhelmingly dependent on oil and gas extraction.* ADJ: oft ADJ *on/upon* n = reliant 2 If one thing is **dependent on** another, the first thing will be affected or determined by the second. ❑ *The treatment of infertility is largely dependent on the ability of couples to pay.* ADJ: v-link ADJ *on/upon* n = contingent ≠ independent 3 → See also **dependant**.

**de|per|son|al|ize** /diːpɜ̲ːʳsənəlaɪz/ **(depersonalizes, depersonalizing, depersonalized)**

> in BRIT, also use **depersonalise**

1 To **depersonalize** a system or a situation means to treat it as if it did not really involve people, or to treat it as if the people involved were not really important. ❑ *It is true that modern weaponry depersonalised war.* VERB V n 2 To **depersonalize** someone means to treat them as if they do not matter because their individual feelings and thoughts are not important. ❑ *She does not feel that the book depersonalises women.* VERB V n

**de|pict** /dɪpɪ̲kt/ **(depicts, depicting, depicted)** 1 To **depict** someone or something means to show or represent them in a work of art such as a drawing or painting. ❑ *...a gallery of pictures depicting Nelson's most famous battles.* VERB V n 2 To **depict** someone or something means to describe them or give an impression of them in writing. ❑ *Margaret Atwood's novel depicts a gloomy, futuristic America... Children's books often depict farmyard animals as gentle, lovable creatures.* VERB = portray V n V n *as* n

**de|pic|tion** /dɪpɪ̲kʃᵊn/ **(depictions)** A **depiction** of something is a picture or a written description of it. N-VAR = portrayal

**de|pila|tory** /dɪpɪ̲lətəri, AM -tɔːri/ **(depilatories)** 1 **Depilatory** substances and processes remove unwanted hair from your body. ADJ: ADJ n 2 A **depilatory** is a depilatory substance. N-COUNT

**de|plete** /dɪpliː̲t/ **(depletes, depleting, depleted)** To **deplete** a stock or amount of something means to reduce it. [FORMAL] ❑ *...substances that deplete the ozone layer.* VERB V n ♦ **de|plet|ed** *...Robert E. Lee's worn and depleted army.* ADJ ♦ **de|ple|tion** /dɪpliː̲ʃᵊn/ *...the depletion of underground water supplies.* N-UNCOUNT: usu with supp

**de|plet|ed ura|nium** **Depleted uranium** is a type of uranium that is used in some bombs. N-UNCOUNT

**de|plor|able** /dɪplɔ̲ːrəbᵊl/ If you say that something is **deplorable**, you think that it is very bad and unacceptable. [FORMAL] ❑ *Many of them live under deplorable conditions.* ADJ = appalling ♦ **de|plor|ably** *The reporters travelling with the President behaved deplorably.* ADV: ADV after v, ADV adj

**de|plore** /dɪplɔ̲ːʳ/ **(deplores, deploring, deplored)** If you say that you **deplore** something, you think it is very wrong or immoral. [FORMAL] ❑ *He deplored the fact that the Foreign Secretary was driven into resignation.* VERB V n

**de|ploy** /dɪplɔ̲ɪ/ **(deploys, deploying, deployed)** To **deploy** troops or military resources means to organize or position them so that they are ready to be used. ❑ *The president said he had no intention of deploying ground troops.* VERB V n

**de|ploy|ment** /dɪplɔ̲ɪmənt/ **(deployments)** The **deployment** of troops, resources, or equipment is the organization and positioning of them so that they are ready for quick action. ❑ *...the deployment of troops into townships.* N-VAR: oft N *of* n

**de|popu|late** /diːpɒ̲pjʊleɪt/ **(depopulates, depopulating, depopulated)** To **depopulate** an area means to greatly reduce the number of people living there. ❑ *The famine threatened to depopulate the continent.* VERB V n ♦ **de|popu|lat|ed** *...a small, rural, and depopulated part of the south-west.* ADJ ♦ **de|popu|la|tion** /diːpɒpjʊle̲ɪʃᵊn/ *...rural depopulation.* N-UNCOUNT

**de|port** /dɪpɔ̲ːʳt/ **(deports, deporting, deported)** If a government **deports** someone, usually someone who is not a citizen of that country, it sends them out of the country because they have committed a crime or because it believes they do not have the right to be there. ❑ *...a government decision earlier this month to deport all illegal immigrants.* VERB V n ♦ **de|por|ta|tion** /diːpɔːʳte̲ɪʃᵊn/ **(deportations)** *...thousands of Albanian migrants facing deportation.* N-VAR

**de|por|tee** /diːpɔːʳtiː̲/ **(deportees)** A **deportee** is someone who is being deported. N-COUNT

**de|port|ment** /dɪpɔ̲ːʳtmənt/ Your **deportment** is the way you behave, especially the way you walk and move. [FORMAL] N-UNCOUNT = bearing

**de|pose** /dɪpo̲ʊz/ **(deposes, deposing, deposed)** If a ruler or political leader **is deposed**, they are forced to give up their position. ❑ *Mr Ben Bella was deposed in a coup in 1965.* VERB: usu passive = oust *be* V-ed

**de|pos|it** /dɪpɒ̲zɪt/ **(deposits, depositing, deposited)** ◆◇◇ 1 A **deposit** is a sum of money which is part of the full price of something, and which you pay when you agree to buy it. ❑ *A £50 deposit is required when ordering, and the balance is due upon delivery.* N-COUNT: usu sing = down payment 2 A **deposit** is a sum of money which you pay when you start renting something. The money is returned to you if you do not damage what you have rented. ❑ *It is common to ask for the equivalent of a month's rent as a deposit.* N-COUNT: usu sing 3 A **deposit** is a sum of money which is in a bank account or savings account, especially a sum which will be left there for some time. N-COUNT 4 A **deposit** is a sum of money which you have to pay if you want to be a candidate in a parliamentary or European election. The money is returned to you if you receive more than a certain percentage of the votes. [BRIT] ❑ *The Tory candidate lost his deposit.* N-COUNT: oft poss N 5 A **deposit** is an amount of a substance that has been left somewhere as a result of a chemical or geological process. ❑ *...underground deposits of gold and diamonds.* N-COUNT: usu with supp 6 To **deposit** someone or something somewhere means to put them or leave them there. ❑ *Someone was seen depositing a packet... Fritz deposited a glass and two bottles of beer in front of Wolfe.* VERB = plant V n V n prep/adv 7 If you **deposit** something somewhere, you put it where it will be safe until it is needed again. ❑ *You are advised to deposit valuables in the hotel safe.* VERB V n prep/adv 8 If you **deposit** a sum of money, you pay it into a bank account or savings account. ❑ *The customer has to deposit a minimum of £100 monthly.* VERB ≠ withdraw V n 9 If a substance **is deposited** somewhere, it is left there as a result of a chemical or geological process. ❑ *The phosphate was deposited by the decay of marine microorganisms.* VERB: usu passive *be* V-ed

**de|pos|it ac|count** **(deposit accounts)** A **deposit account** is a type of bank account where the money in it earns interest. [BRIT] N-COUNT

> in AM, use **savings account**

**depo|si|tion** /de̲pəzɪʃᵊn/ **(depositions)** A **deposition** is a formal written statement, made for example by a witness to a crime, which can be used in a court of law if the witness cannot be present. ❑ *The jury heard 200 pages of depositions.* N-COUNT

**de|posi|tor** /dɪpɒ̲zɪtəʳ/ **(depositors)** A bank's **depositors** are the people who have accounts with that bank. N-COUNT

**de|posi|tory** /dɪpɒ̲zɪtəri/ **(depositories)** A **depository** is a place where objects can be stored safely. N-COUNT

**de|pot** /de̲pəʊ, AM diː̲-/ **(depots)** 1 A **depot** is a place where large amounts of raw materials, equipment, arms, or other supplies are kept until they are needed. ❑ *...food depots. ...a government* N-COUNT = warehouse *arms depot.* [2] N-COUNT A **depot** is a large building or open area where buses or railway engines are kept when they are not being used. [mainly BRIT] [3] N-COUNT A **depot** is a bus station or railway station. [AM] ❑ *...a bus depot in Ozark, Alabama.*

**de|prave** /dɪpreɪv/ **(depraves, depraving, depraved)** VERB = corrupt Something that **depraves** someone makes them morally bad or evil. [FORMAL] ❑ V n *...material likely to deprave or corrupt those who see it.*

**de|praved** /dɪpreɪvd/ ADJ = degenerate **Depraved** actions, things, or people are morally bad or evil. ❑ *...a disturbing and depraved film.*

**de|prav|ity** /dɪprævɪti/ N-UNCOUNT **Depravity** is very dishonest or immoral behaviour. [FORMAL] ❑ *...the absolute depravity that can exist in war.*

**dep|re|cate** /deprɪkeɪt/ **(deprecates, deprecating, deprecated)** VERB If you **deprecate** something, you criticize it. [FORMAL] ❑ V n *He deprecated the low quality of entrants to the profession.*

**dep|re|cat|ing** /deprɪkeɪtɪŋ/ ADJ A **deprecating** attitude, gesture, or remark shows that you think that something is not very good, especially something associated with yourself. [WRITTEN] ❑ *Erica made a little deprecating shrug.* ♦ **dep|re|cat|ing|ly** ADV: ADV after v *He speaks deprecatingly of his father as a lonely man.*

**de|pre|ci|ate** /dɪpriːʃieɪt/ **(depreciates, depreciating, depreciated)** VERB If something such as a currency **depreciates** or if something **depreciates** it, it loses some of its original value. ❑ V *Inflation is rising rapidly; the yuan is depreciating...* V n *The demand for foreign currency depreciates the real value of local currencies...* V *by* amount *During those five years, the pound depreciated by a quarter.* ♦ **de|pre|cia|tion** N-VAR /dɪpriːʃieɪʃən/ **(depreciations)** *...miscellaneous costs, including machinery depreciation and wages.*

**dep|re|da|tion** /deprɪdeɪʃən/ **(depredations)** N-VAR: usu with supp The **depredations** of a person, animal, or force are their harmful actions, which usually involve taking or damaging something. [FORMAL] ❑ *Much of the region's environmental depredation is a result of poor planning.*

**de|press** /dɪpres/ **(depresses, depressing, depressed)** [1] VERB If someone or something **depresses** you, they make you feel sad and disappointed. ❑ V n *I must admit the state of the country depresses me.* [2] VERB If something **depresses** prices, wages, or figures, it causes them to become less. ❑ V n *The stronger U.S. dollar depressed sales.*

**de|pressed** /dɪprest/ [1] ADJ: usu v-link ADJ If you are **depressed**, you are sad and feel that you cannot enjoy anything, because your situation is so difficult and unpleasant. ❑ *She's been very depressed and upset about this whole situation.* [2] ADJ = run-down A **depressed** place or industry does not have enough business or employment to be successful. ❑ *...legislation to encourage investment in depressed areas.*

**de|press|ing** /dɪpresɪŋ/ ADJ Something that is **depressing** makes you feel sad and disappointed. ❑ *Yesterday's unemployment figures were depressing.* ♦ **de|press|ing|ly** ADV: usu ADV adj *It all sounded depressingly familiar to Janet.*

**de|pres|sion** /dɪpreʃən/ **(depressions)** ◆◇◇ [1] N-VAR **Depression** is a mental state in which you are sad and feel that you cannot enjoy anything, because your situation is so difficult and unpleasant. ❑ *Mr Thomas was suffering from depression.* [2] N-COUNT = slump A **depression** is a time when there is very little economic activity, which causes a lot of unemployment and poverty. ❑ *He never forgot the hardships he witnessed during the Great Depression of the 1930s.* [3] N-COUNT = hollow A **depression** in a surface is an area which is lower than the parts surrounding it. ❑ *...an area pockmarked by rain-filled depressions.* [4] N-COUNT A **depression** is a mass of air that has a low pressure and that often causes rain.

**de|pres|sive** /dɪpresɪv/ **(depressives)** [1] ADJ: usu ADJ n **Depressive** means relating to depression or to being depressed. ❑ *He's no longer a depressive character. ...a severe depressive disorder.* [2] N-COUNT A **depressive** is someone who suffers from depression. → See also **manic-depressive**.

**dep|ri|va|tion** /deprɪveɪʃən/ **(deprivations)** N-VAR: oft supp N If you suffer **deprivation**, you do not have or are prevented from having something that you want or need. ❑ *Millions more suffer from serious sleep deprivation caused by long work hours.*

**de|prive** /dɪpraɪv/ **(deprives, depriving, deprived)** VERB If you **deprive** someone **of** something that they want or need, you take it away from them, or you prevent them from having it. ❑ V n *of* n *They've been deprived of the fuel necessary to heat their homes.*

**de|prived** /dɪpraɪvd/ ADJ: usu ADJ n **Deprived** people or people from **deprived** areas do not have the things that people consider to be essential in life, for example acceptable living conditions or education. ❑ *...probably the most severely deprived children in the country.*

**dept (depts)**

✔ in AM, use **dept.**

**Dept** is used as a written abbreviation for **department**, usually in the name of a particular department. ❑ *...the Internal Affairs Dept.*

**depth** /depθ/ **(depths)** ◆◇◇ [1] N-VAR: oft amount *in* N, with poss, N *of* amount The **depth** of something such as a river or hole is the distance downwards from its top surface, or between its upper and lower surfaces. ❑ *The smaller lake ranges from five to fourteen feet in depth... The depth of the shaft is 520 yards... They were detected at depths of more than a kilometre in the sea.* [2] N-VAR: oft amount *in* N, with poss, N *of* amount The **depth** of something such as a cupboard or drawer is the distance between its front surface and its back. [3] N-VAR: usu N *of* n = strength If an emotion is very strongly or intensely felt, you can talk about its **depth**. ❑ *I am well aware of the depth of feeling that exists in Londonderry.* [4] N-UNCOUNT: usu N *of* n = severity The **depth** of a situation is its extent and seriousness. ❑ *The country's leadership had underestimated the depth of the crisis.* [5] N-UNCOUNT: usu N *of* n The **depth** of someone's knowledge is the great amount that they know. ❑ *We felt at home with her and were impressed with the depth of her knowledge.* [6] N-UNCOUNT: also N in pl If you say that someone or something has **depth**, you mean that they have serious and interesting qualities which are not immediately obvious and which you have to think about carefully before you can fully understand them. ❑ *His music lacks depth.* [7] N-PLURAL: the N **The depths** are places that are a long way below the surface of the sea or earth. [LITERARY] ❑ *The ship vanished into the depths.* [8] N-PLURAL: the N *of* n If you talk about **the depths of** an area, you mean the parts of it which are very far from the edge. ❑ *...the depths of the countryside.* [9] N-PLURAL: the N *of* n If you are **in the depths of** an unpleasant emotion, you feel that emotion very strongly. ❑ *I was in the depths of despair when the baby was sick.* [10] N-PLURAL: the N *of* n If something happens in **the depths of** a difficult or unpleasant period of time, it happens in the middle and most severe or intense part of it. ❑ *The country is in the depths of a recession.*

PHRASES [11] PHRASE: PHR after v If you deal with a subject **in depth**, you deal with it very thoroughly and consider all the aspects of it. ❑ *We will discuss these three areas in depth.* [12] PHRASE: usu v-link PHR If you say that someone is **out of** their **depth**, you mean that they are in a situation that is much too difficult for them to be able to cope with it. ❑ *Mr Gibson is clearly intellectually out of his depth.* [13] PHRASE: v-link PHR If you are **out of** your **depth**, you are in water that is deeper than you are tall, with the result that you cannot stand up with your head above water. [14] **to plumb new depths** → see **plumb**. **to plumb the depths** → see **plumb**.

**depth charge (depth charges)** N-COUNT A **depth charge** is a type of bomb which explodes under water and which is used especially to destroy enemy submarines.

**depu|ta|tion** /depjʊteɪʃən/ **(deputations)** N-COUNT = delegation A **deputation** is a small group of people who have been asked to speak to someone on behalf of a larger group of people, especially in order to make a complaint. ❑ *A deputation of elders from the village arrived headed by its chief.*

**de|pute** /dɪpjuːt/ **(deputes, deputing, deputed)** VERB: usu passive
If you **are deputed** to do something, someone tells or allows you to do it on their behalf. [FORMAL] ❑ *A sub-committee was deputed to investigate the claims.* be V-ed to-inf

**depu|tize** /depjʊtaɪz/ **(deputizes, deputizing, deputized)**

in BRIT, also use **deputise**

If you **deputize for** someone, you do something on their behalf, for example attend a meeting. ❑ *I sometimes had to deputise for him in the kitchen... Herr Schulmann cannot be here to welcome you and has asked me to deputize.* VERB V for n V

**depu|ty** /depjʊti/ **(deputies)** ◆◆◇ 1 A **deputy** is the second most important person in an organization such as a business or government department. Someone's deputy often acts on their behalf when they are not there. ❑ *...Jack Lang, France's minister for culture, and his deputy, Catherine Tasca.* N-COUNT: oft N n
2 In some parliaments or law-making bodies, the elected members are called **deputies**. N-COUNT

**de|rail** /diːreɪl/ **(derails, derailing, derailed)**
1 To **derail** something such as a plan or a series of negotiations means to prevent it from continuing as planned. [JOURNALISM] ❑ *The present wave of political killings is the work of people trying to derail peace talks.* VERB V n
2 If a train **is derailed** or if it **derails**, it comes off the track on which it is running. ❑ *Several people were injured today when a train was derailed... No-one knows why the train derailed.* VERB be V-ed V

**de|rail|ment** /diːreɪlmənt/ **(derailments)** A **derailment** is an accident in which a train comes off the track on which it is running. N-VAR

**de|ranged** /dɪreɪndʒd/ Someone who is **deranged** behaves in a wild and uncontrolled way, often as a result of mental illness. ❑ *A deranged man shot and killed 14 people.* ADJ

**de|range|ment** /dɪreɪndʒmənt/ **Derangement** is the state of being mentally ill and unable to think or act in a controlled way. [OLD-FASHIONED] N-UNCOUNT

**der|by** /dɑːʳbi, AM dɜːrbi/ **(derbies)** 1 A **derby** is a sporting event involving teams from the same area or city. [BRIT] ❑ *...a North London derby between Arsenal and Tottenham.* N-COUNT
2 A **derby** is a sports competition or race where there are no restrictions or limits on who can enter. [AM] N-COUNT: oft n N

**de|regu|late** /diːregjʊleɪt/ **(deregulates, deregulating, deregulated)** To **deregulate** something means to remove controls and regulations from it. ❑ *...the need to deregulate the US airline industry.* VERB V n

**de|regu|la|tion** /diːregjʊleɪʃᵊn/ **Deregulation** is the removal of controls and restrictions in a particular area of business or trade. [BUSINESS] ❑ *Since deregulation, banks are permitted to set their own interest rates.* N-UNCOUNT

**der|elict** /derɪlɪkt/ A place or building that is **derelict** is empty and in a bad state of repair because it has not been used or lived in for a long time. ❑ *Her body was found dumped in a derelict warehouse less than a mile from her home.* ADJ

**der|elic|tion** /derɪlɪkʃᵊn/ If a building or a piece of land is in a state of **dereliction**, it is deserted or abandoned. ❑ *The previous owners had rescued the building from dereliction.* N-UNCOUNT

**der|elic|tion of duty** **Dereliction of duty** is deliberate or accidental failure to do what you should do as part of your job. [FORMAL] ❑ *He pleaded guilty to wilful dereliction of duty.* N-UNCOUNT = negligence

**de|ride** /dɪraɪd/ **(derides, deriding, derided)** If you **deride** someone or something, you say that they are stupid or have no value. [FORMAL] ❑ *Opposition MPs derided the Government's response to the crisis.* VERB = ridicule V n

**de ri|gueur** /də rɪgɜːʳ/ If you say that a possession or habit is **de rigueur**, you mean that it is fashionable and therefore necessary for anyone who wants to avoid being considered unfashionable. ❑ *T-shirts now seem almost de rigueur in the West End.* ADJ: v-link ADJ

**de|ri|sion** /dɪrɪʒᵊn/ If you treat someone or something with **derision**, you express contempt for them. ❑ *He tried to calm them, but was greeted with shouts of derision.* N-UNCOUNT = disdain

**de|ri|sive** /dɪraɪsɪv/ A **derisive** noise, expression, or remark expresses contempt. ❑ *There was a short, derisive laugh.* ♦ **de|ri|sive|ly** *Phil's tormentor snorted derisively.* ADJ = contemptuous ADV: ADV with v

**de|ri|sory** /dɪraɪzəri/ 1 If you describe something such as an amount of money as **derisory**, you are emphasizing that it is so small or inadequate that it seems silly or not worth considering. ❑ *She was being paid what I considered a derisory amount of money.* ADJ [disapproval]
2 **Derisory** means the same as **derisive**. ❑ *...derisory remarks about the police.* ADJ: usu ADJ n

**deri|va|tion** /derɪveɪʃᵊn/ **(derivations)** The **derivation** of something, especially a word, is its origin or source. ❑ *The derivation of its name is obscure.* N-VAR: oft N of n, of adj N = origin

**de|riva|tive** /dɪrɪvətɪv/ **(derivatives)** 1 A **derivative** is something which has been developed or obtained from something else. ❑ *...a poppy-seed derivative similar to heroin.* N-COUNT
2 If you say that something is **derivative**, you are criticizing it because it is not new or original but has been developed from something else. ❑ *...their dull, derivative debut album.* ADJ [disapproval]

**de|rive** /dɪraɪv/ **(derives, deriving, derived)**
1 If you **derive** something such as pleasure or benefit **from** a person or from something, you get it from them. [FORMAL] ❑ *Mr Ying is one of those happy people who derive pleasure from helping others.* VERB V n from n/-ing
2 If you say that something such as a word or feeling **derives** or **is derived from** something else, you mean that it comes from that thing. ❑ *Anna's strength is derived from her parents and her sisters... The word Easter derives from Eostre, the pagan goddess of spring.* VERB be V-ed from n V from n

**der|ma|ti|tis** /dɜːʳmətaɪtɪs/ **Dermatitis** is a medical condition which makes your skin red and painful. N-UNCOUNT

**der|ma|tolo|gist** /dɜːʳmətɒlədʒɪst/ **(dermatologists)** A **dermatologist** is a doctor who specializes in the study of skin and the treatment of skin diseases. ♦ **der|ma|tol|ogy** ❑ *...drugs used in dermatology.* N-COUNT N-UNCOUNT

**de|roga|tory** /dɪrɒgətri, AM -tɔːri/ If you make a **derogatory** remark or comment about someone or something, you express your low opinion of them. ❑ *He refused to withdraw derogatory remarks made about his boss.* ADJ: usu ADJ n

**der|rick** /derɪk/ **(derricks)** 1 A **derrick** is a machine that is used to move cargo on a ship by lifting it in the air. N-COUNT
2 A **derrick** is a tower built over an oil well which is used to raise and lower the drill. N-COUNT

**derring-do** /derɪŋ duː/ **Derring-do** is the quality of being bold, often in a rather showy or foolish way. [OLD-FASHIONED] N-UNCOUNT

**der|vish** /dɜːʳvɪʃ/ **(dervishes)** 1 A **dervish** is a member of a Muslim religious group which has a very active and lively dance as part of its worship. N-COUNT
2 If you say that someone is **like a dervish**, you mean that they are turning round and round, waving their arms about, or working very quickly. ❑ *Brian was whirling like a dervish, slapping at the mosquitoes and moaning.* PHRASE: v-link PHR

**de|sali|na|tion** /diːsælɪneɪʃᵊn/ **Desalination** is the process of removing salt from sea water so that it can be used for drinking, or for watering crops. N-UNCOUNT

**des|cant** /deskænt/ **(descants)** A **descant** is a tune which is played or sung above the main tune in a piece of music. N-COUNT

**de|scend** /dɪse̱nd/ **(descends, descending, descended)** 1 If you **descend** a staircase, you move downwards from a higher to a lower level. [FORMAL] ❑ *Things are cooler and more damp as we descend to the cellar... She descended one flight of stairs.* VERB = go down ≠ rise, ascend; V prep; V n
2 When a mood or atmosphere **descends on** a place or on the people there, it affects them by spreading among them. [LITERARY] ❑ *An uneasy calm descended on the area.* VERB = fall; V on/upon/over n
3 If a large group of people arrive to see you, especially if their visit is unexpected or causes you a lot of work, you can say that they **have descended on** you. ❑ *3,000 city officials descended on Capitol Hill to lobby for more money.* VERB; V on/upon n
4 When night, dusk, or darkness **descends**, it starts to get dark. [LITERARY] ❑ *Darkness has now descended and the moon and stars shine hazily in the clear sky.* VERB = fall; V
5 If you say that someone **descends to** behaviour which you consider unacceptable, you are expressing your disapproval of the fact that they do it. ❑ *We're not going to descend to such methods.* VERB [disapproval] = stoop, sink; V to n/-ing
6 When you want to emphasize that the situation that someone is entering is very bad, you can say that they **are descending into** that situation. ❑ *He was ultimately overthrown and the country descended into chaos.* VERB [emphasis] = fall, slide; V into n

**de|scend|ant** /dɪse̱ndənt/ **(descendants)** 1 Someone's **descendants** are the people in later generations who are related to them. ❑ *They are descendants of the original English and Scottish settlers.* N-COUNT: usu pl, usu with poss ≠ ancestor
2 Something modern which developed from an older thing can be called a **descendant of** it. ❑ *His design was a descendant of a 1956 device.* N-COUNT: usu N of n ≠ ancestor

**de|scend|ed** /dɪse̱ndɪd/ 1 A person who is **descended from** someone who lived a long time ago is directly related to them. ❑ *She told us she was descended from some Scottish Lord.* ADJ: v-link ADJ from n
2 An animal that is **descended from** another sort of animal has developed from the original sort. ADJ: v-link ADJ from n

**de|scend|ing** /dɪse̱ndɪŋ/ When a group of things is listed or arranged **in descending order**, each thing is smaller or less important than the thing before it. ❑ *All the other ingredients, including water, have to be listed in descending order by weight.* ADJ: ADJ n ≠ ascending

**de|scent** /dɪse̱nt/ **(descents)** 1 A **descent** is a movement from a higher to a lower level or position. ❑ *...the crash of an Airbus A300 on its descent into Kathmandu airport.* N-VAR ≠ ascent
2 A **descent** is a surface that slopes downwards, for example the side of a steep hill. ❑ *On the descents, cyclists spin past cars, freewheeling downhill at tremendous speed.* N-COUNT ≠ ascent
3 When you want to emphasize that a situation becomes very bad, you can talk about someone's or something's **descent** into that situation. ❑ *...his swift descent from respected academic to struggling small businessman.* N-SING: usu poss N into/from/to n [emphasis] = decline
4 You use **descent** to talk about a person's family background, for example their nationality or social status. [FORMAL] ❑ *All the contributors were of African descent.* N-UNCOUNT: usu of adj N = origin, ancestry

**de|scribe** /dɪskra̱ɪb/ **(describes, describing, described)** ◆◆◆ 1 If you **describe** a person, object, event, or situation, you say what they are like or what happened. ❑ *We asked her to describe what kind of things she did in her spare time... She read a poem by Carver which describes their life together... Just before his death he described seeing their son in a beautiful garden.* VERB; V wh; V n; V -ing
2 If a person **describes** someone or something **as** a particular thing, he or she believes that they are that thing and says so. ❑ *He described it as an extraordinarily tangled and complicated tale... Even his closest allies describe him as forceful, aggressive and determined... He described the meeting as marking a new stage in the peace process.* VERB; V n as n; V n as adj; V n as -ing

**de|scrip|tion** /dɪskrɪ̱pʃən/ **(descriptions)** ◆◇◇ 1 A **description** of someone or something is an account which explains what they are or what they look like. ❑ *Police have issued a description of the man who was aged between fifty and sixty... He has a real gift for vivid description.* N-VAR: oft N of n
2 If something is **of** a particular **description**, it belongs to the general class of items that are mentioned. ❑ *Events of this description occurred daily.* N-SING: of N = kind, type
3 You can say that something is **beyond description**, or that it **defies description**, to emphasize that it is very unusual, impressive, terrible, or extreme. ❑ *His face is weary beyond description.* N-UNCOUNT: oft beyond N [emphasis]

**de|scrip|tive** /dɪskrɪ̱ptɪv/ **Descriptive** language or writing indicates what someone or something is like. ❑ *...his descriptive way of writing.* ADJ

**des|ecrate** /de̱sɪkreɪt/ **(desecrates, desecrating, desecrated)** If someone **desecrates** something which is considered to be holy or very special, they deliberately damage or insult it. ❑ *She shouldn't have desecrated the picture of a religious leader.* VERB; V n
♦ **des|ecra|tion** /de̱sɪkre̱ɪʃən/ *The whole area has been shocked by the desecration of the cemetery.* N-UNCOUNT: oft N of n

**de|seed** /di̱ːsi̱ːd/ **(deseeds, deseeding, deseeded)** also **de-seed.** To **deseed** a fruit or vegetable means to remove all the seeds from it. [BRIT] ❑ *Halve and deseed the peppers.* VERB; V n

**de|seg|re|gate** /di̱ːse̱grɪgeɪt/ **(desegregates, desegregating, desegregated)** To **desegregate** something such as a place, institution, or service means to officially stop keeping the people who use it in separate groups, especially groups that are defined by race. ❑ *...efforts to desegregate sport... The school system itself is not totally desegregated.* VERB = integrate ≠ segregate; V n; V-ed
♦ **de|seg|re|ga|tion** /di̱ːse̱grəge̱ɪʃən/ *Desegregation may be harder to enforce in rural areas.* N-UNCOUNT

**de|sen|si|tize** /di̱ːse̱nsɪtaɪz/ **(desensitizes, desensitizing, desensitized)**

> ✓ in BRIT, also use **desensitise**

To **desensitize** someone **to** things such as pain, anxiety, or other people's suffering, means to cause them to react less strongly to them. ❑ *...the language that is used to desensitize us to the terrible reality of war.* VERB; V n to n

**des|ert** **(deserts, deserting, deserted)** ◆◇◇

> ✓ The noun is pronounced /de̱zəʳt/. The verb is pronounced /dɪzɜ̱ːʳt/ and is hyphenated de|sert.

1 A **desert** is a large area of land, usually in a hot region, where there is almost no water, rain, trees, or plants. ❑ *...the Sahara Desert. ...the burning desert sun.* N-VAR: oft in names after n
2 If people or animals **desert** a place, they leave it and it becomes empty. ❑ *Farmers are deserting their fields and coming here looking for jobs.* VERB; V n
♦ **de|sert|ed** *She led them into a deserted sidestreet.* ADJ = empty
3 If someone **deserts** you, they go away and leave you, and no longer help or support you. ❑ *Mrs Roding's husband deserted her years ago.* VERB = abandon; V n
♦ **de|ser|tion** /dɪzɜ̱ːʳʃən/ **(desertions)** *...her father's desertion.* N-VAR
4 If you **desert** something that you support, use, or are involved with, you stop supporting it, using it, or being involved with it. ❑ *The paper's price rise will encourage readers to desert in even greater numbers... He was pained to see many youngsters deserting kibbutz life... Spaniards are worried about German investors deserting Spain for Eastern Europe.* VERB; V; V n; V n for n
♦ **de|ser|tion** *...a mass desertion of the Party by the electorate.* N-VAR
5 If a quality or skill that you normally have **deserts** you, you suddenly find that you do not have it when you need it or want it. ❑ *Even when he appeared to be depressed, a dry sense of humour never deserted him... She lost the next five games, and the set, as her confidence abruptly deserted her.* VERB = leave; V n; V n
6 If someone **deserts**, or **deserts** a job, especially a job in the armed forces, they leave that job without permission. ❑ *He was a second-lieutenant in the army until he deserted... He deserted from army intelligence last month.* VERB; V; V from n
♦ **de|ser|tion** *The high rate of desertion has added to the army's woes.* N-VAR
7 If you say that someone has got their **just deserts**, you mean that they deserved the unpleasant things that have happened to them, because they did something bad. ❑ *At the end of the book the child's true identity is discovered, and the bad guys get their just deserts.* PHRASE [feelings]

**de|sert|er** /dɪzɜːʳtəʳ/ **(deserters)** A **deserter** is someone who leaves their job in the armed forces without permission. N-COUNT

**des|er|ti|fi|ca|tion** /dɪzɜːʳtɪfɪkeɪʃ°n/ **Desertification** is the process by which a piece of land becomes dry, empty, and unsuitable for growing trees or crops on. ❑ *A third of Africa is under threat of desertification.* N-UNCOUNT

**des|ert is|land** /dezəʳt aɪlənd/ **(desert islands)** A **desert island** is a small tropical island, where nobody lives. N-COUNT

**de|serve** /dɪzɜːʳv/ **(deserves, deserving, deserved)** ◆◇◇ 1 If you say that a person or thing **deserves** something, you mean that they should have it or receive it because of their actions or qualities. ❑ *Government officials clearly deserve some of the blame as well... These people deserve to make more than the minimum wage... I felt I deserved better than that... The Park Hotel has a well-deserved reputation.* VERB V n V to-inf V compar V-ed 2 If you say that someone **got what they deserved**, you mean that they deserved the bad thing that happened to them, and you have no sympathy for them. ❑ *One of them said the two dead joy riders got what they deserved.* PHRASE [feelings]

**de|serv|ed|ly** /dɪzɜːʳvɪdli/ You use **deservedly** to indicate that someone deserved what happened to them, especially when it was something good. ❑ *He deservedly won the Player of the Year award.* ADV: ADV with v, ADV adj/adv, ADV with cl

**de|serv|ing** /dɪzɜːʳvɪŋ/ 1 If you describe a person, organization, or cause as **deserving**, you mean that you think they should be helped. ❑ *The money saved could be used for more deserving causes.* ADJ = worthy 2 If someone is **deserving of** something, they have qualities or achievements which make it right that they should receive it. [FORMAL] ❑ *...artists deserving of public subsidy.* ADJ: v-link ADJ *of* n

**des|ic|cat|ed** /desɪkeɪtɪd/ 1 **Desiccated** things have lost all the moisture that was in them. [FORMAL] ❑ *...desiccated flowers and leaves.* ADJ: usu ADJ n 2 **Desiccated** food has been dried in order to preserve it. ❑ *...desiccated coconut.* ADJ: ADJ n

**des|ic|ca|tion** /desɪkeɪʃ°n/ **Desiccation** is the process of becoming completely dried out. [FORMAL] ❑ *...the disastrous consequences of the desiccation of the wetland.* N-UNCOUNT

**de|sign** /dɪzaɪn/ **(designs, designing, designed)** ◆◆◆ 1 When someone **designs** a garment, building, machine, or other object, they plan it and make a detailed drawing of it from which it can be built or made. ❑ *They wanted to design a machine that was both attractive and practical. ...men wearing specially designed boots.* VERB V n V-ed 2 When someone **designs** a survey, policy, or system, they plan and prepare it, and decide on all the details of it. ❑ *We may be able to design a course to suit your particular needs... A number of very well designed studies have been undertaken.* VERB V n V-ed 3 **Design** is the process and art of planning and making detailed drawings of something. ❑ *He was a born mechanic with a flair for design.* N-UNCOUNT 4 The **design** of something is the way in which it has been planned and made. ❑ *...a new design of clock... BMW is recalling 8,000 cars because of a design fault.* N-UNCOUNT: usu with supp 5 A **design** is a drawing which someone produces to show how they would like something to be built or made. ❑ *They drew up the design for the house in a week.* N-COUNT = plan 6 A **design** is a pattern of lines, flowers, or shapes which is used to decorate something. ❑ *Many pictures have been based on simple geometric designs.* N-COUNT = motif 7 A **design** is a general plan or intention that someone has in their mind when they are doing something. ❑ *Is there some design in having him in the middle?* N-COUNT 8 If something **is designed** for a particular purpose, it is intended for that purpose. ❑ *This project is designed to help landless people... It's not designed for anyone under age eighteen.* V-PASSIVE *be* V-ed to-inf *be* V-ed *for* n

PHRASES 9 If something happens or is done **by design**, someone does it deliberately, rather than by accident. ❑ *The pair met often – at first by chance but later by design.* PHRASE = on purpose 10 If someone **has designs on** something, they want it and are planning to get it, often in a dishonest way. ❑ *His colonel had designs on his wife.* PHRASE: V inflects

**des|ig|nate** **(designates, designating, designated)**

> ✔ The verb is pronounced /dezɪgneɪt/. The adjective is pronounced /dezɪgnət/.

1 When you **designate** someone or something **as** a particular thing, you formally give them that description or name. ❑ *...a man interviewed in one of our studies whom we shall designate as E... There are efforts under way to designate the bridge a historic landmark... I live in Exmoor, which is designated as a national park.* VERB V n *as* n V n n V-ed 2 If something **is designated for** a particular purpose, it is set aside for that purpose. ❑ *Some of the rooms were designated as offices. ...scholarships designated for minorities.* VERB: usu passive *be* V-ed *as*/*for* n V-ed 3 When you **designate** someone **as** something, you formally choose them to do that particular job. ❑ *Designate someone as the spokesperson.* VERB V n *as* n 4 **Designate** is used to describe someone who has been formally chosen to do a particular job, but has not yet started doing it. ❑ *Japan's Prime Minister-designate is completing his Cabinet today.* ADJ: n ADJ

**des|ig|nat|ed driv|er** **(designated drivers)** The **designated driver** in a group of people travelling together is the one who has agreed to drive, or who is insured to drive. N-COUNT: usu sing

**des|ig|na|tion** /dezɪgneɪʃ°n/ **(designations)** A **designation** is a description, name, or title that is given to someone or something. **Designation** is the fact of giving that description, name, or title. [FORMAL] ❑ *...the designation of Madrid as European City of Culture 1992.* N-VAR

**de|sign|er** /dɪzaɪnəʳ/ **(designers)** ◆◇◇ 1 A **designer** is a person whose job is to design things by making drawings of them. ❑ *Carolyne is a fashion designer.* N-COUNT 2 **Designer** clothes or **designer** labels are expensive, fashionable clothes made by a famous designer, rather than being made in large quantities in a factory. ❑ *He wears designer clothes and drives an antique car.* ADJ: ADJ n 3 You can use **designer** to describe things that are worn or bought because they are fashionable. [INFORMAL] ❑ *Designer beers and trendy wines have replaced the good old British pint.* ADJ: ADJ n

**de|sign|er baby** **(designer babies)** also **designer child.** People sometimes refer to a baby that has developed from an embryo with certain desired characteristics as a **designer baby**. [mainly JOURNALISM] N-COUNT

**de|sir|able** /dɪzaɪərəb°l/ 1 Something that is **desirable** is worth having or doing because it is useful, necessary, or popular. ❑ *Prolonged negotiation was not desirable.* ADJ ♦ **de|sir|abil|ity** /dɪzaɪərəbɪlɪti/ *...the desirability of democratic reform.* N-UNCOUNT: usu *the* N *of* n/-ing 2 Someone who is **desirable** is considered to be sexually attractive. ❑ *...the young women whom his classmates thought most desirable.* ADJ ♦ **de|sir|abil|ity** *...Veronica's desirability.* N-UNCOUNT

**de|sire** /dɪzaɪəʳ/ **(desires, desiring, desired)** ◆◆◇ 1 A **desire** is a strong wish to do or have something. ❑ *I had a strong desire to help and care for people... They seem to have lost their desire for life.* N-COUNT: oft N to-inf, N *for* n 2 If you **desire** something, you want it. [FORMAL] ❑ *She had remarried and desired a child with her new husband... But Fred was bored and desired to go home.* VERB: no cont V n V to-inf ♦ **de|sired** *You may find that just threatening this course of action will produce the desired effect.* ADJ: ADJ n 3 **Desire** for someone is a strong feeling of wanting to have sex with them. ❑ *Teenage sex, for instance, may come not out of genuine desire but from a need to get love.* N-UNCOUNT 4 If you say that something **leaves** a lot **to be desired**, you mean that it is not as good as it should be. ❑ *The selection of TV programmes, especially at the weekend, leaves a lot to be desired.* PHRASE: V inflects [disapproval]

**de|sir|ous** /dɪzaɪərəs/ If you are **desirous of** doing something or **desirous of** something, you want to do it very much or want it very much. ADJ: v-link ADJ *of* -ing/n

[FORMAL] ❑ *The enemy is so desirous of peace that he will agree to any terms.*

**de|sist** /dɪzɪst/ **(desists, desisting, desisted)** If you **desist from** doing something, you stop doing it. [FORMAL] ❑ *Ford never desisted from trying to persuade him to return to America.* VERB V from -ing/n

**desk** /desk/ **(desks)** 1 A **desk** is a table, often with drawers, which you sit at to write or work. ◆◆◇ N-COUNT 2 The place in a hotel, hospital, airport, or other building where you check in or obtain information is referred to as a particular **desk**. ❑ *I spoke to the girl on the reception desk.* N-SING: usu supp N 3 A particular department of a broadcasting company, or of a newspaper or magazine company, can be referred to as a particular **desk**. ❑ *Over now to Simon Ingram at the sports desk.* N-SING: supp N

**desk clerk (desk clerks)** A **desk clerk** is someone who works at the main desk in a hotel. [AM] N-COUNT

✔ in BRIT, use **receptionist**

**de|skill** /diːskɪl/ **(deskills, deskilling, deskilled)** If workers **are deskilled**, they no longer need special skills to do their work, especially because of modern methods of production. ❑ *Administrative staff may be deskilled through increased automation and efficiency.* VERB: oft passive be V-ed

**desk|top** /desktɒp/ **(desktops)** also **desk-top.** 1 **Desktop** computers are a convenient size for using on a desk or table, but are not designed to be portable. ❑ *When launched, the Macintosh was the smallest desktop computer ever produced.* ADJ: ADJ n 2 A **desktop** is a desktop computer. N-COUNT 3 The **desktop** of a computer is the display of icons that you see on the screen when the computer is ready to use. N-COUNT

**desk|top pub|lish|ing** **Desktop publishing** is the production of printed materials such as newspapers and magazines using a desktop computer and a laser printer, rather than using conventional printing methods. The abbreviation **DTP** is also used. N-UNCOUNT

**deso|late** /desələt/ 1 A **desolate** place is empty of people and lacking in comfort. ❑ *...a desolate landscape of flat green fields broken by marsh.* ADJ = bleak 2 If someone is **desolate**, they feel very sad, alone, and without hope. [LITERARY] ❑ *He was desolate without her.* ADJ: usu v-link ADJ

**deso|la|tion** /desəleɪʃən/ 1 **Desolation** is a feeling of great unhappiness and hopelessness. ❑ *Kozelek expresses his sense of desolation absolutely without self-pity.* N-UNCOUNT = misery 2 If you refer to **desolation** in a place, you mean that it is empty and frightening, for example because it has been destroyed by a violent force or army. ❑ *We looked out upon a scene of desolation and ruin.* N-UNCOUNT disapproval = devastation

**des|pair** /dɪspeəʳ/ **(despairs, despairing, despaired)** 1 **Despair** is the feeling that everything is wrong and that nothing will improve. ❑ *I looked at my wife in despair. ...feelings of despair or inadequacy.* N-UNCOUNT: also N in pl 2 If you **despair**, you feel that everything is wrong and that nothing will improve. ❑ *'Oh, I despair sometimes,' he says in mock sorrow... He does despair at much of the press criticism.* VERB V V at n 3 If you **despair of** something, you feel that there is no hope that it will happen or improve. If you **despair of** someone, you feel that there is no hope that they will improve. ❑ *He wished to earn a living through writing but despaired of doing so.* VERB V of -ing/n

**des|patch** /dɪspætʃ/ → see **dispatch**.

**des|pe|ra|do** /despərɑːdoʊ/ **(desperadoes** or **desperados)** A **desperado** is someone who does illegal, violent things without worrying about the danger. [OLD-FASHIONED] N-COUNT

**des|per|ate** /despərət/ 1 If you are **desperate**, you are in such a bad situation that you are willing to try anything to change it. ❑ *Troops are needed to help get food into Kosovo where people are in desperate need... He made a desperate attempt to hijack a plane.* ◆ **des|per|ate|ly** *Thousands are desperately trying to leave their battered homes.* ◆◇◇ ADJ ADV: ADV with v 2 If you are **desperate for** something or **desperate to** do something, you want or need it very much indeed. ❑ *They'd been married nearly four years and June was desperate to start a family... People are desperate for him to do something.* ◆ **des|per|ate|ly** *He was a boy who desperately needed affection.* ADJ: v-link ADJ, usu ADJ to-inf, ADJ for n ADV: ADV with v 3 A **desperate** situation is very difficult, serious, or dangerous. ❑ *India's United Nations ambassador said the situation is desperate.* ADJ = dire

**des|pera|tion** /despəreɪʃən/ **Desperation** is the feeling that you have when you are in such a bad situation that you will try anything to change it. ❑ *This feeling of desperation and helplessness was common to most of the refugees.* N-UNCOUNT

**des|pic|able** /dɪspɪkəbəl, AM despɪk-/ If you say that a person or action is **despicable**, you are emphasizing that they are extremely nasty, cruel, or evil. ❑ *The Minister said the bombing was a despicable crime.* ADJ emphasis

**des|pise** /dɪspaɪz/ **(despises, despising, despised)** If you **despise** something or someone, you dislike them and have a very low opinion of them. ❑ *I can never, ever forgive him. I despise him.* VERB V n

**de|spite** /dɪspaɪt/ 1 You use **despite** to introduce a fact which makes the other part of the sentence surprising. ❑ *The National Health Service has visibly deteriorated, despite increased spending... She will stand by husband, despite reports that he sent another woman love notes.* ◆◆◇ PREP: PREP n/-ing = in spite of 2 If you do something **despite yourself** you do it although you did not really intend or expect to. ❑ *Despite myself, Harry's remarks had caused me to stop and reflect.* PREP: PREP pron-refl

**de|spoil** /dɪspɔɪl/ **(despoils, despoiling, despoiled)** To **despoil** a place means to make it less attractive, valuable, or important by taking things away from it or by destroying it. [FORMAL] ❑ *...people who despoil the countryside.* VERB V n

**de|spond|en|cy** /dɪspɒndənsi/ **Despondency** is a strong feeling of unhappiness caused by difficulties which you feel you cannot overcome. ❑ *There's a mood of gloom and despondency in the country.* N-UNCOUNT = dejection

**de|spond|ent** /dɪspɒndənt/ If you are **despondent**, you are very unhappy because you have been experiencing difficulties that you think you will not be able to overcome. ❑ *I feel despondent when my work is rejected.* ◆ **de|spond|ent|ly** *Despondently, I went back and told Bill the news.* ADJ ADV: ADV with v

**des|pot** /despɒt, AM -pət/ **(despots)** A **despot** is a ruler or other person who has a lot of power and who uses it unfairly or cruelly. N-COUNT = tyrant, dictator

**des|pot|ic** /dɪspɒtɪk/ If you say that someone is **despotic**, you are emphasizing that they use their power over other people in a very unfair or cruel way. ❑ *The country was ruled by a despotic tyrant.* ADJ emphasis = tyrannical

**des|pot|ism** /despətɪzəm/ **Despotism** is cruel and unfair government by a ruler or rulers who have a lot of power. N-UNCOUNT = tyranny

**des|sert** /dɪzɜːʳt/ **(desserts)** **Dessert** is something sweet, such as fruit or a pudding, that you eat at the end of a meal. ❑ *She had homemade ice cream for dessert.* N-MASS = sweet, pudding

**dessert|spoon** /dɪzɜːʳtspuːn/ **(dessertspoons)** also **dessert spoon.** 1 A **dessertspoon** is a spoon which is midway between the size of a teaspoon and a tablespoon. You use it to eat desserts. N-COUNT 2 You can refer to an amount of food resting on a dessertspoon as a **dessertspoon** of food. [BRIT] ❑ *...a rounded dessertspoon of flour.* N-COUNT: oft N of n

**dessert|spoon|ful** /dɪzɜːʳtspuːnfʊl/ **(dessertspoonfuls** or **dessertspoonsful)** You can refer to an amount of food resting on a dessertspoon as a **dessertspoonful** of food. [BRIT] ❑ *...a dessertspoonful of olive oil.* N-COUNT: oft N of n

**des|sert wine (dessert wines)** A **dessert wine** is a sweet wine, usually a white wine, that is served with dessert. N-MASS

**de|sta|bi|lize** /diːsteɪbəlaɪz/ **(destabilizes, destabilizing, destabilized)**

in BRIT, also use **destabilise**

To **destabilize** something such as a country or government means to create a situation which reduces its power or influence. ❑ *Their sole aim is to destabilize the Indian government.* VERB V n
♦ **de|sta|bi|li|za|tion** /diːsteɪbəlaɪzeɪʃən/ *...the destabilization of the country.* N-UNCOUNT

**des|ti|na|tion** /destɪneɪʃən/ **(destinations)** The **destination** of someone or something is the place to which they are going or being sent. ❑ *Spain is still our most popular holiday destination... Only half of the emergency supplies have reached their destination.* N-COUNT

**des|tined** /destɪnd/ [1] If something is **destined to** happen or if someone is **destined to** behave in a particular way, that thing seems certain to happen or be done. ❑ *London seems destined to lose more than 2,000 hospital beds... Everyone knew that Muriel was destined for great things.* ADJ: v-link ADJ, ADJ to-inf, ADJ *for* n [2] If someone is **destined for** a particular place, or if goods are **destined for** a particular place, they are travelling towards that place or will be sent to that place. ❑ *...products destined for Saudi Arabia.* ADJ: v-link ADJ *for* n = *bound*

**des|ti|ny** /destɪni/ **(destinies)** [1] A person's **destiny** is everything that happens to them during their life, including what will happen in the future, especially when it is considered to be controlled by someone or something else. ❑ *We are masters of our own destiny.* N-COUNT: usu sing, usu with poss = *fate* [2] **Destiny** is the force which some people believe controls the things that happen to you in your life. ❑ *Is it destiny that brings people together, or is it accident?* N-UNCOUNT = *fate*

**des|ti|tute** /destɪtjuːt, AM -tuːt/ Someone who is **destitute** has no money or possessions. [FORMAL] ❑ *...destitute children who live on the streets.* ADJ

**des|ti|tu|tion** /destɪtjuːʃən, AM -tuː-/ **Destitution** is the state of having no money or possessions. [FORMAL] N-UNCOUNT

**de|stroy** /dɪstrɔɪ/ **(destroys, destroying, destroyed)** ◆◆◇ [1] To **destroy** something means to cause so much damage to it that it is completely ruined or does not exist any more. ❑ *That's a sure recipe for destroying the economy and creating chaos.* VERB V n [2] To **destroy** someone means to ruin their life or to make their situation impossible to bear. ❑ *If I was younger or more naive, the criticism would have destroyed me.* VERB V n [3] If an animal **is destroyed**, it is killed, either because it is ill or because it is dangerous. ❑ *Lindsay was unhurt but the horse had to be destroyed.* VERB: usu passive = *put down* be V-ed [4] → See also **soul-destroying**.

**de|stroy|er** /dɪstrɔɪəʳ/ **(destroyers)** A **destroyer** is a small, heavily armed warship. N-COUNT

**de|struc|tion** /dɪstrʌkʃən/ **Destruction** is the act of destroying something, or the state of being destroyed. ❑ *...an international agreement aimed at halting the destruction of the ozone layer.* ◆◇◇ N-UNCOUNT

**de|struc|tive** /dɪstrʌktɪv/ Something that is **destructive** causes or is capable of causing great damage, harm, or injury. ❑ *...the awesome destructive power of nuclear weapons.* ADJ
♦ **de|struc|tive|ness** *...the size of armies and the destructiveness of their weapons.* N-UNCOUNT
♦ **de|struc|tive|ly** *Power can be used creatively or destructively.* ADV

**des|ul|tory** /desəltri, AM -tɔːri/ Something that is **desultory** is done in an unplanned and disorganized way, and without enthusiasm. [FORMAL] ❑ *The constables made a desultory attempt to keep them away from the barn.* ADJ

**de|tach** /dɪtætʃ/ **(detaches, detaching, detached)** [1] If you **detach** one thing **from** another that it is fixed to, you remove it. If one thing **detaches from** another, it becomes separated from it. [FORMAL] ❑ *Detach the white part of the application form and keep it... It is easy to detach the currants from the stems... There was an accident when the towrope detached from the car.* VERB V n, V n *from* n, V *from* n [2] If you **detach yourself from** something, you become less involved in it or less concerned about it than you used to be. ❑ *It helps them detach themselves from their problems and become more objective.* VERB V pron-refl *from* n

**de|tach|able** /dɪtætʃəbəl/ If a part of an object is **detachable**, it has been made so that it can be removed from the object. ❑ *...a cake tin with a detachable base.* ADJ = *removable*

**de|tached** /dɪtætʃt/ [1] Someone who is **detached** is not personally involved in something or has no emotional interest in it. ❑ *He tries to remain emotionally detached from the prisoners, but fails.* ADJ [2] A **detached** house is one that is not joined to any other house. [mainly BRIT] → See picture on page 1706. ADJ

**de|tach|ment** /dɪtætʃmənt/ **(detachments)** [1] **Detachment** is the feeling that you have of not being personally involved in something or of having no emotional interest in it. ❑ *...a doctor's professional detachment.* N-UNCOUNT [2] A **detachment** is a group of soldiers who are sent away from the main group to do a special job. N-COUNT: oft N *of* n

**de|tail** /diːteɪl/ **(details, detailing, detailed)** ◆◆◇

The pronunciation /dɪteɪl/ is also used in American English.

[1] The **details of** something are its individual features or elements. ❑ *The details of the plan are still being worked out... I recall every detail of the party.* N-COUNT: usu with supp, oft N *of* n [2] **Details** about someone or something are facts or pieces of information about them. ❑ *See the bottom of this page for details of how to apply for this exciting offer.* N-PLURAL: oft N *of* n/wh, adj N [3] A **detail** is a minor point or aspect of something, as opposed to the central ones. ❑ *Only minor details now remain to be settled.* N-COUNT: oft adj N [4] You can refer to the small features of something which are often not noticed as **detail**. ❑ *We like his attention to detail and his enthusiasm.* N-UNCOUNT [5] A **detail** of a picture is a part of it that is printed separately and perhaps made bigger, so that smaller features can be clearly seen. N-COUNT [6] If you **detail** things, you list them or give information about them. ❑ *The report detailed the human rights abuses committed during the war.* VERB V n
PHRASES [7] If someone does not **go into details** about a subject, or does not **go into the detail**, they mention it without explaining it fully or properly. ❑ *He said he had been in various parts of Britain but did not go into details.* PHRASE: V inflects [8] If you examine or discuss something **in detail**, you do it thoroughly and carefully. ❑ *We examine the wording in detail before deciding on the final text.* PHRASE

**de|tailed** /diːteɪld, AM dɪteɪld/ A **detailed** report or plan contains a lot of details. ❑ *Yesterday's letter contains a detailed account of the decisions.* ◆◇◇ ADJ: usu ADJ n

**de|tain** /dɪteɪn/ **(detains, detaining, detained)** [1] When people such as the police **detain** someone, they keep them in a place under their control. [FORMAL] ❑ *The act allows police to detain a suspect for up to 48 hours.* VERB V n [2] To **detain** someone means to delay them, for example by talking to them. [FORMAL] ❑ *Thank you. We won't detain you any further.* VERB V n

**de|tainee** /diːteɪniː/ **(detainees)** A **detainee** is someone who is held prisoner by a government because of his or her political views or activities. N-COUNT

**de|tect** /dɪtekt/ **(detects, detecting, detected)** [1] To **detect** something means to find it or discover that it is present somewhere by using equipment or making an investigation. ❑ *...a sensitive piece of equipment used to detect radiation. ...a device which can detect who is more at risk of a heart attack.* VERB V n, V wh [2] If you **detect** something, you notice it or sense it, even though it is not very obvious. ❑ *Arnold could detect a certain sadness in the old man's face.* VERB = *sense* V n

**de|tect|able** /dɪtektəbəl/ Something that is **detectable** can be noticed or discovered. ❑ *Doctors say the disease is probably inherited but not detectable at birth.* ADJ

**de|tec|tion** /dɪtekʃᵊn/ [1] **Detection** is the act of noticing or sensing something. ❑ *...the early detection of breast cancer.* [2] **Detection** is the discovery of something which is supposed to be hidden. ❑ *They are cheating but are sophisticated enough to avoid detection.* [3] **Detection** is the work of investigating a crime in order to find out what has happened and who committed it. ❑ *The detection rate for motor vehicle theft that year was just 11.7 per cent.*
N-UNCOUNT: oft N *of* n; N-UNCOUNT: oft N *of* n; N-UNCOUNT

**de|tec|tive** /dɪtektɪv/ **(detectives)** [1] A **detective** is someone whose job is to discover what has happened in a crime or other situation and to find the people involved. Some detectives work in the police force and others work privately. ❑ *Detectives are appealing for witnesses who may have seen anything suspicious... She hired a private detective in an attempt to find her daughter.* [2] A **detective** novel or story is one in which a detective tries to solve a crime.
◆◇◇ N-COUNT; ADJ: ADJ n

**de|tec|tor** /dɪtektəʳ/ **(detectors)** A **detector** is an instrument which is used to discover that something is present somewhere, or to measure how much of something there is. ❑ *...a metal detector. ...fire alarms and smoke detectors.*
N-COUNT: oft n N

**de|tente** /deɪtɒnt/ also **détente. Detente** is a state of friendly relations between two countries when previously there had been problems between them. [FORMAL] ❑ *...their desire to pursue a policy of detente.*
N-UNCOUNT: also *a* N

**de|ten|tion** /dɪtenʃᵊn/ **(detentions)** [1] **Detention** is when someone is arrested or put into prison, especially for political reasons. ❑ *...the detention without trial of government critics.* [2] **Detention** is a punishment for naughty schoolchildren, who are made to stay at school after the other children have gone home. ❑ *The teacher kept the boys in detention after school.*
N-UNCOUNT: also N in pl; N-VAR

**de|ten|tion cen|tre (detention centres)**

✔ in AM, use **detention center**

A **detention centre** is a sort of prison, for example a place where people who have entered a country illegally are kept while a decision is made about what to do with them.
N-COUNT

**de|ter** /dɪtɜːʳ/ **(deters, deterring, deterred)** To **deter** someone **from** doing something means to make them not want to do it or continue doing it. ❑ *Supporters of the death penalty argue that it would deter criminals from carrying guns... Arrests and jail sentences have done nothing to deter the protesters.*
VERB = discourage; V n *from* -ing; V n

**de|ter|gent** /dɪtɜːʳdʒᵊnt/ **(detergents) Detergent** is a chemical substance, usually in the form of a powder or liquid, which is used for washing things such as clothes or dishes.
N-MASS

**de|terio|rate** /dɪtɪəriəreɪt/ **(deteriorates, deteriorating, deteriorated)** If something **deteriorates**, it becomes worse in some way. ❑ *There are fears that the situation might deteriorate into full-scale war.* ♦ **de|terio|ra|tion** /dɪtɪəriəreɪʃᵊn/ *...concern about the rapid deterioration in relations between the two countries.*
VERB ≠ improve; V; N-UNCOUNT ≠ improvement

**de|ter|mi|nant** /dɪtɜːʳmɪnənt/ **(determinants)** A **determinant** of something causes it to be of a particular kind or to happen in a particular way. [FORMAL]
N-COUNT: usu with supp

**de|ter|mi|nate** /dɪtɜːʳmɪneɪt/ **Determinate** means fixed and definite. [FORMAL] ❑ *...a contract for the exclusive possession of land for some determinate period.*
ADJ: usu ADJ n ≠ indeterminate

**de|ter|mi|na|tion** /dɪtɜːʳmɪneɪʃᵊn/ **Determination** is the quality that you show when you have decided to do something and you will not let anything stop you. ❑ *Everyone concerned acted with great courage and determination.*
N-UNCOUNT: oft N to-inf

**de|ter|mine** /dɪtɜːʳmɪn/ **(determines, determining, determined)** [1] If a particular factor **determines** the nature of a thing or event, it causes it to be of a particular kind. [FORMAL] ❑ *The size of the chicken pieces will determine the cooking time... What determines whether you are a career success or a failure?* ♦ **de|ter|mi|na|tion** *...the gene which is responsible for male sex determination.* [2] To **determine** a fact means to discover it as a result of investigation. [FORMAL] ❑ *The investigation will determine what really happened... Testing needs to be done to determine the long-term effects on humans... Science has determined that the risk is very small.* [3] If you **determine** something, you decide it or settle it. ❑ *The Baltic people have a right to determine their own future... My aim was first of all to determine what I should do next.* ♦ **de|ter|mi|na|tion (determinations)** *We must take into our own hands the determination of our future.* [4] If you **determine to** do something, you make a firm decision to do it. [FORMAL] ❑ *He determined to rescue his two countrymen... I determined that I would ask him outright.*
◆◆◇ VERB = dictate; V n; V wh; N-UNCOUNT: with supp; VERB = identify; V wh; V n; V that; VERB; V n; V wh; Also V that; N-COUNT: usu sing, usu *the* N *of* n; VERB; V to-inf; V that

**de|ter|mined** /dɪtɜːʳmɪnd/ If you are **determined to** do something, you have made a firm decision to do it and will not let anything stop you. ❑ *His enemies are determined to ruin him... He made determined efforts to overcome the scandal.* ♦ **de|ter|mined|ly** *She shook her head, determinedly.*
◆◇◇ ADJ: oft ADJ to-inf; ADV = resolutely

**de|ter|min|er** /dɪtɜːʳmɪnəʳ/ **(determiners)** In grammar, a **determiner** is a word which is used at the beginning of a noun group to indicate, for example, which thing you are referring to or whether you are referring to one thing or several. Common English determiners are 'a', 'the', 'some', 'this', and 'each'.
N-COUNT

**de|ter|min|ism** /dɪtɜːʳmɪnɪzəm/ **Determinism** is the belief that all actions and events result from other actions, events, or situations, so people cannot in fact choose what to do. [FORMAL] ❑ *I don't believe in historical determinism.*
N-UNCOUNT: oft adj N

**de|ter|min|ist** /dɪtɜːʳmɪnɪst/ **(determinists)** [1] A **determinist** is someone who believes in determinism. [FORMAL] [2] **Determinist** ideas are based on determinism. [FORMAL] ❑ *The determinist doctrines in question maintained that certain people were born to be slaves.*
N-COUNT; ADJ

**de|ter|min|is|tic** /dɪtɜːʳmɪnɪstɪk/ [1] **Deterministic** ideas or explanations are based on determinism. [FORMAL] ❑ *...a deterministic view of human progress.* [2] **Deterministic** forces and factors cause things to happen in a way that cannot be changed. [FORMAL] ❑ *The rise or decline of the United States is not a function of deterministic forces.*
ADJ; ADJ

**de|ter|rence** /dɪterəns, AM -tɜːr-/ **Deterrence** is the prevention of something, especially war or crime, by having something such as weapons or punishment to use as a threat. ❑ *...policies of nuclear deterrence.*
N-UNCOUNT

**de|ter|rent** /dɪterənt, AM -tɜːr-/ **(deterrents)** [1] A **deterrent** is something that prevents people from doing something by making them afraid of what will happen to them if they do it. ❑ *They seriously believe that capital punishment is a deterrent.* [2] A **deterrent** is a weapon or set of weapons designed to prevent enemies from attacking by making them afraid to do so. ❑ *...a nuclear deterrent.* [3] If something has a **deterrent** effect, it has the effect of preventing people from doing certain things. ❑ *...his belief in the deterrent value of capital punishment.*
N-COUNT; N-COUNT; ADJ: ADJ n

**de|test** /dɪtest/ **(detests, detesting, detested)** If you **detest** someone or something, you dislike them very much. ❑ *My mother detested him... Jean detested being photographed.*
VERB = loathe; V n/-ing; V n/-ing

**de|test|able** /dɪtestəbᵊl/ If you say that someone or something is **detestable**, you mean you dislike them very much. [FORMAL] ❑ *I find their views detestable.*
ADJ = loathsome, abhorrent

**de|throne** /diːθroʊn/ **(dethrones, dethroning, dethroned)** If a king, queen, or other powerful person **is dethroned**, they are removed from their position of power. ❑ *He was dethroned and went into exile.*
VERB: usu passive = depose; *be* V-ed

**deto|nate** /detəneɪt/ **(detonates, detonating, detonated)** If someone **detonates** a device such as a bomb, or if it **detonates**, it explodes. ❑ *France is expected to detonate its first nuclear device in the next few days... An explosive device detonated on the roof of the building.*
VERB; V n; V

**deto|na|tion** /detəneɪʃən/ **(detonations)** 1 A **detonation** is a large or powerful explosion. [FORMAL] 2 **Detonation** is the action of causing a device such as a bomb to explode. [FORMAL] ❑ *...accidental detonation of nuclear weapons.*
N-COUNT; N-UNCOUNT

**deto|na|tor** /detəneɪtəʳ/ **(detonators)** A **detonator** is a small amount of explosive or a piece of electrical or electronic equipment which is used to explode a bomb or other explosive device.
N-COUNT

**de|tour** /diːtʊəʳ/ **(detours)** 1 If you make a **detour** on a journey, you go by a route which is not the shortest way, because you want to avoid something such as a traffic jam, or because there is something you want to do on the way. ❑ *He did not take the direct route to his home, but made a detour around the outskirts of the city.* 2 A **detour** is a special route for traffic to follow when the normal route is blocked, for example because it is being repaired. [AM]
N-COUNT; N-COUNT

in BRIT, use **diversion**

**de|tox** /diːtɒks/ **(detoxes, detoxing, detoxed)** 1 **Detox** is treatment given to people who are addicted to drugs or alcohol in order to stop them from being addicted. ❑ *A patient going through acute detox will have an assigned nurse nearby. ...a detox therapist.* 2 A **detox** is a treatment that is intended to remove poisonous or harmful substances from your body. ❑ *Overhaul your body with a cleansing detox... Give yourself a healthy glow on our detox diet.* 3 If someone who is addicted to drugs or alcohol **detoxes**, or if another person **detoxes** them, they undergo treatment which stops them from being addicted. ❑ *...mums trying to detox their kids. ...drugs binges and failed attempts to detox.* 4 If you **detox**, or if something **detoxes** your body, you do something to remove poisonous or harmful substances from your body. ❑ *It might be an idea to detox after the indulgences of Christmas... Honey can help to detox the body.*
N-UNCOUNT: oft N n; N-COUNT: oft N n; VERB; V n; V; VERB; V; V n

**de|toxi|fi|ca|tion** /diːtɒksɪfɪkeɪʃən/ 1 **Detoxification** is treatment given to people who are addicted to drugs or alcohol in order to stop them from being addicted. 2 **Detoxification** is treatment that is intended to remove poisonous or harmful substances from your body. ❑ *Drink at least 2 litres of still mineral water throughout the day to aid detoxification.*
N-UNCOUNT; N-UNCOUNT

**de|toxi|fy** /diːtɒksɪfaɪ/ **(detoxifies, detoxifying, detoxified)** 1 If someone who is addicted to drugs or alcohol **detoxifies**, or if they **are detoxified**, they undergo treatment which stops them from being addicted. ❑ *...drugs which block the affects of heroin use and rapidly detoxify addicts... Queensland heroin users will be able to detoxify rapidly on Naltrexone after a two-year clinical trial of the controversial drug begins in Brisbane this week.* 2 If you **detoxify**, or if something **detoxifies** your body, you do something to remove poisonous or harmful substances from your body. ❑ *Many people have made it a rule to detoxify once a year... Seaweed baths can help to detoxify the body.* 3 To **detoxify** a poisonous substance means to change it chemically so that it is no longer poisonous. ❑ *Vitamin C helps to detoxify pollutants in the body.*
VERB; V n; V; VERB; V; V n; VERB; V n

**de|tract** /dɪtrækt/ **(detracts, detracting, detracted)** If one thing **detracts from** another, it makes it seem less good or impressive. ❑ *The publicity could detract from our election campaign.*
VERB; V *from* n; Also V n *from* n

**de|trac|tor** /dɪtræktəʳ/ **(detractors)** The **detractors** of a person or thing are people who criticize that person or thing. [JOURNALISM] ❑ *This performance will silence many of his detractors.*
N-COUNT: usu pl, usu with poss = critic

**det|ri|ment** /detrɪmənt/ 1 If something happens **to the detriment of** something or **to** a person's **detriment**, it causes harm or damage to them. [FORMAL] ❑ *Children spend too much time on schoolwork, to the detriment of other activities.* 2 If something happens **without detriment to** a person or thing, it does not harm or damage them. [FORMAL]
PHRASE: usu PHR after v, v-link PHR; PHRASE: PHR n

**det|ri|men|tal** /detrɪmentəl/ Something that is **detrimental to** something else has a harmful or damaging effect on it. ❑ *...foods suspected of being detrimental to health.*
ADJ: oft ADJ *to* n = *harmful*

**de|tri|tus** /dɪtraɪtəs/ **Detritus** is the small pieces of rubbish that remain after an event has finished or when something has been used. [FORMAL] ❑ *...the detritus of war.*
N-UNCOUNT: with supp

**deuce** /djuːs, AM duːs/ **(deuces) Deuce** is the score in a game of tennis when both players have forty points. One player has to win two points one after the other to win the game.
N-UNCOUNT: also N in pl

**de|value** /diːvæljuː/ **(devalues, devaluing, devalued)** 1 To **devalue** something means to cause it to be thought less impressive or less deserving of respect. ❑ *They spread tales about her in an attempt to devalue her work.* ♦ **de|valued** *She feels devalued because she knows her husband has had affairs.* 2 To **devalue** the currency of a country means to reduce its value in relation to other currencies. ❑ *India has devalued the Rupee by about eleven per cent.* ♦ **de|valua|tion** /diːvæljueɪʃən/ **(devaluations)** *It will lead to devaluation of a number of European currencies.*
VERB; V n; ADJ; VERB; V n *by* amount; N-VAR

**dev|as|tate** /devəsteɪt/ **(devastates, devastating, devastated)** If something **devastates** an area or a place, it damages it very badly or destroys it totally. ❑ *A few days before, a fire had devastated large parts of Windsor Castle.*
VERB = *ravage, wreck*; V n

**dev|as|tat|ed** /devəsteɪtɪd/ If you are **devastated** by something, you are very shocked and upset by it. ❑ *Teresa was devastated, her dreams shattered.*
ADJ: v-link ADJ

**dev|as|tat|ing** /devəsteɪtɪŋ/ 1 If you describe something as **devastating**, you are emphasizing that it is very harmful or damaging. ❑ *Affairs do have a devastating effect on marriages.* 2 You can use **devastating** to emphasize that something is very shocking, upsetting, or terrible. ❑ *The diagnosis was devastating. She had cancer.* 3 You can use **devastating** to emphasize that something or someone is very impressive. ❑ *...a devastating display of galloping and jumping.* ♦ **dev|as|tat|ing|ly** *Its advertising is devastatingly successful.*
ADJ: usu ADJ n [emphasis]; ADJ [emphasis]; ADJ [emphasis]; ADV: usu ADV adj/-ed

**dev|as|ta|tion** /devəsteɪʃən/ **Devastation** is severe and widespread destruction or damage. ❑ *A huge bomb blast brought chaos and devastation to the centre of Belfast yesterday.*
N-UNCOUNT

**de|vel|op** /dɪveləp/ **(develops, developing, developed)** ♦♦♦ 1 When something **develops**, it grows or changes over a period of time and usually becomes more advanced, complete, or severe. ❑ *It's hard to say at this stage how the market will develop... These clashes could develop into open warfare... Society begins to have an impact on the developing child.* ♦ **de|vel|oped** *Their bodies were well-developed and super fit.* 2 If a problem or difficulty **develops**, it begins to occur. ❑ *A huge row has developed about the pollution emanating from a chemical plant. ...blood clots in his lungs, a problem which developed from a leg injury.* 3 If you say that a country **develops**, you mean that it changes from being a poor agricultural country to being a rich industrial country. ❑ *All countries, it was predicted, would develop and develop fast.* → See also **developed**, **developing**. 4 If you **develop** a business or industry, or if it **develops**, it becomes bigger and more successful. [BUSINESS] ❑ *She won a grant to develop her own business... Over the last few years tourism here has developed considerably.* ♦ **de|vel|oped** *Housing finance is less developed in*
VERB; V; V *into* n; V-ing; ADJ; VERB = *arise*; V; V *from/out of* n; VERB; V; VERB; V n; V; ADJ

*continental Europe.* [5] To **develop** land or property means to make it more profitable, by building houses or factories or by improving the existing buildings. ❑ *Entrepreneurs developed fashionable restaurants and bars in the area.* ♦ **de|vel|oped** *Developed land was to grow from 5.3% to 6.9%.* [6] If you **develop** a habit, reputation, or belief, you start to have it and it then becomes stronger or more noticeable. ❑ *Mr Robinson has developed the reputation of a ruthless cost-cutter.* [7] If you **develop** a skill, quality, or relationship, or if it **develops**, it becomes better or stronger. ❑ *Now you have an opportunity to develop a greater understanding of each other... Their friendship developed through their shared interest in the Arts.* ♦ **de|vel|oped** *...a highly developed instinct for self-preservation.* [8] If you **develop** an illness, or if it **develops**, you become affected by it. ❑ *The test should identify which smokers are most prone to develop lung cancer... A sharp ache developed in her back muscles.* [9] If a piece of equipment **develops** a fault, it starts to have the fault. ❑ *The aircraft made an unscheduled landing after developing an electrical fault.* [10] If someone **develops** a new product, they design it and produce it. ❑ *He claims that several countries have developed nuclear weapons secretly.* [11] If you **develop** an idea, theory, story, or theme, or if it **develops**, it gradually becomes more detailed, advanced, or complex. ❑ *I would like to thank them for allowing me to develop their original idea... The idea of weather forecasting developed incredibly quickly.* [12] To **develop** photographs means to make negatives or prints from a photographic film.

VERB · V n · ADJ · VERB = acquire · V n · VERB · V n · V · ADJ · VERB · V n · V · VERB · V n · VERB · V n · VERB · V n · V · VERB

**de|vel|oped** /dɪveləpt/ ADJ If you talk about **developed** countries or the **developed** world, you mean the countries or the parts of the world that are wealthy and have many industries. ❑ *This scarcity is inevitable in less developed countries.*

**de|vel|op|er** /dɪveləpəʳ/ **(developers)** [1] N-COUNT A **developer** is a person or a company that buys land and builds houses, offices, shops, or factories on it, or buys existing buildings and makes them more modern. [BUSINESS] ❑ *...common land which would have a high commercial value if sold to developers.* [2] N-COUNT: with supp A **developer** is someone who develops something such as an idea, a design, or a product. ❑ *John Bardeen was also co-developer of the theory of superconductivity.*

**de|vel|op|ing** /dɪveləpɪŋ/ ADJ: ADJ n If you talk about **developing** countries or the **developing** world, you mean the countries or the parts of the world that are poor and have few industries. ❑ *In the developing world cigarette consumption is increasing.*

**de|vel|op|ment** /dɪveləpmənt/ **(developments)** ◆◆◆ [1] N-UNCOUNT: with supp, oft N *of* n **Development** is the gradual growth or formation of something. ❑ *...an ideal system for studying the development of the embryo.* [2] N-UNCOUNT: with supp, oft N *of* n **Development** is the growth of something such as a business or an industry. [BUSINESS] ❑ *Education is central to a country's economic development.* [3] N-VAR **Development** is the process or result of making a basic design gradually better and more advanced. ❑ *We are spending $850m on research and development.* [4] N-UNCOUNT: with supp **Development** is the process of making an area of land or water more useful or profitable. ❑ *The talks will focus on economic development of the region.* [5] N-COUNT A **development** is an event or incident which has recently happened and is likely to have an effect on the present situation. ❑ *Police said there had been a significant development in the case.* [6] N-COUNT A **development** is an area of houses or buildings which have been built by property developers.

**de|vel|op|men|tal** /dɪveləpmentᵊl/ ADJ: usu ADJ n **Developmental** means relating to the development of someone or something. ❑ *...the emotional, educational, and developmental needs of the child.*

**de|vel|op|ment bank** **(development banks)** N-COUNT A **development bank** is a bank that provides money for projects in poor countries or areas. [BUSINESS]

**de|vi|ant** /diːviənt/ **(deviants)** [1] ADJ **Deviant** behaviour or thinking is different from what people normally consider to be acceptable. ❑ *...the social reactions to deviant and criminal behaviour.* ♦ **de|vi|ance** /diːviəns/ N-UNCOUNT *...sexual deviance, including the abuse of children.* [2] N-COUNT A **deviant** is someone whose behaviour or beliefs are different from what people normally consider to be acceptable.

**de|vi|ate** /diːvieɪt/ **(deviates, deviating, deviated)** VERB = depart To **deviate from** something means to start doing something different or not planned, especially in a way that causes problems for others. ❑ V *from* n *They stopped you as soon as you deviated from the script.*

**de|via|tion** /diːvieɪʃᵊn/ **(deviations)** N-VAR: oft N *from* n = departure **Deviation** means doing something that is different from what people consider to be normal or acceptable. ❑ *Deviation from the norm is not tolerated.*

**de|vice** /dɪvaɪs/ **(devices)** ◆◇◇ [1] N-COUNT: usu with supp A **device** is an object that has been invented for a particular purpose, for example for recording or measuring something. ❑ *...an electronic device that protects your vehicle 24 hours a day.* [2] N-COUNT A **device** is a method of achieving something. ❑ *They claim that military spending is used as a device for managing the economy.* [3] PHRASE: V inflects If you **leave** someone **to** their **own devices**, you leave them alone to do as they wish. ❑ *Left to his own devices, Osborn is a fluent – and often original – guitarist.*

**dev|il** /devᵊl/ **(devils)** [1] N-PROPER: *the* N = Satan In Judaism, Christianity, and Islam, **the Devil** is the most powerful evil spirit. [2] N-COUNT = demon A **devil** is an evil spirit. ❑ *...the idea of angels with wings and devils with horns and hoofs.* [3] N-COUNT feelings You can use **devil** to emphasize the way you feel about someone. For example, if you call someone a poor **devil**, you are saying that you feel sorry for them. You can call someone you are fond of but who sometimes annoys or irritates you an old **devil** or a little **devil**. [INFORMAL] ❑ *I felt sorry for Blake, poor devil.*

PHRASES [4] PHRASE: v-link PHR If you say that you are **between the devil and the deep blue sea**, you mean that you are in a difficult situation where you have to choose between two equally unpleasant courses of action. [5] PHRASE People say **speak of the devil**, or in British English **talk of the devil**, if someone they have just been talking about appears unexpectedly. ❑ *Well, talk of the devil!* [6] PHRASE emphasis When you want to emphasize how annoyed or surprised you are, you can use an expression such as **what the devil**, **how the devil**, or **why the devil**. [INFORMAL] ❑ *'What the devil's the matter?'*

**dev|il|ish** /devəlɪʃ/ [1] ADJ: usu ADJ n A **devilish** idea or action is cruel or unpleasant. ❑ *...the devilish destructiveness of modern weapons.* [2] ADJ: usu ADJ n emphasis You can use **devilish** to emphasize how extreme or difficult something is. ❑ *...a devilish puzzle.* ♦ **dev|il|ish|ly** ADV *It is devilishly painful.*

**devil-may-care** ADJ: usu ADJ n approval If you say that someone has a **devil-may-care** attitude, you mean that they seem relaxed and do not seem worried about the consequences of their actions.

**dev|il's ad|vo|cate** N-UNCOUNT: also with det If you **play devil's advocate** in a discussion or debate, you express an opinion which you may not agree with but which is very different to what other people have been saying, in order to make the argument more interesting.

**de|vi|ous** /diːviəs/ ADJ disapproval If you describe someone as **devious** you do not like them because you think they are are dishonest and like to keep things secret, often in a complicated way. ❑ *Newman was devious, prepared to say one thing in print and another in private.* ♦ **de|vi|ous|ness** N-UNCOUNT *...the deviousness of drug traffickers.*

**de|vise** /dɪvaɪz/ **(devises, devising, devised)** VERB If you **devise** a plan, system, or machine, you have the idea for it and design it. ❑ V n *We devised a scheme to help him.*

**de|void** /dɪvɔ̲ɪd/ If you say that someone or something is **devoid of** a quality or thing, you are emphasizing that they have none of it. [FORMAL] ❑ *I have never looked on a face that was so devoid of feeling.* ADJ: v-link ADJ *of* n [emphasis] = bereft

**de|vo|lu|tion** /di̲ːvəlu̲ːʃᵊn, de̲v-/ **Devolution** is the transfer of some authority or power from a central organization or government to smaller organizations or government departments. ❑ *...the devolution of power to the regions.* N-UNCOUNT: oft N *of* n

**de|volve** /dɪvɒ̲lv/ **(devolves, devolving, devolved)** If you **devolve** power, authority, or responsibility **to** a less powerful person or group, or if it **devolves upon** them, it is transferred to them. ❑ *...the need to decentralize and devolve power to regional governments... We have made a conscious effort to devolve responsibility... A large portion of this cost devolves upon the patient.* VERB V n *to* n V n V *upon/on* n

**de|vote** /dɪvo̲ʊt/ **(devotes, devoting, devoted)** 1 If you **devote** yourself, your time, or your energy **to** something, you spend all or most of your time or energy on it. ❑ *He decided to devote the rest of his life to scientific investigation... Considerable resources have been devoted to proving him a liar... She gladly gave up her part-time job to devote herself entirely to her art.* VERB = dedicate V n *to* n/-ing V n *to* n/-ing V pron-refl *to* n/-ing 2 If you **devote** a particular proportion of a piece of writing or a speech **to** a particular subject, you deal with the subject in that amount of space or time. ❑ *He devoted a major section of his massive report to an analysis of US aircraft design.* VERB V n *to* n

**de|vot|ed** /dɪvo̲ʊtɪd/ 1 Someone who is **devoted to** a person loves that person very much. ❑ *...a loving and devoted husband... 50 years on, the couple are still devoted to one another.* ADJ: ADJ n, v-link ADJ *to* n = dedicated 2 If you are **devoted to** something, you care about it a lot and are very enthusiastic about it. ❑ *I have personally been devoted to this cause for many years... Joyce Bryt is a devoted Star Trek fan.* ADJ: v-link ADJ *to* n, ADJ n = dedicated 3 Something that is **devoted to** a particular thing deals only with that thing or contains only that thing. ❑ *The shop is devoted to a new range of accessories.* ADJ: v-link ADJ *to* n = dedicated

**devo|tee** /de̲vəti̲ː/ **(devotees)** Someone who is a **devotee of** a subject or activity is very enthusiastic about it. ❑ *Mr Carpenter is obviously a devotee of Britten's music.* N-COUNT: with supp, oft N *of* n = fan

**de|vo|tion** /dɪvo̲ʊʃᵊn/ 1 **Devotion** is great love, affection, or admiration for someone. ❑ *At first she was flattered by his devotion.* N-UNCOUNT: oft poss N 2 **Devotion** is commitment to a particular activity. ❑ *...devotion to the cause of the people and to socialism.* N-UNCOUNT: oft N *to* n = dedication

**de|vo|tion|al** /dɪvo̲ʊʃənᵊl/ **Devotional** activities, writings, or objects relate to religious worship. ❑ *...devotional pictures.* ADJ: ADJ n

**de|vo|tions** /dɪvo̲ʊʃᵊnz/ Someone's **devotions** are the prayers that they say. ❑ *Normally he performs his devotions twice a day.* N-PLURAL: oft poss N

**de|vour** /dɪva̲ʊəʳ/ **(devours, devouring, devoured)** 1 If a person or animal **devours** something, they eat it quickly and eagerly. ❑ *A medium-sized dog will devour at least one can of food per day.* VERB V n 2 If you **devour** a book or magazine, for example, you read it quickly and with great enthusiasm. ❑ *She began devouring newspapers when she was only 12.* VERB V n

**de|vout** /dɪva̲ʊt/ 1 A **devout** person has deep religious beliefs. ❑ *She was a devout Christian.* ADJ ♦ **The devout** are people who are devout. ❑ *...priests instructing the devout.* N-PLURAL: *the* N 2 If you describe someone as a **devout** supporter or a **devout** opponent of something, you mean that they support it enthusiastically or oppose it strongly. ❑ *...devout Marxists.* ADJ: ADJ n

**de|vout|ly** /dɪva̲ʊtli/ 1 **Devoutly** is used to emphasize how sincerely or deeply you hope for something or believe in something. [FORMAL] ❑ *He devoutly hoped it was true.* ADV: ADV with v [emphasis] 2 **Devoutly** is used to emphasize how deep someone's religious beliefs are, or to indicate that something is done in a devout way. ❑ *...a devoutly Buddhist country.* ADV: ADV adj, ADV with v [emphasis]

**dew** /dju̲ː, AM du̲ː/ **Dew** is small drops of water that form on the ground and other surfaces outdoors during the night. ❑ *The dew gathered on the leaves.* N-UNCOUNT

**dewy** /dju̲ːi, AM du̲ːi/ 1 Something that is **dewy** is wet with dew. [LITERARY] ADJ 2 If your skin looks **dewy**, it looks soft and glows healthily. ADJ

**dewy-eyed** If you say that someone is **dewy-eyed**, you are criticizing them because you think that they are unrealistic and think events and situations are better than they really are. ADJ [disapproval]

**dex|ter|ity** /dekste̲rɪti/ **Dexterity** is skill in using your hands, or sometimes your mind. ❑ *...Reid's dexterity on the guitar.* N-UNCOUNT

**dex|ter|ous** /de̲kstrəs/ also **dextrous.** Someone who is **dexterous** is very skilful and clever with their hands. ❑ *As people grow older they generally become less dexterous.* ADJ

**dex|trose** /de̲kstroʊz, AM -roʊs/ **Dextrose** is a natural form of sugar that is found in fruits, honey, and in the blood of animals. N-UNCOUNT

**dia|be|tes** /da̲ɪəbi̲ːtiːz, AM -tɪs/ **Diabetes** is a medical condition in which someone has too much sugar in their blood. N-UNCOUNT

**dia|bet|ic** /da̲ɪəbe̲tɪk/ **(diabetics)** 1 A **diabetic** is a person who suffers from diabetes. ❑ *...an insulin-dependent diabetic.* N-COUNT ♦ **Diabetic** is also an adjective. ❑ *...diabetic patients.* ADJ 2 **Diabetic** means relating to diabetes. ❑ *He found her in a diabetic coma.* ADJ: ADJ n 3 **Diabetic** foods are suitable for diabetics. ADJ: ADJ n

**dia|bol|ic** /da̲ɪəbɒ̲lɪk/ 1 **Diabolic** is used to describe things that people think are caused by or belong to the Devil. [FORMAL] ❑ *...the diabolic forces which lurk in all violence.* ADJ: ADJ n 2 If you describe something as **diabolic**, you are emphasizing that it is very bad, extreme, or unpleasant. [mainly AM] ❑ *Pitt's smile returned, and it was hideously diabolic.* ADJ [emphasis] = diabolical

**dia|boli|cal** /da̲ɪəbɒ̲lɪkᵊl/ If you describe something as **diabolical**, you are emphasizing that it is very bad, extreme, or unpleasant. [INFORMAL] ❑ *It was a diabolical error, a schoolboy error.* ADJ [emphasis] = appalling ♦ **dia|boli|cal|ly** /da̲ɪəbɒ̲lɪkli/ *...diabolically difficult clues.* ADV

**dia|dem** /da̲ɪədem/ **(diadems)** A **diadem** is a small crown with precious stones in it. N-COUNT

**di|ag|nose** /da̲ɪəgnoʊz, AM -noʊs/ **(diagnoses, diagnosing, diagnosed)** If someone or something **is diagnosed as** having a particular illness or problem, their illness or problem is identified. If an illness or problem **is diagnosed**, it is identified. ❑ *The soldiers were diagnosed as having flu... Susan had a mental breakdown and was diagnosed with schizophrenia... In 1894 her illness was diagnosed as cancer... He could diagnose an engine problem simply by listening.* VERB *be* V-ed *as* -ing/adj *be* V-ed *with* n *be* V-ed *as* n V n

**di|ag|no|sis** /da̲ɪəgno̲ʊsɪs/ **(diagnoses)** **Diagnosis** is the discovery and naming of what is wrong with someone who is ill or with something that is not working properly. ❑ *I need to have a second test to confirm the diagnosis.* N-VAR

**di|ag|nos|tic** /da̲ɪəgnɒ̲stɪk/ **Diagnostic** equipment, methods, or systems are used for discovering what is wrong with people who are ill or with things that do not work properly. ❑ *...X-rays and other diagnostic tools.* ADJ: ADJ n

**di|ago|nal** /daɪæ̲gənᵊl/ **(diagonals)** 1 A **diagonal** line or movement goes in a sloping direction, for example, from one corner of a square across to the opposite corner. ❑ *...a pattern of diagonal lines.* ADJ: usu ADJ n ♦ **di|ago|nal|ly** *Vaulting the stile, he headed diagonally across the paddock.* ADV: ADV with v, oft ADV prep 2 A **diagonal** is a line that goes in a sloping direction. ❑ *The bed linen is patterned in stylish checks, stripes, diagonals and triangles.* N-COUNT 3 In geometry, a **diagonal** is a straight line that joins two opposite corners in a flat four-sided shape such as a square. ❑ *Mark five points an equal distance apart along the diagonals.* N-COUNT

**dia|gram** /daɪəgræm/ **(diagrams)** A **diagram** is a simple drawing which consists mainly of lines and is used, for example, to explain how a machine works. ❑ *You can reduce long explanations to simple charts or diagrams.* N-COUNT: usu with supp

**dia|gram|mat|ic** /daɪəgrəmætɪk/ Something that is in **diagrammatic** form is arranged or drawn as a diagram. ❑ *This is the virus in very crude simple diagrammatic form.* ADJ: usu ADJ n

**dial** /daɪəl/ **(dials, dialling, dialled)**

✔ in AM, use **dialing, dialed**

1 A **dial** is the part of a machine or instrument such as a clock or watch which shows you the time or a measurement that has been recorded. ❑ *The luminous dial on the clock showed five minutes to seven.* N-COUNT 2 A **dial** is a control on a device or piece of equipment which you can move in order to adjust the setting, for example to select or change the frequency on a radio or the temperature of a heater. ❑ *He turned the dial on the radio.* N-COUNT 3 On some telephones, especially older ones, **the dial** is the disc on the front that you turn with your finger to choose the number that you want to call. The disc has holes in it, and numbers or letters behind the holes. N-COUNT 4 If you **dial** or if you **dial** a number, you turn the dial or press the buttons on a telephone in order to phone someone. ❑ *He lifted the phone and dialled her number... He dialled, and spoke briefly to the duty officer.* VERB V n V

**dia|lect** /daɪəlekt/ **(dialects)** A **dialect** is a form of a language that is spoken in a particular area. ❑ *In the fifties, many Italians spoke only local dialect... They began to speak rapidly in dialect.* N-COUNT: also *in* N

**dia|lec|tic** /daɪəlektɪk/ **(dialectics)** 1 People refer to the **dialectic** or **dialectics** of a situation when they are referring to the way in which two very different forces or factors work together, and the way in which their differences are resolved. [TECHNICAL or FORMAL] ❑ *...the dialectics of class struggle and of socio-economic change.* N-COUNT: with supp, oft *the* N *of/between* n 2 In philosophy, **dialectics** is a method of reasoning and reaching conclusions by considering theories and ideas together with ones that contradict them. [TECHNICAL] N-UNCOUNT

**dia|lec|ti|cal** /daɪəlektɪkᵊl/ In philosophy, **Dialectical** is used to describe situations, theories, and methods which depend on resolving opposing factors. ❑ *The essence of dialectical thought is division.* ADJ: usu ADJ n

**dial|ling code** **(dialling codes)** A **dialling code** for a particular city or region is the series of numbers that you have to dial before a particular telephone number if you are making a call to that place from a different area. [mainly BRIT] N-COUNT

✔ in AM, use **area code**

**dial|ling tone** **(dialling tones)** The **dialling tone** is the noise which you hear when you pick up a telephone receiver and which means that you can dial the number you want. [BRIT] N-COUNT

✔ in AM, use **dial tone**

**dia|log box** **(dialog boxes)** A **dialog box** is a small area containing information or questions that appears on a computer screen when you are performing particular operations. [COMPUTING] N-COUNT

**dia|logue** /daɪəlɒg, AM -lɔːg/ **(dialogues)** ◆◇◇

✔ in AM, also use **dialog**

1 **Dialogue** is communication or discussion between people or groups of people such as governments or political parties. ❑ *People of all social standings should be given equal opportunities for dialogue.* N-VAR 2 A **dialogue** is a conversation between two people in a book, film, or play. ❑ *The dialogue is amusing but the plot is weak.* N-VAR

**dial tone** **(dial tones)** The **dial tone** is the same as the **dialling tone**. [AM] N-COUNT

**di|aly|sis** /daɪælɪsɪs/ **Dialysis** or **kidney dialysis** is a method of treating kidney failure by using a machine to remove waste material from the kidneys. ❑ *I was on dialysis for seven years before my first transplant.* N-UNCOUNT

**dia|man|te** /daɪəmænti, AM diːəmɑːnteɪ/ also **diamanté**. **Diamante** jewellery is made from small pieces of cut glass which look like diamonds. ❑ *...diamante earrings.* N-UNCOUNT: oft N n

**di|am|eter** /daɪæmɪtəʳ/ **(diameters)** The **diameter** of a round object is the length of a straight line that can be drawn across it, passing through the middle of it. ❑ *...a tube less than a fifth of the diameter of a human hair.* N-COUNT: also *in* N

**dia|met|ri|cal|ly** /daɪəmetrɪkli/ If you say that two things are **diametrically** opposed, you are emphasizing that they are completely different from each other. ADV: ADV adj [emphasis]

**dia|mond** /daɪəmənd/ **(diamonds)** 1 A **diamond** is a hard, bright, precious stone which is clear and colourless. Diamonds are used in jewellery and for cutting very hard substances. ❑ *...a pair of diamond earrings.* N-VAR 2 A **diamond** is a shape with four straight sides of equal length where the opposite angles are the same, but none of the angles is equal to 90°: ◊. ❑ *He formed his hands into the shape of a diamond.* N-COUNT 3 **Diamonds** is one of the four suits of cards in a pack of playing cards. Each card in the suit is marked with one or more red symbols in the shape of a diamond. ❑ *He drew the seven of diamonds.* N-UNCOUNT-COLL ♦ A **diamond** is a playing card of this suit. N-COUNT

**dia|mond ju|bi|lee** **(diamond jubilees)** A **diamond jubilee** is the sixtieth anniversary of an important event. N-COUNT

**dia|per** /daɪəpəʳ/ **(diapers)** A **diaper** is a piece of soft towel or paper, which you fasten round a baby's bottom in order to soak up its urine and faeces. [AM] ❑ *He never changed her diapers, never bathed her.* N-COUNT

✔ in BRIT, use **nappy**

**di|apha|nous** /daɪæfənəs/ **Diaphanous** cloth is very thin and almost transparent. [LITERARY] ❑ *...a diaphanous dress of pale gold.* ADJ: usu ADJ n

**dia|phragm** /daɪəfræm/ **(diaphragms)** 1 Your **diaphragm** is a muscle between your lungs and your stomach. It is used when you breathe. N-COUNT 2 A **diaphragm** is a circular rubber contraceptive device that a woman places inside her vagina. N-COUNT

**dia|rist** /daɪərɪst/ **(diarists)** A **diarist** is a person who records things in a diary which is later published. N-COUNT

**di|ar|rhoea** /daɪəriːə/

✔ in AM, use **diarrhea**

If someone has **diarrhoea**, a lot of liquid faeces comes out of their body because they are ill. N-UNCOUNT

**dia|ry** /daɪəri/ **(diaries)** A **diary** is a book which has a separate space for each day of the year. You use a diary to write down things you plan to do, or to record what happens in your life day by day. ◆◇◇ N-COUNT

**di|as|po|ra** /daɪæspərə/ People who come from a particular nation, or whose ancestors came from it, but who now live in many different parts of the world are sometimes referred to as **the diaspora**. [FORMAL] ❑ *...the history of peoples from the African diaspora.* N-SING: usu *the* N

**dia|tribe** /daɪətraɪb/ **(diatribes)** A **diatribe** is an angry speech or article which is extremely critical of someone's ideas or activities. ❑ *The book is a diatribe against the academic left.* N-COUNT: usu with supp = *tirade*

**dice** /daɪs/ **(dices, dicing, diced)** 1 A **dice** is a small cube which has between one and six spots or numbers on its sides, and which is used in games to provide random numbers. In old-fashioned English, 'dice' was used only as a plural form, and the singular was **die**, but now 'dice' is used as both the singular and the plural form. N-COUNT 2 If you **dice** food, you cut it into small cubes. ❑ *Dice the onion.* VERB V n

**dicey** /daɪsi/ **(dicier, diciest)** Something that is **dicey** is slightly dangerous or uncertain. [BRIT, INFORMAL] ❑ *There was a dicey moment as one of our party made a risky climb up the cliff wall.* *[ADJ]*

**di|choto|my** /daɪkɒtəmi/ **(dichotomies)** If there is a **dichotomy** between two things, there is a very great difference or opposition between them. [FORMAL] ❑ *There is a dichotomy between the academic world and the industrial world.* *[N-COUNT: usu sing, oft N between pl-n]*

**dick** /dɪk/ **(dicks)** A man's **dick** is his penis. [INFORMAL, ⚠ VERY RUDE] *[N-COUNT]*

**dick|er** /dɪkəʳ/ **(dickers, dickering, dickered)** If you say that people **are dickering** about something, you mean that they are arguing or disagreeing about it, often in a way that you think is foolish or unnecessary. [mainly AM] ❑ *Management and labor are dickering over pay and conditions... He may be expecting us to dicker. Don't.* *[V-RECIP; disapproval; pl-n V over/about n; V (non-recip); Also pl-n V]*

**dick|head** /dɪkhed/ **(dickheads)** If someone calls a man a **dickhead**, they are saying that they think he is very stupid. [INFORMAL, RUDE] *[N-COUNT]*

**dic|tate (dictates, dictating, dictated)**

✔ The verb is pronounced /dɪkteɪt, AM dɪkteɪt/. The noun is pronounced /dɪkteɪt/.

1 If you **dictate** something, you say or read it aloud for someone else to write down. ❑ *Sheldon writes every day of the week, dictating his novels in the morning.* *[VERB; V n]* 2 If someone **dictates to** someone else, they tell them what they should do or can do. ❑ *What right has one country to dictate the environmental standards of another?... He cannot be allowed to dictate what can and cannot be inspected... What gives them the right to dictate to us what we should eat?... The officers were more or less able to dictate terms to successive governments.* *[VERB; V n; V wh; V to n wh; V n to n]* 3 If one thing **dictates** another, the first thing causes or influences the second thing. ❑ *The film's budget dictated a tough schedule... Of course, a number of factors will dictate how long an apple tree can survive... Circumstances dictated that they played a defensive rather than attacking game.* *[VERB; V n; V wh; V that]* 4 You say that reason or common sense **dictates that** a particular thing is the case when you believe strongly that it is the case and that reason or common sense will cause other people to agree. ❑ *Commonsense now dictates that it would be wise to sell a few shares.* *[VERB; V that]* 5 A **dictate** is an order which you have to obey. ❑ *Their job is to ensure that the dictates of the Party are followed.* *[N-COUNT: usu with supp, oft N of n]* 6 **Dictates** are principles or rules which you consider to be extremely important. ❑ *We have followed the dictates of our consciences and have done our duty.* *[N-COUNT: usu pl, with supp, usu N of n]*

**dic|ta|tion** /dɪkteɪʃən/ **Dictation** is the speaking or reading aloud of words for someone else to write down. *[N-UNCOUNT]*

**dic|ta|tor** /dɪkteɪtəʳ, AM dɪkteɪt-/ **(dictators)** A **dictator** is a ruler who has complete power in a country, especially power which was obtained by force and is used unfairly or cruelly. *[N-COUNT]*

**dic|ta|tor|ial** /dɪktətɔːriəl/ 1 **Dictatorial** means controlled or used by a dictator. ❑ *He suspended the constitution and assumed dictatorial powers.* *[ADJ]* 2 If you describe someone's behaviour as **dictatorial**, you do not like the fact that they tell people what to do in a forceful and unfair way. ❑ *...his dictatorial management style.* *[ADJ; disapproval]*

**dic|ta|tor|ship** /dɪkteɪtəʳʃɪp/ **(dictatorships)** 1 **Dictatorship** is government by a dictator. ❑ *...a new era of democracy after a long period of military dictatorship in the country.* *[N-VAR]* 2 A **dictatorship** is a country which is ruled by a dictator or by a very strict and harsh government. ❑ *Every country in the region was a military dictatorship.* *[N-COUNT]*

**dic|tion** /dɪkʃən/ Someone's **diction** is how clearly they speak or sing. ❑ *His diction wasn't very good.* *[N-UNCOUNT]*

**dic|tion|ary** /dɪkʃənri, AM -neri/ **(dictionaries)** A **dictionary** is a book in which the words and phrases of a language are listed alphabetically, together with their meanings or their translations in another language. ❑ *...a Welsh-English dictionary.* *[N-COUNT]*

**dic|tum** /dɪktəm/ **(dictums or dicta)** 1 A **dictum** is a saying that describes an aspect of life in an interesting or wise way. ❑ *...the dictum that it is preferable to be roughly right than precisely wrong.* *[N-COUNT: oft N that = saying]* 2 A **dictum** is a formal statement made by someone who has authority. ❑ *...Disraeli's dictum that the first priority of the government must be the health of the people.* *[N-COUNT: oft N that]*

**did** /dɪd/ **Did** is the past tense of **do**.

**di|dac|tic** /daɪdæktɪk/ 1 Something that is **didactic** is intended to teach people something, especially a moral lesson. [FORMAL] ❑ *In totalitarian societies, art exists for didactic purposes.* *[ADJ]* 2 Someone who is **didactic** tells people things rather than letting them find things out or discussing things. [FORMAL] ❑ *He is more didactic in his approach to the learning process.* *[ADJ]*

**did|dle** /dɪdəl/ **(diddles, diddling, diddled)** 1 If someone **diddles** you, they take money from you dishonestly or unfairly. [mainly BRIT, INFORMAL] ❑ *They diddled their insurance company by making a false claim.* *[VERB = con; V n]* 2 If someone **diddles**, they waste time and do not achieve anything. [AM, INFORMAL] ❑ *...if Congress were to just diddle around and not take any action at all.* *[VERB: oft V adv; V around]*

**did|geri|doo** /dɪdʒəriduː/ **(didgeridoos)** A **didgeridoo** is an Australian musical instrument that consists of a long pipe which makes a low sound when you blow into it. *[N-COUNT]*

**didn't** /dɪdənt/ **Didn't** is the usual spoken form of 'did not'.

**die** /daɪ/ **(dies, dying, died)** ◆◆◆ 1 When people, animals, and plants **die**, they stop living. ❑ *A year later my dog died... Sadly, both he and my mother died of cancer... I would die a very happy person if I could stay in music my whole life. ...friends who died young.* *[VERB: no passive; V; V of/from n; V n; V adj]* 2 If a person, animal, or plant **is dying**, they are so ill or so badly injured that they will not live very much longer. ❑ *The elm trees are all dying... Every working day I treat people who are dying from lung diseases caused by smoking.* *[VERB: only cont ≠ recover; V; V of/from n]* 3 If someone **dies** a violent, unnatural, or painful death, they die in a violent, unnatural, or painful way. ❑ *He watched helplessly as his mother died an agonizing death.* *[VERB: no passive; V n]* 4 If a machine or device **dies**, it stops completely, especially after a period of working more and more slowly or inefficiently. [WRITTEN] ❑ *Then suddenly, the engine coughed, spluttered and died.* *[VERB; V]* 5 You can say that you **are dying of** thirst, hunger, boredom, or curiosity to emphasize that you are very thirsty, hungry, bored, or curious. [INFORMAL] ❑ *Order me a pot of tea, I'm dying of thirst.* *[VERB: only cont; emphasis; V of n]* 6 You can say that you **are dying for** something or **are dying to** do something to emphasize that you very much want to have it or do it. [INFORMAL] ❑ *I'm dying for a breath of fresh air... She was dying to talk to Frank.* *[VERB: only cont; emphasis; V for n; V to-inf]* 7 You can use **die** in expressions such as '**I almost died**' or '**I'd die if anything happened**' where you are emphasizing your feelings about a situation, for example to say that it is very shocking, upsetting, embarrassing, or amusing. [INFORMAL, mainly SPOKEN] ❑ *I nearly died when I learned where I was ending up... I nearly died of shame... I thought I'd die laughing.* *[VERB; emphasis; V; V of n; V -ing]* 8 A **die** is a specially shaped or patterned block of metal which is used to press or cut other metal into a particular shape. *[N-COUNT]* 9 → See also **dying**.

**PHRASES** 10 You can say that **the die is cast** to draw attention to the importance of an event or decision which is going to affect your future and which cannot be changed or avoided. *[PHRASE: V inflects]* 11 If you say that habits or attitudes **die hard**, you mean that they take a very long time to disappear or change, so that it may not be possible to get rid of them completely. ❑ *Old habits die hard.* *[PHRASE: V inflects]*

♦ **die away** If a sound **dies away**, it gradually becomes weaker or fainter and finally disappears completely. ❑ *The firing finally began to die away in the late afternoon.* *[PHRASAL VERB = fade away; V P]*

♦ **die down** If something **dies down**, it becomes very much quieter or less intense. ❑ *The controversy is unlikely to die down.* PHRASAL VERB V P

♦ **die out** [1] If something **dies out**, it becomes less and less common and eventually disappears completely. ❑ *We used to believe that capitalism would soon die out.* [2] If something such as a fire or wind **dies out**, it gradually stops burning or blowing. [AM] ❑ *Once the fire has died out, the salvage team will move in.* PHRASAL VERB V P PHRASAL VERB V P

**die|hard** /daɪhɑːʳd/ **(diehards)** also **die-hard.** A **diehard** is someone who is very strongly opposed to change and new ideas, or who is a very strong supporter of a person or idea. N-COUNT: oft N n

**die|sel** /diːzᵊl/ **(diesels)** [1] **Diesel** or **diesel oil** is the heavy oil used in a diesel engine. [2] A **diesel** is a vehicle which has a diesel engine. N-MASS N-COUNT

**die|sel en|gine (diesel engines)** A **diesel engine** is an internal combustion engine in which oil is burnt by very hot air. Diesel engines are used in buses and trucks, and in some trains and cars. N-COUNT

**diet** /daɪət/ **(diets, dieting, dieted)** [1] Your **diet** is the type and range of food that you regularly eat. ❑ *It's never too late to improve your diet. ...a healthy diet rich in fruit and vegetables.* [2] If a doctor puts someone on a **diet**, he or she makes them eat a special type or range of foods in order to improve their health. ❑ *He was put on a diet of milky food.* [3] If you are on a **diet**, you eat special kinds of food or you eat less food than usual because you are trying to lose weight. ❑ *Have you been on a diet? You've lost a lot of weight.* [4] If you **are dieting**, you eat special kinds of food or you eat less food than usual because you are trying to lose weight. ❑ *I've been dieting ever since the birth of my fourth child.* ♦ **diet|ing** *She has already lost around two stone through dieting.* [5] **Diet** drinks or foods have been specially produced so that they do not contain many calories. ❑ *...sugar-free diet drinks.* [6] If you are fed on a **diet of** something, especially something unpleasant or of poor quality, you receive or experience a very large amount of it. ❑ *The radio had fed him a diet of pop songs.* ♦♦◇ N-VAR N-COUNT: usu with supp N-VAR VERB V N-UNCOUNT ADJ: ADJ n N-COUNT: usu N *of* n

**di|etary** /daɪətri, AM -teri/ [1] You can use **dietary** to describe anything that concerns a person's diet. ❑ *Dr Susan Hankinson has studied the dietary habits of more than 50,000 women.* [2] You can use the word **dietary** to describe substances such as fibre and fat that are found in food. ❑ *...a source of dietary fibre.* ADJ: usu ADJ n ADJ: ADJ n

**di|et|er** /daɪətəʳ/ **(dieters)** A **dieter** is someone who is on a diet or who regularly goes on diets. N-COUNT = slimmer

**di|etet|ic** /daɪətetɪk/ **Dietetic** food or drink is food or drink that has been specially produced so that it does not contain many calories. [AM, FORMAL] ❑ *All dietetic meals are low in sugar.* ADJ: ADJ n = diet, low-calorie

**di|eti|cian** /daɪətɪʃᵊn/ **(dieticians)** also **dietitian.** A **dietician** is a person whose job is to give people advice about the kind of food they should eat. Dieticians often work in hospitals. N-COUNT

**dif|fer** /dɪfəʳ/ **(differs, differing, differed)** [1] If two or more things **differ**, they are unlike each other in some way. ❑ *The story he told police differed from the one he told his mother... Management styles differ.* [2] If people **differ** about something, they do not agree with each other about it. ❑ *The two leaders had differed on the issue of sanctions... That is where we differ... Since his retirement, Crowe has differed with the President on several issues.* [3] to **agree to differ** → see **agree**. **'I beg to differ'** → see **beg**. V-RECIP V *from* n pl-n V V-RECIP pl-n V prep pl-n V V *with* n

**dif|fer|ence** /dɪfrəns/ **(differences)** [1] The **difference** between two things is the way in which they are unlike each other. ❑ *That is the fundamental difference between the two societies. ...the vast difference in size.* [2] A **difference** between two quantities is the amount by which one quantity is less than the other. ❑ *The difference is 8532.* [3] If people have their **differences** about something, they disagree about it. ❑ *The two communities are learning how to resolve their differences.* PHRASES [4] If something **makes a difference** or **makes** a lot of **difference**, it affects you and helps you in what you are doing. If something **makes** no **difference**, it does not have any effect on what you are doing. ❑ *Where you live can make such a difference to the way you feel... His retirement won't make any difference to the way we conduct our affairs.* [5] If you **split the difference** with someone, you agree on an amount or price which is halfway between two suggested amounts or prices. ❑ *Shall we split the difference and say $7,500?* [6] If you describe a job or holiday, for example, as a job **with a difference** or a holiday **with a difference**, you mean that the job or holiday is very interesting and unusual. [INFORMAL] ❑ *For a beach resort with a difference, try Key West.* [7] If there is a **difference of opinion** between two or more people or groups, they disagree about something. ❑ *Was there a difference of opinion over what to do with the Nobel Prize money?* ♦♦◇ N-COUNT: usu N prep N-SING N-COUNT: usu pl, oft poss N PHRASE: V inflects PHRASE: V inflects PHRASE: n PHR PHRASE: *difference* inflects

**dif|fer|ent** /dɪfrənt/ [1] If two people or things are **different**, they are not like each other in one or more ways. ❑ *London was different from most European capitals... If he'd attended music school, how might things have been different?... We have totally different views.* ♦ In British English, people sometimes say that one thing is **different to** another. Some people consider this use to be incorrect. ❑ *My approach is totally different to his.* ♦ People sometimes say that one thing is **different than** another. This use is often considered incorrect in British English, but it is acceptable in American English. ❑ *We're not really any different than they are.* ♦ **dif|fer|ent|ly** *Every individual learns differently.* [2] You use **different** to indicate that you are talking about two or more separate and distinct things of the same kind. ❑ *Different countries specialised in different products... The number of calories in different brands of drinks varies enormously.* [3] You can describe something as **different** when it is unusual and not like others of the same kind. ❑ *This recipe is certainly interesting and different.* ♦♦♦ ADJ: oft ADJ *from* n ADJ: v-link ADJ *to* n ADJ: v-link ADJ *than* n/cl ADV ADJ: ADJ n ≠ identical ADJ: v-link ADJ = distinctive

**dif|fer|en|tial** /dɪfərenʃᵊl/ **(differentials)** [1] In mathematics and economics, a **differential** is a difference between two values in a scale. ❑ *Germany and France pledged to maintain the differential between their two currencies.* [2] A **differential** is a difference between things, especially rates of pay. [mainly BRIT] ❑ *During the Second World War, industrial wage differentials in Britain widened.* [3] **Differential** means relating to or using a difference between groups or things. [FORMAL] ❑ *...differential voting rights.* N-COUNT N-COUNT ADJ: ADJ n

**dif|fer|en|ti|ate** /dɪfərenʃieɪt/ **(differentiates, differentiating, differentiated)** [1] If you **differentiate between** things or if you **differentiate** one thing **from** another, you recognize or show the difference between them. ❑ *A child may not differentiate between his imagination and the real world... At this age your baby cannot differentiate one person from another.* [2] A quality or feature that **differentiates** one thing **from** another makes the two things different. ❑ *...distinctive policies that differentiate them from the other parties.* ♦ **dif|fer|en|tia|tion** /dɪfərenʃieɪʃᵊn/ *The differentiation between the two product ranges will increase.* VERB = distinguish V *between* pl-n V n *from* n VERB = distinguish V n *from* n N-UNCOUNT

**dif|fi|cult** /dɪfɪkəlt/ [1] Something that is **difficult** is not easy to do, understand, or deal with. ❑ *The lack of childcare provisions made it difficult for single mothers to get jobs... It was a very difficult decision to make... We're living in difficult times.* [2] Someone who is **difficult** behaves in an unreasonable and unhelpful way. ❑ *I had a feeling you were going to be difficult about this.* ♦♦♦ ADJ: oft *it* v-link ADJ to-inf, *it* v-link ADJ -ing = hard ≠ easy ADJ = awkward

**dif|fi|cul|ty** /dɪfɪkəlti/ **(difficulties)** [1] A **difficulty** is a problem. ❑ *...the difficulty of getting accurate information... The country is facing great eco-* ♦♦◇ N-COUNT

*nomic difficulties.* 2 If you have **difficulty** doing something, you are not able to do it easily. ❑ *Do you have difficulty getting up?* 3 If you are **in difficulty** or **in difficulties**, you are having a lot of problems.
N-UNCOUNT · PHRASE: v-link PHR

**dif|fi|dent** /dɪfɪdənt/ Someone who is **diffident** is rather shy and does not enjoy talking about themselves or being noticed by other people. ❑ *Helen was diffident and reserved.* ♦ **dif|fi|dence** /dɪfɪdəns/ *He entered the room with a certain diffidence.* ♦ **dif|fi|dent|ly** *'Would you,' he asked diffidently, 'like to talk to me about it?'*
ADJ · N-UNCOUNT · ADV: ADV with v

**dif|fuse** **(diffuses, diffusing, diffused)**

> The verb is pronounced /dɪfjuːz/. The adjective is pronounced /dɪfjuːs/.

1 If something such as knowledge or information **is diffused**, or if it **diffuses** somewhere, it is made known over a wide area or to a lot of people. [WRITTEN] ❑ *Over time, the technology is diffused and adopted by other countries. ...an attempt to diffuse new ideas... As agriculture developed, agricultural ideas diffused across Europe.* ♦ **dif|fu|sion** /dɪfjuːʒən/ *...the development and diffusion of ideas.*
VERB = spread · be V-ed · V n · V prep · N-UNCOUNT: with supp

2 To **diffuse** a feeling, especially an undesirable one, means to cause it to weaken and lose its power to affect people. ❑ *The arrival of letters from the Pope did nothing to diffuse the tension.*
VERB = dissipate · V n

3 If something **diffuses** light, it causes the light to spread weakly in different directions. ❑ *Diffusing a light also reduces its power.*
VERB ≠ concentrate · V n

4 To **diffuse** or **be diffused** through something means to move and spread through it. ❑ *It allows nicotine to diffuse slowly and steadily into the bloodstream... The moisture present in all foods absorbs the flavour of the smoke and eventually diffuses that flavour into its interior.* ♦ **dif|fu|sion** *There are data on the rates of diffusion of molecules.*
VERB = permeate · V prep · V n prep · Also V, V n · N-UNCOUNT: with supp

5 Something that is **diffuse** is not directed towards one place or concentrated in one place but spread out over a large area. [WRITTEN] ❑ *...a diffuse community.*
ADJ

6 If you describe something as **diffuse**, you mean that it is vague and difficult to understand or explain. ❑ *His writing is so diffuse and obscure that it is difficult to make out what it is he is trying to say.*
ADJ

**dig** /dɪɡ/ **(digs, digging, dug)** 1 If people or animals **dig**, they make a hole in the ground or in a pile of earth, stones, or rubbish. ❑ *They tried digging in a patch just below the cave... Dig a largish hole and bang the stake in first... Rescue workers are digging through the rubble in search of other victims... They dug for shellfish at low tide.*
◆◇◇ VERB · V · V n · V through n · V for n

2 If you **dig into** something such as a deep container, you put your hand in it to search for something. ❑ *He dug into his coat pocket for his keys.*
VERB = delve · V into/in n

3 If you **dig** one thing **into** another or if one thing **digs into** another, the first thing is pushed hard into the second, or presses hard into it. ❑ *She digs the serving spoon into the moussaka... He could feel the beads digging into his palm.*
VERB · V n into n · V into n

4 If you **dig into** a subject or a store of information, you study it very carefully in order to discover or check facts. ❑ *The enquiry dug deeper into the alleged financial misdeeds of his government... He has been digging into the local archives.*
VERB = probe · V into n · V into n

5 If you **dig yourself out of** a difficult or unpleasant situation, especially one which you caused yourself, you manage to get out of it. ❑ *He's taken these measures to try and dig himself out of a hole.*
VERB · V pron-refl

6 A **dig** is an organized activity in which people dig into the ground in order to discover ancient historical objects. ❑ *He's an archaeologist and has been on a dig in Crete for the past year.*
N-COUNT: oft on N = excavation

7 If you have a **dig at** someone, you say something which is intended to make fun of them or upset them. ❑ *She couldn't resist a dig at Dave after his unfortunate performance.*
N-COUNT: usu N at n = gibe

8 If you give someone a **dig** in a part of their body, you push them with your finger or your elbow, usually as a warning or as a joke.
N-COUNT

9 If you live in **digs**, you live in a room in someone else's house and pay them rent. [BRIT, INFORMAL, OLD-FASHIONED] ❑ *He went to London and lived in digs in Gloucester Road.*
N-PLURAL: oft in N = lodgings

10 **to dig** one's **heels in** → see **heel**.

♦ **dig around** 1 If you **dig around** in a place or container, you search for something in every part of it. ❑ *I went home to dig around in my closets for some old tapes.*
PHRASAL VERB = rummage around · V P in n · Also V P

2 If you **dig around**, you try to find information about someone or something. ❑ *They said, after digging around, the photo was a fake.*
PHRASAL VERB · V P

♦ **dig in** 1 If you **dig** a substance **in**, or **dig** it **into** the soil, you mix it into the soil by digging. ❑ *I usually dig in a small barrow load of compost in late summer... To dig calcium into the soil, he warned, does not help the plant.*
PHRASAL VERB · V P n (not pron) · V n P n

2 When soldiers **dig in** or **dig** themselves **in**, they dig trenches and prepare themselves for an attack by the enemy. ❑ *The battalion went directly to the airport to begin digging in... The enemy must be digging themselves in now ready for the attack... Our forces are dug in along the river.*
PHRASAL VERB · V P · V pron-refl P · V-ed P

3 If someone **digs in**, or **digs into** some food, they start eating eagerly. If you tell someone to **dig in**, you are inviting them to start eating, and encouraging them to eat as much as they want. [INFORMAL] ❑ *'Listen,' said Daisy, digging into her oatmeal... Pull up a chair and dig in!*
PHRASAL VERB = tuck in · V P n · V P

♦ **dig out** 1 If you **dig** someone or something **out of** a place, you get them out by digging or by forcing them from the things surrounding them. ❑ *...digging minerals out of the Earth... She dug out a photograph from under a pile of papers.*
PHRASAL VERB · V n P of n · V P n · Also V n P

2 If you **dig** something **out**, you find it after it has been stored, hidden, or forgotten for a long time. [INFORMAL] ❑ *Recently, I dug out Barstow's novel and read it again... We'll try and dig the number out for you if you want it.*
PHRASAL VERB · V P n (not pron) · V n P

♦ **dig up** 1 If you **dig up** something, you remove it from the ground where it has been buried or planted. ❑ *You would have to dig up the plant yourself... Dig it up once the foliage has died down.*
PHRASAL VERB · V P n (not pron) · V n P

2 If you **dig up** an area of land, you dig holes in it. ❑ *Yesterday they continued the search, digging up the back yard of a police station.*
PHRASAL VERB · V P n · Also V n P

3 If you **dig up** information or facts, you discover something that has not previously been widely known. ❑ *Managers are too expensive and important to spend time digging up market information... His description fits perfectly the evidence dug up by Clyde.*
PHRASAL VERB = unearth · V P n (not pron) · V-ed P · Also V n P

**di|gest** **(digests, digesting, digested)**

> The verb is pronounced /daɪdʒest/. The noun is pronounced /daɪdʒest/.

1 When food **digests** or when you **digest** it, it passes through your body to your stomach. Your stomach removes the substances that your body needs and gets rid of the rest. ❑ *Do not undertake strenuous exercise for a few hours after a meal to allow food to digest... She couldn't digest food properly... Nutrients from the digested food can be absorbed into the blood.*
VERB · V · V n · V-ed

2 If you **digest** information, you think about it carefully so that you understand it. ❑ *They learn well but seem to need time to digest information.*
VERB · V n

3 If you **digest** some unpleasant news, you think about it until you are able to accept it and know how to deal with it. ❑ *All this has upset me. I need time to digest it all.*
VERB · V n

4 A **digest** is a collection of pieces of writing. They are published together in a shorter form than they were originally published. ❑ *...the Middle East Economic Digest.*
N-COUNT

**di|gest|ible** /daɪdʒestɪbəl/ 1 **Digestible** food is food that is easy to digest. ❑ *Bananas are easily digestible.* 2 If a theory or idea is **digestible**, it is easy to understand. ❑ *The book's aim was to make economic theory more digestible.*
ADJ: oft adv ADJ · ADJ = accessible

**di|ges|tion** /daɪdʒestʃən/ **(digestions)** 1 **Digestion** is the process of digesting food. ❑ *No liquids are served with meals because they interfere with digestion.* 2 Your **digestion** is the system in your body which digests your food.
N-UNCOUNT · N-COUNT: usu poss N

**di|ges|tive** /daɪdʒestɪv/ You can describe things that are related to the digestion of food as
ADJ: ADJ n

**digestive**. ❑ *...digestive juices that normally work on breaking down our food.*

**di|ges|tive sys|tem** **(digestive systems)** N-COUNT: usu poss N Your **digestive system** is the set of organs in your body that digest the food you eat.

**dig|ger** /dɪgəʳ/ **(diggers)** N-COUNT A **digger** is a machine that is used for digging. ❑ *...a mechanical digger.*

**digi|cam** /dɪdʒɪkæm/ **(digicams)** N-COUNT A **digicam** is the same as a **digital camera**.

**dig|it** /dɪdʒɪt/ **(digits)** 1 N-COUNT A **digit** is a written symbol for any of the ten numbers from 0 to 9. ❑ *Her telephone number differs from mine by one digit.* 2 N-COUNT A **digit** is a finger, thumb, or toe. [FORMAL]

**digi|tal** /dɪdʒɪtᵊl/ ◆◇◇ 1 ADJ **Digital** systems record or transmit information in the form of thousands of very small signals. ❑ *The new digital technology would allow a rapid expansion in the number of TV channels.* ♦ **digi|tal|ly** ADV *...digitally recorded sound.* 2 ADJ: ADJ n **Digital** devices such as watches or clocks give information by displaying numbers rather than by having a pointer which moves round a dial. Compare **analogue**. ❑ *...a digital display.*

**digi|tal audio tape** N-UNCOUNT **Digital audio tape** is a type of magnetic tape used to make very high quality recordings of sound by recording it in digital form. The abbreviation **DAT** is often used.

**digi|tal cam|era** **(digital cameras)** N-COUNT A **digital camera** is a camera that produces digital images that can be stored on a computer, displayed on a screen, and printed. ❑ *The speed with which digital cameras can take, process and transmit an image is phenomenal.*

**digi|tal ra|dio** **(digital radios)** 1 N-UNCOUNT **Digital radio** is radio in which the signals are transmitted in digital form and decoded by the radio receiver. 2 N-COUNT A **digital radio** is a radio that can receive digital signals. ❑ *Manufacturers are working on a new generation of cheaper digital radios.*

**digi|tal re|cord|ing** **(digital recordings)** 1 N-UNCOUNT **Digital recording** is the process of converting sound or images into numbers. 2 N-COUNT A **digital recording** is a recording made by converting sound or images into numbers.

**digi|tal tele|vi|sion** **(digital televisions)** 1 N-UNCOUNT **Digital television** is television in which the signals are transmitted in digital form and decoded by the television receiver. 2 N-COUNT A **digital television** is a television that can receive digital signals. ❑ *...wide screen digital televisions.*

**digi|tal TV** **(digital TVs)** 1 N-UNCOUNT **Digital TV** is the same as **digital television**. 2 N-COUNT A **digital TV** is the same as a **digital television**.

**dig|it|ize** /dɪdʒɪtaɪz/ **(digitizes, digitizing, digitized)**

✔ in BRIT, also use **digitise**

VERB To **digitize** information means to turn it into a form that can be read easily by a computer. ❑ V n *The picture is digitised by a scanner.*

**dig|ni|fied** /dɪgnɪfaɪd/ ADJ If you say that someone or something is **dignified**, you mean they are calm, impressive and deserve respect. ❑ *He seemed a very dignified and charming man.*

**dig|ni|fy** /dɪgnɪfaɪ/ **(dignifies, dignifying, dignified)** 1 VERB To **dignify** something means to make it impressive. [LITERARY] ❑ V n *Tragic literature dignifies sorrow and disaster.* 2 VERB disapproval If you say that a particular reaction or description **dignifies** something you have a low opinion of, you mean that it makes it appear acceptable. ❑ V n *We won't dignify this kind of speculation with a comment.*

**dig|ni|tary** /dɪgnɪtri, AM -teri/ **(dignitaries)** N-COUNT: usu pl **Dignitaries** are people who are considered to be important because they have a high rank in government or in the Church.

**dig|nity** /dɪgnɪti/ 1 N-UNCOUNT = poise If someone behaves or moves with **dignity**, they are calm, controlled, and admirable. ❑ *...her extraordinary dignity and composure.* 2 N-UNCOUNT: usu with supp If you talk about the **dignity** of people or their lives or activities, you mean that they are valuable and worthy of respect. ❑ *...the sense of human dignity.* 3 N-UNCOUNT = self-respect Your **dignity** is the sense that you have of your own importance and value, and other people's respect for you. ❑ *She still has her dignity.*

**di|gress** /daɪgres/ **(digresses, digressing, digressed)** VERB If you **digress**, you move away from the subject you are talking or writing about and talk or write about something different for a while. ❑ V *I've digressed a little to explain the situation so far, so let me now recap...* V from n *She digressed from her prepared speech to pay tribute to the President.* ♦ **di|gres|sion** /daɪgreʃᵊn/ **(digressions)** N-VAR *The text is dotted with digressions.*

**dike** /daɪk/ → see **dyke**.

**dik|tat** /dɪktæt, AM dɪktɑːt/ **(diktats)** N-VAR disapproval You use **diktat** to refer to something such as a law or government which people have to obey even if they do not agree with it, especially one which seems unfair.

**di|lapi|da|ted** /dɪlæpɪdeɪtɪd/ ADJ = run-down A building that is **dilapidated** is old and in a generally bad condition.

**di|late** /daɪleɪt/ **(dilates, dilating, dilated)** VERB = enlarge When things such as blood vessels or the pupils of your eyes **dilate** or when something **dilates** them, they become wider or bigger. ❑ V *At night, the pupils dilate to allow in more light...* V n *Exercise dilates blood vessels on the surface of the brain.* ♦ **di|lat|ed** ADJ *His eyes seemed slightly dilated.*

**dil|a|tory** /dɪlətri, AM -tɔːri/ ADJ Someone or something that is **dilatory** is slow and causes delay. [FORMAL] ❑ *You might expect politicians to smooth things out when civil servants are being dilatory.*

**dil|do** /dɪldoʊ/ **(dildos)** N-COUNT A **dildo** is an object shaped like a penis, which women can use to get sexual pleasure. [INFORMAL]

**di|lem|ma** /daɪlemə, AM dɪl-/ **(dilemmas)** N-COUNT A **dilemma** is a difficult situation in which you have to choose between two or more alternatives. ❑ *He was faced with the dilemma of whether or not to return to his country.* **on the horns of a dilemma** → see **horn**.

**dil|et|tan|te** /dɪlətænti, AM -tɑːnt/ **(dilettantes** or **dilettanti)** N-COUNT disapproval You can use **dilettante** to talk about someone who seems interested in a subject, especially in art, but who does not really know very much about it. [FORMAL]

**dili|gent** /dɪlɪdʒᵊnt/ ADJ Someone who is **diligent** works hard in a careful and thorough way. ❑ *Meyers is a diligent and prolific worker.* ♦ **dili|gence** /dɪlɪdʒᵊns/ N-UNCOUNT *The police are pursuing their inquiries with great diligence.* ♦ **dili|gent|ly** ADV: ADV with v *The two sides are now working diligently to resolve their differences.*

**dill** /dɪl/ N-UNCOUNT **Dill** is a herb with yellow flowers and a strong sweet smell.

**di|lute** /daɪluːt/ **(dilutes, diluting, diluted)** 1 VERB If a liquid **is diluted** or **dilutes**, it is added to or mixes with water or another liquid, and becomes weaker. ❑ V n prep *If you give your baby juice, dilute it well with cooled, boiled water...* be V-ed *The liquid is then diluted...* V *The poisons seeping from Hanford's contaminated land quickly dilute in the water.* Also V n ♦ **di|lu|tion** N-UNCOUNT *...ditches dug for sewage dilution.* 2 ADJ: usu ADJ n A **dilute** liquid is very thin and weak, usually because it has had water added to it. ❑ *...a dilute solution of bleach.* 3 VERB If someone or something **dilutes** a belief, quality, or value, they make it weaker and less effective. ❑ V n *There was a clear intention to dilute black voting power.* ♦ **di|lu|tion** N-UNCOUNT: oft N of n *...a potentially devastating dilution of earnings per share.*

**di|lu|tion** /daɪluːʃᵊn/ **(dilutions)** N-COUNT A **dilution** is a liquid that has been diluted with water or another liquid, so that it becomes weaker. ❑ *'Aromatherapy oils' are not pure essential oils but dilutions.*

**dim** /dɪm/ **(dimmer, dimmest, dims, dimming, dimmed)** 1 ADJ **Dim** light is not bright. ❑ *She stood waiting, in the dim light.* ♦ **dim|ly** ADV *He followed her* *into a dimly lit kitchen.* ♦ **dim|ness** *...the dimness of an early September evening.* N-UNCOUNT [2] A **dim** place is rather dark because there is not much light in it. ❑ *The room was dim and cool and quiet.* ADJ ♦ **dim|ness** *I squinted to adjust my eyes to the dimness.* N-UNCOUNT [3] A **dim** figure or object is not very easy to see, either because it is in shadow or darkness, or because it is far away. ❑ *Pete's torch picked out the dim figures of Bob and Chang.* ADJ = faint ♦ **dim|ly** *The shoreline could be dimly seen.* ADV: usu ADV with v [4] If you have a **dim** memory or understanding of something, it is difficult to remember or is unclear in your mind. ❑ *It seems that the '60s era of social activism is all but a dim memory.* ADJ: usu ADJ n = hazy ♦ **dim|ly** *Christina dimly recalled the procedure.* ADV: ADV with v, ADV adj [5] If the future of something is **dim**, you have no reason to feel hopeful or positive about it. ❑ *The prospects for a peaceful solution are dim.* ADJ ≠ bright [6] If you describe someone as **dim**, you think that they are stupid. [INFORMAL] ADJ [7] If you **dim** a light or if it **dims**, it becomes less bright. ❑ *Dim the lighting – it is unpleasant to lie with a bright light shining in your eyes... The houselights dimmed.* VERB V n V [8] If your future, hopes, or emotions **dim** or if something **dims** them, they become less good or less strong. ❑ *Their economic prospects have dimmed... Forty eight years of marriage have not dimmed the passion between Bill and Helen.* VERB V V n [9] If your memories **dim** or if something **dims** them, they become less clear in your mind. ❑ *Their memory of what happened has dimmed... The intervening years had dimmed his memory.* VERB V V n [10] to **take a dim view** → see **view**.

**dime** /daɪm/ **(dimes)** A **dime** is an American coin worth ten cents. N-COUNT

**di|men|sion** /daɪmenʃᵊn, dɪm-/ **(dimensions)** [1] A particular **dimension** of something is a particular aspect of it. ❑ *There is a political dimension to the accusations... This adds a new dimension to our work.* N-COUNT: usu with supp = aspect [2] If you talk about the **dimensions** of a situation or problem, you are talking about its extent and size. ❑ *The dimensions of the market collapse were certainly not anticipated.* N-PLURAL: usu with supp = scale [3] A **dimension** is a measurement such as length, width, or height. If you talk about the **dimensions** of an object or place, you are referring to its size and proportions. ❑ *Drilling will continue on the site to assess the dimensions of the new oilfield.* N-COUNT: usu pl, usu N *of* n [4] → See also **fourth dimension**.

**di|men|sion|al** /daɪmenʃənəl, AM dɪm-/ → see **two-dimensional**, **three-dimensional**.

**di|min|ish** /dɪmɪnɪʃ/ **(diminishes, diminishing, diminished)** [1] When something **diminishes**, or when something **diminishes** it, it becomes reduced in size, importance, or intensity. ❑ *The threat of nuclear war has diminished... Federalism is intended to diminish the power of the central state... Universities are facing grave problems because of diminishing resources... This could mean diminished public support for the war.* VERB ≠ increase V V n V-ing V-ed [2] If you **diminish** someone or something, you talk about them or treat them in a way that makes them appear less important than they really are. ❑ *He never put her down or diminished her.* VERB V n

**di|min|ished re|spon|sibil|ity** In law, **diminished responsibility** is a defence which states that someone is not mentally well enough to be totally responsible for their crime. N-UNCOUNT

**di|min|ish|ing re|turns** In economics, **diminishing returns** is a situation in which the increase in production, profits, or benefits resulting from something is less than the money or energy that is invested. N-UNCOUNT

**dimi|nu|tion** /dɪmɪnjuːʃᵊn, AM -nuː-/ A **diminution** of something is its reduction in size, importance, or intensity. [FORMAL] ❑ *...despite a slight diminution in asset value.* N-UNCOUNT: usu N *of/in* n = reduction

**di|minu|tive** /dɪmɪnjʊtɪv/ **(diminutives)** [1] A **diminutive** person or object is very small. ❑ *She noticed a diminutive figure standing at the entrance.* ADJ: usu ADJ n = tiny [2] A **diminutive** is an informal form of a name. For example, 'Jim' and 'Jimmy' are diminutives of 'James'. N-COUNT

**dim|mer** /dɪməʳ/ **(dimmers)** A **dimmer** or a **dimmer switch** is a switch that allows you to gradually change the brightness of an electric light. N-COUNT

**dim|ple** /dɪmpᵊl/ **(dimples)** A **dimple** is a small hollow in someone's cheek or chin, often one that you can see when they smile. ❑ *Bess spoke up, smiling so that her dimples showed.* N-COUNT

**dim|pled** /dɪmpᵊld/ Something that is **dimpled** has small hollows in it. ❑ *...a man with a dimpled chin.* ADJ

**dim|wit** /dɪmwɪt/ **(dimwits)** If you say that someone is a **dimwit**, you mean that they are ignorant and stupid. [INFORMAL] N-COUNT = idiot

**dim-witted** also **dimwitted.** If you describe someone as **dim-witted**, you are saying in quite an unkind way that you do not think they are very clever. [INFORMAL] ADJ = stupid

**din** /dɪn/ A **din** is a very loud and unpleasant noise that lasts for some time. ❑ *They tried to make themselves heard over the din of the crowd.* N-SING = racket

**di|nar** /diːnaːʳ/ **(dinars)** The **dinar** is the unit of money that is used in some north African and Middle Eastern countries, and also in the republics which were part of Yugoslavia. N-COUNT: num N ♦ **The dinar** is also used to refer to the currency system of these countries. N-SING: *the* N

**dine** /daɪn/ **(dines, dining, dined)** When you **dine**, you have dinner. [FORMAL] ❑ *He dines alone most nights... They used to enjoy going out to dine.* VERB: no passive V adv/prep V to **wine and dine** → see **wine**.

**din|er** /daɪnəʳ/ **(diners)** [1] A **diner** is a small cheap restaurant that is open all day. [AM] N-COUNT [2] The people who are having dinner in a restaurant can be referred to as **diners**. ❑ *They sat in a corner, away from other diners.* N-COUNT

**ding-dong** /dɪŋ dɒŋ, AM - dɔːŋ/ **Ding-dong** is used in writing to represent the sound made by a bell. SOUND

**din|ghy** /dɪŋgi/ **(dinghies)** A **dinghy** is a small open boat that you sail or row. N-COUNT

**din|go** /dɪŋgoʊ/ **(dingoes)** A **dingo** is an Australian wild dog. N-COUNT

**din|gy** /dɪndʒi/ **(dingier, dingiest)** [1] A **dingy** building or place is rather dark and depressing, and perhaps dirty. ❑ *Shaw took me to his rather dingy office.* ADJ [2] **Dingy** clothes, curtains, or furnishings look dirty or dull. ❑ *...wallpaper with stripes of dingy yellow.* ADJ: usu ADJ n

**din|ing car** **(dining cars)** A **dining car** is a carriage on a train where passengers can have a meal. N-COUNT

**din|ing room** **(dining rooms)** also **dining-room.** The **dining room** is the room in a house where people have their meals, or a room in a hotel where meals are served. N-COUNT: usu *the* N

**din|ing ta|ble** **(dining tables)** also **dining-table.** A **dining table** is a table that is used for having meals on. N-COUNT

**dinky** /dɪŋki/ [1] If you describe something as **dinky**, you mean that it is attractive and appealing, usually because it is quite small and well-designed. [BRIT, INFORMAL] ❑ *Darby drove a dinky old Fiat sports car.* ADJ [approval] [2] If you describe something as **dinky**, you mean that it is small and unimportant. [AM, INFORMAL] ❑ *The hotels are full up, and the guests have had to go to this dinky little motel way out on Stewart Avenue.* ADJ [disapproval]

**din|ner** /dɪnəʳ/ **(dinners)** [1] **Dinner** is the main meal of the day, usually served in the early part of the evening. ❑ *She invited us to her house for dinner... Would you like to stay and have dinner?* ◆◆◇ N-VAR → See also **TV dinner**. [2] Any meal you eat in the middle of the day can be referred to as **dinner**. N-VAR [3] A **dinner** is a formal social event at which a meal is served. It is held in the evening. ❑ *...a series of official lunches and dinners.* N-COUNT

**din|ner dance** **(dinner dances)** also **dinner-dance.** A **dinner dance** is a social event where a large number of people come to have dinner and to dance. Dinner dances are held in the evening at hotels, restaurants, and social clubs. [BRIT] N-COUNT

**din|ner jack|et** **(dinner jackets)** also **dinner-jacket.** A **dinner jacket** is a jacket, usually black, worn by men for formal social events. [BRIT] N-COUNT

✓ in AM, use **tuxedo**

**din|ner par|ty** **(dinner parties)** A **dinner party** is a social event where a small group of people are invited to have dinner and spend the evening at someone's house. N-COUNT

**din|ner ser|vice** **(dinner services)** A **dinner service** is a set of plates and dishes from which meals are eaten and served. It may also include cups and saucers. [BRIT] N-COUNT

✓ in AM, use **dinnerware set**

**din|ner ta|ble** **(dinner tables)** also **dinner-table.** You can refer to a table as **the dinner table** when it is being used for dinner. [BRIT] ❑ *Sam was left at the dinner table with Peg.* N-COUNT: usu sing, usu *the*/poss N

**din|ner|time** /dɪnəʳtaɪm/ also **dinner time.** **Dinnertime** is the period of the day when most people have their dinner. ❑ *The telephone call came shortly before dinnertime.* N-UNCOUNT: oft prep N

**din|ner|ware** /dɪnəʳweəʳ/ You can refer to the plates and dishes you use during a meal as **dinnerware**. [mainly AM] N-UNCOUNT

**din|ner|ware set** **(dinnerware sets)** A **dinnerware set** is the same as a **dinner service**. [AM] N-COUNT

**di|no|saur** /daɪnəsɔːʳ/ **(dinosaurs)** 1 **Dinosaurs** were large reptiles which lived in prehistoric times. N-COUNT 2 If you refer to an organization as a **dinosaur**, you mean that it is large, inefficient, and out of date. ❑ *...industrial dinosaurs.* N-COUNT disapproval

**dint** /dɪnt/ If you achieve a result **by dint of** something, you achieve it by means of that thing. [WRITTEN] ❑ *He succeeds by dint of sheer hard work.* PREP-PHRASE = by means of

**di|oc|esan** /daɪɒsɪsən/ **Diocesan** means belonging or relating to a diocese. ❑ *...the diocesan synod.* ADJ: ADJ n

**dio|cese** /daɪəsɪs/ **(dioceses)** A **diocese** is the area over which a bishop has control. N-COUNT

**di|ox|ide** /daɪɒksaɪd/ → see **carbon dioxide**.

**di|ox|in** /daɪɒksɪn/ **(dioxins)** **Dioxins** are poisonous chemicals which occur as a by-product of the manufacture of certain weedkillers and disinfectants. N-VAR

**dip** /dɪp/ **(dips, dipping, dipped)** 1 If you **dip** something **in** a liquid, you put it into the liquid for a short time, so that only part of it is covered, and take it out again. ❑ *Quickly dip the base in and out of cold water.* VERB V n into/in n ♦ **Dip** is also a noun. ❑ *One dip into the bottle should do an entire nail.* N-COUNT 2 If you **dip** your hand **into** a container or **dip into** the container, you put your hand into it in order to take something out of it. ❑ *She dipped a hand into the jar of sweets and pulled one out... Watch your fingers as you dip into the pot... Ask the children to guess what's in each container by dipping their hands in.* VERB V n into n, V into n, V n with in 3 If something **dips**, it makes a downward movement, usually quite quickly. ❑ *Blake jumped in expertly; the boat dipped slightly under his weight... The sun dipped below the horizon.* VERB V, V prep ♦ **Dip** is also a noun. ❑ *I noticed little things, a dip of the head, a twitch in the shoulder.* N-COUNT 4 If an area of land, a road, or a path **dips**, it goes down quite suddenly to a lower level. ❑ *The road dipped and rose again. ...a path which suddenly dips down into a tunnel.* VERB V, V adv/prep ♦ **Dip** is also a noun. ❑ *Where the road makes a dip, turn right.* N-COUNT 5 If the amount or level of something **dips**, it becomes smaller or lower, usually only for a short period of time. ❑ *Unemployment dipped to 6.9 per cent last month... The president became more cautious as his popularity dipped.* VERB = fall, V prep/adv, V ♦ **Dip** is also a noun. ❑ *...the current dip in farm spending.* N-COUNT: oft N in n 6 A **dip** is a thick creamy sauce. You dip pieces of raw vegetable or biscuits into the sauce and then eat them. ❑ *Maybe we could just buy some dips. ...prawns with avocado dip.* N-VAR 7 If you have or take a **dip**, you go for a quick swim in the sea, a river, or a swimming pool. ❑ *She flicked through a romantic paperback between occasional dips in the pool.* N-COUNT = swim 8 If you are driving a car and **dip** the headlights, you operate a switch that makes them shine downwards, so that they do not shine directly into the eyes of other drivers. [BRIT] ❑ *He dipped his headlights as they came up behind a slow-moving van... This picture shows the view from a car using normal dipped lights.* VERB V n, V-ed

✓ in AM, use **dim**

9 If you **dip into** a book, you have a brief look at it without reading or studying it seriously. ❑ *...a chance to dip into a wide selection of books on Tibetan Buddhism.* VERB V into n 10 If you **dip into** a sum of money that you had intended to save, you use some of it to buy something or pay for something. ❑ *Just when she was ready to dip into her savings, Greg hastened to her rescue.* VERB V into n 11 → See also **lucky dip**. to **dip** your **toes** → see **toe**.

**Dip.** **Dip.** is a written abbreviation for **diploma**.

**diph|theria** /dɪfθɪəriə, dɪp-/ **Diphtheria** is a dangerous infectious disease which causes fever and difficulty in breathing and swallowing. N-UNCOUNT

**diph|thong** /dɪfθɒŋ, dɪp-/ **(diphthongs)** A **diphthong** is a vowel in which the speaker's tongue changes position while it is being pronounced, so that the vowel sounds like a combination of two other vowels. The vowel sound in 'tail' is a diphthong. N-COUNT

**di|plo|ma** /dɪploʊmə/ **(diplomas)** A **diploma** is a qualification which may be awarded to a student by a university or college, or by a high school in the United States. ❑ *...a new two-year course leading to a diploma in social work.* N-COUNT

**di|plo|ma|cy** /dɪploʊməsi/ 1 **Diplomacy** is the activity or profession of managing relations between the governments of different countries. ❑ *Today's Security Council resolution will be a significant success for American diplomacy.* → See also **shuttle diplomacy**. N-UNCOUNT 2 **Diplomacy** is the skill of being careful to say or do things which will not offend people. ❑ *He stormed off in a fury, and it took all Minnelli's powers of diplomacy to get him to return.* N-UNCOUNT

**dip|lo|mat** /dɪpləmæt/ **(diplomats)** A **diplomat** is a senior official who discusses affairs with another country on behalf of his or her own country, usually working as a member of an embassy. ◆◇◇ N-COUNT

**dip|lo|mat|ic** /dɪpləmætɪk/ 1 **Diplomatic** means relating to diplomacy and diplomats. ❑ *...before the two countries resume full diplomatic relations... Efforts are being made to avert war and find a diplomatic solution.* ◆◇◇ ADJ: usu ADJ n ♦ **dip|lo|mati|cal|ly** /dɪpləmætɪkli/ *...a growing sense of doubt that the conflict can be resolved diplomatically.* ADV: ADV with v, ADV adj 2 Someone who is **diplomatic** is able to be careful to say or do things without offending people. ❑ *She is very direct. I tend to be more diplomatic, I suppose.* ADJ ♦ **dip|lo|mati|cal|ly** *'Their sound is very interesting,' he says, diplomatically.* ADV: ADV with v

**dip|lo|mat|ic bag** **(diplomatic bags)** A **diplomatic bag** is a bag or container in which mail is sent to and from foreign embassies. Diplomatic bags are protected by law, so that they are not opened by anyone except the official or embassy they are addressed to. [BRIT] N-COUNT

✓ in AM, use **diplomatic pouch**

**dip|lo|mat|ic corps** **(diplomatic corps)** The **diplomatic corps** is the group of all the diplomats who work in one city or country. N-COUNT-COLL: usu *the* N

**dip|lo|mat|ic im|mun|ity** **Diplomatic immunity** is the freedom from legal action and from paying taxes that a diplomat has in the country in which he or she is working. ❑ *The em-* N-UNCOUNT bassy official claimed diplomatic immunity and was later released.

**dip|lo|mat|ic pouch** (**diplomatic pouches**) A **diplomatic pouch** is the same as a **diplomatic bag**. [mainly AM] N-COUNT

**dip|lo|mat|ic ser|vice** also **Diplomatic Service. The diplomatic service** is the government department that employs diplomats to work in foreign countries. [mainly BRIT] N-PROPER: the N

☑ in AM, usually use **foreign service**

**dip|py** /dɪpi/ If you describe someone as **dippy**, you mean that they are slightly odd or unusual, but in a way that you find charming and attractive. [INFORMAL] ADJ

**dip|stick** /dɪpstɪk/ (**dipsticks**) A **dipstick** is a metal rod with marks along one end. It is used to measure the amount of liquid in a container, especially the amount of oil in a car engine. N-COUNT

**dire** /daɪəʳ/ [1] **Dire** is used to emphasize how serious or terrible a situation or event is. ❑ *A government split would have dire consequences for domestic peace... He was in dire need of hospital treatment.* ADJ: usu ADJ n [emphasis] = awful, desperate [2] If you describe something as **dire**, you are emphasizing that it is of very low quality. [INFORMAL] ADJ: usu v-link ADJ [emphasis]

**di|rect** /daɪrekt, dɪ-/ (**directs, directing, directed**) ◆◆◆ [1] **Direct** means moving towards a place or object, without changing direction and without stopping, for example in a journey. ❑ *They'd come on a direct flight from Athens.* ADJ: usu ADJ n ≠ indirect ♦ **Direct** is also an adverb. ❑ *You can fly direct to Amsterdam from most British airports.* ADV: ADV after v ♦ **di|rect|ly** *The jumbo jet is due to fly the hostages directly back to London.* ADV: ADV after v [2] If something is in **direct** heat or light, it is strongly affected by the heat or light, because there is nothing between it and the source of heat or light to protect it. ❑ *Medicines should be stored away from direct sunlight.* ADJ: ADJ n [3] You use **direct** to describe an experience, activity, or system which only involves the people, actions, or things that are necessary to make it happen. ❑ *He has direct experience of the process of privatisation... He seemed to be in direct contact with the Boss.* ADJ: usu ADJ n ♦ **Direct** is also an adverb. ❑ *I can deal direct with your Inspector Kimble.* ADV: ADV after v ♦ **di|rect|ly** *We cannot measure pain directly. It can only be estimated.* ADV: ADV with v [4] You use **direct** to emphasize the closeness of a connection between two things. ❑ *They were unable to prove that she died as a direct result of his injection.* ADJ: usu ADJ n [emphasis] ≠ indirect [5] If you describe a person or their behaviour as **direct**, you mean that they are honest and open, and say exactly what they mean. ❑ *He avoided giving a direct answer.* ADJ ≠ indirect ♦ **di|rect|ly** *At your first meeting, explain simply and directly what you hope to achieve.* ADV: ADV after v ♦ **di|rect|ness** *Using 'I' adds directness to a piece of writing.* N-UNCOUNT [6] If you **direct** something **at** a particular thing, you aim or point it at that thing. ❑ *I directed the extinguisher at the fire without effect.* VERB = aim V n at/towards/on n [7] If your attention, emotions, or actions **are directed at** a particular person or thing, you are focusing them on that person or thing. ❑ *The learner's attention needs to be directed to the significant features... Do not be surprised if, initially, she directs her anger at you.* VERB = focus be V-ed to/towards n/-ing V n at n [8] If a remark or look **is directed at** you, someone says something to you or looks at you. ❑ *She could hardly believe the question was directed towards her... The abuse was directed at the TV crews... Arnold directed a meaningful look at Irma.* VERB be V-ed towards n be V-ed at n V n at n [9] If you **direct** someone somewhere, you tell them how to get there. ❑ *Could you direct them to Dr Lamont's office, please?* VERB V n to n [10] When someone **directs** a project or a group of people, they are responsible for organizing the people and activities that are involved. ❑ *Christopher will direct day-to-day operations.* VERB V n ♦ **di|rec|tion** /daɪrekʃᵊn, dɪr-/ *Organizations need clear direction.* N-UNCOUNT [11] When someone **directs** a film, play, or television programme, they are responsible for the way in which it is performed and for telling the actors and assistants what to do. ❑ *He directed various TV shows. ...Miss Birkin's long-held ambition to direct as well as act.* VERB V n V [12] If you **are directed to** do something, someone in authority tells you to do it. [FORMAL] ❑ *They have been directed to give special attention to the problem of poverty... The Bishop directed the faithful to stay at home.* VERB be V-ed to-inf V n to-inf [13] If you are a **direct** descendant of someone, you are related to them through your parents and your grandparents and so on. ❑ *She is a direct descendant of Queen Victoria.* ADJ: ADJ n [14] → See also **direction, directly**.

**di|rect ac|tion Direct action** involves doing something such as going on strike or demonstrating in order to put pressure on an employer or government to do what you want, instead of trying to talk to them. N-UNCOUNT

**di|rect cur|rent** (**direct currents**) A **direct current** is an electric current that always flows in the same direction. The abbreviation **DC** is also used. ❑ *Some kinds of batteries can be recharged by connecting them to a source of direct current.* N-VAR

**di|rect deb|it** (**direct debits**) If you pay a bill by **direct debit**, you give permission for the company who is owed money to transfer the correct amount from your bank account into theirs, usually every month. [mainly BRIT] ❑ *Switch to paying your mortgage by direct debit.* N-VAR

**di|rect dis|course** In grammar, **direct discourse** is speech which is reported by using the exact words that the speaker used. [mainly AM] N-UNCOUNT

☑ in BRIT, usually use **direct speech**

**di|rect hit** (**direct hits**) If a place suffers a **direct hit**, a bomb, bullet, or other missile that has been aimed at it lands exactly in that place, rather than some distance away. ❑ *The dug-outs were secure from everything but a direct hit.* N-COUNT

**di|rec|tion** /daɪrekʃᵊn/ (**directions**) ◆◆◇ [1] A **direction** is the general line that someone or something is moving or pointing in. ❑ *St Andrews was ten miles in the opposite direction... He drove off in the direction of Larry's shop... The instruments will register every change of direction or height.* N-VAR: usu with supp [2] A **direction** is the general way in which something develops or progresses. ❑ *They threatened to walk out if the party did not change direction.* N-VAR: usu with supp [3] **Directions** are instructions that tell you what to do, how to do something, or how to get somewhere. ❑ *I should know by now not to throw away the directions until we've finished cooking.* N-PLURAL: with supp [4] The **direction** of a film, play, or television programme is the work that the director does while it is being made. ❑ *His failures underline the difference between theatre and film direction.* N-UNCOUNT [5] → See also **direct**.

**di|rec|tion|al** /daɪrekʃənᵊl, dɪr-/ [1] If something such as a radio aerial, microphone, or loudspeaker is **directional**, it works most effectively in one direction, rather than equally in all directions at once. [TECHNICAL] ❑ *Dish aerials are highly directional.* ADJ [2] **Directional** means relating to the direction in which something is pointing or going. [TECHNICAL] ❑ *Jets of compressed air gave the aircraft lateral and directional stability.* ADJ: usu ADJ n

**di|rec|tion|less** /daɪrekʃᵊnləs, dɪr-/ If you describe an activity or an organization as **directionless**, you mean that it does not seem to have any point or purpose. If you describe a person as **directionless**, you mean that they do not seem to have any plans or ideas. ❑ *...his seemingly disorganized and directionless campaign.* ADJ = aimless

**di|rec|tive** /daɪrektɪv, dɪr-/ (**directives**) A **directive** is an official instruction that is given by someone in authority. ❑ *Thanks to a new EU directive, insecticide labelling will be more specific.* N-COUNT = ruling

**di|rect|ly** /daɪrektli, dɪr-/ [1] If something is **directly** above, below, or in front of something, it is in exactly that position. ❑ *The naked bulb was directly over his head.* ADV: ADV prep/adv = right [2] If you do one action **directly after** another, you do the second action as soon as the first one is finished. ❑ *Directly after the meeting, a senior cabinet minister spoke to the BBC.* ADV: ADV prep/adv = immediately

3 If something happens **directly**, it happens without any delay. [BRIT, OLD-FASHIONED] ❑ *He will be there directly.* 4 → See also **direct**. — ADV: ADV after v

**di|rect mail** **Direct mail** is a method of marketing which involves companies sending advertising material directly to people who they think may be interested in their products. [BUSINESS] ❑ *...efforts to solicit new customers by direct mail.* — N-UNCOUNT: oft N n

**di|rect mar|ket|ing** **Direct marketing** is the same as **direct mail**. [BUSINESS] ❑ *The direct marketing industry has become adept at packaging special offers.* — N-UNCOUNT: oft N n

**di|rect ob|ject** (**direct objects**) In grammar, the **direct object** of a transitive verb is the noun group which refers to someone or something directly affected by or involved in the action performed by the subject. For example, in 'I saw him yesterday', 'him' is the direct object. Compare **indirect object**. — N-COUNT = object

**di|rec|tor** /daɪre̱ktəʳ, dɪr-/ (**directors**) ◆◆◆ 1 The **director** of a play, film, or television programme is the person who decides how it will appear on stage or screen, and who tells the actors and technical staff what to do. — N-COUNT 2 In some organizations and public authorities, the person in charge is referred to as **the director**. ❑ *...the director of the intensive care unit at Guy's Hospital.* — N-COUNT: oft *the* N 3 The **directors** of a company are its most senior managers, who meet regularly to make important decisions about how it will be run. [BUSINESS] ❑ *He served on the board of directors of a local bank.* — N-COUNT 4 The **director** of an orchestra or choir is the person who is conducting it. [AM] — N-COUNT

☑ in BRIT, use **conductor**

**di|rec|to|rate** /daɪre̱ktərət, dɪr-/ (**directorates**) 1 A **directorate** is a board of directors in a company or organization. [BUSINESS] ❑ *The Bank would be managed by a directorate of professional bankers.* — N-COUNT 2 A **directorate** is a part of a government department which is responsible for one particular thing. ❑ *...the Health and Safety Directorate of the EU.* — N-COUNT: with supp

**di|rec|tor gen|er|al** (**directors general**) The **director general** of a large organization such as the BBC is the person who is in charge of it. — N-COUNT: usu sing

**di|rec|to|rial** /daɪrektɔ̱ːriəl, dɪr-/ **Directorial** means relating to the job of being a film or theatre director. ❑ *...Sam Mendes' directorial debut.* — ADJ: ADJ n

**di|rec|tor|ship** /daɪre̱ktəʳʃɪp, dɪr-/ (**directorships**) A **directorship** is the job or position of a company director. [BUSINESS] ❑ *Barry resigned his directorship in December 1973.* — N-COUNT

**di|rec|tory** /daɪre̱ktəri, dɪr-/ (**directories**) 1 A **directory** is a book which gives lists of facts, for example people's names, addresses, and telephone numbers, or the names and addresses of business companies, usually arranged in alphabetical order. — N-COUNT: oft N *of* n, n N 2 A **directory** is an area of a computer disk which contains one or more files or other directories. ❑ *...a telephone directory.* 3 [COMPUTING] ❑ *This option lets you create new files or directories.* — N-COUNT 4 On the World Wide Web, a **directory** is a list of the subjects that you can find information on. [COMPUTING] ❑ *Yahoo is the oldest and best-known Web directory service.* — N-COUNT

**di|rec|tory en|quiries** **Directory enquiries** is a service which you can telephone to find out someone's telephone number. [BRIT] ❑ *He dialled directory enquiries.* — N-UNCOUNT

☑ in AM, use **information**, **directory assistance**

**di|rect rule** **Direct rule** is a system in which a central government rules an area which has had its own parliament or law-making organization in the past. — N-UNCOUNT

**di|rect speech** In grammar, **direct speech** is speech which is reported by using the exact words that the speaker used. [mainly BRIT] — N-UNCOUNT

☑ in AM, usually use **direct discourse**

**di|rect tax** (**direct taxes**) A **direct tax** is a tax which a person or organization pays directly to the government, for example income tax. — N-COUNT

**di|rect taxa|tion** **Direct taxation** is a system in which a government raises money by means of direct taxes. — N-UNCOUNT

**dirge** /dɜ̱ːʳdʒ/ (**dirges**) A **dirge** is a slow, sad song or piece of music. Dirges are sometimes performed at funerals. — N-COUNT: usu sing

**dirt** /dɜ̱ːʳt/ 1 If there is **dirt** on something, there is dust, mud, or a stain on it. ❑ *I started to scrub off the dirt.* — N-UNCOUNT 2 You can refer to the earth on the ground as **dirt**, especially when it is dusty. ❑ *They all sit on the dirt in the dappled shade of a tree.* — N-UNCOUNT = earth 3 A **dirt** road or track is made from hard earth. A **dirt** floor is made from earth without any cement, stone, or wood laid on it. ❑ *I drove along the dirt road.* — ADJ: ADJ n 4 If you say that you have **the dirt on** someone, you mean that you have information that could harm their reputation or career. [INFORMAL] ❑ *Steve was keen to get all the dirt he could on her.* — N-SING: oft *the* N, N *on* n

PHRASES 5 If someone **dishes the dirt on** you, they say bad things about you, without worrying if they are true or not, or if they will damage your reputation. [mainly BRIT, INFORMAL] ❑ *He dishes the dirt on his buddies.* — PHRASE: V inflects, oft PHR *on* n [disapproval] 6 If you say that someone **treats** you **like dirt**, you are angry with them because you think that they treat you unfairly and with no respect. ❑ *People think they can treat me like dirt!* — PHRASE: V inflects [disapproval]

**dirt bike** (**dirt bikes**) A **dirt bike** is a type of motorbike that is designed to be used on rough ground. — N-COUNT

**dirt-cheap** If you say that something is **dirt-cheap**, you are emphasizing that it is very cheap indeed. [INFORMAL] ❑ *They're always selling off stuff like that dirt cheap.* — ADJ [emphasis]

**dirt-poor** also **dirt poor**. A **dirt-poor** person or place is extremely poor. — ADJ

**dirty** /dɜ̱ːʳti/ (**dirtier, dirtiest, dirties, dirtying, dirtied**) ◆◇◇ 1 If something is **dirty**, it is marked or covered with stains, spots, or mud, and needs to be cleaned. ❑ *She still did not like the woman who had dirty fingernails.* — ADJ = grubby ≠ clean 2 To **dirty** something means to cause it to become dirty. ❑ *He was afraid the dog's hairs might dirty the seats.* — VERB V n 3 If you describe an action as **dirty**, you disapprove of it and consider it unfair, immoral, or dishonest. ❑ *The gunman had been hired by a rival Mafia family to do the dirty deed.* — ADJ: usu ADJ n [disapproval] ♦ **Dirty** is also an adverb. ❑ *Jim Browne is the kind of fellow who can fight dirty.* — ADV: ADV after v 4 If you describe something such as a joke, a book, or someone's language as **dirty**, you mean that it refers to sex in a way that some people find offensive. ❑ *They told dirty jokes and sang raucous ballads.* — ADJ: usu ADJ n ♦ **Dirty** is also an adverb. ❑ *I'm often asked whether the men talk dirty to me. The answer is no.* — ADV: ADV after v 5 **Dirty** is used before words of criticism to emphasize that you do not approve of someone or something. [INFORMAL] ❑ *You dirty liar.* — ADJ: ADJ n [emphasis]

PHRASES 6 If you say that someone **washes** their **dirty linen in public**, you disapprove of their discussing or arguing about unpleasant or private things in front of other people. There are several other forms of this expression, for example **wash** your **dirty laundry in public**, or in American English, **air** your **dirty laundry in public**. ❑ *We shouldn't wash our dirty laundry in public and if I was in his position, I'd say nothing at all.* — PHRASE: V inflects [disapproval] 7 If someone gives you a **dirty look**, they look at you in a way which shows that they are angry with you. [INFORMAL] ❑ *Michael gave him a dirty look and walked out.* — PHRASE: N inflects, PHR after v 8 **Dirty old man** is an expression some people use to describe an older man who they think shows an unnatural interest in sex. — PHRASE: N inflects, usu vlink PHR [disapproval] 9 To **do** someone's **dirty work** means to do a task for them that is dishonest or unpleasant and which they do not want to do themselves. ❑ *As a member of an elite army hit squad, the army would send us out to do their dirty work for them.* — PHRASE: V inflects 10 If you — PHRASE:

say that an expression is **a dirty word** in a particular group of people, you mean it refers to an idea that they strongly dislike or disagree with. ❑ *Marketing became a dirty word at the company.* — v-link PHR

**dirty bomb** **(dirty bombs)** A **dirty bomb** is a nuclear bomb that uses explosives to release radioactive material over a wide area. — N-COUNT

**dirty trick** **(dirty tricks)** You describe the actions of an organization or political group as **dirty tricks** when you think they are using illegal methods to harm the reputation or effectiveness of their rivals. ❑ *He claimed he was the victim of a dirty tricks campaign* — N-COUNT: usu pl

**dis-** /dɪs-/ **Dis-** is added to some words that describe processes, qualities, or states, in order to form words describing the opposite processes, qualities, or states. For example, if you do not agree with someone, you disagree with them; if one thing is not similar to something else, it is dissimilar to it. — PREFIX

**dis|abil|ity** /dɪsəbɪlɪti/ **(disabilities)** [1] A **disability** is a permanent injury, illness, or physical or mental condition that tends to restrict the way that someone can live their life. ❑ *Facilities for people with disabilities are still insufficient.* — N-COUNT [2] **Disability** is the state of being disabled. ❑ *Disability can make extra demands on financial resources.* — N-UNCOUNT

**dis|able** /dɪseɪbᵊl/ **(disables, disabling, disabled)** [1] If an injury or illness **disables** someone, it affects them so badly that it restricts the way that they can live their life. ❑ *She did all this tendon damage and it really disabled her... Although disabled by polio during the Second World War, Proctor was also a first-rate helmsman.* ♦ **dis|abling** *...skin ulcers which are disfiguring and sometimes disabling.* — VERB; V n; V-ed; ADJ [2] If someone or something **disables** a system or mechanism, they stop it working, usually temporarily. ❑ *...if you need to disable a car alarm.* — VERB; V n

**dis|abled** /dɪseɪbᵊld/ Someone who is **disabled** has an illness, injury, or condition that tends to restrict the way that they can live their life, especially by making it difficult for them to move about. ❑ *...practical problems encountered by disabled people in the workplace.* ♦ People who are disabled are sometimes referred to as **the disabled**. ❑ *There are toilet facilities for the disabled.* — ADJ; N-PLURAL: the N

**dis|able|ment** /dɪseɪbᵊlmənt/ **Disablement** is the state of being disabled or the experience of becoming disabled. [FORMAL] ❑ *...permanent total disablement resulting in inability to work.* — N-UNCOUNT

**dis|abuse** /dɪsəbjuːz/ **(disabuses, disabusing, disabused)** If you **disabuse** someone **of** something, you tell them or persuade them that what they believe is in fact untrue. [FORMAL] ❑ *Their view of country people was that they like to please strangers. I did not disabuse them of this notion.* — VERB; V n of n; Also V n

**dis|ad|vant|age** /dɪsədvɑːntɪdʒ, -væn-/ **(disadvantages)** [1] A **disadvantage** is a factor which makes someone or something less useful, acceptable, or successful than other people or things. ❑ *His two main rivals suffer the disadvantage of having been long-term political exiles. ...the advantages and disadvantages of allowing priests to marry.* — N-COUNT: oft N of n; ≠ advantage

PHRASES [2] If you are **at a disadvantage**, you have a problem or difficulty that many other people do not have, which makes it harder for you to be successful. ❑ *The children from poor families were at a distinct disadvantage.* — PHRASE: v-link PHR [3] If something is **to** your **disadvantage** or works **to** your **disadvantage**, it creates difficulties for you. ❑ *A snap election would be to their disadvantage.* — PHRASE: v-link PHR, PHR after v

**dis|ad|van|taged** /dɪsədvɑːntɪdʒd, -væn-/ People who are **disadvantaged** or live in **disadvantaged** areas live in bad conditions and tend not to get a good education or have a reasonable standard of living. ❑ *...the educational problems of disadvantaged children.* ♦ **The disadvantaged** are people who are disadvantaged. — ADJ; = underprivileged; N-PLURAL: the N

**dis|ad|van|ta|geous** /dɪsædvənteɪdʒəs/ Something that is **disadvantageous to** you puts you in a worse position than other people. ❑ *The Second World War started in the most disadvantageous possible way for the western powers.* — ADJ: oft ADJ to/for n; = unfavourable; ≠ advantageous

**dis|af|fect|ed** /dɪsəfektɪd/ **Disaffected** people no longer fully support something such as an organization or political ideal which they previously supported. ❑ *He attracts disaffected voters.* — ADJ

**dis|af|fec|tion** /dɪsəfekʃᵊn/ **Disaffection** is the attitude that people have when they stop supporting something such as an organization or political ideal. ❑ *...people's disaffection with their country and its leaders.* — N-UNCOUNT: oft N with n

**dis|agree** /dɪsəgriː/ **(disagrees, disagreeing, disagreed)** [1] If you **disagree with** someone or **disagree with** what they say, you do not accept that what they say is true or correct. You can also say that two people **disagree**. ❑ *You must continue to see them no matter how much you may disagree with them... They can communicate even when they strongly disagree... 'I think it is inappropriate.' — 'I disagree.'... The two men had disagreed about reincarnation.* — V-RECIP; ≠ agree; V with n; pl-n V; V (non-recip); pl-n V prep [2] If you **disagree with** a particular action or proposal, you disapprove of it and believe that it is wrong. [mainly BRIT] ❑ *I respect the president but I disagree with his decision.* — VERB; ≠ agree; V with n

**dis|agree|able** /dɪsəgriːəbᵊl/ [1] Something that is **disagreeable** is rather unpleasant. ❑ *...a disagreeable odour.* ♦ **dis|agree|ably** /dɪsəgriːəbli/ *The taste is bitter and disagreeably pungent.* — ADJ; ≠ agreeable; ADV: usu ADV adj, also ADV with v [2] Someone who is **disagreeable** is unfriendly or unhelpful. ❑ *He's a shallow, disagreeable man.* — ADJ: usu ADJ n

**dis|agree|ment** /dɪsəgriːmənt/ **(disagreements)** [1] **Disagreement** means objecting to something such as a proposal. ❑ *Britain and France have expressed some disagreement with the proposal.* — N-UNCOUNT: usu N prep; = opposition [2] When there is **disagreement** about something, people disagree or argue about what should be done. ❑ *My instructor and I had a brief disagreement.* — N-VAR: usu with supp, oft in N; = dispute

**dis|al|low** /dɪsəlaʊ/ **(disallows, disallowing, disallowed)** If something **is disallowed**, it is not allowed or accepted officially, because it has not been done correctly. ❑ *England scored again, but the whistle had gone and the goal was disallowed... The Internal Revenue Service sought to disallow the payments.* — VERB; be V-ed; V n

**dis|ap|pear** /dɪsəpɪəʳ/ **(disappears, disappearing, disappeared)** ◆◇◇ [1] If you say that someone or something **disappears**, you mean that you can no longer see them, usually because you or they have changed position. ❑ *The black car drove away from them and disappeared... Clive disappeared into a room by himself.* — VERB; = vanish; V; V prep [2] If someone or something **disappears**, they go away or are taken away somewhere where nobody can find them. ❑ *...a Japanese woman who disappeared thirteen years ago.* — VERB; V [3] If something **disappears**, it stops existing or happening. ❑ *The immediate security threat has disappeared.* — VERB; V

**dis|ap|pear|ance** /dɪsəpɪərəns/ **(disappearances)** [1] If you refer to someone's **disappearance**, you are referring to the fact that nobody knows where they have gone. ❑ *Her disappearance has baffled police.* — N-VAR: oft with poss [2] If you refer to the **disappearance** of an object, you are referring to the fact that it has been lost or stolen. ❑ *Police are investigating the disappearance from council offices of confidential files.* — N-COUNT: usu sing, usu with poss, oft N from n; = loss [3] The **disappearance** of a type of thing, person, or animal is a process in which it becomes less common and finally no longer exists. ❑ *...the virtual disappearance of the red telephone box.* — N-UNCOUNT: usu with supp, oft N of n

**dis|ap|point** /dɪsəpɔɪnt/ **(disappoints, disappointing, disappointed)** If things or people **disappoint** you, they are not as good as you had hoped, or do not do what you hoped they would do. ❑ *She knew that she would disappoint him.* — VERB; = let down; V n

**dis|ap|point|ed** /dɪsəpɔɪntɪd/ ◆◇◇ [1] If you are **disappointed**, you are rather sad because — ADJ: oft ADJ prep, something has not happened or because something is not as good as you had hoped. ❑ *Castlehunters won't be disappointed with the Isle of Man... I was disappointed that Kluge was not there... I was disappointed to see the lack of coverage afforded to this event.* [2] If you are **disappointed in** someone, you are rather sad because they have not behaved as well as you expected them to. ❑ *You should have accepted that. I'm disappointed in you.* — ADJ that, ADJ to-inf; ADJ: v-link ADJ *in* n

**dis|ap|point|ing** /dɪsəpɔɪntɪŋ/ Something that is **disappointing** is not as good or as large as you hoped it would be. ❑ *The wine was excellent, but the food was disappointing.* ♦ **dis|ap|point|ing|ly** *Progress is disappointingly slow.* — ADJ; ADV: ADV adj, ADV with cl

**dis|ap|point|ment** /dɪsəpɔɪntmənt/ **(disappointments)** [1] **Disappointment** is the state of feeling disappointed. ❑ *Despite winning the title, their last campaign ended in great disappointment... Book early to avoid disappointment.* [2] Something or someone that is a **disappointment** is not as good as you had hoped. ❑ *For many, their long-awaited homecoming was a bitter disappointment.* — N-UNCOUNT; N-COUNT

**dis|ap|prov|al** /dɪsəpruːvəl/ If you feel or show **disapproval** of something or someone, you feel or show that you do not approve of them. ❑ *His action had been greeted with almost universal disapproval.* — N-UNCOUNT: oft N *of* n

**dis|ap|prove** /dɪsəpruːv/ **(disapproves, disapproving, disapproved)** If you **disapprove of** something or someone, you feel or show that you do not like them or do not approve of them. ❑ *Most people disapprove of such violent tactics... The Prime Minister made it clear that he disapproved.* — VERB ≠ approve; V *of* n/-ing; V

**dis|ap|prov|ing** /dɪsəpruːvɪŋ/ A **disapproving** action or expression shows that you do not approve of something or someone. ❑ *Janet turned and gave him a disapproving look.* ♦ **dis|ap|prov|ing|ly** *Antonio looked at him disapprovingly.* — ADJ; ADV: ADV after v

**dis|arm** /dɪsɑːʳm/ **(disarms, disarming, disarmed)** [1] To **disarm** a person or group means to take away all their weapons. ❑ *We will agree to disarming troops and leaving their weapons at military positions.* [2] If a country or group **disarms**, it gives up the use of weapons, especially nuclear weapons. ❑ *There has also been a suggestion that the forces in Lebanon should disarm.* [3] If a person or their behaviour **disarms** you, they cause you to feel less angry, hostile, or critical towards them. ❑ *His unease disarmed her.* — VERB; V n; VERB; V; VERB; V n

**dis|arma|ment** /dɪsɑːʳməmənt/ **Disarmament** is the act of reducing the number of weapons, especially nuclear weapons, that a country has. ❑ *...the pace of nuclear disarmament.* — N-UNCOUNT

**dis|arm|ing** /dɪsɑːʳmɪŋ/ If someone or something is **disarming**, they make you feel less angry or hostile. ❑ *Leonard approached with a disarming smile.* ♦ **dis|arm|ing|ly** *He is, as ever, business-like, and disarmingly honest.* — ADJ; ADV: usu ADV adj, also ADV with v

**dis|ar|ray** /dɪsəreɪ/ [1] If people or things are **in disarray**, they are disorganized and confused. ❑ *The nation is in disarray following rioting led by the military.* [2] If things or places are **in disarray**, they are in a very untidy state. ❑ *She was left lying on her side and her clothes were in disarray.* — N-UNCOUNT: oft *in* N = disorder; N-UNCOUNT: oft *in* N

**dis|as|sem|ble** /dɪsəsembəl/ **(disassembles, disassembling, disassembled)** To **disassemble** something means to take it to pieces. [FORMAL] ❑ *You'll have to disassemble the drill.* — VERB = dismantle; V n

**dis|as|so|ci|ate** /dɪsəsoʊʃieɪt/ **(disassociates, disassociating, disassociated)** [1] If you **disassociate yourself from** something or someone, you say or show that you are not connected with them, usually in order to avoid trouble or blame. ❑ *I wish to disassociate myself from this very sad decision.* [2] If you **disassociate** one group or thing **from** another, you separate them. ❑ *...an attempt by the president to disassociate the military from politics.* — VERB = distance ≠ associate; V pron-refl *from* n; VERB; V n *from* n

**dis|as|ter** /dɪzɑːstəʳ, -zæs-/ **(disasters)** [1] A **disaster** is a very bad accident such as an earthquake or a plane crash, especially one in which a lot of people are killed. ❑ *It was the second air disaster in the region in less than two months.* [2] If you refer to something as a **disaster**, you are emphasizing that you think it is extremely bad or unacceptable. ❑ *The whole production was just a disaster!* [3] **Disaster** is something which has very bad consequences for you. ❑ *The government brought itself to the brink of fiscal disaster.* [4] If you say that something is **a recipe for disaster**, you mean that it is very likely to have unpleasant consequences. — ◆◇◇ N-COUNT = tragedy; N-COUNT [emphasis] = catastrophe; N-UNCOUNT = catastrophe; PHRASE: v-link PHR

**dis|as|ter area** **(disaster areas)** [1] A **disaster area** is a part of a country or the world which has been very seriously affected by a disaster such as an earthquake or a flood. ❑ *The region has been declared a disaster area.* [2] If you describe a place, person, or situation as **a disaster area**, you mean that they are in a state of great disorder or failure. [INFORMAL] ❑ *He's a nice old rascal but a disaster area as a politician.* — N-COUNT; N-COUNT: usu sing

**dis|as|trous** /dɪzɑːstrəs, -zæs-/ [1] A **disastrous** event has extremely bad consequences and effects. ❑ *...the recent, disastrous earthquake.* ♦ **dis|as|trous|ly** *The vegetable harvest is disastrously behind schedule... The scheme went disastrously wrong.* [2] If you describe something as **disastrous**, you mean that it was very unsuccessful. ❑ *...their disastrous performance in the general election of 1906.* ♦ **dis|as|trous|ly** *...the company's disastrously timed venture into property.* — ADJ = catastrophic; ADV: ADV adj/prep, ADV with v; ADJ; ADV: ADV adj, ADV with v

**dis|avow** /dɪsəvaʊ/ **(disavows, disavowing, disavowed)** If you **disavow** something, you say that you are not connected with it or responsible for it. [FORMAL] ❑ *Dr. Samuels immediately disavowed the newspaper story.* — VERB = disown, repudiate; V n

**dis|avow|al** /dɪsəvaʊəl/ **(disavowals)** A **disavowal of** something is a statement that you are not connected with it or responsible for it, or that you no longer agree with or believe in it. [FORMAL] ❑ *...a public disavowal of his beliefs.* — N-COUNT: oft N *of* n = repudiation

**dis|band** /dɪsbænd/ **(disbands, disbanding, disbanded)** If someone **disbands** a group of people, or if the group **disbands**, it stops operating as a single unit. ❑ *All the armed groups will be disbanded... The rebels were to have fully disbanded by June the tenth.* — VERB; *be* V-ed; V; Also V n

**dis|be|lief** /dɪsbɪliːf/ **Disbelief** is not believing that something is true or real. ❑ *She looked at him in disbelief.* — N-UNCOUNT: oft *in* N

**dis|be|lieve** /dɪsbɪliːv/ **(disbelieves, disbelieving, disbelieved)** If you **disbelieve** someone or **disbelieve** something that they say, you do not believe that what they say is true. ❑ *There is no reason to disbelieve him.* — VERB ≠ believe; V n; Also V that

**dis|burse** /dɪsbɜːʳs/ **(disburses, disbursing, disbursed)** To **disburse** an amount of money means to pay it out, usually from a fund which has been collected for a particular purpose. [FORMAL] ❑ *The aid will not be disbursed until next year... The bank has disbursed over $350m for the project.* — VERB; *be* V-ed; V n

**dis|burse|ment** /dɪsbɜːʳsmənt/ **(disbursements)** [1] **Disbursement** is the paying out of a sum of money, especially from a fund. [FORMAL] [2] A **disbursement** is a sum of money that is paid out. [FORMAL] — N-UNCOUNT = payment; N-COUNT = payment

**disc** /dɪsk/ **(discs)**

> ✔ The spelling **disk** is also used in American English, mainly for meaning 1.

[1] A **disc** is a flat, circular shape or object. ❑ *Most shredding machines are based on a revolving disc fitted with replaceable blades.* [2] A **disc** is one of the thin, circular pieces of cartilage which separates the bones in your back. ❑ *I had slipped a disc and was frozen in a spasm of pain.* [3] → See also **disk**, **compact disc**, **slipped disc**. — N-COUNT; N-COUNT

**dis|card** /dɪskɑːʳd/ **(discards, discarding, discarded)** If you **discard** something, you get rid of — VERB it because you no longer want it or need it. ❑ *Read the manufacturer's guidelines before discarding the box. ...discarded cigarette butts.* [= dispose of; V n; V-ed]

**dis|cern** /dɪsɜːʳn/ **(discerns, discerning, discerned)** 1 If you can **discern** something, you are aware of it and know what it is. [FORMAL] ❑ *You need a long series of data to be able to discern such a trend... It was hard to discern why this was happening.* [VERB; V n; V wh] 2 If you can **discern** something, you can just see it, but not clearly. [FORMAL] ❑ *Below the bridge we could just discern a narrow, weedy ditch.* [VERB; V n]

**dis|cern|ible** /dɪsɜːʳnəbᵊl/ If something is **discernible**, you can see it or recognize that it exists. [FORMAL] ❑ *Far away the outline of the island is just discernible.* [ADJ]

**dis|cern|ing** /dɪsɜːʳnɪŋ/ If you describe someone as **discerning**, you mean that they are able to judge which things of a particular kind are good and which are bad. ❑ *...tailor-made holidays to suit the more discerning traveller.* [ADJ; approval]

**dis|cern|ment** /dɪsɜːʳnmənt/ **Discernment** is the ability to judge which things of a particular kind are good and which are bad. [N-UNCOUNT = judgment]

**dis|charge** **(discharges, discharging, discharged)**

✓ The verb is pronounced /dɪstʃɑːʳdʒ/. The noun is pronounced /dɪstʃɑːʳdʒ/.

1 When someone **is discharged from** hospital, prison, or one of the armed services, they are officially allowed to leave, or told that they must leave. ❑ *He has a broken nose but may be discharged today... Five days later Henry discharged himself from hospital.* ♦ **Discharge** is also a noun. ❑ *He was given a conditional discharge and ordered to pay compensation.* [VERB; be V-ed; V pron-refl; Also V n; N-VAR] 2 If someone **discharges** their duties or responsibilities, they do everything that needs to be done in order to complete them. [FORMAL] ❑ *...the quiet competence with which he discharged his many college duties.* [VERB; V n] 3 If someone **discharges** a debt, they pay it. [FORMAL] ❑ *The goods will be sold for a fraction of their value in order to discharge the debt.* [VERB; V n] 4 If something **is discharged** from inside a place, it comes out. [FORMAL] ❑ *The resulting salty water will be discharged at sea... The bird had trouble breathing and was discharging blood from the nostrils.* [VERB; be V-ed prep; V n prep] 5 When there is a **discharge** of a substance, the substance comes out from inside somewhere. [FORMAL] ❑ *They develop a fever and a watery discharge from their eyes.* [N-VAR: usu with supp]

**dis|ci|ple** /dɪsaɪpᵊl/ **(disciples)** If you are someone's **disciple**, you are influenced by their teachings and try to follow their example. ❑ *...a disciple of Freud.* [N-COUNT: oft with poss = follower]

**dis|ci|pli|nar|ian** /dɪsɪplɪneəriən/ **(disciplinarians)** If you describe someone as a **disciplinarian**, you mean that they believe in making people obey strict rules of behaviour and in punishing severely anyone who disobeys. ❑ *He has a reputation for being a strict disciplinarian.* [N-COUNT = authoritarian]

**dis|ci|pli|nary** /dɪsɪplɪnəri, AM -neri/ **Disciplinary** bodies or actions are concerned with making sure that people obey rules or regulations and that they are punished if they do not. ❑ *He will now face a disciplinary hearing for having an affair.* [ADJ: ADJ n]

**dis|ci|pline** /dɪsɪplɪn/ **(disciplines, disciplining, disciplined)** ◆◇◇ 1 **Discipline** is the practice of making people obey rules or standards of behaviour, and punishing them when they do not. ❑ *Order and discipline have been placed in the hands of headmasters and governing bodies.* [N-UNCOUNT] 2 **Discipline** is the quality of being able to behave and work in a controlled way which involves obeying particular rules or standards. ❑ *It was that image of calm and discipline that appealed to voters.* [N-UNCOUNT = self-control] 3 If you refer to an activity or situation as a **discipline**, you mean that, in order to be successful in it, you need to behave in a strictly controlled way and obey particular rules or standards. ❑ *The discipline of studying music can help children develop good work habits.* [N-VAR] 4 If someone **is disciplined** for something that they have done wrong, they are punished for it. ❑ *The workman was disciplined by his company but not dismissed... Her husband had at last taken a share in disciplining the boy.* [VERB; be V-ed; V n] 5 If you **discipline yourself** to do something, you train yourself to behave and work in a strictly controlled and regular way. ❑ *Out on the course you must discipline yourself to let go of detailed theory... I'm very good at disciplining myself.* [VERB; V pron-refl to-inf; V pron-refl] 6 A **discipline** is a particular area of study, especially a subject of study in a college or university. [FORMAL] ❑ *We're looking for people from a wide range of disciplines.* [N-COUNT = subject] 7 → See also **self-discipline**.

**dis|ci|plined** /dɪsɪplɪnd/ Someone who is **disciplined** behaves or works in a controlled way. ❑ *For me it meant being very disciplined about how I run my life.* [ADJ]

**disc jock|ey** **(disc jockeys)**

✓ in AM, also use **disk jockey**

A **disc jockey** is someone who plays and introduces CDs on the radio or at a disco. [N-COUNT = DJ]

**dis|claim** /dɪskleɪm/ **(disclaims, disclaiming, disclaimed)** If you **disclaim** knowledge of something or **disclaim** responsibility for something, you say that you did not know about it or are not responsible for it. [FORMAL] ❑ *She disclaims any knowledge of her husband's business.* [VERB = deny; V n]

**dis|claim|er** /dɪskleɪməʳ/ **(disclaimers)** A **disclaimer** is a statement in which a person says that they did not know about something or that they are not responsible for something. [FORMAL] ❑ *The disclaimer asserts that the company won't be held responsible for any inaccuracies.* [N-COUNT]

**dis|close** /dɪskloʊz/ **(discloses, disclosing, disclosed)** If you **disclose** new or secret information, you tell people about it. ❑ *Neither side would disclose details of the transaction... The company disclosed that he will retire in May.* [VERB = reveal; V n; V that]

**dis|clo|sure** /dɪskloʊʒəʳ/ **(disclosures)** **Disclosure** is the act of giving people new or secret information. ❑ *...insufficient disclosure of negative information about the company.* [N-VAR = revelation]

**dis|co** /dɪskoʊ/ **(discos)** A **disco** is a place or event at which people dance to pop music. [N-COUNT]

**dis|cog|ra|phy** /dɪskɒgrəfi/ **(discographies)** A **discography** is a list of all the recordings made by a particular artist or group. [mainly JOURNALISM] [N-COUNT]

**dis|col|our** /dɪskʌləʳ/ **(discolours, discolouring, discoloured)**

✓ in AM, use **discolor**

If something **discolours** or if it **is discoloured** by something else, its original colour changes, so that it looks unattractive. ❑ *A tooth which has been hit hard may discolour... Some oil had seeped out, discolouring the grass.* ♦ **dis|col|oured** *Some of the prints were badly discoloured.* ♦ **dis|col|ora|tion** /dɪskʌləreɪʃᵊn/ *...the discoloration of the soil from acid spills.* [VERB; V; V n; ADJ; N-UNCOUNT]

**dis|com|fit** /dɪskʌmfɪt/ **(discomfits, discomfiting, discomfited)** If you **are discomfited by** something, it causes you to feel slightly embarrassed or confused. [WRITTEN] ❑ *He will be particularly discomfited by the minister's dismissal of his plan... The opposition leader has regularly discomfited him in parliament.* ♦ **dis|com|fit|ed** *Will wanted to do likewise, but felt too discomfited.* [VERB; be V-ed; V n; ADJ: usu v-link ADJ]

**dis|com|fi|ture** /dɪskʌmfɪtʃəʳ/ **Discomfiture** is a feeling of slight embarrassment or confusion. [WRITTEN] [N-UNCOUNT = unease]

**dis|com|fort** /dɪskʌmfəʳt/ **(discomforts)** 1 **Discomfort** is a painful feeling in part of your body when you have been hurt slightly or when you have been uncomfortable for a long time. ❑ *Steve had some discomfort, but no real pain.* [N-UNCOUNT] 2 **Discomfort** is a feeling of worry caused by shame or embarrassment. ❑ *She hears the discomfort in his voice.* [N-UNCOUNT = uneasiness] 3 **Discomforts** are conditions which cause you to feel physically uncomfortable. ❑ *...the discomforts of camping.* [N-COUNT: with supp ≠ comfort]

**dis|con|cert** /dɪskənsɜːʳt/ **(disconcerts, disconcerting, disconcerted)** If something **disconcerts** you, it makes you feel anxious, confused, or embarrassed. ❑ *Antony's wry smile disconcerted Sutcliffe.* ♦ **dis|con|cert|ed** *He was disconcerted to find his fellow diners already seated.*
VERB · V n · ADJ: usu v-link ADJ, oft ADJ to-inf

**dis|con|cert|ing** /dɪskənsɜːʳtɪŋ/ If you say that something is **disconcerting**, you mean that it makes you feel anxious, confused, or embarrassed. ❑ *The reception desk is not at street level, which is a little disconcerting.* ♦ **dis|con|cert|ing|ly** *She looks disconcertingly like a familiar aunt or grandmother.*
ADJ · ADV: usu ADV adj/-ed/prep

**dis|con|nect** /dɪskənekt/ **(disconnects, disconnecting, disconnected)** 1 To **disconnect** a piece of equipment means to separate it from its source of power or to break a connection that it needs in order to work. ❑ *The device automatically disconnects the ignition when the engine is switched off... She ran back to the phone. The line was disconnected.* 2 If you **are disconnected** by a gas, electricity, water, or telephone company, they turn off the connection to your house, usually because you have not paid the bill. ❑ *You will be given three months to pay before you are disconnected.* 3 If you **disconnect** something **from** something else, you separate the two things. ❑ *He disconnected the IV bottle from the overhead hook.*
VERB ≠connect · V n · be V-ed · VERB: usu passive ≠connect · be V-ed · VERB ≠connect · V n from n

**dis|con|nect|ed** /dɪskənektɪd/ **Disconnected** things are not linked in any way. ❑ *...sequences of utterly disconnected events.*
ADJ: usu ADJ n = unconnected

**dis|con|nec|tion** /dɪskənekʃᵊn/ **(disconnections)** The **disconnection** of a gas, water, or electricity supply, or of a telephone, is the act of disconnecting it so that it cannot be used.
N-VAR: oft the N of n

**dis|con|so|late** /dɪskɒnsələt/ Someone who is **disconsolate** is very unhappy and depressed. [WRITTEN] ❑ *He did not have much success, but tried not to get too disconsolate.* ♦ **dis|con|so|late|ly** *Disconsolately, he walked back down the course.*
ADJ = dejected · ADV: ADV with v

**dis|con|tent** /dɪskəntent/ **(discontents) Discontent** is the feeling that you have when you are not satisfied with your situation. ❑ *There are reports of widespread discontent in the capital.*
N-UNCOUNT: also N in pl = dissatisfaction

**dis|con|tent|ed** /dɪskəntentɪd/ If you are **discontented**, you are not satisfied with your situation. ❑ *The government tried to appease discontented workers.*
ADJ: oft ADJ with n = dissatisfied

**dis|con|tinue** /dɪskəntɪnjuː/ **(discontinues, discontinuing, discontinued)** 1 If you **discontinue** something that you have been doing regularly, you stop doing it. [FORMAL] ❑ *Do not discontinue the treatment without consulting your doctor.* 2 If a product **is discontinued**, the manufacturer stops making it. ❑ *The Leica M2 was discontinued in 1967.*
VERB · V n · VERB: usu passive be V-ed

**dis|con|ti|nu|ity** /dɪskɒntɪnjuːɪti, AM -nuː-/ **(discontinuities) Discontinuity** in a process is a lack of smooth or continuous development. [FORMAL] ❑ *There may appear to be discontinuities between broadcasts.*
N-VAR

**dis|con|tinu|ous** /dɪskəntɪnjuəs/ A process that is **discontinuous** happens in stages with intervals between them, rather than continuously.
ADJ = intermittent

**dis|cord** /dɪskɔːʳd/ **Discord** is disagreement and argument between people. [LITERARY]
N-UNCOUNT = conflict

**dis|cord|ant** /dɪskɔːʳdᵊnt/ 1 Something that is **discordant** is strange or unpleasant because it does not fit in with other things. ❑ *His agenda is discordant with ours.* 2 A **discordant** sound or musical effect is unpleasant to hear.
ADJ · ADJ

**dis|co|theque** /dɪskətek/ **(discotheques)** A **discotheque** is the same as a **disco**. [OLD-FASHIONED]
N-COUNT

**dis|count (discounts, discounting, discounted)** ◆◇◇

> Pronounced /dɪskaʊnt/ for meanings 1 and 2, and /dɪskaʊnt/ for meaning 3.

1 A **discount** is a reduction in the usual price of something. ❑ *They are often available at a discount... Full-time staff get a 20 per cent discount.* 2 If a shop or company **discounts** an amount or percentage from something that they are selling, they take the amount or percentage off the usual price. ❑ *This has forced airlines to discount fares heavily in order to spur demand.* 3 If you **discount** an idea, fact, or theory, you consider that it is not true, not important, or not relevant. ❑ *However, traders tended to discount the rumor.*
N-COUNT · VERB · V n · VERB = disregard · V n

**dis|count|er** /dɪskaʊntəʳ/ **(discounters)** A **discounter** is a shop or organization which specializes in selling things very cheaply. Discounters usually sell things in large quantities, or offer only a very limited range of goods.
N-COUNT

**dis|cour|age** /dɪskʌrɪdʒ, AM -kɜːr-/ **(discourages, discouraging, discouraged)** 1 If someone or something **discourages** you, they cause you to lose your enthusiasm about your actions. ❑ *It may be difficult to do at first. Don't let this discourage you.* ♦ **dis|cour|aged** *She was determined not to be too discouraged.* ♦ **dis|cour|ag|ing** *Today's report is rather more discouraging for the economy.* 2 To **discourage** an action or to **discourage** someone **from** doing it means to make them not want to do it. ❑ *...typhoons that discouraged shopping and leisure activities. ...a campaign to discourage children from smoking.*
VERB = dishearten ≠encourage · V n · ADJ: usu v-link ADJ · ADJ: usu v-link ADJ · VERB = deter ≠encourage · V n/-ing · V n from -ing

**dis|cour|age|ment** /dɪskʌrɪdʒmənt, AM -kɜːr-/ **(discouragements)** 1 **Discouragement** is the act of trying to make someone not want to do something. ❑ *He persevered despite discouragement from those around him.* 2 A **discouragement** is something that makes you unwilling to do something because you are afraid of the consequences. ❑ *Uncertainty is a discouragement to investment.*
N-UNCOUNT ≠encouragement · N-COUNT = deterrent ≠encouragement

**dis|course (discourses, discoursing, discoursed)**

> The noun is pronounced /dɪskɔːʳs/. The verb is pronounced /dɪskɔːʳs/.

1 **Discourse** is spoken or written communication between people, especially serious discussion of a particular subject. ❑ *...a tradition of political discourse.* 2 A **discourse** is a serious talk or piece of writing which is intended to teach or explain something. [FORMAL] ❑ *Gates responds with a lengthy discourse on deployment strategy.* 3 If someone **discourses on** something, they talk for a long time about it in a confident way. [FORMAL] ❑ *He discoursed for several hours on French and English prose.* 4 → See also **direct discourse, indirect discourse**.
N-UNCOUNT: usu with supp · N-COUNT · VERB · V prep Also V

**dis|cour|teous** /dɪskɜːʳtiəs/ If you say that someone is **discourteous**, you mean that they are rude and have no consideration for the feelings of other people. [FORMAL]
ADJ: usu v-link ADJ, oft ADJ to n = ill-mannered ≠courteous

**dis|cour|tesy** /dɪskɜːʳtɪsi/ **(discourtesies) Discourtesy** is rude and bad-mannered behaviour. [FORMAL]
N-VAR = rudeness

**dis|cov|er** /dɪskʌvəʳ/ **(discovers, discovering, discovered)** ◆◆◇ 1 If you **discover** something that you did not know about before, you become aware of it or learn of it. ❑ *She discovered that they'd escaped... It was difficult for the inspectors to discover which documents were important... Haskell did not live to discover the deception... It was discovered that the tapes were missing.* 2 If a person or thing **is discovered**, someone finds them, either by accident or because they have been looking for them. ❑ *A few days later his badly beaten body was discovered on a roadside outside the city.* 3 When someone **discovers** a new place, substance, scientific fact, or scientific technique, they are the first person to find it or become aware of it. ❑ *...the first European to discover America... They discovered how to form the image in a thin layer on the surface.* ♦ **dis|cov|er|er (discoverers)** *...the myth of Columbus as the heroic discoverer of the Americas 500 years ago.* 4 If you say that someone **has dis-**
VERB = find out, learn · V that · V wh · V n · it be V-ed that · VERB = find · be V-ed Also V n · VERB · V n · V wh Also V that · N-COUNT: oft N of n · VERB

**covered** a particular activity or subject, you mean that they have tried doing it or studying it for the first time and that they enjoyed it. ❑ *I wish I'd discovered photography when I was younger.* V n
5 When a actor, musician, or other performer who is not well-known **is discovered**, someone recognizes that they have talent and helps them in their career. ❑ *The Beatles were discovered in the early 1960's.* VERB: usu passive; *be* V-ed

**dis|cov|ery** /dɪskʌvəri/ **(discoveries)** ◆◇◇ 1 If someone makes a **discovery**, they become aware of something that they did not know about before. ❑ *I felt I'd made an incredible discovery. ...the discovery that both his wife and son are HIV positive.* N-VAR: usu with supp
2 If someone makes a **discovery**, they are the first person to find or become aware of a place, substance, or scientific fact that no one knew about before. ❑ *In that year, two momentous discoveries were made.* N-VAR: usu with supp
3 If someone makes a **discovery**, they recognize that an actor, musician, or other performer who is not well-known has talent. ❑ *His job is the discovery and promotion of new artists.* N-VAR: usu with supp
4 When the **discovery** of people or objects happens, someone finds them, either by accident or as a result of looking for them. ❑ *...the discovery and destruction by soldiers of millions of marijuana plants.* N-VAR: usu with supp

**dis|cred|it** /dɪskredɪt/ **(discredits, discrediting, discredited)** 1 To **discredit** someone or something means to cause them to lose people's respect or trust. ❑ *...a secret unit within the company that had been set up to discredit its major rival.* VERB; V n
♦ **dis|cred|it|ed** *The previous government is, by now, thoroughly discredited.* ADJ
2 To **discredit** an idea or evidence means to make it appear false or not certain. ❑ *They realized there would be difficulties in discrediting the evidence.* VERB; V n

**dis|cred|it|able** /dɪskredɪtəbᵊl/ **Discreditable** behaviour is not acceptable because people consider it to be shameful and wrong. [FORMAL] ❑ *She had been suspended from her job for discreditable behaviour.* ADJ = improper

**dis|creet** /dɪskriːt/ 1 If you are **discreet**, you are polite and careful in what you do or say, because you want to avoid embarrassing or offending someone. ❑ *They were gossipy and not always discreet.* ADJ
♦ **dis|creet|ly** *I took the phone, and she went discreetly into the living room.* ADV: usu ADV with v
2 If you are **discreet about** something you are doing, you do not tell other people about it, in order to avoid being embarrassed or to gain an advantage. ❑ *She's making a few discreet inquiries with her mother's friends.* ADJ: oft ADJ *about* n
♦ **dis|creet|ly** *Everyone tried discreetly to find out more about him.* ADV: usu ADV with v
3 If you describe something as **discreet**, you approve of it because it is small in size or degree, or not easily noticed. ❑ *She wore discreet jewellery.* ADJ [approval]
♦ **dis|creet|ly** *...stately houses, discreetly hidden behind great avenues of sturdy trees.* ADV: ADV -ed/adj

**dis|crep|an|cy** /dɪskrepənsi/ **(discrepancies)** If there is a **discrepancy between** two things that ought to be the same, there is a noticeable difference between them. ❑ *...the discrepancy between press and radio reports.* N-VAR: usu with supp, oft N *between* pl-n, N *in* n = inconsistency

**dis|crete** /dɪskriːt/ **Discrete** ideas or things are separate and distinct from each other. [FORMAL] ❑ *...instruction manuals that break down jobs into scores of discrete steps.* ADJ: usu ADJ n = separate, distinct

**dis|cre|tion** /dɪskreʃᵊn/ 1 **Discretion** is the quality of behaving in a quiet and controlled way without drawing attention to yourself or giving away personal or private information. [FORMAL] ❑ *Larsson sometimes joined in the fun, but with more discretion.* N-UNCOUNT
2 If someone in a position of authority uses their **discretion** or has **the discretion** to do something in a particular situation, they have the freedom and authority to decide what to do. [FORMAL] ❑ *This committee may want to exercise its discretion to look into those charges.* N-UNCOUNT
3 If something happens **at** someone's **discretion**, it can happen only if they decide to do it or give their permission. [FORMAL] ❑ *We may vary the limit at our discretion and will notify you of any change.* PHRASE: usu PHR after v, v-link PHR

**dis|cre|tion|ary** /dɪskreʃənri, AM -neri/ **Discretionary** things are not fixed by rules but are decided on by people in authority, who consider each individual case. ❑ *Magistrates were given wider discretionary powers.* ADJ: usu ADJ n

**dis|crimi|nate** /dɪskrɪmɪneɪt/ **(discriminates, discriminating, discriminated)** 1 If you can **discriminate between** two things, you can recognize that they are different. ❑ *He is incapable of discriminating between a good idea and a terrible one.* VERB; V *between* pl-n
2 To **discriminate against** a group of people or **in favour of** a group of people means to unfairly treat them worse or better than other groups. ❑ *They believe the law discriminates against women. ...legislation which would discriminate in favour of racial minorities.* VERB; V *against* n; V *in favour of* n

**dis|crimi|nat|ing** /dɪskrɪmɪneɪtɪŋ/ Someone who is **discriminating** has the ability to recognize things that are of good quality. ❑ *More discriminating visitors now tend to shun the area.* ADJ [approval] = discerning

**dis|crimi|na|tion** /dɪskrɪmɪneɪʃᵊn/ 1 **Discrimination** is the practice of treating one person or group of people less fairly or less well than other people or groups. ❑ *She is exempt from sex discrimination laws. ...discrimination against immigrants.* N-UNCOUNT: usu with supp
2 **Discrimination** is knowing what is good or of high quality. ❑ *They cooked without skill and ate without discrimination.* N-UNCOUNT
3 **Discrimination** is the ability to recognize and understand the differences between two things. ❑ *...colour discrimination.* N-UNCOUNT: usu with supp

**dis|crimi|na|tory** /dɪskrɪmɪnətri, AM -tɔːri/ **Discriminatory** laws or practices are unfair because they treat one group of people worse than other groups. ADJ = biased

**dis|cur|sive** /dɪskɜːʳsɪv/ If a style of writing is **discursive**, it includes a lot of facts or opinions that are not necessarily relevant. [FORMAL] ❑ *...a livelier, more candid and more discursive treatment of the subject.* ADJ

**dis|cus** /dɪskəs/ **(discuses)** 1 A **discus** is a heavy circular object which athletes try to throw as far as they can as a sport. N-COUNT
2 **The discus** is the sport of throwing a discus. ❑ *He won the discus at the Montreal Olympics.* N-SING: *the* N

**dis|cuss** /dɪskʌs/ **(discusses, discussing, discussed)** ◆◆◇ 1 If people **discuss** something, they talk about it, often in order to reach a decision. ❑ *I will be discussing the situation with colleagues tomorrow... The cabinet met today to discuss how to respond to the ultimatum.* VERB; V n; V wh-to-inf
2 If you **discuss** something, you write or talk about it in detail. ❑ *I will discuss the role of diet in cancer prevention in Chapter 7.* VERB; V n

**dis|cus|sion** /dɪskʌʃᵊn/ **(discussions)** ◆◆◇ 1 If there is **discussion** about something, people talk about it, often in order to reach a decision. ❑ *There was a lot of discussion about the wording of the report.* N-VAR: oft N *of/about/on* n
● If something is **under discussion**, it is still being talked about and a final decision has not yet been reached. ❑ *'The proposals are still under discussion,' she said.* PHRASE: v-link PHR
2 A **discussion of** a subject is a piece of writing or a lecture in which someone talks about it in detail. ❑ *For a discussion of biology and sexual politics, see chapter 4.* N-COUNT: usu N *of* n
3 A **discussion** document or paper is one that contains information and usually proposals for people to discuss. ADJ: ADJ n

**dis|cus|sion group** **(discussion groups)** A **discussion group** is a group of people who meet regularly to discuss a particular subject. N-COUNT

**dis|dain** /dɪsdeɪn/ **(disdains, disdaining, disdained)** 1 If you feel **disdain for** someone or something, you dislike them because you think that they are inferior or unimportant. ❑ *Janet looked at him with disdain.* N-UNCOUNT: oft N *for* n = contempt, scorn
2 If you **disdain** someone or something, you regard them with disdain. ❑ *Jackie disdained the servants that her millions could buy.* VERB; V n

**dis|dain|ful** /dɪsdeɪnfʊl/ To be **disdainful** means to dislike something or someone because you think they are unimportant or not worth your attention. ❑ *He is highly disdainful of anything to do with the literary establishment.* ♦ **dis|dain|ful|ly** *'We know all about you,' she said disdainfully.*
ADJ: oft ADJ *of* n = scornful, contemptuous; ADV: ADV with v

**dis|ease** /dɪziːz/ **(diseases)** A **disease** is an illness which affects people, animals, or plants, for example one which is caused by bacteria or infection. ❑ *...the rapid spread of disease in the area. ...illnesses such as heart disease.*
◆◆◇ N-VAR

**dis|eased** /dɪziːzd/ Something that is **diseased** is affected by a disease. ❑ *The arteries are diseased and a transplant is the only hope.*
ADJ ≠ healthy

**dis|em|bark** /dɪsɪmbɑːʳk/ **(disembarks, disembarking, disembarked)** When passengers **disembark from** a ship, aeroplane, or bus, they leave it at the end of their journey. [FORMAL] ❑ *I looked towards the plane. Six passengers had already disembarked.* ♦ **dis|em|bar|ka|tion** /dɪsembɑːʳkeɪʃᵊn/ *Disembarkation is at 7.30am.*
VERB; V; Also V *from* n; N-UNCOUNT

**dis|em|bod|ied** /dɪsɪmbɒdid/ 1 **Disembodied** means seeming not to be attached to or to come from anyone. ❑ *A disembodied voice sounded from the back of the cabin.* 2 **Disembodied** means separated from or existing without a body. ❑ *...a disembodied head.*
ADJ: usu ADJ n; ADJ: usu ADJ n

**dis|em|bow|el** /dɪsɪmbaʊəl/ **(disembowels, disembowelling, disembowelled)**

> in AM, use **disemboweling, disemboweled**

To **disembowel** a person or animal means to remove their internal organs, especially their stomach, intestines, and bowels. ❑ *It shows a fox being disembowelled by a pack of hounds.*
VERB = gut; V n

**dis|em|pow|er** /dɪsɪmpaʊəʳ/ **(disempowers, disempowering, disempowered)** If someone or something **disempowers** you, they take away your power or influence. ❑ *She feels that women have been disempowered throughout history.*
VERB: oft passive; *be* V-ed; Also V n, V-ed

**dis|en|chant|ed** /dɪsɪntʃɑːntɪd, -tʃænt-/ If you are **disenchanted with** something, you are disappointed with it and no longer believe that it is good or worthwhile. ❑ *I'm disenchanted with the state of British theatre at the moment.*
ADJ: oft ADJ *with* n = disillusioned

**dis|en|chant|ment** /dɪsɪntʃɑːntmənt, -tʃænt-/ **Disenchantment** is the feeling of being disappointed with something, and no longer believing that it is good or worthwhile. ❑ *There's growing disenchantment with the Government.*
N-UNCOUNT: oft N *with* n = disillusionment

**dis|en|fran|chise** /dɪsɪnfræntʃaɪz/ **(disenfranchises, disenfranchising, disenfranchised)** To **disenfranchise** a group of people means to take away their right to vote, or their right to vote for what they really want. ❑ *...fears of an organized attempt to disenfranchise supporters of Father Aristide. ...the helplessness of disenfranchised minorities.*
VERB; V n; V-ed

**dis|en|gage** /dɪsɪngeɪdʒ/ **(disengages, disengaging, disengaged)** If you **disengage** something, or if it **disengages**, it becomes separate from something which it has been attached to. ❑ *She disengaged the film advance mechanism on the camera... John gently disengaged himself from his sister's tearful embrace... His front brake cable disengaged.*
VERB; V n; V pron-refl *from* n; V

**dis|en|gaged** /dɪsɪngeɪdʒd/ If someone is **disengaged from** something, they are not as involved with it as you would expect.
ADJ: oft ADJ *from* n = detached

**dis|en|gage|ment** /dɪsɪngeɪdʒmənt/ **Disengagement** is a process by which people gradually stop being involved in a conflict, activity, or organization. ❑ *This policy of disengagement from the European war had its critics.*
N-UNCOUNT: oft N *from* n = withdrawal

**dis|en|tan|gle** /dɪsɪntæŋgᵊl/ **(disentangles, disentangling, disentangled)** 1 If you **disentangle** a complicated or confused situation, you make it easier to understand or manage to understand it, by clearly recognizing each separate element. ❑ *In this new book, Harrison brilliantly disentangles complex debates... It's impossible to disentangle the myth from reality.* 2 If you **disentangle** something or someone **from** an undesirable thing or situation, you separate it from that thing or remove it from that situation. ❑ *They are looking at ways to disentangle him from this major policy decision.* 3 If you **disentangle** something, you separate it from things that are twisted around it, or things that it is twisted or knotted around. ❑ *She clawed at the bushes to disentangle herself.*
VERB; V n; V n *from* n; VERB = extricate; V n *from* n; VERB; V n

**dis|equi|lib|rium** /dɪsiːkwɪlɪbriəm/ **Disequilibrium** is a state in which things are not stable or certain, but are likely to change suddenly. [FORMAL] ❑ *There may be a period of disequilibrium as family members adjust to the new baby.*
N-UNCOUNT: also *a* N

**dis|es|tab|lish** /dɪsɪstæblɪʃ/ **(disestablishes, disestablishing, disestablished)** To **disestablish** a church or religion means to take away its official status, so that it is no longer recognized as a national institution. [FORMAL] ❑ *It would be right to disestablish the church.* ♦ **dis|es|tab|lish|ment** /dɪsɪstæblɪʃmənt/ *...Welsh Anglican disestablishment.*
VERB; V n; N-UNCOUNT

**dis|fa|vour** /dɪsfeɪvəʳ/

> in AM, use **disfavor**

If someone or something is **in disfavour**, people dislike or disapprove of them. If someone or something falls **into disfavour**, people start to dislike or disapprove of them. [FORMAL] ❑ *He was in disfavour with the ruling party.*
N-UNCOUNT: usu *in*/*into* N

**dis|fig|ure** /dɪsfɪgəʳ, AM -gjər/ **(disfigures, disfiguring, disfigured)** 1 If someone **is disfigured**, their appearance is spoiled. ❑ *Many of the wounded had been badly disfigured.* ♦ **dis|fig|ured** *She tried not to look at the scarred, disfigured face.* 2 To **disfigure** an object or a place means to spoil its appearance. ❑ *Wind turbines are large and noisy and they disfigure the landscape.*
VERB: usu passive; *be* V-ed; ADJ; VERB; V n

**dis|fig|ure|ment** /dɪsfɪgəʳmənt, AM -gjər-/ **(disfigurements)** A **disfigurement** is something, for example a scar, that spoils a person's appearance. ❑ *He had surgery to correct a facial disfigurement.*
N-VAR: oft supp N

**dis|gorge** /dɪsgɔːʳdʒ/ **(disgorges, disgorging, disgorged)** If something **disgorges** its contents, it empties them out. [WRITTEN] ❑ *The ground had opened to disgorge a boiling stream of molten lava.*
VERB; V n

**dis|grace** /dɪsgreɪs/ **(disgraces, disgracing, disgraced)** 1 If you say that someone is **in disgrace**, you are emphasizing that other people disapprove of them and do not respect them because of something that they have done. ❑ *His vice president also had to resign in disgrace.* 2 If you say that something is **a disgrace**, you are emphasizing that it is very bad or wrong, and that you find it completely unacceptable. ❑ *The way the sales were handled was a complete disgrace.* 3 You say that someone is **a disgrace to** someone else when you want to emphasize that their behaviour causes the other person to feel ashamed. ❑ *Republican leaders called him a disgrace to the party.* 4 If you say that someone **disgraces** someone else, you are emphasizing that their behaviour causes the other person to feel ashamed. ❑ *I have disgraced my family's name... I've disgraced myself by the actions I've taken.*
N-UNCOUNT: oft *in* N [emphasis]; N-SING: *a* N [emphasis] = scandal; N-SING: *a* N, usu N *to* n [emphasis]; VERB [emphasis]; V n; V pron-refl

**dis|graced** /dɪsgreɪst/ You use **disgraced** to describe someone whose bad behaviour has caused them to lose the approval and respect of the public or of people in authority. ❑ *...the disgraced leader of the coup.*
ADJ: usu ADJ n

**dis|grace|ful** /dɪsgreɪsfʊl/ If you say that something such as behaviour or a situation is **disgraceful**, you disapprove of it strongly, and feel that the person or people responsible should be ashamed of it. ❑ *It's disgraceful that they have detained him for so long.* ♦ **dis|grace|ful|ly** *He felt that his brother had behaved disgracefully.*
ADJ: oft *it* v-link ADJ that [disapproval] = shocking, scandalous; ADV: ADV after v, ADV adj/-ed

**dis|grun|tled** /dɪsgrʌntᵊld/ If you are **disgruntled**, you are cross and dissatisfied because
ADJ: oft ADJ *by*/*at*/*over* n

things have not happened the way that you wanted them to happen. ❑ *Disgruntled employees recently called for his resignation.*

**dis|guise** /dɪsgaɪz/ **(disguises, disguising, disguised)** [1] If you are **in disguise**, you are not wearing your usual clothes or you have altered your appearance in other ways, so that people will not recognize you. [N-VAR: oft *in* N] ❑ *You'll have to travel in disguise... He was wearing that ridiculous disguise.* [2] If you **disguise yourself**, you put on clothes which make you look like someone else or alter your appearance in other ways, so that people will not recognize you. [VERB] ❑ *She disguised herself as a man so she could fight on the battlefield.* [V pron-refl *as* n, Also V pron-refl] ♦ **dis|guised** *The extremists entered the building disguised as medical workers.* [ADJ: usu v-link ADJ, oft ADJ *as* n] [3] To **disguise** something means to hide it or make it appear different so that people will not know about it or will not recognize it. [VERB] ❑ *He made no attempt to disguise his agitation.* [V n] ♦ **dis|guised** *This is lust thinly disguised as love.* [ADJ] [4] a **blessing in disguise** → see **blessing**.

**dis|gust** /dɪsgʌst/ **(disgusts, disgusting, disgusted)** [1] **Disgust** is a feeling of very strong dislike or disapproval. [N-UNCOUNT = revulsion] ❑ *He spoke of his disgust at the incident.* [2] To **disgust** someone means to make them feel a strong sense of dislike and disapproval. [VERB] ❑ *He disgusted many with his boorish behaviour.* [V n]

**dis|gust|ed** /dɪsgʌstɪd/ If you are **disgusted**, you feel a strong sense of dislike and disapproval at something. [ADJ: oft ADJ *with/by/at* n, ADJ that = appalled] ❑ *I'm disgusted with the way that he was treated.* ♦ **dis|gust|ed|ly** *'It's a little late for that,' Ritter said disgustedly.* [ADV: ADV with v]

**dis|gust|ing** /dɪsgʌstɪŋ/ [1] If you say that something is **disgusting**, you are criticizing it because it is extremely unpleasant. [ADJ = revolting] ❑ *It tasted disgusting... Smoking is a disgusting habit.* [2] If you say that something is **disgusting**, you mean that you find it completely unacceptable. [ADJ: oft *it* v-link ADJ that = disgraceful] ❑ *It's disgusting that the taxpayer is subsidising this project.*

**dish** /dɪʃ/ **(dishes, dishing, dished)** [1] A **dish** is a shallow container with a wide uncovered top. You eat and serve food from dishes and cook food in them. [◆◇◇ N-COUNT] ❑ *...plastic bowls and dishes.* [2] The contents of a dish can be referred to as a **dish** of something. [N-COUNT: usu N *of* n] ❑ *Nicholas ate a dish of spaghetti.* [3] Food that is prepared in a particular style or combination can be referred to as a **dish**. [N-COUNT] ❑ *There are plenty of vegetarian dishes to choose from.* [4] All the objects that have been used to cook, serve, and eat a meal can be referred to as **the dishes**. [N-PLURAL] ❑ *He'd cooked dinner and washed the dishes.* [5] You can use **dish** to refer to anything that is round and hollow in shape with a wide uncovered top. [N-COUNT: usu with supp] ❑ *...a dish used to receive satellite broadcasts.* [6] → See also **satellite dish**, **side dish**. [7] If you **do the dishes**, you wash the dishes. [PHRASE: V inflects] ❑ *I hate doing the dishes.* [8] to **dish the dirt** → see **dirt**.

♦ **dish out** [1] If you **dish out** something, you distribute it among a number of people. [INFORMAL] [PHRASAL VERB] ❑ *Doctors, not pharmacists, are responsible for dishing out drugs... The council wants to dish the money out to specific projects.* [V P n (not pron), V n P] [2] If someone **dishes out** criticism or punishment, they give it to someone. [INFORMAL] [PHRASAL VERB = dish up] ❑ *Linzi is well qualified to dish out advice.* [V P n, Also V n P] [3] If you **dish out** food, you serve it to people at the beginning of each course of a meal. [INFORMAL] [PHRASAL VERB] ❑ *Here in the dining hall the cooks dish out chicken à la king.* [V P n]

♦ **dish up** If you **dish up** food, you serve it. [INFORMAL] [PHRASAL VERB] ❑ *They dished up a superb meal... I'll dish up and you can grate the Parmesan.* [V P n, V P, Also V n P]

**dis|har|mo|ny** /dɪshɑːʳməni/ When there is **disharmony**, people disagree about important things and this causes an unpleasant atmosphere. [FORMAL] [N-UNCOUNT = conflict ≠harmony] ❑ *...racial disharmony.*

**dish|cloth** /dɪʃklɒθ, AM -klɔːθ/ **(dishcloths)** [1] A **dishcloth** is a cloth used to dry dishes after they have been washed. [N-COUNT = tea-towel] [2] A **dishcloth** is a cloth used for washing dishes, pans, and cutlery. [N-COUNT]

**dis|heart|ened** /dɪshɑːʳtᵊnd/ If you are **disheartened**, you feel disappointed about something and have less confidence or less hope about it than you did before. [ADJ: usu v-link ADJ, oft ADJ *by* n = discouraged] ❑ *He was disheartened by their hostile reaction.*

**dis|heart|en|ing** /dɪshɑːʳtənɪŋ/ If something is **disheartening**, it makes you feel disappointed and less confident or less hopeful. [ADJ]

**di|shev|elled** /dɪʃevᵊld/

✓ in AM, use **disheveled**

If you describe someone's hair, clothes, or appearance as **dishevelled**, you mean that it is very untidy. [ADJ] ❑ *She arrived flushed and dishevelled.*

**dis|hon|est** /dɪsɒnɪst/ If you say that a person or their behaviour is **dishonest**, you mean that they are not truthful or honest and that you cannot trust them. [ADJ: oft *it* v-link ADJ to-inf ≠honest] ❑ *It would be dishonest not to present the data as fairly as possible.* ♦ **dis|hon|est|ly** *The key issue was whether the four defendants acted dishonestly.* [ADV: usu ADV with v]

**dis|hon|es|ty** /dɪsɒnɪsti/ **Dishonesty** is dishonest behaviour. [N-UNCOUNT] ❑ *She accused the government of dishonesty and incompetence.*

**dis|hon|our** /dɪsɒnəʳ/ **(dishonours, dishonouring, dishonoured)**

✓ in AM, use **dishonor**

[1] If you **dishonour** someone, you behave in a way that damages their good reputation. [FORMAL] [VERB] ❑ *It would dishonour my family if I didn't wear the veil.* [V n] [2] **Dishonour** is a state in which people disapprove of you and lose their respect for you. [FORMAL] [N-UNCOUNT = disgrace] ❑ *...a choice between death and dishonour.* [3] If someone **dishonours** an agreement, they refuse to act according to its conditions. [VERB] ❑ *We found that the bank had dishonoured some of our cheques.* [V n]

**dis|hon|our|able** /dɪsɒnərəbᵊl/

✓ in AM, use **dishonorable**

Someone who is **dishonourable** is not honest and does things which you consider to be morally unacceptable. [ADJ = disreputable ≠honourable] ❑ *Mark had done nothing dishonourable.* ♦ **dis|hon|our|ably** /dɪsɒnərəbli/ *He could not bear to be seen to act dishonourably.* [ADV: ADV after v, ADV -ed]

**dish tow|el** **(dish towels)** A **dish towel** is a cloth used to dry dishes after they have been washed. [AM] [N-COUNT]

✓ in BRIT, use **tea towel**

**dish|washer** /dɪʃwɒʃəʳ/ **(dishwashers)** A **dishwasher** is an electrically operated machine that washes and dries plates, saucepans, and cutlery. [N-COUNT]

**dish|water** /dɪʃwɔːtəʳ/ **Dishwater** is water that dishes, pans, and cutlery have been washed in. [N-UNCOUNT]

**dishy** /dɪʃi/ If you describe someone as **dishy**, you mean they are very good looking and attractive; used especially by women about men. [BRIT, INFORMAL] [ADJ]

**dis|il|lu|sion** /dɪsɪluːʒᵊn/ **(disillusions, disillusioning, disillusioned)** [1] If a person or thing **disillusions** you, they make you realize that something is not as good as you thought. [VERB] ❑ *I'd hate to be the one to disillusion him.* [V n] [2] **Disillusion** is the same as **disillusionment**. [N-UNCOUNT: also N in pl] ❑ *There is disillusion with established political parties.*

**dis|il|lu|sioned** /dɪsɪluːʒᵊnd/ If you are **disillusioned with** something, you are disappointed, because it is not as good as you had expected or thought. [ADJ: oft ADJ *with* n = disenchanted] ❑ *I've become very disillusioned with politics.*

**dis|il|lu|sion|ment** /dɪsɪluːʒᵊnmənt/ **Disillusionment** is the disappointment that you feel when you discover that something is not as good as you had expected or thought. [N-UNCOUNT: oft N *with* n = disenchantment] ❑ *...his growing disillusionment with his work.*

**dis|in|cen|tive** /dɪsɪnsentɪv/ **(disincentives)** A **disincentive** is something which discourages people from behaving or acting in a particular [N-VAR: oft N *to* n/-ing, N to-inf = deterrent] way. [FORMAL] ❑ *High marginal tax rates may act as a disincentive to working longer hours.* ≠ incentive

**dis|in|cli|na|tion** /dɪsɪnklɪneɪʃᵊn/ A **disinclination to** do something is a feeling that you do not want to do it. [FORMAL] ❑ *They are showing a marked disinclination to pursue these opportunities.*
N-SING: usu N to-inf = reluctance ≠ inclination

**dis|in|clined** /dɪsɪnklaɪnd/ If you are **disinclined to** do something, you do not want to do it. [FORMAL] ❑ *He was disinclined to talk about himself, especially to his students.*
ADJ: v-link ADJ, usu ADJ to-inf = reluctant, unwilling

**dis|in|fect** /dɪsɪnfekt/ **(disinfects, disinfecting, disinfected)** If you **disinfect** something, you clean it using a substance that kills germs. ❑ *Chlorine is used to disinfect water.*
VERB = sterilize; V n

**dis|in|fect|ant** /dɪsɪnfektənt/ **(disinfectants)** **Disinfectant** is a substance that kills germs. It is used, for example, for cleaning kitchens and bathrooms.
N-MASS = antiseptic

**dis|in|fla|tion** /dɪsɪnfleɪʃᵊn/ **Disinflation** is a reduction in the rate of inflation, especially as a result of government policies.
N-UNCOUNT ≠ inflation

**dis|in|for|ma|tion** /dɪsɪnfəʳmeɪʃᵊn/ If you accuse someone of spreading **disinformation**, you are accusing them of spreading false information in order to deceive people. ❑ *They spread disinformation in order to discredit politicians.*
N-UNCOUNT

**dis|in|genu|ous** /dɪsɪndʒenjuəs/ Someone who is **disingenuous** is slightly dishonest and insincere in what they say. [FORMAL] ❑ *It would be disingenuous to claim that this is great art.*
ADJ: oft *it* v-link ADJ to-inf

♦ **dis|in|genu|ous|ly** *He disingenuously remarked that he knew nothing about strategy.*
ADV: usu ADV with v, also ADV adj

**dis|in|her|it** /dɪsɪnherɪt/ **(disinherits, disinheriting, disinherited)** If you **disinherit** someone such as your son or daughter, you arrange that they will not become the owner of your money and property after your death, usually because they have done something that you do not approve of. ❑ *He threatened to disinherit her if she refused to obey.*
VERB; V n

**dis|in|te|grate** /dɪsɪntɪgreɪt/ **(disintegrates, disintegrating, disintegrated)** 1 If something **disintegrates**, it becomes seriously weakened, and is divided or destroyed. ❑ *During October 1918 the Austro-Hungarian Empire began to disintegrate.*
VERB; V

♦ **dis|in|te|gra|tion** /dɪsɪntɪgreɪʃᵊn/ *...the violent disintegration of Yugoslavia.*
N-UNCOUNT: oft N *of* n

2 If an object or substance **disintegrates**, it breaks into many small pieces or parts and is destroyed. ❑ *At 420mph the windscreen disintegrated completely.*
VERB; V

♦ **dis|in|te|gra|tion** *...the catastrophic disintegration of the aircraft after the explosion.*
N-UNCOUNT

**dis|in|ter** /dɪsɪntɜːʳ/ **(disinters, disinterring, disinterred)** 1 When a dead body **is disinterred**, it is dug up from out of the ground. ❑ *The bones were disinterred and moved to a burial site.*
VERB: usu passive *be* V-ed

2 If you **disinter** something, you start using it again after it has not been used for a long time. [HUMOROUS] ❑ *...the trend for disinterring sixties soul classics for TV commercials.*
VERB; V n

**dis|in|ter|est** /dɪsɪntrəst/ If there is **disinterest in** something, people are not interested in it. ❑ *The fact Liberia has no oil seems to explain foreign disinterest in its internal affairs.*
N-UNCOUNT: oft N *in* n

**dis|in|ter|est|ed** /dɪsɪntrəstɪd/ 1 Someone who is **disinterested** is not involved in a particular situation or not likely to benefit from it and is therefore able to act in a fair and unselfish way. ❑ *Scientists, of course, can be expected to be impartial and disinterested.*
ADJ = impartial

2 If you are **disinterested in** something, you are not interested in it. Some users of English believe that it is not correct to use **disinterested** with this meaning.
ADJ: oft ADJ *in* n = uninterested

**dis|joint|ed** /dɪsdʒɔɪntɪd/ 1 **Disjointed** words, thoughts, or ideas are not presented in a smooth or logical way and are therefore difficult to understand. ❑ *Sally was used to his disjointed, drunken ramblings.*
ADJ = confused

2 **Disjointed** societies, systems, and activities are ones in which the different parts or elements are not as closely connected as they should be or as they used to be. ❑ *...our increasingly fragmented and disjointed society.*
ADJ = divided

**disk** /dɪsk/ **(disks)** also **disc.** In a computer, the **disk** is the part where information is stored. ❑ *The program takes up 2.5 megabytes of disk space.* → See also **disk drive, floppy disk, hard disk.**
N-COUNT: also *on/to* N

**disk drive (disk drives)**

✔ in BRIT, also use **disc drive**

The **disk drive** on a computer is the part that contains the disk or into which a disk can be inserted. The disk drive allows you to read information from the disk and store information on the disk.
N-COUNT

**disk|ette** /dɪsket/ **(diskettes)** A **diskette** is the same as a **floppy disk**.
N-COUNT

**disk jock|ey** → see **disc jockey**.

**dis|like** /dɪslaɪk/ **(dislikes, disliking, disliked)** 1 If you **dislike** someone or something, you consider them to be unpleasant and do not like them. ❑ *We don't serve liver often because so many people dislike it... David began to dislike all his television heroes who smoked.*
VERB; V n; V n

2 **Dislike** is the feeling that you do not like someone or something. ❑ *He made no attempt to conceal his dislike of me.*
N-UNCOUNT

3 Your **dislikes** are the things that you do not like. ❑ *Consider what your likes and dislikes are about your job.*
N-COUNT: usu pl

4 If you **take a dislike to** someone or something, you decide that you do not like them.
PHRASE: V inflects

**dis|lo|cate** /dɪsləkeɪt/ **(dislocates, dislocating, dislocated)** 1 If you **dislocate** a bone or joint in your body, or in someone else's body, it moves out of its proper position in relation to other bones, usually in an accident. ❑ *Harrison dislocated a finger.*
VERB; V n

2 To **dislocate** something such as a system, process, or way of life means to disturb it greatly or prevent it from continuing as normal. ❑ *It would help to end illiteracy and disease, but it would also dislocate a traditional way of life.*
VERB = disrupt; V n

**dis|lo|ca|tion** /dɪsləkeɪʃᵊn/ **(dislocations)** **Dislocation** is a situation in which something such as a system, process, or way of life is greatly disturbed or prevented from continuing as normal. ❑ *Millions of refugees have suffered a total dislocation of their lives.*
N-VAR: oft N *of* n = disruption

**dis|lodge** /dɪslɒdʒ/ **(dislodges, dislodging, dislodged)** 1 To **dislodge** something means to remove it from where it was fixed or held. ❑ *Rainfall had dislodged debris from the slopes of the volcano.*
VERB; V n *from* n; Also V n

2 To **dislodge** a person from a position or job means to remove them from it. ❑ *He may challenge the Prime Minister even if he decides he cannot dislodge her this time.*
VERB; V n

**dis|loy|al** /dɪslɔɪəl/ Someone who is **disloyal to** their friends, family, or country does not support them or does things that could harm them. ❑ *She was so disloyal to her deputy she made his position untenable.*
ADJ: oft ADJ *to* n ≠ loyal

**dis|loy|al|ty** /dɪslɔɪəlti/ **Disloyalty** is disloyal behaviour. ❑ *Charges had already been made against certain officials suspected of disloyalty.*
N-UNCOUNT: oft N *to* n

**dis|mal** /dɪzmᵊl/ 1 Something that is **dismal** is bad in a sad or depressing way. ❑ *It was a dismal failure.*
ADJ

♦ **dis|mal|ly** *He failed dismally in his opening match.*
ADV

2 Something that is **dismal** is sad and depressing, especially in appearance. ❑ *The main part of the hospital is pretty dismal but the children's ward is really lively.*
ADJ = dreary

**dis|man|tle** /dɪsmæntᵊl/ **(dismantles, dismantling, dismantled)** 1 If you **dismantle** a machine or structure, you carefully separate it into its different parts. ❑ *He asked for immediate help from the United States to dismantle the warheads.*
VERB; V n

2 To **dismantle** an organization or system means to cause it to stop functioning by gradually reducing its power or purpose. ❑ *Public services of all kinds are being dismantled.*
VERB; V n

**dis|may** /dɪsmeɪ/ **(dismays, dismaying, dismayed)** 1 **Dismay** is a strong feeling of fear, worry, or sadness that is caused by something un-
N-UNCOUNT: oft *to* N with poss

pleasant and unexpected. [FORMAL] ❑ *Local councillors have reacted with dismay and indignation.* [2] If you **are dismayed** by something, it makes you feel afraid, worried, or sad. [FORMAL] ❑ *The committee was dismayed by what it had been told... The thought that she was crying dismayed him.* ♦ **dis|mayed** *He was dismayed at the cynicism of the youngsters.* VERB be V-ed V n ADJ: usu v-link ADJ, oft ADJ *at* n, ADJ to-inf/that

**dis|mem|ber** /dɪsmembəʳ/ **(dismembers, dismembering, dismembered)** [1] To **dismember** the body of a dead person or animal means to cut or pull it into pieces. ❑ *He then dismembered her, hiding parts of her body in the cellar.* [2] To **dismember** a country or organization means to break it up into smaller parts. ❑ *...Hitler's plans to occupy and dismember Czechoslovakia.* VERB V n VERB V n

**dis|mem|ber|ment** /dɪsmembəʳmənt/ [1] **Dismemberment** is the cutting or pulling into pieces of a body. [2] **Dismemberment** is the breaking up into smaller parts of a country or organization. ❑ *...the case for dismemberment or even abolition of the BBC.* N-UNCOUNT N-UNCOUNT: oft N *of* n

**dis|miss** /dɪsmɪs/ **(dismisses, dismissing, dismissed)** [1] If you **dismiss** something, you decide or say that it is not important enough for you to think about or consider. ❑ *Mr Wakeham dismissed the reports as speculation... I would certainly dismiss any allegations of impropriety by the Labour Party.* [2] If you **dismiss** something **from** your mind, you stop thinking about it. ❑ *I dismissed him from my mind... 'It's been a lovely day,' she said, dismissing the episode.* [3] When an employer **dismisses** an employee, the employer tells the employee that they are no longer needed to do the job that they have been doing. ❑ *...the power to dismiss civil servants who refuse to work.* [4] If you **are dismissed** by someone in authority, they tell you that you can go away from them. ❑ *Two more witnesses were called, heard and dismissed.* [5] When a judge **dismisses** a case against someone, he or she formally states that there is no need for a trial, usually because there is not enough evidence for the case to continue. ❑ *An American judge yesterday dismissed murder charges against Dr Jack Kevorkian. ...their attempt to have the case against them dismissed.* ◆◇◇ VERB = discount V n *as* n V n VERB = banish V n *from* n V n VERB = sack, fire V n VERB be V-ed VERB V n have n V-ed

**dis|mis|sal** /dɪsmɪsᵊl/ **(dismissals)** [1] When an employee is dismissed from their job, you can refer to their **dismissal**. ❑ *...Mr Low's dismissal from his post at the head of the commission.* [2] **Dismissal of** something means deciding or saying that it is not important. ❑ *...their high-handed dismissal of public opinion.* N-VAR: oft with poss N-UNCOUNT: usu N *of* n

**dis|miss|ive** /dɪsmɪsɪv/ If you are **dismissive of** someone or something, you say or show that you think they are not important or have no value. ❑ *Mr Jones was dismissive of the report, saying it was riddled with inaccuracies.* ♦ **dis|miss|ive|ly** *'Forget it,' he replied dismissively.* ADJ: oft ADJ *of* n ADV: usu ADV with v, also ADV adj

**dis|mount** /dɪsmaʊnt/ **(dismounts, dismounting, dismounted)** If you **dismount** from a horse or a bicycle, you get down from it. [FORMAL] ❑ *Emma dismounted and took her horse's bridle.* VERB V

**dis|obedi|ence** /dɪsəbiːdiəns/ **Disobedience** is deliberately not doing what someone tells you to do, or what a rule or law says that you should do. N-UNCOUNT

**dis|obedi|ent** /dɪsəbiːdiənt/ If you are **disobedient**, you deliberately do not do what someone in authority tells you to do, or what a rule or law says that you should do. ❑ *Her tone was that of a parent to a disobedient child.* ADJ ≠ obedient

**dis|obey** /dɪsəbeɪ/ **(disobeys, disobeying, disobeyed)** When someone **disobeys** a person or an order, they deliberately do not do what they have been told to do. ❑ *...a naughty boy who often disobeyed his mother and father... They were threatened with punishment if they disobeyed.* VERB ≠ obey V n V

**dis|or|der** /dɪsɔːʳdəʳ/ **(disorders)** [1] A **disorder** is a problem or illness which affects someone's mind or body. ❑ *...a rare nerve disorder that can cause paralysis of the arms.* [2] **Disorder** is a state of being untidy, badly prepared, or badly organized. ❑ *The emergency room was in disorder.* [3] **Disorder** is violence or rioting in public. ❑ *He called on the authorities to stop public disorder.* N-VAR: usu with supp = complaint N-UNCOUNT: oft *in* N = confusion N-VAR: usu supp N = unrest

**dis|or|dered** /dɪsɔːʳdəʳd/ If you describe something as **disordered**, you mean it is untidy and is not neatly arranged. ❑ *...a disordered heap of mossy branches.* ADJ = messy

**dis|or|der|ly** /dɪsɔːʳdəʳli/ [1] If you describe something as **disorderly**, you mean that it is untidy, irregular, or disorganized. [FORMAL] ❑ *...a large and disorderly room.* [2] If you describe someone as **disorderly**, you mean that they are behaving in a noisy, rude, or violent way in public. You can also describe a place or event as **disorderly** if the people there behave in this way. [FORMAL] ADJ = chaotic ADJ = rowdy

**dis|or|gani|za|tion** /dɪsɔːʳgənaɪzeɪʃᵊn/

☑ in BRIT, also use **disorganisation**

If something is in a state of **disorganization**, it is disorganized. N-UNCOUNT = disarray

**dis|or|gan|ized** /dɪsɔːʳgənaɪzd/

☑ in BRIT, also use **disorganised**

[1] Something that is **disorganized** is in a confused state or is badly planned or managed. ❑ *A report by the state prosecutor described the police action as confused and disorganised.* [2] Someone who is **disorganized** is very bad at organizing things in their life. ❑ *My boss is completely disorganised.* ADJ ≠ organized ADJ ≠ organized

**dis|ori|ent** /dɪsɔːrient/ **(disorients, disorienting, disoriented)**

☑ in BRIT, also use **disorientate**

If something **disorients** you, you lose your sense of direction, or you generally feel lost and uncertain, for example because you are in an unfamiliar environment. ❑ *An overnight stay at a friend's house disorients me.* ♦ **dis|ori|ent|ed** *I feel dizzy and disoriented.* ♦ **dis|ori|ent|ing** *An abrupt change of location can be disorienting.* ♦ **dis|ori|en|ta|tion** /dɪsɔːrienteɪʃᵊn/ *Morris was so stunned by this that he experienced a moment of total disorientation.* VERB = confuse V n ADJ: usu v-link ADJ ADJ N-UNCOUNT

**dis|ori|en|tate** /dɪsɔːrienteɪt/ **(disorientates, disorientating, disorientated)** → see **disorient**.

**dis|own** /dɪsoʊn/ **(disowns, disowning, disowned)** If you **disown** someone or something, you say or show that you no longer want to have any connection with them or any responsibility for them. ❑ *The man who murdered the girl is no son of mine. I disown him.* VERB V n

**dis|par|age** /dɪspærɪdʒ/ **(disparages, disparaging, disparaged)** If you **disparage** someone or something, you speak about them in a way which shows that you do not have a good opinion of them. [FORMAL] ❑ *...Larkin's tendency to disparage literature.* VERB V n

**dis|par|age|ment** /dɪspærɪdʒmənt/ **Disparagement** is the act of speaking about someone or something in a way which shows that you do not have a good opinion of them. [FORMAL] ❑ *Reviewers have been almost unanimous in their disparagement of this book.* N-UNCOUNT: oft N *of* n = denigration

**dis|par|ag|ing** /dɪspærɪdʒɪŋ/ If you are **disparaging** about someone or something, or make **disparaging** comments about them, you say things which show that you do not have a good opinion of them. ❑ *The Minister was alleged to have made disparaging remarks about the rest of the Cabinet.* ♦ **dis|par|ag|ing|ly** *Do not talk disparagingly about your company in public.* ADJ: oft ADJ *about/of* n ADV: ADV with v

**dis|par|ate** /dɪspərət/ [1] **Disparate** things are clearly different from each other in quality or type. [FORMAL] ❑ *Scientists are trying to pull together disparate ideas in astronomy.* [2] A **disparate** thing is made up of very different elements. [FORMAL] ❑ *...a very disparate nation, with enormous regional differences.* ADJ: usu ADJ n ADJ: usu ADJ n = diverse

**dis|par|ity** /dɪspærɪti/ **(disparities)** If there is a **disparity between** two or more things, there is a noticeable difference between them. [FORMAL] ❑ *...the economic disparities between East and West Berlin.*
N-VAR: oft N *between*/*in* pl-n = *difference*

**dis|pas|sion|ate** /dɪspæʃənət/ Someone who is **dispassionate** is calm and reasonable, and not affected by emotions. ❑ *We, as prosecutors, try to be dispassionate about the cases we bring.*
ADJ = *detached*
♦ **dis|pas|sion|ate|ly** *He sets out the facts coolly and dispassionately.*
ADV: ADV with v

**dis|patch** /dɪspætʃ/ **(dispatches, dispatching, dispatched)**

✔ in BRIT, also use **despatch**

[1] If you **dispatch** someone to a place, you send them there for a particular reason. [FORMAL] ❑ *He dispatched scouts ahead... The Italian government was preparing to dispatch 4,000 soldiers to search the island.* ♦ **Dispatch** is also a noun. ❑ *The despatch of the task force is purely a contingency measure.*
VERB = *send*; V n adv/prep; V n to-inf; N-UNCOUNT: usu N *of* n
[2] If you **dispatch** a message, letter, or parcel, you send it to a particular person or destination. [FORMAL] ❑ *The victory inspired him to dispatch a gleeful telegram to Roosevelt... Free gifts are dispatched separately so please allow 28 days for delivery.* ♦ **Dispatch** is also a noun. ❑ *We have 125 cases ready for dispatch.*
VERB = *send*; V n prep/adv; *be* V-ed; Also V n; N-UNCOUNT
[3] A **dispatch** is a special report that is sent to a newspaper or broadcasting organization by a journalist who is in a different town or country. ❑ *...this despatch from our West Africa correspondent.*
N-COUNT = *bulletin*
[4] A **dispatch** is a message or report that is sent, for example, by army officers or government officials to their headquarters. ❑ *I was carrying dispatches from the ambassador.*
N-COUNT
[5] To **dispatch** a person or an animal means to kill them. [OLD-FASHIONED] ❑ *The fox takes his chance with a pack of hounds which may catch him and despatch him immediately.*
VERB; V n

**dis|pel** /dɪspel/ **(dispels, dispelling, dispelled)** To **dispel** an idea or feeling that people have means to stop them having it. ❑ *The President is attempting to dispel the notion that he has neglected the economy.*
VERB; V n

**dis|pen|sable** /dɪspensəbəl/ If someone or something is **dispensable** they are not really needed. ❑ *All those people in the middle are dispensable.*
ADJ: usu v-link ADJ ≠ *indispensable*

**dis|pen|sa|ry** /dɪspensəri/ **(dispensaries)** A **dispensary** is a place, for example in a hospital, where medicines are prepared and given out.
N-COUNT

**dis|pen|sa|tion** /dɪspenseɪʃən/ **(dispensations)** [1] A **dispensation** is special permission to do something that is normally not allowed. ❑ *They were promised dispensation from military service.*
N-VAR
[2] **Dispensation of** something is the issuing of it, especially from a position of authority. [FORMAL] ❑ *...our application of consistent standards in the dispensation of justice.*
N-UNCOUNT: N *of* n

**dis|pense** /dɪspens/ **(dispenses, dispensing, dispensed)** [1] If someone **dispenses** something that they own or control, they give or provide it to a number of people. [FORMAL] ❑ *The Union had already dispensed £40,000 in grants... I thought of myself as a patriarch, dispensing words of wisdom to all my children.*
VERB; V n; V n *to* n
[2] If you obtain a product by getting it out of a machine, you can say that the machine **dispenses** the product. ❑ *For two weeks, the cash machine was unable to dispense money.*
VERB; V n
[3] When a chemist **dispenses** medicine, he or she prepares it, and gives or sells it to the patient or customer. ❑ *Some shops gave wrong or inadequate advice when dispensing homeopathic medicines... Doctors confine themselves to prescribing rather than dispensing.*
VERB; V n; V; Also V n *to* n

♦ **dispense with** If you **dispense with** something, you stop using it or get rid of it completely, especially because you no longer need it. ❑ *Many households have dispensed with their old-fashioned vinyl turntable.*
PHRASAL VERB; V P n

**dis|pens|er** /dɪspensəʳ/ **(dispensers)** A **dispenser** is a machine or container designed so that you can get an item or quantity of something from it in an easy and convenient way. ❑ *...cash dispensers.*
N-COUNT: oft n N

**dis|per|sal** /dɪspɜːʳsəl/ [1] **Dispersal** is the spreading of things over a wide area. ❑ *Plants have different mechanisms of **dispersal** for their spores.*
N-UNCOUNT = *distribution*
[2] The **dispersal of** a crowd involves splitting it up and making the people leave in different directions. ❑ *The police ordered the dispersal of the crowds gathered round the building.*
N-UNCOUNT: oft N *of* n

**dis|perse** /dɪspɜːʳs/ **(disperses, dispersing, dispersed)** [1] When something **disperses** or when you **disperse** it, it spreads over a wide area. ❑ *The oil appeared to be dispersing... The intense currents disperse the sewage.*
VERB; V; V n
[2] When a group of people **disperses** or when someone **disperses** them, the group splits up and the people leave in different directions. ❑ *Police fired shots and used teargas to disperse the demonstrators... The crowd dispersed peacefully after prayers.*
VERB = *break up*; V n; V

**dis|persed** /dɪspɜːʳst/ Things that are **dispersed** are situated in many different places, a long way apart from each other. ❑ *...his widely dispersed businesses.*
ADJ = *scattered*

**dis|per|sion** /dɪspɜːʳʃən/ **Dispersion** is the spreading of people or things over a wide area. [FORMAL] ❑ *The threat will force greater dispersion of their forces.*
N-UNCOUNT: oft N *of* n

**dis|pir|it|ed** /dɪspɪrɪtɪd/ If you are **dispirited**, you have lost your enthusiasm and excitement. ❑ *I left eventually at six o'clock feeling utterly dispirited and depressed.*
ADJ = *dejected*

**dis|pir|it|ing** /dɪspɪrɪtɪŋ/ Something that is **dispiriting** causes you to lose your enthusiasm and excitement. ❑ *It's very dispiriting for anyone to be out of a job.*
ADJ = *disheartening*

**dis|place** /dɪspleɪs/ **(displaces, displacing, displaced)** [1] If one thing **displaces** another, it forces the other thing out of its place, position, or role, and then occupies that place, position, or role itself. ❑ *These factories have displaced tourism as the country's largest source of foreign exchange.*
VERB; V n
[2] If a person or group of people **is displaced**, they are forced to moved away from the area where they live. ❑ *In Europe alone thirty million people were displaced. ...the task of resettling refugees and displaced persons.*
VERB: usu passive; *be* V-ed; V-ed

**dis|placed per|son (displaced persons)** A **displaced person** is someone who has been forced to leave the place where they live, especially because of a war.
N-COUNT

**dis|place|ment** /dɪspleɪsmənt/ [1] **Displacement** is the removal of something from its usual place or position by something which then occupies that place or position. [FORMAL] ❑ *...the displacement of all my energy into caring for the baby.*
N-UNCOUNT
[2] **Displacement** is the forcing of people away from the area or country where they live.
N-UNCOUNT

**dis|play** /dɪspleɪ/ **(displays, displaying, displayed)** ◆◆◇ [1] If you **display** something that you want people to see, you put it in a particular place, so that people can see it easily. ❑ *Among the protesters and war veterans proudly displaying their medals was Aubrey Rose.* ♦ **Display** is also a noun. ❑ *Most of the other artists whose work is on display were his pupils or colleagues.*
VERB = *exhibit*; V n; N-UNCOUNT: oft *on* N
[2] If you **display** something, you show it to people. ❑ *She displayed her wound to the twelve gentlemen of the jury... The chart can then display the links connecting these groups.*
VERB = *show*; V n *to* n; V n
[3] If you **display** a characteristic, quality, or emotion, you behave in a way which shows that you have it. ❑ *He has displayed remarkable courage in his efforts to reform the party.* ♦ **Display** is also a noun. ❑ *Normally, such an outward display of affection is reserved for his mother.*
VERB = *show*; V n; N-VAR: oft N *of* n = *show*
[4] When a computer **displays** information, it shows it on a screen. ❑ *They started out by looking at the computer*
VERB; V n

*screens which display the images.* [5] A **display** is an arrangement of things that have been put in a particular place, so that people can see them easily. ❑ *...a display of your work.* [6] A **display** is a public performance or other event which is intended to entertain people. ❑ *...gymnastic displays.* [7] The **display** on a computer screen is the information that is shown there. The screen itself can also be referred to as the **display**. ❑ *A hard copy of the screen display can also be obtained from a printer.* → See also **liquid crystal display**.
N-COUNT: oft N *of* n
N-COUNT: with supp
N-COUNT: usu sing

**dis|please** /dɪspliːz/ **(displeases, displeasing, displeased)** If something or someone **displeases** you, they make you annoyed or rather angry. ❑ *Not wishing to displease her, he avoided answering the question.*
VERB
V n

**dis|pleased** /dɪspliːzd/ If you are **displeased with** something, you are annoyed or rather angry about it. ❑ *Businessmen are displeased with erratic economic policy-making.*
ADJ: v-link ADJ, oft ADJ *with/at* n, ADJ to-inf

**dis|pleas|ure** /dɪspleʒəʳ/ Someone's **displeasure** is a feeling of annoyance that they have about something that has happened. ❑ *The population has already begun to show its displeasure at the slow pace of change.*
N-UNCOUNT: oft poss N, N *with/at* n

**dis|port** /dɪspɔːʳt/ **(disports, disporting, disported)** If you **disport yourself** somewhere, you amuse yourself there in a happy and energetic way. [HUMOROUS or OLD-FASHIONED] ❑ *...the rich and famous disporting themselves in glamorous places.*
VERB
V pron-refl prep/adv

**dis|pos|able** /dɪspoʊzəbᵊl/ **(disposables)** [1] A **disposable** product is designed to be thrown away after it has been used. ❑ *...disposable nappies suitable for babies up to 8lb.* ♦ Disposable products can be referred to as **disposables**. ❑ *It's estimated that around 80 per cent of babies wear disposables.* [2] Your **disposable** income is the amount of income you have left after you have paid income tax and social security charges. ❑ *Gerald had little disposable income.*
ADJ: usu ADJ n
N-COUNT: usu pl
ADJ: ADJ n

**dis|pos|al** /dɪspoʊzᵊl/ [1] If you have something **at** your **disposal**, you are able to use it whenever you want, and for whatever purpose you want. If you say that you are **at** someone's **disposal**, you mean that you are willing to help them in any way you can. ❑ *Do you have this information at your disposal?... If I can be of service, I am at your disposal.* [2] **Disposal** is the act of getting rid of something that is no longer wanted or needed. ❑ *...methods for the permanent disposal of radioactive wastes.*
PHRASE: usu PHR after v, v-link PHR
N-UNCOUNT: oft n N, N *of* n

**dis|pose** /dɪspoʊz/ **(disposes, disposing, disposed)**

♦ **dispose of** [1] If you **dispose of** something that you no longer want or need, you throw it away. ❑ *...the safest means of disposing of nuclear waste.* [2] If you **dispose of** a problem, task, or question, you deal with it. ❑ *You did us a great favour by disposing of that problem.*
PHRASAL VERB
V P n
PHRASAL VERB = resolve
V P n

**dis|posed** /dɪspoʊzd/ [1] If you are **disposed to** do something, you are willing or eager to do it. [FORMAL] ❑ *I might have been disposed to like him in other circumstances.* [2] You can use **disposed** when you are talking about someone's general attitude or opinion. For example, if you are well or favourably **disposed to** someone or something, you like them or approve of them. [FORMAL] ❑ *I saw that the publishers were well disposed towards my book.*
ADJ: v-link ADJ to-inf = inclined
ADJ: adv ADJ, usu v-link ADJ, usu ADJ *to/towards* n

**dis|po|si|tion** /dɪspəzɪʃᵊn/ **(dispositions)** [1] Someone's **disposition** is the way that they tend to behave or feel. ❑ *The rides are unsuitable for people of a nervous disposition.* [2] A **disposition to** do something is a willingness to do it. [FORMAL] ❑ *This has given him a disposition to consider our traditions critically.* [3] If you refer to **the disposition of** a number of objects, you mean the pattern in which they are arranged or their positions in relation to each other. [FORMAL] [4] The **disposition of** money or property is the act of giving or distributing it to a number of people. [LEGAL] ❑ *Judge Stacks was appointed to oversee the disposition of funds.*
N-COUNT: usu supp N = nature
N-SING: usu N to-inf = inclination
N-SING: *the* N *of* n = arrangement
N-COUNT: N *of* n = distribution

**dis|pos|sess** /dɪspəzes/ **(dispossesses, dispossessing, dispossessed)** If you **are dispossessed of** something that you own, especially land or buildings, it is taken away from you. ❑ *...people who were dispossessed of their land under apartheid... They settled the land, dispossessing many of its original inhabitants... Droves of dispossessed people emigrated to Canada.*
VERB
*be* V-ed *of* n
V n
V-ed
Also V n *of/from* n

**dis|pro|por|tion** /dɪsprəpɔːʳʃᵊn/ **(disproportions)** A **disproportion** is a state in which two things are unequal. [FORMAL] ❑ *...a disproportion in the legal resources available to the two sides.*
N-VAR = imbalance

**dis|pro|por|tion|ate** /dɪsprəpɔːʳʃənət/ Something that is **disproportionate** is surprising or unreasonable in amount or size, compared with something else. ❑ *A disproportionate amount of time was devoted to one topic.* ♦ **dis|pro|por|tion|ate|ly** *...a disproportionately high suicide rate among young prisoners.*
ADJ: oft ADJ *to* n = excessive ≠ proportionate
ADV: ADV group, ADV with v

**dis|prove** /dɪspruːv/ **(disproves, disproving, disproved, disproven)** To **disprove** an idea, belief, or theory means to show that it is not true. ❑ *The statistics to prove or disprove his hypothesis will take years to collect.*
VERB = refute ≠ prove
V n

**dis|pu|ta|tion** /dɪspjʊteɪʃᵊn/ **(disputations)** **Disputation** is discussion on a subject which people cannot agree about. [FORMAL] ❑ *After much legal disputation our right to resign was established.*
N-VAR = debate

**dis|pute** /dɪspjuːt/ **(disputes, disputing, disputed)** ♦♦◇ [1] A **dispute** is an argument or disagreement between people or groups. ❑ *They have won previous pay disputes with the government.* [2] If you **dispute** a fact, statement, or theory, you say that it is incorrect or untrue. ❑ *He disputed the allegations... Nobody disputed that Davey was clever... Some economists disputed whether consumer spending is as strong as the figures suggest.* [3] When people **dispute** something, they fight for control or ownership of it. You can also say that one group of people **dispute** something with another group. ❑ *Russia and Ukraine have been disputing the ownership of the fleet... Fishermen from Bristol disputed fishing rights with the Danes. ...a disputed border region.*
N-VAR: usu with supp, oft N *with/over* n, N *between* pl-n
VERB
V n
V that
V wh
V-RECIP
pl-n V n
V n *with* n
V-ed

PHRASES [4] If two or more people or groups are **in dispute**, they are arguing or disagreeing about something. ❑ *The two countries are in dispute over the boundaries of their coastal waters.* [5] If something is **in dispute**, people are questioning it or arguing about it. ❑ *All those matters are in dispute and it is not for me to decide them.*
PHRASE: v-link PHR, oft PHR *with* n, PHR *over* n
PHRASE: v-link PHR

**dis|quali|fy** /dɪskwɒlɪfaɪ/ **(disqualifies, disqualifying, disqualified)** When someone **is disqualified**, they are officially stopped from taking part in a particular event, activity, or competition, usually because they have done something wrong. ❑ *He was convicted of corruption, and will be disqualified from office for seven years... The stewards conferred and eventually decided to disqualify us.* ♦ **dis|quali|fi|ca|tion** /dɪskwɒlɪfɪkeɪʃᵊn/ **(disqualifications)** *Livingston faces a four-year disqualification from athletics.*
VERB
*be* V-ed *from* n
V n
Also V n *from* n
N-VAR: oft with poss

**dis|qui|et** /dɪskwaɪət/ **(disquiets, disquieting, disquieted)** [1] **Disquiet** is a feeling of worry or anxiety. [FORMAL] ❑ *There is growing public disquiet about the cost of such policing.* [2] If something **disquiets** you, it makes you feel anxious. [FORMAL] ❑ *This information disquieted him.* ♦ **dis|qui|et|ing** *He found her letter disquieting.*
N-UNCOUNT = uneasiness
VERB
V n
ADJ

**dis|qui|si|tion** /dɪskwɪzɪʃᵊn/ **(disquisitions)** A **disquisition** is a detailed explanation of a particular subject. [FORMAL] ❑ *Amanda launched into an authoritative disquisition about contracts.*
N-VAR

**dis|re|gard** /dɪsrɪgɑːʳd/ **(disregards, disregarding, disregarded)** If you **disregard** something, you ignore it or do not take account of it. ❑ *He disregarded the advice of his executives.* ♦ **Disregard**
VERB
V n
N-UNCOUNT

is also a noun. ❑ *Whoever planted the bomb showed a total disregard for the safety of the public.*

**dis|re|pair** /dɪsrɪpeəʳ/ If something is **in disrepair** or is **in a state of disrepair**, it is broken or in bad condition. ❑ *The house was unoccupied and in a bad state of disrepair.* PHRASE: usu v-link PHR

**dis|repu|table** /dɪsrepjʊtəbᵊl/ If you say that someone or something is **disreputable**, you are critical of them because they are not respectable or cannot be trusted. ❑ *...the noisiest and most disreputable bars.* ADJ [disapproval]

**dis|re|pute** /dɪsrɪpjuːt/ If something **is brought into disrepute** or **falls into disrepute**, it loses its good reputation, because it is connected with activities that people do not approve of. ❑ *Such people bring our profession into disrepute.* PHRASE: PHR after v, v-link PHR

**dis|re|spect** /dɪsrɪspekt/ [1] If someone shows **disrespect**, they speak or behave in a way that shows lack of respect for a person, law, or custom. ❑ *...young people with complete disrespect for authority.* N-UNCOUNT: also a N, oft N *for* n ≠ respect [2] You can say **'no disrespect to** someone or something' when you are just about to criticize them, in order to indicate that you are not hostile towards them or admire them for other things. ❑ *No disrespect to John Beck, but the club has been happier since he left.* PHRASE: usu PHR *to* n

**dis|re|spect|ful** /dɪsrɪspektfʊl/ If you are **disrespectful**, you show no respect in the way that you speak or behave to someone. ❑ *...accusations that he had been disrespectful to the Queen.* ADJ: oft ADJ *to/of* n ≠ respectful ♦ **dis|re|spect|ful|ly** *They get angry if they think they are being treated disrespectfully.* ADV: ADV with v

**dis|robe** /dɪsroʊb/ (**disrobes, disrobing, disrobed**) When someone **disrobes**, they remove their clothes. [FORMAL] ❑ *She stood up and began to disrobe, folding each garment neatly.* VERB = undress V

**dis|rupt** /dɪsrʌpt/ (**disrupts, disrupting, disrupted**) If someone or something **disrupts** an event, system, or process, they cause difficulties that prevent it from continuing or operating in a normal way. ❑ *Anti-war protesters disrupted the debate.* VERB V n

**dis|rup|tion** /dɪsrʌpʃᵊn/ (**disruptions**) When there is **disruption** of an event, system, or process, it is prevented from continuing or operating in a normal way. ❑ *The strike is expected to cause delays and disruption to flights from Britain.* N-VAR

**dis|rup|tive** /dɪsrʌptɪv/ To be **disruptive** means to prevent something from continuing or operating in a normal way. ❑ *Alcohol can produce violent, disruptive behavior.* ADJ

**dis|rup|tive tech|nol|ogy** (**disruptive technologies**) A **disruptive technology** is a new technology, such as computers and the Internet, which has a rapid and major effect on technologies that existed before. [BUSINESS] ❑ *...the other great disruptive technologies of the 20th century, such as electricity, the telephone and the car.* N-COUNT

**diss** /dɪs/ (**disses, dissing, dissed**) If someone **disses** you, they criticize you unfairly or speak to you in a way that does not show respect. [INFORMAL] ❑ *He believes that his records speak for themselves and ignores those who diss him.* VERB V n

**dis|sat|is|fac|tion** /dɪssætɪsfækʃᵊn/ (**dissatisfactions**) If you feel **dissatisfaction with** something, you are not contented or pleased with it. ❑ *She has already expressed her dissatisfaction with this aspect of the policy.* N-VAR: oft N *with* n ≠ satisfaction

**dis|sat|is|fied** /dɪssætɪsfaɪd/ If you are **dissatisfied with** something, you are not contented or pleased with it. ❑ *82% of voters are dissatisfied with the way their country is being governed.* ADJ: oft ADJ *with* n

**dis|sect** /daɪsekt, dɪ-/ (**dissects, dissecting, dissected**) [1] If someone **dissects** the body of a dead person or animal, they carefully cut it up in order to examine it scientifically. ❑ *We dissected a frog in biology class.* VERB V n ♦ **dis|sec|tion** /daɪsekʃᵊn, dɪ-/ (**dissections**) *Researchers need a growing supply of corpses for dissection.* N-VAR [2] If someone **dissects** something such as a theory, a situation, or a piece of writing, they consider and talk about each detail of it. ❑ *People want to dissect his work and question his motives.* VERB V n ♦ **dis|sec|tion** (**dissections**) *...her calm, condescending dissection of my proposals.* N-VAR: usu N *of* n

**dis|sem|ble** /dɪsembᵊl/ (**dissembles, dissembling, dissembled**) When people **dissemble**, they hide their real intentions or emotions. [LITERARY] ❑ *Henry was not slow to dissemble when it served his purposes.* VERB V Also V n

**dis|semi|nate** /dɪsemɪneɪt/ (**disseminates, disseminating, disseminated**) To **disseminate** information or knowledge means to distribute it so that it reaches many people or organizations. [FORMAL] ❑ *They disseminated anti-French propaganda.* VERB = propagate V n ♦ **dis|semi|na|tion** /dɪsemɪneɪʃᵊn/ *He promoted the dissemination of scientific ideas.* N-UNCOUNT: usu N *of* n

**dis|sen|sion** /dɪsenʃᵊn/ (**dissensions**) **Dissension** is disagreement and argument. [FORMAL] ❑ *The tax cut issue has caused dissension among administration officials.* N-UNCOUNT: also N in pl = discord

**dis|sent** /dɪsent/ (**dissents, dissenting, dissented**) [1] **Dissent** is strong disagreement or dissatisfaction with a decision or opinion, especially one that is supported by most people or by people in authority. ❑ *He is the toughest military ruler yet and has responded harshly to any dissent.* N-UNCOUNT [2] If you **dissent**, you express disagreement with a decision or opinion, especially one that is supported by most people or by people in authority. [FORMAL] ❑ *Just one of the 10 members dissented... No one dissents from the decision to unify... There are likely to be many dissenting voices.* VERB V V *from* n V-ing

**dis|sent|er** /dɪsentəʳ/ (**dissenters**) **Dissenters** are people who say that they do not agree with something that other people agree with or that is official policy. ❑ *The Party does not tolerate dissenters in its ranks.* N-COUNT

**dis|ser|ta|tion** /dɪsəʳteɪʃᵊn/ (**dissertations**) A **dissertation** is a long formal piece of writing on a particular subject, especially for a university degree. ❑ *He is currently writing a dissertation on the Somali civil war.* N-COUNT: oft N *on* n

**dis|ser|vice** /dɪssɜːʳvɪs/ If you **do** someone or something **a disservice**, you harm them in some way. [FORMAL] ❑ *He said the protesters were doing a disservice to the nation.* N-SING: oft N *to* n

**dis|si|dent** /dɪsɪdənt/ (**dissidents**) [1] **Dissidents** are people who disagree with and criticize their government, especially because it is undemocratic. ❑ *...political dissidents.* N-COUNT [2] **Dissident** people disagree with or criticize their government or a powerful organization they belong to. ❑ *...a dissident Russian novelist.* ADJ: ADJ n

**dis|simi|lar** /dɪsɪmɪləʳ/ If one thing is **dissimilar to** another, or if two things are **dissimilar**, they are very different from each other. ❑ *His methods were not dissimilar to those used by Freud.* ADJ: oft ADJ *to* n ≠ similar ♦ **dis|simi|lar|ity** /dɪsɪmɪlærɪti/ (**dissimilarities**) *One of his main themes is the dissimilarity between parents and children.* N-VAR: oft N *between* pl-n

**dis|simu|late** /dɪsɪmjʊleɪt/ (**dissimulates, dissimulating, dissimulated**) When people **dissimulate**, they hide their true feelings, intentions, or nature. [FORMAL] ❑ *This man was too injured to dissimulate well... They were decked out in tracksuits, seemingly to dissimulate their true function.* VERB = dissemble V V n

**dis|si|pate** /dɪsɪpeɪt/ (**dissipates, dissipating, dissipated**) [1] When something **dissipates** or when you **dissipate** it, it becomes less or becomes less strong until it disappears or goes away completely. [FORMAL] ❑ *The tension in the room had dissipated... He wound down the windows to dissipate the heat.* VERB V V n [2] When someone **dissipates** money, time, or effort, they waste it in a foolish way. [FORMAL] ❑ *He is dissipating his time and energy on too many different things.* VERB V n

**dis|si|pat|ed** /dɪsɪpeɪtɪd/ If you describe someone as **dissipated**, you disapprove of them because they spend a lot of time drinking alcohol ADJ [disapproval] = dissolute and enjoying other physical pleasures, and are probably unhealthy because of this. ❑ *Flynn was still handsome, though dissipated.*

**dis|si|pa|tion** /dɪsɪpeɪʃᵊn/ If someone leads a dissipated life, you can also say that they lead a life of **dissipation**. [LITERARY] N-UNCOUNT = debauchery

**dis|so|ci|ate** /dɪsoʊʃieɪt/ **(dissociates, dissociating, dissociated)** 1 If you **dissociate yourself from** something or someone, you say or show that you are not connected with them, usually in order to avoid trouble or blame. ❑ *It is getting harder for the president to dissociate himself from the scandal.* 2 If you **dissociate** one thing **from** another, you consider the two things as separate from each other, or you separate them. [FORMAL] ❑ *Almost the first lesson they learn is how to dissociate emotion from reason.* ♦ **dis|so|cia|tion** /dɪsoʊsieɪʃᵊn/ *The war between the sexes should not result in their complete dissociation from one another.* VERB; V pron-refl from n; VERB = divorce; V n from n; N-UNCOUNT: oft N from n

**dis|so|lute** /dɪsəluːt/ Someone who is **dissolute** does not care at all about morals and lives in a way that is considered to be wicked and immoral. ADJ disapproval = degenerate

**dis|so|lu|tion** /dɪsəluːʃᵊn/ 1 **Dissolution** is the act of breaking up officially an organization or institution, or of formally ending a parliament. [FORMAL] ❑ *Politicians say it could lead to a dissolution of parliament.* 2 **Dissolution** is the act of officially ending a formal agreement, for example a marriage or a business arrangement. [FORMAL] ❑ *...the statutory requirement for granting dissolution of a marriage.* N-UNCOUNT: also a N, oft N of n; N-UNCOUNT: also a N, oft N of n = termination

**dis|solve** /dɪzɒlv/ **(dissolves, dissolving, dissolved)** 1 If a substance **dissolves** in liquid or if you **dissolve** it, it becomes mixed with the liquid and disappears. ❑ *Heat gently until the sugar dissolves... Dissolve the salt in a little boiled water.* 2 When an organization or institution **is dissolved**, it is officially ended or broken up. ❑ *The committee has been dissolved... The King agreed to dissolve the present commission.* 3 When a parliament **is dissolved**, it is formally ended, so that elections for a new parliament can be held. ❑ *The present assembly will be dissolved on April 30th... Kaifu threatened to dissolve the Parliament and call an election.* 4 When a marriage or business arrangement **is dissolved**, it is officially ended. ❑ *The marriage was dissolved in 1976.* 5 If something such as a problem or feeling **dissolves** or **is dissolved**, it becomes weaker and disappears. ❑ *His new-found optimism dissolved... Lenny still could not dissolve the nagging lump of tension in his chest.* VERB; V; V n; VERB; be V-ed; V n; VERB; be V-ed; V n; VERB: usu passive be V-ed; VERB = dissipate; V; V n

♦ **dissolve into** If you **dissolve into** or **dissolve in** tears or laughter, you begin to cry or laugh, because you cannot control yourself. ❑ *She dissolved into tears at the mention of Munya's name.* PHRASAL VERB; V P n

**dis|so|nance** /dɪsənəns/ **Dissonance** is a lack of agreement or harmony between things. [FORMAL] N-UNCOUNT = discord

**dis|suade** /dɪsweɪd/ **(dissuades, dissuading, dissuaded)** If you **dissuade** someone **from** doing or believing something, you persuade them not to do or believe it. [FORMAL] ❑ *Doctors had tried to dissuade patients from smoking... He considered emigrating, but his family managed to dissuade him.* VERB; V n from -ing/n; V n

**dis|tance** /dɪstəns/ **(distances, distancing, distanced)** ◆◆◇ 1 The **distance between** two points or places is the amount of space between them. ❑ *...the distance between the island and the nearby shore... Everything is within walking distance.* 2 When two things are very far apart, you talk about the **distance** between them. ❑ *The distance wouldn't be a problem.* 3 **Distance** learning or **distance** education involves studying at home and sending your work to a college or university, rather than attending the college or university in person. ❑ *I'm doing a theology degree by distance learning.* 4 When you want to emphasize that two people or things do not have a close relationship or are not the same, you can refer to the **distance between** them. ❑ *There was a vast distance between psychological clues and concrete proof.* 5 If you can see something **in the distance**, you can see it, far away from you. ❑ *We suddenly saw her in the distance.* 6 **Distance** is coolness or unfriendliness in the way that someone behaves towards you. [FORMAL] ❑ *There were periods of sulking, of pronounced distance, of coldness.* 7 If you **distance yourself from** a person or thing, or if something **distances** you **from** them, you feel less friendly or positive towards them, or become less involved with them. ❑ *The author distanced himself from some of the comments in his book... Television may actually be distancing the public from the war.* ♦ **dis|tanced** *Clough felt he'd become too distanced from his fans.* N-VAR: with supp, oft N between pl-n; N-UNCOUNT; ADJ: ADJ n; N-UNCOUNT: usu N between pl-n emphasis; N-SING: in/into the N; N-UNCOUNT: usu with supp ≠ closeness; VERB; V pron-refl from n; V n from n; ADJ: v-link ADJ, ADJ from n

PHRASES 8 If you are **at a distance** from something, or if you see it or remember it **from a distance**, you are a long way away from it in space or time. ❑ *The only way I can cope with my mother is at a distance... Now I can look back on the whole tragedy from a distance of forty years.* 9 If you **keep** your **distance** from someone or something or **keep** them **at a distance**, you do not become involved with them. ❑ *Jay had always tended to keep his girlfriends at a distance.* 10 If you **keep** your **distance** from someone or something, you do not get physically close to them. [OLD-FASHIONED] ❑ *He walked towards the doorway, careful to keep his distance.* PHRASE: PHR after v, v-link PHR; PHRASE: V inflects; PHRASE: V inflects

**dis|tant** /dɪstənt/ 1 **Distant** means very far away. ❑ *The mountains rolled away to a distant horizon. ...the war in that distant land.* 2 You use **distant** to describe a time or event that is very far away in the future or in the past. ❑ *There is little doubt, however, that things will improve in the not too distant future.* 3 A **distant** relative is one who you are not closely related to. ❑ *He's a distant relative of the mayor.* ♦ **dis|tant|ly** *His father's distantly related to the Royal family.* 4 If you describe someone as **distant**, you mean that you find them cold and unfriendly. ❑ *He found her cold, ice-like and distant.* 5 If you describe someone as **distant**, you mean that they are not concentrating on what they are doing because they are thinking about other things. ❑ *There was a distant look in her eyes from time to time, her thoughts elsewhere.* ADJ: usu ADJ n ≠ nearby; ADJ: usu ADJ n = faraway ≠ near; ADJ: usu ADJ n ≠ close; ADV: usu ADV -ed; ADJ: v-link ADJ = aloof; ADJ = faraway

**dis|tant|ly** /dɪstəntli/ 1 **Distantly** means very far away. [LITERARY] ❑ *Distantly, to her right, she could make out the town of Chiffa.* 2 If you are **distantly** aware of something or if you **distantly** remember it, you are aware of it or remember it, but not very strongly. ❑ *She became distantly aware that the light had grown brighter.* 3 → See also **distant**. ADV: ADV -ed, ADV with cl; ADV: ADV adj, ADV with v = vaguely ≠ distinctly

**dis|taste** /dɪsteɪst/ If you feel **distaste for** someone or something, you dislike them and consider them to be unpleasant, disgusting, or immoral. ❑ *He professed a distaste for everything related to money.* N-UNCOUNT: oft N for n = aversion

**dis|taste|ful** /dɪsteɪstfʊl/ If something is **distasteful to** you, you think it is unpleasant, disgusting, or immoral. ❑ *He found it distasteful to be offered drinks before witnessing the execution.* ADJ: oft ADJ to n

**dis|tem|per** /dɪstempəʳ/ 1 **Distemper** is a dangerous and infectious disease that can be caught by animals, especially dogs. 2 **Distemper** is a kind of paint sometimes used for painting walls. N-UNCOUNT; N-UNCOUNT

**dis|tend** /dɪstend/ **(distends, distending, distended)** If a part of your body **is distended**, or if it **distends**, it becomes swollen and unnaturally large. [MEDICAL or FORMAL] ❑ *Through this incision, the abdominal cavity is distended with carbon dioxide gas... The colon, or large intestine, distends and fills with gas.* ♦ **dis|tend|ed** *...an infant with a distended belly.* VERB = swell; be V-ed; V; Also V n; ADJ

**dis|ten|sion** /dɪstenʃᵊn/ also **distention. Distension** is abnormal swelling in a person's or animal's body. [MEDICAL] N-UNCOUNT

**dis|til** /dɪstɪl/ **(distils, distilling, distilled)**

in AM, use **distill**

1 If a liquid such as whisky or water **is distilled**, it is heated until it changes into steam or vapour and then cooled until it becomes liquid again. This is usually done in order to make it pure. ❑ *The whisky had been distilled in 1926 and sat quietly maturing until 1987... You can't actually drink the water from the marshland. But you can distil it.* ♦ **dis|til|la|tion** /dɪstɪleɪʃən/ *Any faults in the original cider stood out sharply after distillation.* 2 If an oil or liquid **is distilled from** a plant, it is produced by a process which extracts the most essential part of the plant. To **distil** a plant means to produce an oil or liquid from it by this process. ❑ *The oil is distilled from the berries of this small tree. ...the art of distilling rose petals.* ♦ **dis|til|la|tion** *...the distillation of rose petals to produce rosewater.* 3 If a thought or idea **is distilled from** previous thoughts, ideas, or experiences, it comes from them. If it **is distilled into** something, it becomes part of that thing. ❑ *Reviews are distilled from articles previously published in the main column... Roy distills these messages into something powerful.* ♦ **dis|til|la|tion** *The material below is a distillation of his work.*

VERB; be V-ed; V n; N-UNCOUNT; VERB; be V-ed *from* n; V n; N-UNCOUNT: usu N *of* n; VERB; be V-ed *from* n; V n *into* n; N-SING: usu N *of* n

**dis|till|er** /dɪstɪlər/ **(distillers)** A **distiller** is a person or a company that makes whisky or a similar strong alcoholic drink by a process of distilling. N-COUNT

**dis|till|ery** /dɪstɪləri/ **(distilleries)** A **distillery** is a place where whisky or a similar strong alcoholic drink is made by a process of distilling. N-COUNT

**dis|tinct** /dɪstɪŋkt/ 1 If something is **distinct from** something else of the same type, it is different or separate from it. ❑ *Engineering and technology are disciplines distinct from one another and from science... This book is divided into two distinct parts.* ♦ **dis|tinct|ly** *...a banking industry with two distinctly different sectors.* 2 If something is **distinct**, you can hear, see, or taste it clearly. ❑ *...to impart a distinct flavor with a minimum of cooking fat.* ♦ **dis|tinct|ly** *I distinctly heard the loudspeaker calling passengers for the Turin-Amsterdam flight.* 3 If an idea, thought, or intention is **distinct**, it is clear and definite. ❑ *Now that Tony was no longer present, there was a distinct change in her attitude.* ♦ **dis|tinct|ly** *I distinctly remember wishing I had not got involved.* 4 You can use **distinct** to emphasize that something is great enough in amount or degree to be noticeable or important. ❑ *Being 6ft 3in tall has some distinct disadvantages!* ♦ **dis|tinct|ly** *His government is looking distinctly shaky.* 5 If you say that you are talking about one thing **as distinct from** another, you are indicating exactly which thing you mean. ❑ *There's a lot of evidence that oily fish, as distinct from fatty meat, has a beneficial effect.*

ADJ: oft ADJ *from* n; ADV: ADV adj; ADJ; ADV: ADV with v; ADJ: usu ADJ n; ADV: ADV with v; ADJ: ADJ n; emphasis; = definite; ADV: ADV adj/-ed; PREP-PHRASE

**dis|tinc|tion** /dɪstɪŋkʃən/ **(distinctions)** 1 A **distinction between** similar things is a difference. ❑ *There are obvious distinctions between the two wine-making areas.* ● If you **draw a distinction** or **make a distinction**, you say that two things are different. ❑ *I did not yet make a distinction between the pleasures of reading and of writing fiction.* 2 **Distinction** is the quality of being very good or better than other things of the same type. [FORMAL] ❑ *Lewis emerges as a composer of distinction and sensitivity.* 3 A **distinction** is a special award or honour that is given to someone because of their very high level of achievement. ❑ *The order was created in 1902 as a special distinction for eminent men and women.* 4 If you say that someone or something has **the distinction of** being something, you are drawing attention to the fact that they have the special quality of being that thing. **Distinction** is normally used to refer to good qualities, but can sometimes also be used to refer to bad qualities. ❑ *He has the distinction of being regarded as the Federal Republic's greatest living writer.*

N-COUNT: usu N *between* pl-n; PHRASE: V inflects, usu PHR *between* pl-n; N-UNCOUNT; N-COUNT = honour; N-SING: oft *the* N *of* n/-ing

**dis|tinc|tive** /dɪstɪŋktɪv/ Something that is **distinctive** has a special quality or feature which makes it easily recognizable and different from other things of the same type. ❑ *His voice was very distinctive.* ♦ **dis|tinc|tive|ly** *...the distinctively fragrant taste of elderflowers.* ♦ **dis|tinc|tive|ness** *His own distinctiveness was always evident at school.*

ADJ; ADV: ADV adj/-ed; N-UNCOUNT: oft with poss

**dis|tin|guish** /dɪstɪŋgwɪʃ/ **(distinguishes, distinguishing, distinguished)** 1 If you can **distinguish** one thing **from** another or **distinguish between** two things, you can see or understand how they are different. ❑ *Could he distinguish right from wrong?... Research suggests that babies learn to see by distinguishing between areas of light and dark... It is necessary to distinguish the policies of two successive governments.* 2 A feature or quality that **distinguishes** one thing **from** another causes the two things to be regarded as different, because only the first thing has the feature or quality. ❑ *There is something about music that distinguishes it from all other art forms... The bird has no distinguishing features.* 3 If you can **distinguish** something, you can see, hear, or taste it although it is very difficult to detect. [FORMAL] ❑ *There were cries, calls. He could distinguish voices.* 4 If you **distinguish yourself**, you do something that makes you famous or important. ❑ *He distinguished himself as a leading constitutional scholar... They distinguished themselves at the Battle of Assaye.*

VERB; V n *from* n; V *between* pl-n; V pl-n; VERB; V n *from* n; V-ing; VERB = discern; V n; VERB; V pron-refl *as* n; V pron-refl

**dis|tin|guish|able** /dɪstɪŋgwɪʃəbəl/ 1 If something is **distinguishable from** other things, it has a quality or feature which makes it possible for you to recognize it and see that it is different. ❑ *...features that make their products distinguishable from those of their rivals.* 2 If something is **distinguishable**, you can see or hear it in conditions when it is difficult to see or hear anything. ❑ *It was getting light and shapes were distinguishable.*

ADJ: usu v-link ADJ, oft ADJ *from* n; ADJ: v-link ADJ = discernible

**dis|tin|guished** /dɪstɪŋgwɪʃt/ 1 If you describe a person or their work as **distinguished**, you mean that they have been very successful in their career and have a good reputation. ❑ *...a distinguished academic family.* 2 If you describe someone as **distinguished**, you mean that they look very noble and respectable. ❑ *He looked very distinguished.*

ADJ = illustrious; ADJ

**dis|tort** /dɪstɔːrt/ **(distorts, distorting, distorted)** 1 If you **distort** a statement, fact, or idea, you report or represent it in an untrue way. ❑ *The media distorts reality; categorises people as all good or all bad.* ♦ **dis|tort|ed** *These figures give a distorted view of the significance for the local economy.* 2 If something you can see or hear **is distorted** or **distorts**, its appearance or sound is changed so that it seems unclear. ❑ *A painter may exaggerate or distort shapes and forms... This caused the sound to distort.* ♦ **dis|tort|ed** *Sound was becoming more and more distorted through the use of hearing aids.*

VERB; V n; ADJ; VERB; V n; V; ADJ

**dis|tor|tion** /dɪstɔːrʃən/ **(distortions)** 1 **Distortion** is the changing of something into something that is not true or not acceptable. ❑ *I think it would be a gross distortion of reality to say that they were motivated by self-interest.* 2 **Distortion** is the changing of the appearance or sound of something in a way that makes it seem strange or unclear. ❑ *Audio signals can be transmitted along cables without distortion.*

N-VAR: usu with supp; disapproval; N-VAR

**dis|tract** /dɪstrækt/ **(distracts, distracting, distracted)** If something **distracts** you or your attention **from** something, it takes your attention away from it. ❑ *Tom admits that playing video games sometimes distracts him from his homework... Don't let yourself be distracted by fashionable theories... A disturbance in the street distracted my attention.*

VERB; V n *from* n; be V-ed; V n

**dis|tract|ed** /dɪstræktɪd/ If you are **distracted**, you are not concentrating on something because you are worried or are thinking about something else. ❑ *She had seemed curiously distracted.* ♦ **dis|tract|ed|ly** *He looked up distractedly. 'Be with you in a second.'*

ADJ; ADV: ADV with v

**dis|tract|ing** /dɪstræktɪŋ/ If you say that something is **distracting**, you mean that it makes it difficult for you to concentrate properly on what you are doing. ❑ *It's distracting to have someone watching me while I work.* ADJ

**dis|trac|tion** /dɪstrækʃən/ **(distractions)** [1] A **distraction** is something that turns your attention away from something you want to concentrate on. ❑ *Total concentration is required with no distractions.* N-VAR: oft N *from* n [2] A **distraction** is an activity which is intended to entertain and amuse you. ❑ *Their national distraction is going to the disco.* N-COUNT = diversion [3] If you say that something or someone **drives** you **to distraction**, you are emphasizing that they annoy you a great deal. ❑ *A very clingy child can drive a parent to distraction.* PHRASE: V inflects [emphasis]

**dis|traught** /dɪstrɔːt/ If someone is **distraught**, they are so upset and worried that they cannot think clearly. ❑ *His distraught parents were being comforted by relatives.* ADJ

**dis|tress** /dɪstres/ **(distresses, distressing, distressed)** [1] **Distress** is a state of extreme sorrow, suffering, or pain. ❑ *Jealousy causes distress and painful emotions.* N-UNCOUNT [2] **Distress** is the state of being in extreme danger and needing urgent help. ❑ *He expressed concern that the ship might be in distress.* N-UNCOUNT: oft *in* N [3] If someone or something **distresses** you, they cause you to be upset or worried. ❑ *The idea of Toni being in danger distresses him enormously.* VERB V n

**dis|tressed** /dɪstrest/ If someone is **distressed**, they are upset or worried. ❑ *I feel very alone and distressed about my problem.* ADJ

**dis|tress|ing** /dɪstresɪŋ/ If something is **distressing**, it upsets you or worries you. ❑ *It is very distressing to see your baby attached to tubes and monitors.* ADJ ♦ **dis|tress|ing|ly** *...a distressingly large bloodstain.* ADV: usu ADV adj

**dis|trib|ute** /dɪstrɪbjuːt/ **(distributes, distributing, distributed)** [1] If you **distribute** things, you hand them or deliver them to a number of people. ❑ *Students shouted slogans and distributed leaflets... In the move most of the furniture was left to the neighbours or distributed among friends.* VERB V n *be* V-ed *among* n [2] When a company **distributes** goods, it supplies them to the shops or businesses that sell them. [BUSINESS] ❑ *We didn't understand how difficult it was to distribute a national paper.* VERB V n [3] If you **distribute** things **among the** members of a group, you share them among those members. ❑ *Immediately after his election he began to distribute major offices among his friends and supporters.* VERB = share out V n *among* n Also V n [4] To **distribute** a substance **over** something means to scatter it over it. [FORMAL] ❑ *Distribute the topping evenly over the fruit.* VERB = scatter V n *over* n [5] → See also **distributed**.

**dis|trib|ut|ed** /dɪstrɪbjuːtɪd/ If things are **distributed** throughout an area, object, or group, they exist throughout it. ❑ *These cells are widely distributed throughout the body.* ADJ: usu v-link ADJ prep/adv, adv ADJ = spread

**dis|tri|bu|tion** /dɪstrɪbjuːʃən/ **(distributions)** ◆◇◇ [1] The **distribution** of things involves giving or delivering them to a number of people or places. ❑ *...the council which controls the distribution of foreign aid. ...emergency food distribution.* N-UNCOUNT: usu with supp [2] The **distribution** of something is how much of it there is in each place or at each time, or how much of it each person has. ❑ *...a more equitable distribution of wealth.* N-VAR: usu with supp = spread

**dis|tri|bu|tion|al** /dɪstrɪbjuːʃənəl/ [1] **Distributional** means relating to the distribution of goods. ❑ *What they're doing is setting up distributional networks.* ADJ: ADJ n [2] **Distributional** effects and policies relate to the share of a country's wealth that different groups of people have. [FORMAL] ❑ *...the distributional effects of free markets, which lead to inequalities in income.* ADJ: ADJ n

**dis|tribu|tive** /dɪstrɪbjuːtɪv/ **Distributive** means relating to the distribution of goods. ❑ *Reorganization is necessary on the distributive side of this industry.* ADJ: ADJ n

**dis|tribu|tor** /dɪstrɪbjʊtəʳ/ **(distributors)** A **distributor** is a company that supplies goods to shops or other businesses. [BUSINESS] ❑ *...Spain's largest distributor of petroleum products.* N-COUNT: usu with supp

**dis|tribu|tor|ship** /dɪstrɪbjʊtəʳʃɪp/ **(distributorships)** A **distributorship** is a company that supplies goods to shops or other businesses, or the right to supply goods to shops and businesses. [BUSINESS] ❑ *...the general manager of an automobile distributorship.* N-COUNT

**dis|trict** /dɪstrɪkt/ **(districts)** ◆◆◇ [1] A **district** is a particular area of a town or country. ❑ *I drove around the business district. ...Nashville's shopping district.* N-COUNT: usu supp N [2] A **district** is an area of a town or country which has been given official boundaries for the purpose of administration. ❑ *...the home of the governor of the district.* N-COUNT: with supp, oft N n

**Dis|trict At|tor|ney** **(District Attorneys)** In the United States, a **District Attorney** is a lawyer who works for a city, state, or federal government and puts on trial people who are accused of crimes. The abbreviation **D.A.** is also used. N-COUNT

**dis|trict nurse** **(district nurses)** In Britain, a **district nurse** is a nurse who goes to people's houses to give them medical treatment and advice. N-COUNT

**dis|trust** /dɪstrʌst/ **(distrusts, distrusting, distrusted)** [1] If you **distrust** someone or something, you think they are not honest, reliable, or safe. ❑ *I don't have any particular reason to distrust them.* VERB = mistrust ≠ trust V n [2] **Distrust** is the feeling of doubt that you have towards someone or something you distrust. ❑ *What he saw there left him with a profound distrust of all political authority.* N-UNCOUNT: also *a* N, oft N *of* n = mistrust

**dis|trust|ful** /dɪstrʌstfʊl/ If you are **distrustful of** someone or something, you think that they are not honest, reliable, or safe. ❑ *Voters are deeply distrustful of all politicians.* ADJ: usu v-link ADJ, oft ADJ *of* n

**dis|turb** /dɪstɜːʳb/ **(disturbs, disturbing, disturbed)** [1] If you **disturb** someone, you interrupt what they are doing and upset them. ❑ *I hope I'm not disturbing you.* VERB V n [2] If something **disturbs** you, it makes you feel upset or worried. ❑ *I dream about him, dreams so vivid that they disturb me for days.* VERB = perturb V n [3] If something **is disturbed**, its position or shape is changed. ❑ *He'd placed his notes in the brown envelope. They hadn't been disturbed... She patted Mona, taking care not to disturb her costume.* VERB *be* V-ed V n [4] If something **disturbs** a situation or atmosphere, it spoils it or causes trouble. ❑ *What could possibly disturb such tranquility?* VERB V n

**dis|turb|ance** /dɪstɜːʳbəns/ **(disturbances)** [1] A **disturbance** is an incident in which people behave violently in public. ❑ *During the disturbance which followed, three Englishmen were hurt.* N-COUNT [2] **Disturbance** means upsetting or disorganizing something which was previously in a calm and well-ordered state. ❑ *The home would cause less disturbance to local residents than a school.* N-UNCOUNT: usu with supp [3] You can use **disturbance** to refer to a medical or psychological problem, when someone's body or mind is not working in the normal way. ❑ *Poor educational performance is related to emotional disturbance.* N-VAR: with supp

**dis|turbed** /dɪstɜːʳbd/ [1] A **disturbed** person is very upset emotionally, and often needs special care or treatment. ❑ *...working with severely emotionally disturbed children.* ADJ [2] You can say that someone is **disturbed** when they are very worried or anxious. ❑ *Doctors were disturbed that less than 30 percent of the patients were women.* ADJ: usu v-link ADJ, oft ADJ that, ADJ to-inf = concerned [3] If you describe a situation or period of time as **disturbed**, you mean that it is unhappy and full of problems. ❑ *...women from disturbed backgrounds.* ADJ: usu ADJ n = troubled

**dis|turb|ing** /dɪstɜːʳbɪŋ/ Something that is **disturbing** makes you feel worried or upset. ❑ *There was something about him she found disturbing.* ADJ ♦ **dis|turb|ing|ly** *...the disturbingly high frequency of racial attacks.* ADV: usu ADV adj, ADV with v

**dis|unit|ed** /dɪsjʊnaɪtɪd/ If a group of people are **disunited**, there is disagreement and division among them. ❑ *...an increasingly disunited party.*
ADJ

**dis|unity** /dɪsjuːnɪti/ **Disunity** is lack of agreement among people which prevents them from working together effectively. [FORMAL] ❑ *He had been accused of promoting disunity within the armed forces.*
N-UNCOUNT ≠ unity

**dis|use** /dɪsjuːs/ If something falls **into disuse**, people stop using it. If something becomes worse as a result of **disuse**, it becomes worse because no one uses it. ❑ *...a church which has fallen into disuse.*
N-UNCOUNT: oft *into* N

**dis|used** /dɪsjuːzd/ A **disused** place or building is empty and is no longer used. ❑ *...a disused airfield near Maidenhead.*
ADJ: usu ADJ n

**ditch** /dɪtʃ/ **(ditches, ditching, ditched)** 1 A **ditch** is a long narrow channel cut into the ground at the side of a road or field. 2 If you **ditch** something that you have or are responsible for, you abandon it or get rid of it, because you no longer want it. [INFORMAL] ❑ *I decided to ditch the sofa bed.* 3 If someone **ditches** someone, they end a relationship with that person. [INFORMAL] ❑ *I can't bring myself to ditch him and start again.* 4 If a pilot **ditches** an aircraft or if it **ditches**, the pilot makes an emergency landing. ❑ *One American pilot was forced to ditch his jet in the Gulf... A survivor was knocked unconscious when the helicopter ditched.* 5 → See also **last-ditch**.
N-COUNT; VERB = dump; V n; VERB = dump; V n; VERB; V n; V

**dith|er** /dɪðəʳ/ **(dithers, dithering, dithered)** When someone **dithers**, they hesitate because they are unable to make a quick decision about something. ❑ *We're still dithering over whether to marry... If you have been dithering about buying shares, now could be the time to do it.*
VERB; V *over* wh/n; V *about* -ing/wh/n

**dit|to** /dɪtoʊ/ In informal English, you can use **ditto** to represent a word or phrase that you have just used in order to avoid repeating it. In written lists, **ditto** can be represented by ditto marks - the symbol " - underneath the word that you want to repeat. ❑ *Lister's dead. Ditto three Miami drug dealers and a lady.*

**dit|ty** /dɪti/ **(ditties)** A **ditty** is a short or light-hearted song or poem. [HUMOROUS or WRITTEN]
N-COUNT

**dit|zy** /dɪtsi/ **(ditzier, ditziest)** also **ditsy**. A **ditzy** person is silly and not very organized. [INFORMAL] ❑ *I sounded like a ditzy blonde!*
ADJ = dizzy

**di|uret|ic** /daɪərετɪk/ **(diuretics)** A **diuretic** is a substance which makes your body increase its production of waste fluids, with the result that you need to urinate more often than usual. [MEDICAL or TECHNICAL] ❑ *Alcohol acts as a diuretic, making you even more dehydrated.* ♦ **Diuretic** is also an adjective. ❑ *Many remedies effective in joint disease are primarily diuretic.*
N-COUNT; ADJ

**di|ur|nal** /daɪ̯ɜːʳnəl/ **Diurnal** means happening or active during the daytime. [FORMAL] ❑ *Kangaroos are diurnal animals.*
ADJ: usu ADJ n ≠ nocturnal

**diva** /diːvə/ **(divas)** You can refer to a successful and famous female opera singer as a **diva**.
N-COUNT

**di|van** /dɪvæn, AM daɪvæn/ **(divans)** 1 A **divan** or **divan bed** is a bed that has a thick base under the mattress. [BRIT] 2 A **divan** is a long soft seat that has no back or arms.
N-COUNT; N-COUNT

**dive** /daɪv/ **(dives, diving, dived)**

> American English sometimes uses the form **dove**, pronounced /doʊv/, for the past tense.

1 If you **dive into** some water, you jump in head-first with your arms held straight above your head. ❑ *He tried to escape by diving into a river... She was standing by a pool, about to dive in... Joanne had just learnt to dive.* ♦ **Dive** is also a noun. ❑ *Pat had earlier made a dive of 80 feet from the Chasm Bridge.* 2 If you **dive**, you go under the surface of the sea or a lake, using special breathing equipment. ❑ *Bezanik is diving to collect marine organisms.* ♦ **Dive** is also a noun. ❑ *This sighting occurred during my dive to a sunken wreck off Sardinia.* 3 When birds and animals **dive**, they go quickly downwards, head-first, through the air or through water. ❑ *...a pelican which had just dived for a fish.* 4 If an aeroplane **dives**, it flies or drops down quickly and suddenly. ❑ *He was killed when his monoplane stalled and dived into the ground.* ♦ **Dive** is also a noun. ❑ *Witnesses said the plane failed to pull out of a dive and smashed down in a field.* 5 If you **dive** in a particular direction or into a particular place, you jump or move there quickly. ❑ *They dived into a taxi.* ♦ **Dive** is also a noun. ❑ *He made a sudden dive for Uncle Jim's legs to try to trip him up.* 6 If you **dive into** a bag or container, you put your hands into it quickly in order to get something out. ❑ *She dived into her bag and brought out a folded piece of paper.* 7 If shares, profits, or figures **dive**, their value falls suddenly and by a large amount. [JOURNALISM] ❑ *If we cut interest rates, the pound would dive... Profits have dived from £7.7m to £7.1m... The shares dived 22p to 338p.* ♦ **Dive** is also a noun. ❑ *Stock prices took a dive.* 8 If you describe a bar or club as a **dive**, you mean it is dirty and dark, and not very respectable. [INFORMAL]
VERB; V *into* n; V *in*; V; N-COUNT; VERB; V; N-COUNT; VERB; V; VERB; V prep/adv; Also V; N-COUNT; VERB = leap; V prep/adv; N-COUNT; VERB; V *into* n; VERB; V; V *from/to/by* amount; V amount; N-COUNT; N-COUNT [disapproval]

**dive-bomb** **(dive-bombs, dive-bombing, dive-bombed)** If a plane **dive-bombs** an area, it suddenly flies down low over it to drop bombs onto it. ❑ *The Russians had to dive-bomb the cities to regain control.*
VERB; V n; Also V

**dive bomb|er** **(dive bombers)** also **dive-bomber**. You can refer to a plane that flies down low over a place in order to drop bombs on it as a **dive bomber**. ❑ *The port had been attacked by German dive bombers for the past five days.*
N-COUNT

**div|er** /daɪvəʳ/ **(divers)** A **diver** is a person who swims under water using special breathing equipment.
N-COUNT

**di|verge** /daɪvɜːʳdʒ, AM dɪ-/ **(diverges, diverging, diverged)** 1 If one thing **diverges from** another similar thing, the first thing becomes different from the second or develops differently from it. You can also say that two things **diverge**. ❑ *His interests increasingly diverged from those of his colleagues... When the aims of the partners begin to diverge, there's trouble.* 2 If one opinion or idea **diverges from** another, they contradict each other or are different. You can also say that two opinions or ideas **diverge**. ❑ *The view of the Estonian government does not diverge that far from Lipmaa's thinking... Needless to say, theory and practice sometimes diverged.* 3 If one road, path, or route **diverges from** another, they lead in different directions after starting from the same place. You can also say that roads, paths, or routes **diverge**. ❑ *...a course that diverged from the Calvert Island coastline... Where three roads diverge take the middle branch.*
V-RECIP; V *from* n; pl-n V; V-RECIP: no cont; V *from* n; pl-n V; V-RECIP ≠ converge; V *from* n; pl-n V

**di|ver|gence** /daɪvɜːʳdʒəns, AM dɪ-/ **(divergences)** A **divergence** is a difference between two or more things, attitudes, or opinions. [FORMAL] ❑ *There's a substantial divergence of opinion within the party.*
N-VAR: usu with supp ≠ convergence

**di|ver|gent** /daɪvɜːʳdʒənt, AM dɪ-/ **Divergent** things are different from each other. [FORMAL] ❑ *...two people who have divergent views on this question.*
ADJ: usu ADJ n

**di|verse** /daɪvɜːʳs, AM dɪ-/ 1 If a group or range of things is **diverse**, it is made up of a wide variety of things. ❑ *...shops selling a diverse range of gifts.* 2 **Diverse** people or things are very different from each other. ❑ *Jones has a much more diverse and perhaps younger audience.*
ADJ = varied; ADJ

**di|ver|si|fy** /daɪvɜːʳsɪfaɪ, AM dɪ-/ **(diversifies, diversifying, diversified)** When an organization or person **diversifies** into other things, or **diversifies** their range of something, they increase the variety of things that they do or make. ❑ *The company's troubles started only when it diversified into new products... Manufacturers have been encouraged to diversify... These firms have been given a tough lesson in the need to diversify their markets.*
VERB = branch out; V *into* n/-ing; V; V n

♦ **di|ver|si|fi|ca|tion** /daɪvɜːʳsɪfɪkeɪʃən, AM dɪ-/ **(diversifications)** *The seminar was to discuss diversification of agriculture.* N-VAR

**di|ver|sion** /daɪvɜːʳʃən, AM dɪvɜːrʒən/ **(diversions)** 1 A **diversion** is an action or event that attracts your attention away from what you are doing or concentrating on. ❑ *The robbers threw smoke bombs to create a diversion.* N-COUNT 2 A **diversion** is an activity that you do for pleasure. [FORMAL] ❑ *Finger painting is very messy but an excellent diversion.* N-COUNT 3 A **diversion** is a special route arranged for traffic to follow when the normal route cannot be used. [BRIT] ❑ *They turned back because of traffic diversions.* N-COUNT

✓ in AM, use **detour**

4 **The diversion of** something involves changing its course or destination. ❑ *...the illegal diversion of profits from secret arms sales.* N-UNCOUNT: the N of n

**di|ver|sion|ary** /daɪvɜːʳʃənri, AM dɪvɜːrʒəneri/ A **diversionary** activity is one intended to attract people's attention away from something which you do not want them to think about, know about, or deal with. ❑ *Fires were started by the prisoners as a diversionary tactic.* ADJ: usu ADJ n

**di|ver|sity** /daɪvɜːʳsɪti, AM dɪ-/ **(diversities)** 1 The **diversity** of something is the fact that it contains many very different elements. ❑ *...the cultural diversity of British society.* N-VAR: usu with supp = variety 2 A **diversity of** things is a range of things which are very different from each other. ❑ *His object is to gather as great a diversity of material as possible.* N-SING: N of n

**di|vert** /daɪvɜːʳt, AM dɪ-/ **(diverts, diverting, diverted)** 1 To **divert** vehicles or travellers means to make them follow a different route or go to a different destination than they originally intended. You can also say that someone or something **diverts from** a particular route or **to** a particular place. [BRIT] ❑ *...Rainham Marshes, east London, where a new bypass will divert traffic from the A13... We diverted a plane to rescue 100 passengers... She insists on diverting to a village close to the airport.* VERB; V n from/to n; V n; V from/to n

✓ in AM, use **detour**

2 To **divert** money or resources means to cause them to be used for a different purpose. ❑ *The government is trying to divert more public funds from west to east.* VERB; V n prep/adv; Also V n 3 To **divert** a phone call means to send it to a different number or place from the one that was dialled by the person making the call. ❑ *He instructed switchboard staff to divert all Laura's calls to him.* VERB; V n prep/adv; Also V n 4 If you say that someone **diverts** your attention from something important or serious, you disapprove of them behaving or talking in a way that stops you thinking about it. ❑ *They want to divert the attention of the people from the real issues.* VERB; [disapproval] = distract; V n prep/adv

**di|vert|ing** /daɪvɜːʳtɪŋ, AM dɪ-/ If you describe something as **diverting**, you mean that it is amusing or entertaining. [OLD-FASHIONED] ADJ = enjoyable

**di|vest** /daɪvest, AM dɪ-/ **(divests, divesting, divested)** 1 If you **divest yourself of** something that you own or are responsible for, you get rid of it or stop being responsible for it. [FORMAL] ❑ *The company divested itself of its oil interests.* VERB = rid; V pron-refl of n 2 If something or someone **is divested of** a particular quality, they lose that quality or it is taken away from them. [FORMAL] ❑ *...in the 1960s, when sexual love had been divested of sin... They have divested rituals of their original meaning.* VERB = strip; be V-ed of n; V n of n

**di|vide** /dɪvaɪd/ **(divides, dividing, divided)** ♦♦◇ 1 When people or things **are divided** or **divide into** smaller groups or parts, they become separated into smaller parts. ❑ *The physical benefits of exercise can be divided into three factors... It will be easiest if we divide them into groups... Divide the pastry in half and roll out each piece... We divide into pairs and each pair takes a region... Bacteria reproduce by dividing and making copies of themselves.* VERB = split; be V-ed into pl-n; V n into pl-n; V n in fraction; V into pl-n; V; Also V n 2 If you **divide** something **among** people or things, you separate it into several parts or quantities which you distribute to the people or things. ❑ *Divide the sauce among 4 bowls.* VERB = share; V n among pl-n 3 If you **divide** a larger number **by** a smaller number or **divide** a smaller number **into** a larger number, you calculate how many times the smaller number can fit exactly into the larger number. ❑ *Measure the floor area of the greenhouse and divide it by six.* VERB; V n by/into num 4 If a border or line **divides** two areas or **divides** an area into two, it keeps the two areas separate from each other. ❑ *...remote border areas dividing Tamil and Muslim settlements. ...the long frontier dividing Mexico from the United States.* VERB = separate; V n; V n from n 5 If people **divide** over something or if something **divides** them, it causes strong disagreement between them. ❑ *She has done more to divide the Conservatives than anyone else... The party is likely to divide along ideological lines.* VERB ≠ unite; V n; V prep 6 A **divide** is a significant distinction between two groups, often one that causes conflict. ❑ *...a deliberate attempt to create a Hindu-Muslim divide in India.* N-COUNT: usu sing, usu with supp = rift 7 A **divide** is a moment in time or a point in a process when there is a complete change from one situation to another. ❑ *The time had come to cross the great divide between formality and truth.* N-COUNT: usu sing, usu with supp = watershed 8 You use **divide and rule** to refer to a policy which is intended to keep someone in a position of power by causing disagreements between people who might otherwise unite against them. ❑ *The government's policies of divide and rule have only contributed to the volatility of the region.* PHRASE [disapproval]

♦ **divide up** 1 If you **divide** something **up**, you separate it into smaller or more useful groups. ❑ *The idea is to divide up the country into four sectors... The Trust needs a new law to divide it up into smaller bodies.* PHRASAL VERB = split up; V P n into pl-n; V n P into pl-n 2 If you **divide** something **up**, you share it out among a number of people or groups in approximately equal parts. ❑ *The aim was to divide up the business, give everyone an equal stake in its future.* PHRASAL VERB; V P n (not pron)

**di|vid|ed high|way** **(divided highways)** A **divided highway** is a road which has two lanes of traffic travelling in each direction with a strip of grass or concrete down the middle to separate the two lots of traffic. [AM] N-COUNT

✓ in BRIT, use **dual carriageway**

**divi|dend** /dɪvɪdend/ **(dividends)** ♦◇◇ 1 A **dividend** is the part of a company's profits which is paid to people who have shares in the company. [BUSINESS] ❑ *The first quarter dividend has been increased by nearly 4 per cent.* N-COUNT 2 If something **pays dividends**, it brings advantages at a later date. ❑ *Steps taken now to maximise your health will pay dividends later on.* PHRASE: V inflects 3 → See also **peace dividend**.

**di|vid|er** /dɪvaɪdəʳ/ **(dividers)** 1 A **divider** is something which forms a barrier between two areas or sets of things. ❑ *A curtain acted as a divider between this class and another.* N-COUNT: usu with supp 2 **Dividers** are an instrument used for measuring lines and for marking points along them. Dividers consist of two pointed arms joined with a hinge. N-PLURAL: also a pair of N

**di|vid|ing line** **(dividing lines)** 1 A **dividing line** is a distinction or set of distinctions which marks the difference between two types of thing or two groups. ❑ *There's a very thin dividing line between joviality and hysteria.* N-COUNT: usu sing, oft N between pl-n 2 **The dividing line** between two areas is the boundary between them. ❑ *...people on both sides of the dividing line between Israel and the occupied territories.* N-SING: oft N between pl-n

**divi|na|tion** /dɪvɪneɪʃən/ **Divination** is the art or practice of discovering what will happen in the future using supernatural means. [FORMAL] N-UNCOUNT

**di|vine** /dɪvaɪn/ **(divines, divining, divined)** 1 You use **divine** to describe something that is provided by or relates to a god or goddess. ❑ *He suggested that the civil war had been a divine punishment.* ♦ **di|vine|ly** *The law was divinely ordained.* ADJ: usu ADJ n; ADV: usu ADV -ed 2 If you **divine** something, you discover or learn it by guessing. [LITERARY] ❑ *...the child's ability to divine the needs of its parents and respond to them... From this he divined that she did not like him much.* VERB; V n; V that; Also V wh

**di|vine right** **(divine rights)** If someone thinks they have a **divine right to** something, they think that it is their right to have it, without making any effort. ❑ *A degree does not give you a divine right to wealth.* [N-COUNT: usu sing]

**div|ing** /daɪvɪŋ/ 1 **Diving** is the activity of working or looking around underwater, using special breathing equipment. ❑ *...equipment and accessories for diving.* [N-UNCOUNT] 2 **Diving** is the sport or activity in which you jump into water head first with your arms held straight above your head, usually from a diving board. [N-UNCOUNT]

**div|ing bell** **(diving bells)** A **diving bell** is a container shaped like a bell, in which people can breathe air while they work under water. [N-COUNT]

**div|ing board** **(diving boards)** A **diving board** is a board high above a swimming pool from which people can dive into the water. [N-COUNT]

**di|vin|ity** /dɪvɪnɪti/ **(divinities)** 1 **Divinity** is the study of religion. [N-UNCOUNT = theology] 2 **Divinity** is the quality of being divine. ❑ *...a lasting faith in the divinity of Christ's word.* [N-UNCOUNT: oft with poss] 3 A **divinity** is a god or goddess. ❑ *The three statues above are probably Roman divinities.* [N-COUNT]

**di|vi|sible** /dɪvɪzɪbᵊl/ If one number is **divisible by** another number, the second number can be divided into the first exactly, with nothing left over. ❑ *Twenty-eight is divisible by seven.* [ADJ: v-link ADJ *by* num]

**di|vi|sion** /dɪvɪʒᵊn/ **(divisions)** ◆◆◇ 1 The **division of** a large unit **into** two or more distinct parts is the act of separating it into these parts. ❑ *...the unification of Germany, after its division into two states at the end of World War Two.* [N-UNCOUNT: oft with poss, oft N *into* pl-n] 2 The **division of** something among people or things is its separation into parts which are distributed among the people or things. ❑ *The current division of labor between workers and management will alter.* [N-UNCOUNT: oft N *of* n *among/between* pl-n] 3 **Division** is the arithmetical process of dividing one number into another number. ❑ *I taught my daughter how to do division at the age of six.* [N-UNCOUNT ≠ multiplication] 4 A **division** is a significant distinction or argument between two groups, which causes the two groups to be considered as very different and separate. ❑ *The division between the prosperous west and the impoverished east remains.* [N-VAR: oft N *between/among* pl-n = divide] 5 In a large organization, a **division** is a group of departments whose work is done in the same place or is connected with similar tasks. ❑ *...the bank's Latin American division.* [N-COUNT: usu supp N] 6 A **division** is a group of military units which fight as a single unit. ❑ *Several armoured divisions are being moved from Germany.* [N-COUNT: usu supp N] 7 In some sports, such as football, baseball, and basketball, a **division** is one of the groups of teams which make up a league. The teams in each division are considered to be approximately the same standard, and they all play against each other during the season. [N-COUNT: usu supp N]

**di|vi|sion|al** /dɪvɪʒənᵊl/ **Divisional** means relating to a division of a large organization or group. ❑ *An alarm links the police station to the divisional headquarters.* [ADJ: ADJ n]

**di|vi|sion sign** **(division signs)** A **division sign** is the symbol œ used between two numbers to show that the first number has to be divided by the second. [N-COUNT]

**di|vi|sive** /dɪvaɪsɪv/ Something that is **divisive** causes unfriendliness and argument between people. ❑ *Abortion has always been a divisive issue.* [ADJ] ♦ **di|vi|sive|ness** *...the divisiveness that has separated Miami's black and Latino communities.* [N-UNCOUNT]

**di|vorce** /dɪvɔːʳs/ **(divorces, divorcing, divorced)** ◆◇◇ 1 A **divorce** is the formal ending of a marriage by law. ❑ *Numerous marriages now end in divorce.* [N-VAR] 2 If a man and woman **divorce** or if one of them **divorces** the other, their marriage is legally ended. ❑ *My parents divorced when I was very young... He and Lillian had got divorced... I am absolutely furious that he divorced me to marry her... Mr Gold is divorcing for the second time... I got divorced when I was about 31.* [V-RECIP: pl-n V, pl-n *get* V-ed, V n, NON-RECIP: V, *get* V-ed] 3 A **divorce of** one thing **from** another, or a divorce **between** two things is a separation between them which is permanent or is likely to be permanent. ❑ *...this divorce of Christian culture from the roots of faith.* [N-SING: usu N *of* n *from* n, N *between* pl-n] 4 If you say that one thing cannot **be divorced from** another, you mean that the two things cannot be considered as different and separate things. ❑ *Good management in the police cannot be divorced from accountability... We have been able to divorce sex from reproduction.* [VERB = dissociate: *be* V-ed *from* n, V n *from* n]

**di|vor|cé** /dɪvɔːʳsi/ **(divorcés)** A **divorcé** is a man who is divorced. [mainly AM] [N-COUNT]

**di|vorced** /dɪvɔːʳst/ 1 Someone who **is divorced** from their former husband or wife has separated from them and is no longer legally married to them. ❑ *He is divorced, with a young son.* [ADJ: oft ADJ *from* n] 2 If you say that one thing **is divorced from** another, you mean that the two things are very different and separate from each other. ❑ *...speculative theories divorced from political reality.* [ADJ: v-link ADJ *from* n = unconnected] 3 If you say that someone **is divorced from** a situation, you mean that they act as if they are not affected by it in any way. ❑ *This just shows how divorced from reality she's become.* [ADJ: v-link ADJ *from* n]

**di|vor|cee** /dɪvɔːʳsiː/ **(divorcees)** A **divorcee** is a person, especially a woman, who is divorced. [N-COUNT]

**di|vor|cée** /dɪvɔːʳsi/ **(divorcées)** A **divorcée** is a woman who is divorced. [mainly AM] [N-COUNT]

**div|ot** /dɪvət/ **(divots)** A **divot** is a small piece of grass and earth which is dug out accidentally, for example by a golf club. [N-COUNT]

**di|vulge** /daɪvʌldʒ, AM dɪ-/ **(divulges, divulging, divulged)** If you **divulge** a piece of secret or private information, you tell it to someone. [FORMAL] ❑ *Officials refuse to divulge details of the negotiations... I do not want to divulge exactly where the village is.* [VERB = reveal, disclose: V n, V wh, Also V n *to* n, V that]

**div|vy** /dɪvi/ **(divvies, divvying, divvied)** If you call someone a **divvy**, you are saying in a humorous way that you think they are rather foolish. [BRIT, INFORMAL] [N-COUNT]

♦ **divvy up** If you **divvy up** something such as money or food, you share it out. [INFORMAL] ❑ *Johnson was free to divvy up his share of the money as he chose.* [PHRASAL VERB = divide: V P n (not pron), Also V n P]

**Di|wa|li** /dɪwɑːli/ also **Divali.** **Diwali** is a Hindu festival held in honour of Lakshmi, the goddess of wealth. It is celebrated in October or November with the lighting of lamps in homes and temples, and with prayers to Lakshmi. [N-UNCOUNT]

**DIY** /diː aɪ waɪ/ **DIY** is the activity of making or repairing things yourself, especially in your home. **DIY** is an abbreviation for 'do-it-yourself'. [BRIT] ❑ *He's useless at DIY. He won't even put up a shelf.* [N-UNCOUNT]

**diz|zy** /dɪzi/ **(dizzier, dizziest, dizzies, dizzying, dizzied)** 1 If you feel **dizzy**, you feel that you are losing your balance and are about to fall. ❑ *Her head still hurt, and she felt slightly dizzy and disoriented.* [ADJ] ♦ **diz|zi|ly** /dɪzɪli/ *Her head spins dizzily as soon as she sits up.* [ADV: usu ADV with v] ♦ **diz|zi|ness** *His complaint causes dizziness and nausea.* [N-UNCOUNT] 2 You can use **dizzy** to describe a woman who is careless and forgets things, but is easy to like. ❑ *She is famed for playing dizzy blondes.* [ADJ: usu ADJ n] 3 If you say that someone has reached **the dizzy heights of** something, you are emphasizing that they have reached a very high level by achieving it. [HUMOROUS] ❑ *I escalated to the dizzy heights of director's secretary.* [PHRASE: usu PHR after v, oft PHR *of* n, emphasis]

**DJ** /diː dʒeɪ/ **(DJs)** also **D.J., dj** 1 A **DJ** is the same as a **disc jockey**. [N-COUNT] 2 A **DJ** is the same as a **dinner jacket**. [BRIT] [N-COUNT]

**DNA** /diː en eɪ/ ◆◇◇ **DNA** is an acid in the chromosomes in the centre of the cells of living things. DNA determines the particular structure and functions of every cell and is responsible for characteristics being passed on from parents to their children. **DNA** is an abbreviation for 'deoxyribonucleic acid'. [N-UNCOUNT]

**DNA finger|print|ing** DNA fingerprinting is the same as **genetic fingerprinting**. N-UNCOUNT

**DNA test** **(DNA tests)** A **DNA test** is a test in which someone's DNA is analysed, for example to see if they have committed a particular crime or are the parent of a particular child. N-COUNT ♦ **DNA test|ing** ❑ *They took samples from his hair for DNA testing.* N-UNCOUNT

> **do**
> ① AUXILIARY VERB USES
> ② OTHER VERB USES
> ③ NOUN USES

①**do** /də, STRONG duː/ **(does, doing, did, done)** ◆◆◆

> **Do** is used as an auxiliary with the simple present tense. **Did** is used as an auxiliary with the simple past tense. In spoken English, negative forms of **do** are often shortened, for example **do not** is shortened to **don't** and **did not** is shortened to **didn't**.

1 **Do** is used to form the negative of main verbs, by putting 'not' after 'do' and before the main verb in its infinitive form, that is the form without 'to'. AUX ❑ *They don't want to work...* AUX neg inf *I did not know Jamie had a knife...* AUX neg inf *It doesn't matter if you win or lose.* AUX neg inf 2 **Do** is used to form questions, by putting the subject after 'do' and before the main verb in its infinitive form, that is the form without 'to'. AUX ❑ *Do you like music?...* AUX n v *What did he say?...* AUX n v *Where does she live?* AUX n v 3 **Do** is used in question tags. AUX ❑ *You know about Andy, don't you?...* cl AUX n *I'm sure they had some of the same questions last year didn't they?* cl AUX n 4 You use **do** when you are confirming or contradicting a statement containing 'do', or giving a negative or positive answer to a question. AUX ❑ *'Did he think there was anything suspicious going on?' — 'Yes, he did.'...* AUX *'Do you have a metal detector?' — 'No, I don't.'.* AUX 5 **Do** is used with a negative to tell someone not to behave in a certain way. AUX: only imper ❑ *Don't be silly...* AUX neg inf *Don't touch that!* 6 **Do** is used to give emphasis to the main verb when there is no other auxiliary. AUX emphasis ❑ *Veronica, I do understand...* AUX inf *You did have a tape recorder with you.* 7 **Do** is used as a polite way of inviting or trying to persuade someone to do something. AUX: only imper ❑ *Do sit down...* AUX inf *Do help yourself to another drink.* 8 **Do** can be used to refer back to another verb group when you are comparing or contrasting two things, or saying that they are the same. VERB ❑ *I make more money than he does...* V *I had fantasies, as do all mothers, about how life would be when my girls were grown...* as V n *Girls receive less health care and less education in the developing world than do boys.* than V n 9 You use **do** after 'so' and 'nor' to say that the same statement is true for two people or groups. VERB ❑ *You know that's true, and so do I...* V n *We don't forget that. Nor does he.* V n

②**do** /duː/ **(does, doing, did, done)** ◆◆◆

> **do** is used in a large number of expressions which are explained under other words in the dictionary. For example, the expression 'easier said than done' is explained at 'easy'.

1 When you **do** something, you take some action or perform an activity or task. **Do** is often used instead of a more specific verb, to talk about a common action involving a particular thing. For example you can say 'do your teeth' instead of 'brush your teeth'. VERB ❑ *I was trying to do some work...* V n *After lunch Elizabeth and I did the washing up...* V n *Dad does the garden.* V n 2 **Do** can be used to stand for any verb group, or to refer back to another verb group, including one that was in a previous sentence. VERB ❑ *What are you doing?...* V n *Think twice before doing anything...* V pron-indef *A lot of people got arrested for looting so they will think before they do it again...* V it *I'm glad they gave me my money back, but I think they did this to shut me up...* V this *The first thing is to get some more food. When we've done that we ought to start again...* V that *Brian counted to twenty and lifted his binoculars. Elena did the same...* V the same *He turned towards the open front door but, as he did so, she pushed past him.* V so 3 You can use **do** in a clause at the beginning of a sentence after words like 'what' and 'all', to give special emphasis to the information that comes at the end of the sentence. VERB emphasis ❑ *All she does is complain...* V n *What I should do is go and see her.* V n 4 If you **do** a particular thing **with** something, you use it in that particular way. VERB ❑ *I was allowed to do whatever I wanted with my life...* V n with n *The technology was good, but you couldn't do much with it.* V amount with n 5 If you **do** something **about** a problem, you take action to try to solve it. VERB ❑ *They refuse to do anything about the real cause of crime: poverty...* V n about n *If an engine packs in, there's not much the engineer can do about it until the plane is back on the ground.* V amount about n 6 If an action or event **does** a particular thing, such as harm or good, it has that result or effect. VERB ❑ *A few bombs can do a lot of damage...* V n *It'll do you good to take a rest.* V n n 7 You can use **do** to talk about the degree to which a person, action, or event affects or improves a particular situation. VERB ❑ *Such incidents do nothing for live music's reputation...* V amount for n *I'd just tried to do what I could for Lou.* V n for n 8 You can talk about what someone or something **does to** a person to mean that they have a very harmful effect on them. VERB ❑ *I saw what the liquor was doing to her.* V to n 9 If you ask someone what they **do**, you want to know what their job or profession is. VERB ❑ *What does your father do?* V n 10 If you **are doing** something, you are busy or active in some way, or have planned an activity for some time in the future. VERB ❑ *Are you doing anything tomorrow night?...* V n *There is nothing to do around here.* V n 11 If you say that someone or something **does** well or badly, you are talking about how successful or unsuccessful they are. VERB ❑ *Connie did well at school and graduated with honours...* V adv *How did I do?* V adv 12 If a person or organization **does** a particular service or product, they provide that service or sell that product. VERB [mainly BRIT] ❑ *They provide design services and do printing and packaging...* V n *They do a good range of herbal tea.* V n 13 You can use **do** when referring to the speed or rate that something or someone achieves or is able to achieve. VERB ❑ *They were doing 70 miles an hour.* V amount 14 If you **do** a subject, author, or book, you study them at school or college. VERB [SPOKEN] ❑ *I'd like to do maths at university.* V n 15 If you **do** a particular person, accent, or role, you imitate that person or accent, or act that role. VERB ❑ *Gina does accents extremely well.* V n 16 If someone **does** drugs, they take illegal drugs. VERB ❑ *I don't do drugs.* V n 17 If you say that something **will do** or **will do** you, you mean that there is enough of it or that it is of good enough quality to meet your requirements or to satisfy you. VERB ❑ *Anything to create a scene and attract attention will do...* V *'What would you like to eat?' — 'Anything'll do me, Eva.'* V n

**PHRASES** 18 If you say that you **could do with** something, you mean that you need it or would benefit from it. PHRASE: V inflects, PHR n/-ing ❑ *I could do with a cup of tea...* *The range could do with being extended.* 19 You can ask someone **what** they **did with** something as another way of asking them where they put it. PHRASE: V inflects, PHR n ❑ *What did you do with that notebook?* 20 If you ask **what** someone or something **is doing** in a particular place, you are asking why they are there. PHRASE: PHR adv/prep ❑ *'Dr Campbell,' he said, clearly surprised. 'What are you doing here?'* 21 If you say that one thing **has** something **to do with** or **is** something **to do with** another thing, you mean that the two things are connected or that the first thing is about the second thing. PHRASE: have/be inflects, PHR n ❑ *Mr Butterfield denies having anything to do with the episode...* *That's none of your business, it has nothing to do with you.*

♦ **do away with** 1 To **do away with** something means to remove it completely or put an end to it. PHRASAL VERB ❑ *The long-range goal must be to do away with nuclear weapons altogether.* V P P n 2 If one person **does away with** another, the first murders PHRASAL VERB the second. If you **do away with yourself**, you kill yourself. [INFORMAL] ❑ *...a woman whose husband had made several attempts to do away with her.* V P P n Also V P P pron-refl

♦ **do for** If you say that you **are done for**, you mean that you are in a terrible and hopeless situation. [INFORMAL] ❑ *We need his help or we're done for, dead and gone, lost.* PHRASAL VERB: usu passive *be* V-ed P

♦ **do in** To **do** someone **in** means to kill them. [INFORMAL] ❑ *Whoever did him in removed a man who was brave as well as ruthless.* PHRASAL VERB = bump off V n P Also V P n

♦ **do out** If a room or building is **done out in** a particular way, it is decorated and furnished in that way. [BRIT] ❑ *...a room newly done out in country-house style.* PHRASAL VERB: usu passive *be* V-ed P prep/adv

♦ **do out of** If you **do** someone **out of** something, you unfairly cause them not to have or get a particular thing that they were expecting to have. [INFORMAL] ❑ *He complains that the others have done him out of his share.* PHRASAL VERB V n P P n

♦ **do over** If you **do** a task **over**, you perform it again from the beginning. [AM] ❑ *If she had the chance to do it over, she would have hired a press secretary.* PHRASAL VERB = do again V n P

♦ **do up** 1 If you **do** something **up**, you fasten it. ❑ *Mari did up the buttons... Keep your scarf on, do your coat up.* PHRASAL VERB V P n V n P 2 If you **do up** an old building, you decorate and repair it so that it is in a better condition. [BRIT] ❑ *Nicholas has bought a barn in Provence and is spending August doing it up.* PHRASAL VERB V n P Also V P n 3 If you say that a person or room **is done up** in a particular way, you mean they are dressed or decorated in that way, often a way that is rather ridiculous or extreme. ❑ *...Beatrice, usually done up like the fairy on the Christmas tree.* PHRASAL VERB: usu passive *be* V-ed prep/adv

♦ **do without** 1 If you **do without** something you need, want, or usually have, you are able to survive, continue, or succeed although you do not have it. ❑ *We can't do without the help of your organisation... We've had a bit more money and that, and the baby doesn't do without.* PHRASAL VERB V P n V P 2 If you say that you could **do without** something, you mean that you would prefer not to have it or it is of no benefit to you. [INFORMAL] ❑ *He could do without her rhetorical questions at five o'clock in the morning.* PHRASAL VERB V P n

③ **do** /duː/ **(dos)** 1 A **do** is a party, dinner party, or other social event. [mainly BRIT, INFORMAL] ❑ *A friend of his is having a do in Stoke.* N-COUNT 2 If someone tells you the **dos and don'ts** of a particular situation, they advise you what you should and should not do in that situation. ❑ *Please advise me on the most suitable colour print film and some dos and don'ts.* PHRASE

**do.** **do.** is an old-fashioned written abbreviation for **ditto**.

**do|able** /duːəbəl/ also **do-able.** If something is **doable**, it is possible to do it. ❑ *Is this project something that you think is doable?*

**d.o.b.** **d.o.b.** is an old-fashioned written abbreviation for **date of birth**, used especially on official forms.

**do|ber|man** /doʊbəʳmən/ **(dobermans)** A **doberman** is a type of large dog with short dark fur. N-COUNT

**doc** /dɒk/ **(docs)** Some people call a doctor **doc**. [INFORMAL] N-VOC; N-COUNT

**doc|ile** /doʊsaɪl, AM dɑːsᵊl/ A person or animal that is **docile** is quiet, not aggressive, and easily controlled. ❑ *...docile, obedient children.* ADJ = placid

♦ **do|cil|ity** /dɒsɪlɪti/ *Her docility had surprised him.* N-UNCOUNT ♦ **doc|ile|ly** *She stood there, docilely awaiting my decision.* ADV: ADV with v

**dock** /dɒk/ **(docks, docking, docked)** 1 A **dock** is an enclosed area in a harbour where ships go to be loaded, unloaded, and repaired. ❑ *She headed for the docks, thinking that Ricardo might be hiding in one of the boats.* N-COUNT: also *in/into* N 2 When a ship **docks** or **is docked**, it is brought into a dock. ❑ *The vessel docked at Liverpool in April 1811... Russian commanders docked a huge aircraft carrier in a Russian port.* VERB V V n 3 When one spacecraft **docks** or **is docked with** another, the two crafts join together in space. ❑ *The space shuttle Atlantis is scheduled to dock with Russia's Mir space station... They have docked a robot module alongside the orbiting space station.* V-RECIP V *with* n V n prep 4 A **dock** is a platform for loading vehicles or trains. [AM] ❑ *The truck left the loading dock with hoses still attached.* N-COUNT 5 A **dock** is a small structure at the edge of water where boats can tie up, especially one that is privately owned. [AM] N-COUNT = jetty 6 In a law court, **the dock** is where the person accused of a crime stands or sits. ❑ *What about the odd chance that you do put an innocent man in the dock?* N-SING: usu *in the* N 7 If you **dock** someone's wages or money, you take some of the money away. If you **dock** someone points in a contest, you take away some of the points that they have. ❑ *He threatens to dock her fee.* VERB V n Also V n n 8 → See also **dry dock**.

**dock|er** /dɒkəʳ/ **(dockers)** A **docker** is a person who works in the docks, loading and unloading ships. [BRIT] N-COUNT

☑ in AM, use **longshoreman**

**dock|et** /dɒkɪt/ **(dockets)** 1 A **docket** is a certificate or ticket which shows the contents of something such as a parcel or cargo, and proves who the goods belong to. [BRIT] N-COUNT 2 A **docket** is a list of cases waiting for trial in a law court. [mainly AM] N-COUNT

**dock|land** /dɒklænd/ **(docklands)** The **dockland** or **docklands** of a town or city is the area around the docks. [BRIT] N-VAR

**dock|side** /dɒksaɪd/ **The dockside** is the part of a dock that is next to the water. N-SING: oft N n

**dock work|er** **(dock workers)** A **dock worker** is a person who works in the docks, loading and unloading ships. N-COUNT

**dock|yard** /dɒkjɑːʳd/ **(dockyards)** A **dockyard** is a place where ships are built, maintained, and repaired. N-COUNT

**doc|tor** /dɒktəʳ/ **(doctors, doctoring, doctored)** ◆◆◇ 1 A **doctor** is someone who is qualified in medicine and treats people who are ill. ❑ *Do not discontinue the treatment without consulting your doctor... Doctor Paige will be here after lunch.* N-COUNT; N-TITLE; N-VOC 2 A **dentist** or **veterinarian** can also be called **doctor**. [AM] N-COUNT; N-TITLE; N-VOC 3 **The doctor's** is used to refer to the surgery or office where a doctor works. ❑ *I have an appointment at the doctors.* N-COUNT: usu sing, *the* N 4 A **doctor** is someone who has been awarded the highest academic or honorary degree by a university. ❑ *He is a doctor of philosophy.* N-COUNT; N-TITLE 5 If someone **doctors** something, they change it in order to deceive people. ❑ *They doctored the prints to make her look as awful as possible.* VERB V n

**doc|tor|al** /dɒktərəl/ A **doctoral** thesis or piece of research is written or done in order to obtain a doctor's degree. ADJ: ADJ n

**doc|tor|ate** /dɒktərət/ **(doctorates)** A **doctorate** is the highest degree awarded by a university. ❑ *He obtained his doctorate in Social Psychology.* N-COUNT

**Doc|tor of Phi|loso|phy** **(Doctors of Philosophy)** A **Doctor of Philosophy** is someone who has a **PhD**. N-COUNT

**doc|tri|naire** /dɒktrɪneəʳ/ If you say that someone is **doctrinaire** or has a **doctrinaire** attitude, you disapprove of them because they have fixed principles which they try to force on other people. [FORMAL] ❑ *He is firm but not doctrinaire.* ADJ [disapproval] = dogmatic

**doc|tri|nal** /dɒktraɪnᵊl, AM dɑːktrɪnᵊl/ **Doctrinal** means relating to doctrines. [FORMAL] ❑ *Doctrinal differences were vigorously debated among religious leaders.* ADJ: usu ADJ n

**doc|trine** /dɒktrɪn/ **(doctrines)** A **doctrine** is a set of principles or beliefs, especially religious ones. ❑ *...the Marxist doctrine of perpetual revolution.* N-VAR: usu with supp, oft N *of* n

**docu|dra|ma** /dɒkjʊdrɑːmə/ **(docudramas)** also **docu-drama.** A **docudrama** is a film based on events that really happened. Docudramas are usually shown on television rather than in cinemas. N-VAR

**docu|ment** **(documents, documenting, documented)** ◆◆◇

> The noun is pronounced /dɒkjəmənt/. The verb is pronounced /dɒkjəment/.

1 A **document** is one or more official pieces of paper with writing on them. ❑ *...a policy document for the Labour Party conference... The policeman wanted to see all our documents.* N-COUNT = paper
2 A **document** is a piece of text or graphics, for example a letter, that is stored as a file on a computer and that you can access in order to read it or change it. [COMPUTING] ❑ *When you are finished typing, remember to save your document.* N-COUNT
3 If you **document** something, you make a detailed record of it in writing or on film or tape. ❑ *He wrote a book documenting his prison experiences.* VERB V n

**docu|men|tary** /dɒkjəmentri/ **(documentaries)** 1 A **documentary** is a television or radio programme, or a film, which shows real events or provides information about a particular subject. ❑ *...a TV documentary on homelessness.* N-COUNT
2 **Documentary** evidence consists of things that are written down. ❑ *We have documentary evidence that they were planning military action.* ADJ: ADJ n

**docu|men|ta|tion** /dɒkjəmenteɪʃən/ **Documentation** consists of documents which provide proof or evidence of something, or are a record of something. ❑ *Passengers must carry proper documentation.* N-UNCOUNT

**docu|soap** /dɒkjəsoʊp/ **(docusoaps)** A **docusoap** is a television programme that shows the daily lives of people who work in a place such as a hospital or an airport, and is broadcast at a regular time each week or day. N-COUNT

**dod|der|ing** /dɒdərɪŋ/ If you refer to someone as a **doddering** old man or woman, you are saying in a disrespectful way that they are old and not strong. ❑ *...a doddering old man making his will before he's too senile.* ADJ: usu ADJ n [disapproval] = decrepit

**dod|dery** /dɒdəri/ Someone who is **doddery** walks in an unsteady way, especially because of old age. ADJ

**dod|dle** /dɒdəl/ If you say that something is **a doddle**, you mean that it is very easy to do. [BRIT, INFORMAL] N-SING: a N = cinch

**dodge** /dɒdʒ/ **(dodges, dodging, dodged)** 1 If you **dodge**, you move suddenly, often to avoid being hit, caught, or seen. ❑ *He dodged amongst the seething crowds of men.* VERB V prep/adv
2 If you **dodge** something, you avoid it by quickly moving aside or out of reach so that it cannot hit or reach you. ❑ *He desperately dodged a speeding car trying to run him down.* VERB = sidestep V n
3 If you **dodge** something, you deliberately avoid thinking about it or dealing with it, often by being deceitful. ❑ *He boasts of dodging military service by feigning illness.* VERB = evade V n ♦ **Dodge** is also a noun. ❑ *This was not just a tax dodge.* N-COUNT: usu supp N

**dodg|em** /dɒdʒəm/ **(dodgems)** A **dodgem** or **dodgem car** is a small electric car with a wide rubber strip all round. People drive dodgems around a special area at an amusement park and sometimes crash into each other for fun. [mainly BRIT, TRADEMARK] N-COUNT: usu pl

> in AM, use **bumper car**

**dodg|er** /dɒdʒəʳ/ **(dodgers)** A **dodger** is someone who avoids doing a duty or paying a charge, for example paying taxes or for train travel. ❑ *...tax dodgers who hide their interest earnings.* ➔ See also **draft dodger**. N-COUNT: usu n N = evader

**dodgy** /dɒdʒi/ **(dodgier, dodgiest)** 1 If you describe someone or something as **dodgy**, you disapprove of them because they seem rather dishonest and unreliable. [BRIT, INFORMAL] ❑ *He was a bit of a dodgy character.* ADJ [disapproval] = suspect
2 If you say that something is **dodgy**, you mean that it seems rather risky, dangerous, or unreliable. [BRIT, INFORMAL] ❑ *Predicting voting trends from economic forecasts is a dodgy business.* ADJ
3 If you say that someone has a **dodgy** heart or knee, for example, you mean that that part of their body is not very strong or healthy. [BRIT, INFORMAL] ❑ *My heart's a bit dodgy.* ADJ

**dodo** /doʊdoʊ/ **(dodos** or **dodoes)** 1 A **dodo** was a very large bird that was unable to fly. Dodos are now extinct. N-COUNT
2 If you refer to someone as a **dodo**, you think they are foolish or silly. [INFORMAL] N-COUNT [disapproval]

**doe** /doʊ/ **(does)** A **doe** is an adult female rabbit, hare, or deer. N-COUNT

**doer** /duːəʳ/ **(doers)** If you refer to someone as a **doer**, you mean that they do jobs promptly and efficiently, without spending a lot of time thinking about them. ❑ *Robertson was a doer, not a thinker.* N-COUNT

**does** /dəz, STRONG dʌz/ **Does** is the third person singular in the present tense of **do**.

**doesn't** /dʌzənt/ **Doesn't** is the usual spoken form of 'does not'. ◆◆◆

**doff** /dɒf, AM dɔːf/ **(doffs, doffing, doffed)** If you **doff** your hat or coat, you take it off. [OLD-FASHIONED] ❑ *The peasants doff their hats.* VERB V n

**dog** /dɒg, AM dɔːg/ **(dogs, dogging, dogged)** ◆◆◇
1 A **dog** is a very common four-legged animal that is often kept by people as a pet or to guard or hunt. There are many different breeds of dog. ❑ *The British are renowned as a nation of dog lovers.* N-COUNT
2 You use **dog** to refer to a male dog, or to the male of some related species such as wolves or foxes. ❑ *Is this a dog or a bitch?* N-COUNT ≠ bitch
3 If someone calls a man a **dog**, they strongly disapprove of him. N-COUNT [disapproval]
4 People use **dog** to refer to something that they consider unsatisfactory or of poor quality. [AM, INFORMAL] N-COUNT [disapproval]
5 If problems or injuries **dog** you, they are with you all the time. ❑ *His career has been dogged by bad luck.* VERB = plague V n
6 ➔ See also **dogged, guide dog, prairie dog, sniffer dog**.
PHRASES 7 You describe something as a **dog's breakfast** or **dog's dinner** in order to express your disapproval of it, for example because it is very untidy, badly organized, or badly done. [BRIT, INFORMAL] PHRASE: v-link PHR, PHR after v [disapproval] = mess
8 You use **dog eat dog** to express your disapproval of a situation where everyone wants to succeed and is willing to harm other people in order to do so. ❑ *It is very much dog eat dog out there.* PHRASE: v-link PHR, PHR n [disapproval] = cut-throat
9 If you say that something **is going to the dogs**, you mean that it is becoming weaker and worse in quality. [INFORMAL] ❑ *They sit in impotent opposition while the country goes to the dogs.* PHRASE: V inflects [disapproval]

**dog-collar** **(dog-collars)** also **dog collar**. 1 A **dog-collar** is a stiff, round, white collar that fastens at the back and that is worn by Christian priests and ministers. [INFORMAL] N-COUNT = clerical collar
2 A **dog-collar** is a collar worn by a dog. N-COUNT

**dog-eared** A book or piece of paper that is **dog-eared** has been used so much that the corners of the pages are turned down or torn. ❑ *...dog-eared copies of ancient history books.* ADJ

**dog|fight** /dɒgfaɪt, AM dɔːg-/ **(dogfights)** also **dog fight**. 1 A **dogfight** is a fight between fighter planes, in which they fly close to one another and move very fast. N-COUNT
2 If you say that organizations or people are involved in a **dogfight**, you mean they are struggling very hard against each other in order to succeed. ❑ *The three leading contenders were locked in a dogfight.* N-COUNT: usu with supp

**dog|fish** /dɒgfɪʃ, AM dɔːg-/ **(dogfish)** A **dogfish** is a small shark. There are several kinds of dogfish. N-COUNT

**dog|ged** /dɒgɪd, AM dɔː-/ If you describe someone's actions as **dogged**, you mean that they are determined to continue with something even if it becomes difficult or dangerous. ❑ *They have gained respect through sheer dogged determination.* ADJ: ADJ n = resolute, persistent ♦ **dog|ged|ly** *She would fight doggedly for her rights as the children's mother.* ADV: usu ADV with v ♦ **dog|ged|ness** *Most of my accomplishments came as the result of sheer doggedness.* N-UNCOUNT

**dog|ger|el** /dɒgərəl, AM dɔː-/ If you refer to a poem as **doggerel**, you are emphasizing that you N-UNCOUNT [disapproval] think it is very bad poetry. ❑ *...fragments of meaningless doggerel.*

**dog|gie** /dɒgi, AM dɔːgi/ **(doggies) Doggie** is a child's word for a dog. N-COUNT

**dog|gie bag (doggie bags)** If you ask for a **doggie bag** in a restaurant, you ask for any food you have not eaten to be put into a bag for you to take home. N-COUNT

**dog|gy** /dɒgi, AM dɔːgi/ **(doggies)** → see **doggie**.

**dog|house** /dɒghaʊs, AM dɔːg-/ **(doghouses)** also **dog-house**. 1 A **doghouse** is a small building made especially for a dog to sleep in. [AM] N-COUNT

✓ in BRIT, use **kennel**

2 If you are **in the doghouse**, people are annoyed or angry with you. [INFORMAL] ❑ *Her husband was in the doghouse for leaving her to cope on her own.* PHRASE: v-link PHR

**dog|leg** /dɒgleg, AM dɔːg-/ **(doglegs)** also **dog-leg**. A **dogleg** is a sharp bend in a road or a path. N-COUNT

**dog|ma** /dɒgmə, AM dɔːg-/ **(dogmas)** If you refer to a belief or a system of beliefs as a **dogma**, you disapprove of it because people are expected to accept that it is true, without questioning it. ❑ *Their political dogma has blinded them to the real needs of the country.* N-VAR: usu with supp [disapproval]

**dog|mat|ic** /dɒgmætɪk, AM dɔːg-/ If you say that someone is **dogmatic**, you are critical of them because they are convinced that they are right, and refuse to consider that other opinions might also be justified. ❑ *Many writers at this time held rigidly dogmatic views.* ♦ **dog|mati|cal|ly** /dɒgmætɪkli, AM dɔːg-/ *He applies the Marxist world view dogmatically to all social phenomena.* ADJ [disapproval] ADV: ADV with v

**dog|ma|tism** /dɒgmətɪzəm, AM dɔːg-/ If you refer to an opinion as **dogmatism**, you are criticizing it for being strongly stated without considering all the relevant facts or other people's opinions. ❑ *We cannot allow dogmatism to stand in the way of progress.* ♦ **dog|ma|tist (dogmatists)** *Intellectuals are becoming unhappy with dogmatists in the party leadership.* N-UNCOUNT [disapproval] N-COUNT

**do-gooder (do-gooders)** If you describe someone as a **do-gooder**, you mean that they do things which they think will help other people, although you think that they are interfering. N-COUNT [disapproval]

**dogs|body** /dɒgzbɒdi, AM dɔːgz-/ **(dogsbodies)** A **dogsbody** is a person who has to do all the boring jobs that nobody else wants to do. [BRIT, INFORMAL] N-COUNT = gofer

**dog tag (dog tags) Dog tags** are metal identification discs that are worn on a chain around the neck by members of the United States armed forces. N-COUNT: usu pl

**dog-tired** If you say that you are **dog-tired**, you are emphasizing that you are extremely tired. [INFORMAL] ❑ *By dusk we were dog-tired and heading for home.* ADJ: v-link ADJ [emphasis]

**dog|wood** /dɒgwʊd, AM dɔːg-/ **(dogwoods)** A **dogwood** is a tree or bush that has groups of small white flowers surrounded by four large leaves. N-VAR

**doi|ly** /dɔɪli/ **(doilies)** A **doily** is a small, round piece of paper or cloth that has a pattern of tiny holes in it. Doilies are put on plates under cakes and sandwiches. N-COUNT

**do|ings** /duːɪŋz/ Someone's **doings** are their activities at a particular time. ❑ *The film chronicles the everyday doings of a group of London schoolchildren.* N-PLURAL: usu with poss

**do-it-yourself Do-it-yourself** is the same as **DIY**. N-UNCOUNT

**Dol|by** /dɒlbi/ **Dolby** is a system which reduces the background noise on electronic cassette players. [TRADEMARK] ❑ *...a cassette deck equipped with Dolby noise reduction.* N-UNCOUNT: oft N n

**dol|drums** /dɒldrəmz/ If an activity or situation is **in the doldrums**, it is very quiet and nothing new or exciting is happening. ❑ *The economy is in the doldrums.* PHRASE: usu v-link PHR

**dole** /doʊl/ 1 **The dole** or **dole** is money that is given regularly by the government to people who are unemployed. [BRIT] N-UNCOUNT: also the N = benefit

✓ in AM, usually use **welfare**

2 Someone who is **on the dole** is registered as unemployed and receives money from the government. [mainly BRIT] ❑ *It's not easy living on the dole.* PHRASE: PHR after v, v-link PHR

✓ in AM, usually use **on welfare**

♦ **dole out** If you **dole** something **out**, you give a certain amount of it to each member of a group. ❑ *I got out my wallet and began to dole out the money.* PHRASAL VERB = dish out V P n (not pron) Also V n P

**dole|ful** /doʊlfʊl/ A **doleful** expression, manner, or voice is depressing and miserable. ❑ *He gave me a long, doleful look.* ♦ **dole|ful|ly** *'I don't know why they left,' he said dolefully.* ADJ = mournful ADV: ADV with v

**dole queue (dole queues)** When people talk about **the dole queue**, they are talking about the state of being unemployed, especially when saying how many people are unemployed. [BRIT] ❑ *Another 29,100 people have joined the dole queue.* N-COUNT

✓ in AM, usually use **unemployment line**

**doll** /dɒl/ **(dolls, dolling, dolled)** A **doll** is a child's toy which looks like a small person or baby. N-COUNT

♦ **doll up** If a woman **dolls** herself **up**, she puts on smart or fashionable clothes in order to try and look attractive for a particular occasion. [INFORMAL] ❑ *We used to doll ourselves up and go into town.* ♦ **dolled up** *She was dolled up for the occasion.* PHRASAL VERB V pron-refl P ADJ: usu v-link ADJ

**dol|lar** /dɒləʳ/ **(dollars)** 1 The **dollar** is the unit of money used in the USA, Canada, Australia, and some other countries. It is represented by the symbol $. A dollar is divided into one hundred smaller units called cents. ❑ *She gets paid seven dollars an hour... The government is spending billions of dollars on new urban rail projects.* ♦ **The dollar** is also used to refer to the American currency system. ❑ *In early trading in Tokyo, the dollar fell sharply against the yen.* 2 If you pay **top dollar** for something, you pay a lot of money for it. [INFORMAL] ❑ *Japanese investors once paid top dollar for the most glamorous hotels in the United States.* ♦♦♦ N-COUNT: usu num N N-SING: the N PHRASE

**dol|lop** /dɒləp/ **(dollops)** A **dollop** of soft or sticky food is a large spoonful of it. [INFORMAL] ❑ *...a dollop of cream.* N-COUNT: usu N of n

**doll's house (doll's houses)**

✓ in AM, use **dollhouse**

A **doll's house** is a toy in the form of a small house, which contains tiny dolls and furniture for children to play with. N-COUNT

**dol|ly** /dɒli/ **(dollies)** A **dolly** is a child's word for a doll. N-COUNT

**dol|phin** /dɒlfɪn/ **(dolphins)** A **dolphin** is a mammal which lives in the sea and looks like a large fish with a pointed mouth. N-COUNT

**dolt** /doʊlt/ **(dolts)** If you call someone a **dolt**, you think they are stupid, or have done something stupid. [INFORMAL] N-COUNT [disapproval] = idiot

**do|main** /doʊmeɪn/ **(domains)** 1 A **domain** is a particular field of thought, activity, or interest, especially one over which someone has control, influence, or rights. [FORMAL] ❑ *...the great experimenters in the domain of art.* 2 On the Internet, a **domain** is a set of addresses that shows, for example, the category or geographical area that an Internet address belongs to. [COMPUTING] N-COUNT: usu with supp N-COUNT

**do|main name (domain names)** A **domain name** is the name of a person's or organization's website on the Internet, for example N-COUNT 'cobuild.collins.co.uk'. [COMPUTING] ❑ *Is the domain name already registered or still available?*

**dome** /doʊm/ **(domes)** 1 A **dome** is a round roof. ❑ *...the dome of St Paul's cathedral.* 2 A **dome** is any object that has a similar shape to a dome. ❑ *...the dome of the hill.* N-COUNT N-COUNT

**domed** /doʊmd/ Something that is **domed** is in the shape of a dome. ❑ *...the great hall with its domed ceiling.* ADJ

**do|mes|tic** /dəmestɪk/ **(domestics)** ◆◆◇ 1 **Domestic** political activities, events, and situations happen or exist within one particular country. ❑ *...over 100 domestic flights a day to 15 UK destinations. ...sales in the domestic market.* ➔ See also **gross domestic product**. ADJ: usu ADJ n ≠ foreign, international ♦ **do|mes|ti|cal|ly** /dəmestɪkli/ *Opportunities will improve as the company expands domestically and internationally.* ADV: ADV after v, ADV -ed/adj, ADV with cl 2 **Domestic** duties and activities are concerned with the running of a home and family. ❑ *...a plan for sharing domestic chores.* ADJ: ADJ n = household 3 **Domestic** items and services are intended to be used in people's homes rather than in factories or offices. ❑ *...domestic appliances.* ADJ: ADJ n = household ≠ industrial 4 A **domestic** situation or atmosphere is one which involves a family and their home. ❑ *It was a scene of such domestic bliss.* ADJ: usu ADJ n 5 A **domestic** animal is one that is not wild and is kept either on a farm to produce food or in someone's home as a pet. ❑ *...a domestic cat.* ADJ ≠ wild 6 A **domestic**, a **domestic help**, or a **domestic worker** is a person who is paid to come to help with the work that has to be done in a house such as the cleaning, washing, and ironing. N-COUNT

**do|mes|ti|cate** /dəmestɪkeɪt/ **(domesticates, domesticating, domesticated)** When people **domesticate** wild animals or plants, they bring them under control and use them to produce food or as pets. ❑ *We domesticated the dog to help us with hunting.* VERB = tame V n

**do|mes|ti|cat|ed** /dəmestɪkeɪtɪd/ Someone who is **domesticated** willingly does household tasks such as cleaning. ❑ *Mum wasn't very domesticated.* ADJ

**do|mes|ti|city** /doʊmestɪsɪti/ **Domesticity** is the state of being at home with your family. ❑ *...a small rebellion against routine and cosy domesticity.* N-UNCOUNT

**do|mes|tic sci|ence** In British schools, **domestic science** was the name used to refer to the subject which involved cookery, sewing, and other household skills. The subject is now referred to as **home economics**, which is also the usual American term. N-UNCOUNT

**do|mes|tic vio|lence** **Domestic violence** is violence that takes place in the home, especially between a husband and wife. ❑ *Women are still the main victims of domestic violence.* N-UNCOUNT

**domi|cile** /dɒmɪsaɪl/ **(domiciles)** Your **domicile** is the place where you live. [FORMAL] N-COUNT: oft with poss = abode

**domi|ciled** /dɒmɪsaɪld/ If you are **domiciled in** a particular place, you live there. [FORMAL] ❑ *Frank is currently domiciled in Berlin.* ADJ: usu v-link ADJ, oft ADJ *in* n

**domi|nance** /dɒmɪnəns/ The **dominance** of a particular person or thing is the fact that they are more powerful, successful, or important than other people or things. ❑ *...an attempt by each group to establish dominance over the other.* N-UNCOUNT: oft N *of/over* n = supremacy

**domi|nant** /dɒmɪnənt/ 1 Someone or something that is **dominant** is more powerful, successful, influential, or noticeable than other people or things. ❑ *...a change which would maintain his party's dominant position in Scotland.* ADJ = pre-eminent 2 A **dominant** gene is one that produces a particular characteristic, whether a person has only one of these genes from one parent, or two genes, one from each parent. Compare **recessive**. [TECHNICAL] ADJ: usu ADJ n

**domi|nate** /dɒmɪneɪt/ **(dominates, dominating, dominated)** ◆◆◇ 1 To **dominate** a situation means to be the most powerful or important person or thing in it. ❑ *The book is expected to dominate the best-seller lists... No single factor appears to dominate.* VERB V n V ♦ **domi|na|tion** /dɒmɪneɪʃᵊn/ *...the domination of the market by a small number of organizations.* N-UNCOUNT 2 If one country or person **dominates** another, they have power over them. ❑ *Women are no longer dominated by the men in their relationships... The countries of Eastern Europe immediately started to dominate.* VERB V n V ♦ **domi|na|tion** *They had five centuries of domination by the Romans.* N-UNCOUNT 3 If a building, mountain, or other object **dominates** an area, it is so large or impressive that you cannot avoid seeing it. ❑ *It's one of the biggest buildings in this area, and it really dominates this whole place.* VERB V n

**domi|nat|ing** /dɒmɪneɪtɪŋ/ A **dominating** person has a very strong personality and influences the people around them. ❑ *She certainly was a dominating figure in politics.* ADJ: usu ADJ n = commanding

**domi|neer|ing** /dɒmɪnɪərɪŋ/ If you say that someone is **domineering**, you disapprove of them because you feel that they try to control other people without any consideration for their feelings or opinions. ❑ *Mick was stubborn and domineering with a very bad temper.* ADJ disapproval = overbearing

**do|min|ion** /dəmɪnjən/ **(dominions)** 1 **Dominion** is control or authority. [FORMAL] ❑ *They truly believe they have dominion over us.* N-COUNT: oft N *over* n 2 A **dominion** is an area of land that is controlled by a ruler. ❑ *The Republic is a dominion of the Brazilian people.* N-COUNT: oft with poss

**domi|no** /dɒmɪnoʊ/ **(dominoes)** 1 **Dominoes** are small rectangular blocks marked with two groups of spots on one side. They are used for playing various games. N-COUNT 2 **Dominoes** is a game in which players put dominoes onto a table in turn. N-UNCOUNT

**domi|no ef|fect** If one event causes another similar event, which in turn causes another event, and so on, you can refer to this as a **domino effect**. ❑ *The domino effect if one train is cancelled is enormous.* N-SING

**don** /dɒn/ **(dons, donning, donned)** 1 If you **don** clothing, you put it on. [WRITTEN] ❑ *The crowd threw petrol bombs at the police, who responded by donning riot gear.* VERB V n 2 A **don** is a lecturer at Oxford or Cambridge University in England. ♦ Lecturers from any university are sometimes referred to as **dons**. [BRIT] N-COUNT N-COUNT

**do|nate** /doʊneɪt/ **(donates, donating, donated)** 1 If you **donate** something **to** a charity or other organization, you give it to them. ❑ *He frequently donates large sums to charity... Others donated secondhand clothes.* VERB V n *to* n V n ♦ **do|na|tion** /doʊneɪʃᵊn/ *...the donation of his collection to the art gallery.* N-UNCOUNT: usu N *of* n 2 If you **donate** your blood or a part of your body, you allow doctors to use it to help someone who is ill. ❑ *...people who are willing to donate their organs for use after death.* VERB V n ♦ **do|na|tion** *...measures aimed at encouraging organ donation.* N-UNCOUNT: usu with supp

**do|na|tion** /doʊneɪʃᵊn/ **(donations)** A **donation** is something which someone gives to a charity or other organization. ❑ *Employees make regular donations to charity.* ➔ See also **donate**. N-COUNT: oft N *to/of/from* n

**done** /dʌn/ ◆◇◇ 1 **Done** is the past participle of **do**. 2 A task or activity that is **done** has been completed successfully. ❑ *When her deal is done, the client emerges with her purchase.* ADJ: v-link ADJ 3 When something that you are cooking is **done**, it has been cooked long enough and is ready. ❑ *As soon as the cake is done, remove it from the oven.* ADJ: v-link ADJ 4 You say '**Done**' when you are accepting a deal, arrangement, or bet that someone has offered to make with you. [SPOKEN] ❑ *'You lead and we'll look for it.' — 'Done.'* CONVENTION formulae 5 If you say that something is **over and done with**, you mean that it is completely finished and you do not have to think about it any more. [SPOKEN] ❑ *Once this is all over and done with you can have a rest.* PHRASE: v-link PHR, PHR after v

**Don Juan** /dɒn dʒuːən/ **(Don Juans)** If you describe a man as a **Don Juan**, you mean he has had sex with many women. N-COUNT

**don|key** /dɒŋki/ **(donkeys)** 1 A **donkey** is an animal which is like a horse but which is smaller and has longer ears. N-COUNT = ass 2 For **donkey's years** means for a very long time. [BRIT, INFORMAL] ❑ *I've been a vegetarian for donkey's years.* PHRASE: prep PHR [emphasis] = ages

**don|key jack|et** **(donkey jackets)** A **donkey jacket** is a thick, warm jacket, usually dark blue with a strip across the shoulders at the back. [BRIT] N-COUNT

**don|key work** If you do **the donkey work**, you do the hard work or the less interesting part of the work that needs to be done. [BRIT, INFORMAL] N-SING: usu *the* N

**don|nish** /dɒnɪʃ/ If you describe a man as **donnish**, you think he is rather serious and intellectual. [mainly BRIT] ADJ

**do|nor** /doʊnəʳ/ **(donors)** 1 A **donor** is someone who gives a part of their body or some of their blood to be used by doctors to help a person who is ill. ❑ *Doctors removed the healthy kidney from the donor.* N-COUNT: oft n N 2 **Donor** organs or parts are organs or parts of the body which people allow doctors to use to help people who are ill. ADJ: ADJ n 3 A **donor** is a person or organization who gives something, especially money, to a charity, organization, or country that needs it. N-COUNT

**do|nor card** **(donor cards)** A **donor card** is a card which people carry in order to make sure that, when they die, their organs are used by doctors to help people who are ill. N-COUNT

**don't** /doʊnt/ **Don't** is the usual spoken form of 'do not'.

**do|nut** /doʊnʌt/ **(donuts)** → see **doughnut**.

**doo|dad** /duːdæd/ **(doodads)** A **doodad** is the same as a **doodah**. [AM, INFORMAL] N-COUNT

**doo|dah** /duːdɑː/ **(doodahs)** You can refer to something, especially an electronic device, as a **doodah** when you do not know exactly what is called. [BRIT, INFORMAL] ❑ *The car has all the latest electronic doodahs.* N-COUNT

**doo|dle** /duːdəl/ **(doodles, doodling, doodled)** 1 A **doodle** is a pattern or picture that you draw when you are bored or thinking about something else. N-COUNT 2 When someone **doodles**, they draw doodles. ❑ *He looked across at Jackson, doodling on his notebook.* VERB V

**doom** /duːm/ **(dooms, dooming, doomed)** 1 **Doom** is a terrible future state or event which you cannot prevent. ❑ *...his warnings of impending doom.* N-UNCOUNT 2 If you have a sense or feeling of **doom**, you feel that things are going very badly and are likely to get even worse. ❑ *Why are people so full of gloom and doom?* N-UNCOUNT 3 If a fact or event **dooms** someone or something **to** a particular fate, it makes certain that they are going to suffer in some way. ❑ *That argument doomed their marriage to failure.* VERB = condemn V n *to* n

**doomed** /duːmd/ 1 If something **is doomed to** happen, or if you **are doomed to** a particular state, something unpleasant is certain to happen, and you can do nothing to prevent it. ❑ *Their plans seemed doomed to failure.* ADJ: v-link ADJ, ADJ *to* n, ADJ to-inf 2 Someone or something that is **doomed** is certain to fail or be destroyed. ❑ *I used to pour time and energy into projects that were doomed from the start.* ADJ

**dooms|day** /duːmzdeɪ/ 1 **Doomsday** is a day or time when you expect something terrible or unpleasant is going to happen. ❑ *...the doomsday scenario of civil war between the two factions.* N-UNCOUNT 2 In the Christian religion, **Doomsday** is the last day of the world, on which God will judge everyone. N-PROPER

**dooms|day cult** **(doomsday cults)** A **doomsday cult** is a religious cult whose members believe that the world is about to end. [mainly JOURNALISM] N-COUNT

**door** /dɔːʳ/ **(doors)** ◆◆◆ 1 A **door** is a piece of wood, glass, or metal, which is moved to open and close the entrance to a building, room, cupboard, or vehicle. ❑ *I knocked at the front door, but there was no answer... The policeman opened the door and looked in.* N-COUNT 2 A **door** is the space in a wall when a door is open. ❑ *She looked through the door of the kitchen. Her daughter was at the stove.* N-COUNT = doorway 3 **Doors** is used in expressions such as **a few doors down** or **three doors up** to refer to a place that is a particular number of buildings away from where you are. [INFORMAL] ❑ *Mrs Cade's house was only a few doors down from her daughter's apartment.* N-PLURAL: amount N *down/up* 4 → See also **next door**.

PHRASES 5 When you **answer the door**, you go and open the door because a visitor has knocked on it or rung the bell. ❑ *Carol answered the door as soon as I knocked.* PHRASE: V inflects 6 If you say that someone gets or does something **by the back door** or **through the back door**, you are criticizing them for doing it secretly and unofficially. ❑ *The government would not allow anyone to sneak in by the back door and seize power by force.* PHRASE: PHR after v [disapproval] 7 If someone **closes the door on** something, they stop thinking about it or dealing with it. ❑ *We never close the door on a successful series.* PHRASE: V inflects: PHR n 8 If people have talks and discussions **behind closed doors**, they have them in private because they want them to be kept secret. ❑ *...decisions taken in secret behind closed doors.* PHRASE: PHR after v, PHR n 9 If someone goes **from door to door** or goes **door to door**, they go along a street calling at each house in turn, for example selling something. ❑ *They are going from door to door collecting money from civilians.* PHRASE: PHR after v, PHR n 10 If you talk about a distance or journey **from door to door** or **door to door**, you are talking about the distance from the place where the journey starts to the place where it finishes. ❑ *...tickets covering the whole journey from door to door.* PHRASE 11 If you say that something helps someone to get their **foot in the door** or their **toe in the door**, you mean that it gives them an opportunity to start doing something new, usually in an area that is difficult to succeed in. ❑ *The bondholding may help the firm get its foot in the door to win the business.* PHRASE: N inflects, PHR after v 12 If someone **shuts the door in** your **face** or **slams the door in** your **face**, they refuse to talk to you or give you any information. ❑ *Did you say anything to him or just shut the door in his face?* PHRASE: V inflects 13 If you **lay** something **at** someone's **door**, you blame them for an unpleasant event or situation. ❑ *The blame is generally laid at the door of the government.* PHRASE: V inflects 14 If someone or something **opens the door to** a good new idea or situation, they introduce it or make it possible. ❑ *This book opens the door to some of the most exciting findings in solid-state physics.* PHRASE: V and N inflect, oft PHR *to* n 15 When you are **out of doors**, you are not inside a building, but in the open air. ❑ *The weather was fine enough for working out of doors.* PHRASE: PHR after v, v-link PHR = outdoors 16 If you **see** someone **to the door**, you go to the door with a visitor when they leave. PHRASE: V inflects 17 If someone **shows** you **the door**, they ask you to leave because they are angry with you. ❑ *Would they forgive and forget – or show him the door?* PHRASE: V inflects 18 **at death's door** → see **death**.

**door|bell** /dɔːʳbel/ **(doorbells)** A **doorbell** is a bell on the outside of a house which you can ring so that the people inside know that you want to see them. → See picture on page 1705. N-COUNT

**door|keeper** /dɔːʳkiːpəʳ/ **(doorkeepers)** A **doorkeeper** is a person whose job is to stand at the door of a building such as a hotel and help people who are going in or out. N-COUNT

**door|knob** /dɔːʳnɒb/ **(doorknobs)** A **doorknob** is a round handle on a door. N-COUNT

**door|man** /dɔːʳmən/ **(doormen)** 1 A **doorman** is a man who stands at the door of a club, prevents unwanted people from coming in, and makes people leave if they cause trouble. N-COUNT = bouncer 2 A **doorman** is a person whose job is to stay by the main entrance of a large building, and help people visiting the building. N-COUNT

**door|mat** /dɔːʳmæt/ **(doormats)** 1 A **doormat** is a mat by a door which people can wipe N-COUNT their shoes on when they enter a house or building. [N-COUNT] [disapproval] 2 If you say that someone is a **doormat**, you are criticizing them because they let other people treat them badly, and do not complain or defend themselves when they are being treated unfairly. [INFORMAL] ❑ *If you always give in to others you will end up feeling like a doormat.*

**door|step** /dɔːʳstep/ **(doorsteps)** [N-COUNT] 1 A **doorstep** is a step in front of a door on the outside of a building. → See picture on page 1705. [PHRASE: v-link PHR, PHR after v] 2 If a place is **on** your **doorstep**, it is very near to where you live. If something happens **on** your **doorstep**, it happens very close to where you live. ❑ *It is all too easy to lose sight of what is happening on our own doorstep.*

**door|stop** /dɔːʳstɒp/ **(doorstops)** [N-COUNT] A **doorstop** is a heavy object that you use to keep a door open.

**door-to-door** → see **door**.

**door|way** /dɔːʳweɪ/ **(doorways)** [N-COUNT] 1 A **doorway** is a space in a wall where a door opens and closes. ❑ *Hannah looked up to see David and another man standing in the doorway.* [N-COUNT] 2 A **doorway** is a covered space just outside the door of a building. ❑ *...homeless people sleeping in shop doorways.*

**dope** /doʊp/ **(dopes, doping, doped)** [N-UNCOUNT] 1 **Dope** is a drug, usually an illegal drug such as marijuana or cocaine. [INFORMAL] [VERB = drug] 2 If someone **dopes** a person or animal or **dopes** their food, they put drugs into their food or force them to take drugs. ❑ *Anyone could have got in and doped the wine...* [V n] *I'd been doped with Somnolin...* [be V-ed with n] *They've got him doped to the eyeballs.* [V-ed] [N-COUNT] [disapproval] 3 If someone calls a person a **dope**, they think that the person is stupid. [INFORMAL]

**doped up** [ADJ: usu v-link ADJ = drugged] If someone is **doped up**, they are in a state where they cannot think clearly because they are under the influence of drugs. [INFORMAL] ❑ *I feel a bit doped up, but I'm okay.*

**dopey** /doʊpi/ [ADJ = groggy] 1 Someone who is **dopey** is sleepy, as though they have been drugged. ❑ *The medicine always made him feel dopey and unable to concentrate.* [ADJ] [disapproval] [= dozy] 2 If you describe someone as **dopey**, you mean that they are rather stupid. [INFORMAL]

**dork** /dɔːʳk/ **(dorks)** [N-COUNT] [disapproval] [= nerd] If you say that someone is a **dork**, you think they dress badly in old-fashioned clothes and behave very awkwardly in social situations. [AM, INFORMAL] ❑ *...their conviction that family holidays were strictly for dorks.*

**dorm** /dɔːʳm/ **(dorms)** [N-COUNT] A **dorm** is the same as a **dormitory**. [INFORMAL]

**dor|mant** /dɔːʳmənt/ [ADJ] Something that is **dormant** is not active, growing, or being used at the present time but is capable of becoming active later on. ❑ *The virus remains dormant in nerve tissue until activated.* ♦ **dor|man|cy** /dɔːʳmənsi/ [N-UNCOUNT] *During dormancy the plants must be kept very dry.*

**dor|mer** /dɔːʳməʳ/ **(dormers)** [N-COUNT] A **dormer** or **dormer window** is a window that is built upright in a sloping roof.

**dor|mi|tory** /dɔːʳmɪtri, AM -tɔːri/ **(dormitories)** [N-COUNT] 1 A **dormitory** is a large bedroom where several people sleep, for example in a boarding school. ❑ *...the boys' dormitory.* [N-COUNT] 2 A **dormitory** is a building in a college or university where students live. [AM] ❑ *She lived in a college dormitory.*

✔ in BRIT, use **hall of residence**

[ADJ: ADJ n] 3 If you refer to a place as a **dormitory** suburb or town, you mean that most of the people who live there travel to work in another, larger town a short distance away. [BRIT]

**dor|mouse** /dɔːʳmaʊs/ **(dormice** /dɔːʳmaɪs/**)** [N-COUNT] A **dormouse** is a small animal that looks like a mouse. It is found in southern England and Wales.

**dor|sal** /dɔːʳsəl/ [ADJ: ADJ n] **Dorsal** means relating to the back of a fish or animal. [TECHNICAL] ❑ *...a dolphin's dorsal fin.*

**DOS** /dɒs/ [N-UNCOUNT] **DOS** is the part of a computer operating system that controls and manages files and programs stored on disk. **DOS** is an abbreviation for 'disk operating system'. [COMPUTING, TRADEMARK] ❑ *Where do I find the instructions to load DOS programs from Windows 98?*

**dos|age** /doʊsɪdʒ/ **(dosages)** [N-COUNT] A **dosage** is the amount of a medicine or drug that someone takes or should take. ❑ *He was put on a high dosage of vitamin C.*

**dose** /doʊs/ **(doses, dosing, dosed)** [N-COUNT: oft N of n] 1 A **dose of** medicine or a drug is a measured amount of it which is intended to be taken at one time. ❑ *One dose of penicillin can wipe out the infection.* [N-COUNT: usu adj N of n] [emphasis] 2 You can refer to an amount of something as a **dose of** that thing, especially when you want to emphasize that there is a great deal of it. ❑ *The West is getting a heavy dose of snow and rain today.* [VERB] 3 If you **dose** a person or animal **with** medicine, you give them an amount of it. ❑ *The doctor fixed the rib, dosed him heavily with drugs, and said he would probably get better...* [V n with n] *I dosed myself with quinine.* [V pron-refl with n] ♦ **Dose up** [PHRASAL VERB] [V n P with n] means the same as **dose**. ❑ *I dosed him up with Valium.*

**dosh** /dɒʃ/ [N-UNCOUNT] **Dosh** is money. [BRIT, INFORMAL] ❑ *...a chap who'd made lots of dosh.*

**doss** /dɒs/ **(dosses, dossing, dossed)** [VERB] If someone **dosses** somewhere, they sleep in a place which is uncomfortable, usually because they have nowhere else to live. [BRIT, INFORMAL] ❑ *...young people dossing in the streets of our cities.* [V prep/adv] ♦ **Doss down** [PHRASAL VERB] [V P prep/adv] means the same as **doss**. ❑ *When we had eaten, we dossed down in the lounge.*

**dos|ser** /dɒsəʳ/ **(dossers)** [N-COUNT] [disapproval] A **dosser** is a city person who does not have a permanent home and sleeps in the streets or in very cheap hotels. [BRIT, INFORMAL]

**doss-house (doss-houses)** also **doss house**, **dosshouse.** [N-COUNT] A **doss-house** is a kind of cheap hotel in a city for people who have no home and very little money. [BRIT, INFORMAL]

✔ in AM, use **flophouse**

**dos|si|er** /dɒsieɪ, -iəʳ/ **(dossiers)** [N-COUNT: oft N of/on n = file] A **dossier** is a collection of papers containing information on a particular event, or on a person such as a criminal or a spy. ❑ *The company is compiling a dossier of evidence to back its allegations.*

**dost** /dʌst/ **Dost** is an old-fashioned second person singular form of the verb 'do'.

**dot** /dɒt/ **(dots, dotting, dotted)** [N-COUNT] 1 A **dot** is a very small round mark, for example one that is used as the top part of the letter 'i', as a full stop, or as a decimal point. [N-COUNT = speck, spot] 2 You can refer to something that you can see in the distance and that looks like a small round mark as a **dot**. ❑ *Soon they were only dots above the hard line of the horizon.* [VERB] 3 When things **dot** a place or an area, they are scattered or spread all over it. ❑ *Small coastal towns dot the landscape.* [V n] 4 → See also **dotted**, **polka dots**.

**PHRASES** [PHRASE = punctually] 5 If you arrive somewhere or do something **on the dot**, you arrive there or do it at exactly the time that you were supposed to. ❑ *They appeared on the dot of 9.50 pm as always.* [PHRASE: Vs inflect] 6 If you say that someone **dots the i's and crosses the t's**, you mean that they pay great attention to every small detail in a task; often used to express your annoyance because such detailed work seems unnecessary and takes a very long time.

**dot|age** /doʊtɪdʒ/ [N-UNCOUNT: usu poss N] If someone is **in** their **dotage**, they are very old and becoming weak. ❑ *Even in his dotage, the Professor still sits on the committee.*

**dot-com (dot-coms)** [N-COUNT] A **dot-com** is a company that does all or most of its business on the Internet. ❑ *In 1999, dot-coms spent more than $1 billion on TV spots.*

**dote** /doʊt/ **(dotes, doting, doted)** [VERB] If you say that someone **dotes on** a person or a thing, you mean that they love or care about them very much and ignore any faults they may have. ❑ *He dotes on his nine-year-old son.* V on/upon n

**doth** /dʌθ/ **Doth** is an old-fashioned third person singular form of the verb 'do'.

**dot|ing** /doʊtɪŋ/ If you say that someone is, for example, a **doting** mother, husband, or friend, you mean that they show a lot of love for someone. ❑ *His doting parents bought him his first racing bike at 13.* ADJ: usu ADJ n

**dot ma|trix print|er** **(dot matrix printers)** also **dot-matrix printer.** A **dot matrix printer** is a computer printer using a device with a series of dots or pins stamped onto it to produce words and numbers. N-COUNT

**dot|ted** /dɒtɪd/ 1 A **dotted** line is a line which is made of a row of dots. ❑ *Cut along the dotted line.* ● If you **sign on the dotted line**, you formally agree to something by signing an official document. ❑ *Once you sign on the dotted line you are committed to that property.* 2 If a place or object is **dotted with** things, it has many of those things scattered over its surface. ❑ *The maps were dotted with the names of small towns.* 3 If things are **dotted around** a place, they can be found in many different parts of that place. ❑ *Many pieces of sculpture are dotted around the house.* 4 → See also **dot**. ADJ: usu ADJ n; PHRASE: V inflects; ADJ: v-link ADJ with n; ADJ: v-link ADJ prep = scattered

**dot|ty** /dɒti/ **(dottier, dottiest)** If you say that someone is **dotty**, you mean that they are slightly mad or likely to do strange things. [mainly BRIT, INFORMAL] ❑ *She was obviously going a bit dotty.* ADJ

**dou|ble** /dʌbᵊl/ **(doubles, doubling, doubled)** ◆◆◇
1 You use **double** to indicate that something includes or is made of two things of the same kind. ❑ *...a pair of double doors into the room from the new entrance hall. ...a lone skier gliding along smooth double tracks.* ADJ: ADJ n
2 You use **double** before a singular noun to refer to two things of the same type that occur together, or that are connected in some way. ❑ *...an extremely nasty double murder.* ADJ: ADJ n
3 If something is **double the** amount or size of another thing, it is twice as large. ❑ *The offer was to start a new research laboratory at double the salary he was then getting.* ♦ **Double** is also a pronoun. ❑ *If they think you're a tourist, they charge you double.* PREDET: PREDET the n = twice ≠ half; PRON
4 You use **double** to describe something which is twice the normal size or can hold twice the normal quantity of something. ❑ *...a double helping of ice cream. ...a large double garage.* ADJ
5 A **double** room is a room intended for two people, usually a couple, to stay or live in. ❑ *...bed and breakfast for £180 for two people in a double room.* ♦ **Double** is also a noun. ❑ *The Great Western Hotel costs around £60 a night for a double.* ADJ: usu ADJ n; N-COUNT
6 A **double** bed is a bed that is wide enough for two people to sleep in. ADJ: ADJ n
7 You use **double** to describe a drink that is twice the normal measure. ❑ *He was drinking his double whiskey too fast and scowling.* ♦ **Double** is also a noun. ❑ *Give me a whisky, a double.* ADJ: ADJ n; N-COUNT
8 **Double** is used when you are spelling a word or telling someone a number to show that a letter or digit is repeated. ❑ *Ring four two double two double two if you'd like to speak to our financial adviser.* ADJ: ADJ n
9 When something **doubles** or when you **double** it, it becomes twice as great in number, amount, or size. ❑ *The number of managers must double to 100 within 3 years... The program will double the amount of money available to help pay for child care.* VERB; V; V n
10 If you refer to someone as a person's **double**, you mean that they look exactly like them. ❑ *Your mother sees you as her double.* N-COUNT: poss N
11 If a person or thing **doubles as** someone or something else, they have a second job or purpose as well as their main one. ❑ *Lots of homes in town double as businesses.* ♦ **Double up** means the same as **double**. ❑ *The lids of the casserole dishes are designed to double up as baking dishes.* VERB; V as n; PHRASAL VERB; V P as n
12 In tennis or badminton, when people play **doubles**, two teams consisting of two players on each team play against each other on the same court. N-UNCOUNT

PHRASES 13 If you are **bent double**, the top half of your body is bent downwards so that your head is close to your knees. ❑ *Pickers are bent double, plucking each flower with lightning speed.* PHRASE: v-link PHR
14 If you **are seeing double**, there is something wrong with your eyes, and you can see two images instead of one. ❑ *I was dizzy, seeing double.* PHRASE: V inflects
15 in **double figures** → see **figure**.

♦ **double back** If you **double back** you go back in the direction that you came from. ❑ *We drove past it and had to double back.* PHRASAL VERB = turn back; V P

♦ **double up** 1 If something **doubles** you **up**, or if you **double up**, you bend your body quickly or violently, for example because you are laughing a lot or because you are feeling a lot of pain. ❑ *...a savage blow in the crutch which doubled him up... They laugh so hard they double up with laughter.* ♦ **Double over** means the same as **double up**. ❑ *Everyone was doubled over in laughter.* 2 → See also **double 11**. PHRASAL VERB; V n P; V P with/in n; PHRASAL VERB; V-ed P

**dou|ble act** **(double acts)** also **double-act.** Two comedians or entertainers who perform together are referred to as a **double act**. Their performance can also be called a **double act**. ❑ *...a famous comedy double act.* N-COUNT

**dou|ble agent** **(double agents)** A **double agent** is someone who works as a spy for a particular country or organization, but who also works for its enemies. N-COUNT

**double-barrelled**

✓ in AM, use **double-barreled**

1 A **double-barrelled** gun has two barrels. ❑ *...a double-barrelled shotgun.* ADJ: ADJ n
2 A **double-barrelled** surname has two parts which are joined by a hyphen, for example 'Miss J. Heydon-Smith'. [BRIT] ADJ: ADJ n
3 **Double-barrelled** is used to describe something such as a plan which has two main parts. [JOURNALISM] ADJ: ADJ n

**dou|ble bass** /dʌbᵊl beɪs/ **(double basses)** also **double-bass.** A **double bass** is the largest instrument in the violin family. N-VAR: oft the N

**dou|ble bill** **(double bills)** also **double-bill.** A **double bill** is a theatre or cinema performance in which there are two shows on the programme. N-COUNT: oft N of n

**dou|ble bind** **(double binds)** If you are **in a double bind**, you are in a very difficult situation, because whatever decision you make will have bad results. ❑ *Women are caught in a double bind, marginalised if they are not wives and mothers, under excessive pressure to be perfect if they are.* N-COUNT: usu sing = catch 22

**double-blind** A **double-blind** study or experiment compares two groups of people, one of which is being tested while the other is not. Neither the people doing the testing nor the members of the two groups know which group is being tested. ❑ *In a double-blind trial, there were definite improvements.* ADJ

**dou|ble bluff** **(double bluffs)** A **double bluff** is an attempt to deceive someone by telling them exactly what you intend to do when you know that they will assume you are lying. [BRIT] ❑ *They suspected this was a double bluff on the part of Cairo Intelligence. ...a continual round of bluff and double bluff.* N-VAR

**double-breasted** A **double-breasted** jacket or suit has two very wide sections at the front of the jacket which fit over one another when you button them up. ADJ: usu ADJ n

**double-check** **(double-checks, double-checking, double-checked)** If you **double-check** something, you examine or test it a second time to make sure that it is completely correct or safe. ❑ *Check and double-check spelling and punctuation... Double-check that the ladder is secure... Don't believe what you are told; double-check with an independent source.* VERB; V n; V that; V with n

**dou|ble chin** **(double chins)** If someone has a **double chin**, they have a fold of fat under their chin, making them look as if they have two chins. N-COUNT: usu sing

**dou|ble cream** **Double cream** is very thick cream. [BRIT] N-UNCOUNT

✓ in AM, use **heavy cream**

**double-cross** (double-crosses, double-crossing, double-crossed) If someone you trust **double-crosses** you, they do something which harms you instead of doing something they had promised to do. [INFORMAL] ❑ *Don't try and double-cross me, Taylor, because I'll kill you.* VERB = betray; V n

**double-dealing** **Double-dealing** is behaviour which is deliberately deceitful. ❑ *Marriages were broken and lives ruined by the revelation of double-dealing.* N-UNCOUNT = betrayal, duplicity

**double-decker** (double-deckers) 1 A **double-decker** or a **double-decker bus** is a bus that has two levels, so that passengers can sit upstairs or downstairs. [mainly BRIT] N-COUNT ≠ single-decker 2 **Double-decker** items or structures have two layers or levels instead of one. ❑ *...a double-decker sandwich.* ADJ: ADJ n

**double-digit** A **double-digit** number is between 10 and 99. ❑ *Australia had 15 years of double-digit inflation.* ADJ: ADJ n

**double-edged** 1 If you say that a comment is **double-edged**, you mean that it has two meanings, so that you are not sure whether the person who said it is being critical or is giving praise. ❑ *Even his praise is double-edged.* ADJ 2 If you say that something is **double-edged**, you mean that its positive effects are balanced by its negative effects, or that its negative effects are greater. ❑ *But tourism is double-edged, boosting the economy but damaging the environment.* ADJ: usu v-link ADJ **a double-edged sword** → see **sword**.

**dou|ble en|ten|dre** /duːbəl ɒntɒndrə/ (double entendres) A **double entendre** is a word or phrase that has two meanings, one of which is rude and often sexual. ❑ *He is a master of the pun and the double entendre.* N-VAR

**dou|ble fault** (double faults) In tennis, if a player serves a **double fault**, they make a mistake with both serves and lose the point. N-COUNT

**double-glaze** (double-glazes, double-glazing, double-glazed) If someone **double-glazes** a house or its windows, they fit windows that have two layers of glass which keeps the inside of the house warmer and quieter. [mainly BRIT] ❑ *The company is now offering to double-glaze the windows for £3,900... We recently had our house double-glazed.* VERB; V n; have n V-ed ♦ **double-glazed** *...double-glazed windows* ADJ

**dou|ble glaz|ing** also **double-glazing**. If someone has **double glazing** in their house, their windows are fitted with two layers of glass. People put in double glazing in order to keep buildings warmer or to keep out noise. [mainly BRIT] N-UNCOUNT

**double-header** (double-headers)

✓ in AM, also use **doubleheader**

A **double-header** is a sporting contest between two teams that involves two separate games being played, often on the same day. [mainly AM] N-COUNT

**dou|ble life** (double lives) If you say that someone is living **a double life**, you mean that they lead two separate and very different lives, and they appear to be a different person in each. ❑ *She threatened to publicly expose his double life if he left her.* N-COUNT: usu sing

**double-park** (double-parks, double-parking, double-parked) If someone **double-parks** their car or their car **double-parks**, they park in a road by the side of another parked car. ❑ *Murray double-parked his car... The car pulled in and double-parked in front of the town hall.* VERB; V n; V

**double-quick** If you say that you will do something **double-quick**, you are emphasizing that you will do it very quickly. [INFORMAL] ❑ *Don't worry. We'll have you out of here double-quick.* ADV: ADV after v [emphasis] ● **In double-quick time** means the same as **double-quick**. ❑ *I was over the fence in double-quick time.* PHRASE: PHR after v

**double|speak** /dʌbəlspiːk/ If you refer to what someone says as **doublespeak**, you are criticizing them for presenting things in a way that is intended to hide the truth or give people the wrong idea. ❑ *...the doublespeak so fluently used by governments and their press offices.* N-UNCOUNT [disapproval]

**dou|ble stand|ard** (double standards) If you accuse a person or institution of applying **double standards** in their treatment of different groups of people, you mean that they unfairly allow more freedom of behaviour to one group than to another. ❑ *Mrs Starky accused the local police of operating double standards.* N-COUNT [disapproval]

**dou|blet** /dʌblɪt/ (doublets) A **doublet** was a short, tight jacket that was worn by men in the fifteenth, sixteenth, and early seventeenth centuries. N-COUNT

**double-take** (double-takes) If you do a **double-take** when you see or hear something strange or surprising, you hesitate for a moment before reacting to it because you wonder if you really saw or heard it. ❑ *I did a double-take when I saw her dressed in biker's gear.* N-COUNT

**double-talk** also **double talk.** If you refer to something someone says as **double-talk**, you mean that it can deceive people or is difficult to understand because it has two possible meanings. N-UNCOUNT

**dou|ble vi|sion** If someone is suffering from **double vision**, they see a single object as two objects, for example because they are ill or have drunk too much alcohol. N-UNCOUNT

**dou|bly** /dʌbli/ 1 You use **doubly** to indicate that there are two aspects or features that are having an influence on a particular situation. ❑ *The new tax and the drop in house values make homeowners feel doubly penalised.* ADV: ADV group, ADV with v 2 You use **doubly** to emphasize that something exists or happens to a greater degree than usual. ❑ *In pregnancy a high fibre diet is doubly important.* ADV: ADV adj/adv [emphasis]

**doubt** /daʊt/ (doubts, doubting, doubted) ◆◆◇ 1 If you have **doubt** or **doubts** about something, you feel uncertain about it and do not know whether it is true or possible. If you say you have **no doubt about** it, you mean that you are certain it is true. ❑ *This raises doubts about the point of advertising... I had my doubts when she started, but she's getting really good... There can be little doubt that he will offend again.* N-VAR: oft N about/as to n, N that = uncertainty 2 If you **doubt** whether something is true or possible, you believe that it is probably not true or possible. ❑ *Others doubted whether that would happen... He doubted if he would learn anything new from Marie... She doubted that the accident could have been avoided.* VERB; V wh; V if; V that 3 If you **doubt** something, you believe that it might not be true or genuine. ❑ *No one doubted his ability.* VERB; V n 4 If you **doubt** someone or **doubt** their word, you think that they may not be telling the truth. ❑ *No one directly involved with the case doubted him.* VERB ≠ trust; V n

PHRASES 5 You say that something is **beyond doubt** or **beyond reasonable doubt** when you are certain that it is true and it cannot be contradicted or disproved. ❑ *A referendum showed beyond doubt that voters wanted independence.* PHRASE: PHR after v, v-link PHR [emphasis] 6 If you are **in doubt** about something, you feel unsure or uncertain about it. ❑ *He is in no doubt as to what is needed... When in doubt, call the doctor.* PHRASE: v-link PHR, oft PHR about/as to n 7 You say **I doubt it** as a response to a question or statement about something that you think is untrue or unlikely. ❑ *'Somebody would have seen her.' — 'I doubt it, not on Monday.'* CONVENTION 8 If you say that something is **in doubt** or **open to doubt**, you consider it to be uncertain or unreliable. ❑ *The outcome was still in doubt... That claim is increasingly open to doubt.* PHRASE: v-link PHR = uncertain 9 You use **no doubt** to emphasize that something seems certain or very likely to you. ❑ *The contract for this will no doubt be widely advertised.* PHRASE: PHR with cl [emphasis] = undoubtedly 10 You use **no doubt** to indicate that you accept the truth of a particular point, but that you do not consider it is important or contradicts the rest of what you are saying. ❑ *No doubt many will regard these as harsh words, but regrettably they are true.* PHRASE: PHR with cl 11 If you say that something is true PHRASE:

without doubt or **without a doubt**, you are emphasizing that it is definitely true. ❑ *Without doubt this was the most important relationship I developed at college.* [12] **the benefit of the doubt** → see **benefit**. **a shadow of a doubt** → see **shadow**. PHR with cl [emphasis] = undoubtedly

**doubt|er** /daʊtəʳ/ **(doubters)** If you refer to people as **doubters**, you mean that they have doubts about something, especially their religious or political system. ❑ *Some doubters fear this news may not be as good as it appears.* N-COUNT: usu pl ≠ believer

**doubt|ful** /daʊtfʊl/ [1] If it is **doubtful that** something will happen, it seems unlikely to happen or you are uncertain whether it will happen. ❑ *For a time it seemed doubtful that he would move at all... It is doubtful whether Tweed, even with his fluent French, passed for one of the locals.* ADJ: usu v-link ADJ, oft *it* v-link ADJ that/wh [2] If you are **doubtful about** something, you feel unsure or uncertain about it. ❑ *I was still very doubtful about the chances for success... Why did he sound so doubtful?* ADJ: usu v-link ADJ, oft ADJ *about* n = dubious ♦ **doubt|ful|ly** *Keeton shook his head doubtfully.* ADV: ADV after v [3] If you say that something is **of doubtful** quality or value, you mean that it is of low quality or value. ❑ *...selling something that is overpriced or of doubtful quality.* ADJ: usu ADJ n [disapproval] = dubious [4] If a sports player is **doubtful for** a match or event, he or she seems unlikely to play, usually because of injury. [JOURNALISM] ADJ: oft ADJ *for* n

**doubt|ing Thomas** /daʊtɪŋ tɒməs/ **(doubting Thomases)** If you describe someone as a **doubting Thomas**, you mean they refuse to believe something until they see definite proof or evidence of it. N-COUNT

**doubt|less** /daʊtləs/ If you say that something is **doubtless** the case, you mean that you think it is probably or almost certainly the case. ❑ *He will doubtless try and persuade his colleagues to change their minds.* ADV: ADV with cl/group

**douche** /duːʃ/ **(douches, douching, douched)** [1] A **douche** is a method of washing the vagina using a stream of water. You also refer to the object which you use to wash the vagina in this way as a **douche**. N-COUNT [2] To **douche** means to wash the vagina using a stream of water. ❑ *Never douche if you are pregnant.* VERB V

**dough** /doʊ/ **(doughs)**

> In meaning 2, **dough** is used in informal American English, and is considered old-fashioned in informal British English.

[1] **Dough** is a fairly firm mixture of flour, water, and sometimes also fat and sugar. It can be cooked to make bread, pastry, and biscuits. ❑ *Roll out the dough into one large circle.* N-MASS [2] You can refer to money as **dough**. ❑ *He worked hard for his dough.* N-UNCOUNT

**dough|nut** /doʊnʌt/ **(doughnuts)**

> in AM, also use **donut**

A **doughnut** is a bread-like cake made from sweet dough that has been cooked in hot fat. N-COUNT

**dough|ty** /daʊti/ If you describe someone as a **doughty** fighter, you mean they are brave, determined, and not easily defeated. [OLD-FASHIONED] ADJ: ADJ n [approval]

**doughy** /doʊi/ If you describe something as **doughy**, you mean that it has a fairly soft texture like dough. ❑ *Add water and mix with a knife to a doughy consistency.* ADJ

**dour** /dʊəʳ, daʊəʳ/ If you describe someone as **dour**, you mean that they are very serious and unfriendly. ❑ *...a dour, taciturn man.* ADJ ♦ **dour|ly** *The old man stared dourly at them.* ADV: usu ADV with v, also ADV adj

**douse** /daʊs/ **(douses, dousing, doused)** also **dowse.** [1] If you **douse** a fire, you stop it burning by pouring a lot of water over it. ❑ *The pumps were started and the crew began to douse the fire with water.* VERB V n [2] If you **douse** someone or something **with** a liquid, you throw a lot of that liquid over them. ❑ *They hurled abuse at their victim as they doused him with petrol.* VERB V n *with/in* n

**dove** **(doves)**

> Pronounced /dʌv/ for meanings 1 and 2, and /doʊv/ for meaning 3.

[1] A **dove** is a bird that looks like pigeon but is smaller and lighter in colour. Doves are often used as a symbol of peace. → See also **turtle dove**. N-COUNT [2] In politics, you can refer to people who support the use of peaceful methods to solve difficult situations as **doves**. Compare **hawk**. ❑ *A split over tactics appears to be emerging between doves and hawks in the party.* N-COUNT [3] In American English, **dove** is sometimes used as the past tense of **dive**.

**dove|cote** /dʌvkɒt, -koʊt/ **(dovecotes)** also **dovecot.** A **dovecote** is a small building or a container for pigeons or doves to live in. N-COUNT

**dove|tail** /dʌvteɪl/ **(dovetails, dovetailing, dovetailed)** If two things **dovetail** or if one thing **dovetails with** another, the two things fit together neatly or have some common characteristics. ❑ *I'm following up a few things that might dovetail. ...an attempt to look for areas where U.S. interests can dovetail with Japanese concerns... It is important that we dovetail our respective interests.* V-RECIP pl-n V V *with* n V pl-n

**dov|ish** /dʌvɪʃ/ also **doveish.** Journalists use **dovish** to describe politicians or governments who are in favour of using peaceful and diplomatic methods to achieve something, rather than using force and violence. ADJ ≠ hawkish

**dowa|ger** /daʊədʒəʳ/ **(dowagers)** [1] You use **dowager** to refer to the wife of a dead duke, emperor, or other man of high rank. ❑ *...the Dowager Countess Spencer... Nobody was allowed to eat in the Empress Dowager's presence.* ADJ: ADJ n, n ADJ ♦ **Dowager** is also a noun. N-COUNT [2] If you describe a woman as a **dowager**, you mean that she is old and rich or looks important. [LITERARY] ❑ *...like stately dowagers on a cruise.* N-COUNT

**dow|dy** /daʊdi/ **(dowdier, dowdiest)** If you describe someone or their clothes as **dowdy**, you mean their clothes are dull and unfashionable. ❑ *Her clothes were clean but dowdy.* ADJ [disapproval] = frumpy

**dow|el** /daʊəl/ **(dowels)** A **dowel** is a short thin piece of wood or metal which is used for joining larger pieces of wood or metal together. N-COUNT

| **down** |
|---|
| ① PREPOSITION AND ADVERB USES |
| ② ADJECTIVE USES |
| ③ VERB USES |
| ④ NOUN USES |

**①down** /daʊn/ ◆◆◆

> **Down** is often used with verbs of movement, such as 'fall' and 'pull', and also in phrasal verbs such as 'bring down' and 'calm down'.

⇛ Please look at category 15 to see if the expression you are looking for is shown under another headword. [1] To go **down** something such as a slope or a pipe means to go towards the ground or to a lower level. ❑ *We're going down a mountain... A man came down the stairs to meet them... The tears began flooding down her cheeks.* PREP ≠ up ♦ **Down** is also an adverb. ❑ *She went down to the kitchen again... She sat on the window seat until they climbed down from the roof.* ADV: ADV after v [2] If you are a particular distance **down** something, you are that distance below the top or surface of it. ❑ *He managed to cling on to a ledge 40ft down the rock face.* PREP: amount PREP n ≠ up ♦ **Down** is also an adverb. ❑ *For the last 18 months miners have cut a face to develop a new shaft 400 metres down.* ADV: amount ADV [3] You use **down** to say that you are looking or facing in a direction that is towards the ground or towards a lower level. ❑ *She was still looking down at her papers... She put her head down, her hands over her face.* ADV: ADV after v ≠ up [4] If you put something **down**, you put it onto a surface. ❑ *Danny put down his glass.* ADV: ADV after v [5] If you go or look **down** something such as a road or river, you go or look along it. If you are **down** a road or river, you are somewhere along it. ❑ *They set off at a* PREP: oft amount PREP n ≠ up

*jog up one street and down another. ...sailing down the river on a barge.* 6 If you are travelling to a particular place, you can say that you are going **down to** that place, especially if you are going towards the south or to a lower level of land. [SPOKEN] ❑ *I went down to L.A. all the way from Seattle.* ADV: ADV after v
7 If an amount of something goes **down**, it decreases. If an amount of something is **down**, it has decreased and is at a lower level than it was. ❑ *Interest rates came down today... Inflation will be down to three percent... My department had a healthy interest in keeping expenses down... The Dow Jones industrial average is down 5 points at 2,913.* ADV: ADV after v, *be* ADV, oft ADV *to/from/by* amount ≠up
**PHRASES** 8 If you say that there are a number of things **down** and a number **to go**, you are saying how many of the things have already been dealt with and how many remain to be dealt with. ❑ *Thirteen months down, twenty-four years to go.* PHRASE: PHR with amount
9 **Down to** a particular detail means including everything, even that detail. **Down to** a particular person means including everyone, even that person. ❑ *...from the chairman right down to the tea ladies.* PREP-PHRASE 10 If you are **down to** a certain amount of something, you have only that amount left. ❑ *The poor man's down to his last £3.* PREP-PHRASE: PREP amount 11 If a situation is **down to** a particular person or thing, it has been caused by that person or thing. [mainly BRIT] ❑ *Any mistakes are entirely down to us.* PREP-PHRASE 12 If someone or something is **down for** a particular thing, it has been arranged that they will do that thing, or that thing will happen. ❑ *Mark had told me that he was down for an interview.* PREP-PHRASE 13 If you pay money **down** on something, you pay part of the money you owe for it. [mainly AM] ❑ *He paid 20 percent down.* → See also **put down**. PREP-PHRASE 14 If people shout '**down with**' something or someone, they are saying that they dislike them and want to get rid of them. [SPOKEN] ❑ *Demonstrators chanted 'down with the rebels'.* PHRASE: PHR n [disapproval] 15 **up and down** → see **up**. **ups and downs** → see **up**.

② **down** /daʊn/ 1 If you are feeling **down**, you are feeling unhappy or depressed. [INFORMAL] ❑ *The old man sounded really down.* ADJ: v-link ADJ = low 2 If something is **down on** paper, it has been written on the paper. ❑ *That date wasn't down on our news sheet.* ADJ: v-link ADJ, usu ADJ *on* n 3 If a piece of equipment, especially a computer system, is **down**, it is temporarily not working because of a fault. Compare **up**. ❑ *The computer's down again.* ADJ: v-link ADJ

③ **down** /daʊn/ **(downs, downing, downed)**
⇛ Please look at category 3 to see if the expression you are looking for is shown under another headword. 1 If you say that someone **downs** food or a drink, you mean that they eat or drink it. ❑ *We downed bottles of local wine.* VERB = consume V n 2 If something or someone **is downed**, they fall to the ground because they have been hurt or damaged in some way. [JOURNALISM] ❑ *Two jet fighters were downed.* VERB *be* V-ed ♦ **down|ing** *...the downing of an airliner, which killed 107 people.* N-UNCOUNT 3 to **down tools** → see **tool**.

④ **down** /daʊn/ 1 **Down** consists of the small, soft feathers on young birds. Down is used to make bed-covers and pillows. ❑ *...goose down.* N-UNCOUNT 2 **Down** is very fine hair. ❑ *The whole plant is covered with fine down.* → See also **downs**. N-UNCOUNT

**down-and-out** **(down-and-outs)** If you describe someone as **down-and-out**, you mean that they have no job and nowhere to live, and they have no real hope of improving their situation. ❑ *...a short story about a down-and-out advertising copywriter.* ADJ: usu ADJ n ♦ **Down-and-out** is also a noun. [BRIT] ❑ *...some poor down-and-out in need of a meal.* N-COUNT

**down-at-heel** also **down at heel.** Something that is **down-at-heel** is in a in bad condition because it has been used too much or has not been looked after properly. If you say that someone is **down-at-heel**, you mean that they are wearing old, worn clothes because they have little money. ❑ *...a down-at-heel disco in central East Berlin. ...a down-at-heel waitress in a greasy New York diner.* ADJ: usu ADJ n = shabby

**down|beat** /daʊnbiːt/ **(downbeats)** 1 If people or their opinions are **downbeat**, they are deliberately casual and not enthusiastic about a situation. ❑ *...a downbeat assessment of 1992's economic prospects.* ADJ: usu ADJ n ≠upbeat 2 If you are feeling **downbeat**, you are feeling depressed and without hope. ❑ *They found him in gloomy, downbeat mood.* ADJ ≠upbeat

**down|cast** /daʊnkɑːst, -kæst/ 1 If you are **downcast**, you are feeling sad and without hope. ❑ *Barbara looked increasingly downcast as defeat loomed.* ADJ: usu v-link ADJ = dejected 2 If your eyes are **downcast**, you are looking towards the ground, usually because you are feeling sad or embarrassed. ❑ *She was silent, her eyes downcast.* ADJ: usu v-link ADJ

**down|er** /daʊnəʳ/ **(downers)** If you describe a situation as **a downer**, you think that it is very depressing. [INFORMAL] ❑ *For divorced people, Christmas can be a downer.* N-COUNT: usu sing, *a* N ● If you are **on a downer**, you are feeling depressed and without hope. [INFORMAL] ❑ *We've been on a bit of a downer since the Liverpool game.* PHRASE: v-link PHR

**down|fall** /daʊnfɔːl/ **(downfalls)** 1 The **downfall** of a successful or powerful person or institution is their loss of success or power. ❑ *His lack of experience had led to his downfall.* N-COUNT: also N in pl, usu with poss ≠rise 2 The thing that was a person's **downfall** caused them to fail or lose power. ❑ *His honesty had been his downfall.* N-COUNT: usu with poss = undoing

**down|grade** /daʊngreɪd/ **(downgrades, downgrading, downgraded)** 1 If something **is downgraded**, it is given less importance than it used to have or than you think it should have. ❑ *The boy's condition has been downgraded from critical to serious.* VERB: usu passive ≠upgrade *be* V-ed 2 If someone **is downgraded**, their job or status is changed so that they become less important or receive less money. ❑ *There was no criticism of her work until after she was downgraded... His superiors suspended him, and then downgraded him.* VERB = demote ≠upgrade *be* V-ed V n

**down|hearted** /daʊnhɑːʳtɪd/ If you are **downhearted**, you are feeling sad and discouraged. ❑ *Max sighed, sounding even more downhearted.* ADJ: usu v-link ADJ = dejected

**down|hill** /daʊnhɪl/ 1 If something or someone is moving **downhill** or is **downhill**, they are moving down a slope or are located towards the bottom of a hill. ❑ *He headed downhill towards the river.* ADV: ADV after v, *be* ADV, ADV *from* n ≠uphill ♦ **Downhill** is also an adjective. ❑ *...downhill ski runs.* ADJ: ADJ n 2 If you say that something **is going downhill**, you mean that it is becoming worse or less successful. ❑ *Since I started to work longer hours things have gone steadily downhill.* ADV: ADV after v, *be* ADV 3 If you say that a task or situation is **downhill** after a particular stage or time, you mean that it is easy to deal with after that stage or time. ❑ *Well, I guess it's all downhill from here.* ADJ: v-link ADJ ≠uphill

**Down|ing Street** /daʊnɪŋ striːt/ **Downing Street** is the street in London in which the Prime Minister and the Chancellor of the Exchequer live. You can also use **Downing Street** to refer to the Prime Minister and his or her officials. ❑ *The Prime Minister arrived back at Downing Street from Paris this morning... Downing Street is taking the French opinion polls very seriously indeed.* N-PROPER

**down|load** /daʊnloʊd/ **(downloads, downloading, downloaded)** To **download** data means to transfer it to or from a computer along a line such as a telephone line, a radio link, or a computer network. [COMPUTING] ❑ *Users can download their material to a desktop PC.* VERB V n

**down|market** /daʊnmɑːʳkɪt/ also **downmarket.** If you describe a product or service as **downmarket**, you think that they are cheap and are not very good in quality. ❑ *It is a downmarket eating house, seating about 60.* ADJ: usu ADJ n ≠upmarket ♦ **Downmarket** is also an adverb. ❑ *Why is the company going downmarket and developing smaller machines?* ADV: ADV after v ≠upmarket

**down pay|ment** **(down payments)** also **downpayment.** If you make a **down payment on** something, you pay only a percentage N-COUNT = deposit of the total cost when you buy it. You then finish paying for it later, usually by paying a certain amount every month.

**down|play** /daʊnpleɪ/ **(downplays, downplaying, downplayed)** If you **downplay** a fact or feature, you try to make people think that it is less important or serious than it really is. ❑ *The government is trying to downplay the violence.* VERB = play down V n

**down|pour** /daʊnpɔːʳ/ **(downpours)** A **downpour** is a sudden and unexpected heavy fall of rain. ❑ *...a sudden downpour of rain.* N-COUNT

**down|right** /daʊnraɪt/ You use **downright** to emphasize unpleasant or bad qualities or behaviour. ❑ *...ideas that would have been downright dangerous if put into practice.* ♦ **Downright** is also an adjective. ❑ *...downright bad manners.* ADV: ADV adj [emphasis] = positively ADJ: ADJ n

**down-river** also **downriver.** Something that is moving **down-river** is moving towards the mouth of a river, from a point further up the river. Something that is **down-river** is towards the mouth of a river. ❑ *By 09.30 we had cast off and were heading down-river. ...a big tourist hotel a few hundred yards down-river... Cologne is not so very far down-river from Mainz.* ♦ **Down-river** is also an adjective. ❑ *...downriver factories dispensing billows of smoke.* ADV: ADV after v, be ADV, n ADV, oft ADV from n ≠ up-river ADJ: ADJ n ≠ up-river

**downs** /daʊnz/ **Downs** are areas of gentle hills with few trees. [BRIT] ❑ *...walking across the downs. ...the Wiltshire downs.* N-PLURAL: oft in names, usu the N

**down|shift** /daʊnʃɪft/ **(downshifts, downshifting, downshifted)** [1] If someone **downshifts**, they leave a job that is well-paid but stressful for a less demanding job and a more enjoyable way of life. [BRIT] ❑ *Lynda now sees many of her clients downshifting in search of a new way of living.* ♦ **down|shift|ing** *The latest lifestyle trend is downshifting.* ♦ **down|shifter** **(downshifters)** *Downshifters are being tempted to leave the sophisticated city and go simple.* [2] If you **downshift** while driving, you change to a lower gear. [mainly AM] ❑ *He downshifted and turned the steering wheel.* VERB V N-UNCOUNT N-COUNT VERB V Also V to n

☑ in BRIT, use **change down**

**down|side** /daʊnsaɪd/ The **downside of** a situation is the aspect of it which is less positive, pleasant, or useful than its other aspects. ❑ *The downside of this approach is a lack of clear leadership.* N-SING: oft the N of n ≠ upside

**down|size** /daʊnsaɪz/ **(downsizes, downsizing, downsized)** To **downsize** something such as a business or industry means to make it smaller. [BUSINESS] ❑ *American manufacturing organizations have been downsizing their factories. ...today's downsized economy. ...a consultant who's helped dozens of companies downsize.* ♦ **down|siz|ing** *...a trend toward downsizing in the personal computer market.* VERB V n V-ed V N-UNCOUNT

**down|spout** /daʊnspaʊt/ **(downspouts)** A **downspout** is a pipe attached to the side of a building, through which water flows from the roof into a drain. [AM] ❑ *He installed rain gutters and downspouts.* N-COUNT = drainpipe

☑ in BRIT, use **drainpipe**

**Down's syn|drome**

☑ in AM, usually use **Down syndrome**

**Down's syndrome** is a disorder that some people are born with. People who have Down's syndrome have a flat forehead and sloping eyes and lower than average intelligence. N-UNCOUNT

**down|stage** /daʊnsteɪdʒ/ When an actor is **downstage** or moves **downstage**, he or she is or moves towards the front part of the stage. [TECHNICAL] ❑ *Krishna stands downstage in the open area.* ♦ **Downstage** is also an adjective. ❑ *...downstage members of the cast.* ADV: ADV after v, be ADV ≠ upstage ADJ: ADJ n

**down|stairs** /daʊnsteəʳz/ [1] If you go **downstairs** in a building, you go down a staircase towards the ground floor. ❑ *Denise went downstairs and made some tea.* [2] If something or someone is **downstairs** in a building, they are on the ground floor or on a lower floor than you. ❑ *The telephone was downstairs in the entrance hall.* [3] **Downstairs** means situated on the ground floor of a building or on a lower floor than you are. ❑ *She repainted the downstairs rooms and closed off the second floor.* [4] **The downstairs** of a building is its lower floor or floors. ❑ *The downstairs of the two little houses had been entirely refashioned.* ADV: ADV after v ≠ upstairs ADV: be ADV, n ADV ≠ upstairs ADJ: ADJ n ≠ upstairs N-SING: the N ≠ upstairs

**down|stream** /daʊnstriːm/ Something that is moving **downstream** is moving towards the mouth of a river, from a point further up the river. Something that is **downstream** is further towards the mouth of a river than where you are. ❑ *We had drifted downstream.* ♦ **Downstream** is also an adjective. ❑ *Breaking the dam could submerge downstream cities such as Wuhan.* ADV: ADV after v, be ADV, n ADV, oft ADV of/from n ≠ upstream ADJ: ADJ n ≠ upstream

**down|swing** /daʊnswɪŋ/ **(downswings)** A **downswing** is a sudden downward movement in something such as an economy, that had previously been improving. ❑ *The manufacturing economy remains on a downswing.* N-COUNT: usu sing

**down|time** /daʊntaɪm/ [1] In industry, **downtime** is the time during which machinery or equipment is not operating. ❑ *On the production line, downtime has been reduced from 55% to 26%.* [2] In computing, **downtime** is time when a computer is not working. [3] **Downtime** is time when people are not working. [mainly AM] ❑ *Downtime in Hollywood can cost a lot of money.* N-UNCOUNT N-UNCOUNT N-UNCOUNT

**down-to-earth** If you say that someone is **down-to-earth**, you approve of the fact that they concern themselves with practical things and actions, rather than with abstract theories. ❑ *...her sincerity and her down-to-earth common sense.* ADJ [approval]

**down|town** /daʊntaʊn/ **Downtown** places are in or towards the centre of a large town or city, where the shops and places of business are. [mainly AM] ❑ *...an office in downtown Chicago.* ♦ **Downtown** is also an adverb. ❑ *By day he worked downtown for American Standard.* ♦ **Downtown** is also a noun. ❑ *...in a large vacant area of the downtown.* ADJ: ADJ n ≠ uptown ADV: ADV after v, be ADV N-UNCOUNT: oft the N

**down|trend** /daʊntrend/ A **downtrend** is a general downward movement in something such as a company's profits or the economy. ❑ *The increase slowed to 0.4 percent, possibly indicating the start of a downtrend.* N-SING ≠ uptrend

**down|trod|den** /daʊntrɒdən/ People who are **downtrodden** are treated very badly by people with power, and do not have the ability or the energy to do anything about it. ❑ *The owner is making huge profits at the expense of downtrodden peasants.* ADJ = oppressed

**down|turn** /daʊntɜːʳn/ **(downturns)** If there is a **downturn** in the economy or in a company or industry, it becomes worse or less successful than it had been. ❑ *They predicted a severe economic downturn.* N-COUNT: oft N in n ≠ upturn

**down un|der** People sometimes refer to Australia and New Zealand as **down under**. [mainly BRIT, INFORMAL] ❑ *For summer skiing down under, there is no better place than New Zealand.* PHRASE: prep PHR, PHR after v

**down|ward** /daʊnwəʳd/ [1] A **downward** movement or look is directed towards a lower place or a lower level. ❑ *...a firm downward movement of the hands.* ➔ See also **downwards**. [2] If you refer to a **downward** trend, you mean that something is decreasing or that a situation is getting worse. ❑ *The downward trend in home ownership is likely to continue.* ADJ: ADJ n ≠ upward ADJ: ADJ n ≠ upward

**down|wards** /daʊnwəʳdz/ also **downward.** [1] If you move or look **downwards**, you move or look towards the ground or a lower level. ❑ *Benedict pointed downwards again with his stick.* [2] If an amount or rate moves **downwards**, it decreases. ❑ *Inflation is moving firmly downwards.* [3] If you want to emphasize that a statement applies to everyone in an organization, you can say ADV: ADV after v, n ADV ≠ upwards ADV: ADV after v ≠ upwards ADV: from n ADV

that it applies from its leader **downwards**. [emphasis] ❑ *...from the Prime Minister downwards.*

**down|wind** /daʊnwɪnd/ If something moves **downwind**, it moves in the same direction as the wind. If something is **downwind**, the wind is blowing towards it. ❑ *He attempted to return downwind to the airfield.* ADV: ADV after v, *be* ADV, oft ADV *of* n ≠ *upwind*

**downy** /daʊni/ **(downier, downiest)** [1] Something that is **downy** is filled or covered with small soft feathers. ❑ *...the warm downy quilt.* ADJ: usu ADJ n [2] Something that is **downy** is covered with very fine hairs. ❑ *...leaves that are often downy underneath.* ADJ = *velvety*

**dow|ry** /daʊəri/ **(dowries)** A woman's **dowry** is the money and goods which, in some cultures, her family gives to the man that she marries. N-COUNT

**dowse** /daʊs/ **(dowses, dowsing, dowsed)** [1] If someone **dowses** for underground water, minerals, or some other substance, they search for it using a special rod. ❑ *He said that dowsing for water is complete nonsense... We dowse oil and ore in South America for big companies. ...a dowsing rod.* VERB V *for* n V n V -ing [2] → see also **douse**.

**doy|en** /dɔɪən, dɔɪen/ **(doyens)** If you refer to a man as **the doyen of** a group or profession, you mean that he is the oldest and most experienced and respected member of it. [FORMAL] ❑ *...the doyen of political interviewers.* N-COUNT: usu sing, usu *the* N *of* n [approval]

**doy|enne** /dɔɪen/ **(doyennes)** If you refer to a woman as **the doyenne of** a group or profession, you mean that she is the oldest and most experienced and respected woman in it. [FORMAL] ❑ *...the doyenne of British fashion.* N-COUNT: usu sing, usu *the* N *of* n [approval]

**doze** /doʊz/ **(dozes, dozing, dozed)** When you **doze**, you sleep lightly or for a short period, especially during the daytime. ❑ *For a while she dozed fitfully.* VERB = *nap* V

♦ **doze off** If you **doze off**, you fall into a light sleep, especially during the daytime. ❑ *I closed my eyes for a minute and must have dozed off.* PHRASAL VERB = *nod off* V P

**doz|en** /dʌzᵊn/ **(dozens)** ♦♦◇

> The plural form is **dozen** after a number, or after a word or expression referring to a number, such as 'several' or 'a few'.

[1] If you have **a dozen** things, you have twelve of them. ❑ *You will be able to take ten dozen bottles free of duty through customs... His chicken eggs sell for $22 a dozen.* NUM: usu *a*/ num NUM [2] You can refer to a group of approximately twelve things or people as **a dozen**. You can refer to a group of approximately six things or people as **half a dozen**. ❑ *In half a dozen words, he had explained the bond that linked them... The riot left four people dead and several dozen injured.* NUM: usu *a*/ num NUM [3] If you refer to **dozens of** things or people, you are emphasizing that there are very many of them. ❑ *...a storm which destroyed dozens of homes and buildings.* QUANT: QUANT *of* pl-n [emphasis] ♦ You can also use **dozens** as a pronoun. ❑ *Just as revealing are Mr Johnson's portraits, of which there are dozens.* PRON

**dozy** /doʊzi/ **(dozier, doziest)** [1] If you are **dozy**, you are feeling sleepy and not very alert. ❑ *Maybe I eat too much and that's what makes me dozy.* ADJ = *drowsy* [2] If you describe someone as **dozy**, you mean they are rather stupid and slow to understand things. [INFORMAL] ADJ [disapproval]

**D Phil** /diː fɪl/ **(D Phils)**

> in AM, use **D. Phil.**

**D Phil** is an abbreviation for **Doctor of Philosophy**.

**Dr** **(Drs)** ♦♦◇

> in AM, use **Dr.**

[1] **Dr** is a written abbreviation for **Doctor**. ❑ *...Dr John Hardy of St Mary's Medical School in London.* [2] **Dr** is used as a written abbreviation for **Drive** when it is part of a street name. ❑ *...6 Queen's Dr.*

**drab** /dræb/ **(drabber, drabbest)** [1] If you describe something as **drab**, you think that it is dull and boring to look at or experience. ❑ *...his drab little office.* ADJ = *dreary* ♦ **drab|ness** *...the dusty drabness of nearby villages.* N-UNCOUNT [2] → See also **dribs and drabs**.

**drach|ma** /drækmə/ **(drachmas)** The **drachma** was the unit of money that was used in Greece. In 2002 it was replaced by the euro. N-COUNT: num N ♦ **The drachma** was also used to refer to the Greek currency system. ❑ *In April 1992 the Greek drachma was the only Community currency not yet part of the EMS exchange-rate mechanism.* N-SING: *the* N

**dra|co|nian** /drəkoʊniən/ **Draconian** laws or measures are extremely harsh and severe. [FORMAL] ❑ *...draconian measures to lower US healthcare costs.* ADJ: usu ADJ n

**draft** /drɑːft, dræft/ **(drafts, drafting, drafted)** ♦◇◇ [1] A **draft** is an early version of a letter, book, or speech. ❑ *I rewrote his rough draft, which was published under my name... I faxed a first draft of this article to him.* N-COUNT: usu with supp [2] When you **draft** a letter, book, or speech, you write the first version of it. ❑ *He drafted a standard letter to the editors.* VERB V n [3] If you **are drafted**, you are ordered to serve in the armed forces, usually for a limited period of time. [mainly AM] ❑ *During the Second World War, he was drafted into the US Army.* VERB: usu passive = *conscript* *be* V-ed *into* n [4] If people **are drafted into** a place, they are moved there to do a particular job. ❑ *Extra police have been drafted into the town after the violence... The manager will make a special plea to draft the player into his squad as a replacement.* VERB *be* V-ed *in/into* n V n *in/into* n [5] **The draft** is the practice of ordering people to serve in the armed forces, usually for a limited period of time. [mainly AM] ❑ *...his effort to avoid the draft.* N-SING: *the* N = *conscription* [6] A **draft** is a written order for payment of money by a bank, especially from one bank to another. ❑ *Ten days later Carmen received a bank draft for a plane ticket.* N-COUNT: oft *by* N [7] → See also **draught**.

**draft dodg|er** **(draft dodgers)** A **draft dodger** is someone who avoids joining the armed forces when normally they would have to join. [mainly AM] N-COUNT [disapproval]

**draftee** /drɑːftiː, dræft-/ **(draftees)** A **draftee** is the same as a **conscript**. [AM] N-COUNT

**drafts|man** **(draftsmen** /drɑːftsmən, dræfts-/**)** → see **draughtsman**.

**drafts|man|ship** /drɑːftsmənʃɪp, dræfts-/ → see **draughtsmanship**.

**drafty** /drɑːfti, dræfti/ → see **draughty**.

**drag** /dræg/ **(drags, dragging, dragged)** ♦◇◇ [1] If you **drag** something, you pull it along the ground, often with difficulty. ❑ *He got up and dragged his chair towards the table.* VERB V n prep/adv [2] To **drag** a computer image means to use the mouse to move the position of the image on the screen, or to change its size or shape. [COMPUTING] ❑ *Use your mouse to drag the pictures to their new size.* VERB V n [3] If someone **drags** you somewhere, they pull you there, or force you to go there by physically threatening you. ❑ *The vigilantes dragged the men out of the vehicles.* VERB V n prep/adv [4] If someone **drags** you somewhere you do not want to go, they make you go there. ❑ *When you can drag him away from his work, he can also be a devoted father.* VERB V n adv/prep [5] If you say that you **drag yourself** somewhere, you are emphasizing that you have to make a very great effort to go there. ❑ *I find it really hard to drag myself out and exercise regularly.* VERB [emphasis] V pron-refl adv/prep [6] If you **drag** your foot or your leg behind you, you walk with great difficulty because you foot or leg is injured in some way. ❑ *He was barely able to drag his poisoned leg behind him.* VERB V n prep [7] If the police **drag** a river or lake, they pull nets or hooks across the bottom of it in order to look for something. ❑ *Yesterday police frogmen dragged a small pond on the Common.* VERB V n [8] If a period of time or an event **drags**, it is very boring and seems to last a long time. ❑ *The minutes dragged past... The pacing was uneven, and the early second act dragged.* VERB V adv V [9] If something is **a drag on** the development or progress of something, it slows it down or makes it more difficult. ❑ *Spending cuts will put a drag on growth.* N-SING: *a* N *on* n [10] If you say that something is **a drag**, N-SING: *a* N, you mean that it is unpleasant or very dull. [INFORMAL] [11] If you take a **drag on** a cigarette or pipe that you are smoking, you take in air through it. [INFORMAL] [12] **Drag** is the wearing of women's clothes by a male entertainer. ● If a man is **in drag**, he is wearing women's clothes. ❑ *The band dressed up in drag.* [13] If you **drag** your **feet** or **drag** your **heels**, you delay doing something or do it very slowly because you do not want to do it. ❑ *The government was dragging its feet.* — oft N to-inf [disapproval]; N-COUNT: oft N *on* n; N-UNCOUNT: oft N n; PHRASE: PHR after v, v-link PHR; PHRASE: V inflects

♦ **drag down** [1] To **drag** someone **down** means to reduce them to an inferior social status or to lower standards of behaviour. ❑ *She dragged him down with her... There were fears he would be dragged down by the scandal.* [2] Something that **drags** you **down** makes you feel weak or depressed. ❑ *I have had really bad bouts of flu that have really dragged me down.* — PHRASAL VERB; V n P (not pron); *be* V-ed P *by* n; PHRASAL VERB; V n P

♦ **drag in** When you are talking, if you **drag in** a subject, you mention something that is not relevant and that other people do not want to discuss. ❑ *They disapproved of my dragging in his wealth.* — PHRASAL VERB = bring up; V P n

♦ **drag into** To **drag** something or someone **into** an event or situation means to involve them in it when it is not necessary or not desirable. ❑ *Why should Carmela have dragged him into the argument?* — PHRASAL VERB; V n P n

♦ **drag on** You say that an event or process **drags on** when you disapprove of the fact that it lasts for longer than necessary. ❑ *The conflict with James has dragged on for two years.* — PHRASAL VERB [disapproval]; V P

♦ **drag out** [1] If you **drag** something **out**, you make it last for longer than is necessary. ❑ *The company was willing to drag out the proceedings for years... Let's get it over with as soon as possible, rather than drag it out.* [2] If you **drag** something **out of** a person, you persuade them to tell you something that they do not want to tell you. ❑ *The families soon discovered that every piece of information had to be dragged out of the authorities.* — PHRASAL VERB = spin out; V P n (not pron); V n P; PHRASAL VERB; V n P *of* n

♦ **drag up** If someone **drags up** an unpleasant event or an old story from the past, they mention it when people do not want to be reminded of it. ❑ *I don't want to go back there and drag up that anger again.* — PHRASAL VERB = bring up; V P n (not pron)

**drag|net** /drægnet/ A **dragnet** is a method used by police to catch suspected criminals. A large number of police officers search a specific area, in the hope that they will eventually find the person they are looking for. ❑ *...a massive police dragnet for two suspected terrorists.* — N-SING: oft n N

**drag|on** /drægən/ **(dragons)** In stories and legends, a **dragon** is an animal like a big lizard. It has wings and claws, and breathes out fire. — N-COUNT

**dragon|fly** /drægənflaɪ/ **(dragonflies)** **Dragonflies** are brightly-coloured insects with long, thin bodies and two sets of wings. Dragonflies are often found near slow-moving water. — N-COUNT

**dra|goon** /drəguːn/ **(dragoons, dragooning, dragooned)** If someone **dragoons** you **into** doing something that you do not want to do, they persuade you to do it even though you try hard not to agree. ❑ *...the history professor who had dragooned me into taking the exam.* — VERB; V n *into* -ing/n

**drain** /dreɪn/ **(drains, draining, drained)** [1] If you **drain** a liquid from a place or object, you remove the liquid by causing it to flow somewhere else. If a liquid **drains** somewhere, it flows there. ❑ *Miners built the tunnel to drain water out of the mines... Now the focus is on draining the water... Springs and rivers that drain into lakes carry dissolved nitrates and phosphates.* [2] If you **drain** a place or object, you dry it by causing water to flow out of it. If a place or object **drains**, water flows out of it until it is dry. ❑ *Vast numbers of people have been mobilised to drain flooded land... The soil drains freely and slugs aren't a problem.* [3] If you **drain** food or if food **drains**, you remove the liquid that it has been in, especially after it has been cooked or soaked in water. ❑ *Drain the pasta well, arrange on four plates and pour over the sauce... Wash the leeks thoroughly and allow them to drain.* [4] A **drain** is a pipe that carries water or sewage away from a place, or an opening in a surface that leads to the pipe. ❑ *Tony built his own house and laid his own drains.* [5] If the colour or the blood **drains** or **is drained from** someone's face, they become very pale. You can also say that someone's face **drains** or **is drained of** colour. [LITERARY] ❑ *Harry felt the colour drain from his face... Thacker's face drained of colour... Jock's face had been suddenly drained of all colour.* [6] If something **drains** you, it leaves you feeling physically and emotionally exhausted. ❑ *My emotional turmoil had drained me.* ♦ **drained** *United left the pitch looking stunned and drained.* ♦ **drain|ing** *This work is physically exhausting and emotionally draining.* [7] If you say that something is **a drain on** an organization's finances or resources, you mean that it costs the organization a large amount of money, and you do not consider that it is worth it. ❑ *...an ultra-modern printing plant, which has been a big drain on resources.* → See also **brain drain**. [8] If you say that a country's or a company's resources or finances **are drained**, you mean that they are used or spent completely. ❑ *The state's finances have been drained by war... The company has steadily drained its cash reserves.* — ◆◇◇ VERB; V n adv/prep; V n; V prep/adv; VERB; V n; V; VERB; V n; V; N-COUNT; VERB; V *from* n; V *of* n; *be* V-ed *of* n; VERB; V n; ADJ; ADJ; N-SING: usu adj N, N *on* n; VERB; *be* V-ed; V n

PHRASES [9] If you say that something **is going down the drain**, you mean that it is being destroyed or wasted. [INFORMAL] ❑ *They were aware that their public image was rapidly going down the drain.* [10] If you say that a business is **going down the drain**, you mean that it is failing financially. [INFORMAL] ❑ *Small local stores are going down the drain.* — PHRASE: usu PHR after v; PHRASE: usu PHR after v

**drain|age** /dreɪnɪdʒ/ **Drainage** is the system or process by which water or other liquids are drained from a place. ❑ *Line the pots with pebbles to ensure good drainage.* — N-UNCOUNT

**drain|board** /dreɪnbɔːʳd/ **(drainboards)** A **drainboard** is the same as a **draining board**. [AM] — N-COUNT: usu *the* N in sing

**drain|ing board** **(draining boards)** The **draining board** is the place on a sink unit where things such as cups, plates, and cutlery are put to drain after they have been washed. [mainly BRIT] — N-COUNT: usu *the* N in sing

✓ in AM, usually use **drainboard**

**drain|pipe** /dreɪnpaɪp/ **(drainpipes)** A **drainpipe** is a pipe attached to the side of a building, through which rainwater flows from the roof into a drain. ❑ *He evaded police by climbing through a window and shinning down a drainpipe.* → See picture on page 1705. — N-COUNT

**drake** /dreɪk/ **(drakes)** A **drake** is a male duck. — N-COUNT

**dram** /dræm/ **(drams)** A **dram** is a small measure of whisky. [mainly SCOTTISH] ❑ *...a dram of whisky... Would you care for a dram?* — N-COUNT: oft N *of* n

**dra|ma** /drɑːmə/ **(dramas)** [1] A **drama** is a serious play for the theatre, television, or radio. ❑ *He acted in radio dramas.* [2] You use **drama** to refer to plays in general or to work that is connected with plays and the theatre, such as acting or producing. ❑ *He knew nothing of Greek drama... She met him when she was at drama school.* [3] You can refer to a real situation which is exciting or distressing as **drama**. ❑ *There was none of the drama and relief of a hostage release.* — ◆◇◇ N-COUNT; N-UNCOUNT; N-VAR

**dra|mat|ic** /drəmætɪk/ [1] A **dramatic** change or event happens suddenly and is very noticeable and surprising. ❑ *A fifth year of drought is expected to have dramatic effects on the California economy.* ♦ **dra|mati|cal|ly** /drəmætɪkli/ *At speeds above 50mph, serious injuries dramatically increase.* [2] A **dramatic** action, event, or situation is exciting and impressive. ❑ *He witnessed many dramatic escapes as people jumped from as high as the fourth floor.* ♦ **dra|mati|cal|ly** *He tipped his head to one side and sighed dramatically.* — ◆◆◇ ADJ: usu ADJ n = striking; ADV: usu ADV with v, also ADV adj; ADJ; ADV: usu ADV with v, also ADV adj

3 You use **dramatic** to describe things connected with or relating to the theatre, drama, or plays. ❑ *...a dramatic arts major in college.* ADJ: ADJ n

**dra|mat|ics** /drəmætɪks/ 1 You use **dramatics** to refer to activities connected with the theatre and drama, such as acting in plays or producing them. ❑ *Angela says she longs to join an amateur dramatics class. ...the university dramatics society.* N-UNCOUNT: usu with supp 2 You talk about **dramatics** to express your disapproval of behaviour which seems to show too much emotion, and which you think is done deliberately in order to impress people. ❑ *...another wearisome outbreak of Nancy's dramatics.* N-PLURAL disapproval

**dra|ma|tis per|so|nae** /dræmətɪs pəʳsoʊnaɪ/ The characters in a play are sometimes referred to as **the dramatis personae**. [TECHNICAL] N-PLURAL: the N

**drama|tist** /dræmətɪst/ **(dramatists)** A **dramatist** is someone who writes plays. N-COUNT

**drama|tize** /dræmətaɪz/ **(dramatizes, dramatizing, dramatized)**

✔ in BRIT, also use **dramatise**

1 If a book or story **is dramatized**, it is written or presented as a play, film, or television drama. ❑ *...an incident later dramatized in the movie 'The Right Stuff'. ...a dramatised version of the novel.* VERB: usu passive; be V-ed; V-ed ♦ **drama|ti|za|tion** /dræmətaɪzeɪʃᵊn/ **(dramatizations)** *...a dramatisation of D H Lawrence's novel, 'Lady Chatterley's Lover.'* N-COUNT: with supp 2 If you say that someone **dramatizes** a situation or event, you mean that they try to make it seem more serious, more important, or more exciting than it really is. ❑ *They have a tendency to show off, to dramatize almost every situation.* VERB disapproval = exaggerate; V n 3 If something that happens or is done **dramatizes** a situation, it focuses people's attention on the situation in a dramatic way. ❑ *The need for change has been dramatized by plummeting bank profits.* VERB = highlight; V n

**drank** /dræŋk/ **Drank** is the past tense of **drink**.

**drape** /dreɪp/ **(drapes, draping, draped)** 1 If you **drape** a piece of cloth somewhere, you place it there so that it hangs down in a casual and graceful way. ❑ *Natasha took the coat and draped it over her shoulders... She had a towel draped around her neck.* VERB = hang; V n prep; V-ed prep 2 If someone or something **is draped in** a piece of cloth, they are loosely covered by it. ❑ *The coffin had been draped in a Union Jack... He draped himself in the Canadian flag and went round the track.* VERB; be V-ed in/with n; V n in/with n 3 If you **drape** a part of your body somewhere, you lay it there in a relaxed and graceful way. ❑ *Nicola slowly draped herself across the couch... He draped his arm over Daniels' shoulder.* VERB; V pron-refl prep; V n prep 4 **Drapes** are pieces of heavy fabric that you hang from the top of a window and can close to keep the light out or stop people looking in. [AM] N-COUNT: usu pl

✔ in BRIT, use **curtains**

**drap|er** /dreɪpəʳ/ **(drapers)** A **draper** is a shopkeeper who sells cloth. [BRIT] N-COUNT

**dra|pery** /dreɪpəri/ **(draperies)** 1 You can refer to cloth, curtains, or clothing hanging in folds as **drapery** or **draperies**. ❑ *In the dining-room the draperies create an atmosphere of elegance.* N-UNCOUNT: also N in pl 2 **Drapery** is cloth that you buy in a shop. [BRIT] ❑ *My mother ran a couple of drapery shops.* N-UNCOUNT: oft N n

✔ in AM, use **dry goods**

**dras|tic** /dræstɪk/ 1 If you have to take **drastic** action in order to solve a problem, you have to do something extreme and basic to solve it. ❑ *Drastic measures are needed to clean up the profession... He's not going to do anything drastic about economic policy.* ADJ = radical 2 A **drastic** change is a very great change. ❑ *...a drastic reduction in the numbers of people dying.* ADJ ♦ **dras|ti|cal|ly** *As a result, services have been drastically reduced.* ADV: ADV with v

**draught** /drɑːft, dræft/ **(draughts)** 1 A **draught** is a current of air that comes into a place in an undesirable way. [BRIT] ❑ *Block draughts around doors and windows.* N-COUNT

✔ in AM, use **draft**

2 **Draught** beer is beer which is kept in barrels rather than bottles. ❑ *Draught beer is available too.* ADJ: usu ADJ n ● Beer that is **on draught** is kept in and served from a barrel rather than a bottle. ❑ *They drink bitter on draught in the local bar.* PHRASE: PHR after v, v-link PHR 3 **Draughts** is a game for two people, played with 24 round pieces on a board. [BRIT] ❑ *He was in the study playing draughts by the fire with Albert.* N-UNCOUNT

✔ in AM, use **checkers**

4 A **draught** is one of the round pieces which are used in the game of draughts. [BRIT] N-COUNT

✔ in AM, use **checker**

**draughts board** **(draughts boards)** also **draught board.** A **draughts board** is a square board for playing draughts, with 64 equal-sized, black and white squares. [BRIT] N-COUNT

✔ in AM, use **checkerboard**

**draughts|man** /drɑːftsmən, dræfts-/ **(draughtsmen)**

✔ in AM, use **draftsman**

A **draughtsman** is someone whose job is to prepare very detailed drawings of machinery, equipment, or buildings. N-COUNT

**draughts|man|ship** /drɑːftsmənʃɪp, dræfts-/

✔ in AM, use **draftsmanship**

**Draughtsmanship** is the ability to draw well or the art of drawing. N-UNCOUNT

**draughty** /drɑːfti, dræfti/ **(draughtier, draughtiest)**

✔ in AM, use **drafty**

A **draughty** room or building has currents of cold air blowing through it, usually because the windows and doors do not fit very well. ADJ

**draw** /drɔː/ **(draws, drawing, drew, drawn)** ♦♦♦

1 When you **draw**, or when you **draw** something, you use a pencil or pen to produce a picture, pattern, or diagram. ❑ *She would sit there drawing with the pencil stub... Draw a rough design for a logo.* VERB = sketch; V; V n ♦ **draw|ing** *I like dancing, singing and drawing.* N-UNCOUNT 2 When a vehicle **draws** somewhere, it moves there smoothly and steadily. ❑ *Claire had seen the taxi drawing away.* VERB; V adv/prep 3 If you **draw** somewhere, you move there slowly. [WRITTEN] ❑ *She drew away and did not smile... When we drew level, he neither slowed down nor accelerated.* VERB; V adv/prep; V adj 4 If you **draw** something or someone in a particular direction, you move them in that direction, usually by pulling them gently. [WRITTEN] ❑ *He drew his chair nearer the fire... He put his arm around Caroline's shoulders and drew her close to him... Wilson drew me aside after an interview.* VERB = pull; V n prep; V n adj; V n with adv 5 When you **draw** a curtain or blind, you pull it across a window, either to cover or to uncover it. ❑ *After drawing the curtains, she lit a candle... Mother was lying on her bed, with the blinds drawn.* VERB; V n; V-ed 6 If someone **draws** a gun, knife, or other weapon, they pull it out of its container and threaten you with it. ❑ *He drew his dagger and turned to face his pursuers.* VERB = take out; V n 7 If an animal or vehicle **draws** something such as a cart, carriage, or another vehicle, it pulls it along. ❑ *...a slow-moving tractor, drawing a trailer.* VERB; V n 8 If you **draw** a deep breath, you breathe in deeply once. ❑ *He paused, drawing a deep breath.* VERB; V n 9 If you **draw on** a cigarette, you breathe the smoke from it into your mouth or lungs. ❑ *He drew on an American cigarette... Her cheeks hollowed as she drew smoke into her lungs.* VERB; V on n; V n into n 10 To **draw** something such as water or energy **from** a particular source means to take it from that source. ❑ *Villagers still have to draw their water from wells.* VERB; V n from n 11 If something that hits you or presses part of your body **draws** blood, it cuts your skin so that it bleeds. ❑ *Any practice that draws blood could increase the risk of getting the virus.* VERB; V n 12 If you **draw** money out of a bank, building society, or savings account, you get it from the ac- VERB

count so that you can use it. ❑ *She was drawing out cash from a cash machine... Companies could not draw money from bank accounts as cash.* [V n with *out*] [V n *from* n] 13 If you **draw** a salary or a sum of money, you receive a sum of money regularly. ❑ *For the first few years I didn't draw any salary at all.* [VERB] [V n] 14 To **draw** something means to choose it or to be given it, as part of a competition, game, or lottery. ❑ *We delved through a sackful of letters to draw the winning name.* [VERB] [V n] ♦ **Draw** is also a noun. ❑ *...the draw for the quarter-finals of the UEFA Cup.* [N-COUNT] 15 A **draw** is a competition where people pay money for numbered or named tickets, then some of those tickets are chosen, and the owners are given prizes. [N-COUNT] 16 To **draw** something **from** a particular thing or place means to take or get it from that thing or place. ❑ *I draw strength from the millions of women who have faced this challenge successfully.* [VERB] [V n *from* n] 17 If you **draw** a particular conclusion, you decide that that conclusion is true. ❑ *He draws two conclusions from this... He says he cannot yet draw any conclusions about the murders.* [VERB] [V n *from* n] [V n] 18 If you **draw** a comparison, parallel, or distinction, you compare or contrast two different ideas, systems, or other things. ❑ *...literary critics drawing comparisons between George Sand and George Eliot.* [VERB] [V n] 19 If you **draw** someone's attention to something, you make them aware of it or make them think about it. ❑ *He was waving his arms to draw their attention... He just wants to draw attention to the plight of the unemployed.* [VERB] [V n] [V n *to* n] 20 If someone or something **draws** a particular reaction, people react to it in that way. ❑ *Such a policy would inevitably draw fierce resistance from farmers. ...an official tour to South Africa which drew angry political reactions.* [VERB] [V n *from* n] [V n] 21 If something such as a film or an event **draws** a lot of people, it is so interesting or entertaining that a lot of people go to it. ❑ *The game is currently drawing huge crowds.* [VERB] [V n] 22 If someone or something **draws** you, it attracts you very strongly. ❑ *He drew and enthralled her... What drew him to the area was its proximity to central London.* [VERB] [V n] [V n *to* n] 23 If someone will not **be drawn** or refuses to **be drawn**, they will not reply to questions in the way that you want them to, or will not reveal information or their opinion. [mainly BRIT] ❑ *The ambassador would not be drawn on questions of a political nature... 'Did he say why?' — 'No, he refuses to be drawn.'* [VERB: with brd-neg, usu passive] [*be* V-ed *on* n] [*be* V-ed] 24 In a game or competition, if one person or team **draws with** another one, or if two people or teams **draw**, they have the same number of points or goals at the end of the game. [mainly BRIT] ❑ *Holland and the Republic of Ireland drew one-one... We drew with Ireland in the first game... Egypt drew two of their matches in Italy.* [V-RECIP = tie] [pl-n V num] [V *with/against* n] [V n (non-recip)] ♦ **Draw** is also a noun. ❑ *We were happy to come away with a draw against Sweden.* [N-COUNT]

☑ in AM, usually use **tie**

25 ➔ See also **drawing**.

PHRASES 26 When an event or period of time **draws to a close** or **draws to an end**, it finishes. ❑ *Another celebration had drawn to its close.* [PHRASE: V inflects] 27 If an event or period of time **is drawing closer** or **is drawing nearer**, it is approaching. ❑ *And all the time next spring's elections are drawing closer.* [PHRASE: V inflects] 28 **to draw a blank** ➔ see **blank**. **to draw the line** ➔ see **line**. **to draw lots** ➔ see **lot**.

♦ **draw in** 1 If you say that the nights, evenings, or days **are drawing in**, you mean that it is becoming dark at an earlier time in the evening, because autumn or winter is approaching. ❑ *The days draw in and the mornings get darker.* [PHRASAL VERB] [V P] 2 If you **draw** someone **in** or **draw** them **into** something you are involved with, you cause them to become involved with it. [BRIT] ❑ *It won't be easy for you to draw him in... Don't let him draw you into his strategy.* [PHRASAL VERB] [V n P] [V n P n] 3 If you **draw in** your breath, you breathe in deeply. If you **draw in** air, you take it into your lungs as you breathe in. ❑ *Rose drew her breath in sharply... Roll the wine around in your mouth, drawing in air at the same time.* [PHRASAL VERB = take in] [V n P] [V P n (not pron)]

♦ **draw into** ➔ see **draw in 2**.

♦ **draw off** If a quantity of liquid **is drawn off** from a larger quantity, it is taken from it, usually by means of a needle or pipe. ❑ *The fluid can be drawn off with a syringe... Doctors drew off a pint of his blood.* [PHRASAL VERB] [*be* V-ed P] [V P n (not pron)] [Also V n P]

♦ **draw on** 1 If you **draw on** or **draw upon** something such as your skill or experience, you make use of it in order to do something. ❑ *He drew on his experience as a yachtsman to make a documentary programme.* [PHRASAL VERB] [V P n] 2 As a period of time **draws on**, it passes and the end of it gets closer. ❑ *As the afternoon drew on we were joined by more of the regulars.* [PHRASAL VERB = wear on] [V P]

♦ **draw out** If you **draw** someone **out**, you make them feel less nervous and more willing to talk. ❑ *Her mother tried every approach to draw her out.* [PHRASAL VERB] [V n P]

♦ **draw up** 1 If you **draw up** a document, list, or plan, you prepare it and write it out. ❑ *They agreed to draw up a formal agreement... He wants his ministers to concentrate on implementing policy, not on drawing it up.* [PHRASAL VERB = formulate] [V P n (not pron)] [V n P] 2 If you **draw up** a chair, you move it nearer to a person or place, for example so that you can watch something or join in with something. ❑ *He drew up a chair and sat down.* [PHRASAL VERB = pull up] [V P n (not pron)] [Also V n P]

♦ **draw upon** ➔ see **draw on 1**.

**draw|back** /drɔːbæk/ **(drawbacks)** A **drawback** is an aspect of something or someone that makes them less acceptable than they would otherwise be. ❑ *He felt the apartment's only drawback was that it was too small.* [N-COUNT = disadvantage]

**draw|bridge** /drɔːbrɪdʒ/ **(drawbridges)** A **drawbridge** is a bridge that can be pulled up, for example to prevent people from getting into a castle or to allow ships to pass underneath it. [N-COUNT]

**drawer** /drɔːə$^{r}$/ **(drawers)** 1 A **drawer** is part of a desk, chest, or other piece of furniture that is shaped like a box and is designed for putting things in. You pull it towards you to open it. ❑ *He opened a drawer in his writing-table.* [N-COUNT] 2 ➔ See also **chest of drawers**.

**draw|ing** /drɔːɪŋ/ **(drawings)** A **drawing** is a picture made with a pencil or pen. ❑ *She did a drawing of me.* ➔ See also **draw**. [N-COUNT: oft N *of* n]

**draw|ing board (drawing boards)**

☑ in AM, use **drawing-board**

1 A **drawing board** is a large flat board, often fixed to a metal frame so that it looks like a desk, on which you place your paper when you are drawing or designing something. [N-COUNT] 2 If you say that you will have to go **back to the drawing board**, you mean that something which you have done has not been successful and that you will have to start again or try another idea. [PHRASE: PHR after v]

**draw|ing pin (drawing pins)** also **drawing-pin.** A **drawing pin** is a short pin with a broad, flat top which is used for fastening papers or pictures to a board, wall, or other surface. [BRIT] [N-COUNT]

☑ in AM, use **thumbtack**

**draw|ing room (drawing rooms)** A **drawing room** is a room, especially a large room in a large house, where people sit and relax, or entertain guests. [FORMAL] [N-COUNT]

**drawl** /drɔːl/ **(drawls, drawling, drawled)** If someone **drawls**, they speak slowly and not very clearly, with long vowel sounds. ❑ *'I guess you guys don't mind if I smoke?' he drawled... He has a deep voice and he drawls slightly.* [VERB] [V with quote] [V] ♦ **Drawl** is also a noun. ❑ *...Jack's southern drawl.* [N-COUNT: with supp]

**drawn** /drɔːn/ 1 **Drawn** is the past participle of **draw**. 2 If someone or their face looks **drawn**, their face is thin and they look very tired, ill, worried, or unhappy. ❑ *She looked drawn and tired when she turned towards me.* [ADJ]

**drawn-out** You can describe something as **drawn-out** when it lasts or takes longer than you would like it to. ❑ *The road to peace will be long and drawn-out.* ADJ = protracted

**draw|string** /drɔːstrɪŋ/ **(drawstrings)** also **draw-string.** A **drawstring** is a cord that goes through an opening, for example at the top of a bag or a pair of trousers. When the cord is pulled tighter, the opening gets smaller. ❑ *...a velvet bag with a drawstring.* N-COUNT: usu sing, oft N n

**dray** /dreɪ/ **(drays)** A **dray** is a large flat cart with four wheels which is pulled by horses. N-COUNT

**dread** /dred/ **(dreads, dreading, dreaded)** 1 If you **dread** something which may happen, you feel very anxious and unhappy about it because you think it will be unpleasant or upsetting. ❑ *I'm dreading Christmas this year... I'd been dreading that the birth would take a long time.* VERB ≠ look forward to; V n/-ing; V that 2 **Dread** is a feeling of great anxiety and fear about something that may happen. ❑ *She thought with dread of the cold winters to come.* N-UNCOUNT 3 **Dread** means terrible and greatly feared. [LITERARY] ❑ *...a more effective national policy to combat this dread disease.* ADJ: usu ADJ n = dreaded 4 → See also **dreaded.** 5 If you say that you **dread to think** what might happen, you mean that you are anxious about it because it is likely to be very unpleasant. ❑ *I dread to think what will happen in the case of a major emergency.* PHRASE: V inflects, usu PHR wh

**dread|ed** /dredɪd/ 1 **Dreaded** means terrible and greatly feared. ❑ *No one knew how to treat this dreaded disease.* ADJ: ADJ n 2 You can use **the dreaded** to describe something that you, or a particular group of people, find annoying, inconvenient, or undesirable. [INFORMAL] ❑ *She's a victim of the dreaded hay fever.* ADJ: ADJ n [feelings]

**dread|ful** /dredfʊl/ 1 If you say that something is **dreadful**, you mean that it is very bad or unpleasant, or very poor in quality. ❑ *They told us the dreadful news.* ADJ = awful, appalling ♦ **dread|ful|ly** *You behaved dreadfully.* ADV: ADV with v 2 **Dreadful** is used to emphasize the degree or extent of something bad. ❑ *We've made a dreadful mistake.* ADJ: ADJ n [emphasis] = terrible ♦ **dread|ful|ly** *He looks dreadfully ill.* ADV: ADV adj, ADV after v 3 If someone **looks** or **feels dreadful**, they look or feel very ill, tired, or upset. ❑ *Are you all right? You look dreadful.* ADJ: feel/look ADJ

**dread|locked** /dredlɒkt/ A **dreadlocked** person has their hair in dreadlocks. [WRITTEN] ❑ *...the dreadlocked Rastafarian, Bob Marley.* ADJ: usu ADJ n

**dread|locks** /dredlɒks/ If someone has **dreadlocks**, their hair is divided into a large number of tight strips, like pieces of rope. Dreadlocks are worn especially by men who are Rastafarians. N-PLURAL

**dream** /driːm/ **(dreams, dreaming, dreamed, dreamt)** ◆◆◇

> ✔ American English uses the form **dreamed** as the past tense and past participle. British English uses either **dreamed** or **dreamt**.

1 A **dream** is an imaginary series of events that you experience in your mind while you are asleep. ❑ *He had a dream about Claire... I had a dream that I was in an old study, surrounded by leather books.* N-COUNT 2 When you **dream**, you experience imaginary events in your mind while you are asleep. ❑ *Ivor dreamed that he was on a bus... She dreamed about her baby.* VERB; V that; V about/of n; Also V 3 You can refer to a situation or event as a **dream** if you often think about it because you would like it to happen. ❑ *He had finally accomplished his dream of becoming a pilot... My dream is to have a house in the country.* N-COUNT: usu with supp = ambition 4 If you often think about something that you would very much like to happen or have, you can say that you **dream of** it. ❑ *As a schoolgirl, she had dreamed of becoming an actress... For most of us, a brand new designer kitchen is something we can only dream about... I dream that my son will attend college and find a good job.* VERB; V of/about n/-ing; V of/about n/-ing; V that 5 You can use **dream** to describe something that you think is ideal or perfect, especially if it is something that you thought you would never be able to have or experience. ❑ *...a dream holiday to Jamaica.* ADJ: ADJ n 6 If you describe something as **a** particular person's **dream**, you think that it would be ideal for that person and that he or she would like it very much. ❑ *Greece is said to be a botanist's dream.* N-SING: poss N 7 If you say that something is **a dream**, you mean that it is wonderful. [INFORMAL] N-SING: a N 8 You can refer to a situation or event that does not seem real as a **dream**, especially if it is very strange or unpleasant. ❑ *When the right woman comes along, this bad dream will be over.* N-COUNT: usu sing, with supp 9 If you say that you **would not dream of** doing something, you are emphasizing that you would never do it because you think it is wrong or is not possible or suitable for you. ❑ *I wouldn't dream of making fun of you.* VERB: with neg [emphasis]; V of -ing/n 10 If you say that you **never dreamed that** something would happen, you are emphasizing that you did not think that it would happen because it seemed very unlikely. ❑ *I never dreamed that I would be able to afford a home here... Who could ever dream of a disaster like this?* VERB: with brd-neg [emphasis]; V that; V of n 11 → See also **pipe dream, wet dream.**

**PHRASES** 12 If you say that you are **in a dream**, you mean that you do not concentrate properly on what you are doing because you are thinking about other things. ❑ *All day long I moved in a dream.* PHRASE: PHR after v, v-link PHR 13 If you say that someone does something **like a dream**, you think that they do it very well. If you say that something happens **like a dream**, you mean that it happens successfully without any problems. ❑ *She cooked like a dream.* PHRASE: PHR after v 14 If you describe someone or something as the person or thing **of** your **dreams**, you mean that you consider them to be ideal or perfect. ❑ *This could be the man of my dreams.* PHRASE: n PHR 15 If you say that you could not imagine a particular thing **in** your **wildest dreams**, you are emphasizing that you think it is extremely strange or unlikely. ❑ *Never in my wildest dreams did I think we could win.* PHRASE: with brd-neg, PHR with cl [emphasis] 16 If you describe something as being **beyond** your **wildest dreams**, you are emphasizing that it is better than you could have imagined or hoped for. ❑ *She had already achieved success beyond her wildest dreams.* PHRASE: n PHR, PHR after v, v-link PHR [emphasis]

♦ **dream up** If you **dream up** a plan or idea, you work it out or create it in your mind. ❑ *I dreamed up a plan to solve both problems at once... His son hadn't dreamed it up.* PHRASAL VERB; V P n (not pron); V n P

**dream|er** /driːməʳ/ **(dreamers)** If you describe someone as a **dreamer**, you mean that they spend a lot of time thinking about and planning for things that they would like to happen but which are improbable or impractical. N-COUNT

**dreami|ly** /driːmɪli/ If you say or do something **dreamily**, you say or do it in a way that shows your mind is occupied with pleasant, relaxing thoughts. ❑ *'They were divine,' she sighs, dreamily.* ADV: usu ADV with v, also ADV adj

**dream|land** /driːmlænd/ If you refer to a situation as **dreamland**, you mean that it represents what someone would like to happen, but that it is completely unrealistic. ❑ *In dreamland we play them in the final.* N-UNCOUNT: also a N

**dream|less** /driːmləs/ A **dreamless** sleep is very deep and peaceful, and without dreams. ❑ *He fell into a deep dreamless sleep.* ADJ: usu ADJ n

**dream|like** /driːmlaɪk/ If you describe something as **dreamlike**, you mean it seems strange and unreal. ❑ *Her paintings have a naive, dreamlike quality.* ADJ = surreal

**dreamt** /dremt/ **Dreamt** is a past tense and past participle of **dream.**

**dream team (dream teams)** A **dream team** is the best possible group of people to be in a sports team or to do a particular job. ❑ *...American basketball's dream team.* N-COUNT

**dream tick|et** If journalists talk about a **dream ticket**, they are referring to two candidates for political positions, for example President and Vice-President, or Prime Minister and Deputy N-SING

Prime Minister, who they think will be extremely successful.

**dreamy** /driːmi/ **(dreamier, dreamiest)** 1 If you say that someone has a **dreamy** expression, you mean that they are not paying attention to things around them and look as if they are thinking about something pleasant. ❑ *His face assumed a sort of dreamy expression.* 2 If you describe something as **dreamy**, you mean that you like it and that it seems gentle and soft, like something in a dream. ❑ *...dreamy shots of beautiful sunsets.* 3 → See also **dreamily**. ADJ / ADJ: usu ADJ n [approval]

**dreary** /drɪəri/ **(drearier, dreariest)** If you describe something as **dreary**, you mean that it is dull and depressing. ❑ *...a dreary little town in the Midwest.* ♦ **dreari|ly** *...a drearily familiar scenario.* ADJ = *dismal* / ADV: ADV adj, ADV with v

**dredge** /dredʒ/ **(dredges, dredging, dredged)** When people **dredge** a harbour, river, or other area of water, they remove mud and unwanted material from the bottom with a special machine in order to make it deeper or to look for something. ❑ *Police have spent weeks dredging the lake but have not found his body.* VERB / V n

♦ **dredge up** 1 If someone **dredges up** a piece of information they learned a long time ago, or if they **dredge up** a distant memory, they manage to remember it. ❑ *...an American trying to dredge up some French or German learned in high school.* 2 If someone **dredges up** a damaging or upsetting fact about your past, they remind you of it or tell other people about it. ❑ *I wouldn't want to dredge up the past... It's the media who keep dredging it up.* PHRASAL VERB / V P n (not pron) / PHRASAL VERB / V P n (not pron) / V n P

**dredg|er** /dredʒəʳ/ **(dredgers)** A **dredger** is a boat which is fitted with a special machine that is used to increase the size of harbours, rivers, and canals. N-COUNT

**dregs** /dregz/ 1 The **dregs** of a liquid are the last drops left at the bottom of a container, together with any solid bits that have sunk to the bottom. ❑ *Colum drained the dregs from his cup.* 2 If you talk about the **dregs of** society or of a community, you mean the people in it who you consider to be the most worthless and bad. ❑ *He sees dissidents as the dregs of society.* N-PLURAL: usu *the* N [disapproval] / N-PLURAL: usu *the* N *of* n [disapproval]

**drench** /drentʃ/ **(drenches, drenching, drenched)** To **drench** something or someone means to make them completely wet. ❑ *They turned fire hoses on the people and drenched them... They were getting drenched by icy water... We were completely drenched and cold.* ♦ **-drenched** *...the rain-drenched streets of the capital.* VERB = *soak* / V n / *get* V-ed / V-ed / COMB in ADJ

**dress** /dres/ **(dresses, dressing, dressed)** 1 A **dress** is a piece of clothing worn by a woman or girl. It covers her body and part of her legs. ❑ *She was wearing a black dress.* 2 You can refer to clothes worn by men or women as **dress**. ❑ *He's usually smart in his dress. ...hundreds of Cambodians in traditional dress.* → See also **evening dress, fancy dress, full dress, morning dress.** 3 When you **dress** or **dress yourself**, you put on clothes. ❑ *He told Sarah to wait while he dressed... Sue had dressed herself neatly for work.* 4 If you **dress** someone, for example a child, you put clothes on them. ❑ *She bathed her and dressed her in clean clothes.* 5 If someone **dresses** in a particular way, they wear clothes of a particular style or colour. ❑ *He dresses in a way that lets everyone know he's got authority.* 6 If you **dress for** something, you put on special clothes for it. ❑ *We don't dress for dinner here.* 7 When someone **dresses** a wound, they clean it and cover it. ❑ *The poor child never cried or protested when I was dressing her wounds.* 8 If you **dress** a salad, you cover it with a mixture of oil, vinegar, and herbs or flavourings. ❑ *Scatter the tomato over, then dress the salad. ... a bowl of dressed salad.* 9 → See also **dressing, dressed.** ♦♦◇ N-COUNT / N-UNCOUNT / VERB / V / V pron-refl / VERB / V n / VERB / V *in* n / VERB / V *for* n / VERB / V n / VERB / V n / V -ed

♦ **dress down** If you **dress down**, you wear clothes that are less smart than usual. ❑ *She dresses down in baggy clothes to avoid hordes of admirers.* PHRASAL VERB / V P

♦ **dress up** 1 If you **dress up** or **dress** yourself **up**, you put on different clothes, in order to make yourself look smarter than usual or to disguise yourself. ❑ *You do not need to dress up for dinner... Little girls dress up as angels for fiestas.* 2 If you **dress** someone **up**, you give them special clothes to wear, in order to make them look smarter or to disguise them. ❑ *Mother loved to dress me up.* 3 If you **dress** something **up**, you try to make it seem more attractive, acceptable, or interesting than it really is. ❑ *Politicians dress up their ruthless ambition as a pursuit of the public good... However you dress it up, a bank only exists to lend money.* 4 → See also **dressed up, dressing-up.** PHRASAL VERB / V P / V P *in/as* n / PHRASAL VERB / V n P / PHRASAL VERB / V P n (not pron) / V n P

**dres|sage** /dresɑːʒ/ **Dressage** is a competition in which horse riders have to make their horse perform controlled movements. N-UNCOUNT

**dress cir|cle The dress circle** is the lowest of the curved rows of seats upstairs in a theatre. N-SING

**dress code (dress codes)** The **dress code** of a place is the rules about what kind of clothes people are allowed to wear there. ❑ *There is a strict dress code: no trainers or jeans.* N-COUNT

**dress-down Fri|day (dress-down Fridays)** In some companies employees are allowed to wear clothes that are less smart than usual on a Friday. This day is known as a **dress-down Friday.** ❑ *But is it really feasible to don sportswear to the office without the excuse of dress-down Friday?* N-COUNT

**dressed** /drest/ 1 If you are **dressed**, you are wearing clothes rather than being naked or wearing your night clothes. If you **get dressed**, you put on your clothes. ❑ *He was fully dressed, including shoes... He went into his bedroom to get dressed.* 2 If you are **dressed** in a particular way, you are wearing clothes of a particular colour or kind. ❑ *...a tall thin woman dressed in black.* → See also **well-dressed.** ♦◇◇ ADJ: usu v-link ADJ / ADJ: v-link ADJ *in*/*as* n, adv ADJ

**dressed up** 1 If someone is **dressed up**, they are wearing special clothes, in order to look smarter than usual or in order to disguise themselves. ❑ *You're all dressed up. Are you going somewhere?* 2 If you say that something is **dressed up as** something else, you mean that someone has tried to make it more acceptable or attractive by making it seem like that other thing. ❑ *He tried to organise things so that the trip would be dressed up as a UN mission.* 3 **dressed up to the nines** → see **nine.** ADJ: usu v-link ADJ / ADJ: v-link ADJ *as*/*in* n [disapproval]

**dress|er** /dresəʳ/ **(dressers)** 1 A **dresser** is a chest of drawers, usually with a mirror on the top. [AM] N-COUNT

in BRIT, use **dressing table**

2 A **dresser** is a piece of furniture which has cupboards or drawers in the lower part and shelves in the top part. It is usually used for storing china. [mainly BRIT] 3 You can use **dresser** to refer to the kind of clothes that a person wears. For example, if you say that someone is a **smart dresser**, you mean that they wear smart clothes. N-COUNT / N-COUNT: adj N

**dress|ing** /dresɪŋ/ **(dressings)** 1 A salad **dressing** is a mixture of oil, vinegar, and herbs or flavourings, which you pour over salad. ❑ *Mix the ingredients for the dressing in a bowl.* 2 A **dressing** is a covering that is put on a wound to protect it while it heals. N-MASS: oft supp N / N-COUNT

**dressing-down** If someone **gives** you **a dressing-down**, they speak angrily to you because you have done something bad or foolish. [INFORMAL] N-SING = *telling off*

**dress|ing gown (dressing gowns)** also **dressing-gown.** A **dressing gown** is a long, loose garment which you wear over your night clothes when you are not in bed. N-COUNT

**dress|ing room (dressing rooms)** also **dressing-room.** 1 A **dressing room** is a N-COUNT room in a theatre where performers can dress and get ready for their performance. [2] A **dressing room** is a room at a sports stadium where players can change and get ready for their game. [BRIT] N-COUNT = changing room

in AM, use **locker room**

**dress|ing ta|ble** **(dressing tables)** also **dressing-table.** A **dressing table** is a small table in a bedroom. It has drawers underneath and a mirror on top. N-COUNT

**dressing-up** also **dressing up.** When children play at **dressing-up**, they put on special or different clothes and pretend to be different people. N-UNCOUNT

**dress|maker** /dresmeɪkəʳ/ **(dressmakers)** A **dressmaker** is a person who makes women's or children's clothes. N-COUNT

**dress|making** /dresmeɪkɪŋ/ **Dressmaking** is the activity or job of making clothes for women or girls. N-UNCOUNT

**dress re|hears|al** **(dress rehearsals)** [1] The **dress rehearsal** of a play, opera, or show is the final rehearsal before it is performed, in which the performers wear their costumes and the lights and scenery are all used as they will be in the performance. N-COUNT [2] You can describe an event as a **dress rehearsal** for a later, more important event when it indicates how the later event will be. ❑ *These elections, you could almost say, are a dress rehearsal for the real elections.* N-COUNT

**dress sense** Someone's **dress sense** is their ability to choose clothes that make them look attractive. ❑ *I've no dress sense at all.* N-UNCOUNT

**dress shirt** **(dress shirts)** A **dress shirt** is a special shirt which men wear on formal occasions. It is worn with a dinner jacket and bow tie. N-COUNT

**dressy** /dresi/ **(dressier, dressiest)** **Dressy** clothes are smart clothes which you wear when you want to look elegant or formal. ADJ

**drew** /druː/ **Drew** is the past tense of **draw**.

**drib|ble** /drɪbəl/ **(dribbles, dribbling, dribbled)**
[1] If a liquid **dribbles** somewhere, or if you **dribble** it, it drops down slowly or flows in a thin stream. ❑ *Sweat dribbled down Hart's face... Dribble the hot mixture slowly into the blender.* VERB = trickle; V prep/adv; V n prep/adv [2] When players **dribble** the ball in a game such as football or basketball, they keep kicking or tapping it quickly in order to keep it moving. ❑ *He dribbled the ball towards Ferris... He dribbled past four defenders... Her dribbling skills look second to none.* VERB; V n; V; V-ing [3] If a person **dribbles**, saliva drops slowly from their mouth. ❑ *...to protect cot sheets when the baby dribbles.* VERB = drool; V [4] **Dribble** is saliva that drops slowly from someone's mouth. ❑ *His clothes are soaked in dribble.* N-UNCOUNT = drool

**dribs and drabs** /drɪbz ən dræbz/ If people or things arrive **in dribs and drabs**, they arrive in small numbers over a period of time rather than arriving all together. [INFORMAL] ❑ *Clients came in dribs and drabs.* PHRASE: PHR after v

**dried** /draɪd/ **Dried** food or milk has had all the water removed from it so that it will last for a long time. ❑ *...an infusion which may be prepared from the fresh plant or the dried herb.* ➔ See also **dry**. ADJ: ADJ n

**dried fruit** **(dried fruits)** **Dried fruit** is fruit that has been preserved by being dried; used especially to refer to currants, raisins, or sultanas, which are kinds of dried grapes. N-VAR

**dried-up** If you describe someone as **dried-up**, you are saying rudely that they are old and dull, and not worth paying attention to. [INFORMAL] ❑ *...her fears of becoming a dried-up old prune.* ➔ See also **dry up**. ADJ: usu ADJ n [disapproval] = withered

**dri|er** /draɪəʳ/ ➔ see **dry, dryer**.

**drift** /drɪft/ **(drifts, drifting, drifted)** ◆◇◇ [1] When something **drifts** somewhere, it is carried there by the movement of wind or water. ❑ *We proceeded to drift on up the river... The waves became rougher as they drifted.* VERB; V adv/prep; V [2] If someone or something **drifts into** a situation, they get into that situation in a way that is not planned or controlled. ❑ *We need to offer young people drifting into crime an alternative set of values... There is a general sense that the country and economy alike are drifting.* VERB; V prep/adv; V [3] If you say that someone **drifts** around, you mean that they travel from place to place without a plan or settled way of life. ❑ *You've been drifting from job to job without any real commitment.* VERB [disapproval]; V prep/adv [4] A **drift** is a movement away from somewhere or something, or a movement towards somewhere or something different. ❑ *...the drift towards the cities.* N-COUNT: usu N prep [5] To **drift** somewhere means to move there slowly or gradually. ❑ *As rural factories shed labour, people drift towards the cities.* VERB; V prep [6] If sounds **drift** somewhere, they can be heard but they are not very loud. ❑ *Cool summer dance sounds are drifting from the stereo indoors.* VERB; V prep/adv [7] If snow **drifts**, it builds up into piles as a result of the movement of the wind. ❑ *The snow, except where it drifted, was only calf-deep.* VERB; V [8] A **drift** is a mass of snow that has built up into a pile as a result of the movement of wind. ❑ *...a nine-foot snow drift.* N-COUNT [9] **The drift of** an argument or speech is the general point that is being made in it. ❑ *Grace was beginning to get his drift.* N-SING: poss N, N of n = gist

♦ **drift off** If you **drift off** to sleep, you gradually fall asleep. ❑ *It was only when he finally drifted off to sleep that the headaches eased.* PHRASAL VERB; V P to n; Also V P

**drift|er** /drɪftəʳ/ **(drifters)** If you describe someone as a **drifter**, you mean that they do not stay in one place or in one job for very long. N-COUNT [disapproval]

**drift|wood** /drɪftwʊd/ **Driftwood** is wood which has been carried onto the shore by the motion of the sea or a river, or which is still floating on the water. N-UNCOUNT

**drill** /drɪl/ **(drills, drilling, drilled)** [1] A **drill** is a tool or machine that you use for making holes. ➔ See picture on page 1709. ❑ *...pneumatic drills. ...a dentist's drill.* N-COUNT [2] When you **drill into** something or **drill** a hole in something, you make a hole in it using a drill. ❑ *He drilled into the wall of Lili's bedroom... I drilled five holes at equal distance.* VERB; V prep; V n [3] When people **drill for** oil or water, they search for it by drilling deep holes in the ground or in the bottom of the sea. ❑ *There have been proposals to drill for more oil... The team is still drilling.* VERB; V for n; V ♦ **drill|ing** *Drilling is due to start early next year.* N-UNCOUNT [4] A **drill** is a way that teachers teach their students something by making them repeat it many times. ❑ *The teacher runs them through a drill – the days of the week, the weather and some counting.* N-COUNT [5] If you **drill** people, you teach them to do something by making them repeat it many times. ❑ *He drills the choir to a high standard.* VERB; V n [6] A **drill** is repeated training for a group of people, especially soldiers, so that they can do something quickly and efficiently. ❑ *The Marines carried out a drill that included 18 ships and 90 aircraft.* N-VAR: oft N n [7] A **drill** is a routine exercise or activity, in which people practise what they should do in dangerous situations. ❑ *...a fire drill. ...air-raid drills.* N-COUNT: oft n N

**dri|ly** /draɪli/ ➔ see **dry**.

**drink** /drɪŋk/ **(drinks, drinking, drank, drunk)** ◆◆◇
[1] When you **drink** a liquid, you take it into your mouth and swallow it. ❑ *He drank his cup of tea... He drank thirstily from the pool under the rock.* VERB; V n; V [2] To **drink** means to drink alcohol. ❑ *He was smoking and drinking too much.* VERB; V ♦ **drink|ing** *She had left him because of his drinking.* N-UNCOUNT [3] A **drink** is an amount of a liquid which you drink. ❑ *I'll get you a drink of water.* N-COUNT: oft N of n [4] A **drink** is an alcoholic drink. ❑ *She felt like a drink after a hard day.* N-COUNT [5] **Drink** is alcohol, such as beer, wine, or whisky. ❑ *Too much drink is bad for your health.* N-UNCOUNT [6] ➔ See also **drinking**. [7] People say **'I'll drink to that'** to show that they agree with and approve of something that someone has just said. [INFORMAL] CONVENTION [feelings]

♦ **drink to** When people **drink to** someone or something, they wish them success, good luck, or good health before having an alcoholic drink. ❑ *Let's drink to his memory, eh?* PHRASAL VERB; V P n

♦ **drink up** When you **drink up** an amount of liquid, you finish it completely. ❑ *Drink up your sherry and we'll go... Drink up, there's time for another.* PHRASAL VERB V P n (not pron) V P

**drink|able** /drɪŋkəbᵊl/ 1 Water that is **drinkable** is clean and safe for drinking. ADJ 2 If you say that a particular wine, beer, or other drink is **drinkable**, you mean that it tastes quite pleasant. ❑ *The food was good and the wine drinkable. ...a very drinkable plonk.* ADJ

**drink-drive** also **drink drive. Drink-drive** means relating to drink-driving. ❑ *He was nearly three times over the drink drive limit.* ADJ: ADJ n

**drink-driver** **(drink-drivers)** also **drink driver.** A **drink-driver** is someone who drives after drinking more than the amount of alcohol that is legally allowed. [BRIT] N-COUNT

☑ in AM, use **drunk driver**

♦ **drink-driving** ❑ *...a drink-driving conviction.* N-UNCOUNT

**drink|er** /drɪŋkəʳ/ **(drinkers)** 1 If someone is a tea **drinker** or a beer **drinker**, for example, they regularly drink tea or beer. ❑ *Are you a coffee drinker?* N-COUNT: supp N 2 If you describe someone as a **drinker**, you mean that they drink alcohol, especially in large quantities. ❑ *I'm not a heavy drinker.* N-COUNT

**drink|ing** /drɪŋkɪŋ/ Someone's **drinking** friends or companions are people they regularly drink alcohol with. → See also **drink**. ADJ: ADJ n

**drink|ing foun|tain** **(drinking fountains)** A **drinking fountain** is a device which supplies water for people to drink in places such as streets, parks, or schools. N-COUNT

**drink|ing wa|ter** **Drinking water** is water which it is safe to drink. N-UNCOUNT

**drip** /drɪp/ **(drips, dripping, dripped)** 1 When liquid **drips** somewhere, or you **drip** it somewhere, it falls in individual small drops. ❑ *Sit your child forward and let the blood drip into a tissue or on to the floor... Amid the trees the sea mist was dripping... The children kept dripping Coke on the carpets.* VERB V prep/adv V V n prep/adv 2 When something **drips**, drops of liquid fall from it. ❑ *A tap in the kitchen was dripping... Lou was dripping with perspiration... He was holding a cloth that dripped pink drops upon the floor.* VERB V V *with* n V n 3 A **drip** is a small individual drop of a liquid. ❑ *Drips of water rolled down the trousers of his uniform.* N-COUNT 4 A **drip** is a piece of medical equipment by which a liquid is slowly passed through a tube into a patient's blood. ❑ *I had a bad attack of pneumonia and spent two days in hospital on a drip.* N-COUNT 5 If you say that something **is dripping with** a particular thing, you mean that it contains a lot of that thing. [LITERARY] ❑ *They were dazed by window displays dripping with diamonds and furs.* VERB: usu cont V *with* n 6 → See also **drip-dry**, **dripping**.

**drip-dry** **Drip-dry** clothes or sheets are made of a fabric that dries free of creases when it is hung up wet. ❑ *...drip-dry shirts.* ADJ

**drip|ping** /drɪpɪŋ/ 1 **Dripping** is the fat which comes out of meat when it is fried or roasted, and which can be used for frying food. N-UNCOUNT 2 If you are **dripping wet**, you are so wet that water is dripping from you. ❑ *We were dripping wet from the spray.* PHRASE: usu v-link PHR = sopping 3 → See also **drip**.

**drip|py** /drɪpi/ If you describe someone as **drippy**, you mean that they are rather stupid and weak. If you describe something such as a book or a type of music as **drippy**, you mean that you think it is rather stupid, dull, and sentimental. [INFORMAL] ❑ *These men look a bit drippy. ...drippy infantile ideas.* ADJ disapproval = wet

**drive** /draɪv/ **(drives, driving, drove, driven)** ◆◆◆ 1 When you **drive** somewhere, you operate a car or other vehicle and control its movement and direction. ❑ *I drove into town and went to a restaurant for dinner... She never learned to drive... Mrs Glick drove her own car and the girls went in Nancy's convertible.* VERB V prep/adv V V n ♦ **driv|ing** *...a qualified driving instructor.* N-UNCOUNT 2 If you **drive** someone somewhere, you take them there in a car or other vehicle. ❑ *His daughter Carly drove him to the train station.* VERB V n prep/adv 3 A **drive** is a journey in a car or other vehicle. ❑ *I thought we might go for a drive on Sunday.* N-COUNT 4 A **drive** is a wide piece of hard ground, or sometimes a private road, that leads from the road to a person's house. N-COUNT = driveway 5 If something **drives** a machine, it supplies the power that makes it work. ❑ *The current flows into electric motors that drive the wheels.* VERB V n 6 You use **drive** to refer to the mechanical part of a computer which reads the data on disks and tapes, or writes data onto them. ❑ *...equipment such as terminals, tape drives or printers.* → See also **disk drive**. N-COUNT: usu supp N 7 If you **drive** something such as a nail **into** something else, you push it in or hammer it in using a lot of effort. ❑ *I used a sledgehammer to drive the pegs into the ground... I held it still and drove in a nail.* VERB V n prep V n with adv 8 In games such as cricket, golf, or football, if a player **drives** a ball somewhere, they kick or hit it there with a lot of force. ❑ *Armstrong drove the ball into the roof of the net.* VERB V n prep/adv Also V n 9 If the wind, rain, or snow **drives** in a particular direction, it moves with great force in that direction. ❑ *Rain drove against the window.* VERB V prep/adv ♦ **driv|ing** *He crashed into a tree in driving rain.* ADJ: ADJ n 10 If you **drive** people or animals somewhere, you make them go to or from that place. ❑ *The last offensive drove thousands of people into Thailand... The smoke also drove mosquitoes away.* VERB V n prep V n with adv 11 To **drive** someone **into** a particular state or situation means to force them into that state or situation. ❑ *The recession and hospital bills drove them into bankruptcy... He nearly drove Elsie mad with his fussing.* VERB V n *into/to* n V n adj 12 The desire or feeling that **drives** a person **to** do something, especially something extreme, is the desire or feeling that causes them to do it. ❑ *More than once, depression drove him to attempt suicide... Jealousy drives people to murder. ...people who are driven by guilt, resentment and anxiety. ...a man driven by a pathological need to win.* VERB V n to-inf V n *to* n *be* V-ed V-ed 13 If you say that someone has **drive**, you mean they have energy and determination. ❑ *John will be best remembered for his drive and enthusiasm.* N-UNCOUNT 14 A **drive** is a very strong need or desire in human beings that makes them act in particular ways. ❑ *...compelling, dynamic sex drives.* N-COUNT 15 A **drive** is a special effort made by a group of people for a particular purpose. ❑ *The ANC is about to launch a nationwide recruitment drive.* N-SING: with supp = campaign 16 **Drive** is used in the names of some streets. ❑ *...23 Queen's Drive, Malvern, Worcestershire.* N-IN-NAMES 17 → See also **driving**. 18 If you ask someone **what** they **are driving at**, you are asking what they are trying to say or what they are saying indirectly. ❑ *It was clear Cohen didn't understand what Millard was driving at.* PHRASE: V inflects 19 to **drive a hard bargain** → see **bargain**.

♦ **drive away** To **drive** people **away** means to make them want to go away or stay away. ❑ *Patrick's boorish rudeness soon drove Monica's friends away... Increased crime is driving away customers.* PHRASAL VERB V n P V P n (not pron)

♦ **drive off** If you **drive** someone or something **off**, you force them to go away and to stop attacking you or threatening you. ❑ *The government drove the guerrillas off with infantry and air strikes... Men drove off the dogs with stones.* PHRASAL VERB V n P V P n

♦ **drive out** To **drive out** something means to make it disappear or stop operating. ❑ *He cut his rates to drive out rivals.* PHRASAL VERB V P n (not pron)

**drive-by** A **drive-by** shooting or a **drive-by** murder involves shooting someone from a moving car. ADJ: ADJ n

**drive-in** **(drive-ins)** A **drive-in** is a restaurant, cinema, or other commercial place which is specially designed so that customers can use the services provided while staying in their cars. ❑ *...fast food drive-ins.* N-COUNT ♦ **Drive-in** is also an adjective. ❑ *...a drive-in movie theater.* ADJ: ADJ n

**driv|el** /drɪvᵊl/ If you describe something that is written or said as **drivel**, you are critical of it N-UNCOUNT disapproval = nonsense because you think it is very silly. ❑ *What absolute drivel!*

**driv|en** /drɪvᵊn/ **Driven** is the past participle of **drive**.

**driv|er** /draɪvəʳ/ **(drivers)** ◆◆◇ 1 N-COUNT The **driver** of a vehicle is the person who is driving it. ❑ *The driver got out of his van. ...a taxi driver.* ➔ See also **back-seat driver**. 2 N-COUNT A **driver** is a computer program that controls a device such as a printer. [COMPUTING] ❑ *...printer driver software.*

**driv|er's li|cense** **(driver's licenses)** N-COUNT A **driver's license** is a card showing that you are qualified to drive because you have passed a driving test. [AM]

☑ in BRIT, use **driving licence**

**driv|er's seat** 1 N-SING: usu *the* N In a vehicle such as a car or a bus, **the driver's seat** is the seat where the person who is driving sits. 2 PHRASE: v-link PHR, PHR after v If you say that someone **is in the driver's seat**, you mean that they are in control in a situation. ❑ *Now he knows he's in the driver's seat and can wait for a better deal.*

**drive shaft** **(drive shafts)** N-COUNT A **drive shaft** is a shaft in a car or other vehicle that transfers power from the gear box to the wheels.

**drive-through** ADJ: ADJ n A **drive-through** shop or restaurant is one where you can buy things without leaving your car. ❑ *...a drive-through burger bar.*

**drive|way** /draɪvweɪ/ **(driveways)** N-COUNT = drive A **driveway** is a piece of hard ground that leads from the road to the front of a house or other building.

**driv|ing** /draɪvɪŋ/ ADJ: ADJ n The **driving** force or idea behind something that happens or is done is the main thing that has a strong effect on it and makes it happen or be done in a particular way. ❑ *Consumer spending was the driving force behind the economic growth in the summer.* ➔ See also **drive**.

**driv|ing li|cence** **(driving licences)** N-COUNT A **driving licence** is a card showing that you are qualified to drive because you have passed a driving test. [BRIT]

☑ in AM, use **driver's license**

**driv|ing range** **(driving ranges)** N-COUNT A **driving range** is an outdoor place where you can practise playing golf.

**driv|ing school** **(driving schools)** N-COUNT A **driving school** is a business that employs instructors who teach people how to drive a car.

**driv|ing seat** 1 N-SING: usu *the* N = driver's seat In a vehicle such as a car or a bus, **the driving seat** is the seat where the person who is driving the vehicle sits. ❑ *He got into the driving seat and started the engine.* 2 PHRASE: usu v-link PHR, PHR after v If you say that someone is **in the driving seat**, you mean that they are in control in a situation. ❑ *At 69 he is as firmly in the driving seat of the company as ever.*

**driz|zle** /drɪzᵊl/ **(drizzles, drizzling, drizzled)** 1 N-UNCOUNT: also *a* N **Drizzle** is light rain falling in fine drops. ❑ *The drizzle had now stopped and the sun was breaking through.* 2 VERB: *it* V If it **is drizzling**, it is raining very lightly. ❑ *Clouds had come down and it was starting to drizzle.*

**driz|zly** /drɪzəli/ ADJ: oft *it* v-link ADJ When the weather is **drizzly**, the sky is dull and grey and it rains steadily but not very hard. ❑ *...a dull, drizzly afternoon... It was dull and slightly drizzly as we left.*

**droll** /droʊl/ ADJ Something or someone that is **droll** is amusing or witty, sometimes in an unexpected way. [WRITTEN] ❑ *The band have a droll sense of humour.*

**drone** /droʊn/ **(drones, droning, droned)** 1 VERB If something **drones**, it makes a low, continuous, dull noise. ❑ *Above him an invisible plane droned* [V] *through the night sky. ...a virtually non-stop droning* [V-ing] *noise in the background.* ♦ N-SING: usu N *of* n **Drone** is also a noun. ❑ *...the constant drone of the motorways.* ♦ N-SING: usu N *of* n **dron|ing** *...the droning of a plane far overhead.* 2 VERB [disapproval] If you say that someone **drones**, you mean that they keep talking about something in a boring way. ❑ *Chambers' voice droned, maddening as an* [V] *insect around his head.* ♦ N-SING **Drone** is also a noun. ❑ *The minister's voice was a relentless drone.*

♦ PHRASAL VERB **Drone on** means the same as **drone**. ❑ *Aunt Maimie's voice droned on...* [V P] *Daniel just drones on about American policy.* [V P *about* n]

♦ **drone on** ➔ see **drone 2**.

**drool** /druːl/ **(drools, drooling, drooled)** 1 VERB [disapproval] To **drool over** someone or something means to look at them with great pleasure, perhaps in an exaggerated or ridiculous way. ❑ *Fashion editors drooled* [V *over* n] *over every item... Advertisers are already drooling at reports* [V prep] *that this might bring 20 million dollars.* 2 VERB If a person or animal **drools**, saliva drops slowly from their mouth. ❑ *My dog Jacques is drooling on my* [V] *shoulder.*

**droop** /druːp/ **(droops, drooping, drooped)** VERB If something **droops**, it hangs or leans downwards with no strength or firmness. ❑ *Crook's eyelids* [V] *drooped and he yawned.* ♦ N-SING: usu N *of* n **Droop** is also a noun. ❑ *...the droop of his shoulders.*

**droopy** /druːpi/ **(droopier, droopiest)** ADJ If you describe something as **droopy**, you mean that it hangs down with no strength or firmness. ❑ *...a tall man with a droopy moustache.*

**drop** /drɒp/ **(drops, dropping, dropped)** ◆◆◇ 1 VERB If a level or amount **drops** or if someone or something **drops** it, it quickly becomes less. ❑ *Temperatures can drop to freezing at night...* [V prep/adv] *His blood pressure had dropped severely...* [V] *He had dropped the price of his London home by £1.25m.* [V n] ♦ N-COUNT: usu sing, oft N *in* n **Drop** is also a noun. ❑ *He was prepared to take a drop in wages.* 2 VERB If you **drop** something, you accidentally let it fall. ❑ *I dropped my glasses and broke them.* [V n] 3 VERB If something **drops onto** something else, it falls onto that thing. If something **drops from** somewhere, it falls from that place. ❑ *He felt hot* [V prep/adv] *tears dropping onto his fingers.* 4 VERB If you **drop** something somewhere or if it **drops** there, you deliberately let it fall there. ❑ *Drop the noodles into* [V n prep/adv] *the water. ...shaped pots that simply drop into their* [V prep/adv] *own container... Bombs drop round us and the floor* [V] *shudders.* ♦ N-UNCOUNT: usu N *of* n **drop|ping** *...the dropping of the first atomic bomb.* 5 VERB If a person or a part of their body **drops** to a lower position, or if they **drop** a part of their body to a lower position, they move to that position, often in a tired and lifeless way. ❑ *Nancy dropped into a nearby chair...* [V prep/adv] *She let her head drop...* [V] *He dropped his hands on to his knees.* [V n prep/adv] 6 VERB: no cont [emphasis] To **drop** is used in expressions such as **to be about to drop** and **to dance until you drop** to emphasize that you are exhausted and can no longer continue doing something. ❑ *She looked* [V] *about to drop.* 7 VERB If a man **drops** his trousers, he pulls them down, usually as a joke or to be rude. ❑ *A couple of boozy revellers dropped their trousers.* [V n] 8 VERB If your voice **drops** or if you **drop** your voice, you speak more quietly. ❑ *Her voice will drop to a* [V *to* n] *dismissive whisper... He dropped his voice and glanced* [V n] *round at the door.* 9 VERB If you **drop** someone or something somewhere, you take them somewhere and leave them there, usually in a car or other vehicle. ❑ *He dropped me outside the hotel.* [V n prep/adv] ♦ PHRASAL VERB **Drop off** means the same as **drop**. ❑ *Just drop me off at* [V n P prep/adv] *the airport... He was dropping off a late birthday present.* [V P n] 10 VERB If you **drop** an idea, course of action, or habit, you do not continue with it. ❑ *The prosecution* [V n] *was forced to drop the case.* ♦ N-UNCOUNT: N *of* n **drop|ping** *This was one of the factors that led to President Suharto's dropping of his previous objections.* 11 VERB: usu passive If someone **is dropped** by a sports team or organization, they are no longer included in that team or employed by that organization. ❑ *The country's captain* [*be* V-ed] *was dropped from the tour party to England.* 12 VERB If you **drop** a game or part of a game in a sports competition, you lose it. ❑ *Oremans has yet* [V n] *to drop a set.* 13 VERB If you **drop** to a lower position in a sports competition, you move to that position. ❑ *Britain has dropped from second to third place* [V prep/adv] *in the league.* 14 N-COUNT: oft N *of* n A **drop of** a liquid is a very small amount of it shaped like a little ball. In informal English, you can also use **drop** when you are referring to a very small amount of something such as a drink. ❑ *...a drop of blue ink... I'll have an-*

*other drop of that Italian milk.* 15 **Drops** are a kind of medicine which you put drop by drop into your ears, eyes, or nose. ❑ *...eye drops.* 16 Fruit or chocolate **drops** are small round sweets with a fruit or chocolate flavour. 17 You use **drop** to talk about vertical distances. For example, a thirty-foot **drop** is a distance of thirty feet between the top of a cliff or wall and the bottom of it. ❑ *There was a sheer drop just outside my window.* N-PLURAL: oft n N / N-COUNT: usu pl, n N / N-COUNT: usu with supp

PHRASES 18 If you **drop a hint**, you give a hint or say something in a casual way. ❑ *If I drop a few hints he might give me a cutting.* 19 If you want someone to **drop the subject**, **drop it**, or **let it drop**, you want them to stop talking about something, often because you are annoyed that they keep talking about it. ❑ *Mary Ann wished he would just drop it.* 20 → See also **air drop**. **to drop dead** → see **dead**. **at the drop of a hat** → see **hat**. **a drop in the ocean** → see **ocean**. PHRASE: V inflects / PHRASE: V inflects

♦ **drop by** If you **drop by**, you visit someone informally. ❑ *She and Danny will drop by later... He dropped by my office this morning.* PHRASAL VERB / V P / V P n

♦ **drop in** If you **drop in on** someone, you visit them informally, usually without having arranged it. ❑ *Why not drop in for a chat?... She spent most of the day dropping in on friends in Edinburgh.* PHRASAL VERB / V P / V P *on* n

♦ **drop off** 1 → see **drop 9**. 2 If you **drop off** to sleep, you go to sleep. [INFORMAL] ❑ *I must have dropped off to sleep... Just as I was dropping off, a strange thought crossed my mind.* 3 If the level of something **drops off**, it becomes less. ❑ *Sales to the British forces are expected to drop off.* PHRASAL VERB / V P *to sleep* / V P / PHRASAL VERB = fall / V P

♦ **drop out** 1 If someone **drops out of** college or a race, for example, they leave it without finishing what they started. ❑ *He'd dropped out of high school at the age of 16... She dropped out after 20 kilometres with stomach trouble.* 2 If someone **drops out**, they reject the accepted ways of society and live outside the usual system. ❑ *She encourages people to keep their jobs rather than dropping out to live in a commune.* → See also **drop-out**. PHRASAL VERB / V P *of* n / V P / PHRASAL VERB [disapproval] / V P

**drop-dead** If you describe someone as, for example, **drop-dead** gorgeous, you mean that they are so gorgeous that people cannot fail to notice them. [INFORMAL] ❑ *She said that Campbell-Black was drop-dead gorgeous.* ♦ **Drop-dead** is also an adjective. ❑ *...the drop-dead glamour of the designer decade.* ADV: ADV adj / ADJ: ADJ n

**drop goal** **(drop goals)** In rugby, a **drop goal** is a goal that a player scores by dropping the ball and kicking it between the posts. N-COUNT

**drop-in** **Drop-in** centres or services provide information and help for people with particular problems, usually on a free and informal basis. ❑ *...a drop-in centre for young mothers.* ADJ: ADJ n

**drop|let** /drɒplət/ **(droplets)** A **droplet** is a very small drop of liquid. ❑ *Droplets of sweat were welling up on his forehead.* N-COUNT: oft N *of* n, n N

**drop-out** **(drop-outs)** also **dropout**. 1 If you describe someone as a **drop-out**, you disapprove of the fact that they have rejected the accepted ways of society, for example by not having a regular job. 2 A **drop-out** is someone who has left school or college before they have finished their studies. ❑ *...high-school drop-outs.* 3 If you refer to the **drop-out** rate, you are referring to the number of people who leave a school or college early, or leave a course or other activity before they have finished it. ❑ *The drop-out rate among students is currently one in three.* N-COUNT [disapproval] / N-COUNT / ADJ: ADJ n

**drop|per** /drɒpəʳ/ **(droppers)** A **dropper** is a small glass tube with a hollow rubber part on one end which you use for drawing up and dropping small amounts of liquid. N-COUNT

**drop|pings** /drɒpɪŋz/ **Droppings** are the faeces of birds and small animals. ❑ *...pigeon droppings.* N-PLURAL

**dross** /drɒs, AM drɔːs/ If you describe something as **dross**, you mean that it is of very poor quality or has no value. [LITERARY] ❑ *I go through phases where everything I write is just dross.* N-UNCOUNT [disapproval] = rubbish

**drought** /draʊt/ **(droughts)** A **drought** is a long period of time during which no rain falls. ❑ *Drought and famines have killed up to two million people here.* N-VAR

**drove** /droʊv/ **Drove** is the past tense of **drive**.

**drov|er** /droʊvəʳ/ **(drovers)** A **drover** is someone whose job is to make sheep or cattle move from one place to another in groups. N-COUNT

**droves** /droʊvz/ If you say that people are going somewhere or doing something **in droves**, you are emphasizing that there is a very large number of them. ❑ *Scientists are leaving the country in droves.* N-PLURAL: usu *in* N, *in* poss N, N *of* n [emphasis]

**drown** /draʊn/ **(drowns, drowning, drowned)** 1 When someone **drowns** or **is drowned**, they die because they have gone or been pushed under water and cannot breathe. ❑ *A child can drown in only a few inches of water... Last night a boy was drowned in the river... He walked into the sea and drowned himself... Dolphins have sometimes been known to save drowning swimmers.* 2 If you say that a person or thing **is drowning in** something, you are emphasizing that they have a very large amount of it, or are completely covered in it. ❑ *...people who gradually find themselves drowning in debt... The potatoes were drowned in chilli.* 3 If something **drowns** a sound, it is so loud that you cannot hear that sound properly. ❑ *Clapping drowned the speaker's words for a moment.* ♦ **Drown out** means the same as **drown**. ❑ *Their cheers drowned out the protests of demonstrators.* 4 If you say that someone **is drowning** their **sorrows**, you mean that they are drinking alcohol in order to forget something sad or upsetting that has happened to them. VERB / V / *be* V-ed / V pron-refl / V-ing / VERB [emphasis] / V *in* n / *be* V-ed / VERB / V n / PHRASAL VERB / V P n (not pron) / PHRASE: V inflects

**drowse** /draʊz/ **(drowses, drowsing, drowsed)** If you **drowse**, you are almost asleep or just asleep. ❑ *Nina drowsed for a while.* VERB = doze / V

**drowsy** /draʊzi/ **(drowsier, drowsiest)** If you feel **drowsy**, you feel sleepy and cannot think clearly. ❑ *He felt pleasantly drowsy and had to fight off the urge to sleep.* ♦ **drowsi|ness** *Big meals during the day cause drowsiness.* ♦ **drowsi|ly** /draʊzɪli/ *'Mm,' she answered drowsily.* ADJ / N-UNCOUNT / ADV: ADV with v

**drub|bing** /drʌbɪŋ/ **(drubbings)** If someone gets **a drubbing**, they are defeated easily. [INFORMAL] N-COUNT: usu sing

**drudge** /drʌdʒ/ **(drudges)** If you describe someone as a **drudge**, you mean they have to work hard at a job which is not very important or interesting. N-COUNT

**drudg|ery** /drʌdʒəri/ You use **drudgery** to refer to jobs and tasks which are boring or unpleasant but which must be done. ❑ *People want to get away from the drudgery of their everyday lives.* N-UNCOUNT

**drug** /drʌg/ **(drugs, drugging, drugged)** 1 A **drug** is a chemical which is given to people in order to treat or prevent an illness or disease. ❑ *The drug will be useful to hundreds of thousands of infected people. ...the drug companies.* 2 **Drugs** are substances that some people take because of their pleasant effects, but which are usually illegal. ❑ *His mother was on drugs, on cocaine... She was sure Leo was taking drugs. ...the problem of drug abuse.* 3 If you **drug** a person or animal, you give them a chemical substance in order to make them sleepy or unconscious. ❑ *She was drugged and robbed.* 4 If food or drink **is drugged**, a chemical substance is added to it in order to make someone sleepy or unconscious when they eat or drink it. ❑ *I wonder now if that drink had been drugged... Anyone could have drugged that wine.* ♦♦♦ N-COUNT / N-COUNT / VERB / V n / VERB / *be* V-ed / V n

**drug ad|dict** **(drug addicts)** A **drug addict** is someone who is addicted to illegal drugs. N-COUNT

**drug|gie** /drʌgi/ **(druggies)** also **druggy**. If you refer to someone as a **druggie** you mean N-COUNT [disapproval] they are involved with or addicted to illegal drugs. [INFORMAL]

**drug|gist** /drʌgɪst/ **(druggists)** 1 A **druggist** is someone who is qualified to sell medicines and drugs ordered by a doctor. [AM] [N-COUNT = pharmacist]

✔ in BRIT, usually use **chemist**

2 A **druggist** or a **druggist's** is a store where medicines and drugs ordered by a doctor are sold. [AM] [N-COUNT: oft *the* N]

✔ in BRIT, usually use **chemist**

**drug|store** /drʌgstɔːʳ/ **(drugstores)** In the United States, a **drugstore** is a shop where drugs and medicines are sold or given out, and where you can buy cosmetics, some household goods, and also drinks and snacks. [N-COUNT: oft *the* N]

**Dru|id** /druːɪd/ **(Druids)** also **druid.** A **Druid** is a priest of the Celtic religion. [N-COUNT]

**drum** /drʌm/ **(drums, drumming, drummed)** ◆◇◇ 1 A **drum** is a musical instrument consisting of a skin stretched tightly over a round frame. You play a drum by beating it with sticks or with your hands. [N-COUNT: oft *the* N] 2 A **drum** is a large cylindrical container which is used to store fuel or other substances. ❑ *...an oil drum.* [N-COUNT: usu with supp] 3 If something **drums on** a surface, or if you **drum** something **on** a surface, it hits it regularly, making a continuous beating sound. ❑ *He drummed his fingers on the leather top of his desk... Rain drummed on the roof of the car.* [VERB; V n *on/against* n; V *on* n] 4 → See also **drumming.** 5 If someone **beats the drum** or **bangs the drum for** something, they support it strongly. [PHRASE: V inflects]

♦ **drum into** If you **drum** something **into** someone, you keep saying it to them until they understand it or remember it. ❑ *Standard examples were drummed into students' heads... They drummed it into her that she was not to tell anyone.* [PHRASAL VERB: usu passive; *be* V-ed P n; V *it* P n that]

♦ **drum out** If someone **is drummed out of** an organization such as the armed forces or a club, they are forced to leave it, usually because they have done something wrong. ❑ *Sailors caught in a drugs scandal are to be drummed out of the service.* [PHRASAL VERB: usu passive; *be* V-ed P P n]

♦ **drum up** If you **drum up** support or business, you try to get it. ❑ *It is to be hoped that he is merely drumming up business.* [PHRASAL VERB; V P n (not pron)]

**drum|beat** /drʌmbiːt/ **(drumbeats)** 1 A **drumbeat** is the sound of a beat on a drum. [N-COUNT] 2 People sometimes describe a series of warnings or continuous pressure on someone to do something as a **drumbeat.** [mainly AM, JOURNALISM] [N-COUNT: oft N *of* n]

**drum kit (drum kits)** A **drum kit** is a set of drums and cymbals. [N-COUNT]

**drum ma|jor (drum majors)** 1 A **drum major** is a sergeant in the army who is in charge of the drummers in a military band, or who leads the band when they are marching. [BRIT] [N-COUNT] 2 A **drum major** is a man who leads a marching band by walking in front of them. [AM] [N-COUNT]

**drum ma|jor|ette (drum majorettes)** A **drum majorette** is a girl or young woman who wears a uniform and carries a stick which at intervals she throws into the air and catches. Drum majorettes march, often in lines, in front of a band as part of a procession. [N-COUNT]

**drum|mer** /drʌməʳ/ **(drummers)** A **drummer** is a person who plays a drum or drums in a band or group. [N-COUNT]

**drum|ming** /drʌmɪŋ/ 1 **Drumming** is the action of playing the drums. [N-UNCOUNT] 2 **Drumming** is the sound or feeling of continuous beating. ❑ *He pointed up to the roof, through which the steady drumming of rain could be heard... His mouth was dry and he felt a drumming in his temples.* [N-UNCOUNT: also *a* N, oft N *of* n]

**drum roll (drum rolls)** also **drumroll.** A **drum roll** is a series of drumbeats that follow each other so quickly that they make a continuous sound. A drum roll is often used to show that someone important is arriving, or to introduce someone. ❑ *A long drum roll introduced the trapeze artists.* [N-COUNT]

**drum|stick** /drʌmstɪk/ **(drumsticks)** 1 A **drumstick** is the lower part of the leg of a bird such as a chicken which is cooked and eaten. [N-COUNT: usu pl] 2 **Drumsticks** are sticks used for beating a drum. [N-COUNT]

**drunk** /drʌŋk/ **(drunks)** 1 Someone who is **drunk** has drunk so much alcohol that they cannot speak clearly or behave sensibly. ❑ *I got drunk and had to be carried home.* [ADJ] 2 A **drunk** is someone who is drunk or frequently gets drunk. ❑ *A drunk lay in the alley.* [N-COUNT] 3 If you are **drunk with** a strong emotion or an experience, you are in a state of great excitement because of it. ❑ *They are currently drunk with success.* [ADJ: v-link ADJ, usu ADJ *with* n] 4 **Drunk** is the past participle of **drink.**

**drunk|ard** /drʌŋkəʳd/ **(drunkards)** A **drunkard** is someone who frequently gets drunk. [N-COUNT]

**drunk driv|er (drunk drivers)** A **drunk driver** is someone who drives after drinking more than the amount of alcohol that is legally allowed. [mainly AM] [N-COUNT]

✔ in BRIT, usually use **drink driver**

♦ **drunk driv|ing** ❑ *...efforts designed to help stop drunk driving.* [N-UNCOUNT]

**drunk|en** /drʌŋkən/ 1 **Drunken** is used to describe events and situations that involve people who are drunk. ❑ *The pain roused him from his drunken stupor.* [ADJ: ADJ n] 2 A **drunken** person is drunk or is frequently drunk. ❑ *Groups of drunken hooligans smashed shop windows and threw stones.* [ADJ: ADJ n] ♦ **drunk|en|ly** *One night Bob stormed drunkenly into her house.* [ADV: ADV with v] ♦ **drunk|en|ness** *He was arrested for drunkenness on his way to the football ground.* [N-UNCOUNT]

**dry** /draɪ/ **(drier** or **dryer, driest, dries, drying, dried)** ◆◆◇ 1 If something is **dry,** there is no water or moisture on it or in it. ❑ *Clean the metal with a soft dry cloth... Pat it dry with a soft towel... Once the paint is dry, apply a coat of the red ochre emulsion paint.* [ADJ ≠ wet, damp] ♦ **dry|ness** *...the parched dryness of the air.* [N-UNCOUNT] 2 When something **dries** or when you **dry** it, it becomes dry. ❑ *Leave your hair to dry naturally whenever possible... Wash and dry the lettuce.* [VERB; V; V n] 3 When you **dry** the dishes after a meal, you wipe the water off the plates, cups, knives, pans, and other things when they have been washed, using a cloth. ❑ *Mrs. Madrigal began drying dishes.* [VERB = wipe; V n] ♦ **Dry up** means the same as **dry.** [BRIT] ❑ *He got up and stood beside Julie, drying up the dishes while she washed.* [PHRASAL VERB; V P n (not pron)] 4 If you say that your skin or hair is **dry,** you mean that it is less oily than, or not as soft as, normal. ❑ *Nothing looks worse than dry, cracked lips.* [ADJ ≠ greasy] ♦ **dry|ness** *Dryness of the skin can also be caused by living in centrally heated homes and offices.* [N-UNCOUNT] 5 If the weather or a period of time is **dry,** there is no rain or there is much less rain than average. ❑ *Exceptionally dry weather over the past year had cut agricultural production.* [ADJ ≠ wet] 6 A **dry** place or climate is one that gets very little rainfall. ❑ *...a hot, dry climate where the sun is shining all the time.* [ADJ: usu ADJ n = arid ≠ wet] ♦ **dry|ness** *He was advised to spend time in the warmth and dryness of Italy.* [N-UNCOUNT] 7 In **the dry** means in a place or at a time that is not damp, wet, or rainy. [mainly BRIT] ❑ *Such cars, however, do grip the road well, even in the dry.* [N-SING: *the* N, usu *in* N ≠ wet] 8 If a river, lake, or well is **dry,** it is empty of water, usually because of hot weather and lack of rain. [ADJ] 9 If an oil well is **dry,** it is no longer producing any oil. [ADJ: usu v-link ADJ] 10 If your mouth or throat is **dry,** it has little or no saliva in it, and so feels very unpleasant, perhaps because you are tense or ill. ❑ *His mouth was dry, he needed a drink.* [ADJ: usu v-link ADJ] ♦ **dry|ness** *Symptoms included frequent dryness in the mouth.* [N-UNCOUNT: usu with supp] 11 If someone has **dry** eyes, there are no tears in their eyes; often used with negatives or in contexts where you are expressing surprise that they are not crying. ❑ *There were few dry eyes in the house when I finished.* [ADJ ≠ moist] 12 If a country, state, or city is **dry,** it has laws or rules which forbid anyone to drink, sell, or buy alcoholic drink. [INFORMAL] ❑ *Gujurat has been a totally dry* [ADJ = teetotal] *state for the past thirty years.* 13 If you say that someone is sucking something **dry** or milking it **dry**, you are criticizing them for taking all the good things from it until there is nothing left. ❑ *He's just milking the company dry.* 14 **Dry** humour is very amusing, but in a subtle and clever way. ❑ *Fulton has retained his dry humour.* ♦ **dri|ly** *'That is surprising.' — 'Hardly,' I said drily.* ♦ **dry|ness** *Her writing has a wry dryness.* 15 If you describe something such as a book, play, or activity as **dry**, you mean that it is dull and uninteresting. ❑ *...dry, academic phrases.* 16 **Dry** bread or toast is plain and not covered with butter or jam. ❑ *For breakfast, they had dry bread and tea.* 17 **Dry** sherry or wine does not have a sweet taste. ❑ *...a glass of chilled, dry white wine.* 18 **high and dry** → see **high**. **home and dry** → see **home**.

ADJ: v n ADJ [disapproval] · ADJ: usu ADJ n [approval] · ADV: ADV with v, ADV adj · N-UNCOUNT · ADJ [disapproval] · ADJ: ADJ n · ADJ ≠ sweet

♦ **dry off** If something **dries off** or if you **dry** it **off**, the moisture on its surface disappears or is removed. ❑ *They are then scrubbed with clean water and left to dry off for an hour or two in a warm room... When the bath water started to cool I got out, dried myself off, and dressed.*

PHRASAL VERB · V P · V n P · Also V P n (not pron)

♦ **dry out** 1 If something **dries out** or **is dried out**, it loses all the moisture that was in it and becomes hard. ❑ *If the soil is allowed to dry out the tree could die... The cold winds dry out your skin very quickly.* 2 If someone **dries out** or **is dried out**, they are cured of addiction to alcohol. [INFORMAL] ❑ *He checked into Cedars Sinai Hospital to dry out.*

PHRASAL VERB · V P · V P n · Also V n P · PHRASAL VERB · V P · Also be V-ed P

♦ **dry up** 1 If something **dries up** or if something **dries** it **up**, it loses all its moisture and becomes completely dry and shrivelled or hard. ❑ *As the day goes on, the pollen dries up and becomes hard... Warm breezes from the South dried up the streets.* ♦ **dried-up** *...a tuft or two of dried-up grass.* 2 If a river, lake, or well **dries up**, it becomes empty of water, usually because of hot weather and a lack of rain. ❑ *Reservoirs are drying up and farmers have begun to leave their land.* ♦ **dried-up** *...a dried-up river bed.* 3 If a supply of something **dries up**, it stops. ❑ *Investment could dry up and that could cause the economy to falter.* 4 If you **dry up** when you are speaking, you stop in the middle of what you were saying, because you cannot think what to say next. ❑ *If you ask her what she's good at she will dry up after two minutes.* 5 → see **dry 3**. 6 → See also **dried-up**, **drying up**.

PHRASAL VERB · V P · V P n · Also V n P · ADJ · PHRASAL VERB · V P · ADJ · PHRASAL VERB · V P · PHRASAL VERB · V P

**dry-clean** (**dry-cleans, dry-cleaning, dry-cleaned**) When things such as clothes **are dry-cleaned**, they are cleaned with a liquid chemical rather than with water. ❑ *Natural-filled duvets must be dry-cleaned by a professional.*

VERB: usu passive · be V-ed

**dry clean|er** (**dry cleaners**) A **dry cleaner** or a **dry cleaner's** is a shop where things can be dry-cleaned.

N-COUNT

**dry-cleaning** also **dry cleaning**. 1 **Dry-cleaning** is the action or work of dry-cleaning things such as clothes. ❑ *He owns a dry-cleaning business.* 2 **Dry-cleaning** is things that have been dry-cleaned, or that are going to be dry-cleaned.

N-UNCOUNT · N-UNCOUNT

**dry dock** (**dry docks**) A **dry dock** is a dock from which water can be removed so that ships or boats can be built or repaired.

N-COUNT

**dry|er** /draɪəʳ/ (**dryers**) also **drier**. A **dryer** is a machine for drying things. There are different kinds of dryer, for examples ones designed for drying clothes, crops, or people's hair or hands. ❑ *...hot air electric hand dryers.* → See also **dry**, **tumble dryer**.

N-COUNT: oft n N

**dry-eyed** If you say that someone is **dry-eyed**, you mean that although they are in a very sad situation they are not actually crying. ❑ *At the funeral she was dry-eyed and composed.*

ADJ ≠ tearful

**dry goods** **Dry goods** are cloth, thread, and other things that are sold at a draper's shop. [AM]

N-PLURAL

✓ in BRIT, use **drapery, haberdashery**

**dry|ing up** When you do **the drying up**, you dry things such as plates, pans, knives, and cups after they have been washed. [BRIT]

N-UNCOUNT: also the N

✓ in AM, use **drying**

**dry land** If you talk about **dry land**, you are referring to land, in contrast to the sea or the air. ❑ *We were glad to be on dry land again.*

N-UNCOUNT: oft on N

**dry rot** **Dry rot** is a serious disease of wood. It is caused by a fungus and causes wood to decay. ❑ *The house was riddled with dry rot.*

N-UNCOUNT

**dry run** (**dry runs**) If you have a **dry run**, you practise something to make sure that you are ready to do it properly. ❑ *The competition is planned as a dry run for the World Cup finals.*

N-COUNT: oft N for n

**dry ski slope** (**dry ski slopes**) or **dry slope** A **dry ski slope** is a slope made of an artificial substance on which you can practise skiing.

N-COUNT

**dry-stone wall** (**dry-stone walls**)

✓ in AM, use **dry wall**

A **dry-stone wall** is a wall that has been built by fitting stones together without using any cement.

N-COUNT

**DTP** /diː tiː piː/ **DTP** is an abbreviation for **desktop publishing**.

**DT's** /diː tiːz/ When alcoholics have **the DT's**, the alcohol causes their bodies to shake and makes them unable to think clearly.

N-PLURAL: the N

**dual** /djuːəl, AM duː-/ **Dual** means having two parts, functions, or aspects. ❑ *...his dual role as head of the party and head of state... Rob may be entitled to dual nationality.*

ADJ: ADJ n

**dual carriage|way** (**dual carriageways**) also **dual-carriageway**. A **dual carriageway** is a road which has two lanes of traffic travelling in each direction with a strip of grass or concrete down the middle to separate the two lots of traffic. [BRIT]

N-VAR

✓ in AM, use **divided highway**

**dual|ism** /djuːəlɪzəm, AM duː-/ **Dualism** is the state of having two main parts or aspects, or the belief that something has two main parts or aspects. [FORMAL] ❑ *...the Gnostic dualism of good and evil struggling for supremacy.*

N-UNCOUNT

**dual|ity** /djuːælɪti, AM duː-/ (**dualities**) A **duality** is a situation in which two opposite ideas or feelings exist at the same time. [FORMAL]

N-VAR

**dub** /dʌb/ (**dubs, dubbing, dubbed**) 1 If someone or something **is dubbed** a particular thing, they are given that description or name. [JOURNALISM] ❑ *...the man whom the Labour opposition dubbed as the 'no change Prime Minister'... At the height of her career, Orson Welles dubbed her 'the most exciting woman in the world'.* 2 If a film or soundtrack in a foreign language **is dubbed**, a new soundtrack is added with actors giving a translation. ❑ *It was dubbed into Spanish for Mexican audiences.*

VERB · V n as n · V n n · VERB: usu passive · be V-ed into n

**du|bi|ous** /djuːbiəs, AM duː-/ 1 If you describe something as **dubious**, you mean that you do not consider it to be completely honest, safe, or reliable. ❑ *This claim seems to us to be rather dubious.* ♦ **du|bi|ous|ly** *Carter was dubiously convicted of shooting three white men in a bar.* 2 If you are **dubious about** something, you are not completely sure about it and have not yet made up your mind about it. ❑ *My parents were dubious about it at first but we soon convinced them.* ♦ **du|bi|ous|ly** *He eyed Coyne dubiously.* 3 If you say that someone has the **dubious** honour or the **dubious** pleasure **of** doing something, you are indicating that what they are doing is not an honour or pleasure at all, but is, in fact, unpleasant or bad. ❑ *Nagy has the dubious honour of being the first athlete to be banned in this way.*

ADJ = questionable · ADV: ADV after v, ADV adj/-ed · ADJ: v-link ADJ, oft ADJ about n = doubtful · ADV · ADJ: ADJ n

**du|cal** /djuːkᵊl, AM duː-/ **Ducal** places or things belong to or are connected with a duke. [FORMAL]

ADJ: ADJ n

**duch|ess** /dʌtʃɪs/ (**duchesses**) A **duchess** is a woman who has the same rank as a duke, or who is a duke's wife or widow. ❑ *...the Duchess of Kent.*

N-COUNT: oft the N of n

**duchy** /dʌtʃi/ **(duchies)** A **duchy** is an area of land that is owned or ruled by a duke. ❑ *...the Duchy of Cornwall.* N-COUNT: oft *the* N *of* n

**duck** /dʌk/ **(ducks, ducking, ducked)** [1] A **duck** is a very common water bird with short legs, a short neck, and a large flat beak. N-VAR ♦ **Duck** is the flesh of this bird when it is eaten as food. N-UNCOUNT ❑ *...honey roasted duck.* [2] If you **duck**, you move your head or the top half of your body quickly downwards to avoid something that might hit you, or to avoid being seen. VERB ❑ *He ducked in time to save his head from a blow from the poker... He ducked his head to hide his admiration... I wanted to duck down and slip past but they saw me.* V / V n / V adv/prep [3] If you **duck** something such as a blow, you avoid it by moving your head or body quickly downwards. VERB = dodge ❑ *Hans deftly ducked their blows.* V n [4] You say that someone **ducks** a duty or responsibility when you disapprove of the fact that they avoid it. [INFORMAL] VERB disapproval ❑ *The Opposition reckons the Health Secretary has ducked all the difficult decisions.* V n [5] → See also **dead duck, lame duck, sitting duck**.

**PHRASES** [6] You say that criticism is **like water off a duck's back** or **water off a duck's back** to emphasize that it is not having any effect on the person being criticized. PHRASE: v-link PHR emphasis [7] If you **take to** something **like a duck to water**, you discover that you are naturally good at it or that you find it very easy to do. PHRASE: V inflects ❑ *She took to mothering like a duck to water.*

♦ **duck out** If you **duck out of** something that you are supposed to do, you avoid doing it. [INFORMAL] PHRASAL VERB = back out ❑ *George ducked out of his forced marriage to a cousin... You can't duck out once you've taken on a responsibility.* V P *of* n / V P

**duck|ling** /dʌklɪŋ/ **(ducklings)** A **duckling** is a young duck. N-COUNT → See also **ugly duckling**.

**duct** /dʌkt/ **(ducts)** [1] A **duct** is a pipe, tube, or channel which carries a liquid or gas. N-COUNT: usu with supp ❑ *...a big air duct in the ceiling.* [2] A **duct** is a tube in your body which carries a liquid such as tears or bile. N-COUNT: with supp ❑ *...tear ducts.*

**dud** /dʌd/ **(duds) Dud** means not working properly or not successful. [INFORMAL] ADJ: ADJ n ❑ *He replaced a dud valve.* ♦ **Dud** is also a noun. N-COUNT ❑ *The mine was a dud.*

**dude** /djuːd, AM duːd/ **(dudes)** A **dude** is a man. [AM, INFORMAL] N-COUNT ❑ *My doctor is a real cool dude.*

**dude ranch (dude ranches)** A **dude ranch** is an American ranch where people can have holidays during which they can do activities such as riding or camping. N-COUNT

**dudg|eon** /dʌdʒᵊn/ If you say that someone is **in high dudgeon**, you are emphasizing that they are very angry or unhappy about something. PHRASE: v-link PHR emphasis ❑ *Washington businesses are in high dudgeon over the plan.*

**due** /djuː, AM duː/ **(dues)** ♦♦◇ [1] If an event is **due to** something, it happens or exists as a direct result of that thing. PREP-PHRASE: v-link PREP n ❑ *The country's economic problems are largely due to the weakness of the recovery.* [2] You can say **due to** to introduce the reason for something happening. Some speakers of English believe that it is not correct to use **due to** in this way. PREP-PHRASE ❑ *Due to the large volume of letters he receives Dave regrets he is unable to answer queries personally.* [3] If something is **due** at a particular time, it is expected to happen, be done, or arrive at that time. ADJ: usu v-link ADJ, oft ADJ to-inf, ADJ prep/adv ❑ *The results are due at the end of the month... Mr Carter is due in London on Monday. ...customers who paid later than twenty days after the due date.* [4] **Due** attention or consideration is the proper, reasonable, or deserved amount of it under the circumstances. ADJ: ADJ n = proper ❑ *After due consideration it was decided to send him away to live with foster parents.* [5] Something that is **due**, or that is **due to** someone, is owed to them, either as a debt or because they have a right to it. ADJ: v-link ADJ, oft ADJ *to* n ❑ *I was sent a cheque for £1,525 and advised that no further pension was due... I've got some leave due to me and I was going to Tasmania for a fortnight.* ♦ **Due** is also a preposition. PREP: oft n PREP n ❑ *He had not taken a summer holiday that year but had accumulated the leave due him.* [6] If someone is **due for** something, that thing is planned to happen or be given to them now, or very soon, often after they have been waiting for it for a long time. ADJ: v-link ADJ *for* n ❑ *He is not due for release until 2020.* ♦ **Due** is also a preposition. PREP ❑ *I reckon I'm due one of my travels.* [7] **Dues** are sums of money that you give regularly to an organization that you belong to, for example a social club or trade union, in order to pay for being a member. N-PLURAL: oft poss N ❑ *Only 18 of the UN's 180 members had paid their dues by the January deadline.* [8] **Due** is used before the words 'north', 'south', 'east', or 'west' to indicate that something is in exactly the direction mentioned. ADV: ADV adv/adj ❑ *They headed due north.*

**PHRASES** [9] If you say that something will happen or take place **in due course**, you mean that you cannot make it happen any quicker and it will happen when the time is right for it. PHRASE: PHR with cl ❑ *In due course the baby was born.* [10] You can say **'to give** him his **due'**, or **'giving** him his **due'** when you are admitting that there are some good things about someone, even though there are things that you do not like about them. PHRASE ❑ *To give Linda her due, she had tried to encourage John in his school work.* [11] You can say **'with due respect'** when you are about to disagree politely with someone. PHRASE: PHR cl politeness ❑ *With all due respect, you're wrong.*

**duel** /djuːəl, AM duː-/ **(duels, duelling, duelled)**

☑ in AM, use **dueling, dueled**

[1] A **duel** is a formal fight between two people in which they use guns or swords in order to settle a quarrel. N-COUNT ❑ *He had killed a man in a duel.* [2] To **duel** means to fight a duel or be involved in a conflict. V-RECIP ❑ *We duelled for two years and Peterson made the most of it, playing us off against each other.* pl-n V *...two silver French duelling pistols.* V-ing

**duet** /djuːet, AM duː-/ **(duets)** A **duet** is a piece of music sung or played by two people. N-COUNT

**duff** /dʌf/ **(duffs, duffing, duffed)** If you describe something as **duff**, you mean it is useless, broken, or of poor quality. [BRIT, INFORMAL] ADJ disapproval ❑ *Sometimes you have to take a duff job when you need the money.*

**duf|fel** /dʌfᵊl/ **(duffels)** [1] A **duffel** is the same as a **duffel coat**. N-COUNT [2] A **duffel** is the same as a **duffel bag**. N-COUNT

**duf|fel bag** /dʌfᵊl bæg/ **(duffel bags)** also **duffle bag.** A **duffel bag** is a bag shaped like a cylinder and made of strong fabric such as canvas. A duffel bag has a string at one end that is used to close the bag and to carry it with. N-COUNT

**duf|fel coat** /dʌfᵊl koʊt/ **(duffel coats)** also **duffle coat.** A **duffel coat** is a heavy coat with a hood and long buttons that fasten with loops. N-COUNT

**duf|fer** /dʌfəʳ/ **(duffers)** If you describe someone as a **duffer**, you mean that they are very bad at doing something. [BRIT, INFORMAL, OLD-FASHIONED] N-COUNT disapproval

**duf|fle** /dʌfᵊl/ → see **duffel bag, duffel coat**.

**dug** /dʌg/ **Dug** is the past tense and past participle of **dig**.

**dug|out** /dʌgaʊt/ **(dugouts)** [1] A **dugout** is a small boat that is made by removing the inside of a log. N-COUNT [2] A **dugout** is a shelter made by digging a hole in the ground and then covering it or tunnelling so that the shelter has a roof over it. N-COUNT

**duke** /djuːk, AM duːk/ **(dukes)** A **duke** is a man with a very high social rank. N-COUNT: oft *the* N *of* n ❑ *...the Queen and the Duke of Edinburgh.*

**duke|dom** /djuːkdəm, AM duːk-/ **(dukedoms)** [1] A **dukedom** is the rank or title of a duke. N-COUNT ❑ *...the present heir to the dukedom.* [2] A **dukedom** is the land owned by a duke. N-COUNT

**dul|cet** /dʌlsɪt/ People often use the expression **dulcet tones** to refer to someone's voice. PHRASE: with poss

[HUMOROUS] ❑ *You hear his dulcet tones on the Radio 1 trailers in the morning.*

**dull** /dʌl/ **(duller, dullest, dulls, dulling, dulled)** 1 If you describe someone or something as **dull**, you mean they are not interesting or exciting. ❑ *I felt she found me boring and dull.* ♦ **dull|ness** *They enjoy anything that breaks the dullness of their routine life.* 2 Someone or something that is **dull** is not very lively or energetic. ❑ *The body's natural rhythms mean we all feel dull and sleepy between 1 and 3pm.* ♦ **dul|ly** *His eyes looked dully ahead.* ♦ **dull|ness** *Did you notice any unusual depression or dullness of mind?* 3 A **dull** colour or light is not bright. ❑ *The stamp was a dull blue colour.* ♦ **dul|ly** *The street lamps gleamed dully through the night's mist.* 4 You say the weather is **dull** when it is very cloudy. ❑ *It's always dull and raining.* 5 **Dull** sounds are not very clear or loud. ❑ *The coffin closed with a dull thud.* ♦ **dul|ly** *He heard his heart thump dully but more quickly.* 6 **Dull** feelings are weak and not intense. ❑ *The pain, usually a dull ache, gets worse with exercise.* ♦ **dul|ly** *His arm throbbed dully.* 7 If a knife or blade is **dull**, it is not sharp. [OLD-FASHIONED] 8 If something **dulls** or if it **is dulled**, it becomes less intense, bright, or lively. ❑ *Her eyes dulled and she gazed blankly... Share prices and trading have been dulled by worries over the war.*
ADJ; disapproval; ≠ interesting; N-UNCOUNT; ADJ; = sluggish; ADV: ADV after v; N-UNCOUNT; ADJ: usu ADJ n; ADV: ADV with v; ADJ; ≠ sunny; ADJ: usu ADJ n; ADV: ADV after v; ADJ: ADJ n; ≠ sharp; ADV; ADJ; = blunt; VERB; V; V n

**dull|ard** /dʌləʳd/ **(dullards)** If you say that someone is a **dullard**, you mean that they are rather boring, unintelligent, and unimaginative. [OLD-FASHIONED]
N-COUNT

**duly** /djuːli, AM duː-/ 1 If you say that something **duly** happened or was done, you mean that it was expected to happen or was requested, and it did happen or it was done. ❑ *Westcott appealed to Waite for an apology, which he duly received.* 2 If something is **duly** done, it is done in the correct way. [FORMAL] ❑ *...the duly elected president of the country.*
ADV: ADV before v; ADV: ADV before v

**dumb** /dʌm/ **(dumber, dumbest, dumbs, dumbing, dumbed)** 1 Someone who is **dumb** is completely unable to speak. ❑ *...a young deaf and dumb man.* 2 If someone is **dumb** on a particular occasion, they cannot speak because they are angry, shocked, or surprised. [LITERARY] ❑ *We were all struck dumb for a minute.* ♦ **dumb|ly** *I shook my head dumbly, not believing him.* 3 If you call a person **dumb**, you mean that they are stupid or foolish. [INFORMAL] ❑ *The questions were set up to make her look dumb.* 4 If you say that something is **dumb**, you think that it is silly and annoying. [AM, INFORMAL] ❑ *I came up with this dumb idea.*
ADJ; = mute; ADJ: v-link ADJ; = speechless; ADV: ADV with v; ADJ; disapproval; ADJ; disapproval; = stupid

♦ **dumb down** If you **dumb down** something, you make it easier for people to understand, especially when this spoils it. ❑ *No one favored dumbing down the magazine.* ♦ **dumb|ing down** *He accused broadcasters of contributing to the dumbing down of America.*
PHRASAL VERB; V P n; Also V n P, V; N-UNCOUNT

**dumb-bell** /dʌmbel/ **(dumb-bells)** also **dumbbell.** A **dumb-bell** is a short bar with weights on either side which people use for physical exercise to strengthen their arm and shoulder muscles.
N-COUNT

**dumb|found** /dʌmfaʊnd/ **(dumbfounds, dumbfounding, dumbfounded)** If someone or something **dumbfounds** you, they surprise you very much. ❑ *This suggestion dumbfounded Joe.*
VERB; = astonish; V n

**dumb|found|ed** /dʌmfaʊndɪd/ If you are **dumbfounded**, you are extremely surprised by something. ❑ *I stood there dumbfounded.*
ADJ: usu v-link ADJ; = astonished

**dumb|struck** /dʌmstrʌk/ If you are **dumbstruck**, you are so shocked or surprised that you cannot speak.
ADJ: usu v-link ADJ; emphasis; = speechless

**dumb wait|er** **(dumb waiters)** also **dumbwaiter.** A **dumb waiter** is a lift used to carry food and dishes from one floor of a building to another.
N-COUNT

**dum-dum** /dʌm dʌm/ **(dum-dums)** A **dum-dum** or a **dum-dum bullet** is a bullet that is very soft or hollow at the front. Dum-dum bullets cause large and serious wounds because they break into small pieces and spread out when they hit someone.
N-COUNT

**dum|my** /dʌmi/ **(dummies)** 1 A **dummy** is a model of a person, often used to display clothes. ❑ *...the bottom half of a shop-window dummy.* 2 You can use **dummy** to refer to things that are not real, but have been made to look or behave as if they are real. ❑ *Dummy patrol cars will be set up beside motorways to frighten speeding motorists.* 3 A baby's **dummy** is a rubber or plastic object that you give the baby to suck so that he or she feels comforted. [BRIT]
N-COUNT; = mannequin; N-COUNT: oft N n; = fake; N-COUNT

✔ in AM, usually use **pacifier**

**dum|my run** **(dummy runs)** A **dummy run** is a trial or test procedure which is carried out in order to see if a plan or process works properly. [BRIT] ❑ *Before we started we did a dummy run.*
N-COUNT; = test run

**dump** /dʌmp/ **(dumps, dumping, dumped)** ◆◇◇ 1 If you **dump** something somewhere, you put it or unload it there quickly and carelessly. [INFORMAL] ❑ *We dumped our bags at the nearby Grand Hotel and hurried towards the market.* 2 If something **is dumped** somewhere, it is put or left there because it is no longer wanted or needed. [INFORMAL] ❑ *The getaway car was dumped near a motorway tunnel... The government declared that it did not dump radioactive waste at sea.* ♦ **dump|ing** *German law forbids the dumping of hazardous waste on German soil.* 3 A **dump** is a place where rubbish is left, for example on open ground outside a town. ❑ *...companies that bring their rubbish straight to the dump.* 4 If you say that a place is a **dump**, you think it is ugly and unpleasant to live in or visit. [INFORMAL] 5 To **dump** something such as an idea, policy, or practice means to stop supporting or using it. [INFORMAL] ❑ *Ministers believed it was vital to dump the poll tax before the election.* 6 If a firm or company **dumps** goods, it sells large quantities of them at prices far below their real value, usually in another country, in order to gain a bigger market share or to keep prices high in the home market. [BUSINESS] ❑ *It produces more than it needs, then dumps its surplus onto the world market.* 7 If you **dump** someone, you end your relationship with them. [INFORMAL] ❑ *I thought he was going to dump me for another girl.* 8 To **dump** computer data or memory means to copy it from one storage system onto another, such as from disk to magnetic tape. [COMPUTING] ❑ *All the data is then dumped into the main computer.* 9 A **dump** is a list of the data that is stored in a computer's memory at a particular time. **Dumps** are often used by computer programmers to find out what is causing a problem with a program. [COMPUTING] ❑ *...a screen dump.*
VERB; V n prep/adv; VERB; be V-ed; V n; N-UNCOUNT; N-COUNT; = tip; N-COUNT; disapproval; VERB; = ditch; V n; VERB; V n; VERB; = ditch; V n; VERB; V n *into* n; N-COUNT

**dump|er truck** **(dumper trucks)** A **dumper truck** is the same as a **dump truck**. [BRIT]
N-COUNT

**dump|ing ground** **(dumping grounds)** If you say that a place is a **dumping ground for** something, usually something unwanted, you mean that people leave or send large quantities of that thing there. ❑ *Eastern Europe is rapidly becoming a dumping-ground for radioactive residues.*
N-COUNT: usu N *for* n, supp N; disapproval

**dump|ling** /dʌmplɪŋ/ **(dumplings)** **Dumplings** are small lumps of dough that are cooked and eaten, either with meat and vegetables or as part of a sweet pudding.
N-VAR

**Dump|ster** /dʌmpstəʳ/ **(Dumpsters)** A **Dumpster** is a large metal container for holding rubbish. [AM, TRADEMARK]
N-COUNT

✔ in BRIT, usually use **skip**

**dump truck** **(dump trucks)** A **dump truck** is a truck whose carrying part can be tipped backwards so that the load falls out.
N-COUNT

**dumpy** /dʌmpi/ If you describe someone as **dumpy**, you mean that they are short and fat, and are usually implying they are unattractive.
ADJ; disapproval

**dun** /dʌn/ Something that is **dun** is a dull grey-brown colour. ❑ *...her dun mare.* COLOUR

**dunce** /dʌns/ **(dunces)** If you say that someone is a **dunce**, you think they are rather stupid because they find it difficult or impossible to learn what someone is trying to teach them. ❑ *Michael may have been a dunce at mathematics, but he was gifted at languages.* N-COUNT [disapproval]

**dune** /djuːn, AM duːn/ **(dunes)** A **dune** is a hill of sand near the sea or in a desert. N-COUNT

**dung** /dʌŋ/ **Dung** is faeces from animals, especially from large animals such as cattle and horses. N-UNCOUNT

**dun|ga|rees** /dʌŋgəriːz/ **Dungarees** are a one-piece garment consisting of trousers, a piece of cloth which covers your chest, and straps which go over your shoulders. In American English, **dungarees** can also refer to jeans. N-PLURAL: also *a pair of* N

**dun|geon** /dʌndʒᵊn/ **(dungeons)** A **dungeon** is a dark underground prison in a castle. N-COUNT

**dunk** /dʌŋk/ **(dunks, dunking, dunked)** If you **dunk** something **in** a liquid, you put it in the liquid, especially for a particular purpose and for a short time. ❑ *Dunk new plants in a bucket of water for an hour or so before planting.* VERB V n *in* n

**dun|no** /dənoʊ/ **Dunno** is sometimes used in written English to represent an informal way of saying 'don't know'. ❑ *'How on earth did she get it?' — 'I dunno.'*

**duo** /djuːoʊ, AM duː-/ **(duos)** [1] A **duo** is two musicians, singers, or other performers who perform together as a pair. ❑ *...a famous dancing and singing duo.* N-COUNT [2] You can refer to two people together as a **duo**, especially when they have something in common. [mainly JOURNALISM] ❑ *...Britain's former golden Olympic duo of Linford Christie and Sally Gunnell.* N-COUNT

**duo|de|nal** /djuːoʊdiːnᵊl, AM duː-/ **Duodenal** means relating to or contained in the duodenum. [MEDICAL] ❑ *...duodenal ulcers.* ADJ: ADJ n

**duo|denum** /djuːoʊdiːnəm, AM duː-/ **(duodenums)** Your **duodenum** is the part of your small intestine that is just below your stomach. [MEDICAL] N-COUNT

**duo|po|ly** /djuːɒpəli/ **(duopolies)** [1] If two companies or people have a **duopoly on** something such as an industry, they share complete control over it and it is impossible for others to become involved in it. [BUSINESS] ❑ *They are no longer part of a duopoly on overseas routes.* N-VAR [2] A **duopoly** is a group of two companies which are the only ones which provide a particular product or service, and which therefore have complete control over an industry. [BUSINESS] ❑ *Their smaller rival is battling to end their duopoly.* N-COUNT

**dupe** /djuːp, AM duːp/ **(dupes, duping, duped)** [1] If a person **dupes** you, they trick you into doing something or into believing something which is not true. ❑ *...a plot to dupe stamp collectors into buying fake rarities... We know some sex offenders dupe the psychologists who assess them.* VERB V n *into* -ing V n [2] A **dupe** is someone who is tricked by someone else. ❑ *He becomes an innocent dupe in a political scandal.* N-COUNT

**du|plex** /djuːpleks, AM duː-/ **(duplexes)** [1] A **duplex** is a house which has been divided into two separate units for two different families or groups of people. [AM] N-COUNT [2] A **duplex** or a **duplex apartment** is a flat or apartment which has rooms on two floors. [AM] N-COUNT

**du|pli|cate** **(duplicates, duplicating, duplicated)**

> ✔ The verb is pronounced /djuːplɪkeɪt, AM duː-/. The noun and adjective are pronounced /djuːplɪkət, AM duː-/.

[1] If you **duplicate** something that has already been done, you repeat or copy it. ❑ *His task will be to duplicate his success overseas here at home.* ♦ **Duplicate** is also a noun. ❑ *Charles scored again, with an exact duplicate of his first goal.* VERB = replicate V n N-COUNT [2] To **duplicate** something which has been written, drawn, or recorded onto tape means to make exact copies of it. ❑ *...a business which duplicates video and cinema tapes for the movie makers.* ♦ **Duplicate** is also a noun. ❑ *I'm on my way to Switzerland, but I've lost my card. I've got to get a duplicate.* VERB = copy V n N-COUNT: also *in* N [3] **Duplicate** is used to describe things that have been made as an exact copy of other things, usually in order to serve the same purpose. ❑ *He let himself in with a duplicate key.* ADJ: ADJ n [4] → See also **duplication**.

**du|pli|ca|tion** /djuːplɪkeɪʃᵊn, AM duː-/ If you say that there has been **duplication** of something, you mean that someone has done a task unnecessarily because it has already been done before. ❑ *...unnecessary duplication of resources.* N-UNCOUNT

**du|plic|it|ous** /djuːplɪsɪtəs, AM duː-/ Someone who is **duplicitous** is deceitful. ❑ *He is a possessive, duplicitous and unreasonable man.* ADJ

**du|plic|ity** /djuːplɪsɪti, AM duː-/ If you accuse someone of **duplicity**, you mean that they are deceitful. [FORMAL] ❑ *Malcolm believed he was guilty of duplicity in his private dealings.* N-UNCOUNT = deceit

**du|rable** /djʊərəbᵊl, AM dʊr-/ Something that is **durable** is strong and lasts a long time without breaking or becoming weaker. ❑ *Bone china is strong and durable.* ♦ **du|rabil|ity** /djʊərəbɪlɪti, AM dʊr-/ *Airlines recommend hard-sided cases for durability.* ADJ N-UNCOUNT

**du|rable goods** or **durables** **Durable goods** or **durables** are goods such as televisions or cars which are expected to last a long time, and are bought infrequently. [mainly AM] N-PLURAL

> ✔ in BRIT, usually use **consumer durables**

**du|ra|tion** /djʊreɪʃᵊn, AM dʊr-/ [1] The **duration of** an event or state is the time during which it happens or exists. ❑ *He was given the task of protecting her for the duration of the trial... Courses are of two years' duration.* N-UNCOUNT: oft *the* N *of* n [2] If you say that something will happen **for the duration**, you mean that it will happen for as long as a particular situation continues. ❑ *His wounds knocked him out of combat for the duration.* PHRASE: PHR after v

**du|ress** /djʊəres, AM dʊr-/ To do something under **duress** means to do it because someone forces you to do it or threatens you. [FORMAL] ❑ *He thought her confession had been made under duress.* N-UNCOUNT: usu *under* N

**Du|rex** /djʊəreks, AM dʊreks/ **(Durex)** A **Durex** is a condom. [TRADEMARK] N-COUNT

**dur|ing** /djʊərɪŋ, AM dʊrɪŋ/ ♦♦♦ [1] If something happens **during** a period of time or an event, it happens continuously, or happens several times between the beginning and end of that period or event. ❑ *Sandstorms are common during the Saudi Arabian winter.* PREP [2] If something develops **during** a period of time, it develops gradually from the beginning to the end of that period. ❑ *Wages have fallen by more than twenty percent during the past two months.* PREP [3] An event that happens **during** a period of time happens at some point or moment in that period. ❑ *During his visit, the Pope will also bless the new hospital.* PREP

**dusk** /dʌsk/ **Dusk** is the time just before night when the daylight has almost gone but when it is not completely dark. ❑ *We arrived home at dusk.* N-UNCOUNT ≠ dawn

**dusky** /dʌski/ [1] **Dusky** means rather dark. [LITERARY] ❑ *He was walking down the road one dusky Friday evening.* ADJ [2] A **dusky** colour is soft rather than bright. [LITERARY] ❑ *...dusky pink carpet.* COMB in COLOUR

**dust** /dʌst/ **(dusts, dusting, dusted)** ♦◇◇ [1] **Dust** is very small dry particles of earth or sand. ❑ *Tanks raise huge trails of dust when they move.* N-UNCOUNT [2] **Dust** is the very small pieces of dirt which you find inside buildings, for example on furniture, floors, or lights. ❑ *I could see a thick layer of dust on the stairs.* N-UNCOUNT [3] **Dust** is a fine powder which consists of very small particles of a substance such as gold, wood, or coal. ❑ *The air is so black with diesel fumes and coal dust, I can barely see.* N-UNCOUNT: oft n N [4] When you **dust** something such as furniture, you remove dust from it, usually using a cloth. ❑ *I vacuumed and dusted the living room... She dusted, she cleaned, and* VERB V n V *she did the washing-up.* ♦ **dust|ing** *I'm very fortunate in that I don't have to do the washing-up or the dusting.* N-UNCOUNT 5 If you **dust** something **with** a fine substance such as powder or if you **dust** a fine substance **onto** something, you cover it lightly with that substance. ❑ *Lightly dust the fish with flour... Dry your feet well and then dust between the toes with baby powder.* VERB V n prep/adv V adv/prep

**PHRASES** 6 If you say that something **has bitten the dust**, you are emphasizing that it no longer exists or that it has failed. [HUMOROUS, INFORMAL] ❑ *In the last 30 years many cherished values have bitten the dust.* PHRASE: V inflects emphasis 7 If you say that something will happen when **the dust settles**, you mean that a situation will be clearer after it has calmed down. If you let **the dust settle** before doing something, you let a situation calm down before you try to do anything else. [INFORMAL] ❑ *Once the dust had settled Beck defended his decision.* PHRASE: V inflects 8 If you say that something **is gathering dust**, you mean that it has been left somewhere and nobody is using it or doing anything with it. ❑ *Many of the machines are gathering dust in basements.* PHRASE: V inflects

♦ **dust off**

✓ in BRIT, also use **dust down**

1 If you say that someone **dusts** something **off** or **dusts** it **down**, you mean they are using an old idea or method, rather than trying something new. ❑ *Critics were busy dusting down the same superlatives they had applied to their first three films.* PHRASAL VERB V P n (not pron) 2 If you say that someone has **dusted himself** or **herself off** or **dusted himself** or **herself down**, you mean that they have managed to recover from a severe problem which has affected their life. ❑ *She dusted herself down and left to build her own career.* PHRASAL VERB V pron-refl P

**dust|bin** /dʌstbɪn/ **(dustbins)** A **dustbin** is a large container with a lid which people put their rubbish in and which is usually kept outside their house. [BRIT] ➔ See picture on page 1705. N-COUNT

✓ in AM, usually use **garbage can**

**dust|cart** /dʌstkɑːʳt/ **(dustcarts)** A **dustcart** is a truck which collects the rubbish from the dustbins outside people's houses. [BRIT] N-COUNT

✓ in AM, usually use **garbage truck**

**dust|er** /dʌstəʳ/ **(dusters)** A **duster** is a cloth which you use for removing dust from furniture, ornaments, or other objects. ➔ See also **feather duster**. N-COUNT

**dust jack|et** **(dust jackets)** also **dust-jacket.** A **dust jacket** is a loose paper cover which is put on a book to protect it. It often contains information about the book and its author. N-COUNT

**dust|man** /dʌstmən/ **(dustmen)** A **dustman** is a person whose job is to empty the rubbish from people's dustbins and take it away to be disposed of. [BRIT] N-COUNT

✓ in AM, use **garbage man**

**dust|pan** /dʌstpæn/ **(dustpans)** A **dustpan** is a small flat container made of metal or plastic. You hold it flat on the floor and put dirt and dust into it using a brush. N-COUNT

**dust sheet** **(dust sheets)** also **dustsheet.** A **dust sheet** is a large cloth which is used to cover objects such as furniture in order to protect them from dust. N-COUNT

**dust storm** **(dust storms)** A **dust storm** is a storm in which strong winds carry a lot of dust. N-COUNT

**dust-up** **(dust-ups)** A **dust-up** is a quarrel that often involves some fighting. [INFORMAL] ❑ *He's now facing suspension after a dust-up with the referee.* N-COUNT = scrap

**dusty** /dʌsti/ **(dustier, dustiest)** 1 If places, roads, or other things outside are **dusty**, they are covered with tiny bits of earth or sand, usually because it has not rained for a long time. ❑ *They started strolling down the dusty road in the moonlight.* ADJ: usu ADJ n 2 If a room, house, or object is **dusty**, it is covered with very small pieces of dirt. ❑ *...a dusty attic.* ADJ

**Dutch** /dʌtʃ/ 1 **Dutch** means belonging or relating to the Netherlands, or to its people, language, or culture. ADJ 2 **The Dutch** are the people of the Netherlands. N-PLURAL: the N 3 **Dutch** is the language that is spoken by the people who live in the Netherlands. N-UNCOUNT

**Dutch cour|age** **Dutch courage** is the courage that you get by drinking alcoholic drinks. [INFORMAL] N-UNCOUNT

**Dutch|man** /dʌtʃmən/ **(Dutchmen)** A **Dutchman** is a man who is a native of the Netherlands. N-COUNT

**du|ti|ful** /djuːtɪfʊl, AM duː-/ If you say that someone is **dutiful**, you mean that they do everything that they are expected to do. ❑ *The days of the dutiful wife, who sacrifices her career for her husband, are over.* ADJ ♦ **du|ti|ful|ly** *The inspector dutifully recorded the date in a large red book.* ADV: ADV with v

**duty** /djuːti, AM duːti/ **(duties)** ◆◆◇ 1 **Duty** is work that you have to do for your job. ❑ *Staff must report for duty at their normal place of work... My duty is to look after the animals.* N-UNCOUNT 2 Your **duties** are tasks which you have to do because they are part of your job. ❑ *I carried out my duties conscientiously.* N-PLURAL 3 If you say that something is your **duty**, you believe that you ought to do it because it is your responsibility. ❑ *I consider it my duty to write to you and thank you.* N-SING: oft with poss 4 **Duties** are taxes which you pay to the government on goods that you buy. ❑ *Import duties still average 30%. ...customs duties.* N-VAR 5 If someone such as a policeman or a nurse is **off duty**, they are not working. If someone is **on duty**, they are working. ❑ *I'm off duty... Extra staff had been put on duty.* PHRASE: PHR after v, v-link PHR

**duty-bound** also **duty bound.** If you say you are **duty-bound** to do something, you are emphasizing that you feel it is your duty to do it. [FORMAL] ❑ *I felt duty bound to help.* ADJ: v-link ADJ to-inf emphasis

**duty-free** **Duty-free** goods are sold at airports or on planes or ships at a cheaper price than usual because you do not have to pay import tax on them. ❑ *...duty-free cigarettes.* ADJ

**duty-free shop** **(duty-free shops)** A **duty-free shop** is a shop, for example at an airport, where you can buy goods at a cheaper price than usual, because no tax is paid on them. N-COUNT

**du|vet** /duːveɪ, AM duːveɪ/ **(duvets)** A **duvet** is a large cover filled with feathers or similar material which you put over yourself in bed instead of a sheet and blankets. [BRIT] N-COUNT = quilt

✓ in AM, use **comforter**

**DVD** /diː viː diː/ **(DVDs)** A **DVD** is a disc on which a film or music is recorded. DVD discs are similar to compact discs but hold a lot more information. **DVD** is an abbreviation for 'digital video disc' or 'digital versatile disc'. ❑ *...a DVD player.* N-COUNT

**DVD-R** /diː viː diː ɑːʳ/ **(DVD-Rs)** A **DVD-R** is a DVD which is capable of recording sound and images, for example from another DVD or from the Internet. **DVD-R** is an abbreviation for 'digital video disc recordable' or 'digital versatile disc recordable'. N-COUNT

**DVD-RW** /diː viː diː ɑːʳ dʌbəljuː/ **(DVD-RWs)** A **DVD-RW** is a DVD which is capable of recording sound and images, for example from another DVD or from the Internet. **CD-RW** is an abbreviation for 'digital video disc rewritable' or 'digital versatile disc rewritable'. N-COUNT

**DVT** /diː viː tiː/ **(DVTs)** **DVT** is a serious medical condition caused by blood clots in the legs moving up to the lungs. **DVT** is an abbreviation for 'deep vein thrombosis'. [MEDICAL] N-VAR

**dwarf** /dwɔːʳf/ **(dwarfs** or **dwarves, dwarfs, dwarfing, dwarfed)** 1 If one person or thing **is dwarfed** by another, the second is so much bigger than the first that it makes them look very small. ❑ *His figure is dwarfed by the huge red McDonald's sign... The US air travel market dwarfs* VERB be V-ed V n that of Britain. [2] **Dwarf** is used to describe varieties or species of plants and animals which are much smaller than the usual size for their kind. ❑ *...dwarf shrubs.* [3] In children's stories, a **dwarf** is an imaginary creature that is like a small man. Dwarfs often have magical powers. [4] In former times, people who were much smaller than normal were called **dwarfs**. [OFFENSIVE, OLD-FASHIONED] — ADJ: ADJ n; N-COUNT; N-COUNT

**dweeb** /dwiːb/ **(dweebs)** If you call someone, especially a man or a boy, a **dweeb**, you are saying in a rather unkind way that you think they are stupid and weak. [AM, INFORMAL] — N-COUNT; disapproval; = drip, nerd

**dwell** /dwel/ **(dwells, dwelling, dwelt or dwelled)** [1] If you **dwell on** something, especially something unpleasant, you think, speak, or write about it a lot or for quite a long time. ❑ *I'd rather not dwell on the past.* [2] If you **dwell** somewhere, you live there. [FORMAL] ❑ *They are concerned for the fate of the forest and the Indians who dwell in it.* [3] → See also **dwelling**. — VERB; V on/upon n; VERB; = live; V prep/adv

**dwell|er** /dweləʳ/ **(dwellers)** A city **dweller** or slum **dweller**, for example, is a person who lives in the kind of place or house indicated. ❑ *The number of city dwellers is growing.* — N-COUNT: supp N

**dwell|ing** /dwelɪŋ/ **(dwellings)** A **dwelling** or a **dwelling place** is a place where someone lives. [FORMAL] ❑ *Some 3,500 new dwellings are planned for the area.* — N-COUNT; = home

**dwelt** /dwelt/ **Dwelt** is the past tense and past participle of **dwell**.

**dwin|dle** /dwɪndᵊl/ **(dwindles, dwindling, dwindled)** If something **dwindles**, it becomes smaller, weaker, or less in number. ❑ *The factory's workforce has dwindled from over 4,000 to a few hundred... He is struggling to come to terms with his dwindling authority.* — VERB; = shrink; V; V-ing

**dye** /daɪ/ **(dyes, dyeing, dyed)** [1] If you **dye** something such as hair or cloth, you change its colour by soaking it in a special liquid. ❑ *The women prepared, spun and dyed the wool.* [2] **Dye** is a substance made from plants or chemicals which is mixed into a liquid and used to change the colour of something such as cloth or hair. ❑ *...bottles of hair dye.* — VERB; V n; N-MASS

**dyed-in-the-wool** If you use **dyed-in-the-wool** to describe someone or their beliefs, you are saying that they have very strong opinions about something, which they refuse to change. ❑ *...a dyed-in-the-wool conservative.* — ADJ: ADJ n

**dy|ing** /daɪɪŋ/ [1] **Dying** is the present participle of **die**. [2] A **dying** person or animal is very ill and likely to die soon. ❑ *...a dying man.* ♦ **The dying** are people who are dying. ❑ *The dead and the dying were everywhere.* [3] You use **dying** to describe something which happens at the time when someone dies, or is connected with that time. ❑ *It'll stay in my mind till my dying day.* [4] The **dying** days or **dying** minutes of a state of affairs or an activity are its last days or minutes. ❑ *The islands were seized by the Soviet army in the dying days of the second world war.* [5] A **dying** tradition or industry is becoming less important and is likely to disappear completely. ❑ *Shipbuilding is a dying business.* — ADJ: ADJ n; N-PLURAL: the N; ADJ: ADJ n; ADJ: ADJ n; = final; ADJ: ADJ n

**dyke** /daɪk/ **(dykes)**

> ✓ The spelling **dike** is also used, especially for meaning 1.

[1] A **dyke** is a thick wall that is built to stop water flooding onto very low-lying land from a river or from the sea. [2] A **dyke** is a lesbian. [INFORMAL, OFFENSIVE] — N-COUNT; N-COUNT

**dy|nam|ic** /daɪnæmɪk/ **(dynamics)** [1] If you describe someone as **dynamic**, you approve of them because they are full of energy or full of new and exciting ideas. ❑ *He seemed a dynamic and energetic leader.* ♦ **dy|nami|cal|ly** /daɪnæmɪkli/ *He's one of the most dynamically imaginative jazz pianists still functioning.* [2] If you describe something as **dynamic**, you approve of it because it is very active and energetic. ❑ *South Asia continues to be the most dynamic economic region in the world.* [3] A **dynamic** process is one that constantly changes and progresses. ❑ *...a dynamic, evolving worldwide epidemic.* ♦ **dy|nami|cal|ly** *Germany has a dynamically growing market at home.* [4] The **dynamic** of a system or process is the force that causes it to change or progress. ❑ *The dynamic of the market demands constant change and adjustment.* [5] The **dynamics** of a situation or group of people are the opposing forces within it that cause it to change. ❑ *...the dynamics of the social system.* [6] **Dynamics** are forces which produce power or movement. [TECHNICAL] [7] **Dynamics** is the scientific study of motion, energy, and forces. — ADJ; approval; ADV: ADV adj/-ed, ADV after v; ADJ; approval; ADJ; ≠ static; ADV: usu ADV adj/-ed; N-COUNT: usu with supp; N-PLURAL: usu with supp; N-UNCOUNT; N-UNCOUNT

**dy|na|mism** /daɪnəmɪzəm/ [1] If you say that someone or something has **dynamism**, you are expressing approval of the fact that they are full of energy or full of new and exciting ideas. ❑ *...a situation that calls for dynamism and new thinking.* [2] If you refer to the **dynamism** of a situation or system, you are referring to the fact that it is changing in an exciting and dramatic way. ❑ *Such changes are indicators of economic dynamism.* — N-UNCOUNT; approval; = energy; N-UNCOUNT; approval

**dy|na|mite** /daɪnəmaɪt/ [1] **Dynamite** is a type of explosive that contains nitroglycerin. ❑ *Fifty yards of track was blown up with dynamite.* [2] If you describe a piece of information as **dynamite**, you think that people will react strongly to it. [INFORMAL] ❑ *Her diaries are political dynamite.* [3] If you describe someone or something as **dynamite**, you think that they are exciting. [INFORMAL] ❑ *The first kiss is dynamite.* — N-UNCOUNT; N-UNCOUNT; N-UNCOUNT; approval

**dy|na|mo** /daɪnəmoʊ/ **(dynamos)** A **dynamo** is a device that uses the movement of a machine or vehicle to produce electricity. — N-COUNT

**dy|nas|tic** /daɪnæstɪk/ **Dynastic** means typical of or relating to a dynasty. ❑ *...dynastic rule.* — ADJ: usu ADJ n

**dyn|as|ty** /dɪnəsti, AM daɪn-/ **(dynasties)** [1] A **dynasty** is a series of rulers of a country who all belong to the same family. ❑ *The Seljuk dynasty of Syria was founded in 1094.* [2] A **dynasty** is a period of time during which a country is ruled by members of the same family. ❑ *...carvings dating back to the Ming dynasty.* [3] A **dynasty** is a family which has members from two or more generations who are important in a particular field of activity, for example in business or politics. ❑ *...the Kennedy dynasty.* — N-COUNT; N-COUNT: with supp; N-COUNT

**d'you** /djuː, dʒuː/ **D'you** is a shortened form of 'do you' or 'did you', used in spoken English. ❑ *What d'you say?*

**dys|en|tery** /dɪsᵊntri, AM -teri/ **Dysentery** is an infection in a person's intestines that causes them to pass a lot of waste, in which blood and mucus are mixed with the person's faeces. — N-UNCOUNT

**dys|func|tion** /dɪsfʌŋkʃən/ **(dysfunctions)** [1] If you refer to a **dysfunction** in something such as a relationship or someone's behaviour, you mean that it is different from what is considered to be normal. [FORMAL] ❑ *...his severe emotional dysfunction was very clearly apparent.* [2] If someone has a physical **dysfunction**, part of their body is not working properly. [MEDICAL] ❑ *...kidney and liver dysfunction.* — N-COUNT; N-VAR

**dys|func|tion|al** /dɪsfʌŋkʃənəl/ **Dysfunctional** is used to describe relationships or behaviour which are different from what is considered to be normal. [FORMAL] ❑ *...the characteristics that typically occur in a dysfunctional family.* — ADJ: usu ADJ n

**dys|lexia** /dɪsleksiə/ If someone suffers from **dyslexia**, they have difficulty with reading because of a slight disorder of their brain. [TECHNICAL] — N-UNCOUNT

**dys|lex|ic** /dɪsleksɪk/ If someone is **dyslexic**, they have difficulty with reading because of a slight disorder of their brain. [TECHNICAL] — ADJ

**dys|pep|sia** /dɪspepsiə, AM -ʃə/ **Dyspepsia** is the same as **indigestion**. [MEDICAL] — N-UNCOUNT

**dys|tro|phy** /dɪstrəfi/ → see **muscular dystrophy**

# E e

**E, e** /iː/ **(E's, e's)** 1 **E** is the fifth letter of the English alphabet. 2 **E** is the drug ecstasy, or a tablet of ecstasy. [INFORMAL] N-VAR N-MASS

**e-** /iː-/ **e-** is used to form words that indicate that something happens on or uses the Internet. **e-** is an abbreviation for 'electronic'. ❑ *...the complete on-line e-store. ...providing e-solutions for business.* PREFIX

**each** /iːtʃ/ 1 If you refer to **each** thing or **each** person in a group, you are referring to every member of the group and considering them as individuals. ❑ *Each book is beautifully illustrated... Each year, hundreds of animals are killed in this way... Blend in the eggs, one at a time, beating well after each one.* ♦ **Each** is also a pronoun. ❑ *...two bedrooms, each with three beds... She began to consult doctors, and each had a different diagnosis.* ♦ **Each** is also an emphasizing pronoun. ❑ *We each have different needs and interests.* ♦ **Each** is also an adverb. ❑ *The children were given one each, handed to them or placed on their plates... They were selling tickets at six pounds each.* ♦ **Each** is also a quantifier. ❑ *He handed each of them a page of photos... Each of these exercises takes one or two minutes to do... The machines, each of which is perhaps five feet in diameter, are not the largest devices in the room.* 2 If you refer to **each one of** the members of a group, you are emphasizing that something applies to every one of them. ❑ *He picked up forty of these publications and read each one of them.* 3 You can refer to **each and every** member **of** a group to emphasize that you mean all the members of that group. ❑ *Each and every person responsible for his murder will be brought to justice... They can't destroy truth without destroying each and every one of us.* 4 You use **each other** when you are saying that each member of a group does something to the others or has a particular connection with the others. ❑ *We looked at each other in silence... Both sides are willing to make allowances for each other's political sensitivities... Uncle Paul and I hardly know each other.* ◆◆◆ DET: DET sing-n; PRON; PRON; ADV: amount ADV; QUANT: QUANT *of* def-pl-n; QUANT: QUANT *of* def-pl-n [emphasis]; PHRASE: PHR n, PHR *of* n [emphasis]; PRON: v PRON, prep PRON

**each way** 1 If you bet money **each way** on the result of a horse race or a dog race, you will win some money if the animal you bet on comes first, second, third, or sometimes fourth. [BRIT] ❑ *In the last race I put £20 each way on two outsiders.* ♦ **Each way** is also an adjective ❑ *...a $10,000 each way bet on Minnehoma at 33-1.* 2 If you say that something is a good **each way** bet, you mean that you think it is a good thing to support or invest in because it is unlikely to fail. [BRIT] ❑ *Large overseas-based trusts are an excellent each way bet. ...a good each way investment.* ADV: ADV after v; ADJ: ADJ n; ADJ: ADJ n

**eager** /iːgəʳ/ 1 If you are **eager to** do or have something, you want to do or have it very much. ❑ *Robert was eager to talk about life in the Army... When my own son was five years old, I became eager for another baby... The low prices still pull in crowds of eager buyers.* ♦ **eager\|ness** *...an eagerness to learn.* 2 If you look or sound **eager**, you look or sound as if you expect something interesting or enjoyable to happen. ❑ *Arty sneered at the crowd of eager faces around him... Her voice was girlish and eager.* ♦ **eager\|ly** *'So what do you think will happen?' he asked eagerly.* ♦ **eager\|ness** *...a woman speaking with breathless eagerness.* ◆◇◇ ADJ: usu v-link ADJ, ADJ to-inf, ADJ *for* n = keen; N-UNCOUNT; ADJ = excited; ADV; N-UNCOUNT = excitement

**eagle** /iːgᵊl/ **(eagles)** 1 An **eagle** is a large bird that lives by eating small animals. 2 If you talk about a person's **eagle eye**, you mean that they are watching someone or something carefully or are very good at noticing things. ❑ *He did the work under the eagle eye of his teacher... The Captain's eagle eye swept the room.* N-COUNT; PHRASE: usu with poss

**eagle-eyed** If you describe someone as **eagle-eyed**, you mean that they watch things very carefully and seem to notice everything. ❑ *Three cannabis plants were found by eagle-eyed police officers.* ADJ

**ear** /ɪəʳ/ **(ears)** 1 Your **ears** are the two parts of your body, one on each side of your head, with which you hear sounds. ❑ *He whispered something in her ear... I'm having my ears pierced.* 2 If you have **an ear for** music or language, you are able to hear its sounds accurately and to interpret them or reproduce them well. ❑ *Moby certainly has a fine ear for a tune... An ear for foreign languages is advantageous.* 3 **Ear** is often used to refer to people's willingness to listen to what someone is saying. ❑ *What would cause the masses to give him a far more sympathetic ear?... They had shut their eyes and ears to everything.* 4 The **ears** of a cereal plant such as wheat or barley are the parts at the top of the stem, which contain the seeds or grains. ◆◇◇ N-COUNT; N-SING: with supp, usu N *for* n; N-COUNT: oft adj N; N-COUNT: usu pl

**PHRASES** 5 If someone says that they are **all ears**, they mean that they are ready and eager to listen. [INFORMAL] 6 If a request **falls on deaf ears** or if the person to whom the request is made **turns a deaf ear to** it, they take no notice of it. ❑ *I hope that our appeals will not fall on deaf ears... He has turned a resolutely deaf ear to American demands for action.* 7 If you **keep** or **have** your **ear to the ground**, you make sure that you find out about the things that people are doing or saying. ❑ *Jobs in manufacturing are relatively scarce but I keep my ear to the ground.* 8 If you **lend an ear** to someone or their problems, you listen to them carefully and sympathetically. ❑ *They are always willing to lend an ear and offer what advice they can.* 9 If you say that something goes **in one ear and out the other**, you mean that someone pays no attention to it, or forgets about it immediately. ❑ *That rubbish goes in one ear and out the other.* 10 If someone says that you will be **out on** your **ear**, they mean that you will be forced to leave a job, an organization or a place suddenly. [INFORMAL] ❑ *We never objected. We'd have been out on our ears looking for another job if we had.* 11 If you **play by ear** or **play** a piece of music **by ear**, you play music by relying on your memory rather than by reading printed music. ❑ *Neil played, by ear, the music he'd heard his older sister practicing.* 12 If you **play it by ear**, you decide what to say or do in a situation by responding to events rather than by following a plan which you have decided on in advance. 13 If you are **up to** your **ears in** something, it is taking up all of your time, attention, or resources. ❑ *He was desperate. He was in debt up to his ears.* 14 **music to** your **ears** → see **music**. **wet behind the ears** → see **wet**. PHRASE: usu v-link PHR; PHRASE: V inflects; PHRASE: V inflects; PHRASE: V inflects; PHRASE: V inflects; PHRASE: N inflects, v-link PHR; PHRASE: V inflects; PHRASE: V inflects; PHRASE: v-link PHR, oft PHR *in* n

**ear\|ache** /ɪəreɪk/ **(earaches)** **Earache** is a pain in the inside part of your ear. N-VAR

**ear|drum** /ɪəʳdrʌm/ **(eardrums)** also **ear drum.** Your **eardrums** are the thin pieces of tightly stretched skin inside each ear, which vibrate when sound waves reach them. [N-COUNT]

**ear|ful** /ɪəʳfʊl/ If you say that you got **an earful**, you mean that someone spoke angrily to you for quite an long time. [INFORMAL] ❑ *I bet Sue gave you an earful when you got home.* [N-SING: *a* N]

**earl** /ɜːʳl/ **(earls)** An **earl** is a British nobleman. ❑ *...the first Earl of Birkenhead.* [N-COUNT: oft N *of* n]

**earl|dom** /ɜːʳldəm/ **(earldoms)** An **earldom** is the rank or title of an earl. [N-COUNT]

**ear|li|er** /ɜːʳliəʳ/ ◆◆◇ [1] **Earlier** is the comparative of **early**. [2] **Earlier** is used to refer to a point or period in time before the present or before the one you are talking about. ❑ *As mentioned earlier, the University supplements this information with an interview... Earlier, it had been hoped to use the indoor track. ...political reforms announced by the President earlier this year... Many years earlier, Grundy had given The Beatles their first television break.* [ADV: ADV with v, ADV with cl, oft amount ADV] ♦ **Earlier** is also an adjective. ❑ *Earlier reports of gunshots have not been substantiated.* [ADJ: ADJ n]

**ear|li|est** /ɜːʳliɪst/ [1] **Earliest** is the superlative of **early**. [2] **At the earliest** means not before the date or time mentioned. ❑ *The first official results are not expected until Tuesday at the earliest.* [PHRASE: cl PHR]

**ear|lobe** /ɪəʳloʊb/ **(earlobes)** also **ear lobe.** Your **earlobes** are the soft parts at the bottom of your ears. [N-COUNT]

**ear|ly** /ɜːʳli/ **(earlier, earliest)** ◆◆◆ [1] **Early** means before the usual time that a particular event or activity happens. ❑ *I knew I had to get up early... Why do we have to go to bed so early?* [ADV: ADV after v ≠ late] ♦ **Early** is also an adjective. ❑ *I decided that I was going to take early retirement... I planned an early night.* [ADJ: ADJ n] [2] **Early** means near the beginning of a day, week, year, or other period of time. ❑ *...in the 1970s and the early 1980s. ...a few weeks in early summer... She was in her early teens. ...the early hours of Saturday morning.* [ADJ: ADJ n ≠ late] ♦ **Early** is also an adverb. ❑ *We'll hope to see you some time early next week. ...early in the season.* [ADV: ADV with cl, ADV n/prep] [3] **Early** means before the time that was arranged or expected. ❑ *She arrived early to secure a place at the front... The first snow came a month earlier than usual.* [ADV: ADV after v ≠ late] ♦ **Early** is also an adjective. ❑ *I'm always early.* [ADJ] [4] **Early** means near the beginning of a period in history, or in the history of something such as the world, a society, or an activity. ❑ *...the early stages of pregnancy. ...Fassbinder's early films... It's too early to declare his efforts a success.* [ADJ: ADJ n] [5] **Early** means near the beginning of something such as a piece of work or a process. ❑ *...the book's early chapters.* [ADJ: ADJ n] ♦ **Early** is also an adverb. ❑ *...an incident which occurred much earlier in the game.* [ADV: ADV with cl, ADV prep] [6] **Early** refers to plants which flower or crop before or at the beginning of the main season. ❑ *...these early cabbages and cauliflowers.* [ADJ: ADJ n] ♦ **Early** is also an adverb. ❑ *...early flowering shrubs.* [ADV: ADV with v] [7] **Early** reports or indications of something are the first reports or indications about it. [FORMAL] ❑ *The early indications look encouraging.* [ADJ: ADJ n]

PHRASES [8] You can use **as early as** to emphasize that a particular time or period is surprisingly early. ❑ *Inflation could fall back into single figures as early as this month.* [PHRASE: PHR n, emphasis] [9] If you say about something that might be true that **it is early days**, you mean that it is too soon for you to be completely sure about it. [INFORMAL] [PHRASE: V inflects]

**ear|ly bird** **(early birds)** [1] An **early bird** is someone who does something or goes somewhere very early, especially very early in the morning. ❑ *We've always been early birds, getting up at 5.30 or 6am.* [N-COUNT] [2] An **early bird** deal or offer is one that is available at a reduced price, but which you must buy earlier than you would normally do. ❑ *Early bird discounts are usually available at the beginning of the season.* [ADJ: ADJ n]

**ear|ly warn|ing** also **early-warning.** An **early warning** system warns people that something bad is likely to happen, for example that a machine is about to stop working, or that a country is being attacked. [ADJ: ADJ n]

**ear|mark** /ɪəʳmɑːʳk/ **(earmarks, earmarking, earmarked)** [1] If resources such as money **are earmarked for** a particular purpose, they are reserved for that purpose. ❑ *...the extra money being earmarked for the new projects... The education department has earmarked £6m for the new school... Some of the money has been earmarked to pay for the re-settlement of people from contaminated areas.* [VERB = set aside; *be* V-ed *for* n; V n *for* n; *be* V-ed to-inf] [2] If something **has been earmarked for** closure or disposal, for example, people have decided that it will be closed or got rid of. ❑ *Their support meant that he was not forced to sell the business which was earmarked for disposal last year.* [VERB: usu passive; *be* V-ed *for* n]

**ear|muffs** /ɪəʳmʌfs/ also **ear muffs. Earmuffs** consist of two thick soft pieces of cloth joined by a band, which you wear over your ears to protect them from the cold or from loud noise. [N-PLURAL: also *a pair of* N]

**earn** /ɜːʳn/ **(earns, earning, earned)** ◆◆◇ [1] If you **earn** money, you receive money in return for work that you do. ❑ *What a lovely way to earn a living.* [VERB; V n] [2] If something **earns** money, it produces money as profit or interest. ❑ *...a current account which earns little or no interest.* [VERB; V n] [3] If you **earn** something such as praise, you get it because you deserve it. ❑ *Companies must earn a reputation for honesty... I think that's earned him very high admiration.* [VERB; V n; V n n]

**earn|er** /ɜːʳnəʳ/ **(earners)** An **earner** is someone or something that earns money or produces profit. ❑ *...a typical wage earner... Sugar is Fiji's second biggest export earner.* [N-COUNT: usu supp N]

**ear|nest** /ɜːʳnɪst/ [1] If something is done or happens **in earnest**, it happens to a much greater extent and more seriously than before. ❑ *Campaigning will begin in earnest tomorrow.* [PHRASE: PHR after v = seriously] [2] **Earnest** people are very serious and sincere in what they say or do, because they think that their actions and beliefs are important. ❑ *Ella was a pious, earnest woman.* [ADJ] ♦ **ear|nest|ness** *He was admired by many for his earnestness.* [N-UNCOUNT] [3] If you are **in earnest**, you are sincere in what you are doing and saying. ❑ *No one could tell whether he was in earnest or in jest.* [PHRASE: usu v PHR, v-link PHR]

**ear|nest|ly** /ɜːʳnɪstli/ [1] If you say something **earnestly**, you say it very seriously, often because you believe that it is important or you are trying to persuade someone else to believe it. ❑ *'Did you?' she asked earnestly.* [ADV: ADV with v] [2] If you do something **earnestly**, you do it in a thorough and serious way, intending to succeed. ❑ *She always listened earnestly as if this might help her to understand.* [ADV: usu ADV with v, also ADV adj] [3] If you **earnestly** hope or wish for something, you hope or wish strongly and sincerely for it. ❑ *I earnestly hope what I learned will serve me well in my new job.* [ADV: ADV before v]

**earn|ings** /ɜːʳnɪŋz/ ◆◇◇ Your **earnings** are the sums of money that you earn by working. ❑ *Average weekly earnings rose by 1.5% in July.* [N-PLURAL = pay, income]

**earnings-related** An **earnings-related** payment or benefit provides higher or lower payments according to the amount a person was earning while working. [BRIT] [ADJ: usu ADJ n]

**ear|phone** /ɪəʳfoʊn/ **(earphones) Earphones** are a small piece of equipment which you wear over or inside your ears so that you can listen to a radio or cassette recorder without anyone else hearing. [N-COUNT: usu pl]

**ear|piece** /ɪəʳpiːs/ **(earpieces)** The **earpiece** of a telephone receiver, hearing aid, or other device is the part that you hold up to your ear or put into your ear. [N-COUNT]

**ear|plug** /ɪəʳplʌg/ **(earplugs)** also **ear plug. Earplugs** are small pieces of a soft material which you put into your ears to keep out noise, water, or cold air. [N-COUNT: usu pl]

**ear|ring** /ɪərɪŋ/ **(earrings) Earrings** are pieces of jewellery which you attach to your ears. [N-COUNT]

**ear|shot** /ɪəʳʃɒt/ If you are **within earshot of** someone or something, you are close enough to be able to hear them. If you are **out of earshot**, you are too far away to hear them. ❑ *It is within earshot of a main road... Mark was out of earshot, walking ahead of them.* — PHRASE: PHR after v, v-link PHR, oft PHR *of* n

**ear-splitting** An **ear-splitting** noise is very loud. ❑ *...ear-splitting screams.* — ADJ: usu ADJ n

**earth** /ɜːʳθ/ ◆◆◇ 1 **Earth** or **the Earth** is the planet on which we live. People usually say **Earth** when they are referring to the planet as part of the universe, and **the Earth** when they are talking about the planet as the place where we live. ❑ *The space shuttle Atlantis returned safely to earth today. ...a fault in the Earth's crust.* — N-PROPER: oft *the* N
2 **The earth** is the land surface on which we live and move about. ❑ *The earth shook and the walls of neighbouring houses fell around them.* — N-SING: *the* N = ground
3 **Earth** is the substance on the land surface of the earth, for example clay or sand, in which plants grow. ❑ *The road winds for miles through parched earth, scrub and cactus.* — N-UNCOUNT = soil
4 The **earth** in an electric plug or piece of electrical equipment is the wire through which electricity can pass into the ground, which makes the equipment safe if something goes wrong with it. [BRIT] ❑ *The earth wire was not connected.* — N-SING

✔ in AM, use **ground**

♦ **earthed** *Light fittings with metal parts should always be earthed.* — ADJ: usu v-link ADJ
5 → See also **down-to-earth**.
PHRASES 6 **On earth** is used for emphasis in questions that begin with words such as 'how', 'why', 'what', or 'where'. It is often used to suggest that there is no obvious or easy answer to the question being asked. ❑ *How on earth did that happen?... What on earth had Luke done?* — PHRASE: quest PHR [emphasis]
7 **On earth** is used for emphasis after some negative noun groups, for example 'no reason'. ❑ *There was no reason on earth why she couldn't have moved in with us... There is no feeling on earth like winning for the first time.* — PHRASE: with neg, n PHR [emphasis]
8 **On earth** is used for emphasis after a noun group that contains a superlative adjective. ❑ *He wanted to be the fastest man on earth.* — PHRASE: adj-superl n PHR [emphasis]
9 If you come **down to earth** or **back to earth**, you have to face the reality of everyday life after a period of great excitement. ❑ *When he came down to earth after his win he admitted: 'It was an amazing feeling'.* — PHRASE: PHR after v
10 If you say that something **cost the earth** or that you **paid the earth** for it, you are emphasizing that it cost a very large amount of money. [INFORMAL] ❑ *It must have cost the earth.* — PHRASE: V inflects [emphasis]
11 **hell on earth** → see **hell**.

**earth|bound** /ɜːʳθbaʊnd/ If something is **earthbound**, it is unable to fly, or is on the ground rather than in the air or in space. ❑ *...earthbound telescopes.* — ADJ

**earth|en** /ɜːʳðᵊn/ 1 **Earthen** containers and objects are made of clay that is baked so that it becomes hard. — ADJ: ADJ n = earthenware
2 An **earthen** floor, bank, or mound is made of hard earth. — ADJ: ADJ n

**earthen|ware** /ɜːʳðᵊnweəʳ/ 1 **Earthenware** bowls, pots, or other objects are made of clay that is baked so that it becomes hard. ❑ *...earthenware pots.* — ADJ: ADJ n = terracotta
2 Earthenware objects are referred to as **earthenware**. ❑ *...colourful Italian china and earthenware.* — N-UNCOUNT = terracotta

**earth|ling** /ɜːʳθlɪŋ/ **(earthlings)** **Earthling** is used in science fiction to refer to human beings who live on the planet Earth. — N-COUNT: usu pl

**earth|ly** /ɜːʳθli/ 1 **Earthly** means happening in the material world of our life on earth and not in any spiritual life or life after death. ❑ *...the need to confront evil during the earthly life.* — ADJ: ADJ n
2 **Earthly** is used for emphasis in phrases such as **no earthly reason**. If you say that there is **no earthly reason why** something should happen, you are emphasizing that there is no reason at all why it should happen. ❑ *There is no earthly reason why they should ever change.* — ADJ: ADJ n [emphasis]

**earth|quake** /ɜːʳθkweɪk/ **(earthquakes)** An **earthquake** is a shaking of the ground caused by movement of the earth's crust. — N-COUNT

**earth-shattering** Something that is **earth-shattering** is very surprising or shocking. ❑ *...earth-shattering news.* — ADJ

**earth|work** /ɜːʳθwɜːʳk/ **(earthworks)** **Earthworks** are large structures of earth that have been built for defence, especially ones which were built a very long time ago. — N-COUNT: usu pl

**earth|worm** /ɜːʳθwɜːʳm/ **(earthworms)** An **earthworm** is a kind of worm which lives in the ground. — N-COUNT

**earthy** /ɜːʳθi/ **(earthier, earthiest)** 1 If you describe someone as **earthy**, you mean that they are open and direct, and talk about subjects which other people avoid or feel ashamed about. ❑ *...his extremely earthy humour.* — ADJ [approval]
♦ **earthi|ness** *He loved Gerard's peasant earthiness.* — N-UNCOUNT
2 If you describe something as **earthy**, you mean it looks, smells, or feels like earth. ❑ *I'm attracted to warm, earthy colours.* — ADJ: usu ADJ n

**ear|wig** /ɪəʳwɪɡ/ **(earwigs)** An **earwig** is a small, thin, brown insect that has a pair of claws at the back end of its body. — N-COUNT

**ease** /iːz/ ◆◇◇ **(eases, easing, eased)** 1 If you do something **with ease**, you do it easily, without difficulty or effort. ❑ *...the ease with which young people could find work.* — PHRASE: PHR after V ≠ difficulty
2 If you talk about the **ease of** a particular activity, you are referring to the way that it has been made easier to do, or to the fact that it is already easy to do. ❑ *For ease of reference, only the relevant extracts of the regulations are included.* — N-UNCOUNT: N *of* n
3 **Ease** is the state of being very comfortable and able to live as you want, without any worries or problems. ❑ *She lived a life of ease.* — N-UNCOUNT = comfort
4 If something unpleasant **eases** or if you **ease** it, it is reduced in degree, speed, or intensity. ❑ *Tensions had eased... I gave him some brandy to ease the pain. ...calls for the easing of sanctions.* — VERB: V, V n, V-ing
5 If you **ease** your **way** somewhere or **ease** somewhere, you move there slowly, carefully, and gently. If you **ease** something somewhere, you move it there slowly, carefully, and gently. ❑ *I eased my way towards the door... She eased back into the chair and nodded... He eased his foot off the accelerator... Leaphorn eased himself silently upward... I eased open the door.* — VERB: V *way* prep/adv, V prep/adv, V n prep/adv, V pron-refl adv/prep, V n with adj
PHRASES 6 If you are **at ease**, you are feeling confident and relaxed, and are able to talk to people without feeling nervous or anxious. If you put someone **at** their **ease**, you make them feel at ease. ❑ *It is essential to feel at ease with your therapist... Both men were unwelcoming, making little attempt to put Kathryn or her companions at their ease.* — PHRASE: v-link PHR, PHR after v
7 If you are **ill at ease**, you feel rather uncomfortable, anxious, or worried. ❑ *He appeared embarrassed and ill at ease with the sustained applause that greeted him.* — PHRASE: usu v-link PHR, PHR after v, oft PHR *with* n
♦ **ease off** If something **eases off**, or a person or thing **eases** it **off**, it is reduced in degree, speed, or intensity. ❑ *These days, the pressure has eased off... Kelly eased off his pace as they reached the elevator.* — PHRASAL VERB: V P, V P n (not pron), Also V n P
♦ **ease up** 1 If something **eases up**, it is reduced in degree, speed, or intensity. ❑ *The rain had eased up.* — PHRASAL VERB: V P
2 If you **ease up**, you start to make less effort. ❑ *He told supporters not to ease up even though he's leading in the presidential race.* — PHRASAL VERB: V P
3 If you **ease up on** someone or something, your behaviour or attitude towards them becomes less severe or strict. [INFORMAL] ❑ *Officials have eased up on the press restrictions.* — PHRASAL VERB: V P *on* n

**easel** /iːzᵊl/ **(easels)** An **easel** is a wooden frame that supports a picture which an artist is painting or drawing. — N-COUNT

**easi|ly** /iːzɪli/ ◆◇◇ 1 You use **easily** to emphasize that something is very likely to happen, or is very likely to be true. ❑ *It could easily be another year before the economy starts to show some improve-* — ADV: usu ADV before v, also ADV n/adj ment. [2] You use **easily** to say that something happens more quickly or more often than is usual or normal. ❑ *He had always cried very easily.* (ADV: ADV after v) [3] → See also **easy**.

**east** /iːst/ also **East.** ◆◆◆ [1] **The east** is the direction where the sun rises. ❑ *...the vast swamps which lie to the east of the River Nile... The principal range runs east to west.* (N-UNCOUNT: also *the* N) [2] **The east of** a place, country, or region is the part which is in the east. ❑ *...a village in the east of the country.* (N-SING: usu *the* N, oft N *of* n) [3] If you go **east**, you travel towards the east. ❑ *To drive, go east on Route 9.* (ADV: ADV after v) [4] Something that is **east of** a place is positioned to the east of it. ❑ *...just east of the center of town.* (ADV: usu ADV *of* n) [5] The **east** edge, corner, or part of a place or country is the part which is towards the east. ❑ *...a low line of hills running along the east coast.* (ADJ: ADJ n) [6] **East** is used in the names of some countries, states, and regions in the east of a larger area ❑ *He had been on safari in East Africa with his son.* (ADJ: ADJ n) [7] An **east** wind is a wind that blows from the east. (ADJ) [8] **The East** is used to refer to the southern and eastern part of Asia, including India, China, and Japan. ❑ *Every so often, a new martial art arrives from the East.* (N-SING: *the* N) [9] → See also **Middle East**, **Far East**.

**east|bound** /iːstbaʊnd/ **Eastbound** roads or vehicles lead to or are travelling towards the east. [FORMAL] ❑ *He caught an eastbound train to Tottenham Court Road.* (ADJ: ADJ n)

**East|er** /iːstəʳ/ **(Easters) Easter** is a Christian festival when Jesus Christ's return to life is celebrated. It is celebrated on a Sunday in March or April. ❑ *'Happy Easter,' he yelled. ...the first Easter morning.* (N-VAR: oft N n)

**East|er egg (Easter eggs)** An **Easter egg** is an egg made of chocolate that is given as a present at Easter. In some countries, Easter eggs are hidden and children then look for them. (N-COUNT)

**east|er|ly** /iːstəʳli/ [1] An **easterly** point, area, or direction is to the east or towards the east. ❑ *He progressed slowly along the coast in an easterly direction.* (ADJ: usu ADJ n) [2] An **easterly** wind is a wind that blows from the east. ❑ *...the cold easterly winds from Scandinavia.* (ADJ: usu ADJ n)

**east|ern** /iːstəʳn/ ◆◆◇ [1] **Eastern** means in or from the east of a region, state, or country. ❑ *...Eastern Europe. ...France's eastern border with Germany.* (ADJ: ADJ n) [2] **Eastern** means coming from or associated with the people or countries of the East, such as India, China, or Japan. ❑ *In many Eastern countries massage was and is a part of everyday life.* (ADJ: ADJ n) → See also **Middle Eastern**.

**east|ern|er** /iːstəʳnəʳ/ **(easterners)** An **easterner** is a person who was born in or who lives in the eastern part of a place or country, especially an American from the East Coast of the USA. [mainly AM] (N-COUNT)

**east|ern|most** /iːstəʳnmoʊst/ The **easternmost** part of an area or the **easternmost** place is the one that is farthest towards the east. [FORMAL] (ADJ: usu ADJ n)

**East|er Sun|day** Easter Sunday is the Sunday in March or April when Easter is celebrated. (N-UNCOUNT)

**East Ger|man (East Germans) East German** is used to describe things that belonged or related to the former German Democratic Republic. (ADJ) ♦ **East Germans** were people from the German Democratic Republic. (N-COUNT)

**east|ward** /iːstwəʳd/ also **eastwards. Eastward** or **eastwards** means towards the east. ❑ *A powerful snow storm is moving eastward... They were pressing on eastwards towards the city's small airfield.* (ADV: usu ADV after v, also n ADV = east) ♦ **Eastward** is also an adjective. ❑ *...the eastward expansion of the City of London.* (ADJ)

**easy** /iːzi/ **(easier, easiest)** ◆◆◆ [1] If a job or action is **easy**, you can do it without difficulty or effort, because it is not complicated and causes no problems. ❑ *The shower is easy to install... This is not an easy task.* (ADJ: oft *it* v-link ADJ to-inf, ADJ to-inf) ♦ **easi|ly** *Dress your child in layers of clothes you can remove easily.* (ADV) [2] If you describe an action or activity as **easy**, you mean that it is done in a confident, relaxed way. If someone is **easy about** something, they feel relaxed and confident about it. ❑ *He was an easy person to talk to. ...when you are both feeling a little easier about the break up of your relationship.* (ADJ: oft ADJ *about* n) ♦ **easi|ly** *They talked amiably and easily about a wide range of topics.* (ADV: ADV with v) [3] If you say that someone has an **easy** life, you mean that they live comfortably without any problems or worries. ❑ *She has not had an easy life.* (ADJ: usu ADJ n ≠ *hard*) [4] If you say that something is **easy** or too **easy**, you are criticizing someone because they have done the most obvious or least difficult thing, and have not considered the situation carefully enough. ❑ *That's easy for you to say... It was all too easy to believe it.* (ADJ: v-link ADJ, oft *it* v-link ADJ to-inf, ADJ to-inf; disapproval) [5] If you describe someone or something as **easy prey** or as an **easy target**, you mean that they can easily be attacked or criticized. ❑ *Tourists have become easy prey... The World Bank, with its poor environmental record, is an easy target for blame.* (ADJ: ADJ n)

**PHRASES** [6] If you tell someone to **go easy on** something, you are telling them to use only a small amount of it. [INFORMAL] ❑ *Go easy on the alcohol.* (PHRASE: V inflects, PHR n) [7] If you tell someone to **go easy on**, or **be easy on**, a particular person, you are telling them not to punish or treat that person very severely. [INFORMAL] ❑ *'Go easy on him,' Sam repeated, opening the door.* (PHRASE: V and ADJ inflect, PHR n) [8] If someone tells you to **take it easy** or **take things easy**, they mean that you should relax and not do very much at all. [INFORMAL] ❑ *It is best to take things easy for a week or two.* (PHRASE: V and ADJ inflect) [9] → See also **easily**.

**easy chair (easy chairs)** An **easy chair** is a large, comfortable padded chair. (N-COUNT)

**easy-going** If you describe someone as **easy-going**, you mean that they are not easily annoyed, worried, or upset, and you think this is a good quality. ❑ *He was easy-going and good-natured.* (ADJ; approval)

**easy lis|ten|ing Easy listening** is gentle, relaxing music. Some people do not like this kind of music because they do not think that it is very interesting or exciting. ❑ *...an easy listening version of the Oasis hit Wonderwall.* (N-UNCOUNT)

**eat** /iːt/ **(eats, eating, ate, eaten)** ◆◆◇ [1] When you **eat** something, you put it into your mouth, chew it, and swallow it. ❑ *She was eating a cheese and ham sandwich... We took our time and ate slowly.* (VERB: V n, V) [2] If you **eat** sensibly or healthily, you eat food that is good for you. ❑ *...a campaign to persuade people to eat more healthily.* (VERB: V adv) [3] If you **eat**, you have a meal. ❑ *Let's go out to eat... We ate lunch together a few times.* (VERB: V, V n) [4] If something **is eating** you, it is annoying or worrying you. [INFORMAL] ❑ *'What the hell's eating you?' he demanded.* (VERB: only cont, V n) [5] If you have someone **eating out of** your **hand**, they are completely under your control. ❑ *She usually has the press eating out of her hand.* (PHRASE: V and N inflect) [6] to **have** your **cake and eat it** → see **cake**. **dog eat dog** → see **dog**. to **eat humble pie** → see **humble**.

♦ **eat away** If one thing **eats away** another or **eats away at** another, it gradually destroys or uses it up. ❑ *Rot is eating away the interior of the house... The recession is eating away at their revenues.* (PHRASAL VERB: V P n (not pron), V P *at* n)

♦ **eat into** [1] If something **eats into** your time or your resources, it uses them, when they should be used for other things. ❑ *Responsibilities at home and work eat into his time.* (PHRASAL VERB: V P n) [2] If a substance such as acid or rust **eats into** something, it destroys or damages its surface. ❑ *Ulcers occur when the stomach's natural acids eat into the lining of the stomach.* (PHRASAL VERB: V P n)

♦ **eat up** [1] When you **eat up** your food, you eat all of it. ❑ *Eat up your lunch... Some seed fell along the footpath, and the birds came and ate it up.* (PHRASAL VERB: V P n (not pron), V n P) [2] If something **eats up** money, time, or resources, it uses them or consumes them in great quantities. ❑ *Health insurance costs are eating up his income.* (PHRASAL VERB: V P n (not pron))

**eat|en** /iːtᵊn/ **Eaten** is the past participle of **eat**.

**eat|en up** If someone is **eaten up with** jealousy, curiosity, or desire, they feel it very intensely. [INFORMAL] ❑ *Don't waste your time being eaten up with envy.* ADJ: v-link ADJ with n

**eat|er** /iːtəʳ/ **(eaters)** You use **eater** to refer to someone who eats in a particular way or who eats particular kinds of food. ❑ *I've never been a fussy eater. ...vegetarians and meat eaters.* N-COUNT: supp N

**eat|ery** /iːtəri/ **(eateries)** An **eatery** is a place where you can buy and eat food. [JOURNALISM] ❑ *...one of the most elegant old eateries in town.* N-COUNT

**eat|ing ap|ple (eating apples)** An **eating apple** is an ordinary apple that is usually eaten raw rather than cooked. N-COUNT ≠cooking apple

**eau de co|logne** /oʊ də kəloʊn/ also **eau de Cologne. Eau de cologne** is a fairly weak, sweet-smelling perfume. N-UNCOUNT = cologne

**eaves** /iːvz/ The **eaves** of a house are the lower edges of its roof. → See picture on page 1705. ❑ *There were icicles hanging from the eaves.* N-PLURAL

**eaves|drop** /iːvzdrɒp/ **(eavesdrops, eavesdropping, eavesdropped)** If you **eavesdrop on** someone, you listen secretly to what they are saying. ❑ *The government illegally eavesdropped on his telephone conversations... The housemaid eavesdropped from behind the kitchen door.* VERB = listen in; V on n; V
♦ **eaves|drop|ping** *...foreign electronic eavesdropping on army communications.* N-UNCOUNT ♦ **eaves|drop|per (eavesdroppers)** *Modern technology enables eavesdroppers to pick up conversations through windows or walls.* N-COUNT

**ebb** /eb/ **(ebbs, ebbing, ebbed)** 1 When the tide or the sea **ebbs**, its level gradually falls. ❑ *When the tide ebbs it's a rock pool inhabited by crustaceans.* VERB; V 2 **The ebb** or the **ebb** tide is one of the regular periods, usually two per day, when the sea gradually falls to a lower level as the tide moves away from the land. ❑ *...the spring ebb tide.* N-COUNT: usu the N 3 If someone's life, support, or feeling **ebbs**, it becomes weaker and gradually disappears. [FORMAL] ❑ *Were there occasions when enthusiasm ebbed?* VERB; V
♦ **Ebb away** means the same as **ebb**. ❑ *Their popular support is ebbing away.* PHRASAL VERB V P
PHRASES 4 If someone or something is **at a low ebb** or **at** their **lowest ebb**, they are not being very successful or profitable. ❑ *...a time when everyone is tired and at a low ebb.* PHRASE: v-link PHR 5 You can use **ebb and flow** to describe the way that something repeatedly increases and decreases or rises and falls. ❑ *...the ebb and flow of feeling and moods.* PHRASE: usu PHR of n

**eb|ony** /ebəni/ 1 **Ebony** is a very hard, heavy, dark-coloured wood. ❑ *...a small ebony cabinet.* N-UNCOUNT: oft N n 2 Something that is **ebony** is a very deep black colour. [LITERARY] ❑ *He had rich, soft ebony hair.* ADJ

**e-book (e-books)** An **e-book** is a book which is produced for reading on a computer screen. **E-book** is an abbreviation for 'electronic book'. ❑ *The new e-books will include a host of Rough Guide titles.* N-COUNT

**ebul|lient** /ɪbʌliənt, -bʊl-/ If you describe someone as **ebullient**, you mean that they are lively and full of enthusiasm or excitement about something. [FORMAL] ❑ *...the ebullient Russian President.* ADJ ♦ **ebul|lience** /ɪbʌliəns, -bʊl-/ *His natural ebullience began to return.* N-UNCOUNT

**e-business (e-businesses)** 1 An **e-business** is a business which uses the Internet to sell goods or services, especially one which does not also have shops or offices that people can visit or phone. [BUSINESS] N-COUNT 2 **E-business** is the buying, selling, and ordering of goods and services using the Internet. [BUSINESS] ❑ *...proven e-business solutions.* N-UNCOUNT: oft N n

**ec|cen|tric** /ɪksentrɪk/ **(eccentrics)** If you say that someone is **eccentric**, you mean that they behave in a strange way, and have habits or opinions that are different from those of most people. ❑ *He is an eccentric character who likes wearing a beret and dark glasses.* ADJ = odd ♦ An **eccentric** is an eccentric person. ❑ *On first impressions it would be easy to dismiss Duke as an eccentric.* N-COUNT ♦ **ec|cen|tri|cal|ly** /ɪksentrɪkli/ *...painters, eccentrically dressed and already half drunk.* ADV

**ec|cen|tri|city** /eksentrɪsɪti/ **(eccentricities)** 1 **Eccentricity** is unusual behaviour that other people consider strange. ❑ *She is unusual to the point of eccentricity.* N-UNCOUNT 2 **Eccentricities** are ways of behaving that people think are strange, or habits or opinions that are different from those of most people. ❑ *We all have our eccentricities.* N-COUNT: usu pl, oft with poss = peculiarity

**ec|cle|si|as|tic** /ɪkliːziæstɪk/ **(ecclesiastics)** An **ecclesiastic** is a priest or clergyman in the Christian Church. [FORMAL] N-COUNT

**ec|cle|si|as|ti|cal** /ɪkliːziæstɪkᵊl/ **Ecclesiastical** means belonging to or connected with the Christian Church. ❑ *My ambition was to travel upwards in the ecclesiastical hierarchy.* ADJ: usu ADJ n

**ECG (ECGs** /iː siː dʒiː/**) ECG** is an abbreviation for **electrocardiogram**. N-VAR

**eche|lon** /eʃəlɒn/ **(echelons)** An **echelon** in an organization or society is a level or rank in it. [FORMAL] ❑ *...the lower echelons of society.* N-COUNT: usu adj N, oft N of n

**echo** /ekoʊ/ **(echoes, echoing, echoed)** 1 An **echo** is a sound which is caused by a noise being reflected off a surface such as a wall. ❑ *He heard nothing but the echoes of his own voice.* ◆◇◇ N-COUNT: oft N of n 2 If a sound **echoes**, it is reflected off a surface and can be heard again after the original sound has stopped. ❑ *His feet echoed on the bare board floor... The bang came suddenly, echoing across the buildings, shattering glass.* VERB = reverberate; V; V prep/adv 3 In a place that **echoes**, a sound is reflected off a surface, and is repeated after the original sound has stopped. ❑ *The room echoed... The corridor echoed with the barking of a dozen dogs. ...the bare stone floors and the echoing hall.* VERB; V; V with/in n; V-ing 4 If you **echo** someone's words, you repeat them or express agreement with their attitude or opinion. ❑ *Their views often echo each other.* VERB; V n 5 A detail or feature which reminds you of something else can be referred to as an **echo**. ❑ *The accident has echoes of past disasters.* N-COUNT: usu N of n 6 If one thing **echoes** another, the first is a copy of a particular detail or feature of the other. ❑ *Pinks and beiges were chosen to echo the colours of the ceiling.* VERB = repeat; V n 7 If something **echoes**, it continues to be discussed and remains important or influential in a particular situation or among a particular group of people. ❑ *The old fable continues to echo down the centuries.* VERB; V prep

**echo|lo|ca|tion** /ekoʊloʊkeɪʃᵊn/ also **echo-location. Echolocation** is a system used by some animals to determine the position of an object by measuring how long it takes for an echo to return from the object. [TECHNICAL] ❑ *Most bats navigate by echolocation.* N-UNCOUNT

**éclair** /ɪkleəʳ, AM eɪk-/ **(éclairs)** also **eclair.** An **éclair** is a long thin cake made of very light pastry, which is filled with cream and usually has chocolate on top. N-COUNT

**ec|lec|tic** /ɪklektɪk/ An **eclectic** collection of objects, ideas, or beliefs is wide-ranging and comes from many different sources. [FORMAL] ❑ *...an eclectic collection of paintings, drawings, and prints.* ADJ = diverse

**ec|lec|ti|cism** /ɪklektɪsɪzəm/ **Eclecticism** is the principle or practice of choosing or involving objects, ideas, and beliefs from many different sources. [FORMAL] ❑ *...her cultural eclecticism.* N-UNCOUNT: usu with supp

**eclipse** /ɪklɪps/ **(eclipses, eclipsing, eclipsed)** 1 An **eclipse of** the sun is an occasion when the moon is between the earth and the sun, so that for a short time you cannot see part or all of the sun. An **eclipse of** the moon is an occasion when the earth is between the sun and the moon, so that for a short time you cannot see part or all of the moon. ❑ *...an eclipse of the sun. ...the total lunar eclipse.* N-COUNT: usu with supp, oft adj N, N of n 2 If one thing **is eclipsed by** a second VERB thing that is bigger, newer, or more important than it, the first thing is no longer noticed because the second thing gets all the attention. ❑ *The gramophone had been eclipsed by new technology such as the compact disc.* = overshadow be V-ed

**eco-** /iːkoʊ-/ **Eco-** combines with nouns and adjectives to form other nouns and adjectives which describe something as being related to ecology. ❑ *...the eco-horror of the North Sea oil spill.* PREFIX

**eco-friendly** **Eco-friendly** products or services are less harmful to the environment than other similar products or services. ❑ *...eco-friendly washing powder.* ADJ: oft ADJ n

**eco|logi|cal** /iːkəlɒdʒɪkəl/ 1 **Ecological** means involved with or concerning ecology. ❑ *Large dams have harmed Siberia's delicate ecological balance.* ♦ **eco|logi|cal|ly** /iːkəlɒdʒɪkli/ *It is very economical to run and ecologically sound.* 2 **Ecological** groups, movements, and people are concerned with preserving the environment and natural resources, so that they can be used in a sensible way, rather than being wasted. ❑ *Ecological groups say that nothing is being done to tackle the problem.* ADJ: ADJ n / ADV / ADJ: ADJ n

**ecolo|gist** /ɪkɒlədʒɪst/ **(ecologists)** 1 An **ecologist** is a person who studies ecology. ❑ *Ecologists argue that the benefits of treating sewage with disinfectants are doubtful.* 2 An **ecologist** is a person who believes that the environment and natural resources should be preserved and used in a sensible way, rather than being wasted. ❑ *In the opinion polls the ecologists reached 20 per cent.* N-COUNT / N-COUNT

**ecol|ogy** /ɪkɒlədʒi/ **(ecologies)** 1 **Ecology** is the study of the relationships between plants, animals, people, and their environment, and the balances between these relationships. ❑ *...a senior lecturer in ecology.* 2 When you talk about the **ecology** of a place, you are referring to the pattern and balance of relationships between plants, animals, people, and the environment in that place. ❑ *...the ecology of the rocky Negev desert in Israel.* N-UNCOUNT / N-VAR: usu with supp

**e-commerce** **E-commerce** is the same as **e-business**. [BUSINESS] ❑ *...the anticipated explosion of e-commerce.* N-UNCOUNT

**eco|nom|ic** /iːkənɒmɪk, ek-/ 1 **Economic** means concerned with the organization of the money, industry, and trade of a country, region, or society. ❑ *...Poland's radical economic reforms... The pace of economic growth is picking up.* ♦ **eco|nomi|cal|ly** /iːkənɒmɪkli, ek-/ *...an economically depressed area... Economically and politically, this affair couldn't come at a worse time.* 2 If something is **economic**, it produces a profit. ❑ *The new system may be more economic but will lead to a decline in programme quality.* ♦♦♦ ADJ: usu ADJ n / ADV: ADV adj/-ed, ADV after v, ADV with cl / ADJ = profitable

**eco|nomi|cal** /iːkənɒmɪkəl, ek-/ 1 Something that is **economical** does not require a lot of money to operate. For example a car that only uses a small amount of petrol is **economical**. ❑ *...plans to trade in their car for something smaller and more economical... It is more economical to wash a full load.* ♦ **eco|nomi|cal|ly** *Services could be operated more efficiently and economically.* 2 Someone who is **economical** spends money sensibly and does not want to waste it on things that are unnecessary. A way of life that is **economical** does not need a lot of money. ❑ *...ideas for economical housekeeping.* 3 **Economical** means using the minimum amount of time, effort, or language that is necessary. ❑ *His gestures were economical, his words generally mild.* ADJ: oft ADJ to-inf, it v-link ADJ to-inf / ADV: ADV after v / ADJ / ADJ: usu v-link ADJ

**eco|nom|ics** /iːkənɒmɪks, ek-/ 1 **Economics** is the study of the way in which money, industry, and trade are organized in a society. ❑ *He gained a first class Honours degree in economics.* → See also **home economics**. 2 The **economics** of a society or industry is the system of organizing money and trade in it. ❑ *...the economics of the third world.* ♦◇◇ N-UNCOUNT / N-UNCOUNT

**econo|mies of scale** **Economies of scale** are the financial advantages that a company gains when it produces large quantities of products. [BUSINESS] ❑ *Car firms are desperate to achieve economies of scale.* N-PLURAL

**econo|mist** /ɪkɒnəmɪst/ **(economists)** An **economist** is a person who studies, teaches, or writes about economics. ♦◇◇ N-COUNT

**econo|mize** /ɪkɒnəmaɪz/ **(economizes, economizing, economized)**

☑ in BRIT, also use **economise**

If you **economize**, you save money by spending it very carefully. ❑ *We're going to have to economize from now on... Hollywood has been talking about economizing on movie budgets.* VERB V / V on n

**econo|my** /ɪkɒnəmi/ **(economies)** 1 An **economy** is the system according to which the money, industry, and trade of a country or region are organized. ❑ *Zimbabwe boasts Africa's most industrialised economy.* 2 A country's **economy** is the wealth that it gets from business and industry. ❑ *The Japanese economy grew at an annual rate of more than 10 per cent.* 3 **Economy** is the use of the minimum amount of money, time, or other resources needed to achieve something, so that nothing is wasted. ❑ *...improvements in the fuel economy of cars.* 4 If you make **economies**, you try to save money by not spending money on unnecessary things. ❑ *They will make economies by hiring fewer part-time workers.* 5 **Economy** services such as travel are cheap and have no luxuries or extras. → see **economy class**. 6 **Economy** is used to describe large packs of goods which are cheaper than normal sized packs. ❑ *...an economy pack containing 150 assorted screws.* 7 If you describe an attempt to save money as **a false economy**, you mean that you have not saved any money as you will have to spend a lot more later. ❑ *A cheap bed can be a false economy.* ♦♦♦ N-COUNT / N-COUNT: usu the N in sing / N-UNCOUNT: with supp / N-COUNT: usu pl / ADJ: ADJ n / ADJ: ADJ n / PHRASE: v-link PHR

**econo|my class** On an aeroplane, an **economy class** ticket or seat is the cheapest available. ❑ *The price includes two economy class airfares from Brisbane to Los Angeles.* ADJ: ADJ n

**economy-class syn|drome** **Economy-class syndrome** is a serious medical condition caused by blood clots in the legs moving up to the lungs; used especially in connection with long-haul flights. ❑ *Lemon juice can help to prevent economy-class syndrome by improving circulation.* N-UNCOUNT

**eco|sys|tem** /iːkoʊsɪstəm, AM ekə-/ **(ecosystems)** An **ecosystem** is all the plants and animals that live in a particular area together with the complex relationship that exists between them and their environment. [TECHNICAL] ❑ *...the forest ecosystem.* N-COUNT

**eco-tourism** **Eco-tourism** is the business of providing holidays and related services which are not harmful to the environment of the area. [BUSINESS] ♦ **eco-tourist** **(eco-tourists)** ❑ *...an environmentally sensitive project to cater for eco-tourists.* N-UNCOUNT / N-COUNT

**eco-warrior** **(eco-warriors)** An **eco-warrior** is someone who spends a lot of time working actively for environmental causes. [BRIT, JOURNALISM] N-COUNT

**ecru** /eɪkruː/ Something that is **ecru** is pale, creamy white in colour. COLOUR

**ec|sta|sy** /ekstəsi/ **(ecstasies)** 1 **Ecstasy** is a feeling of very great happiness. ❑ *...a state of almost religious ecstasy.* 2 **Ecstasy** is an illegal drug which makes people feel happy and energetic. 3 If you are **in ecstasy** about something, you are very excited about it. If you go **into ecstasies**, you become very excited. ❑ *My father was in ecstasy when I won my scholarship... She went into ecstasies over actors.* N-VAR / N-UNCOUNT / PHRASE: N inflects

**ec|stat|ic** /ekstætɪk/ 1 If you are **ecstatic**, you feel very happy and full of excitement. ❑ *His wife gave birth to their first child, and he was ecstatic about it... They were greeted by the cheers of an ecstatic crowd.* ♦ **ec|stati|cal|ly** /ekstætɪkli/ *We are both ecstatically happy.* 2 You can use **ecstatic** ADJ = delirious / ADV / ADJ: ADJ n to describe reactions that are very enthusiastic and excited. For example, if someone receives an **ecstatic** reception or an **ecstatic** welcome, they are greeted with great enthusiasm and excitement. ❑ *They gave an ecstatic reception to the speech.* = *rapturous*

**ec|top|ic** /ektɒpɪk/ An **ectopic** pregnancy occurs when a fertilized egg becomes implanted outside a woman's womb, for example in one of her fallopian tubes. ADJ: usu ADJ n

**ecu|meni|cal** /iːkjuːmenɪkᵊl, ek-/ **Ecumenical** activities, ideas, and movements try to unite different Christian Churches. [FORMAL] ❑ *...ecumenical church services.* ADJ: usu ADJ n

**ecu|men|ism** /ɪkjuːmenɪzəm/ **Ecumenism** is the belief that the different Christian Churches should be as united as possible, and can also be used to refer to actions based on this belief. [FORMAL] N-UNCOUNT

**ec|ze|ma** /eksmə, AM ɪgziːmə/ **Eczema** is a skin disease which makes your skin itch and become sore, rough, and broken. N-UNCOUNT

**-ed**

> Pronounced /-ɪd/ after /t/ or /d/, and /-t/ after one of the following sounds: /p, f, θ, s, tʃ, ʃ, k/. In other cases, it is pronounced /-d/.

1 **-ed** is added to verbs to form their past tense or their past participle. If the verb ends in e, one of the e's is dropped. If the verb ends in y, the y is usually changed to i. ❑ *I posted the letter... He danced well... 'I quite understand,' he replied.* SUFFIX 2 **-ed** is added to nouns to form adjectives that describe someone or something as having a particular feature or features. ❑ *...a fat, bearded man. ...coloured flags.* SUFFIX 3 **-ed** is added to nouns or verbs combined with other words, to form compound adjectives. ❑ *...a cone-shaped container... He wore green-tinted glasses.* SUFFIX

**ed. (eds) ed.** is a written abbreviation for **editor**.

**eddy** /edi/ **(eddies)** An **eddy** is a movement in water or in the air which goes round and round instead of flowing in one continuous direction. N-COUNT

**edge** /edʒ/ **(edges, edging, edged)** ◆◆◇ 1 The **edge** of something is the place or line where it stops, or the part of it that is furthest from the middle. ❑ *We were on a hill, right on the edge of town... She was standing at the water's edge.* N-COUNT: usu with supp 2 The **edge** of something sharp such as a knife or an axe is its sharp or narrow side. ❑ *...the sharp edge of the sword.* N-COUNT: usu with supp 3 If someone or something **edges** somewhere, they move very slowly in that direction. ❑ *He edged closer to the telephone, ready to grab it.* VERB V prep/adv 4 **The edge of** something, especially something bad, is the point at which it may start to happen. ❑ *They have driven the rhino to the edge of extinction.* N-SING: usu *the* N *of* n = *verge, brink* 5 If someone or something has an **edge**, they have an advantage that makes them stronger or more likely to be successful than another thing or person. ❑ *The three days France have to prepare could give them the edge over England... Through superior production techniques they were able to gain the competitive edge.* N-SING: oft N *over* n, N *in* n/-ing = *advantage* 6 If you say that someone or something has **an edge**, you mean that they have a powerful quality. ❑ *Featuring new bands gives the show an edge... Greene's stories had an edge of realism.* N-SING: *a* N 7 If someone's voice has an **edge to** it, it has a sharp, bitter, or emotional quality. ❑ *But underneath the humour is an edge of bitterness.* N-SING: oft N *of* n, N *to* n 8 → See also **cutting edge**, **knife-edge**, **leading edge**.

**PHRASES** 9 If you or your nerves are **on edge**, you are tense, nervous, and unable to relax. ❑ *My nerves were constantly on edge.* PHRASE: usu v-link PHR 10 If you say that someone is **on the edge of** their **seat** or **chair**, you mean that they are very interested in what is happening or what is going to happen. PHRASE: N inflects, usu v-link PHR, v PHR 11 If something **takes the edge off** a situation, usually an unpleasant one, it weakens its effect or intensity. ❑ *A spell of poor health took the edge off her performance.* PHRASE: V inflects, PHR n 12 to **set** your **teeth on edge** → see **tooth**.

♦ **edge out** If someone **edges out** someone else, they just manage to beat them or get in front of them in a game, race, or contest. ❑ *France edged out the British team by less than a second... McGregor's effort was enough to edge Johnson out of the top spot.* PHRASAL VERB V P n (not pron) V n P *of* n Also V n P

**edged** /edʒd/ If something is **edged with** a particular thing, that thing forms a border around it. ❑ *...a large lawn edged with flowers and shrubs.* ADJ: v-link ADJ *with/in* n ♦ **Edged** is also a combining form. ❑ *...a lace-edged handkerchief.* COMB in ADJ

**-edged** /-edʒd/ **-edged** combines with words such as 'sharp', 'raw', and 'dark' to form adjectives which indicate that something such as a play or a piece of writing is very powerful or critical. [JOURNALISM] ❑ *...a sharp-edged satire that puts the Hollywood system under the microscope. ...the raw-edged vitality and daring of these works.* → See also **edge**, **edged**, **hard-edged**. COMB in ADJ

**edge|ways** /edʒweɪz/

> The spelling **edgewise** /edʒwaɪz/ is also used, especially in American English.

If you say that you **cannot get a word in edgeways**, you are complaining that you do not have the opportunity to speak because someone else is talking so much. [INFORMAL] ❑ *He spent all the time talking and they could not get a word in edgeways.* PHRASE: V inflects [disapproval]

**edg|ing** /edʒɪŋ/ **(edgings)** **Edging** is something that is put along the borders or sides of something else, usually to make it look attractive. ❑ *...the satin edging on Randall's blanket.* N-VAR

**edgy** /edʒi/ **(edgier, edgiest)** If someone is **edgy**, they are nervous and anxious, and seem likely to lose control of themselves. [INFORMAL] ❑ *She was nervous and edgy, still chain-smoking.* ADJ = *uptight, tense*

**ed|ible** /edɪbᵊl/ If something is **edible**, it is safe to eat and not poisonous. ❑ *...edible fungi.* ADJ ≠ *inedible*

**edict** /iːdɪkt/ **(edicts)** An **edict** is a command or instruction given by someone in authority. [FORMAL] ❑ *He issued an edict that none of his writings be destroyed.* N-COUNT: oft N that, N *against* n

**edi|fi|ca|tion** /edɪfɪkeɪʃᵊn/ If something is done for your **edification**, it is done to benefit you in some way, for example by teaching you about something. [FORMAL] ❑ *Demonstrations, films, and videotapes are shown for your edification.* N-UNCOUNT: oft with poss

**edi|fice** /edɪfɪs/ **(edifices)** An **edifice** is a large and impressive building. [FORMAL] ❑ *The American consulate was a magnificent edifice in the centre of Bordeaux.* N-COUNT

**edi|fy|ing** /edɪfaɪɪŋ/ 1 If you describe something as **edifying**, you mean that it benefits you in some way, for example by teaching you about something. [FORMAL] ❑ *In the 18th century art was seen, along with music and poetry, as something edifying.* ADJ = *instructive* 2 You say that something is not very **edifying** when you want to express your disapproval or dislike of it, or to suggest that there is something unpleasant or unacceptable about it. ❑ *It all brought back memories of a not very edifying past.* ADJ: with brd-neg [disapproval]

**edit** /edɪt/ **(edits, editing, edited)** ◆◇◇ 1 If you **edit** a text such as an article or a book, you correct and adapt it so that it is suitable for publishing. ❑ *The majority of contracts give the publisher the right to edit a book after it's done. ...an edited version of the speech.* VERB V n V-ed ♦ **edit|ing** *Throughout the editing of this book, we have had much support and encouragement.* N-UNCOUNT 2 If you **edit** a book or a series of books, you collect several pieces of writing by different authors and prepare them for publishing. ❑ *This collection of essays is edited by Ellen Knight... She has edited the media studies quarterly, Screen. ...the Real Sandwich Book, edited by Miriam Polunin.* VERB *be* V-ed *by* n V n V-ed ♦ **edit|ing** *He was certainly not cut out to combine the jobs of editing and writing as a journalist.* N-UNCOUNT 3 If you **edit** a film or a television or radio programme, you choose some of what has been filmed or recorded VERB

and arrange it in a particular order. ❑ *He taught me to edit and splice film... He is editing together excerpts of some of his films.* ♦ **edit|ing** *He sat in on much of the filming and early editing.* [4] Someone who **edits** a newspaper, magazine, or journal is in charge of it. ❑ *I used to edit the college paper in the old days.* [5] An **edit** is the process of examining and correcting a text so that it is suitable for publishing. ❑ *The purpose of the edit is fairly simple – to chop out the boring bits from the original.*
V n; V n with together; N-UNCOUNT; VERB; V n; N-COUNT

♦ **edit out** If you **edit** something **out of** a book or film, you remove it, often because it might be offensive to some people. ❑ *His voice will be edited out of the final film... She edited that line out again.*
PHRASAL VERB = cut; V P n (not pron); V n P

**edi|tion** /ɪdɪʃᵊn/ **(editions)** [1] An **edition** is a particular version of a book, magazine, or newspaper that is printed at one time. ❑ *A paperback edition is now available at bookshops.* [2] An **edition** is the total number of copies of a particular book or newspaper that are printed at one time. ❑ *The second edition was published only in America.* [3] An **edition** is a single television or radio programme that is one of a series about a particular subject. ❑ *They appeared on an edition of BBC2's Arena.*
◆◆◇ N-COUNT: usu supp N; N-COUNT: usu supp N; N-COUNT: with supp = episode

**edi|tor** /edɪtəʳ/ **(editors)** [1] An **editor** is the person who is in charge of a newspaper or magazine and who decides what will be published in each edition of it. [2] An **editor** is a journalist who is responsible for a particular section of a newspaper or magazine. ❑ *Cookery Editor Moyra Fraser takes you behind the scenes.* [3] An **editor** is a person who checks and corrects texts before they are published. ❑ *Your role as editor is important, for you can look at a piece of writing objectively.* [4] An **editor** is a radio or television journalist who reports on a particular type of news. ❑ *...our economics editor, Dominic Harrod.* [5] An **editor** is a person who prepares a film, or a radio or television programme, by selecting some of what has been filmed or recorded and putting it in a particular order. ❑ *She worked at 20th Century Fox as a film editor.* [6] An **editor** is a person who collects pieces of writing by different authors and prepares them for publication in a book or a series of books. ❑ *Michael Rosen is the editor of the anthology.* [7] An **editor** is a computer program that enables you to change and correct stored data. [COMPUTING]
◆◆◇ N-COUNT; N-COUNT: supp N; N-COUNT; N-COUNT: supp N; N-COUNT; N-COUNT; N-COUNT

**edi|to|rial** /edɪtɔːriəl/ **(editorials)** [1] **Editorial** means involved in preparing a newspaper, magazine, or book for publication. ❑ *He has been on the editorial staff of 'Private Eye' since 1963... I went to the editorial board meetings when I had the time.* ♦ **edi|to|ri|al|ly** *Rosie Boycott was not involved editorially with Virago.* [2] **Editorial** means involving the attitudes, opinions, and contents of something such as a newspaper, magazine, or television programme. ❑ *We are not about to change our editorial policy.* ♦ **edi|to|ri|al|ly** *Editorially, they never really became a unique distinct product.* [3] An **editorial** is an article in a newspaper which gives the opinion of the editor or owner on a topic or item of news. ❑ *In an editorial, The Independent suggests the victory could turn nasty.*
◆◇◇ ADJ: ADJ n; ADV; ADJ: ADJ n; ADV: usu ADV after v, ADV with cl; N-COUNT

**edi|to|ri|al|ize** /edɪtɔːriəlaɪz/ **(editorializes, editorializing, editorialized)**

✔ in BRIT, also use **editorialise**

If someone **editorializes**, they express their opinion about something rather than just stating facts; mainly used in contexts where you are talking about journalists and newspapers. ❑ *Other papers have editorialized, criticizing the Czech government for rushing to judgment on this individual.*
VERB; V

**edi|tor|ship** /edɪtəʳʃɪp/ **(editorships)** The **editorship of** a newspaper or magazine is the position of its editor, or his or her work as its editor. ❑ *Under his editorship, the Economist has introduced regular sports coverage.*
N-VAR: oft poss N, N of n

**edu|cate** /edʒʊkeɪt/ **(educates, educating, educated)** [1] When someone, especially a child, **is educated**, he or she is taught at a school or college. ❑ *He was educated at Haslingden Grammar School.* [2] To **educate** people means to teach them better ways of doing something or a better way of living. ❑ *Drinkwise Day is mainly designed to educate people about the destructive effects of alcohol abuse.*
VERB: usu passive; be V-ed; VERB = inform; V n

**edu|cat|ed** /edʒʊkeɪtɪd/ Someone who is **educated** has a high standard of learning. ❑ *He is an educated, amiable and decent man.*
ADJ = learned

**-educated** /-edʒʊkeɪtɪd/ [1] **-educated** combines with nouns and adjectives to form adjectives indicating where someone was educated. ❑ *...the Oxford-educated son of a Liverpool merchant. ...an American-educated lawyer.* [2] **-educated** combines with adverbs to form adjectives indicating how much education someone has had and how good it was. ❑ *Many of the immigrants are well-educated. ...impoverished, undernourished, and ill-educated workers.*
COMB in ADJ; COMB in ADJ

**edu|cat|ed guess** **(educated guesses)** An **educated guess** is a guess which is based on a certain amount of knowledge and is therefore likely to be correct. ❑ *Estimating the right cooking time will always be an educated guess.*
N-COUNT

**edu|ca|tion** /edʒʊkeɪʃᵊn/ **(educations)** [1] **Education** involves teaching people various subjects, usually at a school or college, or being taught. ❑ *They're cutting funds for education.* [2] **Education** of a particular kind involves teaching the public about a particular issue. ❑ *...better health education.* [3] → See also **adult education, further education, higher education.**
◆◆◇ N-VAR; N-UNCOUNT: usu with supp

**edu|ca|tion|al** /edʒʊkeɪʃənᵊl/ [1] **Educational** matters or institutions are concerned with or relate to education. ❑ *...the British educational system. ...pupils with special educational needs.* ♦ **edu|ca|tion|al|ly** *...educationally sound ideas for managing classrooms.* [2] An **educational** experience teaches you something. ❑ *The staff should make sure the kids have an enjoyable and educational day.*
◆◇◇ ADJ: usu ADJ n; ADV; ADJ = instructive

**edu|ca|tion|al|ist** /edʒʊkeɪʃənəlɪst/ **(educationalists)** An **educationalist** is someone who is specialized in the theories and methods of education. [BRIT]
N-COUNT

✔ in AM, use **educator**

**edu|ca|tion|al psy|chol|ogy** **Educational psychology** is the area of psychology that is concerned with the study and assessment of teaching methods, and with helping individual pupils who have educational problems. ♦ **edu|ca|tion|al psy|cholo|gist** **(educational psychologists)** ❑ *An assessment by an independent educational psychologist was essential.*
N-UNCOUNT; N-COUNT

**edu|ca|tion|ist** /edʒʊkeɪʃənɪst/ **(educationists)** An **educationist** is the same as an **educationalist**. [BRIT]
N-COUNT

**edu|ca|tive** /edʒʊkətɪv, AM -keɪt-/ Something that has an **educative** role teaches you something. [FORMAL] ❑ *...the educative value of allowing broadcasters into their courts.*
ADJ

**edu|ca|tor** /edʒʊkeɪtəʳ/ **(educators)** [1] An **educator** is a person who educates people. [AM; also BRIT, FORMAL] [2] An **educator** is someone who is specialized in the theories and methods of education. [mainly AM]
N-COUNT = teacher; N-COUNT

✔ in BRIT, use **educationalist**

**edu|tain|ment** /edʒʊteɪnmənt/ People use **edutainment** to refer to things such as computer games which are designed to be entertaining and educational at the same time. ❑ *...the increased demand for edutainment software.*
N-UNCOUNT

**Ed|ward|ian** /edwɔːdiən/ **Edwardian** means belonging to, connected with, or typical of Britain in the first decade of the 20th century, when Edward VII was King. ❑ *...the Edwardian era.*
ADJ: usu ADJ n

**eel** /iːl/ **(eels)** An **eel** is a long, thin fish that looks like a snake. ♦ **Eel** is the flesh of this fish which is eaten as food. ❑ *...smoked eel.* N-VAR N-UNCOUNT

**eerie** /ɪəri/ **(eerier, eeriest)** If you describe something as **eerie**, you mean that it seems strange and frightening, and makes you feel nervous. ❑ *I walked down the eerie dark path. ...an eerie calm.* ♦ **eeri|ly** /ɪərɪli/ *Monrovia after the fighting is eerily quiet.* ADJ ADV

**ef|face** /ɪfeɪs/ **(effaces, effacing, effaced)** To **efface** something means to destroy or remove it so that it cannot be seen any more. [FORMAL] ❑ *...an event that has helped efface the country's traditional image.* ➔ See also **self-effacing**. VERB V n

**ef|fect** /ɪfekt/ **(effects, effecting, effected)** ◆◆◆
1 The **effect of** one thing **on** another is the change that the first thing causes in the second thing. ❑ *Parents worry about the effect of music on their adolescent's behavior... Even minor head injuries can cause long-lasting psychological effects.* N-VAR: oft N *of/on* n, N *of* -ing, adj N
2 An **effect** is an impression that someone creates deliberately, for example in a place or in a piece of writing. ❑ *The whole effect is cool, light and airy.* N-COUNT = impression
3 A person's **effects** are the things that they have with them at a particular time, for example when they are arrested or admitted to hospital, or the things that they owned when they died. [FORMAL] ❑ *His daughters were collecting his effects.* N-PLURAL: with poss = belongings
4 The **effects** in a film are the specially created sounds and scenery. N-PLURAL
5 If you **effect** something that you are trying to achieve, you succeed in causing it to happen. [FORMAL] ❑ *Prospects for effecting real political change seemed to have taken a major step backwards.* VERB V n
6 ➔ See also **greenhouse effect**, **placebo effect**, **ripple effect**, **side-effect**, **sound effect**, **special effect**.
PHRASES
7 If you say that someone is doing something **for effect**, you mean that they are doing it in order to impress people and to draw attention to themselves. ❑ *The Cockney accent was put on for effect.* PHRASE: PHR after v
8 You add **in effect** to a statement or opinion that is not precisely accurate, but which you feel is a reasonable description or summary of a particular situation. ❑ *That deal would create, in effect, the world's biggest airline.* PHRASE: PHR with cl [vagueness] = effectively
9 If you **put**, **bring**, or **carry** a plan or idea **into effect**, you cause it to happen in practice. ❑ *These and other such measures ought to have been put into effect in 1985.* PHRASE: V inflects = implement
10 If a law or policy **takes effect** or **comes into effect** at a particular time, it officially begins to apply or be valid from that time. If it **remains in effect**, it still applies or is still valid. ❑ *...the ban on new logging permits which will take effect from July... The decision was taken yesterday and will remain in effect until further government instructions.* PHRASE: V inflects
11 You can say that something **takes effect** when it starts to produce the results that are intended. ❑ *The second injection should only have been given once the first drug had taken effect.* PHRASE: V inflects
12 You use **effect** in expressions such as **to good effect** and **to no effect** in order to indicate how successful or impressive an action is. ❑ *Mr Morris feels the museum is using advertising to good effect.* PHRASE: PHR after v
13 You use **to this effect**, **to that effect**, or **to the effect that** to indicate that you have given or are giving a summary of something that was said or written, and not the actual words used. ❑ *A circular to this effect will be issued in the next few weeks.* PHRASE: n PHR
14 If you say that something will happen **with immediate effect** or **with effect from** a particular time, you mean that it will begin to apply or be valid immediately or from the stated time. [BRIT, mainly FORMAL] ❑ *The price of the Saturday edition is going up with effect from 3 November.* PHRASE: PHR after v
15 **cause and effect** ➔ see **cause**.

**ef|fec|tive** /ɪfektɪv/ ◆◆◇
1 Something that is **effective** works well and produces the results that were intended. ❑ *The project looks at how we could be more effective in encouraging students to enter teacher training... Simple antibiotics are effective against this organism. ...an effective public transport system.* ♦ **ef|fec|tive|ly** *...the team roles which you believe to be necessary for the team to function effectively... Services need to be more effectively organised than they are at present.* ♦ **ef|fec|tive|ness** *...the effectiveness of computers as an educational tool.* ADJ: oft ADJ *in* -ing, ADJ *against* n; ADV: usu ADV after v, also ADV -ed; N-UNCOUNT: oft N *of* n
2 **Effective** means having a particular role or result in practice, though not officially or in theory. ❑ *They have had effective control of the area since the security forces left.* ADJ: ADJ n
3 When something such as a law or an agreement becomes **effective**, it begins officially to apply or be valid. ❑ *The new rules will become effective in the next few days.* ADJ: v-link ADJ

**ef|fec|tive|ly** /ɪfektɪvli/ You use **effectively** with a statement or opinion to indicate that it is not accurate in every detail, but that you feel it is a reasonable description or summary of a particular situation. ❑ *The region was effectively independent.* ADV: usu ADV before v, also ADV adj

**ef|fec|tual** /ɪfektʃuəl/ If an action or plan is **effectual**, it succeeds in producing the results that were intended. [FORMAL] ❑ *This is the only effectual way to secure our present and future happiness.* ADJ = effective ≠ ineffectual

**ef|femi|nate** /ɪfemɪnət/ If you describe a man or boy as **effeminate**, you think he behaves, looks, or sounds like a woman or girl. ❑ *...a skinny, effeminate guy in lipstick and earrings.* ADJ [disapproval] ≠ manly

**ef|fer|ves|cent** /efəʳvesᵊnt/
1 An **effervescent** liquid is one that contains or releases bubbles of gas. ❑ *...an effervescent mineral water.* ADJ
2 If you describe someone as **effervescent**, you mean that they are lively, entertaining, enthusiastic, and exciting. ❑ *...an effervescent blonde actress.* ♦ **ef|fer|ves|cence** *He wrote about Gillespie's effervescence, magnetism and commitment.* ADJ [approval] = bubbly, vivacious; N-UNCOUNT

**ef|fete** /ɪfiːt/ If you describe someone as **effete**, you are criticizing them for being weak and powerless. [FORMAL] ❑ *...the charming but effete Russian gentry of the 1840s and 1850s.* ADJ [disapproval]

**ef|fi|ca|cious** /efɪkeɪʃəs/ Something that is **efficacious** is effective. [FORMAL] ❑ *The nasal spray was new on the market and highly efficacious.* ADJ = effective

**ef|fi|ca|cy** /efɪkəsi/ If you talk about the **efficacy** of something, you are talking about its effectiveness and its ability to do what it is supposed to. [FORMAL] ❑ *Recent medical studies confirm the efficacy of a healthier lifestyle.* N-UNCOUNT: usu with poss

**ef|fi|cien|cy** /ɪfɪʃᵊnsi/ **(efficiencies)**
1 **Efficiency** is the quality of being able to do a task successfully, without wasting time or energy. ❑ *There are many ways to increase agricultural efficiency in the poorer areas of the world. ...energy efficiency.* N-UNCOUNT
2 In physics and engineering, **efficiency** is the ratio between the amount of energy a machine needs to make it work, and the amount it produces. [TECHNICAL] N-UNCOUNT: also N in pl

**ef|fi|cient** /ɪfɪʃᵊnt/ ◆◇◇ If something or someone is **efficient**, they are able to do tasks successfully, without wasting time or energy. ❑ *With today's more efficient contraception women can plan their families and careers.* ♦ **ef|fi|cient|ly** *I work very efficiently and am decisive, and accurate in my judgement.* ADJ ADV

**ef|fi|gy** /efɪdʒi/ **(effigies)**
1 An **effigy** is a quickly and roughly made figure, often ugly or amusing, that represents someone you hate or feel contempt for. N-COUNT
2 An **effigy** is a statue or carving of a famous person. [FORMAL] N-COUNT

**eff|ing** /efɪŋ/ Some people use **effing** to emphasize a word or phrase, especially when they are feeling angry or annoyed. [BRIT, RUDE] ADJ: ADJ n [emphasis]

**ef|flu|ent** /efluənt/ **(effluents) Effluent** is liquid waste material that comes out of factories or sewage works. [FORMAL] ❑ *The effluent from the factory was dumped into the river.* N-MASS = waste

**ef|fort** /efəʳt/ **(efforts)** ◆◆◆
1 If you make an **effort to** do something, you try very hard to do it. ❑ *He made no effort to hide his disappointment... Finding a cure requires considerable time and effort. ...his efforts to reform Italian research... Despite the efforts of the United Nations, the problem of drug traffic con-* N-VAR: oft N to-inf

*tinues to grow... But a concerted effort has begun to improve the quality of the urban air.* [2] If you say that someone did something **with effort** or **with an effort**, you mean it was difficult for them to do. [WRITTEN] ❑ *She took a deep breath and sat up slowly and with great effort... With an effort she contained her irritation.* [3] An **effort** is a particular series of activities that is organized by a group of people in order to achieve something. ❑ *...a famine relief effort in Angola.* [4] If you say that something is **an effort**, you mean that an unusual amount of physical or mental energy is needed to do it. ❑ *Even carrying the camcorder while hiking in the forest was an effort.* [5] If you **make the effort to** do something, you do it, even though you need extra energy to do it or you do not really want to. ❑ *I don't get lonely now because I make the effort to see people.*

N-UNCOUNT: usu *with* N, also *a* N = *difficulty*; N-COUNT: usu supp N; N-SING: *a* N = *strain, struggle*; PHRASE: V inflects, oft PHR to-inf

**ef|fort|less** /efərtləs/ [1] Something that is **effortless** is done easily and well. ❑ *In a single effortless motion, he scooped Frannie into his arms.* ♦ **ef|fort|less|ly** *Her son Peter adapted effortlessly to his new surroundings.* [2] You use **effortless** to describe a quality that someone has naturally and does not have to learn. ❑ *She liked him above all for his effortless charm.*

ADJ: usu ADJ n = *easy*; ADV; ADJ: usu ADJ n

**ef|fron|tery** /ɪfrʌntəri/ **Effrontery** is behaviour that is bold, rude, or disrespectful. [FORMAL] ❑ *One could only gasp at the sheer effrontery of the man.*

N-UNCOUNT disapproval

**ef|fu|sion** /ɪfjuːʒᵊn/ **(effusions)** If someone expresses their emotions or ideas with **effusion**, they express them with more enthusiasm and for longer than is usual or expected. ❑ *I did not embarrass her with my effusions.*

N-VAR

**ef|fu|sive** /ɪfjuːsɪv/ If you describe someone as **effusive**, you mean that they express pleasure, gratitude, or approval in a very enthusiastic way. ❑ *He was effusive in his praise for the general.* ♦ **ef|fu|sive|ly** *She greeted them effusively.*

ADJ; ADV

**e-fit** /iːfɪt/ **(e-fits)** also **E-fit.** An **e-fit** is a computer-generated picture of someone who is suspected of a crime. Compare **identikit**, **Photo-fit**. ❑ *Police have released an E-fit picture of the suspected gunman.*

N-COUNT

**EFL** /iː ef el/ **EFL** is the teaching of English to people whose first language is not English. **EFL** is an abbreviation for 'English as a Foreign Language'. ❑ *...an EFL teacher.*

N-UNCOUNT: oft N n

**e.g.** /iː dʒiː/ **e.g.** is an abbreviation that means 'for example'. It is used before a noun, or to introduce another sentence. ❑ *We need helpers of all types, engineers, scientists (e.g. geologists) and teachers.*

**egali|tar|ian** /ɪgælɪteəriən/ **Egalitarian** means supporting or following the idea that all people are equal and should have the same rights and opportunities. ❑ *I still believe in the notion of an egalitarian society.*

ADJ

**egali|tari|an|ism** /ɪgælɪteəriənɪzəm/ **Egalitarianism** is used to refer to the belief that all people are equal and should have the same rights and opportunities, and to actions that are based on this belief.

N-UNCOUNT

**egg** /eg/ **(eggs, egging, egged)** [1] An **egg** is an oval object that is produced by a female bird and which contains a baby bird. Other animals such as reptiles and fish also lay eggs. ❑ *...a baby bird hatching from its egg. ...ant eggs.* [2] In Western countries, **eggs** often means hen's eggs, eaten as food. ❑ *Break the eggs into a shallow bowl and beat them lightly. ...bacon and eggs.* [3] **Egg** is used to refer to an object in the shape of a hen's egg. ❑ *...a chocolate egg.* [4] An **egg** is a cell that is produced in the bodies of female animals and humans. If it is fertilized by a sperm, a baby develops from it. ❑ *It only takes one sperm to fertilize an egg.* [5] → See also **Easter egg**, **nest egg**, **Scotch egg**.

◆◆◇ N-COUNT; N-VAR; N-COUNT: usu supp N; N-COUNT

PHRASES [6] If someone puts **all** their **eggs in one basket**, they put all their effort or resources into doing one thing so that, if it fails, they have no alternatives left. ❑ *The key word here is diversify; don't put all your eggs in one basket.* [7] If someone has **egg on** their **face** or has **egg all over** their **face**, they have been made to look foolish. ❑ *If they take this game lightly they could end up with egg on their faces.* [8] **a chicken and egg situation** → see **chicken**.

PHRASE: usu v PHR; PHRASE: *face* inflects, *have/with* PHR

♦ **egg on** If you **egg** a person **on**, you encourage them to do something, especially something dangerous or foolish. ❑ *He was lifting up handfuls of leaves and throwing them at her. She was laughing and egging him on... They egged each other on to argue and to fight.*

PHRASAL VERB; V n P; V n P to-inf

**egg cup** **(egg cups)** also **eggcup.** An **egg cup** is a small container in which you put a boiled egg while you eat it.

N-COUNT

**egg|head** /eghed/ **(eggheads)** If you think someone is more interested in ideas and theories than in practical actions you can say they are an **egghead**. [INFORMAL] ❑ *The Government was dominated by self-important eggheads.*

N-COUNT disapproval = *boffin*

**egg|nog** /egnɒg/ also **egg nog.** **Eggnog** is a drink made from egg, milk, sugar, spices, and alcohol such as rum or brandy.

N-UNCOUNT

**egg|plant** /egplɑːnt, -plænt/ **(eggplants)** An **eggplant** is a vegetable with a smooth, dark purple skin. [AM]

N-VAR

☑ in BRIT, use **aubergine**

**egg|shell** /egʃel/ **(eggshells)** also **egg shell.** An **eggshell** is the hard covering on the outside of an egg.

N-VAR

**egg tim|er** **(egg timers)** also **egg-timer.** An **egg timer** is a device that measures the time needed to boil an egg.

N-COUNT

**egg whisk** **(egg whisks)** An **egg whisk** is a piece of kitchen equipment used for mixing the different parts of an egg together.

N-COUNT

**ego** /iːgoʊ, egoʊ/ **(egos)** Someone's **ego** is their sense of their own worth. For example, if someone has a large **ego**, they think they are very important and valuable. ❑ *He had a massive ego, never would he admit he was wrong.* → See also **alter ego**, **super-ego**.

N-VAR

**ego|cen|tric** /iːgoʊsentrɪk, eg-/ Someone who is **egocentric** thinks only of themselves and their own wants, and does not consider other people. ❑ *He was egocentric, a man of impulse who expected those around him to serve him.*

ADJ disapproval = *self-centred*

**ego|ism** /iːgoʊɪzəm, eg-/ **Egoism** is the same as **egotism**.

N-UNCOUNT disapproval

**ego|ist** /iːgoʊɪst, eg-/ **(egoists)** An **egoist** is the same as an **egotist**.

N-COUNT disapproval

**ego|is|tic** /iːgoʊɪstɪk, eg-/ **Egoistic** means the same as **egotistic**.

ADJ disapproval

**ego|ma|ni|ac** /iːgoʊmeɪniæk, eg-/ **(egomaniacs)** An **egomaniac** is someone who thinks only of themselves and does not care if they harm other people in order to get what they want. ❑ *Adam is clever, but he's also something of an egomaniac.*

N-COUNT disapproval

**ego|tism** /iːgətɪzəm, eg-/ **Egotism** is the quality of being egotistic.

N-UNCOUNT

**ego|tist** /iːgətɪst, eg-/ **(egotists)** An **egotist** is someone who is egotistic.

N-COUNT disapproval

**ego|tis|tic** /iːgətɪstɪk, eg-/

☑ The form **egotistical** is also used.

Someone who is **egotistic** or **egotistical** behaves selfishly and thinks they are more important than other people. ❑ *Susan and Deborah share an intensely selfish, egotistic streak.*

ADJ disapproval = *self-centred*

**ego trip** **(ego trips)** If you say that someone is **on** an **ego trip**, you are criticizing them for doing something for their own satisfaction and enjoyment, often to show that they think they are more important than other people.

N-COUNT disapproval

**egre|gious** /ɪɡriːdʒəs/ **Egregious** means very bad indeed. [FORMAL] ❑ *...the most egregious abuses of human rights.* ADJ: usu ADJ n = *grievous*

**Egyp|tian** /ɪdʒɪpʃən/ **(Egyptians)** 1 **Egyptian** means belonging or relating to Egypt or to its people, language, or culture. ADJ 2 The **Egyptians** are the people who come from Egypt. N-COUNT 3 **Egyptian** means related to or connected with ancient Egypt. ❑ *...the Egyptian pharaoh.* ADJ 4 The **Egyptians** were the people who lived in ancient Egypt. N-COUNT

**eh** /eɪ/ **Eh** is used in writing to represent a noise that people make as a response in conversation, for example to express agreement or to ask for something to be explained or repeated. ❑ *Let's talk all about it outside, eh?... 'He's um ill in bed.' — 'Eh?' — 'He's ill in bed.'* CONVENTION

**eider|down** /aɪdəʳdaʊn/ **(eiderdowns)** An **eiderdown** is a bed covering, placed on top of sheets and blankets, that is filled with small soft feathers or warm material. [BRIT] N-COUNT = *quilt*

> ✔ in AM, usually use **comforter**

**eight** /eɪt/ **(eights) Eight** is the number 8. ❑ *So far eight workers have been killed.* ◆◆◆ NUM

**eight|een** /eɪtiːn/ **(eighteens) Eighteen** is the number 18. ❑ *He was employed by them for eighteen years.* ◆◆◆ NUM

**eight|eenth** /eɪtiːnθ/ The **eighteenth** item in a series is the one that you count as number eighteen. ❑ *The siege is now in its eighteenth day.* ◆◆◇ ORD

**eighth** /eɪtθ/ **(eighths)** 1 The **eighth** item in a series is the one that you count as number eight. ❑ *...the eighth prime minister of India.* ◆◆◇ ORD 2 An **eighth** is one of eight equal parts of something. ❑ *The Kuban produces an eighth of Russia's grain, meat and milk.* FRACTION

**eighth note (eighth notes)** An **eighth note** is a musical note that has a time value equal to half a quarter note. [AM] N-COUNT

> ✔ in BRIT, use **quaver**

**eighti|eth** /eɪtiəθ/ The **eightieth** item in a series is the one that you count as number eighty. ❑ *Mr Stevens recently celebrated his eightieth birthday.* ◆◆◇ ORD

**eighty** /eɪti/ **(eighties)** 1 **Eighty** is the number 80. ❑ *Eighty horses trotted up the road.* ◆◆◆ NUM 2 When you talk about the **eighties**, you are referring to numbers between 80 and 89. For example, if you are **in** your **eighties**, you are aged between 80 and 89. If the temperature is **in the eighties**, the temperature is between 80 and 89 degrees. ❑ *He was in his late eighties and had become the country's most respected elder statesman.* N-PLURAL 3 **The eighties** is the decade between 1980 and 1989. ❑ *He ran a property development business in the eighties.* N-PLURAL: the N

**eistedd|fod** /aɪstedfɒd, AM -vɑːd/ **(eisteddfods)** An **eisteddfod** is a Welsh festival at which competitions are held in music, poetry, drama, and art. N-COUNT

**either** /aɪðəʳ, iːðəʳ/ 1 You use **either** in front of the first of two or more alternatives, when you are stating the only possibilities or choices that there are. The other alternatives are introduced by 'or'. ❑ *Sightseeing is best done either by tour bus or by bicycles... The former President was demanding that he should be either put on trial or set free... Either she goes or I go.* ◆◆◆ CONJ 2 You use **either** in a negative statement in front of the first of two alternatives to indicate that the negative statement refers to both the alternatives. ❑ *There had been no indication of either breathlessness or any loss of mental faculties right until his death.* CONJ 3 You can use **either** to refer to one of two things, people, or situations, when you want to say that they are both possible and it does not matter which one is chosen or considered. ❑ *There were glasses of champagne and cigars, but not many of either were consumed.* PRON ♦ **Either** is also a quantifier. ❑ *Do either of you smoke or drink heavily?* QUANT ♦ **Either** is also a determiner. ❑ *I don't particularly agree with either group.* DET: DET sing-n 4 You use **either** in a negative statement to refer to each of two things, people, or situations to indicate that the negative statement includes both of them. ❑ *She warned me that I'd never marry or have children. — 'I don't want either.'* PRON: with brd-neg ♦ **Either** is also a quantifier. ❑ *There are no simple answers to either of those questions.* QUANT ♦ **Either** is also a determiner. ❑ *He sometimes couldn't remember either man's name.* DET 5 You use **either** by itself in negative statements to indicate that there is a similarity or connection with a person or thing that you have just mentioned. ❑ *He did not even say anything to her, and she did not speak to him either.* ADV: ADV after v, with brd-neg 6 When one negative statement follows another, you can use **either** at the end of the second one to indicate that you are adding an extra piece of information, and to emphasize that both are equally important. ❑ *Don't agree, but don't argue either.* ADV: ADV after v 7 You can use **either** to introduce a noun that refers to each of two things when you are talking about both of them. ❑ *The basketball nets hung down from the ceiling at either end of the gymnasium.* DET: DET sing-n

**ejacu|late** /ɪdʒækjʊleɪt/ **(ejaculates, ejaculating, ejaculated)** When a man **ejaculates**, sperm comes out through his penis. ❑ *... a tendency to ejaculate quickly.* VERB V ♦ **ejacu|la|tion** /ɪdʒækjʊleɪʃən/ **(ejaculations)** *Each male ejaculation will contain up to 300 million sperm.* N-VAR

**eject** /ɪdʒekt/ **(ejects, ejecting, ejected)** 1 If you **eject** someone **from** a place, you force them to leave. ❑ *Officials used guard dogs to eject the protesters... He was ejected from a restaurant.* VERB V n V n *from* n ♦ **ejec|tion** /ɪdʒekʃən/ **(ejections)** *...the ejection of hecklers from the meeting.* N-VAR = *expulsion* 2 To **eject** something means to remove it or push it out forcefully. ❑ *He aimed his rifle, fired a single shot, then ejected the spent cartridge.* VERB = *expel* V n 3 When a pilot **ejects from** an aircraft, he or she leaves the aircraft quickly using an ejector seat, usually because the plane is about to crash. ❑ *The pilot ejected from the plane and escaped injury.* VERB = *bail out* V *from* n Also V

**ejec|tor seat (ejector seats)** An **ejector seat** is a special seat which can throw the pilot out of a fast military aircraft in an emergency. N-COUNT

**eke** /iːk/ **(ekes, eking, eked)** If you **eke a living** or **eke out an existence**, you manage to survive with very little money. ❑ *That forced peasant farmers to try to eke a living off steep hillsides ... He was eking out an existence on a few francs a day.* PHRASE: V inflects

♦ **eke out** If you **eke out** something, you make your supply of it last as long as possible. ❑ *Many workers can only eke out their redundancy money for about 10 weeks.* PHRASAL VERB V P n (not pron) Also V n P

**elabo|rate (elaborates, elaborating, elaborated)**

> ✔ The adjective is pronounced /ɪlæbərət/. The verb is pronounced /ɪlæbəreɪt/.

1 You use **elaborate** to describe something that is very complex because it has a lot of different parts. ❑ *...an elaborate research project. ...an elaborate ceremony that lasts for eight days.* ADJ: usu ADJ n = *complicated* 2 **Elaborate** plans, systems, and procedures are complicated because they have been planned in very great detail, sometimes too much detail. ❑ *...elaborate efforts at the highest level to conceal the problem. ...an elaborate management training scheme for graduates.* ADJ: usu ADJ n = *complicated* ♦ **elabo|rate|ly** *It was clearly an elaborately planned operation.* ADV 3 **Elaborate** clothing or material is made with a lot of detailed artistic designs. ❑ *He is known for his elaborate costumes.* ADJ: usu ADJ n ♦ **elabo|rate|ly** *...elaborately costumed dolls.* ADV 4 If you **elaborate** a plan or theory, you develop it by making it more complicated and more effective. ❑ *His task was to elaborate policies which would make a market economy compatible with a clean environment.* VERB V n ♦ **elabo|ra|tion** /ɪlæbəreɪʃən/ *...the elaboration of specific policies and mechanisms.* N-UNCOUNT: oft N *of* n 5 If you **elaborate on** something that has been VERB

said, you say more about it, or give more details. ❑ *A spokesman declined to elaborate on a statement released late yesterday... Would you care to elaborate?* V *on* n · V

**élan** /eɪlɑːn/ also **elan.** If you say that someone does something with **élan**, you mean that they do it in an energetic and confident way. [LITERARY] N-UNCOUNT = *panache*

**elapse** /ɪlæps/ **(elapses, elapsing, elapsed)** When time **elapses**, it passes. [FORMAL] ❑ *Forty-eight hours have elapsed since his arrest.* VERB · V

**elas|tic** /ɪlæstɪk/ [1] **Elastic** is a rubber material that stretches when you pull it and returns to its original size and shape when you let it go. Elastic is often used in clothes to make them fit tightly, for example round the waist. ❑ *...a piece of elastic.* N-UNCOUNT [2] Something that is **elastic** is able to stretch easily and then return to its original size and shape. ❑ *Beat it until the dough is slightly elastic.* ADJ [3] If ideas, plans, or policies are **elastic**, they are able to change to suit new circumstances or conditions as they occur. ❑ *...an elastic interpretation of the rules of boxing... If export and import demand is elastic, then the change in trade volumes will operate to remove the surplus.* ADJ = *flexible*

**elas|ti|cat|ed** /ɪlæstɪkeɪtɪd/ If a piece of clothing or part of a piece of clothing is **elasticated**, elastic has been sewn or woven into it to make it fit better and to help it keep its shape. [BRIT] ❑ *...a pink silk jacket with an elasticated waist.* ADJ

✔ in AM, use **elasticized**

**elas|tic band** **(elastic bands)** An **elastic band** is a thin circle of very stretchy rubber that you can put around things in order to hold them together. [mainly BRIT] N-COUNT = *rubber band*

✔ in AM, use **rubber band**

**elas|tici|ty** /iːlæstɪsɪti, ɪlæst-/ The **elasticity** of a material or substance is its ability to return to its original shape, size, and condition after it has been stretched. ❑ *Daily facial exercises help her to retain the skin's elasticity.* N-UNCOUNT

**Elas|to|plast** /ɪlæstəplɑːst/ **(Elastoplasts)** [1] **Elastoplast** is a type of sticky tape that you use to cover small cuts on your body. [BRIT, TRADEMARK] N-VAR

✔ in AM, use **Band-Aid**

[2] If you refer to an **Elastoplast** solution to a problem, you mean that you disapprove of it because you think that it will only be effective for a short period. [BRIT] ❑ *It is only an Elastoplast solution to a far greater constitutional problem.* ADJ: ADJ n [disapproval]

✔ in AM, use **Band-Aid**

**elat|ed** /ɪleɪtɪd/ If you are **elated**, you are extremely happy and excited because of something that has happened. ❑ *I was elated that my second heart bypass had been successful.* ADJ: usu v-link ADJ = *euphoric*

**ela|tion** /ɪleɪʃən/ **Elation** is a feeling of great happiness and excitement about something that has happened. ❑ *His supporters have reacted to the news with elation.* N-UNCOUNT = *euphoria*

**el|bow** /elboʊ/ **(elbows, elbowing, elbowed)** [1] Your **elbow** is the part of your arm where the upper and lower halves of the arm are joined. ❑ *He slipped and fell, badly bruising an elbow.* N-COUNT [2] If you **elbow** people **aside** or **elbow** your **way** somewhere, you push people with your elbows in order to move somewhere. ❑ *They also claim that the security team elbowed aside a steward... Mr Smith elbowed me in the face... Brand elbowed his way to the centre of the group of bystanders.* VERB = *jostle* · V n with *aside* · V n prep · V *way* prep/adv [3] If someone or something **elbows** their **way** somewhere, or **elbows** other people or things **out of the way**, they achieve success by being aggressive and determined. ❑ *Non-state firms gradually elbow aside the inefficient state-owned ones... Environmental concerns will elbow their way right to the top of the agenda.* VERB · V n with *aside/out* · V *way* prep [4] to **rub elbows with** → see **rub**.

**el|bow grease** People use **elbow grease** to refer to the strength and energy that you use when doing physical work like rubbing or polishing. [INFORMAL] ❑ *It took a considerable amount of polish and elbow grease before the brass shone like new.* N-UNCOUNT

**el|bow room** [1] **Elbow room** is the freedom to do what you want to do or need to do in a particular situation. [INFORMAL] ❑ *His speech was designed to give himself more political elbow room.* N-UNCOUNT = *leeway* [2] If there is enough **elbow room** in a place or vehicle, it is not too small or too crowded. [INFORMAL] ❑ *There was not much elbow room in the cockpit of a Snipe.* N-UNCOUNT = *space*

**el|der** /eldəʳ/ **(elders)** [1] **The elder of** two people is the one who was born first. ❑ *...his elder brother. ...the elder of her two daughters.* ADJ: ADJ n, the ADJ, the ADJ *of* n [2] A person's **elder** is someone who is older than them, especially someone quite a lot older. [FORMAL] ❑ *The young have no respect for their elders.* N-COUNT: poss N [3] In some societies, an **elder** is one of the respected older people who have influence and authority. ❑ *...tribal elders.* N-COUNT [4] An **elder** is a bush or small tree which has groups of small white flowers and black berries. N-COUNT

**elder|berry** /eldəʳberi/ **(elderberries)** [1] **Elderberries** are the edible black berries that grow on an elder bush or tree. N-COUNT: usu pl [2] An **elderberry** is an elder bush or tree. N-VAR

**el|der|ly** /eldəʳli/ ◆◇◇ You use **elderly** as a polite way of saying that someone is old. ❑ *...an elderly couple... Many of those most affected are elderly.* ADJ [politeness] ♦ **The elderly** are people who are old. ❑ *The elderly are a formidable force in any election.* N-PLURAL: the N

**el|der states|man** **(elder statesmen)** [1] An **elder statesman** is an old and respected politician or former politician who still has influence because of his or her experience. N-COUNT [2] An experienced and respected member of an organization or profession is sometimes referred to as an **elder statesman**. N-COUNT: usu with supp

**eld|est** /eldɪst/ The **eldest** person in a group is the one who was born before all the others. ❑ *The eldest child was a daughter called Fiona... David was the eldest of three boys... The two eldest are already doing well at Kings Wood.* ADJ

**e-learning** **E-learning** is learning that takes place by means of computers and the Internet. N-UNCOUNT

**elect** /ɪlekt/ **(elects, electing, elected)** ◆◆◇ [1] When people **elect** someone, they choose that person to represent them, by voting for them. ❑ *The people of the Philippines have voted to elect a new president... Manchester College elected him Principal in 1956... The country is about to take a radical departure by electing a woman as its new president.* VERB · V n · V n n · V n *as* n ♦ **elect|ed** *...the country's democratically elected president.* ADJ: ADJ n [2] If you **elect to** do something, you choose to do it. [FORMAL] ❑ *Those electing to smoke will be seated at the rear.* VERB · V to-inf [3] **Elect** is added after words such as 'president' or 'governor' to indicate that a person has been elected to the post but has not officially started to carry out the duties involved. [FORMAL] ❑ *...the date when the president-elect takes office.* ADJ: n ADJ

**elec|tion** /ɪlekʃən/ **(elections)** ◆◆◆ [1] An **election** is a process in which people vote to choose a person or group of people to hold an official position. ❑ *...the first fully free elections for more than fifty years... The final election results will be announced on Friday... Many residents say they have little or no idea who's standing for election.* N-VAR [2] The **election** of a particular person or group of people is their success in winning an election. ❑ *...the election of the Labour government in 1964. ...his election as president... The Democrat candidate is the favorite to win election.* N-UNCOUNT: usu with poss

**elec|tion|eer|ing** /ɪlekʃənɪərɪŋ/ **Electioneering** is the activities that politicians and their supporters carry out in order to persuade people to vote for them or their political party in an elec- N-UNCOUNT tion, for example making speeches and visiting voters.

**elec|tive** /ɪle̱ktɪv/ **(electives)** 1 An **elective** post or committee is one to which people are appointed as a result of winning an election. [FORMAL] ❑ *Buchanan has never held elective office.* ADJ: usu ADJ n
2 **Elective** surgery is surgery that you choose to have before it becomes essential. [FORMAL] ADJ: usu ADJ n
3 An **elective** is a subject which a student can choose to study as part of his or her course. [AM] N-COUNT

in BRIT, use **option**

**elec|tor** /ɪle̱ktəʳ/ **(electors)** 1 An **elector** is a person who has the right to vote in an election. N-COUNT: usu pl = voter
2 An **elector** is a member of the electoral college. People vote for electors in each state to represent them in the presidential elections. [AM] N-COUNT

**elec|tor|al** /ɪle̱ktərəl/ **Electoral** is used to describe things that are connected with elections. ❑ *The Mongolian Democratic Party is campaigning for electoral reform. ...Italy's electoral system of proportional representation.* ◆◇◇ ADJ: ADJ n
♦ **elec|tor|al|ly** *He believed that the policies were both wrong and electorally disastrous.* ADV: ADV adj/-ed, ADV after v, ADV with cl

**elec|tor|al col|lege** **The electoral college** is the system that is used in the United States in presidential elections. The electors in the electoral college act as representatives for each state, and they elect the president and vice-president. [AM] N-SING: the N

**elec|tor|al reg|is|ter** **(electoral registers)** An **electoral register** is an official list of all the people who have the right to vote in an election. [BRIT] ❑ *Many students are not on the electoral register.* N-COUNT: usu the N in sing = electoral roll

**elec|tor|al roll** **(electoral rolls)** An **electoral roll** is the same as an **electoral register**. [BRIT] N-COUNT

**elec|tor|ate** /ɪle̱ktərət/ **(electorates)** The **electorate** of a country or area is all the people in it who have the right to vote in an election. ❑ *He has the backing of almost a quarter of the electorate.* N-COUNT-COLL

**elec|tric** /ɪle̱ktrɪk/ 1 An **electric** device or machine works by means of electricity, rather than using some other source of power. ❑ *...her electric guitar.* ◆◇◇ ADJ: usu ADJ n
2 An **electric** current, voltage, or charge is one that is produced by electricity. ADJ: ADJ n
3 **Electric** plugs, sockets, or power lines are designed to carry electricity. ADJ: ADJ n
4 **Electric** is used to refer to the supply of electricity. [INFORMAL] ❑ *An average electric bill might go up $2 or $3 per month.* ADJ: ADJ n = electricity
5 If you describe the atmosphere of a place or event as **electric**, you mean that people are in a state of great excitement. ❑ *The mood in the hall was electric.* ADJ

**elec|tri|cal** /ɪle̱ktrɪkᵊl/ 1 **Electrical** goods, equipment, or appliances work by means of electricity. ❑ *...shipments of electrical equipment. ...electrical appliances.* ADJ: usu ADJ n
♦ **elec|tri|cal|ly** /ɪle̱ktrɪkli/ *...new electrically-powered vehicles.* ADV: ADV -ed
2 **Electrical** systems or parts supply or use electricity. ADJ: usu ADJ n
3 **Electrical** energy is energy in the form of electricity. ADJ
♦ **elec|tri|cal|ly** ❑ *...electrically charged particles... The researchers stimulated the muscle electrically.* ADV: usu ADV adj
4 **Electrical** industries, engineers, or workers are involved in the production and supply of electricity or electrical goods. ADJ: ADJ n

**elec|tri|cal en|gi|neer** **(electrical engineers)** An **electrical engineer** is a person who uses scientific knowledge to design, construct, and maintain electrical devices. N-COUNT

**elec|tri|cal en|gi|neer|ing** **Electrical engineering** is the designing, constructing, and maintenance of electrical devices. N-UNCOUNT

**elec|tric blan|ket** **(electric blankets)** An **electric blanket** is a blanket with wires inside it which carry an electric current that keeps the blanket warm. N-COUNT

**elec|tric blue** also **electric-blue.** Something that is **electric blue** is very bright blue in colour. COLOUR

**elec|tric chair** **(electric chairs)** **The electric chair** is a method of killing criminals, used especially in the United States, in which a person is strapped to a special chair and killed by a powerful electric current. N-COUNT: usu the N in sing

**elec|tri|cian** /ɪlektrɪ̱ʃᵊn, i̱ːlek-/ **(electricians)** An **electrician** is a person whose job is to install and repair electrical equipment. N-COUNT

**elec|tric|ity** /ɪlektrɪ̱sɪti, i̱ːlek-/ **Electricity** is a form of energy that can be carried by wires and is used for heating and lighting, and to provide power for machines. ❑ *The electricity had been cut off.* ◆◇◇ N-UNCOUNT

**elec|trics** /ɪle̱ktrɪks/ You can refer to a system of electrical wiring as the **electrics**. [BRIT] ❑ *Plumbing and electrics are installed to a high standard.* N-PLURAL

**elec|tric shock** **(electric shocks)** If you get an **electric shock**, you get a sudden painful feeling when you touch something which is connected to a supply of electricity. N-COUNT

**elec|tri|fi|ca|tion** /ɪle̱ktrɪfɪke̱ɪʃᵊn/ The **electrification** of a house, town, or area is the connecting of that place with a supply of electricity. ❑ *...rural electrification.* ➔ See also **electrify**. N-UNCOUNT

**elec|tri|fied** /ɪle̱ktrɪfaɪd/ An **electrified** fence or other barrier has been connected to a supply of electricity, so that a person or animal that touches it will get an electric shock. ❑ *The house was set amid dense trees and surrounded by an electrified fence.* ADJ: ADJ n

**elec|tri|fy** /ɪle̱ktrɪfaɪ/ **(electrifies, electrifying, electrified)** 1 If people **are electrified by** an event or experience, it makes them feel very excited and surprised. ❑ *The world was electrified by his courage and resistance.* VERB: usu passive = thrill be V-ed
♦ **elec|tri|fy|ing** *He gave an electrifying performance.* ADJ
2 When a railway system or railway line **is electrified**, electric cables are put over the tracks, or electric rails are put beside them, so that the trains can be powered by electricity. ❑ *The west-coast line was electrified as long ago as 1974. ...the electrified section of the Lancashire and Yorkshire Railway.* VERB: usu passive be V-ed V-ed

**electro-** /ɪle̱ktroʊ-/ **Electro-** is used to form words that refer to electricity or processes involving electricity. ❑ *...electro-chemical phenomena. ...electro-magnetic energy.* PREFIX

**elec|tro|car|dio|gram** /ɪle̱ktroʊka̱ːʳdioʊgræm/ **(electrocardiograms)** If someone has an **electrocardiogram**, doctors use special equipment to measure the electric currents produced by that person's heart in order to see whether it is working normally. N-COUNT

**elec|tro|cute** /ɪle̱ktrəkjuːt/ **(electrocutes, electrocuting, electrocuted)** 1 If someone **is electrocuted**, they are accidentally killed or badly injured when they touch something connected to a source of electricity. ❑ *Three people were electrocuted by falling power-lines... He accidentally electrocuted himself.* VERB be V-ed V pron-refl
2 If a criminal **is electrocuted**, he or she is executed using electricity. ❑ *He was electrocuted for a murder committed when he was 17.* VERB: usu passive be V-ed
♦ **elec|tro|cu|tion** /ɪle̱ktrəkju̱ːʃᵊn/ **(electrocutions)** *The court sentenced him to death by electrocution.* N-VAR

**elec|trode** /ɪle̱ktroʊd/ **(electrodes)** An **electrode** is a small piece of metal or other substance that is used to take an electric current to or from a source of power, a piece of equipment, or a living body. ❑ *The patient's brain activity is monitored via electrodes taped to the skull.* N-COUNT

**elec|troly|sis** /ɪlektrɒ̱lɪsɪs, i̱ː-/ **Electrolysis** is the process of passing an electric current through a substance in order to produce chemical changes in the substance. [TECHNICAL] N-UNCOUNT

**elec|tro|lyte** /ɪle̱ktrəlaɪt/ **(electrolytes)** N-COUNT An **electrolyte** is a substance, usually a liquid, which electricity can pass through. [TECHNICAL]

**elec|tro|mag|net** /ɪle̱ktroʊmæɡnɪt/ **(electromagnets)** N-COUNT An **electromagnet** is a magnet that consists of a piece of iron or steel surrounded by a coil. The metal becomes magnetic when an electric current is passed through the coil.

**elec|tro|mag|net|ic** /ɪle̱ktroʊmæɡne̱tɪk/ ADJ: usu ADJ n **Electromagnetic** is used to describe the electrical and magnetic forces or effects produced by an electric current. ❑ *...electromagnetic fields.*

**elec|tron** /ɪle̱ktrɒn/ **(electrons)** N-COUNT An **electron** is a tiny particle of matter that is smaller than an atom and has a negative electrical charge. [TECHNICAL]

**elec|tron|ic** /ɪlektrɒ̱nɪk, i̱ː-/ ◆◇◇ 1 ADJ: ADJ n An **electronic** device has transistors or silicon chips which control and change the electric current passing through the device. ❑ *...expensive electronic equipment.* 2 ADJ: usu ADJ n An **electronic** process or activity involves the use of electronic devices. ❑ *...electronic surveillance systems. ...electronic music.* ♦ **elec|troni|cal|ly** ADV: ADV with v *Data is transmitted electronically. ...an electronically controlled dishwasher.*

**elec|tron|ic book** **(electronic books)** N-COUNT An **electronic book** the same as an **e-book**. [COMPUTING]

**elec|tron|ic mail** N-SING **Electronic mail** is the same as **e-mail**.

**elec|tron|ic pub|lish|ing** N-UNCOUNT **Electronic publishing** is the publishing of documents in a form that can be read on a computer, for example as a CD-ROM.

**elec|tron|ics** /ɪlektrɒ̱nɪks/ N-UNCOUNT **Electronics** is the technology of using transistors and silicon chips, especially in devices such as radios, televisions, and computers. ❑ *...Europe's three main electronics companies.*

**elec|tron|ic tag|ging** N-UNCOUNT **Electronic tagging** is a system in which a criminal or suspected criminal has an electronic device attached to them which enables the police to know if they leave a particular area. [BRIT]

**el|egant** /e̱lɪɡənt/ ◆◇◇ 1 ADJ = stylish If you describe a person or thing as **elegant**, you mean that they are pleasing and graceful in appearance or style. ❑ *Patricia looked beautiful and elegant as always. ...an elegant restaurant.* ♦ **el|egance** N-UNCOUNT *...Princess Grace's understated elegance.* ♦ **el|egant|ly** ADV *...a tall, elegantly dressed man with a mustache.* 2 ADJ If you describe a piece of writing, an idea, or a plan as **elegant**, you mean that it is simple, clear, and clever. ❑ *The document impressed me with its elegant simplicity.* ♦ **el|egant|ly** ADV *...an elegantly simple idea.*

**el|egi|ac** /e̱lɪdʒa̱ɪək/ ADJ Something that is **elegiac** expresses or shows sadness. [LITERARY] ❑ *The music has a dreamy, elegiac quality.*

**el|egy** /e̱lɪdʒi/ **(elegies)** N-COUNT An **elegy** is a sad poem, often about someone who has died. ❑ *...a touching elegy for a lost friend.*

**el|ement** /e̱lɪmənt/ **(elements)** ◆◆◇ 1 N-COUNT: usu pl, usu with supp The different **elements** of something are the different parts it contains. ❑ *The exchange of prisoners of war was one of the key elements of the UN's peace plan.* 2 N-COUNT: with supp = factor A particular **element** of a situation, activity, or process is an important quality or feature that it has or needs. ❑ *Fitness has now become an important element in our lives.* 3 N-COUNT: usu pl, supp N When you talk about **elements** within a society or organization, you are referring to groups of people who have similar aims, beliefs, or habits. ❑ *...criminal elements within the security forces. ...the hooligan element.* 4 N-COUNT: usu sing, N *of* n If something has an **element of** a particular quality or emotion, it has a certain amount of this quality or emotion. ❑ *These reports clearly contain elements of propaganda.* 5 N-COUNT ≠compound An **element** is a substance such as gold, oxygen, or carbon that consists of only one type of atom. 6 N-COUNT: usu sing The **element** in an electric fire or water heater is the metal part which changes the electric current into heat. 7 N-PLURAL: *the* N You can refer to the weather, especially wind and rain, as **the elements**. ❑ *The area where most refugees are waiting is exposed to the elements.* 8 PHRASE: v-link PHR If you say that someone is **in** their **element**, you mean that they are in a situation they enjoy. ❑ *My stepmother was in her element, organizing everything.*

**el|ement|al** /e̱lɪme̱ntᵊl/ ADJ = basic **Elemental** feelings and types of behaviour are simple, basic, and forceful. [LITERARY] ❑ *...the elemental life they would be living in this new colony.*

**el|emen|ta|ry** /e̱lɪme̱ntri/ ADJ: usu ADJ n = basic Something that is **elementary** is very simple and basic. ❑ *...elementary computer skills.*

**el|emen|ta|ry school** **(elementary schools)** N-VAR An **elementary school** is a school where children are taught for the first six or sometimes eight years of their education. [mainly AM] ❑ *...the move from elementary school to middle school or junior high.*

**el|ephant** /e̱lɪfənt/ **(elephants)** N-COUNT An **elephant** is a very large animal with a long, flexible nose called a trunk, which it uses to pick up things. Elephants live in India and Africa. ➔ See also **white elephant**.

**el|ephan|tine** /e̱lɪfæ̱ntaɪn/ ADJ [disapproval] If you describe something as **elephantine**, you mean that you think it is large and clumsy. ❑ *...elephantine clumsiness... His legs were elephantine.*

**el|evate** /e̱lɪveɪt/ **(elevates, elevating, elevated)** 1 VERB: usu passive = promote *be* V-ed *to* n When someone or something achieves a more important rank or status, you can say that they **are elevated to** it. [FORMAL] ❑ *He was elevated to the post of prime minister.* ♦ **el|eva|tion** /e̱lɪve̱ɪʃᵊn/ N-UNCOUNT: usu with poss, N *to* n *The Prime Minister is known to favour the elevation of more women to the Cabinet.* 2 VERB V n *to* n If you **elevate** something **to** a higher status, you consider it to be better or more important than it really is. ❑ *Don't elevate your superiors to superstar status.* 3 VERB = raise V n V-ed To **elevate** something means to increase it in amount or intensity. [FORMAL] ❑ *Emotional stress can elevate blood pressure. ...overweight individuals who have elevated cholesterol levels.* 4 VERB V n If you **elevate** something, you raise it above a horizontal level. [FORMAL] ❑ *Jack elevated the gun at the sky.*

**el|evat|ed** /e̱lɪveɪtɪd/ 1 ADJ: usu ADJ n A person, job, or role that is **elevated** is very important or of very high rank. ❑ *His career has blossomed and that has given him a certain elevated status.* 2 ADJ: usu ADJ n If thoughts or ideas are **elevated**, they are on a high moral or intellectual level. ❑ *...the magazine's elevated British tone.* 3 ADJ: usu ADJ n = raised If land or buildings are **elevated**, they are raised up higher than the surrounding area. ❑ *An elevated platform on the stage collapsed during rehearsals.*

**el|eva|tion** /e̱lɪve̱ɪʃᵊn/ **(elevations)** 1 N-COUNT: with supp In architecture, an **elevation** is the front, back, or side of a building, or a drawing of one of these. [TECHNICAL] ❑ *...the addition of two-storey wings on the north and south elevations.* 2 N-COUNT: usu with supp = altitude The **elevation** of a place is its height above sea level. ❑ *We're probably at an elevation of about 13,000 feet above sea level.* 3 N-COUNT An **elevation** is a piece of ground that is higher than the area around it. 4 ➔ See also **elevate**.

**el|eva|tor** /e̱lɪveɪtəʳ/ **(elevators)** N-COUNT An **elevator** is a device that carries people up and down inside buildings. [AM]

☑ in BRIT, use **lift**

**elev|en** /ɪle̱vᵊn/ **(elevens)** ◆◆◆ NUM **Eleven** is the number 11. ❑ *...the Princess and her eleven friends.*

**ele̱ven-plu̱s** also **eleven plus**. N-SING: oft *the* N **The eleven-plus** is an exam which was taken by children in Britain at about the age of eleven, in order to decide which secondary school they should go to. [BRIT]

**elev|en|ses** /ɪle̱vᵊnzɪz/ N-UNCOUNT **Elevenses** is a short break when you have a cup of tea or coffee, and sometimes biscuits, at around eleven o'clock in the morning. [BRIT, INFORMAL]

**elev|enth** /ɪlevənθ/ The **eleventh** item in a series is the one that you count as number eleven. ❑ *We were working on the eleventh floor.* ◆◆◇ ORD

**elev|enth hour** If someone does something **at the eleventh hour**, they do it at the last possible moment. ❑ *He postponed his trip at the eleventh hour. ...last night's eleventh hour agreement.* N-SING: usu *at the* N, N n

**elf** /elf/ **(elves)** In fairy stories, **elves** are small magical beings who play tricks on people. N-COUNT: usu pl

**elf|in** /elfɪn/ If you describe someone as **elfin**, you think that they are attractive because they are small and have delicate features. ❑ *...a little boy with an elfin face.* ADJ: usu ADJ n [approval]

**elic|it** /ɪlɪsɪt/ **(elicits, eliciting, elicited)** [1] If you **elicit** a response or a reaction, you do or say something which makes other people respond or react. ❑ *Mr Norris said he was hopeful that his request would elicit a positive response.* [2] If you **elicit** a piece of information, you get it by asking the right questions. [FORMAL] ❑ *Phone calls elicited no further information.* VERB; V n; VERB; V n

**elide** /ɪlaɪd/ **(elides, eliding, elided)** [1] If you **elide** something, especially a distinction, you leave it out or ignore it. [FORMAL] ❑ *These habits of thinking elide the difference between what is common and what is normal.* [2] In linguistics, if you **elide** a word, you do not pronounce or write it fully. [TECHNICAL] ❑ *He complained about BBC announcers eliding their words.* VERB; V n; VERB = contract; V n

**eli|gible** /elɪdʒɪbəl/ [1] Someone who is **eligible to** do something is qualified or able to do it, for example because they are old enough. ❑ *Almost half the population are eligible to vote in today's election... You could be eligible for a university scholarship.* ♦ **eli|gibil|ity** /elɪdʒəbɪlɪti/ *The rules covering eligibility for benefits changed in the 1980s.* [2] An **eligible** man or woman is not yet married and is thought by many people to be a suitable partner. ❑ *He's the most eligible bachelor in Japan.* ADJ: usu v-link ADJ, usu ADJ *for* n, ADJ to-inf; N-UNCOUNT: oft N *for* n; ADJ: usu ADJ n

**elimi|nate** /ɪlɪmɪneɪt/ **(eliminates, eliminating, eliminated)** [1] To **eliminate** something, especially something you do not want or need, means to remove it completely. [FORMAL] ❑ *The Sex Discrimination Act has not eliminated discrimination in employment... If you think you may be allergic to a food or drink, eliminate it from your diet.* ♦ **elimi|na|tion** /ɪlɪmɪneɪʃən/ *...the prohibition and elimination of chemical weapons.* [2] When a person or team **is eliminated from** a competition, they are defeated and so take no further part in the competition. ❑ *I was eliminated from the 400 metres in the semi-finals... If you are eliminated in the show-jumping then you are out of the complete competition.* [3] If someone says that they **have eliminated** an enemy, they mean that they have killed them. By using the word 'eliminate', they are trying to make the action sound more positive than if they used the word 'kill'. ❑ *He declared war on the government and urged right-wingers to eliminate their opponents.* ◆◇◇ VERB; V n; V n *from* n; N-UNCOUNT: usu N *of* n; V-PASSIVE = knock out; be V-ed *from* n; be V-ed; VERB; V n

**elimi|na|tor** /ɪlɪmɪneɪtəʳ/ **(eliminators)** In sport, an **eliminator** is a game which decides which team or player is to go through to the next stage of a particular competition. [BRIT] ❑ *...a world title eliminator.* N-COUNT: usu n N

☑ in AM, use **elimination game**

**elite** /ɪliːt, eɪ-/ **(elites)** [1] You can refer to the most powerful, rich, or talented people within a particular group, place, or society as the **elite**. ❑ *...a government comprised mainly of the elite... We have a political elite in this country.* [2] **Elite** people or organizations are considered to be the best of their kind. ❑ *...the elite troops of the President's bodyguard.* N-COUNT; ADJ: ADJ n

**elit|ism** /ɪliːtɪzəm, eɪ-/ **Elitism** is the quality or practice of being elitist. ❑ *It became difficult to promote excellence without being accused of elitism.* N-UNCOUNT

**elit|ist** /ɪliːtɪst, eɪ-/ **(elitists)** [1] **Elitist** systems, practices, or ideas favour the most powerful, rich, or talented people within a group, place, or society. ❑ *The legal profession is starting to be less elitist and more representative.* [2] An **elitist** is someone who has elitist ideas or is part of an elite. ❑ *He was an elitist who had no time for the masses.* ADJ [disapproval]; N-COUNT [disapproval]

**elix|ir** /ɪlɪksəʳ/ **(elixirs)** An **elixir** is a liquid that is considered to have magical powers. [LITERARY] ❑ *...the elixir of life.* N-COUNT: oft N *of* n

**Eliza|bethan** /ɪlɪzəbiːθən/ **Elizabethan** means belonging to or connected with England in the second half of the sixteenth century, when Elizabeth the First was Queen. ❑ *...Elizabethan England. ...the Elizabethan theatre.* ADJ: usu ADJ n

**elk** /elk/ **(elks** or **elk)** An **elk** is a type of large deer. Elks have big, flat horns called antlers and are found in Northern Europe, Asia, and North America. Some British speakers use **elk** to refer to the European and Asian varieties of this animal, and **moose** to refer to the North American variety. N-VAR

**el|lipse** /ɪlɪps/ **(ellipses)** An **ellipse** is an oval shape similar to a circle but longer and flatter. ❑ *The Earth orbits in an ellipse.* N-COUNT

**el|lip|sis** /ɪlɪpsɪs/ In linguistics, **ellipsis** means leaving out words rather than repeating them unnecessarily; for example, saying 'I want to go but I can't' instead of 'I want to go but I can't go'. [TECHNICAL] N-UNCOUNT

**el|lip|ti|cal** /ɪlɪptɪkəl/ [1] Something that is **elliptical** has the shape of an ellipse. [FORMAL] ❑ *...the moon's elliptical orbit.* [2] **Elliptical** references to something are indirect rather than clear. [FORMAL] ❑ *...elliptical references to problems best not aired in public.* ♦ **el|lip|ti|cal|ly** /ɪlɪptɪkli/ *He spoke only briefly and elliptically about the mission.* ADJ; ADJ = oblique ≠ direct; ADV: ADV after v

**elm** /elm/ **(elms)** An **elm** is a tree that has broad leaves which it loses in winter. ♦ **Elm** is the wood of this tree. N-VAR; N-UNCOUNT

**elo|cu|tion** /eləkjuːʃən/ **Elocution** lessons are lessons in which someone is taught to speak clearly and in an accent that is considered to be standard and acceptable. N-UNCOUNT

**elon|gate** /iːlɒŋgeɪt, AM ɪlɔːŋ-/ **(elongates, elongating, elongated)** If you **elongate** something or if it **elongates**, you stretch it so that it becomes longer. [FORMAL] ❑ *'Mom,' she intoned, elongating the word... Corn is treated when the stalk starts to elongate.* VERB = lengthen; V n; V

**elon|gat|ed** /iːlɒŋgeɪtɪd, AM ɪlɔːŋ-/ If something is **elongated**, it is very long and thin, often in an unnatural way. ❑ *The light from my candle threw his elongated shadow on the walls.* ADJ

**elope** /ɪloʊp/ **(elopes, eloping, eloped)** When two people **elope**, they go away secretly together to get married. ❑ *My girlfriend Lynn and I eloped... In 1912 he eloped with Frieda von Richthofen.* V-RECIP; pl-n V; V *with* n

**elo|quent** /eləkwənt/ [1] Speech or writing that is **eloquent** is well expressed and effective in persuading people. ❑ *I heard him make a very eloquent speech at that dinner.* ♦ **elo|quence** *...the eloquence of his prose.* ♦ **elo|quent|ly** *Jan speaks eloquently about her art.* [2] A person who is **eloquent** is good at speaking and able to persuade people. ❑ *He was eloquent about his love of books. ...one particularly eloquent German critic.* ♦ **elo|quence** *I wish I'd had the eloquence of Helmut Schmidt.* ADJ; N-UNCOUNT; ADV; ADJ [approval]; N-UNCOUNT

**else** /els/ [1] You use **else** after words such as 'anywhere', 'someone', and 'what', to refer in a vague way to another person, place, or thing. ❑ *If I can't make a living at painting, at least I can teach someone else to paint... We had nothing else to do on those long trips... There's not much else I can say.* ♦ **Else** is also an adverb. ❑ *I never wanted to live anywhere else.* [2] You use **else** after words such as 'everyone', 'everything', and 'everywhere' to refer in a vague way to all the other people, things, or places except the one you are talking about. ❑ *As I try to be truthful, I expect everyone else to be truthful... Cigarettes are in short supply, like everything else here.* ◆◆◆ ADJ: pron-indef/quest ADJ; ADV: adv ADV; ADJ: pron-indef ADJ

♦ **Else** is also an adverb. ❑ *London seems so much dirtier than everywhere else.* ADV: adv ADV

PHRASES [3] You use **or else** after stating a logical conclusion, to indicate that what you are about to say is evidence for that conclusion. ❑ *He must be a good plumber, or else he wouldn't be so busy... Evidently no lessons have been learnt or else the government would not have handled the problem so sloppily.* PHRASE = otherwise

[4] You use **or else** to introduce a statement that indicates the unpleasant results that will occur if someone does or does not do something. ❑ *Make sure you are strapped in very well, or else you will fall out.* PHRASE = otherwise

[5] You use **or else** to introduce the second of two possibilities when you do not know which one is true. ❑ *You are either a total genius or else you must be absolutely raving mad.* PHRASE

[6] **Above all else** is used to emphasize that a particular thing is more important than other things. ❑ *Above all else I hate the cold.* PHRASE: PHR with cl [emphasis]

[7] You can say **'if nothing else'** to indicate that what you are mentioning is, in your opinion, the only good thing in a particular situation. ❑ *If nothing else, you'll really enjoy meeting them.* PHRASE: PHR with cl

[8] You say **'or else'** after a command to warn someone that if they do not obey, you will be angry and may harm or punish them. [SPOKEN] ❑ *He told us to put it right, or else.* PHRASE: cl PHR

**else|where** /elsʰweəʳ/ ◆◇◇ **Elsewhere** means in other places or to another place. ❑ *Almost 80 percent of the state's residents were born elsewhere... But if you are not satisfied then go elsewhere.* ADV: ADV after v, n ADV, ADV with cl, *be* ADV

**ELT** /iː el tiː/ **ELT** is the teaching of English to people whose first language is not English. **ELT** is an abbreviation for 'English Language Teaching'. [mainly BRIT] N-UNCOUNT

**elu|ci|date** /ɪluːsɪdeɪt/ **(elucidates, elucidating, elucidated)** If you **elucidate** something, you make it clear and easy to understand. [FORMAL] ❑ *Haig went on to elucidate his personal principle of war... There was no need for him to elucidate.* VERB = clarify; V n; V

♦ **elu|ci|da|tion** /ɪluːsɪdeɪʃᵊn/ *...Gerald's attempts at elucidation.* N-UNCOUNT

**elude** /ɪluːd/ **(eludes, eluding, eluded)** [1] If something that you want **eludes** you, you fail to obtain it. ❑ *At 62, Brian found the celebrity and status that had eluded him for so long.* VERB: no passive; V n

[2] If you **elude** someone or something, you avoid them or escape from them. ❑ *He eluded the police for 13 years.* VERB; V n

[3] If a fact or idea **eludes** you, you do not succeed in understanding it, realizing it, or remembering it. ❑ *The appropriate word eluded him.* VERB: no passive = escape; V n

**elu|sive** /ɪluːsɪv/ Something or someone that is **elusive** is difficult to find, describe, remember, or achieve. ❑ *In London late-night taxis are elusive and far from cheap.* ADJ ♦ **elu|sive|ness** *...the elusiveness of her character.* N-UNCOUNT

**elves** /elvz/ **Elves** is the plural of **elf**.

**em-** /ɪm-/

> Often pronounced /em-/, particularly in American English.

**Em-** is a form of **en-** that is used before b-, m-, and p-. ❑ *The person who embodies democracy at the local level is the mayor... I want to empower the businessman.* PREFIX

**ema|ci|at|ed** /ɪmeɪsieɪtɪd, -meɪʃ-/ A person or animal that is **emaciated** is extremely thin and weak because of illness or lack of food. ❑ *...horrific television pictures of emaciated prisoners.* ADJ

**e-mail** **(e-mails, e-mailing, e-mailed)** also **E-mail, email.** [1] **E-mail** is a system of sending written messages electronically from one computer to another. **E-mail** is an abbreviation of 'electronic mail'. ❑ *You can contact us by e-mail... Do you want to send an E-mail?... First you need to get an e-mail address.* N-VAR

[2] If you **e-mail** someone, you send them an e-mail. ❑ *Jamie e-mailed me to say he couldn't come... Email your views to sport@times.co.uk* VERB; V n; V n *to* n

**ema|nate** /eməneɪt/ **(emanates, emanating, emanated)** [1] If a quality **emanates from** you, or if you **emanate** a quality, you give people a strong sense that you have that quality. [FORMAL] ❑ *Intelligence and cunning emanated from him... He emanates sympathy.* VERB = radiate; V *from* n; V n

[2] If something **emanates from** somewhere, it comes from there. [FORMAL] ❑ *...reports emanating from America.* VERB; V *from* n

**ema|na|tion** /eməneɪʃᵊn/ **(emanations)** An **emanation** is a form of energy or a mass of tiny particles that comes from something. [FORMAL] N-COUNT

**eman|ci|pate** /ɪmænsɪpeɪt/ **(emancipates, emancipating, emancipated)** If people **are emancipated**, they are freed from unpleasant or unfair social, political, or legal restrictions. [FORMAL] ❑ *Catholics were emancipated in 1792... That war preserved the Union and emancipated the slaves. ...the newly emancipated state.* VERB = liberate; *be* V-ed; V n; V-ed

♦ **eman|ci|pa|tion** /ɪmænsɪpeɪʃᵊn/ *...the emancipation of women.* N-UNCOUNT: oft N *of* n

**eman|ci|pat|ed** /ɪmænsɪpeɪtɪd/ If you describe someone as **emancipated**, you mean that they behave in a less restricted way than is traditional in their society. ❑ *She is an emancipated woman.* ADJ = liberated

**emas|cu|late** /ɪmæskjʊleɪt/ **(emasculates, emasculating, emasculated)** [1] If someone or something **is emasculated**, they have been made weak and ineffective. ❑ *Left-wing dissidents have been emasculated and marginalised... The company tried to emasculate the unions... Since Japan's defeat, the military has remained largely emasculated.* VERB [disapproval] = neuter; *be* V-ed; V n; V-ed

♦ **emas|cu|la|tion** /ɪmæskjʊleɪʃᵊn/ *...the emasculation of fundamental freedoms.* N-UNCOUNT

[2] If a man **is emasculated**, he loses his male role, identity, or qualities. ❑ *Tosh was known to be a man who feared no-one, yet he was clearly emasculated by his girlfriend.* VERB: usu passive [disapproval]; *be* V-ed

**em|balm** /ɪmbɑːm/ **(embalms, embalming, embalmed)** If a dead person **is embalmed**, their body is preserved using special substances. ❑ *His body was embalmed. ...the embalmed body of Lenin.* VERB: usu passive; *be* V-ed; V-ed

**em|bank|ment** /ɪmbæŋkmənt/ **(embankments)** An **embankment** is a thick wall of earth that is built to carry a road or railway over an area of low ground, or to prevent water from a river or the sea from flooding the area. ❑ *They climbed a steep embankment. ...a railway embankment.* N-COUNT: oft in names after n

**em|bar|go** /ɪmbɑːʳgoʊ/ **(embargoes, embargoing, embargoed)** [1] If one country or group of countries imposes an **embargo** against another, it forbids trade with that country. ❑ *The United Nations imposed an arms embargo against the country... He has called on the government to lift its embargo on trade with Vietnam.* N-COUNT: usu with supp = ban

[2] If goods of a particular kind **are embargoed**, people are not allowed to import them from a particular country or export them to a particular country. ❑ *The fruit was embargoed... They embargoed oil shipments to the US. ...embargoed goods.* VERB = ban; *be* V-ed; V n; V-ed

**em|bark** /ɪmbɑːʳk/ **(embarks, embarking, embarked)** [1] If you **embark on** something new, difficult, or exciting, you start doing it. ❑ *He's embarking on a new career as a writer... The government embarked on a programme of radical economic reform.* VERB; V *on/upon* n; V *on/upon* n

[2] When someone **embarks on** a ship, they go on board before the start of a journey. ❑ *They travelled to Portsmouth, where they embarked on the battle cruiser HMS Renown... Bob ordered brigade HQ to embark.* VERB; V *on* n; V

♦ **em|bar|ka|tion** /embɑːʳkeɪʃᵊn/ *Embarkation was scheduled for just after 4 pm.* N-UNCOUNT

**em|bar|rass** /ɪmbærəs/ **(embarrasses, embarrassing, embarrassed)** [1] If something or someone **embarrasses** you, they make you feel shy or ashamed. ❑ *His clumsiness embarrassed him... It embarrassed him that he had no idea of what was going on.* VERB; V n; *it* V n that

[2] If something **embarrasses** a public figure such as a politician or an organization such as a political party, it causes problems for them. ❑ *The Republicans are trying to embarrass the president by thwarting his economic program.* VERB; V n

**em|bar|rassed** /ɪmbærəst/ A person who is **embarrassed** feels shy, ashamed, or guilty about ADJ: usu v-link ADJ something. ❑ *He looked a bit embarrassed. ...an embarrassed silence.*

**em|bar|rass|ing** /ɪmbærəsɪŋ/ [ADJ = uncomfortable, awkward] 1 Something that is **embarrassing** makes you feel shy or ashamed. ❑ *That was an embarrassing situation for me... Men find it embarrassing to be honest.* ♦ **em|bar|rass|ing|ly** [ADV] *Stephens had beaten him embarrassingly easily.* 2 [ADJ: oft ADJ *to* n] Something that is **embarrassing to** a public figure such as a politician or an organization such as a political party causes problems for them. ❑ *He has put the Bonn government in an embarrassing position... The speech was deeply embarrassing to Cabinet ministers.*

**em|bar|rass|ment** /ɪmbærəsmənt/ (**embarrassments**) 1 [N-VAR: oft N prep] **Embarrassment** is the feeling you have when you are embarrassed. ❑ *It is a source of embarrassment to Londoners that the standard of pubs is so low... We apologise for any embarrassment this may have caused.* 2 [N-COUNT: usu with supp] An **embarrassment** is an action, event, or situation which causes problems for a politician, political party, government, or other public group. ❑ *The poverty figures were undoubtedly an embarrassment to the president.* 3 [N-SING: *a* N] [disapproval] If you refer to a person as **an embarrassment**, you mean that you disapprove of them but cannot avoid your connection with them. ❑ *You have been an embarrassment to us from the day Douglas married you.*

**em|bas|sy** /embəsi/ (**embassies**) [◆◇◇] [N-COUNT: oft *the* adj N] An **embassy** is a group of government officials, headed by an ambassador, who represent their government in a foreign country. The building in which they work is also called an **embassy**. ❑ *The American Embassy has already complained... Mr Cohen held discussions at the embassy with one of the rebel leaders.*

**em|bat|tled** /ɪmbætəld/ 1 [ADJ: usu ADJ n = beleaguered] If you describe a person, group, or organization as **embattled**, you mean that they are having a lot of problems or difficulties. ❑ *The embattled president also denied recent claims that he was being held hostage by his own soldiers.* 2 [ADJ: ADJ n] An **embattled** area is one that is involved in the fighting in a war, especially one that is surrounded by enemy forces. ❑ *Both sides say they want to try to reach a political settlement in the embattled north and east of the island.*

**em|bed** /ɪmbed/ (**embeds, embedding, embedded**) 1 [VERB] If an object **embeds itself** in a substance or thing, it becomes fixed there firmly and deeply. ❑ *One of the bullets passed through Andrea's chest before embedding itself in a wall.* [V n *in* n] [Also V n prep] ♦ **em|bed|ded** [ADJ] *There is glass embedded in the cut.* 2 [VERB: usu passive] If something such as an attitude or feeling **is embedded in** a society or system, or in someone's personality, it becomes a permanent and noticeable feature of it. ❑ *This agreement will be embedded in a state treaty to be signed soon.* [*be* V-ed *in* n] ♦ **em|bed|ded** [ADJ: oft ADJ *in* n] *I think that hatred of the other is deeply embedded in our society.*

**em|bel|lish** /ɪmbelɪʃ/ (**embellishes, embellishing, embellished**) 1 [VERB] If something **is embellished with** decorative features or patterns, it has those features or patterns on it and they make it look more attractive. ❑ *The stern was embellished with carvings in red and blue...* [*be* V-ed *with* n] *Ivy leaves embellish the front of the dresser.* [V n] 2 [VERB] If you **embellish** a story, you make it more interesting by adding details which may be untrue. ❑ *I launched into the parable, embellishing the story with invented dialogue and extra details...* [V n] *Irving popularized the story in a dramatic and embellished account.* [V-ed]

**em|bel|lish|ment** /ɪmbelɪʃmənt/ (**embellishments**) [N-VAR] An **embellishment** is a decoration added to something to make it seem more attractive or interesting. ❑ *...Renaissance embellishments. ...public buildings with little bits of decoration and embellishment.*

**em|ber** /embəʳ/ (**embers**) [N-COUNT: usu pl] The **embers** of a fire are small pieces of wood or coal that remain and glow with heat after the fire has finished burning.

**em|bez|zle** /ɪmbezəl/ (**embezzles, embezzling, embezzled**) [VERB] If someone **embezzles** money that their organization or company has placed in their care, they take it and use it illegally for their own purposes. ❑ *One former director embezzled $34 million in company funds.* [V n]

**em|bez|zle|ment** /ɪmbezəlmənt/ [N-UNCOUNT] **Embezzlement** is the crime of embezzling money.

**em|bit|tered** /ɪmbɪtəʳd/ [ADJ] If someone is **embittered**, they feel angry and unhappy because of harsh, unpleasant, and unfair things that have happened to them. ❑ *He had turned into an embittered, hardened adult.*

**em|bla|zoned** /ɪmbleɪzənd/ [ADJ: usu v-link ADJ, usu ADJ *with* n, ADJ *on/across* n] If something is **emblazoned with** a design, words, or letters, they are clearly drawn, printed, or sewn on it. ❑ *The republic's new flag was emblazoned with the ancient symbol of the Greek Macedonian dynasty. ...a T-shirt with 'Mustique' emblazoned on it.*

**em|blem** /embləm/ (**emblems**) 1 [N-COUNT: usu with supp] An **emblem** is a design representing a country or organization. ❑ *...the emblem of the Soviet Union. ...the Red Cross emblem.* 2 [N-COUNT: usu N *of* n = symbol] An **emblem** is something that represents a quality or idea. ❑ *The eagle was an emblem of strength and courage.*

**em|blem|at|ic** /embləmætɪk/ 1 [ADJ: usu v-link ADJ, usu ADJ *of* n = symbolic] If something, such as an object in a picture, is **emblematic of** a particular quality or an idea, it symbolically represents the quality or idea. ❑ *Dogs are emblematic of faithfulness.* 2 [ADJ: usu v-link ADJ *of* n = representative] If you say that something is **emblematic of** a state of affairs, you mean that it is characteristic of it and represents its most typical features. ❑ *The killing in Pensacola is emblematic of a lot of the violence that is happening around the world.*

**em|bodi|ment** /ɪmbɒdimənt/ [N-SING: usu *the* N *of* n] If you say that someone or something is **the embodiment of** a quality or idea, you mean that that is their most noticeable characteristic or the basis of all they do. [FORMAL] ❑ *A baby is the embodiment of vulnerability.*

**em|body** /ɪmbɒdi/ (**embodies, embodying, embodied**) 1 [VERB = represent] To **embody** an idea or quality means to be a symbol or expression of that idea or quality. ❑ *Jack Kennedy embodied all the hopes of the 1960s...* [V n] *That stability was embodied in the Gandhi family.* [*be* V-ed *in/by* n] 2 [VERB] If something **is embodied in** a particular thing, the second thing contains or consists of the first. ❑ *The proposal has been embodied in a draft resolution...* [*be* V-ed *in/by* n] *UK employment law embodies arbitration and conciliation mechanisms for settling industrial disputes.* [V n]

**em|bold|en** /ɪmbəʊldən/ (**emboldens, emboldening, emboldened**) [VERB] If you **are emboldened by** something, it makes you feel confident enough to behave in a particular way. ❑ *The Prime Minister was steadily emboldened by the discovery that he faced no opposition...* [*be* V-ed] *Four days of non-stop demonstrations have emboldened the anti-government protesters.* [V n]

**em|bo|lism** /embəlɪzəm/ (**embolisms**) [N-COUNT: oft adj N] An **embolism** is a serious medical condition that occurs when an artery becomes blocked, usually by a blood clot.

**em|bossed** /ɪmbɒst, AM -bɔːst/ [ADJ: usu v-link ADJ, usu ADJ *with* n] If a surface such as paper or wood is **embossed with** a design, the design stands up slightly from the surface. ❑ *The paper on the walls was pale gold, embossed with swirling leaf designs.*

**em|brace** /ɪmbreɪs/ (**embraces, embracing, embraced**) 1 [V-RECIP = hug] If you **embrace** someone, you put your arms around them and hold them tightly, usually in order to show your love or affection for them. You can also say that two people **embrace**. ❑ *Penelope came forward and embraced her sister...* [V n (non-recip)] *At first people were sort of crying for joy and embracing each other...* [V n (non-recip)] *He threw his arms round her and they embraced passionately.* [pl-n V] ♦ **Embrace** is also a noun. [N-COUNT] ❑ *...a young couple locked in an embrace.* 2 [VERB] If you **embrace** a change, political system, or idea, you accept it and start supporting it or believing in it. [FORMAL] ❑ *He embraces the new information age...* [V n]

*The new rules have been embraced by government watchdog organizations.* V n ♦ **Embrace** is also a noun. N-SING: usu with supp ❑ *The marriage signalled James's embrace of the Catholic faith.* 3 If something **embraces** a group of people, things, or ideas, it includes them in a larger group or category. [FORMAL] VERB ❑ *...a theory that would embrace the whole field of human endeavour.* V n

**em|broi|der** /ɪmbrɔɪdəʳ/ **(embroiders, embroidering, embroidered)** 1 If something such as clothing or cloth **is embroidered with** a design, the design is stitched into it. VERB ❑ *The collar was embroidered with very small red strawberries...* be V-ed with/in n *Matilda was embroidering an altar cloth covered with flowers and birds...* V n *I have a pillow with my name embroidered on it.* V-ed, Also V 2 If you **embroider** a story or account of something, or if you **embroider on** it, you try to make it more interesting by adding details which may be untrue. VERB = embellish ❑ *He told some lies and sometimes just embroidered the truth...* V n *She embroidered on this theme for about ten minutes.* V on n

**em|broi|dery** /ɪmbrɔɪdəri/ **(embroideries)** 1 **Embroidery** consists of designs stitched into cloth. N-VAR ❑ *The shorts had blue embroidery over the pockets.* 2 **Embroidery** is the activity of stitching designs onto cloth. N-UNCOUNT ❑ *She learned sewing, knitting and embroidery.*

**em|broil** /ɪmbrɔɪl/ **(embroils, embroiling, embroiled)** If someone **embroils** you **in** a fight or an argument, they get you deeply involved in it. VERB ❑ *Any hostilities could result in retaliation and further embroil U.N. troops in fighting.* V n in n Also V n

**em|broiled** /ɪmbrɔɪld/ If you become **embroiled in** a fight or argument, you become deeply involved in it. ADJ: v-link ADJ, usu ADJ in n ❑ *The Government insisted that troops would not become embroiled in battles in Bosnia.*

**em|bryo** /embrioʊ/ **(embryos)** 1 An **embryo** is an unborn animal or human being in the very early stages of development. N-COUNT ❑ *...the remarkable resilience of very young embryos.* 2 An **embryo** idea, system, or organization is in the very early stages of development, but is expected to grow stronger. ADJ: ADJ n ❑ *They are an embryo party of government... It was an embryo idea rather than a fully worked proposal.*

**em|bry|ol|ogy** /embriɒlədʒi/ **Embryology** is the scientific study of embryos and their development. N-UNCOUNT ♦ **em|bry|olo|gist** **(embryologists** /embriɒlədʒɪst/**)** N-COUNT ❑ *...a genetic embryologist at the hospital.*

**em|bry|on|ic** /embriɒnɪk/ An **embryonic** process, idea, organization, or organism is one at a very early stage in its development. [FORMAL] ADJ: usu ADJ n ❑ *...Romania's embryonic democracy. ...embryonic plant cells.*

**em|cee** /emsiː/ **(emcees, emceeing, emceed)** 1 An **emcee** is the same as a **master of ceremonies**. [AM] N-COUNT 2 To **emcee** an event or performance of something means to act as master of ceremonies for it. [AM] VERB ❑ *I'm going to be emceeing a costume contest...* V n *That first night I emceed I was absolutely terrified.* V

**em|er|ald** /emərəld/ **(emeralds)** 1 An **emerald** is a precious stone which is clear and bright green. N-COUNT 2 Something that is **emerald** is bright green in colour. COLOUR ❑ *...an emerald valley.*

**emerge** /ɪmɜːʳdʒ/ **(emerges, emerging, emerged)** ◆◆◇ 1 To **emerge** means to come out from an enclosed or dark space such as a room or a vehicle, or from a position where you could not be seen. VERB ❑ *Richard was waiting outside the door as she emerged...* V *The postman emerged from his van soaked to the skin.* V from n *...holes made by the emerging adult beetle.* V-ing 2 If you **emerge from** a difficult or bad experience, you come to the end of it. VERB ❑ *There is growing evidence that the economy is at last emerging from recession.* V from n 3 If a fact or result **emerges** from a period of thought, discussion, or investigation, it becomes known as a result of it. VERB ❑ *...the growing corruption that has emerged in the past few years...* V *It soon emerged that neither the July nor August mortgage repayment had been collected...* it V that *The emerging caution over numbers is perhaps only to be expected.* V-ing 4 If someone or something **emerges as** a particular thing, they become recognized as that thing. [JOURNALISM] VERB ❑ *Vietnam has emerged as the world's third-biggest rice exporter...* V as n *New leaders have emerged.* V 5 When something such as an organization or an industry **emerges**, it comes into existence. [JOURNALISM] VERB ❑ *...the new republic that emerged in October 1917.* V *...the emerging democracies of East-ern Europe.* V-ing

**emer|gence** /ɪmɜːʳdʒəns/ The **emergence** of something is the process or event of its coming into existence. N-UNCOUNT: with supp, usu N of n ❑ *...the emergence of new democracies in East and Central Europe.*

**emer|gen|cy** /ɪmɜːʳdʒənsi/ **(emergencies)** ◆◆◇ 1 An **emergency** is an unexpected and difficult or dangerous situation, especially an accident, which happens suddenly and which requires quick action to deal with it. N-COUNT = crisis ❑ *He deals with emergencies promptly... The hospital will cater only for emergencies.* 2 An **emergency** action is one that is done or arranged quickly and not in the normal way, because an emergency has occurred. ADJ: ADJ n ❑ *The Prime Minister has called an emergency meeting of parliament... She made an emergency appointment.* 3 **Emergency** equipment or supplies are those intended for use in an emergency. ADJ: ADJ n ❑ *The plane is carrying emergency supplies for refugees... They escaped through an emergency exit and called the police.*

**emer|gen|cy brake** **(emergency brakes)** In a vehicle, the **emergency brake** is a brake which the driver operates with his or her hand, and uses, for example, in emergencies or when parking. [mainly AM] N-COUNT

✓ in BRIT, use **handbrake**

**emer|gen|cy room** **(emergency rooms)** The **emergency room** is the room or department in a hospital where people who have severe injuries or sudden illnesses are taken for emergency treatment. The abbreviation **ER** is often used. [mainly AM] N-COUNT

✓ in BRIT, usually use **casualty, A & E**

**emer|gen|cy ser|vices** The **emergency services** are the public organizations whose job is to take quick action to deal with emergencies when they occur, especially the fire brigade, the police, and the ambulance service. N-PLURAL: usu the N

**emer|gent** /ɪmɜːʳdʒənt/ An **emergent** country, political movement, or social group is one that is becoming powerful or coming into existence. [WRITTEN] ADJ: ADJ n ❑ *...an emergent state. ...an emergent nationalist movement.*

**emeri|tus** /ɪmerɪtəs/ **Emeritus** is used with a professional title to indicate that the person bearing it has retired but keeps the title as an honour. ADJ: ADJ n, n ADJ ❑ *...emeritus professor of physics... He will continue as chairman emeritus.*

**emet|ic** /ɪmetɪk/ **(emetics)** 1 An **emetic** is something that is given to someone to swallow, in order to make them vomit. N-COUNT 2 Something that is **emetic** makes you vomit. ADJ

**emi|grant** /emɪgrənt/ **(emigrants)** An **emigrant** is a person who has left their own country to live in another country. Compare **immigrant**. N-COUNT

**emi|grate** /emɪgreɪt/ **(emigrates, emigrating, emigrated)** If you **emigrate**, you leave your own country to live in another country. VERB ❑ *He emigrated to Belgium...* V to n *They planned to emigrate.* V ♦ **emi|gra|tion** /emɪgreɪʃən/ N-UNCOUNT: usu with supp *...the huge emigration of workers to the West.*

**émi|gré** /emɪgreɪ/ **(émigrés)** also **emigre**. An **émigré** is someone who has left their own country and lives in a different country for political reasons. N-COUNT = immigrant ❑ *Several hundred Bosnian refugees and emigres demonstrated outside the main entrance.*

**emi|nence** /emɪnəns/ **Eminence** is the quality of being very well-known and highly respected. N-UNCOUNT ❑ *Many of the pilots were to achieve emi-*

*nence in the aeronautical world... Beveridge was a man of great eminence.*

**emi|nent** /eminənt/ An **eminent** person is well-known and respected, especially because they are good at their profession. ❑ *...an eminent scientist.* ADJ: usu ADJ n

**emi|nent|ly** /eminəntli/ You use **eminently** in front of an adjective describing a positive quality in order to emphasize the quality expressed by that adjective. ❑ *His books on diplomatic history were eminently readable.* ADV: ADV adj/-ed [emphasis] = highly

**emir** /emɪəʳ/ **(emirs)** An **emir** is a Muslim ruler. ❑ *...the Emir of Kuwait.* N-COUNT: usu *the* N

**emir|ate** /emərət, AM ɪmɪərət/ **(emirates)** An **emirate** is a country that is ruled by an emir. N-COUNT: oft in names

**em|is|sary** /emɪsəri, AM -seri/ **(emissaries)** An **emissary** is a representative sent by one government or leader to another. [FORMAL] ❑ *...the President's special emissary to Hanoi.* N-COUNT

**emis|sion** /ɪmɪʃᵊn/ **(emissions)** An **emission of** something such as gas or radiation is the release of it into the atmosphere. [FORMAL] ❑ *The emission of gases such as carbon dioxide should be stabilised at their present level... Sulfur emissions from steel mills become acid rain.* N-VAR

**emit** /ɪmɪt/ **(emits, emitting, emitted)** 1 If something **emits** heat, light, gas, or a smell, it produces it and sends it out by means of a physical or chemical process. [FORMAL] ❑ *The new device emits a powerful circular column of light.* 2 To **emit** a sound or noise means to produce it. [FORMAL] ❑ *Polly blinked and emitted a long, low whistle.* VERB V n VERB V n

**emol|lient** /ɪmɒliənt/ **(emollients)** 1 An **emollient** is a liquid or cream which you put on your skin to make it softer or to reduce pain. [FORMAL] 2 An **emollient** cream or other substance makes your skin softer or reduces pain. [FORMAL] N-MASS ADJ: ADJ n

**emolu|ment** /ɪmɒljumənt/ **(emoluments)** **Emoluments** are money or other forms of payment which a person receives for doing work. [FORMAL] ❑ *He could earn up to £1m a year in salary and emoluments from many directorships.* N-COUNT: usu pl

**emo|ti|con** /ɪmoutɪkɒn/ **(emoticons)** An **emoticon** is a symbol used in e-mail to show how someone is feeling. :-) is an emoticon showing happiness. [COMPUTING] N-COUNT = smiley

**emo|tion** /ɪmouʃᵊn/ **(emotions)** 1 An **emotion** is a feeling such as happiness, love, fear, anger, or hatred, which can be caused by the situation that you are in or the people you are with. ❑ *Happiness was an emotion that Reynolds was having to relearn... Her voice trembled with emotion.* 2 **Emotion** is the part of a person's character that consists of their feelings, as opposed to their thoughts. ❑ *...the split between reason and emotion.* ◆◇◇ N-VAR = feeling N-UNCOUNT

**emo|tion|al** /ɪmouʃənᵊl/ 1 **Emotional** means concerned with emotions and feelings. ❑ *I needed this man's love, and the emotional support he was giving me... Victims are left with emotional problems that can last for life.* ♦ **emo|tion|al|ly** *Are you saying that you're becoming emotionally involved with me?* 2 An **emotional** situation or issue is one that causes people to have strong feelings. ❑ *It's a very emotional issue. How can you advocate selling the ivory from elephants?* ♦ **emo|tion|al|ly** *In an emotionally charged speech, he said he was resigning.* 3 If someone is or becomes **emotional**, they show their feelings very openly, especially because they are upset. ❑ *He is a very emotional man... I don't get as emotional as I once did.* ◆◇◇ ADJ: usu ADJ n = psychological ADV: ADV adj/-ed ADJ = emotive ADV: ADV adj/-ed ADJ

**emo|tion|al capi|tal** When people refer to the **emotional capital** of a company, they mean all the psychological assets and resources of the company, such as how the employees feel about the company. [BUSINESS] ❑ *UK organisations are not nourishing their intellectual and emotional capital.* N-UNCOUNT

**emo|tion|less** /ɪmouʃᵊnləs/ If you describe someone as **emotionless**, you mean that they do not show any feelings or emotions. ADJ ≠ emotional

**emo|tive** /ɪmoutɪv/ An **emotive** situation or issue is likely to make people feel strong emotions. ❑ *Embryo research is an emotive issue.* ADJ: usu ADJ n = emotional

**em|pa|thet|ic** /empəθetɪk/ Someone who is **empathetic** has the ability to share another person's feelings or emotions as if they were their own. [FORMAL] ❑ *...Clinton's skills as an empathetic listener.* ADJ

**em|pa|thize** /empəθaɪz/ **(empathizes, empathizing, empathized)**

☑ in BRIT, also use **empathise**

If you **empathize with** someone, you understand their situation, problems, and feelings, because you have been in a similar situation. ❑ *I clearly empathize with the people who live in those neighborhoods... Parents must make use of their natural ability to empathize.* VERB V with n V

**em|pa|thy** /empəθi/ **Empathy** is the ability to share another person's feelings and emotions as if they were your own. ❑ *Having begun my life in a children's home I have great empathy with the little ones.* N-UNCOUNT: oft N *with/for* n

**em|per|or** /empərəʳ/ **(emperors)** An **emperor** is a man who rules an empire or is the head of state in an empire. N-COUNT; N-TITLE

**em|pha|sis** /emfəsɪs/ **(emphases** /emfəsiːz/**)** 1 **Emphasis** is special or extra importance that is given to an activity or to a part or aspect of something. ❑ *Too much emphasis is placed on research... Grant puts a special emphasis on weather in his paintings.* 2 **Emphasis** is extra force that you put on a syllable, word, or phrase when you are speaking in order to make it seem more important. ❑ *'I might have know it!' Miss Burnett said with emphasis... The emphasis is on the first syllable of the last word.* ◆◇◇ N-VAR: oft N *on* n = stress N-VAR

**em|pha|size** /emfəsaɪz/ **(emphasizes, emphasizing, emphasized)** ◆◇◇

☑ in BRIT, also use **emphasise**

To **emphasize** something means to indicate that it is particularly important or true, or to draw special attention to it. ❑ *But it's also been emphasized that no major policy changes can be expected to come out of the meeting... Discuss pollution with your child, emphasizing how nice a clean street, lawn, or park looks.* VERB V that V how

**em|phat|ic** /ɪmfætɪk/ 1 An **emphatic** response or statement is one made in a forceful way, because the speaker feels very strongly about what they are saying. ❑ *His response was immediate and emphatic... I answered both questions with an emphatic 'Yes'.* 2 If you are **emphatic about** something, you use forceful language which shows that you feel very strongly about what you are saying. ❑ *The rebels are emphatic that this is not a surrender... He is especially emphatic about the value of a precise routine.* 3 An **emphatic** win or victory is one in which the winner has won by a large amount or distance. ❑ *Yesterday's emphatic victory was their fifth in succession.* ADJ ADJ: v-link ADJ, oft ADJ that, ADJ *about* n ADJ: usu ADJ n

**em|phati|cal|ly** /ɪmfætɪkli/ 1 If you say something **emphatically**, you say it in a forceful way which shows that you feel very strongly about what you are saying. ❑ *'No fast food', she said emphatically... Mr Davies has emphatically denied the charges.* 2 You use **emphatically** to emphasize the statement you are making. ❑ *Making people feel foolish is emphatically not my strategy.* ADV: ADV with v ADV: ADV with cl/group [emphasis]

**em|phy|sema** /emfɪsiːmə/ **Emphysema** is a serious medical condition that occurs when the lungs become larger and do not work properly, causing difficulty in breathing. N-UNCOUNT

**em|pire** /empaɪəʳ/ **(empires)** 1 An **empire** is a number of individual nations that are all controlled by the government or ruler of one particular country. ❑ *...the Roman Empire.* 2 You can refer to a group of companies controlled by one person as an **empire**. ❑ *...the big Mondadori publishing empire.* ◆◇◇ N-COUNT N-COUNT: with supp

**em|piri|cal** /ɪmpɪrɪkəl/ **Empirical** evidence or study relies on practical experience rather than theories. ❑ *There is no empirical evidence to support his thesis.* ♦ **em|piri|cal|ly** *...empirically based research... They approached this part of their task empirically.* ADJ: usu ADJ n; ADV: usu ADV adj/-ed, ADV after v

**em|piri|cism** /ɪmpɪrɪsɪzəm/ **Empiricism** is the belief that people should rely on practical experience and experiments, rather than on theories as, a basis for knowledge. [FORMAL] ♦ **em|piri|cist** **(empiricists)** ❑ *He was an unswerving empiricist with little time for theory.* N-UNCOUNT; N-COUNT

**em|place|ment** /ɪmpleɪsmənt/ **(emplacements)** **Emplacements** are specially prepared positions from which a heavy gun can be fired. [TECHNICAL] ❑ *There are gun emplacements every five-hundred yards along the road.* N-COUNT: usu pl, usu supp N

**em|ploy** /ɪmplɔɪ/ **(employs, employing, employed)** ◆◇◇ 1 If a person or company **employs** you, they pay you to work for them. ❑ *The company employs 18 staff... More than 3,000 local workers are employed in the tourism industry... The government counted 27,600,000 employed persons in West Germany.* 2 If you **employ** certain methods, materials, or expressions, you use them. ❑ *The tactics the police are now to employ are definitely uncompromising. ...the approaches and methods employed in the study.* 3 If your time **is employed in** doing something, you are using the time you have to do that thing. ❑ *Your time could be usefully employed in attending to professional matters.* 4 If you are **in the employ of** someone or something, you work for them. [FORMAL] ❑ *Others hinted that he was in the employ of the KGB.* VERB; V n; be V-ed in/as n; V-ed; Also V n to-inf; VERB = use; V n; V-ed; Also V n as n; VERB: usu passive; be V-ed in -ing/n; PHRASE

**em|ploy|able** /ɪmplɔɪəbəl/ Someone who is **employable** has skills or abilities that are likely to make someone want to give them a job. ❑ *People need basic education if they are to become employable. ...employable adults.* ADJ

**em|ployee** /ɪmplɔɪiː/ **(employees)** ◆◆◇ An **employee** is a person who is paid to work for an organization or for another person. ❑ *He is an employee of Fuji Bank. ...a government employee.* N-COUNT

**em|ploy|er** /ɪmplɔɪəʳ/ **(employers)** ◆◇◇ Your **employer** is the person or organization that you work for. ❑ *He had been sent to Rome by his employer... The telephone company is the country's largest employer.* N-COUNT

**em|ploy|ment** /ɪmplɔɪmənt/ ◆◇◇ 1 **Employment** is the fact of having a paid job. ❑ *She was unable to find employment... He regularly drove from his home to his place of employment.* 2 **Employment** is the fact of employing someone. ❑ *...the employment of children under nine.* 3 **Employment** is the work that is available in a country or area. ❑ *...economic policies designed to secure full employment.* N-UNCOUNT; N-UNCOUNT; N-UNCOUNT ≠ unemployment

**em|ploy|ment agen|cy** **(employment agencies)** An **employment agency** is a company whose business is to help people to find work and help employers to find the workers they need. [BUSINESS] N-COUNT

**em|po|rium** /empɔːriəm/ **(emporiums** or **emporia** /empɔːriə/**)** An **emporium** is a store or large shop. [FORMAL] N-COUNT

**em|power** /ɪmpaʊəʳ/ **(empowers, empowering, empowered)** 1 If someone **is empowered to** do something, they have the authority or power to do it. [FORMAL] ❑ *The army is now empowered to operate on a shoot-to-kill basis.* 2 To **empower** someone means to give them the means to achieve something, for example to become stronger or more successful. ❑ *What I'm trying to do is to empower people, to give them ways to help them get well.* VERB = authorize; be V-ed to-inf; VERB; V n

**em|pow|er|ment** /ɪmpaʊəʳmənt/ The **empowerment of** a person or group of people is the process of giving them power and status in a particular situation. ❑ *This government believes very strongly in the empowerment of women.* N-UNCOUNT: oft the N of n

**em|press** /emprɪs/ **(empresses)** An **empress** is a woman who rules an empire or who is the wife of an emperor. N-COUNT; N-TITLE

**emp|ti|ness** /emptinəs/ 1 A feeling of **emptiness** is an unhappy or frightening feeling that nothing is worthwhile, especially when you are very tired or have just experienced something upsetting. ❑ *The result later in life may be feelings of emptiness and depression.* 2 The **emptiness** of a place is the fact that there is nothing in it. ❑ *...the emptiness of the desert.* N-UNCOUNT; N-UNCOUNT

**emp|ty** /empti/ **(emptier, emptiest, empties, emptying, emptied)** ◆◇◇ 1 An **empty** place, vehicle, or container is one that has no people or things in it. ❑ *The room was bare and empty. ...empty cans of lager... The roads were nearly empty of traffic.* 2 An **empty** gesture, threat, or relationship has no real value or meaning. ❑ *His father threatened to throw him out, but he knew it was an empty threat. ...to ensure the event is not perceived as an empty gesture.* 3 If you describe a person's life or a period of time as **empty**, you mean that nothing interesting or valuable happens in it. ❑ *My life was very hectic but empty before I met him.* 4 If you **feel empty**, you feel unhappy and have no energy, usually because you are very tired or have just experienced something upsetting. ❑ *I feel so empty, my life just doesn't seem worth living any more.* 5 If you **empty** a container, or **empty** something out of it, you remove its contents, especially by tipping it up. ❑ *I emptied the ashtray... Empty the noodles and liquid into a serving bowl... He emptied the contents out into the palm of his hand.* 6 If someone **empties** a room or place, or if it **empties**, everyone that is in it goes away. ❑ *The stadium emptied at the end of the first day of athletics. ...a woman who could empty a pub full of drunks just by lifting one fist.* 7 A river or canal that **empties into** a lake, river, or sea flows into it. ❑ *The Washougal empties into the Columbia River near Portland.* 8 **Empties** are bottles or containers which no longer have anything in them. ADJ: oft ADJ of n; ADJ: usu ADJ n; ADJ: usu v-link ADJ; ADJ: usu feel ADJ, also ADJ n; VERB; V n; V n prep; V n with out; VERB; V; V n; VERB; V into n; N-COUNT: usu pl

**empty-handed** If you come away from somewhere **empty-handed**, you have failed to get what you wanted. ❑ *Delegates from the warring sides held a new round of peace talks but went away empty-handed.* ADJ: ADJ after v

**empty-headed** If you describe someone as **empty-headed**, you mean that they are not very intelligent and often do silly things. ADJ

**emu** /iːmjuː/ **(emus** or **emu)** An **emu** is a large Australian bird which cannot fly. N-COUNT

**emu|late** /emjʊleɪt/ **(emulates, emulating, emulated)** If you **emulate** something or someone, you imitate them because you admire them a great deal. [FORMAL] ❑ *Sons are traditionally expected to emulate their fathers.* ♦ **emu|la|tion** /emjʊleɪʃən/ *...a role model worthy of emulation.* VERB; V n; N-UNCOUNT

**emul|si|fi|er** /ɪmʌlsɪfaɪəʳ/ **(emulsifiers)** An **emulsifier** is a substance used in food manufacturing which helps to combine liquids of different thicknesses. N-MASS

**emul|si|fy** /ɪmʌlsɪfaɪ/ **(emulsifies, emulsifying, emulsified)** When two liquids of different thicknesses **emulsify** or when they **are emulsified**, they combine. [TECHNICAL] ❑ *It is the pressure which releases the coffee oils; these emulsify and give the coffee its rich, velvety texture... Whisk the cream into the mixture to emulsify it... Beeswax acts as an emulsifying agent. ...emulsified oil.* VERB; pl-n V; V n; V-ing; V-ed

**emul|sion** /ɪmʌlʃən/ **(emulsions)** 1 **Emulsion** or **emulsion paint** is a water-based paint, which is not shiny when it dries. It is used for painting walls and ceilings. ❑ *...an undercoat of white emulsion paint. ...a dark blue matt emulsion.* 2 An **emulsion** is a liquid or cream which is a mixture of two or more liquids, such as oil and water, which do not naturally mix together. N-MASS; N-MASS

**en-** /ɪn-/

> Pronounced /ɪn-/ or /en-/, especially in American English.

**En-** is added to words to form verbs that describe the process of putting someone into a particular state, condition, or place, or to form adjectives and nouns that describe that process or those states and conditions. ❑ *People with disabilities are now doing many things to enrich their lives. ...the current campaign to enthrone him as our national bard... It is the first enthronement since 1928.* PREFIX

**en|able** /ɪneɪbᵊl/ **(enables, enabling, enabled)** ◆◇◇ [1] If someone or something **enables** you **to** do a particular thing, they give you the opportunity to do it. ❑ *The new test should enable doctors to detect the disease early.* ♦ **en|abling** *Researchers describe it as an enabling technology.* [2] To **enable** something **to** happen means to make it possible for it to happen. ❑ *The hot sun enables the grapes to reach optimum ripeness... The working class is still too small to enable a successful socialist revolution.* [3] To **enable** someone **to** do something means to give them permission or the right to do it. ❑ *The republic's legislation enables young people to do an alternative service.* ♦ **en|abling** *Some protection for victims must be written into the enabling legislation.* VERB; V n to-inf; ADJ; VERB; V n to-inf; V n; VERB; V n to-inf; ADJ: ADJ n

**en|act** /ɪnækt/ **(enacts, enacting, enacted)** [1] When a government or authority **enacts** a proposal, they make it into a law. [TECHNICAL] ❑ *The authorities have failed so far to enact a law allowing unrestricted emigration.* [2] If people **enact** a story or play, they perform it by acting. ❑ *She often enacted the stories told to her by her father.* [3] If a particular event or situation **is enacted**, it happens; used especially to talk about something that has happened before. [JOURNALISM] ❑ *It was a scene which was enacted month after month for eight years.* VERB; V n; VERB; V n; VERB: usu passive; be V-ed

**en|act|ment** /ɪnæktmənt/ **(enactments)** [1] The **enactment of** a law is the process in a parliament or other law-making body by which the law is agreed upon and made official. [TECHNICAL] ❑ *We support the call for the enactment of a Bill of Rights.* [2] The **enactment of** a play or story is the performance of it by an actor or group of actors. [FORMAL] ❑ *The main building was also used for the enactment of mystery plays.* N-VAR: usu N *of* n; N-VAR: usu N *of* n = performance

**enam|el** /ɪnæmᵊl/ **(enamels)** [1] **Enamel** is a substance like glass which can be heated and put onto metal, glass, or pottery in order to decorate or protect it. ❑ *...a white enamel saucepan on the oil stove. ...enamel baths.* [2] **Enamel** is a hard, shiny paint that is used especially for painting metal and wood. ❑ *...enamel polymer paints.* [3] **Enamel** is the hard white substance that forms the outer part of a tooth. N-MASS: oft N n; N-MASS: oft N n; N-UNCOUNT

**enam|elled** /ɪnæmᵊld/

> in AM, use **enameled**

An **enamelled** object is decorated or covered with enamel. ❑ *...enamelled plates.* ADJ: ADJ n

**enam|el|ling** /ɪnæməlɪŋ/

> in AM, use **enameling**

**Enamelling** is the decoration of something such as jewellery with enamel. N-UNCOUNT

**en|am|oured** /ɪnæmərd/

> in AM, use **enamored**

If you are **enamoured of** something, you like or admire it a lot. If you are not **enamoured of** something, you dislike or disapprove of it. [LITERARY] ❑ *I became totally enamored of the wildflowers there... The religious conservatives are not enamoured of the West and its values.* ADJ: usu v-link ADJ, usu ADJ *of/with* n

**en bloc** /ɒn blɒk/ If a group of people do something **en bloc**, they do it all together and at the same time. If a group of people or things are considered **en bloc**, they are considered as a group, rather than separately. ❑ *The selectors should resign en bloc... Now the governors en bloc are demanding far more consultation and rights over contractual approval.* ADV: ADV after v, n ADV = en masse

**en|camped** /ɪnkæmpt/ If people, especially soldiers, are **encamped** somewhere, they have set up camp there. ❑ *He made his way back to the farmyard where his regiment was encamped.* ADJ

**en|camp|ment** /ɪnkæmpmənt/ **(encampments)** An **encampment** is a group of tents or other shelters in a particular place, especially when they are used by soldiers, refugees, or gypsies. ❑ *...a large military encampment.* N-COUNT: usu with supp

**en|cap|su|late** /ɪnkæpsjʊleɪt/ **(encapsulates, encapsulating, encapsulated)** To **encapsulate** particular facts or ideas means to represent all their most important aspects in a very small space or in a single object or event. ❑ *A Wall Street Journal editorial encapsulated the views of many conservatives... His ideas were encapsulated in a book called 'Democratic Ideals and Reality'.* ♦ **en|cap|su|la|tion** /ɪnkæpsjʊleɪʃᵊn/ **(encapsulations)** *...a witty encapsulation of modern America.* VERB; V n; be V-ed *in* n Also V n *in* n; N-COUNT: usu sing, usu N *of* n

**en|case** /ɪnkeɪs/ **(encases, encasing, encased)** If a person or an object **is encased in** something, they are completely covered or surrounded by it. ❑ *When nuclear fuel is manufactured it is encased in metal cans... These weapons also had a heavy brass guard which encased almost the whole hand... The original plan was to encase a small amount of a radioactive substance in a protective steel container.* VERB; be V-ed *in* n; V n; V n *in/with* n

**-ence** /-əns/ or **-ency** /-ənsi/ **-ence** and **-ency** are added to adjectives, usually in place of -ent, to form nouns referring to states, qualities, attitudes, or behaviour. For example, 'affluence' is the state of being affluent. SUFFIX

**en|chant** /ɪntʃɑːnt, -tʃænt/ **(enchants, enchanting, enchanted)** [1] If you **are enchanted by** someone or something, they cause you to have feelings of great delight or pleasure. ❑ *Dena was enchanted by the house... She enchanted you as she has so many others.* ♦ **en|chant|ed** *Don't expect young children to be as enchanted with the scenery as you are.* [2] In fairy stories and legends, to **enchant** someone or something means to put a magic spell on them. ❑ *King Arthur hid his treasures here and Merlin enchanted the cave so that nobody should ever find them. ...Celtic stories of cauldrons and enchanted vessels.* VERB; be V-ed; V n; ADJ; VERB; V n; V-ed

**en|chant|ing** /ɪntʃɑːntɪŋ, -tʃænt-/ If you describe someone or something as **enchanting**, you mean that they are very attractive or charming. ❑ *She's an absolutely enchanting child... The overall effect is enchanting.* ADJ

**en|chant|ment** /ɪntʃɑːntmənt, -tʃænt-/ **(enchantments)** [1] If you say that something has **enchantment**, you mean that it makes you feel great delight or pleasure. Your **enchantment with** something is the fact of your feeling great delight and pleasure because of it. ❑ *The wilderness campsite had its own peculiar enchantment... Percy's enchantment with orchids dates back to 1951.* [2] In fairy stories and legends, an **enchantment** is a magic spell. N-UNCOUNT; N-COUNT = spell

**en|chant|ress** /ɪntʃɑːntrɪs, -tʃænt-/ **(enchantresses)** In fairy stories and legends, an **enchantress** is a woman who uses magic to put spells on people and things. N-COUNT

**en|chi|la|da** /entʃɪlædə/ **(enchiladas)** An **enchilada** consists of a flat piece of bread called a tortilla wrapped round a filling of meat or vegetables and served hot, usually with a sauce. N-COUNT

**en|cir|cle** /ɪnsɜːʳkᵊl/ **(encircles, encircling, encircled)** To **encircle** something or someone means to surround or enclose them, or to go round them. ❑ *A forty-foot-high concrete wall encircles the jail.* VERB = surround; V n

**en|clave** /eŋkleɪv/ **(enclaves)** An **enclave** is an area within a country or a city where people live who have a different nationality or culture from the people living in the surrounding country N-COUNT: usu with supp or city. ❑ *Nagorno-Karabakh is an Armenian enclave inside Azerbaijan.*

**en|close** /ɪnkloʊz/ **(encloses, enclosing, enclosed)** 1 If a place or object **is enclosed** by something, the place or object is inside that thing or completely surrounded by it. ❑ *Samples must be enclosed in two watertight containers... Enclose the pot in a polythene bag. ...the enclosed waters of the Baltic.* 2 If you **enclose** something with a letter, you put it in the same envelope as the letter. ❑ *I have enclosed a cheque for £10... The enclosed leaflet shows how Service Care can ease all your worries.* VERB be V-ed in n V n in n V-ed VERB V n V-ed

**en|closed** /ɪnkloʊzd/ An **enclosed** community of monks or nuns does not have any contact with the outside world. ❑ *...monks and nuns from enclosed orders.* ADJ: usu ADJ n

**en|clo|sure** /ɪnkloʊʒəʳ/ **(enclosures)** An **enclosure** is an area of land that is surrounded by a wall or fence and that is used for a particular purpose. ❑ *This enclosure was so vast that the outermost wall could hardly be seen.* N-COUNT

**en|code** /ɪnkoʊd/ **(encodes, encoding, encoded)** If you **encode** a message or some information, you put it into a code or express it in a different form or system of language. ❑ *The two parties encode confidential data in a form that is not directly readable by the other party.* VERB ≠ decode V n

**en|com|pass** /ɪnkʌmpəs/ **(encompasses, encompassing, encompassed)** 1 If something **encompasses** particular things, it includes them. ❑ *His repertoire encompassed everything from Bach to Schoenberg.* 2 To **encompass** a place means to completely surround or cover it. ❑ *The map shows the rest of the western region, encompassing nine states.* VERB = embrace V n VERB V n

**en|core** /ɒŋkɔːʳ, -kɔːʳ/ **(encores)** An **encore** is a short extra performance at the end of a longer one, which an entertainer gives because the audience asks for it. ❑ *Lang's final encore last night was 'Barefoot'.* N-COUNT

**en|coun|ter** /ɪnkaʊntəʳ/ **(encounters, encountering, encountered)** ◆◇◇ 1 If you **encounter** problems or difficulties, you experience them. ❑ *Every day of our lives we encounter stresses of one kind or another.* 2 If you **encounter** someone, you meet them, usually unexpectedly. [FORMAL] ❑ *Did you encounter anyone in the building?* 3 An **encounter with** someone is a meeting with them, particularly one that is unexpected or significant. ❑ *The author tells of a remarkable encounter with a group of South Vietnamese soldiers.* 4 An **encounter** is a particular type of experience. ❑ *...a sexual encounter. ...his first serious encounter with alcohol.* VERB V n VERB = meet V n N-COUNT: usu with supp N-COUNT: usu with supp

**en|cour|age** /ɪnkʌrɪdʒ, AM -kɜːr-/ **(encourages, encouraging, encouraged)** ◆◆◇ 1 If you **encourage** someone, you give them confidence, for example by letting them know that what they are doing is good and telling them that they should continue to do it. ❑ *When things aren't going well, he encourages me, telling me not to give up.* 2 If someone **is encouraged by** something that happens, it gives them hope or confidence. ❑ *Investors were encouraged by the news.* ♦ **en|cour|aged** *We were very encouraged, after over 17,000 pictures were submitted... I am encouraged that more physicians are asking questions in these meetings and coming to workshops.* 3 If you **encourage** someone **to** do something, you try to persuade them to do it, for example by telling them that it would be a pleasant thing to do, or by trying to make it easier for them to do it. You can also **encourage** an activity. ❑ *Herbie Hancock was encouraged by his family to learn music at a young age... Participation is encouraged at all levels.* 4 If something **encourages** a particular activity or state, it causes it to happen or increase. ❑ *...a natural substance that encourages cell growth... Slow music encourages supermarket-shoppers to browse longer but spend more.* VERB V n VERB: usu passive be V-ed by n ADJ: v-link ADJ, oft ADJ that VERB V n to-inf V n VERB V n V n to-inf

**en|cour|age|ment** /ɪnkʌrɪdʒmənt, AM -kɜːr-/ **(encouragements)** **Encouragement** is the activity of encouraging someone, or something that is said or done in order to encourage them. ❑ *I also had friends who gave me a great deal of encouragement.* N-VAR: oft N of n

**en|cour|ag|ing** /ɪnkʌrɪdʒɪŋ, AM -kɜːr-/ Something that is **encouraging** gives people hope or confidence. ❑ *There are encouraging signs of an artistic revival... The results have been encouraging... It was encouraging that he recognised the dangers facing the company.* ♦ **en|cour|ag|ing|ly** *'You're doing really well,' her midwife said encouragingly.* ADJ: oft it v-link ADJ that ADV: ADV after v, ADV adj, ADV with cl

**en|croach** /ɪnkroʊtʃ/ **(encroaches, encroaching, encroached)** 1 If one thing **encroaches on** another, the first thing spreads or becomes stronger, and slowly begins to restrict the power, range, or effectiveness of the second thing. [FORMAL] ❑ *The new institutions do not encroach on political power... The movie industry had chosen to ignore the encroaching competition of television.* 2 If something **encroaches on** a place, it spreads and takes over more and more of that place. [FORMAL] ❑ *The rhododendrons encroached ever more on the twisting drive... I turned into the dirt road and followed it through encroaching trees and bushes.* VERB disapproval V on/upon n V-ing VERB V on n V-ing

**en|croach|ment** /ɪnkroʊtʃmənt/ **(encroachments)** You can describe the action or process of encroaching on something as **encroachment**. [FORMAL] ❑ *It's a sign of the encroachment of commercialism in medicine.* N-VAR: usu with supp disapproval

**en|crus|ta|tion** /ɪŋkrʌsteɪʃᵊn/ **(encrustations)** An **encrustation** is a hard and thick layer on the surface of something that has built up over a long period of time. N-VAR

**en|crust|ed** /ɪnkrʌstɪd/ If an object is **encrusted with** something, its surface is covered with a layer of that thing. ❑ *...a blue uniform coat that was thickly encrusted with gold loops.* ADJ: oft ADJ with n

**en|crypt** /ɪnkrɪpt/ **(encrypts, encrypting, encrypted)** If a document or piece of information **is encrypted**, it is written in a special code, so that only certain people can read it. ❑ *Account details are encrypted to protect privacy. ...a program that will encrypt the information before sending. ...encrypted signals.* ♦ **en|cryp|tion** /ɪnkrɪpʃᵊn/ *It is currently illegal to export this encryption technology from the US.* VERB be V-ed V n V-ed N-UNCOUNT: oft N n

**en|cum|ber** /ɪnkʌmbəʳ/ **(encumbers, encumbering, encumbered)** If you **are encumbered** by something, it prevents you from moving freely or doing what you want. ❑ *Lead weights and air cylinders encumbered the divers as they walked to the shore... It is still labouring under the debt burden that it was encumbered with in the 1980s.* ♦ **en|cum|bered** *The rest of the world is less encumbered with legislation.* VERB = burden V n be V-ed with n ADJ: v-link ADJ, usu ADJ with/by n

**en|cum|brance** /ɪnkʌmbrəns/ **(encumbrances)** An **encumbrance** is something or someone that encumbers you. [FORMAL] ❑ *Magdalena considered the past an irrelevant encumbrance.* N-COUNT = burden

**-ency** → see **-ence**.

**en|cyc|li|cal** /ɪnsɪklɪkᵊl/ **(encyclicals)** An **encyclical** is an official letter written by the Pope and sent to all Roman Catholic bishops, usually in order to make a statement about the official teachings of the Church. N-COUNT

**en|cy|clo|pedia** /ɪnsaɪkləpiːdiə/ **(encyclopedias)** also **encyclopaedia**. An **encyclopedia** is a book or set of books in which facts about many different subjects or about one particular subject are arranged for reference, usually in alphabetical order. N-COUNT: usu with supp

**en|cy|clo|pedic** /ɪnsaɪkləpiːdɪk/ also **encyclopaedic**. If you describe something as **encyclopedic**, you mean that it is very full, complete, and thorough in the amount of knowledge or information that it has. ❑ *He had an encyclopaedic knowledge of drugs. ...an almost overwhelmingly encyclopaedic volume.* ADJ: usu ADJ n = comprehensive

**end** /end/ **(ends, ending, ended)** ◆◆◆ [1] **The end of** something such as a period of time, an event, a book, or a film is the last part of it or the final point in it. ❑ *The £5 banknote was first issued at the end of the 18th century... The report is expected by the end of the year... You will have the chance to ask questions at the end.*
N-SING: *the* N, usu prep N, N *of* n

[2] When a situation, process, or activity **ends**, or when something or someone **ends** it, it reaches its final point and stops. ❑ *The meeting quickly ended and Steve and I left the room... Talks have resumed to try to end the fighting.*
VERB
V
V n

♦ **end|ing** *The ending of a marriage by death is different in many ways from an ending occasioned by divorce.*
N-SING: usu *the* N *of* n

[3] An **end to** something or the **end of** it is the act or result of stopping it so that it does not continue any longer. ❑ *The French government today called for an end to the violence... I was worried she would walk out or bring the interview to an end... Francis fined him two weeks' wages and said: 'That's the end of the matter.'*
N-COUNT: usu sing, oft N *to/of* n

[4] If you say that someone or something **ends** a period of time in a particular way, you are indicating what the final situation was like. You can also say that a period of time **ends** in a particular way. ❑ *The markets ended the week on a quiet note... The evening ended with a dramatic display of fireworks.*
VERB
V n prep/adv
V prep

[5] If a period of time **ends**, it reaches its final point. ❑ *Its monthly reports on program trading usually come out about three weeks after each month ends... The first figure shows sales for week ending July 27.*
VERB
V
V

[6] If something such as a book, speech, or performance **ends with** a particular thing or the writer or performer **ends** it **with** that thing, its final part consists of the thing mentioned. ❑ *His statement ended with the words: 'Pray for me.'... The book ends on a lengthy description of Hawaii... Dawkins ends his discussion with a call for liberation... The memo ends: 'Please give this matter your most urgent attention.'*
VERB
V *with/on* n
V *with/on* n
V n *with/on* n
V with quote

[7] If a situation or event **ends** in a particular way, it has that particular result. ❑ *The incident could have ended in tragedy... Our conversations ended with him saying he would try to be more understanding... Shares ended 1.7 per cent firmer on the Frankfurt exchange.*
VERB
V *in* n
V *with* n -ing
V adv/adj

[8] The two **ends** of something long and narrow are the two points or parts of it that are furthest away from each other. ❑ *The company is planning to place surveillance equipment at both ends of the tunnel... A typical fluorescent lamp is a tube with metal electrodes at each end.*
N-COUNT: with supp

[9] The **end of** a long, narrow object such as a finger or a pencil is the tip or smallest edge of it, usually the part that is furthest away from you. ❑ *He tapped the ends of his fingers together... She let the long cone of ash hang at the end of her cigarette.*
N-COUNT: usu with supp, oft N *of* n = *tip*

[10] If an object **ends with** or **in** a particular thing, it has that thing on its tip or point, or as its last part. ❑ *It has three pairs of legs, each ending in a large claw.*
VERB
V *with/in* n

[11] A journey, road, or river that **ends** at a particular place stops there and goes no further. ❑ *The road ended at a T-junction.*
VERB
V prep/adv
Also V

[12] **End** is used to refer to either of the two extreme points of a scale, or of something that you are considering as a scale. ❑ *At the other end of the social scale was the grocer, the village's only merchant... The agreement has been criticised by extremist groups on both ends of the political spectrum.*
N-COUNT: with supp, oft N *of* n

[13] The **other end** is one of two places that are connected because people are communicating with each other by telephone or writing, or are travelling from one place to the other. ❑ *When he answered the phone, Ferguson was at the other end... Make sure to meet them at the other end.*
N-COUNT: supp N

[14] If you refer to a particular **end** of a project or piece of work, you mean a part or aspect of it, for example a part of it that is done by a particular person or in a particular place. [SPOKEN] ❑ *You take care of your end, kid, I'll take care of mine.*
N-COUNT: usu sing, usu supp N

[15] An **end** is the purpose for which something is done or towards which you are working. ❑ *The police force is being manipulated for political ends... Now the government is trying another policy designed to achieve the same end.*
N-COUNT: usu supp N

[16] If you say that something **ends** at a particular point, you mean that it is applied or exists up to that point, and no further. ❑ *Helen is also 25 and from Birmingham, but the similarity ends there.*
VERB
V adv/prep

[17] You can refer to someone's death as their **end**, especially when you are talking about the way that they died or might die. [LITERARY] ❑ *Soon after we had spoken to this man he had met a violent end.*
N-COUNT: usu sing, usu supp N

[18] If you **end by** doing something or **end** in a particular state, you do that thing or get into that state even though you did not originally intend to. ❑ *They ended by making themselves miserable... They'll probably end back on the streets.*
VERB
V *by* -ing
V adv/prep

**PHRASES** [19] If someone **ends it all**, they kill themselves. ❑ *He grew suicidal, thinking up ways to end it all.*
PHRASE: V inflects

[20] If you describe something as, for example, the deal **to end all** deals or the film **to end all** films, you mean that it is very important or successful, and that compared to it all other deals or films seem second-rate. ❑ *It was going to be a party to end all parties.*
PHRASE: n PHR n

[21] If something is **at an end**, it has finished and will not continue. ❑ *The recession is definitely at an end.*
PHRASE: v-link PHR

[22] If something **comes to an end**, it stops. ❑ *The cold war came to an end.*
PHRASE: V inflects

[23] You say **at the end of the day** when you are talking about what happens after a long series of events or what appears to be the case after you have considered the relevant facts. [INFORMAL] ❑ *At the end of the day it's up to the Germans to decide.*
PHRASE: PHR with cl

[24] If you **are thrown in at the deep end**, you are put in a completely new situation without any help or preparation. If you **jump in at the deep end**, you go into a completely new situation without any help or preparation. [mainly BRIT] ❑ *It's a superb job. You get thrown in at the deep end and it's all down to you.*
PHRASE: V inflects

[25] You say **in the end** when you are saying what is the final result of a series of events, or what is your final conclusion after considering all the relevant facts. ❑ *I toyed with the idea of calling the police, but in the end I didn't.*
PHRASE: PHR with cl

[26] If you consider something to be **an end in itself**, you do it because it seems desirable and not because it is likely to lead to something else. ❑ *While he had originally traveled in order to study, traveling had become an end in itself.*
PHRASE: usu v-link PHR

[27] If you find it difficult to **make ends meet**, you can only just manage financially because you hardly have enough money for the things you need. ❑ *With Betty's salary they barely made ends meet.*
PHRASE: *make* inflects

[28] **No end** means a lot. [INFORMAL] ❑ *Teachers inform me that Tracey's behaviour has improved no end.*
PHRASE: PHR after v, oft PHR *of* n

[29] When something happens for hours, days, weeks, or years **on end**, it happens continuously and without stopping for the amount of time that is mentioned. ❑ *He is a wonderful companion and we can talk for hours on end.*
PHRASE: pl-n PHR

[30] Something that is **on end** is upright, instead of in its normal or natural position, for example lying down, flat, or on its longest side.
PHRASE: PHR after v

[31] To **put an end to** something means to cause it to stop. ❑ *Only a political solution could put an end to the violence.*
PHRASE: V inflects, PHR n

[32] If a process or person has reached **the end of the road**, they are unable to progress any further. ❑ *Given the results of the vote, is this the end of the road for the hardliners in Congress?*
PHRASE: PHR after v, v-link PHR *for* n

[33] If you say that something bad is **not the end of the world**, you are trying to stop yourself or someone else being so upset by it, by suggesting that it is not the worst thing that could happen. ❑ *Obviously I'd be disappointed if we don't make it, but it wouldn't be the end of the world.*
PHRASE: V inflects, oft *it* v-link PHR if

[34] **the end of** your **tether** → see **tether**. to **burn the candle at both ends** → see **candle**. to **make** your **hair stand on end** → see **hair**. **a means to an end** → see **means**. to **be on the receiving end** → see **receive**. to **get the wrong end of the stick** → see **stick**. to **be at** your **wits' end** → see **wit**.

♦ **end up** [1] If someone or something **ends up** somewhere, they eventually arrive there, usually by accident. ❑ *She fled with her children, moving from neighbour to neighbour and ending up in a friend's cellar.*
PHRASAL VERB = *finish up, wind up*
V P prep/adv

[2] If you **end up** doing something-
PHRASAL VERB

thing or **end up** in a particular state, you do that thing or get into that state even though you did not originally intend to. ❑ *If you don't know what you want, you might end up getting something you don't want... Every time they went dancing they ended up in a bad mood... She could have ended up a millionairess.* [= finish up; V P -ing; V P prep/adv; V P n]

**en|dan|ger** /ɪndeɪndʒəʳ/ **(endangers, endangering, endangered)** To **endanger** something or someone means to put them in a situation where they might be harmed or destroyed completely. ❑ *The debate could endanger the proposed peace talks. ...endangered species such as lynx and wolf.* [VERB; V n; V-ed]

**en|dear** /ɪndɪəʳ/ **(endears, endearing, endeared)** If something **endears** you **to** someone or if you **endear yourself to** them, you become popular with them and well liked by them. ❑ *Their taste for gambling has endeared them to Las Vegas casino owners... He has endeared himself to the American public.* [VERB; V n to n; V pron-refl to n]

**en|dear|ing** /ɪndɪərɪŋ/ If you describe someone's behaviour as **endearing**, you mean that it causes you to feel very fond of them. ❑ *She has such an endearing personality... Henry's lisp is so endearing.* ♦ **en|dear|ing|ly** *He admits endearingly to doubts and hesitations... She is endearingly free of pretensions.* [ADJ: v-link ADJ; ADV: ADV with v, ADV adj]

**en|dear|ment** /ɪndɪəʳmənt/ **(endearments)** An **endearment** is a loving or affectionate word or phrase that you say to someone you love. ❑ *No term of endearment crossed their lips. ...flattering endearments.* [N-VAR]

**en|deav|our** /ɪndevəʳ/ **(endeavours, endeavouring, endeavoured)**

✔ in AM, use **endeavor**

1 If you **endeavour to** do something, you try very hard to do it. [FORMAL] ❑ *I will endeavour to arrange it.* 2 An **endeavour** is an attempt to do something, especially something new or original. [FORMAL] ❑ *His first endeavours in the field were wedding films.* [VERB = strive; V to-inf; N-VAR: usu with supp, oft N to-inf]

**en|dem|ic** /endemɪk/ 1 If a disease or illness is **endemic** in a place, it is frequently found among the people who live there. [TECHNICAL] ❑ *Polio was then endemic among children my age.* [ADJ] 2 If you say that a condition or problem is **endemic**, you mean that it is very common and strong, and cannot be dealt with easily. [WRITTEN] ❑ *Street crime is virtually endemic in large cities. ...powerful radicals with an endemic hatred and fear of the West.* [ADJ]

**end|game** /endgeɪm/ **(endgames)** 1 In chess, **endgame** refers to the final stage of a game, when only a few pieces are left on the board and one of the players must win soon. [N-VAR] 2 Journalists sometimes refer to the final stages of something such as a war, dispute, or contest, as an **endgame**. [JOURNALISM] ❑ *The political endgame is getting closer.* [N-COUNT]

**end|ing** /endɪŋ/ **(endings)** 1 You can refer to the last part of a book, story, play, or film as the **ending**, especially when you are considering the way that the story ends. ❑ *The film has a Hollywood happy ending.* [N-COUNT: oft supp N] 2 The **ending** of a word is the last part of it. ❑ *...common word endings, like 'ing' in walking.* [N-COUNT: with supp] 3 → See also **end**, **nerve ending**.

**en|dive** /endɪv, AM -daɪv/ **(endives)** 1 **Endive** is a type of plant with crisp curly leaves that is eaten in salads. [N-VAR] 2 **Endive** is a type of a plant with crisp bitter leaves that can be cooked or eaten raw in salads. [AM] [N-VAR]

✔ in BRIT, use **chicory**

**end|less** /endləs/ If you say that something is **endless**, you mean that it is very large or lasts for a very long time, and it seems as if it will never stop. ❑ *They turned into an endless street... The war was endless.* ♦ **end|less|ly** *They talk about it endlessly. ...endlessly long arcades of shops.* [ADJ; ADV: ADV after v, ADV adj]

**endo|crine** /endəkraɪn/ The **endocrine** system is the system of glands that produce hormones which go directly into the bloodstream, such as the pituitary or thyroid glands. [MEDICAL] [ADJ: ADJ n]

**en|dorse** /ɪndɔːʳs/ **(endorses, endorsing, endorsed)** 1 If you **endorse** someone or something, you say publicly that you support or approve of them. ❑ *I can endorse their opinion wholeheartedly.* [VERB; V n] 2 If someone's driving licence **is endorsed**, an official record is made on it that they have been found guilty of a driving offence. [BRIT] ❑ *For failing to report the accident, his licence was endorsed... He also had his licence endorsed with eight penalty points.* [V-PASSIVE; be V-ed; have n V-ed] 3 When you **endorse** a cheque, you write your name on the back of it so that it can be paid into someone's bank account. ❑ *The payee of the cheque must endorse the cheque.* [VERB; V n] 4 If you **endorse** a product or company, you appear in advertisements for it. ❑ *The twins endorsed a line of household cleaning products.* [VERB; V n]

**en|dorse|ment** /ɪndɔːʳsmənt/ **(endorsements)** 1 An **endorsement** is a statement or action which shows that you support or approve of something or someone. ❑ *This is a powerful endorsement for his softer style of government.* [N-COUNT: oft N of/for n] 2 An **endorsement** is a note on someone's driving licence saying that they have been found guilty of a driving offence. [BRIT] [N-COUNT] 3 An **endorsement for** a product or company involves appearing in advertisements for it or showing support for it. [N-COUNT]

**en|dow** /ɪndaʊ/ **(endows, endowing, endowed)** 1 You say that someone **is endowed with** a particular desirable ability, characteristic, or possession when they have it by chance or by birth. ❑ *You are endowed with wealth, good health and a lively intellect.* [VERB: usu passive; be V-ed with n] 2 If you **endow** something **with** a particular feature or quality, you provide it with that feature or quality. ❑ *Herbs have been used for centuries to endow a whole range of foods with subtle flavours.* [VERB = imbue; V n with n] 3 If someone **endows** an institution, scholarship, or project, they provide a large amount of money which will produce the income needed to pay for it. ❑ *The ambassador has endowed a $1 million public-service fellowships program.* [VERB; V n] 4 → See also **well-endowed**.

**en|dow|ment** /ɪndaʊmənt/ **(endowments)** 1 An **endowment** is a gift of money that is made to an institution or community in order to provide it with an annual income. ❑ *...the National Endowment for the Arts.* [N-COUNT] 2 If someone has an **endowment** of a particular quality or ability, they possess it naturally. [FORMAL] [N-COUNT: usu with supp] 3 In finance, an **endowment** policy or mortgage is an insurance policy or mortgage which you pay towards each month and which should then provide you with enough money to pay for your house at the end of a fixed period. [BRIT] [N-COUNT: usu N n]

**end prod|uct** **(end products)** The **end product of** something is the thing that is produced or achieved by means of it. ❑ *It is the end product of exhaustive research and development.* [N-COUNT: oft N of n]

**end re|sult** **(end results)** The **end result of** an activity or a process is the final result that it produces. ❑ *The end result of this will be unity.* [N-COUNT: usu the N]

**en|dur|ance** /ɪndjʊərəns, AM -dʊr-/ **Endurance** is the ability to continue with an unpleasant or difficult situation, experience, or activity over a long period of time. ❑ *The exercise obviously will improve strength and endurance.* [N-UNCOUNT]

**en|dure** /ɪndjʊəʳ, AM -dʊr/ **(endures, enduring, endured)** 1 If you **endure** a painful or difficult situation, you experience it and do not avoid it or give up, usually because you cannot. ❑ *The company endured heavy financial losses.* [VERB; V n] 2 If something **endures**, it continues to exist without any loss in quality or importance. ❑ *Somehow the language endures and continues to survive.* ♦ **en|dur|ing** *...the start of an enduring friendship.* [VERB = persist; V; ADJ: usu ADJ n]

**end user** **(end users)** also **end-user**. The **end user** of a product or service is the person that it [N-COUNT] has been designed for, rather than the person who installs or maintains it. ❑ *Try to describe things in a form that the end user can understand.*

**end zone** **(end zones)** In American football, an **end zone** is one of the areas at each end of the field that the ball must cross for a touchdown to be scored. N-COUNT

**en|ema** /enɪmə/ **(enemas)** If someone has an **enema**, a liquid is put into their bottom in order to make them empty their bowels, for example before they have an operation. N-COUNT

**en|emy** /enəmi/ **(enemies)** ◆◇◇ 1 If someone is your **enemy**, they hate you or want to harm you. N-COUNT 2 If someone is your **enemy**, they are opposed to you and to what you think or do. N-COUNT ❑ *The Government's political enemies were quick to pick up on this series of disasters.* 3 **The enemy** is an army or other force that is opposed to you in a war, or a country with which your country is at war. N-SING-COLL: *the* N, N n ❑ *The enemy were pursued for two miles... He searched the skies for enemy bombers.* 4 If one thing is the **enemy of** another thing, the second thing cannot happen or succeed because of the first thing. N-COUNT: usu sing, N *of* n [FORMAL] ❑ *Reform, as we know, is the enemy of revolution.*

**en|er|get|ic** /enəʳdʒetɪk/ 1 If you are **energetic** in what you do, you have a lot of enthusiasm and determination. ADJ ❑ *Blackwell is 59, strong looking and enormously energetic... The next government will play an energetic role in seeking multilateral nuclear disarmament.* ♦ **en|er|geti|cal|ly** /enəʳdʒetɪkli/ ADV: ADV with v *He had worked energetically all day on his new book.* 2 An **energetic** person is very active and does not feel at all tired. An **energetic** activity involves a lot of physical movement and power. ADJ ❑ *Ten year-olds are incredibly energetic.* ♦ **en|er|geti|cal|ly** ADV: ADV with v *Gretchen chewed energetically on the gristled steak.*

**en|er|gize** /enəʳdʒaɪz/ **(energizes, energizing, energized)**

✔ in BRIT, also use **energise**

To **energize** someone means to give them the enthusiasm and determination to do something. VERB ❑ *He helped energize and mobilize millions of people around the nation...* V n *I am completely energized and feeling terrific.* *be* V-ed ♦ **en|er|giz|ing** ADJ *Acupuncture has a harmonizing and energizing effect on mind and body.*

**en|er|gy** /enəʳdʒi/ **(energies)** ◆◆◇ 1 **Energy** is the ability and strength to do active physical things and the feeling that you are full of physical power and life. N-UNCOUNT ❑ *He was saving his energy for next week's race in Belgium.* 2 **Energy** is determination and enthusiasm about doing things. N-UNCOUNT [approval] ❑ *You have drive and energy for those things you are interested in.* 3 Your **energies** are your efforts and attention, which you can direct towards a particular aim. N-COUNT: usu pl, poss N ❑ *She had started to devote her energies to teaching rather than performing.* 4 **Energy** is the power from sources such as electricity and coal that makes machines work or provides heat. N-UNCOUNT: oft N n ❑ *...those who favour nuclear energy... Oil shortages have brought on an energy crisis.*

**energy-efficient** also **energy efficient.** ADJ A device or building that is **energy-efficient** uses relatively little energy to provide the power it needs. ❑ *...energy-efficient light bulbs. ...information on how to make your home more energy efficient.*

**en|er|vat|ed** /enəʳveɪtɪd/ ADJ If you feel **enervated**, you feel tired and weak. [FORMAL]

**en|er|vat|ing** /enəʳveɪtɪŋ/ ADJ Something that is **enervating** makes you feel tired and weak. [FORMAL]

**en|fant ter|ri|ble** /ɒnfɒn teriːblə/ **(enfants terribles)** If you describe someone as an **enfant terrible**, you mean that they are clever but unconventional, and often cause problems or embarrassment for their friends or families. N-COUNT: usu sing, usu *the* N *of* n [LITERARY] ❑ *He was the enfant terrible of British theater.*

**en|fee|bled** /ɪnfiːbəld/ ADJ = *weakened* If someone or something is **enfeebled**, they have become very weak. [FORMAL] ❑ *He finds himself politically enfeebled. ...the already enfeebled newspaper.*

**en|fold** /ɪnfoʊld/ **(enfolds, enfolding, enfolded)** 1 If something **enfolds** an object or person, they cover, surround, or are wrapped around that object or person. VERB [LITERARY] ❑ *Aurora felt the opium haze enfold her...* V n *Wood was now comfortably enfolded in a woolly dressing-gown.* *be* V-ed *in* n Also V n *in* n 2 If you **enfold** someone or something, you hold them close in a very gentle, loving way. VERB [LITERARY] ❑ *Thack came up behind him, enfolding him in his arms.* V n *in* n Also V n

**en|force** /ɪnfɔːʳs/ **(enforces, enforcing, enforced)** 1 If people in authority **enforce** a law or a rule, they make sure that it is obeyed, usually by punishing people who do not obey it. VERB ❑ *Until now,* V n *the government has only enforced the ban with regard to American ships.* 2 To **enforce** something means to force or cause it to be done or to happen. VERB ❑ *They struggled to limit the cost by enforcing a* V n *low-tech specification... David is now living in Beirut* V-ed *again after an enforced absence.*

**en|force|able** /ɪnfɔːʳsəbəl/ ADJ If something such as a law or agreement is **enforceable**, it can be enforced. ❑ *...the creation of legally enforceable contracts.*

**en|force|ment** /ɪnfɔːʳsmənt/ N-UNCOUNT: oft N *of* n If someone carries out the **enforcement of** an act or rule, they enforce it. ❑ *The doctors want stricter enforcement of existing laws, such as those banning sales of cigarettes to children.*

**en|fran|chise** /ɪnfræntʃaɪz/ **(enfranchises, enfranchising, enfranchised)** To **enfranchise** someone means to give them the right to vote in elections. VERB [FORMAL] ❑ *The company voted to enfranchise its 120 women members.* V n

**en|fran|chise|ment** /ɪnfræntʃaɪzmənt/ N-UNCOUNT: oft N *of* n **Enfranchisement** is the condition of someone being enfranchised. [FORMAL] ❑ *...the enfranchisement of the country's blacks.*

**en|gage** /ɪngeɪdʒ/ **(engages, engaging, engaged)** ◆◇◇ 1 If you **engage in** an activity, you do it or are actively involved with it. VERB [FORMAL] ❑ *I have* V *in* n *never engaged in the drug trade.* 2 If something **engages** you or your attention or interest, it keeps you interested in it and thinking about it. VERB ❑ *They never learned skills to engage the attention of* V n *the others.* 3 If you **engage** someone **in** conversation, you have a conversation with them. VERB ❑ *They tried to engage him in conversation.* V n *in* n 4 If you **engage with** something or **with** a group of people, you get involved with that thing or group and feel that you are connected with it or have real contact with it. VERB ❑ *She found it hard to* V *with* n *engage with office life.* ♦ **en|gage|ment** N-UNCOUNT: usu N *with* n *And she, too, suffers from a lack of critical engagement with the literary texts.* 5 If you **engage** someone to do a particular job, you appoint them to do it. VERB [FORMAL] ❑ *We engaged the services of a recognised engineer.* V n 6 When a part of a machine or other mechanism **engages** or when you **engage** it, it moves into a position where it fits into something else. VERB ❑ *Press* V *the lever until you hear the catch engage. ...a lesson in* V n *how to engage the four-wheel drive.* 7 When a military force **engages** the enemy, it attacks them and starts a battle. VERB ❑ *It could engage the enemy be-* V n *yond the range of hostile torpedoes.* 8 ➔ See also **engaged**, **engaging**.

**en|gaged** /ɪngeɪdʒd/ 1 Someone who is **engaged in** or **engaged on** a particular activity is doing that thing. ADJ: v-link ADJ *in/on* n [FORMAL] ❑ *They found the three engaged in target practice. ...the various projects he was engaged on.* 2 When two people are **engaged**, they have agreed to marry each other. ADJ: usu v-link ADJ, oft ADJ *to* n ❑ *We got engaged on my eighteenth birthday.* 3 If a telephone or a telephone line is **engaged**, it is already being used by someone else so that you are unable to speak to the person you are phoning. ADJ: v-link ADJ [BRIT] ❑ *The line is engaged.*

✔ in AM, use **busy**

4 If a public toilet is **engaged**, it is already being used by someone else. [BRIT] ADJ: v-link ADJ

✔ in AM, usually use **occupied**

**en|gage|ment** /ɪngeɪdʒmənt/ **(engagements)** 1 An **engagement** is an arrangement that you have made to do something at a particular time. [FORMAL] ❑ *He had an engagement at a restaurant in Greek Street at eight.* N-COUNT 2 An **engagement** is an agreement that two people have made with each other to get married. ❑ *I've broken off my engagement to Arthur.* N-COUNT: usu sing, usu poss N 3 You can refer to the period of time during which two people are engaged as their **engagement**. N-COUNT: usu sing, usu poss N 4 A military **engagement** is an armed conflict between two enemies. ❑ *The constitution prohibits them from military engagement on foreign soil.* N-VAR 5 → See also **engage**.

**en|gage|ment ring** **(engagement rings)** An **engagement ring** is a ring worn by a woman when she is engaged to be married. N-COUNT

**en|gag|ing** /ɪngeɪdʒɪŋ/ An **engaging** person or thing is pleasant, interesting, and entertaining. ❑ *...one of her most engaging and least known novels... He was engaging company.* ADJ

**en|gen|der** /ɪndʒendəʳ/ **(engenders, engendering, engendered)** If someone or something **engenders** a particular feeling, atmosphere, or situation, they cause it to occur. [FORMAL] ❑ *It helps engender a sense of common humanity.* VERB V n

**en|gine** /endʒɪn/ **(engines)** ◆◆◇ 1 The **engine** of a car or other vehicle is the part that produces the power which makes the vehicle move. ❑ *He got into the driving seat and started the engine. ...an engine failure that forced a jetliner to crash-land in a field.* N-COUNT 2 An **engine** is also the large vehicle that pulls a railway train. ❑ *In 1941, the train would have been pulled by a steam engine.* N-COUNT

**-engined** /-endʒɪnd/ **-engined** combines with other words to show the number or type of engines that something has. ❑ *...the world's biggest twin-engined airliner. ...a petrol-engined Ford Transit.* COMB in ADJ

**en|gi|neer** /endʒɪnɪəʳ/ **(engineers, engineering, engineered)** ◆◇◇ 1 An **engineer** is a person who uses scientific knowledge to design, construct, and maintain engines and machines or structures such as roads, railways, and bridges. → See also **chemical engineer**, **civil engineer**, **electrical engineer**, **sound engineer**. N-COUNT 2 An **engineer** is a person who repairs mechanical or electrical devices. ❑ *They send a service engineer to fix the disk drive.* N-COUNT 3 An **engineer** is a person who is responsible for maintaining the engine of a ship while it is at sea. N-COUNT 4 When a vehicle, bridge, or building **is engineered**, it is planned and constructed using scientific methods. ❑ *Many of Kuwait's spacious freeways were engineered by W S Atkins. ...the car's better designed and engineered rivals.* VERB: usu passive; be V-ed; V-ed 5 If you **engineer** an event or situation, you arrange for it to happen, in a clever or indirect way. ❑ *Some people believe that his murder was engineered by Stalin.* VERB V n

**en|gi|neer|ing** /endʒɪnɪərɪŋ/ ◆◇◇ **Engineering** is the work involved in designing and constructing engines and machinery, or structures such as roads and bridges. **Engineering** is also the subject studied by people who want to do this work. ❑ *...graduates with degrees in engineering.* → See also **chemical engineering**, **civil engineering**, **electrical engineering**, **genetic engineering**. N-UNCOUNT

**en|gine room** **(engine rooms)** 1 On a boat or a ship, the **engine room** is the place where the engines are. N-COUNT 2 If you refer to something as **the engine room of** an organization or institution, you mean it is the most important or influential part of that organization or institution. ❑ *These firms are regarded as the engine room of the British economy.* N-COUNT: oft the N of n

**Eng|lish** /ɪŋglɪʃ/ 1 **English** means belonging or relating to England, or to its people or language. It is also often used to mean belonging or relating to Great Britain, although many people object to this. ♦ **The English** are English people. ADJ; N-PLURAL: the N 2 **English** is the language spoken by people who live in Great Britain and Ireland, the United States, Canada, Australia, and many other countries. N-UNCOUNT

**Eng|lish break|fast** **(English breakfasts)** An **English breakfast** is a breakfast consisting of cooked food such as bacon, eggs, sausages, and tomatoes. It also includes toast and tea or coffee. [BRIT] N-COUNT

**English|man** /ɪŋglɪʃmən/ **(Englishmen)** An **Englishman** is a man who comes from England. N-COUNT

**English|woman** /ɪŋglɪʃwʊmən/ **(Englishwomen)** An **Englishwoman** is a woman who comes from England. N-COUNT

**en|gorged** /ɪngɔːʳdʒd/ Something that is **engorged** is swollen, usually because it has been filled with a particular fluid. ❑ *...the tissues become engorged with blood.* ADJ: oft ADJ with n

**en|grave** /ɪngreɪv/ **(engraves, engraving, engraved)** If you **engrave** something **with** a design or words, or if you **engrave** a design or words **on** it, you cut the design or words into its surface. ❑ *Your wedding ring can be engraved with a personal inscription at no extra cost... Harrods will also engrave your child's name on the side... I'm having 'John Law' engraved on the cap. ...a bottle engraved with her name.* VERB be V-ed with n; V n on/in n; have n V-ed prep; V-ed

**en|graved** /ɪngreɪvd/ If you say that something is **engraved on** your mind or memory or **on** your heart, you are emphasizing that you will never forget it, because it has made a very strong impression on you. ❑ *Her image is engraved upon my heart.* ADJ: v-link ADJ in/on/upon n [emphasis]

**en|grav|er** /ɪngreɪvəʳ/ **(engravers)** An **engraver** is someone who cuts designs or words on metal, glass, or wood. N-COUNT

**en|grav|ing** /ɪngreɪvɪŋ/ **(engravings)** 1 An **engraving** is a picture or design that has been cut into a surface. N-COUNT 2 An **engraving** is a picture that has been printed from a plate on which designs have been cut. ❑ *...a color engraving of oranges and lemons.* N-COUNT

**en|grossed** /ɪngroʊst/ If you are **engrossed in** something, it holds your attention completely. ❑ *Tony didn't notice because he was too engrossed in his work.* ADJ: usu v-link ADJ, usu ADJ in n

**en|gross|ing** /ɪngroʊsɪŋ/ Something that is **engrossing** is very interesting and holds your attention completely. ❑ *He is an engrossing subject for a book.* ADJ [approval]

**en|gulf** /ɪngʌlf/ **(engulfs, engulfing, engulfed)** 1 If one thing **engulfs** another, it completely covers or hides it, often in a sudden and unexpected way. ❑ *A seven-year-old boy was found dead after a landslide engulfed a block of flats... The flat is engulfed in flames.* VERB V n; V n 2 If a feeling or emotion **engulfs** you, you are strongly affected by it. ❑ *...the pain that engulfed him.* VERB V n

**en|hance** /ɪnhɑːns, -hæns/ **(enhances, enhancing, enhanced)** ◆◇◇ To **enhance** something means to improve its value, quality, or attractiveness. ❑ *They'll be keen to enhance their reputation abroad.* VERB V n

**en|hance|ment** /ɪnhɑːnsmənt, -hæns-/ **(enhancements)** The **enhancement of** something is the improvement of it in relation to its value, quality, or attractiveness. [FORMAL] ❑ *He was concerned with the enhancement of the human condition.* N-VAR: usu with supp, oft N of n

**en|hanc|er** /ɪnhɑːnsəʳ, -hæns-/ **(enhancers)** An **enhancer** is a substance or a device which makes a particular thing look, taste, or feel better. ❑ *Cinnamon is an excellent flavour enhancer.* N-COUNT: usu n N

**enig|ma** /ɪnɪgmə/ **(enigmas)** If you describe something or someone as an **enigma**, you mean they are mysterious or difficult to understand. ❑ *Iran remains an enigma for the outside world.* N-COUNT: usu sing = mystery

**en|ig|mat|ic** /enɪgmætɪk/ Someone or something that is **enigmatic** is mysterious and diffi- ADJ cult to understand. ❑ *Haley studied her, an enigmatic smile on his face... She starred in one of Welles's most enigmatic films.* ♦ **en|ig|mati|cal|ly** *'Corbiere didn't deserve this,' she said enigmatically.* ADV: ADV after v, ADV -ed/adj

**en|join** /ɪndʒɔɪn/ **(enjoins, enjoining, enjoined)** [1] If you **enjoin** someone **to** do something, you order them to do it. If you **enjoin** an action or attitude, you order people to do it or have it. [FORMAL] ❑ *She enjoined me strictly not to tell anyone else... It is true that Islam enjoins tolerance; there's no doubt about that... The positive neutrality enjoined on the force has now been overtaken by events.* [2] If a judge **enjoins** someone **from** doing something, they order them not to do it. If a judge **enjoins** an action, they order people not to do it. [AM, FORMAL] ❑ *The judge enjoined Varityper from using the ad in any way. ...a preliminary injunction enjoining the practice.* VERB; V n to-inf; V n; V-ed; VERB; V n *from* -ing/n; V n

**en|joy** /ɪndʒɔɪ/ **(enjoys, enjoying, enjoyed)** ◆◆◇ [1] If you **enjoy** something, you find pleasure and satisfaction in doing it or experiencing it. ❑ *Ross had always enjoyed the company of women... I enjoyed playing cricket.* [2] If you **enjoy yourself**, you do something that you like doing or you take pleasure in the situation that you are in. ❑ *I must say I am really enjoying myself at the moment.* [3] If you **enjoy** something such as a right, benefit, or privilege, you have it. [FORMAL] ❑ *The average German will enjoy 40 days' paid holiday this year.* VERB; V n/-ing; V n/-ing; VERB; V pron-refl; VERB; V n

**en|joy|able** /ɪndʒɔɪəbᵊl/ Something that is **enjoyable** gives you pleasure. ❑ *It was much more enjoyable than I had expected.* ♦ **en|joy|ably** *...an enjoyably nasty thriller. ...the place in which he has enjoyably spent his working life.* ADJ; ADV: ADV adj, ADV with v

**en|joy|ment** /ɪndʒɔɪmənt/ **Enjoyment** is the feeling of pleasure and satisfaction that you have when you do or experience something that you like. ❑ *I apologise if your enjoyment of the movie was spoiled.* N-UNCOUNT: oft N *of* n

**en|large** /ɪnlɑːʳdʒ/ **(enlarges, enlarging, enlarged)** [1] When you **enlarge** something or when it **enlarges**, it becomes bigger. ❑ *...the plan to enlarge Ewood Park into a 30,000 all-seater stadium... The glands in the neck may enlarge.* ♦ **en|larged** *The UN secretary-general yesterday recommended an enlarged peacekeeping force.* [2] If you **enlarge on** something that has been mentioned, you give more details about it. [FORMAL] ❑ *He didn't enlarge on the form that the interim government and assembly would take.* VERB; V n; V; ADJ; VERB = *expand*; V *on/upon* n

**en|large|ment** /ɪnlɑːʳdʒmənt/ **(enlargements)** [1] The **enlargement of** something is the process or result of making it bigger. ❑ *There is insufficient space for enlargement of the buildings.* [2] An **enlargement** is a photograph that has been made bigger. N-UNCOUNT: usu with supp, oft N *of* n; N-COUNT

**en|larg|er** /ɪnlɑʳdʒəʳ/ **(enlargers)** An **enlarger** is a device which makes an image larger. N-COUNT

**en|light|en** /ɪnlaɪtᵊn/ **(enlightens, enlightening, enlightened)** To **enlighten** someone means to give them more knowledge and greater understanding about something. [FORMAL] ❑ *A few dedicated doctors have fought for years to enlighten the profession... If you know what is wrong with her, please enlighten me.* ♦ **en|light|en|ing** *...an enlightening talk on the work done at the animal park.* VERB: no cont; V n; V n; ADJ: usu ADJ n

**en|light|ened** /ɪnlaɪtᵊnd/ If you describe someone or their attitudes as **enlightened**, you mean that they have sensible, modern attitudes and ways of dealing with things. ❑ *Enlightened companies include its human resources in their estimation of the firm's worth.* ADJ: usu ADJ n [approval]

**en|light|en|ment** /ɪnlaɪtᵊnmənt/ [1] **Enlightenment** means the act of enlightening or the state of being enlightened. ❑ *Stella had a moment of enlightenment.* [2] In Buddhism, **enlightenment** is a final spiritual state in which everything is understood and there is no more suffering or desire. ❑ *...a sense of deep peace and spiritual enlightenment.* N-UNCOUNT; N-UNCOUNT

**en|list** /ɪnlɪst/ **(enlists, enlisting, enlisted)** [1] If someone **enlists** or **is enlisted**, they join the army, navy, marines, or air force. ❑ *Michael Hughes of Lackawanna, Pennsylvania, enlisted in the 82nd Airborne 20 years ago... He enlisted as a private in the Mexican War... Three thousand men were enlisted... He decided to enlist.* [2] If you **enlist** the help of someone, you persuade them to help or support you in doing something. ❑ *I had to cut down a tree and enlist the help of seven neighbours to get it out of the garden!... I've read that you've enlisted some 12-year-olds to help out in your campaign.* VERB; V in n; V as n; *be* V-ed; V; VERB; V n; V n to-inf

**en|list|ed** /ɪnlɪstɪd/ An **enlisted** man or woman is a member of the United States armed forces who is below the rank of officer. ADJ: usu ADJ n

**en|list|ment** /ɪnlɪstmənt/ **(enlistments)** [1] **Enlistment** is the act of joining the army, navy, marines, or air force. ❑ *Canadians seek enlistment in the US Marines because they don't see as much opportunity in the Canadian armed forces.* [2] **Enlistment** is the period of time for which someone is a member of one of the armed forces. ❑ *At the end of my term of enlistment I decided to return to civilian life.* N-UNCOUNT: also N in pl; N-VAR = *service*

**en|liv|en** /ɪnlaɪvᵊn/ **(enlivens, enlivening, enlivened)** To **enliven** events, situations, or people means to make them more lively or cheerful. ❑ *Even the most boring meeting was enlivened by Dan's presence.* VERB; V n

**en masse** /ɒn mæs/ If a group of people do something **en masse**, they do it all together and at the same time. ❑ *The people marched en masse.* ADV: ADV after v, n ADV

**en|meshed** /ɪnmeʃt/ If you are **enmeshed in** or **with** something, usually something bad, you are involved in it and cannot easily escape from it. ❑ *All too often they become enmeshed in deadening routines. ...as her life gets enmeshed with Andrew's.* ADJ: v-link ADJ, usu ADJ *in/with* n

**en|mity** /enmɪti/ **(enmities) Enmity** is a feeling of hatred towards someone that lasts for a long time. ❑ *I think there is an historic enmity between them.* N-VAR: usu with supp, oft N *between* pl-n

**en|no|ble** /ɪnoʊbᵊl/ **(ennobles, ennobling, ennobled)** [1] To **ennoble** someone or something means to make them more dignified and morally better. [LITERARY] ❑ *...the enduring fundamental principles of life that ennoble mankind.* ♦ **en|no|bling** *...the ennobling and civilizing power of education.* [2] If someone **is ennobled**, they are made a member of the nobility. [FORMAL] ❑ *...the son of a financier who had been ennobled. ...the newly ennobled Lord Archer.* VERB; V n; ADJ; VERB: usu passive *be* V-ed; V-ed

**en|nui** /ɒnwiː/ **Ennui** is a feeling of being tired, bored, and dissatisfied. [LITERARY] N-UNCOUNT

**enor|mity** /ɪnɔːʳmɪti/ **(enormities)** [1] If you refer to **the enormity of** something that you consider to be a problem or difficulty, you are referring to its very great size, extent, or seriousness. ❑ *I was numbed by the enormity of the responsibility.* [2] If you refer to **the enormity of** an event, you are emphasizing that it is terrible and frightening. ❑ *It makes no sense to belittle the enormity of the disaster which has occurred.* N-UNCOUNT: usu *the* N *of* n; N-UNCOUNT: usu N *of* n [emphasis]

**enor|mous** /ɪnɔːʳməs/ ◆◇◇ [1] Something that is **enormous** is extremely large in size or amount. ❑ *The main bedroom is enormous... There is, of course, an enormous amount to see.* [2] You can use **enormous** to emphasize the great degree or extent of something. ❑ *It was an enormous disappointment.* ♦ **enor|mous|ly** *This book was enormously influential.* ADJ; ADJ: usu ADJ n [emphasis]; ADV: ADV adj, ADV with v

**enough** /ɪnʌf/ ◆◆◆ [1] **Enough** means as much as you need or as much as is necessary. ❑ *They had enough cash for a one-way ticket... There aren't enough tents to shelter them all.* ♦ **Enough** is also an adverb. ❑ *I was old enough to work and earn money... Do you believe that sentences for criminals are tough enough at present?... She graduated with high enough marks to apply for university.* ♦ **Enough** is also a pronoun. ❑ *Although the UK says efforts are* DET: DET n-uncount/pl-n; ADV: adj/adv ADV, ADV after v, oft ADV to-inf; PRON *being made, they are not doing enough.* ♦ **Enough** is also a quantifier. ❑ *All parents worry about whether their child is getting enough of the right foods.* [QUANT: QUANT *of* def-n] ♦ **Enough** is also an adjective. ❑ *It was downright panic – the frozen expressions on the faces of the actors was proof enough of that.* [ADJ: n ADJ] 2 If you say that something is **enough**, you mean that you do not want it to continue any longer or get any worse. ❑ *I met him only the once, and that was enough... I think I have said enough... You've got enough to think about for the moment.* [PRON] ♦ **Enough** is also a quantifier. ❑ *Ann had heard enough of this.* [QUANT: QUANT *of* def-n] ♦ **Enough** is also a determiner. ❑ *I've had enough problems with the police, I don't need this... Would you shut up, please! I'm having enough trouble with these children!* [DET: DET pl-n/ n-uncount] ♦ **Enough** is also an adverb. ❑ *I'm serious, things are difficult enough as they are.* [ADV: adj ADV] 3 You can use **enough** to say that something is the case to a moderate or fairly large degree. ❑ *Winter is a common enough German surname... The rest of the evening passed pleasantly enough.* [ADV: adj/ adv ADV] 4 You use **enough** in expressions such as **strangely enough** and **interestingly enough** to indicate that you think a fact is strange or interesting. ❑ *Strangely enough, the last thing he thought of was his beloved Tanya.* [ADV: adv ADV with cl] 5 If you say that you **have had enough**, you mean that you are unhappy with a situation and you want it to stop. ❑ *I had had enough of other people for one night.* [PHRASE: V inflects, oft PHR *of* n] 6 **fair enough** → see **fair**. **sure enough** → see **sure**.

**en|quire** /ɪnkwaɪəʳ/ → see **inquire**.

**en|quir|er** /ɪnkwaɪərəʳ/ → see **inquirer**.

**en|quiry** /ɪnkwaɪəri/ → see **inquiry**.

**en|rage** /ɪnreɪdʒ/ **(enrages, enraging, enraged)** [VERB] If you **are enraged** by something, it makes you extremely angry. ❑ *He was enraged by news of plans to demolish the pub... He enraged the government by renouncing the agreement.* [*be* V-ed *by* n; V n] ♦ **en|raged** *I began getting more and more enraged at my father.* [ADJ]

**en|rap|ture** /ɪnræptʃəʳ/ **(enraptures, enrapturing, enraptured)** [VERB = enchant] If something or someone **enraptures** you, you think they are wonderful or fascinating. [LITERARY] ❑ *The place at once enraptured me... The 20,000-strong audience listened, enraptured. ...an enraptured audience.* [V n; V-ed; V-ed]

**en|rich** /ɪnrɪtʃ/ **(enriches, enriching, enriched)** 1 To **enrich** something means to improve its quality, usually by adding something to it. ❑ *It is important to enrich the soil prior to planting.* [VERB; V n] ♦ **-enriched** *...with nutrient-enriched water.* [COMB in ADJ] 2 To **enrich** someone means to increase the amount of money that they have. ❑ *He will drain, rather than enrich, the country.* [VERB; V n]

**en|rich|ment** /ɪnrɪtʃmənt/ **Enrichment** is the act of enriching someone or something or the state of being enriched. ❑ *...the enrichment of society.* [N-UNCOUNT: usu with supp]

**en|rol** /ɪnroʊl/ **(enrols, enrolling, enrolled)**

✓ in AM, use **enroll**

If you **enrol** or **are enrolled** at an institution or on a course, you officially join it and pay a fee for it. ❑ *Cherny was enrolled at the University in 1945... She enrolled on a local Women Into Management course... I thought I'd enrol you with an art group at the school.* [VERB; *be* V-ed prep; V prep; V n prep; Also V]

**en|rol|ment** /ɪnroʊlmənt/

✓ in AM, use **enrollment**

**Enrolment** is the act of enrolling at an institution or on a course. ❑ *A fee is charged for each year of study and is payable at enrolment.* [N-UNCOUNT]

**en route** /ɒn ruːt/ → see **route**.

**en|sconced** /ɪnskɒnst/ If you are **ensconced** somewhere, you are settled there firmly or comfortably and have no intention of moving or leaving. ❑ *Brian was ensconced behind the bar.* [ADJ: v-link ADJ prep/ adv]

**en|sem|ble** /ɒnsɒmbᵊl/ **(ensembles)** 1 An **ensemble** is a group of musicians, actors, or dancers who regularly perform together. ❑ *...an ensemble of young musicians.* [N-COUNT: usu sing] 2 An **ensemble of** things or people is a group of things or people considered as a whole rather than as separate individuals. [FORMAL] ❑ *The state is an ensemble of political and social structures.* [N-COUNT: usu sing, oft N *of* n = collection]

**en|shrine** /ɪnʃraɪn/ **(enshrines, enshrining, enshrined)** If something such as an idea or a right **is enshrined in** something such as a constitution or law, it is protected by it. ❑ *His new relationship with Germany is enshrined in a new non-aggression treaty... The apartheid system which enshrined racism in law still existed.* [VERB; *be* V-ed *in* n; V n prep]

**en|shroud** /ɪnʃraʊd/ **(enshrouds, enshrouding, enshrouded)** To **enshroud** something means to cover it completely so that it can no longer be seen. [LITERARY] ❑ *...dispiriting clouds that enshrouded us in twilight. ...the culture of secrecy which enshrouds our politics.* [VERB; V n *in* n; V n]

**en|sign** /ensaɪn, ensᵊn/ **(ensigns)** 1 An **ensign** is a flag flown on a ship to show what country the ship belongs to. [N-COUNT] 2 An **ensign** is a junior officer in the United States Navy. ❑ *He had been a naval ensign stationed off Cuba. ...Ensign Smith.* [N-COUNT; N-TITLE]

**en|slave** /ɪnsleɪv/ **(enslaves, enslaving, enslaved)** 1 To **enslave** someone means to make them into a slave. ❑ *They've been enslaved and had to do what they were told... I'd die myself before I'd let anyone enslave your folk ever again... George was born to an enslaved African mother.* [VERB; *be* V-ed; V n; V-ed] 2 To **enslave** a person or society means to trap them in a situation from which they cannot escape. ❑ *...the various cultures, cults and religions that have enslaved human beings for untold years... It would be a tragedy if both sexes were enslaved to the god of work.* [VERB; V n; *be* V-ed *to* n; Also V n *to* n]

**en|slave|ment** /ɪnsleɪvmənt/ 1 **Enslavement** is the act of making someone into a slave or the state of being a slave. ❑ *...the enslavement of African people.* [N-UNCOUNT: oft N *of* n] 2 **Enslavement** is the state of being trapped in a situation from which it is difficult to escape. ❑ *...the analysis of women's enslavement to appearance.* [N-UNCOUNT: oft poss N, adj N, N *to* n]

**en|snare** /ɪnsneəʳ/ **(ensnares, ensnaring, ensnared)** 1 If you **ensnare** someone, you gain power over them, especially by using dishonest or deceitful methods. ❑ *Feminism is simply another device to ensnare women... We find ourselves ensnared in employment acts which do not help resolve industrial disputes.* [VERB; V n; V-ed] 2 If an animal **is ensnared**, it is caught in a trap. ❑ *The spider must wait for prey to be ensnared on its web.* [VERB; *be* V-ed *on/in* n]

**en|sue** /ɪnsjuː, AM -suː/ **(ensues, ensuing, ensued)** If something **ensues**, it happens immediately after another event, usually as a result of it. ❑ *If the Europeans did not reduce subsidies, a trade war would ensue... A brief but embarrassing silence ensued.* [VERB: no cont = follow; V; V]

**en|su|ing** /ɪnsjuːɪŋ, AM -suː-/ 1 **Ensuing** events happen immediately after other events. ❑ *The ensuing argument had been bitter. ...any ensuing problems.* [ADJ: ADJ n] 2 **Ensuing** months or years follow the time you are talking about. ❑ *The two companies grew tenfold in the ensuing ten years.* [ADJ: det ADJ]

**en suite** /ɒn swiːt/ An **en suite** bathroom is next to a bedroom and can only be reached by a door in the bedroom. An **en suite** bedroom has an en suite bathroom. [BRIT] [ADJ: ADJ n]

✓ in AM, usually use **private bathroom**

**en|sure** /ɪnʃʊəʳ/ **(ensures, ensuring, ensured)** ◆◆◇ [VERB] To **ensure** something, or to **ensure that** something happens, means to make certain that it happens. [FORMAL] ❑ *Britain's negotiators had ensured that the treaty which resulted was a significant change in direction. ...the President's Council, which ensures the supremacy of the National Party.* [V that; V n]

**en|tail** /ɪnteɪl/ **(entails, entailing, entailed)** If one thing **entails** another, it involves it or causes it. [FORMAL] ❑ *Such a decision would entail a huge political risk... I'll never accept parole because that entails me accepting guilt.* [VERB; V n; V n -ing]

**en|tan|gle** /ɪntæŋgəl/ **(entangles, entangling, entangled)** [1] If one thing **entangles itself with** another, the two things become caught together very tightly. ❑ *The blade of the oar had entangled itself with something in the water.* [2] If something **entangles** you **in** problems or difficulties, it causes you to become involved in problems or difficulties from which it is hard to escape. ❑ *Bureaucracy can entangle ventures for months... His tactics were to entangle the opposition in a web of parliamentary procedure.* VERB V n with/in n VERB V n V n in/with n

**en|tan|gled** /ɪntæŋgəld/ [1] If something is **entangled in** something such as a rope, wire, or net, it is caught in it very firmly. ❑ *...a whale that became entangled in crab nets.* [2] If you become **entangled in** problems or difficulties, you become involved in problems or difficulties from which it is hard to escape. ❑ *This case was bound to get entangled in international politics.* ADJ: oft ADJ in/with n ADJ: v-link ADJ, oft ADJ in/with n

**en|tan|gle|ment** /ɪntæŋgəlmənt/ **(entanglements)** [1] An **entanglement** is a complicated or difficult relationship or situation. ❑ *...romantic entanglements. ...a military and political entanglement the Government probably doesn't want.* [2] If things become entangled, you can refer to this as **entanglement**. ❑ *Many dolphins are accidentally killed through entanglement with fishing equipment.* N-COUNT N-VAR

**en|tente** /ɒntɒnt/ **(ententes)** An **entente** or an **entente cordiale** is a friendly agreement between two or more countries. ❑ *The French entente with Great Britain had already been significantly extended.* N-VAR

**en|ter** /entəʳ/ **(enters, entering, entered)** ◆◆◇ [1] When you **enter** a place such as a room or building, you go into it or come into it. [FORMAL] ❑ *He entered the room briskly and stood near the door... As soon as I entered, they stopped and turned my way.* [2] If you **enter** an organization or institution, you start to work there or become a member of it. ❑ *He entered the BBC as a general trainee.* [3] If something new **enters** your mind, you suddenly think about it. ❑ *Dreadful doubts began to enter my mind.* [4] If it does not **enter** your head **to** do, think or say something, you do not think of doing that thing although you should have done. ❑ *It never enters his mind that anyone is better than him... Though she enjoyed flirting with Matt, it had not entered her head to have an affair with him.* [5] If someone or something **enters** a particular situation or period of time, they start to be in it or part of it. ❑ *The war has entered its second month... A million young people enter the labour market each year.* [6] If you **enter** a competition, race, or examination, you officially state that you will compete or take part in it. ❑ *I run so well I'm planning to enter some races... He entered for many competitions, winning several gold medals... To enter, simply complete the coupon on page 150.* [7] If you **enter** someone **for** a race or competition, you officially state that they will compete or take part in it. ❑ *His wife Marie secretly entered him for the Championship. ...some of the 150 projects entered for the awards.* [8] If you **enter** something in a notebook, register, or financial account, you write it down. ❑ *Each week she meticulously entered in her notebooks all sums received... Prue entered the passage in her notebook, then read it aloud again.* [9] To **enter** information **into** a computer or database means to record it there, for example by typing it on a keyboard. ❑ *When a baby is born, they enter that baby's name into the computer... A lot less time is now spent entering the data.* VERB V n V VERB V n VERB = cross V n VERB: with brd-neg it V n that it V n to-inf VERB V n V n VERB V n V for n V VERB V n for n V-ed VERB V n with prep/adv V n prep/adv VERB V n into n V n

♦ **enter into** [1] If you **enter into** something such as an agreement, discussion, or relationship, you become involved in it. You can also say that two people **enter into** something. [FORMAL] ❑ *I have not entered into any financial agreements with them... The United States and Canada may enter into an agreement that would allow easier access to jobs across the border... No correspondence will be entered into.* [2] If one thing **enters into** another, it is a factor in it. [FORMAL] ❑ *There were also other factors that entered into the orchestration.* PHRASAL VERB V P n with n pl-n V n be V-ed P PHRASAL VERB V P n

**en|ter|prise** /entəʳpraɪz/ **(enterprises)** ◆◇◇ [1] An **enterprise** is a company or business, often a small one. [BUSINESS] ❑ *There are plenty of small industrial enterprises.* [2] An **enterprise** is something new, difficult, or important that you do or try to do. ❑ *Horse breeding is indeed a risky enterprise.* [3] **Enterprise** is the activity of managing companies and businesses and starting new ones. [BUSINESS] ❑ *He is still involved in voluntary work promoting local enterprise. ...a national program of subsidies to private enterprise.* [4] **Enterprise** is the ability to think of new and effective things to do, together with an eagerness to do them. ❑ *...the spirit of enterprise worthy of a free and industrious people.* N-COUNT: usu with supp, oft adj N N-COUNT: usu supp N = venture N-UNCOUNT: usu supp N N-UNCOUNT [approval]

**en|ter|prise zone** **(enterprise zones)** An **enterprise zone** is an area, usually a depressed or inner-city area, where the government offers incentives in order to attract new businesses. [BUSINESS] ❑ *Because it is in an enterprise zone, taxes on non-food items are 3.5% instead of the usual 7%.* N-COUNT

**en|ter|pris|ing** /entəʳpraɪzɪŋ/ An **enterprising** person is willing to try out new, unusual ways of doing or achieving something. ❑ *Some enterprising members found ways of reducing their expenses or raising their incomes.* ADJ: usu ADJ n

**en|ter|tain** /entəʳteɪn/ **(entertains, entertaining, entertained)** ◆◇◇ [1] If a performer, performance, or activity **entertains** you, it amuses you, interests you, or gives you pleasure. ❑ *They were entertained by top singers, dancers and celebrities... Children's television not only entertains but also teaches.* ♦ **en|ter|tain|ing** *To generate new money the sport needs to be more entertaining... This is a surprisingly entertaining film.* [2] If you **entertain** people, you provide food and drink for them, for example when you have invited them to your house. ❑ *I don't like to entertain guests anymore... The Monroes continued to entertain extravagantly.* ♦ **en|ter|tain|ing** *...a cosy area for entertaining and relaxing.* [3] If you **entertain** an idea or suggestion, you allow yourself to consider it as possible or as worth thinking about seriously. [FORMAL] ❑ *I feel how foolish I am to entertain doubts... I wouldn't entertain the idea of such an unsociable job.* VERB V n V ADJ VERB V n V N-UNCOUNT VERB V n V n

**en|ter|tain|er** /entəʳteɪnəʳ/ **(entertainers)** An **entertainer** is a person whose job is to entertain audiences, for example by telling jokes, singing, or dancing. ❑ *Some have called him the greatest entertainer of the twentieth century.* N-COUNT

**en|ter|tain|ment** /entəʳteɪnmənt/ **(entertainments)** ◆◇◇ **Entertainment** consists of performances of plays and films, and activities such as reading and watching television, that give people pleasure. ❑ *...the world of entertainment and international stardom.* N-VAR

**en|thral** /ɪnθrɔːl/ **(enthrals, enthralling, enthralled)**

✔ in AM, use **enthrall, enthralls**

If you **are enthralled by** something, you enjoy it and give it your complete attention and interest. ❑ *The passengers were enthralled by the scenery... The fans sat enthralled in the darkened cinema.* VERB be V-ed V-ed

**en|throne** /ɪnθroʊn/ **(enthrones, enthroning, enthroned)** [1] When kings, queens, emperors, or bishops **are enthroned**, they officially take on their role during a special ceremony. [FORMAL] ❑ *Emperor Akihito of Japan has been enthroned in Tokyo... He is expected to be enthroned early next year as the spiritual leader of the Church of England.* [2] If an idea **is enthroned**, it has an important place in people's life or thoughts. [JOURNALISM] ❑ *He was forcing the State to enthrone a particular brand of modernism. ...the religious fundamentalism now enthroned in American life.* VERB: usu passive be V-ed be V-ed as n VERB = enshrine V n V-ed

**en|throne|ment** /ɪnθroʊnmənt/ **(enthronements)** The **enthronement** of a king, queen, emperor, or bishop is a ceremony in which they offi- N-COUNT: usu sing, usu with poss cially take on their role. [FORMAL] ❑ *...the enthronement of their new emperor.*

**en|thuse** /ɪnθjuːz, AM -θuːz/ **(enthuses, enthusing, enthused)** [1] If you **enthuse about** something, you talk about it in a way that shows how excited you are about it. ❑ *Elizabeth David enthuses about the taste, fragrance and character of Provencal cuisine... 'I've found the most wonderful house to buy!' she enthused.* [2] If you **are enthused** by something, it makes you feel excited and enthusiastic. ❑ *I was immediately enthused... Find a hobby or interest which enthuses you.* VERB V about/over n V with quote Also V that VERB be V-ed V n

**en|thu|si|asm** /ɪnθjuːziæzəm, AM -θuː-/ **(enthusiasms)** [1] **Enthusiasm** is great eagerness to be involved in a particular activity which you like and enjoy or which you think is important. ❑ *Their skill, enthusiasm and running has got them in the team.* [2] An **enthusiasm** is an activity or subject that interests you very much and that you spend a lot of time on. ❑ *Draw him out about his current enthusiasms and future plans.* ◆◇◇ N-VAR: oft N for n/-ing N-COUNT: oft with poss = interest

**en|thu|si|ast** /ɪnθjuːziæst, AM -θuː-/ **(enthusiasts)** An **enthusiast** is a person who is very interested in a particular activity or subject and who spends a lot of time on it. ❑ *He is a great sports enthusiast. ...keep-fit enthusiasts.* N-COUNT: usu with supp

**en|thu|si|as|tic** /ɪnθjuːziæstɪk, AM -θuː-/ If you are **enthusiastic about** something, you show how much you like or enjoy it by the way that you behave and talk. ❑ *Tom was very enthusiastic about the place.* ♦ **en|thu|si|as|ti|cal|ly** /ɪnθjuːziæstɪkli, AM -θuː-/ *The announcement was greeted enthusiastically.* ADJ: oft ADJ about n = excited ADV: usu ADV with v, also ADV adj

**en|tice** /ɪntaɪs/ **(entices, enticing, enticed)** To **entice** someone **to** go somewhere or **to** do something means to try to persuade them to go to that place or to do that thing. ❑ *Retailers have tried almost everything to entice shoppers through their doors... They'll entice doctors to move from the cities by paying them better salaries.* VERB = lure V n prep V n to-inf Also V n

**en|tice|ment** /ɪntaɪsmənt/ **(enticements)** An **enticement** is something which makes people want to do a particular thing. ❑ *Among other enticements, they advertized that they would take guests to Ramsgate for the day.* N-VAR = inducement

**en|tic|ing** /ɪntaɪsɪŋ/ Something that is **enticing** is extremely attractive and makes you want to get it or to become involved with it. ❑ *A prospective premium of about 30 per cent on their initial investment is enticing.* ♦ **en|tic|ing|ly** *...laying out their stall enticingly.* ADJ ADV

**en|tire** /ɪntaɪəʳ/ You use **entire** when you want to emphasize that you are referring to the whole of something, for example, the whole of a place, time, or population. ❑ *He had spent his entire life in China as a doctor... There are only 60 swimming pools in the entire country.* ◆◆◇ ADJ: det ADJ emphasis = whole

**en|tire|ly** /ɪntaɪəʳli/ [1] **Entirely** means completely and not just partly. ❑ *...an entirely new approach... Fraud is an entirely different matter... Their price depended almost entirely on their scarcity.* [2] **Entirely** is also used to emphasize what you are saying. ❑ *I agree entirely... Oh, the whole episode was entirely his fault.* ◆◇◇ ADV: ADV adj, ADV with v, ADV with cl/group ADV: ADV with v, ADV group emphasis

**en|tirety** /ɪntaɪərɪti/ If something is used or affected **in** its **entirety**, the whole of it is used or affected. ❑ *The peace plan has not been accepted in its entirety by all parties.* PHRASE: PHR after v

**en|ti|tle** /ɪntaɪtᵊl/ **(entitles, entitling, entitled)** [1] If you **are entitled to** something, you have the right to have it or do it. ❑ *If the warranty is limited, the terms may entitle you to a replacement or refund... There are 23 Clubs throughout the U.S., and your membership entitles you to enjoy all of them.* [2] If the title of something such as a book, film, or painting is, for example, 'Sunrise', you can say that it **is entitled** 'Sunrise'. ❑ *Chomsky's review is entitled 'Psychology and Ideology'. ...a performance entitled 'United States'.* ◆◇◇ VERB V n to n V n to-inf VERB: usu passive be V-ed quote V-ed quote

**en|ti|tle|ment** /ɪntaɪtᵊlmənt/ **(entitlements)** An **entitlement to** something is the right to have it or do it. [FORMAL] ❑ *They lose their entitlement to benefit when they start work.* N-VAR: oft N to n

**en|tity** /ɛntɪti/ **(entities)** An **entity** is something that exists separately from other things and has a clear identity of its own. [FORMAL] ❑ *...the earth as a living entity.* N-COUNT: usu supp N

**en|tomb** /ɪntuːm/ **(entombs, entombing, entombed)** [1] If something **is entombed**, it is buried or permanently trapped by something. [FORMAL] ❑ *The city was entombed in volcanic lava... The Tel, an artificial mountain, entombs Jericho's ancient past.* [2] When a person's dead body **is entombed**, it is buried in a grave or put into a tomb. [FORMAL] ❑ *Neither of them had any idea how long the body had been entombed.* VERB be V-ed in n V n VERB: usu passive be V-ed

**ento|mol|ogy** /ɛntəmɒlədʒi/ **Entomology** is the study of insects. ♦ **ento|molo|gist** /ɛntəmɒlədʒɪst/ **(entomologists)** ❑ *...a research entomologist.* N-UNCOUNT N-COUNT

**en|tou|rage** /ɒnturɑːʒ/ **(entourages)** A famous or important person's **entourage** is the group of assistants, servants, or other people who travel with them. N-COUNT: usu poss N, N of n

**en|trails** /ɛntreɪlz/ The **entrails** of people or animals are their inside parts, especially their intestines. N-PLURAL = innards

**entrance**
① NOUN USES
② VERB USE

① **en|trance** /ɛntrəns/ **(entrances)** [1] The **entrance to** a place is the way into it, for example a door or gate. ❑ *Beside the entrance to the church, turn right... He was driven out of a side entrance with his hand covering his face... A marble entrance hall leads to a sitting room.* [2] You can refer to someone's arrival in a place as their **entrance**, especially when you think that they are trying to be noticed and admired. ❑ *If she had noticed her father's entrance, she gave no indication.* [3] When a performer makes his or her **entrance on to** the stage, he or she comes on to the stage. [4] If you gain **entrance to** a particular place, you manage to get in there. [FORMAL] ❑ *Hewitt had gained entrance to the Hall by pretending to be a heating engineer.* [5] If you gain **entrance to** a particular profession, society, or institution, you are accepted as a member of it. ❑ *Entrance to universities and senior secondary schools was restricted. ...entrance exams for the French civil service.* [6] If you make an **entrance into** a particular activity or system, you succeed in becoming involved in it. ❑ *The acquisition helped BCCI make its entrance into the US market.* ◆◇◇ N-COUNT: oft N to/into/of n = entry N-COUNT: usu sing, usu with poss = entry N-COUNT: usu sing, usu with poss N-UNCOUNT: oft N to n = entry N-UNCOUNT: oft N to/into n N-SING: oft N into n = entry

② **en|trance** /ɪntrɑːns, -træns/ **(entrances, entrancing, entranced)** If something or someone **entrances** you, they cause you to feel delight and wonder, often so that all your attention is taken up and you cannot think about anything else. ❑ *As soon as I met Dick, he entranced me because he has a lovely voice.* ♦ **en|tranced** *For the next three hours we sat entranced as the train made its way up the mountains... He is entranced by the kindness of her smile.* ♦ **en|tranc|ing** *The light reflected off the stone, creating a golden glow he found entrancing.* VERB = enchant V n ADJ: v-link ADJ, ADJ after v, ADJ n ADJ

**en|trance fee** **(entrance fees)** An **entrance fee** is a sum of money which you pay before you go into somewhere such as a cinema or museum, or which you have to pay in order to join an organization or institution. N-COUNT

**en|trance hall** **(entrance halls)** The **entrance hall** of a large house, hotel, or other large building, is the area just inside the main door. → See picture on page 1706. N-COUNT

**en|trant** /ɛntrənt/ **(entrants)** [1] An **entrant** is a person who has recently become a member of an institution such as a university. ❑ *...a young school entrant.* [2] An **entrant** is a person who is N-COUNT: with supp N-COUNT taking part in a competition. ❑ *All items entered for the competition must be the entrant's own work.* = contestant

**en|trap** /ɪntræp/ **(entraps, entrapping, entrapped)** If you **entrap** someone, you trick or deceive them and make them believe or do something wrong. [FORMAL] ❑ *The police have been given extra powers to entrap drug traffickers... He claimed the government had entrapped him into doing something that he would not have done otherwise.* VERB V n V n into n/-ing

**en|trap|ment** /ɪntræpmənt/ **Entrapment** is the practice of arresting someone by using unfair or illegal methods. [LEGAL] ❑ *...allegations of police entrapment.* N-UNCOUNT

**en|treat** /ɪntriːt/ **(entreats, entreating, entreated)** If you **entreat** someone **to** do something, you ask them very politely and seriously to do it. [FORMAL] ❑ *Trevor Steven entreated them to delay their departure... 'Call me Earl!' he entreated... I earnestly entreat that we don't get caught out again.* VERB = implore V n to-inf V with quote V that Also V n

**en|treaty** /ɪntriːti/ **(entreaties)** An **entreaty** is a very polite, serious request. [FORMAL] ❑ *The FA has resisted all entreaties to pledge its support to the campaign.* N-VAR: oft N to n

**en|trée** /ɒntreɪ/ **(entrées)** also **entree.** [1] If you have an **entrée** to a social group, you are accepted and made to feel welcome by them. ❑ *She had an entree into the city's cultivated society.* N-COUNT: oft N into n [2] At restaurants or formal dinners, the **entrée** is the main course, or sometimes a dish before the main course. ❑ *Dinner features a hot entrée of chicken, veal, or lamb.* N-COUNT

**en|trench** /ɪntrentʃ/ **(entrenches, entrenching, entrenched)** If something such as power, a custom, or an idea **is entrenched**, it is firmly established, so that it would be difficult to change it. ❑ *...a series of measures designed to entrench democracy and the rule of law... These dictators have entrenched themselves politically and are difficult to move.* VERB V n V pron-refl ♦ **en|trenched** *The recession remains deeply entrenched.* ADJ

**en|trench|ment** /ɪntrentʃmənt/ **(entrenchments)** [1] **Entrenchments** are a series of long deep holes called trenches which are dug for defence by soldiers in war. N-COUNT: usu pl [2] **Entrenchment** means the firm establishment of a system or your own position in a situation. ❑ *...the entrenchment of democratic norms.* N-UNCOUNT

**en|tre|pre|neur** /ɒntrəprənɜːʳ/ **(entrepreneurs)** An **entrepreneur** is a person who sets up businesses and business deals. [BUSINESS] N-COUNT

**en|tre|pre|neur|ial** /ɒntrəprənɜːriəl/ **Entrepreneurial** means having the qualities that are needed to succeed as an entrepreneur. [BUSINESS] ❑ *...her prodigious entrepreneurial flair.* ADJ: usu ADJ n

**en|tre|pre|neur|ship** /ɒntrəprənɜːʳ/ **Entrepreneurship** is the state of being an entrepreneur, or the activities associated with being an entrepreneur. N-UNCOUNT

**en|tro|py** /entrəpi/ **Entropy** is a state of disorder, confusion, and disorganization. [TECHNICAL] N-UNCOUNT

**en|trust** /ɪntrʌst/ **(entrusts, entrusting, entrusted)** If you **entrust** something important **to** someone or **entrust** them **with** it, you make them responsible for looking after it or dealing with it. ❑ *If parents wanted to entrust their child to the best surgeons, they traveled to Bologna's medical school... He was forced to entrust an assistant with the important task of testing and demonstrating aircraft to prospective customers... They can be entrusted to solve major national problems.* VERB V n to n V n with n be V-ed to-inf

**en|try** /entri/ **(entries)** ♦♦◇ [1] If you gain **entry to** a particular place, you are able to go in. ❑ *Bill was among the first to gain entry to Buckingham Palace when it opened to the public recently... Non-residents were refused entry into the region without authority from their own district... Entry to the museum is free.* N-UNCOUNT: usu N to/into n = entrance ● **No Entry** is used on signs to indicate that you are not allowed to go into a particular area or go through a particular door or gate. PHRASE [2] You can refer to someone's arrival in a place as their **entry**, especially when you think that they are trying to be noticed and admired. ❑ *He made his triumphal entry into Mexico City.* N-COUNT: usu sing, usu with poss = entrance [3] Someone's **entry into** a particular society or group is their joining of it. ❑ *He described Britain's entry into the European Exchange Rate Mechanism as an historic move. ...people who cannot gain entry to the owner-occupied housing sector.* N-UNCOUNT: oft N into/to n = entrance [4] An **entry** in a diary, account book, computer file, or reference book is a short piece of writing in it. ❑ *Violet's diary entry for 20 April 1917 records Brigit admitting to the affair.* N-COUNT [5] An **entry** for a competition is a piece of work, for example a story or drawing, or the answers to a set of questions, which you complete in order to take part in the competition. ❑ *The closing date for entries is 31st December.* N-COUNT [6] Journalists sometimes use **entry** to refer to the total number of people taking part in an event or competition. For example, if a competition has an **entry** of twenty people, twenty people take part in it. ❑ *Prize-money of nearly £90,000 has attracted a record entry of 14 horses from Britain and Ireland... Our competition has attracted a huge entry.* N-SING: with supp, oft N of n [7] **Entry** in a competition is the act of taking part in it. ❑ *Entry to this competition is by invitation only. ...an entry form.* N-UNCOUNT: oft n in/to n [8] The **entry to** a place is the way into it, for example a door or gate. N-COUNT: usu sing = entrance

**entry-level** [1] **Entry-level** is used to describe basic low-cost versions of products such as cars or computers that are suitable for people who have no previous experience or knowledge of them. [BUSINESS] ❑ *Several companies are offering new, entry-level models in hopes of attracting more buyers.* ADJ: usu ADJ n [2] **Entry-level** jobs are suitable for people who do not have previous experience or qualifications in a particular area of work. [BUSINESS] ❑ *Many entry-level jobs were filled by school leavers.* ADJ: usu ADJ n

**entry|way** /entriweɪ/ **(entryways)** An **entryway** is a passage that is used as an entrance to a building. [mainly AM] N-COUNT = entrance

**en|twine** /ɪntwaɪn/ **(entwines, entwining, entwined)** [1] If one thing **is entwined with** another thing, or if you **entwine** two things, the two things are twisted around each other. ❑ *His dazed eyes stare at the eels, which still writhe and entwine... Facing each other, the giraffes were managing to entwine their necks in the most astonishing manner... He entwined his fingers with hers. ...with silk ribbons and flowers entwined in their hair.* V-RECIP pl-n V V pl-n V n with n V-ed Also V with n, V n [2] If two things **entwine** or **are entwined**, they closely resemble or are linked to each other, and they are difficult to separate or identify. ❑ *The book entwines the personal and the political to chart the history of four generations of the family... Once, years ago, he told me our lives should entwine.* VERB V pl-n pl-n V ♦ **en|twined** *...before media manipulation became entwined with management.* ADJ: oft ADJ with n

**E num|ber** /iː nʌmbəʳ/ **(E numbers)** **E numbers** are artificial substances which are added to some foods and drinks to improve their flavour or colour or to make them last longer. They are called **E numbers** because they are represented in Europe by code names which begin with the letter 'E'. [BRIT] N-COUNT

**enu|mer|ate** /ɪnjuːməreɪt, AM -nuː-/ **(enumerates, enumerating, enumerated)** When you **enumerate** a list of things, you name each one in turn. ❑ *I enumerate the work that will have to be done.* VERB = itemize V n

**enun|ci|ate** /ɪnʌnsieɪt/ **(enunciates, enunciating, enunciated)** When you **enunciate** a word or part of a word, you pronounce it clearly. [FORMAL] ❑ *His voice was harsh as he enunciated each word carefully... She enunciates very slowly and carefully.* VERB V n V ♦ **enun|cia|tion** /ɪnʌnsieɪʃᵊn/ *... his grammar always precise, his enunciation always perfect.* N-UNCOUNT

**en|vel|op** /ɪnveləp/ **(envelops, enveloping, enveloped)** If one thing **envelops** another, it covers or surrounds it completely. ❑ *That lovely, rich fragrant smell of the forest enveloped us. ...an enveloping sense of well-being.* VERB V n V-ing

**en|velope** /envəloʊp, ɒn-/ **(envelopes)** 1 An **envelope** is the rectangular paper cover in which you send a letter to someone through the post. N-COUNT
2 If someone **pushes the envelope**, they do something to a greater degree or in a more extreme way than it has ever been done before. ❑ *There's a valuable place for fashion and design that pushes the envelope a bit.* PHRASE: V inflects

**en|vi|able** /enviəbᵊl/ You describe something such as a quality as **enviable** when someone else has it and you wish that you had it too. ❑ *Japan is in the enviable position of having a budget surplus... They have enviable reputations as athletes.* ADJ: usu ADJ n

**en|vi|ous** /enviəs/ If you are **envious of** someone, you want something that they have. ❑ *I don't think I'm envious of your success... Do I sound envious? I pity them, actually. ...envious thoughts.* ADJ: oft ADJ *of* n
♦ **en|vi|ous|ly** *'You haven't changed,' I am often enviously told.* ADV: ADV with v

**en|vi|ron|ment** /ɪnvaɪərənmənt/ **(environments)** ◆◆◇ 1 Someone's **environment** is all the circumstances, people, things, and events around them that influence their life. ❑ *Pupils in our schools are taught in a safe, secure environment... The moral characters of men are formed not by heredity but by environment.* N-VAR
2 Your **environment** consists of the particular natural surroundings in which you live or exist, considered in relation to their physical characteristics or weather conditions. ❑ *...the maintenance of a safe environment for marine mammals.* N-COUNT: usu sing, with supp
3 **The environment** is the natural world of land, sea, air, plants, and animals. ❑ *...persuading people to respect the environment.* N-SING: *the* N

**en|vi|ron|men|tal** /ɪnvaɪərənmentᵊl/ ◆◆◇ 1 **Environmental** means concerned with the protection of the natural world of land, sea, air, plants, and animals. ❑ *...the environmental claims being made for some products... Environmental groups plan to stage public protests during the conference.* ADJ: ADJ n
♦ **en|vi|ron|men|tal|ly** *...the high price of environmentally friendly goods.* ADV: ADV adj
2 **Environmental** means relating to or caused by the surroundings in which someone lives or something exists. ❑ *It protects against environmental hazards such as wind and sun.* ADJ: ADJ n

**en|vi|ron|men|tal|ism** /ɪnvaɪərənmentᵊlɪzəm/ **Environmentalism** is used to describe actions and policies which show a concern with protecting and preserving the natural environment, for example by preventing pollution. N-UNCOUNT

**en|vi|ron|men|tal|ist** /ɪnvaɪərənmentəlɪst/ **(environmentalists)** An **environmentalist** is a person who is concerned with protecting and preserving the natural environment, for example by preventing pollution. N-COUNT

**en|vi|rons** /ɪnvaɪərənz/ The **environs** of a place consist of the area immediately surrounding it. [FORMAL] ❑ *...the environs of Paris... The town and its environs are inviting, with recreational attractions and art museums.* N-PLURAL: with poss

**en|vis|age** /ɪnvɪzɪdʒ/ **(envisages, envisaging, envisaged)** If you **envisage** something, you imagine that it is true, real, or likely to happen. ❑ *He envisages the possibility of establishing direct diplomatic relations in the future... He had never envisaged spending the whole of his working life in that particular job... Personally, I envisage them staying together.* VERB = *imagine, envision* V n; V -ing; V n -ing; Also V that

**en|vi|sion** /ɪnvɪʒᵊn/ **(envisions, envisioning, envisioned)** If you **envision** something, you envisage it. [AM; also BRIT, LITERARY] ❑ *In the future we envision a federation of companies... Most people do stop at this point, not envisioning that there is anything beyond.* VERB = *imagine* V n; V that; Also V wh

**en|voy** /envɔɪ/ **(envoys)** 1 An **envoy** is someone who is sent as a representative from one government or political group to another. N-COUNT: with supp
2 An **envoy** is a diplomat in an embassy who is immediately below the ambassador in rank. N-COUNT

**envy** /envi/ **(envies, envying, envied)** 1 **Envy** is the feeling you have when you wish you could have the same thing or quality that someone else has. ❑ *Gradually he began to acknowledge his feelings of envy towards his mother... They gazed in a mixture of envy and admiration at the beauty of the statue.* N-UNCOUNT
2 If you **envy** someone, you wish that you had the same things or qualities that they have. ❑ *I don't envy the young ones who've become TV superstars and know no other world... He envied Caroline her peace.* VERB V n; V n n
3 If a thing or quality is **the envy of** someone, they wish very much that they could have or achieve it. ❑ *...an economic expansion that was the envy of many other states.* N-SING: *the* N *of* n
4 **green with envy** → see **green**.

**en|zyme** /enzaɪm/ **(enzymes)** An **enzyme** is a chemical substance that is found in living creatures which produces changes in other substances without being changed itself. [TECHNICAL] N-COUNT

**eon** /iːɒn/ → see **aeon**.

**EP** /iː piː/ **(EPs)** An **EP** is a record which lasts for about 8 minutes on each side. **EP** is an abbreviation for 'extended play'. N-COUNT

**ep|aulette** /epəlet/ **(epaulettes)**

☑ in AM, use **epaulet**

**Epaulettes** are decorations worn on the shoulders of certain uniforms, especially military ones. N-COUNT: usu pl

**épée** /eɪpeɪ/ **(épées)** also **epee.** An **épée** is a thin, light sword that is used in the sport of fencing. N-COUNT

**ephem|era** /ɪfemərə/ 1 You can refer to things which last for only a short time as **ephemera**. [LITERARY] N-UNCOUNT
2 **Ephemera** is things people collect such as old postcards, posters, and bus tickets, which were only intended to last a short time when they were produced. ❑ *...tickets and other printed ephemera.* N-UNCOUNT: oft adj N

**ephem|er|al** /ɪfemərəl/ If you describe something as **ephemeral**, you mean that it lasts only for a very short time. [FORMAL] ❑ *He talked about the country's ephemeral unity being shattered by the defeat.* ADJ = *transient*

**epic** /epɪk/ **(epics)** 1 An **epic** is a long book, poem, or film, whose story extends over a long period of time or tells of great events. ❑ *...the Middle High German epic, 'Nibelungenlied', written about 1200... At three hours and 21 minutes, it is an overlong, standard Hollywood epic.* N-COUNT: usu supp N
♦ **Epic** is also an adjective. ❑ *...epic narrative poems... Like 'Gone With The Wind' it's an unashamed epic romance.* ADJ: usu ADJ n
2 Something that is **epic** is very large and impressive. ❑ *...Columbus's epic voyage of discovery.* ADJ: usu ADJ n

**epi|cen|tre** /episentəʳ/ **(epicentres)**

☑ in AM, use **epicenter**

The **epicentre** of an earthquake is the place on the earth's surface directly above the point where it starts, and is the place where it is felt most strongly. ❑ *The earthquake had its epicentre two-hundred kilometres north-east of the capital.* N-COUNT: usu with poss

**epi|cure** /epɪkjʊəʳ/ **(epicures)** An **epicure** is someone who enjoys eating food that is of very good quality, especially unusual or rare food. [FORMAL] N-COUNT = *gourmand*

**epi|cu|rean** /epɪkjʊəriːən/ **Epicurean** food is of very good quality, especially unusual or rare food. [FORMAL] ❑ *...an epicurean dish.* ADJ: usu ADJ n

**epi|dem|ic** /epɪdemɪk/ **(epidemics)** 1 If there is an **epidemic of** a particular disease somewhere, it affects a very large number of people there and spreads quickly to other areas. ❑ *A flu epidemic is sweeping through Moscow. ...a killer epidemic of yellow fever.* N-COUNT: oft n N, N *of* n
2 If an activity that you disapprove of is increasing or spreading rapidly, you can refer to this as an **epidemic of** that activity. ❑ *...an epidemic of serial killings... Drug experts say it could spell the end of the crack epidemic.* N-COUNT: with supp, oft N *of* n [disapproval]

**epi|der|mis** /epɪdɜːʳmɪs/ Your **epidermis** is the thin, protective, outer layer of your skin. [TECHNICAL] N-SING

**epi|dur|al** /epidjʊərəl, AM -dʊr-/ **(epidurals)** N-COUNT An **epidural** is a type of anaesthetic which is injected into a person's spine so that they cannot feel anything from the waist downwards. Epidurals are sometimes given to women when they are giving birth.

**epi|gram** /epɪgræm/ **(epigrams)** N-COUNT An **epigram** is a short saying or poem which expresses an idea in a very clever and amusing way.

**epi|lep|sy** /epɪlepsi/ N-UNCOUNT **Epilepsy** is a brain condition which causes a person to suddenly lose consciousness and sometimes to have fits.

**epi|lep|tic** /epɪleptɪk/ **(epileptics)** 1 ADJ Someone who is **epileptic** suffers from epilepsy. ❑ *He was epileptic and refused to take medication for his condition.* ♦ N-COUNT An **epileptic** is someone who is epileptic. ❑ *His wife is an epileptic.* 2 ADJ: ADJ n An **epileptic** fit is caused by epilepsy. ❑ *He suffered an epileptic fit.*

**epi|logue** /epɪlɒg, AM -lɔːg/ **(epilogues)**

in AM, also use **epilog**

N-COUNT: usu *the* N in sing An **epilogue** is a passage or speech which is added to the end of a book or play as a conclusion.

**Epipha|ny** /ɪpɪfəni/ N-UNCOUNT **Epiphany** is a Christian festival on the 6th of January which celebrates the arrival of the wise men who came to see Jesus Christ soon after he was born.

**epis|co|pal** /ɪpɪskəpəl/ 1 ADJ: ADJ n **Episcopal** means relating to a branch of the Anglican Church in Scotland and the USA. ❑ *...the Scottish Episcopal Church. ...the Episcopal bishop of New York. ...the Protestant Episcopal church.* 2 ADJ: ADJ n **Episcopal** means relating to bishops. [FORMAL] ❑ *...episcopal conferences.*

**Epis|co|pa|li|an** /ɪpɪskəpeɪliən/ **(Episcopalians)** 1 ADJ: ADJ n **Episcopalian** means belonging to the Episcopal Church. 2 N-COUNT An **Episcopalian** is a member of the Episcopal Church.

**epi|sode** /epɪsoʊd/ **(episodes)** 1 N-COUNT: usu with supp You can refer to an event or a short period of time as an **episode** if you want to suggest that it is important or unusual, or has some particular quality. ❑ *This episode is bound to be a deep embarrassment for Washington... Unfortunately it was a rather sordid episode of my life.* 2 N-COUNT: oft N *of* n = *instalment* An **episode** of something such as a series on radio or television or a story in a magazine is one of the separate parts in which it is broadcast or published. ❑ *The final episode will be shown next Sunday.* 3 N-COUNT: usu with supp = *attack* An **episode of** an illness is short period in which a person who suffers from it is affected by it particularly badly. [MEDICAL]

**epi|sod|ic** /epɪsɒdɪk/ ADJ Something that is **episodic** occurs at irregular and infrequent intervals. [FORMAL] ❑ *...episodic attacks of fever.*

**epis|tle** /ɪpɪsəl/ **(epistles)** 1 N-COUNT: supp N An **epistle** is a letter. [LITERARY] 2 N-COUNT: usu N *to* n In the Bible, the **Epistles** are a series of books in the New Testament which were originally written as letters to the early Christians.

**epis|to|lary** /ɪpɪstələri, AM -leri/ ADJ: ADJ n An **epistolary** novel or story is one that is written as a series of letters. [FORMAL]

**epi|taph** /epɪtɑːf, -tæf/ **(epitaphs)** N-COUNT An **epitaph** is a short piece of writing about someone who is dead, often carved on their grave.

**epi|thet** /epɪθet/ **(epithets)** N-COUNT: usu with supp An **epithet** is an adjective or short phrase which is used as a way of criticizing or praising someone. [FORMAL] ❑ *...the religious issue which led to the epithet 'bible-basher'.*

**epito|me** /ɪpɪtəmi/ N-SING: usu *the* N *of* n emphasis If you say that a person or thing is **the epitome of** something, you are emphasizing that they are the best possible example of a particular type of person or thing. [FORMAL] ❑ *Maureen was the epitome of sophistication.*

**epito|mize** /ɪpɪtəmaɪz/ **(epitomizes, epitomizing, epitomized)**

in BRIT, also use **epitomise**

VERB If you say that something or someone **epitomizes** a particular thing, you mean that they are a perfect example of it. ❑ be V-ed *by* n *Lyonnais cooking is epitomized by the so-called 'bouchons'.* V n *...the sleek lift that epitomized the hotel's glossy decor.*

**EPO** /iː piː oʊ/ also **epo.** N-UNCOUNT **EPO** is a drug that can improve performance in sports and is used illegally by some sportspeople. **EPO** is short for 'erythropoietin'.

**epoch** /iːpɒk, AM epək/ **(epochs)** N-COUNT: usu with supp If you refer to a long period of time as an **epoch**, you mean that important events or great changes took place during it. ❑ *The birth of Christ was the beginning of a major epoch of world history.*

**epoch-making** ADJ: usu ADJ n An **epoch-making** change or declaration is considered to be the extremely important because it is likely to have a significant effect on a particular period of time. ❑ *It was meant to sound like an epoch-making declaration. ...the epoch-making changes now taking place in Eastern Europe.*

**epony|mous** /ɪpɒnɪməs/ ADJ: ADJ n An **eponymous** hero or heroine is the character in a play or book whose name is the title of that play or book. [FORMAL]

**epoxy** /ɪpɒksi/ N-UNCOUNT: oft N n **Epoxy** resin or adhesive contains an artificial substance which sets hard when it is heated or when pressure is applied to it.

**Ep|som salts** /epsəm sɔːlts/ N-UNCOUNT **Epsom salts** is a kind of white powder which you can mix with water and drink as a medicine to help you empty your bowels.

**EQ** /iː kjuː/ **(EQs)** N-VAR A person's **EQ** is a measure of their interpersonal and communication skills. **EQ** is an abbreviation for 'emotional quotient'. Compare **IQ**. ❑ *Guy was elected leader and then found to have the highest EQ on a nominal measure.*

**eq|uable** /ekwəbəl/ 1 ADJ If you describe someone as **equable**, you mean that they are calm, cheerful, and fair with other people, even in difficult circumstances. ❑ *He was a man of the most equable temper.* ♦ ADV: ADV after v **eq|uably** *She wasn't prepared to respond equably to Richardson's mood, and she spoke curtly.*

**equal** /iːkwəl/ **(equals, equalling, equalled)** ◆◇◇

in AM, use **equaling, equaled**

1 ADJ: oft ADJ *to* n If two things are **equal** or if one thing is **equal to** another, they are the same in size, number, standard, or value. ❑ *Investors can borrow an amount equal to the property's purchase price. ...in a population having equal numbers of men and women... Research and teaching are of equal importance.* 2 ADJ: usu ADJ n If different groups of people have **equal** rights or are given **equal** treatment, they have the same rights or are treated the same as each other, however different they are. ❑ *We will be justly demanding equal rights at work. ...the commitment to equal opportunities. ...new legislation allowing building societies to compete on equal terms with their competitors.* 3 ADJ: v-link ADJ If you say that people are **equal**, you mean that they have or should have the same rights and opportunities as each other. ❑ *We are equal in every way... At any gambling game, everyone is equal.* 4 N-COUNT: poss N Someone who is your **equal** has the same ability, status, or rights as you have. ❑ *She was one of the boys, their equal... You should have married somebody more your equal.* 5 ADJ: v-link ADJ *to* n If someone is **equal to** a particular job or situation, they have the necessary ability, strength, or courage to deal successfully with it. ❑ *She was determined that she would be equal to any test the corporation put to them.* 6 V-LINK If something **equals** a particular number or amount, it is the same as that amount or the equivalent of that amount. ❑ V amount *9 percent interest less 7 percent inflation equals 2 percent.* 7 VERB To **equal** something or someone means to be as good or as great as them. ❑ V n *The victory equalled Southend's best in history.* 8 PHRASE: PHR with cl If you say '**other things being equal**' or '**all things being equal**' when talking about a possible situation, you mean if nothing unexpected happens or if there are no other factors which affect the situation. ❑ *Other things be-*

*ing equal, most tenants would prefer single to shared rooms.*

**equal|ity** /ɪkwɒlɪti/ **Equality** is the same status, rights, and responsibilities for all the members of a society, group, or family. ❑ *...equality of the sexes.* N-UNCOUNT

**equal|ize** /iːkwəlaɪz/ **(equalizes, equalizing, equalized)**

☑ in BRIT, also use **equalise**

[1] To **equalize** a situation means to give everyone the same rights or opportunities, for example in education, wealth, or social status. ❑ *Such measures are needed to equalize wage rates between countries.* ♦ **equali|za|tion** /iːkwəlaɪzeɪʃᵊn/ *...the equalization of parenting responsibilities between men and women.* [2] In sports such as football, if a player **equalizes**, he or she scores a goal that makes the scores of the two teams equal. [BRIT] ❑ *Keegan equalized with only 16 minutes remaining... They showed little sign of equalising the Portsmouth striker's glorious 55th-minute shot.*

VERB; V n; N-UNCOUNT: also *a* N; VERB; V; V n

**equal|iz|er** /iːkwəlaɪzəʳ/ **(equalizers)** also **equaliser.** In sports such as football, an **equalizer** is a goal or a point that makes the scores of the two teams equal. [BRIT] N-COUNT: usu sing

**equal|ly** /iːkwəli/ [1] **Equally** means in sections, amounts, or spaces that are the same size as each other. ❑ *A bank's local market share tends to be divided equally between the local branch and branches located elsewhere... Try to get into the habit of eating at least three small meals a day, at equally spaced intervals.* [2] **Equally** means to the same degree or extent. ❑ *All these techniques are equally effective... Success doesn't only depend on what you do. What you don't do is equally important.* [3] **Equally** is used to introduce another comment on the same topic, which balances or contrasts with the previous comment. ❑ *They needed his help, but equally they did not trust him.*

◆◇◇ ADV: ADV after v, ADV -ed; ADV: ADV adj/adv, ADV before v; ADV: ADV with cl

**equal op|por|tu|nities** **Equal opportunities** refers to the policy of giving everyone the same opportunities for employment, pay and promotion, without discriminating against particular groups. [BUSINESS] ❑ *The profession's leaders must take action now to promote equal opportunities for all.* N-PLURAL

**equal op|por|tu|nities em|ploy|er** **(equal opportunities employers)** An **equal opportunities employer** is an employer who gives people the same opportunities for employment, pay, and promotion, without discrimination against anyone. [BUSINESS] ❑ *The police force is committed to being an equal opportunities employer.* N-COUNT

**equal sign** **(equal signs)**

☑ in BRIT, also use **equals sign**

An **equal sign** is the sign =, which is used in arithmetic to indicate that two numbers or sets of numbers are equal. N-COUNT

**equa|nim|ity** /ekwənɪmɪti, iːk-/ **Equanimity** is a calm state of mind and attitude to life, so that you never lose your temper or become upset. [FORMAL] ❑ *His sense of humour allowed him to face adversaries with equanimity.* N-UNCOUNT: oft *with* N

**equate** /ɪkweɪt/ **(equates, equating, equated)** If you **equate** one thing **with** another, or if you say that one thing **equates with** another, you believe that they are strongly connected. ❑ *I'm always wary of men wearing suits, as I equate this with power and authority... The author doesn't equate liberalism and conservatism... The principle of hierarchy does not equate to totalitarian terror.* ♦ **equa|tion** *...the equation of gangsterism with business in Coppola's film.*

VERB; V n *with* n; V pl-n; V *to/with* n; N-UNCOUNT: oft N *of* n *with* n

**equa|tion** /ɪkweɪʒᵊn/ **(equations)** [1] An **equation** is a mathematical statement saying that two amounts or values are the same, for example 6x4=12x2. [2] An **equation** is a situation in which two or more parts have to be considered together so that the whole situation can be understood or explained. ❑ *The equation is simple: research breeds new products... New plans have taken chance out of the equation.* [3] → See also **equate**.

N-COUNT; N-COUNT

**equa|tor** /ɪkweɪtəʳ/ **The equator** is an imaginary line around the middle of the earth at an equal distance from the North Pole and the South Pole. N-SING: *the* N

**equa|to|rial** /ekwətɔːriᵊl, AM iː-/ Something that is **equatorial** is near or at the equator. ❑ *...the equatorial island with a hundred and twenty thousand people living there.* ADJ: usu ADJ n

**eq|uer|ry** /ɪkweri, AM ekwəri/ **(equerries)** An **equerry** is an officer of a royal household or court who acts as a personal assistant to a member of the royal family. N-COUNT: oft N *to* n

**eques|trian** /ɪkwestriən/ **Equestrian** means connected with the activity of riding horses. ❑ *...his equestrian skills.* ADJ: usu ADJ n

**eques|tri|an|ism** /ɪkwestriənɪzəm/ **Equestrianism** refers to sports in which people demonstrate their skill at riding and controlling a horse. N-UNCOUNT

**equi|dis|tant** /iːkwɪdɪstənt/ A place that is **equidistant from** two other places is the same distance away from each of these places. ❑ *Horsey is equidistant from Great Yarmouth and Mundesley.* ADJ: usu v-link ADJ, usu ADJ *from/between* n

**equi|lat|eral** /iːkwɪlætərəl/ A shape or figure that is **equilateral** has sides that are all the same length. [TECHNICAL] ❑ *...an equilateral triangle.* ADJ: usu ADJ n

**equi|lib|rium** /iːkwɪlɪbriəm/ **(equilibria)** [1] **Equilibrium** is a balance between several different influences or aspects of a situation. [FORMAL] ❑ *Stocks seesawed ever lower until prices found some new level of equilibrium... For the economy to be in equilibrium, income must equal expenditure.* [2] Someone's **equilibrium** is their normal calm state of mind. ❑ *I paused in the hall to take three deep breaths to restore my equilibrium.*

N-VAR; N-UNCOUNT: oft poss N

**equine** /ekwaɪn, AM iːk-/ **Equine** means connected with or relating to horses. ❑ *...an outbreak of equine influenza.* ADJ: ADJ n

**equi|nox** /iːkwɪnɒks, ek-/ **(equinoxes)** An **equinox** is one of the two days in the year when day and night are of equal length. ❑ *In the Chinese calendar, the Spring Equinox always occurs in the second month.* N-COUNT: oft supp N

**equip** /ɪkwɪp/ **(equips, equipping, equipped)** [1] If you **equip** a person or thing **with** something, you give them the tools or equipment that are needed. ❑ *They become obsessed with trying to equip their vehicles with gadgets to deal with every possible contingency... Owners of restaurants would have to equip them to admit disabled people... The country did not possess the modern guns to equip the reserve army properly.* ♦ **equipped** *...well-equipped research buildings... The greenhouses come equipped with a ventilating system and aluminium screen door.* [2] If something **equips** you for a particular task or experience, it gives you the skills and attitudes you need for it, especially by educating you in a particular way. ❑ *Relative poverty, however, did not prevent Martin from equipping himself with an excellent education... A basic two-hour first aid course would equip you to deal with any of these incidents.* ♦ **equipped** *Some students have emotional problems that teachers feel ill equipped to handle... When they leave school, they will be equipped for obtaining office jobs.*

VERB; V n *with* n; V n to-inf; V n; ADJ; VERB; V n *with* n; V n to-inf; ADJ: v-link ADJ to-inf, v-link ADJ *for* n/-ing

**equip|ment** /ɪkwɪpmənt/ **Equipment** consists of the things which are used for a particular purpose, for example a hobby or job. ❑ *...computers, electronic equipment and machine tools. ...outdoor playing equipment.* ◆◆◇ N-UNCOUNT

**equi|table** /ekwɪtəbᵊl/ Something that is **equitable** is fair and reasonable in a way that gives equal treatment to everyone. ❑ *He has urged them to come to an equitable compromise that gives Hughes his proper due.* ♦ **equi|tably** *...a real attempt to allocate scarce resources more equitably.*

ADJ; ADV: ADV after v, ADV -ed

**equi|ties** /ekwɪtiz/ **Equities** are shares in a company that are owned by people who have a right to vote at the company's meetings and to re- N-PLURAL = *ordinary shares* ceive part of the company's profits after the holders of preference shares have been paid. [BUSINESS] ❑ *Investors have poured money into US equities.* → See also **preference shares.**

**equi|ty** /ekwɪti/ 1 In finance, your **equity** is the sum of your assets, for example the value of your house, once your debts have been subtracted from it. [BUSINESS] ❑ *To capture his equity, Murphy must either sell or refinance. ...a Personal Equity Plan.* → See also **negative equity.** ◆◇◇ N-UNCOUNT 2 **Equity** is the quality of being fair and reasonable in a way that gives equal treatment to everyone. ❑ *We base this call on grounds of social justice and equity.* N-UNCOUNT

**equiva|lence** /ɪkwɪvələns/ If there is **equivalence** between two things, they have the same use, function, size, or value. ❑ *...the equivalence of science and rationality.* N-UNCOUNT

**equiva|lent** /ɪkwɪvələnt/ **(equivalents)** ◆◇◇ 1 If one amount or value is **the equivalent of** another, they are the same. ❑ *The equivalent of two tablespoons of polyunsaturated oils is ample each day... Even the cheapest car costs the equivalent of 70 years' salary for a government worker.* N-SING: oft N *of* n ♦ **Equivalent** is also an adjective. ❑ *A unit is equivalent to a glass of wine or a single measure of spirits... They will react with hostility to the price rises and calls for equivalent wage increases are bound to be heard.* ADJ: oft ADJ *to* n = equal 2 The **equivalent** of someone or something is a person or thing that has the same function in a different place, time, or system. ❑ *...the civil administrator of the West Bank and his equivalent in Gaza. ...the Red Cross emblem, and its equivalent in Muslim countries, the Red Crescent.* N-COUNT: usu with poss = counterpart ♦ **Equivalent** is also an adjective. ❑ *...a decrease of 10% in property investment compared with the equivalent period in 1991.* ADJ 3 You can use **equivalent** to emphasize the great or severe effect of something. ❑ *His party has just suffered the equivalent of a near-fatal heart attack.* N-SING: *the* N *of* n [emphasis]

**equivo|cal** /ɪkwɪvəkəl/ 1 If you are **equivocal**, you are deliberately vague in what you say, because you want to avoid speaking the truth or making a decision. [FORMAL] ❑ *Many were equivocal about the idea... His equivocal response has done nothing to dampen the speculation.* ADJ 2 If something is **equivocal**, it is difficult to understand, interpret, or explain, often because it has aspects that seem to contradict each other. [FORMAL] ❑ *Research in this area is somewhat equivocal... He was tortured by an awareness of the equivocal nature of his position.* ADJ

**equivo|cate** /ɪkwɪvəkeɪt/ **(equivocates, equivocating, equivocated)** When someone **equivocates**, they deliberately use vague language in order to deceive people or to avoid speaking the truth. ❑ *He is equivocating a lot about what is going to happen if and when there are elections... He had asked her once again about her finances. And again she had equivocated.* VERB V *about/over* n V ♦ **equivo|ca|tion** /ɪkwɪvəkeɪʃən/ *Why doesn't the President say so without equivocation?* N-UNCOUNT: usu *without* N

**er** /ɜːʳ/ **Er** is used in writing to represent the sound that people make when they hesitate, especially while they decide what to say next. ❑ *I would challenge the, er, suggestion that we're in third place.*

**ER** /iː ɑːʳ/ **(ERs)** The **ER** is the part of a hospital where people who have severe injuries or sudden illnesses are taken for emergency treatment. **ER** is an abbreviation for 'emergency room'. [AM] N-COUNT

✔ in BRIT, use **casualty, A & E**

**-er** /-əʳ/ 1 You add **-er** to many short adjectives to form comparatives. For example, the comparative of 'nice' is 'nicer'; the comparative of 'happy' is 'happier'. You also add it to some adverbs that do not end in -ly. For example, the comparative of 'soon' is 'sooner'. SUFFIX 2 You add **-er** to verbs to form nouns which refer to a person, animal, or thing that does the action described by the verb; for example a 'reader' is someone who reads and a 'money-saver' is something that saves money. SUFFIX 3 You add **-er** to words to form nouns which refer to a person who is associated or involved with the thing described by the word; for example a 'pensioner' is someone who is entitled to a pension. SUFFIX 4 You add **-er** to nouns to form nouns or adjectives which refer to things with a particular characteristic or feature; for example a 'three-wheeler' is a vehicle with three wheels. SUFFIX 5 You add **-er** to words to form nouns which refer to a person with a particular job. For example, someone who works in a mine is a 'miner'. SUFFIX 6 You add **-er** to the names of some places to form nouns which refer to a person who comes from that place. For example, someone who comes from London is a 'Londoner'. SUFFIX

**era** /ɪərə/ **(eras)** You can refer to a period of history or a long period of time as an **era** when you want to draw attention to a particular feature or quality that it has. ❑ *...the nuclear era... It was an era of austerity.* ◆◇◇ N-COUNT: usu supp N, N *of* n = age

**eradi|cate** /ɪrædɪkeɪt/ **(eradicates, eradicating, eradicated)** To **eradicate** something means to get rid of it completely. [FORMAL] ❑ *They are already battling to eradicate illnesses such as malaria and tetanus... If tedious tasks could be eradicated, the world would be much better place.* VERB = eliminate V n V n ♦ **eradi|ca|tion** /ɪrædɪkeɪʃən/ *He is seen as having made a significant contribution towards the eradication of corruption.* N-UNCOUNT: oft N *of* n

**erase** /ɪreɪz, AM ɪreɪs/ **(erases, erasing, erased)** 1 If you **erase** a thought or feeling, you destroy it completely so that you can no longer remember something or no longer feel a particular emotion. ❑ *They are desperate to erase the memory of that last defeat in Cardiff... Love was a word he'd erased from his vocabulary since Susan's going.* VERB V n V n *from* n 2 If you **erase** sound which has been recorded on a tape or information which has been stored in a computer, you completely remove or destroy it. ❑ *He was in the studio tearfully erasing all the tapes he'd slaved over... It appears the names were accidentally erased from computer disks.* VERB = wipe V n *be* V-ed *from* n 3 If you **erase** something such as writing or a mark, you remove it, usually by rubbing it with a cloth. ❑ *It was unfortunate that she had erased the message.* VERB = rub out V n

**eras|er** /ɪreɪzəʳ, AM -reɪs-/ **(erasers)** An **eraser** is an object, usually a piece of rubber or plastic, which is used for removing something that has been written using a pencil or a pen. [AM; also BRIT, FORMAL] ❑ *...a large, flat, pink India-rubber eraser.* N-COUNT = rubber

**eras|ure** /ɪreɪʒəʳ, AM -reɪʃ-/ The **erasure of** something is the removal, loss, or destruction of it. [FORMAL] ❑ *...a further erasure of the UK's thin manufacturing base.* N-UNCOUNT: oft N *of* n

**ere** /eəʳ/ **Ere** means the same as 'before'. [LITERARY, OLD-FASHIONED] ❑ *Take the water ere the clock strikes twelve.* CONJ

**erect** /ɪrekt/ **(erects, erecting, erected)** 1 If people **erect** something such as a building, bridge, or barrier, they build it or create it. [FORMAL] ❑ *Opposition demonstrators have erected barricades in roads leading to the parliament building... The building was erected in 1900-1901... We all unconsciously erect barriers against intimacy.* VERB = construct V n V n V n 2 If you **erect** a system, a theory, or an institution, you create it. ❑ *Japanese proprietors are erecting a complex infrastructure of political influence throughout America... He erected a new doctrine of precedent.* VERB V n V n 3 People or things that are **erect** are straight and upright. ❑ *Stand reasonably erect, your arms hanging naturally.* ADJ

**erec|tion** /ɪrekʃən/ **(erections)** 1 If a man has an **erection**, his penis is stiff, swollen, and sticking up because he is sexually aroused. N-COUNT 2 The **erection of** something is the act of building it or placing it in an upright position. ❑ *...the erection of temporary fencing to protect hedges under repair.* N-UNCOUNT: oft N *of* n

**er|ga|tive** /ɜːʳgətɪv/ An **ergative** verb is a verb that can be both transitive and intransitive, where the subject of the intransitive verb is the same as the object of the transitive verb. For ex- ADJ ample, 'open' is an ergative verb because you can say 'The door opened' or 'She opened the door'.

**ergo** /ɜːʳɡoʊ/ **Ergo** is sometimes used instead of 'therefore' to introduce a clause in which you mention something that is the consequence or logical result of what you have just said. [FORMAL or LITERARY] ❑ *Neither side would have an incentive to start a war. Ergo, peace would reign.* ADV: ADV with cl = *therefore*

**er|go|nom|ics** /ɜːʳɡənɒmɪks/ **Ergonomics** is the study of how equipment and furniture can be arranged in order that people can do work or other activities more efficiently and comfortably. N-UNCOUNT

**er|mine** /ɜːʳmɪn/ **Ermine** is expensive white fur that comes from small animals called stoats. N-UNCOUNT: oft N n

**erode** /ɪroʊd/ **(erodes, eroding, eroded)** 1 If rock or soil **erodes** or **is eroded** by the weather, sea, or wind, it cracks and breaks so that it is gradually destroyed. ❑ *By 1980, Miami beach had all but totally eroded... Once exposed, soil is quickly eroded by wind and rain.* ♦ **erod|ed** *...the deeply eroded landscape.* 2 If someone's authority, right, or confidence **erodes** or **is eroded**, it is gradually destroyed or removed. [FORMAL] ❑ *His critics say his fumbling of the issue of reform has eroded his authority... America's belief in its own God-ordained uniqueness started to erode.* 3 If the value of something **erodes** or **is eroded** by something such as inflation or age, its value decreases. ❑ *Competition in the financial marketplace has eroded profits... The value of the dollar began to erode rapidly just around this time.* VERB = *wear away* V *be* V-ed ADJ VERB V n V VERB V n V

**erog|enous** /ɪrɒdʒɪnəs/ An **erogenous** part of your body is one where sexual pleasure can be felt or caused. [FORMAL] ❑ *Your body contains many erogenous zones, areas that lead to a feeling of sexual excitement when they are caressed.* ADJ: usu ADJ n

**ero|sion** /ɪroʊʒən/ 1 **Erosion** is the gradual destruction and removal of rock or soil in a particular area by rivers, the sea, or the weather. ❑ *As their roots are strong and penetrating, they prevent erosion. ...erosion of the river valleys. ...soil erosion.* 2 The **erosion of** a person's authority, rights, or confidence is the gradual destruction or removal of them. ❑ *...the erosion of confidence in world financial markets. ...an erosion of presidential power.* 3 The **erosion of** support, values, or money is a gradual decrease in its level or standard. ❑ *...the erosion of moral standards. ...a dramatic erosion of support for the program.* N-UNCOUNT N-UNCOUNT: usu N *of* n N-UNCOUNT: usu N *of* n

**erot|ic** /ɪrɒtɪk/ 1 If you describe something as **erotic**, you mean that it involves sexual feelings or arouses sexual desire. ❑ *It might sound like some kind of wild fantasy, but it wasn't an erotic experience at all. ...photographs of nude women in erotic poses.* ♦ **eroti|cal|ly** /ɪrɒtɪkli/ *The film is shot seductively, erotically.* 2 **Erotic** art shows naked people or sexual acts, and is intended to produce feelings of sexual pleasure. ❑ *Erotic paintings also became a fine art.* ADJ ADV: ADV with v, ADV adj ADJ: ADJ n

**eroti|ca** /ɪrɒtɪkə/ **Erotica** means works of art that show or describe sexual activity, and which are intended to arouse sexual feelings. N-UNCOUNT

**eroti|cism** /ɪrɒtɪsɪzəm/ **Eroticism** is sexual excitement, or the quality of being able to arouse sexual excitement. [FORMAL] ❑ *Almost all of Massenet's works are pervaded with an aura of eroticism.* N-UNCOUNT

**err** /ɜːʳ/ **(errs, erring, erred)** 1 If you **err**, you make a mistake. [FORMAL, OLD-FASHIONED] ❑ *It criticises the main contractor for seriously erring in its original estimates... If you make a threat be sure to carry it out if he errs again.* 2 If you **err on the side of** caution, for example, you decide to act in a cautious way, rather than take risks. ❑ *They may be wise to err on the side of caution... He probably erred on the conservative rather than the generous side.* VERB V *in* n V PHRASE: V inflects

**er|rand** /erənd/ **(errands)** 1 An **errand** is a short trip that you make in order to do a job for someone, for example when you go to a shop to buy something for them. ❑ *She went off on some errand.* 2 If you **run an errand for** someone, you do or get something for them, usually by making a short trip somewhere. ❑ *She was forever running errands for her housebound grandmother.* N-COUNT PHRASE: V inflects

**er|rant** /erənt/ **Errant** is used to describe someone whose actions are considered unacceptable or wrong by other people. For example, an **errant** husband is unfaithful to his wife. [FORMAL] ❑ *Usually his cases involved errant husbands and wandering wives.* ADJ: ADJ n

**er|rat|ic** /ɪrætɪk/ Something that is **erratic** does not follow a regular pattern, but happens at unexpected times or moves along in an irregular way. ❑ *Argentina's erratic inflation rate threatens to upset the plans.* ♦ **er|rati|cal|ly** /ɪrætɪkli/ *Police stopped him for driving erratically.* ADJ = *unpredictable* ADV

**er|ro|neous** /ɪroʊniəs/ Beliefs, opinions, or methods that are **erroneous** are incorrect or only partly correct. ❑ *Some people have the erroneous notion that one can contract AIDS by giving blood... They have arrived at some erroneous conclusions.* ♦ **er|ro|neous|ly** *It had been widely and erroneously reported that Armstrong had refused to give evidence.* ADJ ADV: ADV with v

**er|ror** /erəʳ/ **(errors)** 1 An **error** is something you have done which is considered to be incorrect or wrong, or which should not have been done. ❑ *NASA discovered a mathematical error in its calculations... MPs attacked lax management and errors of judgment.* ◆◇◇ N-VAR: oft N prep

**PHRASES** 2 If you do something **in error** or if it happens **in error**, you do it or it happens because you have made a mistake, especially in your judgment. ❑ *The plane was shot down in error by a NATO missile.* 3 If someone sees **the error of** their **ways**, they realize or admit that they have made a mistake or behaved badly. ❑ *I wanted an opportunity to talk some sense into him and try to make him see the error of his ways.* PHRASE: usu PHR after v PHRASE: PHR after v

**er|satz** /eəʳzæts/ If you describe something as **ersatz**, you dislike it because it is not genuine and is a poor imitation of something better. [WRITTEN] ❑ *...an ersatz Victorian shopping precinct.* ADJ: usu ADJ n disapproval = *fake*

**erst|while** /ɜːʳstʰwaɪl/ You use **erstwhile** to describe someone that used to be the type of person indicated, but no longer is. [FORMAL] ❑ *He fled to America with Phyllis Burton, an erstwhile friend of his wife's.* ADJ: ADJ n = *one-time*

**eru|dite** /erʊdaɪt, AM erjə-/ If you describe someone as **erudite**, you mean that they have or show great academic knowledge. You can also use **erudite** to describe something such as a book or a style of writing. [FORMAL] ❑ *He was never dull, always erudite and well informed. ...an original and highly erudite style.* ADJ

**eru|di|tion** /erʊdɪʃən, AM erjə-/ **Erudition** is great academic knowledge. [FORMAL] ❑ *His erudition was apparently endless.* N-UNCOUNT

**erupt** /ɪrʌpt/ **(erupts, erupting, erupted)** 1 When a volcano **erupts**, it throws out a lot of hot, melted rock called lava, as well as ash and steam. ❑ *The volcano erupted in 1980, devastating a large area of Washington state.* ♦ **erup|tion** /ɪrʌpʃən/ **(eruptions)** *...the volcanic eruption of Tambora in 1815.* 2 If violence or fighting **erupts**, it suddenly begins or gets worse in an unexpected, violent way. [JOURNALISM] ❑ *Heavy fighting erupted there today after a two-day cease-fire.* ♦ **erup|tion** *...this sudden eruption of violence.* 3 When people in a place suddenly become angry or violent, you can say that they **erupt** or that the place **erupts**. [JOURNALISM] ❑ *In Los Angeles, the neighborhood known as Watts erupted into riots.* 4 You say that someone **erupts** when they suddenly have a change in mood, usually becoming quite noisy. ❑ *Then, without warning, she erupts into laughter.* ♦ **erup|tion** *...an eruption of despair.* 5 If your skin **erupts**, sores or spots suddenly appear there. ❑ *At the end of the second week, my skin erupted in pimples.* ♦ **erup|tion** *...eruptions of adolescent acne.* VERB V N-VAR: usu with supp VERB = *break out* V N-COUNT VERB V *into/in* n VERB V *into/in* n N-COUNT VERB V *in/into* n N-COUNT: with supp

**es|ca|late** /eskəleɪt/ **(escalates, escalating, escalated)** If a bad situation **escalates** or if someone or something **escalates** it, it becomes greater in size, seriousness, or intensity. [JOURNALISM] ❑ *Both unions and management fear the dispute could escalate... The protests escalated into five days of rioting... Defeat could cause one side or other to escalate the conflict.* ♦ **es|ca|la|tion** /eskəleɪʃən/ **(escalations)** *The threat of nuclear escalation remains. ...a sudden escalation of violence.*
VERB; V; V *into* n; V n; N-VAR

**es|ca|la|tor** /eskəleɪtəʳ/ **(escalators)** An **escalator** is a moving staircase on which people can go from one level of a building to another.
N-COUNT

**es|ca|lope** /eskəlɒp, AM ɪskɑːləp/ **(escalopes)** An **escalope** is a thin slice of meat without a bone. [mainly BRIT]
N-COUNT: usu with supp

☑ in AM, use **scallop, cutlet**

**es|ca|pade** /eskəpeɪd/ **(escapades)** An **escapade** is an exciting and rather dangerous adventure. ❑ *...the scene of Robin Hood's escapades.*
N-COUNT

**es|cape** /ɪskeɪp/ **(escapes, escaping, escaped)** ◆◆◇
[1] If you **escape from** a place, you succeed in getting away from it. ❑ *A prisoner has escaped from a jail in northern England... They are reported to have escaped to the other side of the border... He was fatally wounded as he tried to escape.* ♦ **es|caped** *Officers mistook Stephen for an escaped prisoner.*
VERB: no passive; V *from* n; V *to* n; V; ADJ
[2] Someone's **escape** is the act of escaping from a particular place or situation. ❑ *The man made his escape.*
N-COUNT: usu poss N
[3] You can say that you **escape** when you survive something such as an accident. ❑ *The two officers were extremely lucky to escape serious injury... The man's girlfriend managed to escape unhurt... He narrowly escaped with his life when suspected right-wing extremists fired shots into his office.* ♦ **Escape** is also a noun. ❑ *I hear you had a very narrow escape on the bridge.*
VERB; V n; V adj; V prep; N-COUNT
[4] If something is an **escape**, it is a way of avoiding difficulties or responsibilities. ❑ *But for me television is an escape. ...an escape from the depressing realities of wartime.*
N-COUNT: usu sing
[5] You can use **escape** to describe things which allow you to avoid difficulties or problems. For example, an **escape route** is an activity or opportunity that lets you improve your situation. An **escape clause** is part of an agreement that allows you to avoid having to do something that you do not want to do. ❑ *We all need the occasional escape route from the boring, routine aspects of our lives... This has, in fact, turned out to be a wonderful escape clause for dishonest employers everywhere.*
ADJ: ADJ n
[6] If something **escapes** you or **escapes** your attention, you do not know about it, do not remember it, or do not notice it. ❑ *It was an actor whose name escapes me for the moment.*
VERB; V n
[7] When gas, liquid, or heat **escapes**, it comes out from a pipe, container, or place. ❑ *Leave a vent open to let some moist air escape.*
VERB; V
[8] ➔ See also **fire escape**.

**es|cape art|ist** **(escape artists)** An **escape artist** is the same as an **escapologist**. [mainly AM]
N-COUNT

**es|capee** /ɪskeɪpiː/ **(escapees)** An **escapee** is a person who has escaped from somewhere, especially from prison.
N-COUNT

**es|cap|ism** /ɪskeɪpɪzəm/ If you describe an activity or type of entertainment as **escapism**, you mean that it makes people think about pleasant things instead of the uninteresting or unpleasant aspects of their life. ❑ *Horoscopes are merely harmless escapism from an ever-bleaker world.*
N-UNCOUNT

**es|cap|ist** /ɪskeɪpɪst/ **Escapist** ideas, activities, or types of entertainment make people think about pleasant or unlikely things instead of the uninteresting or unpleasant aspects of their life. ❑ *...a little escapist fantasy.*
ADJ

**es|ca|polo|gist** /eskəpɒlədʒɪst/ **(escapologists)** An **escapologist** is someone who entertains audiences by being tied up and placed in a dangerous situation, then escaping from it. [BRIT]
N-COUNT

☑ in AM, use **escape artist**

**es|carp|ment** /ɪskɑːʳpmənt/ **(escarpments)** An **escarpment** is a wide, steep slope on a hill or mountain.
N-COUNT

**es|chew** /ɪstʃuː/ **(eschews, eschewing, eschewed)** If you **eschew** something, you deliberately avoid doing it or becoming involved in it. [FORMAL] ❑ *Although he appeared to enjoy a jet-setting life, he eschewed publicity and avoided night-clubs.*
VERB = avoid; V n

**es|cort** **(escorts, escorting, escorted)**

☑ The noun is pronounced /eskɔːʳt/. The verb is pronounced /ɪskɔːʳt/.

[1] An **escort** is a person who travels with someone in order to protect or guard them. ❑ *He arrived with a police escort shortly before half past nine.* ● If someone is taken somewhere **under escort**, they are accompanied by guards, either because they have been arrested or because they need to be protected. ❑ *...a group being taken under police escort to the city outskirts.*
N-COUNT; PHRASE: PHR after v
[2] An **escort** is a person who accompanies another person of the opposite sex to a social event. Sometimes people are paid to be escorts. ❑ *My sister needed an escort for a company dinner.*
N-COUNT
[3] If you **escort** someone somewhere, you accompany them there, usually in order to make sure that they leave a place or get to their destination. ❑ *I escorted him to the door.*
VERB; V n prep/adv

**es|crow** /eskrou/ **Escrow** is money or property which is given to someone, but which is kept by another person until the first person has done a particular thing or met particular requirements. [mainly AM, LEGAL] ❑ *They had $96,000 in their escrow account... His stake has been held in escrow since the start of the year.*
N-UNCOUNT: oft N n; *in* N

**Es|ki|mo** /eskɪmou/ **(Eskimos)** An **Eskimo** is a member of the group of peoples who live in Alaska, Northern Canada, eastern Siberia, and other parts of the Arctic. These peoples now usually call themselves Inuits or Aleuts, and the term Eskimo could cause offence.
N-COUNT = Inuit

**ESL** /iː es el/ **ESL** is taught to people whose native language is not English but who live in a society in which English is the main language or one of the main languages. **ESL** is an abbreviation for 'English as a second language'.

**esopha|gus** /ɪsɒfəgəs/ ➔ see **oesophagus**.

**eso|ter|ic** /iːsouterɪk, AM esə-/ If you describe something as **esoteric**, you mean it is known, understood, or appreciated by only a small number of people. [FORMAL] ❑ *...esoteric knowledge. ...a spoiled aristocrat with pretentious airs and esoteric tastes.*
ADJ

**esp.** **esp.** is a written abbreviation for **especially**.

**ESP** /iː es piː/ [1] **ESP** is the teaching of English to students whose first language is not English but who need it for a particular job, activity, or purpose. **ESP** is an abbreviation for 'English for specific purposes' or 'English for special purposes'. [BRIT]
N-UNCOUNT
[2] **ESP** is an abbreviation for 'extra-sensory perception'.
N-UNCOUNT

**es|pe|cial** /ɪspeʃəl/ **Especial** means unusual or special in some way. [FORMAL] ❑ *The authorities took especial interest in him because of his trade union work.*
ADJ: ADJ n = special

**es|pe|cial|ly** /ɪspeʃəli/ ◆◆◇
[1] You use **especially** to emphasize that what you are saying applies more to one person, thing, or area than to any others. ❑ *Millions of wild flowers colour the valleys, especially in April and May... Re-apply sunscreen every two hours, especially if you have been swimming.*
ADV: ADV with cl/group [emphasis] = particularly
[2] You use **especially** to emphasize a characteristic or quality. ❑ *Babies lose heat much faster than adults, and are especially vulnerable to the cold in their first month.*
ADV: ADV adj/adv [emphasis]

**Es|pe|ran|to** /espərӕntou/ **Esperanto** is an invented language which consists of parts of several European languages, and which was designed
N-UNCOUNT

to help people from different countries communicate with each other.

**es|pio|nage** /espiənɑːʒ/ **Espionage** is the activity of finding out the political, military, or industrial secrets of your enemies or rivals by using spies. [FORMAL] ❑ *The authorities have arrested several people suspected of espionage. ...industrial espionage.* ➔ See also **counter-espionage**. N-UNCOUNT = spying

**es|pla|nade** /esplənei̱d, AM -nɑ̱ːd/ **(esplanades)** The **esplanade**, usually in a town by the sea, is a wide, open road where people walk for pleasure. N-COUNT: usu *the* N in sing

**es|pous|al** /ɪspaʊ̱zəl/ A government's or person's **espousal of** a particular policy, cause, or belief is their strong support of it. [FORMAL] ❑ *...the Slovene leadership's espousal of the popular causes of reform and nationalism.* N-SING: usu poss N *of* n

**es|pouse** /ɪspaʊ̱z/ **(espouses, espousing, espoused)** If you **espouse** a particular policy, cause, or belief, you become very interested in it and give your support to it. [FORMAL] ❑ *She ran away with him to Mexico and espoused the revolutionary cause.* VERB; V n

**es|pres|so** /espre̱soʊ/ **(espressos) Espresso** coffee is made by forcing steam or boiling water through ground coffee beans. ❑ *...Italian espresso coffee.* ♦ An **espresso** is a cup of espresso coffee. N-UNCOUNT; N-COUNT

**es|prit de corps** /espri̱ː də kɔ̱ːr/ **Esprit de corps** is a feeling of loyalty and pride that is shared by the members of a group who consider themselves to be different from other people in some special way. [FORMAL] N-UNCOUNT

**espy** /ɪspaɪ̱/ **(espies, espying, espied)** If you **espy** something, you see or notice it. [OLD-FASHIONED] ❑ *Here, from a window, did Guinevere espy a knight standing in a woodman's cart.* VERB; V n

**Esq.** **Esq.** is used after men's names as a written abbreviation for **esquire**. ❑ *...Harold T. Cranford Esq.*

**es|quire** /ɪskwaɪ̱əʳ, AM e̱skwaɪr/ **Esquire** is a formal title that can be used after a man's name if he has no other title, especially on an envelope that is addressed to him. [OLD-FASHIONED] N-TITLE

**es|say** /e̱seɪ/ **(essays)** 1 An **essay** is a short piece of writing on one particular subject written by a student. ❑ *We asked Jason to write an essay about his hometown and about his place in it.* N-COUNT 2 An **essay** is a short piece of writing on one particular subject that is written by a writer for publication. ❑ *...Thomas Malthus's essay on population.* N-COUNT: oft N *on* n

**es|say|ist** /e̱seɪɪst/ **(essayists)** An **essayist** is a writer who writes essays for publication. N-COUNT

**es|sence** /e̱səns/ **(essences)** 1 The **essence of** something is its basic and most important characteristic which gives it its individual identity. ❑ *The essence of consultation is to listen to, and take account of, the views of those consulted. ...the essence of life.* N-UNCOUNT: usu N *of* n ● You use **in essence** to emphasize that you are talking about the most important or central aspect of an idea, situation, or event. [FORMAL] ❑ *Though off-puttingly complicated in detail, local taxes are in essence simple.* PHRASE: PHR with cl/group [emphasis] ● If you say that something **is of the essence**, you mean that it is absolutely necessary in order for a particular action to be successful. [FORMAL] ❑ *Speed was of the essence in a project of this type.* PHRASE: V inflects = crucial 2 **Essence** is a very concentrated liquid that is used for flavouring food or for its smell. ❑ *...a few drops of vanilla essence.* N-MASS

**es|sen|tial** /ɪse̱nʃəl/ **(essentials)** ◆◆◇ 1 Something that is **essential** is extremely important or absolutely necessary to a particular subject, situation, or activity. ❑ *It was absolutely essential to separate crops from the areas that animals used as pasture... As they must also sprint over short distances, speed is essential... Jordan promised to trim the city budget without cutting essential services.* ADJ: oft *it* v-link ADJ to-inf = crucial 2 The **essentials** are the things that are absolutely necessary for the situation you are in or for the task you are doing. ❑ *The flat contained the basic essentials for bachelor life.* N-COUNT: usu pl 3 The **essential** aspects of something are its most basic or important aspects. ❑ *Most authorities agree that play is an essential part of a child's development... In this trial two essential elements must be proven: motive and opportunity.* ADJ = fundamental 4 The **essentials** are the most important principles, ideas, or facts of a particular subject. ❑ *...the essentials of everyday life, such as eating and exercise.* N-PLURAL

**es|sen|tial|ly** /ɪse̱nʃəli/ ◆◇◇ 1 You use **essentially** to emphasize a quality that someone or something has, and to say that it is their most important or basic quality. [FORMAL] ❑ *It's been believed for centuries that great writers, composers and scientists are essentially quite different from ordinary people... Essentially, vines and grapes need water, heat and light.* ADV: ADV with cl/group [emphasis] = fundamentally 2 You use **essentially** to indicate that what you are saying is mainly true, although some parts of it are wrong or more complicated than has been stated. [FORMAL] ❑ *His analysis of urban use of agricultural land has been proved essentially correct... Essentially, the West has only two options.* ADV: ADV with cl/group, ADV with v [vagueness]

**-est** /-ɪst/ You add **-est** to many short adjectives to form superlatives. For example, the superlative of 'nice' is 'nicest'; the superlative of 'happy' is 'happiest'. You also add it to some adverbs that do not end in -ly. For example, the superlative of 'soon' is 'soonest'. SUFFIX

**es|tab|lish** /ɪstæ̱blɪʃ/ **(establishes, establishing, established)** ◆◆◇ 1 If someone **establishes** something such as an organization, a type of activity, or a set of rules, they create it or introduce it in such a way that it is likely to last for a long time. ❑ *The UN has established detailed criteria for who should be allowed to vote... The School was established in 1989 by an Italian professor.* VERB = set up, found; V n; V n 2 If you **establish** contact with someone, you start to have contact with them. You can also say that two people, groups, or countries **establish** contact. [FORMAL] ❑ *We had already established contact with the museum... Singapore and South Africa have established diplomatic relations.* V-RECIP; V n *with* n; pl-n V 3 If you **establish that** something is true, you discover facts that show that it is definitely true. [FORMAL] ❑ *Medical tests established that she was their child... It will be essential to establish how the money is being spent... An autopsy was being done to establish the cause of death... It was established that the missile had landed on a test range in Australia.* VERB = ascertain; V that; V wh; V n; *it be* V-ed that ♦ **es|tab|lished** *That link is an established medical fact.* ADJ: usu ADJ n 4 If you **establish yourself**, your reputation, or a good quality that you have, you succeed in doing something, and achieve respect or a secure position as a result of this. ❑ *This is going to be the show where up-and-coming comedians will establish themselves... He has established himself as a pivotal figure in US politics... We shall fight to establish our innocence.* VERB; V pron-refl; V pron-refl *as* n; V n; Also V n *as* n

**es|tab|lished** /ɪstæ̱blɪʃt/ If you use **established** to describe something such as an organization, you mean that it is officially recognized or generally approved of because it has existed for a long time. ❑ *Their religious adherence is not to the established church. ...the established names of Paris fashion.* ADJ: usu ADJ n

**es|tab|lish|ment** /ɪstæ̱blɪʃmənt/ **(establishments)** ◆◇◇ 1 The **establishment of** an organization or system is the act of creating it or beginning it. [FORMAL] ❑ *His ideas influenced the establishment of National Portrait Galleries in London and Edinburgh.* N-SING: usu N *of* n = creation 2 An **establishment** is a shop, business, or organization occupying a particular building or place. [FORMAL] ❑ *...a scientific research establishment. ...shops and other commercial establishments.* N-COUNT: usu with supp 3 You refer to the people who have power and influence in the running of a country, society, or organization as **the establishment**. ❑ *Shopkeepers would once have been pillars of the Tory establishment.* N-SING: usu *the* N in sing

**es|tate** /ɪste̱ɪt/ **(estates)** ◆◆◇ 1 An **estate** is a large area of land in the country which is owned by a person, family, or organization. ❑ *...a shoot-* N-COUNT *ing party on Lord Wyville's estate in Yorkshire.* [2] People sometimes use **estate** to refer to a housing estate or an industrial estate. [BRIT] ❑ *He used to live on the estate.* [3] Someone's **estate** is all the money and property that they leave behind them when they die. [LEGAL] ❑ *His estate was valued at $150,000.* [4] → See also **housing estate**, **industrial estate**, **real estate**. N-COUNT N-COUNT: oft poss N

**es|tate agen|cy (estate agencies)** An **estate agency** is a company that sells houses and land for people. [BRIT] N-COUNT

**es|tate agent (estate agents)** An **estate agent** is someone who works for a company that sells houses and land for people. [BRIT] N-COUNT

✔ in AM, use **Realtor**, **real estate agent**

**es|tate car (estate cars)** An **estate car** is a car with a long body, a door at the rear, and space behind the back seats. [BRIT] N-COUNT

✔ in AM, use **station wagon**

**es|teem** /ɪstiːm/ **(esteems, esteeming, esteemed)** [1] **Esteem** is the admiration and respect that you feel towards another person. [FORMAL] ❑ *He is held in high esteem by colleagues in the construction industry.* [2] If you **esteem** someone or something, you respect or admire them. [FORMAL] ❑ *I greatly esteem your message in the midst of our hard struggle.* [3] → See also **self-esteem**. N-UNCOUNT VERB V n

**es|teemed** /ɪstiːmd/ You use **esteemed** to describe someone who you greatly admire and respect. [FORMAL] ❑ *He was esteemed by his neighbours... It is indeed an honour to serve my country in such an esteemed position.* ADJ

**es|thete** /iːsθiːt, AM es-/ → see **aesthete**.

**es|thet|ic** /iːsθetɪk, AM esθ-/ → see **aesthetic**.

**es|ti|mable** /estɪməbᵊl/ If you describe someone or something as **estimable**, you mean that they deserve admiration. [FORMAL] ❑ *...the estimable Miss Cartwright.* ADJ: usu ADJ n = *admirable*

**es|ti|mate (estimates, estimating, estimated)** ◆◆◇

✔ The verb is pronounced /estɪmeɪt/. The noun is pronounced /estɪmət/.

[1] If you **estimate** a quantity or value, you make an approximate judgment or calculation of it. ❑ *Try to estimate how many steps it will take to get to a close object... I estimate that the total cost for treatment will be $12,500... He estimated the speed of the winds from the degree of damage... Some analysts estimate its current popularity at around ten per cent.* ♦ **es|ti|mat|ed** *There are an estimated 90,000 gangsters in the country.* [2] An **estimate** is an approximate calculation of a quantity or value. ❑ *...the official estimate of the election result... This figure is five times the original estimate.* [3] An **estimate** is a judgment about a person or situation which you make based on the available evidence. ❑ *I hadn't been far wrong in my estimate of his grandson's capabilities.* [4] An **estimate** from someone who you employ to do a job for you, such as a builder or a plumber, is a written statement of how much the job is likely to cost. VERB V wh V that V n V n *at* amount ADJ: *a* ADJ amount N-COUNT: usu with supp, oft N *of/for* n N-COUNT: oft with poss, N *of* n N-COUNT

**es|ti|ma|tion** /estɪmeɪʃᵊn/ **(estimations)** [1] Your **estimation** of a person or situation is the opinion or impression that you have formed about them. [FORMAL] ❑ *He has gone down considerably in my estimation.* [2] An **estimation** is an approximate calculation of a quantity or value. ❑ *...estimations of pre-tax profits of £12.25 million.* N-SING: usu with poss N-COUNT: oft N *of* n = *estimate*

**es|tranged** /ɪstreɪndʒd/ [1] An **estranged** wife or husband is no longer living with their husband or wife. [FORMAL] ❑ *...his estranged wife.* [2] If you are **estranged from** your family or friends, you have quarrelled with them and are not communicating with them. [FORMAL] ❑ *Joanna, 30, spent most of her twenties virtually estranged from her father.* [3] If you describe someone as **estranged from** something such as society or their profession, you mean that they no longer seem involved in it. [FORMAL] ❑ *Arran became increasingly estranged from the mainstream of Hollywood.* ADJ: usu ADJ n ADJ: oft ADJ *from* n ADJ: v-link ADJ, usu ADJ *from* n

**es|trange|ment** /ɪstreɪndʒmənt/ **(estrangements)** **Estrangement** is the state of being estranged from someone or the length of time for which you are estranged. [FORMAL] ❑ *The trip will bring to an end years of estrangement between the two countries.* N-VAR

**es|tro|gen** /iːstrədʒᵊn, AM est-/ → see **oestrogen**.

**es|tu|ary** /estʃuri, AM estʃueri/ **(estuaries)** An **estuary** is the wide part of a river where it joins the sea. ❑ *...naval manoeuvres in the Clyde estuary.* N-COUNT; N-IN-NAMES

**e|tailer** /iːteɪləʳ/ **(etailers)** also **e-tailer.** An **etailer** is a person or company that sells products on the Internet. [COMPUTING] ❑ *This company is the biggest wine e-tailer in the UK.* N-COUNT

**e|tailing** /iːteɪlɪŋ/ also **e-tailing. Etailing** is the business of selling products on the Internet. [COMPUTING] ❑ *Electronic retailing has predictably become known as etailing.* N-UNCOUNT

**et al.** /et æl/ **et al.** is used after a name or a list of names to indicate that other people are also involved. It is used especially when referring to books or articles which were written by more than two people. ❑ *...Blough et al.*

**etc** /et setrə/ also **etc. etc** is used at the end of a list to indicate that you have mentioned only some of the items involved and have not given a full list. **etc** is a written abbreviation for 'et cetera'. ❑ *She knew all about my schoolwork, my hospital work etc. ...a packed programme of events – shows, dances, coach tours, sports, etc.* ◆◇◇

**et|cet|era** /etsetrə/ also **et cetera.** → see etc.

**etch** /etʃ/ **(etches, etching, etched)** If a line or pattern **is etched into** a surface, it is cut into the surface by means of acid or a sharp tool. You can also say that a surface **is etched with** a line or pattern. ❑ *Crosses were etched into the walls... The acid etched holes in the crystal surface... Windows are etched with the vehicle identification number... The stained-glass panels are etched and then handpainted using traditional methods.* VERB *be* V-ed *into/in/on* n V n *into/in/on* n *be* V-ed *with* n *be* V-ed

**etch|ing** /etʃɪŋ/ **(etchings)** An **etching** is a picture printed from a metal plate that has had a design cut into it with acid. N-COUNT

**eter|nal** /ɪtɜːʳnᵊl/ [1] Something that is **eternal** lasts for ever. ❑ *Whoever believes in Him shall have eternal life. ...the quest for eternal youth.* ♦ **eter|nal|ly** *She is eternally grateful to her family for their support.* [2] If you describe something as **eternal**, you mean that it seems to last for ever, often because you think it is boring or annoying. ❑ *In the background was that eternal hum.* ADJ ADV: ADV adj, ADV with v ADJ = *interminable, never-ending*

**eter|nal tri|an|gle (eternal triangles)** You use **the eternal triangle** to refer to a relationship involving love and jealousy between two men and a woman or two women and a man. N-COUNT: usu sing

**eter|nity** /ɪtɜːʳnɪti/ [1] **Eternity** is time without an end or a state of existence outside time, especially the state which some people believe they will pass into after they have died. ❑ *I have always found the thought of eternity terrifying.* [2] If you say that a situation lasted for **an eternity**, you mean that it seemed to last an extremely long time, usually because it was boring or unpleasant. ❑ *The war continued for an eternity.* N-UNCOUNT N-SING: *a* N = *age*

**etha|nol** /eθənɒl/ **Ethanol** is another name for **alcohol**. [TECHNICAL] N-UNCOUNT = *ethyl alcohol*

**ether** /iːθəʳ/ **Ether** is a colourless liquid that burns easily. It is used in industry and in medicine as an anaesthetic. ❑ *...a sweetish smell of ether and iodine.* N-UNCOUNT

**ethe|real** /ɪθɪəriəl/ [1] Someone or something that is **ethereal** has a delicate beauty. [FORMAL] ❑ *She's the prettiest, most ethereal romantic heroine in the movies. ...gorgeous, hauntingly ethereal melodies.* [2] **Ethereal** means unrelated to practical things and the real world. [FORMAL] ❑ *...the ethereal nature of romantic fiction.* ADJ ADJ

**eth|ic** /eθɪk/ **(ethics)** [1] **Ethics** are moral beliefs and rules about right and wrong. ❑ *Refugee workers said such action was a violation of medical ethics.* N-PLURAL [2] Someone's **ethics** are the moral principles about right and wrong behaviour which they believe in. ❑ *He told the police that he had thought honestly about the ethics of what he was doing.* N-PLURAL: with supp [3] **Ethics** is the study of questions about what is morally right and wrong. ❑ *...the teaching of ethics and moral philosophy.* N-UNCOUNT [4] An **ethic** of a particular kind is an idea or moral belief that influences the behaviour, attitudes, and philosophy of a group of people. ❑ *...the ethic of public service. ...an indomitable work ethic and determination to succeed.* N-SING: with supp

**ethi|cal** /eθɪkᵊl/ [1] **Ethical** means relating to beliefs about right and wrong. ❑ *...the medical, nursing and ethical issues surrounding terminally-ill people.* ADJ: usu ADJ n ♦ **ethi|cal|ly** /eθɪkli/ *Attorneys are ethically and legally bound to absolute confidentiality.* ADV: ADV adj/-ed, ADV after v [2] If you describe something as **ethical**, you mean that it is morally right or morally acceptable. ❑ *...ethical investment schemes.* ADJ ♦ **ethi|cal|ly** *Mayors want local companies to behave ethically.* ADV: ADV after v

**Ethio|pian** /iːθioʊpiən/ **(Ethiopians)** **Ethiopian** means belonging or relating to Ethiopia, or to its people, language, or culture. ADJ ♦ An **Ethiopian** is an Ethiopian citizen, or a person of Ethiopian origin. N-COUNT

**eth|nic** /eθnɪk/ ◆◇◇ [1] **Ethnic** means connected with or relating to different racial or cultural groups of people. ❑ *...a survey of Britain's ethnic minorities. ...ethnic tensions.* ADJ: usu ADJ n ♦ **eth|ni|cal|ly** /eθnɪkli/ *...a predominantly young, ethnically mixed audience.* ADV: usu ADV -ed/adj [2] You can use **ethnic** to describe people who belong to a particular racial or cultural group but who, usually, do not live in the country where most members of that group live. ❑ *There are still several million ethnic Germans in Russia.* ADJ: ADJ n ♦ **eth|ni|cal|ly** *...a large ethnically Albanian population.* ADV: ADV adj [3] **Ethnic** clothing, music, or food is characteristic of the traditions of a particular ethnic group, and different from what is usually found in modern Western culture. ❑ *...a magnificent range of ethnic fabrics.* ADJ

**eth|nic cleans|ing** **Ethnic cleansing** is the process of using violent methods to force certain groups of people out of a particular area or country. ❑ *In late May, government forces began the 'ethnic cleansing' of the area around the town.* N-UNCOUNT [disapproval]

**eth|nic|ity** /eθnɪsɪti/ **(ethnicities)** **Ethnicity** is the state or fact or belonging to a particular ethnic group. ❑ *He said his ethnicity had not been important to him.* N-VAR

**eth|no|cen|tric** /eθnoʊsentrɪk/ If you describe something as **ethnocentric**, you disagree with it because it is based on the belief that one particular race or nationality of people is superior to all others. ❑ *Her work is open to the criticism that it is ethnocentric.* ADJ [disapproval]

**eth|no|graph|ic** /eθnəgræfɪk/ **Ethnographic** refers to things that are connected with or relate to ethnography. ADJ

**eth|nog|ra|phy** /eθnɒgrəfi/ **Ethnography** is the branch of anthropology in which different cultures are studied and described. N-UNCOUNT

**ethos** /iːθɒs/ An **ethos** is the set of ideas and attitudes that is associated with a particular group of people or a particular type of activity. [FORMAL] ❑ *The whole ethos of the hotel is effortless service. ...the traditional public service ethos.* N-SING: usu with supp

**ethyl al|co|hol** /iːθaɪl ælkəhɒl/ **Ethyl alcohol** is the same as **ethanol**. [TECHNICAL] N-UNCOUNT

**eti|ol|ogy** /iːtiɒlədʒi/ **(etiologies)** also **aetiology**. **The etiology of** a disease or a problem is the study of its causes. ❑ *...the etiology of psychiatric disorder.* N-VAR: oft *the* N *of* n

**eti|quette** /etɪket/ **Etiquette** is a set of customs and rules for polite behaviour, especially among a particular class of people or in a particular profession. ❑ *This was such a great breach of etiquette, he hardly knew what to do.* N-UNCOUNT = protocol

**ety|mo|logi|cal** /etɪməlɒdʒɪkᵊl/ **Etymological** means concerned with or relating to etymology. [FORMAL] ❑ *'Gratification' and 'gratitude' have the same etymological root.* ADJ: usu ADJ n

**ety|mol|ogy** /etɪmɒlədʒi/ **(etymologies)** [1] **Etymology** is the study of the origins and historical development of words. N-UNCOUNT [2] The **etymology** of a particular word is its history. N-COUNT

**EU** /iː juː/ **The EU** is an organization of European countries which have joint policies on matters such as trade, agriculture, and finance. **EU** is an abbreviation for 'European Union'. N-PROPER

**euca|lyp|tus** /juːkəlɪptəs/ **(eucalyptuses** or **eucalyptus)** A **eucalyptus** is an evergreen tree, originally from Australia, that is grown to provide wood, gum, and an oil that is used in medicines. N-VAR: oft N n

**Eucha|rist** /juːkərɪst/ **The Eucharist** is the Christian religious ceremony in which Christ's last meal with his disciples is celebrated by eating bread and drinking wine. N-SING: usu *the* N

**eugen|ics** /juːdʒenɪks/ **Eugenics** is the study of methods to improve the human race by carefully selecting parents who will produce the strongest children. [TECHNICAL] N-UNCOUNT [disapproval]

**eulo|gize** /juːlədʒaɪz/ **(eulogizes, eulogizing, eulogized)**

☑ in AM, also use **eulogise**

[1] If you **eulogize** someone or something, you praise them very highly. [FORMAL] ❑ *Barry Davies eulogized Keegan's part in the operation... Taylor eulogised about Steven's versatility.* VERB = rhapsodize V n V prep [2] If you **eulogize** someone who has died, you make a speech praising them, usually at their funeral. [AM] ❑ *Leaders from around the world eulogized the Egyptian president.* VERB V n

**eulogy** /juːlədʒi/ **(eulogies)** [1] A **eulogy** is a speech or piece of writing that praises someone or something very much. [FORMAL] N-COUNT = tribute [2] A **eulogy** is a speech, usually at a funeral, in which a person who has just died is praised. [AM] N-COUNT

**eunuch** /juːnək/ **(eunuchs)** A **eunuch** is a man who has had his testicles removed. N-COUNT

**euphemism** /juːfəmɪzəm/ **(euphemisms)** A **euphemism** is a polite word or expression that is used to refer to things which people may find upsetting or embarrassing to talk about, for example sex, the human body, or death. ❑ *The term 'early retirement' is nearly always a euphemism for redundancy nowadays.* N-COUNT: oft N *for* n

**euphemis|tic** /juːfəmɪstɪk/ **Euphemistic** language uses polite, pleasant, or neutral words and expressions to refer to things which people may find unpleasant, upsetting, or embarrassing to talk about, for example sex, the human body, or death. ❑ *...a euphemistic way of saying that someone has been lying.* ADJ: usu ADJ n ♦ **euphemis|ti|cal|ly** /juːfəmɪstɪkli/ *...political prisons, called euphemistically 're-education camps'.* ADV: ADV with v

**eupho|ria** /juːfɔːriə/ **Euphoria** is a feeling of intense happiness and excitement. ❑ *There was euphoria after the elections.* N-UNCOUNT: oft N *of/over* n = elation

**euphor|ic** /juːfɒrɪk, AM -fɔːr-/ If you are **euphoric**, you feel intense happiness and excitement. ❑ *It had received euphoric support from the public.* ADJ = elated

**Eura|sian** /jʊəreɪʒᵊn/ **(Eurasians)** [1] **Eurasian** means concerned with or relating to both Europe and Asia. ❑ *...the whole of the Eurasian continent.* ADJ [2] A **Eurasian** is a person who has one European and one Asian parent or whose family comes from both Europe and Asia. N-COUNT ♦ **Eurasian** is also an adjective. ❑ *She married into a leading Eurasian family in Hong Kong.* ADJ

**eureka** /jʊriːkə/ Someone might say '**eureka**' when they suddenly find or realize something, or when they solve a problem. [HUMOROUS, OLD-FASHIONED] ❑ *'Eureka! I've got it!'* EXCLAM

**euro** /jʊ̲ərou/ **(euros)** The **euro** is a unit of currency that is used by the member countries of the European Union which have accepted European monetary union. ❑ *Millions of words have been written about the introduction of the euro... Governments and businesses will start keeping accounts in euros.* N-COUNT: oft *the* N

**Euro-** /jʊ̲ərou-/ **Euro** is used to form words that describe or refer to something which is connected with Europe or with the European Union. ❑ *...German Euro-MPs.* PREFIX

**Euro|bond** /jʊ̲əroubɒnd/ **(Eurobonds)** also **eurobond. Eurobonds** are bonds which are issued in a particular European currency and sold to people from a country with a different currency. N-COUNT

**Euro|cen|tric** /jʊ̲ərousentrɪk/ If you describe something as **Eurocentric**, you disapprove of it because it focuses on Europe and the needs of European people, often with the result that people in other parts of the world suffer in some way. ❑ *...the insultingly Eurocentric bias in the education system.* ADJ [disapproval]

**Euro|crat** /jʊ̲əroukræt/ **(Eurocrats) Eurocrats** are the civil servants and other people who work in the administration of the European Union. [JOURNALISM] N-COUNT

**euro|land** /jʊ̲əroulænd/ also **Euroland. Euroland** is another name for the **eurozone**. ❑ *In much of euroland, inflation is already double the ceiling set by the European Central Bank.* N-UNCOUNT

**Euro|pean** /jʊ̲ərəpi̲ːən/ **(Europeans)** [1] **European** means belonging or relating to, or coming from Europe. ❑ *...in some other European countries.* [2] A **European** is a person who comes from Europe. ADJ: usu ADJ n; N-COUNT

**Euro|pean Un|ion** **The European Union** is an organization of European countries which have joint policies on matters such as trade, agriculture, and finance. N-PROPER = EU

**euro|zone** /jʊ̲ərouzoun/ also **Eurozone. The eurozone** is all those countries that have joined the European single currency, considered as a group. ❑ *Homeowners in the eurozone enjoy cheaper mortgages than we do here in Britain.* N-SING: the N

**eutha|na|sia** /ju̲ːθəne̲ɪziə, AM -ʒə/ **Euthanasia** is the practice of killing someone who is very ill and will never get better in order to end their suffering, usually done at their request or with their consent. N-UNCOUNT

**evacu|ate** /ɪvæ̲kjueɪt/ **(evacuates, evacuating, evacuated)** [1] To **evacuate** someone means to send them to a place of safety, away from a dangerous building, town, or area. ❑ *They were planning to evacuate the seventy American officials still in the country... Since 1951, 18,000 people have been evacuated from the area.* ♦ **evacu|ation** /ɪvæ̲kjue̲ɪʃən/ **(evacuations)** *...the evacuation of the sick and wounded... An evacuation of the city's four-million inhabitants is planned for later this week.* [2] If people **evacuate** a place, they move out of it for a period of time, especially because it is dangerous. ❑ *The fire is threatening about sixty homes, and residents have evacuated the area... Officials ordered the residents to evacuate.* ♦ **evacu|ation (evacuations)** *...the mass evacuation of the Bosnian town of Srebrenica... Burning sulfur from the wreck has forced evacuations from the area.* VERB; V n; be V-ed from; N-VAR; VERB; V n; V; N-VAR

**evac|uee** /ɪvæ̲kjui̲ː/ **(evacuees)** An **evacuee** is someone who has been sent away from a dangerous place to somewhere safe, especially during a war. N-COUNT

**evade** /ɪve̲ɪd/ **(evades, evading, evaded)** [1] If you **evade** something, you find a way of not doing something that you really ought to do. ❑ *By his own admission, he evaded taxes as a Florida real-estate speculator... Delegates accused them of trying to evade responsibility for the failures of the past five years.* [2] If you **evade** a question or a topic, you avoid talking about it or dealing with it. ❑ *Too many companies, she says, are evading the issue.* [3] If you **evade** someone or something, you move so that you can avoid meeting them or avoid being touched or hit. ❑ *She turned and gazed at the river, evading his eyes... He managed to evade capture because of the breakdown of a police computer.* VERB; V n; V n; VERB; V n; VERB; V n; V n

**evalu|ate** /ɪvæ̲ljueɪt/ **(evaluates, evaluating, evaluated)** If you **evaluate** something or someone, you consider them in order to make a judgment about them, for example about how good or bad they are. ❑ *The market situation is difficult to evaluate.* ♦ **evalu|ation** /ɪvæ̲ljue̲ɪʃən/ **(evaluations)** *...the opinions and evaluations of college supervisors... Evaluation is standard practice for all training arranged through the school.* VERB = assess; V n; N-VAR

**evalu|ative** /ɪvæ̲ljuətɪv/ Something that is **evaluative** is based on an assessment of the values, qualities, and significance of a particular person or thing. [FORMAL] ❑ *...ten years of evaluative research.* ADJ

**eva|nes|cent** /e̲vəne̲sənt/ Something that is **evanescent** gradually disappears from sight or memory. [FORMAL or LITERARY] ❑ *...the evanescent scents of summer herbs.* ADJ = ephemeral

**evan|geli|cal** /i̲ːvændʒe̲lɪkəl/ [1] **Evangelical** Christians emphasize the importance of the Bible and the need for personal belief in Christ. ❑ *...an evangelical Christian.* [2] If you describe someone's behaviour as **evangelical**, you mean that it is very enthusiastic. ❑ *With almost evangelical fervour, Marks warns against deliberately seeking a tan.* ADJ; ADJ: usu ADJ n

**evan|gelism** /ɪvæ̲ndʒəlɪzəm/ **Evangelism** is the teaching of Christianity, especially to people who are not Christians. N-UNCOUNT

**evan|gelist** /ɪvæ̲ndʒəlɪst/ **(evangelists)** An **evangelist** is a person who travels from place to place in order to try to convert people to Christianity. ♦ **evan|gelis|tic** ❑ *...an evangelistic meeting at All Saints Church Hall.* N-COUNT; ADJ

**evan|gelize** /ɪvæ̲ndʒəlaɪz/ **(evangelizes, evangelizing, evangelized)**

✔ in BRIT, also use **evangelise**

If someone **evangelizes** a group or area, they try to convert people to their religion, especially Christianity. ❑ *In AD 586 St Kentigern evangelized Tweeddale.* VERB = proselytize; V n; Also V

**evapo|rate** /ɪvæ̲pəreɪt/ **(evaporates, evaporating, evaporated)** [1] When a liquid **evaporates**, or **is evaporated**, it changes from a liquid state to a gas, because its temperature has increased. ❑ *Moisture is drawn to the surface of the fabric so that it evaporates... The water is evaporated by the sun.* ♦ **evapo|ra|tion** /ɪvæ̲pəre̲ɪʃən/ *The soothing, cooling effect is caused by the evaporation of the sweat on the skin.* [2] If a feeling, plan, or activity **evaporates**, it gradually becomes weaker and eventually disappears completely. ❑ *My anger evaporated and I wanted to cry.* VERB; V; be V-ed; Also V n; N-UNCOUNT; VERB; V

**evapo|rat|ed milk** **Evaporated milk** is thick sweet milk that is sold in cans. N-UNCOUNT

**eva|sion** /ɪve̲ɪʒən/ **(evasions)** [1] **Evasion** means deliberately avoiding something that you are supposed to do or deal with. ❑ *Many Koreans were angered at what they saw as an evasion of responsibility... He was arrested for tax evasion.* [2] If you accuse someone of **evasion** when they have been asked a question, you mean that they are deliberately avoiding giving a clear direct answer. ❑ *We want straight answers. No evasions.* N-VAR: usu with supp, oft N *of* n, n N; N-VAR

**eva|sive** /ɪve̲ɪsɪv/ [1] If you describe someone as **evasive**, you mean that they deliberately avoid giving clear direct answers to questions. ❑ *He was evasive about the circumstances of his first meeting with Stanley Dean.* ♦ **eva|sive|ly** *'I can't possibly comment on that,' Paul said evasively.* ♦ **eva|sive|ness** *She looked at him closely to see if his evasiveness was intentional.* [2] If you **take evasive action**, you deliberately move away from someone or something in order to avoid meeting ADJ; ADV: ADV with v; N-UNCOUNT: oft poss N; PHRASE: V inflects them or being hit by them. ❑ *At least four high-flying warplanes had to take evasive action.*

**eve** /iːv/ **(eves) The eve of** a particular event or occasion is the day before it, or the period of time just before it. [JOURNALISM] ❑ *...on the eve of his 27th birthday.* → See also **Christmas Eve**, **New Year's Eve**. N-COUNT: usu sing, usu *the* N *of* n

**even**
① DISCOURSE USES
② ADJECTIVE USES
③ PHRASAL VERB USES

①**even** /iːvᵊn/ [1] You use **even** to suggest that what comes just after or just before it in the sentence is rather surprising. ❑ *He kept calling me for years, even after he got married... Even dark-skinned women should use sunscreens... I cannot come to a decision about it now or even give any indication of my own views... He didn't even hear what I said.* ◆◆◆ ADV: ADV with cl/group, ADV before v

[2] You use **even** with comparative adjectives and adverbs to emphasize a quality that someone or something has. ❑ *It was on television that he made an even stronger impact as an interviewer... Stan was speaking even more slowly than usual.* ADV: ADV compar [emphasis]

PHRASES [3] You use **even if** or **even though** to indicate that a particular fact does not make the rest of your statement untrue. ❑ *Cynthia is not ashamed of what she does, even if she ends up doing something wrong... Even though I'm supposed to be working by myself, there are other people who I can interact with.* PHRASE [4] If one thing happens **even as** something else happens, they both happen at exactly the same time. [LITERARY] ❑ *Even as she said this, she knew it was not quite true.* PHRASE [5] You use **even so** to introduce a surprising fact which relates to what you have just said. [SPOKEN] ❑ *The bus was only half full. Even so, a young man asked Nina if the seat next to her was taken.* PHRASE: PHR with cl = nevertheless [6] You use **even then** to say that something is the case in spite of what has just been stated or whatever the circumstances may be. ❑ *Peace could come only gradually, in carefully measured steps. Even then, it sounds almost impossible to achieve.* PHRASE: PHR with cl

②**even** /iːvᵊn/
⇒ Please look at category 10 to see if the expression you are looking for is shown under another headword. [1] An **even** measurement or rate stays at about the same level. ❑ *How important is it to have an even temperature when you're working?... The brick-built property keeps the temperature at an even level throughout the year.* ADJ: usu ADJ n = constant ♦ **even|ly** *He looked at Ellen, breathing evenly in her sleep.* ADV: usu ADV after v [2] An **even** surface is smooth and flat. ❑ *The tables are fitted with a glass top to provide an even surface.* ADJ = level [3] If there is an **even** distribution or division of something, each person, group, or area involved has an equal amount. ❑ *Divide the dough into 12 even pieces and shape each piece into a ball.* ADJ: usu ADJ n = equal ♦ **even|ly** *The meat is divided evenly and boiled in a stew... The blood vessels in the skin are not evenly distributed around the face and neck.* ADV: ADV after v, ADV -ed = equally [4] An **even** contest or competition is equally balanced between the two sides who are taking part. ❑ *...an even match between eight nations.* ADJ: usu ADJ n ♦ **even|ly** *They must choose between two evenly matched candidates for governor.* ADV: ADV -ed

[5] If your voice is **even**, you are speaking in a very controlled way which makes it difficult for people to tell what your feelings are. [LITERARY] ADJ = steady, calm

[6] An **even** number can be divided exactly by the number two. ADJ: usu ADJ n [7] If there is an **even** chance that something will happen, it is no more likely that it will happen than it will not happen. ❑ *They have a more than even chance of winning the next election.* → See also **evens**. ADJ: ADJ n = fifty-fifty

PHRASES [8] When a company or a person running a business **breaks even**, they make neither a profit nor a loss. [BUSINESS] ❑ *The airline hopes to break even next year and return to profit the following year.* PHRASE: V inflects [9] If you say that you are going to **get even with** someone, you mean that you are going to cause them the same amount of harm or annoyance as they have caused you. [INFORMAL] ❑ *I'm going to get even with you for this... Don't get angry, get even.* PHRASE: V inflects, oft PHR *with* n [10] to **be on an even keel** → see **keel**.

③**even** /iːvᵊn/ **(evens, evening, evened)**

♦ **even out** If something **evens out**, or if you **even** it **out**, the differences between the different parts of it are reduced. ❑ *Relative rates of house price inflation have evened out across the country... Foundation make-up evens out your skin tone and texture.* PHRASAL VERB V P, V P n (not pron)

♦ **even up** To **even up** a contest or game means to make it more equally balanced than it was. ❑ *The nation's electronics industry made important strides this year to even up its balance of trade... I would like to see the championship evened up a little bit more.* PHRASAL VERB V P n (not pron), V-ed P, Also V n P

**even-handed**
in AM, also use **evenhanded**
If someone is **even-handed**, they are completely fair, especially when they are judging other people or dealing with two groups of people. ❑ *...an even-handed approach to the war on drugs.* ADJ = balanced

**eve|ning** /iːvnɪŋ/ **(evenings)** The **evening** is the part of each day between the end of the afternoon and the time when you go to bed. ❑ *All he did that evening was sit around the flat... Supper is from 5.00 to 6.00 in the evening... Towards evening the carnival entered its final stage.* ◆◆◇ N-VAR

**eve|ning class (evening classes)** An **evening class** is a course for adults that is taught in the evening rather than during the day. ❑ *Jackie has been learning flamenco dancing at an evening class for three years.* N-COUNT

**eve|ning dress (evening dresses)**
[1] **Evening dress** consists of the formal clothes that people wear to formal occasions in the evening. N-UNCOUNT [2] An **evening dress** is a special dress, usually a long one, that a woman wears to a formal occasion in the evening. N-COUNT

**eve|ning prim|rose (evening primroses)** **Evening primrose** is a tall plant with yellow flowers that open in the evening. Its seeds are used to make medicine. N-VAR

**evens** /iːvᵊnz/ [1] In a race or contest, if you bet on a horse or competitor that is quoted at **evens**, you will win a sum of money equal to your bet if that horse or competitor wins. [BRIT] ❑ *He won his first race by six lengths at evens... The Martell Cup Chase was won by the evens favourite Toby Tobias.* N-UNCOUNT [2] If there is an **evens** chance that something will happen, it is equally likely that it will happen or will not happen. [BRIT] ❑ *You've then got an evens chance of doubling your money at a stroke.* ADJ: ADJ n = fifty-fifty

**even|song** /iːvᵊnsɒŋ, AM -sɔːŋ/ **Evensong** is the evening service in the Anglican Church. N-UNCOUNT

**event** /ɪvent/ **(events)** [1] An **event** is something that happens, especially when it is unusual or important. You can use **events** to describe all the things that are happening in a particular situation. ❑ *...the events of Black Wednesday... A new book by Grass is always an event.* ◆◆◆ N-COUNT [2] An **event** is a planned and organized occasion, for example a social gathering or a sports match. ❑ *...major sporting events. ...our programme of lectures and social events.* N-COUNT: usu with supp [3] An **event** is one of the races or competitions that are part of an organized occasion such as a sports meeting. ❑ *A solo piper opens Aberdeen Highland Games at 10am and the main events start at 1pm.* N-COUNT

PHRASES [4] You use **in the event of**, **in the event that**, and **in that event** when you are talking about a possible future situation, especially when you are planning what to do if it occurs. ❑ *The bank has agreed to give an immediate refund in the unlikely event of an error being made.* PHRASE [5] You say **in any event** after you have been discussing a situation, in order to indicate that what you are saying is true or possible, in spite of anything that has happened or may happen. ❑ *In any event, the* PHRASE: PHR with cl = anyway

*bowling alley restaurant proved quite acceptable.*
6 You say **in the event** after you have been discussing what could have happened in a particular situation, in order to indicate that you are now describing what actually did happen. [BRIT] ❑ *'Don't underestimate us', Norman Willis warned last year. There was, in the event, little danger of that.* PHRASE: PHR with cl

**even-tempered** If someone is **even-tempered**, they are usually calm and do not easily get angry. ADJ = *equable*

**event|ful** /ɪventfʊl/ If you describe an event or a period of time as **eventful**, you mean that a lot of interesting, exciting, or important things have happened during it. ❑ *Her eventful life included holding senior positions in the Colonial Service.* ADJ

**even|tual** /ɪventʃuəl/ You use **eventual** to indicate that something happens or is the case at the end of a process or period of time. ❑ *The eventual aim is reunification.* ADJ: ADJ n = *ultimate*

**even|tu|al|ity** /ɪventʃuælɪti/ **(eventualities)** An **eventuality** is a possible future event or result, especially one that is unpleasant or surprising. [FORMAL] ❑ *Every eventuality is covered, from running out of petrol to needing water.* N-COUNT: with supp = *contingency*

**even|tu|al|ly** /ɪventʃuəli/ ◆◆◇ 1 **Eventually** means in the end, especially after a lot of delays, problems, or arguments. ❑ *Eventually, the army caught up with him in Latvia... The flight eventually got away six hours late.* ADV: ADV with cl, ADV before v = *finally* 2 **Eventually** means at the end of a situation or process or as the final result of it. ❑ *Eventually your child will leave home to lead her own life as a fully independent adult... She sees the bar as a starting point and eventually plans to run her own chain of country inns.* ADV: ADV with cl, ADV before v = *ultimately*

**ever** /evəʳ/ ◆◆◆

> ☑ **Ever** is an adverb which you use to add emphasis in negative sentences, commands, questions, and conditional structures.

1 **Ever** means at any time. It is used in questions and negative statements. ❑ *I'm not sure I'll ever trust people again... Neither of us had ever skied... Have you ever experienced failure?... I don't know if you ever read any of his books.* ADV: ADV before v, ADV adv ≠ *never* 2 You use **ever** in expressions such as '**did you ever**' and '**have you ever**' to express surprise or shock at something you have just seen, heard, or experienced, especially when you expect people to agree with you. ❑ *Have you ever seen anything like it?... Did you ever hear anyone sound so peculiar?* ADV: in questions, ADV before v [emphasis] 3 You use **ever** after comparatives and superlatives to emphasize the degree to which something is true or when you are comparing a present situation with the past or the future. ❑ *She's got a great voice and is singing better than ever... Japan is wealthier and more powerful than ever before... He feels better than he has ever felt before... This is the most awful evening I can ever remember.* ADV: ADV after compar *than*, ADV after adj-superl [emphasis] 4 You use **ever** to say that something happens more all the time. ❑ *They grew ever further apart.* ADV: ADV adj/adv 5 You can use **ever** for emphasis after 'never'. [INFORMAL] ❑ *I can never, ever, forgive myself.* ADV: ADV before v [emphasis] 6 You use **ever** in questions beginning with words such as 'why', 'when', and 'who' when you want to emphasize your surprise or shock. ❑ *Why ever didn't you tell me?... Who ever heard of a thing like that?* ADV: quest ADV [emphasis] 7 If something has been the case **ever since** a particular time, it has been the case all the time from then until now. ❑ *He's been there ever since you left!... Ever since we moved last year, I worry a lot about whether I can handle this new job.* PHRASE ♦ **Ever** is also an adverb. ❑ *I simply gave in to him, and I've regretted it ever since.* ADV: ADV after v, ADV with cl 8 You use **ever** in the expressions **ever such** and **ever so** to emphasize that someone or something has a particular quality, especially when you are expressing enthusiasm or gratitude. [BRIT, INFORMAL] ❑ *When I met Derek he was ever such a good dancer... I like him ever so much... I'm ever so grateful.* ADV: ADV *such/so* [emphasis] 9 → See also **forever**.

PHRASES 10 You use the expression **all** someone **ever does** when you want to emphasize that they do the same thing all the time, and this annoys you. ❑ *All she ever does is whinge and complain.* PHRASE: V inflects [emphasis] 11 You say **as ever** in order to indicate that something or someone's behaviour is not unusual because it is like that all the time or very often. ❑ *As ever, the meals are primarily fish-based.* PHRASE: PHR with cl 12 **hardly ever** → see **hardly**.

**ever-** /evəʳ-/ You use **ever** in adjectives such as **ever-increasing** and **ever-present**, to show that something exists or continues all the time. ❑ *...the ever-increasing traffic on our roads. ...an ever-changing world of medical information.* COMB in ADJ

**ever|green** /evəʳgriːn/ **(evergreens)** An **evergreen** is a tree or bush which has green leaves all the year round. ❑ *Holly, like ivy and mistletoe, is an evergreen.* N-COUNT ♦ **Evergreen** is also an adjective. ❑ *Plant evergreen shrubs around the end of the month.* ADJ: usu ADJ n

**ever|lasting** /evəʳlɑːstɪŋ, -læst-/ Something that is **everlasting** never comes to an end. ❑ *...a message of peace and everlasting life.* ADJ = *eternal*

**ever more** also **evermore. Ever more** means for all the time in the future. ❑ *They will bitterly regret what they have done for ever more... The editor's decision is final and shall evermore remain so.* ADV: ADV with v, oft *for* ADV

**every** /evri/ ◆◆◆ 1 You use **every** to indicate that you are referring to all the members of a group or all the parts of something and not only some of them. ❑ *Record every expenditure you make. ...recipes for every occasion.* DET: DET sing-n ♦ **Every** is also an adjective. ❑ *His every utterance will be scrutinized.* ADJ: poss ADJ n 2 You use **every** in order to say how often something happens or to indicate that something happens at regular intervals. ❑ *We were made to attend meetings every day... A burglary occurs every three minutes in London... They meet here every Friday morning.* DET 3 You use **every** in front of a number when you are saying what proportion of people or things something happens to or applies to. ❑ *Two out of every three Britons already own a video recorder... About one in every 20 people have clinical depression.* DET: *out of/in/for* DET amount 4 You can use **every** before some nouns, for example 'sign', 'effort', 'reason', and 'intention' in order to emphasize what you are saying. ❑ *The Congressional Budget Office says the federal deficit shows every sign of getting larger... I think that there is every chance that you will succeed... Every care has been taken in compiling this list.* DET: DET sing-n [emphasis] ≠ *no* 5 If you say that someone's **every** whim, wish, or desire will be satisfied, you are emphasizing that everything they want will happen or be provided. ❑ *Dozens of servants had catered to his every whim.* ADJ: poss ADJ n [emphasis]

PHRASES 6 You use **every** in the expressions **every now and then, every now and again, every once in a while**, and **every so often** in order to indicate that something happens occasionally. ❑ *Stir the batter every now and then to keep it from separating... Every so often the horse's heart and lungs are checked.* PHRASE: PHR after v, PHR with cl 7 If something happens **every other day** or **every second day**, for example, it happens one day, then does not happen the next day, then happens the day after that, and so on. You can also say that something happens **every third week, every fourth year**, and so on. ❑ *I went home every other week.* PHRASE: PHR after v, PHR with cl 8 **every bit as** good **as** → see **bit**. **every which way** → see **way**.

**every|body** /evribɒdi/ ◆◆◇ **Everybody** means the same as **everyone**.

**every|day** /evrideɪ/ You use **everyday** to describe something which happens or is used every day, or forms a regular and basic part of your life, so it is not especially interesting or unusual. ❑ *In the course of my everyday life, I had very little contact with teenagers. ...the everyday problems of living in the city.* ADJ: usu ADJ n

**every|man** /evrimæn/ **Everyman** is used to refer to people in general. If you say, for example, that a character in a film or book is an **everyman**, you mean that the character has experiences and emotions that are like those of any or- N-SING dinary person. ❑ *Douglas plays a frustrated American everyman who suddenly loses control under the pressure of daily life.*

**every|one** /evriwʌn/ or **everybody** ◆◆◇ [1] You use **everyone** or **everybody** to refer to all the people in a particular group. ❑ *Everyone in the street was shocked when they heard the news... When everyone else goes home around 5 p.m. Lynn is still hard at work... Not everyone thinks that the government is being particularly generous.* [2] You use **everyone** or **everybody** to refer to all people. ❑ *Everyone feels like a failure at times... You can't keep everybody happy.*

PRON: oft PRON *else* ≠ no one, nobody | PRON ≠ no one, nobody

**every|thing** /evriθɪŋ/ ◆◆◆ [1] You use **everything** to refer to all the objects, actions, activities, or facts in a particular situation. ❑ *He'd gone to Seattle long after everything else in his life had changed... Early in the morning, hikers pack everything that they will need for the day's hike.* [2] You use **everything** to refer to all possible or likely actions, activities, or situations. ❑ *'This should have been decided long before now.' — 'We can't think of everything.'... Noel and I do everything together... Are you doing everything possible to reduce your budget?* [3] You use **everything** to refer to a whole situation or to life in general. ❑ *She says everything is going smoothly... Is everything all right?... Everything's going to be just fine.* [4] If you say that someone or something is **everything**, you mean you consider them to be the most important thing in your life, or the most important thing that there is. ❑ *I love him. He is everything to me... Money isn't everything.* [5] If you say that someone or something has **everything**, you mean they have all the things or qualities that most people consider to be desirable. ❑ *She has everything: beauty, talent, children.*

PRON: oft PRON *else* ≠ nothing | PRON | PRON | PRON: oft PRON *to* n ≠ nothing | PRON

**every|where** /evriʰweəʳ/ ◆◇◇ [1] You use **everywhere** to refer to a whole area or to all the places in a particular area. ❑ *Working people everywhere object to paying taxes... We went everywhere together... Dust is everywhere... People come here from everywhere to see these lights.* [2] You use **everywhere** to refer to all the places that someone goes to. ❑ *Bradley is still accustomed to travelling everywhere in style... Everywhere he went he was introduced as the current United States Open Champion.* [3] You use **everywhere** to emphasize that you are talking about a large number of places, or all possible places. ❑ *I saw her picture everywhere... I looked everywhere. I couldn't find him.* [4] If you say that someone or something is **everywhere**, you mean that they are present in a place in very large numbers. ❑ *There were cartons of cigarettes everywhere.*

ADV: n ADV, ADV after v, *be* ADV, oft *from* ADV, ADV cl/group | ADV: ADV after v, oft ADV cl/prep | ADV: ADV after v, *be* ADV, ADV with cl [emphasis] | ADV: *be* ADV, ADV after v

**evict** /ɪvɪkt/ **(evicts, evicting, evicted)** If someone **is evicted from** the place where they are living, they are forced to leave it, usually because they have broken a law or contract. ❑ *They were evicted from their apartment after their mother became addicted to drugs... In the first week, the city police evicted ten families... If you don't keep up payments you could be evicted.*

VERB: *be* V-ed *from* n | V n | be V-ed | Also V n *from* n

**evic|tion** /ɪvɪkʃᵊn/ **(evictions) Eviction** is the act or process of officially forcing someone to leave a house or piece of land. ❑ *He was facing eviction, along with his wife and family. ...an eviction order.*

N-VAR

**evi|dence** /evɪdəns/ **(evidences, evidencing, evidenced)** ◆◆◇ [1] **Evidence** is anything that you see, experience, read, or are told that causes you to believe that something is true or has really happened. ❑ *Ganley said he'd seen no evidence of widespread fraud... There is a lot of evidence that stress is partly responsible for disease.* [2] **Evidence** is the information which is used in a court of law to try to prove something. Evidence is obtained from documents, objects, or witnesses. [LEGAL] ❑ *The evidence against him was purely circumstantial. ...enough evidence for a successful prosecution.* [3] If you **give evidence** in a court of law or an official enquiry, you officially say what you know about people or events, or describe an occasion at which you were present. ❑ *The forensic scientists who carried out the original tests will be called to give evidence.* [4] If a particular feeling, ability, or attitude **is evidenced by** something or someone, it is seen or felt. [FORMAL] ❑ *He's wise in other ways too, as evidenced by his reason for switching from tennis to golf... She was not calculating and evidenced no specific interest in money.* [5] If someone or something **is in evidence**, they are present and can be clearly seen. ❑ *Few soldiers were in evidence.*

N-UNCOUNT: oft N *of/for* n, N that, N to-inf | N-UNCOUNT: oft N *against* n | PHRASE: V inflects = testify | VERB: *be* V-ed *by* n | V n | PHRASE: V inflects

**evi|dent** /evɪdənt/ [1] If something is **evident**, you notice it easily and clearly. ❑ *His footprints were clearly evident in the heavy dust. ...the best-publicised cases of evident injustice.* [2] You use **evident** to show that you are certain about a situation or fact and your interpretation of it. ❑ *It was evident that she had once been a beauty.* [3] → See also **self-evident**.

ADJ = noticeable | ADJ: oft *it* v-link ADJ that/wh [emphasis] = clear

**evi|dent|ly** /evɪdəntli/ [1] You use **evidently** to say that something is obviously true, for example because you have seen evidence of it yourself. ❑ *The man wore a bathrobe and had evidently just come from the bathroom... The two Russians evidently knew each other.* [2] You use **evidently** to show that you think something is true or have been told something is true, but that you are not sure, because you do not have enough information or proof. ❑ *From childhood, he was evidently at once rebellious and precocious.* [3] You can use **evidently** to introduce a statement or opinion and to emphasize that you feel that it is true or correct. [FORMAL] ❑ *Quite evidently, it has nothing to do with social background.*

ADV: ADV with cl/group, ADV before v = clearly, obviously | ADV: ADV with cl/group, ADV before v = apparently | ADV: ADV with cl [emphasis]

**evil** /iːvᵊl/ **(evils)** ◆◇◇ [1] **Evil** is a powerful force that some people believe to exist, and which causes wicked and bad things to happen. ❑ *There's always a conflict between good and evil in his plays.* [2] **Evil** is used to refer to all the wicked and bad things that happen in the world. ❑ *He could not, after all, stop all the evil in the world.* [3] If you refer to an **evil**, you mean a very unpleasant or harmful situation or activity. ❑ *Higher taxes may be a necessary evil. ...a lecture on the evils of alcohol.* [4] If you describe someone as **evil**, you mean that they are very wicked by nature and take pleasure in doing things that harm other people. ❑ *...the country's most evil terrorists... She's an evil woman.* [5] If you describe something as **evil**, you mean that you think it causes a great deal of harm to people and is morally bad. ❑ *After 1760 few Americans refrained from condemning slavery as evil.* [6] If you describe something as **evil**, you mean that you think it is influenced by the devil. ❑ *I think this is an evil spirit at work.* [7] You can describe a very unpleasant smell as **evil**. ❑ *Both men were smoking evil-smelling pipes.*

N-UNCOUNT ≠ good | N-UNCOUNT | N-COUNT | ADJ | ADJ | ADJ | ADJ

**PHRASES** [8] If someone is putting off **the evil day** or **the evil hour**, they have to do something unpleasant and are trying to avoid doing it for as long as possible. ❑ *You can simply go on putting off the evil day and eventually find yourself smoking as much as ever.* [9] If you have two choices, but think that they are both bad, you can describe the one which is less bad as **the lesser of two evils**, or **the lesser evil**. ❑ *People voted for him as the lesser of two evils.*

PHRASE: usu v PHR | PHRASE

**evil|doer** /iːvᵊlduːəʳ/ **(evildoers)** also **evil-doer**. If you describe someone as an **evildoer**, you mean that they are wicked, and that they deliberately cause harm or suffering to others. [LITERARY or OLD-FASHIONED]

N-COUNT

**evil eye** [1] Some people believe that **the evil eye** is a magical power to cast a spell on someone or something by looking at them, so that bad things happen to them. [2] If someone gives you **the evil eye**, they look at you in an unpleasant way, usually because they dislike you or are jealous of you.

N-SING: *the* N | N-SING: usu *the*

**evince** /ɪvɪns/ **(evinces, evincing, evinced)** If someone or something **evinces** a particular feel-

VERB

ing or quality, they show that feeling or quality, often indirectly. [FORMAL] ❑ *The entire production evinces authenticity and a real respect for the subject matter.* V n

**evis|cer|ate** /ɪvɪsəreɪt/ **(eviscerates, eviscerating, eviscerated)** 1 To **eviscerate** a person or animal means to remove their internal organs, such as their heart, lungs, and stomach. [FORMAL] ❑ *...strangling and eviscerating rabbits for the pot.* VERB V n
2 If you say that something will **eviscerate** an organization or system, you are emphasizing that it will make the organization or system much weaker or much less powerful. [FORMAL] ❑ *Democrats say the petition will eviscerate state government.* VERB emphasis V n

**evo|ca|tion** /iːvəkeɪʃən, ev-/ **(evocations)** An **evocation of** something involves creating an image or impression of it. [FORMAL] ❑ *...a perfect evocation of the period.* N-VAR: usu N *of* n

**evoca|tive** /ɪvɒkətɪv/ If you describe something as **evocative**, you mean that it is good or interesting because it produces pleasant memories, ideas, emotions, and responses in people. [FORMAL] ❑ *Her story is sharply evocative of Italian provincial life.* ♦ **evoca|tive|ly** *...the collection of islands evocatively known as the South Seas.* ADJ: oft ADJ *of* n; ADV: ADV with v, ADV adj

**evoke** /ɪvoʊk/ **(evokes, evoking, evoked)** To **evoke** a particular memory, idea, emotion, or response means to cause it to occur. [FORMAL] ❑ *...the scene evoking memories of those old movies.* VERB V n

**evo|lu|tion** /iːvəluːʃən, ev-/ **(evolutions)** 1 **Evolution** is a process of gradual change that takes place over many generations, during which species of animals, plants, or insects slowly change some of their physical characteristics. ❑ *...the evolution of plants and animals. ...human evolution.* N-UNCOUNT
2 **Evolution** is a process of gradual development in a particular situation or thing over a period of time. [FORMAL] ❑ *...a crucial period in the evolution of modern physics.* N-VAR: usu with supp = development

**evo|lu|tion|ary** /iːvəluːʃənri, AM -neri/ **Evolutionary** means relating to a process of gradual change and development. ❑ *...an evolutionary process. ...a period of evolutionary change.* ADJ: usu ADJ n

**evo|lu|tion|ist** /iːvəluːʃənɪst, ev-/ **(evolutionists)** An **evolutionist** is someone who accepts the scientific theory that all living things evolved from a few simple life forms. N-COUNT

**evolve** /ɪvɒlv/ **(evolves, evolving, evolved)** 1 When animals or plants **evolve**, they gradually change and develop into different forms. ❑ *The bright plumage of many male birds has evolved to attract females... Maize evolved from a wild grass in Mexico. ...when amphibians evolved into reptiles.* VERB V; V *from* n; V *into* n
2 If something **evolves** or you **evolve** it, it gradually develops over a period of time into something different and usually more advanced. ❑ *...a tiny airline which eventually evolved into Pakistan International Airlines... Popular music evolved from folk songs... As medical knowledge evolves, beliefs change... This was when he evolved the working method from which he has never departed.* VERB V *into* n; V *from* n; V; V n

**ewe** /juː/ **(ewes)** A **ewe** is an adult female sheep. N-COUNT

**ewer** /juːəʳ/ **(ewers)** A **ewer** is a large jug with a wide opening. [OLD-FASHIONED] N-COUNT

**ex** /eks/ **(exes)** Someone's **ex** is the person they used to be married to or used to have a romantic or sexual relationship with. [INFORMAL] ❑ *He's different from my ex. ...one of her exes.* N-COUNT: usu poss N

**ex-** /eks-/ **ex-** is added to nouns to show that someone or something is no longer the thing referred to by that noun. For example, a woman's ex-husband is no longer her husband. ❑ *...my ex-wife. ...ex-President Reagan. ...an ex-soldier.* PREFIX

**ex|ac|er|bate** /ɪgzæsəʳbeɪt/ **(exacerbates, exacerbating, exacerbated)** If something **exacerbates** a problem or bad situation, it makes it worse. [FORMAL] ❑ *Longstanding poverty has been exacerbated by racial divisions.* ♦ **ex|ac|er|ba|tion** /ɪgzæsəʳbeɪʃən/ *...the exacerbation of global problems.* VERB = aggravate; V n; N-UNCOUNT: usu *the* N *of* n

**ex|act** /ɪgzækt/ **(exacts, exacting, exacted)** ◆◆◇ 1 **Exact** means correct in every detail. For example, an **exact** copy is the same in every detail as the thing it is copied from. ❑ *I don't remember the exact words... The exact number of protest calls has not been revealed... It's an exact copy of the one which was found in Ann Alice's room.* ♦ **ex|act|ly** *Try to locate exactly where the smells are entering the room... Both drugs will be exactly the same... Barton couldn't remember exactly.* ADJ: usu ADJ n = precise ≠ approximate; ADV: usu ADV with cl/group, also ADV after v
2 You use **exact** before a noun to emphasize that you are referring to that particular thing and no other, especially something that has a particular significance. ❑ *I hadn't really thought about it until this exact moment... It may be that you will feel the exact opposite of what you expected.* ♦ **ex|act|ly** *These are exactly the people who do not vote... He knew exactly what he was doing.* ADJ: ADJ n emphasis; ADV: ADV n/wh = precisely
3 If you describe someone as **exact**, you mean that they are very careful and detailed in their work, thinking, or methods. ❑ *Formal, exact and obstinate, he was also cold, suspicious, touchy and tactless.* ADJ = meticulous
4 When someone **exacts** something, they demand and obtain it from another person, especially because they are in a superior or more powerful position. [FORMAL] ❑ *Already he has exacted a written apology from the chairman of the commission.* VERB V n *from/for* n
5 If someone **exacts** revenge **on** a person, they have their revenge on them. ❑ *She uses the media to help her exact a terrible revenge.* VERB V n
6 If something **exacts** a high price, it has a bad effect on a person or situation. ❑ *The sheer physical effort had exacted a heavy price... The strain of a violent ground campaign will exact a toll on troops.* VERB V n; V n *on* n
7 → See also **exactly**.
8 You say **to be exact** to indicate that you are slightly correcting or giving more detailed information about what you have been saying. ❑ *A small number – five, to be exact – have been bad.* PHRASE: PHR with cl/group

**ex|act|ing** /ɪgzæktɪŋ/ You use **exacting** to describe something or someone that demands hard work and a great deal of care. ❑ *The Duke was not well enough to carry out such an exacting task.* ADJ: usu ADJ n

**ex|acti|tude** /ɪgzæktɪtjuːd, AM -tuːd/ **Exactitude** is the quality of being very accurate and careful. [FORMAL] ❑ *...the precision and exactitude of current genetic mapping.* N-UNCOUNT

**ex|act|ly** /ɪgzæktli/ ◆◇◇ 1 You use **exactly** before an amount, number, or position to emphasize that it is no more, no less, or no different from what you are stating. ❑ *Each corner had a guard tower, each of which was exactly ten meters in height... Agnew's car pulled into the driveway at exactly five o'clock.* ADV: usu ADV num, also ADV prep/adv emphasis = precisely
2 If you say **'Exactly'**, you are agreeing with someone or emphasizing the truth of what they say. If you say **'Not exactly'**, you are telling them politely that they are wrong in part of what they are saying. ❑ *Eve nodded, almost approvingly. 'Exactly.'... 'And you refused?' — 'Well, not exactly. I couldn't say yes.'* ADV: ADV as reply = precisely
3 You use **not exactly** to indicate that a meaning or situation is slightly different from what people think or expect. ❑ *He's not exactly homeless, he just hangs out in this park.* ADV: *not* ADV, usu ADV group vagueness
4 You can use **not exactly** to show that you mean the opposite of what you are saying. ❑ *This was not exactly what I wanted to hear... Sailing is not exactly cheap.* ADV: *not* ADV, usu ADV group emphasis
5 You use **exactly** with a question to show that you disapprove of what the person you are talking to is doing or saying. ❑ *What exactly do you mean?* ADV: ADV with quest disapproval = precisely
6 → See also **exact**.

**ex|act|ness** /ɪgzæktnəs/ **Exactness** is the quality of being very accurate and precise. ❑ *He recalls his native Bombay with cinematic exactness.* N-UNCOUNT: usu with supp

**ex|act sci|ence** If you say that a particular activity is not **an exact science**, you mean that there are no set rules to follow or it does not produce very accurate results. ❑ *Forecasting floods is not an exact science.* N-SING: usu with brd-neg

**ex|ag|ger|ate** /ɪgzædʒəreɪt/ **(exaggerates, exaggerating, exaggerated)** 1 If you **exaggerate**, VERB you indicate that something is, for example, worse or more important than it really is. ❑ [V] *He thinks I'm exaggerating...* [V n] *Sheila admitted that she did sometimes exaggerate the demands of her job.* ♦ **ex|ag|gera|tion** /ɪɡzædʒəreɪʃən/ [N-VAR] **(exaggerations)** *Like many stories about him, it smacks of exaggeration... It would be an exaggeration to call the danger urgent.* [2] [VERB] If something **exaggerates** a situation, quality, or feature, it makes the situation, quality, or feature appear greater, more obvious, or more important than it really is. ❑ [V n] *These figures exaggerate the loss of competitiveness.*

**ex|ag|ger|at|ed** /ɪɡzædʒəreɪtɪd/ [ADJ] Something that is **exaggerated** is or seems larger, better, worse, or more important than it actually needs to be. ❑ *They should be sceptical of exaggerated claims for what such courses can achieve... Western fears, he insists, are greatly exaggerated.* ♦ **ex|ag|ger|at|ed|ly** [ADV: ADV adj/-ed, ADV after v] *...an exaggeratedly feminine appearance... She laughed exaggeratedly at their jokes.*

**ex|alt** /ɪɡzɔːlt/ [VERB] **(exalts, exalting, exalted)** To **exalt** someone or something means to praise them very highly. [FORMAL] ❑ [V n] *His work exalts all those virtues that we, as Americans, are taught to hold dear.*

**ex|al|ta|tion** /eɡzɔːlteɪʃən/ [N-UNCOUNT = exhilaration] **Exaltation** is an intense feeling of great happiness. [FORMAL] ❑ *The city was swept up in the mood of exaltation.* ➔ See also **exalt**.

**ex|alt|ed** /ɪɡzɔːltɪd/ [ADJ: usu ADJ n = lofty] Someone or something that is at an **exalted** level is at a very high level, especially with regard to rank or importance. [FORMAL] ❑ *You must decide how to make the best use of your exalted position.*

**exam** /ɪɡzæm/ **(exams)** [1] [N-COUNT = examination] An **exam** is a formal test that you take to show your knowledge or ability in a particular subject, or to obtain a qualification. ❑ *I don't want to take any more exams... Kate's exam results were excellent.* [2] [N-COUNT = examination] If you have a medical **exam**, a doctor looks at your body, feels it, or does simple tests in order to check how healthy you are. [mainly AM]

**ex|ami|na|tion** /ɪɡzæmɪneɪʃən/ **(examinations)** ♦◇◇ [1] [N-COUNT = exam] An **examination** is a formal test that you take to show your knowledge or ability in a particular subject, or to obtain a qualification. [FORMAL] [2] ➔ See also **examine**.

**ex|am|ine** /ɪɡzæmɪn/ **(examines, examining, examined)** ♦♦◇ [1] [VERB] If you **examine** something, you look at it carefully. ❑ [V n] *He examined her passport and stamped it.* ♦ **ex|ami|na|tion** /ɪɡzæmɪneɪʃən/ [N-VAR = inspection] **(examinations)** *The Navy is to carry out an examination of the wreck tomorrow.* [2] [VERB] If a doctor **examines** you, he or she looks at your body, feels it, or does simple tests in order to check how healthy you are. ❑ [V n] *Another doctor examined her and could still find nothing wrong.* ♦ **ex|ami|na|tion** [N-VAR] *He was later discharged after an examination at Westminster Hospital.* [3] [VERB] If an idea, proposal, or plan **is examined**, it is considered very carefully. ❑ [V n] *The plans will be examined by EU environment ministers.* ♦ **ex|ami|na|tion** [N-VAR] *The proposal requires careful examination and consideration.* [4] [VERB: usu passive] If you **are examined**, you are given a formal test in order to show your knowledge of a subject. ❑ [*be* V-ed] *...learning to cope with the pressures of being judged and examined by our teachers.*

**ex|ami|nee** /ɪɡzæmɪniː/ [N-COUNT] **(examinees)** An **examinee** is someone who is taking an exam. [FORMAL]

**ex|am|in|er** /ɪɡzæmɪnəʳ/ [N-COUNT] **(examiners)** An **examiner** is a person who sets or marks an examination. ➔ See also **medical examiner**. **external examiner** ➔ see **external**.

**ex|am|ple** /ɪɡzɑːmpəl, -zæmp-/ **(examples)** ♦♦♦ [1] [N-COUNT: oft N *of* n] An **example of** something is a particular situation, object, or person which shows that what is being claimed is true. ❑ *The doctors gave numerous examples of patients being expelled from hospital... Listed below are just a few examples of some of the family benefits available.* [2] [N-COUNT: oft N *of* n = illustration] An **example of** a particular class of objects or styles is something that has many of the typical features of such a class or style, and that you consider clearly represents it. ❑ *Symphonies 103 and 104 stand as perfect examples of early symphonic construction.* [3] [PHRASE: PHR with cl/group] You use **for example** to introduce and emphasize something which shows that something is true. ❑ *Take, for example, the simple sentence: 'The man climbed up the hill'... A few simple precautions can be taken, for example ensuring that desks are the right height.* [4] [N-COUNT: oft N *to* n, approval] If you refer to a person or their behaviour as an **example to** other people, you mean that he or she behaves in a good or correct way that other people should copy. ❑ *He is a model professional and an example to the younger lads.* [5] [N-COUNT] In a dictionary entry, an **example** is a phrase or sentence which shows how a particular word is used. ❑ *The examples are unique to this dictionary.*

PHRASES [6] [PHRASE: V inflects] If you **follow** someone's **example**, you behave in the same way as they did in the past, or in a similar way, especially because you admire them. ❑ *Following the example set by her father, she has fulfilled her role and done her duty.* [7] [PHRASE: V inflects, PHR n] To **make an example of** someone who has done something wrong means to punish them severely as a warning to other people not to do the same thing. ❑ *Let us at least see our courts make an example of these despicable criminals.* [8] [PHRASE: V inflects] If you **set an example**, you encourage or inspire people by your behaviour to behave or act in a similar way. ❑ *An officer's job was to set an example.*

**ex|as|per|ate** /ɪɡzɑːspəreɪt, -zæs-/ [VERB] **(exasperates, exasperating, exasperated)** If someone or something **exasperates** you, they annoy you and make you feel frustrated or upset. ❑ [V n] *The sheer futility of it all exasperates her.* ♦ **ex|as|pera|tion** [N-UNCOUNT] /ɪɡzɑːspəreɪʃən, -zæs-/ *Mahoney clenched his fist in exasperation.*

**ex|as|per|at|ed** /ɪɡzɑːspəreɪtɪd, -zæs-/ [ADJ: oft ADJ *by/with/at* n] If you describe a person as **exasperated**, you mean that they are frustrated or angry because of something that is happening or something that another person is doing. ❑ *The president was clearly exasperated by the whole saga.*

**ex|as|per|at|ing** /ɪɡzɑːspəreɪtɪŋ, -zæs-/ [ADJ: usu v-link ADJ] If you describe someone or something as **exasperating**, you mean that you feel angry or frustrated by them or by what they do. ❑ *Hardie could be exasperating to his colleagues.*

**ex|ca|vate** /ekskəveɪt/ **(excavates, excavating, excavated)** [1] [VERB] When archaeologists or other people **excavate** a piece of land, they remove earth carefully from it and look for things such as pots, bones, or buildings which are buried there, in order to discover information about the past. ❑ [V n] *A new Danish expedition is again excavating the site in annual summer digs.* ♦ **ex|ca|va|tion** [N-VAR] /ekskəveɪʃən/ **(excavations)** *...the excavation of a bronze-age boat.* [2] [VERB] To **excavate** means to dig a hole in the ground, for example in order to build there. ❑ [V n] *A contractor was hired to drain the reservoir and to excavate soil from one area for replacement with clay.* ♦ **ex|ca|va|tion** [N-VAR] *...the excavation of canals.*

**ex|ca|va|tor** /ekskəveɪtəʳ/ [N-COUNT] **(excavators)** An **excavator** is a very large machine that is used for digging, for example when people are building something.

**ex|ceed** /ɪksiːd/ **(exceeds, exceeding, exceeded)** [1] [VERB] If something **exceeds** a particular amount or number, it is greater or larger than that amount or number. [FORMAL] ❑ [V n] *Its research budget exceeds $700 million a year...* [V n] *His performance exceeded all expectations.* [2] [VERB] If you **exceed** a limit or rule, you go beyond it, even though you are not supposed to or it is against the law. [FORMAL] ❑ [V n] *He accepts he was exceeding the speed limit.*

**ex|ceed|ing|ly** /ɪksiːdɪŋli/ [ADV: usu ADV adj, also ADV after v] **Exceedingly** means very or very much. [OLD-FASHIONED] ❑ *We had an exceedingly good lunch.*

**ex|cel** /ɪkse̲l/ **(excels, excelling, excelled)** If someone **excels in** something or **excels at** it, they are very good at doing it. ❑ *Caine has always been an actor who excels in irony... Mary was a better rider than either of them and she excelled at outdoor sports... Academically he began to excel... I think Krishnan excelled himself in all departments of his game.* VERB V in n V at n V V pron-refl

**ex|cel|lence** /e̲ksələns/ If someone or something has the quality of **excellence**, they are extremely good in some way. ❑ *...the top US award for excellence in journalism and the arts.* → See also **par excellence**. N-UNCOUNT

**Ex|cel|len|cy** /e̲ksələnsi/ **(Excellencies)** You use expressions such as **Your Excellency** or **His Excellency** when you are addressing or referring to officials of very high rank, for example ambassadors or governors. ❑ *I am reluctant to trust anyone totally, Your Excellency... His excellency the President will be waiting for you in the hall.* N-VOC: poss N; PRON: poss PRON [politeness]

**ex|cel|lent** /e̲ksələnt/ ◆◆◇ [1] Something that is **excellent** is very good indeed. ❑ *The recording quality is excellent... Luckily, Sue is very efficient and does an excellent job as Fred's personal assistant.* ADJ ♦ **ex|cel|lent|ly** *They're both playing excellently.* ADV: ADV after v, ADV adj/-ed [2] Some people say **'Excellent!'** to show that they approve of something. EXCLAM [feelings]

**ex|cept** /ɪkse̲pt/ ◆◆◇ [1] You use **except** to introduce the only thing or person that a statement does not apply to, or a fact that prevents a statement from being completely true. ❑ *I wouldn't have accepted anything except a job in Europe... I don't take any drugs whatsoever, except aspirin for colds.* PREP ♦ **Except** is also a conjunction. ❑ *Freddie would tell me nothing about what he was writing, except that it was to be a Christmas play.* CONJ: oft CONJ that/when/where/if [2] You use **except for** to introduce the only thing or person that prevents a statement from being completely true. ❑ *He hadn't eaten a thing except for one forkful of salad... Everyone was late, except for Richard.* PREP-PHRASE

**ex|cept|ed** /ɪkse̲ptɪd/ You use **excepted** after you have mentioned a person or thing to show that you do not include them in the statement you are making. [FORMAL] ❑ *Jeremy excepted, the men seemed personable.* ADV: n ADV

**ex|cept|ing** /ɪkse̲ptɪŋ/ You use **excepting** to introduce the only thing that prevents a statement from being completely true. [FORMAL] ❑ *The source of meat for much of this region (excepting Japan) has traditionally been the pig.* PREP

**ex|cep|tion** /ɪkse̲pʃᵊn/ **(exceptions)** ◆◇◇ [1] An **exception** is a particular thing, person, or situation that is not included in a general statement, judgment, or rule. ❑ *Few guitarists can sing as well as they can play; Eddie, however, is an exception... There were no floral offerings at the ceremony, with the exception of a single red rose... The law makes no exceptions... With few exceptions, guests are booked for week-long visits.* N-COUNT: oft *with the* N *of* n, *with* N

**PHRASES** [2] If you make a general statement, and then say that something or someone is **no exception**, you are emphasizing that they are included in that statement. ❑ *Marketing is applied to everything these days, and books are no exception... Most people have no real idea how to change to healthy food, and Maureen was no exception.* PHRASE: v-link PHR [emphasis] [3] If you are making a general statement and you say that something is **the exception that proves the rule**, you mean that although it seems to contradict your statement, in most other cases your statement will be true. ❑ *Wine-making and accountants don't usually go together, but Thierry Hasard is an exception that proves the rule.* PHRASE: *exception* and V inflect, usu v-link PHR [4] If you **take exception to** something, you feel offended or annoyed by it, usually with the result that you complain about it. ❑ *He also took exception to having been spied on.* PHRASE: V inflects = object [5] You use **with the exception of** to introduce a thing or person that is not included in a general statement that you are making. ❑ *Yesterday was a day off for everybody, with the exception of Lawrence.* PREP-PHRASE [6] You use **without exception** to emphasize that the statement you are making is true in all cases. ❑ *The vehicles are without exception old, rusty and dented.* PHRASE: PHR with cl/group, PHR after v [emphasis]

**ex|cep|tion|al** /ɪkse̲pʃənᵊl/ [1] You use **exceptional** to describe someone or something that has a particular quality, usually a good quality, to an unusually high degree. ❑ *...children with exceptional ability... His translation is exceptional in its poetic quality.* ADJ [approval] = extraordinary ♦ **ex|cep|tion|al|ly** *He's an exceptionally talented dancer.* ADV: ADV adj/adv [2] **Exceptional** situations and incidents are unusual and only likely to happen very infrequently. [FORMAL] ❑ *School governors have the discretion to allow parents to withdraw pupils in exceptional circumstances.* ADJ = unusual ♦ **ex|cep|tion|al|ly** *Exceptionally, in times of emergency, we may send a team of experts.* ADV: ADV with cl

**ex|cerpt** /e̲ksɜːʳpt/ **(excerpts)** ◆◇◇ An **excerpt** is a short piece of writing or music which is taken from a larger piece. ❑ *...an excerpt from Tchaikovsky's Nutcracker.* N-COUNT: oft N *from* n = extract

**ex|cess** **(excesses)** ◆◇◇

> The noun is pronounced /ɪkse̲s/. The adjective is pronounced /e̲kses/.

[1] An **excess of** something is a larger amount than is needed, allowed, or usual. ❑ *An excess of house plants in a small flat can be oppressive... Polyunsaturated oils are essential for health. Excess is harmful, however.* N-VAR: with supp, usu *a* N *of* n [2] **Excess** is used to describe amounts that are greater than what is needed, allowed, or usual. ❑ *After cooking the fish, pour off any excess fat.* ADJ: ADJ n = surplus [3] **Excess** is behaviour that is unacceptable because it is considered too extreme or immoral. ❑ *She said she was sick of her life of excess. ...adolescent excess.* N-UNCOUNT: also N in pl [4] **Excess** is used to refer to additional amounts of money that need to be paid for services and activities that were not originally planned or taken into account. [FORMAL] ❑ *...a letter demanding an excess fare of £20.* ADJ: ADJ n [5] The **excess** on an insurance policy is a sum of money which the insured person has to pay towards the cost of a claim. The insurance company pays the rest. [BRIT, BUSINESS, TECHNICAL] ❑ *The company wanted £1,800 for a policy with a £400 excess for under-21s.* N-COUNT: usu sing

**PHRASES** [6] **In excess of** means more than a particular amount. [FORMAL] ❑ *Avoid deposits in excess of £20,000 in any one account.* PREP-PHRASE: PREP amount [7] If you do something **to excess**, you do it too much. ❑ *I was reasonably fit, played a lot of tennis, and didn't smoke or drink to excess.* PHRASE: PHR after v [disapproval]

**ex|cess bag|gage** also **excess luggage.** [1] On an aeroplane journey, **excess baggage** is luggage that is larger or weighs more than your ticket allows, so that you have to pay extra to take it on board. N-UNCOUNT [2] You can use **excess baggage** to talk about problems or events from someone's past which you think still worry them, especially when you think these things make it difficult for the person to cope or develop. ❑ *The good thing about these younger players is that they are not carrying any excess baggage from less successful times.* N-UNCOUNT

**ex|ces|sive** /ɪkse̲sɪv/ If you describe the amount or level of something as **excessive**, you disapprove of it because it is more or higher than is necessary or reasonable. ❑ *...the alleged use of excessive force by police... The government says that local authority spending is excessive.* ADJ [disapproval] ♦ **ex|ces|sive|ly** *Managers are also accused of paying themselves excessively high salaries... Mum had started taking pills and drinking excessively.* ADV: ADV adj, ADV with v

**ex|change** /ɪkstʃe̲ɪndʒ/ **(exchanges, exchanging, exchanged)** ◆◆◇ [1] If two or more people **exchange** things of a particular kind, they give them to each other at the same time. ❑ *We exchanged addresses and Christmas cards... He exchanged a quick smile with her then entered the lift.* V-RECIP pl-n V V n with n ♦ **Exchange** is also a noun. ❑ *He ruled out any exchange of prisoners with the militants. ...a frank exchange of views.* N-COUNT: oft N *of* pl-n [2] If you **exchange** something, you replace it with a different thing, especially VERB something that is better or more satisfactory. ❑ *...the chance to sell back or exchange goods... If the car you have leased is clearly unsatisfactory, you can always exchange it for another.* V n / V n for n [3] An **exchange** is a brief conversation, usually an angry one. [FORMAL] ❑ *There've been some bitter exchanges between the two groups.* N-COUNT [4] An **exchange of** fire, for example, is an incident in which people use guns or missiles against each other. ❑ *There was an exchange of fire during which the gunman was wounded.* N-COUNT: oft N of n [5] An **exchange** is an arrangement in which people from two different countries visit each other's country, to strengthen links between them. ❑ *...a series of sporting and cultural exchanges with Seoul... I'm going to go on an exchange visit to Paris.* N-COUNT: usu adj N [6] **The exchange** is the same as the **telephone exchange**. N-COUNT: usu the N [7] → See also **corn exchange**, **foreign exchange**, **stock exchange**. [8] If you do or give something **in exchange for** something else, you do it or give it in order to get that thing. ❑ *It is illegal for public officials to solicit gifts or money in exchange for favors.* PHRASE: usu PHR for n, PHR with cl

**ex|change rate** **(exchange rates)** The **exchange rate** of a country's unit of currency is the amount of another country's currency that you get in exchange for it. ◆◇◇ N-COUNT

**Ex|cheq|uer** /ɪkstʃekəʳ/ **The Exchequer** is the department in the British government which is responsible for receiving, issuing, and accounting for money belonging to the state. N-PROPER: the N

**ex|cise** /eksaɪz/ **(excises, excising, excised)**

> The noun is pronounced /eksaɪz/. The verb is pronounced /ɪksaɪz/.

[1] **Excise** is a tax that the government of a country puts on particular goods, such as cigarettes and alcoholic drinks, which are produced for sale in its own country. ❑ *...this year's rise in excise duties... New car buyers and smokers will be hit by increases in taxes and excise.* N-VAR: usu N n [2] If someone **excises** something, they remove it deliberately and completely. [FORMAL] ❑ *...a personal crusade to excise racist and sexist references in newspapers. ...the question of permanently excising madness from the world.* VERB; V n; V n from n ♦ **ex|ci|sion** /ɪksɪʒən/ **(excisions)** *The authors demanded excision of foreign words.* N-VAR

**ex|cit|able** /ɪksaɪtəbəl/ If you describe someone as **excitable**, you mean that they behave in a rather nervous way and become excited very easily. ❑ *Mary sat beside Elaine, who today seemed excitable.* ADJ ♦ **ex|cit|abil|ity** /ɪksaɪtəbɪlɪti/ *She has always been inclined to excitability.* N-UNCOUNT

**ex|cite** /ɪksaɪt/ **(excites, exciting, excited)** [1] If something **excites** you, it makes you feel very happy, eager, or enthusiastic. ❑ *I only take on work that excites me, even if it means turning down lots of money... Where the show really excites is in the display of avant-garde photography.* VERB; V n; V [2] If something **excites** a particular feeling, emotion, or reaction in someone, it causes them to experience it. ❑ *Daniel's early exposure to motor racing did not excite his interest.* VERB = arouse; V n

**ex|cit|ed** /ɪksaɪtɪd/ [1] If you are **excited**, you are so happy that you cannot relax, especially because you are thinking about something pleasant that is going to happen to you. ❑ *I'm very excited about the possibility of playing for England's first team... I was so excited when I went to sign the paperwork I could hardly write.* ADJ: usu v-link ADJ, oft ADJ about n ♦ **ex|cit|ed|ly** *'You're coming?' he said excitedly. 'That's fantastic! That's incredible!'* ADV: ADV with v [2] If you are **excited**, you are very worried or angry about something, and so you are very alert and cannot relax. ❑ *I don't think there's any reason to get excited about inflation.* ADJ = agitated ♦ **ex|cit|ed|ly** *Larry rose excitedly to the edge of his seat, shook a fist at us and spat.* ADV: ADV with v

**ex|cite|ment** /ɪksaɪtmənt/ **(excitements)** You use **excitement** to refer to the state of being excited, or to something that excites you. ❑ *Everyone is in a state of great excitement.* N-VAR

**ex|cit|ing** /ɪksaɪtɪŋ/ If something is **exciting**, it makes you feel very happy or enthusiastic. ❑ *The race itself is very exciting.* ◆◇◇ ADJ = thrilling

**ex|claim** /ɪkskleɪm/ **(exclaims, exclaiming, exclaimed)** Writers sometimes use **exclaim** to show that someone is speaking suddenly, loudly, or emphatically, often because they are excited, shocked, or angry. ❑ *'He went back to the lab', Iris exclaimed impatiently... He exclaims that it must be a typing error.* VERB = cry; V with quote; V that

**ex|cla|ma|tion** /ekskləmeɪʃən/ **(exclamations)** An **exclamation** is a sound, word, or sentence that is spoken suddenly, loudly, or emphatically and that expresses excitement, admiration, shock, or anger. ❑ *Sue gave an exclamation as we got a clear sight of the house.* N-COUNT

**ex|cla|ma|tion mark** **(exclamation marks)** An **exclamation mark** is the sign ! which is used in writing to show that a word, phrase, or sentence is an exclamation. [BRIT] N-COUNT

> in AM, use **exclamation point**

**ex|clude** /ɪkskluːd/ **(excludes, excluding, excluded)** [1] If you **exclude** someone **from** a place or activity, you prevent them from entering it or taking part in it. ❑ *The Academy excluded women from its classes... Many of the youngsters feel excluded.* VERB; V n from n; V-ed, Also V n [2] If you **exclude** something that has some connection with what you are doing, you deliberately do not use it or consider it. ❑ *They eat only plant foods, and take care to exclude animal products from other areas of their lives... In some schools, Christmas carols are being modified to exclude any reference to Christ.* VERB; V n from n; V n [3] To **exclude** a possibility means to decide or prove that it is wrong and not worth considering. ❑ *I cannot entirely exclude the possibility that some form of pressure was applied to the neck.* VERB: usu with brd-neg; V n [4] To **exclude** something such as the sun's rays or harmful germs means to prevent them physically from reaching or entering a particular place. ❑ *This was intended to exclude the direct rays of the sun.* VERB; V n

**ex|clud|ing** /ɪkskluːdɪŋ/ You use **excluding** before mentioning a person or thing to show that you are not including them in your statement. ❑ *Excluding water, half of the body's weight is protein.* PREP ≠ including

**ex|clu|sion** /ɪkskluːʒən/ **(exclusions)** [1] The **exclusion of** something is the act of deliberately not using, allowing, or considering it. ❑ *It calls for the exclusion of all commercial lending institutions from the college loan program.* N-VAR: oft N of n [2] **Exclusion** is the act of preventing someone from entering a place or taking part in an activity. ❑ *...women's exclusion from political power.* N-UNCOUNT: usu with poss, oft N from n [3] If you do one thing **to the exclusion of** something else, you only do the first thing and do not do the second thing at all. ❑ *Diane had dedicated her life to caring for him to the exclusion of all else.* PHRASE: usu PHR after v, PHR n

**ex|clu|sion|ary** /ɪkskluːʒənri/ Something that is **exclusionary** excludes a particular person or group of people. [FORMAL] ❑ *...exclusionary business practices.* ADJ

**ex|clu|sion zone** **(exclusion zones)** An **exclusion zone** is an area where people are not allowed to go or where they are not allowed to do a particular thing, for example because it would be dangerous. N-COUNT

**ex|clu|sive** /ɪkskluːsɪv/ **(exclusives)** [1] If you describe something as **exclusive**, you mean that it is limited to people who have a lot of money or who belong to a high social class, and is therefore not available to everyone. ❑ *He is already a member of Britain's most exclusive club... The City was criticised for being too exclusive and uncompetitive.* ADJ ♦ **ex|clu|sive|ness** *...a rising middle class, which objected to the exclusiveness of the traditional elite.* N-UNCOUNT ♦ **ex|clu|sivi|ty** /ekskluːsɪvɪti/ *...a company with a reputation for exclusivity.* N-UNCOUNT: oft the N of n [2] Something that is **exclusive** is used or owned by only one person or group, and not shared with anyone else. ❑ *Our group will have exclusive use of a 60-foot boat... Many* ADJ: oft ADJ to n of their cheeses are exclusive to our stores in Britain. 3 If a newspaper, magazine, or broadcasting organization describes one of its reports as **exclusive**, they mean that it is a special report which does not appear in any other publication or on any other channel. ❑ *He told the magazine in an exclusive interview: 'All my problems stem from drink'.* ♦ An **exclusive** is an exclusive article or report. ❑ *Some papers thought they had an exclusive.* 4 If a company states that its prices, goods, or services are **exclusive of** something, that thing is not included in the stated price, although it usually still has to be paid for. ❑ *Skiing weekends cost £58 (exclusive of travel and accommodation).* 5 If two things are **mutually exclusive**, they are separate and very different from each other, so that it is impossible for them to exist or happen together. ❑ *They both have learnt that ambition and successful fatherhood can be mutually exclusive.*

ADJ: usu ADJ n | N-COUNT | ADJ: usu v-link ADJ of n ≠ inclusive | PHRASE: v-link PHR

**ex|clu|sive|ly** /ɪksklu:sɪvli/ **Exclusively** is used to refer to situations or activities that involve only the thing or things mentioned, and nothing else. ❑ *...an exclusively male domain... Instruction in these subjects in undergraduate classes is almost exclusively by lecture.*

ADV: ADV with cl/group, ADV with v

**ex|com|muni|cate** /ekskəmju:nɪkeɪt/ **(excommunicates, excommunicating, excommunicated)** If a Roman Catholic or member of the Orthodox Church **is excommunicated**, it is publicly and officially stated that the person is no longer allowed to be a member of the Church. This is a punishment for some very great wrong that they have done. ❑ *Eventually, he was excommunicated along with his mentor... In 1766 he excommunicated the village for its 'depraved diversion.'* ♦ **ex|com|mu|ni|ca|tion** /ekskəmju:nɪkeɪʃən/ **(excommunications)** *...the threat of excommunication.*

VERB | be V-ed | V n | N-VAR

**ex|co|ri|ate** /ɪkskɔ:rieɪt/ **(excoriates, excoriating, excoriated)** To **excoriate** a person or organization means to criticize them severely, usually in public. [FORMAL] ❑ *He proceeded to excoriate me in front of the nurses.*

VERB = berate | V n

**ex|cre|ment** /ekskrɪmənt/ **Excrement** is the solid waste that is passed out of a person or animal's body through their bowels. [FORMAL] ❑ *The cage smelled of excrement.*

N-UNCOUNT

**ex|cres|cence** /ɪkskresəns/ **(excrescences)** If you describe something such as a building, addition, or development as an **excrescence**, you strongly disapprove of it because you think it is unnecessary, bad, or ugly. [LITERARY] ❑ *...an architectural excrescence... The trade union block vote is an excrescence on democracy.*

N-COUNT: usu with supp, oft N on n [disapproval] = blot

**ex|cre|ta** /ɪkskri:tə/ **Excreta** is the waste matter, such as urine or faeces, which is passed out of a person or animal's body. [TECHNICAL, FORMAL]

N-UNCOUNT

**ex|crete** /ɪkskri:t/ **(excretes, excreting, excreted)** When a person or animal **excretes** waste matter from their body, they get rid of it in faeces, urine, or sweat. [TECHNICAL or FORMAL] ❑ *Your open pores excrete sweat and dirt.* ♦ **ex|cre|tion** /ɪkskri:ʃən/ **(excretions)** *...the excretion of this drug from the body.*

VERB | V n | N-UNCOUNT: also N in pl

**ex|cru|ci|at|ing** /ɪkskru:ʃieɪtɪŋ/ 1 If you describe something as **excruciating**, you are emphasizing that it is extremely painful, either physically or emotionally. ❑ *I was in excruciating pain and one leg wouldn't move.* ♦ **ex|cru|ci|at|ing|ly** *He found the transition to boarding school excruciatingly painful.* 2 If you describe something as **excruciating**, you mean that it is very unpleasant to experience, for example because it is very boring or embarrassing. ❑ *Meanwhile, the boredom is excruciating... There was a moment of excruciating silence.* ♦ **ex|cru|ci|at|ing|ly** *The dialogue is excruciatingly embarrassing.*

ADJ [emphasis] = unbearable | ADV: usu ADV adj, also ADV after v | ADJ | ADV: usu ADV adj, also ADV with v

**ex|cur|sion** /ɪkskɜ:ʳʃən, AM -ʒən/ **(excursions)** 1 You can refer to a short journey as an **excursion**, especially if it is made for pleasure or enjoyment. ❑ *In Bermuda, Sam's father took him on an excursion to a coral barrier.* 2 An **excursion** is a trip or visit to an interesting place, especially one that is arranged or recommended by a holiday company or tourist organization. ❑ *Another pleasant excursion is Malaga, 18 miles away.* 3 If you describe an activity as an **excursion into** something, you mean that it is an attempt to develop or understand something new that you have not experienced before. ❑ *...Radio 3's latest excursion into ethnic music, dance and literature.*

N-COUNT = trip | N-COUNT = outing | N-COUNT: usu N into n, oft poss N

**ex|cus|able** /ɪkskju:zəbəl/ If you say that someone's wrong words or actions are **excusable**, you mean that they can be understood and forgiven. ❑ *I then realised that he had made a simple but excusable historical mistake.*

ADJ = forgivable

**ex|cuse** **(excuses, excusing, excused)** ♦◇◇

✔ The noun is pronounced /ɪkskju:s/. The verb is pronounced /ɪkskju:z/.

1 An **excuse** is a reason which you give in order to explain why something has been done or has not been done, or in order to avoid doing something. ❑ *It is easy to find excuses for his indecisiveness... Once I had had a baby I had the perfect excuse to stay at home... If you stop making excuses and do it you'll wonder what took you so long.* ● If you say that there is **no excuse for** something, you are emphasizing that it should not happen, or expressing disapproval that it has happened. ❑ *There's no excuse for behaviour like that... Solitude was no excuse for sloppiness.* 2 To **excuse** someone or **excuse** their behaviour means to provide reasons for their actions, especially when other people disapprove of these actions. ❑ *He excused himself by saying he was 'forced to rob to maintain my wife and cat'... That doesn't excuse my mother's behaviour.* 3 If you **excuse** someone **for** something wrong that they have done, you forgive them for it. ❑ *Many people might have excused them for shirking some of their responsibilities.* 4 If someone **is excused from** a duty or responsibility, they are told that they do not have to carry it out. ❑ *She is usually excused from her duties during the school holidays... She was excused duties on Saturday.* 5 If you **excuse yourself**, you use a phrase such as 'Excuse me' as a polite way of saying that you are about to leave. ❑ *He excused himself and went up to his room.* 6 You say **'Excuse me'** when you want to politely get someone's attention, especially when you are about to ask them a question. ❑ *Excuse me, but are you Mr Honig?* 7 You use **excuse me** to apologize to someone when you have disturbed or interrupted them. ❑ *Excuse me interrupting, but there's a thing I feel I've got to say.* 8 You use **excuse me** or a phrase such as **if you'll excuse me** as a polite way of indicating that you are about to leave or that you are about to stop talking to someone. ❑ *'Excuse me,' she said to Jarvis, and left the room... Now if you'll excuse me, I've got work to do.* 9 You use **excuse me, but** to indicate that you are about to disagree with someone. [mainly BRIT] ❑ *Excuse me, but I want to know what all this has to do with us.* 10 You say **excuse me** to apologize when you have bumped into someone, or when you need to move past someone in a crowd. 11 You say **excuse me** to apologize when you have done something slightly embarrassing or impolite, such as burping, hiccupping, or sneezing. 12 You say **'Excuse me?'** to show that you want someone to repeat what they have just said. [AM]

N-COUNT: oft N for n/-ing, N to-inf = justification | PHRASE: v-link PHR, oft PHR for n/-ing [disapproval] | VERB = justify | V n by -ing | V n | VERB = forgive | V n for n/-ing | VERB: usu passive | be V-ed from n/-ing | be V-ed n | VERB | V pron-refl | CONVENTION [formulae] | CONVENTION [formulae] | CONVENTION [politeness] | CONVENTION | CONVENTION [formulae] = sorry | CONVENTION [formulae] | CONVENTION [formulae]

✔ in BRIT, usually use **pardon, sorry**

**ex-directory** If a person or their telephone number is **ex-directory**, the number is not listed in the telephone directory, and the telephone company will not give it to people who ask for it. [BRIT]

ADJ

✔ in AM, use **unlisted**

**exec** /ɪgzek/ **(execs) Exec** is an abbreviation for **executive**. N-COUNT

**ex|ecrable** /eksɪkrəbᵊl/ If you describe something as **execrable**, you mean that it is very bad or unpleasant. [FORMAL] ❑ *Accusing us of being disloyal to cover his own sorry behavior is truly execrable. ...an execrable meal.* ADJ = *deplorable*

**ex|ecute** /eksɪkjuːt/ **(executes, executing, executed)** ◆◇◇ 1 To **execute** someone means to kill them as a punishment for a serious crime. ❑ *He was executed by lethal injection earlier today... One group claimed to have executed the American hostage... This boy's father had been executed for conspiring against the throne.* ♦ **ex|ecu|tion** /eksɪkjuːʃᵊn/ **(executions)** *Execution by lethal injection is scheduled for July 30th.* 2 If you **execute** a plan, you carry it out. [FORMAL] ❑ *We are going to execute our campaign plan to the letter.* ♦ **ex|ecu|tion** *US forces are fully prepared for the execution of any action once the order is given by the president.* 3 If you **execute** a difficult action or movement, you successfully perform it. ❑ *The landing was skilfully executed.* 4 When someone **executes** a work of art, they make or produce it, using an idea as a basis. ❑ *Morris executed a suite of twelve drawings in 1978... A well-executed shot of a tall ship is a joy to behold.* ♦ **ex|ecu|tion** *The ideas in the show's presentation were good, but failed in execution.* VERB *be* V-ed, V n, *be* V-ed *for* n/-ing, N-VAR, VERB, V n, N-UNCOUNT, VERB, V n, VERB, V n, V-ed, N-UNCOUNT

**ex|ecu|tion|er** /eksɪkjuːʃənəʳ/ **(executioners)** An **executioner** is a person who has the job of executing criminals. N-COUNT

**ex|ecu|tive** /ɪgzekjʊtɪv/ **(executives)** ◆◆◇ 1 An **executive** is someone who is employed by a business at a senior level. Executives decide what the business should do, and ensure that it is done. ❑ *...an advertising executive. ...Her husband is a senior bank executive.* 2 The **executive** sections and tasks of an organization are concerned with the making of decisions and with ensuring that decisions are carried out. ❑ *A successful job search needs to be as well organised as any other executive task... I don't envisage I will take an executive role, but rather become a consultant on merchandise and marketing.* 3 **Executive** goods are expensive goods designed or intended for executives and other people at a similar social or economic level. ❑ *...an executive briefcase. ...executive cars.* 4 The **executive** committee or board of an organization is a committee within that organization which has the authority to make decisions and ensures that these decisions are carried out. ❑ *He sits on the executive committee that manages Lloyds. ...the executive of the National Union of Students.* 5 **The executive** is the part of the government of a country that is concerned with carrying out decisions or orders, as opposed to the part that makes laws or the part that deals with criminals. ❑ *The government, the executive and the judiciary are supposed to be separate... The matter should be resolved by the executive branch of government.* N-COUNT, ADJ: ADJ n, ADJ: ADJ n, N-SING: *the* N, N n, N-SING: *the* N, N n

**ex|ecu|tor** /ɪgzekjʊtəʳ/ **(executors)** An **executor** is someone whose name you write in your will when you want them to be responsible for dealing with your affairs after your death. [LEGAL] N-COUNT

**ex|egesis** /eksɪdʒiːsɪs/ **(exegeses** /eksɪdʒiːsiːz/**)** An **exegesis** is an explanation and interpretation of a piece of writing, especially a religious piece of writing, after very careful study. [FORMAL] ❑ *...the kind of academic exegesis at which Isaacs excels. ...a substantial exegesis of his work.* N-VAR: usu with supp, oft N *of* n

**ex|em|plar** /ɪgzemplɑːʳ/ **(exemplars)** 1 An **exemplar** is someone or something that is considered to be so good that they should be copied or imitated. [FORMAL] ❑ *They viewed their new building as an exemplar of taste.* 2 An **exemplar** is a typical example of a group or class of things. [FORMAL] ❑ *One of the wittiest exemplars of the technique was M. C. Escher.* N-COUNT: oft N *of* n = *example*, N-COUNT: oft N *of* n

**ex|em|pla|ry** /ɪgzempləri/ 1 If you describe someone or something as **exemplary**, you think they are extremely good. ❑ *Underpinning this success has been an exemplary record of innovation.* 2 An **exemplary** punishment is unusually harsh and is intended to stop other people from committing similar crimes. ❑ *He demanded exemplary sentences for those behind the violence.* ADJ: usu ADJ n, ADJ: usu ADJ n

**ex|em|pli|fy** /ɪgzemplɪfaɪ/ **(exemplifies, exemplifying, exemplified)** If a person or thing **exemplifies** something such as a situation, quality, or class of things, they are a typical example of it. [FORMAL] ❑ *The room's style exemplifies Conran's ideal of 'beauty and practicality'.* VERB, V n

**ex|empt** /ɪgzempt/ **(exempts, exempting, exempted)** 1 If someone or something is **exempt from** a particular rule, duty, or obligation, they do not have to follow it or do it. ❑ *Men in college were exempt from military service.* 2 To **exempt** a person or thing **from** a particular rule, duty, or obligation means to state officially that they are not bound or affected by it. ❑ *South Carolina claimed the power to exempt its citizens from the obligation to obey federal law.* ♦ **ex|emp|tion** /ɪgzempʃᵊn/ **(exemptions)** *...the exemption of employer-provided health insurance from taxation.* ADJ: usu v-link ADJ, usu ADJ *from* n, VERB, V n *from* n, N-VAR: oft N *from* n

**ex|er|cise** /eksəʳsaɪz/ **(exercises, exercising, exercised)** ◆◆◇ 1 If you **exercise** something such as your authority, your rights, or a good quality, you use it or put it into effect. [FORMAL] ❑ *They are merely exercising their right to free speech... Britain has warned travellers to exercise prudence and care.* ♦ **Exercise** is also a noun. ❑ *...the exercise of political and economic power... Leadership does not rest on the exercise of force alone.* 2 When you **exercise**, you move your body energetically in order to get fit and to remain healthy. ❑ *She exercises two or three times a week... Exercising the body does a great deal to improve one's health.* ♦ **Exercise** is also a noun. ❑ *Lack of exercise can lead to feelings of depression and exhaustion.* 3 If a movement or activity **exercises** a part of your body, it keeps it strong, healthy, or in good condition. ❑ *They call rowing the perfect sport. It exercises every major muscle group.* 4 **Exercises** are a series of movements or actions which you do in order to get fit, remain healthy, or practise for a particular physical activity. ❑ *I do special neck and shoulder exercises.* 5 **Exercises** are military activities and operations which are not part of a real war, but which allow the armed forces to practise for a real war. ❑ *General Powell predicted that in the future it might even be possible to stage joint military exercises.* 6 An **exercise** is a short activity or piece of work that you do, for example in school, which is designed to help you learn a particular skill. ❑ *Try working through the opening exercises in this chapter.* 7 If you describe an activity as an **exercise in** a particular quality or result, you mean that it has that quality or result, especially when it was not intended to have it. ❑ *As an exercise in stating the obvious, this could scarcely be faulted... Think what a waste of taxpayers' money the whole exercise was.* 8 If something **exercises** you or your mind, you think or talk about it a great deal, especially because you are worried or concerned about it. ❑ *This has been a major problem exercising the minds of scientists around the world.* VERB, V n, V n, N-SING: N *of* n, VERB, V, V n, N-UNCOUNT, VERB, V n, N-COUNT: usu pl, N-COUNT: usu pl, also *on* N, N-COUNT, N-COUNT: usu sing, usu N *in* n/-ing, VERB, V n

**ex|er|cise bike** **(exercise bikes)** An **exercise bike** is a special bicycle which does not move, so that you can exercise on it at home or at a gym. N-COUNT

**ex|er|cise book** **(exercise books)** An **exercise book** is a small book that students use for writing in. [mainly BRIT] N-COUNT

✔ in AM, usually use **notebook**

**ex|ert** /ɪgzɜːʳt/ **(exerts, exerting, exerted)** 1 If someone or something **exerts** influence, authority, or pressure, they use it in a strong or determined way, especially in order to produce a particular effect. [FORMAL] ❑ *He exerted considerable influence on the thinking of the scientific community on these issues.* 2 If you **exert yourself**, you make a VERB, V n, VERB

great physical or mental effort, or work hard to do something. ❑ *Do not exert yourself unnecessarily.*
V pron-refl
♦ **ex|er|tion (exertions)** *He clearly found the physical exertion exhilarating.*
N-UNCOUNT: also N in pl

**ex|fo|li|ate** /eksfoʊlieɪt/ **(exfoliates, exfoliating, exfoliated)** To **exfoliate** your skin means to remove the dead cells from its surface using something such as a brush or a special cream. ❑ *Exfoliate your back and legs at least once a week.*
VERB
V n
Also V
♦ **ex|fo|li|at|ing** *...a gentle exfoliating cream.*
ADJ
♦ **ex|fo|lia|tion** /eksfoʊlieɪʃᵊn/ *There is little doubt that skin does benefit from exfoliation.*
N-UNCOUNT

**ex gra|tia** /eks greɪʃə/ An **ex gratia** payment is one that is given as a favour or gift and not because it is legally necessary. [mainly BRIT, FORMAL]
ADJ: usu ADJ n

**ex|hale** /eksheɪl/ **(exhales, exhaling, exhaled)** When you **exhale**, you breathe out the air that is in your lungs. [FORMAL] ❑ *Hold your breath for a moment and exhale... Wade exhaled a cloud of smoke and coughed.*
VERB
= breathe out
≠ inhale
V
V n
♦ **ex|ha|la|tion** /ekshəleɪʃᵊn/ **(exhalations)** *Milton let out his breath in a long exhalation.*
N-VAR

**ex|haust** /ɪgzɔːst/ **(exhausts, exhausting, exhausted)** 1 If something **exhausts** you, it makes you so tired, either physically or mentally, that you have no energy left. ❑ *Don't exhaust him.*
◆◇◇
VERB
V n
♦ **ex|haust|ed** *She was too exhausted and distressed to talk about the tragedy.*
ADJ
= worn out
♦ **ex|haust|ing** *It was an exhausting schedule she had set herself.*
ADJ
= gruelling
2 If you **exhaust** something such as money or food, you use or finish it all. ❑ *We have exhausted all our material resources... They said that food supplies were almost exhausted.*
VERB
V n
V-ed
3 If you **have exhausted** a subject or topic, you have talked about it so much that there is nothing more to say about it. ❑ *She and Chantal must have exhausted the subject of babies and clothes.*
VERB
V n
4 The **exhaust** or the **exhaust pipe** is the pipe which carries the gas out of the engine of a vehicle. [mainly BRIT] ➔ See picture on page 1707.
N-COUNT
5 **Exhaust** is the gas or steam that is produced when the engine of a vehicle is running. ❑ *...the exhaust from a car engine... The city's streets are filthy and choked with exhaust fumes.*
N-UNCOUNT: also N in pl

**ex|haus|tion** /ɪgzɔːstʃᵊn/ **Exhaustion** is the state of being so tired that you have no energy left. ❑ *Staff say he is suffering from exhaustion.*
N-UNCOUNT

**ex|haus|tive** /ɪgzɔːstɪv/ If you describe a study, search, or list as **exhaustive**, you mean that it is very thorough and complete. ❑ *This is by no means an exhaustive list but it gives an indication of the many projects taking place.*
ADJ
= comprehensive
♦ **ex|haust|ive|ly** *Hawley said these costs were scrutinised exhaustively by independent accountants.*
ADV: usu ADV with v, also ADV adj

**ex|hib|it** /ɪgzɪbɪt/ **(exhibits, exhibiting, exhibited)** 1 If someone or something shows a particular quality, feeling, or type of behaviour, you can say that they **exhibit** it. [FORMAL] ❑ *He has exhibited symptoms of anxiety and overwhelming worry.*
VERB
= show
V n
2 When a painting, sculpture, or object of interest **is exhibited**, it is put in a public place such as a museum or art gallery so that people can come to look at it. You can also say that animals **are exhibited** in a zoo. ❑ *His work was exhibited in the best galleries in America, Europe and Asia.*
VERB: usu passive
be V-ed
♦ **ex|hi|bi|tion** *Five large pieces of the wall are currently on exhibition in London.*
N-UNCOUNT: usu for/on N
3 When artists **exhibit**, they show their work in public. ❑ *By 1936 she was exhibiting at the Royal Academy.*
VERB
V
4 An **exhibit** is a painting, sculpture, or object of interest that is displayed to the public in a museum or art gallery. ❑ *Shona showed me round the exhibits.*
N-COUNT
5 An **exhibit** is a public display of paintings, sculpture, or objects of interest, for example in a museum or art gallery. [AM] ❑ *...an exhibit at the Metropolitan Museum of Art.*
N-COUNT

✔ in BRIT, use **exhibition**

6 An **exhibit** is an object that a lawyer shows in court as evidence in a legal case.
N-COUNT

**ex|hi|bi|tion** /eksɪbɪʃᵊn/ **(exhibitions)** 1 An **exhibition** is a public event at which pictures, sculptures, or other objects of interest are displayed, for example at a museum or art gallery. ❑ *...an exhibition of expressionist art.*
◆◇◇
N-COUNT
2 An **exhibition of** a particular skilful activity is a display or example of it that people notice or admire. ❑ *He responded in champion's style by treating the fans to an exhibition of power and speed.*
N-SING: N of n
= display
3 ➔ See also **exhibit**.

**ex|hi|bi|tion|ism** /eksɪbɪʃənɪzəm/ **Exhibitionism** is behaviour that tries to get people's attention all the time, and especially behaviour that most people think is silly. ❑ *There is an element of exhibitionism in the parents' performance too.*
N-UNCOUNT
disapproval

**ex|hi|bi|tion|ist** /eksɪbɪʃənɪst/ **(exhibitionists)** An **exhibitionist** is someone who tries to get people's attention all the time by behaving in a way that most people think is silly.
N-COUNT
disapproval

**ex|hibi|tor** /ɪgzɪbɪtəʳ/ **(exhibitors)** An **exhibitor** is a person whose work is being shown in an exhibition. ❑ *Schedules will be sent out to all exhibitors.*
N-COUNT

**ex|hila|rat|ed** /ɪgzɪləreɪtɪd/ If you are **exhilarated by** something, it makes you feel very happy and excited. [FORMAL] ❑ *He felt strangely exhilarated by the brisk, blue morning.*
ADJ: usu v-link ADJ

**ex|hil|arat|ing** /ɪgzɪləreɪtɪŋ/ If you describe an experience or feeling as **exhilarating**, you mean that it makes you feel very happy and excited. ❑ *It was exhilarating to be on the road again and his spirits rose. ...in the exhilarating days of German unification.*
ADJ

**ex|hila|ra|tion** /ɪgzɪləreɪʃᵊn/ **Exhilaration** is a strong feeling of excitement and happiness.
N-UNCOUNT

**ex|hort** /ɪgzɔːʳt/ **(exhorts, exhorting, exhorted)** If you **exhort** someone **to** do something, you try hard to persuade or encourage them to do it. [FORMAL] ❑ *Kennedy exhorted his listeners to turn away from violence... He exhorted his companions, 'Try to accomplish your aim with diligence'.*
VERB
= urge
V n to-inf
V n with quote
♦ **ex|hor|ta|tion** /egzɔːʳteɪʃᵊn/ **(exhortations)** *Foreign funds alone are clearly not enough, nor are exhortations to reform.*
N-VAR

**ex|hume** /ekshjuːm, AM ɪgzuːm/ **(exhumes, exhuming, exhumed)** If a dead person's body **is exhumed**, it is taken out of the ground where it is buried, especially so that it can be examined in order to find out how the person died. [FORMAL] ❑ *His remains have been exhumed from a cemetery in Queen's, New York City.*
VERB: usu passive
be V-ed
♦ **ex|hu|ma|tion** /egzjuːmeɪʃᵊn/ **(exhumations)** *Detectives ordered the exhumation when his wife said she believed he had been killed.*
N-VAR

**exi|gen|cy** /eksɪdʒᵊnsi/ **(exigencies)** The **exigencies of** a situation or a job are the demands or difficulties that you have to deal with as part of it. [FORMAL] ❑ *...the exigencies of a wartime economy.*
N-COUNT: usu pl, usu N of n

**ex|ile** /eksaɪl, egz-/ **(exiles, exiling, exiled)** 1 If someone is living **in exile**, they are living in a foreign country because they cannot live in their own country, usually for political reasons. ❑ *He is now living in exile in Egypt... He returned from exile earlier this year. ...after nearly six years of exile... During his exile, he also began writing books.*
◆◇◇
N-UNCOUNT: usu prep N
2 If someone **is exiled**, they are living in a foreign country because they cannot live in their own country, usually for political reasons. ❑ *His wife had been widowed, then exiled from South Africa... They threatened to exile her in southern Spain. ...Haiti's exiled president.*
VERB
be V-ed from n
V n
V-ed
3 An **exile** is someone who has been exiled.
N-COUNT
4 If you say that someone **has been exiled from** a particular place or situation, you mean that they have been sent away from it or removed from it against their will. ❑ *He has been exiled from the first team and forced to play in third team matches.*
VERB: usu passive
= banish
be V-ed from n
♦ **Exile** is also a noun. ❑ *Rovers lost 4-1 and began their long exile from the First Division.*
N-UNCOUNT: oft N from n

**ex|ist** /ɪgzɪst/ **(exists, existing, existed)** 1 If something **exists**, it is present in the world as a real thing. ❑ *He thought that if he couldn't see something, it didn't exist... Research opportunities exist in a wide range of pure and applied areas of entomology.* 2 To **exist** means to live, especially under difficult conditions or with very little food or money. ❑ *I was barely existing. ...the problems of having to exist on unemployment benefit.* ◆◆◇ VERB: no cont V V VERB V V *on* n

**ex|ist|ence** /ɪgzɪstəns/ **(existences)** 1 The **existence** of something is the fact that it is present in the world as a real thing. ❑ *...the existence of other galaxies... The Congress of People's Deputies in effect voted itself out of existence... Public worries about accidents are threatening the very existence of the nuclear power industry.* 2 You can refer to someone's way of life as an **existence**, especially when they live under difficult conditions. ❑ *You may be stuck with a miserable existence for the rest of your life.* ◆◇◇ N-UNCOUNT: usu with supp N-COUNT: with supp

**ex|ist|ent** /ɪgzɪstənt/ You can describe something as **existent** when it exists. [FORMAL] ❑ *Their remedy lay within the range of existent technology.* → See also **non-existent**. ADJ = existing

**ex|is|ten|tial** /egzɪstenʃᵊl/ 1 **Existential** means relating to human existence and experience. [FORMAL] ❑ *Existential questions requiring religious answers still persist.* 2 You use **existential** to describe fear, anxiety, and other feelings that are caused by thinking about human existence and death. [FORMAL] ❑ *'What if there's nothing left at all?' he cries, lost in some intense existential angst.* ADJ: ADJ n ADJ: ADJ n

**ex|is|ten|tial|ism** /egzɪstenʃəlɪzəm/ **Existentialism** is a philosophy which stresses the importance of human experience, and says that everyone is responsible for the results of their own actions. [TECHNICAL] N-UNCOUNT

**ex|is|ten|tial|ist** /egzɪstenʃəlɪst/ **(existentialists)** 1 An **existentialist** is a person who agrees with the philosophy of existentialism. 2 If you describe a person or their philosophy as **existentialist**, you mean that their beliefs are based on existentialism. ❑ *...existentialist theories.* N-COUNT ADJ

**ex|ist|ing** /ɪgzɪstɪŋ/ **Existing** is used to describe something which is now present, available, or in operation, especially when you are contrasting it with something which is planned for the future. ❑ *...the need to improve existing products and develop new lines... Existing timbers are replaced or renewed.* ◆◇◇ ADJ: ADJ n

**exit** /egzɪt, eksɪt/ **(exits, exiting, exited)** 1 The **exit** is the door through which you can leave a public building. ❑ *He picked up the case and walked towards the exit... There's a fire exit by the downstairs ladies room.* 2 An **exit** on a motorway or highway is a place where traffic can leave it. ❑ *Take the A422 exit at Old Stratford.* 3 If you refer to someone's **exit**, you are referring to the way that they left a room or building, or the fact that they left it. [FORMAL] ❑ *I made a hasty exit and managed to open the gate.* 4 If you refer to someone's **exit**, you are referring to the way that they left a situation or activity, or the fact that they left it. [FORMAL] ❑ *...after England's exit from the European Championship... They suggested that she make a dignified exit in the interest of the party.* 5 If you **exit** from a room or building, you leave it. [FORMAL] ❑ *She exits into the tropical storm... As I exited the final display, I entered a hexagonal room... She walked into the front door of a store and exited from the rear.* 6 If you **exit** a computer program or system, you stop running it. [COMPUTING] ❑ *I can open other applications without having to exit WordPerfect.* ♦ **Exit** is also a noun. ❑ *Press Exit to return to your document.* N-COUNT N-COUNT: with supp N-COUNT: usu adj N = departure N-COUNT: oft N *from* n = departure VERB V V n V *from* n VERB V n N-SING

**exit visa** **(exit visas)** An **exit visa** is an official stamp in someone's passport, or an official document, which allows them to leave the country that they are visiting or living in. N-COUNT

**exo|dus** /eksədəs/ If there is an **exodus of** people from a place, a lot of people leave that place at the same time. ❑ *The medical system is facing collapse because of an exodus of doctors.* N-SING: oft N *of* n

**ex of|fi|cio** /eks ɒfɪʃiou/ **Ex officio** is used to describe something such as a rank or privilege that someone is entitled to because of the job or position they have. [FORMAL] ❑ *...ex officio members of the Advisory Council. ...an ex-officio degree.* ADJ: ADJ n

**ex|on|er|ate** /ɪgzɒnəreɪt/ **(exonerates, exonerating, exonerated)** If a court, report, or person in authority **exonerates** someone, they officially say or show that that person is not responsible for something wrong or unpleasant that has happened. [FORMAL] ❑ *The official report basically exonerated everyone... An investigation exonerated the school from any blame.* ♦ **ex|on|era|tion** /ɪgzɒnəreɪʃᵊn/ *They expected complete exoneration for their clients.* VERB V n V n *from* n N-UNCOUNT

**ex|or|bi|tant** /ɪgzɔːʳbɪtənt/ If you describe something such as a price or fee as **exorbitant**, you are emphasizing that it is much greater than it should be. ❑ *Exorbitant housing prices have created an acute shortage of affordable housing for the poor.* ♦ **ex|or|bi|tant|ly** *...exorbitantly high salaries.* ADJ emphasis = excessive ADV

**ex|or|cism** /eksɔːʳsɪzəm/ **(exorcisms)** **Exorcism** is the removing of evil spirits from a person or place by the use of prayer. ❑ *The exorcism was broadcast on television.* N-VAR

**ex|or|cist** /eksɔːʳsɪst/ **(exorcists)** An **exorcist** is someone who performs exorcisms. N-COUNT

**ex|or|cize** /eksɔːʳsaɪz/ **(exorcizes, exorcizing, exorcized)**

in BRIT, also use **exorcise**

1 If you **exorcize** a painful or unhappy memory, you succeed in removing it from your mind. ❑ *He confronted his childhood trauma and tried to exorcise the pain.* 2 To **exorcize** an evil spirit or to **exorcize** a place or person means to force the spirit to leave the place or person by means of prayers and religious ceremonies. ❑ *They came to our house and exorcised me.* VERB V n VERB V n

**ex|ot|ic** /ɪgzɒtɪk/ Something that is **exotic** is unusual and interesting, usually because it comes from or is related to a distant country. ❑ *...brilliantly coloured, exotic flowers... She flits from one exotic location to another.* ♦ **ex|oti|cal|ly** *...exotically beautiful scenery.* ADJ ADV

**ex|oti|ca** /ɪgzɒtɪkə/ You use **exotica** to refer to objects which you think are unusual and interesting, usually because they come from or are related to a distant country. N-PLURAL

**ex|oti|cism** /ɪgzɒtɪsɪzəm/ **Exoticism** is the quality of seeming unusual or interesting, usually because of associations with a distant country. N-UNCOUNT

**ex|pand** /ɪkspænd/ **(expands, expanding, expanded)** 1 If something **expands** or **is expanded**, it becomes larger. ❑ *Engineers noticed that the pipes were not expanding as expected... We have to expand the size of the image. ...a rapidly expanding universe. ...strips of expanded polystyrene.* 2 If something such as a business, organization, or service **expands**, or if you **expand** it, it becomes bigger and includes more people, goods, or activities. [BUSINESS] ❑ *The popular ceramics industry expanded towards the middle of the 19th century... Health officials are proposing to expand their services by organising counselling.* ◆◇◇ VERB V V n V-ing V-ed VERB V V n

♦ **expand on** or **expand upon** If you **expand on** or **expand upon** something, you give more information or details about it when you write or talk about it. ❑ *The president used today's speech to expand on remarks he made last month.* PHRASAL VERB V P n

**ex|panse** /ɪkspæns/ **(expanses)** An **expanse of** something, usually sea, sky, or land, is a very large amount of it. ❑ *...a vast expanse of grassland.* N-COUNT: usu N *of* n

**ex|pan|sion** /ɪkspænʃᵊn/ **(expansions)** **Expansion** is the process of becoming greater in size, number, or amount. ❑ *...the rapid expansion of private health insurance. ...a new period of economic expansion.* ◆◇◇ N-VAR: oft N *of* n = growth

**ex|pan|sion|ary** /ɪkspænʃənri/ 1 **Expansionary** economic policies are intended to expand the economy of a country. [ADJ: usu ADJ n] 2 **Expansionary** policies or actions are intended to increase the amount of land that a particular country rules. [ADJ: usu ADJ n] [disapproval] ❑ *...America's concerns about Soviet expansionary objectives.*

**ex|pan|sion|ism** /ɪkspænʃənɪzəm/ If you refer to a country's **expansionism**, you disapprove of its policy of increasing its land or power. [N-UNCOUNT] [disapproval] ❑ *Soviet expansionism was considered a real threat.*

**ex|pan|sion|ist** /ɪkspænʃənɪst/ If you describe a country or organization as **expansionist**, you disapprove of it because it has a policy of increasing its land or power. [ADJ] [disapproval] ❑ *...the intended victim of his expansionist foreign policy.*

**ex|pan|sive** /ɪkspænsɪv/ 1 If something is **expansive**, it covers or includes a large area or many things. [FORMAL] [ADJ: ADJ n] ❑ *...an expansive grassy play area... They have played an expansive style of rugby.* 2 If you are **expansive**, you talk a lot, or are friendly or generous, because you are feeling happy and relaxed. [ADJ] ❑ *He was becoming more expansive as he relaxed.* ♦ **ex|pan|sive|ly** *'I'm here to make them feel good,' he says expansively.* [ADV: usu ADV with v] 3 If you describe something such as a period of time or an economy as **expansive**, you mean that it is associated with growth or expansion. [ADJ: usu ADJ n] ❑ *An active and expansive market economy is a necessary condition for progress.*

**ex|pat** /ekspæt/ **(expats)** An **expat** is the same as an **expatriate**. [BRIT, INFORMAL] [N-COUNT]

**ex|pat|ri|ate** /ekspætriət, -peɪt-/ **(expatriates)** An **expatriate** is someone who is living in a country which is not their own. [N-COUNT] ❑ *...British expatriates in Spain.* ♦ **Expatriate** is also an adjective. [ADJ: ADJ n] ❑ *The French military is preparing to evacuate women and children of expatriate families.*

**ex|pect** /ɪkspekt/ **(expects, expecting, expected)** ◆◆◆ 1 If you **expect** something **to** happen, you believe that it will happen. [VERB] ❑ *...a council workman who expects to lose his job in the next few weeks...* [V to-inf] *The talks are expected to continue until tomorrow...* [V n to-inf] *Few expected that he would declare his candidacy for the Democratic nomination for the presidency...* [V that] *It is expected that the new owner will change the yacht's name...* [it be V-ed that] *They expect a gradual improvement in sales of new cars.* [V n] 2 If you **are expecting** something or someone, you believe that they will be delivered to you or come to you soon, often because this has been arranged earlier. [VERB: usu cont] ❑ *I wasn't expecting a visitor...* [V n] *We were expecting him home again any day now.* [V adv n] 3 If you **expect** something, or **expect** a person **to** do something, you believe that it is your right to have that thing, or the person's duty to do it for you. [VERB] ❑ *He wasn't expecting our hospitality...* [V n] *I do expect to have some time to myself in the evenings...* [V to-inf] *I wasn't expecting you to help...* [V n to-inf] *Is this a rational thing to expect of your partner, or not?...* [V n of n] *She realizes now she expected too much of Helen.* [V amount of n] 4 If you tell someone not to **expect** something, you mean that the thing is unlikely to happen as they have planned or imagined, and they should not hope that it will. [VERB: with brd-neg] ❑ *Don't expect an instant cure...* [V n] *You cannot expect to like all the people you work with...* [V to-inf] *Don't expect me to come and visit you there.* [V n to-inf] 5 If you say that a woman **is expecting** a baby, or that she **is expecting**, you mean that she is pregnant. [VERB: only cont] ❑ *She was expecting another baby...* [V n] *I hear Dawn's expecting again.* [V] 6 You say '**I expect**' to suggest that a statement is probably correct, or a natural consequence of the present situation, although you have no definite knowledge. [SPOKEN] [PHRASE: PHR that, PHR so/not] ❑ *I expect you can guess what follows... I expect you're tired... 'Will Joe be here at Christmas?' — 'I expect so.'.*

**ex|pec|tan|cy** /ɪkspektənsi/ **Expectancy** is the feeling or hope that something exciting, interesting, or good is about to happen. [N-UNCOUNT = anticipation] ❑ *The supporters had a tremendous air of expectancy.* ➔ See also **life expectancy**.

**ex|pec|tant** /ɪkspektənt/ 1 If someone is **expectant**, they are excited because they think something interesting is about to happen. [ADJ] ❑ *An expectant crowd gathered... She turned to me with an expectant look on her face.* ♦ **ex|pect|ant|ly** *The others waited, looking at him expectantly.* [ADV: ADV after v] 2 An **expectant** mother or father is someone whose baby is going to be born soon. [ADJ: ADJ n]

**ex|pec|ta|tion** /ekspekteɪʃən/ **(expectations)** ◆◇◇ 1 Your **expectations** are your strong hopes or beliefs that something will happen or that you will get something that you want. [N-UNCOUNT: also N in pl] ❑ *Students' expectations were as varied as their expertise... The car has been General Motors' most visible success story, with sales far exceeding expectations.* 2 A person's **expectations** are strong beliefs which they have about the proper way someone should behave or something should happen. [N-COUNT: usu pl] ❑ *Stephen Chase had determined to live up to the expectations of the Company.*

**ex|pec|to|rant** /ɪkspektərənt/ **(expectorants)** An **expectorant** is a cough medicine that helps you to cough up mucus from your lungs. [MEDICAL] [N-COUNT]

**ex|pedi|en|cy** /ɪkspiːdiənsi/ **Expediency** means doing what is convenient rather than what is morally right. [FORMAL] [N-UNCOUNT = convenience] ❑ *This was a matter less of morals than of expediency.*

**ex|pedi|ent** /ɪkspiːdiənt/ **(expedients)** 1 An **expedient** is an action that achieves a particular purpose, but may not be morally right. [N-COUNT: usu sing, oft N of -ing] ❑ *Surgical waiting lists were reduced by the simple expedient of striking off all patients awaiting varicose vein operations.* 2 If it is **expedient to** do something, it is useful or convenient to do it, even though it may not be morally right. [ADJ: oft it v-link ADJ to-inf] ❑ *Governments frequently ignore human rights abuses in other countries if it is politically expedient to do so.*

**ex|pedite** /ekspɪdaɪt/ **(expedites, expediting, expedited)** If you **expedite** something, you cause it to be done more quickly. [FORMAL] [VERB = speed up] ❑ *We tried to help you expedite your plans.* [V n]

**ex|pedi|tion** /ekspɪdɪʃən/ **(expeditions)** 1 An **expedition** is an organized journey that is made for a particular purpose such as exploration. [N-COUNT: oft N to n] ❑ *...Byrd's 1928 expedition to Antarctica.* 2 You can refer to a group of people who are going on an expedition as an **expedition**. [N-COUNT] ❑ *Forty-three members of the expedition were killed.* 3 An **expedition** is a short journey or trip that you make for pleasure. [N-COUNT = trip] ❑ *...a fishing expedition.*

**ex|pedi|tion|ary force** /ekspɪdɪʃənri fɔːʳs, AM -neri/ **(expeditionary forces)** An **expeditionary force** is a group of soldiers who are sent to fight in a foreign country. [MILITARY] [N-COUNT]

**ex|pedi|tious** /ekspɪdɪʃəs/ **Expeditious** means quick and efficient. [FORMAL] [ADJ] ❑ *The judge said that arbitration was a fair and expeditious decision-making process.* ♦ **ex|pedi|tious|ly** *The matter has certainly been handled expeditiously by the authorities.* [ADV: ADV with v]

**ex|pel** /ɪkspel/ **(expels, expelling, expelled)** 1 If someone **is expelled from** a school or organization, they are officially told to leave because they have behaved badly. [VERB: usu passive] ❑ *More than five-thousand secondary school students have been expelled for cheating.* [be V-ed] *...a boy expelled from school for making death threats to his teacher.* [V-ed] 2 If people **are expelled from** a place, they are made to leave it, often by force. [VERB] ❑ *An American academic was expelled from the country yesterday...* [be V-ed] *They were told at first that they should simply expel the refugees.* [V n] 3 To **expel** something means to force it out from a container or from your body. [VERB] ❑ *As the lungs exhale this waste, gas is expelled into the atmosphere.* [V n]

**ex|pend** /ɪkspend/ **(expends, expending, expended)** To **expend** something, especially energy, time, or money, means to use it or spend it. [FORMAL] [VERB] ❑ *Children expend a lot of energy and may need more high-energy food than adults.* [V n]

**ex|pend|able** /ɪkspe̲ndəbᵊl/ If you regard someone or something as **expendable**, you think it is acceptable to get rid of them, abandon them, or allow them to be destroyed when they are no longer needed. [FORMAL] ❑ *Once our services cease to be useful to them, we're expendable... During the recession, training budgets were seen as an expendable luxury.* ADJ

**ex|pendi|ture** /ɪkspe̲ndɪtʃəʳ/ **(expenditures)** 1 **Expenditure** is the spending of money on something, or the money that is spent on something. [FORMAL] ❑ *Policies of tax reduction must lead to reduced public expenditure... They should cut their expenditure on defence.* N-VAR 2 **Expenditure of** something such as time or energy is the using of that thing for a particular purpose. [FORMAL] ❑ *The financial rewards justified the expenditure of effort.* N-UNCOUNT: N *of* n

**ex|pense** /ɪkspe̲ns/ **(expenses)** ◆◇◇ 1 **Expense** is the money that something costs you or that you need to spend in order to do something. ❑ *He's bought a specially big TV at vast expense so that everyone can see properly... It was not a fortune but would help to cover household expenses.* N-VAR
2 **Expenses** are amounts of money that you spend while doing something in the course of your work, which will be paid back to you afterwards. [BUSINESS] ❑ *As a member of the International Olympic Committee her fares and hotel expenses were paid by the IOC... Can you claim this back on expenses?* N-PLURAL: oft poss N
**PHRASES** 3 If you do something **at** someone's **expense**, they provide the money for it. ❑ *Should architects continue to be trained for five years at public expense?* PHRASE: PHR after v 4 If someone laughs or makes a joke **at** your **expense**, they do it to make you seem foolish. ❑ *I think he's having fun at our expense.* PHRASE: PHR after v 5 If you achieve something **at the expense of** someone, you do it in a way which might cause them some harm or disadvantage. ❑ *According to this study, women have made notable gains at the expense of men.* PHRASE: PHR after v, PHR n 6 If you say that someone does something **at the expense of** another thing, you are expressing concern at the fact that they are not doing the second thing, because the first thing uses all their resources. ❑ *The orchestra has more discipline now, but at the expense of spirit.* PHRASE: PHR after v, PHR n [disapproval] 7 If you **go to the expense of** doing something, you do something which costs a lot of money. If you **go to** great **expense to** do something, you spend a lot of money in order to achieve it. ❑ *Why go to the expense of buying an electric saw when you can hire one?* PHRASE: V inflects, oft PHR *of* -ing, PHR to-inf

**ex|pense ac|count (expense accounts)** An **expense account** is an arrangement between an employer and an employee which allows the employee to spend the company's money on things relating to their job, for example travelling or looking after clients. [BUSINESS] ❑ *He put Elizabeth's motel bill and airfare on his expense account. ...expense account lunches.* N-COUNT

**ex|pen|sive** /ɪkspe̲nsɪv/ If something is **expensive**, it costs a lot of money. ❑ *Wine's so expensive in this country... I get very nervous because I'm using a lot of expensive equipment.* ◆◆◇ ADJ = costly ≠ inexpensive ♦ **ex|pen|sive|ly** *She was expensively dressed, with fine furs and jewels.* ADV: ADV -ed, ADV after v ≠ cheaply

**ex|peri|ence** /ɪkspɪ̲əriəns/ **(experiences, experiencing, experienced)** ◆◆◆ 1 **Experience** is knowledge or skill in a particular job or activity, which you have gained because you have done that job or activity for a long time. ❑ *He has also had managerial experience on every level... He's counting on his mother to take care of the twins for him; she's had plenty of experience with them.* → See also **work experience**. N-UNCOUNT: usu with supp 2 **Experience** is used to refer to the past events, knowledge, and feelings that make up someone's life or character. ❑ *I should not be in any danger here, but experience has taught me caution... She had learned from experience to take little rests in between her daily routine.* N-UNCOUNT 3 An **experience** is something that you do or that happens to you, especially something important that affects you. ❑ *His only experience of gardening so far proved immensely satisfying... Many of his clients are unbelievably nervous, usually because of a bad experience in the past.* N-COUNT: usu with supp 4 If you **experience** a particular situation, you are in that situation or it happens to you. ❑ *We had never experienced this kind of holiday before and had no idea what to expect.* VERB V n 5 If you **experience** a feeling, you feel it or are affected by it. ❑ *Widows seem to experience more distress than do widowers.* ♦ **Experience** is also a noun. ❑ *...the experience of pain.* VERB V n N-SING: *the* N *of* n

**ex|pe|ri|enced** /ɪkspɪ̲əriənst/ If you describe someone as **experienced**, you mean that they have been doing a particular job or activity for a long time, and therefore know a lot about it or are very skilful at it. ❑ *...lawyers who are experienced in these matters... It's a team packed with experienced and mature professionals.* ADJ: oft ADJ *in* n/-ing

**ex|peri|en|tial** /ɪkspɪ̲əriẹnʃᵊl/ **Experiential** means relating to or resulting from experience. [FORMAL] ❑ *Learning has got to be active and experiential.* ADJ

**ex|peri|ment (experiments, experimenting, experimented)** ◆◇◇

> The noun is pronounced /ɪkspe̲rɪmənt/. The verb is pronounced /ɪkspe̲rɪment/.

1 An **experiment** is a scientific test which is done in order to discover what happens to something in particular conditions. ❑ *The astronauts are conducting a series of experiments to learn more about how the body adapts to weightlessness... This question can be answered only by experiment.* N-VAR 2 If you **experiment with** something or **experiment on** it, you do a scientific test on it in order to discover what happens to it in particular conditions. ❑ *In 1857 Mendel started experimenting with peas in his monastery garden... The scientists have already experimented at each other's test sites.* VERB V *with/on* n V ♦ **ex|peri|men|ta|tion** /ɪkspe̲rɪmenteɪ̲ʃᵊn/ *...the ethical aspects of animal experimentation.* N-UNCOUNT ♦ **ex|peri|ment|er (experimenters)** *When the experimenters repeated the tests on themselves, they observed an exactly opposite effect.* N-COUNT 3 An **experiment** is the trying out of a new idea or method in order to see what it is like and what effects it has. ❑ *As an experiment, we bought Ted a watch.* N-VAR
4 To **experiment** means to try out a new idea or method to see what it is like and what effects it has. ❑ *...if you like cooking and have the time to experiment... He believes that students should be encouraged to experiment with bold ideas.* VERB V V *with* n ♦ **ex|peri|men|ta|tion** *Decentralization and experimentation must be encouraged.* N-UNCOUNT

**ex|peri|men|tal** /ɪkspe̲rɪme̲ntᵊl/
1 Something that is **experimental** is new or uses new ideas or methods, and might be modified later if it is unsuccessful. ❑ *...an experimental air conditioning system... The technique is experimental, but the list of its practitioners is growing.* ADJ 2 **Experimental** means using, used in, or resulting from scientific experiments. ❑ *...the main techniques of experimental science.* ADJ: ADJ n ♦ **ex|peri|men|tal|ly** *...an ecology laboratory, where communities of species can be studied experimentally under controlled conditions.* ADV: ADV with v 3 An **experimental** action is done in order to see what it is like, or what effects it has. ❑ *The British Sports Minister is reported to be ready to argue for an experimental lifting of the ban.* ADJ: usu ADJ n ♦ **ex|peri|men|tal|ly** *This system is being tried out experimentally at many universities.* ADV: ADV with v

**ex|pert** /e̲kspɜːʳt/ **(experts)** ◆◆◇ 1 An **expert** is a person who is very skilled at doing something or who knows a lot about a particular subject. ❑ *...a yoga expert. ...an expert on trade in that area.* N-COUNT: oft n N, N *on* n = specialist
2 Someone who is **expert at** doing something is very skilled at it. ❑ *The Japanese are expert at lowering manufacturing costs.* ADJ: oft ADJ *at* -ing ♦ **ex|pert|ly** *Shopkeepers expertly rolled spices up in bay leaves.* ADV: ADV with v 3 If you say ADJ: ADJ n

that someone has **expert** hands or an **expert** eye, you mean that they are very skilful or experienced in using their hands or eyes for a particular purpose. ❑ *When the horse suffered a back injury Harvey cured it with his own expert hands.* [4] **Expert** advice or help is given by someone who has studied a subject thoroughly or who is very skilled at a particular job. ❑ *We'll need an expert opinion.* ADJ: ADJ n

**ex|per|tise** /ekspɜːʳtiːz/ **Expertise** is special skill or knowledge that is acquired by training, study, or practice. ❑ *The problem is that most local authorities lack the expertise to deal sensibly in this market.* N-UNCOUNT

**ex|pi|ate** /ekspieɪt/ **(expiates, expiating, expiated)** If you **expiate** guilty feelings or bad behaviour, you do something to indicate that you are sorry for what you have done. [FORMAL] ❑ *It seemed that Alice was expiating her father's sins with her charity work.* ♦ **ex|pia|tion** /ekspieɪʃᵊn/ *...an often painful process of evaluation and expiation.* VERB; V n; Also V *for* n; N-UNCOUNT

**ex|pi|ra|tion** /ekspɪreɪʃᵊn/ **The expiration of** a fixed period of time is its ending. [FORMAL] ❑ *...a few hours before the expiration of the midnight deadline.* N-UNCOUNT: oft *the* N *of* n

**ex|pire** /ɪkspaɪəʳ/ **(expires, expiring, expired)** When something such as a contract, deadline, or visa **expires**, it comes to an end or is no longer valid. ❑ *He had lived illegally in the United States for five years after his visitor's visa expired.* VERB = *run out*; V

**ex|pi|ry** /ɪkspaɪəri/ The **expiry of** something such as a contract, deadline, or visa is the time that it comes to an end or stops being valid. ❑ *...the expiry of a fixed term contract... Make a note of credit card numbers and check expiry dates.* N-UNCOUNT: oft N *of* n, N n

**ex|plain** /ɪkspleɪn/ **(explains, explaining, explained)** ◆◆◇ [1] If you **explain** something, you give details about it or describe it so that it can be understood. ❑ *Not every judge, however, has the ability to explain the law in simple terms... Don't sign anything until your solicitor has explained the contract to you... Professor Griffiths explained how the drug appears to work... 'He and Mrs Stein have a plan,' she explained... I explained that each person has different ideas of what freedom is.* [2] If you **explain** something that has happened, you give people reasons for it, especially in an attempt to justify it. ❑ *'Let me explain, sir.' — 'Don't tell me about it. I don't want to know.'... Before she ran away, she left a note explaining her actions... Hospital discipline was broken. Amy would have to explain herself... Explain why you didn't telephone... The receptionist apologized for the delay, explaining that it had been a hectic day.* VERB; V n; V n *to* n; V wh; V with quote; V that, Also V, V *to* n that/wh; VERB; V; V n; V pron-refl; V why; V that; Also V n *to* n, V with quote

♦ **explain away** If someone **explains away** a mistake or a bad situation they are responsible for, they try to indicate that it is unimportant or that it is not really their fault. ❑ *He evaded her questions about the war and tried to explain away the atrocities... I had noticed blood on my husband's clothing but he explained it away.* PHRASAL VERB; V P n (not pron); V n P

**ex|pla|na|tion** /ekspləneɪʃᵊn/ **(explanations)** ◆◇◇ [1] If you give an **explanation** of something that has happened, you give people reasons for it, especially in an attempt to justify it. ❑ *She told the court she would give a full explanation of the prosecution's decision on Monday... 'It's my ulcer,' he added by way of explanation.* [2] If you say there is an **explanation for** something, you mean that there is a reason for it. ❑ *The deputy airport manager said there was no apparent explanation for the crash... It's the only explanation I can think of.* [3] If you give an **explanation of** something, you give details about it or describe it so that it can be understood. ❑ *Haig was immediately impressed by Charteris's expertise and by his lucid explanation of the work.* N-COUNT: also *of/in* N; N-COUNT: oft N *for* n = *reason*; N-COUNT: oft N *of* n

**ex|plana|tory** /ɪksplænətəri, AM -tɔːri/ **Explanatory** statements or theories are intended to make people understand something by describing it or giving the reasons for it. [FORMAL] ❑ *These statements are accompanied by a series of explanatory notes.* ADJ: usu ADJ n

**ex|ple|tive** /ɪkspliːtɪv/ **(expletives)** An **expletive** is a rude word or expression such as 'Damn!' which you say when you are annoyed, excited, or in pain. [FORMAL] N-COUNT = *swear word*

**ex|pli|cable** /ɪksplɪkəbᵊl, AM eksplɪk-/ If something is **explicable**, it can be explained and understood because it is logical or sensible. [FORMAL] ❑ *The older I grow, the stranger and less explicable the world appears to me.* ADJ

**ex|pli|cate** /eksplɪkeɪt/ **(explicates, explicating, explicated)** To **explicate** something means to explain it and make it clear. [FORMAL] ❑ *We shall have to explicate its basic assumptions before we can assess its implications.* ♦ **ex|pli|ca|tion** /eksplɪkeɪʃᵊn/ **(explications)** *The jury listened to his impassioned explication of article 306... McKen criticises the lack of explication of what the term 'areas' means.* VERB; V n; N-VAR

**ex|plic|it** /ɪksplɪsɪt/ [1] Something that is **explicit** is expressed or shown clearly and openly, without any attempt to hide anything. ❑ *...sexually explicit scenes in films and books. ...explicit references to age in recruitment advertising.* ♦ **ex|plic|it|ly** *The play was the first commercially successful work dealing explicitly with homosexuality.* ♦ **ex|plic|it|ness** *When the book was published, the energy and explicitness caught the popular imagination.* [2] If you are **explicit about** something, you speak about it very openly and clearly. ❑ *He was explicit about his intention to overhaul the party's internal voting system.* ♦ **ex|plic|it|ly** *She has been talking very explicitly about AIDS to these groups.* ADJ = *overt* ≠ *implicit*; ADV: ADV with v, ADV adj; N-UNCOUNT; ADJ: v-link ADJ, oft ADJ *about* n; ADV: ADV with v

**ex|plode** /ɪkspləʊd/ **(explodes, exploding, exploded)** ◆◇◇ [1] If an object such as a bomb **explodes** or if someone or something **explodes** it, it bursts loudly and with great force, often causing damage or injury. ❑ *They were clearing up when the second bomb exploded... A school bus was hit by gunfire which exploded the fuel tank.* [2] If someone **explodes**, they express strong feelings suddenly and violently. ❑ *Do you fear that you'll burst into tears or explode with anger in front of her?... 'What happened!' I exploded... George caught the look and decided that Bess had better leave before she exploded.* [3] If something **explodes**, it increases suddenly and rapidly in number or intensity. ❑ *The population explodes to 40,000 during the tourist season... Investment by Japanese firms has exploded.* [4] If someone **explodes** a theory or myth, they prove that it is wrong or impossible. ❑ *Electricity privatisation has exploded the myth of cheap nuclear power.* VERB; V; V n; VERB; V *with* n; V with quote; V; VERB; V *to* n; V; VERB; V n

**ex|ploit** **(exploits, exploiting, exploited)** ◆◇◇

> ✓ The verb is pronounced /ɪksplɔɪt/. The noun is pronounced /eksplɔɪt/.

[1] If you say that someone **is exploiting** you, you think that they are treating you unfairly by using your work or ideas and giving you very little in return. ❑ *Critics claim he exploited black musicians for personal gain. ...the plight of the exploited sugar cane workers.* ♦ **ex|ploi|ta|tion** /eksplɔɪteɪʃᵊn/ *Extra payments should be made to protect the interests of the staff and prevent exploitation.* [2] If you say that someone **is exploiting** a situation, you disapprove of them because they are using it to gain an advantage for themselves, rather than trying to help other people or do what is right. ❑ *The government and its opponents compete to exploit the troubles to their advantage.* ♦ **ex|ploi|ta|tion** *...the exploitation of the famine by local politicians.* [3] If you **exploit** something, you use it well, and achieve something or gain an advantage from it. ❑ *Cary is hoping to exploit new opportunities in Europe.* [4] To **exploit** resources or raw materials means to develop them and use them for industry or commercial activities. ❑ *I think we're being very short sighted in not exploiting our own coal.* ♦ **ex|ploi|ta|tion** *...the planned exploitation of its potential oil and natural gas reserves.* [5] If you refer to someone's **ex-** VERB; V n; V-ed; N-UNCOUNT; VERB [disapproval]; V n; N-SING: N *of* n; VERB; V n; VERB; V n; N-UNCOUNT: usu N *of* n; N-COUNT:

**ploits**, you mean the brave, interesting, or amusing things that they have done. ❑ *His wartime exploits were later made into a film.* usu pl, with poss

**ex|ploit|able** /ɪksplɔɪtəbᵊl/ [1] If something is **exploitable**, it can be used or developed to make a profit. ❑ *Exploitable raw materials were in short supply... Of 27 new wells drilled, 16 have proved exploitable.* ADJ [2] An **exploitable** situation can be used by someone to their own advantage. ❑ *Your hope was I'd make some exploitable mistake.* ADJ

**ex|ploita|tive** /ɪksplɔɪtətɪv/ If you describe something as **exploitative**, you disapprove of it because it treats people unfairly by using their work or ideas for its own advantage, and giving them very little in return. [FORMAL] ❑ *The expansion of Western capitalism incorporated the Third World into an exploitative world system.* ADJ disapproval

**ex|ploit|er** /ɪksplɔɪtəʳ/ **(exploiters)** If you refer to people as **exploiters**, you disapprove of them because they exploit other people in an unfair and cruel way. [FORMAL] N-COUNT disapproval

**ex|plora|tory** /ɪksplɒrətri, AM -plɔːrətɔːri/ **Exploratory** actions are done in order to discover something or to learn the truth about something. ❑ *Exploratory surgery revealed her liver cancer.* ADJ

**ex|plore** /ɪksplɔːʳ/ **(explores, exploring, explored)** ◆◇◇ [1] If you **explore** a place, you travel around it to find out what it is like. ❑ *After exploring the old part of town there is a guided tour of the cathedral... We've come to this country, let's explore!* VERB V n V ♦ **ex|plo|ra|tion** /ekspləreɪʃᵊn/ **(explorations)** *We devote several days to the exploration of the magnificent Maya sites of Copan.* N-VAR [2] If you **explore** an idea or suggestion, you think about it or comment on it in detail, in order to assess it carefully. ❑ *The film explores the relationship between artist and instrument.* VERB = investigate V n ♦ **ex|plo|ra|tion** *I looked forward to the exploration of their theories.* N-VAR [3] If people **explore** an area **for** a substance such as oil or minerals, they study the area and do tests on the land to see whether they can find it. ❑ *Central to the operation is a mile-deep well, dug originally to explore for oil.* VERB V *for* n ♦ **ex|plo|ra|tion** *Oryx is a Dallas-based oil and gas exploration and production concern.* N-UNCOUNT [4] If you **explore** something with your hands or fingers, you touch it to find out what it feels like. ❑ *He explored the wound with his finger, trying to establish its extent.* VERB V n

**ex|plor|er** /ɪksplɔːrəʳ/ **(explorers)** An **explorer** is someone who travels to places about which very little is known, in order to discover what is there. N-COUNT

**ex|plo|sion** /ɪksploʊʒᵊn/ **(explosions)** ◆◇◇ [1] An **explosion** is a sudden, violent burst of energy, for example one caused by a bomb. ❑ *After the second explosion, all of London's main train and subway stations were shut down... Three people have been killed in a bomb explosion in northwest Spain.* N-COUNT = blast [2] **Explosion** is the act of deliberately causing a bomb or similar device to explode. ❑ *Bomb disposal experts blew up the bag in a controlled explosion.* N-VAR [3] An **explosion** is a large rapid increase in the number or amount of something. ❑ *The study also forecast an explosion in the diet soft-drink market... The spread of the suburbs has triggered a population explosion among America's deer.* N-COUNT: with supp [4] An **explosion** is a sudden violent expression of someone's feelings, especially anger. ❑ *Every time they met, Myra anticipated an explosion.* N-COUNT = outburst [5] An **explosion** is a sudden and serious political protest or violence. ❑ *...the explosion of protest and violence sparked off by the killing of seven workers.* N-COUNT

**ex|plo|sive** /ɪksploʊsɪv/ **(explosives)** [1] An **explosive** is a substance or device that can cause an explosion. ❑ *...one-hundred-and-fifty pounds of Semtex explosive.* N-VAR [2] Something that is **explosive** is capable of causing an explosion. ❑ *The explosive device was timed to go off at the rush hour.* ADJ ♦ **ex|plo|sive|ly** *Hydrogen is explosively flammable when mixed with oxygen.* ADV: ADV adj, ADV after v [3] An **explosive** growth is a sudden, rapid increase in the size or quantity of something. ❑ *The explosive growth in casinos is one of the most conspicuous signs of Westernisation.* ADJ ♦ **ex|plo|sive|ly** *These transactions grew explosively in the early 1980s.* ADV: ADV after v, ADV adj [4] An **explosive** situation is likely to have difficult, serious, or dangerous effects. ❑ *He appeared to be treating the potentially explosive situation with some sensitivity... Nobody knows what explosive arguments the future of Europe will bring.* ADJ: usu ADJ n ♦ **ex|plo|sive|ly** *A referendum next year would coincide explosively with the election campaign.* ADV: ADV after v [5] If you describe someone as **explosive**, you mean that they tend to express sudden violent anger. ❑ *He's inherited his father's explosive temper.* ADJ = fiery ♦ **ex|plo|sive|ly** *'Are you mad?' David asked explosively.* ADV: ADV after v, ADV adj [6] A sudden loud noise can be described as **explosive**. ❑ *He made a loud, explosive noise of disgust. ...an explosive drumbeat.* ADJ ♦ **ex|plo|sive|ly** *The sound of her own chewing and swallowing were explosively loud.* ADV: ADV adj, ADV after v

**expo** /ekspoʊ/ **(expos)** also **Expo.** An **expo** is a large event where goods, especially industrial goods, are displayed. ❑ *...the 1995 Queensland Computer Expo.* N-COUNT: usu with supp, oft in names

**ex|po|nent** /ɪkspoʊnənt/ **(exponents)** [1] An **exponent of** an idea, theory, or plan is a person who supports and explains it, and who tries to persuade other people that it is a good idea. [FORMAL] ❑ *...a leading exponent of test-tube baby techniques.* N-COUNT: usu N *of* n = advocate [2] An **exponent of** a particular skill or activity is a person who is good at it. ❑ *...the great exponent of expressionist dance, Kurt Jooss.* N-COUNT: with supp

**ex|po|nen|tial** /ekspənenʃᵊl/ **Exponential** means growing or increasing very rapidly. [FORMAL] ❑ *The policy tried to check the exponential growth of public expenditure.* ADJ: usu ADJ n ♦ **ex|po|nen|tial|ly** *The quantity of chemical pollutants has increased exponentially.* ADV: ADV after v

**ex|port** **(exports, exporting, exported)** ◆◆◇

| |
|---|
| ✓ The verb is pronounced /ɪkspɔːʳt/. The noun is pronounced /ekspɔːʳt/. |

[1] To **export** products or raw materials means to sell them to another country. ❑ *The nation also exports beef... They expect the antibiotic products to be exported to Southeast Asia and Africa... To earn foreign exchange we must export.* VERB ≠ import V n *be* V-ed *to* n V ♦ **Export** is also a noun. ❑ *...the production and export of cheap casual wear. ...illegal arms exports.* Also V n *to* n N-UNCOUNT: also N in pl [2] **Exports** are goods which are sold to another country and sent there. ❑ *He did this to promote American exports... Ghana's main export is cocoa.* N-COUNT ≠ import [3] To **export** something means to introduce it into another country or make it happen there. ❑ *It has exported inflation at times. ...hecklers who said the deal would export jobs to Mexico.* VERB ≠ import V n V n *to* n [4] In computing, if you **export** files or information from one type of software into another type, you change their format so that they can be used in the new software. ❑ *Files can be exported in ASCII or PCX formats.* VERB ≠ import *be* V-ed Also V n

**ex|port|able** /ɪkspɔːʳtəbᵊl/ **Exportable** products are suitable for being exported. ❑ *They are reliant on a very limited number of exportable products.* ADJ

**ex|port|er** /ekspɔːʳtəʳ, ɪkspɔːʳtəʳ/ **(exporters)** An **exporter** is a country, firm, or person that sells and sends goods to another country. ❑ *France is the world's second-biggest exporter of agricultural products.* N-COUNT: usu with supp ≠ importer

**ex|pose** /ɪkspoʊz/ **(exposes, exposing, exposed)** ◆◇◇ [1] To **expose** something that is usually hidden means to uncover it so that it can be seen. ❑ *Lowered sea levels exposed the shallow continental shelf beneath the Bering Sea. ...the exposed brickwork.* VERB V n V-ed [2] To **expose** a person or situation means to reveal that they are bad or immoral in some way. ❑ *The Budget does expose the lies ministers were telling a year ago... He has simply been exposed as an adulterer and a fool.* VERB V n *be* V-ed *as* n/adj [3] If someone **is exposed to** something dangerous or unpleasant, they are put in a situation in which it might affect them. ❑ *They had not been exposed to most diseases* VERB *be* V-ed *to* n

*common to urban populations... A wise mother never exposes her children to the slightest possibility of danger. ...people exposed to high levels of radiation.* V n *to* n V-ed
4 If someone **is exposed to** an idea or feeling, usually a new one, they are given experience of it, or introduced to it. ❑ *...local people who've not been exposed to glimpses of Western life before... These units exposed children to many viewpoints of a given issue.* VERB *be* V-ed *to* n V n *to* n
5 A man who **exposes himself** shows people his genitals in a public place, usually because he is mentally or emotionally disturbed. ❑ *Smith admitted indecently exposing himself on Wimbledon Common.* VERB V pron-refl

**ex|po|sé** /ekspo͟ʊzeɪ, AM e̲kspoʊze͟ɪ/ **(exposés)** An **exposé** is a film or piece of writing which reveals the truth about a situation or person, especially something involving shocking facts. ❑ *The movie is an exposé of prison conditions in the South.* N-COUNT: oft N *of* n

**ex|posed** /ɪkspo͟ʊzd/ If a place is **exposed**, it has no natural protection against bad weather or enemies, for example because it has no trees or is on very high ground. ❑ *...an exposed hillside in Connecticut.* ADJ

**ex|po|si|tion** /e̲kspəzɪʃᵊn/ **(expositions)**
1 An **exposition of** an idea or theory is a detailed explanation or account of it. [FORMAL] ❑ *The fullest exposition of Coleridge's thought can be found in the Statesman's Manual.* N-COUNT: oft N *of* n
2 An **exposition** is an exhibition in which something such as goods or works of art are shown to the public. ❑ *...an art exposition.* N-COUNT = exhibition

**ex|pos|tu|late** /ɪkspɒ̲stʃʊleɪt/ **(expostulates, expostulating, expostulated)** If you **expostulate**, you express strong disagreement with someone. [FORMAL] ❑ *'For heaven's sake!' Dot expostulated. 'They're cheap and they're useful.'... For a moment I thought she was going to expostulate... His family expostulated with him.* VERB = remonstrate V with quote V V *with* n

**ex|po|sure** /ɪkspo͟ʊʒəʳ/ **(exposures)** ◆◇◇
1 **Exposure to** something dangerous means being in a situation where it might affect you. ❑ *Exposure to lead is known to damage the brains of young children.* N-UNCOUNT: usu N *to* n
2 **Exposure** is the harmful effect on your body caused by very cold weather. ❑ *He was suffering from exposure and shock but his condition was said to be stable.* N-UNCOUNT
3 The **exposure** of a well-known person is the revealing of the fact that they are bad or immoral in some way. ❑ *...the exposure of Anthony Blunt as a former Soviet spy.* N-UNCOUNT: usu with poss
4 **Exposure** is publicity that a person, company, or product receives. ❑ *All the candidates have been getting an enormous amount of exposure on television and in the press.* N-UNCOUNT = publicity
5 In photography, an **exposure** is a single photograph. [TECHNICAL] ❑ *Larger drawings tend to require two or three exposures to cover them.* N-COUNT
6 In photography, the **exposure** is the amount of light that is allowed to enter a camera when taking a photograph. [TECHNICAL] ❑ *Against a deep blue sky or dark storm-clouds, you may need to reduce the exposure.* N-VAR

**ex|pound** /ɪkspa͟ʊnd/ **(expounds, expounding, expounded)** If you **expound** an idea or opinion, you give a clear and detailed explanation of it. [FORMAL] ❑ *Schmidt continued to expound his views on economics and politics.* ♦ **Expound on** means the same as **expound**. ❑ *Lawrence expounded on the military aspects of guerrilla warfare.* VERB = explain V n PHRASAL VERB V P n

**ex|press** /ɪkspre̲s/ **(expresses, expressing, expressed)** ◆◆◇
1 When you **express** an idea or feeling, or **express yourself**, you show what you think or feel. ❑ *He expressed grave concern at American attitudes... He expresses himself easily in English.* VERB V n V pron-refl
2 If an idea or feeling **expresses itself** in some way, it can be clearly seen in someone's actions or in its effects on a situation. ❑ *The anxiety of the separation often expresses itself as anger towards the child for getting lost.* VERB = manifest V pron-refl prep
3 In mathematics, if you **express** a quantity or mathematical problem in a particular way, you write it using particular symbols, figures, or equations. [TECHNICAL] ❑ *It is expressed as a percentage.* VERB V n prep
4 An **express** command or order is one that is clearly and deliberately stated. [FORMAL] ❑ *The ship was sunk on express orders from the Prime Minister.* ♦ **ex|press|ly** *He has expressly forbidden her to go out on her own.* ADJ: ADJ n = explicit ADV: ADV before v
5 If you refer to an **express** intention or purpose, you are emphasizing that it is a deliberate and specific one that you have before you do something. ❑ *I had obtained my first camera for the express purpose of taking railway photographs.* ♦ **ex|press|ly** *...projects expressly designed to support cattle farmers.* ADJ: ADJ n emphasis = specific ADV: ADV before v, ADV prep/to-inf
6 **Express** is used to describe special services which are provided by companies or organizations such as the Post Office, in which things are sent or done faster than usual for a higher price. ❑ *A special express service is available by fax... It was sent to us by express mail.* ♦ **Express** is also an adverb. ❑ *Send it express.* ADJ: ADJ n ADV
7 An **express** or an **express** train is a fast train which stops at very few stations. ❑ *Punctually at 7.45, the express to Kuala Lumpur left Singapore station.* N-COUNT: oft N *to/for* n

**ex|pres|sion** /ɪkspre̲ʃᵊn/ **(expressions)** ◆◇◇
1 The **expression of** ideas or feelings is the showing of them through words, actions, or artistic activities. ❑ *Laughter is one of the most infectious expressions of emotion. ...the rights of the individual to freedom of expression... Her concern has now found expression in the new environmental protection act.* N-VAR: usu N *of* n
2 Your **expression** is the way that your face looks at a particular moment. It shows what you are thinking or feeling. ❑ *Levin sat there, an expression of sadness on his face.* N-VAR: usu with supp, oft poss N
3 **Expression** is the showing of feeling when you are acting, singing, or playing a musical instrument. ❑ *I don't sing perfectly in tune, but I think I put more expression into my lyrics than a lot of other singers do.* N-UNCOUNT
4 An **expression** is a word or phrase. ❑ *She spoke in a quiet voice but used remarkably coarse expressions.* N-COUNT

**ex|pres|sion|ism** /ɪkspre̲ʃənɪzəm/ **Expressionism** is a style of art, literature, and music which uses symbols and exaggeration to represent emotions, rather than representing physical reality. N-UNCOUNT

**ex|pres|sion|ist** /ɪkspre̲ʃənɪst/ **(expressionists)**
1 An **expressionist** is an artist, writer, or composer who uses the style of expressionism. N-COUNT
2 **Expressionist** artists, writers, composers, or works use the style of expressionism. ❑ *...an extraordinary collection of expressionist paintings.* ADJ: usu ADJ n

**ex|pres|sion|less** /ɪkspre̲ʃᵊnləs/ If you describe someone's face as **expressionless**, you mean that they are not showing their feelings. ADJ

**ex|pres|sive** /ɪkspre̲sɪv/ If you describe a person or their behaviour as **expressive**, you mean that their behaviour clearly indicates their feelings or intentions. ❑ *You can train people to be more expressive. ...her small, usually expressive face.* ♦ **ex|pres|sive|ly** *He moved his hands expressively.* ♦ **ex|pres|sive|ness** *Crying is part of our natural expressiveness.* ADJ ADV: ADV with v N-UNCOUNT

**ex|press|way** /ɪkspre̲sweɪ/ **(expressways)** An **expressway** is a wide road that is specially designed so that a lot of traffic can move along it very quickly. It is usually divided, so that traffic travelling in one direction is separated from the traffic travelling in the opposite direction. N-COUNT

**ex|pro|pri|ate** /ekspro͟ʊprieɪt/ **(expropriates, expropriating, expropriated)** If a government or other authority **expropriates** someone's property, they take it away from them for public use. [LEGAL] ❑ *The Bolsheviks expropriated the property of the landowners.* ♦ **ex|pro|pria|tion** /ekspro͟ʊprie͟ɪʃᵊn/ **(expropriations)** *...the expropriation of property... Ownership is not clear because of expropriations in the Nazi era.* VERB V n N-VAR: oft N *of* n

**ex|pul|sion** /ɪkspʌ̲lʃᵊn/ **(expulsions)**
1 **Expulsion** is when someone is forced to leave a school, university, or organization. ❑ *Her hatred of authority led to her expulsion from high school. ...the high number of school expulsions.* N-VAR: usu with supp
2 **Expulsion** is when someone is forced to leave a place. [FORMAL] ❑ *...the expulsion of Yemeni workers. ...a new wave of* N-VAR: usu with supp

*mass expulsions.* [3] **Expulsion** is when something is forced out from your body. [FORMAL] ❑ *...their expulsion from the digestive tract.* N-UNCOUNT: usu with supp

**ex|punge** /ɪkspʌndʒ/ **(expunges, expunging, expunged)** If you **expunge** something, you get rid of it completely, because it causes problems or bad feelings. [FORMAL] ❑ *The revolutionaries expunged domestic opposition... The experience was something he had tried to expunge from his memory... His name was expunged from the record books.* VERB V n V n *from* n V n *from* n

**ex|pur|gate** /ekspəʳgeɪt/ **(expurgates, expurgating, expurgated)** If someone **expurgates** a piece of writing, they remove parts of it before it is published because they think those parts will offend or shock people. [FORMAL] ❑ *He heavily expurgated the work in its second edition.* ♦ **ex|pur|gat|ed** *It was first published in 1914 in a highly expurgated version.* VERB = censor V n ADJ

**ex|quis|ite** /ɪkskwɪzɪt, ekskwɪzɪt/ Something that is **exquisite** is extremely beautiful or pleasant, especially in a delicate way. ❑ *The Indians brought in exquisite beadwork to sell... Mr Zhang's photography is exquisite.* ♦ **ex|quis|ite|ly** *...exquisitely crafted dolls' houses.* ADJ ADV: usu ADV adj/-ed

**ex-serviceman** **(ex-servicemen)** An **ex-serviceman** is a man who used to be in a country's army, navy, or air force. [BRIT] N-COUNT

✓ in AM, use **veteran**

**ext.** **Ext.** is the written abbreviation for **extension** when it is used to refer to a particular telephone number. N-VAR: N num

**ex|tant** /ekstænt, ekstənt/ If something is **extant**, it is still in existence, in spite of being very old. [FORMAL] ❑ *Two fourteenth-century manuscripts of this text are still extant... The oldest extant document is dated 1492.* ADJ = surviving

**ex|tem|po|rize** /ɪkstempəraɪz/ **(extemporizes, extemporizing, extemporized)**

✓ in BRIT, also use **extemporise**

If you **extemporize**, you speak, act, or perform something immediately, without rehearsing or preparing it beforehand. [FORMAL] ❑ *He completely departed from the text and extemporized in a very energetic fashion.* VERB = improvise V

**ex|tend** /ɪkstend/ **(extends, extending, extended)** ◆◆◇ [1] If you say that something, usually something large, **extends for** a particular distance or **extends from** one place **to** another, you are indicating its size or position. ❑ *The caves extend for some 18 kilometres... The main stem will extend to around 12ft, if left to develop naturally... Our personal space extends about 12 to 18 inches around us... The high-speed train service is planned to extend from Paris to Bordeaux... The new territory would extend over one-fifth of Canada's land mass.* VERB V *for* amount V *to* amount V amount V *from* n *to* n V *over* n [2] If an object **extends from** a surface or place, it sticks out from it. ❑ *A shelf of land extended from the escarpment.* VERB V *from* n [3] If an event or activity **extends over** a period of time, it continues for that time. ❑ *...a playing career in first-class cricket that extended from 1894 to 1920... The courses are based on a weekly two-hour class, extending over a period of 25 weeks.* VERB V *from* n *to* n V *over* n Also V *to* n [4] If something **extends to** a group of people, things, or activities, it includes or affects them. ❑ *The service also extends to wrapping and delivering gifts... His influence extends beyond the TV viewing audience.* VERB V *to* n/-ing V *beyond* n [5] If you **extend** something, you make it longer or bigger. ❑ *This year they have introduced three new products to extend their range... The building was extended in 1500. ...an extended exhaust pipe.* VERB V n V n V-ed [6] If a piece of equipment or furniture **extends**, its length can be increased. ❑ *... a table which extends to accommodate extra guests... The table extends to 220cm.* VERB V V *to* amount [7] If you **extend** something, you make it last longer than before or end at a later date. ❑ *They have extended the deadline by twenty-four hours. ...an extended contract.* VERB V n V-ed [8] If you **extend** something **to** other people or things, you make it include or affect more people or things. ❑ *It might be possible to extend the technique to other crop plants.* VERB V n *to* n [9] If someone **extends** their hand, they stretch out their arm and hand to shake hands with someone. ❑ *The man extended his hand: 'I'm Chuck'.* VERB = stretch out V n

**ex|tend|able** /ɪkstendəbᵊl/ Something that is **extendable** can be made longer. ❑ *These were hung in place with extendable rods.* ADJ: usu ADJ n

**ex|tend|ed** /ɪkstendɪd/ If something happens for an **extended** period of time, it happens for a long period of time. ❑ *Obviously, any child who receives dedicated teaching over an extended period is likely to improve.* ➔ See also **extend**. ADJ: ADJ n = lengthy

**ex|tend|ed fami|ly** **(extended families)** An **extended family** is a family group which includes relatives such as uncles, aunts, and grandparents, as well as parents, children, and brothers and sisters. ❑ *The pregnant woman in such a community has the support of all the womenfolk in her extended family.* N-COUNT

**ex|ten|sion** /ɪkstenʃᵊn/ **(extensions)** [1] An **extension** is a new room or building which is added to an existing building or group of buildings. N-COUNT [2] An **extension** is a new section of a road or rail line that is added to an existing road or line. ❑ *...the Jubilee Line extension.* N-COUNT: usu with supp [3] An **extension** is an extra period of time for which something lasts or is valid, usually as a result of official permission. ❑ *He first entered Britain on a six-month visa, and was given a further extension of six months.* N-COUNT [4] Something that is an **extension of** something else is a development of it that includes or affects more people, things, or activities. ❑ *Many Filipinos see the bases as an extension of American colonial rule.* N-COUNT: usu N *of* n [5] An **extension** is a telephone line that is connected to the switchboard of a company or institution, and that has its own number. The written abbreviation **ext.** is also used. ❑ *She can get me on extension 308.* N-COUNT: also N num [6] An **extension** is a part which is connected to a piece of equipment in order to make it reach something further away. ❑ *...a 30-foot extension cord.* N-COUNT

**ex|ten|sive** /ɪkstensɪv/ ◆◇◇ [1] Something that is **extensive** covers or includes a large physical area. ❑ *...an extensive tour of Latin America... When built, the palace and its grounds were more extensive than the city itself.* ♦ **ex|ten|sive|ly** *Mark, however, needs to travel extensively with his varied business interests.* ADJ ADV: ADV after v [2] Something that is **extensive** covers a wide range of details, ideas, or items. ❑ *Developments in South Africa receive extensive coverage in The Sunday Telegraph... The facilities available are very extensive.* ♦ **ex|ten|sive|ly** *All these issues have been extensively researched in recent years.* ADJ ADV: ADV after v, ADV adj/-ed [3] If something is **extensive**, it is very great. ❑ *The blast caused extensive damage, shattering the ground-floor windows... The security forces have extensive powers of search and arrest.* ♦ **ex|ten|sive|ly** *Hydrogen is used extensively in industry for the production of ammonia.* ADJ ADV: ADV after v, ADV -ed

**ex|tent** /ɪkstent/ ◆◇◇ [1] If you are talking about how great, important, or serious a difficulty or situation is, you can refer to **the extent of** it. ❑ *The government itself has little information on the extent of industrial pollution... The full extent of the losses was disclosed yesterday.* N-SING: with supp, usu *the* N *of* n [2] **The extent of** something is its length, area, or size. ❑ *Their commitment was only to maintain the extent of forests, not their biodiversity.* N-SING: with supp, usu *the* N *of* n

PHRASES [3] You use expressions such as **to a large extent**, **to some extent**, or **to a certain extent** in order to indicate that something is partly true, but not entirely true. ❑ *It was and, to a large extent, still is a good show... To some extent this was the truth.* PHRASE: PHR with cl [vagueness] [4] You use expressions such as **to what extent**, **to that extent**, or **to the extent that** when you are discussing how true a statement is, or in what ways it is true. ❑ *It's still not clear to what extent this criticism is originating from within the ruling party... To that extent they helped bring about their own destruction.* PHRASE [vagueness] [5] You use expres- PHRASE sions such as **to the extent of**, **to the extent that**, or **to such an extent that** in order to emphasize that a situation has reached a difficult, dangerous, or surprising stage. ❑ *He said he didn't like the president, but not to the extent of wanting to kill him.* [emphasis]

**ex|tenu|at|ing** /ɪkstenjueɪtɪŋ/ If you say that there are **extenuating** circumstances for a bad situation or wrong action, you mean that there are reasons or factors which partly excuse it. [FORMAL] ❑ *The defendants decide to admit their guilt, but insist that there are extenuating circumstances.* ADJ: usu ADJ n = mitigating

**ex|te|ri|or** /ɪkstɪəriəʳ/ **(exteriors)** 1 The **exterior** of something is its outside surface. ❑ *In one ad the viewer scarcely sees the car's exterior... The exterior of the building was elegant and graceful.* N-COUNT: usu sing = outside 2 You can refer to someone's usual appearance or behaviour as their **exterior**, especially when it is very different from their real character. ❑ *According to Mandy, Pat's tough exterior hides a shy and sensitive soul.* N-COUNT: usu sing, usu with supp, oft poss N = facade 3 You use **exterior** to refer to the outside parts of something or things that are outside something. ❑ *The exterior walls were made of pre-formed concrete.* ADJ: ADJ n = outer, outside

**ex|ter|mi|nate** /ɪkstɜːʳmɪneɪt/ **(exterminates, exterminating, exterminated)** To **exterminate** a group of people or animals means to kill all of them. ❑ *A huge effort was made to exterminate the rats.* VERB V n ♦ **ex|ter|mi|na|tion** /ɪkstɜːʳmɪneɪʃᵊn/ *...the extermination of hundreds of thousands of their countrymen.* N-UNCOUNT: oft N *of* n, N n

**ex|ter|mi|na|tor** /ɪkstɜːʳmɪneɪtəʳ/ **(exterminators)** An **exterminator** is a person whose job is to kill animals such as rats or mice, because they are annoying or dangerous. N-COUNT

**ex|ter|nal** /ɪkstɜːʳnᵊl/ 1 **External** is used to indicate that something is on the outside of a surface or body, or that it exists, happens, or comes from outside. ❑ *...a much reduced heat loss through external walls. ...internal and external allergic reactions.* ADJ: usu ADJ n ≠ internal ♦ **ex|ter|nal|ly** *Vitamins can be applied externally to the skin. ...externally imposed conditions.* ADV: usu ADV with v 2 **External** means involving or intended for foreign countries. ❑ *...the commissioner for external affairs. ...Jamaica's external debt. ...the republic's external borders.* ADJ: ADJ n ♦ **ex|ter|nal|ly** *...protecting the value of the mark both internally and externally.* ADV: usu ADV after v 3 **External** means happening or existing in the world in general and affecting you in some way. ❑ *...a reaction to external events... Such events occur only when the external conditions are favorable.* ADJ: ADJ n 4 **External** experts, for example **external examiners**, come into an organization from outside in order to do a particular job fairly and impartially, or to check that a particular job was done properly. [mainly BRIT] ADJ: ADJ n = outside ♦ **ex|ter|nal|ly** ❑ *There must be externally moderated tests.* ADV: ADV -ed 5 If medicine is **for external use**, it is intended to be used only on the outside of your body, and not to be eaten or drunk. PHRASE: v-link PHR, PHR after v

**ex|ter|nal|ize** /ɪkstɜːʳnəlaɪz/ **(externalizes, externalizing, externalized)**

> ✔ in BRIT, also use **externalise**

If you **externalize** your ideas or feelings, you express them openly, in words or actions. [FORMAL] ❑ *These are people who tend to externalize blame when anything goes wrong at work.* VERB ≠ internalize V n

**ex|ter|nals** /ɪkstɜːʳnəlz/ When you talk about **externals**, you are referring to the features of a situation that are obvious but not important or central. ❑ *All that the tourists see are the externals of our faith.* N-PLURAL

**ex|tinct** /ɪkstɪŋkt/ 1 A species of animal or plant that is **extinct** no longer has any living members, either in the world or in a particular place. ❑ *It is 250 years since the wolf became extinct in Britain.* ADJ 2 If a particular kind of worker, way of life, or type of activity is **extinct**, it no longer exists, because of changes in society. ❑ *Herbalism had become an all but extinct skill in the Western world.* ADJ 3 An **extinct** volcano is one that does not erupt or is not expected to erupt any more. ❑ *Its tallest volcano, long extinct, is Olympus Mons.* ADJ

**ex|tinc|tion** /ɪkstɪŋkʃᵊn/ 1 The **extinction** of a species of animal or plant is the death of all its remaining living members. ❑ *An operation is beginning to try to save a species of crocodile from extinction.* N-UNCOUNT 2 If someone refers to the **extinction** of a way of life or type of activity, they mean that the way of life or activity stops existing. ❑ *The loggers say their jobs are faced with extinction because of declining timber sales.* N-UNCOUNT

**ex|tin|guish** /ɪkstɪŋgwɪʃ/ **(extinguishes, extinguishing, extinguished)** 1 If you **extinguish** a fire or a light, you stop it burning or shining. [FORMAL] ❑ *It took about 50 minutes to extinguish the fire.* VERB = put out V n 2 If something **extinguishes** a feeling or idea, it destroys it. ❑ *The message extinguished her hopes of Richard's return.* VERB V n

**ex|tin|guish|er** /ɪkstɪŋgwɪʃəʳ/ **(extinguishers)** An **extinguisher** is the same as a **fire extinguisher**. N-COUNT

**ex|tol** /ɪkstoʊl/ **(extols, extolling, extolled)** If you **extol** something or someone, you praise them enthusiastically. ❑ *Now experts are extolling the virtues of the humble potato.* VERB V n

**ex|tort** /ɪkstɔːʳt/ **(extorts, extorting, extorted)** If someone **extorts** money **from** you, they get it from you using force, threats, or other unfair or illegal means. ❑ *Corrupt government officials were extorting money from him... Her kidnapper extorted a £175,000 ransom for her release.* VERB = extract V n *from* n V n

**ex|tor|tion** /ɪkstɔːʳʃᵊn/ **Extortion** is the crime of obtaining something from someone, especially money, by using force or threats. ❑ *He has been charged with extortion and abusing his powers.* N-UNCOUNT

**ex|tor|tion|ate** /ɪkstɔːʳʃᵊnət/ If you describe something such as a price as **extortionate**, you are emphasizing that it is much greater than it should be. ADJ [emphasis] = outrageous

**ex|tor|tion|ist** /ɪkstɔːʳʃᵊnɪst/ **(extortionists)** An **extortionist** is a person who commits the crime of obtaining something from someone by using force or threats. N-COUNT

**ex|tra** /ekstrə/ **(extras)** ◆◆◇ 1 You use **extra** to describe an amount, person, or thing that is added to others of the same kind, or that can be added to others of the same kind. ❑ *Police warned motorists to allow extra time to get to work... Extra staff have been taken on to cover busy periods... There's an extra blanket in the bottom drawer of the cupboard.* ADJ: ADJ n = additional 2 If something is **extra**, you have to pay more money for it in addition to what you are already paying for something. ❑ *The price of your meal is extra.* ADJ: v-link ADJ ♦ **Extra** is also a pronoun. ❑ *Many of the additional features now cost extra.* PRON ♦ **Extra** is also an adverb. ❑ *You may be charged 10% extra for this service.* ADV 3 **Extras** are additional amounts of money that are added to the price that you have to pay for something. ❑ *There are no hidden extras.* N-COUNT: usu pl 4 **Extras** are things which are not necessary in a situation, activity, or object, but which make it more comfortable, useful, or enjoyable. ❑ *Optional extras include cooking tuition at a top restaurant.* N-COUNT: usu pl 5 The **extras** in a film are the people who play unimportant parts, for example as members of a crowd. N-COUNT 6 You can use **extra** in front of adjectives and adverbs to emphasize the quality that they are describing. [INFORMAL] ❑ *I'd have to be extra careful... What makes a magnificent garden extra special?* ADV: ADV adj/adv [emphasis] = especially 7 to **go the extra mile** → see **mile**.

**extra-** /ekstrə-/ **extra-** is used to form adjectives indicating that something is outside something or is not part of it. [FORMAL] ❑ *The move was extra-constitutional... They competed for power through a combination of parliamentary and extra-parliamentary methods... The report says torture was widespread, as were extra-judicial executions by government troops.* PREFIX

**ex|tract (extracts, extracting, extracted)**

The verb is pronounced /ɪkstræ̲kt/. The noun is pronounced /e̲kstrækt/.

1 To **extract** a substance means to obtain it from something else, for example by using industrial or chemical processes. ❑ *...the traditional method of pick and shovel to extract coal... Citric acid can be extracted from the juice of oranges, lemons, limes or grapefruit. ...looking at the differences in the extracted DNA.* ♦ **ex|trac|tion** *Petroleum engineers plan and manage the extraction of oil.* 2 If you **extract** something **from** a place, you take it out or pull it out. ❑ *He extracted a small notebook from his hip pocket... Patterson went straight to the liquor cabinet and extracted a bottle of Scotch.* 3 When a dentist **extracts** a tooth, they remove it from the patient's mouth. ❑ *A dentist may decide to extract the tooth to prevent recurrent trouble... She is to go and have a tooth extracted at 3 o'clock today.* ♦ **ex|trac|tion (extractions)** *In those days, dentistry was basic. Extractions were carried out without anaesthetic.* 4 If you say that someone **extracts** something, you disapprove of them because they take it for themselves to gain an advantage. ❑ *He sought to extract the maximum political advantage from the cut in interest rates.* 5 If you **extract** information or a response **from** someone, you get it from them with difficulty, because they are unwilling to say or do what you want. ❑ *He made the mistake of trying to extract further information from our director.* 6 If you **extract** a particular piece of information, you obtain it from a larger amount or source of information. ❑ *I've simply extracted a few figures... Britain's trade figures can no longer be extracted from export-and-import documentation at ports.* 7 If part of a book or text **is extracted from** a particular book, it is printed or published. [JOURNALISM] ❑ *This material has been extracted from 'Collins Good Wood Handbook'.* 8 An **extract from** a book or piece of writing is a small part of it that is printed or published separately. ❑ *Read this extract from an information booklet about the work of an airline cabin crew.* 9 An **extract** is a substance that has been obtained from something else, for example by means of a chemical or industrial process. ❑ *Blend in the lemon extract, lemon peel and walnuts.* 10 → See also **yeast extract**.

VERB; V n; be V-ed from n; V-ed; N-UNCOUNT; VERB; V n from n; V n; VERB; V n; have n V-ed; N-VAR; VERB; disapproval; V n from n; VERB; V n from n; VERB; V n; be V-ed from n; V-PASSIVE; be V-ed from n; N-COUNT: usu N from n = excerpt; N-MASS: oft n N

**ex|trac|tion** /ɪkstræ̲kʃᵊn/ If you say, for example, that someone is **of** French **extraction**, you mean that they or their family originally came from France. [FORMAL] ❑ *Her real father was of Italian extraction.* — N-UNCOUNT: with supp = origin, descent

**ex|trac|tor** /ɪkstræ̲ktəʳ/ **(extractors)** 1 An **extractor** or **extractor fan** is a device that is fixed to a window or wall to draw smells, steam, or hot air out of a room. [mainly BRIT] — N-COUNT

in AM, use **ventilator**

2 An **extractor** is a device that squeezes liquid out of something. ❑ *...a juice extractor.* — N-COUNT: with supp

**extra|cur|ricu|lar** /e̲kstrə kərɪ̲kjʊləʳ/

in BRIT, also use **extra-curricular**

1 **Extracurricular** activities are activities for students that are not part of their course. [FORMAL] ❑ *Each child had participated in extracurricular activities at school. ...extra-curricular sport.* — ADJ: ADJ n
2 **Extracurricular** activities are activities that someone does that are not part of their normal work. [INFORMAL] ❑ *The money he made from these extra-curricular activities enabled him to pursue other ventures.* — ADJ: ADJ n

**extra|dite** /e̲kstrədaɪt/ **(extradites, extraditing, extradited)** If someone **is extradited**, they are officially sent back to their own or another country to be tried for a crime that they have been accused of. [FORMAL] ❑ *He was extradited to Britain from the Irish Republic to face explosives charges... The authorities refused to extradite him.* ♦ **extra|di|tion** /e̲kstrədɪ̲ʃᵊn/ **(extraditions)** *A New York court turned down the British government's request for his extradition... There were no plans to reopen extradition proceedings against him.* — VERB; be V-ed to/from n; V n; N-VAR

**extra-marital** also **extramarital.** An **extra-marital** affair is a sexual relationship between a married person and another person who is not their husband or wife. ❑ *Her husband has admitted having an extra-marital affair.* — ADJ: usu ADJ n

**extra-mural** also **extramural. Extra-mural** courses are courses at a college or university which are taken mainly by part-time students. — ADJ: usu ADJ n

**extra|neous** /ɪkstre̲ɪniəs/ **Extraneous** things are not relevant or essential to the situation you are involved in or the subject you are talking about. [FORMAL] ❑ *We ought not to bring in extraneous matters in trying to find a basis for a settlement.* — ADJ: usu ADJ n

**extraor|di|naire** /ekstrɔ̲ːʳdɪne̲əʳ/ If you describe someone as being, for example, a musician **extraordinaire**, you are saying in a slightly humorous way that you think they are an extremely good musician. ❑ *...George Kuchar, film-maker extraordinaire.* — ADJ: n ADJ

**extraor|di|nary** /ɪkstrɔ̲ːʳdənri, AM -neri/ ◆◇◇
1 If you describe something or someone as **extraordinary**, you mean that they have some extremely good or special quality. ❑ *We've made extraordinary progress as a society in that regard... The task requires extraordinary patience and endurance... Rozhdestvensky is an extraordinary musician.* ♦ **extraor|di|nari|ly** /ɪkstrɔ̲ːʳdənrɪli, AM -nerɪli/ *Michael is extraordinarily disciplined.* 2 If you describe something as **extraordinary**, you mean that it is very unusual or surprising. ❑ *What an extraordinary thing to happen!... His decision to hold talks is extraordinary because it could mean the real end of the war.* ♦ **extraor|di|nari|ly** *Apart from the hair, he looked extraordinarily unchanged... Extraordinarily, the favourites for the title lie at the bottom of the table.* 3 An **extraordinary** meeting is arranged specially to deal with a particular situation or problem, rather than happening regularly. [FORMAL] ❑ *...at an extraordinary meeting of the sport's ruling body.*

ADJ: usu ADJ n; approval = exceptional, remarkable, amazing; ADV: ADV adj = exceptionally; ADJ; emphasis = remarkable; ADV: ADV adj/adv, ADV with cl = remarkably; ADJ: ADJ n

**ex|trapo|late** /ɪkstræ̲pᵊleɪt/ **(extrapolates, extrapolating, extrapolated)** If you **extrapolate from** known facts, you use them as a basis for general statements about a situation or about what is likely to happen in the future. [FORMAL] ❑ *Extrapolating from his American findings, he reckons about 80% of these deaths might be attributed to smoking... It is unhelpful to extrapolate general trends from one case.* ♦ **ex|trapo|la|tion** /ɪkstræ̲pəle̲ɪʃᵊn/ **(extrapolations)** *His estimate of half a million HIV positive cases was based on an extrapolation of the known incidence of the virus.* — VERB; V from n; V n from n; N-VAR

**extra-sensory perception** also **extrasensory perception. Extra-sensory perception** means knowing without using your ordinary senses such as sight and hearing. Some people believe this is possible. The abbreviation **ESP** is also used. — N-UNCOUNT

**extra|ter|res|trial** /e̲kstrətɪre̲striəl/ **(extraterrestrials)** also **extra-terrestrial.**
1 **Extraterrestrial** means happening, existing, or coming from somewhere beyond the planet Earth. [FORMAL] ❑ *NASA has started a 10-year search for extraterrestrial intelligence. ...extraterrestrial rocks.* — ADJ: usu ADJ n
2 **Extraterrestrials** are living creatures that some people think exist or may exist in another part of the universe. — N-COUNT

**ex|tra time** If a game of football, hockey, or basketball goes into **extra time**, the game continues for a set period after it would usually have ended because both teams have the same score. [BRIT] ❑ *Cambridge won 2-0 after extra time.* — N-UNCOUNT

in AM, use **overtime**

**ex|trava|gance** /ɪkstræ̲vəgəns/ **(extravagances)** 1 **Extravagance** is the spending of more money than is reasonable or than you can afford. ❑ *...gross mismanagement and financial ex-* — N-UNCOUNT travagance... *When the company went under, tales of his extravagance surged through the industry.* [2] An **extravagance** is something that you spend money on but cannot really afford. ❑ *Her only extravagance was horses.* N-COUNT

**ex|trava|gant** /ɪkstrævəgənt/ [1] Someone who is **extravagant** spends more money than they can afford or uses more of something than is reasonable. ❑ *We are not extravagant; restaurant meals are a luxury and designer clothes are out.* ♦ **ex|trava|gant|ly** *Jeff had shopped extravagantly for presents for the whole family.* [2] Something that is **extravagant** costs more money than you can afford or uses more of something than is reasonable. ❑ *Her Aunt Sallie gave her an uncharacteristically extravagant gift. ...her extravagant lifestyle.* ♦ **ex|trava|gant|ly** *By supercar standards, though, it is not extravagantly priced for a beautifully engineered machine.* [3] **Extravagant** behaviour is extreme behaviour that is often done for a particular effect. ❑ *He was extravagant in his admiration of Hellas... They may make extravagant shows of generosity.* ♦ **ex|trava|gant|ly** *...extravagantly bizarre clothes.* [4] **Extravagant** claims or ideas are unrealistic or impractical. ❑ *They have to compete by adorning their products with ever more extravagant claims... Don't be afraid to consider apparently extravagant ideas.* ADJ; ADV: ADV with v; ADJ; ADV: ADV adj/-ed; ADJ; ADV: ADV with v, ADV adj; ADJ: usu ADJ n [disapproval] = wild

**ex|trava|gan|za** /ɪkstrævəgænzə/ **(extravaganzas)** An **extravaganza** is a very elaborate and expensive show or performance. ❑ *...a magnificent firework extravaganza. ...an all-night musical extravaganza.* N-COUNT: usu sing, with supp = spectacular

**ex|treme** /ɪkstriːm/ **(extremes)** ◆◇◇ [1] **Extreme** means very great in degree or intensity. ❑ *The girls were afraid of snakes and picked their way along with extreme caution. ...people living in extreme poverty. ...the author's extreme reluctance to generalise.* ADJ: usu ADJ n = great
[2] You use **extreme** to describe situations and behaviour which are much more severe or unusual than you would expect, especially when you disapprove of them because of this. ❑ *The extreme case was Poland, where 29 parties won seats... It is hard to imagine Lineker capable of anything so extreme.* ADJ [disapproval] [3] You use **extreme** to describe opinions, beliefs, or political movements which you disapprove of because they are very different from those that most people would accept as reasonable or normal. ❑ *This extreme view hasn't captured popular opinion. ...the racist politics of the extreme right.* ADJ: usu ADJ n [disapproval] ≠ moderate [4] You can use **extremes** to refer to situations or types of behaviour that have opposite qualities to each other, especially when each situation or type of behaviour has such a quality to the greatest degree possible. ❑ *...a 'middle way' between the extremes of success and failure... They can withstand extremes of temperature and weather without fading or cracking.* N-COUNT: usu pl, oft N *of* n [5] The **extreme** end or edge of something is its furthest end or edge. ❑ *...the room at the extreme end of the corridor. ...winds from the extreme north.* ADJ: ADJ n = far
**PHRASES** [6] If a person **goes to extremes** or **takes** something **to extremes**, they do or say something in a way that people consider to be unacceptable, unreasonable, or foolish. ❑ *The police went to the extremes of installing the most advanced safety devices in the man's house... The doctor told me not to mention dieting to her in case she took it to the extreme.* PHRASE: V and N inflect [7] You use **in the extreme** after an adjective in order to emphasize what you are saying, especially when you want to indicate that it is something which is undesirable or very surprising. [FORMAL] ❑ *It is proving controversial in the extreme.* PHRASE: adj PHR [emphasis]

**ex|treme|ly** /ɪkstriːmli/ ◆◆◇ You use **extremely** in front of adjectives and adverbs to emphasize that the specified quality is present to a very great degree. ❑ *These headaches are extremely common... Three of them are working extremely well.* ADV: ADV adj/adv [emphasis] = exceedingly, very

**ex|tre|mis** /ɪkstriːmɪs/ → see **in extremis**.

**ex|trem|ism** /ɪkstriːmɪzəm/ **Extremism** is the behaviour or beliefs of extremists. ❑ *Greater demands were being placed on the police by growing violence and left and right-wing extremism.* N-UNCOUNT

**ex|trem|ist** /ɪkstriːmɪst/ **(extremists)** [1] If you describe someone as an **extremist**, you disapprove of them because they try to bring about political change by using violent or extreme methods. ❑ *The country needs a strong intelligence service to counter espionage and foreign extremists... A previously unknown extremist group has said it carried out Friday's bomb attack. ...a marked rise in extremist violence.* N-COUNT [disapproval] [2] If you say that someone has **extremist** views, you disapprove of them because they believe in bringing about change by using violent or extreme methods. ADJ: usu ADJ n [disapproval]

**ex|trem|ity** /ɪkstremɪti/ **(extremities)** [1] The **extremity** of something is its furthest end or edge. [FORMAL] ❑ *...a small port on the north-western extremity of the Iberian peninsula. ...the extremities of the aeroplane.* N-COUNT: with supp [2] Your **extremities** are the end parts of your body, especially your hands and feet. ❑ *He found that his extremities grew cold.* N-PLURAL: oft with poss [3] The **extremity of** a situation or **of** someone's behaviour is the degree to which it is severe, unusual, or unacceptable. ❑ *In spite of the extremity of her seclusion she was sane... In the past, the region had been protected by its forbidding geography and the extremities of its climate.* N-UNCOUNT: also N in pl, oft N *of* n

**ex|tri|cate** /ekstrɪkeɪt/ **(extricates, extricating, extricated)** [1] If you **extricate yourself** or another person **from** a difficult or serious situation, you free yourself or the other person from it. ❑ *It represents a last ditch attempt by the country to extricate itself from its economic crisis... She tugged on Hart's arm to extricate him from the circle of men with whom he'd been talking.* VERB = free; V pron-refl *from* n; V n *from* n [2] If you **extricate** someone or something from a place where they are trapped or caught, you succeed in freeing them. [FORMAL] ❑ *He endeavoured to extricate the car, digging with his hands in the blazing sunshine.* VERB = free; V n

**ex|trin|sic** /ɪkstrɪnzɪk, AM -sɪk/ **Extrinsic** reasons, forces, or factors exist outside the person or situation they affect. [FORMAL] ❑ *Nowadays there are fewer extrinsic pressures to get married.* ADJ: ADJ n = external ≠ intrinsic

**extro|vert** /ekstrəvɜːʳt/ **(extroverts)** Someone who is **extrovert** is very active, lively, and friendly. [mainly BRIT] ❑ *...his extrovert personality.* ♦ An **extrovert** is someone who is extrovert. ❑ *He was a showman, an extrovert who revelled in controversy.* ADJ; N-COUNT ≠ introvert

✓ in AM, usually use **extroverted**

**extro|vert|ed** /ekstrəvɜːʳtɪd/ Someone who is **extroverted** is very active, lively, and friendly. [mainly AM] ❑ *Some young people who were easy-going and extroverted as children become self-conscious in early adolescence.* ADJ ≠ introverted

✓ in BRIT, usually use **extrovert**

**ex|trude** /ɪkstruːd/ **(extrudes, extruding, extruded)** If a substance **is extruded**, it is forced or squeezed out through a small opening. [TECHNICAL] ❑ *These crystals are then embedded in a plastic, and the plastic is extruded as a wire... I work in the extruded tube business.* VERB: usu passive; *be* V-ed; V-ed

**ex|tru|sion** /ɪkstruːʒᵊn/ **(extrusions)** **Extrusion** is the act or process of extruding something. [TECHNICAL] N-VAR

**exu|ber|ance** /ɪgzjuːbərəns, AM -zuːb-/ **Exuberance** is behaviour which is energetic, excited, and cheerful. ❑ *Her burst of exuberance and her brightness overwhelmed me.* N-UNCOUNT

**exu|ber|ant** /ɪgzjuːbərənt, AM -zuːb-/ If you are **exuberant**, you are full of energy, excitement, and cheerfulness. ❑ *...an exuberant young girl who decided to become a screen actress.* ♦ **exu|ber|ant|ly** *They both laughed exuberantly.* ADJ; ADV

**ex|ude** /ɪgzjuːd, AM -zuːd/ **(exudes, exuding, exuded)** [1] If someone **exudes** a quality or feeling, or if it **exudes**, they show that they have it to a great extent. [FORMAL] ❑ *The guerrillas exude* VERB = radiate; V n

*confidence. Every town, they say, is under their control... A dogged air of confidence exuded.* V
2 If something **exudes** a liquid or smell or if a liquid or smell **exudes from** it, the liquid or smell comes out of it slowly and steadily. [FORMAL] ❑ *Nearby was a factory which exuded a pungent smell. ...the fluid that exudes from the cane toad's back.* VERB; V n; V *from* n

**ex|ult** /ɪgzʌlt/ **(exults, exulting, exulted)** If you **exult in** a triumph or success that you have had, you feel and show great happiness and pleasure because of it. [WRITTEN] ❑ *He was exulting in a win at the show earlier that day... Some individual investors exulted at the record... I exulted and wept for joy... 'This is what I've longed for during my entire career,' Kendall exulted.* VERB; V *in/at* n; V *in/at* n; V; V with quote
♦ **ex|ul|ta|tion** /egzʌlteɪʃən/ ❑ *I felt a tremendous sense of relief and exultation.* N-UNCOUNT

**ex|ult|ant** /ɪgzʌltənt/ If you are **exultant**, you feel very happy and proud about something you have done. [FORMAL] ❑ *An exultant party leader said: 'He will be an excellent MP.'* ADJ; = *jubilant*
♦ **ex|ult|ant|ly** *'We cannot lose the war!' he shouted exultantly.* ADV: ADV with v

**eye** /aɪ/ **(eyes, eyeing** or **eying, eyed)** ◆◆◆ 1 Your **eyes** are the parts of your body with which you see. ❑ *I opened my eyes and looked... Maria's eyes filled with tears. ...a tall, thin white-haired lady with piercing dark brown eyes... He is now blind in one eye.* N-COUNT: oft poss N in pl
2 If you **eye** someone or something in a particular way, you look at them carefully in that way. ❑ *Sally eyed Claire with interest... Martin eyed the bottle at Marianne's elbow.* VERB; V n prep/adv; V n
3 You use **eye** when you are talking about a person's ability to judge things or about the way in which they are considering or dealing with things. ❑ *William was a man of discernment, with an eye for quality... Their chief negotiator turned his critical eye on the United States... He first learnt to fish under the watchful eye of his grandmother.* N-COUNT: usu sing, with supp, oft *a* N *for* n
4 An **eye** on a potato is one of the dark spots from which new stems grow. N-COUNT
5 An **eye** is a small metal loop which a hook fits into, as a fastening on a piece of clothing. N-COUNT
6 The **eye** of a needle is the small hole at one end which the thread passes through. N-COUNT
7 **The eye of** a storm, tornado, or hurricane is the centre of it. ❑ *The eye of the hurricane hit Florida just south of Miami.* N-SING: *the* N *of* n
8 → See also **black eye**, **private eye**, **shut-eye**.

**PHRASES** 9 If you say that something happens **before** your **eyes**, **in front of** your **eyes**, or **under** your **eyes**, you are emphasizing that it happens where you can see it clearly and often implying that it is surprising or unpleasant. ❑ *A lot of them died in front of our eyes.* PHRASE: usu PHR after v, v-link PHR; emphasis
10 If you **cast** your **eye** or **run** your **eye** over something, you look at it or read it quickly. ❑ *I would be grateful if he could cast an expert eye over it and tell me what he thought of it.* PHRASE: V inflects, PHR prep
11 If something **catches** your **eye**, you suddenly notice it. ❑ *As she turned back, a movement across the lawn caught her eye.* → See also **eye-catching**. PHRASE: V inflects
12 If you **catch** someone's **eye**, you do something to attract their attention, so that you can speak to them. ❑ *I tried to catch Chrissie's eye to find out what she was playing at.* PHRASE: V inflects
13 To **clap eyes on** someone or something, or **set** or **lay eyes on** them, means to see them. [INFORMAL] ❑ *That's probably the most bare and bleak island I've ever had the misfortune to clap eyes on... What was he doing when you last set eyes on him?* PHRASE: V inflects, oft after superl, oft with brd-neg
14 If you **make eye contact with** someone, you look at them at the same time as they look at you, so that you are both aware that you are looking at each other. If you **avoid eye contact with** someone, you deliberately do not look straight at them because you feel awkward or embarrassed. ❑ *She was looking at me across the room, and we made eye contact several times... I spent a fruitless ten minutes walking up and down the high street, desperately avoiding eye contact with passers-by.* PHRASE: PHR after v
15 If you **close** your **eyes to** something bad or if you **shut** your **eyes to** it, you ignore it. ❑ *Most governments must simply be shutting their eyes to the problem.* PHRASE: V inflects, PHR n
16 If you **cry** your **eyes out**, you cry very hard. [INFORMAL] PHRASE: V inflects
17 If there is something **as far as the eye can see**, there is a lot of it and you cannot see anything else beyond it. ❑ *There are pine trees as far as the eye can see.* PHRASE
18 If you say that someone **has an eye for** something, you mean that they are good at noticing it or making judgments about it. ❑ *Susan has a keen eye for detail, so each dress is beautifully finished off.* PHRASE: V inflects
19 You use expressions such as **in** his **eyes** or **to** her **eyes** to indicate that you are reporting someone's opinion and that other people might think differently. ❑ *The other serious problem in the eyes of the new government is communalism... Richard Dorrington was, in their eyes, a very sensible and reliable man.* PHRASE: PHR with cl-group
20 If you **keep** your **eyes open** or **keep an eye out for** someone or something, you watch for them carefully. [INFORMAL] ❑ *I ask the mounted patrol to keep their eyes open... You and your friends keep an eye out – if there's any trouble we'll make a break for it.* PHRASE: V inflects, oft PHR *for* n
21 If you **keep an eye on** something or someone, you watch them carefully, for example to make sure that they are satisfactory or safe, or not causing trouble. ❑ *I'm sure you will appreciate that we must keep a careful eye on all our running costs... I went for a run there, keeping an eye on the children the whole time.* PHRASE: V inflects, PHR n
22 You say **'there's more to** this **than meets the eye'** when you think a situation is not as simple as it seems to be. ❑ *This whole business is very puzzling. There is a lot more to it than meets the eye.* PHRASE
23 If something, especially something surprising or impressive, **meets** your **eyes**, you see it. ❑ *The first sight that met my eyes on reaching the front door was the church enveloped in flames.* PHRASE: V inflects
24 If you say that **all eyes are on** something or that the **eyes of the world are on** something, you mean that everyone is paying careful attention to it and what will happen. [JOURNALISM] ❑ *All eyes will be on tomorrow's vote... The eyes of the world were now on the police.* PHRASE: V inflects, PHR n
25 If someone **has** their **eye on** you, they are watching you carefully to see what you do. ❑ *As the boat plodded into British waters and up the English Channel, Customs had their eye on her.* PHRASE: V inflects, PHR n
26 If you **have** your **eye on** something, you want to have it. [INFORMAL] ❑ *...if you're saving up for a new outfit you've had your eye on.* PHRASE: V inflects, PHR n
27 If you say that you did something **with** your **eyes open** or **with** your **eyes wide open**, you mean that you knew about the problems and difficulties that you were likely to have. ❑ *We want all our members to undertake this trip responsibly, with their eyes open.* PHRASE: PHR after v
28 If something **opens** your **eyes**, it makes you aware that something is different from the way that you thought it was. ❑ *Watching your child explore the world about her can open your eyes to delights long forgotten.* PHRASE: V inflects, oft PHR *to* n
29 If you **see eye to eye with** someone, you agree with them and have the same opinions and views. ❑ *Yuriko saw eye to eye with Yul on almost every aspect of the production.* PHRASE: V inflects, PHR *with* n, pl-n PHR
30 When you **take** your **eyes off** the thing you have been watching or looking at, you stop looking at it. ❑ *She took her eyes off the road to glance at me.* PHRASE: V inflects, PHR n
31 If someone sees or considers something **through** your **eyes**, they consider it in the way that you do, from your point of view. ❑ *She tried to see things through his eyes.* PHRASE: PHR after v
32 If you say that you are **up to** your **eyes in** something, you are emphasizing that you have a lot of it to deal with, and often that you are very busy. [INFORMAL] ❑ *I am up to my eyes in work.* PHRASE: v-link PHR, usu PHR *in* n; emphasis
33 **the apple of** your **eye** → see **apple**. to **turn a blind eye** → see **blind**. to **feast** your **eyes** → see **feast**. **in** your **mind's eye** → see **mind**. the **naked eye** → see **naked**. to **pull the wool over** someone's **eyes** → see **wool**.

♦ **eye up** If someone **eyes** you **up**, they look at you in a way that shows they consider you attractive. [BRIT, INFORMAL] ❑ *...a slob who eyes up the women and makes lewd comments... The women sit in the corner and men eye them up.* PHRASAL VERB; = *ogle*; V P n (not pron); V n P

**eye|ball** /aɪbɔːl/ **(eyeballs, eyeballing, eyeballed)** 1 Your **eyeballs** are your whole eyes, rather than just the part which can be seen between your eyelids. N-COUNT 2 If you **eyeball** someone or something, you stare at them. [INFORMAL] ❑ *The guard eyeballed him pretty hard despite his pass.* VERB V n

**PHRASES** 3 If you are **eyeball to eyeball with** someone, you are in their presence and involved in a meeting, dispute, or contest with them. You can also talk about having an **eyeball to eyeball** meeting or confrontation. [INFORMAL] ❑ *...proposals that the two armies end their eyeball to eyeball confrontation and withdraw.* PHRASE: PHR after v, v-link PHR, PHR n, oft PHR *with* n = face to face 4 You use **up to** the **eyeballs** to emphasize that someone is in an undesirable state to a very great degree. [INFORMAL] ❑ *He is out of a job and up to his eyeballs in debt.* PHRASE: usu v-link PHR, adj/-ed PHR, PHR *in* n [emphasis]

**eye|brow** /aɪbraʊ/ **(eyebrows)** 1 Your **eyebrows** are the lines of hair which grow above your eyes. N-COUNT: usu pl, oft poss N 2 If something causes you to **raise an eyebrow** or to **raise** your **eyebrows**, it causes you to feel surprised or disapproving. ❑ *An intriguing item on the news pages caused me to raise an eyebrow over my morning coffee.* PHRASE: V inflects

**eye-catching** Something that is **eye-catching** is very noticeable. ❑ *...a series of eye-catching ads.* ADJ = striking

**-eyed** /-aɪd/ **-eyed** combines with adjectives to form adjectives which indicate the colour, shape, or size of a person's eyes, or indicate the kind of expression that they have. ❑ *...a blonde-haired, blue-eyed little girl... She watched open-eyed as the plane took off.* COMB in ADJ

**eye drops** **Eye drops** are a kind of medicine that you put in your eyes one drop at a time. N-PLURAL

**eye|ful** /aɪfʊl/ **(eyefuls)** If you get an **eyeful of** something, especially of something that you would not normally see, you are able to get a good look at it. [INFORMAL] ❑ *Then she bent over and gave him an eyeful of her tattoos.* N-COUNT: usu sing, oft N *of* n

**eye|glasses** /aɪglɑːsɪz/ **Eyeglasses** are two lenses in a frame that some people wear in front of their eyes in order to help them see better. [AM] N-PLURAL

✔ in BRIT, usually use **glasses**

**eye|lash** /aɪlæʃ/ **(eyelashes)** Your **eyelashes** are the hairs which grow on the edges of your eyelids. N-COUNT: usu pl

**eye|let** /aɪlɪt/ **(eyelets)** An **eyelet** is a small hole with a metal or leather ring round it which is made in cloth, for example a sail. You can put cord, rope, or string through it. N-COUNT

**eye|lid** /aɪlɪd/ **(eyelids)** Your **eyelids** are the two pieces of skin which cover your eyes when they are closed. **not bat an eyelid** → see **bat**. N-COUNT: usu pl

**eye|liner** /aɪlaɪnəʳ/ **(eyeliners)**

✔ in AM, use **eye-liner**

**Eyeliner** is a special kind of pencil which some women use on the edges of their eyelids next to their eyelashes in order to look more attractive. N-MASS

**eye-opener** **(eye-openers)** If you describe something as an **eye-opener**, you mean that it surprises you and that you learn something new from it. [INFORMAL] ❑ *Writing these scripts has been quite an eye-opener to me. It proves that one can do anything if the need is urgent.* N-COUNT: usu sing, usu *a* N = revelation

**eye patch** **(eye patches)** An **eye patch** is a piece of material which you wear over your eye when you have damaged or injured it. N-COUNT

**eye|piece** /aɪpiːs/ **(eyepieces)** The **eyepiece** of a microscope or telescope is the piece of glass at one end, where you put your eye in order to look through the instrument. N-COUNT

**eye shad|ow** **(eye shadows)** also **eye-shadow.** **Eye shadow** is a substance which you can paint on your eyelids in order to make them a different colour. N-MASS

**eye|sight** /aɪsaɪt/ Your **eyesight** is your ability to see. ❑ *He suffered from poor eyesight and could no longer read properly.* N-UNCOUNT: usu supp N

**eye sock|et** **(eye sockets)** Your **eye sockets** are the two hollow parts on either side of your face, where your eyeballs are. N-COUNT

**eye|sore** /aɪsɔːʳ/ **(eyesores)** You describe a building or place as an **eyesore** when it is extremely ugly and you dislike it or disapprove of it. ❑ *Poverty leads to slums, which are an eyesore and a health hazard.* N-COUNT: usu sing [disapproval]

**eye strain** If you suffer from **eye strain**, you feel pain around your eyes or at the back of your eyes, because you are very tired or should be wearing glasses. N-UNCOUNT

**eye teeth** If you say that you would **give** your **eye teeth for** something, you mean that you want it very much and you would do anything to get it. [INFORMAL] ❑ *She has the job most of us would give our eye teeth for.* PHRASE: V inflects

**eye|wear** /aɪweəʳ/ **Eyewear** is sometimes used to talk about glasses and sunglasses. N-UNCOUNT

**eye|witness** /aɪwɪtnəs/ **(eyewitnesses)** An **eyewitness** is a person who was present at an event and can therefore describe it, for example in a law court. ❑ *Eyewitnesses say the police then opened fire on the crowd. ...dramatic eye-witness accounts of the fighting.* N-COUNT

**ey|rie** /ɪəri, AM eri/ **(eyries)**

✔ in AM, use **aerie**

1 If you refer to a place such as a house or a castle as an **eyrie**, you mean it is built high up and is difficult to reach. [LITERARY] ❑ *...marooned in my 48th floor eyrie in the sky.* N-COUNT: with supp 2 An **eyrie** is the nest of a bird of prey such as an eagle, and is usually built high up in the mountains. N-COUNT

**e-zine** /iːziːn/ **(e-zines)** An **e-zine** is a website which contains the kind of articles, pictures, and advertisements that you would find in a magazine. N-COUNT

# F f

**F, f** /ef/ **(F's, f's)** 1 N-VAR **F** is the sixth letter of the English alphabet. 2 N-VAR In music, **F** is the fourth note in the scale of C major. 3 **f.** is an abbreviation for 'following'. It is written after a page or line number to indicate that you are referring to both the page or line mentioned and the one after it. You use **ff.** when you are referring to the page or line mentioned and two or more pages or lines after it.

**fab** /fæb/ ADJ [emphasis] = great If you say that something is **fab**, you are emphasizing that you think it is very good. [INFORMAL] ❑ *The dancing is fab.*

**fa|ble** /feɪbəl/ **(fables)** 1 N-VAR A **fable** is a story which teaches a moral lesson. Fables sometimes have animals as the main characters. ❑ *...the fable of the tortoise and the hare... Each tale has the timeless quality of fable.* 2 N-VAR = myth You can describe a statement or explanation that is untrue but that many people believe as **fable**. ❑ *Is reincarnation fact or fable? ...little-known horticultural facts and fables.*

**fa|bled** /feɪbəld/ ADJ: ADJ n = legendary If you describe a person or thing as **fabled**, especially someone or something remarkable, you mean that they are well known because they are often talked about or a lot of stories are told about them. ❑ *...the fabled city of Troy.*

**fab|ric** /fæbrɪk/ **(fabrics)** ◆◇◇ 1 N-MASS **Fabric** is cloth or other material produced by weaving together cotton, nylon, wool, silk, or other threads. Fabrics are used for making things such as clothes, curtains, and sheets. ❑ *...small squares of red cotton fabric... Whatever your colour scheme, there's a fabric to match.* 2 N-SING: with supp, usu *the* N *of* n The **fabric** of a society or system is its basic structure, with all the customs and beliefs that make it work successfully. ❑ *The fabric of society has been deeply damaged by the previous regime.* 3 N-SING: usu *the* N *of* n The **fabric** of a building is its walls, roof, and the materials with which it is built. ❑ *Condensation will eventually cause the fabric of the building to rot away.*

**fab|ri|cate** /fæbrɪkeɪt/ **(fabricates, fabricating, fabricated)** 1 VERB If someone **fabricates** information, they invent it in order to deceive people. ❑ *All four claim that officers fabricated evidence against them...* [V n] *Eleven key officials were hanged on fabricated charges.* [V-ed] ♦ **fab|ri|ca|tion** /fæbrɪkeɪʃən/ N-VAR = invention **(fabrications)** *She described the interview with her in an Italian magazine as a 'complete fabrication'... This story is total fabrication.* 2 VERB = manufacture If something **is fabricated from** different materials or substances, it is made out of those materials or substances. ❑ *All the tools are fabricated from high quality steel.* [be V-ed *from* n] *...a plant which fabricates airplane components.* [V n] [Also V n *from* n]

**fabu|lous** /fæbjʊləs/ ADJ [emphasis] = wonderful If you describe something as **fabulous**, you are emphasizing that you like it a lot or think that it is very good. [INFORMAL] ❑ *This is a fabulous album. It's fresh, varied, fun... The scenery and weather were fabulous.*

**fa|cade** /fəsɑːd/ **(facades)** also **façade.** 1 N-COUNT The **facade** of a building, especially a large one, is its front wall or the wall that faces the street. 2 N-SING: oft N *of* n = show, semblance A **facade** is an outward appearance which is deliberately false and gives you a wrong impression about someone or something. ❑ *They hid the troubles plaguing their marriage behind a facade of family togetherness.*

| **face** |
|---|
| ① NOUN USES |
| ② VERB AND PHRASAL VERB USES |

① **face** /feɪs/ **(faces)** ◆◆◆

⇛ Please look at category 25 to see if the expression you are looking for is shown under another headword. 1 N-COUNT: oft poss N Your **face** is the front part of your head from your chin to the top of your forehead, where your mouth, eyes, nose, and other features are. ❑ *A strong wind was blowing right in my face... He was going red in the face and breathing with difficulty... She had a beautiful face.* 2 N-COUNT: poss N, adj N If your **face** is happy, sad, or serious, for example, the expression on your face shows that you are happy, sad, or serious. ❑ *He was walking around with a sad face... The priest frowned into the light, his face puzzled.* 3 N-COUNT: with supp, oft N *of* n The **face** of a cliff, mountain, or building is a vertical surface or side of it. ❑ *...the north face of the Eiger... He scrambled 200 feet up the cliff face.* 4 N-COUNT The **face** of a clock or watch is the surface with the numbers or hands on it, which shows the time. 5 N-SING: *the* N *of* n If you say that **the face of** an area, institution, or field of activity is changing, you mean its appearance or nature is changing. ❑ *...the changing face of the British countryside.* 6 N-SING: *the* adj N *of* n If you refer to something as **the** particular **face of** an activity, belief, or system, you mean that it is one particular aspect of it, in contrast to other aspects. ❑ *Who ever thought people would see Arsenal as the acceptable face of football?* 7 N-UNCOUNT If you lose **face**, you do something which makes you appear weak and makes people respect or admire you less. If you do something in order to save **face**, you do it in order to avoid appearing weak and losing people's respect or admiration. ❑ *To cancel the airport would mean a loss of face for the present governor... She claimed they'd been in love, but I sensed she was only saying this to save face.* 8 → See also **about-face**, **face value**, **poker face**.

PHRASES 9 PHRASE: V inflects [emphasis] If you say that someone can do something **until** they are **blue in the face**, you are emphasizing that however much they do it, it will not make any difference. ❑ *You can criticise him until you're blue in the face, but you'll never change his personality.* 10 PHRASE: PHR after v, v-link PHR If someone or something is **face down**, their face or front points downwards. If they are **face up**, their face or front points upwards. ❑ *All the time Stephen was lying face down and unconscious in the bath tub... Charles laid down his cards face up.* 11 PHRASE: n PHR, usu after adj-super/brd-neg [emphasis] You can use the expression '**on the face of the earth**' to mean 'in the whole world', when you are making or emphasizing a statement that you are making or making a very exaggerated statement. ❑ *No human being on the face of the earth could do anything worse than what he did.* 12 PHRASE: PHR after v, PHR n, oft PHR *with* n If you come **face to face** with someone, you meet them and can talk to them or look at them directly. ❑ *We were strolling into the town when we came face to face with Jacques Dubois... It was the first face-to-face meeting between the two men.* 13 PHRASE: PHR after v, PHR n If you come **face to face with** a difficulty or reality, you cannot avoid it and have to deal with it. ❑ *Eventually, he came face to face with discrimination again.* 14 PHRASE: V inflects, PHR n If an action or belief **flies in the face of** accepted ideas or rules, it seems to completely oppose or contradict them. ❑ *...scien-*

*tific principles that seem to fly in the face of common sense.* 15 If you take a particular action or attitude **in the face of** a problem or difficulty, you respond to that problem or difficulty in that way. ❑ *The Prime Minister has called for national unity in the face of the violent anti-government protests.* PREP-PHRASE

16 If you have **a long face**, you look very unhappy or serious. ❑ *He came to me with a very long face.* PHRASE: N inflects

17 If you **make a face**, you show a feeling such as dislike or disgust by putting an exaggerated expression on your face, for example by sticking out your tongue. In British English, you can also say **pull a face.** ❑ *Opening the door, she made a face at the musty smell... Kathryn pulled a face at Thomas behind his back.* PHRASE: V and N inflect, oft PHR *at* n

18 You say **on the face of it** when you are describing how something seems when it is first considered, in order to suggest that people's opinion may change when they know or think more about the subject. ❑ *It is, on the face of it, difficult to see how the West could radically change its position.* PHRASE: PHR with cl

19 If you **put a brave face on** a bad situation or **put on a brave face,** you try not to show how disappointed or upset you are about the situation. In American English you can also say **put on a good face.** ❑ *Friends will see you are putting on a brave face and might assume you've got over your grief... Scientists are putting a good face on the troubles.* PHRASE: V inflects, oft PHR n

20 You can say that someone **has set** their **face against** something to indicate that they are opposed to it, especially when you want to suggest that they are wrong. [mainly BRIT] ❑ *This Government has set its face against putting up income tax.* PHRASE: V inflects, PHR n/-ing

21 If you **show** your **face** somewhere, you go there and see people, although you are not welcome, are rather unwilling to go, or have not been there for some time. ❑ *I felt I ought to show my face at her father's funeral.* PHRASE: V inflects, PHR adv/prep

22 If you manage to keep **a straight face**, you manage to look serious, although you want to laugh. ❑ *What went through Tom's mind I can't imagine, but he did manage to keep a straight face... You have to wonder how anyone could say that seriously and with a straight face.* PHRASE: PHR after v, *with* PHR

23 If you say something **to** someone's **face**, you say it openly in their presence. ❑ *Her opponent called her a liar to her face.* PHRASE: PHR after v

24 If a feeling **is written all over** your **face** or **is written across** your **face**, it is very obvious to other people from your expression. ❑ *Relief and gratitude were written all over his face... I could just see the pain written across her face.* PHRASE: V inflects

25 to **shut the door in** someone's **face** → see **door**. to **have egg on** your **face** → see **egg**. to **cut off** your **nose to spite** your **face** → see **nose**. **a slap in the face** → see **slap**.

**②face** /feɪs/ **(faces, facing, faced)** ◆◆◆

⇛ Please look at category 8 to see if the expression you are looking for is shown under another headword. 1 If someone or something **faces** a particular thing, person, or direction, they are positioned opposite them or are looking in that direction. ❑ *They stood facing each other... The garden faces south.* VERB V n V adv/prep

2 If you **face** someone or something, you turn so that you are looking at them. ❑ *She stood up from the table and faced him... Stand up. Face the wall.* VERB V n V n

3 If you have to **face** a person or group, you have to stand or sit in front of them and talk to them, although it may be difficult and unpleasant. ❑ *Christie looked relaxed and calm as he faced the press.* VERB V n

4 If you **face** or **are faced** with something difficult or unpleasant, or if it **faces** you, it is going to affect you and you have to deal with it. ❑ *Williams faces life in prison if convicted of attempted murder... We are faced with a serious problem.* VERB V n *be* V-ed *with* n

5 If you **face** the truth or **face** the facts, you accept that something is true. If you **face** someone with the truth or with the facts, you try to make them accept that something is true. ❑ *Although your heart is breaking, you must face the truth that a relationship has ended... He accused the Government of refusing to face facts about the economy... He called a family conference and faced them with the problems.* VERB V n V n V n *with* n

◆ **Face up to** means the same as **face.** ❑ *I have grown up now and I have to face up to my responsibilities.* PHRASAL VERB V P P n

6 If you **cannot face** something, you do not feel able to do it because it seems so difficult or unpleasant. ❑ *My children want me with them for Christmas Day, but I can't face it... I couldn't face seeing anyone.* VERB: with neg V n/-ing V n/-ing

7 You use the expression **'let's face it'** when you are stating a fact or making a comment about something which you think the person you are talking to may find unpleasant or be unwilling to admit. ❑ *She was always attracted to younger men. But, let's face it, who is not?* PHRASE: PHR with cl

8 **face the music** → see **music**.

◆ **face down** If you **face** someone **down**, you oppose them or defeat them by being confident and looking at them boldly. [mainly AM] ❑ *He's confronted crowds before and faced them down.* PHRASAL VERB V n P Also V P n (not pron)

◆ **face up to** → see **face 5**.

**face|cloth** /feɪsklɒθ, AM -klɔːθ/ **(facecloths)** also **face cloth.** A **facecloth** is the same as a **face flannel** or **washcloth**. [mainly BRIT] N-COUNT

**face cream (face creams) Face cream** is a thick substance that you rub into your face in order to keep it soft. N-MASS

**-faced** /-feɪst/ **-faced** combines with adjectives to form other adjectives that describe someone's face or expression. ❑ *...a slim, thin-faced man... The committee walked out, grim-faced and shocked.* → See also **ashen-faced, bare-faced, po-faced, poker-faced, red-faced, shame-faced, straight-faced, two-faced.** COMB in ADJ

**face flan|nel (face flannels)** A **face flannel** is a small cloth made of towelling which you use for washing yourself. [BRIT] N-COUNT

✔ in AM, usually use **washcloth**

**face|less** /feɪsləs/ If you describe someone or something as **faceless**, you dislike them because they are uninteresting and have no character. ❑ *Ordinary people are at the mercy of faceless bureaucrats.* ADJ: usu ADJ n disapproval

**face|lift** /feɪslɪft/ **(facelifts)** also **face-lift.** 1 If you give a place or thing **a facelift**, you do something to make it look better or more attractive. ❑ *Nothing gives a room a faster facelift than a coat of paint.* N-COUNT: usu sing

2 A **facelift** is an operation in which a surgeon tightens the skin on someone's face in order to make them look younger. N-COUNT

**face mask (face masks)** 1 A **face mask** is a device that you wear over your face, for example to prevent yourself from breathing bad air or from spreading germs, or to protect your face when you are in a dangerous situation. N-COUNT

2 A **face mask** is the same as a **face pack**. [mainly AM] N-COUNT

**face pack (face packs)** A **face pack** is a thick substance which you spread on your face, allow to dry for a short time, and then remove, in order to clean your skin thoroughly. [BRIT] N-COUNT

✔ in AM, use **face mask**

**face pow|der (face powders) Face powder** is a very fine soft powder that you can put on your face in order to make it look smoother. N-MASS = powder

**face-saver (face-savers)** A **face-saver** is an action or excuse which prevents damage to your reputation or the loss of people's respect for you. [JOURNALISM] N-COUNT

**face-saving** A **face-saving** action is one which prevents damage to your reputation or the loss of people's respect for you. ❑ *The decision appears to be a face-saving compromise which will allow the government to remain in office.* ADJ: ADJ n

**fac|et** /fæsɪt, -set/ **(facets)** 1 A **facet of** something is a single part or aspect of it. ❑ *The caste system shapes nearly every facet of Indian life.* N-COUNT: oft N *of* n

2 The **facets** of a diamond or other precious stone are the flat surfaces that have been cut on its outside. N-COUNT

**fa|cetious** /fəsiːʃəs/ If you say that someone is being **facetious**, you are criticizing them because they are making humorous remarks or saying things that they do not mean in a situation where they ought to be serious. ❑ *The woman eyed him coldly. 'Don't be facetious,' she said.* ADJ disapproval = *flippant*

**face to face** → see **face**.

**face value** [1] The **face value** of things such as coins, paper money, investment documents, or tickets is the amount of money that they are worth, and that is written on them. ❑ *Tickets were selling at twice their face value.* N-SING [2] If you take something **at face value**, you accept it and believe it without thinking about it very much, even though it might untrue. ❑ *Public statements from the various groups involved should not necessarily be taken at face value.* PHRASE: PHR after v

**fa|cial** /feɪʃəl/ **(facials)** [1] **Facial** means appearing on or being part of your face. ❑ *Cross didn't answer; his facial expression didn't change... I ended up in hospital with facial injuries.* ADJ: ADJ n [2] A **facial** is a sort of beauty treatment in which someone's face is massaged, and creams and other substances are rubbed into it. N-COUNT

**fa|cie** /feɪʃi/ → see **prima facie**.

**fac|ile** /fæsaɪl, AM -səl/ If you describe someone's arguments or suggestions as **facile**, you are criticizing them because their ideas are too simple and indicate a lack of careful, intelligent thinking. ❑ *The subject of racism is admittedly too complex for facile summarization.* ADJ disapproval = *simplistic*

**fa|cili|tate** /fəsɪlɪteɪt/ **(facilitates, facilitating, facilitated)** To **facilitate** an action or process, especially one that you would like to happen, means to make it easier or more likely to happen. ❑ *The new airport will facilitate the development of tourism... He argued that the economic recovery had been facilitated by his tough stance.* VERB = *aid, assist* V n V n

**fa|cili|ta|tor** /fəsɪlɪteɪtər/ **(facilitators)** A **facilitator** is a person or organization that helps another person or organization to do or to achieve a particular thing. [FORMAL] N-COUNT

**fa|cil|ity** /fəsɪlɪti/ **(facilities)** [1] **Facilities** are buildings, pieces of equipment, or services that are provided for a particular purpose. ❑ *What recreational facilities are now available?... The problem lies in getting patients to a medical facility as soon as possible.* ◆◆◇ N-COUNT: usu pl, usu with supp [2] A **facility** is something such as an additional service provided by an organization or an extra feature on a machine which is useful but not essential. ❑ *It is very useful to have an overdraft facility.* N-COUNT: with supp, oft n N, N to-inf

**fac|ing** /feɪsɪŋ/ **Facing** is fabric which is stitched inside the edges of a piece of clothing in order to make them look neat and strengthen them. N-UNCOUNT

**fac|simi|le** /fæksɪmɪli/ **(facsimiles)** [1] A **facsimile of** something is an copy or imitation of it. [FORMAL] ❑ *...a facsimile edition of Beethoven's musical manuscripts.* N-COUNT: oft N *of* n, N n [2] A **facsimile** is the same as a **fax**. [FORMAL] N-COUNT

**fact** /fækt/ **(facts)** [1] You use **the fact that** after some verbs or prepositions, especially in expressions such as **in view of the fact that, apart from the fact that**, and **despite the fact that**, to link the verb or preposition with a clause. ❑ *His chances do not seem good in view of the fact that the Chief Prosecutor has already voiced his public disapproval... We have to lie and hide the fact that I have an illness.* ◆◆◆ PHRASE: prep PHR cl, v PHR cl [2] You use **the fact that** instead of a simple that-clause either for emphasis or because the clause is the subject of your sentence. ❑ *The fact that he had left her of his own accord proved to me that everything he'd said was true.* PHRASE: PHR cl, oft v PHR cl, prep PHR cl [3] You use **in fact, in actual fact**, or **in point of fact** to indicate that you are giving more detailed information about what you have just said. ❑ *We've had a pretty bad time while you were away. In fact, we very nearly split up this time... He apologised as soon as he realised what he had done. In actual fact he wrote a nice little note to me.* PHRASE: PHR with cl [4] You use **in fact, in actual fact**, or **in point of fact** to introduce or draw attention to a comment that modifies, contradicts, or contrasts with a previous statement. ❑ *That sounds rather simple, but in fact it's very difficult... Why had she ever trusted her? In point of fact she never had, she reminded herself.* PHRASE: PHR with cl = *actually* [5] When you refer to something as a **fact** or as **fact**, you mean that you think it is true or correct. ❑ *...a statement of verifiable historical fact... How much was fact and how much fancy no one knew.* N-VAR [6] **Facts** are pieces of information that can be discovered. ❑ *There is so much information you can almost effortlessly find the facts for yourself... His opponent swamped him with facts and figures... The lorries always left in the dead of night when there were few witnesses around to record the fact.* N-COUNT [7] You use **as a matter of fact** to introduce a statement that gives more details about what has just been said, or an explanation of it, or something that contrasts with it. ❑ *It's not that difficult. As a matter of fact, it's quite easy... 'I guess you haven't eaten yet.' — 'As a matter of fact, I have,' said Hunter.* PHRASE: PHR with cl = *actually* [8] If you say that you know something **for a fact**, you are emphasizing that you are completely certain that it is true. ❑ *I know for a fact that Graham has kept in close touch with Alan.* PHRASE: PHR after v emphasis [9] You use **the fact is** or **the fact of the matter is** to introduce and draw attention to a summary or statement of the most important point about what you have been saying. ❑ *The fact is blindness hadn't stopped the children doing many of the things that sighted children enjoy... The fact of the matter is that student finances are stretched.* PHRASE: V inflects, PHR cl

**fact-finding** A **fact-finding** mission or visit is one whose purpose is to get information about a particular situation, especially for an official group. ❑ *A UN fact-finding mission is on its way to the region.* ADJ: ADJ n

**fac|tion** /fækʃən/ **(factions)** [1] A **faction** is an organized group of people within a larger group, which opposes some of the ideas of the larger group and fights for its own ideas. ❑ *A peace agreement will be signed by the leaders of the country's warring factions.* ◆◇◇ N-COUNT [2] **Faction** is also used to describe argument and disagreement within a group of people. ❑ *Faction and self-interest appear to be the norm.* N-UNCOUNT

**fac|tion|al** /fækʃənəl/ **Factional** arguments or disputes involve two or more small groups from within a larger group. ❑ *...factional disputes between the various groups that make up the leadership.* ADJ: usu ADJ n

**fac|tion|al|ism** /fækʃənəlɪzəm/ **Factionalism** refers to arguments or disputes between two or more small groups from within a larger group. ❑ *There has been a substantial amount of factionalism within the movement.* N-UNCOUNT

**fact of life (facts of life)** [1] You say that something which is not pleasant is a **fact of life** when there is nothing you can do to change it so you must accept it. ❑ *Stress is a fact of life from time to time for all of us.* N-COUNT [2] If you tell a child about **the facts of life**, you tell him or her about sexual intercourse and how babies are born. ❑ *There comes a time when children need to know more than the basic facts of life.* N-PLURAL: *the* N

**fac|tor** /fæktər/ **(factors, factoring, factored)** [1] A **factor** is one of the things that affects an event, decision, or situation. ❑ *Physical activity is an important factor in maintaining fitness.* ◆◆◇ N-COUNT [2] If an amount increases by **a factor of** two, for example, or by **a factor of** eight, then it becomes two times bigger or eight times bigger. ❑ *The cost of butter quadrupled and bread prices increased by a factor of five.* N-COUNT: usu sing, usu *a* N *of* num [3] You can use **factor** to refer to a particular level on a scale of measurement. ❑ *...suncream with a protection factor of 8.* N-SING: usu *a* N *of* num [4] A **factor** of a whole number is a smaller whole number which can be multiplied with another whole N-COUNT number to produce the first whole number. [TECHNICAL]

♦ **factor in** or **factor into** If you **factor** a particular cost or element **into** a calculation you are making, or if you **factor** it **in**, you include it. [mainly AM] ❑ *Using a computer model they factored in the costs of transplants for those women who die... You'd better consider this and factor this into your decision making.* PHRASAL VERB V P n (not pron) V n P n Also V n P

**fac|to|ry** /fæktri/ **(factories)** A **factory** is a large building where machines are used to make large quantities of goods. ❑ *He owned furniture factories in New York State.* ◆◆◇ N-COUNT: oft n N

**fac|to|ry farm|ing** **Factory farming** is a system of farming which involves keeping animals indoors, often with very little space, and giving them special foods so that they grow more quickly or produce more eggs or milk. [mainly BRIT] N-UNCOUNT

**fac|to|ry floor** **The factory floor** refers to the workers in a factory, as opposed to the managers. It can also refer to the area where they work. ❑ *He had worked on the factory floor for 16 years.* N-SING: the N

**fac|to|ry out|let** **(factory outlets)** or **factory shop** A **factory outlet** is a shop where a factory sells damaged or out-of-date goods directly to customers at reduced prices. N-COUNT: oft N n

**fac|to|ry ship** **(factory ships)** A **factory ship** is a large fishing boat which has equipment for processing the fish that are caught, for example by cleaning or freezing them, before it returns to port. N-COUNT

**fac|to|tum** /fæktoutəm/ **(factotums)** A **factotum** is a servant who is employed to do a wide variety of jobs for someone. [FORMAL] N-COUNT

**fact sheet** **(fact sheets)** A **fact sheet** is a short, printed document with information about a particular subject, especially a summary of information that has been given on a radio or television programme. N-COUNT

**fac|tual** /fæktʃuəl/ Something that is **factual** is concerned with facts or contains facts, rather than giving theories or personal interpretations. ❑ *The editorial contained several factual errors... Any comparison that is not strictly factual runs the risk of being interpreted as subjective.* ♦ **fac|tu|al|ly** *I learned that a number of statements in my talk were factually wrong.* ADJ ADV: ADV adj/-ed, ADV after v

**fac|ul|ty** /fækəlti/ **(faculties)** [1] Your **faculties** are your physical and mental abilities. ❑ *He was drunk and not in control of his faculties... It is also a myth that the faculty of hearing is greatly increased in blind people.* [2] A **faculty** is a group of related departments in some universities, or the people who work in them. [BRIT] ❑ *...the Faculty of Social and Political Sciences.* [3] A **faculty** is all the teaching staff of a university or college, or of one department. [AM] ❑ *The faculty agreed on a change in the requirements... How can faculty improve their teaching so as to encourage creativity? ...eminent Stanford faculty members.* N-COUNT: usu pl, oft poss N, N of n N-VAR N-VAR: oft N n

**fad** /fæd/ **(fads)** You use **fad** to refer to an activity or topic of interest that is very popular for a short time, but which people become bored with very quickly. ❑ *Hamnett does not believe environmental concern is a passing fad.* N-COUNT = craze

**fad|dish** /fædɪʃ/ If you describe something as **faddish**, you mean that it has no real value and that it will not remain popular for very long. ❑ *...faddish footwear.* ADJ

**fad|dy** /fædi/ If you describe someone as **faddy**, you mean that they have very strong likes and dislikes, especially about what they eat, which you think are rather silly. [BRIT] ❑ *My boys have always been faddy eaters.* ADJ [disapproval] = fussy

**fade** /feɪd/ **(fades, fading, faded)** [1] When a coloured object **fades** or when the light **fades** it, it gradually becomes paler. ❑ *All colour fades – especially under the impact of direct sunlight... No matter how soft the light is, it still plays havoc, fading carpets and curtains in every room. ...fading portraits of the Queen and Prince Philip.* ♦ **fad|ed** *...a girl in a faded dress. ...faded painted signs on the sides of some of the buildings.* [2] When light **fades**, it slowly becomes less bright. When a sound **fades**, it slowly becomes less loud. ❑ *Seaton lay on his bed and gazed at the ceiling as the light faded... The sound of the last bomber's engines faded into the distance.* [3] When something that you are looking at **fades**, it slowly becomes less bright or clear until it disappears. ❑ *They observed the comet for 70 days before it faded from sight... They watched the familiar mountains fade into the darkness.* ♦ **Fade away** means the same as **fade**. ❑ *We watched the harbour and then the coastline fade away into the morning mist.* [4] If memories, feelings, or possibilities **fade**, they slowly become less intense or less strong. ❑ *Sympathy for the rebels, the government claims, is beginning to fade. ...fading memories of better days.* ◆◇◇ VERB V V n V-ing ADJ VERB V V into n VERB V from/into n PHRASAL VERB V P into n Also V P VERB V V-ing

♦ **fade out** [1] When something **fades out**, it slowly becomes less noticeable or less important until it disappears completely. ❑ *He thought her campaign would probably fade out soon in any case.* [2] When light, an image or a sound **fades out**, it disappears after gradually becoming weaker. ❑ *You'll need to be able to project two images onto the screen as the new one fades in and the old image fades out.* PHRASAL VERB = fizzle out V P Also V P of n PHRASAL VERB V P Also V P of n

**fae|cal** /fiːkəl/

☑ in AM, use **fecal**

**Faecal** means referring or relating to faeces. [FORMAL] ❑ *One of the ways the parasite spreads is through fecal matter.* ADJ

**fae|ces** /fiːsiːz/

☑ in AM, use **feces**

**Faeces** is the solid waste substance that people and animals get rid of from their body by passing it through the anus. [FORMAL] N-UNCOUNT

**faff** /fæf/ **(faffs, faffing, faffed)**

♦ **faff about** or **faff around** If you say that someone is **faffing about** or **faffing around**, you mean that they are doing things in a disorganized way and not achieving very much. [BRIT, INFORMAL] ❑ *It was annoying to watch them faffing around when a more direct response was required.* PHRASAL VERB V P

**fag** /fæg/ **(fags)** [1] A **fag** is a cigarette. [mainly BRIT, INFORMAL] [2] A **fag** is a homosexual. [mainly AM, INFORMAL, OFFENSIVE] N-COUNT N-COUNT

**fag end** **(fag ends)** also **fag-end.** [1] A **fag end** is the last part of a cigarette, which people throw away when they have smoked the rest. [BRIT, INFORMAL] [2] If you refer to the **fag end** of something, you mean the last part of it, especially when you consider this part boring or unimportant. [INFORMAL] ❑ *He never had much confidence in his judgement at the fag-end of the working day.* N-COUNT = butt N-COUNT: usu sing, N of n

**fag|got** /fægət/ **(faggots)** A **faggot** is a homosexual man. [AM, INFORMAL, OFFENSIVE] N-COUNT

**Fahr|en|heit** /færənhaɪt/ **Fahrenheit** is a scale for measuring temperature, in which water freezes at 32 degrees and boils at 212 degrees. It is represented by the symbol °F. ❑ *By mid-morning, the temperature was already above 100 degrees Fahrenheit.* ♦ **Fahrenheit** is also a noun. ❑ *He was asked for the boiling point of water in Fahrenheit.* ADJ: n/num ADJ N-UNCOUNT

**fail** /feɪl/ **(fails, failing, failed)** [1] If you **fail** to do something that you were trying to do, you are unable to do it or do not succeed in doing it. ❑ *The Workers' Party failed to win a single governorship... He failed in his attempt to take control of the company... Many of us have tried to lose weight and failed miserably... The truth is, I'm a failed comedy writer really.* [2] If an activity, attempt, or plan **fails**, it is not successful. ❑ *We tried to develop plans for them to get along, which all failed miserably... He was afraid the revolution they had started would fail... After a failed military offensive, all government troops* ◆◆◆ VERB ≠ succeed V to-inf V in n V V-ed VERB ≠ succeed V V V-ed *and police were withdrawn from the island.* 3 VERB If someone or something **fails** to do a particular thing that they should have done, they do not do it. [FORMAL] ❑ V to-inf *Some schools fail to set any homework... The bomb failed to explode.* V to-inf 4 VERB If something **fails**, it stops working properly, or does not do what it is supposed to do. ❑ V *The lights mysteriously failed, and we stumbled around in complete darkness...* V *In fact many food crops failed because of the drought.* 5 VERB If a business, organization, or system **fails**, it becomes unable to continue in operation or in existence. [BUSINESS] ❑ V *So far this year, 104 banks have failed.* V-ed *...a failed hotel business...* V-ing *Who wants to buy a computer from a failing company?* 6 VERB If something such as your health or a physical quality **is failing**, it is becoming gradually weaker or less effective. ❑ V *He was 58, and his health was failing rapidly...* V-ing *An apparently failing memory is damaging for a national leader.* 7 VERB If someone **fails** you, they do not do what you had expected or trusted them to do. ❑ V n *...communities who feel that the political system has failed them.* 8 VERB If someone **fails in** their duty or **fails in** their responsibilities, they do not do everything that they have a duty or a responsibility to do. ❑ V *in* n *If we did not report what was happening in the country, we would be failing in our duty.* 9 VERB If a quality or ability that you have **fails** you, or if it **fails**, it is not good enough in a particular situation to enable you to do what you want to do. ❑ V n *For once, the artist's fertile imagination failed him...* V *Their courage failed a few steps short and they came running back.* 10 VERB ≠pass If someone **fails** a test, examination, or course, they perform badly in it and do not reach the standard that is required. ❑ V n *I lived in fear of failing my end-of-term exams.* ♦ N-COUNT **Fail** is also a noun. ❑ *It's the difference between a pass and a fail.* 11 VERB ≠pass If someone **fails** you in a test, examination, or course, they judge that you have not reached a high enough standard in it. ❑ V n *...the two men who had failed him during his first year of law school.*

**PHRASES** 12 PHRASE: PHR with cl You say **if all else fails** to suggest what could be done in a certain situation if all the other things you have tried are unsuccessful. ❑ *If all else fails, I could always drive a truck.* 13 PHRASE: PHR with cl [emphasis] You use **without fail** to emphasize that something always happens. ❑ *He attended every meeting without fail.* 14 PHRASE: PHR with cl [emphasis] You use **without fail** to emphasize an order or a promise. ❑ *On the 30th you must without fail hand in some money for Alex.*

**fail|ing** /feɪlɪŋ/ **(failings)** 1 N-COUNT: usu pl, oft with poss = shortcoming The **failings** of someone or something are their faults or unsatisfactory features. ❑ *Like many in Russia, she blamed the country's failings on futile attempts to catch up with the West.* 2 PHRASE: PHR with cl/group You say **failing that** to introduce an alternative, in case what you have just said is not possible. ❑ *Find someone who will let you talk things through, or failing that, write down your thoughts.*

**fail-safe** also **failsafe.** ADJ: usu ADJ n Something that is **fail-safe** is designed or made in such a way that nothing dangerous can happen if a part of it goes wrong. ❑ *The camera has a built-in failsafe device which prevents it from working if the right signals aren't received.*

**fail|ure** /feɪljəʳ/ **(failures)** ♦♦◇ 1 N-UNCOUNT ≠success **Failure** is a lack of success in doing or achieving something, especially in relation to a particular activity. ❑ *This policy is doomed to failure... Three attempts on the British 200-metre record also ended in failure. ...feelings of failure.* 2 N-COUNT ≠success If something is **a failure**, it is not a success. ❑ *The marriage was a failure and they both wanted to be free of it... His six-year transition programme has by no means been a complete failure.* 3 N-COUNT ≠success If you say that someone is **a failure**, you mean that they have not succeeded in a particular activity, or that they are unsuccessful at everything they do. ❑ *Elgar received many honors and much acclaim and yet he often considered himself a failure.* 4 N-UNCOUNT: N to-inf, oft poss N Your **failure to** do a particular thing is the fact that you do not do it, even though you were expected to do it. ❑ *...their failure to get the product mix right.* 5 N-VAR: with supp, oft n N If there is a **failure** of something, for example a machine or part of the body, it goes wrong and stops working or developing properly. ❑ *There were also several accidents mainly caused by engine failures on take-off... He was being treated for kidney failure.* 6 N-VAR: with supp = collapse If there is a **failure** of a business or bank, it is no longer able to continue operating. [BUSINESS] ❑ *Business failures rose 16% last month.*

**faint** /feɪnt/ **(fainter, faintest, faints, fainting, fainted)** 1 ADJ: usu ADJ n A **faint** sound, colour, mark, feeling, or quality has very little strength or intensity. ❑ *He became aware of the soft, faint sounds of water dripping... He could see faint lines in her face... There was still the faint hope deep within him that she might never need to know.* ♦ ADV: usu ADV after v, also ADV adj = slightly **faint|ly** *He was already asleep in the bed, which smelled faintly of mildew... She felt faintly ridiculous.* 2 ADJ: ADJ n A **faint** attempt at something is one that is made without proper effort and with little enthusiasm. ❑ *Caroline made a faint attempt at a laugh... A faint smile crossed the Monsignor's face and faded quickly.* ♦ ADV: ADV after v **faint|ly** *John smiled faintly and shook his head.* 3 VERB = pass out If you **faint**, you lose consciousness for a short time, especially because you are hungry, or because of pain, heat, or shock. ❑ V *She suddenly fell forward on to the table and fainted...* V *I thought he'd faint when I kissed him.* ♦ N-COUNT: oft *in a* N **Faint** is also a noun. ❑ *She slumped to the ground in a faint.* 4 ADJ: v-link ADJ Someone who is **faint** feels weak and unsteady as if they are about to lose consciousness. ❑ *Other signs of angina are nausea, sweating, feeling faint and shortness of breath.*

**faint|est** /feɪntɪst/ ADJ: ADJ n, with neg [emphasis] = slightest, remotest You can use **faintest** for emphasis in negative statements. For example, if you say that someone hasn't the **faintest** idea what to do, you are emphasizing that they do not know what to do. ❑ *I haven't the faintest idea how to care for a snake.*

**faint-hearted** also **fainthearted.** 1 ADJ If you describe someone or their behaviour as **faint-hearted**, you mean that they are not very confident and do not take strong action because they are afraid of failing. ❑ *This is no time to be faint-hearted.* 2 PHRASE: usu v-link PHR If you say that something is **not for the faint-hearted**, you mean that it is an extreme or very unusual example of its kind, and is not suitable for people who like only safe and familiar things. ❑ *It's a film about a serial killer and not for the faint-hearted.*

**fair** /feəʳ/ **(fairer, fairest, fairs)** ♦♦◇ 1 ADJ: oft *it* v-link ADJ to-inf Something or someone that is **fair** is reasonable, right, and just. ❑ *It didn't seem fair to leave out her father... Do you feel they're paying their fair share?... Independent observers say the campaign's been very much fairer than expected... An appeals court had ruled that they could not get a fair trial in Los Angeles.* ♦ ADV: usu ADV after v, also ADV -ed **fair|ly** *...demonstrating concern for employees and solving their problems quickly and fairly... In a society where water was precious, it had to be shared fairly between individuals.* 2 ADJ: ADJ n A **fair** amount, degree, size, or distance is quite a large amount, degree, size, or distance. ❑ *My neighbours across the street travel a fair amount... My mother's brother lives a fair distance away so we don't see him and his family very often.* 3 ADJ: ADJ n = reasonable A **fair** guess or idea about something is one that is likely to be correct. ❑ *It's a fair guess to say that the damage will be extensive... I have a fair idea of how difficult things can be.* 4 ADJ = adequate If you describe someone or something as **fair**, you mean that they are average in standard or quality, neither very good nor very bad. ❑ *Reimar had a fair command of English.* 5 ADJ Someone who is **fair**, or who has **fair** hair, has light-coloured hair. ❑ *Both children were very like Robina, but were much fairer than she was.* ♦ COMB in ADJ **Fair** is also a combining form. ❑ *...a tall, fair-haired Englishman.* 6 ADJ **Fair** skin is very pale and usually burns easily. ❑ *It's important to protect my fair skin from the sun.* ♦ COMB in ADJ **Fair** is also a combining form. ❑ *Fair-skinned people who spend a great deal of time in the sun have the greatest risk of skin cancer.* 7 ADJ When the weather is **fair**, it is quite sunny and not raining. [FORMAL] ❑ *Weather conditions were fair.* [= fine] 8 A county, state, or country **fair** is an event where there are, for example, displays of goods and animals, and amusements, games, and competitions. [N-COUNT: usu n N] 9 A **fair** is an event at which people display and sell goods, especially goods of a particular type. ❑ *...an antiques fair.* ➔ See also **craft fair, trade fair**. [N-COUNT: oft n N]

PHRASES 10 You use **fair enough** when you want to say that a statement, decision, or action seems reasonable to a certain extent, but that perhaps there is more to be said or done. [mainly SPOKEN] ❑ *If you don't like it, fair enough, but that's hardly a justification to attack the whole thing.* [PHRASE: PHR with cl] 11 If you say that someone **plays fair**, you mean that they behave or act in a reasonable and honest way. ❑ *The government is not playing fair, one union official told me.* [PHRASE: V inflects] 12 If you say that someone won a competition **fair and square**, you mean that they won honestly and without cheating. ❑ *There are no excuses. We were beaten fair and square.* [PHRASE: PHR after v]

**fair game** If you say that someone is **fair game**, you mean that it is acceptable to criticize or attack them, usually because of the way that they behave. ❑ *Politicians were always considered fair game by cartoonists.* [N-UNCOUNT]

**fair|ground** /fɛəʳgraʊnd/ **(fairgrounds)** A **fairground** is an area of land where a fair is held. [N-COUNT]

**fair|ly** /fɛəʳli/ ◆◇◇ 1 **Fairly** means to quite a large degree. For example, if you say that something is **fairly** old, you mean that it is old but not very old. ❑ *Both ships are fairly new... We did fairly well but only fairly well.* [ADV: ADV adj/adv = quite] 2 You use **fairly** instead of 'very' to add emphasis to an adjective or adverb without making it sound too forceful. ❑ *Were you always fairly bright at school?... I'll have no income and no home and will need a job fairly badly.* [ADV: ADV adj/adv, vagueness = pretty] 3 ➔ See also **fair**.

**fair-minded** A **fair-minded** person always tries to be fair and reasonable, and always listens to other people's opinions. ❑ *She is one of the most fair-minded people I know.* [ADJ: oft ADJ n]

**fair|ness** /fɛəʳnəs/ **Fairness** is the quality of being reasonable, right, and just. ❑ *...concern about the fairness of the election campaign.* [N-UNCOUNT]

**fair play** If you refer to someone's attitude or behaviour as **fair play**, you approve of it because it shows respect and sympathy towards everyone, even towards people who are thought to be wrong or to deserve punishment. ❑ *...a legal system that is unmatched anywhere in the world for its justice and sense of fair play.* [N-UNCOUNT, approval]

**fair sex** also **fairer sex.** If a man talks about **the fair sex**, he is referring to women in general. [OLD-FASHIONED] [N-SING: the N]

**fair trade** **Fair trade** is the practice of buying goods directly from producers in developing countries at a fair price. ❑ *...fair trade coffee.* [N-UNCOUNT: oft N n]

**fair|way** /fɛəʳweɪ/ **(fairways)** **The fairway** on a golf course is the long strip of short grass between each tee and green. [N-COUNT: usu the N]

**fair-weather** You use **fair-weather** to refer to someone who offers help to someone, or who takes part in a particular activity, only when it is easy or pleasant for them to do so. ❑ *...a fair-weather friend.* [ADJ: ADJ n, disapproval]

**fairy** /fɛəri/ **(fairies)** 1 A **fairy** is an imaginary creature with magical powers. Fairies are often represented as small people with wings. [N-COUNT] 2 If someone describes a man as a **fairy**, they mean that he is a homosexual and they disapprove of this. [OFFENSIVE, OLD-FASHIONED] [N-COUNT, disapproval]

**fairy god|mother** If you call a woman your **fairy godmother**, you are saying in a slightly humorous way that she has been very helpful in your life, often at times when you thought you had problems that could not be solved. [N-SING: poss N]

**fairy|land** /fɛərilænd/ **(fairylands)** 1 **Fairyland** is the imaginary place where fairies live. [N-UNCOUNT] 2 If you describe a place as a **fairyland**, you mean that it has a delicate beauty. ❑ *If you came with me to one of my toy shops, you'd think you were stepping into a fairyland.* [N-VAR]

**fairy lights** **Fairy lights** are small, coloured electric lights that are hung up as decorations, for example on a Christmas tree. [BRIT] [N-PLURAL]

**fairy sto|ry** **(fairy stories)** A **fairy story** is the same as a **fairy tale**. [N-COUNT]

**fairy tale** **(fairy tales)** also **fairytale.** A **fairy tale** is a story for children involving magical events and imaginary creatures. ❑ *She was like a princess in a fairy tale.* [N-COUNT]

**fait ac|com|pli** /feɪt əkɒmpli, AM -ækɔːmpliː/ **(faits accomplis)** If something is **a fait accompli**, it has already been decided or done and cannot be changed. [FORMAL] ❑ *They became increasingly annoyed that they were being presented with a fait accompli.* [N-COUNT: usu sing]

**faith** /feɪθ/ **(faiths)** ◆◇◇ 1 If you have **faith in** someone or something, you feel confident about their ability or goodness. ❑ *She had placed a great deal of faith in Mr Penleigh... People have lost faith in the British Parliament.* [N-UNCOUNT: usu N *in* n = confidence] 2 A **faith** is a particular religion, for example Christianity, Buddhism, or Islam. ❑ *England shifted officially from a Catholic to a Protestant faith in the 16th century.* [N-COUNT: also no det, usu adj N] 3 **Faith** is strong religious belief in a particular God. ❑ *Umberto Eco's loss of his own religious faith is reflected in his novels.* [N-UNCOUNT]

PHRASES 4 If you **break faith with** someone you made a promise to or something you believed in, you stop acting in a way that supports them. ❑ *If we don't, we're breaking faith with our people!* [PHRASE: V inflects] 5 If you do something **in good faith**, you seriously believe that what you are doing is right, honest, or legal, even though this may not be the case. ❑ *This report was published in good faith but we regret any confusion which may have been caused.* [PHRASE: PHR after v] 6 If you **keep faith with** someone you have made a promise to or something you believe in, you continue to support them even when it is difficult to do so. ❑ *He has made one of the most powerful American films of the year by keeping faith with his radical principles.* [PHRASE: V inflects, PHR n] 7 ➔ See also **article of faith, leap of faith**.

**faith|ful** /feɪθfʊl/ 1 Someone who is **faithful to** a person, organization, idea, or activity remains firm in their belief in them or support for them. ❑ *She had been faithful to her promise to guard this secret... Older Americans are among this country's most faithful voters.* [ADJ: oft ADJ *to* n] ♦ **The faithful** are people who are faithful to someone or something. ❑ *He spends his time making speeches at factories or gatherings of the Party faithful.* [N-PLURAL: the N] ♦ **faith|ful|ly** *He has since 1965 faithfully followed and supported every twist and turn of government policy.* [ADV: ADV with v] 2 Someone who is **faithful to** their husband, wife, or lover does not have a sexual relationship with anyone else. ❑ *She insisted that she had remained faithful to her husband.* [ADJ: oft ADJ *to* n ≠ unfaithful] 3 A **faithful** account, translation, or copy of something represents or reproduces the original accurately. ❑ *Colin Welland's screenplay is faithful to the novel.* [ADJ: oft ADJ *to* n] ♦ **faith|ful|ly** *When I adapt something I translate from one meaning to another as faithfully as I can.* [ADV: ADV with v]

**faith|ful|ly** /feɪθfʊli/ When you start a formal or business letter with 'Dear Sir' or 'Dear Madam', you write **Yours faithfully** before your signature at the end. [BRIT] ➔ See also **faithful**. [CONVENTION]

✔ in AM, use **Sincerely yours**

**faith heal|er** **(faith healers)** A **faith healer** is someone who believes they can treat and heal sick people using prayer or supernatural powers. [N-COUNT]

**faith heal|ing** also **faith-healing. Faith healing** is the treatment of a sick person by someone who believes that they are able to heal people through prayer or a supernatural power. [N-UNCOUNT]

**faith|less** /feɪθləs/ If you say that someone is **faithless**, you mean that they are disloyal or dis- [ADJ] honest. ❑ *She decided to divorce her increasingly faithless and unreliable husband.*

**fake** /feɪk/ **(fakes, faking, faked)** ADJ: usu ADJ n [1] A **fake** fur or a **fake** painting, for example, is a fur or painting that has been made to look valuable or genuine, usually in order to deceive people. ❑ *The bank manager is said to have issued fake certificates.* N-COUNT ♦ A **fake** is something that is fake. ❑ *It is filled with famous works of art, and every one of them is a fake.*
VERB [2] If someone **fakes** something, they try to make it look valuable or genuine, although in fact it is not. V n ❑ *He faked his own death last year to collect on a $1 million insurance policy.* V-ed ...*faked evidence.*
N-COUNT = fraud [3] Someone who is a **fake** is not what they claim to be, for example because they do not have the qualifications that they claim to have. VERB [4] If you **fake** a feeling, emotion, or reaction, you pretend that you are experiencing it when you are not. V n ❑ *Jon faked nonchalance...* V n *Maturity and emotional sophistication can't be faked.*

**fal|con** /fɔːlkən, fælk-/ **(falcons)** N-COUNT A **falcon** is a bird of prey that can be trained to hunt other birds and animals.

**fal|con|er** /fɔːlkənəʳ, fælk-/ **(falconers)** N-COUNT A **falconer** is someone who trains and uses falcons for hunting.

**fal|con|ry** /fɔːlkənri, fælk-/ N-UNCOUNT **Falconry** is the skill of training falcons to hunt, and the sport of using them to hunt.

**fall** /fɔːl/ **(falls, falling, fell, fallen)** ◆◆◆ VERB [1] If someone or something **falls**, they move quickly downwards onto or towards the ground, by accident or because of a natural force. V prep ❑ *Her father fell into the sea after a massive heart attack...* V *Bombs fell in the town...* V out/off *I ought to seal the boxes up. I don't want the books falling out...* V-ing *Twenty people were injured by falling masonry.* N-COUNT: oft N from n ♦ **Fall** is also a noun. ❑ *The helmets are designed to withstand impacts equivalent to a fall from a bicycle.* VERB [2] If a person or structure that is standing somewhere **falls**, they move from their upright position, so that they are then lying on the ground. V ❑ *The woman gripped the shoulders of her man to stop herself from falling...* V prep/adv *We watched buildings fall on top of people and pets...* V prep/adv *He lost his balance and fell backwards.* N-COUNT ♦ **Fall** is also a noun. ❑ *Mrs Briscoe had a bad fall last week.* PHRASAL VERB ♦ **Fall down** means the same as **fall**. V P ❑ *I hit him so hard he fell down...* V P *Children jumped from upper floors as the building fell down around them.* ADJ: ADJ n ♦ **fall|en** *A number of roads have been blocked by fallen trees.* VERB [3] When rain or snow **falls**, it comes down from the sky. V ❑ *Winds reached up to 100mph in some places with an inch of rain falling within 15 minutes.* N-COUNT: N of n ♦ **Fall** is also a noun. ❑ *One night there was a heavy fall of snow.* → See also **rainfall**, **snowfall**. VERB [4] If you **fall** somewhere, you allow yourself to drop there in a hurried or disorganized way, often because you are very tired. V prep ❑ *Totally exhausted, he tore his clothes off and fell into bed.* VERB = drop ≠ rise [5] If something **falls**, it decreases in amount, value, or strength. V by n ❑ *Output will fall by 6%...* V to/from n *Her weight fell to under seven stones...* V amount *Between July and August, oil product prices fell 0.2 per cent...* V *The number of prosecutions has stayed static and the rate of convictions has fallen.* V-ing ...*a time of falling living standards and emerging mass unemployment.* N-COUNT: usu sing ♦ **Fall** is also a noun. ❑ *There was a sharp fall in the value of the pound.* VERB [6] If a powerful or successful person **falls**, they suddenly lose their power or position. V ❑ *There's a danger of the government falling because it will lose its majority...* V from n *The moment Mrs Thatcher fell from power has left a lasting imprint on the world's memory.* N-SING: with poss ≠ rise ♦ **Fall** is also a noun. ❑ *Following the fall of the military dictator in March, the country has had a civilian government.* VERB [7] If a place **falls** in a war or election, an enemy army or a different political party takes control of it. V to n ❑ *Croatian army troops retreated from northern Bosnia and the area fell to the Serbs...* V *With the announcement 'Paphos has fallen!' a cheer went up from the assembled soldiers.* N-SING: usu N of n ♦ **Fall** is also a noun. ❑ ...*the fall of Rome.* VERB [8] If someone **falls** in battle, they are killed. [LITERARY] V ❑ *Another wave of troops followed the first, running past those who had fallen.* V-LINK [9] You can use **fall** to show that someone or something passes into another state. For example, if someone **falls ill**, they become ill, and if something **falls into disrepair**, it is then in a state of disrepair. V in/into/out of n ❑ *It is almost impossible to visit Florida without falling in love with the state...* V adj *I took Moira to the cinema, where she fell asleep...* V n *Almost without exception these women fall victim to exploitation.* VERB [10] If you say that something or someone **falls into** a particular group or category, you mean that they belong in that group or category. V into n ❑ *The problems generally fall into two categories...* V into n *Both women fall into the highest-risk group.* VERB [11] If the responsibility or blame for something **falls on** someone, they have to take the responsibility or the blame for it. [WRITTEN] V on n ❑ *That responsibility falls on the local office of the United Nations High Commissioner for Refugees.* VERB [12] If a celebration or other special event **falls on** a particular day or date, it happens to be on that day or date. V on n ❑ ...*the oddly named Quasimodo Sunday which falls on the first Sunday after Easter.* VERB [13] When light or shadow **falls** on something, it covers it. V across/over/on n ❑ *Nancy, out of the corner of her eye, saw the shadow that suddenly fell across the doorway.* VERB [14] If someone's hair or a garment **falls** in a certain way, it hangs downwards in that way. V prep/adv ❑ ...*a slender boy with black hair falling across his forehead.* VERB [15] If you say that someone's eyes **fell on** something, you mean they suddenly noticed it. [WRITTEN] V on/upon n ❑ *As he laid the flowers on the table, his eye fell upon a note in Grace's handwriting.* VERB [16] When night or darkness **falls**, night begins and it becomes dark. V ❑ *As darkness fell outside, they sat down to eat at long tables.* N-PLURAL; N-IN-NAMES [17] You can refer to a waterfall as **the falls**. ❑ ...*panoramic views of the falls.* ...*Niagara Falls.* N-VAR [18] **Fall** is the season between summer and winter when the weather becomes cooler. [AM] ❑ *He was elected judge in the fall of 1991... The Supreme Court will not hear the case until next fall.*

☑ in BRIT, use **autumn**

[19] → See also **fallen**. PHRASE: V inflects [20] To **fall to pieces**, or in British English to **fall to bits**, means the same as to **fall apart**. ❑ *At that point the radio handset fell to pieces.* [21] to **fall on** your **feet** → see **foot**. to **fall foul of** → see **foul**. to **fall flat** → see **flat**. to **fall from grace** → see **grace**. to **fall into place** → see **place**. to **fall short** → see **short**. to **fall into** the **trap** → see **trap**. to **fall by the wayside** → see **wayside**.

♦ **fall apart** PHRASAL VERB [1] If something **falls apart**, it breaks into pieces because it is old or badly made. V P ❑ *The work was never finished and bit by bit the building fell apart.* PHRASAL VERB = break down [2] If an organization or system **falls apart**, it becomes disorganized or unable to work effectively, or breaks up into its different parts. V P ❑ *Europe's monetary system is falling apart...* V P *I've tried everything to stop our marriage falling apart.* PHRASAL VERB = crack up [3] If you say that someone **is falling apart**, you mean that they are becoming emotionally disturbed and are unable to think calmly or to deal with the difficult or unpleasant situation that they are in. [INFORMAL] V P ❑ *I was falling apart. I wasn't getting any sleep.*

♦ **fall away** PHRASAL VERB [1] If something **falls away** from the thing it is attached to, it breaks off. V P from n Also V P ❑ *Officials say that one or two engines fell away from the plane shortly after takeoff.* PHRASAL VERB [2] If you say that land **falls away**, you mean it slopes downwards from a particular point. V P ❑ *On either side of the tracks the ground fell away sharply.* PHRASAL VERB = fall off [3] If the degree, amount, or size of something **falls away**, it decreases. V P ❑ *His coalition may hold a clear majority but this could quickly fall away.*

♦ **fall back** PHRASAL VERB [1] If you **fall back**, you move backwards a short distance away from someone or something. V P ❑ *He fell back in embarrassment when he saw that Ross had no hair at all...* V P from n *The congregation fell back from them slightly as they entered.* PHRASAL VERB [2] If an army **falls back** during a battle or war, it withdraws. ❑ *The Prussian garrison at Charleroi was falling back.* V P

♦ **fall back on** If you **fall back on** something, you do it or use it after other things have failed. ❑ *Unable to defeat him by logical discussion, she fell back on her old habit of criticizing his speech... When necessary, instinct is the most reliable resource you can fall back on.* PHRASAL VERB V P P n V P P n

♦ **fall behind** [1] If you **fall behind**, you do not make progress or move forward as fast as other people. ❑ *Evans had rheumatic fever, missed school and fell behind... Boris is falling behind all the top players.* [2] If you **fall behind** with something or let it **fall behind**, you do not do it or produce it when you should, according to an agreement or schedule. ❑ *He faces losing his home after falling behind with the payments... Thousands of people could die because the relief effort has fallen so far behind... Construction work fell behind schedule.* PHRASAL VERB V P V P n PHRASAL VERB V P *with* n V P V P n

♦ **fall down** [1] → see **fall 2**. [2] If an argument, organization, or person **falls down on** a particular point, they are weak or unsatisfactory on that point. ❑ *Service was outstandingly friendly and efficient, falling down on only one detail... That is where his argument falls down.* PHRASAL VERB = *fail* V P *on* n V P

♦ **fall for** [1] If you **fall for** someone, you are strongly attracted to them and start loving them. ❑ *He was fantastically handsome – I just fell for him right away.* [2] If you **fall for** a lie or trick, you believe it or are deceived by it. ❑ *It was just a line to get you out here, and you fell for it!* PHRASAL VERB V P n PHRASAL VERB V P n

♦ **fall in** If a roof or ceiling **falls in**, it collapses and falls to the ground. ❑ *Part of my bedroom ceiling has fallen in.* PHRASAL VERB = *cave in* V P

♦ **fall into** If you **fall into** conversation or a discussion with someone, usually someone you have just met, you start having a conversation or discussion with them. ❑ *Over breakfast at my motel, I fell into conversation with the owner of a hardware shop.* PHRASAL VERB V P n

♦ **fall off** [1] If something **falls off**, it separates from the thing to which it was attached and moves towards the ground. ❑ *When your exhaust falls off, you have to replace it.* [2] If the degree, amount, or size of something **falls off**, it decreases. ❑ *Unemployment is rising again and retail buying has fallen off.* → See also **falling-off**. PHRASAL VERB = *drop off* V P PHRASAL VERB V P

♦ **fall on** If you **fall on** something when it arrives or appears, you eagerly seize it or welcome it. ❑ *They fell on the sandwiches with alacrity.* PHRASAL VERB V P n

♦ **fall out** [1] If something such as a person's hair or a tooth **falls out**, it comes out. ❑ *Her hair started falling out as a result of radiation treatment.* [2] If you **fall out** with someone, you have an argument and stop being friendly with them. You can also say that two people **fall out**. ❑ *She fell out with her husband... Mum and I used to fall out a lot.* [3] → See also **fallout**. PHRASAL VERB V P PHRASAL VERB V P *with* n pl-n V P

♦ **fall over** If a person or object that is standing **falls over**, they accidentally move from their upright position so that they are then lying on the ground or on the surface supporting them. ❑ *If he drinks more than two glasses of wine he falls over.* PHRASAL VERB V P

♦ **fall through** If an arrangement, plan, or deal **falls through**, it fails to happen. ❑ *They wanted to turn the estate into a private golf course and offered £20 million, but the deal fell through.* PHRASAL VERB V P

♦ **fall to** [1] If a responsibility, duty, or opportunity **falls to** someone, it becomes their responsibility, duty, or opportunity. ❑ *He's been very unlucky that no chances have fallen to him... It fell to me to get rid of them.* [2] If someone **falls to** doing something, they start doing it. [WRITTEN] ❑ *When she had departed, they fell to fighting among themselves.* PHRASAL VERB V P n *it* V P n to-inf PHRASAL VERB V P -ing

**fal|la|cious** /fəleɪʃəs/ If an idea, argument, or reason is **fallacious**, it is wrong because it is based on a fallacy. [FORMAL] ❑ *Their main argument is fallacious.* ADJ

**fal|la|cy** /fæləsi/ **(fallacies)** A **fallacy** is an idea which many people believe to be true, but which is in fact false because it is based on incorrect information or reasoning. ❑ *It's a fallacy that the affluent give relatively more to charity than the less prosperous.* N-VAR: oft N that, N *of* n/-ing

**fall|back** /fɔːlbæk/ Someone's **fallback** position is what they will do if their plans do not succeed, or if something unexpected happens. [JOURNALISM] ❑ *Yesterday's vote itself was a retreat from an earlier fallback position.* ADJ: ADJ n

**fall|en** /fɔːlən/ [1] **Fallen** is the past participle of **fall**. [2] **The fallen** are soldiers who have died in battle. [LITERARY] ❑ *Work began on establishing the cemeteries as permanent memorials to the fallen.* [3] → See also **fall**. N-PLURAL: the N = *dead*

**fall guy** **(fall guys)** If someone is the **fall guy**, they are blamed for something which they did not do or which is not their fault. [INFORMAL] ❑ *He claims he was made the fall guy for the affair.* N-COUNT = *scapegoat*

**fal|lible** /fælɪbᵊl/ If you say that someone or something is **fallible**, you mean that they are not perfect and are likely to make mistakes or to fail in what they are doing. [FORMAL] ❑ *They are only human and all too fallible.* ♦ **fal|libil|ity** /fælɪbɪlɪti/ *Errors may have been made due to human fallibility.* ADJ ≠ *infallible* N-UNCOUNT: usu with supp

**falling-off** If there is a **falling-off** of an activity, there is a decrease in its amount or intensity. ❑ *There has been a falling-off in box office income and other earnings.* N-SING: N *of/in* n = *decline*

**fal|lo|pian tube** /fəloʊpiən tjuːb, AM - tuːb/ **(fallopian tubes)** A woman's **fallopian tubes** are the two tubes in her body along which eggs pass from her ovaries to her womb. N-COUNT

**fall|out** /fɔːlaʊt/ [1] **Fallout** is the radiation that affects a particular place or area after a nuclear explosion has taken place. ❑ *They were exposed to radioactive fallout during nuclear weapons tests.* [2] If you refer to the **fallout from** something that has happened, you mean the unpleasant consequences that follow it. ❑ *Grundy lost his job in the fallout from the incident.* N-UNCOUNT N-UNCOUNT: oft N *from* n

**fal|low** /fæloʊ/ [1] **Fallow** land has been dug or ploughed but nothing has been planted in it, especially so that its quality or strength has a chance to improve. ❑ *The fields lay fallow.* [2] A **fallow** period is a time when very little is being achieved. ❑ *There followed something of a fallow period professionally, until a job came up in the summer.* ADJ ADJ: usu ADJ n

**fal|low deer** **(fallow deer)** A **fallow deer** is a small deer that has a reddish coat which develops white spots in summer. N-COUNT

**false** /fɔːls/ [1] If something is **false**, it is incorrect, untrue, or mistaken. ❑ *It was quite clear the President was being given false information by those around him... You do not know whether what you're told is true or false... His sister said he had deliberately given the hospital a false name and address.* ♦ **false|ly** *...a man who is falsely accused of a crime.* [2] You use **false** to describe objects which are artificial but which are intended to look like the real thing or to be used instead of the real thing. ❑ *...a set of false teeth.* [3] If you describe a person or their behaviour as **false**, you are criticizing them for being insincere or for hiding their real feelings. ❑ *'Thank you,' she said with false enthusiasm.* ♦ **false|ly** *He was falsely jovial, with his booming, mirthless laugh... 'This food is divine,' they murmur, falsely.* ◆◇◇ ADJ ≠ *true* ADV: ADV with v ADJ: usu ADJ n = *artificial* ≠ *real* ADJ disapproval ≠ *genuine* ADV: ADV adj, ADV after v

**false alarm** **(false alarms)** When you think something dangerous is about to happen, but then discover that you were mistaken, you can say that it was a **false alarm**. ❑ *...a bomb threat that turned out to be a false alarm.* N-COUNT

**false|hood** /fɔːlshʊd/ **(falsehoods)** [1] **Falsehood** is the quality or fact of being untrue or of being a lie. ❑ *She called the verdict a victory of truth over falsehood.* [2] A **falsehood** is a lie. N-UNCOUNT ≠ *truth* N-COUNT

[FORMAL] ❑ *He accused them of knowingly spreading falsehoods about him.*

**false move** You use **one false move** to introduce the very bad or serious consequences which will result if someone makes a mistake, even a very small one. ❑ *One false move and I knew Sarah would be dead.* PHRASE

**false positive** (**false positives**) A **false positive** is a mistaken result of a scientific test. For example, if the result of a pregnancy test is a false positive, it indicates that a woman is pregnant when she is not. ❑ *...a high rate of false positive results.* N-COUNT: oft N n

**false start** (**false starts**) 1 A **false start** is an attempt to start something, such as a speech, project, or plan, which fails because you were not properly prepared or ready to begin. ❑ *Any economic reform, he said, faced false starts and mistakes.* N-COUNT 2 If there is a **false start** at the beginning of a race, one of the competitors moves before the person who starts the race has given the signal. N-COUNT

**falsetto** /fɔːlsetoʊ/ (**falsettos**) If a man sings or speaks **in a falsetto**, his voice is high-pitched, and higher than a man's normal voice. ❑ *He sang to himself in a soft falsetto. ...a falsetto voice.* N-COUNT: usu sing, oft in N, N n

**falsify** /fɔːlsɪfaɪ/ (**falsifies, falsifying, falsified**) If someone **falsifies** something, they change it or add untrue details to it in order to deceive people. ❑ *The charges against him include fraud, bribery, and falsifying business records.* VERB V n ♦ **falsification** /fɔːlsɪfɪkeɪʃən/ (**falsifications**) *...recent concern about the falsification of evidence in court.* N-VAR: usu N of n

**falter** /fɔːltəʳ/ (**falters, faltering, faltered**) 1 If something **falters**, it loses power or strength in an uneven way, or no longer makes much progress. ❑ *Normal life is at a standstill, and the economy is faltering.* VERB V 2 If you **falter**, you lose your confidence and stop doing something or start making mistakes. ❑ *I have not faltered in my quest for a new future.* VERB V

**faltering** /fɔːltərɪŋ/ A **faltering** attempt, effort, or movement is uncertain because the person doing it is nervous or weak, or does not really know what to do. ❑ *Leaning on Jon, Michael took faltering steps to the bathroom.* ADJ = hesitant

**fame** /feɪm/ If you achieve **fame**, you become very well-known. ❑ *The film earned him international fame. ...her rise to fame and fortune as a dramatist.* N-UNCOUNT
**claim to fame** → see **claim**.

**famed** /feɪmd/ If people, places, or things are **famed for** a particular thing, they are very well known for it. ❑ *The city is famed for its outdoor restaurants. ...the famed Brazilian photographer Sebastiao Salgado.* ADJ: oft ADJ for n = renowned

**familial** /fəmɪliəl/ **Familial** means relating to families in general, or typical of a family. [FORMAL] ❑ *Gerard also took on wider familial responsibilities.* ADJ: usu ADJ n

**familiar** /fəmɪliəʳ/ ◆◇◇ 1 If someone or something is **familiar** to you, you recognize them or know them well. ❑ *He talked of other cultures as if they were more familiar to him than his own... They are already familiar faces on our TV screens. ...the familiar names of long-established local firms.* ADJ: oft ADJ to n ♦ **familiarity** /fəmɪliærɪti/ *Tony was unnerved by the uncanny familiarity of her face.* N-UNCOUNT 2 If you are **familiar with** something, you know or understand it well. ❑ *Lesinko is quite familiar with Central Television. He worked there for 25 years.* ADJ: v-link ADJ with n ♦ **familiarity** *The enemy would always have the advantage of familiarity with the rugged terrain.* N-UNCOUNT: usu N with n 3 If someone you do not know well behaves in a **familiar** way towards you, they treat you very informally in a way that you might find offensive. ❑ *The driver of that taxi-cab seemed to me familiar to the point of impertinence.* ADJ [disapproval] ♦ **familiarity** *She needed to control her surprise at the easy familiarity with which her host greeted the head waiter.* N-UNCOUNT ♦ **familiarly** *'Gerald, isn't it?' I began familiarly.* ADV

**familiarity** /fəmɪliærɪti/ **Familiarity** is used especially in the expression **familiarity breeds contempt** to say that if you know a person or situation very well, you can easily lose respect for that person or become careless in that situation. → See also **familiar**. PHRASE: V inflects

**familiarize** /fəmɪliəraɪz/ (**familiarizes, familiarizing, familiarized**)

✓ in BRIT, also use **familiarise**

If you **familiarize** yourself **with** something, or if someone **familiarizes** you **with** it, you learn about it and start to understand it. ❑ *I was expected to familiarise myself with the keyboard... The goal of the experiment was to familiarize the people with the new laws.* VERB V pron-refl with n, V n with n

**familiarly** /fəmɪljəʳli/ If you say that something or someone is **familiarly known as** a particular thing or **familiarly called** a particular thing, you are giving the name that people use informally to refer to it. ❑ *...Ann Hamilton's father, familiarly known as 'Dink'.* PHRASE

**family** /fæmɪli/ (**families**) ◆◆◆ 1 A **family** is a group of people who are related to each other, especially parents and their children. ❑ *There's room in there for a family of five... His family are completely behind him, whatever he decides... To him the family is the core of society... Does he have any family?* N-COUNT-COLL 2 When people talk about a **family**, they sometimes mean children. ❑ *They decided to start a family. ...couples with large families.* N-COUNT-COLL 3 When people talk about their **family**, they sometimes mean their ancestors. ❑ *Her family came to Los Angeles at the turn of the century. ...the history of mental illness in the family.* N-COUNT-COLL 4 You can use **family** to describe things that belong to a particular family. ❑ *He returned to the family home... I was working in the family business.* ADJ: ADJ n 5 You can use **family** to describe things that are designed to be used or enjoyed by both parents and children. ❑ *It had been designed as a family house... A wedding is a family event.* ADJ: ADJ n 6 A **family** of animals or plants is a group of related species. ❑ *...foods in the cabbage family, such as Brussels sprouts.* N-COUNT: with supp

**family doctor** (**family doctors**) A **family doctor** is a doctor who does not specialize in any particular area of medicine, but who has a medical practice in which he or she treats all types of illness. [BRIT] N-COUNT: oft poss N = GP

**family man** (**family men**) 1 **A family man** is a man who is very fond of his wife and children and likes to spend a lot of time with them. ❑ *I'm very much a family man and need to be close to those I love.* N-COUNT 2 **A family man** is a man who has a wife and children. ❑ *I am a family man with a mortgage.* N-COUNT

**family name** (**family names**) Your **family name** is your surname. N-COUNT

**family planning** **Family planning** is the practice of using contraception to control the number of children you have. ❑ *...a family planning clinic.* N-UNCOUNT: oft N n

**family tree** (**family trees**) A **family tree** is a chart that shows all the people in a family over many generations and their relationship to one another. N-COUNT

**famine** /fæmɪn/ (**famines**) **Famine** is a situation in which large numbers of people have little or no food, and many of them die. ❑ *Thousands of refugees are trapped by war, drought and famine... The civil war is obstructing distribution of famine relief by aid agencies.* N-VAR

**famished** /fæmɪʃt/ If you are **famished**, you are very hungry. [INFORMAL] ❑ *Isn't dinner ready? I'm famished.* ADJ: usu v-link ADJ = starving

**famous** /feɪməs/ ◆◆◇ Someone or something that is **famous** is very well known. ❑ *New Orleans is famous for its cuisine. ...England's most famous landscape artist, John Constable.* ADJ: oft ADJ for n

**famously** /feɪməsli/ 1 You use **famously** to refer to a fact that is well known, usually be- ADV: usu ADV adj, also ADV with v cause it is remarkable or extreme. ❑ *Authors are famously ignorant about the realities of publishing.* [2] If you get on or get along **famously** with someone, you are very friendly with each other and enjoy meeting and being together. [INFORMAL, OLD-FASHIONED] ❑ *I got on famously with Leary from the first time we met.* ADV: ADV after v

**fan** /fæn/ **(fans, fanning, fanned)** ◆◆◇ [1] If you are a **fan** of someone or something, especially a famous person or a sport, you like them very much and are very interested in them. ❑ *As a boy he was a Manchester United fan... I am a great fan of rave music.* N-COUNT: usu n N, N *of* n [2] A **fan** is a flat object that you hold in your hand and wave in order to move the air and make yourself feel cooler. N-COUNT [3] If you **fan** yourself or your face when you are hot, you wave a fan or other flat object in order to make yourself feel cooler. ❑ *She would have to wait in the truck, fanning herself with a piece of cardboard... Mo kept bringing me out refreshments and fanning me as it was that hot.* VERB V pron-refl V n [4] A **fan** is a piece of electrical or mechanical equipment with blades that go round and round. It keeps a room or machine cool or gets rid of unpleasant smells. ❑ *He cools himself in front of an electric fan. ...an extractor fan.* N-COUNT: oft supp N [5] If you **fan** a fire, you wave something flat next to it in order to make it burn more strongly. If a wind **fans** a fire, it blows on it and makes it burn more strongly. ❑ *During the afternoon, hot winds fan the flames.* VERB V n [6] If someone **fans** an emotion such as fear, hatred, or passion, they deliberately do things to make people feel the emotion more strongly. ❑ *He said students were fanning social unrest with their violent protests.* VERB = fuel V n [7] to **fan the flames** → see **flame**. **the shit hit the fan** → see **shit**.

♦ **fan out** If a group of people or things **fan out**, they move forwards away from a particular point in different directions. ❑ *The main body of British, American, and French troops had fanned out to the west.* PHRASAL VERB = spread out V P

**fa|nat|ic** /fənætɪk/ **(fanatics)** [1] If you describe someone as a **fanatic**, you disapprove of them because you consider their behaviour or opinions to be very extreme, for example in the way they support particular religious or political ideas. ❑ *I am not a religious fanatic but I am a Christian.* N-COUNT [disapproval] = extremist [2] If you say that someone is a **fanatic**, you mean that they are very enthusiastic about a particular activity, sport, or way of life. ❑ *Both Rod and Phil are football fanatics.* N-COUNT: usu n N = enthusiast [3] **Fanatic** means the same as **fanatical**. ADJ

**fa|nati|cal** /fənætɪkᵊl/ If you describe someone as **fanatical**, you disapprove of them because you consider their behaviour or opinions to be very extreme. ❑ *As a boy he was a fanatical patriot.* ADJ [disapproval]

**fa|nati|cism** /fənætɪsɪzəm/ **Fanaticism** is fanatical behaviour or the quality of being fanatical. ❑ *...a protest against intolerance and religious fanaticism.* N-UNCOUNT [disapproval] = extremism

**fan belt (fan belts)** In a car engine, the **fan belt** is the belt that drives the fan which keeps the engine cool. N-COUNT

**fan|ci|er** /fænsiəʳ/ **(fanciers)** An animal or plant **fancier** is a person who breeds animals or plants of a particular type or who is very interested in them. ❑ *...pigeon fanciers.* → See also **fancy**. N-COUNT: supp N

**fan|ci|ful** /fænsɪfʊl/ If you describe an idea as **fanciful**, you disapprove of it because you think it comes from someone's imagination, and is therefore unrealistic or unlikely to be true. ❑ *...fanciful ideas about Martian life... Designing silicon chips to mimic human organs sounds fanciful.* ADJ [disapproval]

**fan club (fan clubs)** A **fan club** is an organized group of people who all admire the same person or thing, for example a pop singer or pop group. Members of the fan club receive information and can take part in activities such as trips to concerts. N-COUNT

| **fancy** |
|---|
| ① WANTING, LIKING, OR THINKING |
| ② ELABORATE OR EXPENSIVE |

**① fan|cy** /fænsi/ **(fancies, fancying, fancied)** ◆◇◇ [1] If you **fancy** something, you want to have it or to do it. [mainly BRIT, INFORMAL] ❑ *What do you fancy doing, anyway?... I just fancied a drink.* VERB V -ing V n [2] A **fancy** is a liking or desire for someone or something, especially one that does not last long. ❑ *She did not suspect that his interest was just a passing fancy.* N-COUNT: usu with supp = whim [3] If you **fancy** someone, you feel attracted to them, especially in a sexual way. [INFORMAL] ❑ *I think he thinks I fancy him or something.* VERB V n [4] If you **fancy yourself as** a particular kind of person or fancy **yourself** doing a particular thing, you like the idea of being that kind of person or doing that thing. ❑ *So you fancy yourself as the boss someday?... I didn't fancy myself wearing a kilt.* VERB V pron-refl *as* n V pron-refl -ing [5] If you say that someone **fancies themselves as** a particular kind of person, you mean that they think, often wrongly, that they have the good qualities which that kind of person has. ❑ *She fancies herself a bohemian. ...a flighty young woman who really fancies herself.* VERB V pron-refl n V pron-refl [6] If you say that you **fancy** a particular competitor or team in a competition, you think they will win. [BRIT] ❑ *You have to fancy Bath because they are the most consistent team... I fancy England to win.* VERB V n V n to-inf [7] You say '**fancy**' or '**fancy that**' when you want to express surprise or disapproval. ❑ *It was very tasteless. Fancy talking like that so soon after his death... 'Fancy that!' smiled Conti.* EXCLAM [feelings]

PHRASES [8] If you **take a fancy to** someone or something, you start liking them, usually for no understandable reason. ❑ *Sylvia took quite a fancy to him.* PHRASE: V inflects, PHR n/-ing [9] If something **takes** your **fancy** or **tickles** your **fancy**, you like it a lot when you see it or think of it. ❑ *She makes most of her own clothes, copying any fashion which takes her fancy.* PHRASE: V inflects

**② fan|cy** /fænsi/ **(fancier, fanciest)** [1] If you describe something as **fancy**, you mean that it is special, unusual, or elaborate, for example because it has a lot of decoration. ❑ *It was packaged in a fancy plastic case with attractive graphics. ...fancy jewellery.* ADJ: usu ADJ n [2] If you describe something as **fancy**, you mean that it is very expensive or of very high quality, and you often dislike it because of this. [INFORMAL] ❑ *They sent me to a fancy private school.* ADJ: usu ADJ n

**fan|cy dress Fancy dress** is clothing that you wear for a party at which everyone tries to look like a famous person or a person from a story, from history, or from a particular profession. ❑ *Guests were told to come in fancy dress.* N-UNCOUNT: oft N n

**fancy-free footloose and fancy-free** → see **footloose**.

**fan|dan|go** /fændæŋgoʊ/ **(fandangos)** A **fandango** is a Spanish dance in which two people dance very close together. N-COUNT: oft *the* N

**fan|fare** /fænfeəʳ/ **(fanfares)** [1] A **fanfare** is a short, loud tune played on trumpets or other similar instruments to announce a special event. ❑ *The ceremony opened with a fanfare of trumpets.* N-COUNT [2] If something happens with a **fanfare**, it happens or is announced with a lot of publicity. If something happens without a **fanfare**, it happens without a lot of fuss or publicity. [JOURNALISM] ❑ *...a fanfare of publicity.* N-VAR: oft N *of* n

**fang** /fæŋ/ **(fangs) Fangs** are the two long, sharp, upper teeth that some animals have. ❑ *The cobra sank its venomous fangs into his hand.* N-COUNT: usu pl

**fan|light** /fænlaɪt/ **(fanlights)** A **fanlight** is a small window over a door or above another window. N-COUNT

**fan|ny** /fæni/ **(fannies)** [1] Someone's **fanny** is their bottom. [AM, INFORMAL, RUDE] N-COUNT: usu poss N [2] A woman's **fanny** is her genitals. [BRIT, INFORMAL, ⚠ VERY RUDE] N-COUNT: usu poss N

**fan|ta|sia** /fænteɪziə, AM -ʒə/ **(fantasias)** A **fantasia** is a piece of music that is not written in a traditional or fixed form. [TECHNICAL] N-COUNT: usu sing

**fan|ta|sist** /fæntəzɪst/ **(fantasists)** A **fantasist** is someone who constantly tells lies about their life and achievements in order to make them sound more exciting than they really are. ❑ *Singleton was a fantasist who claimed to have a karate blackbelt.* N-COUNT

**fan|ta|size** /fæntəsaɪz/ **(fantasizes, fantasizing, fantasized)**

✓ in BRIT, also use **fantasise**

1 If you **fantasize** about an event or situation that you would like to happen, you give yourself pleasure by imagining that it is happening, although it is untrue or unlikely to happen. ❑ *I fantasised about writing music... Her husband died in 1967, although she fantasised that he was still alive.* VERB V about n/-ing V that

2 If someone **fantasizes**, they try to excite themselves sexually by imagining a particular person or situation. ❑ *Research has shown that men are likely to fantasize far more frequently than women... I tried to fantasize about Christine: those wondering blue eyes, that coppery red hair of hers.* VERB V V about/over n Also V n

**fan|tas|tic** /fæntæstɪk/

✓ The form **fantastical** is also used for meaning 3.

1 If you say that something is **fantastic**, you are emphasizing that you think it is very good or that you like it a lot. [INFORMAL] ❑ *I have a fantastic social life... I thought she was fantastic.* ADJ emphasis = great 2 A **fantastic** amount or quantity is an extremely large one. ❑ *...fantastic amounts of money.* ADJ: ADJ n ♦ **fan|tas|ti|cal|ly** /fæntæstɪkli/ *...a fantastically expensive restaurant.* ADV: ADV adj/adv 3 You describe something as **fantastic** or **fantastical** when it seems strange and wonderful or unlikely. ❑ *Unlikely and fantastic legends grew up around a great many figures, both real and fictitious... The book has many fantastical aspects.* ADJ

**fan|ta|sy** /fæntəzi/ **(fantasies)** also **phantasy**. ◆◇◇ 1 A **fantasy** is a pleasant situation or event that you think about and that you want to happen, especially one that is unlikely to happen. ❑ *...fantasies of romance and true love.* N-COUNT = dream 2 You can refer to a story or situation that someone creates from their imagination and that is not based on reality as **fantasy**. ❑ *The film is more of an ironic fantasy than a horror story.* N-VAR 3 **Fantasy** is the activity of imagining things. ❑ *...a world of imagination, passion, fantasy, reflection.* N-UNCOUNT

**fan|zine** /fænziːn/ **(fanzines)** A **fanzine** is a magazine for people who are fans of, for example, a particular pop group or football team. Fanzines are written by people who are fans themselves, rather than by professional journalists. N-COUNT

**FAO** You use **FAO** when addressing a letter or parcel to a particular person. **FAO** is a written abbreviation for 'for the attention of'. ❑ *Send the coupon with your deposit to House Beautiful Weekend, FAO Heidi Ross.*

**FAQ** /fæk/ **(FAQs) FAQ** is used especially on websites to refer to questions about computers and the Internet. **FAQ** is an abbreviation for 'frequently asked questions'. N-PLURAL

**far** /fɑːʳ/ ◆◆◆

> **Far** has two comparatives, **farther** and **further**, and two superlatives, **farthest** and **furthest**. **Farther** and **farthest** are used mainly in sense 1, and are dealt with here. **Further** and **furthest** are dealt with in separate entries.

1 If one place, thing, or person is **far** away from another, there is a great distance between them. ❑ *I know a nice little Italian restaurant not far from here... They came from as far away as Florida... Both of my sisters moved even farther away from home... They lay in the cliff top grass with the sea stretching out far below... Is it far?* ADV: ADV after v, v-link ADV, usu ADV prep/adv ≠near 2 If you ask **how far** a place is, you are asking what distance it is from you or from another place. If you ask **how far** someone went, you are asking what distance they travelled, or what place they reached. ❑ *How far is Pawtucket from Providence?... How far is it to Malcy?... How far can you throw?... You can only judge how high something is when you know how far away it is... She followed the tracks as far as the road.* ADV: how ADV, as/so ADV as, ADV-compar than 3 When there are two things of the same kind in a place, **the far** one is the one that is a greater distance from you. ❑ *He had wandered to the far end of the room.* ADJ: ADJ n ≠near

4 You can use **far** to refer to the part of an area or object that is the greatest distance from the centre in a particular direction. For example, **the far** north **of** a country is the part of it that is the greatest distance to the north. ❑ *I wrote the date at the far left of the blackboard.* ADJ: ADJ n 5 A time or event that is **far** away in the future or the past is a long time from the present or from a particular point in time. ❑ *...hidden conflicts whose roots lie far back in time... I can't see any farther than the next six months... The first day of term, which seemed so far away at the start of the summer holidays, is looming.* ADV: ADV after v, v-link ADV, usu ADV adv/prep

6 You can use **far** to talk about the extent or degree to which something happens or is true. ❑ *How far did the film tell the truth about Barnes Wallis?* ADV: ADV with v, usu how ADV 7 You can talk about how **far** someone or something gets to describe the progress that they make. ❑ *Discussions never progressed very far... Think of how far we have come in a little time... I don't think Mr Cavanagh would get far with that trick.* ADV: ADV with v, oft how ADV 8 You can talk about how **far** a person or action goes to describe the degree to which someone's behaviour or actions are extreme. ❑ *It's still not clear how far the Russian parliament will go to implement its own plans... This time he's gone too far.* ADV: ADV with v 9 You can use **far** to mean 'very much' when you are comparing two things and emphasizing the difference between them. For example, you can say that something is **far better** or **far worse** than something else to indicate that it is very much better or worse. You can also say that something is, for example, **far too big** to indicate that it is very much too big. ❑ *Women who eat plenty of fresh vegetables are far less likely to suffer anxiety or depression... The police say the response has been far better than expected... These trials are simply taking far too long.* ADV: usu ADV compar, ADV too adj/adv, also ADV adv/prep emphasis 10 You can describe people with extreme left-wing or right-wing political views as the **far** left or the **far** right. ❑ *Anti-racist campaigners are urging the Government to ban all far-Right groups.* ADJ: ADJ n = extreme

11 You can use **far** in expressions like '**as far as I know**' and '**so far as I remember**' to indicate that you are not absolutely sure of the statement you are about to make or have just made, and you may be wrong. ❑ *It only lasted a couple of years, as far as I know... So far as I am aware, no proper investigation has ever been carried out into the subject.* ADV: as/so ADV as vagueness

PHRASES 12 You use the expression **far and away** when you are comparing something or someone with others of the same kind, in order to emphasize how great the difference is between them. For example, you can say that something is **far and away the best** to indicate that it is definitely the best. ❑ *He's still far and away the best we have.* PHRASE: PHR the adj-superl emphasis = easily 13 You use the expression **by far** when you are comparing something or someone with others of the same kind, in order to emphasize how great the difference is between them. For example, you can say that something is **by far the best** or **the best by far** to indicate that it is definitely the best. ❑ *By far the most important issue for them is unemployment... It was better by far to be clear-headed.* PHRASE: PHR with-compar/superl emphasis 14 If you say that something is **far from** a particular thing or **far from** being the case, you are emphasizing that it is not that particular thing or not at all the case, especially when people expect or assume that it is. ❑ *It was obvious that much of what they recorded was far from the truth... Far from being relaxed, we both felt so uncomfortable we hardly spoke... It is still far from clear exactly what the Thais intend to do.* PHRASE: PHR n/-ing/adj, oft v-link PHR emphasis 15 You can use the expression '**far from it**' to emphasize a negative PHRASE emphasis statement that you have just made. ❑ *Being dyslexic does not mean that one is unintelligent. Far from it.* [16] You say **far be it from me** to disagree, or **far be it from me** to criticize, when you are disagreeing or criticizing and you want to appear less hostile. ❑ *Far be it from me to criticise, but shouldn't their mother take a share of the blame?* PHRASE: PHR to-inf [17] If you say that something is good **as far as it goes** or true **so far as it goes**, you mean that it is good or true only to a limited extent. ❑ *His plan for tax relief is fine as far as it goes but will not be sufficient to get the economy moving again.* PHRASE: PHR with cl [18] If you say that someone **will go far**, you mean that they will be very successful in their career. ❑ *I was very impressed with the talent of Michael Ball. He will go far.* PHRASE [19] Someone or something that is **far gone** is in such a bad state or condition that not much can be done to help or improve them. ❑ *In his last few days the pain seemed to have stopped, but by then he was so far gone that it was no longer any comfort... Many of the properties are in a desperate state but none is too far gone to save.* PHRASE: v-link PHR [20] Someone or something that is **not far wrong**, **not far out**, or **not far off** is almost correct or almost accurate. ❑ *I hadn't been far wrong in my estimate... Robertson is not far off her target.* PHRASE: v-link PHR, oft PHR *in* n [21] You can use the expression '**as far as I can see**' when you are about to state your opinion of a situation, or have just stated it, to indicate that it is your personal opinion. ❑ *As far as I can see there are only two reasons for such an action.* PHRASE: PHR with cl [22] If you say that something only goes **so far** or can only go **so far**, you mean that its extent, effect, or influence is limited. ❑ *Their loyalty only went so far... The church can only go so far in secular matters.* PHRASE: PHR after v [23] If you tell or ask someone what has happened **so far**, you are telling or asking them what has happened up until the present point in a situation or story, and often implying that something different might happen later. ❑ *It's been quiet so far... So far, they have met with no success.* PHRASE: PHR with cl [24] You can say **so far so good** to express satisfaction with the way that a situation or activity is progressing, developing, or happening. PHRASE [feelings] [25] If people come from **far and wide**, they come from a large number of places, some of them far away. If things spread **far and wide**, they spread over a very large area or distance. [WRITTEN] ❑ *Volunteers came from far and wide... His fame spread far and wide.* PHRASE: *from* PHR, PHR after v [26] If you say that someone **won't go far wrong** or **can't go far wrong** with a particular thing or course of action, you mean that it is likely to be successful or satisfactory. ❑ *If you remember these three golden rules you won't go far wrong.* PHRASE [27] **as far as** I am **concerned** → see **concern**. **a far cry from** → see **cry**. **in so far as** → see **insofar as**. **near and far** → see **near**.

**far|away** /fɑːrəweɪ/ also **far-away**. A **faraway** place is a long distance from you or from a particular place. ❑ *They have just returned from faraway places with wonderful stories to tell.* ADJ: ADJ n = distant

**farce** /fɑːʳs/ **(farces)** [1] A **farce** is a humorous play in which the characters become involved in complicated and unlikely situations. N-COUNT [2] **Farce** is the style of acting and writing that is typical of farces. ❑ *The plot often borders on farce.* N-UNCOUNT [3] If you describe a situation or event as a **farce**, you mean that it is so disorganized or ridiculous that you cannot take it seriously. ❑ *The elections have been reduced to a farce.* N-SING: also no det [disapproval]

**far|ci|cal** /fɑːʳsɪkᵊl/ If you describe a situation or event as **farcical**, you mean that it is so silly or extreme that you are unable to take it seriously. ❑ *...a farcical nine months' jail sentence imposed yesterday on a killer.* ADJ [disapproval]

**fare** /feəʳ/ **(fares, faring, fared)** [1] A **fare** is the money that you pay for a journey that you make, for example, in a bus, train, or taxi. ❑ *He could barely afford the railway fare. ...taxi fares.* ◆◇◇ N-COUNT [2] The **fare** at a restaurant or café is the type of food that is served there. [WRITTEN] ❑ *The fare has much improved since Hugh has taken charge of the kitchen. ...traditional Portuguese fare in a traditional setting.* N-UNCOUNT [3] If you say that someone or something **fares** well or badly, you are referring to the degree of success they achieve in a particular situation or activity. ❑ *It is unlikely that the marine industry will fare any better in September.* VERB = do V adv

**Far East** The **Far East** is used to refer to all the countries of Eastern Asia, including China, Japan, North and South Korea, and Indochina. N-PROPER: *the* N

**fare|well** /feəʳwel/ **(farewells)** **Farewell** means the same as **goodbye**. [LITERARY, OLD-FASHIONED] ◆ **Farewell** is also a noun. ❑ *They said their farewells there at the cafe.* CONVENTION N-COUNT

**far-fetched** If you describe a story or idea as **far-fetched**, you are criticizing it because you think it is unlikely to be true or practical. ❑ *The storyline was too far-fetched and none of the actors was particularly good.* ADJ [disapproval] = unrealistic

**far-flung** **(farther-flung, farthest-flung)** **Far-flung** places are a very long distance away from where you are or from important places. ❑ *Ferries are a lifeline to the far-flung corners of Scotland. ...one of the farthest-flung outposts of the old Roman Empire.* ADJ: ADJ n = remote

**farm** /fɑːʳm/ **(farms, farming, farmed)** [1] A **farm** is an area of land, together with the buildings on it, that is used for growing crops or raising animals, usually in order to sell them. ❑ *Farms in France are much smaller than those in the United States or even Britain.* ◆◆◇ N-COUNT [2] If you **farm** an area of land, you grow crops or keep animals on it. ❑ *They farmed some of the best land in Scotland... He has lived and farmed in the area for 46 years.* VERB V n V [3] A mink **farm** or a fish **farm**, for example, is a place where a particular kind of animal or fish is bred and kept in large quantities in order to be sold. ❑ *...trout fresh from a local trout farm.* N-COUNT: n N

**farm|er** /fɑːʳməʳ/ **(farmers)** A **farmer** is a person who owns or manages a farm. ◆◆◇ N-COUNT

**farm|ers' mar|ket** **(farmers' markets)** also **farmers market**. A **farmers' market** is a market where food growers sell their produce directly to the public. N-COUNT

**farm|hand** /fɑːʳmhænd/ **(farmhands)** also **farm hand**. A **farmhand** is a person who is employed to work on a farm. N-COUNT

**farm|house** /fɑːʳmhaʊs/ **(farmhouses)** also **farm house**. A **farmhouse** is the main house on a farm, usually where the farmer lives. N-COUNT

**farm|ing** /fɑːʳmɪŋ/ **Farming** is the activity of growing crops or keeping animals on a farm. N-UNCOUNT

**farm|land** /fɑːʳmlænd/ **(farmlands)** **Farmland** is land which is farmed, or which is suitable for farming. N-UNCOUNT: also N in pl

**farm|yard** /fɑːʳmjɑːʳd/ **(farmyards)** On a farm, the **farmyard** is an area of land near the farmhouse which is enclosed by walls or buildings. N-COUNT

**far off** **(further off, furthest off)** [1] If you describe a moment in time as **far off**, you mean that it is a long time from the present, either in the past or the future. ❑ *In those far off days it never entered anyone's mind that she could be Prime Minister... Agreement is even further off.* ADJ = distant [2] If you describe something as **far off**, you mean that it is a long distance from you or from a particular place. ❑ *...stars in far-off galaxies.* ADJ ◆ **Far off** is also an adverb. ❑ *The band was playing far off in their blue and yellow uniforms.* ADV: ADV after v

**far out** also **far-out**. If you describe something as **far out**, you mean that it is very strange or extreme. [INFORMAL] ❑ *Fantasies cannot harm you, no matter how bizarre or far out they are.* ADJ: usu v-link ADJ

**far|ra|go** /fərɑːgoʊ/ **(farragoes** or **farragos)** If you describe something as a **farrago**, you are critical of it because you think it is a confused mixture of different types of things. [FORMAL] ❑ *His own books and memoirs are a farrago of half-truth and outright invention.* N-COUNT: oft N *of* n [disapproval] = hotch-potch

**far-reaching** If you describe actions, events, or changes as **far-reaching**, you mean that they have a very great influence and affect a great number of things. ❑ *The economy is in danger of collapse unless far-reaching reforms are implemented.*
ADJ = *sweeping*

**far|ri|er** /færiəʳ/ **(farriers)** A **farrier** is a person who fits horseshoes onto horses.
N-COUNT

**far-sighted** 1 If you describe someone as **far-sighted**, you admire them because they understand what is likely to happen in the future, and therefore make wise decisions and plans. ❑ *Haven't far-sighted economists been telling us for some time now that in the future we will work less, not more?*
ADJ [approval]

2 **Far-sighted** people cannot see things clearly that are close to them, and therefore need to wear glasses. [AM]
ADJ ≠ *near-sighted*

✔ in BRIT, usually use **long-sighted**

**fart** /fɑːʳt/ **(farts, farting, farted)** If someone **farts**, air is forced out of their body through their anus. [INFORMAL, RUDE] ❑ *He'd been farting all night.*
VERB V

♦ **Fart** is also a noun. ❑ *...a loud fart.*
N-COUNT

**far|ther** /fɑːʳðəʳ/ **Farther** is a comparative form of **far**.

**far|thest** /fɑːʳðɪst/ **Farthest** is a superlative form of **far**.

**far|thing** /fɑːʳðɪŋ/ **(farthings)** A **farthing** was a small British coin which was worth a quarter of an old penny.
N-COUNT

**fas|cia** /feɪʃə/ **(fascias)** 1 In a car, **the fascia** is the part surrounding the instruments and dials. [BRIT, FORMAL]
N-COUNT: usu sing

✔ in AM, use **instrument panel**

2 The **fascia** on a shop front is the flat surface above the shop window, on which the name of the shop is written. [BRIT]
N-COUNT: usu sing

**fas|ci|nate** /fæsɪneɪt/ **(fascinates, fascinating, fascinated)** If something **fascinates** you, it interests and delights you so much that your thoughts tend to concentrate on it. ❑ *Politics fascinated Franklin's father... She fascinated him, both on and off stage.*
VERB V n V n

**fas|ci|nat|ed** /fæsɪneɪtɪd/ If you are **fascinated by** something, you find it very interesting and attractive, and your thoughts tend to concentrate on it. ❑ *I sat on the stairs and watched, fascinated... A new generation of scientists became fascinated by dinosaurs.*
ADJ: usu v-link ADJ, oft ADJ *by/with* n

**fas|ci|nat|ing** /fæsɪneɪtɪŋ/ If you describe something as **fascinating**, you find it very interesting and attractive, and your thoughts tend to concentrate on it. ❑ *Madagascar is the most fascinating place I have ever been to... Her perceptions and intuitions about human nature were fascinating.*
ADJ

**fas|ci|na|tion** /fæsɪneɪʃᵊn/ **(fascinations)** 1 **Fascination** is the state of being greatly interested in or delighted by something. ❑ *I've had a lifelong fascination with the sea and with small boats.*
N-UNCOUNT: oft N *with/of/for* n

2 A **fascination** is something that fascinates people. ❑ *...a series focusing on the fascinations of the British Museum.*
N-COUNT

**fas|cism** /fæʃɪzəm/ **Fascism** is a set of right-wing political beliefs that includes strong control of society and the economy by the state, a powerful role for the armed forces, and the stopping of political opposition.
N-UNCOUNT

**fas|cist** /fæʃɪst/ **(fascists)** 1 You use **fascist** to describe organizations, ideas, or systems which follow the principles of fascism. ❑ *...the threatening nature of fascist ideology.*
ADJ: usu ADJ n

♦ A **fascist** is someone who has fascist views.
N-COUNT

2 If you refer to someone as a **fascist**, you are expressing disapproval of the fact that they have extreme views on something, and do not tolerate alternative views. ❑ *...the so-called health fascists who would meddle in their lives and regulate their calorie intake.*
N-COUNT [disapproval]

**fash|ion** /fæʃᵊn/ **(fashions, fashioning, fashioned)** ◆◆◇ 1 **Fashion** is the area of activity that involves styles of clothing and appearance. ❑ *There are 20 full-colour pages of fashion for men... The fashion world does not mind what the real world thinks.*
N-UNCOUNT

2 A **fashion** is a style of clothing or a way of behaving that is popular at a particular time. ❑ *Queen Mary started the fashion for blue and white china in England... He stayed at the top through all changes and fashions in pop music.*
N-COUNT: oft *the* N

3 If you do something **in** a particular **fashion** or **after** a particular **fashion**, you do it in that way. ❑ *There is another drug called DHE that works in a similar fashion... It is happening in this fashion because of the obstinacy of one woman.* ➔ See also **parrot-fashion**.
N-SING: with supp = *manner*

4 If you **fashion** an object or a work of art, you make it. [FORMAL] ❑ *Stone Age settlers fashioned necklaces from sheep's teeth.* 5 ➔ See also **old-fashioned**.
VERB V n

PHRASES 6 If you say that something was done **after a fashion**, you mean that it was done, but not very well. ❑ *She was educated – after a fashion – at home... He knew the way, after a fashion.*
PHRASE

7 If something is **in fashion**, it is popular and approved of at a particular time. If it is **out of fashion**, it is not popular or approved of. ❑ *That sort of house is back in fashion... Marriage seems to be going out of fashion.*
PHRASE

**fash|ion|able** /fæʃənəbᵊl/ Something or someone that is **fashionable** is popular or approved of at a particular time. ❑ *It became fashionable to eat certain kinds of fish... Chelsea Harbour is renowned for its fashionable restaurants.*
ADJ

♦ **fash|ion|ably** *...women who are perfectly made up and fashionably dressed.*
ADV: usu ADV adj/-ed

**fash|ion vic|tim** **(fashion victims)** A **fashion victim** is someone who thinks that being fashionable is more important than looking nice, and as a result often wears very fashionable clothes that do not suit them or that make them look silly.
N-COUNT [disapproval]

**fast** /fɑːst, fæst/ **(faster, fastest, fasts, fasting, fasted)** ◆◆◇ 1 **Fast** means happening, moving, or doing something at great speed. You also use **fast** in questions or statements about speed. ❑ *...fast cars with flashing lights and sirens... Brindley was known as a very, very fast driver... The party aims to attract votes from the business and professional communities, which want a faster pace of political reform... The only question is how fast the process will be.*
ADJ = *quick* ≠ *slow*

♦ **Fast** is also an adverb. ❑ *They work terrifically fast... It would be nice to go faster and break the world record... Barnes also knows that he is fast running out of time... How fast were you driving?... How fast would the disease develop?*
ADV: ADV with v = *quickly* ≠ *slowly*

2 You use **fast** to say that something happens without any delay. ❑ *When you've got a crisis like this you need professional help – fast!... We'd appreciate your leaving as fast as possible.*
ADV: ADV after v = *soon, swiftly*

♦ **Fast** is also an adjective. ❑ *That would be an astonishingly fast action on the part of the Congress.*
ADJ: ADJ n = *swift*

3 If a watch or clock is **fast**, it is showing a time that is later than the real time. ❑ *That clock's an hour fast.*
ADJ: v-link ADJ

4 If you hold something **fast**, you hold it tightly and firmly. If something is stuck **fast**, it is stuck very firmly and cannot move. ❑ *She climbed the staircase cautiously, holding fast to the rail... The tanker is stuck fast on the rocks.*
ADV: ADV after v = *firmly*

5 If you hold **fast** to a principle or idea, or if you stand **fast**, you do not change your mind about it, even though people are trying to persuade you to. ❑ *We can only try to hold fast to the age-old values of honesty, decency and concern for others... He told supporters to stand fast over the next few vital days.*
ADV: ADV after v = *firm*

6 If colours or dyes are **fast**, they do not come out of the fabrics they are used on when they get wet. ❑ *The fabric was ironed to make the colours fast.*
ADJ: usu v-link ADJ

7 If you **fast**, you eat no food for a period of time, usually for either religious or medical reasons, or as a protest. ❑ *I fasted for a day and half and asked God to help me.*
VERB V

♦ **Fast** is also a noun. ❑ *The fast is broken at sunset, traditionally with dates and water.*
N-COUNT

♦ **fast|ing** *...the Muslim holy month of fasting and prayer.*
N-UNCOUNT

8 Someone who is **fast asleep** is completely asleep. ❑ *When he went upstairs five minutes later, she was fast asleep.*
PHRASE: v-link PHR, PHR after v

9 to **make a fast buck** ➔ see **buck**.

**fast-breeder re|ac|tor** **(fast-breeder reactors)** A **fast-breeder reactor** or a **fast-breeder** is a kind of nuclear reactor that produces more plutonium than it uses. N-COUNT

**fas|ten** /fɑːsᵊn, fæs-/ **(fastens, fastening, fastened)** [1] When you **fasten** something, you close it by means of buttons or a strap, or some other device. If something **fastens** with buttons or straps, you can close it in this way. ❑ *She got quickly into her Mini and fastened the seat-belt... Her long fair hair was fastened at the nape of her neck by an elastic band. ...the dress, which fastens with a long back zip.* VERB = do up; V n; *be* V-ed prep; V prep [2] If you **fasten** one thing **to** another, you attach the first thing to the second, for example with a piece of string or tape. ❑ *There were no instructions on how to fasten the carrying strap to the box.* Also V n prep; VERB = attach; V n prep/adv [3] → See also **fastening**.

**fas|ten|er** /fɑːsənəʳ, fæs-/ **(fasteners)** A **fastener** is a device such as a button, zip, or small hook that fastens something, especially clothing. N-COUNT

**fas|ten|ing** /fɑːsənɪŋ, fæs-/ **(fastenings)** A **fastening** is something such as a clasp or zip that you use to fasten something and keep it shut. ❑ *The sundress has a neat back zip fastening.* N-COUNT: oft n N

**fast food** **Fast food** is hot food, such as hamburgers and chips, that you obtain from particular types of restaurant, and which is served quickly after you order it. ❑ *James works as assistant chef at a fast food restaurant.* N-UNCOUNT: oft n N

**fast for|ward** **(fast forwards, fast forwarding, fast forwarded)** also **fast-forward.** [1] When you **fast forward** the tape in a video or tape recorder or when you **fast forward**, you make the tape go forwards. Compare **rewind**. ❑ *Just fast forward the video... He fast-forwarded the tape past the explosion... The urge to fast-forward is almost irresistible.* VERB; V n; V n prep/adv; V; Also V prep/adv [2] If you put a video or cassette tape **on fast forward**, you make the tape go forwards. Compare **rewind**. ❑ *Before recording onto a new tape, wind it on fast forward, then rewind.* N-UNCOUNT: oft *on* N

**fas|tidi|ous** /fæstɪdiəs/ [1] If you say that someone is **fastidious**, you mean that they pay great attention to detail because they like everything to be very neat, accurate, and in good order. ❑ *...her fastidious attention to historical detail... He was fastidious about his appearance.* ADJ = meticulous [2] If you say that someone is **fastidious**, you mean that they are concerned about keeping clean to an extent that many people consider to be excessive. ❑ *Be particularly fastidious about washing your hands before touching food.* ADJ ♦ **fas|tidi|ous|ly** *Ernestine kept her daughters fastidiously clean.* ADV

**fast lane** **(fast lanes)** [1] On a motorway, **the fast lane** is the part of the road where the vehicles that are travelling fastest go. [mainly BRIT] N-COUNT: usu *the* N [2] If someone is living **in the fast lane**, they have a very busy, exciting life, although they sometimes seem to take a lot of risks. ❑ *..a tale of life in the fast lane.* N-SING: usu *the* N

**fast|ness** /fɑːstnəs, fæst-/ **(fastnesses)** A **fastness** is a place, such as a castle, which is considered safe because it is difficult to reach or easy to defend against attack. [LITERARY] ❑ *They could have withdrawn into the mountain fastness of Eryri.* N-COUNT: with supp

**fast track** **(fast tracks, fast tracking, fast tracked)** also **fast-track.** [1] The **fast track to** a particular goal, especially in politics or in your career, is the quickest route to achieving it. ❑ *Many Croats and Slovenes saw independence as the fast track to democracy.* N-SING: oft N *to* n, N n [2] To **fast track** something means to make it happen or progress faster or earlier than normal. ❑ *A Federal Court case had been fast tracked to Wednesday... Woodward has fast-tracked a number of youngsters into the line-up since he became coach.* VERB; *be* V-ed; V n

**fat** /fæt/ **(fatter, fattest, fats)** [1] If you say that a person or animal is **fat**, you mean that they have a lot of flesh on their body and that they weigh too much. You usually use the word **fat** when you think that this is a bad thing. ❑ *I could eat what I liked without getting fat... After five minutes, the fat woman in the seat in front of me was asleep.* ♦◆◇ ADJ disapproval = overweight ≠ thin ♦ **fat|ness** *No one knows whether a child's tendency towards fatness is inherited or due to the food he eats.* N-UNCOUNT [2] **Fat** is the extra flesh that animals and humans have under their skin, which is used to store energy and to help keep them warm. ❑ *Because you're not burning calories, everything you eat turns to fat.* N-UNCOUNT [3] **Fat** is a solid or liquid substance obtained from animals or vegetables, which is used in cooking. ❑ *When you use oil or fat for cooking, use as little as possible. ...vegetable fats, such as coconut oil and palm oil.* N-MASS [4] **Fat** is a substance contained in foods such as meat, cheese, and butter which forms an energy store in your body. ❑ *An easy way to cut the amount of fat in your diet is to avoid eating red meats... Most low-fat yogurts are about 40 calories per 100g.* N-MASS [5] A **fat** object, especially a book, is very thick or wide. ❑ *...'Europe in Figures', a fat book published on September 22nd.* ADJ = thick ≠ thin, slim [6] A **fat** profit or fee is a large one. [INFORMAL] ❑ *They are set to make a big fat profit.* ADJ: ADJ n [7] If you say that there is **fat chance of** something happening, you mean that you do not believe that it will happen. [INFORMAL, mainly SPOKEN] ❑ *'Would your car be easy to steal?' — 'Fat chance. I've got a device that shuts down the gas and ignition.'* PHRASE: oft PHR *of* n feelings

**fa|tal** /feɪtᵊl/ [1] A **fatal** action has very undesirable effects. ❑ *It would clearly be fatal for Europe to quarrel seriously with America... He made the fatal mistake of compromising early... It would deal a fatal blow to his fading chances of success.* ADJ ♦ **fa|tal|ly** *Failure now could fatally damage his chances in the future.* ADV: ADV with v [2] A **fatal** accident or illness causes someone's death. ❑ *A hospital spokesman said she had suffered a fatal heart attack.* ADJ ♦ **fa|tal|ly** *The dead soldier is reported to have been fatally wounded in the chest.* ADV: usu ADV with v

**fa|tal|ism** /feɪtəlɪzəm/ **Fatalism** is a feeling that you cannot control events or prevent unpleasant things from happening, especially when this feeling stops you from making decisions or making an effort. ❑ *There's a certain mood of fatalism now among the radicals.* N-UNCOUNT = resignation

**fa|tal|is|tic** /feɪtəlɪstɪk/ If someone is **fatalistic about** something, especially an unpleasant event or situation, they feel that they cannot change or control it, and therefore that there is no purpose in trying. ❑ *People we spoke to today were really rather fatalistic about what's going to happen.* ADJ: oft ADJ *about* n = resigned

**fa|tal|ity** /fətælɪti/ **(fatalities)** A **fatality** is a death caused by an accident or by violence. [FORMAL] ❑ *Drunk driving fatalities have declined more than 10 percent over the past 10 years.* N-COUNT

**fat cat** **(fat cats)** If you refer to a businessman or politician as a **fat cat**, you are indicating that you disapprove of the way they use their wealth and power. [INFORMAL, BUSINESS] ❑ *...the fat cats who run the bank.* N-COUNT disapproval

**fate** /feɪt/ **(fates)** [1] **Fate** is a power that some people believe controls and decides everything that happens, in a way that cannot be prevented or changed. You can also refer to **the fates**. ❑ *I see no use quarrelling with fate. ...the fickleness of fate... It was just one of those times when you wonder whether the fates conspire against you.* ♦◇◇ N-UNCOUNT: also N in pl [2] A person's or thing's **fate** is what happens to them. ❑ *The Russian Parliament will hold a special session later this month to decide his fate... He seems for a moment to be again holding the fate of the country in his hands... The Casino, where she had often danced, had suffered a similar fate.* N-COUNT: oft with poss = destiny [3] If something **seals** a person's or thing's **fate**, it makes it certain that they will fail or that something unpleasant will happen to them. ❑ *The call for a boycott could be enough to seal the fate of next week's general election.* PHRASE: V inflects [4] to **tempt fate** → see **tempt**.

**fat|ed** /feɪtɪd/ If you say that a person is **fated to** do something, or that something is **fated**, you mean that it seems to have been decided by fate before it happens, and nothing can be done ADJ: oft ADJ to-inf = doomed to avoid or change it. ❑ *He was fated not to score. ...stories of desperation, fated love, treachery and murder.* → See also **ill-fated**.

**fate|ful** /feɪtfʊl/ If an action or a time when something happened is described as **fateful**, it is considered to have an important, and often very bad, effect on future events. ❑ *It was a fateful decision, one which was to break the Government.* ADJ: usu ADJ n = momentous

**fa|ther** /fɑːðəʳ/ **(fathers, fathering, fathered)** ◆◆◆ 1 Your **father** is your male parent. You can also call someone your **father** if he brings you up as if he was this man. ❑ *His father was a painter... He would be a good father to my children. ...Mr Stoneman, a father of five.* N-FAMILY 2 When a man **fathers** a child, he makes a woman pregnant and their child is born. ❑ *She claims Mark fathered her child... He fathered at least three children by the wives of other men.* VERB V n V n by n 3 The man who invented or started something is sometimes referred to as the **father of** that thing. ❑ *...Max Dupain, regarded as the father of modern photography.* N-COUNT: N of n 4 In some Christian churches, priests are addressed or referred to as **Father**. N-VOC; N-TITLE; N-COUNT

**Father Christ|mas** **Father Christmas** is the name given to an imaginary old man with a long white beard and a red coat. Traditionally, young children in many countries are told that he brings their Christmas presents. [BRIT] N-PROPER = Santa Claus

☑ in AM, use **Santa Claus**

**fa|ther fig|ure (father figures)** also **father-figure.** If you describe someone as a **father figure**, you mean that you feel able to turn to that person for advice and support in the same way that you might turn to your father. ❑ *She believed her daughter needed a father-figure... He became a father figure to the whole company.* N-COUNT

**father|hood** /fɑːðəʳhʊd/ **Fatherhood** is the state of being a father. ❑ *...the joys of fatherhood.* N-UNCOUNT

**father-in-law (fathers-in-law)** Someone's **father-in-law** is the father of their husband or wife. N-COUNT: usu poss N

**father|land** /fɑːðəʳlænd/ **(fatherlands)** If someone is very proud of the country where they or their ancestors were born, they sometimes refer to it as the **fatherland**. The word **fatherland** is particularly associated with Germany. ❑ *They were willing to serve the fatherland in its hour of need.* N-COUNT: usu sing

**fa|ther|less** /fɑːðəʳləs/ You describe children as **fatherless** when their father has died or does not live with them. ❑ *...widows and fatherless children... They were left fatherless.* ADJ

**fa|ther|ly** /fɑːðəʳli/ **Fatherly** feelings or actions are like those of a kind father. ❑ *His voice filled with fatherly concern.* ADJ: usu ADJ n

**Fa|ther's Day** **Father's Day** is the third Sunday in June, when children give cards and presents to their fathers to show that they love them. N-UNCOUNT

**fath|om** /fæðəm/ **(fathoms, fathoming, fathomed)** 1 A **fathom** is a measurement of 1.8 metres or 6 feet, used when referring to the depth of water. ❑ *We sailed into the bay and dropped anchor in five fathoms of water.* N-COUNT: oft num N 2 If you cannot **fathom** something, you are unable to understand it, although you think carefully about it. ❑ *I really couldn't fathom what Steiner was talking about... Jeremy's passive attitude was hard to fathom.* ♦ **Fathom out** means the same as **fathom**. ❑ *We're trying to fathom out what's going on... I'm having difficulty using my video editing equipment and can't fathom out the various connections.* VERB: no cont, oft with brd-neg V wh V n PHRASAL VERB V P wh V P n (not pron) Also V n P

**fath|om|less** /fæðəmləs/ Something that is **fathomless** cannot be measured or understood because it gives the impression of being very deep, mysterious, or complicated. ❑ *...the fathomless space of the universe... The silence was fathomless and overwhelming.* ADJ

**fa|tigue** /fətiːg/ **(fatigues)** 1 **Fatigue** is a feeling of extreme physical or mental tiredness. ❑ *She continued to have severe stomach cramps, aches, fatigue, and depression... Clarke says his team could have lasted another 15 days before fatigue would have begun to take a toll.* N-UNCOUNT 2 You can say that people are suffering from a particular kind of **fatigue** when they have been doing something for a long time and feel they can no longer continue to do it. ❑ *...compassion fatigue caused by endless TV and celebrity appeals. ...the result of four months of battle fatigue.* N-UNCOUNT: with supp, usu n N 3 **Fatigues** are clothes that soldiers wear when they are fighting or when they are doing routine jobs. ❑ *He never expected to return home wearing US combat fatigues.* N-PLURAL 4 **Fatigue** in metal or wood is a weakness in it that is caused by repeated stress. Fatigue can cause the metal or wood to break. ❑ *The problem turned out to be metal fatigue in the fuselage.* N-UNCOUNT: usu n N

**fa|tigued** /fətiːgd/ If you are feeling **fatigued**, you are suffering from extreme physical or mental tiredness. ADJ: usu v-link ADJ

**fa|tigu|ing** /fətiːgɪŋ/ Something that is **fatiguing** makes you feel extremely physically or mentally tired. ❑ *Jet travel is undeniably fatiguing.* ADJ: usu v-link ADJ

**fat|ten** /fætᵊn/ **(fattens, fattening, fattened)** 1 If an animal **is fattened**, or if it **fattens**, it becomes fatter as a result of eating more. ❑ *The cattle are being fattened for slaughter... The creature continued to grow and fatten.* VERB be V-ed V Also V n 2 If you say that someone **is fattening** something such as a business or its profits, you mean that they are increasing the value of the business or its profits, in a way that you disapprove of. [BUSINESS] ❑ *They have kept the price of sugar artificially high and so fattened the company's profits.* VERB disapproval V n ♦ **Fatten up** means the same as **fatten**. ❑ *The Government is making the taxpayer pay to fatten up a public sector business for private sale.* PHRASAL VERB V P n (not pron) Also V n P

♦ **fatten up** To **fatten up** an animal or person means to make them fatter, by forcing or encouraging them to eat more food. ❑ *They fattened up ducks and geese... You're too skinny – we'll have to fatten you up.* → See also **fatten 2**. PHRASAL VERB V P n (not pron) V n P

**fat|ten|ing** /fætənɪŋ/ Food that is **fattening** is considered to make people fat easily. ❑ *Some foods are more fattening than others.* ADJ

**fat|ty** /fæti/ **(fattier, fattiest)** 1 **Fatty** food contains a lot of fat. ❑ *Don't eat fatty food or chocolates... The report dispels the myth that Northerners have a fattier diet than people in the south.* ADJ: usu ADJ n 2 **Fatty** acids or **fatty** tissues, for example, contain or consist of fat. ❑ *...fatty acids... The woman lost about 1.8kg of fatty tissue during the week's fast.* ADJ: ADJ n

**fatu|ous** /fætʃuəs/ If you describe a person, action, or remark as **fatuous**, you think that they are extremely silly, showing a lack of intelligence or thought. [FORMAL] ❑ *The Chief was left speechless by this fatuous remark.* ADJ disapproval = idiotic

**fat|wa** /fætwɑː/ **(fatwas)** also **fatwah.** A **fatwa** is a religious order issued by a Muslim leader. N-COUNT

**fau|cet** /fɔːsɪt/ **(faucets)** A **faucet** is a device that controls the flow of a liquid or gas from a pipe or container. Sinks and baths have faucets attached to them. [AM] ❑ *She turned off the faucet and dried her hands.* N-COUNT

☑ in BRIT, usually use **tap**

**fault** /fɔːlt/ **(faults, faulting, faulted)** ◆◇◇ 1 If a bad or undesirable situation is your **fault**, you caused it or are responsible for it. ❑ *There was no escaping the fact: it was all his fault... A few borrowers will find themselves in trouble with their repayments through no fault of their own.* N-SING: with poss 2 A **fault** is a mistake in what someone is doing or in what they have done. ❑ *It is a big fault to think that you can learn how to manage people in business school.* N-COUNT: usu with supp = error, mistake 3 A **fault** in someone or something is a weakness in them or something that is not perfect. ❑ *His manners had always made her blind to his faults. ...a short delay due to a minor technical fault.* N-COUNT: usu with supp, oft poss N = failing, flaw 4 If you **cannot fault** someone, you cannot find any reason for criticizing them or the things that they are doing. ❑ *You can't fault them for lack of invention...* VERB: with brd-neg V n for n/-ing

*It is hard to fault the way he runs his own operation.* V n
[5] A **fault** is a large crack in the surface of the earth. ❑ *...the San Andreas Fault.* N-COUNT [6] A **fault** in tennis is a service that is wrong according to the rules. N-COUNT

PHRASES [7] If someone or something is **at fault**, they are to blame or are responsible for a particular situation that has gone wrong. ❑ *He could never accept that he had been at fault.* PHRASE: v-link PHR [8] If you **find fault with** something or someone, you look for mistakes and complain about them. ❑ *I was disappointed whenever the cook found fault with my work.* PHRASE: V inflects, usu PHR *with* n
[9] If you say that someone has a particular good quality **to a fault**, you are emphasizing that they have more of this quality than is usual or necessary. ❑ *Jefferson was generous to a fault... Others will tell you that she is modest to a fault, funny, clever and warm.* PHRASE: usu adj PHR [emphasis]

**fault|less** /fɔːltləs/ Something that is **faultless** is perfect and has no mistakes at all. ❑ *...Mary Thomson's faultless and impressive performance on the show... Hans's English was faultless.* ♦ **fault|less|ly** *Howard was faultlessly dressed in a dark blue suit.* ADJ = flawless; ADV: ADV with v, ADV adj

**fault line (fault lines)** [1] A **fault line** is a long crack in the surface of the earth. Earthquakes usually occur along fault lines. N-COUNT = fault [2] A **fault line** in a system or process is an area of it that seems weak and likely to cause problems or failure. ❑ *These issues have created a stark fault line within the Peace Process.* N-COUNT = weakness

**faulty** /fɔːlti/ [1] A **faulty** piece of equipment has something wrong with it and is not working properly. ❑ *The money will be used to repair faulty equipment.* ADJ [2] If you describe someone's argument or reasoning as **faulty**, you mean that it is wrong or contains mistakes, usually because they have not been thinking in a logical way. ❑ *Their interpretation was faulty – they had misinterpreted things.* ADJ = flawed

**faun** /fɔːn/ **(fauns)** A **faun** is an imaginary creature which is like a man with goat's legs and horns. N-COUNT

**fau|na** /fɔːnə/ **(faunas)** Animals, especially the animals in a particular area, can be referred to as **fauna**. [TECHNICAL] ❑ *...the flora and fauna of the African jungle... Brackish waters generally support only a small range of faunas.* N-COUNT-COLL

**faux pas** /foʊ pɑː/ **(faux pas)** A **faux pas** is a socially embarrassing action or mistake. [FORMAL] ❑ *It was not long before I realised the enormity of my faux pas.* N-COUNT = gaffe, blunder

**fava bean** /fɑvə biːn/ **(fava beans)** **Fava beans** are flat round beans that are light green in colour and are eaten as a vegetable. [AM] N-COUNT: usu pl

☑ in BRIT, use **broad beans**

**fave** /feɪv/ **(faves)** [1] Your **fave** thing or person of a particular type is the one you like the most. [JOURNALISM, BRIT, INFORMAL] ❑ *Vote for your fave song by dialing 0906 474 8000.* ADJ: ADJ n [2] A **fave** is a thing or person of a particular type that you like the most. [JOURNALISM, BRIT, INFORMAL] ❑ *...old faves like 'Summer Babe' and 'Debris Slide'.* N-COUNT

**fa|vour** /feɪvəʳ/ **(favours, favouring, favoured)** ◆◆◇

☑ in AM, use **favor**

[1] If you regard something or someone with **favour**, you like or support them. ❑ *It remains to be seen if the show will still find favour with a 1990s audience... No one would look with favour on the continuing military rule... He has won favour with a wide range of interest groups.* N-UNCOUNT [2] If you **do** someone **a favour**, you do something for them even though you do not have to. ❑ *I've come to ask you to do me a favour.* N-COUNT [3] If you **favour** something, you prefer it to the other choices available. ❑ *The French say they favour a transition to democracy... He favours bringing the UN into touch with 'modern realities'.* VERB V n V -ing
[4] If you **favour** someone, you treat them better or in a kinder way than you treat other people. ❑ *The Government came under fire yesterday for favouring elitist arts groups in the South-east.* VERB V n

PHRASES [5] If you are **in favour of** something, you support it and think that it is a good thing. ❑ *I wouldn't be in favour of income tax cuts... Yet this is a Government which proclaims that it is all in favour of openness... The vote passed with 111 in favour and 25 against.* PHRASE: oft v-link PHR, PHR *of* n [6] If someone makes a judgment **in** your **favour**, they say that you are right about something. ❑ *If the commission rules in Mr Welch's favour the case will go to the European Court of Human Rights.* PHRASE: PHR after v [7] If something is **in** your **favour**, it helps you or gives you an advantage. ❑ *Firms are trying to shift the balance of power in the labour market back in their favour.* PHRASE: n PHR, PHR after v, v-link PHR [8] If one thing is rejected **in favour of** another, the second thing is done or chosen instead of the first. ❑ *The policy was rejected in favour of a more cautious approach.* PHRASE: PHR n, usu PHR after v [9] If someone or something is **in favour**, people like or support them. If they are **out of favour**, people no longer like or support them. PHRASE: v-link PHR

**fa|vour|able** /feɪvərəbᵊl/

☑ in AM, use **favorable**

[1] If your opinion or your reaction is **favourable** to something, you agree with it and approve of it. ❑ *His recently completed chapel for Fitzwilliam is attracting favourable comment... The commission is cautiously favourable to Austrian membership, foreseeing few economic problems.* ADJ: ADJ n, v-link ADJ *to* n [2] If something makes a **favourable** impression on you or is **favourable to** you, you like it and approve of it. ❑ *His ability to talk tough while eating fast made a favourable impression on his dining companions... These terms were favourable to India.* ADJ: oft ADJ *to* n = positive, good [3] **Favourable** conditions make something more likely to succeed or seem more attractive. ❑ *It's believed the conditions in which the elections are being held are too favourable to the government. ...favourable weather conditions.* ADJ: oft ADJ *to* n/-ing
[4] If you make a **favourable** comparison between two things, you say that the first is better than or as good as the second. ❑ *The film bears favourable technical comparison with Hollywood productions costing 10 times as much.* ADJ: usu ADJ n

**fa|vour|ite** /feɪvərɪt/ **(favourites)** ◆◆◇

☑ in AM, use **favorite**

[1] Your **favourite** thing or person of a particular type is the one you like most. ❑ *...a bottle of his favourite champagne... Her favourite writer is Hans Christian Andersen.* ♦ **Favourite** is also a noun. ❑ *The Liverpool Metropole is my favourite.* ● If you refer to something as an **old favourite**, you mean that it has been in existence for a long time and everyone knows it or likes it. ❑ *Everyone must be familiar with the old favourite among roses, Crystal Palace.* ADJ: ADJ n; N-COUNT: usu with poss; PHRASE [2] If you describe one person as the **favourite** of another, you mean that the second person likes the first person a lot and treats them with special kindness. ❑ *...Robert Carr, Earl of Somerset, a favourite of King James I... The Prime Minister is no favourite of the tabloids.* N-COUNT: usu with poss [3] The **favourite** in a race or contest is the competitor that is expected to win. In a team game, the team that is expected to win is referred to as the **favourites**. ❑ *The Belgian Cup has been won by the favourites F.C. Liege.* N-COUNT: usu *the* N

**fa|vour|it|ism** /feɪvərɪtɪzəm/

☑ in AM, use **favoritism**

If you accuse someone of **favouritism**, you disapprove of them because they unfairly help or favour one person or group much more than another. ❑ *Maria loved both the children. There was never a hint of favouritism.* N-UNCOUNT [disapproval] = bias

**fawn** /fɔːn/ **(fawns, fawning, fawned)** [1] **Fawn** is a pale yellowish-brown colour. ❑ *...a light fawn coat.* COLOUR [2] A **fawn** is a very young deer. ❑ *The fawn ran to the top of the ridge.* N-COUNT [3] If you say that someone **fawns over** a powerful or rich person, you disapprove of them because they flatter that person and like to be with him or her. ❑ *People fawn over you when you're famous... Nauseatingly fawning journalism that's all it is.* VERB [disapproval] V *over/on/around* n V-ing

**fax** /fæks/ **(faxes, faxing, faxed)** 1 A **fax** or a **fax machine** is a piece of equipment used to copy documents by sending information electronically along a telephone line, and to receive copies that are sent in this way. ❑ *...a modern reception desk with telephone and fax... These days, cartoonists send in their work by fax.* N-COUNT: also *by* N 2 If you **fax** a document to someone, you send it from one fax machine to another. ❑ *I faxed a copy of the agreement to each of the investors... Did you fax him a reply?... Pop it in the post, or get your secretary to fax it... I faxed 10 hotels in the area to check room size.* VERB V n *to* n V n n V n V n 3 You can refer to a copy of a document that is transmitted by a fax machine as a **fax**. ❑ *I sent him a long fax, saying I didn't need any help.* N-COUNT

**faze** /feɪz/ **(fazes, fazed)** If something **fazes** you, it surprises, shocks, or frightens you, so that you do not know what to do. [INFORMAL] ❑ *Big concert halls do not faze Melanie.* VERB: no cont, oft with brd-neg V n

**FBI** /ef biː aɪ/ **The FBI** is a government agency in the United States that investigates crimes in which a national law is broken or in which the country's security is threatened. **FBI** is an abbreviation for 'Federal Bureau of Investigation'. N-PROPER: *the* N

**fe|al|ty** /fiːəlti/ In former times, if someone swore **fealty** to their ruler, they promised to be loyal to him or her. N-UNCOUNT = *allegiance*

**fear** /fɪəʳ/ **(fears, fearing, feared)** ◆◆◆ 1 **Fear** is the unpleasant feeling you have when you think that you are in danger. ❑ *I was sitting on the floor shivering with fear. ...boyhood memories of sickness and fear of the dark.* N-VAR: oft N *of* n/-ing 2 If you **fear** someone or something, you are frightened because you think that they will harm you. ❑ *Many people fear change because they do not like the old ways to be disrupted.* VERB V n 3 A **fear** is a thought that something unpleasant might happen or might have happened. ❑ *These youngsters are motivated not by a desire to achieve, but by fear of failure... Then one day his worst fears were confirmed.* N-VAR: with supp, oft N *of* n/-ing, N that 4 If you **fear** something unpleasant or undesirable, you are worried that it might happen or might have happened. ❑ *She had feared she was going down with pneumonia or bronchitis... More than two million refugees have fled the area, fearing attack by loyalist forces.* VERB V that V n 5 If you say that there is a **fear that** something unpleasant or undesirable will happen, you mean that you think it is possible or likely. ❑ *There is a fear that the freeze on bank accounts could prove a lasting deterrent to investors.* N-VAR: oft N that, N *of* n/-ing 6 If you **fear for** someone or something, you are very worried because you think that they might be in danger. ❑ *Carla fears for her son... He fled on Friday, saying he feared for his life.* VERB V *for* n V *for* n 7 If you have **fears for** someone or something, you are very worried because you think that they might be in danger. ❑ *He also spoke of his fears for the future of his country's culture.* N-VAR: N *for* n 8 You say that you **fear** that a situation is the case when the situation is unpleasant or undesirable, and when you want to express sympathy, sorrow, or regret about it. [FORMAL] ❑ *I fear that a land war now looks very probable... 'Is anything left at all?' — 'I fear not.'* VERB = *regret* V that V *so/not*

PHRASES 9 If you are **in fear of** doing or experiencing something unpleasant or undesirable, you are very worried that you might have to do it or experience it. ❑ *The elderly live in fear of assault and murder.* PHRASE: PHR n/-ing, usu v-link PHR, PHR after v 10 If you take a particular course of action **for fear of** something, you take the action in order to prevent that thing happening. ❑ *She was afraid to say anything to them for fear of hurting their feelings.* PHRASE: PHR n/-ing, PHR with cl 11 You use **'no fear'** to emphasize that you do not want to do something. [BRIT, INFORMAL] ❑ *When I asked him if he wanted to change his mind, William said 'No fear.'* CONVENTION emphasis

**fear|ful** /fɪəʳfʊl/ 1 If you are **fearful of** something, you are afraid of it. [FORMAL] ❑ *Bankers were fearful of a world banking crisis... I had often been very fearful, very angry, and very isolated.* ADJ: usu v-link ADJ, oft ADJ *of* n, ADJ that 2 You use **fearful** to emphasize how serious or bad a situation is. [FORMAL] ❑ *...the fearful consequences which might flow from unilateral military moves.* ADJ: ADJ n emphasis = *dreadful* 3 **Fearful** is used to emphasize that something is very bad. [INFORMAL, OLD-FASHIONED] ❑ *You gave me a fearful shock!* ADJ: ADJ n emphasis

**fear|less** /fɪəʳləs/ If you say that someone is **fearless**, you mean that they are not afraid at all, and you admire them for this. ❑ *...his fearless campaigning for racial justice.* ADJ approval

**fear|some** /fɪəʳsəm/ **Fearsome** is used to describe things that are frightening, for example because of their large size or extreme nature. ❑ *He had developed a fearsome reputation for intimidating people. ...a fearsome array of weapons.* ADJ = *formidable*

**fea|sible** /fiːzəbᵊl/ If something is **feasible**, it can be done, made, or achieved. ❑ *She questioned whether it was feasible to stimulate investment in these regions.* ADJ: oft ADJ to-inf ♦ **fea|sibil|ity** /fiːzəbɪlɪti/ *The committee will study the feasibility of setting up a national computer network.* N-UNCOUNT: oft N *of* n

**feast** /fiːst/ **(feasts, feasting, feasted)** 1 A **feast** is a large and special meal. ❑ *Lunch was a feast of meat and vegetables, cheese, yoghurt and fruit, with unlimited wine... The fruit was often served at wedding feasts.* N-COUNT = *banquet* 2 If you **feast on** a particular food, you eat a large amount of it with great enjoyment. ❑ *They feasted well into the afternoon on mutton and corn stew.* VERB V *on* n 3 If you **feast**, you take part in a feast. ❑ *Only a few feet away, their captors feasted in the castle's banqueting hall.* VERB V ♦ **feast|ing** *The feasting, drinking, dancing and revelry continued for several days.* N-UNCOUNT 4 A **feast** is a day or time of the year when a special religious celebration takes place. ❑ *The Jewish feast of Passover began last night.* N-COUNT = *festival* 5 If you **feast** your **eyes on** something, you look at it for a long time with great attention because you find it very attractive. ❑ *She stood feasting her eyes on the view.* PHRASE: V inflects

**feat** /fiːt/ **(feats)** If you refer to an action, or the result of an action, as a **feat**, you admire it because it is an impressive and difficult achievement. ❑ *A racing car is an extraordinary feat of engineering.* N-COUNT approval

**feath|er** /feðəʳ/ **(feathers)** 1 A bird's **feathers** are the soft covering on its body. Each **feather** consists of a lot of smooth hairs on each side of a thin stiff centre. ❑ *...a hat that she had made herself from black ostrich feathers. ...a feather bed.* → See also **feathered**. N-COUNT 2 to **ruffle** someone's **feathers** → see **ruffle**.

**feath|er boa** → see **boa**.

**feath|er dust|er** **(feather dusters)** A **feather duster** is a stick with a bunch of real or artificial feathers attached to one end. It is used for dusting and cleaning things. N-COUNT

**feath|ered** /feðəʳd/ 1 If you describe something as **feathered**, you mean that it has feathers on it. ❑ *...the ceremonial feathered hat worn by Hong Kong's governor.* ADJ 2 Birds are sometimes referred to as **our feathered friends**. PHRASE

**feather|weight** /feðəʳweɪt/ **(featherweights)** A **featherweight** is a professional boxer who weighs between 53.5 and 57 kilograms, which is one of the lowest weight ranges. N-COUNT

**feath|ery** /feðəri/ 1 If something is **feathery**, it has an edge divided into a lot of thin parts so that it looks soft. ❑ *The foliage was soft and feathery.* ADJ 2 **Feathery** is used to describe things that are soft and light. ❑ *...flurries of small, feathery flakes of snow.* ADJ

**fea|ture** /fiːtʃəʳ/ **(features, featuring, featured)** ◆◆◇ 1 A **feature of** something is an interesting or important part or characteristic of it. ❑ *Patriotic songs have long been a feature of Kuwaiti life... The spacious gardens are a special feature of this property.* N-COUNT: with supp, oft N *of* n 2 Your **features** are your eyes, nose, mouth, and other parts of your face. ❑ *His features seemed to change... Her features were strongly defined.* N-PLURAL: usu poss N 3 When something such as a film or exhibition **features** a particular person or thing, they are an VERB = *include* important part of it. ❑ *It's a great movie and it features a Spanish actor who is going to be a world star within a year... This spectacular event, now in its 5th year, features a stunning catwalk show.* V n V n [4] If someone or something **features in** something such as a show, exhibition, or magazine, they are an important part of it. ❑ *Jon featured in one of the show's most thrilling episodes.* VERB V *in/on* n [5] A **feature** is a special article in a newspaper or magazine, or a special programme on radio or television. ❑ *...a special feature on the fund-raising project.* N-COUNT: oft N *on* n [6] A **feature** or a **feature** film or movie is a full-length film about a fictional situation, as opposed to a short film or a documentary. ❑ *...the first feature-length cartoon, Snow White and the Seven Dwarfs.* N-COUNT: usu N n [7] A geographical **feature** is something noticeable in a particular area of country, for example a hill, river, or valley. N-COUNT

**fea|ture|less** /fiːtʃəʳləs/ If you say that something is **featureless**, you mean that it has no interesting features or characteristics. ❑ *Malone looked out at the grey-green featureless landscape.* ADJ = nondescript

**Feb.** **Feb.** is a written abbreviation for **February**.

**fe|brile** /fiːbraɪl/ **Febrile** behaviour is intensely and nervously active. [LITERARY] ❑ *The news plunged the nation into a febrile, agitated state.* ADJ = feverish

**Feb|ru|ary** /febjuəri, AM -jueri/ **(Februaries)** **February** is the second month of the year in the Western calendar. ❑ *He joined the Army in February 1943... His exhibition opens on 5 February... Last February the tribunal agreed he had been the victim of racial discrimination.* N-VAR

**fe|cal** /fiːkəl/ → see **faecal**.

**fe|ces** /fiːsiːz/ → see **faeces**.

**feck|less** /fekləs/ If you describe someone as **feckless**, you mean that they lack determination or strength, and are unable to do anything properly. [FORMAL] ❑ *He regarded the young man as feckless and irresponsible.* ADJ disapproval = incompetent

**fe|cund** /fiːkənd, fek-/ [1] Land or soil that is **fecund** is able to support the growth of a large number of strong healthy plants. [FORMAL] ❑ *The pampas are still among the most fecund lands in the world.* ADJ [2] If you describe something as **fecund**, you approve of it because it produces a lot of good or useful things. [FORMAL] ❑ *It has now become clear how extraordinarily fecund a decade was the 1890s.* ADJ approval = productive

**fed** /fed/ **(feds)** [1] **Fed** is the past tense and past participle of **feed**. See also **fed up**. [2] The **feds** are federal agents, for example of the American security agency, the FBI, or of the Bureau of Alcohol, Tobacco, and Firearms. [AM, INFORMAL] N-COUNT: usu pl

**fed|er|al** /fedərəl/ **(federals)** [1] A **federal** country or system of government is one in which the different states or provinces of the country have important powers to make their own laws and decisions. ❑ *Five of the six provinces are to become autonomous regions in a new federal system of government.* ◆◆◇ ADJ: ADJ n [2] Some people use **federal** to describe a system of government which they disapprove of, in which the different states or provinces are controlled by a strong central government. ❑ *He does not believe in a federal Europe with centralising powers.* ADJ: ADJ n disapproval [3] **Federal** also means belonging or relating to the national government of a federal country rather than to one of the states within it. ❑ *The federal government controls just 6% of the education budget. ...a federal judge.* ADJ: ADJ n ♦ **fed|er|al|ly** *...residents of public housing and federally subsidized apartments.* ADV: ADV -ed [4] **Federals** are the same as **feds**. N-COUNT

**fed|er|al|ism** /fedərəlɪzəm/ **Federalism** is belief in or support for a federal system of government, or this system itself. ❑ *They argue that the amendment undermines Canadian federalism.* N-UNCOUNT

**fed|er|al|ist** /fedərəlɪst/ **(federalists)** Someone or something that is **federalist** believes in, supports, or follows a federal system of government. ❑ *...the federalist idea of Europe.* ADJ ♦ **Federalist** is also a noun. ❑ *Many Quebeckers are federalists.* N-COUNT

**fed|er|at|ed** /fedəreɪtɪd/ **Federated** states or societies are ones that have joined together for a common purpose. ❑ *Whether to stay in the federated state or become independent is a decision that has to be made by the people.* ADJ: ADJ n, v-link ADJ *to* n

**fed|era|tion** /fedəreɪʃən/ **(federations)** [1] A **federation** is a federal country. ❑ *...the Russian Federation.* ◆◇◇ N-COUNT [2] A **federation** is a group of societies or other organizations which have joined together, usually because they share a common interest. ❑ *...the British Athletic Federation... The organization emerged from a federation of six national agencies.* N-COUNT: usu with supp, oft in names

**fe|do|ra** /fɪdɔːrə/ **(fedoras)** A **fedora** is a type of hat which has a brim and is made from a soft material such as velvet. N-COUNT

**fed up** If you are **fed up**, you are unhappy, bored, or tired of something, especially something that you have been experiencing for a long time. [INFORMAL] ❑ *He had become fed up with city life... I'm just fed up and I don't know what to do.* ADJ: v-link ADJ, oft ADJ *with/of* n/-ing

**fee** /fiː/ **(fees)** [1] A **fee** is a sum of money that you pay to be allowed to do something. ❑ *He hadn't paid his television licence fee.* ◆◆◇ N-COUNT [2] A **fee** is the amount of money that a person or organization is paid for a particular job or service that they provide. ❑ *Find out how much your surveyor's and solicitor's fees will be.* N-COUNT

**fee|ble** /fiːbəl/ **(feebler, feeblest)** [1] If you describe someone or something as **feeble**, you mean that they are weak. ❑ *He told them he was old and feeble and was not able to walk so far... The feeble light of a tin lamp.* ADJ ♦ **fee|bly** *His left hand moved feebly at his side.* ADV: ADV with v [2] If you describe something that someone says as **feeble**, you mean that it is not very good or convincing. ❑ *This is a particularly feeble argument.* ADJ = weak ♦ **fee|bly** *I said 'Sorry', very feebly, feeling rather embarrassed.* ADV: ADV with v = weakly

**feed** /fiːd/ **(feeds, feeding, fed)** [1] If you **feed** a person or animal, you give them food to eat and sometimes actually put it in their mouths. ❑ *We brought along pieces of old bread and fed the birds... In that part of the world you can feed cattle on almost any green vegetable or fruit... He spooned the ice cream into a cup and fed it to her.* ◆◆◇ VERB V n V n *on/with* n V n *to* n Also V pron-refl ♦ **Feed** is also a noun. [mainly BRIT] ❑ *She's had a good feed.* N-COUNT ♦ **feed|ing** *The feeding of dairy cows has undergone a revolution.* N-UNCOUNT [2] To **feed** a family or a community means to supply food for them. ❑ *Feeding a hungry family can be expensive . ...a food reserve large enough to feed the Sudanese population for many months.* VERB V n V n [3] When an animal **feeds**, it eats or drinks something. ❑ *After a few days the caterpillars stopped feeding... Slugs feed on decaying plant and animal material.* VERB V V *on/off* n [4] When a baby **feeds**, or when you **feed** it, it drinks breast milk or milk from a bottle. ❑ *When a baby is thirsty, it feeds more often... I knew absolutely nothing about handling or feeding a baby.* VERB V V n [5] Animal **feed** is food given to animals, especially farm animals. ❑ *The grain just rotted and all they could use it for was animal feed. ...poultry feed.* N-MASS: usu n N [6] To **feed** something to a place, means to supply it to that place in a steady flow. ❑ *...blood vessels that feed blood to the brain. ...gas fed through pipelines.* VERB V n prep V n prep [7] If you **feed** something **into** a container or piece of equipment, you put it into it. ❑ *She was feeding documents into a paper shredder.* VERB V n prep [8] If someone **feeds** you false or secret information, they deliberately tell it to you. ❑ *He was surrounded by people who fed him ghastly lies... At least one British officer was feeding him with classified information.* VERB V n n V n *with* n Also V n *to* n [9] If you **feed** a plant, you add substances to it to make it grow well. ❑ *Feed plants to encourage steady growth.* VERB V n [10] If one thing **feeds on** another, it becomes stronger as a result of the other thing's existence. ❑ *The drinking and the guilt fed on each other.* VERB V *on* n [11] To **feed** information **into** a computer means to gradually put it into it. ❑ *An automatic weather station feeds information on wind direction to the computer.* VERB V n *into/to* n [12] to **bite the hand that**

**feeds** you → see **bite**. **mouths to feed** → see **mouth**.

**feed|back** /fiːdbæk/ 1 If you get **feedback on** your work or progress, someone tells you how well or badly you are doing, and how you could improve. If you get good feedback you have worked or performed well. ❑ *Continue to ask for feedback on your work... I was getting great feedback from my boss.* [N-UNCOUNT: oft N prep] 2 **Feedback** is the unpleasant high-pitched sound produced by a piece of electrical equipment when part of the signal that comes out goes back into it. [N-UNCOUNT]

**feed|er** /fiːdəʳ/ **(feeders)** 1 A **feeder** road, railway, or river is a smaller one that leads to a more important one. [ADJ: ADJ n] 2 **Feeder** airline and railway services connect major routes and local destinations. ❑ *...a feeder to British Airways's transatlantic destinations.* [N-COUNT: usu N n] 3 A **feeder** school or team provides students or players for a larger or more important one. [N-COUNT: oft N n] 4 A **feeder** is a container that you fill with food for birds or animals. [N-COUNT: oft n N]

**feed|ing bot|tle** **(feeding bottles)** also **feeding-bottle.** A **feeding bottle** is a plastic bottle with a special rubber top through which a baby can suck milk or other liquids. [mainly BRIT] [N-COUNT]

☑ in AM, use **nursing bottle**

**feed|ing ground** **(feeding grounds)** The **feeding ground** of a group of animals or birds, is the place where they find food and eat. ❑ *The mud is a feeding ground for large numbers of birds.* [N-COUNT: usu with supp]

**feel** /fiːl/ **(feels, feeling, felt)** ◆◆◆ 1 If you **feel** a particular emotion or physical sensation, you experience it. ❑ *I am feeling very depressed... I will always feel grateful to that little guy... I remember feeling sick... Suddenly I felt a sharp pain in my shoulder... You won't feel a thing... I felt as if all my strength had gone... I felt like I was being kicked in the teeth every day.* [V-LINK; V adj; V adj; V adj; V n; V n; V as if; V like] 2 If you talk about how an experience or event **feels**, you talk about the emotions and sensations connected with it. ❑ *It feels good to have finished a piece of work... The speed at which everything moved felt strange... Within five minutes of arriving back from holiday, it feels as if I've never been away... It felt like I'd had two babies instead of one.* [V-LINK: no cont; *it* V adj to-inf/that; V adj; *it* V as if; *it* V like] 3 If you talk about how an object **feels**, you talk about the physical quality that you notice when you touch or hold it. For example, if something **feels** soft, you notice that it is soft when you touch it. ❑ *The metal felt smooth and cold... The ten-foot oars felt heavy and awkward... When the clay feels like putty, it is ready to use.* ♦ **Feel** is also a noun. ❑ *He remembered the feel of her skin... Linen raincoats have a crisp, papery feel.* [V-LINK: no cont; V adj; V adj; V *like* n; N-SING: usu with supp] 4 If you talk about how the weather **feels**, you describe the weather, especially the temperature or whether or not you think it is going to rain or snow. ❑ *It felt wintry cold that day.* [V-LINK: no cont; *it* V adj; Also *it* V like/as if] 5 If you **feel** an object, you touch it deliberately with your hand, so that you learn what it is like, for example what shape it is or whether it is rough or smooth. ❑ *The doctor felt his head... When dry, feel the surface and it will no longer be smooth... Feel how soft the skin is in the small of the back... Her eyes squeezed shut, she felt inside the tin, expecting it to be bare.* [VERB; V n; V n; V wh; V prep/adv] 6 If you can **feel** something, you are aware of it because it is touching you. ❑ *Through several layers of clothes I could feel his muscles... He felt her leg against his.* [VERB: no cont; V n; V n prep/adv] 7 If you **feel** something happening, you become aware of it because of the effect it has on your body. ❑ *She felt something being pressed into her hands... He felt something move beside him... She felt herself lifted from her feet... Tremors were felt 250 miles away.* [VERB; V n -ing; V n inf; V pron-refl -ed, *be* V-ed] 8 If you **feel yourself** doing something or being in a particular state, you are aware that something is happening to you which you are unable to control. ❑ *I felt myself blush... If at any point you feel yourself becoming tense, make a conscious effort to relax... I actually felt my heart quicken.* [VERB; V pron-refl inf; V n inf; Also V n -ing] 9 If you **feel** the presence of someone or something, you become aware of them, even though you cannot see or hear them. ❑ *He felt her eyes on him... Suddenly, I felt a presence behind me... I could feel that a man was watching me very intensely... He almost felt her wincing at the other end of the telephone.* [VERB: no cont = sense; V n; V that; V n -ing] 10 If you **feel** that something is the case, you have a strong idea in your mind that it is the case. ❑ *I feel that not enough is being done to protect the local animal life... I feel certain that it will all turn out well... She felt herself to be part of a large business empire... I never felt myself a real child of the sixties.* [VERB: no cont; V that; V adj that; V n to-inf; V pron-refl n] 11 If you **feel** that you should do something, you think that you should do it. ❑ *I feel I should resign... He felt that he had to do it... You need not feel obliged to contribute... They felt under no obligation to maintain their employees.* [VERB: no cont; V that; V that; V -ed to-inf; V *under* n] 12 If you talk about how you **feel about** something, you talk about your opinion, attitude, or reaction to it. ❑ *We'd like to know what you feel about abortion... She feels guilty about spending less time lately with her two kids... He feels deep regret about his friend's death.* [VERB: no cont; V *about* n; V adj/adv *about* n; V n *about* n] 13 If you **feel like** doing something or having something, you want to do it or have it because you are in the right mood for it and think you would enjoy it. ❑ *Neither of them felt like going back to sleep... Could we take a walk? I feel like a little exercise.* [VERB; V *like* -ing/n; V *like* -ing/n] 14 If you **feel** the effect or result of something, you experience it. ❑ *The charity is still feeling the effects of revelations about its one-time president... The real impact will be felt in the developing world.* [VERB; V n; V n] 15 The **feel** of something, for example a place, is the general impression that it gives you. ❑ *The room has a warm, cosy feel.* [N-SING: with supp] ● If you **get the feel of** something, for example a place or a new activity, you become familiar with it. ❑ *He wanted to get the feel of the place.* [PHRASE: V inflects, PHR n] 16 → See also **feeling**, **felt**. **feel free** → see **free**.

♦ **feel for** 1 If you **feel for** something, for example in the dark, you try to find it by moving your hand around until you touch it. ❑ *I felt for my wallet and papers in my inside pocket... I slumped down in my usual armchair and felt around for the newspaper.* [PHRASAL VERB; V P n; V adv/prep P n] 2 If you **feel for** someone, you have sympathy for them. ❑ *She cried on the phone and was very upset and I really felt for her.* [PHRASAL VERB; V P n]

**feel|er** /fiːləʳ/ **(feelers)** 1 An insect's **feelers** are the two thin stalks on its head with which it touches and senses things around it. [N-COUNT: usu pl = *antenna*] 2 If you **put out feelers**, you make careful, quiet contacts with people in order to get information from them, or to find out what their reaction will be to a suggestion. ❑ *When vacancies occur, the office puts out feelers to the universities.* [N-PLURAL]

**feel-good** also **feelgood.** 1 A **feel-good** film is a film which presents people and life in a way which makes the people who watch it feel happy and optimistic. ❑ *...a bright and enjoyable feelgood romance.* [ADJ: ADJ n] 2 When journalists refer to **the feel-good factor**, they mean that people are feeling hopeful and optimistic about the future. ❑ *There were obvious signs of the feel-good factor in the last survey taken in the wake of the election result.* [PHRASE]

**feel|ing** /fiːlɪŋ/ **(feelings)** ◆◆◇ 1 A **feeling** is an emotion, such as anger or happiness. ❑ *It gave me a feeling of satisfaction... I think our main feeling would be of an immense gratitude... He was unable to contain his own destructive feelings.* [N-COUNT: usu with supp, oft N *of* n] 2 Your **feelings** about something are the things that you think and feel about it, or your attitude towards it. ❑ *She has strong feelings about the alleged growth in violence against female officers... I think that sums up the feelings of most discerning and intelligent Indians... He made no real secret of his feelings to his friends.* [N-PLURAL: with supp, oft with poss, oft N *about* n/-ing] 3 When you refer to someone's **feelings**, you are talking about the things that might embarrass, offend, or upset them. For example, if you hurt someone's **feelings**, you upset them by something that you say or do. ❑ *He was afraid of hurting my feelings... He has no respect, no regard for anyone's feelings.* [N-PLURAL: usu poss N] 4 **Feeling** is a way of thinking and reacting to things which is emotional and not planned rather than logical and practical. ❑ *He* [N-UNCOUNT = *emotion*] *was prompted to a rare outburst of feeling. ...a voice that trembles with feeling.* 5 **Feeling** for someone is love, affection, sympathy, or concern for them. ❑ *Thomas never lost his feeling for Harriet... It's incredible that Peter can behave with such stupid lack of feeling.* — N-UNCOUNT: oft N *for* n

6 If you have a **feeling** of hunger, tiredness, or other physical sensation, you experience it. ❑ *I also had a strange feeling in my neck... He experienced feelings of claustrophobia from being in a small place.* — N-COUNT: usu with supp, oft N *of* n

7 **Feeling** in part of your body is the ability to experience the sense of touch in this part of the body. ❑ *After the accident he had no feeling in his legs.* — N-UNCOUNT

8 If you have **a feeling that** something is the case or **that** something is going to happen, you think that is probably the case or that it is probably going to happen. ❑ *I have a feeling that everything will come right for us one day... You have a feeling about people, and I just felt she was going to be good.* — N-COUNT: usu with supp, oft N *about* n, N that

9 **Feeling** is used to refer to a general opinion that a group of people has about something. ❑ *There is still some feeling in the art world that the market for such works may be declining... It seemed that anti-Fascist feeling was not being encouraged.* — N-UNCOUNT: with supp, oft N that

10 If you have a **feeling of** being in a particular situation, you feel that you are in that situation. ❑ *I had the terrible feeling of being left behind to bring up the baby while he had fun.* — N-SING: N *of* -ing

11 If you have **a feeling for** something, you have an understanding of it or a natural ability to do it. ❑ *Try to get a feeling for the people who live here... You seem to have a feeling for drawing.* — N-SING: *a* N *for* n

12 If something such as a place or book creates a particular kind of **feeling**, it creates a particular kind of atmosphere. ❑ *That's what we tried to portray in the book, this feeling of opulence and grandeur.* — N-SING: with supp

13 → See also **feel**.

PHRASES 14 **Bad feeling** or **ill feeling** is bitterness or anger which exists between people, for example after they have had an argument. ❑ *There's been some bad feeling between the two families.* — PHRASE: oft PHR *between* n

15 **Hard feelings** are feelings of anger or bitterness towards someone who you have had an argument with or who has upset you. If you say '**no hard feelings**', you are making an agreement with someone not to be angry or bitter about something. ❑ *I don't want any hard feelings between our companies... He held out his large hand. 'No hard feelings, right?'* — PHRASE

16 You say '**I know the feeling**' to show that you understand or feel sorry about a problem or difficult experience that someone is telling you about. [SPOKEN] — CONVENTION [feelings]

17 If you **have mixed feelings** about something or someone, you feel uncertain about them because you can see both good and bad points about them. — PHRASE: V inflects, usu PHR *about* n

**feel|ing|ly** /fiːlɪŋli/ If someone says something **feelingly**, they say it in a way which shows that they have very strong feelings about what they are saying. ❑ *'It's what I want,' she said feelingly.* — ADV: ADV after v = *emotionally*

**fee-paying** **Fee-paying** is used to talk about institutions or services which people have to pay to use, especially ones which are often provided free. ❑ *...fee-paying schools. ...fee-paying postgraduate students.* — ADJ: usu ADJ n

**feet** /fiːt/ **Feet** is the plural of **foot**.

**feign** /feɪn/ **(feigns, feigning, feigned)** If someone **feigns** a particular feeling, attitude, or physical condition, they try to make other people think that they have it or are experiencing it, although this is not true. [FORMAL] ❑ *One morning, I didn't want to go to school, and decided to feign illness... 'Giles phoned this morning,' Mirella said with feigned indifference.* — VERB = *affect*; V n; V-ed; Also V to-inf

**feint** /feɪnt/ **(feints, feinting, feinted)** In sport or military conflict, if someone **feints**, they make a brief movement in a different direction from the one they intend to follow, as a way of confusing or deceiving their opponent. ❑ *I feinted to the left, then to the right... They feinted and concentrated forces against the most fortified line of the enemy side.* — VERB; V prep/adv; V

**feisty** /faɪsti/ If you describe someone as **feisty**, you mean that they are tough, independent, and spirited, often when you would not expect them to be, for example because they are old or ill. ❑ *At 66, she was as feisty as ever.* — ADJ = *spunky*

**fe|lici|tous** /fɪlɪsɪtəs/ If you describe a remark or idea as **felicitous**, you approve of it because it seems particularly suitable in the circumstances. [FORMAL] ❑ *Her prose style is not always felicitous; she tends to repetition.* — ADJ [approval]

**fe|lic|ity** /fɪlɪsɪti/ 1 **Felicity** is great happiness and pleasure. [LITERARY] ❑ *...joy and felicity.* — N-UNCOUNT

2 **Felicity** is the quality of being good, pleasant, or desirable. [LITERARY] ❑ *...his conversational manner and easy verbal felicity.* — N-UNCOUNT

**fe|line** /fiːlaɪn/ **(felines)** 1 **Feline** means belonging or relating to the cat family. — ADJ: ADJ n

2 A **feline** is an animal that belongs to the cat family. ❑ *The 14lb feline is so fat she can hardly walk.* — N-COUNT = *cat*

3 You can use **feline** to describe someone's appearance or movements if they are elegant or graceful in a way that makes you think of a cat. [LITERARY] ❑ *She moves with feline grace.* — ADJ: usu ADJ n = *catlike*

**fell** /fel/ **(fells, felling, felled)** 1 **Fell** is the past tense of **fall**. 2 If trees **are felled**, they are cut down. ❑ *Badly infected trees should be felled and burned.* — VERB: usu passive *be* V-ed

3 If you **fell** someone, you knock them down, for example in a fight. ❑ *...a blow on the forehead which felled him to the ground.* — VERB; V n

4 **in one fell swoop** → see **swoop**.

**fel|la** /felə/ **(fellas)** also **feller.** You can refer to a man as a **fella**. [INFORMAL] ❑ *He's an intelligent man and a nice fella.* — N-COUNT: usu with supp = *fellow*

**fel|la|tio** /fəleɪʃiəʊ/ **Fellatio** is oral sex which involves someone using their mouth to stimulate their partner's penis. — N-UNCOUNT

**fel|low** /feləʊ/ **(fellows)** ◆◆◇ 1 You use **fellow** to describe people who are in the same situation as you, or people you feel you have something in common with. ❑ *She discovered to her pleasure, a talent for making her fellow guests laugh... Even in jail, my fellow inmates treated me with kindness.* — ADJ: ADJ n

2 A **fellow** is a man or boy. [INFORMAL, OLD-FASHIONED] ❑ *By all accounts, Rodger would appear to be a fine fellow.* — N-COUNT = *chap*

3 Your **fellows** are the people who you work with, do things with, or who are like you in some way. [FORMAL] ❑ *People looked out for one another and were concerned about the welfare of their fellows.* — N-PLURAL: poss N

4 A **fellow of** an academic or professional association is someone who is a specially elected member of it, usually because of their work or achievements or as a mark of honour. ❑ *...the fellows of the Zoological Society of London.* — N-COUNT: usu N *of* n

**fel|low feel|ing** also **fellow-feeling. Fellow feeling** is sympathy and friendship that exists between people who have shared similar experiences or difficulties. — N-UNCOUNT

**fel|low|ship** /feləʊʃɪp/ **(fellowships)** 1 A **fellowship** is a group of people that join together for a common purpose or interest. ❑ *...the National Schizophrenia Fellowship... At Merlin's instigation, Arthur founds the Fellowship of the Round Table.* — N-COUNT: with supp

2 A **fellowship** at a university is a post which involves research work. ❑ *He was offered a research fellowship at Clare College.* — N-COUNT

3 **Fellowship** is a feeling of friendship that people have when they are talking or doing something together and sharing their experiences. ❑ *...a sense of community and fellowship.* — N-UNCOUNT = *companionship*

**fel|on** /felən/ **(felons)** A **felon** is a person who is guilty of committing a felony. [LEGAL] ❑ *He's a convicted felon.* — N-COUNT

**felo|ny** /feləni/ **(felonies)** In countries where the legal system distinguishes between very serious crimes and less serious ones, a **felony** is a very serious crime such as armed robbery. [LEGAL] ❑ *He pleaded guilty to six felonies.* — N-COUNT

**felt** /felt/ 1 **Felt** is the past tense and past participle of **feel**. 2 **Felt** is a thick cloth made from wool or other fibres packed tightly together. — N-UNCOUNT

**felt-tip** **(felt-tips)** A **felt-tip** or a **felt-tip pen** is a pen which has a piece of fibre at the end that the ink comes through. N-COUNT

**fem.** **fem.** is a written abbreviation for **female** or **feminine**.

**fe|male** /fiːmeɪl/ **(females)** 1 Someone who is **female** is a woman or a girl. ❑ *...a sixteen-piece dance band with a female singer... Only 13 per cent of consultants are female.* ◆◆◇ ADJ ≠male 2 Women and girls are sometimes referred to as **females** when they are being considered as a type. ❑ *Hay fever affects males more than females.* N-COUNT ≠male 3 **Female** matters and things relate to, belong to, or affect women rather than men. ❑ *...female infertility. ...a purveyor of female undergarments.* ADJ: ADJ n ≠male 4 You can refer to any creature that can lay eggs or produce babies from its body as a **female**. ❑ *Each female will lay just one egg in April or May.* ♦ **Female** is also an adjective. ❑ *...the scent given off by the female aphid to attract the male.* N-COUNT ≠male ADJ ≠male 5 A **female** flower or plant contains the part that will become the fruit when it is fertilized. ❑ *Figs have male and female flowers.* ADJ: usu ADJ n ≠male

**femi|nine** /femɪnɪn/ 1 **Feminine** qualities and things relate to or are considered typical of women, in contrast to men. ❑ *...male leaders worrying about their women abandoning traditional feminine roles. ...a manufactured ideal of feminine beauty.* ADJ: usu ADJ n = female ≠masculine 2 Someone or something that is **feminine** has qualities that are considered typical of women, especially being pretty or gentle. ❑ *I've always been attracted to very feminine, delicate women... The bedroom has a light, feminine look.* ADJ approval ≠masculine 3 In some languages, a **feminine** noun, pronoun, or adjective has a different form from a masculine or neuter one, or behaves in a different way. ADJ

**femi|nin|ity** /femɪnɪnɪti/ 1 A woman's **femininity** is the fact that she is a woman. ❑ *...the drudgery behind the ideology of motherhood and femininity.* N-UNCOUNT ≠masculinity 2 **Femininity** means the qualities that are considered to be typical of women. ❑ *...this courageous German tennis star's unique blend of strength and femininity.* N-UNCOUNT ≠masculinity

**femi|nism** /femɪnɪzəm/ **Feminism** is the belief and aim that women should have the same rights, power, and opportunities as men. ❑ *...Barbara Johnson, that champion of radical feminism.* N-UNCOUNT

**femi|nist** /femɪnɪst/ **(feminists)** 1 A **feminist** is a person who believes in and supports feminism. ❑ *Only 16 per cent of young women in a 1990 survey considered themselves feminists.* N-COUNT 2 **Feminist** groups, ideas, and activities are involved in feminism. ❑ *...the concerns addressed by the feminist movement.* ADJ: ADJ n

**femi|nize** /femɪnaɪz/ **(feminizes, feminizing, feminized)**

> ✓ in BRIT, also use **feminise**

To **feminize** something means to make it into something that involves mainly women or is thought suitable for or typical of women. [FORMAL] ❑ *...their governments' policies of feminizing low-paid factory work. ...a feminised pinstriped suit.* VERB V n V-ed

**femme fa|tale** /fæm fətɑːl/ **(femmes fatales)** If a woman has a reputation as a **femme fatale**, she is considered to be very attractive sexually, and likely to cause problems for any men who are attracted to her. N-COUNT: usu sing

**fe|mur** /fiːməʳ/ **(femurs)** Your **femur** is the large bone in the upper part of your leg. N-COUNT

**fen** /fen/ **(fens)** **Fen** is used to refer to an area of low, flat, wet land, especially in the east of England. ❑ *...the flat fen lands near Cambridge.* N-VAR

**fence** /fens/ **(fences, fencing, fenced)** 1 A **fence** is a barrier between two areas of land, made of wood or wire supported by posts. ➔ See picture on page 1705. ❑ *Villagers say the fence would restrict public access to the hills.* ◆◇◇ N-COUNT 2 If you **fence** an area of land, you surround it with a fence. ❑ *The first task was to fence the wood to exclude sheep... Thomas was playing in a little fenced area full of sand.* VERB V n V-ed 3 A **fence** in show jumping or horse racing is an obstacle or barrier that horses have to jump over. N-COUNT

PHRASES 4 If one country tries to **mend fences with** another, it tries to end a disagreement or quarrel with the other country. You can also say that two countries **mend fences**. ❑ *Washington was last night doing its best to mend fences with the Europeans, saying it understood their concerns.* PHRASE: V inflects, PHR *with* n, pl-n PHR 5 If you **sit on the fence**, you avoid supporting a particular side in a discussion or argument. ❑ *They are sitting on the fence and refusing to commit themselves.* PHRASE: V inflects

♦ **fence in** 1 If you **fence** something **in**, you surround it completely with a fence. ❑ *He plans to fence in about 100 acres of his ranch five miles north of town.* PHRASAL VERB V P n 2 If you **are fenced in** by someone or something, they are so close to you that you are unable to move or leave. ❑ *She was basically fenced in by what the military wanted to do... He put his hand on the post behind her so that he had her fenced in and could look down on her.* PHRASAL VERB: usu passive *be* V-ed P V-ed P

**fenc|ing** /fensɪŋ/ 1 **Fencing** is a sport in which two competitors fight each other using very thin swords. The ends of the swords are covered and the competitors wear protective clothes, so that they do not hurt each other. N-UNCOUNT 2 Materials such as wood or wire that are used to make fences are called **fencing**. ❑ *...old wooden fencing.* N-UNCOUNT

**fend** /fend/ **(fends, fending, fended)** If you have to **fend for** yourself, you have to look after yourself without relying on help from anyone else. ❑ *The woman and her young baby had been thrown out and left to fend for themselves.* VERB V *for* pron-refl

♦ **fend off** 1 If you **fend off** unwanted questions, problems, or people, you stop them from affecting you or defend yourself from them, but often only for a short time and without dealing with them completely. ❑ *He looked relaxed and determined as he fended off questions from the world's Press... He had struggled to pay off creditors but couldn't fend them off any longer.* PHRASAL VERB V P n (not pron) V n P 2 If you **fend off** someone who is attacking you, you use your arms or something such as a stick to defend yourself from their blows. ❑ *He raised his hand to fend off the blow.* PHRASAL VERB = ward off V P n (not pron) Also V n P

**fend|er** /fendəʳ/ **(fenders)** 1 A **fender** is a low metal wall built around a fireplace, which stops any coals that fall out of the fire from rolling onto the carpet. ❑ *...a brass fender.* N-COUNT = guard 2 A **fender** is the same as a **fireguard**. N-COUNT 3 The **fenders** of a car are the parts of the body over the wheels. [AM] ➔ See picture on page 1707. N-COUNT

> ✓ in BRIT, use **wing**

4 The **fender** of a car is a bar at the front or back that protects the car if it bumps into something. [AM] N-COUNT

> ✓ in BRIT, use **bumper**

5 The **fenders** of a boat are objects which hang against the outside and protect it from damage when it comes next to a harbour wall or another boat. N-COUNT

**feng shui** /fʌŋ ʃweɪ/ **Feng shui** is a Chinese art which is based on the belief that the way you arrange things within a building, and within the rooms of that building, can affect aspects of your life such as how happy and successful you are. N-UNCOUNT

**fen|nel** /fenᵊl/ **Fennel** is a plant with a crisp rounded base and feathery leaves. It can be eaten as a vegetable or the leaves can be used as a herb. N-UNCOUNT

**fe|ral** /ferəl, fɪər-/ **Feral** animals are wild animals that are not owned or controlled by anyone, especially ones that belong to species which are normally owned and kept by people. [FORMAL] ❑ *...feral cats.* ADJ: usu ADJ n ≠domesticated

**fer|ment** **(ferments, fermenting, fermented)**

> ✓ The noun is pronounced /fɜːʳment/. The verb is pronounced /fəʳment/.

1 **Ferment** is excitement and trouble caused by N-UNCOUNT = turmoil

change or uncertainty. ❑ *The whole country has been in a state of political ferment for some months.* 2 If a food, drink, or other natural substance **ferments**, or if it **is fermented**, a chemical change takes place in it so that alcohol is produced. This process forms part of the production of alcoholic drinks such as wine and beer. ❑ *The dried grapes are allowed to ferment until there is no sugar left and the wine is dry... To serve the needs of bakers, manufacturers ferment the yeast to produce a more concentrated product.* ♦ **fer|men|ta|tion** /fɜːʳmenteɪʃᵊn/ *Yeast is essential for the fermentation that produces alcohol.* VERB; V; V n; N-UNCOUNT

**fern** /fɜːʳn/ **(ferns)** A **fern** is a plant that has long stems with feathery leaves and no flowers. There are many types of fern. N-VAR

**fe|ro|cious** /fəroʊʃəs/ 1 A **ferocious** animal, person, or action is very fierce and violent. ❑ *...a ferocious guard-dog... The police had had to deal with some of the most ferocious violence ever seen on the streets of London.* 2 A **ferocious** war, argument, or other form of conflict involves a great deal of anger, bitterness, and determination. ❑ *Fighting has been ferocious... A ferocious battle to select a new parliamentary candidate is in progress.* 3 If you describe actions or feelings as **ferocious**, you mean that they are intense and determined. ❑ *Lindbergh was startled at the ferocious depth of anti-British feeling.* ADJ = fierce; ADJ; ADJ

**fe|roc|ity** /fərɒsɪti/ The **ferocity** of something is its fierce or violent nature. ❑ *The armed forces seem to have been taken by surprise by the ferocity of the attack.* N-UNCOUNT

**fer|ret** /ferɪt/ **(ferrets, ferreting, ferreted)** 1 A **ferret** is a small, fierce animal which is used for hunting rabbits and rats. 2 If you **ferret** about for something, you look for it in a lot of different places or in a place where it is hidden. [BRIT, INFORMAL] ❑ *She nonetheless continued to ferret about for possible jobs... She ferreted among some papers.* N-COUNT; VERB = search; V about/around; V prep

♦ **ferret out** If you **ferret out** some information, you discover it by searching for it very thoroughly. [INFORMAL] ❑ *The team is trying to ferret out missing details... I leave it to the reader to ferret these out.* PHRASAL VERB = unearth; V P n (not pron); V n P

**Fer|ris wheel** /ferɪs wiːl/ **(Ferris wheels)** also **ferris wheel.** A **Ferris wheel** is a very large upright wheel with carriages around the edge of it which people can ride in. Ferris wheels are often found at theme parks or funfairs. [AM] N-COUNT

☑ in BRIT, use **big wheel**

**fer|rous** /ferəs/ **Ferrous** means containing or relating to iron. ❑ *...ferrous metals. ...ferrous chloride.* ADJ: ADJ n

**fer|rule** /feruːl, AM -rᵊl/ **(ferrules)** A **ferrule** is a metal or rubber cap that is fixed onto the end of a stick or post in order to prevent it from splitting or wearing down. [FORMAL] N-COUNT

**fer|ry** /feri/ **(ferries, ferrying, ferried)** 1 A **ferry** is a boat that transports passengers and sometimes also vehicles, usually across rivers or short stretches of sea. ❑ *They had recrossed the River Gambia by ferry.* 2 If a vehicle **ferries** people or goods, it transports them, usually by means of regular journeys between the same two places. ❑ *Every day, a plane arrives to ferry guests to and from Bird Island Lodge... It was still dark when five coaches started to ferry the miners the 140 miles from the Silverhill colliery... A helicopter ferried in more soldiers to help in the search.* N-COUNT: also *by* N; VERB = transport; V n prep/adv; V n amount; V n with adv; Also V n

**fer|ry|boat** /feriboʊt/ **(ferryboats)** A **ferryboat** is a boat used as a ferry. N-COUNT

**fer|tile** /fɜːʳtaɪl, AM -tᵊl/ 1 Land or soil that is **fertile** is able to support the growth of a large number of strong healthy plants. ❑ *...fertile soil. ...the rolling fertile countryside of East Cork.* ♦ **fer|til|ity** /fɜːʳtɪlɪti/ *He was able to bring large sterile acreages back to fertility.* 2 A **fertile** mind or imagination is able to produce a lot of good, original ideas. ❑ *...a product of Flynn's fertile imagination.* 3 A situation or environment that is **fertile** in relation to a particular activity or feeling encourages the activity or feeling. ❑ *...a fertile breeding ground for this kind of violent racism.* 4 A person or animal that is **fertile** is able to reproduce and have babies or young. ❑ *The operation cannot be reversed to make her fertile again.* ♦ **fer|til|ity** *Doctors will tell you that pregnancy is the only sure test for fertility.* ADJ = rich; N-UNCOUNT; ADJ: usu ADJ n; ADJ: ADJ n; ADJ ≠ infertile, sterile; N-UNCOUNT ≠ infertility, sterility

**fer|ti|lize** /fɜːʳtɪlaɪz/ **(fertilizes, fertilizing, fertilized)**

☑ in BRIT, also use **fertilise**

1 When an egg from the ovary of a woman or female animal **is fertilized**, a sperm from the male joins with the egg, causing a baby or young animal to begin forming. A female plant **is fertilized** when its reproductive parts come into contact with pollen from the male plant. ❑ *Certain varieties cannot be fertilised with their own pollen. ...the normal sperm levels needed to fertilise the female egg... Pregnancy begins when the fertilized egg is implanted in the wall of the uterus.* ♦ **fer|ti|li|za|tion** /fɜːʳtɪlaɪzeɪʃᵊn/ *The average length of time from fertilization until birth is about 266 days.* 2 To **fertilize** land means to improve its quality in order to make plants grow well on it, by spreading solid animal waste or a chemical mixture on it. ❑ *The faeces contain nitrogen and it is that which fertilises the desert soil. ...chemically fertilized fields.* VERB; *be* V-ed *with* n; V n; V-ed; N-UNCOUNT; VERB = enrich; V n; V-ed

**fer|ti|liz|er** /fɜːʳtɪlaɪzəʳ/ **(fertilizers)**

☑ in BRIT, also use **fertiliser**

**Fertilizer** is a substance such as solid animal waste or a chemical mixture that you spread on the ground in order to make plants grow more successfully. ❑ *...farming without any purchased chemical, fertilizer or pesticide.* N-MASS

**fer|vent** /fɜːʳvᵊnt/ A **fervent** person has or shows strong feelings about something, and is very sincere and enthusiastic about it. ❑ *...a fervent admirer of Morisot's work. ...the fervent hope that matters will be settled promptly.* ♦ **fer|vent|ly** *Their claims will be fervently denied.* ADJ: usu ADJ n = ardent; ADV: usu ADV with v, also ADV adj

**fer|vour** /fɜːʳvəʳ/

☑ in AM, use **fervor**

**Fervour** for something is a very strong feeling for or belief in it. [FORMAL] ❑ *They were concerned only with their own religious fervour.* N-UNCOUNT: usu with supp = enthusiasm

**fes|ter** /festəʳ/ **(festers, festering, festered)** 1 If you say that a situation, problem, or feeling **is festering**, you disapprove of the fact that it is being allowed to grow more unpleasant or full of anger, because it is not being properly recognized or dealt with. ❑ *Resentments are starting to fester. ...festering wounds of the legacy of British imperialism.* 2 If a wound **festers**, it becomes infected, making it worse. ❑ *The wound is festering, and gangrene has set in... Many of the children are afflicted by festering sores.* VERB [disapproval]; V; V-ing; VERB; V; V-ing

**fes|ti|val** /festɪvᵊl/ **(festivals)** 1 A **festival** is an organized series of events such as musical concerts or drama productions. ❑ *Numerous Umbrian towns hold their own summer festivals of music, theatre, and dance... There are over 350 films in the Edinburgh Film Festival this year.* 2 A **festival** is a day or time of the year when people have a holiday from work and celebrate some special event, often a religious event. ❑ *...the Hindu festival of Diwali.* ◆◆◇ N-COUNT; N-COUNT

**fes|tive** /festɪv/ 1 Something that is **festive** is special, colourful, or exciting, especially because of a holiday or celebration. ❑ *The town has a festive holiday atmosphere.* 2 **Festive** means relating to a holiday or celebration, especially Christmas. ❑ *The factory was due to shut for the festive period.* ADJ: usu ADJ n; ADJ: ADJ n

**fes|tive sea|son** People sometimes refer to the Christmas period as **the festive season**. N-SING: usu *the* N = Christmas

**fes|tiv|ity** /festɪvɪti/ **(festivities)** 1 **Festivity** is the celebration of something in a happy way. ❑ *There was a general air of festivity and abandon.* 2 **Festivities** are events that are organized in or- N-UNCOUNT; N-COUNT:

der to celebrate something. ❑ *The festivities included a huge display of fireworks.* usu pl

**fes|toon** /festuːn/ **(festoons, festooning, festooned)** If something **is festooned with**, for example, lights, balloons, or flowers, large numbers of these things are hung from it or wrapped around it, especially in order to decorate it. ❑ *The temples are festooned with lights.*
VERB: usu passive = bedeck; be V-ed with/in n

**feta** /fetə/ **Feta** is a type of salty white cheese made from goats' or sheep's milk. It is traditionally made in Greece.
N-UNCOUNT

**fe|tal** /fiːtᵊl/ → see **foetal**.

**fetch** /fetʃ/ **(fetches, fetching, fetched)** 1 If you **fetch** something or someone, you go and get them from the place where they are. ❑ *Sylvia fetched a towel from the bathroom... Fetch me a glass of water... The caddie ran over to fetch something for him.* 2 If something **fetches** a particular sum of money, it is sold for that amount. ❑ *The painting is expected to fetch between two and three million pounds.* 3 → See also **far-fetched, fetching**.
1 VERB = get; V n; V n n; V n for n. 2 VERB = go for; V n

**fetch|ing** /fetʃɪŋ/ If you describe someone or something as **fetching**, you think that they look very attractive. ❑ *Sue was sitting up in bed, looking very fetching in a flowered bedjacket.*
ADJ

**fete** /feɪt/ **(fetes, feting, feted)** also **fête.** 1 A **fete** is an event that is usually held outdoors and includes competitions, entertainments, and the selling of used and home-made goods. 2 If someone **is feted**, they are celebrated, welcomed, or admired by the public. ❑ *Anouska Hempel, the British dress designer, was feted in New York this week at a spectacular dinner.*
1 N-COUNT. 2 VERB: usu passive; be V-ed

**fet|id** /fetɪd, fiː-/

✔ in BRIT, also use **foetid**

**Fetid** water or air has a very strong unpleasant smell. [FORMAL] ❑ *...the fetid river of waste. ...the fetid stench of vomit.*
ADJ: usu ADJ n = stinking

**fet|ish** /fetɪʃ/ **(fetishes)** 1 If someone has a **fetish**, they have an unusually strong liking or need for a particular object or activity, as a way of getting sexual pleasure. ❑ *...rubber and leather fetishes. ...fetish wear for sexual arousal.* 2 If you say that someone has a **fetish** for doing something, you disapprove of the fact that they do it very often or enjoy it very much. ❑ *What began as a post-war fetish for sunbathing is rapidly developing into a world health crisis.* 3 In some cultures, a **fetish** is an object, especially a carved object, which is considered to have religious importance or magical powers.
1 N-COUNT: oft n N. 2 N-COUNT: usu with supp [disapproval]. 3 N-COUNT

**fet|ish|ism** /fetɪʃɪzəm/ **Fetishism** involves a person having a strong liking or need for a particular object or activity which gives them sexual pleasure and excitement.
N-UNCOUNT

**fet|ish|ist** /fetɪʃɪst/ **(fetishists)** A **fetishist** is a person who has a strong liking or need for a particular object or activity in order to experience sexual pleasure and excitement. ❑ *...a foot fetishist.*
N-COUNT: usu n N

**fet|lock** /fetlɒk/ **(fetlocks)** A horse's **fetlock** is the back part of its leg, just above the hoof.
N-COUNT

**fet|ter** /fetəʳ/ **(fetters, fettering, fettered)** 1 If you say that you **are fettered** by something, you dislike it because it prevents you from behaving or moving in a free and natural way. [LITERARY] ❑ *...a private trust which would not be fettered by bureaucracy... The black mud fettered her movements.* 2 You can use **fetters** to refer to things such as rules, traditions, or responsibilities that you dislike because they prevent you from behaving in the way you want. [LITERARY]
1 VERB [disapproval] = hamper; be V-ed; V n. 2 N-PLURAL: usu with supp, oft N of n [disapproval] = constraints

**fet|tle** /fetᵊl/ If you say that someone or something is **in fine fettle**, you mean that they are in very good health or condition. [INFORMAL] ❑ *You seem in fine fettle.*
PHRASE: v-link PHR, PHR after v

**fe|tus** /fiːtəs/ → see **foetus**.

**feud** /fjuːd/ **(feuds, feuding, feuded)** 1 A **feud** is a quarrel in which two people or groups remain angry with each other for a long time, although they are not always fighting or arguing. ❑ *...a long and bitter feud between the state government and the villagers.* 2 If one person or group **feuds with** another, they have a quarrel that lasts a long time. You can also say that two people or groups **feud**. ❑ *He feuded with his ex-wife... Their families had feuded since their teenage daughters quarrelled two years ago.*
1 N-COUNT = vendetta. 2 V-RECIP; V with n; pl-n V

**feu|dal** /fjuːdᵊl/ **Feudal** means relating to the system or the time of feudalism. ❑ *...the emperor and his feudal barons.*
ADJ: ADJ n

**feu|dal|ism** /fjuːdəlɪzəm/ **Feudalism** was a system in which people were given land and protection by people of higher rank, and worked and fought for them in return.
N-UNCOUNT

**fe|ver** /fiːvəʳ/ **(fevers)** 1 If you have a **fever** when you are ill, your body temperature is higher than usual and your heart beats faster. ❑ *My Uncle Jim had a high fever... Symptoms of the disease include fever and weight loss.* → See also **hay fever, rheumatic fever, scarlet fever**. 2 A **fever** is extreme excitement or nervousness about something. ❑ *Angie waited in a fever of excitement.*
1 N-VAR. 2 N-COUNT: usu with supp = frenzy

**fe|ver blis|ter** **(fever blisters)** **Fever blisters** are small sore spots that sometimes appear on or near someone's lips and nose when they have a cold. [AM]
N-COUNT

✔ in BRIT, usually use **cold sore**

**fe|vered** /fiːvəʳd/ 1 **Fevered** is used to describe feelings of great excitement, and the activities that result from them. [WRITTEN] ❑ *Meg was in a state of fevered anticipation. ...fevered speculation over the leadership.* 2 If a person is **fevered**, or they have a **fevered** brow, they are suffering from a fever. [LITERARY] ❑ *...her fevered brow.*
1 ADJ: usu ADJ n = feverish. 2 ADJ: usu ADJ n

**fe|ver|ish** /fiːvərɪʃ/ 1 **Feverish** activity is done extremely quickly, often in a state of nervousness or excitement because you want to finish it as soon as possible. ❑ *Hours of feverish activity lay ahead. The tents had to be erected, the stalls set up.* 2 **Feverish** emotion is characterized by extreme nervousness or excitement. ❑ *...a state of feverish excitement.* 3 If you are **feverish**, you are suffering from a fever. ❑ *A feverish child refuses to eat and asks only for cold drinks... She looked feverish, her eyes glistened.* ♦ **fe|ver|ish|ly** *He slept feverishly all afternoon and into the night.*
1 ADJ = frantic. 2 ADJ: ADJ n. 3 ADJ. ADV: ADV with v, ADV adj

**fe|ver pitch** If something is at **fever pitch**, it is in an extremely active or excited state. ❑ *Campaigning is reaching fever pitch for elections on November 6.*
N-UNCOUNT: oft at N

**few** /fjuː/ **(fewer, fewest)** 1 You use **a few** to indicate that you are talking about a small number of people or things. You can also say **a very few**. ❑ *I gave a dinner party for a few close friends... Here are a few more ideas to consider... She was silent for a few seconds.* ♦ **Few** is also a pronoun. ❑ *Doctors work an average of 90 hours a week, while a few are on call for up to 120 hours... A strict diet is appropriate for only a few.* ♦ **Few** is also a quantifier. ❑ *There are many ways eggs can be prepared; here are a few of them. ...a little tea-party I'm giving for a few of the teachers.* 2 You use **few** after adjectives and determiners to indicate that you are talking about a small number of things or people. ❑ *The past few weeks of her life had been the most pleasant she could remember. ...in the last few chapters... A train would pass through there every few minutes at that time of day.* 3 You use **few** to indicate that you are talking about a small number of people or things. You can use 'so', 'too' and 'very' in front of **few**. ❑ *She had few friends, and was generally not very happy... Few members planned to vote for him... Very few firms collect the tax, even when they're required to do so by law.* ♦ **Few** is also a pronoun. ❑ *The trouble is that few want to buy, despite the knockdown prices on offer. ...a true singing and songwriting talent that few suspected.* ♦ **Few** is also a quantifier. ❑ *Few of the volunteers had military experience.* ♦ **Few** is also an adjective. ❑ *...spending*
◆◆◆ 1 DET: DET pl-n; PRON; QUANT: QUANT of def-pl-n. 2 ADJ: adj/det ADJ n. 3 DET: DET pl-n ≠ many; PRON; QUANT: QUANT of def-pl-n; ADJ

*her few waking hours in front of the TV... His memories of his father are few.* [4] **The few** means a small set of people considered as separate from the majority, especially because they share a particular opportunity or quality that the others do not have. ❑ *This should not be an experience for the few. ...a system built on academic excellence for the few.* N-SING: *the* N

**PHRASES** [5] You use **as few as** before a number to suggest that it is surprisingly small. ❑ *One study showed that even as few as ten cigarettes a day can damage fertility.* PHRASE: PHR num [emphasis] [6] Things that are **few and far between** are very rare or do not happen very often. ❑ *In this economic climate new ideas were few and far between.* PHRASE: v-link PHR [emphasis] = rare [7] You use **no fewer than** to emphasize that a number is surprisingly large. ❑ *No fewer than thirteen foreign ministers attended the session.* PHRASE: PHR num [emphasis]

**fey** /feɪ/ If you describe someone as **fey**, you mean that they behave in a shy, childish, or unpredictable way, and you are often suggesting that this is unnatural or insincere. [LITERARY] ❑ *Her fey charm and eccentric ways were legendary.* ADJ = whimsical

**fez** /fez/ **(fezzes)** A **fez** is a round, red hat with no brim and a flat top. N-COUNT

**ff.** [1] In a book or magazine, when **ff.** is written it refers to the page or line mentioned and two or more pages or lines after it. ❑ *...p. 173 ff.* [2] In a piece of music, **ff** is a written abbreviation for **fortissimo**.

**fi|an|cé** /fiɒnseɪ, AM fiːɑːnseɪ/ **(fiancés)** A woman's **fiancé** is the man to whom she is engaged to be married. N-COUNT: usu poss N

**fi|an|cée** /fiɒnseɪ, AM fiːɑːnseɪ/ **(fiancées)** A man's **fiancée** is the woman to whom he is engaged to be married. N-COUNT: usu poss N

**fi|as|co** /fiæskoʊ/ **(fiascos)** If you describe an event or attempt to do something as a **fiasco**, you are emphasizing that it fails completely. ❑ *The blame for the Charleston fiasco did not lie with him... It was a bit of a fiasco.* N-COUNT: usu with supp [emphasis] = debacle

**fiat** /fiːæt, faɪ-/ **(fiats)** If something is done **by fiat**, it is done because of an official order given by someone in authority. [FORMAL] ❑ *He has tried to impose solutions to the country's problems by fiat.* N-COUNT: also *by* N

**fib** /fɪb/ **(fibs, fibbing, fibbed)** [1] A **fib** is a small, unimportant lie. [INFORMAL] ❑ *She told innocent fibs like anyone else.* N-COUNT [2] If someone **is fibbing**, they are telling lies. [INFORMAL] ❑ *He laughs loudly when I accuse him of fibbing.* VERB V

**fi|bre** /faɪbəʳ/ **(fibres)**

✔ in AM, use **fiber**

[1] A **fibre** is a thin thread of a natural or artificial substance, especially one that is used to make cloth or rope. ❑ *If you look at the paper under a microscope you will see the fibres. ...a variety of coloured fibres.* N-COUNT [2] A particular **fibre** is a type of cloth or other material that is made from or consists of threads. ❑ *The ball is made of rattan – a natural fibre.* N-VAR [3] **Fibre** consists of the parts of plants or seeds that your body cannot digest. Fibre is useful because it makes food pass quickly through your body. ❑ *Most vegetables contain fibre.* N-UNCOUNT [4] A **fibre** is a thin piece of flesh like a thread which connects nerve cells in your body or which muscles are made of. ❑ *...the nerve fibres.* N-COUNT

**fibre|glass** /faɪbəʳglɑːs, -glæs/

✔ in AM, use **fiberglass**

[1] **Fibreglass** is plastic strengthened with short, thin threads of glass. N-UNCOUNT [2] **Fibreglass** is a material made from short, thin threads of glass which can be used to stop heat escaping. N-UNCOUNT

**fi|bre op|tics**

✔ The spelling **fiber optics** is also used in American English. The form **fibre optic** is used as a modifier.

[1] **Fibre optics** is the use of long thin threads of glass to carry information in the form of light. N-UNCOUNT [2] **Fibre optic** means relating to or involved in fibre optics. ❑ *...fibre optic cables.* ADJ: ADJ n

**fi|broid** /faɪbrɔɪd/ **(fibroids)** **Fibroids** are lumps of fibrous tissue that form in a woman's womb, often causing pain. [MEDICAL] N-COUNT: usu pl

**fi|brous** /faɪbrəs/ A **fibrous** object or substance contains a lot of fibres or fibre, or looks as if it does. ❑ *...fibrous tissue.* ADJ: usu ADJ n

**fibu|la** /fɪbjʊlə/ **(fibulae)** Your **fibula** is the outer bone of the two bones in the lower part of your leg. [MEDICAL] N-COUNT

**fick|le** /fɪkᵊl/ [1] If you describe someone as **fickle**, you disapprove of them because they keep changing their mind about what they like or want. ❑ *The group has been notoriously fickle in the past.* ♦ **fick|le|ness** *...the fickleness of businessmen and politicians.* ADJ [disapproval] N-UNCOUNT: usu N *of* n [2] If you say that something is **fickle**, you mean that it often changes and is unreliable. ❑ *Orta's weather can be fickle.* ADJ

**fic|tion** /fɪkʃᵊn/ **(fictions)** [1] **Fiction** refers to books and stories about imaginary people and events, rather than books about real people or events. ❑ *Immigrant tales have always been popular themes in fiction... Diana is a writer of historical fiction.* → See also **science fiction**. N-UNCOUNT: also N in pl [2] A statement or account that is **fiction** is not true. ❑ *The truth or fiction of this story has never been truly determined.* N-UNCOUNT ≠ truth, fact [3] If something is a **fiction**, it is not true, although people sometimes pretend that it is true. ❑ *The idea that the United States could harmoniously accommodate all was a fiction.* N-COUNT ≠ fact

**fic|tion|al** /fɪkʃənᵊl/ **Fictional** characters or events occur only in stories, plays, or films and never actually existed or happened. ❑ *It is drama featuring fictional characters.* ADJ: usu ADJ n = fictitious, imaginary

**fic|tion|al|ize** /fɪkʃənəlaɪz/ **(fictionalizes, fictionalizing, fictionalized)**

✔ in BRIT, also use **fictionalise**

To **fictionalize** an account of something that really happened means to tell it as a story, with some details changed or added. ❑ *We had to fictionalize names. ...a fictionalised account of a true and horrific story.* VERB V n V-ed

**fic|ti|tious** /fɪktɪʃəs/ [1] **Fictitious** is used to describe something that is false or does not exist, although some people claim that it is true or exists. ❑ *We're interested in the source of these fictitious rumours.* ADJ: usu ADJ n [2] A **fictitious** character, thing, or event occurs in a story, play, or film but never really existed or happened. ❑ *The persons and events portrayed in this production are fictitious.* ADJ = fictional, imaginary

**fid|dle** /fɪdᵊl/ **(fiddles, fiddling, fiddled)** [1] If you **fiddle with** an object, you keep moving it or touching it with your fingers. ❑ *Harriet fiddled with a pen on the desk.* VERB V *with* n [2] If you **fiddle with** something, you change it in minor ways. ❑ *She told Whistler that his portrait of her was finished and to stop fiddling with it.* VERB V *with* n [3] If you **fiddle with** a machine, you adjust it. ❑ *He turned on the radio and fiddled with the knob until he got a talk show.* VERB V *with* n [4] If someone **fiddles** financial documents, they alter them dishonestly so that they get money for themselves. [BRIT, INFORMAL] ❑ *He's been fiddling the books.* VERB V n [5] Some people call violins **fiddles**, especially when they are used to play folk music. ❑ *Hardy as a young man played the fiddle at local dances.* N-VAR: oft *the* N = violin

**PHRASES** [6] Someone who is as **fit as a fiddle** is very healthy and full of energy. ❑ *I'm as fit as a fiddle – with energy to spare.* PHRASE: v-link PHR [7] If you **play second fiddle** to someone, your position is less important than theirs in something that you are doing together. ❑ *She hated the thought of playing second fiddle to Rose.* PHRASE: V inflects, oft PHR *to* n

♦ **fiddle around**

✔ in BRIT, also use **fiddle about**

[1] If you **fiddle around** or **fiddle about** with a machine, you do things to it to try and make it work. ❑ *Two of them got out to fiddle around with the* PHRASAL VERB = tinker V P *with* n

*engine.* [2] If you say that someone is **fiddling around with** or **fiddling about with** something, you mean that they are changing it in a way that you disapprove of. ❑ *Right now in Congress, they're fiddling around with the budget and so on.* *Also V P PHRASAL VERB disapproval; V P P n*

**fid|dler** /fɪdləʳ/ **(fiddlers)** A **fiddler** is someone who plays the violin, especially one who plays folk music. *N-COUNT = violinist*

**fid|dling** /fɪdəlɪŋ/ [1] **Fiddling** is the practice of getting money dishonestly by altering financial documents. [BRIT, INFORMAL] ❑ *Salomon's fiddling is likely to bring big trouble for the firm.* *N-UNCOUNT* [2] Violin playing, especially in folk music, is sometimes referred to as **fiddling**. *N-UNCOUNT* [3] You can describe something as **fiddling** if it is small, unimportant, or difficult to do. ❑ *...the daunting amount of fiddling technical detail.* *ADJ: usu ADJ n*

**fid|dly** /fɪdəli/ **(fiddlier, fiddliest)** Something that is **fiddly** is difficult to do or use because it involves small or complicated objects. [BRIT] ❑ *It was a time-consuming and fiddly job... Fish can be fiddly to cook.* *ADJ: oft ADJ to-inf*

**fi|del|ity** /fɪdelɪti/ [1] **Fidelity** is loyalty to a person, organization, or set of beliefs. [FORMAL] ❑ *I had to promise fidelity to the Queen.* *N-UNCOUNT: oft N to n = loyalty* [2] **Fidelity** is being loyal to your husband, wife, or partner by not having a sexual relationship with anyone else. ❑ *Wanting fidelity implies you're thinking about a major relationship.* *N-UNCOUNT ≠ infidelity* [3] The **fidelity** of something such as a report or translation is the degree to which it is accurate. [FORMAL] ❑ *...the fidelity of these early documents.* *N-UNCOUNT: with poss, oft N to n = accuracy*

**fidg|et** /fɪdʒɪt/ **(fidgets, fidgeting, fidgeted)** [1] If you **fidget**, you keep moving your hands or feet slightly or changing your position slightly, for example because you are nervous, bored, or excited. ❑ *Brenda fidgeted in her seat.* *VERB V* ♦ **Fidget around** and **fidget about** mean the same as **fidget**. ❑ *There were two new arrivals, fidgeting around, waiting to ask questions.* *PHRASAL VERB V P* [2] If you **fidget with** something, you keep moving it or touching it with your fingers with small movements, for example because you are nervous or bored. ❑ *He fidgeted with his tie.* *VERB = fiddle; V with n*

**fidg|ety** /fɪdʒɪti/ Someone who is **fidgety** keeps fidgeting, for example because they are nervous or bored. *ADJ*

**fi|du|ci|ary** /fɪduːʃiəri/ **Fiduciary** is used to talk about things which relate to a trust, or to the people who are in charge of a trust. [LEGAL] ❑ *They have a case against their directors for breach of fiduciary duty.* *ADJ: usu ADJ n*

**fief** /fiːf/ **(fiefs)** In former times, a **fief** was a piece of land given to someone by their lord, to whom they had a duty to provide particular services in return. *N-COUNT*

**field** /fiːld/ **(fields, fielding, fielded)** ◆◆◇ [1] A **field** is an area of grass, for example in a park or on a farm. A **field** is also an area of land on which a crop is grown. ❑ *...a field of wheat... They went for walks together in the fields.* *N-COUNT* [2] A sports **field** is an area of grass where sports are played. ❑ *...a football field... Gavin Hastings was helped from the field with ankle injuries.* *N-COUNT* [3] A **field** is an area of land or sea bed under which large amounts of a particular mineral have been found. ❑ *...an extensive natural gas field in Alaska.* *N-COUNT: usu supp N* [4] A magnetic, gravitational, or electric **field** is the area in which that particular force is strong enough to have an effect. ❑ *Some people are worried that electromagnetic fields from electric power lines could increase the risk of cancer.* *N-COUNT: usu supp N* [5] A particular **field** is a particular subject of study or type of activity. ❑ *Exciting artistic breakthroughs have recently occurred in the fields of painting, sculpture and architecture... Each of the authors of the tapes is an expert in his field.* *N-COUNT: usu with supp* [6] A **field** is an area of a computer's memory or a program where data can be entered, edited, or stored. [COMPUTING] ❑ *Go to a site like Yahoo! Finance and enter 'AOL' in the Get Quotes field.* *N-COUNT* [7] You can refer to the area where fighting or other military action in a war takes place as **the field** or **the field of battle**. ❑ *We never defeated them on the field of battle. ...the need for politicians to leave day-to-day decisions to commanders in the field.* *N-COUNT: usu the N, oft N of n* [8] Your **field** of vision or your visual **field** is the area that you can see without turning your head. ❑ *Our field of vision is surprisingly wide.* *N-COUNT: with supp* [9] **The field** is a way of referring to all the competitors taking part in a particular race or sports contest. ❑ *Going into the fourth lap, the two most broadly experienced riders led the field.* *N-COUNT-COLL: usu sing, the N* [10] You use **field** to describe work or study that is done in a real, natural environment rather than in a theoretical way or in controlled conditions. ❑ *I also conducted a field study among the boys about their attitude to relationships... Our teachers took us on field trips to observe plants and animals, firsthand.* *ADJ: ADJ n* [11] In a game of cricket, baseball, or rounders, the team that **is fielding** is trying to catch the ball, while the other team is trying to hit it. ❑ *When we are fielding, the umpires keep looking at the ball.* *VERB: usu cont V* [12] If you say that someone **fields** a question, you mean that they answer it or deal with it, usually successfully. [JOURNALISM] ❑ *He was later shown on television, fielding questions.* *VERB V n* [13] If a sports team **fields** a particular number or type of players, the players are chosen to play for the team on a particular occasion. ❑ *England intend fielding their strongest team in next month's World Youth Championship.* *VERB V n* [14] If a candidate in an election is representing a political party, you can say that the party **is fielding** that candidate. [JOURNALISM] ❑ *There are signs that the new party aims to field candidates in elections scheduled for February next year.* *VERB = put up; V n* [15] → See also **coalfield**, **minefield**, **playing field**, **snowfield**.

**PHRASES** [16] If someone **is having a field day**, they are very busy doing something that they enjoy, even though it may be hurtful for other people. ❑ *In our absence the office gossips are probably having a field day.* *PHRASE: V inflects* [17] Work or study that is done **in the field** is done in a real, natural environment rather than in a theoretical way or in controlled conditions. ❑ *The zoo is doing major conservation work, both in captivity and in the field.* *PHRASE: usu PHR after v* [18] If you say that someone **leads the field** in a particular activity, you mean that they are better, more active, or more successful than everyone else who is involved in it. ❑ *When it comes to picking up awards they lead the field by miles.* *PHRASE: V inflects* [19] If someone **plays the field**, they have a number of different romantic or sexual relationships. [INFORMAL] ❑ *He gave up playing the field and married a year ago.* *PHRASE: V inflects*

**field|er** /fiːldəʳ/ **(fielders)** A **fielder** is a player in cricket, baseball, or rounders who is fielding or one who has a particular skill at fielding. ❑ *The fielders crouch around the batsman's wicket.* *N-COUNT*

**field event (field events)** A **field event** is an athletics contest such as the high jump or throwing the discus or javelin, rather than a race. *N-COUNT*

**field-glasses** also **field glasses**. **Field-glasses** are the same as **binoculars**. [FORMAL] *N-PLURAL: also a pair of N*

**field hand (field hands)** A **field hand** is someone who is employed to work on a farm. [mainly AM] *N-COUNT*

**field hock|ey** **Field hockey** is an outdoor game played on a grass field between two teams of 11 players who use long curved sticks to hit a small ball and try to score goals. [AM] *N-UNCOUNT: oft N n*

✓ in BRIT, use **hockey**

**field mar|shal (field marshals)** also **field-marshal**. A **field marshal** is an officer in the army who has the highest rank. *N-COUNT; N-TITLE*

**field mouse (field mice)** also **fieldmouse**. A **field mouse** is a mouse with a long tail that lives in fields and woods. *N-COUNT*

**field sport (field sports)** Hunting, shooting birds, and fishing with a rod are referred to as *N-COUNT: usu pl*

**field sports** when they are done mainly for pleasure.

**field-test (field-tests, field-testing, field-tested)** also **field test.** If you **field-test** a new piece of equipment, you test it in a real, natural environment. ❑ *We've field-tested them ourselves and are happy that they work.* VERB V n

**field|work** /fiːldwɜːʳk/ also **field work.** **Fieldwork** is the gathering of information about something in a real, natural environment, rather than in a place of study such as a laboratory or classroom. ❑ *...anthropological fieldwork.* N-UNCOUNT

**fiend** /fiːnd/ **(fiends)** [1] If you describe someone as a **fiend**, you mean that they are extremely wicked or cruel. [WRITTEN] ❑ *A tearful husband repeated calls for help in catching the fiend who battered his wife.* N-COUNT = monster [2] **Fiend** can be used after a noun to refer to a person who is very interested in the thing mentioned, and enjoys having a lot of it or doing it often. ❑ *...if you're a heavy coffee drinker or strong-tea fiend.* N-COUNT: n N

**fiend|ish** /fiːndɪʃ/ [1] A **fiendish** plan, action, or device is very clever or imaginative. [INFORMAL] ❑ *...a fiendish plot.* ♦ **fiend|ish|ly** *This figure is reached by a fiendishly clever equation.* ADJ: usu ADJ n = devilish ADV: usu ADV adj [2] A **fiendish** problem or task is very difficult and challenging. [INFORMAL] ❑ *...the fiendish difficulty of the questions.* ♦ **fiend|ish|ly** *America's trade laws are fiendishly complex.* ADJ: ADJ n ADV: ADV adj [3] A **fiendish** person enjoys being cruel. ❑ *This was a fiendish act of wickedness.* ADJ: usu ADJ n

**fierce** /fɪəʳs/ **(fiercer, fiercest)** [1] A **fierce** animal or person is very aggressive or angry. ❑ *They look like the teeth of some fierce animal.* ♦ **fierce|ly** *'I don't know,' she said fiercely.* ◆◇◇ ADJ = ferocious ADV [2] **Fierce** feelings or actions are very intense or enthusiastic, or involve great activity. ❑ *Competition has been fierce to win a stake in Skoda... The town was captured after a fierce battle with rebels at the weekend... He inspires fierce loyalty in his friends.* ♦ **fierce|ly** *He has always been ambitious and fiercely competitive.* ADJ ADV: ADV adj, ADV with v [3] **Fierce** conditions are very intense, great, or strong. ❑ *The climbers were trapped by a fierce storm which went on for days.* ADJ

**fiery** /faɪəri/ **(fieriest)** [1] If you describe something as **fiery**, you mean that it is burning strongly or contains fire. [LITERARY] ❑ *A helicopter crashed in a fiery explosion in Vallejo.* ADJ: usu ADJ n [2] You can use **fiery** for emphasis when you are referring to bright colours such as red or orange. [LITERARY] ❑ *A large terracotta pot planted with Busy Lizzie provides a fiery bright red display.* ADJ: usu ADJ n [emphasis] [3] If you describe food or drink as **fiery**, you mean that it has a very strong hot or spicy taste. [WRITTEN] ❑ *A fiery combination of chicken, chillies and rice.* ADJ: usu ADJ n [4] If you describe someone as **fiery**, you mean that they express very strong emotions, especially anger, in their behaviour or speech. [WRITTEN] ADJ: usu ADJ n

**fi|es|ta** /fiestə/ **(fiestas)** A **fiesta** is a time of public entertainment and parties, usually on a special religious holiday, especially in Spain or Latin America. N-COUNT

**fife** /faɪf/ **(fifes)** A **fife** is a musical instrument like a small flute. N-COUNT

**fif|teen** /fɪftiːn/ **(fifteens)** **Fifteen** is the number 15. ❑ *In India, there are fifteen official languages.* ◆◆◆ NUM

**fif|teenth** /fɪftiːnθ/ The **fifteenth** item in a series is the one that you count as number fifteen. ❑ *...the invention of the printing press in the fifteenth century.* ◆◆◇ ORD

**fifth** /fɪfθ/ **(fifths)** [1] The **fifth** item in a series is the one that you count as number five. ❑ *Joe has recently returned from his fifth trip to Australia.* ◆◆◇ ORD [2] A **fifth** is one of five equal parts of something. ❑ *India spends over a fifth of its budget on defence.* FRACTION

**fifth col|umn|ist** **(fifth columnists)** A **fifth columnist** is someone who secretly supports and helps the enemies of the country or organization they are in. N-COUNT = traitor

**fif|ti|eth** /fɪftiəθ/ The **fiftieth** item in a series is the one that you count as number fifty. ❑ *He retired in 1970, on his fiftieth birthday.* ◆◆◇ ORD

**fif|ty** /fɪfti/ **(fifties)** [1] **Fifty** is the number 50. ◆◆◆ NUM [2] When you talk about the **fifties**, you are referring to numbers between 50 and 59. For example, if you are **in** your **fifties**, you are aged between 50 and 59. If the temperature is **in the fifties**, the temperature is between 50 and 59 degrees. ❑ *I probably look as if I'm in my fifties rather than my seventies.* N-PLURAL [3] **The fifties** is the decade between 1950 and 1959. ❑ *He began performing in the early fifties.* N-PLURAL: the N

**fifty-fifty** [1] If something such money or property is divided or shared **fifty-fifty** between two people, each person gets half of it. [INFORMAL] ❑ *The proceeds of the sale are split fifty-fifty.* ♦ **Fifty-fifty** is also an adjective. ❑ *The new firm was owned on a fifty-fifty basis by the two parent companies.* ADV: ADV after v ADJ [2] If there is a **fifty-fifty** chance of something happening, it is equally likely to happen as it is not to happen. [INFORMAL] ❑ *You've got a fifty-fifty chance of being right.* ADJ: usu ADJ n

**fig** /fɪg/ **(figs)** [1] A **fig** is a soft sweet fruit that grows in hot countries. It is full of tiny seeds and is often eaten dried. N-COUNT [2] A **fig** or a **fig tree** is a tree on which figs grow. N-COUNT

**fig.** [1] In books and magazines, **fig.** is used as an abbreviation for **figure** in order to tell the reader which picture or diagram is being referred to. ❑ *Draw the basic outlines in black felt-tip pen (see fig. 4).* [2] In some dictionaries and language books, **fig.** is used as an abbreviation for **figurative**.

**fight** /faɪt/ **(fights, fighting, fought)** [1] If you **fight** something unpleasant, you try in a determined way to prevent it or stop it happening. ❑ *More units to fight forest fires are planned... I've spent a lifetime fighting against racism and prejudice.* ◆◆◆ VERB V n V against n ♦ **Fight** is also a noun. ❑ *...the fight against drug addiction.* N-COUNT: oft N against n [2] If you **fight** for something, you try in a determined way to get it or achieve it. ❑ *Our Government should be fighting for an end to food subsidies... I told him how we had fought to hold on to the company... The team has fought its way to the cup final.* VERB V for n V to-inf V way prep/adv ♦ **Fight** is also a noun. ❑ *I too am committing myself to continue the fight for justice.* N-COUNT: usu N for n = battle [3] If an army or group **fights** a battle with another army or group, they oppose each other with weapons. You can also say that two armies or groups **fight** a battle. ❑ *The two men fought a battle over land and water rights... In the latest incident at the weekend police fought a gun battle with a gang which used hand grenades against them... The Sioux had always fought other tribes for territorial rights.* V-RECIP pl-n V n over/for n V n with n V n for/over n Also pl-n V, V n [4] If a person or army **fights** in a battle or a war, they take part in it. ❑ *He fought in the war and was taken prisoner by the Americans... If I were a young man I would sooner go to prison than fight for this country... My father did leave his university to fight the Germans... Last month rebels fought their way into the capital.* ➔ See also **dogfight**. ♦ **fight|ing** *More than nine hundred people have died in the fighting.* VERB V V for n V n V way prep/adv N-UNCOUNT [5] If one person **fights** with another, or **fights** them, the two people hit or kick each other because they want to hurt each other. You can also say that two people **fight**. ❑ *As a child she fought with her younger sister... I did fight him, I punched him but it was like hitting a wall... He wrenched the crutch from Jacob, who didn't fight him for it... I refuse to act that way when my kids fight... You get a lot of unruly drunks fighting each other.* ♦ **Fight** is also a noun. ❑ *He had had a fight with Smith and bloodied his nose.* V-RECIP V with n V n V n for n pl-n V pl-n V pron-recip N-COUNT: oft N with n [6] If one person **fights** with another, or **fights** them, they have an angry disagreement or quarrel. You can also say that two people **fight**. [INFORMAL] ❑ *She was always fighting with him... Gwendolen started fighting her teachers... Mostly, they fight about paying bills.* ♦ **Fight** is also a noun. ❑ *We think maybe he took off because he had a big fight with his dad the night before.* V-RECIP = quarrel, argue V with n V n, pl-n V about/over n N-COUNT [7] If you **fight** your way to a place, you move towards it with VERB = battle great difficulty, for example because there are a lot of people or obstacles in your way. ❑ *I fought my way into a carriage just before the doors closed.* [8] A **fight** is a boxing match. ❑ *The referee stopped the fight.* [9] To **fight** means to take part in a boxing match. ❑ *In a few hours' time one of the world's most famous boxers will be fighting in Britain for the first time... I'd like to fight him because he's undefeated and I want to be the first man to beat him... I'd like to fight him for the title.* [10] If you **fight** an election, you are a candidate in the election and try to win it. ❑ *The former party treasurer helped raise almost £40 million to fight the election campaign.* [11] You can use **fight** to refer to a contest such as an election or a sports match. [JOURNALISM] ❑ *...the fight for power between the two parties.* [12] If you **fight** a case or a court action, you make a legal case against someone in a very determined way, or you put forward a defence when a legal case is made against you. ❑ *Watkins sued the Army and fought his case in various courts for 10 years... The newspaper is fighting a damages action brought by the actress.* [13] **Fight** is the desire or ability to keep fighting. ❑ *I thought that we had a lot of fight in us.* [14] If you **fight** an emotion or desire, you try very hard not to feel it, show it, or act on it, but do not always succeed. ❑ *I desperately fought the urge to giggle... He fought with the urge to smoke one of the cigars he'd given up awhile ago... He fought to be patient with her.*

V way prep/adv; N-COUNT = bout; VERB; V; V n; V n for n; VERB; V n; N-COUNT: usu sing = contest; VERB; V n; V n; N-UNCOUNT; VERB; V n; V with n; V to-inf

PHRASES [15] If you describe someone as **fighting fit**, you are emphasizing that they are very fit or healthy. [BRIT] ❑ *After a good night's sleep I feel fighting fit again.* [16] Someone who **is fighting for** their **life** is making a great effort to stay alive, either when they are being physically attacked or when they are very ill. ❑ *He is still fighting for his life in hospital.* [17] to **fight a losing battle** → see **battle**.

PHRASE: v-link PHR [emphasis]; PHRASE: V inflects

♦ **fight back** [1] If you **fight back** against someone or something that is attacking or harming you, you resist them actively or attack them. ❑ *The teenage attackers fled when the two men fought back... We should take some comfort from the ability of the judicial system to fight back against corruption.* [2] If you **fight back** an emotion or a desire, you try very hard not to feel it, show it, or act on it. ❑ *She fought back the tears.*

PHRASAL VERB; V P; V P against n; PHRASAL VERB; V P n, Also V n P

♦ **fight off** [1] If you **fight off** something, for example an illness or an unpleasant feeling, you succeed in getting rid of it and in not letting it overcome you. ❑ *Unfortunately these drugs are quite toxic and hinder the body's ability to fight off infection... All day she had fought off the impulse to telephone Harry.* [2] If you **fight off** someone who has attacked you, you fight with them, and succeed in making them go away or stop attacking you. ❑ *The woman fought off the attacker.*

PHRASAL VERB = resist; V P n (not pron); V P n Also V n P; PHRASAL VERB; V P n, Also V n P

♦ **fight out** If two people or groups **fight** something **out**, they fight or argue until one of them wins. ❑ *Instead of retaliating, he walks away leaving his team-mates to fight it out... Malcolm continued to fight it out with Julien from his self-imposed exile in Paris.*

PHRASAL VERB; pl-n V it P; V it P with n Also pl-n V P n (not pron), V P n with n

**fight|back** /faɪtbæk/ A **fightback** is an effort made by a person or group of people to get back into a strong position when they seem likely to lose something such as an election or an important sports match. [BRIT, JOURNALISM] ❑ *The West Indies have staged a dramatic fightback on the first day of the fifth test.* N-SING

✔ in AM, use **comeback**

**fight|er** /faɪtəʳ/ **(fighters)** [1] A **fighter** or a **fighter plane** is a fast military aircraft that is used for destroying other aircraft. [2] If you describe someone as a **fighter**, you approve of them because they continue trying to achieve things in spite of great difficulties or opposition. ❑ *From the start it was clear this tiny girl was a real fighter.* [3] A **fighter** is a person who physically fights another person, especially a professional boxer. ❑ *...a tough little street fighter.* [4] → See also **fire fighter**, **freedom fighter**, **prize fighter**.

◆◇◇ N-COUNT; N-COUNT [approval]; N-COUNT

**fig leaf** **(fig leaves)** [1] A **fig leaf** is a large leaf which comes from the fig tree. A fig leaf is sometimes used in painting and sculpture to cover the genitals of a naked body. [2] People sometimes refer disapprovingly to something which is intended to hide or prevent an embarrassing situation as a **fig leaf**. [JOURNALISM] ❑ *This deal is little more than a fig leaf for the continued destruction of the landscape.*

N-COUNT; N-COUNT: usu with supp [disapproval]

**fig|ment** /fɪgmənt/ **(figments)** If you say that something is a **figment of** someone's **imagination**, you mean that it does not really exist and that they are just imagining it. ❑ *The attack wasn't just a figment of my imagination.* PHRASE: Ns inflect, usu v-link PHR

**fig|ura|tive** /fɪgərətɪv, AM -gjər-/ [1] If you use a word or expression in a **figurative** sense, you use it with a more abstract or imaginative meaning than its ordinary literal one. ❑ *...an event that will change your route – in both the literal and figurative sense.* ♦ **fig|ura|tive|ly** *Europe, with Germany literally and figuratively at its centre, is still at the start of a remarkable transformation.* [2] **Figurative** art is a style of art in which people and things are shown in a realistic way. ❑ *His career spanned some 50 years and encompassed both abstract and figurative painting.*

ADJ: usu ADJ n ≠ literal; ADV: ADV with cl/group, ADV with v; ADJ: usu ADJ n ≠ abstract

**fig|ure** /fɪgəʳ, AM -gjər/ **(figures, figuring, figured)** [1] A **figure** is a particular amount expressed as a number, especially a statistic. ❑ *It would be very nice if we had a true figure of how many people in this country haven't got a job... It will not be long before the inflation figure starts to fall... New Government figures predict that one in two marriages will end in divorce.* [2] A **figure** is any of the ten written symbols from 0 to 9 that are used to represent a number. [3] An amount or number that is in single **figures** is between zero and nine. An amount or number that is in double **figures** is between ten and ninety-nine. You can also say, for example, that an amount or number is in three **figures** when it is between one hundred and nine hundred and ninety-nine. ❑ *Inflation, which has usually been in single figures, is running at more than 12%... Crawley, with 14, was the only other player to reach double figures.* [4] You refer to someone that you can see as a **figure** when you cannot see them clearly or when you are describing them. ❑ *She waited, standing on the bridge, until his figure vanished against the grey backdrop of the Palace.* [5] In art, a **figure** is a person in a drawing or a painting, or a statue of a person. ❑ *...a life-size bronze figure of a brooding, hooded woman.* [6] Your **figure** is the shape of your body. ❑ *Take pride in your health and your figure... Janet was a natural blonde with a good figure.* [7] Someone who is referred to as a **figure** of a particular kind is a person who is well-known and important in some way. ❑ *The movement is supported by key figures in the three main political parties.* [8] If you say that someone is, for example, a mother **figure** or a hero **figure**, you mean that other people regard them as the type of person stated or suggested. ❑ *Sometimes young lads just need to turn to a mother figure for a bit of a chat and reassurance.* [9] In books and magazines, the diagrams which help to show or explain information are referred to as **figures**. ❑ *If you look at a world map (see Figure 1) you can identify the major wine-producing regions.* [10] In geometry, a **figure** is a shape, especially a regular shape. [TECHNICAL] ❑ *Draw a pentagon, a regular five-sided figure.* [11] If you **figure** that something is the case, you think or guess that it is the case. [INFORMAL] ❑ *She figured that both she and Ned had learned a lot from the experience.* [12] If you say **'That figures'** or **'It figures'**, you mean that the fact referred to is not surprising. [INFORMAL] ❑ *When I finished, he said, 'Yeah. That figures'.* [13] If a person or thing **figures in** something,

◆◆◆ N-COUNT; N-COUNT = digit; N-PLURAL: adj/num N; N-COUNT: usu with supp, oft N of n; N-COUNT; N-COUNT: with supp, oft poss/adj N; N-COUNT: with supp; N-COUNT: with supp, usu n N, N of n; N-COUNT: also N num; N-COUNT: usu supp N; VERB; V that; VERB; that/it V Also it V that; VERB:

they appear in or are included in it. ❑ *Human rights violations figured prominently in the report.* no passive V *in* n Also V *as* n

♦ **figure on** If you **figure on** something, you plan that it will happen or assume that it will happen when making your plans. [INFORMAL] ❑ *Jack worked as hard as he could to build his business, but he hadn't figured on a few obstacles.* PHRASAL VERB = *reckon on* V P n/-ing

♦ **figure out** If you **figure out** a solution to a problem or the reason for something, you succeed in solving it or understanding it. [INFORMAL] ❑ *It took them about one month to figure out how to start the equipment... They're trying to figure out the politics of this whole situation... I don't have to be a detective to figure that out.* PHRASAL VERB = *work out* V P wh/that V P n (not pron) V n P

**-figure** **-figure** combines with a number, usually 'five', 'six', or 'seven', to form adjectives which say how many figures are in a number. These adjectives usually describe a large amount of money. For example, a six-figure sum is between 100,000 and 999,999. ❑ *Columbia Pictures paid him a six-figure sum for the film rights.* COMB in ADJ: ADJ n

**fig|ure eight** **(figure eights)** A **figure eight** is the same as a **figure of eight**. [AM] N-COUNT

**figure|head** /fɪɡəʳhed, AM -ɡjəʳ-/ **(figureheads)** [1] If someone is the **figurehead** of an organization or movement, they are recognized as being its leader, although they have little real power. ❑ *The President will be little more than a figurehead.* N-COUNT [2] A **figurehead** is a large wooden model of a person that was put just under the pointed front of a sailing ship in former times. N-COUNT

**figure-hugging** **Figure-hugging** clothes fit very close to the body of the person who is wearing them. **Figure-hugging** is usually used to describe clothes worn by women. ADJ

**fig|ure of eight** **(figures of eight)** A **figure of eight** is something that has the shape of the number 8, for example a knot or a movement done by a skater. [BRIT] N-COUNT

☑ in AM, usually use **figure eight**

**fig|ure of speech** **(figures of speech)** A **figure of speech** is an expression or word that is used with a metaphorical rather than a literal meaning. ❑ *Of course I'm not. It was just a figure of speech.* N-COUNT

**fig|ure skat|ing** **Figure skating** is skating in an attractive pattern, usually with spins and jumps included. N-UNCOUNT

**figu|rine** /fɪɡəriːn, AM -ɡjər-/ **(figurines)** A **figurine** is a small ornamental model of a person. N-COUNT

**fila|ment** /fɪləmənt/ **(filaments)** A **filament** is a very thin piece or thread of something, for example the piece of wire inside a light bulb. N-COUNT

**filch** /fɪltʃ/ **(filches, filching, filched)** If you say that someone **filches** something, you mean they steal it, especially when you do not consider this to be a very serious crime. [INFORMAL] ❑ *I filched some notes from his wallet.* VERB = *swipe* V n

**file** /faɪl/ **(files, filing, filed)** [1] A **file** is a box or a folded piece of heavy paper or plastic in which letters or documents are kept. ❑ *He sat behind a table on which were half a dozen files. ...a file of insurance papers.* ◆◆◇ N-COUNT [2] A **file** is a collection of information about a particular person or thing. ❑ *We already have files on people's tax details, mortgages and poll tax... You must record and keep a file of all expenses.* N-COUNT: oft N *of/on* n [3] If you **file** a document, you put it in the correct file. ❑ *They are all filed alphabetically under author.* VERB V n [4] In computing, a **file** is a set of related data that has its own name. N-COUNT [5] If you **file** a formal or legal accusation, complaint, or request, you make it officially. ❑ *A number of them have filed formal complaints against the police... I filed for divorce on the grounds of adultery a few months later.* VERB V n V *for* n [6] When someone **files** a report or a news story, they send or give it to their employer. ❑ *Catherine Bond filed that report for the BBC from Nairobi.* VERB V n [7] When a group of people **files** somewhere, they walk one behind the other in a line. ❑ *Slowly, people filed into the room and sat down.* VERB V prep/adv [8] A **file** is a hand tool which is used for rubbing hard objects to make them smooth, shape them, or cut through them. N-COUNT [9] If you **file** an object, you smooth it, shape it, or cut it with a file. ❑ *Manicurists are skilled at shaping and filing nails.* VERB V n [10] → See also **nail file**, **rank and file**.

PHRASES [11] Something that is **on file** or **on** someone's **files** is recorded or kept in a file or in a collection of information. ❑ *His fingerprints were on file in Washington... We'll keep your details on file... It is one of the most desperate cases on her files.* PHRASE: v-link PHR, PHR after v [12] A group of people who are walking or standing **in single file** are in a line, one behind the other. ❑ *We were walking in single file to the lake.* PHRASE: PHR after v

**fil|ial** /fɪliəl/ You can use **filial** to describe the duties, feelings, or relationships which exist between a son or daughter and his or her parents. [FORMAL] ❑ *His father would accuse him of neglecting his filial duties.* ADJ: ADJ n

**fili|bus|ter** /fɪlɪbʌstəʳ/ **(filibusters, filibustering, filibustered)** [1] A **filibuster** is a long slow speech made to use up time so that a vote cannot be taken and a law cannot be passed. [mainly AM] ❑ *Senator Seymour has threatened a filibuster to block the bill.* N-COUNT [2] If a politician **filibusters**, he or she makes a long slow speech in order to use up time so that a vote cannot be taken and a law cannot be passed. [mainly AM] ❑ *They simply threatened to filibuster until the Senate adjourns... A group of senators plans to filibuster a measure that would permit drilling in Alaska.* VERB V V n

**fili|gree** /fɪlɪɡriː/ The word **filigree** is used to refer to delicate ornamental designs made with gold or silver wire. N-UNCOUNT: oft N n

**fil|ing cabi|net** **(filing cabinets)** A **filing cabinet** is a piece of office furniture, usually made of metal, which has drawers in which files are kept. N-COUNT

**fil|ings** /faɪlɪŋz/ [1] **Filings** are very small pieces of a substance, especially a metal, that are produced when it is filed or cut. ❑ *...iron filings. ...metal filings.* N-PLURAL: usu n N [2] Court **filings** are cases filed in a court of law. [AM, AUSTRALIAN] ❑ *In court filings, they argued that the settlement was inadequate.* N-COUNT: usu plural

**Fili|pi|no** /fɪlɪpiːnoʊ/ **(Filipinos)** [1] **Filipino** means belonging or relating to the Philippines, or to its people or culture. ADJ [2] A **Filipino** is a person who comes from the Philippines. N-COUNT

**fill** /fɪl/ **(fills, filling, filled)** [1] If you **fill** a container or area, or if it **fills**, an amount of something enters it that is enough to make it full. ❑ *Fill a saucepan with water and bring to a slow boil... She made sandwiches, filled a flask and put sugar in... The boy's eyes filled with tears... While the bath was filling, he padded about in his underpants.* ◆◆◇ VERB ≠ *empty* V n *with* n V n V *with* n V ♦ **Fill up** means the same as **fill**. ❑ *Pass me your cup, Amy, and I'll fill it up for you... Warehouses at the frontier between the two countries fill up with sacks of rice and flour.* PHRASAL VERB V n P V P *with* n Also V P, V P n (not pron) [2] If something **fills** a space, it is so big, or there are such large quantities of it, that there is very little room left. ❑ *He cast his eyes at the rows of cabinets that filled the enormous work area... The text fills 231 pages.* VERB V n V n ♦ **Fill up** means the same as **fill**. ❑ *...the complicated machines that fill up today's laboratories.* PHRASAL VERB V P n Also V n P ♦ **filled** *...four museum buildings filled with historical objects.* ADJ: v-link ADJ *with* n ♦ **-filled** *...the flower-filled courtyard of an old Spanish colonial house.* COMB in ADJ [3] If you **fill** a crack or hole, you put a substance into it in order to make the surface smooth again. ❑ *Fill small holes with wood filler in a matching colour... The gravedigger filled the grave.* VERB V n *with* n V n ♦ **Fill in** means the same as **fill**. ❑ *If any cracks have appeared in the tart case, fill these in with raw pastry.* PHRASAL VERB V n P Also V P n [4] If a sound, smell, or light **fills** a space, or the air, it is very strong or noticeable. ❑ *In the parking lot of the school, the siren filled the air... All the light bars were turned on which filled the room with these rotating beams of light.* VERB V n V n *with* n ♦ **-filled** *...those whose work forces them to be in dusty or smoke-filled environments.* COMB in ADJ [5] If something **fills** you **with** an emotion, or if an emotion **fills** you, you experience this emotion VERB strongly. ❑ *I admired my father, and his work filled me with awe and curiosity... He looked at me without speaking, and for the first time I could see the pride that filled him.* [6] If you **fill** a period of time with a particular activity, you spend the time in this way. ❑ *If she wants a routine to fill her day, let her do community work.* ♦ **Fill up** means the same as **fill**. ❑ *On Thursday night she went to her yoga class, glad to have something to fill up the evening.* [7] If something **fills** a need or a gap, it puts an end to this need or gap by existing or being active. ❑ *She brought him a sense of fun, of gaiety that filled a gap in his life.* [8] If something **fills** a role, position, or function, they have that role or position, or perform that function, often successfully. ❑ *Dena was filling the role of diplomat's wife with the skill she had learned over the years.* [9] If a company or organization **fills** a job vacancy, they choose someone to do the job. If someone **fills** a job vacancy, they accept a job that they have been offered. ❑ *One problem not mentioned is the unemployed may not have the skills to fill the vacancies on offer... A vacancy has arisen which I intend to fill.* [10] When a dentist **fills** someone's tooth, he or she puts a filling in it. ❑ *It is almost impossible to find a dentist who will fill a tooth on the National Health.* [11] If you **fill** an order or a prescription, you provide the things that are asked for. [mainly AM] ❑ *A pharmacist can fill any prescription if, in his or her judgment, the prescription is valid.* [12] to **fill the bill** → see **bill**.

V n *with* n / V n / VERB / V n, Also V n *with* n / PHRASAL VERB / V P n, Also V n P / VERB / V n / VERB = *perform* / V n / VERB / V n / V n / VERB / V n / VERB / V n

♦ **fill in** [1] If you **fill in** a form or other document requesting information, you write information in the spaces on it. [mainly BRIT] ❑ *If you want your free copy of the Patients' Charter fill this form in... Fill in the coupon and send it first class to the address shown.*

PHRASAL VERB = *fill out* / V n P / V P n (not pron)

☑ in AM, usually use **fill out**

[2] If you **fill in** a shape, you cover the area inside the lines with colour or shapes so that none of the background is showing. ❑ *When you have both filled in your patterns, you may want to share these with each other... With a lip pencil, outline lips and fill them in.* [3] If you **fill** someone **in**, you give them more details about something that you know about. [INFORMAL] ❑ *I didn't give Reid all the details yet – I'll fill him in... He filled her in on Wilbur Kantor's visit.* [4] If you **fill in** for someone, you do the work or task that they normally do because they are unable to do it. ❑ *Vice-presidents' wives would fill in for first ladies.* [5] If you **are filling in** time, you are using time that is available by doing something that is not very important. ❑ *That's not a career. She's just filling in time until she gets married.* [6] → See also **fill 3**.

PHRASAL VERB / V P n (not pron) / V n P / PHRASAL VERB / V n P / V n P *on* n / PHRASAL VERB = *stand in* / V P *for* n / PHRASAL VERB: usu passive / V P n (not pron)

♦ **fill out** [1] If you **fill out** a form or other document requesting information, you write information in the spaces on it. [mainly AM] ❑ *Fill out the application carefully, and keep copies of it.*

PHRASAL VERB = *fill in* / V P n (not pron) Also V n P

☑ in BRIT, usually use **fill in**

[2] If a fairly thin person **fills out**, they become fatter. ❑ *A girl may fill out before she reaches her full height.*

PHRASAL VERB / V P

♦ **fill up** [1] If you **fill up** or **fill** yourself **up** with food, you eat so much that you do not feel hungry. ❑ *Fill up on potatoes, bread and pasta, which are high in carbohydrate and low in fat... When you are happy about yourself you won't need to fill yourself up with food.* [2] A type of food that **fills** you **up** makes you feel that you have eaten a lot, even though you have only eaten a small amount. ❑ *Potatoes fill us up without overloading us with calories.* [3] → See also **fill 1, 2, 6**.

PHRASAL VERB / V P *on/with* n / V pron-refl P *with* n / PHRASAL VERB / V n P

**fill|er** /fɪləʳ/ **(fillers)** [1] **Filler** is a substance used for filling cracks or holes, especially in walls, car bodies, or wood. [2] You can describe something as a **filler** when it is being used or done because there is a need for something and nothing better is available. [INFORMAL] [3] → See also **stocking filler**.

N-MASS / N-COUNT = *stopgap*

**fil|let** /fɪlɪt, AM fɪleɪ/ **(fillets, filleting, filleted)** [1] **Fillet** is a strip of meat, especially beef, that has no bones in it. ❑ *...fillet of beef with shallots. ...chicken breast fillets. ...fillet steak.* [2] A **fillet** of fish is the side of a fish with the bones removed. ❑ *...anchovy fillets... I ordered a fine fillet of salmon.* [3] When you **fillet** fish or meat, you prepare it by taking the bones out. ❑ *Don't be afraid to ask your fishmonger to fillet flat fish.*

N-VAR: usu with supp, also N n / N-COUNT: usu with supp / VERB / V n

**fill|ing** /fɪlɪŋ/ **(fillings)** [1] A **filling** is a small amount of metal or plastic that a dentist puts in a hole in a tooth to prevent further decay. ❑ *The longer your child can go without needing a filling, the better.* [2] The **filling** in something such as a cake, pie, or sandwich is a substance or mixture that is put inside it. ❑ *Spread some of the filling over each pancake.* [3] The **filling** in a piece of soft furniture or in a cushion is the soft substance inside it. ❑ *...second-hand sofas with old-style foam fillings.* [4] Food that is **filling** makes you feel full when you have eaten it. ❑ *Although it is tasty, crab is very filling.*

N-COUNT / N-MASS / N-MASS / ADJ

**fill|ing sta|tion** **(filling stations)** A **filling station** is a place where you can buy petrol and oil for your car. [mainly BRIT]

N-COUNT

☑ in AM, usually use **gas station**

**fil|lip** /fɪlɪp/ **(fillips)** If someone or something gives a **fillip** to an activity or person, they suddenly encourage or improve them. [WRITTEN] ❑ *The news gave a fillip to the troubled telecommunications sector.*

N-COUNT: usu sing, oft N *to/for* n = *boost*

**fil|ly** /fɪli/ **(fillies)** A **filly** is a young female horse.

N-COUNT

**film** /fɪlm/ **(films, filming, filmed)** [1] A **film** consists of moving pictures that have been recorded so that they can be shown at the cinema or on television. A film tells a story, or shows a real situation. [mainly BRIT] ❑ *Everything about the film was good. Good acting, good story, good fun.*

◆◆◆ N-COUNT = *movie*

☑ in AM, use **movie**

[2] If you **film** something, you use a camera to take moving pictures which can be shown on a screen or on television. ❑ *He had filmed her life story... Considering the restrictions under which she filmed, I think she did a commendable job.* [3] **Film** of something is moving pictures of a real event that are shown on television or on a screen. ❑ *They have seen news film of families queueing in Russia to buy a loaf of bread.* [4] A **film** is the narrow roll of plastic that is used in a camera to take photographs. ❑ *The photographers had already shot a dozen rolls of film.* [5] The making of cinema films, considered as a form of art or a business, can be referred to as **film** or **films**. [mainly BRIT] ❑ *Film is a business with limited opportunities for actresses... She wanted to set up her own company to invest in films.* [6] A **film of** powder, liquid, or oil is a very thin layer of it. ❑ *The sea is coated with a film of raw sewage.* [7] Plastic **film** is a very thin sheet of plastic used to wrap and cover things. [BRIT] ❑ *Cover with plastic film and refrigerate for 24 hours.*

VERB / V n / V / N-UNCOUNT = *footage* / N-VAR / N-UNCOUNT: also N in pl / N-COUNT: usu sing, usu with supp / N-UNCOUNT: usu adj N

☑ in AM, use **plastic wrap, Saran wrap**

→ See also **clingfilm**.

**film|ic** /fɪlmɪk/ **Filmic** means related to films. [FORMAL] ❑ *...a new filmic style.*

ADJ: ADJ n

**film|ing** /fɪlmɪŋ/ **Filming** is the activity of making a film including the acting, directing, and camera shots. ❑ *Filming was due to start next month.*

N-UNCOUNT

**film-maker** **(film-makers)** also **filmmaker.** A **film-maker** is someone involved in making films, in particular a director or producer. [mainly BRIT]

N-COUNT

**film noir** /fɪlm nwɑːʳ/ **(films noir) Film noir** refers to a type of film or a style of film-making which shows the world as a dangerous or depressing place where many people suffer, especially because of the greed or cruelty of others. ❑ *...a remake of the 1947 film noir classic, Kiss of Death.*

N-VAR

**fi|lm star** **(film stars)** A **film star** is a famous actor or actress who appears in films. [mainly BRIT] N-COUNT

in AM, use **movie star**

**filmy** /fɪlmi/ **(filmier, filmiest)** A **filmy** fabric or substance is very thin and almost transparent. ❑ *...filmy nightgowns.* ADJ: usu ADJ n = *diaphanous*

**filo** /fiːloʊ/ or **filo pastry** **Filo** or **filo pastry** is a type of light pastry made of thin layers. It is traditionally used in Greek cooking. N-UNCOUNT

**Filo|fax** /faɪləfæks/ **(Filofaxes)** A **Filofax** is a type of personal filing system in the form of a small book with pages that can easily be added or removed. [TRADEMARK] N-COUNT

**fil|ter** /fɪltəʳ/ **(filters, filtering, filtered)** [1] To **filter** a substance means to pass it through a device which is designed to remove certain particles contained in it. ❑ *The best prevention for cholera is to boil or filter water, and eat only well-cooked food.* VERB V n
[2] A **filter** is a device through which a substance is passed when it is being filtered. ❑ *...a paper coffee filter.* N-COUNT [3] A **filter** is a device through which sound or light is passed and which blocks or reduces particular sound or light frequencies. ❑ *You might use a yellow filter to improve the clarity of a hazy horizon.* N-COUNT [4] If light or sound **filters into** a place, it comes in weakly or slowly, either through a partly covered opening, or from a long distance away. ❑ *Light filtered into my kitchen through the soft, green shade of the cherry tree.* VERB V into/through n
[5] When news or information **filters** through to people, it gradually reaches them. ❑ *It took months before the findings began to filter through to the politicians... News of the attack quickly filtered through the college. ...as indications filter in from polling stations. ...the horror stories which were beginning to filter out of Germany.* VERB V through to n V through n V in V out of n [6] A traffic **filter** is a traffic signal or lane which controls the movement of traffic wanting to turn left or right. [BRIT] N-COUNT

♦ **filter out** To **filter out** something from a substance or from light means to remove it by passing the substance or light through something acting as a filter. ❑ *Children should have glasses which filter out UV rays... Plants and trees filter carbon dioxide out of the air and produce oxygen.* PHRASAL VERB V P n V n P of/from n Also V n P

**fil|ter tip** **(filter tips)** A **filter tip** is a small device at the end of a cigarette that reduces the amount of dangerous substances that pass into the smoker's body. **Filter tips** are cigarettes that are manufactured with these devices. N-COUNT

**filth** /fɪlθ/ [1] **Filth** is a disgusting amount of dirt. ❑ *Thousands of tons of filth and sewage pour into the Ganges every day.* N-UNCOUNT = *muck* [2] People refer to words or pictures, usually ones relating to sex, as **filth** when they think they are very disgusting and rude. ❑ *The dialogue was all filth and innuendo.* N-UNCOUNT [disapproval]

**filthy** /fɪlθi/ **(filthier, filthiest)** [1] Something that is **filthy** is very dirty indeed. ❑ *He never washed, and always wore a filthy old jacket.* ADJ = *grimy* [2] If you describe something as **filthy**, you mean that you think it is morally very unpleasant and disgusting, sometimes in a sexual way. ❑ *The play was full of filthy foul language.* ADJ [disapproval] [3] **filthy rich** → see **rich**.

**fil|tra|tion** /fɪltreɪʃᵊn/ **Filtration** is the process of filtering a substance. ❑ *This enzyme makes the filtration of beer easier. ...water filtration systems.* N-UNCOUNT

**fin** /fɪn/ **(fins)** [1] A fish's **fins** are the flat objects which stick out of its body and help it to swim and keep its balance. N-COUNT [2] A **fin** on something such as an aeroplane, rocket, or bomb is a flat part which sticks out and which is intended to help control its movement. N-COUNT

**fi|nal** /faɪnᵊl/ **(finals)** [1] In a series of events, things, or people, the **final** one is the last one. ❑ *Astronauts will make a final attempt today to rescue a communications satellite from its useless orbit... This is the fifth and probably final day of testimony before the Senate Judiciary Committee... On the last Saturday in September, I received a final letter from Clive.* ◆◆◆ ADJ: det ADJ = *last*
[2] **Final** means happening at the end of an event or series of events. ❑ *The countdown to the Notting Hill Carnival is in its final hours.* ADJ: ADJ n [3] If a decision or someone's authority is **final**, it cannot be changed or questioned. ❑ *The judges' decision is final... The White House has the final say.* ADJ [4] The **final** is the last game or contest in a series and decides who is the winner. ❑ *...the Scottish Cup Final.* → See also **quarter-final**, **semi-final**. N-COUNT [5] The **finals** of a sporting tournament consist of a smaller tournament that includes only players or teams that have won earlier games. The finals decide the winner of the whole tournament. ❑ *Poland know they have a chance of qualifying for the World Cup Finals.* N-PLURAL [6] When a student takes his or her **finals**, he or she takes the last and most important examinations in a university or college course. ❑ *Anna sat her finals in the summer.* N-PLURAL: oft poss N

**fi|na|le** /fɪnɑːli, -næli/ **(finales)** **The finale** of a show, piece of music, or series of shows is the last part of it or the last one of them, especially when this is exciting or impressive. ❑ *... the finale of Shostakovich's Fifth Symphony... Tonight's show is the grand finale of a month-long series of events.* N-COUNT: usu with supp

**fi|nal|ise** /faɪnəlaɪz/ → see **finalize**.

**fi|nal|ist** /faɪnəlɪst/ **(finalists)** A **finalist** is someone who reaches the last stages of a competition or tournament by doing well or winning in its earlier stages. ❑ *The twelve finalists will be listed in the Sunday Times.* N-COUNT

**fi|nal|ity** /faɪnælɪti/ **Finality** is the quality of being final and impossible to change. If you say something with **finality**, you say it in a way that shows that you have made up your mind about something and do not want to discuss it further. [FORMAL] ❑ *Young children have difficulty grasping the finality of death.* N-UNCOUNT: oft N of n

**fi|nal|ize** /faɪnəlaɪz/ **(finalizes, finalizing, finalized)**

in BRIT, also use **finalise**

If you **finalize** something such as a plan or an agreement, you complete the arrangements for it, especially by discussing it with other people. ❑ *Negotiators from the three countries finalized the agreement in August... They have not finalized the deal with the government.* VERB V n V n with n

**fi|nal|ly** /faɪnəli/ [1] You use **finally** to suggest that something happens after a long period of time, usually later than you wanted or expected it to happen. ❑ *The food finally arrived at the end of last week and distribution began... Finally, after ten hours of negotiations, the gunman gave himself up.* ◆◆◇ ADV: ADV before v, ADV with cl = *at last*
[2] You use **finally** to indicate that something is last in a series of actions or events. ❑ *The action slips from comedy to melodrama and finally to tragedy.* ADV: ADV with cl/group = *lastly*
[3] You use **finally** in speech or writing to introduce a final point, question, or topic. ❑ *And finally, a word about the winner and runner-up.* ADV: ADV with cl = *in conclusion*

**fi|nance** /faɪnæns, fɪnæns/ **(finances, financing, financed)** [1] When someone **finances** something such as a project or a purchase, they provide the money that is needed to pay for them. ❑ *The fund has been used largely to finance the construction of federal prisons... Government expenditure is financed by taxation and by borrowing.* ♦ **Finance** is also a noun. ❑ *A United States delegation is in Japan seeking finance for a major scientific project.* ◆◆◇ VERB = *fund* V n be V-ed by n N-UNCOUNT
[2] **Finance** is the commercial or government activity of managing money, debt, credit, and investment. ❑ *...a major player in the world of high finance... The report recommends an overhaul of public finances... A former Finance Minister and five senior civil servants are accused of fraud.* N-UNCOUNT: also N in pl [3] You can refer to the amount of money that you have and how well it is organized as your **finances**. ❑ *Be prepared for unexpected news concerning your finances... Finance is usually the biggest problem for students.* N-UNCOUNT: also N in pl, oft with poss

**fi|nance com|pa|ny** **(finance companies)** A **finance company** is a business which lends money to people and charges them interest while they pay it back. [BUSINESS] N-COUNT

**fi|nan|cial** /faɪnænʃᵊl, fɪn-/ ◆◆◆ [ADJ: usu ADJ n] **Financial** means relating to or involving money. ❑ *The company is in financial difficulties. ...the government's financial advisers.* ♦ **fi|nan|cial|ly** [ADV] *She would like to be more financially independent.*

**fi|nan|cial ad|vis|er** (**financial advisers**) [N-COUNT] A **financial adviser** is someone whose job it is to advise people about financial products and services. [BUSINESS]

**fi|nan|cial con|sult|ant** (**financial consultants**) [N-COUNT] A **financial consultant** is the same as a **financial adviser**. [BUSINESS]

**fi|nan|cial ser|vices**

> The form **financial service** is used as a modifier.

[N-PLURAL] A company or organization that provides **financial services** is able to help you do things such as make investments or buy a pension or mortgage. [BUSINESS] ❑ *...voluntary organisations that provide independent advice to consumers on financial services. ...financial service companies.*

**fi|nan|cial year** (**financial years**) [N-COUNT: usu sing, usu with supp = *fiscal year*] A **financial year** is a period of twelve months, used by government, business, and other organizations in order to calculate their budgets, profits, and losses. [BRIT, BUSINESS] ❑ *...33,000 possible job losses in the coming financial year.*

> in AM, use **fiscal year**

**fi|nan|ci|er** /faɪnænsiəʳ, fɪn-/ (**financiers**) [N-COUNT] A **financier** is a person, company, or government that provides money for projects or businesses. [BUSINESS]

**finch** /fɪntʃ/ (**finches**) [N-COUNT] A **finch** is a small bird with a short strong beak.

**find** /faɪnd/ (**finds, finding, found**) ◆◆◆ 1 [VERB] If you **find** someone or something, you see them or learn where they are. ❑ *The police also found a pistol...* [V n] *I wonder if you could find me a deck of cards?* [V n n, Also V n *for* n] 2 [VERB] If you **find** something that you need or want, you succeed in achieving or obtaining it. ❑ *So far* [V n] *they have not found a way to fight the virus... He has to apply for a permit and we have to find him a job...* [V n n] *Does this mean that they haven't found a place for him?* [V n *for* n] 3 [V-PASSIVE] If something **is found** in a particular place or thing, it exists in that place. ❑ *Fibre is found in cereal foods, beans, fruit and vegetables.* [*be* V-ed] 4 [VERB] If you **find** someone or something in a particular situation, they are in that situation when you see them or come into contact with them. ❑ *They found her walking alone and depressed on the beach...* [V n -ing] *She returned to her east London home to find her back door forced open...* [V n -ed] *Thrushes are a protected species so you will not find them on any menu.* [V n prep/adv] 5 [VERB] If you **find yourself** doing something, you are doing it without deciding or intending to do it. ❑ *It's not the first time that you've found yourself in this situation...* [V pron-refl prep/adv] *I found myself having more fun than I had had in years...* [V pron-refl -ing] *It all seemed so far away from here that he found himself quite unable to take it in.* [V pron-refl adj] 6 [VERB] If you **find** that something is the case, you become aware of it or realize that it is the case. ❑ *The two biologists found, to their surprise, that both groups of birds survived equally well...* [V that] *At my age I would find it hard to get another job...* [V *it* adj to-inf] *We find her evidence to be based on a degree of oversensitivity...* [V n to-inf] *I've never found my diet a problem.* [V n n] 7 [VERB] When a court or jury decides that a person on trial is guilty or innocent, you say that the person **has been found** guilty or not guilty. ❑ *She was found guilty of manslaughter and put on probation for two years...* [*be* V-ed adj] *When they found us guilty, I just went blank.* [V n adj] 8 [VERB] You can use **find** to express your reaction to someone or something. ❑ *We're sure you'll find it exciting!...* [V n adj] *I find it ludicrous that nothing has been done to protect passengers from fire...* [V *it* adj that] *But you'd find him a good worker if you showed him what to do.* [V n n] 9 [VERB] If you **find** a feeling such as pleasure or comfort **in** a particular thing or activity, you experience the feeling mentioned as a result of this thing or activity. ❑ *How could anyone find pleasure in hunting and killing this beautiful creature?...* [V n *in* -ing] *I was too tired and frightened to find comfort in that familiar promise.* [V n *in* n] 10 [VERB] If you **find** the time or money **to** do something, you succeed in making or obtaining enough time or money to do it. ❑ *I was just finding more time to write music...* [V n] *My sister helped me find the money for a private operation.* [V n] 11 [N-COUNT: usu adj N] If you describe someone or something that has been discovered as a **find**, you mean that they are valuable, interesting, good, or useful. ❑ *Another of his lucky finds was a pair of candle-holders... His discovery was hailed as the botanical find of the century.* 12 → See also **finding**, **found**.

PHRASES 13 [PHRASE: V inflects, oft PHR prep/adv] If you **find** your **way** somewhere, you successfully get there by choosing the right way to go. ❑ *After a while I pulled myself to my feet and found my way to the street.* 14 [PHRASE: V inflects, PHR adv/prep] If something **finds** its **way** somewhere, it comes to that place, especially by chance. ❑ *It is one of the very few Michelangelos that have found their way out of Italy.* 15 to **find fault with** → see **fault**. to **find** one's **feet** → see **foot**.

♦ **find out** 1 [PHRASAL VERB = *discover*] If you **find** something **out**, you learn something that you did not already know, especially by making a deliberate effort to do so. ❑ *It makes you want to watch the next episode to find out what's going to happen...* [V P wh] *I was relieved to find out that my problems were due to a genuine disorder...* [V P that] *Yesterday, the men's families held a news conference in their campaign to find out the truth...* [V P n (not pron)] *As soon as we found this out, we closed the ward.* [V n P] 2 [PHRASAL VERB] If you **find** someone **out**, you discover that they have been doing something dishonest. ❑ *Her face was so grave, I wondered for a moment if she'd found me out.* [V n P]

**find|er** /faɪndəʳ/ (**finders**) [N-COUNT] You can refer to someone who finds something as the **finder** of that thing. ❑ *The finder of a wallet who takes it home may be guilty of theft.*

**fin de siè|cle** /fæn də siekla/ also **fin-de-siècle.** [ADJ: ADJ n] **Fin de siècle** is used to describe something that is thought to be typical of the end of the nineteenth century, especially when it is considered stylish or exaggerated. [WRITTEN] ❑ *...fin de siècle decadence.*

**find|ing** /faɪndɪŋ/ (**findings**) 1 [N-COUNT: usu pl, usu with supp] Someone's **findings** are the information they get or the conclusions they come to as the result of an investigation or some research. ❑ *We hope that manufacturers will take note of the findings and improve their products accordingly.* 2 [N-COUNT: usu pl, usu with poss] The **findings** of a court are the decisions that it reaches after a trial or an investigation. ❑ *The government hopes the court will announce its findings before the end of the month.*

> **fine**
> ① ADJECTIVE USES
> ② PUNISHMENT

① **fine** /faɪn/ (**finer, finest**) ◆◆◇ 1 [ADJ: usu ADJ n] You use **fine** to describe something that you admire and think is very good. ❑ *There is a fine view of the countryside... This is a fine book. ...London's finest art deco cinema.* ♦ **fine|ly** [ADV: ADV -ed] *They are finely engineered boats.* 2 [ADJ: v-link ADJ] If you say that you are **fine**, you mean that you are in good health or reasonably happy. ❑ *Lina is fine and sends you her love and best wishes.* 3 [ADJ: usu v-link ADJ, oft *it* v-link ADJ to-inf] If you say that something is **fine**, you mean that it is satisfactory or acceptable. ❑ *The skiing is fine... Everything was going to be just fine... It's fine to ask questions as we go along, but it's better if you wait until we have finished.* ♦ **Fine** is also an adverb. [ADV] ❑ *All the instruments are working fine.* 4 [CONVENTION formulae] You say **'fine'** or **'that's fine'** to show that you do not object to an arrangement, action, or situation that has been suggested. ❑ *If competition is the best way to achieve it, then, fine... If you don't want to give it to me, that's fine, I don't mind.* 5 [ADJ: usu ADJ n ≠ *coarse*] Something that is **fine** is very delicate, narrow, or small. ❑ *The heat scorched the fine hairs on her arms.* ♦ **fine|ly** [ADV: ADV with v] *Chop the ingredients finely and mix them together.* 6 [ADJ: usu ADJ n] **Fine** objects or clothing are of good quality, delicate, and expensive. ❑ *We waited in our fine clothes.* 7 [ADJ:] A **fine** detail or distinction is very delicate, small, or exact. ❑ *The market likes the broad outline but is reserving judgment on the fine detail.* ♦ **fine|ly** *They had to take the finely balanced decision to let the visit proceed.* ♦ **fine|ness** *...a sense of quality and fineness of detail.* [8] A **fine** person is someone you consider good, moral, and worth admiring. ❑ *He was an excellent journalist and a very fine man.* [9] When the weather is **fine**, the sun is shining and it is not raining. ❑ *He might be doing a spot of gardening if the weather is fine.*

usu ADJ n / ADV: usu ADV -ed, also ADV after v / N-UNCOUNT: oft N *of* n / ADJ: usu ADJ n / approval / ADJ

**② fine** /faɪn/ **(fines, fining, fined)** [1] A **fine** is a punishment in which a person is ordered to pay a sum of money because they have done something illegal or broken a rule. [2] If someone **is fined**, they are punished by being ordered to pay a sum of money because they have done something illegal or broken a rule. ❑ *She was fined £300 and banned from driving for one month... An east London school has set a precedent by fining pupils who break the rules.*

◆◇◇ N-COUNT / VERB / *be* V-ed / V n

**fine art** **(fine arts)** [1] Painting and sculpture, in which objects are produced that are beautiful rather than useful, can be referred to as **fine art** or as the **fine arts**. ❑ *He deals in antiques and fine art. ...the university of Cairo's faculty of fine arts.* [2] If you **have got** something **down to a fine art**, you are able to do it in a very skilful or efficient way because you have had a lot of experience of doing it.

N-UNCOUNT: also N in pl / PHRASE: V inflects

**fine print** In a contract or agreement, the **fine print** is the same as the **small print**.

N-UNCOUNT: usu *the* N

**fin|ery** /faɪnəri/ If someone is dressed in their **finery**, they are wearing the elegant and impressive clothes and jewellery that they wear on special occasions. [LITERARY] ❑ *...the guests in all their finery.*

N-UNCOUNT

**fi|nesse** /fɪnes/ If you do something with **finesse**, you do it with great skill and style. ❑ *...handling momentous diplomatic challenges with tact and finesse.*

N-UNCOUNT

**fine-tooth comb** also **fine tooth comb.** If you say that you will **go over** something **with a fine-tooth comb** or **go through** something **with a fine-tooth comb**, you are emphasizing that you will search it thoroughly or examine it very carefully.

PHRASE: V inflects / emphasis

**fine-tune** **(fine-tunes, fine-tuning, fine-tuned)** If you **fine-tune** something, you make very small and precise changes to it in order to make it as successful or effective as it possibly can be. ❑ *We do not try to fine-tune the economy on the basis of short-term predictions.* ♦ **fine-tuning** *There's a lot of fine-tuning to be done yet.*

VERB / V n / N-UNCOUNT

**fin|ger** /fɪŋgəʳ/ **(fingers, fingering, fingered)** [1] Your **fingers** are the four long thin parts at the end of each hand. ❑ *She suddenly held up a small, bony finger and pointed across the room... She ran her fingers through her hair... There was a ring on each of his fingers.* → See also **light-fingered**. [2] The **fingers** of a glove are the parts that a person's fingers fit into. [3] A **finger of** something such as smoke or land is an amount of it that is shaped rather like a finger. ❑ *...a thin finger of land that separates Pakistan from the former Soviet Union... Cover the base with a single layer of sponge fingers.* → See also **fish finger**. [4] If you **finger** something, you touch or feel it with your fingers. ❑ *He fingered the few coins in his pocket... Self-consciously she fingered the emeralds at her throat.*

◆◆◇ N-COUNT / N-COUNT: usu pl / N-COUNT: N *of* n, n N = strip / VERB / V n / V n

**PHRASES** [5] If you **get your fingers burned** or **burn your fingers**, you suffer because something you did or were involved in was a failure or a mistake. ❑ *He has had his fingers burnt by deals that turned out badly... Mr Walesa burned his fingers by promising he would give every Pole 100m zlotys to start a business.* [6] If you **cross** your **fingers**, you put one finger on top of another and hope for good luck. If you say that someone **is keeping their fingers crossed**, you mean they are hoping for good luck. ❑ *I'm keeping my fingers crossed that they turn up soon.* [7] If you say that someone did not **lay a finger on** a particular person or thing, you are emphasizing that they did not touch or harm them at all. ❑ *I must make it clear I never laid a finger on her.* [8] If you say that a person does not **lift a finger** or **raise a finger** to do something, especially to help someone, you are critical of them because they do nothing. ❑ *She never lifted a finger around the house... They will not lift a finger to help their country.* [9] If you **point the finger at** someone or **point an accusing finger at** someone, you blame them or accuse them of doing wrong. ❑ *He said he wasn't pointing an accusing finger at anyone in the government or the army.* [10] If you tell someone to **pull** their **finger out** or to **get** their **finger out**, you are telling them rudely that you want them to start doing some work or making an effort. [BRIT, INFORMAL] ❑ *Isn't it about time that you pulled your finger out?* [11] If you **put** your **finger on** something, for example a reason or problem, you see and identify exactly what it is. ❑ *He could never quite put his finger on who or what was responsible for all this.* [12] If someone or something **slips through** your **fingers**, you just fail to catch them, get them, or keep them. ❑ *Money has slipped through his fingers all his life... You mustn't allow a golden opportunity to slip through your fingers or you will regret it later.* [13] to **have green fingers** → see **green**. **finger on the pulse** → see **pulse**.

PHRASE: V inflects / PHRASE: V inflects / PHRASE: V inflects, / usu with brd-neg, PHR n / emphasis / PHRASE: V inflects, with brd-neg / disapproval / PHRASE: V inflects, PHR n / PHRASE: V inflects / disapproval / PHRASE: V inflects, PHR n/wh / PHRASE: V inflects

**fin|ger|ing** /fɪŋgərɪŋ/ **Fingering** is the method of using the most suitable finger to play each note when you are playing a musical instrument, especially the piano.

N-UNCOUNT

**finger|mark** /fɪŋgəʳmɑːʳk/ **(fingermarks)** A **fingermark** is a mark which is made when someone puts a dirty or oily finger onto a clean surface.

N-COUNT

**finger|nail** /fɪŋgəʳneɪl/ **(fingernails)** also **finger-nail.** Your **fingernails** are the thin hard areas at the end of each of your fingers.

N-COUNT = nail

**finger|print** /fɪŋgəʳprɪnt/ **(fingerprints, fingerprinting, fingerprinted)** [1] **Fingerprints** are marks made by a person's fingers which show the lines on the skin. Everyone's fingerprints are different, so they can be used to identify criminals. ❑ *The detective discovered no fewer than 35 fingerprints.* ● If the police **take** someone's **fingerprints**, they make that person press their fingers onto a pad covered with ink, and then onto paper, so that they know what that person's fingerprints look like. ❑ *They were photographed and had their fingerprints taken.* [2] If someone **is fingerprinted**, the police take their fingerprints. ❑ *He took her to jail, where she was fingerprinted and booked.*

N-COUNT: usu pl / PHRASE: V inflects / VERB: usu passive *be* V-ed

**finger|tip** /fɪŋgəʳtɪp/ **(fingertips)** also **finger-tip.** [1] Your **fingertips** are the ends of your fingers. ❑ *The fat and flour are rubbed together with the fingertips as for pastry.* [2] If you say that something is **at** your **fingertips**, you approve of the fact that you can reach it easily or that it is easily available to you. ❑ *I had the information at my fingertips and hadn't used it.*

N-COUNT: usu pl / PHRASE / approval

**finger|tip search** **(fingertip searches)** When the police carry out a **fingertip search** of a place, they examine it for evidence in a very detailed way. ❑ *Officers continued a fingertip search of the area yesterday.*

N-COUNT: oft N of n

**fin|icky** /fɪnɪki/ If you say that someone is **finicky**, you mean that they are worried about small details and are difficult to please. ❑ *Even the most finicky eater will find something appetizing here.*

ADJ / disapproval / = picky

**fin|ish** /fɪnɪʃ/ **(finishes, finishing, finished)** [1] When you **finish** doing or dealing with something, you do or deal with the last part of it, so that there is no more for you to do or deal with. ❑ *As soon as he'd finished eating, he excused himself... Mr Gould was given a standing ovation and loud cheers when he finished his speech.* ♦ **Finish up** means the same as **finish**. [AM] ❑ *We waited a few*

◆◆◇ VERB / V n/-ing / V n/-ing / PHRASAL VERB / V P n (not pron) *minutes outside his office while he finished up his meeting.* [2] When you **finish** something that you are making or producing, you reach the end of making or producing it, so that it is complete. ❑ *The consultants had been working to finish a report this week.* ♦ **Finish off** and, in American English, **finish up** mean the same as **finish**. ❑ *Now she is busy finishing off a biography of Queen Caroline. ...the amount of stuff required to finish up a movie.* VERB = complete V n PHRASAL VERB V P n (not pron) V P n (not pron)

[3] When something such as a course, film, or sale **finishes**, especially at a planned time, it ends. ❑ *The teaching day finishes at around 4pm... When a play finishes its run, many of the costumes are hired out to amateur dramatics companies and schools.* VERB = end V at/on/by n V n Also V

[4] You say that someone or something **finishes** a period of time or an event in a particular way to indicate what the final situation was like. You can also say that a period of time or an event **finishes** in a particular way. ❑ *The two of them finished by kissing each other goodbye... The evening finished with the welcoming of three new members... The American dollar finished the day up against foreign currencies... The last track finishes this compilation beautifully.* VERB V by -ing V with n V n adj/adv V n adj/adv

[5] If someone **finishes** second, for example, in a race or competition, they are in second place at the end of the race or competition. ❑ *He finished second in the championship four years in a row.* VERB V ord/prep

[6] To **finish** means to reach the end of saying something. ❑ *Her eyes flashed, but he held up a hand. 'Let me finish.'* VERB V

[7] **The finish** of something is the end of it or the last part of it. ❑ *I intend to continue it and see the job through to the finish... From start to finish he believed in me, often more than I did myself.* N-SING: the N, with poss = end

[8] The **finish** of a race is the end of it. ❑ *Win a trip to see the finish of the Tour de France!... The replays of the close finish showed Ottey finished ahead of the Olympic champion.* N-COUNT

[9] If the surface of something that has been made has a particular kind of **finish**, it has the appearance or texture mentioned. ❑ *The finish and workmanship of the woodwork was excellent.* N-COUNT: usu with supp

[10] → See also **finished**.

[11] If you add **the finishing touches** to something, you add or do the last things that are necessary to complete it. ❑ *Right up until the last minute, workers were still putting the finishing touches on the pavilions.* PHRASE: N inflects

♦ **finish off** [1] If you **finish off** something that you have been eating or drinking, you eat or drink the last part of it with the result that there is none left. ❑ *Kelly finished off his coffee... He took the bottle from her hands and finished it off in one long swallow.* PHRASAL VERB V P n (not pron) V n P

[2] If someone **finishes off** a person or thing that is already badly injured or damaged, they kill or destroy them. ❑ *They meant to finish her off, swiftly and without mercy.* PHRASAL VERB V n P

[3] → see **finish 2**.

♦ **finish up** [1] If you **finish up** in a particular place or situation, you are in that place or situation after doing or experiencing several things. ❑ *They had met by chance at university and finished up getting married... He's probably going to finish up in jail for business fraud.* PHRASAL VERB = end up, wind up V P -ing V P prep

[2] If you **finish up** something that you have been eating or drinking, you eat or drink the last part of it. ❑ *Finish up your drinks now, please.* PHRASAL VERB V P n (not pron) Also V n P

[3] → See also **finish 1, 2**.

♦ **finish with** If you **finish with** someone or something, you stop dealing with them, being involved with them, or being interested in them. ❑ *My boyfriend was threatening to finish with me.* PHRASAL VERB V P n

**fin|ished** /fɪnɪʃt/ [1] Someone who is **finished with** something is no longer doing it or dealing with it or is no longer interested in it. ❑ *One suspects he will be finished with boxing.* ADJ: v-link ADJ with n

[2] Something that is **finished** no longer exists or is no longer happening. ❑ *I go back on the dole when the shooting season's finished.* ADJ: v-link ADJ = over

[3] Someone or something that is **finished** is no longer important, powerful, or effective. ❑ *Her power over me is finished... He confessed: 'I thought I was finished.'* ADJ: v-link ADJ

**fin|ish|ing line** **(finishing lines)** or **finish line** In a race, the **finishing line** is the place on the track or course where the race officially ends. N-COUNT

**fin|ish|ing school** **(finishing schools)** A **finishing school** is a private school where rich or upper-class young women are taught manners and other social skills that are considered to be suitable for them. ❑ *...a Swiss finishing school. ...where the Princess of Wales attended finishing school.* N-VAR

**fi|nite** /faɪnaɪt/ [1] Something that is **finite** has a definite fixed size or extent. [FORMAL] ❑ *Only a finite number of situations can arise... The fossil fuels (coal and oil) are finite resources.* ADJ ≠ infinite

[2] A **finite** clause is a clause based on a verb group which indicates tense, such as 'went', 'is waiting', or 'will be found', rather than on an infinitive or a participle. Compare **non-finite**. ADJ: usu ADJ n

**Finn** /fɪn/ **(Finns)** The **Finns** are the people of Finland. N-COUNT

**Finn|ish** /fɪnɪʃ/ [1] **Finnish** means belonging or relating to Finland or to its people, language, or culture. ADJ [2] **Finnish** is the language spoken in Finland. N-UNCOUNT

**fir** /fɜːʳ/ **(firs)** A **fir** or a **fir tree** is a tall evergreen tree that has thin needle-like leaves. N-VAR

| fire |
|---|
| ① BURNING, HEAT, OR ENTHUSIASM |
| ② SHOOTING OR ATTACKING |
| ③ DISMISSAL |

① **fire** /faɪəʳ/ **(fires, firing, fired)** ◆◆◇

⇛ Please look at category 13 to see if the expression you are looking for is shown under another headword. [1] **Fire** is the hot, bright flames produced by things that are burning. ❑ *They saw a big flash and a huge ball of fire reaching hundreds of feet into the sky... Many students were trapped by smoke and fire on an upper floor.* N-UNCOUNT

[2] **Fire** or a **fire** is an occurrence of uncontrolled burning which destroys buildings, forests, or other things. ❑ *87 people died in a fire at the Happy Land Social Club... A forest fire is sweeping across portions of north Maine this evening... Much of historic Rennes was destroyed by fire in 1720.* N-VAR

[3] A **fire** is a burning pile of wood, coal, or other fuel that you make, for example to use for heat, light, or cooking. ❑ *There was a fire in the grate... After the killing, he calmly lit a fire to destroy evidence.* N-COUNT

[4] A **fire** is a device that uses electricity or gas to give out heat and warm a room. [mainly BRIT] ❑ *The gas fire was still alight.* N-COUNT: oft n N

☑ in AM, usually use **heater**

[5] When a pot or clay object **is fired**, it is heated at a high temperature in a special oven, as part of the process of making it. ❑ *After the pot is dipped in this mixture, it is fired.* VERB be V-ed

[6] When the engine of a motor vehicle **fires**, an electrical spark is produced which causes the fuel to burn and the engine to work. ❑ *The engine fired and we moved off.* VERB V

[7] If you **fire** someone **with** enthusiasm, you make them feel very enthusiastic. If you **fire** someone's imagination, you make them feel interested and excited. ❑ *...the potential to fire the imagination of an entire generation... It was Allen who fired this rivalry with real passion... Both his grandfathers were fired with an enthusiasm for public speaking.* VERB V n V n with n be V-ed with n

[8] You can use **fire** to refer in an approving way to someone's energy and enthusiasm. ❑ *I went to hear him speak and was very impressed. He seemed so full of fire.* N-UNCOUNT [approval] = passion

PHRASES [9] If an object or substance **catches fire**, it starts burning. ❑ *The aircraft caught fire soon after take-off.* PHRASE: V inflects

[10] If something is **on fire**, it is burning and being damaged or destroyed by an uncontrolled fire. ❑ *The captain radioed that the ship was on fire.* PHRASE: v-link PHR = burning

[11] If you say that someone **is playing with fire**, you mean that they are doing something dangerous that may result in great harm for them and cause many problems. PHRASE: V inflects

❑ *Schulte warned government and industrial leaders that those who even venture to think about mass layoffs are playing with fire.* 12 If you **set fire to** something or if you **set** it **on fire**, you start it burning in order to damage or destroy it. ❑ *They set fire to vehicles outside that building... Lightning set several buildings on fire.* 13 to **have irons on the fire** → see **iron**. **like a house on fire** → see **house**. **there's no smoke without fire** → see **smoke**. PHRASE: V inflects

**②fire** /faɪəʳ/ **(fires, firing, fired)** ◆◆◇

⇛ Please look at category 13 to see if the expression you are looking for is shown under another headword. 1 If someone **fires** a gun or a bullet, or if they **fire**, a bullet is sent from a gun that they are using. ❑ *Seven people were wounded when soldiers fired rubber bullets to disperse crowds... The gun was fired and Beaton was wounded a second time... Seventeen people were killed when security forces fired on demonstrators... They were firing. I screamed at them to stop.* ♦ **fir|ing** *The firing continued even while the protestors were fleeing.* 2 You can use **fire** to refer to the shots fired from a gun or guns. ❑ *His car was raked with fire from automatic weapons... The two were reportedly killed in an exchange of fire during a police raid.* 3 If you **fire** an arrow, you send it from a bow. ❑ *He fired an arrow into a clearing in the forest.* 4 If you **fire** questions at someone, you ask them a lot of questions very quickly, one after another. ❑ *They were bombarded by more than 100 representatives firing questions on pollution.* VERB; V n; V n; V *on* n; V; N-UNCOUNT; N-UNCOUNT = gunfire; VERB = shoot V n; VERB; V n

**PHRASES** 5 If you **draw fire** for something that you have done, you cause people to criticize you or attack you because of it. ❑ *The council recently drew fire for its intervention in the dispute.* 6 If someone **holds** their **fire** or **holds fire**, they stop shooting or they wait before they start shooting. ❑ *Devereux ordered his men to hold their fire until the ships got closer.* 7 If you **hold fire** in a situation, you delay before taking action. ❑ *Observers reckon the Bank of England will hold fire until nearer the Budget.* 8 If you are in the **line of fire**, you are in a position where someone is aiming their gun at you. If you move into their **line of fire**, you move into a position between them and the thing they were aiming at. ❑ *He cheerfully blows away any bad guy stupid enough to get in his line of fire... The man and his son had been pushed into the line of fire by their captors.* 9 If you **open fire on** someone, you start shooting at them. ❑ *Then without warning, the troops opened fire on the crowd.* 10 If you **return fire** or you **return** someone's **fire**, you shoot back at someone who has shot at you. ❑ *The soldiers returned fire after being attacked.* 11 If you come **under fire** or are **under fire**, someone starts shooting at you. ❑ *The Belgians fell back as the infantry came under fire.* 12 If you come **under fire from** someone or are **under fire**, they criticize you strongly. ❑ *The president's plan first came under fire from critics who said he hadn't included enough spending cuts.* 13 to **fire from the hip** → see **hip**. PHRASE: V inflects; PHRASE: V inflects; PHRASE: V inflects = hold back; PHRASE; PHRASE: V inflects, oft PHR *on* n; PHRASE: V inflects; PHRASE: usu v PHR, v-link PHR; PHRASE: usu v PHR, v-link PHR

♦ **fire away** If someone wants to say or ask something, you can say **'fire away'** as a way of showing that you are ready for them to speak. [INFORMAL] ❑ *'May I ask you something?' — 'Sure. Fire away.'* PHRASAL VERB: only imper; V P

♦ **fire off** 1 If you **fire off** a shot, you send a bullet or other missile from a gun. ❑ *A gunman fired off a volley of shots into the air. ...an illustration of a guy firing a huge cannon off into the distance.* 2 If you **fire off** a letter, question, or remark, you send or say it very quickly, often as part of a series. ❑ *He immediately fired off an angry letter to his ministry colleagues.* PHRASAL VERB; V P n (not pron); V n P; PHRASAL VERB; V P n (not pron)

**③fire** /faɪəʳ/ **(fires, firing, fired)** If an employer **fires** you, they dismiss you from your job. ❑ *If he hadn't been so good at the rest of his job, I probably would have fired him... She was sent a box of chocolates along with a letter saying she was fired.* ♦ **fir|ing** *There was yet another round of firings.* VERB = sack; V n; V n; N-COUNT

**fire alarm** **(fire alarms)** A **fire alarm** is a device that makes a noise, for example with a bell, to warn people when there is a fire. N-COUNT

**fire|arm** /faɪərɑːʳm/ **(firearms)** **Firearms** are guns. [FORMAL] ❑ *He was also charged with illegal possession of firearms... He was jailed for firearms offences.* N-COUNT: usu pl

**fire|ball** /faɪəʳbɔːl/ **(fireballs)** A **fireball** is a ball of fire, for example one at the centre of a nuclear explosion. N-COUNT

**fire|bomb** /faɪəʳbɒm/ **(firebombs, firebombing, firebombed)** 1 A **firebomb** is a type of bomb which is designed to cause fires. 2 To **firebomb** a building, vehicle, or place means to set fire to it using a firebomb. ❑ *Protestors firebombed the embassy building yesterday.* ♦ **fire|bombing** **(firebombings)** *The homes bore evidence of firebombing.* N-COUNT; VERB; V n; N-VAR

**fire|brand** /faɪəʳbrænd/ **(firebrands)** If you describe someone as a **firebrand**, especially someone who is very active in politics, you mean that they are always trying to make people take strong action. ❑ *...his reputation as a young firebrand.* N-COUNT

**fire|break** /faɪəʳbreɪk/ **(firebreaks)** also **fire break**. A **firebreak** is an area of open land in a wood or forest that has been created to stop a fire from spreading. N-COUNT

**fire bri|gade** **(fire brigades)** The **fire brigade** is an organization which has the job of putting out fires; used especially to refer to the people who actually fight the fires. ❑ *Get everyone out and call the fire brigade.* N-COUNT-COLL: usu *the* N

**fire|cracker** /faɪəʳkrækəʳ/ **(firecrackers)** A **firecracker** is a firework that makes several loud bangs when it is lit. N-COUNT

**-fired** /-faɪəʳd/ **-fired** combines with nouns which refer to fuels to form adjectives which describe power stations, machines, or devices that operate by means of that fuel. ❑ *...coal-fired power stations... Most of the food is cooked on a large wood-fired oven.* COMB in ADJ: usu ADJ n

**fire de|part|ment** **(fire departments)** The **fire department** is an organization which has the job of putting out fires. [AM] N-COUNT-COLL: usu *the* N

✓ in BRIT, use **fire service**

**fire drill** **(fire drills)** When there is a **fire drill** in a particular building, the people who work or live there practise what to do if there is a fire. N-VAR

**fire-eater** **(fire-eaters)** **Fire-eaters** are performers who put flaming rods into their mouths in order to entertain people. N-COUNT

**fire en|gine** **(fire engines)** A **fire engine** is a large vehicle which carries firefighters and equipment for putting out fires. [BRIT] N-COUNT

✓ in AM, usually use **fire truck**

**fire es|cape** **(fire escapes)** also **fire-escape**. A **fire escape** is a metal staircase on the outside of a building, which can be used to escape from the building if there is a fire. N-COUNT

**fire ex|tin|guish|er** **(fire extinguishers)** also **fire-extinguisher**. A **fire extinguisher** is a metal cylinder which contains water or chemicals at high pressure which can put out fires. N-COUNT

**fire|fight** /faɪəʳfaɪt/ **(firefights)** A **firefight** is a battle in a war which involves the use of guns rather than bombs or any other sort of weapon. [JOURNALISM] ❑ *U.S. Marines had a firefight with local gunmen this morning.* N-COUNT

**fire|fighter** /faɪəʳfaɪtəʳ/ **(firefighters)** also **fire fighter**, **fire-fighter**. **Firefighters** are people whose job is to put out fires. N-COUNT: usu pl = fireman

**fire|fighting** /faɪəʳfaɪtɪŋ/ also **fire fighting**, **fire-fighting**. **Firefighting** is the work of putting out fires. ❑ *There was no fire-fighting equipment.* N-UNCOUNT: oft N n

**fire|fly** /faɪəʳflaɪ/ **(fireflies)** also **fire fly.** A **firefly** is a type of beetle that produces light from its body. N-COUNT

**fire|guard** /faɪəʳgɑːʳd/ **(fireguards)** also **fire-guard.** A **fireguard** is a screen made of strong wire that you put round a fire so that people cannot accidentally burn themselves. N-COUNT

**fire hy|drant** **(fire hydrants)** also **fire-hydrant.** A **fire hydrant** is a pipe in the street from which fire fighters can obtain water for putting out a fire. N-COUNT

**fire|light** /faɪəʳlaɪt/ **Firelight** is the light that comes from a fire. ❑ *In the firelight his head gleamed with sweat.* N-UNCOUNT: also *the* N

**fire|man** /faɪəʳmən/ **(firemen)** A **fireman** is a person, usually a man, whose job is to put out fires. N-COUNT

**fire|place** /faɪəʳpleɪs/ **(fireplaces)** In a room, the **fireplace** is the place where a fire can be lit and the area on the wall and floor surrounding this place. N-COUNT

**fire|power** /faɪəʳpaʊəʳ/ The **firepower** of an army, ship, tank, or aircraft is the amount of ammunition it can fire. ❑ *America has enough firepower in the area to mount sustained air strikes.* N-UNCOUNT

**fire|proof** /faɪəʳpruːf/ Something that is **fireproof** cannot be damaged by fire. ❑ *...fireproof clothing.* ADJ

**fire-retardant** **Fire-retardant** substances make the thing that they are applied to burn more slowly. ❑ *...fire-retardant foam.* ADJ = flame-retardant

**fire sale** **(fire sales)** [1] A **fire sale** is an event in which goods are sold cheaply because the shop or storeroom they were in has been damaged by fire. N-COUNT [2] If you describe a sale of goods or other assets as a **fire sale**, you mean that everything is being sold very cheaply. ❑ *They're likely to hold big fire sales to liquidate their inventory.* N-COUNT: oft N n

**fire ser|vice** **(fire services)** **The fire service** is an organization which has the job of putting out fires. [BRIT] ❑ *Crowds of youths prevented the fire service from dealing with the blaze.* N-COUNT-COLL: usu *the* N

☑ in AM, use **fire department**

**fire|side** /faɪəʳsaɪd/ **(firesides)** If you sit by **the fireside** in a room, you sit near the fire. ❑ *...winter evenings by the fireside. ...cosy fireside chats.* N-COUNT: usu sing

**fire sta|tion** **(fire stations)** A **fire station** is a building where fire engines are kept, and where firefighters wait until they are called to put out a fire. N-COUNT

**fire|storm** /faɪəʳstɔːʳm/ **(firestorms)** also **fire storm.** [1] A **firestorm** is a fire that is burning uncontrollably, usually in a place that has been bombed. N-COUNT [2] If you say that there is a **firestorm of** protest or criticism, you are emphasizing that there is a great deal of very fierce protest or criticism. [AM] ❑ *The speech has resulted in a firestorm of controversy.* N-COUNT: usu with supp [emphasis]

**fire truck** **(fire trucks)** A **fire truck** is a large vehicle which carries fire fighters and equipment for putting out fires. [AM, AUSTRALIAN] N-COUNT

☑ in BRIT, usually use **fire engine**

**fire|wall** /faɪəʳwɔːl/ **(firewalls)** A **firewall** is a computer system or program that automatically prevents an unauthorized person from gaining access to a computer when it is connected to a network such as the Internet. [COMPUTING] ❑ *New technology should provide a secure firewall against hackers.* N-COUNT

**fire|wood** /faɪəʳwʊd/ **Firewood** is wood that has been cut into pieces so that it can be burned on a fire. N-UNCOUNT

**fire|work** /faɪəʳwɜːʳk/ **(fireworks)** **Fireworks** are small objects that are lit to entertain people on special occasions. They contain chemicals and burn brightly or attractively, often with a loud noise, when you light them. ❑ *...a firework display.* N-COUNT: usu pl

**fir|ing line** **(firing lines)** also **firing-line.** [1] If you are **in the firing line** in a conflict, you are in a position where someone is aiming their gun at you. ❑ *Any hostages in the firing line would have been sacrificed.* N-COUNT: usu *the* N in sing, usu prep N [2] If you say that someone is **in the firing line**, you mean that they are being criticized, blamed, or attacked for something. ❑ *Foreign banks are in the firing line too.* N-SING: *the* N, usu *in/out of* N

**fir|ing squad** **(firing squads)** A **firing squad** is a group of soldiers who are ordered to shoot and kill a person who has been found guilty of committing a crime. ❑ *He was executing by firing squad.* N-COUNT: also *by* N

**firm** /fɜːʳm/ **(firms, firmer, firmest)** [1] A **firm** is an organization which sells or produces something or which provides a service which people pay for. ❑ *The firm's employees were expecting large bonuses. ...a firm of heating engineers.* ◆◆◆ N-COUNT = company [2] If something is **firm**, it does not change much in shape when it is pressed but is not completely hard. ❑ *Fruit should be firm and in excellent condition... Choose a soft, medium or firm mattress to suit their individual needs.* ADJ ≠ soft [3] If something is **firm**, it does not shake or move when you put weight or pressure on it, because it is strongly made or securely fastened. ❑ *If you have to climb up, use a firm platform or a sturdy ladder.* ADJ = secure ♦ **firm|ly** *The front door is locked and all the windows are firmly shut.* ADV: ADV -ed, ADV after v [4] If someone's grip is **firm** or if they perform a physical action in a **firm** way, they do it with quite a lot of force or pressure but also in a controlled way. ❑ *The quick handshake was firm and cool... He managed to grasp the metal, get a firm grip of it and heave his body upwards.* ADJ = strong ♦ **firm|ly** *She held me firmly by the elbow and led me to my aisle seat.* ADV: ADV after v [5] If you describe someone as **firm**, you mean they behave in a way that shows that they are not going to change their mind, or that they are the person who is in control. ❑ *She had to be firm with him. 'I don't want to see you again.'... Perhaps they need the guiding hand of a firm father figure.* ADJ: oft ADJ *with* n ♦ **firm|ly** *'A good night's sleep is what you want,' he said firmly.* ADV: ADV with v [6] A **firm** decision or opinion is definite and unlikely to change. ❑ *He made a firm decision to leave Fort Multry by boat... It is my firm belief that an effective partnership approach between police and the public is absolutely necessary.* ADJ: usu ADJ n = definite ♦ **firm|ly** *He is firmly convinced that it is vital to do this.* ADV: ADV -ed, ADV after v [7] **Firm** evidence or information is based on facts and so is likely to be true. ❑ *There's unlikely to be firm news about the convoy's progress for some time.* ADJ: ADJ n = hard, definite [8] You use **firm** to describe control or a basis or position when it is strong and unlikely to be ended or removed. ❑ *Although the Yakutians are a minority, they have firm control of the territory.* ADJ: usu ADJ n = secure ♦ **firm|ly** *This tradition is also firmly rooted in the past.* ADV: ADV -ed, ADV after v [9] If a price, value, or currency is **firm**, it is not decreasing in value or amount. ❑ *Cotton prices remain firm and demand is strong... The shares held firm at 280p.* ADJ = steady ♦ **firm|ness** *...the firmness of the dollar against other currencies.* N-UNCOUNT: usu N *of* n [10] If someone **stands firm**, they refuse to change their mind about something. ❑ *The council is standing firm against the barrage of protest.* PHRASE: V inflects

♦ **firm up** [1] If you **firm up** something or if it **firms up**, it becomes firmer and more solid. ❑ *This treatment helps tone the body, firm up muscles and tighten the skin... I now go swimming five times a week, which helps firm me up... The mixture will seem too wet at this stage, but it will firm up when chilled.* PHRASAL VERB V P n (not pron) V n P V P [2] If you **firm** something **up** or if it **firms up**, it becomes clearer, stronger, or more definite. ❑ *Looking to the future, the Government will firm up their plans for a cleaner, greener, safer Britain... At least the bank situation had firmed up.* PHRASAL VERB V P n (not pron) V P [3] If a financial institution **firms up** the price or value of something, they take action to protect and maintain its price or value. ❑ *OPEC has agreed to freeze its global oil production slightly in order to firm up crude prices.* Also V n P PHRASAL VERB V P n (not pron)

**fir|ma|ment** /fɜːʳməmənt/ [1] **The firmament** is the sky or heaven. [LITERARY] ❑ *There are* N-SING: *the* N *no stars in the firmament.* 2 If you talk about **the firmament** in a particular organization or field of activity, you mean the top of it. ❑ *He was rich, and a rising star in the political firmament.* N-SING: *the* N, usu with supp

**firm|ware** /fɜːʳmweəʳ/ In computer systems, **firmware** is a set of commands which are stored on a chip rather than as part of a program, because the computer uses them very often. [COMPUTING] N-UNCOUNT

**first** /fɜːʳst/ **(firsts)** ◆◆◆ 1 The **first** thing, person, event, or period of time is the one that happens or comes before all the others of the same kind. ❑ *She lost 16 pounds in the first month of her diet. ...the first few flakes of snow... Two years ago Johnson came first in the one hundred metres at Seoul.* ORD ≠ *last* ♦ **First** is also a pronoun. ❑ *The second paragraph startled me even more than the first... He put me through a series of exercises to improve my car control. The first was to drive on simulated ice.* PRON 2 If you do something **first**, you do it before anyone else does, or before you do anything else. ❑ *I do not remember who spoke first, but we all expressed the same opinion... First, tell me what you think of my products... Routine questions first, if you don't mind.* ADV: ADV with v, ADV with cl/group 3 When something happens or is done for the **first** time, it has never happened or been done before. ❑ *This is the first time she has experienced disappointment... It was the first occasion when they had both found it possible to keep a rendezvous.* ORD ♦ **First** is also an adverb. ❑ *Anne and Steve got engaged two years after they had first started going out.* ADV: ADV with v 4 An event that is described as **a first** has never happened before and is important or exciting. ❑ *It is a first for New York. An outdoor exhibition of Fernando Botero's sculpture on Park Avenue.* N-SING: *a* N, oft N *for* n 5 **The first** you hear of something or **the first** you know about it is the time when you first become aware of it. ❑ *We heard it on the TV last night – that was the first we heard of it.* PRON: *the* PRON that 6 You use **first** when you are talking about what happens in the early part of an event or experience, in contrast to what happens later. ❑ *When he first came home he wouldn't say anything about what he'd been doing.* ADV: ADV before v = *initially* ♦ **First** is also an ordinal. ❑ *She told him that her first reaction was disgust.* ORD: usu poss ORD 7 In order to emphasize your determination not to do a particular thing, you can say that rather than do it, you would do something else **first**. ❑ *Marry that fat son of a fat cattle dealer? She would die first!* ADV: ADV after v [emphasis] 8 You use **first** when you are about to give the first in a series of items. ❑ *Certain guidelines can be given. First, have a heating engineer check the safety of the system.* ADV: ADV with cl/group 9 The **first** thing, person, or place in a line is the one that is nearest to you or nearest to the front. ❑ *Before him, in the first row, sat the President... First in the queue were two Japanese students.* ORD ≠ *last* 10 You use **first** to refer to the best or most important thing or person of a particular kind. ❑ *The first duty of any government must be to protect the interests of the taxpayers... Imagine winning the local lottery first prize of £5,000.* ORD 11 **First** is used in the title of the job or position of someone who has a higher rank than anyone else with the same basic job title. ❑ *...the First Lord of the Admiralty. ...the first mate of a British tanker.* ORD 12 In British universities, a **first** is an honours degree of the highest standard. ❑ *...an Oxford Blue who took a First in Constitutional History.* N-COUNT: oft N *in* n

**PHRASES** 13 You use **first of all** to introduce the first of a number of things that you want to say. ❑ *The cut in the interest rates has not had very much impact in California for two reasons. First of all, banks are still afraid to loan.* PHRASE: PHR with cl/group 14 You use **at first** when you are talking about what happens in the early stages of an event or experience, or just after something else has happened, in contrast to what happens later. ❑ *At first, he seemed surprised by my questions... I had some difficulty at first recalling why we were there.* PHRASE: PHR with cl = *initially* 15 If you say that someone or something **comes first** for a particular person, you mean they treat or consider that person or thing as more important than anything else. ❑ *There's no time for boyfriends, my career comes first.* PHRASE: V inflects 16 If you learn or experience something **at first hand**, you experience it yourself or learn it directly rather than being told about it by other people. ❑ *He arrived in Natal to see at first hand the effects of the recent heavy fighting.* PHRASE: PHR after v 17 If you say that you **do not know the first thing about** something, you are emphasizing that you know absolutely nothing about it. ❑ *You don't know the first thing about farming.* PHRASE: V inflects [emphasis] 18 If you **put** someone or something **first**, you treat or consider them as more important than anything else. ❑ *Somebody has to think for the child and put him first.* PHRASE: V inflects 19 You say '**first things first**' when you are talking about something that should be done or dealt with before anything else because it is the most important. ❑ *Let's see if we can't find something to set the mood. First things first; some music.* PHRASE 20 **first and foremost** → see **foremost**.

**-first** /-fɜːʳst/ **-first** combines with nouns like 'head' and 'feet' to indicate that someone moves with the part that is mentioned pointing in the direction in which they are moving. ❑ *He overbalanced and fell head first.* COMB in ADV: ADV after v

**first aid** **First aid** is simple medical treatment given as soon as possible to a person who is injured or who suddenly becomes ill. ❑ *There are many emergencies which need prompt first aid treatment. ...a first aid kit.* N-UNCOUNT: oft N n

**first born** also **first-born.** Someone's **first born** is their first child. ❑ *She was my first-born.* N-SING: oft N n

**first-class** also **first class.** 1 If you describe something or someone as **first-class**, you mean that they are extremely good and of the highest quality. ❑ *The food was first-class... She has a first-class brain and is a damned good writer.* ADJ = *first-rate* 2 You use **first-class** to describe something that is in the group that is considered to be of the highest standard. ❑ *He officially announced his retirement from first-class cricket yesterday... Harriet graduated with a first class degree in literature.* ADJ: ADJ n 3 **First-class** accommodation on a train, aeroplane, or ship is the best and most expensive type of accommodation. ❑ *He won himself two first-class tickets to fly to Dublin. ...first-class passengers.* ADJ: ADJ n ♦ **First-class** is also an adverb. ❑ *She had never flown first class before.* ADV: ADV after v ♦ **First-class** is the first-class accommodation on a train, aeroplane, or ship. ❑ *He paid for and was assigned a cabin in first class.* N-UNCOUNT 4 In Britain, **first-class** postage is the quicker and more expensive type of postage. In the United States, **first-class** postage is the type of postage that is used for sending letters and postcards. ❑ *Two first class stamps, please.* ADJ: ADJ n ♦ **First-class** is also an adverb. ❑ *It took six days to arrive despite being posted first class.* ADV: ADV after v

**first cous|in** **(first cousins)** Someone's **first cousin** is the same as their **cousin**. Compare **second cousin**. N-COUNT: oft with poss

**first de|gree** **(first degrees)** People who have gained a higher qualification after completing a basic university degree such as a BA or a BSc refer to that basic degree as their **first degree**. ❑ *He was born in Zimbabwe where he completed his first degree in economics.* N-COUNT

**first-degree** 1 In the United States, **first-degree** is used to describe crimes that are considered to be the most serious of their kind. For example, **first-degree** murder is when a murder is planned before it is carried out. ❑ *He pleaded guilty to a charge of first-degree robbery.* ADJ: ADJ n 2 A **first-degree** burn is one of the least severe kind, where only the surface layer of the skin has been burnt. ADJ: ADJ n

**first ever** also **first-ever.** Something that is the **first ever** one of its kind has never happened before. ❑ *It's the first-ever meeting between leaders of the two countries.* ADJ: usu ADJ n

**first floor** **(first floors)** 1 **The first floor** of a building is the floor immediately above the one at ground level. [BRIT] N-COUNT: usu *the* N in sing

in AM, use **second floor**

2 **The first floor** of a building is the one at ground level. [AM] N-COUNT: usu *the* N in sing

in BRIT, use **ground floor**

**first fruits** **The first fruits of** a project or activity are the earliest results or profits. ❑ *The deal is one of the first fruits of a liberalization of foreign investment law.* N-PLURAL: usu N *of* n

**first hand** also **first-hand, firsthand.** 1 **First hand** information or experience is gained or learned directly, rather than from other people or from books. ❑ *School trips give children firsthand experience not available in the classroom.* ADJ: ADJ n ♦ **First-hand** is also an adverb. ❑ *We've been through Germany and seen first-hand what's happening there.* ADV: ADV after v 2 **at first hand** → see **first**.

**first lady** **(first ladies)** **The First Lady** in a country or state is the wife of the president or state governor, or a woman who performs the official duties normally performed by the wife. N-COUNT: usu *the* N in sing

**first lan|guage** **(first languages)** Someone's **first language** is the language that they learned first and speak best; used especially when someone speaks more than one language. N-COUNT

**first|ly** /fɜːʳstli/ You use **firstly** in speech or writing when you want to give a reason, make a point, or mention an item that will be followed by others connected with it. ❑ *The programme is now seven years behind schedule as a result, firstly of increased costs, then of technical problems.* ADV: ADV with cl/group

**First Min|is|ter** **(First Ministers)** In the Scottish Assembly and the Northern Ireland Assembly, the **First Minister** is the leader of the ruling party. N-COUNT: usu *the* N; N-TITLE; N-VOC

**first name** **(first names)** Your **first name** is the first of the names that were given to you when you were born. You can also refer to all of your names except your surname as your **first names**. ❑ *Her first name was Mary. I don't know what her surname was.* N-COUNT: usu poss N ● If two people are **on first-name terms**, they know each other well enough to call each other by their first names, rather than having to use a more formal title. ❑ *The two were said to have been on first-name terms.* PHRASE: usu v-link PHR, oft PHR *with* n

**first night** **(first nights)** The **first night** of a show, play, or performance is the first public performance of it. N-COUNT: oft N n

**first of|fend|er** **(first offenders)** A **first offender** is a person who has been found guilty of a crime for the first time. N-COUNT

**first-past-the-post** A **first-past-the-post** system for choosing members of parliament or other representatives is one in which the candidate who gets most votes wins. [BRIT] ADJ: ADJ n

**first per|son** A statement **in the first person** is a statement about yourself, or about yourself and someone else. The subject of a statement like this is 'I' or 'we'. ❑ *He tells the story in the first person.* N-SING: *the* N

**first-rate** also **first rate.** If you say that something or someone is **first-rate**, you mean that they are extremely good and of the highest quality. ❑ *People who used his service knew they were dealing with a first-rate professional.* ADJ [approval] = *first-class*

**first school** **(first schools)** A **first school** is a school for children aged between five and eight or nine. [BRIT] N-COUNT

**First Sec|re|tary** **(First Secretaries)** The **First Secretary** of the Welsh Assembly is the leader of the ruling party. N-COUNT: usu *the* N; N-TITLE; N-VOC

**first-timer** **(first-timers)** A **first-timer** is someone who does something for the first time. ❑ *Gabrielle entered this year's charts faster than any first-timer before her.* N-COUNT

**First World** The most prosperous and industrialized parts of the world are sometimes referred to as **the First World**. Compare **Third World**. [BUSINESS] ❑ *Although South Africa has many of the attributes of the first world - some good infrastructure, millions of rich people - it is still not part of that world. ...wealthy First World countries.* N-PROPER: *the* N, N n

**First World War** **The First World War** or **the First War** is the war that was fought between 1914 and 1918 in Europe. N-PROPER: *the* N

**fir tree** **(fir trees)** A **fir tree** is the same as a **fir**. N-COUNT

**fis|cal** /fɪskəl/ **Fiscal** is used to describe something that relates to government money or public money, especially taxes. ❑ *...in 1987, when the government tightened fiscal policy.* ◆◇◇ ADJ: ADJ n = *financial* ♦ **fis|cal|ly** *The scheme would be fiscally dangerous... Many members are determined to prove that they are fiscally responsible.* ADV: usu ADV adj, also ADV after v → See also **procurator fiscal**.

**fis|cal year** **(fiscal years)** The **fiscal year** is the same as the **financial year**. [BUSINESS] ❑ *...the budget for the coming fiscal year.* N-COUNT: usu sing, usu with supp

**fish** /fɪʃ/ **(fish** or **fishes, fishes, fishing, fished)** ◆◆◇

The form **fish** is usually used for the plural, but **fishes** can also be used.

1 A **fish** is a creature that lives in water and has a tail and fins. There are many different kinds of fish. ❑ *I was chatting to an islander who had just caught a fish... The fish were counted and an average weight recorded.* N-COUNT 2 **Fish** is the flesh of a fish eaten as food. ❑ *Does dry white wine go best with fish?* N-UNCOUNT 3 If you **fish**, you try to catch fish, either for food or as a form of sport or recreation. ❑ *Brian remembers learning to fish in the River Cam.* VERB V 4 If you **fish** a particular area of water, you try to catch fish in it. ❑ *On Saturday we fished the River Arno.* VERB V n 5 If you say that someone is **fishing for** information or praise, you disapprove of the fact that they are trying to get it from someone in an indirect way. ❑ *He didn't want to create the impression that he was fishing for information... 'Lucinda, you don't have to talk to him!' Mike shouted. 'He's just fishing.'* VERB [disapproval] = *angle* V *for* n V 6 → See also **fishing**. 7 If you tell someone that **there are plenty more fish in the sea**, you are comforting them by saying that although their relationship with someone has failed, there are many other people they can have relationships with. [INFORMAL] PHRASE

♦ **fish out** If you **fish** something **out** from somewhere, you take or pull it out, often after searching for it for some time. [INFORMAL] ❑ *She fished out a pair of David's socks for her cold feet.* PHRASAL VERB V P n (not pron) Also V n P

**fish and chip shop** **(fish and chip shops)** In Britain, a **fish and chip shop** is a shop which sells hot food such as fish and chips, fried chicken, sausages, and meat pies. The food is cooked in the shop and people take it away to eat at home or in the street. N-COUNT = *chippy*

**fish cake** **(fish cakes)** also **fishcake.** A **fish cake** is a mixture of fish and potato that is made into a flat round shape, covered in breadcrumbs, and fried. N-COUNT

**fisher|man** /fɪʃəʳmən/ **(fishermen)** A **fisherman** is a person who catches fish as a job or for sport. N-COUNT

**fish|ery** /fɪʃəri/ **(fisheries)** 1 **Fisheries** are areas of the sea where fish are caught in large quantities for commercial purposes. ❑ *...the fisheries off Newfoundland.* N-COUNT: usu pl 2 A **fishery** is a place where fish are bred and reared. N-COUNT

**fish fin|ger** **(fish fingers)** also **fishfinger.** **Fish fingers** are small long pieces of fish covered in breadcrumbs. They are usually sold in frozen form. [mainly BRIT] N-COUNT: usu pl

**fish|ing** /fɪʃɪŋ/ **Fishing** is the sport, hobby, or business of catching fish. ❑ *Despite the poor weather the fishing has been pretty good. ...a fishing boat.* ◆◇◇ N-UNCOUNT

**fish|ing rod** **(fishing rods)** also **fishing-rod.** A **fishing rod** is a long thin pole which has a line N-COUNT and hook attached to it and which is used for catching fish.

**fish|ing tack|le** also **fishing-tackle.** N-UNCOUNT **Fishing tackle** consists of all the equipment that is used in the sport of fishing, such as fishing rods, lines, hooks, and bait.

**fish knife** **(fish knives)** N-COUNT A **fish knife** is a knife that you use when you eat fish. It has a wide flat blade and does not have a sharp edge.

**fish|monger** /fɪʃmʌŋgəʳ/ **(fishmongers)** 1 N-COUNT A **fishmonger** is a shopkeeper who sells fish. [mainly BRIT] 2 N-COUNT: oft *the* N **The fishmonger** or **the fishmonger's** is a shop where fish is sold. [mainly BRIT] ❑ *Purchase your oysters from a reputable fishmonger.*

**fish|net** /fɪʃnet/ N-UNCOUNT: usu N n **Fishnet** tights or stockings are made from a stretchy fabric which has wide holes between its threads, rather like the holes in a fishing net.

**fish slice** **(fish slices)** also **fish-slice.** N-COUNT A **fish slice** is a kitchen tool which consists of a flat part with narrow holes in it attached to a handle. It is used for turning or serving fish or other food that is cooked in a frying pan. [BRIT] ➔ See picture on page 1710.

☑ in AM, use **spatula**

**fish|wife** /fɪʃwaɪf/ **(fishwives)** N-COUNT [disapproval] If you say that someone is behaving like a **fishwife**, you mean that they are shouting a great deal and behaving in a very unpleasant and bad-tempered way. [mainly BRIT]

**fishy** /fɪʃi/ 1 ADJ A **fishy** taste or smell reminds you of fish. 2 ADJ = *suspicious* If you describe a situation as **fishy**, you feel that someone is not telling the truth or behaving completely honestly. [INFORMAL] ❑ *There seems to be something fishy going on.*

**fis|sion** /fɪʃᵊn/ N-UNCOUNT Nuclear **fission** is the splitting of the nucleus of an atom to produce a large amount of energy or cause a large explosion.

**fis|sure** /fɪʃəʳ/ **(fissures)** N-COUNT A **fissure** is a deep crack in something, especially in rock or in the ground.

**fist** /fɪst/ **(fists)** N-COUNT Your hand is referred to as your **fist** when you have bent your fingers in towards the palm in order to hit someone, to make an angry gesture, or to hold something. ❑ *Angry protestors with clenched fists shouted their defiance... Gary clutched a penny in his fist.*

**fist|ful** /fɪstfʊl/ **(fistfuls)** N-COUNT: usu N *of* n A **fistful of** things is the number of them that you can hold in your fist. ❑ *Mandy handed him a fistful of coins.*

**fisti|cuffs** /fɪstikʌfs/ N-UNCOUNT **Fisticuffs** is fighting in which people try to hit each other with their fists. [HUMOROUS or OLD-FASHIONED]

**fit**

① BEING RIGHT OR GOING IN THE RIGHT PLACE
② HEALTHY
③ UNCONTROLLABLE MOVEMENTS OR EMOTIONS

**① fit** /fɪt/ **(fits, fitting, fitted)** ◆◆◇

☑ In American English the form **fit** is used in the present tense and sometimes also as the past tense and past participle of the verb.

⇛ Please look at category 13 to see if the expression you are looking for is shown under another headword. 1 VERB If something **fits**, it is the right size and shape to go onto a person's body or onto a particular object. ❑ *The sash, kimono, and other garments were made to fit a child...* (V n) *She has to go to the men's department to find trousers that fit at the waist...* (V prep/adv) *Line a tin with lightly-greased greaseproof paper, making sure the corners fit well.* (V prep/adv) 2 N-SING: adj N If something is a good **fit**, it fits well. ❑ *Eventually he was happy that the sills and doors were a reasonably good fit.* 3 VERB: usu passive If you **are fitted for** a particular piece of clothing, you try it on so that the person who is making it can see where it needs to be altered. ❑ *She was being fitted for her wedding dress.* (be V-ed *for* n) 4 VERB If something **fits** somewhere, it can be put there or is designed to be put there. ❑ *...a pocket computer which is small enough to fit into your pocket...* (V prep/adv) *He folded his long legs to fit under the table.* (V prep/adv) 5 VERB If you **fit** something into a particular space or place, you put it there. ❑ *She fitted her key in the lock...* (V n prep/adv) *When the crown has been made you go back and the dentist will fit it into place.* (V n prep/adv) 6 VERB If you **fit** something somewhere, you attach it there, or put it there carefully and securely. ❑ *Fit hinge bolts to give extra support to the door lock...* (V n) *Peter had built the overhead ladders, and the next day he fitted them to the wall.* (V n prep) 7 VERB If something **fits** something else or **fits** into it, it goes together well with that thing or is able to be part of it. ❑ *Her daughter doesn't fit the current feminine ideal...* (V n) *Fostering is a full-time job and you should carefully consider how it will fit into your career...* (V *in/into* n) *There's something about the way he talks of her that doesn't fit.* (V) 8 VERB = *match* You can say that something **fits** a particular person or thing when it is appropriate or suitable for them or it. ❑ *The punishment must always fit the crime.* (V n) 9 ADJ: oft ADJ *for* n, ADJ to-inf, ADJ n to-inf, ADJ n *for* n If something is **fit** for a particular purpose, it is suitable for that purpose. ❑ *Of the seven bicycles we had, only two were fit for the road. ...safety measures intended to reassure consumers that the meat is fit to eat.* 10 ADJ: oft ADJ to-inf, ADJ *for* n, ADJ n *for* n, ADJ n to-inf If someone is **fit** to do something, they have the appropriate qualities or skills that will allow them to do it. ❑ *You're not fit to be a mother!... He was not a fit companion for their skipper.* ♦ **fit|ness** N-UNCOUNT: N *for* n, N to-inf *There is a debate about his fitness for the highest office.* 11 VERB If something **fits** someone for a particular task or role, it makes them good enough or suitable for it. [FORMAL] ❑ *...a man whose past experience fits him for the top job in education...* (V n *for* n) *It is not a person's gender that fits them to be a vicar but what is in their hearts.* (V n to-inf) 12 PHRASE: V inflects [disapproval] If you say that someone **sees fit to** do something, you mean that they are entitled to do it, but that you disapprove of their decision to do it. [FORMAL] ❑ *He's not a friend, yet you saw fit to lend him money.* 13 ➔ See also **fitted**, **fitting**. **fit the bill** ➔ see **bill**. to **fit like a glove** ➔ see **glove**. **not in a fit state** ➔ see **state**.

♦ **fit in** 1 PHRASAL VERB If you manage to **fit** a person or task **in**, you manage to find time to deal with them. ❑ *We work long hours both outside and inside the home and we rush around trying to fit everything in...* (V n P) *I find that I just can't fit in regular domestic work.* (V P n (not pron)) 2 PHRASAL VERB If you **fit in** as part of a group, you seem to belong there because you are similar to the other people in it. ❑ *She was great with the children and fitted in beautifully.* (V P) 3 PHRASAL VERB If you say that someone or something **fits in**, you understand how they form part of a particular situation or system. ❑ *He knew where I fitted in and what he had to do to get the best out of me...* (V P) *This fits in with what you've told me.* (V P *with* n)

♦ **fit into** 1 PHRASAL VERB If you **fit into** a particular group, you seem to belong there because you are similar to the other people in it. ❑ *It's hard to see how he would fit into the team.* (V P n (not pron)) 2 PHRASAL VERB If something **fits into** a particular situation or system, that seems to be the right place for it. ❑ *Most film locations broadly fit into two categories; those on private property and those in a public place.* (V P n)

♦ **fit out**

☑ in BRIT, also use **fit up**

PHRASAL VERB = *kit out* If you **fit** someone or something **out**, or you **fit** them **up**, you provide them with equipment and other things that they need. ❑ *We helped to fit him out for a trip to the Baltic...* (V n P *for* n) *They spent 18 million pounds fitting out the London headquarters.* (V P n (not pron), Also V n P)

♦ **fit up** 1 PHRASAL VERB = *frame* If someone **fits** another person **up**, they try to make it seem that that person is responsible for a crime. [BRIT, INFORMAL] ❑ *Mr Stone said inmates who had given evidence were trying to 'fit him up'...* (V n P) *There can never be any legitimate basis for police officers to fit up suspects they 'know' to be guilty.* (V P n (not pron)) 2 ➔ See also **fit out**.

**② fit** /fɪt/ **(fitter, fittest)** ◆◇◇

⇛ Please look at category 2 to see if the expression

you are looking for is shown under another headword. [1] Someone who is **fit** is healthy and physically strong. ❑ *An averagely fit person can master easy ski runs within a few days.* ♦ **fit|ness** *Squash was once thought to offer all-round fitness.* [2] **fit as a fiddle** → see **fiddle**. **fighting fit** → see **fight**.
ADJ ≠unfit
N-UNCOUNT: oft N n

**③fit** /fɪt/ **(fits)** [1] If someone has a **fit** they suddenly lose consciousness and their body makes uncontrollable movements. ❑ *About two in every five epileptic fits occur during sleep.* [2] If you have a **fit of** coughing or laughter, you suddenly start coughing or laughing in an uncontrollable way. ❑ *Halfway down the cigarette she had a fit of coughing.* [3] If you do something in a **fit of** anger or panic, you are very angry or afraid when you do it. ❑ *Pattie shot Tom in a fit of jealous rage.* [4] If you say that someone will **have a fit** when they hear about something, you mean that they will be very angry or shocked. [INFORMAL] ❑ *He'd have a fit if he knew what we were up to!* [5] Something that happens **in fits and starts** or **by fits and starts** keeps happening and then stopping again. ❑ *My slimming attempts tend to go in fits and starts... Military technology advances by fits and starts.*
N-COUNT = seizure
N-COUNT: with supp, N *of* n
N-COUNT: N *of* n
PHRASE: V inflects = go mad
PHRASE: PHR after v

**fit|ful** /fɪtfʊl/ Something that is **fitful** happens for irregular periods of time or occurs at irregular times, rather than being continuous. ❑ *Colin drifted off into a fitful sleep.*
ADJ ≠continuous

**fit|ted** /fɪtɪd/ [1] A **fitted** piece of clothing is designed so that it is the same size and shape as your body rather than being loose. ❑ *...baggy trousers with fitted jackets.* [2] A **fitted** piece of furniture, for example a cupboard, is designed to fill a particular space and is fixed in place. ❑ *I've re-carpeted our bedroom and added fitted wardrobes.* [3] A **fitted** carpet is cut to the same shape as a room so that it covers the floor completely. ❑ *...fitted carpets, central heating and double glazing.* [4] A **fitted** sheet has the corners sewn so that they fit over the corners of the mattress and do not have to be folded.
ADJ: usu ADJ n
ADJ: usu ADJ n
ADJ: ADJ n
ADJ: ADJ n

**fit|ter** /fɪtəʳ/ **(fitters)** A **fitter** is a person whose job is to put together, adjust, or install machinery or equipment. ❑ *George was a fitter at the shipyard.*
N-COUNT

**fit|ting** /fɪtɪŋ/ **(fittings)** [1] A **fitting** is one of the smaller parts on the outside of a piece of equipment or furniture, for example a handle or a tap. ❑ *...brass light fittings. ...industrial fittings for kitchen and bathroom.* [2] **Fittings** are things such as ovens or heaters, that are fitted inside a building, but can be removed if necessary. [3] Something that is **fitting** is right or suitable. ❑ *A solitary man, it was perhaps fitting that he should have died alone.* ♦ **fit|ting|ly** *...the four-storeyed, and fittingly named, High House.* [4] If someone has a **fitting**, they try on a piece of clothing that is being made for them to see if it fits. ❑ *She lunched and shopped and went for fittings for clothes she didn't need.*
N-COUNT: usu with supp
N-PLURAL
ADJ = appropriate
ADV: ADV adj, ADV before v, ADV with cl
N-COUNT

**-fitting** /-fɪtɪŋ/ **-fitting** combines with adjectives or adverbs such as 'close', 'loose', or 'tightly' to show that something is the size indicated in relation to the thing it is on, in, or next to. ❑ *...loose-fitting night clothes. ...glass bottles with tight-fitting caps.*
COMB in ADJ

**five** /faɪv/ **(fives)** [1] **Five** is the number 5. ❑ *Eric Edward Bullus was born in Peterborough, the second of five children.* [2] → See also **high five**.
◆◆◆ NUM

**fiv|er** /faɪvəʳ/ **(fivers)** [1] A **fiver** is a five pound note. [BRIT, INFORMAL] [2] A **fiver** is a five dollar bill. [AM, INFORMAL]
N-COUNT
N-COUNT

**fix** /fɪks/ **(fixes, fixing, fixed)** [1] If something **is fixed** somewhere, it is attached there firmly or securely. ❑ *It is fixed on the wall... He fixed a bayonet to the end of his rifle.* [2] If you **fix** something, for example a date, price, or policy, you decide and say exactly what it will be. ❑ *He's going to fix a time when I can see him... The prices of milk and cereals, are fixed annually.* [3] If you **fix** something for someone, you arrange for it to happen or you organize it for them. ❑ *I've fixed it for you to see Bonnie Lachlan... It's fixed. He's going to meet us at the airport... They thought that their relatives would be able to fix the visas... He vanished after you fixed him with a job... We fixed for the team to visit our headquarters... They'd fixed yesterday that Mike'd be in late today.* [4] If you **fix** something which is damaged or which does not work properly, you repair it. ❑ *He cannot fix the electricity... If something is broken, we get it fixed.* [5] If you **fix** a problem or a bad situation, you deal with it and make it satisfactory. ❑ *It's not too late to fix the problem, although time is clearly getting short... Fixing a 40-year-old wrong does not mean, however, that history can be undone.* [6] You can refer to a solution to a problem as a **fix**. [INFORMAL] ❑ *Many of those changes could just be a temporary fix.* → See also **quick fix**. [7] If you **fix** your eyes **on** someone or something or if your eyes **fix on** them, you look at them with complete attention. ❑ *She fixes her steel-blue eyes on an unsuspecting local official... Her soft brown eyes fixed on Kelly... The child kept her eyes fixed on the wall behind him.* [8] If someone or something **is fixed in** your mind, you remember them well, for example because they are very important, interesting, or unusual. ❑ *Leonard was now fixed in his mind... Amy watched the child's intent face eagerly, trying to fix it in her mind.* [9] If someone **fixes** a gun, camera, or radar **on** something, they point it at that thing. ❑ *The US crew fixed its radar on the Turkish ship.* [10] If you get **a fix on** someone or something, you have a clear idea or understanding of them. [INFORMAL] ❑ *It's been hard to get a steady fix on what's going on.* [11] If you **fix** some food or a drink for someone, you make it or prepare it for them. ❑ *Sarah fixed some food for us... Let me fix you a drink... Scotty stayed behind to fix lunch.* [12] If you **fix** your hair, clothes, or make-up, you arrange or adjust them so you look neat and tidy, showing you have taken care with your appearance. [INFORMAL] ❑ *'I've got to fix my hair,' I said and retreated to my bedroom.* [13] If someone **fixes** a race, election, contest, or other event, they make unfair or illegal arrangements or use deception to affect the result. ❑ *They offered opposing players bribes to fix a decisive league match against Valenciennes. ...this week's report of match-fixing.* ♦ **Fix** is also a noun. ❑ *It's all a fix, a deal they've made.* [14] If you accuse someone of **fixing** prices, you accuse them of making unfair arrangements to charge a particular price for something, rather than allowing market forces to decide it. [BUSINESS] ❑ *...a suspected cartel that had fixed the price of steel for the construction market... The company is currently in dispute with the government over price fixing.* [15] An injection of an addictive drug such as heroin can be referred to as a **fix**. [INFORMAL] [16] You can use **fix** to refer to an amount of something which a person gets or wants and which helps them physically or psychologically to survive. [INFORMAL] ❑ *The trouble with her is she needs her daily fix of publicity. ...a quick energy fix.* [17] If you say that you **are fixing to** do something, you mean that you are planning or intending to do it. [AM, INFORMAL] ❑ *I'm fixing to go to graduate school.* [18] → See also **fixed**, **fixings**.
◆◇◇ VERB = fasten
*be* V-ed prep/adv
V n prep/adv
VERB = set
V n
V n
VERB
V *it for* n to-inf
*be* V-ed
V n
V n *with* n
V *for* n to-inf
V that
VERB = mend
V n, *get/have* n V-ed
VERB
V n
V-ing
N-COUNT: usu adj N
VERB
V n *on* n
V *on* n
V-ed
VERB
*be* V-ed *in* n
V n *in* n
VERB
V n *on* n
N-SING: *a* N *on* n
VERB
V n *for* n
V n n
V n
VERB: no passive
V n
VERB disapproval = rig
V n
V-ing
N-COUNT
VERB disapproval
V n
V-ing
N-COUNT
N-COUNT: with supp, oft N *of* n, n N
VERB: only cont
V to-inf

♦ **fix on** If you **fix on** a particular thing, you decide that it is the one you want and will have. ❑ *The Vietnamese government has fixed on May 19th to celebrate his anniversary.*
PHRASAL VERB
V P n

♦ **fix up** [1] If you **fix** something **up**, you arrange it. ❑ *I fixed up an appointment to see her.* [2] If you **fix** something **up**, you do work that is necessary in order to make it more suitable or attractive. ❑ *I've fixed up Matthew's old room.* [3] If you **fix** someone **up with** something they need, you provide it for them. ❑ *He was fixed up with a job.*
PHRASAL VERB
V P n
Also V n P
PHRASAL VERB = do up
V P n
Also V n P
PHRASAL VERB
V n P *with* n
Also V n P

**fix|at|ed** /fɪkseɪtɪd, fɪkseɪtɪd/ If you accuse someone of being **fixated on** a particular thing,
ADJ: v-link ADJ *on/with/by* n

you mean that they think about it to an extreme and excessive degree. ❑ *But by then the administration wasn't paying attention, for top officials were fixated on Kuwait.*

**fixa|tion** /fɪkseɪʃᵊn/ **(fixations)** If you accuse a person of having **a fixation on** something or someone, you mean they think about a particular subject or person to an extreme and excessive degree. ❑ *The country's fixation on the war may delay a serious examination of domestic needs.* N-COUNT: usu sing, usu with supp

**fixa|tive** /fɪksətɪv/ **(fixatives)** **Fixative** is a liquid used to preserve the surface of things such as a drawings or photographs. N-MASS

**fixed** /fɪkst/ ◆◇◇ [1] You use **fixed** to describe something which stays the same and does not or cannot vary. ❑ *They issue a fixed number of shares that trade publicly... Tickets will be printed with fixed entry times... Many restaurants offer fixed-price menus.* ADJ: usu ADJ n = set [2] If you say that someone has **fixed** ideas or opinions, you mean that they do not often change their ideas and opinions, although perhaps they should. ❑ *...people who have fixed ideas about things.* ADJ: usu ADJ n ≠ flexible [3] If someone has a **fixed** smile on their face, they are smiling even though they do not feel happy or pleased. ❑ *I had to go through the rest of the evening with a fixed smile on my face.* ADJ [4] Someone who is of **no fixed address**, or in British English **no fixed abode**, does not have a permanent place to live. [FORMAL] ❑ *They are not able to get a job interview because they have no fixed address... He's of no fixed abode and we found him on the streets.* PHRASE: of/with PHR, v PHR [5] ➔ See also **fix**.

**fixed as|set** **(fixed assets)** **Fixed assets** are assets which a company uses on a continuous basis, such as property and machinery. [BUSINESS] ❑ *Investment in fixed assets is an important vehicle for ensuring that the latest technology is available to business.* N-COUNT

**fix|ed|ly** /fɪksɪdli/ If you stare **fixedly** at someone or something, you look at them steadily and continuously for a period of time. [LITERARY] ❑ *I stared fixedly at the statue.* ADV: ADV after v = intently

**fix|er** /fɪksəʳ/ **(fixers)** If someone is a **fixer**, he or she is the sort of person who solves problems and gets things done. [JOURNALISM] ❑ *John Wakeham seems certain to become the fixer the Prime Minister will need at election time.* N-COUNT

**fix|ings** /fɪksɪŋz/ [1] **Fixings** are extra items that are used to decorate or complete something, especially a meal. [AM] ❑ *He bought a hot dog and had it covered with all the fixings.* N-PLURAL [2] **Fixings** are items such as nails and screws which are used to fix things such as furniture together. ❑ *Have you got all the screws and fixings you need?* N-PLURAL

**fix|ity** /fɪksɪti/ If you talk about the **fixity of** something, you talk about the fact that it does not change or weaken. [WRITTEN] ❑ *She believed in the fixity of the class system.* N-UNCOUNT: oft N of n

**fix|ture** /fɪkstʃəʳ/ **(fixtures)** [1] **Fixtures** are pieces of furniture or equipment, for example baths and sinks, which are fixed inside a house or other building and which stay there if you move. ❑ *...a detailed list of what fixtures and fittings are included in the purchase price.* N-COUNT: usu pl [2] A **fixture** is a sports event which takes place on a particular date. [BRIT] ❑ *City won this fixture 3-0 last season.* N-COUNT [3] If you describe someone or something as **a fixture in** a particular place or occasion, you mean that they always seem to be there. ❑ *She was a fixture in New York's nightclubs... The cordless kettle may now be a fixture in most kitchens.* N-COUNT: usu N in n

**fizz** /fɪz/ **(fizzes, fizzing, fizzed)** [1] If a drink **fizzes**, it produces lots of little bubbles of gas and makes a sound like a long 's'. ❑ *After a while their mother was back, holding a tray of glasses that fizzed.* VERB V ♦ **Fizz** is also a noun. ❑ *I wonder if there's any fizz left in the lemonade.* N-UNCOUNT [2] If something such as an engine **fizzes**, it makes a sound like a long 's'. ❑ *When I started the engine it sparked, fizzed and went dead.* VERB V [3] If you say that someone puts **fizz** into something, you mean that they make it more interesting or exciting. ❑ *A Brazilian public relations firm has brought some fizz into his campaign.* N-UNCOUNT = sparkle

**fiz|zle** /fɪzᵊl/ **(fizzles, fizzling, fizzled)** If something **fizzles**, it ends in a weak or disappointing way after starting off strongly. ❑ *Our relationship fizzled into nothing.* ♦ **Fizzle out** means the same as **fizzle**. ❑ *The railway strike fizzled out on its second day as drivers returned to work.* VERB V into/to n Also V PHRASAL VERB = peter out V P

**fizzy** /fɪzi/ **(fizzier, fizziest)** **Fizzy** drinks are drinks that contain small bubbles of carbon dioxide. They make a sound like a long 's' when you pour them. [BRIT] ❑ *...fizzy water. ...a can of fizzy drink.* ADJ: usu ADJ n

✓ in AM, use **carbonated**

**fjord** /fjɔːʳd, fiːɔːʳd/ **(fjords)** also **fiord.** A **fjord** is a strip of sea that comes into the land between high cliffs, especially in Norway. N-COUNT: oft in names after n

**flab** /flæb/ If you say that someone has **flab**, you mean they have loose flesh on their body because they are rather fat, especially when you are being critical of them. ❑ *Don had a hefty roll of flab overhanging his waistband.* N-UNCOUNT [disapproval]

**flab|ber|gast|ed** /flæbəʳgɑːstɪd, -gæst-/ If you say that you are **flabbergasted**, you are emphasizing that you are extremely surprised. ❑ *Everybody was flabbergasted when I announced I was going to emigrate to Australia.* ADJ: usu v-link ADJ, oft ADJ by n, ADJ to-inf [emphasis]

**flab|by** /flæbi/ **(flabbier, flabbiest)** [1] **Flabby** people are rather fat, with loose flesh over their bodies. ❑ *This exercise is brilliant for getting rid of flabby tums.* ADJ [disapproval] [2] If you describe something as **flabby**, you are criticizing it for being disorganized or wasteful. ❑ *You hear talk about American business being flabby.* ADJ [disapproval] ≠ lean

**flac|cid** /flæsɪd, flæksɪd/ You use **flaccid** to describe a part of someone's body when it is unpleasantly soft and not hard or firm. ❑ *I picked up her wrist. It was limp and flaccid.* ADJ = limp

**flag** /flæg/ **(flags, flagging, flagged)** ◆◇◇ [1] A **flag** is a piece of cloth which can be attached to a pole and which is used as a sign, signal, or symbol of something, especially of a particular country. ❑ *The Marines climbed to the roof of the embassy building to raise the American flag... They had raised the white flag in surrender.* N-COUNT [2] Journalists sometimes refer to the **flag** of a particular country or organization as a way of referring to the country or organization itself and its values or power. ❑ *Joining John Whitaker will be his brother Michael also riding under the British flag.* N-COUNT: with supp, usu adj N, N of n [3] If you **flag** or if your spirits **flag**, you begin to lose enthusiasm or energy. ❑ *His enthusiasm was in no way flagging... By 4,000m he was beginning to flag.* VERB V V [4] ➔ See also **flagged**. [5] If you **fly the flag**, you show that you are proud of your country, or that you support a particular cause, especially when you are in a foreign country or when few other people do. PHRASE: V inflects

♦ **flag down** If you **flag down** a vehicle, especially a taxi, you wave at it as a signal for the driver to stop. ❑ *They flagged down a passing family who stopped to help them... Marlette was already out of the door, flagging down a taxi.* PHRASAL VERB = hail V P n (not pron) V n P

**flag day** **(flag days)** In Britain, a **flag day** is a day on which people collect money for a charity from people in the street. They are given a small sticker to wear to show that they have given money. N-COUNT

**Flag Day** In the United States, **Flag Day** is the 14th of June, the anniversary of the day in 1777 when the Stars and Stripes became the official U.S. flag. N-UNCOUNT

**flag|el|la|tion** /flædʒəleɪʃᵊn/ **Flagellation** is the act of beating yourself or someone else, usually as a religious punishment. [FORMAL] N-UNCOUNT

**flagged** /flægd/ A **flagged** path or area of ground is covered with large, flat, square pieces of stone. ADJ

**flag|on** /flægən/ **(flagons)** 1 A **flagon** is a wide bottle in which liquids such as wine are sold. N-COUNT
2 A **flagon** is a jug with a narrow neck in which wine or another drink is served. N-COUNT

**flag|pole** /flægpoʊl/ **(flagpoles)** A **flagpole** is a tall pole on which a flag can be displayed. ❑ *The new Namibian flag was hoisted up the flagpole.* N-COUNT

**fla|grant** /fleɪgrənt/ You can use **flagrant** to describe an action, situation, or someone's behaviour that you find extremely bad or shocking in a very obvious way. ❑ *The judge called the decision 'a flagrant violation of international law'.* ADJ: ADJ n [disapproval] = blatant
♦ **fla|grant|ly** *It is a situation where basic human rights are being flagrantly abused.* ADV: usu ADV with v, also ADV adj

**flag|ship** /flægʃɪp/ **(flagships)** 1 A **flagship** is the most important ship in a fleet of ships, especially the one on which the commander of the fleet is sailing. N-COUNT 2 The **flagship** of a group of things that are owned or produced by a particular organization is the most important one. ❑ *The company plans to open a flagship store in New York this month.* N-COUNT: oft with poss

**flag|staff** /flægstɑːf, -stæf/ **(flagstaffs)** A **flagstaff** is the same as a **flagpole**. N-COUNT

**flag|stone** /flægstoʊn/ **(flagstones)** **Flagstones** are large, flat, square pieces of stone which are used for covering a path or area of ground. N-COUNT: usu pl

**flag-waving** You can use **flag-waving** to refer to the expression of feelings for a country in a loud or exaggerated way, especially when you disapprove of this. ❑ *The real costs of the war have been ignored in the flag-waving of recent months.* N-UNCOUNT [disapproval]

**flail** /fleɪl/ **(flails, flailing, flailed)** If your arms or legs **flail** or if you **flail** them about, they wave about in an energetic but uncontrolled way. ❑ *His arms were flailing in all directions... He gave a choked cry, flailed his arms wildly for a moment, and then went over the edge.* VERB V, V n ♦ **Flail around** means the same as **flail**. ❑ *He starting flailing around and hitting Vincent in the chest.* PHRASAL VERB V P

**flair** /fleəʳ/ 1 If you have **a flair for** a particular thing, you have a natural ability to do it well. ❑ *...a friend who has a flair for languages.* N-SING: N *for* n = talent, gift 2 If you have **flair**, you do things in an original, interesting, and stylish way. ❑ *Their work has all the usual punch, panache and flair you'd expect.* N-UNCOUNT [approval] = style, panache

**flak** /flæk/ If you get a lot of **flak** from someone, they criticize you severely. If you take the **flak**, you get the blame for something. [INFORMAL] ❑ *The President is getting a lot of flak for that.* N-UNCOUNT

**flake** /fleɪk/ **(flakes, flaking, flaked)** 1 A **flake** is a small thin piece of something, especially one that has broken off a larger piece. ❑ *Large flakes of snow began swiftly to fall. ...oat flakes.* N-COUNT: usu with supp, oft N *of* n, n N 2 If something such as paint **flakes**, small thin pieces of it come off. ❑ *They can see how its colours have faded and where paint has flaked.* VERB V ♦ **Flake off** means the same as **flake**. ❑ *The surface corrosion was worst where the paint had flaked off.* PHRASAL VERB V P

**flak jack|et** **(flak jackets)** A **flak jacket** is a thick sleeveless jacket that soldiers and policemen sometimes wear to protect themselves against bullets. N-COUNT

**flaky** /fleɪki/ 1 Something that is **flaky** breaks easily into small thin pieces or tends to come off in small thin pieces. ❑ *...a small patch of red, flaky skin.* ADJ 2 If you describe an idea, argument, or person as **flaky**, you mean that they are rather eccentric and unreliable. [INFORMAL] ❑ *He wondered if the idea wasn't just a little too flaky, a little too outlandish.* ADJ [disapproval]

**flam|boy|ant** /flæmbɔɪənt/ If you say that someone or something is **flamboyant**, you mean that they are very noticeable, stylish, and exciting. ❑ *Freddie Mercury was a flamboyant star of the British hard rock scene.* ADJ ♦ **flam|boy|ance** *Campese was his usual mixture of flamboyance and flair.* N-UNCOUNT

**flame** /fleɪm/ **(flames, flaming, flamed)** 1 A **flame** is a hot bright stream of burning gas that comes from something that is burning. ❑ *The heat from the flames was so intense that roads melted. ...a huge ball of flame.* N-VAR 2 A **flame** is an e-mail message which severely criticizes or attacks someone. [COMPUTING, INFORMAL] ❑ *The best way to respond to a flame is to ignore it.* N-COUNT ♦ **Flame** is also a verb. ❑ *Ever been flamed?* VERB V n 3 → See also **flaming**, **old flame**.
PHRASES 4 If something **bursts into flames** or **bursts into flame**, it suddenly starts burning strongly. ❑ *She managed to scramble out of the vehicle as it burst into flames.* PHRASE: V inflects 5 If someone or something **fans the flames** of a situation or feeling, usually a bad one, they make it more intense or extreme in some way. ❑ *He accused the Tories of 'fanning the flames of extremism'.* PHRASE: V inflects 6 If something **goes up in flames**, it starts to burn strongly and is destroyed. ❑ *Fires broke out everywhere, the entire city went up in flames.* PHRASE: V inflects 7 Something that is **in flames** is on fire. PHRASE: v-link PHR

**fla|men|co** /fləmeŋkoʊ/ **(flamencos)** **Flamenco** is a Spanish dance that is danced to a special type of guitar music. N-VAR

**flame|proof** /fleɪmpruːf/ also **flame-proof.** **Flameproof** cooking dishes can withstand direct heat, so they can be used, for example, on top of a cooker or stove, or under a grill. ADJ: usu ADJ n

**flame-retardant** **Flame-retardant** is the same as **fire-retardant**. ADJ

**flame-thrower** **(flame-throwers)** also **flame thrower.** A **flame-thrower** is a gun that can send out a stream of burning liquid and that is used as a weapon or for clearing plants from an area of ground. N-COUNT

**flam|ing** /fleɪmɪŋ/ 1 **Flaming** is used to describe something that is burning and producing a lot of flames. ❑ *The plane, which was full of fuel, scattered flaming fragments over a large area.* ADJ: usu ADJ n = blazing 2 Something that is **flaming** red or orange is bright red or orange in colour. ❑ *He has flaming red hair.* ADJ: ADJ n 3 A **flaming** row or a **flaming** temper, for example, is a very angry row or a very bad temper. ❑ *She has had a flaming row with her lover.* ADJ: ADJ n [emphasis]

**fla|min|go** /fləmɪŋgoʊ/ **(flamingos** or **flamingoes)** A **flamingo** is a bird with pink feathers, long thin legs, a long neck, and a curved beak. Flamingos live near water in warm countries. N-COUNT

**flam|mable** /flæməbᵊl/ **Flammable** chemicals, gases, cloth, or other things catch fire and burn easily. ❑ *...flammable liquids such as petrol or paraffin.* ADJ = inflammable

**flan** /flæn/ **(flans)** A **flan** is a food that has a base and sides of pastry or sponge cake. The base is filled with fruit or savoury food. N-VAR

**flange** /flændʒ/ **(flanges)** A **flange** is a projecting edge on an object. Its purpose is to strengthen the object or to connect it to another object. N-COUNT

**flank** /flæŋk/ **(flanks, flanking, flanked)** 1 An animal's **flank** is its side, between the ribs and the hip. ❑ *He put his hand on the dog's flank.* N-COUNT 2 A **flank** of an army or navy force is one side of it when it is organized for battle. ❑ *The assault element, led by Captain Ramirez, opened up from their right flank.* N-COUNT 3 The side of anything large can be referred to as its **flank**. ❑ *They continued along the flank of the mountain.* N-COUNT: usu N *of* n 4 If something **is flanked by** things, it has them on both sides of it, or sometimes on one side of it. ❑ *The altar was flanked by two Christmas trees... Bookcases flank the bed.* VERB *be* V-ed *by* n, V n

**flan|nel** /flænᵊl/ **(flannels)** 1 **Flannel** is a soft cloth, usually made of cotton or wool, that is used for making clothes. ❑ *He wore a faded red flannel shirt.* N-UNCOUNT: oft N n 2 A **flannel** is a small cloth that you use for washing yourself. [BRIT] N-COUNT

✓ in AM, use **washcloth**

**flap** /flæp/ **(flaps, flapping, flapped)** 1 If something such as a piece of cloth or paper **flaps** or if you **flap** it, it moves quickly up and down or from side to side. ❑ *Grey sheets flapped on the* VERB = flutter V *clothes line... They would flap bath towels from their balconies as they chatted.* V n [2] If a bird or insect **flaps** its wings or if its wings **flap**, the wings move quickly up and down. ❑ *The bird flapped its wings furiously... A pigeon emerges, wings flapping noisily, from the tower.* VERB V pl-n V [3] If you **flap** your arms, you move them quickly up and down as if they were the wings of a bird. ❑ *...a kid running and flapping her arms.* VERB V n [4] A **flap** of cloth or skin, for example, is a flat piece of it that can move freely up and down or from side to side because it is held or attached by only one edge. ❑ *He drew back the tent flap and strode out into the blizzard. ...a loose flap of skin.* N-COUNT: usu with supp [5] A **flap** on the wing of an aircraft is an area along the edge of the wing that can be raised or lowered to control the movement of the aircraft. ❑ *...the sudden slowing as the flaps were lowered.* N-COUNT

**flap|jack** /flæpdʒæk/ **(flapjacks)** [1] **Flapjacks** are thick biscuits made from oats, butter, and syrup. [BRIT] N-VAR [2] **Flapjacks** are thin, flat, circular pieces of cooked batter made of milk, flour, and eggs. Flapjacks are usually rolled up or folded and eaten hot with a sweet or savoury filling. [AM] N-COUNT = *pancake*

**flare** /fleəʳ/ **(flares, flaring, flared)** [1] A **flare** is a small device that produces a bright flame. Flares are used as signals, for example on ships. ❑ *...a ship which had fired a distress flare.* N-COUNT [2] If a fire **flares**, the flames suddenly become larger. ❑ *Camp fires flared like beacons in the dark.* VERB V ♦ **Flare up** means the same as **flare**. ❑ *Don't spill too much fat on the barbecue as it could flare up.* PHRASAL VERB V P [3] If something such as trouble, violence, or conflict **flares**, it starts or becomes more violent. ❑ *Even as the President appealed for calm, trouble flared in several American cities.* VERB V ♦ **Flare up** means the same as **flare**. ❑ *Dozens of people were injured as fighting flared up.* PHRASAL VERB V P [4] If people's tempers **flare**, they get angry. ❑ *Tempers flared and harsh words were exchanged.* VERB V [5] If someone's nostrils **flare** or if they **flare** them, their nostrils become wider, often because the person is angry or upset. ❑ *I turned to Jacky, my nostrils flaring in disgust... He stuck out his tongue and flared his nostrils.* VERB V V n [6] If something such as a dress **flares**, it spreads outwards at one end to form a wide shape. ❑ *...a simple black dress, cut to flare from the hips.* VERB V [7] **Flares** are trousers that are very wide at the bottom. N-PLURAL: also *a pair of* N [8] → See also **flared**.

♦ **flare up** If a disease or injury **flares up**, it suddenly returns or becomes painful again. ❑ *Students often find that their acne flares up before and during exams.* PHRASAL VERB V P → See also **flare 2, 3, flare-up**.

**flared** /fleəʳd/ **Flared** skirts or trousers are wider at the bottom or at the end of the legs than at the top. ❑ *In the 1970s they all had flared trousers.* ADJ: usu ADJ n

**flare-up** **(flare-ups)** If there is a **flare-up** of violence or of an illness, it suddenly starts or gets worse. ❑ *There's been a flare-up of violence in South Africa.* N-COUNT: usu *a* N *of/in* n

**flash** /flæʃ/ **(flashes, flashing, flashed)** ◆◇◇ [1] A **flash** is a sudden burst of light or of something shiny or bright. ❑ *A sudden flash of lightning lit everything up for a second... The wire snapped at the wall plug with a blue flash and the light fused... A jay emerged from the juniper bush in a flash of blue feathers.* N-COUNT: usu with supp [2] If a light **flashes** or if you **flash** a light, it shines with a sudden bright light, especially as quick, regular flashes of light. ❑ *Lightning flashed among the distant dark clouds... He lost his temper after a driver flashed her headlights as he overtook... He saw the flashing lights of the highway patrol car in his driving mirror.* VERB V V n V-ing [3] You talk about **a flash of** something when you are saying that it happens very suddenly and unexpectedly. ❑ *'What did Moira tell you?' Liz demanded with a flash of anger... The essays could do with a flash of wit or humor.* N-COUNT: with supp, N *of* n = *burst* [4] If something **flashes** past or by, it moves past you so fast that you cannot see it properly. ❑ *It was a busy road, cars flashed by every few minutes.* VERB V prep/adv [5] If something **flashes through** or **into** your mind, you suddenly think about it. ❑ *A ludicrous thought flashed through Harry's mind.* VERB V *through/into* n [6] If you **flash** something such as an identity card, you show it to people quickly and then put it away again. [INFORMAL] ❑ *Halim flashed his official card, and managed to get hold of a soldier to guard the Land Rover.* VERB V n [7] If a picture or message **flashes up on** a screen, or if you **flash** it **onto** a screen, it is displayed there briefly or suddenly, and often repeatedly. ❑ *The figures flash up on the scoreboard... The words 'Good Luck' were flashing on the screen... Researchers flash two groups of different letters onto a computer screen... The screen flashes a message: Try again... A list of items is repeatedly flashed up on the screen.* VERB V *up* V prep V n prep V n *be* V-ed *up* Also V n *up* [8] If you **flash** news or information to a place, you send it there quickly by computer, satellite, or other system. ❑ *They had told their offices to flash the news as soon as it broke... This is, of course, international news and soon it was being flashed around the world.* VERB V n *be* V-ed prep/adv Also V n prep/adv [9] If you **flash** a look or a smile at someone, you suddenly look at them or smile at them. [WRITTEN] ❑ *I flashed a look at Sue... Meg flashed Cissie a grateful smile.* VERB V n *at* n V n n [10] If someone's eyes **flash**, they suddenly show a strong emotion, especially anger. [LITERARY] ❑ *Her dark eyes flashed and she spoke rapidly.* VERB V [11] **Flash** is the use of special bulbs to give more light when taking a photograph. ❑ *He was one of the first people to use high speed flash in bird photography.* N-UNCOUNT: oft N n [12] A **flash** is the same as a **flashlight**. [AM, INFORMAL] ❑ *Stopping to rest, Pete shut off the flash.* N-COUNT [13] If you describe something as **flash**, you mean that it looks expensive, fashionable, and new. [INFORMAL] ❑ *...a flash uptown restaurant... You can go for a 'rostrum' system, which sounds flash, but can be assembled quite cheaply.* ADJ

PHRASES [14] If you describe an achievement or success as **a flash in the pan**, you mean that it is unlikely to be repeated and is not an indication of future achievements or success. ❑ *People will be looking in to see how good we are now and whether our success has just been a flash in the pan.* PHRASE: usu v-link PHR disapproval = *one-off* [15] If you say that something happens **in a flash**, you mean that it happens suddenly and lasts only a very short time. ❑ *The answer had come to him in a flash... It was done in a flash.* PHRASE: usu PHR after v [16] If you say that someone reacts to something **quick as a flash**, you mean that they react to it extremely quickly. ❑ *Quick as a flash, the man said, 'I have to, don't I?'* PHRASE

♦ **flash back** If your mind **flashes back** to something in the past, you remember it or think of it briefly or suddenly. ❑ *His mind kept flashing back to the previous night.* PHRASAL VERB V P *to* n → See also **flashback**.

**flash|back** /flæʃbæk/ **(flashbacks)** [1] In a film, novel, or play, a **flashback** is a scene that returns to events in the past. ❑ *There is even a flashback to the murder itself.* N-COUNT: oft N *to* n [2] If you have a **flashback** to a past experience, you have a sudden and very clear memory of it. ❑ *He has recurring flashbacks to the night his friends died.* N-COUNT: oft N *to* n

**flash|bulb** /flæʃbʌlb/ **(flashbulbs)** also **flash bulb.** A **flashbulb** is a small bulb that can be fixed to a camera. It makes a bright flash of light so that you can take photographs indoors. N-COUNT

**flash card** **(flash cards)** also **flashcard. Flash cards** are cards which are sometimes used in the teaching of reading or a foreign language. Each card has words or a picture on it. N-COUNT

**flash|er** /flæʃəʳ/ **(flashers)** A **flasher** is a man who deliberately exposes his genitals to people in public places, especially in front of women. [INFORMAL] N-COUNT

**flash flood** **(flash floods)** A **flash flood** is a sudden rush of water over dry land, usually caused by a great deal of rain. N-COUNT

**flash|gun** /flæʃgʌn/ **(flashguns)** A **flashgun** is a device that you can attach to, or that is part of, a camera. It makes bright flashes of light so that you can take photographs indoors. N-COUNT

**flash|light** /flæʃlaɪt/ **(flashlights)** A **flashlight** is a small electric light which gets its power from batteries and which you can carry in your N-COUNT: also *by* N = *torch* hand. [mainly AM] ❑ *Len studied it a moment in the beam of his flashlight.*

☑ in BRIT, use **torch**

**flash|point** /flæʃpɔɪnt/ **(flashpoints)** 1 N-VAR A **flashpoint** is the moment at which a conflict, especially a political conflict, suddenly gets worse and becomes violent. ❑ *The immediate flashpoint was Wednesday's big rally in the city centre.* 2 N-COUNT A **flashpoint** is a place which people think is dangerous because political trouble may start there and then spread to other towns or countries. ❑ *The more serious flashpoints are outside the capital.*

**flashy** /flæʃi/ **(flashier, flashiest)** ADJ disapproval If you describe a person or thing as **flashy**, you mean they are smart and noticeable, but in a rather vulgar way. [INFORMAL] ❑ *He was much less flashy than his brother.*

**flask** /flɑːsk, flæsk/ **(flasks)** 1 N-COUNT A **flask** is a bottle which you use for carrying drinks around with you. ❑ *He took out a metal flask from a canvas bag.* ♦ N-COUNT: N *of* n A **flask** of liquid is the flask and the liquid which it contains. ❑ *There's some sandwiches here and a flask of coffee.* 2 N-COUNT A **flask** is a bottle or other container which is used in science laboratories and industry for holding liquids. ❑ *...flasks for the transport of spent fuel.* 3 → See also **hip flask, vacuum flask.**

**flat** /flæt/ **(flats, flatter, flattest)** ◆◆◇ 1 N-COUNT: also N num = apartment A **flat** is a set of rooms for living in, usually on one floor and part of a larger building. A flat usually includes a kitchen and bathroom. [mainly BRIT] ❑ *Sara lives with her husband and children in a flat in central London... It started a fire in a block of flats... Later on, Victor from flat 10 called.*

☑ in AM, usually use **apartment**

2 ADJ Something that is **flat** is level, smooth, or even, rather than sloping, curved, or uneven. ❑ *Tiles can be fixed to any surface as long as it's flat, firm and dry... After a moment his right hand moved across the cloth, smoothing it flat... The sea was calm, perfectly flat.* 3 ADJ: ADJ n, v-link ADJ, ADJ after v **Flat** means horizontal and not upright. ❑ *Two men near him threw themselves flat... As heartburn is usually worse when you're lying down in bed, you should avoid lying flat.* 4 ADJ: usu ADJ n = shallow A **flat** object is not very tall or deep in relation to its length and width. ❑ *Ellen is walking down the drive with a square flat box balanced on one hand.* 5 ADJ: ADJ n, v-link ADJ, ADJ after v **Flat** land is level, with no high hills or other raised parts. ❑ *To the north lie the flat and fertile farmlands of the Solway plain... The landscape became wider, flatter and very scenic.* 6 N-COUNT: usu pl, usu n N A low flat area of uncultivated land, especially an area where the ground is soft and wet, can be referred to as **flats** or a **flat**. ❑ *The salt marshes and mud flats attract large numbers of waterfowl.* 7 N-COUNT: usu sing, the N *of* n You can refer to one of the broad flat surfaces of an object as **the flat of** that object. ❑ *He slammed the counter with the flat of his hand. ...eight cloves of garlic crushed with the flat of a knife.* 8 ADJ: usu ADJ n **Flat** shoes have no heels or very low heels. ❑ *People wear slacks, sweaters, flat shoes, and all manner of casual attire for travel.* ♦ N-PLURAL **Flats** are flat shoes. [AM] ❑ *His mother looked ten years younger in jeans and flats.* 9 ADJ A **flat** tyre, ball, or balloon does not have enough air in it. 10 N-COUNT A **flat** is a tyre that does not have enough air in it. ❑ *Then, after I finally got back on the highway, I developed a flat.* 11 ADJ ≠ fizzy A drink that is **flat** is no longer fizzy. ❑ *Could this really stop the champagne from going flat?* 12 ADJ A **flat** battery has lost some or all of its electrical charge. [mainly BRIT] ❑ *His car alarm had been going off for two days and, as a result, the battery was flat.*

☑ in AM, use **dead**

13 ADJ If you have **flat** feet, the arches of your feet are too low. ❑ *The condition of flat feet runs in families.* 14 ADJ: ADJ n A **flat** denial or refusal is definite and firm, and is unlikely to be changed. ❑ *The Foreign Ministry has issued a flat denial of any involvement.* ♦ ADV: ADV with v, ADV adj **flat|ly** *He flatly refused to discuss it.* 15 ADJ: num n ADJ emphasis If you say that something happened, for example, in ten seconds **flat** or ten minutes **flat**, you are emphasizing that it happened surprisingly quickly and only took ten seconds or ten minutes. ❑ *You're sitting behind an engine that'll move you from 0 to 60mph in six seconds flat.* 16 ADJ: ADJ n = fixed ≠ variable A **flat** rate, price, or percentage is one that is fixed and which applies in every situation. ❑ *Fees are charged at a flat rate, rather than on a percentage basis... Sometimes there's a flat fee for carrying out a particular task.* 17 ADJ = sluggish If trade or business is **flat**, it is slow and inactive, rather than busy and improving or increasing. ❑ *During the first eight months of this year, sales of big pickups were up 14% while car sales stayed flat.* 18 ADJ If you describe something as **flat**, you mean that it is dull and not exciting or interesting. ❑ *The past few days have seemed comparatively flat and empty.* 19 ADJ You use **flat** to describe someone's voice when they are saying something without expressing any emotion. ❑ *'Whatever you say,' he said in a deadly flat voice. 'I'll sit here and wait.'... Her voice was flat, with no question or hope in it.* ♦ ADV: ADV after v **flat|ly** *I know you,' he said flatly, matter-of-fact, neutral in tone.* 20 ADJ: n ADJ ≠ sharp **Flat** is used after a letter representing a musical note to show that the note should be played or sung half a tone lower than the note which otherwise matches that letter. **Flat** is often represented by the symbol ♭ after the letter. ❑ *...Schubert's B flat Piano Trio (Opus 99).* 21 ADV: ADV after v If someone sings **flat** or if a musical instrument is **flat**, their singing or the instrument is slightly lower in pitch than it should be. ❑ *She had a distressing tendency to sing flat.* ♦ ADJ **Flat** is also an adjective. ❑ *He had been fired because his singing was flat.*

**PHRASES** 22 PHRASE: v-link PHR emphasis If you say that something is **as flat as a pancake**, you are emphasizing that it is completely flat. ❑ *My home state of Illinois is flat as a pancake.* 23 PHRASE: V inflects, oft PHR *on* n If you **fall flat** on your face, you fall over. ❑ *A man walked in off the street and fell flat on his face, unconscious.* 24 PHRASE: V inflects = fail If an event or attempt **falls flat** or **falls flat on** its **face**, it is unsuccessful. ❑ *Liz meant it as a joke but it fell flat... If it wasn't for the main actress, Ellen Barkin, the plot would have fallen flat on its face.* 25 PHRASE: v-link PHR emphasis = skint If you say that you are **flat broke**, you mean that you have no money at all. [INFORMAL] ❑ *Two years later he is flat broke and on the dole.* 26 PHRASE: PHR after v, PHR n If you do something **flat out**, you do it as fast or as hard as you can. ❑ *Everyone is working flat out to try to trap those responsible... They hurtled across the line in a flat-out sprint.* 27 PHRASE: PHR n/adj, PHR with v emphasis You use **flat out** to emphasize that something is completely the case. [mainly AM, INFORMAL] ❑ *That allegation is a flat-out lie.* 28 PHRASE **On the flat** means on level ground. ❑ *He had angina and was unable to walk for more than 200 yards on the flat.* 29 **in a flat spin** → see **spin**.

**flat|bed** /flætbed/ **(flatbeds)**

☑ The form **flatbed truck** is also used, especially in American English.

N-COUNT: oft N n A **flatbed** is a truck that has a long flat platform with no sides.

**flat cap** **(flat caps)** N-COUNT A **flat cap** is the same as a **cloth cap**. [mainly BRIT]

**flat|fish** /flætfɪʃ/ **(flatfish)** N-VAR **Flatfish** are sea fish with flat wide bodies, for example plaice or sole.

**flat-footed** 1 ADJ: v-link ADJ, ADJ n, ADJ after v If you are **flat-footed**, the arches of your feet are too low. ❑ *He told me I was flat-footed.* 2 ADJ: ADJ n, v-link ADJ, ADJ after v disapproval If you describe a person or action as **flat-footed**, you think they are clumsy, awkward, or foolish. ❑ *...flat-footed writing... The government could be caught flat-footed.*

**flat|mate** /flætmeɪt/ **(flatmates)** also **flat-mate.** N-COUNT: usu poss N Someone's **flatmate** is a person who shares a flat with them. [BRIT]

☑ in AM, use **roommate**

**flat pack** **(flat packs)** also **flat-pack.** N-COUNT: usu N n **Flat pack** furniture is furniture such as shelves and cupboards which you buy as a number of separate pieces and assemble yourself. [BRIT]

**flat rac|ing** **Flat racing** is horse racing which does not involve jumping over fences. N-UNCOUNT

**flat|ten** /flætᵊn/ **(flattens, flattening, flattened)**
1 If you **flatten** something or if it **flattens**, it becomes flat or flatter. ❑ *He carefully flattened the wrappers and put them between the leaves of his book... The dog's ears flattened slightly as Cook spoke his name. ...the pitiful shacks built of cardboard boxes, corrugated iron sheets and flattened oil drums.* ♦ **Flatten out** means the same as **flatten**. ❑ *The hills flattened out just south of the mountain... Peel off the blackened skin, flatten the pepper out and trim it into edible pieces.* 2 To **flatten** something such as a building, town, or plant means to destroy it by knocking it down or crushing it. ❑ *...explosives capable of flattening a five-storey building. ...areas of flattened corn.* 3 If you **flatten yourself against** something, you press yourself flat against it, for example to avoid getting in the way or being seen. ❑ *He flattened himself against a brick wall as I passed.* 4 If you **flatten** someone, you make them fall over by hitting them violently. ❑ *'I've never seen a woman flatten someone like that,' said a crew member. 'She knocked him out cold.'*
VERB V n V V-ed PHRASAL VERB V P V n P Also V P n (not pron) VERB V n V-ed VERB V pron-refl *against/on* n VERB V n

**flat|ter** /flætəʳ/ **(flatters, flattering, flattered)**
1 If someone **flatters** you, they praise you in an exaggerated way that is not sincere, because they want to please you or to persuade you to do something. ❑ *I knew she was just flattering me. ...a story of how the president flattered and feted him into taking his side.* 2 If you **flatter yourself that** something good is the case, you believe that it is true, although others may disagree. If someone says to you **'you're flattering yourself'** or **'don't flatter yourself'**, they mean that they disagree with your good opinion of yourself. ❑ *I flatter myself that this campaign will put an end to the war... You flatter yourself. Why would we go to such ludicrous lengths?* 3 If something **flatters** you, it makes you appear more attractive. ❑ *Orange and khaki flatter those with golden skin tones... My philosophy of fashion is that I like to make clothes that flatter.* 4 → See also **flat**, **flattered**, **flattering**.
VERB [disapproval] V n V n *into* -ing VERB V pron-refl that V pron-refl VERB V n V

**flat|tered** /flætəʳd/ If you are **flattered** by something that has happened, you are pleased about it because it makes you feel important or special. ❑ *She was flattered by Roberto's long letter... I am flattered that they should be so supportive.* ADJ: v-link ADJ, oft ADJ *by* n, ADJ that/to-inf

**flat|ter|ing** /flætərɪŋ/ 1 If something is **flattering**, it makes you appear more attractive. ❑ *Some styles are so flattering that they instantly become classics... It wasn't a very flattering photograph.* 2 If someone's remarks are **flattering**, they praise you and say nice things about you. ❑ *There were pleasant and flattering obituaries about him.* ADJ ADJ

**flat|tery** /flætəri/ **Flattery** consists of flattering words or behaviour. ❑ *He is ambitious and susceptible to flattery.* N-UNCOUNT [disapproval]

**flatu|lence** /flætʃʊləns/ **Flatulence** is too much gas in a person's intestines, which causes an uncomfortable feeling. N-UNCOUNT = wind

**flat|ware** /flætweəʳ/ You can refer to the knives, forks, and spoons that you eat your food with as **flatware**. [AM] N-UNCOUNT
✔ in BRIT, use **cutlery**

**flaunt** /flɔːnt/ **(flaunts, flaunting, flaunted)**
1 If you say that someone **flaunts** their possessions, abilities, or qualities, you mean that they display them in a very obvious way, especially in order to try to obtain other people's admiration. ❑ *They drove around in Rolls-Royces, openly flaunting their wealth.* 2 If you say that someone **is flaunting themselves**, you disapprove of them because they are behaving in a very confident way, or in a way that is intended to attract sexual attention. ❑ *...tourists flaunting themselves in front of the castle guards in bra and shorts.*
VERB [disapproval] = show off V n VERB [disapproval] V pron-refl

**flau|tist** /flɔːtɪst/ **(flautists)** A **flautist** is someone who plays the flute. [mainly BRIT] N-COUNT
✔ in AM, usually use **flutist**

**fla|vour** /fleɪvəʳ/ **(flavours, flavouring, flavoured)** ◆◇◇
✔ in AM, use **flavor**
1 The **flavour** of a food or drink is its taste. ❑ *This cheese has a crumbly texture with a strong flavour... I always add some paprika for extra flavour.* 2 If something is orange **flavour** or beef **flavour**, it is made to taste of orange or beef. ❑ *...salt and vinegar flavour crisps. ...now available in three new flavours.* 3 If you **flavour** food or drink, you add something to it to give it a particular taste. ❑ *Flavour your favourite dishes with exotic herbs and spices... Lime preserved in salt is a north African speciality which is used to flavour chicken dishes.* 4 If something gives you a **flavour of** a subject, situation, or event, it gives you a general idea of what it is like. ❑ *The book gives you a flavour of what alternative therapy is about.*
N-VAR N-COUNT: oft n N VERB V n *with* n V n N-SING: oft *a* N *of* n = taste

**fla|voured** /fleɪvəʳd/
✔ in AM, use **flavored**
If a food is **flavoured**, various ingredients have been added to it so that it has a distinctive flavour. ❑ *...meat flavoured with herbs... Many of these recipes are highly flavoured.* ADJ: oft ADJ *with* n

**-flavoured** /-fleɪvəʳd/
✔ in AM, use **-flavored**
**-flavoured** is used after nouns such as strawberry and chocolate to indicate that a food or drink is flavoured with strawberry or chocolate. ❑ *...strawberry-flavoured sweets. ...fruit-flavored sparkling water.* COMB in ADJ: usu ADJ n

**fla|vour|ing** /fleɪvərɪŋ/ **(flavourings)**
✔ in AM, use **flavoring**
**Flavourings** are substances that are added to food or drink to give it a particular taste. ❑ *Our range of herbal teas contain no preservatives, colourings or artificial flavourings. ...lemon flavoring.* N-VAR

**fla|vour|less** /fleɪvəʳləs/
✔ in AM, use **flavorless**
**Flavourless** food is uninteresting because it does not taste strongly of anything. ADJ

**fla|vour|some** /fleɪvəʳsəm/
✔ in AM, use **flavorsome**
**Flavoursome** food has a strong, pleasant taste and is good to eat. ADJ [approval]

**flaw** /flɔː/ **(flaws)** 1 A **flaw in** something such as a theory or argument is a mistake in it, which causes it to be less effective or valid. ❑ *Almost all of these studies have serious flaws.* 2 A **flaw in** someone's character is an undesirable quality that they have. ❑ *The only flaw in his character seems to be a short temper.* 3 A **flaw in** something such as a pattern or material is a fault in it that should not be there.
N-COUNT: oft N *in* n N-COUNT: oft N *in* n = defect, failing N-COUNT = imperfection

**flawed** /flɔːd/ Something that is **flawed** has a mark, fault, or mistake in it. ❑ *These tests were so seriously flawed as to render the results meaningless.* ADJ

**flaw|less** /flɔːləs/ If you say that something or someone is **flawless**, you mean that they are extremely good and that there are no faults or problems with them. ❑ *She attributed her flawless complexion to the moisturiser she used... Discovery's takeoff this morning from Cape Canaveral was flawless.* ♦ **flaw|less|ly** *Each stage of the battle was carried off flawlessly.* ADJ = perfect ADV: ADV with v, ADV adj

**flax** /flæks/ **Flax** is a plant with blue flowers. Its stem is used for making thread, rope, and cloth, and its seeds are used for making linseed oil. N-UNCOUNT

**flax|en** /flæksᵊn/ **Flaxen** hair is pale yellow in colour. [LITERARY] ADJ: ADJ n

**flay** /fleɪ/ **(flays, flaying, flayed)** When someone **flays** an animal or person, they remove their skin, usually when they are dead. ❑ *They had to flay the great, white, fleecy animals and cut them up for food.* VERB V n

**flea** /fliː/ **(fleas)** A **flea** is a very small jumping insect that has no wings and feeds on the blood of humans or animals. N-COUNT

**flea mar|ket** **(flea markets)** A **flea market** is an outdoor market which sells cheap used goods and sometimes also very old furniture. N-COUNT

**flea|pit** /fliːpɪt/ **(fleapits)** also **flea-pit.** If you refer to a cinema or theatre as a **fleapit**, you mean that it is old and does not look very clean or tidy. [BRIT, HUMOROUS, INFORMAL] N-COUNT [disapproval]

**fleck** /flek/ **(flecks)** **Flecks** are small marks on a surface, or objects that look like small marks. ❑ *His hair is dark grey with flecks of ginger.* N-COUNT: usu pl, oft N *of* n = speck

**flecked** /flekt/ Something that is **flecked** with something is marked or covered with small bits of it. ❑ *His hair was increasingly flecked with grey.* ♦ **Flecked** is also a combining form. ❑ *He was attired in a plain, mud-flecked uniform.* ADJ: oft ADJ *with* n = speckled; COMB in ADJ

**fled** /fled/ **Fled** is the past tense and past participle of **flee**.

**fledg|ling** /fledʒlɪŋ/ **(fledglings)** 1 A **fledgling** is a young bird that has its feathers and is learning to fly. N-COUNT 2 You use **fledgling** to describe a person, organization, or system that is new or without experience. ❑ *...the sound practical advice he gave to fledgling writers. ...Russia's fledgling democracy.* ADJ: ADJ n

**flee** /fliː/ **(flees, fleeing, fled)** If you **flee from** something or someone, or **flee** a person or thing, you escape from them. [WRITTEN] ❑ *He slammed the bedroom door behind him and fled... He fled to Costa Rica to avoid military service. ...refugees fleeing persecution or torture... Thousands have been compelled to flee the country in makeshift boats.* ◆◇◇ VERB: no passive; V; V prep/adv; V n; V n

**fleece** /fliːs/ **(fleeces, fleecing, fleeced)** 1 A sheep's **fleece** is the coat of wool that covers it. N-COUNT 2 A **fleece** is the wool that is cut off one sheep in a single piece. N-COUNT 3 If you **fleece** someone, you get a lot of money from them by tricking them or charging them too much. [INFORMAL] ❑ *She claims he fleeced her out of thousands of pounds.* VERB = swindle; V n *out of* n; Also V n 4 **Fleece** is a soft warm artificial fabric. A **fleece** is also a jacket or other garment made from this fabric. N-VAR

**fleecy** /fliːsi/ 1 **Fleecy** clothes, blankets, or other objects are made of a soft light material. ❑ *...fleecy walking jackets.* ADJ: usu ADJ n 2 Something that is **fleecy** is light and soft in appearance. ❑ *It was a lovely afternoon with a blue sky and a few fleecy white clouds.* ADJ

**fleet** /fliːt/ **(fleets)** 1 A **fleet** is a group of ships organized to do something together, for example to fight battles or to catch fish. ❑ *...restaurants supplied by local fishing fleets.* ◆◇◇ N-COUNT: usu supp N 2 A **fleet** of vehicles is a group of them, especially when they all belong to a particular organization or business, or when they are all going somewhere together. ❑ *With its own fleet of trucks, the company delivers most orders overnight.* N-COUNT: oft N *of* n

**fleet|ing** /fliːtɪŋ/ **Fleeting** is used to describe something which lasts only for a very short time. ❑ *The girls caught only a fleeting glimpse of the driver... She wondered for a fleeting moment if he would put his arm around her.* ♦ **fleet|ing|ly** *A smile passed fleetingly across his face.* ADJ: usu ADJ n = brief; ADV: usu ADV with v, also ADV adj

**Fleet Street** **Fleet Street** is used to refer to British national newspapers and to the journalists who work for them. ❑ *He was the highest-paid sub-editor in Fleet Street. ...Fleet Street journalists.* N-PROPER

**Flem|ish** /flemɪʃ/ 1 **Flemish** means belonging or relating to the region of Flanders in northern Europe, or to its people, language, or culture. ADJ 2 **Flemish** is a language spoken in Belgium. N-UNCOUNT

**flesh** /fleʃ/ **(fleshes, fleshing, fleshed)** 1 **Flesh** is the soft part of a person's or animal's body between the bones and the skin. ❑ *...maggots which eat away dead flesh. ...the pale pink flesh of trout and salmon.* N-UNCOUNT 2 You can use **flesh** to refer to human skin and the human body, especially when you are considering it in a sexual way. ❑ *...the sins of the flesh.* N-UNCOUNT 3 The **flesh** of a fruit or vegetable is the soft inside part of it. ❑ *Cut the flesh from the olives and discard the stones.* N-UNCOUNT

PHRASES 4 You use **flesh and blood** to emphasize that someone has human feelings or weaknesses, often when contrasting them with machines. ❑ *I'm only flesh and blood, like anyone else.* PHRASE [emphasis] 5 If you say that someone is your **own flesh and blood**, you are emphasizing that they are a member of your family. ❑ *The kid, after all, was his own flesh and blood. He deserved a second chance.* PHRASE: usu v-link PHR [emphasis] 6 If something **makes** your **flesh creep** or **makes** your **flesh crawl**, it makes you feel disgusted, shocked or frightened. ❑ *It makes my flesh creep to think of it... I was heading on a secret mission that made my flesh crawl.* PHRASE: *make* inflects 7 If you meet or see someone **in the flesh**, you actually meet or see them, rather than, for example, seeing them in a film or on television. ❑ *The first thing viewers usually say when they see me in the flesh is 'You're smaller than you look on TV.'* PHRASE: usu PHR after v, v-link PHR

♦ **flesh out** If you **flesh out** something such as a story or plan, you add details and more information to it. ❑ *He talked with him for an hour and a half, fleshing out the details of his original five-minute account.* PHRASAL VERB; V P n (not pron); Also V n P

**flesh-coloured**

☑ in AM, use **flesh-colored**

Something that is **flesh-coloured** is yellowish pink in colour. ADJ

**flesh wound** **(flesh wounds)** A **flesh wound** is a wound that breaks the skin but does not damage the bones or any of the body's important internal organs. N-COUNT

**fleshy** /fleʃi/ 1 If you describe someone as **fleshy**, you mean that they are slightly too fat. ❑ *He was well-built, but too fleshy to be impressive.* ADJ 2 **Fleshy** parts of the body or **fleshy** plants are thick and soft. ❑ *...fleshy fruits like apples, plums, pears, peaches.* ADJ

**flew** /fluː/ **Flew** is the past tense of **fly**.

**flex** /fleks/ **(flexes, flexing, flexed)** 1 A **flex** is an electric cable containing two or more wires that is connected to an electrical appliance. [mainly BRIT] N-VAR

☑ in AM, use **cord**

2 If you **flex** your muscles or parts of your body, you bend, move, or stretch them for a short time in order to exercise them. ❑ *He slowly flexed his muscles and tried to stand.* VERB; V n 3 to **flex** your **muscles** → see **muscle**.

**flex|ible** /fleksɪbᵊl/ 1 A **flexible** object or material can be bent easily without breaking. ❑ *...brushes with long, flexible bristles.* ◆◇◇ ADJ = pliable ♦ **flexi|bil|ity** /fleksɪbɪlɪti/ *The flexibility of the lens decreases with age.* N-UNCOUNT 2 Something or someone that is **flexible** is able to change easily and adapt to different conditions and circumstances as they occur. ❑ *Look for software that's flexible enough for a range of abilities. ...flexible working hours.* ADJ [approval] = adaptable ♦ **flexi|bil|ity** *The flexibility of distance learning would be particularly suited to busy managers.* N-UNCOUNT

**flexi|time** /fleksitaɪm/

☑ in AM, use **flextime**

**Flexitime** is a system that allows employees to vary the time that they start or finish work, provided that an agreed total number of hours are spent at work. [BUSINESS] N-UNCOUNT

**flick** /flɪk/ **(flicks, flicking, flicked)** 1 If something **flicks** in a particular direction, or if someone **flicks** it, it moves with a short, sudden movement. ❑ *His tongue flicked across his lips... He flicked his cigarette out of the window.* ♦ **Flick** is also a noun. ❑ *...a flick of a paintbrush.* VERB; V prep/adv; V n prep/adv; N-COUNT: oft *a* N *of* n 2 If you **flick** something away, or off something else, you remove it with a quick movement of your hand or finger. ❑ *Shirley flicked a speck of fluff from the sleeve of her black suit... Alan stretched out his hand and flicked the letter away.* VERB; V n *from/off* n; V n *away* 3 If you **flick** something VERB such as a whip or a towel, or **flick** something with it, you hold one end of it and move your hand quickly up and then forward, so that the other end moves. ❑ *He helped her up before flicking the reins...* V n *She sighed and flicked a dishcloth at the counter.* V n prep ♦ **Flick** is also a noun. ❑ *...a flick of the whip.* N-COUNT [4] If you **flick** a switch, or **flick** an electrical appliance on or off, you press the switch sharply so that it moves into a different position and works the equipment. VERB ❑ *He flicked a light-switch on the wall beside the door...* V n *Sam was flicking a flashlight on and off.* V n with *on/off* [5] If you **flick through** a book or magazine, you turn its pages quickly, for example to get a general idea of its contents or to look for a particular item. If you **flick through** television channels, you continually change channels very quickly, for example using a remote control. VERB ❑ *She was flicking through some magazines on a table.* V *through* n ♦ **Flick** is also a noun. ❑ *I thought I'd have a quick flick through some recent issues.* N-SING: *a* N

**flick|er** /flɪkəʳ/ **(flickers, flickering, flickered)** [1] If a light or flame **flickers**, it shines unsteadily. VERB ❑ *A television flickered in the corner.* V ♦ **Flicker** is also a noun. N-COUNT ❑ *Looking through the cabin window I saw the flicker of flames.* [2] If you experience **a flicker of** emotion, you feel that emotion only for a very short time, and not very strongly. N-COUNT: usu sing, oft N *of* n ❑ *He felt a flicker of regret... He looked at me, a flicker of amusement in his cold eyes.* [3] If something **flickers**, it makes very slight, quick movements. VERB ❑ *In a moment her eyelids flickered, then opened...* V *A few moments later Mrs Tenney's eyelids flickered open.* V adj

**flick-knife** **(flick-knives)** also **flick knife.** A **flick-knife** is a knife with a blade in the handle that springs out when a button is pressed. [BRIT] N-COUNT

✓ in AM, use **switchblade**

**fli|er** /flaɪəʳ/ → see **flyer**.

**flight** /flaɪt/ **(flights)** ◆◆◇ [1] A **flight** is a journey made by flying, usually in an aeroplane. N-COUNT ❑ *The flight will take four hours.* [2] You can refer to an aeroplane carrying passengers on a particular journey as a particular **flight**. N-COUNT: also N num ❑ *I'll try to get on the flight down to Karachi tonight... BA flight 286 was two hours late.* [3] **Flight** is the action of flying, or the ability to fly. N-UNCOUNT ❑ *These hawks are magnificent in flight, soaring and circling for long periods... Supersonic flight could become a routine form of travel in the 21st century.* [4] A **flight of** birds is a group of them flying together. N-COUNT: N *of* n ❑ *A flight of green parrots shot out of the cedar forest.* [5] **Flight** is the act of running away from a dangerous or unpleasant situation or place. N-UNCOUNT: oft *in* N ❑ *The family was often in flight, hiding out in friends' houses. ...her hurried flight from the palace in a cart.* [6] A **flight of** steps or stairs is a set of steps or stairs that lead from one level to another without changing direction. N-COUNT: usu N *of* n ❑ *We walked in silence up a flight of stairs and down a long corridor.* [7] If someone **takes flight**, they run away from an unpleasant situation or place. PHRASE: V inflects = flee ❑ *He was told of the raid and decided to take flight immediately.*

**flight at|tend|ant** **(flight attendants)** On an aeroplane, the **flight attendants** are the people whose job is to look after the passengers and serve their meals. N-COUNT

**flight deck** **(flight decks)** also **flight-deck.** [1] On an aircraft carrier, **the flight deck** is the flat open surface on the deck where aircraft take off and land. N-COUNT [2] On a large aeroplane, **the flight deck** is the area at the front where the pilot works and where all the controls are. N-COUNT

**flight|less** /flaɪtləs/ A **flightless** bird or insect is unable to fly because it does not have the necessary type of wings. ADJ: ADJ n

**flight lieu|ten|ant** **(flight lieutenants)** also **flight-lieutenant.** In the British air force, a **flight lieutenant** is an officer of the rank below squadron leader. N-COUNT; N-TITLE

**flight of capi|tal** When people lose confidence in a particular economy or market and withdraw their investment from it, you can refer to a **flight of capital** from that economy or market. [BUSINESS] N-SING ❑ *TI has seen its shares suffer because of a flight of capital to telecom and Internet-related businesses.*

**flight re|cord|er** **(flight recorders)** On an aeroplane, the **flight recorder** is the same as the **black box**. N-COUNT

**flighty** /flaɪti/ **(flightier, flightiest)** If you say that someone is **flighty**, you disapprove of them because they are not very serious or reliable and keep changing from one activity, idea, or partner to another. ADJ disapproval ❑ *Isabelle was a frivolous little fool, vain and flighty.*

**flim|sy** /flɪmzi/ **(flimsier, flimsiest)** [1] A **flimsy** object is weak because it is made of a weak material, or is badly made. ADJ ❑ *...a flimsy wooden door. ...a pair of flimsy shoes.* [2] **Flimsy** cloth or clothing is thin and does not give much protection. ADJ ❑ *...a very flimsy pink chiffon nightgown.* [3] If you describe something such as evidence or an excuse as **flimsy**, you mean that it is not very good or convincing. ADJ = weak, unconvincing ❑ *The charges were based on very flimsy evidence.*

**flinch** /flɪntʃ/ **(flinches, flinching, flinched)** [1] If you **flinch**, you make a small sudden movement, especially when something surprises you or hurts you. VERB: usu neg ❑ *Murat had looked into the eyes of the firing squad without flinching...* V *The sharp surface of the rock caught at her skin, making her flinch.* V [2] If you **flinch from** something unpleasant, you are unwilling to do it or think about it, or you avoid doing it. VERB ❑ *The world community should not flinch in the face of this challenge...* V *He has never flinched from harsh financial decisions.* V *from* n

**fling** /flɪŋ/ **(flings, flinging, flung)** [1] If you **fling** something somewhere, you throw it there using a lot of force. VERB ❑ *The woman flung the cup at him...* V n prep/adv *He once seized my knitting, flinging it across the room.* V n prep/adv [2] If you **fling yourself** somewhere, you move or jump there suddenly and with a lot of force. VERB ❑ *He flung himself to the floor.* V pron-refl prep/adv [3] If you **fling** a part of your body in a particular direction, especially your arms or head, you move it there suddenly. VERB = throw ❑ *She flung her arms around my neck and kissed me.* V n prep/adv [4] If you **fling** someone to the ground, you push them very roughly so that they fall over. VERB ❑ *The youth got him by the front of his shirt and flung him to the ground.* V n prep/adv [5] If you **fling** something into a particular place or position, you put it there in a quick or angry way. VERB ❑ *Peter flung his shoes into the corner.* V n prep/adv [6] If you **fling yourself into** a particular activity, you do it with a lot of enthusiasm and energy. VERB ❑ *She flung herself into her career.* V pron-refl *into* n [7] If two people have **a fling**, they have a brief sexual relationship. [INFORMAL] N-COUNT: oft N *with* n = affair ❑ *She claims she had a brief fling with him 30 years ago.* [8] **Fling** can be used instead of 'throw' in many expressions that usually contain 'throw'.

**flint** /flɪnt/ **(flints)** [1] **Flint** is a very hard greyish-black stone that was used in former times for making tools. N-UNCOUNT ❑ *...a flint arrowhead. ...eyes the colour of flint.* [2] A **flint** is a small piece of flint which can be struck with a piece of steel to produce sparks. N-COUNT

**flint|lock** /flɪntlɒk/ **(flintlocks)** A **flintlock** gun is a type of gun that was used in former times. It is fired by pressing a trigger which causes a spark struck from a flint to light gunpowder. N-COUNT: oft N n

**flinty** /flɪnti/ If you describe a person or someone's character or expression as **flinty**, you mean they are harsh and show no emotion. ADJ = stony ❑ *...her flinty stare. ...a man of flinty determination.*

**flip** /flɪp/ **(flips, flipping, flipped)** [1] If you **flip** a device on or off, or if you **flip** a switch, you turn it on or off by pressing the switch quickly. VERB = flick ❑ *Then he walked out, flipping the lights off...* V n with *on/off* *He flipped the timer switch.* V n [2] If you **flip** through the pages of a book, for example, you quickly turn over the pages in order to find a particular one or to get an idea of the contents. VERB ❑ *He was flipping* V *through* n

*through a magazine in the living room... He flipped the pages of the diary and began reading the last entry.* V n
3 If something **flips** over, or if you **flip** it over or into a different position, it moves or is moved into a different position. ❑ *The plane then flipped over and burst into flames... He flipped it neatly on to the plate.* VERB V adv/prep V n prep/adv
4 If you **flip** something, especially a coin, you use your thumb to make it turn over and over, as it goes through the air. ❑ *I pulled a coin from my pocket and flipped it.* VERB = toss V n
5 If you say that someone is being **flip**, you disapprove of them because you think that what they are saying shows they are not being serious enough about something. ❑ *...a flip answer... The tone of the book is sometimes too flip.* ADJ disapproval

**flip chart** (flip charts) also **flipchart.** A **flip chart** is a stand with large sheets of paper which is used when presenting information at a meeting. N-COUNT

**flip-flop** (flip-flops, flip-flopping, flip-flopped) 1 **Flip-flops** are open shoes which are held on your feet by a strap that goes between your toes. [mainly BRIT] N-PLURAL

✔ in AM, usually use **thongs**

2 If you say that someone, especially a politician, **flip-flops** on a decision, you are critical of them because they change their decision, so that they do or think the opposite. [mainly AM, INFORMAL] ❑ *He has been criticized for flip-flopping on several key issues... He seemed so sure of his decision, how could he flip-flop so dramatically now?* ♦ **Flip-flop** is also a noun. ❑ *The President's flip-flops on taxes made him appear indecisive.* VERB disapproval V on n V N-COUNT

**flip|pant** /flɪpənt/ If you describe a person or what they say as **flippant**, you are criticizing them because you think they are not taking something as seriously as they should. ❑ *Don't be flippant, damn it! This is serious!... He now dismisses that as a flippant comment.* ADJ disapproval = flip, glib

**flip|per** /flɪpəʳ/ (flippers) 1 **Flippers** are flat pieces of rubber that you can wear on your feet to help you swim more quickly, especially underwater. 2 The **flippers** of an animal that lives in water, for example a seal or a penguin, are the two or four flat limbs which it uses for swimming. N-COUNT: usu pl N-COUNT: usu pl

**flip|ping** /flɪpɪŋ/ Some people use **flipping** to emphasize what they are saying, especially when they are annoyed. [BRIT, INFORMAL, SPOKEN] ❑ *This is such a flipping horrible picture.* ♦ **Flipping** is also an adjective. ❑ *I even washed the flipping bed sheets yesterday.* ADV: ADV adj emphasis = flaming ADJ: ADJ n

**flip side** also **flipside.** 1 **The flip side** of a record is the side that does not have the main song on it. ❑ *'What's on the flip side?'* 2 **The flip side** of a situation consists of the less obvious or less pleasant aspects of it. ❑ *The trade deficit is the flip side of a rapidly expanding economy.* N-SING: the N N-SING

**flirt** /flɜːʳt/ (flirts, flirting, flirted) 1 If you **flirt with** someone, you behave as if you are sexually attracted to them, in a playful or not very serious way. ❑ *Dad's flirting with all the ladies, or they're all flirting with him, as usual... He flirts outrageously.* ♦ **flir|ta|tion** /flɜːʳteɪʃᵊn/ (flirtations) *...a professor who has a flirtation with a student... She was aware of his attempts at flirtation.* 2 Someone who is a **flirt** likes to flirt a lot. 3 If you **flirt with** the idea of something, you consider it but do not do anything about it. ❑ *Di Pietro, 45, has been flirting with the idea of a political career.* ♦ **flir|ta|tion** *...the ruling party's brief flirtation with economic liberalism.* V-RECIP V with n V (non-recip) N-VAR: oft N with n N-COUNT VERB V with n N-VAR

**flir|ta|tious** /flɜːʳteɪʃəs/ Someone who is **flirtatious** behaves towards someone else as if they are sexually attracted to them, usually not in a very serious way. ❑ *He was dashing, self-confident and flirtatious.* ADJ

**flir|ty** /flɜːʳti/ 1 If you describe someone as **flirty**, you mean that they behave towards people in a way which suggests they are sexually attracted to them, usually in a playful or not very serious way. ❑ *She is amazingly flirty and sensual... She had an appealing flirty smile.* 2 **Flirty** clothes are feminine and sexy. ADJ ADJ

**flit** /flɪt/ (flits, flitting, flitted) 1 If you **flit** around or **flit** between one place and another, you go to lots of places without staying for very long in any of them. ❑ *Laura flits about New York hailing taxis at every opportunity... He spends his time flitting between Florence, Rome and Bologna.* 2 If someone **flits from** one thing or situation **to** another, they move or turn their attention from one to the other very quickly. ❑ *She flits from one dance partner to another... He's prone to flit between subjects with amazing ease.* 3 If something such as a bird or a bat **flits** about, it flies quickly from one place to another. ❑ *...the parrot that flits from tree to tree.* 4 If an expression **flits across** your face or an idea **flits through** your mind, it is there for a short time and then goes again. ❑ *He was unable to prevent a look of interest from flitting across his features... Images and memories of the evening flitted through her mind.* VERB V prep/adv V prep/adv VERB V from n to n V prep VERB V prep/adv VERB V across n V through n

**float** /floʊt/ (floats, floating, floated) 1 If something or someone **is floating** in a liquid, they are in the liquid, on or just below the surface, and are being supported by it. You can also **float** something on a liquid. ❑ *They noticed fifty and twenty dollar bills floating in the water. ...barges floating quietly by the grassy river banks... They'll spend some time floating boats in the creek.* 2 Something that **floats** lies on or just below the surface of a liquid when it is put in it and does not sink. ❑ *Empty things float.* 3 A **float** is a light object that is used to help someone or something float. 4 A **float** is a small object attached to a fishing line which floats on the water and moves when a fish has been caught. 5 Something that **floats** in or through the air hangs in it or moves slowly and gently through it. ❑ *The white cloud of smoke floated away.* 6 If you **float** a project, plan, or idea, you suggest it for others to think about. ❑ *The French had floated the idea of placing the diplomatic work in the hands of the UN.* 7 If a company director **floats** their company, they start to sell shares in it to the public. [BUSINESS] ❑ *He floated his firm on the stock market... The advisers are delaying the key decision on whether to float 60 per cent or 100 per cent of the shares.* 8 If a government **floats** its country's currency or allows it to **float**, it allows the currency's value to change freely in relation to other currencies. [BUSINESS] ❑ *A decision by the Finns to float their currency sent a shudder through the foreign exchanges... 59 per cent of people believed the pound should be allowed to float freely.* 9 A **float** is a truck on which displays and people in special costumes are carried in a festival procession. → See also **milk float.** 10 A **float** is a small amount of coins and notes of low value that someone has before they start selling things so that they are able to give customers change if necessary. [BRIT] ◆◇◇ VERB V in n V prep/adv V n Also V n prep/adv VERB ≠ sink V N-COUNT N-COUNT VERB V prep/adv VERB V n VERB V n on n V n VERB V n V N-COUNT N-SING

♦ **float around** A rumour or idea that **is floating around** is often heard or talked about. ❑ *There are still some unfounded fears floating around out there about cancer being contagious.* PHRASAL VERB V P

**float|ing vot|er** (floating voters) A **floating voter** is a person who is not a firm supporter of any political party, and whose vote in an election is difficult to predict. [mainly BRIT] N-COUNT

✔ in AM, use **swing voter**

**flock** /flɒk/ (flocks, flocking, flocked) 1 A **flock of** birds, sheep, or goats is a group of them. ❑ *They kept a small flock of sheep... They are gregarious birds and feed in flocks.* 2 You can refer to a group of people or things as a **flock of** them to emphasize that there are a lot of them. ❑ *These cases all attracted flocks of famous writers. ...his flock of advisers.* 3 If people **flock to** a particular place or event, a very large number of them go there, usually because it is pleasant or interesting. ❑ *The public have flocked to the show... The criticisms* N-COUNT-COLL: usu N of n N-COUNT-COLL: N of n emphasis VERB V to n *will not stop people flocking to see the film... His greatest wish must be that huge crowds flock into the beautiful park.* — V to-inf; V prep/adv

**floe** /fləʊ/ → see **ice floe**.

**flog** /flɒg/ **(flogs, flogging, flogged)** [1] If someone tries to **flog** something, they try to sell it. [BRIT, INFORMAL] ❑ *They are trying to flog their house.* — VERB; V n
[2] If someone **is flogged**, they are hit very hard with a whip or stick as a punishment. ❑ *In these places people starved, were flogged, were clubbed to death... Flog them soundly.* ♦ **flog|ging (floggings)** *He was sentenced to a flogging and life imprisonment.* — VERB; be V-ed; V n; N-VAR
[3] If you say that someone **is flogging a dead horse**, you mean that they are trying to achieve something impossible. [INFORMAL] — PHRASE: V inflects

**flood** /flʌd/ **(floods, flooding, flooded)** ◆◇◇ [1] If there is a **flood**, a large amount of water covers an area which is usually dry, for example when a river flows over its banks or a pipe bursts. ❑ *More than 70 people were killed in the floods, caused when a dam burst... This is the type of flood dreaded by cavers... Over 25 people drowned when a schoolbus tried to cross a river and flood waters swept through.* — N-VAR
[2] If something such as a river or a burst pipe **floods** an area that is usually dry or if the area **floods**, it becomes covered with water. ❑ *The Chicago River flooded the city's underground tunnel system... The kitchen flooded.* ♦ **flood|ed** *People have been mobilised to build defences and drain flooded land as heavy rains continue to fall.* — VERB; V n; V; ADJ
[3] If a river **floods**, it overflows, especially after very heavy rain. ❑ *...the relentless rain that caused twenty rivers to flood... Many streams have flooded their banks, making some roads impassable.* — VERB = overflow; V; V n
[4] If you say that a **flood of** people or things arrive somewhere, you are emphasizing that a very large number of them arrive there. ❑ *The administration is trying to stem the flood of refugees out of Haiti and into Florida... He received a flood of letters from irate constituents.* — N-COUNT: usu N *of* n; [emphasis]; = tide, torrent
[5] If you say that people or things **flood** into a place, you are emphasizing that they arrive there in large numbers. ❑ *Enquiries flooded in from all over the world. ...the refugees flooding out of Kosovo.* — VERB; [emphasis]; = pour; V prep/adv; V prep/adv
[6] If you **flood** a place **with** a particular type of thing, or if a particular type of thing **floods** a place, the place becomes full of so many of them that it cannot hold or deal with any more. ❑ *...a policy aimed at flooding Europe with exports... German cameras at knockdown prices flooded the British market.* ♦ **flood|ed** *...the danger of Europe becoming flooded with low-cost agricultural imports.* — VERB = saturate; V n *with* n; V n; ADJ
[7] If an emotion, feeling, or thought **floods** you, you suddenly feel it very intensely. If feelings or memories **flood back**, you suddenly remember them very clearly. [LITERARY] ❑ *A wave of happiness flooded me... Mary Ann was flooded with relief ... It was probably the shock which had brought all the memories flooding back.* — VERB; V n; be V-ed *with* n; V adv
[8] If light **floods** a place or **floods** into it, it suddenly fills it. ❑ *The afternoon light flooded the little rooms... Morning sunshine flooded in through the open curtains.* — VERB; V n; V prep/adv
[9] → See also **flash flood**.
[10] If you say that someone was in **floods of tears** or in a **flood of tears**, you are emphasizing that they were crying with great intensity because they were very upset. ❑ *They said goodbye in a flood of tears.* — PHRASE: *flood* inflects, usu *in* PHR; [emphasis]

♦ **flood out** If people, places, or things **are flooded out**, the water from a flood makes it impossible for people to stay in that place or to use that thing. ❑ *Train lines were flooded out... The river flooded them out every few years.* — PHRASAL VERB; be V-ed P; V n P

**flood|gates** /flʌdgeɪts/ If events **open the floodgates** to something, they make it possible for that thing to happen much more often or much more seriously than before. ❑ *A decision against the cigarette companies could open the floodgates to many more lawsuits.* — PHRASE: V inflects, usu PHR *to/for* n

**flood|ing** /flʌdɪŋ/ If **flooding** occurs, an area of land that is usually dry is covered with water after heavy rain or after a river or lake flows over its banks. ❑ *The flooding, caused by three days of torrential rain, is the worst in sixty-five years.* — N-UNCOUNT

**flood|light** /flʌdlaɪt/ **(floodlights, floodlighting, floodlit)** [1] **Floodlights** are very powerful lamps that are used outside to light public buildings, sports grounds, and other places at night. — N-COUNT: usu pl
[2] If a building or place **is floodlit**, it is lit by floodlights. ❑ *In the evening the facade is floodlit... A police helicopter hovered above, floodlighting the area.* — VERB; be V-ed; V n

**flood plain (flood plains)** also **floodplain.** A **flood plain** is a flat area on the edge of a river, where the ground consists of soil, sand, and rock left by the river when it floods. — N-COUNT

**floor** /flɔːʳ/ **(floors, flooring, floored)** ◆◆◇ [1] **The floor** of a room is the part of it that you walk on. ❑ *Jack's sitting on the floor watching TV... We painted the wooden floor with a white stain.* — N-COUNT: usu *the* N in sing
[2] A **floor** of a building is all the rooms that are on a particular level. ❑ *It is on the fifth floor of the hospital... They occupied the first two floors of the tower.* — N-COUNT: usu supp N = storey
[3] The ocean **floor** is the ground at the bottom of an ocean. The valley **floor** is the ground at the bottom of a valley. — N-COUNT: usu sing, with supp, oft n N
[4] The place where official debates and discussions are held, especially between members of parliament, is referred to as **the floor**. ❑ *The issues were debated on the floor of the House.* — N-COUNT: usu *the* N in sing
[5] In a debate or discussion, **the floor** is the people who are listening to the arguments being put forward but who are not among the main speakers. ❑ *The president is taking questions from the floor.* — N-SING-COLL: *the* N
[6] **The floor** of a stock exchange is the large open area where trading is done. ❑ *...the dealing floor at Standard Chartered Bank.* — N-COUNT: usu sing, with supp
[7] **The floor** in a place such as a club or disco is the area where people dance. — N-COUNT
[8] If you **are floored by** something, you are unable to respond to it because you are so surprised by it. ❑ *He was floored by the announcement... He seemed floored by a string of scandals.* — VERB: usu passive; be V-ed; V-ed
[9] → See also **floored**, **flooring**, **dance floor**, **first floor**, **ground floor**, **shop floor**.

PHRASES [10] If you **take the floor**, you start speaking in a debate or discussion. If you **are given the floor**, you are allowed to do this. ❑ *Ministers took the floor to denounce the decision to suspend constitutional rule... Only members would be given the floor.* — PHRASE: V inflects
[11] If you **take to the floor**, you start dancing at a dance or disco. ❑ *The happy couple and their respective parents took to the floor.* — PHRASE: V inflects
[12] If you say that prices or sales have fallen **through the floor**, you mean that they have suddenly decreased. ❑ *Property prices have dropped through the floor.* — PHRASE: PHR after v
[13] If you **wipe the floor with** someone, you defeat them completely in a competition or discussion. [INFORMAL] ❑ *He could wipe the floor with the Prime Minister.* — PHRASE: V inflects, PHR n
[14] → See also **factory floor**.

**floor|board** /flɔːʳbɔːʳd/ **(floorboards)** **Floorboards** are the long pieces of wood that a wooden floor is made up of. — N-COUNT: usu pl

**floored** /flɔːʳd/ A room or part of a room that is **floored with** a particular material has a floor made of that material. ❑ *The aisle was floored with ancient bricks.* ♦ **Floored** is also a combining form. ❑ *They had to cross the large marble-floored hall.* — ADJ; COMB in ADJ

**floor|ing** /flɔːrɪŋ/ **(floorings)** **Flooring** is a material that is used to make the floor of a room. ❑ *Quarry tiles are a popular kitchen flooring.* — N-MASS

**floor lamp (floor lamps)** A **floor lamp** is a tall electric light which stands on the floor in a living room. [AM] — N-COUNT

✔ in BRIT, use **standard lamp**

**floor show (floor shows)** also **floorshow.** A **floor show** is a series of performances by dancers, singers, or comedians at a night club. — N-COUNT

**floo|zy** /fluːzi/ **(floozies)** If you refer to a woman as a **floozy**, you disapprove of her sexual behaviour and the fact that she wears vulgar clothes. [INFORMAL, OLD-FASHIONED] — N-COUNT; [disapproval]

**flop** /flɒp/ **(flops, flopping, flopped)** [1] If you **flop** into a chair, for example, you sit down suddenly and heavily because you are so tired. ❑ *Bunbury flopped down upon the bed and rested his* — VERB = collapse; V prep/adv tired feet... She flopped, exhausted, on to a sofa. [2] If something **flops** onto something else, it falls there heavily or untidily. ❑ *The briefcase flopped onto the desk... His hair flopped over his left eye.* [3] If something is a **flop**, it is completely unsuccessful. [INFORMAL] ❑ *It is the public who decide whether a film is a hit or a flop.* [4] If something **flops**, it is completely unsuccessful. [INFORMAL] ❑ *The film flopped badly at the box office.* V prep/adv VERB V prep/adv V prep/adv N-COUNT: oft adj N = failure VERB V

**flop|house** /flɒphaʊs/ **(flophouses)** A **flophouse** is a kind of cheap hotel in a city for people who have no home and very little money. [AM, INFORMAL] N-COUNT

☑ in BRIT, use **doss-house**

**flop|py** /flɒpi/ Something that is **floppy** is loose rather than stiff, and tends to hang downwards. ❑ *...the girl with the floppy hat and glasses.* ADJ

**flop|py disk** **(floppy disks)**

☑ in BRIT, also use **floppy disc**

A **floppy disk** is a small magnetic disk that is used for storing computer data and programs. Floppy disks are used especially with personal computers. N-COUNT

**flo|ra** /flɔːrə/ You can refer to plants as **flora**, especially the plants growing in a particular area. [FORMAL] ❑ *...the variety of food crops and flora which now exists in Dominica.* N-UNCOUNT-COLL

**flo|ral** /flɔːrəl/ [1] A **floral** fabric or design has flowers on it. ❑ *...a bright yellow floral fabric.* [2] You can use **floral** to describe something that contains flowers or is made of flowers. ❑ *...eye-catching floral arrangements.* ADJ: usu ADJ n ADJ: ADJ n

**flo|ret** /flɒrɪt/ **(florets)** [1] On a flowering plant, a **floret** is a small flower that is part of a larger flower. [2] On vegetables such as broccoli and cauliflower, a **floret** is one of the small, flower-shaped pieces which make up the part of the vegetable that you eat. ➔ See picture on page 1712. N-COUNT N-COUNT

**flor|id** /flɒrɪd, AM flɔːr-/ [1] If you describe something as **florid**, you disapprove of the fact that it is complicated and extravagant rather than plain and simple. ❑ *...florid language.* [2] Someone who is **florid** always has a red face. ❑ *Jacobs was a stout, florid man.* ADJ [disapproval] = ornate ADJ

**flor|in** /flɒrɪn, AM flɔːr-/ **(florins)** A **florin** was a British coin that was worth two shillings. N-COUNT

**flo|rist** /flɒrɪst, AM flɔːr-/ **(florists)** [1] A **florist** is a shopkeeper who arranges and sells flowers and sells house plants. [2] A **florist** or a **florist's** is a shop where flowers and house plants are sold. N-COUNT N-COUNT: oft the N

**floss** /flɒs, AM flɔːs/ **(flosses, flossing, flossed)** [1] You can use **floss** to refer to fine soft threads of some kind. ❑ *Craft Resources also sells yarn and embroidery floss.* ➔ See also **candyfloss**, **dental floss**. [2] When you **floss**, you use a special kind of strong string to clean between your teeth and gums. ❑ *Brush your teeth after each meal and floss daily... She was flossing her teeth at the time.* N-UNCOUNT VERB V V n

**flo|ta|tion** /floʊteɪʃən/ **(flotations)** [1] The **flotation** of a company is the selling of shares in it to the public. [BUSINESS] [2] A **flotation** compartment helps something to float because it is filled with air or gas. N-VAR ADJ: ADJ n

**flo|til|la** /flətɪlə/ **(flotillas)** A **flotilla** is a group of small ships, usually military ships. N-COUNT

**flot|sam** /flɒtsəm/ [1] **Flotsam** is rubbish, for example bits of wood and plastic, that is floating on the sea or has been left by the sea on the shore. ❑ *The water was full of flotsam and refuse.* [2] You can use **flotsam and jetsam** to refer to small or unimportant items that are found together, especially ones that have no connection with each other. ❑ *...cornflake packets, bottles, and all the flotsam and jetsam of the kitchen.* N-UNCOUNT PHRASE

**flounce** /flaʊns/ **(flounces, flouncing, flounced)** [1] If you **flounce** somewhere, you walk there quickly with exaggerated movements, in a way that shows you are annoyed or upset. ❑ *She flounced out of my room in a huff... She will flounce and argue when asked to leave the room.* [2] A **flounce** is a piece of cloth that has been sewn into folds and put around the edge of something, for example a skirt, dress, tablecloth, or curtain. ❑ *...a gown with a flounce round the hem.* VERB V adv/prep V N-COUNT = frill

**floun|der** /flaʊndəʳ/ **(flounders, floundering, floundered)** [1] If something **is floundering**, it has many problems and may soon fail completely. ❑ *What a pity that his career was left to flounder... The economy was floundering.* [2] If you say that someone **is floundering**, you are criticizing them for not making decisions or for not knowing what to say or do. ❑ *Right now, you've got a president who's floundering, trying to find some way to get his campaign jump-started... I know that you're floundering around, trying to grasp at any straw.* [3] If you **flounder** in water or mud, you move in an uncontrolled way, trying not to sink. ❑ *Three men were floundering about in the water.* VERB = founder V V VERB [disapproval] = dither V V around VERB V adv/prep Also V

**flour** /flaʊəʳ/ **(flours, flouring, floured)** [1] **Flour** is a white or brown powder that is made by grinding grain. It is used to make bread, cakes, and pastry. [2] If you **flour** cooking equipment or food, you cover it with flour. ❑ *Lightly flour a rolling pin... Remove the dough from the bowl and put it on a floured surface.* N-MASS VERB V n V-ed

**flour|ish** /flʌrɪʃ, AM flɜːr-/ **(flourishes, flourishing, flourished)** [1] If something **flourishes**, it is successful, active, or common, and developing quickly and strongly. ❑ *Business flourished and within six months they were earning 18,000 roubles a day.* ♦ **flour|ish|ing** *London quickly became a flourishing port.* [2] If a plant or animal **flourishes**, it grows well or is healthy because the conditions are right for it. ❑ *The plant flourishes particularly well in slightly harsher climes.* ♦ **flour|ish|ing** *Britain has the largest and most flourishing fox population in Europe.* [3] If you **flourish** an object, you wave it about in a way that makes people notice it. ❑ *He flourished the glass to emphasize the point.* ♦ **Flourish** is also a noun. ❑ *He took his peaked cap from under his arm with a flourish and pulled it low over his eyes.* [4] If you do something **with a flourish**, you do in a showy way so that people notice it. VERB = thrive ≠ flounder V ADJ VERB = thrive V ADJ VERB V n N-COUNT N-COUNT

**floury** /flaʊəri/ [1] Something that is **floury** is covered with flour or tastes of flour. ❑ *She wiped her floury hands on her apron. ...floury scones.* [2] **Floury** potatoes go soft round the edges and break up when they are cooked. ADJ ADJ: usu ADJ n

**flout** /flaʊt/ **(flouts, flouting, flouted)** If you **flout** something such as a law, an order, or an accepted way of behaving, you deliberately do not obey it or follow it. ❑ *...illegal campers who persist in flouting the law.* VERB = defy ≠ observe, respect V n

**flow** /floʊ/ **(flows, flowing, flowed)** [1] If a liquid, gas, or electrical current **flows** somewhere, it moves there steadily and continuously. ❑ *A stream flowed gently down into the valley... The current flows into electric motors that drive the wheels. ...compressor stations that keep the gas flowing.* ♦ **Flow** is also a noun. ❑ *It works only in the veins, where the blood flow is slower.* [2] If a number of people or things **flow** from one place to another, they move there steadily in large groups, usually without stopping. ❑ *Large numbers of refugees continue to flow from the troubled region into the no-man's land.* ♦ **Flow** is also a noun. ❑ *She watched the frantic flow of cars and buses along the street.* [3] If information or money **flows** somewhere, it moves freely between people or organizations. ❑ *A lot of this information flowed through other police departments... An interest rate reduction is needed to get more money flowing.* ♦ **Flow** is also a noun. ❑ *...the opportunity to control the flow of information.* ➔ See also **cash flow**. ◆◆◇ VERB V adv/prep V adv/prep V N-VAR: with supp VERB V prep/adv N-VAR: with supp VERB V prep/adv V N-VAR: with supp

PHRASES [4] Someone who is **in full flow** is talking easily and continuously and seems likely to go on talking for some time. ❑ *He had been replying for some 40 minutes already and was still in full flow.* [5] If you say that an activity, or the person who is performing the activity, is **in full flow**, you mean PHRASE: v-link PHR PHRASE: v-link PHR that the activity has started and is being carried out with a great deal of energy and enthusiasm. ❑ *Lunch at Harry's Bar was in full flow when Irene made a splendid entrance.* 6 If you **go with the flow**, you let things happen or let other people tell you what to do, rather than trying to control what happens yourself. ❑ *There's nothing I can do about the problem, so I might as well go with the flow.* PHRASE: V inflects

**flow chart** (flow charts) A **flow chart** or a **flow diagram** is a diagram which represents the sequence of actions in a particular process or activity. N-COUNT

**flow|er** /flaʊəʳ/ (flowers, flowering, flowered) ◆◆◇
1 A **flower** is the part of a plant which is often brightly coloured, grows at the end of a stem, and only survives for a short time. ❑ *Each individual flower is tiny. ...large, purplish-blue flowers.* N-COUNT
2 A **flower** is a stem of a plant that has one or more flowers on it and has been picked, usually with others, for example to give as a present or to put in a vase. ❑ *...a bunch of flowers sent by a new admirer.* N-COUNT: usu pl
3 **Flowers** are small plants that are grown for their flowers as opposed to trees, shrubs, and vegetables. ❑ *...a lawned area surrounded by plants and flowers... The flower garden will be ablaze with colour every day.* N-COUNT: usu pl
4 When a plant or tree **flowers**, its flowers appear and open. ❑ *Several of these rhododendrons will flower this year for the first time.* VERB V
5 When something **flowers**, for example a political movement or a relationship, it gets stronger and more successful. ❑ *Their relationship flowered.* VERB = blossom V
6 When a plant is **in flower** or when it has come **into flower**, its flowers have appeared and opened. PHRASE: usu v-link PHR, PHR after v
7 → See also **flowered**.

**flow|er ar|rang|ing** **Flower arranging** is the art or hobby of arranging cut flowers in a way which makes them look attractive. N-UNCOUNT

**flower|bed** /flaʊəʳbed/ (flowerbeds) also **flower bed**. A **flowerbed** is an area of ground in a garden or park which has been specially prepared so that flowers can be grown in it. → See picture on page 1705. N-COUNT

**flow|ered** /flaʊəʳd/ **Flowered** paper or cloth has a pattern of flowers on it. ❑ *She was wearing a pretty flowered cotton dress.* ADJ: ADJ n = floral

**flow|er|ing** /flaʊərɪŋ/ 1 **The flowering of** something such as an idea or artistic style is the development of its popularity and success. ❑ *...the flowering of creative genius.* N-UNCOUNT: usu N of n
2 **Flowering** shrubs, trees, or plants are those which produce noticeable flowers. ADJ: ADJ n

**flower|pot** /flaʊəʳpɒt/ (flowerpots) also **flower pot**. A **flowerpot** is a container that is used for growing plants. N-COUNT = plant pot

**flow|er pow|er** **Flower power** is an old-fashioned way of referring to hippies and the culture associated with hippies in the late 1960s and early 1970s. ❑ *...the era of flower power.* N-UNCOUNT

**flow|ery** /flaʊəri/ 1 A **flowery** smell is strong and sweet, like flowers. ❑ *Amy thought she caught the faintest drift of Isabel's flowery perfume.* ADJ
2 **Flowery** cloth, paper, or china has a lot of flowers printed or painted on it. ❑ *The baby, dressed in a flowery jumpsuit, waved her rattle.* ADJ: usu ADJ n = floral
3 **Flowery** speech or writing contains long or literary words and expressions. ❑ *They were using uncommonly flowery language.* ADJ = florid

**flown** /floʊn/ **Flown** is the past participle of **fly**.

**fl. oz.** **fl. oz.** is a written abbreviation for **fluid ounce**.

**flu** /fluː/ **Flu** is an illness which is similar to a bad cold but more serious. It often makes you feel very weak and makes your muscles hurt. ❑ *I got flu... He had come down with the flu.* N-UNCOUNT: also the N

**fluc|tu|ate** /flʌktʃueɪt/ (fluctuates, fluctuating, fluctuated) If something **fluctuates**, it changes a lot in an irregular way. ❑ *Body temperature can fluctuate if you are ill. ...the fluctuating price of oil.* VERB V V-ing
♦ **fluc|tua|tion** /flʌktʃueɪʃᵊn/ (fluctuations) *Don't worry about tiny fluctuations in your weight... The calculations do not take into account any fluctuation in the share price.* N-VAR: usu N in/of n

**flue** /fluː/ (flues) A **flue** is a pipe or long tube that acts as a chimney, taking smoke away from a device such as a heater, fire, or cooker. N-COUNT

**flu|ent** /fluːənt/ 1 Someone who is **fluent in** a particular language, can speak the language easily and correctly. You can also say that someone speaks **fluent** French, Chinese, or some other language. ❑ *She studied eight foreign languages but is fluent in only six of them... He speaks fluent Russian.* ADJ: oft ADJ in n
♦ **flu|en|cy** *To work as a translator, you need fluency in at least one foreign language.* N-UNCOUNT
♦ **flu|ent|ly** *He spoke three languages fluently.* ADV
2 If your speech, reading, or writing is **fluent**, you speak, read, or write easily, smoothly, and clearly with no mistakes. ❑ *He had emerged from being a hesitant and unsure candidate into a fluent debater.* ADJ
♦ **flu|en|cy** *His son was praised for speeches of remarkable fluency.* N-UNCOUNT
♦ **flu|ent|ly** *Alex didn't read fluently till he was nearly seven.* ADV: ADV with v

**fluff** /flʌf/ **Fluff** consists of soft threads or fibres in the form of small, light balls or lumps. For example, you can refer to the fur of a small animal as **fluff**. ❑ *She noticed some bits of fluff on the sleeve of her sweater.* N-UNCOUNT: oft n of N

**fluffy** /flʌfi/ (fluffier, fluffiest) 1 If you describe something such as a towel or a toy animal as **fluffy**, you mean that it is very soft. ❑ *...fluffy white towels... It's a very fluffy kind of wool.* ADJ
2 A cake or other food that is **fluffy** is very light because it has a lot of air in it. ❑ *Cream together the margarine and sugar until light and fluffy.* ADJ

**flu|id** /fluːɪd/ (fluids) 1 A **fluid** is a liquid. [FORMAL] ❑ *The blood vessels may leak fluid, which distorts vision... Make sure that you drink plenty of fluids. ...fluid retention.* N-MASS
2 **Fluid** movements or lines or designs are smooth and graceful. ❑ *The forehand stroke should be fluid and well balanced.* ADJ
3 A situation that is **fluid** is unstable and is likely to change often. ADJ: usu v-link ADJ = changeable

**flu|id ounce** (fluid ounces) A **fluid ounce** is a measurement of liquid. There are twenty fluid ounces in a British pint, and sixteen in an American pint. N-COUNT: num N, oft N of n

**fluke** /fluːk/ (flukes) If you say that something good is a **fluke**, you mean that it happened accidentally rather than by being planned or arranged. [INFORMAL] ❑ *The discovery was something of a fluke... By sheer fluke, one of the shipowner's employees was in the city.* N-COUNT: usu sing, also by N

**flum|mox** /flʌməks/ (flummoxes, flummoxing, flummoxed) If someone **is flummoxed** by something, they are confused by it and do not know what to do or say. ❑ *The two leaders were flummoxed by the suggestion.* VERB: usu passive be V-ed
♦ **flum|moxed** *No wonder Josef was feeling a bit flummoxed.* ADJ

**flung** /flʌŋ/ **Flung** is the past tense and past participle of **fling**.

**flunk** /flʌŋk/ (flunks, flunking, flunked) If you **flunk** an exam or a course, you fail to reach the required standard. [mainly AM, INFORMAL] ❑ *Your son is upset because he flunked a history exam.* VERB = fail V n

**flunk|ey** /flʌŋki/ (flunkeys) also **flunky**.
1 Someone who refers to a servant as a **flunkey** is expressing their dislike for a job that involves doing things for an employer that ordinary people do for themselves. N-COUNT disapproval = lackey
2 If you refer to someone as a **flunkey**, you disapprove of the fact that they associate themselves with someone who is powerful and carry out small, unimportant jobs for them in the hope of being rewarded. N-COUNT disapproval = hanger-on

**fluo|res|cent** /flʊəresᵊnt/ 1 A **fluorescent** surface, substance, or colour has a very bright appearance when light is directed onto it, as if it is actually shining itself. ❑ *...a piece of fluorescent tape.* ADJ: usu ADJ n
♦ **fluo|res|cence** *...the green fluorescence it gives off under ultraviolet radiation.* N-UNCOUNT
2 A **fluorescent** light shines with a very hard, bright ADJ: usu ADJ n

light and is usually in the form of a long strip. ❑ *...fluorescent light tubes.*

**fluori|da|tion** /flʊərɪdeɪʃᵊn/ N-UNCOUNT **Fluoridation** is the action or process of adding fluoride to a water supply. ❑ *...fluoridation of the water supply.*

**fluo|ride** /flʊəraɪd/ N-UNCOUNT **Fluoride** is a mixture of chemicals that is sometimes added to drinking water and toothpaste because it is considered to be good for people's teeth.

**fluo|rine** /flʊəriːn/ N-UNCOUNT **Fluorine** is a pale yellow, poisonous gas. It is used in the production of uranium and other chemicals.

**flur|ry** /flʌri, AM flɜːri/ **(flurries)** 1 N-COUNT: usu N *of* n A **flurry** of something such as activity or excitement is a short intense period of it. ❑ *...a flurry of diplomatic activity aimed at ending the war.* 2 N-COUNT: oft N *of* n A **flurry** of something such as snow is a small amount of it that suddenly appears for a short time and moves in a quick, swirling way.

**flush** /flʌʃ/ **(flushes, flushing, flushed)** 1 VERB If you **flush**, your face goes red because you are hot or ill, or because you are feeling a strong emotion such as embarrassment or anger. ❑ V *Do you sweat a lot or flush a lot?...* V colour *He turned away embarrassed, his face flushing red.* ♦ N-COUNT **Flush** is also a noun. ❑ *There was a slight flush on his cheeks.* ♦ ADJ: oft ADJ *with* n **flushed** *Her face was flushed with anger.* 2 VERB When someone **flushes** a toilet after using it, they fill the toilet bowl with water in order to clean it, usually by pressing a handle or pulling a chain. You can also say that a toilet **flushes.** ❑ V n *She flushed the toilet and went back in the bedroom.* V *...the sound of the toilet flushing.* ♦ N-COUNT: usu sing **Flush** is also a noun. ❑ *He heard the flush of a toilet.* 3 VERB If you **flush** something **down** the toilet, you get rid of it by putting it into the toilet bowl and flushing the toilet. ❑ V n *down* n *He was found trying to flush banknotes down the toilet.* 4 VERB = cleanse If you **flush** a part of your body, you clean it or make it healthier by using a large amount of liquid to get rid of dirt or harmful substances. ❑ V n *Flush the eye with clean cold water for at least 15 minutes.* ♦ PHRASAL VERB **Flush out** means the same as **flush.** ❑ V P n (not pron) Also V n P *...an 'alternative' therapy that gently flushes out the colon to remove toxins.* 5 VERB If you **flush** dirt or a harmful substance **out** of a place, you get rid of it by using a large amount of liquid. ❑ V n with *out* *That won't flush out all the sewage, but it should unclog some stinking drains.* 6 VERB If you **flush** people or animals **out** of a place where they are hiding, you find or capture them by forcing them to come out of that place. ❑ V n *out of* n *They flushed them out of their hiding places...* V n with *out* *The Guyana Defence Force is engaged in flushing out illegal Brazilian miners operating in the country.* 7 ADJ: v-link ADJ, oft ADJ *with* n = level If one object or surface is **flush with** another, they are at the same height or distance from something else, so that they form a single smooth surface. ❑ *Make sure the tile is flush with the surrounding tiles.* 8 N-SING: N *of* n **The flush of** something is an intense feeling of excitement or pleasure that you have when you are experiencing it and for a short time afterwards. ❑ *...the first flush of young love. ...in the flush of victory.*

♦ **flush out** → see **flush 4**.

**flushed** /flʌʃt/ ADJ: v-link ADJ *with* n If you say that someone is **flushed with** success or pride you mean that they are very excited by their success or pride. ❑ *Grace was flushed with the success of the venture.*

**flus|ter** /flʌstəʳ/ **(flusters, flustering, flustered)** VERB If you **fluster** someone, you make them feel nervous and confused by rushing them and preventing them from concentrating on what they are doing. ❑ *be* V-ed *The General refused to be flustered...* V n *She was a very calm person. Nothing could fluster her.* ♦ ADJ: usu v-link ADJ **flus|tered** *She was so flustered that she forgot her reply.*

**flute** /fluːt/ **(flutes)** N-VAR: oft *the* N A **flute** is a musical instrument of the woodwind family. You play it by blowing over a hole near one end while holding it sideways to your mouth.

**flut|ed** /fluːtɪd/ ADJ: usu ADJ n = grooved Something that is **fluted** has shallow curves cut into it. ❑ *...the fluted wooden post of the porch.*

**flut|ing** /fluːtɪŋ/ ADJ If you describe someone's voice as **fluting**, you mean that it goes up and down a lot, and usually that it is high pitched. ❑ *Her voice, small and fluting, stopped abruptly. ...a fluting and melodic Scottish accent.*

**flut|ist** /fluːtɪst/ **(flutists)** N-COUNT A **flutist** is someone who plays the flute. [AM]

in BRIT, use **flautist**

**flut|ter** /flʌtəʳ/ **(flutters, fluttering, fluttered)** 1 VERB If something thin or light **flutters**, or if you **flutter** it, it moves up and down or from side to side with a lot of quick, light movements. ❑ V *Her chiffon skirt was fluttering in the night breeze.* V n *...a butterfly fluttering its wings.* V-ing *...the fluttering white lace handkerchief.* ♦ N-COUNT **Flutter** is also a noun. ❑ *...a flutter of white cloth.* 2 VERB If something light such as a small bird or a piece of paper **flutters** somewhere, it moves through the air with small quick movements. ❑ V adv/prep *The paper fluttered to the floor...* V *The birds were active, whirring and fluttering among the trees.* 3 N-COUNT: oft N *on* n = bet If you have **a flutter**, you have a small bet on something such as a horse race. [BRIT, INFORMAL] ❑ *I had a flutter on five horses.*

**flux** /flʌks/ N-UNCOUNT: oft *in* N If something is in **a** state **of flux**, it is constantly changing. ❑ *Education remains in a state of flux which will take some time to settle down.*

**fly** /flaɪ/ **(flies, flying, flew, flown)** ◆◆◆ 1 N-COUNT A **fly** is a small insect with two wings. There are many kinds of flies, and the most common are black in colour. 2 VERB When something such as a bird, insect, or aircraft **flies**, it moves through the air. ❑ V prep/adv Also V *The planes flew through the clouds... The bird flew away.* 3 VERB If you **fly** somewhere, you travel there in an aircraft. ❑ V prep/adv *He flew back to London... Mr Baker flew in from Moscow.* 4 VERB When someone **flies** an aircraft, they control its movement in the air. ❑ V n *Parker had successfully flown both aircraft...* V n prep/adv V *He flew a small plane to Cuba... His inspiration to fly came even before he joined the Army.* ♦ N-UNCOUNT **fly|ing** *...a flying instructor.* 5 VERB To **fly** someone or something somewhere means to take or send them there in an aircraft. ❑ V n adv/prep *The relief supplies are being flown from a warehouse in Pisa.* 6 VERB If something such as your hair **is flying** about, it is moving about freely and loosely in the air. ❑ V adv/prep *His long, uncovered hair flew back in the wind...* V *She was running down the stairs, her hair flying.* 7 VERB If you **fly** a flag or if it **is flying**, you display it at the top of a pole. ❑ V n *They flew the flag of the African National Congress...* V *A flag was flying on the new military HQ.* 8 VERB emphasis If you say that someone or something **flies** in a particular direction, you are emphasizing that they move there with a lot of speed or force. ❑ V prep/adv *I flew downstairs.* 9 N-COUNT The front opening on a pair of trousers is referred to as the **fly**, or in British English the **flies**. It usually consists of a zip or row of buttons behind a band of cloth. 10 → See also **flying**, **tsetse fly**.

PHRASES 11 PHRASE: with brd-neg, V inflects emphasis If you say that someone wouldn't **hurt a fly** or wouldn't **harm a fly**, you are emphasizing that they are very kind and gentle. ❑ *...a lovely girl, who would not have harmed a fly.* 12 PHRASE: V inflects If you **let fly**, you attack someone, either physically by hitting them, or with words by insulting them. ❑ *A simmering row ended with her letting fly with a stream of obscenities.* 13 PHRASE: V inflects, PHR after v If you **send** someone or something **flying** or if they **go flying**, they move through the air and fall down with a lot of force. ❑ *The blow sent the young man flying.* 14 PHRASE: v-link PHR If you say that you would like to be **a fly on the wall** in a situation that does not involve you, you mean that you would like to see or hear what happens in that situation. ❑ *What I'd give to be a fly on the wall when Davis finds out what's happened to his precious cargo.* → See also **fly-on-the-wall.** 15 **as the crow flies** → see **crow**. **to fly in the face of** → see **face**. **to fly**

**the flag** → see **flag**. to **fly off the handle** → see **handle**. a **fly in the ointment** → see **ointment**. **pigs might fly** → see **pig**. **sparks fly** → see **spark**. **time flies** → see **time**.

♦ **fly at** If you **fly at** someone, you attack them, either physically by hitting them, or with words by insulting them. ❑ *She flew at him for making a very anti-British remark.* [PHRASAL VERB = let fly at; V P n]

♦ **fly into** If you **fly into** a bad temper or a panic, you suddenly become very angry or anxious and show this in your behaviour. ❑ *Losing a game would cause him to fly into a rage.* [PHRASAL VERB; V P n]

**fly|away** /flaɪəweɪ/ **Flyaway** hair is very soft and fine. [WRITTEN] [ADJ: usu ADJ n]

**fly|by** /flaɪbaɪ/ **(flybys)** also **fly-by.** A **flyby** is a flight made by an aircraft or a spacecraft over a particular place in order to record details about it. [N-COUNT]

**fly-by-night** A **fly-by-night** businessman is someone who wants to make money very quickly, without caring about the quality or honesty of the service they offer. [INFORMAL] ❑ *...fly-by-night operators who fail to complete jobs.* [ADJ: ADJ n; disapproval; = cowboy]

**fly-drive** On a **fly-drive** holiday, you travel part of the way to your destination by aeroplane, and collect a hired car at the airport so that you can drive the rest of the way. ❑ *...a fly-drive break in New Zealand.* [ADJ: ADJ n]

**fly|er** /flaɪəʳ/ **(flyers)** also **flier.** 1 A **flyer** is a pilot of an aircraft. [N-COUNT] 2 You can refer to someone who travels by aeroplane as a **flyer**. ❑ *...regular business flyers. ...nervous fliers.* [N-COUNT: usu supp N] 3 A **flyer** is a small printed notice which is used to advertise a particular company, service, or event. [N-COUNT] 4 → See also **high-flyer**.

**fly-fishing** also **fly fishing. Fly-fishing** is a method of fishing in which a silk or nylon model of a small winged insect is used as bait. [N-UNCOUNT]

**fly|ing** /flaɪɪŋ/ 1 A **flying** animal has wings and is able to fly. ❑ *...species of flying insects.* [ADJ: ADJ n] 2 If someone or something **gets off to a flying start**, or **makes a flying start**, they start very well, for example in a race or a new job. ❑ *Advertising revenue in the new financial year has got off to a flying start.* [PHRASE: V inflects]

**fly|ing doc|tor** **(flying doctors)** A **flying doctor** is a doctor, especially in Australia, who travels by aircraft to visit patients who live in distant or isolated areas. [N-COUNT]

**fly|ing fish** **(flying fish** or **flying fishes)** **Flying fish** are a type of fish that live in warm seas. They have large fins that enable them to move forward in the air when they jump out of the water. [N-VAR]

**fly|ing sau|cer** **(flying saucers)** A **flying saucer** is a round, flat object which some people say they have seen in the sky and which they believe to be a spacecraft from another planet. [OLD-FASHIONED] [N-COUNT]

**Fly|ing Squad** **The Flying Squad** is a group of police officers who are always ready to travel quickly to the scene of a serious crime. [BRIT] [N-PROPER-COLL: the N]

**fly|ing vis|it** **(flying visits)** A **flying visit** is a visit that only lasts a very short time. [N-COUNT]

**fly|leaf** /flaɪliːf/ **(flyleaves)** The **flyleaf** of a book is a page at the front that has nothing printed on it, or just the title and the author's name. [N-COUNT]

**fly-on-the-wall** A **fly-on-the-wall** documentary is made by filming people as they do the things they normally do, rather than by interviewing them or asking them to talk directly to the camera. ❑ *...a fly-on-the-wall documentary about the Queen's life.* **a fly on the wall** → see **fly**. [ADJ: ADJ n]

**fly|over** /flaɪoʊvəʳ/ **(flyovers)** 1 A **flyover** is a structure which carries one road over the top of another road. [BRIT] [N-COUNT]

> in AM, use **overpass**

2 A **flyover** is the same as a **flypast**. [AM] [N-COUNT]

**fly|past** /flaɪpɑːst, -pæst/ **(flypasts)** also **fly-past.** A **flypast** is a flight by a group of aircraft in a special formation which takes place on a ceremonial occasion or as a display. [BRIT] [N-COUNT]

> in AM, use **flyover**

**fly|weight** /flaɪweɪt/ **(flyweights)** A **flyweight** is a boxer who weighs 112 pounds or less. [N-COUNT]

**fly|wheel** /flaɪʰwiːl/ **(flywheels)** A **flywheel** is a heavy wheel that is part of some engines. It regulates the engine's rotation, making it operate at a steady speed. [N-COUNT]

**FM** /ef em/ **FM** is a method of transmitting radio waves that can be used to broadcast high quality sound. **FM** is an abbreviation for 'frequency modulation'.

**FMCG** /ef em siː dʒiː/ **(FMCGs)** **FMCGs** are inexpensive products that people usually buy on a regular basis, such as supermarket foods or toiletries. **FMCG** is an abbreviation for 'fast-moving consumer goods'. [BUSINESS] [N-COUNT]

**foal** /foʊl/ **(foals, foaling, foaled)** 1 A **foal** is a very young horse. [N-COUNT] 2 When a female horse **foals**, it gives birth. ❑ *The mare is due to foal today.* [VERB; V]

**foam** /foʊm/ **(foams)** 1 **Foam** consists of a mass of small bubbles that are formed when air and a liquid are mixed together. ❑ *The water curved round the rocks in great bursts of foam.* [N-UNCOUNT = froth] 2 **Foam** is used to refer to various kinds of manufactured products which have a soft, light texture like a thick liquid. ❑ *...shaving foam.* [N-MASS = cream] 3 **Foam** or **foam rubber** is soft rubber full of small holes which is used, for example, to make mattresses and cushions. ❑ *...modern three-piece suites filled with foam rubber... We had given him a large foam mattress to sleep on.* [N-MASS] 4 If a liquid **foams**, it is full of small bubbles and keeps moving slightly. ❑ *I let the water run into it and we watched as it foamed and bubbled. ...ravines with foaming rivers rushing through them.* [VERB = froth; V; V-ing]

**foamy** /foʊmi/ A **foamy** liquid has a mass of small bubbles on its surface or consists of a mass of bubbles. ❑ *...foamy waves... Whisk the egg whites until they are foamy but not stiff.* [ADJ = frothy]

**fob** /fɒb/ **(fobs, fobbing, fobbed)** In former times, a **fob** was a short chain or piece of cloth which fastened a man's watch to his clothing. [N-COUNT]

♦ **fob off** If someone **fobs** you **off**, they tell you something just to stop you asking questions. ❑ *I've asked her about it but she fobs me off... Don't be fobbed off with excuses.* [PHRASAL VERB; disapproval; V n P; be V-ed P with n]

**fo|cal** /foʊkᵊl/ 1 **Focal** is used to describe something that relates to the point where a number of rays or lines meet. ❑ *...the focal plane of the telescope.* [ADJ: ADJ n] 2 **Focal** is used to describe something that is very important. ❑ *...one of the focal centres of the Far East.* [ADJ: ADJ n]

**fo|cal point** **(focal points)** The **focal point** of something is the thing that people concentrate on or pay most attention to. ❑ *...the focal point for the town's many visitors – the Royal Shakespeare Theatre.* [N-COUNT]

**fo'c'sle** /foʊksl/ → see **forecastle**.

**fo|cus** /foʊkəs/ **(foci** /foʊsaɪ/**, focuses, focusing, focused)** ♦♦◇

> The spellings **focusses, focussing, focussed** are also used. The plural of the noun can be either **foci** or **focuses**.

1 If you **focus on** a particular topic or if your attention **is focused on** it, you concentrate on it and think about it, discuss it, or deal with it, rather than dealing with other topics. ❑ *He is currently focusing on assessment and development... Many of the papers focus their attention on the controversy surrounding the Foreign Secretary.* [VERB = concentrate; V on n; V n on n] 2 **The focus** of something is the main topic or main thing that it is concerned with. ❑ *The new system is the focus of controversy... Her children are the main focus of her life.* [N-COUNT: usu sing, usu with supp] 3 Your **focus** on something is the special attention that you pay it. ❑ *IBM has also shifted its focus from mainframes to personal computers.* [N-COUNT: usu sing, usu with supp, oft N on n] 4 If you say that something has a **focus**, you mean that you can see a purpose in it. ❑ *Some-* [N-UNCOUNT]

*how, though, their latest album has a focus that the others have lacked.* 5 If you **focus** your eyes or if your eyes **focus**, your eyes adjust so that you can clearly see the thing that you want to look at. If you **focus** a camera, telescope, or other instrument, you adjust it so that you can see clearly through it. ❑ *Kelly couldn't focus his eyes well enough to tell if the figure was male or female... His eyes slowly began to focus on what looked like a small dark ball... He found the binoculars and focused them on the boat... Had she kept the camera focused on the river bank she might have captured a vital scene.* — VERB; V n; V *on* n; V n *on* n; V-ed; Also V

6 You use **focus** to refer to the fact of adjusting your eyes or a camera, telescope, or other instrument, and to the degree to which you can see clearly. ❑ *His focus switched to the little white ball.* — N-UNCOUNT

7 If you **focus** rays of light on a particular point, you pass them through a lens or reflect them from a mirror so that they meet at that point. ❑ *Magnetic coils focus the electron beams into fine spots.* — VERB; V n prep

8 The **focus** of a number of rays or lines is the point at which they meet. [TECHNICAL] — N-COUNT

**PHRASES** 9 If an image or a camera, telescope, or other instrument is **in focus**, the edges of what you see are clear and sharp. ❑ *Pictures should be in focus, with realistic colours and well composed groups.* — PHRASE: v-link PHR, PHR after v

10 If something is **in focus**, it is being discussed or its purpose and nature are clear. ❑ *This aggression is the real issue the world should be concerned about. We want to keep that in focus.* — PHRASE: v-link PHR, PHR after v

11 If an image or a camera, telescope, or other instrument is **out of focus**, the edges of what you see are unclear. ❑ *In some of the pictures the subjects are out of focus while the background is sharp.* — PHRASE: v-link PHR, PHR after v

**fo|cused** /foʊkəst/ also **focussed.** If you describe someone or something as **focused**, you approve of the fact that they have a clear and definite purpose. ❑ *I spent the next year just wandering. I wasn't focused.* — ADJ: usu v-link ADJ [approval]

**fo|cus group** **(focus groups)** A **focus group** is a specially selected group of people who are intended to represent the general public. Focus groups have discussions in which their opinions are recorded as a form of market research. — N-COUNT

**fod|der** /fɒdəʳ/ 1 **Fodder** is food that is given to cows, horses, and other animals. ❑ *The alfalfa plant is widely used as animal fodder.* — N-UNCOUNT = feed

2 If you say that something is **fodder** for a particular purpose, you mean that it is useful for that purpose and perhaps nothing else. ❑ *The press conference simply provided more fodder for another attack on his character.* — N-UNCOUNT: usu with supp [disapproval]

**foe** /foʊ/ **(foes)** Someone's **foe** is their enemy. [WRITTEN] — N-COUNT

**foe|tal** /fiːtᵊl/ also **fetal.** **Foetal** is used to describe something that relates to or is like a foetus. ❑ *...an early stage of foetal development.* — ADJ: ADJ n

**foet|id** /fiːtɪd/ → see **fetid**.

**foe|tus** /fiːtəs/ **(foetuses)** also **fetus.** A **foetus** is an animal or human being in its later stages of development before it is born. — N-COUNT

**fog** /fɒg/ **(fogs)** 1 When there is **fog**, there are tiny drops of water in the air which form a thick cloud and make it difficult to see things. ❑ *The crash happened in thick fog... These ocean fogs can last for days.* — N-VAR

2 A **fog** is an unpleasant cloud of something such as smoke inside a building or room. ❑ *...a fog of stale cigarette smoke.* — N-SING: usu N *of* n

3 You can use **fog** to refer to a situation which stops people from being able to notice things, understand things, or think clearly. ❑ *The most basic facts about him are lost in a fog of mythology... Synchronizing these attacks may be difficult in the fog of war... His mind was in a fog when he finally got up.* — N-SING: oft *in* N, N *of* n

**fog bank** **(fog banks)** A **fog bank** is an area of thick fog, especially at sea. — N-COUNT

**fog|bound** /fɒgbaʊnd/ also **fog-bound.** If you are **fogbound** in a place or if the place is **fogbound**, thick fog makes it dangerous or impossible to go anywhere. ❑ *He was fog-bound at London airport. ...a fogbound motorway.* — ADJ

**fo|gey** /foʊgi/ **(fogies** or **fogeys)** also **fogy.** If you describe someone as a **fogey** or an **old fogey**, you mean that they are boring and old-fashioned. [INFORMAL] ❑ *I don't want to sound like I'm some old fogy.* — N-COUNT [disapproval]

**fog|gy** /fɒgi/ **(foggier, foggiest)** 1 When it is **foggy**, there is fog. ❑ *Conditions were damp and foggy after morning sleet.* — ADJ: oft *it* v-link ADJ

2 If you say that you **haven't the foggiest** or you **haven't the foggiest idea**, you are emphasizing that you do not know something. [INFORMAL] ❑ *I did not have the foggiest idea what he meant.* — PHRASE: V inflects [emphasis]

**fog|horn** /fɒghɔːʳn/ **(foghorns)** also **fog horn.** A **foghorn** is a piece of equipment that makes a loud noise and is used to warn ships about the position of land and other ships in fog. — N-COUNT

**foi|ble** /fɔɪbᵊl/ **(foibles)** A **foible** is a habit or characteristic that someone has which is considered rather strange, foolish, or bad but which is also considered unimportant. ❑ *...human foibles and weaknesses.* — N-COUNT = quirk

**foie gras** /fwɑː grɑː/ **Foie gras** is a food made from the livers of geese that were specially fed so that their livers became very large. — N-UNCOUNT

**foil** /fɔɪl/ **(foils, foiling, foiled)** 1 **Foil** consists of sheets of metal as thin as paper. It is used to wrap food in. ❑ *Pour cider around the meat and cover with foil. ...aluminium foil.* — N-UNCOUNT

2 If you **foil** someone's plan or attempt to do something, for example to commit a crime, you succeed in stopping them from doing what they want. [JOURNALISM] ❑ *A brave police chief foiled an armed robbery on a jewellers' by grabbing the raiders' shotgun.* — VERB = thwart; V n

3 If you refer to one thing or person as **a foil for** another, you approve of the fact that they contrast with each other and go well together, often in a way that makes the second thing or person seem better or less harmful. ❑ *He thought of her serenity as a foil for his intemperance... A cold beer is the perfect foil for a curry.* — N-COUNT: usu sing, N *for* n [approval] = complement

**foist** /fɔɪst/ **(foists, foisting, foisted)**

♦ **foist on** If you say that someone **foists** something **on** you, or **foists** it **upon** you, you dislike the way that they force you to listen to it or experience it. ❑ *I don't see my role as foisting my beliefs on them... What this amounts to is foisting onto women the responsibility for reducing 'the opportunities for crime' by changing their behaviour.* — PHRASAL VERB [disapproval]; V n P n; V P n n (not pron)

**fold** /foʊld/ **(folds, folding, folded)** 1 If you **fold** something such as a piece of paper or cloth, you bend it so that one part covers another part, often pressing the edge so that it stays in place. ❑ *He folded the paper carefully... Fold the omelette in half. ...a folded towel.* — ◆◇◇ VERB; V n; V n prep/adv; V-ed

2 A **fold** in a piece of paper or cloth is a bend that you make in it when you put one part of it over another part and press the edge. ❑ *Make another fold and turn the ends together.* — N-COUNT = crease

3 The **folds** in a piece of cloth are the curved shapes which are formed when it is not hanging or lying flat. ❑ *The priest fumbled in the folds of his gown.* — N-COUNT: usu pl

4 If a piece of furniture or equipment **folds** or if you can **fold** it, you can make it smaller by bending or closing parts of it. ❑ *The back of the bench folds forward to make a table... This portable seat folds flat for easy storage... Check if you can fold the buggy. ...a folding beach chair.* — VERB; V adv/prep; V adj; V n; V-ing; Also V n adj

♦ **Fold up** means the same as **fold**. ❑ *When not in use it folds up out of the way... Fold the ironing board up so that it is flat.* — PHRASAL VERB; V P; V n P

5 If you **fold** your arms or hands, you bring them together and cross or link them, for example over your chest. ❑ *Meer folded his arms over his chest and turned his head away... Mrs Ringrose sat down and folded her hands in her lap.* — VERB; V n; V n

6 If a business or organization **folds**, it is unsuccessful and has to close. [mainly BRIT, BUSINESS] ❑ *2,500 small businesses were folding each week.* — VERB; V

7 When someone joins an organization or group, you can say that they have come into **the fold**. — N-SING: *the*/poss N,

When they leave the organization or group, you can say that they leave **the fold**. ❑ *The EU wanted to bring the US back into the fold... He might find it difficult to return to the family fold when he realizes his mistake.* [usu *the* supp N]

♦ **fold in** or **fold into** In cooking, if you **fold in** an ingredient or **fold** it **into** the other ingredients, you mix it very gently into the other ingredients. ❑ *Fold in the flour... Fold the cream into the egg yolk mixture.* [PHRASAL VERB] [V P n (not pron)] [V n P n]

♦ **fold up** If you **fold** something **up**, you make it into a smaller, neater shape by folding it, usually several times. ❑ *She folded it up, and tucked it into her purse... He folded up his paper and put it away.* ➔ See also **fold 4**, **fold-up**. [PHRASAL VERB] [≠ *unfold*] [V n P] [V P n (not pron)]

**-fold** /-foʊld/ **-fold** combines with numbers to form adverbs which say how much an amount has increased by. For example, if an amount increases fourfold, it is four times greater than it was originally. ❑ *By the late eighties their number had grown fourfold... Pretax profit surged almost twelvefold.* [SUFFIX]

♦ **-fold** also combines with numbers to form adjectives. ❑ *One survey revealed a threefold increase in breast cancer.* [ADJ: ADJ n]

**fold|er** /foʊldəʳ/ **(folders)** 1 A **folder** is a thin piece of cardboard in which you can keep loose papers. [N-COUNT] 2 A **folder** is a group of files that are stored together on a computer. [N-COUNT]

**fold-up** A **fold-up** piece of furniture or equipment is one that is specially designed so that it can be folded into a smaller shape in order to be stored. [ADJ: ADJ n]

**fo|li|age** /foʊliɪdʒ/ The leaves of a plant are referred to as its **foliage**. ❑ *...shrubs with grey or silver foliage.* [N-UNCOUNT]

**fo|lic acid** /foʊlɪkæsɪd/ **Folic acid** is one of the B group of vitamins. It is found in green vegetables and fruit. [N-UNCOUNT]

**fo|lio** /foʊlioʊ/ **(folios)** A **folio** is a book made with paper of a large size, used especially in the early centuries of European printing. ❑ *Richard told me of three 16th-century folio volumes on alchemy.* [N-COUNT]

**folk** /foʊk/ **(folks)** ◆◇◇

> ✔ **folk** can also be used as the plural form for meaning 1.

1 You can refer to people as **folk** or **folks**. ❑ *Country folk can tell you that there are certain places which animals avoid. ...old folks.* [N-PLURAL: usu with supp] [= *people*] 2 You can refer to your close family, especially your mother and father, as your **folks**. [INFORMAL] ❑ *I've been avoiding my folks lately.* [N-PLURAL: usu poss N] 3 You can use **folks** as a term of address when you are talking to several people. [INFORMAL] ❑ *This is it, folks: the best record guide in the business.* [N-VOC] 4 **Folk** art and customs are traditional or typical of a particular community or nation. ❑ *...traditional Chinese folk medicine.* [ADJ: ADJ n] 5 **Folk** music is music which is traditional or typical of a particular community or nation. ❑ *...Irish folk music.* [ADJ: ADJ n] ♦ **Folk** is also a noun. ❑ *...a variety of music including classical, jazz, and folk.* [N-UNCOUNT] 6 **Folk** can be used to describe something that relates to the beliefs and opinions of ordinary people. ❑ *Jack was a folk hero in the Greenwich Village bars.* [ADJ: ADJ n]

**folk|lore** /foʊklɔːʳ/ **Folklore** is the traditional stories, customs, and habits of a particular community or nation. ❑ *In Chinese folklore the bat is an emblem of good fortune.* [N-UNCOUNT]

**folk song (folk songs)** also **folksong**. A **folk song** is a traditional song that is typical of a particular community or nation. [N-COUNT]

**folk|sy** /foʊksi/ 1 If you describe something as **folksy**, you mean that it is simple and has a style characteristic of folk craft and tradition. You sometimes use **folksy** to show disapproval of something because it seems unsophisticated. ❑ *...folksy country furniture.* [ADJ: usu ADJ n] 2 If you describe someone as **folksy**, you mean that they are friendly and informal in their behaviour. [AM] ❑ *...an elderly, folksy postman.* [ADJ: usu ADJ n] [approval]

**fol|li|cle** /fɒlɪkəl/ **(follicles)** A **follicle** is one of the small hollows in the skin which hairs grow from. [N-COUNT]

**fol|low** /fɒloʊ/ **(follows, following, followed)** ◆◆◆

1 If you **follow** someone who is going somewhere, you move along behind them because you want to go to the same place. ❑ *We followed him up the steps into a large hall... Please follow me, madam... They took him into a small room and I followed.* [VERB] [V n prep/adv] [V n] [V] [Also V *after* n]

2 If you **follow** someone who is going somewhere, you move along behind them without their knowledge, in order to catch them or find out where they are going. ❑ *She realized that the Mercedes was following her... I think we're being followed.* [VERB] [= *trail*] [V n] [V n]

3 If you **follow** someone to a place where they have recently gone and where they are now, you go to join them there. ❑ *He followed Janice to New York, where she was preparing an exhibition.* [VERB] [V n *to* n]

4 An event, activity, or period of time that **follows** a particular thing happens or comes after that thing, at a later time. ❑ *...the rioting and looting that followed the verdict... Other problems may follow... Eyewitnesses spoke of a noise followed by a huge red light.* [VERB] [V n] [V] [V-ed]

5 If you **follow** one thing **with** another, you do or say the second thing after you have done or said the first thing. ❑ *Her first major role was in Martin Scorsese's 'Goodfellas' and she followed this with a part in Spike Lee's 'Jungle Fever'.* [VERB] [V n *with* n] ♦ **Follow up** means the same as **follow**. ❑ *The book proved such a success that the authors followed it up with 'The Messianic Legacy'.* [PHRASAL VERB] [V n P *with* n] [Also V P n (not pron) *with* n]

6 If it **follows** that a particular thing is the case, that thing is a logical result of something else being true or being the case. ❑ *Just because a bird does not breed one year, it does not follow that it will fail the next... If the explanation is right, two things follow... It is easy to see the conclusions described in the text follow from this equation.* [VERB] [*it* V that] [V] [V *from* n]

7 If you refer to the words that **follow** or **followed**, you are referring to the words that come next or came next in a piece of writing or speech. ❑ *What follows is an eye-witness account... There followed a list of places where Hans intended to visit... General analysis is followed by five case studies.* [VERB] [V] [*there* V n] [*be* V-ed *by* n]

8 If you **follow** a path, route, or set of signs, you go somewhere using the path, route, or signs to direct you. ❑ *If they followed the road, they would be certain to reach a village... I followed the signs to Metrocity.* [VERB] [V n] [V n prep/adv]

9 If something such as a path or river **follows** a particular route or line, it goes along that route or line. ❑ *Our route follows the Pacific coast through densely populated neighbourhoods.* [VERB] [V n]

10 If you **follow** something with your eyes, or if your eyes **follow** it, you watch it as it moves or you look along its route or course. ❑ *Ann's eyes followed a police car as it drove slowly past.* [VERB] [V n]

11 Something that **follows** a particular course of development happens or develops in that way. ❑ *His release turned out to follow the pattern set by that of the other six hostages.* [VERB] [V n]

12 If you **follow** advice, an instruction, or a recipe, you act or do something in the way that it indicates. ❑ *Take care to follow the instructions carefully.* [VERB] [V n]

13 If you **follow** what someone else has done, you do it too because you think it is a good thing or because you want to copy them. ❑ *His admiration for the athlete did not extend to the point where he would follow his example in taking drugs... Where eastern Germany goes the rest will surely follow.* [VERB] [V n] [V]

14 If you **follow** someone in what you do, you do the same thing or job as they did previously. ❑ *He followed his father and became a surgeon... Anni-Frid's son has followed her into the music business.* [VERB] [V n] [V n *into* n]

15 If you are able to **follow** something such as an explanation or the story of a film, you understand it as it continues and develops. ❑ *Can you follow the plot so far?... I'm afraid I don't follow.* [VERB] [= *understand*] [V n] [V]

16 If you **follow** something, you take an interest in it and keep informed about what happens. ❑ *...the millions of people who follow football because they genuinely love it... She was following Laura's pro-* [VERB] [V n] [V n]

*gress closely.* [17] If you **follow** a particular religion or political belief, you have that religion or belief. ❑ *'Do you follow any particular religion?' — 'Yes, we're all Hindus.'* [VERB; V n] [18] → See also **following**.

PHRASES [19] You use **as follows** in writing or speech to introduce something such as a list, description, or explanation. ❑ *The winners are as follows: E. Walker; R. Foster; R. Gates; A. Mackintosh... This can be done if you proceed as follows.* [PHRASE: v-link PHR, PHR after v] [20] You use **followed by** to say what comes after something else in a list or ordered set of things. ❑ *Potatoes are still the most popular food, followed by white bread.* [PHRASE: PHR n] [21] After mentioning one course of a meal, you can mention the next course by saying what you will have **to follow** or what there will be **to follow**. ❑ *He decided on roast chicken and vegetables, with apple pie to follow.* [PHRASE: n PHR] [22] **to follow in** someone's **footsteps** → see **footstep**. **to follow** your **nose** → see **nose**. **to follow suit** → see **suit**.

♦ **follow through** If you **follow through** an action, plan, or idea or **follow through with** it, you continue doing or thinking about it until you have done everything possible. ❑ *The leadership has been unwilling to follow through the implications of these ideas... I was trained to be an actress but I didn't follow it through... He decided to follow through with his original plan.* [PHRASAL VERB = pursue; V P n (not pron); V n P; V P *with* n/-ing; Also V P, V P *on* n]

♦ **follow up** If you **follow up** something that has been said, suggested, or discovered, you try to find out more about it or take action about it. ❑ *State security police are following up several leads... An officer took a statement from me, but no one's bothered to follow it up.* → See also **follow 5**, **follow-up**. [PHRASAL VERB = investigate; V P n (not pron); V n P]

**fol|low|er** /fɒləʊəʳ/ **(followers)** A **follower** of a particular person, group, or belief is someone who supports or admires this person, group, or belief. ❑ *...the Democratic Party's most loyal followers.* → See also **camp follower**. [N-COUNT: usu with poss = supporter]

**fol|low|ing** /fɒləʊɪŋ/ **(followings)** ◆◆◇

[1] **Following** a particular event means after that event. ❑ *In the centuries following Christ's death, Christians genuinely believed the world was about to end... Following a day of medical research, the conference focused on educational practices.* [PREP] [2] The **following** day, week, or year is the day, week, or year after the one you have just mentioned. ❑ *We went to dinner the following Monday evening... The following year she joined the Royal Opera House.* [ADJ: det ADJ ≠ previous]

[3] You use **following** to refer to something that you are about to mention. ❑ *Write down the following information: name of product, type, date purchased and price... The method of helping such patients is explained in the following chapters.* [ADJ: det ADJ] ♦ **The following** refers to the thing or things that you are about to mention. ❑ *Do you use any of the following? Pager, Answering machine, Mobile phone, Car phone.* [PRON: *the* PRON] [4] A person or organization that has a **following** has a group of people who support or admire their beliefs or actions. ❑ *Australian rugby league enjoys a huge following in New Zealand.* [N-COUNT: with supp, usu adj N] [5] If a boat or vehicle has a **following** wind, the wind is moving in the same direction as the boat or vehicle. [ADJ: ADJ n]

**follow-on** A **follow-on** is something that is done to continue or add to something done previously. ❑ *This course for bridge players with some experience is intended as a follow-on to the Beginners' course.* [N-SING: also no det, usu N *to* n]

**follow-through** **(follow-throughs)** [1] A **follow-through** is something that completes an action or a planned series of actions. ❑ *...the task of finding a durable solution to the refugee problem as a follow-through to the very temporary measures.* [N-UNCOUNT: also *a* N, oft N prep] [2] A **follow-through** is a movement that completes an action such as hitting a ball. ❑ *Focus on making a short, firm follow-through.* [N-VAR]

**follow-up** **(follow-ups)** A **follow-up** is something that is done to continue or add to something done previously. ❑ *They are recording a follow-up to their successful 1989 album... One man was arrested during the raid and another during a follow-up operation.* [N-VAR: oft N n]

**fol|ly** /fɒli/ **(follies)** [1] If you say that a particular action or way of behaving is **folly** or a **folly**, you mean that it is foolish. ❑ *It's sheer folly to build nuclear power stations in a country that has dozens of earthquakes every year.* [N-VAR: oft N *of* n/-ing, *it* v-link N to-inf] [2] A **folly** is a small tower or other unusual building that is built as a decoration in a large garden or park, especially in Britain in former times. [N-COUNT]

**fo|ment** /fəʊment/ **(foments, fomenting, fomented)** If someone or something **foments** trouble or violent opposition, they cause it to develop. [FORMAL] ❑ *They accused strike leaders of fomenting violence.* [VERB = incite; V n]

**fond** /fɒnd/ **(fonder, fondest)** [1] If you are **fond of** someone, you feel affection for them. ❑ *I am very fond of Michael... She was especially fond of a little girl named Betsy.* [ADJ: v-link ADJ *of* n] ♦ **fond|ness** *...a great fondness for children.* [N-UNCOUNT] [2] You use **fond** to describe people or their behaviour when they show affection. ❑ *...a fond father... He gave him a fond smile.* [ADJ: ADJ n] ♦ **fond|ly** *Liz saw their eyes meet fondly across the table.* [ADV: ADV after v] [3] If you are **fond of** something, you like it or you like doing it very much. ❑ *He was fond of marmalade... She is fond of collecting rare carpets.* [ADJ: v-link ADJ *of* n/-ing] ♦ **fond|ness** *I've always had a fondness for jewels.* [N-UNCOUNT: usu N *for* n/-ing] [4] If you have **fond** memories of someone or something, you remember them with pleasure. ❑ *I have very fond memories of living in our village.* [ADJ: ADJ n = pleasant] ♦ **fond|ly** *My dad took us there when I was about four and I remembered it fondly.* [ADV: ADV with v] [5] You use **fond** to describe hopes, wishes, or beliefs which you think are foolish because they seem unlikely to be fulfilled. ❑ *My fond hope is that we will be ready by Christmastime.* [ADJ: ADJ n] ♦ **fond|ly** *I fondly imagined that surgery meant a few stitches and an overnight stay in hospital.* [ADV: ADV with v]

**fon|dant** /fɒndənt/ **Fondant** is a sweet paste made from sugar and water. ❑ *...fondant cakes.* [N-UNCOUNT: oft N n]

**fon|dle** /fɒndəl/ **(fondles, fondling, fondled)** If you **fondle** someone or something, you touch them gently with a stroking movement, usually in a sexual way. ❑ *He tried to kiss her and fondle her.* [VERB; V n]

**fon|due** /fɒndjuː, AM -duː/ **(fondues)** A **fondue** is a sauce made from melted cheese into which you dip bread, or a pot of hot oil into which you dip pieces of meat or vegetables. [N-VAR]

**font** /fɒnt/ **(fonts)** [1] In printing, a **font** is a set of characters of the same style and size. [N-COUNT] [2] In a church, a **font** is a bowl which holds the water used for baptisms. [N-COUNT]

**food** /fuːd/ **(foods)** ◆◆◆ [1] **Food** is what people and animals eat. ❑ *Enjoy your food. ...supplies of food and water. ...emergency food aid. ...frozen foods.* → See also **convenience food**, **fast food**, **health food**, **junk food**, **wholefood**. [N-MASS]

PHRASES [2] If you are **off** your **food**, you do not want to eat, usually because you are ill. ❑ *It's not like you to be off your food.* [PHRASE: v-link PHR] [3] If you give someone **food for thought**, you make them think carefully about something. ❑ *Lord Fraser's speech offers much food for thought.* [PHRASE: usu PHR after v]

**food chain** **(food chains)** The **food chain** is a series of living things which are linked to each other because each thing feeds on the one next to it in the series. ❑ *The whole food chain is affected by the over use of chemicals in agriculture.* [N-COUNT: usu sing]

**foodie** /fuːdi/ **(foodies)** also **foody**. **Foodies** are people who enjoy cooking and eating different kinds of food. [INFORMAL] ❑ *Other neighbourhoods in the city offer foodies a choice of Chinese, Portuguese or Greek food.* [N-COUNT]

**food mix|er** **(food mixers)** also **food-mixer**. A **food mixer** is a piece of electrical equipment that is used to mix food such as cake mixture. [N-COUNT]

**food poi|son|ing** If you get **food poisoning**, you become ill because you have eaten food that has gone bad. [N-UNCOUNT]

**food pro|ces|sor (food processors)** A **food processor** is a piece of electrical equipment that is used to mix, chop, or beat food, or to make it into a liquid. N-COUNT

**food stamp (food stamps)** In the United States, **food stamps** are official vouchers that are given to people with low incomes to be exchanged for food. N-COUNT: usu pl

**food|stuff** /fuːdstʌf/ **(foodstuffs)** **Foodstuffs** are substances which people eat. ❑ *...basic foodstuffs such as sugar, cooking oil and cheese.* N-VAR: usu pl

**food value (food values)** The **food value** of a particular food is a measure of how good it is for you, based on its level of vitamins, minerals, or calories. N-VAR

**foody** /fuːdi/ → see **foodie**.

**fool** /fuːl/ **(fools, fooling, fooled)** 1 If you call someone a **fool**, you are indicating that you think they are not at all sensible and show a lack of good judgment. ❑ *'You fool!' she shouted... He'd been a fool to get involved with her!* ◆◇◇ N-COUNT disapproval = idiot 2 **Fool** is used to describe an action or person that is not at all sensible and shows a lack of good judgment. [mainly AM, INFORMAL] ❑ *What a damn fool thing to do!.* ADJ: ADJ n disapproval 3 If someone **fools** you, they deceive or trick you. ❑ *Art dealers fool a lot of people... Don't be fooled by his appearance... They tried to fool you into coming after us.* VERB = trick, con V n V n V n into -ing 4 If you say that a person **is fooling with** something or someone, you mean that the way they are behaving is likely to cause problems. ❑ *What are you doing fooling with such a staggering sum of money?* VERB V with n

**PHRASES** 5 If you **make a fool of** someone, you make them seem silly by telling people about something stupid that they have done, or by tricking them. ❑ *Your brother is making a fool of you... He'd been made a fool of.* PHRASE: V and N inflect 6 If you **make a fool of** yourself, you behave in a way that makes other people think that you are silly or lacking in good judgment. ❑ *He was drinking and making a fool of himself.* PHRASE: V and N inflect 7 If you say to someone '**More fool** you' when they tell you what they have done or what they plan to do, you are indicating that you think that it is silly and shows a lack of judgment. [BRIT] ❑ *Most managers couldn't care less about information technology. More fool them.* PHRASE disapproval 8 If you **play the fool** or **act the fool**, you behave in a playful, childish, and foolish way, usually in order to make other people laugh. ❑ *They used to play the fool together, calling each other silly names and giggling.* PHRASE: V inflects

♦ **fool about** → see **fool around 3**.

♦ **fool around** 1 If you **fool around**, you behave in a silly, dangerous, or irresponsible way. ❑ *They were fooling around on an Army firing range... Have you been fooling around with something you shouldn't?* PHRASAL VERB V P V P with n 2 If someone **fools around** with another person, especially when one of them is married, they have a casual sexual relationship. ❑ *Never fool around with the clients' wives... Her husband was fooling around.* PHRASAL VERB V P with n V P 3 If you **fool around**, you behave in a playful, childish, and silly way, often in order to make people laugh. In British English, you can also say you **fool about**. ❑ *Stop fooling about, man... They fooled around for the camera.* PHRASAL VERB = mess about V P V P

**fool|hardy** /fuːlhɑːʳdi/ If you describe behaviour as **foolhardy**, you disapprove of it because it is extremely risky. ❑ *When he tested an early vaccine on himself, some described the act as foolhardy.* ADJ: oft *it* v-link ADJ to-inf disapproval

**fool|ish** /fuːlɪʃ/ 1 If someone's behaviour or action is **foolish**, it is not sensible and shows a lack of good judgment. ❑ *It would be foolish to raise hopes unnecessarily... It is foolish to risk skin cancer.* ADJ: oft *it* v-link ADJ to-inf ♦ **fool|ish|ly** *He admitted that he had acted foolishly.* ADV: usu ADV with v ♦ **fool|ish|ness** *They don't accept any foolishness when it comes to spending money.* N-UNCOUNT 2 If you look or feel **foolish**, you look or feel so silly or ridiculous that people are likely to laugh at you. ❑ *I didn't want him to look foolish and be laughed at.* ADJ: usu v-link ADJ = ridiculous ♦ **fool|ish|ly** *He saw me standing there, grinning foolishly at him.* ADV: ADV after v

**fool|proof** /fuːlpruːf/ Something such as a plan or a machine that is **foolproof** is so well designed, easy to understand, or easy to use that it cannot go wrong or be used wrongly. ❑ *The system is not 100 per cent foolproof... I spent the day working out a foolproof plan to save him.* ADJ

**fools|cap** /fuːlzkæp/ **Foolscap** is paper which is about 34 centimetres by 43 centimetres in size. [mainly BRIT] N-UNCOUNT

**fool's gold** 1 **Fool's gold** is a substance that is found in rock and that looks very like gold. N-UNCOUNT 2 If you say that a plan for getting money is **fool's gold**, you mean that it is foolish to carry it out because you are sure that it will fail or cause problems. ❑ *The British establishment seems to be off on another quest for fool's gold.* N-UNCOUNT disapproval

**fool's para|dise** If you say that someone is living in **a fool's paradise**, you are criticizing them because they are not aware that their present happy situation is likely to change and get worse. ❑ *...living in a fool's paradise of false prosperity.* N-SING: *a* N disapproval

**foot** /fʊt/ **(feet)** 1 Your **feet** are the parts of your body that are at the ends of your legs, and that you stand on. ❑ *She stamped her foot again. ...a foot injury. ...his aching arms and sore feet.* ◆◆◆ N-COUNT ♦ **-footed** *She was bare-footed. ...pink-footed geese.* COMB in ADJ 2 **The foot of** something is the part that is farthest from its top. ❑ *David called to the children from the foot of the stairs... A single word at the foot of a page caught her eye.* N-SING: usu *the* N *of* n = bottom ≠head, top 3 **The foot of** a bed is the end nearest to the feet of the person lying in it. ❑ *Friends stood at the foot of the bed, looking at her with serious faces.* N-SING: usu *the* N *of* n ≠head 4 A **foot** is a unit for measuring length, height, or depth, and is equal to 12 inches or 30.48 centimetres. When you are giving measurements, the form 'foot' is often used as the plural instead of the plural form 'feet'. ❑ *This beautiful and curiously shaped lake lies at around fifteen thousand feet... He occupies a cell 10 foot long, 6 foot wide and 10 foot high... I have to give my height in feet and inches.* N-COUNT: usu num N, oft num N adj 5 A **foot** brake or **foot** pump is operated by your foot rather than by your hand. ❑ *I tried to reach the foot brakes but I couldn't.* ADJ: ADJ n 6 A **foot** patrol or **foot** soldiers walk rather than travelling in vehicles or on horseback. ❑ *Paratroopers and foot-soldiers entered the building on the government's behalf.* ADJ: ADJ n 7 → See also **footing**.

**PHRASES** 8 If you get **cold feet about** something, you become nervous or frightened about it because you think it will fail. ❑ *The Government is getting cold feet about the reforms.* PHRASE: V inflects, oft PHR *about* n 9 If you say that someone **is finding** their **feet** in a new situation, you mean that they are starting to feel confident and to deal with things successfully. ❑ *I don't know anyone in England but I am sure I will manage when I find my feet.* PHRASE: V inflects 10 If you say that someone has their **feet on the ground**, you approve of the fact that they have a sensible and practical attitude towards life, and do not have unrealistic ideas. ❑ *In that respect he needs to keep his feet on the ground and not get carried away... Kevin was always level-headed with both feet on the ground.* PHRASE: usu v PHR approval 11 If you go somewhere **on foot**, you walk, rather than using any form of transport. ❑ *We rowed ashore, then explored the island on foot for the rest of the day.* PHRASE 12 If you are **on** your **feet**, you are standing up. ❑ *Everyone was on their feet applauding wildly.* PHRASE: usu v-link PHR 13 If you say that someone or something is **on** their **feet** again after an illness or difficult period, you mean that they have recovered and are back to normal. ❑ *He said they all needed to work together to put the country on its feet again.* PHRASE: v-link PHR, PHR after v 14 If you say that someone always **falls** or **lands on** their **feet**, you mean that they are always successful or lucky, although they do not seem to achieve this by their own efforts. ❑ *He has good looks and charm, and always falls on his feet.* PHRASE: V inflects

15 If you say that someone **has one foot in the grave**, you mean that they are very old or very ill and will probably die soon. [INFORMAL] PHRASE: V inflects 16 If you say, in British English, **the boot is on the other foot** or, mainly in American English, **the shoe is on the other foot**, you mean that a situation has been reversed completely, so that the person who was in the better position before is now in the worse one. PHRASE: V inflects ❑ *You're not in a position to remove me. The boot is now on the other foot.* 17 If someone **puts** their **foot down**, they use their authority in order to stop something happening. PHRASE: V inflects ❑ *He had planned to go skiing on his own in March but his wife had decided to put her foot down.* 18 If someone **puts** their **foot down** when they are driving, they drive as fast as they can. PHRASE: V inflects ❑ *I asked the driver to put his foot down for Nagchukha.* 19 If someone **puts** their **foot in it** or **puts** their **foot in** their **mouth**, they accidentally do or say something which embarrasses or offends people. [INFORMAL] PHRASE: V inflects ❑ *Our chairman has really put his foot in it, poor man, though he doesn't know it.* 20 If you **put** your **feet up**, you relax or have a rest, especially by sitting or lying with your feet supported off the ground. PHRASE: V inflects = rest ❑ *After supper he'd put his feet up and read. It was a pleasant prospect.* 21 If you never **put a foot wrong**, you never make any mistakes. PHRASE: V inflects, with brd-neg ❑ *When he's around, we never put a foot wrong.* 22 If you say that someone **sets foot** in a place, you mean that they enter it or reach it, and you are emphasizing the significance of their action. If you say that someone **never sets foot** in a place, you are emphasizing that they never go there. PHRASE: V inflects, oft with brd-neg [emphasis] ❑ *...the day the first man set foot on the moon... A little later I left that place and never set foot in Texas again.* 23 If someone has to **stand on** their **own two feet**, they have to be independent and manage their lives without help from other people. PHRASE: V inflects ❑ *My father didn't mind whom I married, so long as I could stand on my own two feet and wasn't dependent on my husband.* 24 If you get or rise **to** your **feet**, you stand up. PHRASE: v PHR ❑ *Malone got to his feet and followed his superior out of the suite... He sprang to his feet and ran outside.* 25 If someone **gets off on the wrong foot** in a new situation, they make a bad start by doing something in completely the wrong way. PHRASE: V inflects ❑ *Even though they called the election and had been preparing for it for some time, they got off on the wrong foot.* 26 to **foot the bill** → see **bill**. **foot in the door** → see **door**. **drag** your **feet** → see **drag**. to **vote with** your **feet** → see **vote**.

**foot|age** /fʊtɪdʒ/ **Footage** of a particular event is a film of it or the part of a film which shows this event. N-UNCOUNT ❑ *They are planning to show exclusive footage from this summer's festivals.*

**foot-and-mouth dis|ease** **Foot-and-mouth disease** or **foot-and-mouth** is a serious and highly infectious disease that affects cattle, sheep, pigs, and goats. N-UNCOUNT

**foot|ball** /fʊtbɔːl/ **(footballs)** ◆◆◇ 1 **Football** is a game played by two teams of eleven players using a round ball. Players kick the ball to each other and try to score goals by kicking the ball into a large net. [BRIT] N-UNCOUNT = soccer ❑ *Several boys were still playing football on the waste ground. ...Arsenal Football Club. ...Italian football fans.*

☑ in AM, use **soccer**

2 **Football** is a game played by two teams of eleven players using an oval ball. Players carry the ball in their hands or throw it to each other as they try to score goals that are called touchdowns. [AM] N-UNCOUNT ❑ *Two blocks beyond our school was a field where boys played football... This year's national college football championship was won by Princeton.*

☑ in BRIT, use **American football**

3 A **football** is a ball that is used for playing football. N-COUNT

**foot|ball|er** /fʊtbɔːləʳ/ **(footballers)** A **footballer** is a person who plays football, especially as a profession. [BRIT] N-COUNT

☑ in AM, use **soccer player**

**foot|balling** /fʊtbɔːlɪŋ/ **Footballing** means relating to the playing of football. [BRIT] ADJ: ADJ n ❑ *My two years at Farnham were the best of my footballing life.*

**foot|ball pools** If you do **the football pools**, you take part in a gambling competition in which people try to win money by guessing the results of football matches. [BRIT] N-PLURAL: the N = pools

**foot|bridge** /fʊtbrɪdʒ/ **(footbridges)** A **footbridge** is a narrow bridge for people travelling on foot. N-COUNT

**foot-dragging** **Foot-dragging** is the action of deliberately slowing down a plan or process. N-UNCOUNT [disapproval] ❑ *Their bargaining position with America was weakened by their foot-dragging over the Gulf.*

**-footed** /-fʊtid/ **-footed** combines with words such as 'heavy' or 'light' to form adjectives which indicate how someone moves or walks. COMB in ADJ ❑ *...a slim, light-footed little man... He was a nimble-footed boy of ten.* → See also **foot**, **flat-footed**, **sure-footed**.

**foot|er** /fʊtəʳ/ **(footers)** A **footer** is text such as a name or page number that can be automatically displayed at the bottom of each page of a printed document. Compare **header**. [COMPUTING] N-COUNT

**foot|fall** /fʊtfɔːl/ **(footfalls)** A **footfall** is the sound that is made by someone walking each time they take a step. [LITERARY] N-COUNT ❑ *She heard the priest's familiar, flat footfall on the staircase.*

**foot|hills** /fʊthɪlz/ The **foothills** of a mountain or a range of mountains are the lower hills or mountains around its base. N-PLURAL: oft N of n ❑ *Pasadena lies in the foothills of the San Gabriel mountains.*

**foot|hold** /fʊthoʊld/ **(footholds)** 1 A **foothold** is a strong or favourable position from which further advances or progress may be made. N-COUNT: oft adj N, N in n ❑ *If British business is to have a successful future, companies must establish a firm foothold in Europe.* 2 A **foothold** is a place such as a small hole or area of rock where you can safely put your foot when climbing. N-COUNT: oft adj N, N on n ❑ *He lowered his legs until he felt he had a solid foothold on the rockface beneath him.*

**footie** /fʊti/ also **footy**. **Footie** is the same as **football**. [BRIT, INFORMAL] N-UNCOUNT ❑ *...footie fans. ...a game of footie.*

**foot|ing** /fʊtɪŋ/ 1 If something is put **on** a particular **footing**, it is defined, established, or changed in a particular way, often so that it is able to develop or exist successfully. N-UNCOUNT: with supp, usu on N = basis ❑ *The new law will put official corruption on the same legal footing as treason.* 2 If you are **on** a particular kind of **footing** with someone, you have that kind of relationship with them. N-UNCOUNT: with supp, usu on N = basis ❑ *They decided to put their relationship on a more formal footing... They are now trying to compete on an equal footing.* 3 If a country or armed force is **on a war footing**, it is ready to fight a war. PHRASE: v-link PHR, PHR after v ❑ *The president placed the republic on a war footing.* 4 You refer to your **footing** when you are referring to your position and how securely your feet are placed on the ground. For example, if you lose your **footing**, your feet slip and you fall. N-UNCOUNT: poss N ❑ *He was cautious of his footing, wary of the edge... He lost his footing and slid into the water.*

**foot|lights** /fʊtlaɪts/ In a theatre, **the footlights** are the row of lights along the front of the stage. N-PLURAL

**foot|locker** /fʊtlɒkəʳ/ **(footlockers)** also **foot locker**. A **footlocker** is a large box for keeping personal possessions in, especially one that is placed at the end of a bed. [AM] N-COUNT

**foot|loose** /fʊtluːs/ 1 If you describe someone as **footloose**, you mean that they have no responsibilities or commitments, and are therefore free to do what they want and go where they ADJ want. ❑ *People that are single tend to be more footloose.* 2 If you describe someone as **footloose and fancy-free**, you mean that they are not married or in a similar relationship, and you therefore consider them to have very few responsibilities or commitments. PHRASE: usu v-link PHR

**foot|man** /fʊtmən/ **(footmen)** A **footman** is a male servant who typically does jobs such as opening doors or serving food, and who often wears a special uniform. N-COUNT

**foot|note** /fʊtnoʊt/ **(footnotes)** 1 A **footnote** is a note at the bottom of a page in a book which provides more detailed information about something that is mentioned on that page. N-COUNT 2 If you refer to what you are saying as a **footnote**, you mean that you are adding some information that is related to what has just been mentioned. ❑ *As a footnote, I should add that there was one point on which his bravado was more than justified.* N-COUNT 3 If you describe an event as a **footnote**, you mean that it is fairly unimportant although it will probably be remembered. ❑ *I'm afraid that his name will now become a footnote in history.* N-COUNT

**foot|path** /fʊtpɑːθ, -pæθ/ **(footpaths)** A **footpath** is a path for people to walk on, especially in the countryside. N-COUNT

**foot|plate** /fʊtpleɪt/ **(footplates)** On a steam train, **the footplate** is the place where the driver and fireman stand. [mainly BRIT] N-COUNT: usu *the* N in sing

**foot|print** /fʊtprɪnt/ **(footprints)** A **footprint** is a mark in the shape of a foot that a person or animal makes in or on a surface. N-COUNT

**foot|sie** /fʊtsi/ If someone **plays footsie with** you, they touch your feet with their own feet, for example under a table, often as a playful way of expressing their romantic or sexual feelings towards you. [INFORMAL] PHRASE: V inflects, usu PHR *with* n

**foot sol|dier** **(foot soldiers)** The **foot soldiers** of a particular organization are people who seem unimportant and who do not have a high position but who do a large amount of very important and often very boring work. N-COUNT

**foot|sore** /fʊtsɔːʳ/ If you are **footsore**, you have sore or tired feet after walking a long way. ADJ

**foot|step** /fʊtstep/ **(footsteps)** 1 A **footstep** is the sound or mark that is made by someone walking each time their foot touches the ground. ❑ *I heard footsteps outside.* N-COUNT: usu pl 2 If you **follow in** someone's **footsteps**, you do the same things as they did earlier. ❑ *My father is extremely proud that I followed in his footsteps and became a doctor.* PHRASE: V inflects

**foot|stool** /fʊtstuːl/ **(footstools)** A **footstool** is a small low stool that you can rest your feet on when you are sitting in a chair. N-COUNT

**foot|wear** /fʊtweəʳ/ **Footwear** refers to things that people wear on their feet, for example shoes and boots. ❑ *Some footballers get paid millions for endorsing footwear.* N-UNCOUNT

**foot|work** /fʊtwɜːʳk/ 1 **Footwork** is the way in which you move your feet, especially in sports such as boxing, football, or tennis, or in dancing. ❑ *This exercise improves your coordination, balance, timing and footwork.* N-UNCOUNT: usu supp N 2 If you refer to someone's **footwork** in a difficult situation, you mean the clever way they deal with it. ❑ *In the end, his brilliant legal footwork paid off.* N-UNCOUNT: supp N

**fop|pish** /fɒpɪʃ/ If you describe a man as **foppish**, you disapprove of the fact that he dresses in beautiful, expensive clothes and is very proud of his appearance. [OLD-FASHIONED] ADJ [disapproval]

**for** /fəʳ, STRONG fɔːʳ/ ◆◆◆

> In addition to the uses shown below, **for** is used after some verbs, nouns, and adjectives in order to introduce extra information, and in phrasal verbs such as 'account for' and 'make up for'. It is also used with some verbs that have two objects in order to introduce the second object.

1 If something is **for** someone, they are intended to have it or benefit from it. ❑ *Isn't that enough for you?... I have some free advice for you. ...a table for two... Your mother is only trying to make things easier for you... What have you got for me this morning, Patrick?... He wanted all the running of the business for himself.* PREP 2 If you work or do a job **for** someone, you are employed by them. ❑ *I knew he worked for a security firm... Have you had any experience writing for radio? ...a buyer for one of the largest chain stores in the south.* PREP 3 If you speak or act **for** a particular group or organization, you represent them. ❑ *She appears nightly on the television news, speaking for the State Department. ...the spokesman for the Democrats.* PREP 4 If someone does something **for** you, they do it so that you do not have to do it. ❑ *If your pharmacy doesn't stock the product you want, have them order it for you... He picked the bracelet up for me.* PREP 5 If you feel a particular emotion **for** someone, you feel it on their behalf. ❑ *This is the best thing you've ever done – I am so happy for you!... He felt a great sadness for this little girl.* PREP: adj/n PREP 6 If you feel a particular emotion **for** someone or something, they are the object of that emotion, and you feel it when you think about them. ❑ *John, I'm sorry for Steve, but I think you've made the right decisions... Mack felt a pitiless contempt for her.* PREP: adj/n PREP 7 You use **for** after words such as 'time', 'space', 'money', or 'energy' when you say how much there is or whether there is enough of it in order to be able to do or use a particular thing. ❑ *Many new trains have space for wheelchair users... It would take three to six hours for a round trip... Chris couldn't even raise the energy for a smile.* PREP 8 If something is **for** sale, hire, or use, it is available to be sold, hired, or used. ❑ *...fishmongers displaying freshwater fish for sale. ...a room for rent. ...a comfortable chair, suitable for use in the living room.* PREP 9 You use **for** when you state or explain the purpose of an object, action, or activity. ❑ *...drug users who use unsterile equipment for injections of drugs... The knife for cutting sausage was sitting in the sink. ...economic aid for the future reconstruction of the country.* PREP: PREP n/-ing 10 You use **for** after nouns expressing reason or cause. ❑ *He's soon to make a speech in parliament explaining his reasons for going... The county hospital could find no physical cause for Sumner's problems... He has now been formally given the grounds for his arrest.* PREP: n PREP n/-ing 11 **For** is used in conditional sentences, in expressions such as **'if not for'** and **'were it not for'**, to introduce the only thing which prevents the main part of the sentence from being true. ❑ *If not for John, Brian wouldn't have learned the truth... The earth would be a frozen ball if it were not for the radiant heat of the sun... She might have forgotten her completely had it not been for recurrent nightmares.* PREP 12 You use **for** to say how long something lasts or continues. ❑ *The toaster remained on for more than an hour... For a few minutes she sat on her bed watching the clock... They talked for a bit.* PREP: PREP amount 13 You use **for** to say how far something extends. ❑ *We drove on for a few miles... Great clouds of black smoke were rising for several hundred feet or so.* PREP: PREP amount 14 If something is bought, sold, or done **for** a particular amount of money, that amount of money is its price. ❑ *We got the bus back to Tange for 30 cents... The Martins sold their house for about 1.4 million pounds... The doctor was prepared to do the operation for a large sum.* PREP: PREP amount 15 If something is planned **for** a particular time, it is planned to happen then. ❑ *...the Welsh Boat Show, planned for July 30 – August 1... Marks & Spencer will be unveiling its latest fashions for autumn and winter.* PREP 16 If you do something **for** a particular occasion, you do it on that occasion or to celebrate that occasion. ❑ *He asked his daughter what she would like for her birthday... I'll be home for Christmas.* PREP 17 If you leave **for** a particular place or if you take a bus, train, plane, or boat **for** a place, you are going there. ❑ *They would be leaving for Rio early the next morning.* PREP 18 You use **for** when you make a statement about something in order to say how it af- PREP

fects or relates to someone, or what their attitude to it is. ❑ *What matters for most scientists is money and facilities... For her, books were as necessary to life as bread... It would be excellent experience for him to travel a little.* [19] After some adjective, noun, and verb phrases, you use **for** to introduce the subject of the action indicated by the following infinitive verb. ❑ *It might be possible for a single woman to be accepted as a foster parent... I had made arrangements for my affairs to be dealt with by one of my children... He held out his glass for an old waiter to refill.* PREP: PREP n to-inf

[20] You use **for** when you say that an aspect of something or someone is surprising in relation to other aspects of them. ❑ *He was tall for an eight-year-old... He had too much money for a young man.* PREP

[21] If you say that you are **for** a particular activity, you mean that this is what you want or intend to do. ❑ *Right, who's for a toasted sandwich then?... 'What'll it be?' Paul said. — 'I'm for halibut.'* PREP: v-link PREP n/-ing

[22] If you say that something is **not for** you, you mean that you do not enjoy it or that it is not suitable for you. [INFORMAL] ❑ *Wendy decided the sport was not for her.* PREP: with neg [23] If it is **for** you **to** do something, it is your responsibility or right to do it. ❑ *I wish you would come back to Washington with us, but that's for you to decide... It is not for me to arrange such matters.* PREP: PREP n to-inf [24] If you are **for** something, you agree with it or support it. ❑ *Are you for or against public transport?... I'm for a government that the people respect and that respects the people.* PREP: v-link PREP n/-ing ≠ against

[25] You use **for** after words such as 'argue', 'case', 'evidence', or 'vote' in order to introduce the thing that is being supported or proved. ❑ *Another union has voted for industrial action in support of a pay claim... The case for nuclear power is impressive... We have no real, objective, scientific evidence for our belief.* PREP: n/v PREP n ≠ against ♦ **For** is also an adverb. ❑ *833 delegates voted for, and only 432 against.* ADV: ADV after v [26] **For** is the preposition that is used after some nouns, adjectives, or verbs in order to introduce more information or to indicate what a quality, thing, or action relates to. ❑ *Reduced-calorie cheese is a great substitute for cream cheese... Car park owners should be legally responsible for protecting vehicles... Be prepared for both warm and cool weather... Make sure you have ample time to prepare for the new day ahead.* PREP: n/adj/v PREP n/-ing [27] To be named **for** someone means to be given the same name as them. [AM] ❑ *The Brady Bill is named for former White House Press Secretary James Brady.* PREP

✔ in BRIT, use **after**

[28] You use **for** with 'every' when you are stating a ratio, to introduce one of the things in the ratio. ❑ *For every farm job that is lost, two or three other jobs in the area are put at risk... Where there had been one divorce for every 100 marriages before the war, now there were five.* PREP [29] You can use **for** in expressions such as **pound for pound** or **mile for mile** when you are making comparisons between the values or qualities of different things. ❑ *...the Antarctic, mile for mile one of the planet's most lifeless areas... He insists any tax cut be matched dollar-for-dollar with cuts in spending.* PREP: n PREP n [30] If a word or expression has the same meaning as another word or expression, you can say that the first one is another word or expression **for** the second one. ❑ *The technical term for sunburn is erythema.* PREP [31] You use **for** in a piece of writing when you mention information which will be found somewhere else. ❑ *For further information on the life of William James Sidis, see Amy Wallace, 'The Prodigy'.* PREP

**PHRASES** [32] If you say that you are **all for** doing something, you agree or strongly believe that it should be done, but you are also often suggesting that other people disagree with you or that there are practical difficulties. ❑ *He is all for players earning what they can while they are in the game... I was all for it, but Wolfe said no.* PHRASE: v-link PHR, PHR -ing/n [33] If you **are in for it** or, in British English, if you **are for it**, you are likely to get into trouble because of something you have done. [INFORMAL] PHRASE: V inflects [34] You use expressions such as **for the first time** and **for the last time** when you are talking about how often something has happened before. ❑ *He was married for the second time, this time to a Belgian... For the first time in my career, I was failing.* PHRASE: PHR with cl [35] **as for** → see **as**. **but for** → see **but**. **for all** → see **all**.

**for|age** /fɒrɪdʒ, AM fɔːr-/ **(forages, foraging, foraged)** [1] If someone **forages for** something, they search for it in a busy way. ❑ *They were forced to forage for clothing and fuel.* VERB V for n [2] When animals **forage**, they search for food. ❑ *We disturbed a wild boar that had been foraging by the roadside... The cat forages for food.* VERB V V for n

**for|ay** /fɒreɪ, AM fɔːreɪ/ **(forays)** [1] If you make a **foray into** a new or unfamiliar type of activity, you start to become involved in it. ❑ *Emporio Armani, the Italian fashion house, has made a discreet foray into furnishings. ...her first forays into politics.* N-COUNT: oft poss N, usu N into n [2] You can refer to a short journey that you make as a **foray** if it seems to involve excitement or risk, for example because it is to an unfamiliar place or because you are looking for a particular thing. ❑ *Most guests make at least one foray into the town.* N-COUNT: usu N into/to n [3] If a group of soldiers make a **foray into** enemy territory, they make a quick attack there, and then return to their own territory. ❑ *These base camps were used by the PKK guerrillas to make forays into Turkey.* N-COUNT: oft N into n = raid

**for|bade** /fəʳbæd, -beɪd/ **Forbade** is the past tense of **forbid**.

**for|bear** /fɔːʳbeəʳ/ **(forbears, forbearing, forbore, forborne)** If you **forbear to** do something, you do not do it although you have the opportunity or the right to do it. [FORMAL] ❑ *I forbore to comment on this... Protesters largely forbore from stone-throwing and vandalism.* VERB V to-inf V from -ing/n

**for|bear|ance** /fɔːʳbeərəns/ If you say that someone has shown **forbearance**, you admire them for behaving in a calm and sensible way about something that they have a right to be very upset or angry about. [FORMAL] ❑ *All the Greenpeace people behaved with impressive forbearance and dignity.* N-UNCOUNT [approval]

**for|bear|ing** /fɔːʳbeərɪŋ/ Someone who is **forbearing** behaves in a calm and sensible way at a time when they would have a right to be very upset or angry. [FORMAL] ADJ [approval] = tolerant

**for|bid** /fəʳbɪd/ **(forbids, forbidding, forbade, forbidden)** [1] If you **forbid** someone **to** do something, or if you **forbid** an activity, you order that it must not be done. ❑ *They'll forbid you to marry... Brazil's constitution forbids the military use of nuclear energy.* VERB = prohibit V n to-inf V n [2] If something **forbids** a particular course of action or state of affairs, it makes it impossible for the course of action or state of affairs to happen. ❑ *His own pride forbids him to ask Arthur's help... Custom forbids any modernisation.* VERB V n to-inf V n [3] **God forbid** → see **god**. **heaven forbid** → see **heaven**.

**for|bid|den** /fəʳbɪdᵊn/ [1] If something is **forbidden**, you are not allowed to do it or have it. ❑ *Smoking was forbidden everywhere... It is forbidden to drive faster than 20mph.* ADJ: usu v-link ADJ, oft it v-link ADJ to-inf [2] A **forbidden** place is one that you are not allowed to visit or enter. ❑ *This was a forbidden area for foreigners.* ADJ: usu ADJ n [3] **Forbidden** is used to describe things that people strongly disapprove of or feel guilty about, and that are not often mentioned or talked about. ❑ *The war was a forbidden subject... Divorce? It was such a forbidden word.* ADJ: usu ADJ n = taboo

**for|bid|den fruit** **(forbidden fruits)** **Forbidden fruit** is a source of pleasure that involves breaking a rule or doing something that you are not supposed to do. ❑ *...the forbidden fruit of an illicit romance.* N-VAR

**for|bid|ding** /fəʳbɪdɪŋ/ If you describe a person, place, or thing as **forbidding**, you mean they have a severe, unfriendly, or threatening appearance. ❑ *There was something a little severe and forbidding about her face. ...a huge, forbidding building.* ADJ

**force** /fɔːʳs/ **(forces, forcing, forced)** ◆◆◆ [1] VERB If someone **forces** you **to** do something, they make you do it even though you do not want to, for example by threatening you. ❑ *He was forced to resign by Russia's conservative parliament... I cannot force you in this. You must decide... They were grabbed by three men who appeared to force them into a car.* V n to-inf V n V n prep/adv [2] VERB If a situation or event **forces** you to do something, it makes it necessary for you to do something that you would not otherwise have done. ❑ *A back injury forced her to withdraw from Wimbledon... He turned right, down a dirt road that forced him into four-wheel drive... She finally was forced to the conclusion that she wouldn't get another paid job in her field.* V n to-inf V n *into/to/out of* n V n *into/to/out of* n [3] VERB = impose If someone **forces** something **on** or **upon** you, they make you accept or use it when you would prefer not to. ❑ *To force this agreement on the nation is wrong.* V n *on/upon* n [4] VERB If you **force** something into a particular position, you use a lot of strength to make it move there. ❑ *They were forcing her head under the icy waters, drowning her.* V n prep/adv [5] VERB If someone **forces** a lock, a door, or a window, they break the lock or fastening in order to get into a building without using a key. ❑ *That evening police forced the door of the flat and arrested Mr Roberts... He tried to force the window open but it was jammed shut.* V n V n adj [6] N-UNCOUNT If someone uses **force** to do something, or if it is done by **force**, strong and violent physical action is taken in order to achieve it. ❑ *The government decided against using force to break-up the demonstrations. ...the guerrillas' efforts to seize power by force.* [7] N-UNCOUNT **Force** is the power or strength which something has. ❑ *The force of the explosion shattered the windows of several buildings.* [8] N-COUNT: with supp, oft N *in/behind* n If you refer to someone or something as a **force** in a particular type of activity, you mean that they have a strong influence on it. ❑ *For years the army was the most powerful political force in the country... One of the driving forces behind this recent expansion is the growth of services.* [9] N-UNCOUNT: oft N *of* n The **force of** something is the powerful effect or quality that it has. ❑ *He changed our world through the force of his ideas.* [10] N-COUNT: usu pl, usu with supp You can use **forces** to refer to processes and events that do not appear to be caused by human beings, and are therefore difficult to understand or control. ❑ *...the protection of mankind against the forces of nature: epidemics, predators, floods, hurricanes... The principle of market forces was applied to some of the countries most revered institutions.* [11] N-VAR In physics, a **force** is the pulling or pushing effect that something has on something else. ❑ *...the earth's gravitational force. ...protons and electrons trapped by magnetic forces in the Van Allen belts.* [12] N-UNCOUNT: N num **Force** is used before a number to indicate a wind of a particular speed or strength, especially a very strong wind. ❑ *Northerly winds will increase to force six by midday.* [13] VERB If you **force** a smile or a laugh, you manage to smile or laugh, but with an effort because you are unhappy. ❑ *Joe forced a smile, but underneath he was a little disturbed... 'Why don't you offer me a drink?' he asked, with a forced smile.* V n V-ed [14] N-COUNT: usu pl **Forces** are groups of soldiers or military vehicles that are organized for a particular purpose. ❑ *...the deployment of American forces in the region.* [15] N-PLURAL **The forces** means the army, the navy, or the air force, or all three. ❑ *The more senior you become in the forces, the more likely you are to end up in a desk job.* [16] N-SING: det N **The force** is sometimes used to mean the police force. ❑ *It was hard for a police officer to make friends outside the force.* [17] → See also **air force**, **armed forces**, **labour force**, **peacekeeping**, **task force**, **tour de force**, **workforce**.

**PHRASES** [18] PHRASE: usu *from/by* PHR If you do something **from force of habit**, you do it because you have always done it in the past, rather than because you have thought carefully about it. ❑ *Unconsciously, by force of habit, she plugged the coffee pot in.* [19] PHRASE: v-link PHR A law, rule, or system that is **in force** exists or is being used. ❑ *Although the new tax is already in force, you have until November to lodge an appeal.* [20] PHRASE: PHR after v When people do something **in force**, they do it in large numbers. ❑ *Voters turned out in force for their first taste of multi-party elections.* [21] PHRASE: V inflects, pl-n PHR, PHR *with* n If you **join forces with** someone, you work together in order to achieve a common aim or purpose. ❑ *William joined forces with businessman Nicholas Court to launch the new vehicle.* [22] PHRASE: V inflects, oft PHR *through/into* n If you **force** your **way through** or **into** somewhere, you have to push or break things that are in your way in order to get there. ❑ *The miners were armed with clubs as they forced their way through a police cordon... He forced his way into a house shouting for help.* [23] **to force** someone's **hand** → see **hand**.

♦ **force back** PHRASAL VERB = fight back If you **force back** an emotion or desire, you manage, with an effort, not to experience it. ❑ *Nancy forced back tears. She wasn't going to cry in front of all those people.* V P n (not pron) Also V n P

**forced** /fɔːʳst/ [1] ADJ: ADJ n A **forced** action is something that you do because someone else makes you do it. ❑ *A system of forced labour was used on the cocoa plantations.* [2] ADJ: ADJ n A **forced** action is something that you do because circumstances make it necessary. ❑ *He made a forced landing on a highway.* [3] ADJ ≠ natural If you describe something as **forced**, you mean it does not happen naturally and easily. ❑ *...a forced smile... She called him darling. It sounded so forced.*

**force-feed** **(force-feeds, force-feeding, force-fed)** VERB If you **force-feed** a person or animal, you make them eat or drink by pushing food or drink down their throat. ❑ *Production of the foie gras pâté involves force-feeding geese and ducks so that their livers swell.* V n

**force|ful** /fɔːʳsfʊl/ [1] ADJ [approval] If you describe someone as **forceful**, you approve of them because they express their opinions and wishes in a strong, emphatic, and confident way. ❑ *He was a man of forceful character, with considerable insight and diplomatic skills.* ♦ **force|ful|ly** ADV: ADV with v *Mrs. Dambar was talking very rapidly and somewhat forcefully.* ♦ **force|ful|ness** N-UNCOUNT *She had inherited her father's forcefulness.* [2] ADJ = powerful Something that is **forceful** has a very powerful effect and causes you to think or feel something very strongly. ❑ *It made a very forceful impression on me... For most people a heart attack is a forceful reminder that they are mortal.* ♦ **force|ful|ly** ADV: ADV with v *Daytime television tended to remind her too forcefully of her own situation.* [3] ADJ = powerful A **forceful** point or argument in a discussion is one that is good, valid, and convincing.

**for|ceps** /fɔːʳseps/ N-PLURAL: also *a pair of* N **Forceps** are an instrument consisting of two long narrow arms. Forceps are used by a doctor to hold things.

**for|cible** /fɔːʳsɪbᵊl/ ADJ: usu ADJ n **Forcible** action involves physical force or violence. ❑ *Reports are coming in of the forcible resettlement of villagers from the countryside into towns.*

**ford** /fɔːʳd/ **(fords, fording, forded)** [1] N-COUNT A **ford** is a shallow place in a river or stream where it is possible to cross safely without using a boat. [2] VERB If you **ford** a river or stream, you cross it without using a boat, usually at a shallow point. ❑ *They were guarding the bridge, so we forded the river.* V n

**fore** /fɔːʳ/ [1] PHRASE: PHR after v If someone or something comes **to the fore** in a particular situation or group, they become important or popular. ❑ *A number of low-budget independent films brought new directors and actors to the fore.* [2] ADJ: ADJ n = front **Fore** is used to refer to parts at the front of an animal, ship, or aircraft. ❑ *There had been no direct damage in the fore part of the ship.*

**fore|arm** /fɔːrɑːʳm/ **(forearms)** N-COUNT: oft poss N Your **forearm** is the part of your arm between your elbow and your wrist.

**fore|armed** /fɔːʳwɔːʳnd/ PHRASE If you say **'Forewarned is forearmed'**, you are saying that if you know about a problem or situation in advance, you will be able to deal with it when you need to.

**fore|bear** /fɔːʳbeəʳ/ **(forebears)** Your **forebears** are your ancestors. [LITERARY] ❑ *I'll come back to the land of my forebears.* N-COUNT: usu with poss = forefather

**fore|bod|ing** /fɔːʳboʊdɪŋ/ **(forebodings)** **Foreboding** is a strong feeling that something terrible is going to happen. ❑ *His triumph was overshadowed by an uneasy sense of foreboding.* N-VAR

**fore|cast** /fɔːʳkɑːst, -kæst/ **(forecasts, forecasting, forecasted)** ◆◇◇

> ✔ The forms **forecast** and **forecasted** can both be used for the past tense and past participle.

1 A **forecast** is a statement of what is expected to happen in the future, especially in relation to a particular event or situation. ❑ *...a forecast of a 2.25 per cent growth in the economy... He delivered his election forecast... The weather forecast is better for today.* N-COUNT: usu with supp 2 If you **forecast** future events, you say what you think is going to happen in the future. ❑ *They forecast a humiliating defeat for the Prime Minister... He forecasts that average salary increases will remain around 4 per cent.* VERB V n V that 3 ➔ See also **weather forecast**.

**fore|cast|er** /fɔːʳkɑːstəʳ, -kæst-/ **(forecasters)** A **forecaster** is someone who uses detailed knowledge about a particular activity in order to work out what they think will happen in that activity in the future. ❑ *Some of the nation's top economic forecasters say the economic recovery is picking up speed.* ➔ See also **weather forecaster**. N-COUNT

**fore|cas|tle** /foʊksl/ **(forecastles)** or **fo'c'sle** **The forecastle** is the part at the front of a ship where the sailors live. N-COUNT: usu *the* N in sing

**fore|close** /fɔːʳkloʊz/ **(forecloses, foreclosing, foreclosed)** If the person or organization that lent someone money **forecloses**, they take possession of a property that was bought with the borrowed money, for example because regular repayments have not been made. [BUSINESS] ❑ *The bank foreclosed on the mortgage for his previous home.* VERB V *on* n Also V

**fore|clo|sure** /fɔːʳkloʊʒəʳ/ **(foreclosures)** **Foreclosure** is when someone who has lent money to a person or organization so that they can buy property takes possession of the property because the money has not been repaid. [BUSINESS] ❑ *If homeowners can't keep up the payments, they face foreclosure... If interest rates go up, won't foreclosures rise?* N-VAR

**fore|court** /fɔːʳkɔːʳt/ **(forecourts)** The **forecourt** of a large building or petrol station is the open area at the front of it. [mainly BRIT] ❑ *I locked the bike in the forecourt of the Kirey Hotel.* N-COUNT: oft N *of* n, n N

**fore|deck** /fɔːʳdek/ **(foredecks)** **The foredeck** is the part of the deck at the front of a ship. N-COUNT: usu N SING, *the* N

**fore|father** /fɔːʳfɑːðəʳ/ **(forefathers)** Your **forefathers** are your ancestors, especially your male ancestors. [LITERARY] ❑ *They were determined to go back to the land of their forefathers.* N-COUNT: usu pl, usu poss N = forebear

**fore|finger** /fɔːʳfɪŋgəʳ/ **(forefingers)** Your **forefinger** is the finger that is next to your thumb. ❑ *He took the pen between his thumb and forefinger.* N-COUNT: oft poss N

**fore|foot** /fɔːʳfʊt/ **(forefeet)** A four-legged animal's **forefeet** are its two front feet. N-COUNT: usu pl

**fore|front** /fɔːʳfrʌnt/ 1 If you are at **the forefront** of a campaign or other activity, you have a leading and influential position in it. ❑ *They have been at the forefront of the campaign for political change.* N-SING: *the* N, usu *at/in/to* N, N *of/in* n/-ing 2 If something is **at the forefront of** people's minds or attention, they think about it a lot because it is particularly important to them. ❑ *The pension issue was not at the forefront of his mind in the spring of 1985.* N-SING: *the* N, usu *at/in/to* N *of* n

**fore|go** /fɔːʳgoʊ/ **(foregoes, foregoing, forewent, foregone)** also **forgo**. If you **forego** something, you decide to do without it, although you would like it. [FORMAL] ❑ *Keen skiers are happy to forego a summer holiday to go skiing.* VERB = do without V n

**fore|going** /fɔːʳgoʊɪŋ, fɔːʳgoʊ-/ You can refer to what has just been stated or mentioned as **the foregoing**. [FORMAL] ❑ *You might think from the foregoing that the French want to phase accents out. Not at all.* PRON: *the* PRON ♦ **Foregoing** is also an adjective. ❑ *The foregoing paragraphs were written in 1985.* ADJ: ADJ n

**fore|gone** /fɔːʳgɒn/ 1 **Foregone** is the past participle of **forego**. 2 If you say that a particular result is **a foregone conclusion**, you mean you are certain that it will happen. ❑ *Most voters believe the result is a foregone conclusion.* PHRASE: usu v-link PHR, oft *it* v-link PHR that

**fore|ground** /fɔːʳgraʊnd/ **(foregrounds)** 1 **The foreground** of a picture or scene you are looking at is the part or area of it that appears nearest to you. ❑ *He is the bowler-hatted figure in the foreground of Orpen's famous painting.* N-VAR: oft *in the* N ≠ background 2 If something or someone is **in the foreground**, or comes **to the foreground**, they receive a lot of attention. ❑ *This is another worry that has come to the foreground in recent years.* N-SING: usu *the* N, oft *in/to* N

**fore|hand** /fɔːʳhænd/ **(forehands)** A **forehand** is a shot in tennis or squash in which the palm of your hand faces the direction in which you are hitting the ball. ❑ *Agassi saw his chance and, with another lightning forehand, reached match point.* N-COUNT

**fore|head** /fɒrɪd, fɔːʳhed/ **(foreheads)** Your **forehead** is the area at the front of your head between your eyebrows and your hair. N-COUNT: oft poss N = brow

**for|eign** /fɒrɪn, AM fɔːr-/ ◆◆◆ 1 Something or someone that is **foreign** comes from or relates to a country that is not your own. ❑ *...in Frankfurt, where a quarter of the population is foreign... She was on her first foreign holiday without her parents. ...a foreign language... It is the largest ever private foreign investment in the Bolivian mining sector.* ADJ 2 In politics and journalism, **foreign** is used to describe people, jobs, and activities relating to countries that are not the country of the person or government concerned. ❑ *...the German foreign minister... I am the foreign correspondent in Washington of La Tribuna newspaper of Honduras. ...the effects of US foreign policy in the 'free world'.* ADJ: ADJ n 3 A **foreign** object is something that has got into something else, usually by accident, and should not be there. [FORMAL] ❑ *The patient's immune system would reject the transplanted organ as a foreign object.* ADJ: usu ADJ n 4 Something that is **foreign to** a particular person or thing is not typical of them or is unknown to them. ❑ *The very notion of price competition is foreign to many schools.* ADJ: usu v-link ADJ *to* n

**for|eign body** **(foreign bodies)** A **foreign body** is an object that has come into something else, usually by accident, and should not be in it. [FORMAL] ❑ *...a foreign body in the eye.* N-COUNT

**for|eign|er** /fɒrɪnəʳ, AM fɔːr-/ **(foreigners)** A **foreigner** is someone who belongs to a country that is not your own. ❑ *They are discouraged from becoming close friends with foreigners.* ◆◇◇ N-COUNT

**for|eign ex|change** **(foreign exchanges)** 1 **Foreign exchanges** are the institutions or systems involved with changing one currency into another. ❑ *On the foreign exchanges, the US dollar is up point forty-five.* N-PLURAL 2 **Foreign exchange** is used to refer to foreign currency that is obtained through the foreign exchange system. ❑ *...an important source of foreign exchange. ...foreign-exchange traders.* N-UNCOUNT: oft N n

**For|eign Of|fice** **(Foreign Offices)** **The Foreign Office** is the government department, especially in Britain, which has responsibility for the government's dealings and relations with foreign governments. ❑ *...a Foreign Office spokesman.* N-COUNT: *the* N, oft N n

**for|eign ser|vice** **The foreign service** is the government department that employs diplomats to work in foreign countries. [AM] N-SING: *the* N

> ✔ in BRIT, use **diplomatic service**

**fore|knowl|edge** /fɔːʳnɒlɪdʒ/ If you have **foreknowledge of** an event or situation, you have some knowledge of it before it actually hap- N-UNCOUNT: oft N *of* n pens. ❑ *She has maintained that the General had foreknowledge of the plot.*

**fore|leg** /fɔːʳleg/ **(forelegs)** A four-legged animal's **forelegs** are its two front legs.
N-COUNT: usu pl

**fore|lock** /fɔːʳlɒk/ **(forelocks)** 1 A **forelock** is a piece of hair that falls over your forehead. People often used to pull their forelocks to show respect for other people of a higher class than they were. 2 If you say that a person **tugs their forelock** to another person, you are criticizing them for showing too much respect to the second person or being unnecessarily worried about their opinions. [mainly BRIT]
N-COUNT
PHRASE: V and N inflect, oft PHR *to* n [disapproval]

**fore|man** /fɔːʳmən/ **(foremen)** 1 A **foreman** is a person, especially a man, in charge of a group of workers. ❑ *He still visited the dairy daily, but left most of the business details to his manager and foreman.* 2 The **foreman** of a jury is the person who is chosen as their leader. ❑ *There was applause from the public gallery as the foreman of the jury announced the verdict.*
N-COUNT
N-COUNT

**fore|most** /fɔːʳmoʊst/ 1 The **foremost** thing or person in a group is the most important or best. ❑ *He was one of the world's foremost scholars of ancient Indian culture.* 2 You use **first and foremost** to emphasize the most important quality of something or someone. ❑ *It is first and foremost a trade agreement.*
ADJ
PHRASE: PHR n/prep, PHR with cl, PHR after v [emphasis]

**fore|name** /fɔːʳneɪm/ **(forenames)** Your **forename** is your first name. Your **forenames** are your names other than your surname. [FORMAL]
N-COUNT: oft poss N = *first name*

**fore|noon** /fɔːʳnuːn/ The **forenoon** is the morning. [OLD-FASHIONED]
N-SING

**fo|ren|sic** /fərensɪk/ **(forensics)** 1 **Forensic** is used to describe the work of scientists who examine evidence in order to help the police solve crimes. ❑ *They were convicted on forensic evidence alone... Forensic experts searched the area for clues.* 2 **Forensics** is the use of scientific techniques to solve crimes. ❑ *...the newest advances in forensics. ...federal forensics legislation.*
ADJ: ADJ n
N-UNCOUNT

**fore|play** /fɔːʳpleɪ/ **Foreplay** is activity such as kissing and stroking when it takes place before sexual intercourse.
N-UNCOUNT

**fore|run|ner** /fɔːʳrʌnəʳ/ **(forerunners)** If you describe a person or thing as the **forerunner of** someone or something similar, you mean they existed before them and either influenced their development or were a sign of what was going to happen. ❑ *...a machine which, in some respects, was the forerunner of the modern helicopter.*
N-COUNT: oft N *of* n = *precursor*

**fore|see** /fɔːʳsiː/ **(foresees, foreseeing, foresaw, foreseen)** If you **foresee** something, you expect and believe that it will happen. ❑ *He did not foresee any problems... He could never have foreseen that one day his books would sell in millions.*
VERB = *predict* V n V that Also V wh

**fore|see|able** /fɔːʳsiːəbᵊl/ 1 If a future event is **foreseeable**, you know that it will happen or that it can happen, because it is a natural or obvious consequence of something else that you know. ❑ *It seems to me that this crime was foreseeable and this death preventable.*
ADJ = *predictable*

**PHRASES** 2 If you say that something will happen **for the foreseeable future**, you think that it will continue to happen for a long time. ❑ *Profit and dividend growth looks like being above average for the foreseeable future.* 3 If you say that something will happen **in the foreseeable future** you mean that you think it will happen fairly soon. ❑ *So, might they finally have free elections in the foreseeable future?*
PHRASE: usu PHR after v, PHR with cl
PHRASE: usu PHR after v, PHR with cl

**fore|shad|ow** /fɔːʳʃædoʊ/ **(foreshadows, foreshadowing, foreshadowed)** If something **foreshadows** an event or situation, it suggests that it will happen. ❑ *The disappointing sales figures foreshadow more redundancies.*
VERB V n

**fore|shore** /fɔːʳʃɔːʳ/ **(foreshores)** Beside the sea, a lake, or a wide river, **the foreshore** is the part of the shore which is between the highest and lowest points reached by the water.
N-COUNT: usu sing

**fore|short|en** /fɔːʳʃɔːʳtᵊn/ **(foreshortens, foreshortening, foreshortened)** To **foreshorten** someone or something means to draw them, photograph them, or see them from an unusual angle so that the parts of them that are furthest away seem smaller than they really are. ❑ *She could see herself in the reflecting lenses, which had grotesquely foreshortened her.*
VERB V n

**fore|sight** /fɔːʳsaɪt/ Someone's **foresight** is their ability to see what is likely to happen in the future and to take appropriate action. ❑ *He was later criticised for his lack of foresight... They had the foresight to invest in new technology.*
N-UNCOUNT [approval]

**fore|skin** /fɔːʳskɪn/ **(foreskins)** A man's **foreskin** is the skin that covers the end of his penis.
N-VAR

**for|est** /fɒrɪst, AM fɔːr-/ **(forests)** 1 A **forest** is a large area where trees grow close together. ❑ *Parts of the forest are still dense and inaccessible. ...25 million hectares of forest.* 2 A **forest** of tall or narrow objects is a group of them standing or sticking upright. [LITERARY] ❑ *They descended from the plane into a forest of microphones and cameras.*
◆◇◇ N-VAR
N-COUNT: with supp, usu N *of* n

**fore|stall** /fɔːʳstɔːl/ **(forestalls, forestalling, forestalled)** If you **forestall** someone, you realize what they are likely to do and prevent them from doing it. ❑ *Large numbers of police were in the square to forestall any demonstrations.*
VERB = *stop* V n

**for|est|ed** /fɒrɪstɪd, AM fɔːr-/ A **forested** area is an area covered in trees growing closely together. ❑ *...a thickly forested valley... Only 8 per cent of Britain is forested.*
ADJ

**for|est|er** /fɒrɪstəʳ, AM fɔːr-/ **(foresters)** A **forester** is a person whose job is to look after the trees in a forest and to plant new ones.
N-COUNT

**for|est|ry** /fɒrɪstri, AM fɔːr-/ **Forestry** is the science or skill of growing and taking care of trees in forests, especially in order to obtain wood.
N-UNCOUNT

**fore|taste** /fɔːʳteɪst/ **(foretastes)** If you describe an event as **a foretaste of** a future situation, you mean that it suggests to you what that future situation will be like. ❑ *It was a foretaste of things to come.*
N-COUNT: usu *a* N *of* n = *indication*

**fore|tell** /fɔːʳtel/ **(foretells, foretelling, foretold)** If you **foretell** a future event, you predict that it will happen. [LITERARY] ❑ *...prophets who have foretold the end of the world.*
VERB V n Also V that/wh

**fore|thought** /fɔːʳθɔːt/ If you act with **forethought**, you think carefully before you act about what will be needed, or about what the consequences will be. ❑ *With a little forethought many accidents could be avoided.*
N-UNCOUNT

**fore|told** /fɔːʳtoʊld/ **Foretold** is the past tense and past participle of **foretell**.

**for|ever** /fərevəʳ/ also **for ever.** 1 If you say that something will happen or continue **forever**, you mean that it will always happen or continue. ❑ *I think that we will live together forever... I will forever be grateful for his considerable input.* 2 If something has gone or changed **forever**, it has gone or changed completely and permanently. ❑ *The old social order was gone forever... Their lives changed forever.* 3 If you say that something takes **forever** or lasts **forever**, you are emphasizing that it takes or lasts a very long time, or that it seems to. [INFORMAL] ❑ *The drive seemed to take forever.*
ADV: ADV with v
ADV: ADV after v
ADV: ADV after v [emphasis]

**fore|warn** /fɔːʳwɔːʳn/ **(forewarns, forewarning, forewarned)** If you **forewarn** someone **about** something, you warn them in advance that it is going to happen. ❑ *The Macmillan Guide had forewarned me of what to expect.* **forewarned is forearmed** → see **forearmed**.
VERB = *alert* V n *of/about* n Also V n that, V n

**fore|went** /fɔːʳwent/ **Forewent** is the past tense of **forego**.

**fore|word** /fɔːʳwɜːʳd/ **(forewords)** The **foreword** to a book is an introduction by the author or by someone else.
N-COUNT: oft N *to* n

**forex** /fɒreks/ **Forex** is an abbreviation for **foreign exchange**. ❑ *...the forex market.*
N-UNCOUNT

**for|feit** /fɔːʳfɪt/ **(forfeits, forfeiting, forfeited)** 1 If you **forfeit** something, you lose it or are forced to give it up because you have broken a rule or done something wrong. ❑ *He was ordered to forfeit more than £1.5m in profits... He argues that murderers forfeit their own right to life.* 2 If you **forfeit** something, you give it up willingly, especially so that you can achieve something else. ❑ *He has forfeited a lucrative fee but feels his well-being is more important.* 3 A **forfeit** is something that you have to give up because you have done something wrong. ❑ *That is the forfeit he must pay.*
VERB; V n; V n; VERB; V n; N-COUNT = penalty

**for|fei|ture** /fɔːʳfɪtʃəʳ/ **(forfeitures)** **Forfeiture** is the action of forfeiting something. [LEGAL] ❑ *...the forfeiture of illegally obtained profits... Both face maximum forfeitures of about $1.2 million.*
N-VAR: oft N *of* n

**for|gave** /fəʳgeɪv/ **Forgave** is the past tense of **forgive**.

**forge** /fɔːʳdʒ/ **(forges, forging, forged)** 1 If one person or institution **forges** an agreement or relationship with another, they create it with a lot of hard work, hoping that it will be strong or lasting. ❑ *The Prime Minister is determined to forge a good relationship with America's new leader... They agreed to forge closer economic ties... The programme aims to forge links between higher education and small businesses... The Community was trying to forge a common foreign and security policy.* 2 If someone **forges** something such as a banknote, a document, or a painting, they copy it or make it so that it looks genuine, in order to deceive people. ❑ *She alleged that Taylor had forged her signature on the form... They used forged documents to leave the country.* ♦ **forg|er** **(forgers)** *...the most prolific art forger in the country.* 3 A **forge** is a place where someone makes metal goods and equipment by heating pieces of metal and then shaping them. ❑ *...the blacksmith's forge. ...Woodbury Blacksmith & Forge Co.* 4 If someone **forges** an object out of metal, they heat the metal and then hammer and bend it into the required shape. ❑ *To forge a blade takes great skill.*
V-RECIP; V n *with* n; pl-n V n; NON-RECIP: V n *between* pl-n; V n; VERB; V n; V-ed; N-COUNT; N-COUNT: oft in names; VERB; V n

♦ **forge ahead** If you **forge ahead** with something, you continue with it and make a lot of progress with it. ❑ *He again pledged to forge ahead with his plans for reform... The two companies forged ahead, innovating and expanding.*
PHRASAL VERB; V P *with* n; V P

**for|gery** /fɔːʳdʒəri/ **(forgeries)** 1 **Forgery** is the crime of forging money, documents, or paintings. ❑ *He was found guilty of forgery.* 2 You can refer to a forged document, banknote, or painting as a **forgery**. ❑ *The letter was a forgery.*
N-UNCOUNT; N-COUNT

**for|get** /fəʳget/ **(forgets, forgetting, forgot, forgotten)** ◆◆◇ 1 If you **forget** something or **forget** how to do something, you cannot think of it or think how to do it, although you knew it or knew how to do it in the past. ❑ *Sometimes I improvise and change the words because I forget them... She forgot where she left the car and it took us two days to find it.* 2 If you **forget** something or **forget** to do it, you fail to think about it or fail to remember to do it, for example because you are thinking about other things. ❑ *She never forgets her daddy's birthday... She forgot to lock her door one day and two men got in... Don't forget that all dogs need a supply of fresh water to drink... She forgot about everything but the sun and the wind and the salt spray.* 3 If you **forget** something that you had intended to bring with you, you do not bring it because you did not think about it at the right time. ❑ *Once when we were going to Paris, I forgot my passport.* 4 If you **forget** something or someone, you deliberately put them out of your mind and do not think about them any more. ❑ *I hope you will forget the bad experience you had today... I found it very easy to forget about Sumner... She tried to forget that sometimes she heard them quarrelling.* 5 You say '**Forget it**' in reply to someone as a way of telling them not to worry or bother about something, or as an emphatic way of saying no to a suggestion. [SPOKEN] ❑ *'Sorry, Liz. I think I was a bit rude to you.' — 'Forget it, but don't do it again!'... 'You want more?' roared Claire. 'Forget it, honey.'* 6 You say **not forgetting** a particular thing or person when you want to include them in something that you have already talked about. ❑ *The first thing is to support as many shows as one can, not forgetting the small local ones.*
VERB ≠ remember; V n; V wh; VERB ≠ remember; V n; V to-inf; V that; V *about* n; VERB; V n; Also V *about* n; VERB; V n; V *about* n; V that; CONVENTION formulae; PHRASE: PHR n

**for|get|ful** /fəʳgetfʊl/ Someone who is **forgetful** often forgets things. ❑ *My mother has become very forgetful and confused recently.*
ADJ = absent-minded

**forget-me-not** **(forget-me-nots)** A **forget-me-not** is a small plant with tiny blue flowers.
N-COUNT

**for|get|table** /fəʳgetəbəl/ If you describe something or someone as **forgettable**, you mean that they do not have any qualities that make them special, unusual, or interesting. ❑ *He has acted in three forgettable action films.*
ADJ ≠ unforgettable

**for|giv|able** /fəʳgɪvəbəl/ If you say that something bad is **forgivable**, you mean that you can understand it and can forgive it in the circumstances. ❑ *Is infidelity ever forgivable?*
ADJ ≠ unforgivable

**for|give** /fəʳgɪv/ **(forgives, forgiving, forgave, forgiven)** 1 If you **forgive** someone who has done something bad or wrong, you stop being angry with them and no longer want to punish them. ❑ *Hopefully she'll understand and forgive you, if she really loves you... She'd find a way to forgive him for the theft of the money... Still, for those flashes of genius, you can forgive him anything.* 2 If you say that someone could **be forgiven for** doing something, you mean that they were wrong or mistaken, but not seriously, because many people would have done the same thing in those circumstances. ❑ *Looking at the figures, you could be forgiven for thinking the recession is already over.* 3 **Forgive** is used in polite expressions and apologies like '**forgive me**' and '**forgive my ignorance**' when you are saying or doing something that might seem rude, silly, or complicated. ❑ *Forgive me, I don't mean to insult you... I do hope you'll forgive me but I've got to leave... 'Forgive my manners,' she said calmly. 'I neglected to introduce myself.'* 4 If an organization such as a bank **forgives** someone's debt, they agree not to ask for that money to be repaid. ❑ *The American Congress has agreed to forgive Egypt's military debt.*
VERB; V n; V n *for* n/-ing; V n n; Also V; V-PASSIVE; *be* V-ed *for* -ing/n; VERB politeness; V n; V n; V n; VERB; V n

**for|give|ness** /fəʳgɪvnəs/ If you ask for **forgiveness**, you ask to be forgiven for something wrong that you have done. ❑ *I offered up a short prayer for forgiveness. ...a spirit of forgiveness and national reconciliation.*
N-UNCOUNT

**for|giv|ing** /fəʳgɪvɪŋ/ Someone who is **forgiving** is willing to forgive. ❑ *Voters can be remarkably forgiving of presidents who fail to keep their campaign promises.*
ADJ

**for|go** /fɔːʳgoʊ/ → see **forego**.

**for|got** /fəʳgɒt/ **Forgot** is the past tense of **forget**.

**for|got|ten** /fəʳgɒtən/ **Forgotten** is the past participle of **forget**.

**fork** /fɔːʳk/ **(forks, forking, forked)** 1 A **fork** is a tool used for eating food which has a row of three or four long metal points at the end. → See picture on page 1710. ❑ *...knives and forks.* 2 If you **fork** food **into** your mouth or **onto** a plate, you put it there using a fork. ❑ *Ann forked some fish into her mouth... He forked an egg onto a piece of bread and folded it into a sandwich.* 3 A garden **fork** is a tool used for breaking up soil which has a row of three or four long metal points at the end. 4 A **fork** in a road, path, or river is a point at which it divides into two parts and forms a 'Y' shape. ❑ *We arrived at a fork in the road... The road divides; you should take the right fork.* 5 If a road, path, or river **forks**, it forms a fork. ❑ *Beyond the village the road forked... The path dipped down to a sort of cove, and then it forked in two directions.* 6 → See also **tuning fork**.
N-COUNT; VERB; V n *into/onto* n; N-COUNT; N-COUNT: usu with supp; VERB: no cont; V; V prep/adv

♦ **fork out** If you **fork out for** something, you spend a lot of money on it. [INFORMAL] ❑ *He*
PHRASAL VERB = cough up

*will have to fork out for private school fees for Nina... You don't ask people to fork out every time they drive up the motorways... Britons fork out more than a billion pounds a year on toys.* V P *for/on* n / V P / V P n *for/on* n

**forked** /fɔːʳkt/ Something that divides into two parts and forms a 'Y' shape can be described as **forked**. ❑ *Jaegers are swift black birds with long forked tails.* ADJ: usu ADJ n

**forked light|ning** **Forked lightning** is lightning that divides into two or more parts near the ground. N-UNCOUNT

**fork|ful** /fɔːʳkfʊl/ **(forkfuls)** You can refer to an amount of food on a fork as a **forkful of** food. ❑ *I put a forkful of fillet steak in my mouth.* N-COUNT: usu N *of* n

**fork|lift truck** /fɔːʳklɪftrʌk/ **(forklift trucks)**

☑ in BRIT, also use **fork-lift truck**

A **forklift truck** or a **forklift** is a small vehicle with two movable parts on the front that are used to lift heavy loads. N-COUNT

**for|lorn** /fɔːʳlɔːʳn/ 1 If someone is **forlorn**, they feel alone and unhappy. [LITERARY] ❑ *One of the demonstrators sat forlorn on the pavement.* ADJ: ADJ n, v-link ADJ, ADJ after v 2 A **forlorn** hope or attempt is one that you think has no chance of success. ❑ *Peasants have left the land in the forlorn hope of finding a better life in cities.* ADJ: usu ADJ n

**form** /fɔːʳm/ **(forms, forming, formed)** ◆◆◆ 1 A **form of** something is a type or kind of it. ❑ *He contracted a rare form of cancer... Doctors are willing to take some form of industrial action... I am against hunting in any form.* N-COUNT: with supp, oft N *of* n 2 When something can exist or happen in several possible ways, you can use **form** to refer to one particular way in which it exists or happens. ❑ *Valleys often take the form of deep canyons... They received a benefit in the form of a tax reduction.* N-COUNT: with supp, oft N *of* n 3 When a particular shape **forms** or **is formed**, people or things move or are arranged so that this shape is made. ❑ *A queue forms outside Peter's study... They formed a circle and sang 'Auld Lang Syne'... The General gave orders for the cadets to form into lines.* VERB / V / V n / V *into* n / Also V n *into* n 4 The **form** of something is its shape. ❑ *...the form of the body.* N-COUNT: with supp 5 You can refer to something that you can see as a **form** if you cannot see it clearly, or if its outline is the clearest or most striking aspect of it. ❑ *She thought she'd never been so glad to see his bulky form.* N-COUNT: usu with supp 6 If something is arranged or changed so that it becomes similar to a thing with a particular structure or function, you can say that it **forms** that thing. ❑ *These panels folded up to form a screen some five feet tall.* VERB / V n 7 If something consists of particular things, people, or features, you can say that they **form** that thing. ❑ *Cereals form the staple diet of an enormous number of people around the world.* VERB / V n 8 If you **form** an organization, group, or company, you start it. ❑ *They tried to form a study group on human rights... They formed themselves into teams.* VERB / V n / V pron-refl *into* n 9 When something natural **forms** or **is formed**, it begins to exist and develop. ❑ *The stars must have formed 10 to 15 billion years ago... Huge ice sheets were formed.* VERB / V / *be* V-ed 10 If you **form** a relationship, a habit, or an idea, or if it **forms**, it begins to exist and develop. ❑ *This should help him form lasting relationships... An idea formed in his mind.* VERB / V n / V 11 If you say that something **forms** a person's character or personality, you mean that it has a strong influence on them and causes them to develop in a particular way. ❑ *Anger at injustice formed his character.* VERB = mould / V n 12 In sport, **form** refers to the ability or success of a person or animal over a period of time. ❑ *His form this season has been brilliant.* N-UNCOUNT: usu supp N 13 A **form** is a paper with questions on it and spaces marked where you should write the answers. Forms usually ask you to give details about yourself, for example when you are applying for a job or joining an organization. ❑ *You will be asked to fill in a form with details of your birth and occupation. ...application forms.* N-COUNT 14 → See also **sixth form**.

**PHRASES** 15 If you say that it is **bad form** to behave in a particular way, you mean that it is rude and impolite. [BRIT, OLD-FASHIONED] ❑ *It was thought bad form to discuss business on social occasions.* PHRASE: usu PHR after v, v-link PHR 16 If you say that someone is **in good form**, you mean that they seem healthy and cheerful. [BRIT] PHRASE: v-link PHR 17 If you say that someone is **off form**, you think they are not performing as well as they usually do. [BRIT] PHRASE: v-link PHR = below par 18 If you say that someone is **on form**, you think that they are performing their usual activity very well. [BRIT] ❑ *Robert Redford is back on form in his new movie 'Sneakers'.* PHRASE: v-link PHR 19 When something **takes form**, it develops or begins to be visible. ❑ *As plans took form in her mind, she realized the need for an accomplice... The face of Mrs Lisbon took form in the dimness.* PHRASE: V inflects 20 If someone or something behaves **true to form**, they do what is expected and is typical of them. ❑ *My luck was running true to form... True to form, she kept her guests waiting for more than 90 minutes.* PHRASE: v PHR, PHR with cl

**for|mal** /fɔːʳməl/ **(formals)** ◆◆◇ 1 **Formal** speech or behaviour is very correct and serious rather than relaxed and friendly, and is used especially in official situations. ❑ *He wrote a very formal letter of apology to Douglas... Business relationships are necessarily a bit more formal.* ADJ ≠ informal ♦ **for|mal|ly** *He took her back to Vincent Square in a taxi, saying goodnight formally on the doorstep.* ADV: ADV with v ♦ **for|mal|ity** *Lillith's formality and seriousness amused him.* N-UNCOUNT 2 A **formal** action, statement, or request is an official one. ❑ *UN officials said a formal request was passed to American authorities... No formal announcement had been made.* ADJ: ADJ n ≠ informal ♦ **for|mal|ly** *Diplomats haven't formally agreed to Anderson's plan.* ADV: ADV with v 3 **Formal** occasions are special occasions at which people wear smart clothes and behave according to a set of accepted rules. ❑ *One evening the film company arranged a formal dinner after the play.* ADJ: usu ADJ n ≠ informal ♦ **Formal** is also a noun. ❑ *...a wide array of events, including school formals and speech nights, weddings, and balls.* N-COUNT 4 **Formal** clothes are very smart clothes that are suitable for formal occasions. ❑ *They wore ordinary ties instead of the more formal high collar and cravat.* ADJ: ADJ n ≠ informal, casual ♦ **for|mal|ly** *It was really too warm for her to dress so formally.* ADV: ADV after v, ADV -ed 5 **Formal** education or training is given officially, usually in a school, college, or university. ❑ *Leroy didn't have any formal dance training.* ADJ: ADJ n ♦ **for|mal|ly** *Mr Dawe was the ancient, formally trained head gardener.* ADV: ADV -ed 6 → See also **formality**.

**for|mal|de|hyde** /fɔːʳmældihaɪd/ **Formaldehyde** is a strong-smelling gas, used especially to preserve parts of animals or plants for biological study. N-UNCOUNT

**for|mal|ise** /fɔːʳməlaɪz/ → see **formalize**.

**for|mal|ism** /fɔːʳməlɪzəm/ **Formalism** is a style, especially in art, in which great attention is paid to the outward form or appearance rather than to the inner reality or significance of things. N-UNCOUNT ♦ **for|mal|ist** ❑ *...art based on formalist principles.* ADJ: ADJ n

**for|mal|ity** /fɔːʳmælɪti/ **(formalities)** 1 If you say that an action or procedure is just a **formality**, you mean that it is done only because it is normally done, and that it will not have any real effect on the situation. ❑ *With the Cold War almost over, the talks were a mere formality.* N-COUNT 2 **Formalities** are formal actions or procedures that are carried out as part of a particular activity or event. ❑ *They are whisked through the immigration and customs formalities in a matter of minutes.* N-COUNT: usu pl 3 → See also **formal**.

**for|mal|ize** /fɔːʳməlaɪz/ **(formalizes, formalizing, formalized)**

☑ in BRIT, also use **formalise**

If you **formalize** a plan, idea, arrangement, or system, you make it formal and official. ❑ *A recent treaty signed by Russia, Canada and Japan formalized an agreement to work together to stop the pirates.* VERB / V n

**for|mat** /fɔːʳmæt/ **(formats, formatting, formatted)** 1 The **format** of something is the way or order in which it is arranged and presented. ❑ *I had met with him to explain the format of the programme and what we had in mind. ...a large-format book.* N-COUNT 2 The **format** of a piece of computer soft- N-COUNT ware or a musical recording is the type of equipment on which it is designed to be used or played. For example, possible formats for a musical recording are CD and cassette. ❑ *His latest album is available on all formats.* [3] To **format** a computer disk means to run a program so that the disk can be written on. [COMPUTING] [4] To **format** a piece of computer text or graphics means to arrange the way in which it appears when it is printed or is displayed on a screen. [COMPUTING] ❑ *When text is saved from a Web page, it is often very badly formatted with many short lines.* VERB: V n / VERB / V n

**for|ma|tion** /fɔːʳmeɪʃᵊn/ **(formations)** [1] **The formation of** something is the starting or creation of it. ❑ *...the formation of a new government.* [2] **The formation of** an idea, habit, relationship, or character is the process of developing and establishing it. ❑ *My profession had an important influence in the formation of my character and temperament.* [3] If people or things are **in formation**, they are arranged in a particular pattern as they move. ❑ *He was flying in formation with seven other jets.* [4] A rock or cloud **formation** is rock or cloud of a particular shape or structure. ❑ *...a vast rock formation shaped like a pillar... Enormous cloud formations formed a purple mass.* N-UNCOUNT: with supp, usu *the* N *of* n / N-UNCOUNT: with supp = development / N-COUNT: also *a* N, usu *in* N / N-COUNT: n N

**forma|tive** /fɔːʳmətɪv/ A **formative** period of time or experience is one that has an important and lasting influence on a person's character and attitudes. ❑ *She was born in Barbados but spent her formative years in east London.* ADJ: usu ADJ n

**for|mer** /fɔːʳməʳ/ ◆◆◆ [1] **Former** is used to describe someone who used to have a particular job, position, or role, but no longer has it. ❑ *...former President Richard Nixon... He pleaded not guilty to murdering his former wife.* [2] **Former** is used to refer to countries which no longer exist or whose boundaries have changed. ❑ *...the former Soviet Union. ...the former Yugoslavia.* [3] **Former** is used to describe something which used to belong to someone or which used to be a particular thing. ❑ *...the former home of Sir Christopher Wren. ...a former monastery.* [4] **Former** is used to describe a situation or period of time which came before the present one. [FORMAL] ❑ *He would want you to remember him as he was in former years.* [5] When two people, things, or groups have just been mentioned, you can refer to the first of them as **the former**. ❑ *Given the choice between a pure white T-shirt and a more expensive, dirty cream one, most people can be forgiven for choosing the former.* ADJ: ADJ n / ADJ: ADJ n / ADJ: ADJ n / ADJ: ADJ n / PRON: *the* PRON ≠ latter

**for|mer|ly** /fɔːʳməʳli/ If something happened or was true **formerly**, it happened or was true in the past. ❑ *He had formerly been in the Navy. ...east Germany's formerly state-controlled companies.* ADV: ADV with cl/group, ADV before v

**For|mi|ca** /fɔːʳmaɪkə/ **Formica** is a hard plastic that is used for covering surfaces such as kitchen tables or counters. [TRADEMARK] N-UNCOUNT

**for|mi|dable** /fɔːʳmɪdəbᵊl, fəʳmɪd-/ If you describe something or someone as **formidable**, you mean that you feel slightly frightened by them because they are very great or impressive. ❑ *We have a formidable task ahead of us... Marsalis has a formidable reputation in both jazz and classical music.* ADJ

**form|less** /fɔːʳmləs/ Something that is **formless** does not have a clear or definite structure or shape. ❑ *A series of largely formless images rushed across the screen.* ADJ = amorphous

**for|mu|la** /fɔːʳmjʊlə/ **(formulae** /fɔːʳmjʊliː/ **or formulas)** ◆◇◇ [1] A **formula** is a plan that is invented in order to deal with a particular problem. ❑ *It is difficult to imagine how the North and South could ever agree on a formula to unify the divided peninsula. ...a peace formula.* [2] A **formula for** a particular situation, usually a good one, is a course of action or a combination of actions that is certain or likely to result in that situation. ❑ *Clever exploitation of the latest technology would be a sure formula for success.* [3] A **formula** is a group of letters, numbers, or other symbols which represents a scientific or mathematical rule. ❑ *He developed a mathematical formula describing the distances of the planets from the Sun.* [4] In science, the **formula** for a substance is a list of the amounts of various substances which make up that substance, or an indication of the atoms that it is composed of. [5] **Formula** is a powder which you mix with water to make artificial milk for babies. ❑ *...bottles of formula.* N-COUNT: usu with supp / N-SING: N *for* n = recipe / N-COUNT / N-COUNT / N-UNCOUNT

**for|mu|laic** /fɔːʳmjʊleɪɪk/ If you describe a way of saying or doing something as **formulaic**, you are criticizing it because it is not original and has been used many times before in similar situations. ❑ *His paintings are contrived and formulaic.* ADJ [disapproval] = conventional

**for|mu|late** /fɔːʳmjʊleɪt/ **(formulates, formulating, formulated)** [1] If you **formulate** something such as a plan or proposal, you invent it, thinking about the details carefully. ❑ *Little by little, he formulated his plan for escape.* [2] If you **formulate** a thought, opinion, or idea, you express it or describe it using particular words. ❑ *I was impressed by the way he could formulate his ideas.* VERB = devise / V n / VERB = articulate / V n

**for|mu|la|tion** /fɔːʳmjʊleɪʃᵊn/ **(formulations)** [1] The **formulation** of something such as a medicine or a beauty product is the way in which different ingredients are combined to make it. You can also say that the finished product is a **formulation**. ❑ *There have been problems with the formulation of the vaccine... You can buy a formulation containing royal jelly, pollen and vitamin C.* [2] The **formulation** of something such as a policy or plan is the process of creating or inventing it. ❑ *...the process of policy formulation and implementation.* [3] A **formulation** is the way in which you express your thoughts and ideas. ❑ *This is a far weaker formulation than is in the draft resolution which is being proposed.* N-VAR / N-UNCOUNT / N-VAR

**for|ni|cate** /fɔːʳnɪkeɪt/ **(fornicates, fornicating, fornicated)** To **fornicate** means to have sex with someone you are not married to. [FORMAL] V-RECIP: pl-n V, V *with* n, V (non-recip)

♦ **for|ni|ca|tion** /fɔːʳnɪkeɪʃᵊn/ ❑ *Fornication is a crime in some American states.* N-UNCOUNT

**for|sake** /fəʳseɪk/ **(forsakes, forsaking, forsook** /fəʳsʊk/**, forsaken)** [1] If you **forsake** someone, you leave them when you should have stayed, or stop you helping them or looking after them. [LITERARY] ❑ *I still love him and I would never forsake him.* [2] If you **forsake** something, you stop doing it, using it, or having it. [LITERARY] ❑ *He doubted their claim to have forsaken military solutions to the civil war.* VERB [disapproval] / V n / VERB / V n

**for|sak|en** /fəʳseɪkᵊn/ [1] A **forsaken** place is not lived in, used, or looked after. [LITERARY] ❑ *The delta region of the Rio Grande river was a forsaken land of thickets and swamps.* [2] → See also **godforsaken**. ADJ: ADJ n

**for|swear** /fɔːʳsweəʳ/ **(forswears, forswearing, forswore, forsworn)** If you **forswear** something, you promise that you will stop doing it, having it, or using it. [FORMAL or LITERARY] ❑ *The party was offered a share of government if it forswore violence.* VERB = renounce / V n

**for|sythia** /fɔːʳsaɪθiə, AM -sɪθ-/ **(forsythias)** **Forsythia** is a bush whose yellow flowers appear in the spring before the leaves have grown. N-VAR

**fort** /fɔːʳt/ **(forts)** [1] A **fort** is a strong building or a place with a wall or fence around it where soldiers can stay and be safe from the enemy. [2] If you **hold the fort** for someone, or, in American English, if you **hold down the fort**, you look after things for them while they are somewhere else or are busy doing something else. ❑ *His business partner is holding the fort while he is away.* N-COUNT; N-IN-NAMES / PHRASE: V inflects, oft PHR *for* n

**forte** /fɔːʳteɪ, AM fɔːrt/ **(fortes)**

> ✔ Pronounced /fɔːrt/ for meaning 1 in American English.

[1] You can say that a particular activity is your **forte** if you are very good at it. ❑ *Originality was never his forte.* [2] A piece of music that is played **forte** is played loudly. [TECHNICAL] N-COUNT: usu sing, poss N / ADV: ADV after v

**forth** /fɔːʳθ/ ◆◇◇

> In addition to the uses shown below, **forth** is also used in the phrasal verbs 'put forth' and 'set forth'.

[1] When someone goes **forth** from a place, they leave it. [LITERARY] ❑ *Go forth into the desert.* [ADV: ADV after v] [2] If one thing brings **forth** another, the first thing produces the second. [LITERARY] ❑ *My reflections brought forth no conclusion.* [ADV: ADV after v] [3] When someone or something is brought **forth**, they are brought to a place or moved into a position where people can see them. [LITERARY] ❑ *Pilate ordered Jesus to be brought forth.* [ADV: ADV after v; = out] [4] **back and forth** → see **back**. to **hold forth** → see **hold**.

**forth|com|ing** /fɔːʳθkʌmɪŋ/ [1] A **forthcoming** event is planned to happen soon. ❑ *...his opponents in the forthcoming elections.* [ADJ: ADJ n] [2] If something that you want, need, or expect is **forthcoming**, it is given to you or it happens. [FORMAL] ❑ *They promised that the money would be forthcoming... We must first see some real evidence. So far it has not been forthcoming.* [ADJ: v-link ADJ] [3] If you say that someone is **forthcoming**, you mean that they willingly give information when you ask them. [ADJ: usu v-link ADJ]

**forth|right** /fɔːʳθraɪt/ If you describe someone as **forthright**, you admire them because they show clearly and strongly what they think and feel. [ADJ; approval; = outspoken]

**forth|with** /fɔːʳθwɪθ/ **Forthwith** means immediately. [FORMAL] ❑ *I could have you arrested forthwith!* [ADV: ADV with v]

**for|ti|eth** /fɔːʳtiəθ/ The **fortieth** item in a series is the one that you count as number forty. ❑ *It was the fortieth anniversary of the death of the composer.* [◆◆◇ ORD]

**for|ti|fi|ca|tion** /fɔːʳtɪfɪkeɪʃᵊn/ **(fortifications)** **Fortifications** are buildings, walls, or ditches that are built to protect a place and make it more difficult to attack. ❑ *The government has started building fortifications along its eastern border.* → See also **fortify**. [N-COUNT: usu pl; = defence]

**for|ti|fied wine** **(fortified wines)** **Fortified wine** is an alcoholic drink such as sherry or port that is made by mixing wine with a small amount of brandy or strong alcohol. [N-MASS]

**for|ti|fy** /fɔːʳtɪfaɪ/ **(fortifies, fortifying, fortified)** [1] To **fortify** a place means to make it stronger and more difficult to attack, often by building a wall or ditch round it. ❑ *...British soldiers working to fortify an airbase in Bahrain.* [VERB; V n] [2] If food or drink **is fortified**, another substance is added to it to make it healthier or stronger. ❑ *It has also been fortified with vitamin C. ...fortified cereal products.* [VERB: usu passive; be V-ed with n; V-ed]

**for|tis|si|mo** /fɔːʳtɪsɪmoʊ/ A piece of music that is played **fortissimo** is played very loudly. [TECHNICAL] [ADV: ADV after v]

**for|ti|tude** /fɔːʳtɪtjuːd, AM -tuːd/ If you say that someone has shown **fortitude**, you admire them for being brave, calm, and uncomplaining when they have experienced something unpleasant or painful. [FORMAL] ❑ *He suffered a long series of illnesses with tremendous dignity and fortitude.* [N-UNCOUNT; approval; = courage, grit]

**fort|night** /fɔːʳtnaɪt/ **(fortnights)** A **fortnight** is a period of two weeks. [mainly BRIT] ❑ *I hope to be back in a fortnight.* [N-COUNT]

**fort|night|ly** /fɔːʳtnaɪtli/ A **fortnightly** event or publication happens or appears once every two weeks. [BRIT] ❑ *...an exciting new fortnightly magazine.* [ADJ: ADJ n] ♦ **Fortnightly** is also an adverb. ❑ *They recently put my rent up and I pay it fortnightly.* [ADV: ADV after v]

> ✔ in AM, use **biweekly**

**for|tress** /fɔːʳtrɪs/ **(fortresses)** A **fortress** is a castle or other large strong building, or a well-protected place, which is intended to be difficult for enemies to enter. ❑ *...a 13th-century fortress.* [N-COUNT]

**for|tui|tous** /fɔːʳtjuːɪtəs, AM -tuː-/ You can describe something as **fortuitous** if it happens, by chance, to be very successful or pleasant. ❑ *Their success is the result of a fortuitous combination of circumstances.* [ADJ; = lucky]

**for|tu|nate** /fɔːʳtʃʊnɪt/ If you say that someone or something is **fortunate**, you mean that they are lucky. ❑ *He was extremely fortunate to survive... It was fortunate that the water was shallow... She is in the fortunate position of having plenty of choice.* [ADJ: oft ADJ to-inf, ADJ *in* -ing, it v-link ADJ that; = lucky; ≠ unfortunate]

**for|tu|nate|ly** /fɔːʳtʃʊnɪtli/ **Fortunately** is used to introduce or indicate a statement about an event or situation that is good. ❑ *Fortunately, the weather that winter was reasonably mild.* [ADV: ADV with cl, oft ADV *for* n; = luckily; ≠ unfortunately]

**for|tune** /fɔːʳtʃuːn/ **(fortunes)** [1] You can refer to a large sum of money as **a fortune** or a small **fortune** to emphasize how large it is. ❑ *We had to eat out all the time. It ended up costing a fortune... He made a small fortune in the London property boom.* [◆◇◇ N-COUNT; emphasis] [2] Someone who has a **fortune** has a very large amount of money. ❑ *He made his fortune in car sales... Having spent his rich wife's fortune, the Major ended up in a debtors' prison.* [N-COUNT: oft poss N] [3] **Fortune** or good **fortune** is good luck. Ill **fortune** is bad luck. ❑ *Government ministers are starting to wonder how long their good fortune can last.* [N-UNCOUNT] [4] If you talk about someone's **fortunes** or the **fortunes** of something, you are talking about the extent to which they are doing well or being successful. ❑ *The electoral fortunes of the Liberal Democratic party may decline... The company had to do something to reverse its sliding fortunes.* [N-PLURAL: with poss] [5] When someone **tells** your **fortune**, they tell you what they think will happen to you in the future, which they say is shown, for example, by the lines on your hand. [PHRASE: V inflects]

**for|tune cookie** **(fortune cookies)** A **fortune cookie** is a sweet, crisp cake which contains a piece of paper which is supposed to say what will happen to you in the future. Fortune cookies are often served in Chinese restaurants. [N-COUNT]

**fortune-teller** **(fortune-tellers)** A **fortune-teller** is a person who tells you what they think will happen to you in the future, after looking at something such as the lines on your hand. [N-COUNT]

**for|ty** /fɔːʳti/ **(forties)** [1] **Forty** is the number 40. [◆◆◆ NUM] [2] When you talk about the **forties**, you are referring to numbers between 40 and 49. For example, if you are **in** your **forties**, you are aged between 40 and 49. If the temperature is **in the forties**, the temperature is between 40 and 49 degrees. ❑ *He was a big man in his forties, smartly dressed in a suit and tie.* [N-PLURAL] [3] **The forties** is the decade between 1940 and 1949. ❑ *Steel cans were introduced sometime during the forties.* [N-PLURAL: the N]

**fo|rum** /fɔːrəm/ **(forums)** A **forum** is a place, situation, or group in which people exchange ideas and discuss issues, especially important public issues. ❑ *Members of the council agreed that it still had an important role as a forum for discussion.* [N-COUNT: with supp, oft N *for* n/-ing]

**for|ward** /fɔːʳwəʳd/ **(forwards, forwarding, forwarded)** ◆◆◇

> In addition to the uses shown below, **forward** is also used in phrasal verbs such as 'bring forward' and 'look forward to'. In British English, **forwards** is often used as an adverb instead of **forward** in senses 1, 3, and 6.

[1] If you move or look **forward**, you move or look in a direction that is in front of you. In British English, you can also move or look **forwards**. ❑ *He came forward with his hand out. 'Mr and Mrs Selby?' he enquired... She fell forwards on to her face.* [ADV: ADV after v; ≠ backwards] [2] **Forward** means in a position near the front of something such as a building or a vehicle. ❑ *The best seats are in the aisle and as far forward as possible... The other car had a 3-inch lower driving seat and had its engine mounted further forward.* [ADV: be ADV, ADV after v] ♦ **Forward** is also an adjective. ❑ *Reinforcements were needed to allow more troops to move to forward positions.* [ADJ: ADJ n] [3] If you say that someone looks **forward**, [ADV:]

you approve of them because they think about what will happen in the future and plan for it. In British English, you can also say that someone looks **forwards**. ❑ *Now the leadership wants to look forward, and to outline a strategy for the rest of the century... People should forget and look forwards... Manchester United has always been a forward-looking club.* ♦ **Forward** is also an adjective. ❑ *The university system requires more forward planning.* [4] If you put a clock or watch **forward**, you change the time shown on it so that it shows a later time, for example when the time changes to summer time or daylight saving time. ❑ *When we put the clocks forward in March we go into British Summer Time.* [5] When you are referring to a particular time, if you say that something was true **from** that time **forward**, you mean that it became true at that time, and continued to be true afterwards. ❑ *Velazquez's work from that time forward was confined largely to portraits of the royal family.* [6] You use **forward** to indicate that something progresses or improves. In British English, you can also use **forwards**. ❑ *And by boosting economic prosperity in Mexico, Canada and the United States, it will help us move forward on issues that concern all of us... They just couldn't see any way forward... Space scientists and astronomers have taken another step forwards.* [7] If something or someone is put **forward**, or comes **forward**, they are suggested or offered as suitable for a particular purpose. ❑ *Over the years several similar theories have been put forward... Next month the Commission is to bring forward its first proposals for action... He was putting himself forward as a Democrat... Investigations have ground to a standstill because no witnesses have come forward.* [8] If a letter or message **is forwarded to** someone, it is sent to the place where they are, after having been sent to a different place earlier. ❑ *When he's out on the road, office calls are forwarded to the cellular phone in his truck... We will forward your letters to him.* [9] In football, basketball, or hockey, a **forward** is a player whose usual position is in the opponents' half of the field, and whose usual job is to attack or score goals. → See also **centre-forward**. [10] **backwards and forwards** → see **backwards**.

usu ADV after v, also ADV adj [approval] · ADJ: ADJ n · ADV: ADV after v · ADV: *from* n ADV = *on* · ADV: ADV after v, n ADV · ADV: ADV after v · VERB · *be* V-ed *from/to* n · V n, *from/to* n · Also V n · N-COUNT

**for|ward|ing ad|dress** **(forwarding addresses)** A **forwarding address** is an address that you give to someone when you go and live somewhere else so that they can send your mail on to you. ❑ *The former owner had not left any forwarding address.* N-COUNT

**forward-looking** If you describe a person or organization as **forward-looking**, you approve of the fact that they think about the future or have modern ideas. ADJ [approval]

**for|wards** /fɔːʳwəʳdz/ → see **forward**.

**for|went** /fɔːʳwent/ **Forwent** is the past tense of **forgo**.

**fos|sil** /fɒsəl/ **(fossils)** A **fossil** is the hard remains of a prehistoric animal or plant that are found inside a rock. N-COUNT

**fos|sil fuel** **(fossil fuels)** also **fossil-fuel**. **Fossil fuel** is fuel such as coal or oil that is formed from the decayed remains of plants or animals. N-MASS

**fos|sil|ize** /fɒsɪlaɪz/ **(fossilizes, fossilizing, fossilized)**

✓ in BRIT, also use **fossilise**

[1] If the remains of an animal or plant **fossilize** or **are fossilized**, they become hard and form fossils, instead of decaying completely. ❑ *The most important parts, the flowers, rarely fossilise... The survival of the proteins depends on the way in which bones are fossilised. ...fossilized dinosaur bones.* [2] If you say that ideas, attitudes, or ways of behaving **have fossilized** or **have been fossilized**, you are criticizing the fact that they are fixed and unlikely to change, in spite of changing situations or circumstances. ❑ *What they seem to want to do in fact is fossilize the particular environment in which people live and work... Needs change while policies fossilize.* ♦ **fos|sil|ized** *...these fossilized organisations.*

VERB · V · *be* V-ed · V-ed · VERB [disapproval] · V n · V · ADJ

**fos|ter** /fɒstəʳ, AM fɔːst-/ **(fosters, fostering, fostered)** [1] **Foster** parents are people who officially take a child into their family for a period of time, without becoming the child's legal parents. The child is referred to as their **foster** child. ❑ *Little Jack was placed with foster parents.* [2] If you **foster** a child, you take it into your family for a period of time, without becoming its legal parent. ❑ *She has since gone on to find happiness by fostering more than 100 children.* [3] To **foster** something such as an activity or idea means to help it to develop. ❑ *He said that developed countries had a responsibility to foster global economic growth to help new democracies.*

ADJ: ADJ n · VERB · V n · VERB · V n

**fought** /fɔːt/ **Fought** is the past tense and past participle of **fight**.

**foul** /faʊl/ **(fouler, foulest, fouls, fouling, fouled)** [1] If you describe something as **foul**, you mean it is dirty and smells or tastes unpleasant. ❑ *...foul polluted water... The smell was quite foul.* [2] **Foul** language is offensive and contains swear words or rude words. ❑ *He was sent off for using foul language in a match last Sunday... He had a foul mouth.* [3] If someone has a **foul** temper or is in a **foul** mood, they become angry or violent very suddenly and easily. ❑ *Collins was in a foul mood even before the interviews began.* [4] **Foul** weather is unpleasant, windy, and stormy. [5] If an animal **fouls** a place, it drops faeces onto the ground. ❑ *It is an offence to let your dog foul a footpath.* [6] In a game or sport, if a player **fouls** another player, they touch them or block them in a way which is not allowed according to the rules. ❑ *Middlesbrough's Jimmy Phillips was sent off for fouling Steve Tilson.* [7] A **foul** is an act in a game or sport that is not allowed according to the rules. ❑ *He picked up his first booking for a 45th-minute foul on Bull.* ♦ **Foul** is also an adjective. ❑ *...a foul tackle.* [8] If you **fall foul of** someone or **run foul of** them, you do something which gets you into trouble with them. [mainly BRIT] ❑ *He had fallen foul of the FBI.*

ADJ = *disgusting* · ADJ: usu ADJ n = *filthy* · ADJ: usu ADJ n = *bad* · ADJ · VERB · V n · VERB · V n · N-COUNT: oft N *on* n · ADJ: ADJ n · PHRASE: V inflects, PHR n

**foul-mouthed** If you describe someone as **foul-mouthed**, you disapprove of them because they use offensive words or say very rude things. ADJ [disapproval]

**foul play** [1] **Foul play** is criminal violence or activity that results in a person's death. ❑ *The report says it suspects foul play was involved in the deaths of two journalists.* [2] **Foul play** is unfair or dishonest behaviour, especially during a sports game. ❑ *Players were warned twice for foul play.* N-UNCOUNT · N-UNCOUNT

**foul-up** **(foul-ups)** A **foul-up** is something that has gone badly wrong as a result of someone's mistakes or carelessness. [INFORMAL] ❑ *A series of technical foul-ups delayed the launch of the new product.* N-COUNT = *bungle*

**found** /faʊnd/ **(founds, founding, founded)** ◆◇◇ [1] **Found** is the past tense and past participle of **find**. [2] When an institution, company, or organization **is founded** by someone or by a group of people, they get it started, often by providing the necessary money. ❑ *The Independent Labour Party was founded in Bradford on January 13, 1893... He founded the Centre for Journalism Studies at University College Cardiff... The business, founded by Dawn and Nigel, suffered financial setbacks.* ♦ **foun|da|tion** /faʊndeɪʃən/ *...the 150th anniversary of the foundation of Kew Gardens.* ♦ **found|ing** *I have been a member of The Sunday Times Wine Club since its founding in 1973.* [3] When a town, important building, or other place **is founded** by someone or by a group of people, they cause it to be built. ❑ *The town was founded in 1610.* [4] → See also **founded**, **founding**.

VERB = *set up, establish* · *be* V-ed · V n · V-ed · N-SING: with poss · N-SING: with poss · VERB: usu passive · *be* V-ed

**foun|da|tion** /faʊndeɪʃən/ **(foundations)** ◆◇◇ [1] **The foundation of** something such as a belief or way of life is the things on which it is based. ❑ *The issue strikes at the very foundation of our community... This laid the foundations for later modern*

N-COUNT: usu *the* N *of/for* n

*economic growth.* ● If an event **shakes the foundations** of a society or a system of beliefs, it causes great uncertainty and makes people question their most deeply held beliefs. ❑ *The destruction of war and the death of millions of young people shook the foundations of Western idealism.* [2] The **foundations** of a building or other structure are the layer of bricks or concrete below the ground that it is built on. [3] A **foundation** is an organization which provides money for a special purpose such as research or charity. ❑ *...the National Foundation for Educational Research.* [4] If a story, idea, or argument has **no foundation**, there are no facts to prove that it is true. ❑ *The allegations were without foundation... Each complaint is analysed very closely, and if it has no foundation it is rejected.* [5] **Foundation** is a skin-coloured cream that you put on your face before putting on the rest of your make-up. [6] → See also **found**.
PHRASE: V inflects
N-PLURAL
N-COUNT
N-UNCOUNT: with brd-neg
N-MASS

**foun|da|tion course** **(foundation courses)** A **foundation course** is a course that you do at some colleges and universities in order to prepare yourself for a longer or more advanced course. [BRIT]
N-COUNT

✔ in AM, use **basic course**

**foun|da|tion stone** **(foundation stones)** [1] A **foundation stone** is a large block of stone built into a large public building near the bottom. It is often involved in a ceremony for the opening of the building, and has writing on it recording this. [mainly BRIT] ❑ *The Princess of Wales laid the foundation stone for the extension to the Cathedral.*
N-COUNT: oft with poss

✔ in AM, use **cornerstone**

[2] The **foundation stone of** something is the basic, important thing which its existence or success depends on. ❑ *...these foundation stones of the future: education, training, research, development.*
N-COUNT: usu N *of* n

**found|ed** /faʊndɪd/ If something is **founded on** a particular thing, it is based on it. ❑ *The criticisms are founded on facts as well as on convictions.* → See also **found**.
ADJ: v-link ADJ *on* n

**found|er** /faʊndəʳ/ **(founders, foundering, foundered)** [1] The **founder** of an institution, organization, or building is the person who got it started or caused it to be built, often by providing the necessary money. ❑ *He was one of the founders of the university's medical faculty.* [2] If something such as a plan or project **founders**, it fails because of a particular point, difficulty, or problem. ❑ *The talks have foundered, largely because of the reluctance of some members of the government to do a deal with criminals.*
◆◇◇
N-COUNT: usu with poss
VERB = fail
V

**found|er mem|ber** **(founder members)** A **founder member** of a club, group, or organization is one of the first members, often one who was involved in setting it up. [BRIT]
N-COUNT: usu N *of* n

✔ in AM, use **charter member**

**found|ing** /faʊndɪŋ/ **Founding** means relating to the starting of a particular institution or organization. ❑ *The committee held its founding congress in the capital, Riga... He is founding director of The Conservation Foundation.* → See also **found**.
ADJ: ADJ n

**found|ing fa|ther** **(founding fathers)** [1] The **founding father** of an institution, organization, or idea is the person who sets it up or who first develops it. [LITERARY] [2] The **Founding Fathers** of the United States were the members of the American Constitutional Convention of 1787.
N-COUNT: oft N *of* n = founder
N-PROPER-PLURAL

**found|ling** /faʊndlɪŋ/ **(foundlings)** A **foundling** is a baby that has been abandoned by its parents, often in a public place, and that has then been found by someone. [OLD-FASHIONED]
N-COUNT

**found|ry** /faʊndri/ **(foundries)** A **foundry** is a place where metal or glass is melted and formed into particular shapes.
N-COUNT

**fount** /faʊnt/ **(founts)** If you describe a person or thing as **the fount of** something, you are saying that they are an important source or supply of it. [LITERARY] ❑ *To the young boy his father was the fount of all knowledge.*
N-COUNT: usu sing, N *of* n = source

**foun|tain** /faʊntɪn/ **(fountains)** [1] A **fountain** is an ornamental feature in a pool or lake which consists of a long narrow stream of water that is forced up into the air by a pump. [2] A **fountain of** a liquid is an amount of it which is sent up into the air and falls back. [LITERARY] ❑ *The volcano spewed a fountain of molten rock 650 feet in the air.*
N-COUNT
N-COUNT: usu N *of* n = jet

**foun|tain pen** **(fountain pens)** A **fountain pen** is a pen which uses ink that you have drawn up inside it from a bottle.
N-COUNT

**four** /fɔːʳ/ **(fours)** [1] **Four** is the number 4. ❑ *Judith is married with four children.* [2] If you are **on all fours**, your knees, feet, and hands are on the ground. ❑ *She crawled on all fours over to the window.*
◆◆◆
NUM
PHRASE: PHR after v, v-link PHR

**four-letter word** **(four-letter words)** A **four-letter word** is a short word that people consider to be rude or offensive, usually because it refers to sex or other bodily functions.
N-COUNT = swear word

**four-poster bed** **(four-poster beds)** A **four-poster bed** or a **four-poster** is a large old-fashioned bed that has a tall post at each corner and curtains that can be drawn around it.
N-COUNT

**four|some** /fɔːʳsəm/ **(foursomes)** A **foursome** is a group of four people or things. ❑ *The London-based foursome are set to release their fourth single this month.*
N-COUNT-COLL

**four-square** also **foursquare.** To stand **four-square** behind someone or something means to be firm in your support of that person or thing. ❑ *They stood four-square behind their chief, and they would not accept pressure on him to resign.*
ADJ: v-link ADJ prep

**four|teen** /fɔːʳtiːn/ **(fourteens)** **Fourteen** is the number 14. ❑ *I'm fourteen years old.*
◆◆◆
NUM

**four|teenth** /fɔːʳtiːnθ/ The **fourteenth** item in a series is the one that you count as number fourteen. ❑ *The Festival, now in its fourteenth year, has become a major international jazz event.*
◆◆◇
ORD

**fourth** /fɔːʳθ/ **(fourths)** [1] The **fourth** item in a series is the one that you count as number four. ❑ *Last year's winner Greg Lemond of the United States is in fourth place.* [2] A **fourth** is one of four equal parts of something. [AM] ❑ *Three-fourths of the public say they favor a national referendum on the issue.*
◆◆◇
ORD
FRACTION

✔ in BRIT, use **quarter**

**fourth di|men|sion** In physics, **the fourth dimension** is time. The other three dimensions, which exist in space, are length, width, and height. [TECHNICAL]
N-SING: the N

**fourth|ly** /fɔːʳθli/ You say **fourthly** when you want to make a fourth point or give a fourth reason for something. ❑ *Fourthly, the natural enthusiasm of the student teachers should be maintained.*
ADV: ADV with cl

**fourth of|fi|cial** **(fourth officials)** In football, the **fourth official** is an official who assists the referee and assistant referees from the side of the pitch.
N-COUNT

**Fourth of July** In the United States, **the Fourth of July** is a public holiday when people celebrate the Declaration of Independence in 1776. ❑ *...a Fourth of July picnic.*
N-SING: usu the N

**four-wheel drive** **(four-wheel drives)** A **four-wheel drive** is a vehicle in which all four wheels receive power from the engine to help with steering. This makes the vehicle easier to drive on rough roads or surfaces such as sand or snow.
N-COUNT

**fowl** /faʊl/ **(fowls** or **fowl)** A **fowl** is a bird, especially one that can be eaten as food, such as a duck or a chicken. ❑ *Carve the fowl into 8 pieces.*
N-COUNT

**fox** /fɒks/ **(foxes, foxing, foxed)** [1] A **fox** is a wild animal which looks like a dog and has reddish-brown fur, a pointed face and ears, and a thick tail. Foxes eat smaller animals. [2] If you **are foxed** by something, you cannot understand it or solve it. [mainly BRIT] ❑ *I admit I was foxed for*
N-COUNT
VERB
be V-ed

some time... Only once did we hit on a question which foxed one of the experts. V n

**fox|glove** /fɒksglʌv/ **(foxgloves)** A **foxglove** is a tall plant that has pink or white flowers shaped like bells growing up its stem. N-VAR

**fox|hole** /fɒkshoʊl/ **(foxholes)** A **foxhole** is a small hole which soldiers dig as a shelter from the enemy and from which they can shoot. N-COUNT

**fox|hound** /fɒkshaʊnd/ **(foxhounds)** A **foxhound** is a type of dog that is trained to hunt foxes. N-COUNT

**fox-hunting** also **foxhunting. Fox-hunting** is a sport in which people riding horses chase a fox across the countryside. Dogs called hounds are used to find the fox. N-UNCOUNT

**fox|trot** /fɒkstrɒt/ **(foxtrots)** The **foxtrot** is a type of dance which involves a combination of long slow steps and short fast steps. N-COUNT: usu sing

**foxy** /fɒksi/ **(foxier, foxiest)** 1 If you describe someone as **foxy**, you mean that they are deceitful in a clever, secretive way. ❑ *He had wary, foxy eyes.* ADJ = crafty 2 If a man calls a woman **foxy**, he means that she is physically attractive. [mainly AM, INFORMAL] ADJ

**foy|er** /fɔɪəʳ, fwaɪeɪ/ **(foyers)** The **foyer** is the large area where people meet or wait just inside the main doors of a building such as a theatre, cinema, or hotel. N-COUNT = lobby

**Fr**

> ✔ The spelling **Fr.** is used in American English for meaning 2.

1 **Fr** is a written abbreviation for **French** or **franc**. 2 **Fr** is a written abbreviation for **Father** when it is used in titles before the name of a Catholic priest.

**fra|cas** /frækɑː, AM freɪkəs/ A **fracas** is a rough, noisy quarrel or fight. N-SING = brawl

**frac|tal** /fræktᵊl/ **(fractals)** In geometry, a **fractal** is a shape made up of parts that are the same shape as itself and are of smaller and smaller sizes. N-COUNT: oft N n

**frac|tion** /frækʃᵊn/ **(fractions)** 1 A **fraction of** something is a tiny amount or proportion of it. ❑ *She hesitated for a fraction of a second before responding... I opened my eyes just a fraction.* N-COUNT: oft N *of* n 2 A **fraction** is a number that can be expressed as a proportion of two whole numbers. For example, ½ and ⅓ are both fractions. ❑ *The students had a grasp of decimals, percentages and fractions.* N-COUNT

**frac|tion|al** /frækʃənᵊl/ If something is **fractional**, it is very small in size or degree. ❑ *...a fractional hesitation.* ADJ: usu ADJ n ♦ **frac|tion|al|ly** /frækʃənli/ *Murphy, Sinclair's young team-mate, was fractionally behind him.* ADV: ADV group

**frac|tious** /frækʃəs/ If you describe someone as **fractious**, you disapprove of them because they become upset or angry very quickly about small unimportant things. ❑ *Nancy was in a fractious mood... The children were predictably fractious.* ADJ [disapproval]

**frac|ture** /fræktʃəʳ/ **(fractures, fracturing, fractured)** 1 A **fracture** is a slight crack or break in something, especially a bone. ❑ *At least one-third of all women over ninety have sustained a hip fracture.* N-COUNT 2 If something such as a bone **is fractured** or **fractures**, it gets a slight crack or break in it. ❑ *You've fractured a rib, maybe more than one...* VERB V n *One strut had fractured and been crudely repaired in several places...* V *He suffered a fractured skull.* V-ed 3 If something such as an organization or society **is fractured** or **fractures**, it splits into several parts or stops existing. [FORMAL] ❑ *His policy risks fracturing the coalition...* VERB V n *It might be a society that could fracture along class lines.* V

**frag|ile** /frædʒaɪl, AM -dʒᵊl/ 1 If you describe a situation as **fragile**, you mean that it is weak or uncertain, and unlikely to be able to resist strong pressure or attack. [JOURNALISM] ❑ *The fragile economies of several southern African nations could be irreparably damaged... His overall condition remained fragile.* ADJ = unstable ♦ **fra|gil|ity** /frədʒɪlɪti/ *By mid-1988 there were clear indications of the extreme fragility of the Right-wing coalition.* N-UNCOUNT: oft N *of* n 2 Something that is **fragile** is easily broken or damaged. ❑ *He leaned back in his fragile chair.* ADJ ≠ sturdy ♦ **fra|gil|ity** *Older drivers are more likely to be seriously injured because of the fragility of their bones.* N-UNCOUNT: oft N *of* n

**frag|ment** **(fragments, fragmenting, fragmented)**

> ✔ The noun is pronounced /frægmənt/. The verb is pronounced /frægment/.

1 A **fragment of** something is a small piece or part of it. ❑ *...fragments of metal in my shoulder... She read everything, digesting every fragment of news. ...glass fragments.* N-COUNT: oft N *of* n = piece 2 If something **fragments** or **is fragmented**, it breaks or separates into small pieces or parts. ❑ *The clouds fragmented and out came the sun...* VERB V *Fierce rivalries have traditionally fragmented the region.* V n ♦ **frag|men|ta|tion** /frægmenteɪʃᵊn/ *...the extraordinary fragmentation of styles on the music scene.* N-UNCOUNT: oft N *of* n

**frag|men|tary** /frægməntəri, AM -teri/ Something that is **fragmentary** is made up of small or unconnected pieces. ❑ *Any action on the basis of such fragmentary evidence would be foolish.* ADJ

**fra|grance** /freɪgrəns/ **(fragrances)** 1 A **fragrance** is a pleasant or sweet smell. ❑ *...a shrubby plant with a strong characteristic fragrance. ...the fragrance of his cologne.* N-VAR: usu with supp 2 **Fragrance** is a pleasant-smelling liquid which people put on their bodies to make themselves smell nice. ❑ *The advertisement is for a male fragrance.* N-MASS = perfume

**fra|grant** /freɪgrənt/ Something that is **fragrant** has a pleasant, sweet smell. ❑ *...fragrant oils and perfumes... The air was fragrant with the smell of orange blossoms.* ADJ: oft ADJ *with* n

**frail** /freɪl/ **(frailer, frailest)** 1 Someone who is **frail** is not very strong or healthy. ❑ *She lay in bed looking particularly frail.* ADJ = weak 2 Something that is **frail** is easily broken or damaged. ❑ *The frail craft rocked as he clambered in.* ADJ = fragile

**frail|ty** /freɪlti/ **(frailties)** 1 If you refer to the **frailties** or **frailty** of people, you are referring to their weaknesses. ❑ *...the frailties of human nature. ...a triumph of will over human frailty.* N-VAR 2 **Frailty** is the condition of having poor health. ❑ *She died after a long period of increasing frailty.* N-UNCOUNT

**frame** /freɪm/ **(frames, framing, framed)** ◆◇◇ 1 The **frame** of a picture or mirror is the wood, metal, or plastic that is fitted around it, especially when it is displayed or hung on a wall. ❑ *Estelle kept a photograph of her mother in a silver frame on the kitchen mantelpiece. ...a pair of picture frames.* N-COUNT 2 The **frame** of an object such as a building, chair, or window is the arrangement of wooden, metal, or plastic bars between which other material is fitted, and which give the object its strength and shape. ❑ *He supplied housebuilders with modern timber frames... We painted our table to match the window frame in the bedroom.* N-COUNT 3 The **frames** of a pair of glasses are all the metal or plastic parts of it, but not the lenses. ❑ *He was wearing new spectacles with gold wire frames.* N-COUNT: usu pl 4 You can refer to someone's body as their **frame**, especially when you are describing the general shape of their body. ❑ *Their belts are pulled tight against their bony frames.* N-COUNT: oft poss N 5 A **frame** of cinema film is one of the many separate photographs that it consists of. ❑ *Standard 8mm projects at 16 frames per second.* N-COUNT 6 When a picture or photograph **is framed**, it is put in a frame. ❑ *The picture is now ready to be mounted and framed...* VERB: usu passive *be* V-ed *On the wall is a large framed photograph.* V-ed 7 If an object **is framed** by a particular thing, it is surrounded by that thing in a way that makes the object more striking or attractive to look at. ❑ *The swimming pool is framed by tropical gardens.* VERB: usu passive *be* V-ed prep 8 If someone **frames** an innocent person, they make other people think that that person is guilty of a crime, by lying or inventing evidence. [INFORMAL] ❑ *I need to* VERB V n

*find out who tried to frame me.* 9 If someone is **in the frame for** something such as a job or position, they are being considered for it. ❑ *We need a win to keep us in the frame for the title.* 10 ➔ See also **cold frame**.
PHRASE = *in the running*

**frame of mind** **(frames of mind)** Your **frame of mind** is the mood that you are in, which causes you to have a particular attitude to something. ❑ *Lewis was not in the right frame of mind to continue.*
N-COUNT: usu sing, with supp

**frame of ref|er|ence** **(frames of reference)** A **frame of reference** is a particular set of beliefs or ideas on which you base your judgment of things. ❑ *We know we're dealing with someone with a different frame of reference.*
N-COUNT: usu with supp

**frame-up** **(frame-ups)** A **frame-up** is a situation where someone pretends that an innocent person has committed a crime by deliberately lying or inventing evidence. [INFORMAL] ❑ *He was innocent and the victim of a frame-up.*
N-COUNT

**frame|work** /freɪmwɜːʳk/ **(frameworks)** 1 A **framework** is a particular set of rules, ideas, or beliefs which you use in order to deal with problems or to decide what to do. ❑ *... within the framework of federal regulations.*
N-COUNT: usu adj N, N *of* n
2 A **framework** is a structure that forms a support or frame for something. ❑ *...wooden shelves on a steel framework.*
N-COUNT: usu supp N

**franc** /fræŋk/ **(francs)** The **franc** was the unit of currency that was used in France and Belgium, before it was replaced by the euro. It is also the unit of currency in some other countries where French is spoken. ❑ *The price of grapes had shot up to 32 francs a kilo.*
N-COUNT: num N
♦ **The franc** was used to refer to the currency systems of France and Belgium, before it was replaced by the **euro**. It is also used to refer to the currency systems of some other countries where French is spoken. ❑ *The Swiss franc has remained surprisingly strong.*
N-SING: *the* N

**fran|chise** /fræntʃaɪz/ **(franchises, franchising, franchised)** 1 A **franchise** is an authority that is given by an organization to someone, allowing them to sell its goods or services or to take part in an activity which the organization controls. [BUSINESS] ❑ *...fast-food franchises... Talk to other franchise holders and ask them what they think of the parent company.*
N-COUNT: oft n N, N *to* n, N n
2 If a company **franchises** its business, it sells franchises to other companies, allowing them to sell its goods or services. [BUSINESS] ❑ *She has recently franchised her business... It takes hundreds of thousands of dollars to get into the franchised pizza business.*
VERB
V n
V-ed
♦ **fran|chis|ing** *One of the most important aspects of franchising is the reduced risk of business failure it offers to franchisees.*
N-UNCOUNT
3 **Franchise** is the right to vote in an election, especially one in which people elect a parliament. ❑ *...the introduction of universal franchise... The 1867 Reform Act extended the franchise to much of the male working class.*
N-UNCOUNT: also *the* N

**fran|chi|see** /fræntʃaɪziː/ **(franchisees)** A **franchisee** is a person or group of people who buy a particular franchise. [BUSINESS]
N-COUNT

**fran|chi|ser** /fræntʃaɪzəʳ/ **(franchisers)** A **franchiser** is an organization which sells franchises. [BUSINESS]
N-COUNT

**Franco-** /fræŋkoʊ-/ 1 **Franco-** occurs in words connected with France and the French language. For example, a Francophile is someone who likes France and French culture.
PREFIX
2 **Franco-** combines with adjectives indicating nationality to form adjectives which describe something connected with relations between France and another country. ❑ *Ministers expressed broad support for the Franco-German plan.*
COMB in ADJ: ADJ n

**Fran|co|phone** /fræŋkoʊfoʊn/ **(Francophones)** A **Francophone** is someone who speaks French, especially someone who speaks it as their first language. [FORMAL]
N-COUNT: oft N n

**frank** /fræŋk/ **(franker, frankest, franks, franking, franked)** 1 If someone is **frank**, they state or express things in an open and honest way. ❑ *'It is clear that my client has been less than frank with me,' said his lawyer... They had a frank discussion about the issue.*
ADJ: oft ADJ *about/with* n = *candid*
♦ **frank|ly** *He now frankly admits that much of his former playboy lifestyle was superficial.*
ADV: ADV with v
♦ **frank|ness** *The reaction to his frankness was hostile.*
N-UNCOUNT: oft with poss
2 When a letter or parcel **is franked**, it is marked with a symbol that shows that the proper charge has been paid or that no stamp is needed. ❑ *The letter was franked in London on August 6. ...a self-addressed, franked envelope.*
VERB: usu passive
*be* V-ed
V-ed

**frank|fur|ter** /fræŋkfɜːʳtəʳ/ **(frankfurters)** A **frankfurter** is a type of smoked sausage.
N-COUNT

**frank|in|cense** /fræŋkɪnsens/ **Frankincense** is a substance which is obtained from a tree and which smells pleasant when it is burned. It is used especially in religious ceremonies.
N-UNCOUNT

**frank|ly** /fræŋkli/ You use **frankly** when you are expressing an opinion or feeling to emphasize that you mean what you are saying, especially when the person you are speaking to may not like it. ❑ *'You don't give a damn about my feelings, do you.' — 'Quite frankly, I don't.'... Frankly, Thomas, this question of your loan is beginning to worry me.* ➔ See also **frank**.
ADV: ADV with cl, ADV adj/-ed [emphasis]

**fran|tic** /fræntɪk/ 1 If you are **frantic**, you are behaving in a wild and uncontrolled way because you are frightened or worried. ❑ *A bird had been locked in and was by now quite frantic.*
ADJ
♦ **fran|ti|cal|ly** /fræntɪkli/ *She clutched frantically at Emily's arm.*
ADV: ADV with v
2 If an activity is **frantic**, things are done quickly and in an energetic but disorganized way, because there is very little time. ❑ *A busy night in the restaurant can be frantic in the kitchen.*
ADJ
♦ **fran|ti|cal|ly** *We have been frantically trying to save her life.*
ADV: ADV with v

**fra|ter|nal** /frətɜːʳnəl/ 1 **Fraternal** actions show strong links of friendship between two people or groups of people. [FORMAL] ❑ *...the fraternal assistance of our colleagues and comrades.*
ADJ: usu ADJ n
2 **Fraternal** twins are twins born from two eggs, so they are not exactly the same. They look different from each other and may be different sexes.
ADJ: usu ADJ n

**fra|ter|nity** /frətɜːʳnɪti/ **(fraternities)** 1 **Fraternity** refers to friendship and support between people who feel they are closely linked to each other. [FORMAL] ❑ *Bob needs the fraternity of others who share his mission.*
N-UNCOUNT
2 You can refer to people who have the same profession or the same interests as a particular **fraternity**. ❑ *...the spread of stolen guns among the criminal fraternity. ...the sailing fraternity.*
N-COUNT: usu supp N = *set*
3 In the United States, a **fraternity** is a society of male university or college students.
N-COUNT

**frat|er|nize** /frætəʳnaɪz/ **(fraternizes, fraternizing, fraternized)**

✔ in BRIT, also use **fraternise**

If you **fraternize with** someone, you associate with them in a friendly way. ❑ *At these conventions, executives fraternized with the key personnel of other banks... Mrs Zuckerman does not fraternize widely... The recession has created an atmosphere where disparate groups fraternise in an atmosphere of mutual support.*
V-RECIP = *mix*
V *with* n
V (non-recip)
pl-n V

**frat|ri|cid|al** /frætrɪsaɪdəl/ A **fratricidal** war or conflict is one in which people kill members of their own society or social group. [FORMAL]
ADJ: ADJ n

**frat|ri|cide** /frætrɪsaɪd/ If someone commits **fratricide**, they kill their brother. [FORMAL]
N-UNCOUNT

**fraud** /frɔːd/ **(frauds)** 1 **Fraud** is the crime of gaining money or financial benefits by a trick or by lying. ❑ *He was jailed for two years for fraud and deception... Tax frauds are dealt with by the Inland Revenue.*
◆◇◇ N-VAR
2 A **fraud** is something or someone that deceives people in a way that is illegal or dishonest. ❑ *He believes many 'psychics' are frauds who rely on perception and subtle deception.*
N-COUNT
3 If you call someone or something a **fraud**, you are criticizing them because you think that they are not genuine, or are less good than they claim or appear to be. ❑ *...all those fashion frauds who think*
N-COUNT [disapproval]

*they are being original by raiding the tired old styles of the '60s.*

**fraud squad** **(fraud squads)** The **fraud squad** is a part of a police force whose job is to investigate crimes involving fraud. N-COUNT: oft N n

**fraud|ster** /frɔːdstəʳ/ **(fraudsters)** A **fraudster** is someone who commits the crime of fraud. [mainly BRIT] N-COUNT

**fraudu|lent** /frɔːdʒʊlənt/ A **fraudulent** activity is deliberately deceitful, dishonest, or untrue. ❑ *...fraudulent claims about being a nurse.* ADJ: usu ADJ n ♦ **fraudu|lent|ly** *The report concludes that I acted neither fraudulently nor improperly.* ADV: ADV with v

**fraught** /frɔːt/ 1 If a situation or action is **fraught with** problems or risks, it is filled with them. ❑ *The earliest operations employing this technique were fraught with dangers.* ADJ: v-link ADJ *with* n 2 If you say that a situation or action is **fraught**, you mean that it is worrying or difficult. ❑ *It has been a somewhat fraught day.* ADJ

**fray** /freɪ/ **(frays, fraying, frayed)** 1 If something such as cloth or rope **frays**, or if something **frays** it, its threads or fibres start to come apart from each other and spoil its appearance. ❑ *The fabric is very fine or frays easily... The stitching had begun to fray at the edges... Her washing machine tends to fray edges on intricate designs. ...fraying edges in the stair carpet... He wore frayed jeans and cowboy shirts.* VERB V V *at* n V n V-ing V-ed 2 If your nerves or your temper **fray**, or if something **frays** them, you become nervous or easily annoyed because of mental strain and anxiety. ❑ *Tempers began to fray as the two teams failed to score... This kind of living was beginning to fray her nerves.* VERB V V n 3 **The fray** is an exciting or challenging activity, situation, or argument that you are involved in. ❑ *There will have to be a second round of voting when new candidates can enter the fray... He would be inspiring young people to get into the political fray.* N-SING: *the* N

**freak** /friːk/ **(freaks, freaking, freaked)** 1 A **freak** event or action is one that is a very unusual or extreme example of its type. ❑ *Weir broke his leg in a freak accident playing golf.* ADJ: ADJ n 2 If you describe someone as a particular kind of **freak**, you are emphasizing that they are very enthusiastic about a thing or activity, and often seem to think about nothing else. [INFORMAL] ❑ *Oat bran became the darling of health freaks last year. ...computer freaks.* ➔ See also **control freak**. N-COUNT: n N = *fanatic* 3 People are sometimes referred to as **freaks** when their behaviour or attitude is very different from that of the majority of people. ❑ *Not so long ago, transsexuals were regarded as freaks.* N-COUNT disapproval 4 If you refer to someone as a **freak**, you mean that they are physically abnormal in some way. This use could cause offence. N-COUNT disapproval

♦ **freak out** If someone **freaks out**, or if something **freaks** them **out**, they suddenly feel extremely surprised, upset, angry, or confused. ❑ *I remember the first time I went onstage. I freaked out completely... I think our music freaks people out sometimes... It sort of frightens me. I guess I am kind of freaked out by it.* PHRASAL VERB V P V n P *be* V-ed P Also V P n (not pron)

**freak|ish** /friːkɪʃ/ Something that is **freakish** is remarkable because it is not normal or natural. ❑ *...his freakish voice varying from bass to soprano.* ADJ: usu ADJ n

**freaky** /friːki/ **(freakier, freakiest)** If someone or something is **freaky**, they are very unusual in some way. [INFORMAL] ❑ *This guy bore a really freaky resemblance to Jones.* ADJ = *weird*

**freck|le** /frekᵊl/ **(freckles) Freckles** are small light brown spots on someone's skin, especially on their face. ❑ *He had short ginger-coloured hair and freckles.* N-COUNT: usu pl

**freck|led** /frekᵊld/ If a part of your body is **freckled**, it has freckles on it. ❑ *...a slight man with auburn hair and a freckled face.* ADJ

**free** /friː/ **(freer, freest, frees, freeing, freed)** ♦♦♦ 1 If something is **free**, you can have it or use it without paying for it. ❑ *The seminars are free, with lunch provided. ...a free brochure with details of gift vouchers.* **free of charge** ➔ see **charge**. ADJ 2 Someone or something that is **free** is not restricted, controlled, or limited, for example by rules, customs, or other people. ❑ *The government will be free to pursue its economic policies... The elections were free and fair... Economists argued that freer markets would quickly revive the region's economy... He fears that until state subsidies are removed, Russia will never have a truly free press... Dogs were allowed to roam free and 48 sheep were killed.* ADJ: oft ADJ to-inf ♦ **free|ly** *They cast their votes freely and without coercion on election day... Merchandise can now circulate freely among the EU countries.* ADV: ADV with v 3 If you **free** someone of something that is unpleasant or restricting, you remove it from them. ❑ *The 30-year-old star is trying to free himself from his recording contract.* VERB V n *of/from* n 4 Someone who is **free** is no longer a prisoner or a slave. ❑ *More than ninety prisoners have been set free so far under a government amnesty.* ADJ: ADJ n, v-link ADJ, ADJ after v 5 To **free** a prisoner or a slave means to let them go or release them from prison. ❑ *Israel is set to free more Lebanese prisoners... The act had a specific intent, to protect freed slaves from white mobs.* VERB V n V-ed 6 If someone or something is **free of** or **free from** an unpleasant thing, they do not have it or they are not affected by it. ❑ *...a future far more free of fear... The filtration system provides the crew with clean air free from fumes.* ADJ: v-link ADJ *of/from* n 7 A sum of money or type of goods that is **free of** tax or duty is one that you do not have to pay tax on. ➔ See also **duty-free**, **interest-free**, **tax-free**. ADJ: v-link ADJ *of* n 8 To **free** someone or something means to make them available for a task or function that they were previously not available for. ❑ *Toolbelts free both hands and lessen the risk of dropping hammers... His deal with Disney will run out shortly, freeing him to pursue his own project... There were more civilians working for the police, freeing officers from desk jobs.* VERB V n V n to-inf V n *from/of/for* n ♦ **Free up** means the same as **free**. ❑ *It can handle even the most complex graphic jobs, freeing up your computer for other tasks.* PHRASAL VERB V P n Also V n P 9 If you have a **free** period of time or are **free** at a particular time, you are not working or occupied then. ❑ *She spent her free time shopping... I am always free at lunchtime.* ADJ 10 If something such as a table or seat is **free**, it is not being used or occupied by anyone, or is not reserved for anyone to use. ❑ *There was only one seat free on the train.* ADJ 11 If you get something **free** or if it gets **free**, it is no longer trapped by anything or attached to anything. ❑ *He pulled his arm free, and strode for the door... The shark was writhing around wildly, trying to get free.* ADJ: v n ADJ, v-link ADJ, oft ADJ *of* n 12 If you **free** someone or something, you remove them from the place in which they have been trapped or become fixed. ❑ *It took firemen two hours to cut through the drive belt to free him.* VERB V n 13 When someone is using one hand or arm to hold or move something, their other hand or arm is referred to as their **free** one. ❑ *He snatched up the receiver and his free hand groped for the switch on the bedside lamp.* ADJ: ADJ n 14 If you say that someone is **free with** something such as advice or money, you mean that they give a lot of it, sometimes when it is not wanted. ❑ *They weren't always so free with their advice... They would often be free with criticism, some of it unjustified.* ADJ: v-link ADJ *with* n disapproval

**PHRASES** 15 You say '**feel free**' when you want to give someone permission to do something, in a very willing way. [INFORMAL] ❑ *If you have any questions at all, please feel free to ask me.* PHRASE: oft PHR to-inf formulae 16 If you do something or get something **for free**, you do it without being paid or get it without having to pay for it. [INFORMAL] ❑ *I wasn't expecting you to do it for free.* PHRASE: PHR after v 17 to **give** someone **a free hand** ➔ see **hand**.

♦ **free up** 1 ➔ see **free 8**. 2 To **free up** a market, economy, or system means to make it operate with fewer restrictions and controls. ❑ *...policies for freeing up markets and extending competition.* PHRASAL VERB V P n (not pron) Also V n P

**-free** /-friː/ **-free** combines with nouns to form adjectives that indicate that something does COMB in ADJ not have the thing mentioned, or has only a little of it. For example, sugar-free drinks do not contain any sugar, and lead-free petrol is made using only a small amount of lead. ❑ *...a salt-free diet.*

**free agent** **(free agents)** [1] If you say that someone is a **free agent**, you are emphasizing that they can do whatever they want to do, because they are not responsible to anyone or for anyone. ❑ *We are not free agents; we abide by the decisions of our president.* [2] If a sports player is a **free agent**, he or she is free to sign a contract with any team. [AM] N-COUNT N-COUNT

**free and easy** also **free-and-easy.** Someone or something that is **free and easy** is casual and informal. ❑ *...the free and easy atmosphere of these cafés.* ADJ = *easy-going, laid-back*

**free|bie** /friːbi/ **(freebies)** A **freebie** is something that you are given, usually by a company, without having to pay for it. [INFORMAL] N-COUNT

**free|dom** /friːdəm/ **(freedoms)** [1] **Freedom** is the state of being allowed to do what you want to do. **Freedoms** are instances of this. ❑ *...freedom of speech... They want greater political freedom... Today we have the freedom to decide our own futures... The United Nations Secretary-General has spoken of the need for individual freedoms and human rights.* [2] When prisoners or slaves are set free or escape, they gain their **freedom.** ❑ *...the agreement worked out by the UN, under which all hostages and detainees would gain their freedom.* [3] **Freedom from** something you do not want means not being affected by it. ❑ *...all the freedom from pain that medicine could provide. ...freedom from government control.* [4] **The freedom of** a particular city is a special honour which is given to a famous person who is connected with that city, or to someone who has performed some special service for the city. ◆◆◇ N-UNCOUNT: also N in pl; N-UNCOUNT: oft poss N = *liberty*; N-UNCOUNT: N *from* n; N-SING: *the* N *of* n

**free|dom fight|er** **(freedom fighters)** If you refer to someone as a **freedom fighter**, you mean that they belong to a group that is trying to change the government of their country using violent methods, and you agree with or approve of this. N-COUNT [approval]

**free en|ter|prise** **Free enterprise** is an economic system in which businesses compete for profit without much government control. [BUSINESS] N-UNCOUNT

**free fall** **(free falls)** also **free-fall.** [1] If the value or price of something goes **into free fall**, it starts to fall uncontrollably. [JOURNALISM] ❑ *Sterling went into free fall... The price did a free fall.* [2] In parachuting, **free fall** is the part of the jump before the parachute opens. N-VAR: oft *into/in* N; N-UNCOUNT

**free-floating** **Free-floating** things or people are able to move freely and are not controlled or directed by anything. ❑ *...a system of free-floating exchange rates.* ADJ: ADJ n

**Free|fone** /friːfoʊn/ also **freefone, freephone.** A **Freefone** telephone number is one which you can dial without having to pay for the call. [BRIT, TRADEMARK] ❑ *...London's Freefone emergency housing helpline.* N-UNCOUNT: usu N num, N n

✔ in AM, use **toll-free**

**free-for-all** **(free-for-alls)** [1] A **free-for-all** is a situation in which several people or groups are trying to get something for themselves and there are no controls on how they do it. [2] A **free-for-all** is a disorganized fight or argument which lots of people join in. N-SING; N-COUNT

**free form** also **free-form.** A **free form** work of art or piece of music has not been created according to a standard style or convention. ❑ *...free-form jazz.* ADJ: ADJ n

**free|hand** /friːhænd/ A **freehand** drawing is drawn without using instruments such as a ruler or a pair of compasses. ❑ *...freehand sketches.* ♦ **Freehand** is also an adverb. ❑ *Use a template or stencil or simply do it freehand.* ADJ: ADJ n; ADV: ADV after v

**free|hold** /friːhoʊld/ **(freeholds)** [1] If you have the **freehold** of a building or piece of land, it is yours for life and there are no conditions regarding your ownership. ❑ *People owning leasehold homes will be given a new right to buy the freehold of their property.* [2] If a building or piece of land is **freehold**, you can own it for life. ❑ *The property register will also say whether the property is freehold or leasehold.* N-VAR; ADJ

**free|holder** /friːhoʊldəʳ/ **(freeholders)** A **freeholder** is someone who owns the freehold to a particular piece of land. N-COUNT

**free house** **(free houses)** In Britain, a **free house** is a pub which is not owned by a particular company and so can sell whatever beers it chooses. N-COUNT

**free kick** **(free kicks)** In a game of football, when there is a **free kick**, the ball is given to a member of one side to kick because a member of the other side has broken a rule. N-COUNT

**free|lance** /friːlɑːns, -læns/ **(freelances, freelancing, freelanced)** [1] Someone who does **freelance** work or who is, for example, a **freelance** journalist or photographer is not employed by one organization, but is paid for each piece of work they do by the organization they do it for. [BUSINESS] ❑ *Michael Cross is a freelance journalist... She had a baby and decided to go freelance.* ♦ **Freelance** is also an adverb. ❑ *He is now working freelance from his home in Hampshire.* [2] A **freelance** is the same as a **freelancer.** [3] If you **freelance**, you do freelance work. ❑ *She has freelanced as a writer and researcher.* ADJ: usu ADJ n; ADV: ADV after v; N-COUNT; VERB V *as* n Also V

**free|lancer** /friːlɑːnsəʳ, -læns-/ **(freelancers)** A **freelancer** is someone who does freelance work. N-COUNT

**free|loader** /friːloʊdəʳ/ **(freeloaders)** If you refer to someone as a **freeloader**, you disapprove of them because they take advantage of other people's kindness, for example by accepting food or accommodation from them, without giving anything in return. [INFORMAL] N-COUNT [disapproval]

**free love** A belief in **free love** is the belief that it is acceptable and good to have sexual relationships without marrying, often several relationships at the same time. [OLD-FASHIONED] N-UNCOUNT

**free|ly** /friːli/ [1] **Freely** means many times or in large quantities. ❑ *We have referred freely to his ideas. ...the United States, where consumer goods are freely available.* [2] If you can talk **freely**, you can talk without needing to be careful about what you say. ❑ *She wondered whether he had someone to whom he could talk freely.* [3] If someone gives or does something **freely**, they give or do it willingly, without being ordered or forced to do it. ❑ *Danny shared his knowledge freely with anyone interested... Williams freely admits he lives for racing.* [4] If something or someone moves **freely**, they move easily and smoothly, without any obstacles or resistance. ❑ *You must allow the clubhead to swing freely.* [5] → See also **free.** ADV: ADV after v, ADV adj; ADV: ADV after v; ADV: ADV with v; ADV: ADV after v

**free|man** /friːmən/ **(freemen)** Someone who is a **freeman of** a particular city has been given a special honour by that city, known as the freedom of the city. ❑ *Peter was made a Freeman of the City of London.* N-COUNT: usu N *of* n

**free mar|ket** **(free markets)** A **free market** is an economic system in which business organizations decide things such as prices and wages, and are not controlled by the government. [BUSINESS] ❑ *...the creation of a free market. ...free market economies.* N-COUNT: usu sing

**free-marketeer** **(free-marketeers)** A **free-marketeer** is someone, especially a politician, who is in favour of letting market forces control the economy. [BUSINESS] N-COUNT

**Free|mason** /friːmeɪsᵊn/ **(Freemasons)** A **Freemason** is a man who is a member of a large secret society. Freemasons promise to help each N-COUNT other, and use a system of secret signs in order to recognize each other.

**free|masonry** /friːmeɪsənri/ 1 **Freemasonry** is the organization of the Freemasons and their beliefs and practices. [N-UNCOUNT] ❑ *He was very active in Freemasonry.* 2 **Freemasonry** is the friendly feeling that exists between people who are of the same kind or who have the same interests. [N-UNCOUNT: also *a* N, usu with supp] ❑ *...the freemasonry of sailors.*

**free pass** **(free passes)** A **free pass** is an official document that allows a person to travel or to enter a particular building without having to pay. [N-COUNT]

**free|phone** /friːfoʊn/ → see **Freefone**.

**free port** **(free ports)** A **free port** is a port or airport where goods can be brought in from foreign countries without payment of duty if they are going to be exported again. [BUSINESS] [N-COUNT]

**Free|post** /friːpoʊst/ **Freepost** is a system in Britain which allows you to send mail to certain organizations without paying for the postage. 'Freepost' is written on the envelope as part of the address. [TRADEMARK] [N-UNCOUNT]

**freer** /friːər/ **Freer** is the comparative of **free**.

**free radi|cal** **(free radicals)** **Free radicals** are atoms that contain one or more unpaired electrons. Free radicals are believed to be a cause of ageing, heart disease, and some cancers. [TECHNICAL] [N-COUNT: usu pl]

**free-range** **Free-range** means relating to a system of keeping animals in which they can move and feed freely on an area of open ground. [ADJ: usu ADJ n] ❑ *...free-range eggs.*

**free|sia** /friːʒə/ **(freesias)** **Freesias** are small plants with yellow, pink, white, or purple flowers that are shaped like tubes. [N-VAR]

**free spir|it** **(free spirits)** If you describe someone as a **free spirit**, you admire them because they are independent and live as they want to live rather than in a conventional way. [N-COUNT] [approval]

**fre|est** /friːɪst/ **Freest** is the superlative of **free**.

**free-standing** A **free-standing** piece of furniture or other object is not fixed to anything, or stands on its own away from other things. [ADJ] ❑ *...a free-standing cooker.*

**free|style** /friːstaɪl/ **Freestyle** is used to describe sports competitions, especially in swimming, wrestling, and skiing, in which competitors can use any style or method that they like when they take part. [ADJ: ADJ n] ❑ *...the 100m freestyle swimming event.* ♦ **Freestyle** is also a noun. [N-SING] ❑ *She won the 800 metres freestyle.*

**free-thinker** **(free-thinkers)** If you refer to someone as a **free-thinker**, you admire them because they work out their own ideas rather than accepting generally accepted views. [N-COUNT] [approval]

**free-to-air** **Free-to-air** television programmes and channels are broadcast to all televisions and do not require a subscription or payment. [ADJ: usu ADJ n] ♦ **Free to air** is also an adverb. [ADV] ❑ *For a change, the fight will be televised free to air on the Fox Network.*

**free|ware** /friːweər/ **Freeware** is computer software that you can use without payment. [COMPUTING] [N-UNCOUNT] ❑ *Is there a freeware program that I can use to produce my own clip art?*

**free|way** /friːweɪ/ **(freeways)** A **freeway** is a major road that has been specially built for fast travel over long distances. Freeways have several lanes and special places where traffic gets on and leaves. [AM] [N-COUNT] ❑ *The speed limit on the freeway is 55mph. ...Boston's freeway system.*

✓ in BRIT, usually use **motorway**

**free|wheel** /friːhwiːl/ **(freewheels, freewheeling, freewheeled)** also **free-wheel.** If you **freewheel**, you travel, usually downhill, on a bicycle without using the pedals, or in a vehicle without using the engine. [VERB] ❑ *He freewheeled back down the course.* [V adv/prep, Also V]

**free|wheeling** /friːhwiːlɪŋ/ also **free-wheeling.** If you refer to someone's **freewheeling** lifestyle or attitudes, you mean that they behave in a casual, relaxed way without feeling restricted by rules or accepted ways of doing things. [ADJ: usu ADJ n] ❑ *He has given up his freewheeling lifestyle to settle down with his baby daughter.*

**free will** 1 If you believe in **free will**, you believe that people have a choice in what they do and that their actions have not been decided in advance by God or by any other power. [N-UNCOUNT] ❑ *...the free will of the individual.* 2 If you do something **of** your **own free will**, you do it by choice and not because you are forced to do it. [PHRASE: PHR after v] ❑ *Would Bethany return of her own free will, as she had promised?*

**freeze** /friːz/ **(freezes, freezing, froze, frozen)** ◆◇◇
1 If a liquid or a substance containing a liquid **freezes**, or if something **freezes** it, it becomes solid because of low temperatures. [VERB] ❑ *If the temperature drops below 0°C, water freezes...* [V] *The ground froze solid.* [V adj] *...the discovery of how to freeze water at higher temperatures.* [V n] *...frozen puddles.* [V-ed] 2 If you **freeze** something such as food, you preserve it by storing it at a temperature below freezing point. You can also talk about how well food **freezes**. [VERB] ❑ *You can freeze the soup at this stage...* [V n] *Most fresh herbs will freeze successfully.* [V adv] 3 When **it freezes** outside, the temperature falls below freezing point. [VERB] ❑ *What if it rained and then froze all through those months?* [it V] ♦ **Freeze** is also a noun. [N-COUNT] ❑ *The trees were damaged by a freeze in December.* 4 If you **freeze**, you feel extremely cold. [VERB] ❑ *The windows didn't fit at the bottom so for a while we froze even in the middle of summer.* [V] 5 If someone who is moving **freezes**, they suddenly stop and become completely still and quiet. [WRITTEN] [VERB] ❑ *She froze when the beam of the flashlight struck her.* [V] 6 If the government or a company **freeze** things such as prices or wages, they state officially that they will not allow them to increase for a fixed period of time. [BUSINESS] [VERB] ❑ *They want the government to freeze prices.* [V n] ♦ **Freeze** is also a noun. [N-COUNT: with supp] ❑ *A wage freeze was imposed on all staff earlier this month.* 7 If a government **freezes** a plan or process, they state officially that they will not allow it to continue for a period of time. [VERB] ❑ *Britain has already frozen its aid programme...* [V n] *Diplomatic relations were frozen until August this year.* [V n] ♦ **Freeze** is also a noun. [N-COUNT: with supp] ❑ *...a freeze in nuclear weapons programs.* 8 If someone in authority **freezes** something such as a bank account, fund, or property, they obtain a legal order which states that it cannot be used or sold for a particular period of time. [BUSINESS] [VERB] ❑ *The governor's action freezes 300,000 accounts...* [V n] *Under these laws, he said, Mr. Rice's assets could have been frozen.* [V n] ♦ **Freeze** is also a noun. [N-COUNT: with supp] ❑ *...a freeze on private savings.* 9 → See also **freezing, frozen.**

♦ **freeze out** If you **freeze** someone **out of** an activity or situation, you prevent them from being involved in it by creating difficulties or by being unfriendly. [PHRASAL VERB = squeeze out] ❑ *Other traders did everything they could to freeze us out of the business.* [V n P *of* n, Also V n P]

♦ **freeze over** If something **freezes over**, it becomes covered with a layer of ice or other frozen substance. [PHRASAL VERB] ❑ *The air temperature was well below freezing, and lakes and rivers froze over...* [V P] *The lakes are still frozen over.* [V-ed P]

♦ **freeze up** If something **freezes up** or if something **freezes** it **up**, it becomes completely covered or blocked with ice. [PHRASAL VERB = ice up] ❑ *...lavatories that often freeze up in winter...* [V P] *Ice could freeze up their torpedo release mechanisms.* [V P n (not pron), Also V n P]

**freeze-dried** **Freeze-dried** food has been preserved by a process of rapid freezing and drying. [ADJ] ❑ *...freeze-dried instant mashed potato. ...freeze-dried coffee granules.*

**freeze-frame** **(freeze-frames)** A **freeze-frame** from a film is an individual picture from it, produced by stopping the film or video tape at that point. [N-COUNT]

**freez|er** /friːzəʳ/ **(freezers)** A **freezer** is a large container like a fridge in which the temperature is kept below freezing point so that you can store food inside it for long periods. N-COUNT

**freez|ing** /friːzɪŋ/ [1] If you say that something is **freezing** or **freezing cold**, you are emphasizing that it is very cold. ❑ *The cinema was freezing. ...a freezing January afternoon.* [2] If you say that you are **freezing** or **freezing cold**, you emphasizing that you feel very cold. ❑ *'You must be freezing,' she said.* [3] **Freezing** means the same as **freezing point**. ❑ *It's 15 degrees below freezing.* [4] → See also **freeze**. ADJ emphasis; ADJ: v-link ADJ emphasis; N-UNCOUNT

**freez|ing point** **(freezing points)** also **freezing-point.** [1] **Freezing point** is 0° Celsius, the temperature at which water freezes. Freezing point is often used when talking about the weather. ❑ *The temperature remained below freezing point throughout the day.* [2] The **freezing point** of a particular substance is the temperature at which it freezes. N-UNCOUNT: usu *above/below/to* N; N-COUNT: usu with poss

**freight** /freɪt/ **(freights, freighting, freighted)** [1] **Freight** is the movement of goods by lorries, trains, ships, or aeroplanes. ❑ *France derives 16% of revenue from air freight.* [2] **Freight** is goods that are transported by lorries, trains, ships, or aeroplanes. ❑ *90% of managers wanted to see more freight carried by rail.* [3] When goods **are freighted**, they are transported in large quantities over a long distance. ❑ *From these ports the grain is freighted down to Addis Ababa.* N-UNCOUNT; N-UNCOUNT; VERB: usu passive *be* V-ed adv/prep

**freight car** **(freight cars)** On a train, a **freight car** is a large container in which goods are transported. [mainly AM] N-COUNT

**freight|er** /freɪtəʳ/ **(freighters)** A **freighter** is a large ship or aeroplane that is designed for carrying freight. N-COUNT

**freight train** **(freight trains)** A **freight train** is a train on which goods are transported. N-COUNT

**French** /frentʃ/ [1] **French** means belonging or relating to France, or its people, language, or culture. [2] **The French** are the people who come from France. [3] **French** is the language spoken by people who live in France and in parts of some other countries, including Belgium, Canada, and Switzerland. ❑ *The villagers spoke French.* ADJ; N-PLURAL; N-UNCOUNT

**French bean** **(French beans)** **French beans** are narrow green beans that are eaten as a vegetable. They grow on a tall climbing plant and are the cases that contain the seeds of the plant. [BRIT] N-COUNT: usu pl

> in AM, use **string beans**

**French bread** **French bread** is white bread which is baked in long, thin loaves. N-UNCOUNT

**French Ca|na|dian** **(French Canadians)** also **French-Canadian.** [1] **French Canadian** means belonging or relating to people who come from the part of Canada where French is spoken. [2] **French Canadians** are Canadians whose native language is French. ADJ; N-COUNT

**French door** **(French doors)** **French doors** are the same as **French windows**. N-COUNT: usu pl

**French dress|ing** **French dressing** is a thin sauce made of oil, vinegar, salt, and spices which you put on salad. N-UNCOUNT

**French fries** **French fries** are long, thin pieces of potato fried in oil or fat. N-PLURAL

**French horn** **(French horns)** A **French horn** is a musical instrument of the brass family. It is shaped like a long metal tube with one wide end, wound round in a circle. You play the French horn by blowing into it and moving valves in order to obtain different notes. N-VAR: oft *the* N = horn

**French|man** /frentʃmən/ **(Frenchmen)** A **Frenchman** is a man who comes from France. N-COUNT

**French pol|ish** **French polish** is a type of varnish which is painted onto wood so that the wood has a hard shiny surface. N-UNCOUNT

**French win|dow** **(French windows)** **French windows** are a pair of glass doors which you go through into a garden or onto a balcony. N-COUNT: usu pl = French door

**French|woman** /frentʃwʊmən/ **(Frenchwomen)** A **Frenchwoman** is a woman who comes from France. N-COUNT

**fre|net|ic** /frɪnetɪk/ If you describe an activity as **frenetic**, you mean that it is fast and energetic, but rather uncontrolled. ❑ *...the frenetic pace of life in New York.* ADJ = frantic

**fren|zied** /frenzid/ **Frenzied** activities or actions are wild, excited, and uncontrolled. ❑ *...the frenzied activity of the general election... The man was stabbed to death in a frenzied attack.* ADJ: usu ADJ n

**frenzy** /frenzi/ **(frenzies)** **Frenzy** or a **frenzy** is great excitement or wild behaviour that often results from losing control of your feelings. ❑ *The country was gripped by a frenzy of nationalism.* N-VAR: oft N *of* n

**fre|quen|cy** /friːkwənsi/ **(frequencies)** [1] The **frequency** of an event is the number of times it happens during a particular period. ❑ *The frequency of Kara's phone calls increased rapidly... The tanks broke down with increasing frequency.* [2] In physics, the **frequency** of a sound wave or a radio wave is the number of times it vibrates within a specified period of time. ❑ *You can't hear waves of such a high frequency. ...a frequency of 24 kilohertz. ...low frequency waves.* N-UNCOUNT; N-VAR

**fre|quent** **(frequents, frequenting, frequented)** ◆◆◇

> The adjective is pronounced /friːkwənt/. The verb is pronounced /frɪkwent/.

[1] If something is **frequent**, it happens often. ❑ *Bordeaux is on the main Paris-Madrid line so there are frequent trains... He is a frequent visitor to the house.* ♦ **fre|quent|ly** *Iron and folic acid supplements are frequently given to pregnant women.* [2] If someone **frequents** a particular place, they regularly go there. [FORMAL] ❑ *I hear he frequents the Cajun restaurant in Hampstead.* ADJ; ADV: usu ADV with v; VERB V n

**fres|co** /freskoʊ/ **(frescoes** or **frescos)** A **fresco** is a picture that is painted on a plastered wall when the plaster is still wet. → See also **alfresco**. N-COUNT

**fresh** /freʃ/ **(fresher, freshest)** [1] A **fresh** thing or amount replaces or is added to a previous thing or amount. ❑ *He asked Strathclyde police, which carried out the original investigation, to make fresh inquiries... I need a new challenge and a fresh start somewhere else.* [2] Something that is **fresh** has been done, made, or experienced recently. ❑ *There were no fresh car tracks or footprints in the snow... With the memory of the bombing fresh in her mind, Eleanor became increasingly agitated.* [3] **Fresh** food has been picked or produced recently, and has not been preserved, for example by being frozen or put in a tin. ❑ *...locally caught fresh fish. ...fresh fruit.* [4] If you describe something as **fresh**, you like it because it is new and exciting. ❑ *These designers are full of fresh ideas. ...a fresh image.* [5] If you describe something as **fresh**, you mean that it is pleasant, bright, and clean in appearance. ❑ *Gingham fabrics always look fresh and pretty.* [6] If something smells, tastes, or feels **fresh**, it is clean or cool. ❑ *The air was fresh and for a moment she felt revived.* [7] **Fresh** water is water that is not salty, for example the water from rivers or lakes. [8] If you say that the weather is **fresh**, you mean that it is fairly cold and windy. ❑ *It was a fine, fresh summer morning... Outside the breeze was fresh and from the north.* [9] If you feel **fresh**, you feel full of energy and enthusiasm. ❑ *It's vital we are as fresh as possible for those matches.* [10] **Fresh** paint is not yet dry. [AM] ◆◆◇ ADJ: ADJ n = new; ADJ; ADJ; ADJ = original; ADJ; ADJ: usu ADJ n; ADJ; ADJ; ADJ: usu v-link ADJ; ADJ

> in BRIT, use **wet**

[11] If you are **fresh from** a particular place or experience, you have just come from that place or you have just had that experience. You can also say that someone is **fresh out of** a place. ❑ *I returned to the office, fresh from Heathrow... From what* ADJ: v-link ADJ *from/out of* n = straight

*I've heard he started wheeling and dealing fresh out of college.*

**fresh-** /freʃ-/ **Fresh-** is added to past participles in order to form adjectives which describe something as having been recently made or done. ❑ *...a vase of fresh-cut flowers. ...a meadow of fresh-mown hay.* COMB in ADJ: ADJ n

**fresh air** You can describe the air outside as **fresh air**, especially when you mean that it is good for you because it does not contain dirt or dangerous substances. ❑ *'Let's take the baby outside,' I suggested. 'We all need some fresh air.'* N-UNCOUNT: also *the* N

**fresh|en** /freʃᵊn/ **(freshens, freshening, freshened)** If the wind **freshens**, it becomes stronger and colder. ❑ *The wind had freshened.* VERB V

♦ **freshen up** [1] If you **freshen** something **up**, you make it clean and pleasant in appearance or smell. ❑ *A thorough brushing helps to freshen up your mouth... My room needed a lick of paint to freshen it up.* PHRASAL VERB V P n (not pron) V n P [2] If you **freshen up**, you wash your hands and face and make yourself look neat and tidy. ❑ *After Martine had freshened up, they went for a long walk.* PHRASAL VERB V P

**fresh|er** /freʃəʳ/ **(freshers)** [1] **Fresher** is the comparative form of **fresh**. [2] **Freshers** are students who have just started their first year at university or college. [BRIT, INFORMAL] N-COUNT: usu pl

☑ in AM, use **freshmen**

**fresh|ly** /freʃli/ If something is **freshly** made or done, it has been recently made or done. ❑ *...freshly baked bread. ...freshly cut grass.* ADV: ADV -ed = recently

**fresh|man** /freʃmən/ **(freshmen)** In America, a **freshman** is a student who is in his or her first year at university or college. N-COUNT

**fresh|water** /freʃwɔːtəʳ/ A **freshwater** lake contains water that is not salty, usually in contrast to the sea. **Freshwater** creatures live in water that is not salty. ❑ *...Lake Balaton, the largest freshwater lake in Europe... The perch is a freshwater fish.* ADJ: ADJ n

**fret** /fret/ **(frets, fretting, fretted)** [1] If you **fret** about something, you worry about it. ❑ *I was working all hours and constantly fretting about everyone else's problems... But congressional staffers fret that the project will eventually cost billions more... Don't fret, Mary. This is all some crazy mistake.* VERB = worry V about/over n V that V [2] The **frets** on a musical instrument such as a guitar are the raised lines across its neck. N-COUNT

**fret|ful** /fretfʊl/ If someone is **fretful**, they behave in a way that shows that they worried or unhappy about something. ❑ *Don't assume your baby automatically needs feeding if she's fretful.* ADJ

**fret|work** /fretwɜːʳk/ **Fretwork** is wood or metal that has been decorated by cutting bits of it out to make a pattern. N-UNCOUNT: oft N n

**Freud|ian** /frɔɪdiən/ **Freudian** means relating to the ideas and methods of the psychiatrist Freud, especially to his ideas about people's subconscious sexual feelings. ❑ *...the Freudian theory about daughters falling in love with their father.* ADJ: usu ADJ n

**Freud|ian slip** **(Freudian slips)** If someone accidentally says something that reveals their subconscious feelings, especially their sexual feelings, this is referred to as a **Freudian slip**. N-COUNT

**Fri.** **Fri.** is a written abbreviation for **Friday**.

**fri|ar** /fraɪəʳ/ **(friars)** A **friar** is a member of one of several Catholic religious orders. N-COUNT

**fric|tion** /frɪkʃᵊn/ **(frictions)** [1] If there is **friction** between people, there is disagreement and argument between them. ❑ *Sara sensed that there had been friction between her children.* N-UNCOUNT: also N in pl = conflict [2] **Friction** is the force that makes it difficult for things to move freely when they are touching each other. ❑ *The pistons are graphite-coated to reduce friction.* N-UNCOUNT

**Fri|day** /fraɪdeɪ, -di/ **(Fridays)** **Friday** is the day after Thursday and before Saturday. ❑ *Mr Cook is intending to go to the Middle East on Friday... Friday 6 November... I get home at half seven on a Friday.* N-VAR

**fridge** /frɪdʒ/ **(fridges)** A **fridge** is a large metal container which is kept cool, usually by electricity, so that food that is put in it stays fresh. [mainly BRIT] N-COUNT = refrigerator

☑ in AM, use **refrigerator**

**friend** /frend/ **(friends)** [1] A **friend** is someone who you know well and like, but who is not related to you. ❑ *I had a long talk about this with my best friend... She never was a close friend of mine. ...Sara's old friend, Ogden.* ◆◆◆ N-COUNT [2] If you are **friends with** someone, you are their friend and they are yours. ❑ *I still wanted to be friends with Alison... We remained good friends... Sally and I became friends.* N-PLURAL: oft N *with* n [3] The **friends of** a country, cause, organization, or a famous politician are the people and organizations who help and support them. ❑ *...The Friends of Birmingham Royal Ballet.* N-PLURAL; N-IN-NAMES [4] If one country refers to another as a **friend**, they mean that the other country is not an enemy of theirs. ❑ *The president said that Japan is now a friend and international partner.* N-COUNT = ally [5] If you **make friends with** someone, you begin a friendship with them. You can also say that two people **make friends**. ❑ *He has made friends with the kids on the street... He had made a friend of both girls.* PHRASE: V inflects, usu PHR *with* n

**friend|less** /frendləs/ Someone who is **friendless** has no friends. ❑ *The boy was unhappy because he thought he was friendless.* ADJ

**friend|ly** /frendli/ **(friendlier, friendliest, friendlies)** [1] If someone is **friendly**, they behave in a pleasant, kind way, and like to be with other people. ❑ *Godfrey had been friendly to me. ...a man with a pleasant, friendly face... Robert has a friendly relationship with all of his customers. ...a friendly atmosphere... Your cat isn't very friendly.* ◆◇◇ ADJ ♦ **friend|li|ness** *She also loves the friendliness of the people.* N-UNCOUNT [2] If you are **friendly with** someone, you like each other and enjoy spending time together. ❑ *I'm friendly with his mother.* ADJ: v-link ADJ, usu ADJ *with* n [3] You can describe another country or their government as **friendly** when they have good relations with your own country rather than being an enemy. ❑ *...a worsening in relations between the two previously friendly countries.* ADJ [4] In sport, a **friendly** is a match which is not part of a competition, and is played for entertainment or practice, often without any serious effort to win. [BRIT] ❑ *Athletic Bilbao agreed to play a friendly at Real Sociedad.* N-COUNT ♦ **Friendly** is also an adjective. ❑ *Austria beat Hungary 3-nil in a friendly match at Salzburg on Wednesday.* ADJ: ADJ n

☑ in AM, use **exhibition game**

**-friendly** /-frendli/ [1] **-friendly** combines with nouns to form adjectives which describe things that are not harmful to the specified part of the natural world. ❑ *Palm oil is environment-friendly. ...ozone-friendly fridges.* COMB in ADJ [2] **-friendly** combines with nouns to form adjectives which describe things which are intended for or suitable for the specified person, especially things that are easy for them to understand, appreciate, or use. ❑ *...customer-friendly banking facilities.* ➔ See also **user-friendly**. COMB in ADJ

**friend|ly so|ci|ety** **(friendly societies)** A **friendly society** is an organization to which people regularly pay small amounts of money and which then gives them money when they retire or when they are ill. [BRIT] N-COUNT

**friend|ship** /frendʃɪp/ **(friendships)** [1] A **friendship** is a relationship between two or more friends. ❑ *She struck up a close friendship with Desiree during the week of rehearsals... After seven years of friendship, she still couldn't tell when he was kidding.* ◆◇◇ N-VAR [2] You use **friendship** to refer in a general way to the state of being friends, or the feelings that friends have for each other. ❑ *...a hobby which led to a whole new world of friendship and adventure.* N-UNCOUNT [3] **Friendship** is a relationship between two countries in which they help and support each N-VAR = goodwill other. ❑ *The President set the targets for the future to promote friendship with East Europe.*

**frieze** /friːz/ **(friezes)** A **frieze** is a decoration high up on the walls of a room or just under the roof of a building. It consists of a long panel of carving or a long strip of paper with a picture or pattern on it. [N-COUNT]

**frig|ate** /frɪgət/ **(frigates)** A **frigate** is a fairly small ship owned by the navy that can move at fast speeds. Frigates are often used to protect other ships. [N-COUNT]

**frig|ging** /frɪgɪŋ/ **Frigging** is used by some people to emphasize what they are saying, especially when they are angry or annoyed about something. [INFORMAL, RUDE] [ADJ: ADJ n; emphasis]

**fright** /fraɪt/ **(frights)** 1 **Fright** is a sudden feeling of fear, especially the fear that you feel when something unpleasant surprises you. ❑ *The steam pipes rattled suddenly, and Franklin uttered a shriek and jumped with fright... The birds smashed into the top of their cages in fright... To hide my fright I asked a question.* [N-UNCOUNT] 2 **A fright** is an experience which makes you suddenly afraid. ❑ *The snake picked up its head and stuck out its tongue which gave everyone a fright... The last time you had a real fright, you nearly crashed the car.* [N-COUNT: usu sing = scare] 3 If a person or animal **takes fright** at something, they are suddenly frightened by it, and want to run away or to stop doing what they are doing. ❑ *An untrained horse had taken fright at the sound of gunfire... When costs soared, the studio took fright and recalled the company from Rome.* [PHRASE: V inflects]

**fright|en** /fraɪtᵊn/ **(frightens, frightening, frightened)** 1 If something or someone **frightens** you, they cause you to suddenly feel afraid, anxious, or nervous. ❑ *He knew that Soli was trying to frighten him, so he smiled to hide his fear... Most children are frightened by the sight of blood.* [VERB = scare; V n; V n] 2 If something **frightens the life out of** you, **frightens the wits out of** you, or **frightens** you **out of your wits**, it causes you to feel suddenly afraid or gives you a very unpleasant shock. ❑ *Fairground rides are intended to frighten the life out of you.* [PHRASE: V inflects; emphasis]

♦ **frighten away** or **frighten off** 1 If you **frighten away** a person or animal or **frighten** them **off**, you make them afraid so that they run away or stay some distance away from you. ❑ *The fishermen said the company's seismic survey was frightening away fish... He fired into the air, hoping that the noise would frighten them off.* [PHRASAL VERB = scare off; V P n (not pron); V n P] 2 To **frighten** someone **away** or **frighten** them **off** means to make them nervous so that they decide not to become involved with a particular person or activity. ❑ *Building society repossessions have frightened buyers off... The government is convinced that the bombers want to frighten away foreign investors.* [PHRASAL VERB = scare off; V n P; V P n (not pron)]

♦ **frighten off** → see **frighten away**.

**fright|ened** /fraɪtᵊnd/ If you are **frightened**, you are anxious or afraid, often because of something that has just happened or that you think may happen. ❑ *She was frightened of flying... Miriam was too frightened to tell her family what had happened.* [ADJ: oft v-link ADJ *of* n/-ing, ADJ to-inf]

**fright|en|ing** /fraɪtənɪŋ/ If something is **frightening**, it makes you feel afraid, anxious, or nervous. ❑ *It was a very frightening experience and they were very courageous... The number of youngsters involved in crime is frightening.* [ADJ = alarming] ♦ **fright|en|ing|ly** *The country is frighteningly close to possessing nuclear weapons.* [ADV: usu ADV adj]

**fright|ful** /fraɪtfʊl/ 1 **Frightful** means very bad or unpleasant. [OLD-FASHIONED] ❑ *My father was unable to talk about the war, it was so frightful.* [ADJ = terrible] 2 **Frightful** is used to emphasize the extent or degree of something, usually something bad. [INFORMAL, OLD-FASHIONED] ❑ *He got himself into a frightful muddle.* [ADJ: ADJ n; emphasis = dreadful]

**frig|id** /frɪdʒɪd/ 1 **Frigid** means extremely cold. [FORMAL] ❑ *A snowstorm hit the West today, bringing with it frigid temperatures.* [ADJ = icy] 2 If a woman is **frigid**, she finds it difficult to become sexually aroused. You can often use frigid to show disapproval. ❑ *My husband says I am frigid.* [ADJ: usu v-link ADJ] ♦ **fri|gid|ity** /frɪdʒɪdɪti/ *...an inability to experience orgasm (often called frigidity).* [N-UNCOUNT]

**frill** /frɪl/ **(frills)** 1 A **frill** is a long narrow strip of cloth or paper with many folds in it, which is attached to something as a decoration. ❑ *...net curtains with frills.* [N-COUNT] 2 If you describe something as having **no frills**, you mean that it has no extra features, but is acceptable or good if you want something simple. ❑ *This booklet restricts itself to facts without frills.* [N-COUNT: usu with brd-neg, usu pl; approval]

**frilled** /frɪld/ A **frilled** item of clothing is decorated with a frill or frills. [ADJ: ADJ n]

**frilly** /frɪli/ **Frilly** items of clothing or fabric have a lot of frills on them. ❑ *...maids in frilly aprons.* [ADJ: usu ADJ n]

**fringe** /frɪndʒ/ **(fringes)** 1 A **fringe** is hair which is cut so that it hangs over your forehead. [BRIT] [N-COUNT]

✔ in AM, use **bangs**

2 A **fringe** is a decoration attached to clothes, or other objects such as curtains, consisting of a row of hanging strips or threads. ❑ *The jacket had leather fringes.* [N-COUNT] 3 To be **on the fringe** or **the fringes of** a place means to be on the outside edge of it, or to be in one of the parts that are farthest from its centre. ❑ *...black townships located on the fringes of the city... They lived together in a mixed household on the fringe of a campus.* [N-COUNT: usu *on the* N *of* n] 4 **The fringe** or **the fringes of** an activity or organization are its less important, least typical, or most extreme parts, rather than its main and central part. ❑ *The party remained on the fringe of the political scene until last year.* [N-COUNT: usu pl, *the* N *of* n] 5 **Fringe** groups or events are less important or popular than other related groups or events. ❑ *The monarchists are a small fringe group who quarrel fiercely among themselves.* [ADJ: ADJ n]

**fringe ben|efit** **(fringe benefits)** 1 **Fringe benefits** are extra things that some people get from their job in addition to their salary, for example a car. [BUSINESS] [N-COUNT: usu pl] 2 The **fringe benefits** of doing something are the extra advantages which you get from it, although you may not have expected them and they were not the main reason for doing it. ❑ *His support was one of the nicest fringe benefits of pursuing this research.* [N-COUNT: oft N *of* -ing/n = bonus]

**fringed** /frɪndʒd/ 1 **Fringed** clothes, curtains, or lampshades are decorated with fringes. ❑ *Emma wore a fringed scarf round her neck.* [ADJ: ADJ n] 2 If a place or object **is fringed with** something, that thing forms a border around it or is situated along its edges. ❑ *Her eyes were large and brown and fringed with incredibly long lashes.* [ADJ: v-link ADJ *with* n = edged]

**frip|pery** /frɪpəri/ **(fripperies)** If you refer to something as **frippery**, you mean that it is silly or unnecessary, and only done or worn for pleasure. [mainly BRIT] ❑ *...all the fripperies with which the Edwardian woman indulged herself. ...a sombre display, with no frills or frippery.* [N-UNCOUNT: also N in pl; disapproval]

**Fris|bee** /frɪzbi/ **(Frisbees)** A **frisbee** is a light plastic disc that one person throws to another as a game. [TRADEMARK] [N-COUNT]

**frisk** /frɪsk/ **(frisks, frisking, frisked)** If someone **frisks** you, they search you, usually with their hands in order to see if you are hiding a weapon or something else such as drugs in your clothes. ❑ *Drago pushed him up against the wall and frisked him.* [VERB = body-search; V n]

**frisky** /frɪski/ **(friskier, friskiest)** A **frisky** animal or person is energetic and playful, and may be difficult to control. ❑ *His horse was feeling frisky, and he had to hold the reins tightly.* [ADJ = spirited]

**fris|son** /friːsɒn, AM friːsoʊn/ **(frissons)** A **frisson** is a short, sudden feeling of excitement or [N-COUNT: usu with supp, oft N *of* n] fear. [LITERARY] ❑ *A frisson of apprehension rippled round the theatre.*

**frit|ter** /frɪtəʳ/ **(fritters, frittering, frittered)** N-COUNT: usu n N **Fritters** are round pieces of fruit, vegetables, or meat that are dipped in batter and fried. ❑ *...apple fritters.*

♦ **fritter away** PHRASAL VERB = squander If someone **fritters away** time or money, they waste it on unimportant or unnecessary things. V P n (not pron) V n P ❑ *The firm soon started frittering away the cash it was generating... I seem to fritter my time away at coffee mornings.*

**fri|vol|ity** /frɪvɒlɪti/ **(frivolities)** N-VAR If you refer to an activity as a **frivolity**, you think that it is amusing and rather silly, rather than serious and sensible. ❑ *There is a serious message at the core of all this frivolity... He was one of my most able pupils, but far too easily distracted by frivolities.*

**frivo|lous** /frɪvələs/ 1 ADJ If you describe someone as **frivolous**, you mean they behave in a silly or light-hearted way, rather than being serious and sensible. ❑ *I just decided I was a bit too frivolous to be a doctor.* 2 ADJ disapproval If you describe an activity as **frivolous**, you disapprove of it because it is not useful and wastes time or money. ❑ *The group says it wants politicians to stop wasting public money on what it believes are frivolous projects.*

**frizz** /frɪz/ N-UNCOUNT **Frizz** is frizzy hair. ❑ *Manic brushing will only cause frizz.*

**friz|zy** /frɪzi/ **(frizzier, frizziest)** ADJ **Frizzy** hair is very tightly curled. ❑ *Carol's hair had a slightly frizzy perm.*

**fro** /froʊ/ **to and fro** → see **to**.

**frock** /frɒk/ **(frocks)** N-COUNT A **frock** is a woman's or girl's dress. [OLD-FASHIONED]

**frock coat** **(frock coats)** also **frock-coat.** N-COUNT A **frock coat** was a long coat that was worn by men in the 19th century.

**frog** /frɒg, AM frɔːg/ **(frogs)** 1 N-COUNT A **frog** is a small creature with smooth skin, big eyes, and long back legs which it uses for jumping. Frogs usually live near water. 2 N-COUNT **Frogs** is sometimes used to refer to French people. This use could cause offence. [INFORMAL]

**frog|man** /frɒgmən, AM frɔːg-/ **(frogmen)** N-COUNT = diver A **frogman** is someone whose job involves diving and working underwater, especially in order to mend or search for something. Frogmen wear special rubber suits and shoes, and carry equipment to help them to breathe underwater.

**frog-march** **(frog-marches, frog-marching, frog-marched)** also **frogmarch.** VERB If you **are frog-marched** somewhere, someone takes you there by force, holding you by the arms or another part of your body so that you have to walk along with them. *be* V-ed prep/adv V n prep/adv ❑ *He was frog-marched through the kitchen and out into the yard... They arrested the men and frog-marched them to the local police station.*

**frog|spawn** /frɒgspɔːn, AM frɔːg-/ also **frog spawn.** N-UNCOUNT **Frogspawn** is a soft substance like jelly which contains the eggs of a frog.

**fro-ing** → see **to-ing and fro-ing**.

**frol|ic** /frɒlɪk/ **(frolics, frolicking, frolicked)** VERB When people or animals **frolic**, they play or move in a lively, happy way. V ❑ *...lambs frolicking in the fields.*

**from** /frəm, STRONG frɒm, AM frʌm/ ♦♦♦

> In addition to the uses shown below, **from** is used in phrasal verbs such as 'date from' and 'grow away from'.

1 PREP If something comes **from** a particular person or thing, or if you get something **from** them, they give it to you or they are the source of it. ❑ *He appealed for information from anyone who saw the attackers. ...an anniversary present from his wife... The results were taken from six surveys... The dirt from the fields drifted like snow.* 2 PREP Someone who comes **from** a particular place lives in that place or originally lived there. Something that comes **from** a particular place was made in that place. ❑ *Katy Jones is nineteen and comes from Birmingham. ...wines from Coteaux d'Aix-en-Provence.* 3 PREP A person **from** a particular organization works for that organization. ❑ *...a representative from the Israeli embassy.*

4 PREP If someone or something moves or is moved **from** a place, they leave it or are removed, so that they are no longer there. ❑ *The guests watched as she fled from the room.* 5 PREP If you take one thing or person **from** another, you move that thing or person so that they are no longer with the other or attached to the other. ❑ *In many bone transplants, bone can be taken from other parts of the patient's body... Remove the bowl from the ice and stir in the cream.* 6 PREP If you take something **from** an amount, you reduce the amount by that much. ❑ *The £103 is deducted from Mrs Adams' salary every month... Three from six leaves three.* 7 PREP **From** is used in expressions such as **away from** or **absent from** to say that someone or something is not present in a place where they are usually found. ❑ *Her husband worked away from home a lot... Jo was absent from the house all the next day.*

8 PREP If you return **from** a place or an activity, you return after being in that place or doing that activity. ❑ *...a group of men travelling home from a darts match.* 9 PREP If you are back **from** a place or activity, you have left it and have returned to your former place. ❑ *Our economics correspondent, James Morgan, is just back from Germany... One afternoon when I was home from school, he asked me to come to see a movie with him.* 10 PREP: PREP n, PREP prep, PREP adv If you see or hear something **from** a particular place, you are in that place when you see it or hear it. ❑ *Visitors see the painting from behind a plate glass window.* 11 PREP: v PREP n If something hangs or sticks out **from** an object, it is attached to it or held by it. ❑ *Hanging from his right wrist is a heavy gold bracelet. ...large fans hanging from ceilings... He saw the corner of a magazine sticking out from under the blanket.* 12 PREP: amount PREP n You can use **from** when giving distances. For example, if a place is fifty miles **from** another place, the distance between the two places is fifty miles. ❑ *The centre of the town is 4 kilometres from the station... How far is it from here?* 13 PREP If a road or railway line goes **from** one place to another, you can travel along it between the two places. ❑ *...the road from St Petersburg to Tallinn.* 14 PREP: v PREP n = out of **From** is used, especially in the expression **made from**, to say what substance has been used to make something. ❑ *...bread made from white flour. ...a luxurious resort built from the island's native coral stone.* 15 PREP You can use **from** when you are talking about the beginning of a period of time. ❑ *Breakfast is available to fishermen from 6 a.m... From 1922 till 1925 she lived in Prague.* 16 PREP: PREP n/-ing You say **from** one thing **to** another when you are stating the range of things that are possible, or when saying that the range of things includes everything in a certain category. ❑ *Over 150 companies will be there, covering everything from finance to fixtures and fittings.* 17 PREP If something changes **from** one thing **to** another, it stops being the first thing and becomes the second thing. ❑ *The expression on his face changed from sympathy to surprise... Unemployment has fallen from 7.5 to 7.2%.* 18 PREP: PREP n/-ing You use **from** after some verbs and nouns when mentioning the cause of something. ❑ *The problem simply resulted from a difference of opinion... He is suffering from eye ulcers, brought on by the intense light in Australia... They really do get pleasure from spending money on other people... Most of the wreckage from the 1985 quake has been cleared.* 19 PREP You use **from** when you are giving the reason for an opinion. ❑ *She knew from experience that Dave was about to tell her the truth... He sensed from the expression on her face that she had something to say.* 20 PREP **From** is used after verbs with meanings such as 'protect', 'free', 'keep', and 'prevent' to introduce the action that does not happen, or that someone does not want to happen. ❑ *Such laws could protect the consumer from harmful*

or dangerous remedies... 300 tons of Peruvian mangoes were kept from entering France.

**fro|mage frais** /frɒmɑːʒ freɪ/ **(fromage frais)** **Fromage frais** is a thick, creamy dessert that is made from milk and often flavoured with fruit. A **fromage frais** is a small pot of fromage frais. N-VAR

**frond** /frɒnd/ **(fronds)** A **frond** is a long leaf which has an edge divided into lots of thin parts. ❑ *...palm fronds.* N-COUNT: usu with supp

**front** /frʌnt/ **(fronts, fronting, fronted)** ◆◆◆ 1 **The front of** something is the part of it that faces you, or that faces forward, or that you normally see or use. ❑ *One man sat in an armchair, and the other sat on the front of the desk... Stand at the front of the line... Her cotton dress had ripped down the front.* N-COUNT: usu sing, oft *the* N *of* n ≠ back 2 **The front of** a building is the side or part of it that faces the street. ❑ *Attached to the front of the house, there was a large veranda.* N-COUNT: usu sing, oft *the* N *of* n 3 A person's or animal's **front** is the part of their body between their head and their legs that is on the opposite side to their back. ❑ *If you lie your baby on his front, he'll lift his head and chest up.* N-SING: poss N ≠ back 4 **Front** is used to refer to the side or part of something that is towards the front or nearest to the front. ❑ *I went out there on the front porch... She was only six and still missing her front teeth... Children may be tempted to climb into the front seat while the car is in motion.* ADJ: ADJ n ≠ back 5 The **front** page of a newspaper is the outside of the first page, where the main news stories are printed. ❑ *The Guardian's front page carries a photograph of the two foreign ministers... The violence in the Gaza Strip makes the front page of most of the newspapers.* ➔ See also **front-page**. ADJ: ADJ n 6 **The front** is a road next to the sea in a seaside town. [BRIT] ❑ *Amy went out for a last walk along the sea front.* N-SING: *the* N = promenade 7 In a war, the **front** is a line where two opposing armies are facing each other. ❑ *Sonja's husband is fighting at the front.* ➔ See also **front line**. N-COUNT: usu *the* N in sing 8 If you say that something is happening on a particular **front**, you mean that it is happening with regard to a particular situation or field of activity. ❑ *We're moving forward on a variety of fronts.* N-COUNT 9 If someone puts on a particular kind of **front**, they pretend to have a particular quality. ❑ *Michael kept up a brave front both to the world and in his home.* N-COUNT: usu adj N 10 An organization or activity that is **a front for** one that is illegal or secret is used to hide it. ❑ *...a firm later identified by the police as a front for crime syndicates.* N-COUNT: usu N *for* n = cover 11 In relation to the weather, a **front** is a line where a mass of cold air meets a mass of warm air. ❑ *A very active cold front brought dramatic weather changes to Kansas on Wednesday.* N-COUNT 12 A building or an area of land that **fronts** a particular place or **fronts onto** it is next to it and faces it. ❑ *...real estate, which includes undeveloped land fronting the city convention center... There are some delightful Victorian houses fronting onto the pavement. ...quaint cottages fronted by lawns and flowerbeds.* VERB = face V n V *onto* n V-ed 13 The person who **fronts** an organization is the most senior person in it. [BRIT] ❑ *He fronted a formidable band of fighters... The commission, fronted by Sir Isaac Hayatali, was set up in June 1992.* VERB = head V n V-ed

☑ in AM, use **head**

PHRASES 14 If a person or thing is **in front**, they are ahead of others in a moving group, or further forward than someone or something else. ❑ *Officers will crack down on lunatic motorists who speed or drive too close to the car in front... 'What's with this guy?' demanded an American voice in the row in front.* PHRASE 15 Someone who is **in front** in a competition or contest at a particular point is winning at that point. ❑ *Richard Dunwoody is in front in the jockeys' title race... Some preliminary polls show him out in front.* PHRASE: PHR after v, v-link PHR = leading 16 If someone or something is **in front of** a particular thing, they are facing it, ahead of it, or close to the front part of it. ❑ *She sat down in front of her dressing-table mirror to look at herself... Something darted out in front of my car, and my car hit it... A police car was parked in front of the house.* PREP-PHRASE 17 If you do or say something **in front of** someone else, you do or say it when they are present. ❑ *They never argued in front of their children... He has been brought up not to swear in front of women.* PREP-PHRASE 18 **On the home front** or **on the domestic front** means with regard to your own country rather than foreign countries. [JOURNALISM] ❑ *Its present economic ills on the home front are largely the result of overspending... On the domestic front, the president got his way with his budget proposals.* PHRASE: PHR with cl

**front|age** /frʌntɪdʒ/ **(frontages)** A **frontage** of a building is a wall which faces a public place such as a street or a river. ❑ *The restaurant has a river frontage.* N-COUNT: also no det

**front|al** /frʌntᵊl/ 1 **Frontal** means relating to or involving the front of something, for example the front of an army, a vehicle, or the brain. [FORMAL] ❑ *Military leaders are not expecting a frontal assault by the rebels... He pioneered the surgical technique called frontal lobotomy.* ADJ: usu ADJ n 2 ➔ See also **full-frontal**.

**front bench** **(front benches)** In Britain, **the front bench** or people who sit on **the front bench** are members of Parliament who are ministers in the Government or who hold official positions in an opposition party. ❑ *Some of the Government front bench still believe our relationship with the US is paramount.* N-COUNT-COLL

**front|bencher** /frʌntbentʃəʳ/ **(frontbenchers)** In Britain, a **frontbencher** is a member of Parliament who is a minister in the Government or who holds an official position in an opposition party. N-COUNT: usu supp N

**front burn|er** If an issue is **on the front burner**, it receives a lot of attention because it is considered to be more urgent or important than other issues. ❑ *It helps to put an important issue back on the front burner.* N-SING: usu *on the* N ≠ back burner

**front door** **(front doors)** The **front door** of a house or other building is the main door, which is usually in the wall that faces a street. ➔ See picture on page 1705. N-COUNT

**fron|tier** /frʌntɪəʳ, -tɪəʳ/ **(frontiers)** 1 A **frontier** is a border between two countries. [BRIT] ❑ *It wasn't difficult then to cross the frontier.* N-COUNT

☑ in AM, usually use **border**

2 When you are talking about the western part of America before the twentieth century, you use **frontier** to refer to the area beyond the part settled by Europeans. ❑ *...a far-flung outpost on the frontier.* N-COUNT 3 **The frontiers** of something, especially knowledge, are the limits to which it extends. ❑ *...pushing back the frontiers of science. ...technological frontiers.* N-COUNT: usu pl, usu N *of* n, adj N

**fron|tis|piece** /frʌntɪspiːs/ **(frontispieces)** The **frontispiece** of a book is a picture at the beginning, opposite the page with the title on. N-COUNT: usu sing

**front line** **(front lines)** also **front-line**. 1 **The front line** is the place where two opposing armies are facing each other and where fighting is going on. ❑ *...a massive concentration of soldiers on the front line.* N-COUNT: usu *the* N 2 A **front line** state shares a border with a country that it is at war with or is in conflict with. ❑ *...the front-line states bordering South Africa.* ADJ: ADJ n 3 Someone who is **in the front line** has to play a very important part in defending or achieving something. ❑ *Information officers are in the front line of putting across government policies.* PHRASE: v-link PHR, PHR after v

**front man** **(front men)** If you say that someone is a **front man** for a group or organization, you mean that their role is to represent and give a good impression of it to the public, especially when it is not very respectable or popular. ❑ *He is the company's front man in Washington.* N-COUNT: oft N *for* n [disapproval]

**front-page** A **front-page** article or picture appears on the front page of a newspaper because it is very important or interesting. ❑ *...a front-page article in last week's paper.* ADJ: ADJ n

**front-runner** **(front-runners)** In a competition or contest, the **front-runner** is the person who seems most likely to win it. ❑ *Neither of the front-runners in the presidential election is a mainstream politician.* N-COUNT = favourite

**frost** /frɒst, AM frɔːst/ **(frosts)** When there is **frost** or a **frost**, the temperature outside falls below freezing point and the ground becomes covered in ice crystals. ❑ *There is frost on the ground and snow is forecast... The wind had veered to north, bringing clear skies and a keen frost.* N-VAR

**frost|bite** /frɒstbaɪt, AM frɔːst-/ **Frostbite** is a condition in which parts of your body, such as your fingers or toes, become seriously damaged as a result of being very cold. ❑ *The survivors suffered from frostbite.* N-UNCOUNT

**frost|bitten** /frɒstbɪtᵊn, AM frɔːst-/ If a person or a part of their body is **frostbitten**, they are suffering from frostbite. ADJ

**frost|ed** /frɒstɪd, AM frɔːst-/ [1] **Frosted** glass is glass that you cannot see through clearly. ❑ *The top half of the door to his office was of frosted glass.* ADJ [2] **Frosted** means covered with frost. ❑ *...the frosted trees.* ADJ [3] **Frosted** means covered with something that looks like frost. ❑ *...frosted blue eye shadow.* ADJ [4] **Frosted** means covered with icing. [AM] ❑ *...a plate of frosted cupcakes.* ADJ

✔ in BRIT, usually use **iced**

**frost|ing** /frɒstɪŋ, AM frɔːst-/ **Frosting** is a sweet substance made from powdered sugar that is used to cover and decorate cakes. [AM] ❑ *...a huge pastry with green frosting on it.* N-UNCOUNT

✔ in BRIT, usually use **icing**

**frosty** /frɒsti, AM frɔːsti/ **(frostier, frostiest)** [1] If the weather is **frosty**, the temperature is below freezing. ❑ *...sharp, frosty nights.* ADJ [2] You describe the ground or an object as **frosty** when it is covered with frost. ❑ *The street was deserted except for a cat lifting its paws off the frosty stones.* ADJ

**froth** /frɒθ, AM frɔːθ/ **(froths, frothing, frothed)** [1] **Froth** is a mass of small bubbles on the surface of a liquid. ❑ *...the froth of bubbles on the top of a glass of beer... The froth is blown away.* N-UNCOUNT = foam [2] If a liquid **froths**, small bubbles appear on its surface. ❑ *The sea froths over my feet... Add a little of the warmed milk and allow to froth a little.* VERB V prep V [3] If you refer to an activity or object as **froth**, you disapprove of it because it appears exciting or attractive, but has very little real value or importance. ❑ *No substance at all, just froth.* N-UNCOUNT [disapproval]

**frothy** /frɒθi, AM frɔːθi/ **(frothier, frothiest)** A **frothy** liquid has lots of bubbles on its surface. ❑ *...frothy milk shakes.* ADJ: usu ADJ n

**frown** /fraʊn/ **(frowns, frowning, frowned)** When someone **frowns**, their eyebrows become drawn together, because they are annoyed, worried, or puzzled, or because they are concentrating. ❑ *Nancy shook her head, frowning... He frowned at her anxiously. ...a frowning man.* ♦ **Frown** is also a noun. ❑ *There was a deep frown on the boy's face.* VERB V, V at n V-ing N-COUNT

♦ **frown upon** or **frown on** If something **is frowned upon** or **is frowned on** people disapprove of it. ❑ *This practice is frowned upon as being wasteful... Many teachers frown on such practices.* PHRASAL VERB *be* V-ed P, V P n (not pron)

**froze** /froʊz/ **Froze** is the past tense of **freeze**.

**fro|zen** /froʊzᵊn/ [1] **Frozen** is the past participle of **freeze**. [2] If the ground is **frozen** it has become very hard because the weather is very cold. ❑ *It was bitterly cold now and the ground was frozen hard. ...the frozen bleakness of the Far North.* ADJ [3] **Frozen** food has been preserved by being kept at a very low temperature. ❑ *...frozen desserts like ice cream.* ADJ: usu ADJ n [4] If you say that you are **frozen**, or a part of your body is **frozen**, you are emphasizing that you feel very cold. ❑ *He put one hand up to his frozen face.* ADJ [emphasis] ● **Frozen stiff** means the same as **frozen**. ❑ *It was cold and damp; he pulled up his collar and was aware of being frozen stiff.* PHRASE: v-link PHR

**fruc|tose** /frʊktoʊz/ **Fructose** is a sweet substance which occurs naturally in fruit and vegetables. It is sometimes used to make food sweeter. N-UNCOUNT

**fru|gal** /fruːgᵊl/ [1] People who are **frugal** or who live **frugal** lives do not eat much or spend much money on themselves. ❑ *She lives a frugal life.* ADJ ♦ **fru|gal|ity** *We must practise the strictest frugality and economy.* N-UNCOUNT ♦ **fru|gal|ly** *We lived fairly frugally... He frugally saved various bits of the machine in carefully marked boxes.* ADV: ADV with v [2] A **frugal** meal is small and not expensive. ❑ *The diet was frugal: cheese and water, rice and beans.* ADJ

**fruit** /fruːt/ **(fruit** or **fruits; fruits, fruiting, fruited)** ◆◆◇ [1] **Fruit** or a **fruit** is something which grows on a tree or bush and which contains seeds or a stone covered by a substance that you can eat. ❑ *Fresh fruit and vegetables provide fibre and vitamins. ...bananas and other tropical fruits... Try to eat at least one piece of fruit a day.* N-VAR [2] If a plant **fruits**, it produces fruit. ❑ *The scientists will study the variety of trees and observe which are fruiting.* VERB V [3] **The fruits** or **the fruit of** someone's work or activity are the good things that result from it. ❑ *The team have really worked hard and Mansell is enjoying the fruits of that labour... The findings are the fruit of more than three years research.* N-COUNT: usu *the* N *of* n [4] ➔ See also **dried fruit**, **forbidden fruit**, **kiwi fruit**, **passion fruit**.

PHRASES [5] If the effort that you put into something or a particular way of doing something **bears fruit**, it is successful and produces good results. ❑ *He was naturally disappointed when the talks failed to bear fruit.* PHRASE: V inflects [6] **The first fruits** or **the first fruit** of a project or activity are its earliest results or profits. ❑ *This project is one of the first fruits of commercial co-operation between the two countries.* PHRASE: oft PHR *of* n

**fruit bowl** **(fruit bowls)** A **fruit bowl** is a large bowl in which fruit is kept and displayed. N-COUNT

**fruit|cake** /fruːtkeɪk/ **(fruitcakes)** also **fruit cake.** [1] A **fruitcake** is a cake that contains raisins, currants, and other dried fruit. N-VAR [2] If you refer to someone as a **fruitcake**, you mean that they are mad or that their behaviour is very strange. [INFORMAL] N-COUNT [disapproval]

**fruit cock|tail** **(fruit cocktails)** **Fruit cocktail** is a mixture of pieces of different kinds of fruit eaten as part of a meal. N-VAR

**fruit fly** **(fruit flies)** **Fruit flies** are very small flies which eat fruit and rotting plants. N-COUNT

**fruit|ful** /fruːtfʊl/ [1] Something that is **fruitful** produces good and useful results. ❑ *We had a long, happy, fruitful relationship... The talks had been fruitful, but much remained to be done.* ADJ = productive ♦ **fruit|ful|ly** *...taking their skills where they can be applied most fruitfully.* ADV: ADV with v [2] **Fruitful** land or trees produce a lot of crops. ❑ *...a landscape that was fruitful and lush.* ADJ = fertile

**frui|tion** /fruɪʃᵊn/ If something comes **to fruition**, it starts to succeed and produce the results that were intended or hoped for. [FORMAL] ❑ *These plans take time to come to fruition.* N-UNCOUNT: usu *to* N

**fruit|less** /fruːtləs/ **Fruitless** actions, events, or efforts do not achieve anything at all. ❑ *It was a fruitless search... Talks have so far have been fruitless.* ADJ = unproductive

**fruit ma|chine** **(fruit machines)** A **fruit machine** is a machine used for gambling. You put money into it and if a particular combination of symbols, especially fruit, appears, you win money. [BRIT] N-COUNT

✔ in AM, use **slot machine**

**fruit sal|ad** **(fruit salads)** **Fruit salad** is a mixture of pieces of different kinds of fruit. It is usually eaten as a dessert. N-VAR

**fruity** /fruːti/ **(fruitier, fruitiest)** [1] Something that is **fruity** smells or tastes of fruit. ❑ *This shampoo smells fruity and leaves the hair beautifully silky. ...a lovely rich fruity wine.* ADJ [2] A **fruity** voice or laugh is pleasantly rich and deep. ❑ *Jerrold laughed again, a solid, fruity laugh.* ADJ: usu ADJ n

**frumpy** /frʌmpi/ If you describe a woman or her clothes as **frumpy**, you mean that her clothes are dull and not fashionable. ❑ *I looked so frumpy next to these women.* ADJ [disapproval] = dowdy

**frus|trate** /frʌstreɪt, AM frʌstreɪt/ **(frustrates, frustrating, frustrated)** ◆◇◇ 1 If something **frustrates** you, it upsets or angers you because you are unable to do anything about the problems it creates. ❑ *These questions frustrated me... Doesn't it frustrate you that audiences in the theatre are so restricted?* VERB V n V n ♦ **frus|trat|ed** *Roberta felt frustrated and angry. ...voters who are frustrated with the council.* ADJ: usu v-link ADJ ♦ **frus|tra|tion** /frʌstreɪʃᵊn/ **(frustrations)** *The results show the level of frustration among hospital doctors. ...a man fed up with the frustrations of everyday life.* N-VAR 2 If someone or something **frustrates** a plan or attempt to do something, they prevent it from succeeding. ❑ *The government has deliberately frustrated his efforts to gain work permits for his foreign staff. ...her frustrated attempt to become governor.* VERB V n V-ed

**frus|trat|ing** /frʌstreɪtɪŋ/ Something that is **frustrating** annoys you or makes you angry because you cannot do anything about the problems it causes. ❑ *The current situation is very frustrating for us. ...It is a frustrating and difficult time for Pat.* ADJ ♦ **frus|trat|ing|ly** *Poverty and unemployment are frustratingly hard to tackle.* ADV

**fry** /fraɪ/ **(fries, frying, fried)** ◆◇◇ 1 When you **fry** food, you cook it in a pan that contains hot fat or oil. ❑ *Fry the breadcrumbs until golden brown. ...fried rice.* VERB V n V-ed 2 **Fry** are very small, young fish. N-PLURAL 3 **Fries** are the same as **French fries**. N-PLURAL 4 → See also **small fry**.

**fry|er** /fraɪəʳ/ **(fryers)** A **fryer** is a type of deep pan which you can use to fry food in hot oil. N-COUNT: oft n N

**fry|ing pan** **(frying pans)** A **frying pan** is a flat metal pan with a long handle, in which you fry food. → See picture on page 1710. N-COUNT

**fry-up** **(fry-ups)** A **fry-up** is a meal consisting of a mixture of foods such as sausages, bacon, and eggs that have been fried. [BRIT, INFORMAL] N-COUNT

**ft** **ft** is a written abbreviation for **feet** or **foot**. ❑ *Flying at 1,000 ft, he heard a peculiar noise from the rotors. ...an area of 2,750 sq ft.*

**fuch|sia** /fjuːʃə/ **(fuchsias)** A **fuchsia** is a plant or a small bush which has pink, purple, or white flowers. The flowers hang downwards, with their outer petals curved backwards. N-VAR

**fuck** /fʌk/ **(fucks, fucking, fucked)**

> **Fuck** is a rude and offensive word which you should avoid using.

1 **Fuck** is used to express anger or annoyance. [⚠ VERY RUDE] EXCLAM [feelings] 2 To **fuck** someone means to have sex with them. [⚠ VERY RUDE] V-RECIP ♦ **Fuck** is also a noun. N-COUNT 3 **Fuck all** is used to mean 'nothing at all'. [⚠ VERY RUDE] PHRASE [emphasis]

♦ **fuck off** Telling someone to **fuck off** is an insulting way of telling them to go away. [⚠ VERY RUDE] PHRASAL VERB: usu imper, V P

♦ **fuck up** If you **fuck** something **up**, you make a mistake or do something badly. [⚠ VERY RUDE] PHRASAL VERB: V n P, V P n (not pron)

**fuck|er** /fʌkəʳ/ **(fuckers)** If someone calls a person a **fucker**, they are insulting them. [⚠ VERY RUDE] N-COUNT [disapproval]

**fuck|ing** /fʌkɪŋ/ **Fucking** is used by some people to emphasize a word or phrase, especially when they are feeling angry or annoyed. [⚠ VERY RUDE] ADJ: ADJ n; ADV: ADV adj [emphasis]

**fud|dled** /fʌdᵊld/ Someone who is **fuddled** cannot think clearly, for example because they are very tired or slightly drunk. ❑ *Fuddled by brandy, her brain fumbled over the events of the night.* ADJ

**fuddy-duddy** /fʌdi dʌdi/ **(fuddy-duddies)** If you describe someone as a **fuddy-duddy**, you are criticizing or making fun of them because they are old-fashioned in their appearance or attitudes. [OLD-FASHIONED] ❑ *He didn't want all those old fuddy-duddies around.* N-COUNT [disapproval]

**fudge** /fʌdʒ/ **(fudges, fudging, fudged)** 1 **Fudge** is a soft brown sweet that is made from butter, cream, and sugar. N-UNCOUNT 2 If you **fudge** something, you avoid making a clear and definite decision, distinction, or statement about it. ❑ *Both have fudged their calculations and avoided specifics.* VERB V n

**fuel** /fjuːəl/ **(fuels, fuelling, fuelled)** ◆◆◇

> in AM, use **fueling, fueled**

1 **Fuel** is a substance such as coal, oil, or petrol that is burned to provide heat or power. ❑ *They ran out of fuel. ...industrial research into cleaner fuels.* N-MASS 2 To **fuel** a situation means to make it become worse or more intense. ❑ *The result will inevitably fuel speculation about the Prime Minister's future... The economic boom was fueled by easy credit.* VERB = feed V n be V-ed 3 If something **adds fuel to** a conflict or debate, or **adds fuel to the fire**, it makes the conflict or debate more intense. ❑ *His comments are bound to add fuel to the debate... The decision to raise tariffs on imports will only add fuel to the fire.* PHRASE: V inflects

**fuel in|jec|tion** **Fuel injection** is a system in the engines of some vehicles which forces fuel directly into the part of the engine where it is burned. N-UNCOUNT

**fuelled** /fjuːəld/

> in AM, use **fueled**

A machine or vehicle that **is fuelled by** a particular substance works by burning that substance. ❑ *It is less polluting than power stations fuelled by oil, coal and gas.* ADJ: v-link ADJ by n

**fuel rod** **(fuel rods)** **Fuel rods** are metal tubes containing nuclear fuel. They are used in some nuclear reactors. N-COUNT

**fug** /fʌg/ People refer to the atmosphere somewhere as **a fug** when it is smoky and smelly and there is no fresh air. [mainly BRIT] ❑ *...the fug of cigarette smoke.* N-SING: oft N of n

**fu|gi|tive** /fjuːdʒɪtɪv/ **(fugitives)** A **fugitive** is someone who is running away or hiding, usually in order to avoid being caught by the police. ❑ *...the fugitive train robber.* N-COUNT

**fugue** /fjuːg/ **(fugues)** A **fugue** is a piece of music that begins with a simple tune which is then repeated by other voices or instrumental parts with small variations. [TECHNICAL] N-COUNT

**-ful** /-fʊl/ **(-fuls)** You use **-ful** to form nouns that refer to the quantity of a substance that an object contains or can contain. For example, a handful of sand is the amount of sand that you can hold in your hand. ❑ *...a spoonful of brown sugar.* SUFFIX

**ful|crum** /fʊlkrəm/ If you say that someone or something is **the fulcrum** of an activity or situation, you mean that they have a very important effect on what happens. [FORMAL] ❑ *The decision is the strategic fulcrum of the Budget.* N-SING: oft N of n = pivot

**ful|fil** /fʊlfɪl/ **(fulfils** or **fulfills, fulfilling, fulfilled)** also **fulfill.** ◆◇◇ 1 If you **fulfil** something such as a promise, dream, or hope, you do what you said or hoped you would do. ❑ *President Kaunda fulfilled his promise of announcing a date for the referendum.* VERB = carry out V n 2 To **fulfil** a task, role, or requirement means to do or be what is required, necessary, or expected. ❑ *Without them you will not be able to fulfil the tasks you have before you... All the necessary conditions were fulfilled.* VERB V n V n 3 If something **fulfils** you, or if you **fulfil yourself**, you feel happy and satisfied with what you are doing or with what you have achieved. ❑ *The war was the biggest thing in her life and nothing after that quite fulfilled her... They don't like the idea that women can fulfil themselves without the assistance of a man.* VERB = satisfy V n V pron-refl ♦ **ful|filled** *I feel more fulfilled doing this than I've ever done.* ADJ ♦ **ful|fil|ling** *...a fulfilling career... I found it all very fulfilling.* ADJ

**ful|fil|ment** /fʊlfɪlmənt/ also **fulfillment.** 1 **Fulfilment** is a feeling of satisfaction that you get from doing or achieving something, especially something useful. ❑ *...professional fulfilment.* N-UNCOUNT = satisfaction

2 **The fulfilment of** a promise, threat, request, hope, or duty is the event or act of it happening or being made to happen. ❑ *Visiting Angkor was the fulfilment of a childhood dream.* N-UNCOUNT: usu N *of* n = *realization*

**full** /fʊl/ **(fuller, fullest)** 1 If something is **full**, it contains as much of a substance or as many objects as it can. ❑ *Once the container is full, it stays shut until you turn it clockwise. ...a full tank of petrol.* ◆◆◆ ADJ ≠ *empty*
2 If a place or thing **is full of** things or people, it contains a large number of them. ❑ *The case was full of clothes... The streets are still full of debris from two nights of rioting. ...a useful recipe leaflet full of ideas for using the new cream.* ADJ: v-link ADJ *of* n = *filled* 3 If someone or something **is full of** a particular feeling or quality, they have a lot of it. ❑ *I feel full of confidence and so open to possibilities... Mom's face was full of pain. ...an exquisite mousse, incredibly rich and full of flavour.* ADJ: v-link ADJ *of* n 4 You say that a place or vehicle is **full** when there is no space left in it for any more people or things. ❑ *The main car park was full when I left about 10.45... They stay here a few hours before being sent to refugee camps, which are now almost full... The bus was completely full, and lots of people were standing.* ADJ: usu v-link ADJ 5 If your hands or arms are **full**, you are carrying or holding as much as you can carry. ❑ *Sylvia entered, her arms full of packages... People would go into the store and come out with their arms full.* ADJ: v-link ADJ 6 If you feel **full**, you have eaten or drunk so much that you do not want anything else. ❑ *It's healthy to eat when I'm hungry and to stop when I'm full.* ADJ: v-link ADJ ♦ **full|ness** *High fibre diets give the feeling of fullness.* N-UNCOUNT 7 You use **full** before a noun to indicate that you are referring to all the details, things, or people that it can possibly include. ❑ *Full details will be sent to you once your application has been accepted... May I have your full name?* ADJ: ADJ n = *complete*
8 **Full** is used to describe a sound, light, or physical force which is being produced with the greatest possible power or intensity. ❑ *From his study came the sound of Mahler, playing at full volume... Then abruptly he revved the engine to full power.* ADJ: ADJ n ♦ **Full** is also an adverb. ❑ *...a two-seater Lotus, parked with its headlamps full on.* ADV: ADV adv 9 You use **full** to emphasize the completeness, intensity, or extent of something. ❑ *We should conserve oil and gas by making full use of other energy sources... Television cameras are carrying the full horror of this war into homes around the world... The lane leading to the farm was in full view of the house windows.* ADJ: ADJ n [emphasis] 10 A **full** statement or report contains a lot of information and detail. ❑ *Mr Primakov gave a full account of his meeting with the President. ...the enormous detail in this very full document.* ADJ: usu ADJ n 11 If you say that someone has or leads a **full** life, you approve of the fact that they are always busy and do a lot of different things. ❑ *You will be successful in whatever you do and you will have a very full and interesting life.* ADJ: usu ADJ n [approval]
12 You use **full** to emphasize the force or directness with which someone or something is hit or looked at. ❑ *She kissed him full on the mouth.* ADV: ADV prep [emphasis]
13 You use **full** to refer to something which gives you all the rights, status, or importance for a particular position or activity, rather than just some of them. ❑ *How did the meeting go, did you get your full membership?* ADJ: ADJ n 14 A **full** flavour is strong and rich. ❑ *Italian plum tomatoes have a full flavour, and are best for cooking.* ADJ: ADJ n 15 If you describe a part of someone's body as **full**, you mean that it is rounded and rather large. ❑ *The Juno Collection specialises in large sizes for ladies with a fuller figure. ...his strong chin, his full lips, his appealing mustache.* ADJ: usu ADJ n
16 A **full** skirt or sleeve is wide and has been made from a lot of fabric. ❑ *My wedding dress has a very full skirt.* ADJ: usu ADJ n ♦ **full|ness** *The coat has raglan sleeves, and is cut to give fullness at the back.* N-UNCOUNT
17 When there is a **full** moon, the moon appears as a bright, complete circle. ADJ: usu ADJ n
**PHRASES** 18 You say that something has been done or described **in full** when everything that was necessary has been done or described. ❑ *The medical experts have yet to report in full.* PHRASE: PHR after v = *fully* 19 If you say that a person **knows full well** that something is true, especially something unpleasant, you are emphasizing that they are definitely aware of it, although they may behave as if they are not. ❑ *He knew full well he'd be ashamed of himself later.* PHRASE: V inflects [emphasis]
20 Something that is done or experienced **to the full** is done to as great an extent as is possible. ❑ *She probably has a good mind, which should be used to the full.* PHRASE: PHR after v 21 to **be full of beans** → see **bean**. **full blast** → see **blast**. to **come full circle** → see **circle**. to **have** your **hands full** → see **hand**. **in full swing** → see **swing**.

**full-back** **(full-backs)** also **fullback.** In rugby or football, a **full-back** is a defending player whose position is towards the goal which their team is defending. N-COUNT

**full-blooded** **Full-blooded** behaviour and actions are carried out with great commitment and enthusiasm. ❑ *Experts are agreed that full-blooded market reform is the only way to save the economy.* ADJ: ADJ n ≠ *half-hearted*

**full-blown** **Full-blown** means having all the characteristics of a particular type of thing or person. ❑ *Before becoming a full-blown director, he worked as the film editor on Citizen Kane.* ADJ: ADJ n

**full board** also **full-board.** If the price at a hotel includes **full board**, it includes all your meals. [mainly BRIT] N-UNCOUNT

**full dress** Someone who is **in full dress** is wearing all the clothes needed for a ceremony or formal occasion. N-UNCOUNT

**full-flavoured**

✓ in AM, use **full-flavored**

**Full-flavoured** food or wine has a pleasant fairly strong taste. ADJ

**full-fledged** **Full-fledged** means the same as **fully fledged**. ADJ

**full-frontal** also **full frontal.** 1 If there is **full-frontal** nudity in a photograph or film, you can see the whole of the front part of someone's naked body, including the genitals. ❑ *Why is full-frontal male nudity still so scarce in films?* ADJ: usu ADJ n 2 If you use **full-frontal** to describe someone's criticism or way of dealing with something, you are emphasizing that it is very strong and direct. ❑ *The Tories believe a full-frontal attack on the opposition leader is their best hope.* ADJ: usu ADJ n [emphasis]

**full-grown** An animal or plant that is **full-grown** has reached its full adult size and stopped growing. ❑ *...a full-grown male orang-utan.* ADJ

**full house** **(full houses)** If a theatre has **a full house** for a particular performance, it has as large an audience as it can hold. ❑ *...playing to a full house.* N-COUNT

**full-length** 1 A **full-length** book, record, or film is the normal length, rather than being shorter than normal. ❑ *...his first full-length recording in well over a decade.* ADJ: ADJ n 2 A **full-length** coat or skirt is long enough to reach the lower part of a person's leg, almost to the ankles. A full-length sleeve reaches a person's wrist. ADJ: ADJ n 3 **Full-length** curtains or other furnishings reach to the floor. ADJ: ADJ n
4 A **full-length** mirror or painting shows the whole of a person. ADJ: ADJ n 5 Someone who is lying **full-length**, is lying down flat and stretched out. ❑ *She stretched herself out full-length.* ADV: ADV after v

**full marks** If you get **full marks** in a test or exam, you get everything right and gain the maximum number of marks. [BRIT] ❑ *Most people in fact got full marks in one question and zero in the other.* N-PLURAL

✓ in AM, use **a perfect score**

**full monty** /fʊl mɒnti/ You use **the full monty** to describe something that impresses you because it includes everything that you could possibly expect it to include. [BRIT, INFORMAL] ❑ *There was everything from simple piano to a full orchestral finish. The full monty.* N-SING: *the* N [approval]

**full|ness** /fʊlnəs/ [1] → see **full**. [2] If you say that something will happen **in the fullness of time**, you mean that it will eventually happen after a long time or after a long series of events. [WRITTEN] ❑ *...a mystery that will be revealed in the fullness of time.* PHRASE: PHR with cl, PHR after v

**full-on** **Full-on** is used to describe things or activities that have all the characteristics of their type, or are done in the strongest or most extreme way possible. [INFORMAL] ❑ *What they were really good at was full-on rock'n'roll.* ADJ

**full-page** A **full-page** advertisement, picture, or article in a newspaper or magazine uses a whole page. ADJ: ADJ n

**full-scale** [1] **Full-scale** means as complete, intense, or great in extent as possible. ❑ *...the possibility of a full-scale nuclear war.* ADJ: ADJ n ≠ *limited* [2] A **full-scale** drawing or model is the same size as the thing that it represents. ❑ *...working, full-scale prototypes.* ADJ: ADJ n

**full-size** or **full-sized** A **full-size** or **full-sized** model or picture is the same size as the thing or person that it represents. ❑ *I made a full-size cardboard model.* ADJ: ADJ n

**full stop** **(full stops)** A **full stop** is the punctuation mark . which you use at the end of a sentence when it is not a question or exclamation. [BRIT] N-COUNT

✔ in AM, use **period**

**full-strength** → see **strength**.

**full-throated** A **full-throated** sound coming from someone's mouth, such as a shout or a laugh, is very loud. ❑ *...full-throated singing.* ADJ: ADJ n

**full-time** also **full time.** [1] **Full-time** work or study involves working or studying for the whole of each normal working week rather than for part of it. ❑ *...a full-time job. ...full-time staff.* ADJ: usu ADJ n ≠ *part-time* ♦ **Full-time** is also an adverb. ❑ *Deirdre works full-time.* ADV: ADV after v [2] In games such as football, **full-time** is the end of a match. [BRIT] ❑ *The score at full-time was Arsenal 1, Sampdoria 1.* N-UNCOUNT

**full-timer** **(full-timers)** A **full-timer** is someone who works full-time. ❑ *The company employs six full-timers and one part-time worker.* N-COUNT

**full up** also **full-up.** [1] Something that is **full up** has no space left for any more people or things. ❑ *The prisons are all full up.* ADJ: v-link ADJ [2] If you are **full up** you have eaten or drunk so much that you do not want to eat or drink anything else. [INFORMAL] ADJ: v-link ADJ

**ful|ly** /fʊli/ ◆◆◇ [1] **Fully** means to the greatest degree or extent possible. ❑ *She was fully aware of my thoughts... I don't fully agree with that.* ADV: ADV adj, ADV with v [2] You use **fully** to say that a process is completely finished. ❑ *He had still not fully recovered.* ADV: ADV with v [3] If you describe, answer, or deal with something **fully**, you leave out nothing that should be mentioned or dealt with. ❑ *Major elements of these debates are discussed more fully later in this book.* ADV: ADV with v [4] **Fully** is used to emphasize how great an amount is. [WRITTEN] ❑ *Fully 30% of the poor could not even afford access to illegal shanties.* ADV: ADV amount [emphasis]

**ful|ly fledged** also **fully-fledged. Fully fledged** means complete or fully developed. ❑ *Hungary is to have a fully-fledged Stock Exchange from today.* ADJ: ADJ n

**ful|mi|nate** /fʊlmɪneɪt, fʌl-/ **(fulminates, fulminating, fulminated)** If you **fulminate against** someone or something, you criticize them angrily. [FORMAL] ❑ *They all fulminated against the new curriculum.* VERB V *against/about* n

**ful|some** /fʊlsəm/ If you describe expressions of praise, apology, or gratitude as **fulsome**, you disapprove of them because they are exaggerated and elaborate, so that they sound insincere. ❑ *Newspapers have been fulsome in their praise of the former president.* ADJ [disapproval] = *extravagant*

**fum|ble** /fʌmbəl/ **(fumbles, fumbling, fumbled)** [1] If you **fumble for** something or **fumble with** something, you try and reach for it or hold it in a clumsy way. ❑ *She crept from the bed and fumbled for her dressing gown.* VERB V *for/with/in* n [2] When you are trying to say something, if you **fumble** for the right words, you speak in a clumsy and unclear way. ❑ *I fumbled for something to say... He fumbled his lines, not knowing what he was going to say.* VERB V *for* n, V n, Also V

**fume** /fjuːm/ **(fumes, fuming, fumed)** [1] **Fumes** are the unpleasant and often unhealthy smoke and gases that are produced by fires or by things such as chemicals, fuel, or cooking. ❑ *...car exhaust fumes.* N-PLURAL [2] If you **fume** over something, you express annoyance and anger about it. ❑ *He was still fuming over the remark... 'It's monstrous!' Jackie fumed.* VERB V *over/at/about* n, V with quote

**fu|mi|gate** /fjuːmɪgeɪt/ **(fumigates, fumigating, fumigated)** If you **fumigate** something, you get rid of germs or insects from it using special chemicals. ❑ *...fruit which has been treated with insecticide and fumigated.* VERB V n ♦ **fu|mi|ga|tion** /fjuːmɪgeɪʃən/ *Methods of control involved poisoning and fumigation.* N-UNCOUNT

**fun** /fʌn/ ◆◆◇ [1] You refer to an activity or situation as **fun** if you think it is pleasant and enjoyable and it causes you to feel happy. ❑ *It was such a success and we had so much fun doing it... It could be fun to watch them... You still have time to join in the fun.* N-UNCOUNT [2] If you say that someone is **fun**, you mean that you enjoy being with them because they say and do interesting or amusing things. ❑ *Liz was wonderful fun to be with.* N-UNCOUNT [approval] [3] If you describe something as a **fun** thing, you mean that you think it is enjoyable. If you describe someone as a **fun** person, you mean that you enjoy being with them. [INFORMAL] ❑ *It was a fun evening... What a fun person he is!* ADJ: ADJ n = *entertaining*

PHRASES [4] Someone who is a **figure of fun** is considered ridiculous, so that people laugh at them or make jokes about them. PHRASE: *figure* inflects, v-link PHR [5] If you do something **for fun** or **for the fun of it**, you do it in order to enjoy yourself rather than because it is important or necessary. ❑ *I took my M. A. just for fun really... He had just come for the fun of it.* PHRASE: PHR after v [6] If you do something **in fun**, you do it as a joke or for amusement, without intending to cause any harm. ❑ *Don't say such things, even in fun.* PHRASE: PHR after v, v-link PHR [7] If you **make fun of** someone or something or **poke fun at** them, you laugh at them, tease them, or make jokes about them in a way that causes them to seem ridiculous. ❑ *Don't make fun of me... She poked fun at people's shortcomings.* PHRASE: V inflects, PHR n

**func|tion** /fʌŋkʃən/ ◆◆◇ **(functions, functioning, functioned)** [1] The **function** of something or someone is the useful thing that they do or are intended to do. ❑ *The main function of the merchant banks is to raise capital for industry.* N-COUNT: with supp = *purpose, role* [2] If a machine or system **is functioning**, it is working or operating. ❑ *The authorities say the prison is now functioning normally.* VERB V [3] If someone or something **functions as** a particular thing, they do the work or fulfil the purpose of that thing. ❑ *On weekdays, one third of the room functions as workspace.* VERB V *as* n [4] A **function** is a series of operations that a computer performs, for example when a single key or a combination of keys is pressed. N-COUNT [5] If you say that one thing is **a function of** another, you mean that its amount or nature depends on the other thing. [FORMAL] ❑ *Investment is a function of the interest rate.* N-COUNT: usu sing, N *of* n [6] A **function** is a large formal dinner or party. N-COUNT

**func|tion|al** /fʌŋkʃənəl/ [1] **Functional** things are useful rather than decorative. ❑ *...modern, functional furniture... The decor is functional.* ADJ [2] **Functional** means relating to the way in which something works or operates, or relating to how useful it is. ❑ *...rules defining the territorial boundaries and functional limits of the local state.* ADJ: ADJ n [3] **Functional** equipment works or operates in the way that it is supposed to. ❑ *We have fully functional smoke alarms on all staircases.* ADJ = *operational*

**func|tion|al|ism** /fʌŋkʃənəlɪzəm/ **Functionalism** is the idea that the most important as- N-UNCOUNT pect of something, especially the design of a building or piece of furniture, is how it is going to be used or its usefulness. [TECHNICAL]

**func|tion|al|ity** /fʌŋkʃənælɪti/ The **functionality** of a computer or other machine is how useful it is or how many functions it can perform. ❑ *It is significantly more compact than any comparable laptop, with no loss in functionality.* N-UNCOUNT

**func|tion|ary** /fʌŋkʃənəri, AM -neri/ **(functionaries)** A **functionary** is a person whose job is to do administrative work, especially for a government or a political party. [FORMAL] N-COUNT

**func|tion key** **(function keys)** **Function keys** are the keys along the top of a computer keyboard, usually numbered from F1 to F12. Each key is designed to make a particular thing happen when you press it. [COMPUTING] ❑ *Just hit the F5 function key to send and receive your e-mails.* N-COUNT

**fund** /fʌnd/ **(funds, funding, funded)** ◆◆◆ 1 **Funds** are amounts of money that are available to be spent, especially money that is given to an organization or person for a particular purpose. ❑ *The concert will raise funds for research into Aids. ...government funds.* → See also **fund-raising**. N-PLURAL 2 A **fund** is an amount of money that is collected or saved for a particular purpose. ❑ *...a scholarship fund for undergraduate engineering students.* → See also **trust fund**. N-COUNT: oft n N 3 When a person or organization **funds** something, they provide money for it. ❑ *The airport is being privately funded by a construction group. ...a new privately funded scheme.* VERB = finance V n V-ed ♦ **-funded** *...government-funded institutions.* COMB in ADJ 4 If you have a **fund of** something, you have a lot of it. ❑ *He is possessed of an extraordinary fund of energy.* N-COUNT: N *of* n

**fun|da|men|tal** /fʌndəmentəl/ ◆◇◇ 1 You use **fundamental** to describe things, activities, and principles that are very important or essential. They affect the basic nature of other things or are the most important element upon which other things depend. ❑ *Our constitution embodies all the fundamental principles of democracy... A fundamental human right is being withheld from these people.* ADJ: usu ADJ n = basic 2 You use **fundamental** to describe something which exists at a deep and basic level, and is therefore likely to continue. ❑ *But on this question, the two leaders have very fundamental differences.* ADJ: usu ADJ n = profound 3 If one thing **is fundamental to** another, it is absolutely necessary to it, and the second thing cannot exist, succeed, or be imagined without it. ❑ *The method they pioneered remains fundamental to research into the behaviour of nerve cells.* ADJ: v-link ADJ *to* n = vital 4 You can use **fundamental** to show that you are referring to what you consider to be the most important aspect of a situation, and that you are not concerned with less important details. ❑ *The fundamental problem lies in their inability to distinguish between reality and invention.* ADJ: ADJ n = basic

**fun|da|men|tal|ism** /fʌndəmentəlɪzəm/ **Fundamentalism** is the belief in the original form of a religion or theory, without accepting any later ideas. ❑ *Religious fundamentalism was spreading in the region.* N-UNCOUNT ♦ **fun|da|men|tal|ist** **(fundamentalists)** *He will try to satisfy both wings of the party, the fundamentalists and the realists. ...fundamentalist Christians.* N-COUNT: oft N n

**fun|da|men|tal|ly** /fʌndəmentəli/ 1 You use **fundamentally** for emphasis when you are stating an opinion, or when you are making an important or general statement about something. ❑ *Fundamentally, women like him for his sensitivity and charming vulnerability... He can be very charming, but he is fundamentally a bully.* ADV: ADV with cl/group [emphasis] = basically 2 You use **fundamentally** to indicate that something affects or relates to the deep, basic nature of something. ❑ *He disagreed fundamentally with the President's judgment... Environmentalists say the treaty is fundamentally flawed.* ADV: ADV with v = profoundly

**fun|da|men|tals** /fʌndəmentəlz/ **The fundamentals** of something are its simplest, most important elements, ideas, or principles, in contrast to more complicated or detailed ones. ❑ *...teaching small children the fundamentals of road safety... They agree on fundamentals, like the need for further political reform.* N-PLURAL: usu *the* N, oft N *of* n = basics

**fund|ing** /fʌndɪŋ/ **Funding** is money which a government or organization provides for a particular purpose. ❑ *They hope for government funding for the scheme... Many colleges have seen their funding cut.* ◆◇◇ N-UNCOUNT

**fund|rais|er** /fʌndreɪzəʳ/ **(fundraisers)** also **fund-raiser.** 1 A **fundraiser** is an event which is intended to raise money for a particular purpose, for example, for a charity. ❑ *Organize a fundraiser for your church.* N-COUNT 2 A **fundraiser** is someone who works to raise money for a particular purpose, for example, for a charity. ❑ *Sir Anthony was a keen fundraiser for the Liberal Democrats.* N-COUNT

**fund-raising** also **fundraising. Fund-raising** is the activity of collecting money to support a charity or political campaign or organization. ❑ *Encourage her to get involved in fund-raising for charity.* N-UNCOUNT

**fu|ner|al** /fjuːnərəl/ **(funerals)** A **funeral** is the ceremony that is held when the body of someone who has died is buried or cremated. ❑ *His funeral will be on Thursday at Blackburn Cathedral... He was given a state funeral.* N-COUNT

**fu|ner|al di|rec|tor** **(funeral directors)** A **funeral director** is a person whose job is to arrange funerals. N-COUNT

**fu|ner|al home** **(funeral homes)** A **funeral home** is a place where a funeral director works and where dead people are prepared for burial or cremation. N-COUNT

**fu|ner|al par|lour** **(funeral parlours)** A **funeral parlour** is a place where a funeral director works and where dead people are prepared for burial or cremation. [BRIT] N-COUNT

☑ in AM, use **funeral home**

**fu|ner|ary** /fjuːnərəri, AM -reri/ **Funerary** means relating to funerals, burials, or cremations. [FORMAL] ❑ *...funerary monuments.* ADJ: ADJ n

**fu|nereal** /fjuːnɪəriəl/ A **funereal** tone, atmosphere, or colour is very sad and serious and would be suitable for a funeral. ❑ *He addressed the group in funereal tones.* ADJ: usu ADJ n = solemn

**fun|fair** /fʌnfeəʳ/ **(funfairs)** A **funfair** is an event held in a park or field at which people pay to ride on various machines for amusement or try to win prizes in games. The people who organize and operate it usually take it from one place to another. [BRIT] N-COUNT = fair

☑ in AM, use **carnival**

**fun|gal** /fʌŋgəl/ **Fungal** means caused by, consisting of, or relating to fungus. ❑ *Athlete's foot is a fungal infection.* ADJ: usu ADJ n

**fun|gi** /fʌŋgiː, fʌndʒaɪ/ **Fungi** is the plural of **fungus**.

**fun|gi|cide** /fʌŋgɪsaɪd, fʌndʒ-/ **(fungicides)** A **fungicide** is a chemical that can be used to kill fungus or to prevent it from growing. N-MASS

**fun|gus** /fʌŋgəs/ **(fungi)** A **fungus** is a plant that has no flowers, leaves, or green colouring, such as a mushroom or a toadstool. Other types of fungus such as mould are extremely small and look like a fine powder. N-MASS

**fu|nicu|lar** /fjuːnɪkjʊləʳ/ A **funicular** or a **funicular railway** is a type of railway which goes up a very steep hill or mountain. A machine at the top of the slope pulls the carriage up the rails by a steel rope. N-SING

**funk** /fʌŋk/ **Funk** is a style of dance music based on jazz and blues, with a strong, repeated bass part. ❑ *...a mixture of experimental jazz, soul and funk.* N-UNCOUNT

**funky** /fʌŋki/ **(funkier, funkiest)** 1 **Funky** jazz, blues, or pop music has a very strong, repeat- ADJ ed bass part. ❑ *It's a funky sort of rhythm.* [2] If you describe something or someone as **funky**, you like them because they are unconventional or unusual. [mainly AM, INFORMAL] ❑ *It had a certain funky charm, I guess, but it wasn't much of a place to raise a kid.* ADJ approval

**fun|nel** /fʌnəl/ **(funnels, funnelling, funnelled)**

✓ in AM, use **funneling, funneled**

[1] A **funnel** is an object with a wide, circular top and a narrow short tube at the bottom. Funnels are used to pour liquids into containers which have a small opening, for example bottles. → See picture on page 1710. N-COUNT [2] A **funnel** is a metal chimney on a ship or railway engine powered by steam. ❑ *...a merchantman with three masts and two funnels.* N-COUNT [3] You can describe as a **funnel** something that is narrow, or narrow at one end, through which a substance flows and is directed. ❑ *These fires create convection funnels, and throw a lot of particles into the upper atmosphere.* N-COUNT [4] If something **funnels** somewhere or **is funnelled** there, it is directed through a narrow space. ❑ *The winds came from the north, across the plains, funnelling down the valley... High tides in the North Sea were funnelled down into the English Channel by a storm.* VERB V adv/prep *be* V-ed adv/prep Also V n adv/prep [5] If you **funnel** money, goods, or information from one place or group to another, you cause it to be sent there as it becomes available. ❑ *Its Global Programme on AIDS funnelled money from donors to governments.* VERB = *channel* V n prep/adv

**fun|ni|ly** /fʌnɪli/ You use **funnily enough** to indicate that, although something is surprising, it is true or really happened. ❑ *Funnily enough I can remember what I had for lunch on July 5th, 1906, but I've forgotten what I had for breakfast today.* PHRASE: PHR with cl = *oddly*

**fun|ny** /fʌni/ **(funnier, funniest, funnies)** ◆◇◇ [1] Someone or something that is **funny** is amusing and likely to make you smile or laugh. ❑ *Wade was smart and not bad-looking, and he could be funny when he wanted to... I'll tell you a funny story.* ADJ = *amusing, comical* [2] If you describe something as **funny**, you think it is strange, surprising, or puzzling. ❑ *Children get some very funny ideas sometimes!... There's something funny about him... It's funny how love can come and go.* ADJ: oft *it* v-link ADJ how/that = *odd, curious* [3] If you feel **funny**, you feel slightly ill. [INFORMAL] ❑ *My head had begun to ache and my stomach felt funny.* ADJ: usu *feel* ADJ [4] **The funnies** are humorous drawings or a series of humorous drawings in a newspaper or magazine. [AM, INFORMAL] N-PLURAL: *the* N

**fun|ny bone** **(funny bones)** Your **funny bone** is the soft part of your elbow which gives you an uncomfortable feeling on your skin if it is hit. [INFORMAL] N-COUNT: usu sing

**funny|man** /fʌnimæn/ **(funnymen)** A **funnyman** is a male **comedian**. [JOURNALISM] ❑ *...Hollywood funnyman Billy Crystal.* N-COUNT: usu sing

**fun run** **(fun runs)** A **fun run** is a long distance race which anyone can take part in. Fun runs are often held to raise money for charity. [BRIT, AUSTRALIAN] N-COUNT

**fur** /fɜːʳ/ **(furs)** [1] **Fur** is the thick and usually soft hair that grows on the bodies of many mammals. ❑ *This creature's fur is short, dense and silky.* N-MASS [2] **Fur** is the fur-covered skin of an animal that is used to make clothing or small carpets. ❑ *She had on a black coat with a fur collar. ...the trading of furs from Canada.* N-VAR: oft N n [3] A **fur** is a coat made from real or artificial fur, or a piece of fur worn round your neck. ❑ *There were women in furs and men in comfortable overcoats.* N-COUNT [4] **Fur** is an artificial fabric that looks like fur and is used, for example, to make clothing, soft toys, and seat covers. N-MASS

**fu|ri|ous** /fjʊəriəs/ [1] Someone who is **furious** is extremely angry. ❑ *He is furious at the way his wife has been treated... I am furious that it has taken so long to uncover what really happened.* ADJ: usu v-link ADJ, oft ADJ *at/with* n, ADJ that ♦ **fu|ri|ous|ly** *He stormed out of the apartment, slamming the door furiously behind him.* ADV: usu ADV with v [2] **Furious** is also used to describe something that is done with great energy, effort, speed, or violence. ❑ *A furious gunbattle ensued.* ♦ **fu|ri|ous|ly** *Officials worked furiously to repair the centre court.* ADJ: usu ADJ n ADV: usu ADV with v

**furl** /fɜːʳl/ **(furls, furling, furled)** When you **furl** something made of fabric such as an umbrella, sail, or flag, you roll or fold it up because it is not going to be used. ❑ *An attempt was made to furl the headsail. ...a furled umbrella.* VERB V n V-ed

**fur|long** /fɜːʳlɒŋ, AM -lɔːŋ/ **(furlongs)** A **furlong** is a unit of length that is equal to 220 yards or 201.2 metres. N-COUNT: usu num N

**fur|lough** /fɜːʳloʊ/ **(furloughs, furloughing, furloughed)** [1] If workers are given **furlough**, they are told to stay away from work for a certain period because there is not enough for them to do. [AM] ❑ *This could mean a massive furlough of government workers.* N-VAR [2] If people who work for a particular organization **are furloughed**, they are given a furlough. [AM] ❑ *We regret to inform you that you are being furloughed indefinitely... The factories have begun furloughing hundreds of workers.* VERB = *lay off* *be* V-ed V n [3] When soldiers are given **furlough**, they are given official permission to leave the area where they are based or are fighting, for a certain period. [AM] ❑ *I was at home on furlough.* N-VAR

✓ in BRIT, use **leave**

**fur|nace** /fɜːʳnɪs/ **(furnaces)** A **furnace** is a container or enclosed space in which a very hot fire is made, for example to melt metal, burn rubbish, or produce steam. N-COUNT

**fur|nish** /fɜːʳnɪʃ/ **(furnishes, furnishing, furnished)** [1] If you **furnish** a room or building, you put furniture and furnishings into it. ❑ *Many proprietors try to furnish their hotels with antiques.* VERB V n *with* n Also V n [2] If you **furnish** someone **with** something, you provide or supply it. [FORMAL] ❑ *They'll be able to furnish you with the rest of the details.* VERB V n *with* n

**fur|nished** /fɜːʳnɪʃt/ [1] A **furnished** room or house is available to be rented together with the furniture in it. ADJ [2] When you say that a room or house is **furnished** in a particular way, you are describing the kind or amount of furniture that it has in it. ❑ *We took tea by lamplight in his sparsely furnished house.* ADJ: adv ADJ

**fur|nish|ings** /fɜːʳnɪʃɪŋz/ The **furnishings** of a room or house are the furniture, curtains, carpets, and decorations such as pictures. N-PLURAL

**fur|ni|ture** /fɜːʳnɪtʃəʳ/ **Furniture** consists of large objects such as tables, chairs, or beds that are used in a room for sitting or lying on or for putting things on or in. ❑ *Each piece of furniture in their home suited the style of the house.* ◆◇◇ N-UNCOUNT

**fu|ro|re** /fjʊrɔːri, fjʊərɔːʳ/

✓ in AM, use **furor**

A **furore** is a very angry or excited reaction by people to something. ❑ *The disclosure has already caused a furore among MPs.* N-SING: usu with supp, oft adj N, N *over* n = *uproar*

**fur|ri|er** /fʌriəʳ, AM fɜːr-/ **(furriers)** A **furrier** is a person who makes or sells clothes made from fur. N-COUNT

**fur|row** /fʌroʊ, AM fɜːr-/ **(furrows, furrowing, furrowed)** [1] A **furrow** is a long, thin line in the earth which a farmer makes in order to plant seeds or to allow water to flow along. N-COUNT [2] A **furrow** is a deep, fairly wide line in the surface of something. ❑ *Dirt bike trails crisscrossed the grassy furrows.* N-COUNT [3] A **furrow** is a deep fold or line in the skin of someone's face. ❑ *...the deep furrows that marked the corners of his mouth.* N-COUNT = *wrinkle* [4] If someone **furrows** their brow or forehead or if it **furrows**, deep folds appear in it because the person is annoyed, unhappy, or confused. [WRITTEN] ❑ *My bank manager furrowed his brow, fingered his calculator and finally pronounced 'Aha!'... Midge's forehead furrowed as she saw that several were drinking... Fatigue and stress quickly result in a dull complexion and a furrowed brow.* VERB = *crease* V n V V-ed [5] If you say that someone **ploughs** a particular **furrow** or **ploughs** their **own furrow**, you mean that their activities or in- PHRASE: V inflects terests are different or isolated from those of other people. [BRIT] ❑ *The government is more than adept at ploughing its own diplomatic furrow.*

**fur|ry** /fɜːri/ 1 A **furry** animal is covered with thick, soft hair. ❑ *...the coyote's furry tail.* ADJ: usu ADJ n
2 If you describe something as **furry**, you mean that it has a soft rough texture like fur. ❑ *...his herringbone tweed coat with its furry lining.* ADJ: usu ADJ n

**fur|ther** /fɜːʳðəʳ/ **(furthers, furthering, furthered)** ◆◆◆

> **Further** is a comparative form of **far**. It is also a verb.

1 **Further** means to a greater extent or degree. ❑ *Inflation is below 5% and set to fall further... The rebellion is expected to further damage the country's image... The government's economic policies have further depressed living standards.* ADV: ADV with v 2 If you go or get **further with** something, or take something **further**, you make some progress. ❑ *They lacked the scientific personnel to develop the technical apparatus much further.* ADV: ADV with v 3 If someone goes **further** in a discussion, they make a more extreme statement or deal with a point more thoroughly. ❑ *On February 7th the Post went further, claiming that Mr Wood had grabbed and kissed another 13 women... To have a better comparison, we need to go further and address such issues as repairs and insurance.* ADV: ADV after v 4 A **further** thing, number of things, or amount of something is an additional thing, number of things, or amount. ❑ *His speech provides further evidence of his increasingly authoritarian approach... There was nothing further to be done for this man.* ADJ: ADJ n, pron-indef ADJ = more 5 **Further** means a greater distance than before or than something else. ❑ *Now we live further away from the city centre... He came to a halt at a crossroads fifty yards further on... Further to the south are some of the island's loveliest unspoilt coves.* ADV: ADV adv/prep 6 **Further** is used in expressions such as '**further back**' and '**further ahead**' to refer to a point in time that is earlier or later than the time you are talking about. ❑ *Looking still further ahead, by the end of the next century world population is expected to be about ten billion.* ADV: ADV adv/prep 7 If you **further** something, you help it to progress, to be successful, or to be achieved. ❑ *Education needn't only be about furthering your career.* VERB V n 8 You use **further** to introduce a statement that relates to the same general topic and that gives additional information or makes an additional point. [FORMAL] ❑ *Dodd made no appeal of his death sentence and, further, instructed his attorney to sue anyone who succeeds in delaying his execution.* ADV: ADV with cl = moreover 9 **Further to** is used in letters in expressions such as '**further to your letter**' or '**further to our conversation**', in order to indicate what you are referring to in the letter. [BRIT, FORMAL] ❑ *Further to your letter, I agree that there are some presentational problems, politically speaking.* PREP-PHRASE

**fur|ther|ance** /fɜːʳðərəns/ The **furtherance of** something is the activity of helping it to be successful or be achieved. [FORMAL] ❑ *The thing that matters is the furtherance of research in this country.* N-UNCOUNT: N of n = advancement

**fur|ther edu|ca|tion** **Further education** is the education of people who have left school but who are not at a university or a college of education. [mainly BRIT] ❑ *Most further-education colleges offer A-level courses.* N-UNCOUNT

> ✔ in AM, use **continuing education**

**further|more** /fɜːʳðəʳmɔː/ **Furthermore** is used to introduce a piece of information or opinion that adds to or supports the previous one. [FORMAL] ❑ *Furthermore, they claim that any such interference is completely ineffective.* ADV: ADV with cl = moreover

**further|most** /fɜːʳðəʳmoʊst/ The **furthermost** one of a number of similar things is the one that is the greatest distance away from a place. ❑ *We walked to the furthermost point and then sat on the sand dunes.* ADJ: ADJ n

**fur|thest** /fɜːʳðɪst/

> **Furthest** is a superlative form of **far**.

1 **Furthest** means to a greater extent or degree than ever before or than anything or anyone else. ❑ *The south of England, where prices have fallen furthest, will remain the weakest market... These institutional reforms have gone furthest in Poland.* ADV: ADV with v
2 **Furthest** means at a greater distance from a particular point than anyone or anything else, or for a greater distance than anyone or anything else. ❑ *The risk of thunder is greatest in those areas furthest from the coast... Amongst those who have travelled furthest to take part in the Festival are a group from Northern Ireland.* ADV: n ADV, ADV after v, be ADV, ADV prep/adv ♦ **Furthest** is also an adjective. ❑ *...the furthest point from earth that any controlled spacecraft has ever been.* ADJ: ADJ n

**fur|tive** /fɜːʳtɪv/ If you describe someone's behaviour as **furtive**, you disapprove of them behaving as if they want to keep something secret or hidden. ❑ *With a furtive glance over her shoulder, she unlocked the door and entered the house.* ADJ [disapproval]

**fury** /fjʊəri/ **Fury** is violent or very strong anger. ❑ *She screamed, her face distorted with fury and pain.* N-UNCOUNT = rage

**fuse** /fjuːz/ **(fuses, fusing, fused)** 1 A **fuse** is a safety device in an electric plug or circuit. It contains a piece of wire which melts when there is a fault so that the flow of electricity stops. ❑ *The fuse blew as he pressed the button to start the motor... Remove the circuit fuse before beginning electrical work.* N-COUNT 2 When an electric device **fuses** or when you **fuse** it, it stops working because of a fault. [BRIT] ❑ *The wire snapped at the wall plug and the light fused... Rainwater had fused the bulbs.* VERB V V n 3 A **fuse** is a device on a bomb or firework which delays the explosion so that people can move a safe distance away. ❑ *A bomb was deactivated at the last moment, after the fuse had been lit.* N-COUNT 4 When things **fuse** or **are fused**, they join together physically or chemically, usually to become one thing. You can also say that one thing **fuses** with another. ❑ *The skull bones fuse between the ages of fifteen and twenty-five... Conception occurs when a single sperm fuses with an egg... Manufactured glass is made by fusing various types of sand... Their solution was to isolate specific clones of B cells and fuse them with cancer cells... The flakes seem to fuse together and produce ice crystals.* V-RECIP pl-n V V with n V pl-n V n with n pl-n V together 5 If something **fuses** two different qualities, ideas, or things, or if they **fuse**, they join together, especially in order to form a pleasing or satisfactory combination. ❑ *His music of that period fused the rhythms of jazz with classical forms... What they have done is fuse two different types of entertainment, the circus and the rock concert... Past and present fuse.* V-RECIP = combine V n with n V pl-n pl-n V Also V with n

PHRASES 6 If you **blow a fuse**, you suddenly become very angry and are unable to stay calm. [INFORMAL] ❑ *For all my experience, I blew a fuse in the quarter-final and could have been sent off.* PHRASE: V inflects 7 If someone or something **lights the fuse** of a particular situation or activity, they suddenly get it started. ❑ *Hopes for an early cut in German interest rates lit the market's fuse early on.* PHRASE: V inflects 8 If you say that someone **has a short fuse** or is **on a short fuse** you mean that they are quick to react angrily when something goes wrong. ❑ *I have a very short fuse and a violent temper.* PHRASE: V inflects

**fuse box** **(fuse boxes)** **The fuse box** is the box that contains the fuses for all the electric circuits in a building. It is usually fixed to a wall. N-COUNT: oft the N in sing

**fused** /fjuːzd/ If an electric plug or circuit is **fused**, it has a fuse in it. ADJ

**fu|selage** /fjuːzɪlɑːʒ/ **(fuselages)** The **fuselage** is the main body of an aeroplane, missile, or rocket. It is usually cylindrical in shape. N-COUNT

**fu|sil|lade** /fjuːzɪleɪd, AM -lɑːd/ A **fusillade of** shots or objects is a large number of them fired or thrown at the same time. [FORMAL] ❑ *Both were killed in a fusillade of bullets fired at close range.* N-SING: usu N of n

**fu|sion** /fjuːʒᵊn/ **(fusions)** 1 A **fusion of** different qualities, ideas, or things is something new that is created by joining them together. ❑ *His previous fusions of jazz, pop and African melodies have proved highly successful.* N-COUNT: oft N *of* pl-n
2 The **fusion** of two or more things involves joining them together to form one thing. ❑ *His final reform was the fusion of regular and reserve forces.* N-VAR: oft N *of* pl-n
3 In physics, **fusion** is the process in which atomic particles combine and produce a large amount of nuclear energy. ❑ *...research into nuclear fusion.* N-UNCOUNT

**fuss** /fʌs/ **(fusses, fussing, fussed)** 1 **Fuss** is anxious or excited behaviour which serves no useful purpose. ❑ *I don't know what all the fuss is about... He just gets down to work without any fuss.* N-SING: also no det
2 If you **fuss**, you worry or behave in a nervous, anxious way about unimportant matters or rush around doing unnecessary things. ❑ *Carol fussed about getting me a drink... My wife was fussing over the food and clothing we were going to take... A team of waiters began fussing around the table... 'Stop fussing,' he snapped.* VERB; V *about*; V *over* n; V prep; V
3 If you **fuss over** someone, you pay them a lot of attention and do things to make them happy or comfortable. ❑ *Auntie Hilda and Uncle Jack couldn't fuss over them enough.* VERB; V *over* n
PHRASES 4 If you **make a fuss** or **kick up a fuss** about something, you become angry or excited about it and complain. [INFORMAL] ❑ *I kick up a fuss if my wife wants to spend time alone.* PHRASE: V inflects
5 If you **make a fuss of** someone, you pay them a lot of attention and do things to make them happy or comfortable. [BRIT] ❑ *When I arrived my nephews made a big fuss of me.* PHRASE: V inflects, PHR n

**fussed** /fʌst/ If you say you **are not fussed** about something, you mean you do not mind about it or do not mind what happens. [BRIT, INFORMAL] ❑ *I'm not fussed as long as we get where we want to go.* ADJ: with brd-neg, v-link ADJ = *bothered*

**fussy** /fʌsi/ **(fussier, fussiest)** 1 Someone who is **fussy** is very concerned with unimportant details and is difficult to please. ❑ *She is not fussy about her food... Her aunt was small, with a rather fussy manner.* ADJ: oft ADJ *about* n; disapproval
2 If you describe things such as clothes and furniture as **fussy**, you are criticizing them because they are too elaborate or detailed. ❑ *We are not very keen on floral patterns and fussy designs.* ADJ; disapproval

**fus|ty** /fʌsti/ **(fustier, fustiest)** 1 If you describe something or someone as **fusty**, you disapprove of them because they are old-fashioned in attitudes or ideas. ❑ *The fusty old establishment refused to recognise the demand for popular music.* ADJ; disapproval
2 A **fusty** place or thing has a smell that is not fresh or pleasant. ❑ *...fusty old carpets.* ADJ: usu ADJ n

**fu|tile** /fjuːtaɪl, AM -tᵊl/ If you say that something is **futile**, you mean there is no point in doing it, usually because it has no chance of succeeding. ❑ *He brought his arm up in a futile attempt to ward off the blow... It would be futile to sustain his life when there is no chance of any improvement.* ADJ: oft *it* v-link ADJ to-inf = *pointless*

**fu|til|ity** /fjuːtɪlɪti/ **Futility** is a total lack of purpose or usefulness. ❑ *...the injustice and futility of terrorism.* N-UNCOUNT: oft N *of* n/-ing

**fu|ton** /fuːtɒn/ **(futons)** A **futon** is a piece of furniture which consists of a thin mattress on a low wooden frame which can be used as a bed or folded up to make a chair. N-COUNT

**fu|ture** /fjuːtʃəʳ/ **(futures)** ◆◆◆ 1 **The future** is the period of time that will come after the present, or the things that will happen then. ❑ *The spokesman said no decision on the proposal was likely in the immediate future... He was making plans for the future... I had little time to think about what the future held for me.* N-SING: *the* N ≠ *past*
2 **Future** things will happen or exist after the present time. ❑ *She said if the world did not act conclusively now, it would only bequeath the problem to future generations... Meanwhile, the domestic debate on Denmark's future role in Europe rages on. ...the future King and Queen.* ADJ: ADJ n
**for future reference** → see **reference**.
3 Someone's **future**, or **the future of** something, is what will happen to them or what they will do after the present time. ❑ *His future as prime minister depends on the outcome of the elections. ...a proposed national conference on the country's political future.* N-COUNT: usu sing, usu with supp
4 If you say that someone or something has **a future**, you mean that they are likely to be successful or to survive. ❑ *These abandoned children have now got a future... There's no future in this relationship.* N-COUNT: usu *a* N in sing
5 When people trade in **futures**, they buy stocks and shares, commodities such as coffee or oil, or foreign currency at a price that is agreed at the time of purchase for items which are delivered some time in the future. [BUSINESS] ❑ *This report could spur some buying in corn futures when the market opens today.* N-PLURAL: usu with supp
6 In grammar, the **future** tense of a verb is the one used to talk about things that are going to happen. In English, this applies to verb groups consisting of 'will' or 'shall' and the base form of a verb. The **future perfect** tense of a verb is used to talk about things that will have happened at some time in the future. ADJ: ADJ n
7 You use **in future** when saying what will happen from now on, which will be different from what has previously happened. The form **in the future** is sometimes used instead, especially in American English. ❑ *I asked her to be more careful in future... In the future, Mr. Fernandes says, he won't rely on others to handle this.* PHRASE

**fu|tur|ism** /fjuːtʃərɪzəm/ **Futurism** was a modern artistic and literary movement in the early twentieth century. N-UNCOUNT

**fu|tur|ist** /fjuːtʃərɪst/ **(futurists)** 1 **Futurists** were artists and writers who were followers of futurism. N-COUNT
2 A **futurist** is someone who makes predictions about what is going to happen, on the basis of facts about what is happening now. [mainly AM] N-COUNT = *futurologist*

**fu|tur|is|tic** /fjuːtʃərɪstɪk/ 1 Something that is **futuristic** looks or seems very modern and unusual, like something from the future. ❑ *The theatre is a futuristic steel and glass structure. ...futuristic cars.* ADJ
2 A **futuristic** film or book tells a story that is set in the future, when things are different. ❑ *...the futuristic hit film, 'Terminator 2'.* ADJ: ADJ n

**fu|tur|ol|ogy** /fjuːtʃərɒlədʒi/ **Futurology** is the activity of trying to predict what is going to happen, on the basis of facts about what is happening now. ❑ *The way a good investor does really well is by engaging in successful futurology.* N-UNCOUNT
♦ **fu|tur|olo|gist** /fjuːtʃərɒlədʒɪst/ **(futurologists)** *In his March 1984 report Wanger analyzed some predictions made by futurologists in 1972.* N-COUNT

**fuzz** /fʌz/ 1 **Fuzz** is a mass of short, curly hairs. N-UNCOUNT: also *a* N
2 **The fuzz** are the police. [INFORMAL, OLD-FASHIONED] N-PLURAL: usu *the* N

**fuzzy** /fʌzi/ **(fuzzier, fuzziest)** 1 **Fuzzy** hair sticks up in a soft, curly mass. ❑ *He had fuzzy black hair and bright black eyes.* ADJ
2 If something is **fuzzy**, it has a covering that feels soft and like fur. ❑ *...fuzzy material.* ADJ
3 A **fuzzy** picture, image, or sound is unclear and hard to see or hear. ❑ *A couple of fuzzy pictures have been published. ...fuzzy bass lines.* ADJ
4 If you or your thoughts are **fuzzy**, you are confused and cannot think clearly. ❑ *He had little patience for fuzzy ideas.* ADJ ≠ *clear*
5 You describe something as **fuzzy** when it is vague and not clearly defined. ❑ *The border between science fact and science fiction gets a bit fuzzy.* ADJ = *hazy*
6 **Fuzzy** logic is a type of computer logic that is supposed to imitate the way that humans think, for example by adapting to changing circumstances rather than always following the same procedure. ADJ: ADJ n

# G g

**G, g** /dʒiː/ **(G's, g's)** G is the seventh letter of the English alphabet. N-VAR

**gab** /gæb/ If someone has **the gift of the gab**, they are able to speak easily and confidently, and to persuade people. Also **the gift of gab**, mainly in American English. ❑ *They are naturally good salesmen with the gift of the gab.* PHRASE [approval]

**gab|ar|dine** /gæbəʳdiːn, AM -diːn/ **(gabardines)**

in BRIT, also use **gaberdine**

1 **Gabardine** is a fairly thick cloth which is used for making coats, suits, and other clothes. N-UNCOUNT: also N in pl, oft N n
2 A **gabardine** is a coat made from gabardine. N-COUNT

**gab|ble** /gæbəl/ **(gabbles, gabbling, gabbled)** If you **gabble**, you say things so quickly that it is difficult for people to understand you. [INFORMAL] ❑ *Marcello sat on his knee and gabbled excitedly... She gabbles on about drug dealers and journalists... The soldiers gabbled something and pointed at the door.* VERB = babble; V; V adv; V n, Also V with quote

**ga|ble** /geɪbəl/ **(gables)** A **gable** is the triangular part at the top of the end wall of a building, between the two sloping sides of the roof. → See picture on page 1705. N-COUNT

**ga|bled** /geɪbəld/ A **gabled** building or roof has a gable. ADJ: usu ADJ n

**gad** /gæd/ **(gads, gadding, gadded)** If you **gad about**, you go to a lot of different places looking for amusement or entertainment. [INFORMAL] ❑ *Don't think you'll keep me here while you gad about.* VERB; V about/out

**gad|fly** /gædflaɪ/ **(gadflies)** If you refer to someone as a **gadfly**, you believe that they deliberately annoy or challenge other people, especially people in authority. N-COUNT

**gadg|et** /gædʒɪt/ **(gadgets)** A **gadget** is a small machine or device which does something useful. You sometimes refer to something as a **gadget** when you are suggesting that it is complicated and unnecessary. ❑ *...kitchen gadgets including toasters, kettles and percolators. ...the latest gadget for the technology obsessed: pocket-sized computers that you write on with a pen.* N-COUNT: usu with supp

**gadg|et|ry** /gædʒɪtri/ **Gadgetry** is small machines or devices which do something useful. ❑ *...a passion for the latest electronic gadgetry.* N-UNCOUNT: oft adj N

**Gael|ic** /geɪlɪk, gælɪk/ 1 **Gaelic** is a language spoken by people in parts of Scotland and Ireland. ❑ *We weren't allowed to speak Gaelic at school.* ♦ **Gaelic** is also an adjective. ❑ *...the Gaelic language.* 2 **Gaelic** means coming from or relating to Scotland and Ireland, especially the parts where Gaelic is spoken. ❑ *...an evening of Gaelic music and drama.* N-UNCOUNT; ADJ: usu ADJ n; ADJ: usu ADJ n

**gaff** /gæf/ **(gaffs)** 1 On a boat, a **gaff** is a pole which is attached to a mast in order to support a particular kind of sail. 2 A **gaff** is a pole with a point or hook at one end, which is used for catching large fish. 3 → See also **gaffe**. N-COUNT: oft N n; N-COUNT

**gaffe** /gæf/ **(gaffes)** also **gaff.** 1 A **gaffe** is a stupid or careless mistake, for example when you say or do something that offends or upsets people. ❑ *He made an embarrassing gaffe at the convention last weekend. ...social gaffes committed by high-ranking individuals.* 2 If you **blow the gaffe** or **blow the gaff**, you tell someone something that other people wanted you to keep secret. [BRIT, INFORMAL] N-COUNT = blunder; PHRASE: V inflects

**gaf|fer** /gæfəʳ/ **(gaffers)** People use **gaffer** to refer to the the person in charge of the workers at a place of work such as a factory. [BRIT, INFORMAL] ❑ *The gaffer said he'd been fined for not doing the contract on time.* N-COUNT: usu *the* N in sing; N-VOC = boss

**gag** /gæg/ **(gags, gagging, gagged)** 1 A **gag** is something such as a piece of cloth that is tied around or put inside someone's mouth in order to stop them from speaking. ❑ *His captors had put a gag of thick leather in his mouth.* 2 If someone **gags** you, they tie a piece of cloth around your mouth in order to stop you from speaking or shouting. ❑ *I gagged him with a towel.* 3 If a person **is gagged** by someone in authority, they are prevented from expressing their opinion or from publishing certain information. ❑ *Judges must not be gagged.* 4 If you **gag**, you cannot swallow and nearly vomit. ❑ *I knelt by the toilet and gagged.* 5 A **gag** is a joke. [INFORMAL] ❑ *...a gag about policemen giving evidence in court.* 6 If you say that someone **is gagging for** something or **is gagging to** do something, you are emphasizing that they want to have it or do it very much. [INFORMAL] ❑ *Girls everywhere are gagging for a car like this... There are thousands of students absolutely gagging to come to this university.* N-COUNT; VERB; V n; VERB [disapproval]; *be* V-ed; VERB; V; N-COUNT: usu with supp; VERB: only cont; V *for* n; V to-inf

**gaga** /gɑːgɑː/ 1 If you say that someone is **gaga**, you mean that they cannot think clearly any more, especially because they are old. [INFORMAL] ❑ *If you don't keep your brain working you go gaga.* 2 If someone goes **gaga** over a person or thing, they like them very much. [INFORMAL] ❑ *My daughter is just gaga over men with hairy chests.* ADJ: v-link ADJ = dotty; ADJ: v-link ADJ = crazy

**gag|gle** /gægəl/ **(gaggles)** You can use **gaggle** to refer to a group of people, especially if they are noisy or disorganized. ❑ *A gaggle of journalists sit in a hotel foyer waiting impatiently.* N-COUNT-COLL: usu N *of* n [disapproval]

**gai|ety** /geɪɪti/ **Gaiety** is a feeling, attitude, or atmosphere of liveliness and fun. ❑ *Music rang out adding to the gaiety and life of the market.* N-UNCOUNT = joyfulness

**gai|ly** /geɪli/ 1 If you do something **gaily**, you do it in a lively, happy way. ❑ *Magda laughed gaily.* 2 Something that is **gaily** coloured or **gaily** decorated is coloured or decorated in a bright, pretty way. ❑ *He put on a gaily coloured shirt. ...gaily painted front doors.* ADV: ADV with v; ADV: ADV -ed = brightly

**gain** /geɪn/ **(gains, gaining, gained)** 1 If a person or place **gains** something such as an ability or quality, they gradually get more of it. ❑ *Students can gain valuable experience by working on the campus radio or magazine... While it has lost its tranquility, the area has gained in liveliness.* 2 If you **gain from** something such as an event or situation, you get some advantage or benefit from it. ❑ *The company didn't disclose how much it expects to gain from the two deals... There is absolutely nothing to be gained by feeling bitter... It is sad that a major company should try to gain from other people's suffering.* 3 To **gain** something such as weight or speed means to have an increase in that particular thing. ❑ *Some people do gain weight after they stop smoking... She gained some 25lb in weight during her pregnancy.* ♦ **Gain** is also a noun. ❑ *Excessive weight gain doesn't do you any good.* 4 If you **gain** something, you obtain it, especially after a lot of ◆◆◇ VERB; V n; V *in* n; VERB; V n *from/by* n/-ing; V n *from/by* n/-ing; V *from* n; VERB ≠ lose; V n; V amount; N-VAR: usu with supp; VERB = obtain

hard work or effort. ❑ *They realise that passing exams is no longer enough to gain a place at university.* V n

**PHRASES** 5 If you do something **for gain**, you do it in order to get some advantage or profit for yourself, and for no other reason. [FORMAL] ❑ *...buying art solely for financial gain.* PHRASE: PHR after v [disapproval] 6 If something such as an idea or an ideal **gains ground**, it gradually becomes more widely known or more popular. ❑ *The Christian right has been steadily gaining ground in state politics.* PHRASE: V inflects 7 If you do something in order to **gain time**, you do it in order to give yourself enough time to think of an excuse or a way out of a difficult situation. ❑ *I hoped to gain time by keeping him talking.* PHRASE: V inflects, oft PHR to-inf

♦ **gain on** If you **gain on** someone or something that is moving in front of you, you gradually get closer to them. ❑ *The Mercedes began to gain on the van.* PHRASAL VERB V P n

**gain|er** /geɪnəʳ/ **(gainers)** A **gainer** is a person or organization who gains something from a particular situation. ❑ *Overall, there were more losers than gainers.* N-COUNT: oft adj N ≠ loser

**gain|ful** /geɪnfʊl/ If you are in **gainful** employment, you have a job for which you are paid. [FORMAL] ❑ *...opportunities for gainful employment.* ADJ: ADJ n ♦ **gain|ful|ly** *Both her parents were gainfully employed.* ADV: ADV -ed

**gain|say** /geɪnseɪ/ **(gainsays, gainsaying, gainsaid)** If there is no **gainsaying** something, it is true or obvious and everyone would agree with it. [FORMAL] ❑ *There is no gainsaying the fact that they have been responsible for a truly great building.* VERB: with brd-neg = deny V n

**gait** /geɪt/ **(gaits)** A particular kind of **gait** is a particular way of walking. [WRITTEN] ❑ *His movements were clumsy, and his gait peculiarly awkward.* N-COUNT: usu sing, usu with supp

**gal** /gæl/ **(gals)** **Gal** is used in written English to represent the word 'girl' as it is pronounced in a particular accent. ❑ *...a Southern gal who wants to make it in the movies.* N-COUNT; N-VOC

**gal** also **gal.** **gal** is a written abbreviation for **gallon** or **gallons**. ❑ *Diesel cost 60p/gal in some places.*

**gala** /gɑːlə, AM geɪlə/ **(galas)** A **gala** is a special public celebration, entertainment, performance, or festival. ❑ *...a gala evening at the Royal Opera House.* N-COUNT: oft N n

**ga|lac|tic** /gəlæktɪk/ **Galactic** means relating to galaxies. ADJ: ADJ n

**gal|axy** /gæləksi/ **(galaxies)** also **Galaxy.** 1 A **galaxy** is an extremely large group of stars and planets that extends over many billions of light years. ❑ *Astronomers have discovered a distant galaxy.* N-COUNT 2 **The Galaxy** is the extremely large group of stars and planets to which the Earth and the Solar System belong. ❑ *The Galaxy consists of 100 billion stars.* N-PROPER: the N 3 If you talk about **a galaxy of** people from a particular profession, you mean a group of them who are all famous or important. ❑ *He is one of a small galaxy of Dutch stars on German television.* N-SING: N of n = array

**gale** /geɪl/ **(gales)** 1 A **gale** is a very strong wind. ❑ *...forecasts of fierce gales over the next few days.* N-COUNT 2 You can refer to the loud noise made by a lot of people all laughing at the same time as a **gale of** laughter or **gales of** laughter. [WRITTEN] ❑ *This was greeted with gales of laughter from the audience.* N-COUNT: N of n

**gale-force** A **gale-force** wind is a very strong wind. ADJ: ADJ n

**gall** /gɔːl/ **(galls, galling, galled)** 1 If you say that someone has **the gall to** do something, you are criticizing them for behaving in a rude or disrespectful way. ❑ *She had the gall to suggest that I might supply her with information about what Steve was doing.* N-UNCOUNT: oft the N of n, the N to-inf [disapproval] = nerve 2 If someone's action **galls** you, it makes you feel very angry or annoyed, often because it is unfair to you and you cannot do anything about it. ❑ *It must have galled him that Bardo thwarted each of these measures... It was their serenity which galled her most.* VERB it V n that V n ♦ **gall|ing** *It was especially galling to be criticised by this scoundrel.* ADJ: usu v-link ADJ 3 A **gall** is a growth on the surface of a plant that is caused by an insect, disease, fungus, or injury. N-COUNT

**gal|lant** /gælənt/

✔ Also pronounced /gəlænt/ for meaning 3.

1 If someone is **gallant**, they behave bravely and honourably in a dangerous or difficult situation. [OLD-FASHIONED] ❑ *The gallant soldiers lost their lives so that peace might reign again.* ADJ = brave ♦ **gal|lant|ly** *The town responded gallantly to the War.* ADV 2 A **gallant** effort or fight is one in which someone tried very hard to do something difficult, although in the end they failed. [WRITTEN] ❑ *He died at the age of 82, after a gallant fight against illness.* ADJ: ADJ n [approval] = valiant, brave 3 If a man is **gallant**, he is kind, polite, and considerate towards women. [OLD-FASHIONED] ❑ *Douglas was a complex man, thoughtful, gallant, and generous.* ADJ = courteous ♦ **gal|lant|ly** *He gallantly kissed Marie's hand as we prepared to leave.* ADV: ADV with v

**gal|lant|ry** /gæləntri/ 1 **Gallantry** is bravery shown by someone who is in danger, for example when they are fighting in a war. [FORMAL] ❑ *For his gallantry he was awarded a Victoria Cross.* N-UNCOUNT = bravery 2 **Gallantry** is kind, polite, and considerate behaviour towards other people, especially women. [FORMAL] ❑ *It's that time of year again, when thoughts turn to romance and gallantry.* N-UNCOUNT = courtesy

**gall blad|der** **(gall bladders)** Your **gall bladder** is the organ in your body which contains bile and is next to your liver. N-COUNT

**gal|leon** /gæliən/ **(galleons)** A **galleon** is a sailing ship with three masts. Galleons were used mainly in the fifteenth to seventeenth centuries. N-COUNT

**gal|lery** /gæləri/ **(galleries)** ◆◇◇ 1 A **gallery** is a place that has permanent exhibitions of works of art in it. ❑ *...an art gallery. ...the National Gallery.* N-COUNT; N-IN-NAMES 2 A **gallery** is a privately owned building or room where people can look at and buy works of art. ❑ *The painting is in the gallery upstairs.* N-COUNT 3 A **gallery** is an area high above the ground at the back or at the sides of a large room or hall. ❑ *A crowd already filled the gallery.* N-COUNT 4 **The gallery** in a theatre or concert hall is an area high above the ground that usually contains the cheapest seats. ❑ *They had been forced to find cheap tickets in the gallery.* N-COUNT: usu the N in sing ● If you **play to the gallery**, you do something in public in a way which you hope will impress people. ❑ *...but I must tell you that in my opinion you're both now playing to the gallery.* PHRASE: V inflects

**gal|ley** /gæli/ **(galleys)** 1 On a ship or aircraft, the **galley** is the kitchen. N-COUNT 2 In former times, a **galley** was a ship with sails and a lot of oars, which was often rowed by slaves or prisoners. N-COUNT

**Gal|lic** /gælɪk/ **Gallic** means the same as **French**. You sometimes use **Gallic** to describe ideas, feelings, or actions that you think are very typical of France and French people. ❑ *The proposal has provoked howls of Gallic indignation.* ADJ: usu ADJ n

**gal|li|vant** /gælɪvænt/ **(gallivants, gallivanting, gallivanted)** Someone who **is gallivanting around** goes to a lot of different places looking for amusement and entertainment. [OLD-FASHIONED] ❑ *A girl's place is in the home, not gallivanting around and filling her head with nonsense.* VERB = gad V prep/adv Also V

**gal|lon** /gælən/ **(gallons)** A **gallon** is a unit of measurement for liquids that is equal to eight pints. In Britain, it is equal to 4.564 litres. In America, it is equal to 3.785 litres. ❑ *...80 million gallons of water a day. ...a gasoline tax of 4.3 cents a gallon.* N-COUNT: oft N of n

**gal|lop** /gæləp/ **(gallops, galloping, galloped)** 1 When a horse **gallops**, it runs very fast so that all four legs are off the ground at the same time. If you **gallop** a horse, you make it gallop. ❑ *The horses galloped away... Staff officers galloped fine horses down the road.* VERB V adv/prep V n prep/adv 2 If you **gallop**, you ride a horse that is galloping. ❑ *Major Winston galloped into the distance.* VERB V prep/adv 3 A **gallop** is a ride on a horse N-SING that is galloping. ❑ *I was forced to attempt a gallop.* [4] If something such as a process **gallops**, it develops very quickly and is often difficult to control. ❑ *In spite of the recession, profits have galloped ahead. ...galloping inflation.* [5] If you **gallop**, you run somewhere very quickly. ❑ *They are galloping around the garden playing football.* [6] If you do something **at a gallop**, you do it very quickly. ❑ *I read the book at a gallop.*

VERB; V adv; V-ing; VERB; V prep; PHRASE: PHR after v

**gal|lows** /gæloʊz/ **(gallows)** A **gallows** is a wooden frame used to execute criminals by hanging. N-COUNT

**gall|stone** /gɔːlstoʊn/ **(gallstones)** A **gallstone** is a small, painful lump which can develop in your gall bladder. N-COUNT

**ga|lore** /gəlɔːʳ/ You use **galore** to emphasize that something you like exists in very large quantities. [INFORMAL, WRITTEN] ❑ *You'll be able to win prizes galore. ...a popular resort with beaches galore.* ADJ: n ADJ; emphasis

**ga|loshes** /gəlɒʃɪz/ **Galoshes** are waterproof shoes, usually made of rubber, which you wear over your ordinary shoes to prevent them getting wet. N-PLURAL

**gal|va|nize** /gælvənaɪz/ **(galvanizes, galvanizing, galvanized)**

✓ in BRIT, also use **galvanise**

To **galvanize** someone means to cause them to take action, for example by making them feel very excited, afraid, or angry. ❑ *The aid appeal has galvanised the German business community... They have been galvanised into collective action – militarily, politically and economically.* VERB = stir; V n; be V-ed *into* n/-ing; Also V n *into* n/-ing

**gal|va|nized** /gælvənaɪzd/

✓ in BRIT, also use **galvanised**

**Galvanized** metal, especially iron and steel, has been covered with zinc in order to protect it from rust and other damage. ❑ *...corrosion-resistant galvanized steel. ...75mm galvanised nails.* ADJ: usu ADJ n

**gam|bit** /gæmbɪt/ **(gambits)** [1] A **gambit** is an action or set of actions, which you carry out in order to try to gain an advantage in a situation or game. ❑ *He sees the proposal as more of a diplomatic gambit than a serious defense proposal... Campaign strategists are calling the plan a clever political gambit.* N-COUNT: usu with supp = ploy, tactic [2] A **gambit** is a remark which you make to someone in order to start or continue a conversation with them. ❑ *His favourite opening gambit is: 'You are so beautiful, will you be my next wife?'... Bernard made no response to Tom's conversational gambits.* N-COUNT: usu with supp

**gam|ble** /gæmbᵊl/ **(gambles, gambling, gambled)** [1] A **gamble** is a risky action or decision that you take in the hope of gaining money, success, or an advantage over other people. ❑ *...the French president's risky gamble in calling a referendum.* N-COUNT = risk [2] If you **gamble on** something, you take a risky action or decision in the hope of gaining money, success, or an advantage over other people. ❑ *Few firms will be willing to gamble on new products... They are not prepared to gamble their careers on this matter... Who wants to gamble with the life of a friend?* VERB; V *on* n/-ing; V n *on* n; V *with* n [3] If you **gamble** an amount of money, you bet it in a game such as cards or on the result of a race or competition. People who **gamble** usually do it frequently. ❑ *Most people visit Las Vegas to gamble their hard-earned money... John gambled heavily on the horses... Britain is the only country in Europe that allows minors to gamble... He gambled away his family estate on a single throw of the dice.* VERB; V n; V *on* n; V; V n with *away*

**gam|bler** /gæmbləʳ/ **(gamblers)** [1] A **gambler** is someone who gambles regularly, for example in card games or horse racing. N-COUNT [2] If you describe someone as a **gambler**, you mean that they are ready to take risks in order to gain advantages or success. ❑ *He had never been afraid of failure: he was a gambler, ready to go off somewhere else and start all over again.* N-COUNT

**gam|bling** /gæmblɪŋ/ **Gambling** is the act or activity of betting money, for example in card games or on horse racing. ❑ *Gambling is a form of entertainment. ...gambling casinos.* N-UNCOUNT

**gam|bol** /gæmbᵊl/ **(gambols, gambolling, gambolled)**

✓ in AM, use **gamboling, gamboled**

If animals or people **gambol**, they run or jump about in a playful way. ❑ *...the sight of newborn lambs gambolling in the fields.* VERB; V prep/adv

**game** /geɪm/ **(games)** [1] A **game** is an activity or sport usually involving skill, knowledge, or chance, in which you follow fixed rules and try to win against an opponent or to solve a puzzle. ❑ *...the wonderful game of football. ...a playful game of hide-and-seek. ...a video game.* ◆◆◆ N-COUNT [2] A **game** is one particular occasion on which a game is played. ❑ *It was the first game of the season... He regularly watched our games from the stands... We won three games against Australia.* N-COUNT = match [3] A **game** is a part of a match, for example in tennis or bridge, consisting of a fixed number of points. ❑ *She won six games to love in the second set. ...the last three points of the second game.* N-COUNT [4] **Games** are an organized event in which competitions in several sports take place. ❑ *...the 2000 Olympic Games at Sydney.* N-PLURAL [5] **Games** are organized sports activities that children do at school. [BRIT] ❑ *At his grammar school he is remembered for being bad at games but good in debates.* N-PLURAL = sport [6] Someone's **game** is the degree of skill or the style that they use when playing a particular game. ❑ *Once I was through the first set my game picked up.* N-SING: usu poss N [7] You can describe a situation that you do not treat seriously as a **game**. ❑ *Many people regard life as a game: you win some, you lose some.* N-COUNT [8] You can use **game** to describe a way of behaving in which a person uses a particular plan, usually in order to gain an advantage for himself or herself. ❑ *Until now, the Americans have been playing a very delicate political game.* N-COUNT: usu with supp [9] Wild animals or birds that are hunted for sport and sometimes cooked and eaten are referred to as **game**. ❑ *...men who shot game for food.* N-UNCOUNT [10] If you are **game for** something, you are willing to do something new, unusual, or risky. ❑ *After all this time he still had new ideas and was game to try them... He said he's game for a similar challenge next year.* ADJ: v-link ADJ, oft ADJ to-inf, ADJ *for* n [11] → See also **gamely**.

PHRASES [12] If someone or something **gives the game away**, they reveal a secret or reveal their feelings, and this puts them at a disadvantage. ❑ *The faces of the two conspirators gave the game away.* PHRASE: V inflects [13] If you are **new to** a particular **game**, you have not done a particular activity or been in a particular situation before. ❑ *Don't forget that she's new to this game and will take a while to complete the task.* PHRASE: v-link PHR [14] If you beat someone **at** their **own game**, you use the same methods that they have used, but more successfully, so that you gain an advantage over them. ❑ *He must anticipate the maneuvers of the other lawyers and beat them at their own game... The police knew that to trap the killer they had to play him at his own game.* PHRASE: PHR after v [15] If you say that someone is **playing games** or **playing silly games**, you mean that they are not treating a situation seriously and you are annoyed with them. ❑ *'Don't play games with me' he thundered... From what I know of him he doesn't play silly games.* PHRASE: V inflects; disapproval [16] If you say that someone **has raised** their **game**, you mean that they have begun to perform better, usually because they were under pressure to do so. ❑ *The world No. 9 had to raise his game to see off a strong challenge from Dale... As it expands its services around the continent, the competition it offers should force the other airlines to raise their game.* PHRASE [17] If you say **the game is up**, you mean that someone's secret plans or activities have been revealed and therefore must stop because they cannot succeed. ❑ *Some thought they would hold out until Sunday. The realists knew that the game was already up.* PHRASE: V inflects

**game bird (game birds) Game birds** are birds which are shot for food or for sport. N-COUNT: usu pl

**Game|boy** /geɪmbɔɪ/ **(Gameboys)** A **Gameboy** is a small portable computer that is specially designed for people to play games on. [TRADEMARK] N-VAR

**game|keeper** /geɪmkiːpəʳ/ **(gamekeepers)** A **gamekeeper** is a person who takes care of the wild animals or birds that are kept on someone's land for hunting. N-COUNT

**game|ly** /geɪmli/ If you do something **gamely**, you do it bravely or with a lot of effort. ❑ *He gamely defended his organisation's decision.* ADV: ADV with v = *resolutely*

**game park** **(game parks)** A **game park** is a large area of land, especially in Africa, where wild animals can live safely. N-COUNT = *game reserve*

**game plan** **(game plans)** also **game-plan.** [1] In sport, a team's **game plan** is their plan for winning a match. ❑ *Leeds kept quiet, stuck to their game plan and quietly racked up the points.* N-COUNT: usu poss N [2] Someone's **game plan** is the actions they intend to take and the policies they intend to adopt in order to achieve a particular thing. ❑ *If he has a game plan for winning the deal, only he understands it... He is unlikely to alter his game plan.* N-COUNT: oft poss N

**game|play** /geɪmpleɪ/ The **gameplay** of a computer game is the way that it is designed and the skills that you need in order to play it. ❑ *On PC, the game had it all – imaginative storyline and characters, challenging gameplay, superb graphics.* N-UNCOUNT

**gamer** /geɪməʳ/ **(gamers)** A **gamer** is someone who plays computer games. N-COUNT

**game re|serve** **(game reserves)** A **game reserve** is a large area of land, especially in Africa, where wild animals can live safely. N-COUNT = *game park*

**game show** **(game shows)** **Game shows** are television programmes on which people play games in order to win prizes. ❑ *Being a good game-show host means getting to know your contestants.* N-COUNT

**games|man|ship** /geɪmzmənʃɪp/ **Gamesmanship** is the art or practice of winning a game by clever methods which are not against the rules but are very close to cheating. ❑ *...a remarkably successful piece of diplomatic gamesmanship.* N-UNCOUNT

**gam|ete** /gæmiːt/ **(gametes)** **Gamete** is the name for the two types of male and female cell that join together to make a new creature. [TECHNICAL] N-COUNT

**gam|ine** /gæmiːn/ If you describe a girl or a woman as **gamine**, you mean that she is attractive in a boyish way. ❑ *She had a gamine charm which men found irresistibly attractive.* ADJ: usu ADJ n = *boyish* ♦ **Gamine** is also a noun. ❑ *...a snub-nosed gamine.* N-SING

**gam|ing** /geɪmɪŋ/ [1] **Gaming** means the same as **gambling**. ❑ *...offences connected with vice, gaming and drugs. ...the most fashionable gaming club in London.* N-UNCOUNT: oft N n [2] **Gaming** is the activity of playing computer games. ❑ *Online gaming allows players from around the world to challenge each other.* N-UNCOUNT

**gam|ma** /gæmə/ **(gammas)** **Gamma** is the third letter of the Greek alphabet. N-VAR

**gam|ma rays** **Gamma rays** are a type of electromagnetic radiation that has a shorter wavelength and higher energy than X-rays. N-PLURAL

**gam|mon** /gæmən/ **Gammon** is smoked or salted meat, similar to bacon, from the back leg or the side of a pig. [BRIT] N-UNCOUNT

**gam|ut** /gæmət/ [1] **The gamut of** something is the complete range of things of that kind, or a wide variety of things of that kind. ❑ *As the story unfolded throughout the past week, I experienced the gamut of emotions: shock, anger, sadness, disgust, confusion.* N-SING: usu *the* N *of* n = *range* [2] To **run the gamut of** something means to include, express, or experience all the different things of that kind, or a wide variety of them. ❑ *The show runs the gamut of 20th century design.* PHRASE: V inflects

**gan|der** /gændəʳ/ **(ganders)** A **gander** is a male goose. N-COUNT

**gang** /gæŋ/ **(gangs, ganging, ganged)** ◆◇◇ [1] A **gang** is a group of people, especially young people, who go around together and often deliberately cause trouble. ❑ *During the fight with a rival gang he lashed out with his flick knife... Gang members were behind a lot of the violence... He was attacked by a gang of youths.* N-COUNT: oft N *of* n [2] A **gang** is a group of criminals who work together to commit crimes. ❑ *Police were hunting for a gang who had allegedly stolen fifty-five cars. ...an underworld gang. ...a gang of masked robbers.* N-COUNT [3] **The gang** is a group of friends who frequently meet. [INFORMAL] ❑ *Come on over, we've got lots of the old gang here.* N-SING: usu *the* N [4] A **gang** is a group of workers who do physical work together. ❑ *...a gang of labourers.* N-COUNT: oft N *of* n

♦ **gang up** If people **gang up on** someone, they unite against them for a particular reason, for example in a fight or argument. [INFORMAL] ❑ *Harrison complained that his colleagues ganged up on him... All the other parties ganged up to keep them out of power... All the girls in my class seemed to gang up against me.* PHRASAL VERB V P *on* n V P to-inf V P *against* n

**gang|buster** /gæŋbʌstəʳ/ **(gangbusters)** If something is **going gangbusters**, it is going strongly and doing very well. If someone **comes on like gangbusters**, they behave very energetically and sometimes aggressively. [AM] ❑ *The economy was still going gangbusters... The team, who struggled early, came on like gangbusters at precisely the right time.* PHRASE: Vs inflect

**gang|land** /gæŋlænd/ **Gangland** is used to describe activities or people that are involved in organized crime. ❑ *It's been suggested they were gangland killings. ...one of Italy's top gangland bosses.* ADJ: ADJ n

**gan|gling** /gæŋglɪŋ/ **Gangling** is used to describe a young person, especially a man, who is tall, thin, and clumsy in their movements. ❑ *His gangling, awkward gait has earned him the name Spiderman. ...his gangling, bony frame.* ADJ: ADJ n

**gan|gly** /gæŋgli/ If you describe someone as **gangly**, you mean that they are tall and thin and have a slightly awkward or clumsy manner. ADJ: usu ADJ n = *gangling*

**gang|plank** /gæŋplæŋk/ **(gangplanks)** **The gangplank** is a short bridge or platform that can be placed between the side of a ship or boat and the shore, so that people can get on or off. N-COUNT: usu *the* N in sing = *gangway*

**gang rape** **(gang rapes, gang raping, gang raped)** also **gang-rape.** If a woman **is gang raped**, several men force her to have sex with them. ❑ *For five hours, the women were gang-raped.* VERB: usu passive *be* V-ed Also V n ♦ **Gang rape** is also a noun. N-COUNT

**gan|grene** /gæŋgriːn/ **Gangrene** is the decay that can occur in a part of a person's body if the blood stops flowing to it, for example as a result of illness or injury. ❑ *Once gangrene has developed the tissue is dead.* N-UNCOUNT

**gan|gre|nous** /gæŋgrɪnəs/ **Gangrenous** is used to describe a part of a person's body that has been affected by gangrene. ❑ *...patients with gangrenous limbs.* ADJ

**gang|sta** /gæŋstə/ or **gangsta rap** **Gangsta** or **gangsta rap** is a form of rap music in which the words often refer to crime and violence. N-UNCOUNT

**gang|ster** /gæŋstəʳ/ **(gangsters)** A **gangster** is a member of an organized group of violent criminals. N-COUNT

**gang|way** /gæŋweɪ/ **(gangways)** **The gangway** is the passage between rows of seats, for example in a theatre or aircraft, for people to walk along. [BRIT] ❑ *A man in the gangway suddenly stood up to reach for something in the overhead locker.* N-COUNT: usu *the* N in sing = *aisle*

**gan|net** /gænɪt/ **(gannets)** **Gannets** are large white sea birds that live on cliffs. N-COUNT

**gan|try** /gæntri/ **(gantries)** A **gantry** is a high metal structure that supports a set of road signs, railway signals, or other equipment. ❑ *On top of the gantry the American flag flew. ...the lighting gantries.* N-COUNT

**gaol** /dʒeɪl/ **(gaols, gaoling, gaoled)** → see **jail**.

**gaol|er** /dʒeɪləʳ/ **(gaolers)** → see **jailer**.

**gap** /gæp/ **(gaps)** [1] A **gap** is a space between two things or a hole in the middle of something solid. ❑ *He pulled the thick curtains together, leaving just a narrow gap. ...the wind tearing through gaps in the window frames.* [2] A **gap** is a period of time when you are not busy or when you stop doing something that you normally do. ❑ *There followed a gap of four years, during which William joined the Army.* [3] If there is something missing from a situation that prevents it being complete or satisfactory, you can say that there is a **gap**. ❑ *We need more young scientists to fill the gap left by a wave of retirements expected over the next decade... Like a good businessman, Stewart identified a gap in the market.* [4] A **gap between** two groups of people, things, or sets of ideas is a big difference between them. ❑ *...the gap between rich and poor... America's trade gap widened... Britain needs to bridge the technology gap between academia and industry.* — ◆◇◇ N-COUNT; N-COUNT: oft N *of* n = break; N-COUNT: usu with supp; N-COUNT: with supp, oft N *between* pl-n

**gape** /geɪp/ **(gapes, gaping, gaped)** [1] If you **gape**, you look at someone or something in surprise, usually with an open mouth. ❑ *His secretary stopped taking notes to gape at me. ...a grotesque face with its gaping mouth.* [2] If you say that something such as a hole or a wound **gapes**, you are emphasizing that it is big or wide. ❑ *The front door was missing. A hole gaped in the roof.* ♦ **gap|ing** *The aircraft took off with a gaping hole in its fuselage. ...a gaping wound in her back.* — VERB; V *at* n; V-ing; VERB [emphasis]; V; ADJ: usu ADJ n

**gap-fill** **(gap-fills)** In language teaching, a **gap-fill** test is an exercise in which words are removed from a text and replaced with spaces. The learner has to fill each space with the missing word or a suitable word. — N-COUNT: usu N n = cloze

**gap-toothed** If you describe a person or their smile as **gap-toothed**, you mean that some of that person's teeth are missing. ❑ *...a broad, gap-toothed grin.* — ADJ: usu ADJ n

**gap year** A **gap year** is a period of time during which a student takes a break from studying after they have finished school and before they start college or university. [BRIT] ❑ *I went around the world in my gap year.* — N-SING

**gar|age** /gærɑːʒ, -rɪdʒ, AM gərɑːʒ/ **(garages)** [1] A **garage** is a building in which you keep a car. A garage is often built next to or as part of a house. → See picture on page 1705. [2] A **garage** is a place where you can get your car repaired. In Britain, you can also buy fuel for your car, or buy cars. ❑ *Nancy took her car to a local garage.* — N-COUNT; N-COUNT; N-IN-NAMES

**gar|age sale** **(garage sales)** If you have a **garage sale**, you sell things such as clothes, toys and household items that you do not want, usually in your garage. [mainly AM] — N-COUNT

**garb** /gɑːʳb/ Someone's **garb** is the clothes they are wearing, especially when these are unusual. [WRITTEN] ❑ *...a familiar figure in civilian garb... He wore the garb of a scout, not a general.* — N-UNCOUNT: oft *in* adj N, oft with poss = attire

**gar|bage** /gɑːʳbɪdʒ/ [1] **Garbage** is rubbish, especially waste from a kitchen. [mainly AM] ❑ *...a garbage bag. ...rotting piles of garbage.* [2] If someone says that an idea or opinion is **garbage**, they are emphasizing that they believe it is untrue or unimportant. [INFORMAL] ❑ *I personally think this is complete garbage... Furious government officials branded her story 'garbage'.* — N-UNCOUNT; N-UNCOUNT [disapproval] = rubbish

**gar|bage can** **(garbage cans)** A **garbage can** is a container that you put rubbish into. [AM] → See picture on page 1705. ❑ *A bomb planted in a garbage can exploded early today.* — N-COUNT

☑ in BRIT, use **dustbin**

**gar|bage col|lec|tor** **(garbage collectors)** A **garbage collector** is a person whose job is to take people's garbage away. [AM] — N-COUNT

☑ in BRIT, use **dustman**

**gar|bage dis|pos|al** **(garbage disposals)** A **garbage disposal** or a **garbage disposal unit** is a small machine in the kitchen sink that breaks down waste matter so that it does not block the sink. [AM] — N-COUNT

☑ in BRIT, use **waste disposal**

**gar|bage man** **(garbage men)** A **garbage man** is the same as a **garbage collector**. [AM] — N-COUNT

**gar|bage truck** **(garbage trucks)** A **garbage truck** is a large truck which collects the garbage from outside people's houses. [AM] — N-COUNT

☑ in BRIT, use **dustcart**

**garbed** /gɑːʳbd/ If someone is **garbed in** particular clothes, they are wearing those clothes. [LITERARY] ❑ *He was garbed in sweater, tweed jacket, and flying boots.* ♦ **Garbed** is also a combining form. ❑ *...the small blue-garbed woman with a brown wrinkled face.* — ADJ: v-link ADJ *in* n; COMB in ADJ: usu ADJ n

**gar|bled** /gɑːʳbᵊld/ A **garbled** message or report contains confused or wrong details, often because it is spoken by someone who is nervous or in a hurry. ❑ *The Coastguard needs to decipher garbled messages in a few minutes. ...his own garbled version of the El Greco story.* — ADJ

**gar|den** /gɑːʳdᵊn/ **(gardens, gardening, gardened)** [1] In British English, a **garden** is a piece of land next to a house, with flowers, vegetables, other plants, and often grass. In American English, the usual word is **yard**, and a **garden** refers only to land which is used for growing flowers and vegetables. ❑ *...the most beautiful garden on Earth.* [2] If you **garden**, you do work in your garden such as weeding or planting. ❑ *Jim gardened at the homes of friends on weekends.* ♦ **gar|den|ing** *I have taken up gardening again.* [3] **Gardens** are places like a park that have areas of plants, trees, and grass, and that people can visit and walk around. ❑ *The Gardens are open from 10.30am until 5pm. ...Kensington Gardens.* [4] **Gardens** is sometimes used as part of the name of a street. ❑ *He lives at 9, Acacia Gardens.* — ◆◆◇ N-COUNT; VERB; V; N-UNCOUNT; N-PLURAL; N-IN-NAMES

**gar|den cen|tre** **(garden centres)** A **garden centre** is a large shop, usually with an outdoor area, where you can buy things for your garden such as plants and gardening tools. [BRIT] — N-COUNT

**gar|den|er** /gɑːʳdənəʳ/ **(gardeners)** [1] A **gardener** is a person who is paid to work in someone else's garden. [2] A **gardener** is someone who enjoys working in their own garden growing flowers or vegetables. ❑ *...enthusiastic amateur gardeners.* — N-COUNT; N-COUNT

**gar|denia** /gɑːʳdiːniə/ **(gardenias)** A **gardenia** is a type of large, white, or yellow flower with a very pleasant smell. A **gardenia** is also the bush on which these flowers grow. — N-COUNT

**gar|den|ing leave** If someone who leaves their job is given **gardening leave**, they continue to receive their salary and in return they agree not to work for anyone else for a period of time. [BRIT, BUSINESS] ❑ *The settlement means that the three executives can return from gardening leave and start their new jobs.* — N-UNCOUNT

**gar|den par|ty** **(garden parties)** A **garden party** is a formal party that is held out of doors, especially in a large private garden, during the afternoon. — N-COUNT: usu sing

**garden-variety** You can use **garden-variety** to describe something you think is ordinary and not special in any way. [mainly AM] ❑ *The experiment itself is garden-variety science.* — ADJ: usu ADJ n

☑ in BRIT, usually use **common-or-garden**

**gar|gan|tuan** /gɑːʳgæntʃuən/ If you say that something is **gargantuan**, you are emphasizing that it is very large. [WRITTEN] ❑ *...a marketing event of gargantuan proportions. ...a gargantuan corruption scandal.* — ADJ: usu ADJ n [emphasis] = huge, colossal

**gar|gle** /gɑːʳgᵊl/ **(gargles, gargling, gargled)** If you **gargle**, you wash your mouth and throat by filling your mouth with a liquid, tipping your head back and using your throat to blow bubbles through the liquid, and finally spitting it out. — VERB

❑ *Try gargling with salt water as soon as a cough begins... Neil noisily gargled something medicinal.* V / V n

**gar|goyle** /gɑːʳgɔɪl/ **(gargoyles)** A **gargoyle** is a decorative stone carving on old buildings. It is usually shaped like the head of a strange and ugly creature, and water drains through it from the roof of the building. N-COUNT

**gar|ish** /geərɪʃ/ You describe something as **garish** when you dislike it because it is very bright in an unattractive, showy way. ❑ *They climbed the garish purple-carpeted stairs. ...the restaurant's garish, illuminated signs.* ♦ **gar|ish|ly** *...a garishly patterned three-piece suite.* ADJ disapproval = gaudy / ADV: ADV adj/-ed

**gar|land** /gɑːʳlənd/ **(garlands)** A **garland** is a circular decoration made from flowers and leaves. People sometimes wear garlands of flowers on their heads or around their necks. ❑ *They wore garlands of summer flowers in their hair.* N-COUNT: usu pl, oft N *of* n

**gar|lic** /gɑːʳlɪk/ **Garlic** is the small, white, round bulb of a plant that is related to the onion plant. Garlic has a very strong smell and taste and is used in cooking. ❑ *...a clove of garlic.* N-UNCOUNT

**gar|licky** /gɑːʳlɪki/ Something that is **garlicky** tastes or smells of garlic. ❑ *...a garlicky salad. ...garlicky breath.* ADJ: usu ADJ n

**gar|ment** /gɑːʳmənt/ **(garments)** A **garment** is a piece of clothing; used especially in contexts where you are talking about the manufacture or sale of clothes. ❑ *Many of the garments have the customers' name tags sewn into the linings.* N-COUNT

**gar|ner** /gɑːʳnəʳ/ **(garners, garnering, garnered)** If someone **has garnered** something useful or valuable, they have gained it or collected it. [FORMAL] ❑ *Durham had garnered three times as many votes as Carey... He has garnered extensive support for his proposals.* VERB = acquire / V n / V n

**gar|net** /gɑːʳnɪt/ **(garnets)** A **garnet** is a hard, shiny stone that is used in making jewellery. Garnets can be red, yellow, or green in colour. N-COUNT

**gar|nish** /gɑːʳnɪʃ/ **(garnishes, garnishing, garnished)** [1] A **garnish** is a small amount of salad, herbs, or other food that is used to decorate cooked or prepared food. ❑ *...a garnish of chopped raw onion, tomato and fresh coriander... Reserve some watercress for garnish.* N-VAR [2] If you **garnish** cooked or prepared food, you decorate it with a garnish. ❑ *She had finished the vegetables and was garnishing the roast.* VERB / V n

**gar|ret** /gærɪt/ **(garrets)** A **garret** is a small room at the top of a house. N-COUNT

**gar|ri|son** /gærɪsᵊn/ **(garrisons, garrisoning, garrisoned)** [1] A **garrison** is a group of soldiers whose task is to guard the town or building where they live. ❑ *...a five-hundred man French army garrison.* N-COUNT-COLL [2] A **garrison** is the buildings which the soldiers live in. ❑ *The approaches to the garrison have been heavily mined.* N-COUNT [3] To **garrison** a place means to put soldiers there in order to protect it. You can also say that soldiers **are garrisoned** in a place. ❑ *British troops still garrisoned the country... No other soldiers were garrisoned there. ...the large, heavily garrisoned towns.* VERB / V n / *be* V-ed / V-ed

**gar|rotte** /gərɒt/ **(garrottes, garrotting, garrotted)** [1] If someone **is garrotted**, they are killed by having something such as a piece of wire or cord pulled tightly round their neck. ❑ *The two guards had been garrotted.* VERB / *be* V-ed / Also V n [2] A **garrotte** is a piece of wire or cord used to garrotte someone. N-COUNT

**gar|ru|lous** /gærələs/ If you describe someone as **garrulous**, you mean that they talk a great deal, especially about unimportant things. ❑ *...a garrulous old woman.* ADJ

**gar|ter** /gɑːʳtəʳ/ **(garters)** A **garter** is a piece of elastic worn round the top of a stocking or sock in order to prevent it from slipping down. N-COUNT

**gar|ter belt** **(garter belts)** A **garter belt** is a piece of underwear for women that is used for holding up stockings. [AM] N-COUNT

✔ in BRIT, use **suspender belt**

**gas** /gæs/ **(gases, gasses, gassing, gassed)** ◆◆◇

✔ The form **gases** is the plural of the noun. The form **gasses** is the third person singular of the verb.

[1] **Gas** is a substance like air that is neither liquid nor solid and burns easily. It is used as a fuel for cooking and heating. ❑ *Coal is actually cheaper than gas... Shell signed a contract to develop oil and gas reserves near Archangel.* N-UNCOUNT [2] A **gas** is any substance that is neither liquid nor solid, for example oxygen or hydrogen. ❑ *Helium is a very light gas. ...a huge cloud of gas and dust from the volcanic eruption.* N-VAR [3] **Gas** is a poisonous gas that can be used as a weapon. ❑ *...mustard gas... The problem was that the exhaust gases contain many toxins.* N-MASS [4] **Gas** is a gas used for medical purposes, for example to make patients feel less pain or go to sleep during an operation. [INFORMAL] ❑ *...an anaesthetic gas used by many dentists.* N-MASS [5] **Gas** is the fuel which is used to drive motor vehicles. [AM] ❑ *...a tank of gas. ...gas stations.* N-UNCOUNT = gasoline

✔ in BRIT, use **petrol**

[6] To **gas** a person or animal means to kill them by making them breathe poisonous gas. ❑ *Her husband ran a pipe from her car exhaust to the bedroom in an attempt to gas her.* VERB / V n [7] → See also **gas chamber**, **gas mask**, **greenhouse gas**, **laughing gas**, **natural gas**, **tear gas**. [8] If you **step on the gas** when you are driving a vehicle, you go faster. [mainly AM, INFORMAL] PHRASE: V inflects

✔ in BRIT, use **step on it**

**gas cham|ber** **(gas chambers)** A **gas chamber** is a room that has been specially built so that it can be filled with poisonous gas in order to kill people or animals. N-COUNT

**gas|eous** /gæsiəs, geɪʃəs/ You use **gaseous** to describe something which is in the form of a gas, rather than a solid or liquid. ❑ *Freon exists both in liquid and gaseous states.* ADJ: usu ADJ n

**gas fire** **(gas fires)** A **gas fire** is a fire that produces heat by burning gas. N-COUNT

**gas guz|zler** **(gas guzzlers)** also **gas-guzzler.** If you say that a car is a **gas guzzler** you mean that it uses a lot of fuel and is not cheap to run. [AM, INFORMAL] N-COUNT

**gash** /gæʃ/ **(gashes, gashing, gashed)** [1] A **gash** is a long, deep cut in your skin or in the surface of something. ❑ *There was an inch-long gash just above his right eye.* N-COUNT [2] If you **gash** something, you accidentally make a long and deep cut in it. ❑ *He gashed his leg while felling trees.* VERB / V n

**gas|ket** /gæskɪt/ **(gaskets)** A **gasket** is a flat piece of soft material that you put between two joined surfaces in a pipe or engine in order to make sure that gas and oil cannot escape. N-COUNT

**gas|light** /gæshouldəʳ/ **(gaslights)** also **gas light.** A **gaslight** is a lamp that produces light by burning gas. ♦ **Gaslight** is also the light that the lamp produces. ❑ *He would show his collection by gaslight.* N-COUNT / N-UNCOUNT

**gas|man** /gæsmæn/ **(gasmen)** **The gasman** is a man who works for a gas company, repairing gas appliances in people's houses, or checking how much gas they have used. [BRIT, INFORMAL] N-COUNT: usu *the* N in sing

**gas mask** **(gas masks)** A **gas mask** is a device that you wear over your face in order to protect yourself from poisonous gases. N-COUNT

**gaso|line** /gæsəliːn/ **Gasoline** is the same as **petrol**. [AM] N-UNCOUNT

**gasp** /gɑːsp, gæsp/ **(gasps, gasping, gasped)** [1] A **gasp** is a short quick breath of air that you take in through your mouth, especially when you are surprised, shocked, or in pain. ❑ *An audible gasp went round the court as the jury announced the verdict... She gave a small gasp of pain.* N-COUNT: usu with supp [2] When you **gasp**, you take a short quick breath through your mouth, especially when you are surprised, VERB shocked, or in pain. ❑ *She gasped for air and drew in a lungful of water... I heard myself gasp and cry out.* V for n / V

[3] You describe something as **the last gasp** to emphasize that it is the final part of something or happens at the last possible moment. ❑ *...the last gasp of a dying system of censorship.* PHRASE: usu PHR of n, PHR n [emphasis]

**gas pe|dal** **(gas pedals)** **The gas pedal** is another name for the **accelerator**. [mainly AM] → See picture on page 1708. N-COUNT: usu *the* N

**gas ring** **(gas rings)** A **gas ring** is a metal device on top of a cooker or stove, where you can burn gas in order to cook food on it. [BRIT] N-COUNT

☑ in AM, use **burner**

**gas sta|tion** **(gas stations)** A **gas station** is a place where you can buy fuel for your car. [AM] N-COUNT

☑ in BRIT, use **petrol station**

**gas|sy** /gæsi/ **(gassier, gassiest)** Something that is **gassy** contains a lot of bubbles or gas. ❑ *The champagne was sweet and too gassy.* ADJ

**gas|tric** /gæstrɪk/ You use **gastric** to describe processes, pain, or illnesses that occur in someone's stomach. [MEDICAL] ❑ *He suffered from diabetes and gastric ulcers.* ADJ: ADJ n

**gas|tro|en|teri|tis** /gæstroʊentəraɪtɪs/ also **gastro-enteritis. Gastroenteritis** is an illness in which the lining of your stomach and intestines becomes swollen and painful. [MEDICAL] N-UNCOUNT

**gas|tro|in|tes|ti|nal** /gæstroʊɪntestɪnəl/ **Gastrointestinal** means relating to the stomach and intestines. [MEDICAL] ADJ: ADJ n

**gas|tro|nome** /gæstrənoʊm/ **(gastronomes)** A **gastronome** is someone who enjoys preparing and eating good food, especially unusual or expensive food. [FORMAL] N-COUNT = gourmet

**gas|tro|nom|ic** /gæstrənɒmɪk/ **Gastronomic** is used to describe things that are concerned with good food. [FORMAL] ❑ *Paris is the gastronomic capital of the world... She is sampling gastronomic delights along the Riviera.* ADJ: ADJ n

**gas|trono|my** /gæstrɒnəmi/ **Gastronomy** is the activity and knowledge involved in preparing and appreciating good food. [FORMAL] ❑ *Burgundy has always been a major centre of gastronomy.* N-UNCOUNT

**gas|works** /gæswɜːʳks/ **(gasworks)** also **gas works.** A **gasworks** is a factory where gas is made, usually from coal, so that it can be used as a fuel. N-COUNT

**gate** /geɪt/ **(gates)** ◆◇◇ [1] A **gate** is a structure like a door which is used at the entrance to a field, a garden, or the grounds of a building. → See picture on page 1705. ❑ *He opened the gate and started walking up to the house.* N-COUNT [2] In an airport, a **gate** is a place where passengers leave the airport and get on their aeroplane. ❑ *Passengers with hand luggage can go straight to the departure gate to check in there.* N-COUNT [3] **Gate** is used in the names of streets in Britain that are in a place where there once was a gate into a city. ❑ *...9 Palace Gate.* N-IN-NAMES [4] The **gate** at a sporting event such as a football match or baseball game is the total number of people who attend it. ❑ *Their average gate is less than 23,000.* N-COUNT

**ga|teau** /gætoʊ/ **(gateaux)** A **gateau** is a very rich, elaborate cake, especially one with cream in it. [mainly BRIT] ❑ *...a large slice of gateau. ...a huge selection of gateaux, cakes and pastries.* N-VAR

**gate|crash** /geɪtkræʃ/ **(gatecrashes, gatecrashing, gatecrashed)** If someone **gatecrashes** a party or other social event, they go to it, even though they have not been invited. ❑ *Scores of people tried desperately to gatecrash the party... He had gatecrashed but he was with other people we knew and there was no problem.* VERB / V n / V

♦ **gate|crash|er** **(gatecrashers)** *Panic set in as gatecrashers tried to force their way through the narrow doors and corridors.* N-COUNT

**gat|ed com|mu|nity** **(gated communities)** A **gated community** is an area of houses and sometimes shops that is surrounded by a wall or fence and has an entrance that is guarded. [mainly AM] N-COUNT

**gate|house** /geɪthaʊs/ **(gatehouses)** A **gatehouse** is a small house next to a gate on the edge of a park or country estate. N-COUNT

**gate|keeper** /geɪtkiːpəʳ/ **(gatekeepers)** A **gatekeeper** is a person who is in charge of a gate and who allows people through it. N-COUNT

**gate mon|ey** **Gate money** is the total amount of money that is paid by the people who go to a sports match or other event. [mainly BRIT] N-UNCOUNT

**gate|post** /geɪtpoʊst/ **(gateposts)** A **gatepost** is a post in the ground which a gate is hung from, or which it is fastened to when it is closed. N-COUNT

**gate|way** /geɪtweɪ/ **(gateways)** [1] A **gateway** is an entrance where there is a gate. ❑ *He walked across the park and through a gateway.* N-COUNT [2] A **gateway to** somewhere is a place which you go through because it leads you to a much larger place. ❑ *Lyons is the gateway to the Alps for motorists driving out from Britain.* N-COUNT: usu N *to* n [3] If something is a **gateway to** a job, career, or other activity, it gives you the opportunity to make progress or get further success in that activity. ❑ *The prestigious title offered a gateway to success in the highly competitive world of modelling.* N-COUNT: with supp, usu N *to* n [4] In computing, a **gateway** connects different computer networks so that information can be passed between them. [COMPUTING] N-COUNT

**gate|way drug** **(gateway drugs)** A **gateway drug** is a drug such as cannabis that is believed by some people to lead to the use of more harmful drugs such as heroin or cocaine. N-COUNT

**gath|er** /gæðəʳ/ **(gathers, gathering, gathered)** ◆◆◇ [1] If people **gather** somewhere or if someone **gathers** people somewhere, they come together in a group. ❑ *In the evenings, we gathered around the fireplace and talked... The man signalled for me to gather the children together.* VERB = assemble, collect / V prep/adv / V n with together [2] If you **gather** things, you collect them together so that you can use them. ❑ *I suggest we gather enough firewood to last the night... She stood up and started gathering her things together.* VERB = collect / V n / V n together ♦ **Gather up** means the same as **gather**. ❑ *When Sutcliffe had gathered up his papers, he went out... He gathered the leaves up off the ground.* PHRASAL VERB / V P n (not pron) / V n P [3] If you **gather** information or evidence, you collect it, especially over a period of time and after a lot of hard work. ❑ *...a private detective using a hidden tape recorder to gather information.* VERB = collect, amass / V n [4] If something **gathers** speed, momentum, or force, it gradually becomes faster or more powerful. ❑ *Demands for his dismissal have gathered momentum in recent weeks... The raft gathered speed as the current dragged it toward the falls.* VERB = gain / V n / V n [5] When you **gather** something such as your strength, courage, or thoughts, you make an effort to prepare yourself to do something. ❑ *You must gather your strength for the journey.* VERB = muster / V n ♦ **Gather up** means the same as **gather**. ❑ *She was gathering up her courage to approach him when he called to her.* PHRASAL VERB / V P n (not pron) / Also V n P [6] You use **gather** in expressions such as '**I gather**' and '**as far as I can gather**' to introduce information that you have found out, especially when you have found it out in an indirect way. ❑ *I gather his report is highly critical of the trial judge... 'He speaks English,' she said to Graham. 'I gathered that.'... From what I could gather, he was trying to raise money by organising festivals.* VERB / V that / V n / V n [7] to **gather dust** → see **dust**.

♦ **gather up** → see **gather 2, 5**.

**gath|er|er** /gæðərəʳ/ **(gatherers)** A **gatherer** is someone who collects or gathers a particular thing. ❑ *...professional intelligence gatherers.* N-COUNT: usu n N

**gath|er|ing** /gæðərɪŋ/ **(gatherings)** [1] A **gathering** is a group of people meeting together for a particular purpose. ❑ *...the twenty-second annual gathering of the South Pacific Forum.* N-COUNT [2] If there is **gathering** darkness, the light is gradually decreasing, usually because it is nearly night. ❑ *The* ADJ: ADJ n lighthouse beam was quite distinct in the gathering dusk. → See also **gather**.

**gator** /geɪtəʳ/ **(gators)** also **'gator.** A **gator** is the same as an **alligator**. [AM, INFORMAL] N-COUNT

**gauche** /goʊʃ/ If you describe someone as **gauche**, you mean that they are awkward and uncomfortable in the company of other people. ❑ *We're all a bit gauche when we're young... She was a rather gauche, provincial creature.* ADJ = awkward

**gau|cho** /gaʊtʃoʊ/ **(gauchos)** A **gaucho** is a South American cowboy. N-COUNT

**gaudy** /gɔːdi/ **(gaudier, gaudiest)** If something is **gaudy**, it is very brightly-coloured and showy. ❑ *...her gaudy orange-and-purple floral hat.* ADJ disapproval = garish

**gauge** /geɪdʒ/ **(gauges, gauging, gauged)** 1 If you **gauge** the speed or strength of something, or if you gauge an amount, you measure or calculate it, often by using a device of some kind. ❑ *He gauged the wind at over thirty knots... Distance is gauged by journey time rather than miles.* VERB V n V n 2 A **gauge** is a device that measures the amount or quantity of something and shows the amount measured. ❑ *...temperature gauges. ...pressure gauges.* N-COUNT: oft n N 3 If you **gauge** people's actions, feelings, or intentions in a particular situation, you carefully consider and judge them. ❑ *...as he gauged possible enemy moves and his own responses.* VERB = assess V n 4 A **gauge of** someone's feelings or a situation is a fact or event that can be used to judge them. ❑ *The index is the government's chief gauge of future economic activity.* N-SING: usu N *of* n = measure 5 A **gauge** is the distance between the two rails on a railway line. ❑ *...a narrow gauge railway.* N-COUNT: usu n N 6 A **gauge** is the thickness of something, especially metal or wire. N-COUNT

**gaunt** /gɔːnt/ 1 If someone looks **gaunt**, they look very thin, usually because they have been very ill or worried. ❑ *Looking gaunt and tired, he denied there was anything to worry about.* ADJ = drawn 2 If you describe a building as **gaunt**, you mean it is very plain and unattractive. [LITERARY] ❑ *Above on the hillside was a large, gaunt, grey house.* ADJ: ADJ n

**gaunt|let** /gɔːntlɪt/ **(gauntlets)** 1 **Gauntlets** are long, thick, protective gloves. ❑ *...a pair of black leather driving gauntlets.* N-COUNT: usu pl

PHRASES 2 If you **pick up the gauntlet** or **take up the gauntlet**, you accept the challenge that someone has made. ❑ *She picked up the gauntlet in her incisive Keynote Address to the Conference... Whoever decides to take up the gauntlet and challenge the Prime Minister will have a tough battle.* PHRASE: V inflects 3 If you **run the gauntlet**, you go through an unpleasant experience in which a lot of people criticize or attack you. ❑ *The trucks tried to drive to the British base, running the gauntlet of marauding bands of gunmen.* PHRASE: V inflects, oft PHR *of* n 4 If you **throw down the gauntlet to** someone, you say or do something that challenges them to argue or compete with you. ❑ *Luxury car firm Jaguar has thrown down the gauntlet to competitors by giving the best guarantee on the market.* PHRASE: V inflects, oft PHR *to* n

**gauze** /gɔːz/ **Gauze** is a type of light, soft cloth with tiny holes in it. ❑ *Strain the juice through a piece of gauze or a sieve.* N-UNCOUNT

**gauzy** /gɔːzi/ **Gauzy** material is light, soft, and thin, so that you can see through it. ❑ *...thin, gauzy curtains.* ADJ: ADJ n

**gave** /geɪv/ **Gave** is the past tense of **give**.

**gav|el** /gævəl/ **(gavels)** A **gavel** is a small wooden hammer that the person in charge of a law court, an auction, or a meeting bangs on a table to get people's attention. N-COUNT: usu sing, oft poss N

**gawd** /gɔːd/ **Gawd** is used to represent the word 'God' pronounced in a particular accent or tone of voice, especially to show that someone is bored, irritated, or shocked. [INFORMAL, WRITTEN] ❑ *I thought, oh my gawd!* EXCLAM

**gawk** /gɔːk/ **(gawks, gawking, gawked)** To **gawk at** someone or something means to stare at them in a rude, stupid, or unthinking way. [INFORMAL] ❑ *The youth continued to gawk at her and did not answer... Tens of thousands came to gawk.* VERB V at n V

**gawky** /gɔːki/ If you describe someone, especially a young person, as **gawky**, you mean they are awkward and clumsy. ❑ *...a gawky lad with spots.* ADJ = gangling

**gawp** /gɔːp/ **(gawps, gawping, gawped)** To **gawp** means the same as to **gawk**. [BRIT, INFORMAL] ❑ *At weekends the roads are jammed with holidaymakers coming to gawp at the parade... Thorpe could only stand and gawp.* VERB V at n V

**gay** /geɪ/ **(gays, gayer, gayest)** 1 A **gay** person is homosexual. ❑ *The quality of life for gay men has improved over the last two decades. ...the gay community.* ♦ **Gays** are homosexual people, especially homosexual men. ❑ *More importantly, gays have proved themselves to be style leaders.* ♦ **gay|ness** *...Mike's admission of his gayness.* ◆◆◇ ADJ: usu ADJ n ≠ straight N-PLURAL N-UNCOUNT 2 A **gay** person is fun to be with because they are lively and cheerful. [OLD-FASHIONED] ❑ *I am happy and free, in good health, gay and cheerful.* ADJ 3 A **gay** object is brightly coloured and pretty to look at. [OLD-FASHIONED] ❑ *I like gay, relaxing paintings.* ADJ = cheerful

**gaze** /geɪz/ **(gazes, gazing, gazed)** 1 If you **gaze at** someone or something, you look steadily at them for a long time, for example because you find them attractive or interesting, or because you are thinking about something else. ❑ *She stood gazing at herself in the mirror... Sitting in his wicker chair, he gazed reflectively at the fire.* VERB V at n V at n 2 You can talk about someone's **gaze** as a way of describing how they are looking at something, especially when they are looking steadily at it. [WRITTEN] ❑ *She felt increasingly uncomfortable under the woman's steady gaze... The interior was shielded from the curious gaze of passersby.* N-COUNT: usu sing, usu with poss 3 If someone or something is **in the public gaze**, they are receiving a lot of attention from the general public. ❑ *You won't find a couple more in the public gaze than Michael and Lizzie.* PHRASE: oft v-link PHR

**ga|zebo** /gəziːboʊ, AM -zeɪ-/ **(gazebos)** A **gazebo** is a small building with open sides. Gazebos are often put up in gardens so that people can sit in them to enjoy the view. N-COUNT

**ga|zelle** /gəzel/ **(gazelles)** A **gazelle** is a type of small African or Asian deer. Gazelles move very quickly and gracefully. N-COUNT

**ga|zette** /gəzet/ **(gazettes)** 1 **Gazette** is often used in the names of newspapers. ❑ *...the Arkansas Gazette.* N-IN-NAMES: n N 2 In Britain, a **gazette** is an official publication in which information such as honours, public appointments, and important decisions are announced. N-COUNT: oft adj N

**gaz|et|teer** /gæzɪtɪəʳ/ **(gazetteers)** A **gazetteer** is a book or a part of a book which lists and describes places. N-COUNT

**ga|zump** /gəzʌmp/ **(gazumps, gazumping, gazumped)** If you **are gazumped** by someone, they agree to sell their house to you, but then sell it to someone else who offers to pay a higher price. [BRIT, INFORMAL] ❑ *In France you cannot be gazumped.* ♦ **ga|zump|ing** *During the 1980s property boom, gazumping was common.* VERB: usu passive *be* V-ed N-UNCOUNT

**GB** /dʒiː biː/ **GB** is an abbreviation for **Great Britain**. N-PROPER

**GBH** /dʒiː biː eɪtʃ/ **GBH** is an abbreviation for **grievous bodily harm**. [BRIT, INFORMAL] N-UNCOUNT

**GCSE** /dʒiː siː es iː/ **(GCSEs) GCSEs** are British educational qualifications which schoolchildren take when they are fifteen or sixteen years old. **GCSE** is an abbreviation for 'General Certificate of Secondary Education'. ❑ *She quit school as soon as she had taken her GCSEs. ...GCSE candidates.* N-VAR

**gdn** **(gdns) gdn** is a written abbreviation for **garden**, for example in addresses, or in advertisements for houses that are for sale. ❑ *The Piazza, Covent Gdn, WC2. ...flat, private gdn, close to station.*

**GDP** /dʒiː diː piː/ **(GDPs)** In economics, a country's **GDP** is the total value of goods and ser- ◆◇◇ N-VAR vices produced within a country in a year, not including its income from investments in other countries. **GDP** is an abbreviation for 'gross domestic product'. Compare **GNP**.

**gear** /gɪəʳ/ **(gears, gearing, geared)** [1] The **gears** on a machine or vehicle are a device for changing the rate at which energy is changed into motion. ❑ *On hills, he must use low gears... The car was in fourth gear... He put the truck in gear and drove on.* [2] The **gear** involved in a particular activity is the equipment or special clothing that you use. ❑ *About 100 officers in riot gear were needed to break up the fight. ...fishing gear... They helped us put our gear back into the van.* [3] **Gear** means clothing. [INFORMAL] ❑ *I used to wear trendy gear but it just looked ridiculous.* [4] If someone or something **is geared to** or **towards** a particular purpose, they are organized or designed in order to achieve that purpose. ❑ *Colleges are not always geared to the needs of mature students... My training was geared towards winning gold in Munich.*
◆◇◇ N-COUNT; N-UNCOUNT; N-UNCOUNT; V-PASSIVE; be V-ed to n; be V-ed towards -ing

♦ **gear up** If someone **is gearing up for** a particular activity, they are preparing to do it. If they **are geared up to** do a particular activity, they are prepared to do it. ❑ *...another indication that the Government is gearing up for an election... The factory was geared up to make 1,100 cars a day.*
PHRASAL VERB: usu passive; V P for/to n; be V-ed P to-inf

**gear|box** /gɪəʳbɒks/ **(gearboxes)** A **gearbox** is the system of gears in an engine or vehicle. N-COUNT

**gear lev|er** **(gear levers)** or **gear stick** A **gear lever** or a **gear stick** is the lever that you use to change gear in a car or other vehicle. [BRIT] → See picture on page 1708. N-COUNT

☑ in AM, usually use **gearshift**

**gear|shift** /gɪəʳʃɪft/ **(gearshifts)** also **gear shift.** In a vehicle, the **gearshift** is the same as the **gear lever**. [mainly AM] → See picture on page 1708. N-COUNT

**gear stick** → see **gear lever**.

**gee** /dʒiː/ People sometimes say **gee** to emphasize a reaction or remark. [AM, INFORMAL] ❑ *Gee, it's hot... Gee thanks, Stan.* EXCLAM [emphasis]

**geek** /giːk/ **(geeks)** If you call someone, usually a man or boy, a **geek**, you are saying in an unkind way that they are stupid, awkward, or weak. [INFORMAL] N-COUNT [disapproval] = nerd

**geeky** /giːki/ If you describe someone as **geeky**, you think they look or behave like a geek. ADJ

**geese** /giːs/ **Geese** is the plural of **goose**.

**gee whiz** /dʒiː ʰwɪz/ also **gee whizz.** [1] People sometimes say **gee whiz** in order to express a strong reaction to something or to introduce a remark or response. [AM, INFORMAL] ❑ *Gee whiz, they carried on and on, they loved the evening.* [2] You use **gee whiz** to describe something that is new, exciting, and impressive, but that is perhaps more complicated or showy than it needs to be. [mainly AM, INFORMAL] ❑ *The trend now is towards 'lifestyle' electronics – black, shiny gee-whiz things that people like to own.*
EXCLAM [feelings]; ADJ: ADJ n

**gee|zer** /giːzəʳ/ **(geezers)** Some people use **geezer** to refer to a man. [mainly BRIT, INFORMAL, OLD-FASHIONED] ❑ *...an old bald geezer in a posh raincoat.* N-COUNT = bloke

**Geiger coun|ter** /gaɪgəʳ kaʊntəʳ/ **(Geiger counters)** A **Geiger counter** is a device which finds and measures radioactivity. N-COUNT

**gei|sha** /geɪʃə/ **(geishas)** A **geisha** is a Japanese woman who is specially trained in music, dancing, and the art of conversation. Her job is to entertain men. N-COUNT

**gel** /dʒel/ **(gels, gelling, gelled)**

☑ The spelling **jell** is usually used in American English and is sometimes used in British English for meanings 1 and 2.

[1] If people **gel with** each other, or if two groups of people **gel**, they work well together because their skills and personalities fit together well. ❑ *They have gelled very well with the rest of the side... There were signs on Saturday that the team is starting to gel at last... Their partnership gelled and scriptwriting for television followed.* [2] If a vague shape, thought, or creation **gels**, it becomes clearer or more definite. ❑ *Even if her interpretation has not yet gelled into a satisfying whole, she displays real musicianship... It was not until 1974 that his ability to write gelled again.* [3] **Gel** is a thick jelly-like substance, especially one used to keep your hair in a particular style.
V-RECIP; V with n; V; V (non-recip); VERB; V into n; V; N-MASS

**gela|tine** /dʒelɪtiːn, AM -tᵊn/ **(gelatines)** also **gelatin. Gelatine** is a clear tasteless powder that is used to make liquids become firm, for example when you are making desserts such as jelly. N-MASS

**ge|lati|nous** /dʒɪlætɪnəs/ **Gelatinous** substances or mixtures are wet and sticky. ❑ *Pour a cup of the gelatinous mixture into the blender.* ADJ

**geld|ing** /geldɪŋ/ **(geldings)** A **gelding** is a male horse that has been castrated. N-COUNT

**gel|ig|nite** /dʒelɪgnaɪt/ **Gelignite** is a type of explosive. N-UNCOUNT

**gem** /dʒem/ **(gems)** [1] A **gem** is a jewel or stone that is used in jewellery. ❑ *...a gold mask inset with emeralds and other gems.* [2] If you describe something or someone as a **gem**, you mean that they are especially pleasing, good, or helpful. [INFORMAL] ❑ *...a gem of a hotel, Castel Clara... Miss Famous, as she was called, was a gem.*
N-COUNT; N-COUNT: oft N of n

**Gemi|ni** /dʒemɪnaɪ, AM -niː/ **(Geminis)** [1] **Gemini** is one of the twelve signs of the zodiac. Its symbol is a pair of twins. People who are born approximately between 21st May and 20th June come under this sign. [2] A **Gemini** is a person whose sign of the zodiac is Gemini.
N-UNCOUNT; N-COUNT

**gem|stone** /dʒemstoʊn/ **(gemstones)** A **gemstone** is a jewel or stone used in jewellery. N-COUNT = gem

**Gen.** **Gen.** is a written abbreviation for **General**. ❑ *Gen. de Gaulle sensed that nuclear weapons would fundamentally change international relations.*

**gen|darme** /ʒɒndɑːʳm/ **(gendarmes)** A **gendarme** is a member of the French police force. N-COUNT

**gen|der** /dʒendəʳ/ **(genders)** [1] A person's **gender** is the fact that they are male or female. ❑ *Women are sometimes denied opportunities solely because of their gender. ...groups that are traditionally discriminated against on grounds of gender, colour, race, or age.* [2] You can refer to all male people or all female people as a particular **gender**. ❑ *While her observations may be true about some men, they could hardly apply to the entire gender. ...the different abilities and skills of the two genders.* [3] In grammar, the **gender** of a noun, pronoun, or adjective is whether it is masculine, feminine, or neuter. A word's gender can affect its form and behaviour. In English, only personal pronouns such as 'she', reflexive pronouns such as 'itself', and possessive determiners such as 'his' have gender. ❑ *In both Welsh and Irish the word for 'moon' is of feminine gender.*
N-VAR = sex; N-COUNT = sex; N-VAR

**gender-bender** **(gender-benders)** People sometimes use **gender-bender** to refer to a man who dresses or behaves like a woman, or a woman who dresses or behaves like a man. [INFORMAL] N-COUNT [disapproval]

♦ **gender-bending** ❑ *...a gender-bending production of the ballet Swan Lake with lines of male swans.* ADJ: ADJ n

**gene** /dʒiːn/ **(genes)** A **gene** is the part of a cell in a living thing which controls its physical characteristics, growth, and development. ◆◇◇ N-COUNT

**ge|neal|ogy** /dʒiːniælədʒi/ **Genealogy** is the study of the history of families, especially through studying historical documents to discover the relationships between particular people and their families. N-UNCOUNT ♦ **ge|nea|logi|cal** /dʒiːniəlɒdʒɪkᵊl/ ❑ *...genealogical research on his family.* ADJ: ADJ n

**gen|era** /dʒenərə/ **Genera** is the plural of **genus**.

**gen|er|al** /dʒenrəl/ **(generals)** [1] A **general** is a high-ranking officer in the armed forces, usually in the army. ❑ *The General's visit to Sarajevo* ◆◆◆ N-COUNT; N-TITLE; N-VOC is part of preparations for the deployment of extra troops. [2] If you talk about the **general** situation somewhere or talk about something in **general** terms, you are describing the situation as a whole rather than considering its details or exceptions. ❑ *The figures represent a general decline in employment. ...the general deterioration of English society.* ● If you describe something **in general terms**, you describe it without giving details. ❑ *She recounted in very general terms some of the events of recent months.* [3] You use **general** to describe several items or activities when there are too many of them or when they are not important enough to mention separately. ❑ *£2,500 for software is soon swallowed up in general costs... His firm took over the planting and general maintenance of the park last March.* [4] You use **general** to describe something that involves or affects most people, or most people in a particular group. ❑ *The project should raise general awareness about bullying.* [5] If you describe something as **general**, you mean that it is not restricted to any one thing or area. ❑ *...a general ache radiating from the back of the neck. ...a general sense of well-being. ...raising the level of general physical fitness.* [6] **General** is used to describe a person's job, usually as part of their title, to indicate that they have complete responsibility for the administration of an organization or business. [BUSINESS] ❑ *He joined Sanders Roe, moving on later to become General Manager.* [7] → See also **generally**.

ADJ: ADJ n | PHRASE | ADJ: ADJ n | ADJ: ADJ n | ADJ: ADJ n | ADJ: ADJ n

**PHRASES** [8] You use **in general** to indicate that you are talking about something as a whole, rather than about part of it. ❑ *I think we need to improve our educational system in general... She had a confused idea of life in general.* [9] You say **in general** to indicate that you are referring to most people or things in a particular group. ❑ *People in general will support us... She enjoys a sterling reputation in law enforcement circles and among the community in general.* [10] You say **in general** to indicate that a statement is true in most cases. ❑ *In general, it was the better-educated voters who voted Yes in the referendum.*

PHRASE: n PHR | PHRASE: n PHR | PHRASE: PHR with cl = on the whole

**gen|er|al elec|tion** **(general elections)** ◆◇◇ [1] In Britain, a **general election** is an election where everyone votes for people to represent them in Parliament. [2] In the United States, a **general election** is a local, state, or national election where the candidates have been selected by a primary election. Compare **primary**.

N-COUNT | N-COUNT

**gen|er|al|ise** /dʒenrəlaɪz/ → see **generalize**.

**gen|er|al|ity** /dʒenəræ̱lɪti/ **(generalities)** [1] A **generality** is a general statement that covers a range of things, rather than being concerned with specific instances. [FORMAL] ❑ *I'll start with some generalities and then examine a few specific examples... He avoided this tricky question and talked in generalities.* [2] The **generality** of a statement or description is the fact that it is a general one, rather than a specific, detailed one. ❑ *That there are problems with this kind of definition is hardly surprising, given its level of generality.*

N-COUNT | N-UNCOUNT

**gen|er|ali|za|tion** /dʒenrəlaɪze̱ɪʃᵊn/ **(generalizations)**

in BRIT, also use **generalisation**

A **generalization** is a statement that seems to be true in most situations or for most people, but that may not be completely true in all cases. ❑ *He is making sweeping generalisations to get his point across... The evaluation of conduct involves some amount of generalization.*

N-VAR

**gen|er|al|ize** /dʒenrəlaɪz/ **(generalizes, generalizing, generalized)**

in BRIT, also use **generalise**

[1] If you **generalize**, you say something that seems to be true in most situations or for most people, but that may not be completely true in all cases. ❑ *'In my day, children were a lot better behaved'. — 'It's not true, you're generalizing'... It's hard to generalize about Cole Porter because he wrote so many great songs that were so varied.* [2] If you **generalize** something such as an idea, you apply it more widely than its original context, as if it was true in many other situations. ❑ *A child first labels the household pet cat as a 'cat' and then generalises this label to other animals that look like it.*

VERB | V | V prep | VERB | V n across/to n

**gen|er|al|ized** /dʒenrəlaɪzd/

in BRIT, also use **generalised**

[1] **Generalized** means involving many different things, rather than one or two specific things. ❑ *...a generalised discussion about admirable singers. ...generalised feelings of inadequacy.* [2] You use **generalized** to describe medical conditions or problems which affect the whole of someone's body, or the whole of a part of their body. [MEDICAL] ❑ *She experienced an increase in generalized aches and pains. ...generalised muscle disorders.*

ADJ: usu ADJ n = general ≠ specific | ADJ: usu ADJ n

**gen|er|al knowl|edge** **General knowledge** is knowledge about many different things, as opposed to detailed knowledge about one particular subject.

N-UNCOUNT

**gen|er|al|ly** /dʒenrəli/ ◆◆◇ [1] You use **generally** to give a summary of a situation, activity, or idea without referring to the particular details of it. ❑ *University teachers generally have admitted a lack of enthusiasm about their subjects... Speaking generally, the space enterprise has served astronomy well.* [2] You use **generally** to say that something happens or is used on most occasions but not on every occasion. ❑ *As women we generally say and feel too much about these things... It is generally true that the darker the fruit the higher its iron content... The warmer a place is, generally speaking, the more types of plants and animals it will usually support.*

ADV: ADV with cl/group, ADV with v | ADV: ADV with cl/group, ADV with v = usually

**gen|er|al prac|tice** **(general practices)** [1] When a doctor is in **general practice**, he or she treats sick people at a surgery or office, or visits them at home, and does not specialize in a particular type of medicine. ❑ *In recent years, doctors have been trained specifically for general practice.* ♦ **General practice** is also a noun. ❑ *The sample was selected from the medical records of two general practices.* [2] When lawyers deal with all kinds of legal matters, rather than specializing in one kind of law, you can say they have a **general practice** or are **in general practice**. [mainly AM]

N-UNCOUNT | N-COUNT | N-UNCOUNT

**gen|er|al prac|ti|tion|er** **(general practitioners)** A **general practitioner** is the same as a **GP**. [BRIT, FORMAL]

N-COUNT

**gen|er|al pub|lic** You can refer to the people in a society as **the general public**, especially when you are contrasting people in general with a small group. ❑ *These charities depend on the compassionate feelings and generosity of the general public... Unemployment is 10 percent among the general public and about 40 percent among North African immigrants.*

N-SING-COLL: the N

**gen|er|al strike** **(general strikes)** A **general strike** is a situation where most or all of the workers in a country are on strike and are refusing to work.

N-COUNT

**gen|er|ate** /dʒenəreɪt/ **(generates, generating, generated)** ◆◇◇ [1] To **generate** something means to cause it to begin and develop. ❑ *The Employment Minister said the reforms would generate new jobs. ...the excitement generated by the changes in Eastern Europe.* [2] To **generate** a form of energy or power means to produce it. ❑ *The company, New England Electric, burns coal to generate power.*

VERB = create | V n | V-ed | VERB | V n

**gen|era|tion** /dʒenəre̱ɪʃᵊn/ **(generations)** ◆◆◇ [1] A **generation** is all the people in a group or country who are of a similar age, especially when they are considered as having the same experiences or attitudes. ❑ *...the younger generation of Party members... David Mamet has long been considered the leading American playwright of his generation.* [2] A **generation** is the period of time, usually

N-COUNT: with supp | N-COUNT

considered to be about thirty years, that it takes for children to grow up and become adults and have children of their own. ❑ *Within a generation flight has become the method used by many travellers.* [3] You can use **generation** to refer to a stage of development in the design and manufacture of machines or equipment. ❑ *...a new generation of IBM/Apple computers.* [4] **Generation** is used to indicate how long members of your family have had a particular nationality. For example, second generation means that you were born in the country you live in, but your parents were not. ❑ *...second generation Asians in Britain.* [5] **Generation** is also the production of a form of energy or power from fuel or another source of power such as water. ❑ *Japan has announced plans for a sharp rise in its nuclear power generation.*

N-COUNT: N *of* n — ADJ: ord ADJ n — N-UNCOUNT: with supp

**gen|era|tion|al** /dʒenəreɪʃənəl/ **Generational** means relating to a particular generation, or to the relationship between particular generations. ❑ *People's lifestyles are usually fixed by generational habits and fashions.* — ADJ: usu ADJ n

**gen|era|tion gap** (**generation gaps**) If you refer to the **generation gap**, you are referring to a difference in attitude and behaviour between older people and younger people, which may cause them to argue or may prevent them from understanding each other fully. — N-COUNT

**gen|era|tive** /dʒenərətɪv/ [1] If something is **generative**, it is capable of producing something or causing it to develop. [FORMAL] ❑ *...the generative power of the sun.* [2] In linguistics, **generative** is used to describe linguistic theories or models which are based on the idea that a single set of rules can explain how all the possible sentences of a language are formed. [TECHNICAL] — ADJ — ADJ: ADJ n

**gen|era|tor** /dʒenəreɪtəʳ/ (**generators**) [1] A **generator** is a machine which produces electricity. [2] A **generator of** something is a person, organization, product, or situation which produces it or causes it to happen. ❑ *The US economy is still an impressive generator of new jobs... The company has been a very good cash generator.* — N-COUNT — N-COUNT: with supp, oft N *of* n

**ge|ner|ic** /dʒɪnerɪk/ (**generics**) [1] You use **generic** to describe something that refers or relates to a whole class of similar things. ❑ *Parmesan is a generic term used to describe a family of hard Italian cheeses.* ♦ **ge|neri|cal|ly** *I will refer to child abuse generically (which includes physical, sexual, and emotional abuse and neglect). ...something generically called 'rock 'n' roll'.* [2] A **generic** drug or other product is one that does not have a trademark and that is known by a general name, rather than the manufacturer's name. ❑ *They encourage doctors to prescribe cheaper generic drugs instead of more expensive brand names.* ♦ **Generic** is also a noun. ❑ *The program saved $11 million in 1988 by substituting generics for brand-name drugs.* [3] People sometimes use **generic** to refer to something that is exactly typical of the kind of thing mentioned, and that has no special or unusual characteristics. ❑ *...generic California apartments, the kind that have white walls and white drapes and were built five years ago.* — ADJ: usu ADJ n ≠ specific — ADV: usu ADV after v, ADV -ed/adj, also ADV with cl — ADJ: usu ADJ n ≠ branded — N-COUNT — ADJ: ADJ n = archetypal

**gen|er|os|ity** /dʒenərɒsɪti/ If you refer to someone's **generosity**, you mean that they are generous, especially in doing or giving more than is usual or expected. ❑ *There are stories about his generosity, the massive amounts of money he gave to charities. ...a man of great generosity of spirit.* — N-UNCOUNT ≠ meanness

**gen|er|ous** /dʒenərəs/ [1] A **generous** person gives more of something, especially money, than is usual or expected. ❑ *German banks are more generous in their lending... The gift is generous by any standards.* ♦ **gen|er|ous|ly** *We would like to thank all the judges who gave so generously of their time.* [2] A **generous** person is friendly, helpful, and willing to see the good qualities in someone or something. ❑ *He was always generous in sharing his enormous knowledge... He was generous enough to congratulate his successor on his decision.* ♦ **gen|er|ous|ly** *The students generously gave them instruction in social responsibility.* [3] A **generous** amount of something is much larger than is usual or necessary. ❑ *...a generous six weeks of annual holiday... He should be able to keep his room tidy with the generous amount of storage space.* ♦ **gen|er|ous|ly** *...a generously sized sitting room... Season the steaks generously with salt and pepper before cooking.* — ◆◇◇ ADJ ≠ mean — ADV: ADV with v — ADJ — ADV: ADV with v — ADJ — ADV: ADV -ed, ADV after v

**gen|esis** /dʒenɪsɪs/ The **genesis** of something is its beginning, birth, or creation. [FORMAL] ❑ *The project had its genesis two years earlier.* — N-SING: usu with poss = origin

**gene thera|py** **Gene therapy** is the use of genetic material to treat disease. — N-UNCOUNT

**ge|net|ic** /dʒɪnetɪk/ You use **genetic** to describe something that is concerned with genetics or with genes. ❑ *Cystic fibrosis is the most common fatal genetic disease in the United States.* ♦ **ge|neti|cal|ly** /dʒɪnetɪkli/ *Some people are genetically predisposed to diabetes.* — ADJ — ADV: usu ADV adj

**ge|neti|cal|ly modi|fied** **Genetically modified** plants and animals have had one or more genes changed, for example so that they resist pests and diseases better. **Genetically modified** food contains ingredients made from genetically modified plants or animals. The abbreviation **GM** is often used. ❑ *Top supermarkets are to ban many genetically modified foods.* — ADJ: usu ADJ n

**ge|net|ic en|gi|neer|ing** **Genetic engineering** is the science or activity of changing the genetic structure of an animal, plant, or other organism in order to make it stronger or more suitable for a particular purpose. ❑ *Scientists have used genetic engineering to protect tomatoes against the effects of freezing.* — N-UNCOUNT

**ge|net|ic finger|print|ing** **Genetic fingerprinting** is a method of identifying people using the genetic material in their bodies. — N-SING

**ge|neti|cist** /dʒɪnetɪsɪst/ (**geneticists**) A **geneticist** is a person who studies or specializes in genetics. — N-COUNT

**ge|net|ics** /dʒɪnetɪks/ **Genetics** is the study of heredity and how qualities and characteristics are passed on from one generation to another by means of genes. — N-UNCOUNT

**gen|ial** /dʒiːniəl/ Someone who is **genial** is kind and friendly. ❑ *Bob was always genial and welcoming... He was a warm-hearted friend and genial host.* ♦ **gen|ial|ly** *'If you don't mind,' Mrs. Dambar said genially.* ♦ **ge|ni|al|ity** /dʒiːniælɪti/ *He soon recovered his habitual geniality.* — ADJ [approval] = amiable — ADV — N-UNCOUNT

**ge|nie** /dʒiːni/ (**genies**) [1] In stories from Arabia and Persia, a **genie** is a spirit which appears and disappears by magic and obeys the person who controls it. [2] If you say that **the genie is out of the bottle** or that someone **has let the genie out of the bottle**, you mean that something has happened which has made a great and permanent change in people's lives, especially a bad change. — N-COUNT — PHRASE: V inflects

**geni|tal** /dʒenɪtᵊl/ (**genitals**) [1] Someone's **genitals** are their external sexual organs. [2] **Genital** means relating to a person's external sexual organs. ❑ *Keep the genital area clean.* — N-PLURAL — ADJ: ADJ n

**geni|ta|lia** /dʒenɪteɪliə/ A person's or animal's **genitalia** are their external sexual organs. [FORMAL] — N-PLURAL

**geni|tive** /dʒenɪtɪv/ In the grammar of some languages, **the genitive**, or **the genitive case**, is a noun case which is used mainly to show possession. In English grammar, a noun or name with 's added to it, for example 'dog's' or 'Anne's', is sometimes called **the genitive form**. — N-SING: *the* N

**ge|ni|us** /dʒiːniəs/ (**geniuses**) [1] **Genius** is very great ability or skill in a particular subject or activity. ❑ *This is the mark of her real genius as a designer... The man had genius and had made his mark in the aviation world... Its title is a stroke of genius.* [2] A **genius** is a highly talented, creative, or in- — N-UNCOUNT — N-COUNT telligent person. ❑ *Chaplin was not just a genius, he was among the most influential figures in film history.*

**geno|cid|al** /dʒenəsaɪdᵊl/ **Genocidal** means relating to genocide or carrying out genocide. ❑ *They have been accused of genocidal crimes.* ADJ: usu ADJ n

**geno|cide** /dʒenəsaɪd/ **Genocide** is the deliberate murder of a whole community or race. ❑ *They have alleged that acts of genocide and torture were carried out.* N-UNCOUNT

**ge|nome** /dʒiːnoʊm/ **(genomes)** In biology and genetics, a **genome** is the particular number and combination of certain chromosomes necessary to form the single nucleus of a living cell. [TECHNICAL] N-COUNT

**ge|nom|ic** /dʒɪnɒmɪk/ **Genomic** means relating to genomes. [TECHNICAL] ❑ *...genomic research.* ADJ: ADJ n

**ge|nom|ics** /dʒɪnɒmɪks/ **Genomics** is the study of genomes. [TECHNICAL] ❑ *...the genomics revolution.* N-SING

**gen|re** /ʒɒnrə/ **(genres)** A **genre** is a particular type of literature, painting, music, film, or other art form which people consider as a class because it has special characteristics. [FORMAL] ❑ *...his love of films and novels in the horror genre.* N-COUNT

**gent** /dʒent/ **(gents)** 1 **Gent** is an informal and old-fashioned word for **gentleman**. ❑ *Mr Blake was a gent. He knew how to behave.* N-COUNT 2 People sometimes refer to a public toilet for men as **the gents**. [BRIT, INFORMAL] N-SING-COLL: usu *the* N 3 **Gents** is used when addressing men in an informal, humorous way, especially in the expression 'ladies and gents'. [HUMOROUS, INFORMAL] ❑ *Don't be left standing, ladies and gents, while a bargain slips past your eyes.* N-VOC

**gen|teel** /dʒentiːl/ 1 A **genteel** person is respectable and well-mannered, and comes or seems to come from a high social class. ❑ *It was a place to which genteel families came in search of health and quiet. ...two maiden ladies with genteel manners and voices.* ADJ ≠common 2 A **genteel** place or area is quiet and traditional, but may also be old-fashioned and dull. ❑ *...the genteel towns of Winchester and Chichester.* ADJ: usu ADJ n

**gen|tian** /dʒenʃᵊn/ **(gentians)** A **gentian** is a small plant with a blue or purple flower shaped like a bell which grows in mountain regions. N-COUNT

**Gen|tile** /dʒentaɪl, AM -tᵊl/ **(Gentiles)** also **gentile.** A **Gentile** is a person who is not Jewish. N-COUNT ♦ **Gentile** is also an adjective. ❑ *...a flood of Jewish and Gentile German refugees.* ADJ: usu ADJ n

**gen|til|ity** /dʒentɪlɪti/ **Gentility** is the fact or appearance of belonging to a high social class. ❑ *The hotel has an air of faded gentility.* N-UNCOUNT

**gen|tle** /dʒentᵊl/ **(gentler, gentlest)** ◆◇◇ 1 Someone who is **gentle** is kind, mild, and calm. ❑ *My son was a quiet and gentle man who liked sports and enjoyed life... Michael's voice was gentle and consoling.* ADJ ♦ **gen|tly** *She smiled gently at him... 'I'm sorry to disturb you,' Webb said gently.* ADV: ADV with v ♦ **gen|tle|ness** *...the gentleness with which she treated her pregnant mother.* N-UNCOUNT 2 **Gentle** actions or movements are performed in a calm and controlled manner, with little force. ❑ *...a gentle game of tennis... His movements were gentle and deliberate.* ADJ ♦ **gen|tly** *Patrick took her gently by the arm and led her to a chair.* ADV 3 If you describe the weather, especially the wind, as **gentle**, you mean it is pleasant and calm and not harsh or violent. ❑ *The blustery winds dropped to a gentle breeze.* ADJ ♦ **gen|tly** *Light warm airs blew gently out of the south-east.* ADV: ADV with v 4 A **gentle** slope or curve is not steep or severe. ❑ *...gentle, rolling meadows.* ADJ ♦ **gen|tly** *With its gently rolling green hills it looks like Tuscany.* ADV: ADV after v, ADV adj 5 A **gentle** heat is a fairly low heat. ❑ *Cook for 30 minutes over a gentle heat.* ADJ ♦ **gen|tly** *Add the onion and cook gently for about 5 minutes.* ADV: ADV with v

**gentle|man** /dʒentᵊlmən/ **(gentlemen)** 1 A **gentleman** is a man who comes from a family of high social standing. ❑ *...this wonderful portrait of English gentleman Joseph Greenway.* ◆◇◇ N-COUNT 2 If you say that a man is a **gentleman**, you mean he is polite and educated, and can be trusted. ❑ *He was always such a gentleman.* N-COUNT 3 You can address men as **gentlemen**, or refer politely to them as **gentlemen**. ❑ *This way, please, ladies and gentlemen... It seems this gentleman was waiting for the doctor.* N-COUNT; N-VOC politeness

**gentle|man|ly** /dʒentᵊlmənli/ If you describe a man's behaviour as **gentlemanly**, you approve of him because he has good manners. ❑ *He was respected by all who knew him for his kind and gentlemanly consideration.* ADJ: usu ADJ n approval

**gentle|woman** /dʒentᵊlwʊmən/ **(gentlewomen)** A **gentlewoman** is a woman of high social standing, or a woman who is cultured, educated, and well-mannered. [OLD-FASHIONED] N-COUNT

**gen|tri|fy** /dʒentrɪfaɪ/ **(gentrifies, gentrifying, gentrified)** When a street or area **is gentrified**, it becomes a more expensive place to live because wealthy people move into the area and buy the houses where people with less money used to live. ❑ *The local neighbourhood, like so many areas of Manhattan, is gradually being gentrified.* VERB: usu passive be V-ed ♦ **gen|tri|fi|ca|tion** /dʒentrɪfɪkeɪʃᵊn/ *...the gentrification of the area.* N-UNCOUNT

**gen|try** /dʒentri/ The **gentry** are people of high social status or high birth. [mainly BRIT, OLD-FASHIONED] ❑ *Most of the country estates were built by the landed gentry during the late 19th century.* N-PLURAL

**genu|flect** /dʒenjʊflekt/ **(genuflects, genuflecting, genuflected)** 1 If you **genuflect**, you bend one or both knees and bow, especially in church, as a sign of respect. [FORMAL] ❑ *He genuflected in front of the altar.* VERB V 2 You can say that someone **is genuflecting to** something when they are giving it a great deal of attention and respect, especially if you think it does not deserve this. [mainly JOURNALISM] ❑ *They refrained from genuflecting to the laws of political economy.* VERB disapproval = bow down V *to* n Also V prep

**genu|ine** /dʒenjuɪn/ 1 **Genuine** is used to describe people and things that are exactly what they appear to be, and are not false or an imitation. ❑ *There was a risk of genuine refugees being returned to Vietnam. ...genuine leather... They're convinced the picture is genuine.* ◆◇◇ ADJ: usu ADJ n ≠fake 2 **Genuine** refers to things such as emotions that are real and not pretended. ❑ *There was genuine joy in this room... If this offer is genuine I will gladly accept it.* ADJ = sincere ♦ **genu|ine|ly** *He was genuinely surprised.* ADV ♦ **genu|ine|ness** *He needed at least three days to assess the genuineness of their intentions.* N-UNCOUNT: usu with supp 3 If you describe a person as **genuine**, you approve of them because they are honest, truthful, and sincere in the way they live and in their relationships with other people. ❑ *She is very caring and very genuine.* ADJ approval ♦ **genu|ine|ness** *I have no doubt about their genuineness.* N-UNCOUNT

**ge|nus** /dʒenəs, AM dʒiː-/ **(genera** /dʒenərə/**)** A **genus** is a class of similar things, especially a group of animals or plants that includes several closely related species. [TECHNICAL] N-COUNT

**geo-** /dʒiːoʊ-/ **Geo-** is used at the beginning of words that refer to the whole of the world or to the Earth's surface. ❑ *...geo-politics. ...the Geophysical Institute.* PREFIX

**ge|og|ra|pher** /dʒiɒgrəfəʳ/ **(geographers)** A **geographer** is a person who studies geography or is an expert in it. N-COUNT

**geo|graphi|cal** /dʒiːəgræfɪkᵊl/

> The form **geographic** /dʒiːəgræfɪk/ is also used.

**Geographical** or **geographic** means concerned with or relating to geography. ❑ *...a vast geographical area.* ADJ: usu ADJ n ♦ **geo|graphi|cal|ly** /dʒiːəgræfɪkli/ *It is geographically more diverse than any other continent.* ADV

**ge|og|ra|phy** /dʒiɒgrəfi/ 1 **Geography** is the study of the countries of the world and of such things as the land, seas, climate, towns, and population. N-UNCOUNT 2 The **geography** of a place is the way that features such as rivers, mountains, N-UNCOUNT: usu with poss towns, or streets are arranged within it. ❑ *...policemen who knew the local geography.*

**geo|logi|cal** /dʒiːəlɒdʒɪkᵊl/ **Geological** means relating to geology. ❑ *...a lengthy geological survey.* ♦ **geo|logi|cal|ly** /dʒiːəlɒdʒɪkli/ *At least 10,000 of these hectares are geologically unsuitable for housing.* ADJ: usu ADJ n / ADV

**ge|ol|ogy** /dʒiɒlədʒi/ [1] **Geology** is the study of the Earth's structure, surface, and origins. ❑ *He was visiting professor of geology at the University of Jordan.* ♦ **ge|olo|gist** **(geologists)** *Geologists have studied the way that heat flows from the earth.* N-UNCOUNT / N-COUNT
[2] The **geology** of an area is the structure of its land, together with the types of rocks and minerals that exist within it. ❑ *...an expert on the geology of southeast Asia.* N-UNCOUNT: usu with poss

**geo|met|ric** /dʒiːəmetrɪk/

> The form **geometrical** /dʒiːəmetrɪkᵊl/ is also used.

[1] **Geometric** or **geometrical** patterns or shapes consist of regular shapes or lines. ❑ *Geometric designs were popular wall decorations in the 14th century.* ♦ **geo|met|ri|cal|ly** /dʒiːəmetrɪkli/ *...a few geometrically planted trees.* ADJ: usu ADJ n / ADV
[2] **Geometric** or **geometrical** means relating to or involving the principles of geometry. ❑ *Euclid was trying to convey his idea of a geometrical point.* ADJ: usu ADJ n

**ge|om|etry** /dʒiɒmɪtri/ [1] **Geometry** is the branch of mathematics concerned with the properties and relationships of lines, angles, curves, and shapes. ❑ *...the very ordered way in which mathematics and geometry describe nature.* N-UNCOUNT
[2] The **geometry** of an object is its shape or the relationship of its parts to each other. ❑ *They have tinkered with the geometry of the car's nose.* N-UNCOUNT: usu with poss

**geo|physi|cal** /dʒiːoʊfɪzɪkᵊl/ **Geophysical** means relating to geophysics. ADJ: usu ADJ n

**geo|physi|cist** /dʒiːoʊfɪzɪsɪst/ **(geophysicists)** A **geophysicist** is someone who studies or specializes in geophysics. N-COUNT

**geo|phys|ics** /dʒiːoʊfɪzɪks/ **Geophysics** is the branch of geology that uses physics to examine the earth's structure, climate, and oceans. N-UNCOUNT

**geo|po|liti|cal** /dʒiːoʊpəlɪtɪkᵊl/ **Geopolitical** means relating to or concerned with geopolitics. ❑ *Hungary and Poland have suffered before because of their unfortunate geopolitical position on the European map.* ADJ: usu ADJ n

**geo|poli|tics** /dʒiːoʊpɒlɪtɪks/ **Geopolitics** is concerned with politics and the way that geography affects politics or relations between countries. N-UNCOUNT

**Geor|gian** /dʒɔːʳdʒᵊn/ **Georgian** means belonging to or connected with Britain in the eighteenth and early nineteenth centuries, during the reigns of King George I to King George IV. ❑ *...the restoration of his Georgian house.* ADJ

**ge|ra|nium** /dʒɪreɪniəm/ **(geraniums)** A **geranium** is a plant with red, pink, or white flowers. N-COUNT

**ger|bil** /dʒɜːʳbɪl/ **(gerbils)** A **gerbil** is a small, furry animal that is often kept as a pet. N-COUNT

**geri|at|ric** /dʒeriætrɪk/ **(geriatrics)** [1] **Geriatric** is used to describe things relating to the illnesses and medical care of old people. [MEDICAL] ❑ *There is a question mark over the future of geriatric care... The geriatric patients will be moved out.* ADJ: ADJ n
[2] **Geriatrics** is the study of the illnesses that affect old people and the medical care of old people. N-UNCOUNT
[3] If you describe someone as a **geriatric**, you are implying that they are old and that their mental or physical condition is poor. This use could cause offence. ❑ *He will complain about having to spend time with such a boring bunch of geriatrics. ...how can it be acceptable to have a load of geriatric judges deciding what should happen?* N-COUNT: oft N n [disapproval]

**germ** /dʒɜːʳm/ **(germs)** [1] A **germ** is a very small organism that causes disease. ❑ *Chlorine is widely used to kill germs. ...a germ that destroyed hundreds of millions of lives.* N-COUNT
[2] The **germ of** something such as an idea is something which developed or might develop into that thing. ❑ *The germ of an idea took root in Rosemary's mind.* N-SING: N of n
[3] → See also **wheatgerm**.

**Ger|man** /dʒɜːʳmən/ **(Germans)** [1] **German** means belonging or relating to Germany. ♦ A **German** is a person who comes from Germany. ADJ / N-COUNT
[2] **German** is the language used in Germany, Austria, and parts of Switzerland. ❑ *I heard a very angry man talking in German.* N-UNCOUNT

**ger|mane** /dʒɜːʳmeɪn/ Something that is **germane to** a situation or idea is connected with it in an important way. [FORMAL] ❑ *...the suppression of a number of documents which were very germane to the case... Fenton was a good listener, and his questions were germane.* ADJ: oft ADJ to n = relevant

**Ger|man|ic** /dʒɜːʳmænɪk/ [1] If you describe someone or something as **Germanic**, you think that their appearance or behaviour is typical of German people or things. ❑ *He asked in his Germanic English if I was enjoying France.* ADJ
[2] **Germanic** is used to describe the ancient culture and language of the peoples of northern Europe. ❑ *...the Germanic tribes of pre-Christian Europe.* ADJ

**Ger|man mea|sles** **German measles** is a disease which causes you to have a cough, a sore throat, and red spots on your skin. N-UNCOUNT = rubella

**ger|mi|nate** /dʒɜːʳmɪneɪt/ **(germinates, germinating, germinated)** [1] If a seed **germinates** or if it **is germinated**, it starts to grow. ❑ *Some seed varieties germinate fast, so check every day or so... First, the researchers germinated the seeds.* ♦ **ger|mi|na|tion** /dʒɜːʳmɪneɪʃᵊn/ *The poor germination of your seed could be because the soil was too cold.* VERB / V / V n / N-UNCOUNT: usu with supp
[2] If an idea, plan, or feeling **germinates**, it comes into existence and begins to develop. ❑ *He wrote to Eliot about a 'big book' that was germinating in his mind.* VERB / V / Also V into n

**germ war|fare** **Germ warfare** is the use of germs in a war in order to cause disease in enemy troops, or to destroy crops that they might use as food. ❑ *...an international treaty banning germ warfare.* N-UNCOUNT

**ger|on|tol|ogy** /dʒerəntɒlədʒi/ **Gerontology** is the study of the process by which we get old, how our bodies change, and the problems that old people have. N-UNCOUNT

**ger|ry|man|der|ing** /dʒerimændərɪŋ/ **Gerrymandering** is the act of altering political boundaries in order to give an unfair advantage to one political party or group of people. N-UNCOUNT [disapproval]

**ger|und** /dʒerʌnd/ **(gerunds)** A **gerund** is a noun formed from a verb which refers to an action, process, or state. In English, gerunds end in '-ing', for example 'running' and 'thinking'. N-COUNT

**ge|stalt** /gəʃtælt/ In psychology, a **gestalt** is something that has particular qualities when you consider it as a whole which are not obvious when you consider only the separate parts of it. [TECHNICAL] N-SING

**ges|ta|tion** /dʒesteɪʃᵊn/ [1] **Gestation** is the process in which babies grow inside their mother's body before they are born. [TECHNICAL] ❑ *...the seventeenth week of gestation... The gestation period can be anything between 95 and 150 days.* N-UNCOUNT
[2] **Gestation** is the process in which an idea or plan develops. [FORMAL] ❑ *...the prolonged period of gestation of this design.* N-UNCOUNT = development

**ges|ticu|late** /dʒestɪkjʊleɪt/ **(gesticulates, gesticulating, gesticulated)** If you **gesticulate**, you make movements with your arms or hands, often while you are describing something that is difficult to express in words. [mainly WRITTEN] ❑ *A man with a paper hat upon his head was gesticulating wildly... The architect was gesticulating at a hole in the ground.* ♦ **ges|ticu|la|tion** /dʒestɪkjʊleɪʃᵊn/ **(gesticulations)** *We communicated mainly by signs, gesticulation and mime.* VERB / V / V prep / N-UNCOUNT: also N in pl

**ges|ture** /dʒestʃəʳ/ **(gestures, gesturing, gestured)** ◆◇◇ 1 N-COUNT A **gesture** is a movement that you make with a part of your body, especially your hands, to express emotion or information. ❑ *Sarah made a menacing gesture with her fist... He throws his hands open in a gesture which clearly indicates his relief.* 2 N-COUNT: oft N *of* n A **gesture** is something that you say or do in order to express your attitude or intentions, often something that you know will not have much effect. ❑ *He questioned the government's commitment to peace and called on it to make a gesture of good will.* 3 VERB If you **gesture**, you use movements of your hands or head in order to tell someone something or draw their attention to something. ❑ *I gestured towards the boathouse, and he looked inside... He gestures, gesticulates, and moves with the grace of a dancer.* V prep, V

**get**
① CHANGING, CAUSING, MOVING, OR REACHING
② OBTAINING, RECEIVING, OR CATCHING
③ PHRASES AND PHRASAL VERBS

① **get** /get/ **(gets, getting, got** or **gotten)** ◆◆◆

✔ In most of its uses **get** is a fairly informal word. **Gotten** is an American form of the past tense and past participle.

1 V-LINK You use **get** with adjectives to mean 'become'. For example, if someone **gets cold**, they become cold, and if they **get angry**, they become angry. ❑ *The boys were getting bored... There's no point in getting upset... From here on, it can only get better.* V adj, V adj, V adj 2 V-LINK **Get** is used with expressions referring to states or situations. For example, to **get into trouble** means to start being in trouble. ❑ *Half the pleasure of an evening out is getting ready... Perhaps I shouldn't say that – I might get into trouble... How did we get into this recession, and what can we do to get out of it?* V adj, V prep/adv, V prep/adv 3 VERB To **get** someone or something into a particular state or situation means to cause them to be in it. ❑ *I don't know if I can get it clean... What got me interested was looking at an old New York Times... Brian will get them out of trouble.* V n adj, V n adj, V n prep 4 VERB = persuade If you **get** someone **to** do something, you cause them to do it by asking, persuading, or telling them to do it. ❑ *...a long campaign to get US politicians to take the Aids epidemic more seriously... How did you get him to pose for this picture?* V n to-inf, V n to-inf 5 VERB If you **get** something done, you cause it to be done. ❑ *I might benefit from getting my teeth fixed... It was best to get things done quickly.* V n -ed, V n -ed 6 VERB To **get** somewhere means to move there. ❑ *I got off the bed and opened the door... I heard David yelling and telling them to get back.* V prep/adv, V prep/adv 7 VERB When you **get** to a place, you arrive there. ❑ *Generally I get to work at 9.30am... It was dark by the time she got home.* V to n, V adv 8 VERB To **get** something or someone into a place or position means to cause them to move there. ❑ *Mack got his wallet out... The UN was supposed to be getting aid to where it was most needed.* V n with adv, V n prep 9 AUX **Get** is often used in place of 'be' as an auxiliary verb to form passives. ❑ *Does she ever get asked for her autograph?... A pane of glass got broken.* AUX -ed, AUX -ed 10 VERB If you **get to** do something, you eventually or gradually reach a stage at which you do it. ❑ *No one could figure out how he got to be so wealthy.* V to-inf 11 VERB If you **get to** do something, you manage to do it or have the opportunity to do it. ❑ *Do you get to see him often?... They get to stay in nice hotels.* V to-inf, V to-inf 12 VERB You can use **get** in expressions like **get moving**, **get going**, and **get working** when you want to tell people to begin moving, going, or working quickly. ❑ *I aim to be off the lake before dawn, so let's get moving.* V -ing 13 VERB If you **get to** a particular stage in your life or in something you are doing, you reach that stage. ❑ *We haven't got to the stage of a full-scale military conflict... If she gets that far, Jane may get legal aid to take her case to court... It got to the point where I was so ill I was waiting to die.* V to n, V adv, *it* V *to* n 14 VERB You can use **get** to talk about the progress that you are making. For example, if you say that you **are getting somewhere**, you mean that you are making progress, and if you say that something **won't get** you **anywhere**, you mean it will not help you to progress at all. ❑ *Radical factions say the talks are getting nowhere and they want to withdraw... My perseverance was getting me somewhere.* V adv, V n adv 15 V-LINK When **it gets to** a particular time, it is that time. If **it is getting towards** a particular time, it is approaching that time. ❑ *It got to after 1am and I was exhausted... It was getting towards evening when we got back... It's getting late.* *it* V *to* n, *it* V *towards* n, *it* V adj 16 VERB If something that has continued for some time **gets to** you, it starts causing you to suffer. ❑ *That's the first time I lost my cool in 20 years in this job. This whole thing's getting to me.* V *to* n 17 VERB: no passive If something **gets** you, it annoys you. [INFORMAL] ❑ *What gets me is the attitude of so many of the people.* V n

② **get** /get/ **(gets, getting, got** or **gotten)** ◆◆◆ 1 VERB If you **get** something that you want or need, you obtain it. ❑ *I got a job at the sawmill... He had been having trouble getting a hotel room... I asked him to get me some information.* V n, V n n, Also V n *for* n 2 VERB If you **get** something, you receive it or are given it. ❑ *I'm getting a bike for my birthday... He gets a lot of letters from women.* V n, V n 3 VERB If you **get** someone or something, you go and bring them to a particular place. ❑ *I came down this morning to get the newspaper... Go and get me a large brandy... Go and get your daddy for me.* V n, V n n, V n *for* n 4 VERB If you **get** a meal, you prepare it. ❑ *She was getting breakfast as usual.* V n 5 VERB If you **get** a particular result, you obtain it from some action that you take, or from a calculation or experiment. ❑ *You could run that race again and get a different result each time... What do you get if you multiply six by nine?* V n, V n 6 VERB If you **get** a particular price **for** something that you sell, you obtain that amount of money by selling it. ❑ *He can't get a good price for his crops.* V n *for* n 7 VERB If you **get** the time or opportunity to do something, you have the time or opportunity to do it. ❑ *You get time to think in prison... Whenever I get the chance I go to Maxim's for dinner.* V n, V n 8 VERB If you **get** an idea, impression, or feeling, you begin to have that idea, impression, or feeling as you learn or understand more about something. ❑ *I get the feeling that you're an honest man... The study is an attempt to get a better idea of why people live where they do.* V n, V n 9 VERB If you **get** a feeling or benefit from an activity or experience, the activity or experience gives you that feeling or benefit. ❑ *Charles got a shock when he saw him... She gets enormous pleasure out of working freelance.* V n, V n *out of/from* n/-ing 10 VERB = obtain If you **get** a look, view, or glimpse of something, you manage to see it. ❑ *Young men climbed on buses and fences to get a better view... Crowds shouted and pushed to get a glimpse of their hero.* V n, V n 11 VERB If a place **gets** a particular type of weather, it has that type of weather. ❑ *Riyadh got 25 mm of rain in just 12 hours... Northern Kentucky is likely to get snow mixed with sleet.* V n, V n 12 VERB If you **get** a joke or **get** the point of something that is said, you understand it. ❑ *Did you get that joke, Ann? I'll explain later... You don't seem to get the point.* V n, V n 13 VERB If you **get** an illness or disease, you become ill with it. ❑ *When I was five I got measles.* V n 14 VERB When you **get** a train, bus, plane, or boat, you leave a place on a particular train, bus, plane, or boat. ❑ *What time are you getting your train?* V n 15 VERB If you **get** a person or animal, you succeed in catching, killing, or hitting them. ❑ *Take it easy. We've got him. He's not going to kill anyone else.* V n 16 → See also **getting**, **got**.

③ **get** /get/ **(gets, getting, got** or **gotten)** ◆◆◆ 1 PHRASE: v-link PHR, PHR after v You can say that something is, for example, **as good as you can get** to mean that it is as good as it is possible for that thing to be. ❑ *Consort has a population of 714 and is about as rural and isolated as you can get.* 2 PHRASE: PHR n emphasis If you say **you can't get away from** something or **there is no getting away from** something, you are emphasizing that it is true, even though people might prefer it not to be true. [INFORMAL] ❑ *There is no getting away from the* *fact that he is on the left of the party.* [3] If you **get away from it all**, you have a holiday in a place that is very different from where you normally live and work. [PHRASE: V inflects] ❑ *...the ravishing island of Ischia, where rich Italians get away from it all.* [4] **Get** is used in rude expressions like **get stuffed** and **get lost** to express contempt, disagreement, or refusal to do something. [RUDE] [CONVENTION] [feelings] [5] You can say, for example, '**How lucky can you get?**' or '**How stupid can you get?**' to show your surprise that anyone could be as lucky or stupid as the person that you are talking about. [INFORMAL] [PHRASE] [feelings] ❑ *I mean, how crazy can you get?* [6] You can use **you get** instead of 'there is' or 'there are' to say that something exists, happens, or can be experienced. [SPOKEN] [PHRASE: PHR n] ❑ *You get a lot of things like that now don't you... That's where you get some differences of opinion.*

♦ **get about** [1] If you **get about**, you go to different places and visit different people. [PHRASAL VERB] ❑ *So you're getting about a bit again? Not shutting yourself away?* [V P] [2] The way that someone **gets about** is the way that they walk or go from one place to another. [PHRASAL VERB] ❑ *She was finding it increasingly difficult to get about.* [V P] [3] If news **gets about**, it becomes well known as a result of being told to lots of people. [mainly BRIT] [PHRASAL VERB = get around] ❑ *The story had soon got about that he had been suspended.* [V P]

♦ **get across** When an idea **gets across** or when you **get** it **across**, you succeed in making other people understand it. [PHRASAL VERB = get over] ❑ *Officers felt their point of view was not getting across to ministers...* [V P *to* n] *I had created a way to get my message across while using as few words as possible.* [V n P]

♦ **get ahead** If you want to **get ahead**, you want to be successful in your career. [PHRASAL VERB = get on] ❑ *He wanted safety, security, a home, and a chance to get ahead.* [V P]

♦ **get along** [1] If you **get along with** someone, you have a friendly relationship with them. You can also say that two people **get along**. [PHRASAL VERB = get on] ❑ *It's impossible to get along with him...* [V P *with* n] *They seemed to be getting along fine.* [pl-n V P] [2] **Get along** means the same as **get by**. [PHRASAL VERB = manage, survive] ❑ *You can't get along without water.* [V P prep]

♦ **get around**

> ☑ in BRIT, also use **get round**

[1] To **get around** a problem or difficulty means to overcome it. [PHRASAL VERB = get over] ❑ *None of these countries has found a way yet to get around the problem of the polarization of wealth.* [V P n] [2] If you **get around** a rule or law, you find a way of doing something that the rule or law is intended to prevent, without actually breaking it. [PHRASAL VERB] ❑ *Although tobacco ads are prohibited, companies get around the ban by sponsoring music shows.* [V P n] [3] If news **gets around**, it becomes well known as a result of being told to lots of people. [PHRASAL VERB = get about] ❑ *They threw him out because word got around that he was taking drugs...* [V P that] *I'll see that it gets round that you've arrived.* [it V P that] [4] If you **get around** someone, you persuade them to allow you to do or have something by pleasing them or flattering them. [PHRASAL VERB] ❑ *Max could always get round her.* [V P n] [5] If you **get around**, you visit a lot of different places as part of your way of life. [PHRASAL VERB] ❑ *He claimed to be a journalist, and he got around.* [V P]

♦ **get around to**

> ☑ in BRIT, also use **get round to**

When you **get around to** doing something that you have delayed doing or have been too busy to do, you finally do it. [PHRASAL VERB] ❑ *I said I would write to you, but as usual I never got around to it.* [V P P n/-ing]

♦ **get at** [1] To **get at** something means to succeed in reaching it. [PHRASAL VERB] ❑ *A goat was standing up against a tree on its hind legs, trying to get at the leaves.* [V P n] [2] If you **get at** the truth about something, you succeed in discovering it. [PHRASAL VERB = find out] ❑ *We want to get at the truth. Who killed him? And why?* [V P n] [3] If you ask someone what they **are getting at**, you are asking them to explain what they mean, usually because you think that they are being unpleasant or are suggesting something that is untrue. [PHRASAL VERB: usu cont] ❑ *'What are you getting at now?' demanded Rick.* [V P]

♦ **get away** [1] If you **get away**, you succeed in leaving a place or a person's company. [PHRASAL VERB = escape] ❑ *She'd gladly have gone anywhere to get away from the cottage...* [V P *from* n] *I wanted a divorce. I wanted to get away.* [V P] [2] If you **get away**, you go away for a period of time in order to have a holiday. [PHRASAL VERB] ❑ *He is too busy to get away.* [V P] [3] When someone or something **gets away**, or when you **get** them **away**, they escape. [PHRASAL VERB] ❑ *Dr Dunn was apparently trying to get away when he was shot...* [V P] *I wanted to get her away to somewhere safe.* [V n P]

♦ **get away with** If you **get away with** doing something wrong or risky, you do not suffer any punishment or other bad consequences because of it. [PHRASAL VERB] ❑ *The criminals know how to play the system and get away with it.* [V P P n/-ing]

♦ **get back** [1] If someone or something **gets back to** a state they were in before, they are then in that state again. [PHRASAL VERB] ❑ *Then life started to get back to normal...* [V P *to/into* n] *I couldn't get back to sleep.* [2] If you **get back to** a subject that you were talking about before, you start talking about it again. [PHRASAL VERB = return] ❑ *It wasn't until we had sat down to eat that we got back to the subject of Tom Halliday.* [V P *to/onto* n] [3] If you **get** something **back** after you have lost it or after it has been taken from you, you then have it again. [PHRASAL VERB] ❑ *You have 14 days in which you can cancel the contract and get your money back.* [V n P] [4] If you **get back at** someone or **get** them **back**, you do something unpleasant to them in order to have revenge for something unpleasant that they did to you. [INFORMAL] [PHRASAL VERB] ❑ *The divorce process should not be used as a means to get back at your former partner...* [V P *at* n] *I'm going to get you back so badly you'll never to be able to show your face again.* [V n P]

♦ **get back to** If you **get back to** an activity, you start doing it again after you have stopped doing it. [PHRASAL VERB] ❑ *I think I ought to get back to work.* [V P P n]

♦ **get by** If you can **get by** with what you have, you can manage to live or do things in a satisfactory way. [PHRASAL VERB = survive, manage] ❑ *I'm a survivor. I'll get by...* [V P] *Melville managed to get by on a small amount of money.* [V P *on* n]

♦ **get down** [1] If something **gets** you **down**, it makes you unhappy. [PHRASAL VERB] ❑ *At times when my work gets me down, I like to fantasize about being a farmer.* [V n P] [2] If you **get down**, you lower your body until you are sitting, kneeling, or lying on the ground. [PHRASAL VERB] ❑ *She got down on her hands and knees on the floor...* [V P *on* n] *'Get down!' she yelled. 'Somebody's shooting!'* [V P] [3] If you **get** something **down**, especially something that someone has just said, you write it down. [PHRASAL VERB] ❑ *The idea has been going around in my head for quite a while and now I am getting it down on paper.* [V n P] [Also V P n (not pron)] [4] If you **get** food or medicine **down**, you swallow it, especially with difficulty. [INFORMAL] [PHRASAL VERB] ❑ *I bit into a hefty slab of bread and cheese. When I had got it down I started talking.* [V n P] [Also V P n (not pron)]

♦ **get down to** If you **get down to** something, especially something that requires a lot of attention, you begin doing it. [PHRASAL VERB] ❑ *With the election out of the way, the government can get down to business.* [V P P n]

♦ **get in** [1] If a political party or a politician **gets in**, they are elected. [PHRASAL VERB] ❑ *If the Conservatives got in they might decide to change it.* [V P] [2] If you **get** something **in**, you manage to do it at a time when you are very busy doing other things. [PHRASAL VERB] ❑ *I plan to get a few lessons in.* [V n P] [3] To **get** crops or the harvest **in** means to gather them from the land and take them to a particular place. [PHRASAL VERB] ❑ *We didn't get the harvest in until Christmas, there was so much snow.* [V n P] [4] When a train, bus, or plane **gets in**, it arrives. [PHRASAL VERB] ❑ *We would have come straight here, except our flight got in too late.* [V P]

♦ **get into** [1] If you **get into** a particular kind of work or activity, you manage to become involved in it. [PHRASAL VERB] ❑ *He was eager to get into politics.* [V P n] [2] If you **get into** a school, college, or university, [PHRASAL VERB] you are accepted there as a student. ❑ *I was working hard to get into Cambridge.* [V P n] [3] If you ask what has **got into** someone, you mean that they are behaving very differently from the way they usually behave. [INFORMAL] ❑ *What has got into you today? Why are you behaving like this?* [PHRASAL VERB] [V P n]

♦ **get off** [1] If someone who has broken a law or rule **gets off**, they are not punished, or are given only a very small punishment. ❑ *He is likely to get off with a small fine.* [PHRASAL VERB] [V P with n] [2] If you **get off**, you leave a place because it is time to leave. ❑ *At eight I said 'I'm getting off now.'* [PHRASAL VERB] [V P] [3] If you tell someone to **get off** a piece of land or a property, you are telling them to leave, because they have no right to be there and you do not want them there. ❑ *I told you. Get off the farm.* [PHRASAL VERB] [V P n] [4] You can tell someone to **get off** when they are touching something and you do not want them to. ❑ *I kept telling him to get off... 'Get off me!' I screamed.* [PHRASAL VERB] [V P] [V P n]

♦ **get on** [1] If you **get on with** someone, you like them and have a friendly relationship with them. ❑ *The host fears the guests won't get on... What are your neighbours like? Do you get on with them?* [PHRASAL VERB = get along] [pl-n V P] [V P with n] [2] If you **get on with** something, you continue doing it or start doing it. ❑ *Jane got on with her work... Let's get on.* [PHRASAL VERB] [V P with n] [V P] [3] If you say how someone **is getting on**, you are saying how much success they are having with what they are trying to do. ❑ *Livy's getting on very well in Russian. She learns very quickly... When he came back to see me I asked how he had got on.* [PHRASAL VERB] [V P adv] [V P adv] [4] If you try to **get on**, you try to be successful in your career. [mainly BRIT] ❑ *Politics is seen as a man's world. It is very difficult for women to get on.* [PHRASAL VERB] [V P] [5] If someone **is getting on**, they are getting old. [INFORMAL] ❑ *I'm nearly 31 and that's getting on a bit for a footballer.* [PHRASAL VERB: usu cont] [V P]

♦ **get on to** [1] If you **get on to** a topic when you are speaking, you start talking about it. ❑ *We got on to the subject of relationships.* [PHRASAL VERB] [V P P n] [2] If you **get on to** someone, you contact them in order to ask them to do something or to give them some information. [mainly BRIT] ❑ *I got on to him and explained some of the things I had been thinking of.* [PHRASAL VERB] [V P P n]

♦ **get out** [1] If you **get out**, you leave a place because you want to escape from it, or because you are made to leave it. ❑ *They probably wanted to get out of the country... I told him to leave and get out.* [PHRASAL VERB] [V P of n] [V P] [2] If you **get out**, you go to places and meet people, usually in order to have a more enjoyable life. ❑ *Get out and enjoy yourself, make new friends.* [PHRASAL VERB = go out] [V P] [3] If you **get out of** an organization or a commitment, you withdraw from it. ❑ *I wanted to get out of the group, but they wouldn't let me... Getting out of the contract would be no problem.* [PHRASAL VERB] [V P of n] [V P of n] [Also V P] [4] If news or information **gets out**, it becomes known. ❑ *If word got out now, a scandal could be disastrous... Once the news gets out that Armenia is in a very critical situation, I think the world will respond.* [PHRASAL VERB] [V P] [V P that]

♦ **get out of** If you **get out of** doing something that you do not want to do, you succeed in avoiding doing it. ❑ *It's amazing what people will do to get out of paying taxes.* [PHRASAL VERB] [V P P -ing/n]

♦ **get over** [1] If you **get over** an unpleasant or unhappy experience or an illness, you recover from it. ❑ *It took me a very long time to get over the shock of her death.* [PHRASAL VERB] [V P n] [2] If you **get over** a problem or difficulty, you overcome it. ❑ *How would they get over that problem, he wondered?* [PHRASAL VERB = get around] [V P n] [3] If you **get** your message **over to** people, they hear and understand it. ❑ *We have got to get the message over to the young that smoking isn't cool.* [PHRASAL VERB = get across] [V n P to n]

♦ **get over with** If you want to **get** something unpleasant **over with**, you want to do it or finish experiencing it quickly, since you cannot avoid it. ❑ *The sooner we start, the sooner we'll get it over with.* [PHRASAL VERB] [V n P P]

♦ **get round** → see **get around**.

♦ **get round to** → see **get around to**.

♦ **get through** [1] If you **get through** a task or an amount of work, especially when it is difficult, you complete it. ❑ *I think you can get through the first two chapters.* [PHRASAL VERB] [V P n] [2] If you **get through** a difficult or unpleasant period of time, you manage to live through it. ❑ *It is hard to see how people will get through the winter.* [PHRASAL VERB = survive] [V P n] [3] If you **get through** a large amount of something, you use it. [mainly BRIT] ❑ *You'll get through at least ten nappies a day.* [PHRASAL VERB] [V P n] [4] If you **get through to** someone, you succeed in making them understand something that you are trying to tell them. ❑ *An old friend might well be able to get through to her and help her... The message was finally getting through to him.* [PHRASAL VERB] [V P to n] [V P to n] [Also V P] [5] If you **get through to** someone, you succeed in contacting them on the telephone. ❑ *Look, I can't get through to this number... I've been trying to ring up all day and I couldn't get through.* [PHRASAL VERB] [V P to n] [V P] [6] If you **get through** an examination or **get through**, you pass it. [mainly BRIT] ❑ *Did you have to get through an entrance examination?* [PHRASAL VERB] [V P n] [Also V P] [7] If a law or proposal **gets through**, it is officially approved by something such as a parliament or committee. ❑ *...if his referendum law failed to get through... Such a radical proposal would never get through parliament.* [PHRASAL VERB = go through] [V P] [V P n]

♦ **get together** [1] When people **get together**, they meet in order to discuss something or to spend time together. ❑ *This is the only forum where East and West can get together.* → See also **get-together**. [PHRASAL VERB] [V P] [2] If you **get** something **together**, you organize it. ❑ *Paul and I were getting a band together, and we needed a new record deal.* [PHRASAL VERB] [V n P] [3] If you **get** an amount of money **together**, you succeed in getting all the money that you need in order to pay for something. ❑ *Now you've finally got enough money together to put down a deposit on your dream home.* [PHRASAL VERB = scrape together] [V n P]

♦ **get up** [1] When someone who is sitting or lying down **gets up**, they rise to a standing position. ❑ *I got up and walked over to where he was.* [PHRASAL VERB = stand up] [V P] [2] When you **get up**, you get out of bed. ❑ *They have to get up early in the morning.* [PHRASAL VERB] [V P] [3] → See also **get-up**.

♦ **get up to** If you say that someone **gets up to** something, you mean that they do it and you do not approve of it. [BRIT, mainly SPOKEN] ❑ *They get up to all sorts behind your back.* [PHRASAL VERB] [disapproval] [V P P n]

**get|away** /getəweɪ/ **(getaways)** also **get-away.** [1] If someone makes a **getaway**, they leave a place quickly, especially after committing a crime or when trying to avoid someone. ❑ *They made their getaway along a pavement on a stolen motorcycle. ...the burglar's getaway car.* [N-COUNT: usu sing, oft N n] [2] A **getaway** is a short holiday somewhere. [INFORMAL] ❑ *Weekend tours are ideal for families who want a short getaway.* [N-COUNT = break]

**get|ting** /getɪŋ/ [1] **Getting** is the present participle of **get**. [2] **Getting on for** means the same as **nearly**. [BRIT, mainly SPOKEN] ❑ *I've been trying to give up smoking for getting on for two years now... It was getting on for two o'clock.* [PREP-PHRASE]

**get-together** **(get-togethers)** A **get-together** is an informal meeting or party, usually arranged for a particular purpose. ❑ *...a get-together I had at my home.* [N-COUNT]

**get-up** **(get-ups)** If you refer to a set of clothes as a **get-up**, you think that they are unusual or ridiculous. [INFORMAL] ❑ *Naturally he couldn't work in this get-up.* [N-COUNT] [disapproval]

**gey|ser** /giːzəʳ, AM gaɪzəʳ/ **(geysers)** A **geyser** is a hole in the Earth's surface from which hot water and steam are forced out, usually at irregular intervals of time. [N-COUNT]

**Gha|na|ian** /gɑːneɪən/ **(Ghanaians)** Something that is **Ghanaian** belongs or relates to Ghana or to its people. ♦ **Ghanaians** are people who are Ghanaian. [ADJ] [N-COUNT]

**ghast|ly** /gɑːstli, gæstli/ If you describe someone or something as **ghastly**, you mean that you find them very unpleasant. [INFORMAL] ❑ *...a* [ADJ = awful] *mother accompanied by her ghastly unruly child... It was the worst week of my life. It was ghastly.*

**ghee** /giː/ **Ghee** is a hard fat that is obtained by heating butter made from the milk of a cow or a buffalo. Ghee is used in Indian cooking. N-UNCOUNT

**gher|kin** /gɜːʳkɪn/ **(gherkins) Gherkins** are small green cucumbers that have been preserved in vinegar. N-COUNT

**ghet|to** /getoʊ/ **(ghettos** or **ghettoes)** A **ghetto** is a part of a city in which many poor people or many people of a particular race, religion, or nationality live separately from everyone else. ❑ *...the black ghettos of New York and Los Angeles.* N-COUNT

**ghet|to blast|er (ghetto blasters)** also **ghetto-blaster.** A **ghetto blaster** is a large portable radio and cassette player with built-in speakers, especially one that is played loudly in public by young people. [mainly BRIT, INFORMAL] N-COUNT

☑ in AM, use **boom box**

**ghost** /goʊst/ **(ghosts, ghosting, ghosted)** [1] A **ghost** is the spirit of a dead person that someone believes they can see or feel. ❑ *...the ghost of Marie Antoinette... The village is haunted by the ghosts of the dead children.* N-COUNT: oft N *of* n [2] The **ghost of** something, especially of something bad that has happened, is the memory of it. ❑ *...the ghost of anti-Americanism.* N-COUNT: N *of* n [3] If there is a **ghost of** something, that thing is so faint or weak that it hardly exists. ❑ *He gave the ghost of a smile... The sun was warm and there was just a ghost of a breeze from the north-west.* N-SING: N *of* n [4] If a book or other piece of writing **is ghosted**, it is written by a writer for another person, for example a politician or sportsman, who then publishes it as his or her own work. ❑ *I published his autobiography, which was very competently ghosted by a woman journalist from the Daily Mail... I ghosted his weekly rugby column for the Telegraph.* VERB = ghost-write; *be* V-ed; V n [5] If someone **does not stand** or **does not have a ghost of a chance** of doing something, they have very little chance of succeeding in it. [INFORMAL] ❑ *He doesn't stand a ghost of a chance of selling the house.* PHRASE: v PHR, with neg

**ghost|ly** /goʊstli/ [1] Something that is **ghostly** seems unreal or unnatural and may be frightening because of this. ❑ *The moon shone, shedding a ghostly light on the fields. ...Sonia's ghostly laughter.* ADJ: usu ADJ n [2] A **ghostly** presence is the ghost or spirit of a dead person. ❑ *...the ghostly presences which haunt these islands.* ADJ: ADJ n

**ghost sto|ry (ghost stories)** A **ghost story** is a story about ghosts. N-COUNT

**ghost town (ghost towns)** A **ghost town** is a town which used to be busy and wealthy but is now poor and deserted. ❑ *Mogadishu is said to be a virtual ghost town, deserted by two-thirds of its residents.* N-COUNT

**ghost-write (ghost-writes, ghost-writing, ghost-wrote, ghost-written)** also **ghostwrite.** If a book or other piece of writing **is ghost-written**, it is written by a writer for another person, for example a politician or sportsman, who then publishes it as his or her own work. ❑ *Articles were ghost-written by company employees.* VERB: usu passive = ghost; *be* V-ed

**ghost writ|er (ghost writers)** also **ghostwriter.** A **ghost writer** is someone who writes a book or other published work instead of the person who is named as the author. N-COUNT

**ghoul** /guːl/ **(ghouls)** A **ghoul** is an imaginary evil spirit. **Ghouls** are said to steal bodies from graves and eat them. N-COUNT

**ghoul|ish** /guːlɪʃ/ [1] **Ghoulish** people and things show an unnatural interest in things such as human suffering, death, or dead bodies. ❑ *They are there only to satisfy their ghoulish curiosity.* ADJ: usu ADJ n [disapproval] [2] Something that is **ghoulish** looks or behaves like a ghoul. ❑ *...the ghoulish apparitions at the window.* ADJ: usu ADJ n

**GHQ** /dʒiː eɪtʃ kjuː/ **GHQ** is used to refer to the place where the people who organize military forces or a military operation work. **GHQ** is an abbreviation for 'General Headquarters'. [MILITARY] ❑ *...the dispatches he was carrying from GHQ to the Eighth Army.* N-UNCOUNT

**GI** /dʒiː aɪ/ **(GIs)** A **GI** is a soldier in the United States army. N-COUNT

**gi|ant** /dʒaɪənt/ **(giants)** [1] Something that is described as **giant** is much larger or more important than most others of its kind. ❑ *...Italy's giant car maker, Fiat. ...a giant oak table. ...a giant step towards unification with the introduction of monetary union.* ◆◇◇ ADJ: ADJ n = huge [2] **Giant** is often used to refer to any large, successful business organization or country. [JOURNALISM] ❑ *...Japanese electronics giant Sony. ...one of Germany's industrial giants, Daimler-Benz.* N-COUNT: usu n N [3] A **giant** is an imaginary person who is very big and strong, especially one mentioned in old stories. ❑ *...a Nordic saga of giants.* N-COUNT [4] You can refer to someone, especially a man, as a **giant**, if they seem important or powerful or if they are big and strong. ❑ *The biggest man in the patrol, a giant of a man, lifted Mattie on to his shoulders.* N-COUNT: usu *a* N *of* n [5] You can refer to someone such as a famous musician or writer as a **giant**, if they are regarded as one of the most important or successful people in their field. ❑ *He was without question one of the giants of Japanese literature.* N-COUNT: usu N *of* n; N-COUNT

**giant-killer (giant-killers)** also **giant killer.** A **giant-killer** is a sportsman, sportswoman, or team that unexpectedly beats a much stronger opponent. [mainly BRIT, JOURNALISM] ❑ *Giant-killers Yeovil became the most successful non-league club in history with their 5-2 win at Torquay.* N-COUNT

**giant-killing (giant-killings)** In sport, when a weaker team or competitor beats a much stronger, well-known team or competitor, their success is sometimes called a **giant-killing**. [mainly BRIT, JOURNALISM] ❑ *Scarborough are aiming to pull off a repeat of their giant-killing act against Chelsea three years ago.* N-COUNT: usu N n

**giant-sized** An object that is **giant-sized** is much bigger than objects of its kind usually are. ❑ *...a giant-sized TV.* ADJ: usu ADJ n

**gib|ber** /dʒɪbəʳ/ **(gibbers, gibbering, gibbered)** If you say that someone **is gibbering**, you mean that they are talking very fast and in a confused manner. [INFORMAL] ❑ *Everyone is gibbering insanely, nerves frayed as showtime approaches... I was a gibbering wreck by this stage.* VERB = babble; V; V-ing

**gib|ber|ish** /dʒɪbərɪʃ/ If you describe someone's words or ideas as **gibberish**, you mean that they do not make any sense. ❑ *When he was talking to a girl he could hardly speak, and when he did speak he talked gibberish.* N-UNCOUNT = nonsense

**gib|bet** /dʒɪbɪt/ **(gibbets)** A **gibbet** is a **gallows.** [OLD-FASHIONED] N-COUNT

**gib|bon** /gɪbən/ **(gibbons)** A **gibbon** is an ape with very long arms and no tail that lives in southern Asia. N-COUNT

**gibe** /dʒaɪb/ → see **jibe**.

**gib|lets** /dʒɪblɪts/ **Giblets** are the parts such as the heart and liver that you remove from inside a chicken or other bird before you cook and eat it. Some people cook the giblets separately to make soup or a sauce. N-PLURAL

**gid|dy** /gɪdi/ **(giddier, giddiest)** [1] If you feel **giddy**, you feel unsteady and think that you are about to fall over, usually because you are not well. ❑ *He felt giddy and light-headed.* ADJ = dizzy ♦ **gid|di|ness** *A wave of giddiness swept over her.* N-UNCOUNT [2] If you feel **giddy with** delight or excitement, you feel so happy or excited that you find it hard to think or act normally. ❑ *Anthony was giddy with self-satisfaction... Being there gave me a giddy pleasure.* ADJ ♦ **gid|di|ness** *There's almost a giddiness surrounding the talks in Houston.* N-UNCOUNT

**gift** /gɪft/ **(gifts)** [1] A **gift** is something that you give someone as a present. ❑ *...a gift of $50.00... They believed the unborn child was a gift from God. ...gift shops.* ◆◇◇ N-COUNT [2] If someone has a **gift for** doing something, they have a natural ability N-COUNT: oft N *for/of* -ing/n for doing it. ❑ *As a youth he discovered a gift for teaching... Her grandmother had the gift of making people happy.*

**gift|ed** /gɪftɪd/ [1] Someone who is **gifted** has a natural ability to do something well. ❑ *...one of the most gifted players in the world... He was witty, amusing and gifted with a sharp business brain.* ADJ [2] A **gifted** child is much more intelligent or talented than average. ❑ *...a state program for gifted children.* ADJ

**gift-wrapped** A **gift-wrapped** present is wrapped in pretty paper. ADJ: usu ADJ n

**gig** /gɪg/ **(gigs, gigging, gigged)** [1] A **gig** is a live performance by someone such as a musician or a comedian. [INFORMAL] ❑ *The two bands join forces for a gig at the Sheffield Arena on November 28... He supplemented his income with occasional comedy gigs.* N-COUNT = show [2] When musicians or other performers **gig**, they perform live in public. [INFORMAL] ❑ *By the time he was 15, Scott had gigged with a handful of well-known small bands.* VERB V

**gi|ga|byte** /gɪgəbaɪt/ **(gigabytes)** In computing, a **gigabyte** is one thousand and twenty-four megabytes. N-COUNT

**gi|gan|tic** /dʒaɪgæntɪk/ If you describe something as **gigantic**, you are emphasizing that it is extremely large in size, amount, or degree. ❑ *...gigantic rocks... A gigantic task of national reconstruction awaits us.* ADJ [emphasis] = colossal

**gig|gle** /gɪgəl/ **(giggles, giggling, giggled)** [1] If someone **giggles**, they laugh in a childlike way, because they are amused, nervous, or embarrassed. ❑ *Both of the girls began to giggle... 'I beg your pardon?' she giggled. ...a giggling little girl.* VERB V V with quote V-ing ♦ **Giggle** is also a noun. ❑ *She gave a little giggle.* N-COUNT [2] If you say that someone has **the giggles**, you mean they cannot stop giggling. ❑ *I was so nervous I got the giggles... She had a fit of the giggles.* N-PLURAL: the N [3] If you say that something is **a giggle**, you mean it is fun or is amusing. [mainly BRIT, INFORMAL] ❑ *I might buy one for a friend's birthday as a giggle.* N-SING: a N

**gig|gly** /gɪgəli/ Someone who is **giggly** keeps laughing in a childlike way, because they are amused, nervous, or drunk. ❑ *Ray was very giggly and joking all the time. ...giggly girls.* ADJ

**gigo|lo** /dʒɪgəloʊ/ **(gigolos)** A **gigolo** is a man who is paid to be the lover of a rich and usually older woman. N-COUNT: usu sing [disapproval]

**gild** /gɪld/ **(gilds, gilding, gilded)** If you **gild** a surface, you cover it in a thin layer of gold or gold paint. ❑ *Carve the names and gild them. ...gilded statues.* VERB V n V-ed

**gild|ing** /gɪldɪŋ/ **Gilding** is a layer of gold or gold paint that is put on something. N-UNCOUNT

**gill** /gɪl/ **(gills) Gills** are the organs on the sides of fish and other water creatures through which they breathe. N-COUNT: usu pl

**gilt** /gɪlt/ **(gilts)** [1] A **gilt** object is covered with a thin layer of gold or gold paint. ❑ *...marble columns and gilt spires.* ADJ: usu ADJ n [2] **Gilts** are gilt-edged stocks or securities. [BRIT, BUSINESS] N-COUNT

**gilt-edged Gilt-edged** stocks or securities are issued by the government for people to invest in for a fixed period of time at a fixed rate of interest. [BRIT, BUSINESS] ADJ: ADJ n

**gim|let** /gɪmlɪt/ If you say that someone has **gimlet** eyes, you mean that they look at people or things very carefully, and seem to notice every detail. [WRITTEN] ❑ *'Have you read the whole book?' she asks, gimlet-eyed.* ADJ: ADJ n

**gim|me** /gɪmi/ **Gimme** is sometimes used in written English to represent the words 'give me' when they are pronounced informally. ❑ *'Gimme a break, kid! You know how much those things cost?'*

**gim|mick** /gɪmɪk/ **(gimmicks)** A **gimmick** is an unusual and unnecessary feature or action whose purpose is to attract attention or publicity. ❑ *It is just a public relations gimmick... The exhibition is informative, up to date, and mercifully free of gimmicks.* N-COUNT [disapproval]

**gim|mick|ry** /gɪmɪkri/ If you describe features or actions as **gimmickry**, you mean they are not necessary or useful, and their only purpose is to attract attention or publicity. ❑ *Privatisation and gimmickry are not the answer to improving Britain's rail service.* N-UNCOUNT [disapproval]

**gim|micky** /gɪmɪki/ If you describe something as **gimmicky**, you think it has features which are not necessary or useful, and whose only purpose is to attract attention or publicity. [INFORMAL] ❑ *The campaign was gimmicky, but it had a serious side to it.* ADJ [disapproval]

**gin** /dʒɪn/ **(gins) Gin** is a strong colourless alcoholic drink made from grain and juniper berries. N-MASS ♦ A **gin** is a glass of gin. ❑ *...another gin and tonic.* N-COUNT

**gin|ger** /dʒɪndʒəʳ/ [1] **Ginger** is the root of a plant that is used to flavour food. It has a sweet spicy flavour and is often sold in powdered form. N-UNCOUNT [2] **Ginger** is used to describe things that are orangey-brown in colour. ❑ *She was a mature lady with dyed ginger hair.* COLOUR

**gin|ger ale (ginger ales) Ginger ale** is a fizzy non-alcoholic drink flavoured with ginger, which is often mixed with an alcoholic drink. ❑ *I live mostly on coffee and ginger ale.* N-MASS ♦ A glass of ginger ale can be referred to as a **ginger ale**. N-COUNT

**gin|ger beer (ginger beers) Ginger beer** is a fizzy drink that is made from syrup and ginger and is sometimes slightly alcoholic. N-MASS ♦ A glass of ginger beer can be referred to as a **ginger beer**. N-COUNT

**ginger|bread** /dʒɪndʒəʳbred/ **Gingerbread** is a sweet biscuit or cookie that is flavoured with ginger. It is often made in the shape of a man or an animal. N-UNCOUNT

**gin|ger group (ginger groups)** A **ginger group** is a group of people who have similar ideas and who work together, especially within a larger organization, to try to persuade others to accept their ideas. [BRIT] ❑ *I set up a ginger group on the environment.* N-COUNT: usu sing

**gin|ger|ly** /dʒɪndʒəʳli/ If you do something **gingerly**, you do it in a careful manner, usually because you expect it to be dangerous, unpleasant, or painful. [WRITTEN] ❑ *I drove gingerly past the security check points.* ADV: ADV with v = cautiously

**gin|gery** /dʒɪndʒəri/ Something, especially hair, that is **gingery** is slightly ginger in colour. ADJ

**ging|ham** /gɪŋəm/ **Gingham** is cotton cloth which has a woven pattern of small squares, usually in white and one other colour. ❑ *...a gingham apron. ...gingham check shorts.* N-UNCOUNT

**gin|seng** /dʒɪnseŋ/ **Ginseng** is the root of a plant found in China, Korea, and America which some people believe is good for your health. N-UNCOUNT

**gip|sy** /dʒɪpsi/ → see **gypsy**.

**gi|raffe** /dʒɪrɑːf, -ræf/ **(giraffes)** A **giraffe** is a large African animal with a very long neck, long legs, and dark patches on its body. N-COUNT

**gird** /gɜːʳd/ **(girds, girding, girded)** If you **gird yourself for** a battle or contest, you prepare yourself for it. [LITERARY] ❑ *With audiences in the US falling for the first time in a generation, Hollywood is girding itself for recession.* VERB V pron-refl for n to **gird** your **loins** → see **loin**.

**gird|er** /gɜːʳdəʳ/ **(girders)** A **girder** is a long, thick piece of steel or iron that is used in the framework of buildings and bridges. N-COUNT

**gir|dle** /gɜːʳdəl/ **(girdles, girdling, girdled)** A **girdle** is a piece of women's underwear that fits tightly around the stomach and hips. N-COUNT

**girl** /gɜːʳl/ **(girls)** [1] A **girl** is a female child. ❑ *...an eleven year old girl... I must have been a horrid little girl.* ◆◆◆ N-COUNT [2] You can refer to someone's daughter as a **girl**. ❑ *We had a little girl.* N-COUNT [3] Young women are often referred to as **girls**. This use could cause offence. ❑ *...a pretty twenty-year old girl.* N-COUNT [4] Some people refer to a man's girlfriend as his **girl**. [INFORMAL] ❑ *I've been with my girl for nine years.* N-COUNT

**girl band** **(girl bands)** A **girl band** is a band consisting of young women who sing pop music and dance. N-COUNT

**girl|friend** /gɜːʳlfrend/ **(girlfriends)** ◆◇◇ **1** Someone's **girlfriend** is a girl or woman with whom they are having a romantic or sexual relationship. ❑ *He had been going out with his girlfriend for seven months... Has he got a girlfriend?* N-COUNT: oft poss N **2** A **girlfriend** is a female friend. ❑ *I met a girlfriend for lunch.* N-COUNT

**Girl Guide** **(Girl Guides)** also **girl guide.** **1** In Britain, the Guides used to be called **the Girl Guides.** N-PROPER-COLL: the N **2** In Britain, a **Girl Guide** was a girl who was a member of the Girl Guides. N-COUNT = Guide

**girl|hood** /gɜːʳlhʊd/ **Girlhood** is the period of a female person's life during which she is a girl. ❑ *She had shared responsibility for her brother since girlhood... Her girlhood dream had been to study painting.* N-UNCOUNT: oft poss N

**girlie** /gɜːʳli/ **(girlies)** also **girly.** **1** **Girlie** magazines or calendars show photographs of naked or almost naked women which are intended to please men. [INFORMAL] ADJ: ADJ n **2** **Girlie** things are suitable for girls or women rather than men or boys. [INFORMAL] ❑ *She swapped her plain suit for an absurdly girlie dress... I'm a very girlie person while Polly is one of the lads.* ADJ disapproval **3** Some people refer to women as **girlies**, especially when they think they are not as intelligent or able as men. [BRIT, INFORMAL] ❑ *They think we're just a bunch of girlies who don't know what we're doing.* N-COUNT disapproval

**girl|ish** /gɜːʳlɪʃ/ If you describe a woman as **girlish**, you mean she behaves, looks, or sounds like a young girl, for example because she is shy, excited, or lively. ❑ *She gave a little girlish giggle.* ADJ: usu ADJ n

**Girl Scout** **(Girl Scouts)** **1** In the United States, **the Girl Scouts** is an organization similar to **the Guides.** N-PROPER-COLL: the N **2** In the United States, a **Girl Scout** is a girl who is a member of the Girl Scouts. N-COUNT

**giro** /dʒaɪərou/ **(giros)** also **Giro.** **1** In Britain, a **giro** or a **giro cheque** is a cheque that is given by the government to a person who is unemployed or ill. ❑ *He lived on an invalidity pension which came as a weekly giro.* N-COUNT **2** **Giro** is a system in which banks and post offices transfer money directly from one bank account to another using computers. [BRIT] ❑ *There will be no further costs as long as the bank is part of the giro network.* N-UNCOUNT

**girth** /gɜːʳθ/ **(girths)** **1** The **girth** of an object, for example a person's or an animal's body, is its width or thickness, considered as the measurement around its circumference. [FORMAL] ❑ *A girl he knew had upset him by commenting on his increasing girth.* N-VAR: with supp, oft poss N **2** A **girth** is a leather strap which is fastened firmly around the middle of a horse to keep the saddle or load in the right place. N-COUNT

**gist** /dʒɪst/ **The gist of** a speech, conversation, or piece of writing is its general meaning. ❑ *He related the gist of his conversation to Naseby.* N-SING: the N of n

**git** /gɪt/ **(gits)** If you refer to another person as a **git**, you mean you dislike them and find them annoying. [BRIT, OFFENSIVE] N-COUNT: usu adj N disapproval

**give**
① USED WITH NOUNS DESCRIBING ACTIONS
② TRANSFERRING
③ OTHER USES, PHRASES, AND PHRASAL VERBS

① **give** /gɪv/ **(gives, giving, gave, given)** ◆◆◆ **1** You can use **give** with nouns that refer to physical actions. The whole expression refers to the performing of the action. For example, **She gave a smile** means almost the same as 'She smiled'. ❑ *She stretched her arms out and gave a great yawn... He reached for her hand and gave it a reassuring squeeze.* VERB: no cont; V n; V n n **2** You use **give** to say that a person does something for another person. For example, if you **give** someone a lift, you take them somewhere in your car. ❑ *I gave her a lift back out to her house... He was given mouth-to-mouth resuscitation... Sophie asked her if she would like to come and give art lessons.* VERB; V n n; V n n; V n **3** You use **give** with nouns that refer to information, opinions, or greetings to indicate that something is communicated. For example, if you **give** someone some news, you tell it to them. ❑ *He gave no details... Would you like to give me your name?... He asked me to give his regards to all of you... He gave the cause of death as multiple injuries.* VERB; V n; V n n; V n *to* n; V n *as* n **4** You use **give** to say how long you think something will last or how much you think something will be. ❑ *A BBC poll gave the Labour Party a 12 per cent lead.* VERB; V n n **5** People use **give** in expressions such as **I don't give a damn** to show that they do not care about something. [INFORMAL] ❑ *They don't give a damn about the state of the country.* VERB: no cont, no passive, with brd-neg; feelings; V n **6** If someone or something **gives** you a particular idea or impression, it causes you to have that idea or impression. ❑ *They gave me the impression that they were doing exactly what they wanted in life... The examiner's final report does not give an accurate picture.* VERB; V n n; V n **7** If someone or something **gives** you a particular physical or emotional feeling, it makes you experience it. ❑ *He gave me a shock... It will give great pleasure to the many thousands of children who visit the hospital each year.* VERB; V n n; V n *to* n; Also V n **8** If you **give** a performance or speech, you perform or speak in public. ❑ *Kotto gives a stupendous performance... I am sure you remember Mrs Butler who gave us such an interesting talk last year.* VERB; V n; V n n **9** If you **give** something thought or attention, you think about it, concentrate on it, or deal with it. ❑ *I've been giving it some thought... Priority will be given to those who apply early.* VERB; V n n; V n *to* n/-ing **10** If you **give** a party or other social event, you organize it. ❑ *That evening, I gave a dinner party for a few close friends.* VERB = have; V n

② **give** /gɪv/ **(gives, giving, gave, given)** ◆◆◆ **1** If you **give** someone something that you own or have bought, you provide them with it, so that they have it or can use it. ❑ *They gave us T-shirts and stickers... He gave money to the World Health Organisation to help defeat smallpox... Americans are still giving to charity despite hard economic times.* VERB; V n n; V n *to* n; V *to* n **2** If you **give** someone something that you are holding or that is near you, you pass it to them, so that they are then holding it. ❑ *Give me that pencil... He pulled a handkerchief from his pocket and gave it to him.* VERB; V n n; V n *to* n **3** To **give** someone or something a particular power or right means to allow them to have it. ❑ *...a citizen's charter giving rights to gays... The draft would give the president the power to appoint the central bank's chairman.* VERB = grant; V n *to* n; V n n

③ **give** /gɪv/ **(gives, giving, gave, given)** ◆◆◆ ➾ Please look at category 7 to see if the expression you are looking for is shown under another headword. **1** If something **gives**, it collapses or breaks under pressure. ❑ *My knees gave under me.* VERB; V **2** You say that you **are given to** understand or believe that something is the case when you do not want to say how you found out about it, or who told you. [FORMAL] ❑ *We were given to understand that he was ill.* V-PASSIVE vagueness; *be* V-ed to-inf **3** → See also **given.**

**PHRASES** **4** You use **give me** to say that you would rather have one thing than another, especially when you have just mentioned the thing that you do not want. ❑ *I've never had anything barbecued and I don't want it. Give me a good roast dinner any day.* PHRASE: PHR n **5** If you say that something requires **give and take**, you mean that people must compromise or co-operate for it to be successful. ❑ *...a happy relationship where there's a lot of give and take.* PHRASE **6** **Give or take** is used to indicate that an amount is approximate. For example, if you say that something is fifty years old, **give or take** a few years, you mean that it is approximately fifty years old. ❑ *They grow to a height of 12 ins – give or take a couple of inches.* PHRASE: PHR amount **7** to **give the game away** → see **game.** to **give notice** → see **notice.** to **give rise to** → see **rise.** to **give way** → see **way.**

♦ **give away** [1] If you **give away** something that you own, you give it to someone, rather than selling it, often because you no longer want it. ❑ *He was giving his collection away for nothing... We have six copies of the book to give away.* [2] If someone **gives away** an advantage, they accidentally cause their opponent or enemy to have that advantage. ❑ *We gave away a silly goal.* [3] If you **give away** information that should be kept secret, you reveal it to other people. ❑ *She would give nothing away... They felt like they were giving away company secrets.* [4] To **give** someone or something **away** means to show their true nature or identity, which is not obvious. ❑ *Although they are pretending hard to be young, grey hair and cellulite give them away.* [5] In a Christian wedding ceremony, if someone **gives** the bride **away**, they officially present her to her husband. This is traditionally done by the bride's father.

PHRASAL VERB ≠ keep; V n P; V P n (not pron); PHRASAL VERB = throw away; V P n; Also V n P; PHRASAL VERB; V n P; V P n (not pron); PHRASAL VERB; V n P; PHRASAL VERB: V n P

♦ **give back** If you **give** something **back**, you return it to the person who gave it to you. ❑ *I gave the textbook back to him... You gave me back the projector... I gave it back politely.*

PHRASAL VERB; V n P *to* n; V n P n (not pron); V n P

♦ **give in** [1] If you **give in**, you admit that you are defeated or that you cannot do something. ❑ *All right. I give in. What did you do with the ship?* [2] If you **give in**, you agree to do something that you do not want to do. ❑ *I pressed my parents until they finally gave in and registered me for skating classes... Officials say they won't give in to the workers' demands.*

PHRASAL VERB; V P; PHRASAL VERB; V P; V P *to* n

♦ **give off** or **give out** If something **gives off** or **gives out** a gas, heat, or a smell, it produces it and sends it out into the air. ❑ *...natural gas, which gives off less carbon dioxide than coal.*

PHRASAL VERB; V P n (not pron)

♦ **give out** [1] If you **give out** a number of things, you distribute them among a group of people. ❑ *There were people at the entrance giving out leaflets.* [2] If you **give out** information, you make it known to people. ❑ *He wouldn't give out any information... How often do you give your phone number out?* [3] If a piece of equipment or part of the body **gives out**, it stops working. ❑ *All machines give out eventually... One of his lungs gave out entirely.* [4] → see **give off**.

PHRASAL VERB = hand out; V P n; Also V n P; PHRASAL VERB; V P n (not pron); V n P; PHRASAL VERB; V P; V P

♦ **give over to** or **give up to** If something **is given over** or **given up to** a particular use, it is used entirely for that purpose. ❑ *Much of the garden was given over to vegetables.*

PHRASAL VERB: usu passive; *be* V-ed P P n

♦ **give up** [1] If you **give up** something, you stop doing it or having it. ❑ *Coastguards had given up all hope of finding the two divers alive. ...smokers who give up before 30.* [2] If you **give up**, you decide that you cannot do something and stop trying to do it. ❑ *After a fruitless morning sitting at his desk he had given up.* [3] If you **give up** your job, you resign from it. ❑ *She gave up her job to join her husband's campaign... He is thinking of giving up teaching.* [4] If you **give up** something that you have or that you are entitled to, you allow someone else to have it. ❑ *Georgia refuses to give up any territory... One of the men with him gave up his place on the bench.* [5] If you **give yourself up**, you let the police or other people know where you are, after you have been hiding from them. ❑ *A 28-year-old man later gave himself up and will appear in court today.*

PHRASAL VERB; V P n/-ing; V P; PHRASAL VERB; V P; PHRASAL VERB; V P n/-ing (not pron); PHRASAL VERB; V P n (not pron); PHRASAL VERB; V pron-refl P

♦ **give up on** If you **give up on** something or someone, you decide that you will never succeed in doing what you want to with them, and you stop trying to. ❑ *He urged them not to give up on peace efforts... My teachers gave up on me.*

PHRASAL VERB; V P P n; V P P n

♦ **give up to** → see **give over to**.

**give-and-take** → see **give**.

**give|away** /gɪvəweɪ/ **(giveaways)** also **give-away.** [1] A **giveaway** is something that makes you realize the truth about a particular person or situation. ❑ *The only giveaway was the look of amusement in her eyes.* [2] A **giveaway** is something that a company or organization gives to someone, usually in order to encourage people to buy a particular product. ❑ *Next week TODAY is celebrating with a great giveaway of FREE garden seeds.*

N-SING; N-COUNT

**giv|en** /gɪvᵊn/ ♦◇◇ [1] **Given** is the past participle of **give**. [2] If you talk about, for example, any **given** position or a **given** time, you mean the particular position or time that you are discussing. ❑ *In chess there are typically about 36 legal moves from any given board position... Over a given period, the value of shares will rise and fall.* [3] **Given** is used when indicating a possible situation in which someone has the opportunity or ability to do something. For example, **given the chance** means 'if I had the chance'. ❑ *Write down the sort of thing you would like to do, given the opportunity... Given patience, successful breeding of this species can be achieved.* [4] If you say **given that** something is the case, you mean taking that fact into account. ❑ *Usually, I am sensible with money, as I have to be, given that I don't earn that much.* [5] If you say **given** something, you mean taking that thing into account. ❑ *Given the uncertainty over Leigh's future I was left with little other choice.* [6] If you are **given to** doing something, you often do it. [FORMAL] ❑ *I am not very given to emotional displays.*

ADJ: det ADJ = particular; PREP; PHRASE = considering; PREP; ADJ: v-link ADJ *to* -ing/n

**giv|en name (given names)** A **given name** is a person's first name, which they are given at birth in addition to their surname. [FORMAL]

N-COUNT: oft with poss = first name

**giv|er** /gɪvəʳ/ **(givers)** You can refer to a person or organization that gives or supplies a particular thing as a **giver** of that thing. ❑ *Germany is the largest giver of aid among the wealthy countries of the West.* ♦ **Giver** is also a combining form. ❑ *...if the money-givers do not have specific projects in view.*

N-COUNT; COMB in N-COUNT

**giz|mo** /gɪzmoʊ/ **(gizmos)** A **gizmo** is a device or small machine which performs a particular task, usually in a new and efficient way. People often use **gizmo** to refer to a device or machine when they do not know what it is really called. [INFORMAL] ❑ *...a plastic gizmo for holding a coffee cup on the dashboard.*

N-COUNT: usu with supp

**gla|cé** /glæseɪ, AM -seɪ/ **Glacé** fruits are fruits that have been preserved in a thick sugary syrup and then dried. ❑ *...pieces of glacé cherry.*

ADJ: ADJ n

**gla|cial** /gleɪʃᵊl/ [1] **Glacial** means relating to or produced by glaciers or ice. [TECHNICAL] ❑ *...a true glacial landscape with U-shaped valleys.* [2] If you say that a person, action, or atmosphere is **glacial**, you mean that they are very unfriendly or hostile. ❑ *Inside the jeep the atmosphere was glacial.* [3] If you say that something moves or changes at a **glacial** pace, you are emphasizing that it moves or changes very slowly. [4] If you describe someone, usually a woman, as **glacial**, you mean they are very beautiful and elegant, but do not show their feelings. ❑ *Her glacial beauty is magnetic.*

ADJ: usu ADJ n; ADJ [disapproval] = frosty, icy; ADJ: usu ADJ n [emphasis]; ADJ: usu ADJ n

**gla|cia|tion** /gleɪsieɪʃᵊn/ **(glaciations)** In geology, **glaciation** is the process by which the land is covered by glaciers. **Glaciations** are periods when this happens. [TECHNICAL]

N-VAR

**glaci|er** /glæsiəʳ, AM gleɪʃəʳ/ **(glaciers)** A **glacier** is an extremely large mass of ice which moves very slowly, often down a mountain valley.

N-COUNT

**glad** /glæd/ ♦◇◇ [1] If you are **glad** about something, you are happy and pleased about it. ❑ *I'm glad I relented in the end... The people seem genuinely glad to see you... I ought to be glad about what happened... I'd be glad if the boys slept a little longer so I could do some ironing.* ♦ **glad|ly** *Mallarmé gladly accepted the invitation.* ♦ **glad|ness** *...a night of joy and gladness.* [2] If you say that you will be **glad to** do something, usually for someone else, you mean that you are willing and eager to do it. ❑ *I'll be glad to show you everything... We should be glad to answer any questions.* ♦ **glad|ly** *The counselors will gladly baby-sit during their free time.*

ADJ: v-link ADJ, oft ADJ that, ADJ to-inf, ADJ *of/about* n; ADV; N-UNCOUNT; ADJ: v-link ADJ to-inf [feelings] = happy; ADV: ADV with v

**glad|den** /glædᵊn/ **(gladdens, gladdening, gladdened)** [1] If you say that something **gladdens** someone's **heart**, you mean that it makes them feel pleased and hopeful. [WRITTEN] ❑ *...a*

PHRASE: V and N inflect

*conclusion that should gladden the hearts of all animal-rights activists.* [2] If something **gladdens** you, it makes you feel happy and pleased. [LITERARY] ❑ *Charles's visit surprised him and gladdened him.* VERB ≠sadden V n

**glade** /gleɪd/ **(glades)** A **glade** is a grassy space without trees in a wood or forest. [LITERARY] N-COUNT

**gladia|tor** /glædieɪtəʳ/ **(gladiators)** [1] In the time of the Roman Empire, a **gladiator** was a man who had to fight against other men or wild animals in order to entertain an audience. N-COUNT [2] You can refer to a sports player or a performer as a **gladiator** in order to emphasize how brave or dangerous their actions are. [JOURNALISM] ❑ *As the gladiators rolled away from the starting gates, a gasp went up when the Scottish cyclist's left foot clicked out of the pedal.* N-COUNT emphasis

**gladio|lus** /glædioʊləs/ **(gladioli)** A **gladiolus** is a type of plant with long thin leaves and several large brightly coloured flowers. N-COUNT

**glad rags** You can refer to clothes that you wear to parties and other special occasions as your **glad rags**. [INFORMAL] N-PLURAL

**glam** /glæm/ **Glam** is short for glamorous. [BRIT, INFORMAL] ❑ *She was always glam. She looked like a star.* ADJ

**glam|or** /glæməʳ/ → see **glamour**.

**glam|or|ize** /glæməraɪz/ **(glamorizes, glamorizing, glamorized)**

in BRIT, also use **glamorise**

If someone **glamorizes** something, they make it look or seem more attractive than it really is, especially in a film, book, or programme. ❑ *Filmmakers have often been accused of glamorizing organized crime. ...a glamorised view of the past.* VERB disapproval V n V-ed

**glam|or|ous** /glæmərəs/ If you describe someone or something as **glamorous**, you mean that they are more attractive, exciting, or interesting than ordinary people or things. ❑ *...some of the world's most beautiful and glamorous women... The south coast is less glamorous but full of clean and attractive hotels.* ADJ

**glam|our** /glæməʳ/

in AM, also use **glamor**

**Glamour** is the quality of being more attractive, exciting, or interesting than ordinary people or things. ❑ *...the glamour of show biz.* N-UNCOUNT

**glance** /glɑːns, glæns/ **(glances, glancing, glanced)** ◆◇◇ [1] If you **glance at** something or someone, you look at them very quickly and then look away again immediately. ❑ *He glanced at his watch... I glanced back.* VERB V prep/adv [2] If you **glance through** or **at** a newspaper, report, or book, you spend a short time looking at it without reading it very carefully. ❑ *I picked up the phone book and glanced through it... I never even glanced at the political page of a daily paper.* VERB V through/at n [3] A **glance** is a quick look at someone or something. ❑ *Trevor and I exchanged a glance.* N-COUNT

**PHRASES** [4] If you see something **at a glance**, you see or recognize it immediately, and without having to think or look carefully. ❑ *One could tell at a glance that she was a compassionate person.* PHRASE [5] If you say that something is true or seems to be true **at first glance**, you mean that it seems to be true when you first see it or think about it, but that your first impression may be wrong. ❑ *At first glance, organic farming looks much more expensive for the farmer.* PHRASE: PHR with cl [6] If you **steal a glance at** someone or something, you look at them quickly so that nobody sees you looking. ❑ *He stole a glance at the clock behind her.* PHRASE: V and N inflect, oft PHR at n

♦ **glance off** If an object **glances off** something, it hits it at an angle and bounces away in another direction. ❑ *My fist glanced off his jaw.* PHRASAL VERB V P n

**glanc|ing** /glɑːnsɪŋ, glæns-/ A **glancing** blow is one that hits something at an angle rather than from directly in front. ❑ *The car struck him a glancing blow on the forehead.* ADJ: ADJ n

**gland** /glænd/ **(glands)** A **gland** is an organ in the body which produces chemical substances for the body to use or get rid of. ❑ *...the hormones secreted by our endocrine glands. ...sweat glands.* N-COUNT: usu supp N

**glan|du|lar** /glændʒʊləʳ/ **Glandular** means relating to or affecting your glands. [TECHNICAL] ❑ *...the amount of fat and glandular tissue in the breasts.* ADJ: usu ADJ n

**glan|du|lar fe|ver** **Glandular fever** is a disease which causes swollen glands, fever, and a sore throat. [mainly BRIT] N-UNCOUNT

in AM, use **mononucleosis**

**glare** /gleəʳ/ **(glares, glaring, glared)** [1] If you **glare at** someone, you look at them with an angry expression on your face. ❑ *The old woman glared at him... Jacob glared and muttered something. ...glaring eyes.* VERB V at n V V-ing [2] A **glare** is an angry, hard, and unfriendly look. ❑ *His glasses magnified his irritable glare.* N-COUNT [3] If the sun or a light **glares**, it shines with a very bright light which is difficult to look at. ❑ *The sunlight glared. ...glaring searchlight beams.* VERB V V-ing [4] **Glare** is very bright light that is difficult to look at. ❑ *...the glare of a car's headlights... Special-purpose glasses reduce glare.* N-UNCOUNT: usu with supp [5] If someone is in **the glare of** publicity or public attention, they are constantly being watched and talked about by a lot of people. ❑ *Norma is said to dislike the glare of publicity... She attacked police in the full glare of TV cameras.* N-SING: the N of n

**glar|ing** /gleərɪŋ/ If you describe something bad as **glaring**, you are emphasizing that it is very obvious and easily seen or noticed. ❑ *I never saw such a glaring example of misrepresentation.* ADJ: usu ADJ n emphasis = blatant ♦ **glar|ing|ly** *It was glaringly obvious... He told a glaringly different story.* → See also **glare**. ADV

**glas|nost** /glæznɒst/ **Glasnost** is a policy of making a government more open and democratic. The word **glasnost** was originally used to describe the policies of President Gorbachev in the former Soviet Union in the 1980s. N-UNCOUNT

**glass** /glɑːs, glæs/ **(glasses)** ◆◆◇ [1] **Glass** is a hard transparent substance that is used to make things such as windows and bottles. ❑ *...a pane of glass. ...a sliding glass door.* N-UNCOUNT [2] A **glass** is a container made from glass, which you can drink from and which does not have a handle. ❑ *Grossman raised the glass to his lips.* ♦ The contents of a glass can be referred to as a **glass of** something. ❑ *...a glass of milk.* N-COUNT N-COUNT: usu N of n [3] **Glass** is used to mean objects made of glass, for example drinking containers and bowls. ❑ *There's a glittering array of glass to choose from at markets.* N-UNCOUNT [4] **Glasses** are two lenses in a frame that some people wear in front of their eyes in order to help them see better. ❑ *He took off his glasses.* N-PLURAL [5] → See also **dark glasses**, **magnifying glass**.

**glass ceil|ing** **(glass ceilings)** When people refer to a **glass ceiling**, they are talking about the attitudes and traditions in a society that prevent women from rising to the top jobs. [JOURNALISM] ❑ *In her current role she broke through the glass ceiling as the first woman to reach senior management level in the company.* N-COUNT: usu sing

**glassed-in** A **glassed-in** room or building has large windows instead of walls. ADJ: usu ADJ n

**glass fi|bre**

in AM, use glass fiber

**Glass fibre** is another name for **fibreglass**. N-UNCOUNT

**glass|house** /glɑːshaʊs, glæs-/ **(glasshouses)** A **glasshouse** is a **greenhouse**, especially a large one which is used for the commercial production of fruit, flowers, or vegetables. [mainly BRIT] N-COUNT

**glass|ware** /glɑːsweəʳ, glæs-/ **Glassware** consists of objects made of glass, such as bowls, drinking containers, and ornaments. N-UNCOUNT

**glassy** /glɑːsi, glæsi/ If you describe something as **glassy**, you mean that it is very smooth and shiny, like glass. [WRITTEN] ❑ *The water was glassy. ...glassy green pebbles.* ADJ

**glau|co|ma** /glɔːkoʊmə, AM glaʊ-/ **Glaucoma** is an eye disease which can cause people to go gradually blind. N-UNCOUNT

**glaze** /gleɪz/ **(glazes, glazing, glazed)** 1 A **glaze** is a thin layer of liquid which is put on a piece of pottery and becomes hard and shiny when the pottery is heated in a very hot oven. ❑ *...hand-painted French tiles with decorative glazes.* N-COUNT 2 A **glaze** is a thin layer of beaten egg, milk, or other liquid that you spread onto food in order to make the surface shine and look attractive. ❑ *Brush the glaze over the top and sides of the hot cake.* N-COUNT 3 When you **glaze** food such as bread or pastry, you spread a layer of beaten egg, milk, or other liquid onto it before you cook it in order to make its surface shine and look attractive. ❑ *Glaze the pie with beaten egg.* VERB V n

♦ **glaze over** If your eyes **glaze over**, they become dull and lose all expression, usually because you are bored or are thinking about something else. ❑ *...movie actors whose eyes glaze over as soon as the subject wavers from themselves.* PHRASAL VERB V P

**glazed** /gleɪzd/ 1 If you describe someone's eyes as **glazed**, you mean that their expression is dull or dreamy, usually because they are tired or are having difficulty concentrating on something. ❑ *Doctors with glazed eyes sat chain-smoking in front of a television set... There was a glazed look in her eyes.* ADJ: usu ADJ n 2 **Glazed** pottery is covered with a thin layer of a hard shiny substance. ADJ: usu ADJ n 3 A **glazed** window or door has glass in it. ADJ

**gla|zi|er** /gleɪziəʳ, AM -ʒər/ **(glaziers)** A **glazier** is someone whose job is fitting glass into windows and doors. N-COUNT

**gleam** /gliːm/ **(gleams, gleaming, gleamed)** 1 If an object or a surface **gleams**, it reflects light because it is shiny and clean. ❑ *His black hair gleamed in the sun. ...a gleaming red sports car.* VERB V V-ing 2 You can refer to the light reflected from something as a **gleam**. [LITERARY] ❑ *...the gleam of the dark river... In the light from the hall, her hair had a golden gleam.* N-SING 3 If your eyes **gleam**, they look bright and show that you are excited or happy. [WRITTEN] VERB = glisten, shine 4 A **gleam of** something is a faint sign of it. ❑ *There was a gleam of hope for a peaceful settlement.* N-COUNT: N *of* n = glimmer

**glean** /gliːn/ **(gleans, gleaning, gleaned)** If you **glean** something such as information or knowledge, you learn or collect it slowly and patiently, and perhaps indirectly. ❑ *At present we're gleaning information from all sources... 10,000 pages of evidence were gleaned from hundreds and hundreds of interviews.* VERB = gather V n *from* n V n

**glee** /gliː/ **Glee** is a feeling of happiness and excitement, often caused by someone else's misfortune. ❑ *There was much glee among journalists over the leaked letter.* N-UNCOUNT: oft *with* N = delight

**glee|ful** /gliːfʊl/ Someone who is **gleeful** is happy and excited, often because of someone else's bad luck. [WRITTEN] ❑ *He took an almost gleeful delight in showing how wrong they can be.* ADJ ♦ **glee|ful|ly** *I spent the rest of their visit gleefully boring them with tedious details.* ADV: ADV with v

**glen** /glen/ **(glens)** A **glen** is a deep, narrow valley, especially in the mountains of Scotland or Ireland. N-COUNT: oft in names

**glib** /glɪb/ If you describe what someone says as **glib**, you disapprove of it because it implies that something is simple or easy, or that there are no problems involved, when this is not the case. ❑ *...the glib talk of 'past misery'... Mr. Lewis takes an insufferably glib attitude toward it all.* ADJ [disapproval] ♦ **glib|ly** *We talk glibly of equality of opportunity.* ADV: ADV with v

**glide** /glaɪd/ **(glides, gliding, glided)** 1 If you **glide** somewhere, you move silently and in a smooth and effortless way. ❑ *Waiters glide between tightly packed tables bearing trays of pasta.* VERB V prep/adv 2 When birds or aeroplanes **glide**, they float on air currents. ❑ *Our only companion is the wandering albatross, which glides effortlessly and gracefully behind the yacht.* VERB V prep/adv

**glid|er** /glaɪdəʳ/ **(gliders)** A **glider** is an aircraft without an engine, which flies by floating on air currents. N-COUNT

**glid|ing** /glaɪdɪŋ/ **Gliding** is the sport or activity of flying in a glider. N-UNCOUNT

**glim|mer** /glɪməʳ/ **(glimmers, glimmering, glimmered)** 1 If something **glimmers**, it produces or reflects a faint, gentle, often unsteady light. ❑ *The moon glimmered faintly through the mists. ...the glimmering ocean.* VERB V V-ing 2 A **glimmer** is a faint, gentle, often unsteady light. ❑ *In the east there is the slightest glimmer of light.* N-COUNT = flicker 3 A **glimmer of** something is a faint sign of it. ❑ *Despite an occasional glimmer of hope, this campaign has not produced any results... He is celebrating his first glimmer of success.* N-COUNT: N *of* n

**glim|mer|ing** /glɪmərɪŋ/ **(glimmerings)** A **glimmering of** something is a faint sign of it. ❑ *...a glimmering of understanding. ...the first glimmerings of civilization.* N-COUNT: N *of* n

**glimpse** /glɪmps/ **(glimpses, glimpsing, glimpsed)** 1 If you get a **glimpse of** someone or something, you see them very briefly and not very well. ❑ *Some of the fans had waited 24 hours outside the Hyde Park Hotel to catch a glimpse of their heroine.* N-COUNT: usu N *of* n 2 If you **glimpse** someone or something, you see them very briefly and not very well. ❑ *She glimpsed a group of people standing on the bank of a river.* VERB V n 3 A **glimpse of** something is a brief experience of it or an idea about it that helps you understand or appreciate it better. ❑ *As university campuses become increasingly multi-ethnic, they offer a glimpse of the conflicts society will face tomorrow. ...a glimpse into the future.* N-COUNT: usu N *of* n

**glint** /glɪnt/ **(glints, glinting, glinted)** 1 If something **glints**, it produces or reflects a quick flash of light. [WRITTEN] ❑ *The sea glinted in the sun... Sunlight glinted on his spectacles.* VERB = glisten V V *on/off* n 2 A **glint** is a quick flash of light. [WRITTEN] ❑ *...a glint of silver. ...glints of sunlight.* N-COUNT: usu N *of* n

**glis|ten** /glɪsᵊn/ **(glistens, glistening, glistened)** If something **glistens**, it shines, usually because it is wet or oily. ❑ *The calm sea glistened in the sunlight... Darcy's face was white and glistening with sweat.* VERB V V *with* n

**glitch** /glɪtʃ/ **(glitches)** A **glitch** is a problem which stops something from working properly or being successful. [INFORMAL] ❑ *Manufacturing glitches have limited the factory's output.* N-COUNT = hitch, problem

**glit|ter** /glɪtəʳ/ **(glitters, glittering, glittered)** 1 If something **glitters**, light comes from or is reflected off different parts of it. ❑ *The bay glittered in the sunshine... The Palace glittered with lights.* VERB = sparkle V V prep 2 **Glitter** consists of tiny shining pieces of metal. It is glued to things for decoration. ❑ *Decorate the tunic with sequins or glitter.* N-UNCOUNT 3 You can use **glitter** to refer to superficial attractiveness or to the excitement connected with something. ❑ *She was blinded by the glitter and the glamour of her own life.* N-UNCOUNT

**glit|te|ra|ti** /glɪtərɑːti/ The **glitterati** are rich and famous people such as actors and rock stars. [JOURNALISM] ❑ *The glitterati of Hollywood are flocking to Janet Vaughan's nail salon.* N-PLURAL

**glit|ter|ing** /glɪtərɪŋ/ You use **glittering** to indicate that something is very impressive or successful. ❑ *...a brilliant school pupil destined for a glittering academic career. ...a glittering array of celebrities.* ADJ: ADJ n

**glit|tery** /glɪtəri/ Something that is **glittery** shines with a lot of very small points of light. ❑ *...a gold suit and a glittery bow tie.* ADJ

**glitz** /glɪts/ You use **glitz** to refer to something that is exciting and attractive in a showy way. ❑ *...the glitz of Beverly Hills.* N-UNCOUNT

**glitzy** /glɪtsi/ **(glitzier, glitziest)** Something that is **glitzy** is exciting and attractive in a showy way. ❑ *...Aspen, Colorado, one of the glitziest ski resorts in the world.* ADJ

**gloat** /gloʊt/ **(gloats, gloating, gloated)** If someone **is gloating**, they are showing pleasure at their own success or at other people's failure in an arrogant and unpleasant way. ❑ *Anti-abortionists are gloating over the court's decision... This is nothing to gloat about.* VERB [disapproval] V over/about n Also V

**glob** /glɒb/ **(globs)** A **glob of** something soft or liquid is a small round amount of it. [INFORMAL] ❑ *...oily globs of soup.* N-COUNT: usu N of n = blob

**glob|al** /gloʊbᵊl/ [1] You can use **global** to describe something that happens in all parts of the world or affects all parts of the world. ❑ *...a global ban on nuclear testing... On a global scale, AIDS may well become the leading cause of infant death.* ◆◇◇ ADJ: usu ADJ n = worldwide ♦ **glob|al|ly** *...a globally familiar trade name.* ADV [2] A **global** view or vision of a situation is one in which all the different aspects of it are considered. ❑ *...the global view, the ability to make wider decisions based on a knowledge of all the facts, not just some of them. ...a global vision of contemporary societies.* ADJ: usu ADJ n

**glob|al|ize** /gloʊbəlaɪz/ **(globalizes, globalizing, globalized)**

✔ in BRIT, also use **globalise**

When industry **globalizes** or **is globalized**, companies from one country link with companies from another country in order to do business with them. [BUSINESS] ❑ *As the world becomes more complex, some things do, of course, standardize and globalize... Companies will come together because of the sheer costs involved in globalising their businesses.* VERB V V n ♦ **glob|ali|za|tion** /gloʊbəlaɪzeɪʃᵊn/ *Trends toward the globalization of industry have dramatically affected food production in California.* N-UNCOUNT

**glob|al po|si|tion|ing sys|tem** **(global positioning systems)** A **global positioning system** is a system that uses signals from satellites to find out the position of an object. The abbreviation **GPS** is also used. N-COUNT

**glob|al reach** When people talk about the **global reach** of a company or industry, they mean its ability to have customers in many different parts of the world. [BUSINESS] ❑ *The company does not yet have the global reach of its bigger competitors... It would have to grow by acquisitions or joint ventures to achieve global reach.* N-SING

**glob|al vil|lage** People sometimes refer to the world as a **global village** when they want to emphasize that all the different parts of the world form one community linked together by electronic communications, especially the Internet. ❑ *Now that we are all part of the global village, everyone becomes a neighbour.* N-SING

**glob|al warm|ing** **Global warming** is the gradual rise in the earth's temperature caused by high levels of carbon dioxide and other gases in the atmosphere. ❑ *The threat of global warming will eventually force the US to slow down its energy consumption.* N-UNCOUNT

**globe** /gloʊb/ **(globes)** [1] You can refer to the world as **the globe** when you are emphasizing how big it is or that something happens in many different parts of it. ❑ *...bottles of beer from every corner of the globe... 70% of our globe's surface is water.* N-SING: usu the N = planet [2] A **globe** is a ball-shaped object with a map of the world on it. It is usually fixed on a stand. ❑ *...a globe of the world... Three large globes stand on the floor.* N-COUNT [3] Any ball-shaped object can be referred to as a **globe**. ❑ *The overhead light was covered now with a white globe.* N-COUNT: usu with supp

**globe ar|ti|choke** **(globe artichokes)** → see **artichoke**.

**globe-trot** **(globe-trots, globe-trotting, globe-trotted)** also **globetrot**. If someone spends their time **globe-trotting**, they spend a lot of time travelling to different parts of the world. [INFORMAL] ❑ *The son of a diplomat, he has spent much of his life globe-trotting.* VERB: usu cont V ♦ **globe-trotting** *...globe-trotting academic superstars.* ADJ ♦ **globe-trotter** **(globe-trotters)** *TV globe-trotter Alan Whicker was nearly burned alive by an angry mob in Egypt.* N-COUNT

**globu|lar** /glɒbjʊləʳ/ A **globular** object is shaped like a ball. [FORMAL] ❑ *The globular seed capsule contains numerous small seeds.* ADJ: usu ADJ n

**glob|ule** /glɒbjuːl/ **(globules)** **Globules of** a liquid or of a soft substance are tiny round particles of it. ❑ *...globules of saliva... Our bone marrow contains fat in the form of small globules.* N-COUNT: usu pl, oft N of n = droplet

**glock|en|spiel** /glɒkənʃpiːl/ **(glockenspiels)** A **glockenspiel** is a musical instrument which consists of metal bars of different lengths arranged like the keyboard of a piano. You play the glockenspiel by hitting the bars with wooden hammers. N-COUNT: oft the N

**gloom** /gluːm/ [1] **The gloom** is a state of near darkness. ❑ *...the gloom of a foggy November morning... I was peering about me in the gloom.* N-SING: the N, oft in/into N [2] **Gloom** is a feeling of sadness and lack of hope. ❑ *...the deepening gloom over the economy.* N-UNCOUNT: also a N

**gloomy** /gluːmi/ **(gloomier, gloomiest)** [1] If a place is **gloomy**, it is almost dark so that you cannot see very well. ❑ *Inside it's gloomy after all that sunshine. ...this huge gloomy church.* ADJ [2] If people are **gloomy**, they are unhappy and have no hope. ❑ *Miller is gloomy about the fate of the serious playwright in America.* ADJ = despondent ♦ **gloomi|ly** *He tells me gloomily that he has been called up for army service.* ADV: ADV with v [3] If a situation is **gloomy**, it does not give you much hope of success or happiness. ❑ *...a gloomy picture of an economy sliding into recession... Officials say the outlook for next year is gloomy.* ADJ = grim

**glo|ri|fied** /glɔːrɪfaɪd/ You use **glorified** to indicate that something is less important or impressive than its name suggests. ❑ *Sometimes they tell me I'm just a glorified waitress.* ADJ: ADJ n

**glo|ri|fy** /glɔːrɪfaɪ/ **(glorifies, glorifying, glorified)** To **glorify** something means to praise it or make it seem good or special, usually when it is not. ❑ *This magazine in no way glorifies gangs. ...the banning of songs glorifying war and racism.* VERB V n V n ♦ **glo|ri|fi|ca|tion** /glɔːrɪfɪkeɪʃᵊn/ *...the glorification of violence.* N-UNCOUNT

**glo|ri|ous** /glɔːriəs/ [1] Something that is **glorious** is very beautiful and impressive. ❑ *She had missed the glorious blooms of the Mediterranean spring. ...a glorious Edwardian opera house.* ADJ = magnificent ♦ **glo|ri|ous|ly** *...gloriously embroidered costumes.* ADV: usu ADV adj [2] If you describe something as **glorious**, you are emphasizing that it is wonderful and it makes you feel very happy. ❑ *The win revived glorious memories of his championship-winning days... We opened the windows and let in the glorious evening air.* ADJ [emphasis] = wonderful ♦ **glo|ri|ous|ly** *...her gloriously happy love life.* ADV [3] A **glorious** career, victory, or occasion involves great fame or success. ❑ *Harrison had a glorious career spanning more than six decades.* ADJ ♦ **glo|ri|ous|ly** *But the mission was successful, gloriously successful.* ADV: usu ADV adj [4] **Glorious** weather is hot and sunny. ❑ *I got dressed and emerged into glorious sunshine... The sun was out again, and it was a glorious day.* ADJ ♦ **glo|ri|ous|ly** *For a change, it was a gloriously sunny day.* ADV: ADV adj

**glo|ry** /glɔːri/ **(glories, glorying, gloried)** [1] **Glory** is the fame and admiration that you gain by doing something impressive. ❑ *Walsham had his moment of glory when he won a 20km race. ...we were still basking in the glory of our Championship win.* N-UNCOUNT [2] A person's **glories** are the occasions when they have done something people greatly admire which makes them famous. ❑ *The album sees them re-living past glories but not really breaking any new ground.* N-PLURAL: with supp [3] **The glory of** something is its great beauty or impressive nature. ❑ *The glory of the idea blossomed in his mind.* N-UNCOUNT: with poss, usu the N of n [4] **The glories of** a culture or place are the things that people admire most about it. ❑ *...a tour of Florence, to enjoy the artistic glories of the Italian Renaissance.* N-COUNT: usu pl, with supp, usu the N of n [5] If you **glory in** a situation or activity, you enjoy it very much. ❑ *The workers were glorying in their new-found freedom.* VERB = revel V in n [6] If you go out **in a blaze of glory**, you do something very dramatic at the end of your career or your life which makes you famous. PHRASE: oft in PHR

❑ *I am never going back to prison. I am going to make national news headlines and go out in a blaze of glory.*

**gloss** /glɒs, AM glɔːs/ **(glosses, glossing, glossed)** [1] A **gloss** is a bright shine on the surface of something. ❑ *Rain produced a black gloss on the asphalt.* N-SING = sheen [2] **Gloss** is an appearance of attractiveness or good quality which sometimes hides less attractive features or poor quality. ❑ *Television commercials might seem more professional but beware of mistaking the gloss for the content.* N-UNCOUNT [3] If you put **a gloss on** a bad situation, you try to make it seem more attractive or acceptable by giving people a false explanation or interpretation of it. ❑ *He used his diary to put a fine gloss on the horrors the regime perpetrated.* N-SING: *a* N, usu N *on* n [4] **Gloss** is the same as **gloss paint**. N-MASS [5] **Gloss** is a type of shiny make-up. ❑ *She brushed gloss on to her eyelids. ...lip glosses.* N-MASS [6] If you **gloss** a difficult word or idea, you provide an explanation of it. ❑ *Older editors glossed 'drynke' as 'love-potion'.* VERB V n *as* n

♦ **gloss over** If you **gloss over** a problem, a mistake, or an embarrassing moment, you try and make it seem unimportant by ignoring it or by dealing with it very quickly. ❑ *Some foreign governments appear happy to gloss over continued human rights abuses.* PHRASAL VERB V P n (not pron)

**glos|sa|ry** /glɒsəri, AM glɔːs-/ **(glossaries)** A **glossary** of special, unusual, or technical words or expressions is an alphabetical list of them giving their meanings, for example at the end of a book on a particular subject. N-COUNT

**glossies** /glɒsiz, AM glɔːs-/ The **glossies** are expensive magazines which are printed on thick, shiny paper. [BRIT, INFORMAL] N-PLURAL

**gloss paint** **Gloss paint** is paint that forms a shiny surface when it dries. N-UNCOUNT

**glossy** /glɒsi, AM glɔːsi/ **(glossier, glossiest)** [1] **Glossy** means smooth and shiny. ❑ *...glossy black hair... The leaves were dark and glossy.* ADJ [2] You can describe something as **glossy** if you think that it has been designed to look attractive but has little practical value or may have hidden faults. ❑ *...a glossy new office... British TV commercials are glossy and sophisticated.* ADJ [3] **Glossy** magazines, leaflets, books, and photographs are produced on expensive, shiny paper. ❑ *...a glossy magazine called 'Women Today'.* ADJ: ADJ n

**glove** /glʌv/ **(gloves)** [1] **Gloves** are pieces of clothing which cover your hands and wrists and have individual sections for each finger. You wear gloves to keep your hands warm or dry or to protect them. ❑ *...a pair of white cotton gloves.* N-COUNT [2] If you say that something **fits like a glove**, you are emphasizing that it fits exactly. PHRASE: V inflects [emphasis] [3] → See also **kid gloves**. **hand in glove** → see **hand**.

**glove com|part|ment** **(glove compartments)** or **glove box** The **glove compartment** in a car is a small cupboard or shelf below the front windscreen. → See picture on page 1708. N-COUNT

**gloved** /glʌvd/ A **gloved** hand has a glove on it. [mainly WRITTEN] ADJ: usu ADJ n

**glow** /gloʊ/ **(glows, glowing, glowed)** [1] A **glow** is a dull, steady light, for example the light produced by a fire when there are no flames. ❑ *...the cigarette's red glow... The rising sun casts a golden glow over the fields.* N-COUNT: usu sing [2] A **glow** is a pink colour on a person's face, usually because they are healthy or have been exercising. ❑ *The moisturiser gave my face a healthy glow that lasted all day.* N-SING: usu *a* N [3] If you feel a **glow of** satisfaction or achievement, you have a strong feeling of pleasure because of something that you have done or that has happened. ❑ *Exercise will give you a glow of satisfaction at having achieved something... He felt a glow of pride in what she had accomplished.* N-SING: oft N *of* n [4] If something **glows**, it produces a dull, steady light. ❑ *The night lantern glowed softly in the darkness... Even the mantel above the fire glowed white.* VERB V V adj [5] If a place **glows with** a colour or a quality, it is bright, attractive, and colourful. ❑ *Used together these colours will make your interiors glow with warmth and vitality. ...carved wood bathed in glowing colors and gold leaf.* VERB V *with* n V-ing Also V [6] If something **glows**, it looks bright because it is reflecting light. ❑ *The instruments glowed in the bright orange light... The fall foliage glowed red and yellow in the sunlight.* VERB V V adj [7] If someone's skin **glows**, it looks pink because they are healthy or excited, or have been doing physical exercise. ❑ *Her freckled skin glowed with health again. ...a glowing complexion.* VERB V *with* n V-ing [8] If someone **glows with** an emotion such as pride or pleasure, the expression on their face shows how they feel. ❑ *The expectant mothers that Amy had encountered positively glowed with pride.* VERB V *with* n [9] → See also **glowing**.

**glow|er** /glaʊəʳ/ **(glowers, glowering, glowered)** If you **glower at** someone or something, you look at them angrily. ❑ *He glowered at me but said nothing... He glowered and glared, but she steadfastly refused to look his way.* VERB = glare V *at* n V

**glow|er|ing** /glaʊərɪŋ/ [1] If you describe a person as **glowering**, you mean they look angry and bad tempered. [WRITTEN] ❑ *...his glowering good looks.* ADJ: usu ADJ n [2] If you describe a place as **glowering**, you mean that it looks dark and threatening. [WRITTEN] ❑ *...glowering castle walls.* ADJ: usu ADJ n

**glow|ing** /gloʊɪŋ/ A **glowing** description or opinion about someone or something praises them highly or supports them strongly. ❑ *The media has been speaking in glowing terms of the relationship between the two countries.* → See also **glow**. ADJ: usu ADJ n

♦ **glow|ing|ly** *Wallis spoke glowingly about players like Chapman.* ADV

**glow-worm** **(glow-worms)** A **glow-worm** is a type of beetle which produces light from its body. N-COUNT

**glu|cose** /gluːkoʊz, -oʊs/ **Glucose** is a type of sugar that gives you energy. N-UNCOUNT

**glue** /gluː/ **(glues, glueing** or **gluing, glued)** [1] **Glue** is a sticky substance used for joining things together, often for repairing broken things. ❑ *...a tube of glue. ...high quality glues.* N-MASS [2] If you **glue** one object to another, you stick them together using glue. ❑ *Glue the fabric around the window... The pieces are then glued together.* VERB V n prep/adv *be* V-ed together V-PASSIVE [3] If you say that someone **is glued to** something, you mean that they are giving it all their attention. ❑ *They are all glued to the Olympic Games.* *be* V-ed *to* n

**glue sniff|ing** **Glue sniffing** is the practice of breathing the vapour from glue in order to become intoxicated. N-UNCOUNT = solvent abuse

**glum** /glʌm/ **(glummer, glummest)** Someone who is **glum** is sad and quiet because they are disappointed or unhappy about something. ❑ *She was very glum and was obviously missing her children.* ADJ: usu v-link ADJ = despondent

♦ **glum|ly** *When Eleanor returned, I was still sitting glumly on the settee.* ADV: ADV with v

**glut** /glʌt/ **(gluts, glutting, glutted)** [1] If there is a **glut of** something, there is so much of it that it cannot all be sold or used. ❑ *There's a glut of agricultural products in Western Europe. ...a world oil glut.* N-COUNT: usu sing, usu with supp = surplus [2] If a market **is glutted with** something, there is a glut of that thing. [BUSINESS] ❑ *The region is glutted with hospitals... Soldiers returning from the war had glutted the job market.* VERB *be* V-ed *with* n V n

**glu|ta|mate** /gluːtəmeɪt/ → see **monosodium glutamate**.

**glu|ten** /gluːtᵊn/ **Gluten** is a substance found in cereal grains such as wheat. N-UNCOUNT

**glu|ti|nous** /gluːtɪnəs/ Something that is **glutinous** is very sticky. ❑ *The sauce was glutinous and tasted artificial. ...soft and glutinous mud.* ADJ

**glut|ton** /glʌtᵊn/ **(gluttons)** [1] If you think that someone eats too much and is greedy, you can say they are a **glutton**. ❑ *I can't control my eating. It's hard when people don't understand and call you a glutton.* N-COUNT [disapproval] [2] If you say that someone is a **glutton for** something, you mean that they enjoy or need it very much. ❑ *He was a glutton for hard work... Ivy must be a glutton for punishment.* N-COUNT: N *for* n

**glut|ton|ous** /glʌtənəs/ If you think that someone eats too much and is greedy, you can ADJ say they are **gluttonous**. ❑ *...a selfish, gluttonous and lazy person.*

**glut|tony** /glʌtəni/ **Gluttony** is the act or habit of eating too much and being greedy. N-UNCOUNT

**glyc|er|ine** /glɪsərɪn/

in AM, usually use **glycerin**

**Glycerine** is a thick, sweet, colourless liquid that is used especially in making medicine, explosives, and antifreeze for cars. N-UNCOUNT

**gm** **(gm** or **gms) gm** is a written abbreviation for **gram**. ❑ *...450 gm (1 lb) mixed soft summer fruits.*

**GM** /dʒiː em/ 1 **GM** crops have had one or more genes changed, for example in order to make them resist pests better. **GM** food contains ingredients made from GM crops. **GM** is an abbreviation for 'genetically modified'. [mainly BRIT] ❑ *Many of us may be eating food containing GM ingredients without realising it.* ADJ 2 In Britain, **GM** schools receive money directly from the government rather than from a local authority. **GM** is an abbreviation for 'grant-maintained'. ❑ *GM schools receive better funding than other state schools.* ADJ

**GM-free** **GM-free** products or crops are products or crops that do not contain any genetically modified material. ❑ *...GM-free soya. ...food that is meant to be GM-free.* ADJ

**GMO** /dʒiː em oʊ/ **(GMOs)** A **GMO** is an animal, plant, or other organism whose genetic structure has been changed by genetic engineering. **GMO** is an abbreviation for 'genetically modified organism'. N-COUNT

**GMT** /dʒiː em tiː/ **GMT** is the standard time in Great Britain which is used to calculate the time in the rest of the world. **GMT** is an abbreviation for 'Greenwich Mean Time'. ❑ *New Mexico is seven hours behind GMT.*

**gnarled** /nɑːʳld/ 1 A **gnarled** tree is twisted and strangely shaped because it is old. ❑ *...a large and beautiful garden full of ancient gnarled trees.* ADJ 2 A person who is **gnarled** looks very old because their skin has lines on it or their body is bent. If someone has **gnarled** hands, their hands are twisted as a result of old age or illness. ❑ *...gnarled old men... His hands were gnarled with arthritis.* ADJ

**gnash** /næʃ/ **(gnashes, gnashing, gnashed)** If you say that someone **is gnashing** their **teeth**, you mean they are angry or frustrated about something. ❑ *If you couldn't attend either of the concerts and are currently gnashing your teeth at having missed out, don't despair.* PHRASE: V inflects

**gnat** /næt/ **(gnats)** A **gnat** is a very small flying insect that bites people and usually lives near water. N-COUNT

**gnaw** /nɔː/ **(gnaws, gnawing, gnawed)** 1 If people or animals **gnaw** something or **gnaw at** it, they bite it repeatedly. ❑ *Woodlice attack living plants and gnaw at the stems... Melanie gnawed a long, painted fingernail.* VERB = chew; V *at/on* n; V n 2 If a feeling or thought **gnaws at** you, it causes you to keep worrying. [WRITTEN] ❑ *Doubts were already gnawing away at the back of his mind... Mary Ann's exhilaration gave way to gnawing fear.* VERB = nag; V *at* n; V-ing

**gnoc|chi** /nɒki/ **Gnocchi** are a type of pasta consisting of small round balls made from flour and sometimes potato. N-PLURAL

**gnome** /noʊm/ **(gnomes)** In children's stories, a **gnome** is an imaginary creature that is like a tiny old man with a beard and pointed hat. In Britain people sometimes have small statues of gnomes in their gardens. N-COUNT

**gno|mic** /noʊmɪk/ A **gnomic** remark is brief and seems wise but is difficult to understand. [WRITTEN] ❑ *...the somewhat gnomic utterances of John Maynard Keynes in his General Theory.* ADJ: usu ADJ n

**GNP** /dʒiː en piː/ **(GNPs)** In economics, a country's **GNP** is the total value of all the goods produced and services provided by that country in one year. **GNP** is an abbreviation for 'gross national product'. Compare **GDP**. ❑ *By 1973 the government deficit equalled thirty per cent of GNP.* ◆◇◇ N-VAR

**gnu** /nuː/ **(gnus)** A **gnu** is a large African deer. N-COUNT

**GNVQ** /dʒiː en viː kjuː/ **(GNVQs)** In Britain, **GNVQs** are qualifications in practical subjects such as business, design, and information technology. **GNVQ** is an abbreviation for 'general national vocational qualification'. ❑ *We have a 90 cent pass rate for GNVQs.* N-COUNT

**go**

① MOVING OR LEAVING
② LINK VERB USES
③ OTHER VERB USES, NOUN USES, AND PHRASES
④ PHRASAL VERBS

① **go** /goʊ/ **(goes, going, went, gone)** ◆◆◆

In most cases the past participle of **go** is **gone**, but occasionally you use 'been': see **been**.

1 When you **go** somewhere, you move or travel there. ❑ *We went to Rome... Gladys had just gone into the kitchen... I went home at the weekend... It took us an hour to go three miles.* VERB; V prep/adv; V amount 2 When you **go**, you leave the place where you are. ❑ *Let's go... She's going tomorrow.* VERB; V 3 You use **go** to say that someone leaves the place where they are and does an activity, often a leisure activity. ❑ *We went swimming very early... Maybe they've just gone shopping... He went for a walk.* VERB; V -ing; V -ing; V *for* n 4 When you **go to** do something, you move to a place in order to do it and you do it. You can also **go and** do something, and in American English, you can **go** do something. However, you always say that someone **went and** did something. ❑ *His second son, Paddy, had gone to live in Canada... I must go and see this film... Go ask whoever you want.* VERB; V to-inf; V *and* v; V inf 5 If you **go to** school, work, or church, you attend it regularly as part of your normal life. ❑ *She will have to go to school... His son went to a top university in America.* VERB; V *to* n; V *to* n 6 When you say where a road or path **goes**, you are saying where it begins or ends, or what places it is in. ❑ *There's a mountain road that goes from Blairstown to Millbrook Village.* VERB = lead; V prep/adv 7 You can use **go** in expressions such as **'don't go telling everybody'**, in order to express disapproval of the kind of behaviour you mention, or to tell someone not to behave in that way. ❑ *You don't have to go running upstairs every time she rings... Don't you go thinking it was your fault.* VERB: with brd-neg; V -ing; V -ing 8 You can use **go** with words like 'further' and 'beyond' to show the degree or extent of something. ❑ *He went even further in his speech to the conference... Some physicists have gone so far as to suggest that the entire Universe is a sort of gigantic computer.* VERB; V adv/prep; V adv/prep 9 If you say that a period of time **goes** quickly or slowly, you mean that it seems to pass quickly or slowly. ❑ *The weeks go so quickly!* VERB = pass; V adv 10 If you say where money **goes**, you are saying what it is spent on. ❑ *Most of my money goes on bills... The money goes to projects chosen by the wider community.* VERB; V prep/adv; V prep/adv 11 If you say that something **goes to** someone, you mean that it is given to them. ❑ *A lot of credit must go to the chairman and his father... The job went to Yuri Skokov, a capable administrator.* VERB; V *to* n; V *to* n 12 If someone **goes on** television or radio, they take part in a television or radio programme. ❑ *The Turkish president has gone on television to defend stringent new security measures... We went on the air, live, at 7.30.* VERB; V *on* n; V *on* n 13 If something **goes**, someone gets rid of it. ❑ *The Institute of Export now fears that 100,000 jobs will go... If people stand firm against the tax, it is only a matter of time before it has to go.* VERB; V; V 14 If someone **goes**, they leave their job, usually because they are forced to. ❑ *He had made a humiliating tactical error and he had to go.* VERB; V 15 If something **goes into** something else, it is put in it as one of the parts or elements that form it. ❑ *...the really interesting ingredients that go into the dishes that we all love to eat.* VERB; V *into/in* n 16 If some- VERB

thing **goes** in a particular place, it fits in that place or should be put there because it is the right size or shape. ❑ *He was trying to push it through the hole and it wouldn't go. ...This knob goes here.* (V; V prep/adv)

17 VERB If something **goes** in a particular place, it belongs there or should be put there, because that is where you normally keep it. ❑ *The shoes go on the shoe shelf... 'Where does everything go?'* (V prep/adv; V prep/adv)

18 VERB If you say that one number **goes into** another number a particular number of times, you are dividing the second number by the first. ❑ *Six goes into thirty five times.* (V *into* num)

19 VERB = *fail* If one of a person's senses, such as their sight or hearing, **is going**, it is getting weak and they may soon lose it completely. [INFORMAL] ❑ *His eyes are going; he says he has glaucoma... Lately he'd been making mistakes; his nerve was beginning to go.* (V; V)

20 VERB If something such as a light bulb or a part of an engine **is going**, it is no longer working properly and will soon need to be replaced. ❑ *I thought it looked as though the battery was going.* (V)

② **go** /gəʊ/ **(goes, going, went, gone)** ◆◆◆

1 V-LINK You can use **go** to say that a person or thing changes to another state or condition. For example, if someone **goes crazy**, they become crazy, and if something **goes green**, it changes colour and becomes green. ❑ *I'm going bald... You'd better serve it to them before it goes cold... 50,000 companies have gone out of business.* (V adj; V adj; V prep)

2 V-LINK You can use **go** when indicating whether or not someone wears or has something. For example, if someone **goes barefoot**, they do not wear any shoes. ❑ *The baby went naked on the beach... But if you arm the police won't more criminals go armed?* (V adj; V adj)

3 V-LINK You can use **go** before adjectives beginning with 'un-' to say that something does not happen. For example, if something **goes unheard**, nobody hears it. ❑ *As President, he affirmed that no tyranny went unnoticed.* (V -ed)

③ **go** /gəʊ/ **(goes, going, went, gone)** ◆◆◆

1 VERB You use **go** to talk about the way something happens. For example, if an event or situation **goes well**, it is successful. ❑ *She says everything is going smoothly... How did it go at the hairdresser's?* (V adv; V adv)

2 VERB If a machine or device **is going**, it is working. ❑ *What about my copier? Can you get it going again?... I said, 'My car won't go in fog'.* (V; V)

3 VERB If a bell **goes**, it makes a noise, usually as a signal for you to do something. ❑ *The bell went for the break.* (V)

4 V-RECIP If something **goes with** something else, or if two things **go together**, they look or taste nice together. ❑ *I was searching for a pair of grey gloves to go with my new gown... I can see that some colours go together and some don't... Wear something else. This won't go.* (V *with* n; pl-n V *together*; V (non-recip))

5 VERB You use **go** to introduce something you are quoting. For example, you say **the story goes** or **the argument goes** just before you quote all or part of it. ❑ *The story goes that she went home with him that night... The story goes like this... As the saying goes, 'There's no smoke without fire.'* (V that; V prep; V with quote)

6 VERB You use **go** when indicating that something makes or produces a sound. For example, if you say that something **goes 'bang'**, you mean it produces the sound 'bang'. ❑ *She stopped in front of a painting of a dog and she started going 'woof woof'... The button on his jeans went POP.* (V with sound; V with sound)

7 VERB You can use **go** instead of 'say' when you are quoting what someone has said or what you think they will say. [INFORMAL] ❑ *They say 'Tom, shut up' and I go 'No, you shut up'... He goes to me: 'Oh, what do you want now?'* (V with quote; V *to* n with quote)

8 N-COUNT: oft N *at* n/-ing A **go** is an attempt at doing something. ❑ *I always wanted to have a go at football... She won on her first go... Her hair was bright orange. It took us two goes to get the colour right.*

9 N-COUNT: poss N = *turn* If it is your **go** in a game, it is your turn to do something, for example to play a card or move a piece. ❑ *I'm two behind you but it's your go... Now whose go is it?*

10 → See also **going, gone**.

PHRASES

11 PHRASE: V inflects, PHR to-inf, PHR *for* n If you **go all out to** do something or **go all out for** something, you make the greatest possible effort to do it or get it. [INFORMAL] ❑ *They will go all out to get exactly what they want... They're ready to go all out for the Premier League title next season.*

12 PHRASE: PHR with cl You use expressions like **as things go** or **as children go** when you are describing one person or thing and comparing them with others of the same kind. [INFORMAL] ❑ *This is a straightforward case, as these things go... He's good company, as small boys go.*

13 PHRASE: PHR after v If you do something **as** you **go along**, you do it while you are doing another thing, without preparing it beforehand. ❑ *Learning how to become a parent takes time. It's a skill you learn as you go along.*

14 PHRASE: Vs inflect disapproval If you say that someone **has gone and done** something, you are expressing your annoyance at the foolish thing they have done. [INFORMAL] ❑ *Well, he's gone and done it again, hasn't he?... Somebody goes and does something mindless like that and just destroys everything for you.*

15 CONVENTION You say **'Go for it'** to encourage someone to increase their efforts to achieve or win something. [INFORMAL]

16 PHRASE: V inflects, PHR n If someone **has a go at** you, they criticize you, often in a way that you feel is unfair. [mainly BRIT, INFORMAL] ❑ *Some people had a go at us for it, which made us more angry.*

17 CONVENTION If someone says **'Where do we go from here?'** they are asking what should be done next, usually because a problem has not been solved in a satisfactory way.

18 PHRASE: V inflects, PHR n If you say that someone **is making a go of** something such as a business or relationship, you mean that they are having some success with it. ❑ *I knew we could make a go of it and be happy.*

19 PHRASE: usu v-link PHR, PHR after v If you say that someone is always **on the go**, you mean that they are always busy and active. [INFORMAL] ❑ *I got a new job this year where I am on the go all the time.*

20 PHRASE: V inflects, usu PHR after v If you **have** something **on the go**, you have started it and are busy doing it. ❑ *Do you like to have many projects on the go at any one time?*

21 PHRASE: amount PHR If you say that there are a particular number of things **to go**, you mean that they still remain to be dealt with. ❑ *I still had another five operations to go.*

22 PHRASE: amount PHR, oft PHR prep If you say that there is a certain amount of time **to go**, you mean that there is that amount of time left before something happens or ends. ❑ *There is a week to go until the elections.*

23 PHRASE: n PHR If you are in a café or restaurant and ask for an item of food **to go**, you mean that you want to take it away with you and not eat it there. [mainly AM] ❑ *Large fries to go.*

✔ in BRIT, use **to take out, to take away**

④ **go** /gəʊ/ **(goes, going, went, gone)** ◆◆◆

♦ **go about** 1 PHRASAL VERB The way you **go about** a task or problem is the way you approach it and deal with it. ❑ *I want him back, but I just don't know how to go about it.* (V P n/-ing)

2 PHRASAL VERB When you **are going about** your normal activities, you are doing them. ❑ *We were simply going about our business when we were pounced upon by these police officers.* (V P n)

3 PHRASAL VERB = *go around* If you **go about** in a particular way, you behave or dress in that way, often as part of your normal life. ❑ *He used to go about in a black cape... He went about looking ill and unhappy.* (V P prep; V P -ing)

♦ **go after** PHRASAL VERB If you **go after** something, you try to get it, catch it, or hit it. ❑ *We're not going after civilian targets.* (V P n)

♦ **go against** 1 PHRASAL VERB If a person or their behaviour **goes against** your wishes, beliefs, or expectations, their behaviour is the opposite of what you want, believe in, or expect. ❑ *Changes are being made here which go against my principles and I cannot agree with them.* (V P n)

2 PHRASAL VERB If a decision, vote, or result **goes against** you, you do not get the decision, vote, or result that you wanted. ❑ *The prime minister will resign if the vote goes against him.* (V P n)

♦ **go ahead** 1 PHRASAL VERB If someone **goes ahead with** something, they begin to do it or make it, especially after planning, promising, or asking permission to do it. ❑ *The district board will vote today on whether to go ahead with the plan.* (V P *with* n)

2 PHRASAL VERB If a process or an organized event **goes ahead**, it takes place or is carried out. ❑ *The event will go ahead as planned in Sheffield next summer.* (V P)

♦**go along** [1] If you **go along to** a meeting, event, or place, you attend or visit it. PHRASAL VERB ❑ *I went along to the meeting...* V P to n *You should go along and have a look.* V P and inf [2] If you describe how something **is going along**, you describe how it is progressing. PHRASAL VERB: usu cont ❑ *Things were going along fairly well.* V P adv

♦**go along with** [1] If you **go along with** a rule, decision, or policy, you accept it and obey it. PHRASAL VERB ❑ *Whatever the majority decided I was prepared to go along with.* V P P n [2] If you **go along with** a person or an idea, you agree with them. PHRASAL VERB ❑ *'I don't think a government has properly done it for about the past twenty-five years.' — 'I'd go along with that.'* V P P n

♦**go around**

✓ in BRIT, also use **go round**

[1] If you **go around to** someone's house, you go to visit them at their house. PHRASAL VERB ❑ *I asked them to go around to the house to see if they were there...* V P to n *Mike went round to see them.* V P to-inf [2] If you **go around** in a particular way, you behave or dress in that way, often as part of your normal life. PHRASAL VERB = go about ❑ *I had got in the habit of going around with bare feet...* V P prep *If they went around complaining publicly, they might not find it so easy to get another job.* V P -ing Also V P adj [3] If a piece of news or a joke **is going around**, it is being told by many people in the same period of time. PHRASAL VERB ❑ *There's a nasty sort of rumour going around about it.* V P [4] If there is enough of something **to go around**, there is enough of it to be shared among a group of people, or to do all the things for which it is needed. PHRASAL VERB ❑ *Eventually we will not have enough water to go around.* V P

♦**go away** [1] If you **go away**, you leave a place or a person's company. PHRASAL VERB ❑ *I think we need to go away and think about this.* V P [2] If you **go away**, you leave a place and spend a period of time somewhere else, especially as a holiday. PHRASAL VERB ❑ *Why don't you and I go away this weekend?* V P

♦**go back** [1] If something **goes back to** a particular time in the past, it was made or started at that time. PHRASAL VERB = date back ❑ *The feud with the Catholics goes back to the 11th century...* V P to n *Our association with him goes back four years.* V P n [2] If someone **goes back to** a time in the past, they begin to discuss or consider events that happened at that time. PHRASAL VERB ❑ *If you go back to 1960, you'll find that very few jobs were being created.* V P to n Also V P n

♦**go back on** If you **go back on** a promise or agreement, you do not do what you promised or agreed to do. PHRASAL VERB ❑ *The budget crisis has forced the President to go back on his word.* V P P n

♦**go back to** [1] If you **go back to** a task or activity, you start doing it again after you have stopped doing it for a period of time. PHRASAL VERB ❑ *I now look forward to going back to work as soon as possible...* V P P n/-ing *Amy went back to studying.* V P P n/-ing [2] If you **go back to** a particular point in a lecture, discussion, or book, you start to discuss it. PHRASAL VERB ❑ *Let me just go back to the point I was making.* V P P n

♦**go before** [1] Something that **has gone before** has happened or been discussed at an earlier time. PHRASAL VERB ❑ *This is a rejection of most of what has gone before.* V P [2] To **go before** a judge, tribunal, or court of law means to be present there as part of an official or legal process. PHRASAL VERB ❑ *The case went before Mr Justice Henry on December 23 and was adjourned.* V P n

♦**go by** [1] If you say that time **goes by**, you mean that it passes. PHRASAL VERB = go on ❑ *My grandmother was becoming more and more sad and frail as the years went by.* V P [2] If you **go by** something, you use it as a basis for a judgment or action. PHRASAL VERB ❑ *If they prove that I was wrong, then I'll go by what they say.* V P n

♦**go down** [1] If a price, level, or amount **goes down**, it becomes lower or less than it was. PHRASAL VERB = fall ❑ *Income from sales tax went down...* V P *Crime has gone down 70 percent in the last five years...* V P amount *Average life expectancy went down from about 70 to 67.* V P from/to/by n [2] If you **go down on** your knees or **on** all fours, you lower your body until it is supported by your knees, or by your hands and knees. PHRASAL VERB = get down ❑ *I went down on my knees and prayed for guidance.* V P on n [3] In sport, if a person or team **goes down**, they are defeated in a match or contest. PHRASAL VERB = lose ❑ *They went down 2-1 to Australia.* V P num Also V P [4] If you say that a remark, idea, or type of behaviour **goes down** in a particular way, you mean that it gets a particular kind of reaction from a person or group of people. PHRASAL VERB ❑ *Solicitors advised their clients that a tidy look went down well with the magistrates.* V P adv [5] When the sun **goes down**, it goes below the horizon. PHRASAL VERB = set ❑ *...the glow left in the sky after the sun has gone down.* V P [6] If a ship **goes down**, it sinks. If a plane **goes down**, it crashes out of the sky. PHRASAL VERB ❑ *Their aircraft went down during a training exercise.* V P [7] If a computer **goes down**, it stops functioning temporarily. PHRASAL VERB ❑ *The main computers went down for 30 minutes.* V P

♦**go down as** If you say that an event or action will **go down as** a particular thing, you mean that it will be regarded, remembered, or recorded as that thing. PHRASAL VERB ❑ *It will go down as one of the highlights of my career.* V P P n

♦**go down with** If you **go down with** an illness or a disease, you catch it. [INFORMAL] PHRASAL VERB ❑ *Three members of the band went down with flu.* V P P n

♦**go for** [1] If you **go for** a particular thing or way of doing something, you choose it. PHRASAL VERB ❑ *People tried to persuade him to go for a more gradual reform programme.* V P n [2] If you **go for** someone or something, you like them very much. [INFORMAL] PHRASAL VERB ❑ *I tend to go for large dark men.* V P n [3] If you **go for** someone, you attack them. PHRASAL VERB ❑ *Pantieri went for him, gripping him by the throat.* V P n [4] If you say that a statement you have made about one person or thing also **goes for** another person or thing, you mean that the statement is also true of this other person or thing. PHRASAL VERB ❑ *It is illegal to dishonour bookings; that goes for restaurants as well as customers.* V P n [5] If something **goes for** a particular price, it is sold for that amount. PHRASAL VERB = fetch ❑ *Some old machines go for as much as 35,000 pounds.*

♦**go in** If the sun **goes in**, a cloud comes in front of it and it can no longer be seen. [BRIT] PHRASAL VERB ≠ come out ❑ *The sun went in, and the breeze became cold.* V P

♦**go in for** If you **go in for** a particular activity, you decide to do it as a hobby or interest. PHRASAL VERB ❑ *They go in for tennis and bowls.* V P P n

♦**go into** [1] If you **go into** something, you describe or examine it fully or in detail. PHRASAL VERB ❑ *It was a private conversation and I don't want to go into details about what was said.* V P n [2] If you **go into** something, you decide to do it as your job or career. PHRASAL VERB ❑ *Mr Pok has now gone into the tourism business.* V P n [3] If an amount of time, effort, or money **goes into** something, it is spent or used to do it, get it, or make it. PHRASAL VERB ❑ *Is there a lot of effort and money going into this sort of research?* V P n

♦**go off** [1] If you **go off** someone or something, you stop liking them. [BRIT, INFORMAL] PHRASAL VERB ❑ *'Why have they gone off him now?' — 'It could be something he said.'...* V P n *I started to go off the idea.* V P n [2] If an explosive device or a gun **goes off**, it explodes or fires. PHRASAL VERB ❑ *A few minutes later the bomb went off, destroying the vehicle.* V P [3] If an alarm bell **goes off**, it makes a sudden loud noise. PHRASAL VERB ❑ *Then the fire alarm went off. I just grabbed my clothes and ran out.* V P [4] If an electrical device **goes off**, it stops operating. PHRASAL VERB ❑ *As the water came in the windows, all the lights went off.* V P [5] If you say how an organized event **went off**, you are saying whether everything happened in the way that was planned or hoped. PHRASAL VERB ❑ *The meeting went off all right.* V P adv/prep [6] Food or drink that **has gone off** has gone bad. [BRIT] PHRASAL VERB ❑ *Don't eat that! It's mouldy. It's gone off!* V P

♦**go off with** [1] If someone **goes off with** another person, they leave their husband, wife, or lover and have a relationship with that person. PHRASAL VERB ❑ *I suppose Carolyn went off with some man she'd fallen in love with.* V P P n [2] If someone **goes off with** something that belongs to another person, they leave and take it with them. PHRASAL VERB ❑ *He's gone off with my passport.* V P P n

♦ **go on** [1] If you **go on** doing something, or **go on with** an activity, you continue to do it. ❑ *Unemployment is likely to go on rising this year... I'm all right here. Go on with your work... I don't want to leave, but I can't go on.* [2] If something **is going on**, it is happening. ❑ *I don't know what's going on.* [3] If a process or institution **goes on**, it continues to happen or exist. ❑ *The population failed to understand the necessity for the war to go on.* [4] If you say that a period of time **goes on**, you mean that it passes. ❑ *Renewable energy will become progressively more important as time goes on.* [5] If you **go on to** do something, you do it after you have done something else. ❑ *Alliss retired from golf in 1969 and went on to become a successful broadcaster.* [6] If you **go on to** a place, you go to it from the place that you have reached. ❑ *He goes on to Holland tomorrow.* [7] If you **go on**, you continue saying something or talking about something. ❑ *Meer cleared his throat several times before he went on... 'Go on,' Chee said. 'I'm interested.'* [8] If you **go on about** something, or in British English **go on at** someone, you continue talking about the same thing, often in an annoying way. [INFORMAL] ❑ *Expectations have been raised with the Government going on about choice and market forces... She's always going on at me to have a baby.* [9] You say **'Go on'** to someone to persuade or encourage them to do something. [INFORMAL] ❑ *Go on, it's fun.* [10] If you talk about the information you have **to go on**, you mean the information you have available to base an opinion or judgment on. ❑ *But you have to go on the facts... There's not much to go on.* [11] If an electrical device **goes on**, it begins operating. ❑ *A light went on at seven every evening.*

PHRASAL VERB = carry on; V P -ing; V P *with* n; V P; PHRASAL VERB; V P; PHRASAL VERB; V P; PHRASAL VERB = go by; V P; PHRASAL VERB; V P to-inf; PHRASAL VERB; V P prep/adv; PHRASAL VERB; V P; V P with quote; PHRASAL VERB; V P *about* n; V P *at* n to-inf; Also V P *at* n; PHRASAL VERB: only imper; V P; PHRASAL VERB; V P n; V P n; PHRASAL VERB = come on; V P

♦ **go out** [1] If you **go out**, you leave your home in order to do something enjoyable, for example to go to a party, a bar, or the cinema. ❑ *I'm going out tonight.* [2] If you **go out with** someone, the two of you spend time together socially, and have a romantic or sexual relationship. ❑ *I once went out with a French man... They've only been going out for six weeks.* [3] If you **go out to** do something, you make a deliberate effort to do it. ❑ *You do not go out to injure opponents... It will be a marvellous occasion and they should go out and enjoy it.* [4] If a light **goes out**, it stops shining. ❑ *The bedroom light went out after a moment.* [5] If something that is burning **goes out**, it stops burning. ❑ *The fire seemed to be going out.* [6] If a message **goes out**, it is announced, published, or sent out to people. ❑ *Word went out that a column of tanks was on its way.* [7] When a television or radio programme **goes out**, it is broadcast. [BRIT] ❑ *The series goes out at 10.30pm, Fridays, on Channel 4.* [8] When the tide **goes out**, the water in the sea gradually moves back to a lower level. ❑ *The tide was going out.* [9] You can say **'My heart goes out to him'** or **'My sympathy goes out to her'** to express the strong sympathy you have for someone in a difficult or unpleasant situation. ❑ *My heart goes out to Mrs Adams and her fatherless children.*

PHRASAL VERB ≠ stay in; V P; PHRASAL VERB; V P *with* n; pl-n V P; PHRASAL VERB; V P to-inf; V P *and* inf; PHRASAL VERB; V P; PHRASAL VERB; V P; PHRASAL VERB; V P; PHRASAL VERB; V P; PHRASAL VERB ≠ come in; V P; PHRASE: V inflects; feelings

♦ **go out for** To **go out for** something means to try to do it or be chosen for it. [AM] ❑ *You should go out for Supreme Court justice.*

PHRASAL VERB = try out for; V P P n

♦ **go out of** If a quality or feeling **goes out of** someone or something, they no longer have it. ❑ *The fun had gone out of it.*

PHRASAL VERB; V P P n

♦ **go over** If you **go over** a document, incident, or problem, you examine, discuss, or think about it very carefully. ❑ *I won't know how successful it is until an accountant has gone over the books.*

PHRASAL VERB; V P n

♦ **go over to** [1] If someone or something **goes over to** a different way of doing things, they change to it. ❑ *The Armed Forces could do away with conscription and go over to a volunteer system.* [2] If you **go over to** a group or political party, you join them after previously belonging to an opposing group or party. ❑ *Only a small number of tanks and paratroops have gone over to his side.*

PHRASAL VERB; V P P n; PHRASAL VERB; V P P n

♦ **go round** → see **go around**.

♦ **go through** [1] If you **go through** an experience or a period of time, especially an unpleasant or difficult one, you experience it. ❑ *He was going through a very difficult time... South Africa was going through a period of irreversible change.* [2] If you **go through** a lot of things such as papers or clothes, you look at them, usually in order to sort them into groups or to search for a particular item. ❑ *It was evident that someone had gone through my possessions.* [3] If you **go through** a list, story, or plan, you read or check it from beginning to end. ❑ *Going through his list of customers is a massive job.* [4] When someone **goes through** a routine, procedure, or series of actions, they perform it in the way they usually do. ❑ *Every night, they go through the same routine: he throws open the bedroom window, she closes it.* [5] If a law, agreement, or official decision **goes through**, it is approved by a parliament or committee. ❑ *The bill might have gone through if the economy was growing.*

PHRASAL VERB; V P n; V P n; PHRASAL VERB; V P n; PHRASAL VERB; V P n; PHRASAL VERB; V P n; PHRASAL VERB = get through; V P

♦ **go through with** If you **go through with** an action you have decided on, you do it, even though it may be very unpleasant or difficult for you. ❑ *Richard pleaded for Belinda to reconsider and not to go through with the divorce.*

PHRASAL VERB; V P P n

♦ **go towards** If an amount of money **goes towards** something, it is used to pay part of the cost of that thing. ❑ *One per cent of total public spending should eventually go towards the arts... Under the new approach more money will go towards improving the standard of training.*

PHRASAL VERB; V P n/-ing; V P n/-ing

♦ **go under** [1] If a business or project **goes under**, it becomes unable to continue in operation or in existence. [BUSINESS] ❑ *If one firm goes under it could provoke a cascade of bankruptcies.* [2] If a boat, ship, or person in a sea or river **goes under**, they sink below the surface of the water. ❑ *The ship went under, taking with her all her crew.*

PHRASAL VERB = collapse; V P; PHRASAL VERB = sink; V P

♦ **go up** [1] If a price, amount, or level **goes up**, it becomes higher or greater than it was. ❑ *Interest rates went up... The cost has gone up to $1.95 a minute... Prices have gone up 61 percent since deregulation.* [2] When a building, wall, or other structure **goes up**, it is built or fixed in place. ❑ *He noticed a new building going up near Whitaker Park.* [3] If something **goes up**, it explodes or starts to burn, usually suddenly and with great intensity. ❑ *I was going to get out of the building in case it went up... The hotel went up in flames.* [4] If a shout or cheer **goes up**, it is made by a lot of people together. ❑ *A cheer went up from the other passengers.*

PHRASAL VERB = rise; V P; V P *to/from/by* n; V P amount; PHRASAL VERB; V P; PHRASAL VERB; V P; V P *in* n; PHRASAL VERB; V P

♦ **go with** [1] If one thing **goes with** another thing, the two things officially belong together, so that if you get one, you also get the other. ❑ *...the lucrative $250,000 salary that goes with the job.* [2] If one thing **goes with** another thing, it is usually found or experienced together with the other thing. ❑ *For many women, the status which goes with being a wife is important.*

PHRASAL VERB = accompany; V P n; PHRASAL VERB; V P n

♦ **go without** If you **go without** something that you need or usually have or do, you do not get it or do it. ❑ *I have known what it is like to go without food for days... The embargo won't hurt us because we're used to going without.*

PHRASAL VERB; V P n/-ing; V P

**goad** /goʊd/ **(goads, goading, goaded)** If you **goad** someone, you deliberately make them feel angry or irritated, often causing them to react by doing something. ❑ *He wondered if the psychiatrist was trying to goad him into some unguarded response... Charles was always goading me.* ♦ **Goad** is also a noun. ❑ *His opposition acted as a goad to her determination to succeed.*

VERB; V n *into* n/-ing; V n; N-COUNT

**go-ahead** [1] If you give someone or something **the go-ahead**, you give them permission to start doing something. ❑ *The Greek government today gave the go-ahead for five major road schemes... Don't do any major repair work until you get the go-*

N-SING: *the* N

*ahead from your insurers.* 2 A **go-ahead** person or organization tries hard to succeed, often by using new methods. ❑ *Fairview Estate is one of the oldest and the most go-ahead wine producers in South Africa.* — ADJ: ADJ n

**goal** /goʊl/ **(goals)** 1 In games such as football, netball or hockey, the **goal** is the space into which the players try to get the ball in order to score a point for their team. ❑ *David Seaman was back in the Arsenal goal after breaking a knuckle.* — ◆◆◇ N-COUNT

2 In games such as football or hockey, a **goal** is when a player gets the ball into the goal, or the point that is scored by doing this. ❑ *They scored five goals in the first half of the match... The scorer of the winning goal.* — N-COUNT

3 Something that is your **goal** is something that you hope to achieve, especially when much time and effort will be needed. ❑ *It's a matter of setting your own goals and following them... The goal is to raise as much money as possible.* — N-COUNT = aim, objective

**goalie** /goʊli/ **(goalies)** A **goalie** is the same as a **goalkeeper**. [INFORMAL] — N-COUNT

**goal|keeper** /goʊlkiːpəʳ/ **(goalkeepers)** A **goalkeeper** is the player in a sports team whose job is to guard the goal. — N-COUNT

**goal|keeping** /goʊlkiːpɪŋ/ In games such as football and hockey, **goalkeeping** refers to the activity of guarding the goal. ❑ *They were thankful for the excellent goalkeeping of John Lukic.* — N-UNCOUNT

**goal|less** /goʊlləs/ In football, a **goalless** draw is a game which ends without any goals having been scored. ❑ *The fixture ended in a goalless draw... The semi-final finished goalless after extra time.* — ADJ

**goal line** **(goal lines)** also **goal-line.** In games such as football and rugby, a **goal line** is one of the lines at each end of the field. — N-COUNT

**goal|mouth** /goʊlmaʊθ/ **(goalmouths)** In football, the **goalmouth** is the area just in front of the goal. — N-COUNT

**goal|post** /goʊlpoʊst/ **(goalposts)** also **goal post.** 1 A **goalpost** is one of the two upright wooden posts that are connected by a crossbar and form the goal in games such as football and rugby. — N-COUNT

2 If you accuse someone of **moving the goalposts**, you mean that they have changed the rules in a situation or an activity, in order to gain an advantage for themselves and to make things difficult for other people. ❑ *They seem to move the goal posts every time I meet the conditions which are required.* — PHRASE: V inflects [disapproval]

**goat** /goʊt/ **(goats)** A **goat** is a farm animal or a wild animal that is about the size of a sheep. Goats have horns, and hairs on their chin which resemble a beard. — N-COUNT

**goat cheese** **(goat cheeses)** also **goat's cheese. Goat cheese** is cheese made from goat's milk. — N-MASS

**goatee** /goʊtiː/ **(goatees)** A **goatee** is a very short pointed beard that covers a man's chin but not his cheeks. — N-COUNT

**gob** /gɒb/ **(gobs, gobbing, gobbed)** 1 A person's **gob** is their mouth. [BRIT, INFORMAL, RUDE] ❑ *Shut your gob.* — N-COUNT

2 A **gob of** a thick, unpleasant liquid is a small amount of it. [INFORMAL] ❑ *...a gob of spit.* — N-COUNT: N *of* n

3 If someone **gobs**, they **spit**. [BRIT, INFORMAL] ❑ *At a concert in Leeds, some punks gobbed at them and threw beer cans.* — VERB V prep Also V

**gob|bet** /gɒbɪt/ **(gobbets)** 1 A **gobbet of** something soft, especially food, is a small lump or piece of it. ❑ *...gobbets of meat.* — N-COUNT

2 A **gobbet of** information is a small piece of it. — N-COUNT

**gob|ble** /gɒbᵊl/ **(gobbles, gobbling, gobbled)** If you **gobble** food, you eat it quickly and greedily. ❑ *Pete gobbled all the beef stew.* — VERB V n

♦ **Gobble down** and **gobble up** mean the same as **gobble**. ❑ *There were dangerous beasts in the river that might gobble you up.* — PHRASAL VERB V n P Also V P n (not pron)

♦ **gobble down** → see **gobble**.

♦ **gobble up** 1 If an organization **gobbles up** a smaller organization, it takes control of it or destroys it. ❑ *Banc One of Ohio has built an empire in the mid-west by gobbling up smaller banks.* — PHRASAL VERB V P n (not pron) Also V n P

2 To **gobble up** something such as money means to use or waste a lot of it. ❑ *The firm's expenses gobbled up 44% of revenues.* — PHRASAL VERB V P n (not pron) Also V n P

3 → See also **gobble**.

**gob|ble|dy|gook** /gɒbᵊldiguːk/ also **gobbledegook.** If you describe a speech or piece of writing as **gobbledygook**, you are criticizing it for seeming like nonsense and being very technical or complicated. [INFORMAL] ❑ *When he asked questions, the answers came back in Wall Street gobbledygook.* — N-UNCOUNT [disapproval]

**go-between** **(go-betweens)** A **go-between** is a person who takes messages between people who are unable or unwilling to meet each other. ❑ *He will act as a go-between to try and work out an agenda.* — N-COUNT = intermediary

**gob|let** /gɒblɪt/ **(goblets)** A **goblet** is a type of cup without handles and usually with a long stem. — N-COUNT

**gob|lin** /gɒblɪn/ **(goblins)** In fairy stories, a **goblin** is a small, ugly creature which usually enjoys causing trouble. — N-COUNT

**gob|smacked** /gɒbsmækt/ If you say that you were **gobsmacked** by something, you are emphasizing how surprised you were by it. [BRIT, INFORMAL] ❑ *I was really gobsmacked when I saw your picture of a model wearing a hat with a toy airplane on it.* — ADJ [emphasis] = stunned

**god** /gɒd/ **(gods)** 1 The name **God** is given to the spirit or being who is worshipped as the creator and ruler of the world, especially by Jews, Christians, and Muslims. ❑ *He believes in God... God bless you.* — ◆◆◇ N-PROPER

2 People sometimes use **God** in exclamations to emphasize something that they are saying, or to express surprise, fear, or excitement. This use could cause offence. ❑ *God, how I hated him!... Oh my God he's shot somebody.* — CONVENTION [emphasis]

3 In many religions, a **god** is one of the spirits or beings that are believed to have power over a particular part of the world or nature. ❑ *...Pan, the God of nature. ...Zeus, king of the gods.* — N-COUNT

4 Someone who is admired very much by a person or group of people, and who influences them a lot, can be referred to as a **god**. ❑ *To his followers he was a god.* — N-COUNT

5 → See also **act of God**.

**PHRASES** 6 If you say **God forbid**, you are expressing your hope that something will not happen. ❑ *If, God forbid, something goes wrong, I don't know what I would do.* — PHRASE: PHR with cl [feelings]

7 You can say **God knows, God only knows**, or **God alone knows** to emphasize that you do not know something. ❑ *Gunga spoke God knows how many languages... God alone knows what she thinks.* — PHRASE: PHR wh [emphasis]

8 If someone says **God knows** in reply to a question, they mean that they do not know the answer. ❑ *'Where is he now?' 'God knows.'* — PHRASE [emphasis]

9 The term **a man of God** is sometimes used to refer to Christian priests or ministers. — PHRASE

10 If someone uses such expressions as **what in God's name, why in God's name**, or **how in God's name**, they are emphasizing how angry, annoyed, or surprised they are. [INFORMAL] ❑ *What in God's name do you expect me to do?... Why in God's name did you have to tell her?* — PHRASE [emphasis]

11 If someone **plays God**, they act as if they have unlimited power and can do anything they want. ❑ *You have no right to play God in my life!* — PHRASE: V inflects [disapproval]

12 You can use **God** in expressions such as **I hope to God**, or **I wish to God**, or **I swear to God**, in order to emphasize what you are saying. ❑ *I hope to God they are paying you well... I wish to God I hadn't met you.* — PHRASE: usu v PHR that [emphasis]

13 If you say **God willing**, you are saying that something will happen if all goes well. ❑ *God willing, there will be a breakthrough.* — PHRASE

14 **honest to God** → see **honest. in the lap of the gods** → see **lap. for God's sake** → see **sake. thank God** → see **thank**.

**god-awful** also **godawful.** If someone says that something is **god-awful**, they think it is very unpleasant. This word could cause offence. [INFORMAL] — ADJ: usu ADJ n [emphasis]

**god|child** /gɒdtʃaɪld/ **(godchildren)** In the Christian religion, your **godchild** is a person that you promise to help bring up in the Christian faith. N-COUNT: usu with poss

**god|dammit** /gɒddæmɪt/ also **god-damnit, goddamn it.** Some people say **goddammit** when they are angry or irritated. This use could cause offence. [INFORMAL] EXCLAM [feelings]

**god|damn** /gɒdæm/ also **goddam, god-damned.** Some people use **goddamn** when they are angry, surprised, or excited. This use could cause offence. [INFORMAL] ♦ **Goddamn** is also an adverb. ADJ: ADJ n [feelings] ADV: ADV adj

**god|damned** /gɒdæmd/ **Goddamned** means the same as **goddamn**. This use could cause offence. [INFORMAL] ADJ: usu ADJ n

**god|daughter** /gɒddɔːtəʳ/ **(goddaughters)** also **god-daughter.** A **goddaughter** is a female godchild. N-COUNT: usu with poss

**god|dess** /gɒdes/ **(goddesses)** In many religions, a **goddess** is a female spirit or being that is believed to have power over a particular part of the world or nature. ❑ *...Diana, the goddess of war.* N-COUNT

**god|father** /gɒdfɑːðəʳ/ **(godfathers)** 1 A **godfather** is a male godparent. N-COUNT 2 A powerful man who is at the head of a criminal organization is sometimes referred to as a **godfather**. ❑ *...the feared godfather of the Mafia.* N-COUNT 3 You can refer to a man who started or developed something such as a style of music as the **godfather of** that thing. [JOURNALISM] ❑ *...the godfather of soul, James Brown.* N-COUNT: N *of* n

**God-fearing** A **God-fearing** person is religious and behaves according to the moral rules of their religion. ❑ *They brought up their children to be God-fearing Christians.* ADJ: usu ADJ n

**god|forsaken** /gɒdfəʳseɪkən/ also **God-forsaken.** If you say that somewhere is a **god-forsaken** place, you dislike it a lot because you find it very boring and depressing. ❑ *I don't want to stay here, in this job and in this God-forsaken country.* ADJ: ADJ n [disapproval]

**God|head** /gɒdhed/ **The Godhead** is the essential nature of God. N-SING: usu *the* N

**god|less** /gɒdləs/ If you say that a person or group of people is **godless**, you disapprove of them because they do not believe in God. ❑ *...a godless and alienated society.* ♦ **god|less|ness** *...his assaults on the godlessness of America.* ADJ: usu ADJ n [disapproval] N-UNCOUNT

**god|like** /gɒdlaɪk/ A **godlike** person or a person with **godlike** qualities is admired or respected very much as if he or she were perfect. ❑ *His energy and talent elevate him to godlike status... They were godlike in their wisdom and compassion.* ADJ: usu ADJ n

**god|li|ness** /gɒdlinəs/ 1 **Godliness** is the quality of being godly. N-UNCOUNT 2 If someone says that **cleanliness is next to godliness**, they are referring to the idea that people have a moral duty to keep themselves and their homes clean. PHRASE

**god|ly** /gɒdli/ A **godly** person is someone who is deeply religious and shows obedience to the rules of their religion. ❑ *...a learned and godly preacher.* ADJ: usu ADJ n

**god|mother** /gɒdmʌðəʳ/ **(godmothers)** A **godmother** is a female godparent. N-COUNT: usu with poss

**god|parent** /gɒdpeərənt/ **(godparents)** In the Christian religion, if you are the **godparent** of a younger person, you promise to help bring them up in the Christian faith. N-COUNT: usu with poss

**god|send** /gɒdsend/ If you describe something as **a godsend**, you are emphasizing that it helps you very much. ❑ *Pharmacists are a godsend when you don't feel sick enough to call the doctor.* N-SING: *a* N [emphasis]

**god|son** /gɒdsʌn/ **(godsons)** A **godson** is a male godchild. N-COUNT: usu with poss

**God|speed** /gɒdspiːd/ also **godspeed.** The term **Godspeed** is sometimes used in order to wish someone success and safety, especially if they are about to go on a long and dangerous journey. [FORMAL] ❑ *I know you will join me in wishing them Godspeed.* CONVENTION

**-goer** /-goʊəʳ/ **(-goers) -goer** is added to words such as 'theatre', 'church', and 'film' to form nouns which describe people who regularly go to that type of place or event. ❑ *They are regular church-goers. ...excited party-goers.* COMB in N-COUNT

**go|fer** /goʊfəʳ/ **(gofers)** A **gofer** is a person whose job is to do simple and rather boring tasks for someone. [INFORMAL] N-COUNT = dogsbody

**go-getter** **(go-getters)** If someone is a **go-getter**, they are very energetic and eager to succeed. N-COUNT [approval]

**gog|gle** /gɒgəl/ **(goggles, goggling, goggled)** 1 If you **goggle at** something, you stare at it with your eyes wide open, usually because you are surprised by it. ❑ *She goggled at me... He goggled in bewilderment.* VERB = gape V *at* n V 2 **Goggles** are large glasses that fit closely to your face around your eyes to protect them from such things as water, wind, or dust. N-PLURAL: also *a pair of* N

**goggle-eyed** 1 If you say that someone is **goggle-eyed**, you mean that they are very surprised or interested by something. ❑ *Johnson stared goggle-eyed at Kravis' sumptuous quarters.* ADJ: ADJ n, ADJ after v, v-link ADJ = wide-eyed 2 If you say that someone is **goggle-eyed**, you mean they watch television a lot. [BRIT, INFORMAL] ADJ [disapproval]

**go-go** 1 A **go-go** dancer is a young woman whose job involves dancing to pop music in nightclubs wearing very few clothes. ADJ: ADJ n 2 A **go-go** period of time is a time when people make a lot of money and businesses are growing. A **go-go** company is very energetic and is growing fast. [mainly AM, BUSINESS] ❑ *Current economic activity is markedly slower than during the go-go years of the mid to late 1980s... It will be a go-go business with pre-tax profits forecast to climb from £152m last year to £200m.* ADJ: ADJ n

**going** /goʊɪŋ/ ◆◆◆ 1 If you say that something **is going to** happen, you mean that it will happen in the future, usually quite soon. ❑ *I think it's going to be successful... You're going to enjoy this... I'm going to have to tell him the truth... Are they going to be alright?* PHRASE 2 You say that you **are going to** do something to express your intention or determination to do it. ❑ *I'm going to go to bed... He announced that he's going to resign... I was not going to compromise.* PHRASE 3 You use **the going** to talk about how easy or difficult it is to do something. You can also say that something is, for example, **hard going** or **tough going**. ❑ *He has her support to fall back on when the going gets tough... Though the talks had been hard going at the start, they had become more friendly.* N-UNCOUNT: *the* N, adj N 4 In horse racing and horse riding, when you talk about **the going**, you are talking about the condition of the surface the horses are running on. ❑ *The going was soft; some horses found it hard work.* N-UNCOUNT: oft *the* N 5 The **going** rate or the **going** salary is the usual amount of money that you expect to pay or receive for something. ❑ *She says that's the going rate for a house this big... That's about half the going price on world oil markets.* ADJ: ADJ n 6 → See also **go**.

PHRASES 7 If someone or something **has** a lot **going for** them, they have a lot of advantages. ❑ *This area has a lot going for it... I wish I could show you the things you've got going for you.* PHRASE: V inflects, PHR n 8 When you **get going**, you start doing something or start a journey, especially after a delay. ❑ *Now what about that shopping list? I've got to get going.* PHRASE: V inflects 9 If you say that someone should do something **while the going is good**, you are advising them to do it while things are going well and they still have the opportunity, because you think it will become much more difficult to do. ❑ *People are leaving in their thousands while the going is good.* PHRASE: V inflects 10 If you **keep going**, you continue doing things or doing a particular thing. ❑ *I like to keep going. I hate to sit still.* PHRASE: V inflects 11 If you can **keep going** with the money you have, you can manage to live on it. ❑ *Things were difficult, and we needed her wages to keep going.* PHRASE: V inflects 12 If you say that something PHRASE:

is enough **to be going on with**, you mean that it is enough for your needs at the moment, although you will need something better at some time in the future. [mainly BRIT] ❑ *It was a good enough description for Mattie to be going on with.* usu PHR after v
13 You can use **going on** before a number to say that something has almost reached that number. For example, you can say that someone is **going on 40** to indicate that they are nearly 40. PHRASE: PHR num
14 → See also **comings and goings**. **going concern** → see **concern**.

**-going** /-gouɪŋ/ 1 **-going** is added to nouns such as 'theatre', 'church', and 'film' to form nouns which describe the activity of going to that type of place or event. ❑ *...his party-going days as a student.* COMB in N-UNCOUNT: oft N n 2 **-going** is added to nouns such as 'ocean', 'sea', and 'road' to form adjectives which describe vehicles that are designed for that type of place. ❑ *...one of the largest ocean-going liners in the world.* COMB: COMB in ADJ: usu ADJ n 3 **-going** is added to nouns that refer to directions to form adjectives which describe things that are moving in that direction. ❑ *The material can absorb outward-going radiation from the Earth.* COMB: COMB in ADJ: usu ADJ n 4 → See also **easy-going**, **ongoing**, **outgoing**, **thoroughgoing**.

**going-over** 1 If you give someone or something a **going-over**, you examine them thoroughly. [INFORMAL] ❑ *Michael was given a complete going-over and then treated for glandular fever.* N-SING 2 A **going-over** is a violent attack on or criticism of someone. [BRIT, INFORMAL] ❑ *He gets a terrible going-over in these pages.* N-SING

**goings-on** If you describe events or activities as **goings-on**, you mean that they are strange, interesting, amusing, or dishonest. ❑ *The girl had found out about the goings-on in the factory.* N-PLURAL

**goi|tre** /gɔɪtəʳ/ **(goitres)**

✓ in AM, also use **goiter**

**Goitre** is a disease of the thyroid gland that makes a person's neck very swollen. N-VAR

**go-kart** **(go-karts)** also **go-cart**. A **go-kart** is a very small motor vehicle with four wheels, used for racing. N-COUNT

**go-karting** **Go-karting** is the sport of racing or riding on go-karts. N-UNCOUNT

**gold** /gould/ **(golds)** 1 **Gold** is a valuable, yellow-coloured metal that is used for making jewellery and ornaments, and as an international currency. ❑ *...a sapphire set in gold... The price of gold was going up. ...gold coins.* ◆◆◇ N-UNCOUNT 2 **Gold** is jewellery and other things that are made of gold. ❑ *We handed over all our gold and money.* N-UNCOUNT 3 Something that is **gold** is a bright yellow colour, and is often shiny. ❑ *I'd been wearing Michel's black and gold shirt.* COLOUR 4 A **gold** is the same as a **gold medal**. [INFORMAL] ❑ *His ambition was to win gold at the Atlanta Games in 1996... This Saturday the British star is going for gold in the Winter Olympics.* N-VAR

PHRASES 5 If you say that a child is being **as good as gold**, you are emphasizing that they are behaving very well and are not causing you any problems. ❑ *The boys were as good as gold on our walk.* PHRASE: v-link PHR, PHR after v [emphasis] 6 If you say that someone has **a heart of gold**, you are emphasizing that they are very good and kind to other people. ❑ *They are all good boys with hearts of gold. They would never steal.* PHRASE: *heart* inflects, v PHR, *with* PHR [emphasis]
7 → See also **fool's gold**. **to strike gold** → see **strike**. **worth** one's **weight in gold** → see **weight**.

**gold card** **(gold cards)** A **gold card** is a special type of credit card that gives you extra benefits such as a higher spending limit. N-COUNT

**gold-digger** **(gold-diggers)** also **gold digger**. A **gold-digger** is a person who has a relationship with someone who is rich in order to get money or expensive things from them. N-COUNT [disapproval]

**gold dust** 1 **Gold dust** is gold in the form of a fine powder. N-UNCOUNT 2 If you say that a type of thing is **like gold dust** or is **gold dust**, you mean that it is very difficult to obtain, usually because everyone wants it. [BRIT] ❑ *Tickets were like gold dust.* N-UNCOUNT

**gold|en** /gouldᵊn/ 1 Something that is **golden** is bright yellow in colour. ❑ *She combed and arranged her golden hair. ...an endless golden beach.* ◆◇◇ ADJ 2 **Golden** things are made of gold. ❑ *...a golden chain with a golden locket.* ADJ: usu ADJ n 3 If you describe something as **golden**, you mean it is wonderful because it is likely to be successful and rewarding, or because it is the best of its kind. ❑ *He says there's a golden opportunity for peace which must be seized.* ADJ: ADJ n 4 If you refer to a man as a **golden boy** or a woman as a **golden girl**, you mean that they are especially popular and successful. ❑ *When the movie came out the critics went wild, hailing Tarantino as the golden boy of the 1990s.* PHRASE

**gold|en age** **(golden ages)** A **golden age** is a period of time during which a very high level of achievement is reached in a particular field of activity, especially in art or literature. ❑ *You grew up in the golden age of American children's books.* N-COUNT: oft N *of* n

**gold|en goal** **(golden goals)** In some football matches, a **golden goal** is the first goal scored in extra time, which wins the match for the team that scores it. [BRIT] N-COUNT

**gold|en good|bye** **(golden goodbyes)** A **golden goodbye** is the same as a **golden handshake.** [BUSINESS] N-COUNT

**gold|en hand|shake** **(golden handshakes)** A **golden handshake** is a large sum of money that a company gives to an employee when he or she leaves, as a reward for long service or good work. [BUSINESS] N-COUNT

**gold|en hel|lo** **(golden hellos)** A **golden hello** is a sum of money that a company offers to a person in order to persuade them to join the company. [BUSINESS] ❑ *Most people recognise the need to pay a golden hello to attract the best.* N-COUNT

**gold|en ju|bi|lee** **(golden jubilees)** A **golden jubilee** is the 50th anniversary of an important or special event. ❑ *The company is celebrating its golden jubilee.* N-COUNT

**gold|en oldie** **(golden oldies)** People sometimes refer to something that is still successful or popular even though it is quite old as a **golden oldie**. [INFORMAL] N-COUNT

**gold|en para|chute** **(golden parachutes)** A **golden parachute** is an agreement to pay a large amount of money to a senior executive of a company if they are forced to leave. [BUSINESS] ❑ *Golden parachutes entitle them to a full year's salary if they get booted out of the company.* N-COUNT

**gold|en rule** **(golden rules)** A **golden rule** is a principle you should remember because it will help you to be successful. ❑ *Hanson's golden rule is to add value to whatever business he buys.* N-COUNT

**gold|en syr|up** **Golden syrup** is a sweet food in the form of a thick, sticky, yellow liquid. [BRIT] N-UNCOUNT

**gold|en wed|ding** **(golden weddings)** A **golden wedding** or a **golden wedding anniversary** is the 50th anniversary of a wedding. N-COUNT

**gold|field** /gouldfiːld/ **(goldfields)** A **goldfield** is an area of land where gold is found. N-COUNT

**gold|fish** /gouldfɪʃ/ **(goldfish)** **Goldfish** are small gold or orange fish which are often kept as pets. N-COUNT

**gold leaf** **Gold leaf** is gold that has been beaten flat into very thin sheets and is used for decoration, for example to form the letters on the cover of a book. N-UNCOUNT

**gold med|al** **(gold medals)** A **gold medal** is a medal made of gold which is awarded as first prize in a contest or competition. N-COUNT

**gold mine** also **goldmine.** If you describe something such as a business or idea as a **gold mine**, you mean that it produces large profits. ❑ *The programme was a gold mine for small production companies.* N-SING

**gold-plated** Something that is **gold-plated** is covered with a very thin layer of gold. ❑ *...marble bathrooms with gold-plated taps.* ADJ

**gold-rimmed** **Gold-rimmed** glasses have gold-coloured frames. ADJ: usu ADJ n

**gold rush** **(gold rushes)** A **gold rush** is a situation when a lot of people suddenly go to a place where gold has been discovered. N-COUNT

**gold|smith** /gouldsmɪθ/ **(goldsmiths)** A **goldsmith** is a person whose job is making jewellery and other objects using gold. N-COUNT

**golf** /gɒlf/ **Golf** is a game in which you use long sticks called clubs to hit a small, hard ball into holes that are spread out over a large area of grassy land. ◆◇◇ N-UNCOUNT

**golf ball** **(golf balls)** A **golf ball** is a small, hard white ball which people use when they are playing golf. N-COUNT

**golf club** **(golf clubs)** 1 A **golf club** is a long, thin, metal stick with a piece of wood or metal at one end that you use to hit the ball in golf. N-COUNT 2 A **golf club** is a social organization which provides a golf course and a building to meet in for its members. N-COUNT

**golf course** **(golf courses)** also **golf-course**. A **golf course** is a large area of grass which is specially designed for people to play golf on. N-COUNT

**golf|er** /gɒlfəʳ/ **(golfers)** A **golfer** is a person who plays golf for pleasure or as a profession. N-COUNT

**golf|ing** /gɒlfɪŋ/ 1 **Golfing** is used to describe things that involve the playing of golf or that are used while playing golf. ❑ *He was wearing a cream silk shirt and a tartan golfing cap. ...a golfing holiday in Spain.* ADJ: ADJ n 2 **Golfing** is the activity of playing golf. ❑ *You can play tennis or go golfing.* N-UNCOUNT

**gol|ly** /gɒli/ 1 Some people say **golly** to indicate that they are very surprised by something. [INFORMAL, OLD-FASHIONED] ❑ *'Golly,' he says, 'Isn't it exciting!'* EXCLAM [feelings] 2 Some people say **by golly** to emphasize that something did happen or should happen. [INFORMAL, OLD-FASHIONED] ❑ *By golly we can do something about it this time.* EXCLAM [emphasis]

**gon|do|la** /gɒndələ/ **(gondolas)** A **gondola** is a long narrow boat that is used especially in Venice. It has a flat bottom and curves upwards at both ends. A person stands at one end of the boat and uses a long pole to move and steer it. N-COUNT

**gone** /gɒn, AM gɔːn/ 1 **Gone** is the past participle of **go**. ◆◆◇ 2 When someone is **gone**, they have left the place where you are and are no longer there. When something is **gone**, it is no longer present or no longer exists. ❑ *He's already been gone four hours!... By morning the smoke will be all gone.* ADJ: v-link ADJ 3 If you say it is **gone** a particular time, you mean it is later than that time. [BRIT, INFORMAL] ❑ *It was just gone 7 o'clock this evening when I finished.* PREP = after, past

**gon|er** /gɒnəʳ, AM gɔːn-/ **(goners)** If you say that someone is a **goner**, you mean that they are about to die, or are in such danger that nobody can save them. [INFORMAL] ❑ *She fell so heavily I thought she was a goner.* N-COUNT

**gong** /gɒŋ, AM gɔːŋ/ **(gongs)** A **gong** is a large, flat, circular piece of metal that you hit with a hammer to make a sound like a loud bell. Gongs are sometimes used as musical instruments, or to give a signal that it is time to do something. ❑ *On the stroke of seven, a gong summons guests into the dining-room.* N-COUNT

**gon|na** /gɒnə, AM gɔːnə/ **Gonna** is used in written English to represent the words 'going to' when they are pronounced informally. ❑ *Then what am I gonna do?*

**gon|or|rhoea** /gɒnəriːə/

✔ in AM, use **gonorrhea**

**Gonorrhoea** is a sexually transmitted disease. N-UNCOUNT

**goo** /guː/ You can use **goo** to refer to any thick, sticky substance, for example mud or paste. [INFORMAL] ❑ *...a sticky goo of pineapple and coconut.* N-UNCOUNT

**good** /gʊd/ **(better, best)** 1 **Good** means pleasant or enjoyable. ❑ *We had a really good time together... I know they would have a better life here... There's nothing better than a good cup of hot coffee... It's so good to hear your voice after all this time.* ◆◆◆ ADJ ≠ bad 2 **Good** means of a high quality, standard, or level. ❑ *Exercise is just as important to health as good food... His parents wanted Raymond to have the best possible education. ...good quality furniture.* ADJ ≠ poor 3 If you are **good at** something, you are skilful and successful at doing it. ❑ *He was very good at his work... I'm not very good at singing... He is one of the best players in the world... I always played football with my older brother because I was good for my age.* ADJ: oft ADJ at n/-ing ≠ bad, poor 4 If you describe a piece of news, an action, or an effect as **good**, you mean that it is likely to result in benefit or success. ❑ *On balance biotechnology should be good news for developing countries... I had the good fortune to be selected... This is not a good example to set other children... I think the response was good.* ADJ: usu ADJ n ≠ bad 5 A **good** idea, reason, method, or decision is a sensible or valid one. ❑ *They thought it was a good idea to make some offenders do community service... There is good reason to doubt this... Could you give me some advice on the best way to do this?* ADJ: usu ADJ n ≠ bad, poor 6 If you say that **it is good that** something should happen or **good to** do something, you mean it is desirable, acceptable, or right. ❑ *I think it's good that some people are going... It is always best to choose organically grown foods if possible.* ADJ: usu v-link ADJ, oft it v-link ADJ that/to-inf ≠ bad 7 A **good** estimate or indication of something is an accurate one. ❑ *We have a fairly good idea of what's going on... This is a much better indication of what a school is really like... Laboratory tests are not always a good guide to what happens in the world.* ADJ: usu ADJ n ≠ poor 8 If you get a **good** deal or a **good** price when you buy or sell something, you receive a lot in exchange for what you give. ❑ *Whether such properties are a good deal will depend on individual situations... The merchandise is reasonably priced and offers exceptionally good value.* ADJ: usu ADJ n 9 If something is **good for** a person or organization, it benefits them. ❑ *Rain water was once considered to be good for the complexion... Nancy chose the product because it is better for the environment.* ADJ: v-link ADJ for n = beneficial ≠ bad 10 If something is done for **the good** of a person or organization, it is done in order to benefit them. ❑ *Furlaud urged him to resign for the good of the country... I'm only telling you this for your own good!* N-SING: with poss = benefit 11 If someone or something is **no good** or is **not any good**, they are not satisfactory or are of a low standard. ❑ *If the weather's no good then I won't take any pictures... I was never any good at maths.* N-UNCOUNT: with brd-neg 12 If you say that doing something is **no good** or does **not** do **any good**, you mean that doing it is not of any use or will not bring any success. ❑ *It's no good worrying about it now... We gave them water and kept them warm, but it didn't do any good... There is no way to measure these effects; the chances are it did some good.* N-UNCOUNT: usu with brd-neg 13 **Good** is what is considered to be right according to moral standards or religious beliefs. ❑ *Good and evil may co-exist within one family.* N-UNCOUNT ≠ evil 14 Someone who is **good** is morally correct in their attitudes and behaviour. ❑ *The president is a good man... For me to think I'm any better than a homeless person on the street is ridiculous.* ADJ ≠ bad 15 Someone, especially a child, who is **good** obeys rules and instructions and behaves in a socially correct way. ❑ *The children were very good... I'm going to be a good boy now... Both boys had good manners, politely shaking hands.* ADJ ≠ bad 16 Someone who is **good** is kind and thoughtful. ❑ *You are good to me... Her good intentions were thwarted almost immediately.* ADJ 17 Someone who is in a **good** mood is cheerful and pleasant to be with. ❑ *People were in a pretty good mood... He exudes natural charm and good humour... A relaxation session may put you in a better frame of mind.* ADJ: usu ADJ n ≠ bad 18 If people are **good** friends, they get on well together and are very close. ❑ *She and Gavin are good friends... She's my best friend, and I really love her.* ADJ: ADJ n 19 A person's **good** eye, arm, or leg is the one that is healthy ADJ: ADJ n ≠ bad and strong, if the other one is injured or weak. 20 You use **good** to emphasize the great extent or degree of something. ❑ *We waited a good fifteen minutes... This whole thing's got a good bit more dangerous.* ADJ: a ADJ n emphasis 21 You say **'Good'** or **'Very good'** to express pleasure, satisfaction, or agreement with something that has been said or done, especially when you are in a position of authority. ❑ *'Are you all right?' — 'I'm fine.' — 'Good. So am I.'... Oh good, Tom's just come in.* CONVENTION 22 → See also **best**, **better**, **goods**.

PHRASES 23 **'As good as'** can be used to mean 'almost.' ❑ *His career is as good as over... The vote as good as kills the chance of real reform.* PHRASE: v-link PHR adj/-ed/v = practically 24 If you say that something will **do** someone **good**, you mean that it will benefit them or improve them. ❑ *The outing will do me good... It's probably done you good to get away for a few hours... You don't do anybody any good by getting yourself arrested.* PHRASE: V inflects, oft it PHR if/to-inf 25 If something changes or disappears **for good**, it never changes back or comes back as it was before. ❑ *The days of big-time racing at Herne Hill had gone for good... A few shots of this drug cleared up the disease for good.* PHRASE: PHR after v 26 People say **'Good for you'** to express approval of your actions. ❑ *'He has a girl now, who he lives with.' — 'Good for him.'* CONVENTION feelings 27 If you say **it's a good thing**, or in British English **it's a good job, that** something is the case, you mean that it is fortunate. ❑ *It's a good thing you aren't married... It's a good job it happened here rather than on the open road.* PHRASE: V inflects 28 If you **make good** some damage, a loss, or a debt, you try to repair the damage, replace what has been lost, or repay the debt. ❑ *It may cost several billion roubles to make good the damage.* PHRASE: V inflects, PHR n = put right 29 If someone **makes good** a threat or promise or **makes good on** it, they do what they have threatened or promised to do. [mainly AM] ❑ *Certain that he was going to make good his threat to kill her, she lunged for the gun... He was confident the allies would make good on their pledges.* PHRASE: V inflects, PHR n, PHR on n 30 If you say that something or someone is **as good as new**, you mean that they are in a very good condition or state, especially after they have been damaged or ill. ❑ *I only ever use that on special occasions so it's as good as new... In a day or so he will be as good as new.* PHRASE: usu v-link PHR 31 You use **good old** before the name of a person, place, or thing when you are referring to them in an affectionate way. ❑ *Good old Harry. Reliable to the end.* PHRASE: PHR n feelings 32 **good deal** → see **deal**. **in good faith** → see **faith**. **so far so good** → see **far**. **good as gold** → see **gold**. **good gracious** → see **gracious**. **good grief** → see **grief**. **good heavens** → see **heaven**. **good job** → see **job**. **good lord** → see **lord**. **for good measure** → see **measure**. **the good old days** → see **old**. **in good shape** → see **shape**. to **stand** someone **in good stead** → see **stead**. **in good time** → see **time**. **too good to be true** → see **true**.

**good after|noon** You say **'Good afternoon'** when you are greeting someone in the afternoon. [FORMAL] CONVENTION formulae

**good|bye** /gʊdbaɪ/ **(goodbyes)** also **good-bye.** 1 You say **'Goodbye'** to someone when you or they are leaving, or at the end of a telephone conversation. CONVENTION formulae 2 When you say your **goodbyes**, you say something such as 'Goodbye' when you leave. ❑ *He said his goodbyes knowing that a long time would pass before he would see his child again... I said a hurried goodbye and walked home in the cold.* N-COUNT: usu supp N

PHRASES 3 When you **say goodbye to** someone, you say something such as 'Goodbye', 'Bye', or 'See you', when you or they are leaving. You can also **wave goodbye to** someone. ❑ *He left without saying goodbye... He wanted to say goodbye to you... They came to the front door to wave goodbye.* PHRASE: V inflects, oft PHR to n 4 If you **say goodbye** or **wave goodbye to** something that you want or usually have, you accept that you are not going to have it. ❑ *He has probably said goodbye to his last chance of Olympic gold... We can wave goodbye to the sort of protection that people at work need and deserve.* PHRASE: V inflects, PHR n 5 to **kiss** something **goodbye** → see **kiss**.

**good day** People sometimes say **'Good day'** instead of 'Hello' or 'Goodbye'. [OLD-FASHIONED] ❑ *Well, I'd better be off. Good day to you.* CONVENTION formulae

**good eve|ning** You say **'Good evening'** when you are greeting someone in the evening. [FORMAL] CONVENTION formulae

**good-for-nothing** **(good-for-nothings)** If you describe someone as **good-for-nothing**, you think that they are lazy or irresponsible. ❑ *...a good-for-nothing fourteen-year-old son who barely knows how to read and count.* ADJ: ADJ n ♦ **Good-for-nothing** is also a noun. ❑ *...lazy good-for-nothings.* N-COUNT

**Good Fri|day** **Good Friday** is the day on which Christians remember the crucifixion of Jesus Christ. It is the Friday before Easter Sunday. N-UNCOUNT

**good guy** **(good guys)** You can refer to the good characters in a film or story as the **good guys**. You can also refer to the **good guys** in a situation in real life. [mainly AM, INFORMAL] ❑ *There was a fine line between the good guys and the bad guys.* N-COUNT: usu pl = goody ≠ bad guy

☑ in BRIT, use **goodies**

**good-humoured**

☑ in AM, use **good-humored**

A **good-humoured** person or atmosphere is pleasant and cheerful. ❑ *Charles was brave and remarkably good-humoured... It was a good humoured conference.* ADJ

**goodie** /gʊdi/ → see **goody**.

**good-looking** **(better-looking, best-looking)** Someone who is **good-looking** has an attractive face. ❑ *Cassandra noticed him because he was good-looking. ...a good-looking woman.* ADJ

**good|ly** /gʊdli/ A **goodly** amount or part of something is a fairly large amount or part of it, often more than was expected. [FORMAL] ❑ *Laski spent a goodly part of his lecturing life in American universities.* ADJ: ADJ n = substantial

**good morn|ing** You say **'Good morning'** when you are greeting someone in the morning. [FORMAL] CONVENTION formulae

**good-natured** A **good-natured** person or animal is naturally friendly and does not get angry easily. ❑ *He was good natured about it, he didn't fuss.* ADJ

**good|ness** /gʊdnəs/ 1 People sometimes say **'goodness'** or **'my goodness'** to express surprise. ❑ *Goodness, I wonder if he knows... My goodness, he's earned millions in his career.* **for goodness sake** → see **sake**. **thank goodness** → see **thank**. EXCLAM feelings 2 **Goodness** is the quality of being kind, helpful, and honest. ❑ *He retains a faith in human goodness.* N-UNCOUNT

**good|night** /gʊdnaɪt/ also **good night.** 1 You say **'Goodnight'** to someone late in the evening before one of you goes home or goes to sleep. CONVENTION formulae 2 If you **say goodnight to** someone or **kiss** them **goodnight**, you say something such as 'Goodnight' to them or kiss them before one of you goes home or goes to sleep. ❑ *Eleanor went upstairs to say goodnight to the children... Both men rose to their feet and kissed her goodnight. ...a goodnight kiss.* PHRASE

**goods** /gʊdz/ ◆◆◇ 1 **Goods** are things that are made to be sold. ❑ *Money can be exchanged for goods or services. ...a wide range of consumer goods.* N-PLURAL 2 Your **goods** are the things that you own and that can be moved. ❑ *All his worldly goods were packed into a neat checked carrier bag... You can give your unwanted goods to charity.* N-PLURAL: usu poss adj N

**goods train** **(goods trains)** A **goods train** is a train that transports goods and not people. [BRIT] N-COUNT

☑ in AM, use **freight train**

**good-tempered** A **good-tempered** person or animal is naturally friendly and pleasant and ADJ = good-natured does not easily get angry or upset. ❑ *He was a happy, good-tempered child. ...a horse which is quiet and good tempered.*

**good|will** /gʊdwɪl/ [1] **Goodwill** is a friendly or helpful attitude towards other people, countries, or organizations. ❑ *I invited them to dinner, a gesture of goodwill... They depend on the goodwill of visitors to pick up rubbish.* N-UNCOUNT [2] The **goodwill** of a business is something such as its good reputation, which increases the value of the business. [BUSINESS] ❑ *We do not want to lose the goodwill built up over 175 years.* N-UNCOUNT

**goody** /gʊdi/ **(goodies)** also **goodie.** [1] You can refer to pleasant, exciting, or attractive things as **goodies**. [INFORMAL] ❑ *...a little bag of goodies.* N-COUNT: usu pl [2] You can refer to the heroes or the morally good characters in a film or story as the **goodies**. You can also refer to the **goodies** in a situation in real life. [BRIT, INFORMAL] ❑ *...the thriller, a genre which depends on goodies and baddies.* N-COUNT: usu pl = good guy ≠ baddy

☑ in AM, usually use **good guys**

**goody bag** **(goody bags)** A **goody bag** is a bag of little gifts, often given away by manufacturers in order to encourage people to try their products. [INFORMAL] N-COUNT

**goody-goody** **(goody-goodies)** If you call someone a **goody-goody**, you mean they behave extremely well in order to please people in authority. [INFORMAL] N-COUNT [disapproval]

**goo|ey** /guːi/ **(gooier, gooiest)** If you describe a food or other substance as **gooey**, you mean that it is very soft and sticky. [INFORMAL] ❑ *...a lovely, gooey, sticky mess.* ADJ

**goof** /guːf/ **(goofs, goofing, goofed)** [1] If you **goof** or **goof up**, you make a silly mistake. [INFORMAL] ❑ *We goofed last week at the end of our interview with singer Annie Ross.* ♦ **Goof** is also a noun. ❑ *But was it, in fact, a hideous goof?* VERB V Also V adv N-COUNT [2] If you call someone a **goof**, you think they are silly. [INFORMAL] ❑ *I could write for TV as well as any of those goofs.* N-COUNT [disapproval] = fool, idiot

**goofy** /guːfi/ **(goofier, goofiest)** If you describe someone or something as **goofy**, you think they are rather silly or ridiculous. [INFORMAL] ❑ *...a goofy smile.* ADJ

**goog|ly** /guːgli/ **(googlies)** When a cricketer bowls a **googly**, he or she spins the ball and makes it bounce in a different direction from the direction that the batsman is expecting. N-COUNT

**goon** /guːn/ **(goons)** [1] A **goon** is a person who is paid to hurt or threaten people. [AM, INFORMAL] ❑ *He and the other goon began to beat me up.* N-COUNT [2] If you call someone a **goon**, you think they behave in a silly way. [OLD-FASHIONED] N-COUNT [disapproval]

**goose** /guːs/ **(geese)** [1] A **goose** is a large bird that has a long neck and webbed feet. Geese are often farmed for their meat. N-COUNT [2] **Goose** is the meat from a goose that has been cooked. ❑ *...roast goose.* N-UNCOUNT [3] → See also **wild goose chase**.

**goose|berry** /gʊzbəri, AM guːsberi/ **(gooseberries)** A **gooseberry** is a small green fruit that has a sharp taste and is covered with tiny hairs. N-COUNT

**goose bumps** If you get **goose bumps**, the hairs on your skin stand up so that it is covered with tiny bumps. You get goose bumps when you are cold, frightened, or excited. N-PLURAL = goose pimples

**goose pim|ples** **Goose pimples** are the same as **goose bumps**. N-PLURAL

**goose-step** **(goose-steps, goose-stepping, goose-stepped)** When soldiers **goose-step**, they lift their legs high and do not bend their knees as they march. ❑ *...photos of soldiers goose-stepping beside fearsome missiles.* VERB V

**go|pher** /goʊfəʳ/ **(gophers)** [1] A **gopher** is a small animal which looks a bit like a rat and lives in holes in the ground. Gophers are found in Canada and the USA. N-COUNT [2] In computing, **Gopher** is a program that collects information for you from many databases across the Internet. N-PROPER; also N-COUNT

**gore** /gɔːʳ/ **(gores, goring, gored)** [1] If someone **is gored** by an animal, they are badly wounded by its horns or tusks. ❑ *Carruthers had been gored by a rhinoceros... He was gored to death in front of his family.* VERB: usu passive be V-ed be V-ed to n [2] **Gore** is blood from a wound that has become thick. ❑ *There were pools of blood and gore on the pavement.* N-UNCOUNT

**gorge** /gɔːʳdʒ/ **(gorges, gorging, gorged)** [1] A **gorge** is a deep, narrow valley with very steep sides, usually where a river passes through mountains or an area of hard rock. N-COUNT = ravine [2] If you **gorge on** something or **gorge yourself on** it, you eat lots of it in a very greedy way. ❑ *I could spend each day gorging on chocolate. ...teenagers gorging themselves on ice-cream sundaes.* VERB V on n V pron-refl on n

**gor|geous** /gɔːʳdʒəs/ [1] If you say that something is **gorgeous**, you mean that it gives you a lot of pleasure or is very attractive. [INFORMAL] ❑ *...gorgeous mountain scenery... It's a gorgeous day... Some of the Renaissance buildings are gorgeous.* ADJ = beautiful ♦ **gor|geous|ly** *She has a gorgeously warm speaking voice.* ADV: ADV adj/-ed [2] If you describe someone as **gorgeous**, you mean that you find them very sexually attractive. [INFORMAL] ❑ *The cosmetics industry uses gorgeous women to sell its skincare products... All the girls in my house are mad about Ryan, they think he's gorgeous.* ADJ [3] If you describe things such as clothes and colours as **gorgeous**, you mean they are bright, rich, and impressive. ❑ *...a red-haired man in the gorgeous uniform of a Marshal of the Empire.* ADJ: usu ADJ n ♦ **gor|geous|ly** *...gorgeously embroidered clothing.* ADV: ADV adj/-ed

**go|ril|la** /gərɪlə/ **(gorillas)** A **gorilla** is a very large ape. It has long arms, black fur, and a black face. N-COUNT

**gorm|less** /gɔːʳmləs/ If you say that someone is **gormless**, you think that they are stupid because they do not understand things very well. [BRIT, INFORMAL] ADJ [disapproval]

**gorse** /gɔːʳs/ **Gorse** is a dark green bush that grows in Europe. It has small yellow flowers and sharp prickles. N-UNCOUNT

**gory** /gɔːri/ **(gorier, goriest)** **Gory** situations involve people being injured or dying in a horrible way. ❑ *...the gory details of Mayan human sacrifices. ...the gory death scenes.* ADJ: usu ADJ n

**gosh** /gɒʃ/ Some people say '**Gosh**' when they are surprised. [OLD-FASHIONED] ❑ *Gosh, there's a lot of noise.* EXCLAM

**gos|ling** /gɒzlɪŋ/ **(goslings)** A **gosling** is a baby goose. N-COUNT

**go-slow** **(go-slows)** A **go-slow** is a protest by workers in which they deliberately work slowly in order to cause problems for their employers. [BRIT] N-COUNT

☑ in AM, use **slowdown**

**gos|pel** /gɒspᵊl/ **(gospels)** [1] In the New Testament of the Bible, the **Gospels** are the four books which describe the life and teachings of Jesus Christ. ❑ *...the parable in St Matthew's Gospel. ...an illustrated and illuminated manuscript of the four gospels.* N-COUNT; N-IN-NAMES [2] In the Christian religion, **the gospel** refers to the message and teachings of Jesus Christ, as explained in the New Testament. ❑ *I didn't shirk my duties. I visited the sick and I preached the gospel.* N-SING: the N [3] You can use **gospel** to refer to a particular way of thinking that a person or group believes in very strongly and that they try to persuade others to accept. ❑ *...the gospel according to my mom.* N-COUNT: usu N of n, N according to n-proper [4] **Gospel** or **gospel music** is a style of religious music that uses strong rhythms and vocal harmony. It is especially popular among black Christians in the southern United States of America. ❑ *I had to go to church, so I grew up singing gospel... The group perform variations on soul and gospel music.* N-UNCOUNT [5] If you take something **as gospel**, or **as gospel truth**, you believe that it is completely true. ❑ *The results were not to be taken as gospel... He wouldn't say this if it weren't the gospel truth.* N-UNCOUNT: usu as N

**gos|sa|mer** /gɒsəməʳ/ You use **gossamer** to indicate that something is very light, thin, or deli- ADJ: ADJ n cate. [LITERARY] ❑ *...the daring gossamer dresses of sheer black lace.*

**gos|sip** /gɒsɪp/ **(gossips, gossiping, gossiped)** 1 **Gossip** is informal conversation, often about other people's private affairs. ❑ *There has been much gossip about the possible reasons for his absence... Don't you like a good gossip?* (N-UNCOUNT: also a N) 2 If you **gossip with** someone, you talk informally, especially about other people or local events. You can also say that two people **gossip**. ❑ *We spoke, debated, gossiped into the night... Eva gossiped with Sarah... Mrs Lilywhite never gossiped.* (V-RECIP; pl-n V; V with n; V (non-recip)) 3 If you describe someone as a **gossip**, you mean that they enjoy talking informally to people about the private affairs of others. ❑ *He was a vicious gossip.* (N-COUNT; disapproval)

**gos|sip col|umn** **(gossip columns)** A **gossip column** is a part of a newspaper or magazine where the activities and private lives of famous people are discussed. ❑ *The jet-setting couple made frequent appearances in the gossip columns.* (N-COUNT) ♦ **gos|sip col|umn|ist** **(gossip columnists)** *...a Hollywood gossip columnist.* (N-COUNT)

**gos|sipy** /gɒsɪpi/ 1 If you describe a book or account as **gossipy**, you mean it is informal and full of interesting but often unimportant news or information about people. ❑ *...a chatty, gossipy account of Forster's life.* (ADJ: usu ADJ n) 2 If you describe someone as **gossipy**, you are critical of them because they talk about other people's private lives a great deal. ❑ *...gossipy old women.* (ADJ: usu ADJ n; disapproval)

**got** /gɒt/ 1 **Got** is the past tense and past participle of **get**. ◆◆◆

PHRASES 2 You use **have got** to say that someone has a particular thing, or to mention a quality or characteristic that someone or something has. In informal American English, people sometimes just use 'got'. [SPOKEN] ❑ *I've got a coat just like this... She hasn't got a work permit... Have you got any ideas?... Every city's got its good and bad points... After a pause he asked, 'You got any identification?'* (PHRASE: have inflects, PHR n = have) 3 You use **have got to** when you are saying that something is necessary or must happen in the way stated. In informal American English, the 'have' is sometimes omitted. [SPOKEN] ❑ *I'm not happy with the situation, but I've just got to accept it... There has got to be a degree of flexibility... See, you got to work very hard.* (PHRASE = must) 4 People sometimes use **have got to** in order to emphasize that they are certain that something is true, because of the facts or circumstances involved. In informal American English, the 'have' is sometimes omitted. [SPOKEN] ❑ *We'll do what we got to do.* (PHRASE; emphasis = must)

**gotcha** /gɒtʃə/ **Gotcha** is used in written English to represent the words 'got you' when they are pronounced informally. ❑ *'Gotcha there, didn't I?'* (INTERJ)

**Goth|ic** /gɒθɪk/ 1 **Gothic** architecture and religious art was produced in the Middle Ages. Its features include tall pillars, high curved ceilings, and pointed arches. ❑ *...a vast, lofty Gothic cathedral. ...Gothic stained glass windows.* (ADJ: usu ADJ n) 2 In **Gothic** stories, strange, mysterious adventures happen in dark and lonely places such as graveyards and old castles. ❑ *This novel is not science fiction, nor is it Gothic horror.* (ADJ: usu ADJ n)

**got|ta** /gɒtə/ **Gotta** is used in written English to represent the words 'got to' when they are pronounced informally, with the meaning 'have to' or 'must'. ❑ *Prices are high and our kids gotta eat.*

**got|ten** /gɒtᵊn/ **Gotten** is the past participle of **get** in American English. → See also **ill-gotten gains**.

**gouge** /gaʊdʒ/ **(gouges, gouging, gouged)** If you **gouge** something, you make a hole or a long cut in it, usually with a pointed object. ❑ *He gouged her cheek with a screwdriver.* (VERB; V n prep)

♦ **gouge out** To **gouge out** a piece or part of something means to cut, dig, or force it from the surrounding surface. You can also **gouge out** a hole in the ground. ❑ *He has accused her of threatening to gouge his eyes out. ...stripping off the soil and gouging out gold or iron ore.* (PHRASAL VERB; V n P; V P n (not pron))

**gourd** /gʊəʳd, gɔːʳd/ **(gourds)** 1 A **gourd** is a large round fruit with a hard skin. You can also use **gourd** to refer to the plant on which this fruit grows. (N-COUNT) 2 A **gourd** is a container made from the hard dry skin of a gourd fruit. Gourds are often used to carry water or for decoration. (N-COUNT)

**gour|mand** /gʊəʳmɒnd/ **(gourmands)** A **gourmand** is a person who enjoys eating and drinking in large amounts. [FORMAL] ❑ *The food here satisfies gourmands rather than gourmets.* (N-COUNT; disapproval)

**gour|met** /gʊəʳmeɪ/ **(gourmets)** 1 **Gourmet** food is nicer or more unusual or sophisticated than ordinary food, and is often more expensive. ❑ *Flavored coffee is sold at gourmet food stores and coffee shops... The couple share a love of gourmet cooking. ...a gourmet dinner.* (ADJ: ADJ n) 2 A **gourmet** is someone who enjoys good food, and who knows a lot about food and wine. (N-COUNT)

**gout** /gaʊt/ **Gout** is a disease which causes people's joints to swell painfully, especially in their toes. (N-UNCOUNT)

**Gov.** **(Govs)** **Gov.** is a written abbreviation for **Governor**. ❑ *...Gov. Thomas Kean of New Jersey.* (N-TITLE)

**gov|ern** /gʌvəʳn/ **(governs, governing, governed)** ◆◇◇ 1 To **govern** a place such as a country, or its people, means to be officially in charge of the place, and to have responsibility for making laws, managing the economy, and controlling public services. ❑ *They go to the polls on Friday to choose the people they want to govern their country... Their citizens are very thankful they are not governed by a dictator.* (VERB = rule; V n; V n) 2 If a situation or activity **is governed by** a particular factor, rule, or force, it is controlled by that factor, rule, or force. ❑ *Marine insurance is governed by a strict series of rules and regulations... The government has altered the rules governing eligibility for unemployment benefit.* (VERB; be V-ed by n; V n)

**gov|ern|ance** /gʌvəʳnəns/ 1 The **governance** of a country is the way in which it is governed. [FORMAL] ❑ *They believe that a fundamental change in the governance of Britain is the key to all other necessary changes.* (N-UNCOUNT) 2 The **governance** of a company or organization is the way in which it is managed. [FORMAL] ❑ *...a dramatic move away from the traditional view of governance in American education.* (N-UNCOUNT)

**gov|er|ness** /gʌvəʳnes/ **(governesses)** A **governess** is a woman who is employed by a family to live with them and educate their children. (N-COUNT)

**gov|ern|ing** /gʌvəʳnɪŋ/ A **governing** body or organization is one which controls a particular activity. ❑ *The league became the governing body for amateur fencing in the U.S.* (ADJ: ADJ n = ruling)

**gov|ern|ment** /gʌvəʳnmənt/ **(governments)** ◆◆◆ 1 The **government** of a country is the group of people who are responsible for governing it. ❑ *The Government has insisted that confidence is needed before the economy can improve. ...democratic governments in countries like Britain and the US. ...fighting between government forces and left-wing rebels.* (N-COUNT-COLL) 2 **Government** consists of the activities, methods, and principles involved in governing a country or other political unit. ❑ *The first four years of government were completely disastrous. ...our system of government.* (N-UNCOUNT)

**gov|ern|men|tal** /gʌvəʳnmentᵊl/ **Governmental** means relating to a particular government, or to the practice of governing a country. ❑ *...a governmental agency for providing financial aid to developing countries.* (ADJ: ADJ n)

**gov|er|nor** /gʌvəʳnəʳ/ **(governors)** ◆◆◇ 1 In some systems of government, a **governor** is a person who is in charge of the political administration of a region or state. ❑ *He was governor of the province in the late 1970s... Governor William Livingston addressed the New Jersey Assembly.* (N-COUNT; N-TITLE) 2 A **governor** is a member of a committee which controls an organization such as a school or a (N-COUNT) hospital. ❑ *Governors are using the increased powers given to them to act against incompetent headteachers. ...the chairman of the BBC board of governors.* 3 In some British institutions, the **governor** is the most senior official, who is in charge of the institution. ❑ *The incident was reported to the prison governor.* N-COUNT

**Governor-General** **(Governors-General)** A **Governor-General** is a person who is sent to a former British colony as the chief representative of Britain. [BRIT] ❑ *...the former Governor-General of New Zealand.* N-COUNT: oft *the* N *of* n

**gov|er|nor|ship** /gʌvnəʳʃɪp/ **(governorships)** The **governorship** of a particular country or state is the position of being its governor. **Governorship** is also used to refer to the period of time a particular person spends being the governor of a country or state. ❑ *The governorship went to a Democrat, Mrs Anne Richards.* N-COUNT

**govt** **govt** is a written abbreviation for **government**.

**gown** /gaʊn/ **(gowns)** 1 A **gown** is a dress, usually a long dress, which women wear on formal occasions. ❑ *The new ball gown was a great success. ...wedding gowns.* N-COUNT 2 A **gown** is a loose black garment worn on formal occasions by people such as lawyers and academics. ❑ *...an old headmaster in a flowing black gown.* N-COUNT

**GP** /dʒiː piː/ **(GPs)** A **GP** is a doctor who does not specialize in any particular area of medicine, but who has a medical practice in which he or she treats all types of illness. **GP** is an abbreviation for 'general practitioner'. ❑ *Her husband called their local GP.* ◆◇◇ N-COUNT: oft poss N

**GPS** /dʒiː piː es/ **(GPSs)** **GPS** is an abbreviation for **global positioning system**. ❑ *GPS operates best near the equator. ...a GPS receiver.* N-COUNT

**grab** /græb/ **(grabs, grabbing, grabbed)** ◆◇◇ 1 VERB If you **grab** something, you take it or pick it up suddenly and roughly. ❑ *I managed to grab her hand...* V n *I grabbed him by the neck of his jersey.* V n *by/round* n 2 VERB If you **grab at** something, you try to grab it. ❑ *He was clumsily trying to grab at Alfred's arms.* V *at* n ♦ **Grab** is also a noun. N-COUNT: usu sing, N *for/at* n ❑ *I made a grab for the knife... Mr Penrose made a grab at his collar.* 3 VERB If you **grab** someone who is walking past, you succeed in getting their attention. [INFORMAL] V n ❑ *Grab that waiter, Mary Ann.* 4 VERB If you **grab** someone's attention, you do something in order to make them notice you. ❑ *I jumped on the wall to grab the attention of the crowd.* V n 5 VERB If you **grab** something such as food, drink, or sleep, you manage to get some quickly. [INFORMAL] ❑ *Grab a beer.* V n 6 VERB = seize If you **grab** something such as a chance or opportunity, or **grab at** it, you take advantage of it eagerly. ❑ *She grabbed the chance of a job interview...* V n *He grabbed at the opportunity to buy his castle.* V *at* n 7 N-COUNT: usu sing, N *for* n A **grab for** something such as power or fame is an attempt to gain it. ❑ *...a grab for personal power.* 8 → See also **smash-and-grab**. to **grab hold of** → see **hold**. 9 PHRASE: usu v-link PHR If something is **up for grabs**, it is available to anyone who is interested. [INFORMAL] ❑ *The famous Ritz hotel is up for grabs for £100m.*

**grab bag** **(grab bags)** 1 N-COUNT A **grab bag** is a game in which you take a prize out of a container full of hidden prizes. [AM]

✔ in BRIT, use **lucky dip**

2 N-COUNT: usu N *of* n A **grab bag of** things, ideas, or people is a varied group of them. ❑ *...a fascinating grab-bag of documents about the life of Liszt.*

**grace** /greɪs/ **(graces, gracing, graced)** 1 N-UNCOUNT: usu with supp If someone moves with **grace**, they move in a smooth, controlled, and attractive way. ❑ *He moved with the grace of a trained boxer.* 2 N-UNCOUNT If someone behaves with **grace**, they behave in a pleasant, polite, and dignified way, even when they are upset or being treated unfairly. ❑ *The new King seemed to be carrying out his duties with grace and due decorum.* 3 N-PLURAL: oft adj N The **graces** are the ways of behaving and doing things which are considered polite and well-mannered. ❑ *She didn't fit in and she had few social graces.* 4 N-UNCOUNT: usu supp N **Grace** is used in expressions such as **a day's grace** and **a month's grace** to say that you are allowed that amount of extra time before you have to finish something. ❑ *She wanted a couple of days' grace to get the maisonette cleaned before she moved in... We have only a few hours' grace before the soldiers come.* 5 VERB If you say that something **graces** a place or a person, you mean that it makes them more attractive. [FORMAL] ❑ *He went to the beautiful old Welsh dresser that graced this homely room...* V n *Her shoulders were graced with mink and her fingers sparkled with diamonds.* *be* V-ed *with/by* n 6 N-UNCOUNT In Christianity and some other religions, **grace** is the kindness that God shows to people because he loves them. ❑ *It was only by the grace of God that no one died.* 7 N-VAR When someone says **grace** before or after a meal, they say a prayer in which they thank God for the food and ask Him to bless it. ❑ *Leo, will you say grace?* 8 N-VOC; N-PROPER: det-poss N You use expressions such as **Your Grace** and **His Grace** when you are addressing or referring to a duke, duchess, or archbishop. ❑ *Your Grace, I have a great favour to ask of you.* 9 → See also **coup de grace**, **saving grace**.

PHRASES 10 PHRASE: V inflects If someone **falls from grace**, they suddenly stop being successful or popular. [mainly WRITTEN] ❑ *All went well at first, and I was in high favour; but presently I fell from grace.* 11 PHRASE: V inflects, PHR to-inf approval If someone **has the** good **grace to** do something, they are polite enough or honest enough to do it. ❑ *He did not even have the grace to apologise... Many of us do stupid things in our youth, but we should have the good grace to admit them.* 12 PHRASE: PHR after v If you do something unpleasant **with good grace** or **with a good grace**, you do it cheerfully and without complaining. If you do something **with bad grace** or **with a bad grace**, you do it unwillingly and without enthusiasm. ❑ *He accepted the decision with good grace, and wished me the very best of luck... With appallingly bad grace I packed up and we drove north.*

**grace|ful** /greɪsfʊl/ 1 ADJ Someone or something that is **graceful** moves in a smooth and controlled way which is attractive to watch. ❑ *His movements were so graceful they seemed effortless. ...graceful ballerinas.* ♦ **grace|ful|ly** ADV: ADV with v *She stepped gracefully onto the stage.* 2 ADJ Something that is **graceful** is attractive because it has a pleasing shape or style. ❑ *His handwriting, from earliest young manhood, was flowing and graceful.* ♦ **grace|ful|ly** ADV: ADV adj/-ed *She loved the gracefully high ceiling, with its white-painted cornice.* 3 ADJ If a person's behaviour is **graceful**, it is polite, kind, and pleasant, especially in a difficult situation. ❑ *Aubrey could think of no graceful way to escape Corbet's company... He was charming, cheerful, and graceful under pressure.* ♦ **grace|ful|ly** ADV: ADV with v *We managed to decline gracefully.*

**grace|less** /greɪsləs/ 1 ADJ ≠ graceful Something that is **graceless** is unattractive and not at all interesting or charming. ❑ *It was a massive, graceless house.* 2 ADJ A **graceless** movement is clumsy and uncontrolled. ❑ *...a graceless pirouette.* ♦ **grace|less|ly** ADV: ADV with v *He dropped gracelessly into a chair opposite her.* 3 ADJ If you describe someone as **graceless**, you mean that their behaviour is impolite. ❑ *She couldn't stand his blunt, graceless manner.* ♦ **grace|less|ly** ADV: ADV with v *The task fell to Mr Harris to deliver this bad news. It was gracelessly done.*

**gra|cious** /greɪʃəs/ 1 ADJ = courteous If you describe someone, especially someone you think is superior to you, as **gracious**, you mean that they are very well-mannered and pleasant. [FORMAL] ❑ *She is a lovely and gracious woman.* 2 ADJ If you describe the behaviour of someone in a position of authority as **gracious**, you mean that they behave in a polite and considerate way. [FORMAL] ❑ *She closed with a gracious speech of thanks.* ♦ **gra|cious|ly** ADV: ADV with v *Hospitality at the Presidential guest house was graciously declined.* 3 ADJ: You use **gracious** to describe the comfortable way of life of wealthy people. ❑ *He drove through the gracious suburbs with the swimming pools and tennis courts.* [4] Some people say **good gracious** or **goodness gracious** in order to express surprise or annoyance. ❑ *Good gracious, look at that specimen will you?* usu ADJ n EXCLAM feelings

**grad** /græd/ **(grads)** A **grad** is a **graduate**. [mainly AM, INFORMAL] N-COUNT: oft N n

**gra|da|tion** /grədeɪʃən, AM greɪd-/ **(gradations)** **Gradations** are small differences or changes in things. [FORMAL] ❑ *But TV images require subtle gradations of light and shade.* N-COUNT: usu pl, with supp

**grade** /greɪd/ **(grades, grading, graded)** [1] If something **is graded**, its quality is judged, and it is often given a number or a name that indicates how good or bad it is. ❑ *Dust masks are graded according to the protection they offer... South Point College does not grade the students' work. ...a three-tier grading system.* [2] The **grade** of a product is its quality, especially when this has been officially judged. ❑ *...a good grade of plywood. ...a grade II listed building.* ♦ **Grade** is also a combining form. ❑ *...weapons-grade plutonium. ...aviation fuel and high-grade oil.* [3] Your **grade** in an examination or piece of written work is the mark you get, usually in the form of a letter or number, that indicates your level of achievement. ❑ *What grade are you hoping to get?... There was a lot of pressure on you to obtain good grades.* [4] Your **grade** in a company or organization is your level of importance or your rank. ❑ *Staff turnover is particularly high among junior grades.* [5] In the United States, a **grade** is a group of classes in which all the children are of a similar age. When you are six years old you go into the first grade and you leave school after the twelfth grade. ❑ *Mr White teaches first grade in south Georgia.* [6] A **grade** is a slope. [AM] ❑ *She drove up a steep grade and then began the long descent into the desert.* ◆◇◇ VERB be V-ed V n V-ing N-COUNT: with supp, oft adj N, N num COMB in ADJ N-COUNT: with supp, oft adj N, N num N-COUNT: with supp N-COUNT: usu with supp, oft ord N N-COUNT

✔ in BRIT, use **gradient**

[7] Someone's **grade** is their military rank. [AM] ❑ *I was a naval officer, lieutenant junior grade.* [8] If someone **makes the grade**, they succeed, especially by reaching a particular standard. ❑ *She had a strong desire to be a dancer but failed to make the grade.* N-COUNT PHRASE: V inflects

**grade cross|ing** **(grade crossings)** A **grade crossing** is a place where a railroad track crosses a road at the same level. [AM] N-COUNT

✔ in BRIT, use **level crossing**

**grad|ed read|er** **(graded readers)** A **graded reader** is a story which has been adapted for people learning to read or learning a foreign language. Graded readers avoid using difficult grammar and vocabulary. N-COUNT

**-grader** /-greɪdər/ **(-graders)** **-grader** combines with words such as 'first' and 'second' to form nouns which refer to a child or young person who is in a particular grade in the American education system. ❑ *...a sixth-grader at the Latta School.* COMB in N-COUNT

**grade school** **(grade schools)** In the United States, a **grade school** is the same as an **elementary school**. ❑ *I was just in grade school at the time, but I remember it perfectly.* N-VAR: oft *in* N

**gra|di|ent** /greɪdiənt/ **(gradients)** A **gradient** is a slope, or the degree to which the ground slopes. [BRIT] ❑ *...a gradient of 1 in 3... The courses are long and punishing, with steep gradients.* N-COUNT

✔ in AM, usually use **grade**

**grad|ual** /grædʒuəl/ A **gradual** change or process occurs in small stages over a long period of time, rather than suddenly. ❑ *Losing weight is a slow, gradual process... You can expect her progress at school to be gradual rather than brilliant.* ADJ

**gradu|al|ly** /grædʒuəli/ If something changes or is done **gradually**, it changes or is done in small stages over a long period of time, rather than suddenly. ❑ *Electricity lines to 30,000 homes were gradually being restored yesterday... Gradually we learned to cope.* ◆◇◇ ADV: ADV with v

**gradu|ate** **(graduates, graduating, graduated)** ◆◇◇

✔ The noun is pronounced /grædʒuət/. The verb is pronounced /grædʒueɪt/.

[1] In Britain, a **graduate** is a person who has successfully completed a degree at a university or college and has received a certificate that shows this. ❑ *In 1973, the first Open University graduates received their degrees. ...graduates in engineering.* [2] In the United States, a **graduate** is a student who has successfully completed a course at a high school, college, or university. ❑ *The top one-third of all high school graduates are entitled to an education at the California State University.* [3] In Britain, when a student **graduates** from university, they have successfully completed a degree course. ❑ *She graduated in English and Drama from Manchester University.* [4] In the United States, when a student **graduates**, they complete their studies successfully and leave their school or university. You can also say that a school or university **graduates** a student or students. ❑ *When the boys graduated from high school, Ann moved to a small town in Vermont... In 1986, American universities graduated a record number of students with degrees in computer science.* [5] If you **graduate from** one thing **to** another, you go from a less important job or position to a more important one. ❑ *From commercials she quickly graduated to television shows.* N-COUNT: usu with supp, oft N *in/from/of* n N-COUNT: usu supp N VERB V prep Also V VERB V prep V n Also V VERB = progress V *to/from* n

**gradu|at|ed** /grædʒueɪtɪd/ [1] **Graduated** means increasing by regular amounts or grades. ❑ *The US military wants to avoid the graduated escalation that marked the Vietnam War.* [2] **Graduated** jars are marked with lines and numbers which show particular measurements. ❑ *...a graduated tube marked in millimetres.* ADJ: ADJ n ADJ: ADJ n

**gradu|ate school** **(graduate schools)** In the United States, a **graduate school** is a department in a university or college where postgraduate students are taught. ❑ *She was in graduate school, studying for a master's degree in social work.* N-VAR

**gradu|ate stu|dent** **(graduate students)** In the United States, a **graduate student** is a student with a first degree from a university who is studying or doing research at a more advanced level. [AM] N-COUNT

✔ in BRIT, use **postgraduate**

**gradua|tion** /grædʒueɪʃən/ **(graduations)** [1] **Graduation** is the successful completion of a course of study at a university, college, or school, for which you receive a degree or diploma. ❑ *They asked what his plans were after graduation.* [2] A **graduation** is a special ceremony at university, college, or school, at which degrees and diplomas are given to students who have successfully completed their studies. ❑ *...the graduation ceremony at Yale... At my brother's high school graduation the students recited a poem.* [3] A **graduation** is a line or number on a container or measuring instrument which marks a particular measurement. ❑ *...medicine bottles with graduations on them.* N-UNCOUNT N-COUNT: usu sing, oft N n N-COUNT

**graf|fi|ti** /grəfiːti/ **Graffiti** is words or pictures that are written or drawn in public places, for example on walls or posters. ❑ *There's no vandalism, no graffiti, no rubbish left lying about.* N-UNCOUNT-COLL

**graft** /grɑːft, græft/ **(grafts, grafting, grafted)** [1] A **graft** is a piece of healthy skin or bone, or a healthy organ, which is attached to a damaged part of your body by a medical operation in order to replace it. ❑ *I am having a skin graft on my arm soon.* [2] If a piece of healthy skin or bone or a healthy organ **is grafted onto** a damaged part of your body, it is attached to that part of your body by a medical operation. ❑ *The top layer of skin has to be grafted onto the burns.* [3] If a part of one plant or tree **is grafted** onto another plant or tree, they are joined together so that they will become one plant or tree, often in order to produce a new variety. ❑ *Pear trees are grafted on quince* N-COUNT: oft supp N VERB: usu passive be V-ed *onto/on* n VERB be V-ed *on/onto* n *rootstocks.* 4 If you **graft** one idea or system **on to** another, you try to join one to the other. ❑ *The Japanese tried to graft their own methods on to this different structure.* 5 **Graft** means hard work. [BRIT, INFORMAL] ❑ *His career has been one of hard graft.* 6 In politics, **graft** is used to refer to the activity of using power or authority to obtain money dishonestly. [mainly AM] ❑ *...another politician accused of graft.* VERB; V n *onto* n; N-UNCOUNT; N-UNCOUNT

**Grail** /greɪl/ 1 **The Grail** or **the Holy Grail** is the cup that was used by Jesus Christ at the Last Supper. In medieval times, many people tried to find the Grail without success. 2 If you describe something as a **grail** or a **holy grail**, you mean that someone is trying very hard to obtain or achieve it. ❑ *The discovery is being hailed as The Holy Grail of astronomy.* N-PROPER; N-SING: oft *the* N *of* n

**grain** /greɪn/ **(grains)** 1 A **grain of** wheat, rice, or other cereal crop is a seed from it. ❑ *...a grain of wheat. ...rice grains.* 2 **Grain** is a cereal crop, especially wheat or corn, that has been harvested and is used for food or in trade. ❑ *...a bag of grain. ...the best grains.* 3 A **grain of** something such as sand or salt is a tiny hard piece of it. ❑ *...a grain of sand.* ♦ **-grained** *...coarse-grained salt.* 4 A **grain of** a quality is a very small amount of it. ❑ *There's more than a grain of truth in that.* 5 **The grain** of a piece of wood is the direction of its fibres. You can also refer to the pattern of lines on the surface of the wood as **the grain**. ❑ *Brush the paint generously over the wood in the direction of the grain.* ♦ **-grained** *...a hard, heavy, straight-grained wood.* 6 If you say that an idea or action **goes against the grain**, you mean that it is very difficult for you to accept it or do it, because it conflicts with your previous ideas, beliefs, or principles. ❑ *Privatisation goes against the grain of their principle of opposition to private ownership of industry.* ◆◇◇ N-COUNT: usu with supp; N-MASS; N-COUNT; COMB in ADJ; N-SING: N *of* n; N-SING: *the* N; COMB in ADJ; PHRASE: V inflects

**grain el|eva|tor** **(grain elevators)** A **grain elevator** is a building in which grain such as corn is stored and which contains machinery for moving the grain. [AM] N-COUNT

**grainy** /greɪni/ 1 A **grainy** photograph looks as if it is made up of lots of spots, which make the lines or shapes in it difficult to see. ❑ *...grainy black and white photos.* 2 **Grainy** means having a rough surface or texture, or containing small bits of something. ❑ *...the grainy tree trunk... Do not use a grainy mustard.* ADJ; ADJ: usu ADJ n ≠ smooth

**gram** /græm/ **(grams)**

✔ in BRIT, also use **gramme**

A **gram** is a unit of weight. One thousand grams are equal to one kilogram. ❑ *A football weighs about 400 grams.* N-COUNT

**-gram** /-græm/ **(-grams)** **-gram** combines with nouns to form other nouns which refer to someone who dresses up in order to a bring a message to someone else, as a practical joke. ❑ *Now he has only six or seven kissogram girls on his books.* COMB in N-COUNT

**gram|mar** /græməʳ/ **(grammars)** 1 **Grammar** is the ways that words can be put together in order to make sentences. ❑ *He doesn't have mastery of the basic rules of grammar. ...the difference between Sanskrit and Tibetan grammar.* 2 Someone's **grammar** is the way in which they obey or do not obey the rules of grammar when they write or speak. ❑ *His vocabulary was sound and his grammar excellent. ...a deterioration in spelling and grammar among teenagers.* 3 A **grammar** is a book that describes the rules of a language. ❑ *...an advanced English grammar.* 4 A particular **grammar** is a particular theory that is intended to explain the rules of a language. ❑ *Transformational grammars are more restrictive.* N-UNCOUNT; N-UNCOUNT: oft supp N; N-COUNT; N-VAR: with supp

**gram|mar|ian** /grəmeəriən/ **(grammarians)** A **grammarian** is someone who studies the grammar of a language and writes books about it or teaches it. N-COUNT

**gram|mar school** **(grammar schools)** A **grammar school** is a school in Britain for children aged between eleven and eighteen who have a high academic ability. ❑ *He is in the third year at Leeds Grammar School.* N-VAR; N-IN-NAMES

**gram|mati|cal** /grəmætɪkᵊl/ 1 **Grammatical** is used to indicate that something relates to grammar. ❑ *Should the teacher present grammatical rules to students? ...common grammatical errors.* ♦ **gram|mati|cal|ly** *...grammatically correct language.* 2 If someone's language is **grammatical**, it is considered correct because it obeys the rules of grammar. ❑ *...a new test to determine whether students can write grammatical English.* ♦ **gram|mati|cal|ly** *One in five undergraduates cannot write grammatically.* ADJ: ADJ n; ADV: ADV adj/-ed; ADJ; ADV: ADV after v

**gramme** /græm/ ➔ see **gram**.

**gramo|phone** /græməfoʊn/ **(gramophones)** A **gramophone** is an old-fashioned type of record player. [mainly BRIT] ❑ *...a wind-up gramophone with a big horn. ...gramophone records.* N-COUNT

✔ in AM, usually use **phonograph**

**gran** /græn/ **(grans)** Some people refer to or address their grandmother as **gran**. [BRIT, INFORMAL] ❑ *My gran's given us some apple jam.* N-FAMILY

**grana|ry** /grænəri/ **(granaries)** 1 A **granary** is a building which is used for storing grain. 2 In Britain, **Granary** bread contains whole grains of wheat. [TRADEMARK] N-COUNT; ADJ: ADJ n

**grand** /grænd/ **(grander, grandest, grands)** ◆◆◇

✔ The form **grand** is used as the plural for meaning 8.

1 If you describe a building or a piece of scenery as **grand**, you mean that its size or appearance is very impressive. ❑ *...this grand building in the center of town... The scenery of South Island is on a grand scale.* 2 **Grand** plans or actions are intended to achieve important results. ❑ *The grand design of Europe's monetary union is already agreed.* 3 People who are **grand** think they are important or socially superior. ❑ *He is grander and even richer than the Prince of Wales.* 4 If you describe an activity or experience as **grand**, you mean that it is very pleasant and enjoyable. ❑ *The dinner was a grand success... He was having a grand time meeting new sorts of people.* 5 You can describe someone or something as **grand** when you admire or approve of them very much. [INFORMAL, SPOKEN] ❑ *He was a grand bloke.* 6 A **grand** total is one that is the final amount or the final result of a calculation. ❑ *It came to a grand total of £220,329.* 7 **Grand** is often used in the names of buildings such as hotels, especially when they are very large. ❑ *They stayed at The Grand Hotel, Budapest.* 8 A **grand** is a thousand dollars or a thousand pounds. [INFORMAL] ❑ *They're paying you ten grand now for those adaptations of old plays.* 9 ➔ See also **grandly**. ADJ = majestic; ADJ; ADJ [disapproval]; ADJ = great; ADJ [approval] = great, wonderful; ADJ: ADJ n; ADJ: ADJ n; N-COUNT: usu *a*/num N

**gran|dad** /grændæd/ **(grandads)** also **granddad.** Your **grandad** is your grandfather. [INFORMAL] ❑ *My grandad is 85.* N-FAMILY

**gran|dad|dy** /grændædi/ **(grandaddies)** also **granddaddy.** Some people refer to or address their grandfather as **grandaddy**. [AM, INFORMAL] N-FAMILY

**grand|child** /græntʃaɪld/ **(grandchildren)** Someone's **grandchild** is the child of their son or daughter. ❑ *Mary loves her grandchildren.* N-COUNT: oft poss N

**grand|dad** /grændæd/ ➔ see **grandad**.

**grand|daughter** /grændɔːtəʳ/ **(granddaughters)** Someone's **granddaughter** is the daughter of their son or daughter. ❑ *...a drawing of my granddaughter Amelia.* N-COUNT: usu with poss

**gran|dee** /grændiː/ **(grandees)** 1 In the past, a **grandee** was a Spanish prince of the highest rank. 2 You can refer to someone, especially a politician, who is upper class and has a lot of influence as a **grandee**. [mainly BRIT] ❑ *He is a former defence secretary of the United States and a grandee of the Democratic Party.* N-COUNT; N-COUNT

**gran|deur** /grændʒəʳ/ 1 If something such as a building or a piece of scenery has **grandeur**, it is impressive because of its size, its beauty, or its power. ❑ *...the grandeur and natural beauty of South America.* 2 Someone's **grandeur** is the great importance and social status that they have, or think they have. ❑ *He is wholly concerned with his own grandeur.* 3 **delusions of grandeur** → see **delusion**.
N-UNCOUNT: oft *the* N *of* n = *splendour, magnificence*; N-UNCOUNT: oft poss N

**grand|father** /grændfɑːðəʳ/ **(grandfathers)** Your **grandfather** is the father of your father or mother. ❑ *His grandfather was a professor.* N-FAMILY

**grand|father clock** **(grandfather clocks)** A **grandfather clock** is an old-fashioned type of clock in a tall wooden case which stands upright on the floor. N-COUNT

**gran|dilo|quent** /grændɪləkwənt/ **Grandiloquent** language or behaviour is very formal, literary, or exaggerated, and is used by people when they want to seem important. [FORMAL] ADJ [disapproval]

**gran|di|ose** /grændious/ If you describe something as **grandiose**, you mean it is bigger or more elaborate than necessary. ❑ *Not one of Kim's grandiose plans has even begun.* ADJ [disapproval]

**grand jury** **(grand juries)** A **grand jury** is a jury, usually in the United States, which considers a criminal case in order to decide if someone should be tried in a court of law. ❑ *They have already given evidence before a grand jury in Washington.* N-COUNT

**grand|ly** /grændli/ 1 You say that someone speaks or behaves **grandly** when they are trying to impress other people. ❑ *He grandly declared that 'international politics is a struggle for power'.* 2 You use **grandly** in expressions such as 'grandly named' or 'grandly called' to say that the name of a place or thing makes it sound much more impressive than it really is. [mainly BRIT] ❑ *Lucille's home was very grandly called a chateau, though in truth it was nothing more than a large moated farm.*
ADV: usu ADV with v, also ADV adj [disapproval]; ADV: ADV adj, ADV before v

**grand|ma** /grænmɑː/ **(grandmas)** Your **grandma** is your grandmother. [INFORMAL] ❑ *Grandma was from Scotland.* N-FAMILY

**Grand|master** /grændmɑːstəʳ, -mæst-/ **(Grandmasters)** In chess, a **Grandmaster** is a player who has achieved a very high standard in tournaments. N-COUNT; N-TITLE

**grand|mother** /grænmʌðəʳ/ **(grandmothers)** Your **grandmother** is the mother of your father or mother. ❑ *My grandmothers are both widows.* N-FAMILY

**grand|pa** /grænpɑː/ **(grandpas)** Your **grandpa** is your grandfather. [INFORMAL] ❑ *Grandpa was not yet back from the war.* N-FAMILY

**grand|parent** /grænpeərənt/ **(grandparents)** Your **grandparents** are the parents of your father or mother. ❑ *Tammy was raised by her grandparents.* N-COUNT: usu pl, oft poss N

**grand pia|no** **(grand pianos)** A **grand piano** is a large piano whose strings are set horizontally to the ground. Grand pianos are used especially for giving concerts and making recordings. N-COUNT

**Grand Prix** /grɒn priː, AM grænd -/ **(Grands Prix** or **Grand Prix)** A **Grand Prix** is one of a series of races for very powerful racing cars; also used sometimes in the names of competitions in other sports. ❑ *He never won the British Grand Prix.* N-COUNT: usu with supp

**Grand Slam** **(Grand Slams)** 1 In sport, a **Grand Slam** tournament is a major one. ❑ *...her 39 Grand Slam titles.* ♦ **Grand Slam** is also a noun. ❑ *It's my first Grand Slam and I was hoping to make a good impression.* 2 If someone wins a **Grand Slam**, they win all the major tournaments in a season in a particular sport, for example in rugby or tennis. ❑ *They won the Grand Slam in 1990.*
ADJ: ADJ n; N-COUNT; N-COUNT

**grand|son** /grænsʌn/ **(grandsons)** Someone's **grandson** is the son of their son or daughter. ❑ *My grandson's birthday was on Tuesday.* N-COUNT: oft with poss

**grand|stand** /grændstænd/ **(grandstands)** A **grandstand** is a covered stand with rows of seats for people to sit on at sporting events. N-COUNT

**grand|stand|ing** /grændstændɪŋ/ **Grandstanding** means behaving in a way that makes people pay attention to you instead of thinking about more important matters. [mainly AM] ❑ *Opponents of the measure say it's political grandstanding that could prove devastating to the economy.* N-UNCOUNT

**Grand Tour** **(Grand Tours)** also **grand tour**. **The Grand Tour** was a journey round the main cities of Europe that young men from rich families used to make as part of their education. N-COUNT

**gran|ite** /grænɪt/ **(granites)** **Granite** is a very hard rock used in building. N-MASS

**gran|ny** /græni/ **(grannies)** also **grannie**. Some people refer to their grandmother as **granny**. [INFORMAL] ❑ *...my old granny.* N-FAMILY

**grant** /grɑːnt, grænt/ **(grants, granting, granted)** ◆◆◇ 1 A **grant** is an amount of money that a government or other institution gives to an individual or to an organization for a particular purpose such as education or home improvements. ❑ *They'd got a special grant to encourage research... Unfortunately, my application for a grant was rejected.* 2 If someone in authority **grants** you something, or if something **is granted to** you, you are allowed to have it. [FORMAL] ❑ *France has agreed to grant him political asylum... It was a Labour government which granted independence to India and Pakistan... Permission was granted a few weeks ago.* 3 If you **grant that** something is true, you accept that it is true, even though your opinion about it does not change. ❑ *The magistrates granted that the charity was justified in bringing the action.* ● You use '**I grant you**' or '**I'll grant you**' to say that you accept something is true, even though your opinion about it does not change. ❑ *He took a risk, I'll grant you. But when you think about it, the risk was pretty small.*
N-COUNT; VERB = *give*, V n n, V n *to* n, *be* V-ed; VERB, V that; PHRASE: oft PHR that

PHRASES 4 If you say that someone **takes** you **for granted**, you are complaining that they benefit from your help, efforts, or presence without showing that they are grateful. ❑ *The officials felt taken for granted and grumbled loudly.* 5 If you **take** something **for granted**, you believe that it is true or accept it as normal without thinking about it. ❑ *I was amazed that virtually all the things I took for granted up north just didn't happen in London.* 6 If you **take it for granted that** something is the case, you believe that it is true or you accept it as normal without thinking about it. ❑ *He seemed to take it for granted that he should speak as a representative.*
PHRASE: *take* inflects; PHRASE: *take* inflects; PHRASE: *take* inflects, PHR that

**grant|ed** /grɑːntɪd, græntɪd/ You use **granted** or **granted that** at the beginning of a clause to say that something is true, before you make a comment on it. ❑ *Granted that the firm has not broken the law, is the law what it should be?* ♦ **Granted** is also an adverb. ❑ *Granted, he doesn't look too bad for his age, but I don't fancy him.*
CONJ; ADV: ADV with cl

**grant-maintained** In Britain, a **grant-maintained school** is one which receives money directly from the national government rather than from a local authority. The abbreviation **GM** is also used. ADJ: usu ADJ n

**granu|lar** /grænjʊləʳ/ **Granular** substances are composed of a lot of granules, or feel or look as if they are composed of a lot of granules. ❑ *...a granular fertiliser.* ADJ: usu ADJ n

**granu|lat|ed sug|ar** /grænjʊleɪtɪd ʃʊgəʳ/ **Granulated sugar** is sugar that is in the form of grains, and is usually white. N-UNCOUNT

**gran|ule** /grænjuːl/ **(granules)** **Granules** are small round pieces of something. ❑ *She was spooning coffee granules into cups.* N-COUNT: usu pl, oft supp N

**grape** /greɪp/ **(grapes)** 1 **Grapes** are small green or dark purple fruit which grow in bunches. Grapes can be eaten raw, used for making wine, or dried. → See picture on page 1711. 2 If you describe someone's attitude as **sour grapes**, you mean that they say something is worthless or undesirable because they want it themselves but can-
N-COUNT; PHRASE: usu v-link PHR, PHR after v

not have it. ❑ *These accusations have been going on for some time now, but it is just sour grapes.*

**grape|fruit** /greɪpfruːt/ **(grapefruit** or **grapefruits)** A **grapefruit** is a large, round, yellow fruit, similar to an orange, that has a sharp, slightly bitter taste. N-VAR

**grape|vine** /greɪpvaɪn/ If you hear or learn something **on the grapevine**, you hear it or learn it in casual conversation with other people. ❑ *He'd doubtless heard rumours on the grapevine... I had heard through the grapevine that he was quite critical of what we were doing.* N-SING: usu *on/through the* N

**graph** /grɑːf, græf/ **(graphs)** A **graph** is a mathematical diagram which shows the relationship between two or more sets of numbers or measurements. N-COUNT

**graph|ic** /græfɪk/ **(graphics)** 1 If you say that a description or account of something unpleasant is **graphic**, you are emphasizing that it is clear and detailed. ❑ *The descriptions of sexual abuse are graphic. ...graphic scenes of drug taking.* ADJ emphasis = explicit ♦ **graphi|cal|ly** /græfɪkli/ *Here, graphically displayed, was confirmation of the entire story.* ADV: ADV with v 2 **Graphic** means concerned with drawing or pictures, especially in publishing, industry, or computing. ❑ *...fine and graphic arts.* ADJ: ADJ n 3 **Graphics** is the activity of drawing or making pictures, especially in publishing, industry, or computing. ❑ *...a computer manufacturer which specialises in graphics.* N-UNCOUNT 4 **Graphics** are drawings and pictures that are composed using simple lines and sometimes strong colours. ❑ *The articles are noticeably shorter with strong headlines and graphics... The Agriculture Department today released a new graphic to replace the old symbol.* N-COUNT: usu pl

**graphi|cal** /græfɪkəl/ A **graphical** representation of something uses graphs or similar images to represent statistics or figures. ❑ *A graphical representation of results is shown in figure 1.* ADJ: ADJ n

**graph|ic de|sign** **Graphic design** is the art of designing advertisements, magazines, and books by combining pictures and words. ❑ *...the graphic design department.* N-UNCOUNT

**graph|ic de|sign|er** **(graphic designers)** A **graphic designer** is a person who designs advertisements, magazines, and books by combining pictures and words. N-COUNT

**graph|ite** /græfaɪt/ **Graphite** is a soft black substance that is a form of carbon. It is used in pencils and electrical equipment. N-UNCOUNT

**graph|ol|ogy** /græfɒlədʒi/ **Graphology** is the study of people's handwriting in order to discover what sort of personality they have. N-UNCOUNT

**graph pa|per** **Graph paper** is paper that has small squares printed on it so that you can use it for drawing graphs. N-UNCOUNT

**grap|ple** /græpəl/ **(grapples, grappling, grappled)** 1 If you **grapple with** a problem or difficulty, you try hard to solve it. ❑ *The economy is just one of several critical problems the country is grappling with.* VERB = wrestle V with n 2 If you **grapple with** someone, you take hold of them and struggle with them, as part of a fight. You can also say that two people **grapple**. ❑ *He was grappling with an alligator in a lagoon... They grappled desperately for control of the weapon.* V-RECIP V with n pl-n V

**grasp** /grɑːsp, græsp/ **(grasps, grasping, grasped)** 1 If you **grasp** something, you take it in your hand and hold it very firmly. ❑ *He grasped both my hands... She was trying to grasp at something.* → See also **grasping**. VERB V n V *at* n 2 A **grasp** is a very firm hold or grip. ❑ *His hand was taken in a warm, firm grasp.* N-SING: with supp 3 If you say that something is **in** someone's **grasp**, you disapprove of the fact that they possess or control it. If something slips **from** your **grasp**, you lose it or lose control of it. ❑ *The people in your grasp are not guests, they are hostages... She allowed victory to slip from her grasp. ...the task of liberating a number of states from the grasp of tyrants.* N-SING: with poss, oft *in/from* N 4 If you **grasp** something that is complicated or difficult to understand, you understand it. ❑ *The Government has not yet grasped the seriousness of the crisis... He instantly grasped that Stephen was talking about his wife.* VERB V n V that 5 A **grasp of** something is an understanding of it. ❑ *They have a good grasp of foreign languages.* N-SING: with supp, usu N *of* N 6 If you say that something is **within** someone's **grasp**, you mean that it is very likely that they will achieve it. ❑ *Peace is now within our grasp.* PHRASE: v-link PHR

**grasp|ing** /grɑːspɪŋ, græsp-/ If you describe someone as **grasping**, you are criticizing them for wanting to get and keep as much money as possible, and for being unwilling to spend it. ❑ *...a greedy grasping drug-ridden individual.* ADJ disapproval

**grass** /grɑːs, græs/ **(grasses, grassing, grassed)** ◆◇◇ 1 **Grass** is a very common plant consisting of large numbers of thin, spiky, green leaves that cover the surface of the ground. ❑ *Small things stirred in the grass around the tent... The lawn contained a mixture of grasses.* N-MASS 2 If you talk about **the grass**, you are referring to an area of ground that is covered with grass, for example in your garden. ❑ *I'm going to cut the grass.* N-SING: usu *the* N 3 **Grass** is the same as **marijuana**. [INFORMAL] N-UNCOUNT 4 If you say that one person **grasses on** another, the first person tells the police or other authorities about something criminal or wrong which the second person has done. [BRIT, INFORMAL] ❑ *His wife wants him to grass on the members of his own gang... He was repeatedly attacked by other inmates, who accused him of grassing.* VERB disapproval = inform V *on* n V ♦ **Grass up** means the same as **grass**. ❑ *How many of them are going to grass up their own kids to the police?* PHRASAL VERB V P n Also V n P 5 A **grass** is someone who tells the police or other authorities about criminal activities that they know about. [BRIT, INFORMAL] N-COUNT disapproval = informer 6 If you say **the grass is greener** somewhere else, you mean that other people's situations always seem better or more attractive than your own, but may not really be so. ❑ *He was very happy with us but wanted to see if the grass was greener elsewhere.* PHRASE: V inflects

♦ **grass over** If an area of ground **is grassed over**, grass is planted all over it. ❑ *The asphalt playgrounds have been grassed over or sown with flowers.* PHRASAL VERB: usu passive *be* V-ed P

♦ **grass up** → see **grass 4**.

**grass|hopper** /grɑːshɒpəʳ, græs-/ **(grasshoppers)** A **grasshopper** is an insect with long back legs that jumps high into the air and makes a high, vibrating sound. N-COUNT

**grass|land** /grɑːslænd, græs-/ **(grasslands)** **Grassland** is land covered with wild grass. ❑ *...areas of open grassland.* N-UNCOUNT: also N in pl, usu supp N

**grass roots** also **grass-roots, grassroots.** The **grass roots** of an organization or movement are the ordinary people who form the main part of it, rather than its leaders. ❑ *You have to join the party at grass-roots level.* N-PLURAL: oft N n

**grassy** /grɑːsi, græs-/ **(grassier, grassiest)** A **grassy** area of land is covered in grass. ❑ *Its buildings are half-hidden behind grassy banks.* ADJ: usu ADJ n

**gra|ta** /grɑːtə/ → see **persona non grata**.

**grate** /greɪt/ **(grates, grating, grated)** 1 A **grate** is a framework of metal bars in a fireplace, which holds the coal or wood. ❑ *A wood fire burned in the grate.* N-COUNT 2 If you **grate** food such as cheese or carrots, you rub it over a metal tool called a grater so that the food is cut into very small pieces. ❑ *Grate the cheese into a mixing bowl. ...grated carrot.* VERB V n V-ed 3 When something **grates**, it rubs against something else making a harsh, unpleasant sound. ❑ *His chair grated as he got to his feet... The gun barrel grated against the floor.* VERB V V *against/on* n 4 If something such as someone's behaviour **grates on** you or **grates**, it makes you feel annoyed. ❑ *His manner always grated on me... What truly grates is the painful banter.* VERB V *on* n V 5 → See also **grating**.

**grate|ful** /greɪtfʊl/ If you are **grateful for** something that someone has given you or done ADJ: usu v-link ADJ, usu ADJ *to* n,

for you, you have warm, friendly feelings towards them and wish to thank them. ❑ *She was grateful to him for being so good to her... I should like to extend my grateful thanks to all the volunteers.* ♦ **grate|ful|ly** *'That's kind of you, Sally,' Claire said gratefully.*
ADJ *for* n/-ing
ADV: ADV with v

**grat|er** /greɪtəʳ/ **(graters)** A **grater** is a kitchen tool which has a rough surface that you use for cutting food into very small pieces. ➔ See picture on page 1710.
N-COUNT

**grati|fy** /grætɪfaɪ/ **(gratifies, gratifying, gratified)** 1 If you **are gratified** by something, it gives you pleasure or satisfaction. [FORMAL] ❑ *Mr. Dambar was gratified by his response.* ♦ **grati|fied** *He was gratified to hear that his idea had been confirmed... They were gratified that America kept its promise.* ♦ **grati|fy|ing** *We took a chance and we've won. It's very gratifying.* ♦ **grati|fi|ca|tion** /grætɪfɪkeɪʃən/ *He is waiting for them to recognise him and eventually they do, much to his gratification.*
VERB *be* V-ed Also V n
ADJ: oft ADJ to-inf, ADJ that
ADJ
N-UNCOUNT

2 If you **gratify** your own or another person's desire, you do what is necessary to please yourself or them. [FORMAL] ❑ *We gratified our friend's curiosity.* ♦ **grati|fi|ca|tion** *...sexual gratification.*
VERB = satisfy V n
N-UNCOUNT

**grat|in** /grætæŋ/ **(gratins)** A **gratin** is a dish containing vegetables or sometimes meat or fish. It is covered with cheese or cheese sauce and baked in the oven. ❑ *...fresh salmon with potato and cheese gratin.*
N-VAR

**grat|ing** /greɪtɪŋ/ **(gratings)** 1 A **grating** is a flat metal frame with rows of bars across it, which is fastened over a window or over a hole in a wall or the ground. ❑ *...an open grating in the sidewalk.*
N-COUNT

2 A **grating** sound is harsh and unpleasant. ❑ *She recognized the grating voice of Dr. Sarnoff.*
ADJ: usu ADJ n

**gra|tis** /grætɪs, grɑːt-/ If something is done or provided **gratis**, it does not have to be paid for. ❑ *David gives the first consultation gratis.* ♦ **Gratis** is also an adjective. ❑ *What I did for you was free, gratis, you understand?*
ADV: ADV after v = free
ADJ

**grati|tude** /grætɪtjuːd, AM -tuːd/ **Gratitude** is the state of feeling grateful. ❑ *I wish to express my gratitude to Kathy for her immense practical help.*
N-UNCOUNT: oft N *for/to* n

**gra|tui|tous** /grətjuːɪtəs, AM -tuː-/ If you describe something as **gratuitous**, you mean that it is unnecessary, and often harmful or upsetting. ❑ *There's too much crime and gratuitous violence on TV. ...his insistence on offering gratuitous advice.* ♦ **gra|tui|tous|ly** *They wanted me to change the title to something less gratuitously offensive.*
ADJ
ADV: ADV adj, ADV with v

**gra|tu|ity** /grətjuːɪti, AM -tuː-/ **(gratuities)** 1 A **gratuity** is a gift of money to someone who has done something for you. [FORMAL] ❑ *The porter expects a gratuity.* 2 A **gratuity** is a large gift of money that is given to someone when they leave their job, especially when they leave the armed forces. [BRIT, FORMAL] ❑ *He is taking a gratuity from the Navy.*
N-COUNT = tip
N-COUNT

**grave** **(graves, graver, gravest)** ◆◇◇

✔ Pronounced /greɪv/, except for meaning 5, when it is pronounced /grɑːv/.

1 A **grave** is a place where a dead person is buried. ❑ *They used to visit her grave twice a year.*
N-COUNT

2 You can refer to someone's death as their **grave** or to death as **the grave**. ❑ *...drinking yourself to an early grave... Most men would rather go to the grave than own up to feelings of dependency.*
N-COUNT: oft *to* N, oft poss/adj N

3 A **grave** event or situation is very serious, important, and worrying. ❑ *He said that the situation in his country is very grave... I have grave doubts that the documents tell the whole story.* ♦ **grave|ly** *They had gravely impaired the credibility of the government.*
ADJ
ADV: ADV adj, ADV with v

4 A **grave** person is quiet and serious in their appearance or behaviour. ❑ *William was up on the roof for some time and when he came down he looked grave.* ♦ **grave|ly** *'I think I've covered that business more than adequately,' he said gravely.*
ADJ
ADV: ADV with v, ADV adj

5 In some languages such as French, a **grave** accent is a symbol that is placed over a vowel in a word to show how the vowel is pronounced. For example, the word 'mère' has a grave accent over the first 'e'.
ADJ: ADJ n

6 If you say that someone who is dead would **turn in** their **grave at** something that is happening now, you mean that they would be very shocked or upset by it, if they were alive. ❑ *Darwin must be turning in his grave at the thought of what is being perpetrated in his name.* 7 **from the cradle to the grave** ➔ see **cradle**.
PHRASE: V and N inflect

**grave|digger** /greɪvdɪgəʳ/ **(gravediggers)** A **gravedigger** is a person whose job is to dig the graves in which dead people can be buried.
N-COUNT

**grav|el** /grævəl/ **Gravel** consists of very small stones. It is often used to make paths. ❑ *...a gravel path leading to the front door.*
N-UNCOUNT: oft N n

**grav|elled** /grævəld/

✔ in AM, use **graveled**

A **gravelled** path, road, or area has a surface made of gravel.
ADJ: ADJ n

**grav|el|ly** /grævəli/ 1 A **gravelly** voice is low and rather rough and harsh. ❑ *There's a triumphant note in his gravelly voice.* 2 A **gravelly** area of land is covered in or full of small stones. ❑ *Water runs through the gravelly soil very quickly.*
ADJ: usu ADJ n
ADJ

**grave|side** /greɪvsaɪd/ **(gravesides)** You can refer to the area around a grave as the **graveside**, usually when you are talking about the time when someone is buried. ❑ *Both women wept at his graveside.*
N-COUNT: usu sing, oft *at* N

**grave|stone** /greɪvstoun/ **(gravestones)** A **gravestone** is a large stone with words carved into it, which is placed on a grave.
N-COUNT = tombstone, headstone

**grave|yard** /greɪvjɑːʳd/ **(graveyards)** 1 A **graveyard** is an area of land, sometimes near a church, where dead people are buried. ❑ *They made their way to a graveyard to pay their traditional respects to the dead.* 2 If you call a place a **graveyard of** particular things, you mean that there are many broken or unwanted things of that kind there. ❑ *This had once been the greatest port in the world, now it was a graveyard of rusting cranes.*
N-COUNT
N-COUNT: usu sing, oft N *of* n [disapproval]

**grave|yard shift** **(graveyard shifts)** If someone works **the graveyard shift**, they work during the night. [mainly AM]
N-COUNT: usu *the* N

**gravi|tas** /grævɪtæs/ If you say that someone has **gravitas**, you mean that you respect them because they seem serious and intelligent. [FORMAL] ❑ *He is pale, dark, and authoritative, with the gravitas you might expect of a Booker prize winner.*
N-UNCOUNT

**gravi|tate** /grævɪteɪt/ **(gravitates, gravitating, gravitated)** If you **gravitate towards** a particular place, thing, or activity, you are attracted by it and go to it or get involved in it. ❑ *Traditionally young Asians in Britain have gravitated towards medicine, law and engineering.*
VERB V *towards/to* n

**gravi|ta|tion** /grævɪteɪʃən/ In physics, **gravitation** is the force which causes objects to be attracted towards each other because they have mass. [TECHNICAL]
N-UNCOUNT

**gravi|ta|tion|al** /grævɪteɪʃənəl/ **Gravitational** means relating to or resulting from the force of gravity. [TECHNICAL] ❑ *If a spacecraft travels faster than 11 km a second, it escapes the earth's gravitational pull.*
ADJ: ADJ n

**grav|ity** /grævɪti/ 1 **Gravity** is the force which causes things to drop to the ground. ❑ *Arrows would continue to fly forward forever in a straight line were it not for gravity, which brings them down to earth.* ➔ See also **centre of gravity**. 2 The **gravity of** a situation or event is its extreme importance or seriousness. ❑ *They deserve punishment which matches the gravity of their crime... Not all acts of vengeance are of equal gravity.* 3 The **gravity** of someone's behaviour or speech is the extremely serious way in which they behave or speak. ❑ *There was an appealing gravity to everything she said.*
N-UNCOUNT
N-UNCOUNT: oft N *of* n
N-UNCOUNT

**gra|vy** /greɪvi/ **(gravies)** **Gravy** is a sauce made from the juices that come from meat when it cooks.
N-MASS

**gra|vy boat (gravy boats)** A **gravy boat** is a long narrow jug that is used to serve gravy. N-COUNT

**gra|vy train (gravy trains)** If an organization or person earns a lot of money without doing much work, you can say that they are **on the gravy train**. [JOURNALISM] ❑ *We were disgusted when bosses awarded themselves a massive pay rise. How can they get on the gravy train, but ask us to take a wage freeze?* N-COUNT: oft *on the* N [disapproval]

**gray** /greɪ/ → see **grey**.

**gray|ing** /greɪɪŋ/ → see **greying**.

**graze** /greɪz/ **(grazes, grazing, grazed)** 1 When animals **graze** or **are grazed**, they eat the grass or other plants that are growing in a particular place. You can also say that a field **is grazed** by animals. ❑ *Five cows graze serenely around a massive oak... The hills have been grazed by sheep because they were too steep to be ploughed... Several horses grazed the meadowland. ...a large herd of grazing animals.* VERB V be V-ed V n V -ing 2 If you **graze** a part of your body, you injure your skin by scraping against something. ❑ *I had grazed my knees a little.* VERB V n ♦ **grazed** *...grazed arms and legs.* ADJ 3 A **graze** is a small wound caused by scraping against something. N-COUNT 4 If something **grazes** another thing, it touches that thing lightly as it passes by. ❑ *A bullet had grazed his arm.* VERB V n

**graz|ing** /greɪzɪŋ/ **Grazing** or **grazing land** is land on which animals graze. ❑ *He had nearly a thousand acres of grazing and arable land.* N-UNCOUNT

**GRE** /dʒiː ɑːr iː/ The **GRE** is the examination which you have to pass to be able to join most graduate degree courses in the United States. **GRE** is an abbreviation for 'Graduate Record Examination'. N-PROPER

**grease** /griːs/ **(greases, greasing, greased)** 1 **Grease** is a thick, oily substance which is put on the moving parts of cars and other machines in order to make them work smoothly. ❑ *...grease-stained hands.* N-UNCOUNT = oil 2 If you **grease** a part of a car, machine, or device, you put grease on it in order to make it work smoothly. ❑ *I greased front and rear hubs and adjusted the brakes.* VERB = oil V n 3 **Grease** is an oily substance that is produced by your skin. ❑ *His hair is thick with grease.* N-UNCOUNT 4 **Grease** is animal fat that is produced by cooking meat. You can use **grease** for cooking. ❑ *He could smell the bacon grease.* N-UNCOUNT 5 If you **grease** a dish, you put a small amount of fat or oil around the inside of it in order to prevent food sticking to it during cooking. ❑ *Grease two sturdy baking sheets and heat the oven to 400 degrees... Place the frozen rolls on a greased baking tray.* VERB V n V-ed 6 → See also **elbow grease**.

**grease|paint** /griːspeɪnt/ **Greasepaint** is an oily substance used by actors as make-up. N-UNCOUNT

**grease|proof pa|per** /griːspruːf peɪpəʳ/ **Greaseproof paper** is a special kind of paper which does not allow fat or oil to pass through it. It is mainly used in cooking or to wrap food. [BRIT] N-UNCOUNT

✔ in AM, use **wax paper**

**greasy** /griːsi, -zi/ **(greasier, greasiest)** Something that is **greasy** has grease on it or in it. ❑ *...the problem of greasy hair... He propped his elbows upon a greasy counter.* ADJ

**greasy spoon (greasy spoons)** A **greasy spoon** is a small, cheap, unattractive café that serves mostly fried food. [INFORMAL] N-COUNT

**great** /greɪt/ **(greater, greatest, greats)** ◆◆◆ 1 You use **great** to describe something that is very large. **Great** is more formal than **big**. ❑ *The room had a great bay window. ...a great hall as long and high as a church.* ADJ: ADJ n 2 **Great** means large in amount or degree. ❑ *I'll take great care of it... Benjamin Britten did not live to a great age.* ADJ 3 You use **great** to describe something that is important, famous, or exciting. ❑ *...the great cultural achievements of the past... America can be great again.* ADJ ♦ **great|ness** *A nation must take certain risks to achieve greatness.* N-UNCOUNT 4 You can describe someone who is successful and famous for their actions, knowledge, or skill as **great**. ❑ *Wes Hall was once one of the West Indies' great cricketers. ...the great George Padmore.* ADJ: usu ADJ n ♦ **great|ness** *Abraham Lincoln achieved greatness.* N-UNCOUNT 5 The **greats** in a particular subject or field of activity are the people who have been most successful or famous in it. [JOURNALISM] ❑ *...all the greats of Hollywood. ...cycling's all-time greats.* N-PLURAL: with supp 6 The **greats** of popular modern music are records that have been successful and that continue to be popular. [JOURNALISM] ❑ *...a medley of rock'n'roll greats.* N-PLURAL 7 If you describe someone or something as **great**, you approve of them or admire them. [INFORMAL] ❑ *Arturo has this great place in Cazadero... They're a great bunch of guys... I think she's great.* ADJ [approval] 8 If you **feel great**, you feel very healthy, energetic, and enthusiastic. ❑ *I feel just great.* ADJ: *feel* ADJ 9 You use **great** in order to emphasize the size or degree of a characteristic or quality. ❑ *...a great big Italian wedding. ...her sense of colour and great eye for detail.* ADJ [emphasis] 10 You say **great** in order to emphasize that you are pleased or enthusiastic about something. ❑ *Oh great! That'll be good for Fergus.* EXCLAM [feelings] 11 You say **great** in order to emphasize that you are angry or annoyed about something. ❑ *'Oh great,' I thought. 'Just what I need.'* EXCLAM [feelings] 12 **Great** is used as part of the name of a species of plant or animal when there is another species of the same plant or animal which is smaller and has different characteristics. ❑ *...the great white shark.* → See also **greater**. N-IN-NAMES

**great-** /greɪt-/ **Great-** is used before some nouns that refer to relatives. Nouns formed in this way refer to a relative who is a further generation away from you. For example, your great-aunt is the aunt of one of your parents. ❑ *...Davis's great-grandmother.* PREFIX

**Great Brit|ain** /greɪt brɪtᵊn/ **Great Britain** is the island consisting of England, Scotland, and Wales, which together with Northern Ireland makes up the United Kingdom. N-PROPER = GB

**great|coat** /greɪtkoʊt/ **(greatcoats)** also **great coat.** A **greatcoat** is a long thick coat that is worn especially as part of a uniform. ❑ *...an army greatcoat.* N-COUNT

**great|er** /greɪtəʳ/ 1 **Greater** is the comparative of **great**. 2 **Greater** is used with the name of a large city to refer to the city together with the surrounding urban and suburban area. ❑ *...Greater London.* ADJ: ADJ n 3 **Greater** is used with the name of a country to refer to a larger area which includes that country and other land which used to belong to it, or which some people believe should belong to it. ❑ *...greater Syria.* ADJ: ADJ n

**great|ly** /greɪtli/ You use **greatly** to emphasize the degree or extent of something. [FORMAL] ❑ *People would benefit greatly from a pollution-free vehicle... We were greatly honoured that Sheik Hasina took the trouble to visit us.* ADV: ADV with v, ADV adj [emphasis]

**grebe** /griːb/ **(grebes)** A **grebe** is a type of water bird. N-COUNT

**Gre|cian** /griːʃᵊn/ **Grecian** is used to describe something which is in the style of things from ancient Greece. ❑ *...elegant Grecian columns.* ADJ: usu ADJ n

**greed** /griːd/ **Greed** is the desire to have more of something, such as food or money, than is necessary or fair. ❑ *...an insatiable greed for personal power... I get fed up with other people's greed.* N-UNCOUNT

**greedy** /griːdi/ **(greedier, greediest)** If you describe someone as **greedy**, you mean that they want to have more of something such as food or money than is necessary or fair. ❑ *He attacked greedy bosses for awarding themselves big rises... She is greedy and selfish.* ADJ ♦ **greedi|ly** *Livy ate the pasties greedily and with huge enjoyment.* ADV: ADV with v

**Greek** /griːk/ **(Greeks)** 1 **Greek** means belonging or relating to Greece. ADJ 2 A **Greek** is a person who comes from Greece. N-COUNT 3 **Greek** is the language used in Greece. ❑ *I had to learn Greek.* N-UNCOUNT

[4] **Greek** or **Ancient Greek** was the language used in Greece in ancient times. N-UNCOUNT

**green** /griːn/ **(greens, greener, greenest)** ◆◆◆
[1] **Green** is the colour of grass or leaves. ❑ *...shiny red and green apples... Yellow and green together make a pale green.* COLOUR [2] A place that is **green** is covered with grass, plants, and trees and not with houses or factories. ❑ *Cairo has only thirteen square centimetres of green space for each inhabitant.* ADJ ♦ **green|ness** *...the lush greenness of the river valleys.* N-UNCOUNT [3] **Green** issues and political movements relate to or are concerned with the protection of the environment. ❑ *The power of the Green movement in Germany has made that country a leader in the drive to recycle more waste materials.* ADJ: ADJ n [4] If you say that someone or something is **green**, you mean they harm the environment as little as possible. ❑ *...trying to persuade governments to adopt greener policies.* ADJ ♦ **green|ness** *A Swiss company offers to help environmental investors by sending teams round factories to ascertain their greenness.* N-UNCOUNT [5] **Greens** are members of green political movements. ❑ *The Greens see themselves as a radical alternative to the two major British political parties.* N-COUNT: usu pl [6] A **green** is a smooth, flat area of grass around a hole on a golf course. ❑ *...the 18th green.* N-COUNT [7] A **green** is an area of land covered with grass, especially in a town or in the middle of a village. ❑ *...the village green.* N-COUNT [8] **Green** is used in the names of places that contain or used to contain an area of grass. ❑ *...Bethnal Green.* N-IN-NAMES: n N [9] You can refer to the cooked leaves of vegetables such as spinach or cabbage as **greens**. N-PLURAL [10] If you say that someone is **green**, you mean that they have had very little experience of life or a particular job. ❑ *He was a young lad, very green, very immature.* ADJ

**PHRASES** [11] If you say that someone is **green with envy**, you mean that they are very envious indeed. PHRASE: v-link PHR [12] If someone has **green fingers**, they are very good at gardening and their plants grow well. [BRIT] ❑ *You don't need green fingers to fill your home with lush leaves.* PHRASE

✓ in AM, use **a green thumb**

[13] to **give** someone **the green light** → see **light**.

**green|back** /griːnbæk/ **(greenbacks)** A **greenback** is a banknote such as a dollar bill. [AM, INFORMAL] N-COUNT

**green bean** **(green beans)** **Green beans** are long narrow beans that are eaten as a vegetable. N-COUNT: usu pl

**green belt** **(green belts)** A **green belt** is an area of land with fields or parks around a town or city, where people are not allowed to build houses or factories by law. N-COUNT

**Green Be|ret** **(Green Berets)** A **Green Beret** is a British or American **commando**. [INFORMAL] N-COUNT

**green card** **(green cards)** A **green card** is a document showing that someone who is not a citizen of the United States has permission to live and work there. ❑ *Nicollette married Harry so she could get a green card.* N-COUNT

**green|ery** /griːnəri/ Plants that make a place look attractive are referred to as **greenery**. ❑ *They have ordered a bit of greenery to brighten up the new wing at Guy's Hospital.* N-UNCOUNT

**green|field** /griːnfiːld/ **Greenfield** is used to refer to land that has not been built on before. ❑ *The Government has ruled out the building of a new airport on a greenfield site.* ADJ: ADJ n

**green|fly** /griːnflaɪ/ **(greenfly** or **greenflies)** **Greenfly** are small green winged insects that damage plants. N-COUNT

**green|gage** /griːngeɪdʒ/ **(greengages)** A **greengage** is a greenish-yellow plum with a sweet taste. N-COUNT

**green|grocer** /griːngroʊsəʳ/ **(greengrocers)**
[1] A **greengrocer** is a shopkeeper who sells fruit and vegetables. [mainly BRIT] N-COUNT [2] A **greengrocer** or a **greengrocer's** is a shop where fruit and vegetables are sold. [mainly BRIT] N-COUNT: oft *the* N

**green|house** /griːnhaʊs/ **(greenhouses)**
[1] A **greenhouse** is a glass building in which you grow plants that need to be protected from bad weather. N-COUNT [2] **Greenhouse** means relating to or causing the greenhouse effect. ADJ: ADJ n

**green|house ef|fect** **The greenhouse effect** is the problem caused by increased quantities of gases such as carbon dioxide in the air. These gases trap the heat from the sun, and cause a gradual rise in the temperature of the Earth's atmosphere. N-SING

**green|house gas** **(greenhouse gases)** **Greenhouse gases** are the gases which are responsible for causing the greenhouse effect. The main greenhouse gas is carbon dioxide. N-VAR

**green|ing** /griːnɪŋ/ The **greening of** a person or organization means that the person or organization is becoming more aware of environmental issues. [JOURNALISM] ❑ *But the country has been slow to react to the 'greening' of the rest of Europe.* N-SING: also no det, oft N *of* n

**green|ish** /griːnɪʃ/ **Greenish** means slightly green in colour. ❑ *...his cold greenish eyes.* ADJ ♦ **Greenish** is also a combining form. ❑ *...greenish-yellow flowers.* COMB in COLOUR

**green|mail** /griːnmeɪl/ **Greenmail** is when a company buys enough shares in another company to threaten a takeover and makes a profit if the other company buys back its shares at a higher price. [mainly AM, BUSINESS] ❑ *Family control would prevent any hostile takeover or greenmail attempt.* N-UNCOUNT

**green on|ion** **(green onions)** **Green onions** are small onions with long green leaves. [mainly AM] N-COUNT = *scallion*

✓ in BRIT, usually use **spring onions**

**Green Pa|per** **(Green Papers)** In Britain, a **Green Paper** is a document containing ideas about a particular subject that is published by the Government so that people can discuss them before any decisions are made. N-COUNT

**Green Par|ty** **The Green Party** is a political party that is particularly concerned about protecting the environment. N-PROPER

**green pep|per** **(green peppers)** A **green pepper** is an unripe pepper that is used in cooking or eaten raw in salads. N-COUNT

**green revo|lu|tion** also **Green Revolution.** **The green revolution** is the increase in agricultural production that has been made possible by the use of new types of crops and new farming methods, especially in developing countries. N-SING

**green|room** /griːnruːm/ **(greenrooms)** also **green room.** A **greenroom** is a room in a theatre or television studio where performers can rest. N-COUNT

**green sal|ad** **(green salads)** A **green salad** is a salad made mainly with lettuce and other green vegetables. N-VAR

**Green|wich Mean Time** /grenɪtʃ miːn taɪm/ → see **GMT**.

**greeny** /griːni/ **Greeny** means slightly green in colour. ❑ *...greeny sea water.* ADJ ♦ **Greeny** is also a combining form. ❑ *...a lightweight, greeny-grey wool suit.* COMB in COLOUR

**greet** /griːt/ **(greets, greeting, greeted)**
[1] When you **greet** someone, you say 'Hello' or shake hands with them. ❑ *She liked to be home to greet Steve when he came in from school.* VERB V n [2] If something **is greeted** in a particular way, people react to it in that way. ❑ *The European Court's decision has been greeted with dismay by fishermen... It is unlikely that this suggestion will be greeted enthusiastically in the Baltic States.* VERB: usu passive be V-ed *with/by* n be V-ed adv [3] If you **are greeted by** something, it is the first thing you notice in a particular place. [WRITTEN] ❑ *I was greeted by a shocking sight... The savoury smell greeted them as they went through the door.* VERB be V-ed *by* n V n

**greet|ing** /griːtɪŋ/ **(greetings)** A **greeting** is something friendly that you say or do when you meet someone. ❑ *They exchanged greetings... He raised a hand in greeting.* N-VAR

**greet|ings card** **(greetings cards)**
☑ in AM, use **greeting card**
A **greetings card** is a folded card with a picture on the front and greetings inside that you give or send to someone, for example on their birthday. N-COUNT

**gre|gari|ous** /grɪgeəriəs/ 1 Someone who is **gregarious** enjoys being with other people. ❑ *She is such a gregarious and outgoing person.* ADJ
2 **Gregarious** animals or birds normally live in large groups. ❑ *Snow geese are very gregarious birds.* ADJ

**grem|lin** /gremlɪn/ **(gremlins)** A **gremlin** is a tiny imaginary evil spirit that people say is the cause of a problem, especially in a machine, which they cannot explain properly or locate. ❑ *The microphones went dead as if the technical gremlins had struck again.* N-COUNT

**gre|nade** /grɪneɪd/ **(grenades)** A **grenade** or a **hand grenade** is a small bomb that can be thrown by hand. ❑ *A hand grenade was thrown at an army patrol.* N-COUNT

**grew** /gruː/ **Grew** is the past tense of **grow**.

**grey** /greɪ/ **(greyer, greyest)** ◆◆◇
☑ in AM, use **gray**
1 **Grey** is the colour of ashes or of clouds on a rainy day. ❑ *...a grey suit.* COLOUR
2 You use **grey** to describe the colour of people's hair when it changes from its original colour, usually as they get old. ❑ *...my grey hair... Eddie was going grey.* ADJ
3 If the weather is **grey**, there are many clouds in the sky and the light is dull. ❑ *It was a grey, wet April Sunday.* ♦ **grey|ness** *...winter's greyness.* ADJ; N-UNCOUNT
4 If you describe a situation as **grey**, you mean that it is dull, unpleasant, or difficult. ❑ *Brazilians look gloomily forward to a New Year that even the president admits will be grey and cheerless.* ♦ **grey|ness** *In this new world of greyness there is an attempt to remove all risks.* ADJ = bleak; N-UNCOUNT
5 If you describe someone or something as **grey**, you think that they are boring and unattractive, and very similar to other things or other people. ❑ *...little grey men in suits.* ♦ **grey|ness** *Journalists are frustrated by his apparent greyness.* ADJ [disapproval]; N-UNCOUNT: with supp
6 Journalists sometimes use **grey** to describe things concerning old people. ❑ *There was further evidence of grey consumer power last week, when Ford revealed a car designed with elderly people in mind.* ADJ

**grey area** **(grey areas)**
☑ in AM, use **gray area**
If you refer to something as a **grey area**, you mean that it is unclear, for example because nobody is sure how to deal with it or who is responsible for it, or it falls between two separate categories of things. ❑ *At the moment, the law on compensation is very much a grey area. ...that gray area between blue-collar laborers and white-collar professionals.* N-COUNT

**grey|hound** /greɪhaʊnd/ **(greyhounds)** A **greyhound** is a dog with a thin body and long thin legs, which can run very fast. Greyhounds sometimes run in races and people bet on them. N-COUNT

**grey|ing** /greɪɪŋ/
☑ in AM, use **graying**
If someone has **greying** hair, there is a lot of grey hair mixed with the person's natural colour. ❑ *He was a smallish, greying man, with a wrinkly face.* ADJ: usu ADJ n

**grey|ish** /greɪɪʃ/
☑ in AM, use **grayish**
**Greyish** means slightly grey in colour. ❑ *The building was of greyish plaster and looked old.* ♦ **Greyish** is also a combining form. ❑ *...greyish-green leaves.* ADJ; COMB in COLOUR

**grey mar|ket** **(grey markets)**
☑ in AM, use **gray market**
1 **Grey market** goods are bought unofficially and then sold to customers at lower prices than usual. [BUSINESS] ❑ *Grey-market perfumes and toiletries are now commonly sold by mail.* N-SING: oft N n, the N
2 **Grey market** shares are sold to investors before they have been officially issued. [BUSINESS] ❑ *At one point last week shares in the grey market touched 230p.* N-SING: oft N n, the N

**grey mat|ter**
☑ in AM, use **gray matter**
You can refer to your intelligence or your brains as **grey matter**. [INFORMAL] ❑ *...an unsolved mathematical equation which has caused his grey matter to work overtime.* N-UNCOUNT

**grid** /grɪd/ **(grids)** 1 A **grid** is something which is in a pattern of straight lines that cross over each other, forming squares. On maps the grid is used to help you find a particular thing or place. ❑ *...a grid of ironwork. ...a grid of narrow streets... Many canals were built along map grid lines.* → See also **cattle grid**. N-COUNT
2 A **grid** is a network of wires and cables by which sources of power, such as electricity, are distributed throughout a country or area. ❑ *...breakdowns in communications and electric power grids.* N-COUNT
3 **The grid** or **the starting grid** is the starting line on a car-racing track. ❑ *The Ferrari of Alain Prost will be second on the grid.* N-COUNT

**grid|dle** /grɪdᵊl/ **(griddles)** A **griddle** is a round, flat, heavy piece of metal which is placed on a cooker or fire and used for cooking. N-COUNT

**grid|iron** /grɪdaɪəʳn/ American football is sometimes referred to as **gridiron**. [AM] ❑ *...the greatest quarterback in gridiron history.* N-UNCOUNT

**grid|lock** /grɪdlɒk/ 1 **Gridlock** is the situation that exists when all the roads in a particular place are so full of vehicles that none of them can move. ❑ *The streets are wedged solid with near-constant traffic gridlock.* N-UNCOUNT
2 You can use **gridlock** to refer to a situation in an argument or dispute when neither side is prepared to give in, so no agreement can be reached. ❑ *He agreed that these policies will lead to gridlock in the future.* N-UNCOUNT = deadlock

**grief** /griːf/ **(griefs)** 1 **Grief** is a feeling of extreme sadness. ❑ *...a huge outpouring of national grief for the victims of the shootings... Their grief soon gave way to anger.* N-VAR
2 If something **comes to grief**, it fails. If someone **comes to grief**, they fail in something they are doing, and may be hurt. ❑ *So many marriages have come to grief over lack of money... He was driving a Mercedes racer at 100 mph and almost came to grief.* PHRASE: V inflects
3 Some people say **'Good grief'** when they are surprised or shocked. ❑ *'He's been arrested for theft and burglary.' — 'Good grief!'* EXCLAM [feelings]

**grief-stricken** If someone is **grief-stricken**, they are extremely sad about something that has happened. [FORMAL] ❑ *...the grief-stricken family... The Queen was grief-stricken over his death.* ADJ

**griev|ance** /griːvᵊns/ **(grievances)** If you have a **grievance** about something that has happened or been done, you believe that it was unfair. ❑ *They had a legitimate grievance... The main grievance of the drivers is the imposition of higher fees for driving licences. ...a deep sense of grievance.* N-VAR: usu with supp

**grieve** /griːv/ **(grieves, grieving, grieved)** 1 If you **grieve over** something, especially someone's death, you feel very sad about it. ❑ *He's grieving over his dead wife and son... I didn't have any time to grieve... Margery's grieving family battled to come to terms with their loss.* VERB; V prep; V; V-ing
2 If you **are grieved by** something, it makes you unhappy or upset. ❑ *He was deeply grieved by the sufferings of the common people... I was grieved to hear of the suicide of James... It grieved me to see the poor man in such distress.* VERB; be V-ed by/at n; be V-ed to-inf; it V n to-inf

**griev|ous** /griːvəs/ 1 If you describe something such as a loss as **grievous**, you mean that it is extremely serious or worrying in its effects. ❑ *Their loss would be a grievous blow to our engineering industries... Mr Morris said the victims had suffered from a very grievous mistake.* ♦ **griev|ous|ly** *Birds, sea-life and the coastline all suffered grievously.* ADJ: usu ADJ n; ADV: ADV with v

2 A **grievous** injury to your body is one that causes you great pain and suffering. ❑ *He survived in spite of suffering grievous injuries.* ♦ **griev|ous|ly** *Nelson Piquet, three times world champion, was grievously injured.* ADJ: usu ADJ n; ADV: ADV with v, ADV adj

**griev|ous bodi|ly harm** If someone is accused of **grievous bodily harm**, they are accused of causing very serious physical injury to someone. The abbreviation **GBH** is often used. [LEGAL] ❑ *They were both found guilty of causing grievous bodily harm.* N-UNCOUNT

**grif|fin** /grɪfɪn/ **(griffins)** also **griffon.** In mythology, a **griffin** is a winged creature with the body of a lion and the head of an eagle. N-COUNT

**grill** /grɪl/ **(grills, grilling, grilled)** 1 A **grill** is a part of a stove which produces strong heat to cook food that has been placed underneath it. [BRIT] ❑ *Place the omelette under a gentle grill until the top is set.* N-COUNT

in AM, use **broiler**

2 A **grill** is a flat frame of metal bars on which food can be cooked over a fire. N-COUNT 3 When you **grill** food, or when it **grills**, you cook it using very strong heat directly above or below it. [BRIT] VERB ❑ *Grill the meat for 20 minutes each side...* V n *Apart from peppers and aubergines, many other vegetables grill well.* V adv *...grilled chicken.* V-ed

in AM, use **broil**

♦ **grill|ing** *The breast can be cut into portions for grilling.* N-UNCOUNT 4 If you **grill** someone **about** something, you ask them a lot of questions for a long period of time. [INFORMAL] VERB ❑ *Grill your travel agent about the facilities for families with children...* V n *about/on* n *The police grilled him for hours.* V n ♦ **grill|ing (grillings)** *They gave him a grilling about the implications of a united Europe.* N-COUNT 5 A **grill** is a restaurant that serves grilled food. N-COUNT

**grille** /grɪl/ **(grilles)** also **grill.** A **grille** is a framework of metal bars or wire which is placed in front of a window or a piece of machinery, in order to protect it or to protect people. N-COUNT

**grim** /grɪm/ **(grimmer, grimmest)** 1 A situation or piece of information that is **grim** is unpleasant, depressing, and difficult to accept. ❑ *They painted a grim picture of growing crime... There was further grim economic news yesterday... The mood could not have been grimmer.* ADJ ♦ **grim|ness** *...an unrelenting grimness of tone.* N-UNCOUNT 2 A place that is **grim** is unattractive and depressing in appearance. ❑ *...the tower blocks on the city's grim edges.* ADJ

3 If a person or their behaviour is **grim**, they are very serious, usually because they are worried about something. [WRITTEN] ❑ *She was a grim woman with a turned-down mouth... Her expression was grim and unpleasant.* ADJ 4 If you say that something is **grim**, you think that it is very bad, ugly, or depressing. [INFORMAL] ❑ *Things were pretty grim for a time.* ADJ

**gri|mace** /grɪmeɪs, grɪməs/ **(grimaces, grimacing, grimaced)** If you **grimace**, you twist your face in an ugly way because you are annoyed, disgusted, or in pain. [WRITTEN] ❑ *She started to sit up, grimaced, and sank back weakly against the pillow...* V *She grimaced at Cerezzi, then turned to Brenda.* V *at* n ♦ **Grimace** is also a noun. ❑ *He took another drink of his coffee. 'Awful,' he said with a grimace.* VERB; N-COUNT

**grime** /graɪm/ **Grime** is dirt which has collected on the surface of something. ❑ *Kelly got the grime off his hands before rejoining her in the kitchen.* N-UNCOUNT

**Grim Reap|er The Grim Reaper** is an imaginary character who represents death. He looks like a skeleton, wears a long, black cloak with a hood, and carries a scythe. N-SING: *the* N

**grimy** /graɪmi/ **(grimier, grimiest)** Something that is **grimy** is very dirty. ❑ *...a grimy industrial city.* ADJ

**grin** /grɪn/ **(grins, grinning, grinned)** 1 When you **grin**, you smile broadly. ❑ *He grins, delighted at the memory...* V *Sarah tried several times to catch Philip's eye, but he just grinned at her.* V *at* n *...a statue of a grinning old man cutting the throat of a deer.* V-ing VERB 2 A **grin** is a broad smile. ❑ *She came out of his office with a big grin on her face... Bobby looked at her with a sheepish grin.* N-COUNT: oft adj N 3 If you **grin and bear it**, you accept a difficult or unpleasant situation without complaining because you know there is nothing you can do to make things better. ❑ *They cannot stand the sight of each other, but they will just have to grin and bear it.* PHRASE: Vs inflect

**grind** /graɪnd/ **(grinds, grinding, ground)** 1 If you **grind** a substance such as corn, you crush it between two hard surfaces or with a machine until it becomes a fine powder. ❑ *Store the peppercorns in an airtight container and grind the pepper as you need it.* V n *...the odor of fresh ground coffee.* V-ed VERB ♦ **Grind up** means the same as **grind**. ❑ *He makes his own paint, grinding up the pigment with a little oil.* PHRASAL VERB: V P n (not pron) 2 If you **grind** something **into** a surface, you press and rub it hard into the surface using small circular or sideways movements. ❑ *'Well,' I said, grinding my cigarette nervously into the granite step.* VERB: V n prep ● If you **grind** your **teeth**, you rub your upper and lower teeth together as though you are chewing something. ❑ *If you know you're grinding your teeth, particularly at night, see your dentist.* PHRASE: V inflects; V n 3 If you **grind** something, you make it smooth or sharp by rubbing it against a hard surface. ❑ *...a shop where they grind knives...* V n *The tip can be ground to a much sharper edge to cut smoother and faster.* *be* V-ed *to* n VERB 4 If a vehicle **grinds** somewhere, it moves there very slowly and noisily. ❑ *Tanks had crossed the border at five fifteen and were grinding south.* VERB: V adv/prep 5 The **grind of** a machine is the harsh, scraping noise that it makes, usually because it is old or is working too hard. ❑ *The grind of heavy machines could get on their nerves.* N-SING: oft N *of* n 6 If you refer to routine tasks or activities as **the grind**, you mean they are boring and take up a lot of time and effort. [INFORMAL] ❑ *The daily grind of government is done by Her Majesty's Civil Service.* N-SING: oft adj N disapproval 7 → See also **grinding**.

PHRASES 8 If a country's economy or something such as a process **grinds to a halt**, it gradually becomes slower or less active until it stops. ❑ *The peace process has ground to a halt while Israel struggles to form a new government.* PHRASE: V inflects 9 If a vehicle **grinds to a halt**, it stops slowly and noisily. ❑ *The tanks ground to a halt after a hundred yards because the fuel had been siphoned out.* PHRASE: V inflects 10 to have **an axe to grind** → see **axe**. to **come to a grinding halt** → see **grinding**.

♦ **grind down** If you say that someone **grinds** you **down**, you mean that they treat you very harshly and cruelly, reducing your confidence or your will to resist them. ❑ *There are people who want to humiliate you and grind you down.* PHRASAL VERB: V n P

♦ **grind on** If you say that something **grinds on**, you disapprove of the fact that it continues to happen in the same way for a long time. ❑ *Civil war in the Sudan has been grinding on for nine years.* PHRASAL VERB disapproval: V P

♦ **grind up** → see **grind 1**.

**grind|er** /graɪndəʳ/ **(grinders)** 1 In a kitchen, a **grinder** is a device for crushing food such as coffee or meat into small pieces or into a powder. ❑ *...an electric coffee grinder.* N-COUNT: oft n N 2 A **grinder** is a machine or tool for sharpening, smoothing, or polishing the surface of something. N-COUNT: oft supp N

**grind|ing** /graɪndɪŋ/ 1 If you describe a bad situation as **grinding**, you mean it never gets better, changes, or ends. ❑ *Their grandfather had left his village in order to escape the grinding poverty.* ADJ: ADJ n ♦ **grind|ing|ly** *Nursing was ill-paid and grindingly hard work.* ADV: ADV adj 2 If you say that something comes **to a grinding halt**, you are emphasizing that it stops very suddenly, especially before it was meant to. ❑ *A car will come to a grinding halt if you put water in the petrol tank.* PHRASE: PHR after v emphasis 3 → See also **grind**.

**grind|stone** /graɪndstoʊn/ **(grindstones)** A **grindstone** is a large round stone that turns like N-COUNT a wheel and is used for sharpening knives and tools.

**grin|go** /grɪŋgoʊ/ **(gringos) Gringo** is sometimes used by people from Latin America to refer to people from other countries, especially the United States and Britain. This word could cause offence. N-COUNT

**grip** /grɪp/ **(grips, gripping, gripped)** ◆◇◇ 1 If you **grip** something, you take hold of it with your hand and continue to hold it firmly. ❑ *She gripped the rope.* VERB V n 2 A **grip** is a firm, strong hold on something. ❑ *His strong hand eased the bag from her grip.* N-COUNT: oft poss N 3 Someone's **grip on** something is the power and control they have over it. ❑ *The president maintains an iron grip on his country... Tony Blair last night tightened his grip on Labour mps with new powers to root out trouble-makers.* N-SING: with supp, oft N *on* n 4 If something **grips** you, it affects you very strongly. ❑ *The entire community has been gripped by fear.* VERB V n 5 If you **are gripped by** something such as a story or a series of events, your attention is concentrated on it and held by it. ❑ *The nation is gripped by the dramatic story.* VERB: usu passive *be* V-ed ♦ **grip|ping** *The film turned out to be a gripping thriller.* ADJ 6 If things such as shoes or car tyres have **grip**, they do not slip. ❑ *...a new way of reinforcing rubber which gives car tyres better grip.* N-UNCOUNT 7 A **grip** is a bag that is smaller than a suitcase, and that you use when you are travelling. N-COUNT

PHRASES 8 If you **get to grips with** a problem or if you **come to grips with** it, you consider it seriously, and start taking action to deal with it. ❑ *The government's first task is to get to grips with the economy.* PHRASE: V inflects, PHR n 9 If you **get a grip** on yourself, you make an effort to control or improve your behaviour or work. PHRASE: V inflects 10 If a person, group, or place is **in the grip of** something, they are being severely affected by it. ❑ *Britain is still in the grip of recession. ...a region in the grip of severe drought.* PHRASE: v-link PHR, PHR n 11 If you **lose** your **grip**, you become less efficient and less confident, and less able to deal with things. PHRASE: V inflects 12 If you say that someone has a **grip on reality**, you mean they recognize the true situation and do not have mistaken ideas about it. ❑ *Shakur loses his fragile grip on reality and starts blasting away at friends and foe alike.* PHRASE: usu PHR after v

**gripe** /graɪp/ **(gripes, griping, griped)** 1 If you say that someone **is griping**, you mean they are annoying you because they keep on complaining about something. [INFORMAL] ❑ *Why are football players griping when the average salary is half a million dollars?... They were always griping about high prices.* VERB [disapproval] = grumble, whinge V V *about* n ♦ **grip|ing** *Still, the griping went on.* N-UNCOUNT 2 A **gripe** is a complaint about something. [INFORMAL] ❑ *My only gripe is that one main course and one dessert were unavailable.* N-COUNT = grumble, whinge

**grip|ing** /graɪpɪŋ/ A **griping** pain is a sudden, sharp pain in your stomach or bowels. ADJ: ADJ n

**gris|ly** /grɪzli/ **(grislier, grisliest)** Something that is **grisly** is extremely unpleasant, and usually involves death and violence. ❑ *...two horrifically grisly murders.* ADJ: usu ADJ n = gruesome

**grist** /grɪst/ If you say that something is **grist to the mill**, you mean that it is useful for a particular purpose or helps support someone's point of view. PHRASE: v-link PHR, oft PHR *of/for* n

**gris|tle** /grɪsᵊl/ **Gristle** is a tough, rubbery substance found in meat, especially in meat of poor quality, which is unpleasant to eat. N-UNCOUNT

**grit** /grɪt/ **(grits, gritting, gritted)** 1 **Grit** is very small pieces of stone. It is often put on roads in winter to make them less slippery. ❑ *He felt tiny bits of grit and sand peppering his knees.* N-UNCOUNT 2 If someone has **grit**, they have the determination and courage to continue doing something even though it is very difficult. ❑ *You've got to admire her grit.* N-UNCOUNT 3 If you **grit** your **teeth**, you press your upper and lower teeth tightly together, usually because you are angry about something. ❑ *Gritting my teeth, I did my best to stifle one or two remarks... 'It is clear that my client has been less than frank with me,' said his lawyer, through gritted teeth.* VERB V n V-ed 4 If you **grit** your **teeth**, you make up your mind to carry on even if the situation is very difficult. ❑ *There is going to be hardship, but we have to grit our teeth and get on with it.* PHRASE: V inflects

**grit|ty** /grɪti/ **(grittier, grittiest)** 1 Something that is **gritty** contains grit, is covered with grit, or has a texture like that of grit. ❑ *The sheets fell on the gritty floor, and she just let them lie.* ADJ 2 Someone who is **gritty** is brave and determined. ❑ *We have to prove how gritty we are. ...a gritty determination to avoid humiliation.* ADJ 3 A **gritty** description of a tough or unpleasant situation shows it in a very realistic way. ❑ *...gritty social comment.* ADJ: usu ADJ n

**griz|zled** /grɪzᵊld/ A **grizzled** person or a person with **grizzled** hair has hair that is grey or partly grey. ADJ: usu ADJ n

**griz|zly** /grɪzli/ **(grizzlies)** 1 A **grizzly** or a **grizzly bear** is a large, fierce, greyish-brown bear. ❑ *...two grizzly bear cubs.* N-COUNT 2 → See also **grisly**.

**groan** /groʊn/ **(groans, groaning, groaned)** 1 If you **groan**, you make a long, low sound because you are in pain, or because you are upset or unhappy about something. ❑ *Slowly, he opened his eyes. As he did so, he began to groan with pain... They glanced at the man on the floor, who began to groan... She was making small groaning noises.* VERB = moan V *with* n V V-ing ♦ **Groan** is also a noun. ❑ *She heard him let out a pitiful, muffled groan... As his ball flew wide, there was a collective groan from the stands.* N-COUNT = moan 2 If you **groan** something, you say it in a low, unhappy voice. ❑ *'My leg – I think it's broken,' Eric groaned.* VERB V with quote 3 If you **groan about** something, you complain about it. ❑ *His parents were beginning to groan about the price of college tuition.* VERB V *about* n ♦ **Groan** is also a noun. ❑ *Listen sympathetically to your child's moans and groans about what she can't do.* N-COUNT 4 If wood or something made of wood **groans**, it makes a loud sound when it moves. ❑ *The timbers groan and creak and the floorboards shift.* VERB V 5 If you say that something such as a table **groans under** the weight of food, you are emphasizing that there is a lot of food on it. ❑ *The bar counter groans under the weight of huge plates of the freshest fish. ...a table groaning with food.* VERB [emphasis] V *under/with* n V-ing 6 If you say that someone or something **is groaning under** the weight of something, you think there is too much of that thing. ❑ *Consumers were groaning under the weight of high interest rates.* VERB: usu cont [disapproval] V *under* n

**gro|cer** /groʊsəʳ/ **(grocers)** 1 A **grocer** is a shopkeeper who sells foods such as flour, sugar, and tinned foods. N-COUNT 2 A **grocer** or a **grocer's** is a shop where foods such as flour, sugar, and tinned foods are sold. [mainly BRIT] N-COUNT: oft *the* N

**gro|cery** /groʊsəri/ **(groceries)** 1 A **grocery** or a **grocery store** is a grocer's shop. [mainly AM] N-COUNT 2 **Groceries** are foods you buy at a grocer's or at a supermarket such as flour, sugar, and tinned foods. N-PLURAL

**grog** /grɒg/ **Grog** is a drink made by mixing a strong spirit, such as rum or whisky, with water. N-UNCOUNT

**grog|gy** /grɒgi/ **(groggier, groggiest)** If you feel **groggy**, you feel weak and rather ill. [INFORMAL] ❑ *She was feeling a bit groggy when I saw her.* ADJ: usu v-link ADJ

**groin** /grɔɪn/ **(groins)** Your **groin** is the front part of your body between your legs. N-COUNT

**groom** /gruːm/ **(grooms, grooming, groomed)** 1 A **groom** is the same as a **bridegroom**. ❑ *...the bride and groom.* N-COUNT 2 A **groom** is someone whose job is to look after the horses in a stable and to keep them clean. N-COUNT 3 If you **groom** an animal, you clean its fur, usually by brushing it. ❑ *The horses were exercised and groomed with special care.* VERB V n 4 If you **are groomed for** a special job, someone prepares you for it by teaching you the skills you will need. ❑ *George was already being groomed for the top job... Marshall was groomed to run the family companies.* VERB: usu passive *be* V-ed *for* n *be* V-ed to-inf

**groomed** /gruːmd/ You use **groomed** in expressions such as **well groomed** and **badly groomed** to say how neat, clean, and smart a ADJ: usu adv ADJ person is. ❑ *...a very well groomed man... She always appeared perfectly groomed.*

**groom|ing** /gruːmɪŋ/ **Grooming** refers to the things that people do to keep themselves clean and make their face, hair, and skin look nice. ❑ *...a growing concern for personal grooming.* N-UNCOUNT: oft N n

**groove** /gruːv/ **(grooves)** A **groove** is a deep line cut into a surface. ❑ *Their wheels left grooves in the ground.* N-COUNT

**grooved** /gruːvd/ Something that is **grooved** has grooves on its surface. ❑ *The inscriptions are fresh and deep-grooved.* ADJ

**groovy** /gruːvi/ **(groovier, grooviest)** If you describe something as **groovy**, you mean that it is attractive, fashionable, or exciting. [INFORMAL, OLD-FASHIONED] ❑ *...the grooviest club in London.* ADJ

**grope** /group/ **(gropes, groping, groped)** [1] If you **grope for** something that you cannot see, you try to find it by moving your hands around in order to feel it. ❑ *With his left hand he groped for the knob, turned it, and pulled the door open... Bunbury groped in his breast pocket for his wallet.* VERB = fumble V for n V adv/prep [2] If you **grope** your **way** to a place, you move there, holding your hands in front of you and feeling the way because you cannot see anything. ❑ *I didn't turn on the light, but groped my way across the room.* VERB = feel V way prep/adv [3] If you **grope for** something, for example the solution to a problem, you try to think of it, when you have no real idea what it could be. ❑ *She groped for a simple word to express a simple idea.* VERB V for n ♦ **grop|ing** **(gropings)** *They continue their groping towards a constitutional settlement.* N-VAR [4] If one person **gropes** another, they touch or take hold of them in a rough, sexual way. [INFORMAL] ❑ *He would try to grope her breasts and put his hand up her skirt.* VERB disapproval V n ♦ **Grope** is also a noun. ❑ *She even boasted of having a grope in a cupboard with a 13-year-old.* N-COUNT

**gross** /grous/ **(grosser, grossest, grosses, grossing, grossed)** ◆◇◇

✔ The plural of the number is **gross**.

[1] You use **gross** to describe something unacceptable or unpleasant to a very great amount, degree, or intensity. ❑ *The company were guilty of gross negligence. ...an act of gross injustice.* ADJ: ADJ n ♦ **gross|ly** *Funding of education had been grossly inadequate for years... She was grossly overweight.* ADV: ADV -ed/adj [2] If you say that someone's speech or behaviour is **gross**, you think it is very rude or unacceptable. ❑ *He abused the Admiral in the grossest terms... I feel disgusted and wonder how I could ever have been so gross.* ADJ disapproval [3] If you describe something as **gross**, you think it is very unpleasant. [INFORMAL] ❑ *They had a commercial on the other night for Drug Free America that was so gross I thought Daddy was going to faint... He wears really gross holiday outfits.* ADJ disapproval [4] If you describe someone as **gross**, you mean that they are extremely fat and unattractive. ❑ *I only resist things like chocolate if I feel really gross.* ADJ: v-link ADJ disapproval [5] **Gross** means the total amount of something, especially money, before any has been taken away. ❑ *...a fixed rate account guaranteeing 10.4% gross interest or 7.8% net until October.* ADJ: ADJ n ♦ **Gross** is also an adverb. ❑ *Interest is paid gross, rather than having tax deducted. ...a father earning £20,000 gross a year.* ADV: ADV after v [6] **Gross** means the total amount of something, after all the relevant amounts have been added together. ❑ *National Savings gross sales in June totalled £709 million.* ADJ: ADJ n [7] **Gross** means the total weight of something, including its container or wrapping. ADJ: ADJ n [8] If a person or a business **grosses** a particular amount of money, they earn that amount of money before tax has been taken away. [BUSINESS] ❑ *So far the films have grossed more than £590 million.* VERB V n [9] A **gross** is a group of 144 things. ❑ *He ordered twelve gross of the disks.* NUM: usu a/num NUM

**gross do|mes|tic prod|uct** **(gross domestic products)** A country's **gross domestic product** is the total value of all the goods it has produced and the services it has provided in a particular year, not including its income from investments in other countries. [BUSINESS] N-VAR = GDP

**gross na|tion|al prod|uct** **(gross national products)** A country's **gross national product** is the total value of all the goods it has produced and the services it has provided in a particular year, including its income from investments in other countries. [BUSINESS] N-VAR = GNP

**gro|tesque** /groutesk/ **(grotesques)** [1] You say that something is **grotesque** when it is so unnatural, unpleasant, and exaggerated that it upsets or shocks you. ❑ *...the grotesque disparities between the wealthy few and nearly everyone else. ...a country where grotesque abuses are taking place.* ADJ ♦ **gro|tesque|ly** *He called it the most grotesquely tragic experience that he's ever had.* ADV [2] If someone or something is **grotesque**, they are very ugly. ❑ *They tried to avoid looking at his grotesque face and his crippled body.* ADJ = hideous ♦ **gro|tesque|ly** *...grotesquely deformed beggars.* ADV: ADV adj/-ed [3] A **grotesque** is a person who is very ugly in a strange or unnatural way, especially one in a novel or painting. ❑ *Grass's novels are peopled with outlandish characters: grotesques, clowns, scarecrows, dwarfs.* N-COUNT

**grot|to** /grɒtou/ **(grottoes** or **grottos)** A **grotto** is a small cave with interesting or attractively shaped rocks. ❑ *Water trickles through an underground grotto.* N-COUNT

**grot|ty** /grɒti/ **(grottier, grottiest)** If you describe something as **grotty**, you mean that it is unpleasant or of poor quality and you dislike it strongly. [BRIT, INFORMAL] ❑ *...a grotty little flat in Camden.* ADJ disapproval

**grouch** /grautʃ/ **(grouches)** [1] A **grouch** is someone who is always complaining in a bad-tempered way. [INFORMAL] ❑ *He's an old grouch but she puts up with him.* N-COUNT disapproval [2] A **grouch** is a bad-tempered complaint. [INFORMAL] ❑ *One of the biggest grouches is the new system of payment.* N-COUNT = gripe

**grouchy** /grautʃi/ If someone is **grouchy**, they are very bad-tempered and complain a lot. [INFORMAL] ❑ *Your grandmother has nothing to stop her from being bored, grouchy and lonely.* ADJ disapproval

**ground** /graund/ **(grounds, grounding, grounded)** ◆◆◆ [1] **The ground** is the surface of the earth. ❑ *Forty or fifty women were sitting cross-legged on the ground... We slid down the roof and dropped to the ground.* N-SING: the N ● Something that is **below ground** is under the earth's surface or under a building. Something that is **above ground** is on top of the earth's surface. ❑ *People were making for the air-raid shelters below ground.* PHRASE [2] If you say that something takes place **on the ground**, you mean it takes place on the surface of the earth and not in the air. ❑ *Coordinating airline traffic on the ground is as complicated as managing the traffic in the air.* N-SING: oft N n [3] **The ground** is the soil and rock on the earth's surface. ❑ *The ground had eroded. ...the marshy ground of the river delta.* N-SING: usu the N [4] You can refer to land as **ground**, especially when it has very few buildings or when it is considered to be special in some way. ❑ *...a stretch of waste ground... This memorial stands on sacred ground.* N-UNCOUNT: usu with supp [5] You can use **ground** to refer to an area of land, sea, or air which is used for a particular activity. ❑ *...Indian hunting grounds... The best fishing grounds are around the islands.* N-COUNT: supp N [6] A **ground** is an area of land which is specially designed and made for playing sport or for some other activity. In American English **grounds** is also used. ❑ *...the city's football ground. ...a parade ground.* N-COUNT: supp N [7] The **grounds** of a large or important building are the garden or area of land which surrounds it. ❑ *...the palace grounds. ...the grounds of the University.* N-PLURAL: usu with supp, oft N of n, n N [8] You can use **ground** to refer to a place or situation in which particular methods or ideas can develop and be successful. ❑ *The company has maintained its reputation as the developing ground for new techniques... Colonialism is especially fertile ground for nationalist ideas.* N-VAR: with supp, oft N for n [9] You can use **ground** in expressions such as **on shaky ground** and **the same ground** to refer to a par- N-UNCOUNT: supp N, oft on adj N ticular subject, area of experience, or basis for an argument. ❑ *Sensing she was on shaky ground, Marie changed the subject... The French are on solid ground when they argue that competitiveness is no reason for devaluation... It's often necessary to go over the same ground more than once.* 10 **Ground** is used in expressions such as **gain ground**, **lose ground**, and **give ground** in order to indicate that someone gets or loses an advantage. [JOURNALISM] ❑ *There are signs that the party is gaining ground in the latest polls... The US dollar lost more ground.* N-UNCOUNT

11 If something is **grounds for** a feeling or action, it is a reason for it. If you do something **on the grounds** of a particular thing, that thing is the reason for your action. ❑ *In the interview he gave some grounds for optimism... The court overturned that decision on the grounds that the Prosecution had withheld crucial evidence... Owen was against it, on the grounds of expense.* N-VAR: N *for* n, *on* N with supp

12 If an argument, belief, or opinion **is grounded** in something, that thing is used to justify it. ❑ *Her argument was grounded in fact... They believe the soul is immortal, grounding this belief on the Divine nature of the human spirit.* VERB = base; *be* V-ed *in/on* n; V n *in/on* n

13 If an aircraft or its passengers **are grounded**, they are made to stay on the ground and are not allowed to take off. ❑ *The civil aviation minister ordered all the planes to be grounded... A hydrogen leak forced NASA to ground the space shuttle.* VERB; *be* V-ed; V n

14 When parents **ground** a child, they forbid them to go out and enjoy themselves for a period of time, as a punishment. ❑ *Thompson grounded him for a month, and banned television.* VERB; V n

15 If a ship or boat **is grounded** or if it **grounds**, it touches the bottom of the sea, lake, or river it is on, and is unable to move off. ❑ *Residents have been told to stay away from the region where the ship was grounded... The boat finally grounded on a soft, underwater bank. ...a grounded oil tanker.* VERB; *be* V-ed; V; V-ed

16 The **ground** in an electric plug or piece of electrical equipment is the wire through which electricity passes into the ground and which makes the equipment safe. [AM] N-COUNT: usu sing

☑ in BRIT, use **earth**

17 **Ground** meat has been cut into very small pieces in a machine. [mainly AM] ❑ *...ground beef. ...The sausages are made of coarsely ground pork.* ADJ

☑ in BRIT, usually use **minced**

18 **Ground** is the past tense and past participle of **grind**. 19 → See also **grounding**, **home ground**.

**PHRASES** 20 If you **break new ground**, you do something completely different or you do something in a completely different way. ❑ *Gellhorn may have broken new ground when she filed her first report on the Spanish Civil War.* PHRASE: V inflects; approval

21 If you say that a town or building **is burnt to the ground** or **is razed to the ground**, you are emphasizing that it has been completely destroyed by fire. ❑ *The town was razed to the ground after the French Revolution.* PHRASE: V inflects; emphasis

22 If two people or groups find **common ground**, they agree about something, especially when they do not agree about other things. PHRASE

23 If you **go to ground**, you hide somewhere where you cannot easily be found. [BRIT] ❑ *Citizens of East Beirut went to ground in basements and shelters.* PHRASE: V inflects

24 The **middle ground** between two groups, ideas, or plans involves things which do not belong to either of these groups, ideas, or plans but have elements of each, often in a less extreme form. ❑ *She seems to have found a middle ground in which mutual support, rather than complete dependency, is possible.* PHRASE: oft PHR *between* n

25 If something such as a project gets **off the ground**, it begins or starts functioning. ❑ *We help small companies to get off the ground.* PHRASE: PHR after v, v-link PHR

26 If you **prepare the ground for** a future event, course of action, or development, you make it easier for it to happen. ❑ *...a political initiative which would prepare the ground for war.* PHRASE: V inflects

27 If you **shift** your **ground** or **change** your **ground**, you change the basis on which you are arguing. PHRASE: V inflects

28 If you **stand** your **ground** or **hold** your **ground**, you continue to support a particular argument or to have a particular opinion when other people are opposing you or trying to make you change your mind. ❑ *The spectacle of Sakharov standing his ground and speaking his mind gave me hope.* PHRASE: V inflects

29 If you **stand** your **ground** or **hold** your **ground**, you do not run away from a situation, but face it bravely. ❑ *She had to force herself to stand her ground when she heard someone approaching.* PHRASE: V inflects

30 If you say that something such as a job or piece of clothing **suits** someone **down to the ground**, you mean that it is completely suitable or right for them. [BRIT, INFORMAL] PHRASE: V inflects; emphasis

31 If people or things of a particular kind are **thin on the ground**, there are very few of them. [mainly BRIT] ❑ *Good managers are often thin on the ground.* PHRASE: v-link PHR

32 to **have** one's **ear to the ground** → see **ear**.

**ground|bait** /graʊndbeɪt/ **Groundbait** is food that you throw on to a river or lake when you are fishing in order to attract the fish. N-UNCOUNT

**ground|break|ing** /graʊndbreɪkɪŋ/ also **ground-breaking.** You use **groundbreaking** to describe things which you think are significant because they provide new and positive ideas, and influence the way people think about things. ❑ *...his groundbreaking novel on homosexuality. ...groundbreaking research.* ADJ: usu ADJ n

**ground|cloth** /graʊndklɒθ/ **(groundcloths)** A **groundcloth** is a piece of waterproof material which you put on the ground to sleep on when you are camping. [AM] N-COUNT

☑ in BRIT, use **groundsheet**

**ground crew** **(ground crews)** At an airport, the people who look after the planes when they are on the ground are called the **ground crew**. ❑ *The airport ground crew tried to dissuade the pilot from taking off.* N-COUNT-COLL

**ground floor** **(ground floors)** The **ground floor** of a building is the floor that is level or almost level with the ground outside. [BRIT] ❑ *She showed him around the ground floor of the empty house... Jenny now lives in a terraced ground floor flat.* N-COUNT: usu *the* N in sing

☑ in AM, use **first floor**

**ground|hog** /graʊndhɒg, AM -hɔːg/ **(groundhogs)** A **groundhog** is a type of small animal with reddish-brown fur that is found in North America. N-COUNT = woodchuck

**ground|ing** /graʊndɪŋ/ If you have a **grounding in** a subject, you know the basic facts or principles of that subject, especially as a result of a particular course of training or instruction. ❑ *The degree provides a thorough grounding in both mathematics and statistics.* N-SING: oft N *in* n

**ground|less** /graʊndləs/ If you say that a fear, accusation, or story is **groundless**, you mean that it is not based on evidence and is unlikely to be true or valid. ❑ *Fears that the world was about to run out of fuel proved groundless... A ministry official described the report as groundless.* ADJ: usu v-link ADJ

**ground lev|el** If something is **at ground level**, it is at the same level as the ground, as opposed to being higher up or below the surface. ❑ *The hotel is set on three floors. There's a bar and cafe at ground level... The remaining block of woodland is cut down to ground level.* N-UNCOUNT: oft prep N

**ground|nut** /graʊndnʌt/ **(groundnuts)** A **groundnut** is a **peanut**. [mainly BRIT] N-COUNT

**ground plan** **(ground plans)** 1 In British English, a **ground plan** is a plan of the ground floor of a building. In American English, a **ground plan** is a plan of any floor of a building. N-COUNT 2 A **ground plan** is a basic plan for future action. N-COUNT

**ground rent** **(ground rents)** **Ground rent** is rent that is paid by the owner of a flat or house to the owner of the land on which it is built. [mainly BRIT] N-VAR

**ground rule** **(ground rules)** The **ground rules** for something are the basic principles on which N-COUNT: usu pl, oft N *for/of* n future action will be based. ❑ *The panel says the ground rules for the current talks should be maintained.*

**ground|sheet** /graʊndʃiːt/ **(groundsheets)** A **groundsheet** is a piece of waterproof material which you put on the ground to sleep on when you are camping. [BRIT] N-COUNT

✓ in AM, use **groundcloth**

**grounds|keeper** /graʊndzkiːpəʳ/ **(groundskeepers)** A **groundskeeper** is the same as a **groundsman**. [AM] N-COUNT

**grounds|man** /graʊndzmən/ **(groundsmen)** A **groundsman** is a person whose job is to look after a park or sports ground. [BRIT] N-COUNT

✓ in AM, use **groundskeeper**

**ground staff** 1 The people who are paid to maintain a sports ground are called the **ground staff**. ❑ *The ground staff do all they can to prepare the pitch.* 2 At an airport, the **ground staff** are the employees of aeroplane companies who do not fly with the planes, but who work in the airport helping passengers and providing information. ❑ *There had been a strike amongst British Airways ground staff.* N-COUNT-COLL N-COUNT-COLL

**ground|swell** /graʊndswel/ A sudden growth of public feeling or support for something is often called a **groundswell**. [JOURNALISM] ❑ *There is undoubtedly a groundswell of support for the idea of a strong central authority... The groundswell of opinion is in favour of a referendum.* N-SING: with supp, usu N *of* n

**ground|water** /graʊndwɔːtəʳ/ **Groundwater** is water that is found under the ground. Groundwater has usually passed down through the soil and become trapped by rocks. N-UNCOUNT

**ground|work** /graʊndwɜːʳk/ **The groundwork for** something is the early work on it which forms the basis for further work. ❑ *Yesterday's meeting was to lay the groundwork for the task ahead.* N-SING: *the* N, oft *the* N *for* n

**group** /gruːp/ **(groups, grouping, grouped)** ◆◆◆ 1 A **group of** people or things is a number of people or things which are together in one place at one time. ❑ *The trouble involved a small group of football supporters... The students work in groups on complex problems.* 2 A **group** is a set of people who have the same interests or aims, and who organize themselves to work or act together. ❑ *...the Minority Rights Group... Members of an environmental group are staging a protest inside a chemical plant.* 3 A **group** is a set of people, organizations, or things which are considered together because they have something in common. ❑ *She is among the most promising players in her age group... As a group, today's old people are still relatively deprived.* 4 A **group** is a number of separate commercial or industrial firms which all have the same owner. [BUSINESS] ❑ *The group made a pre-tax profit of £1.05 million. ...a French-based insurance group.* 5 A **group** is a number of musicians who perform together, especially ones who play popular music. ❑ *At school he played bass in a pop group called The Urge. ...Billy Bragg's backing group.* 6 If a number of things or people **are grouped together** or **group together**, they are together in one place or within one organization or system. ❑ *The fact sheets are grouped into seven sections... The G-7 organization groups together the world's seven leading industrialized nations... We want to encourage them to group together to act as a big purchaser.* 7 → See also **grouping**, **blood group**, **ginger group**, **pressure group**. N-COUNT-COLL: oft N *of* n; N-COUNT: usu supp N; N-COUNT: usu supp N; N-COUNT: usu supp N; N-COUNT = band; VERB *be* V-ed prep, V pl-n with *together*, V *together*, Also V n prep

**groupie** /gruːpi/ **(groupies)** A **groupie** is someone, especially a young woman, who is a fan of a particular pop group, singer, or other famous person, and follows them around. N-COUNT

**group|ing** /gruːpɪŋ/ **(groupings)** A **grouping** is a set of people or things that have something in common. ❑ *There were two main political groupings pressing for independence.* N-COUNT: usu with supp

**group thera|py** Group therapy is a form of psychiatric treatment in which a group of people discuss their problems with each other. N-UNCOUNT

**grouse** /graʊs/ **(grouses, grousing, groused)**

✓ The form **grouse** is used as the plural for meaning 1.

1 A **grouse** is a wild bird with a round body. Grouse are often shot for sport and can be eaten. ❑ *The party had been to the grouse moors that morning.* ♦ **Grouse** is the flesh of this bird eaten as food. ❑ *The menu included roast grouse.* 2 If you **grouse**, you complain. ❑ *'How come we never know what's going on?' he groused... When they groused about the parking regulations, they did it with good humor.* 3 A **grouse** is a complaint. ❑ *There have been grouses about the economy, interest rates and house prices.* N-COUNT: oft N n; N-UNCOUNT; VERB V with quote, V *about* n, Also V that, V; N-COUNT

**grout** /graʊt/ **(grouts, grouting, grouted)** 1 **Grout** is a thin mixture of sand, water, and cement or lime, which is used to fill in the spaces between tiles that are fixed to a wall. 2 If you **grout** the tiles on a wall, you use grout to fill in the spaces between the tiles. ❑ *Make sure that your tiles are thoroughly grouted and sealed.* N-UNCOUNT; VERB *be* V-ed, Also V n

**grove** /groʊv/ **(groves)** 1 A **grove** is a group of trees that are close together. ❑ *...an olive grove.* 2 **Grove** is often used as part of the name of a street. [mainly BRIT] ❑ *...47 Canada Grove, Bognor Regis.* N-COUNT: usu with supp; N-IN-NAMES

**grov|el** /grɒvᵊl/ **(grovels, grovelling, grovelled)**

✓ in AM, use **groveling, groveled**

1 If you say that someone **grovels**, you think they are behaving too respectfully towards another person, for example because they are frightened or because they want something. ❑ *I don't grovel to anybody... Speakers have been shouted down, classes disrupted, teachers made to grovel. ...a letter of grovelling apology.* 2 If you **grovel**, you crawl on the ground, for example in order to find something. ❑ *We grovelled around the club on our knees.* VERB [disapproval] V *to/before* n, V, V-ing; VERB V prep/adv, Also V

**grow** /groʊ/ **(grows, growing, grew, grown)** ◆◆◆ 1 When people, animals, and plants **grow**, they increase in size and change physically over a period of time. ❑ *We stop growing at maturity.* 2 If a plant or tree **grows** in a particular place, it is alive there. ❑ *The station had roses growing at each end of the platform.* 3 If you **grow** a particular type of plant, you put seeds or young plants in the ground and look after them as they develop. ❑ *I always grow a few red onions.* 4 When someone's hair **grows**, it gradually becomes longer. Your nails also **grow**. ❑ *Then the hair began to grow again and I felt terrific.* 5 If someone **grows** their hair, or **grows** a beard or moustache, they stop cutting their hair or shaving so that their hair becomes longer. You can also **grow** your nails. ❑ *I'd better start growing my hair.* 6 If someone **grows** mentally, they change and develop in character or attitude. ❑ *They began to grow as persons.* 7 You use **grow** to say that someone or something gradually changes until they have a new quality, feeling, or attitude. ❑ *I grew a little afraid of the guy next door... He grew to love his work.* 8 If an amount, feeling, or problem **grows**, it becomes greater or more intense. ❑ *Opposition grew and the government agreed to negotiate. ...a growing number of immigrants.* 9 If one thing **grows into** another, it develops or changes until it becomes that thing. ❑ *The boys grew into men... This political row threatens to grow into a full blown crisis.* 10 If something such as an idea or a plan **grows out of** something else, it develops from it. ❑ *The idea for this book grew out of conversations with Philippa Brewster.* 11 If the economy or a business **grows**, it increases in wealth, size, or importance. [BUSINESS] ❑ *The economy continues to grow. ...a fast growing business.* 12 If someone **grows** a business, they take actions that will cause it to increase in wealth, size, or importance. [BUSINESS] VERB V; VERB V; VERB V n; VERB V; VERB V n; VERB V; V-LINK V adj, V to-inf; VERB V, V-ing; VERB V *into* n, V *into* n; VERB V *out of* n; VERB V, V-ing; VERB

❑ *To grow the business, he needs to develop management expertise and innovation across his team.* V n [13] If a crystal **grows**, or if a scientist **grows** it, it forms from a solution. VERB ❑ *...crystals that grow in cavities in the rock...* V *We tried to grow some copper sulphate crystals with our children.* V n [14] ➔ See also **grown**.

♦ **grow apart** If people who have a close relationship **grow apart**, they gradually start to have different interests and opinions from each other, and their relationship starts to fail. PHRASAL VERB ❑ *He and his wife grew apart...* pl-n V P *It sounds as if you have grown apart from Tom.* V P *from* n

♦ **grow into** When a child **grows into** an item of clothing, they become taller or bigger so that it fits them properly. PHRASAL VERB ❑ *It's a bit big, but she'll soon grow into it.* V P n

♦ **grow on** If someone or something **grows on** you, you start to like them more and more. PHRASAL VERB ❑ *Slowly and strangely, the place began to grow on me.* V P n

♦ **grow out of** [1] If you **grow out of** a type of behaviour or an interest, you stop behaving in that way or having that interest, as you develop or change. PHRASAL VERB = outgrow ❑ *Most children who stammer grow out of it.* V P P n [2] When a child **grows out of** an item of clothing, they become so tall or big that it no longer fits them properly. PHRASAL VERB = outgrow ❑ *You've grown out of your shoes again.* V P P n

♦ **grow up** [1] When someone **grows up**, they gradually change from being a child into being an adult. PHRASAL VERB ❑ *She grew up in Tokyo.* V P ➔ See also **grown-up**. [2] If you tell someone to **grow up**, you are telling them to stop behaving in a silly or childish way. [INFORMAL] PHRASAL VERB: usu imper [disapproval] ❑ *It's time you grew up.* V P [3] If something **grows up**, it starts to exist and then becomes larger or more important. PHRASAL VERB ❑ *A variety of heavy industries grew up alongside the port.* V P

**grow|er** /groʊəʳ/ **(growers)** A **grower** is a person who grows large quantities of a particular plant or crop in order to sell them. N-COUNT: usu supp N ❑ *...England's apple growers.*

**grow|ing pains** [1] If a person or organization suffers from **growing pains**, they experience temporary difficulties and problems at the beginning of a particular stage of development. N-PLURAL: usu with poss ❑ *There's some sympathy for this new country's growing pains, but that sympathy is fast wearing out.* [2] If children suffer from **growing pains**, they have pain in their muscles or joints that is caused by unusually fast growth. N-PLURAL

**grow|ing sea|son (growing seasons)** The **growing season** in a particular country or area is the period in each year when the weather and temperature is right for plants and crops to grow. N-COUNT: usu sing

**growl** /graʊl/ **(growls, growling, growled)** [1] When a dog or other animal **growls**, it makes a low noise in its throat, usually because it is angry. VERB ❑ *The dog was biting, growling and wagging its tail.* V ♦ **Growl** is also a noun. N-COUNT ❑ *The bear exposed its teeth in a muffled growl.* [2] If someone **growls** something, they say something in a low, rough, and angry voice. VERB [WRITTEN] ❑ *His fury was so great he could hardly speak.* V n *He growled some unintelligible words at Pete...* *'I should have killed him,' Sharpe growled.* V with quote ♦ **Growl** is also a noun. N-COUNT ❑ *...with an angry growl of contempt for her own weakness.*

**grown** /groʊn/ A **grown** man or woman is one who is fully developed and mature, both physically and mentally. ADJ: ADJ n ❑ *Few women can understand a grown man's love of sport... Dad, I'm a grown woman. I know what I'm doing.* ➔ See also **full-grown**.

**grown-up (grown-ups)**

✔ The spelling **grownup** is also used. The syllable **up** is not stressed when it is a noun.

[1] A **grown-up** is an adult; used by or to children. N-COUNT = adult ❑ *Tell children to tell a grown-up if they're being bullied.* [2] Someone who is **grown-up** is physically and mentally mature and no longer depends on their parents or another adult. ADJ ❑ *I have grown-up children who're doing well.* [3] If you say that someone is **grown-up**, you mean that they behave in an adult way, often when they are in fact still a child. ADJ: usu v-link ADJ ❑ *She's very grown-up.* [4] **Grown-up** things seem suitable for or typical of adults. ADJ = adult [INFORMAL] ❑ *Her songs tackle grown-up subjects... She talked in a grown-up manner.*

**growth** /groʊθ/ **(growths)** ♦♦◇ [1] The **growth of** something such as an industry, organization, or idea is its development in size, wealth, or importance. N-UNCOUNT: oft N *of* n ❑ *...the growth of nationalism. ...Japan's enormous economic growth. ...high growth rates.* [2] The **growth** in something is the increase in it. N-UNCOUNT: also *a* N, oft supp N, N *in* n, N *of* amount ❑ *A steady growth in the popularity of two smaller parties may upset the polls... The area has seen a rapid population growth... The market has shown annual growth of 20 per cent for several years.* [3] A **growth** industry, area, or market is one which is increasing in size or activity. ADJ: ADJ n [BUSINESS] ❑ *Computers and electronics are growth industries and need skilled technicians... Real estate lending has become the biggest growth area for American banks.* [4] Someone's **growth** is the development and progress of their character. N-UNCOUNT: usu supp N ❑ *...the child's emotional and intellectual growth.* [5] **Growth** in a person, animal, or plant is the process of increasing in physical size and development. N-UNCOUNT: usu with supp ❑ *...hormones which control fertility and body growth... Cells divide and renew as part of the human growth process.* [6] You can use **growth** to refer to plants which have recently developed or which developed at the same time. N-VAR ❑ *This helps to ripen new growth and makes it flower profusely.* [7] A **growth** is a lump that grows inside or on a person, animal, or plant, and that is caused by a disease. N-COUNT ❑ *This type of surgery could even be used to extract cancerous growths.*

**grub** /grʌb/ **(grubs, grubbing, grubbed)** [1] A **grub** is a young insect which has just come out of an egg and looks like a short fat worm. N-COUNT [2] **Grub** is food. N-UNCOUNT [INFORMAL] ❑ *Get yourself some grub and come and sit down.* [3] If you **grub** around, you search for something. VERB V adv/prep ❑ *I simply cannot face grubbing through all this paper.*

**grub|by** /grʌbi/ **(grubbier, grubbiest)** [1] A **grubby** person or object is rather dirty. ADJ ❑ *His white coat was grubby and stained. ...kids with grubby faces.* [2] If you call an activity or someone's behaviour **grubby**, you mean that it is not completely honest or respectable. ADJ [disapproval] ❑ *...the grubby business of politics.*

**grudge** /grʌdʒ/ **(grudges)** If you have or bear a **grudge against** someone, you have unfriendly feelings towards them because of something they did in the past. N-COUNT: oft N *against* n ❑ *He appears to have a grudge against certain players... There is no doubt it was an accident and I bear no grudges.*

**grudge match (grudge matches)** You can call a contest between two people or groups a **grudge match** when they dislike each other. N-COUNT ❑ *This is something of a grudge match against a long-term enemy.*

**grudg|ing** /grʌdʒɪŋ/ A **grudging** feeling or action is felt or done very unwillingly. ADJ: usu ADJ n = reluctant ❑ *He even earned his opponents' grudging respect... There seems to be a grudging acceptance of the situation.* ♦ **grudg|ing|ly** *The film studio grudgingly agreed to allow him to continue working.* ADV: ADV with v = reluctantly

**gru|el** /gruːəl/ **Gruel** is a food made by boiling oats with water or milk. N-UNCOUNT

**gru|el|ling** /gruːəlɪŋ/

✔ in AM, use **grueling**

A **gruelling** activity is extremely difficult and tiring to do. ADJ = exhausting ❑ *He had complained of exhaustion after his gruelling schedule over the past week... This flight was more gruelling than I had expected.*

**grue|some** /gruːsəm/ Something that is **gruesome** is extremely unpleasant and shocking. ADJ: usu ADJ n = grisly ❑ *There has been a series of gruesome murders in the capital.* ♦ **grue|some|ly** *He has spent periods in* ADV:

*prison, where he was gruesomely tortured. ...a gruesomely compelling series of interviews.* ADV adj, ADV with v

**gruff** /grʌf/ 1 A **gruff** voice sounds low and rough. ❑ *He picked up the phone expecting to hear the chairman's gruff voice.* ADJ ♦ **gruff|ly** *'Well, never mind now,' he said gruffly.* ADV 2 If you describe someone as **gruff**, you mean that they seem rather unfriendly or bad-tempered. ❑ *His gruff exterior concealed one of the kindest hearts.* ADJ

**grum|ble** /grʌmbəl/ **(grumbles, grumbling, grumbled)** 1 If someone **grumbles**, they complain about something in a bad-tempered way. VERB = moan, whinge ❑ *I shouldn't grumble about Mum – she's lovely really...* V about/at n *Taft grumbled that the law so favored the criminal that trials seemed like a game of chance...* V that *'This is inconvenient,' he grumbled...* V with quote *It's simply not in her nature to grumble.* V ♦ **Grumble** is also a noun. ❑ *My grumble is with the structure and organisation of the material.* N-COUNT ♦ **grum|bling** **(grumblings)** *There have been grumblings about the party leader.* N-VAR 2 If something **grumbles**, it makes a low continuous sound. [LITERARY] VERB ❑ *It was quiet now, the thunder had grumbled away to the west...* V adv/prep *The dogs made a noise, a rough, grumbling sound.* V-ing, Also V ♦ **Grumble** is also a noun. ❑ *One could often hear, far to the east, the grumble of guns.* N-SING: usu N *of* n

**grumpy** /grʌmpi/ **(grumpier, grumpiest)** If you say that someone is **grumpy**, you mean that they are bad-tempered and miserable. ❑ *Some folk think I'm a grumpy old man.* ADJ ♦ **grumpi|ly** *'I know, I know,' said Ken, grumpily, without looking up.* ADV: ADV with v

**grunge** /grʌndʒ/ 1 **Grunge** is the name of a fashion and of a type of music. **Grunge** fashion involves wearing clothes which look old and untidy. **Grunge** music is played on guitars and is very loud. N-UNCOUNT: oft N n 2 **Grunge** is dirt. [AM, INFORMAL] N-UNCOUNT ♦ **grungy** ❑ *...grungy motel rooms.* ADJ

**grunt** /grʌnt/ **(grunts, grunting, grunted)** 1 If you **grunt**, you make a low sound, especially because you are annoyed or not interested in something. VERB ❑ *The driver grunted, convinced that Michael was completely crazy...* V *'Rubbish,' I grunted...* V with quote *He grunted his thanks.* V n ♦ **Grunt** is also a noun. ❑ *Their replies were no more than grunts of acknowledgement.* N-COUNT: oft N *of* n 2 When an animal **grunts**, it makes a low rough noise. VERB ❑ *...the sound of a pig grunting.* V

**GSM** /dʒiː es em/ **GSM** is a digital mobile telephone system, used across Europe and in other parts of the world. **GSM** is an abbreviation for 'global system for mobile communication'. ❑ *There has been consistent growth in GSM mobile subscribers.* N-UNCOUNT

**G-string** /dʒiː strɪŋ/ **(G-strings)** A **G-string** is a narrow band of cloth that is worn between a person's legs to cover his or her sexual organs, and that is held up by a narrow string round the waist. N-COUNT

**gua|ca|mo|le** /gwɑːkəmoʊli/ **Guacamole** is a cold food from Mexico made of crushed avocados and other ingredients such as tomatoes and chillis. N-UNCOUNT

**gua|no** /gwɑːnoʊ/ **Guano** is the faeces of sea birds and bats. It is used as a fertilizer. N-UNCOUNT

**guar|an|tee** /gærəntiː/ **(guarantees, guaranteeing, guaranteed)** ♦♦◇ 1 If one thing **guarantees** another, the first is certain to cause the second thing to happen. VERB ❑ *Surplus resources alone do not guarantee growth.* V n *...a man whose fame guarantees that his calls will nearly always be returned.* V that, Also V n n 2 Something that is a **guarantee of** something else makes it certain that it will happen or that it is true. N-COUNT: oft N *of* n, N that ❑ *A famous old name on a firm is not necessarily a guarantee of quality... There is still no guarantee that a formula could be found.* 3 If you **guarantee** something, you promise that it will definitely happen, or that you will do or provide it for someone. VERB ❑ *Most states guarantee the right to free and adequate education...* V n *All students are guaranteed campus accommodation for their first year...* *be* V-ed n *We guarantee that you will find a community with which to socialise...* V that *We guarantee to refund your money if you are not delighted with your purchase.* V to-inf *...a guaranteed income of £3.6 million.* V-ed ♦ **Guarantee** is also a noun. ❑ *The Editor can give no guarantee that they will fulfil their obligations... California's state Constitution includes a guarantee of privacy.* N-COUNT: oft N that, N *of* n 4 A **guarantee** is a written promise by a company to replace or repair a product free of charge if it has any faults within a particular time. N-COUNT: also *under* N ❑ *Whatever a guarantee says, when something goes wrong, you can still claim your rights from the shop... It was still under guarantee.* 5 If a company **guarantees** its product or work, they provide a guarantee for it. VERB ❑ *Some builders guarantee their work...* V n *All Dreamland's electric blankets are guaranteed for three years.* V n 6 A **guarantee** is money or something valuable which you give to someone to show that you will do what you have promised. N-COUNT: usu N *of* n/-ing ❑ *Males between 18 and 20 had to leave a deposit as a guarantee of returning to do their military service.*

**guar|an|teed** /gærəntiːd/ If you say that something is **guaranteed to** happen, you mean that you are certain that it will happen. ADJ: v-link ADJ, usu ADJ to-inf, *it* v-link ADJ that ❑ *Reports of this kind are guaranteed to cause anxiety... It's guaranteed that my colleagues think I'm deranged... Success is not guaranteed.* → See also **guarantee**.

**guar|an|tor** /gærəntɔːʳ/ **(guarantors)** A **guarantor** is a person who gives a guarantee or who is bound by one. [LEGAL] N-COUNT

**guard** /gɑːʳd/ **(guards, guarding, guarded)** ♦♦◇ 1 If you **guard** a place, person, or object, you stand near them in order to watch and protect them. VERB ❑ *Gunmen guarded homes near the cemetery with shotguns.* V n *...the heavily guarded courtroom.* V-ed 2 If you **guard** someone, you watch them and keep them in a particular place to stop them from escaping. VERB ❑ *Marines with rifles guarded them...* V n *He is being guarded by a platoon of police.* *be* V-ed *by* n 3 A **guard** is someone such as a soldier, police officer, or prison officer who is guarding a particular place or person. N-COUNT ❑ *The prisoners overpowered their guards and locked them in a cell.* 4 A **guard** is a specially organized group of people, such as soldiers or policemen, who protect or watch someone or something. N-SING-COLL ❑ *We have a security guard around the whole area... A heavily armed guard of police have sealed off the city centre.* 5 On a train, a **guard** is a person whose job is to travel on the train in order to help passengers, check tickets, and make sure that the train travels safely and on time. [BRIT] N-COUNT

✔ in AM, use **conductor**

6 If you **guard** some information or advantage that you have, you try to protect it or keep it for yourself. VERB ❑ *He closely guarded her identity.* V n *...a threat to the country's jealously guarded unity.* V-ed 7 A **guard** is a protective device which covers a part of someone's body or a dangerous part of a piece of equipment. N-COUNT: usu with supp ❑ *...the chin guard of my helmet... A blade guard is fitted to protect the operator.* 8 Some regiments in the British Army, or the soldiers in them, are referred to as **Guards**. N-IN-NAMES ❑ *...the Grenadier Guards.* 9 → See also **guarded**, **bodyguard**, **coastguard**, **lifeguard**, **old guard**.

PHRASES 10 If someone **catches** you **off guard**, they surprise you by doing something you do not expect. If something **catches** you **off guard**, it surprises you by happening when you are not expecting it. PHRASE: V inflects ❑ *Charm the audience and catch them off guard... The invitation had caught me off guard.* 11 If you **lower** your **guard**, **let** your **guard down** or **drop** your **guard**, you relax when you should be careful and alert, often with unpleasant consequences. PHRASE: V inflects ❑ *The ANC could not afford to lower its guard until everything had been carried out... You can't let your guard down.* 12 If you **mount guard** or if you **mount a guard**, you organize people to watch or protect a person or place. PHRASE: V and N inflect ❑ *They've even mounted guard outside the main hotel in the capital.* 13 If you are **on** your **guard** or **on guard**, you are being very careful because you think a situation might become difficult or dangerous. PHRASE: usu v-link PHR ❑ *The police have questioned him thoroughly,* *and he'll be on his guard... He is constantly on guard against any threat of humiliation.* 14 If someone is **on guard**, they are on duty and responsible for guarding a particular place or person. ❑ *Police were on guard at Barnet town hall.* PHRASE: usu v-link PHR 15 If you **stand guard**, you stand near a particular person or place because you are responsible for watching or protecting them. ❑ *One young policeman stood guard outside the locked embassy gates.* PHRASE: V inflects 16 If someone is **under guard**, they are being guarded. ❑ *Three men were arrested and one was under guard in hospital.* PHRASE: v-link PHR, PHR after v

♦ **guard against** If you **guard against** something, you are careful to prevent it from happening, or to avoid being affected by it. ❑ *The armed forces were on high alert to guard against any retaliation.* PHRASAL VERB V P n

**guard dog** **(guard dogs)** A **guard dog** is a fierce dog that has been specially trained to protect a particular place. N-COUNT

**guard|ed** /gɑːʳdɪd/ If you describe someone as **guarded**, you mean that they are careful not to show their feelings or give away information. ❑ *The boy gave him a guarded look... He seemed less guarded, more relaxed.* ADJ ♦ **guard|ed|ly** *'I am happy, so far,' he says guardedly... They are guardedly optimistic that the market is on the road to recovery.* ADV: usu ADV with v, ADV adj, also ADV with cl

**guard|ian** /gɑːʳdiən/ **(guardians)** 1 A **guardian** is someone who has been legally appointed to look after the affairs of another person, for example a child or someone who is mentally ill. N-COUNT: usu with poss 2 The **guardian of** something is someone who defends and protects it. ❑ *The National Party is lifting its profile as socially conservative guardian of traditional values.* N-COUNT: usu N *of* n

**guard|ian an|gel** **(guardian angels)** A **guardian angel** is a spirit who is believed to protect and guide a particular person. N-COUNT

**guardi|an|ship** /gɑːʳdiənʃɪp/ **Guardianship** is the position of being a guardian. ❑ *...depriving mothers of the guardianship of their children.* N-UNCOUNT: usu with poss

**guard of hon|our** **(guards of honour)** A **guard of honour** is an official parade of troops, usually to celebrate or honour a special occasion, such as the visit of a head of state. [BRIT] N-COUNT

> ✔ in AM, use **honor guard**

**guard|rail** /gɑːʳdreɪl/ **(guardrails)** also **guard rail.** A **guardrail** is a railing that is placed along the edge of something such as a staircase, path, or boat, so that people can hold onto it or so that they do not fall over the edge. N-COUNT

**guards|man** /gɑːʳdzmən/ **(guardsmen)** also **Guardsman.** 1 In Britain, a **guardsman** is a soldier who is a member of one of the regiments of Guards. N-COUNT 2 In the United States, a **guardsman** is a soldier who is a member of the National Guard. N-COUNT

**guard's van** **(guard's vans)** The **guard's van** of a train is a small carriage or part of a carriage in which the guard travels. [BRIT] N-COUNT

**gua|va** /gwɑːvə/ **(guavas)** A **guava** is a round yellow tropical fruit with pink or white flesh and hard seeds. N-VAR

**gu|ber|na|to|rial** /guːbəʳnətɔːriəl/ **Gubernatorial** means relating to or connected with the post of governor. ❑ *...a well-known Dallas lawyer and former Texas gubernatorial candidate.* ADJ: ADJ n

**guer|ril|la** /gərɪlə/ **(guerrillas)** also **guerilla.** A **guerrilla** is someone who fights as part of an unofficial army, usually against an official army or police force. ❑ *The guerrillas threatened to kill their hostages. ...a guerrilla war.* ♦◇◇ N-COUNT: oft N n

**guess** /ges/ **(guesses, guessing, guessed)** 1 If you **guess** something, you give an answer or provide an opinion which may not be true because you do not have definite knowledge about the matter concerned. ❑ *The suit was faultless: Wood guessed that he was a very successful publisher or a banker... You can only guess at what mental suffering they endure... Paula reached for her camera, guessed distance and exposure, and shot two frames... Guess what I did for the whole of the first week... If she guessed wrong, it meant twice as many meetings the following week.* ♦♦◇ VERB V that V *at* n/wh V n V wh V adv 2 If you **guess that** something is the case, you correctly form the opinion that it is the case, although you do not have definite knowledge about it. ❑ *By now you will have guessed that I'm back in Ireland... He should have guessed what would happen... Someone might have guessed our secret and passed it on.* VERB V that V wh V n 3 A **guess** is an attempt to give an answer or provide an opinion which may not be true because you do not have definite knowledge about the matter concerned. ❑ *My guess is that the chance that these vaccines will work is zero... He'd taken her pulse and made a guess at her blood pressure... Well, we can hazard a guess at the answer.* N-COUNT: oft N that, N *at* n, N *as to* n/wh

**PHRASES** 4 If you say that something is **anyone's guess** or **anybody's guess**, you mean that no-one can be certain about what is really true. [INFORMAL] ❑ *Just when this will happen is anyone's guess.* PHRASE: v-link PHR 5 You say **at a guess** to indicate that what you are saying is only an estimate or what you believe to be true, rather than being a definite fact. ❑ *At a guess he's been dead for two days.* PHRASE: PHR with cl [vagueness] 6 You say **I guess** to show that you are slightly uncertain or reluctant about what you are saying. [mainly AM, INFORMAL] ❑ *I guess she thought that was pretty smart... I guess he's right... 'I think you're being paranoid.' — 'Yeah. I guess so.'* PHRASE: PHR with cl, PHR *so/not* [vagueness] 7 If someone **keeps** you **guessing**, they do not tell you what you want to know. ❑ *The author's intention is to keep everyone guessing until the bitter end.* PHRASE: V inflects 8 You say **guess what** to draw attention to something exciting, surprising, or interesting that you are about to say. [INFORMAL] ❑ *Guess what, I just got my first part in a movie.* CONVENTION

**guess|ti|mate** /gestɪmət/ **(guesstimates)** A **guesstimate** is an approximate calculation which is based mainly or entirely on guessing. [INFORMAL] N-COUNT = guess

**guess|work** /geswɜːʳk/ **Guesswork** is the process of trying to guess or estimate something without knowing all the facts or information. ❑ *The question of who planted the bomb remains a matter of guesswork.* N-UNCOUNT

**guest** /gest/ **(guests)** 1 A **guest** is someone who is visiting you or is at an event because you have invited them. ❑ *She was a guest at the wedding... Their guests sipped drinks on the veranda.* ♦♦◇ N-COUNT 2 A **guest** is someone who visits a place or organization or appears on a radio or television show because they have been invited to do so. ❑ *...a frequent chat show guest... Dr Gerald Jeffers is the guest speaker... They met when she made a guest appearance in the hit TV show Minder.* N-COUNT 3 A **guest** is someone who is staying in a hotel. ❑ *I was the only hotel guest... Hotels operate a collection service for their guests from the airports.* N-COUNT 4 If you say **be my guest** to someone, you are giving them permission to do something. ❑ *If anybody wants to work on this, be my guest.* CONVENTION

**guest book** **(guest books)** A **guest book** is a book in which guests write their names and addresses when they have been staying in someone's house or in a hotel. N-COUNT

**guest house** **(guest houses)** also **guesthouse.** 1 A **guest house** is a small hotel. [BRIT] N-COUNT 2 A **guest house** is a small house in the grounds of a large house, where visitors can stay. [AM] N-COUNT

**guest of hon|our** **(guests of honour)**

> ✔ in AM, use **guest of honor**

If you say that someone is the **guest of honour** at a dinner or other social occasion, you mean that they are the most important guest. N-COUNT: usu sing

**guest room** **(guest rooms)** A **guest room** is a bedroom in a house or hotel for visitors or guests to sleep in. N-COUNT

**guest work|er** **(guest workers)** A **guest worker** is a person, especially one from a poor country, who lives and works in a different country for a period. N-COUNT

**guff** /gʌf/ If you say that what someone has said or written is **guff**, you think that it is nonsense. [INFORMAL] N-UNCOUNT [disapproval]

**guf|faw** /gʌfɔːˈ/ **(guffaws, guffawing, guffawed)** 1 A **guffaw** is a very loud laugh. ❑ *He bursts into a loud guffaw.* N-COUNT 2 To **guffaw** means to laugh loudly. ❑ *As they guffawed loudly, the ticket collector arrived... 'Ha, ha,' everyone guffawed. 'It's one of Viv's shock tactics.'* VERB V V with quote Also V *at* n

**guid|ance** /gaɪdᵊns/ **Guidance** is help and advice. ❑ *...an opportunity for young people to improve their performance under the guidance of professional coaches... The nation looks to them for guidance.* N-UNCOUNT: oft *the* N *of* n, supp N

**guid|ance coun|se|lor** **(guidance counselors)**

✓ in BRIT, use **guidance counsellor**

A **guidance counselor** is a person who works in a school giving students advice about careers and personal problems. [mainly AM] N-COUNT

**guid|ance sys|tem** **(guidance systems)** The **guidance system** of a missile or rocket is the device which controls its course. ❑ *The guidance systems didn't work and the missile couldn't hit its target.* N-COUNT

**guide** /gaɪd/ **(guides, guiding, guided)** ◆◆◇ 1 A **guide** is a book that gives you information or instructions to help you do or understand something. ❑ *Our 10-page guide will help you to change your life for the better. ...the Pocket Guide to Butterflies of Britain and Europe.* N-COUNT; N-IN-NAMES = guidebook 2 A **guide** is a book that gives tourists information about a town, area, or country. ❑ *The Rough Guide to Paris lists accommodation for as little as £25 a night.* N-COUNT; N-IN-NAMES = guidebook 3 A **guide** is someone who shows tourists around places such as museums or cities. ❑ *We've arranged a walking tour of the city with your guide.* N-COUNT 4 If you **guide** someone around a city, museum, or building, you show it to them and explain points of interest. ❑ *...a young Egyptologist who guided us through tombs and temples with enthusiasm... There will be guided walks around the site.* → See also **guided tour**. VERB V n adv/prep V-ed 5 A **guide** is someone who shows people the way to a place in a difficult or dangerous region. ❑ *The mountain people say that, with guides, the journey can be done in fourteen days.* N-COUNT 6 A **guide** is something that can be used to help you plan your actions or to form an opinion about something. ❑ *As a rough guide, a horse needs 2.5 per cent of his body weight in food every day... When selecting fresh fish, let your taste buds be your guide.* N-COUNT: usu sing 7 If you **guide** someone somewhere, you go there with them in order to show them the way. ❑ *He took the bewildered Elliott by the arm and guided him out.* VERB = lead V n adv/prep 8 If you **guide** a vehicle somewhere, you control it carefully to make sure that it goes in the right direction. ❑ *Captain Shelton guided his plane down the runway and took off.* VERB V n adv/prep 9 If something **guides** you somewhere, it gives you the information you need in order to go in the right direction. ❑ *They sailed across the Baltic and North Seas with only a compass to guide them.* VERB V n 10 If something or someone **guides** you, they influence your actions or decisions. ❑ *He should have let his instinct guide him... My mother, whose guiding principle in life was doing right, had a far greater influence on me.* VERB V n V-ing 11 If you **guide** someone through something that is difficult to understand or to achieve, you help them to understand it or to achieve success in it. ❑ *...a free helpline to guide businessmen through the maze of EU grants.* VERB V n adv/prep

**Guide** **(Guides)** 1 In Britain, **the Guides** is an organization for girls which teaches them to become practical and independent. The Guides used to be called the Girl Guides. In the United States, there is a similar organization called the **Girl Scouts**. N-PROPER-COLL: *the* N 2 In Britain, a **Guide** is a girl who is a member of the Guides. N-COUNT

**guide|book** /gaɪdbʊk/ **(guidebooks)** also **guide book.** 1 A **guidebook** is a book that gives tourists information about a town, area, or country. N-COUNT = guide 2 A **guidebook** is a book that gives you information or instructions to help you do or understand something. ❑ *In 1987 Congressional Quarterly published a series of guidebooks to American politics.* N-COUNT = guide

**guid|ed mis|sile** **(guided missiles)** A **guided missile** is a missile whose direction can be controlled while it is in the air. N-COUNT

**guide dog** **(guide dogs)** A **guide dog** is a dog that has been trained to lead a blind person. [mainly BRIT] N-COUNT

✓ in AM, usually use **seeing-eye dog**

**guid|ed tour** **(guided tours)** If someone takes you on a **guided tour of** a place, they show you the place and tell you about it. N-COUNT: oft N *of* n

**guid|ed writ|ing** In language teaching, when students do **guided writing** activities, they are given an outline in words or pictures to help them write. ❑ *...some guided writing tasks.* N-UNCOUNT: oft N n

**guide|line** /gaɪdlaɪn/ **(guidelines)** 1 If an organization issues **guidelines on** something, it issues official advice about how to do it. ❑ *The government should issue clear guidelines on the content of religious education... The accord also lays down guidelines for the conduct of American drug enforcement agents.* N-COUNT: usu pl 2 A **guideline** is something that can be used to help you plan your actions or to form an opinion about something. ❑ *The effects of the sun can be significantly reduced if we follow certain guidelines.* N-COUNT

**guild** /gɪld/ **(guilds)** A **guild** is an organization of people who do the same job. ❑ *...the Writers' Guild of America.* N-COUNT: oft in names, N *of* n

**guil|der** /gɪldəʳ/ **(guilders)** A **guilder** was a unit of money that was used in the Netherlands. In 2002 it was replaced by the euro. ♦ **The guilder** was also used to refer to the Dutch currency system. ❑ *During the turmoil in the foreign-exchange markets the guilder remained strong.* N-COUNT: num N N-SING: *the* N

**guild|hall** /gɪldhɔːl/ **(guildhalls)** In Britain, a **guildhall** is a building near the centre of a town where members of a guild used to meet in former times. N-COUNT

**guile** /gaɪl/ **Guile** is the quality of being good at deceiving people in a clever way. ❑ *I love children's innocence and lack of guile.* N-UNCOUNT

**guile|less** /gaɪlləs/ If you describe someone as **guileless**, you mean that they behave openly and truthfully and do not try to deceive people. [WRITTEN] ❑ *Daphne was so guileless that Claire had no option but to believe her.* ADJ [approval]

**guil|lo|tine** /gɪlətiːn/ **(guillotines, guillotining, guillotined)** 1 A **guillotine** is a device used to execute people, especially in France in the past. A sharp blade was raised up on a frame and dropped onto the person's neck. ❑ *One after the other Danton, Robespierre and the rest went to the guillotine.* N-COUNT: also *by* N 2 If someone **is guillotined**, they are killed with a guillotine. ❑ *After Marie Antoinette was guillotined, her lips moved in an attempt to speak.* VERB: usu passive *be* V-ed 3 A **guillotine** is a device used for cutting paper. N-COUNT

**guilt** /gɪlt/ 1 **Guilt** is an unhappy feeling that you have because you have done something wrong or think that you have done something wrong. ❑ *Her emotions had ranged from anger to guilt in the space of a few seconds... Some cancer patients experience strong feelings of guilt.* N-UNCOUNT 2 **Guilt** is the fact that you have done something wrong or illegal. ❑ *The trial is concerned only with the determination of guilt according to criminal law... You weren't convinced of Mr Matthews' guilt.* N-UNCOUNT

**guilt com|plex** **(guilt complexes)** If you say that someone has a **guilt complex** about something, you mean that they feel very guilty about it, in a way that you consider is exaggerated, unreasonable, or unnecessary. N-COUNT disapproval

**guilt-ridden** If a person is **guilt-ridden**, they feel very guilty about something. ❑ *In the first week of January, thousands of guilt-ridden people signed up for fitness courses or embarked on diets.* ADJ

**guilty** /gɪlti/ **(guiltier, guiltiest)** [1] If you feel **guilty**, you feel unhappy because you think that you have done something wrong or have failed to do something which you should have done. ❑ *I feel so guilty, leaving all this to you... When she saw me she looked guilty.* ♦ **guilti|ly** *He glanced guiltily over his shoulder.* [2] **Guilty** is used of an action or fact that you feel guilty about. ❑ *Many may be keeping it a guilty secret... I leave with a guilty sense of relief.* **guilty conscience** → see **conscience**. [3] If someone is **guilty of** a crime or offence, they have committed that crime or offence. ❑ *They were found guilty of murder... He pleaded guilty to causing actual bodily harm.* [4] If someone is **guilty of** doing something wrong, they have done that thing. ❑ *He claimed Mr Brooke had been guilty of a 'gross error of judgment'... They will consider whether or not he has been guilty of serious professional misconduct.* ◆◇◇ ADJ: usu v-link ADJ, oft ADJ *about* n ADV: ADV with v ADJ: ADJ n ADJ: oft ADJ *of* n/-ing ADJ: oft ADJ *of* n/-ing

**guinea** /gɪni/ **(guineas)** A **guinea** is an old British unit of money that was worth £1.05. Guineas are still sometimes used, for example in auctions. N-COUNT

**guinea fowl** **(guinea fowl)** A **guinea fowl** is a large grey African bird that is often eaten as food. N-COUNT

**guinea pig** **(guinea pigs)** also **guinea-pig.** [1] If someone is used as a **guinea pig** in an experiment, something is tested on them that has not been tested on people before. ❑ *...a human guinea pig... Nearly 500,000 pupils are to be guinea pigs in a trial run of the new 14-plus exams.* [2] A **guinea pig** is a small furry animal without a tail. Guinea pigs are often kept as pets. N-COUNT N-COUNT

**guise** /gaɪz/ **(guises)** You use **guise** to refer to the outward appearance or form of someone or something, which is often temporary or different from their real nature. ❑ *He turned up at a fancy dress Easter dance in the guise of a white rabbit.* N-COUNT: with supp, oft *in/under the* N *of* n

**gui|tar** /gɪtɑːʳ/ **(guitars)** A **guitar** is a musical instrument with six strings and a long neck. You play the guitar by plucking or strumming the strings. ◆◇◇ N-VAR: oft *the* N

**gui|tar|ist** /gɪtɑːrɪst/ **(guitarists)** A **guitarist** is someone who plays the guitar. N-COUNT

**gu|lag** /guːlæg/ **(gulags)** A **gulag** is a prison camp where conditions are extremely bad and the prisoners are forced to work very hard. The name **gulag** comes from the prison camps in the former Soviet Union. N-COUNT

**gulch** /gʌltʃ/ **(gulches)** A **gulch** is a long narrow valley with steep sides which has been made by a stream flowing through it. [mainly AM] ❑ *...California Gulch.* N-COUNT: oft in names

**gulf** /gʌlf/ **(gulfs)** [1] A **gulf** is an important or significant difference between two people, things, or groups. ❑ *Within society, there is a growing gulf between rich and poor. ...the gulf between rural and urban life.* [2] A **gulf** is a large area of sea which extends a long way into the surrounding land. ❑ *Hurricane Andrew was last night heading into the Gulf of Mexico.* N-COUNT: oft N *between* pl-n N-COUNT

**Gulf** **The Gulf** is used to refer to the Arabian Gulf, the Persian Gulf and the surrounding countries. ❑ *...the Gulf crisis. ...the Gulf war. ...the oil wells of the Gulf.* N-PROPER: *the* N, oft N n

**gull** /gʌl/ **(gulls)** A **gull** is a common sea bird. N-COUNT

**gul|let** /gʌlɪt/ **(gullets)** Your **gullet** is the tube which goes from your mouth to your stomach. N-COUNT

**gul|ley** /gʌli/ → see **gully**.

**gul|lible** /gʌlɪbᵊl/ If you describe someone as **gullible**, you mean they are easily tricked because they are too trusting. ❑ *I'm so gullible I would have believed him.* ♦ **gul|li|bil|ity** /gʌləbɪlɪti/ *Was she taking part of the blame for her own gullibility?* ADJ N-UNCOUNT: oft with poss

**gul|ly** /gʌli/ **(gullies)** also **gulley.** A **gully** is a long narrow valley with steep sides. ❑ *The bodies of the three climbers were located at the bottom of a steep gully.* N-COUNT

**gulp** /gʌlp/ **(gulps, gulping, gulped)** [1] If you **gulp** something, you eat or drink it very quickly by swallowing large quantities of it at once. ❑ *She quickly gulped her tea.* [2] If you **gulp**, you swallow air, often making a noise in your throat as you do so, because you are nervous or excited. [WRITTEN] ❑ *I gulped, and then proceeded to tell her the whole story... 'I'm sorry,' he gulped.* [3] If you **gulp** air, you breathe in a large amount of air quickly through your mouth. ❑ *She gulped air into her lungs... He slumped back, gulping for air.* [4] A **gulp of** air, food, or drink, is a large amount of it that you swallow at once. ❑ *I took in a large gulp of air... When his whisky came he drank half of it in one gulp.* VERB V n VERB V V with quote VERB V n *into* n V *for* n N-COUNT: oft N *of* n

♦ **gulp down** If you **gulp down** food or drink, you quickly eat or drink it all by swallowing large quantities of it at once. ❑ *She gulped down a mouthful of coffee... He'd gulped it down in one bite.* PHRASAL VERB V P n V n P

**gum** /gʌm/ **(gums, gumming, gummed)** [1] **Gum** is a substance, usually tasting of mint, which you chew for a long time but do not swallow. → See also **bubblegum**, **chewing gum**. [2] Your **gums** are the areas of firm, pink flesh inside your mouth, which your teeth grow out of. ❑ *The toothbrush gently removes plaque without damaging the gums. ...gum disease.* [3] **Gum** is a type of glue that is used to stick two pieces of paper together. [mainly BRIT] ❑ *He was holding up a pound note that had been torn in half and stuck together with gum.* ♦ **gummed** *...gummed labels.* [4] If two things are **gummed together**, they are stuck together. [BRIT] ❑ *It is a mild infection in which a baby's eyelashes can become gummed together.* N-MASS N-COUNT: usu pl N-MASS ADJ: usu ADJ n ADJ = stuck

**gum|ball** /gʌmbɔːl/ **(gumballs)** **Gumballs** are round, brightly coloured balls of chewing gum. [mainly AM] N-COUNT

**gum|bo** /gʌmboʊ/ **(gumbos)** [1] **Gumbo** is a type of soup or stew from the southern United States. It can be made with meat or fish, and usually contains okra. [2] In parts of the United States, **gumbo** is another name for **okra**. N-VAR N-UNCOUNT

**gum|boot** /gʌmbuːt/ **(gumboots)** **Gumboots** are long rubber boots which you wear to keep your feet dry. [BRIT, OLD-FASHIONED] N-COUNT: usu pl = wellington

**gum|drop** /gʌmdrɒp/ **(gumdrops)** A **gumdrop** is a chewy sweet which feels like firm rubber and usually tastes of fruit. N-COUNT

**gum|my** /gʌmi/ Something that is **gummy** is sticky. ❑ *My eyes are gummy.* ADJ = sticky

**gump|tion** /gʌmpʃᵊn/ [1] If someone has **gumption**, they are able to think what it would be sensible to do in a particular situation, and they do it. [INFORMAL] ❑ *Surely anyone with marketing gumption should be able to sell good books at any time of year.* [2] If someone has **the gumption to** do something, they are brave enough to do it. ❑ *He suspected that deep down, she admired him for having the gumption to disagree with her.* N-UNCOUNT N-UNCOUNT: oft *the* N to-inf

**gum tree** **(gum trees)** A **gum tree** is a tree such as a eucalyptus that produces gum. N-COUNT

**gun** /gʌn/ **(guns, gunning, gunned)** [1] A **gun** is a weapon from which bullets or other things are fired. ❑ *He produced a gun and he came into the house... The inner-city has guns and crime and drugs and deprivation. ...gun control laws.* [2] A **gun** or a **starting gun** is an object like a gun that is used to make a noise to signal the start of a race. ❑ *The starting gun blasted and they were off.* [3] To **gun** an engine or a vehicle means to make it start or go faster by pressing on the accelerator pedal. [mainly AM] ❑ *He gunned his engine and drove off.* [4] → See ◆◆◇ N-COUNT N-COUNT VERB V n also **airgun**, **machine-gun**, **shotgun**, **sub-machine gun**.

PHRASES 5 If you come out **with guns blazing** or **with all guns blazing**, you put all your effort and energy into trying to achieve something. ❑ *The company came out with guns blazing.* PHRASE: PHR after v 6 If you **jump the gun**, you do something before everyone else or before the proper or right time. [INFORMAL] ❑ *It wasn't due to be released until September 10, but some booksellers have jumped the gun and decided to sell it early.* PHRASE: V inflects 7 If you **stick to** your **guns**, you continue to have your own opinion about something even though other people are trying to tell you that you are wrong. [INFORMAL] ❑ *He should have stuck to his guns and refused to meet her.* PHRASE: V inflects

♦ **gun down** If someone **is gunned down**, they are shot and severely injured or killed. [JOURNALISM] ❑ *He had been gunned down and killed at point-blank range.* PHRASAL VERB: usu passive *be* V-ed P

♦ **gun for** If someone **is gunning for** you, they are trying to find a way to harm you or cause you trouble. [INFORMAL] ❑ *You knew that they were gunning for you, but did you ever imagine that it would be as bad as this?* PHRASAL VERB: only cont V P n

**gun|boat** /gʌnbout/ **(gunboats)** A **gunboat** is a small ship which has several large guns fixed on it. N-COUNT

**gun con|trol** **Gun control** refers to the laws that restrict the possession and use of guns. ❑ *France has tight gun-control laws for handguns, but not for hunting rifles.* N-UNCOUNT: oft N n

**gun dog** **(gun dogs)** also **gundog.** A **gun dog** is a dog that has been trained to work with a hunter or gamekeeper, especially to find and carry back birds or animals that have been shot. N-COUNT

**gun|fight** /gʌnfaɪt/ **(gunfights)** A **gunfight** is a fight between people using guns. N-COUNT ♦ **gun|fighter** **(gunfighters)** ❑ *Eastwood plays retired gunfighter Will Munny.* N-COUNT

**gun|fire** /gʌnfaɪəʳ/ **Gunfire** is the repeated shooting of guns. ❑ *The sound of gunfire and explosions grew closer.* N-UNCOUNT

**gunge** /gʌndʒ/ You use **gunge** to refer to a soft, sticky substance, especially if it is unpleasant. [BRIT, INFORMAL] ❑ *He had painted the floors with some kind of black gunge.* N-UNCOUNT = *gunk*

**gung ho** /gʌŋ hou/ also **gung-ho.** If you say that someone is **gung ho**, you mean that they are very enthusiastic or eager to do something, for example to fight in a battle. [INFORMAL] ❑ *He has warned some of his more gung ho generals about the consequences of an invasion... Senate Republicans are less gung-ho about tax cuts.* ADJ

**gunk** /gʌŋk/ You use **gunk** to refer to any soft sticky substance, especially if it is unpleasant. [INFORMAL] N-UNCOUNT = *gunge*

**gun|man** /gʌnmən/ **(gunmen)** A **gunman** is a man who uses a gun to commit a crime such as murder or robbery. [JOURNALISM] ❑ *Two policemen were killed when gunmen opened fire on their car.* N-COUNT

**gun|ner** /gʌnəʳ/ **(gunners)** A **gunner** is an ordinary soldier in an artillery regiment. N-COUNT

**gun|nery** /gʌnəri/ **Gunnery** is the activity of firing large guns. [MILITARY, TECHNICAL] ❑ *During the war the area was used for gunnery practice.* N-UNCOUNT: usu N n

**gun|point** /gʌnpɔɪnt/ If you are held **at gunpoint**, someone is threatening to shoot and kill you if you do not obey them. ❑ *She and her two daughters were held at gunpoint by a gang who burst into their home.* PHRASE: PHR after v

**gun|powder** /gʌnpaudəʳ/ **Gunpowder** is an explosive substance which is used to make fireworks or cause explosions. N-UNCOUNT

**gun-runner** **(gun-runners)**

✔ in AM, use **gunrunner**

A **gun-runner** is someone who takes or sends guns into a country secretly and illegally. N-COUNT

**gun-running** **Gun-running** is the activity of taking or sending guns into a country secretly and illegally. N-UNCOUNT

**gun|ship** /gʌnʃɪp/ **(gunships)** → see **helicopter gunship**.

**gun|shot** /gʌnʃɒt/ **(gunshots)** 1 **Gunshot** is used to refer to bullets that are fired from a gun. ❑ *They had died of gunshot wounds. ...avoiding the volleys of gunshot.* N-UNCOUNT: usu N n 2 A **gunshot** is the firing of a gun or the sound of a gun being fired. ❑ *A balloon popped, sounding like a gunshot.* N-COUNT

**gun-shy** If someone is **gun-shy**, they are nervous or afraid. ❑ *The electric-power industry is gun-shy about building more large plants.* ADJ: usu v-link ADJ

**gun|slinger** /gʌnslɪŋəʳ/ **(gunslingers)** A **gunslinger** is someone, especially a criminal, who uses guns in fighting. N-COUNT

**gun|smith** /gʌnsmɪθ/ **(gunsmiths)** A **gunsmith** is someone who makes and repairs guns. N-COUNT

**gup|py** /gʌpi/ **(guppies)** A **guppy** is a small, brightly-coloured tropical fish. N-COUNT

**gur|gle** /gɜːʳgᵊl/ **(gurgles, gurgling, gurgled)** 1 If water **is gurgling**, it is making the sound that it makes when it flows quickly and unevenly through a narrow space. ❑ *...a narrow stone-edged channel along which water gurgles unseen.* VERB V adv/prep ♦ **Gurgle** is also a noun. ❑ *We could hear the swish and gurgle of water against the hull.* N-COUNT 2 If someone, especially a baby, **is gurgling**, they are making a sound in their throat similar to the gurgling of water. ❑ *Henry gurgles happily in his baby chair.* VERB V ♦ **Gurgle** is also a noun. ❑ *There was a gurgle of laughter on the other end of the line.* N-COUNT

**gur|ney** /gɜːni/ **(gurneys)** A **gurney** is a bed on wheels that is used in hospitals for moving sick or injured people. [AM] N-COUNT

✔ in BRIT, use **trolley**

**guru** /guːruː/ **(gurus)** 1 A **guru** is a person who some people regard as an expert or leader. ❑ *Fashion gurus dictate crazy ideas such as squeezing oversized bodies into tight trousers.* N-COUNT: oft n N 2 A **guru** is a religious and spiritual leader and teacher, especially in Hinduism. N-COUNT; N-TITLE

**gush** /gʌʃ/ **(gushes, gushing, gushed)** 1 When liquid **gushes** out of something, or when something **gushes** a liquid, the liquid flows out very quickly and in large quantities. ❑ *Piping-hot water gushed out... A supertanker continues to gush oil off the coast of Spain.* VERB V adv/prep V n 2 A **gush of** liquid is a sudden, rapid flow of liquid, or a quantity of it that suddenly flows out. ❑ *I heard a gush of water.* N-SING: usu N *of* n 3 If someone **gushes**, they express their admiration or pleasure in an exaggerated way. ❑ *'Oh, it was brilliant,' he gushes... He gushed about his love for his wife.* VERB V with quote V prep ♦ **gush|ing** *He delivered a gushing speech.* ADJ

**gussy** /gʌsi/ **(gussies, gussying, gussied)**

♦ **gussy up** If someone **is gussied up**, they are dressed very smartly. If something **is gussied up**, it is made more interesting or attractive. [mainly AM, INFORMAL] ❑ *They all got gussied up. ...plans to gussy up the venues, offering better food and games arcades.* PHRASAL VERB V-ed P V P n (not pron) Also V pron P

**gust** /gʌst/ **(gusts, gusting, gusted)** 1 A **gust** is a short, strong, sudden rush of wind. ❑ *A gust of wind drove down the valley... A hurricane-force gust blew off part of a church tower.* N-COUNT: oft N *of* n 2 When the wind **gusts**, it blows with short, strong, sudden rushes. ❑ *The wind gusted again... The wind gusted up to 164 miles an hour.* VERB V V prep/adv 3 If you feel a **gust of** emotion, you feel the emotion suddenly and intensely. ❑ *...a small gust of pleasure.* N-COUNT: N *of* n

**gus|to** /gʌstou/ If you do something **with gusto**, you do it with energetic and enthusiastic enjoyment. ❑ *Hers was a minor part, but she played it with gusto.* N-UNCOUNT: usu *with* N [approval]

**gusty** /gʌsti/ **Gusty** winds are very strong and irregular. ❑ *Weather forecasts predict more hot weather, gusty winds and lightning strikes.* ADJ: usu ADJ n

**gut** /gʌt/ **(guts, gutting, gutted)** [1] A person's or animal's **guts** are all the organs inside them. ❑ *By the time they finish, the crewmen are standing ankle-deep in fish guts.* N-PLURAL [2] When someone **guts** a dead animal or fish, they prepare it for cooking by removing all the organs from inside it. ❑ *It is not always necessary to gut the fish prior to freezing.* VERB V n [3] **The gut** is the tube inside the body of a person or animal through which food passes while it is being digested. N-SING: the/poss N [4] **Guts** is the will and courage to do something which is difficult or unpleasant, or which might have unpleasant results. [INFORMAL] ❑ *The new Chancellor has the guts to push through unpopular tax increases.* N-UNCOUNT [5] A **gut** feeling is based on instinct or emotion rather than reason. ❑ *Let's have your gut reaction to the facts as we know them.* N-SING: usu N n [6] You can refer to someone's stomach as their **gut**, especially when it is very large and sticks out. [INFORMAL] ❑ *His gut sagged out over his belt.* → See also **beer gut**. N-COUNT: usu sing [7] To **gut** a building means to destroy the inside of it so that only its outside walls remain. ❑ *Over the weekend, a firebomb gutted a building where 60 people lived... A factory stands gutted and deserted.* VERB V n V-ed [8] **Gut** is string made from part of the stomach of an animal. Traditionally, it is used to make the strings of sports rackets or musical instruments such as violins. N-UNCOUNT [9] → See also **gutted**.

PHRASES [10] If you **hate** someone's **guts**, you dislike them very much indeed. [INFORMAL] ❑ *We hate each other's guts.* PHRASE: V inflects [emphasis] [11] If you say that you **are working** your **guts out** or **slogging** your **guts out**, you are emphasizing that you are working as hard as you can. [INFORMAL] ❑ *Most have worked their guts out and made sacrifices.* PHRASE: V inflects [emphasis]

**gut|less** /gʌtləs/ If you describe someone as **gutless**, you think they have a weak character and lack courage or determination. ❑ *By attacking me, by attacking my wife, he has proved himself to be a gutless coward.* ADJ [disapproval]

**gutsy** /gʌtsi/ **(gutsier, gutsiest)** If you describe someone as **gutsy**, you mean they show courage or determination. [INFORMAL] ❑ *I've always been drawn to tough, gutsy women... They admired his gutsy and emotional speech.* ADJ [approval]

**gut|ted** /gʌtɪd/ If you are **gutted**, you feel extremely disappointed or depressed about something that has happened. [BRIT, INFORMAL] ❑ *Birmingham City supporters will be absolutely gutted if he leaves the club.* ADJ: v-link ADJ

**gut|ter** /gʌtəʳ/ **(gutters)** [1] **The gutter** is the edge of a road next to the pavement, where rain water collects and flows away. ❑ *It is supposed to be washed down the gutter and into the city's vast sewerage system.* N-COUNT: usu the N [2] A **gutter** is a plastic or metal channel fixed to the lower edge of the roof of a building, which rain water drains into. → See picture on page 1705. ❑ *Did you fix the gutter?* N-COUNT [3] If someone is **in the gutter**, they are very poor and live in a very bad way. ❑ *Instead of ending up in jail or in the gutter he was remarkably successful.* N-SING: the N [4] → See also **gutter press**.

**gut|ter|ing** /gʌtərɪŋ/ **Guttering** consists of the plastic or metal channels fixed to the lower edge of the roof of a building, which rain water drains into. N-UNCOUNT

**gut|ter press** You can refer to newspapers and magazines which print mainly stories about sex and crime as **the gutter press**. [BRIT] ❑ *The gutter press has held the royals up to ridicule.* N-SING: the N [disapproval]

✓ in AM, use **scandal sheets**

**gut|tur|al** /gʌtərᵊl/ **Guttural** sounds are harsh sounds that are produced at the back of a person's throat. ❑ *Joe had a low, guttural voice with a mid-Western accent.* ADJ

**gut-wrenching** **Gut-wrenching** events or experiences make you feel extremely shocked or upset. [mainly JOURNALISM] ❑ *Going to court can be an expensive, time consuming and gut wrenching experience that is best avoided.* ADJ

**guv** /gʌv/ **Guv** is sometimes used to address a man, especially a customer or someone you are doing a service for. [BRIT, INFORMAL, SPOKEN] ❑ *Hey, thanks, guv.* N-VOC

**guvnor** /gʌvnəʳ/ **(guvnors)** also **guv'nor.** **Guvnor** is sometimes used to refer to or address a man who is in a position of authority over you, for example your employer or father. [BRIT, INFORMAL] N-COUNT; N-VOC

**guy** /gaɪ/ **(guys)** [1] A **guy** is a man. [INFORMAL] ❑ *I was working with a guy from Manchester.* → See also **wise guy**. ◆◆◇ N-COUNT [2] Americans sometimes address a group of people, whether they are male or female, as **guys** or **you guys**. [INFORMAL] ❑ *Hi, guys. How are you doing?... Mom wants to know if you guys still have that two-person tent.* N-VOC; N-PLURAL: you N

**Guy Fawkes Night** /gaɪ fɔːks naɪt/ In Britain, **Guy Fawkes Night** is the evening of 5th November, when many people have parties with bonfires and fireworks. It began as a way of remembering the attempt by Guy Fawkes to blow up the Houses of Parliament in 1605. Guy Fawkes Night is often referred to as 'Bonfire Night'. N-UNCOUNT = Bonfire Night

**guy rope** **(guy ropes)** A **guy rope** is a rope or wire that has one end fastened to a tent or pole and the other end fixed to the ground, so that it keeps the tent or pole in position. N-COUNT = guy

**guz|zle** /gʌzᵊl/ **(guzzles, guzzling, guzzled)** [1] If you **guzzle** something, you drink it or eat it quickly and greedily. [INFORMAL] ❑ *Melissa had guzzled gin and tonics like they were lemonade.* VERB V n Also V [2] If you say that a vehicle **guzzles** fuel, you mean that it uses a lot of it in a way that is wasteful and unnecessary. ❑ *The plane was deafeningly noisy, guzzled fuel, and left a trail of smoke.* VERB V n ♦ **-guzzling** *The boom of the 1980s led to a taste for petrol-guzzling cars. ...big energy-guzzling houses.* → See also **gas guzzler**. COMB in ADJ: ADJ n

**gym** /dʒɪm/ **(gyms)** [1] A **gym** is a club, building, or large room, usually containing special equipment, where people go to do physical exercise and get fit. ❑ *While the lads are golfing, I work out in the gym. ...the school gym.* N-COUNT [2] **Gym** is the activity of doing physical exercises in a gym, especially at school. [INFORMAL] ❑ *...gym classes.* N-UNCOUNT: oft N n

**gym|kha|na** /dʒɪmkɑːnə/ **(gymkhanas)** A **gymkhana** is an event in which people ride horses in competition. N-COUNT

**gym|na|sium** /dʒɪmneɪziəm/ **(gymnasiums** or **gymnasia** /dʒɪmneɪziə/**)** A **gymnasium** is the same as a **gym**. [FORMAL] N-COUNT

**gym|nast** /dʒɪmnæst/ **(gymnasts)** A **gymnast** is someone who is trained in gymnastics. N-COUNT

**gym|nas|tics** /dʒɪmnæstɪks/

✓ The form **gymnastic** is used as a modifier.

[1] **Gymnastics** consists of physical exercises that develop your strength, co-ordination, and ease of movement. ❑ *...the British Amateur Gymnastics Association.* N-UNCOUNT [2] **Gymnastic** is used to describe things relating to gymnastics. ❑ *...gymnastic exercises.* ADJ: ADJ n [3] You can use **gymnastics** to refer to activities which require skills such as speed and adaptability. ❑ *Hers is the kind of voice that excels at vocal gymnastics.* N-UNCOUNT: adj N

**gy|nae|col|ogy** /gaɪnɪkɒlədʒi/

✓ in AM, use **gynecology**

**Gynaecology** is the branch of medical science which deals with women's diseases and medical conditions. N-UNCOUNT ♦ **gy|nae|colo|gist** **(gynaecologists)** ❑ *Gynaecologists at Aberdeen Maternity Hospital have successfully used the drug on 60 women.* N-COUNT ♦ **gy|nae|co|logi|cal** /gaɪnɪkəlɒdʒɪkᵊl/ *Breast examination is a part of a routine gynaecological examination.* ADJ: ADJ n

**gyp|sum** /dʒɪpsəm/ **Gypsum** is a soft white substance which looks like chalk and which is used to make plaster of Paris. N-UNCOUNT

**gyp|sy** /dʒɪpsi/ **(gypsies)** also **gipsy.** A **gypsy** is a member of a race of people who travel from place to place, usually in caravans, rather than living in one place. N-COUNT ♦ **Gypsy** is also an adjective. ADJ: usu ADJ n ❑ *...the largest gypsy community of any country.*

**gy|rate** /dʒaɪreɪt, AM dʒaɪreɪt/ **(gyrates, gyrating, gyrated)** [1] If you **gyrate**, you dance or move your body quickly with circular movements. VERB ❑ *The woman began to gyrate to the music.* V *...a room stuffed full of gasping, gyrating bodies.* V-ing ♦ **gy|ra|tion** /dʒaɪreɪʃən/ **(gyrations)** *Prince continued his enthusiastic gyrations on stage.* N-COUNT: usu pl [2] To **gyrate** means to turn round and round in a circle, usually very fast. VERB ❑ *The aeroplane was gyrating about the sky in a most unpleasant fashion.* V prep Also V [3] If things such as prices or currencies **gyrate**, they move up and down in a rapid and uncontrolled way. VERB [JOURNALISM] ❑ *Interest rates began to gyrate up towards 20 per cent in 1980 and then down and up again.* V adv/prep Also V ♦ **gy|ra|tion** *...the gyrations of the currency markets.* N-COUNT: usu pl, with supp

**gy|ro|scope** /dʒaɪrəskoʊp/ **(gyroscopes)** A **gyroscope** is a device that contains a disc turning on an axis that can turn freely in any direction, so that the disc maintains the same position whatever the position or movement of the surrounding structure. N-COUNT

# H h

**H, h** /eɪtʃ/ **(H's, h's)** **H** is the eighth letter of the English alphabet.

**ha** /hɑː/ also **hah.** **Ha** is used in writing to represent a noise that people make to show they are surprised, annoyed, or pleased about something. ❑ *Ha! said Wren. Think I'd trust you?* ➔ See also **ha ha**. EXCLAM

**ha.** **ha.** is a written abbreviation for **hectare**.

**ha|beas cor|pus** /heɪbiəs kɔːʳpəs/ **Habeas corpus** is a law that states that a person cannot be kept in prison unless they have first been brought before a court of law, which decides whether it is legal for them to be kept in prison. N-UNCOUNT

**hab|er|dash|er** /hæbəʳdæʃəʳ/ **(haberdashers)** 1 A **haberdasher** or a **haberdasher's** is a shop where small articles for sewing are sold. [BRIT] N-COUNT 2 A **haberdasher** is a shopkeeper who makes and sells men's clothes. [AM] N-COUNT

✔ in BRIT, use **tailor**

3 A **haberdasher** or a **haberdasher's** is a shop where men's clothes are sold. [AM] N-COUNT

✔ in BRIT, use **tailor, tailor's**

**hab|er|dash|ery** /hæbəʳdæʃəri/ **(haberdasheries)** 1 **Haberdashery** is small articles for sewing, such as buttons, zips, and thread, which are sold in a haberdasher's shop. [BRIT] N-UNCOUNT

✔ in AM, use **notions**

2 **Haberdashery** is men's clothing sold in a shop. [AM] N-UNCOUNT 3 A **haberdashery** is a shop selling haberdashery. N-COUNT

**hab|it** /hæbɪt/ **(habits)** ◆◇◇ 1 A **habit** is something that you do often or regularly. ❑ *He has an endearing habit of licking his lips when he's nervous... Many people add salt to their food out of habit, without even tasting it first. ...a survey on eating habits in the UK.* N-VAR: oft N *of* -ing 2 A **habit** is an action which is considered bad that someone does repeatedly and finds it difficult to stop doing. ❑ *A good way to break the habit of eating too quickly is to put your knife and fork down after each mouthful... After twenty years as a chain smoker Mr Nathe has given up the habit.* N-COUNT: oft N *of* -ing 3 A drug **habit** is an addiction to a drug such as heroin or cocaine. ❑ *She became a prostitute in order to pay for her cocaine habit.* N-COUNT: supp N 4 A **habit** is a piece of clothing shaped like a long loose dress, which a nun or monk wears. N-COUNT

PHRASES 5 If you say that someone is **a creature of habit**, you mean that they usually do the same thing at the same time each day, rather than doing new and different things. PHRASE: *creature* inflects, usu v-link PHR 6 If you are **in the habit of** doing something, you do it regularly or often. If you **get into the habit of** doing something, you begin to do it regularly or often. ❑ *They were in the habit of giving two or three dinner parties a month... I got into the habit of calling in on Gloria on my way home from work.* PHRASE: v-link PHR -ing 7 If you **make a habit of** doing something, you do it regularly or often. ❑ *You can phone me at work as long as you don't make a habit of it.* PHRASE: V inflects, PHR -ing/n

**hab|it|able** /hæbɪtəbəl/ If a place is **habitable**, it is good enough for people to live in. ❑ *Making the house habitable was a major undertaking.* ADJ

**habi|tat** /hæbɪtæt/ **(habitats)** The **habitat** of an animal or plant is the natural environment in which it normally lives or grows. ❑ *In its natural habitat, the hibiscus will grow up to 25ft.* N-VAR: usu supp N

**habi|ta|tion** /hæbɪteɪʃən/ **(habitations)** **Habitation** is the activity of living somewhere. [FORMAL] ❑ *The recent survey found that 20 per cent of private-rented dwellings are unfit for human habitation.* N-UNCOUNT

**ha|bitu|al** /həbɪtʃuəl/ 1 A **habitual** action, state, or way of behaving is one that someone usually does or has, especially one that is considered to be typical or characteristic of them. ❑ *If bad posture becomes habitual, you risk long-term effects.* ADJ ♦ **ha|bitu|al|ly** *His mother had a long term patient who habitually flew into rages.* ADV: ADV with v, ADV adj 2 You use **habitual** to describe someone who usually or often does a particular thing. ❑ *...the home secretary's plans for minimum sentences for habitual criminals.* ADJ: ADJ n

**ha|bitu|at|ed** /həbɪtʃueɪtɪd/ If you are **habituated to** something, you have become used to it. [FORMAL] ❑ *People in the area are habituated to the idea of learning from the person above how to do the work.* ADJ: usu v-link ADJ, usu ADJ *to* n

**ha|bitué** /həbɪtʃueɪ/ **(habitués)** Someone who is a **habitué of** a particular place often visits that place. [FORMAL] ❑ *Kiki and Man Ray, who lived just down the street, were habitués of this bar.* N-COUNT: usu with supp, oft N *of* n

**hack** /hæk/ **(hacks, hacking, hacked)** 1 If you **hack** something or **hack** at it, you cut it with strong, rough strokes using a sharp tool such as an axe or knife. ❑ *An armed gang barged onto the train and began hacking and shooting anyone in sight... Some were hacked to death with machetes... Matthew desperately hacked through the leather.* VERB V n, *be* V-ed, V prep/adv, V prep 2 If you **hack** your **way** through an area such as a jungle or **hack** a **path** through it, you move forward, cutting back the trees or plants that are in your way. ❑ *We undertook the task of hacking our way through the jungle.* VERB V n prep/adv 3 If you **hack at** or **hack** something which is too large, too long, or too expensive, you reduce its size, length, or cost by cutting out or getting rid of large parts of it. ❑ *He hacked away at the story, eliminating one character entirely.* VERB V adv/prep, Also V n 4 If you refer to a professional writer, such as a journalist, as a **hack**, you disapprove of them because they write for money without worrying very much about the quality of their writing. ❑ *...tabloid hacks, always eager to find victims in order to sell newspapers.* N-COUNT [disapproval] 5 If you refer to a politician as a **hack**, you disapprove of them because they are too loyal to their party and perhaps do not deserve the position they have. ❑ *Far too many party hacks from the old days still hold influential jobs.* N-COUNT: oft supp N [disapproval] 6 If someone **hacks into** a computer system, they break into the system, especially in order to get secret information. ❑ *The saboteurs had demanded money in return for revealing how they hacked into the systems.* VERB V *into* n ♦ **hack|ing** *...the common and often illegal art of computer hacking.* N-UNCOUNT 7 If you say that someone **can't hack it** or **couldn't hack it**, you mean that they do not or did not have the qualities needed to do a task or cope with a situation. [INFORMAL] ❑ *You have to be strong and confident and never give the slightest impression that you can't hack it.* PHRASE 8 ➔ See also **hacking**.

**hack|er** /hækəʳ/ **(hackers)** 1 A computer **hacker** is someone who tries to break into com- N-COUNT puter systems, especially in order to get secret information. [2] A computer **hacker** is someone who uses a computer a lot, especially so much that they have no time to do anything else. [N-COUNT]

**hack|ing** /hækɪŋ/ A **hacking** cough is a dry, painful cough with a harsh, unpleasant sound. ➔ See also **hack**. [ADJ: ADJ n]

**hack|ing jack|et** **(hacking jackets)** A **hacking jacket** is a jacket made of a woollen cloth called tweed. Hacking jackets are often worn by people who go horse riding. [mainly BRIT] [N-COUNT]

**hack|les** /hækəlz/ If something **raises** your **hackles** or makes your **hackles rise**, it makes you feel angry and hostile. [PHRASE: V inflects]

**hack|neyed** /hæknid/ If you describe something such as a saying or an image as **hackneyed**, you think it is no longer likely to interest, amuse or affect people because it has been used, seen, or heard many times before. ❑ *Power corrupts and absolute power absolutely corrupts. That's the old hackneyed phrase, but it's true.* [ADJ]

**hack|saw** /hæksɔː/ **(hacksaws)** A **hacksaw** is a small saw used for cutting metal. [N-COUNT]

**had**

> The auxiliary verb is pronounced /həd/, STRONG hæd/. For the main verb, and for the meanings 2 to 5, the pronunciation is /hæd/.

[1] **Had** is the past tense and past participle of **have**. [2] **Had** is sometimes used instead of 'if' to begin a clause which refers to a situation that might have happened but did not. For example, the clause 'had he been elected' means the same as 'if he had been elected'. ❑ *Had he succeeded, he would have acquired a monopoly... Had I known what the problem was, we could have addressed it.* [AUX] [AUX n -ed] [AUX n -ed]

**PHRASES** [3] If you **have been had**, someone has tricked you, for example by selling you something at too high a price. [INFORMAL] ❑ *If your customer thinks he's been had, you have to make him happy.* [PHRASE: *be* inflects]

[4] If you say that someone **has had it**, you mean they are in very serious trouble or have no hope of succeeding. [INFORMAL] ❑ *Unless she loses some weight, she's had it.* [PHRASE: AUX inflects] [5] If you say that you **have had it**, you mean that you are very tired of something or very annoyed about it, and do not want to continue doing it or it to continue happening. [INFORMAL] ❑ *I've had it. Let's call it a day.* [PHRASE: AUX inflects]

**had|dock** /hædək/ **(haddock)** **Haddock** are a type of edible sea fish that are found in the North Atlantic. [N-VAR]

**Ha|des** /heɪdiːz/ In Greek mythology, **Hades** was a place under the earth where people went after they died. [N-PROPER = *the underworld*]

**hadn't** /hædənt/ **Hadn't** is the usual spoken form of 'had not'.

**haemo|glo|bin** /hiːməgloʊbɪn/

> in AM, use **hemoglobin**

**Haemoglobin** is the red substance in blood, which combines with oxygen and carries it around the body. [N-UNCOUNT]

**haemo|philia** /hiːməfɪliə/

> in AM, use **hemophilia**

**Haemophilia** is a medical condition in which a person's blood does not thicken or clot properly when they are injured, so they continue bleeding. [N-UNCOUNT]

**haemo|phili|ac** /hiːməfɪliæk/ **(haemophiliacs)**

> in AM, use **hemophiliac**

A **haemophiliac** is a person who suffers from haemophilia. [N-COUNT]

**haem|or|rhage** /hemərɪdʒ/ **(haemorrhages, haemorrhaging, haemorrhaged)**

> in AM, use **hemorrhage**

[1] A **haemorrhage** is serious bleeding inside a person's body. ❑ *Shortly after his admission into hospital he had a massive brain haemorrhage and died... These drugs will not be used if hemorrhage is the cause of the stroke.* [N-VAR] [2] If someone **is haemorrhaging**, there is serious bleeding inside their body. ❑ *I haemorrhaged badly after the birth of all three of my sons... If this is left untreated, one can actually haemorrhage to death.* ♦ **haem|or|rhag|ing** *A post mortem showed he died from shock and haemorrhaging.* [VERB] [V] [V to n] [N-UNCOUNT] [3] A **haemorrhage of** people or resources is a rapid loss of them from a group or place, seriously weakening its position. ❑ *He said the move would definitely stem the haemorrhage of talent and enterprise from the colony.* [N-SING: N *of* n] [4] To **haemorrhage** people or resources means to lose them rapidly and become weak. You can also say that people or resources **haemorrhage** from a place or organization. ❑ *Venice is haemorrhaging the very resource which could save it: its own people... The figures showed that cash was haemorrhaging from the conglomerate.* [VERB] [V n] [V *from* n]

**haem|or|rhoid** /hemərɔɪdz/ **(haemorrhoids)**

> in AM, use **hemorrhoids**

**Haemorrhoids** are painful swellings that can appear in the veins inside the anus. [MEDICAL] [N-COUNT: usu pl = *piles*]

**hag** /hæg/ **(hags)** If someone refers to a woman as a **hag**, they mean that she is ugly, old, and unpleasant. [OFFENSIVE] [N-COUNT] [disapproval]

**hag|gard** /hægəʳd/ Someone who looks **haggard** has a tired expression and shadows under their eyes, especially because they are ill or have not had enough sleep. ❑ *He was pale and a bit haggard.* [ADJ]

**hag|gis** /hægɪs/ **(haggises)** A **haggis** is a large sausage, usually shaped like a ball, which is made from minced sheep's meat contained inside the skin from a sheep's stomach. **Haggis** is traditionally made and eaten in Scotland. [N-VAR]

**hag|gle** /hægəl/ **(haggles, haggling, haggled)** If you **haggle**, you argue about something before reaching an agreement, especially about the cost of something that you are buying. ❑ *Ella taught her how to haggle with used furniture dealers... Meanwhile, as the politicians haggle, the violence worsens... Of course he'll still haggle over the price.* ♦ **hag|gling** *After months of haggling, they recovered only three-quarters of what they had lent.* [V-RECIP] [V *with* n] [pl-n V] [V (non-recip)] [N-UNCOUNT]

**hah** /hɑː/ ➔ see **ha**.

**ha ha** or **ha ha ha** [1] **Ha ha** is used in writing to represent the sound that people make when they laugh. ❑ *I dropped my bag at the officer's feet. The bank notes fell out. 'Ha ha ha!' he laughed. 'Got no money, uh?'* [EXCLAM] [2] People sometimes say '**ha ha**' to show that they are not amused by what you have said, or do not believe it. [SPOKEN] ❑ *He said 'vegetarians unite', and I looked at him and said 'yeah, ha ha'.* [EXCLAM]

**hail** /heɪl/ **(hails, hailing, hailed)** [1] If a person, event, or achievement **is hailed as** important or successful, they are praised publicly. ❑ *Faulkner has been hailed as the greatest American novelist of his generation... US magazines hailed her as the greatest rock'n'roll singer in the world.* [VERB: usu passive] [*be* V-ed *as* n] [V n *as* n] [2] **Hail** consists of small balls of ice that fall like rain from the sky. ❑ *...a sharp short-lived storm with heavy hail.* [N-UNCOUNT] [3] When **it hails**, hail falls like rain from the sky. ❑ *It started to hail, huge great stones.* [VERB] [*it* V] [4] A **hail of** things, usually small objects, is a large number of them that hit you at the same time and with great force. ❑ *The victim was hit by a hail of bullets.* [N-SING: N *of* n] [5] Someone who **hails from** a particular place was born there or lives there. [FORMAL] ❑ *I hail from Brighton.* [VERB] [V *from* n] [6] If you **hail** a taxi, you wave at it in order to stop it because you want the driver to take you somewhere. ❑ *I hurried away to hail a taxi.* [VERB] [V n]

**Hail Mary** **(Hail Marys)** A **Hail Mary** is a prayer to the Virgin Mary that is said by Roman Catholics. [N-COUNT]

**hail|stone** /heɪlstoʊn/ **(hailstones)** **Hailstones** are small balls of ice that fall like rain from the sky. [N-COUNT: usu pl]

**hail|storm** /heɪlstɔːʳm/ **(hailstorms)** also **hail storm.** A **hailstorm** is a storm during which it hails. N-COUNT

**hair** /heəʳ/ **(hairs)** [1] Your **hair** is the fine threads that grow in a mass on your head. ❑ *I wash my hair every night. ...a girl with long blonde hair... I get some grey hairs but I pull them out.* ◆◆◇ N-VAR: usu supp N
[2] **Hair** is the short, fine threads that grow on different parts of your body. ❑ *The majority of men have hair on their chest... It tickled the hairs on the back of my neck.* N-VAR
[3] **Hair** is the threads that cover the body of an animal such as a dog, or make up a horse's mane and tail. ❑ *I am allergic to cat hair. ...dog hairs on the carpet.* N-VAR
PHRASES [4] If you **let** your **hair down**, you relax completely and enjoy yourself. ❑ *...the world-famous Oktoberfest, a time when everyone in Munich really lets their hair down.* PHRASE: V inflects
[5] Something that **makes** your **hair stand on end** shocks or frightens you very much. ❑ *This was the kind of smile that made your hair stand on end.* PHRASE: V inflects
[6] If you say that someone has **not a hair out of place**, you are emphasizing that they are extremely smart and neatly dressed. ❑ *She had a lot of make-up on and not a hair out of place.* PHRASE emphasis
[7] If you say that someone faced with a shock or a problem **does not turn a hair**, you mean that they do not show any surprise or fear, and remain completely calm. ❑ *No one seems to turn a hair at the thought of the divorced Princess marrying.* PHRASE: V inflects
[8] If you say that someone **is splitting hairs**, you mean that they are making unnecessary distinctions between things when the differences between them are so small they are not important. ❑ *Don't split hairs. You know what I'm getting at.* PHRASE: V inflects

**hair|brush** /heəʳbrʌʃ/ **(hairbrushes)** A **hairbrush** is a brush that you use to brush your hair. N-COUNT

**hair care** also **haircare. Hair care** is all the things people do to keep their hair clean, healthy-looking, and attractive. ❑ *...an American maker of hair-care products.* N-UNCOUNT

**hair|cut** /heəʳkʌt/ **(haircuts)** [1] If you have a **haircut**, someone cuts your hair for you. ❑ *Your hair is all right; it's just that you need a haircut.* N-COUNT
[2] A **haircut** is the style in which your hair has been cut. ❑ *Who's that guy with the funny haircut?* N-COUNT

**hair|do** /heəʳduː/ **(hairdos)** A **hairdo** is the style in which your hair has been cut and arranged. [INFORMAL] N-COUNT = hairstyle

**hair|dresser** /heəʳdresəʳ/ **(hairdressers)** [1] A **hairdresser** is a person who cuts, colours, and arranges people's hair. N-COUNT
[2] A **hairdresser** or a **hairdresser's** is a shop where a hairdresser works. N-COUNT

**hair|dressing** /heəʳdresɪŋ/ **Hairdressing** is the job or activity of cutting, colouring, and arranging people's hair. N-UNCOUNT

**hair|dry|er** /heəʳdraɪəʳ/ **(hairdryers)** also **hairdrier.** A **hairdryer** is a machine that you use to dry your hair. N-COUNT

**-haired** /-heəʳd/ **-haired** combines with adjectives to describe the length, colour, or type of hair that someone has. ❑ *He was a small, dark-haired man.* COMB in ADJ

**hair|grip** /heəʳgrɪp/ **(hairgrips)** also **hair-grip.** A **hairgrip** is a small piece of metal or plastic bent back on itself, which you use to hold your hair in position. [mainly BRIT] N-COUNT = hairpin
✓ in AM, use **bobby pin**

**hair|less** /heəʳləs/ A part of your body that is **hairless** has no hair on it. ADJ ≠ hairy

**hair|line** /heəʳlaɪn/ **(hairlines)** [1] Your **hairline** is the edge of the area where your hair grows on your head. ❑ *Joanne had a small dark birthmark near her hairline.* N-COUNT: usu sing, oft poss N
[2] A **hairline** crack or gap is very narrow or fine. ❑ *He suffered a hairline fracture of the right index finger.* ADJ: ADJ n

**hair|net** /heəʳnet/ **(hairnets)** A **hairnet** is a small net that some women wear over their hair in order to keep it tidy. N-COUNT

**hair|piece** /heəʳpiːs/ **(hairpieces)** A **hairpiece** is a piece of false hair that some people wear on their head if they are bald or if they want to make their own hair seem longer or thicker. N-COUNT

**hair|pin** /heəʳpɪn/ **(hairpins)** [1] A **hairpin** is a small piece of metal or plastic bent back on itself which someone uses to hold their hair in position. N-COUNT = hairgrip
[2] A **hairpin** is the same as a **hairpin bend**. N-COUNT

**hair|pin bend** **(hairpin bends)** A **hairpin bend** or a **hairpin** is a very sharp bend in a road, where the road turns back in the opposite direction. N-COUNT

**hair-raising** A **hair-raising** experience, event, or story is very frightening but can also be exciting. ❑ *...hair-raising rides at funfairs.* ADJ

**hair's breadth** A **hair's breadth** is a very small degree or amount. ❑ *The dollar fell to within a hair's breadth of its all-time low.* N-SING: a N

**hair shirt** **(hair shirts)** [1] A **hair shirt** is a shirt made of rough uncomfortable cloth which some religious people used to wear to punish themselves. N-COUNT
[2] If you say that someone is wearing a **hair shirt**, you mean that they are trying to punish themselves to show they are sorry for something they have done. ❑ *No one is asking you to put on a hair shirt and give up all your luxuries.* N-COUNT

**hair|spray** /heəʳspreɪ/ **(hairsprays) Hairspray** is a sticky substance that you spray out of a can onto your hair in order to hold it in place. N-MASS

**hair|style** /heəʳstaɪl/ **(hairstyles)** Your **hairstyle** is the style in which your hair has been cut or arranged. ❑ *I think her new short hairstyle looks simply great.* N-COUNT

**hair|stylist** /heəʳstaɪlɪst/ **(hairstylists)** also **hair stylist.** A **hairstylist** is someone who cuts and arranges people's hair, especially in order to get them ready for a photograph or film. N-COUNT

**hair-trigger** If you describe something as **hair-trigger**, you mean that it is likely to change very violently and suddenly. ❑ *His boozing, arrogance, and hair-trigger temper have often led him into ugly nightclub brawls... A hair-trigger situation has been created which could lead to an outbreak of war at any time.* ADJ: ADJ n

**hairy** /heəri/ **(hairier, hairiest)** [1] Someone or something that is **hairy** is covered with hairs. ❑ *He was wearing shorts which showed his long, muscular, hairy legs.* ADJ
[2] If you describe a situation as **hairy**, you mean that it is exciting, worrying, and rather frightening. [INFORMAL] ❑ *His driving was a bit hairy.* ADJ

**hake** /heɪk/ **(hake)** A **hake** is a type of large edible sea fish. ♦ **Hake** is this fish eaten as food. N-VAR N-UNCOUNT

**halal** /həlɑːl/ **Halal** meat is meat from animals that have been killed according to Muslim law. ❑ *...a halal butcher's shop* N-UNCOUNT: usu N n

**hal|cy|on** /hælsiən/ A **halcyon** time is a time in the past that was peaceful or happy. [LITERARY] ❑ *It was all a far cry from those halcyon days in 1990, when he won three tournaments on the European tour.* ADJ: ADJ n

**hale** /heɪl/ If you describe people, especially people who are old, as **hale**, you mean that they are healthy. [OLD-FASHIONED] ❑ *She is remarkable and I'd like to see her remain hale and hearty for years yet.* ADJ: usu v-link ADJ

**half** /hɑːf, AM hæf/ **(halves** /hɑːvz, AM hævz/ **)** ◆◆◆
[1] **Half of** an amount or object is one of two equal parts that together make up the whole number, amount, or object. ❑ *They need an extra two and a half thousand pounds to complete the project... More than half of all households report incomes above £35,000... Cut the tomatoes in half vertically.* FRACTION
♦ **Half** is also a predeterminer. ❑ *We just sat and talked for half an hour or so... They had only received half the money promised.* PREDET
♦ **Half** is also an adjective. ❑ *...a half measure of fresh lemon juice... Steve barely said a handful of words during the first half hour.* ADJ: ADJ n
[2] You use **half** to say that something is only partly the case or happens to only a limited ex- ADV: ADV adj, ADV before v

tent. ❑ *His eyes were half closed... His refrigerator frequently looked half empty... She'd half expected him to withdraw from the course.* [3] In games such as football, rugby, and basketball, matches are divided into two equal periods of time which are called **halves**. ❑ *The only goal was scored by Jakobsen early in the second half.* [4] A **half** is a half-price bus or train ticket for a child. [BRIT] [5] You use **half** to say that someone has parents of different nationalities. For example, if you are **half** German, one of your parents is German but the other is not. ❑ *She was half Italian and half English.* [6] You use **half past** to refer to a time that is thirty minutes after a particular hour. ❑ *'What time were you planning lunch?' — 'Half past twelve, if that's convenient.'.* [7] **Half** means the same as **half past**. [BRIT, INFORMAL] ❑ *They are supposed to be here at about half four.* [8] You can use **half** before an adjective describing an extreme quality, as a way of emphasizing and exaggerating something. [INFORMAL] ❑ *He felt half dead with tiredness.* ♦ **Half** can also be used in this way with a noun referring to a long period of time or a large quantity. ❑ *I thought about you half the night... He wouldn't know what he was saying half the time.* [9] **Half** is sometimes used in negative statements, with a positive meaning, to emphasize a particular fact or quality. For example, if you say **'he isn't half lucky'**, you mean that he is very lucky. [BRIT, INFORMAL] ❑ *You don't half sound confident... 'There'd been a tremendous amount of poverty around and presumably this made some impact then.' — 'Oh not half.'* [10] You use **not half** or **not half as** to show that you do not think something is as good or impressive as it is meant to be. ❑ *You're not half the man you think you are.*

N-COUNT: usu ord N · N-COUNT · ADV: ADV adj · PREP-PHRASE: usu PREP num · PREP: PREP num · ADV: ADV adj [emphasis] · PREDET · ADV: with neg, usu ADV before v, ADV adj/adv, ADV n, also ADV as reply [emphasis] · ADV: with neg, ADV n, ADV *as/so* adj [emphasis]

**PHRASES** [11] When you use an expression such as **a problem and a half** or **a meal and a half**, you are emphasizing that your reaction to it is either very favourable or very unfavourable. ❑ *It becomes clear that Montgomerie has a job and half on his hands.* [12] If you say that someone never **does things by halves**, you mean that they always do things very thoroughly. ❑ *In Italy they rarely do things by halves. Designers work thoroughly, producing the world's most wearable clothes in the most beautiful fabrics.* [13] If two people **go halves**, they divide the cost of something equally between them. ❑ *He's constantly on the phone to his girlfriend. We have to go halves on the phone bill which drives me mad.* [14] **half the battle** → see **battle**.

PHRASE: usu v-link PHR [emphasis] · PHRASE: with brd-neg, V inflects · PHRASE: V inflects, oft PHR *on* n

**half-baked** If you describe an idea or plan as **half-baked**, you mean that it has not been properly thought out, and so is stupid or impractical. ❑ *This is another half-baked scheme that isn't going to work.*
ADJ: usu ADJ n [disapproval]

**half board** If you stay at a hotel and have **half board**, your breakfast and evening meal are included in the price of your stay at the hotel, but not your lunch. [mainly BRIT]
N-UNCOUNT

**half-brother** (**half-brothers**) Someone's **half-brother** is a boy or man who has either the same mother or the same father as they have.
N-COUNT

**half-caste** (**half-castes**) Someone who is **half-caste** has parents who come from different races. [mainly BRIT, OFFENSIVE]
ADJ

**half-day** (**half-days**) also **half day**. A **half-day** is a day when you work only in the morning or in the afternoon, but not all day.
N-COUNT

**half-hearted** If someone does something in a **half-hearted** way, they do it without any real effort, interest, or enthusiasm. ❑ *Joanna had made one or two half-hearted attempts to befriend Graham's young wife.* ♦ **half-heartedly** *I can't do anything half-heartedly. I have to do everything 100 per cent.*
ADJ · ADV: ADV with v

**half-life** (**half-lives**) also **half life**. The **half-life** of a radioactive substance is the amount of time that it takes to lose half its radioactivity.
N-COUNT

**half-mast** If a flag is flying **at half-mast**, it is flying from the middle of the pole, not the top, to show respect and sorrow for someone who has just died.
PHRASE: usu PHR after v

**half meas|ure** (**half measures**) also **half-measure**. If someone refers to policies or actions as **half measures**, they are critical of them because they think that they are not forceful enough and are therefore of little value. ❑ *They have already declared their intention to fight on rather than settle for half-measures.*
N-COUNT: usu pl [disapproval]

**half note** (**half notes**) A **half note** is a musical note that has a time value equal to two quarter notes. [AM]
N-COUNT

✔ in BRIT, use **minim**

**half|penny** /heɪpni/ (**halfpennies** or **halfpence** /heɪpəns/) A **halfpenny** was a small British coin which was worth half a penny.
N-COUNT

**half-price** [1] If something is **half-price**, it costs only half what it usually costs. ❑ *Main courses are half price from 12.30pm to 2pm... Mind you, a half-price suit still cost $400... We can get in half-price.* [2] If something is sold **at** or **for half-price**, it is sold for only half of what it usually costs. ❑ *By yesterday she was selling off stock at half price... They normally charge three hundred pounds but we got it for half price.*
ADJ: v-link ADJ, ADJ n, ADJ after v · N-UNCOUNT: usu *at/for* N

**half-sister** (**half-sisters**) Someone's **half-sister** is a girl or woman who has either the same mother or the same father as they have.
N-COUNT: oft poss N

**half-term** (**half-terms**) also **half term**. **Half-term** is a short holiday in the middle of a school term. [BRIT] ❑ *There was no play school at half term, so I took them both to the cinema. ...the half-term holidays.*
N-VAR: oft *at* N

**half-timbered** **Half-timbered** is used to describe old buildings that have wooden beams showing in the brick and plaster walls, both on the inside and the outside of the building.
ADJ

**half-time** **Half-time** is the short period of time between the two parts of a sporting event such as a football, rugby, or basketball game, when the players have a short rest.
N-UNCOUNT

**half-truth** (**half-truths**) also **half truth**. If you describe statements as **half-truths**, you mean that they are only partly based on fact and are intended or likely to deceive people. ❑ *The article had been full of errors and half truths.*
N-COUNT

**half|way** /hɑːfweɪ, AM hæf-/ also **half-way**. [1] **Halfway** means in the middle of a place or between two points, at an equal distance from each of them. ❑ *Half-way across the car-park, he noticed she was walking with her eyes closed... He was halfway up the ladder.* [2] **Halfway** means in the middle of a period of time or of an event. ❑ *By then, it was October and we were more than halfway through our tour.* ♦ **Halfway** is also an adjective. ❑ *Welsh international Matthew Postle was third fastest at the halfway point.* [3] If you **meet** someone **halfway**, you accept some of the points they are making so that you can come to an agreement with them. ❑ *The Democrats are willing to meet the president halfway.* [4] **Halfway** means reasonably. [INFORMAL] ❑ *You need hard currency to get anything halfway decent.*
ADV: usu ADV prep/adv, also ADV after v · ADV: ADV prep/adv · ADJ: ADJ n · PHRASE: V inflects · ADV: ADV adj

**half|way house** (**halfway houses**) [1] A **halfway house** is an arrangement or thing that has some of the qualities of two different things. ❑ *A halfway house between the theatre and cinema is possible. Olivier created one in his imaginative 'Henry V' in 1945.* [2] A **halfway house** is a home for people such as former prisoners, mental patients, or drug addicts who can stay there for a limited period of time to get used to life outside prison or hospital.
N-SING · N-COUNT

**half|wit** /hɑːfwɪt, AM hæf-/ (**halfwits**) also **half-wit**. [1] If you describe someone as a **halfwit**, you think that they have behaved in a stupid, silly, or irresponsible way. [INFORMAL] [2] A **halfwit** is a person who has little intelligence. [OLD-FASHIONED]
N-COUNT [disapproval] = *fool* · N-COUNT

**half-witted** If you describe someone as **half-witted**, you think they are very stupid, silly, or irresponsible. [INFORMAL] ADJ disapproval

**half-yearly** 1 **Half-yearly** means happening in the middle of a calendar year or a financial year. [BRIT] ❑ *...the Central Bank's half-yearly report on the state of the economy.* ADJ: ADJ n

in AM, use **semiannual**

2 A company's **half-yearly** profits are the profits that it makes in six months. [BRIT] ❑ *The company announced a half-yearly profit of just £2 million.* ADJ: ADJ n

in AM, use **semiannual**

3 **Half-yearly** means happening twice a year, with six months between each event. [BRIT] ❑ *...half-yearly payments.* ADJ: usu ADJ n

in AM, use **semiannual**

**hali|but** /hælɪbət/ **(halibut)** A **halibut** is a large flat fish. ♦ **Halibut** is this fish eaten as food. N-VAR N-UNCOUNT

**hali|to|sis** /hælɪtoʊsɪs/ If someone has **halitosis**, their breath smells unpleasant. [FORMAL] N-UNCOUNT

**hall** /hɔːl/ **(halls)** 1 The **hall** in a house or flat is the area just inside the front door, into which some of the other rooms open. [BRIT] → See picture on page 1706. ◆◇◇ N-COUNT

in AM, use **entrance hall**

2 A **hall** in a building is a long passage with doors into rooms on both sides of it. [mainly AM] N-COUNT

in BRIT, use **hallway**

3 A **hall** is a large room or building which is used for public events such as concerts, exhibitions, and meetings. ❑ *We picked up our conference materials and filed into the lecture hall.* → See also **city hall**, **town hall**. N-COUNT: oft n N 4 If students live **in hall** in British English, or **in a hall** in American English, they live in a university or college building called a **hall of residence**. N-COUNT: also prep N 5 **Hall** is sometimes used as part of the name of a large house in the country. ❑ *He died at Holly Hall, his wife's family home.* N-IN-NAMES 6 → See also **entrance hall**, **music hall**.

**hal|le|lu|jah** /hælɪluːjə/ also **alleluia**. 1 **Hallelujah** is used in religious songs and worship as an exclamation of praise and thanks to God. EXCLAM 2 People sometimes say **'Hallelujah!'** when they are pleased that something they have been waiting a long time for has finally happened. ❑ *Hallelujah! College days are over!* EXCLAM

**hall|mark** /hɔːlmɑːʳk/ **(hallmarks)** 1 The **hallmark** of something or someone is their most typical quality or feature. ❑ *It's a technique that has become the hallmark of Amber Films.* N-COUNT: usu with poss 2 A **hallmark** is an official mark put on things made of gold, silver, or platinum that indicates the quality of the metal, where the object was made, and who made it. N-COUNT

**hal|lo** /hæloʊ/ → see **hello**.

**hall of fame** **(halls of fame)** 1 If you say that someone is a member of a particular **hall of fame**, you mean that they are one of the most famous people in that area of activity. ❑ *Vivienne Westwood has scaled the heights of fashion's hall of fame.* N-SING: with supp 2 In the United States, a **hall of fame** is a type of museum where people can see things relating to famous people who are connected with a particular area of activity. N-COUNT

**hall of resi|dence** **(halls of residence)** **Halls of residence** are buildings with rooms or flats, usually built by universities or colleges, in which students live during the term. [mainly BRIT] N-COUNT

in AM, use **dormitory**, **residence hall**

**hal|lowed** /hæloʊd/ 1 **Hallowed** is used to describe something that is respected and admired, usually because it is old, important, or has a good reputation. ❑ *They protested that there was no place for a school of commerce in their hallowed halls of learning.* ADJ: ADJ n 2 **Hallowed** is used to describe something that is considered to be holy. ❑ *...hallowed ground.* ADJ: ADJ n

**Hal|low|een** /hæloʊwiːn/ also **Hallowe'en.** **Halloween** is the night of the 31st of October and is traditionally said to be the time when ghosts and witches can be seen. On Halloween, children often dress up as ghosts and witches. N-UNCOUNT

**hal|lu|ci|nate** /həluːsɪneɪt/ **(hallucinates, hallucinating, hallucinated)** If you **hallucinate**, you see things that are not really there, either because you are ill or because you have taken a drug. ❑ *Hunger made him hallucinate.* VERB V Also V that

**hal|lu|ci|na|tion** /həluːsɪneɪʃᵊn/ **(hallucinations)** A **hallucination** is the experience of seeing something that is not really there because you are ill or have taken a drug. ❑ *The drug induces hallucinations at high doses.* N-VAR

**hal|lu|ci|na|tory** /həluːsɪnətri, AM -tɔːri/ **Hallucinatory** is used to describe something that is like a hallucination or is the cause of a hallucination. ❑ *It was an unsettling show. There was a hallucinatory feel from the start.* ADJ: usu ADJ n

**hal|lu|cino|gen** /həluːsɪnədʒen/ **(hallucinogens)** A **hallucinogen** is a substance such as a drug which makes you hallucinate. N-COUNT

**hal|lu|ci|no|gen|ic** /həluːsɪnədʒenɪk/ A **hallucinogenic** drug is one that makes you hallucinate. ADJ: usu ADJ n

**hall|way** /hɔːlweɪ/ **(hallways)** 1 A **hallway** in a building is a long passage with doors into rooms on both sides of it. N-COUNT 2 A **hallway** in a house or flat is the area just inside the front door, into which some of the other rooms open. [BRIT] N-COUNT

in AM, use **entrance hall**

**halo** /heɪloʊ/ **(haloes** or **halos)** 1 A **halo** is a circle of light that is shown in pictures round the head of a holy figure such as a saint or angel. N-COUNT 2 A **halo** is a circle of light round a person or thing, or something that looks like a circle of light. ❑ *The sun had a faint halo round it.* N-COUNT: oft N *of* n

**halt** /hɔːlt/ **(halts, halting, halted)** 1 When a person or a vehicle **halts** or when something **halts** them, they stop moving in the direction they were going and stand still. ❑ *They halted at a short distance from the house... She held her hand out flat, to halt him.* ◆◇◇ VERB V V n 2 When something such as growth, development, or activity **halts** or when you **halt** it, it stops completely. ❑ *Striking workers halted production at the auto plant yesterday... The flow of assistance to Vietnam's fragile economy from its ideological allies has virtually halted.* VERB V n V 3 **'Halt!'** is a military order to stop walking or marching and stand still. ❑ *The colonel ordered 'Halt!'* VERB: only imper V

PHRASES 4 If someone **calls a halt to** something such as an activity, they decide not to continue with it or to end it immediately. ❑ *The Russian government had called a halt to the construction of a new project in the Rostov region.* PHRASE: V inflects, oft PHR *to* n 5 If someone or something comes **to a halt**, they stop moving. ❑ *The elevator creaked to a halt at the ground floor.* PHRASE: PHR after v 6 If something such as growth, development, or activity **comes** or **grinds to a halt** or **is brought to a halt**, it stops completely. ❑ *Her political career came to a halt in December 1988.* PHRASE: PHR after v

**hal|ter** /hɔːltəʳ/ **(halters)** A **halter** is a piece of leather or rope that is fastened round the head of a horse so that it can be led easily. N-COUNT

**hal|ter|neck** /hɔːltəʳnek/ **(halternecks)** A piece of clothing with a **halterneck** has a strap that goes around the back of the neck, rather than a strap over each shoulder. ♦ **Halterneck** is also an adjective. ❑ *...a halterneck evening dress.* N-COUNT ADJ: ADJ n

**halt|ing** /hɔːltɪŋ/ If you speak or do something in a **halting** way, you speak or do it slowly and with a lot of hesitation, usually because you are uncertain about what to say or do next. ❑ *In a halting voice she said that she wished to make a statement.* ♦ **halt|ing|ly** *She spoke haltingly of her deep upset and hurt.* ADJ ADV: ADV with v

**halve** /hɑːv, AM hæv/ **(halves, halving, halved)** 1 When you **halve** something or when it **halves**, it is reduced to half its previous size or VERB amount. ❑ *Dr Lee believes that men who exercise can halve their risk of cancer of the colon... Meanwhile, sales of vinyl records halved in 1992 to just 6.7m.* V n / V

2 If you **halve** something, you divide it into two equal parts. ❑ *Halve the pineapple and scoop out the inside.* VERB / V n 3 **Halves** is the plural of **half**.

**ham** /hæm/ **(hams, hamming, hammed)** 1 **Ham** is meat from the top of the back leg of a pig, specially treated so that it can be kept for a long period of time. ❑ *...ham sandwiches.* N-VAR 2 If actors or actresses **ham it up**, they exaggerate every emotion and gesture when they are acting, often deliberately because they think that the audience will be more amused. ❑ *Thrusting themselves into the spirit of the farce, they ham it up like mad.* PHRASE: V inflects

**ham|burg|er** /hæmbɜːʳgəʳ/ **(hamburgers)** A **hamburger** is minced meat which has been shaped into a flat circle. Hamburgers are fried or grilled and then eaten, often in a bread roll. N-COUNT

**ham-fisted** If you describe someone as **ham-fisted**, you mean that they are clumsy, especially in the way that they use their hands. ❑ *They can be made in minutes by even the most ham-fisted cooks.* ADJ

**ham|let** /hæmlɪt/ **(hamlets)** A **hamlet** is a very small village. N-COUNT

**ham|mer** /hæməʳ/ **(hammers, hammering, hammered)** 1 A **hammer** is a tool that consists of a heavy piece of metal at the end of a handle. It is used, for example, to hit nails into a piece of wood or a wall, or to break things into pieces. → See picture on page 1709. ❑ *He used a hammer and chisel to chip away at the wall.* N-COUNT 2 If you **hammer** an object such as a nail, you hit it with a hammer. ❑ *To avoid damaging the tree, hammer a wooden peg into the hole... Builders were still hammering outside the window.* ♦ **Hammer in** means the same as **hammer**. ❑ *The workers kneel on the ground and hammer the small stones in.* ♦ **ham|mer|ing** *The noise of hammering was dulled by the secondary glazing.* VERB / V n prep/adv / V / Also V n / PHRASAL VERB / V n P / Also V P n (not pron) / N-UNCOUNT 3 If you **hammer on** a surface, you hit it several times in order to make a noise, or to emphasize something you are saying when you are angry. ❑ *We had to hammer and shout before they would open up... A crowd of reporters was hammering on the door... He hammered his two clenched fists on the table.* ♦ **ham|mer|ing** *As he said it, there was a hammering outside.* VERB = pound / V / V *on* n / V n *on* n / N-SING 4 If you **hammer** something such as an idea **into** people or you **hammer at** it, you keep repeating it forcefully so that it will have an effect on people. ❑ *He hammered it into me that I had not suddenly become a rotten goalkeeper... Recent advertising campaigns from the industry have hammered at these themes.* VERB / V n *into* n / V *at* n 5 If you say that someone **hammers** another person, you mean that they attack, criticize, or punish the other person severely. [mainly BRIT] ❑ *The report hammers the private motorist.* ♦ **ham|mer|ing** *Parents have taken a terrible hammering.* VERB / V n / N-SING 6 If you say that businesses **are being hammered**, you mean that they are being unfairly harmed, for example by a change in taxes or by bad economic conditions. [BRIT] ❑ *The company has been hammered by the downturn in the construction and motor industries.* V-PASSIVE / *be* V-ed 7 In sports, if you say that one player or team **hammered** another, you mean that the first player or team defeated the second completely and easily. [BRIT, JOURNALISM] ❑ *He hammered the young Austrian player in four straight sets.* ♦ **ham|mer|ing** *Our cricketers are suffering their ritual hammering at the hands of the Aussies.* VERB = thrash / V n / N-SING 8 In athletics, a **hammer** is a heavy weight on a piece of wire, which the athlete throws as far as possible. ♦ **The hammer** also refers to the sport of throwing the hammer. N-COUNT / N-SING: *the* N

PHRASES 9 If you say that someone **was going at** something **hammer and tongs**, you mean that they were doing it with great enthusiasm or energy. ❑ *He loved gardening. He went at it hammer and tongs as soon as he got back from work.* PHRASE: PHR after v 10 If you say that something goes, comes, or is **under the hammer**, you mean that it is going to be sold at an auction. ❑ *Ian Fleming's original unpublished notes are to go under the hammer at London auctioneers Sotheby's.* PHRASE: PHR after v

♦ **hammer away** 1 If you **hammer away at** a task or activity, you work at it constantly and with great energy. ❑ *Palmer kept hammering away at his report.* PHRASAL VERB / V P *at* n 2 If you **hammer away at** an idea or subject, you keep talking about it, especially because you disapprove of it. ❑ *They also hammered away at Labor's plans to raise taxes.* PHRASAL VERB / V P *at* n

♦ **hammer in** → see **hammer 2**.

♦ **hammer out** If people **hammer out** an agreement or treaty, they succeed in producing it after a long or difficult discussion. ❑ *I think we can hammer out a solution.* PHRASAL VERB / V P n (not pron) / Also V n P

**ham|mock** /hæmək/ **(hammocks)** A **hammock** is a piece of strong cloth or netting which is hung between two supports and used as a bed. N-COUNT

**ham|per** /hæmpəʳ/ **(hampers, hampering, hampered)** 1 If someone or something **hampers** you, they makes it difficult for you to do what you are trying to do. ❑ *The bad weather hampered rescue operations.* VERB / V n 2 A **hamper** is a basket containing food of various kinds that is given to people as a present. N-COUNT 3 A **hamper** is a large basket with a lid, used especially for carrying food in. N-COUNT

**ham|ster** /hæmstəʳ/ **(hamsters)** A **hamster** is a small furry animal which is similar to a mouse, and which is often kept as a pet. N-COUNT

**ham|string** /hæmstrɪŋ/ **(hamstrings, hamstringing, hamstrung)** 1 A **hamstring** is a length of tissue or tendon behind your knee which joins the muscles of your thigh to the bones of your lower leg. ❑ *Webster has not played since suffering a hamstring injury in the opening game.* N-COUNT 2 If you **hamstring** someone, you make it very difficult for them to take any action. ❑ *If he becomes the major opposition leader, he could hamstring a conservative-led coalition.* VERB / V n

**hand**
① NOUN USES AND PHRASES
② VERB USES

①**hand** /hænd/ **(hands)** ◆◆◆

⇛ Please look at category 49 to see if the expression you are looking for is shown under another headword. 1 Your **hands** are the parts of your body at the end of your arms. Each hand has four fingers and a thumb. ❑ *I put my hand into my pocket and pulled out the letter... Sylvia, camera in hand, asked, 'Where do we go first?'* N-COUNT 2 The **hand** of someone or something is their influence in an event or situation. ❑ *The hand of the military authorities can be seen in the entire electoral process.* N-SING: with poss 3 If you say that something is **in** a particular person's **hands**, you mean that they are looking after it, own it, or are responsible for it. ❑ *He is leaving his north London business in the hands of a colleague... We're in safe hands.* N-PLURAL: usu *in/into* N 4 If you ask someone for **a hand** with something, you are asking them to help you in what you are doing. ❑ *Come and give me a hand in the garden.* N-SING: *a* N, oft N *with* n 5 A **hand** is someone, usually a man, who does hard physical work, for example in a factory or on a farm, as part of a group of people who all do similar work. ❑ *He now works as a farm hand.* N-COUNT: usu with supp 6 If someone asks an audience to give someone **a hand**, they are asking the audience to clap loudly, usually before or after that person performs. ❑ *Let's give 'em a big hand.* N-SING: *a* N 7 If a man asks for a woman's **hand in marriage**, he asks her or her parents for permission to marry her. [OLD-FASHIONED] ❑ *He came to ask Usha's father for her hand in marriage.* N-COUNT: usu sing, poss N, oft N *in* n 8 In a game of cards, your **hand** is the set of cards that you are holding in your hand at a particular time or the cards that are dealt to you at the beginning of the game. ❑ *He carefully inspected his hand.* N-COUNT 9 A **hand** is a measurement of four inches, which is used for measuring the height of a horse from its front feet to its shoulders. ❑ *I had a very good 14.2 hands pony, called Brandy.* N-COUNT: usu num N 10 The **hands** of a N-COUNT clock or watch are the thin pieces of metal or plastic that indicate what time it is.

**PHRASES** 11 If something is **at hand**, **near at hand**, or **close at hand**, it is very near in place or time. ❑ *Having the right equipment at hand will be enormously helpful.* PHRASE: PHR after v, v-link PHR

12 If someone experiences a particular kind of treatment, especially unpleasant treatment, **at the hands of** a person or organization, they receive it from them. ❑ *The civilian population were suffering greatly at the hands of the security forces.* PREP-PHRASE: PREP n

13 If you do something **by hand**, you do it using your hands rather than a machine. ❑ *Each pleat was stitched in place by hand.* PHRASE: PHR after v = *manually*

14 When something **changes hands**, its ownership changes, usually because it is sold to someone else. ❑ *The firm has changed hands many times over the years.* PHRASE: V inflects

15 If you have someone **eating out of** your **hand**, they are completely under your control. ❑ *Parker could have customers eating out of his hand.* PHRASE: V and N inflect

16 If you **force** someone's **hand**, you force them to act sooner than they want to, or to act in public when they would prefer to keep their actions secret. ❑ *He blamed the press for forcing his hand.* PHRASE: V and N inflect

17 If you **have** your **hands full with** something, you are very busy because of it. ❑ *She had her hands full with new arrivals.* PHRASE: V inflects, oft PHR *with* n

18 If someone gives you **a free hand**, they give you the freedom to use your own judgment and to do exactly as you wish. ❑ *He gave Stephanie a free hand in the decoration.* PHRASE: PHR after v

19 If you **get** your **hands on** something or **lay** your **hands on** something, you manage to find it or obtain it, usually after some difficulty. [INFORMAL] ❑ *Patty began reading everything she could get her hands on.* PHRASE: V inflects, PHR n

20 If you work **hand in glove with** someone, you work very closely with them. ❑ *The UN inspectors work hand in glove with the Western intelligence agencies.* PHRASE: usu PHR *with* n

21 If two people are **hand in hand**, they are holding each other's nearest hand, usually while they are walking or sitting together. People often do this to show their affection for each other. ❑ *I saw them making their way, hand in hand, down the path.* PHRASE: usu PHR after v, PHR with cl

22 If two things **go hand in hand**, they are closely connected and cannot be considered separately from each other. ❑ *For us, research and teaching go hand in hand.* PHRASE: usu PHR after v, v-link PHR, oft PHR *with* n

23 If you **have a hand in** something such as an event or activity, you are involved in it. ❑ *He thanked all who had a hand in his release.* PHRASE: V inflects, PHR n

24 If you say that someone such as the ruler of a country treats people **with a heavy hand**, you are criticizing them because they are very strict and severe with them. ❑ *Henry and Richard both ruled with a heavy hand.* PHRASE: usu *with* PHR [disapproval]

25 If two people **are holding hands**, they are holding each other's nearest hand, usually while they are walking or sitting together. People often do this to show their affection for each other. ❑ *She approached a young couple holding hands on a bench.* PHRASE: V inflects, pl-n PHR, PHR *with* n

26 If you ask someone to **hold** your **hand** at an event that you are worried about, you ask them to support you by being there with you. [INFORMAL] ❑ *I don't need anyone to hold my hand.* PHRASE: V and N inflect

27 In a competition, if someone has games or matches **in hand**, they have more games or matches left to play than their opponent and therefore have the possibility of scoring more points. [BRIT] ❑ *Wales are three points behind Romania in the group but have a game in hand.* PHRASE: n PHR

28 If you have time or money **in hand**, you have more time or money than you need. [BRIT] ❑ *Hughes finished with 15 seconds in hand.* PHRASE: usu *with* amount PHR

29 The job or problem **in hand** is the job or problem that you are dealing with at the moment. ❑ *The business in hand was approaching some kind of climax.* PHRASE: n PHR, v-link PHR

30 If a situation is **in hand**, it is under control. ❑ *The Olympic organisers say that matters are well in hand.* PHRASE: v-link PHR, PHR after v

31 If you **lend** someone **a hand**, you help them. ❑ *I'd be glad to lend a hand.* PHRASE: V inflects

32 If you tell someone to **keep** their **hands off** something or to **take** their **hands off** it, you are telling them in a rather aggressive way not to touch it or interfere with it. ❑ *Keep your hands off my milk.* PHRASE: V inflects, PHR n

33 If you do not know something **off hand**, you do not know it without having to ask someone else or look it up in a book. [SPOKEN] ❑ *I can't think of any off hand.* PHRASE: usu with brd-neg, PHR after v

34 If you have a problem or responsibility **on** your **hands**, you have to deal with it. If it is **off** your **hands**, you no longer have to deal with it. ❑ *They now have yet another drug problem on their hands... She would like the worry of dealing with her affairs taken off her hands.* PHRASE: PHR after v

35 If someone or something is **on hand**, they are near and able to be used if they are needed. ❑ *The Bridal Department will have experts on hand to give you all the help and advice you need.* PHRASE: PHR after v, v-link PHR = *available*

36 You use **on the one hand** to introduce the first of two contrasting points, facts, or ways of looking at something. It is always followed later by **on the other hand** or 'on the other'. ❑ *On the one hand, if the body doesn't have enough cholesterol, we would not be able to survive. On the other hand, if the body has too much cholesterol, the excess begins to line the arteries.* PHRASE: PHR with cl

37 You use **on the other hand** to introduce the second of two contrasting points, facts, or ways of looking at something. ❑ *Well, all right, hospitals lose money. But, on the other hand, if people are healthy, don't think of it as losing money; think of it as saving lives.* PHRASE

38 If a person or a situation gets **out of hand**, you are no longer able to control them. ❑ *His drinking had got out of hand.* PHRASE: v-link PHR

39 If you dismiss or reject something **out of hand**, you do so immediately and do not consider believing or accepting it. ❑ *I initially dismissed the idea out of hand.* PHRASE: PHR after v

40 If you **play into** someone's **hands**, you do something which they want you to do and which places you in their power. [JOURNALISM] ❑ *He is playing into the hands of racists.* PHRASE: V inflects

41 If you **show** your **hand**, you show how much power you have and the way you intend to act. ❑ *He has grown more serious about running for president, although he refuses to show his hand.* PHRASE: V and N inflect

42 If you **take** something or someone **in hand**, you take control or responsibility over them, especially in order to improve them. ❑ *I hope that Parliament will soon take the NHS in hand.* PHRASE: V inflects

43 If you say that your **hands are tied**, you mean that something is preventing you from acting in the way that you want to. ❑ *Politicians are always saying that they want to help us but their hands are tied.* PHRASE: V inflects

44 If you have something **to hand** or **near to hand**, you have it with you or near you, ready to use when needed. ❑ *You may want to keep this brochure safe, so you have it to hand whenever you may need it.* PHRASE: PHR after v, v-link PHR

45 If you **try** your **hand at** an activity, you attempt to do it, usually for the first time. ❑ *After he left school, he tried his hand at a variety of jobs – bricklayer, cinema usher, coal man.* PHRASE: V and N inflect, usu PHR *at* n/-ing

46 If you **turn** your **hand to** something such as a practical activity, you learn about it and do it for the first time. ❑ *...a person who can turn his hand to anything.* PHRASE: V and N inflect, PHR n

47 If you **wash** your **hands of** someone or something, you refuse to be involved with them any more or to take responsibility for them. ❑ *He seems to have washed his hands of the job.* PHRASE: V inflects, PHR n

48 If you **win hands down**, you win very easily. PHRASE: V inflects

49 → See also **hand-to-mouth**. **with** one's **bare hands** → see **bare**. to **overplay** one's **hand** → see **overplay**. to **shake** someone's **hand** → see **shake**. to **shake hands** → see **shake**.

②**hand** /hænd/ **(hands, handing, handed)** ◆◆◇ 1 If you **hand** something **to** someone, you pass it to them. ❑ *He handed me a little rectangle of white paper... He took a thick envelope from an inside pocket and handed it to me.* VERB: V n n, V n *to* n

2 You say things such as **'You have to hand it to her'** or **'You've got to hand it to them'** when you admire someone for their skills or achievements and you think they deserve a lot of praise. [INFORMAL] ❑ *You've got to hand it to Melissa, she certainly gets around.* PHRASE [approval]

### ♦ hand around

✔ in BRIT, also use **hand round**

If you **hand around** or **hand round** something such as food, you pass it from one person to an- PHRASAL VERB = *distribute* other in a group. ❑ *John handed round the plate of sandwiches... Dean produced another bottle and handed it round.* V P n (not pron) V n P

♦ **hand back** If you **hand back** something that you have borrowed or taken from someone, you return it to them. ❑ *The management handed back his few possessions... He took a saxophone from the Salvation Army but was caught and had to hand it back... He handed the book back to her... He unlocked her door and then handed her back the key.* PHRASAL VERB = give back; V P n (not pron) V n P; V n P *to* n; V n P n Also V P n *to* n

♦ **hand down** [1] If you **hand down** something such as knowledge, a possession, or a skill, you give or leave it to people who belong to a younger generation. ❑ *The idea of handing down his knowledge from generation to generation is important to McLean.* [2] When a particular decision **is handed down** by someone in authority, it is given by them. [JOURNALISM] ❑ *Tougher sentences are being handed down these days... She is expected soon to hand down a ruling.* PHRASAL VERB = pass on; V P n (not pron) Also V n P; PHRASAL VERB; *be* V-ed P; V P n (not pron) Also V n P

♦ **hand in** [1] If you **hand in** something such as homework or something that you have found, you give it to a teacher, police officer, or other person in authority. ❑ *I'm supposed to have handed in a first draft of my dissertation... My advice to anyone who finds anything on a bus is to hand it in to the police.* [2] If you **hand in** your notice or resignation, you tell your employer, in speech or in writing, that you no longer wish to work for them. ❑ *I handed my notice in on Saturday... All eighty opposition members of parliament have handed in their resignation.* PHRASAL VERB; V P n (not pron) V n P; PHRASAL VERB; V n P; V P n (not pron)

♦ **hand on** If you **hand** something **on**, you give it or transfer it to another person, often someone who replaces you. ❑ *The government is criticised for not handing on information about missing funds... His chauffeur-driven car and company mobile phone will be handed on to his successor.* PHRASAL VERB = pass on; V P n (not pron); *be* V-ed P *to* n

♦ **hand out** [1] If you **hand** things **out** to people, you give one or more to each person in a group. ❑ *One of my jobs was to hand out the prizes.* [2] When people in authority **hand out** something such as advice or permission to do something, they give it. ❑ *I listened to a lot of people handing out a lot of advice.* [3] ➔ See also **handout**. PHRASAL VERB = give out; V P n (not pron); PHRASAL VERB; V P n (not pron)

♦ **hand over** [1] If you **hand** something **over** to someone, you pass it to them. ❑ *He also handed over a letter of apology from the Prime Minister... 'I've got his card.' Judith said, handing it over.* [2] When you **hand over** someone such as a prisoner to someone else, you give the control of and responsibility for them to that other person. ❑ *They would just catch the robbers and hand them over to the police.* [3] If you **hand over to** someone or **hand** something **over to** them, you give them the responsibility for dealing with a particular situation or problem. ❑ *The present leaders have to decide whether to stand down and hand over to a younger generation... I wouldn't dare hand this project over to anyone else.* PHRASAL VERB; V P n (not pron); V n P; PHRASAL VERB; V n P *to* n; PHRASAL VERB; V P *to* n; V n P *to* n Also V n P, V P n (not pron)

♦ **hand round** ➔ see **hand around**.

**hand-** /hænd-/ **Hand-** combines with past participles to indicate that something has been made by someone using their hands or using tools rather than by machines. ❑ *...handcrafted jewelry. ...handbuilt cars.* COMB in ADJ: COMB -ed

**hand|bag** /hændbæg/ **(handbags)** A **handbag** is a small bag which a woman uses to carry things such as her money and keys in when she goes out. N-COUNT

**hand|ball** /hændbɔːl/ also **hand-ball.** [1] In Britain, **handball** is a team sport in which the players try to score goals by throwing or hitting a large ball with their hand. [2] In the United States and some other countries, **handball** is a sport in which players try to score points by hitting a small ball against a wall with their hand. [3] **Handball** is the act of touching the ball with your hand during a football game, which is not allowed. [BRIT] ❑ *He got sent off for deliberate handball in the 32nd minute.* N-UNCOUNT; N-UNCOUNT; N-UNCOUNT: also *a* N

**hand|bill** /hændbɪl/ **(handbills)** A **handbill** is a small printed notice which is used to advertise a particular company, service, or event. N-COUNT

**hand|book** /hændbʊk/ **(handbooks)** A **handbook** is a book that gives you advice and instructions about a particular subject, tool, or machine. N-COUNT: usu with supp = manual

**hand|brake** /hændbreɪk/ **(handbrakes)** also **hand brake.** In a vehicle, the **handbrake** is a brake which the driver operates with his or her hand, for example when parking. [mainly BRIT] ➔ See picture on page 1708. N-COUNT

✔ in AM, usually use **emergency brake**

**hand|cart** /hændkɑːʳt/ **(handcarts)** also **hand-cart.** A **handcart** is a small cart with two wheels which is pushed or pulled along and is used for transporting goods. N-COUNT

**hand|clap** /hændklæp/ **(handclaps)** If a group of people give a **handclap**, they clap their hands. ❑ *...the crowd's slow handclap.* N-COUNT

**hand|cuff** /hændkʌf/ **(handcuffs, handcuffing, handcuffed)** [1] **Handcuffs** are two metal rings which are joined together and can be locked round someone's wrists, usually by the police during an arrest. ❑ *He was led away to jail in handcuffs.* [2] If you **handcuff** someone, you put handcuffs around their wrists. ❑ *They tried to handcuff him but, despite his injuries, he fought his way free.* N-PLURAL: also *a pair of* N; VERB; V n

**-hander** /-hændəʳ/ **(-handers) -hander** combines with words like 'two' or 'three' to form nouns which indicate how many people are involved in a particular activity, especially a play or a film. [mainly BRIT] ❑ *...a two-hander play... Williams's play is a tense contemporary three-hander about two murderers and a bank-robber.* ➔ See also **left-hander, right-hander**. COMB in N-COUNT: oft N n

**hand|ful** /hændfʊl/ **(handfuls)** [1] A **handful of** people or things is a small number of them. ❑ *He surveyed the handful of customers at the bar.* [2] A **handful of** something is the amount of it that you can hold in your hand. ❑ *She scooped up a handful of sand and let it trickle through her fingers.* [3] If you say that someone, especially a child, is a **handful**, you mean that they are difficult to control. [INFORMAL] ❑ *Zara can be a handful sometimes.* N-SING: usu N *of* n; N-COUNT: usu N *of* n; N-SING

**hand gre|nade** **(hand grenades)** A **hand grenade** is the same as a **grenade**. N-COUNT

**hand|gun** /hændgʌn/ **(handguns)** also **hand gun.** A **handgun** is a gun that you can hold, carry, and fire with one hand. N-COUNT

**hand-held** **(hand-helds)** also **handheld.** A **hand-held** device such as a camera or a computer is small and light enough to be used while you are holding it. ❑ *Saivonsac shot the entire film with a hand-held camera.* ♦ **Hand-held** is also a noun. ❑ *Users will be able to use their hand-helds to check their bank accounts.* ADJ: usu ADJ n; N-COUNT

**hand|hold** /hændhoʊld/ **(handholds)** A **handhold** is a small hole or hollow in something such as rock or a wall that you can put your hand in if you are trying to climb it. ❑ *I found handholds and hoisted myself along.* N-COUNT

**handi|cap** /hændikæp/ **(handicaps, handicapping, handicapped)** [1] A **handicap** is a physical or mental disability. ❑ *He lost his leg when he was ten, but learnt to overcome his handicap.* [2] A **handicap** is an event or situation that places you at a disadvantage and makes it harder for you to do something. ❑ *Being a foreigner was not a handicap.* [3] If an event or a situation **handicaps** someone or something, it places them at a disadvantage. ❑ *Greater levels of stress may seriously handicap some students.* [4] In golf, a **handicap** is an advantage given to someone who is not a good player, in order to make the players more equal. As you improve, your handicap gets lower. ❑ *I see your handicap is down from 16 to 12.* [5] In horse racing, a **handicap** is a race in which some com- N-COUNT; N-COUNT; VERB; V n; N-COUNT; N-COUNT petitors are given a disadvantage of extra weight in an attempt to give everyone an equal chance of winning.

**handi|capped** /hændikæpt/ Someone who is **handicapped** has a physical or mental disability that prevents them living a totally normal life. Many people who have a disability find this word offensive. ❑ *I work two days a week teaching handicapped kids to fish... Alex was mentally handicapped.* ADJ
♦ Some people refer to people who are handicapped as **the handicapped**. ❑ *...measures to prevent discrimination against the handicapped.* N-PLURAL: the N

**handi|craft** /hændikrɑːft, -kræft/ **(handicrafts)** 1 **Handicrafts** are activities such as embroidery and pottery which involve making things with your hands in a skilful way. N-COUNT: usu pl 2 **Handicrafts** are the objects that are produced by people doing handicrafts. ❑ *She sells handicrafts to the tourists.* N-COUNT: usu pl

**handi|work** /hændiwɜːʳk/ You can refer to something that you have done or made yourself as your **handiwork**. ❑ *The architect stepped back to admire his handiwork.* N-UNCOUNT: usu with poss

**hand|ker|chief** /hæŋkəʳtʃɪf/ **(handkerchiefs)** A **handkerchief** is a small square piece of fabric which you use for blowing your nose. N-COUNT

**han|dle** /hændᵊl/ **(handles, handling, handled)** ♦♦◊
1 A **handle** is a small round object or a lever that is attached to a door and is used for opening and closing it. ❑ *I turned the handle and found the door was open.* N-COUNT 2 A **handle** is the part of an object such as a tool, bag, or cup that you hold in order to be able to pick up and use the object. ➔ See picture on page 1710. ❑ *The handle of a cricket bat protruded from under his arm. ...a broom handle.* N-COUNT 3 If you say that someone can **handle** a problem or situation, you mean that they have the ability to deal with it successfully. ❑ *To tell the truth, I don't know if I can handle the job.* VERB V n 4 If you talk about the way that someone **handles** a problem or situation, you mention whether or not they are successful in achieving the result they want. ❑ *I think I would handle a meeting with Mr. Siegel very badly.* VERB V n adv ♦ **han|dling** *The family has criticized the military's handling of Robert's death.* N-UNCOUNT: usu N of n 5 If you **handle** a particular area of work, you have responsibility for it. ❑ *She handled travel arrangements for the press corps during the presidential campaign.* VERB V n 6 When you **handle** something such as a weapon, vehicle, or animal, you use it or control it, especially by using your hands. ❑ *I had never handled an automatic.* VERB V n 7 If something such as a vehicle **handles** well, it is easy to use or control. ❑ *His ship had handled like a dream!* VERB V adv/prep 8 When you **handle** something, you hold it or move it with your hands. ❑ *Wear rubber gloves when handling cat litter.* VERB V n 9 If you have **a handle on** a subject or problem, you have a way of approaching it that helps you to understand it or deal with it. [INFORMAL] ❑ *When you have got a handle on your anxiety you can begin to control it.* N-SING: a N on n 10 If you **fly off the handle**, you suddenly and completely lose your temper. [INFORMAL] ❑ *He flew off the handle at the slightest thing.* PHRASE: V inflects

**handle|bar** /hændᵊlbɑːʳ/ **(handlebars)** The **handlebar** or **handlebars** of a bicycle consist of a curved metal bar with handles at each end which are used for steering. ➔ See picture on page 1708. N-COUNT

**handle|bar mous|tache** **(handlebar moustaches)** also **handlebar mustache.** A **handlebar moustache** is a long thick moustache with curled ends. N-COUNT

**han|dler** /hændləʳ/ **(handlers)** 1 A **handler** is someone whose job is to be in charge of and control an animal. ❑ *Fifty officers, including frogmen and dog handlers, are searching for her.* N-COUNT: usu supp N 2 A **handler** is someone whose job is to deal with a particular type of object. ❑ *...baggage handlers at Gatwick airport.* N-COUNT: usu n N

**hand lug|gage** When you travel by air, your **hand luggage** is the luggage you have with you in the plane, rather than the luggage that is carried in the hold. N-UNCOUNT

**hand|made** /hændmeɪd/ also **hand-made.** 1 **Handmade** objects have been made by someone using their hands or using tools rather than by machines. ❑ *As they're handmade, each one varies slightly. ...handmade chocolates.* ADJ 2 If something **is handmade**, it is made by someone using their hands or using tools rather than by machines. ❑ *The beads they use are handmade in the Jura mountains in central France.* V-PASSIVE be V-ed

**hand|maiden** /hændmeɪdᵊn/ **(handmaidens)** 1 A **handmaiden** is a female servant. [LITERARY, OLD-FASHIONED] N-COUNT 2 If one thing is the **handmaiden of** another, the first thing helps the second or makes it possible. [FORMAL] ❑ *The fear is that science could become the handmaiden of industry.* N-COUNT: N of/to n

**hand-me-down** **(hand-me-downs)** 1 **Hand-me-downs** are things, especially clothes, which have been used by someone else before you and which have been given to you for your use. ❑ *Edward often wore Andrew's hand-me-downs.* N-COUNT: usu pl 2 **Hand-me-down** is used to describe things, especially clothes, which have been used by someone else before you and which have been given to you for your use. ❑ *Most of the boys wore hand-me-down military shirts from their fathers.* ADJ: ADJ n

**hand|out** /hændaʊt/ **(handouts)** 1 A **handout** is a gift of money, clothing, or food, which is given free to poor people. ❑ *Each family is being given a cash handout of six thousand rupees.* N-COUNT 2 If you call money that is given to someone a **handout**, you disapprove of it because you believe that the person who receives it has done nothing to earn or deserve it. ❑ *...the tendency of politicians to use money on vote-buying handouts rather than on investment in the future.* N-COUNT disapproval 3 A **handout** is a document which contains news or information about something and which is given, for example, to journalists or members of the public. ❑ *Official handouts describe the Emperor as 'particularly noted as a scholar'.* N-COUNT 4 A **handout** is a paper containing a summary of information or topics which will be dealt with in a lecture or talk. N-COUNT

**hand|over** /hændoʊvəʳ/ **(handovers)** The **handover of** something is when possession or control of it is given by one person or group of people to another. ❑ *The handover is expected to be completed in the next ten years.* N-COUNT: usu sing, oft N of n

**hand-pick** **(hand-picks, hand-picking, hand-picked)** also **handpick.** If someone **is hand-picked**, they are very carefully chosen by someone in authority for a particular purpose or a particular job. ❑ *He was hand-picked for this job by the Admiral... Sokagakkai was able to hand-pick his successor.* VERB be V-ed V n

**hand|rail** /hændreɪl/ **(handrails)** A **handrail** is a long piece of metal or wood which is fixed near stairs or places where people could slip and fall, and which people can hold on to for support. N-COUNT

**hand|set** /hændset/ **(handsets)** 1 The **handset** of a telephone is the part that you hold next to your face in order to speak and listen. N-COUNT 2 You can refer to a device such as the remote control of a television or stereo as a **handset**. N-COUNT

**hands-free** A **hands-free** telephone or other device can be used without being held in your hand. ADJ: ADJ n

**hand|shake** /hændʃeɪk/ **(handshakes)** If you give someone a **handshake**, you take their right hand with your own right hand and hold it firmly or move it up and down, as a sign of greeting or to show that you have agreed about something such as a business deal. ➔ See also **golden handshake**. N-COUNT

**hand|some** /hænsəm/ 1 A **handsome** man has an attractive face with regular features. ❑ *...a tall, dark, handsome sheep farmer.* ADJ = good-looking 2 A ADJ

**handsome** woman has an attractive appearance with features that are large and regular rather than small and delicate. ❑ *...an extremely handsome woman with a beautiful voice.* ADJ: ADJ n 3 A **handsome** sum of money is a large or generous amount. [FORMAL] ❑ *They will make a handsome profit on the property.* ♦ **hand|some|ly** ADV: ADV with v *He was rewarded handsomely for his efforts.* ADJ: ADJ n 4 If someone has a **handsome** win or a **handsome** victory, they get many more points or votes than their opponent. ❑ *The opposition won a handsome victory in the election.* ♦ **hand|some|ly** ADV: ADV after v *The car ran perfectly to the finish, and we won handsomely.*

**hands-on** ADJ: usu ADJ n **Hands-on** experience or work involves actually doing a particular thing, rather than just talking about it or getting someone else to do it. ❑ *Ninety-nine per cent of primary pupils now have hands-on experience of computers.*

**hand|stand** /hændstænd/ **(handstands)** N-COUNT If you do a **handstand**, you balance yourself upside down on your hands with your body and legs straight up in the air.

**hand-to-hand** also **hand to hand.** ADJ: ADJ n **Hand-to-hand** fighting is fighting where the people are very close together, using either their hands or weapons such as knives. ❑ *There was, reportedly, hand-to-hand combat in the streets.*

**hand-to-mouth** ADJ A **hand-to-mouth** existence is a way of life in which you have hardly enough food or money to live on. ❑ *The worst-paid live a hand-to-mouth existence without medical or other benefits.* ♦ **Hand-to-mouth** is also an adverb. ADV: ADV after v ❑ *...penniless students living hand-to-mouth.*

**hand tool** **(hand tools)** N-COUNT **Hand tools** are fairly simple tools which you use with your hands, and which are usually not powered.

**hand|wash** /hændwɒʃ/ **(handwashes, handwashing, handwashed)** VERB: V n If you **handwash** something, you wash it by hand rather than in a washing machine.

**hand|writing** /hændraɪtɪŋ/ N-UNCOUNT: oft poss N Your **handwriting** is your style of writing with a pen or pencil. ❑ *The address was in Anna's handwriting.*

**hand|written** /hændrɪtᵊn/ ADJ A piece of writing that is **handwritten** is one that someone has written using a pen or pencil rather than by typing it.

**handy** /hændi/ **(handier, handiest)**
1 ADJ Something that is **handy** is useful. ❑ *Credit cards can be handy – they mean you do not have to carry large sums of cash.* 2 PHRASE: V inflects If something **comes in handy**, it is useful in a particular situation. ❑ *The $20 check came in very handy.* 3 ADJ: usu v-link ADJ A thing or place that is **handy** is nearby and therefore easy to get or reach. ❑ *It would be good to have a pencil and paper handy.* 4 ADJ: v-link ADJ *with* n Someone who is **handy with** a particular tool is skilful at using it. [INFORMAL] ❑ *If you're handy with a needle you could brighten up your sweater with giant daisies.*

**handy|man** /hændimæn/ **(handymen)** N-COUNT A **handyman** is a man who earns money by doing small jobs for people such as making and repairing things in their houses. You can also describe a man who is good at making or repairing things in his home as a **handyman**.

**hang** /hæŋ/ **(hangs, hanging, hung, hanged)** ◆◆◇

> The form **hung** is used as the past tense and past participle. The form **hanged** is used as the past tense for meaning 5.

1 VERB If something **hangs** in a high place or position, or if you **hang** it there, it is attached there so it does not touch the ground. ❑ *Notices painted on sheets hang at every entrance.* V prep/adv *...small hanging lanterns...* V-ing *They saw a young woman come out of the house to hang clothes on a line.* V n prep/adv ♦ **Hang up** means the same as **hang**. PHRASAL VERB ❑ *I found his jacket, which was hanging up in the hallway...* V P *Some prisoners climbed onto the roof and hung up a banner.* V P n Also V n P 2 VERB If a piece of clothing or fabric **hangs** in a particular way or position, that is how it is worn or arranged. ❑ *...a ragged fur coat that hung down to her calves.* V adv/prep 3 VERB If something **hangs** loose or **hangs** open, it is partly fixed in position, but is not firmly held, supported, or controlled, often in such a way that it moves freely. ❑ *...her long golden hair which hung loose about her shoulders.* V adj 4 VERB: usu passive If something such as a wall **is hung with** pictures or other objects, they are attached to it. ❑ *The walls were hung with huge modern paintings.* *be* V-ed *with* n 5 VERB If someone **is hanged** or if they **hang**, they are killed, usually as a punishment, by having a rope tied around their neck and the support taken away from under their feet. ❑ *The five were expected to be hanged at 7 am on Tuesday...* *be* V-ed *It is right that their murderers should hang...* V *He hanged himself two hours after arriving at a mental hospital.* V pron-refl ♦ **hang|ing** **(hangings)** N-VAR *Four steamboat loads of spectators came to view a hanging in New Orleans.* 6 VERB If something such as someone's breath or smoke **hangs** in the air, it remains there without appearing to move or change position. ❑ *His breath was hanging in the air before him.* V prep/adv 7 VERB If a possibility **hangs over** you, it worries you and makes your life unpleasant or difficult because you think it might happen. ❑ *A constant threat of unemployment hangs over thousands of university researchers.* V *over* n 8 → See also **hanging, hung.**

PHRASES 9 PHRASE: V inflects: PHR n If you **get the hang of** something such as a skill or activity, you begin to understand or realize how to do it. [INFORMAL] ❑ *It's a bit tricky at first till you get the hang of it.* 10 PHRASE: V inflects If you tell someone to **hang in there** or to **hang on in there**, you are encouraging them to keep trying to do something and not to give up even though it might be difficult. [INFORMAL] ❑ *Hang in there and you never know what you might achieve.* 11 to **hang by a thread** → see **thread.**

♦ **hang around**

> in BRIT, also use **hang about, hang round**

1 PHRASAL VERB If you **hang around**, **hang about**, or **hang round**, you stay in the same place doing nothing, usually because you are waiting for something or someone. [INFORMAL] ❑ *He got sick of hanging around waiting for me...* V P -ing *On Saturdays we hang about in the park.* V P *...those people hanging round the streets at 6 am with nowhere to go.* V P n 2 PHRASAL VERB If you **hang around**, **hang about**, or **hang round** with someone or in a particular place, you spend a lot of time with that person or in that place. [INFORMAL] ❑ *They usually hung around together most of the time...* V P *together* *Helen used to hang round with the boys.* V P *with* n *...the usual young crowd who hung around the cafe day in and day out.* V P n

♦ **hang back** 1 PHRASAL VERB If you **hang back**, you move or stay slightly behind a person or group, usually because you are nervous about something. ❑ *I saw him step forward momentarily but then hang back, nervously massaging his hands.* V P 2 PHRASAL VERB If a person or organization **hangs back**, they do not do something immediately. ❑ *They will then hang back on closing the deal...* V P *on* n *Even his closest advisers believe he should hang back no longer.* V P

♦ **hang on** 1 PHRASAL VERB = hold on If you ask someone to **hang on**, you ask them to wait or stop what they are doing or saying for a moment. [INFORMAL] ❑ *Can you hang on for a minute?...* V P *Hang on a sec. I'll come with you.* V P n 2 PHRASAL VERB If you **hang on**, you manage to survive, achieve success, or avoid failure in spite of great difficulties or opposition. ❑ *Manchester United hung on to take the Cup.* V P 3 PHRASAL VERB If you **hang on to** or **hang onto** something that gives you an advantage, you succeed in keeping it for yourself, and prevent it from being taken away or given to someone else. ❑ *The British driver was unable to hang on to his lead...* V P *to* n *The company has been struggling to hang onto its sales force.* V P n 4 PHRASAL VERB = cling If you **hang on to** or **hang onto** something, you hold it very tightly, for example to stop it falling or to support yourself. ❑ *She was conscious of a second man hanging on to the rail.* V P *to* n *...a flight stewardess who helped save the life of a pilot by hanging onto his legs...* V P n *He hangs on tightly, his arms around my neck.* V P 5 PHRASAL VERB If you

**hang on to** or **hang onto** something, you keep it for a longer time than you would normally expect. [INFORMAL] ❑ *You could, alternatively, hang onto it in the hope that it will be worth millions in 10 years time... In the present climate, owners are hanging on to old ships.* 6 If one thing **hangs on** another, it depends on it in order to be successful. ❑ *Much hangs on the success of the collaboration between the Group of Seven governments and Brazil.* V P n; V P *to* n; PHRASAL VERB = *depend*; V P n

♦ **hang out** 1 If you **hang out** clothes that you have washed, you hang them on a clothes line to dry. ❑ *I was worried I wouldn't be able to hang my washing out.* 2 If you **hang out** in a particular place or area, you go and stay there for no particular reason, or spend a lot of time there. [mainly AM, INFORMAL] ❑ *I often used to hang out in supermarkets... We can just hang out and have a good time.* → See also **hangout**. PHRASAL VERB; V n P; Also V P n; PHRASAL VERB; V P adv/prep; V P

♦ **hang round** → see **hang around**.

♦ **hang up** 1 → see **hang 1**. 2 If you **hang up** or you **hang up** the phone, you end a phone call. If you **hang up on** someone you are speaking to on the phone, you end the phone call suddenly and unexpectedly. ❑ *Mum hung up the phone... Don't hang up!... He said he'd call again, and hung up on me.* 3 You can use **hang up** to indicate that someone stops doing a particular sport or activity that they have regularly done over a long period. For example, when a footballer **hangs up** his boots, he stops playing football. ❑ *Keegan announced he was hanging up his boots for good.* 4 → See also **hang-up**, **hung up**. PHRASAL VERB; V P n (not pron); V P, V P *on* n; PHRASAL VERB; V P n (not pron); Also V n P

**hang|ar** /hæŋəʳ/ **(hangars)** A **hangar** is a large building in which aircraft are kept. N-COUNT

**hang|dog** /hæŋdɒg, AM -dɔːg/ also **hang-dog**. If you say that someone has a **hangdog** expression on their face, you mean that they look sad, and often guilty or ashamed. ADJ: usu ADJ n

**hang|er** /hæŋəʳ/ **(hangers)** A **hanger** is the same as a **coat hanger**. N-COUNT

**hanger-on** **(hangers-on)** If you describe someone as a **hanger-on**, you are critical of them because they are trying to be friendly with a richer or more important person, especially in order to gain an advantage for themselves. ❑ *For every one or two talented people in any group of artists, there are hordes of talentless hangers-on.* N-COUNT [disapproval]

**hang-glider** **(hang-gliders)** also **hang glider**. A **hang-glider** is a type of glider, made from large piece of cloth fixed to a frame. It is used to fly from high places, with the pilot hanging underneath. N-COUNT

**hang-gliding** **Hang-gliding** is the activity of flying in a hang-glider. N-UNCOUNT

**hang|ing** /hæŋɪŋ/ **(hangings)** A **hanging** is a large piece of cloth that you put as a decoration on a wall. N-COUNT: usu with supp

**hang|ing bas|ket** **(hanging baskets)** A **hanging basket** is a basket with small ropes or chains attached so that it can be hung from a hook. Hanging baskets are usually used for displaying plants or storing fruit and vegetables. N-COUNT

**hang|man** /hæŋmæn/ **(hangmen)** A **hangman** is a man whose job is to execute people by hanging them. N-COUNT

**hang|out** /hæŋaʊt/ **(hangouts)** If a place is a **hangout** for a particular group of people, they spend a lot of time there because they can relax and meet other people there. [INFORMAL] ❑ *By the time he was sixteen, Malcolm already knew most of London's teenage hangouts.* N-COUNT: with supp = *haunt*

**hang|over** /hæŋoʊvəʳ/ **(hangovers)** 1 If someone wakes up with a **hangover**, they feel sick and have a headache because they have drunk a lot of alcohol the night before. 2 Something that is a **hangover from** the past is an idea or way of behaving which people used to have in the past but which people no longer generally have. ❑ *As a hangover from rationing, they mixed butter and margarine.* N-COUNT; N-COUNT: with supp, usu N *from* n

**hang-up** **(hang-ups)** If you have a **hang-up** about something, you have a feeling of fear, anxiety, or embarrassment about it. [INFORMAL] ❑ *I don't have any hang-ups about my body.* N-COUNT = *inhibition*

**hank** /hæŋk/ **(hanks)** A **hank of** wool, rope, or string is a length of it which has been loosely wound. N-COUNT: oft N *of* n

**hank|er** /hæŋkəʳ/ **(hankers, hankering, hankered)** If you **hanker after** something, you want it very much. ❑ *I hankered after a floor-length brown suede coat.* VERB; V *after/for* n; Also V to-inf

**hank|er|ing** /hæŋkərɪŋ/ **(hankerings)** A **hankering for** something is a desire or longing for it. ❑ *From time to time we all get a hankering for something a little different.* N-COUNT: usu N *for/after* n, N to-inf

**hanky** /hæŋki/ **(hankies)** also **hankie**. A **hanky** is the same as a handkerchief. [INFORMAL] N-COUNT

**hanky-panky** /hæŋki pæŋki/ **Hanky-panky** is used to refer to sexual activity between two people, especially when this is regarded as improper or not serious. [HUMOROUS, INFORMAL] ❑ *Does this mean no hanky-panky after lights out?* N-UNCOUNT

**han|som** /hænsəm/ **(hansoms)** In former times, a **hansom** or a **hansom cab** was a horse-drawn carriage with two wheels and a fixed hood. N-COUNT

**Ha|nuk|kah** /hɑːnʊkə/ also **Hanukah**. **Hanukkah** is a Jewish festival that celebrates the rededication of the Temple in Jerusalem in 165 B.C. It begins in November or December and lasts for eight days. N-UNCOUNT = *Chanukah*

**hap|haz|ard** /hæphæzəʳd/ If you describe something as **haphazard**, you are critical of it because it is not at all organized or is not arranged according to a plan. ❑ *The investigation does seem haphazard.* ♦ **hap|haz|ard|ly** *She looked at the books jammed haphazardly in the shelves.* ADJ [disapproval]; ADV: usu ADV with v

**hap|less** /hæpləs/ A **hapless** person is unlucky. [FORMAL] ❑ *...his hapless victim.* ADJ: ADJ n

**hap|pen** /hæpən/ **(happens, happening, happened)** 1 Something that **happens** occurs or is done without being planned. ❑ *We cannot say for sure what will happen.* 2 If something **happens**, it occurs as a result of a situation or course of action. ❑ *She wondered what would happen if her parents found her... He trotted to the truck and switched on the ignition. Nothing happened.* 3 When something, especially something unpleasant, **happens to** you, it takes place and affects you. ❑ *If we had been spotted at that point, I don't know what would have happened to us.* 4 If you **happen to** do something, you do it by chance. If **it happens that** something is the case, it occurs by chance. ❑ *We happened to discover we had a friend in common... If it happens that I'm wanted badly somewhere, my mother will take the call and phone through to me here.* 5 You use **as it happens** in order to introduce a statement, especially one that is rather surprising. ❑ *She called Amy to see if she had any idea of her son's whereabouts. As it happened, Amy had.* ◆◆◆; VERB; V; VERB; V; V; VERB; V *to* n; VERB; V to-inf; *it* V that; PHRASE: V inflects, PHR with cl

**hap|pen|ing** /hæpənɪŋ/ **(happenings)** **Happenings** are things that happen, often in a way that is unexpected or hard to explain. ❑ *The Budapest office plans to hire freelance reporters to cover the latest happenings.* N-COUNT: usu pl, usu with supp

**hap|pen|stance** /hæpənstæns/ If you say that something happened **by happenstance**, you mean that it happened because of certain circumstances, although it was not planned by anyone. [WRITTEN] ❑ *I came to live at the farm by happenstance.* N-UNCOUNT: also *a* N, oft *by* N

**hap|pi|ly** /hæpɪli/ You can add **happily** to a statement to indicate that you are glad that something happened or is true. ❑ *Happily, his neck injuries were not serious.* → See also **happy**. ADV: ADV with cl = *fortunately*

**hap|py** /hæpi/ **(happier, happiest)** 1 Someone who is **happy** has feelings of pleasure, usually because something nice has happened or because they feel satisfied with their life. ❑ *Marina was a confident, happy child... I'm just happy to be back running.* ♦ **hap|pi|ly** *Albert leaned back happily* ◆◆◇; ADJ; ADV: usu ADV with v and lit a cigarette. ♦ **hap|pi|ness** *I think mostly she was looking for happiness.* N-UNCOUNT 2 A **happy** time, place, or relationship is full of happy feelings and pleasant experiences, or has an atmosphere in which people feel happy. ❑ *It had always been a happy place... We have a very happy marriage.* ADJ: usu ADJ n 3 If you are **happy about** a situation or arrangement, you are satisfied with it, for example because you think that something is being done in the right way. ❑ *If you are not happy about a repair, go back and complain... He's happy that I deal with it myself.* ADJ: v-link ADJ, ADJ *about/with* n/-ing, ADJ that, ADJ to-inf 4 If you say you are **happy to** do something, you mean that you are very willing to do it. ❑ *I'll be happy to answer any questions if there are any.* ADJ: v-link ADJ, usu ADJ to-inf ♦ **hap|pi|ly** *If I've caused any offence over something I have written, I will happily apologise.* ADV: ADV with v = *gladly* 5 **Happy** is used in greetings and other conventional expressions to say that you hope someone will enjoy a special occasion. ❑ *Happy Birthday!... Happy Easter!* **many happy returns** → see **return**. ADJ: ADJ n 6 A **happy** coincidence is one that results in something pleasant or helpful happening. ❑ *By happy coincidence, Robert met Richard and Julia and discovered they were experiencing similar problems.* ADJ: ADJ n

**happy-go-lucky** Someone who is **happy-go-lucky** enjoys life and does not worry about the future. ADJ = *easy going*

**hap|py hour** **(happy hours)** In a pub, **happy hour** is a period when drinks are sold more cheaply than usual to encourage people to come to the pub. N-VAR

**hara-kiri** /hærə kɪri/ In former times, if a Japanese man committed **hara-kiri**, he killed himself by cutting his own stomach open, in order to avoid dishonour. N-UNCOUNT

**ha|rangue** /həræŋ/ **(harangues, haranguing, harangued)** If someone **harangues** you, they try to persuade you to accept their opinions or ideas in a forceful way. VERB ❑ *An argument ensued, with various band members joining in and haranguing Simpson and his girlfriend for over two hours.* V n

**har|ass** /hærəs, həræs/ **(harasses, harassing, harassed)** If someone **harasses** you, they trouble or annoy you, for example by attacking you repeatedly or by causing you as many problems as they can. VERB ❑ *A woman reporter complained one of them sexually harassed her in the locker room.* V n

**har|assed** /hærəst, həræst/ If you are **harassed**, you are anxious and tense because you have too much to do or too many problems to cope with. ❑ *This morning, looking harassed and drawn, Lewis tendered his resignation.* ADJ

**har|ass|ment** /hærəsmənt, həræs-/ **Harassment** is behaviour which is intended to trouble or annoy someone, for example repeated attacks on them or attempts to cause them problems. ❑ *The party has accused the police of harassment.* N-UNCOUNT: oft adj N

**har|bin|ger** /hɑːʳbɪndʒəʳ/ **(harbingers)** Something that is a **harbinger of** something else, especially something bad, is a sign that it is going to happen. [LITERARY] ❑ *The November air stung my cheeks, a harbinger of winter.* N-COUNT: usu N *of* n

**har|bour** /hɑːʳbəʳ/ **(harbours, harbouring, harboured)** ◆◇◇

> in AM, use **harbor**

1 A **harbour** is an area of the sea at the coast which is partly enclosed by land or strong walls, so that boats can be left there safely. ❑ *She led us to a room with a balcony overlooking the harbour.* N-COUNT; N-IN-NAMES 2 If you **harbour** an emotion, thought, or secret, you have it in your mind over a long period of time. VERB ❑ *He might have been murdered by a former client or someone harbouring a grudge.* V n 3 If a person or country **harbours** someone who is wanted by the police, they let them stay in their house or country and offer them protection. VERB ❑ *Accusations of harbouring suspects were raised against the former Hungarian leadership.* V n

**har|bour|master** /hɑːʳbəʳmɑːstəʳ, -mæs-/ **(harbourmasters)** also **harbour master.**

> in AM, use **harbormaster** or **harbor master**

A **harbourmaster** is the official in charge of a harbour. N-COUNT

**hard** /hɑːʳd/ **(harder, hardest)** ◆◆◆ 1 Something that is **hard** is very firm and stiff to touch and is not easily bent, cut, or broken. ADJ ≠ *soft* ❑ *He shuffled his feet on the hard wooden floor... Something cold and hard pressed into the back of his neck.* ♦ **hard|ness** *He felt the hardness of the iron railing press against his spine.* N-UNCOUNT: oft with poss 2 Something that is **hard** is very difficult to do or deal with. ❑ *It's hard to tell what effect this latest move will have... Our traveller's behaviour on the journey is hard to explain... That's a very hard question.* ADJ: oft *it* v-link ADJ to-inf, ADJ to-inf = *difficult* ≠ *easy* 3 If you work **hard** doing something, you are very active or work intensely, with a lot of effort. ❑ *I'll work hard. I don't want to let him down... Am I trying too hard?* ADV: ADV after v ♦ **Hard** is also an adjective. ❑ *I admired him as a true scientist and hard worker.* ADJ: ADJ n 4 **Hard** work involves a lot of activity and effort. ❑ *Coping with three babies is very hard work... Their work is hard and unglamorous, and most people would find it boring.* ADJ 5 If you look, listen, or think **hard**, you do it carefully and with a great deal of attention. ❑ *You had to listen hard to hear the old man breathe.* ADV: ADV after v ♦ **Hard** is also an adjective. ❑ *It might be worth taking a long hard look at your frustrations and resentments.* ADJ: usu ADJ n 6 If you strike or take hold of something **hard**, you strike or take hold of it with a lot of force. ❑ *I kicked a dustbin very hard and broke my toe.* ADV: ADV after v ♦ **Hard** is also an adjective. ❑ *He gave her a hard push which toppled her backwards into an armchair.* ADJ: ADJ n 7 You can use **hard** to indicate that something happens intensely and for a long time. ❑ *I've never seen Terry laugh so hard... It was snowing hard by then.* ADV: ADV after v 8 If a person or their expression is **hard**, they show no kindness or sympathy. ❑ *His father was a hard man.* ADJ: usu ADJ n ≠ *gentle* 9 If you are **hard on** someone, you treat them severely or unkindly. ❑ *Don't be so hard on him.* ADJ: v-link ADJ *on* n ♦ **Hard** is also an adverb. ❑ *He said the security forces would continue to crack down hard on the protestors.* ADV: ADV after v 10 If you say that something is **hard on** a person or thing, you mean it affects them in a way that is likely to cause them damage or suffering. ❑ *The grey light was hard on the eyes... These last four years have been hard on them.* ADJ: v-link ADJ *on* n 11 If you have a **hard** life or a **hard** period of time, your life or that period is difficult and unpleasant for you. ❑ *It had been a hard life for her... Those were hard times.* ADJ = *tough* ♦ **hard|ness** *In America, people don't normally admit to the hardness of life.* N-UNCOUNT: N *of* n 12 **Hard** evidence or facts are definitely true and do not need to be questioned. ❑ *There are probably fewer hard facts about the life of Henry Purcell than that of any other great composer since the Renaissance.* ADJ: ADJ n 13 **Hard** water contains a lot of calcium compounds that stop soap making bubbles and sometimes appear as a deposit in kettles and baths. ADJ ≠ *soft* 14 **Hard** drugs are very strong illegal drugs such as heroin or cocaine. ADJ: ADJ n ≠ *soft*

PHRASES 15 If you feel **hard done by**, you feel that you have not been treated fairly. [BRIT] ❑ *The hall porter was feeling hard done by at having to extend his shift.* PHRASE: v-link PHR 16 If you say that something is **hard going**, you mean it is difficult and requires a lot of effort. ❑ *The talks had been hard going at the start.* PHRASE: usu v-link PHR 17 To be **hard hit by** something means to be affected very severely by it. ❑ *California's been particularly hard hit by the recession.* PHRASE: usu v-link PHR 18 If someone **plays hard to get**, they pretend not to be interested in another person or in what someone is trying to persuade them to do. ❑ *I wanted her and she was playing hard to get.* PHRASE: V inflects 19 If someone is **hard put to** do something or, in British English if they are **hard pushed to** do something, they have great difficulty doing it. ❑ *Mr Morton is undoubtedly cleverer than Mr Kirkby, but he will be hard put to match his popularity.* PHRASE: usu v-link PHR to-inf 20 If PHRASE:

you **take** something **hard**, you are very upset or depressed by it. ❑ *Maybe I just took it too hard.* V inflects

**hard and fast** If you say that there are no **hard and fast** rules, or that there is no **hard and fast** information about something, you are indicating that there are no fixed or definite rules or facts. ❑ *There are no hard and fast rules, but rather traditional guidelines as to who pays for what.* ADJ: usu with brd-neg, usu ADJ n = definite

**hard|back** /hɑːʳdbæk/ **(hardbacks)** A **hardback** is a book which has a stiff hard cover. Compare **paperback**. ❑ *His autobiography has sold more than 36,000 copies in hardback.* N-COUNT: also *in* N

**hard|ball** /hɑːʳdbɔːl/ If someone **plays hardball**, they will do anything that is necessary to achieve or get what they want, even if this involves being harsh or unfair. [mainly AM] ❑ *She is playing hardball in a world dominated by men 20 years her senior.* PHRASE

**hard-bitten** If you describe someone as **hard-bitten**, you are critical of them because they do not show much emotion or have much sympathy for other people, usually because they have experienced many unpleasant things. ❑ *...a cynical hard-bitten journalist.* ADJ: usu ADJ n [disapproval] = tough

**hard|board** /hɑːʳdbɔːʳd/ **Hardboard** is a material which is made by pressing very small pieces of wood very closely together to form a thin, slightly flexible sheet. N-UNCOUNT

**hard-boiled** also **hard boiled.** [1] A **hard-boiled** egg has been boiled in its shell until the whole of the inside is solid. ADJ [2] You use **hard-boiled** to describe someone who is tough and does not show much emotion. ❑ *She's hard-boiled, tough and funny.* ADJ

**hard cash** **Hard cash** is money in the form of notes and coins as opposed to a cheque or a credit card. N-UNCOUNT

**hard ci|der** **Hard cider** is an alcoholic drink that is made from apples. [AM] N-UNCOUNT

✓ in BRIT, use **cider**

**hard copy** **(hard copies)** A **hard copy** of a document is a printed version of it, rather than a version that is stored on a computer. ❑ *...eight pages of hard copy.* N-VAR

**hard core** **Hard core** consists of pieces of broken stone that are used as a base on which to build roads. [mainly BRIT] N-UNCOUNT

**hard-core** also **hardcore, hard core.** [1] You can refer to the members of a group who are the most committed to its activities or who are the most involved in them as a **hard core of** members or as the **hard-core** members. ❑ *We've got a hard core of customers that have stood by us... A hard-core group of right-wing senators had hoped to sway their colleagues.* N-SING: oft N *of* n, N n [2] **Hard-core** pornography shows sex in a very detailed way, or shows very violent or unpleasant sex. Compare **soft-core**. ADJ: ADJ n

**hard|cover** /hɑːʳdkʌvəʳ/ **(hardcovers)** A **hardcover** is a book which has a stiff hard cover. Compare **softcover**. [AM] N-COUNT: also *in* N

✓ in BRIT, use **hardback**

**hard cur|ren|cy** **(hard currencies)** A **hard currency** is one which is unlikely to lose its value and so is considered to be a good one to have or to invest in. ❑ *The government is running short of hard currency to pay for imports.* N-VAR

**hard disk** **(hard disks)** A computer's **hard disk** is a stiff magnetic disk on which data and programs can be stored. N-COUNT

**hard-drinking** If you describe someone as a **hard-drinking** person, you mean that they frequently drink large quantities of alcohol. ADJ: ADJ n

**hard-edged** If you describe something such as a style, play, or article as **hard-edged**, you mean you admire it because it is powerful, critical, or unsentimental. ❑ *...hard-edged drama.* ADJ [approval] = uncompromising

**hard|en** /hɑːʳdᵊn/ **(hardens, hardening, hardened)** [1] When something **hardens** or when you **harden** it, it becomes stiff or firm. ❑ *Mould the mixture into shape while hot, before it hardens... Give the cardboard two or three coats of varnish to harden it.* VERB V V n [2] When an attitude or opinion **hardens** or **is hardened**, it becomes harsher, stronger, or fixed. ❑ *Their action can only serve to harden the attitude of landowners... The bitter split which has developed within Solidarity is likely to harden further into separation.* VERB V n V ♦ **hard|en|ing** *...a hardening of the government's attitude towards rebellious parts of the army.* N-SING: usu N *of* n [3] When prices and economies **harden**, they become much more stable than they were. ❑ *Property prices are just beginning to harden again.* VERB V [4] When events **harden** people or when people **harden**, they become less easily affected emotionally and less sympathetic and gentle than they were before. ❑ *Her years of drunken bickering hardened my heart... All of a sudden my heart hardened against her.* VERB V n V *against* n [5] If you say that someone's face or eyes **harden**, you mean that they suddenly look serious or angry. ❑ *His smile died and the look in his face hardened.* VERB V

**hard|ened** /hɑːʳdᵊnd/ If you describe someone as **hardened**, you mean that they have had so much experience of something bad or unpleasant that they are no longer affected by it in the way that other people would be. ❑ *...hardened criminals. ...hardened politicians.* ADJ: usu ADJ n

**hard hat** **(hard hats)** A **hard hat** is a hat made from a hard material, which people wear to protect their heads on building sites or in factories, or when riding a horse. N-COUNT

**hard-headed** You use **hard-headed** to describe someone who is practical and determined to get what they want or need, and who does not allow emotions to affect their actions. ❑ *...a hard-headed and shrewd businesswoman.* ADJ = tough

**hard-hearted** If you describe someone as **hard-hearted**, you disapprove of the fact that they have no sympathy for other people and do not care if people are hurt or made unhappy. ❑ *You would have to be pretty hard-hearted not to feel something for him.* ADJ [disapproval] = unfeeling

**hard-hitting** If you describe a report or speech as **hard-hitting**, you like the way it talks about difficult or serious matters in a bold and direct way. [JOURNALISM] ❑ *In a hard-hitting speech to the IMF, he urged third world countries to undertake sweeping reforms.* ADJ: usu ADJ n [approval]

**hard la|bour**

✓ in AM, use **hard labor**

**Hard labour** is hard physical work which people have to do as punishment for a crime. ❑ *The sentence of the court was twelve years' hard labour, to be served in a British prison.* N-UNCOUNT

**hard left** also **hard-left.** You use **hard left** to describe those members of a left wing political group or party who have the most extreme political beliefs. [mainly BRIT] ❑ *...the hard-left view that foreign forces should not have been sent.* N-SING: *the* N, oft N n

✓ in AM, usually use **far left**

**hard|line** /hɑːʳdlaɪn/ also **hard-line.** If you describe someone's policy or attitude as **hardline**, you mean that it is strict or extreme, and they refuse to change it. ❑ *The United States has taken a lot of criticism for its hard-line stance.* ADJ

**hard|liner** /hɑːʳdlaɪnəʳ/ **(hardliners)** The **hardliners** in a group such as a political party are the people who support a strict, fixed set of ideas that are often extreme, and who refuse to accept any change in them. ❑ *Unionist hardliners warned the U.S. President he would not be welcome.* ◆◇◇ N-COUNT: usu pl

**hard luck** [1] If you say that someone had some **hard luck**, or that a situation was **hard luck on** them, you mean that something bad happened to them and you are implying that it was not their fault. [INFORMAL] ❑ *We had a bit of hard luck this season.* N-UNCOUNT = bad luck [2] If someone says that a bad situation affecting you is just your **hard luck**, N-UNCOUNT: poss N = tough luck they do not care about it or think you should be helped, often because they think it is your fault. [INFORMAL] ❑ *The shop assistants didn't really want to discuss the matter, saying it was just my hard luck.* [3] You can say '**hard luck**' to someone to show that you are sorry they have not got or done something that they had wanted to get or do. [INFORMAL] ❑ *Hard luck, chaps, but don't despair too much.* CONVENTION [feelings] = *tough luck*

**hard|ly** /hɑːʳdli/ [1] You use **hardly** to modify a statement when you want to emphasize that it is only a small amount or detail which makes it true, and that therefore it is best to consider the opposite statement as being true. ❑ *I hardly know you... Their two faces were hardly more than eighteen inches apart.* ◆◆◇ ADV: ADV before v, ADV group, oft ADV amount [emphasis] = *scarcely, barely* [2] You use **hardly** in expressions such as **hardly ever**, **hardly any**, and **hardly anyone** to mean almost never, almost none, or almost no-one. ❑ *We ate chips every night, but hardly ever had fish... Most of the others were so young they had hardly any experience.* ADV: ADV *ever/any* [3] You use **hardly** before a negative statement in order to emphasize that something is usually true or usually happens. ❑ *Hardly a day goes by without a visit from someone.* ADV: ADV n [emphasis] = *scarcely* [4] When you say you can **hardly** do something, you are emphasizing that it is very difficult for you to do it. ❑ *My garden was covered with so many butterflies that I could hardly see the flowers.* ADV: *can/could* ADV inf [emphasis] [5] If you say **hardly** had one thing happened when something else happened, you mean that the first event was followed immediately by the second. ❑ *He had hardly collected the papers on his desk when the door burst open.* ADV: ADV before v = *no sooner* [6] You use **hardly** to mean 'not' when you want to suggest that you are expecting your listener or reader to agree with your comment. ❑ *We have not seen the letter, so we can hardly comment on it.* ADV: ADV before v, ADV group [7] You use '**hardly**' to mean 'no', especially when you want to express surprise or annoyance at a statement that you disagree with. [SPOKEN] ❑ *'They all thought you were marvellous!' — 'Well, hardly.'.* CONVENTION

**hard-nosed** You use **hard-nosed** to describe someone who is tough and realistic, and who takes decisions on practical grounds rather than emotional ones. [INFORMAL] ❑ *If nothing else, Doug is a hard-nosed businessman.* ADJ: usu ADJ n = *unsentimental*

**hard of hear|ing** Someone who is **hard of hearing** is not able to hear properly. ADJ: usu v-link ADJ

**hard porn** **Hard porn** is pornography that shows sex in a very detailed way, or shows very violent or unpleasant sex. N-UNCOUNT

**hard-pressed** also **hard pressed.** [1] If someone is **hard-pressed**, they are under a great deal of strain and worry, usually because they have not got enough money. [JOURNALISM] ❑ *The region's hard-pressed consumers are spending less on luxuries.* ADJ [2] If you will be **hard-pressed to** do something, you will have great difficulty doing it. ❑ *This year the airline will be hard-pressed to make a profit.* ADJ: v-link ADJ to-inf

**hard right** also **hard-right.** You use **hard right** to describe those members of a right wing political group or party who have the most extreme political beliefs. [mainly BRIT] ❑ *...the appearance of hard-right political groupings.* N-SING: *the* N, oft N n

✔ in AM, usually use **far right**

**hard sell** A **hard sell** is a method of selling in which the salesperson puts a lot of pressure on someone to make them buy something. ❑ *...a double-glazing firm whose hard-sell techniques were exposed by a consumer programme.* N-SING: oft N n

**hard|ship** /hɑːʳdʃɪp/ **(hardships)** **Hardship** is a situation in which your life is difficult or unpleasant, often because you do not have enough money. ❑ *Many people are suffering economic hardship... One of the worst hardships is having so little time to spend with one's family.* N-VAR

**hard shoul|der** **(hard shoulders)** The **hard shoulder** is the area at the side of a motorway or other road where you are allowed to stop if your car breaks down. [mainly BRIT] N-COUNT: usu *the* N in sing

✔ in AM, use **shoulder**

**hard up** also **hard-up.** If you are **hard up**, you have very little money. [INFORMAL] ❑ *Her parents were very hard up.* ADJ ≠ *well-off*

**hard|ware** /hɑːʳdweəʳ/ [1] In computer systems, **hardware** refers to the machines themselves as opposed to the programs which tell the machines what to do. Compare **software**. N-UNCOUNT [2] Military **hardware** is the machinery and equipment that is used by the armed forces, such as tanks, aircraft, and missiles. N-UNCOUNT: usu adj N [3] **Hardware** refers to tools and equipment that are used in the home and garden, for example saucepans, screwdrivers, and lawnmowers. N-UNCOUNT

**hard|ware store** **(hardware stores)** A **hardware store** is a shop where articles for the house and garden such as tools, nails, and pans are sold. N-COUNT

**hard-wearing** also **hard wearing.** Something that is **hard-wearing** is strong and well-made so that it lasts for a long time and stays in good condition even though it is used a lot. [mainly BRIT] ❑ *...hard-wearing cotton shirts.* ADJ

✔ in AM, use **long-wearing**

**hard-wired** also **hardwired.** [1] A **hard-wired** part of a computer forms part of its hardware. ADJ [2] If an ability, approach, or type of activity is **hard-wired into** the brain, it is a basic one and cannot be changed. ❑ *Others think that the rules for what is 'musical' are hard-wired in our brains to some degree.* ADJ

**hard-won** If you describe something that someone has gained or achieved as **hard-won**, you mean that they worked hard to gain or achieve it. ❑ *The dispute could destroy Australia's hard-won reputation for industrial stability.* ADJ: usu ADJ n

**hard|wood** /hɑːʳdwʊd/ **(hardwoods)** **Hardwood** is wood such as oak, teak, and mahogany, which is very strong and hard. ❑ *...hardwood floors.* N-MASS: oft N n ≠ *softwood*

**hard-working** also **hardworking.** If you describe someone as **hard-working**, you mean that they work very hard. ❑ *He was hardworking and energetic.* ADJ

**har|dy** /hɑːʳdi/ **(hardier, hardiest)** [1] Plants that are **hardy** are able to survive cold weather. ❑ *The silver-leaved varieties of cyclamen are not quite as hardy.* ♦ **har|di|ness** *...the hardiness of other species that have blue flowers.* ADJ N-UNCOUNT [2] People and animals that are **hardy** are strong and able to cope with difficult conditions. ❑ *It should not surprise us that such an environment has produced a hardy and independent people.* ♦ **har|di|ness** *...the hardiness, endurance, and courage of my companions.* ADJ N-UNCOUNT [3] If you describe a group of people as **hardy**, you mean that they have been very patient or loyal, or have been trying hard to do something in difficult conditions. ❑ *...the ten hardy supporters who had made the trek to Dublin from Riga.* ADJ: usu ADJ n

**hare** /heəʳ/ **(hares, haring, hared)** [1] A **hare** is an animal like a rabbit but larger with long ears, long legs, and a small tail. N-VAR [2] If you **hare off** somewhere, you go there very quickly. [BRIT, INFORMAL] ❑ *...an over-protective mother who keeps haring off to ring the babysitter.* VERB V adv/prep

**hare-brained** also **harebrained.** You use **hare-brained** to describe a scheme or theory which you consider to be very foolish and which you think is unlikely to be successful or true. ❑ *This isn't the first hare-brained scheme he's had.* ADJ: usu ADJ n [disapproval] = *crackpot*

**har|em** /hɑːriːm, AM herəm/ **(harems)** If a man, especially a Muslim, has several wives or sexual partners living in his house, they can be referred to as his **harem**. N-COUNT

**hari|cot bean** /hærɪkoʊ biːn/ **(haricot beans)** **Haricot beans** are small white beans that are eaten as a vegetable. They are often sold dried rather than fresh. [BRIT] N-COUNT: usu pl

**hark** /hɑːʳk/ **(harks, harking, harked)**
♦ **hark back to** 1 If you say that one thing **harks back to** another thing in the past, you mean it is similar to it or takes it as a model. ❑ *...pitched roofs, which hark back to the Victorian era.* 2 When people **hark back to** something in the past, they remember it or remind someone of it. ❑ *The result devastated me at the time. Even now I hark back to it.* PHRASAL VERB V P P n PHRASAL VERB V P P n

**har|lequin** /hɑːʳlɪkwɪn/ You use **harlequin** to describe something that has a lot of different colours, often in a diamond pattern. [WRITTEN] ❑ *...the striking harlequin floor.* ADJ: ADJ n

**har|lot** /hɑːʳlət/ **(harlots)** If someone describes a woman as a **harlot**, they disapprove of her because she is a prostitute, or because she looks or behaves like a prostitute. [OFFENSIVE, OLD-FASHIONED] N-COUNT disapproval

**harm** /hɑːʳm/ **(harms, harming, harmed)** 1 To **harm** a person or animal means to cause them physical injury, usually on purpose. ❑ *The hijackers seemed anxious not to harm anyone.* 2 **Harm** is physical injury to a person or an animal which is usually caused on purpose. ❑ *All dogs are capable of doing harm to human beings.* 3 To **harm** a thing, or sometimes a person, means to damage them or make them less effective or successful than they were. ❑ *...a warning that the product may harm the environment.* 4 **Harm** is the damage to something which is caused by a particular course of action. ❑ *To cut taxes would probably do the economy more harm than good.* ◆◇◇ VERB = injure, hurt V n N-UNCOUNT: oft N *to* n VERB = damage, ruin V n N-UNCOUNT

PHRASES 5 If you say that someone or something **will come to no harm** or that **no harm will come to** them, you mean that they will not be hurt or damaged in any way. ❑ *There is always a lifeguard to ensure that no one comes to any harm.* 6 If you say **it does no harm to** do something or **there is no harm in** doing something, you mean that it might be worth doing, and you will not be blamed for doing it. ❑ *They are not always willing to take on untrained workers, but there's no harm in asking.* 7 If you say that there is **no harm done**, you are telling someone not to worry about something that has happened because it has not caused any serious injury or damage. ❑ *There, now, you're all right. No harm done.* 8 If someone is put **in harm's way**, they are caused to be in a dangerous situation. ❑ *These men were never told how they'd been put in harm's way.* 9 If someone or something is **out of harm's way**, they are in a safe place away from danger or from the possibility of being damaged. ❑ *For parents, it is an easy way of keeping their children entertained, or simply out of harm's way.* PHRASE: V inflects PHRASE: V inflects PHRASE: usu v-link PHR PHRASE: PHR after v, v-link PHR PHRASE: v-link PHR, PHR after v

**harm|ful** /hɑːʳmfʊl/ Something that is **harmful** has a bad effect on something else, especially on a person's health. ❑ *...the harmful effects of smoking... It believed the affair was potentially harmful to British aviation.* ADJ: oft ADJ *to* n = damaging ≠ harmless

**harm|less** /hɑːʳmləs/ 1 Something that is **harmless** does not have any bad effects, especially on people's health. ❑ *Industry has been working at developing harmless substitutes for these gases... This experiment was harmless to the animals.* ♦ **harm|less|ly** *Another missile exploded harmlessly outside the town.* 2 If you describe someone or something as **harmless**, you mean that they are not important and therefore unlikely to annoy other people or cause trouble. ❑ *He seemed harmless enough... I would not want to deny them a harmless pleasure.* ♦ **harm|less|ly** *It started harmlessly enough, with a statement from the Secretary of State for Social Security.* ADJ = safe ≠ harmful ADV: ADV with v ADJ ADV: ADV after v

**har|mon|ic** /hɑːʳmɒnɪk/ **Harmonic** means composed, played, or sung using two or more notes which sound right and pleasing together. ADJ: usu ADJ n

**har|moni|ca** /hɑːʳmɒnɪkə/ **(harmonicas)** A **harmonica** is a small musical instrument. You play the harmonica by moving it across your lips and blowing and sucking air through it. N-COUNT: oft *the* N = mouth organ

**har|mo|ni|ous** /hɑːʳmoʊniəs/ 1 A **harmonious** relationship, agreement, or discussion is friendly and peaceful. ❑ *Their harmonious relationship resulted in part from their similar goals.* ♦ **har|mo|ni|ous|ly** *To live together harmoniously as men and women is indeed an achievement.* 2 Something that is **harmonious** has parts which go well together and which are in proportion to each other. ❑ *...a harmonious balance of mind, body, and spirit.* ♦ **har|mo|ni|ous|ly** *...a pure, harmoniously proportioned face. ...stone paths that blend harmoniously with the scenery.* 3 Musical notes that are **harmonious** produce a pleasant sound when played together. ❑ *...the mysterious skill involved in producing harmonious sounds.* ADJ = amicable ADV: ADV after v ADJ ADV: ADV adj, ADV after v ADJ

**har|mo|nize** /hɑːʳmənaɪz/ **(harmonizes, harmonizing, harmonized)**

in BRIT, also use **harmonise**

1 If two or more things **harmonize with** each other, they fit in well with each other. ❑ *...slabs of pink and beige stone that harmonize with the carpet... Barbara White and her mother like to listen to music together, though their tastes don't harmonize.* 2 When governments or organizations **harmonize** laws, systems, or regulations, they agree in a friendly way to make them the same or similar. ❑ *How far will members have progressed towards harmonising their economies?* ♦ **har|mo|ni|za|tion** /hɑːʳmənaɪzeɪʃən/ *Air France pilots called a strike over the European harmonisation of their working hours.* 3 When people **harmonize**, they sing or play notes which are different from the main tune but which sound nice with it. ❑ *Bremer and Garland harmonize on the title song, 'Meet Me in St. Louis'.* V-RECIP V *with* n pl-n V VERB V n N-UNCOUNT: usu with supp VERB V

**har|mo|ny** /hɑːʳməni/ **(harmonies)** 1 If people are living **in harmony with** each other, they are living together peacefully rather than fighting or arguing. ❑ *We must try to to live in peace and harmony with ourselves and those around us.* 2 **Harmony** is the pleasant combination of different notes of music played at the same time. ❑ *...complex vocal harmonies. ...singing in harmony.* 3 The **harmony** of something is the way in which its parts are combined into a pleasant arrangement. ❑ *...the ordered harmony of the universe.* N-UNCOUNT N-VAR N-UNCOUNT

**har|ness** /hɑːʳnɪs/ **(harnesses, harnessing, harnessed)** 1 If you **harness** something such as an emotion or natural source of energy, you bring it under your control and use it. ❑ *Turkey plans to harness the waters of the Tigris and Euphrates rivers for big hydro-electric power projects.* 2 A **harness** is a set of straps which fit under a person's arms and fasten round their body in order to keep a piece of equipment in place or to prevent the person moving from a place. 3 A **harness** is a set of leather straps and metal links fastened round a horse's head or body so that the horse can have a carriage, cart, or plough fastened to it. 4 If a horse or other animal **is harnessed**, a harness is put on it, especially so that it can pull a carriage, cart, or plough. ❑ *On Sunday the horses were harnessed to a heavy wagon for a day-long ride over the Border.* VERB V n N-COUNT N-COUNT VERB: usu passive be V-ed *to* n

**harp** /hɑːʳp/ **(harps, harping, harped)** A **harp** is a large musical instrument consisting of a row of strings stretched from the top to the bottom of a frame. You play the harp by plucking the strings with your fingers. N-VAR: oft *the* N

♦ **harp on** If you say that someone **harps on** a subject, or **harps on about** it, you mean that they keep on talking about it in a way that other people find annoying. ❑ *Jones harps on this theme more than on any other... She concentrated on the good parts of her trip instead of harping on about the bad.* PHRASAL VERB V P n V P *about* n

**harp|ist** /hɑːʳpɪst/ **(harpists)** A **harpist** is someone who plays the harp. N-COUNT

**har|poon** /hɑːʳpuːn/ **(harpoons, harpooning, harpooned)** 1 A **harpoon** is a long pointed N-COUNT weapon with a long rope attached to it, which is fired or thrown by people hunting whales or large sea fish. [2] To **harpoon** a whale or large fish means to hit it with a harpoon. ❑ *Norwegian whalers said yesterday they had harpooned a female minke whale.* VERB V n

**harp|si|chord** /hɑːʳpsɪkɔːʳd/ **(harpsichords)** A **harpsichord** is an old-fashioned musical instrument rather like a small piano. When you press the keys, the strings are pulled, rather than being hit by hammers as in a piano. N-VAR: oft *the* N

**har|py** /hɑːʳpi/ **(harpies)** [1] In classical mythology, **the harpies** were creatures with the bodies of birds and the faces of women. They flew quickly and were cruel and greedy. N-COUNT: usu pl, oft *the* N [2] If you refer to a woman as a **harpy**, you mean that she is very cruel or violent. [LITERARY] ❑ *...a snobby, scheming harpy who sells off the family silverware.* N-COUNT [disapproval]

**har|ri|dan** /hærɪdən/ **(harridans)** If you call a woman a **harridan**, you mean that she is unpleasant and speaks too forcefully. [FORMAL] ❑ *She was a mean old harridan.* N-COUNT [disapproval]

**har|row** /hæroʊ/ **(harrows)** A **harrow** is a piece of farm equipment consisting of a row of blades fixed to a heavy frame. When it is pulled over ploughed land, the blades break up large lumps of soil. N-COUNT

**har|row|ing** /hæroʊɪŋ/ A **harrowing** experience is extremely upsetting or disturbing. ❑ *You've had a harrowing time this past month.* ADJ: usu ADJ n

**har|ry** /hæri/ **(harries, harrying, harried)** If someone **harries** you, they keep bothering you or trying to get something from you. ❑ *He is increasingly active in harrying the government in late-night debates.* VERB = badger, harass V n ♦ **har|ried** *...harried businessmen scurrying from one crowded office to another.* ADJ = harassed

**harsh** /hɑːʳʃ/ **(harsher, harshest)** [1] **Harsh** climates or conditions are very difficult for people, animals, and plants to live in. ❑ *The weather grew harsh, chilly and unpredictable.* ADJ = severe ≠ mild ♦ **harsh|ness** *...the harshness of their living conditions.* N-UNCOUNT = severity [2] **Harsh** actions or speech are unkind and show no understanding or sympathy. ❑ *He said many harsh and unkind things about his opponents.* ADJ = cruel ♦ **harsh|ly** *She's been told that her husband is being harshly treated in prison.* ADV: ADV with v ♦ **harsh|ness** *...treating him with great harshness.* N-UNCOUNT = severity [3] Something that is **harsh** is so hard, bright, or rough that it seems unpleasant or harmful. ❑ *Tropical colours may look rather harsh in our dull northern light.* ADJ ♦ **harsh|ness** *...as the wine ages, losing its bitter harshness.* N-UNCOUNT [4] **Harsh** voices and sounds are ones that are rough and unpleasant to listen to. ❑ *It's a pity she has such a loud harsh voice.* ADJ ≠ soft, gentle ♦ **harsh|ly** *Chris laughed harshly.* ADV: ADV with v ♦ **harsh|ness** *Then in a tone of abrupt harshness, he added, 'Open these trunks!'.* N-UNCOUNT [5] If you talk about **harsh** realities or facts, or the **harsh** truth, you are emphasizing that they are true or real, although they are unpleasant and people try to avoid thinking about them. ❑ *The harsh truth is that luck plays a big part in who will live or die.* ADJ [emphasis] = bitter

**har|vest** /hɑːʳvɪst/ **(harvests, harvesting, harvested)** [1] **The harvest** is the gathering of a crop. ❑ *There were about 300 million tons of grain in the fields at the start of the harvest.* N-SING: *the* N [2] A **harvest** is the crop that is gathered in. ❑ *Millions of people are threatened with starvation as a result of drought and poor harvests.* N-COUNT [3] When you **harvest** a crop, you gather it in. ❑ *Many farmers are refusing to harvest the cane. ...freshly harvested beetroot.* VERB V n V-ed ♦ **har|vest|ing** *...war is hampering harvesting and the distribution of food aid.* N-UNCOUNT

**har|vest|er** /hɑːʳvɪstəʳ/ **(harvesters)** [1] A **harvester** is a machine which cuts and often collects crops such as wheat, maize, or vegetables. → See also **combine harvester**. N-COUNT [2] You can refer to a person who cuts, picks, or gathers crops as a **harvester**. N-COUNT

**har|vest fes|ti|val** **(harvest festivals)** A **harvest festival** is a Christian church service held every autumn to thank God for the harvest. [mainly BRIT] N-VAR

**has**

> ✔ The auxiliary verb is pronounced /həz, STRONG hæz/. The main verb is usually pronounced /hæz/.

**Has** is the third person singular of the present tense of **have**.

**has-been** **(has-beens)** If you describe someone as a **has-been**, you are indicating in an unkind way that they were important or respected in the past, but they are not now. ❑ *...the so-called experts and various has-beens who foist opinions on us.* N-COUNT [disapproval]

**hash** /hæʃ/ [1] If you **make a hash of** a job or task, you do it very badly. [INFORMAL] ❑ *The Government made a total hash of things and squandered a fortune.* PHRASE: V inflects, PHR n/-ing [2] **Hash** is **hashish**. [INFORMAL] N-UNCOUNT

**hash browns** also **hashed browns**. **Hash browns** or **hashed browns** are potatoes that have been chopped into small pieces, formed into small cakes, and cooked on a grill or in a frying pan. N-PLURAL

**hash|ish** /hæʃiːʃ/ **Hashish** is an illegal drug made from the hemp plant which some people smoke like a cigarette to make them feel relaxed. [OLD-FASHIONED] N-UNCOUNT

**hasn't** /hæzᵊnt/ **Hasn't** is the usual spoken form of 'has not'.

**hasp** /hɑːsp hæsp/ **(hasps)** A **hasp** is a flat piece of metal with a long hole in it, fastened to the edge of a door or lid. To close the door or lid, you push the hasp over a metal loop fastened to the other part and put a lock through the loop. N-COUNT

**has|sle** /hæsᵊl/ **(hassles, hassling, hassled)** [1] A **hassle** is a situation that is difficult and involves problems, effort, or arguments with people. [INFORMAL] ❑ *I don't think it's worth the money or the hassle. ...a day spent travelling, with all the usual hassles at airport check-in.* N-VAR [2] If someone **hassles** you, they cause problems for you, often by repeatedly telling you or asking you to do something, in an annoying way. [INFORMAL] ❑ *Then my husband started hassling me.* VERB V n

**has|sock** /hæsək/ **(hassocks)** A **hassock** is a cushion for kneeling on in a church. [mainly BRIT] N-COUNT

**hast** /hæst/ **Hast** is an old-fashioned second person singular form of the verb 'have'. It is used with 'thou' which is an old-fashioned form of 'you'.

**haste** /heɪst/ [1] **Haste** is the quality of doing something quickly, sometimes too quickly so that you are careless and make mistakes. ❑ *In their haste to escape the rising water, they dropped some expensive equipment.* N-UNCOUNT [2] If you do something **in haste**, you do it quickly and hurriedly, and sometimes carelessly. ❑ *Don't act in haste or be hot-headed.* PHRASE: PHR after v

**has|ten** /heɪsᵊn/ **(hastens, hastening, hastened)** [1] If you **hasten** an event or process, often an unpleasant one, you make it happen faster or sooner. ❑ *But if he does this, he may hasten the collapse of his own country.* VERB = speed up V n [2] If you **hasten to** do something, you are quick to do it. ❑ *She more than anyone had hastened to sign the contract.* VERB V to-inf [3] If you **hasten to** say something, you quickly add something to what you have just said in order to prevent it being misunderstood. ❑ *He hastened to assure me that there was nothing traumatic to report.* VERB V to-inf

**has|ty** /heɪsti/ **(hastier, hastiest)** [1] A **hasty** movement, action, or statement is sudden, and often done in reaction to something that has just happened. ❑ *One company is giving its employees airplane tickets in the event they need to make a hasty escape.* ADJ: usu ADJ n = swift, quick ♦ **hasti|ly** /heɪstɪli/ *'It may be satisfying, but it's not fun.' 'No, I'm sure it's not,' said Virginia hastily. 'I didn't mean that.'* ADV: ADV with v = swiftly [2] A **hasty** event or action is one that is completed more quickly than normal. ❑ *After the hasty meal, the men had moved forward to take up their positions.* ADJ: usu ADJ n = quick, hurried ♦ **hasti|ly** *He said* ADV:

*good night hastily, promising that he would phone Hans in the morning.* ADV with v = hurriedly [3] If you describe a person or their behaviour as **hasty**, you mean that they are acting too quickly, without thinking carefully, for example because they are angry. ADJ disapproval = rash ❑ *A number of the United States' allies had urged him not to take a hasty decision.* ♦ **hasti|ly** *I decided that nothing should be done hastily, that things had to be sorted out carefully.* ADV: ADV with v

**hat** /hæt/ **(hats)** [1] A **hat** is a head covering, often with a brim round it, which is usually worn out of doors to give protection from the weather. ◆◇◇ N-COUNT [2] If you say that someone is wearing a particular **hat**, you mean that they are performing a particular role at that time. If you say that they wear several **hats**, you mean that they have several roles or jobs. N-COUNT: with supp ❑ *...putting on my nationalistic hat. ...various problems, including too many people wearing too many hats.*

**PHRASES** [3] If you say that you are ready to do something **at the drop of a hat**, you mean that you are willing to do it immediately, without hesitating. PHRASE: PHR after v ❑ *India is one part of the world I would go to at the drop of a hat.* [4] If you tell someone to **keep** a piece of information **under** their **hat**, you are asking them not to tell anyone else about it. PHRASE: V inflects ❑ *Look, if I tell you something, will you promise to keep it under your hat?* [5] If you say that something or someone is **old hat**, you mean that they have existed or been known for a long time, and they have become uninteresting and boring. PHRASE: v-link PHR ❑ *The younger generation tell me that religion is 'old hat' and science has proved this.* [6] In British English, if you **pass the hat around**, you collect money from a group of people, for example in order to give someone a present. In American English, you just say **pass the hat**. PHRASE: V inflects ❑ *Professors are passing the hat to help staff in their department.* [7] If you say that you **take** your **hat off to** someone, you mean that you admire them for something that they have done. PHRASE: V inflects, PHR n approval ❑ *I take my hat off to Mr Clarke for taking this action.* [8] To **pull** something **out of the hat** means to do something unexpected which helps you to succeed, often when you are failing. PHRASE: V inflects ❑ *Southampton had somehow managed to pull another Cup victory out of the hat.* [9] In competitions, if you say that the winners will be drawn or picked **out of the hat**, you mean that they will be chosen randomly, so everyone has an equal chance of winning. PHRASE: PHR after v ❑ *The first 10 correct entries drawn out of the hat will win a pair of tickets, worth £20 each.* [10] to **knock** something **into a cocked hat** → see **cocked hat**.

**hat|box** /hætbɒks/ **(hatboxes)** A **hatbox** is a cylindrical box in which a hat can be carried and stored. N-COUNT

**hatch** /hætʃ/ **(hatches, hatching, hatched)** [1] When a baby bird, insect, or other animal **hatches**, or when it **is hatched**, it comes out of its egg by breaking the shell. VERB ❑ *As soon as the two chicks hatch, they leave the nest burrow... The young disappeared soon after they were hatched.* V, be V-ed [2] When an egg **hatches** or when a bird, insect, or other animal **hatches** an egg, the egg breaks open and a baby comes out. VERB ❑ *The eggs hatch after a week or ten days... During these periods the birds will lie on the cage floor as if trying to lay or hatch eggs.* V, V n [3] If you **hatch** a plot or a scheme, you think of it and work it out. VERB ❑ *He has accused opposition parties of hatching a plot to assassinate the Pope.* V n [4] A **hatch** is an opening in the deck of a ship, through which people or cargo can go. You can also refer to the door of this opening as a **hatch**. N-COUNT ❑ *He stuck his head up through the hatch.* [5] A **hatch** is an opening in a ceiling or a wall, especially between a kitchen and a dining room, which you can pass something such as food through. [mainly BRIT] N-COUNT [6] If someone **battens down the hatches**, they prepare themselves so that they will be able to survive a coming difficulty or crisis. PHRASE: V inflects ❑ *Many firms are battening down the hatches and preparing to ride out the storm.*

**hatch|back** /hætʃbæk/ **(hatchbacks)** A **hatchback** is a car with an extra door at the back which opens upwards. N-COUNT

**hatch|ery** /hætʃəri/ **(hatcheries)** A **hatchery** is a place where people control the hatching of eggs, especially fish eggs. N-COUNT

**hatch|et** /hætʃɪt/ **(hatchets)** [1] A **hatchet** is a small axe that you can hold in one hand. N-COUNT [2] If two people **bury the hatchet**, they become friendly again after a quarrel or disagreement. PHRASE: V inflects

**hatch|et job (hatchet jobs)** To do a **hatchet job on** someone or something means to say or write something mentioning many bad things about them, which harms their reputation. [INFORMAL] N-COUNT: usu sing, oft N on n ❑ *Unfortunately, his idea of bold journalism was a hatchet job, portraying the staff in a negative light.*

**hatch|et man (hatchet men)** You can refer to someone who makes changes in an organization by getting rid of lots of people as a **hatchet man**, especially if you think they do so in an unnecessarily harsh way. [INFORMAL] N-COUNT disapproval

**hatch|way** /hætʃweɪ/ **(hatchways)** A **hatchway** is the same as a hatch. N-COUNT

**hate** /heɪt/ **(hates, hating, hated)** [1] If you **hate** someone or something, you have an extremely strong feeling of dislike for them. ◆◇◇ VERB = detest, loathe ≠ love ❑ *Most people hate him, but they don't dare to say so, because he still rules the country.* V n ♦ **Hate** is also a noun. N-UNCOUNT = hatred ❑ *I was 17 and filled with a lot of hate.* ♦ **hat|ed** *He's probably the most hated man in this county.* ADJ: ADJ n = detested [2] If you say that you **hate** something such as a particular activity, you mean that you find it very unpleasant. VERB: no cont = dislike ≠ love, like ❑ *Ted hated parties, even gatherings of people he liked individually... He hates to be interrupted during training... He hated coming home to the empty house... I hate it when people accuse us of that... I would hate him to think I'm trying to trap him... She hates me having any fun and is quite jealous and spoiled.* V n, V to-inf, V -ing, V it wh, V n to-inf, V n -ing [3] You can use **hate** in expressions such as **'I hate to trouble you'** or **'I hate to bother you'** when you are apologizing to someone for interrupting them or asking them to do something. VERB: no cont politeness ❑ *I hate to rush you but I have another appointment later on.* V to-inf [4] You can use **hate** in expressions such as **'I hate to say it'** or **'I hate to tell you'** when you want to express regret about what you are about to say, because you think it is unpleasant or should not be the case. VERB: no cont feelings ❑ *I hate to admit it, but you were right.* V to-inf [5] to **hate** someone's **guts** → see **gut**. [6] You can use **hate** in expressions such as **'I hate to see'** or **'I hate to think'** when you are emphasizing that you find a situation or an idea unpleasant. VERB: no cont emphasis ❑ *I just hate to see you doing this to yourself.* V to-inf [7] You can use **hate** in expressions such as **'I'd hate to think'** when you hope that something is not true or that something will not happen. VERB: no cont ❑ *I'd hate to think my job would not be secure if I left it temporarily.* V to-inf

**hate cam|paign (hate campaigns)** A **hate campaign** is a series of actions which are intended to harm or upset someone, or to make other people have a low opinion of them. N-COUNT: usu sing ❑ *The media has waged a virulent hate campaign against her.*

**hate crime (hate crimes)** A **hate crime** is a crime, especially against people such as homosexuals and members of ethnic minorities, that is motivated by feelings of hatred. N-COUNT

**hate|ful** /heɪtfʊl/ [1] Someone or something that is **hateful** is extremely bad or unpleasant. [OLD-FASHIONED] ADJ = horrid ❑ *I'm sorry. That was a hateful thing to say.* [2] Someone who is **hateful** hates someone else. ADJ ❑ *These are not necessarily hateful, malicious people.*

**hate mail** also **hate-mail.** If someone receives **hate mail**, they receive unpleasant or threatening letters. N-UNCOUNT

**hat|er** /heɪtəʳ/ **(haters)** If you call someone a **hater of** something, you mean that they strongly N-COUNT: N of n dislike that thing. ❑ *Braccio was a hater of idleness.* ♦ **Hater** is also a combining form. ❑ *He was reputed to be a woman-hater.* [COMB in N-COUNT]

**hath** /hæθ/ **Hath** is an old-fashioned third person singular form of the verb 'have'.

**hat|pin** /hætpɪn/ **(hatpins)** A **hatpin** is a metal pin which can be pushed through a woman's hat and through her hair to keep the hat in position. [N-COUNT]

**ha|tred** /heɪtrɪd/ **(hatreds)** **Hatred** is an extremely strong feeling of dislike for someone or something. ❑ *Her hatred of them would never lead her to murder.* [N-UNCOUNT: also N in pl, oft N *of/for* n = hate ≠ love]

**hat-trick** **(hat-tricks)** A **hat-trick** is a series of three achievements, especially in a sports event, for example three goals scored by the same person in a football game. [N-COUNT]

**haugh|ty** /hɔːti/ You use **haughty** to describe someone's behaviour or appearance when you disapprove of the fact that they seem to be very proud and to think that they are better than other people. ❑ *He spoke in a haughty tone.* [ADJ: usu ADJ n] [disapproval] ♦ **haugh|ti|ly** /hɔːtɪli/ *Toni looked at him rather haughtily.* [ADV: usu ADV with v, also ADV adj]

**haul** /hɔːl/ **(hauls, hauling, hauled)** 1 If you **haul** something which is heavy or difficult to move, you move it using a lot of effort. ❑ *A crane had to be used to haul the car out of the stream... She hauled up her bedroom window and leaned out.* [VERB] [V n prep/adv] [V adv n] 2 If someone **is hauled before** a court or someone in authority, they are made to appear before them because they are accused of having done something wrong. ❑ *He was hauled before the managing director and fired.* [VERB: usu passive] [*be* V-ed *before* n] ♦ **Haul up** means the same as **haul**. ❑ *He was hauled up before the Board of Trustees.* [PHRASAL VERB: usu passive] 3 A **haul** is a quantity of things that are stolen, or a quantity of stolen or illegal goods found by police or customs. ❑ *The size of the drugs haul shows that the international trade in heroin is still flourishing.* [N-COUNT: with supp] 4 If you say that a task or a journey is a **long haul**, you mean that it takes a long time and a lot of effort. ❑ *Revitalising the Romanian economy will be a long haul.* → See also **long-haul**. [PHRASE]

**haul|age** /hɔːlɪdʒ/ **Haulage** is the business of transporting goods by road. [mainly BRIT] ❑ *The haulage company was a carrier of machine parts to Turkey.* [N-UNCOUNT: usu with supp]

**haul|er** /hɔːləʳ/ **(haulers)** A **hauler** is the same as a **haulier**. [AM] [N-COUNT]

**haul|ier** /hɔːliəʳ/ **(hauliers)** A **haulier** is a company or a person that transports goods by road. [BRIT] [N-COUNT]

✓ in AM, use **hauler**

**haunch** /hɔːntʃ/ **(haunches)** 1 If you get down **on** your **haunches**, you lower yourself towards the ground so that your legs are bent under you and you are balancing on your feet. ❑ *Edgar squatted on his haunches.* [PHRASE: v PHR] 2 The **haunches** of an animal or person are the area of the body which includes the bottom, the hips, and the tops of the legs. [N-COUNT: usu pl]

**haunt** /hɔːnt/ **(haunts, haunting, haunted)** 1 If something unpleasant **haunts** you, you keep thinking or worrying about it over a long period of time. ❑ *The decision to leave her children now haunts her.* [VERB] [V n] 2 Something that **haunts** a person or organization regularly causes them problems over a long period of time. ❑ *The stigma of being a bankrupt is likely to haunt him for the rest of his life.* [VERB] [V n] 3 A place that is the **haunt** of a particular person is one which they often visit because they enjoy going there. ❑ *The Channel Islands are a favourite summer haunt for UK and French yachtsmen alike.* [N-COUNT: with supp] 4 A ghost or spirit that **haunts** a place or a person regularly appears in the place, or is seen by the person and frightens them. ❑ *His ghost is said to haunt some of the rooms, banging a toy drum.* [VERB] [V n]

**haunt|ed** /hɔːntɪd/ 1 A **haunted** building or other place is one where a ghost regularly appears. ❑ *Tracy said the cabin was haunted. ...a haunted house.* [ADJ] 2 Someone who has a **haunted** expression looks very worried or troubled. ❑ *She looked so haunted, I almost didn't recognize her.* [ADJ]

**haunt|ing** /hɔːntɪŋ/ **Haunting** sounds, images, or words remain in your thoughts because they are very beautiful or sad. ❑ *...the haunting calls of wild birds in the mahogany trees.* [ADJ: usu ADJ n] ♦ **haunt|ing|ly** *Each one of these ancient towns is hauntingly beautiful.* [ADV: usu ADV adj]

**haute cou|ture** /oʊt kuːtjʊəʳ/ **Haute couture** refers to the designing and making of high-quality fashion clothes, or to the clothes themselves. [FORMAL] [N-UNCOUNT]

**hau|teur** /oʊtɜːʳ, AM hoʊtʊr/ You can use **hauteur** to describe behaviour which you think is proud and arrogant. [FORMAL] ❑ *Once, she had been put off by his hauteur.* [N-UNCOUNT] [disapproval]

**have**

① AUXILIARY VERB USES
② USED WITH NOUNS DESCRIBING ACTIONS
③ OTHER VERB USES AND PHRASES
④ MODAL PHRASES

**①have** /həv, STRONG hæv/ **(has, having, had)** ◆◆◆

In spoken English, forms of **have** are often shortened, for example **I have** is shortened to **I've** and **has not** is shortened to **hasn't**.

1 You use the forms **have** and **has** with a past participle to form the present perfect tense of verbs. ❑ *Alex has already gone... My term hasn't finished yet... What have you found so far?... Frankie hasn't been feeling well for a long time.* [AUX] [AUX -ed] [AUX *been* -ing] 2 You use the form **had** with a past participle to form the past perfect tense of verbs. ❑ *When I met her, she had just returned from a job interview.* [AUX] [AUX -ed] 3 **Have** is used in question tags. ❑ *You haven't sent her away, have you?* [AUX] [cl AUX n] 4 You use **have** when you are confirming or contradicting a statement containing 'have', 'has', or 'had', or answering a question. ❑ *'Have you been to York before?' — 'Yes we have.'* [AUX] [AUX] 5 The form **having** with a past participle can be used to introduce a clause in which you mention an action which had already happened before another action began. ❑ *He arrived in San Francisco, having left New Jersey on January 19th.* [AUX] [AUX -ed]

**②have** /hæv/ **(has, having, had)** ◆◆◆

**Have** is used in combination with a wide range of nouns, where the meaning of the combination is mostly given by the noun.

1 You can use **have** followed by a noun to talk about an action or event, when it would be possible to use the same word as a verb. For example, you can say **'I had a look at the photos'** instead of 'I looked at the photos.' ❑ *I went out and had a walk around... She rested for a while, then had a wash and changed her clothes... I'll have a think about that.* [VERB: no passive] [V n] [V n] [V n] 2 In normal spoken or written English, people use **have** with a wide range of nouns to talk about actions and events, often instead of a more specific verb. For example people are more likely to say **'we had ice cream'** or **'he's had a shock'** than 'we ate ice cream', or 'he's suffered a shock'. ❑ *Come and have a meal with us tonight... She had an operation on her knee at the clinic... His visit had a great effect on them.* [VERB: no passive] [V n] [V n] [V n]

**③have** /hæv/ **(has, having, had)** ◆◆◆

For meanings 1-4, people often use **have got** in spoken British English or **have gotten** in spoken American English, instead of **have**. In this case, **have** is pronounced as an auxiliary verb. For more information and examples of the use of 'have got' and 'have gotten', see **got**.

⇒ Please look at category 19 to see if the expression you are looking for is shown under another headword. [1] You use **have** to say that someone or something owns a particular thing, or when you are mentioning one of their qualities or characteristics. ❑ *Oscar had a new bicycle... I want to have my own business... You have beautiful eyes... Do you have any brothers and sisters?... I have no doubt at all in my own mind about this... Have you any valuables anywhere else in the house?* [2] If you **have** something **to** do, you are responsible for doing it or must do it. ❑ *He had plenty of work to do... I have some important calls to make.* [3] You can use **have** instead of 'there is' to say that something exists or happens. For example, you can say **'you have no alternative'** instead of 'there is no alternative', or **'he had a good view from his window'** instead of 'there was a good view from his window'. ❑ *He had two tenants living with him... We haven't any shops on the island.* [4] If you **have** something such as a part of your body in a particular position or state, it is in that position or state. ❑ *Mary had her eyes closed... As I was working, I had the radio on... He had his hand on Maria's shoulder.* [5] If you **have** something done, someone does it for you or you arrange for it to be done. ❑ *I had your rooms cleaned and aired... You've had your hair cut, it looks great.* [6] If someone **has** something unpleasant happen to them, it happens to them. ❑ *We had our money stolen... The dance hall once even had its roof blown off in World War II.* [7] If you **have** someone do something, you persuade, cause, or order them to do it. ❑ *The bridge is not as impressive as some guides would have you believe... Mr Gower had had us all working so hard.* [8] If someone **has** you **by** a part of your body, they are holding you there and they are trying to hurt you or force you to go somewhere. ❑ *When the police came, Larry had him by the ear and was beating his head against the pavement.* [9] If you **have** something from someone, they give it to you. ❑ *You can have my ticket... I had comments from people in all age groups.* [10] If you **have** an illness or disability, you suffer from it. ❑ *I had a headache... He might be having a heart attack.* [11] If a woman **has** a baby, she gives birth to it. If she **is having** a baby, she is pregnant. ❑ *My wife has just had a baby boy.* [12] You can use **have** in expressions such as **'I won't have it'** or **'I'm not having that'**, to mean that you will not allow or put up with something. ❑ *I'm not having any of that nonsense... I will not have the likes of you dragging down my reputation.*

VERB: no passive; V n; V n adv/prep; VERB: no passive; V n to-inf; V n to-inf; VERB: no passive; V n; V n; VERB: no passive; V n adj/adv/prep; VERB: no passive; V n -ed; VERB: no passive; V n -ed; VERB: no passive; V n inf; V n -ing; VERB: no passive; V n *by* n; VERB: no passive; V n; V n; VERB: no passive; V n; V n; VERB: no passive; V n; VERB: with neg; V n; V n -ing

**PHRASES** [13] You can use **has it** in expressions such as **'rumour has it that'** or **'as legend has it'** when you are quoting something that you have heard, but you do not necessarily think it is true. ❑ *Rumour has it that tickets were being sold for £300.* [14] If someone **has it in for** you, they do not like you and they want to make life difficult for you. [INFORMAL] ❑ *He's always had it in for the Dawkins family.* [15] If you **have it in** you, you have abilities and skills which you do not usually use and which only show themselves in a difficult situation. ❑ *'You were brilliant!' he said. 'I didn't know you had it in you.'* [16] To **have it off with** someone or **have it away with** someone means to have sex with them. [BRIT, INFORMAL, RUDE] [17] If you **are having** someone **on**, you are pretending that something is true when it is not true, for example as a joke or in order to tease them. [BRIT, INFORMAL] ❑ *Malone's eyes widened. 'You're having me on, Liam.'* [18] If you **have it out** or **have things out with** someone, you discuss a problem or disagreement very openly with them, even if it means having an argument, because you think this is the best way to solve the problem. ❑ *Why not have it out with your critic, discuss the whole thing face to face?* [19] to **be had** → see **had**. to **have had it** → see **had**.

PHRASE: V inflects, oft PHR that [vagueness]; PHRASE: V inflects, PHR n; PHRASE: V inflects, PHR pron, oft PHR pron to-inf; PHRASE: V inflects, PHR *with* n, pl-n V; PHRASE: *be* inflects; PHRASE: V inflects, oft PHR *with* n

④ **have** /hæv, hæf/ **(has, having, had)** [1] You use **have to** when you are saying that something is necessary or required, or must happen. If you do not **have to** do something, it is not necessary or required. ❑ *He had to go to Germany... They didn't have to pay tax.* [2] You can use **have to** in order to say that you feel certain that something is true or will happen. ❑ *There has to be some kind of way out.*

◆◆◆ PHRASE = must; PHRASE = must

**ha|ven** /heɪvᵊn/ **(havens)** A **haven** is a place where people or animals feel safe, secure, and happy. ❑ *...Lake Baringo, a freshwater haven for a mixed variety of birds.* → See also **safe haven**.

N-COUNT: oft N *for/of* n = refuge

**have-nots** If you refer to two groups of people as **haves and have-nots**, you mean that the first group are very wealthy and the second group are very poor. You can also refer generally to poor people as **have-nots**.

PHRASE

**haven't** /hævᵊnt/ **Haven't** is the usual spoken form of 'have not'.

**hav|er|sack** /hævəʳsæk/ **(haversacks)** A **haversack** is a canvas bag that is usually worn over one shoulder. [mainly BRIT]

N-COUNT

**haves** /hævz/ **haves and have-nots** → see **have-nots**.

**hav|oc** /hævək/ [1] **Havoc** is great disorder, and confusion. ❑ *Rioters caused havoc in the centre of the town.* [2] If one thing **plays havoc with** another or **wreaks havoc on** it, it prevents it from continuing or functioning as normal, or damages it. ❑ *The weather played havoc with airline schedules.*

N-UNCOUNT; PHRASE: V inflects, PHR n

**haw** /hɔː/ **(haws, hawing, hawed)** [1] **Haws** are the red berries produced by hawthorn trees in autumn. [2] Writers sometimes use **'haw haw'** to show that one of their characters is laughing, especially in a rather unpleasant or superior way. ❑ *Look at the plebs! Getting all muddy! Haw haw haw!* [3] If you **hem and haw**, or in British English **hum and haw**, you take a long time to say something because you cannot think of the right words, or because you are not sure what to say. ❑ *Tim hemmed and hawed, but finally told his boss the truth.*

N-COUNT; EXCLAM; PHRASE: Vs inflect

**hawk** /hɔːk/ **(hawks, hawking, hawked)** [1] A **hawk** is a large bird with a short, hooked beak, sharp claws, and very good eyesight. Hawks catch and eat small birds and animals. [2] In politics, if you refer to someone as a **hawk**, you mean that they believe in using force and violence to achieve something, rather than using more peaceful or diplomatic methods. Compare **dove**. ❑ *Both hawks and doves have expanded their conditions for ending the war.* [3] If someone **hawks** goods, they sell them by walking through the streets or knocking at people's houses, and asking people to buy them. [OLD-FASHIONED] ❑ *...vendors hawking trinkets.* [4] You can say that someone **is hawking** something if you do not like the forceful way in which they are asking people to buy it. ❑ *Developers will be hawking cut-price flats and houses.* [5] If you **watch** someone **like a hawk**, you observe them very carefully, usually to make sure that they do not make a mistake or do something you do not want them to do.

N-COUNT; N-COUNT ≠ dove; VERB = peddle; V n; VERB [disapproval]; V n; PHRASE: V inflects

**hawk|er** /hɔːkəʳ/ **(hawkers)** You can use **hawker** to refer to a person who tries to sell things by calling at people's homes or standing in the street, especially when you do not approve of this activity.

N-COUNT [disapproval]

**hawk|ish** /hɔːkɪʃ/ Journalists use **hawkish** to describe politicians or governments who are in favour of using force to achieve something, rather than using peaceful and diplomatic methods. ❑ *He is one of the most hawkish members of the new cabinet.*

ADJ ≠ dovish

**haws|er** /hɔːzəʳ/ **(hawsers)** A **hawser** is a large heavy rope, especially one used on a ship.

N-COUNT

**haw|thorn** /hɔːθɔːʳn/ **(hawthorns)** A **hawthorn** is a small tree which has sharp thorns and produces white or pink flowers.

N-VAR

**hay** /heɪ/ [1] **Hay** is grass which has been cut and dried so that it can be used to feed animals. ❑ *...bales of hay.* N-UNCOUNT [2] If you say that someone **is making hay** or **is making hay while the sun shines**, you mean that they are taking advantage of a situation that is favourable to them while they have the chance to. ❑ *We knew that war was coming, and were determined to make hay while we could.* PHRASE: V inflects

**hay fe|ver** If someone is suffering from **hay fever**, they sneeze and their eyes itch, because they are allergic to grass or flowers. N-UNCOUNT

**hay|stack** /heɪstæk/ **(haystacks)** [1] A **haystack** is a large, solid pile of hay, often covered with a straw roof to protect it, which is left in the field until it is needed. N-COUNT [2] If you are trying to find something and say that it is like looking for **a needle in a haystack**, you mean that you are very unlikely indeed to find it. PHRASE

**hay|wire** /heɪwaɪəʳ/ If something goes **haywire**, it goes out of control or starts doing the wrong thing. [INFORMAL] ❑ *Many Americans think their legal system has gone haywire.* ADJ: v-link ADJ

**haz|ard** /hæzəʳd/ **(hazards, hazarding, hazarded)** [1] A **hazard** is something which could be dangerous to you, your health or safety, or your plans or reputation. ❑ *A new report suggests that chewing-gum may be a health hazard.* N-COUNT: oft N *to/for* n, N *of* n [2] If you **hazard** someone or something, you put them into a situation which might be dangerous for them. [mainly WRITTEN] ❑ *He could not believe that, had the Englishman known how much he was at risk, he would have hazarded his grandson.* VERB V n [3] If you **hazard** or if you **hazard a guess**, you make a suggestion about something which is only a guess and which you know might be wrong. ❑ *I would hazard a guess that they'll do fairly well in the next election.* VERB V n

**haz|ard|ous** /hæzəʳdəs/ Something that is **hazardous** is dangerous, especially to people's health or safety. ❑ *They have no way to dispose of the hazardous waste they produce.* ADJ = dangerous ≠ safe

**haze** /heɪz/ **(hazes)** [1] **Haze** is light mist, caused by particles of water or dust in the air, which prevents you from seeing distant objects clearly. Haze often forms in hot weather. ❑ *They vanished into the haze near the horizon.* N-VAR [2] If there is a **haze of** something such as smoke or steam, you cannot see clearly through it. [LITERARY] ❑ *Dan smiled at him through a haze of smoke and steaming coffee.* N-SING: usu N *of* n

**ha|zel** /heɪzəl/ **(hazels)** [1] A **hazel** is a small tree which produces nuts that you can eat. N-VAR [2] **Hazel** eyes are greenish-brown in colour. COLOUR

**hazel|nut** /heɪzəlnʌt/ **(hazelnuts)** **Hazelnuts** are nuts from a hazel tree, which can be eaten. N-COUNT

**hazy** /heɪzi/ **(hazier, haziest)** [1] **Hazy** weather conditions are those in which things are difficult to see, because of light mist, hot air, or dust. ❑ *The air was thin and crisp, filled with hazy sunshine and frost.* ADJ ≠ clear [2] If you are **hazy about** ideas or details, or if they are **hazy**, you are uncertain or confused about them. ❑ *I'm a bit hazy about that... I have only a hazy memory of what he was really like.* ADJ ≠ clear [3] If things seem **hazy**, you cannot see things clearly, for example because you are feeling ill. ❑ *My vision has grown so hazy.* ADJ

**H-bomb** **(H-bombs)** An **H-bomb** is a bomb in which energy is released from hydrogen atoms. N-COUNT

**he** /hi, STRONG hiː/ ◆◆◆

> **He** is a third person singular pronoun. **He** is used as the subject of a verb.

[1] You use **he** to refer to a man, boy, or male animal. ❑ *He could never quite remember all our names... Our dog Rex did all sorts of tricks. I cried when he died.* PRON [2] In written English, **he** is sometimes used to refer to a person without saying whether that person is a man or a woman. Some people dislike this use and prefer to use 'he or she' or 'they'. ❑ *The teacher should encourage the child to proceed as far as he can, and when he is stuck, ask for help.* PRON

**H.E.** **H.E.** is a written abbreviation for **His Excellency** or **Her Excellency** and is used in the title of an important official such as an ambassador. ❑ *...H.E. the Italian Ambassador.* N-TITLE

**head** /hed/ **(heads, heading, headed)** ◆◆◆

> **Head** is used in a large number of expressions which are explained under other words in the dictionary. For example, the expression 'off the top of your head' is explained at 'top'.

[1] Your **head** is the top part of your body, which has your eyes, mouth, and brain in it. ❑ *She turned her head away from him... He took a puff on his pipe and shook his head.* N-COUNT [2] You can use **head** to refer to your mind and your mental abilities. ❑ *...an exceptional analyst who could do complex maths in his head.* N-COUNT [3] The **head of** a line of people or vehicles is the front of it, or the first person or vehicle in the line. ❑ *...the head of the queue.* N-SING: with supp [4] If someone or something **heads** a line or procession, they are at the front of it. ❑ *The parson, heading the procession, had just turned right towards the churchyard.* VERB V n [5] If something **heads** a list or group, it is at the top of it. ❑ *Running a business heads the list of ambitions among the 1,000 people interviewed by Good Housekeeping magazine.* VERB V n [6] The **head** of something is the highest or top part of it. ❑ *...the head of the stairs... Every day a different name was placed at the head of the chart.* N-SING: usu N *of* n = top [7] The **head** of something long and thin is the end which is wider than or a different shape from the rest, and which is often considered to be the most important part. ➔ See picture on page 1709. ❑ *Keep the head of the club the same height throughout the swing.* N-COUNT: usu with supp [8] The **head** of a school is the teacher who is in charge. [mainly BRIT] N-COUNT [9] The **head** of a company or organization is the person in charge of it and in charge of the people in it. ❑ *Heads of government from more than 100 countries gather in Geneva tomorrow. ...the head waiter.* N-COUNT: with supp [10] If you **head** a department, company, or organization, you are the person in charge of it. ❑ *...Michael Williams, who heads the department's Office of Civil Rights. ...the ruling Socialist Party, headed by Dr Franz Vranitzky.* VERB V n V-ed [11] The **head** on a glass of beer is the layer of small bubbles that form on the top of the beer. N-COUNT: usu sing [12] If you have a bad **head**, you have a headache. [BRIT, INFORMAL] ❑ *I had a terrible head and was extraordinarily drunk.* N-COUNT: usu sing, with supp [13] If you toss a coin and it comes down **heads**, you can see the side of the coin which has a picture of a head on it. ❑ *'We might toss up for it,' suggested Ted. 'If it's heads, then we'll talk.'... Heads or tails?* ADV: *be* ADV, ADV after v [14] If you **are heading** for a particular place, you are going towards that place. In American English, you can also say that you **are headed** for a particular place. ❑ *He headed for the bus stop... It is not clear how many of them will be heading back to Saudi Arabia tomorrow... She and her child boarded a plane headed to where her family lived.* VERB V *for* n V adv/prep V-ed [15] If something or someone **is heading for** a particular result, the situation they are in is developing in a way that makes that result very likely. In American English, you can also say that something or someone **is headed for** a particular result. ❑ *The latest talks aimed at ending the civil war appear to be heading for deadlock... The centuries-old ritual seems headed for extinction.* VERB V *for/towards* n V-ed [16] If a piece of writing **is headed** a particular title, it has that title written at the beginning of it. ❑ *One chapter is headed, 'Beating the Test'.* VERB: usu passive *be* V-ed quote [17] If you **head** a ball in football, you hit it with your head in order to make it go in a particular direction. ❑ *He headed the ball across the face of the goal.* VERB V n prep/adv [18] ➔ See also **heading**.

PHRASES [19] You use **a head** or **per head** after stating a cost or amount in order to indicate that that cost or amount is for each person in a par- PHRASE: amount PHR ticular group. ❑ *This simple chicken dish costs less than £1 a head.* [20] **From head to foot** means all over your body. ❑ *Colin had been put into a bath and been scrubbed from head to foot.* [21] If you have **a head for** something, you can deal with it easily. For example, if you have **a head for figures**, you can do arithmetic easily, and if you have **a head for heights**, you can climb to a great height without feeling afraid. ❑ *I don't have a head for business.* [22] If you **get** a fact or idea **into** your **head**, you suddenly realize or think that it is true and you usually do not change your opinion about it. ❑ *Once they get an idea into their heads, they never give up.* [23] If you say that someone has **got** something **into** their **head**, you mean that they have finally understood or accepted it, and you are usually criticizing them because it has taken them a long time to do this. ❑ *Managers have at last got it into their heads that they can no longer accept inefficient operations.* [24] If alcoholic drink **goes to** your **head**, it makes you feel drunk. ❑ *That wine was strong, it went to your head.* [25] If you say that something such as praise or success **goes to** someone's **head**, you are criticizing them because you think that it makes them too proud or confident. ❑ *Ford is definitely not a man to let a little success go to his head.* [26] If you are **head over heels** or **head over heels in love**, you are very much in love. [27] If you **keep** your **head**, you remain calm in a difficult situation. If you **lose** your **head**, you panic or do not remain calm in a difficult situation. ❑ *She was able to keep her head and not panic... She lost her head and started screaming at me.* [28] If you **knock** something **on the head**, you stop it. [BRIT, INFORMAL] ❑ *When we stop enjoying ourselves we'll knock it on the head.* [29] Phrases such as **laugh** your **head off** and **scream** your **head off** can be used to emphasize that someone is laughing or screaming a lot or very loudly. ❑ *He carried on telling a joke, laughing his head off.* [30] If you say that someone is **off** their **head**, you think that their ideas or behaviour are very strange, foolish, or dangerous. [mainly BRIT, INFORMAL] ❑ *He's gone completely off his head.* [31] If you **stand** an idea or argument **on its head** or **turn** it **on its head**, you think about it or treat it in a completely new and different way. ❑ *Their relationship turned the standard notion of marriage on its head.* [32] If something such as an idea, joke, or comment goes **over** someone's **head**, it is too difficult for them to understand. ❑ *I admit that a lot of the ideas went way over my head.* [33] If someone does something **over** another person's **head**, they do it without asking them or discussing it with them, especially when they should do so because the other person is in a position of authority. ❑ *He was reprimanded for trying to go over the heads of senior officers.* [34] If you say that something unpleasant or embarrassing **rears its ugly head** or **raises its ugly head**, you mean that it occurs, often after not occurring for some time. ❑ *There was a problem which reared its ugly head about a week after she moved back in.* [35] If you **stand on** your **head**, you balance upside down with the top of your head and your hands on the ground. [36] If you say that you cannot **make head nor tail of** something or you cannot **make head or tail of** it, you are emphasizing that you cannot understand it at all. [INFORMAL] ❑ *I couldn't make head nor tail of the damn film.* [37] If somebody **takes it into** their **head to** do something, especially something strange or foolish, they suddenly decide to do it. ❑ *He suddenly took it into his head to go out to Australia to stay with his son.* [38] If a problem or disagreement **comes to a head** or **is brought to a head**, it becomes so bad that something must be done about it. ❑ *These problems came to a head in September when five of the station's journalists were sacked.* [39] If two or more people **put** their **heads together**, they talk about a problem they have and try to solve it. ❑ *So everyone put their heads together and eventually an amicable arrangement was reached.* [40] If you **keep** your **head above water**, you just avoid getting into difficulties; used especially to talk about business. ❑ *We are keeping our head above water, but our cash flow position is not too good.* [41] If you say that **heads will roll** as a result of something bad that has happened, you mean that people will be punished for it, especially by losing their jobs. ❑ *The group's problems have led to speculation that heads will roll.*

PHRASE: oft *be* V-ed PHR [emphasis]
PHRASE: *have/with* PHR, PHR n
PHRASE: V and N inflect
PHRASE: V and N inflect
PHRASE: V and N inflect
PHRASE: V and N inflect [disapproval]
PHRASE: v PHR, v-link PHR
PHRASE: V and N inflect
PHRASE: V inflects
PHRASE: N inflects [emphasis]
PHRASE: N inflects, usu v-link PHR [disapproval]
PHRASE: V inflects
PHRASE: v-link PHR, PHR after v
PHRASE: v-link PHR, PHR after v
PHRASE: V inflects
PHRASE: V and N inflect
PHRASE: usu with brd-neg, V inflects, PHR n
PHRASE: V and N inflect, usu PHR to-inf
PHRASE: V inflects
PHRASE: V inflects
PHRASE: V inflects
PHRASE: V inflects

♦ **head off** [1] If you **head off** a person, animal, or vehicle, you move to a place in front of them in order to capture them or make them change the direction they are moving in. ❑ *He changed direction swiftly, turned into the hallway and headed her off.* [2] If you **head** something **off**, especially something unpleasant, you take action before it is expected to happen in order to prevent it from happening. ❑ *He would ask Congress to intervene and head off a strike... You have to be good at spotting trouble on the way and heading it off.*

PHRASAL VERB
V n P
Also V P n (not pron)
PHRASAL VERB
V P n (not pron)
V n P

♦ **head up** The person who **heads up** a group, organization, or activity is the leader of it. ❑ *Judge Frederick Lacey headed up the investigation... We asked ourselves what we wanted from our management structure and who we wanted to head it up.*

PHRASAL VERB
V P n (not pron)
V n P

**head|ache** /hedeɪk/ **(headaches)** [1] If you have a **headache**, you have a pain in your head. ❑ *I have had a terrible headache for the last two days.* [2] If you say that something is a **headache**, you mean that it causes you difficulty or worry. ❑ *The airline's biggest headache is the increase in the price of aviation fuel.*

N-COUNT
N-COUNT = *problem*

**head|band** /hedbænd/ **(headbands)** also **head band.** A **headband** is a narrow strip of material which you can wear around your head across your forehead, for example to keep hair or sweat out of your eyes.

N-COUNT

**head|board** /hedbɔːʳd/ **(headboards)** A **headboard** is an upright board at the end of a bed where you lay your head.

N-COUNT

**head boy** **(head boys)** The **head boy** of a school is the boy who is the leader of the prefects and who often represents the school on public occasions. [BRIT]

N-COUNT

**head-butt** **(head-butts, head-butting, head-butted)** also **headbutt.** If someone **head-butts** you, they hit you with the top of their head. ❑ *He was said to have head-butted one policeman and stamped on another's hand.* ♦ **Head-butt** is also a noun. ❑ *The cuts on Colin's head could only have been made by head-butts.*

VERB
V n
N-COUNT

**head count** **(head counts)** If you do a **head count**, you count the number of people present. You can also use **head count** to talk about the number of people that are present at an event, or that an organization employs.

N-COUNT

**head|dress** /heddres/ **(headdresses)** also **head-dress.** A **headdress** is something that is worn on a person's head for decoration.

N-COUNT

**head|er** /hedəʳ/ **(headers)** [1] In football, a **header** is the act of hitting the ball in a particular direction with your head. [2] A **header** is text such as a name or a page number that can be automatically displayed at the top of each page of a printed document. Compare **footer**. [COMPUTING]

N-COUNT
N-COUNT

**head-first** also **headfirst.** If you move **head-first** in a particular direction, your head is the part of your body that is furthest forward as you are moving. ❑ *He had apparently fallen head-first down the stairwell.*

ADV: ADV after v

**head|gear** /hedgɪəʳ/ also **head gear.** You use **headgear** to refer to hats or other things worn on the head.

N-UNCOUNT

**head girl** **(head girls)** The **head girl** of a school is the girl who is the leader of the prefects and who often represents the school on public occasions. [BRIT]

N-COUNT

**head|hunt** /hedhʌnt/ **(headhunts, headhunting, headhunted)** If someone who works for a particular company **is headhunted**, they leave that company because another company has approached them and offered them another job with better pay and higher status. ❑ *He was headhunted by Barkers last October to build an advertising team... They may headhunt her for the vacant position of Executive Producer.* VERB be V-ed V n

**head|hunter** /hedhʌntəʳ/ **(headhunters)** also **head-hunter.** A **headhunter** is a person who tries to persuade someone to leave their job and take another job which has better pay and more status. N-COUNT

**head|ing** /hedɪŋ/ **(headings)** A **heading** is the title of a piece of writing, which is written or printed at the top of the page. ❑ *...helpful chapter headings.* → See also **head**. N-COUNT

**head|lamp** /hedlæmp/ **(headlamps)** A **headlamp** is the same as a headlight. [BRIT] N-COUNT

**head|land** /hedlənd/ **(headlands)** A **headland** is a narrow piece of land which sticks out from the coast into the sea. N-COUNT

**head|less** /hedləs/ If the body of a person or animal is **headless**, the head has been cut off. ADJ

**head|light** /hedlaɪt/ **(headlights)** A vehicle's **headlights** are the large powerful lights at the front. → See picture on page 1707. N-COUNT

**head|line** /hedlaɪn/ **(headlines, headlining, headlined)** ◆◇◇ [1] A **headline** is the title of a newspaper story, printed in large letters at the top of the story, especially on the front page. ❑ *The Daily Mail has the headline 'The Voice of Conscience'.* N-COUNT [2] **The headlines** are the main points of the news which are read on radio or television. ❑ *I'm Claudia Polley with the news headlines.* N-PLURAL [3] If a newspaper or magazine article **is headlined** a particular thing, that is the headline that introduces it. ❑ *The article was headlined 'Tell us the truth'.* VERB: usu passive be V-ed quote [4] If someone **headlines** a show, they are the main performer in it. VERB [5] Someone or something that **hits the headlines** or **grabs the headlines** gets a lot of publicity from the media. ❑ *El Salvador first hit the world headlines at the beginning of the 1980s.* PHRASE: V inflects

**headline-grabbing** A **headline-grabbing** statement or activity is one that is intended to attract a lot of attention, especially from the media. ❑ *...a series of headline-grabbing announcements.* ADJ: usu ADJ n

**head|lin|er** /hedlaɪnəʳ/ **(headliners)** A **headliner** is the main performer or group of performers in a show. ❑ *We have introduced singers like Madeline Bell as headliners and I think the club is beginning to take off.* N-COUNT

**head|long** /hedlɒŋ, AM -lɔːŋ/ [1] If you move **headlong** in a particular direction, you move there very quickly. ❑ *He ran headlong for the open door.* ADV: ADV after v [2] If you fall or move **headlong**, you fall or move with your head furthest forward. ❑ *She missed her footing and fell headlong down the stairs.* ADV: ADV after v [3] If you rush **headlong into** something, you do it quickly without thinking carefully about it. ❑ *Do not leap headlong into decisions.* ADV: ADV after v ♦ **Headlong** is also an adjective. ❑ *...the headlong rush to independence.* ADJ: ADJ n

**head|man** /hedmən/ **(headmen)** A **headman** is the chief or leader of a tribe in a village. N-COUNT

**head|master** /hedmɑːstəʳ, -mæst-/ **(headmasters)** A **headmaster** is a man who is the head teacher of a school. [mainly BRIT] N-COUNT

**head|mistress** /hedmɪstrɪs/ **(headmistresses)** A **headmistress** is a woman who is the head teacher of a school. [mainly BRIT] N-COUNT

**head of state** **(heads of state)** A **head of state** is the leader of a country, for example a president, king, or queen. N-COUNT

**head-on** [1] If two vehicles hit each other **head-on**, they hit each other with their fronts pointing towards each other. ❑ *Pulling out to overtake, the car collided head-on with a van.* ADV: ADV after v ♦ **Head-on** is also an adjective. ❑ *Their car was in a head-on smash with an articulated lorry.* ADJ: ADJ n [2] A **head-on** conflict or approach is direct, without any attempt to compromise or avoid the issue. ❑ *The only victors in a head-on clash between the president and the assembly would be the hardliners on both sides.* ADJ: ADJ n ♦ **Head-on** is also an adverb. ❑ *Once again, I chose to confront the issue head-on.* ADV: ADV after v

**head|phones** /hedfoʊnz/ **Headphones** are a pair of padded speakers which you wear over your ears in order to listen to a radio, CD player, or tape recorder without other people hearing it. N-PLURAL: also *a pair of* N

**head|quartered** /hedkwɔːʳtəʳd/ If an organization **is headquartered in** a particular place, that is where its main offices are. ❑ *The company is headquartered in Chicago.* V-PASSIVE be V-ed *in/at* n

**head|quarters** /hedkwɔːʳtəʳz/ The **headquarters** of an organization are its main offices. ❑ *...fraud squad officers from London's police headquarters.* ◆◇◇ N-SING-COLL = HQ

**head|rest** /hedrest/ **(headrests)** A **headrest** is the part of the back of a seat on which you can lean your head, especially one on the front seat of a car. N-COUNT

**head|room** /hedruːm/ **Headroom** is the amount of space below a roof or bridge. ❑ *The forecabin, with 6ft headroom, also has plenty of room to stand and get dressed.* N-UNCOUNT

**head|scarf** /hedskɑːʳf/ **(headscarves)** also **head scarf.** [1] A **headscarf** is a head covering which Muslim women wear. N-COUNT [2] A **headscarf** is a small square scarf which some women wear round their heads, for example to keep it tidy. [BRIT] N-COUNT

**head|set** /hedset/ **(headsets)** [1] A **headset** is a small pair of headphones that you can use for listening to a radio or recorded music, or for using a telephone. N-COUNT [2] A **headset** is a piece of equipment that you wear on your head so you can see computer images or images from a camera in front of your eyes. N-COUNT

**head|ship** /hedʃɪp/ **(headships)** A **headship** is the position of being the head of a school, college, or department. ❑ *I feel sure you'll be offered the headship.* N-COUNT

**head start** **(head starts)** If you have a **head start on** other people, you have an advantage over them in something such as a competition or race. ❑ *A good education gives your child a head start in life.* N-COUNT: usu sing, oft N *on/over* n

**head|stone** /hedstoʊn/ **(headstones)** A **headstone** is a large stone which stands at one end of a grave, usually with the name of the dead person carved on it. N-COUNT = *gravestone, tombstone*

**head|strong** /hedstrɒŋ, AM -strɔːŋ/ If you refer to someone as **headstrong**, you are slightly critical of the fact that they are determined to do what they want. ❑ *He's young, very headstrong, but he's a good man underneath.* ADJ = *stubborn, wilful*

**head teach|er** **(head teachers)** also **headteacher.** A **head teacher** is a teacher who is in charge of a school. [BRIT] N-COUNT = *head*

**head-to-head** **(head-to-heads)** [1] A **head-to-head** contest or competition is one in which two people or groups compete directly against each other. ❑ *He won a head-to-head battle with NF leader Jean-Marie Le Pen.* ADJ: usu ADJ n ♦ **Head-to-head** is also an adverb. ❑ *Canadian business cannot compete head-to-head with American business.* ADV: v ADV [2] A **head-to-head** is a head-to-head contest or competition. ❑ *...a head-to-head between the champion and the aspiring champion.* N-COUNT: usu sing

**head|way** /hedweɪ/ If you **make headway**, you progress towards achieving something. ❑ *There was concern in the city that police were making little headway in the investigation.* PHRASE: oft with brd-neg, V inflects = *progress*

**head|wind** /hedwɪnd/ **(headwinds)** also **head-wind.** A **headwind** is a wind which blows in the opposite direction to the one in which you are moving. N-COUNT

**head|word** /hedwɜːʳd/ **(headwords)** In a dictionary, a **headword** is a word which is followed by an explanation of its meaning. N-COUNT

**heady** /hedi/ **(headier, headiest)** A **heady** drink, atmosphere, or experience strongly affects your senses, for example by making you feel drunk or excited. ❑ *...in the heady days just after their marriage.* ADJ: usu ADJ n

**heal** /hiːl/ **(heals, healing, healed)** ◆◇◇ 1 When a broken bone or other injury **heals** or when something **heals** it, it becomes healthy and normal again. ❑ *Within six weeks the bruising had gone, but it was six months before it all healed... Therapies like acupuncture do work and many people have been healed by them.* VERB V, V n 2 If you **heal** something such as a rift or a wound, or if it **heals**, the situation is put right so that people are friendly or happy again. ❑ *Today Sophie and her sister have healed the family rift and visit their family every weekend... The psychological effects on the United States were immense and in Washington the wounds have still not fully healed.* VERB V n, V

**heal|er** /hiːləʳ/ **(healers)** A **healer** is a person who heals people, especially a person who heals through prayer and religious faith. N-COUNT

**health** /helθ/ ◆◆◆ 1 A person's **health** is the condition of their body and the extent to which it is free from illness or is able to resist illness. ❑ *Caffeine is bad for your health.* N-UNCOUNT: oft with poss 2 **Health** is a state in which a person is not suffering from any illness and is feeling well. ❑ *In hospital they nursed me back to health.* N-UNCOUNT 3 The **health** of something such as an organization or a system is its success and the fact that it is working well. ❑ *There's no way to predict the future health of the banking industry.* N-UNCOUNT = prosperity

**health care work|er (health care workers)** A **health care worker** is someone who works in a hospital or health centre. N-COUNT

**health cen|tre (health centres)**

| ✓ in AM, use **health center** |

A **health centre** is a building in which a group of doctors have offices or surgeries where their patients can visit them. N-COUNT = surgery

**health club (health clubs)** A **health club** is a private club that people go to in order to do exercise and have beauty treatments. N-COUNT

**health farm (health farms)** A **health farm** is a hotel where people go to get fitter or lose weight by exercising and eating special food. [mainly BRIT] N-COUNT

| ✓ in AM, use **spa** |

**health food (health foods) Health foods** are natural foods without artificial ingredients which people buy because they consider them to be good for them. N-MASS: oft N n

**health|ful** /helθfʊl/ Something that is **healthful** is good for your health. ❑ *Does the college cafeteria provide a healthful diet?* ADJ = healthy

**health visi|tor (health visitors)** In Britain, a **health visitor** is a nurse whose job is to visit people in their homes and offer advice on matters such as how to look after very young babies or people with physical disabilities. N-COUNT

**healthy** /helθi/ **(healthier, healthiest)** ◆◇◇ 1 Someone who is **healthy** is well and is not suffering from any illness. ❑ *Most of us need to lead more balanced lives to be healthy and happy.* ADJ ♦ **healthi|ly** /helθɪli/ *What I really want is to live healthily for as long as possible.* ADV: usu ADV after v 2 If a feature or quality that you have is **healthy**, it makes you look well or shows that you are well. ❑ *...the glow of healthy skin.* ADJ: usu ADJ n 3 Something that is **healthy** is good for your health. ❑ *...a healthy diet.* ADJ: usu ADJ n 4 A **healthy** organization or system is successful. ❑ *...an economically healthy socialist state.* ADJ: usu ADJ n 5 A **healthy** amount of something is a large amount that shows success. ❑ *He predicts a continuation of healthy profits in the current financial year.* ADJ: usu ADJ n = substantial 6 If you have a **healthy** attitude about something, you show good sense. ❑ *She has a refreshingly healthy attitude to work.* ADJ: oft *it* v-link ADJ to-inf

**heap** /hiːp/ **(heaps, heaping, heaped)** 1 A **heap of** things is a pile of them, especially a pile arranged in a rather untidy way. ❑ *...a heap of bricks... He has dug up the tiles that cover the floor and left them in a heap.* N-COUNT: oft N *of* n 2 If you **heap** things somewhere, you arrange them in a large pile. ❑ *Mrs. Madrigal heaped more carrots onto Michael's plate.* ♦ **Heap up** means the same as **heap**. ❑ *Off to one side, the militia was heaping up wood for a bonfire.* VERB V n prep/adv PHRASAL VERB V P n Also V n P 3 If you **heap** praise or criticism **on** someone or something, you give them a lot of praise or criticism. ❑ *The head of the navy heaped scorn on both the methods and motives of the conspirators.* VERB V n *on/upon* n 4 **Heaps of** something or a **heap of** something is a large quantity of it. [INFORMAL] ❑ *You have heaps of time... I got in a heap of trouble.* QUANT: QUANT *of* n-uncount/pl-n = load

**PHRASES** 5 Someone who is **at the bottom of the heap** or **at the top of the heap** is low down or high up in society or an organization. ❑ *Ordinary workers in state industry, once favoured, suddenly found themselves at the bottom of the heap.* PHRASE: usu v-link PHR, PHR after v 6 If someone collapses **in a heap**, they fall heavily and untidily and do not move. ❑ *The young footballer collapsed in a heap after a heavy tackle.* PHRASE: v PHR, v-link PHR

**heaped** /hiːpt/ 1 A **heaped** spoonful has the contents of the spoon piled up above the edge. ❑ *Add one heaped tablespoon of salt.* ADJ: ADJ n 2 A container or a surface that is **heaped with** things has a lot of them in it or on it in a pile, often so many that it cannot hold any more. ❑ *The large desk was heaped with papers.* ADJ: v-link ADJ *with* n

**hear** /hɪəʳ/ **(hears, hearing, heard** /hɜːʳd/**)** ◆◆◆ 1 When you **hear** a sound, you become aware of it through your ears. ❑ *She heard no further sounds... They heard the protesters shout: 'No more fascism!'... And then we heard the bells ringing out... I'm not hearing properly.* VERB V n, V n inf, V n -ing, V 2 If you **hear** something such as a lecture or a piece of music, you listen to it. ❑ *You can hear commentary on the match in about half an hour's time... I don't think you've ever heard Doris talking about her emotional life before... I'd love to hear it played by a professional orchestra.* VERB V n, V n -ing, V n -ed 3 If you say that you can **hear** someone saying something, you mean that you are able to imagine hearing it. ❑ *Can't you just hear John Motson now?... 'I was hot,' I could still hear Charlotte say with her delicious French accent.* VERB: no cont V n, V n inf 4 When a judge or a court of law **hears** a case, or evidence in a case, they listen to it officially in order to make a decision about it. [FORMAL] ❑ *The jury have heard evidence from defence witnesses.* VERB V n 5 If you **hear from** someone, you receive a letter or telephone call from them. ❑ *Drop us a line, it's always great to hear from you.* VERB V *from* n 6 In a debate or discussion, if you **hear from** someone, you listen to them giving their opinion or information. ❑ *What are you hearing from people there?* VERB V *from* n 7 If you **hear** some news or information about something, you find out about it by someone telling you, or from the radio or television. ❑ *My mother heard of this school through Leslie... He had heard that the trophy had been sold... I had waited to hear the result.* VERB V *of/about* n, V that, V n 8 If you **have heard of** something or someone, you know about them, but not in great detail. ❑ *Many people haven't heard of reflexology. ...people who, maybe, had hardly heard the word till a year or two ago.* VERB: no cont V *of* n, V n

**PHRASES** 9 If you say that you **have heard** something **before**, you mean that you are not interested in it, or do not believe it, or are not surprised about it, because you already know about it or have experienced it. ❑ *Furness shrugs wearily. He has heard it all before.* PHRASE: V inflects 10 During political debates and public meetings, people sometimes say **'Hear hear!'** to express their agreement with what the speaker is saying. [BRIT, FORMAL] CONVENTION formulae 11 If you say that you **can't hear yourself think**, you are complaining and emphasizing that there is a lot of noise, and that it is disturbing you or prevent- PHRASE: usu with brd-neg emphasis ing you from doing something. [INFORMAL] ❑ *For God's sake shut up. I can't hear myself think!.* 12 If you say that you **won't hear of** someone doing something, you mean that you refuse to let them do it. ❑ *I've always wanted to be an actor but Dad wouldn't hear of it.* PHRASE: PHR n

♦ **hear out** If you **hear** someone **out**, you listen to them without interrupting them until they have finished saying everything that they want to say. ❑ *Perhaps, when you've heard me out, you'll appreciate the reason for secrecy... He shows keen interest in his friends, hearing out their problems and offering counsel.* PHRASAL VERB V n P V P n (not pron)

**hear|er** /hɪərəʳ/ **(hearers)** Your **hearers** are the people who are listening to you speak. [FORMAL] N-COUNT = listener

**hear|ing** /hɪərɪŋ/ **(hearings)** 1 A person's or animal's **hearing** is the sense which makes it possible for them to be aware of sounds. ❑ *His mind still seemed clear and his hearing was excellent.* 2 A **hearing** is an official meeting which is held in order to collect facts about an incident or problem. ❑ *The judge adjourned the hearing until next Tuesday.* 3 → See also **hard of hearing**. ◆◇◇ N-UNCOUNT: oft poss N; N-COUNT

**PHRASES** 4 If someone gives you **a fair hearing** or **a hearing**, they listen to you when you give your opinion about something. ❑ *Weber gave a fair hearing to anyone who held a different opinion.* 5 If someone says something **in** your **hearing** or **within** your **hearing**, you can hear what they say because they are with you or near you. ❑ *No one spoke disparagingly of her father in her hearing.* PHRASE: usu PHR after v; PHRASE: usu PHR after v

**hear|ing aid** **(hearing aids)** A **hearing aid** is a device which people with hearing difficulties wear in their ear to enable them to hear better. N-COUNT

**hear|ing dog** **(hearing dogs)** **Hearing dogs** are dogs that have been specially trained to help deaf people. N-COUNT

**hear|say** /hɪəʳseɪ/ **Hearsay** is information which you have been told but do not know to be true. ❑ *Much of what was reported to them was hearsay.* N-UNCOUNT

**hearse** /hɜːʳs/ **(hearses)** A **hearse** is a large car that carries the coffin at a funeral. N-COUNT

**heart** /hɑːʳt/ **(hearts)** 1 Your **heart** is the organ in your chest that pumps the blood around your body. People also use **heart** to refer to the area of their chest that is closest to their heart. ❑ *The bullet had passed less than an inch from Andrea's heart.* 2 You can refer to someone's **heart** when you are talking about their deep feelings and beliefs. [LITERARY] ❑ *Alik's words filled her heart with pride.* 3 You use **heart** when you are talking about someone's character and attitude towards other people, especially when they are kind and generous. ❑ *She loved his brilliance and his generous heart.* 4 **The heart of** something is the most central and important part of it. → See picture on page 1712. ❑ *The heart of the problem is supply and demand.* 5 **The heart of** a place is its centre. ❑ *...a busy dentists' practice in the heart of London's West End.* 6 A **heart** is a shape that is used as a symbol of love: ♥. ❑ *...heart-shaped chocolates.* 7 **Hearts** is one of the four suits in a pack of playing cards. Each card in the suit is marked with one or more red symbols in the shape of a heart. ♦ A **heart** is a playing card of this suit. ◆◆◇ N-COUNT; N-COUNT: usu with poss; N-VAR: usu adj N in sing [approval]; N-SING: N *of* n = crux; N-SING: usu N *of* n; N-COUNT; N-UNCOUNT-COLL; N-COUNT

**PHRASES** 8 If you feel or believe something **with all** your **heart**, you feel or believe it very strongly. ❑ *My own family I loved with all my heart.* 9 If you say that someone is a particular kind of person **at heart**, you mean that that is what they are really like, even though they may seem very different. ❑ *He was a gentle boy at heart.* 10 If you say that someone has your interests or your welfare **at heart**, you mean that they are concerned about you and that is why they are doing something. 11 If someone **breaks** your **heart**, they make you very sad and unhappy, usually because they end a love affair or close relationship with you. [LITERARY] 12 If something **breaks** your **heart**, it makes you feel very sad and depressed, especially because people are suffering but you can do nothing to help them. ❑ *It really breaks my heart to see them this way.* 13 If you say that someone has a **broken heart**, you mean that they are very sad, for example because a love affair has ended unhappily. [LITERARY] ❑ *She never recovered from her broken heart.* 14 If you know something such as a poem **by heart**, you have learned it so well that you can remember it without having to read it. ❑ *Mack knew this passage by heart.* 15 If someone has a **change of heart**, their attitude towards something changes. ❑ *Several brokers have had a change of heart about prospects for the company.* PHRASE: PHR after v, PHR with cl [emphasis]; PHRASE: PHR with cl; PHRASE: usu *have* n PHR; PHRASE: V and N inflect; PHRASE: V and N inflect, oft PHR to-inf; PHRASE: N inflects; PHRASE: PHR after v; PHRASE: *change* inflects

16 If something such as a subject or project is **close to** your **heart** or **near to** your **heart**, it is very important to you and you are very interested in it and concerned about it. ❑ *Animal welfare is a subject very close to my heart.* 17 If you can do something **to** your **heart's content**, you can do it as much as you want. ❑ *I was delighted to be able to eat my favorite dishes to my heart's content.* PHRASE: N inflects, oft v-link PHR; PHRASE: PHR after v

18 You can say '**cross my heart**' when you want someone to believe that you are telling the truth. You can also ask '**cross your heart?**', when you are asking someone if they are really telling the truth. [SPOKEN] ❑ *And I won't tell any of the other girls anything you tell me about it. I promise, cross my heart.* 19 If you say something **from the heart** or **from the bottom of** your **heart**, you sincerely mean what you say. ❑ *He spoke with confidence, from the heart.* 20 If something **gives** you **heart**, it makes you feel more confident or happy about something. ❑ *It gave me heart to see one thug get what he deserves.* 21 If you want to do something but do **not have the heart to** do it, you do not do it because you know it will make someone unhappy or disappointed. ❑ *We knew all along but didn't have the heart to tell her.* 22 If you believe or know something **in** your **heart of hearts**, that is what you really believe or think, even though it may sometimes seem that you do not. ❑ *I know in my heart of hearts that I am the right man for that mission.* 23 If your **heart isn't in** the thing you are doing, you have very little enthusiasm for it, usually because you are depressed or are thinking about something else. ❑ *I tried to learn some lines but my heart wasn't really in it.* CONVENTION; PHRASE: PHR after v = sincerely; PHRASE: V inflects; PHRASE: V inflects, usu PHR to-inf; PHRASE: PHR after v, PHR with cl; PHRASE: V and N inflect, PHR n/-ing

24 If you **lose heart**, you become sad and depressed and are no longer interested in something, especially because it is not progressing as you would like. ❑ *He appealed to his countrymen not to lose heart.* 25 If your **heart is in** your **mouth**, you feel very excited, worried, or frightened. ❑ *My heart was in my mouth when I walked into her office.* PHRASE: V inflects; PHRASE: V and Ns inflect

26 If you **open** your **heart** or **pour out** your **heart** to someone, you tell them your most private thoughts and feelings. ❑ *She opened her heart to millions yesterday and told how she came close to suicide.* 27 If you say that someone's **heart is in the right place**, you mean that they are kind, considerate, and generous, although you may disapprove of other aspects of their character. ❑ *He is a bit of a tearaway but his heart is in the right place.* PHRASE: V and N inflect, usu PHR *to* n; PHRASE: *heart* and V inflect

28 If you have **set** your **heart on** something, you want it very much or want to do it very much. ❑ *He had always set his heart on a career in the fine arts.* 29 If you **wear** your **heart on** your **sleeve**, you openly show your feelings or emotions rather than keeping them hidden. 30 If you put your **heart and soul into** something, you do it with a great deal of enthusiasm and energy. PHRASE: V and N inflect, PHR n/-ing; PHRASE: V and N inflect; PHRASE [emphasis]

31 If you **take heart from** something, you are encouraged and made to feel optimistic by it. 32 If you **take** something **to heart**, for example someone's behaviour, you are deeply affected and upset by it. ❑ *If someone says something critical I take it to heart.* PHRASE: V inflects, oft PHR *from* n; PHRASE: V inflects

**heart|ache** /hɑːʳteɪk/ **(heartaches)** also **heart-ache. Heartache** is very great sadness and emotional suffering. ❑ *...after suffering the heartache of her divorce from her first husband.* N-VAR

**heart at|tack** **(heart attacks)** If someone has a **heart attack**, their heart begins to beat very irregularly or stops completely. ❑ *He died of a heart attack brought on by overwork.* N-COUNT

**heart|beat** /hɑːʳtbiːt/ Your **heartbeat** is the regular movement of your heart as it pumps blood around your body. N-SING: oft poss N

**heart|break** /hɑːʳtbreɪk/ **(heartbreaks)** **Heartbreak** is very great sadness and emotional suffering, especially after the end of a love affair or close relationship. N-VAR

**heart|breaking** /hɑːʳtbreɪkɪŋ/ Something that is **heartbreaking** makes you feel extremely sad and upset. ❑ *This year we won't even be able to buy presents for our grandchildren. It's heartbreaking.* ADJ

**heart|broken** /hɑːʳtbroʊkən/ Someone who is **heartbroken** is very sad and emotionally upset. ❑ *Was your daddy heartbroken when they got a divorce?* ADJ

**heart|burn** /hɑːʳtbɜːʳn/ **Heartburn** is a painful burning sensation in your chest, caused by indigestion. N-UNCOUNT

**-hearted** /-hɑːʳtɪd/ **-hearted** combines with adjectives such as 'kind' or 'cold' to form adjectives which indicate that someone has a particular character or personality or is in a particular mood. ❑ *They are now realising just how much they owe to kind-hearted strangers.* COMB in ADJ

**heart|en** /hɑːʳtᵊn/ **(heartens, heartening, heartened)** If someone **is heartened by** something, it encourages them and makes them cheerful. ❑ *He will have been heartened by the telephone opinion poll published yesterday... The news heartened everybody.* ♦ **heart|ened** *I feel heartened by her progress.* ♦ **heart|en|ing** *This is heartening news.* VERB = cheer; be V-ed; V n; ADJ; ADJ

**heart fail|ure** **Heart failure** is a serious medical condition in which someone's heart does not work as well as it should, sometimes stopping completely so that they die. N-UNCOUNT

**heart|felt** /hɑːʳtfelt/ **Heartfelt** is used to describe a deep or sincere feeling or wish. ❑ *My heartfelt sympathy goes out to all the relatives.* ADJ: usu ADJ n = sincere

**hearth** /hɑːʳθ/ **(hearths)** The **hearth** is the floor of a fireplace, which sometimes extends into the room. N-COUNT

**hearth rug** **(hearth rugs)** also **hearthrug.** A **hearth rug** is a rug which is put in front of a fireplace. N-COUNT

**heart|land** /hɑːʳtlænd/ **(heartlands)** [1] Journalists use **heartland** or **heartlands** to refer to the area or region where a particular set of activities or beliefs is most significant. ❑ *...his six-day bus tour around the industrial heartland of America.* N-COUNT: with supp, oft adj N, N *of* n [2] The most central area of a country or continent can be referred to as its **heartland** or **heartlands**. [WRITTEN] ❑ *For many, the essence of French living is to be found in the rural heartlands.* N-COUNT: with supp

**heart|less** /hɑːʳtləs/ If you describe someone as **heartless**, you mean that they are cruel and unkind, and have no sympathy for anyone or anything. ❑ *I couldn't believe they were so heartless.* ADJ = cruel, callous ≠ kind, kind-hearted

**heart-rending** also **heartrending.** You use **heart-rending** to describe something that causes you to feel great sadness and pity. ❑ *...heart-rending pictures of refugees.* ADJ: usu ADJ n

**heart|strings** /hɑːʳtstrɪŋz/ If you say that someone or something tugs at your **heartstrings**, you mean that they cause you to feel strong emotions, usually sadness or pity. ❑ *She knows exactly how to tug at readers' heartstrings.* N-PLURAL: oft with poss

**heart-throb** **(heart-throbs)** If you describe a man as a **heart-throb**, you mean that he is physically very attractive, so that a lot of women fall in love with him. N-COUNT

**heart-to-heart** **(heart-to-hearts)** A **heart-to-heart** is a conversation between two people, especially close friends, in which they talk freely about their feelings or personal problems. ❑ *I've had a heart-to-heart with him.* N-COUNT: oft N n

**heart-warming** Something that is **heart-warming** causes you to feel happy, usually because something nice has happened to people. ❑ *...the heart-warming story of enemies who discover a shared humanity.* ADJ = cheering

**hearty** /hɑːʳti/ **(heartier, heartiest)** [1] **Hearty** people or actions are loud, cheerful, and energetic. ❑ *Wade was a hearty, bluff, athletic sort of guy... He gave a hearty laugh.* ♦ **hearti|ly** *He laughed heartily.* [2] **Hearty** feelings or opinions are strongly felt or strongly held. ❑ *With the last sentiment, Arnold was in hearty agreement.* ♦ **hearti|ly** *Most Afghans are heartily sick of war and violence.* [3] A **hearty** meal is large and very satisfying. ❑ *The men ate a hearty breakfast.* ♦ **hearti|ly** *He ate heartily but would drink only beer.* ADJ; ADV: ADV after v; ADJ: usu ADJ n; ADV: ADV with v, ADV adj; ADJ: usu ADJ n; ADV: ADV after v

**heat** /hiːt/ **(heats, heating, heated)** ◆◆◇ [1] When you **heat** something, you raise its temperature, for example by using a flame or a special piece of equipment. ❑ *Meanwhile, heat the tomatoes and oil in a pan. ...heated swimming pools.* VERB; V n; V-ed [2] **Heat** is warmth or the quality of being hot. ❑ *The seas store heat and release it gradually during cold periods.* N-UNCOUNT [3] **The heat** is very hot weather. ❑ *As an asthmatic, he cannot cope with the heat and humidity.* N-UNCOUNT [4] The **heat** of something is the temperature of something that is warm or that is being heated. ❑ *Adjust the heat of the barbecue by opening and closing the air vents.* N-UNCOUNT: with supp [5] You use **heat** to refer to a source of heat, for example a cooking ring or the heating system of a house. ❑ *Immediately remove the pan from the heat.* N-SING [6] You use **heat** to refer to a state of strong emotion, especially of anger or excitement. ❑ *It was all done in the heat of the moment and I have certainly learned by my mistake.* N-UNCOUNT: oft N *of* n [7] **The heat of** a particular activity is the point when there is the greatest activity or excitement. ❑ *Last week, in the heat of the election campaign, the Prime Minister left for America.* N-SING: the N *of* n [8] A **heat** is one of a series of races or competitions. The winners of a heat take part in another race or competition, against the winners of other heats. ❑ *...the heats of the men's 100m breaststroke.* → See also **dead heat.** N-COUNT [9] When a female animal is **on heat** in British English, or **in heat** in American English, she is in a state where she is ready to mate with a male animal, as this will probably result in her becoming pregnant. PHRASE: v-link PHR

♦ **heat up** [1] When you **heat** something **up**, especially food which has already been cooked and allowed to go cold, you make it hot. ❑ *Freda heated up a pie for me.* PHRASAL VERB = warm up; V P n (not pron) [2] When a situation **heats up**, things start to happen much more quickly and with increased interest and excitement among the people involved. ❑ *Then in the last couple of years, the movement for democracy began to heat up.* PHRASAL VERB = hot up ≠ cool off; V P [3] When something **heats up**, it gradually becomes hotter. ❑ *In the summer her mobile home heats up like an oven.* PHRASAL VERB ≠ cool down; V P

**heat|ed** /hiːtɪd/ [1] A **heated** discussion or quarrel is one where the people involved are angry and excited. ❑ *It was a very heated argument and they were shouting at each other.* ADJ ≠ calm [2] If someone gets **heated about** something, they get angry and excited about it. ❑ *You will understand that people get a bit heated about issues such as these.* ♦ **heat|ed|ly** *The crowd continued to argue heatedly about the best way to tackle the problem.* ADJ: v-link ADJ *about*/*over* n; ADV: ADV with v

**heat|er** /hiːtəʳ/ **(heaters)** A **heater** is a piece of equipment or a machine which is used to raise the temperature of something, especially of the air inside a room or a car. N-COUNT

**heath** /hiːθ/ **(heaths)** A **heath** is an area of open land covered with rough grass or heather and with very few trees or bushes. [BRIT] N-COUNT

**hea|then** /hiːðən/ **(heathens)** [1] **Heathen** means having no religion, or belonging to a religion that is not Christianity, Judaism, or Islam. [OLD-FASHIONED] ♦ **The heathen** are heathen people. ❑ *They first set out to convert the heathen.* ADJ: usu ADJ n; N-PLURAL: the N

2 People sometimes refer to other people who have no religion as **heathens**, especially if they do not like the way they behave as a result of this. [OLD-FASHIONED] [N-COUNT, disapproval]

**heath|er** /heðəʳ/ **Heather** is a low, spreading plant with small purple, pink, or white flowers. **Heather** grows wild in Europe on high land with poor soil. [N-UNCOUNT]

**heat|ing** /hiːtɪŋ/ 1 **Heating** is the process of heating a building or room, considered especially from the point of view of how much this costs. ❑ *You can still find cottages for £150 a week, including heating. ...heating bills.* [N-UNCOUNT] 2 **Heating** is the system and equipment that is used to heat a building. ❑ *I wish I knew how to turn on the heating.* [N-UNCOUNT] → See also **central heating**.

**heat stroke** also **heatstroke**. **Heat stroke** is the same as **sunstroke**. [N-UNCOUNT]

**heat|wave** /hiːtweɪv/ **(heatwaves)** also **heat wave**. A **heatwave** is a period of time during which the weather is much hotter than usual. [N-COUNT]

**heave** /hiːv/ **(heaves, heaving, heaved)** 1 If you **heave** something heavy or difficult to move somewhere, you push, pull, or lift it using a lot of effort. ❑ *It took five strong men to heave the statue up a ramp and lower it into place.* [VERB: V n prep/adv] ♦ **Heave** is also a noun. ❑ *It took only one heave to hurl him into the river.* [N-COUNT] 2 If something **heaves**, it moves up and down with large regular movements. ❑ *His chest heaved, and he took a deep breath.* [VERB: V] 3 If you **heave**, or if your stomach **heaves**, you vomit or feel sick. ❑ *My stomach heaved and I felt sick.* [VERB: V] 4 If you **heave** a **sigh**, you give a big sigh. ❑ *Mr Collier heaved a sigh and got to his feet.* [VERB: V n] 5 to heave **a sigh of relief** → see **sigh**.

**heav|en** /hevən/ **(heavens)** ◆◇◇ 1 In some religions, **heaven** is said to be the place where God lives, where good people go when they die, and where everyone is always happy. It is usually imagined as being high up in the sky. [N-PROPER = paradise] 2 You can use **heaven** to refer to a place or situation that you like very much. [INFORMAL] ❑ *We went touring in Wales and Ireland. It was heaven.* [N-UNCOUNT = paradise] 3 **The heavens** are the sky. [OLD-FASHIONED] ❑ *He walked out into the middle of the road, looking up at the heavens.* [N-PLURAL: the N = sky, skies] 4 → See also **seventh heaven**.

**PHRASES** 5 You say **'Heaven forbid!'** to emphasize that you very much hope that something will not happen. [SPOKEN] ❑ *Heaven forbid that he should leave because of me!* [PHRASE: PHR that, emphasis] 6 You say **'Good heavens!'** or **'Heavens!'** to express surprise or to emphasize that you agree or disagree with someone. [SPOKEN] ❑ *Good Heavens! That explains a lot!.* [EXCLAM, feelings] 7 You say **'Heaven help** someone' when you are worried that something bad is going to happen to them, often because you disapprove of what they are doing or the way they are behaving. [SPOKEN] ❑ *If this makes sense to our leaders, then heaven help us all.* [PHRASE: PHR n, disapproval] 8 You can say **'Heaven knows'** to emphasize that you do not know something, or that you find something very surprising. [SPOKEN] ❑ *Heaven knows what they put in it.* [PHRASE: PHR wh, emphasis] 9 You can say **'Heaven knows'** to emphasize something that you feel or believe very strongly. [SPOKEN] ❑ *Heaven knows they have enough money.* [PHRASE: PHR with cl, emphasis] 10 If **the heavens open**, it suddenly starts raining very heavily. ❑ *The match had just begun when the heavens opened and play was suspended.* [PHRASE: V inflects] 11 **for heaven's sake** → see **sake**. **thank heavens** → see **thank**.

**heav|en|ly** /hevənli/ 1 **Heavenly** things are things that are connected with the religious idea of heaven. ❑ *...heavenly beings whose function it is to serve God.* [ADJ: usu ADJ n] 2 Something that is **heavenly** is very pleasant and enjoyable. [INFORMAL] ❑ *The idea of spending two weeks with him may seem heavenly.* [ADJ = blissful]

**heav|en|ly body** **(heavenly bodies)** A **heavenly body** is a planet, star, moon, or other natural object in space. [N-COUNT]

**heaven-sent** also **heaven sent**. You use **heaven-sent** to describe something such as an opportunity which is unexpected, but which is very welcome because it occurs at just the right time. ❑ *It will be a heaven-sent opportunity to prove himself.* [ADJ: usu ADJ n]

**heav|en|ward** /hevᵊnwəʳd/ also **heavenwards**. **Heavenward** means towards the sky or to heaven. [WRITTEN] ❑ *He rolled his eyes heavenward in disgust.* [ADV: ADV after v = upward]

**heavi|ly** /hevɪli/ If someone says something **heavily**, they say it in a slow way which shows a feeling such as sadness, tiredness, or annoyance. ❑ *'I didn't even think about her,' he said heavily.* [ADV: ADV after v ≠ lightly] → See also **heavy**.

**heavy** /hevi/ **(heavier, heaviest, heavies)** ◆◆◇ 1 Something that is **heavy** weighs a lot. ❑ *These scissors are awfully heavy... The mud stuck to her boots, making her feet heavy and her legs tired.* [ADJ ≠ light] ♦ **heavi|ness** *...a sensation of warmth and heaviness in the muscles.* [N-UNCOUNT] 2 You use **heavy** to ask or talk about how much someone or something weighs. ❑ *How heavy are you?... Protons are nearly 2000 times as heavy as electrons.* [ADJ: how ADJ, as ADJ as, ADJ-compar than] 3 **Heavy** means great in amount, degree, or intensity. ❑ *Heavy fighting has been going on... He worried about her heavy drinking... The traffic along Fitzjohn's Avenue was heavy.* [ADJ: usu ADJ n] ♦ **heavi|ly** *It has been raining heavily all day.* [ADV: ADV after v, ADV -ed/adj] ♦ **heavi|ness** *...the heaviness of the blood loss.* [N-UNCOUNT] 4 Someone or something that is **heavy** is solid in appearance or structure, or is made of a thick material. ❑ *He was short and heavy.* [ADJ ≠ light] ♦ **heavi|ly** *He was a big man of about forty, wide-shouldered and heavily built.* [ADV: ADV -ed] 5 A **heavy** meal is large in amount and often difficult to digest. ❑ *He had been feeling drowsy, the effect of an unusually heavy meal.* [ADJ = filling ≠ light] 6 Something that is **heavy with** things is full of them or loaded with them. [LITERARY] ❑ *The air is heavy with moisture.* [ADJ: v-link ADJ with n] 7 If a person's breathing is **heavy**, it is very loud and deep. ❑ *Her breathing became slow and heavy.* [ADJ ≠ light, shallow] ♦ **heavi|ly** *She sank back on the pillow and closed her eyes, breathing heavily as if asleep.* [ADV: ADV after v] 8 A **heavy** movement or action is done with a lot of force or pressure. ❑ *...a heavy blow on the back of the skull.* [ADJ: ADJ n ≠ gentle] ♦ **heavi|ly** *I sat down heavily on the ground beside the road.* [ADV: ADV after v] 9 A **heavy** machine or piece of military equipment is very large and very powerful. ❑ *...government militia backed by tanks and heavy artillery.* [ADJ: ADJ n] 10 If you describe a period of time or a schedule as **heavy**, you mean it involves a lot of work. ❑ *It's been a heavy day and I'm tired.* [ADJ: usu ADJ n = busy] 11 **Heavy** work requires a lot of strength or energy. ❑ *The business is thriving and Philippa employs two full-timers for the heavy work.* [ADJ: usu ADJ n] 12 If you say that something is **heavy on** another thing, you mean that it uses a lot of that thing or too much of that thing. ❑ *Tanks are heavy on fuel and destructive to roads.* [ADJ: v-link ADJ on n] 13 Air or weather that is **heavy** is unpleasantly still, hot, and damp. ❑ *The outside air was heavy and moist and sultry.* [ADJ = oppressive] 14 If your heart is **heavy**, you are sad about something. [LITERARY] ❑ *Mr Maddison handed over his resignation letter with a heavy heart.* [ADJ ≠ light] 15 A situation that is **heavy** is serious and difficult to cope with. [INFORMAL] ❑ *I don't want any more of that heavy stuff.* [ADJ = serious] 16 A **heavy** is a large strong man who is employed to protect a person or place, often by using violence. [INFORMAL] ❑ *They had employed heavies to evict shop squatters from neighbouring sites.* [N-COUNT] 17 **to make heavy weather of** something → see **weather**. **a heavy hand** → see **hand**.

**heavy cream** **Heavy cream** is very thick cream. [AM] [N-UNCOUNT]

in BRIT, use **double cream**

**heavy-duty** A **heavy-duty** piece of equipment is very strong and can be used a lot. ❑ *...a heavy duty polythene bag.* [ADJ: usu ADJ n]

**heavy-handed** If you say that someone's behaviour is **heavy-handed**, you mean that they [ADJ, disapproval] are too forceful or too rough. ❑ *...heavy-handed police tactics.*

**heavy in|dus|try** **(heavy industries)** **Heavy industry** is industry in which large machines are used to produce raw materials or to make large objects. N-VAR ≠ light industry

**heavy met|al** **(heavy metals)** 1 **Heavy metal** is a type of very loud rock music with a fast beat. ❑ *...a German heavy metal band named The Scorpions.* N-UNCOUNT: oft N n 2 A **heavy metal** is a metallic element with a high density. Many heavy metals are poisonous. [TECHNICAL] N-COUNT

**heavy-set** Someone who is **heavy-set** has a large solid body. ADJ = thick-set

**heavy|weight** /heviweɪt/ **(heavyweights)** 1 A **heavyweight** is a boxer weighing more than 175 pounds and therefore in the heaviest class. N-COUNT 2 If you refer to a person or organization as a **heavyweight**, you mean that they have a lot of influence, experience, and importance in a particular field, subject, or activity. ❑ *He was a political heavyweight.* N-COUNT: oft supp N

**He|brew** /hiːbruː/ 1 **Hebrew** is a language that was spoken by Jews in former times. A modern form of Hebrew is spoken now in Israel. ❑ *He is a fluent speaker of Hebrew.* N-UNCOUNT 2 **Hebrew** means belonging to or relating to the Hebrew language or people. ❑ *...the respected Hebrew newspaper Haarez.* ADJ

**heck** /hek/ 1 People sometimes say '**heck!**' when they are slightly irritated or surprised. [INFORMAL] ❑ *Heck, if you don't like it, don't vote for him.* EXCLAM [feelings]

PHRASES 2 People use **a heck of** to emphasize how big something is or how much of it there is. [INFORMAL] ❑ *They're spending a heck of a lot of money... The truth is, I'm in one heck of a mess.* PHRASE: PHR n [emphasis] 3 You use **the heck** in expressions such as '**what the heck**' and '**how the heck**' in order to emphasize a question, especially when you are puzzled or annoyed. [INFORMAL] ❑ *What the heck's that?... The question was, where the heck was he?* PHRASE: quest PHR [emphasis] 4 You say '**what the heck**' to indicate that you do not care about a bad aspect of an action or situation. [INFORMAL] ❑ *What the heck, I thought, I'll give it a whirl.* PHRASE: PHR with cl [feelings]

**heck|le** /hekᵊl/ **(heckles, heckling, heckled)** If people in an audience **heckle** public speakers or performers, they interrupt them, for example by making rude remarks. ❑ *They heckled him and interrupted his address with angry questions... A small group of youths stayed behind to heckle and shout abuse.* VERB; V n; V ♦ **Heckle** is also a noun. ❑ *The offending comment was in fact a heckle from an audience member.* N-COUNT ♦ **heck|ling** *The ceremony was disrupted by unprecedented heckling and slogan-chanting.* N-UNCOUNT ♦ **heck|ler** /heklәʳ/ **(hecklers)** *As he began his speech, a heckler called out asking for his opinion on gun control.* N-COUNT

**hec|tare** /hekteәʳ/ **(hectares)** A **hectare** is a measurement of an area of land which is equal to 10,000 square metres, or 2.471 acres. N-COUNT: usu num N

**hec|tic** /hektɪk/ A **hectic** situation is one that is very busy and involves a lot of rushed activity. ❑ *Despite his hectic work schedule, Benny has rarely suffered poor health.* ADJ = busy

**hec|tor** /hektәʳ/ **(hectors, hectoring, hectored)** If you say that someone **is hectoring** you, you do not like the way they are trying to make you do something by bothering you and talking to you aggressively. ❑ *I suppose you'll hector me until I phone him.* VERB [disapproval] = bully; V n ♦ **hec|tor|ing** *In a loud, hectoring tone, Alan told us that he wasn't going to waste time discussing nonsense.* ADJ: usu ADJ n = bullying

**he'd** /hɪd, hiːd/ 1 **He'd** is the usual spoken form of 'he had', especially when 'had' is an auxiliary verb. ❑ *He'd never learnt to read.* 2 **He'd** is a spoken form of 'he would'. ❑ *He'd come into the clubhouse every day.*

**hedge** /hedʒ/ **(hedges, hedging, hedged)** 1 A **hedge** is a row of bushes or small trees, usually along the edge of a garden, field, or road. ➔ See picture on page 1705. N-COUNT 2 If you **hedge against** something unpleasant or unwanted that might affect you, especially losing money, you do something which will protect you from it. ❑ *You can hedge against redundancy or illness with insurance... Today's clever financial instruments make it possible for firms to hedge their risks.* VERB; V against n; V n 3 Something that is a **hedge against** something unpleasant will protect you from its effects. ❑ *Gold is traditionally a hedge against inflation.* N-COUNT: N against n 4 If you **hedge**, you avoid answering a question or committing yourself to a particular action or decision. ❑ *They hedged in answering various questions about the operation... 'I can't give you an answer now,' he hedged.* VERB; V; V with quote 5 If you **hedge** your **bets**, you reduce the risk of losing a lot by supporting more than one person or thing in a situation where they are opposed to each other. ❑ *Hawker Siddeley tried to hedge its bets by diversifying into other fields.* PHRASE: V inflects

♦ **hedge about** or **hedge around** If you say that something such as an offer **is hedged about** or **is hedged around with** rules or conditions, you mean that there are a lot of rules or conditions. ❑ *The offer was hedged around with conditions... Many reduced fares are hedged around with restrictions.* PHRASAL VERB; be V-ed P with n; be V-ed P with n

**hedge fund** **(hedge funds)** A **hedge fund** is an investment fund that invests large amounts of money using methods that involve a lot of risk. [BUSINESS] N-COUNT

**hedge|hog** /hedʒhɒg, AM -hɔːg/ **(hedgehogs)** A **hedgehog** is a small brown animal with sharp spikes covering its back. N-COUNT

**hedge|row** /hedʒroʊ/ **(hedgerows)** A **hedgerow** is a row of bushes, trees, and plants, usually growing along a bank bordering a country lane or between fields. N-VAR

**he|don|ism** /hiːdәnɪzәm/ **Hedonism** is the belief that gaining pleasure is the most important thing in life. [FORMAL] N-UNCOUNT

**he|don|ist** /hiːdәnɪst/ **(hedonists)** A **hedonist** is someone who believes that having pleasure is the most important thing in life. [FORMAL] N-COUNT

**he|don|is|tic** /hiːdәnɪstɪk/ **Hedonistic** means relating to hedonism. [FORMAL] ❑ *...the hedonistic pleasures of the South.* ADJ

**heed** /hiːd/ **(heeds, heeding, heeded)** 1 If you **heed** someone's advice or warning, you pay attention to it and do what they suggest. [FORMAL] ❑ *But few at the conference in London last week heeded his warning.* VERB; V n 2 If you **take heed of** what someone says or if you **pay heed to** them, you pay attention to them and consider carefully what they say. [FORMAL] ❑ *But what if the government takes no heed?* PHRASE: V inflects, oft PHR to/of n

**heed|less** /hiːdlәs/ If you are **heedless of** someone or something, you do not take any notice of them. [FORMAL] ❑ *Heedless of time or any other consideration, they began to search the underwater cave... She was rummaging through the letters, scattering them about the table in her heedless haste.* ADJ: oft ADJ of n

**heel** /hiːl/ **(heels)** 1 Your **heel** is the back part of your foot, just below your ankle. N-COUNT 2 The **heel** of a shoe is the raised part on the bottom at the back. ❑ *...the shoes with the high heels.* N-COUNT 3 **Heels** are women's shoes that are raised very high at the back. ❑ *...two well-dressed ladies in high heels. ...the old adage that you shouldn't wear heels with trousers.* N-PLURAL 4 The **heel** of a sock or stocking is the part that covers your heel. N-COUNT 5 The **heel of** your hand is the rounded pad at the bottom of your palm. N-COUNT: N of n 6 ➔ See also **Achilles heel**.

PHRASES 7 If you **bring** someone **to heel**, you force them to obey you. ❑ *It's still not clear how the president will use his power to bring the republics to heel.* PHRASE: V inflects 8 If you **dig** your **heels in** or **dig in** your **heels**, you refuse to do something such as change your opinions or plans, especially when someone is trying very hard to make you do so. ❑ *It was really the British who, by digging their heels in, prevented* PHRASE: V inflects *any last-minute deal.* 9 If you say that one event follows **hard on the heels of** another or **hot on the heels of** another, you mean that one happens very quickly or immediately after another. ❑ *Unfortunately, bad news has come hard on the heels of good.* 10 If you say that someone is **hot on** your **heels**, you are emphasizing that they are chasing you and are not very far behind you. ❑ *They sped through the American southwest with the law hot on their heels.* 11 If you are **kicking** your **heels**, you are having to wait around with nothing to do, so that you get bored or impatient. [BRIT, INFORMAL] ❑ *The authorities wouldn't grant us permission to fly all the way down to San Francisco, so I had to kick my heels at Tunis Airport.* 12 If you **turn on** your **heel** or **spin on** your **heel**, you suddenly turn round, especially because you are angry or surprised. ❑ *He simply turned on his heel and walked away.* 13 **head over heels** → see **head**. to **drag** your **heels** → see **drag**. PHRASE: PHR after v, PHR n / PHRASE: usu v-link PHR emphasis / PHRASE: V inflects / PHRASE: V inflects

**hefty** /hefti/ **(heftier, heftiest)** 1 **Hefty** means large in size, weight, or amount. [INFORMAL] ❑ *She was quite a hefty woman... If he is found guilty he faces a hefty fine.* 2 A **hefty** movement is done with a lot of force. [INFORMAL] ❑ *Lambert gave Luckwell a hefty shove to send him on his way.* ADJ: usu ADJ n / ADJ: usu ADJ n

**he|gemo|ny** /hɪgeməni, AM -dʒem-/ **Hegemony** is a situation in which one country, organization, or group has more power, control, or importance than others. [FORMAL] N-UNCOUNT

**heif|er** /hefəʳ/ **(heifers)** A **heifer** is a young cow that has not yet had a calf. N-COUNT

**height** /haɪt/ **(heights)** 1 The **height** of a person or thing is their size or length from the bottom to the top. ❑ *I am 5'6" in height... The wave here has a length of 250 feet and a height of 10 feet... He was a man of medium height.* 2 **Height** is the quality of being tall. ❑ *She admits that her height is intimidating for some men.* 3 A particular **height** is the distance that something is above the ground or above something else mentioned. ❑ *...a test in which a 6.3 kilogram weight was dropped on it from a height of 1 metre.* 4 A **height** is a high position or place above the ground. ❑ *I'm not afraid of heights.* 5 When an activity, situation, or organization is **at** its **height**, it is at its most successful, powerful, or intense. ❑ *During the early sixth century emigration from Britain to Brittany was at its height.* 6 If you say that something is **the height of** a particular quality, you are emphasizing that it has that quality to the greatest degree possible. ❑ *The hip-hugging black and white polka-dot dress was the height of fashion.* 7 If something reaches great **heights**, it becomes very extreme or intense. ❑ *...the mid-1980s, when house prices rose to absurd heights.* ◆◇◇ N-VAR: oft with poss, amount *in* N, N *of* amount / N-UNCOUNT / N-VAR / N-COUNT / N-SING: *at* N with poss = peak / N-SING: *the* N *of* n emphasis / N-PLURAL: with supp, oft adj N, N *of* n

**height|en** /haɪtᵊn/ **(heightens, heightening, heightened)** If something **heightens** a feeling or if the feeling **heightens**, the feeling increases in degree or intensity. ❑ *The move has heightened tension in the state... Cross's interest heightened. ...a heightened awareness of the dangers that they now face.* VERB = intensify / V n / V / V-ed

**hei|nous** /heɪnəs/ If you describe something such as a crime as **heinous**, you mean that it is extremely evil or horrible. [FORMAL] ❑ *They are capable of the most heinous acts.* ADJ: usu ADJ n = evil, monstrous

**heir** /eəʳ/ **(heirs)** An **heir** is someone who has the right to inherit a person's money, property, or title when that person dies. ❑ *...the heir to the throne.* N-COUNT: oft with poss, oft N *to* n

**heir ap|par|ent** **(heirs apparent)** **The heir apparent to** a particular job or position is the person who is expected to have it after the person who has it now. [JOURNALISM] N-COUNT: usu sing, oft *the* N *to* n, poss N

**heir|ess** /eərɪs/ **(heiresses)** An **heiress** is a woman or girl who has the right to inherit property or a title, or who has inherited it, especially when this involves great wealth. ❑ *...the heiress to a jewellery empire.* N-COUNT: oft N *to* n

**heir|loom** /eəʳluːm/ **(heirlooms)** An **heirloom** is an ornament or other object that has belonged to a family for a very long time and that has been handed down from one generation to another. N-COUNT

**heist** /haɪst/ **(heists)** A **heist** is a robbery, especially one in which money, jewellery, or art is stolen. [JOURNALISM] N-COUNT: oft n N

**held** /held/ **Held** is the past tense and past participle of **hold**.

**heli|cop|ter** /helɪkɒptəʳ/ **(helicopters)** A **helicopter** is an aircraft with long blades on top that go round very fast. It is able to stay still in the air and to move straight upwards or downwards. ◆◇◇ N-COUNT

**heli|cop|ter gun|ship** **(helicopter gunships)** A **helicopter gunship** is a helicopter with large guns attached to it. N-COUNT

**heli|pad** /helipæd/ **(helipads)** A **helipad** is a place where helicopters can land and take off. N-COUNT

**heli|port** /helipɔːʳt/ **(heliports)** A **heliport** is an airport for helicopters. N-COUNT

**he|lium** /hiːliəm/ **Helium** is a very light gas that is colourless and has no smell. N-UNCOUNT

**he|lix** /hiːlɪks/ **(helixes)** A **helix** is a spiral shape or form. [TECHNICAL] N-COUNT

**hell** /hel/ **(hells)** 1 In some religions, **hell** is the place where the Devil lives, and where wicked people are sent to be punished when they die. Hell is usually imagined as being under the ground and full of flames. 2 If you say that a particular situation or place is **hell**, you are emphasizing that it is extremely unpleasant. ❑ *...the hell of the Siberian labor camps.* 3 **Hell** is used by some people when they are angry or excited, or when they want to emphasize what they are saying. ❑ *'Hell, no!' the doctor snapped.* ◆◇◇ N-PROPER; N-COUNT / N-VAR emphasis = misery / EXCLAM emphasis

PHRASES 4 You can use **as hell** after adjectives or some adverbs to emphasize the adjective or adverb. [INFORMAL] ❑ *The men might be armed, but they sure as hell weren't trained.* 5 If you say that a place or a situation is **hell on earth** or **a hell on earth**, you are emphasizing that it is extremely unpleasant or that it causes great suffering. ❑ *She believed she would die in the snake-infested sand dunes. She said: 'It was hell on earth'.* 6 If someone does something **for the hell of it**, or **just for the hell of it**, they do it for fun or for no particular reason. [INFORMAL] ❑ *Managers seem to be spending millions just for the hell of it.* 7 You can use **from hell** after a noun when you are emphasizing that something or someone is extremely unpleasant or evil. [INFORMAL] ❑ *He's a child from hell.* 8 If you tell someone to **go to hell**, you are angrily telling them to go away and leave you alone. [INFORMAL, RUDE] ❑ *'Well, you can go to hell!' He swept out of the room.* 9 If you say that someone can **go to hell**, you are emphasizing angrily that you do not care about them and that they will not stop you doing what you want. [INFORMAL, RUDE] ❑ *Peter can go to hell. It's my money and I'll leave it to who I want.* 10 If you say that someone **is going hell for leather**, you are emphasizing that they are doing something or are moving very quickly and perhaps carelessly. [INFORMAL] ❑ *The first horse often goes hell for leather, hits a few fences but gets away with it.* 11 Some people say **like hell** to emphasize that they strongly disagree with you or are strongly opposed to what you say. [INFORMAL] ❑ *'I'll go myself.' — 'Like hell you will!'* 12 Some people use **like hell** to emphasize how strong an action or quality is. [INFORMAL] ❑ *It hurts like hell.* 13 If you describe a place or situation as a **living hell**, you are emphasizing that it is extremely unpleasant. [INFORMAL] ❑ *School is a living hell for some children.* 14 If you say that **all hell breaks loose**, you are emphasizing that a lot of arguing or fighting suddenly starts. [INFORMAL] ❑ *He had an affair, I found out and then all hell broke loose.* 15 If you talk about **a hell of a lot of** PHRASE: adj PHR emphasis / PHRASE: oft v-link PHR emphasis = living hell / PHRASE: usu PHR with cl, PHR after v, n PHR / PHRASE: n PHR emphasis / PHRASE feelings / PHRASE emphasis / PHRASE: usu v PHR emphasis / PHRASE: usu PHR cl emphasis / PHRASE: PHR after v emphasis / PHRASE: v-link PHR emphasis / PHRASE: V inflects emphasis / PHRASE:

something, or **one hell of a lot of** something, you mean that there is a large amount of it. [INFORMAL] ❑ *The manager took a hell of a lot of money out of the club.* 16 Some people use **a hell of** or **one hell of** to emphasize that something is very good, very bad, or very big. [INFORMAL] ❑ *Whatever the outcome, it's going to be one hell of a fight.* 17 Some people use **the hell out of** for emphasis after verbs such as 'scare', 'irritate', and 'beat'. [INFORMAL] ❑ *I patted the top of her head in the condescending way I knew irritated the hell out of her.* 18 If you say **there'll be hell to pay**, you are emphasizing that there will be serious trouble. [INFORMAL] ❑ *There would be hell to pay when Ferguson and Tony found out about it.* 19 To **play hell with** something means to have a bad effect on it or cause great confusion. In British English, you can also say that one person or thing **plays merry hell with** another. [INFORMAL] ❑ *Lord Beaverbrook, to put it bluntly, played hell with the war policy of the R.A.F.* 20 If you say that someone **raises hell**, you are emphasizing that they protest strongly and angrily about a situation in order to persuade other people to correct it or improve it. [INFORMAL] ❑ *The only way to preserve democracy is to raise hell about its shortcomings.* 21 People sometimes use **the hell** for emphasis in questions, after words such as 'what', 'where', and 'why', often in order to express anger. [INFORMAL, RUDE] ❑ *Where the hell have you been?* 22 If you **go through hell**, or if someone **puts** you **through hell**, you have a very difficult or unpleasant time. [INFORMAL] ❑ *All of you seem to have gone through hell making this record.* 23 If you say you **hope to hell** or **wish to hell that** something is true, you are emphasizing that you strongly hope or wish it is true. [INFORMAL] ❑ *I hope to hell you're right.* 24 If you say that you will do something **come hell or high water**, you are emphasizing that you are determined to do it, in spite of the difficulties involved. ❑ *I've always managed to get into work come hell or high water.* 25 You can say '**what the hell**' when you decide to do something in spite of the doubts that you have about it. [INFORMAL] ❑ *What the hell, I thought, at least it will give the lazy old man some exercise.* 26 If you say '**to hell with**' something, you are emphasizing that you do not care about something and that it will not stop you from doing what you want to do. [INFORMAL] ❑ *To hell with this, I'm getting out of here.*

usu PHR *of* n/-ing [emphasis] — PHRASE: PHR n [emphasis] — PHRASE: v PHR n [emphasis] — PHRASE: V inflects [emphasis] — PHRASE: V inflects, usu PHR *with* n — PHRASE: V inflects [emphasis] — PHRASE: quest PHR [emphasis] — PHRASE: V inflects — PHRASE: V inflects, PHR that [emphasis] — PHRASE: usu PHR after v [emphasis] — PHRASE [feelings] — PHRASE: PHR n [emphasis]

**he'll** /hɪl, hiːl/ **He'll** is the usual spoken form of 'he will'. ❑ *By the time he's twenty he'll know everyone worth knowing in Washington.*

**hell-bent** also **hellbent.** If you say that someone is **hell-bent on** doing something, you are emphasizing that they are determined to do it, even if this causes problems or difficulties for other people. ❑ *He accused Ford of being hell-bent on achieving its cuts by whatever means.* — ADJ: usu v-link ADJ, usu ADJ *on* -ing/n [emphasis]

**Hel|len|ic** /helenɪk, -liː-/ **Hellenic** is used to describe the people, language, and culture of Ancient Greece. — ADJ: usu ADJ n

**hell|hole** /helhoʊl/ **(hellholes)** If you call a place a **hellhole**, you mean that it is extremely unpleasant, usually because it is dirty and uncomfortable. ❑ *...stuck in this hellhole of a jail.* — N-COUNT

**hell|ish** /helɪʃ/ You describe something as **hellish** to emphasize that it is extremely unpleasant. [INFORMAL] ❑ *The atmosphere in Washington is hellish.* — ADJ [emphasis]

**hel|lo** /heloʊ/ **(hellos)** also **hallo, hullo.** ◆◇◇ 1 You say '**Hello**' to someone when you meet them. ❑ *Hello, Trish... Do you want to pop your head in and say hallo to my girlfriend?* ♦ **Hello** is also a noun. ❑ *The salesperson greeted me with a warm hello.* 2 You say '**Hello**' to someone at the beginning of a telephone conversation, either when you answer the phone or before you give your name or say why you are phoning. ❑ *A moment later, Cohen picked up the phone. 'Hello?'* 3 You can call '**hello**' to attract someone's attention. ❑ *Very softly, she called out: 'Hallo? Who's there?'* — CONVENTION [formulae]; N-COUNT; CONVENTION [formulae]; CONVENTION

**hell-raiser** **(hell-raisers)** If you describe someone as a **hell-raiser**, you mean that they often behave in a wild and unacceptable way, especially because they have drunk too much alcohol. [INFORMAL] — N-COUNT

**hell|uva** /heləvə/ Some people say **a helluva** or **one helluva** to emphasize that something is very good, very bad, or very big. [INFORMAL] ❑ *It taught me a helluva lot about myself... The man did one helluva job getting it all together.* — ADJ: *a/one* ADJ n [emphasis] = *a hell of a, one hell of a*

**helm** /helm/ **(helms)** 1 The **helm** of a boat or ship is the part that is used to steer it. 2 You can say that someone is at **the helm** when they are leading or running a country or organization. ❑ *He has been at the helm of Lonrho for 31 years.* — N-COUNT: usu sing; N-SING: *the* N

**hel|met** /helmɪt/ **(helmets)** A **helmet** is a hat made of a strong material which you wear to protect your head. → See also **crash helmet**. — N-COUNT

**helms|man** /helmzmən/ **(helmsmen)** The **helmsman** of a boat is the person who is steering it. — N-COUNT

**help** /help/ **(helps, helping, helped)** ◆◆◆ 1 If you **help** someone, you make it easier for them to do something, for example by doing part of the work for them or by giving them advice or money. ❑ *He has helped to raise a lot of money... You can of course help by giving them a donation directly... If you're not willing to help me, I'll find somebody who will.* ♦ **Help** is also a noun. ❑ *Thanks very much for your help... Always ask the pharmacist for help.* 2 If you say that something **helps**, you mean that it makes something easier to do or get, or that it improves a situation to some extent. ❑ *The right style of swimsuit can help to hide, minimise or emphasise what you want it to... Building more motorways and by-passes will help the environment by reducing pollution and traffic jams in towns and cities... Understanding these rare molecules will help chemists to find out what is achievable... I could cook your supper, though, if that would help.* 3 If you **help** someone go somewhere or move in some way, you give them support so that they can move more easily. ❑ *Martin helped Tanya over the rail... She helped her sit up in bed so she could hold her baby.* 4 If you say that someone or something has been **a help** or has been some **help**, you mean that they have helped you to solve a problem. ❑ *The books were not much help.* 5 **Help** is action taken to rescue a person who is in danger. You shout '**help!**' when you are in danger in order to attract someone's attention so that they can come and rescue you. ❑ *He was screaming for help... 'Help!' I screamed, turning to run.* 6 In computing, **help**, or the **help** menu, is a file that gives you information and advice, for example about how to use a particular program. [COMPUTING] ❑ *If you get stuck, click on Help.* 7 If you **help yourself to** something, you serve yourself or you take it for yourself. If someone tells you to **help yourself**, they are telling you politely to serve yourself anything you want or to take anything you want. ❑ *There's bread on the table. Help yourself... Just help yourself to leaflets.* 8 If someone **helps themselves to** something, they steal it. [INFORMAL] ❑ *Has somebody helped himself to some film star's diamonds?* 9 → See also **helping**.

VERB: V to-inf/inf; V; V n — N-UNCOUNT = assistance — VERB: V to-inf/inf; V n; V n to-inf/inf; V — VERB: V n prep/adv; V n inf/to-inf — N-SING: *a* N, also no det — N-UNCOUNT — N-UNCOUNT — VERB: V pron-refl; V pron-refl *to* n — VERB: V pron-refl *to* n

**PHRASES** 10 If you **can't help** the way you feel or behave, you cannot control it or stop it happening. You can also say that you **can't help yourself**. ❑ *I can't help feeling sorry for the poor man.* 11 If you say you **can't help** thinking something, you are expressing your opinion in an indirect way, often because you think it seems rude. ❑ *I can't help feeling that this may just be another of her schemes.* 12 If someone or something **is of help**, they make a situation easier or better. ❑ *Can I be of help to you?*

PHRASE: V inflects, PHR -ing, PHR *it*, PHR pron-refl, PHR n — PHRASE: V inflects, PHR -ing, PHR *but* inf [vagueness] — PHRASE: V inflects

♦ **help out** If you **help** someone **out**, you help them by doing some work for them or by — PHRASAL VERB lending them some money. ❑ *I help out with the secretarial work... All these presents came to more money than I had, and my mother had to help me out... He thought you'd been brought in from Toronto to help out the local police.* V P *with* n / V n P / V P n (not pron) Also V P

**help|er** /helpəʳ/ **(helpers)** A **helper** is a person who helps another person or group with a job they are doing. N-COUNT = *assistant*

**help|ful** /helpfʊl/ 1 If you describe someone as **helpful**, you mean that they help you in some way, such as doing part of your job for you or by giving you advice or information. ❑ *The staff in the London office are helpful but only have limited information.* ♦ **help|ful|ly** *They had helpfully provided us with instructions on how to find the house.* ♦ **help|ful|ness** *The level of expertise and helpfulness is far higher in smaller shops.* 2 If you describe information or advice as **helpful**, you mean that it is useful for you. ❑ *The following information may be helpful to readers.* 3 Something that is **helpful** makes a situation more pleasant or more easy to tolerate. ❑ *It is often helpful to have your spouse in the room when major news is expected.* ADJ / ADV: ADV with v / N-UNCOUNT / ADJ ≠ *unhelpful* / ADJ: oft *it* v-link ADJ to-inf, ADJ *for* n/-ing, ADJ *in* -ing/n

**help|ing** /helpɪŋ/ **(helpings)** 1 A **helping of** food is the amount of it that you get in a single serving. ❑ *She gave them extra helpings of ice cream.* 2 You can refer to an amount of something, especially a quality, as a **helping of** that thing. [INFORMAL] ❑ *It took a generous helping of entrepreneurial confidence to persevere during this incident.* N-COUNT: usu with supp, oft N *of* n, adj N / N-COUNT: N *of* n, usu adj N *of* n = *amount*

**help|less** /helpləs/ If you are **helpless**, you do not have the strength or power to do anything useful or to control or protect yourself. ❑ *Parents often feel helpless, knowing that all the cuddles in the world won't stop the tears.* ♦ **help|less|ly** *Their son watched helplessly as they vanished beneath the waves.* ♦ **help|less|ness** *I remember my feelings of helplessness.* ADJ: oft ADJ to-inf, ADJ *with* n / ADV: usu ADV with v / N-UNCOUNT

**help|line** /helplaɪn/ **(helplines)** A **helpline** is a special telephone service that people can call to get advice about a particular subject. N-COUNT

**help|mate** /helpmeɪt/ **(helpmates)** If you say that one person is another person's **helpmate**, you mean that they help the other person in their life or work, especially by doing boring but necessary jobs for them such as cooking and cleaning. [OLD-FASHIONED] N-COUNT

**helter-skelter** /heltəʳ skeltəʳ/ You use **helter-skelter** to describe something that is hurried and disorganized, especially when things happen very quickly, one after the other. ❑ *He now faces another crisis in his helter-skelter existence.* ♦ **Helter-skelter** is also an adverb. ❑ *...a panic-stricken crowd running helter-skelter to get away from the tear gas.* ADJ: ADJ n / ADV: ADV after v

**hem** /hem/ **(hems, hemming, hemmed)** 1 A **hem** on something such as a piece of clothing is an edge that is folded over and stitched down to prevent threads coming loose. The **hem** of a skirt or dress is the bottom edge. 2 If you **hem** something, you form a hem along its edge. ❑ *Turn under and hem the outer edges.* 3 **hem and haw** → see **haw**. N-COUNT / VERB V n

♦ **hem in** 1 If a place **is hemmed in by** mountains or **by** other places, it is surrounded by them. ❑ *Manchester is hemmed in by greenbelt countryside and by housing and industrial areas.* 2 If someone **is hemmed in** or if someone **hems** them **in**, they are prevented from moving or changing, for example because they are surrounded by people or obstacles. ❑ *The company's competitors complain that they are hemmed in by rigid legal contracts.* PHRASAL VERB: usu passive *be* V-ed P *by* n / PHRASAL VERB *be* V-ed P *by* n Also V n P

**he-man** **(he-men)** A **he-man** is a strong and very masculine man. [INFORMAL] N-COUNT

**hemi|sphere** /hemɪsfɪəʳ/ **(hemispheres)** 1 A **hemisphere** is one half of the earth. ❑ *...the northern hemisphere.* 2 A **hemisphere** is one half of the brain. N-COUNT: usu supp N / N-COUNT: usu supp N

**hem|line** /hemlaɪn/ **(hemlines)** The **hemline** of a dress or skirt is its lower edge. People sometimes use **hemline** to talk about how long a dress or skirt is. ❑ *Mickey favoured tight skirts with a hemline at the knee.* N-COUNT

**hem|lock** /hemlɒk/ **Hemlock** is a poisonous plant. N-UNCOUNT

**hemo|glo|bin** /hiːməgloʊbɪn/ → see **haemoglobin**.

**hemo|philia** /hiːməfɪliə/ → see **haemophilia**.

**hemo|phili|ac** /hiːməfɪliæk/ → see **haemophiliac**.

**hem|or|rhage** /hemərɪdʒ/ → see **haemorrhage**.

**hem|or|rhoid** /hemərɔɪd/ → see **haemorrhoid**.

**hemp** /hemp/ **Hemp** is a plant used for making rope or the drug marijuana. N-UNCOUNT

**hen** /hen/ **(hens)** 1 A **hen** is a female chicken. People often keep hens in order to eat them or sell their eggs. 2 The female of any bird can be referred to as a **hen**. N-COUNT / N-COUNT

**hence** /hens/ 1 You use **hence** to indicate that the statement you are about to make is a consequence of what you have just said. [FORMAL] ❑ *The trade imbalance is likely to rise again in 1990. Hence a new set of policy actions will be required soon.* 2 You use **hence** in expressions such as '**several years hence**' or '**six months hence**' to refer to a time in the future, especially a long time in the future. [FORMAL] ❑ *The gases that may be warming the planet will have their main effect many years hence.* ADV: ADV cl/group = *therefore, thus* / ADV: amount ADV

**hence|forth** /hensfɔːʳθ/ **Henceforth** means from this time onwards. [FORMAL] ❑ *Henceforth, parties which fail to get 5% of the vote will not be represented in parliament.* ADV: ADV with cl

**hence|forward** /hensfɔːʳwəʳd/ **Henceforward** means from this time on. [FORMAL] ❑ *Henceforward France and Britain had a common interest.* ADV: ADV with cl = *henceforth, from now on*

**hench|man** /hentʃmən/ **(henchmen)** If you refer to someone as another person's **henchman**, you mean that they work for or support the other person, especially by doing unpleasant, violent, or dishonest things on their behalf. N-COUNT: usu poss N [disapproval] = *heavy*

**hen|house** /henhaʊs/ **(henhouses)** A **henhouse** is a special building where hens are kept. N-COUNT

**hen|na** /henə/ **Henna** is a reddish-brown dye that is made from the leaves of a shrub. It is used especially for colouring hair or skin. N-UNCOUNT

**hen night** **(hen nights)** A **hen night** is a party for a woman who is getting married very soon, to which only women are invited. [BRIT] N-COUNT

**hen par|ty** **(hen parties)** A **hen party** is a party to which only women are invited. [BRIT] N-COUNT

**hen-pecked** also **henpecked**. You use **hen-pecked** to describe a man when you disapprove of the fact that his wife, or another woman, is always telling him what to do or telling him that he has done something wrong. [INFORMAL] ADJ: usu ADJ n [disapproval]

**hepa|ti|tis** /hepətaɪtɪs/ **Hepatitis** is a serious disease which affects the liver. N-UNCOUNT

**hep|tath|lon** /heptæθlɒn/ **(heptathlons)** The **heptathlon** is an athletics competition for women in which each athlete competes in seven different events. N-COUNT

**her** /həʳ, STRONG hɜːʳ/ ◆◆◆

> **Her** is a third person singular pronoun. **Her** is used as the object of a verb or a preposition. **Her** is also a possessive determiner.

1 You use **her** to refer to a woman, girl, or female animal. ❑ *I went in the room and told her I had something to say to her... I really thought I'd lost her. Everybody kept asking me, 'Have you found your cat?'* PRON: v PRON, prep PRON

♦ **Her** is also a possessive determiner. ❑ *Liz travelled round the world for a year with her boyfriend James.* [2] In written English, **her** is sometimes used to refer to a person without saying whether that person is a man or a woman. Some people dislike this use and prefer to use 'him or her' or 'them'. ❑ *Talk to your baby, play games, and show her how much you enjoy her company.* ♦ **Her** is also a possessive determiner. ❑ *The non-drinking, non smoking model should do nothing which would risk her reputation.* [3] **Her** is sometimes used to refer to a country or nation. [FORMAL or WRITTEN] ♦ **Her** is also a possessive determiner. ❑ *Our reporter looks at reactions to Britain's apparently deep-rooted distrust of her EU partner.* DET / PRON: v PRON, prep PRON / DET / PRON: v PRON, prep PRON / DET

**her|ald** /herəld/ **(heralds, heralding, heralded)** [1] Something that **heralds** a future event or situation is a sign that it is going to happen or appear. [FORMAL] ❑ *...the sultry evening that heralded the end of the baking hot summer.* [2] Something that is a **herald of** a future event or situation is a sign that it is going to happen or appear. [FORMAL] ❑ *I welcome the report as a herald of more freedom, not less.* [3] If an important event or action **is heralded by** people, announcements are made about it so that it is publicly known and expected. [FORMAL] ❑ *Janet Jackson's new album has been heralded by a massive media campaign... Tonight's clash between Real Madrid and Arsenal is being heralded as the match of the season.* [4] In former times, a **herald** was a person who delivered and announced important messages. VERB: V n / N-COUNT: N *of* n / VERB: usu passive, *be* V-ed *by* n, *be* V-ed *as* n / N-COUNT

**he|ral|dic** /hərældɪk/ **Heraldic** means relating to heraldry. ❑ *...religious and heraldic symbols.* ADJ: ADJ n

**her|ald|ry** /herəldri/ **Heraldry** is the study of coats of arms and of the history of the families who are entitled to have them. N-UNCOUNT

**herb** /hɜːʳb, AM ɜːʳb/ **(herbs)** A **herb** is a plant whose leaves are used in cooking to add flavour to food, or as a medicine. N-COUNT

**her|ba|ceous** /hɜːʳbeɪʃəs, AM ɜːʳb-/ **Herbaceous** plants have green stems, not hard, woody stems. ADJ: ADJ n

**her|ba|ceous bor|der** **(herbaceous borders)** A **herbaceous border** is a flower bed containing a mixture of plants that flower every year. [BRIT] N-COUNT

**herb|al** /hɜːʳbəl, AM ɜːʳb-/ **(herbals)** **Herbal** means made from or using herbs. ❑ *...herbal remedies for colds.* ADJ: ADJ n

**herb|al|ism** /hɜːʳbəlɪzəm, AM ɜːʳb-/ **Herbalism** is the practice of using herbs to treat illnesses. N-UNCOUNT

**herb|al|ist** /hɜːʳbəlɪst, AM ɜːʳb-/ **(herbalists)** A **herbalist** is a person who grows or sells herbs that are used in medicine. N-COUNT

**herbi|cide** /hɜːʳbɪsaɪd, AM ɜːʳb-/ **(herbicides)** A **herbicide** is a chemical that is used to destroy plants, especially weeds. N-MASS

**her|bi|vore** /hɜːʳbɪvɔːʳ, AM ɜːʳb-/ **(herbivores)** A **herbivore** is an animal that only eats plants. N-COUNT

**her|cu|lean** /hɜːʳkjʊliːən/ also **Herculean.** A **herculean** task or ability is one that requires extremely great strength or effort. [LITERARY] ❑ *...his herculean efforts to bring peace to our troubled island.* ADJ: usu ADJ n = formidable

**herd** /hɜːʳd/ **(herds, herding, herded)** [1] A **herd** is a large group of animals of one kind that live together. ❑ *...large herds of elephant and buffalo.* [2] If you say that someone has joined **the herd** or follows **the herd**, you are criticizing them because you think that they behave just like everyone else and do not think for themselves. ❑ *They are individuals; they will not follow the herd.* [3] If you **herd** people somewhere, you make them move there in a group. ❑ *He began to herd the prisoners out.* [4] If you **herd** animals, you make them move along as a group. ❑ *Stefano used a motor cycle to herd the sheep... A boy herded half a dozen camels down towards the water trough.* N-COUNT: oft n N, N *of* n / N-SING: *the* N, disapproval = pack / VERB: V n prep/adv / VERB: V n, V n prep/adv

**herds|man** /hɜːʳdzmən/ **(herdsmen)** A **herdsman** is a man who looks after a herd of animals such as cattle or goats. N-COUNT

**here** /hɪəʳ/ ◆◆◆ [1] You use **here** when you are referring to the place where you are. ❑ *I'm here all by myself and I know I'm going to get lost... Well, I can't stand here chatting all day. ...the growing number of skiers that come here.* [2] You use **here** when you are pointing towards a place that is near you, in order to draw someone else's attention to it. ❑ *...if you will just sign here... Come and sit here, Lauren.* [3] You use **here** in order to indicate that the person or thing that you are talking about is near you or is being held by you. ❑ *My friend here writes for radio.* [4] If you say that you are **here to** do something, that is your role or function. ❑ *I'm not here to listen to your complaints.* [5] You use **here** in order to draw attention to something or someone who has just arrived in the place where you are, or to draw attention to the place you have just arrived at. ❑ *'Mr Cummings is here,' she said, holding the door open.* [6] You use **here** to refer to a particular point or stage of a situation or subject that you have come to or that you are dealing with. ❑ *The book goes into recent work in greater detail than I have attempted here.* [7] You use **here** to refer to a period of time, a situation, or an event that is present or happening now. ❑ *Here is your opportunity to acquire a luxurious one bedroom home.* [8] You use **here** at the beginning of a sentence in order to draw attention to something or to introduce something. ❑ *Now here's what I want you to do.* [9] You use **here** when you are offering or giving something to someone. ❑ *Here's some letters I want you to sign... Here's your cash.* ADV: *be* ADV, ADV after v, prep ADV ≠ there / ADV: ADV after v, prep ADV, *be* ADV / ADV: n ADV, ADV after v / ADV: *be* ADV to-inf / ADV: ADV with *be*, ADV before v / ADV: *it* v-link ADV that, ADV with v, ADV with cl / ADV: ADV before v, ADV with *be* / ADV: ADV *be* n/wh / ADV: ADV *be* n

PHRASES [10] You say '**here** we **are**' or '**here** you **are**' when the statement that you are making about someone's character or situation is unexpected. ❑ *Here you are, saying these terrible things.* [11] You say '**here we are**' when you have just found something that you have been looking for. ❑ *I rummaged through the drawers and came up with Amanda's folder. 'Here we are.'* [12] You say '**here goes**' when you are about to do or say something difficult or unpleasant. ❑ *Dr Culver nervously muttered 'Here goes,' and gave the little girl an injection.* [13] You use expressions such as '**here we go**' and '**here we go again**' in order to indicate that something is happening again in the way that you expected, especially something unpleasant. [INFORMAL] ❑ *At first, he was told he was too young and I thought, 'Oh, boy, here we go again.'.* [14] You use **here and now** to emphasize that something is happening at the present time, rather than in the future or past, or that you would like it to happen at the present time. ❑ *I'm a practicing physician trying to help people here and now.* [15] If something happens **here and there**, it happens in several different places. ❑ *I do a bit of teaching here and there.* [16] You use expressions such as '**here's to us**' and '**here's to your new job**' before drinking a toast in order to wish someone success or happiness. ❑ *Tony smiled and lifted his glass. 'Here's to you, Amy.'* PHRASE: V inflects, PHR with cl / CONVENTION / CONVENTION / PHRASE / PHRASE emphasis / PHRASE: PHR with cl, PHR after v / CONVENTION formulae

**here|abouts** /hɪərəbaʊts/ You use **hereabouts** to indicate that you are talking about something near you or in the same area as you. ❑ *It's a bit chilly and empty hereabouts.* ADV: ADV after v, n ADV = here

**here|after** /hɪərɑːftəʳ, -æft-/ [1] **Hereafter** means from this time onwards. [FORMAL, WRITTEN] ❑ *I realised how hard life was going to be for me hereafter.* [2] In legal documents and in written English, **hereafter** is used to introduce information about an abbreviation that will be used in the rest of the text to refer to the person or thing just mentioned. ❑ *Michel Foucault (1972), The Archaeology of Knowledge; hereafter this text will be abbreviated as AK.* [3] **The hereafter** is sometimes used to refer to the time after you have died, or to the life which some people believe you have after you ADV: ADV with cl = henceforth, from now on / ADV: ADV with cl / N-SING: usu *the* N have died. ❑ *...belief in the hereafter.* ♦ **Hereafter** is also an adjective. ❑ *...the life hereafter.* ADJ: n ADJ

**here|by** /hɪəʳbaɪ/ You use **hereby** when officially or formally saying what you are doing. [FORMAL] ❑ *I hereby sentence you for life after all the charges against you have been proven true.* ADV: ADV before v

**he|redi|tary** /hɪredɪtri/ [1] A **hereditary** characteristic or illness is passed on to a child from its parents before it is born. ❑ *In men, hair loss is hereditary.* ADJ [2] A title or position in society that is **hereditary** is one that is passed on as a right from parent to child. ❑ *...the position of the head of state is hereditary.* ADJ

**he|red|ity** /hɪredɪti/ **Heredity** is the process by which features and characteristics are passed on from parents to their children before the children are born. ❑ *Heredity is not a factor in causing the cancer.* N-UNCOUNT

**here|in** /hɪərɪn/ [1] **Herein** means in this document, text, or book. [FORMAL, WRITTEN] ❑ *The statements and views expressed herein are those of the author and are not necessarily those of the Wilson Centre.* ADV: ADV after v, n ADV [2] You can use **herein** to refer back to the situation or fact you have just mentioned, when saying it is something such as a problem or reason for something. [FORMAL, WRITTEN] ❑ *The point is that people grew unaccustomed to thinking and acting in a responsible and independent way. Herein lies another big problem.* ADV: ADV cl

**her|esy** /herɪsi/ **(heresies)** [1] **Heresy** is a belief or action that most people think is wrong, because it disagrees with beliefs that are generally accepted. ❑ *It might be considered heresy to suggest such a notion.* N-VAR [2] **Heresy** is a belief or action which seriously disagrees with the principles of a particular religion. ❑ *He said it was a heresy to suggest that women should not conduct services.* N-VAR

**her|etic** /herɪtɪk/ **(heretics)** [1] A **heretic** is someone whose beliefs or actions are considered wrong by most people, because they disagree with beliefs that are generally accepted. ❑ *He was considered a heretic and was ridiculed and ostracized for his ideas.* N-COUNT [2] A **heretic** is a person who belongs to a particular religion, but whose beliefs or actions seriously disagree with the principles of that religion. N-COUNT

**he|reti|cal** /hɪretɪkᵊl/ [1] A belief or action that is **heretical** is one that most people think is wrong because it disagrees with beliefs that are generally accepted. ❑ *I made the then heretical suggestion that it might be cheaper to design new machines.* ADJ [2] A belief or action that is **heretical** is one that seriously disagrees with the principles of a particular religion. ❑ *The Church regards spirit mediums and people claiming to speak to the dead as heretical.* ADJ

**here|to|fore** /hɪəʳtuːfɔːʳ/ **Heretofore** means 'before this time' or 'up to now'. [mainly AM, FORMAL] ❑ *They reported that clouds are an important and heretofore uninvestigated contributor to the climate.* ADV: usu ADV with v, also ADV adj, ADV with cl = *hitherto, previously*

**here|with** /hɪəʳwɪð/ **Herewith** means with this document, text, or book. You can use **herewith** in a letter to say that you are enclosing something with it. [FORMAL, WRITTEN] ❑ *...the 236 revolutionary prisoners whose names are listed herewith... I return herewith your papers.* ADV: usu ADV with v, also n ADV, ADV n, ADV with cl

**her|it|age** /herɪtɪdʒ/ **(heritages)** A country's **heritage** is all the qualities, traditions, or features of life there that have continued over many years and have been passed on from one generation to another. ❑ *The historic building is as much part of our heritage as the paintings.* N-VAR: usu with supp, oft poss N

**her|maph|ro|dite** /hɜːʳmæfrədaɪt/ **(hermaphrodites)** A **hermaphrodite** is a person, animal, or flower that has both male and female reproductive organs. N-COUNT

**her|met|ic** /hɜːʳmetɪk/ [1] If a container has a **hermetic** seal, the seal is very tight so that no air can get in or out. [TECHNICAL] ADJ: ADJ n = *airtight* ♦ **her|meti|cal|ly** /hɜːʳmetɪkli/ ❑ *The batteries are designed to be leak-proof and hermetically sealed.* ADV: ADV -ed, ADV after v [2] You use **hermetic** to describe something which you disapprove of because it seems to be totally separate from other people and things in society. [WRITTEN] ❑ *Its film industry operates in its own curiously hermetic way... Their work is more cosily hermetic than ever.* ADJ [disapproval]

**her|mit** /hɜːʳmɪt/ **(hermits)** A **hermit** is a person who lives alone, away from people and society. N-COUNT

**her|nia** /hɜːʳniə/ **(hernias)** A **hernia** is a medical condition which is often caused by strain or injury. It results in one of your internal organs sticking through a weak point in the surrounding tissue. N-VAR

**hero** /hɪərou/ **(heroes)** [1] The **hero** of a book, play, film, or story is the main male character, who usually has good qualities. ❑ *The hero of Doctor Zhivago dies in 1929.* ◆◇◇ N-COUNT ≠ *villain* [2] A **hero** is someone, especially a man, who has done something brave, new, or good, and who is therefore greatly admired by a lot of people. ❑ *He called Mr Mandela a hero who had inspired millions.* N-COUNT [3] If you describe someone as your **hero**, you mean that you admire them a great deal, usually because of a particular quality or skill that they have. ❑ *My boyhood hero was Bobby Charlton.* N-COUNT: usu sing, with poss = *idol*

**he|ro|ic** /hɪrouɪk/ **(heroics)** [1] If you describe a person or their actions as **heroic**, you admire them because they show extreme bravery. ❑ *His heroic deeds were celebrated in every corner of India.* ADJ: usu ADJ n = *courageous* ♦ **he|roi|cal|ly** /hɪrouɪkli/ *He had acted heroically during the liner's evacuation.* ADV: ADV with v [2] If you describe an action or event as **heroic**, you admire it because it involves great effort or determination to succeed. ❑ *The company has made heroic efforts at cost reduction.* ADJ [approval] ♦ **he|roi|cal|ly** *Single parents cope heroically in doing the job of two people.* ADV: usu ADV with v, also ADV adj [3] **Heroic** means being or relating to the hero of a story. ❑ *...the book's central, heroic figure.* ADJ: usu ADJ n [4] **Heroics** are actions involving bravery, courage, or determination. ❑ *...the man whose aerial heroics helped save the helicopter pilot.* N-PLURAL [5] If you describe someone's actions or plans as **heroics**, you think that they are foolish or dangerous because they are too difficult or brave for the situation in which they occur. [SPOKEN] ❑ *He said his advice was: 'No heroics, stay within the law'.* N-PLURAL: usu with brd-neg [disapproval]

**hero|in** /herouɪn/ **Heroin** is a powerful drug which some people take for pleasure, but which they can become addicted to. N-UNCOUNT

**hero|ine** /herouɪn/ **(heroines)** [1] The **heroine** of a book, play, film, or story is the main female character, who usually has good qualities. ❑ *The heroine is a senior TV executive.* N-COUNT [2] A **heroine** is a woman who has done something brave, new, or good, and who is therefore greatly admired by a lot of people. ❑ *The national heroine of the day was Xing Fen, winner of the first Gold medal of the Games.* N-COUNT [3] If you describe a woman as your **heroine**, you mean that you admire her greatly, usually because of a particular quality or skill that she has. ❑ *My heroine was Elizabeth Taylor.* N-COUNT: usu sing, with poss = *idol*

**hero|ism** /herouɪzəm/ **Heroism** is great courage and bravery. ❑ *...individual acts of heroism.* N-UNCOUNT

**her|on** /herən/ **(herons)** A **heron** is a large bird which has long legs and a long beak, and which eats fish. N-COUNT

**hero-worship** **(hero-worships, hero-worshipping, hero-worshipped)**

✔ The noun is also spelled **hero worship**.

[1] **Hero-worship** is a very great admiration of someone and a belief that they are special or perfect. ❑ *Singer Brett Anderson inspires old-fashioned hero-worship.* N-UNCOUNT [2] If you **hero-worship** someone, you admire them a great deal and think they are special or perfect. ❑ *He was amused by the way younger actors started to hero-worship and copy him.* VERB V n

**her|pes** /hɜːpiːz/ **Herpes** is a disease which causes painful red spots to appear on the skin. N-UNCOUNT

**her|ring** /herɪŋ/ **(herring** or **herrings)** A **herring** is a long silver-coloured fish. Herring live in large groups in the sea. N-VAR ♦ **Herring** is a piece of this fish eaten as food. → See also **red herring**. N-UNCOUNT

**herring|bone** /herɪŋboʊn/ **Herringbone** is a pattern used in fabrics or brickwork which looks like parallel rows of zigzag lines. N-UNCOUNT: oft N n

**hers** /hɜːʳz/

> **Hers** is a third person possessive pronoun.

1 You use **hers** to indicate that something belongs or relates to a woman, girl, or female animal. PRON ❑ *His hand as it shook hers was warm and firm... He'd never seen eyes as green as hers... Professor Camm was a great friend of hers.* 2 In written English, **hers** is sometimes used to refer to a person without saying whether that person is a man or a woman. Some people dislike this use and prefer to use 'his or hers' or 'theirs'. PRON ❑ *The author can report other people's results which more or less agree with hers.* 3 **Hers** is sometimes used to refer to a country or nation. [FORMAL or WRITTEN] PRON

**her|self** /həʳself/ ♦♦♦

> **Herself** is a third person singular reflexive pronoun. **Herself** is used when the object of a verb or preposition refers to the same person as the subject of the verb, except in meaning 3.

1 You use **herself** to refer to a woman, girl, or female animal. PRON: v PRON, prep PRON ❑ *She let herself out of the room... Jennifer believes she will move out on her own when she is financially able to support herself... Robin didn't feel good about herself.* 2 In written English, **herself** is sometimes used to refer to a person without saying whether that person is a man or a woman. Some people dislike this use and prefer to use 'himself or herself' or 'themselves'. PRON ❑ *How can anyone blame her for actions for which she feels herself to be in no way responsible?* 3 **Herself** is sometimes used to refer to a country or nation. [FORMAL or WRITTEN] PRON ❑ *Britain's dream of herself began to fade.* 4 You use **herself** to emphasize the person or thing that you are referring to. **Herself** is sometimes used instead of 'her' as the object of a verb or preposition. PRON [emphasis] ❑ *She's so beautiful herself... She herself was not a keen gardener.*

**he's** /hɪz, hiːz/ **He's** is the usual spoken form of 'he is' or 'he has', especially when 'has' is an auxiliary verb. ❑ *He's working maybe twenty-five hours a week.*

**hesi|tant** /hezɪtᵊnt/ If you are **hesitant about** doing something, you do not do it quickly or immediately, usually because you are uncertain, embarrassed, or worried. ADJ: oft ADJ *about* n, ADJ to-inf ❑ *She was hesitant about coming forward with her story.* ♦ **hesi|tan|cy** /hezɪtənsi/ N-UNCOUNT = reluctance ❑ *A trace of hesitancy showed in Dr. Stockton's eyes.* ♦ **hesi|tant|ly** ADV: ADV with v ❑ *'Would you do me a favour?' she asked hesitantly.*

**hesi|tate** /hezɪteɪt/ **(hesitates, hesitating, hesitated)** 1 If you **hesitate**, you do not speak or act for a short time, usually because you are uncertain, embarrassed, or worried about what you are going to say or do. VERB ❑ *The telephone rang. Catherine hesitated, debating whether to answer it.* V ♦ **hesi|ta|tion** /hezɪteɪʃᵊn/ **(hesitations)** N-VAR ❑ *Asked if he would go back, Mr Searle said after some hesitation, 'I'll have to think about that'.* 2 If you **hesitate to** do something, you delay doing it or are unwilling to do it, usually because you are not certain it would be right. If you do not **hesitate to** do something, you do it immediately. VERB ❑ *Some parents hesitate to take these steps because they suspect that their child is exaggerating.* V to-inf 3 You can use **hesitate** in expressions such as '**don't hesitate to call me**' or '**don't hesitate to contact us**' when you are telling someone that they should do something as soon as it needs to be done and should not worry about disturbing other people. VERB: only imper, with neg ❑ *In the event of difficulties, please do not hesitate to contact our Customer Service Department.* V to-inf

**hesi|ta|tion** /hezɪteɪʃᵊn/ **(hesitations)** 1 **Hesitation** is an unwillingness to do something, or a delay in doing it, because you are uncertain, worried, or embarrassed about it. N-VAR: oft N *in* -ing ❑ *He promised there would be no more hesitations in pursuing reforms. ...the prime minister's hesitation to accept a ceasefire.* → See also **hesitate**.
PHRASES 2 If you say that you **have no hesitation in** doing something, you are emphasizing that you will do it immediately or willingly because you are certain that it is the right thing to do. PHRASE: V inflects, usu PHR *in* -ing [emphasis] ❑ *The board said it had no hesitation in unanimously rejecting the offer.* 3 If you say that someone does something **without hesitation**, you are emphasizing that they do it immediately and willingly. PHRASE: usu PHR after v, PHR with cl [emphasis] ❑ *The great majority of players would, of course, sign the contract without hesitation.*

**hes|sian** /hesiən, AM heʃən/ **Hessian** is a thick, rough fabric that is used for making sacks. [mainly BRIT] N-UNCOUNT

> in AM, use **burlap**

**hetero|dox** /hetərədɒks/ **Heterodox** beliefs, opinions, or ideas are different from the accepted or official ones. [FORMAL] ADJ = unorthodox

**hetero|geneous** /hetərədʒiːniəs/ A **heterogeneous** group consists of many different types of things or people. [FORMAL] ADJ: usu ADJ n = diverse ≠ homogeneous ❑ *...a rather heterogeneous collection of studies from diverse origins.*

**hetero|sex|ual** /hetəroʊsekʃuəl/ **(heterosexuals)** 1 A **heterosexual** relationship is a sexual relationship between a man and a woman. ADJ: usu ADJ n 2 Someone who is **heterosexual** is sexually attracted to people of the opposite sex. ADJ ♦ **Heterosexual** is also a noun. N-COUNT ❑ *In Denmark the age of consent is fifteen for both heterosexuals and homosexuals.* ♦ **hetero|sexu|al|ity** /hetəroʊsekʃuælɪti/ N-UNCOUNT ❑ *...a challenge to the assumption that heterosexuality was 'normal'.*

**het up** /het ʌp/ If you get **het up about** something, you get very excited, angry, or anxious about it. [INFORMAL] ADJ: v-link ADJ, oft ADJ *about* n = worked up

**heu|ris|tic** /hjʊərɪstɪk/ 1 A **heuristic** method of learning involves discovery and problem-solving, using reasoning and past experience. [TECHNICAL] ADJ 2 A **heuristic** computer program uses rules based on previous experience in order to solve a problem, rather than using a mathematical procedure. [COMPUTING] ADJ → See also **algorithm**.

**hew** /hjuː/ **(hews, hewing, hewed, hewed** or **hewn)** 1 If you **hew** stone or wood, you cut it, for example with an axe. [OLD-FASHIONED] VERB = chop ❑ *He felled, peeled and hewed his own timber.* V n 2 If something **is hewn from** stone or wood, it is cut from stone or wood. [LITERARY, OLD-FASHIONED] VERB: usu passive = cut ❑ *...the rock from which the lower chambers and subterranean passageways have been hewn. ...medieval monasteries hewn out of the rockface.* be V-ed from/out of n V-ed 3 → See also **rough-hewn**.

**hexa|gon** /heksəgən, AM -gɑːn/ **(hexagons)** A **hexagon** is a shape that has six straight sides. N-COUNT

**hex|ago|nal** /heksægənᵊl/ A **hexagonal** object or shape has six straight sides. ADJ

**hey** /heɪ/ In informal situations, you say or shout '**hey**' to attract someone's attention, or to show surprise, interest, or annoyance. CONVENTION [feelings] ❑ *'Hey! Look out!' shouted Patty.*

**hey|day** /heɪdeɪ/ Someone's **heyday** is the time when they are most powerful, successful, or popular. N-SING: with poss ❑ *In its heyday, the studio's boast was that it had more stars than there are in heaven.*

**HGH** /eɪtʃ dʒiː eɪtʃ/ **HGH** is an abbreviation for **human growth hormone**.

**hi** /haɪ/ In informal situations, you say '**hi**' to greet someone. ◆◇◇ CONVENTION [formulae] ❑ *'Hi, Liz,' she said shyly as she came into the room.*

**hia|tus** /haɪeɪtəs/ A **hiatus** is a pause in which nothing happens, or a gap where something is missing. [FORMAL] ❑ *Diplomatic efforts to reach a settlement resume today after a two-week hiatus.* N-SING: usu with supp, oft N *in/of* n

**hi|ber|nate** /haɪbəʳneɪt/ **(hibernates, hibernating, hibernated)** Animals that **hibernate** spend the winter in a state like a deep sleep. ❑ *Dormice hibernate from October to May.* VERB V

**hi|bis|cus** /hɪbɪskəs, AM haɪ-/ **(hibiscus)** A **hibiscus** is a tropical bush that has large, brightly-coloured bell-shaped flowers. N-VAR

**hic|cup** /hɪkʌp/ **(hiccups, hiccuping** or **hiccupping, hiccuped** or **hiccupped)** also **hiccough.**
[1] You can refer to a small problem or difficulty as a **hiccup**, especially if it does not last very long or is easily put right. ❑ *A recent sales hiccup is nothing to panic about.* N-COUNT: usu with supp, oft n N, N *in* n [2] When you have **hiccups**, you make repeated sharp sounds in your throat, often because you have been eating or drinking too quickly. ❑ *A young baby may frequently get a bout of hiccups during or soon after a feed.* N-UNCOUNT: also *the* N [3] A **hiccup** is a sound of the kind that you make when you have hiccups. N-COUNT [4] When you **hiccup**, you make repeated sharp sounds in your throat. ❑ *She was still hiccuping from the egg she had swallowed whole.* VERB V

**hick** /hɪk/ **(hicks)** If you refer to someone as a **hick**, you are saying in a rude way that you think they are uneducated and stupid because they come from the countryside. [INFORMAL] N-COUNT: oft N n [disapproval]

**hid** /hɪd/ **Hid** is the past tense of **hide**.

**hid|den** /hɪdᵊn/ [1] **Hidden** is the past participle of **hide**. [2] **Hidden** facts, feelings, activities, or problems are not easy to notice or discover. ❑ *Under all the innocent fun, there are hidden dangers, especially for children.* ADJ [3] A **hidden** place is difficult to find. ❑ *As you descend, suddenly you see at last the hidden waterfall.* ADJ

**hid|den agen|da** **(hidden agendas)** If you say that someone has a **hidden agenda**, you are criticizing them because you think they are secretly trying to achieve or cause a particular thing, while they appear to be doing something else. ❑ *He accused foreign nations of having a hidden agenda to harm French influence.* N-COUNT [disapproval]

**hide** /haɪd/ **(hides, hiding, hid, hidden)** [1] If you **hide** something or someone, you put them in a place where they cannot easily be seen or found. ❑ *He hid the bicycle in the hawthorn hedge...* *They could see that I was terrified, and hid me until the coast was clear.* ◆◇◇ VERB = conceal V n V n [2] If you **hide** or if you **hide yourself**, you go somewhere where you cannot easily be seen or found. ❑ *At their approach the little boy scurried away and hid...* *They hid themselves behind a tree.* VERB V V pron-refl [3] If you **hide** your face, you press your face against something or cover your face with something, so that people cannot see it. ❑ *She hid her face under the collar of his jacket and she started to cry.* VERB V n [4] If you **hide** what you feel or know, you keep it a secret, so that no one knows about it. ❑ *Lee tried to hide his excitement.* VERB V n [5] If something **hides** an object, it covers it and prevents it from being seen. ❑ *The man's heavy moustache hid his upper lip completely.* VERB V n [6] A **hide** is a place which is built to look like its surroundings. Hides are used by people who want to watch or photograph animals and birds without being seen by them. [mainly BRIT] N-COUNT

✔ in AM, use **blind**

[7] A **hide** is the skin of a large animal such as a cow, horse, or elephant, which can be used for making leather. ❑ *...the process of tanning animal hides.* N-VAR = skin [8] → See also **hidden, hiding.**

**hide-and-seek** **Hide-and-seek** is a children's game in which one player covers his or her eyes until the other players have hidden themselves, and then he or she tries to find them. N-UNCOUNT

**hide|away** /haɪdəweɪ/ **(hideaways)** A **hideaway** is a place where you go to hide or to get away from other people. ❑ *The bandits fled to a remote mountain hideaway.* N-COUNT

**hide|bound** /haɪdbaʊnd/ If you describe someone or something as **hidebound**, you are criticizing them for having old-fashioned ideas or ways of doing things and being unwilling or unlikely to change. ❑ *The men are hidebound and reactionary...* *The economy was hidebound by public spending and private monopolies.* ADJ: oft ADJ *by* n [disapproval]

**hid|eous** /hɪdiəs/ [1] If you say that someone or something is **hideous**, you mean that they are very ugly or unattractive. ❑ *She saw a hideous face at the window and screamed.* ADJ = monstrous, horrible [2] You can describe an event, experience, or action as **hideous** when you mean that it is very unpleasant, painful, or difficult to bear. ❑ *His family was subjected to a hideous attack by the gang.* ADJ = horrendous

**hid|eous|ly** /hɪdiəsli/ [1] You use **hideously** to emphasize that something is very ugly or unattractive. ❑ *Everything here is hideously ugly.* ADV: usu ADV adj/-ed, also ADV after v [emphasis] [2] You can use **hideously** to emphasize that something is very unpleasant or unacceptable. ❑ *...a hideously complex program.* ADV: ADV adj/-ed [emphasis]

**hide|out** /haɪdaʊt/ **(hideouts)** A **hideout** is a place where someone goes secretly because they do not want anyone to find them, for example if they are running away from the police. N-COUNT

**hid|ing** /haɪdɪŋ/ **(hidings)** [1] If someone is **in hiding**, they have secretly gone somewhere where they cannot be seen or found. ❑ *Gray is thought to be in hiding near the France/Italy border...* *The duchess is expected to come out of hiding to attend the ceremony.* N-UNCOUNT: prep N [2] If you give someone a **hiding**, you punish them by hitting them many times. [INFORMAL] N-COUNT = beating [3] If you say that someone who is trying to achieve something is **on a hiding to nothing**, you are emphasizing that they have absolutely no chance of being successful. [BRIT, INFORMAL] ❑ *As regards commercial survival, a car manufacturer capable of making only 50,000 cars a year is on a hiding to nothing.* PHRASE: v-link PHR [emphasis]

**hid|ing place** **(hiding places)** A **hiding place** is a place where someone or something can be hidden, or where they are hiding. N-COUNT

**hi|er|ar|chi|cal** /haɪərɑːʳkɪkᵊl/ A **hierarchical** system or organization is one in which people have different ranks or positions, depending on how important they are. ❑ *...the traditional hierarchical system of military organization.* ADJ: usu ADJ n

**hi|er|ar|chy** /haɪərɑːʳki/ **(hierarchies)** [1] A **hierarchy** is a system of organizing people into different ranks or levels of importance, for example in society or in a company. ❑ *Like most other American companies with a rigid hierarchy, workers and managers had strictly defined duties.* N-VAR: usu with supp [2] The **hierarchy** of an organization such as the Church is the group of people who manage and control it. N-COUNT-COLL: with supp [3] A **hierarchy of** ideas and beliefs involves organizing them into a system or structure. [FORMAL] ❑ *...the notion of 'cultural imperialism' implies a hierarchy of cultures, some of which are stronger than others.* N-COUNT: usu N *of* n

**hi|ero|glyph** /haɪərəglɪf/ **(hieroglyphs)** **Hieroglyphs** are symbols in the form of pictures, which are used in some writing systems, especially those of ancient Egypt. N-COUNT = hieroglyphics

**hi|ero|glyph|ics** /haɪərəglɪfɪks/ **Hieroglyphics** are symbols in the form of pictures which are used in some writing systems, for example those of ancient Egypt. N-PLURAL = hieroglyphs

**hi-fi** /haɪ faɪ/ **(hi-fis)** A **hi-fi** is a set of equipment on which you play CDs and tapes, and which produces stereo sound of very good quality. N-VAR

**higgledy-piggledy** /hɪgᵊldi pɪgᵊldi/ If you say that things are **higgledy-piggledy**, you mean that they are very disorganized and untidy. [INFORMAL] ❑ *Books are often stacked in higgledy-piggledy piles on the floor.* ADJ = jumbled, untidy ♦ **Higgledy-piggledy** is also an adverb. ❑ *A whole valley of boulders tossed higgledy-piggledy as though by some giant.* ADV: ADV after v

**high** /haɪ/ **(higher, highest, highs)** ◆◆◆

1 Something that is **high** extends a long way from the bottom to the top when it is upright. You do not use **high** to describe people, animals, or plants. ❑ *...a house, with a high wall all around it... Mount Marcy is the highest mountain in the Adirondacks. ...high-heeled shoes... The gate was too high for a man of his age to climb.* — ADJ ≠ low
♦ **High** is also an adverb. ❑ *...wagons packed high with bureaus, bedding, and cooking pots.* — ADV: ADV after v

2 You use **high** to talk or ask about how much something upright measures from the bottom to the top. ❑ *...an elegant bronze horse only nine inches high... Measure your garage: how high is the door?* — ADJ: amount ADJ, n ADJ, how ADJ, as ADJ as, ADJ-compar than

3 If something is **high**, it is a long way above the ground, above sea level, or above a person or thing. ❑ *I looked down from the high window... In Castel Molo, high above Taormina, you can sample the famous almond wine made there.* — ADJ: oft ADJ prep ≠ low
♦ **High** is also an adverb. ❑ *...being able to run faster or jump higher than other people.* — ADV: ADV after v
● If something is **high up**, it is a long way above the ground, above sea level, or above a person or thing. ❑ *We saw three birds circling very high up.* — PHRASE: oft PHR prep

4 You can use **high** to indicate that something is great in amount, degree, or intensity. ❑ *The European country with the highest birth rate is Ireland... Official reports said casualties were high... Commercialisation has given many sports a higher profile.* — ADJ ≠ low
♦ **High** is also an adverb. ❑ *He expects the unemployment figures to rise even higher in coming months.* — ADV: ADV after v
● You can use phrases such as **'in the high 80s'** to indicate that a number or level is, for example, more than 85 but not as much as 90. — PHRASE ≠ low

5 If a food or other substance is **high in** a particular ingredient, it contains a large amount of that ingredient. ❑ *Don't indulge in rich sauces, fried food and thick pastry as these are high in fat.* — ADJ: v-link ADJ in n ≠ low

6 If something reaches a **high of** a particular amount or degree, that is the greatest it has ever been. ❑ *Traffic from Jordan to Iraq is down to a dozen loaded lorries a day, compared with a high of 200 a day... Sales of Russian vodka have reached an all-time high.* — N-COUNT: oft N of amount ≠ low

7 If you say that something is a **high** priority or is **high on** your list, you mean that you consider it to be one of the most important things you have to do or deal with. ❑ *The Labour Party has not made the issue a high priority... Economic reform is high on the agenda.* — ADJ: oft ADJ on n ≠ low

8 Someone who is **high in** a particular profession or society, or has a **high** position, has a very important position and has great authority and influence. ❑ *Was there anyone particularly high in the administration who was an advocate of a different policy? ...corruption in high places.* — ADJ: v-link ADJ in n, ADJ n
● Someone who is **high up in** a profession or society has a very important position. ❑ *His cousin is somebody quite high up in the navy.* — PHRASE: oft PHR in n

9 You can use **high** to describe something that is advanced or complex. ❑ *Neither Anna nor I are interested in high finance.* — ADJ: ADJ n

10 If you aim **high**, you try to obtain or to achieve the best that you can. ❑ *You should not be afraid to aim high in the quest for an improvement in your income.* — ADV: ADV after v

11 If someone has a **high** reputation, or people have a **high** opinion of them, people think they are very good in some way, for example at their work. ❑ *She has always had a high reputation for her excellent short stories... People have such high expectations of you.* — ADJ ≠ low

12 If the quality or standard of something is **high**, it is very good indeed. ❑ *His team were of the highest calibre.* — ADJ

13 If someone has **high** principles, they are morally good. ❑ *He was a man of the highest principles.* — ADJ: usu ADJ n

14 A **high** sound or voice is close to the top of a particular range of notes. ❑ *Her high voice really irritated Maria.* — ADJ ≠ low

15 When a river is **high**, it contains much more water than usual. ❑ *The waters of the Yangtze River are dangerously high for the time of year.* — ADJ ≠ low

16 If your spirits are **high**, you feel happy and excited. ❑ *Her spirits were high with the hope of seeing Nick in minutes rather than hours.* — ADJ ≠ low

17 If someone is **high on** drink or drugs, they are affected by the alcoholic drink or drugs they have taken. [INFORMAL] ❑ *He was too high on drugs and alcohol to remember them.* — ADJ: v-link ADJ, usu ADJ on n

18 A **high** is a feeling or mood of great excitement or happiness. [INFORMAL] — N-COUNT

**PHRASES** 19 If you say that something came from **on high**, you mean that it came from a person or place of great authority. ❑ *Orders had come from on high that extra care was to be taken during this week.* — PHRASE: usu from PHR

20 If you say that you were left **high and dry**, you are emphasizing that you were left in a difficult situation and were unable to do anything about it. ❑ *Schools with better reputations will be flooded with applications while poorer schools will be left high and dry.* — PHRASE: PHR after v, v-link PHR [emphasis]

21 If you refer to the **highs and lows of** someone's life or career, you are referring to both the successful or happy times, and the unsuccessful or bad times. — PHRASE: oft PHR of n

22 If you say that you looked **high and low** for something, you are emphasizing that you looked for it in every place that you could think of. — PHRASE: PHR after v [emphasis]

23 **in high dudgeon** → see **dudgeon**. **come hell or high water** → see **hell**. to **be high time** → see **time**.

**-high** /-haɪ/ **-high** combines with words such as 'knee' or 'shoulder' to indicate that someone or something reaches as high as the point that is mentioned. ❑ *The grass was knee-high.* — COMB in ADJ

**high and mighty** If you describe someone as **high and mighty**, you disapprove of them because they consider themselves to be very important and are confident that they are always right. ❑ *I think you're a bit too high and mighty yourself.* — ADJ [disapproval] = arrogant

**high|born** /haɪbɔːʳn/ also **high-born.** If someone is **highborn**, their parents are members of the nobility. [OLD-FASHIONED] — ADJ

**high|brow** /haɪbraʊ/ **(highbrows)** 1 If you say that a book or discussion is **highbrow**, you mean that it is intellectual, academic, and is often difficult to understand. ❑ *He presents his own highbrow literary programme.* — ADJ ≠ lowbrow
2 If you describe someone as **highbrow**, you mean that they are interested in serious subjects of a very intellectual nature, especially when these are difficult to understand. ❑ *Highbrow critics sniff that the programme was 'too sophisticated' to appeal to most viewers.* — ADJ: usu ADJ n ≠ lowbrow

**high chair (high chairs)** also **highchair.** A **high chair** is a chair with long legs for a small child to sit in while they are eating. — N-COUNT

**high-class** If you describe something as **high-class**, you mean that it is of very good quality or of superior social status. ❑ *...a high-class jeweller's.* — ADJ: usu ADJ n

**high com|mand (high commands)** The **high command** is the group that consists of the most senior officers in a nation's armed forces. — N-COUNT-COLL: oft supp N

**High Com|mis|sion (High Commissions)** A **High Commission** is the office where a High Commissioner and his or her staff work, or the group of officials who work there. — N-COUNT: oft the adj N

**High Com|mis|sion|er (High Commissioners)** 1 A **High Commissioner** is a senior representative who is sent by one Commonwealth country to live in another in order to work as an ambassador. — N-COUNT: oft the adj N
2 A **High Commissioner** is the head of an international commission. ❑ *...the United Nations High Commissioner for Refugees.* — N-COUNT: usu N for n, supp N

**High Court (High Courts)** In England and Wales, the **High Court** is a court of law which deals with very serious or important cases. — N-COUNT: usu sing

**high-end** **High-end** products, especially electronic products, are the most expensive of their kind. ❑ *...high-end personal computers and computer workstations.* — ADJ

**high|er** /haɪəʳ/ A **higher** degree or diploma is a qualification of an advanced standard or level. ❑ *...a higher diploma in hotel management.* → See also **high**. — ADJ: ADJ n

**high|er edu|ca|tion** **Higher education** is education at universities and colleges. — ◆◇◇ N-UNCOUNT

**higher-up (higher-ups)** A **higher-up** is an important person who has a lot of authority and influence. [AM, INFORMAL] — N-COUNT

✔ in BRIT, use **high-up**

**high ex|plo|sive** **(high explosives)** **High explosive** is an extremely powerful explosive substance. N-VAR

**high|fa|lu|tin** /haɪfəluːtɪn/ People sometimes use **highfalutin** to describe something that they think is being made to sound complicated or important in order to impress people. [INFORMAL, OLD-FASHIONED] ❑ *This isn't highfalutin art-about-art. It's marvellous and adventurous stuff.* ADJ [disapproval] = pretentious

**high five** **(high fives)** also **high-five.** If you give someone a **high five**, you put your hand up and hit their open hand with yours, especially after a victory or as a greeting. N-COUNT

**high-flier** → see **high-flyer**.

**high-flown** **High-flown** language is very grand, formal, or literary. ADJ: usu ADJ n [disapproval]

**high-flyer** **(high-flyers)** also **high flyer, high-flier.** A **high-flyer** is someone who has a lot of ability and is likely to be very successful in their career. N-COUNT

**high-flying** A **high-flying** person is successful or is likely to be successful in their career. ❑ *...her high-flying newspaper-editor husband.* ADJ: usu ADJ n

**high ground** 1 If a person or organization has **the high ground** in an argument or dispute, that person or organization has an advantage. [JOURNALISM] ❑ *The President must seek to regain the high ground in the political debate.* N-SING: the N, oft the adj N 2 If you say that someone has taken **the moral high ground**, you mean that they consider that their policies and actions are morally superior to the policies and actions of their rivals. ❑ *The Republicans took the moral high ground with the message that they were best equipped to manage the authority.* PHRASE: PHR after v

**high-handed** If you say that someone is **high-handed**, you disapprove of them because they use their authority in an unnecessarily forceful way without considering other people's feelings. ❑ *He wants to be seen as less bossy and high-handed.* ADJ [disapproval] ♦ **high-handedness** *They have been accused of secrecy and high-handedness in their dealings.* N-UNCOUNT

**high-heeled** **High-heeled** shoes are women's shoes that have high heels. ADJ: ADJ n ≠ flat

**high heels** You can refer to high-heeled shoes as **high heels**. N-PLURAL

**high-impact** 1 **High-impact** exercise puts a lot of stress on your body. ❑ *...high-impact aerobics.* ADJ: usu ADJ n ≠ low-impact 2 **High-impact** materials are very strong. ❑ *The durable high-impact plastic case is water resistant to 100 feet.* ADJ: usu ADJ n

**high jinks** **High jinks** is lively, excited behaviour in which people do things for fun. [INFORMAL, OLD-FASHIONED] N-UNCOUNT-COLL

**high jump** **The high jump** is an athletics event which involves jumping over a raised bar. N-SING: usu the N

**high|lands** /haɪləndz/ **Highlands** are mountainous areas of land. N-PLURAL

**high life** You use **the high life** to refer to an exciting and luxurious way of living that involves a great deal of entertainment, going to parties, and eating good food. ❑ *...the Hollywood high life.* N-SING: also no det

**high|light** /haɪlaɪt/ **(highlights, highlighting, highlighted)** ◆◇◇ 1 If someone or something **highlights** a point or problem, they emphasize it or make you think about it. ❑ *Two events have highlighted the tensions in recent days.* VERB V n 2 To **highlight** a piece of text means to mark it in a different colour, either with a special type of pen or on a computer screen. ❑ *...the relevant maps with the route highlighted in yellow.* VERB V n 3 The **highlights of** an event, activity, or period of time are the most interesting or exciting parts of it. ❑ *...a match that is likely to prove one of the highlights of the tournament.* N-COUNT: oft N of n 4 **Highlights** in a person's hair are narrow lighter areas made by dyeing or sunlight. N-PLURAL

**high|light|er** /haɪlaɪtə^r/ **(highlighters)** 1 **Highlighter** is a pale-coloured cosmetic that someone puts above their eyes or on their cheeks to emphasize the shape of their face. N-MASS 2 A **highlighter** is a pen with brightly-coloured ink that is used to mark parts of a document. N-COUNT

**high|ly** /haɪli/ ◆◆◇ 1 **Highly** is used before some adjectives to mean 'very'. ❑ *Mr Singh was a highly successful salesman. ...the highly controversial nuclear energy programme.* ADV: ADV adj = extremely 2 You use **highly** to indicate that someone has an important position in an organization or set of people. ❑ *...a highly placed government advisor.* ADV: ADV -ed 3 If someone is **highly** paid, they receive a large salary. ❑ *He was the most highly paid member of staff.* ADV: ADV -ed 4 If you think **highly** of something or someone, you think they are very good indeed. ❑ *...one of the most highly regarded chefs in the French capital.* ADV: ADV after v, ADV -ed

**high|ly strung** also **highly-strung.**

✔ in AM, use **high-strung**

If someone is **highly strung**, they are very nervous and easily upset. ADJ = sensitive

**high mass** also **High Mass. High mass** is a church service held in a Catholic church in which there is more ceremony than in an ordinary mass. N-UNCOUNT

**high-minded** If you say that someone is **high-minded**, you think they have strong moral principles. ❑ *The President's hopes for the country were high-minded, but too vague.* ADJ

**High|ness** /haɪnɪs/ **(Highnesses)** Expressions such as '**Your Highness**' or '**His Highness**' are used to address or refer to a member of the royal family other than a king or queen. ❑ *That would be best, Your Highness.* N-VOC: poss N; PRON: poss PRON [politeness]

**high noon** 1 **High noon** means the same as noon. [LITERARY] N-UNCOUNT 2 Journalists sometimes use **high noon** to refer to a crisis or event which is likely to decide finally what is going to happen in a conflict or situation. ❑ *It looks like high noon for the nation's movie theaters, now we are in the age of the home video.* N-UNCOUNT: usu with supp, oft N for/of n

**high-octane** You can use **high-octane** to emphasize that something is very exciting or intense. [JOURNALISM] ❑ *...a high-octane performance.* ADJ: ADJ n

**high-performance** A **high-performance** car or other product goes very fast or does a lot. ❑ *...the thrill of taking an expensive high-performance car to its limits.* ADJ: ADJ n

**high-pitched** A **high-pitched** sound is shrill and high in pitch. ❑ *A woman squealed in a high-pitched voice.* ADJ = piercing

**high point** **(high points)** **The high point** of an event or period of time is the most exciting or enjoyable part of it. ❑ *The high point of this trip was a day at the races in Balgriffin.* N-COUNT: usu with supp, oft N of/in n = highlight

**high-powered** 1 A **high-powered** machine or piece of equipment is very powerful and efficient. ❑ *...high powered lasers.* ADJ: usu ADJ n 2 Someone who is **high-powered** or has a **high-powered** job has a very important and responsible job which requires a lot of ability. ❑ *I had a very high-powered senior job in publishing.* ADJ: usu ADJ n

**high priest** **(high priests)** If you call a man the **high priest of** a particular thing, you are saying in a slightly mocking way that he is considered by people to be expert in that thing. ❑ *...the high priest of cheap periodical fiction.* N-COUNT: usu N of n

**high priest|ess** **(high priestesses)** If you call a woman the **high priestess of** a particular thing, you are saying in a slightly mocking way that she is considered by people to be expert in that thing. ❑ *...the American high priestess of wit.* N-COUNT: usu N of n

**high-profile** A **high-profile** person or a **high-profile** event attracts a lot of attention or publicity. ❑ *...the high-profile reception being given to Mr Arafat.* ADJ: usu ADJ n

**high-ranking** A **high-ranking** person has an important position in a particular organization. ❑ *...a high-ranking officer in the medical corps.* ADJ: ADJ n

**high-rise** **(high-rises)** **High-rise** buildings are modern buildings which are very tall and have ADJ: ADJ n many levels or floors. ❑ *...high-rise office buildings.* ♦ A **high-rise** is a high-rise building. ❑ *That big high-rise above us is where Brian lives.* N-COUNT

**high road** [1] A **high road** is a main road. [BRIT] N-COUNT: usu sing

☑ in AM, use **highway**

[2] If you say that someone is taking **the high road** in a situation, you mean that they are taking the most positive and careful course of action. [mainly AM] ❑ *US diplomats say the president is likely to take the high road in his statements about trade.* N-SING: usu *the* N

**high-roller** **(high-rollers)** also **high roller.** **High rollers** are people who are very rich and who spend money in an extravagant or risky way, especially by gambling. [JOURNALISM] N-COUNT

**high school** **(high schools)** [1] In Britain, a **high school** is a school for children aged between eleven and eighteen. ❑ *...Sunderland High School.* N-VAR; N-IN-NAMES [2] In the United States, a **high school** is a school for children usually aged between fourteen and eighteen. ❑ *...an 18-year-old inner-city kid who dropped out of high school.* N-VAR; N-IN-NAMES

**high seas** **The high seas** is used to refer to the sea. [LITERARY] ❑ *...battles on the high seas.* N-PLURAL: *the* N

**high sea|son** The **high season** is the time of year when a place has most tourists or visitors. [BRIT] ❑ *A typical high-season week in a chalet costs about £470.* N-SING: also no det ≠ *low season*

**high so|ci|ety** You can use **high society** to refer to people who come from rich and important families. N-UNCOUNT

**high-sounding** You can use **high-sounding** to describe language and ideas which seem very grand and important, especially when you think they are not really important. ❑ *...high-sounding decrees designed to impress foreigners and attract foreign capital.* ADJ: usu ADJ n [disapproval]

**high-spirited** Someone who is **high-spirited** is very lively and easily excited. ADJ ≠ *placid*

**high spot** **(high spots)** The **high spot of** an event or activity is the most exciting or enjoyable part of it. ❑ *Rough weather would have denied us a landing on the island, for me the high spot of the entire cruise.* N-COUNT: oft N *of* n = *highlight*

**high street** **(high streets)** [1] The **high street** of a town is the main street where most of the shops and banks are. [mainly BRIT] N-COUNT; N-IN-NAMES

☑ in AM, use **Main Street**

[2] **High street** banks and businesses are companies which have branches in the main shopping areas of most towns. [mainly BRIT] ❑ *The scanners are available from high street stores.* ADJ: ADJ n

**high sum|mer** **High summer** is the middle of summer. N-UNCOUNT

**high tea** **(high teas)** In Britain, some people have a meal called **high tea** in the late afternoon instead of having dinner or supper later in the evening. [OLD-FASHIONED] N-VAR

**high-tech** also **high tech**, **hi tech.** **High-tech** activities or equipment involve or result from the use of high technology. ❑ *...the latest high-tech medical gadgetry.* ADJ: usu ADJ n

**high tech|nol|ogy** **High technology** is the practical use of advanced scientific research and knowledge, especially in relation to electronics and computers, and the development of new advanced machines and equipment. N-UNCOUNT

**high-tension** A **high-tension** electricity cable is one which is able to carry a very powerful current. ADJ: ADJ n

**high tide** At the coast, **high tide** is the time when the sea is at its highest level because the tide is in. N-UNCOUNT ≠ *low tide*

**high trea|son** **High treason** is a very serious crime which involves putting your country or its head of state in danger. N-UNCOUNT

**high-up** **(high-ups)** [1] A **high-up** is an important person who has a lot of authority and influence. [BRIT, INFORMAL] N-COUNT

☑ in AM, use **higher-up**

[2] **high up** → see **high**.

**high wa|ter** **High water** is the time at which the water in a river or sea is at its highest level as a result of the tide. ❑ *Fishing is possible for a couple of hours either side of high water.* **come hell or high water** → see **hell**. N-UNCOUNT = *high tide*

**high-water mark** also **high water mark.** [1] **The high-water mark** is the level reached in a particular place by the sea at high tide or by a river in flood. N-SING: *the* N [2] The **high-water mark of** a process is its highest or most successful stage of achievement. ❑ *This was almost certainly the high-water mark of her career.* N-SING: with supp, oft N *of/for* n

**high|way** /haɪweɪ/ **(highways)** A **highway** is a main road, especially one that connects towns or cities. [mainly AM] ❑ *I crossed the highway, dodging the traffic.* N-COUNT

**High|way Code** In Britain, **the Highway Code** is an official book published by the Department of Transport, which contains the rules which tell people how to use public roads safely. N-SING: *the* N

**highway|man** /haɪweɪmən/ **(highwaymen)** In former times, **highwaymen** were people who stopped travellers and robbed them. N-COUNT

**high wire** **(high wires)** also **high-wire.** [1] A **high wire** is a length of rope or wire stretched tight high above the ground and used for balancing acts. N-COUNT = *tightrope* [2] Journalists talk about a person being on a **high wire** or performing a **high-wire** act when he or she is dealing with a situation in which it would be easy to do the wrong thing. ❑ *This year's Budget looks set to be a precarious high-wire act for the Chancellor.* N-SING: oft N n

**hi|jack** /haɪdʒæk/ **(hijacks, hijacking, hijacked)** [1] If someone **hijacks** a plane or other vehicle, they illegally take control of it by force while it is travelling from one place to another. ❑ *Two men tried to hijack a plane on a flight from Riga to Murmansk... The hijacked plane exploded in a ball of fire.* VERB V n V-ed ♦ **Hijack** is also a noun. ❑ *Every minute during the hijack seemed like a week.* N-COUNT ♦ **hi|jack|ing** **(hijackings)** *Car hijackings are running at a rate of nearly 50 a day.* N-COUNT [2] If you say that someone **has hijacked** something, you disapprove of the way in which they have taken control of it when they had no right to do so. ❑ *A peaceful demonstration had been hijacked by anarchists intent on causing trouble.* VERB [disapproval] V n

**hi|jack|er** /haɪdʒækəʳ/ **(hijackers)** A **hijacker** is a person who hijacks a plane or other vehicle. N-COUNT

**hike** /haɪk/ **(hikes, hiking, hiked)** [1] A **hike** is a long walk in the country, especially one that you go on for pleasure. N-COUNT = *walk* [2] If you **hike**, you go for a long walk in the country. ❑ *You could hike through the Fish River Canyon... We plan to hike the Samaria Gorge.* VERB V prep/adv V n ♦ **hik|ing** *...heavy hiking boots.* N-UNCOUNT: oft N n [3] A **hike** is a sudden or large increase in prices, rates, taxes, or quantities. [INFORMAL] ❑ *...a sudden 1.75 per cent hike in Italian interest rates.* N-COUNT: usu supp N [4] To **hike** prices, rates, taxes, or quantities means to increase them suddenly or by a large amount. [INFORMAL] ❑ *It has now been forced to hike its rates by 5.25 per cent.* VERB = *raise* V n ♦ **Hike up** means the same as **hike.** ❑ *The insurers have started hiking up premiums by huge amounts... Big banks were hiking their rates up.* PHRASAL VERB V P n (not pron) V n P

**hik|er** /haɪkəʳ/ **(hikers)** A **hiker** is a person who is going for a long walk in the countryside for pleasure. N-COUNT

**hi|lari|ous** /hɪleəriəs/ If something is **hilarious**, it is extremely funny and makes you laugh a lot. ❑ *We thought it was hilarious when we first heard about it.* ADJ ♦ **hi|lari|ous|ly** *She found it hilariously funny.* ADV: usu ADV adj, ADV with v

**hi|lar|ity** /hɪlærɪti/ **Hilarity** is great amusement and laughter. N-UNCOUNT

**hill** /hɪl/ **(hills)** 1 A **hill** is an area of land that is higher than the land that surrounds it. ❑ *We trudged up the hill to the stadium. ...Maple Hill.* 2 If you say that someone is **over the hill**, you are saying rudely that they are old and no longer fit, attractive, or capable of doing useful work. [INFORMAL] ❑ *He doesn't take kindly to suggestions that he is over the hill.* ◆◇◇ N-COUNT; N-IN-NAMES PHRASE: usu v-link PHR [disapproval]

**hill|bil|ly** /hɪlbɪli/ **(hillbillies)** If you refer to someone as a **hillbilly**, you are saying in a fairly rude way that you think they are uneducated and stupid because they come from the countryside. [AM, INFORMAL] N-COUNT [disapproval]

**hill|ock** /hɪlək/ **(hillocks)** A **hillock** is a small hill. N-COUNT

**hill|side** /hɪlsaɪd/ **(hillsides)** A **hillside** is the sloping side of a hill. N-COUNT

**hill|top** /hɪltɒp/ **(hilltops)** A **hilltop** is the top of a hill. N-COUNT: oft N n

**hilly** /hɪli/ **(hillier, hilliest)** A **hilly** area has many hills. ❑ *The areas where the fighting is taking place are hilly and densely wooded.* ADJ

**hilt** /hɪlt/ **(hilts)** 1 The **hilt** of a sword, dagger, or knife is its handle. 2 **To the hilt** and **up to the hilt** mean to the maximum extent possible or as fully as possible. [INFORMAL] ❑ *The men who wield the power are certainly backing him to the hilt.* N-COUNT PHRASE: usu PHR after v [emphasis]

**him** /hɪm/ ◆◆◆

> **Him** is a third person singular pronoun. **Him** is used as the object of a verb or a preposition.

1 You use **him** to refer to a man, boy, or male animal. ❑ *John's aunt died suddenly and left him a surprisingly large sum... Is Sam there? Let me talk to him... My brother had a lovely dog. I looked after him for about a week.* 2 In written English, **him** is sometimes used to refer to a person without saying whether that person is a man or a woman. Some people dislike this use and prefer to use 'him or her' or 'them'. ❑ *If the child sees the word 'hear', we should show him that this is the base word in 'hearing' and 'hears'.* PRON: v PRON, prep PRON PRON: v PRON, prep PRON

**him|self** /hɪmself/ ◆◆◆

> **Himself** is a third person singular reflexive pronoun. **Himself** is used when the object of a verb or preposition refers to the same person as the subject of the verb, except in meaning 3.

1 You use **himself** to refer to a man, boy, or male animal. ❑ *He poured himself a whisky and sat down in the chair... A driver blew up his car and himself after being stopped at a police checkpoint... William went away muttering to himself.* 2 In written English, **himself** is sometimes used to refer to a person without saying whether that person is a man or a woman. Some people dislike this use and prefer to use 'himself or herself' or 'themselves'. ❑ *The child's natural way of expressing himself is play.* 3 You use **himself** to emphasize the person or thing that you are referring to. **Himself** is sometimes used instead of 'him' as the object of a verb or preposition. ❑ *The Prime Minister himself is on a visit to Peking.* PRON: v PRON, prep PRON PRON: v PRON, prep PRON PRON [emphasis]

**hind** /haɪnd/ An animal's **hind** legs are at the back of its body. ❑ *Suddenly the cow kicked up its hind legs.* ADJ: ADJ n

**hin|der** /hɪndəʳ/ **(hinders, hindering, hindered)** 1 If something **hinders** you, it makes it more difficult for you to do something or make progress. ❑ *Further investigation was hindered by the loss of all documentation on the case.* 2 If something **hinders** your movement, it makes it difficult for you to move forward or move around. ❑ *A thigh injury increasingly hindered her mobility.* VERB V n VERB V n

**Hin|di** /hɪndi/ **Hindi** is a language that is spoken by people in northern India. It is also one of the official languages of India. N-UNCOUNT

**hind|quarters** /haɪndkwɔːʳtəz/ also **hind quarters.** The **hindquarters** of a four-legged animal are its back part, including its two back legs. N-PLURAL: oft with poss

**hin|drance** /hɪndrəns/ **(hindrances)** 1 A **hindrance** is a person or thing that makes it more difficult for you to do something. ❑ *The higher rates have been a hindrance to economic recovery.* 2 **Hindrance** is the act of hindering someone or something. ❑ *They boarded their flight to Paris without hindrance.* N-COUNT: oft N *to* n ≠ *help* N-UNCOUNT

**hind|sight** /haɪndsaɪt/ **Hindsight** is the ability to understand and realize something about an event after it has happened, although you did not understand or realize it at the time. ❑ *With hindsight, we'd all do things differently.* N-UNCOUNT: oft *with*/*in* N

**Hin|du** /hɪnduː, hɪnduː/ **(Hindus)** 1 A **Hindu** is a person who believes in Hinduism and follows its teachings. 2 **Hindu** is used to describe things that belong or relate to Hinduism. ❑ *...a Hindu temple.* N-COUNT ADJ: usu ADJ n

**Hin|du|ism** /hɪnduːɪzəm/ **Hinduism** is an Indian religion. It has many gods and teaches that people have another life on earth after they die. N-UNCOUNT

**hinge** /hɪndʒ/ **(hinges, hinging, hinged)** A **hinge** is a piece of metal, wood, or plastic that is used to join a door to its frame or to join two things together so that one of them can swing freely. ❑ *The top swung open on well-oiled hinges.* N-COUNT

♦ **hinge on** Something that **hinges on** one thing or event depends entirely on it. ❑ *The plan hinges on a deal being struck with a new company.* PHRASAL VERB V P n/-ing/wh

**hinged** /hɪndʒd/ Something that is **hinged** is joined to another thing, or joined together, by means of a hinge. ❑ *The mirror was hinged to a surrounding frame.* ADJ

**hint** /hɪnt/ **(hints, hinting, hinted)** 1 A **hint** is a suggestion about something that is made in an indirect way. ❑ *The Minister gave a strong hint that the government were thinking of introducing tax concessions for mothers... I'd dropped a hint about having an exhibition of his work up here.* ● If you **take a hint**, you understand something that is suggested to you indirectly. ❑ *'I think I hear the telephone ringing.' — 'Okay, I can take a hint.'* 2 If you **hint at** something, you suggest it in an indirect way. ❑ *She suggested a trip to the shops and hinted at the possibility of a treat of some sort... The President hinted he might make some changes in the government.* 3 A **hint** is a helpful piece of advice, usually about how to do something. ❑ *Here are some helpful hints to make your journey easier.* 4 A **hint of** something is a very small amount of it. ❑ *She added only a hint of vermouth to the gin.* ◆◇◇ N-COUNT: oft N that PHRASE: V inflects VERB V *at* n V that N-COUNT: usu supp N = *tip* N-SING: N *of* n = *trace*

**hinter|land** /hɪntəʳlænd/ **(hinterlands)** The **hinterland** of a stretch of coast or a large river is the area of land behind it or around it. ❑ *...the French Mediterranean coast and its hinterland.* N-COUNT: usu sing, usu with supp

**hip** /hɪp/ **(hips, hipper, hippest)** 1 Your **hips** are the two areas at the sides of your body between the tops of your legs and your waist. ❑ *Tracey put her hands on her hips and sighed.* ♦ **-hipped** *He is broad-chested and narrow-hipped.* 2 You refer to the bones between the tops of your legs and your waist as your **hips**. 3 If you say that someone is **hip**, you mean that they are very modern and follow all the latest fashions, for example in clothes and ideas. [INFORMAL] ❑ *...a hip young character with tight-cropped blond hair and stylish glasses.* 4 If a large group of people want to show their appreciation or approval of someone, one of them says '**Hip hip**' and they all shout '**hooray**'. 5 If you say that someone **shoots from the hip** or **fires from the hip**, you mean that they react to situations or give their opinion very quickly, without stopping to think. ❑ *Judges don't have to shoot from the hip. They have the leisure to think, to decide.* ◆◇◇ N-COUNT: oft poss N COMB in ADJ N-COUNT: oft poss N ADJ = *trendy*, *cool* EXCLAM PHRASE: V inflects

**hip flask** **(hip flasks)** A **hip flask** is a small metal container in which brandy, whisky, or other spirits can be carried. N-COUNT

**hip-hop** **Hip-hop** is a form of popular culture which started among young black people in the United States in the 1980s. It includes rap music and graffiti art. N-UNCOUNT: oft N n

**hip|pie** /hɪpi/ **(hippies)** also **hippy**. **Hippies** were young people in the 1960s and 1970s who rejected conventional ways of living, dressing, and behaving, and tried to live a life based on peace and love. Hippies often had long hair and many took drugs. N-COUNT

**hip|po** /hɪpoʊ/ **(hippos)** A **hippo** is a hippopotamus. [INFORMAL] N-COUNT

**Hip|po|crat|ic oath** /hɪpəkrætɪk oʊθ/ **The Hippocratic oath** is a formal promise made by recently-qualified doctors that they will follow the standards set by their profession and try to preserve life. N-SING: *the* N

**hippo|pota|mus** /hɪpəpɒtəməs/ **(hippopotamuses)** A **hippopotamus** is a very large African animal with short legs and thick, hairless skin. Hippopotamuses live in and near rivers. N-COUNT

**hip|py** /hɪpi/ → see **hippie**.

**hip|ster** /hɪpstəʳ/ **(hipsters)** [1] If you refer to someone as a **hipster**, you mean that they are very fashionable, often in a way that you think is rather silly. [HUMOROUS] N-COUNT [2] **Hipsters** are trousers which are designed so that the highest part of them is around your hips, rather than around your waist. [mainly BRIT] N-PLURAL: oft N n

**hire** /haɪəʳ/ **(hires, hiring, hired)** ◆◇◇ [1] If you **hire** someone, you employ them or pay them to do a particular job for you. VERB ❑ *Sixteen of the contestants have hired lawyers and are suing the organisers...* V n *The rest of the staff have been hired on short-term contracts...* V *He will be in charge of all hiring and firing at PHA.* V-ing *...the mystery assassin (who turned out to be a hired killer).* V-ed [2] If you **hire** something, you pay money to the owner so that you can use it for a period of time. [mainly BRIT] VERB ❑ *To hire a car you must produce a passport and a current driving licence...* V n *Her hired car was found abandoned at Beachy Head.* V-ed

☑ in AM, usually use **rent**

[3] You use **hire** to refer to the activity or business of hiring something. [mainly BRIT] N-UNCOUNT: usu n N, N *of* n, N n ❑ *They booked our hotel, and organised car hire.*

☑ in AM, usually use **rental**

[4] If something is **for hire**, it is available for you to hire. [mainly BRIT] PHRASE: usu v-link PHR ❑ *Fishing tackle is available for hire.*

☑ in AM, usually use **for rent**

♦ **hire out** If you **hire out** something such as a car or a person's services, you allow them to be used in return for payment. PHRASAL VERB ❑ *Companies hiring out narrow boats report full order books.* V P n (not pron) Also V n P

**hire|ling** /haɪəʳlɪŋ/ **(hirelings)** If you refer to someone as a **hireling**, you disapprove of them because they do not care who they work for and they are willing to do illegal or immoral things as long as they are paid. N-COUNT [disapproval]

**hire pur|chase** **Hire purchase** is a way of buying goods gradually. You make regular payments until you have paid the full price and the goods belong to you. The abbreviation **HP** is often used. [BRIT] N-UNCOUNT: oft N n ❑ *...buying a car on hire purchase.*

☑ in AM, usually use **installment plan**

**hir|sute** /hɜːʳsjuːt, AM -suːt/ If a man is **hirsute**, he is hairy. [FORMAL] ADJ

**his** ◆◆◆

☑ The determiner is pronounced /hɪz/. The pronoun is pronounced /hɪz/.

**His** is a third person singular possessive determiner. **His** is also a possessive pronoun.

[1] You use **his** to indicate that something belongs or relates to a man, boy, or male animal. DET ❑ *Brian splashed water on his face, then brushed his teeth... He spent a large part of his career in Hollywood... The dog let his head thump on the floor again.* ♦ **His** is also a possessive pronoun. PRON ❑ *Anna reached out her hand to him and clasped his.* [2] In written English, **his** is sometimes used to refer to a person without saying whether that person is a man or a woman. Some people dislike this use and prefer to use 'his or her' or 'their'. DET ❑ *Formerly, the relations between a teacher and his pupils were dominated by fear on the part of the pupils.* ♦ **His** is also a possessive pronoun. PRON ❑ *The student going to art or drama school will be very enthusiastic about further education. His is not a narrow mind, but one eager to grasp every facet of anything he studies.*

**His|pan|ic** /hɪspænɪk/ **(Hispanics)** A **Hispanic** person is a citizen of the United States of America who originally came from Latin America, or whose family originally came from Latin America. ADJ ❑ *...a group of Hispanic doctors in Washington.* ♦ A **Hispanic** is someone who is Hispanic. N-COUNT

**hiss** /hɪs/ **(hisses, hissing, hissed)** [1] To **hiss** means to make a sound like a long 's'. VERB ❑ *The tires of Lenny's bike hissed over the wet pavement as he slowed down...* V prep *My cat hissed when I stepped on its tail...* V *Caporelli made a small hissing sound of irritation.* V-ing ♦ **Hiss** is also a noun. N-COUNT ❑ *...the hiss of water running into the burnt pan.* ♦ **hiss|ing** N-UNCOUNT *...a steady hissing from above my head.* [2] If you **hiss** something, you say it forcefully in a whisper. VERB ❑ *'Now, quiet,' my mother hissed...* V with quote *'Stay here,' I hissed at her.* V *at/to* n with quote [3] If people **hiss at** someone such as a performer or a person making a speech, they express their disapproval or dislike of that person by making long loud 's' sounds. VERB ❑ *One had to listen hard to catch the words of the President's speech as the delegates booed and hissed...* V *Some local residents whistled and hissed at them as they entered.* V *at* n Also V n ♦ **Hiss** is also a noun. N-COUNT: usu pl = *hissing* ❑ *After a moment the barracking began. First came hisses, then shouts.*

**his|to|rian** /hɪstɔːriən/ **(historians)** A **historian** is a person who specializes in the study of history, and who writes books and articles about it. N-COUNT

**his|tor|ic** /hɪstɒrɪk, AM -tɔːr-/ ◆◇◇ Something that is **historic** is important in history, or likely to be considered important at some time in the future. ADJ: usu ADJ n ❑ *...the historic changes in Eastern Europe.*

**his|tori|cal** /hɪstɒrɪkəl, AM -tɔːr-/ ◆◇◇ [1] **Historical** people, situations, or things existed in the past and are considered to be a part of history. ADJ: ADJ n ❑ *...an important historical figure. ...the historical impact of Western capitalism on the world.* ♦ **his|tori|cal|ly** ADV *Historically, royal marriages have been cold, calculating affairs.* [2] **Historical** books, films, or pictures describe or represent people, situations, or things that existed in the past. ADJ: ADJ n ❑ *He is writing a historical novel about nineteenth-century France.* [3] **Historical** information, research, and discussion is related to the study of history. ADJ: ADJ n ❑ *...historical records. ...modern historical research.* [4] If you look at an event within a **historical** context, you look at what was happening at that time and what had happened previously, in order to judge the event and its importance. ADJ: ADJ n ❑ *It was this kind of historical context that Morris brought to his work.*

**his|to|ry** /hɪstəri/ **(histories)** ◆◆◆ [1] You can refer to the events of the past as **history**. You can also refer to the past events which concern a particular topic or place as its history. N-UNCOUNT: usu with supp ❑ *The Catholic Church has played a prominent role throughout Polish history. ...the most evil mass killer in history. ...the history of Birmingham.* ● Someone who **makes history** does something that is considered to be important and significant in the development of the world or of a particular society. PHRASE: V inflects ❑ *Willy Brandt made history by visiting East Germany in 1970.* ● If someone or something **goes down in history**, people in the future remember them because of particular actions that they have done or because of particular events that have happened. PHRASE: V inflects ❑ *Bradley will go down* *in history as Los Angeles' longest serving mayor.* 2 (N-UNCOUNT) **History** is a subject studied in schools, colleges, and universities that deals with events that have happened in the past. 3 (N-COUNT: with supp, oft N *of* n) A **history** is an account of events that have happened in the past. ❑ *...his magnificent history of broadcasting in Canada.* 4 (N-COUNT: usu sing, usu *a* N *of* n/-ing) If a person or a place has **a history of** something, it has been very common or has happened frequently in their past. ❑ *He had a history of drink problems.* 5 (N-COUNT: with poss) Someone's **history** is the set of facts that are known about their past. ❑ *He couldn't get a new job because of his medical history.* 6 (N-UNCOUNT) If you say that an event, thing, or person is **history**, you mean that they are no longer important. ❑ *The Charlottetown agreement is history.* 7 (PHRASE) If you are telling someone about an event and say **the rest is history**, you mean that you do not need to tell them what happened next because everyone knows about it already. ❑ *We met at college, the rest is history.* 8 → See also **natural history**.

**his|tri|on|ic** /hɪstriɒnɪk/ (ADJ: usu ADJ n; disapproval) If you refer to someone's behaviour as **histrionic**, you are critical of it because it is very dramatic, exaggerated, and insincere. ❑ *Dorothea let out a histrionic groan.*

**his|tri|on|ics** /hɪstriɒnɪks/ (N-PLURAL; disapproval) If you disapprove of someone's dramatic and exaggerated behaviour, you can describe it as **histrionics**. ❑ *When I explained everything to my mum and dad, there were no histrionics.*

**hit** /hɪt/ **(hits, hitting)** ◆◆◆

> ✔ The form **hit** is used in the present tense and is the past and present participle.

1 (VERB = strike) If you **hit** someone or something, you deliberately touch them with a lot of force, with your hand or an object held in your hand. ❑ (V n) *Find the exact grip that allows you to hit the ball hard...* (V n) *Police at the scene said Dr Mahgoub had been hit several times in the head.* 2 (VERB = strike; V n) When one thing **hits** another, it touches it with a lot of force. ❑ *The car had apparently hit a traffic sign before skidding out of control.* 3 (VERB) If a bomb or missile **hits** its target, it reaches it. ❑ (V n) *The hospital had been hit with heavy artillery fire.* ♦ (N-COUNT) **Hit** is also a noun. ❑ *First a house took a direct hit and then the rocket exploded.* 4 (VERB) If something **hits** a person, place, or thing, it affects them very badly. [JOURNALISM] ❑ (V n) *The plan to charge motorists £75 a year to use the motorway is going to hit me hard...* (V n) *About two-hundred people died in the earthquake which hit northern Peru.* 5 (VERB) When a feeling or an idea **hits** you, it suddenly affects you or comes into your mind. ❑ (*it* V n that) *It hit me that I had a choice...* (V n) *Then the answer hit me. It had been staring me in the face.* 6 (VERB) If you **hit** a particular high or low point on a scale of something such as success or health, you reach it. [JOURNALISM] ❑ (V n) *Oil prices hit record levels yesterday.* 7 (N-COUNT: oft N n ≠ flop) If a CD, film, or play is a **hit**, it is very popular and successful. ❑ *The song became a massive hit in 1945.* 8 (N-COUNT) A **hit** is a single visit to a website. [COMPUTING] ❑ *Our small company has had 78,000 hits on its Internet pages.* 9 (N-COUNT) If someone who is searching for information on the Internet gets a **hit**, they find a website where there is that information. 10 (PHRASE: V inflects, pl-n PHR, PHR *with* n) If two people **hit it off**, they like each other and become friendly as soon as they meet. [INFORMAL] ❑ *They hit it off straight away, Daddy and Walter.* 11 to **hit the headlines** → see **headline**. to **hit home** → see **home**. to **hit the nail on the head** → see **nail**. to **hit the road** → see **road**. to **hit the roof** → see **roof**.

♦ **hit back** 1 (PHRASAL VERB) If you **hit back** when someone hits you, or **hit** them **back**, you hit them in return. ❑ (V P) *Some violent men beat up their sons, until the boys are strong enough to hit back...* (V n P) *If somebody hit me, I'd hit him back.* 2 (PHRASAL VERB = strike back) If you **hit back at** someone who has criticized or harmed you, you criticize or harm them in return. [JOURNALISM] ❑ (V P *at* n) *The President has hit back at those who have criticised his economic reforms...* (V P) *British Rail immediately hit back with their own cheap fares scheme.*

♦ **hit on** or **hit upon** 1 (PHRASAL VERB = stumble on; V P n) If you **hit on** an idea or a solution to a problem, or **hit upon** it, you think of it. ❑ *After running through the numbers in every possible combination, we finally hit on a solution.* 2 (PHRASAL VERB) If someone **hits on** you, they speak or behave in a way that shows they want to have a sexual relationship with you. [INFORMAL] ❑ (V P n) *She was hitting on me and I was surprised and flattered.*

♦ **hit out** 1 (PHRASAL VERB = lash out) If you **hit out at** someone, you try to hit them, although you may miss them. [mainly BRIT] ❑ (V P *at* n) *I used to hit out at my husband and throw things at him...* (V P) *I had never punched anybody in my life but I hit out and gave him a black eye.* 2 (PHRASAL VERB = lash out) If you **hit out** at someone or something, you criticize them strongly because you do not agree with them. [JOURNALISM] ❑ (V P *at/against* n) *The President took the opportunity to hit out at what he sees as foreign interference...* (V P) *Brazilian soccer boss Carlos Parreira hit out angrily last night after his side were barred from training at Wembley.*

♦ **hit upon** → see **hit on**.

**hit and miss** also **hit-and-miss.** (ADJ) If something is **hit and miss** or **hit or miss**, it is sometimes successful and sometimes not. ❑ *Farming can be very much a hit-and-miss affair.*

**hit-and-run** 1 (ADJ: ADJ n) A **hit-and-run** accident is an accident in which the driver of a vehicle hits someone and then drives away without stopping. ❑ *...a hit-and-run driver in a stolen car.* 2 (ADJ: ADJ n) A **hit-and-run** attack on an enemy position relies on surprise and speed for its success. ❑ *The rebels appear to be making hit-and-run guerrilla style attacks on military targets.*

**hitch** /hɪtʃ/ **(hitches, hitching, hitched)** 1 (N-COUNT = snag) A **hitch** is a slight problem or difficulty which causes a short delay. ❑ *After some technical hitches the show finally got under way... The five-hour operation went without a hitch.* 2 (VERB) If you **hitch**, **hitch** a lift, or **hitch** a ride, you hitchhike. [INFORMAL] ❑ (V n) *There was no garage in sight, so I hitched a lift into town...* (V) *Jean-Phillippe had hitched all over Europe in the 1960s.* 3 (VERB) If you **hitch** something **to** something else, you hook it or fasten it there. ❑ (V n *onto/to* n) *Last night we hitched the horse to the cart and moved here.* 4 (PHRASE: V inflects) If you **get hitched**, you get married. [INFORMAL] ❑ *The report shows that fewer couples are getting hitched.*

**hitch|hike** /hɪtʃhaɪk/ **(hitchhikes, hitchhiking, hitchhiked)** (VERB) If you **hitchhike**, you travel by getting lifts from passing vehicles without paying. ❑ (V prep/adv) *Neff hitchhiked to New York during his Christmas vacation...* (V) *They had an eighty-mile journey and decided to hitch-hike.* ♦ (N-COUNT) **hitch|hiker (hitchhikers)** *On my way to Vancouver one Friday night I picked up a hitchhiker.*

**hi tech** → see **high-tech**.

**hith|er** /hɪðəʳ/ 1 (ADV: ADV after v) **Hither** means to the place where you are. [OLD-FASHIONED] ❑ *He has sent hither swarms of officers to harass our people.* 2 (PHRASE: PHR after v) **Hither and thither** means in many different directions or places, and in a disorganized way. In American English, the expression **hither and yon** is sometimes used. ❑ *Refugees run hither and thither in search of safety. ...the awful amount of time I spend moving things hither and yon every year!*

**hither|to** /hɪðəʳtuː/ (ADV: ADV after v, ADV with cl, ADV adj/-ed) You use **hitherto** to indicate that something was true up until the time you are talking about, although it may no longer be the case. [FORMAL] ❑ *The polytechnics have hitherto been at an unfair disadvantage in competing for pupils and money.*

**hit list (hit lists)** 1 (N-COUNT: oft poss N, N *of* n) If someone has a **hit list of** people or things, they are intending to take action concerning those people or things. ❑ *Some banks also have a hit list of people whom they threaten to sue for damages.* 2 (N-COUNT) A **hit list** is a list that someone makes of people they intend to have killed.

**hit|man** /hɪtmæn/ **(hitmen)** also **hit man.** (N-COUNT) A **hitman** is a man who is hired by someone in order to kill another person.

**hit or miss** → see **hit and miss.**

**hit pa|rade** **The hit parade** is the list of CDs which have sold most copies over the previous week or month. [OLD-FASHIONED] — N-SING: the N = charts

**hit|ter** /hɪtəʳ/ **(hitters)** [1] In sports, you can use **hitter** to say how good someone is at hitting the ball. ❑ *The Georgian, aged 19, is not one of the game's big hitters.* — N-COUNT: adj N [2] If you refer to someone such as a politician or a businessman as a heavy **hitter** or a big **hitter**, you mean that they are powerful and influential. ❑ *...friendships with heavy hitters like European industrialist Carlo De Benedetti.* — N-COUNT: adj N

**HIV** /eɪtʃ aɪ viː/ [1] **HIV** is a virus which reduces people's resistance to illness and can cause AIDS. **HIV** is an abbreviation for 'human immunodeficiency virus'. — ◆◇◇ N-UNCOUNT: oft N n [2] If someone is **HIV positive**, they are infected with the HIV virus, and may develop AIDS. If someone is **HIV negative**, they are not infected with the virus. — PHRASE: v-link PHR

**hive** /haɪv/ **(hives, hiving, hived)** [1] A **hive** is a structure in which bees are kept, which is designed so that the beekeeper can collect the honey that they produce. — N-COUNT [2] If you describe a place as a **hive of** activity, you approve of the fact that there is a lot of activity there or that people are busy working there. ❑ *In the morning the house was a hive of activity.* — N-COUNT: N of n [approval] [3] **Hives** is a condition in which patches of your skin become red and very uncomfortable and itchy. — N-UNCOUNT

♦ **hive off** If someone **hives off** part of a business, they transfer it to new ownership, usually by selling it. [mainly BRIT] ❑ *Klockner plans to hive off its loss-making steel businesses.* — PHRASAL VERB; V P n (not pron)

**hiya** /haɪjə/ You can say '**hiya**' when you are greeting someone. [INFORMAL] ❑ *Hiya. How are you?* — CONVENTION [formulae] = hi

**HM** /eɪtʃ em/ **HM** is the written abbreviation for **Her** or **His Majesty** or **Her** or **His Majesty's**. It is used as part of the name of some British government organizations, or as part of a person's title. ❑ *...HM the Queen. ...his enlistment in HM Armed Forces. ...HM Chief Inspector of Fire Services.*

**h'm** also **hm. H'm** is used in writing to represent a noise that people make when they are hesitating, for example because they are thinking about something.

**HMS** /eɪtʃ em es/ **HMS** is used before the names of ships in the British Royal Navy. **HMS** is an abbreviation for 'Her Majesty's Ship' or 'His Majesty's Ship'. ❑ *...launching HMS Warrior.* — N-IN-NAMES: N n

**HNC** /eɪtʃ en siː/ **(HNCs)** An **HNC** is a group of examinations in technical subjects which you can take at a British college. **HNC** is an abbreviation for 'Higher National Certificate'. ❑ *...passing his HNC in computer studies.* — N-VAR

**hoard** /hɔːʳd/ **(hoards, hoarding, hoarded)** [1] If you **hoard** things such as food or money, you save or store them, often in secret, because they are valuable or important to you. ❑ *They've begun to hoard food and gasoline and save their money... Consumers did not spend and create jobs; they hoarded.* — VERB; V n; V ♦ **hoard|er (hoarders)** *Most hoarders have favorite hiding places.* — N-COUNT [2] A **hoard** is a store of things that you have saved and that are valuable or important to you or you do not want other people to have. ❑ *The case involves a hoard of silver and jewels valued at up to $40m.* — N-COUNT: oft N of n = cache

**hoard|ing** /hɔːʳdɪŋ/ **(hoardings)** A **hoarding** is a very large board at the side of a road or on the side of a building, which is used for displaying advertisements and posters. [BRIT] ❑ *An advertising hoarding on the platform caught her attention.* — N-COUNT

☑ in AM, usually use **billboard**

**hoarse** /hɔːʳs/ **(hoarser, hoarsest)** If your voice is **hoarse** or if you are **hoarse**, your voice sounds rough and unclear, for example because your throat is sore. ❑ *'So what do you think?' she said in a hoarse whisper.* — ADJ ♦ **hoarse|ly** *'Thank you,' Maria said hoarsely.* — ADV ♦ **hoarse|ness** *Hoarseness is very common in the winter season.* — N-UNCOUNT

**hoary** /hɔːri/ If you describe a problem or subject as **hoary**, you mean that it is old and familiar. ❑ *...the hoary old myth that women are unpredictable.* — ADJ: usu ADJ n

**hoax** /hoʊks/ **(hoaxes)** A **hoax** is a trick in which someone tells people a lie, for example that there is a bomb somewhere when there is not, or that a picture is genuine when it is not. ❑ *He denied making the hoax call but was convicted after a short trial.* — N-COUNT: usu with supp, oft N n

**hoax|er** /hoʊksəʳ/ **(hoaxers)** A **hoaxer** is someone who carries out a hoax. [mainly BRIT] — N-COUNT

**hob** /hɒb/ **(hobs)** A **hob** is a surface on top of a cooker or set into a work surface, which can be heated in order to cook things on it. [BRIT] — N-COUNT

☑ in AM, use **burner**

**hob|ble** /hɒbᵊl/ **(hobbles, hobbling, hobbled)** [1] If you **hobble**, you walk in an awkward way with small steps, for example because your foot is injured. ❑ *He got up slowly and hobbled over to the coffee table... The swelling had begun to go down, and he was able, with pain, to hobble.* — VERB; V adv/prep; V [2] To **hobble** something or someone means to make it more difficult for them to be successful or to achieve what they want. ❑ *The poverty of 10 million citizens not only demeans our society but its cost also hobbles our economy.* — VERB; V n

**hob|by** /hɒbi/ **(hobbies)** A **hobby** is an activity that you enjoy doing in your spare time. ❑ *My hobbies are letter writing, football, music, photography, and tennis.* — N-COUNT = pastime

**hobby-horse** **(hobby-horses)** also **hobbyhorse.** You describe a subject or idea as your **hobby-horse** if you have strong feelings on it and like talking about it whenever you have the opportunity. ❑ *Honesty is a favourite hobby-horse for Courau.* — N-COUNT

**hob|by|ist** /hɒbiɪst/ **(hobbyists)** You can refer to person who is very interested in a particular hobby and spends a lot of time on it as a **hobbyist**. — N-COUNT

**hob|nob** /hɒbnɒb/ **(hobnobs, hobnobbing, hobnobbed)** If you disapprove of the way in which someone is spending a lot of time with a group of people, especially rich and powerful people, you can say that he or she **is hobnobbing with** them. [INFORMAL] ❑ *This gave Bill an opportunity to hobnob with the company's president, board chairman, and leading executives.* — VERB [disapproval]; V with n; Also V

**hobo** /hoʊboʊ/ **(hobos** or **hoboes)** [1] A **hobo** is a person who has no home, especially one who travels from place to place and gets money by begging. [AM] — N-COUNT

☑ in BRIT, use **tramp**

[2] A **hobo** is a worker, especially a farm worker, who goes from place to place in order to find work. [AM] — N-COUNT

**hock** /hɒk/ **(hocks)** [1] A **hock** is a piece of meat from above the foot of an animal, especially a pig. — N-COUNT: usu n N

**PHRASES** [2] If someone is **in hock**, they are in debt. ❑ *Even company directors on £100,000 a year can be deeply in hock to the banks.* — PHRASE: v-link PHR, oft PHR to n [3] If you are **in hock to** someone, you feel you have to do things for them because they have given you money or support. ❑ *It is almost impossible for the prime minister to stand above the factions. He always seems in hock to one or another.* — PHRASE: v-link PHR n

**hock|ey** /hɒki/ [1] **Hockey** is an outdoor game played between two teams of 11 players who use long curved sticks to hit a small ball and try to score goals. [BRIT] ❑ *She played hockey for the national side. ...the British hockey team.* — N-UNCOUNT: oft N n

☑ in AM, usually use **field hockey**

[2] **Hockey** is a game played on ice between two teams of 11 players who use long curved sticks to — N-UNCOUNT: oft N n

hit a small rubber disk, called a puck, and try to score goals. [AM]

in BRIT, usually use **ice hockey**

**hocus-pocus** /hoʊkəs poʊkəs/ If you describe something as **hocus-pocus**, you disapprove of it because you think it is false and intended to trick or deceive people. N-UNCOUNT disapproval = trickery

**hod** /hɒd/ **(hods)** A **hod** is a container that is used by a building worker for carrying bricks. N-COUNT

**hodge|podge** /hɒdʒpɒdʒ/ also **hodge-podge.** A **hodgepodge** is an untidy mixture of different types of things. [mainly AM, INFORMAL] ❑ *...a hodgepodge of maps, small tools, and notebooks.* N-SING: usu with supp, oft N *of* n = jumble

in BRIT, usually use **hotch-potch**

**hoe** /hoʊ/ **(hoes, hoeing, hoed)** 1 A **hoe** is a gardening tool with a long handle and a small square blade, which you use to remove small weeds and break up the surface of the soil. N-COUNT 2 If you **hoe** a field or crop, you use a hoe on the weeds or soil there. ❑ *I have to feed the chickens and hoe the potatoes... Today he was hoeing in the vineyard.* VERB V n V

**hog** /hɒg, AM hɔːg/ **(hogs, hogging, hogged)** 1 A **hog** is a pig. In British English, **hog** usually refers to a large male pig that has been castrated, but in American English it can refer to any kind of pig. N-COUNT 2 If you **hog** something, you take all of it in a greedy or impolite way. [INFORMAL] ❑ *Have you done hogging the bathroom?* VERB V n 3 → See also **road hog**. 4 If you **go the whole hog**, you do something bold or extravagant in the most complete way possible. [INFORMAL] ❑ *Well, I thought, I've already lost half my job, I might as well go the whole hog and lose it completely.* PHRASE: V inflects

**Hog|ma|nay** /hɒgmənei/ **Hogmanay** is New Year's Eve in Scotland and the celebrations that take place there at that time. N-UNCOUNT

**hog|wash** /hɒgwɒʃ, AM hɔːg-/ If you describe what someone says as **hogwash**, you think it is nonsense. [INFORMAL] ❑ *Sugar said it was a 'load of hogwash' that he was not interested in football.* N-UNCOUNT disapproval = rubbish

**ho ho** /hoʊ hoʊ/ or **ho ho ho** **Ho ho** is used in writing to represent the sound that people make when they laugh. ❑ *'Ha ha, ho ho,' he chortled.* EXCLAM

**ho hum** /hoʊ hʌm/ also **ho-hum.** 1 You can use **ho hum** when you want to show that you think something is not interesting, remarkable, or surprising in any way. [INFORMAL] ❑ *My general reaction to this news might be summed up as 'ho-hum'.* PHRASE feelings 2 You can say **ho hum** to show that you accept an unpleasant situation because it is not very serious. [INFORMAL] ❑ *Ho hum, another nice job down the drain.* EXCLAM feelings

**hoi pol|loi** /hɔɪ pəlɔɪ/ If someone refers to **the hoi polloi**, they are referring in a humorous or rather rude way to ordinary people, in contrast to rich, well-educated, or upper-class people. ❑ *Monstrously inflated costs are designed to keep the hoi polloi at bay.* N-PLURAL

**hoist** /hɔɪst/ **(hoists, hoisting, hoisted)** 1 If you **hoist** something heavy somewhere, you lift it or pull it up there. ❑ *Hoisting my suitcase on to my shoulder, I turned and headed toward my hotel... Grabbing the side of the bunk, he hoisted himself to a sitting position.* VERB V n prep/adv V pron-refl prep/adv 2 If something heavy **is hoisted** somewhere, it is lifted there using a machine such as a crane. ❑ *A twenty-foot steel pyramid is to be hoisted into position on top of the tower... Then a crane hoisted him on to the platform.* VERB *be* V-ed prep/adv V n prep/adv 3 A **hoist** is a machine for lifting heavy things. N-COUNT 4 If you **hoist** a flag or a sail, you pull it up to its correct position by using ropes. ❑ *A group of youths hoisted their flag on top of the disputed monument.* VERB V n 5 **hoist with** your **own petard** → see **petard**.

**ho|kum** /hoʊkəm/ If you describe something as **hokum**, you think it is nonsense. [INFORMAL] ❑ *The book is enjoyable hokum.* N-UNCOUNT = nonsense

**hold**

① PHYSICALLY TOUCHING, SUPPORTING, OR CONTAINING
② HAVING OR DOING
③ CONTROLLING OR REMAINING
④ PHRASES
⑤ PHRASAL VERBS

**① hold** /hoʊld/ **(holds, holding, held)** ◆◆◆
1 When you **hold** something, you carry or support it, using your hands or your arms. ❑ *Hold the knife at an angle... He held the pistol in his right hand.* VERB V n prep/adv V n ♦ **Hold** is also a noun. ❑ *He released his hold on the camera.* N-COUNT: usu sing 2 **Hold** is used in expressions such as **grab hold of**, **catch hold of**, and **get hold of**, to indicate that you close your hand tightly around something, for example to stop something moving or falling. ❑ *I was woken up by someone grabbing hold of my sleeping bag... A doctor and a nurse caught hold of his arms.* N-UNCOUNT: N *of* n 3 When you **hold** someone, you put your arms round them, usually because you want to show them how much you like them or because you want to comfort them. ❑ *She wished he would hold her close to him.* VERB V n adv Also V n 4 If you **hold** someone in a particular position, you use force to keep them in that position and stop them from moving. ❑ *He then held the man in an armlock until police arrived... I'd got two nurses holding me down.* VERB V n prep V n with adv Also V n 5 A **hold** is a particular way of keeping someone in a position using your own hands, arms, or legs. ❑ *...use of an unauthorized hold on a handcuffed suspect.* N-COUNT 6 When you **hold** a part of your body, you put your hand on or against it, often because it hurts. ❑ *Soon she was crying bitterly about the pain and was holding her throat.* VERB V n 7 When you **hold** a part of your body in a particular position, you put it into that position and keep it there. ❑ *Hold your hands in front of your face... He walked at a rapid pace with his back straight and his head held erect.* VERB V n prep/adv V-ed Also V n adj 8 If one thing **holds** another in a particular position, it keeps it in that position. ❑ *...the wooden wedge which held the heavy door open... They used steel pins to hold everything in place.* VERB V n with adv V n prep 9 If one thing is used to **hold** another, it is used to store it. ❑ *Two knife racks hold her favourite knives.* VERB = store V n 10 In a ship or aeroplane, a **hold** is a place where cargo or luggage is stored. ❑ *A fire had been reported in the cargo hold.* N-COUNT: oft n N 11 If a place **holds** something, it keeps it available for reference or for future use. ❑ *The Small Firms Service holds an enormous amount of information on any business problem.* VERB V n 12 If something **holds** a particular amount of something, it can contain that amount. ❑ *One CD-ROM disk can hold over 100,000 pages of text.* VERB: no cont V n 13 If a vehicle **holds** the road well, it remains in close contact with the road and can be controlled safely and easily. ❑ *I thought the car held the road really well.* VERB V n adv Also V n 14 → See also **holding**.

**② hold** /hoʊld/ **(holds, holding, held)** ◆◆◆

**Hold** is often used to indicate that someone or something has the particular thing, characteristic, or attitude that is mentioned. Therefore it takes most of its meaning from the word that follows it.

1 **Hold** is used with words and expressions indicating an opinion or belief, to show that someone has a particular opinion or believes that something is true. ❑ *He holds certain expectations about the teacher's role... Current thinking holds that obesity is more a medical than a psychological problem... The public, meanwhile, hold architects in low esteem. ...a widely held opinion.* VERB: no cont V n V that V n *in* n V-ed 2 **Hold** is used with words such as 'fear' or 'mystery' to indicate someone's feelings towards something, as if those feelings were a characteristic of the thing itself. ❑ *Death doesn't hold any fear for me... It held more mystery than even the darkest jungle.* VERB: no passive V n *for* n V n 3 **Hold** is used with nouns such as 'office', 'power', and 'responsibility' to indicate that someone has a particular position VERB

of power or authority. ❑ *She has never held ministerial office.* [V n] **4** **Hold** is used with nouns such as 'permit', 'degree', or 'ticket' to indicate that someone has a particular document that allows them to do something. [VERB] ❑ *He did not hold a firearm certificate... Passengers holding tickets will receive refunds.* [V n] [V n] **5** **Hold** is used with nouns such as 'party', 'meeting', 'talks', 'election', and 'trial' to indicate that people are organizing a particular activity. [VERB] ❑ *The German sports federation said it would hold an investigation.* [V n] ♦ **hold|ing** *They also called for the holding of multi-party general elections.* [N-UNCOUNT: N *of* n] **6** **Hold** is used with nouns such as 'conversation', 'interview', and 'talks' to indicate that two or more people meet and discuss something. [V-RECIP] ❑ *The Prime Minister, is holding consultations with his colleagues to finalise the deal... The engineer and his son held frequent consultations concerning technical problems... They can't believe you can even hold a conversation.* [V n *with* n] [pl-n V] [V n (non-recip)] **7** **Hold** is used with nouns such as 'shares' and 'stock' to indicate that someone owns a particular proportion of a business. [VERB] ❑ *The group said it continues to hold 1,774,687 Vons shares.* [V n] → See also **holding**. **8** **Hold** is used with words such as 'lead' or 'advantage' to indicate that someone is winning or doing well in a contest. [VERB] ❑ *He continued to hold a lead in Angola's presidential race.* [V n] **9** **Hold** is used with nouns such as 'attention' or 'interest' to indicate that what you do or say keeps someone interested or listening to you. [VERB = keep] ❑ *If you want to hold someone's attention, look them directly in the eye but don't stare.* [V n] **10** If you **hold** someone responsible, liable, or accountable for something, you will blame them if anything goes wrong. [VERB] ❑ *It's impossible to hold any individual responsible.* [V n adj]

③**hold** /hoʊld/ **(holds, holding, held)** ◆◆◆ **1** If someone **holds** you in a place, they keep you there as a prisoner and do not allow you to leave. [VERB] ❑ *The inside of a van was as good a place as any to hold a kidnap victim... Somebody is holding your wife hostage... Japan had originally demanded the return of two seamen held on spying charges.* [V n] [V n n] [V-ed] **2** If people such as an army or a violent crowd **hold** a place, they control it by using force. [VERB] ❑ *Demonstrators have been holding the square since Sunday.* [V n] **3** If you have a **hold over** someone, you have power or control over them, for example because you know something about them you can use to threaten them or because you are in a position of authority. [N-SING: usu N *over/on* n] ❑ *He had ordered his officers to keep an exceptionally firm hold over their men.* **4** If you ask someone to **hold**, or to **hold the line**, when you are answering a telephone call, you are asking them to wait for a short time, for example so that you can find the person they want to speak to. [VERB: no passive = hold on] ❑ *Could you hold the line and I'll just get my pen... A telephone operator asked him to hold.* [V n] [V] **5** If you **hold** telephone calls for someone, you do not allow people who phone to speak to that person, but take messages instead. [VERB] ❑ *He tells his secretary to hold his calls.* [V n] **6** If something **holds** at a particular value or level, or **is held** there, it is kept at that value or level. [VERB] ❑ *OPEC production is holding at around 21.5 million barrels a day... The Prime Minister yesterday ruled out Government action to hold down petrol prices... The final dividend will be held at 20.7p, after an 8 per cent increase. ...provided the pound holds its value against the euro.* [V prep/adv/adj] [V n with adv] [V n prep/adj] [V n] **7** If you **hold** a sound or musical note, you continue making it. [VERB] ❑ *...a voice which hit and held every note with perfect ease and clarity.* [V n] **8** If you **hold** something such as a train, a lift, or an elevator, you delay it. [VERB] ❑ *A London Underground spokesman defended the decision to hold the train until police arrived.* [V n] **9** If an offer or invitation still **holds**, it is still available for you to accept. [VERB] ❑ *Does your offer still hold?* [V] **10** If a good situation **holds**, it continues and does not get worse or fail. [VERB] ❑ *Our luck couldn't hold for ever... Would the weather hold?* [V] [V] **11** If an argument or theory **holds**, it is true or valid, even after close examination. [VERB] ❑ *Today, most people think that argument no longer holds.* [V] ♦ **Hold up** means the same as **hold**. [PHRASAL VERB] ❑ *Democrats say arguments against the bill won't hold up.* [V P] **12** If part of a structure **holds**, it does not fall or break although there is a lot of force or pressure on it. [VERB] ❑ *How long would the roof hold?* [V] **13** If laws or rules **hold**, they exist and remain in force. [VERB] ❑ *These laws also hold for universities.* [V] **14** If you **hold to** a promise or to high standards of behaviour, you keep that promise or continue to behave according to those standards. [VERB = stick to] [FORMAL] ❑ *Will the President be able to hold to this commitment?* [V *to* n] **15** If someone or something **holds** you **to** a promise or **to** high standards of behaviour, they make you keep that promise or those standards. [VERB] ❑ *Don't hold me to that.* [V n *to* n]

④**hold** /hoʊld/ **(holds, holding, held)** ◆◆◆
⇒ Please look at category 13 to see if the expression you are looking for is shown under another headword. **1** If you **hold forth on** a subject, you speak confidently and for a long time about it, especially to a group of people. [PHRASE: V inflects, oft PHR *on* n] ❑ *Barry was holding forth on politics.* **2** If you **get hold of** an object or information, you obtain it, usually after some difficulty. [PHRASE: V inflects, PHR n] ❑ *It is hard to get hold of guns in this country.* **3** If you **get hold of** a fact or a subject, you learn about it and understand it well. [PHRASE: V inflects, PHR n] [BRIT, INFORMAL] ❑ *He first had to get hold of some basic facts.* **4** If you **get hold of** someone, you manage to contact them. [PHRASE: V inflects, PHR n] ❑ *The only electrician we could get hold of was miles away.* **5** If you say '**Hold it**', you are telling someone to stop what they are doing and to wait. [CONVENTION = stop] ❑ *Hold it! Don't move!* **6** If you put something **on hold**, you decide not to do it, deal with it, or change it now, but to leave it until later. [PHRASE: PHR after v, v-link PHR] ❑ *He put his retirement on hold until he had found a solution.* **7** If you **hold** your **own**, you are able to resist someone who is attacking or opposing you. [PHRASE: V inflects] ❑ *The Frenchman held his own against the challenger.* **8** If you can do something well enough to **hold** your **own**, you do not appear foolish when you are compared with someone who is generally thought to be very good at it. [PHRASE: V inflects, oft PHR *against* n] ❑ *She can hold her own against almost any player.* **9** If you **hold still**, you do not move. [PHRASE: V inflects] ❑ *Can't you hold still for a second?* **10** If something **takes hold**, it gains complete control or influence over a person or thing. [PHRASE: V inflects, oft PHR *of* n] ❑ *She felt a strange excitement taking hold of her.* **11** If you **hold tight**, you put your hand round or against something in order to prevent yourself from falling over. [PHRASE: V inflects, oft PHR prep = hang on] A bus driver might say '**Hold tight!**' to you if you are standing on a bus when it is about to move. ❑ *He held tight to the rope.* **12** If you **hold tight**, you do not immediately start a course of action that you have been planning or thinking about. [PHRASE: V inflects] ❑ *The unions are urging members to hold tight until a national deal is struck.* **13** to **hold** something **at bay** → see **bay**. to **hold** your **breath** → see **breath**. to **hold** something **in check** → see **check**. to **hold court** → see **court**. to **hold fast** → see **fast**. to **hold the fort** → see **fort**. to **hold** your **ground** → see **ground**. to **hold** your **peace** → see **peace**. to **hold** someone **to ransom** → see **ransom**. to **hold sway** → see **sway**. to **hold** your **tongue** → see **tongue**.

⑤**hold** /hoʊld/ **(holds, holding, held)** ◆◆◆
♦ **hold against** If you **hold** something **against** someone, you let their actions in the past influence your present attitude towards them and cause you to deal severely or unfairly with them. [PHRASAL VERB] ❑ *Bernstein lost the case, but never held it against Grundy.* [V n P n]

♦ **hold back** **1** If you **hold back** or if something **holds** you **back**, you hesitate before you do something because you are not sure whether it is the right thing to do. [PHRASAL VERB] ❑ *The administration had several reasons for holding back... Melancholy and mistrust of men hold her back.* [V P] [V n P] **2** To **hold** someone or something **back** means to prevent someone from doing something, or to prevent something from happening. [PHRASAL VERB] ❑ *Stagnation in home sales is holding back economic recovery... Jake wanted to wake up, but* [V P n (not pron)] [V n P] *sleep held him back.* 3 If you **hold** something **back**, you keep it in reserve to use later. [PHRASAL VERB] [V P n (not pron)] [Also V n P] ❑ *Farmers apparently hold back produce in the hope that prices will rise.* 4 If you **hold** something **back**, you do not include it in the information you are giving about something. [PHRASAL VERB] [V n P] ❑ *You seem to be holding something back.* 5 If you **hold back** something such as tears or laughter, or if you **hold back**, you make an effort to stop yourself from showing how you feel. [PHRASAL VERB] [V P n] [V P] [Also V n P] ❑ *She kept trying to hold back her tears... I was close to tears with frustration, but I held back.*

♦ **hold down** 1 If you **hold down** a job or a place in a team, you manage to keep it. [PHRASAL VERB: oft with brd-neg] [V P n (not pron)] [Also V n P] ❑ *He never could hold down a job... Constant injury problems had made it tough for him to hold down a regular first team place.* 2 If you **hold** someone **down**, you keep them under control and do not allow them to have much freedom or power or many rights. [PHRASAL VERB] [V P n (not pron)] ❑ *Everyone thinks there is some vast conspiracy wanting to hold down the younger generation.*

♦ **hold in** If you **hold in** an emotion or feeling, you do not allow yourself to express it, often making it more difficult to deal with. [PHRASAL VERB] [V P n (not pron)] [V n P] ❑ *Depression can be traced to holding in anger... Go ahead and cry. Don't hold it in.*

♦ **hold off** 1 If you **hold off** doing something, you delay doing it or delay making a decision about it. [PHRASAL VERB] [V P -ing] [V P] ❑ *The hospital staff held off taking Rosenbaum in for an X-ray... They have threatened military action but held off until now.* 2 If you **hold off** a challenge in a race or competition, you do not allow someone to pass you. [PHRASAL VERB] [V P n (not pron)] ❑ *Between 1987 and 1990, Steffi Graf largely held off Navratilova's challenge for the crown.*

♦ **hold on** or **hold onto** 1 If you **hold on**, or **hold onto** something, you keep your hand on it or around it, for example to prevent the thing from falling or to support yourself. [PHRASAL VERB] [V P *to* n] [V P n] [V P] ❑ *His right arm was extended up beside his head, still holding on to a coffee cup... He was struggling to hold onto a rock on the face of the cliff... Despite her aching shoulders, Nancy held on.* 2 If you **hold on**, you manage to achieve success or avoid failure in spite of great difficulties or opposition. [PHRASAL VERB] [V P] ❑ *This Government deserved to lose power a year ago. It held on.* 3 If you ask someone to **hold on**, you are asking them to wait for a short time. [SPOKEN] [PHRASAL VERB = hang on] [V P] ❑ *The manager asked him to hold on while he investigated.*

♦ **hold on to** or **hold onto** 1 If you **hold on to** something that gives you an advantage, you succeed in keeping it for yourself, and prevent it from being taken away or given to someone else. [PHRASAL VERB] [V P P n] [V P n] ❑ *Firms are now keen to hold on to the people they recruit. ...a politician who knew how to hold onto power.* 2 If you **hold on to** something, you keep it for a longer time than would normally be expected. [PHRASAL VERB = keep] [V P P n] [V P n] ❑ *Do you think you could hold on to that report for the next day or two?... People hold onto letters for years and years.* 3 If you **hold on to** your beliefs, ideas, or principles, you continue to believe in them and do not change or abandon them if others try to influence you or if circumstances cause you to doubt them. [PHRASAL VERB] [V P P n] ❑ *He was imprisoned for 19 years yet held on to his belief in his people.*

♦ **hold out** 1 If you **hold out** your hand or something you have in your hand, you move your hand away from your body, for example to shake hands with someone. [PHRASAL VERB] [V P n (not pron)] ❑ *'I'm Nancy Drew,' she said, holding out her hand.* 2 If you **hold out for** something, you refuse to accept something which you do not think is good enough or large enough, and you continue to demand more. [PHRASAL VERB] [V P *for* n] [V P] ❑ *I should have held out for a better deal... He can only hold out a few more weeks.* 3 If you say that someone **is holding out on** you, you think that they are refusing to give you information that you want. [INFORMAL] [PHRASAL VERB] [V P *on* n] ❑ *He had always believed that kids could sense it when you held out on them.* 4 If you **hold out**, you manage to resist an enemy or opponent in difficult circumstances and refuse to give in. [PHRASAL VERB] [V P] ❑ *One prisoner was still holding out on the roof of the jail.* 5 If you **hold out** hope of something happening, you hope that in the future something will happen as you want it to. [PHRASAL VERB] [V P n (not pron)] ❑ *He still holds out hope that they could be a family again.*

♦ **hold over** 1 If you **hold** something **over** someone, you use it in order to threaten them or make them do what you want. [PHRASAL VERB] [V n P n] ❑ *Did Laurie know something, and hold it over Felicity?* 2 If something **is held over**, it does not happen or it is not dealt with until a future date. [PHRASAL VERB] [*be* V-ed P] [V n P] [Also V P n (not pron)] ❑ *Further voting might be held over until tomorrow... We would have held the story over until the next day.*

♦ **hold together** If you **hold** a group of people **together**, you help them to live or work together without arguing, although they may have different aims, attitudes, or interests. [PHRASAL VERB] [V n P] [V P n (not pron)] [V P] ❑ *Her 13-year-old daughter is holding the family together. ...the political balance which holds together the government... The coalition will never hold together for six months.*

♦ **hold up** 1 If you **hold up** your hand or something you have in your hand, you move it upwards into a particular position and keep it there. [PHRASAL VERB] [V P n] [V n P] ❑ *She held up her hand stiffly... Hold it up so that we can see it.* 2 If one thing **holds up** another, it is placed under the other thing in order to support it and prevent it from falling. [PHRASAL VERB] [V P n (not pron)] [V n P] ❑ *Mills have iron pillars all over the place holding up the roof... Her legs wouldn't hold her up.* 3 To **hold up** a person or process means to make them late or delay them. [PHRASAL VERB = delay] [V n P] [V P n (not pron)] ❑ *Why were you holding everyone up?... Continuing violence could hold up progress towards reform.* 4 If someone **holds up** a place such as a bank or a shop, they point a weapon at someone there to make them give them money or valuable goods. [PHRASAL VERB = rob] [V P n] [Also V n P] ❑ *A thief ran off with hundreds of pounds yesterday after holding up a petrol station.* 5 If you **hold up** something such as someone's behaviour, you make it known to other people, so that they can criticize or praise it. [PHRASAL VERB] [*be* V-ed P *as* n] [Also V n P *as* n] ❑ *He had always been held up as an example to the younger ones.* 6 If something such as a type of business **holds up** in difficult conditions, it stays in a reasonably good state. [PHRASAL VERB] [V P] ❑ *Children's wear is one area that is holding up well in the recession.* 7 If an argument or theory **holds up**, it is true or valid, even after close examination. [PHRASAL VERB = stand up] ❑ *I'm not sure if the argument holds up, but it's stimulating.* 8 → See also **hold-up**.

♦ **hold with** If you do not **hold with** an activity or action, you do not approve of it. [PHRASAL VERB: with brd-neg] [V P n] ❑ *I don't hold with the way they do things nowadays.*

**hold|all** /hoʊldɔːl/ **(holdalls)** also **hold-all**. [N-COUNT] A **holdall** is a strong bag which you use to carry your clothes and other things, for example when you are travelling. [mainly BRIT]

✓ in AM, usually use **carryall**

**hold|er** /hoʊldəʳ/ **(holders)** ◆◇◇ 1 A **holder** is someone who owns or has something. [N-COUNT: n N, N *of* n] ❑ *This season the club has had 73,500 season-ticket holders.* 2 A **holder** is a container in which you put an object, usually in order to protect it or to keep it in place. [N-COUNT: usu n N] ❑ *...a toothbrush holder.*

**hold|ing** /hoʊldɪŋ/ **(holdings)** 1 If you have a **holding** in a company, you own shares in it. [BUSINESS] [N-COUNT: with supp = investment] ❑ *That would increase Olympia & York's holding to 35%.* 2 A **holding** operation or action is a temporary one that is intended to keep a situation under control and to prevent it from becoming worse. [ADJ: ADJ n] ❑ *A garden is, at best, a holding operation against nature.*

**hold|ing com|pa|ny** **(holding companies)** [N-COUNT] A **holding company** is a company that has enough shares in one or more other companies to be able to control the other companies. [BUSINESS]

**hold|out** /hoʊldaʊt/ **(holdouts)** [N-COUNT] A **holdout** is someone who refuses to agree or act with other people in a particular situation and by doing so stops the situation from progressing or being resolved. [AM] ❑ *France has been the holdout in trying to negotiate an end to the dispute.*

**hold-up** **(hold-ups)** [1] A **hold-up** is a situation in which someone is threatened with a weapon in order to make them hand over money or valuables. N-COUNT [2] A **hold-up** is something which causes a delay. N-COUNT [3] A **hold-up** is the stopping or very slow movement of traffic, sometimes caused by an accident which happened earlier. N-COUNT ❑ *They arrived late due to a motorway hold-up.*

**hole** /həʊl/ **(holes, holing, holed)** ◆◆◇ [1] A **hole** is a hollow space in something solid, with an opening on one side. N-COUNT ❑ *He took a shovel, dug a hole, and buried his once-prized possessions. ...a 60ft hole.* [2] A **hole** is an opening in something that goes right through it. N-COUNT: oft N *in* n ❑ *These tiresome creatures eat holes in the leaves. ...kids with holes in the knees of their jeans.* [3] A **hole** is the home or hiding place of a mouse, rabbit, or other small animal. N-COUNT ❑ *...a rabbit hole.* [4] A **hole in** a law, theory, or argument is a fault or weakness that it has. N-COUNT: oft N *in* n ❑ *There were some holes in that theory, some unanswered questions.* [5] A **hole** is also one of the nine or eighteen sections of a golf course. N-COUNT ❑ *I played nine holes with Gary Player today.* [6] A **hole** is one of the places on a golf course that the ball must drop into, usually marked by a flag. N-COUNT

PHRASES [7] If you say that you **need** something or someone **like a hole in the head**, you are emphasizing that you do not want them and that they would only add to the problems that you already have. PHRASE: V inflects [emphasis] [INFORMAL] ❑ *We need more folk heroes like we need a hole in the head.* [8] If you say that you are **in a hole**, you mean that you are in a difficult or embarrassing situation. PHRASE: v-link PHR [INFORMAL] ❑ *He admitted that the government was in 'a dreadful hole'.* [9] If you get **a hole in one** in golf, you get the golf ball into the hole with a single stroke. PHRASE: usu v PHR [10] If you **pick holes in** an argument or theory, you find weak points in it so that it is no longer valid. PHRASE: V inflects [INFORMAL] ❑ *He then goes on to pick holes in the article before reaching his conclusion.*

♦ **hole up** If you **hole up** somewhere, you hide or shut yourself there, usually so that people cannot find or disturb you. PHRASAL VERB [INFORMAL] ❑ *His creative process involves holing up in his Paris flat with the phone off the hook.* V P

**holed up** If you are **holed up** somewhere, you are hiding or staying there, usually so that other people cannot find or disturb you. ADJ: v-link ADJ [INFORMAL] ❑ *If he had another well-stocked hideaway like this, he could stay holed up for months.*

**hole-in-the-wall** A **hole-in-the-wall** machine is a machine built into the wall of a bank or other building, which allows people to take out money from their bank account by using a special card. N-SING: usu N n = *cash dispenser* [BRIT, INFORMAL]

✓ in AM, use **ATM**

**holi|day** /hɒlɪdeɪ/ **(holidays, holidaying, holidayed)** ◆◆◇ [1] A **holiday** is a period of time during which you relax and enjoy yourself away from home. People sometimes refer to their holiday as their **holidays**. N-COUNT: also *on/from* N [BRIT] ❑ *We rang Duncan to ask where he was going on holiday... Ischia is a popular seaside holiday resort... We're going to Scotland for our holidays.*

✓ in AM, use **vacation**

[2] A **holiday** is a day when people do not go to work or school because of a religious or national festival. N-COUNT: usu with supp ❑ *New Year's Day is a public holiday throughout Britain.* → See also **bank holiday**.
[3] **The holidays** are the time when children do not have to go to school. N-PLURAL: usu *the* N, oft n N [BRIT] ❑ *...the first day of the school holidays.*

✓ in AM, use **vacation**

[4] If you have a particular number of days' or weeks' **holiday**, you do not have to go to work for that number of days or weeks. N-UNCOUNT [BRIT] ❑ *Every worker will be entitled to four weeks' paid holiday a year.*

✓ in AM, use **vacation**

[5] If you **are holidaying** in a place away from home, you are on holiday there. VERB: oft cont V prep/adv [BRIT] ❑ *Sampling the local cuisine is one of the delights of holidaying abroad.*

✓ in AM, use **vacation**

**holi|day camp** **(holiday camps)** In Britain, a **holiday camp** is a place which provides holiday accommodation and entertainment for large numbers of people. N-COUNT

**holi|day|maker** /hɒlɪdeɪmeɪkəʳ/ **(holidaymakers)** A **holidaymaker** is a person who is away from their home on holiday. N-COUNT [BRIT]

✓ in AM, use **vacationer**

**holi|day rep** **(holiday reps)** A **holiday rep** is someone employed by a holiday company to help look after people when they are on holiday. N-COUNT = *travel rep, tour rep* [BRIT]

**holier-than-thou** If you describe someone as **holier-than-thou**, you disapprove of them because they seem to believe that they are more religious or have better moral qualities than anyone else. ADJ [disapproval] = *self-righteous* ❑ *He has always sounded holier-than-thou.*

**ho|li|ness** /həʊlinəs/ [1] **Holiness** is the state or quality of being holy. N-UNCOUNT: usu with supp ❑ *We were immediately struck by this city's holiness.* [2] You say **Your Holiness** or **His Holiness** when you address or refer respectfully to the Pope or to leaders of some other religions. N-VOC: poss N; PRON: poss PRON [politeness] ❑ *The President received His Holiness at the White House.*

**ho|lism** /həʊlɪzəm/ **Holism** is the belief that everything in nature is connected in some way. N-UNCOUNT [FORMAL]

**ho|lis|tic** /həʊlɪstɪk/ **Holistic** means based on the principles of holism. ADJ: usu ADJ n [FORMAL] ❑ *...practitioners of holistic medicine.*

**hol|ler** /hɒləʳ/ **(hollers, hollering, hollered)** If you **holler**, you shout loudly. VERB = *shout, yell* [mainly AM, INFORMAL] ❑ *The audience whooped and hollered... 'Watch out!' he hollered... The passengers hollered for help.* V; V with quote; V *at/for* n ♦ **Holler** is also a noun. N-COUNT ❑ *On the ship's deck, after the whoops and hollers, the butchering begins.* ♦ **Holler out** means the same as **holler**. PHRASAL VERB ❑ *I hollered out the names... I heard him holler out, 'Somebody bombed the Church.'* V P n; V P with quote

**hol|low** /hɒləʊ/ **(hollows, hollowing, hollowed)** [1] Something that is **hollow** has a space inside it, as opposed to being solid all the way through. ADJ ❑ *...a hollow tree. ...a hollow cylinder.* [2] A surface that is **hollow** curves inwards. ADJ ❑ *He looked young, dark and sharp-featured, with hollow cheeks.* [3] A **hollow** is a hole inside a tree. N-COUNT ❑ *I made my home there, in the hollow of a dying elm.* [4] A **hollow** is an area that is lower than the surrounding surface. N-COUNT: oft N *of/in/between* n ❑ *Below him the town lay warm in the hollow of the hill.* [5] If you describe a statement, situation, or person as **hollow**, you mean they have no real value, worth, or effectiveness. ADJ: usu ADJ n ❑ *Any threat to bring in the police is a hollow one.* ♦ **hol|low|ness** N-UNCOUNT: oft N *of/behind* n *One month before the deadline we see the hollowness of these promises.* [6] If someone gives a **hollow** laugh, they laugh in a way that shows that they do not really find something amusing. ADJ: ADJ n ❑ *Murray Pick's hollow laugh had no mirth in it.* [7] A **hollow** sound is dull and echoing. ADJ: ADJ n ❑ *...the hollow sound of a gunshot.* [8] If something **is hollowed**, its surface is made to curve inwards or downwards. VERB: usu passive ❑ *The mule's back was hollowed by the weight of its burden. ...her high, elegantly hollowed cheekbones.* *be* V-ed; V-ed

**hol|ly** /hɒli/ **(hollies)** **Holly** is an evergreen tree or shrub which has hard, shiny leaves with sharp points, and red berries in winter. N-VAR

**Hol|ly|wood** /hɒliwʊd/ You use **Hollywood** to refer to the American film industry that is based in Hollywood, California. N-PROPER: oft N n ❑ *...a major Hollywood studio.*

**holo|caust** /hɒləkɔːst/ **(holocausts)** [1] A **holocaust** is an event in which there is a lot of destruction and many people are killed, especially one caused by war. N-VAR ❑ *A nuclear holocaust seemed a very real possibility in the '50s.* [2] **The Holocaust** N-SING: *the* N is used to refer to the killing by the Nazis of millions of Jews during the Second World War.

**holo|gram** /hɒləgræm/ **(holograms)** A **hologram** is a three-dimensional photographic image created by laser beams. [N-COUNT]

**hols** /hɒlz/ Some people refer to their holidays as their **hols.** [BRIT, INFORMAL] ❑ *Where did you go for your hols?* [N-PLURAL: usu supp N = holidays]

**hol|ster** /hoʊlstəʳ/ **(holsters)** A **holster** is a holder for a small gun, which is worn on a belt around someone's waist or on a strap around their shoulder. [N-COUNT]

**holy** /hoʊli/ **(holier, holiest)** 1 If you describe something as **holy**, you mean that it is considered to be special because it is connected with God or a particular religion. ❑ *To them, as to all Tibetans, this is a holy place.* [◆◇◇ ADJ: usu ADJ n] 2 A **holy** person is a religious leader or someone who leads a religious life. [ADJ] 3 → See also **holier-than-thou**.

**Holy Com|mun|ion** **Holy Communion** is the most important religious service in the Christian church, in which people share bread and wine as a symbol of the Last Supper and the death of Christ. [N-UNCOUNT]

**Holy Father** In the Catholic Church, **the Holy Father** is the Pope. [N-PROPER: the N]

**Holy Ghost** **The Holy Ghost** is the same as the **Holy Spirit**. [N-PROPER: the N]

**holy of holies** /hoʊli əv hoʊliz/ A **holy of holies** is a place that is so sacred that only particular people are allowed to enter; often used in informal English to refer humorously to a place where only a few special people can go. ❑ *...the holy of holies in the Temple. ...the Aldeburgh Festival, the holy of holies in the contemporary music scene.* [N-SING]

**holy or|ders** also **Holy Orders.** Someone who is in **holy orders** is a member of the Christian clergy. ❑ *He took holy orders in 1935.* [N-PLURAL]

**Holy Spir|it** In the Christian religion, **the Holy Spirit** is one of the three aspects of God, together with God the Father and God the Son. [N-PROPER: the N = Holy Ghost]

**Holy Week** In the Christian religion, **Holy Week** is the week before Easter, when Christians remember the events leading up to the death of Christ. [N-UNCOUNT]

**hom|age** /hɒmɪdʒ/ **Homage** is respect shown towards someone or something you admire, or to a person in authority. ❑ *Palace has released two marvellous films that pay homage to our literary heritage.* [N-UNCOUNT: usu N to n]

> **home**
> ① NOUN, ADJECTIVE, AND ADVERB USES
> ② PHRASAL VERB USES

**① home** /hoʊm/ **(homes)** 1 Someone's **home** is the house or flat where they live. ❑ *Last night they stayed at home and watched TV. ...his home in Hampstead. ...the allocation of land for new homes.* [◆◆◆ N-COUNT: oft poss N, also at N] 2 You can use **home** to refer in a general way to the house, town, or country where someone lives now or where they were born, often to emphasize that they feel they belong in that place. ❑ *She gives frequent performances of her work, both at home and abroad... His father worked away from home for much of Jim's first five years... Warwick is home to some 550 international students.* [N-UNCOUNT] 3 **Home** means to or at the place where you live. ❑ *His wife wasn't feeling too well and she wanted to go home... Hi, Mom, I'm home!.* [ADV: ADV after v, be ADV] 4 **Home** means made or done in the place where you live. ❑ *...cheap but healthy home cooking... All you have to do is make a home video.* [ADJ: ADJ n] 5 **Home** means relating to your own country as opposed to foreign countries. ❑ *Europe's software companies still have a growing home market.* [ADJ: ADJ n = domestic] 6 A **home** is a large house or institution where a number of people live and are looked after, instead of living in their own houses or flats. They usually live there because they are too old or ill to look after themselves or for their families to care for them. ❑ *...an old people's home.* [N-COUNT] 7 You can refer to a family unit as a **home**. ❑ *She had, at any rate, provided a peaceful and loving home for Harriet.* [N-COUNT] 8 If you refer to the **home of** something, you mean the place where it began or where it is most typically found. ❑ *This south-west region of France is the home of claret.* [N-SING: with supp, usu N of n] 9 If you find a **home for** something, you find a place where it can be kept. ❑ *The equipment itself is getting smaller, neater and easier to find a home for.* [N-COUNT: oft N for n] 10 If you press, drive, or hammer something **home**, you explain it to people as forcefully as possible. ❑ *It is now up to all of us to debate this issue and press home the argument.* [ADV: ADV after v] 11 When a sports team plays **at home**, they play a game on their own ground, rather than on the opposing team's ground. ❑ *I scored in both games against Barcelona; we drew at home and beat them away.* ♦ **Home** is also an adjective. ❑ *All three are Chelsea fans, and attend all home games.* [N-UNCOUNT: usu at N] [ADJ: ADJ n ≠ away]

PHRASES 12 If you feel **at home**, you feel comfortable in the place or situation that you are in. ❑ *He spoke very good English and appeared pleased to see us, and we soon felt quite at home.* [PHRASE: v-link PHR] 13 To **bring** something **home to** someone means to make them understand how important or serious it is. ❑ *Their sobering conversation brought home to everyone present the serious and worthwhile work the Red Cross does.* [PHRASE: V inflects, usu PHR to n] 14 If you say that someone is, in British English **home and dry**, or in American English **home free**, you mean that they have been successful or that they are certain to be successful. ❑ *The prime minister and the moderates are not yet home and dry.* [PHRASE: v-link PHR] 15 If a situation or what someone says **hits home** or **strikes home**, people accept that it is real or true, even though it may be painful for them to realize. ❑ *Did the reality of war finally hit home?* [PHRASE: V inflects] 16 You can say **a home from home** in British English or **a home away from home** in American English to refer to a place in which you are as comfortable as in your own home. ❑ *Many cottages are a home from home, offering microwaves, dishwashers, tvs and videos.* [PHRASE: usu v-link PHR] [approval] 17 If you say to a guest **'Make yourself at home'**, you are making them feel welcome and inviting them to behave in an informal, relaxed way. [CONVENTION] [politeness] 18 If you say that something is **nothing to write home about**, you mean that it is not very interesting or exciting. [INFORMAL] ❑ *So a dreary Monday afternoon in Walthamstow is nothing to write home about, right?* [PHRASE: v-link PHR] 19 If something that is thrown or fired **strikes home**, it reaches its target. [WRITTEN] ❑ *Only two torpedoes struck home.* [PHRASE: V inflects]

**② home** /hoʊm/ **(homes, homing, homed)**

♦ **home in** 1 If you **home in on** one particular aspect of something, you give all your attention to it. ❑ *The critics immediately homed in on the group's newly-elected members.* [PHRASAL VERB: V P on n] 2 If something such as a missile **homes in on** something else, it is aimed at that thing and moves towards it. ❑ *Two rockets homed in on it from behind without a sound.* [PHRASAL VERB: V P on n] → See also **homing**.

**home birth** **(home births)** If a woman has a **home birth**, she gives birth to her baby at home rather than in a hospital. [N-VAR]

**home|boy** /hoʊmbɔɪ/ **(homeboys)** A **homeboy** is a boy or man from the same area as you, especially one from the same social group as you. [AM, INFORMAL] [N-COUNT]

**home-brew** **Home-brew** is beer or wine that is made in someone's home, rather than in a brewery. [N-UNCOUNT]

**home|coming** /hoʊmkʌmɪŋ/ **(homecomings)** 1 Your **homecoming** is your return to your home or your country after being away for a long time. ❑ *Her homecoming was tinged with sadness.* [N-VAR: oft poss N] 2 **Homecoming** is a day or weekend each year when former students of a particular school, college, or university go back to it to meet each other again and go to dances and sports matches. [AM] [N-UNCOUNT]

**Home Coun|ties** also **home counties.** The **Home Counties** are the counties which surround London. N-PROPER-PLURAL: *the* N

**home eco|nom|ics** **Home economics** is a school subject dealing with how to run a house well and efficiently. N-UNCOUNT

**home field** **(home fields)** A sports team's **home field** is their own playing field, as opposed to that of other teams. [AM] N-COUNT

☑ in BRIT, use **home ground**

**home|girl** /hoʊmgɜːʳl/ **(homegirls)** A **homegirl** is a girl or woman from the same area as you, especially one from the same social group as you. [AM, INFORMAL] N-COUNT

**home ground** **(home grounds)** [1] A sports team's **home ground** is their own playing field, as opposed to that of other teams. [BRIT] N-VAR

☑ in AM, use **home field**

[2] If you say that someone is **on** their **home ground**, you mean that they are in or near where they work or live, and feel confident and secure because of this. ❑ *Although he was on home ground, his campaign had been rocked by adultery allegations.* PHRASE: v-link PHR, PHR after v

**home-grown** **Home-grown** fruit and vegetables have been grown in your garden, rather than on a farm, or in your country rather than abroad. ADJ: usu ADJ n

**home help** **(home helps)** A **home help** is a person who is employed to visit sick or old people at home and help with their cleaning or cooking. [mainly BRIT] N-COUNT

**home|land** /hoʊmlænd/ **(homelands)** [1] Your **homeland** is your native country. [mainly WRITTEN] ❑ *Many are planning to return to their homeland.* N-COUNT: usu poss N [2] The **homelands** were regions within South Africa in which black South Africans had a limited form of self-government. N-COUNT

**home|less** /hoʊmləs/ **Homeless** people have nowhere to live. ❑ *...the growing number of homeless families... Hundreds were made homeless.* ◆◇◇ ADJ ♦ **The homeless** are people who are homeless. ❑ *...shelters for the homeless.* N-PLURAL: *the* N ♦ **home|less|ness** *The only way to solve homelessness is to provide more homes.* N-UNCOUNT

**home|ly** /hoʊmli/ [1] If you describe a room or house as **homely**, you like it because you feel comfortable and relaxed there. [mainly BRIT] ❑ *We try and provide a very homely atmosphere.* ADJ [approval] = *cosy*

☑ in AM, usually use **homey**

[2] If you describe a woman as **homely**, you mean that she has a warm, comforting manner and looks like someone who would enjoy being at home and running a family. [BRIT] ❑ *Mrs Jones was a pleasant, homely person with a ready smile.* ADJ [3] If you say that someone is **homely**, you mean that they are not very attractive to look at. [AM] ❑ *The man was homely and overweight.* ADJ = *plain*

**home-made** Something that is **home-made** has been made in someone's home, rather than in a shop or factory. ❑ *The bread, pastry and mayonnaise are home-made... A home-made bomb exploded during the disturbances.* ADJ

**home|maker** /hoʊmmeɪkəʳ/ **(homemakers)** A **homemaker** is a woman who spends a lot of time looking after her home and family. If you describe a woman as a **homemaker**, you usually mean that she does not have another job. N-COUNT

**Home Of|fice** **The Home Office** is the department of the British Government which is responsible for things such as the police, broadcasting, and making decisions about people who want to come to live in Britain. N-PROPER: usu *the* N

**homeo|path** /hoʊmioʊpæθ/ **(homeopaths)**

☑ in BRIT, also use **homoeopath**

A **homeopath** is someone who treats illness by homeopathy. N-COUNT

**homeo|path|ic** /hoʊmioʊpæθɪk/

☑ in BRIT, also use **homoeopathic**

**Homeopathic** means relating to or used in homeopathy. ❑ *...homeopathic remedies.* ADJ: usu ADJ n

**homeopa|thy** /hoʊmiɒpəθi/

☑ in BRIT, also use **homoeopathy**

**Homeopathy** is a way of treating an illness in which the patient is given very small amounts of a drug that produces signs of the illness in healthy people. N-UNCOUNT

**home own|er** **(home owners)** also **homeowner.** A **home owner** is a person who owns the house or flat that they live in. N-COUNT

**home page** **(home pages)** also **homepage.** On the Internet, a person's or organization's **home page** is the main page of information about them, which often contains links to other pages about them. N-COUNT

**home rule** If a country or region has **home rule**, it has its own independent government and laws. N-UNCOUNT

**Home Sec|re|tary** **(Home Secretaries)** The **Home Secretary** is the member of the British government who is in charge of the Home Office. N-COUNT: usu *the* N in sing

**home shop|ping** **Home shopping** is shopping that people do by ordering goods from their homes, using catalogues, television channels, or computers. ❑ *...America's most successful home-shopping channel.* N-UNCOUNT: oft N n

**home|sick** /hoʊmsɪk/ If you are **homesick**, you feel unhappy because you are away from home and are missing your family, friends, and home very much. ❑ *She's feeling a little homesick.* ADJ: usu v-link ADJ ♦ **home|sick|ness** *There were inevitable bouts of homesickness.* N-UNCOUNT

**home|spun** /hoʊmspʌn/ [1] You use **homespun** to describe opinions or ideas that are simple and not based on special knowledge. ❑ *The book is simple homespun philosophy.* ADJ: usu ADJ n [2] **Homespun** clothes are made from cloth that has been made at home, rather than in a factory. N-UNCOUNT: usu N n

**home|stead** /hoʊmsted/ **(homesteads)** [1] A **homestead** is a farmhouse, together with the land around it. N-COUNT [2] In United States history, a **homestead** was a piece of government land in the west, which was given to someone so they could settle there and develop a farm. [AM] N-COUNT

**home stretch**

☑ in BRIT, also use **home straight**

[1] **The home stretch** or **the home straight** is the last part of a race. ❑ *Holmes matched Boulmerka stride for stride down the home straight to finish second.* N-SING: *the* N [2] You can refer to the last part of any activity that lasts for a long time as **the home stretch** or **the home straight**, especially if the activity is difficult or boring. ❑ *...as his two hours of banter, quips and anecdotes goes into the home straight.* N-SING: *the* N

**home|town** /hoʊmtaʊn/ **(hometowns)** also **home town.** Someone's **hometown** is the town where they live or the town that they come from. N-COUNT: with poss

**home truth** **(home truths)** **Home truths** are unpleasant facts that you learn about yourself, usually from someone else. [BRIT] ❑ *We held a team meeting and a few home truths were spelled out.* N-COUNT: usu pl

**home|ward** /hoʊmwəʳd/ also **homewards.** [1] If you are on a **homeward** journey, you are on a journey towards your home. ❑ *She is ready for her homeward journey.* ADJ: ADJ n [2] If you are travelling **homeward** or **homewards**, you are travelling towards your home. ❑ *John drove homeward through the lanes.* ADV: ADV after v

**home|ward bound** People or things that are **homeward bound** are on their way home. ❑ *I'd be homeward bound even before Grant arrived.* ADJ

**home|work** /hoʊmwɜːʳk/ [1] **Homework** is school work that teachers give to pupils to do at home in the evening or at the weekend. ❑ *Have you done your homework, Gemma?* [2] If you **do** your **homework**, you find out what you need to know in preparation for something. ❑ *Before you go near a stockbroker, do your homework.* N-UNCOUNT N-UNCOUNT

**homey** /hoʊmi/ If you describe a room or house as **homey**, you like it because you feel comfortable and relaxed there. [mainly AM, INFORMAL] ❑ *...a large, homey dining room.* ADJ approval = cosy

in BRIT, usually use **homely**

**homi|ci|dal** /hɒmɪsaɪdᵊl/ **Homicidal** is used to describe someone who is dangerous because they are likely to kill someone. ❑ *That man is a homicidal maniac.* ADJ: usu ADJ n

**homi|cide** /hɒmɪsaɪd/ **(homicides) Homicide** is the illegal killing of a person. [mainly AM] ❑ *The police arrived at the scene of the homicide.* N-VAR

in BRIT, usually use **murder**

**homi|ly** /hɒmɪli/ **(homilies)** A **homily** is a speech or piece of writing in which someone complains about the state of something or tells people how they ought to behave. [FORMAL] ❑ *...a receptive audience for his homily on moral values.* N-COUNT

**hom|ing** /hoʊmɪŋ/ [1] A weapon or piece of equipment that has a **homing** system is able to guide itself to a target or to give out a signal that guides people to it. ❑ *All the royal cars are fitted with electronic homing devices.* [2] An animal that has a **homing** instinct has the ability to remember and return to a place where it has been in the past. ❑ *Then the pigeons flew into thick fog, and the famous homing instinct failed.* ADJ: ADJ n ADJ: ADJ n

**hom|ing pi|geon (homing pigeons)** A **homing pigeon** is a pigeon that is trained to return to a particular place, especially in races with other pigeons. N-COUNT

**homoeo|path** /hoʊmioʊpæθ/ → see **homeopath**.

**homoeo|path|ic** /hoʊmioʊpæθɪk/ → see **homeopathic**.

**homoeopa|thy** /hoʊmiɒpəθi/ → see **homeopathy**.

**homo|erot|ic** /hɒmoʊɪrɒtɪk/ **Homoerotic** is used to describe things such as films, literature, and images intended to be sexually appealing to homosexual men. ADJ

**homo|genei|ty** /hɒmədʒəniːɪti, hoʊ-/ **Homogeneity** is the quality of being homogeneous. [FORMAL] N-UNCOUNT = uniformity

**homo|geneous** /hɒmədʒiːniəs, hoʊ-/ also **homogenous. Homogeneous** is used to describe a group or thing which has members or parts that are all the same. [FORMAL] ❑ *The unemployed are not a homogeneous group.* ADJ

**ho|mog|enize** /həmɒdʒənaɪz/ **(homogenizes, homogenizing, homogenized)**

in BRIT, also use **homogenise**

If something **is homogenized**, it is changed so that all its parts are similar or the same, especially in a way that is undesirable. ❑ *Even Brussels bureaucrats can't homogenize national cultures and tastes.* VERB disapproval V n

**ho|mog|enized** /həmɒdʒənaɪzd/

in BRIT, also use **homogenised**

**Homogenized** milk is milk where the fat has been broken up so that it is evenly distributed. ADJ

**ho|mog|enous** /həmɒdʒənəs/ **Homogenous** means the same as **homogeneous**. ADJ

**homo|pho|bia** /hɒməfoʊbiə/ **Homophobia** is a strong and unreasonable dislike of homosexual people, especially homosexual men. N-UNCOUNT

**ho|mo|pho|bic** /hɒməfoʊbɪk/ **Homophobic** means involving or related to a strong and unreasonable dislike of homosexual people, especially homosexual men. ADJ

**homo|phone** /hɒməfoʊn/ **(homophones)** In linguistics, **homophones** are words with different meanings which are pronounced in the same way but are spelled differently. For example, 'write' and 'right' are homophones. N-COUNT

**homo sa|pi|ens** /hoʊmoʊ sæpienz/ **Homo sapiens** is used to refer to modern human beings as a species, in contrast to other species of ape or animal, or earlier forms of human. [TECHNICAL] ❑ *What distinguishes homo sapiens from every other living creature is the mind.* N-UNCOUNT

**homo|sex|ual** /hɒmoʊsekʃuəl, AM hoʊ-/ **(homosexuals)** [1] A **homosexual** relationship is a sexual relationship between people of the same sex. [2] Someone who is **homosexual** is sexually attracted to people of the same sex. ❑ *A fraud trial involving two homosexual lawyers was abandoned.* ◆◇◇ ADJ: usu ADJ n ADJ

♦ **Homosexual** is also a noun. ❑ *The judge said that discrimination against homosexuals is deplorable.* N-COUNT

♦ **homo|sex|ual|ity** /hɒmoʊsekʃuælɪti, AM hoʊm-/ *...a place where gays could openly discuss homosexuality.* N-UNCOUNT

**Hon.** /ɒn/ **Hon.** is an abbreviation for **honourable** and **honorary** when they are used as part of a person's title. N-TITLE

**hone** /hoʊn/ **(hones, honing, honed)** [1] If you **hone** something, for example a skill, technique, idea, or product, you carefully develop it over a long period of time so that it is exactly right for your purpose. ❑ *Leading companies spend time and money on honing the skills of senior managers.* [2] If you **hone** a blade, weapon, or tool, you sharpen it on a stone or with a special device. [TECHNICAL] ❑ *...four grinding wheels for honing fine edged tools and implements. ...a thin, honed blade.* VERB V n VERB = sharpen V n V-ed

**hon|est** /ɒnɪst/ [1] If you describe someone as **honest**, you mean that they always tell the truth, and do not try to deceive people or break the law. ❑ *I know she's honest and reliable.* ◆◇◇ ADJ

♦ **hon|est|ly** *She fought honestly for a just cause and for freedom.* [2] If you are **honest** in a particular situation, you tell the complete truth or give your sincere opinion, even if this is not very pleasant. ❑ *I was honest about what I was doing... He had been honest with her and she had tricked him!.* ADV: ADV after v ADJ = frank

♦ **hon|est|ly** *It came as a shock to hear an old friend speak so honestly about Ted.* [3] You say '**honest**' before or after a statement to emphasize that you are telling the truth and that you want people to believe you. [INFORMAL] ❑ *I'm not sure, honest.* ADV: ADV with v ADV: ADV with cl emphasis

**PHRASES** [4] Some people say '**honest to God**' to emphasize their feelings or to emphasize that something is really true. [INFORMAL] ❑ *I wish we weren't doing this, Lillian, honest to God, I really do.* [5] You can say '**to be honest**' before or after a statement to indicate that you are telling the truth about your own opinions or feelings, especially if you think these will disappoint the person you are talking to. ❑ *To be honest the house is not quite our style.* PHRASE: PHR with cl, PHR n emphasis PHRASE: PHR with cl feelings

**hon|est bro|ker (honest brokers)** If a person or country acts as an **honest broker**, they try to help people resolve a dispute or arrange a deal by talking to all sides and finding out what they want, without favouring any one side. ❑ *Canada's prime minister will be hoping to play honest broker in the row between the United States and Japan.* N-COUNT: usu sing

**hon|est|ly** /ɒnɪstli/ [1] You use **honestly** to emphasize that you are referring to your, or someone else's, true beliefs or feelings. ❑ *But did you honestly think we wouldn't notice?* [2] You use **honestly** to emphasize that you are telling the truth and that you want people to believe you. [SPOKEN] ❑ *Honestly, I don't know anything about it.* [3] You use **honestly** to indicate that you are annoyed or impatient. [SPOKEN] ❑ *Honestly, Nev! Must you be quite so crude!* [4] → See also **honest**. ADV: ADV before v emphasis ADV: ADV with cl emphasis ADV: ADV with cl feelings = really

**hon|es|ty** /ɒnɪsti/ **Honesty** is the quality of being honest. ❑ *They said the greatest virtues in a politician were integrity, correctness and honesty.* N-UNCOUNT

• You say **in all honesty** when you are saying something that might be disappointing or upsetting, and you want to soften its effect by emphasizing your sincerity. ❑ *In all honesty, aren't there already far too many pages of scientific research published every week?* PHRASE: PHR with cl [emphasis]

**hon|ey** /hʌni/ **(honeys)** [1] **Honey** is a sweet, sticky, yellowish substance that is made by bees. N-VAR [2] You call someone **honey** as a sign of affection. [mainly AM] ❑ *Honey, I don't really think that's a good idea.* N-VOC

**honey|bee** /hʌnibiː/ **(honeybees)** A **honeybee** is a bee that makes honey. N-COUNT

**honey|comb** /hʌnikoʊm/ **(honeycombs)** A **honeycomb** is a wax structure consisting of rows of six-sided spaces where bees store their honey. N-VAR

**hon|eyed** /hʌnid/ [1] You can describe someone's voice or words as **honeyed** when they are very pleasant to listen to, especially if you want to suggest that they are insincere. ❑ *His gentle manner and honeyed tones reassured Andrew.* ADJ: usu ADJ n [2] You can describe something as **honeyed** when it tastes or smells of honey, or is the pale yellowish colour of honey. [LITERARY] ❑ *I could smell the honeyed ripeness of melons and peaches. ...a warm, honeyed light.* ADJ: usu ADJ n

**honey|moon** /hʌnimuːn/ **(honeymoons, honeymooning, honeymooned)** [1] A **honeymoon** is a holiday taken by a man and a woman who have just got married. N-COUNT [2] When a recently-married couple **honeymoon** somewhere, they go there on their honeymoon. ❑ *They honeymooned in Venice.* VERB; V [3] You can use **honeymoon** to refer to a period of time after the start of a new job or new government when everyone is pleased with the person or people concerned and is nice to them. ❑ *Brett is enjoying a honeymoon period with both press and public.* N-COUNT: usu with supp

**honey|pot** /hʌnipɒt/ **(honeypots)** [1] If you describe something as a **honeypot**, you mean that it is very desirable or very popular. ❑ *...traditional tourist honeypots such as London, Bath, Edinburgh, and York.* N-COUNT [2] If something attracts people **like bees to a honeypot** or **like bees round a honeypot**, it attracts people in large numbers. ❑ *This is the show that attracts computer industry people like bees to a honeypot.* PHRASE

**honey|suckle** /hʌnisʌk$^{ə}$l/ **(honeysuckles)** **Honeysuckle** is a climbing plant with sweet-smelling yellow, pink, or white flowers. N-VAR

**honey|trap** /hʌnitræp/ **(honeytraps)** A **honeytrap** is a situation in which someone is tricked into immoral or illegal sexual behaviour so that their behaviour can be publicly exposed. N-COUNT

**honk** /hɒŋk/ **(honks, honking, honked)** If you **honk** the horn of a vehicle or if the horn **honks**, you make the horn produce a short loud sound. ❑ *Drivers honked their horns in solidarity with the peace marchers... Horns honk. An angry motorist shouts.* VERB = hoot; V n; V ♦ **Honk** is also a noun. ❑ *She pulled to the right with a honk.* N-COUNT

**honky-tonk** /hɒŋki tɒŋk/ **(honky-tonks)** [1] A **honky-tonk** is a cheap bar or nightclub. [AM] ❑ *...little honky-tonk bars in Texas.* N-COUNT: oft N n [2] **Honky-tonk** is the kind of piano music that was formerly played in honky-tonks. ❑ *...the beat of honky-tonk pianos.* N-UNCOUNT: oft N n

**hon|or** /ɒnə$^{r}$/ → see **honour**.

**hon|or|able** /ɒnərəb$^{ə}$l/ → see **honourable**.

**hono|rar|ium** /ɒnəreəriəm/ **(honoraria** /ɒnəreəriə/ or **honorariums)** An **honorarium** is a fee that someone receives for doing something which is not a normal part of their job, for example giving a talk. N-COUNT

**hon|or|ary** /ɒnərəri, AM -reri/ [1] An **honorary** title or membership of a group is given to someone without their needing to have the necessary qualifications, usually because of their public achievements. ❑ *...an honorary member of the Golf Club.* ADJ: ADJ n [2] **Honorary** is used to describe an official job that is done without payment. ❑ *...the honorary secretary of the Cheshire Beekeepers' Association.* ADJ: ADJ n

**hon|or guard** An **honor guard** is a group of troops who formally greet or accompany someone special such as a visiting head of state. [AM] N-SING

☑ in BRIT, use **guard of honour**

**hon|or|if|ic** /ɒnərɪfɪk/ An **honorific** title or way of talking is used to show respect or honour to someone. [FORMAL] ❑ *He was given the honorific title of national chairman.* ADJ: ADJ n

**hon|our** /ɒnə$^{r}$/ **(honours, honouring, honoured)** ♦◇◇

☑ in AM, use **honor**

[1] **Honour** means doing what you believe to be right and being confident that you have done what is right. ❑ *I do not believe I can any longer serve with honour as a member of your government.* N-UNCOUNT [2] An **honour** is a special award that is given to someone, usually because they have done something good or because they are greatly respected. ❑ *He was showered with honours – among them an Oscar.* N-COUNT [3] If someone **is honoured**, they are given public praise or an award for something they have done. ❑ *Two American surgeons were last week honoured with the Nobel Prize for Medicine and Physiology.* VERB: usu passive; be V-ed [4] If you describe doing or experiencing something as an **honour**, you mean you think it is something special and desirable. ❑ *Five other cities had been competing for the honour of staging the Games.* N-SING: oft N of -ing, it v-link N to-inf [5] If you say that you **would be honoured to** do something, you are saying very politely and formally that you would be pleased to do it. If you say that you **are honoured by** something, you are saying that you are grateful for it and pleased about it. ❑ *Peter Alliss says he would be honoured to be asked... It's a very flattering offer, and I'm honoured by your confidence in me.* V-PASSIVE [politeness]; be V-ed to-inf; be V-ed [6] To **honour** someone means to treat them or regard them with special attention and respect. ❑ *Her Majesty later honoured the Headmaster with her presence at lunch... Those right-wing people who most honour their monarch see no reason for any apology.* VERB; V n with n; V n ♦ **hon|oured** *Mrs Patrick Campbell was an honoured guest.* ADJ: ADJ n [7] If you **honour** an arrangement or promise, you do what you said you would do. ❑ *The two sides agreed to honour a new ceasefire.* VERB; V n [8] **Honours** is a type of university degree which is of a higher standard than a pass or ordinary degree. ❑ *...an honours degree in business studies.* N-UNCOUNT: usu N n [9] Judges, and mayors in the United States, are sometimes called **your honour** or referred to as **his honour** or **her honour**. ❑ *I bring this up, your honor, because I think it is important to understand the background of the defendant.* N-VOC: poss N; PRON: poss PRON [10] → See also **guest of honour**, **lap of honour**, **maid of honour**.

PHRASES [11] If someone **does the honours** at a social occasion or public event, they act as host or perform some official function. [INFORMAL] ❑ *A well-known television personality did the honours at the official opening of the show.* PHRASE: V inflects [12] If something is arranged **in honour of** a particular event, it is arranged in order to celebrate that event. ❑ *The Foundation is holding a dinner at the Museum of American Art in honour of the opening of their new show.* PREP-PHRASE [13] If something is arranged or happens **in** someone's **honour**, it is done specially to show appreciation of them. ❑ *He will attend an outdoor concert in his honour in the centre of Paris.* PHRASE: n PHR, PHR after v, PHR with cl

**hon|our|able** /ɒnrəb$^{ə}$l/

☑ in AM, use **honorable**

[1] If you describe people or actions as **honourable**, you mean that they are good and deserve to be respected and admired. ❑ *I believe he was an honourable man, dedicated to the people and his union... However, their intentions are honourable.* ADJ ♦ **hon|our|ably** /ɒnrəbli/ *He also felt she had not behaved honorably in the leadership election.* ADV: usu ADV with v [2] **Honourable** is used as a title before the ADJ: the ADJ n-proper

names of some members of the nobility, judges, and some other officials. ❑ *...the Honourable Mr Justice Swinton Thomas.*

**hon|our|able men|tion** **(honourable mentions)**

☑ in AM, use **honorable mention**

N-COUNT If something that you do in a competition is given an **honourable mention**, it receives special praise from the judges although it does not actually win a prize.

**hon|ours list** **(honours lists)** N-COUNT: usu *the* N in sing, oft supp N In Britain, **the honours list** is the list of people who have been selected to receive titles or awards from the Queen because of their achievements. ❑ *He has been made an MBE in the New Year Honours list.*

**Hons** /ɒnz/ In Britain, **Hons** is an abbreviation for **Honours**, used after the names of some university degrees, mainly first degrees. ❑ *...Kevin P Kearns, BA (Hons), University of Liverpool.*

**hooch** /huːtʃ/ N-UNCOUNT **Hooch** is strong alcoholic drink. [INFORMAL]

**hood** /hʊd/ **(hoods)** 1 N-COUNT A **hood** is a part of a coat which you can pull up to cover your head. It is in the shape of a triangular bag attached to the neck of the coat at the back. 2 N-COUNT The **hood** of a car is the metal cover over the engine at the front. [AM] → See picture on page 1707.

☑ in BRIT, use **bonnet**

3 N-COUNT: usu n N A cooker **hood** is an electrical device fitted over a cooker above head height, and containing an extractor fan and usually a light.

**hood|ed** /hʊdɪd/ 1 ADJ: usu ADJ n A **hooded** piece of clothing or furniture has a hood. ❑ *...a blue, hooded anorak.* 2 ADJ: ADJ n If someone has **hooded** eyes, their eyelids always look as though they are partly closed. 3 ADJ: ADJ n A **hooded** person is wearing a hood or a piece of clothing pulled down over their face, so they are difficult to recognize. ❑ *The class was held hostage by a hooded gunman.*

**hood|lum** /huːdləm/ **(hoodlums)** N-COUNT A **hoodlum** is a violent criminal, especially one who is a member of a group. [INFORMAL]

**hood|wink** /hʊdwɪŋk/ **(hoodwinks, hoodwinking, hoodwinked)** VERB = con V n If someone **hoodwinks** you, they trick or deceive you. ❑ *People expect others to be honest, which is why conmen find it so easy to hoodwink people.*

**hoof** /huːf/ **(hoofs** or **hooves)** N-COUNT: usu pl The **hooves** of an animal such as a horse are the hard lower parts of its feet. ❑ *The horses' hooves often could not get a proper grip.*

**hoof|er** /huːfəʳ/ **(hoofers)** N-COUNT A **hoofer** is a dancer, especially one who dances in musicals. [INFORMAL]

**hoo-ha** /huːhɑː/ N-SING: also no det If there is a **hoo-ha**, there is a lot of fuss about something. [INFORMAL] ❑ *Schulman is a little tired of the hoo-ha about the all-women team.*

**hook** /hʊk/ **(hooks, hooking, hooked)** ◆◇◇ 1 N-COUNT A **hook** is a bent piece of metal or plastic that is used for catching or holding things, or for hanging things up. ❑ *One of his jackets hung from a hook. ...curtain hooks.* 2 VERB If you **hook** one thing **to** another, you attach it there using a hook. If something **hooks** somewhere, it can be hooked there. ❑ *Paul hooked his tractor to the car and pulled it to safety.* (V n *to/onto* n) *...one of those can openers that hooked onto the wall.* (V *onto* n, Also V n prep, V prep) 3 VERB If you **hook** your arm, leg, or foot round an object, you place it like a hook round the object in order to move it or hold it. ❑ *She latched on to his arm, hooking her other arm around a tree.* (V n prep) 4 VERB If you **hook** a fish, you catch it with a hook on the end of a line. ❑ *At the first cast I hooked a huge fish.* (V n) 5 N-COUNT: usu adj N A **hook** is a short sharp blow with your fist that you make with your elbow bent, usually in a boxing match. ❑ *Lewis desperately needs to keep clear of Ruddock's big left hook.* 6 VERB If you **are hooked into** something, or **hook into** something, you get involved with it. [mainly AM] ❑ *I'm guessing again now because I'm not hooked into the political circles...* (*be/get* V-ed *into* n) *Eager to hook into a career but can't find one right for you?* (V *into* n) 7 VERB If you **hook into** the Internet, you make a connection with the Internet on a particular occasion so that you can use it. ❑ *...an interactive media tent where people will be able to hook into the internet.* (V *into* n) ♦ PHRASAL VERB **Hook up** means the same as **hook**. ❑ *...a UK firm that lets Britons hook up to the Internet.* (V P *to* n)

**PHRASES** 8 PHRASE: V inflects If someone gets **off the hook** or is let **off the hook**, they manage to get out of the awkward or unpleasant situation that they are in. [INFORMAL] ❑ *His opponents have no intention of letting him off the hook until he agrees to leave office immediately.* 9 PHRASE: PHR after v If you take a phone **off the hook**, you take the receiver off the part that it normally rests on, so that the phone will not ring. 10 PHRASE: V inflects If your phone **is ringing off the hook**, so many people are trying to telephone you that it is ringing constantly. [AM] ❑ *Since war broke out, the phones at donation centers have been ringing off the hook.* 11 **by hook or by crook** → see **crook**. **hook, line, and sinker** → see **sinker**.

♦ **hook up** 1 → see **hook 7**. 2 PHRASAL VERB When someone **hooks up** a computer or other electronic machine, they connect it to other similar machines or to a central power supply. ❑ *...technicians who hook up computer systems and networks...* (V P n (not pron)) *He brought it down, hooked it up, and we got the generator going.* (V n P) *...if the machine is hooked up to an apartment's central wiring system.* (*be* V-ed P *to* n)

**hooked** /hʊkt/ 1 ADJ: usu ADJ n If you describe something as **hooked**, you mean that it is shaped like a hook. ❑ *He was thin and tall, with a hooked nose.* 2 ADJ: v-link ADJ, oft ADJ *on* n If you are **hooked on** something, you enjoy it so much that it takes up a lot of your interest and attention. [INFORMAL] ❑ *Many of the leaders have become hooked on power and money.* 3 ADJ: v-link ADJ, oft ADJ *on* n If you are **hooked on** a drug, you are addicted to it. [INFORMAL] ❑ *He spent a number of years hooked on cocaine, heroin and alcohol.*

**hook|er** /hʊkəʳ/ **(hookers)** N-COUNT A **hooker** is a prostitute. [mainly AM, INFORMAL]

**hook-up** **(hook-ups)** N-COUNT: usu supp N A **hook-up** is a connection between two places, systems, or pieces of equipment. ❑ *Water and electric hook-ups are available and facilities are good.*

**hooky** /hʊki/ also **hookey**. PHRASE: V inflects If a child **plays hooky**, they stay away from school without permission. [mainly AM, INFORMAL]

☑ in BRIT, use **play truant**

**hoo|li|gan** /huːlɪgən/ **(hooligans)** N-COUNT disapproval If you describe people, especially young people, as **hooligans**, you are critical of them because they behave in a noisy and violent way in a public place. ❑ *...riots involving football hooligans.*

**hoo|li|gan|ism** /huːlɪgənɪzəm/ N-UNCOUNT **Hooliganism** is the behaviour and actions of hooligans. ❑ *...police investigating football hooliganism.*

**hoop** /huːp/ **(hoops)** 1 N-COUNT A **hoop** is a large ring made of wood, metal, or plastic. 2 PHRASE: V inflects If someone makes you **jump through hoops**, they make you do lots of difficult or boring things in order to please them or achieve something. ❑ *He had the duty receptionist almost jumping through hoops for him. But to no avail.*

**hooped** /huːpt/ ADJ: ADJ n If something is **hooped**, it is decorated with hoops or horizontal stripes, or it contains hoops as part of its structure. [mainly BRIT] ❑ *...a hooped arbour of iron rods. ...red hooped sleeves.*

**hoo|ray** /hʊreɪ/ EXCLAM People sometimes shout **'Hooray!'** when they are very happy and excited about something. **hip hip hooray** → see **hip**.

**hoot** /huːt/ **(hoots, hooting, hooted)** 1 VERB If you **hoot** the horn on a vehicle or if it **hoots**, it makes a loud noise on one note. [mainly BRIT] ❑ *I never hoot my horn when I pick a girl up for a date...* (V n) *Somewhere in the distance a siren hooted...* (V) *I can be very rude to motorists who hoot at me.* (V *at* n)

♦ **Hoot** is also a noun. ❑ *Mortlake strode on, ignoring the car, in spite of a further warning hoot.* N-COUNT

☑ in AM, usually use **honk, toot**

[2] If you **hoot**, you make a loud high-pitched noise when you are laughing or showing disapproval. ❑ *The protesters chanted, blew whistles and hooted at the name of Governor Pete Wilson.* ♦ **Hoot** is also a noun. ❑ *His confession was greeted with derisive hoots.* VERB; V; N-COUNT: usu with supp [3] When an owl **hoots**, it makes a sound like a long 'oo'. ❑ *Out in the garden an owl hooted suddenly.* VERB; V [4] If you say that you **don't give a hoot** or **don't care two hoots about** something, you are emphasizing that you do not care at all about it. [INFORMAL] ❑ *Alan doesn't care two hoots about Irish politics.* PHRASE: V inflects, oft PHR *about*/*for* n, PHR wh; emphasis

**hoot|er** /huːtəʳ/ **(hooters)** A **hooter** is a device such as a horn that makes a hooting noise. [BRIT, OLD-FASHIONED] N-COUNT

**hoo|ver** /huːvəʳ/ **(hoovers, hoovering, hoovered)** [1] A **Hoover** is a vacuum cleaner. [BRIT, TRADEMARK] N-COUNT [2] If you **hoover** a room or a carpet, you clean it using a vacuum cleaner. [BRIT] ❑ *She hoovered the study and the sitting-room.* VERB; V n ♦ **hoo|ver|ing** *I finished off the hoovering upstairs.* N-UNCOUNT: also *the* N

**hooves** /huːvz/ **Hooves** is a plural of **hoof**.

**hop** /hɒp/ **(hops, hopping, hopped)** [1] If you **hop**, you move along by jumping on one foot. ❑ *I hopped down three steps... Malcolm hopped rather than walked.* ♦ **Hop** is also a noun. ❑ *'This really is a catchy rhythm, huh?' he added, with a few little hops.* VERB; V prep/adv; V; N-COUNT [2] When birds and some small animals **hop**, they move along by jumping on both feet. ❑ *A small brown fawn hopped across the trail in front of them.* ♦ **Hop** is also a noun. ❑ *The rabbit got up, took four hops and turned round.* VERB; V prep/adv; N-COUNT [3] If you **hop** somewhere, you move there quickly or suddenly. [INFORMAL] ❑ *My wife and I were the first to arrive and hopped on board.* VERB = *jump*; V prep/adv [4] A **hop** is a short, quick journey, usually by plane. [INFORMAL] ❑ *It is a three-hour drive from Geneva but can be reached by a 20-minute hop in a private helicopter.* N-COUNT [5] **Hops** are flowers that are dried and used for making beer. N-COUNT: usu pl [6] If you are caught **on the hop**, you are surprised by someone doing something when you were not expecting them to and so you are not prepared for it. [BRIT, INFORMAL] ❑ *His plans almost caught security chiefs and hotel staff on the hop.* PHRASE: usu PHR after v

**hope** /hoʊp/ **(hopes, hoping, hoped)** ♦♦♦ [1] If you **hope** that something is true, or if you **hope** for something, you want it to be true or to happen, and you usually believe that it is possible or likely. ❑ *She had decided she must go on as usual, follow her normal routine, and hope and pray... He hesitates before leaving, almost as though he had been hoping for conversation... I hope to get a job within the next two weeks... The researchers hope that such a vaccine could be available in about ten years' time... 'We'll speak again.' — 'I hope so.'* VERB; V; V for n; V to-inf; V that; V *so*/*not* [2] If you say that you cannot **hope for** something, or if you talk about the only thing that you can **hope to** get, you mean that you are in a bad situation, and there is very little chance of improving it. ❑ *Things aren't ideal, but that's the best you can hope for. ...these mountains, which no one can hope to penetrate.* ♦ **Hope** is also a noun. ❑ *The only hope for underdeveloped countries is to become, as far as possible, self-reliant.* VERB: with brd-neg; V for n; V to-inf; N-VAR [3] **Hope** is a feeling of desire and expectation that things will go well in the future. ❑ *But Kevin hasn't given up hope of being fit... Consumer groups still hold out hope that the president will change his mind.* N-UNCOUNT [4] If someone wants something to happen, and considers it likely or possible, you can refer to their **hopes of** that thing, or to their **hope that** it will happen. ❑ *They have hopes of increasing trade between the two regions... The delay in the programme has dashed Japan's hopes of commercial success in space.* N-COUNT: with supp, oft N *of* n/-ing, N that [5] If you think that the help or success of a particular person or thing will cause you to be successful or to get what you want, you can refer to them as your **hope**. ❑ *Roemer represented the best hope for a businesslike climate in Louisiana.* N-COUNT: with supp

PHRASES [6] If you are in a difficult situation and do something and **hope for the best**, you hope that everything will happen in the way you want, although you know that it may not. ❑ *Some companies are cutting costs and hoping for the best.* PHRASE: V inflects [7] If you tell someone not to **get** their **hopes up**, or not to **build** their **hopes up**, you are warning them that they should not become too confident of progress or success. ❑ *There is no reason for people to get their hopes up over this mission.* PHRASE: V inflects [8] If you say that someone has **not** got **a hope in hell of** doing something, you are emphasizing that they will not be able to do it. [INFORMAL] ❑ *Everybody knows they haven't got a hope in hell of forming a government anyway.* PHRASE: PHR after v, v-link PHR, oft PHR *of* -ing; emphasis [9] If you have **high hopes** or **great hopes that** something will happen, you are confident that it will happen. ❑ *I had high hopes that Derek Randall might play an important part.* PHRASE: PHR after v, v-link PHR, usu PHR that, PHR *of* n/-ing, PHR *for* n [10] If you **hope against hope that** something will happen, you hope that it will happen, although it seems impossible. ❑ *She glanced about the hall, hoping against hope that Richard would be waiting for her.* PHRASE: V inflects, usu PHR that [11] You use '**I hope**' in expressions such as '**I hope you don't mind**' and '**I hope I'm not disturbing you**', when you are being polite and want to make sure that you have not offended someone or disturbed them. ❑ *I hope you don't mind me coming to see you... I hope I haven't said anything to upset you.* PHRASE: PHR with cl; politeness [12] You say '**I hope**' when you want to warn someone not to do something foolish or dangerous. ❑ *I hope you won't be too harsh with the girl.* PHRASE: PHR with cl, PHR *not* [13] If you do one thing **in the hope of** another thing happening, you do it because you think it might cause or help the other thing to happen, which is what you want. ❑ *He was studying in the hope of being admitted to an engineering college.* PHRASE: PHR after v, PHR *of* -ing, PHR that [14] If you **live in hope** that something will happen, you continue to hope that it will happen, although it seems unlikely, and you realize that you are being foolish. ❑ *My mother bought lots of tickets and lived in hope of winning the prize.* PHRASE: V inflects, oft PHR that, PHR *of* -ing [15] If you say '**Some hope**', or '**Not a hope**', you think there is no possibility that something will happen, although you may want it to happen. [INFORMAL] ❑ *The industry reckons it will see orders swell by 10% this financial year. Some hope.* CONVENTION; feelings

**hoped-for** **Hoped-for** is used to describe something that people would like to happen, and which they usually think is likely or possible. [JOURNALISM] ❑ *The hoped-for economic recovery in Britain did not arrive.* ADJ: ADJ n

**hope|ful** /hoʊpfʊl/ **(hopefuls)** [1] If you are **hopeful**, you are fairly confident that something that you want to happen will happen. ❑ *I am hopeful this misunderstanding will be rectified very quickly.* ♦ **hope|ful|ly** *'Am I welcome?' He smiled hopefully, leaning on the door.* ADJ: usu v-link ADJ, oft ADJ that, ADJ *of* n/-ing; ADV: ADV with v [2] If something such as a sign or event is **hopeful**, it makes you feel that what you want to happen will happen. ❑ *The result of the election in is yet another hopeful sign that peace could come to the Middle East.* ADJ [3] A **hopeful** action is one that you do in the hope that you will get what you want to get. ❑ *We've chartered the aircraft in the hopeful anticipation that the government will allow them to leave.* ADJ: ADJ n [4] If you refer to someone as a **hopeful**, you mean that they are hoping and trying to achieve success in a particular career, election, or competition. ❑ *His soccer skills continue to be put to good use in his job as football coach to young hopefuls.* N-COUNT

**hope|ful|ly** /hoʊpfʊli/ You say **hopefully** when mentioning something that you hope will happen. Some careful speakers of English think that this use of **hopefully** is not correct, but it is very frequently used. ❑ *Hopefully, you won't have any problems after reading this.* ADV: ADV with cl/group

**hope|less** /hoʊpləs/ [1] If you feel **hopeless**, you feel very unhappy because there seems ADJ to be no possibility of a better situation or success. ❑ *He had not heard her cry before in this uncontrolled, hopeless way... The economic crisis makes jobs almost impossible to find and even able pupils feel hopeless about job prospects.* ♦ **hope|less|ly** *I looked around hopelessly.* ♦ **hope|less|ness** *She had a feeling of hopelessness about the future.* [2] Someone or something thing that is **hopeless** is certain to fail or be unsuccessful. ❑ *I don't believe your situation is as hopeless as you think. If you love each other, you'll work it out.* [3] If someone is **hopeless at** something, they are very bad at it. [INFORMAL] ❑ *I'd be hopeless at working for somebody else.* [4] You use **hopeless** to emphasize how bad or inadequate something or someone is. ❑ *Argentina's economic policies were a hopeless mess.* ♦ **hope|less|ly** *Harry was hopelessly lost.* ADV: ADV after v, ADV prep; N-UNCOUNT; ADJ; ADJ: oft ADJ *at* n; ADJ emphasis; ADV: usu ADV adj/-ed/prep, also ADV after v

**hop|per** /hɒpəʳ/ **(hoppers)** A **hopper** is a large cone-shaped device into which substances such as grain, coal, or animal food can be put and from which they can be released when required. N-COUNT

**hop|scotch** /hɒpskɒtʃ/ **Hopscotch** is a children's game which involves jumping between squares which are drawn on the ground. N-UNCOUNT

**horde** /hɔːʳd/ **(hordes)** If you describe a crowd of people as a **horde**, you mean that the crowd is very large and excited and, often, rather frightening or unpleasant. ❑ *This attracts hordes of tourists to Las Vegas.* N-COUNT: usu N *of* n

**ho|ri|zon** /həraɪzᵊn/ **(horizons)** [1] **The horizon** is the line in the far distance where the sky seems to meet the land or the sea. ❑ *A grey smudge appeared on the horizon. That must be Calais, thought Fay... The sun had already sunk below the horizon.* [2] Your **horizons** are the limits of what you want to do or of what you are interested or involved in. ❑ *As your horizons expand, these new ideas can give a whole new meaning to life.* [3] If something is **on the horizon**, it is almost certainly going to happen or be done quite soon. ❑ *With breast cancer, as with many common diseases, there is no obvious breakthrough on the horizon.* N-SING: usu *the* N; N-COUNT: usu pl; PHRASE

**hori|zon|tal** /hɒrɪzɒntᵊl, AM hɔːr-/ **(horizontals)** [1] Something that is **horizontal** is flat and level with the ground, rather than at an angle to it. ❑ *The board consists of vertical and horizontal lines.* ♦ **Horizontal** is also a noun. ❑ *Do not raise your left arm above the horizontal.* ♦ **hori|zon|tal|ly** *The wind was cold and drove the snow at him almost horizontally.* [2] A **horizontal** is a line or structure that is horizontal. ❑ *The undulating planes of the countryside provide relief from the hard horizontals and verticals of the urban scene.* ADJ; N-SING: *the* N; ADV: ADV with v, ADV -ed; N-COUNT

**hor|mo|nal** /hɔːʳmoʊnᵊl/ **Hormonal** means relating to or involving hormones. ❑ *...our individual hormonal balance.* ADJ: usu ADJ n

**hor|mone** /hɔːʳmoʊn/ **(hormones)** A **hormone** is a chemical, usually occurring naturally in your body, that makes an organ of your body do something. N-COUNT

**hor|mone re|place|ment thera|py** If a woman has **hormone replacement therapy**, she takes the hormone oestrogen, usually in order to control the symptoms of the menopause. The abbreviation **HRT** is often used. N-UNCOUNT: usu N n

**horn** /hɔːʳn/ **(horns)** [1] On a vehicle such as a car, the **horn** is the device that makes a loud noise as a signal or warning. → See picture on page 1708. ❑ *He sounded the car horn.* [2] The **horns** of an animal such as a cow or deer are the hard pointed things that grow from its head. [3] **Horn** is the hard substance that the horns of animals are made of. Horn is sometimes used to make objects such as spoons, buttons, or ornaments. → See also **horn-rimmed**. [4] A **horn** is a musical instrument of the brass family. It is a long circular metal tube, wide at one end, which you play by blowing. [5] A **horn** is a simple musical instrument consisting of a metal tube that is wide at one end and narrow at the other. You play it by blowing into it. ❑ *...a hunting horn.* [6] → See also **shoehorn**. N-COUNT: oft supp N; N-COUNT: usu pl; N-UNCOUNT; N-COUNT: oft *the* N; N-COUNT

PHRASES [7] If you **blow** your **own horn**, you boast about yourself. [mainly AM] [8] If two people **lock horns**, they argue about something. ❑ *During his six years in office, Seidman has often locked horns with lawmakers.* [9] If you are **on the horns of a dilemma**, you have to choose between two things, both of which are unpleasant or difficult. ❑ *The bird is caught on the horns of a dilemma. Should it attack the predator, even though it then risks its own life? Or should it get out while the going is good?* [10] If someone **pulls in** their **horns** or **draws in** their **horns**, they start behaving more cautiously than they did before, especially by spending less money. ❑ *Customers are drawing in their horns at a time of high interest rates.* [11] to **take the bull by the horns** → see **bull**. PHRASE; PHRASE: V inflects, pl-n PHR; PHRASE: PHR after v; PHRASE: V inflects

**horned** /hɔːʳnd/ **Horned** animals have horns, or parts of their bodies that look like horns. ❑ *...horned cattle. ...the call of a horned lark.* ADJ: usu ADJ n

**hor|net** /hɔːʳnɪt/ **(hornets)** [1] A **hornet** is a large wasp. Hornets live in nests and have a powerful sting. [2] If you say that someone has stirred up **a hornet's nest**, you mean that they have done something which has caused a lot of argument or trouble. N-COUNT; PHRASE: usu PHR after v

**horn|pipe** /hɔːʳnpaɪp/ **(hornpipes)** A **hornpipe** is a lively dance which was traditionally danced by sailors. N-COUNT

**horn-rimmed** **Horn-rimmed** glasses have plastic frames that look as though they are made of horn. ADJ: ADJ n

**horny** /hɔːʳni/ **(hornier, horniest)** [1] If you describe someone as **horny**, you mean that they are sexually aroused or that they easily become sexually aroused. [INFORMAL] ❑ *...horny adolescent boys.* [2] Something that is **horny** is hard, strong, and made of horn or of a hard substance like horn. ❑ *His fingernails had grown long, and horny.* ADJ = randy; ADJ

**horo|scope** /hɒrəskoʊp, AM hɔːr-/ **(horoscopes)** Your **horoscope** is a prediction of events which some people believe will happen to you in the future. Horoscopes are based on the position of the stars when you were born. N-COUNT

**hor|ren|dous** /hərendəs, AM hɔːr-/ [1] Something that is **horrendous** is very unpleasant or shocking. ❑ *He described it as the most horrendous experience of his life.* [2] Some people use **horrendous** to describe something that is so big or great that they find it extremely unpleasant. [INFORMAL] ❑ *...the usually horrendous traffic jams.* ♦ **hor|ren|dous|ly** *Many outings can now be horrendously expensive for parents with a young family.* ADJ = horrific; ADJ = dreadful; ADV: usu ADV adj/-ed, also ADV after v

**hor|ri|ble** /hɒrɪbᵊl, AM hɔːr-/ [1] If you describe something or someone as **horrible**, you do not like them at all. [INFORMAL] ❑ *The record sounds horrible. ...a horrible small boy.* ♦ **hor|ri|bly** /hɒrɪbli, AM hɔːr-/ *When trouble comes they behave selfishly and horribly.* [2] You can call something **horrible** when it causes you to feel great shock, fear, and disgust. ❑ *Still the horrible shrieking came out of his mouth.* ♦ **hor|ri|bly** *A two-year-old boy was horribly murdered there.* [3] **Horrible** is used to emphasize how bad something is. ❑ *That seems like a horrible mess that will drag on for years.* ♦ **hor|ri|bly** *Our plans have all gone horribly wrong... You got horribly drunk.* ADJ; ADV: ADV with v; ADJ = terrible; ADV: ADV with v; ADJ: ADJ n emphasis = awful; ADV: ADV with v, ADV adj

**hor|rid** /hɒrɪd, AM hɔːr-/ [1] If you describe something as **horrid**, you mean that it is very unpleasant indeed. [INFORMAL] ❑ *What a horrid smell!* [2] If you describe someone as **horrid**, you mean that they behave in a very unpleasant way towards other people. [INFORMAL] ❑ *I must have been a horrid little girl.* ADJ = horrible; ADJ: oft ADJ *to* n = horrible

**hor|rif|ic** /hərɪfɪk, AM hɔːr-/ [1] If you describe a physical attack, accident, or injury as **horrific**, you mean that it is very bad, so that people are shocked when they see it or think about it. ❑ *I have never seen such horrific injuries.* ADJ = horrendous

♦ **hor|rifi|cal|ly** *He had been horrifically assaulted before he died.* ADV: ADV with v
[2] If you describe something as **horrific**, you mean that it is so big that it is extremely unpleasant. ❑ *...piling up horrific extra amounts of money on top of your original debt.* ADJ = horrendous
♦ **hor|rifi|cal|ly** *Opera productions are horrifically expensive.* ADV: ADV adj

**hor|ri|fy** /hɒrɪfaɪ, AM hɔːr-/ **(horrifies, horrifying, horrified)** If someone **is horrified**, they feel shocked or disgusted, usually because of something that they have seen or heard. ❑ *His family were horrified by the change. ...a crime trend that will horrify all parents.* ♦ **hor|ri|fied** *When I saw these figures I was horrified.* VERB = appal; be V-ed; V n; ADV

**hor|ri|fy|ing** /hɒrɪfaɪɪŋ/ If you describe something as **horrifying**, you mean that it is shocking or disgusting. ❑ *These were horrifying experiences... The scale of the problem is horrifying.* ♦ **hor|ri|fy|ing|ly** *...horrifyingly high levels of infant mortality.* ADJ = appalling; ADV: ADV adj, ADV with v

**hor|ror** /hɒrəʳ, AM hɔːr-/ **(horrors)** ◆◇◇ [1] **Horror** is a feeling of great shock, fear, and worry caused by something extremely unpleasant. ❑ *As I watched in horror the boat began to power away from me.* N-UNCOUNT = terror
[2] If you have a **horror of** something, you are afraid of it or dislike it very much. ❑ *...his horror of death.* N-SING: N of n
[3] The **horror of** something, especially something that hurts people, is its very great unpleasantness. ❑ *...the horror of this most bloody of civil wars.* N-SING: oft N of n
[4] You can refer to extremely unpleasant or frightening experiences as **horrors**. ❑ *Can you possibly imagine all the horrors we have undergone since I last wrote you?* N-COUNT: usu pl
[5] A **horror** film or story is intended to be very frightening. ❑ *...a psychological horror film.* ADJ: ADJ n
[6] You can refer to an account of a very unpleasant experience or event as a **horror** story. ❑ *...a horror story about lost luggage while flying.* ADJ: ADJ n

**horror-stricken** /hɒrəʳstrɪkən/ **Horror-stricken** means the same as **horror-struck**. ADJ

**horror-struck** If you describe someone as **horror-struck** or **horror-stricken**, you mean that they feel very great horror at something that has happened. ❑ *'What is the matter with Signora Anna?' he whispered, horror-struck at her vacant face.* ADJ = appalled

**hors d'oeu|vre** /ɔːʳdɜːʳv/ **(hors d'oeuvres)** **Hors d'oeuvres** are small amounts of food that are served before the main part of a meal. N-VAR

**horse** /hɔːʳs/ **(horses)** ◆◆◇ [1] A **horse** is a large animal which people can ride. Some horses are used for pulling ploughs and carts. ❑ *A small man on a grey horse had appeared.* N-COUNT
[2] When you talk about **the horses**, you mean horse races in which people bet money on the horse which they think will win. [INFORMAL] ❑ *He still likes to bet on the horses.* N-PLURAL: the N, usu on the N
[3] A vaulting **horse** is a tall piece of gymnastics equipment for jumping over. N-COUNT
[4] If you hear something **from the horse's mouth**, you hear it from someone who knows that it is definitely true. ❑ *He has got to hear it from the horse's mouth. Then he can make a judgment as to whether his policy is correct or not.* PHRASE: v PHR
[5] → See also **clothes horse**, **dark horse**, **rocking horse**, **seahorse**.

**horse|back** /hɔːʳsbæk/ [1] If you do something **on horseback**, you do it while riding a horse. ❑ *In remote mountain areas, voters arrived on horseback.* N-UNCOUNT: usu on/by N
[2] A **horseback** ride is a ride on a horse. ❑ *...a horseback ride into the mountains.* ADJ: ADJ n
♦ **Horseback** is also an adverb. ❑ *Many people in this area ride horseback.* ADV

**horse|back rid|ing** **Horseback riding** is the activity of riding a horse, especially for enjoyment or as a form of exercise. [AM] N-UNCOUNT

☑ in BRIT, use **horse riding**

**horse|box** /hɔːʳsbɒks/ **(horseboxes)** also **horse box.** A **horsebox** is a vehicle which is used to take horses from one place to another. [mainly BRIT] N-COUNT

**horse chest|nut** **(horse chestnuts)** also **horse-chestnut.** [1] A **horse chestnut** is a large tree which has leaves with several pointed parts and shiny reddish-brown nuts called conkers that grow in cases with points on them. N-COUNT
[2] **Horse chestnuts** are the nuts of a horse chestnut tree. They are more commonly called **conkers**. N-COUNT

**horse-drawn** also **horsedrawn.** A **horse-drawn** carriage, cart, or other vehicle is one that is pulled by one or more horses. ❑ *...a horse-drawn open-topped carriage.* ADJ: ADJ n

**horse|hair** /hɔːʳsheəʳ/ **Horsehair** is hair from the tails or manes of horses and was used in the past to fill mattresses and furniture such as armchairs. N-UNCOUNT: oft N n

**horse|man** /hɔːʳsmən/ **(horsemen)** A **horseman** is a man who is riding a horse, or who rides horses well. ❑ *Gerald was a fine horseman.* N-COUNT: usu with supp

**horse|man|ship** /hɔːʳsmənʃɪp/ **Horsemanship** is the ability to ride horses well. N-UNCOUNT

**horse|play** /hɔːʳspleɪ/ **Horseplay** is rough play in which people push and hit each other, or behave in a silly way. [OLD-FASHIONED] N-UNCOUNT

**horse|power** /hɔːʳspaʊəʳ/ **Horsepower** is a unit of power used for measuring how powerful an engine is. ❑ *...a 300-horsepower engine.* N-UNCOUNT: usu num N

**horse rac|ing** also **horse-racing, horseracing.** **Horse racing** is a sport in which horses ridden by people called jockeys run in races, sometimes jumping over fences. N-UNCOUNT

**horse|radish** /hɔːʳsrædɪʃ/ [1] **Horseradish** is a small white vegetable that is the root of a crop. It has a very strong sharp taste and is often made into a sauce. N-UNCOUNT
[2] **Horseradish** or **horseradish sauce** is a sauce made from horseradish. It is often eaten with roast beef. N-UNCOUNT

**horse rid|ing** also **horse-riding.** **Horse riding** is the activity of riding a horse, especially for enjoyment or as a form of exercise. [BRIT] N-UNCOUNT

☑ in AM, use **horseback riding**

**horse|shoe** /hɔːʳsʃuː/ **(horseshoes)** [1] A **horseshoe** is a piece of metal shaped like a U, which is fixed with nails to the bottom of a horse's foot in order to protect it. N-COUNT
[2] A **horseshoe** is an object in the shape of a horseshoe which is used as a symbol of good luck, especially at a wedding. N-COUNT

**horse show** **(horse shows)** A **horse show** is a sporting event in which people riding horses compete in order to demonstrate their skill and control. N-COUNT

**horse-trading** also **horsetrading.** [1] If you describe discussions or negotiations as **horse-trading**, you disapprove of them because they are unofficial and involve compromises. [BRIT, mainly JOURNALISM] ❑ *...the anger and distaste many people feel at the political horse-trading involved in forming a government.* N-UNCOUNT [disapproval]
[2] When negotiation or bargaining is forceful and shows clever and careful judgment, you can describe it as **horse-trading**. [AM] N-UNCOUNT

**horse|whip** /hɔːʳshwɪp/ **(horsewhips, horsewhipping, horsewhipped)** also **horse-whip.** [1] A **horsewhip** is a long, thin piece of leather on the end of a short, stiff handle. It is used to train and control horses. N-COUNT
[2] If someone **horsewhips** an animal or a person, they hit them several times with a horsewhip in order to hurt or punish them. ❑ *These young louts deserve to be horse-whipped.* VERB; V n

**horse|woman** /hɔːʳswʊmən/ **(horsewomen)** A **horsewoman** is a woman who is riding a horse, or who rides horses well. ❑ *She developed into an excellent horsewoman.* N-COUNT

**horsey** /hɔːʳsi/ also **horsy.** [1] Someone who is **horsey** likes horses a lot and spends a lot of time with them. [INFORMAL] ❑ *...a very horsey family.* ADJ
[2] If you describe a woman as **horsey**, you are saying in a rather rude way that her face ADJ [disapproval]

reminds you of a horse, for example because it is long and thin.

**hor|ti|cul|tur|al** /hɔːʳtɪkʌltʃərəl/ **Horticultural** means concerned with horticulture. ❑ *...Monkton horticultural show.* — *ADJ: usu ADJ n*

**hor|ti|cul|tur|al|ist** /hɔːʳtɪkʌltʃərəlɪst/ **(horticulturalists)** A **horticulturalist** is a person who grows flowers, fruit, and vegetables, especially as their job. — *N-COUNT*

**hor|ti|cul|ture** /hɔːʳtɪkʌltʃəʳ/ **Horticulture** is the study and practice of growing plants. — *N-UNCOUNT*

**hose** /hoʊz/ **(hoses, hosing, hosed)** 1 A **hose** is a long, flexible pipe made of rubber or plastic. Water is directed through a hose in order to do things such as put out fires, clean cars, or water gardens. ❑ *You've left the garden hose on.* — *N-COUNT* 2 A **hose** is a pipe made of rubber or plastic, along which a liquid or gas flows, for example from one part of an engine to another. ❑ *Water in the engine compartment is sucked away by a hose.* — *N-COUNT* 3 If you **hose** something, you wash or water it using a hose. ❑ *We wash our cars and hose our gardens without even thinking of the water that uses.* — *VERB; V n*

♦ **hose down** When you **hose** something or someone **down**, you clean them using a hose. ❑ *In one driveway a chauffeur wearing rubber boots was hosing down a limousine... When the children come in covered in sand you can just hose them down.* — *PHRASAL VERB; V P n (not pron); V n P*

**hose|pipe** /hoʊzpaɪp/ **(hosepipes)** A **hosepipe** is a hose that people use to water their gardens or wash their cars. [mainly BRIT] — *N-COUNT = hose*

**ho|siery** /hoʊziəri, AM -ʒəri/ You use **hosiery** to refer to tights, stockings, and socks, especially when they are on sale in shops. [FORMAL] — *N-UNCOUNT*

**hos|pice** /hɒspɪs/ **(hospices)** A **hospice** is a special hospital for people who are dying, where their practical and emotional needs are dealt with as well as their medical needs. — *N-COUNT; N-IN-NAMES*

**hos|pi|table** /hɒspɪtəbəl, hɒspɪt-/ 1 A **hospitable** person is friendly, generous, and welcoming to guests or people they have just met. ❑ *The locals are hospitable and welcoming.* — *ADJ* 2 A **hospitable** climate or environment is one that encourages the existence or development of particular people or things. ❑ *Even in summer this place did not look exactly hospitable.* — *ADJ*

**hos|pi|tal** /hɒspɪtəl/ **(hospitals)** A **hospital** is a place where people who are ill are looked after by nurses and doctors. ❑ *...a children's hospital with 120 beds... A couple of weeks later my mother went into hospital.* — *◆◆◆ N-VAR*

**hos|pi|tal|ity** /hɒspɪtælɪti/ 1 **Hospitality** is friendly, welcoming behaviour towards guests or people you have just met. ❑ *Every visitor to Georgia is overwhelmed by the kindness, charm and hospitality of the people.* — *N-UNCOUNT* 2 **Hospitality** is the food, drink, and other privileges which some companies provide for their visitors or clients at major sporting or other public events. ❑ *...corporate hospitality tents.* — *N-UNCOUNT*

**hos|pi|tal|ize** /hɒspɪtəlaɪz/ **(hospitalizes, hospitalizing, hospitalized)**

> ✔ in BRIT, also use **hospitalise**

If someone **is hospitalized**, they are sent or admitted to hospital. ❑ *Most people do not have to be hospitalized for asthma or pneumonia.* — *VERB: usu passive be V-ed*

♦ **hos|pi|tali|za|tion** /hɒspɪtəlaɪzeɪʃən/ *Occasionally hospitalization is required to combat dehydration.* — *N-UNCOUNT*

**host** /hoʊst/ **(hosts, hosting, hosted)** 1 The **host** at a party is the person who has invited the guests and provides the food, drink, or entertainment. ❑ *Apart from my host, I didn't know a single person there.* — *◆◆◆ N-COUNT* 2 If someone **hosts** a party, dinner, or other function, they have invited the guests and provide the food, drink, or entertainment. ❑ *Tonight she hosts a ball for 300 guests.* — *VERB; V n* 3 A country, city, or organization that is the **host** of an event provides the facilities for that event to take place. ❑ *Barcelona was chosen to be host of the 1992 Olympic games.* — *N-COUNT: oft N n* 4 If a country, city, or organization **hosts** an event, they provide the facilities for the event to take place. ❑ *Cannes hosts the annual film festival.* — *VERB; V n* 5 If a person or country **plays host to** an event or an important visitor, they host the event or the visit. ❑ *The Prime Minister played host to French Premier Jacques Chirac.* — *PHRASE: V inflects* 6 The **host** of a radio or television show is the person who introduces it and talks to the people who appear in it. ❑ *I am host of a live radio programme.* — *N-COUNT: usu with supp = presenter* 7 The person who **hosts** a radio or television show introduces it and talks to the people who appear in it. ❑ *She also hosts a show on St Petersburg Radio.* — *VERB; V n* 8 A **host of** things is a lot of them. ❑ *A host of problems may delay the opening of the Channel Tunnel.* — *QUANT = multitude* 9 A **host** or a **host computer** is the main computer in a network of computers, which controls the most important files and programs. — *N-COUNT: oft N n* 10 The **host** of a parasite is the plant or animal which it lives on or inside and from which it gets its food. [TECHNICAL] ❑ *When the eggs hatch the larvae eat the living flesh of the host animal.* — *N-COUNT: oft N n* 11 **The Host** is the bread which is used to represent the body of Christ in Christian church services such as Holy Communion. [TECHNICAL] — *N-COUNT: usu sing, the N*

**hos|tage** /hɒstɪdʒ/ **(hostages)** 1 A **hostage** is someone who has been captured by a person or organization and who may be killed or injured if people do not do what that person or organization demands. — *◆◆◇ N-COUNT* 2 If someone **is taken hostage** or **is held hostage**, they are captured and kept as a hostage. ❑ *He was taken hostage while on his first foreign assignment as a television journalist.* — *PHRASE: V inflects* 3 If you say you are **hostage to** something, you mean that your freedom to take action is restricted by things that you cannot control. ❑ *With the reduction in foreign investments, the government will be even more a hostage to the whims of the international oil price.* — *N-VAR: N to n*

**hos|tel** /hɒstəl/ **(hostels)** A **hostel** is a large house where people can stay cheaply for a short period of time. Hostels are usually owned by local government authorities or charities. [mainly BRIT] → See also **youth hostel**. — *N-COUNT*

**hos|tel|ry** /hɒstəlri/ **(hostelries)** A **hostelry** is a pub or a hotel. [BRIT, FORMAL] — *N-COUNT*

**host|ess** /hoʊstɪs/ **(hostesses)** 1 The **hostess** at a party is the woman who has invited the guests and provides the food, drink, or entertainment. ❑ *The hostess introduced them.* — *N-COUNT* 2 A **hostess** at a night club or dance hall is a woman who is paid by a man to be with him for the evening. — *N-COUNT*

**hos|tile** /hɒstaɪl, AM -təl/ 1 If you are **hostile to** another person or an idea, you disagree with them or disapprove of them, often showing this in your behaviour. ❑ *Many people felt he would be hostile to the idea of foreign intervention... The West has gradually relaxed its hostile attitude to this influential state.* — *ADJ: oft ADJ to/towards n* 2 Someone who is **hostile** is unfriendly and aggressive. ❑ *Drinking may make a person feel relaxed and happy, or it may make her hostile, violent, or depressed.* — *ADJ = aggressive* 3 **Hostile** situations and conditions make it difficult for you to achieve something. ❑ *If this round of talks fails, the world's trading environment is likely to become increasingly hostile.* — *ADJ* 4 A **hostile** takeover bid is one that is opposed by the company that is being bid for. [BUSINESS] ❑ *Kingfisher launched a hostile bid for Dixons.* — *ADJ* 5 In a war, you use **hostile** to describe your enemy's forces, organizations, weapons, land, and activities. ❑ *The city is encircled by a hostile army.* — *ADJ: ADJ n = enemy*

**hos|til|ities** /hɒstɪlɪtiz/ You can refer to fighting between two countries or groups who are at war as **hostilities**. [FORMAL] ❑ *The authorities have urged people to stock up on fuel in case hostilities break out.* — *N-PLURAL*

**hos|til|ity** /hɒstɪlɪti/ 1 **Hostility** is unfriendly or aggressive behaviour towards people or ideas. ❑ *The last decade has witnessed a serious rise in the levels of racism and hostility to Black and ethnic* — *N-UNCOUNT: oft N to/towards n* *groups.* [2] Your **hostility to** something you do not approve of is your opposition to it. ❑ *There is hostility among traditionalists to this method of teaching history.* N-UNCOUNT: usu N *to/towards* n

**hot** /hɒt/ **(hotter, hottest, hots, hotting, hotted)** ◆◆◇ [1] Something that is **hot** has a high temperature. ❑ *When the oil is hot, add the sliced onion... What he needed was a hot bath and a good sleep.* ADJ ≠cold, cool [2] **Hot** is used to describe the weather or the air in a room or building when the temperature is high. ❑ *It was too hot even for a gentle stroll... It was a hot, humid summer day.* ADJ ≠chilly, cold [3] If you are **hot**, you feel as if your body is at an unpleasantly high temperature. ❑ *I was too hot and tired to eat more than a few mouthfuls.* ADJ: usu v-link ADJ ≠cold [4] You can say that food is **hot** when it has a strong, burning taste caused by chillies, pepper, or ginger. ❑ *...hot curries. ...a dish that's spicy but not too hot.* ADJ = spicy ≠mild [5] A **hot** issue or topic is one that is very important at the present time and is receiving a lot of publicity. [JOURNALISM] ❑ *The role of women in war has been a hot topic of debate in America since the Gulf conflict.* ADJ: usu ADJ n [6] **Hot** news is new, recent, and fresh. [INFORMAL] ❑ *...eight pages of the latest movies, video releases and the hot news from Tinseltown.* ADJ: usu ADJ n [7] You can use **hot** to describe something that is very exciting and that many people want to see, use, obtain, or become involved with. [INFORMAL] ❑ *The hottest show in town was the Monet Exhibition at the Art Institute.* ADJ: usu ADJ n [8] You can use **hot** to describe something that no one wants to deal with, often because it has been illegally obtained and is very valuable or famous. [INFORMAL] ❑ *If too much publicity is given to the theft of important works, the works will become too hot to handle and be destroyed.* ADJ: usu v-link ADJ [9] You can describe a situation that is created by a person's behaviour or attitude as **hot** when it is unpleasant and difficult to deal with. [INFORMAL] ❑ *When the streets get too hot for them, they head south in one stolen car after another.* ADJ: usu v-link ADJ [10] A **hot** contest is one that is intense and involves a great deal of activity and determination. [INFORMAL] ❑ *It took hot competition from abroad, however, to show us just how good Scottish cashmere really is.* ADJ: usu ADJ n = fierce [11] If a person or team is the **hot** favourite, people think that they are the one most likely to win a race or competition. ❑ *Atlantic City is the hot favourite to stage the fight.* ADJ: ADJ n [12] Someone who has a **hot** temper gets angry very quickly and easily. ❑ *His hot temper was making it increasingly difficult for others to work with him.* → See also **hot-tempered**. ADJ: usu ADJ n

**PHRASES** [13] If someone **blows hot and cold**, they keep changing their attitude towards something, sometimes being very enthusiastic and at other times expressing no interest at all. ❑ *The media, meanwhile, has blown hot and cold on the affair.* PHRASE: V inflects, oft PHR *on/over/about* n [14] If you are **hot and bothered**, you are so worried and anxious that you cannot think clearly or behave sensibly. ❑ *Ray was getting very hot and bothered about the idea.* PHRASE: v-link PHR, oft PHR *about* n [15] If you say that one person **has the hots for** another, you mean that they feel a strong sexual attraction to that person. [INFORMAL] ❑ *I've had the hots for him ever since he came to college.* PHRASE: V inflects

♦ **hot up** When something **hots up**, it becomes more active or exciting. [BRIT] ❑ *The bars rarely hot up before 1am.* PHRASAL VERB V P

**hot air** If you say that someone's claims or promises are just **hot air**, you are criticizing them because they are made mainly to impress people and have no real value or meaning. [INFORMAL] ❑ *His justification for the merger was just hot air.* N-UNCOUNT [disapproval]

**hot-air balloon** **(hot-air balloons)** A **hot-air balloon** is a large balloon with a basket underneath in which people can travel. The balloon is filled with hot air in order to make it float in the air. N-COUNT

**hot|bed** /hɒtbed/ **(hotbeds)** If you say that somewhere is a **hotbed of** an undesirable activity, you are emphasizing that a lot of the activity is going on there or being started there. ❑ *...a state now known worldwide as a hotbed of racial intolerance.* N-COUNT: with supp, usu N *of* n [emphasis]

**hot-blooded** If you describe someone as **hot-blooded**, you mean that they are very quick to express their emotions, especially anger and love. ❑ *Both of these dancers knew full well why they attracted the attentions of two hot-blooded young men.* ADJ: usu ADJ n ≠cold-blooded

**hot but|ton** **(hot buttons)** A **hot button** is a subject or problem that people have very strong feelings about. [mainly AM, JOURNALISM] ❑ *Abortion is still one of the hot button issues of US life.* N-COUNT: oft N n

**hotch-potch** /hɒtʃ pɒtʃ/ also **hotchpotch.** A **hotch-potch** is an untidy mixture of different types of things. [BRIT] ❑ *The palace is a complete hotch-potch of architectural styles.* N-SING: usu with supp, oft N *of* n = jumble

☑ in AM, use **hodgepodge**

**hot-desk** **(hot-desks, hot-desking, hot-desked)** If employees **hot-desk**, they are not assigned particular desks and work at any desk that is available. [BUSINESS] ❑ *Some ministers will have to hot-desk until more accommodation can be found.* ♦ **hot-desking** *I think that very few employees prefer hot-desking to having a fixed desk.* VERB V N-UNCOUNT

**hot dog** **(hot dogs)** A **hot dog** is a long bread roll with a hot sausage inside it. N-COUNT

**ho|tel** /hoʊtel/ **(hotels)** A **hotel** is a building where people stay, for example on holiday, paying for their rooms and meals. ◆◆◇ N-COUNT

**ho|tel|ier** /hoʊteliəʳ, AM oʊteljeɪ/ **(hoteliers)** A **hotelier** is a person who owns or manages a hotel. N-COUNT

**hot flash** **(hot flashes)** A **hot flash** is the same as a **hot flush**. [AM] N-COUNT

**hot flush** **(hot flushes)** A **hot flush** is a sudden hot feeling in the skin which women often experience at the time of their menopause. [mainly BRIT] N-COUNT

☑ in AM, use **hot flash**

**hot-foot** **(hot-foots, hot-footing, hot-footed)** also **hotfoot.** If you **hot-foot it** somewhere, you go there in a hurry. [INFORMAL] ❑ *...a group of actors hot-footing it for the bar.* VERB V *it* adv/prep

**hot|head** /hɒthed/ **(hotheads)** If you refer to someone as a **hothead**, you are criticizing them for acting too quickly, without thinking of the consequences. N-COUNT [disapproval]

**hot-headed** If you describe someone as **hot-headed**, you are criticizing them for acting too quickly, without thinking of the consequences. ADJ [disapproval]

**hot|house** /hɒthaʊs/ **(hothouses)** [1] A **hothouse** is a heated building, usually made of glass, in which plants and flowers can be grown. N-COUNT [2] You can refer to a situation or place as a **hothouse** when there is intense activity, especially intellectual or emotional activity. ❑ *...the reputation of the College as a hothouse of novel ideas.* N-COUNT: oft N n, N *of* n

**hot key** **(hot keys)** A **hot key** is a key, or a combination of keys, on a computer keyboard that you can press in order to make something happen, without having to type the full instructions. [COMPUTING] N-COUNT

**hot|line** /hɒtlaɪn/ **(hotlines)** also **hot line.** [1] A **hotline** is a telephone line that the public can use to contact an organization about a particular subject. Hotlines allow people to obtain information from an organization or to give the organization information. ❑ *...a telephone hotline for gardeners seeking advice.* N-COUNT [2] A **hotline** is a special, direct telephone line between the heads of government in different countries. ❑ *They have discussed setting up a military hotline between Hanoi and Bangkok.* N-COUNT

**hot link** **(hot links)** A **hot link** is a word or phrase in a hypertext document that can be selected in order to access additional information. [COMPUTING] N-COUNT

**hot|ly** /hɒtli/ 1 If people discuss, argue, or say something **hotly**, they speak in a lively or angry way, because they feel strongly. ❑ *The bank hotly denies any wrongdoing.* ADV: ADV with v = vehemently
2 If you are being **hotly** pursued, someone is trying hard to catch you and is close behind you. ❑ *He'd snuck out of America hotly pursued by the CIA.* ADV: ADV with v = closely

**hot|plate** /hɒtpleɪt/ **(hotplates)** 1 A **hotplate** is a flat surface, usually on top of a cooker or stove, that you heat in order to cook food on it. [mainly BRIT] N-COUNT
2 A **hotplate** is a portable device that you use for cooking food or keeping it warm. N-COUNT

**hot|pot** /hɒtpɒt/ **(hotpots)** also **hot-pot.** A **hotpot** is a mixture of meat and vegetables cooked slowly in liquid in the oven. [mainly BRIT] ❑ *...lamb hotpot.* N-VAR = stew, casserole

**hot po|ta|to** **(hot potatoes)** If you describe a problem or issue as a **hot potato**, you mean that it is very difficult and nobody wants to deal with it. [INFORMAL] N-COUNT

**hot rod** **(hot rods)** A **hot rod** is a fast car used for racing, especially an old car fitted with a new engine. [INFORMAL] N-COUNT

**hot seat** If you are **in the hot seat**, you are responsible for making important and difficult decisions. [INFORMAL] ❑ *He is to remain in the hot seat as chief executive.* PHRASE: usu *in/into* PHR

**hot|shot** /hɒtʃɒt/ **(hotshots)** If you refer to someone as a **hotshot**, you mean they are very good at a particular job and are going to be very successful. ❑ *...a bunch of corporate hotshots.* N-COUNT: oft N n

**hot spot** **(hot spots)** also **hotspot.** 1 You can refer to an exciting place where there is a lot of activity or entertainment as a **hot spot**. [INFORMAL] ❑ *...a popular and lively package tour hotspot.* N-COUNT
2 You can refer to an area where there is fighting or serious political trouble as a **hot spot**. [JOURNALISM] ❑ *There were many hot spots in the region, where fighting had been going on.* N-COUNT

**hot stuff** If you think that someone or something is **hot stuff**, you find them exciting or sexually attractive. [INFORMAL] ❑ *His love letters were hot stuff, apparently.* N-UNCOUNT

**hot-tempered** If you describe someone as **hot-tempered**, you think they get angry very quickly and easily. ADJ

**hot tub** **(hot tubs)** A **hot tub** is a very large, round bath which several people can sit in together. N-COUNT

**hot-water bot|tle** **(hot-water bottles)** also **hot water bottle.** A **hot-water bottle** is a rubber container that you fill with hot water and put in a bed to make it warm. N-COUNT

**hot-wire** **(hot-wires, hot-wiring, hot-wired)** If someone, especially a thief, **hot-wires** a car, they start its engine using a piece of wire rather than the key. ❑ *A youth was inside the car, attempting to hot-wire it.* VERB V n

**hou|mous** /huːməs/ also **humous, hummus.** **Houmous** is a smooth food made from chick peas which people usually eat with bread or vegetables. N-UNCOUNT

**hound** /haʊnd/ **(hounds, hounding, hounded)** 1 A **hound** is a type of dog that is often used for hunting or racing. N-COUNT
2 If someone **hounds** you, they constantly disturb or speak to you in an annoying or upsetting way. ❑ *Newcomers are constantly hounding them for advice.* VERB V n
3 If someone **is hounded out of** a job or place, they are forced to leave it, often because other people are constantly criticizing them. ❑ *There is a general view around that he has been hounded out of office by the press.* VERB: usu passive *be* V-ed *out of/from* n

**hour** /aʊəʳ/ **(hours)** ◆◆◆ 1 An **hour** is a period of sixty minutes. ❑ *They waited for about two hours... I only slept about half an hour that night. ...a twenty-four hour strike.* N-COUNT
2 People say that something takes or lasts **hours** to emphasize that it takes or lasts a very long time, or what seems like a very long time. ❑ *Getting there would take hours.* N-PLURAL emphasis
3 A clock that strikes **the hour** strikes when it is exactly one o'clock, two o'clock, and so on. N-SING: the N
4 You can refer to a particular time or moment as a particular **hour**. [LITERARY] ❑ *...the hour of his execution.* N-SING: with supp = time
5 If you refer, for example, to someone's **hour of** need or **hour of** happiness, you are referring to the time in their life when they are or were experiencing that condition or feeling. [LITERARY] ❑ *...the darkest hour of my professional life.* N-COUNT: with supp
6 You can refer to the period of time during which something happens or operates each day as the **hours** during which it happens or operates. ❑ *...the hours of darkness... Phone us on this number during office hours.* N-PLURAL: with supp
7 If you refer to the **hours** involved in a job, you are talking about how long you spend each week doing it and when you do it. ❑ *I worked quite irregular hours.* N-PLURAL
8 → see **eleventh hour, lunch hour, rush hour.**

PHRASES 9 If you do something **after hours**, you do it outside normal business hours or the time when you are usually at work. ❑ *...a local restaurant where steel workers unwind after hours.* → See also **after-hours.** PHRASE: PHR after v, PHR n
10 If you say that something happens **at all hours of** the day or night, you disapprove of it happening at the time that it does or as often as it does. ❑ *She didn't want her fourteen-year-old daughter coming home at all hours of the morning.* PHRASE: PHR after v disapproval
11 If something happens **in the early hours** or **in the small hours**, it happens in the early morning after midnight. ❑ *Gibbs was arrested in the early hours of yesterday morning.* PHRASE
12 If something happens **on the hour**, it happens every hour at, for example, nine o'clock, ten o'clock, and so on, and not at any number of minutes past an hour. PHRASE: PHR after v
13 Something that happens **out of hours** happens at a time that is not during the usual hours of business or work. [mainly BRIT] ❑ *Teachers refused to run out of hours sports matches because they weren't being paid.* PHRASE: PHR after v, PHR n

**hour|glass** /aʊəʳglɑːs/ **(hourglasses)** also **hour glass.** An **hourglass** is a device that was used to measure the passing of an hour. It has two round glass sections linked by a narrow channel, and contains sand which takes an hour to flow from the top section into the lower one. N-COUNT

**hour|ly** /aʊəʳli/ 1 An **hourly** event happens once every hour. ❑ *He flipped on the radio to get the hourly news broadcast.* ♦ **Hourly** is also an adverb. ❑ *The hospital issued press releases hourly.* ADJ: ADJ n; ADV: ADV after v
2 Your **hourly** earnings are the money that you earn in one hour. ❑ *They have little prospect of finding new jobs with the same hourly pay.* ADJ: ADJ n

**house** **(houses, housing, housed)** ◆◆◆

> ✔ Pronounced /haʊs/ for the noun and adjective, and /haʊz/ for the verb. The form **houses** is pronounced /haʊzɪz/.

1 A **house** is a building in which people live, usually the people belonging to one family. ❑ *She has moved to a smaller house. ...her parents' house in Warwickshire.* N-COUNT
2 You can refer to all the people who live together in a house as **the house**. ❑ *If he set his alarm clock for midnight, it would wake the whole house.* N-SING: usu *the* N = household
3 **House** is used in the names of types of places where people go to eat and drink. ❑ *...a steak house. ...an old Salzburg coffee house.* N-COUNT: n N
4 **House** is used in the names of types of companies, especially ones which publish books, lend money, or design clothes. ❑ *Many of the clothes come from the world's top fashion houses... Eventually she was fired from her job at a publishing house.* N-COUNT: n N
5 **House** is sometimes used in the names of office buildings and large private homes or expensive houses. [mainly BRIT] ❑ *I was to go to the very top floor of Bush House in Aldwych. ...Harewood House near Leeds.* N-IN-NAMES: n N
6 You can refer to the two main bodies of Britain's parliament and the United States of America's legislature as **the House** or a **House**. ❑ *Some members of the House and Senate worked all day yesterday.* N-COUNT
7 A **house** is a family which has been or will be important for many generations, especially the family of a king or N-COUNT: with supp

queen. ❑ *...the House of Windsor.* [8] The **house** is the part of a theatre, cinema, or other place of entertainment where the audience sits. You can also refer to the audience at a particular performance as the **house**. ❑ *They played in front of a packed house.* N-COUNT [9] A restaurant's **house** wine is the cheapest wine it sells, which is not listed by name on the wine list. ❑ *Tweed ordered a carafe of the house wine.* ADJ: ADJ n [10] To **house** someone means to provide a house or flat for them to live in. ❑ *Part III of the Housing Act 1985 imposes duties on local authorities to house homeless people... Regrettably we have to house families in these inadequate flats.* VERB V n V n adv/prep [11] A building or container that **houses** something is the place where it is located or from where it operates. ❑ *The château itself is open to the public and houses a museum of motorcycles and cars.* VERB: no cont V n [12] If you say that a building **houses** a number of people, you mean that is the place where they live or where they are staying. ❑ *The building will house twelve boys and eight girls.* VERB: no cont = accommodate V n [13] → See also **boarding house**, **chapter house**, **clearing house**, **council house**, **doll's house**, **full house**, **open house**, **opera house**, **public house**, **Wendy house**, **White House**.

PHRASES [14] If a person or their performance or speech **brings the house down**, the audience claps, laughs, or shouts loudly because the performance or speech is very impressive or amusing. [INFORMAL] ❑ *It's really an amazing dance. It just always brings the house down.* PHRASE: V inflects [15] If two people **get on like a house on fire**, they quickly become close friends, for example because they have many interests in common. [INFORMAL] PHRASE: V inflects [16] If you are given something in a restaurant or bar **on the house**, you do not have to pay for it. ❑ *The owner knew about the engagement and brought them glasses of champagne on the house.* PHRASE: v-link PHR, PHR after v [17] If someone **gets** their **house in order**, **puts** their **house in order**, or **sets** their **house in order**, they arrange their affairs and solve their problems. ❑ *Some think Stempel's departure will help the company get its financial house in order.* PHRASE: V inflects

**house ar|rest** If someone is **under house arrest**, they are officially ordered not to leave their home, because they are suspected of being involved in an illegal activity. N-UNCOUNT: usu *under* N

**house|boat** /haʊsboʊt/ **(houseboats)** A **houseboat** is a small boat on a river or canal which people live in. N-COUNT

**house|bound** /haʊsbaʊnd/ Someone who is **housebound** is unable to go out of their house, usually because they are ill or cannot walk far. ❑ *If you are housebound, you can arrange for a home visit from a specialist adviser.* ADJ: usu v-link ADJ

**house|boy** /haʊsbɔɪ/ **(houseboys)** A **houseboy** is a man or boy who cleans and does other jobs in someone else's house. [OLD-FASHIONED] N-COUNT

**house|break|er** /haʊsbreɪkəʳ/ **(housebreakers)** A **housebreaker** is someone who enters another person's house by force, for example by breaking the locks or windows, in order to steal their possessions. N-COUNT = burglar

**house|break|ing** /haʊsbreɪkɪŋ/ **Housebreaking** is the crime of entering another person's house by force, for example by breaking the locks or windows, in order to steal their possessions. N-UNCOUNT = burglary

**house|coat** /haʊskoʊt/ **(housecoats)** A **housecoat** is a long loose piece of clothing that some women wear over their underwear or nightclothes when they are at home during the day. N-COUNT = dressing gown

**house guest** **(house guests)** A **house guest** is a person who is staying at someone's house for a period of time. N-COUNT

**house|hold** /haʊshoʊld/ **(households)** [1] A **household** is all the people in a family or group who live together in a house. ❑ *...growing up in a male-only household.* ◆◇◇ N-COUNT [2] The **household** is your home and everything that is connected with looking after it. ❑ *...household chores.* N-SING: oft N n [3] Someone or something that is a **household** name or word is very well known. ❑ *Today, fashion designers are household names.* ADJ: ADJ n

**house|holder** /haʊshoʊldəʳ/ **(householders)** The **householder** is the person who owns or rents a particular house. ❑ *Millions of householders are eligible to claim the new council tax benefit.* N-COUNT

**house|husband** /haʊshʌzbənd/ **(househusbands)** also **house husband.** A **househusband** is a married man who does not have a paid job, but instead looks after his home and children. N-COUNT

**house|keeper** /haʊski:pəʳ/ **(housekeepers)** A **housekeeper** is a person whose job is to cook, clean, and look after a house for its owner. N-COUNT

**house|keeping** /haʊski:pɪŋ/ [1] **Housekeeping** is the work and organization involved in running a home, including the shopping and cleaning. ❑ *I thought that cooking and housekeeping were unimportant, easy tasks.* N-UNCOUNT [2] **Housekeeping** is the money that you use to buy food, cleaning materials, and other things that you need in your home. [BRIT] ❑ *...the housekeeping money Jim gave her each week.* N-UNCOUNT: oft N n

**house lights** In a theatre or cinema, when **the house lights** dim or go down, the lights where the audience sits are switched off. When **the house lights** come up, the lights are switched on. N-PLURAL: *the* N

**house|maid** /haʊsmeɪd/ **(housemaids)** A **housemaid** is a female servant who does cleaning and other work in someone's house. N-COUNT

**house|man** /haʊsmən/ **(housemen)** [1] A **houseman** is a doctor who has a junior post in a hospital and usually sleeps there. [BRIT] N-COUNT

☑ in AM, use **intern**

[2] A **houseman** is a man who is a servant in a house. [AM] N-COUNT

☑ in BRIT, use **manservant**

**house|master** /haʊsmɑːstəʳ, -mæs-/ **(housemasters)** A **housemaster** is a male teacher who is in charge of one of the houses in a school. [mainly BRIT] N-COUNT

**house|mate** /haʊsmeɪt/ **(housemates)** Your **housemate** is someone who shares a house with you. You do not use 'housemate' to refer to members of your family or your boyfriend or girlfriend. N-COUNT: usu poss N

**House of Com|mons** **The House of Commons** is the part of parliament in Britain or Canada whose members are elected. The building where they meet is also called **the House of Commons**. ❑ *The House of Commons has overwhelmingly rejected demands to bring back the death penalty for murder.* N-PROPER: *the* N

**house of God** **(houses of God)** A Christian church is sometimes referred to as a **house of God**. N-COUNT

**House of Lords** **The House of Lords** is the part of the parliament in Britain whose members have not been elected. The building where they meet is also called **the House of Lords**. ❑ *The legislation has twice been rejected by the House of Lords.* N-PROPER: *the* N

**House of Rep|re|senta|tives** **The House of Representatives** is the less powerful of the two parts of Congress in the United States, or the equivalent part of the system of government in some other countries. ❑ *The House of Representatives approved a new budget plan.* N-PROPER: *the* N

**house own|er** **(house owners)** also **houseowner.** A **house owner** is a person who owns a house. N-COUNT

**house par|ty** **(house parties)** A **house party** is a party held at a big house in the country, usually at a weekend, where the guests stay for a few days. N-COUNT

**house plant** **(house plants)** also **houseplant.** A **house plant** is a plant which is grown in a pot indoors. N-COUNT = pot plant

**house|proud** /haʊspraʊd/ also **house-proud.** Someone who is **houseproud** spends a lot of time cleaning and decorating their house, because they want other people to admire it. [mainly BRIT] ADJ

**house|room** /haʊsruːm/ also **house room.** If you say that you wouldn't **give** something **houseroom**, you are emphasizing that you do not want it or do not like it at all. [mainly BRIT] PHRASE: V inflects, with brd-neg emphasis

**Houses of Par|lia|ment** In Britain, **the Houses of Parliament** are the British parliament, which consists of two parts, the House of Commons and the House of Lords. The buildings where the British parliament does its work are also called **the Houses of Parliament.** ❑ *...issues aired in the Houses of Parliament.* N-PROPER-COLL: the N

**house-to-house** also **house to house.** A **house-to-house** activity involves going to all the houses in an area one after another. ❑ *Security officers have carried out a number of house-to-house searches.* ♦ **House-to-house** is also an adverb. ❑ *They're going house to house, rounding up the residents.* ADJ: ADJ n = door-to-door; ADV: ADV after v

**house|wares** /haʊsweəʳz/ Some shops and manufacturers refer to objects on sale for use in your house as **housewares**, especially objects related to cooking and cleaning. N-PLURAL

**house|warm|ing** /haʊswɔːʳmɪŋ/ **(housewarmings)** also **house-warming.** A **housewarming** is a party that you give for friends when you have just moved to a new house. ❑ *I'm so sorry I missed the housewarming. ...a housewarming party.* N-COUNT: oft N n

**house|wife** /haʊswaɪf/ **(housewives)** A **housewife** is a married woman who does not have a paid job, but instead looks after her home and children. N-COUNT

**house|work** /haʊswɜːʳk/ **Housework** is the work such as cleaning, washing, and ironing that you do in your home. N-UNCOUNT

**hous|ing** /haʊzɪŋ/ You refer to the buildings in which people live as **housing** when you are talking about their standard, price, or availability. ❑ *...a shortage of affordable housing.* ♦♦◇ N-UNCOUNT = accommodation

**hous|ing as|so|cia|tion** **(housing associations)** A **housing association** is an organization which owns houses and helps its members to rent or buy them more cheaply than on the open market. [BRIT] N-COUNT

**hous|ing ben|efit** **(housing benefits)** In Britain, **housing benefit** is money that the government gives to people with no income or very low incomes to pay for part or all of their rent. N-UNCOUNT: also N in pl

**hous|ing de|vel|op|ment** **(housing developments)** A **housing development** is the same as a **housing estate**. N-COUNT

**hous|ing es|tate** **(housing estates)** A **housing estate** is a large number of houses or flats built close together at the same time. [BRIT] N-COUNT

**hous|ing proj|ect** **(housing projects)** A **housing project** is a group of homes for poorer families which is funded and controlled by the local government. [AM] N-COUNT

**hove** /hoʊv/ **Hove** is the past tense and past participle of **heave** in one of its meanings.

**hov|el** /hɒvᵊl, AM hʌv-/ **(hovels)** 1 A **hovel** is a small hut, especially one which is dirty or needs a lot of repair. ❑ *They lived in a squalid hovel for the next five years.* N-COUNT 2 You describe a house, room, or flat as a **hovel** to express your disapproval or dislike of it because it is dirty, untidy, and in poor condition. ❑ *I went for a living-in job, but the room I was given was a hovel.* N-COUNT disapproval = dump

**hov|er** /hɒvəʳ, AM hʌv-/ **(hovers, hovering, hovered)** 1 To **hover** means to stay in the same position in the air without moving forwards or backwards. Many birds and insects can hover by moving their wings very quickly. ❑ *Beautiful butterflies hovered above the wild flowers.* VERB V 2 If you **hover**, you stay in one place and move slightly in a nervous way, for example because you cannot decide what to do. ❑ *Judith was hovering in the doorway... With no idea of what to do for my next move, my hand hovered over the board.* VERB V, V prep/adv 3 If you **hover**, you are in an uncertain situation or state of mind. ❑ *She hovered on the brink of death for three months as doctors battled to save her.* VERB V prep/adv 4 If a something such as a price, value, or score **hovers** around a particular level, it stays at more or less that level and does not change much. ❑ *In September 1989 the exchange rate hovered around 140 yen to the dollar.* VERB V prep/adv

**hover|craft** /hɒvəʳkrɑːft, AM hʌvəʳkræft/ **(hovercraft)** A **hovercraft** is a vehicle that can travel across land and water. It floats above the land or water on a cushion of air. N-COUNT: also by N

**how** /haʊ/ ♦♦♦

✔ The conjunction is pronounced /haʊ/.

1 You use **how** to ask about the way in which something happens or is done. ❑ *How do I make payments into my account?... How do you manage to keep the place so tidy?... How are you going to plan for the future?* ♦ **How** is also a conjunction. ❑ *I don't want to know how he died... I didn't know how to tell you.* QUEST; CONJ 2 You use **how** after certain adjectives and verbs to introduce a statement or fact, often something that you remember or expect other people to know about. ❑ *It's amazing how people collect so much stuff over the years... It's important to become acutely aware of how your eating ties in with your stress level.* CONJ 3 You use **how** to ask questions about the quantity or degree of something. ❑ *How much money are we talking about?... How many full-time staff have we got?... How long will you be staying?... How old is your son now?... How fast were you driving?... He was asked how serious the situation had become.* QUEST: QUEST much/many, QUEST adj/adv 4 You use **how** when you are asking someone whether something was successful or enjoyable. ❑ *How was your trip down to Orlando?... I wonder how Sam got on with him.* QUEST 5 You use **how** to ask about someone's health or to find out someone's news. ❑ *Hi! How are you doing?... How's Rosie?... How's the job?* QUEST 6 **'How do you do'** is a polite way of greeting someone when you meet them for the first time. CONVENTION formulae 7 You use **how** to emphasize the degree to which something is true. ❑ *I didn't realize how heavy that shopping was going to be... Franklin told them all how happy he was to be in Britain again.* ADV: ADV adj/adv emphasis 8 You use **how** in exclamations to emphasize an adjective, adverb, or statement. ❑ *How strange that something so simple as a walk on the beach could suddenly mean so much.* ADV: ADV adj/adv/cl emphasis 9 You use **how** in expressions such as **'How can you...'** and **'How could you...'** to indicate that you disapprove of what someone has done or that you find it hard to believe. ❑ *How can you drink so much beer, Luke?... How could he be so indiscreet?* QUEST: QUEST can/could disapproval 10 You use **how** in expressions such as **'how about...'** or **'how would you like...'** when you are making an offer or a suggestion. ❑ *How about a cup of coffee?... You want Jeannie to make the appointment for you? How about the end of next week?* QUEST 11 If you ask someone **'How about you?'** you are asking them what they think or want. ❑ *Well, I enjoyed that. How about you two?* CONVENTION

**PHRASES** 12 You use **how about** to introduce a new subject which you think is relevant to the conversation you have been having. ❑ *Are your products and services competitive? How about marketing?* PHRASE: PHR n 13 You ask **'How come?'** or **'How so?'** when you are surprised by something and are asking why it happened or was said. [INFORMAL] ❑ *'They don't say a single word to each other.' — 'How come?'* PHRASE: oft PHR cl

**how|dy** /haʊdi/ **'Howdy'** is an informal way of saying 'Hello'. [AM, DIALECT] CONVENTION formulae

**how|ever** /haʊe̲vəʳ/ ◆◆◆ ADV: ADV with cl [1] You use **however** when you are adding a comment which is surprising or which contrasts with what has just been said. ❑ *This was not an easy decision. It is, however, a decision that we feel is dictated by our duty... Some of the food crops failed. However, the cotton did quite well.* ADV: ADV adj/adv, ADV *many/much* [emphasis] [2] You use **however** before an adjective or adverb to emphasize that the degree or extent of something cannot change a situation. ❑ *You should always strive to achieve more, however well you have done before... However hard she tried, nothing seemed to work.* CONJ [3] You use **however** when you want to say that it makes no difference how something is done. ❑ *However we adopt healthcare reform, it isn't going to save major amounts of money... Wear your hair however you want.* ADV: ADV *many/much*, ADV adv [vagueness] [4] You use **however** in expressions such as **or however long it takes** and **or however many there were** to indicate that the figure you have just mentioned may not be accurate. ❑ *Wait 30 to 60 minutes or however long it takes.* QUEST [emphasis] = *how* [5] You can use **however** to ask in an emphatic way how something has happened which you are very surprised about. Some speakers of English think that this form is incorrect and prefer to use 'how ever'. ❑ *However did you find this place in such weather?*

**how|itz|er** /haʊ̲ɪtsəʳ/ N-COUNT **(howitzers)** A **howitzer** is a large gun with a short barrel, which fires shells high up into the air so that they will drop down onto the target.

**howl** /haʊ̲l/ **(howls, howling, howled)** VERB [1] If an animal such as a wolf or a dog **howls**, it makes a long, loud, crying sound. V ❑ *Somewhere in the streets beyond a dog suddenly howled, baying at the moon.* N-COUNT ♦ **Howl** is also a noun. ❑ *The dog let out a savage howl and, wheeling round, flew at him.* VERB [2] If a person **howls**, they make a long, loud cry expressing pain, anger, or unhappiness. V ❑ *He howled like a wounded animal as blood spurted from the gash.* N-COUNT ♦ **Howl** is also a noun. ❑ *With a howl of rage, he grabbed the neck of a broken bottle and advanced.* VERB [3] When the wind **howls**, it blows hard and makes a loud noise. V ❑ *The wind howled all night, but I slept a little...* V-ing *It sank in a howling gale.* VERB [4] If you **howl** something, you say it in a very loud voice. [INFORMAL] V with quote ❑ *'Get away, get away, get away' he howled...* V n *The crowd howled its approval.* VERB [5] If you **howl with** laughter, you laugh very loudly. V *with* n ❑ *Joe, Pink, and Booker howled with delight...* V *The crowd howled, delirious.* N-COUNT ♦ **Howl** is also a noun. ❑ *His stories caused howls of laughter.*

**howl|er** /haʊ̲ləʳ/ N-COUNT = *blunder* **(howlers)** A **howler** is a stupid mistake. [mainly BRIT, INFORMAL] ❑ *I felt as if I had made an outrageous howler.*

**hp** **hp** is an abbreviation for **horsepower**.

**HP** /eɪtʃ pi̲ː/ N-UNCOUNT: oft *on* N **HP** is an abbreviation for **hire purchase**. [BRIT] ❑ *I have never bought anything on HP.*

**HQ** /eɪtʃ kju̲ː/ N-VAR **(HQs)** **HQ** is an abbreviation for **headquarters**. ❑ *...the European Commission's luxurious HQ.*

**hr** **(hrs)** **hr** is a written abbreviation for **hour**. ❑ *Let this cook on low for another 1 hr 15 mins.*

**HR** /eɪtʃ ɑ̲ːr/ In a company or other organization, the **HR** department is the department with responsibility for the recruiting, training, and welfare of the staff. **HR** is an abbreviation for 'human resources'. [BUSINESS]

**HRH** /eɪtʃ ɑːr eɪ̲tʃ/ N-TITLE **HRH** is an abbreviation for 'His Royal Highness' or 'Her Royal Highness' when it is used as part of the title of a prince or princess.

**HRT** /eɪtʃ ɑːʳ ti̲ː/ N-UNCOUNT **HRT** is given to women and involves taking the hormone oestrogen, usually in order to control the symptoms of the menopause. **HRT** is an abbreviation for 'hormone replacement therapy'.

**HTML** /eɪtʃ tiː em e̲l/ N-UNCOUNT **HTML** is a system of codes for producing documents for the Internet. **HTML** is an abbreviation for 'hypertext markup language'. [COMPUTING]

**HTTP** /eɪtʃ tiː tiː pi̲ː/ N-UNCOUNT **HTTP** is a way of formatting and transmitting messages on the Internet. **HTTP** is an abbreviation for 'hypertext transfer protocol'. [COMPUTING]

**hub** /hʌ̲b/ **(hubs)** N-COUNT: usu with supp, oft N *of* n = *centre* [1] You can describe a place as a **hub of** an activity when it is a very important centre for that activity. ❑ *The island's social hub is the Cafe Sport.* N-COUNT: oft N *of* n [2] The **hub** of a wheel is the part at the centre.

**hub|bub** /hʌ̲bʌb/ **(hubbubs)** N-VAR: oft N *of* n [1] A **hubbub** is a noise made by a lot of people all talking or shouting at the same time. [WRITTEN] ❑ *There was a hubbub of excited conversation from over a thousand people.* N-SING: also no det [2] You can describe a situation where there is great confusion or excitement as a **hubbub**. ❑ *In all the hubbub over the election, one might be excused for missing yesterday's announcement.*

**hub|by** /hʌ̲bi/ N-COUNT: usu poss N **(hubbies)** You can refer to a woman's husband as her **hubby**. [INFORMAL, OLD-FASHIONED]

**hub|cap** /hʌ̲bkæp/ N-COUNT **(hubcaps)** also **hub cap.** A **hubcap** is a metal or plastic disc that covers and protects the centre of a wheel on a car, truck, or other vehicle. → See picture on page 1707.

**hu|bris** /hju̲ːbrɪs/ N-UNCOUNT = *arrogance* If you accuse someone of **hubris**, you are accusing them of arrogant pride. [FORMAL] ❑ *...a tale of how an honourable man pursuing honourable goals was afflicted with hubris and led his nation towards catastrophe.*

**huck|ster** /hʌ̲kstəʳ/ N-COUNT [disapproval] **(hucksters)** If you refer to someone as a **huckster**, you are criticizing them for trying to sell useless or worthless things in a dishonest or aggressive way. [AM]

**hud|dle** /hʌ̲dᵊl/ **(huddles, huddling, huddled)** VERB = *hunch* [1] If you **huddle** somewhere, you sit, stand, or lie there holding your arms and legs close to your body, usually because you are cold or frightened. V prep/adv ❑ *She huddled inside the porch as she rang the bell...* V-ed *Myrtle sat huddled on the side of the bed, weeping.* VERB [2] If people **huddle together** or **huddle round** something, they stand, sit, or lie close to each other, usually because they all feel cold or frightened. V adv/prep ❑ *Tired and lost, we huddled together...* V-ed *The survivors spent the night huddled around bonfires.* V-RECIP [3] If people **huddle** in a group, they gather together to discuss something quietly or secretly. pl-n V ❑ *Off to one side, Sticht, Macomber, Jordan, and Kreps huddled to discuss something...* V *with* n *The president has been huddling with his most senior aides...* V-ed *Mrs Clinton was huddled with advisers at her headquarters.* N-COUNT: oft N *of* n [4] A **huddle** is a small group of people or things that are standing very close together or lying on top of each other, usually in a disorganized way. ❑ *We lay there: a huddle of bodies, gasping for air.*

**hue** /hju̲ː/ N-COUNT = *shade* [1] A **hue** is a colour. [LITERARY] ❑ *The same hue will look different in different light.* PHRASE [2] If people raise a **hue and cry** about something, they protest angrily about it. [WRITTEN] ❑ *Just as the show ended, he heard a huge hue and cry outside.*

**huff** /hʌ̲f/ **(huffs, huffing, huffed)** VERB [1] If you **huff**, you indicate that you are annoyed or offended about something, usually by the way that you say something. V with quote ❑ *'This', huffed Mr Buthelezi, 'was discrimination.'* PHRASE: PHR after v, v-link PHR [2] If someone is **in a huff**, they are behaving in a bad-tempered way because they are annoyed and offended. [INFORMAL] ❑ *After the row in a pub he drove off in a huff.*

**huffy** /hʌ̲fi/ ADJ Someone who is **huffy** is obviously annoyed or offended about something. [INFORMAL] ❑ *I, in my turn, became embarrassed and huffy and told her to take the money back.* ADV: ADV with v ♦ **huffi|ly** /hʌ̲fɪli/ *'I appreciate your concern for my feelings,' Bess said huffily, 'but I'm a big girl now'.*

**hug** /hʌ̲g/ **(hugs, hugging, hugged)** V-RECIP = *embrace* [1] When you **hug** someone, you put your arms around them and hold them tightly, for example because you like them or are pleased to see them. You can also say that two people **hug** each other or that they **hug**. ❑ *She had hugged him exuberantly and invited him to dinner the next day... We hugged and kissed.* ♦ **Hug** is also a noun. ❑ *Syvil leapt out of the back seat, and gave him a hug.* [2] If you **hug** something, you hold it close to your body with your arms tightly round it. ❑ *Shaerl trudged toward them, hugging a large box... She hugged her legs tight to her chest.* [3] Something that **hugs** the ground or a stretch of land or water stays very close to it. [WRITTEN] ❑ *The road hugs the coast for hundreds of miles.* [4] → See also **bear hug**. — V n; (non-recip) pl-n V; N-COUNT; VERB; V n; V n adv/prep; VERB; V n

**huge** /hjuːdʒ/ **(huger, hugest)** [1] Something or someone that is **huge** is extremely large in size. ❑ *...a tiny little woman with huge black glasses.* [2] Something that is **huge** is extremely large in amount or degree. ❑ *I have a huge number of ties because I never throw them away.* ♦ **huge|ly** *In summer this hotel is a hugely popular venue for wedding receptions.* [3] Something that is **huge** exists or happens on a very large scale, and involves a lot of different people or things. ❑ *Another team is looking at the huge problem of debts between companies.* — ◆◆◇; ADJ = massive ≠ tiny; ADJ = enormous; ADV: ADV adj, ADV with v = enormously; ADJ = enormous ≠ tiny

**-hugging** /-hʌgɪŋ/ **-hugging** combines with nouns to form adjectives which describe an item of clothing that fits very tightly and clearly reveals the shape of your body. ❑ *...a figure-hugging dress.* — COMB in ADJ: usu ADJ n

**huh** /hʌ, hɜː/ **Huh** is used in writing to represent a noise that people make at the end of a question if they want someone to agree with them or if they want someone to repeat what they have just said. **Huh** is also used to show that someone is surprised or not impressed. ❑ *Can we just get on with it, huh?*

**hulk** /hʌlk/ **(hulks)** [1] The **hulk of** something is the large, ruined remains of it. ❑ *...the ruined hulk of the old church tower.* [2] You use **hulk** to describe anything which is large and seems threatening to you. ❑ *I followed his big hulk into the house.* — N-COUNT: oft N *of* n; N-COUNT: usu with supp

**hulk|ing** /hʌlkɪŋ/ You use **hulking** to describe a person or object that is extremely large, heavy, or slow-moving, especially when they seem threatening in some way. ❑ *When I woke up there was a hulking figure staring down at me.* — ADJ: ADJ n

**hull** /hʌl/ **(hulls)** The **hull** of a boat or tank is the main body of it. ❑ *The hull had suffered extensive damage to the starboard side.* — N-COUNT

**hul|la|ba|loo** /hʌləbəluː/ A **hullabaloo** is a lot of noise or fuss made by people who are angry or excited about something. [INFORMAL] ❑ *I was scared by the hullabaloo over my arrival.* — N-SING = rumpus

**hul|lo** /hʌloʊ/ → see **hello**.

**hum** /hʌm/ **(hums, humming, hummed)** [1] If something **hums**, it makes a low continuous noise. ❑ *The birds sang, the bees hummed... There was a low humming sound in the sky.* ♦ **Hum** is also a noun. ❑ *...the hum of traffic.* [2] When you **hum** a tune, you sing it with your lips closed. ❑ *She was humming a merry little tune... He hummed to himself as he opened the trunk.* [3] If you say that a place **hums**, you mean that it is full of activity. ❑ *The place is really beginning to hum... On Saturday morning, the town hums with activity and life.* [4] **Hum** is sometimes used to represent the sound people make when they are not sure what to say. ❑ *Hum, I am sorry but I thought you were French.* [5] → See also **ho hum**. **hum and haw** → see **haw**. — VERB; V, V-ing; N-SING: oft *the* N *of* n; VERB; V n; V; VERB; V; V *with* n; CONVENTION

**hu|man** /hjuːmən/ **(humans)** [1] **Human** means relating to or concerning people. ❑ *...the human body. ...human history.* [2] You can refer to people as **humans**, especially when you are comparing them with animals or machines. ❑ *Its rate of growth was fast – much more like that of an ape than that of a human.* [3] **Human** feelings, weaknesses, or errors are ones that are typical of humans rather than machines. ❑ *...an ever growing risk of human error.* — ◆◆◆; ADJ: ADJ n; N-COUNT; ADJ

**hu|man be|ing (human beings)** A **human being** is a man, woman, or child. — N-COUNT

**hu|mane** /hjuːmeɪn/ [1] **Humane** people act in a kind, sympathetic way towards other people and animals, and try to do them as little harm as possible. ❑ *In the mid-nineteenth century, Dorothea Dix began to campaign for humane treatment of the mentally ill.* ♦ **hu|mane|ly** *Our horse had to be humanely destroyed after breaking his right foreleg.* [2] **Humane** values and societies encourage people to act in a kind and sympathetic way towards others, even towards people they do not agree with or like. ❑ *...the humane values of socialism.* — ADJ; ADV: ADV with v; ADJ

**hu|man growth hor|mone (human growth hormones)** **Human growth hormone** is a hormone that is used to help short people, especially short children, to grow taller. The abbreviation **HGH** is also used. — N-VAR

**hu|man in|ter|est** If something such as a news story has **human interest**, people are likely to find it interesting because it gives interesting details about the person or people involved. ❑ *...a human interest story.* — N-UNCOUNT: oft N n

**hu|man|ise** /hjuːmənaɪz/ → see **humanize**.

**hu|man|ism** /hjuːmənɪzəm/ **Humanism** is the belief that people can achieve happiness and live well without religion. ♦ **hu|man|ist (humanists)** ❑ *He is a practical humanist, who believes in the dignity of mankind.* — N-UNCOUNT; N-COUNT

**hu|man|ist|ic** /hjuːmənɪstɪk/ A **humanistic** idea, condition, or practice relates to humanism. ❑ *Religious values can often differ greatly from humanistic morals.* — ADJ: usu ADJ n

**hu|mani|tar|ian** /hjuːmænɪteəriən/ If a person or society has **humanitarian** ideas or behaviour, they try to avoid making people suffer or they help people who are suffering. ❑ *Air bombardment raised criticism on the humanitarian grounds that innocent civilians might suffer.* — ADJ: usu ADJ n

**hu|mani|tari|an|ism** /hjuːmænɪteəriənɪzəm/ **Humanitarianism** is humanitarian ideas or actions. — N-UNCOUNT

**hu|man|ity** /hjuːmænɪti/ **(humanities)** [1] All the people in the world can be referred to as **humanity**. ❑ *They face charges of committing crimes against humanity.* [2] A person's **humanity** is their state of being a human being, rather than an animal or an object. [FORMAL] ❑ *...a man who's almost lost his humanity in his bitter hatred of his rivals.* [3] **Humanity** is the quality of being kind, thoughtful, and sympathetic towards others. ❑ *Her speech showed great maturity and humanity.* [4] **The humanities** are the subjects such as history, philosophy, and literature which are concerned with human ideas and behaviour. ❑ *...students majoring in the humanities.* — N-UNCOUNT; N-UNCOUNT: with poss; N-UNCOUNT; N-PLURAL: oft *the* N

**hu|man|ize** /hjuːmənaɪz/ **(humanizes, humanizing, humanized)**

✔ in BRIT, also use **humanise**

If you **humanize** a situation or condition, you improve it by changing it in a way which makes it more suitable and pleasant for people. ❑ *Jo Robinson began by humanizing the waiting time at the health centre with tea-making and toys for children.* — VERB; V n

**human|kind** /hjuːmənkaɪnd/ **Humankind** is the same as **mankind**. — N-UNCOUNT

**hu|man|ly** /hjuːmənli/ If something is **humanly possible**, it is possible for people to do it. ❑ *She has gained a reputation for creating books as perfect as is humanly possible.* — PHRASE: v-link PHR, pron-indef PHR, *as* PHR

**hu|man na|ture** **Human nature** is the natural qualities and ways of behaviour that most people have. ❑ *It seems to be human nature to worry.* — N-UNCOUNT

**hu|man race** **The human race** is the same as **mankind**. ❑ *Can the human race carry on expanding and growing the same way that it is now?* — N-SING: *the* N

**hu|man re|sources** In a company or other organization, the department of **human resources** is the department with responsibility for the recruiting, training, and welfare of the staff. The abbreviation **HR** is often used. [BUSINESS] N-UNCOUNT = personnel

**hu|man rights** **Human rights** are basic rights which many societies believe that all people should have. ◆◇◇ N-PLURAL

**hu|man shield** If a group of people are used as a **human shield** in a battle or war, they are put in a particular place so that the enemy will be unwilling to attack that place and harm them. N-SING

**hum|ble** /hʌmbᵊl/ **(humbler, humblest, humbles, humbling, humbled)** 1 A **humble** person is not proud and does not believe that they are better than other people. ❑ *He gave a great performance, but he was very humble.* ♦ **hum|bly** *'I'm a lucky man, undeservedly lucky,' he said humbly.* ADJ ≠proud; ADV: ADV with v
2 People with low social status are sometimes described as **humble**. ❑ *Spyros Latsis started his career as a humble fisherman in the Aegean.* ADJ: usu ADJ n = lowly
3 A **humble** place or thing is ordinary and not special in any way. ❑ *There are restaurants, both humble and expensive, that specialize in them.* ADJ
4 People use **humble** in a phrase such as **in my humble opinion** as a polite way of emphasizing what they think, even though they do not feel humble about it. ❑ *It is, in my humble opinion, perhaps the best steak restaurant in Great Britain.* ♦ **hum|bly** *So may I humbly suggest we all do something next time.* ADJ politeness = modest; ADV: ADV before v
5 If you **eat humble pie**, you speak or behave in a way which tells people that you admit you were wrong about something. ❑ *Anson was forced to eat humble pie and publicly apologise to her.* PHRASE: V inflects
6 If you **humble** someone who is more important or powerful than you, you defeat them easily. ❑ *Honda won fame in the 1980s as the little car company that humbled the industry giants.* VERB: V n
7 If something or someone **humbles** you, they make you realize that you are not as important or good as you thought you were. ❑ *Ted's words humbled me.* ♦ **hum|bled** *I came away very humbled and recognizing that I, for one, am not well-informed.* ♦ **hum|bling** *Giving up an addiction is a humbling experience.* VERB: V n; ADJ; ADJ

**hum|bug** /hʌmbʌg/ If you describe someone's language or behaviour as **humbug**, you mean that it is dishonest or insincere. ❑ *There was all the usual humbug and obligatory compliments from ministers.* N-UNCOUNT disapproval

**hum|ding|er** /hʌmdɪŋəʳ/ **(humdingers)** If you describe someone or something as a **humdinger**, you mean that they are very impressive, exciting, or enjoyable. [INFORMAL] ❑ *It should be a humdinger of a match... His latest novel is a humdinger.* N-COUNT: usu sing, oft *a* N *of* n approval

**hum|drum** /hʌmdrʌm/ If you describe someone or something as **humdrum**, you mean that they are ordinary, dull, or boring. ❑ *...her lawyer husband, trapped in a humdrum but well-paid job.* ADJ disapproval

**hu|mid** /hjuːmɪd/ You use **humid** to describe an atmosphere or climate that is very damp, and usually very hot. ❑ *Visitors can expect hot and humid conditions.* ADJ = sticky, heavy ≠dry

**hu|midi|fi|er** /hjuːmɪdɪfaɪəʳ/ **(humidifiers)** A **humidifier** is a machine for increasing the amount of moisture in the air. N-COUNT

**hu|mid|ity** /hjuːmɪdɪti/ 1 You say there is **humidity** when the air feels very heavy and damp. ❑ *The heat and humidity were insufferable.* N-UNCOUNT
2 **Humidity** is the amount of water in the air. ❑ *The humidity is relatively low.* N-UNCOUNT

**hu|mili|ate** /hjuːmɪlieɪt/ **(humiliates, humiliating, humiliated)** To **humiliate** someone means to say or do something which makes them feel ashamed or stupid. ❑ *She had been beaten and humiliated by her husband... His teacher continually humiliates him in maths lessons.* ♦ **hu|mili|at|ed** *I have never felt so humiliated in my life.* VERB: *be* V-ed, V n; ADJ

**hu|mili|at|ing** /hjuːmɪlieɪtɪŋ/ If something is **humiliating**, it embarrasses you and makes you feel ashamed and stupid. ❑ *The Conservatives have suffered a humiliating defeat.* ♦ **hu|mili|at|ing|ly** *Thousands of men struggled humiliatingly for jobs... He was caught cheating during the Seoul Olympics and humiliatingly stripped of his title.* ADJ = crushing; ADV: usu ADV after v, ADV adj/-ed, also ADV with cl

**hu|milia|tion** /hjuːmɪlieɪʃᵊn/ **(humiliations)** 1 **Humiliation** is the embarrassment and shame you feel when someone makes you appear stupid, or when you make a mistake in public. ❑ *She faced the humiliation of discussing her husband's affair.* N-UNCOUNT
2 A **humiliation** is an occasion or a situation in which you feel embarrassed and ashamed. ❑ *The result is a humiliation for the prime minister.* N-COUNT

**hu|mil|ity** /hjuːmɪlɪti/ Someone who has **humility** is not proud and does not believe they are better than other people. ❑ *...a deep sense of humility.* N-UNCOUNT ≠pride

**humming|bird** /hʌmɪŋbɜːʳd/ **(hummingbirds)** A **hummingbird** is a small brightly coloured bird found in America, especially Central and South America. It has a long thin beak and powerful narrow wings that can move very fast. N-COUNT

**hum|mock** /hʌmək/ **(hummocks)** A **hummock** is a small raised area of ground, like a very small hill. N-COUNT = hillock

**hum|mus** /hʊməs/ → see **houmous**.

**hu|mong|ous** /hjuːmɒŋgəs/ also **humungous.** If you describe something or someone as **humongous**, you are emphasizing that they are very large or important. [INFORMAL] ❑ *We had a humongous row just because she left... Barbra Streisand is such a humungous star.* ADJ emphasis

**hu|mor** /hjuːməʳ/ → see **humour**.

**hu|mor|ist** /hjuːmərɪst/ **(humorists)** A **humorist** is a writer who specializes in writing amusing things. ❑ *...a political humorist.* N-COUNT

**hu|mor|ous** /hjuːmərəs/ If someone or something is **humorous**, they are amusing, especially in a clever or witty way. ❑ *He was quite humorous, and I liked that about him.* ♦ **hu|mor|ous|ly** *He looked at me humorously as he wrestled with the door.* ADJ; ADV: ADV with v, ADV adj

**hu|mour** /hjuːməʳ/ **(humours, humouring, humoured)** ◆◇◇

✔ in AM, use **humor**

1 You can refer to the amusing things that people say as their **humour**. ❑ *Her humour and determination were a source of inspiration to others.* → See also **sense of humour**. N-UNCOUNT: supp N
2 **Humour** is a quality in something that makes you laugh, for example in a situation, in someone's words or actions, or in a book or film. ❑ *She felt sorry for the man but couldn't ignore the humour of the situation.* N-UNCOUNT
3 If you are **in** a good **humour**, you feel cheerful and happy, and are pleasant to people. If you are **in** a bad **humour**, you feel bad-tempered and unhappy, and are unpleasant to people. ❑ *Christina was still not clear why he had been in such ill humour.* N-VAR: supp N = temper
4 If you do something with good **humour**, you do it cheerfully and pleasantly. ❑ *Hugo bore his illness with great courage and good humour.* N-UNCOUNT: adj N
5 If you **humour** someone who is behaving strangely, you try to please them or pretend to agree with them, so that they will not become upset. ❑ *She disliked Dido but was prepared to tolerate her for a weekend in order to humour her husband.* VERB: V n

**hu|mour|less** /hjuːməʳləs/

✔ in AM, use **humorless**

If you accuse someone of being **humourless**, you mean that they are very serious about everything and do not find things amusing. ❑ *He was a straight-faced, humourless character.* ADJ disapproval = solemn

**hump** /hʌmp/ **(humps, humping, humped)** 1 A **hump** is a small hill or raised area. ❑ *The path goes over a large hump by a tree before running near a road.* N-COUNT = mound
2 A camel's **hump** is the large lump on its back. N-COUNT
3 A **hump** is a large lump on a person's back, usually caused by illness or old age. N-COUNT: oft poss N
4 If you **hump** something heavy, you carry it VERB

from one place to another with great difficulty. [BRIT, INFORMAL] ❑ *Charlie humped his rucksack up the stairs to his flat.* 5 If someone **gets the hump**, they get very annoyed about something. [BRIT, INFORMAL] ❑ *Fans just get the hump when they lose.* = lug; V n prep/adv; PHRASE: V inflects

**hump|back** /hʌmpbæk/ **(humpbacks)** A **humpback** or a **humpback whale** is a large whale with a curved back. N-COUNT

**hump|backed bridge** **(humpbacked bridges)** A **humpbacked bridge** or **humpback bridge** is a short and very curved bridge with a shape similar to a semi-circle. [mainly BRIT] N-COUNT

**humped** /hʌmpt/ If someone is **humped**, their back is bent so that their shoulders are further forward than usual and their head hangs down. ❑ *I was humped like an old lady.* ADJ

**hu|mung|ous** /hjuːmʌŋgəs/ ➔ see **humongous**.

**hu|mus** /huːməs/ **Humus** is the part of soil which consists of dead plants that have begun to decay. N-UNCOUNT

**hunch** /hʌntʃ/ **(hunches, hunching, hunched)** 1 If you have a **hunch** about something, you are sure that it is correct or true, even though you do not have any proof. [INFORMAL] ❑ *I had a hunch that Susan and I would work well together.* 2 If you **hunch** forward, you raise your shoulders, put your head down, and lean forwards, often because you are cold, ill, or unhappy. ❑ *He got out his map of Yorkshire and hunched over it to read the small print.* 3 If you **hunch** your shoulders, you raise them and lean forwards slightly. ❑ *Wes hunched his shoulders and leaned forward on the edge of the counter.* N-COUNT; VERB; V adv/prep; VERB; V n

**hunch|back** /hʌntʃbæk/ **(hunchbacks)** A **hunchback** is someone who has a large lump on their back because their spine is curved. [OFFENSIVE, OLD-FASHIONED] N-COUNT

**hunched** /hʌntʃt/ If you are **hunched**, or **hunched up**, you are leaning forwards with your shoulders raised and your head down, often because you are cold, ill, or unhappy. ❑ *A solitary hunched figure emerged from Number Ten.* ADJ

**hun|dred** /hʌndrəd/ **(hundreds)** ◆◆◆

> ✔ The plural form is **hundred** after a number, or after a word or expression referring to a number, such as 'several' or 'a few'.

1 **A hundred** or **one hundred** is the number 100. ❑ *According to one official more than a hundred people have been arrested.* 2 If you refer to **hundreds of** things or people, you are emphasizing that there are very many of them. ❑ *Hundreds of tree species face extinction.* ♦ You can also use **hundreds** as a pronoun. ❑ *Hundreds have been killed in the fighting and thousands made homeless.* 3 You can use **a hundred per cent** or **one hundred per cent** to emphasize that you agree completely with something or that it is completely right or wrong. [INFORMAL] ❑ *Are you a hundred per cent sure it's your neighbour?* NUM: usu *a*/num NUM; QUANT: QUANT *of* pl-n; emphasis; PRON; PHRASE: PHR adj, PHR after v; emphasis; = absolutely

**hun|dredth** /hʌndrədθ/ **(hundredths)** ◆◆◇ 1 The **hundredth** item in a series is the one that you count as number one hundred. ❑ *The bank celebrates its hundredth anniversary in December.* 2 A **hundredth of** something is one of a hundred equal parts of it. ❑ *Mitchell beat Lewis by three-hundredths of a second.* ORD; FRACTION

**hundred|weight** /hʌndrədweɪt/ **(hundredweights)**

> ✔ The plural form is **hundredweight** after a number.

A **hundredweight** is a unit of weight that is equal to 112 pounds in Britain and to 100 pounds in the United States. ❑ *...a hundredweight of coal.* N-COUNT: oft N *of* n

**hung** /hʌŋ/ 1 **Hung** is the past tense and past participle of most of the senses of **hang**. 2 A **hung** jury is the situation that occurs when a jury is unable to reach a decision because there is not a clear majority of its members in favour of any one decision. In British English you can also talk about a **hung** parliament or a **hung** council. ❑ *In the event of a hung Parliament he would still fight for everything in the manifesto.* ADJ: usu ADJ n

**Hun|gar|ian** /hʌŋgeəriən/ **(Hungarians)** 1 **Hungarian** means belonging or relating to Hungary, or to its people, language, or culture. ❑ *...the Hungarian government.* 2 A **Hungarian** is a Hungarian citizen, or a person of Hungarian origin. 3 **Hungarian** is the language spoken by people who live in Hungary. ADJ: usu ADJ n; N-COUNT: usu pl; N-UNCOUNT

**hun|ger** /hʌŋgəʳ/ **(hungers, hungering, hungered)** 1 **Hunger** is the feeling of weakness or discomfort that you get when you need something to eat. ❑ *Hunger is the body's signal that levels of blood sugar are too low... The nutritionally balanced menus are designed to help you lose up to a pound a day without hunger pangs.* 2 **Hunger** is a severe lack of food which causes suffering or death. ❑ *Three hundred people in this town are dying of hunger every day.* 3 If you have a **hunger for** something, you want or need it very much. [WRITTEN] ❑ *Geffen has a hunger for success that seems bottomless.* 4 If you say that someone **hungers for** something or **hungers after** it, you are emphasizing that they want it very much. [FORMAL] ❑ *But Jules was not eager for classroom learning, he hungered for adventure.* N-UNCOUNT; N-UNCOUNT = starvation; N-SING: also no det, with supp, oft N *for* n = craving; VERB emphasis; V *for/after* n

**hun|ger strike** **(hunger strikes)** If someone goes **on hunger strike** or goes **on a hunger strike**, they refuse to eat as a way of protesting about something. ❑ *The protesters have been on hunger strike for 17 days.* ♦ **hun|ger strik|er** **(hunger strikers)** *The five hunger strikers in London called off their strike and celebrated the good news.* N-VAR; N-COUNT

**hung|over** /hʌŋoʊvəʳ/ also **hung-over**, **hung over**. Someone who is **hungover** is unwell because they drank too much alcohol on the previous day. ❑ *He was still hungover on the 25-minute bus drive to work the following morning.* ADJ: usu v-link ADJ

**hun|gry** /hʌŋgri/ **(hungrier, hungriest)** 1 When you are **hungry**, you want some food because you have not eaten for some time and have an uncomfortable or painful feeling in your stomach. ❑ *My friend was hungry, so we drove to a shopping mall to get some food.* ♦ **hun|gri|ly** /hʌŋgrɪli/ *James ate hungrily.* 2 If people **go hungry**, they do not have enough food to eat. ❑ *Leonidas' family had been poor, he went hungry for years.* 3 If you say that someone is **hungry** for something, you are emphasizing that they want it very much. [LITERARY] ❑ *I left Oxford in 1961 hungry to be a critic.* ♦ **Hungry** is also a combining form. ❑ *...power-hungry politicians.* ♦ **hun|gri|ly** *He looked at her hungrily. What eyes! What skin!* ADJ ≠ full; ADV: ADV with v; PHRASE: V inflects; ADJ: usu v-link ADJ *for* n, v-link ADJ to-inf emphasis; COMB in ADJ; ADV: ADV with v

**hung up** If you say that someone is **hung up about** a particular person or thing, you are criticizing them for thinking or worrying too much about that person or thing. [INFORMAL] ❑ *It was a time when people weren't so hung-up about health.* ADJ: v-link ADJ, usu ADJ *about/on* n; disapproval

**hunk** /hʌŋk/ **(hunks)** 1 A **hunk of** something is a large piece of it. ❑ *...a thick hunk of bread.* 2 If you refer to a man as a **hunk**, you mean that he is big, strong, and sexually attractive. [INFORMAL] ❑ *...a blond, blue-eyed hunk.* N-COUNT: usu N *of* n; N-COUNT approval

**hunk|er** /hʌŋkəʳ/ **(hunkers, hunkering, hunkered)**

♦ **hunker down** 1 If you **hunker down**, you bend your knees so that you are in a low position, balancing on your feet. [AM] ❑ *Betty hunkered down on the floor... He ended up hunkering down beside her.* 2 If you say that someone **hunkers down**, you mean that they are trying to avoid doing things that will make them noticed or put them in danger. [AM] ❑ *Their strategy for the moment is to hunker down and let the fuss die down.* PHRASAL VERB = squat; V P *on* n; V P *beside* n; PHRASAL VERB = lie low; V P

**hunt** /hʌnt/ **(hunts, hunting, hunted)** ◆◇◇ 1 If you **hunt for** something or someone, you try to find them by searching carefully or thoroughly. ❑ *A forensic team was hunting for clues.* ♦ **Hunt** is also a VERB = search; V *for* n; N-COUNT noun. ❑ *The couple had helped in the hunt for the toddlers.* = search [2] If you **hunt** a criminal or an enemy, you search for them in order to catch or harm them. ❑ *Detectives have been hunting him for seven months.* ♦ **Hunt** is also a noun. ❑ *Despite a nation-wide hunt for the kidnap gang, not a trace of them was found.* VERB V n Also V *for* n N-COUNT: usu sing, oft N *for* n [3] When people or animals **hunt**, they chase and kill wild animals for food or as a sport. ❑ *As a child I learned to hunt and fish... He got up at four and set out on foot to hunt black grouse.* ♦ **Hunt** is also a noun. ❑ *He set off for a nineteen-day moose hunt in Nova Scotia.* VERB V V n Also V *for* n N-COUNT: oft n N [4] In Britain, when people **hunt**, they ride horses over fields with dogs called hounds and try to catch and kill foxes, as a sport. ❑ *She liked to hunt as often as she could.* ♦ **Hunt** is also a noun. ❑ *The hunt was held on land owned by the Duke of Marlborough.* VERB V Also V n N-COUNT [5] In Britain, a **hunt** is a group of people who meet regularly to hunt foxes. N-COUNT [6] If a team or competitor is **in the hunt for** something, they still have a chance of winning it. ❑ *We're still in the hunt for the League title and we want to go all the way in the Cup.* PHRASE: usu v-link PHR *for* [7] → See also **hunting**, **witch-hunt**.

♦ **hunt down** If you **hunt down** a criminal or an enemy, you find them after searching for them. ❑ *Last December they hunted down and killed one of the gangsters... It took her four months to hunt him down.* PHRASAL VERB V P n (not pron) V n P

♦ **hunt out** If you **hunt out** something that is hidden or difficult to find, you search for it and eventually find it. ❑ *I'll try and hunt out the information you need... American consumers are accustomed to hunting out bargains.* PHRASAL VERB = dig out V P n (not pron) Also V n P

**hunt|er** /hʌntəʳ/ **(hunters)** [1] A **hunter** is a person who hunts wild animals for food or as a sport. ❑ *The hunters stalked their prey.* ◆◇◇ N-COUNT [2] People who are searching for things of a particular kind are often referred to as **hunters**. ❑ *...job-hunters. ...treasure hunters.* → See also **bargain hunter**, **headhunter**. N-COUNT: n N = seeker

**hunter-gatherer** **(hunter-gatherers)** **Hunter-gatherers** were people who lived by hunting and collecting food rather than by farming. There are still groups of hunter-gatherers living in some parts of the world. N-COUNT

**hunt|ing** /hʌntɪŋ/ [1] **Hunting** is the chasing and killing of wild animals by people or other animals, for food or as a sport. ❑ *Deer hunting was banned in Scotland in 1959.* N-UNCOUNT [2] **Hunting** is the activity of searching for a particular thing. ❑ *Jobclub can help you with job hunting.* ♦ **Hunting** is also a combining form. ❑ *Lee has divided his time between flat-hunting and travelling.* N-UNCOUNT: n N COMB in N-UNCOUNT

**hunt|ing ground** **(hunting grounds)** [1] If you say that a place is a good **hunting ground for** something, you mean that people who have a particular interest are likely to find something that they want there. ❑ *Other people's weddings are the perfect hunting ground for ideas.* N-COUNT: oft N *for* n [2] A **hunting ground** is an area where people or animals chase and kill wild animals for food or as a sport. N-COUNT

**hunt sabo|teur** **(hunt saboteurs)** A **hunt saboteur** is someone who tries to stop a hunt from taking place or being successful because they believe it is cruel to the animal being hunted. N-COUNT

**hunts|man** /hʌntsmən/ **(huntsmen)** A **huntsman** is a person who hunts wild animals, especially one who hunts foxes on horseback using dogs. N-COUNT

**hur|dle** /hɜːʳdᵊl/ **(hurdles, hurdling, hurdled)** [1] A **hurdle** is a problem, difficulty, or part of a process that may prevent you from achieving something. ❑ *Two-thirds of candidates fail at this first hurdle and are packed off home.* N-COUNT: usu supp N = obstacle [2] **Hurdles** is a race in which people have to jump over a number of obstacles, that are also called hurdles. You can use **hurdles** to refer to one or more races. ❑ *Davis won the 400m. hurdles in a new Olympic time of 49.3 sec.* N-COUNT-COLL [3] If you **hurdle**, you jump over something while you are running. ❑ *He crossed the lawn and hurdled the short fence... She learnt to hurdle by leaping over bales of hay on her family's farm.* VERB V n V

**hur|dler** /hɜːʳdləʳ/ **(hurdlers)** A **hurdler** is an athlete who takes part in hurdles races. N-COUNT

**hurl** /hɜːʳl/ **(hurls, hurling, hurled)** [1] If you **hurl** something, you throw it violently and with a lot of force. ❑ *Groups of angry youths hurled stones at police... Simon caught the grenade and hurled it back... Gangs rioted last night, breaking storefront windows and hurling rocks and bottles.* VERB V n prep V n with adv V n [2] If you **hurl** abuse or insults **at** someone, you shout insults at them aggressively. ❑ *How would you handle being locked in the back of a cab while the driver hurled abuse at you?* VERB V n *at* n Also V n

**hurly-burly** /hɜːʳli bɜːʳli/ If you talk about **the hurly-burly of** a situation, you are emphasizing how noisy or busy it is. ❑ *No one expects him to get involved in the hurly-burly of campaigning.* N-SING: usu *the* N, oft N *of* n [emphasis]

**hur|ray** /hʊreɪ/ also **hurrah.** → see **hooray**.

**hur|ri|cane** /hʌrɪkən, AM hɜːrɪkeɪn/ **(hurricanes)** A **hurricane** is an extremely violent wind or storm. N-COUNT

**hur|ried** /hʌrid, AM hɜːr-/ [1] A **hurried** action is done quickly, because you do not have much time to do it in. ❑ *...a hurried breakfast.* ♦ **hur|ried|ly** *...students hurriedly taking notes.* ADJ: usu ADJ n ADV: ADV with v [2] A **hurried** action is done suddenly, in reaction to something that has just happened. ❑ *Downing Street denied there had been a hurried overnight redrafting of the text.* ♦ **hur|ried|ly** *The moment she saw it, she blushed and hurriedly left the room.* ADJ: usu ADJ n ADV: ADV with v [3] Someone who is **hurried** does things more quickly than they should because they do not have much time to do them. ❑ *Parisians on the street often looked worried, hurried and unfriendly.* ADJ: usu v-link ADJ = rushed

**hur|ry** /hʌri, AM hɜːri/ **(hurries, hurrying, hurried)** [1] If you **hurry** somewhere, you go there as quickly as you can. ❑ *Claire hurried along the road... Bob hurried to join him, and they rode home together.* VERB V prep/adv V [2] If you **hurry to** do something, you start doing it as soon as you can, or try to do it quickly. ❑ *Mrs Hardie hurried to make up for her tactlessness by asking her guest about his holiday... There was no longer any reason to hurry.* VERB V to-inf V [3] If you are **in a hurry to** do something, you need or want to do something quickly. If you do something **in a hurry**, you do it quickly or suddenly. ❑ *Kate was in a hurry to grow up, eager for knowledge and experience.* N-SING: usu *in a* N, oft N to-inf [4] To **hurry** something means the same as to **hurry up** something. ❑ *...The President's attempt to hurry the process of independence.* VERB V n [5] If you **hurry** someone to a place or into a situation, you try to make them go to that place or get into that situation quickly. ❑ *They say they are not going to be hurried into any decision... I don't want to hurry you.* VERB = rush V n prep/adv V n

**PHRASES** [6] If you say to someone '**There's no hurry**' or '**I'm in no hurry**' you are telling them that there is no need for them to do something immediately. ❑ *I'll need to talk with you, but there's no hurry.* PHRASE [7] If you are **in no hurry to** do something, you are very unwilling to do it. ❑ *I love it at St Mirren so I'm in no hurry to go anywhere.* PHRASE: PHR after v, PHR to-inf, PHR *for* n

♦ **hurry along** → see **hurry up 2**.

♦ **hurry up** [1] If you tell someone to **hurry up**, you are telling them do something more quickly than they were doing. ❑ *Franklin told Howe to hurry up and take his bath; otherwise, they'd miss their train... Hurry up with that coffee, will you.* PHRASAL VERB V P V P *with* n [2] If you **hurry** something **up** or **hurry** it **along**, you make it happen faster or sooner than it would otherwise have done. ❑ *...if you want to hurry up the application process... Petter saw no reason to hurry the divorce along.* PHRASAL VERB = speed up V P n (not pron) V n P

**hurt** /hɜːʳt/ **(hurts, hurting, hurt)** [1] If you **hurt yourself** or **hurt** a part of your body, you feel pain because you have injured yourself. ❑ *Yasin had seriously hurt himself while trying to escape from the police... He had hurt his back in an accident.* ◆◆◇ VERB V pron-refl V n [2] If a part of your body **hurts**, you feel pain there. ❑ *His collar bone only hurt when he lifted* VERB V his arm. 3 If you are **hurt**, you have been injured. ❑ *His comrades asked him if he was hurt... They were dazed but did not seem to be badly hurt.* ADJ: usu v-link ADJ 4 If you **hurt** someone, you cause them to feel pain. ❑ *I didn't mean to hurt her, only to keep her still... Ouch. That hurt.* VERB V n V 5 If someone **hurts** you, they say or do something that makes you unhappy. ❑ *He is afraid of hurting Bessy's feelings... What hurts most is the betrayal, the waste.* VERB V n V 6 If you are **hurt**, you are upset because of something that someone has said or done. ❑ *Yes, I was hurt, jealous.* ADJ 7 If you say that you **are hurting**, you mean that you are experiencing emotional pain. ❑ *I am lonely and I am hurting.* VERB: only cont V 8 To **hurt** someone or something means to have a bad effect on them or prevent them from succeeding. ❑ *The combination of hot weather and decreased water supplies is hurting many industries.* VERB = damage V n 9 A feeling of **hurt** is a feeling that you have when you think that you have been treated badly or judged unfairly. ❑ *I was full of jealousy and hurt.* N-VAR = pain 10 If you say **'It won't hurt to** do something' or **'It never hurts to** do something', you are recommending an action which you think is helpful or useful. [INFORMAL] ❑ *It wouldn't hurt you to be a bit more serious.* PHRASE: V inflects, usu PHR to-inf

**hurt|ful** /hɜːʳtfʊl/ If you say that someone's comments or actions are **hurtful**, you mean that they are unkind and upsetting. ❑ *Her comments can only be hurtful to Mrs Green's family.* ADJ = upsetting

**hurt|le** /hɜːʳtᵊl/ **(hurtles, hurtling, hurtled)** If someone or something **hurtles** somewhere, they move there very quickly, often in a rough or violent way. ❑ *A pretty young girl came hurtling down the stairs.* VERB = career, dash V prep

**hus|band** /hʌzbənd/ **(husbands)** A woman's **husband** is the man she is married to. ❑ *Eva married her husband Jack in 1957.* ◆◆◆ N-COUNT: oft poss N

**hus|band|ry** /hʌzbəndri/ **Husbandry** is farming animals, especially when it is done carefully and well. N-UNCOUNT

**hush** /hʌʃ/ **(hushes, hushing, hushed)** 1 You say **'Hush!'** to someone when you are asking or telling them to be quiet. ❑ *Hush, my love, it's all right.* CONVENTION 2 If you **hush** someone or if they **hush**, they stop speaking or making a noise. ❑ *She tried to hush her noisy father... I had to box Max's ears to get him to hush.* VERB V n V 3 You say there is a **hush** in a place when everything is quiet and peaceful, or suddenly becomes quiet. ❑ *A hush fell over the crowd and I knew something terrible had happened.* N-SING: also no det = silence

♦ **hush up** If someone **hushes** something **up**, they prevent other people from knowing about it. ❑ *The scandal has been discussed by the politburo, although the authorities have tried to hush it up... The Ministry desperately tried to hush up the whole affair.* PHRASAL VERB = cover up V n P V P n (not pron)

**hushed** /hʌʃt/ 1 A **hushed** place is peaceful and much quieter and calmer than usual. ❑ *The house seemed muted, hushed as if it had been deserted.* ADJ = quiet ≠ noisy 2 A **hushed** voice or **hushed** conversation is very quiet. ❑ *We discussed the situation in hushed whispers.* ADJ: usu ADJ n

**hush-hush** Something that is **hush-hush** is secret and not to be discussed with other people. [INFORMAL] ❑ *Apparently there's a very hush-hush project under way up north.* ADJ = secret

**hush mon|ey** If a person is paid **hush money**, someone gives them money not to reveal information they have which could be damaging or embarrassing. [INFORMAL] N-UNCOUNT

**husk** /hʌsk/ **(husks)** A **husk** is the outer covering of a grain or a seed. N-COUNT

**husky** /hʌski/ **(huskier, huskiest, huskies)** 1 If someone's voice is **husky**, it is low and rather rough, often in an attractive way. ❑ *His voice was husky with grief. ...Dietrich's deep, husky voice.* ADJ ♦ **huski|ly** *'Ready?' I asked huskily.* ADV: ADV after v 2 If you describe a man as **husky**, you think that he is tall, strong, and attractive. [INFORMAL] ❑ *...a very husky young man, built like a football player.* ADJ: usu ADJ n 3 A **husky** is a strong, furry dog, which is used to pull sledges across snow. N-COUNT

**hus|sy** /hʌsi, AM hʌzi/ **(hussies)** If someone refers to a girl or woman as a **hussy**, they are criticizing her for behaving in a shocking or immoral way. [HUMOROUS, OLD-FASHIONED] N-COUNT [disapproval]

**hus|tings** /hʌstɪŋz/ The political campaigns and speeches before an election are sometimes referred to as **the hustings**. [mainly BRIT] ❑ *With only days to go before elections in Pakistan, candidates are battling it out at the hustings.* N-PLURAL: usu *the* N

**hus|tle** /hʌsᵊl/ **(hustles, hustling, hustled)** 1 If you **hustle** someone, you try to make them go somewhere or do something quickly, for example by pulling or pushing them along. ❑ *The guards hustled Harry out of the car.* VERB V n prep/adv 2 If you **hustle**, you go somewhere or do something as quickly as you can. ❑ *You'll have to hustle if you're to get home for supper... They had finished the exam and the teacher was hustling to get the papers gathered up.* VERB V V to-inf 3 If someone **hustles**, they try to earn money or gain an advantage from a situation, often by using dishonest or illegal means. [mainly AM] ❑ *We're expected to hustle and fight for what we want... I hustled some tickets from a magazine and off we went.* VERB V V n *from* n 4 **Hustle** is busy, noisy activity. ❑ *Shell Cottage provides the perfect retreat from the hustle and bustle of London.* N-UNCOUNT = bustle

**hus|tler** /hʌsləʳ/ **(hustlers)** 1 If you refer to someone as a **hustler**, you mean that they try to earn money or gain an advantage from situations they are in by using dishonest or illegal methods. [INFORMAL] ❑ *...an insurance hustler.* N-COUNT [disapproval] 2 A **hustler** is a prostitute, especially a male prostitute. [INFORMAL] N-COUNT

**hut** /hʌt/ **(huts)** 1 A **hut** is a small house with only one or two rooms, especially one which is made of wood, mud, grass, or stones. N-COUNT 2 A **hut** is a small wooden building in someone's garden, or a temporary building used by builders or repair workers. N-COUNT = shed

**hutch** /hʌtʃ/ **(hutches)** A **hutch** is a wooden structure that rabbits or other small pet animals are kept in. N-COUNT

**hya|cinth** /haɪəsɪnθ/ **(hyacinths)** A **hyacinth** is a plant with a lot of small, sweet-smelling flowers growing closely around a single stem. It grows from a bulb and the flowers are usually blue, pink, or white. N-COUNT

**hy|brid** /haɪbrɪd/ **(hybrids)** 1 A **hybrid** is an animal or plant that has been bred from two different species of animal or plant. [TECHNICAL] ❑ *All these brightly coloured hybrids are so lovely in the garden.* N-COUNT ♦ **Hybrid** is also an adjective. ❑ *...the hybrid maize seed.* ADJ: ADJ n 2 You can use **hybrid** to refer to anything that is a mixture of other things, especially two other things. ❑ *...a hybrid of solid and liquid fuel.* N-COUNT ♦ **Hybrid** is also an adjective. ❑ *...a hybrid system.* ADJ: ADJ n

**hy|brid|ize** /haɪbrɪdaɪz/ **(hybridizes, hybridizing, hybridized)**

in BRIT, also use **hybridise**

If one species of plant or animal **hybridizes with** another, the species reproduce together to make a hybrid. You can also say that you **hybridize** one species of plant or animal **with** another. [TECHNICAL] ❑ *All sorts of colours will result as these flowers hybridise freely... Wild boar readily hybridises with the domestic pig... Hybridising the two species will reduce the red to orange... Some people will take the seeds and hybridize the resulting plants with others of their own.* V-RECIP pl-n V V *with* n V pl-n V n *with* n

**hy|drant** /haɪdrənt/ **(hydrants)** → see **fire hydrant**.

**hy|drate** /haɪdreɪt/ **(hydrates, hydrating, hydrated)** 1 A **hydrate** is a chemical compound that contains water. ❑ *...aluminium hydrate.* N-MASS: usu n/adj N 2 If a substance **hydrates** your skin, it makes it softer and less dry. ❑ *After-sun products will cool and hydrate your skin.* VERB = moisturize V n

**hy|drau|lic** /haɪdrɒlɪk, AM -drɔːl-/ **Hydraulic** equipment or machinery involves or is operated by a fluid that is under pressure, such as water or oil. ❑ *The boat has no fewer than five hydraulic pumps.* ♦ **hy|drau|li|cal|ly** *...hydraulically operated pistons for raising and lowering the blade.* ADJ: ADJ n / ADV: ADV with v

**hy|drau|lics** /haɪdrɒlɪks, AM -drɔːl-/ **Hydraulics** is the study and use of systems that work using hydraulic pressure. N-UNCOUNT

**hydro|car|bon** /haɪdroʊkɑːʳbᵊn/ **(hydrocarbons)** A **hydrocarbon** is a chemical compound that is a mixture of hydrogen and carbon. N-COUNT

**hydro|chlo|ric acid** /haɪdrəklɒrɪk æsɪd/ **Hydrochloric acid** is a colourless, strong acid containing hydrogen and chlorine. N-UNCOUNT

**hydro|elec|tric** /haɪdroʊɪlektrɪk/ also **hydro-electric. Hydroelectric** means relating to or involving electricity made from the energy of running water. ADJ: ADJ n

**hydro|elec|tric|ity** /haɪdroʊɪlektrɪsɪti/ also **hydro-electricity. Hydroelectricity** is electricity made from the energy of running water. N-UNCOUNT

**hydro|foil** /haɪdrəfɔɪl/ **(hydrofoils)** A **hydrofoil** is a boat which can travel partly out of the water on a pair of flat parts like wings. You can also refer to the flat parts as **hydrofoils**. N-COUNT

**hydro|gen** /haɪdrədʒᵊn/ **Hydrogen** is a colourless gas that is the lightest and commonest element in the universe. N-UNCOUNT

**hydro|gen bomb** **(hydrogen bombs)** A **hydrogen bomb** is a nuclear bomb in which energy is released from hydrogen atoms. N-COUNT

**hydro|gen per|ox|ide** **Hydrogen peroxide** is a chemical that is often used to make hair lighter or to kill germs. N-UNCOUNT

**hydro|plane** /haɪdrəpleɪn/ **(hydroplanes)** A **hydroplane** is a speedboat which rises out of the water when it is travelling fast. N-COUNT

**hydro|thera|py** /haɪdroʊθerəpi/ **Hydrotherapy** is a method of treating people with some diseases or injuries by making them swim or do exercises in water. N-UNCOUNT

**hy|ena** /haɪiːnə/ **(hyenas)** A **hyena** is an animal that looks rather like a dog and makes a sound which is similar to a human laugh. Hyenas live in Africa and Asia. N-COUNT

**hy|giene** /haɪdʒiːn/ **Hygiene** is the practice of keeping yourself and your surroundings clean, especially in order to prevent illness or the spread of diseases. ❑ *Be extra careful about personal hygiene.* N-UNCOUNT = cleanliness

**hy|gien|ic** /haɪdʒiːnɪk, AM haɪdʒienɪk/ Something that is **hygienic** is clean and unlikely to cause illness. ❑ *...a white, clinical-looking kitchen that was easy to keep clean and hygienic.* ADJ

**hy|gien|ist** /haɪdʒiːnɪst/ **(hygienists)** A **hygienist** or a **dental hygienist** is a person who is trained to clean people's teeth and to give them advice on how to look after their teeth and gums. N-COUNT

**hy|men** /haɪmen/ **(hymens)** A **hymen** is a piece of skin that often covers part of a girl's or woman's vagina and breaks, usually when she has sex for the first time. [MEDICAL] N-COUNT

**hymn** /hɪm/ **(hymns)** 1 A **hymn** is a religious song that Christians sing in church. ❑ *I like singing hymns. ...a hymn book.* 2 If you describe a film, book, or speech as a **hymn to** something, you mean that it praises or celebrates that thing. [mainly JOURNALISM] ❑ *...a hymn to freedom and rebellion.* N-COUNT / N-COUNT: N *to* n

**hym|nal** /hɪmnᵊl/ **(hymnals)** A **hymnal** is a book of hymns. [FORMAL] N-COUNT

**hype** /haɪp/ **(hypes, hyping, hyped)** 1 **Hype** is the use of a lot of publicity and advertising to make people interested in something such as a product. ❑ *We are certainly seeing a lot of hype by some companies.* 2 To **hype** a product means to advertise or praise it a lot. ❑ *We had to hype the film to attract the financiers.* ♦ **Hype up** means the same as **hype**. ❑ *The media seems obsessed with hyping up individuals or groups.* N-UNCOUNT: usu supp N disapproval / VERB disapproval V n / PHRASAL VERB V P n (not pron)

♦ **hype up** To **hype** someone **up** means to deliberately make them very excited about something. ❑ *Everyone at school used to hype each other up about men all the time.* ➔ See also **hype 2**. PHRASAL VERB V n P Also V P n (not pron)

**hyped up** also **hyped-up.** If someone is **hyped up** about something, they are very excited or anxious about it. [INFORMAL] ❑ *We were both so hyped up about buying the house, we could not wait to get in there.* ADJ

**hy|per** /haɪpəʳ/ If someone is **hyper**, they are very excited and energetic. [INFORMAL] ❑ *I was incredibly hyper. I couldn't sleep.* ADJ: usu v-link ADJ = hyperactive

**hyper-** /haɪpəʳ-/ **Hyper-** is used to form adjectives that describe someone as having a lot or too much of a particular quality. ❑ *I hated my father. He was hyper-critical and mean... He is one of those lean, hyper-fit people.* PREFIX

**hyper|ac|tive** /haɪpəræktɪv/ Someone who is **hyperactive** is unable to relax and is always moving about or doing things. ❑ *His research was used in planning treatments for hyperactive children.* ♦ **hyper|ac|tiv|ity** /haɪpəræktɪvɪti/ *...an extreme case of hyperactivity.* ADJ / N-UNCOUNT

**hyper|bo|le** /haɪpɜːʳbəli/ If someone uses **hyperbole**, they say or write things that make something sound much more impressive than it really is. [TECHNICAL or FORMAL] ❑ *...the hyperbole that portrays him as one of the greatest visionaries in the world.* N-UNCOUNT

**hyper|bol|ic** /haɪpəʳbɒlɪk/ If you describe language as **hyperbolic**, you mean that it makes something sound much more impressive than it really is. [TECHNICAL or FORMAL] ADJ: usu ADJ n

**hyper|in|fla|tion** /haɪpərɪnfleɪʃᵊn/ also **hyper-inflation. Hyperinflation** is very severe inflation. N-UNCOUNT

**hyper|link** /haɪpəʳlɪŋk/ **(hyperlinks, hyperlinking, hyperlinked)** 1 In an HTML document, a **hyperlink** is a link to another part of the document or to another document. Hyperlinks are shown as words with a line under them. [COMPUTING] 2 If a document or file **is hyperlinked**, it contains hyperlinks. [COMPUTING] ❑ *The database is fully hyperlinked both within the database and to thousands of external links.* N-COUNT / VERB: usu passive *be* V-ed

**hyper|mar|ket** /haɪpəʳmɑːʳkɪt/ **(hypermarkets)** A **hypermarket** is a very large supermarket. [mainly BRIT] N-COUNT

**hyper|sen|si|tive** /haɪpəʳsensɪtɪv/ 1 If you say that someone is **hypersensitive**, you mean that they get annoyed or offended very easily. ❑ *Student teachers were hypersensitive to any criticism of their performance.* 2 Someone who is **hypersensitive** is extremely sensitive to certain drugs or chemicals. [MEDICAL] ADJ: oft ADJ *to/about* n = touchy / ADJ: oft ADJ *to* n

**hyper|ten|sion** /haɪpəʳtenʃᵊn/ **Hypertension** is a medical condition in which a person has very high blood pressure. N-UNCOUNT

**hyper|text** /haɪpəʳtekst/ In computing, **hypertext** is a way of connecting pieces of text so that you can go quickly and directly from one to another. [COMPUTING] N-UNCOUNT

**hy|per|ven|ti|late** /haɪpəʳventɪleɪt/ **(hyperventilates, hyperventilating, hyperventilated)** If someone **hyperventilates**, they begin to breathe very fast in an uncontrollable way, usually because they are very frightened, tired, or excited. ❑ *I hyperventilate when they come near me with the needle.* ♦ **hyper|ven|ti|la|tion** /haɪpəʳventɪleɪʃᵊn/ *Several notable researchers are studying the effects of hyperventilation.* VERB V / N-UNCOUNT

**hy|phen** /haɪfᵊn/ **(hyphens)** A **hyphen** is the punctuation sign used to join words together to make a compound, as in 'left-handed'. People also use a hyphen to show that the rest of a word is on the next line. N-COUNT

**hy|phen|at|ed** /haɪfəneɪtɪd/ A word that is **hyphenated** is written with a hyphen between ADJ two or more of its parts. ❑ *...hyphenated names such as Wong-Shong or Li-Wong.*

**hyp|no|sis** /hɪpnoʊsɪs/ [1] **Hypnosis** is a state in which a person seems to be asleep but can still see, hear, or respond to things said to them. ❑ *Bevin is now an adult and has re-lived her birth experience under hypnosis.* N-UNCOUNT [2] **Hypnosis** is the art or practice of hypnotizing people. N-UNCOUNT = hypnotism

**hyp|no|thera|pist** /hɪpnoʊθerəpɪst/ **(hypnotherapists)** A **hypnotherapist** is a person who treats people by using hypnotherapy. N-COUNT

**hyp|no|thera|py** /hɪpnoʊθerəpi/ **Hypnotherapy** is the practice of hypnotizing people in order to help them with a mental or physical problem, for example to help them give up smoking. N-UNCOUNT

**hyp|not|ic** /hɪpnɒtɪk/ [1] If someone is in a **hypnotic** state, they have been hypnotized. ❑ *The hypnotic state actually lies somewhere between being awake and being asleep.* ADJ: usu ADJ n [2] Something that is **hypnotic** holds your attention or makes you feel sleepy, often because it involves repeated sounds, pictures, or movements. ❑ *His songs are often both hypnotic and reassuringly pleasant.* ADJ

**hyp|no|tise** /hɪpnətaɪz/ → see **hypnotize**.

**hyp|no|tism** /hɪpnətɪzəm/ **Hypnotism** is the practice of hypnotizing people. N-UNCOUNT = hypnosis ♦ **hyp|no|tist (hypnotists)** ❑ *He was put into a trance by a police hypnotist.* N-COUNT

**hyp|no|tize** /hɪpnətaɪz/ **(hypnotizes, hypnotizing, hypnotized)**

in BRIT, also use **hypnotise**

[1] If someone **hypnotizes** you, they put you into a state in which you seem to be asleep but can still see, hear, or respond to things said to you. ❑ *A hypnotherapist will hypnotize you and will stop you from smoking.* VERB V n [2] If you **are hypnotized by** someone or something, you are so fascinated by them that you cannot think of anything else. ❑ *He's hypnotized by that black hair and that white face... Davey sat as if hypnotized by Nick's voice.* VERB: usu passive = mesmerize *be* V-ed V-ed

**hypo|chon|dria** /haɪpəkɒndriə/ If someone suffers from **hypochondria**, they continually worry about their health and imagine that they are ill, although there is really nothing wrong with them. N-UNCOUNT

**hypo|chon|dri|ac** /haɪpəkɒndriæk/ **(hypochondriacs)** A **hypochondriac** is a person who continually worries about their health, although there is really nothing wrong with them. N-COUNT

**hy|poc|ri|sy** /hɪpɒkrɪsi/ **(hypocrisies)** If you accuse someone of **hypocrisy**, you mean that they pretend to have qualities, beliefs, or feelings that they do not really have. ❑ *He accused newspapers of hypocrisy in their treatment of the story.* N-VAR [disapproval] ≠ sincerity

**hypo|crite** /hɪpəkrɪt/ **(hypocrites)** If you accuse someone of being a **hypocrite**, you mean that they pretend to have qualities, beliefs, or feelings that they do not really have. N-COUNT [disapproval]

**hypo|criti|cal** /hɪpəkrɪtɪkəl/ If you accuse someone of being **hypocritical**, you mean that they pretend to have qualities, beliefs, or feelings that they do not really have. ❑ *It would be hypocritical to say I travel at 70mph simply because that is the law.* ADJ [disapproval] ≠ sincere

**hypo|der|mic** /haɪpədɜːʳmɪk/ **(hypodermics)** A **hypodermic** needle or syringe is a medical instrument with a hollow needle, which is used to give injections. ♦ **Hypodermic** is also a noun. ❑ *He held up a hypodermic to check the dosage.* ADJ: ADJ n N-COUNT

**hy|pot|enuse** /haɪpɒtənjuːz, AM -nuːs/ **(hypotenuses)** **The hypotenuse** of a right-angled triangle is the side opposite its right angle. [TECHNICAL] N-COUNT: usu *the* N

**hypo|ther|mia** /haɪpoʊθɜːʳmiə/ If someone has **hypothermia**, their body temperature has become dangerously low as a result of being in severe cold for a long time. [MEDICAL] N-UNCOUNT

**hy|poth|esis** /haɪpɒθɪsɪs/ **(hypotheses)** A **hypothesis** is an idea which is suggested as a possible explanation for a particular situation or condition, but which has not yet been proved to be correct. [FORMAL] ❑ *Work will now begin to test the hypothesis in rats.* N-VAR = theory

**hy|poth|esize** /haɪpɒθɪsaɪz/ **(hypothesizes, hypothesizing, hypothesized)**

in BRIT, also use **hypothesise**

If you **hypothesize that** something will happen, you say that you think that thing will happen because of various facts you have considered. [FORMAL] ❑ *To explain this, they hypothesise that galaxies must contain a great deal of missing matter which cannot be detected... I have long hypothesized a connection between these factors.* VERB V that V n Also V

**hypo|theti|cal** /haɪpəθetɪkəl/ If something is **hypothetical**, it is based on possible ideas or situations rather than actual ones. ❑ *Let's look at a hypothetical situation in which Carol, a recovering cocaine addict, gets invited to a party. ...a purely hypothetical question.* ADJ = theoretical ♦ **hypo|theti|cal|ly** /haɪpəθetɪkli/ *He was invariably willing to discuss the possibilities hypothetically.* ADV: usu ADV with v, ADV with cl, also ADV adj

**hys|ter|ec|to|my** /hɪstərektəmi/ **(hysterectomies)** A **hysterectomy** is a surgical operation to remove a woman's womb. N-COUNT

**hys|te|ria** /hɪstɪəriə, AM -ster-/ [1] **Hysteria** among a group of people is a state of uncontrolled excitement, anger, or panic. ❑ *No one could help getting carried away by the hysteria.* N-UNCOUNT [2] A person who is suffering from **hysteria** is in a state of violent and disturbed emotion as a result of shock. [MEDICAL] ❑ *By now, she was screaming, completely overcome with hysteria.* N-UNCOUNT

**hys|teri|cal** /hɪsterɪkəl/ [1] Someone who is **hysterical** is in a state of uncontrolled excitement, anger, or panic. ❑ *Police and bodyguards had to protect him as the almost hysterical crowds struggled to approach him.* ADJ ♦ **hys|teri|cal|ly** /hɪsterɪkli/ *I don't think we can go round screaming hysterically: 'Ban these dogs. Muzzle all dogs.'* ADV: ADV with v, ADV adj/adv [2] Someone who is **hysterical** is in a state of violent and disturbed emotion that is usually a result of shock. ❑ *I suffered bouts of really hysterical depression.* ADJ ♦ **hys|teri|cal|ly** *I was curled up on the floor in a corner sobbing hysterically.* ADV [3] **Hysterical** laughter is loud and uncontrolled. [INFORMAL] ❑ *I had to rush to the loo to avoid an attack of hysterical giggles.* ADJ: usu ADJ n ♦ **hys|teri|cal|ly** *She says she hasn't laughed as hysterically since she was 13.* ADV: ADV with v [4] If you describe something or someone as **hysterical**, you think that they are very funny and they make you laugh a lot. [INFORMAL] ❑ *Paul Mazursky was Master of Ceremonies, and he was pretty hysterical.* ADJ ♦ **hys|teri|cal|ly** *It wasn't supposed to be a comedy but I found it hysterically funny.* ADV: ADV adj

**hys|ter|ics** /hɪsterɪks/ [1] If someone is **in hysterics** or is having **hysterics**, they are in a state of uncontrolled excitement, anger, or panic. [INFORMAL] ❑ *I'm sick of your having hysterics, okay?* N-PLURAL: oft *in* N [2] If someone is **in hysterics** or is having **hysterics**, they are in a state of violent and disturbed emotion that is usually a result of shock. ❑ *It was such a shock I had hysterics.* N-PLURAL: oft *in* N = hysteria [3] You can say that someone is **in hysterics** or is having **hysterics** when they are laughing loudly in an uncontrolled way. [INFORMAL] ❑ *He'd often have us all in absolute hysterics.* N-PLURAL: oft *in* N

# I i

**I, i** /aɪ/ **(I's, i's) I** is the ninth letter of the English alphabet. N-VAR

**I** /aɪ/ ◆◆◆ A speaker or writer uses **I** to refer to himself or herself. **I** is a first person singular pronoun. **I** is used as the subject of a verb. ❑ *Jim and I are getting married... She liked me, I think.* PRON: PRON v

**-ian** ➔ see **-an**.

**ibid** ◆◇◇ **Ibid** is used in books and journals to indicate that a piece of text taken from somewhere else is from the same source as the previous piece of text. CONVENTION

**-ibility** /-ɪbɪlɪti/ **(-ibilities) -ibility** replaces '-ible' at the end of adjectives to form nouns referring to the state or quality described by the adjective. ❑ *...its commitment to increase the accessibility of the arts... Check your eligibility for State benefits.* SUFFIX

**ice** /aɪs/ ◆◆◇ **(ices, icing, iced)** 1 **Ice** is frozen water. ❑ *Glaciers are moving rivers of ice. ...a bitter lemon with ice.* N-UNCOUNT 2 If you **ice** a cake, you cover it with icing. ❑ *I've iced and decorated the cake.* VERB V n 3 ➔ See also **iced**, **icing**.

PHRASES 4 If you **break the ice** at a party or meeting, or in a new situation, you say or do something to make people feel relaxed and comfortable. ➔ See also **ice-breaker**. PHRASE: V inflects 5 If you say that something **cuts no ice with** you, you mean that you are not impressed or influenced by it. ❑ *That sort of romantic attitude cuts no ice with money-men.* PHRASE: V inflects, oft PHR *with* n 6 If someone puts a plan or project **on ice**, they delay doing it. ❑ *The deal was put on ice for three months.* PHRASE: PHR after v, v-link PHR 7 If you say that someone is **on thin ice** or **is skating on thin ice**, you mean that they are doing something risky which may have serious or unpleasant consequences. ❑ *I had skated on thin ice and, so far, got away with it.* PHRASE

**Ice Age The Ice Age** was a period of time lasting many thousands of years, during which a lot of the earth's surface was covered with ice. N-PROPER: *the* N

**ice|berg** /aɪsbɜːʳg/ **(icebergs)** An **iceberg** is a large tall mass of ice floating in the sea. **the tip of the iceberg** ➔ see **tip**. N-COUNT

**ice-blue Ice-blue** is a very pale blue colour. [LITERARY] COLOUR

**ice|box** /aɪsbɒks/ **(iceboxes)** also **ice-box.** An **icebox** is the same as a **refrigerator**. [AM, OLD-FASHIONED] N-COUNT

**ice-breaker (ice-breakers)** also **icebreaker.** 1 An **ice-breaker** is a large ship which sails through frozen waters, breaking the ice as it goes, in order to create a passage for other ships. N-COUNT 2 An **ice-breaker** is something that someone says or does in order to make it easier for people have never met before to talk to each other. ❑ *This exercise can be quite a useful ice-breaker for new groups.* N-COUNT

**ice buck|et (ice buckets)** An **ice bucket** is a container which holds ice cubes or cold water and ice. You can use it to provide ice cubes to put in drinks, or to put bottles of wine in and keep the wine cool. N-COUNT

**ice cap (ice caps)** also **ice-cap. The ice caps** are the thick layers of ice and snow that cover the North and South Poles. N-COUNT: usu *the* N

**ice-cold** 1 If you describe something as **ice-cold**, you are emphasizing that it is very cold. ❑ *...delicious ice-cold beer.* ADJ 2 If you describe someone as **ice-cold**, you are emphasizing that they do not allow their emotions to affect them or that they lack feeling and friendliness. ❑ *...the gunman's ice-cold stare.* ADJ

**ice-cool** If you describe someone as **ice-cool**, you admire them because they are calm and do not show emotion in difficult situations. [JOURNALISM] ❑ *The ice-cool driver has built a reputation for pulling out his best performances under pressure.* ADJ: usu ADJ n approval

**ice cream (ice creams)** also **ice-cream.** 1 **Ice cream** is a very cold sweet food which is made from frozen cream or a substance like cream and has a flavour such as vanilla, chocolate, or strawberry. ❑ *I'll get you some ice cream.* N-MASS 2 An **ice cream** is an amount of ice cream sold in a small container or a cone made of thin biscuit. ❑ *Do you want an ice cream?* N-COUNT

**ice cube (ice cubes)** An **ice cube** is a small square block of ice that you put into a drink in order to make it cold. N-COUNT

**iced** /aɪst/ 1 An **iced** drink has been made very cold, often by putting ice in it. ❑ *...iced tea.* ADJ: ADJ n 2 An **iced** cake is covered with a layer of icing. ❑ *We were all given little iced cakes.* ADJ: usu ADJ n

**ice floe (ice floes)** An **ice floe** is a large area of ice floating in the sea. N-COUNT

**ice hock|ey** also **ice-hockey. Ice hockey** is a game played on ice between two teams of 11 players who use long curved sticks to hit a small rubber disk, called a puck, and try to score goals. [mainly BRIT] N-UNCOUNT

☑ in AM, usually use **hockey**

**Ice|land|er** /aɪsləndəʳ/ **(Icelanders)** An **Icelander** is a person who comes from Iceland. N-COUNT

**Ice|land|ic** /aɪslændɪk/ 1 Something that is **Icelandic** belongs or relates to Iceland, to its people, or to its language. ADJ 2 **Icelandic** is the official language of Iceland. N-UNCOUNT

**ice lol|ly (ice lollies)** also **ice-lolly.** An **ice lolly** is a piece of flavoured ice or ice cream on a stick. [BRIT] N-COUNT

☑ in AM, use **Popsicle**

**ice pack (ice packs)** An **ice pack** is a bag full of ice which is used to cool parts of the body when they are injured or painful. N-COUNT

**ice pick (ice picks)** also **icepick.** An **ice pick** is a small pointed tool that you use for breaking ice. N-COUNT

**ice rink (ice rinks)** An **ice rink** is a level area of ice, usually inside a building, that has been made artificially and kept frozen so that people can skate on it. N-COUNT

**ice sheet (ice sheets)** An **ice sheet** is a large thick area of ice, especially one that exists for a long time. N-COUNT

**ice-skate (ice-skates) Ice-skates** are boots with a thin metal bar underneath that people wear to move quickly on ice. N-COUNT

**ice skat|er (ice skaters)** An **ice skater** is someone who skates on ice. N-COUNT

**ice-skating** also **ice skating.** If you go **ice-skating**, you move about on ice wearing ice-skates. This activity is also a sport. ❑ *They took me ice-skating on a frozen lake.* VERB: only cont V ♦ **Ice-skating** is also a noun. ❑ *I love watching ice-skating on television.* N-UNCOUNT = *skating*

**ice wa|ter** Ice water is very cold water served as a drink. [AM] N-UNCOUNT

**ici|cle** /aɪsɪkəl/ **(icicles)** An **icicle** is a long pointed piece of ice hanging down from a surface. It forms when water comes slowly off the surface, and freezes as it falls. N-COUNT

**ic|ing** /aɪsɪŋ/ 1 **Icing** is a sweet substance made from powdered sugar that is used to cover and decorate cakes. ❑ *...a birthday cake with yellow icing.* N-UNCOUNT 2 If you describe something as **the icing on the cake**, you mean that it makes a good thing even better, but it is not essential. ❑ *The third goal was the icing on the cake.* PHRASE: v-link PHR

**ic|ing sug|ar** **Icing sugar** is very fine white sugar that is used for making icing and sweets. [BRIT] N-UNCOUNT

in AM, usually use **confectioners' sugar**

**-icity** /-ɪsɪti/ **(-icities)** **-icity** replaces '-ic' at the end of adjectives to form nouns referring to the state, quality, or behaviour described by the adjective. ❑ *...if someone disputes the authenticity of the document... He soon exhibited signs of eccentricity.* SUFFIX

**icky** /ɪki/ 1 If you describe something as **icky**, you mean that it is too emotional or sentimental. [mainly AM, INFORMAL] ❑ *They've even got one of those icky photos of themselves on the bedside table.* ADJ disapproval 2 If you describe a substance as **icky**, you mean that it is disgustingly sticky. [mainly AM, INFORMAL] ❑ *She could feel something icky on her fingers.* ADJ disapproval

**icon** /aɪkɒn/ **(icons)** 1 If you describe something or someone as an **icon**, you mean that they are important as a symbol of a particular thing. ❑ *Only Marilyn has proved as enduring a fashion icon.* N-COUNT: usu with supp 2 An **icon** is a picture of Christ, his mother, or a saint painted on a wooden panel. N-COUNT 3 An **icon** is a picture on a computer screen representing a particular computer function. If you want to use it, you move the cursor onto the icon using a mouse. [COMPUTING] N-COUNT

**icon|ic** /aɪkɒnɪk/ An **iconic** image or thing is important or impressive because it seems to be a symbol of something. [FORMAL] ❑ *The ads helped Nike to achieve iconic status.* ADJ

**icono|clast** /aɪkɒnəklæst/ **(iconoclasts)** If you describe someone as an **iconoclast**, you mean that they often criticize beliefs and things that are generally accepted by society. [FORMAL] N-COUNT

**icono|clas|tic** /aɪkɒnəklæstɪk/ If you describe someone or their words or ideas as **iconoclastic**, you mean that they contradict established beliefs. [FORMAL] ❑ *Is it utopian to hope that such iconoclastic ideas will gain ground?* ADJ

**ico|no|gra|phy** /aɪkənɒgrəfi/ The **iconography** of a group of people consists of the symbols, pictures, and objects which represent their ideas and way of life. ❑ *...the iconography of revolutionary posters. ...religious iconography.* N-UNCOUNT

**icy** /aɪsi/ **(icier, iciest)** 1 If you describe something as **icy** or **icy cold**, you mean that it is extremely cold. ❑ *An icy wind blew hard across the open spaces.* ADJ 2 An **icy** road has ice on it. ADJ 3 If you describe a person or their behaviour as **icy**, you mean that they are not affectionate or friendly, and they show their dislike or anger in a quiet, controlled way. ❑ *His response was icy.* ADJ disapproval = cold ≠ warm ♦ **ici|ly** *'Have you finished?' he asked icily.* ADV: ADV after v, ADV adj

**ID** /aɪ diː/ **(IDs)** If you have **ID** or an **ID**, you are carrying a document such as an identity card or driver's licence which proves that you are a particular person. ❑ *I had no ID on me so I couldn't prove I was the owner of the car.* N-VAR = identification

**I'd** /aɪd/ 1 **I'd** is the usual spoken form of 'I had', especially when 'had' is an auxiliary verb. ❑ *I felt absolutely certain that I'd seen her before.* 2 **I'd** is the usual spoken form of 'I would'. ❑ *There are some questions I'd like to ask.*

**idea** /aɪdiːə/ **(ideas)** ◆◆◆ 1 An **idea** is a plan, suggestion, or possible course of action. ❑ *It's a good idea to plan ahead... I really like the idea of helping people... She told me she'd had a brilliant idea.* N-COUNT: oft adj N, N to-inf, N of n/-ing 2 An **idea** is an opinion or belief about what something is like or should be like. ❑ *Some of his ideas about democracy are entirely his own. ...the idea that reading too many books ruins your eyes.* N-COUNT: usu N about/on/of n, N that 3 If someone gives you an **idea of** something, they give you information about it without being very exact or giving a lot of detail. ❑ *This table will give you some idea of how levels of ability can be measured... If you cannot remember the exact date give a rough idea of when it was.* N-SING: N of n/wh 4 If you have an **idea** of something, you know about it to some extent. ❑ *No one has any real idea how much the company will make next year.* N-SING: with supp 5 If you have an **idea that** something is the case, you think that it may be the case, although you are not certain. ❑ *I had an idea that he joined the army later, but I may be wrong.* N-SING: N that vagueness 6 **The idea** of an action or activity is its aim or purpose. ❑ *The idea is to encourage people to get to know their neighbours.* N-SING: the N = objective 7 If you have the **idea of** doing something, you intend to do it. ❑ *He sent for a number of books he admired with the idea of re-reading them.* N-COUNT: N of -ing/n = intention 8 You can use **idea** in expressions such as **I've no idea** or **I haven't the faintest idea** to emphasize that you do not know something. ❑ *'Is she coming by coach?' — 'Well I've no idea.'* N-SING: with brd-neg emphasis 9 If someone **gets the idea**, they understand how to do something or they understand what you are telling them. [INFORMAL] ❑ *It isn't too difficult once you get the idea.* PHRASE: V inflects

**ideal** /aɪdiːəl/ **(ideals)** ◆◇◇ 1 An **ideal** is a principle, idea, or standard that seems very good and worth trying to achieve. ❑ *The party has drifted too far from its socialist ideals.* N-COUNT: oft N of n 2 Your **ideal of** something is the person or thing that seems to you to be the best possible example of it. ❑ *...the Japanese ideal of beauty.* N-SING: oft poss N 3 The **ideal** person or thing for a particular task or purpose is the best possible person or thing for it. ❑ *She decided that I was the ideal person to take over the job.* ADJ = perfect 4 An **ideal** society or world is the best possible one that you can imagine. ❑ *We do not live in an ideal world.* ADJ: ADJ n

**ideal|ise** /aɪdiːəlaɪz/ → see **idealize**.

**ideal|ism** /aɪdiːəlɪzəm/ **Idealism** is the beliefs and behaviour of someone who has ideals and who tries to base their behaviour on these ideals. ❑ *She never lost her respect for the idealism of the 1960s.* N-UNCOUNT ♦ **ideal|ist** **(idealists)** *He is not such an idealist that he cannot see the problems.* N-COUNT

**ideal|is|tic** /aɪdiəlɪstɪk/ If you describe someone as **idealistic**, you mean that they have ideals, and base their behaviour on these ideals, even though this may be impractical. ❑ *Idealistic young people died for the cause.* ADJ

**ideal|ize** /aɪdiːəlaɪz/ **(idealizes, idealizing, idealized)**

in BRIT, also use **idealise**

If you **idealize** something or someone, you think of them, or represent them to other people, as being perfect or much better than they really are. ❑ *People idealize the past.* VERB: V n ♦ **ideal|ized** *...an idealised image of how a parent should be.* ADJ: usu ADJ n ♦ **ideali|za|tion** /aɪdiːəlaɪzeɪʃən/ **(idealizations)** *...Marie's idealisation of her dead husband.* N-VAR

**ideal|ly** /aɪdiːəli/ 1 If you say that **ideally** a particular thing should happen or be done, you mean that this is what you would like to happen or be done, but you know that this is may not be possible or practical. ❑ *People should, ideally, eat much less fat.* ADV: ADV with cl/group = preferably 2 If you say that someone or something is **ideally** suited, **ideally** located, or **ideally** qualified, you mean that they are as well suited, located, or qualified as they could possibly be. ❑ *They were an extremely happy couple, ideally suited.* ADV: usu ADV -ed, also ADV after v = perfectly

**iden|ti|cal** /aɪdentɪkəl/ Things that are **identical** are exactly the same. ❑ *The two parties fought the last election on almost identical manifestos.* ADJ: oft ADJ to/with n ♦ **iden|ti|cal|ly** /aɪdentɪkli/ *...nine identically dressed female dancers.* ADV: usu ADV -ed/adj

**iden|ti|cal twin** **(identical twins)** **Identical twins** are twins of the same sex who look exactly the same. N-COUNT: usu pl

**iden|ti|fi|able** /aɪdentɪfaɪəbᵊl/ Something or someone that is **identifiable** can be recognized. ❑ *In the corridor were four dirty, ragged bundles, just identifiable as human beings.* ADJ: oft ADJ *as/by/from* n = recognizable

**iden|ti|fi|ca|tion** /aɪdentɪfɪkeɪʃᵊn/ **(identifications)** [1] The **identification** of something is the recognition that it exists, is important, or is true. ❑ *Early identification of a disease can prevent death and illness.* N-VAR: oft N *of* n [2] Your **identification** of a particular person or thing is your ability to name them because you know them or recognize them. ❑ *He's made a formal identification of the body.* N-VAR [3] If someone asks you for some **identification**, they want to see something such as a driving licence, which proves who you are. ❑ *The woman who was on passport control asked me if I had any further identification.* N-UNCOUNT = ID [4] The **identification of** one person or thing **with** another is the close association of one with the other. ❑ *...the identification of Spain with Catholicism.* N-VAR: usu N *of* n *with* n = association [5] **Identification with** someone or something is the feeling of sympathy and support for them. ❑ *Marilyn had an intense identification with animals.* N-UNCOUNT: N *with* n = empathy

**iden|ti|fy** /aɪdentɪfaɪ/ **(identifies, identifying, identified)** ◆◆◇ [1] If you can **identify** someone or something, you are able to recognize them or distinguish them from others. ❑ *There are a number of distinguishing characteristics by which you can identify a Hollywood epic.* VERB; V n [2] If you **identify** someone or something, you name them or say who or what they are. ❑ *Police have already identified around 10 murder suspects... The reporters identified one of the six Americans as an Army Specialist.* VERB = name; V n; V n *as* n/-ing [3] If you **identify** something, you discover or notice its existence. ❑ *Scientists claim to have identified natural substances with cancer-combating properties.* VERB = discover; V n [4] If a particular thing **identifies** someone or something, it makes them easy to recognize, by making them different in some way. ❑ *She wore a little nurse's hat on her head to identify her... His boots and purple beret identify him as commanding the Scottish Paratroops.* VERB = distinguish; V n; V n *as* -ing/n [5] If you **identify with** someone or something, you feel that you understand them or their feelings and ideas. ❑ *She would only play a role if she could identify with the character.* VERB; V *with* n [6] If you **identify** one person or thing **with** another, you think that they are closely associated or involved in some way. ❑ *She hates playing the sweet, passive women that audiences identify her with... The candidates all want to identify themselves with reform.* VERB = associate; V n *with* n; V pron-refl *with* n

**iden|ti|kit** /aɪdentɪkɪt/ **(identikits)** also **Identikit.** An **identikit** or an **identikit picture** is a drawing of the face of someone the police want to question. It is made from descriptions given to them by witnesses to a crime. Compare **e-fit**, **Photofit**. [mainly BRIT, TRADEMARK] N-COUNT

**iden|tity** /aɪdentɪti/ **(identities)** ◆◇◇ [1] Your **identity** is who you are. ❑ *Abu is not his real name, but it's one he uses to disguise his identity.* N-COUNT: with poss [2] The **identity** of a person or place is the characteristics they have that distinguish them from others. ❑ *I wanted a sense of my own identity.* N-VAR: usu with supp, oft with poss, adj N

**iden|tity card** **(identity cards)** An **identity card** is a card with a person's name, photograph, date of birth, and other information on it. In some countries, people are required to carry identity cards in order to prove who they are. N-COUNT

**iden|tity pa|rade** **(identity parades)** At an **identity parade**, a witness to a crime tries to identify the criminal from among a line of people. [BRIT] N-COUNT

☑ in AM, usually use **line-up**

**ideo|gram** /ɪdioʊgræm/ **(ideograms)** [1] An **ideogram** is a sign or symbol that represents a particular idea or thing rather than a word. The writing systems of Japan and China, for example, use ideograms. N-COUNT [2] In languages such as English which are written using letters and words, an **ideogram** is a sign or symbol that can be used to represent a particular word. %, @, and & are examples of ideograms. N-COUNT

**ideo|logi|cal** /aɪdiəlɒdʒɪkᵊl/ **Ideological** means relating to principles or beliefs. ❑ *Others left the party for ideological reasons.* ADJ: usu ADJ n ♦ **ideo|logi|cal|ly** /aɪdiəlɒdʒɪkli/ *...an ideologically sound organisation.* ADV: ADV adj/-ed, ADV with cl, ADV after v

**ideolo|gist** /aɪdiɒlədʒɪst/ **(ideologists)** An **ideologist** is someone who develops or supports a particular ideology. N-COUNT

**ideo|logue** /aɪdiəlɒg, AM -lɔːg/ **(ideologues)** An **ideologue** is the same as an **ideologist**. [FORMAL] N-COUNT

**ideol|ogy** /aɪdiɒlədʒi/ **(ideologies)** An **ideology** is a set of beliefs, especially the political beliefs on which people, parties, or countries base their actions. ❑ *...capitalist ideology.* N-VAR

**id|io|cy** /ɪdiəsi/ **(idiocies)** If you refer to something as **idiocy**, you mean that you think it is very stupid. ❑ *...the idiocy of continuing government subsidies for environmentally damaging activities.* N-VAR: oft N *of* n/-ing = lunacy

**idi|om** /ɪdiəm/ **(idioms)** [1] A particular **idiom** is a particular style of something such as music, dance, or architecture. [FORMAL] ❑ *McCartney was also keen to write in a classical idiom, rather than a pop one.* N-COUNT: usu sing, with supp = style [2] An **idiom** is a group of words which have a different meaning when used together from the one they would have if you took the meaning of each word separately. [TECHNICAL] ❑ *Proverbs and idioms may become worn with overuse.* N-COUNT = phrase [3] **Idiom** of a particular kind is the language that people use at a particular time or in a particular place. [FORMAL] ❑ *...her command of the Chinese idiom.* N-UNCOUNT

**idio|mat|ic** /ɪdioʊmætɪk/ **Idiomatic** language uses words in a way that sounds natural to native speakers of the language. ❑ *...her remarkable command of idiomatic English.* ADJ: usu ADJ n

**idio|syn|cra|sy** /ɪdioʊsɪŋkrəsi/ **(idiosyncrasies)** If you talk about the **idiosyncrasies** of someone or something, you are referring to their rather unusual habits or characteristics. ❑ *Everyone has a few little idiosyncrasies.* N-VAR: usu with poss = eccentricity, peculiarity

**idio|syn|crat|ic** /ɪdioʊsɪŋkrætɪk/ If you describe someone's actions or characteristics as **idiosyncratic**, you mean that they are rather unusual. ❑ *...a highly idiosyncratic personality.* ADJ = eccentric

**id|iot** /ɪdiət/ **(idiots)** If you call someone an **idiot**, you are showing that you think they are very stupid or have done something very stupid. ❑ *I knew I'd been an idiot to stay there.* N-COUNT [disapproval] = fool

**id|iot box** The **idiot box** is the television. [mainly BRIT, INFORMAL] N-SING: *the* N

☑ in AM, use **boob tube**

**idi|ot|ic** /ɪdiɒtɪk/ If you call someone or something **idiotic**, you mean that they are very stupid or silly. ❑ *What an idiotic thing to say!* ADJ [disapproval] = ridiculous ♦ **idi|oti|cal|ly** /ɪdiɒtɪkli/ *...his idiotically romantic views.* ADV

**idle** /aɪdᵊl/ **(idles, idling, idled)** [1] If people who were working are **idle**, they have no jobs or work. ❑ *Employees have been idle almost a month because of shortages.* ADJ: v-link ADJ [2] If machines or factories are **idle**, they are not working or being used. ❑ *Now the machine is lying idle.* ADJ: v-link ADJ [3] If you say that someone is **idle**, you disapprove of them because they are not doing anything and you think they should be. ❑ *...idle bureaucrats who spent the day reading newspapers.* ADJ [disapproval] ♦ **idle|ness** *Idleness is a very bad thing for human nature.* N-UNCOUNT ♦ **idly** *We were not idly sitting around.* ADV: ADV with v [4] **Idle** is used to describe something that you do for no particular reason, often because you have nothing better to do. ❑ *Brian kept up the idle chatter for another five minutes.* ADJ: ADJ n ♦ **idly** *We talked idly about magazines and baseball.* ADV: ADV with v, ADV adj [5] You refer to an **idle** threat or boast when you do not think the person making it will or can do what they say. ADJ: ADJ n = empty

❑ *It was more of an idle threat than anything.* 6 To **idle** a factory or other place of work means to close it down because there is no work to do or because the workers are on strike. [AM, BUSINESS] ❑ *...idled assembly plants.* VERB V-ed Also V n

in BRIT, usually use **shut down**

7 To **idle** workers means to stop them working. [AM, BUSINESS] ❑ *The strike has idled about 55,000 machinists.* VERB V n

in BRIT, use **lay off**

8 If an engine or vehicle **is idling**, the engine is running slowly and quietly because it is not in gear, and the vehicle is not moving. ❑ *Beyond a stand of trees a small plane idled.* VERB V

**idler** /aɪdləʳ/ **(idlers)** If you describe someone as an **idler**, you are criticizing them because you think they are lazy and should be working. ❑ *The Duke resents being seen as a moneyed idler.* N-COUNT disapproval = loafer

**idol** /aɪdəl/ **(idols)** 1 If you refer to someone such as a film, pop, or sports star as an **idol**, you mean that they are greatly admired or loved by their fans. ❑ *A great cheer went up from the crowd as they caught sight of their idol.* N-COUNT: usu with supp 2 An **idol** is a statue or other object that is worshipped by people who believe that it is a god. N-COUNT 3 If you refer to someone as a **fallen idol**, you mean that they have lost people's respect and admiration because of something bad that they have done. PHRASE: N inflects

**idola|try** /aɪdɒlətri/ 1 Someone who practises **idolatry** worships idols. [FORMAL] N-UNCOUNT 2 If you refer to someone's admiration for a particular person as **idolatry**, you think it is too great and uncritical. [FORMAL] ❑ *Their affection for her soon increased almost to idolatry.* N-UNCOUNT disapproval

**idol|ize** /aɪdəlaɪz/ **(idolizes, idolizing, idolized)**

in BRIT, also use **idolise**

If you **idolize** someone, you admire them very much. ❑ *Naomi idolised her father as she was growing up.* VERB = worship V n

**id|yll** /ɪdɪl, AM aɪdəl/ **(idylls)**

in AM, also use **idyl**

If you describe a situation as an **idyll**, you mean that it is idyllic. ❑ *She finds that the sleepy town she moves to isn't the rural idyll she imagined.* N-COUNT

**idyl|lic** /ɪdɪlɪk, AM aɪd-/ If you describe something as **idyllic**, you mean that it is extremely pleasant, simple, and peaceful without any difficulties or dangers. ❑ *...an idyllic setting for a summer romance.* ADJ

**i.e.** /aɪ iː/ **i.e.** is used to introduce a word or sentence which makes what you have just said clearer or gives details. ❑ *...strategic points – i.e. airports or military bases.*

**-ied** → see **-ed**.

**-ier** → see **-er**.

**-iest** → see **-est**.

**if** /ɪf/ ◆◆◆

Often pronounced /ɪf/ at the beginning of the sentence.

1 You use **if** in conditional sentences to introduce the circumstances in which an event or situation might happen, might be happening, or might have happened. ❑ *She gets very upset if I exclude her from anything... You can go if you want... If you went into town, you'd notice all the pubs have loud jukeboxes... Do you have a knack for coming up with ideas? If so, we would love to hear from you.* CONJ 2 You use **if** in indirect questions where the answer is either 'yes' or 'no'. ❑ *He asked if I had left with you, and I said no... I wonder if I might have a word with Mr Abbot?* CONJ = whether 3 You use **if** to suggest that something might be slightly different from what you are stating in the main part of the sentence, for example that there might be slightly more or less of a particular quality. ❑ *Sometimes, that standard is quite difficult, if not impossible, to achieve... I'm working on my fitness and I will be ready in a couple of weeks, if not sooner.* CONJ: with neg 4 You use **if**, usually with 'can', 'could', 'may', or 'might', at a point in a conversation when you are politely trying to make a point, change the subject, or interrupt another speaker. ❑ *If I could just make another small point about the weightlifters in the Olympics.* CONJ 5 You use **if** at or near the beginning of a clause when politely asking someone to do something. ❑ *I wonder if you'd be kind enough to give us some information, please?* CONJ politeness 6 You use **if** to introduce a subordinate clause in which you admit a fact which you regard as less important than the statement in the main clause. ❑ *If there was any disappointment it was probably temporary.* CONJ

PHRASES 7 You use **if not** in front of a word or phrase to indicate that your statement does not apply to that word or phrase, but to something closely related to it that you also mention. ❑ *She understood his meaning, if not his words, and took his advice.* PHRASE 8 You use **if ever** with past tenses when you are introducing a description of a person or thing, to emphasize how appropriate it is. ❑ *I became a distraught, worried mother, a useless role if ever there was one.* PHRASE emphasis 9 You use **if only** with past tenses to introduce what you think is a fairly good reason for doing something, although you realize it may not be a very good one. ❑ *She writes me often, if only to scold me because I haven't written to her.* PHRASE 10 You use **if only** to express a wish or desire, especially one that cannot be fulfilled. ❑ *If only you had told me that some time ago.* PHRASE feelings 11 You use **as if** when you are making a judgment about something that you see or notice. Your belief or impression might be correct, or it might be wrong. ❑ *The whole room looks as if it has been lovingly put together over the years.* PHRASE 12 You use **as if** to describe something or someone by comparing them with another thing or person. ❑ *He points two fingers at his head, as if he were holding a gun.* PHRASE 13 You use **as if** to emphasize that something is not true. [SPOKEN] ❑ *Getting my work done! My God! As if it mattered.* PHRASE emphasis 14 You use **'if anything'** to introduce something which strengthens or changes the meaning of the statement you have just made, but only in a small or unimportant way. ❑ *Living together didn't harm our friendship. If anything it strengthened it.* PHRASE: PHR with cl 15 You use **'It's not as if'** to introduce a statement which, if it were true, might explain something puzzling, although in fact it is not true. ❑ *I am surprised by the fuss she's making. It's not as if my personality has changed.* PHRASE: V inflects 16 You say **'if I were you'** to someone when you are giving them advice. ❑ *If I were you, Mrs Gretchen, I just wouldn't worry about it.* PHRASE: PHR with cl

**if|fy** /ɪfi/ 1 If you say that something is **iffy**, you mean that it is not very good in some way. [INFORMAL] ❑ *If your next record's a bit iffy, you're forgotten.* ADJ = dodgy 2 If something is **iffy**, it is uncertain. [INFORMAL] ❑ *His political future has looked iffy for most of this year.* ADJ = doubtful

**-ify** /-ifaɪ/ **(-ifies, -ifying, -ified)** **-ify** is used at the end of verbs that refer to making something or someone different in some way. ❑ *More needs to be done to simplify the process of registering to vote... Water can be purified by boiling for five minutes.* SUFFIX

**ig|loo** /ɪgluː/ **(igloos)** **Igloos** are dome-shaped houses built from blocks of snow by the Inuit people. N-COUNT

**ig|ne|ous** /ɪgniəs/ In geology, **igneous** rocks are rocks that were once so hot that they were liquid. [TECHNICAL] ADJ: ADJ n

**ig|nite** /ɪgnaɪt/ **(ignites, igniting, ignited)** 1 When you **ignite** something or when it **ignites**, it starts burning or explodes. ❑ *The bombs ignited a fire which destroyed some 60 houses... The blasts were caused by pockets of methane gas that ignited.* VERB V n V 2 If something or someone **ignites** your feelings, they cause you to have very strong feelings about something. [LITERARY] ❑ *There was one teacher who really ignited my interest in words.* VERB V n

**ig|ni|tion** /ɪgnɪʃᵊn/ **(ignitions)** 1 In a car engine, the **ignition** is the part where the fuel is ignited. → See picture on page 1708. ❑ *The device automatically disconnects the ignition.* N-VAR 2 Inside a car, **the ignition** is the part where you turn the key so that the engine starts. N-SING: the N 3 **Ignition** is the process of something starting to burn. ❑ *The ignition of methane gas killed eight men.* N-UNCOUNT

**ig|no|ble** /ɪgnoʊbᵊl/ If you describe something as **ignoble**, you mean that it is bad and something to be ashamed of. [FORMAL] ❑ *...ignoble thoughts.* ADJ disapproval

**ig|no|mini|ous** /ɪgnəmɪniəs/ If you describe an experience or action as **ignominious**, you mean it is embarrassing because it shows a great lack of success. [FORMAL] ❑ *...their ignominious defeat.* ADJ = humiliating ♦ **ig|no|mini|ous|ly** *Their soldiers had to retreat ignominiously after losing hundreds of lives.* ADV: ADV with v

**ig|no|miny** /ɪgnəmɪni/ **Ignominy** is shame or public disgrace. [FORMAL] ❑ *...the ignominy of being made redundant.* N-UNCOUNT: oft N of n/-ing

**ig|no|ra|mus** /ɪgnəreɪməs/ **(ignoramuses)** If you describe someone as an **ignoramus**, you are being critical of them because they do not have the knowledge you think they ought to have. [FORMAL] N-COUNT disapproval

**ig|no|rance** /ɪgnərəns/ **Ignorance of** something is lack of knowledge about it. ❑ *I am embarrassed by my complete ignorance of history.* N-UNCOUNT: oft N of/about n

**ig|no|rant** /ɪgnərənt/ 1 If you describe someone as **ignorant**, you mean that they do not know things they should know. If someone is **ignorant of** a fact, they do not know it. ❑ *People don't like to ask questions for fear of appearing ignorant.* ADJ: oft ADJ of/about n 2 People are sometimes described as **ignorant** when they do something that is not polite or kind. Some people think that it is not correct to use **ignorant** with this meaning. ADJ

**ig|nore** /ɪgnɔːʳ/ **(ignores, ignoring, ignored)** ♦♦◊ 1 If you **ignore** someone or something, you pay no attention to them. ❑ *She said her husband ignored her.* VERB V n 2 If you say that an argument or theory **ignores** an important aspect of a situation, you are criticizing it because it fails to consider that aspect or to take it into account. ❑ *Such arguments ignore the question of where ultimate responsibility lay.* VERB = overlook V n

**igua|na** /ɪgjuɑːnə, AM ɪgwɑːnə/ **(iguanas)** An **iguana** is a type of large lizard found in America. N-COUNT

**ikon** /aɪkɒn/ → see **icon**.

**il-**

> Usually pronounced /ɪl/ before an unstressed syllable, and /ɪl/ before a stressed syllable.

**Il-** is added to words that begin with the letter 'l' to form words with the opposite meaning. ❑ *...an awful illegible signature... He could face a charge of illegally importing weapons.* PREFIX

**ilk** /ɪlk/ If you talk about people or things **of** the same **ilk**, you mean people or things of the same type as a person or thing that has been mentioned. ❑ *He currently terrorises politicians and their ilk on 'Newsnight'... Where others of his ilk have battled against drugs, Gabriel's problems have centred on his marriage.* N-SING: supp N = kind

**ill** /ɪl/ **(ills)** ♦♦◊ 1 Someone who is **ill** is suffering from a disease or a health problem. ❑ *In November 1941 Payne was seriously ill with pneumonia.* ADJ: usu v-link ADJ ♦ People who are ill in some way can be referred to as, for example, **the** mentally **ill**. ❑ *I used to work with the mentally ill.* N-PLURAL: the adv N 2 Difficulties and problems are sometimes referred to as **ills**. [FORMAL] ❑ *His critics maintain that he's responsible for many of Algeria's ills.* N-COUNT: usu pl, usu with supp 3 **Ill** is evil or harm. [LITERARY] ❑ *They say they mean you no ill.* N-UNCOUNT 4 **Ill** means the same as 'badly'. [FORMAL] ❑ *The company's conservative instincts sit ill with competition.* ADV: ADV with v 5 You can use **ill** in front of some nouns to indicate that you are referring to something harmful or unpleasant. [FORMAL] ❑ *She had brought ill luck into her family.* ADJ: ADJ n = bad

PHRASES 6 If you say that someone **can ill afford to** do something, or **can ill afford** something, you mean that they must prevent it from happening because it would be harmful or embarrassing to them. [FORMAL] ❑ *It's possible he won't play but I can ill afford to lose him.* PHRASE: PHR to-inf, PHR n 7 If you **fall ill** or **are taken ill**, you suddenly become ill. ❑ *Shortly before Christmas, he was mysteriously taken ill.* PHRASE: V inflects 8 to **speak ill of** someone → see **speak**.

**ill-** /ɪl-/ **Ill-** is added to words, especially adjectives and past participles, to add the meaning 'badly' or 'inadequately'. For example, 'ill-written' means badly written. ❑ *...ill-disciplined children.* COMB in ADJ

**I'll** /aɪl/ **I'll** is the usual spoken form of 'I will' or 'I shall'. ❑ *I'll be leaving town in a few weeks.*

**ill-advised** If you describe something that someone does as **ill-advised**, you mean that it is not sensible or wise. ❑ *They would be ill-advised to do this.* ADJ: oft ADJ to-inf

**ill at ease** also **ill-at-ease.** → see **ease**.

**ill-bred** If you say that someone is **ill-bred**, you mean that they have bad manners. ADJ disapproval = uncouth

**ill-conceived** If you describe a plan or action as **ill-conceived**, you mean that it is likely to fail or have bad consequences because it has not been thought about carefully enough. ❑ *...an ill-conceived plan to close the coal mine.* ADJ

**ill-considered** If you describe something that someone says or does as **ill-considered**, you mean that it is not sensible or not appropriate. ❑ *He made some ill-considered remarks about the cost.* ADJ

**ill-defined** If you describe something as **ill-defined**, you mean that its exact nature or extent is not as clear as it should be or could be. ❑ *...staff with ill-defined responsiblities.* ADJ

**ill ef|fects** also **ill-effects.** If something has **ill effects**, it causes problems or damage. ❑ *Some people are still suffering ill effects from the contamination of their water.* N-PLURAL

**il|legal** /ɪliːgᵊl/ **(illegals)** ♦◊◊ 1 If something is **illegal**, the law says that it is not allowed. ❑ *It is illegal to intercept radio messages. ...illegal drugs.* ADJ: oft it v-link ADJ to-inf ♦ **il|legal|ly** *They were yesterday convicted of illegally using a handgun.* ADV: ADV with v ♦ **il|legal|ity** /ɪlɪgælɪti/ **(illegalities)** *There is no evidence of illegality.* N-VAR 2 **Illegal** immigrants or workers have travelled into a country or are working without official permission. ADJ: ADJ n ♦ Illegal immigrants or workers are sometimes referred to as **illegals**. ❑ *...a clothing factory where many illegals worked.* N-COUNT

**il|leg|ible** /ɪledʒɪbᵊl/ Writing that is **illegible** is so unclear that you cannot read it. ADJ

**il|legiti|ma|cy** /ɪlɪdʒɪtɪməsi/ **Illegitimacy** is the state of being born of parents who were not married to each other. ❑ *Illegitimacy rates are soaring.* N-UNCOUNT

**il|legiti|mate** /ɪlɪdʒɪtɪmət/ 1 A person who is **illegitimate** was born of parents who were not married to each other. ADJ 2 **Illegitimate** is used to describe activities and institutions that are not in accordance with the law or with accepted standards of what is right. ❑ *The election was dismissed as illegitimate by the opposition.* ADJ

**ill-equipped** Someone who is **ill-equipped to** do something does not have the ability, the qualities, or the equipment necessary to do it. ❑ *Universities were ill-equipped to meet the massive intake of students.* ADJ: oft ADJ to-inf, ADJ for n

**ill-fated** If you describe something as **ill-fated**, you mean that it ended or will end in an unsuccessful or unfortunate way. ❑ *England's footballers are back home after their ill-fated trip to Algeria.* ADJ: usu ADJ n

**ill-fitting** An **ill-fitting** piece of clothing does not fit the person who is wearing it properly. ❑ *He wore an ill-fitting green corduroy suit.* ADJ: ADJ n

**ill-founded** Something that is **ill-founded** is not based on any proper proof or evidence. ❑ *Suspicion and jealousy, however ill-founded, can poison a marriage.* ADJ

**ill-gotten gains** **Ill-gotten gains** are things that someone has obtained in a dishonest or illegal way. ❑ *But many leaders have invested their ill-gotten gains in several different countries.* N-PLURAL

**ill health** Someone who suffers from **ill health** has an illness or keeps being ill. ❑ *He was forced to retire because of ill health.* N-UNCOUNT

**il|lib|er|al** /ɪlɪbərᵊl/ If you describe someone or something as **illiberal**, you are critical of them because they do not allow or approve of much freedom or choice of action. ❑ *...illiberal legislation.* ADJ [disapproval]

**il|lic|it** /ɪlɪsɪt/ An **illicit** activity or substance is not allowed by law or the social customs of a country. ❑ *Dante clearly condemns illicit love.* ADJ: usu ADJ n

**il|lit|era|cy** /ɪlɪtərəsi/ **Illiteracy** is the state of not knowing how to read or write. N-UNCOUNT

**il|lit|er|ate** /ɪlɪtərət/ **(illiterates)** [1] Someone who is **illiterate** does not know how to read or write. ❑ *A large percentage of the population is illiterate.* ♦ An **illiterate** is someone who is illiterate. ❑ *...an educational centre for illiterates.* ADJ; N-COUNT [2] If you describe someone as musically, technologically, or economically **illiterate**, you mean that they do not know much about music, technology, or economics. ADJ: usu adv ADJ

**ill-mannered** If you describe someone as **ill-mannered**, you are critical of them because they are impolite or rude. [FORMAL] ❑ *Chantal would have considered it ill-mannered to show surprise.* ADJ [disapproval] = bad-mannered ≠ well-mannered

**ill|ness** /ɪlnəs/ **(illnesses)** [1] **Illness** is the fact or experience of being ill. ❑ *If your child shows any signs of illness, take her to the doctor... Mental illness is still a taboo subject.* ◆◇◇ N-UNCOUNT [2] An **illness** is a particular disease such as measles or pneumonia. ❑ *She returned to her family home to recover from an illness.* N-COUNT

**il|logi|cal** /ɪlɒdʒɪkᵊl/ If you describe an action, feeling, or belief as **illogical**, you are critical of it because you think that it does not result from a logical and ordered way of thinking. ❑ *It is illogical to oppose the repatriation of economic migrants.* ADJ: oft it v-link ADJ to-inf [disapproval] = irrational, unreasonable ♦ **il|logi|cal|ly** /ɪlɒdʒɪkli/ *Illogically, I felt guilty.* ADV

**ill-prepared** If you are **ill-prepared for** something, you have not made the correct preparations for it, for example because you are not expecting it to happen. ❑ *The government was ill-prepared for the problems it now faces.* ADJ: usu v-link ADJ, oft ADJ *for* n, ADJ to-inf

**ill-starred** If you describe something or someone as **ill-starred**, you mean that they were unlucky or unsuccessful. [LITERARY] ❑ *...an ill-starred attempt to create jobs in Northern Ireland.* ADJ: usu ADJ n

**ill-tempered** If you describe someone as **ill-tempered**, you mean they are angry or hostile, and you may be implying that this is unreasonable. [FORMAL] ❑ *It was a day of tense and often ill-tempered debate.* ADJ

**ill-timed** If you describe something as **ill-timed**, you mean that it happens or is done at the wrong time, so that it is damaging or rude. ❑ *He argued that the tax cut was ill-timed.* ADJ = inopportune

**ill-treat** **(ill-treats, ill-treating, ill-treated)** If someone **ill-treats** you, they treat you badly or cruelly. ❑ *They thought Mr Smith had been ill-treating his wife.* VERB = mistreat, abuse V n

**ill-treatment** **Ill-treatment** is harsh or cruel treatment. ❑ *Ill-treatment of animals remains commonplace.* N-UNCOUNT = abuse

**il|lu|mi|nate** /ɪluːmɪneɪt/ **(illuminates, illuminating, illuminated)** [1] To **illuminate** something means to shine light on it and to make it brighter and more visible. [FORMAL] ❑ *No streetlights illuminated the street.* VERB V n [2] If you **illuminate** something that is unclear or difficult to understand, you make it clearer by explaining it carefully or giving information about it. [FORMAL] ❑ *They use games and drawings to illuminate their subject.* VERB V n ♦ **il|lu|mi|nat|ing** *His autobiography provides an illuminating insight into his mind.* ADJ: oft it v-link ADJ to-inf

**il|lu|mi|nat|ed** /ɪluːmɪneɪtɪd/ Something that is **illuminated** is lit up, usually by electric lighting. ❑ *...an illuminated sign.* ADJ

**il|lu|mi|na|tion** /ɪluːmɪneɪʃᵊn/ **(illuminations)** [1] **Illumination** is the lighting that a place has. [FORMAL] ❑ *The only illumination came from a small window high in the opposite wall.* N-UNCOUNT [2] **Illuminations** are coloured lights which are put up in towns, especially at Christmas, in order to make them look attractive, especially at night. [mainly BRIT] ❑ *...the famous Blackpool illuminations.* N-PLURAL

**il|lu|mine** /ɪluːmɪn/ **(illumines, illumining, illumined)** To **illumine** something means the same as to **illuminate** it. [LITERARY] ❑ *The interchange of ideas illumines the debate... By night, the perimeter wire was illumined by lights.* VERB V n V n

**il|lu|sion** /ɪluːʒᵊn/ **(illusions)** [1] An **illusion** is a false idea or belief. ❑ *No one really has any illusions about winning the war.* N-VAR: oft N that, N *of* n/-ing [2] An **illusion** is something that appears to exist or be a particular thing but does not actually exist or is in reality something else. ❑ *Floor-to-ceiling windows can give the illusion of extra height.* N-COUNT: oft N *of* n/-ing

**il|lu|sion|ist** /ɪluːʒənɪst/ **(illusionists)** An **illusionist** is a performer who makes it seem that strange or impossible things are happening, for example that a person has disappeared or been cut in half. N-COUNT

**il|lu|so|ry** /ɪluːzəri, -səri/ If you describe something as **illusory**, you mean that although it seems true or possible, it is in fact false or impossible. ❑ *His freedom is illusory.* ADJ

**il|lus|trate** /ɪləstreɪt/ **(illustrates, illustrating, illustrated)** [1] If you say that something **illustrates** a situation that you are drawing attention to, you mean that it shows that the situation exists. ❑ *The example of the United States illustrates this point... The incident graphically illustrates how parlous their position is... The case also illustrates that some women are now trying to fight back.* ◆◇◇ VERB = demonstrate V n V wh V that [2] If you use an example, story, or diagram to **illustrate** a point, you use it show that what you are saying is true or to make your meaning clearer. ❑ *Let me give another example to illustrate this difficult point... Throughout, she illustrates her analysis with excerpts from discussions.* VERB V n V n *with* n ♦ **il|lus|tra|tion** /ɪləstreɪʃᵊn/ *Here, by way of illustration, are some extracts from our new catalogue.* N-UNCOUNT: usu prep N [3] If you **illustrate** a book, you put pictures, photographs or diagrams into it. ❑ *She went on to art school and is now illustrating a book... He has illustrated the book with black-and-white photographs.* VERB V n V n *with* n ♦ **il|lus|trat|ed** *The book is beautifully illustrated throughout.* ADJ ♦ **il|lus|tra|tion** *...the world of children's book illustration.* N-UNCOUNT

**il|lus|tra|tion** /ɪləstreɪʃᵊn/ **(illustrations)** [1] An **illustration** is an example or a story which is used to make a point clear. ❑ *...a perfect illustration of the way Britain absorbs and adapts external influences.* ◆◇◇ N-COUNT: oft N *of* n [2] An **illustration** in a book is a picture, design, or diagram. ❑ *She looked like a princess in a nineteenth-century illustration.* N-COUNT [3] → See also **illustrate**.

**il|lus|tra|tive** /ɪləstrətɪv/ If you use something as an **illustrative** example, or for **illustrative** purposes, you use it to show that what you are saying is true or to make your meaning clearer. [FORMAL] ❑ *A second illustrative example was taken from The Observer newspaper.* ADJ: oft ADJ *of* n

**il|lus|tra|tor** /ɪləstreɪtəʳ/ **(illustrators)** An **illustrator** is an artist who draws pictures and diagrams for books and magazines. N-COUNT

**il|lus|tri|ous** /ɪlʌstriəs/ If you describe someone as an **illustrious** person, you mean that they are extremely well known because they have a high position in society or they have done something impressive. ❑ *...his long and illustrious career.* ADJ: usu ADJ n = distinguished

**ill will** also **ill-will.** **Ill will** is unfriendly or hostile feelings that you have towards someone. ❑ *He didn't bear anyone any ill will.* N-UNCOUNT = animosity

**ill wind** You can describe an unfortunate event as an **ill wind** if someone benefits from it. The expression occurs in the proverb 'It's an ill wind that blows nobody any good'. ❑ *But it's an ill wind; I recovered and married one of my nurses from that hospital.* N-SING: usu *a* N

**im-**

> Usually pronounced /ɪm-/ before an unstressed syllable, and /ɪm-/ before a stressed syllable.

**Im-** is added to words that begin with 'm', 'p', or 'b' to form words with the opposite meaning. ❑ *He implied that we were emotionally immature... Don't stare at me – it's impolite!... The illness is triggered by a chemical imbalance in the brain.* PREFIX

**I'm** /aɪm/ **I'm** is the usual spoken form of 'I am'. ❑ *I'm sorry... I'm already late for my next appointment.*

**im|age** /ɪmɪdʒ/ **(images)** ◆◆◇ 1 If you have an **image** of something or someone, you have a picture or idea of them in your mind. ❑ *The image of art theft as a gentleman's crime is outdated.* N-COUNT: usu with supp 2 The **image** of a person, group, or organization is the way that they appear to other people. ❑ *The tobacco industry has been trying to improve its image.* N-COUNT: oft with poss 3 An **image** is a picture of someone or something. [FORMAL] ❑ *...photographic images of young children.* N-COUNT 4 An **image** is a poetic description of something. [FORMAL] ❑ *The natural images in the poem are meant to be suggestive of realities beyond themselves.* N-COUNT 5 If you **are the image of** someone else, you look very much like them. ❑ *Marianne's son was the image of his father.* PHRASE: V inflects 6 → See also **mirror image**. **spitting image** → see **spit**.

**im|age|ry** /ɪmɪdʒri/ 1 You can refer to the descriptions in something such as a poem or song, and the pictures they create in your mind, as its **imagery**. [FORMAL] ❑ *...the nature imagery of the ballad.* N-UNCOUNT 2 You can refer to pictures and representations of things as **imagery**, especially when they act as symbols. [FORMAL] ❑ *This is an ambitious and intriguing movie, full of striking imagery.* N-UNCOUNT

**im|agi|nable** /ɪmædʒɪnəbəl/ 1 You use **imaginable** after a superlative such as 'best' or 'worst' to emphasize that something is extreme in some way. ❑ *...their imprisonment under some of the most horrible circumstances imaginable.* ADJ: adj-superl n ADJ, adj-superl ADJ n [emphasis] = conceivable 2 You use **imaginable** after a word like 'every' or 'all' to emphasize that you are talking about all the possible examples of something. You use **imaginable** after 'no' to emphasize that something does not have the quality mentioned. ❑ *Parents encourage every activity imaginable.* ADJ: ADJ n, n ADJ [emphasis] = possible

**im|agi|nary** /ɪmædʒɪnəri, AM -neri/ An **imaginary** person, place, or thing exists only in your mind or in a story, and not in real life. ❑ *Lots of children have imaginary friends.* ADJ: usu ADJ n

**im|agi|na|tion** /ɪmædʒɪneɪʃən/ **(imaginations)** ◆◇◇ 1 Your **imagination** is the ability that you have to form pictures or ideas in your mind of things that are new and exciting, or things that you have not experienced. ❑ *Antonia is a woman with a vivid imagination... The Government approach displays a lack of imagination.* N-VAR 2 Your **imagination** is the part of your mind which allows you to form pictures or ideas of things that do not necessarily exist in real life. ❑ *Long before I ever went there, Africa was alive in my imagination.* N-COUNT: usu with supp

PHRASES 3 If you say that someone or something **captured** your **imagination**, you mean that you thought they were interesting or exciting when you saw them or heard them for the first time. ❑ *Italian football captured the imagination of the nation last season.* PHRASE: V inflects 4 If you say that something **stretches** your **imagination**, you mean that it is good because it makes you think about things that you had not thought about before. ❑ *Their films are exciting and really stretch the imagination.* PHRASE: V inflects [approval] 5 not **by any stretch of the imagination** → see **stretch**.

**im|agi|na|tive** /ɪmædʒɪnətɪv/ If you describe someone or their ideas as **imaginative**, you are praising them because they are easily able to think of or create new or exciting things. ❑ *...an imaginative writer.* ADJ [approval] = inventive ♦ **im|agi|na|tive|ly** *The hotel is decorated imaginatively and attractively.* ADV: ADV with v

**im|ag|ine** /ɪmædʒɪn/ **(imagines, imagining, imagined)** ◆◆◇ 1 If you **imagine** something, you think about it and your mind forms a picture or idea of it. ❑ *He could not imagine a more peaceful scene... Can you imagine how she must have felt when Mary Brent turned up with me in tow?... Imagine you're lying on a beach, listening to the steady rhythm of waves lapping the shore... I can't imagine you being unfair to anyone, Leigh.* VERB V n/-ing V wh V that V n -ing/prep 2 If you **imagine** that something is the case, you think that it is the case. ❑ *I imagine you're referring to Jean-Paul Sartre... 'Was he meeting someone?' — 'I imagine so.'* VERB = suppose V that V *so/not* 3 If you **imagine** something, you think that you have seen, heard, or experienced that thing, although actually you have not. ❑ *I realised that I must have imagined the whole thing.* VERB = dream V n Also V that

**im|ag|ing** /ɪmɪdʒɪŋ/ **Imaging** is the process of forming images that represent things such as sound waves, temperature, chemicals, or electrical activity. [TECHNICAL] ❑ *...thermal imaging cameras.* N-UNCOUNT

**im|ag|in|ings** /ɪmædʒɪnɪŋz/ **Imaginings** are things that you think you have seen or heard, although they have not. [LITERARY] N-PLURAL

**imam** /ɪmɑːm/ **(imams)** In Islam, an **imam** is a religious leader, especially the leader of a Muslim community or the person who leads the prayers in a mosque. N-COUNT

**IMAX** /aɪmæks/ **IMAX** is a system for showing films on very large screens with very clear sound and pictures. [TRADEMARK] ❑ *...a new IMAX cinema.* N-UNCOUNT: oft N n

**im|bal|ance** /ɪmbæləns/ **(imbalances)** If there is an **imbalance** in a situation, the things involved are not the same size, or are not the right size in proportion to each other. ❑ *...the imbalance between the two sides in this war.* N-VAR: oft N *in/between* pl-n

**im|bal|anced** /ɪmbælənst/ If you describe a situation as **imbalanced**, you mean that the elements within it are not evenly or fairly arranged. ❑ *...the present imbalanced structure of world trade.* ADJ = uneven

**im|becile** /ɪmbɪsiːl, AM -səl/ **(imbeciles)** 1 If you call someone an **imbecile**, you are showing that you think they are stupid or have done something stupid. ❑ *I don't want to deal with these imbeciles any longer.* N-COUNT [disapproval] = idiot 2 **Imbecile** means stupid. ❑ *It was an imbecile thing to do.* ADJ: ADJ n

**im|bibe** /ɪmbaɪb/ **(imbibes, imbibing, imbibed)** 1 To **imbibe** alcohol means to drink it. [FORMAL, often HUMOROUS] ❑ *They were used to imbibing enormous quantities of alcohol... No one believes that current nondrinkers should be encouraged to start imbibing.* VERB V n V 2 If you **imbibe** ideas or arguments, you listen to them, accept them, and believe that they are right or true. [FORMAL] ❑ *As a clergyman's son he'd imbibed a set of mystical beliefs from the cradle.* VERB = absorb V n

**im|bro|glio** /ɪmbroʊlioʊ/ **(imbroglios)** An **imbroglio** is a very confusing or complicated situation. [LITERARY] N-COUNT: usu with supp

**im|bue** /ɪmbjuː/ **(imbues, imbuing, imbued)** If someone or something **is imbued** with an idea, feeling, or quality, they become filled with it. [FORMAL] ❑ *As you listen, you notice how every single word is imbued with a breathless sense of wonder. ...men who can imbue their hearers with enthusiasm.* VERB = infuse be V-ed *with* n V n *with* n ♦ **im|bued** *...a Guards officer imbued with a military sense of duty and loyalty.* ADJ: v-link ADJ *with* n

**IMF** /aɪ em ef/ **The IMF** is an international agency which tries to promote trade and improve economic conditions in poorer countries, sometimes by lending them money. **IMF** is an abbreviation for 'International Monetary Fund'. ◆◇◇ N-PROPER: *the* N

**IMHO** **IMHO** is the written abbreviation for 'in my humble opinion', mainly used in text messages and e-mails. [COMPUTING]

**imi|tate** /ɪmɪteɪt/ **(imitates, imitating, imitated)** [1] If you **imitate** someone, you copy what they do or produce. ❑ *...a genuine German musical which does not try to imitate the American model.* VERB V n
[2] If you **imitate** a person or animal, you copy the way they speak or behave, usually because you are trying to be funny. ❑ *Clarence screws up his face and imitates the Colonel again.* VERB = mimic V n

**imi|ta|tion** /ɪmɪteɪʃən/ **(imitations)** [1] An **imitation** of something is a copy of it. ❑ *...the most accurate imitation of Chinese architecture in Europe.* N-COUNT: oft N *of* n [2] **Imitation** means copying someone else's actions. ❑ *They discussed important issues in imitation of their elders.* N-UNCOUNT: oft *in* N *of* n [3] **Imitation** things are not genuine but are made to look as if they are. ❑ *...a complete set of Dickens bound in imitation leather.* ADJ: ADJ n [4] If someone does an **imitation of** another person, they copy the way they speak or behave, sometimes in order to be funny. ❑ *He gave his imitation of Queen Elizabeth's royal wave.* N-COUNT: usu N *of* n = impersonation

**imi|ta|tive** /ɪmɪtətɪv, AM -teɪt-/ People and animals who are **imitative** copy others' behaviour. ❑ *Babies of eight to twelve months are generally highly imitative.* ADJ

**imi|ta|tor** /ɪmɪteɪtə^r/ **(imitators)** An **imitator** is someone who copies what someone else does, or copies the way they speak or behave. ❑ *He doesn't take chances; that's why he's survived and most of his imitators haven't. ...a group of Elvis imitators.* N-COUNT

**im|macu|late** /ɪmækjʊlət/ [1] If you describe something as **immaculate**, you mean that it is extremely clean, tidy, or neat. ❑ *Her front room was kept immaculate.* ♦ **im|macu|late|ly** *As always he was immaculately dressed.* ADJ = pristine ADV [2] If you say that something is **immaculate**, you are emphasizing that it is perfect, without any mistakes or bad parts at all. ❑ *The goalkeeper's performance was immaculate.* ♦ **im|macu|late|ly** *The orchestra plays immaculately.* ADJ [emphasis] = flawless ADV: ADV with v

**im|ma|nent** /ɪmənənt/ If you say that a quality is **immanent** in a particular thing, you mean that the thing has that quality, and cannot exist or be imagined without it. [FORMAL] ADJ

**im|ma|teri|al** /ɪmətɪəriəl/ If you say that something is **immaterial**, you mean that it is not important or not relevant. ❑ *Whether we like him or not is immaterial.* ADJ: v-link ADJ = irrelevant

**im|ma|ture** /ɪmətjʊə^r, AM -tʊr/ [1] Something or someone that is **immature** is not yet completely grown or fully developed. ❑ *She is emotionally immature.* ♦ **im|ma|tu|rity** /ɪmətjʊərɪti, AM -tʊr-/ *In spite of some immaturity in the figure drawing and painting, it showed real imagination.* ADJ N-UNCOUNT [2] If you describe someone as **immature**, you are being critical of them because they do not behave in a sensible or responsible way. ❑ *She's just being childish and immature.* ♦ **im|ma|tu|rity** *...his immaturity and lack of social skills.* ADJ [disapproval] N-UNCOUNT

**im|meas|ur|able** /ɪmeʒərəbəl/ If you describe something as **immeasurable**, you are emphasizing how great it is. [FORMAL] ❑ *His contribution is immeasurable.* ADJ [emphasis]

**im|meas|ur|ably** /ɪmeʒərəbli/ You use **immeasurably** to emphasize the degree or extent of a process or quality. [FORMAL] ❑ *They have improved immeasurably since their arrival.* ADV: ADV with v, ADV adj [emphasis] = infinitely

**im|medi|acy** /ɪmiːdiəsi/ The **immediacy** of an event or situation is the quality that it has which makes it seem important or exciting because it is happening at the present time. ❑ *Do they understand the immediacy of the crisis?* N-UNCOUNT: oft N *of* n

**im|medi|ate** /ɪmiːdiət/ [1] An **immediate** result, action, or reaction happens or is done without any delay. ❑ *These tragic incidents have had an immediate effect... My immediate reaction was just disgust.* ◆◇◇ ADJ: usu ADJ n = instant [2] **Immediate** needs and concerns exist at the present time and must be dealt with quickly. ❑ *Relief agencies say the immediate problem is not a lack of food, but transportation.* ADJ: usu ADJ n = pressing [3] The **immediate** person or thing comes just before or just after another person or thing in a sequence. ❑ *His immediate superior, General Geichenko, had singled him out for special mention.* ADJ: ADJ n [4] You use **immediate** to describe an area or position that is next to or very near a particular place or person. ❑ *Only a handful had returned to work in the immediate vicinity.* ADJ: ADJ n [5] Your **immediate** family are the members of your family who are most closely related to you, for example your parents, children, brothers, and sisters. ADJ: ADJ n

**im|medi|ate|ly** /ɪmiːdiətli/ [1] If something happens **immediately**, it happens without any delay. ❑ *He immediately flung himself to the floor... Ingrid answered Peter's letter immediately.* ◆◆◇ ADV: ADV with v
[2] If something is **immediately** obvious, it can be seen or understood without any delay. ❑ *The cause of the accident was not immediately apparent.* ADV: ADV adj = instantly
[3] **Immediately** is used to indicate that someone or something is closely and directly involved in a situation. ❑ *The man immediately responsible for this misery is the province's governor.* ADV: ADV adj/-ed [4] **Immediately** is used to emphasize that something comes next, or is next to something else. ❑ *She always sits immediately behind the driver.* ADV: ADV prep/adj = directly [5] If one thing happens **immediately** something else happens, it happens after that event, without any delay. [mainly BRIT] ❑ *Immediately I've done it I feel completely disgusted with myself.* CONJ

**im|memo|ri|al** /ɪmɪmɔːriəl/ If you say that something has been happening **since time immemorial** or **from time immemorial**, you are emphasizing that it has been happening for many centuries. [LITERARY] ❑ *It has remained virtually unchanged since time immemorial.* PHRASE [emphasis]

**im|mense** /ɪmens/ If you describe something as **immense**, you mean that it is extremely large or great. ❑ *...an immense cloud of smoke... With immense relief I stopped running.* ♦ **im|men|si|ty** /ɪmensɪti/ *The immensity of the universe is difficult to grasp.* ADJ: usu ADJ n = enormous N-UNCOUNT: usu N *of* n

**im|mense|ly** /ɪmensli/ You use **immensely** to emphasize the degree or extent of a quality, feeling, or process. ❑ *I enjoyed this movie immensely.* ADV: usu ADV adj, also ADV after v [emphasis]

**im|merse** /ɪmɜː^rs/ **(immerses, immersing, immersed)** [1] If you **immerse** yourself in something that you are doing, you become completely involved in it. ❑ *Since then I've lived alone and immersed myself in my career.* ♦ **im|mersed** *He's really becoming immersed in his work.* VERB V pron-refl *in* n ADJ: v-link ADJ *in* n [2] If something **is immersed** in a liquid, someone puts it into the liquid so that it is completely covered. ❑ *The electrodes are immersed in liquid.* VERB: usu passive *be* V-ed *in* n

**im|mer|sion** /ɪmɜː^rʃən/ [1] Someone's **immersion in** a subject is their complete involvement in it. ❑ *...long-term assignments that allowed them total immersion in their subjects.* N-UNCOUNT: N *in* n
[2] **Immersion** of something in a liquid means putting it into the liquid so that it is completely covered. ❑ *The wood had become swollen from prolonged immersion.* N-UNCOUNT: oft N *in* n

**im|mi|grant** /ɪmɪgrənt/ **(immigrants)** An **immigrant** is a person who has come to live in a country from some other country. Compare **emigrant**. ❑ *...illegal immigrants. ...immigrant visas.* ◆◇◇ N-COUNT

**im|mi|grate** /ɪmɪgreɪt/ **(immigrates, immigrating, immigrated)** If someone **immigrates** to a particular country, they come to live or work in that country, after leaving the country where they were born. ❑ *...a Russian-born professor who had immigrated to the United States... He immigrated from Ulster in 1848... 10,000 people are expected to immigrate in the next two years.* VERB: no passive V *to* n V *from* n V

**im|mi|gra|tion** /ɪmɪgreɪʃən/ [1] **Immigration** is the coming of people into a country in order to live and work there. ❑ *The government has decided to tighten its immigration policy.* ◆◇◇ N-UNCOUNT
[2] **Immigration** or **immigration control** is the place at a port, airport, or international border N-UNCOUNT

where officials check the passports of people who wish to come into the country.

**im|mi|nent** /ɪmɪnənt/ [ADJ] If you say that something is **imminent**, especially something unpleasant, you mean it is almost certain to happen very soon. ❑ *There appeared no imminent danger.* ♦ **im|mi|nence** [N-UNCOUNT: usu N *of* n] *The imminence of war was on everyone's mind.*

**im|mo|bile** /ɪmoʊbaɪl, AM -bᵊl/ 1 [ADJ: usu v-link ADJ = motionless] Someone or something that is **immobile** is completely still. ❑ *Joe remained as immobile as if he had been carved out of rock.* ♦ **im|mo|bil|ity** /ɪmoʊbɪlɪti/ [N-UNCOUNT] *Hyde maintained the rigid immobility of his shoulders.* 2 [ADJ: usu v-link ADJ] Someone or something that is **immobile** is unable to move or unable to be moved. ❑ *A riding accident left him immobile.* ♦ **im|mo|bil|ity** [N-UNCOUNT] *Again, the pain locked me into immobility.*

**im|mo|bi|lize** /ɪmoʊbɪlaɪz/ **(immobilizes, immobilizing, immobilized)**

✓ in BRIT, also use **immobilise**

[VERB] To **immobilize** something or someone means to stop them from moving or operating. ❑ [V n] *...a car alarm system that immobilises the engine.*

**im|mo|bi|liz|er** /ɪmoʊbɪlaɪzəʳ/ **(immobilizers)**

✓ in BRIT, also use **immobiliser**

[N-COUNT] An **immobilizer** is a device on a car which prevents it from starting unless a special key is used, so that no one can steal the car.

**im|mod|er|ate** /ɪmɒdərət/ [ADJ: usu ADJ n; disapproval; = excessive] If you describe something as **immoderate**, you disapprove of it because it is too extreme. [FORMAL] ❑ *He launched an immoderate tirade on Turner.*

**im|mod|est** /ɪmɒdɪst/ 1 [ADJ: usu ADJ n] If you describe someone's behaviour as **immodest**, you mean that it shocks or embarrasses you because you think that it is rude. 2 [ADJ: usu v-link ADJ; disapproval; = boastful; ≠ modest] If you say that someone is **immodest**, you disapprove of the way in which they often say how good, important, or clever they are. ❑ *He could become ungraciously immodest about his own capacities.*

**im|mor|al** /ɪmɒrᵊl, AM -mɔːr-/ [ADJ; disapproval] If you describe someone or their behaviour as **immoral**, you believe that their behaviour is morally wrong. ❑ *...those who think that birth control and abortion are immoral.* ♦ **im|mo|ral|ity** /ɪməræ̱lɪti/ [N-UNCOUNT] *...a reflection of our society's immorality.*

**im|mor|tal** /ɪmɔ̱ːʳtᵊl/ **(immortals)** 1 [ADJ] Someone or something that is **immortal** is famous and likely to be remembered for a long time. ❑ *...Wuthering Heights, Emily Bronte's immortal love story.* ♦ [N-COUNT: usu pl] An **immortal** is someone who is immortal. ❑ *He called Moore 'one of the immortals of soccer'.* ♦ **im|mor|tal|ity** /ɪmɔːʳtæ̱lɪti/ [N-UNCOUNT] *Some people want to achieve immortality through their works.* 2 [ADJ; ≠ mortal] Someone or something that is **immortal** will live or last for ever and never die or be destroyed. ❑ *The pharaohs were considered gods and therefore immortal.* ♦ [N-COUNT: usu pl] An **immortal** is an immortal being. ❑ *...porcelain figurines of the Chinese immortals.* ♦ **im|mor|tal|ity** [N-UNCOUNT] *The Greeks accepted belief in the immortality of the soul.* 3 [ADJ: ADJ n] If you refer to someone's **immortal** words, you mean that what they said is well-known, and you are usually about to quote it. ❑ *...Roosevelt's immortal words, 'Speak softly and carry a big stick.'*

**im|mor|tal|ize** /ɪmɔ̱ːʳtəlaɪz/ **(immortalizes, immortalizing, immortalized)**

✓ in BRIT, also use **immortalise**

[VERB] If someone or something **is immortalized** in a story, film, or work of art, they appear in it, and will be remembered for it. [WRITTEN] ❑ [*be* V-ed] *The town of Whitby was immortalised in Bram Stoker's famous Dracula story...* [V n] *D H Lawrence immortalised her in his novel 'Women in Love'.*

**im|mov|able** /ɪmu̱ːvəbᵊl/ 1 [ADJ: usu ADJ n] An **immovable** object is fixed and cannot be moved. 2 [ADJ: usu v-link ADJ; = resolute] If someone is **immovable** in their attitude to something, they will not change their mind. ❑ *On one issue, however, she was immovable.*

**im|mune** /ɪmju̱ːn/ ◆◇◇ 1 [ADJ: v-link ADJ, usu ADJ *to* n] If you are **immune to** a particular disease, you cannot be affected by it. ❑ *Most adults are immune to Rubella.* ♦ **im|mun|ity** /ɪmju̱ːnɪti/ [N-UNCOUNT: oft N *to* n] *Birds in outside cages develop immunity to airborne bacteria.* 2 [ADJ: v-link ADJ, usu ADJ *to* n] If you are **immune to** something that happens or is done, you are not affected by it. ❑ *Football is not immune to economic recession.* 3 [ADJ: v-link ADJ, usu ADJ *from* n] Someone or something that is **immune from** a particular process or situation is able to escape it. ❑ *Members of the Bundestag are immune from prosecution for corruption.* ♦ **im|mun|ity** [N-UNCOUNT] *The police are offering immunity to witnesses.* → See also **diplomatic immunity**.

**im|mune sys|tem** **(immune systems)** [N-COUNT: usu sing] Your **immune system** consists of all the organs and processes in your body which protect you from illness and infection.

**im|mun|ize** /ɪmjʊnaɪz/ **(immunizes, immunizing, immunized)**

✓ in BRIT, also use **immunise**

[VERB: usu passive] If people or animals **are immunized**, they are made immune to a particular disease, often by being given an injection. ❑ [*be* V-ed *against* n] *We should require that every student is immunized against hepatitis B...* [*be* V-ed] *The monkeys had been immunized with a vaccine made from infected cells...* [*have* n V-ed] *All parents should have their children immunized.* ♦ **im|mun|iza|tion** /ɪmjʊnaɪze̱ɪʃᵊn/ **(immunizations)** [N-VAR] *...universal immunization against childhood diseases.*

**im|mu|table** /ɪmju̱ːtəbᵊl/ [ADJ] Something that is **immutable** will never change or cannot be changed. [FORMAL] ❑ *...the eternal and immutable principles of right and wrong.*

**imp** /ɪmp/ **(imps)** 1 [N-COUNT = sprite] In fairy stories, an **imp** is a small, magical creature that often causes trouble in a playful way. 2 [N-COUNT] People sometimes refer to a naughty child as an **imp**. [INFORMAL]

**im|pact** **(impacts, impacting, impacted)** ◆◆◇

✓ The noun is pronounced /ɪmpækt/. The verb is pronounced /ɪmpæ̱kt/.

1 [N-COUNT: usu sing, oft N *on* n] The **impact** that something has **on** a situation, process, or person is a sudden and powerful effect that it has on them. ❑ *They say they expect the meeting to have a marked impact on the future of the country... When an executive comes into a new job, he wants to quickly make an impact.* 2 [N-VAR] An **impact** is the action of one object hitting another, or the force with which one object hits another. ❑ *The plane is destroyed, a complete wreck: the pilot must have died on impact.* 3 [VERB] To **impact on** a situation, process, or person means to affect them. ❑ [V *on/upon* n] *Such schemes mean little unless they impact on people.* [V n] *...the potential for women to impact the political process.* 4 [VERB] If one object **impacts on** another, it hits it with great force. [FORMAL] ❑ [V *on/upon/with* n] *...the sharp tinkle of metal impacting on stone...* [V n] *When a large object impacts the Earth, it makes a crater.*

**im|pair** /ɪmpe̱əʳ/ **(impairs, impairing, impaired)** [VERB] If something **impairs** something such as an ability or the way something works, it damages it or makes it worse. [FORMAL] ❑ [V n] *Consumption of alcohol impairs your ability to drive a car or operate machinery.* ♦ **im|paired** [ADJ] *The blast left him with permanently impaired hearing.*

**-impaired** /-ɪmpe̱əʳd/ [COMB in ADJ] You use **-impaired** in adjectives where you are describing someone with a particular disability. For example, someone who is **hearing-impaired** has a disability affecting their hearing, and someone who is **visually-impaired** has a disability affecting their sight. ❑ *More than 1 in 20 of the population is hearing-impaired to some extent.* ♦ [COMB in N-PLURAL: *the* N] **The hearing-impaired** or **the visually-impaired** are people with disabilities affecting their hearing or sight. ❑ *...giving a voice to the speech-impaired.*

**im|pair|ment** /ɪmpe̱əʳmənt/ **(impairments)** [N-VAR: usu with supp] If someone has an **impairment**, they have a condition which prevents their eyes, ears, or brain from working properly. ❑ *He has a visual impairment in the right eye.*

**im|pale** /ɪmpeɪl/ **(impales, impaling, impaled)** [VERB] To **impale** something on a pointed object means to cause the point to go into it or through it. ❑ *Researchers observed one bird impale a rodent on a cactus.* [V n *on* n; Also V n, V n *with* n]

**im|part** /ɪmpɑːʳt/ **(imparts, imparting, imparted)** 1 If you **impart** information **to** people, you tell it to them. [FORMAL] ❑ *The ability to impart knowledge and command respect is the essential qualification for teachers... I am about to impart knowledge to you that you will never forget.* [VERB = convey; V n; V n *to* n] 2 To **impart** a particular quality to something means to give it that quality. [FORMAL] ❑ *She managed to impart great elegance to the unpretentious dress she was wearing.* [VERB; V n *to* n]

**im|par|tial** /ɪmpɑːʳʃəl/ Someone who is **impartial** is not directly involved in a particular situation, and is therefore able to give a fair opinion or decision about it. ❑ *Careers officers offer impartial advice to all pupils.* [ADJ ≠ partial, biased] ♦ **im|par|tial|ity** /ɪmpɑːʳʃiælɪti/ *...a justice system lacking impartiality by democratic standards.* [N-UNCOUNT] ♦ **im|par|tial|ly** *He has vowed to oversee the elections impartially.* [ADV: ADV with v]

**im|pass|able** /ɪmpɑːsəbəl, -pæs-/ If a road, path, or route is **impassable**, it is impossible to travel over because it is blocked or in bad condition. [ADJ]

**im|passe** /æmpæs, ɪm-/ If people are in a difficult position in which it is impossible to make any progress, you can refer to the situation as an **impasse**. ❑ *The company says it has reached an impasse in negotiations with the union.* [N-SING = deadlock]

**im|pas|sioned** /ɪmpæʃənd/ An **impassioned** speech or piece of writing is one in which someone expresses their strong feelings about an issue in a forceful way. [JOURNALISM or WRITTEN] ❑ *He made an impassioned appeal for peace.* [ADJ: usu ADJ n = fervent]

**im|pas|sive** /ɪmpæsɪv/ If someone is **impassive** or their face is **impassive**, they are not showing any emotion. [WRITTEN] ❑ *He searched Hill's impassive face for some indication that he understood.* [ADJ] ♦ **im|pas|sive|ly** *The lawyer looked impassively at him and said nothing.* [ADV: ADV with v]

**im|pa|tient** /ɪmpeɪʃənt/ 1 If you are **impatient**, you are annoyed because you have to wait too long for something. ❑ *The big clubs are becoming increasingly impatient at the rate of progress.* [ADJ: v-link ADJ] ♦ **im|pa|tient|ly** *People have been waiting impatiently for a chance to improve the situation.* [ADV: ADV with v] ♦ **im|pa|tience** /ɪmpeɪʃəns/ *There is considerable impatience with the slow pace of political change.* [N-UNCOUNT] 2 If you are **impatient**, you are easily irritated by things. ❑ *Beware of being too impatient with others.* [ADJ] ♦ **im|pa|tient|ly** *'Come on, David,' Harry said impatiently.* [ADV: ADV with v] ♦ **im|pa|tience** *There was a hint of impatience in his tone.* [N-UNCOUNT] 3 If you are **impatient to** do something or **impatient for** something to happen, you are eager to do it or for it to happen and do not want to wait. ❑ *He was impatient to get home.* [ADJ: v-link ADJ, ADJ to-inf, ADJ *for* n] ♦ **im|pa|tience** *She showed impatience to continue the climb.* [N-UNCOUNT: N to-inf, N *for* n]

**im|peach** /ɪmpiːtʃ/ **(impeaches, impeaching, impeached)** If a court or a group in authority **impeaches** a president or other senior official, it charges them with committing a crime which makes them unfit for office. ❑ *...an opposition move to impeach the President.* [VERB; V n]

**im|peach|ment** /ɪmpiːtʃmənt/ **(impeachments)** The **impeachment** of a senior official is their trial for a crime which makes them unfit for office. ❑ *There are grounds for impeachment.* [N-VAR]

**im|pec|cable** /ɪmpekəbəl/ If you describe something such as someone's behaviour or appearance as **impeccable**, you are emphasizing that it is perfect and has no faults. ❑ *She had impeccable taste in clothes.* [ADJ; emphasis] ♦ **im|pec|cably** /ɪmpekəbli/ *He was impeccably polite.* [ADV]

**im|pecu|ni|ous** /ɪmpɪkjuːniəs/ Someone who is **impecunious** has very little money. [FORMAL] [ADJ = poor]

**im|pede** /ɪmpiːd/ **(impedes, impeding, impeded)** If you **impede** someone or something, you make their movement, development, or progress difficult. [FORMAL] ❑ *Fallen rock is impeding the progress of rescue workers.* [VERB = hinder, hamper; V n]

**im|pedi|ment** /ɪmpedɪmənt/ **(impediments)** 1 Something that is an **impediment to** a person or thing makes their movement, development, or progress difficult. [FORMAL] ❑ *He was satisfied there was no legal impediment to the marriage.* [N-COUNT: oft N *to* n, also *without* N = obstacle] 2 Someone who has a speech **impediment** has a disability which makes speaking difficult. [N-COUNT]

**im|pel** /ɪmpel/ **(impels, impelling, impelled)** When something such as an emotion **impels** you **to** do something, it affects you so strongly that you feel forced to do it. ❑ *...the courage and competitiveness which impels him to take risks.* [VERB = force, compel; V n to-inf]

**im|pend|ing** /ɪmpendɪŋ/ An **impending** event is one that is going to happen very soon. [FORMAL] ❑ *On the morning of the expedition I awoke with a feeling of impending disaster.* [ADJ: ADJ n]

**im|pen|etrable** /ɪmpenɪtrəbəl/ 1 If you describe something such as a barrier or a forest as **impenetrable**, you mean that it is impossible or very difficult to get through. ❑ *...the Caucasus range, an almost impenetrable barrier between Europe and Asia.* [ADJ: usu ADJ n] 2 If you describe something such as a book or a theory as **impenetrable**, you are emphasizing that it is impossible or very difficult to understand. ❑ *His books are notoriously impenetrable.* [ADJ; emphasis; = incomprehensible] ♦ **im|pen|etrably** *...impenetrably detailed reports on product sales.* [ADV: ADV adj]

**im|pera|tive** /ɪmperətɪv/ **(imperatives)** 1 If it is **imperative** that something is done, that thing is extremely important and must be done. [FORMAL] ❑ *It was imperative that he act as naturally as possible.* [ADJ: usu v-link ADJ = vital] 2 An **imperative** is something that is extremely important and must be done. [FORMAL] ❑ *The most important political imperative is to limit the number of US casualties.* [N-COUNT: usu with supp] 3 In grammar, a clause that is in **the imperative**, or in **the imperative** mood, contains the base form of a verb and usually has no subject. Examples are 'Go away' and 'Please be careful'. Clauses of this kind are typically used to tell someone to do something. [N-SING: *the* N] 4 An **imperative** is a verb in the base form that is used, usually without a subject, in an imperative clause. [N-COUNT]

**im|per|cep|tible** /ɪmpəʳseptɪbəl/ Something that is **imperceptible** is so small that it is not noticed or cannot be seen. ❑ *Brian's hesitation was almost imperceptible.* [ADJ] ♦ **im|per|cep|tibly** /ɪmpərseptɪbli/ *The disease develops gradually and imperceptibly.* [ADV: usu ADV with v, also ADV adj]

**im|per|fect** /ɪmpɜːʳfɪkt/ 1 Something that is **imperfect** has faults and is not exactly as you would like it to be. [FORMAL] ❑ *We live in an imperfect world.* [ADJ ≠ perfect] ♦ **im|per|fect|ly** *This effect was imperfectly understood by designers at that time.* [ADV: usu ADV -ed/adj] 2 In grammar, **the imperfect** or **the imperfect** tense of a verb is used to describe continuous situations or repeated actions in the past. Examples are 'I was reading' and 'they were eating'. [N-SING: *the* N]

**im|per|fec|tion** /ɪmpəʳfekʃən/ **(imperfections)** 1 An **imperfection in** someone or something is a fault, weakness, or undesirable feature that they have. ❑ *He concedes that there are imperfections in the socialist system.* [N-VAR = flaw, failing] 2 An **imperfection in** something is a small mark or damaged area which may spoil its appearance. ❑ *...imperfections in the cloth.* [N-COUNT = flaw, blemish]

**im|perial** /ɪmpɪəriəl/ 1 **Imperial** is used to refer to things or people that are or were connected with an empire. ❑ *...the Imperial Palace in Tokyo.* [ADJ: ADJ n] 2 The **imperial** system of measurement uses inches, feet, and yards to measure length, ounces [ADJ: ADJ n] and pounds to measure weight, and pints and gallons to measure volume.

**im|peri|al|ism** /ɪmpɪə̲riəlɪzəm/ **Imperialism** is a system in which a rich and powerful country controls other countries, or a desire for control over other countries. N-UNCOUNT

**im|peri|al|ist** /ɪmpɪə̲riəlɪst/ **(imperialists)** **Imperialist** means relating to or based on imperialism. ❑ *The developed nations have all benefited from their imperialist exploitation.* ♦ An **imperialist** is someone who has imperialist views. ADJ: usu ADJ n / N-COUNT

**im|peri|al|is|tic** /ɪmpɪə̲riəlɪ̲stɪk/ If you describe a country as **imperialistic**, you disapprove of it because it wants control over other countries. ADJ [disapproval]

**im|per|il** /ɪmpe̲rɪl/ **(imperils, imperilling, imperilled)**

> in AM, use **imperiling**, **imperiled**

Something that **imperils** you puts you in danger. [FORMAL] ❑ *You imperilled the lives of other road users by your driving.* VERB = endanger V n

**im|peri|ous** /ɪmpɪə̲riəs/ If you describe someone as **imperious**, you mean that they have a proud manner and expect to be obeyed. [WRITTEN] ❑ *Her attitude is imperious at times.* ♦ **im|peri|ous|ly** *Imperiously she beckoned me out of the room.* ADJ = haughty / ADV: ADV with v

**im|per|ish|able** /ɪmpe̲rɪʃəbᵊl/ Something that is **imperishable** cannot disappear or be destroyed. [LITERARY] ❑ *My memories are within me, imperishable.* ADJ

**im|per|ma|nent** /ɪmpɜ̲ːʳmənənt/ Something that is **impermanent** does not last for ever. [FORMAL] ❑ *We are reminded just how small and how impermanent we are.* ♦ **im|per|ma|nence** /ɪmpɜ̲ːʳmənəns/ *He was convinced of the impermanence of his work.* ADJ = transient ≠ permanent / N-UNCOUNT

**im|per|meable** /ɪmpɜ̲ːʳmiəbᵊl/ Something that is **impermeable** will not allow fluid to pass through it. [FORMAL] ❑ *The canoe is made from an impermeable wood.* ADJ = waterproof

**im|per|son|al** /ɪmpɜ̲ːʳsənᵊl/ [1] If you describe a place, organization, or activity as **impersonal**, you mean that it is not very friendly and makes you feel unimportant because it involves or is used by a large number of people. ❑ *Before then many children were cared for in large impersonal orphanages.* [2] If you describe someone's behaviour as **impersonal**, you mean that they do not show any emotion about the person they are dealing with. ❑ *We must be as impersonal as a surgeon with his knife.* ♦ **im|per|son|al|ly** *The doctor treated Ted gently but impersonally.* [3] An **impersonal** room or statistic does not give any information about the character of the person to whom it belongs or relates. ❑ *The rest of the room was neat and impersonal.* ADJ [disapproval] / ADJ / ADV / ADJ

**im|per|son|ate** /ɪmpɜ̲ːʳsəneɪt/ **(impersonates, impersonating, impersonated)** If someone **impersonates** a person, they pretend to be that person, either to deceive people or to make people laugh. ❑ *He was returned to prison in 1977 for impersonating a police officer.* ♦ **im|per|sona|tion** /ɪmpɜ̲ːʳsəne̲ɪʃᵊn/ **(impersonations)** *She did impersonations of his teachers.* VERB V n / N-COUNT: oft N of n

**im|per|sona|tor** /ɪmpɜ̲ːʳsəneɪtəʳ/ **(impersonators)** An **impersonator** is a stage performer who impersonates famous people. N-COUNT = impressionist

**im|per|ti|nence** /ɪmpɜ̲ːʳtɪnəns/ **(impertinences)** If someone talks or behaves in a rather impolite and disrespectful way, you can call this behaviour **impertinence** or **an impertinence**. ❑ *He was punished for his impertinence.* N-VAR = impudence, cheek

**im|per|ti|nent** /ɪmpɜ̲ːʳtɪnənt/ If someone talks or behaves in a rather impolite and disrespectful way, you can say that they are being **impertinent**. ❑ *Would it be impertinent to ask where exactly you were?* ADJ: oft it v-link ADJ to-inf = impudent, cheeky

**im|per|turb|able** /ɪmpəʳtɜ̲ːʳbəbᵊl/ If you describe someone as **imperturbable**, you mean that they remain calm, even in disturbing or dangerous situations. [WRITTEN] ❑ *Thomas, of course, was cool and aloof and imperturbable.* ADJ

**im|per|vi|ous** /ɪmpɜ̲ːʳviəs/ [1] If you are **impervious to** someone's actions, you are not affected or influenced by them. ❑ *She seems almost impervious to the criticism from all sides.* [2] Something that is **impervious to** water, heat, or a particular object is able to resist it or stop it passing through it. ❑ *The floorcovering you select will need to be impervious to water.* ADJ: usu v-link ADJ, usu ADJ to n / ADJ: oft ADJ to n = impermeable

**im|petu|os|ity** /ɪmpe̲tʃuɒ̲sɪti/ **Impetuosity** is the quality of being impetuous. ❑ *With characteristic impetuosity, he announced he was leaving school.* N-UNCOUNT

**im|petu|ous** /ɪmpe̲tʃuəs/ If you describe someone as **impetuous**, you mean that they are likely to act quickly and suddenly without thinking or being careful. ❑ *He was young and impetuous.* ADJ = rash, impulsive

**im|petus** /ɪ̲mpɪtəs/ Something that gives a process **impetus** or an **impetus** makes it happen or progress more quickly. ❑ *This decision will give renewed impetus to the economic regeneration of east London.* N-UNCOUNT: also a N, oft N for n = stimulus

**im|pinge** /ɪmpɪ̲ndʒ/ **(impinges, impinging, impinged)** Something that **impinges on** you affects you to some extent. [FORMAL] ❑ *...the cuts in defence spending that have impinged on two of the region's largest employers.* VERB = impact V on/upon n

**im|pi|ous** /ɪ̲mpiəs/ If you describe someone as **impious**, you mean that they show a lack of respect for religious things. [FORMAL] ADJ = irreverent

**imp|ish** /ɪ̲mpɪʃ/ If you describe someone or their behaviour as **impish**, you mean that they are rather disrespectful or naughty in a playful way. ❑ *Gillespie is well known for his impish sense of humour.* ♦ **imp|ish|ly** *He smiled at me impishly.* ADJ / ADV

**im|plac|able** /ɪmplæ̲kəbᵊl/ If you say that someone is **implacable**, you mean that they have very strong feelings of hostility or disapproval which nobody can change. ❑ *...the threat of invasion by a ruthless and implacable enemy.* ♦ **im|plac|ably** *His union was implacably opposed to the privatization of the company.* ADJ / ADV: usu ADV -ed/adj, also ADV after v

**im|plant** **(implants, implanting, implanted)**

> The verb is pronounced /ɪmplɑ̲ːnt, -plæ̲nt/. The noun is pronounced /ɪ̲mplɑːnt, -plænt/.

[1] To **implant** something into a person's body means to put it there, usually by means of a medical operation. ❑ *Two days later, they implanted the fertilized eggs back inside me. ...a surgically implanted birth-control device.* ♦ **im|plan|ta|tion** /ɪmplɑːnte̲ɪʃᵊn, -plæn-/ *The embryos were tested to determine their sex prior to implantation.* [2] An **implant** is something that is implanted into a person's body. ❑ *A woman can choose to have breast implants.* [3] When an egg or embryo **implants in** the womb, it becomes established there and can then develop. ❑ *Non-identical twins are the result of two fertilised eggs implanting in the uterus at the same time.* ♦ **im|plan|ta|tion** *...the 11 days required to allow for normal implantation of a fertilized egg.* [4] If you **implant** an idea or attitude **in** people, you make it become accepted or believed. ❑ *The speech implanted a dangerous prejudice in their minds... He is devoting much of his energy to implanting an element of distrust in the community.* VERB V n adv/prep V-ed / N-UNCOUNT / N-COUNT / VERB V in n Also V / N-UNCOUNT / VERB = sow V n in/into n V n

**im|plau|sible** /ɪmplɔ̲ːzɪbᵊl/ If you describe something as **implausible**, you believe that it is unlikely to be true. ❑ *I had to admit it sounded like an implausible excuse.* ♦ **im|plau|sibly** *They are, rather implausibly, close friends.* ADJ / ADV

**im|ple|ment** **(implements, implementing, implemented)** ◆◇◇

> The verb is pronounced /ɪ̲mplɪment/. The noun is pronounced /ɪ̲mplɪmənt/.

[1] If you **implement** something such as a plan, you ensure that what has been planned is done. VERB = carry out

❑ *The government promised to implement a new system to control financial loan institutions.* [V n] ♦ **im|ple|men|ta|tion** /ɪmplɪmənteɪʃən/ *Very little has been achieved in the implementation of the peace agreement signed last January.* [N-UNCOUNT: oft N *of* n] 2 An **implement** is a tool or other piece of equipment. [FORMAL] ❑ *...writing implements.* [N-COUNT]

**im|pli|cate** /ɪmplɪkeɪt/ **(implicates, implicating, implicated)** To **implicate** someone means to show or claim that they were involved in something wrong or criminal. [VERB] ❑ *He was obliged to resign when one of his own aides was implicated in a financial scandal...* [V n *in* n] *He didn't find anything in the notebooks to implicate Stu.* [V n] → See also **implicated**. ♦ **im|pli|ca|tion** *...his implication in a murder.* [N-UNCOUNT]

**im|pli|cat|ed** /ɪmplɪkeɪtɪd/ If someone or something is **implicated in** a crime or a bad situation, they are involved in it or responsible for it. [ADJ: v-link ADJ, usu ADJ *in* n] ❑ *The President was implicated in the cover-up and forced to resign.* → See also **implicate**.

**im|pli|ca|tion** /ɪmplɪkeɪʃən/ **(implications)** ◆◇◇ 1 **The implications of** something are the things that are likely to happen as a result. [N-COUNT: usu pl, oft N *of/for* n = consequence] ❑ *The Attorney General was aware of the political implications of his decision to prosecute... The low level of current investment has serious implications for future economic growth.* 2 **The implication** of a statement, event, or situation is what it implies or suggests is the case. [N-COUNT = inference] ❑ *The implication was obvious: vote for us or it will be very embarrassing for you.* ● If you say that something is the case **by implication**, you mean that a statement, event, or situation implies that it is the case. [PHRASE: PHR with cl/group] ❑ *His authority and, by implication, that of his management team is under threat.* 3 → See also **implicate**.

**im|plic|it** /ɪmplɪsɪt/ 1 Something that is **implicit** is expressed in an indirect way. [ADJ ≠ explicit] ❑ *This is seen as an implicit warning not to continue with military action.* ♦ **im|plic|it|ly** *The jury implicitly criticised the government by their verdict.* [ADV: ADV with v] 2 If a quality or element is **implicit in** something, it is involved in it or is shown by it. [FORMAL] [ADJ: v-link ADJ *in* n] ❑ *...the delays implicit in formal council meetings.* 3 If you say that someone has an **implicit** belief or faith in something, you mean that they have complete faith in it and no doubts at all. [ADJ: usu ADJ n = absolute] ❑ *He had implicit faith in the noble intentions of the Emperor.* ♦ **im|plic|it|ly** *I trust him implicitly.* [ADV: ADV after v]

**im|plode** /ɪmploʊd/ **(implodes, imploding, imploded)** 1 If something **implodes**, it collapses into itself in a sudden and violent way. [VERB] ❑ *The engine imploded.* [V] 2 If something such as an organization or a system **implodes**, it suddenly ends completely because it cannot deal with the problems it is experiencing. [VERB = collapse] ❑ *...the possibility that the party may implode in opposition.* [V]

**im|plore** /ɪmplɔːr/ **(implores, imploring, implored)** If you **implore** someone **to** do something, you ask them to do it in a forceful, emotional way. [VERB = beg] ❑ *Opposition leaders this week implored the president to break the deadlock...* [V n to-inf] *'Tell me what to do!' she implored him.* [V n with quote]

**im|plor|ing** /ɪmplɔːrɪŋ/ An **imploring** look, cry, or letter shows that you very much want someone to do something and are afraid they may not do it. [ADJ: ADJ n = pleading] ❑ *Frank looked at Jim with imploring eyes.* ♦ **im|plor|ing|ly** *Michael looked at him imploringly, eyes brimming with tears.* [ADV: ADV after v]

**im|ply** /ɪmplaɪ/ **(implies, implying, implied)** ◆◇◇ 1 If you **imply that** something is the case, you say something which indicates that it is the case in an indirect way. [VERB = suggest] ❑ *'Are you implying that I have something to do with those attacks?' she asked...* [V that] *She felt undermined by the implied criticism.* [V-ed] [Also V n] 2 If an event or situation **implies** that something is the case, it makes you think it likely that it is the case. [VERB = suggest] ❑ *Exports in June rose 1.5%, implying that the economy was stronger than many investors had realized...* [V that] *A 'frontier-free' Europe implies a greatly increased market for all economic operators.* [V n]

**im|po|lite** /ɪmpəlaɪt/ If you say that someone is **impolite**, you mean that they are rather rude and do not have good manners. [ADJ: oft *it* v-link ADJ to-inf ≠ polite] ❑ *It is impolite to ask too many questions.*

**im|pon|der|able** /ɪmpɒndərəbəl/ **(imponderables)** An **imponderable** is something unknown which it is difficult or impossible to estimate or make correct guesses about. [N-COUNT] ❑ *They are speculating on the imponderables of the future.*

**im|port** **(imports, importing, imported)** ◆◆◇

> The verb is pronounced /ɪmpɔːrt/. The noun is pronounced /ɪmpɔːrt/.

1 To **import** products or raw materials means to buy them from another country for use in your own country. [VERB ≠ export] ❑ *Britain last year spent nearly £5000 million more on importing food than selling abroad...* [V n] *To import from Russia, a Ukrainian firm needs Russian roubles.* [V *from* n] *...imported goods from India.* [V-ed] ♦ **Import** is also a noun. [N-UNCOUNT: also N in pl] ❑ *Germany, however, insists on restrictions on the import of Polish coal.* ♦ **im|por|ta|tion** /ɪmpɔːrteɪʃən/ *...restrictions concerning the importation of birds.* [N-UNCOUNT: usu N *of* n] 2 **Imports** are products or raw materials bought from another country for use in your own country. [N-COUNT: usu pl] ❑ *...farmers protesting about cheap imports.* 3 The **import** of something is its importance. [FORMAL] [N-UNCOUNT = consequence] ❑ *Such arguments are of little import.* 4 If you **import** files or information into one type of software from another type, you open them in a format that can be used in the new software. [COMPUTING] [VERB ≠ export] ❑ *You can import files from Microsoft Word 5.1 or MacWrite II.* [V n] 5 The **import** of something is its meaning, especially when the meaning is not clearly expressed. [FORMAL] [N-SING: with poss] ❑ *I have already spoken about the import of his speech.*

**im|por|tance** /ɪmpɔːrtəns/ ◆◇◇ 1 The **importance** of something is its quality of being significant, valued, or necessary in a particular situation. [N-UNCOUNT: oft N *of* n] ❑ *We have always stressed the importance of economic reform... Safety is of paramount importance.* 2 **Importance** means having influence, power, or status. [N-UNCOUNT]

**im|por|tant** /ɪmpɔːrtənt/ ◆◆◆ 1 Something that is **important** is very significant, is highly valued, or is necessary. [ADJ: oft ADJ *to* n, *it* v-link ADJ to-inf/that] ❑ *The planned general strike represents an important economic challenge to the government... It's important to answer her questions as honestly as you can... It was important that he rest.* ♦ **im|por|tant|ly** *I was hungry, and, more importantly, my children were hungry.* [ADV] 2 Someone who is **important** has influence or power within a society or a particular group. [ADJ] ❑ *...an important figure in the media world.*

**im|port|er** /ɪmpɔːrtər/ **(importers)** An **importer** is a country, firm, or person that buys goods from another country for use in their own country. [N-COUNT: oft N *of* n] ❑ *...an importer of exotic food.*

**im|por|tu|nate** /ɪmpɔːrtʃʊnət/ If you describe someone as **importunate**, you think they are annoying because they keep trying to get something from you. [FORMAL] [ADJ] [disapproval] [= troublesome] ❑ *His secretary shielded him from importunate visitors.*

**im|por|tune** /ɪmpɔːrtjuːn, AM -tuːn/ **(importunes, importuning, importuned)** If someone **importunes** another person, they ask them for something or ask them to do something, in an annoying way. [FORMAL] [VERB] [disapproval] [= pester] ❑ *One can no longer walk the streets without seeing beggars importuning passers by.* [V n] [Also V n to-inf, V n *for* n]

**im|pose** /ɪmpoʊz/ **(imposes, imposing, imposed)** ◆◆◇ 1 If you **impose** something **on** people, you use your authority to force them to accept it. [VERB] ❑ *Britain imposed fines on airlines which bring in passengers without proper papers...* [V n *on* n] *Many companies have imposed a pay freeze...* [V n] *The conditions imposed on volunteers were stringent.* [V-ed] ♦ **im|po|si|tion** /ɪmpəzɪʃən/ *...the imposition of a ban on cycling in the city centre.* [N-UNCOUNT: oft N *of* n] 2 If you **impose** your opinions or beliefs **on** other people, you try and make people accept them as a rule or as a model to copy. [VERB] ❑ *Parents of either sex should beware of imposing their* [V n *on* n] own tastes on their children. 3 If something **imposes** strain, pressure, or suffering **on** someone, it causes them to experience it. ❑ *The filming imposed an additional strain on her.* VERB = inflict; V n *on* n

4 If someone **imposes on** you, they unreasonably expect you to do something for them which you do not want to do. ❑ *I was afraid you'd simply feel we were imposing on you.* VERB; V *on/upon* n ♦ **im|po|si|tion** **(impositions)** *I know this is an imposition. But please hear me out.* N-COUNT

5 If someone **imposes themselves on** you, they force you to accept their company although you may not want to. ❑ *I didn't want to impose myself on my married friends.* VERB; V pron-refl *on* n

**im|pos|ing** /ɪmpoʊzɪŋ/ If you describe someone or something as **imposing**, you mean that they have an impressive appearance or manner. ❑ *...the imposing wrought-iron gates at the entrance to the estate.* ADJ

**im|pos|sible** /ɪmpɒsɪbᵊl/ ◆◆◇ 1 Something that is **impossible** cannot be done or cannot happen. ❑ *It was impossible for anyone to get in because no one knew the password... He thinks the tax is impossible to administer... Keller is good at describing music – an almost impossible task to do well.* ADJ: oft *it* v-link ADJ to-inf/that, ADJ to-inf ≠ possible ♦ **The impossible** is something which is impossible. ❑ *They were expected to do the impossible.* N-SING: *the* N ♦ **im|pos|sibly** *Mathematical physics is an almost impossibly difficult subject.* ADV: ADV adj ♦ **im|pos|sibil|ity** /ɪmpɒsɪbɪlɪti/ **(impossibilities)** *...the impossibility of knowing absolute truth.* N-VAR: oft *the* N *of* n

2 An **impossible** situation or an **impossible** position is one that is very difficult to deal with. ❑ *The Government was now in an almost impossible position.* ADJ: ADJ n = hopeless

3 If you describe someone as **impossible**, you are annoyed that their bad behaviour or strong views make them difficult to deal with. ❑ *The woman is impossible, thought Frannie.* ADJ [disapproval] = intolerable

**im|pos|tor** /ɪmpɒstəʳ/ **(impostors)** also **imposter.** Someone who is an **impostor** is dishonestly pretending to be someone else in order to gain an advantage. ❑ *He was an imposter, who masqueraded as a doctor.* N-COUNT

**im|po|tence** /ɪmpətəns/ 1 **Impotence** is a lack of power to influence people or events. ❑ *...a sense of impotence in the face of deplorable events.* N-UNCOUNT = powerlessness

2 **Impotence** is a man's sexual problem in which his penis fails to get hard or stay hard. ❑ *Impotence affects 10 million men in the US alone.* N-UNCOUNT

**im|po|tent** /ɪmpətənt/ 1 If someone feels **impotent**, they feel that they have no power to influence people or events. ❑ *The aggression of a bully leaves people feeling hurt, angry and impotent.* ADJ = powerless

2 If a man is **impotent**, he is unable to have sex normally, because his penis fails to get hard or stay hard. ADJ: usu v-link ADJ

**im|pound** /ɪmpaʊnd/ **(impounds, impounding, impounded)** If something **is impounded** by policemen, customs officers or other officials, they officially take possession of it because a law or rule has been broken. ❑ *The ship was impounded under the terms of the UN trade embargo... The police moved in, arrested him and impounded the cocaine.* VERB = confiscate; *be* V-ed; V n

**im|pov|er|ish** /ɪmpɒvərɪʃ/ **(impoverishes, impoverishing, impoverished)** 1 Something that **impoverishes** a person or a country makes them poor. ❑ *We need to reduce the burden of taxes that impoverish the economy. ...a society impoverished by wartime inflation.* VERB; V n; V-ed ♦ **im|pov|er|ished** *...an attempt to lure businesses into impoverished areas.* ADJ

2 A person or thing that **impoverishes** something makes it worse in quality. ❑ *...plants that impoverish the soil quickly.* VERB; V n

**im|pov|er|ish|ment** /ɪmpɒvərɪʃmənt/ **Impoverishment** is the state or process of being impoverished. ❑ *National isolation can only cause economic and cultural impoverishment.* N-UNCOUNT

**im|prac|ti|cable** /ɪmpræktɪkəbᵊl/ If something such as a course of action is **impracticable**, it is impossible to do. ❑ *Such measures would be highly impracticable and almost impossible to apply.* ADJ: usu v-link ADJ

**im|prac|ti|cal** /ɪmpræktɪkᵊl/ 1 If you describe an object, idea, or course of action as **impractical**, you mean that it is not sensible or realistic, and does not work well in practice. ❑ *It became impractical to make a business trip by ocean liner.* ADJ: usu v-link ADJ, oft *it* v-link ADJ to-inf ≠ practical

2 If you describe someone as **impractical**, you mean that they do not have the abilities or skills to do practical work such as making, repairing, or organizing things. ❑ *Geniuses are supposed to be eccentric and hopelessly impractical.* ADJ: usu v-link ADJ ≠ practical

**im|pre|ca|tion** /ɪmprɪkeɪʃᵊn/ **(imprecations)** An **imprecation** is something rude, angry, or hostile that is said to or about someone. [FORMAL] N-VAR

**im|pre|cise** /ɪmprɪsaɪs/ Something that is **imprecise** is not clear, accurate, or precise. ❑ *The charges were vague and imprecise.* ADJ

**im|pre|ci|sion** /ɪmprɪsɪʒᵊn/ **Imprecision** is the quality of being imprecise. ❑ *This served to hide the confusion and imprecision in their thinking.* N-UNCOUNT

**im|preg|nable** /ɪmpregnəbᵊl/ 1 If you describe a building or other place as **impregnable**, you mean that it cannot be broken into or captured. ❑ *The old Dutch fort with its thick high walls looks virtually impregnable.* ADJ = impenetrable

2 If you say that a person or group is **impregnable**, or their position is **impregnable**, you think they cannot be defeated by anyone. ❑ *The Bundesbank's seemingly impregnable position has begun to weaken.* ADJ = unassailable

**im|preg|nate** /ɪmpregneɪt, AM ɪmpreg-/ **(impregnates, impregnating, impregnated)** 1 If someone or something **impregnates** a thing **with** a substance, they make the substance spread through it and stay in it. ❑ *Undercover officers found drug-making equipment used to impregnate paper with LSD.* VERB; V n *with* n ♦ **-impregnated** *...nicotine-impregnated chewing gum.* COMB in ADJ

2 When a man or a male animal **impregnates** a female, he makes her pregnant. [FORMAL] ❑ *Norman's efforts to impregnate her failed.* VERB; V n

**im|pre|sa|rio** /ɪmprɪsɑːrioʊ/ **(impresarios)** An **impresario** is a person who arranges for plays, concerts, and other entertainments to be performed. N-COUNT

**im|press** /ɪmpres/ **(impresses, impressing, impressed)** ◆◇◇ 1 If something **impresses** you, you feel great admiration for it. ❑ *What impressed him most was their speed... Cannon's film impresses on many levels.* VERB; V n; V ♦ **im|pressed** *I was very impressed by one young man at my lectures.* ADJ: v-link ADJ

2 If you **impress** something **on** someone, you make them understand its importance or degree. ❑ *I had always impressed upon the children that if they worked hard they would succeed in life... I've impressed upon them the need for more professionalism... I impressed on him what a huge honour he was being offered.* VERB; V *on/upon* n that; V *on/upon* n n; V *on/upon* n wh

3 If something **impresses itself on** your mind, you notice and remember it. ❑ *But this change has not yet impressed itself on the minds of the British public.* VERB; V pron-refl *on* n

4 If someone or something **impresses** you **as** a particular thing, usually a good one, they gives you the impression of being that thing. ❑ *Billy Sullivan had impressed me as a fine man.* VERB; V n *as* n/-ing

**im|pres|sion** /ɪmpreʃᵊn/ **(impressions)** ◆◇◇ 1 Your **impression** of a person or thing is what you think they are like, usually after having seen or heard them. Your **impression** of a situation is what you think is going on. ❑ *What were your first impressions of college?... My impression is that they are totally out of control.* N-COUNT: oft poss N, N *of* n, N that

2 If someone gives you a particular **impression**, they cause you to believe that something is the case, often when it is not. ❑ *I don't want to give the impression that I'm running away from the charges.* N-SING: usu with supp, oft N that, N *of* n

3 An **impression** is an amusing imitation of someone's behaviour or way of talking, usually someone well-known. ❑ *He did impressions of Sean Connery and James Mason.* N-COUNT: oft N *of* n = impersonation

4 An **impression** of an object is a mark or outline that it has left after being pressed hard onto a surface. ❑ *...the world's oldest fossil impressions of plant life.* N-COUNT

PHRASES [5] If someone or something **makes an impression**, they have a strong effect on people or a situation. ❑ *The aid coming in has made no impression on the horrific death rates.*
PHRASE: V inflects

[6] If you are **under the impression that** something is the case, you believe that it is the case, usually when it is not actually the case. ❑ *He had apparently been under the impression that a military coup was in progress.*
PHRASE: v-link PHR, usu PHR that

**im|pres|sion|able** /ɪmpreʃənəbᵊl/ Someone who is **impressionable**, usually a young person, is not very critical and is therefore easy to influence. ❑ *The law is intended to protect young and impressionable viewers.*
ADJ

**Im|pres|sion|ism** /ɪmpreʃənɪzəm/ **Impressionism** is a style of painting developed in France between 1870 and 1900 which concentrated on showing the effects of light on things rather than on clear and exact detail.
N-UNCOUNT

**im|pres|sion|ist** /ɪmpreʃənɪst/ **(impressionists)** An **impressionist** is an entertainer who does amusing imitations of well-known people.
N-COUNT

**Im|pres|sion|ist (Impressionists)** [1] An **Impressionist** is an artist who painted in the style of Impressionism. ❑ *...the French Impressionists.*
N-COUNT

[2] An **Impressionist** painting is by an Impressionist or is in the style of Impressionism.
ADJ: ADJ n

**im|pres|sion|is|tic** /ɪmpreʃənɪstɪk/ An **impressionistic** work of art or piece of writing shows the artist's or writer's impressions of something rather than giving clear details. ❑ *His paintings had become more impressionistic as his eyesight dimmed.*
ADJ

**im|pres|sive** /ɪmpresɪv/ Something that is **impressive** impresses you, for example because it is great in size or degree, or is done with a great deal of skill. ❑ *It is an impressive achievement.*
◆◇◇ ADJ

♦ **im|pres|sive|ly** *...an impressively bright and energetic American woman called Cathie Gould.*
ADV: ADV adj, ADV with v

**im|pri|ma|tur** /ɪmprɪmɑːtəʳ/ **(imprimaturs)** If something such as a product has someone's **imprimatur**, that person has given it their official approval, for example by allowing their name to be shown on it. ❑ *...a tennis racket bearing Andre Agassi's imprimatur.*
N-COUNT: usu poss N

**im|print (imprints, imprinting, imprinted)**

> ✔ The noun is pronounced /ɪmprɪnt/. The verb is pronounced /ɪmprɪnt/.

[1] If something leaves an **imprint** on a place or on your mind, it has a strong and lasting effect on it. ❑ *The city bears the imprint of Japanese investment.*
N-COUNT: usu sing, usu N *of/on* n

[2] When something **is imprinted on** your memory, it is firmly fixed in your memory so that you will not forget it. ❑ *The skyline of domes and minarets was imprinted on my memory... He repeated the names, as if to imprint them in his mind.*
VERB *be* V-ed *on/in* n; V n *on/in* n

[3] An **imprint** is a mark or outline made by the pressure of one object on another. ❑ *The ground still bore the imprints of their feet.*
N-COUNT

[4] If a surface **is imprinted with** a mark or design, that mark or design is printed on the surface or pressed into it. ❑ *Stationery can be imprinted with your logo.*
VERB: usu passive *be* V-ed *with/on* n

**im|pris|on** /ɪmprɪzᵊn/ **(imprisons, imprisoning, imprisoned)** If someone **is imprisoned**, they are locked up or kept somewhere, usually in prison as a punishment for a crime or for political opposition. ❑ *The local priest was imprisoned for 18 months on charges of anti-state agitation... Dutch colonial authorities imprisoned him for his part in the independence movement.*
VERB *be* V-ed; V n

**im|pris|on|ment** /ɪmprɪzᵊnmənt/ **Imprisonment** is the state of being imprisoned. ❑ *She was sentenced to seven years' imprisonment.*
N-UNCOUNT

**im|prob|able** /ɪmprɒbəbᵊl/ [1] Something that is **improbable** is unlikely to be true or to happen. ❑ *...a highly improbable coincidence.*
ADJ: oft *it* v-link ADJ that = unlikely ≠ probable

♦ **im|prob|abil|ity** /ɪmprɒbəbɪlɪti/ **(improbabilities)** *...the improbability of such an outcome.*
N-VAR

[2] If you describe something as **improbable**, you mean it is strange, unusual, or ridiculous. ❑ *On the face of it, their marriage seems an improbable alliance.*
ADJ = unlikely

♦ **im|prob|ably** *The sea is an improbably pale turquoise.*
ADV: ADV adj, ADV with v, ADV with cl

**im|promp|tu** /ɪmprɒmptjuː, AM -tuː/ An **impromptu** action is one that you do without planning or organizing it in advance. ❑ *This afternoon the Palestinians held an impromptu press conference.*
ADJ: usu ADJ n

**im|prop|er** /ɪmprɒpəʳ/ [1] **Improper** activities are illegal or dishonest. [FORMAL] ❑ *25 officers were investigated following allegations of improper conduct during the murder inquiry.*
ADJ

♦ **im|prop|er|ly** *I acted neither fraudulently nor improperly.*
ADV: ADV with v

[2] **Improper** conditions or methods of treatment are not suitable or good enough for a particular purpose. [FORMAL] ❑ *The improper use of medicine could lead to severe adverse reactions.*
ADJ: ADJ n = inappropriate

♦ **im|prop|er|ly** *The study confirmed many reports that doctors were improperly trained.*
ADV: ADV with v

[3] If you describe someone's behaviour as **improper**, you mean that it is rude or shocking. [OLD-FASHIONED] ❑ *He would never be improper, he is always the perfect gentleman.*
ADJ disapproval = indecent

**im|pro|pri|ety** /ɪmprəpraɪɪti/ **(improprieties)** **Impropriety** is improper behaviour. [FORMAL] ❑ *He resigned amid allegations of financial impropriety.*
N-VAR

**im|prov** /ɪmprɒv/ **Improv** is acting or singing in which someone invents the words or music as they speak. **Improv** is an abbreviation for 'improvisation'. [INFORMAL]
N-UNCOUNT

**im|prove** /ɪmpruːv/ **(improves, improving, improved)** [1] If something **improves** or if you **improve** it, it gets better. ❑ *Both the texture and condition of your hair should improve... Time won't improve the situation.*
◆◆◇ VERB V; V n

[2] If a skill you have **improves** or you **improve** a skill, you get better at it. ❑ *Their French has improved enormously... He said he was going to improve his football.*
VERB V; V n

[3] If you **improve** after an illness or an injury, your health gets better or you get stronger. ❑ *He had improved so much the doctor had cut his dosage.*
VERB = recover V

[4] If you **improve on** a previous achievement of your own or of someone else, you achieve a better standard or result. ❑ *We need to improve on our performance against France.*
VERB V *on* n

**im|prove|ment** /ɪmpruːvmənt/ **(improvements)** [1] If there is an **improvement in** something, it becomes better. If you make **improvements to** something, you make it better. ❑ *...the dramatic improvements in organ transplantation in recent years.*
◆◇◇ N-VAR

[2] If you say that something is **an improvement on** a previous thing or situation, you mean that it is better than that thing. ❑ *The new Prime Minister is an improvement on his predecessor.*
N-COUNT: usu sing, oft N *on* n

**im|pro|vise** /ɪmprəvaɪz/ **(improvises, improvising, improvised)** [1] If you **improvise**, you make or do something using whatever you have or without having planned it in advance. ❑ *You need a wok with a steaming rack for this; if you don't have one, improvise... The vet had improvised a harness. ...an improvised stone shelter.*
VERB V; V n; V-ed

♦ **im|provi|sa|tion** /ɪmprəvaɪzeɪʃᵊn, AM -vɪz-/ **(improvisations)** *Funds were not abundant and clever improvisation was necessary.*
N-VAR

[2] When performers **improvise**, they invent music or words as they play, sing, or speak. ❑ *I asked her what the piece was and she said, 'Oh, I'm just improvising'... Uncle Richard intoned a chapter from the Bible and improvised a prayer... I think that the art of a storyteller is to take the story and improvise on it.*
VERB V; V n; V *on* n

♦ **im|provi|sa|tion (improvisations)** *...an improvisation on 'Jingle Bells'.*
N-VAR: oft N *on* n

**im|pru|dent** /ɪmpruːdᵊnt/ If you describe someone's behaviour as **imprudent**, you think it is not sensible or carefully thought out. [FORMAL] ❑ *...an imprudent investment.*
ADJ = unwise

**im|pu|dent** /ɪmpjʊdənt/ If you describe someone as **impudent**, you mean they are rude or disrespectful, or do something they have no right to do. [FORMAL] ❑ *Some of them were impudent*
ADJ disapproval = cheeky

and insulting. ♦ **im|pu|dence** *One sister had the impudence to wear the other's clothes.* N-UNCOUNT = cheek

**im|pugn** /ɪmpjuːn/ **(impugns, impugning, impugned)** If you **impugn** something such as someone's motives or integrity, you imply that they are not entirely honest or honourable. [FORMAL] ❑ *The Secretary's letter questions my veracity and impugns my motives.* VERB V n

**im|pulse** /ɪmpʌls/ **(impulses)** 1 An **impulse** is a sudden desire to do something. ❑ *Unable to resist the impulse, he glanced at the sea again.* N-VAR: oft N to-inf 2 An **impulse** is a short electrical signal that is sent along a wire or nerve or through the air, usually as one of a series. N-COUNT 3 An **impulse** buy or **impulse** purchase is something that you decide to buy when you see it, although you had not planned to buy it. ❑ *The curtains were an impulse buy.* ADJ: ADJ n 4 If you do something **on impulse**, you suddenly decide to do it, without planning it. ❑ *Sean's a fast thinker, and he acts on impulse.* PHRASE: PHR after v

**im|pul|sive** /ɪmpʌlsɪv/ If you describe someone as **impulsive**, you mean that they do things suddenly without thinking about them carefully first. ❑ *He is too impulsive to be a responsible prime minister.* ADJ ♦ **im|pul|sive|ly** *He studied her face for a moment, then said impulsively: 'Let's get married'.* ADV: ADV with v ♦ **im|pul|sive|ness** *The president's impulsiveness often worries his advisers.* N-UNCOUNT

**im|pu|nity** /ɪmpjuːnɪti/ If you say that someone does something **with impunity**, you disapprove of the fact that they are not punished for doing something bad. ❑ *These gangs operate with apparent impunity.* PHRASE: PHR after v [disapproval]

**im|pure** /ɪmpjʊəʳ/ A substance that is **impure** is not of good quality because it has other substances mixed with it. ADJ

**im|pu|rity** /ɪmpjʊərɪti/ **(impurities)** 1 **Impurities** are substances that are present in small quantities in another substance and make it dirty or of an unacceptable quality. ❑ *The air in the factory is filtered to remove impurities.* N-COUNT: usu pl 2 **Impurity** is the state of being no longer pure, especially sexually pure. N-UNCOUNT

**im|pute** /ɪmpjuːt/ **(imputes, imputing, imputed)** If you **impute** something such as blame or a crime **to** someone, you say that they are responsible for it or are the cause of it. [FORMAL] ❑ *It is grossly unfair to impute blame to the United Nations.* VERB = attribute V n to n

**in**

① POSITION OR MOVEMENT
② INCLUSION OR INVOLVEMENT
③ TIME AND NUMBERS
④ STATES AND QUALITIES
⑤ OTHER USES AND PHRASES

**① in** ♦♦♦

The preposition is pronounced /ɪn/. The adverb is pronounced /ɪn/.

In addition to the uses shown below, **in** is used after some verbs, nouns, and adjectives in order to introduce extra information. **In** is also used with verbs of movement such as 'walk' and 'push', and in phrasal verbs such as 'give in' and 'dig in'.

1 Someone or something that is **in** something else is enclosed by it or surrounded by it. If you put something **in** a container, you move it so that it is enclosed by the container. ❑ *He was in his car. ...clothes hanging in the wardrobe.* PREP 2 If something happens **in** a place, it happens there. ❑ *We spent a few days in a hotel... He had intended to take a holiday in America.* PREP 3 If you **are in**, you are present at your home or place of work. ❑ *My flatmate was in at the time.* ADV: be ADV ≠out 4 When someone comes **in**, they enter a room or building. ❑ *She looked up anxiously as he came in... They shook hands and went in.* ADV: ADV after v 5 If a train, boat, or plane has come **in** or is **in**, it has arrived at a station, port, or airport. ❑ *We'd be watching every plane coming in from Melbourne... Look. The train's in. We'll have to run for it now.* ADV: ADV after v, be ADV 6 When the sea or tide comes **in**, the sea moves towards the shore rather than away from it. ❑ *She thought of the tide rushing in, covering the wet sand.* ADV: ADV after v, be ADV ≠out 7 Something that is **in** a window, especially a shop window, is just behind the window so that you can see it from outside. ❑ *There was a camera for sale in the window.* PREP 8 When you see something **in** a mirror, the mirror shows an image of it. ❑ *I couldn't bear to see my reflection in the mirror.* PREP 9 If you are dressed **in** a piece of clothing, you are wearing it. ❑ *He was a big man, smartly dressed in a suit and tie.* PREP: oft -ed PREP n 10 Something that is covered or wrapped **in** something else has that thing over or round its surface. ❑ *His legs were covered in mud.* PREP: oft -ed PREP n 11 If there is something such as a crack or hole **in** something, there is a crack or hole on its surface. ❑ *There was a deep crack in the ceiling above him.* PREP

**② in** /ɪn/ ♦♦♦ 1 If something is **in** a book, film, play, or picture, you can read it or see it there. ❑ *Don't stick too precisely to what it says in the book.* PREP 2 If you are **in** something such as a play or a race, you are one of the people taking part. ❑ *Alf offered her a part in the play he was directing... More than fifteen thousand people took part in the memorial service.* PREP 3 Something that is **in** a group or collection is a member of it or part of it. ❑ *The New England team are the worst in the league.* PREP 4 You use **in** to specify a general subject or field of activity. ❑ *...those working in the defence industry. ...future developments in medicine.* PREP

**③ in** /ɪn/ ♦♦♦ 1 If something happens **in** a particular year, month, or other period of time, it happens during that time. ❑ *...that early spring day in April 1949... Export orders improved in the last month... In the evening, the people assemble in the mosques.* PREP 2 If something happens **in** a particular situation, it happens while that situation is going on. ❑ *His father had been badly wounded in the last war. ...issues you struggle with in your daily life.* PREP 3 If you do something **in** a particular period of time, that is how long it takes you to do it. ❑ *He walked two hundred and sixty miles in eight days.* PREP: PREP amount 4 If something will happen **in** a particular length of time, it will happen after that length of time. ❑ *I'll have some breakfast ready in a few minutes... They'll be back in six months.* PREP: PREP amount 5 You use **in** to indicate roughly how old someone is. For example, if someone is **in** their fifties, they are between 50 and 59 years old. ❑ *...young people in their twenties.* PREP: PREP poss pl-num 6 You use **in** to indicate roughly how many people or things do something. ❑ *...men who came there in droves.* PREP: oft PREP num 7 You use **in** to express a ratio, proportion, or probability. ❑ *Last year, one in five boys left school without a qualification.* PREP: num PREP num

**④ in** /ɪn/ ♦♦♦ 1 If something or someone is **in** a particular state or situation, that is their present state or situation. ❑ *The economy was in trouble... Dave was in a hurry to get back to work... Their equipment was in poor condition.* PREP: v-link PREP n 2 You use **in** to indicate the feeling or desire which someone has when they do something, or which causes them to do it. ❑ *Simpson looked at them in surprise... Chris was weeping in anger and grief.* PREP 3 If a particular quality or ability is **in** you, you naturally have it. ❑ *Violence is not in his nature.* PREP: oft PREP pron to-inf 4 You use **in** when saying that someone or something has a particular quality. ❑ *He had all the qualities I was looking for in a partner... 'I don't agree,' she said, surprised at the strength in her own voice.* PREP 5 You use **in** to indicate how someone is expressing something. ❑ *Information is given to the patient verbally and in writing. ...lessons in languages other than Spanish.* PREP 6 You use **in** in expressions such as **in a row** or **in a ball** to describe the arrangement or shape of something. ❑ *The cards need to be laid out in two rows... Her ear, shoulder and hip are in a straight line.* PREP 7 If something is **in** a particular colour, it has that colour. ❑ *...white flowers edged in pink.* PREP: oft -ed PREP colour

8 You use **in** to specify which feature or aspect of something you are talking about. ❑ *The movie is nearly two hours in length... There is a big difference in the amounts that banks charge. ...a real increase in the standard of living.* PREP

**⑤ in** **(ins)** ◆◆◆

> Pronounced /ɪn/ for meanings 1 and 3 to 8, and /ɪn/ for meaning 2.

1 If you say that something is **in**, or is the **in** thing, you mean it is fashionable or popular. [INFORMAL] ❑ *A few years ago jogging was the in thing.* ADJ

2 You use **in** with a present participle to indicate that when you do something, something else happens as a result. ❑ *In working with others, you find out more about yourself.* PREP: PREP -ing

PHRASES 3 If you say that someone **is in for** a shock or a surprise, you mean that they are going to experience it. ❑ *You might be in for a shock at the sheer hard work involved.* PHRASE: V inflects, PHR n 4 If someone **has it in for** you, they dislike you and try to cause problems for you. [INFORMAL] ❑ *The other kids had it in for me.* PHRASE: V inflects, PHR n 5 If you are **in on** something, you are involved in it or know about it. ❑ *I don't know. I wasn't in on that particular argument.* PREP-PHRASE: v-link PREP n, v n PREP n 6 If you **are in with** a person or group, they like you and accept you, and are likely to help you. [INFORMAL] PHRASE: PHR n 7 You use **in that** to introduce an explanation of a statement you have just made. ❑ *I'm lucky in that I've got four sisters.* PHRASE 8 The **ins and outs** of a situation are all the detailed points and facts about it. ❑ *...the ins and outs of high finance.* PHRASE: usu *the* PHR *of* n/-ing

**in.** **in.** is a written abbreviation for **inch**. The plural can be 'in.' or 'ins'. ❑ *...30.4 x 25.4 cm (12 x 10 in)... It is 24 ins wide and 16 ins high.*

**in-**

> Usually pronounced /ɪn-/ before an unstressed syllable, and /ɪn-/ before a stressed syllable.

**In-** is added to some words to form words with the opposite meaning. For example, something that is incorrect is not correct. ❑ *...incomplete answers. ...women who are insecure about themselves.* PREFIX

**in|abil|ity** /ɪnəbɪlɪti/ If you refer to someone's **inability to** do something, you are referring to the fact that they are unable to do it. ❑ *Her inability to concentrate could cause an accident.* N-UNCOUNT: usu N to-inf, usu with poss ≠ ability

**in|ac|ces|sible** /ɪnəksesɪbəl/ 1 An **inaccessible** place is very difficult or impossible to reach. ❑ *...the remote, inaccessible areas of the Andes rainforests.* ADJ: oft ADJ *to* n ♦ **in|ac|ces|sibil|ity** /ɪnəksesɪbɪlɪti/ *Its inaccessibility makes food distribution difficult.* N-UNCOUNT 2 If something is **inaccessible**, you are unable to see, use, or buy it. ❑ *Ninety-five per cent of its magnificent collection will remain inaccessible to the public.* ADJ: usu v-link ADJ, oft ADJ *to* n = unavailable ♦ **in|ac|ces|sibil|ity** *...the problem of inaccessibility of essential goods.* N-UNCOUNT: oft N *of* n 3 Someone or something that is **inaccessible** is difficult or impossible to understand or appreciate. ❑ *...using language that is inaccessible to working people.* ADJ: usu v-link ADJ, oft ADJ *to* n [disapproval] ♦ **in|ac|ces|sibil|ity** *...the inaccessibility of his literature.* N-UNCOUNT

**in|ac|cu|ra|cy** /ɪnækjʊrəsi/ **(inaccuracies)** The **inaccuracy** of a statement or measurement is the fact that it is not accurate or correct. ❑ *He was disturbed by the inaccuracy of the answers.* N-VAR ≠ accuracy

**in|ac|cu|rate** /ɪnækjʊrət/ If a statement or measurement is **inaccurate**, it is not accurate or correct. ❑ *The book is both inaccurate and exaggerated.* ADJ ≠ accurate ♦ **in|ac|cu|rate|ly** *He claimed his remarks had been reported inaccurately.* ADV: ADV with v

**in|ac|tion** /ɪnækʃən/ If you refer to someone's **inaction**, you disapprove of the fact that they are doing nothing. ❑ *He is bitter about the inaction of the other political parties.* N-UNCOUNT: oft with poss [disapproval]

**in|ac|tive** /ɪnæktɪv/ Someone or something that is **inactive** is not doing anything or is not working. ❑ *He certainly was not politically inactive.* ADJ ≠ active ♦ **in|ac|tiv|ity** /ɪnæktɪvɪti/ *The players have comparatively long periods of inactivity.* N-UNCOUNT ≠ activity

**in|ad|equa|cy** /ɪnædɪkwəsi/ **(inadequacies)** 1 The **inadequacy** of something is the fact that there is not enough of it, or that it is not good enough. ❑ *...the inadequacy of the water supply.* N-VAR: oft *the* N *of* n = deficiency ≠ adequacy 2 If someone has feelings of **inadequacy**, they feel that they do not have the qualities and abilities necessary to do something or to cope with life in general. ❑ *...his deep-seated sense of inadequacy.* N-UNCOUNT = accidentally

**in|ad|equate** /ɪnædɪkwət/ 1 If something is **inadequate**, there is not enough of it or it is not good enough. ❑ *Supplies of food and medicines are inadequate.* ADJ = deficient ≠ adequate ♦ **in|ad|equate|ly** *The projects were inadequately funded.* ADV: ADV with v 2 If someone feels **inadequate**, they feel that they do not have the qualities and abilities necessary to do something or to cope with life in general. ❑ *I still feel inadequate, useless and mixed up.* ADJ: usu v-link ADJ

**in|ad|mis|si|ble** /ɪnədmɪsɪbəl/ 1 **Inadmissible** evidence cannot be used in a court of law. ❑ *The judge ruled that the evidence was inadmissible.* ADJ ≠ admissible 2 If you say that something that someone says or does is **inadmissible**, you think that it is totally unacceptable. ❑ *He said the use of force would be inadmissible.* ADJ: usu v-link ADJ [disapproval]

**in|ad|vert|ent** /ɪnədvɜːʳtənt/ An **inadvertent** action is one that you do without realizing what you are doing. ❑ *The government has said it was an inadvertent error.* ADJ = unintentional ≠ deliberate ♦ **in|ad|vert|ent|ly** *I inadvertently pressed the wrong button.* ADV: ADV with v

**in|ad|vis|able** /ɪnədvaɪzəbəl/ A course of action that is **inadvisable** should not be carried out because it is not wise or sensible. ❑ *For three days, it was inadvisable to leave the harbour.* ADJ: oft *it* v-link ADJ to-inf = unwise ≠ advisable

**in|al|ien|able** /ɪneɪljənəbəl/ If you say that someone has an **inalienable** right to something, you are emphasizing that they have a right to it which cannot be changed or taken away. [FORMAL] ❑ *He said the republic now had an inalienable right to self-determination.* ADJ: usu ADJ n [emphasis]

**in|ane** /ɪneɪn/ If you describe someone's behaviour or actions as **inane**, you think they are very silly or stupid. ❑ *He always had this inane grin.* ADJ [disapproval] = idiotic ♦ **in|ane|ly** *He lurched through the bar, grinning inanely.* ADV: ADV after v ♦ **in|an|ity** /ɪnænɪti/ *...the inanity of the conversation.* N-UNCOUNT

**in|ani|mate** /ɪnænɪmət/ An **inanimate** object is one that has no life. ❑ *He thought of the baby almost as an inanimate object.* ADJ ≠ animate

**in|ap|pli|cable** /ɪnəplɪkəbəl, AM ɪnæplɪk-/ Something that is **inapplicable** to what you are talking about is not relevant or appropriate to it. ❑ *His theory was inapplicable to many underdeveloped economies.* ADJ: usu v-link ADJ, oft ADJ *to* n = irrelevant ≠ applicable

**in|ap|pro|pri|ate** /ɪnəproʊpriət/ 1 Something that is **inappropriate** is not useful or suitable for a particular situation or purpose. ❑ *There is no suggestion that clients have been sold inappropriate policies.* ADJ ≠ appropriate ♦ **in|ap|pro|pri|ate|ly** *He was dressed inappropriately for the heat in a dark suit.* ADV: ADV with v 2 If you say that someone's speech or behaviour in a particular situation is **inappropriate**, you are criticizing it because you think it is not suitable for that situation. ❑ *I feel the remark was inappropriate for such a serious issue.* ADJ: oft ADJ *for* n, *it* v-link ADJ to-inf [disapproval] ♦ **in|ap|pro|pri|ate|ly** *You have the law on your side if the bank is acting inappropriately.* ADV: ADV with v, ADV adj

**in|ar|ticu|late** /ɪnɑːʳtɪkjʊlət/ If someone is **inarticulate**, they are unable to express themselves easily or well in speech. ❑ *Inarticulate and rather shy, he had always dreaded speaking in public.* ADJ ≠ articulate

**in|as|much as** /ɪnəzmʌtʃ æz/ You use **inasmuch as** to introduce a statement which explains something you have just said, and adds to it. [FORMAL] ❑ *This was a good decision inasmuch as it worked for you.* PHRASE = insofar as

**in|at|ten|tion** /ɪnətenʃən/ A person's **inattention** is their lack of attention. ❑ *Vital evidence had been lost through a moment's inattention.* N-UNCOUNT ≠ attention

**in|at|ten|tive** /ɪnətentɪv/ Someone who is **inattentive** is not paying complete attention to a person or thing, which often causes an accident or problems.
ADJ ≠ attentive

**in|audible** /ɪnɔːdɪbəl/ If a sound is **inaudible**, you are unable to hear it. ❑ *His voice was almost inaudible.*
ADJ ≠ audible

**in|augu|ral** /ɪnɔːgjʊrəl/ An **inaugural** meeting or speech is the first meeting of a new organization or the first speech by the new leader of an organization or a country. ❑ *In his inaugural address, the President appealed for unity.*
ADJ: ADJ n

**in|augu|rate** /ɪnɔːgjʊreɪt/ **(inaugurates, inaugurating, inaugurated)** 1 When a new leader **is inaugurated**, they are formally given their new position at an official ceremony. ❑ *The new President will be inaugurated on January 20.* ♦ **in|augu|ra|tion** /ɪnɔːgjʊreɪʃən/ **(inaugurations)** *...the inauguration of the new Governor.*
VERB: usu passive; be V-ed; N-VAR: oft N *of* n, N n

2 When a new building or institution **is inaugurated**, it is declared open in a formal ceremony. ❑ *A new centre for research on toxic waste was inaugurated today at Imperial College.* ♦ **in|augu|ra|tion** *They later attended the inauguration of the University.*
VERB: usu passive = open; be V-ed; N-COUNT: usu N *of* n

3 If you **inaugurate** a new system or service, you start it. [FORMAL] ❑ *Pan Am inaugurated the first scheduled international flight.*
VERB; V n

**in|aus|pi|cious** /ɪnɔːspɪʃəs/ An **inauspicious** event is one that gives signs that success is unlikely. [FORMAL] ❑ *The meeting got off to an inauspicious start when he was late.*
ADJ: usu ADJ n ≠ auspicious

**in|board** /ɪnbɔːʳd/ An **inboard** motor or engine is inside a boat rather than attached to the outside.
ADJ: ADJ n ≠ outboard

**in|born** /ɪnbɔːʳn/ **Inborn** qualities are natural ones which you are born with. ❑ *He had an inborn talent for languages.*
ADJ: usu ADJ n = innate, inbred

**in|bound** /ɪnbaʊnd/ An **inbound** flight is one that is arriving from another place. ❑ *...a special inbound flight from Honduras.*
ADJ: usu ADJ n ≠ outbound

**in|bred** /ɪnbred/ 1 **Inbred** means the same as **inborn**. ❑ *...behaviour patterns that are inbred.*
ADJ = innate, inborn

2 People who are **inbred** have ancestors who are all closely related to each other. ❑ *The whole population is so inbred that no genetic differences remain.*
ADJ: usu v-link ADJ

**in|breed|ing** /ɪnbriːdɪŋ/ **Inbreeding** is the repeated breeding of closely related animals or people. ❑ *In the 19th century, inbreeding nearly led to the extinction of the royal family.*
N-UNCOUNT

**in|built** /ɪnbɪlt/ also **in-built**. An **inbuilt** quality is one that someone has from the time they were born or that something has from the time it was produced. [mainly BRIT] ❑ *The children had this inbuilt awareness that not everyone was as lucky as they were.*
ADJ: usu ADJ n

> in AM, usually use **built-in**

**inc.** In written advertisements, **inc.** is an abbreviation for **including**. ❑ *...a two-night break for £210 per person, inc. breakfast and dinner.*
= incl.

**Inc.** **Inc.** is an abbreviation for **Incorporated** when it is used after a company's name. [AM, BUSINESS] ❑ *...BP America Inc.*
◆◇◇

**in|cal|cu|lable** /ɪnkælkjʊləbəl/ Something that is **incalculable** cannot be calculated or estimated because it is so great. ❑ *He warned that the effects of any war would be incalculable.*
ADJ = inestimable

**in|can|des|cent** /ɪnkændesənt/ 1 **Incandescent** substances or devices give out a lot of light when heated. [TECHNICAL] ❑ *...incandescent gases.*
ADJ

2 If you describe someone or something as **incandescent**, you mean that they are very lively and impressive. [LITERARY] ❑ *Gill had an extraordinary, incandescent personality.* ♦ **in|can|des|cence** *She burned with an incandescence that had nothing to do with her looks.*
ADJ: usu ADJ n; N-UNCOUNT

3 If you say that someone is **incandescent with** rage, you mean that they are extremely angry. [LITERARY] ❑ *It makes me incandescent with fury.*
ADJ: oft ADJ *with* n

**in|can|ta|tion** /ɪnkænteɪʃən/ **(incantations)** An **incantation** is a series of words that a person says or sings as a magic spell. [FORMAL] ❑ *...strange prayers and incantations.*
N-COUNT = chant

**in|ca|pable** /ɪnkeɪpəbəl/ 1 Someone who is **incapable of** doing something is unable to do it. ❑ *She seemed incapable of taking decisions.*
ADJ: v-link ADJ *of* -ing/n ≠ capable

2 An **incapable** person is weak or stupid. ❑ *He lost his job for allegedly being incapable.*
ADJ ≠ capable

**in|ca|paci|tate** /ɪnkəpæsɪteɪt/ **(incapacitates, incapacitating, incapacitated)** If something **incapacitates** you, it weakens you in some way, so that you cannot do certain things. [FORMAL] ❑ *A serious fall incapacitated the 68-year-old congressman.* ♦ **in|ca|paci|tat|ed** *He is incapacitated and can't work.*
VERB; V n; ADJ: usu v-link ADJ

**in|ca|pac|ity** /ɪnkəpæsɪti/ The **incapacity of** a person, society, or system **to** do something is their inability to do it. [FORMAL] ❑ *...Europe's incapacity to take collective action.*
N-UNCOUNT: oft with poss, oft N to-inf = inability

**in|car|cer|ate** /ɪnkɑːʳsəreɪt/ **(incarcerates, incarcerating, incarcerated)** If people **are incarcerated**, they are kept in a prison or other place. [FORMAL] ❑ *They were incarcerated for the duration of the war... It can cost $40,000 to $50,000 to incarcerate a prisoner for a year.* ♦ **in|car|cera|tion** *...her mother's incarceration in a psychiatric hospital.*
VERB = imprison; be V-ed; V n; N-UNCOUNT = imprisonment

**in|car|nate** **(incarnates, incarnating, incarnated)**

> The adjective is pronounced /ɪnkɑːʳnɪt/. The verb is pronounced /ɪnkɑːʳneɪt/.

1 If you say that someone is a quality **incarnate**, you mean that they represent that quality or are typical of it in an extreme form. ❑ *She is evil incarnate.*
ADJ: n ADJ = personified

2 You use **incarnate** to say that something, especially a god or spirit, is represented in human form. ❑ *Why should God become incarnate as a male?*
ADJ: v-link ADJ, n ADJ, ADJ n

3 If you say that a quality **is incarnated** in a person, you mean that they represent that quality or are typical of it in an extreme form. ❑ *The iniquities of the regime are incarnated in one man. ...a writer who incarnates the changing consciousness of the Americas.*
VERB = embody; be V-ed *in* n; V n

4 If you say that someone or something **is incarnated** in a particular form, you mean that they appear on earth in that form. ❑ *The god Vishnu was incarnated on earth as a king.*
VERB: usu passive; be V-ed prep

**in|car|na|tion** /ɪnkɑːʳneɪʃən/ **(incarnations)** 1 If you say that someone is the **incarnation of** a particular quality, you mean that they represent that quality or are typical of it in an extreme form. ❑ *The regime was the very incarnation of evil.*
N-COUNT: N *of* n = embodiment

2 An **incarnation** is an instance of being alive on earth in a particular form. Some religions believe that people have several incarnations in different forms. ❑ *She began recalling a series of previous incarnations.*
N-COUNT

**in|cau|tious** /ɪnkɔːʃəs/ If you say that someone is **incautious**, you are criticizing them because they do or say something without thinking or planning. [FORMAL] ♦ **in|cau|tious|ly** ❑ *Incautiously, Crook had asked where she was.*
ADJ: usu ADJ n [disapproval] = rash; ADV: ADV with v

**in|cen|di|ary** /ɪnsendiəri, AM -eri/ **(incendiaries)** 1 **Incendiary** weapons or attacks are ones that cause large fires. ❑ *Five incendiary devices were found in her house.*
ADJ: ADJ n

2 An **incendiary** is an incendiary bomb. ❑ *A shower of incendiaries struck the Opera House.*
N-COUNT

**in|cense** **(incenses, incensing, incensed)**

> The noun is pronounced /ɪnsens/. The verb is pronounced /ɪnsens/.

1 **Incense** is a substance that is burned for its sweet smell, often as part of a religious ceremony.
N-UNCOUNT

2 If you say that something **incenses** you, you mean that it makes you extremely angry. ❑ *This proposal will incense conservation campaigners.* ♦ **in|censed** *Mum was incensed at his lack of compassion.*
VERB = enrage; V n; ADJ: usu v-link ADJ, oft ADJ *at/by* n, ADJ that

**in|cen|tive** /ɪnsentɪv/ **(incentives)** If something is an **incentive to** do something, it encourages you to do it. ❑ *There is little or no incentive to adopt such measures.* [N-VAR: oft N to-inf = inducement]

**in|cep|tion** /ɪnsepʃᵊn/ The **inception** of an institution or activity is the start of it. [FORMAL] ❑ *Since its inception the company has produced 53 different aircraft designs.* [N-UNCOUNT: with poss]

**in|ces|sant** /ɪnsesᵊnt/ An **incessant** process or activity is one that continues without stopping. ❑ *...incessant rain.* ♦ **in|ces|sant|ly** *Dee talked incessantly.* [ADJ: usu ADJ n = constant ≠ intermittent] [ADV: usu ADV with v]

**in|cest** /ɪnsest/ **Incest** is the crime of two members of the same family having sexual intercourse, for example a father and daughter, or a brother and sister. [N-UNCOUNT]

**in|ces|tu|ous** /ɪnsestʃuəs/ 1 An **incestuous** relationship is one involving sexual intercourse between two members of the same family, for example a father and daughter, or a brother and sister. ❑ *They accused her of an incestuous relationship with her father.* [ADJ] 2 If you describe a group of people as **incestuous**, you disapprove of the fact that they are not interested in ideas or people from outside the group. ❑ *Its inhabitants are a close and incestuous lot.* [ADJ] [disapproval]

**inch** /ɪntʃ/ **(inches, inching, inched)** 1 An **inch** is an imperial unit of length, approximately equal to 2.54 centimetres. There are twelve inches in a foot. ❑ *...18 inches below the surface.* [◆◇◇ N-COUNT: num N, oft N *of* n] 2 To **inch** somewhere or to **inch** something somewhere means to move there very slowly and carefully, or to make something do this. ❑ *...a climber inching up a vertical wall of rock... He inched the van forward... An ambulance inched its way through the crowd.* [VERB] [V prep/adv] [V n prep/adv] [V *way* prep/adv]

**PHRASES** 3 If you say that someone looks **every inch** a certain type of person, you are emphasizing that they look exactly like that kind of person. ❑ *He looks every inch the City businessman.* [PHRASE: v-link PHR n] [emphasis] 4 If someone or something moves **inch by inch**, they move very slowly and carefully. ❑ *The car moved forward inch by inch.* [PHRASE: PHR after v] [emphasis]

**in|cho|ate** /ɪnkoʊɪt/ If something is **inchoate**, it is recent or new, and vague or not yet properly developed. [FORMAL] ❑ *His dreams were senseless and inchoate.* [ADJ = unformed]

**in|ci|dence** /ɪnsɪdəns/ **(incidences)** **The incidence of** something bad, such as a disease, is the frequency with which it occurs, or the occasions when it occurs. ❑ *The incidence of breast cancer increases with age.* [N-VAR]

**in|ci|dent** /ɪnsɪdənt/ **(incidents)** An **incident** is something that happens, often something that is unpleasant. [FORMAL] ❑ *These incidents were the latest in a series of disputes between the two nations.* [◆◆◇ N-COUNT: also *without* N]

**in|ci|den|tal** /ɪnsɪdentᵊl/ If one thing is **incidental** to another, it is less important than the other thing or is not a major part of it. ❑ *The playing of music proved to be incidental to the main business of the evening.* [ADJ: oft ADJ *to* n]

**in|ci|den|tal|ly** /ɪnsɪdentli/ 1 You use **incidentally** to introduce a point which is not directly relevant to what you are saying, often a question or extra information that you have just thought of. ❑ *'I didn't ask you to come. Incidentally, why have you come?'* [ADV: ADV with cl] 2 If something occurs only **incidentally**, it is less important than another thing or is not a major part of it. ❑ *The letter mentioned my great-aunt and uncle only incidentally.* [ADV: ADV with v]

**in|ci|den|tal mu|sic** In a film, play, or television programme, **incidental music** is music that is played to create a particular atmosphere. [N-UNCOUNT]

**in|ci|dent room** **(incident rooms)** An **incident room** is a room used by the police while they are dealing with a major crime or accident. [BRIT] ❑ *Police have set up an incident room as they begin to investigate this morning's fire.* [N-COUNT: usu sing]

**in|cin|er|ate** /ɪnsɪnəreɪt/ **(incinerates, incinerating, incinerated)** When authorities **incinerate** rubbish or waste material, they burn it completely in a special container. ❑ *The government is trying to stop hospitals incinerating their own waste.* [VERB] [V n] ♦ **in|cin|era|tion** /ɪnsɪnəreɪʃᵊn/ *...banning the incineration of lead batteries.* [N-UNCOUNT]

**in|cin|era|tor** /ɪnsɪnəreɪtəʳ/ **(incinerators)** An **incinerator** is a special large container for burning rubbish at a very high temperature. [N-COUNT]

**in|cipi|ent** /ɪnsɪpiənt/ An **incipient** situation or quality is one that is starting to happen or develop. [FORMAL] ❑ *...an incipient economic recovery.* [ADJ: ADJ n = impending]

**in|cise** /ɪnsaɪz/ **(incises, incising, incised)** If an object **is incised** with a design, the design is carefully cut into the surface of the object with a sharp instrument. [FORMAL] ❑ *After the surface is polished, a design is incised or painted. ...a set of chairs incised with Grecian scrolls.* [VERB: usu passive] [*be* V-ed] [V-ed]

**in|ci|sion** /ɪnsɪʒᵊn/ **(incisions)** An **incision** is a sharp cut made in something, for example by a surgeon who is operating on a patient. ❑ *The technique involves making a tiny incision in the skin.* [N-COUNT = opening, cut]

**in|ci|sive** /ɪnsaɪsɪv/ You use **incisive** to describe a person, their thoughts, or their speech when you approve of their ability to think and express their ideas clearly, briefly, and forcefully. ❑ *...a shrewd operator with an incisive mind.* [ADJ] [approval]

**in|ci|sor** /ɪnsaɪzəʳ/ **(incisors)** Your **incisors** are the teeth at the front of your mouth which you use for biting into food. [N-COUNT]

**in|cite** /ɪnsaɪt/ **(incites, inciting, incited)** If someone **incites** people **to** behave in a violent or illegal way, they encourage people to behave in that way, usually by making them excited or angry. ❑ *He incited his fellow citizens to take their revenge... The party agreed not to incite its supporters to violence... They pleaded guilty to possessing material likely to incite racial hatred.* [VERB] [V n to-inf] [V n *to* n] [V n]

**in|cite|ment** /ɪnsaɪtmənt/ **(incitements)** If someone is accused of **incitement to** violent or illegal behaviour, they are accused of encouraging people to behave in that way. ❑ *British law forbids incitement to murder.* [N-VAR: oft N *to* n]

**incl.** 1 In written advertisements, **incl.** is an abbreviation for **including**. ❑ *...only £19.95 (incl. VAT and delivery).* [= inc.] 2 In written advertisements, **incl.** is an abbreviation for **inclusive**. ❑ *Open 19th July-6th September, Sun to Thurs incl.*

**in|clem|ent** /ɪnklemənt/ **Inclement** weather is unpleasantly cold or stormy. [FORMAL] [ADJ ≠ clement]

**in|cli|na|tion** /ɪnklɪneɪʃᵊn/ **(inclinations)** An **inclination** is a feeling that makes you want to act in a particular way. ❑ *He had neither the time nor the inclination to think of other things.* [N-VAR: usu with supp, oft N to-inf, oft with brd-neg]

**in|cline** **(inclines, inclining, inclined)**

> ✔ The verb is pronounced /ɪnklaɪn/. The noun is pronounced /ɪnklaɪn/.

1 If you **incline to** think or act in a particular way, or if something **inclines** you **to** it, you are likely to think or act in that way. [FORMAL] ❑ *I incline to the view that he is right. ...the factors which incline us towards particular beliefs... Many end up as team leaders, which inclines them to co-operate with the bosses... Those who fail incline to blame the world for their failure.* [VERB] [V *to/towards* n] [V n *to/towards* n] [V n to-inf] [V to-inf] 2 If you **incline** your head, you bend your neck so that your head is leaning forward. [WRITTEN] ❑ *Jack inclined his head very slightly.* [VERB] [V n] 3 An **incline** is land that slopes at an angle. [FORMAL] ❑ *He came to a halt at the edge of a steep incline.* [N-COUNT = slope]

**in|clined** /ɪnklaɪnd/ 1 If you are **inclined to** behave in a particular way, you often behave in that way, or you want to do so. ❑ *Nobody felt inclined to argue with Smith... If you are so inclined, you can watch TV.* [ADJ: v-link ADJ, ADJ to-inf, ADJ *to* n, *so* ADJ] 2 If you say that you are **inclined to** have a particular opinion, you mean that you hold this opinion but you are not expressing it strongly. ❑ *I am inclined to agree with Alan.* [ADJ: v-link ADJ to-inf] [vagueness] 3 Someone who is mathematically **inclined** or artistically **inclined**, for example, has a [ADJ: adv ADJ] natural talent for mathematics or art. ❑ *...the needs of academically inclined pupils.* 4 → See also **incline**.

**in|clude** /ɪnkluːd/ **(includes, including, included)** [◆◆◆] 1 If one thing **includes** another thing, it has the other thing as one of its parts. [VERB: V n] ❑ *The trip has been extended to include a few other events.* 2 If someone or something **is included in** a large group, system, or area, they become a part of it or are considered a part of it. [VERB: be V-ed in n, V n in n] ❑ *I had worked hard to be included in a project like this... The President is expected to include this idea in his education plan.*

**in|clud|ed** /ɪnkluːdɪd/ [◆◆◇] You use **included** to emphasize that a person or thing is part of the group of people or things that you are talking about. [ADJ: n ADJ, v-link ADJ; emphasis] ❑ *All of us, myself included, had been totally committed to the Party... Food is included in the price.*

**in|clud|ing** /ɪnkluːdɪŋ/ [◆◆◆] You use **including** to introduce examples of people or things that are part of the group of people or things that you are talking about. [PREP: PREP n/-ing; ≠ excluding] ❑ *Stars including Joan Collins are expected to attend.*

**in|clu|sion** /ɪnkluːʒᵊn/ **(inclusions)** **Inclusion** is the act of making a person or thing part of a group or collection. [N-VAR: usu with poss] ❑ *...a confident performance which justified his inclusion in the team.*

**in|clu|sive** /ɪnkluːsɪv/ 1 If a price is **inclusive**, it includes all the charges connected with the goods or services offered. If a price is **inclusive of** postage and packing, it includes the charge for this. [ADJ: oft ADJ of n] ❑ *...all prices are inclusive of delivery. ...an inclusive price of £32.90.* ♦ **Inclusive** is also an adverb. [ADV: amount ADV] ❑ *...a special introductory offer of £5,995 fully inclusive.* → See also **all-inclusive**. 2 After stating the first and last item in a set of things, you can add **inclusive** to make it clear that the items stated are included in the set. [ADJ: n ADJ] ❑ *Training will commence on 5 October, running from Tuesday to Saturday inclusive.* 3 If you describe a group or organization as **inclusive**, you mean that it allows all kinds of people to belong to it, rather than just one kind of person. [ADJ; ≠ exclusive] ❑ *The academy is far more inclusive now than it used to be.*

**in|cog|ni|to** /ɪnkɒgniːtoʊ/ Someone who is **incognito** is using a false name or wearing a disguise, in order not to be recognized or identified. [ADJ: v-link ADJ, ADJ after v] ❑ *Hotel inspectors have to travel incognito.*

**in|co|her|ent** /ɪnkoʊhɪərənt/ 1 If someone is **incoherent**, they are talking in a confused and unclear way. [ADJ; ≠ coherent] ❑ *The man was almost incoherent with fear.* ♦ **in|co|her|ence** [N-UNCOUNT] *Beth's incoherence told Amy that something was terribly wrong.* ♦ **in|co|her|ent|ly** [ADV: ADV with v] *He collapsed on the floor, mumbling incoherently.* 2 If you say that something such as a policy is **incoherent**, you are criticizing it because the different parts of it do not fit together properly. [ADJ; disapproval; ≠ coherent] ❑ *...an incoherent set of objectives.* ♦ **in|co|her|ence** [N-UNCOUNT: oft N of n] *...the general incoherence of government policy.*

**in|come** /ɪnkʌm/ **(incomes)** [◆◆◇] A person's or organization's **income** is the money that they earn or receive, as opposed to the money that they have to spend or pay out. [N-VAR] ❑ *Many families on low incomes will be unable to afford to buy their own home.*

**in|comer** /ɪnkʌməʳ/ **(incomers)** An **incomer** is someone who has recently come to live in a particular place or area. [mainly BRIT] [N-COUNT]

**in|come sup|port** In Britain, **income support** is money that the government gives regularly to people with no income or very low incomes. [N-UNCOUNT]

**in|come tax** **(income taxes)** **Income tax** is a certain percentage of your income that you have to pay regularly to the government. [N-VAR]

**in|com|ing** /ɪnkʌmɪŋ/ 1 An **incoming** message or phone call is one that you receive. [ADJ: ADJ n; ≠ outgoing] ❑ *We keep a tape of incoming calls.* 2 An **incoming** plane or passenger is one that is arriving at a place. [ADJ: ADJ n; ≠ outgoing] ❑ *The airport was closed for incoming flights.* 3 An **incoming** official or government is one that has just been appointed or elected. [ADJ: ADJ n; ≠ outgoing] ❑ *...the problems confronting the incoming government.*

**in|com|mu|ni|ca|do** /ɪnkəmjuːnɪkɑːdoʊ/ 1 If someone is being kept **incommunicado**, they are not allowed to talk to anyone outside the place where they are. [ADJ: usu v n ADJ] ❑ *He was held incommunicado in prison for ten days before being released without charge.* 2 If someone is **incommunicado**, they do not want to be disturbed, or are in a place where they cannot be contacted. [ADJ: v-link ADJ] ❑ *Yesterday she was incommunicado, putting the finishing touches to her autobiography.*

**in|com|pa|rable** /ɪnkɒmprəbᵊl/ 1 If you describe someone or something as **incomparable**, you mean that they are extremely good or impressive. [ADJ] ❑ *...a play starring the incomparable Edith Evans.* 2 You use **incomparable** to emphasize that someone or something has a good quality to a great degree. [FORMAL] [ADJ: ADJ n; emphasis; = superlative] ❑ *...an area of incomparable beauty.*

**in|com|pa|rably** /ɪnkɒmprəbli/ You can use **incomparably** to mean 'very much' when you are comparing two things and emphasizing the difference between them. [FORMAL] [ADV: ADV compar; emphasis; = infinitely] ❑ *...his incomparably brilliant love songs.*

**in|com|pat|ible** /ɪnkəmpætɪbᵊl/ 1 If one thing or person is **incompatible with** another, they are very different in important ways, and do not suit each other or agree with each other. [ADJ: usu v-link ADJ, oft ADJ with n; ≠ compatible] ❑ *They feel strongly that their religion is incompatible with the political system.* ♦ **in|com|pat|ibil|ity** /ɪnkəmpætɪbɪlɪti/ [N-UNCOUNT: usu N between/of/with n] *Incompatibility between the mother's and the baby's blood groups may cause jaundice.* 2 If one type of computer or computer system is **incompatible with** another, they cannot use the same programs or be linked up together. [ADJ: oft ADJ with n; ≠ compatible] ❑ *This made its mini-computers incompatible with its mainframes.*

**in|com|pe|tence** /ɪnkɒmpɪtəns/ If you refer to someone's **incompetence**, you are criticizing them because they are unable to do their job or a task properly. [N-UNCOUNT; disapproval; ≠ competence] ❑ *The incompetence of government officials is appalling.*

**in|com|pe|tent** /ɪnkɒmpɪtənt/ **(incompetents)** If you describe someone as **incompetent**, you are criticizing them because they are unable to do their job or a task properly. [ADJ; disapproval; ≠ competent] ❑ *He wants the power to sack incompetent teachers.* ♦ An **incompetent** is someone who is incompetent. [N-COUNT] ❑ *I'm surrounded by incompetents!*

**in|com|plete** /ɪnkəmpliːt/ Something that is **incomplete** is not yet finished, or does not have all the parts or details that it needs. [ADJ; ≠ complete] ❑ *The clearing of rubbish and drains is still incomplete.*

**in|com|pre|hen|sible** /ɪnkɒmprɪhensɪbᵊl/ Something that is **incomprehensible** is impossible to understand. [ADJ] ❑ *...incomprehensible mathematics puzzles.*

**in|com|pre|hen|sion** /ɪnkɒmprɪhenʃᵊn/ **Incomprehension** is the state of being unable to understand something or someone. [N-UNCOUNT] ❑ *Rosie had a look of incomprehension on her face.*

**in|con|ceiv|able** /ɪnkənsiːvəbᵊl/ If you describe something as **inconceivable**, you think it is very unlikely to happen or be true. [ADJ: usu v-link ADJ, oft it v-link ADJ that; = unthinkable] ❑ *It was inconceivable to me that Toby could have been my attacker.*

**in|con|clu|sive** /ɪnkənkluːsɪv/ 1 If research or evidence is **inconclusive**, it has not proved anything. [ADJ; ≠ conclusive] ❑ *Research has so far proved inconclusive.* 2 If a contest or conflict is **inconclusive**, it is not clear who has won or who is winning. [ADJ] ❑ *The past two elections were inconclusive.*

**in|con|gru|ity** /ɪnkɒŋgruːɪti/ **(incongruities)** The **incongruity** of something is its strangeness when considered together with other aspects of a situation. [FORMAL] [N-VAR: oft N of n] ❑ *She smiled at the incongruity of the question.*

**in|con|gru|ous** /ɪnkɒŋgruəs/ Someone or something that is **incongruous** seems strange [ADJ] when considered together with other aspects of a situation. [FORMAL] ❑ *She was small and fragile and looked incongruous in an army uniform.* ♦ **in|con|gru|ous|ly** *...buildings perched incongruously in a high green valley.* ADV: ADV after v, ADV adj/-ed

**in|con|sequen|tial** /ɪnkɒnsɪkwenʃəl/ Something that is **inconsequential** is not important. ❑ *...a constant reminder of just how insignificant and inconsequential their lives were.* ADJ = unimportant

**in|con|sid|er|able** /ɪnkənsɪdərəbəl/ If you describe an amount or quality as **not inconsiderable**, you are emphasizing that it is, in fact, large or present to a large degree. ❑ *The production costs are a not inconsiderable £8 million.* ADJ: with neg, usu ADJ n [emphasis]

**in|con|sid|er|ate** /ɪnkənsɪdərət/ If you accuse someone of being **inconsiderate**, you mean that they do not take enough care over how their words or actions will affect other people. ❑ *Motorists were criticised for being inconsiderate to pedestrians.* ADJ [disapproval] ≠ considerate

**in|con|sist|en|cy** /ɪnkənsɪstənsi/ **(inconsistencies)** 1 If you refer to someone's **inconsistency**, you are criticizing them for not behaving in the same way every time a similar situation occurs. ❑ *His worst fault was his inconsistency.* N-UNCOUNT [disapproval] ≠ consistency 2 If there are **inconsistencies** in two statements, one cannot be true if the other is true. ❑ *We were asked to investigate the alleged inconsistencies in his evidence.* N-VAR

**in|con|sist|ent** /ɪnkənsɪstənt/ 1 If you describe someone as **inconsistent**, you are criticizing them for not behaving in the same way every time a similar situation occurs. ❑ *You are inconsistent and unpredictable.* ADJ [disapproval] ≠ consistent 2 Someone or something that is **inconsistent** does not stay the same, being sometimes good and sometimes bad. ❑ *We had a terrific start to the season, but recently we've been inconsistent.* ADJ ≠ consistent 3 If two statements are **inconsistent**, one cannot possibly be true if the other is true. ❑ *The evidence given in court was inconsistent with what he had previously told them.* ADJ: oft ADJ *with* n ≠ consistent 4 If something is **inconsistent with** a set of ideas or values, it does not fit in well with them or match them. ❑ *This legislation is inconsistent with what they call Free Trade.* ADJ: v-link ADJ *with* n ≠ consistent

**in|con|sol|able** /ɪnkənsoʊləbəl/ If you say that someone is **inconsolable**, you mean that they are very sad and cannot be comforted. ❑ *When my mother died I was inconsolable.* ADJ

**in|con|spicu|ous** /ɪnkənspɪkjuəs/ 1 Someone who is **inconspicuous** does not attract attention to themselves. ❑ *I'll try to be as inconspicuous as possible.* ♦ **in|con|spicu|ous|ly** *I sat inconspicuously in a corner.* ADJ = unobtrusive ≠ conspicuous; ADV: ADV after v 2 Something that is **inconspicuous** is not easily seen or does not attract attention because it is small, ordinary, or hidden away. ❑ *...an inconspicuous grey building.* ADJ = unobtrusive ≠ conspicuous

**in|con|ti|nence** /ɪnkɒntɪnəns/ **Incontinence** is the inability to prevent urine or faeces coming out of your body. ❑ *Incontinence is not just a condition of old age.* N-UNCOUNT

**in|con|ti|nent** /ɪnkɒntɪnənt/ Someone who is **incontinent** is unable to prevent urine or faeces coming out of their body. ❑ *His diseased bladder left him incontinent.* ADJ

**in|con|tro|vert|ible** /ɪnkɒntrəvɜːʳtɪbəl/ **Incontrovertible** evidence or facts are absolutely certain and cannot be shown to be wrong. ❑ *We have incontrovertible evidence of what took place.* ♦ **in|con|tro|vert|ibly** *No solution is incontrovertibly right.* ADJ = indisputable; ADV

**in|con|ven|ience** /ɪnkənviːniəns/ **(inconveniences, inconveniencing, inconvenienced)** 1 If someone or something causes **inconvenience**, they cause problems or difficulties. ❑ *We apologize for any inconvenience caused during the repairs.* N-VAR 2 If someone **inconveniences** you, they cause problems or difficulties for you. ❑ *He promised to be quick so as not to inconvenience them any further.* VERB V n

**in|con|ven|ient** /ɪnkənviːniənt/ Something that is **inconvenient** causes problems or difficulties for someone. ❑ *Can you come at 10.30? I know it's inconvenient for you, but I must see you.* ♦ **in|con|ven|ient|ly** *The Oriental is a comfortable hotel, but rather inconveniently situated.* ADJ: oft ADJ *for* n ≠ convenient; ADV ≠ conveniently

**in|cor|po|rate** /ɪnkɔːʳpəreɪt/ **(incorporates, incorporating, incorporated)** 1 If one thing **incorporates** another thing, it includes the other thing. [FORMAL] ❑ *The new cars will incorporate a number of major improvements.* VERB = contain; V n 2 If someone or something **is incorporated into** a large group, system, or area, they become a part of it. [FORMAL] ❑ *The agreement would allow the rebels to be incorporated into a new national police force... The party vowed to incorporate environmental considerations into all its policies.* ♦ **in|cor|po|ra|tion** /ɪnkɔːʳpəreɪʃən/ *...the incorporation of Piedmont Airlines and PSA into US Air.* VERB; *be* V-ed *into* n; V n *into* n; N-UNCOUNT: usu N *of* n *into* n

**In|cor|po|rated** /ɪnkɔːʳpəreɪtɪd/ **Incorporated** is used after a company's name to show that it is a legally established company in the United States. [AM, BUSINESS] ❑ *...MCA Incorporated.* ADJ: n ADJ

**in|cor|rect** /ɪnkərekt/ 1 Something that is **incorrect** is wrong and untrue. ❑ *He denied that his evidence about the telephone call was incorrect.* ♦ **in|cor|rect|ly** *The magazine suggested incorrectly that he was planning to retire.* ADJ: oft *it* v-link ADJ to-inf ≠ correct; ADV: ADV with v 2 Something that is **incorrect** is not the thing that is required or is most suitable in a particular situation. ❑ *...injuries caused by incorrect posture.* ♦ **in|cor|rect|ly** *He was told that the doors had been fitted incorrectly.* ADJ: usu ADJ n ≠ correct; ADV: ADV with v

**in|cor|ri|gible** /ɪnkɒrɪdʒəbəl, AM -kɔːr-/ If you tell someone they are **incorrigible**, you are saying, often in a humorous way, that they have faults which will never change. ❑ *'Sue, you are incorrigible!'... Gamblers are incorrigible optimists.* ADJ

**in|cor|rupt|ible** /ɪnkərʌptɪbəl/ If you describe someone as **incorruptible**, you approve of the fact that they cannot be persuaded or paid to do things that they should not do. ❑ *He was a sound businessman, totally reliable and incorruptible.* ADJ [approval]

**in|crease** **(increases, increasing, increased)** ◆◆◆

> ✔ The verb is pronounced /ɪnkriːs/. The noun is pronounced /ɪnkriːs/.

1 If something **increases** or you **increase** it, it becomes greater in number, level, or amount. ❑ *The population continues to increase... Japan's industrial output increased by 2%... The company has increased the price of its cars.* VERB ≠ decrease; V; V *by/from/to* amount, V n 2 If there is an **increase in** the number, level, or amount of something, it becomes greater. ❑ *...a sharp increase in productivity.* N-COUNT: oft N *in* n, N *of* amount = rise 3 If something is **on the increase**, it is happening more often or becoming greater in number or intensity. ❑ *Crime is on the increase.* PHRASE: v-link PHR

**in|creas|ing|ly** /ɪnkriːsɪŋli/ You can use **increasingly** to indicate that a situation or quality is becoming greater in intensity or more common. ❑ *He was finding it increasingly difficult to make decisions... Increasingly, their goals have become more radical.* ◆◆◇ ADV: ADV adj, ADV with v, ADV with cl

**in|cred|ible** /ɪnkredɪbəl/ 1 If you describe something or someone as **incredible**, you like them very much or are impressed by them, because they are extremely or unusually good. ❑ *The wildflowers will be incredible after this rain.* ♦ **in|cred|ibly** /ɪnkredɪbli/ *Their father was incredibly good-looking.* ◆◇◇ ADJ [approval] = fantastic; ADV: ADV adj/adv 2 If you say that something is **incredible**, you mean that it is very unusual or surprising, and you cannot believe it is really true, although it may be. ❑ *It seemed incredible that people would still want to play football during a war.* ♦ **in|cred|ibly** *Incredibly, some people don't like the name.* ADJ: oft *it* v-link ADJ that ≠ credible; ADV: usu ADV with cl 3 You use **incredible** to emphasize the degree, amount, or intensity of something. ❑ *It's incredible how much Francesca wants her father's approval.* ♦ **in|cred|ibly** *The tour was incredibly hard work.* ADJ: usu ADJ n v-link ADJ [emphasis]; ADV: ADV adj/adv

**in|cre|du|lity** /ɪnkrɪdjuːlɪti, AM -duːl-/ If someone reacts with **incredulity** to something, N-UNCOUNT = disbelief they are unable to believe it because it is very surprising or shocking. ❑ *The announcement has been met with incredulity.*

**in|credu|lous** /ɪnkre̲dʒʊləs/ ADJ If someone is **incredulous**, they are unable to believe something because it is very surprising or shocking. ❑ *'He made you do it?' Her voice was incredulous.* ♦ **in|credu|lous|ly** ADV: ADV with v *'You told Pete?' Rachel said incredulously. 'I can't believe it!'*

**in|cre|ment** /ɪ̲nkrɪmənt/ **(increments)** 1 N-COUNT: oft N *in/of* n An **increment in** something or **in** the value of something is an amount by which it increases. [FORMAL] ❑ *The average yearly increment in labour productivity in industry was 4.5 per cent.* 2 N-COUNT An **increment** is an amount by which your salary automatically increases after a fixed period of time. [FORMAL] ❑ *Many teachers qualify for an annual increment.*

**in|cre|men|tal** /ɪ̲nkrɪme̲ntəl/ ADJ: usu ADJ n **Incremental** is used to describe something that increases in value or worth, often by a regular amount. [FORMAL] ❑ *...our ability to add production capacity at relatively low incremental cost.*

**in|crimi|nate** /ɪnkrɪ̲mɪneɪt/ **(incriminates, incriminating, incriminated)** VERB If something **incriminates** you, it suggests that you are responsible for something bad, especially a crime. ❑ V n *He claimed that the drugs had been planted to incriminate him...* V pron-refl *They are afraid of incriminating themselves and say no more than is necessary.* ♦ **in|crimi|nat|ing** ADJ: usu ADJ n *Police had reportedly searched his flat and found incriminating evidence.*

**in|cu|bate** /ɪ̲nkjʊbeɪt/ **(incubates, incubating, incubated)** 1 VERB When birds **incubate** their eggs, they keep the eggs warm until the baby birds come out. ❑ V n *The birds returned to their nests and continued to incubate the eggs.* Also V ♦ **in|cu|ba|tion** N-UNCOUNT /ɪ̲nkjʊbeɪ̲ʃən/ *Male albatrosses share in the incubation of eggs.* 2 VERB When a germ in your body **incubates** or **is incubated**, it develops for a period of time before it starts making you feel ill. ❑ V *The virus can incubate for up to ten days after the initial infection.* Also V n ♦ **in|cu|ba|tion** N-UNCOUNT: usu N n *The illness has an incubation period of up to 11 days.*

**in|cu|ba|tor** /ɪ̲nkjʊbeɪtər/ **(incubators)** 1 N-COUNT An **incubator** is a piece of hospital equipment which helps weak or small babies to survive. It consists of a transparent container in which the oxygen and temperature levels can be controlled. 2 N-COUNT An **incubator** is a piece of equipment used to keep eggs or bacteria at the correct temperature for them to develop.

**in|cul|cate** /ɪ̲nkʌlkeɪt, AM ɪnkʌ̲l-/ **(inculcates, inculcating, inculcated)** VERB = *instil* If you **inculcate** an idea or opinion **in** someone's mind, you teach it to them by repeating it until it is fixed in their mind. [FORMAL] ❑ V n *in* n *We have tried to inculcate a feeling of citizenship in youngsters...* V n *with* n *The aim is to inculcate business people with an appreciation of different cultures...* V n *Great care was taken to inculcate the values of nationhood and family.*

**in|cum|bent** /ɪnkʌ̲mbənt/ **(incumbents)** 1 N-COUNT An **incumbent** is someone who holds an official post at a particular time. [FORMAL] ❑ *In general, incumbents have a 94 per cent chance of being re-elected.* ♦ **Incumbent** is also an adjective. ADJ: ADJ n ❑ *...the only candidate who defeated an incumbent senator.* 2 ADJ: *it* v-link ADJ *upon/on* n to-inf If it is **incumbent upon** you **to** do something, it is your duty or responsibility to do it. [FORMAL] ❑ *It is incumbent upon all of us to make an extra effort.*

**in|cur** /ɪnkɜ̲ːr/ **(incurs, incurring, incurred)** VERB = *sustain* If you **incur** something unpleasant, it happens to you because of something you have done. [WRITTEN] ❑ V n *The government had also incurred huge debts.* V-ed *...the terrible damage incurred during the past decade.*

**in|cur|able** /ɪnkjʊ̲ərəbəl/ 1 ADJ If someone has an **incurable** disease, they cannot be cured of it. ❑ *He is suffering from an incurable skin disease.* ♦ **in|cur|ably** /ɪnkjʊ̲ərəbli/ ADV: ADV adj *...youngsters who are disabled, or incurably ill.* 2 ADJ: ADJ n You can use **incurable** to indicate that someone has a particular quality or attitude and will not change. ❑ *Poor old William is an incurable romantic.* ♦ **in|cur|ably** ADV: ADV adj *I know you think I'm incurably nosey.*

**in|cur|sion** /ɪnkɜ̲ːrʃən, -ʒən/ **(incursions)** 1 N-COUNT: oft N *into* n If there is an **incursion into** a country, enemy soldiers suddenly enter it. [FORMAL] ❑ *...armed incursions into border areas by rebel forces.* 2 N-COUNT: oft N *of* n If someone or something enters an area where you would not expect them to be, or where they have not been found before, you can call this an **incursion**, especially when you disapprove of their presence. [FORMAL] ❑ *...her disastrous incursion into the property market.*

**in|debt|ed** /ɪnde̲tɪd/ 1 ADJ: v-link ADJ *to* n If you say that you are **indebted to** someone for something, you mean that you are very grateful to them for something. ❑ *I am deeply indebted to him for his help.* ♦ **in|debt|ed|ness** N-UNCOUNT *Mortimer recounted his indebtedness to her in his autobiography.* 2 ADJ: usu ADJ n **Indebted** countries, organizations, or people are ones that owe money to other countries, organizations, or people. ❑ *America's treasury secretary identified the most heavily indebted countries.* ♦ **in|debt|ed|ness** N-UNCOUNT: usu with supp *The company has reduced its indebtedness to just $15 million.*

**in|de|cen|cy** /ɪndi̲ːsənsi/ 1 N-UNCOUNT If you talk about the **indecency** of something or someone, you are indicating that you find them morally or sexually offensive. ❑ *...the indecency of their language.* 2 N-UNCOUNT In law, an act of **indecency** is an illegal sexual act. ❑ *They were found guilty of acts of gross indecency.*

**in|de|cent** /ɪndi̲ːsənt/ 1 ADJ = *obscene* If you describe something as **indecent**, you mean that it is shocking and offensive, usually because it relates to sex or nakedness. ❑ *He accused Mrs Moore of making an indecent suggestion.* ♦ **in|de|cent|ly** ADV: ADV with v, ADV adj *...an indecently short skirt.* 2 ADJ If you describe the speed or amount of something as **indecent**, you are indicating, often in a humorous way, that it is much quicker or larger than is usual or desirable. ❑ *The opposition says the legislation was drafted with indecent haste.* ♦ **in|de|cent|ly** ADV *...an indecently large office.*

**in|de̲cent as|sa̲ult** N-UNCOUNT **Indecent assault** is the crime of attacking someone in a way which involves touching or threatening them sexually, but not forcing them to have sexual intercourse.

**in|de̲cent ex|po̲|sure** N-UNCOUNT **Indecent exposure** is a criminal offence that is committed when someone exposes their genitals in public.

**in|de|ci|pher|able** /ɪndɪsa̲ɪfərəbəl/ ADJ If writing or speech is **indecipherable**, you cannot understand what the words are. ❑ *Maggie's writing was virtually indecipherable... He uttered little indecipherable sounds.*

**in|de|ci|sion** /ɪ̲ndɪsɪ̲ʒən/ N-UNCOUNT If you say that someone suffers from **indecision**, you mean that they find it very difficult to make decisions. ❑ *After months of indecision, the government gave the plan the go-ahead on Monday.*

**in|de|ci|sive** /ɪndɪsa̲ɪsɪv/ 1 ADJ ≠ *decisive* If you say that someone is **indecisive**, you mean that they find it very difficult to make decisions. ❑ *He was criticised as a very weak and indecisive leader.* ♦ **in|de|ci|sive|ness** N-UNCOUNT: oft with poss *The mayor was criticized by radical reformers for his indecisiveness.* 2 ADJ = *inconclusive* An **indecisive** result in a contest or election is one which is not clear or definite. ❑ *The outcome of the battle was indecisive.*

**in|deed** /ɪndi̲ːd/ ◆◆◇ 1 ADV: ADV with v, ADV with cl/group [emphasis] You use **indeed** to confirm or agree with something that has just been said. ❑ *Later, he admitted that the payments had indeed been made... 'Did you know him?' — 'I did indeed.'... 'That's a topic which has come to the fore very much recently.' — 'Indeed.'* 2 ADV: ADV with cl [emphasis] You use **indeed** to introduce a further comment or statement which strengthens the point you have already made. ❑ *We have nothing against diversity; indeed, we want* *more of it.* 3 You use **indeed** at the end of a clause to give extra force to the word 'very', or to emphasize a particular word. ❑ *The engine began to sound very loud indeed.* ADV: adj ADV [emphasis]

**in|de|fati|gable** /ɪndɪfætɪgəbᵊl/ You use **indefatigable** to describe someone who never gets tired of doing something. [FORMAL] ❑ *His indefatigable spirit helped him to cope with his illness.* ADJ = untiring, tireless
♦ **in|de|fati|gab|ly** /ɪndɪfætɪgəbli/ *She worked indefatigably and enthusiastically to interest the young in music.* ADV: ADV with v, ADV adj

**in|de|fen|sible** /ɪndɪfensɪbᵊl/ 1 If you say that a statement, action, or idea is **indefensible**, you mean that it cannot be justified or supported because it is completely wrong or unacceptable. ❑ *She described the new policy as 'morally indefensible'.* ADJ ≠ defensible 2 Places or buildings that are **indefensible** cannot be defended if they are attacked. ❑ *The checkpoint was abandoned as militarily indefensible.* ADJ

**in|de|fin|able** /ɪndɪfaɪnəbᵊl/ An **indefinable** quality or feeling cannot easily be described. [WRITTEN] ❑ *There was something indefinable in her eyes.* ADJ

**in|defi|nite** /ɪndefɪnɪt/ 1 If you describe a situation or period as **indefinite**, you mean that people have not decided when it will end. ❑ *The trial was adjourned for an indefinite period.* ADJ: usu ADJ n 2 Something that is **indefinite** is not exact or clear. ❑ *...at some indefinite time in the future.* ADJ

**in|defi|nite ar|ti|cle** **(indefinite articles)** The words 'a' and 'an' are sometimes called **the indefinite article**. N-COUNT

**in|defi|nite|ly** /ɪndefɪnɪtli/ If a situation will continue **indefinitely**, it will continue for ever or until someone decides to change it or end it. ❑ *The visit has now been postponed indefinitely.* ADV: ADV with v

**in|defi|nite pro|noun** **(indefinite pronouns)** An **indefinite pronoun** is a pronoun such as 'someone', 'anything', or 'nobody', which you use to refer in a general way to a person or thing. N-COUNT

**in|del|ible** /ɪndelɪbᵊl/ If you say that something leaves an **indelible** impression, you mean that it is very unlikely to be forgotten. ❑ *My visit to India in 1986 left an indelible impression on me.* ADJ: usu ADJ n
♦ **in|del|ibly** *The horrors he experienced are imprinted, perhaps indelibly, in his brain.* ADV: ADV with v

**in|deli|cate** /ɪndelɪkət/ If something or someone is **indelicate**, they are rude or embarrassing. [FORMAL] ❑ *She really could not touch upon such an indelicate subject.* ADJ

**in|dem|ni|fy** /ɪndemnɪfaɪ/ **(indemnifies, indemnifying, indemnified)** To **indemnify** someone against something bad happening means to promise to protect them, especially financially, if it happens. [FORMAL] ❑ *They agreed to indemnify the taxpayers against any loss... It doesn't have the money to indemnify everybody.* VERB V n against n V n

**in|dem|nity** /ɪndemnɪti/ **(indemnities)** 1 If something provides **indemnity**, it provides insurance or protection against damage or loss. [FORMAL] ❑ *Political exiles had not been given indemnity from prosecution.* N-UNCOUNT 2 An **indemnity** is an amount of money paid to someone because of some damage or loss they have suffered. [FORMAL] ❑ *The government paid the family an indemnity for the missing pictures.* N-VAR

**in|dent** /ɪndent/ **(indents, indenting, indented)** When you **indent** a line of writing, you start it further away from the edge of the paper than all the other lines. ❑ *Indent the second line.* VERB V n

**in|den|ta|tion** /ɪndenteɪʃᵊn/ **(indentations)** 1 An **indentation** is the space at the beginning of a line of writing when it starts further away from the edge of the paper than all the other lines. N-COUNT 2 An **indentation** is a shallow hole or cut in the surface or edge of something. ❑ *Using a knife, make slight indentations around the edges of the pastry.* N-COUNT

**in|dent|ed** /ɪndentɪd/ If something is **indented**, its edge or surface is uneven because parts of it have been worn away or cut away. ADJ

**in|den|tured** /ɪndentʃəʳd/ In the past, an **indentured** worker was one who was forced to work for someone for a period of time, because of an agreement made by people in authority. ADJ: usu ADJ n

**in|de|pend|ence** /ɪndɪpendəns/ ◆◆◇ 1 If a country has or gains **independence**, it has its own government and is not ruled by any other country. ❑ *In 1816, Argentina declared its independence from Spain.* N-UNCOUNT 2 Someone's **independence** is the fact that they do not rely on other people. ❑ *He was afraid of losing his independence.* N-UNCOUNT: oft poss N

**In|de|pend|ence Day** A country's **Independence Day** is the day on which its people celebrate their independence from another country that ruled them in the past. In the United States, Independence Day is celebrated each year on 4th July. ❑ *He died on Independence Day, 1831.* N-UNCOUNT

**in|de|pend|ent** /ɪndɪpendənt/ **(independents)** ◆◆◆ 1 If one thing or person is **independent of** another, they are separate and not connected, so the first one is not affected or influenced by the second. ❑ *Your questions should be independent of each other... Two independent studies have been carried out.* ADJ: oft ADJ of/from n ♦ **in|de|pen|dent|ly** *...several people working independently in different areas of the world. The commission will operate independently of ministers.* ADV: usu ADV with v, also ADV adj, oft ADV of/from n 2 If someone is **independent**, they do not need help or money from anyone else. ❑ *Phil was now much more independent of his parents... She would like to be financially independent.* ADJ: oft ADJ of/from n ♦ **in|de|pen|dent|ly** *We aim to help disabled students to live and study independently.* ADV: ADV after v, ADV adj/-ed 3 **Independent** countries and states are not ruled by other countries but have their own government. ❑ *Papua New Guinea became independent from Australia in 1975.* ADJ: oft ADJ from/of n 4 An **independent** organization or other body is one that controls its own finances and operations, rather than being controlled by someone else. ❑ *...an independent television station.* ADJ: ADJ n 5 An **independent** school does not receive money from the government or local council, but from the fees paid by its students' parents or from charities. [BRIT] ❑ *He taught chemistry at a leading independent school.* ADJ: usu ADJ n ≠ state 6 An **independent** inquiry or opinion is one that involves people who are not connected with a particular situation, and should therefore be fair. ❑ *The government ordered an independent inquiry into the affair.* ADJ: ADJ n 7 An **independent** politician is one who does not represent any political party. ❑ *There's been a late surge of support for an independent candidate.* ADJ: usu ADJ n ♦ An **independent** is an independent politician. N-COUNT

**in|de|scrib|able** /ɪndɪskraɪbəbᵊl/ You use **indescribable** to emphasize that a quality or condition is very intense or extreme, and therefore cannot be properly described. ❑ *...her indescribable joy when it was confirmed her son was alive.* ADJ [emphasis] = inexpressible
♦ **in|de|scrib|ably** /ɪndɪskraɪbəbli/ *...indescribably filthy conditions.* ADV: ADV adj

**in|de|struct|ible** /ɪndɪstrʌktɪbᵊl/ If something is **indestructible**, it is very strong and cannot be destroyed. ❑ *This type of plastic is almost indestructible.* ADJ

**in|de|ter|mi|na|cy** /ɪndɪtɜːʳmɪnəsi/ The **indeterminacy** of something is its quality of being uncertain or vague. [FORMAL] ❑ *...the indeterminacy of language.* N-UNCOUNT

**in|de|ter|mi|nate** /ɪndɪtɜːʳmɪnət/ If something is **indeterminate**, you cannot say exactly what it is. ❑ *I hope to carry on for an indeterminate period.* ADJ: usu ADJ n = indefinite

**in|dex** /ɪndeks/ **(indices, indexes, indexing, indexed)** ◆◇◇

> ✓ The usual plural is **indexes**, but the form **indices** can be used for meaning 1.

1 An **index** is a system by which changes in the value of something and the rate at which it N-COUNT: with supp

changes can be recorded, measured, or interpreted. ❑ *...the UK retail price index. ...economic indices.*
2 An **index** is an alphabetical list that is printed at the back of a book and tells you on which pages important topics are referred to. ❑ *There's even a special subject index.* N-COUNT
3 If you **index** a book or a collection of information, you make an alphabetical list of the items in it. ❑ *This vast archive has been indexed and made accessible to researchers... She's indexed the book by author, by age, and by illustrator.* VERB be V-ed V n
4 If a quantity or value **is indexed to** another, a system is arranged so that it increases or decreases whenever the other one increases or decreases. ❑ *Minimum pensions and wages are to be indexed to inflation.* VERB: usu passive be V-ed to n
5 → See also **card index**.

**in|dex card** **(index cards)** An **index card** is a small card on which you can write information. Index cards are kept in a box, arranged in order. N-COUNT

**in|dex fin|ger** **(index fingers)** Your **index finger** is the finger that is next to your thumb. N-COUNT = forefinger

**index-linked** **Index-linked** pensions or payments change as inflation or the cost of living changes. [mainly BRIT] ADJ

**In|dian** /ɪndiən/ **(Indians)** 1 **Indian** means belonging or relating to India, or to its people or culture. ❑ *...the Indian government.* ADJ: usu ADJ n
2 An **Indian** is an Indian citizen, or a person of Indian origin. N-COUNT
3 **Indians** are the people who lived in North, South, or Central America before Europeans arrived, or people related to them. The usual name for them now is **Native Americans**. [OLD-FASHIONED] N-COUNT
4 → See also **Anglo-Indian**.

**In|dian sum|mer** **(Indian summers)** You can refer to a period of unusually warm and sunny weather during the autumn as an **Indian summer**. N-COUNT

**in|di|cate** /ɪndɪkeɪt/ **(indicates, indicating, indicated)** ◆◆◇
1 If one thing **indicates** another, the first thing shows that the second is true or exists. ❑ *A survey of retired people has indicated that most are independent and enjoying life... Our vote today indicates a change in United States policy... This indicates whether remedies are suitable for children.* VERB V that V n V wh
2 If you **indicate** an opinion, an intention, or a fact, you mention it in an indirect way. ❑ *Mr Rivers has indicated that he may resign... U.S. authorities have not yet indicated their monetary policy plans.* VERB V that V n
3 If you **indicate** something to someone, you show them where it is, especially by pointing to it. [FORMAL] ❑ *He indicated a chair. 'Sit down.'* VERB V n
4 If one thing **indicates** something else, it is a sign of that thing. ❑ *Dreams can help indicate your true feelings.* VERB V n
5 If a technical instrument **indicates** something, it shows a measurement or reading. ❑ *The needles that indicate your height are at the top right-hand corner... The temperature gauge indicated that it was boiling.* VERB = show V n V that
6 When drivers **indicate**, they make lights flash on one side of their vehicle to show that they are going to turn in that direction. [mainly BRIT] ❑ *He told us when to indicate and when to change gear.* VERB = signal V Also V n

☑ in AM, use **signal**

**in|di|ca|tion** /ɪndɪkeɪʃᵊn/ **(indications)** An **indication** is a sign which suggests, for example, what people are thinking or feeling. ❑ *All the indications are that we are going to receive reasonable support from abroad... He gave no indication that he was ready to compromise.* ◆◇◇ N-VAR = sign

**in|dica|tive** /ɪndɪkətɪv/ 1 If one thing is **indicative of** another, it suggests what the other thing is likely to be. [FORMAL] ❑ *The result was indicative of a strong retail market.* ADJ: usu v-link ADJ, usu ADJ of n/wh
2 In grammar, a clause that is in **the indicative**, or in **the indicative mood**, has a subject followed by a verb group. Examples are 'I'm hungry' and 'She was followed'. Clauses of this kind are typically used to make statements. N-SING: the N

**in|di|ca|tor** /ɪndɪkeɪtəʳ/ **(indicators)** 1 An **indicator** is a measurement or value which gives you an idea of what something is like. ❑ *...vital economic indicators, such as inflation, growth and the trade gap.* N-COUNT: usu with supp
2 A car's **indicators** are the flashing lights that tell you when it is going to turn left or right. [mainly BRIT] → See picture on page 1707. N-COUNT

☑ in AM, usually use **turn signals**

**in|di|ces** /ɪndɪsiːz/ **Indices** is a plural form of **index**.

**in|dict** /ɪndaɪt/ **(indicts, indicting, indicted)** If someone **is indicted for** a crime, they are officially charged with it. [mainly AM, LEGAL] ❑ *He was later indicted on corruption charges... She has been indicted for possessing cocaine.* VERB: usu passive be V-ed on n be V-ed for -ing/n

**in|dict|ment** /ɪndaɪtmənt/ **(indictments)**
1 If you say that one thing is **an indictment of** another thing, you mean that it shows how bad the other thing is. ❑ *It's a sad indictment of society that policemen are regarded as easy targets by thugs.* N-COUNT: oft N of n
2 An **indictment** is a formal accusation that someone has committed a crime. [mainly AM, LEGAL] ❑ *Prosecutors may soon seek an indictment on racketeering and fraud charges.* N-VAR: oft N against n = charge

**in|die** /ɪndi/ **(indies)** 1 **Indie** music refers to rock or pop music produced by new bands working with small, independent record companies. [mainly BRIT] ❑ *...a multi-racial indie band.* ADJ: ADJ n ≠ mainstream
♦ An **indie** is an indie band or record company. N-COUNT ≠ major
2 **Indie** films are produced by small independent companies rather than by major studios. [mainly BRIT] ❑ *...the indie movie Happiness.* ADJ: ADJ n
♦ An **indie** is an indie film or film company. N-COUNT

**in|dif|fer|ence** /ɪndɪfərəns/ If you accuse someone of **indifference to** something, you mean that they have a complete lack of interest in it. ❑ *...his callous indifference to the plight of his son.* N-UNCOUNT: oft N to n

**in|dif|fer|ent** /ɪndɪfərənt/ 1 If you accuse someone of being **indifferent to** something, you mean that they have a complete lack of interest in it. ❑ *People have become indifferent to the suffering of others.* ADJ: oft ADJ to n
♦ **in|dif|fer|ent|ly** *'Not that it matters,' said Tench indifferently.* ADV: ADV after v
2 If you describe something or someone as **indifferent**, you mean that their standard or quality is not very good, and often quite bad. ❑ *She had starred in several very indifferent movies.* ADJ = mediocre
♦ **in|dif|fer|ent|ly** *...an eight-year-old girl who reads tolerably and writes indifferently.* ADV: ADV with v

**in|dig|enous** /ɪndɪdʒɪnəs/ **Indigenous** people or things belong to the country in which they are found, rather than coming there or being brought there from another country. [FORMAL] ❑ *...the country's indigenous population.* ADJ = native

**in|di|gent** /ɪndɪdʒənt/ Someone who is **indigent** is very poor. [FORMAL] ADJ

**in|di|gest|ible** /ɪndɪdʒestɪbᵊl/ 1 Food that is **indigestible** cannot be digested easily. ❑ *Fried food is very indigestible.* ADJ ≠ digestible
2 If you describe facts or ideas as **indigestible**, you mean that they are difficult to understand, complicated, and dull. ❑ *...a dense, indigestible and wordy book.* ADJ [disapproval]

**in|di|ges|tion** /ɪndɪdʒestʃᵊn/ If you have **indigestion**, you have pains in your stomach and chest that are caused by difficulties in digesting food. N-UNCOUNT

**in|dig|nant** /ɪndɪgnənt/ If you are **indignant**, you are shocked and angry, because you think that something is unjust or unfair. ❑ *He is indignant at suggestions that they were secret agents.* ADJ: oft ADJ at/about n/-ing, ADJ that
♦ **in|dig|nant|ly** *'That is not true,' Erica said indignantly.* ADV: ADV with v

**in|dig|na|tion** /ɪndɪgneɪʃᵊn/ **Indignation** is the feeling of shock and anger which you have when you think that something is unjust or unfair. ❑ *She was filled with indignation at the conditions under which miners were forced to work.* N-UNCOUNT

**in|dig|nity** /ɪndɪgnɪti/ **(indignities)** If you talk about **the indignity of** doing something, you mean that it makes you feel embarrassed or unimportant. [FORMAL] ❑ *Later, he suffered the indignity of having to flee angry protesters.* N-VAR: oft the N of -ing/n = humiliation

**in|di|go** /ɪndɪgoʊ/ Something that is **indigo** is dark purplish blue in colour. COLOUR

**in|di|rect** /ɪndaɪrekt, -dɪr-/ [1] An **indirect** result or effect is not caused immediately and obviously by a thing or person, but happens because of something else that they have done. ❑ *Businesses are feeling the indirect effects from the recession that's going on elsewhere.* ♦ **in|di|rect|ly** *Drugs are indirectly responsible for the violence.* [2] An **indirect** route or journey does not use the shortest or easiest way between two places. ❑ *The goods went by a rather indirect route.* [3] **Indirect** remarks and information suggest something or refer to it, without actually mentioning it or stating it clearly. ❑ *His remarks amounted to an indirect appeal for economic aid.* ♦ **in|di|rect|ly** *He referred indirectly to the territorial dispute.* ADJ: usu ADJ n ≠ direct; ADV: usu ADV adj, ADV with v, also ADV with cl; ADJ ≠ direct; ADJ; ADV: ADV with v

**in|di|rect dis|course** **Indirect discourse** is the same as **indirect speech**. [AM] N-UNCOUNT

**in|di|rect ob|ject** **(indirect objects)** An **indirect object** is an object which is used with a transitive verb to indicate who benefits from an action or gets something as a result. For example, in 'She gave him her address', 'him' is the indirect object. Compare **direct object**. N-COUNT

**in|di|rect ques|tion** **(indirect questions)** An **indirect question** is the same as a **reported question**. [mainly BRIT] N-COUNT

**in|di|rect speech** **Indirect speech** is speech which tells you what someone said, but does not use the person's actual words: for example, 'They said you didn't like it', 'I asked him what his plans were', and 'Citizens complained about the smoke'. [mainly BRIT] N-UNCOUNT

✔ in AM, usually use **indirect discourse**

**in|di|rect tax** **(indirect taxes)** An **indirect tax** is a tax on goods and services which is added to their price. Compare **direct tax**. N-COUNT

**in|di|rect taxa|tion** **Indirect taxation** is a system in which a government raises money by means of indirect taxes. N-UNCOUNT

**in|dis|ci|pline** /ɪndɪsɪplɪn/ If you refer to **indiscipline** in a group or team, you disapprove of the fact that they do not behave in a controlled way as they should. ❑ *There is growing evidence of indiscipline among the troops.* N-UNCOUNT [disapproval] ≠ discipline

**in|dis|creet** /ɪndɪskriːt/ If you describe someone as **indiscreet**, you mean that they do or say things in public which they should only do or say secretly or in private. ❑ *He is notoriously indiscreet about his private life.* ADJ ≠ discreet

**in|dis|cre|tion** /ɪndɪskreʃᵊn/ **(indiscretions)** If you talk about someone's **indiscretion**, you mean that they have done or said something that is risky, careless, or likely to upset people. ❑ *Occasionally they paid for their indiscretion with their lives.* N-VAR

**in|dis|crimi|nate** /ɪndɪskrɪmɪnət/ If you describe an action as **indiscriminate**, you are critical of it because it does not involve any careful thought or choice. ❑ *The indiscriminate use of fertilisers is damaging to the environment.* ♦ **in|dis|crimi|nate|ly** *The men opened fire indiscriminately.* ADJ [disapproval] ≠ selective; ADV: usu ADV with v, also ADV adj

**in|dis|pen|sable** /ɪndɪspensəbᵊl/ If you say that someone or something is **indispensable**, you mean that they are absolutely essential and other people or things cannot function without them. ❑ *She was becoming indispensable to him.* ADJ: oft ADJ *to* n = essential ≠ dispensable

**in|dis|posed** /ɪndɪspoʊzd/ If you say that someone is **indisposed**, you mean that they are not available because they are ill, or for a reason that you do not want to reveal. [FORMAL] ❑ *The speaker was regrettably indisposed.* ADJ: usu v-link ADJ = unwell

**in|dis|put|able** /ɪndɪspjuːtəbᵊl/ If you say that something is **indisputable**, you are emphasizing that it is true and cannot be shown to be untrue. ❑ *It is indisputable that birds in the UK are harbouring this illness.* ADJ: oft *it* v-link ADJ that [emphasis] = undeniable

**in|dis|tinct** /ɪndɪstɪŋkt/ Something that is **indistinct** is unclear and difficult to see, hear, or recognize. ❑ *The lettering is fuzzy and indistinct.* ♦ **in|dis|tinct|ly** *He speaks so indistinctly that many listeners haven't a clue what he is saying.* ADJ ≠ distinct; ADV: ADV after v

**in|dis|tin|guish|able** /ɪndɪstɪŋgwɪʃəbᵊl/ If one thing is **indistinguishable from** another, the two things are so similar that it is difficult to know which is which. ❑ *Replica weapons are indistinguishable from the real thing.* ADJ: usu v-link ADJ, oft ADJ *from* n

**in|di|vid|ual** /ɪndɪvɪdʒuᵊl/ **(individuals)** ◆◆◇ [1] **Individual** means relating to one person or thing, rather than to a large group. ❑ *They wait for the group to decide rather than making individual decisions... Aid to individual countries would be linked to progress towards democracy.* ♦ **in|di|vid|ual|ly** *...cheeses which come in individually wrapped segments.* [2] An **individual** is a person. ❑ *...anonymous individuals who are doing good things within our community.* [3] If you describe someone or something as **individual**, you mean that you admire them because they are very unusual and do not try to imitate other people or things. ❑ *It was really all part of her very individual personality.* ADJ: ADJ n; ADV: usu ADV with v, ADV adj, also ADV with cl; N-COUNT; ADJ [approval]

**in|di|vidu|al|ism** /ɪndɪvɪdʒuɪzəm/ [1] You use **individualism** to refer to the behaviour of someone who likes to think and do things in their own way, rather than imitating other people. ❑ *He is struck by what he calls the individualism of American officers.* [2] **Individualism** is the belief that economics and politics should not be controlled by the state. ❑ *...the strong individualism in their political culture.* N-UNCOUNT; N-UNCOUNT

**in|di|vidu|al|ist** /ɪndɪvɪdʒʊlɪst/ **(individualists)** [1] If you describe someone as an **individualist**, you mean that they like to think and do things in their own way, rather than imitating other people. ❑ *Individualists say that you should be able to wear what you want.* [2] **Individualist** means relating to the belief that economics and politics should not be controlled by the state. ❑ *...a party committed to individualist values.* ♦ An **individualist** is a person with individualist views. ❑ *They share with earlier individualists a fear of collectivism.* N-COUNT; ADJ: usu ADJ n; N-COUNT

**in|di|vidu|al|is|tic** /ɪndɪvɪdʒʊlɪstɪk/ If you say that someone is **individualistic**, you mean that they like to think and do things in their own way, rather than imitating other people. You can also say that a society is **individualistic** if it encourages people to behave in this way. ❑ *Most artists are very individualistic.* ADJ

**in|di|vidu|al|ity** /ɪndɪvɪdʒuælɪti/ The **individuality** of a person or thing consists of the qualities that make them different from other people or things. ❑ *People should be free to express their individuality.* N-UNCOUNT

**in|di|vidu|al|ize** /ɪndɪvɪdʒʊlaɪz/ **(individualizes, individualizing, individualized)**

✔ in BRIT, also use **individualise**

To **individualize** a thing or person means to make them different from other things or people and to give them a recognizable identity. [FORMAL] ❑ *You can individualize a document by adding comments in the margins.* VERB; V n

**in|di|vis|ible** /ɪndɪvɪzɪbᵊl/ If you say that something is **indivisible**, you mean that it cannot be divided into different parts. ❑ *Far from being separate, the mind and body form an indivisible whole.* ADJ ≠ divisible

**Indo-** /ɪndoʊ-/ **Indo-** combines with nationality adjectives to form adjectives which describe something as connected with both India and another country. ❑ *...Indo-Pakistani talks.* PREFIX

**in|doc|tri|nate** /ɪndɒktrɪneɪt/ **(indoctrinates, indoctrinating, indoctrinated)** If people **are indoctrinated**, they are taught a particular belief with the aim that they will reject other beliefs. ❑ *They have been completely indoctrinated... I wouldn't say that she was trying to indoctrinate us.* VERB [disapproval] = brainwash; *be* V-ed; V n

♦ **in|doc|tri|na|tion** /ɪndɒktrɪneɪʃᵊn/ *...political indoctrination classes.* N-UNCOUNT

**in|do|lence** /ɪndələns/ **Indolence** means laziness. [FORMAL] N-UNCOUNT

**in|do|lent** /ɪndələnt/ Someone who is **indolent** is lazy. [FORMAL] ADJ

**in|domi|table** /ɪndɒmɪtəbᵊl/ If you say that someone has an **indomitable** spirit, you admire them because they never give up or admit that they have been defeated. [FORMAL] ❑ *...a woman of indomitable will.* ADJ approval

**In|do|nesian** /ɪndəniːʒən/ **(Indonesians)** 1 **Indonesian** means belonging or relating to Indonesia, or to its people or culture. ADJ 2 An **Indonesian** is an Indonesian citizen, or a person of Indonesian origin. N-COUNT 3 **Indonesian** is the national language of Indonesia. N-UNCOUNT

**in|door** /ɪndɔːʳ/ **Indoor** activities or things are ones that happen or are used inside a building and not outside. ❑ *...an indoor market.* ADJ: ADJ n ≠ outdoor

**in|doors** /ɪndɔːʳz/ If something happens **indoors**, it happens inside a building. ❑ *I think perhaps we should go indoors.* ADV: be ADV, ADV after v ≠ outdoors

**in|du|bi|table** /ɪndjuːbɪtəbᵊl, AM -duːb-/ You use **indubitable** to describe something when you want to emphasize that it is definite and cannot be doubted. [FORMAL] ❑ *His brilliance renders this film an indubitable classic.* ADJ emphasis = undeniable ♦ **in|du|bi|tably** *His behaviour was indubitably ill-judged.* ADV

**in|duce** /ɪndjuːs, AM -duːs-/ **(induces, inducing, induced)** 1 To **induce** a state or condition means to cause it. ❑ *Doctors said surgery could induce a heart attack. ...an economic crisis induced by high oil prices.* VERB V n V-ed 2 If you **induce** someone **to** do something, you persuade or influence them to do it. ❑ *More than 4,000 teachers were induced to take early retirement.* VERB = persuade be V-ed to-inf 3 If a doctor or nurse **induces** labour or birth, they cause a pregnant woman to start giving birth by using drugs or other medical means. [MEDICAL] ❑ *He might decide that it is best to induce labour.* VERB V n

**-induced** /-ɪndjuːst, AM -duːs-/ **-induced** combines with nouns to form adjectives which indicate that a state, condition, or illness is caused by a particular thing. ❑ *...stress-induced disorders. ...a drug-induced hallucination.* COMB in ADJ

**in|duce|ment** /ɪndjuːsmənt, AM -duːs-/ **(inducements)** If someone is offered an **inducement to** do something, they are given or promised gifts or benefits in order to persuade them to do it. ❑ *They offer every inducement to foreign businesses to invest in their states.* N-COUNT: oft N to-inf = incentive

**in|duct** /ɪndʌkt/ **(inducts, inducting, inducted)** If someone **is inducted into** a particular job, rank, or position, they are given the job, rank, or position in a formal ceremony. [FORMAL] ❑ *Six new members have been inducted into the Provincial Cabinet... She inducts Nina into the cult.* VERB be V-ed into n V n into n

**in|duc|tion** /ɪndʌkʃᵊn/ **(inductions)** 1 **Induction** is a procedure or ceremony for introducing someone to a new job, organization, or way of life. ❑ *...an induction course for new members.* N-VAR: oft with poss, N to/into n 2 **Induction** is a method of reasoning in which you use individual ideas or facts to give you a general rule or conclusion. [FORMAL] N-UNCOUNT 3 → See also **induce**.

**in|duc|tive** /ɪndʌktɪv/ **Inductive** reasoning is based on the process of induction. ADJ

**in|dulge** /ɪndʌldʒ/ **(indulges, indulging, indulged)** 1 If you **indulge in** something or if you **indulge yourself**, you allow yourself to have or do something that you know you will enjoy. ❑ *Only rarely will she indulge in a glass of wine... He returned to Britain so that he could indulge his passion for football... You can indulge yourself without spending a fortune.* VERB V in n V n V pron-refl Also V 2 If you **indulge** someone, you let them have or do what they want, even if this is not good for them. ❑ *He did not agree with indulging children.* VERB = spoil V n

**in|dul|gence** /ɪndʌldʒᵊns/ **(indulgences)** **Indulgence** means treating someone with special kindness, often when it is not a good thing. ❑ *The king's indulgence towards his sons angered the business community.* N-VAR

**in|dul|gent** /ɪndʌldʒᵊnt/ If you are **indulgent**, you treat a person with special kindness, often in a way that is not good for them. ❑ *His indulgent mother was willing to let him do anything he wanted.* ADJ ♦ **in|dul|gent|ly** *Ned smiled at him indulgently.* ADV: usu ADV with v, also ADV adj

**in|dus|trial** /ɪndʌstriəl/ ♦♦◇ 1 You use **industrial** to describe things which relate to or are used in industry. ❑ *...industrial machinery and equipment. ...a link between industrial chemicals and cancer.* ADJ: usu ADJ n 2 An **industrial** city or country is one in which industry is important or highly developed. ❑ *...ministers from leading western industrial countries.* ADJ: usu ADJ n

**in|dus|trial ac|tion** If workers take **industrial action**, they join together and do something to show that they are unhappy with their pay or working conditions, for example refusing to work. [mainly BRIT] ❑ *Prison officers have decided to take industrial action.* N-UNCOUNT

**in|dus|trial es|tate** **(industrial estates)** An **industrial estate** is an area which has been specially planned for a lot of factories. [BRIT] N-COUNT

☑ in AM, use **industrial park**

**in|dus|tri|al|ise** /ɪndʌstriəlaɪz/ → see **industrialize**.

**in|dus|tri|al|ism** /ɪndʌstriəlɪzəm/ **Industrialism** is the state of having an economy based on industry. N-UNCOUNT

**in|dus|tri|al|ist** /ɪndʌstriəlɪst/ **(industrialists)** An **industrialist** is a powerful businessman who owns or controls large industrial companies or factories. ❑ *...prominent Japanese industrialists.* N-COUNT

**in|dus|tri|al|ize** /ɪndʌstriəlaɪz/ **(industrializes, industrializing, industrialized)**

☑ in BRIT, also use **industrialise**

When a country **industrializes** or **is industrialized**, it develops a lot of industries. ❑ *Energy consumption rises as countries industrialise... Stalin's methods had industrialized the Russian economy.* VERB V V n ♦ **in|dus|tri|ali|za|tion** /ɪndʌstriəlaɪzeɪʃᵊn/ *Industrialization began early in Spain.* N-UNCOUNT

**in|dus|tri|al|ized** /ɪndʌstriəlaɪzd/ ♦◇◇

☑ in BRIT, also use **industrialised**

An **industrialized** area or place is one which has a lot of industries. ❑ *Industrialized countries must reduce carbon dioxide emissions.* ADJ: ADJ n

**in|dus|trial park** **(industrial parks)** An **industrial park** is the same as an **industrial estate**. [AM] N-COUNT

**in|dus|trial re|la|tions** **Industrial relations** refers to the relationship between employers and employees in industry, and the political decisions and laws that affect it. [BUSINESS] ❑ *The offer is seen as an attempt to improve industrial relations.* N-PLURAL

**in|dus|tri|ous** /ɪndʌstriəs/ If you describe someone as **industrious**, you mean they work very hard. ❑ *She was an industrious and willing worker.* ADJ = hard-working ♦ **in|dus|tri|ous|ly** *Maggie paints industriously all through the summer.* ADV: ADV with v

**in|dus|try** /ɪndəstri/ **(industries)** ♦♦♦ 1 **Industry** is the work and processes involved in collecting raw materials, and making them into products in factories. ❑ *British industry suffers through insufficient investment in research.* N-UNCOUNT 2 A particular **industry** consists of all the people and activities involved in making a particular product or providing a particular service. ❑ *...the motor vehicle and textile industries.* N-COUNT: oft n N 3 If you refer to a social or political activity as an **industry**, you are criticizing it because you think it involves a lot of people in unnecessary or useless work. ❑ *Some Afro-Caribbeans are rejecting the whole race relations indus-* N-COUNT: usu sing, the supp N disapproval *try.* [4] **Industry** is the fact of working very hard. [FORMAL] ❑ *No one doubted his ability, his industry or his integrity.* [5] → See also **captain of industry, cottage industry, service industry.** N-UNCOUNT

**ine|bri|at|ed** /ɪniːbrieɪtɪd/ Someone who is **inebriated** has drunk too much alcohol. [FORMAL] ❑ *Scott was obviously inebriated by the time the dessert was served.* ADJ

**in|ed|ible** /ɪnedɪbəl/ If you say that something is **inedible**, you mean you cannot eat it, for example because it tastes bad or is poisonous. ❑ *Detainees complained of being given food which is inedible.* ADJ ≠ edible

**in|ef|fable** /ɪnefəbəl/ You use **ineffable** to say that something is so great or extreme that it cannot be described in words. [FORMAL] ❑ *...the ineffable sadness of many of the portraits.* ADJ: usu ADJ n = indescribable
♦ **in|ef|fably** /ɪnefəbli/ *...his ineffably powerful brain.* ADV: usu ADV adj

**in|ef|fec|tive** /ɪnɪfektɪv/ If you say that something is **ineffective**, you mean that it has no effect on a process or situation. ❑ *Economic reform will continue to be painful and ineffective.* ADJ ≠ effective
♦ **in|ef|fec|tive|ness** *...the ineffectiveness of some of the police's anti-crime strategies.* N-UNCOUNT

**in|ef|fec|tual** /ɪnɪfektʃuəl/ If someone or something is **ineffectual**, they fail to do what they are expected to do or are trying to do. ❑ *The mayor had become ineffectual in the struggle to clamp down on drugs.* ADJ ♦ **in|ef|fec|tu|al|ly** *Her voice trailed off ineffectually.* ADV

**in|ef|fi|cient** /ɪnɪfɪʃənt/ **Inefficient** people, organizations, systems, or machines do not use time, energy, or other resources in the best way. ❑ *Their communication systems are inefficient in the extreme.* ADJ ≠ efficient ♦ **in|ef|fi|cien|cy** **(inefficiencies)** *...the inefficiency of the distribution system.* N-VAR
♦ **in|ef|fi|cient|ly** *Energy prices have been kept low, so energy is used inefficiently.* ADV: ADV with v

**in|el|egant** /ɪnelɪgənt/ If you say that something is **inelegant**, you mean that it is not attractive or graceful. ❑ *The grand piano has been replaced with a small, inelegant electric model.* ADJ ≠ elegant

**in|eli|gible** /ɪnelɪdʒəbəl/ If you are **ineligible for** something, you are not qualified for it or entitled to it. [FORMAL] ❑ *They were ineligible to remain in the USA.* ADJ: usu v-link ADJ, oft ADJ *for* n, ADJ to-inf ≠ eligible

**in|eluc|table** /ɪnɪlʌktəbəl/ You use **ineluctable** to describe something that cannot be stopped, escaped, or ignored. [FORMAL] ❑ *...Malthus's theories about the ineluctable tendency of populations to exceed resources.* ADJ: usu ADJ n = inescapable

**in|ept** /ɪnept/ If you say that someone is **inept**, you are criticizing them because they do something with a complete lack of skill. ❑ *He was inept and lacked the intelligence to govern.* ADJ [disapproval] ≠ skilful

**in|epti|tude** /ɪneptɪtjuːd, AM -tuːd/ If you refer to someone's **ineptitude**, you are criticizing them because they do something with a complete lack of skill. ❑ *...the tactical ineptitude of the allied commander.* N-UNCOUNT [disapproval] ≠ skill

**in|equal|ity** /ɪnɪkwɒlɪti/ **(inequalities)** **Inequality** is the difference in social status, wealth, or opportunity between people or groups. ❑ *People are concerned about social inequality.* N-VAR ≠ equality

**in|equi|table** /ɪnekwɪtəbəl/ If you say that something is **inequitable**, you are criticizing it because it is unfair or unjust. [FORMAL] ❑ *The welfare system is grossly inequitable and inefficient.* ADJ [disapproval] ≠ equitable

**in|equi|ty** /ɪnekwɪti/ **(inequities)** If you refer to the **inequity** of something, you are criticizing it because it is unfair or unjust. [FORMAL] ❑ *Social imbalance worries him more than inequity of income.* N-VAR [disapproval] = inequality

**in|eradi|cable** /ɪnɪrædɪkəbəl/ You use **ineradicable** to emphasize that a quality, fact, or situation is permanent and cannot be changed. [FORMAL] ❑ *Divorce is a permanent, ineradicable fact of modern life.* ADJ: usu ADJ n [emphasis]

**in|ert** /ɪnɜːʳt/ [1] Someone or something that is **inert** does not move at all. ❑ *He covered the inert body with a blanket.* ADJ [2] If you describe something as **inert**, you are criticizing it because it is not very lively or interesting. ❑ *The novel itself remains oddly inert.* ADJ [disapproval] [3] An **inert** substance is one which does not react with other substances. [TECHNICAL] ❑ *...inert gases like neon and argon.* ADJ

**in|er|tia** /ɪnɜːʳʃə/ [1] If you have a feeling of **inertia**, you feel very lazy and unwilling to move or be active. ❑ *...her inertia, her lack of energy.* N-UNCOUNT = lethargy [2] **Inertia** is the tendency of a physical object to remain still or to continue moving, unless a force is applied to it. [TECHNICAL] N-UNCOUNT

**in|es|cap|able** /ɪnɪskeɪpəbəl/ If you describe a fact, situation, or activity as **inescapable**, you mean that it is difficult not to notice it or be affected by it. ❑ *The economic logic of reform is inescapable.* ADJ = unavoidable ♦ **in|es|cap|ably** /ɪnɪskeɪpəbli/ *It is inescapably clear that they won't turn round.* ADV

**in|es|sen|tial** /ɪnɪsenʃəl/ If something is **inessential**, you do not need it. [FORMAL] ❑ *We have omitted footnotes which we judged inessential to the text.* ADJ = superfluous ≠ essential

**in|es|ti|mable** /ɪnestɪməbəl/ If you describe the value, benefit, or importance of something as **inestimable**, you mean that it is extremely great and cannot be calculated. [FORMAL] ❑ *Human life is of inestimable value.* ADJ: usu ADJ n = incalculable

**in|evi|tabil|ity** /ɪnevɪtəbɪlɪti/ **(inevitabilities)** The **inevitability** of something is the fact that it is certain to happen and cannot be prevented or avoided. ❑ *We are all bound by the inevitability of death.* N-VAR: oft N *of* n

**in|evi|table** /ɪnevɪtəbəl/ If something is **inevitable**, it is certain to happen and cannot be prevented or avoided. ❑ *If the case succeeds, it is inevitable that other trials will follow... The defeat had inevitable consequences for British policy.* ◆◇◇ ADJ: oft *it* v-link ADJ that = unavoidable ♦ **The inevitable** is something which is inevitable. ❑ *'It's just delaying the inevitable,' he said.* N-SING: *the* N

**in|evi|tably** /ɪnevɪtəbli/ If something will **inevitably** happen, it is certain to happen and cannot be prevented or avoided. ❑ *Technological changes will inevitably lead to unemployment.* ADV: usu ADV with v, also ADV with cl, ADV adj = unavoidably

**in|ex|act** /ɪnɪgzækt/ Something that is **inexact** is not precise or accurate. ❑ *Forecasting was an inexact science.* ADJ ≠ exact

**in|ex|cus|able** /ɪnɪkskjuːzəbəl/ If you say that something is **inexcusable**, you are emphasizing that it cannot be justified or tolerated because it is extremely bad. ❑ *He said the killing of innocent people was inexcusable.* ADJ [emphasis] = unpardonable ♦ **in|ex|cus|ably** /ɪnɪkskjuːzəbli/ *She had been inexcusably careless.* ADV

**in|ex|haust|ible** /ɪnɪgzɔːstəbəl/ If there is an **inexhaustible** supply of something, there is so much of it that it cannot all be used up. ❑ *She has an inexhaustible supply of enthusiasm.* ADJ = endless

**in|exo|rable** /ɪneksərəbəl/ You use **inexorable** to describe a process which cannot be prevented from continuing or progressing. [FORMAL] ❑ *...the seemingly inexorable rise in unemployment.* ADJ: usu ADJ n = relentless
♦ **in|exo|rably** /ɪneksərəbli/ *Spending on health is growing inexorably.* ADV: ADV with v

**in|ex|pen|sive** /ɪnɪkspensɪv/ Something that is **inexpensive** does not cost very much. ❑ *...a variety of good inexpensive restaurants.* ADJ = cheap ≠ expensive

**in|ex|pe|ri|ence** /ɪnɪkspɪəriəns/ If you refer to someone's **inexperience**, you mean that they have little knowledge or experience of a particular situation or activity. ❑ *Critics attacked the youth and inexperience of his staff.* N-UNCOUNT ≠ experience

**in|ex|pe|ri|enced** /ɪnɪkspɪəriənst/ If you are **inexperienced**, you have little knowledge or experience of a particular situation or activity. ❑ *Routine tasks are often delegated to inexperienced young doctors.* ADJ ≠ experienced

**in|ex|pert** /ɪnekspɜːʳt/ If you describe someone or something as **inexpert**, you mean that they show a lack of skill. ❑ *He was too inexperienced and too inexpert to succeed. ...inexpert needlework.* ADJ ≠ expert

**in|ex|pli|cable** /ɪnɪksplɪkəbᵊl/ If something is **inexplicable**, you cannot explain why it happens or why it is true. ❑ *For some inexplicable reason, all the investors decided to pull out.* ♦ **in|ex|pli|cably** /ɪnɪksplɪkəbli/ *She suddenly and inexplicably announced her retirement.* ADJ = incomprehensible; ADV: usu ADV with v

**in|ex|press|ible** /ɪnɪkspresɪbᵊl/ An **inexpressible** feeling cannot be expressed in words because it is so strong. [FORMAL] ❑ *He felt a sudden inexpressible loneliness.* ADJ = indescribable

**in ex|tre|mis** /ɪn ɪkstriːmɪs/ If someone or something is **in extremis**, they are in a very difficult situation and have to use extreme methods. [FORMAL] ❑ *The use of antibiotics is permitted only in extremis.* PHRASE: PHR with v

**in|ex|tri|cable** /ɪnɪkstrɪkəbᵊl, ɪnekstrɪk-/ If there is an **inextricable** link between things, they cannot be considered separately. [FORMAL] ❑ *Meetings are an inextricable part of business.* ADJ = inseparable

**in|ex|tri|cably** /ɪnekstrɪkəbᵊli/ If two or more things are **inextricably** linked, they cannot be considered separately. [FORMAL] ❑ *Religion was for her inextricably linked with life itself.* ADV: ADV with v

**in|fal|lible** /ɪnfælɪbᵊl/ If a person or thing is **infallible**, they are never wrong. ❑ *Although he was experienced, he was not infallible.* ♦ **in|fal|libil|ity** /ɪnfælɪbɪlɪti/ *...exaggerated views of the infallibility of science.* ADJ ≠ fallible; N-UNCOUNT

**in|fa|mous** /ɪnfəməs/ **Infamous** people or things are well-known because of something bad. [FORMAL] ❑ *He was infamous for his anti-feminist attitudes.* ADJ: usu ADJ n, also v-link ADJ for n, v-link ADJ = notorious

**in|fa|my** /ɪnfəmi/ **Infamy** is the state of being infamous. [FORMAL] ❑ *...one of the greatest acts of infamy in history.* N-UNCOUNT = notoriety

**in|fan|cy** /ɪnfənsi/ [1] **Infancy** is the period of your life when you are a very young child. ❑ *...the development of the mind from infancy onwards.* N-UNCOUNT: usu poss N, prep N [2] If something is **in its infancy**, it is new and has not developed very much. ❑ *Computing science was still in its infancy.* N-UNCOUNT: usu in poss N

**in|fant** /ɪnfənt/ **(infants)** [1] An **infant** is a baby or very young child. [FORMAL] ❑ *...young mums with infants in prams. ...the infant mortality rate in Britain.* N-COUNT: oft N n [2] **Infants** are children between the ages of five and seven, who go to an infant school. [BRIT] N-COUNT: usu pl ♦ You use **the infants** to refer to a school or class for such children. ❑ *You've been my best friend ever since we started in the infants.* N-UNCOUNT: the N [3] **Infant** means designed especially for very young children. ❑ *...an infant carrier in the back of a car.* ADJ: ADJ n [4] An **infant** organization or system is new and has not developed very much. ❑ *The infant company was based in Germany.* ADJ: ADJ n

**in|fan|ti|cide** /ɪnfæntɪsaɪd/ **Infanticide** is the crime of killing a young child. N-UNCOUNT

**in|fan|tile** /ɪnfəntaɪl/ [1] **Infantile** behaviour or illnesses are typical of very young children. [FORMAL] ❑ *...infantile aggression.* ADJ: ADJ n [2] If you accuse someone or something of being **infantile**, you think that they are foolish and childish. ❑ *This kind of humour is infantile and boring.* ADJ [disapproval] = childish

**in|fan|try** /ɪnfəntri/ **Infantry** are soldiers who fight on foot rather than in tanks or on horses. ❑ *...an infantry division.* N-UNCOUNT-COLL

**in|fantry|man** /ɪnfəntrimən/ **(infantrymen)** An **infantryman** is a soldier who fights on foot. N-COUNT

**in|fant school** **(infant schools)** In Britain, an **infant school** is a school for children between the ages of five and seven. N-VAR

**in|fatu|at|ed** /ɪnfætʃueɪtɪd/ If you are **infatuated with** a person or thing, you have strong feelings of love or passion for them which make you unable to think clearly or sensibly about them. ❑ *He was utterly infatuated with her.* ADJ: oft ADJ with n = obsessed

**in|fat|ua|tion** /ɪnfætʃueɪʃᵊn/ **(infatuations)** If you have an **infatuation** for a person or thing, you have strong feelings of love or passion for them which make you unable to think clearly or sensibly about them. ❑ *...his infatuation with bull-fighting.* N-VAR = obsession

**in|fect** /ɪnfekt/ **(infects, infecting, infected)** ♦◇◇ [1] To **infect** people, animals, or plants means to cause them to have a disease or illness. ❑ *A single mosquito can infect a large number of people. ...people infected with HIV.* VERB; V n; V-ed ♦ **in|fec|tion** /ɪnfekʃᵊn/ *...plants that are resistant to infection.* N-UNCOUNT [2] To **infect** a substance or area means to cause it to contain harmful germs or bacteria. ❑ *The birds infect the milk. ...a virus which is spread mainly by infected blood.* VERB = contaminate; V n; V-ed [3] When people, places, or things **are infected** by a feeling or influence, it spreads to them. ❑ *For an instant I was infected by her fear... He thought they might infect others with their bourgeois ideas... His urge for revenge would never infect her.* VERB; be V-ed by n; V n with n; V n [4] If a virus **infects** a computer, it affects the computer by damaging or destroying programs. [COMPUTING] ❑ *This virus infected thousands of computers within days.* VERB; V n

**in|fect|ed** /ɪnfektɪd/ An **infected** place is one where germs or bacteria are causing a disease to spread among people or animals. ❑ *In heavily infected areas, half the population become blind.* ADJ: ADJ n

**in|fec|tion** /ɪnfekʃᵊn/ **(infections)** An **infection** is a disease caused by germs or bacteria. ❑ *Ear infections are common in pre-school children.* → See also **infect**. ♦◇◇ N-COUNT

**in|fec|tious** /ɪnfekʃəs/ [1] A disease that is **infectious** can be caught by being near a person who has it. Compare **contagious**. ❑ *...infectious diseases such as measles.* ADJ [2] If a feeling is **infectious**, it spreads to other people. ❑ *She radiates an infectious enthusiasm for everything she does.* ADJ

**in|fec|tive** /ɪnfektɪv/ **Infective** means related to infection or likely to cause infection. [FORMAL] ❑ *...a mild and very common infective disease of children.* ADJ: usu ADJ n

**in|fer** /ɪnfɜːʳ/ **(infers, inferring, inferred)** [1] If you **infer** that something is the case, you decide that it is true on the basis of information that you already have. ❑ *I inferred from what she said that you have not been well... By measuring the motion of the galaxies in a cluster, astronomers can infer the cluster's mass.* VERB = deduce; V that; V n [2] Some people use **infer** to mean 'imply', but many people consider this use to be incorrect. ❑ *The police inferred that they found her behaviour rather suspicious.* VERB; V that

**in|fer|ence** /ɪnfərəns/ **(inferences)** [1] An **inference** is a conclusion that you draw about something by using information that you already have about it. ❑ *There were two inferences to be drawn from her letter.* N-COUNT = conclusion [2] **Inference** is the act of drawing conclusions about something on the basis of information that you already have. ❑ *It had an extremely tiny head and, by inference, a tiny brain.* N-UNCOUNT

**in|fe|ri|or** /ɪnfɪəriəʳ/ **(inferiors)** [1] Something that is **inferior** is not as good as something else. ❑ *The cassettes were of inferior quality... If children were made to feel inferior to other children their confidence declined.* ADJ: oft ADJ to n ≠ superior [2] If one person is regarded as **inferior to** another, they are regarded as less important because they have less status or ability. ❑ *He preferred the company of those who were intellectually inferior to himself.* ADJ: oft ADJ to n ≠ superior ♦ **Inferior** is also a noun. ❑ *A gentleman should always be civil, even to his inferiors.* N-COUNT ♦ **in|fe|ri|or|ity** /ɪnfɪəriɒrɪti, AM -ɔːr-/ *I found it difficult to shake off a sense of social inferiority.* N-UNCOUNT

**in|fe|ri|or|ity com|plex** **(inferiority complexes)** Someone who has an **inferiority complex** feels that they are of less worth or importance than other people. N-COUNT

**in|fer|nal** /ɪnfɜːʳnᵊl/ [1] **Infernal** is used to emphasize that something is very annoying or unpleasant. [OLD-FASHIONED] ❑ *The post office is shut, which is an infernal bore.* ADJ: ADJ n [emphasis] [2] **Infernal** is used to describe things that relate to hell. [LITERARY] ❑ *...the goddess of the infernal regions.* ADJ: ADJ n

**in|fer|no** /ɪnfɜːʳnoʊ/ **(infernos)** If you refer to a fire as an **inferno**, you mean that it is burning N-COUNT: usu sing fiercely and causing great destruction. [JOURNALISM] ❑ *Rescue workers fought to get to victims inside the inferno.*

**in|fer|tile** /ɪnfɜːʳtaɪl, AM -tᵊl/ ADJ ≠ fertile [1] A person or animal that is **infertile** is unable to produce babies. ❑ *According to one survey, one woman in eight is infertile.* ♦ **in|fer|til|ity** /ɪnfɜːʳtɪlɪti/ N-UNCOUNT *Male infertility is becoming commonplace.* [2] ADJ ≠ fertile **Infertile** soil is of poor quality so that plants cannot grow in it. ❑ *The polluted waste is often dumped, making the surrounding land infertile.*

**in|fest** /ɪnfest/ **(infests, infesting, infested)** [1] VERB When creatures such as insects or rats **infest** plants or a place, they are present in large numbers and cause damage. ❑ V n *...pests like aphids which infest cereal crops.* ♦ **in|fest|ed** ADJ *The prison is infested with rats.* ♦ **-infested** COMB in ADJ *...the rat-infested slums where the plague flourished.* ♦ **in|fes|ta|tion** N-VAR: oft n N, N *of* n /ɪnfesteɪʃᵊn/ **(infestations)** *The premises were treated for cockroach infestation.* [2] VERB disapproval = overrun If you say that people or things you disapprove of or regard as dangerous **are infesting** a place, you mean that there are large numbers of them in that place. ❑ V n *Crime and drugs are infesting the inner cities.* ♦ **in|fest|ed** ADJ *The road further south was infested with bandits.* ♦ **-infested** COMB in ADJ *...the shark-infested waters of the Great Barrier Reef.*

**in|fi|del** /ɪnfɪdᵊl/ **(infidels)** N-COUNT disapproval If one person refers to another as an **infidel**, the first person is hostile towards the second person because that person has a different religion or has no religion. [LITERARY] ❑ *...a holy war, to drive the infidels and the non-believers out of this holy land.* ♦ **Infidel** is also an adjective. ADJ: ADJ n ❑ *He promised to continue the fight against infidel forces.*

**in|fi|del|ity** /ɪnfɪdelɪti/ **(infidelities)** N-VAR **Infidelity** occurs when a person who is married or in a steady relationship has sex with another person. ❑ *George ignored his partner's infidelities.*

**in|fighting** /ɪnfaɪtɪŋ/ also **in-fighting.** N-UNCOUNT **In-fighting** is quarrelling and competition between members of the same group or organization. ❑ *...in-fighting between right-wingers and moderates in the party.*

**in|fill** /ɪnfɪl/ **(infills, infilling, infilled)** VERB To **infill** a hollow place or gap means to fill it. [mainly BRIT] ❑ be V-ed *The entrance to the cave was infilled by the landowner...* V *It is wise to start infilling with a layer of gravel for drainage.* Also V n

☑ in AM, use **fill in**

**in|fil|trate** /ɪnfɪltreɪt/ **(infiltrates, infiltrating, infiltrated)** [1] VERB If people **infiltrate** a place or organization, or **infiltrate into** it, they enter it secretly in order to spy on it or influence it. ❑ V n *Activists had infiltrated the student movement...* V *into/from* n *A reporter tried to infiltrate into the prison.* ♦ **in|fil|tra|tion** N-VAR /ɪnfɪltreɪʃᵊn/ **(infiltrations)** *...an inquiry into alleged infiltration by the far left group.* [2] VERB To **infiltrate** people **into** a place or organization means to get them into it secretly in order to spy on it or influence it. ❑ V n *into* n *Some countries have infiltrated their agents into the Republic.*

**in|fil|tra|tor** /ɪnfɪltreɪtəʳ/ **(infiltrators)** N-COUNT An **infiltrator** is a person who has infiltrated a place or organization.

**infin.** **Infin.** is an abbreviation for **infinitive**.

**in|fi|nite** /ɪnfɪnɪt/ [1] ADJ emphasis If you describe something as **infinite**, you are emphasizing that it is extremely great in amount or degree. ❑ *...an infinite variety of landscapes... The choice is infinite.* ♦ **in|fi|nite|ly** ADV: ADV adj/adv *His design was infinitely better than anything I could have done.* [2] ADJ Something that is **infinite** has no limit, end, or edge. ❑ *Obviously, no company has infinite resources.* ♦ **in|fi|nite|ly** ADV: ADV with v *A centimeter can be infinitely divided into smaller units.*

**in|fini|tesi|mal** /ɪnfɪnɪtesɪmᵊl/ ADJ = tiny Something that is **infinitesimal** is extremely small. [FORMAL] ❑ *...mineral substances present in infinitesimal amounts in the soil.*

**in|fini|tive** /ɪnfɪnɪtɪv/ **(infinitives)** N-COUNT The **infinitive** of a verb is the basic form, for example 'do', 'be', 'take', and 'eat'. The infinitive is often used with 'to' in front of it.

**in|fi|ni|tum** /ɪnfɪnaɪtəm/ → see **ad infinitum**.

**in|fin|ity** /ɪnfɪnɪti/ [1] N-UNCOUNT: also *a* N *of* n **Infinity** is a number that is larger than any other number and can never be given an exact value. ❑ *These permutations multiply towards infinity.* [2] N-UNCOUNT **Infinity** is a point that is further away than any other point and can never be reached. ❑ *...the darkness of a starless night stretching to infinity.*

**in|firm** /ɪnfɜːʳm/ ADJ A person who is **infirm** is weak or ill, and usually old. [FORMAL] ❑ *...her aging, infirm husband.* ♦ **The infirm** N-PLURAL: *the* N are people who are infirm. ❑ *We are here to protect and assist the weak and infirm.* ♦ **in|fir|mity** /ɪnfɜːʳmɪti/ **(infirmities)** N-VAR *In spite of his age and infirmity, he still writes plays and novels.*

**in|fir|ma|ry** /ɪnfɜːʳməri/ **(infirmaries)** N-COUNT; N-IN-NAMES Some hospitals are called **infirmaries**. ❑ *Mrs Hardie had been taken to the infirmary in an ambulance.*

**in|flame** /ɪnfleɪm/ **(inflames, inflaming, inflamed)** VERB If something **inflames** a situation or **inflames** people's feelings, it makes people feel even more strongly about something. [JOURNALISM] ❑ V n *The General holds the rebels responsible for inflaming the situation.*

**in|flamed** /ɪnfleɪmd/ ADJ If part of your body is **inflamed**, it is red or swollen, usually as a result of an infection, injury, or illness. [FORMAL] ❑ *Symptoms include red, itchy and inflamed skin.*

**in|flam|mable** /ɪnflæməbᵊl/ ADJ = flammable An **inflammable** material or chemical catches fire and burns easily. ❑ *...a highly inflammable liquid.*

**in|flam|ma|tion** /ɪnfləmeɪʃᵊn/ **(inflammations)** N-VAR An **inflammation** is a painful redness or swelling of a part of your body that results from an infection, injury, or illness. [FORMAL] ❑ *The drug can cause inflammation of the liver.*

**in|flam|ma|tory** /ɪnflæmətəri, AM -tɔːri/ [1] ADJ disapproval If you accuse someone of saying or doing **inflammatory** things, you mean that what they say or do is likely to make people react very angrily. ❑ *...nationalist policies that are too drastic and inflammatory.* [2] ADJ: ADJ n An **inflammatory** condition or disease is one in which the patient suffers from inflammation. [FORMAL] ❑ *...the inflammatory reactions that occur in asthma.*

**in|flat|able** /ɪnfleɪtəbᵊl/ **(inflatables)** [1] ADJ: usu ADJ n An **inflatable** object is one that you fill with air when you want to use it. ❑ *The children were playing on the inflatable castle.* [2] N-COUNT An **inflatable** is an inflatable object, especially a small boat.

**in|flate** /ɪnfleɪt/ **(inflates, inflating, inflated)** [1] VERB If you **inflate** something such as a balloon or tyre, or if it **inflates**, it becomes bigger as it is filled with air or a gas. ❑ V n *Stuart jumped into the sea and inflated the liferaft...* V *Don's lifejacket had failed to inflate.* [2] VERB = increase If you say that someone **inflates** the price of something, or that the price **inflates**, you mean that the price increases. ❑ V n *The promotion of a big release can inflate a film's final cost...* V *Clothing prices have not inflated as much as automobiles.* ♦ **in|flat|ed** ADJ *They had to buy everything at inflated prices at the ranch store.* [3] VERB If someone **inflates** the amount or effect of something, they say it is bigger, better, or more important than it really is, usually so that they can profit from it. ❑ V n *They inflated clients' medical treatment to defraud insurance companies.*

**in|fla|tion** /ɪnfleɪʃᵊn/ ◆◆◇ N-UNCOUNT **Inflation** is a general increase in the prices of goods and services in a country. [BUSINESS] ❑ *...rising unemployment and high inflation. ...an inflation rate of only 2.2%.*

**in|fla|tion|ary** /ɪnfleɪʃənri, AM -neri/ ADJ: usu ADJ n **Inflationary** means connected with inflation or causing inflation. [BUSINESS] ❑ *The bank is worried about mounting inflationary pressures.*

**in|flect** /ɪnflekt/ **(inflects, inflecting, inflected)** VERB: V If a word **inflects**, its ending or form changes in order to show its grammatical function. If a language **inflects**, it has words in it that inflect. ♦ **in|flect|ed** ADJ ❑ *...Sanskrit, a highly inflected language.*

**-inflected** /-ɪnflektɪd/ 1 COMB in ADJ **-inflected** is used to form adjectives describing someone's voice or accent. [LITERARY] ❑ *'Sergeant, I should like a word with you,' said the newcomer, in a pleasantly-inflected baritone.* 2 COMB in ADJ **-inflected** is used to form adjectives describing the style of a piece of music or a performance. [JOURNALISM] ❑ *...his attacking, gospel-inflected vocal style.*

**in|flec|tion** /ɪnflekʃ^ən/ **(inflections)** 1 N-VAR An **inflection** in someone's voice is a change in its tone or pitch as they are speaking. [WRITTEN] ❑ *The man's voice was devoid of inflection.* 2 N-VAR In grammar, an **inflection** is a change in the form of a word that shows its grammatical function, for example a change that makes a noun plural or makes a verb into the past tense.

**in|flex|ible** /ɪnfleksɪb^əl/ 1 ADJ = rigid ≠ flexible Something that is **inflexible** cannot be altered in any way, even if the situation changes. ❑ *Workers insisted the new system was too inflexible.* ♦ **in|flex|ibil|ity** N-UNCOUNT /ɪnfleksɪbɪlɪti/ *The snag about an endowment mortgage is its inflexibility.* 2 ADJ disapproval ≠ flexible If you say that someone is **inflexible**, you are criticizing them because they refuse to change their mind or alter their way of doing things. ❑ *His opponents viewed him as stubborn, dogmatic, and inflexible.* ♦ **in|flex|ibil|ity** N-UNCOUNT: oft with poss *Joyce was irritated by the inflexibility of her colleagues.*

**in|flex|ion** /ɪnflekʃ^ən/ → see **inflection**.

**in|flict** /ɪnflɪkt/ **(inflicts, inflicting, inflicted)** VERB To **inflict** harm or damage **on** someone or something means to make them suffer it. ❑ *Rebels say they have inflicted heavy casualties on government forces...* (V n *on* n) *The dog then attacked her, inflicting serious injuries.* (V n) ♦ **in|flic|tion** N-UNCOUNT: usu N *of* n /ɪnflɪkʃ^ən/ *...without the unnecessary or cruel infliction of pain.*

**in-flight** ADJ: ADJ n also **inflight. In-flight** services are ones that are provided on board an aeroplane. ❑ *...an inflight magazine.*

**in|flow** /ɪnfloʊ/ **(inflows)** N-COUNT: usu N *of* n ≠ outflow If there is an **inflow of** money or people into a place, a large amount of money or people move into a place. ❑ *The Swiss wanted to discourage an inflow of foreign money.*

**in|flu|ence** /ɪnfluəns/ **(influences, influencing, influenced)** ◆◆◇ 1 N-UNCOUNT: oft N *over* n **Influence** is the power to make other people agree with your opinions or do what you want. ❑ *He denies exerting any political influence over them... The government should continue to use its influence for the release of all hostages.* 2 VERB If you **influence** someone, you use your power to make them agree with you or do what you want. ❑ *He is trying to improperly influence a witness...* (V n) *My dad influenced me to do electronics.* (V n to-inf) 3 N-COUNT: usu with supp To have an **influence on** people or situations means to affect what they do or what happens. ❑ *Van Gogh had a major influence on the development of modern painting.* 4 VERB If someone or something **influences** a person or situation, they have an effect on that person's behaviour or that situation. ❑ *We became the best of friends and he influenced me deeply...* (V n) *They still influence what's played on the radio.* (V wh) 5 N-COUNT: usu sing, usu adj N, oft N *on* n Someone or something that is a good or bad **influence on** people has a good or bad effect on them. ❑ *I thought Sue would be a good influence on you.* 6 PHRASE: PHR n, usu v-link PHR, PHR after v If you are **under the influence of** someone or something, you are being affected or controlled by them. ❑ *He was arrested on suspicion of driving under the influence of alcohol.*

**in|flu|en|tial** /ɪnfluenʃ^əl/ ADJ: oft ADJ *in* -ing Someone or something that is **influential** has a lot of influence over people or events. ❑ *He had been influential in shaping economic policy. ...one of the most influential books ever written.*

**in|flu|en|za** /ɪnfluenzə/ N-UNCOUNT **Influenza** is the same as **flu**. [FORMAL]

**in|flux** /ɪnflʌks/ **(influxes)** N-COUNT: usu sing, oft N *of* n An **influx of** people or things into a place is their arrival there in large numbers. ❑ *...problems caused by the influx of refugees.*

**info** /ɪnfoʊ/ N-UNCOUNT **Info** is information. [INFORMAL] ❑ *For more info phone 414-3935.*

**info|bahn** /ɪnfoʊbɑːn/ N-SING: *the* N **The infobahn** means the same as the information **superhighway**.

**in|fo|mer|cial** /ɪnfoʊmɜːʳʃ^əl/ **(infomercials)** N-COUNT An **infomercial** is a television programme in which a famous person gives information about a company's products or services, or a politician gives his or her opinions. The word is formed from 'information' and 'commercial'.

**in|form** /ɪnfɔːʳm/ **(informs, informing, informed)** ◆◇◇ 1 VERB If you **inform** someone **of** something, you tell them about it. ❑ *They would inform him of any progress they had made...* (V n *of* n) *My daughter informed me that she was pregnant...* (V n that) *'I just added a little soy sauce,' he informs us.* (V n with quote) 2 VERB If someone **informs on** a person, they give information about the person to the police or another authority, which causes the person to be suspected or proved guilty of doing something bad. ❑ *Thousands of American citizens have informed on these organized crime syndicates.* (V *on* n) 3 VERB If a situation or activity **is informed** by an idea or a quality, that idea or quality is very noticeable in it. [FORMAL] ❑ *All great songs are informed by a certain sadness and tension...* (be V-ed *by* n) *The concept of the Rose continued to inform the poet's work.* (V n)

**in|for|mal** /ɪnfɔːʳm^əl/ 1 ADJ: usu v-link ADJ ≠ formal **Informal** speech or behaviour is relaxed and friendly rather than serious, very correct, or official. ❑ *She is refreshingly informal.* ♦ **in|for|mal|ly** ADV: ADV after v *She was always there at half past eight, chatting informally to the children.* ♦ **in|for|mal|ity** N-UNCOUNT /ɪnfɔːʳmælɪti/ *He was overwhelmed by their friendly informality.* 2 ADJ ≠ formal An **informal** situation is one which is relaxed and friendly and not very serious or official. ❑ *The house has an informal atmosphere.* 3 ADJ = casual ≠ formal **Informal** clothes are casual and suitable for wearing when you are relaxing, but not on formal occasions. ❑ *For lunch, dress is informal.* ♦ **in|for|mal|ly** ADV *Everyone dressed informally in shorts or jeans.* 4 ADJ: usu ADJ n You use **informal** to describe something that is done unofficially or casually without planning. ❑ *The two leaders will retire to Camp David for informal discussions.* ♦ **in|for|mal|ly** ADV *He began informally to handle Ted's tax affairs for him.*

**in|form|ant** /ɪnfɔːʳmənt/ **(informants)** 1 N-COUNT An **informant** is someone who gives another person a piece of information. [FORMAL] 2 N-COUNT An **informant** is the same as an **informer**.

**in|for|ma|tion** /ɪnfəʳmeɪʃ^ən/ ◆◆◆ 1 N-UNCOUNT: oft N *about/on* n **Information** about someone or something consists of facts about them. ❑ *Pat refused to give her any information about Sarah... Each centre would provide information on technology and training. ...an important piece of information.* 2 N-UNCOUNT = data **Information** consists of the facts and figures that are stored and used by a computer program. [COMPUTING] ❑ *Pictures are scanned into a form of digital information that computers can recognize.* 3 N-UNCOUNT **Information** is a service which you can telephone to find out someone's telephone number. [AM]

☑ in BRIT, use **directory enquiries**

**in|for|ma|tion|al** /ɪnfəʳmeɪʃən^əl/ ADJ: ADJ n **Informational** means relating to information. [JOURNALISM] ❑ *...the informational needs of school-age children.*

**in|for|ma|tion tech|nol|ogy** N-UNCOUNT **Information technology** is the theory and practice of using computers to store and analyse information. The abbreviation **IT** is often used. ❑ *...the information technology industry.*

**in|forma|tive** /ɪnfɔːʳmətɪv/ ADJ Something that is **informative** gives you useful information. ❑ *The adverts are not very informative.*

**in|formed** /ɪnfɔːʳmd/ [1] Someone who is **informed** knows about a subject or what is happening in the world. ❑ *Informed people know the company is shaky. ...the importance of keeping the public properly informed.* → See also **well-informed.** [2] When journalists talk about **informed** sources, they mean people who are likely to give correct information because of their private or special knowledge. ❑ *According to informed sources, those taken into custody include at least one major-general.* [3] An **informed** guess or decision is one that likely to be good, because it is based on definite knowledge or information. ❑ *We are able to make more informed choices about how we use drugs.* [4] → See also **inform.**
ADJ / ADJ: ADJ n / ADJ: ADJ n

**in|form|er** /ɪnfɔːʳməʳ/ **(informers)** An **informer** is a person who tells the police that someone has done something illegal. ❑ *...two men suspected of being police informers.*
N-COUNT

**info|tain|ment** /ɪnfoʊteɪnmənt/ **Infotainment** is used to refer to radio or television programmes that are intended both to entertain people and to give information. The word is formed from 'information' and 'entertainment'.
N-UNCOUNT

**infra|red** /ɪnfrə red/ also **infra-red.** [1] **Infrared** radiation is similar to light but has a longer wavelength, so we cannot see it without special equipment. [2] **Infrared** equipment detects infrared radiation. ❑ *...searching with infra-red scanners for weapons and artillery.*
ADJ: ADJ n / ADJ: ADJ n

**infra|struc|ture** /ɪnfrəstrʌktʃəʳ/ **(infrastructures)** The **infrastructure** of a country, society, or organization consists of the basic facilities such as transport, communications, power supplies, and buildings, which enable it to function. ❑ *...investment in infrastructure.*
N-VAR

**in|fre|quent** /ɪnfriːkwənt/ If something is **infrequent**, it does not happen often. ❑ *...John's infrequent visits to London.* ♦ **in|fre|quent|ly** *The bridge is used infrequently.*
ADJ = rare / ADV: usu ADV with v, also ADV with cl/group

**in|fringe** /ɪnfrɪndʒ/ **(infringes, infringing, infringed)** [1] If someone **infringes** a law or a rule, they break it or do something which disobeys it. ❑ *The film exploited his image and infringed his copyright.* [2] If something **infringes** people's rights, it interferes with these rights and does not allow people the freedom they are entitled to. ❑ *They rob us, they infringe our rights, they kill us... It's starting to infringe on our personal liberties.*
VERB / V n / VERB / V n / V *on* n

**in|fringe|ment** /ɪnfrɪndʒmənt/ **(infringements)** [1] An **infringement** is an action or situation that interferes with your rights and the freedom you are entitled to. ❑ *...infringement of privacy... They see it as an infringement on their own freedom of action.* [2] An **infringement of** a law or rule is the act of breaking it or disobeying it. ❑ *There might have been an infringement of the rules.*
N-VAR: usu N *of/on* n / N-VAR: usu N *of* n

**in|furi|ate** /ɪnfjʊəriett/ **(infuriates, infuriating, infuriated)** If something or someone **infuriates** you, they make you extremely angry. ❑ *Jimmy's presence had infuriated Hugh... It infuriates us to have to deal with this particular mayor.* ♦ **in|furi|at|ed** *I was absolutely infuriated with him.*
VERB / V n / *it* V n to-inf / Also *it* V n that / ADJ: usu v-link ADJ

**in|furi|at|ing** /ɪnfjʊərieɪtɪŋ/ Something that is **infuriating** annoys you very much. ❑ *I was in the middle of typing when Robert rang. It was infuriating!* ♦ **in|furi|at|ing|ly** *This book is infuriatingly repetitious.*
ADJ = maddening / ADV: usu ADV adj, also ADV with v

**in|fuse** /ɪnfjuːz/ **(infuses, infusing, infused)** To **infuse** a quality **into** someone or something, or to **infuse** them **with** a quality, means to fill them with it. [FORMAL] ❑ *Many of the girls seemed to be infused with excitement on seeing the snow... A union would infuse unnecessary conflict into the company's employee relations.*
VERB / *be* V-ed *with* n / V n *into* n / Also V n *with* n

**in|fu|sion** /ɪnfjuːʒᵊn/ **(infusions)** If there is an **infusion** of one thing into another, the first thing is added to the other thing and makes it stronger or better. [FORMAL] ❑ *He brought a tremendous infusion of hope to the people.*
N-VAR: usu N *of* n

**-ing** /-ɪŋ/ [1] **-ing** is added to verbs to form present participles. Present participles are used with auxiliary verbs to make continuous tenses. They are also used like adjectives, describing a person or thing as doing something. ❑ *He was walking along the street... Children sit round small tables, talking to each other... It was worth it to see all those smiling faces.* [2] **-ing** is added to verbs to form uncount nouns referring to activities. ❑ *Gardening is very popular in Britain... This campaign is one of the most successful in the history of advertising.*
SUFFIX / SUFFIX

**in|gen|ious** /ɪndʒiːniəs/ Something that is **ingenious** is very clever and involves new ideas, methods, or equipment. ❑ *...a truly ingenious invention.* ♦ **in|gen|ious|ly** *The roof has been ingeniously designed to provide solar heating.*
ADJ / ADV: usu ADV with v, also ADV adj

**in|ge|nue** /ænʒeɪnjuː/ **(ingenues)** also **ingénue.** An **ingenue** is a young, innocent girl in a play or film, or an actress who plays the part of young, innocent girls. [FORMAL] ❑ *I don't want any more ingenue roles.*
N-COUNT: usu sing

**in|genu|ity** /ɪndʒənjuːɪti, AM -nuː-/ **Ingenuity** is skill at working out how to achieve things or skill at inventing new things. ❑ *Inspecting the nest may require some ingenuity.*
N-UNCOUNT

**in|genu|ous** /ɪndʒenjuəs/ If you describe someone as **ingenuous**, you mean that they are innocent, trusting, and honest. [FORMAL] ❑ *He seemed far too ingenuous for a reporter.* ♦ **in|genu|ous|ly** *Somewhat ingenuously, he explains how the crime may be accomplished.*
ADJ ≠ disingenuous / ADV: ADV with v, ADV adj

**in|gest** /ɪndʒest/ **(ingests, ingesting, ingested)** When animals or plants **ingest** a substance, they take it into themselves, for example by eating or absorbing it. [TECHNICAL] ❑ *...side effects occurring in fish that ingest this substance.* ♦ **in|ges|tion** /ɪndʒestʃən/ *Every ingestion of food can affect our mood or thinking processes.*
VERB / V n / N-UNCOUNT

**in|glo|ri|ous** /ɪnglɔːriəs/ If you describe something as **inglorious**, you mean that it is something to be ashamed of. ❑ *James wouldn't have accepted such an inglorious outcome.* ♦ **in|glo|ri|ous|ly** *If fighting worsens, the troops might be reinforced, or ingloriously withdrawn.*
ADJ: usu ADJ n / ADV: ADV with v

**in|got** /ɪŋgət/ **(ingots)** An **ingot** is a lump of metal, usually shaped like a brick. ❑ *...gold ingots.*
N-COUNT: oft n N

**in|grained** /ɪngreɪnd/ **Ingrained** habits and beliefs are difficult to change or remove. ❑ *Morals tend to be deeply ingrained.*
ADJ

**in|gra|ti|ate** /ɪngreɪʃieɪt/ **(ingratiates, ingratiating, ingratiated)** If someone tries to **ingratiate themselves with** you, they do things to try and make you like them. ❑ *Many politicians are trying to ingratiate themselves with her.*
VERB [disapproval] / V pron-refl *with* n

**in|gra|ti|at|ing** /ɪngreɪʃieɪtɪŋ/ If you describe someone or their behaviour as **ingratiating**, you mean that they try to make people like them. ❑ *He said this with an ingratiating smile.*
ADJ [disapproval]

**in|grati|tude** /ɪngrætɪtjuːd, AM -tuːd/ **Ingratitude** is lack of gratitude for something that has been done for you. ❑ *The Government could expect only ingratitude from the electorate.*
N-UNCOUNT ≠ gratitude

**in|gre|di|ent** /ɪngriːdiənt/ **(ingredients)** ◆◇◇ [1] **Ingredients** are the things that are used to make something, especially all the different foods you use when you are cooking a particular dish. ❑ *Mix in the remaining ingredients.* [2] An **ingredient** of a situation is one of the essential parts of it. ❑ *The meeting had all the ingredients of high political drama.*
N-COUNT / N-COUNT: oft N *of/in* n

**in|grown** /ɪngroʊn/ or **ingrowing** /ɪngroʊɪŋ/ An **ingrown** toenail, or in British English an **ingrowing** toenail, is one which is growing into your toe, often causing you pain.
ADJ

**in|hab|it** /ɪnhæbɪt/ **(inhabits, inhabiting, inhabited)** If a place or region **is inhabited** by a group of people or a species of animal, those people or animals live there. ❑ *The valley is inhabited by the Dani tribe. ...the people who inhabit these islands. ...a land primarily inhabited by nomads.*
VERB / *be* V-ed / V n / V-ed

**in|hab|it|ant** /ɪnhæbɪtənt/ **(inhabitants)** The **inhabitants** of a place are the people who live there. ❑ *...the inhabitants of Glasgow.* N-COUNT: usu pl

**in|ha|la|tion** /ɪnhəleɪʃən/ **(inhalations)** 1 **Inhalation** is the process or act of breathing in, taking air and sometimes other substances into your lungs. [FORMAL] ❑ *...a complete cycle of inhalation and exhalation... They were taken to hospital suffering from smoke inhalation... Take several deep inhalations.* N-VAR ≠ exhalation 2 An **inhalation** is a treatment for colds and other illnesses in which you dissolve substances in hot water and breathe in the vapour. ❑ *Inhalations can soothe and control the cough.* N-COUNT

**in|hale** /ɪnheɪl/ **(inhales, inhaling, inhaled)** When you **inhale**, you breathe in. When you **inhale** something such as smoke, you take it into your lungs when you breathe in. ❑ *He took a long slow breath, inhaling deeply... He was treated for the effects of inhaling smoke.* VERB ≠ exhale; V; V n

**in|hal|er** /ɪnheɪləʳ/ **(inhalers)** An **inhaler** is a small device that helps you to breathe more easily if you have asthma or a bad cold. You put it in your mouth and breathe in deeply, and it sends a small amount of a drug into your lungs. N-COUNT

**in|her|ent** /ɪnherənt, -hɪər-/ The **inherent** qualities of something are the necessary and natural parts of it. ❑ *Stress is an inherent part of dieting. ...the dangers inherent in an outbreak of war.* ADJ: usu ADJ n = intrinsic

♦ **in|her|ent|ly** *Aeroplanes are not inherently dangerous.* ADV: usu ADV adj

**in|her|it** /ɪnherɪt/ **(inherits, inheriting, inherited)** 1 If you **inherit** money or property, you receive it from someone who has died. ❑ *He has no son to inherit his land. ...paintings that he inherited from his father. ...people with inherited wealth.* VERB; V n; V n *from* n; V-ed 2 If you **inherit** something such as a task, problem, or attitude, you get it from the people who used to have it, for example because you have taken over their job or been influenced by them. ❑ *The government inherited an impossible situation from its predecessors.* VERB; V n *from* n 3 If you **inherit** a characteristic or quality, you are born with it, because your parents or ancestors also had it. ❑ *We inherit from our parents many of our physical characteristics... Her children have inherited her love of sport... Stammering is probably an inherited defect.* VERB; V n *from* n; V n; V-ed

**in|her|it|ance** /ɪnherɪtəns/ **(inheritances)** 1 An **inheritance** is money or property which you receive from someone who has died. ❑ *She feared losing her inheritance to her stepmother.* N-VAR 2 If you get something such as job, problem, or attitude from someone who used to have it, you can refer to this as an **inheritance**. ❑ *...the situation that was Truman's inheritance as President.* N-COUNT: usu sing, with supp, oft with poss 3 Your **inheritance** is the particular characteristics or qualities which your family or ancestors had and which you are born with. ❑ *Eye colour shows your genetic inheritance.* N-SING: also no det, with supp

**in|her|it|ance tax** **(inheritance taxes)** An **inheritance tax** is a tax which has to be paid on the money and property of someone who has died. N-COUNT

**in|heri|tor** /ɪnherɪtəʳ/ **(inheritors)** The **inheritors** of something such as a tradition are the people who live or arrive after it has been established and are able to benefit from it. ❑ *...the proud inheritors of the Prussian military tradition.* N-COUNT: usu pl, usu N *of* n

**in|hib|it** /ɪnhɪbɪt/ **(inhibits, inhibiting, inhibited)** 1 If something **inhibits** an event or process, it prevents it or slows it down. ❑ *The high cost of borrowing is inhibiting investment by industry in new equipment.* VERB; V n 2 To **inhibit** someone **from** doing something means to prevent them from doing it, although they want to do it or should be able to do it. ❑ *It could inhibit the poor from getting the medical care they need.* VERB; V n *from* -ing/n

**in|hib|it|ed** /ɪnhɪbɪtɪd/ If you say that someone is **inhibited**, you mean they find it difficult to behave naturally and show their feelings, and that you think this is a bad thing. ❑ *We are rather inhibited about touching each other.* ADJ: oft ADJ *about* n/-ing [disapproval] ≠ uninhibited

**in|hi|bi|tion** /ɪnɪbɪʃən/ **(inhibitions)** **Inhibitions** are feelings of fear or embarrassment that make it difficult for you to behave naturally. ❑ *The whole point about dancing is to stop thinking and lose all your inhibitions.* N-VAR

**in|hos|pi|table** /ɪnhɒspɪtəbəl/ 1 An **inhospitable** place is unpleasant to live in. ❑ *...the earth's most inhospitable regions.* ADJ: usu ADJ n ≠ hospitable 2 If someone is **inhospitable**, they do not make people welcome when they visit. ADJ ≠ hospitable

**in-house** **In-house** work or activities are done by employees of an organization or company, rather than by workers outside the organization or company. ❑ *A lot of companies do in-house training.* ADJ

♦ **In-house** is also an adverb. ❑ *The magazine is still produced in-house.* ADV

**in|hu|man** /ɪnhjuːmən/ 1 If you describe treatment or an action as **inhuman**, you mean that it is extremely cruel. ❑ *The detainees are often held in cruel and inhuman conditions.* ADJ: usu ADJ n 2 If you describe someone or something as **inhuman**, you mean that they are strange or bad because they do not seem human in some way. ❑ *...inhuman shrieks that chilled my heart.* ADJ

**in|hu|mane** /ɪnhjʊmeɪn/ If you describe something as **inhumane**, you mean that it is extremely cruel. ❑ *He was kept under inhumane conditions.* ADJ ≠ humane

**in|hu|man|ity** /ɪnhjʊmænɪti/ **(inhumanities)** You can describe extremely cruel actions as **inhumanity**. ❑ *...the inhumanity of war.* N-UNCOUNT: also N in pl, oft N *of* n

**in|imi|cal** /ɪnɪmɪkəl/ Conditions that are **inimical to** something make it difficult for that thing to exist or do well. [FORMAL] ❑ *...goals inimical to Western interests.* ADJ: usu v-link ADJ, usu ADJ *to* n

**in|imi|table** /ɪnɪmɪtəbəl/ You use **inimitable** to describe someone, especially a performer, when you like or admire them because of their special qualities. [FORMAL] ❑ *He makes his own point in his own inimitable way.* ADJ: usu ADJ n [approval] = unique

**in|iqui|tous** /ɪnɪkwɪtəs/ If you describe something as **iniquitous**, you mean that it is very unfair or morally bad. [FORMAL] ❑ *...an iniquitous fine.* ADJ: usu ADJ n

**in|iquity** /ɪnɪkwɪti/ **(iniquities)** You can refer to wicked actions or very unfair situations as **iniquity**. [FORMAL] ❑ *He rails against the iniquities of capitalism.* N-VAR

**ini|tial** /ɪnɪʃəl/ **(initials, initialling, initialled)** ◆◇◇

✔ in AM, use **initialing, initialed**

1 You use **initial** to describe something that happens at the beginning of a process. ❑ *The initial reaction has been excellent.* ADJ: ADJ n 2 **Initials** are the capital letters which begin each word of a name. For example, if your full name is Michael Dennis Stocks, your initials will be M.D.S. ❑ *...a silver Porsche car with her initials JB on the side.* N-COUNT: usu pl, oft poss N 3 If someone **initials** an official document, they write their initials on it, for example to show that they have seen it or that they accept or agree with it. ❑ *Would you mind initialing this voucher?* VERB; V n

**ini|tial|ly** /ɪnɪʃəli/ **Initially** means soon after the beginning of a process or situation, rather than in the middle or at the end of it. ❑ *Forecasters say the gales may not be as bad as they initially predicted.* ◆◇◇ ADV: ADV with v, ADV with cl/group = originally

**ini|ti|ate** /ɪnɪʃieɪt/ **(initiates, initiating, initiated)** 1 If you **initiate** something, you start it or cause it to happen. ❑ *They wanted to initiate a discussion on economics.* VERB; V n 2 If you **initiate** someone **into** something, you introduce them to a particular skill or type of knowledge and teach them about it. ❑ *He initiated her into the study of other cultures.* VERB; V n *into* n; Also V n 3 If someone **is initiated into** something such as a religion, secret society, or social group, they become a member of it by taking part in ceremonies at which they learn its special knowledge VERB or customs. ❑ *In many societies, young people are formally initiated into their adult roles. ...the ceremony that initiated members into the Order.* be V-ed into n; V n into n; Also V n

**ini|tia|tion** /ɪnɪʃieɪʃᵊn/ **(initiations)** [1] The **initiation** of something is the starting of it. ❑ *They announced the initiation of a rural development programme.* N-UNCOUNT: usu the N of n [2] Someone's **initiation into** a particular group is the act or process by which they officially become a member, often involving special ceremonies. ❑ *This was my initiation into the peace movement.* N-VAR: oft N into n, N n

**ini|tia|tive** /ɪnɪʃətɪv/ **(initiatives)** ◆◇◇ [1] An **initiative** is an important act or statement that is intended to solve a problem. ❑ *Government initiatives to help young people have been inadequate... There's talk of a new peace initiative.* N-COUNT: usu with supp, oft N to-inf [2] In a fight or contest, if you have **the initiative**, you are in a better position than your opponents to decide what to do next. ❑ *We have the initiative; we intend to keep it.* N-SING: the N [3] If you have **initiative**, you have the ability to decide what to do next and to do it, without needing other people to tell you what to do. ❑ *She was disappointed by his lack of initiative.* N-UNCOUNT [4] If you **take the initiative** in a situation, you are the first person to act, and are therefore able to control the situation. ❑ *We must take the initiative in the struggle to end the war.* PHRASE: V inflects

**ini|tia|tor** /ɪnɪʃieɪtəʳ/ **(initiators)** The **initiator** of a plan or process is the person who was responsible for thinking of it or starting it. ❑ *...one of the major initiators of the tumultuous changes in Eastern Europe.* N-COUNT: oft N of n

**in|ject** /ɪndʒe̲kt/ **(injects, injecting, injected)** [1] To **inject** someone with a substance such as a medicine means to put it into their body using a device with a needle called a syringe. ❑ *His son was injected with strong drugs... The technique consists of injecting healthy cells into the muscles... He needs to inject himself once a month.* VERB: be V-ed with n, V n into n, V pron-refl; Also V n, V n with n [2] If you **inject** a new, exciting, or interesting quality **into** a situation, you add it. ❑ *She kept trying to inject a little fun into their relationship.* VERB: V n into n [3] If you **inject** money or resources **into** a business or organization, you provide more money or resources for it. [BUSINESS] ❑ *He has injected £5.6 billion into the health service.* VERB: V n into n

**in|jec|tion** /ɪndʒe̲kʃᵊn/ **(injections)** [1] If you have an **injection**, a doctor or nurse puts a medicine into your body using a device with a needle called a syringe. ❑ *They gave me an injection to help me sleep.* N-COUNT: also by N [2] An **injection of** money or resources into an organization is the act of providing it with more more money or resources, to help it become more efficient or profitable. [BUSINESS] ❑ *An injection of cash is needed to fund some of these projects.* N-COUNT: with supp, oft N of n

**in|ju|di|cious** /ɪndʒudɪʃəs/ If you describe a person or something that they have done as **injudicious**, you are critical of them because they have shown very poor judgment. [FORMAL] ❑ *He blamed injudicious comments by bankers for last week's devaluation.* ADJ; disapproval; = ill-advised, unwise

**in|junc|tion** /ɪndʒʌŋkʃᵊn/ **(injunctions)** [1] An **injunction** is a court order, usually one telling someone not to do something. [LEGAL] ❑ *He took out a court injunction against the newspaper demanding the return of the document.* N-COUNT: usu with supp [2] An **injunction to** do something is an order or strong request to do it. [FORMAL] ❑ *We hear endless injunctions to build a sense of community among staff.* N-COUNT: with supp, oft N to n, to-inf

**in|jure** /ɪ̲ndʒəʳ/ **(injures, injuring, injured)** If you **injure** a person or animal, you damage some part of their body. ❑ *A number of bombs have exploded, seriously injuring at least five people. ...stiff penalties for motorists who kill, maim, and injure.* VERB: V n; V

**in|jured** /ɪ̲ndʒəʳd/ ◆◇◇ [1] An **injured** person or animal has physical damage to part of their body, usually as a result of an accident or fighting. ❑ *The other injured man had a superficial stomach wound... Many of them will have died because they were so badly injured.* ADJ ♦ **The injured** are people who are injured. ❑ *Army helicopters tried to evacuate the injured.* N-PLURAL: the N [2] If you have **injured** feelings, you feel upset because you believe someone has been unfair or unkind to you. ❑ *...a look of injured pride.* ADJ = hurt

**in|jured par|ty** **(injured parties)** The **injured party** in a court case or dispute about unfair treatment is the person who says they were unfairly treated. [LEGAL] ❑ *The injured party got some compensation.* N-COUNT: usu the N = victim

**in|ju|ri|ous** /ɪndʒʊ̲əriəs/ Something that is **injurious to** someone or **to** their health or reputation is harmful or damaging to them. [FORMAL] ❑ *...substances that are injurious to health.* ADJ: oft ADJ to n = damaging, detrimental

**in|ju|ry** /ɪ̲ndʒəri/ **(injuries)** ◆◆◇ [1] An **injury** is damage done to a person's or an animal's body. ❑ *Four police officers sustained serious injuries in the explosion... The two other passengers escaped serious injury.* N-VAR [2] If someone suffers **injury to** their feelings, they are badly upset by something. If they suffer **injury to** their reputation, their reputation is seriously harmed. [LEGAL] ❑ *She was awarded £3,500 for injury to her feelings.* N-VAR: oft N to n [3] **to add insult to injury** → see **insult**.

**in|ju|ry time** **Injury time** is the period of time added to the end of a football game because play was stopped during the match when players were injured. [mainly BRIT] N-UNCOUNT

**in|jus|tice** /ɪndʒʌ̲stɪs/ **(injustices)** [1] **Injustice** is a lack of fairness in a situation. ❑ *They'll continue to fight injustice.* N-VAR [2] If you say that someone has **done** you **an injustice**, you mean that they have been unfair in the way that they have judged you or treated you. ❑ *The article does them both an injustice.* PHRASE: V inflects

**ink** /ɪŋk/ **(inks)** **Ink** is the coloured liquid used for writing or printing. ❑ *The letter was handwritten in black ink.* N-MASS

**ink|ling** /ɪ̲ŋklɪŋ/ **(inklings)** If you have **an inkling of** something, you have a vague idea about it. ❑ *I had no inkling of his real purpose until much later.* N-COUNT: usu sing, usu N of n/wh, N that/wh

**ink|well** /ɪ̲ŋkwel/ **(inkwells)** An **inkwell** is a container for ink on a desk. N-COUNT

**inky** /ɪ̲ŋki/ [1] **Inky** means black or very dark blue. [LITERARY] ❑ *The moon was rising in the inky sky.* ADJ: usu ADJ n ♦ **Inky** is also a combining form. ❑ *...looking out over an inky blue ocean.* COMB in COLOUR [2] If something is **inky**, it is covered in ink. ❑ *...inky fingers.* ADJ

**in|laid** /ɪnle̲ɪd/ An object that is **inlaid** has a design on it which is made by putting materials such as wood, gold, or silver into the surface of the object. ❑ *...a box delicately inlaid with little triangles.* ADJ: oft ADJ with n

**in|land**

✔ The adverb is pronounced /ɪnlæ̲nd/. The adjective is pronounced /ɪ̲nlænd/.

[1] If something is situated **inland**, it is away from the coast, towards or near the middle of a country. If you go **inland**, you go away from the coast, towards the middle of a country. ❑ *The vast majority live further inland... The car turned away from the coast and headed inland.* ADV: be ADV, ADV after v, oft amount ADV [2] **Inland** areas, lakes, and places are not on the coast, but in or near the middle of a country. ❑ *...a rather quiet inland town.* ADJ: ADJ n

**In|land Rev|enue** In Britain, **the Inland Revenue** is the government authority which collects income tax and some other taxes. N-PROPER

**In|land Rev|enue Ser|vice** In the United States, **the Inland Revenue Service** is the government authority which collects taxes. The abbreviation **IRS** is often used. N-PROPER: the N

**in-laws** Your **in-laws** are the parents and close relatives of your husband or wife. N-PLURAL: usu poss N

**in|lay** /ɪ̲nleɪ/ **(inlays)** An **inlay** is a design or pattern on an object which is made by putting materials such as wood, gold, or silver into the surface of the object. ❑ *...an inlay of medieval glass.* N-VAR

**in|let** /ɪnlet/ **(inlets)** An **inlet** is a narrow strip of water which goes from a sea or lake into the land. ❑ *...a sheltered inlet.* N-COUNT

**in|mate** /ɪnmeɪt/ **(inmates)** The **inmates** of a prison or mental hospital are the prisoners or patients who are living there. N-COUNT

**in|most** /ɪnmoʊst/ **Inmost** means the same as **innermost**. ❑ *He knew in his inmost heart that he was behaving badly.* ADJ: ADJ n

**inn** /ɪn/ **(inns)** An **inn** is a small hotel or pub, usually an old one. [OLD-FASHIONED] ❑ *...the Waterside Inn.* N-COUNT; N-IN-NAMES

**in|nards** /ɪnəʳdz/ The **innards** of a person or animal are the organs inside their body. [INFORMAL] N-PLURAL: usu with poss

**in|nate** /ɪneɪt/ An **innate** quality or ability is one which a person is born with. ❑ *Americans have an innate sense of fairness.* ADJ: usu ADJ n = natural ♦ **in|nate|ly** *I believe everyone is innately psychic.* ADV: ADV adj

**in|ner** /ɪnəʳ/ ◆◇◇ [1] The **inner** parts of something are the parts which are contained or are enclosed inside the other parts, and which are closest to the centre. ❑ *Wade stepped inside and closed the inner door behind him.* ADJ: ADJ n ≠ outer [2] Your **inner** feelings are feelings which you have but do not show to other people. ❑ *Loving relationships will give a child an inner sense of security.* ADJ: ADJ n

**in|ner child** Some psychologists refer to a person's childish feelings as his or her **inner child**. ❑ *For me, recovery has been all about finding my inner child and accepting her.* N-SING: oft poss N

**in|ner cir|cle** **(inner circles)** An **inner circle** is a small group of people within a larger group who have a lot of power, influence, or special information. ❑ *...Mr Blair's inner circle of advisers.* N-COUNT: usu sing, oft N *of* n

**in|ner city** **(inner cities)** You use **inner city** to refer to the areas in or near the centre of a large city where people live and where there are often social and economic problems. ❑ *...helping kids deal with the fear of living in the inner city.* N-COUNT

**inner|most** /ɪnəʳmoʊst/ [1] Your **innermost** thoughts and feelings are your most personal and secret ones. ❑ *...revealing a company's innermost secrets.* ADJ: ADJ n = inmost [2] The **innermost** thing is the one that is nearest to the centre. ❑ *...the innermost part of the eye.* ADJ: ADJ n ≠ outermost

**in|ner tube** **(inner tubes)** An **inner tube** is a rubber tube containing air which is inside a car tyre or a bicycle tyre. N-COUNT

**in|ning** /ɪnɪŋ/ **(innings)** An **inning** is one of the nine periods that a standard baseball game is divided into. Each team is at bat once in each inning. ◆◇◇ N-COUNT

**in|nings** /ɪnɪŋz/ **(innings)** An **innings** is a period in a game of cricket during which a particular team or player is batting. ❑ *The home side were all out for 50 in their second innings.* N-COUNT

**innit** /ɪnɪt/ **Innit** can be used at the end of a statement to make it into a question. It is a way of saying 'isn't it'. [INFORMAL, SPOKEN] ❑ *The record's great, innit?*

**inn|keeper** /ɪnkiːpəʳ/ **(innkeepers)** An **innkeeper** is someone who owns or manages a small hotel or pub. [OLD-FASHIONED] N-COUNT

**in|no|cence** /ɪnəsəns/ [1] **Innocence** is the quality of having no experience or knowledge of the more complex or unpleasant aspects of life. ❑ *...the sweet innocence of youth.* N-UNCOUNT [2] If someone proves their **innocence**, they prove that they are not guilty of a crime. ❑ *He claims he has evidence which could prove his innocence.* N-UNCOUNT: oft poss N ≠ guilt

**in|no|cent** /ɪnəsənt/ **(innocents)** [1] If someone is **innocent**, they did not commit a crime which they have been accused of. ❑ *He was sure that the man was innocent of any crime... The police knew from day one that I was innocent.* ◆◇◇ ADJ: oft ADJ *of* n ≠ guilty [2] If someone is **innocent**, they have no experience or knowledge of the more complex or unpleasant aspects of life. ❑ *They seemed so young and innocent.* ADJ = naive ♦ An **innocent** is someone who is innocent. ❑ *Ian was a hopeless innocent where women were concerned.* N-COUNT ♦ **in|no|cent|ly** *The baby gurgled innocently on the bed.* ADV: usu ADV with v [3] **Innocent** people are those who are not involved in a crime or conflict, but are injured or killed as a result of it. ❑ *All those wounded were innocent victims.* ADJ: usu ADJ n [4] An **innocent** question, remark, or comment is not intended to offend or upset people, even if it does so. ❑ *It was a perfectly innocent question.* ADJ = harmless

**in|no|cent|ly** /ɪnəsəntli/ If you say that someone does or says something **innocently**, you mean that they are pretending not to know something about a situation. ❑ *I caught Chrissie's eye, but she only smiled back at me innocently.* ➔ See also **innocent**. ADV: ADV with v

**in|nocu|ous** /ɪnɒkjuəs/ Something that is **innocuous** is not at all harmful or offensive. [FORMAL] ❑ *Both mushrooms look innocuous but are in fact deadly.* ADJ = harmless

**in|no|vate** /ɪnəveɪt/ **(innovates, innovating, innovated)** To **innovate** means to introduce changes and new ideas in the way something is done or made. ❑ *...his constant desire to innovate and experiment.* VERB V Also V n

**in|no|va|tion** /ɪnəveɪʃən/ **(innovations)** [1] An **innovation** is a new thing or a new method of doing something. ❑ *The vegetarian burger was an innovation which was rapidly exported to Britain.* N-COUNT [2] **Innovation** is the introduction of new ideas, methods, or things. ❑ *We must promote originality and encourage innovation.* N-UNCOUNT

**in|no|va|tive** /ɪnəveɪtɪv/ [1] Something that is **innovative** is new and original. ❑ *...products which are more innovative than those of their competitors.* ADJ [2] An **innovative** person introduces changes and new ideas. ❑ *He was one of the most creative and innovative engineers of his generation.* ADJ

**in|no|va|tor** /ɪnəveɪtəʳ/ **(innovators)** An **innovator** is someone who introduces changes and new ideas. ❑ *He is an innovator in this field.* N-COUNT

**in|no|va|tory** /ɪnəveɪtəri, AM -tɔːri/ **Innovatory** means the same as **innovative**. [mainly BRIT] ❑ *Only the opening sequence could claim to be genuinely innovatory.* ADJ

**in|nu|en|do** /ɪnjuendoʊ/ **(innuendoes** or **innuendos)** **Innuendo** is indirect reference to something rude or unpleasant. ❑ *The report was based on rumours, speculation, and innuendo.* N-VAR

**in|nu|mer|able** /ɪnjuːmərəbəl, AM -nuː-/ **Innumerable** means very many, or too many to be counted. [FORMAL] ❑ *He has invented innumerable excuses, told endless lies.* ADJ: usu ADJ n = countless, endless

**in|ocu|late** /ɪnɒkjʊleɪt/ **(inoculates, inoculating, inoculated)** To **inoculate** a person or animal means to inject a weak form of a disease into their body as a way of protecting them against the disease. ❑ *...a program to inoculate every child in the state... His dogs were inoculated against rabies.* VERB = vaccinate V n *be* V-ed *against* n ♦ **in|ocu|la|tion** /ɪnɒkjʊleɪʃən/ **(inoculations)** *This may eventually lead to routine inoculation of children.* N-VAR: oft N *against* n

**in|of|fen|sive** /ɪnəfensɪv/ If you describe someone or something as **inoffensive**, you mean that they are not unpleasant or unacceptable in any way, but are perhaps rather dull. ❑ *He's a mild inoffensive man.* ADJ ≠ offensive

**in|op|er|able** /ɪnɒpərəbəl/ An **inoperable** medical condition is one that cannot be cured by a surgical operation. [FORMAL] ❑ *He was diagnosed with inoperable lung cancer.* ADJ

**in|op|era|tive** /ɪnɒpərətɪv/ An **inoperative** rule, principle, or tax is one that does not work any more or that cannot be made to work. [FORMAL] ADJ

**in|op|por|tune** /ɪnɒpəʳtjuːn, AM -tuːn/ If you describe something as **inopportune** or if you say that it happens at an **inopportune** time, you mean that it happens at an unfortunate or unsuitable time, and causes trouble or embarrassment ADJ because of this. ❑ *The dismissals came at an inopportune time.*

**in|or|di|nate** /ɪnɔːʳdɪnɪt/ If you describe something as **inordinate**, you are emphasizing that it is unusually or excessively great in amount or degree. [FORMAL] ❑ *They spend an inordinate amount of time talking.* ♦ **in|or|di|nate|ly** *He is inordinately proud of his wife's achievements.* ADJ: usu ADJ n [emphasis] ADV: usu ADV adj/-ed

**in|or|gan|ic** /ɪnɔːʳgænɪk/ **Inorganic** substances are substances such as stone and metal that do not come from living things. ❑ *...roofing made from organic and inorganic fibres.* ADJ: usu ADJ n ≠ *organic*

**in-patient** **(in-patients)** also **inpatient**. An **in-patient** is someone who stays in hospital while they receive their treatment. ♦ **In-patient** is also an adjective. ❑ *...inpatient hospital care.* N-COUNT ≠ *out-patient* ADJ: ADJ n

**in|put** /ɪnput/ **(inputs, inputting)**

> The form **input** is used in the present tense and is the past tense and past participle.

1 **Input** consists of information or resources that a group or project receives. ❑ *We listen to our employees and value their input.* N-VAR 2 **Input** is information that is put into a computer. [COMPUTING] N-UNCOUNT ≠ *output* 3 If you **input** information into a computer, you feed it in, for example by typing it on a keyboard. [COMPUTING] ❑ *All this information had to be input onto the computer.* VERB *be* V-ed *onto* n

**in|put de|vice** **(input devices)** An **input device** is a piece of computer equipment such as a keyboard which enables you to put information into a computer. [COMPUTING] N-COUNT

**input/output** 1 **Input/output** refers to the information that is passed into or out of a computer. [COMPUTING] N-UNCOUNT 2 **Input/output** refers to the hardware or software that controls the passing of information into or out of a computer. [COMPUTING] ❑ *... an input/output system.* N-UNCOUNT

**in|quest** /ɪnkwest/ **(inquests)** 1 When an **inquest** is held, a public official hears evidence about someone's death in order to find out the cause. ❑ *The inquest into their deaths opened yesterday in Enniskillen.* N-COUNT: oft N *into* n 2 You can refer to an investigation by the people involved into the causes of a defeat or failure as an **inquest**. ❑ *His plea came last night as party chiefs held an inquest into the election disaster.* N-COUNT: usu sing, usu N *into* n = *inquiry*

**in|quire** /ɪnkwaɪəʳ/ **(inquires, inquiring, inquired)** also **enquire**. 1 If you **inquire** about something, you ask for information about it. [FORMAL] ❑ *'Is something wrong?' he enquired... 'Who are you?' he enquired of the first man... I rang up to inquire about train times... He inquired whether there had been any messages for him... He was so impressed that he inquired the young shepherd's name.* VERB V with quote V *of* n with quote V *about* n V wh, V n Also V *for* n, V *of* n wh, V 2 If you **inquire into** something, you investigate it carefully. ❑ *Inspectors were appointed to inquire into the affairs of the company.* VERB V *into* n/wh

♦ **inquire after** If you **inquire after** someone, you ask how they are or what they are doing. [FORMAL] ❑ *Elsie called to inquire after my health.* PHRASAL VERB = *ask after* V P n (not pron)

**in|quir|er** /ɪnkwaɪərəʳ/ **(inquirers)** also **enquirer**. 1 An **inquirer** is a person who asks for information about something or someone. [FORMAL] ❑ *I send each inquirer a packet of information.* N-COUNT 2 **Inquirer** is used in the names of some newspapers and magazines. ❑ *...the National Enquirer.* N-IN-NAMES: *the* supp N

**in|quir|ing** /ɪnkwaɪərɪŋ/ also **enquiring**. 1 If you have an **inquiring** mind, you have a great interest in learning new things. ❑ *All this helps children to develop an inquiring attitude to learning.* ADJ: ADJ n 2 If someone has an **inquiring** expression on their face, they are showing that they want to know something. [WRITTEN] ❑ *...an enquiring glance.* ADJ: ADJ n = *questioning* ♦ **in|quir|ing|ly** *She looked at me inquiringly. 'Well?'* ADV

**in|quiry** /ɪnkwaɪəri/ **(inquiries)** ◆◇◇

> The spelling **enquiry** is also used. **Inquiry** is sometimes pronounced /ɪŋkwɪri/ in American English.

1 An **inquiry** is a question which you ask in order to get some information. ❑ *He made some inquiries and discovered she had gone to the Continent.* N-COUNT 2 An **inquiry** is an official investigation. ❑ *The Democratic Party has called for an independent inquiry into the incident.* N-COUNT 3 **Inquiry** is the process of asking about or investigating something in order to find out more about it. ❑ *The investigation has suddenly switched to a new line of inquiry.* N-UNCOUNT 4 → See also **court of inquiry**.

**in|qui|si|tion** /ɪnkwɪzɪʃən/ **(inquisitions)** An **inquisition** is an official investigation, especially one which is very thorough and uses harsh methods of questioning. N-COUNT

**in|quisi|tive** /ɪnkwɪzɪtɪv/ An **inquisitive** person likes finding out about things, especially secret things. ❑ *Barrow had an inquisitive nature.* ♦ **in|quisi|tive|ly** *Molly looked at Ann inquisitively. 'Where do you want to go?'* ♦ **in|quisi|tive|ness** *I liked children, loved their innocence and their inquisitiveness.* ADJ ADV: ADV after v N-UNCOUNT

**in|quisi|tor** /ɪnkwɪzɪtəʳ/ **(inquisitors)** An **inquisitor** is someone who is asking someone else a series of questions, especially in a rather hostile way or as part of an inquisition. N-COUNT

**in|quisi|to|rial** /ɪnkwɪzɪtɔːriəl/ If you describe something or someone as **inquisitorial**, you mean they resemble things or people in an inquisition. ❑ *The next hearings will be structured differently in order to minimize the inquisitorial atmosphere.* ADJ

**in|roads** /ɪnroʊdz/ If one thing **makes inroads into** another, the first thing starts affecting or destroying the second. ❑ *In Italy, as elsewhere, television has made deep inroads into cinema.* PHRASE: V inflects, usu PHR *into* n

**in|sane** /ɪnseɪn/ 1 Someone who is **insane** has a mind that does not work in a normal way, with the result that their behaviour is very strange. ❑ *Some people simply can't take it and they just go insane.* ADJ: usu v-link ADJ = *mad* 2 If you describe a decision or action as **insane**, you think it is very foolish or excessive. ❑ *I said, 'Listen, this is completely insane.'* ADJ [disapproval] ♦ **in|sane|ly** *I would be insanely jealous if Bill left me for another woman.* ADV: usu ADV adj, also ADV with v

**in|sani|tary** /ɪnsænɪtri, AM -teri/ If something such as a place is **insanitary**, it is so dirty that it is likely to have a bad effect on people's health. [FORMAL] ❑ *...the insanitary conditions of slums... British prisons remain disgracefully crowded and insanitary.* ADJ = *unhygienic*

**in|san|ity** /ɪnsænɪti/ 1 **Insanity** is the state of being insane. ❑ *The defence pleaded insanity, but the defendant was found guilty and sentenced.* N-UNCOUNT = *madness* 2 If you describe a decision or an action as **insanity**, you think it is very foolish. ❑ *...the final financial insanity of the 1980s.* N-UNCOUNT: usu with supp, oft N *of* n [disapproval]

**in|sa|tiable** /ɪnseɪʃəbəl/ If someone has an **insatiable** desire for something, they want as much of it as they can possibly get. ❑ *The public has an insatiable appetite for stories about the famous.* ADJ = *voracious*

**in|scribe** /ɪnskraɪb/ **(inscribes, inscribing, inscribed)** 1 If you **inscribe** words **on** an object, you write or carve the words on the object. ❑ *Some galleries commemorate donors by inscribing their names on the walls. ...stone slabs inscribed with Buddhist texts.* VERB V n *on* n V-ed *on/with* n 2 If you **inscribe** something in the front of a book or on a photograph, you write it there, often before giving it to someone. ❑ *On the back I had inscribed the words: 'Here's to Great Ideas! John'... The book is inscribed: To John Arlott from Laurie Lee.* VERB V n V-ed quote

**in|scrip|tion** /ɪnskrɪpʃən/ **(inscriptions)** 1 An **inscription** is writing carved into something made of stone or metal, for example a gravestone or medal. ❑ *The medal bears the inscription 'For distinguished service'.* N-COUNT 2 An **inscription** is something written by hand in the front of a book or on a photograph. ❑ *The inscription reads: 'To Emma, with love from Harry'.* N-COUNT

**in|scru|table** /ɪnskruːtəbᵊl/ If a person or their expression is **inscrutable**, it is very hard to know what they are really thinking or what they mean. ❑ *In public he remained inscrutable.* ADJ

**in|sect** /ɪnsekt/ **(insects)** An **insect** is a small animal that has six legs. Most insects have wings. Ants, flies, butterflies, and beetles are all insects. N-COUNT

**in|sec|ti|cide** /ɪnsektɪsaɪd/ **(insecticides) Insecticide** is a chemical substance that is used to kill insects. ❑ *Spray the plants with insecticide.* N-MASS

**in|secure** /ɪnsɪkjʊəʳ/ [1] If you are **insecure**, you lack confidence because you think that you are not good enough or are not loved. ❑ *Most mothers are insecure about their performance as mothers.* ADJ: usu v-link ADJ ≠confident ♦ **in|secu|rity** /ɪnsɪkjʊərɪti/ **(insecurities)** *She is always assailed by self-doubt and emotional insecurity.* N-VAR [2] Something that is **insecure** is not safe or protected. ❑ *...low-paid, insecure jobs.* ADJ ≠secure ♦ **in|secu|rity** *Crime creates feelings of insecurity in the population.* N-UNCOUNT

**in|semi|nate** /ɪnsemɪneɪt/ **(inseminates, inseminating, inseminated)** [1] To **inseminate** a woman or female animal means to put a male's sperm into her in order to make her pregnant. ❑ *The gadget is used to artificially inseminate cows.* VERB V n ♦ **in|semi|na|tion** /ɪnsemɪneɪʃᵊn/ *The sperm sample is checked under the microscope before insemination is carried out.* N-UNCOUNT [2] → See also **artificial insemination**.

**in|sen|si|tive** /ɪnsensɪtɪv/ [1] If you describe someone as **insensitive**, you are criticizing them for being unaware of or unsympathetic to other people's feelings. ❑ *I feel my husband is very insensitive about my problem.* ADJ disapproval ≠sensitive ♦ **in|sen|si|tiv|ity** /ɪnsensɪtɪvɪti/ *I was ashamed at my insensitivity towards her.* N-UNCOUNT [2] Someone who is **insensitive to** a situation or to a need does not think or care about it. ❑ *Women's and Latino organizations that say he is insensitive to civil rights.* ADJ: usu ADJ *to* n ♦ **in|sen|si|tiv|ity** *...insensitivity to the environmental consequences.* N-UNCOUNT [3] Someone who is **insensitive to** a physical sensation is unable to feel it. ❑ *He had become insensitive to cold.* ADJ: usu v-link ADJ *to* n

**in|sepa|rable** /ɪnseprəbᵊl/ [1] If one thing is **inseparable from** another, the things are so closely connected that they cannot be considered separately. ❑ *He firmly believes liberty is inseparable from social justice.* ADJ: oft ADJ *from* n ♦ **in|sepa|rably** *In his mind, religion and politics were inseparably intertwined.* ADV: usu ADV -ed, also ADV after v [2] If you say that two people are **inseparable**, you are emphasizing that they are very good friends and spend a great deal of time together. ❑ *She and Kristin were inseparable.* ADJ emphasis

**in|sert (inserts, inserting, inserted)**

> ✓ The verb is pronounced /ɪnsɜːʳt/. The noun is pronounced /ɪnsɜːʳt/.

[1] If you **insert** an object **into** something, you put the object inside it. ❑ *He took a small key from his pocket and slowly inserted it into the lock... Wait for a couple of minutes with your mouth closed before inserting the thermometer.* VERB V n *into* n V n ♦ **in|ser|tion** /ɪnsɜːʳʃᵊn/ **(insertions)** *...the first experiment involving the insertion of a new gene into a human being.* N-VAR [2] If you **insert** a comment into a piece of writing or a speech, you include it. ❑ *They joined with the monarchists to insert a clause calling for a popular vote on the issue.* VERB V n Also V n *into/in* n ♦ **in|ser|tion** *He recorded an item for insertion in the programme.* N-VAR [3] An **insert** is something that is inserted somewhere, especially an advertisement on a piece of paper that is placed between the pages of a book or magazine. N-COUNT

**in-service** If people working in a particular profession are given **in-service** training, they attend special courses to improve their skills or to learn about new developments in their field. ❑ *...in-service courses for teachers.* ADJ: ADJ n

**in|set** /ɪnset/ **(insets)** [1] Something that is **inset with** a decoration or piece of material has the decoration or material set inside it. ❑ *...a gold pendant, inset with a diamond.* ADJ: usu v-link ADJ, oft ADJ *with* n [2] An **inset** is a small picture, diagram, or map that is inside a larger one. ❑ *I frequently paint between 10 and 20 insets for my murals.* N-COUNT

**in|shore**

> ✓ The adverb is pronounced /ɪnʃɔːʳ/. The adjective is pronounced /ɪnʃɔːʳ/.

If something is **inshore**, it is in the sea but quite close to the land. If something moves **inshore**, it moves from the sea towards the land. ❑ *A barge was close inshore about a hundred yards away.* ADV: *be* ADV, ADV after v ≠offshore ♦ **Inshore** is also an adjective. ❑ *...inshore reefs and islands.* ADJ: ADJ n ≠offshore

**in|side** /ɪnsaɪd/ **(insides)** ♦♦◇

> ✓ The preposition is usually pronounced /ɪnsaɪd/.

> The form **inside of** can also be used as a preposition. This form is more usual in American English.

[1] Something or someone that is **inside** a place, container, or object is in it or is surrounded by it. ❑ *Inside the passport was a folded slip of paper... There is a telephone inside the entrance hall.* PREP ≠outside ♦ **Inside** is also an adverb. ❑ *The couple chatted briefly on the doorstep before going inside... Inside, clouds of cigarette smoke swirled.* ADV: ADV after v, *be* ADV, *from* ADV, n ADV, ADV with cl ♦ **Inside** is also an adjective. ❑ *...four-berth inside cabins with en suite bathroom and shower.* ADJ: ADJ n [2] The **inside** of something is the part or area that its sides surround or contain. ❑ *The doors were locked from the inside... I painted the inside of the house.* N-COUNT: usu *the* N in sing ≠outside ♦ **Inside** is also an adjective. ❑ *The popular papers all have photo features on their inside pages.* ADJ: ADJ n ♦ **Inside** is also an adverb. ❑ *The potato cakes should be crisp outside and meltingly soft inside.* ADV: adj ADV [3] You can say that someone is **inside** when they are in prison. [INFORMAL] ❑ *He's been inside three times.* ADV: *be* ADV, ADV after v [4] On a wide road, the **inside** lane is the one closest to the edge of the road. Compare **outside**. [BRIT] ❑ *I was driving at seventy miles an hour on the inside lane on the motorway.* ADJ: ADJ n = nearside ≠outside ♦ **Inside** is also a noun. ❑ *I overtook Charlie on the inside.* N-SING: *the* N, oft *on the* N ≠outside

> ✓ in AM, use **slow lane**

[5] **Inside** information is obtained from someone who is involved in a situation and therefore knows a lot about it. ❑ *Sloane used inside diplomatic information to make himself rich.* ADJ: ADJ n [6] If you are **inside** an organization, you belong to it. ❑ *75 per cent of chief executives come from inside the company.* PREP ♦ **Inside** is also an adjective. ❑ *...a recent book about the inside world of pro football.* ADJ: ADJ n ♦ **Inside** is also a noun. ❑ *McAvoy was convinced he could control things from the inside but he lost control.* N-SING: *the* N [7] Your **insides** are your internal organs, especially your stomach. [INFORMAL] N-PLURAL: usu poss N [8] If you say that someone has a feeling **inside**, you mean that they have it but have not expressed it. ❑ *There is nothing left inside – no words, no anger, no tears.* ADV: ADV after v, n ADV ♦ **Inside** is also a preposition. ❑ *He felt a great weight of sorrow inside him.* PREP: usu n PREP pron ♦ **Inside** is also a noun. ❑ *What is needed is a change from the inside, a real change in outlook and attitude.* N-SING: *the* N [9] If you do something **inside** a particular time, you do it before the end of that time. ❑ *They should have everything working inside an hour.* PREP: PREP amount = within

PHRASES [10] If something such as a piece of clothing is **inside out**, the part that is normally inside now faces outwards. ❑ *Her umbrella blew inside out.* PHRASE: PHR after v [11] If you say that you know something or someone **inside out**, you are emphasizing that you know them extremely well. ❑ *He knew the game inside out.* PHRASE: v n PHR emphasis

**in|sid|er** /ɪnsaɪdəʳ/ **(insiders)** An **insider** is someone who is involved in a situation and who knows more about it than other people. ❑ *An insider said, 'Katharine has told friends it is time to end her career.'* N-COUNT

**in|sid|er trad|ing** also **insider dealing**. **Insider trading** or **insider dealing** is the illegal buying or selling of a company's shares by some- N-UNCOUNT one who has secret or private information about the company. [BUSINESS]

**in|sidi|ous** /ɪnsɪdiəs/ Something that is **insidious** is unpleasant or dangerous and develops gradually without being noticed. ❑ *The changes are insidious, and will not produce a noticeable effect for 15 to 20 years.* ♦ **in|sidi|ous|ly** *Delusions are sometimes insidiously destructive.* ADJ; ADV: usu ADV adj

**in|sight** /ɪnsaɪt/ **(insights)** 1 If you gain **insight** or an **insight into** a complex situation or problem, you gain an accurate and deep understanding of it. ❑ *The project would give scientists new insights into what is happening to the earth's atmosphere.* 2 If someone has **insight**, they are able to understand complex situations. ❑ *He was a man with considerable insight.* N-VAR: usu N *into* n; N-UNCOUNT

**in|sight|ful** /ɪnsaɪtfʊl/ If you describe a person or their remarks as **insightful**, you mean that they show a very good understanding of people and situations. ❑ *She offered some really interesting, insightful observations.* ADJ [approval] = astute, shrewd

**in|sig|nia** /ɪnsɪgniə/ **(insignia)** An **insignia** is a design or symbol which shows that a person or object belongs to a particular organization, often a military one. ❑ *The red star was the national insignia of the USSR.* N-COUNT = emblem

**in|sig|nifi|cance** /ɪnsɪgnɪfɪkəns/ **Insignificance** is the quality of being insignificant. ❑ *The cost pales into insignificance when compared with the damage done to his reputation.* N-UNCOUNT ≠ significance

**in|sig|nifi|cant** /ɪnsɪgnɪfɪkənt/ Something that is **insignificant** is unimportant, especially because it is very small. ❑ *In 1949 Bonn was a small, insignificant city.* ADJ ≠ significant

**in|sin|cere** /ɪnsɪnsɪəʳ/ If you say that someone is **insincere**, you are being critical of them because they say things they do not really mean, usually pleasant, admiring, or encouraging things. ❑ *Some people are so terribly insincere you can never tell if they are telling the truth.* ♦ **in|sin|cer|ity** /ɪnsɪnserɪti/ *Too many superlatives lend a note of insincerity.* ADJ [disapproval] ≠ sincere; N-UNCOUNT ≠ sincerity

**in|sinu|ate** /ɪnsɪnjueɪt/ **(insinuates, insinuating, insinuated)** 1 If you say that someone **insinuates** that something bad is the case, you mean that they say it in an indirect way. ❑ *The libel claim followed an article which insinuated that the President was lying.* ♦ **in|sin|ua|tion** /ɪnsɪnjueɪʃᵊn/ **(insinuations)** *He speaks with rage of insinuations that there's a 'gay mafia' in Hollywood.* 2 If you say that someone **insinuates themselves into** a particular situation, you mean that they manage very cleverly, and perhaps dishonestly, to get into that situation. ❑ *He gradually insinuated himself into her life.* VERB [disapproval] = imply; V that; N-VAR; VERB [disapproval] = worm; V pron-refl *into* n; Also V n prep

**in|sinu|at|ing** /ɪnsɪnjueɪtɪŋ/ If you describe someone's words or voice as **insinuating**, you mean that they are saying in an indirect way that something bad is the case. ❑ *Marcus kept making insinuating remarks.* ADJ [disapproval]

**in|sip|id** /ɪnsɪpɪd/ 1 If you describe food or drink as **insipid**, you dislike it because it has very little taste. ❑ *It tasted indescribably bland and insipid, like warmed cardboard.* 2 If you describe someone or something as **insipid**, you mean they are dull and boring. ❑ *On the surface she seemed meek, rather insipid.* ADJ [disapproval] = bland, flavourless; ADJ [disapproval]

**in|sist** /ɪnsɪst/ **(insists, insisting, insisted)** ◆◆◇ 1 If you **insist that** something should be done, you say so very firmly and refuse to give in about it. If you **insist on** something, you say firmly that it must be done or provided. ❑ *My family insisted that I should not give in, but stay and fight... She insisted on being present at all the interviews... I didn't want to join in, but Kenneth insisted.* 2 If you **insist** that something is the case, you say so very firmly and refuse to say otherwise, even though other people do not believe you. ❑ *The president insisted that he was acting out of compassion, not opportunism... 'It's not that difficult,' she insists... Crippen insisted on his innocence.* VERB; V that; V *on* -ing/n; V; VERB; V that; V with quote; V *on* n

**in|sist|ence** /ɪnsɪstəns/ Someone's **insistence** on something is the fact that they insist that it should be done or insist that it is the case. ❑ *...Raeder's insistence that naval uniform be worn.* N-UNCOUNT: oft N *on* -ing/n, N that

**in|sist|ent** /ɪnsɪstənt/ 1 Someone who is **insistent** keeps insisting that a particular thing should be done or is the case. ❑ *Stalin was insistent that the war would be won and lost in the machine shops.* ♦ **in|sist|ent|ly** *'What is it?' his wife asked again, gently but insistently.* 2 An **insistent** noise or rhythm keeps going on for a long time and holds your attention. ❑ *...the insistent rhythms of the Caribbean and Latin America.* ADJ: oft ADJ that, ADJ *on* n/-ing; ADV: ADV with v; ADJ = unrelenting

**in situ** /ɪn sɪtjuː, AM - sɪtuː/ If something remains **in situ**, especially while something is done to it, it remains where it is. [FORMAL] ❑ *Major works of painting, sculpture, mosaic and architecture were examined in situ in Venice.* ♦ **In situ** is also an adjective. ❑ *...technical data derived from laboratory and in-situ experimentation.* ADV: ADV after v; ADJ: ADJ n

**in|so|far as** /ɪnsəfɑːr æz/ You use **insofar as** to introduce a statement which explains and adds to something you have just said. [FORMAL] ❑ *Looking back helps insofar as it helps you learn from your mistakes.* PHRASE = inasmuch as

**in|sole** /ɪnsoʊl/ **(insoles)** The **insoles** of a pair of shoes are the soft layer of material inside each one, which the soles of your feet rest on. N-COUNT: usu pl

**in|so|lent** /ɪnsələnt/ If you say that someone is being **insolent**, you mean they are being rude to someone they ought to be respectful to. ❑ *...her insolent stare.* ♦ **in|so|lence** *Pupils could be excluded from school for insolence.* ADJ; N-UNCOUNT

**in|sol|uble** /ɪnsɒljʊbᵊl/ 1 An **insoluble** problem is so difficult that it is impossible to solve. ❑ *I pushed the problem aside; at present it was insoluble.* 2 If a substance is **insoluble**, it does not dissolve in a liquid. ❑ *Carotenes are insoluble in water and soluble in oils and fats.* ADJ; ADJ ≠ soluble

**in|sol|ven|cy** /ɪnsɒlvᵊnsi/ **(insolvencies)** **Insolvency** is the state of not having enough money to pay your debts. [BUSINESS, FORMAL] ❑ *...companies on the brink of insolvency.* N-VAR

**in|sol|vent** /ɪnsɒlvᵊnt/ A person or organization that is **insolvent** does not have enough money to pay their debts. [BUSINESS, FORMAL] ❑ *The bank was declared insolvent.* ADJ: usu v-link ADJ

**in|som|nia** /ɪnsɒmniə/ Someone who suffers from **insomnia** finds it difficult to sleep. N-UNCOUNT

**in|som|ni|ac** /ɪnsɒmniæk/ **(insomniacs)** An **insomniac** is a person who finds it difficult to sleep. N-COUNT

**in|sou|ci|ance** /ɪnsuːsiəns/ **Insouciance** is lack of concern shown by someone about something which they might be expected to take more seriously. [FORMAL] ❑ *He replied with characteristic insouciance: 'So what?'* N-UNCOUNT = nonchalance

**in|sou|ci|ant** /ɪnsuːsiənt/ An **insouciant** action or quality shows someone's lack of concern about something which they might be expected to take more seriously. [FORMAL] ❑ *Programme-makers seem irresponsibly insouciant about churning out violence.* ADJ = nonchalant

**Insp.** **Insp.** is the written abbreviation for **Inspector** when it is used as a title. ❑ *...Insp John Downs.* N-TITLE

**in|spect** /ɪnspekt/ **(inspects, inspecting, inspected)** ◆◇◇ 1 If you **inspect** something, you look at every part of it carefully in order to find out about it or check that it is all right. ❑ *Elaine went outside to inspect the playing field.* ♦ **in|spec|tion** /ɪnspekʃᵊn/ **(inspections)** *He had completed his inspection of the doors.* 2 When an official **inspects** a place or a group of people, they visit it and check it carefully, for example in order to find out whether regulations are being obeyed. ❑ *The Public Utilities Commission inspects us once a year.* VERB = examine; V n; N-VAR; VERB; V n

♦ **in|spec|tion** *Officers making a routine inspection of the vessel found fifty kilograms of the drug.* N-VAR

**in|spec|tor** /ɪnspektəʳ/ **(inspectors)** ◆◇◇ 1 An **inspector** is a person, usually employed by a government agency, whose job is to find out whether people are obeying official regulations. ❑ *The mill was finally shut down by state safety inspectors.* N-COUNT 2 In Britain, an **inspector** is an officer in the police who is higher in rank than a sergeant and lower in rank than a superintendent. ❑ *I got on the phone to Inspector Joplin at Scotland Yard.* N-COUNT; N-TITLE; N-VOC 3 In the United States, an **inspector** is an officer in the police who is next in rank to a superintendent or police chief. ❑ *...San Francisco police inspector Tony Camileri.* N-COUNT; N-TITLE; N-VOC

**in|spec|tor|ate** /ɪnspektərət/ **(inspectorates)** An **inspectorate** is a group of inspectors who work on the same issue or area. ❑ *...the Nuclear Installations Inspectorate.* N-COUNT: usu with supp

**in|spi|ra|tion** /ɪnspɪreɪʃən/ **(inspirations)** 1 **Inspiration** is a feeling of enthusiasm you get from someone or something, which gives you new and creative ideas. ❑ *My inspiration comes from poets like Baudelaire and Jacques Prévert.* N-UNCOUNT 2 If you describe someone or something good as **an inspiration**, you mean that they make you or other people want to do or achieve something. ❑ *Powell's unusual journey to high office is an inspiration to millions.* N-SING: an N, oft N *to* n [approval] 3 If something or someone is the **inspiration** for a particular book, work of art, or action, they are the source of the ideas in it or act as a model for it. ❑ *India's myths and songs are the inspiration for her books.* N-SING: oft the N *for/behind* n 4 If you suddenly have an **inspiration**, you suddenly think of an idea of what to do or say. ❑ *Alison had an inspiration.* N-COUNT

**in|spi|ra|tion|al** /ɪnspɪreɪʃənəl/ Something that is **inspirational** provides you with inspiration. ❑ *Gandhi was an inspirational figure.* ADJ [approval]

**in|spire** /ɪnspaɪəʳ/ **(inspires, inspiring, inspired)** 1 If someone or something **inspires** you **to** do something new or unusual, they make you want to do it. ❑ *Our challenge is to motivate those voters and inspire them to join our cause.* VERB V n to-inf 2 If someone or something **inspires** you, they give you new ideas and a strong feeling of enthusiasm. ❑ *Jimi Hendrix inspired a generation of guitarists.* VERB V n 3 If a book, work of art, or action **is inspired by** something, that thing is the source of the idea for it. ❑ *The book was inspired by a real person, namely Tamara de Treaux. ...a murder inspired by the nationalist conflicts now wrecking the country.* VERB: usu passive be V-ed *by* n V-ed ♦ **-inspired** *...Mediterranean-inspired ceramics in bright yellow and blue.* COMB in ADJ 4 Someone or something that **inspires** a particular emotion or reaction in people makes them feel this emotion or reaction. ❑ *The car's performance quickly inspires confidence.* VERB V n

**in|spir|ing** /ɪnspaɪərɪŋ/ Something or someone that is **inspiring** is exciting and makes you feel strongly interested and enthusiastic... ❑ *She was one of the most inspiring people I've ever met.* ADJ

**Inst.** **Inst.** is a written abbreviation for **Institute** or **Institution**. ❑ *...the Liverpool Inst. of Higher Ed.* N-IN-NAMES

**in|stabil|ity** /ɪnstəbɪlɪti/ **(instabilities)** **Instability** is the quality of being unstable. ❑ *...unpopular policies, which resulted in social discontent and political instability.* N-UNCOUNT: also N in pl ≠ stability

**in|stall** /ɪnstɔːl/ **(installs, installing, installed)** ◆◇◇ also **instal.** 1 If you **install** a piece of equipment, you fit it or put it somewhere so that it is ready to be used. ❑ *They had installed a new phone line in the apartment.* VERB V n ♦ **in|stal|la|tion** *Hundreds of lives could be saved if the installation of alarms was more widespread.* N-UNCOUNT: oft N *of* n 2 If someone **is installed** in a new job or important position, they are officially given the job or position, often in a special ceremony. ❑ *A new Catholic bishop was installed in Galway yesterday... Professor Sawyer was formally installed as President last Thursday... The army has promised to install a new government within a week.* VERB be V-ed, be V-ed *as* n, V n ♦ **in|stal|la|tion** *He sent a letter inviting Naomi to attend his installation as chief of his tribe.* N-UNCOUNT: oft with poss, N *as* n 3 If you **install yourself** in a particular place, you settle there and make yourself comfortable. [FORMAL] ❑ *Before her husband's death she had installed herself in a modern villa.* VERB V pron-refl prep/adv

**in|stal|la|tion** /ɪnstəleɪʃən/ **(installations)** An **installation** is a place that contains equipment and machinery which are being used for a particular purpose. ❑ *...a nuclear installation.* → See also **install**. N-COUNT: usu supp N

**in|stall|ment plan** **(installment plans)** An **installment plan** is a way of buying goods gradually. You make regular payments to the seller until, after some time, you have paid the full price and the goods belong to you. [AM] N-COUNT

✓ in BRIT, use **hire purchase**

**in|stal|ment** /ɪnstɔːlmənt/ **(instalments)**

✓ in AM, use **installment**

1 If you pay for something in **instalments**, you pay small sums of money at regular intervals over a period of time, rather than paying the whole amount at once. ❑ *The first instalment of £1 per share is payable on application.* N-COUNT 2 An **instalment** of a story or plan is one of its parts that are published or carried out separately one after the other. ❑ *...the disappointing third instalment of the Highlander series.* N-COUNT = part

**in|stance** /ɪnstəns/ **(instances)** ◆◆◇ 1 You use **for instance** to introduce a particular event, situation, or person that is an example of what you are talking about. ❑ *There are a number of improvements; for instance, both mouse buttons can now be used.* PHRASE: PHR with cl/group 2 An **instance** is a particular example or occurrence of something. ❑ *...an investigation into a serious instance of corruption.* N-COUNT 3 You say **in the first instance** to mention something that is the first step in a series of actions. ❑ *In the first instance your child will be seen by an ear, nose and throat specialist.* PHRASE: PHR with cl

**in|stant** /ɪnstənt/ **(instants)** ◆◇◇ 1 An **instant** is an extremely short period of time. ❑ *For an instant, Catherine was tempted to flee... The pain disappeared in an instant.* N-COUNT: usu sing = moment 2 If you say that something happens **at** a particular **instant**, you mean that it happens at exactly the time you have been referring to, and you are usually suggesting that it happens quickly or immediately. ❑ *At that instant the museum was plunged into total darkness.* N-SING: with supp, usu *at/in* N = moment 3 To do something **the instant** something else happens means to do it immediately. ❑ *I had bolted the door the instant I had seen the bat.* PHRASE [emphasis] 4 You use **instant** to describe something that happens immediately. ❑ *He had taken an instant dislike to Mortlake.* ADJ: usu ADJ n = immediate ♦ **in|stant|ly** *The man was killed instantly.* ADV: ADV with v, ADV adj 5 **Instant** food is food that you can prepare very quickly, for example by just adding water. ❑ *...instant coffee.* ADJ: ADJ n

**in|stan|ta|neous** /ɪnstənteɪniəs/ Something that is **instantaneous** happens immediately and very quickly. ❑ *His death was instantaneous because both bullets hit the heart.* ADJ = immediate ♦ **in|stan|ta|neous|ly** *Airbags inflate instantaneously on impact.* ADV: ADV with v

**in|stant re|play** **(instant replays)** An **instant replay** is a repeated showing, usually in slow motion, of an event that has just been on television. [AM] N-COUNT

✓ in BRIT, use **action replay**

**in|stead** /ɪnsted/ ◆◆◇ 1 If you do one thing **instead of** another, you do the first thing and not the second thing, as the result of a choice or a change of behaviour. ❑ *They raised prices and cut production, instead of cutting costs... Instead of going to work thinking that it will be totally boring, try to be positive.* PREP-PHRASE: PREP n/-ing 2 If you do not do something, but do something else **instead**, you do the second thing and not the first thing, as the result of a choice or a change of behaviour. ❑ *My husband asked why I* ADV: ADV with cl *couldn't just forget about dieting all the time and eat normally instead.*

**in|step** /ɪnstep/ **(insteps)** Your **instep** is the middle part of your foot, where it arches upwards. N-COUNT

**in|sti|gate** /ɪnstɪgeɪt/ **(instigates, instigating, instigated)** Someone who **instigates** an event causes it to happen. ❑ *Jenkinson instigated a refurbishment of the old gallery.* ♦ **in|sti|ga|tion** /ɪnstɪgeɪʃᵊn/ *The talks are taking place at the instigation of Germany.* VERB = initiate V n N-UNCOUNT: usu *at/on* N with poss

**in|sti|ga|tor** /ɪnstɪgeɪtəʳ/ **(instigators)** The **instigator** of an event is the person who causes it to happen. ❑ *He was accused of being the main instigator of the coup.* N-COUNT: oft N *of* n

**in|stil** /ɪnstɪl/ **(instils, instilling, instilled)**

in AM, use **instill**

If you **instil** an idea or feeling in someone, especially over a period of time, you make them think it or feel it. ❑ *They hope that their work will instil a sense of responsibility in children... The motive of the executions would be to instil fear.* VERB V n *in/into* n V n

**in|stinct** /ɪnstɪŋkt/ **(instincts)** 1 **Instinct** is the natural tendency that a person or animal has to behave or react in a particular way. ❑ *I didn't have as strong a maternal instinct as some other mothers... He always knew what time it was, as if by instinct.* 2 If you have an **instinct for** something, you are naturally good at it or able to do it. ❑ *Farmers are increasingly losing touch with their instinct for managing the land.* 3 If it is your **instinct to** do something, you feel that it is right to do it. ❑ *I should've gone with my first instinct, which was not to do the interview.* 4 **Instinct** is a feeling that you have that something is the case, rather than an opinion or idea based on facts. ❑ *He seems so honest and genuine and my every instinct says he's not.* N-VAR N-COUNT: oft N *for* n/-ing, N to-inf = aptitude N-VAR: usu with poss, oft N to-inf N-VAR: oft N that = intuition

**in|stinc|tive** /ɪnstɪŋktɪv/ An **instinctive** feeling, idea, or action is one that you have or do without thinking or reasoning. ❑ *It's an absolutely instinctive reaction – if a child falls you pick it up.* ♦ **in|stinc|tive|ly** *Jane instinctively knew all was not well with her 10-month old son.* ADJ = natural ADV: ADV with v

**in|stinc|tual** /ɪnstɪŋktʃuəl/ An **instinctual** feeling, action, or idea is one based on instinct. [WRITTEN] ❑ *The relationship between a parent and a child is instinctual and stems from basic human nature.* ADJ = instinctive

**in|sti|tute** /ɪnstɪtjuːt, AM -tuːt/ **(institutes, instituting, instituted)** ◆◆◇ 1 An **institute** is an organization set up to do a particular type of work, especially research or teaching. You can also use **institute** to refer to the building the organization occupies. ❑ *...an elite research institute devoted to computer software.* 2 If you **institute** a system, rule, or course of action, you start it. [FORMAL] ❑ *We will institute a number of measures to better safeguard the public.* N-COUNT; N-IN-NAMES VERB V n

**in|sti|tu|tion** /ɪnstɪtjuːʃᵊn, AM -tuː-/ **(institutions)** ◆◆◇ 1 An **institution** is a large important organization such as a university, church, or bank. ❑ *The Hong Kong Bank is Hong Kong's largest financial institution.* 2 An **institution** is a building where certain people are looked after, for example people who are mentally ill or children who have no parents. ❑ *Larry has been in an institution since he was four.* 3 An **institution** is a custom or system that is considered an important or typical feature of a particular society or group, usually because it has existed for a long time. ❑ *I believe in the institution of marriage.* 4 The **institution** of a new system is the act of starting it or bringing it in. ❑ *There was never an official institution of censorship in Albania.* N-COUNT; N-IN-NAMES N-COUNT; N-IN-NAMES N-COUNT: usu N *of* n N-UNCOUNT: usu N *of* n

**in|sti|tu|tion|al** /ɪnstɪtjuːʃənᵊl, AM -tuː-/ 1 **Institutional** means relating to a large organization, for example a university, bank, or church. ❑ *The share price will be determined by bidding from institutional investors.* 2 **Institutional** means relating to a building where people are looked after or held. ❑ *Outside the protected environment of institutional care he could not survive.* 3 An **institutional** value or quality is considered an important and typical feature of a particular society or group, usually because it has existed for a long time. ❑ *...social and institutional values.* ADJ: ADJ n ADJ: ADJ n ADJ: ADJ n

**in|sti|tu|tion|al|ize** /ɪnstɪtjuːʃənəlaɪz, AM -tuː-/ **(institutionalizes, institutionalizing, institutionalized)**

in BRIT, also use **institutionalise**

1 If someone such as a sick, mentally ill, or old person **is institutionalized**, they are sent to stay in a special hospital or home, usually for a long period. ❑ *She became seriously ill and had to be institutionalized for a lengthy period. ...institutionalized children with medical problems.* ♦ **in|sti|tu|tion|ali|za|tion** /ɪnstɪtjuːʃənəlaɪzeɪʃᵊn, AM -tuː-/ *Institutionalization was necessary when his wife became both blind and violent.* 2 To **institutionalize** something means to establish it as part of a culture, social system, or organization. ❑ *The goal is to institutionalize family planning into community life... In the first century there was no such thing as institutionalized religion.* ♦ **in|sti|tu|tion|ali|za|tion** *...the institutionalization of social change.* VERB: usu passive be V-ed V-ed N-UNCOUNT VERB V n V-ed N-UNCOUNT

**in-store** also **instore. In-store** facilities are facilities that are available within a department store, supermarket or other large shop. ❑ *...in-store banking. ...an instore bakery.* ♦ **In-store** is also an adverb. ❑ *Ask in-store for details.* ADJ: usu ADJ n ADV: ADV after v

**in|struct** /ɪnstrʌkt/ **(instructs, instructing, instructed)** 1 If you **instruct** someone to do something, you formally tell them to do it. [FORMAL] ❑ *The family has instructed solicitors to sue Thomson for compensation... 'Go and have a word with her, Ken,' Webb instructed... I want you to instruct them that they've got three months to get the details sorted out.* 2 Someone who **instructs** people **in** a subject or skill teaches it to them. ❑ *He instructed family members in nursing techniques.* VERB V n to-inf V with quote V n that Also V n with quote VERB V n *in/on* n Also V

**in|struc|tion** /ɪnstrʌkʃᵊn/ **(instructions)** ◆◇◇ 1 An **instruction** is something that someone tells you to do. ❑ *Two lawyers were told not to leave the building but no reason for this instruction was given.* 2 If someone gives you **instruction** in a subject or skill, they teach it to you. [FORMAL] ❑ *Each candidate is given instruction in safety.* 3 **Instructions** are clear and detailed information on how to do something. ❑ *Always read the instructions before you start taking the medicine.* N-COUNT N-UNCOUNT: usu with supp N-PLURAL

**in|struc|tion|al** /ɪnstrʌkʃənᵊl/ **Instructional** books or films are meant to teach people something or to offer them help with a particular problem. ❑ *...instructional material designed to help you with your lifestyle.* ADJ: usu ADJ n

**in|struc|tive** /ɪnstrʌktɪv/ Something that is **instructive** gives useful information. ❑ *...an entertaining and instructive documentary.* ADJ: oft *it* v-link ADJ to-inf = informative

**in|struc|tor** /ɪnstrʌktəʳ/ **(instructors)** An **instructor** is someone who teaches a skill such as driving or skiing. In American English, **instructor** can also be used to refer to a schoolteacher or to a university teacher of low rank. ❑ *...tuition from an approved driving instructor.* N-COUNT: oft n N

**in|stru|ment** /ɪnstrəmənt/ **(instruments)** ◆◇◇ 1 An **instrument** is a tool or device that is used to do a particular task, especially a scientific task. ❑ *...instruments for cleaning and polishing teeth... The environment itself will at the same time be measured by about 60 scientific instruments.* 2 A musical **instrument** is an object such as a piano, guitar, or flute, which you play in order to produce music. ❑ *Learning a musical instrument introduces a child to an understanding of music.* 3 An **instrument** is a device that is used for making measurements of something such as speed, height, or sound, for example on a ship or plane or in a car. ❑ *...crucial instruments on the control panel.* 4 Something that is an **instrument** for achieving a particular aim is used by people to achieve that aim. ❑ *The veto has* N-COUNT: usu with supp N-COUNT: oft supp N N-COUNT: oft supp N N-COUNT: oft N *of* n *been a traditional instrument of diplomacy for centuries.* [5] → See also **stringed instrument**, **wind instrument**.

**in|stru|men|tal** /ɪnstrəme̲ntᵊl/ **(instrumentals)** [1] Someone or something that is **instrumental in** a process or event helps to make it happen. ❑ *In his first years as chairman he was instrumental in raising the company's wider profile.* ADJ: usu v-link ADJ, oft ADJ *in* -ing/n
[2] **Instrumental** music is performed by instruments and not by voices. ❑ *...a cassette recording of vocal and instrumental music.* ♦ **Instrumentals** are pieces of instrumental music. ❑ *The last track on the CD is an instrumental.* ADJ: ADJ n; N-COUNT: usu pl

**in|stru|men|tal|ist** /ɪnstrəme̲ntəlɪst/ **(instrumentalists)** An **instrumentalist** is someone who plays a musical instrument. N-COUNT = *musician*

**in|stru|men|ta|tion** /ɪnstrəmente̲ɪʃᵊn/ **Instrumentation** is a group or collection of instruments, usually ones that are part of the same machine. ❑ *Basic flight instrumentation was similar on both planes.* N-UNCOUNT

**in|stru|ment pan|el** **(instrument panels)** The **instrument panel** of a plane, car, or machine is the panel where the dials and switches are located. N-COUNT

**in|sub|or|di|nate** /ɪnsəbɔ̲ːʳdɪnət/ If you say that someone is **insubordinate**, you mean that they do not obey someone of higher rank. [FORMAL] ❑ *In industry, a worker who is grossly insubordinate is threatened with discharge.* ADJ

**in|sub|or|di|na|tion** /ɪnsəbɔːʳdɪne̲ɪʃᵊn/ **Insubordination** is a refusal to obey someone of higher rank. [FORMAL] ❑ *Hansen and his partner were fired for insubordination.* N-UNCOUNT

**in|sub|stan|tial** /ɪnsəbstæ̲nʃᵊl/ Something that is **insubstantial** is not large, solid, or strong. ❑ *Mars has an insubstantial atmosphere, consisting almost entirely of carbon dioxide.* ADJ

**in|suf|fer|able** /ɪnsʌ̲frəbᵊl/ If you say that someone or something is **insufferable**, you are emphasizing that they are very unpleasant or annoying. [FORMAL] ❑ *He was an insufferable bore.* ♦ **in|suf|fer|ably** /ɪnsʌ̲frəbli/ *His letters are insufferably dull.* ADJ [emphasis] = *unbearable*; ADV: ADV adj

**in|suf|fi|cient** /ɪnsəfɪ̲ʃᵊnt/ Something that is **insufficient** is not large enough in amount or degree for a particular purpose. [FORMAL] ❑ *He decided there was insufficient evidence to justify criminal proceedings.* ♦ **in|suf|fi|cien|cy** /ɪnsəfɪ̲ʃᵊnsi/ *Late miscarriages are usually not due to hormonal insufficiency.* ♦ **in|suf|fi|cient|ly** *Food that is insufficiently cooked can lead to food poisoning.* ADJ: oft ADJ to-inf, ADJ *for* n = *inadequate*; N-UNCOUNT; ADV: ADV adj/-ed

**in|su|lar** /ɪ̲nsjʊləʳ, AM -sə-/ If you say that someone is **insular**, you are being critical of them because they are unwilling to meet new people or to consider new ideas. ❑ *...the old image of the insular, xenophobic Brit.* ♦ **in|su|lar|ity** /ɪnsjʊlæ̲rɪti, AM -sə-/ *But at least they have started to break out of their old insularity.* ADJ [disapproval]; N-UNCOUNT

**in|su|late** /ɪ̲nsjʊleɪt, AM -sə-/ **(insulates, insulating, insulated)** [1] If a person or group **is insulated from** the rest of society or from outside influences, they are protected from them. ❑ *They wonder if their community is no longer insulated from big city problems... Their wealth had insulated them from reality.* ♦ **in|su|la|tion** *They lived in happy insulation from brutal facts.* VERB = *shield*; be V-ed *from*/*against* n; V n *from*/*against* n; N-UNCOUNT
[2] To **insulate** something such as a building means to protect it from cold or noise by covering it or surrounding it in a thick layer. ❑ *It will take almost 25 years to insulate the homes of the six million households that require this assistance... Is there any way we can insulate our home from the noise?... Are your hot and cold water pipes well insulated?* VERB; V n; V n *from*/*against* n; V-ed
[3] If a piece of equipment **is insulated**, it is covered with rubber or plastic to prevent electricity passing through it and giving the person using it an electric shock. ❑ *In order to make it safe, the element is electrically insulated.* VERB; be V-ed

**in|su|la|tion** /ɪnsjʊle̲ɪʃᵊn, AM -sə-/ **Insulation** is a thick layer of a substance that keeps something warm, especially a building. ❑ *High electricity bills point to a poor heating system or bad insulation.* → See also **insulate**. N-UNCOUNT

**in|su|la|tor** /ɪ̲nsjʊleɪtəʳ, AM -sə-/ **(insulators)** An **insulator** is a material that insulates something. ❑ *Fat is an excellent insulator against the cold.* N-COUNT: usu sing

**in|su|lin** /ɪ̲nsjʊlɪn, AM -sə-/ **Insulin** is a substance that most people produce naturally in their body and which controls the level of sugar in their blood. ❑ *In diabetes the body produces insufficient insulin.* N-UNCOUNT

**in|sult** **(insults, insulting, insulted)**

> ✔ The verb is pronounced /ɪnsʌ̲lt/. The noun is pronounced /ɪ̲nsʌlt/.

[1] If someone **insults** you, they say or do something that is rude or offensive. ❑ *I did not mean to insult you.* ♦ **in|sult|ed** *I would be a bit insulted if he said anything like that.* VERB; V n; ADJ: usu v-link ADJ
[2] An **insult** is a rude remark, or something a person says or does which insults you. ❑ *Their behaviour was an insult to the people they represent.* N-COUNT: oft N *to* n
[3] You say **to add insult to injury** when mentioning an action or fact that makes an unfair or unacceptable situation even worse. PHRASE: V inflects, PHR with cl

**in|sult|ing** /ɪnsʌ̲ltɪŋ/ Something that is **insulting** is rude or offensive. ❑ *The article was insulting to the families of British citizens.* ♦ **in|sult|ing|ly** *Anthony laughed loudly and insultingly.* ADJ: oft ADJ *to* n = *offensive*; ADV: ADV with v, ADV adj

**in|su|per|able** /ɪnsu̲ːpərəbᵊl/ A problem that is **insuperable** cannot be dealt with successfully. [FORMAL] ❑ *...an insuperable obstacle to negotiations.* ADJ = *insurmountable*

**in|sup|port|able** /ɪnsəpɔ̲ːʳtəbᵊl/ If you say that something is **insupportable**, you mean that it cannot be coped with or accepted. [FORMAL] ❑ *Too much spending on rearmament would place an insupportable burden on the nation's productive capacity... Life without Anna had no savour, was tedious, insupportable.* ADJ = *intolerable*

**in|sur|ance** /ɪnʃʊ̲ərəns/ **(insurances)** ◆◆◇
[1] **Insurance** is an arrangement in which you pay money to a company, and they pay money to you if something unpleasant happens to you, for example if your property is stolen or damaged, or if you get a serious illness. ❑ *The insurance company paid out for the stolen jewellery and silver... We recommend that you take out travel insurance on all holidays.* N-VAR: oft N n
[2] If you do something as **insurance against** something unpleasant happening, you do it to protect yourself in case the unpleasant thing happens. ❑ *The country needs a defence capability as insurance against the unexpected.* N-VAR: usu N *against* n

**in|sur|ance ad|just|er** **(insurance adjusters)** An **insurance adjuster** is the same as a **claims adjuster**. [AM, BUSINESS] N-COUNT

> ✔ in BRIT, use **loss adjuster**

**in|sure** /ɪnʃʊ̲əʳ/ **(insures, insuring, insured)** [1] If you **insure** yourself or your property, you pay money to an insurance company so that, if you become ill or if your property is damaged or stolen, the company will pay you a sum of money. ❑ *For protection against unforeseen emergencies, you insure your house, your furnishings and your car... Think carefully before you insure against accident, sickness and redundancy... We automatically insure your belongings against fire and theft.* VERB; V n; V *against*/*for* n, V n *against*/*for* n
[2] If you **insure yourself against** something unpleasant that might happen in the future, you do something to protect yourself in case it happens, or to prevent it happening. ❑ *He insured himself against failure by treating only people he was sure he could cure... All the electronics in the world cannot insure against accidents, though.* VERB; V pron-refl *against* n; V *against* n
[3] → See also **ensure**.

**in|sured** /ɪnʃʊ̲əʳd/ **(insured)** **The insured** is the person who is insured by a particular policy. [LEGAL] ❑ *Once the insured has sold his policy, he naturally loses all rights to it.* N-COUNT: usu sing, *the* N

**in|sur|er** /ɪnʃʊərəʳ/ **(insurers)** An **insurer** is a company that sells insurance. [BUSINESS] [N-COUNT]

**in|sur|gen|cy** /ɪnsɜːʳdʒənsi/ **(insurgencies)** An **insurgency** is a violent attempt to oppose a country's government carried out by citizens of that country. [FORMAL] ❑ *He has led a violent armed insurgency for 15 years.* [N-VAR = uprising, insurrection]

**in|sur|gent** /ɪnsɜːʳdʒənt/ **(insurgents) Insurgents** are people who are fighting against the government or army of their own country. [FORMAL] ❑ *By early yesterday, the insurgents had taken control of the country's main military air base.* [N-COUNT: usu pl = rebel]

**in|sur|mount|able** /ɪnsəʳmaʊntəbəl/ A problem that is **insurmountable** is so great that it cannot be dealt with successfully. ❑ *The crisis doesn't seem like an insurmountable problem.* [ADJ = insuperable]

**in|sur|rec|tion** /ɪnsərekʃən/ **(insurrections)** An **insurrection** is violent action that is taken by a large group of people against the rulers of their country, usually in order to remove them from office. [FORMAL] ❑ *They were plotting to stage an armed insurrection.* [N-VAR = uprising, insurgency]

**int.** **Int.** is an abbreviation for **internal** or for **international**.

**in|tact** /ɪntækt/ Something that is **intact** is complete and has not been damaged or changed. ❑ *Most of the cargo was left intact after the explosion.* [ADJ: usu v-link ADJ]

**in|take** /ɪnteɪk/ **(intakes)** 1 Your **intake** of a particular kind of food, drink, or air is the amount that you eat, drink, or breathe in. ❑ *Your intake of alcohol should not exceed two units per day.* [N-SING: with supp, oft N *of* n] 2 The people who are accepted into an organization or place at a particular time are referred to as a particular **intake**. ❑ *...one of this year's intake of students.* [N-COUNT: usu sing, with supp, oft N *of* n]

**in|tan|gible** /ɪntændʒɪbəl/ **(intangibles)** Something that is **intangible** is abstract or is hard to define or measure. ❑ *There are intangible benefits beyond a rise in the share price.* [ADJ] ♦ You can refer to intangible things as **intangibles**. ❑ *Women workers place more importance on intangibles such as a sense of achievement.* [N-PLURAL]

**in|te|ger** /ɪntɪdʒəʳ/ **(integers)** In mathematics, an **integer** is an exact whole number such as 1, 7, or 24 as opposed to a number with fractions or decimals. [TECHNICAL] [N-COUNT]

**in|te|gral** /ɪntɪgrəl/ Something that is an **integral** part of something is an essential part of that thing. ❑ *Rituals and festivals form an integral part of every human society.* [ADJ: oft ADJ *to* n = basic, fundamental]

**in|te|grate** /ɪntɪgreɪt/ **(integrates, integrating, integrated)** ◆◇◇ 1 If someone **integrates** into a social group, or **is integrated** into it, they behave in such a way that they become part of the group or are accepted into it. [VERB] ❑ *He didn't integrate successfully into the Italian way of life...* [V *into/with* n] *Integrating the kids with the community, finding them a role, is essential...* [V n *into/with* n] *The way Swedes integrate immigrants is, she feels, 100% more advanced...* [V n] *If they want to integrate, that's fine with me.* [V] ♦ **in|te|grat|ed** *He thinks we are living in a fully integrated, supportive society.* [ADJ] ♦ **in|te|gra|tion** /ɪntɪgreɪʃən/ *...the integration of disabled people into mainstream society.* [N-UNCOUNT: oft N *of* n] 2 When races **integrate** or when schools and organizations **are integrated**, people who are black or belong to ethnic minorities can join white people in their schools and organizations. [AM] [VERB] ❑ *Schools came to us because they wanted to integrate...* [V] *Encouraging teacher transfer would not, by itself, integrate the teaching corps.* [V n] ♦ **in|te|grat|ed** *...a black honor student in Chicago's integrated Lincoln Park High School.* [ADJ: ADJ n] ♦ **in|te|gra|tion** *Lots of people in Chicago don't see that racial border. They see progress towards integration.* [N-UNCOUNT] 3 If you **integrate** one thing **with** another, or one thing **integrates with** another, the two things become closely linked or form part of a whole idea or system. You can also say that two things **integrate**. [V-RECIP] ❑ *Integrating the pound with other European currencies could cause difficulties...* [V n *with* n] *Ann wanted the conservatory to integrate with the kitchen...* [V *with* n] *Little attempt was made to integrate the parts into a coherent whole...* [V pl-n *into* n] *Talks will now begin about integrating the activities of both companies.* [V pl-n. Also pl-n V] ♦ **in|te|grat|ed** *There is, he said, a lack of an integrated national transport policy.* [ADJ] ♦ **in|te|gra|tion** *With Germany, France has been the prime mover behind closer European integration.* [N-UNCOUNT: usu with supp, oft adj N]

**in|te|grat|ed** /ɪntɪgreɪtɪd/ An **integrated** institution is intended for use by all races or religious groups. ❑ *We believe that pupils of integrated schools will have more tolerant attitudes.* → See also **integrate**. [ADJ: usu ADJ n ≠ segregated]

**in|te|grat|ed cir|cuit** **(integrated circuits)** An **integrated circuit** is a very small electronic circuit printed on a single silicon chip. [TECHNICAL] [N-COUNT]

**in|teg|rity** /ɪntegrɪti/ 1 If you have **integrity**, you are honest and firm in your moral principles. ❑ *I have always regarded him as a man of integrity.* [N-UNCOUNT] 2 The **integrity** of something such as a group of people or a text is its state of being a united whole. [FORMAL] ❑ *Separatist movements are a threat to the integrity of the nation.* [N-UNCOUNT: with poss]

**in|tel|lect** /ɪntɪlekt/ **(intellects)** 1 **Intellect** is the ability to understand or deal with ideas and information. ❑ *Do the emotions develop in parallel with the intellect?* [N-VAR] 2 **Intellect** is the quality of being very intelligent or clever. ❑ *Her intellect is famed far and wide.* [N-VAR: oft poss N]

**in|tel|lec|tual** /ɪntɪlektʃuəl/ **(intellectuals)** ◆◇◇ 1 **Intellectual** means involving a person's ability to think and to understand ideas and information. ❑ *High levels of lead could damage the intellectual development of children.* [ADJ: ADJ n] ♦ **in|tel|lec|tual|ly** *...intellectually satisfying work.* [ADV: usu ADV adj/-ed] 2 An **intellectual** is someone who spends a lot of time studying and thinking about complicated ideas. ❑ *...teachers, artists and other intellectuals.* [N-COUNT] ♦ **Intellectual** is also an adjective. ❑ *They were very intellectual and witty.* [ADJ]

**in|tel|lec|tu|al|ize** /ɪntɪlektʃuəlaɪz/ **(intellectualizes, intellectualizing, intellectualized)**

✔ in BRIT, also use **intellectualise**

If someone **intellectualizes** a subject or issue, they consider it in an intellectual way, often when this is not appropriate. ❑ *I tended to mistrust my emotions and intellectualize everything.* [VERB] [V n]

**in|tel|li|gence** /ɪntelɪdʒəns/ ◆◇◇ 1 **Intelligence** is the quality of being intelligent or clever. ❑ *She's a woman of exceptional intelligence.* [N-UNCOUNT] 2 **Intelligence** is the ability to think, reason, and understand instead of doing things automatically or by instinct. ❑ *Nerve cells, after all, do not have intelligence of their own.* [N-UNCOUNT] 3 **Intelligence** is information that is gathered by the government or the army about their country's enemies and their activities. ❑ *Why was military intelligence so lacking?* [N-UNCOUNT]

**in|tel|li|gent** /ɪntelɪdʒənt/ ◆◇◇ 1 A person or animal that is **intelligent** has the ability to think, understand, and learn things quickly and well. ❑ *Susan's a very bright and intelligent woman who knows her own mind.* [ADJ] ♦ **in|tel|li|gent|ly** *They are incapable of thinking intelligently about politics.* [ADV: ADV with v, ADV adj] 2 Something that is **intelligent** has the ability to think and understand instead of doing things automatically or by instinct. ❑ *An intelligent computer will be an indispensable diagnostic tool for doctors.* [ADJ]

**in|tel|li|gent|sia** /ɪntelɪdʒentsiə/ The **intelligentsia** in a country or community are the most educated people there, especially those interested in the arts, philosophy, and politics. [N-SING-COLL: usu *the* N]

**in|tel|li|gi|ble** /ɪntelɪdʒɪbəl/ Something that is **intelligible** can be understood. ❑ *The language of Darwin was intelligible to experts and non-experts alike.* [ADJ: oft ADJ *to* n ≠ unintelligible]

**in|tem|per|ate** /ɪntempərət/ If you describe someone's words as **intemperate**, you are critical of them because they are too forceful and uncontrolled. [FORMAL] ❑ *The tone of the article is intemperate.* [ADJ] [disapproval] [= extreme]

**in|tend** /ɪnte̱nd/ **(intends, intending, intended)** ◆◆◇ 1 If you **intend** to do something, you have decided or planned to do it. ❑ *She intends to do A levels and go to university... I didn't intend coming to Germany to work... We had always intended that the new series would be live.* 2 If something **is intended** for a particular purpose, it has been planned to fulfil that purpose. If something **is intended** for a particular person, it has been planned to be used by that person or to affect them in some way. ❑ *This money is intended for the development of the tourist industry... Columns are usually intended in architecture to add grandeur and status... Originally, Hatfield had been intended as a leisure complex.* 3 If you **intend** a particular idea or feeling in something that you say or do, you want to express it or want it to be understood. ❑ *He didn't intend any sarcasm... Burke's response seemed a little patronizing, though he undoubtedly hadn't intended it that way... This sounds like a barrage of accusation – I don't intend it to be... I think he intended it as a put-down comment.*

VERB · V to-inf · V -ing · V that · VERB: usu passive · *be* V-ed *for* n · *be* V-ed to-inf · *be* V-ed *as* n · VERB = mean · V n · V n n · V n to-inf · V n prep

**in|tend|ed** /ɪnte̱ndɪd/ You use **intended** to describe the thing you are trying to achieve or person you are trying to affect. ❑ *The intended target had been a military building.*

ADJ: ADJ n

**in|tense** /ɪnte̱ns/ ◆◇◇ 1 **Intense** is used to describe something that is very great or extreme in strength or degree. ❑ *He was sweating from the intense heat... His threats become more intense, agitated, and frequent.* ♦ **in|tense|ly** *The fast-food business is intensely competitive.* ♦ **in|ten|sity** /ɪnte̱nsɪti/ **(intensities)** *The attack was anticipated but its intensity came as a shock.* 2 If you describe an activity as **intense**, you mean that it is very serious and concentrated, and often involves doing a great deal in a short time. ❑ *The battle for third place was intense.* 3 If you describe the way someone looks at you as **intense**, you mean that they look at you very directly and seem to know what you are thinking or feeling. ❑ *I felt so self-conscious under Luke's mother's intense gaze.* ♦ **in|tense|ly** *He sipped his drink, staring intensely at me.* 4 If you describe a person as **intense**, you mean that they appear to concentrate very hard on everything that they do, and they feel and show their emotions in a very extreme way. ❑ *I know he's an intense player, but he does enjoy what he's doing.* ♦ **in|ten|sity** *His intensity and the ferocity of his feelings alarmed me.*

ADJ · ADV · N-VAR: usu with poss · ADJ · ADJ = piercing · ADV: ADV with v · ADJ · N-UNCOUNT

**in|ten|si|fi|er** /ɪnte̱nsɪfaɪəʳ/ **(intensifiers)** In grammar, an **intensifier** is a word such as 'very' or 'extremely' which you can put in front of an adjective or adverb in order to make its meaning stronger. [TECHNICAL]

N-COUNT

**in|ten|si|fy** /ɪnte̱nsɪfaɪ/ **(intensifies, intensifying, intensified)** If you **intensify** something or if it **intensifies**, it becomes greater in strength, amount, or degree. ❑ *Britain is intensifying its efforts to secure the release of the hostages... The conflict is almost bound to intensify.* ♦ **in|ten|si|fi|ca|tion** /ɪnte̱nsɪfɪkeɪʃən/ *The country was on the verge of collapse because of the intensification of violent rebel attacks.*

VERB = increase · V n · V · N-UNCOUNT

**in|ten|sive** /ɪnte̱nsɪv/ 1 **Intensive** activity involves concentrating a lot of effort or people on one particular task in order to try to achieve a great deal in a short time. ❑ *...several days and nights of intensive negotiations.* ♦ **in|ten|sive|ly** *Ruth's parents opted to educate her intensively at home.* 2 **Intensive** farming involves producing as many crops or animals as possible from your land, usually with the aid of chemicals. ❑ *...intensive methods of rearing poultry.* ♦ **in|ten|sive|ly** *Will they farm the rest of their land less intensively?*

ADJ: usu ADJ n · ADV: ADV with v · ADJ: usu ADJ n · ADV: ADV with v

**-intensive** /-ɪntensɪv/ **-intensive** combines with nouns to form adjectives which indicate that an industry or activity involves the use of a lot of a particular thing. ❑ *...the development of capital-intensive farming.*

COMB in ADJ

**in|ten|sive care** If someone is **in intensive care**, they are being given extremely thorough care in a hospital because they are very ill or very badly injured. ❑ *She spent the night in intensive care after the operation.*

N-UNCOUNT: usu *in* N

**in|tent** /ɪnte̱nt/ **(intents)** 1 If you are **intent on** doing something, you are eager and determined to do it. ❑ *The rebels are obviously intent on keeping up the pressure.* 2 If someone does something in an **intent** way, they pay great attention to what they are doing. [WRITTEN] ❑ *She looked from one intent face to another.* ♦ **in|tent|ly** *He listened intently, then slammed down the phone.* 3 A person's **intent** is their intention to do something. [FORMAL] ❑ *...a strong statement of intent on arms control.* 4 You say **to all intents and purposes** to suggest that a situation is not exactly as you describe it but the effect is the same as if it were. ❑ *To all intents and purposes he was my father.*

ADJ: v-link ADJ *on/upon* -ing/n · ADJ: oft ADJ *on/upon* n · ADV: ADV after v · N-VAR · PHRASE: usu PHR with cl

**in|ten|tion** /ɪnte̱nʃən/ **(intentions)** ◆◇◇ 1 An **intention** is an idea or plan of what you are going to do. ❑ *Beveridge announced his intention of standing for parliament... Unfortunately, his good intentions never seemed to last long.* 2 If you say that you **have no intention of** doing something, you are emphasizing that you are not going to do it. If you say that you **have every intention of** doing something, you are emphasizing that you intend to do it. ❑ *We have no intention of buying American jets.*

N-VAR: oft N *of* -ing, N to-inf · PHRASE: V inflects, PHR -ing · emphasis

**in|ten|tion|al** /ɪnte̱nʃənəl/ Something that is **intentional** is deliberate. ❑ *How can I blame him? It wasn't intentional.* ♦ **in|ten|tion|al|ly** *I've never intentionally hurt anyone.*

ADJ = deliberate ≠ accidental · ADV: ADV with v, ADV adj

**in|ter** /ɪntɜ̱ːʳ/ **(inters, interring, interred)** When a dead person **is interred**, they are buried. [FORMAL] ❑ *...the spot where his bones were originally interred.*

VERB · *be* V-ed · Also V n

**inter-** /ɪntəʳ-/ **Inter-** combines with adjectives and nouns to form adjectives indicating that something connects two or more places, things, or groups of people. For example, intergovernmental relations are relations between governments. ❑ *He hopes to be able to announce a date for inter-party talks. ...a policy of encouraging interracial marriage.*

PREFIX

**inter|act** /ɪntəræ̱kt/ **(interacts, interacting, interacted)** 1 When people **interact with** each other or **interact**, they communicate as they work or spend time together. ❑ *While the other children interacted and played together, Ted ignored them. ...rhymes and songs to help parents interact with their babies.* ♦ **inter|ac|tion** /ɪntəræ̱kʃən/ **(interactions)** *...our experience of informal social interaction among adults.* 2 When people **interact with** computers, or when computers **interact with** other machines, information or instructions are exchanged. ❑ *Millions of people want new, simplified ways of interacting with a computer... There will be a true global village in which telephones, computers and televisions interact.* ♦ **inter|ac|tion** **(interactions)** *...experts on human-computer interaction.* 3 When one thing **interacts with** another or two things **interact**, the two things affect each other's behaviour or condition. ❑ *You have to understand how cells interact... Atoms within the fluid interact with the minerals that form the grains.* ♦ **inter|ac|tion** *...the interaction between physical and emotional illness.*

V-RECIP · pl-n V · V *with* n · N-VAR: oft N prep · VERB · V *with* n · pl-n V · N-VAR: usu with supp · V-RECIP · pl-n V · V *with* n · N-VAR: oft N prep

**inter|ac|tive** /ɪntəræ̱ktɪv/ 1 An **interactive** computer program or television system is one which allows direct communication between the user and the machine. ❑ *This will make videogames more interactive than ever.* ♦ **in|ter|ac|tiv|ity** /ɪntərækt̠ɪvɪti/ *...cable broadcast companies that offer interactivity.* 2 If you describe a group of people or their activities as **interactive**, you mean that the people communicate with each other. ❑ *...flexible, interactive teaching in the classroom.*

ADJ · N-UNCOUNT · ADJ

**in|ter alia** /ɪntər eɪliə/ You use **inter alia**, meaning 'among other things', when you want to say that there are other things involved apart from the one you are mentioning. [FORMAL] ❑ *...a collector who had, inter alia, 900 engraved gems, 59 marble busts, and over 2,500 coins and medals.* PHRASE: PHR with cl

**inter|cede** /ɪntəʳsiːd/ **(intercedes, interceding, interceded)** If you **intercede** with someone, you try to persuade them to forgive someone or end their disagreement with them. [FORMAL] ❑ *They asked my father to intercede with the king on their behalf... It has also asked Britain and the United States to intercede.* VERB; V with n; V

**inter|cept** /ɪntəʳsept/ **(intercepts, intercepting, intercepted)** If you **intercept** someone or something that is travelling from one place to another, you stop them before they get to their destination. ❑ *Gunmen intercepted him on his way to the airport.* ♦ **inter|cep|tion** /ɪntəʳsepʃən/ **(interceptions)** *...the interception of a ship off the west coast of Scotland.* VERB; V n; N-VAR

**inter|cep|tor** /ɪntəʳseptəʳ/ **(interceptors)** An **interceptor** is an aircraft or ground-based missile system designed to intercept and attack enemy planes. N-COUNT

**inter|ces|sion** /ɪntəʳseʃən/ **(intercessions)** **Intercession** is the act of interceding with someone. [FORMAL] ❑ *His intercession could be of help to the tribe.* N-VAR

**inter|change** **(interchanges, interchanging, interchanged)**

> The noun is pronounced /ɪntəʳtʃeɪndʒ/. The verb is pronounced /ɪntəʳtʃeɪndʒ/.

1 If there is an **interchange** of ideas or information among a group of people, each person talks about his or her ideas or gives information to the others. ❑ *What made the meeting exciting was the interchange of ideas from different disciplines.* N-VAR: with supp, usu N of n = exchange

2 If you **interchange** one thing **with** another, or you **interchange** two things, each thing takes the place of the other or is exchanged for the other. You can also say that two things **interchange**. ❑ *She likes to interchange her furnishings at home with the stock in her shop... Your task is to interchange words so that the sentence makes sense. ...the point where the illusions of the stage and reality begin to interchange.* ♦ **Interchange** is also a noun. ❑ *...the interchange of matter and energy at atomic or sub-atomic levels.* V-RECIP; V n with n; V pl-n; pl-n V; Also V with n; N-VAR: oft N of n

3 An **interchange** on a motorway, freeway, or road is a place where it joins a main road or another motorway or freeway. N-COUNT: usu n N = junction

**inter|change|able** /ɪntəʳtʃeɪndʒəbəl/ Things that are **interchangeable** can be exchanged with each other without it making any difference. ❑ *Every part on the new models is interchangeable with those on the original.* ♦ **in|ter|change|ably** *These expressions are often used interchangeably, but they do have different meanings.* ADJ: oft ADJ with n; ADV: ADV after v

**inter|col|legi|ate** /ɪntəʳkəliːdʒət/ **Intercollegiate** means involving or related to more than one college or university. [AM] ❑ *...the first intercollegiate gymnastics team championship.* ADJ: ADJ n ≠ intramural

**inter|com** /ɪntəʳkɒm/ **(intercoms)** An **intercom** is a small box with a microphone which is connected to a loudspeaker in another room. You use it to talk to the people in the other room. N-COUNT

**inter|con|nect** /ɪntəʳkənekt/ **(interconnects, interconnecting, interconnected)** Things that **interconnect** or **are interconnected** are connected to or with each other. You can also say that one thing **interconnects with** another. ❑ *The causes are many and may interconnect... Their lives interconnect with those of celebrated figures of the late eighteenth-century. ...a dense network of nerve fibres that interconnects neurons in the brain.* V-RECIP; pl-n V; V with n; V n; Also V n with n

**inter|con|nec|tion** /ɪntəʳkənekʃən/ **(interconnections)** If you say that there is an **interconnection** between two or more things, you mean that they are very closely connected. [FORMAL] ❑ *...the alarming interconnection of drug abuse and AIDS infection.* N-VAR: oft N between pl-n

**inter|con|ti|nen|tal** /ɪntəʳkɒntɪnentəl/ **Intercontinental** is used to describe something that exists or happens between continents. ❑ *...intercontinental flights.* ADJ: ADJ n

**inter|course** /ɪntəʳkɔːʳs/ 1 **Intercourse** is the act of having sex. [FORMAL] ❑ *...sexual intercourse... We didn't have intercourse.* N-UNCOUNT 2 Social **intercourse** is communication between people as they spend time together. [OLD-FASHIONED] ❑ *There was social intercourse between the old and the young.* N-UNCOUNT: usu adj N

**inter|cut** /ɪntəʳkʌt/ **(intercuts, intercutting)**

> The form **intercut** is used in the present tense and is the past tense and past participle.

If a film **is intercut with** particular images, those images appear regularly throughout the film. [TECHNICAL] ❑ *The film is set in a night club and intercut with images of gangland London... He intercuts scenes of Rex getting more and more desperate with scenes of the abductor with his family.* VERB; be V-ed with n; V n with n

**inter|de|pend|ence** /ɪntəʳdɪpendəns/ **Interdependence** is the condition of a group of people or things that all depend on each other. ❑ *...the interdependence of nations.* N-UNCOUNT

**inter|de|pend|ent** /ɪntəʳdɪpendənt/ People or things that are **interdependent** all depend on each other. ❑ *We live in an increasingly interdependent world.* ADJ

**inter|dict** **(interdicts, interdicting, interdicted)**

> The verb is pronounced /ɪntəʳdɪkt/. The noun is pronounced /ɪntəʳdɪkt/.

1 If an armed force **interdicts** something or someone, they stop them and prevent them from moving. If they **interdict** a route, they block it or cut it off. [AM, FORMAL] ❑ *Troops could be ferried in to interdict drug shipments.* ♦ **inter|dic|tion** **(interdictions)** *...increased drug interdiction efforts by the military and Coast Guard.* VERB = intercept; V n; N-VAR

2 An **interdict** is an official order that something must not be done or used. [FORMAL] ❑ *The National Trust has placed an interdict on jet-skis in Dorset, Devon and Cornwall.* N-COUNT = ban

**inter|dis|ci|pli|nary** /ɪntəʳdɪsɪplɪnəri, AM -plɪneri/ **Interdisciplinary** means involving more than one academic subject. ❑ *...interdisciplinary courses combining psychology, philosophy and linguistics.* ADJ: usu ADJ n

**in|ter|est** /ɪntrəst, -tərest/ **(interests, interesting, interested)** ◆◆◆

1 If you have an **interest in** something, you want to learn or hear more about it. ❑ *There has been a lively interest in the elections in the last two weeks... His parents tried to discourage his interest in music, but he persisted... Food was of no interest to her at all.* N-UNCOUNT: also a N

2 Your **interests** are the things that you enjoy doing. ❑ *Encourage your child in her interests and hobbies even if they're things that you know little about.* N-COUNT

3 If something **interests** you, it attracts your attention so that you want to learn or hear more about it or continue doing it. ❑ *That passage interested me because it seems to parallel very closely what you're doing in the novel... It may interest you to know that Miss Woods, the housekeeper, witnessed the attack.* VERB; V n; it V n to-inf

4 If you are trying to persuade someone to buy or do something, you can say that you are trying to **interest** them **in** it. ❑ *In the meantime I can't interest you in a new car, I suppose?* VERB; V n in n/-ing

5 If something is in the **interests** of a particular person or group, it will benefit them in some way. ❑ *Did those directors act in the best interests of their club?* N-COUNT: usu pl, usu in N with poss

6 You can use **interests** to refer to groups of people who you think use their power or money to benefit themselves. ❑ *The government accused unnamed 'foreign interests' of inciting the trouble.* N-COUNT: usu pl, supp N

7 A person or organization that has **interests** in a company or in a particular type of business owns shares in this company or this type of business. [BUSINESS] ❑ *Disney will retain a 51 percent controlling interest in the venture.* N-COUNT: usu with supp

8 If a person, country, or organization has an **interest in** a N-COUNT: usu N in n/-ing

possible event or situation, they want that event or situation to happen because they are likely to benefit from it. ❑ *The West has an interest in promoting democratic forces in Eastern Europe.* 9 **Interest** is extra money that you receive if you have invested a sum of money. **Interest** is also the extra money that you pay if you have borrowed money or are buying something on credit. ❑ *Does your current account pay interest?* 10 → See also **interested**, **interesting**, **compound interest**, **self-interest**, **vested interest**. 11 If you do something **in the interests of** a particular result or situation, you do it in order to achieve that result or maintain that situation. ❑ *...a call for all businessmen to work together in the interests of national stability.* to have someone's interests **at heart** → see **heart**. N-UNCOUNT: oft N n; PHRASE: N inflects, PHR n

**in|ter|est|ed** /ɪntrestɪd/ 1 If you are **interested in** something, you think it is important and want to learn more about it or spend time doing it. ❑ *I thought she might be interested in Paula's proposal... I'd be interested to meet her.* 2 An **interested** party or group of people is affected by or involved in a particular event or situation. ❑ *All the interested parties eventually agreed to the idea.* 3 → See also **self-interested**. ◆◆◇ ADJ: usu v-link ADJ, oft ADJ *in* n/-ing, ADJ to-inf; ADJ: ADJ n

**interest-free** An **interest-free** loan has no interest charged on it. ❑ *He was offered a £10,000 interest-free loan.* ♦ **Interest-free** is also an adverb. ❑ *Customers allowed the banks to use their money interest-free.* ADJ: usu ADJ n; ADV: ADV after v

**in|ter|est|ing** /ɪntrestɪŋ/ If you find something **interesting**, it attracts your attention, for example because you think it is exciting or unusual. ❑ *It was interesting to be in a different environment... His third album is by far his most interesting.* ◆◇◇ ADJ: oft *it* v-link ADJ to-inf/that

**in|ter|est|ing|ly** /ɪntrestɪŋli/ You use **interestingly** to introduce a piece of information that you think is interesting or unexpected. ❑ *Interestingly enough, a few weeks later, Benjamin remarried.* ADV: ADV with cl

**in|ter|est rate** (**interest rates**) The **interest rate** is the amount of interest that must be paid. It is expressed as a percentage of the amount that is borrowed or gained as profit. ❑ *The Finance Minister has renewed his call for lower interest rates.* N-COUNT

**inter|face** /ɪntəʳfeɪs/ (**interfaces, interfacing, interfaced**) 1 The **interface** between two subjects or systems is the area in which they affect each other or have links with each other. ❑ *...a witty exploration of that interface between bureaucracy and the working world.* 2 If you refer to the user **interface** of a particular piece of computing software, you are talking about its presentation on screen and how easy it is to operate. [COMPUTING] ❑ *...the development of better user interfaces.* 3 In computing and electronics, an **interface** is an electrical circuit which links one machine, especially a computer, with another. [TECHNICAL] 4 If one thing **interfaces with** another, or if two things **interface**, they have connections with each other. If you **interface** one thing **with** another, you connect the two things. [TECHNICAL or FORMAL] ❑ *...the way we interface with the environment... The different components all have to interface smoothly... He had interfaced all this machinery with a master computer.* N-COUNT; N-COUNT: usu n N; N-COUNT; V-RECIP; V *with* n; pl-n V; V n *with* n; Also V pl-n

**inter|fere** /ɪntəʳfɪəʳ/ (**interferes, interfering, interfered**) 1 If you say that someone **interferes in** a situation, you mean they get involved in it although it does not concern them and their involvement is not wanted. ❑ *I wish everyone would stop interfering and just leave me alone... The UN cannot interfere in the internal affairs of any country.* 2 Something that **interferes with** a situation, activity, or process has a damaging effect on it. ❑ *Smoking and drinking interfere with your body's ability to process oxygen.* VERB [disapproval]; V; V *in/with* n; VERB; V *with* n

**inter|fer|ence** /ɪntəʳfɪərəns/ 1 **Interference** by a person or group is their unwanted or unnecessary involvement in something. ❑ *Airlines will be able to set cheap fares without interference from the government.* 2 When there is **interference**, a radio signal is affected by other radio waves or electrical activity so that it cannot be received properly. ❑ *...electrical interference.* N-UNCOUNT: oft N *in/with* n, N *from* n [disapproval]; N-UNCOUNT

**inter|fer|ing** /ɪntəʳfɪərɪŋ/ If you describe someone as **interfering**, you are criticizing them because they try to get involved in other people's affairs or to give them advice, especially when the advice is not wanted. ❑ *...interfering neighbours.* ADJ: ADJ n [disapproval] = meddling

**in|ter|im** /ɪntərɪm/ 1 **Interim** is used to describe something that is intended to be used until something permanent is done or established. ❑ *She was sworn in as head of an interim government in March. ...an interim report.* 2 **In the interim** means until a particular thing happens or until a particular thing happened. [FORMAL] ❑ *But, in the interim, we obviously have a duty to maintain law and order.* ◆◇◇ ADJ: ADJ n; PHRASE: PHR with cl

**in|te|ri|or** /ɪntɪəriəʳ/ (**interiors**) 1 The **interior** of something is the inside part of it. ❑ *The boat's interior badly needed painting.* 2 You use **interior** to describe something that is inside a building or vehicle. ❑ *The interior walls were painted green.* 3 The **interior** of a country or continent is the central area of it. ❑ *The Yangzi river would give access to much of China's interior.* 4 A country's **interior** minister, ministry, or department deals with affairs within that country, such as law and order. ❑ *The French Interior Minister has intervened in a scandal over the role of a secret police force.* 5 A country's minister or ministry of **the interior** deals with affairs within that country, such as law and order. ❑ *An official from the Ministry of the Interior said six people had died.* ◆◇◇ N-COUNT: oft with poss; ADJ: ADJ n; N-SING: oft *the* N, oft with poss; ADJ: ADJ n; N-SING

**in|te|ri|or deco|ra|tion** **Interior decoration** is the decoration of the inside of a house. N-UNCOUNT

**in|te|ri|or deco|ra|tor** (**interior decorators**) An **interior decorator** is a person who is employed to design and decorate the inside of people's houses. N-COUNT

**in|te|ri|or de|sign** **Interior design** is the art or profession of designing the decoration for the inside of a house. N-UNCOUNT

**in|te|ri|or de|sign|er** (**interior designers**) An **interior designer** is a person who is employed to design the decoration for the inside of people's houses. N-COUNT

**inter|ject** /ɪntəʳdʒekt/ (**interjects, interjecting, interjected**) If you **interject** something, you say it and interrupt someone else who is speaking. [FORMAL] ❑ *'Surely there's something we can do?' interjected Palin... He listened thoughtfully, interjecting only the odd word.* VERB; V with quote; V n; Also V

**inter|jec|tion** /ɪntəʳdʒekʃᵊn/ (**interjections**) 1 An **interjection** is something you say which interrupts someone else who is speaking. ❑ *...the moronic and insensitive interjections of the disc jockey.* 2 In grammar, an **interjection** is a word or expression which you use to express a strong feeling such as surprise, pain, or horror. N-COUNT; N-COUNT

**inter|laced** /ɪntəʳleɪst/ If things are **interlaced**, parts of one thing go over, under, or between parts of another. [WRITTEN] ❑ *During my whole report, he sat with his eyes closed and his fingers interlaced. ...languid women, their flowing locks interlaced with flowers and vines.* ADJ: oft ADJ *with* n = entwined

**inter|link** /ɪntəʳlɪŋk/ (**interlinks, interlinking, interlinked**) Things that **are interlinked** or **interlink** are linked with each other in some way. ❑ *Those two processes are very closely interlinked... The question to be addressed is interlinked with the question of human rights. ...a more integrated transport network, with bus, rail, and ferry services all interlinking.* V-RECIP = interconnect; *be* V-ed; *be* V-ed *with* n; pl-n V

**inter|lock** /ɪntəʳlɒk/ (**interlocks, interlocking, interlocked**) 1 Things that **interlock** or **are interlocked** go between or through each other so that they are linked. ❑ *The parts interlock... Interlock your fingers behind your back.* 2 If systems, situations, or plans **are interlocked** or **interlock**, V-RECIP; pl-n V; V pl-n; V-RECIP they are very closely connected. ❑ *The problems of Israel, Lebanon, and the Gulf were tightly interlocked... The tragedies begin to interlock... Your girlfriend's fear seems to interlock with your fear.* be V-ed / pl-n V / V with n / Also V pl-n

**inter|locu|tor** /ɪntəʳlɒkjʊtəʳ/ **(interlocutors)** 1 Your **interlocutor** is the person with whom you are having a conversation. [FORMAL] ❑ *Owen had the habit of staring motionlessly at his interlocutor.* N-COUNT: oft poss N 2 If a person or organization has a role as an **interlocutor** in talks or negotiations, they take part or act as a representative in them. [FORMAL] ❑ *...key interlocutors in the Middle East conference.* N-COUNT

**inter|lop|er** /ɪntəʳloʊpəʳ/ **(interlopers)** If you describe someone as an **interloper**, you mean that they have come into a situation or a place where they are not wanted or do not belong. ❑ *She had no wish to share her father with any outsider and regarded us as interlopers.* N-COUNT disapproval = intruder

**inter|lude** /ɪntəʳluːd/ **(interludes)** An **interlude** is a short period of time when an activity or situation stops and something else happens. ❑ *Superb musical interludes were provided by Sinclair.* N-COUNT

**inter|mar|riage** /ɪntəʳmærɪdʒ/ **(intermarriages)** **Intermarriage** is marriage between people from different social, racial, or religious groups. ❑ *...intermarriage between members of the old and new ruling classes.* N-UNCOUNT: also N in pl, oft N between pl-n

**inter|mar|ry** /ɪntəʳmæri/ **(intermarries, intermarrying, intermarried)** When people from different social, racial, or religious groups **intermarry**, they marry each other. You can also say that one group **intermarries with** another group. ❑ *They were allowed to intermarry... Some of the traders settled and intermarried with local women.* V-RECIP / pl-n V / V with n

**inter|medi|ary** /ɪntəʳmiːdiəri/ **(intermediaries)** An **intermediary** is a person who passes messages or proposals between two people or groups. ❑ *She wanted him to act as an intermediary in the dispute with Moscow.* N-COUNT = go-between

**inter|medi|ate** /ɪntəʳmiːdiət/ **(intermediates)** 1 An **intermediate** stage, level, or position is one that occurs between two other stages, levels, or positions. ❑ *You should consider breaking the journey with intermediate stopovers at airport hotels.* ADJ: usu ADJ n 2 **Intermediate** learners of something have some knowledge or skill but are not yet advanced. ❑ *The Badminton Club holds coaching sessions for beginners and intermediate players on Friday evenings.* ADJ ♦ An **intermediate** is an intermediate learner. ❑ *The ski school coaches beginners, intermediates, and advanced skiers.* N-COUNT

**in|ter|ment** /ɪntɜːʳmənt/ **(interments)** The **interment** of a dead person is their burial. [FORMAL] N-VAR = burial

**in|ter|mi|nable** /ɪntɜːʳmɪnəbəl/ If you describe something as **interminable**, you are emphasizing that it continues for a very long time and indicating that you wish it was shorter or would stop. ❑ *...an interminable meeting.* ADJ emphasis = endless ♦ **in|ter|mi|nably** *He talked to me interminably about his first wife.* ADV: usu ADV after v

**inter|min|gle** /ɪntəʳmɪŋgəl/ **(intermingles, intermingling, intermingled)** When people or things **intermingle**, they mix with each other. [FORMAL] ❑ *This allows the two cultures to intermingle without losing their separate identities. ...an opportunity for them to intermingle with the citizens of other countries.* V-RECIP / pl-n V / V with n ♦ **inter|min|gled** *The ethnic populations are so intermingled that there's bound to be conflict.* ADJ: usu v-link ADJ

**inter|mis|sion** /ɪntəʳmɪʃən/ **(intermissions)** An **intermission** is a short break between two parts of a film, concert, or show. ❑ *...during the intermission of the musical 'Steppin' Out'.* N-COUNT = interval, interlude ♦ In American English, you can also use **intermission** to refer to a short break between two parts of a game, or say that something happens at, after, or during **intermission**. ❑ *Fraser did not perform until after intermission.* N-COUNT: also prep N

**inter|mit|tent** /ɪntəʳmɪtənt/ Something that is **intermittent** happens occasionally rather than continuously. ❑ *After three hours of intermittent rain, the game was abandoned.* ADJ = sporadic ♦ **in|ter|mit|tent|ly** *The talks went on intermittently for three years.* ADV: usu ADV with v

**in|tern** **(interns, interning, interned)**

> The verb is pronounced /ɪntɜːʳn/. The noun is pronounced /ɪntɜːʳn/.

1 If someone **is interned**, they are put in prison or in a prison camp for political reasons. ❑ *He was interned as an enemy alien at the outbreak of the Second World War.* VERB: usu passive be V-ed 2 An **intern** is an advanced student or a recent graduate, especially in medicine, who is being given practical training under supervision. [AM] N-COUNT

**in|ter|nal** /ɪntɜːʳnəl/ 1 **Internal** is used to describe things that exist or happen inside a country or organization. ❑ *The country stepped up internal security... We now have a Europe without internal borders.* ◆◇◇ ADJ: ADJ n ♦ **in|ter|nal|ly** *The state is not a unified and internally coherent entity.* ADV 2 **Internal** is used to describe things that exist or happen inside a particular person, object, or place. ❑ *...massive internal bleeding... Some of the internal walls of my house are made of plasterboard.* ADJ: ADJ n ♦ **in|ter|nal|ly** *Evening primrose oil is used on the skin as well as taken internally.* ADV: usu ADV with v, also ADV with cl, ADV adj

**in|ter|nal com|bus|tion en|gine** **(internal combustion engines)** An **internal combustion engine** is an engine that creates its energy by burning fuel inside itself. Most cars have internal combustion engines. N-COUNT

**in|ter|nal|ize** /ɪntɜːʳnəlaɪz/ **(internalizes, internalizing, internalized)**

> in BRIT, also use **internalise**

If you **internalize** something such as a belief or a set of values, you make it become part of your attitude or way of thinking. [FORMAL] ❑ *Over time she internalized her parents' attitudes.* VERB / V n ♦ **in|ter|nali|za|tion** /ɪntɜːʳnəlaɪzeɪʃən/ *...my internalisation of hatred, disgust and fear.* N-UNCOUNT: usu with poss

**inter|na|tion|al** /ɪntəʳnæʃənəl/ **(internationals)** 1 **International** means between or involving different countries. ❑ *...an international agreement against exporting arms to that country. ...emergency aid from the international community.* ◆◆◆ ADJ: usu ADJ n ♦ **inter|na|tion|al|ly** *There are only two internationally recognised certificates in Teaching English as a Foreign Language.* ADV: usu ADV adj/-ed, also ADV with cl, ADV after v 2 In sport, an **international** is a game that is played between teams representing two different countries. [BRIT] ❑ *...the midweek international against England.* N-COUNT 3 An **international** is a member of a country's sports team. [BRIT] ❑ *...a former England international.* N-COUNT: usu n N

**inter|na|tion|al|ism** /ɪntəʳnæʃənəlɪzəm/ **Internationalism** is the belief that countries should work with, help, and be friendly with one another. N-UNCOUNT

**inter|na|tion|al|ist** /ɪntəʳnæʃənəlɪst/ **(internationalists)** If someone has **internationalist** beliefs or opinions, they believe that countries should work with, help, and be friendly with one another. ❑ *...a more genuinely internationalist view of US participation in peace-keeping.* ADJ

**inter|na|tion|al|ize** /ɪntəʳnæʃənəlaɪz/ **(internationalizes, internationalizing, internationalized)**

> in BRIT, also use **internationalise**

If an issue or a crisis is **internationalized**, it becomes the concern of many nations throughout the world. [JOURNALISM] ❑ *A very real danger exists of the conflict becoming internationalised... They have been trying to internationalise the Kashmir problem.* VERB / be V-ed / V n ♦ **inter|na|tion|ali|za|tion** /ɪntəʳnæʃənəlaɪzeɪʃən/ *...the increasing internationalization of business.* N-UNCOUNT

**inter|na|tion|al re|la|tions** The political relationships between different countries are referred to as **international relations**. ❑ *...peaceful and friendly international relations.* N-PLURAL

**inter|necine** /ɪntəʳniːsaɪn, AM -siːn/ An **internecine** conflict, war, or quarrel is one which takes place between opposing groups within a country or organization. [FORMAL] ADJ: ADJ n

**in|ternee** /ɪntɜːʳniː/ **(internees)** An **internee** is a person who has been put in prison for political reasons. N-COUNT

**In|ter|net** /ɪntəʳnet/ also **internet. The Internet** is the computer network which allows computer users to connect with computers all over the world, and which carries e-mail. N-PROPER: *the* N

**In|ter|net ca|fé** **(Internet cafés)** An **Internet café** is a café with computers where people can pay to use the Internet. N-COUNT = *cybercafé*

**in|tern|ment** /ɪntɜːʳnmənt/ **Internment** is the practice of putting people in prison for political reasons. ❑ *They called for the return of internment without trial for terrorists.* N-UNCOUNT

**in|tern|ship** /ɪntɜːʳnʃɪp/ **(internships)** An **internship** is the position held by an intern, or the period of time when someone is an intern. [AM] N-COUNT

**inter|per|son|al** /ɪntəʳpɜːʳsənəl/ **Interpersonal** means relating to relationships between people. ❑ *Training in interpersonal skills is essential.* ADJ: ADJ n

**inter|play** /ɪntəʳpleɪ/ The **interplay between** two or more things or people is the way that they have an effect on each another or react to each other. ❑ *...the interplay of political, economic, social and cultural factors.* N-UNCOUNT: usu N *between/ of* pl-n = *interaction*

**in|ter|po|late** /ɪntɜːʳpəleɪt/ **(interpolates, interpolating, interpolated)** If you **interpolate** a comment into a conversation or some words into a piece of writing, you put it in as an addition. [FORMAL] ❑ *Williams interpolated much spurious matter... These odd assertions were interpolated into the manuscript some time after 1400.* VERB = *insert*; V n; *be* V-ed *into* n

**in|ter|po|la|tion** /ɪntɜːʳpəleɪʃən/ **(interpolations)** An **interpolation** is an addition to a piece of writing. [FORMAL] ❑ *The interpolation appears to have been inserted very soon after the original text was finished.* N-COUNT = *addition*

**inter|pose** /ɪntəʳpoʊz/ **(interposes, interposing, interposed)** If you **interpose** something **between** two people or things, you place it between them. [FORMAL] ❑ *Police had to interpose themselves between the two rival groups... The work interposes a glass plate between two large circular mirrors.* VERB; V pron-refl *between* pl-n; V n *between* pl-n

**in|ter|pret** /ɪntɜːʳprɪt/ **(interprets, interpreting, interpreted)** 1 If you **interpret** something in a particular way, you decide that this is its meaning or significance. ❑ *The whole speech might well be interpreted as a coded message to the Americans... The judge quite rightly says that he has to interpret the law as it's been passed... Both approaches agree on what is depicted in the poem, but not on how it should be interpreted.* 2 If you **interpret** what someone is saying, you translate it immediately into another language. ❑ *The chambermaid spoke little English, so her husband came with her to interpret... Interpreters found they could not interpret half of what he said.* VERB; V n *as* n; V n; V n adv/prep; VERB; V; V n

**in|ter|pre|ta|tion** /ɪntɜːʳprɪteɪʃən/ **(interpretations)** 1 An **interpretation** of something is an opinion about what it means. ❑ *The opposition Conservative Party put a different interpretation on the figures.* 2 A performer's **interpretation** of something such as a piece of music or a role in a play is the particular way in which they choose to perform it. ❑ *...her full-bodied interpretation of the role of Micaela.* N-VAR; N-COUNT: with supp

**in|ter|pre|ta|tive** /ɪntɜːʳprɪtətɪv/ → see **interpretive**.

**in|ter|pret|er** /ɪntɜːʳprɪtəʳ/ **(interpreters)** An **interpreter** is a person whose job is to translate what someone is saying into another language. ❑ *Aristide spoke to the press through an interpreter.* N-COUNT

**in|ter|pre|tive** /ɪntɜːʳprɪtɪv/ or **interpretative** You use **interpretive** to describe something that provides an interpretation. [FORMAL] ❑ *History is an interpretive process.* ADJ: ADJ n

**inter|reg|num** /ɪntəʳregnəm/ An **interregnum** is a period between the end of one person's time as ruler or leader and the coming to power of the next ruler or leader. [FORMAL] N-SING

**inter|re|late** /ɪntəʳrɪleɪt/ **(interrelates, interrelating, interrelated)** If two or more things **interrelate**, there is a connection between them and they have an effect on each other. ❑ *The body and the mind interrelate... Each of these cells have their specific jobs to do, but they also interrelate with each other. ...the way in which we communicate and interrelate with others... All things are interrelated.* V-RECIP = *interconnect*; pl-n V; pl-n V *with* pron-recip; V *with* n; V-ed

**inter|re|la|tion|ship** /ɪntəʳrɪleɪʃənʃɪp/ **(interrelationships)** An **interrelationship** is a close relationship between two or more things or people. ❑ *...the interrelationships between unemployment, crime, and imprisonment.* N-COUNT: oft N *between/ of* pl-n

**in|ter|ro|gate** /ɪnterəgeɪt/ **(interrogates, interrogating, interrogated)** If someone, especially a police officer, **interrogates** someone, they question them thoroughly for a long time in order to get some information from them. ❑ *I interrogated everyone even slightly involved.* ♦ **in|ter|ro|ga|tor** **(interrogators)** *I was well aware of what my interrogators wanted to hear.* VERB = *question*; V n; N-COUNT: oft poss N

**in|ter|ro|ga|tion** /ɪnterəgeɪʃən/ **(interrogations)** An **interrogation** is the act of interrogating someone. ❑ *...the right to silence in police interrogations.* N-VAR

**in|ter|roga|tive** /ɪntərɒgətɪv/ **(interrogatives)** 1 An **interrogative** gesture or tone of voice shows that you want to know the answer to a question. [WRITTEN] ❑ *Donovan cocked an interrogative eye at his companion, who nodded in reply.* 2 In grammar, a clause that is in **the interrogative**, or in the **interrogative** mood, has its subject following 'do', 'be', 'have', or a modal verb. Examples are 'When did he get back?' and 'Are you all right?'. Clauses of this kind are typically used to ask questions. 3 In grammar, an **interrogative** is a word such as 'who', 'how', or 'why', which can be used to ask a question. ADJ: usu ADJ n = *questioning*; N-SING: *the* N; N-COUNT

**in|ter|rupt** /ɪntərʌpt/ **(interrupts, interrupting, interrupted)** 1 If you **interrupt** someone who is speaking, you say or do something that causes them to stop. ❑ *Turkin tapped him on the shoulder. 'Sorry to interrupt, Colonel.'... He tried to speak, but she interrupted him.* ♦ **in|ter|rup|tion** /ɪntərʌpʃən/ **(interruptions)** *The sudden interruption stopped Beryl in mid-flow.* 2 If someone or something **interrupts** a process or activity, they stop it for a period of time. ❑ *He has rightly interrupted his holiday in Spain to return to London.* ♦ **in|ter|rup|tion** *...interruptions in the supply of food and fuel.* 3 If something **interrupts** a line, surface, or view, it stops it from being continuous or makes it look irregular. ❑ *Taller plants interrupt the views from the house.* VERB; V; V n; N-VAR; VERB; V n; N-VAR: oft N *in/to* n; VERB; V n

**inter|sect** /ɪntəʳsekt/ **(intersects, intersecting, intersected)** 1 If two or more lines or roads **intersect**, they meet or cross each other. You can also say that one line or road **intersects** another. ❑ *The orbit of this comet intersects the orbit of the Earth... The circles will intersect in two places.* 2 If one thing **intersects with** another or if two things **intersect**, the two things have a connection at a particular point. ❑ *...the ways in which historical events intersect with individual lives... Their histories intersect.* 3 If a place, area, or surface **is intersected by** things such as roads or lines, they cross it. ❑ *The city is intersected by three main waterways.* V-RECIP; V n; pl-n V; V-RECIP = *overlap*; V *with* n; pl-n V; VERB: usu passive = *cross*; *be* V-ed

**inter|sec|tion** /ɪntəʳsekʃən/ **(intersections)** An **intersection** is a place where roads or other lines meet or cross. ❑ *...at the intersection of two main canals. ...a busy highway intersection.* N-COUNT: oft N *of/ with* n = *junction*

**inter|sperse** /ɪntəʳspɜːʳs/ **(intersperses, interspersing, interspersed)** If you **intersperse** one group of things **with** another or **among** another, you put or include the second things between or VERB among the first things. ❑ *Originally the intention was to intersperse the historical scenes with modern ones.* V n with n

**inter|spersed** /ɪntəʳspɜːʳst/ If one group of things are **interspersed with** another or **interspersed among** another, the second things occur between or among the first things. ❑ *...bursts of gunfire, interspersed with single shots.* ADJ: v-link ADJ prep, usu ADJ with n, ADJ among n

**inter|state** /ɪntəʳsteɪt/ **(interstates)** [1] **Interstate** means between states, especially the states of the United States. ❑ *...interstate highways.* ADJ: ADJ n [2] In the United States, an **interstate** is a major road linking states. ❑ *...the southbound lane of Interstate 75.* N-COUNT: also N num

**inter|stel|lar** /ɪntəʳstelər/ **Interstellar** means between the stars. [FORMAL] ❑ *...interstellar space.* ADJ: ADJ n

**inter|twine** /ɪntəʳtwaɪn/ **(intertwines, intertwining, intertwined)** [1] If two or more things **are intertwined** or **intertwine**, they are closely connected with each other in many ways. ❑ *Their destinies are intertwined... Three major narratives intertwine within Foucault's text, 'Madness and Civilisation'... He intertwines personal reminiscences with the story of British television... Her fate intertwined with his.* V-RECIP = interweave; be V-ed; pl-n V; V n with n; V with n; Also V pl-n [2] If two things **intertwine**, they are twisted together or go over and under each other. ❑ *Trees, undergrowth and creepers intertwined, blocking our way... The towels were embroidered with their intertwined initials.* V-RECIP = entwine; pl-n V; V-ed; Also V with n

**in|ter|val** /ɪntəʳvəl/ **(intervals)** [1] An **interval** between two events or dates is the period of time between them. ❑ *The ferry service has restarted after an interval of 12 years.* N-COUNT: oft N of n = gap [2] An **interval** during a film, concert, show, or game is a short break between two of the parts. [mainly BRIT] ❑ *During the interval, wine was served.* N-COUNT

✔ in AM, usually use **intermission**

**PHRASES** [3] If something happens **at intervals**, it happens several times with gaps or pauses in between. ❑ *She woke him for his medicines at intervals throughout the night.* PHRASE: PHR with v [4] If things are placed **at** particular **intervals**, there are spaces of a particular size between them. ❑ *Several red and white barriers marked the road at intervals of about a mile.* PHRASE: PHR with v

**inter|vene** /ɪntəʳviːn/ **(intervenes, intervening, intervened)** [1] If you **intervene in** a situation, you become involved in it and try to change it. ❑ *The situation calmed down when police intervened... The Government is doing nothing to intervene in the crisis.* VERB; V; V in n [2] If you **intervene**, you interrupt a conversation in order to add something to it. ❑ *Hattie intervened and told me to stop it... 'I've told you he's not here,' Irena intervened.* VERB; V; V with quote [3] If an event **intervenes**, it happens suddenly in a way that stops, delays, or prevents something from happening. ❑ *The South African mailboat arrived on Friday mornings unless bad weather intervened.* VERB; V

**inter|ven|ing** /ɪntəʳviːnɪŋ/ [1] An **intervening** period of time is one that separates two events or points in time. ❑ *During those intervening years Bridget had married her husband Robert.* ADJ: ADJ n [2] An **intervening** object or area comes between two other objects or areas. ❑ *They had scoured the intervening miles of moorland.* ADJ: ADJ n

**inter|ven|tion** /ɪntəʳvenʃən/ **(interventions)** ◆◇◇ **Intervention** is the act of intervening in a situation. ❑ *...the role of the United States and its intervention in the internal affairs of many countries. ...military interventions.* N-VAR: oft N in n

**inter|ven|tion|ist** /ɪntəʳvenʃənɪst/ **(interventionists)** **Interventionist** policies are policies which show an organization's desire to become involved in a problem or a crisis which does not concern it directly. [JOURNALISM] ❑ *...the interventionist industrial policy of the Wilson government.* ADJ ≠ laissez-faire ♦ An **interventionist** is someone who supports interventionist policies. [JOURNALISM] N-COUNT

**inter|view** /ɪntəʳvjuː/ **(interviews, interviewing, interviewed)** ◆◆◇ [1] An **interview** is a formal meeting at which someone is asked questions in order to find out if they are suitable for a job or a course of study. ❑ *The interview went well... Not everyone who writes in can be invited for interview.* N-VAR: oft N for n [2] If you **are interviewed** for a particular job or course of study, someone asks you questions about yourself to find out if you suitable for it. ❑ *When Wardell was interviewed, he was impressive, and on that basis, he was hired.* VERB: usu passive; be V-ed [3] An **interview** is a conversation in which a journalist puts questions to someone such as a famous person or politician. ❑ *Allan gave an interview to the Chicago Tribune newspaper last month.* N-COUNT [4] When a journalist **interviews** someone such as a famous person, they ask them a series of questions. ❑ *I seized the chance to interview Chris Hani about this issue.* VERB; V n [5] When the police **interview** someone, they ask them questions about a crime that has been committed. ❑ *The police interviewed the driver, but had no evidence to go on.* VERB = question; V n

**inter|viewee** /ɪntəʳvjuiː/ **(interviewees)** An **interviewee** is a person who is being interviewed. N-COUNT

**inter|view|er** /ɪntəʳvjuəʳ/ **(interviewers)** An **interviewer** is a person who is asking someone questions at an interview. N-COUNT

**inter|weave** /ɪntəʳwiːv/ **(interweaves, interweaving, interwove, interwoven)** If two or more things **are interwoven** or **interweave**, they are very closely connected or are combined with each other. ❑ *For these people, land is inextricably interwoven with life itself... Complex family relationships interweave with a murder plot in this ambitious new novel... The programme successfully interweaves words and pictures... Social structures are not discrete objects; they overlap and interweave.* V-RECIP = intertwine; be V-ed with n; V with n; V pl-n; pl-n V; Also V n with n

**in|tes|ti|nal** /ɪntestɪnəl/ **Intestinal** means relating to the intestines. [FORMAL] ADJ: ADJ n

**in|tes|tine** /ɪntestɪn/ **(intestines)** Your **intestines** are the tubes in your body through which food passes when it has left your stomach. ❑ *This area is always tender to the touch if the intestines are not functioning properly.* N-COUNT

**in|ti|ma|cy** /ɪntɪməsi/ [1] **Intimacy** between two people is a very close personal relationship between them. ❑ *...a means of achieving intimacy with another person.* N-UNCOUNT: oft N with/between n [2] You sometimes use **intimacy** to refer to sex or a sexual relationship. ❑ *The truth was he did not feel like intimacy with any woman.* N-UNCOUNT

**in|ti|mate** **(intimates, intimating, intimated)**

✔ The adjective is pronounced /ɪntɪmət/. The verb is pronounced /ɪntɪmeɪt/.

[1] If you have an **intimate** friendship with someone, you know them very well and like them a lot. ❑ *I discussed with my intimate friends whether I would immediately have a baby.* ADJ: usu ADJ n ♦ **in|ti|mate|ly** *He did not feel he had got to know them intimately.* ADV: ADV after v, ADV -ed [2] If two people are in an **intimate** relationship, they are involved with each other in a loving or sexual way. ❑ *...their intimate moments with their boyfriends.* ADJ: usu ADJ n ♦ **in|ti|mate|ly** *You have to be willing to get to know yourself and your partner intimately.* ADV: ADV after v [3] An **intimate** conversation or detail, for example, is very personal and private. ❑ *He wrote about the intimate details of his family life.* ADJ: usu ADJ n = private ♦ **in|ti|mate|ly** *It was the first time they had attempted to talk intimately.* ADV: ADV after v [4] If you use **intimate** to describe an occasion or the atmosphere of a place, you like it because it is quiet and pleasant, and seems suitable for close conversations between friends. ❑ *...an intimate candlelit dinner for two.* ADJ: usu ADJ n approval [5] An **intimate** connection between ideas or organizations, for example, is a very strong link between them. ❑ *...an intimate connection between madness and wisdom.* ADJ: usu ADJ n ♦ **in|ti|mate|ly** *Property and equities are intimately connected in Hong Kong.* ADV: ADV after v [6] An **intimate** knowledge of something is a deep and detailed knowledge of it. ❑ *Richard surprised me with his intimate knowledge of Kierkegaard and Schopenhauer.* ADJ: usu ADJ n = thorough

♦ **in|ti|mate|ly** *...a golden age of musicians whose work she knew intimately.* [7] If you **intimate** something, you say it in an indirect way. [FORMAL] ❑ *He went on to intimate that he was indeed contemplating a shake-up of the company... He had intimated to the French and Russians his readiness to come to a settlement.* ADV: usu ADV after v; VERB = hint; V that; V to n n; Also V n

**in|ti|ma|tion** /ɪntɪmeɪʃən/ **(intimations)** An **intimation** is an indirect suggestion or sign that something is likely to happen or be true. [FORMAL] ❑ *I did not have any intimation that he was going to resign.* N-COUNT: usu N of n, N that

**in|timi|date** /ɪntɪmɪdeɪt/ **(intimidates, intimidating, intimidated)** If you **intimidate** someone, you deliberately make them frightened enough to do what you want them to do. ❑ *Jones had set out to intimidate and dominate Paul... Attempts to intimidate people into voting for the governing party did not work.* ♦ **in|timi|da|tion** /ɪntɪmɪdeɪʃən/ *...an inquiry into allegations of intimidation during last week's vote.* VERB; V n; V n into -ing; N-UNCOUNT

**in|timi|dat|ed** /ɪntɪmɪdeɪtɪd/ Someone who feels **intimidated** feels frightened and lacks confidence because of the people they are with or the situation they are in. ❑ *Women can come in here and not feel intimidated.* ADJ: usu v-link ADJ

**in|timi|dat|ing** /ɪntɪmɪdeɪtɪŋ/ If you describe someone or something as **intimidating**, you mean that they are frightening and make people lose confidence. ❑ *He was a huge, intimidating figure.* ADJ: usu ADJ n

**into** /ɪntuː/ ♦♦♦

> ✓ Pronounced /ɪntuː/ or /ɪntuː/, particularly before pronouns and for meaning 14.

> In addition to the uses shown below, **into** is used after some verbs and nouns in order to introduce extra information. **Into** is also used with verbs of movement, such as 'walk' and 'push', and in phrasal verbs such as 'enter into' and 'talk into'.

[1] If you put one thing **into** another, you put the first thing inside the second. ❑ *Combine the remaining ingredients and put them into a dish... Until the 1980s almost all olives were packed into jars by hand.* PREP = in

[2] If you go **into** a place or vehicle, you move from being outside it to being inside it. ❑ *I have no idea how he got into Iraq... He got into bed and started to read.* PREP

[3] If one thing goes **into** another, the first thing moves from the outside to the inside of the second thing, by breaking or damaging the surface of it. ❑ *The rider came off and the handlebar went into his neck.* PREP

[4] If one thing gets **into** another, the first thing enters the second and becomes part of it. ❑ *Poisonous smoke had got into the water supply.* PREP

[5] If you are walking or driving a vehicle and you bump **into** something or crash **into** something, you hit it accidentally. ❑ *A train plowed into the barrier at the end of the platform.* PREP

[6] When you get **into** a piece of clothing, you put it on. ❑ *She could change into a different outfit in two minutes.* PREP

[7] If someone or something gets **into** a particular state, they start being in that state. ❑ *I slid into a depression.* PREP: v PREP n, n PREP n

[8] If you talk someone **into** doing something, you persuade them to do it. ❑ *Gerome tried to talk her into taking an apartment in Paris.* PREP: v n PREP n/-ing

[9] If something changes **into** something else, it then has a new form, shape, or nature. ❑ *...his attempt to turn a nasty episode into a joke.* PREP

[10] If something is cut or split **into** a number of pieces or sections, it is divided so that it becomes several smaller pieces or sections. ❑ *Sixteen teams are taking part, divided into four groups.* PREP

[11] An investigation **into** a subject or event is concerned with that subject or event. ❑ *The concert will raise funds for research into Aids.* PREP: n PREP n

[12] If you move or go **into** a particular career or business, you start working in it. ❑ *In the early 1990s, it was easy to get into the rental business.* PREP

[13] If something continues **into** a period of time, it continues until after that period of time has begun. ❑ *He had three children, and lived on into his sixties.* PREP

[14] If you are very interested in something and like it very much, you can say that you are **into** it. [INFORMAL] ❑ *I'm into electronics myself.* PREP: v-link PREP n

**in|tol|er|able** /ɪntɒlərəbəl/ If you describe something as **intolerable**, you mean that it is so bad or extreme that no one can bear it or tolerate it. ❑ *They felt this would put intolerable pressure on them.* ♦ **in|tol|er|ably** /ɪntɒlərəbli/ *...intolerably cramped conditions.* ADJ = unbearable ≠ tolerable; ADV

**in|tol|er|ance** /ɪntɒlərəns/ **Intolerance** is unwillingness to let other people act in a different way or hold different opinions from you. ❑ *...his intolerance of any opinion other than his own.* N-UNCOUNT: usu with supp [disapproval] ≠ tolerance

**in|tol|er|ant** /ɪntɒlərənt/ If you describe someone as **intolerant**, you mean that they do not accept behaviour and opinions that are different from their own. ❑ *...intolerant attitudes toward non-Catholics.* ADJ: oft v-link ADJ of n [disapproval] ≠ tolerant

**in|to|na|tion** /ɪntəneɪʃən/ **(intonations)** Your **intonation** is the way that your voice rises and falls as you speak. ❑ *His voice had a very slight German intonation.* N-VAR

**in|tone** /ɪntoʊn/ **(intones, intoning, intoned)** If you **intone** something, you say it in a slow and serious way, with most of the words at one pitch. [WRITTEN] ❑ *He quietly intoned several prayers... 'But Jesus is here!' the priest intoned.* VERB = chant; V n; V with quote

**in|toxi|cat|ed** /ɪntɒksɪkeɪtɪd/ [1] Someone who is **intoxicated** is drunk. [FORMAL] ❑ *He appeared intoxicated, police said.* ADJ

[2] If you are **intoxicated by** or **with** something such as a feeling or an event, you are so excited by it that you find it hard to think clearly and sensibly. [LITERARY] ❑ *They seem to have become intoxicated by their success.* ADJ: v-link ADJ by/with n

**in|toxi|cat|ing** /ɪntɒksɪkeɪtɪŋ/ [1] **Intoxicating** drink contains alcohol and can make you drunk. [FORMAL] ❑ *...intoxicating liquor.* ADJ: usu ADJ n

[2] If you describe something as **intoxicating**, you mean that it makes you feel a strong sense of excitement or happiness. [LITERARY] ❑ *...the intoxicating fragrance of lilies.* ADJ

**in|toxi|ca|tion** /ɪntɒksɪkeɪʃən/ [1] **Intoxication** is the state of being drunk. [FORMAL] ❑ *Intoxication interferes with memory and thinking, speech and coordination.* N-UNCOUNT

[2] You use **intoxication** to refer to a quality that something has that makes you feel very excited. [LITERARY] ❑ *...the intoxication of greed and success.* N-UNCOUNT: oft N of n

**in|trac|table** /ɪntræktəbəl/ [1] **Intractable** people are very difficult to control or influence. [FORMAL] ❑ *What may be done to reduce the influence of intractable opponents?* ADJ: usu ADJ n

[2] **Intractable** problems or situations are very difficult to deal with. [FORMAL] ❑ *The economy still faces intractable problems.* ADJ: usu ADJ n

**intra|mu|ral** /ɪntrəmjʊərəl/ **Intramural** activities happen within one college or university, rather than between different colleges or universities. [AM] ❑ *...a comprehensive, well-supported program of intramural sports.* ADJ: ADJ n ≠ intercollegiate

**in|tra|net** /ɪntrənet/ **(intranets)** An **intranet** is a network of computers, similar to the Internet, within a particular company or organization. N-COUNT

**in|tran|si|gence** /ɪntrænsɪdʒəns/ If you talk about someone's **intransigence**, you mean that they refuse to behave differently or to change their attitude to something. [FORMAL] ❑ *He often appeared angry and frustrated by the intransigence of both sides.* N-UNCOUNT: usu with poss [disapproval] ≠ flexibility

**in|tran|si|gent** /ɪntrænsɪdʒənt/ If you describe someone as **intransigent**, you mean that they refuse to behave differently or to change their attitude to something. [FORMAL] ❑ *They put pressure on the Government to change its intransigent stance.* ADJ [disapproval] ≠ flexible

**in|tran|si|tive** /ɪntrænsɪtɪv/ An **intransitive** verb does not have an object. ADJ ≠ transitive

**intra|venous** /ɪntrəviːnəs/ **Intravenous** foods or drugs are given to sick people through their veins, rather than their mouths. [MEDICAL] ❑ *...an intravenous drip.* ♦ **intra|venous|ly** *Premature babies have to be fed intravenously.*
ADJ: ADJ n
ADV: ADV after v

**in tray** **(in trays)** also **in-tray.** An **in tray** is a shallow container used in offices to put letters and documents in before they are dealt with. Compare **out tray**.
N-COUNT ≠ out tray

**in|trep|id** /ɪntrepɪd/ An **intrepid** person acts in a brave way. ❑ *...an intrepid space traveller.*
ADJ: usu ADJ n = fearless

**in|tri|ca|cy** /ɪntrɪkəsi/ **(intricacies)** 1 **Intricacy** is the state of being made up of many small parts or details. ❑ *The price depends on the intricacy of the work.* 2 The **intricacies** of something are its complicated details. ❑ *Rose explained the intricacies of the job.*
N-UNCOUNT: usu N of n = complexity
N-PLURAL: usu N of n

**in|tri|cate** /ɪntrɪkət/ You use **intricate** to describe something that has many small parts or details. ❑ *...intricate patterns and motifs.* ♦ **in|tri|cate|ly** *...intricately carved sculptures.*
ADJ: usu ADJ n ≠ simple
ADV

**in|trigue** **(intrigues, intriguing, intrigued)**

> The noun is pronounced /ɪntriːg/. The verb is pronounced /ɪntriːg/.

1 **Intrigue** is the making of secret plans to harm or deceive people. ❑ *...political intrigue. ...a powerful story of intrigue, passion and betrayal.* 2 If something, especially something strange, **intrigues** you, it interests you and you want to know more about it. ❑ *The novelty of the situation intrigued him.*
N-VAR: usu with supp
VERB = fascinate
V n

**in|trigued** /ɪntriːgd/ If you are **intrigued by** something, especially something strange, it interests you and you want to know more about it. ❑ *I would be intrigued to hear others' views.*
ADJ: usu v-link ADJ, oft ADJ by n, ADJ to-inf

**in|tri|guing** /ɪntriːgɪŋ/ If you describe something as **intriguing**, you mean that it is interesting or strange. ❑ *This intriguing book is both thoughtful and informative.* ♦ **in|tri|guing|ly** *...the intriguingly-named newspaper Le Canard Enchainé (The Chained Duck).*
ADJ: usu ADJ n = fascinating
ADV: ADV adj, ADV with v

**in|trin|sic** /ɪntrɪnsɪk/ If something has **intrinsic** value or **intrinsic** interest, it is valuable or interesting because of its basic nature or character, and not because of its connection with other things. [FORMAL] ❑ *The paintings have no intrinsic value except as curiosities.* ♦ **in|trin|si|cal|ly** /ɪntrɪnsɪkli/ *Sometimes I wonder if people are intrinsically evil.*
ADJ: ADJ n
ADV: ADV adj, ADV with cl

**in|tro** /ɪntroʊ/ **(intros)** The **intro** to a song, programme, or book is the first part, which comes before the main part. [INFORMAL] ❑ *...the keyboard intro to The Who's 'Won't Get Fooled Again'.*
N-COUNT: oft N to n

**intro|duce** /ɪntrədjuːs, AM -duːs/ **(introduces, introducing, introduced)** ◆◆◇ 1 To **introduce** something means to cause it to enter a place or exist in a system for the first time. ❑ *The Government has introduced a number of other money-saving moves... The word 'Pagoda' was introduced to Europe by the 17th century Portuguese.* ♦ **intro|duc|tion** *He is best remembered for the introduction of the moving assembly-line.* 2 If you **introduce** someone **to** something, you cause them to learn about it or experience it for the first time. ❑ *He introduced us to the delights of natural food.* ♦ **intro|duc|tion** *His introduction to League football would have been gentler if he had started at a smaller club.* 3 If you **introduce** one person **to** another, or you **introduce** two people, you tell them each other's names, so that they can get to know each other. If you **introduce yourself** to someone, you tell them your name. ❑ *Tim, may I introduce you to my uncle's secretary, Mary Waller?... Someone introduced us and I sat next to him... Let me introduce myself.* ♦ **intro|duc|tion** **(introductions)** *With considerable shyness, Elaine performed the introductions.* 4 The person who **introduces** a television or radio programme speaks at the beginning of it, and often between the different items in it, in order to explain what the programme or the items are about. ❑ *'Health Matters' is introduced by Dick Oliver on BBC World Service.*
VERB
V n
be V-ed into/to n
N-VAR: usu N of n
VERB
V n to n
N-SING: usu N to n
VERB
V n to n
V pl-n
V pron-refl
N-VAR
VERB = present
be V-ed by n
Also V n

**intro|duc|tion** /ɪntrədʌkʃən/ **(introductions)** 1 The **introduction to** a book or talk is the part that comes at the beginning and tells you what the rest of the book or talk is about. ❑ *Ellen Malos, in her introduction to 'The Politics of Housework', provides a summary of the debates.* 2 If you refer to a book as an **introduction to** a particular subject, you mean that it explains the basic facts about that subject. ❑ *On balance, the book is a friendly, down-to-earth introduction to physics.* 3 → See also **introduce**.
N-COUNT: oft N to n
N-COUNT: usu N to n, oft in names

**intro|duc|tory** /ɪntrədʌktəri/ 1 An **introductory** remark, talk, or part of a book gives a small amount of general information about a particular subject, often before a more detailed explanation. ❑ *...an introductory course in religion and theology.* 2 An **introductory** offer or price on a new product is something such as a free gift or a low price that is meant to attract new customers. [BUSINESS] ❑ *...just out on the shelves at an introductory price of £2.99.*
ADJ: ADJ n
ADJ: ADJ n

**intro|spec|tion** /ɪntrəspekʃən/ **Introspection** is the examining of your own thoughts, ideas, and feelings. ❑ *He had always had his moments of quiet introspection.*
N-UNCOUNT

**intro|spec|tive** /ɪntrəspektɪv/ **Introspective** people spend a lot of time examining their own thoughts, ideas, and feelings.
ADJ

**intro|vert** /ɪntrəvɜːʳt/ **(introverts)** 1 An **introvert** is a quiet, shy person who finds it difficult to talk to people. 2 **Introvert** means the same as **introverted**. ❑ *The music students here are a very introvert lot.*
N-COUNT ≠ extrovert
ADJ

**intro|vert|ed** /ɪntrəvɜːʳtɪd/ **Introverted** people are quiet and shy and find it difficult to talk to other people. ❑ *Machen was a lonely, introverted child.*
ADJ ≠ extroverted

**in|trude** /ɪntruːd/ **(intrudes, intruding, intruded)** 1 If you say that someone **is intruding into** a particular place or situation, you mean that they are not wanted or welcome there. ❑ *The press has been blamed for intruding into people's personal lives in an unacceptable way... I hope I'm not intruding.* 2 If something **intrudes on** your mood or your life, it disturbs it or has an unwanted effect on it. ❑ *Do you feel anxious when unforeseen incidents intrude on your day?... There are times when personal feelings cannot be allowed to intrude.* 3 If someone **intrudes into** a place, they go there even though they are not allowed to be there. ❑ *The officer on the scene said no one had intruded into the area.*
VERB
V into/on/upon n
V
VERB
V on/into/upon n
V
VERB
V into/onto n

**in|trud|er** /ɪntruːdəʳ/ **(intruders)** An **intruder** is a person who goes into a place where they are not supposed to be.
N-COUNT

**in|tru|sion** /ɪntruːʒən/ **(intrusions)** 1 If someone disturbs you when you are in a private place or having a private conversation, you can call this event an **intrusion**. ❑ *I hope you don't mind this intrusion, Jon.* 2 An **intrusion** is something that disturbs your mood or your life in a way you do not like. ❑ *I felt it was a grotesque intrusion into our lives.*
N-VAR
N-VAR: oft N into n

**in|tru|sive** /ɪntruːsɪv/ Something that is **intrusive** disturbs your mood or your life in a way you do not like. ❑ *The cameras were not an intrusive presence.*
ADJ

**in|tu|it** /ɪntjuːɪt, AM -tuː-/ **(intuits, intuiting, intuited)** If you **intuit** something, you guess what it is on the basis of your intuition or feelings, rather than on the basis of knowledge. [FORMAL] ❑ *They would confidently intuit your very thoughts... He was probably right to intuit that it was universal.*
VERB
V n
V that

**in|tui|tion** /ɪntjuɪʃən, AM -tu-/ **(intuitions)** Your **intuition** or your **intuitions** are unexplained feelings you have that something is true even when you have no evidence or proof of it. ❑ *Her intuition was telling her that something was wrong.*
N-VAR = instinct

**in|tui|tive** /ɪntjuːətɪv, AM -tuː-/ If you have an **intuitive** idea or feeling about something, you feel that it is true although you have no evidence or proof of it. ❑ *A positive pregnancy test soon confirmed her intuitive feelings.* ♦ **in|tui|tive|ly** *He seemed to know intuitively that I must be missing my mother.* ADJ: usu ADJ n = instinctive; ADV: ADV with v, ADV adj

**Inu|it** /ɪnjuɪt/ **(Inuits** or **Inuit)** The **Inuit** are a race of people descended from the original people of Eastern Canada and Greenland. N-COUNT

**in|un|date** /ɪnʌndeɪt/ **(inundates, inundating, inundated)** [1] If you say that you **are inundated with** things such as letters, demands, or requests, you are emphasizing that you receive so many of them that you cannot deal with them all. ❑ *Her office was inundated with requests for tickets... They have inundated me with fan letters.* [2] If an area of land **is inundated**, it becomes covered with water. ❑ *Their neighborhood is being inundated by the rising waters of the Colorado River.* VERB emphasis = swamp be V-ed with n; V n with n; Also V n; VERB: usu passive = flood be V-ed

**in|ured** /ɪnjʊəʳd/ If you are **inured to** something unpleasant, you have become used to it so that it no longer affects you. [FORMAL] ❑ *Doctors become inured to death.* ADJ: v-link ADJ to n

**in|vade** /ɪnveɪd/ **(invades, invading, invaded)** [1] To **invade** a country means to enter it by force with an army. ❑ *In autumn 1944 the allies invaded the Italian mainland at Anzio and Salerno... The Romans and the Normans came to Britain as invading armies.* [2] If you say that people or animals **invade** a place, you mean that they enter it in large numbers, often in a way that is unpleasant or difficult to deal with. ❑ *People invaded the streets in victory processions almost throughout the day.* [3] to **invade** someone's **privacy** → see **privacy**. VERB V n; V-ing; Also V; VERB; V n

**in|vad|er** /ɪnveɪdəʳ/ **(invaders)** [1] **Invaders** are soldiers who are invading a country. ❑ *The invaders were only finally crushed when troops overcame them at Glenshiel in June 1719.* [2] You can refer to a country or army that has invaded or is about to invade another country as an **invader**. ❑ *...action against a foreign invader.* N-COUNT: usu pl; N-COUNT: usu sing

**in|va|lid** **(invalids)**

> ✔ The noun is pronounced /ɪnvəlɪd/. The adjective is pronounced /ɪnvælɪd/ and is hyphenated in|val|id.

[1] An **invalid** is someone who needs to be cared for because they have an illness or disability. ❑ *I hate being treated as an invalid.* [2] If an action, procedure, or document is **invalid**, it cannot be accepted, because it breaks the law or some official rule. ❑ *The trial was stopped and the results declared invalid.* [3] An **invalid** argument or conclusion is wrong because it is based on a mistake. ❑ *We think that those arguments are rendered invalid by the hard facts on the ground.* N-COUNT; ADJ; ADJ

**in|vali|date** /ɪnvælɪdeɪt/ **(invalidates, invalidating, invalidated)** [1] To **invalidate** something such as an argument, conclusion, or result means to prove that it is wrong or cause it to be wrong. ❑ *Any form of physical activity will invalidate the results.* [2] If something **invalidates** something such as a law, contract, or election, it causes it to be considered illegal. ❑ *An official decree invalidated the vote in the capital.* VERB V n; VERB V n

**in|va|lid|ity** /ɪnvəlɪdɪti/ **Invalidity** is the state of being an invalid. ❑ *I live on an invalidity pension.* N-UNCOUNT

**in|valu|able** /ɪnvæljəbᵊl/ If you describe something as **invaluable**, you mean that it is extremely useful. ❑ *I was able to gain invaluable experience over that year... The research should prove invaluable in the study of linguistics.* ADJ: oft ADJ in n/-ing, ADJ to n

**in|vari|able** /ɪnveəriəbᵊl/ You use **invariable** to describe something that never changes. ❑ *It was his invariable custom to have one whisky before his supper.* ADJ: usu ADJ n = unchanging

**in|vari|ably** /ɪnveəriəbli/ If something **invariably** happens or is **invariably** true, it always happens or is always true. ❑ *They almost invariably get it wrong.* ADV: ADV with v, ADV with cl/group

**in|va|sion** /ɪnveɪʒᵊn/ **(invasions)** [1] If there is an **invasion** of a country, a foreign army enters it by force. ❑ *...seven years after the Roman invasion of Britain.* [2] If you refer to the arrival of a large number of people or things as an **invasion**, you are emphasizing that they are unpleasant or difficult to deal with. ❑ *...this year's annual invasion of flies, wasps and ants.* [3] If you describe an action as an **invasion**, you disapprove of it because it affects someone or something in a way that is not wanted. ❑ *Is reading a child's diary always a gross invasion of privacy?* ◆◇◇ N-VAR: usu with supp, oft adj N, N of n; N-VAR: oft N of n; N-VAR: usu N of n disapproval

**in|va|sive** /ɪnveɪsɪv/ [1] You use **invasive** to describe something undesirable which spreads very quickly and which is very difficult to stop from spreading. ❑ *They found invasive cancer during a routine examination.* [2] An **invasive** medical procedure involves operating on a patient or examining the inside of their body. ADJ: usu ADJ n; ADJ: usu ADJ n

**in|vec|tive** /ɪnvektɪv/ **Invective** is rude and unpleasant things that people shout at people they hate or are angry with. [FORMAL] ❑ *A woman had hurled racist invective at the family.* N-UNCOUNT: usu with supp

**in|veigh** /ɪnveɪ/ **(inveighs, inveighing, inveighed)** If you **inveigh against** something, you criticize it strongly. [FORMAL] ❑ *A lot of his writings inveigh against luxury and riches.* VERB V against n

**in|vei|gle** /ɪnveɪgᵊl/ **(inveigles, inveigling, inveigled)** If you **inveigle** someone **into** doing something, you cleverly persuade them to do it when they do not really want to. [FORMAL] ❑ *She inveigles Paco into a plot to swindle Tania out of her savings.* VERB = cajole V n into n/-ing

**in|vent** /ɪnvent/ **(invents, inventing, invented)** [1] If you **invent** something such as a machine or process, you are the first person to think of it or make it. ❑ *He invented the first electric clock.* [2] If you **invent** a story or excuse, you try to make other people believe that it is true when in fact it is not. ❑ *I stood still, trying to invent a plausible excuse.* VERB V n; VERB V n

**in|ven|tion** /ɪnvenʃᵊn/ **(inventions)** [1] An **invention** is a machine, device, or system that has been invented by someone. ❑ *The spinning wheel was a Chinese invention.* [2] **Invention** is the act of inventing something that has never been made or used before. ❑ *...the invention of the telephone.* [3] If you refer to someone's account of something as an **invention**, you think that it is untrue and that they have made it up. ❑ *The story was certainly a favourite one, but it was undoubtedly pure invention.* [4] **Invention** is the ability to invent things or to have clever and original ideas. ❑ *...his great powers of invention.* N-COUNT; N-UNCOUNT: oft N of n; N-VAR = fabrication; N-UNCOUNT = creativity

**in|ven|tive** /ɪnventɪv/ An **inventive** person is good at inventing things or has clever and original ideas. ❑ *It inspired me to be more inventive with my own cooking.* ♦ **in|ven|tive|ness** *He has surprised us before with his inventiveness.* ADJ = creative; N-UNCOUNT

**in|ven|tor** /ɪnventəʳ/ **(inventors)** An **inventor** is a person who has invented something, or whose job is to invent things. ❑ *...Alexander Graham Bell, the inventor of the telephone.* N-COUNT

**in|ven|tory** /ɪnvᵊntri, AM -tɔːri/ **(inventories)** [1] An **inventory** is a written list of all the objects in a particular place. ❑ *Before starting, he made an inventory of everything that was to stay.* [2] An **inventory** is a supply or stock of something. [AM] ❑ *...one inventory of twelve sails for each yacht.* N-COUNT; N-VAR

**in|verse** /ɪnvɜːʳs/ [1] If there is an **inverse** relationship between two things, one of them becomes larger as the other becomes smaller. ❑ *The tension grew in inverse proportion to the distance from their final destination.* ♦ **in|verse|ly** *The size of the nebula at this stage is inversely proportional to its mass.* [2] **The inverse** of something is its exact opposite. [FORMAL] ❑ *There is no sign that you bothered to consider the inverse of your logic.* ♦ **Inverse** is ADJ: usu ADJ n ≠ direct; ADV: ADV adj/-ed, ADV after v; N-SING: the N, usu N of n; ADJ: ADJ n also an adjective. ❑ *The hologram can be flipped to show the inverse image.*

**in|ver|sion** /ɪnvɜːʳʃᵊn, -ʒᵊn/ **(inversions)** When there is an **inversion** of something, it is changed into its opposite. [FORMAL] ❑ *...a scandalous inversion of the truth.* N-VAR: usu N *of* n

**in|vert** /ɪnvɜːʳt/ **(inverts, inverting, inverted)** 1 If you **invert** something, you turn it the other way up or back to front. [FORMAL] ❑ *Invert the cake onto a cooling rack. ...a black inverted triangle.* VERB V n V-ed 2 If you **invert** something, you change it to its opposite. [FORMAL] ❑ *They may be hoping to invert the presumption that a defendant is innocent until proved guilty. ...a telling illustration of inverted moral values.* VERB V n V-ed

**in|ver|tebrate** /ɪnvɜːʳtɪbrət/ **(invertebrates)** An **invertebrate** is a creature that does not have a spine, for example an insect, a worm, or an octopus. [TECHNICAL] ♦ **Invertebrate** is also an adjective. ❑ *...invertebrate creatures.* N-COUNT ADJ

**in|vert|ed com|mas** 1 **Inverted commas** are punctuation marks that are used in writing to show where speech or a quotation begins and ends. They are usually written or printed as ' ' or " ". Inverted commas are also sometimes used around the titles of books, plays, or songs, or around a word or phrase that is being discussed. [BRIT] N-PLURAL

✔ in AM, use **quotation marks**

2 If you say **in inverted commas** after a word or phrase, you are indicating that it is inaccurate or unacceptable in some way, or that you are quoting someone else. [BRIT] ❑ *They're asked to make objective, in inverted commas, evaluations of these statements.* PHRASE

**in|vest** /ɪnvest/ **(invests, investing, invested)** ◆◇◇ 1 If you **invest in** something, or if you **invest** a sum of money, you use your money in a way that you hope will increase its value, for example by paying it into a bank, or buying shares or property. ❑ *They intend to invest directly in shares... He invested all our profits in gold shares... When people buy houses they're investing a lot of money.* VERB V *in* n V n *in* n V n 2 When a government or organization **invests in** something, it gives or lends money for a purpose that it considers useful or profitable. ❑ *...the British government's failure to invest in an integrated transport system. ...the European Investment Bank, which invested £100 million in Canary Wharf... Why does Japan invest, on average, twice as much capital per worker per year than the United States?* VERB V *in* n V n *in* n V n Also V 3 If you **invest in** something useful, you buy it, because it will help you to do something more efficiently or more cheaply. ❑ *The company invested thousands in an electronic order-control system... The easiest way to make ice cream yourself is to invest in an ice cream machine.* VERB V n *in* n V *in* n 4 If you **invest** time or energy **in** something, you spend a lot of time or energy on something that you consider to be useful or likely to be successful. ❑ *I would rather invest time in Rebecca than in the kitchen.* VERB V n *in* n 5 To **invest** someone **with** rights or responsibilities means to give them those rights or responsibilities legally or officially. [FORMAL] ❑ *The constitution had invested him with certain powers.* VERB V n *with* n

**in|ves|ti|gate** /ɪnvestɪgeɪt/ **(investigates, investigating, investigated)** ◆◆◇ If someone, especially an official, **investigates** an event, situation, or claim, they try to find out what happened or what is the truth. ❑ *Gas officials are investigating the cause of an explosion which badly damaged a house in Hampshire... Police are still investigating how the accident happened.* ♦ **in|ves|ti|ga|tion** /ɪnvestɪgeɪʃᵊn/ **(investigations)** *He ordered an investigation into the affair.* VERB V n V wh Also V N-VAR: oft N *into* n

**in|ves|ti|gative** /ɪnvestɪgətɪv, AM -geɪt-/ **Investigative** work, especially journalism, involves investigating things. ❑ *...an investigative reporter.* ADJ: usu ADJ n

**in|ves|ti|ga|tor** /ɪnvestɪgeɪtəʳ/ **(investigators)** An **investigator** is someone who carries out investigations, especially as part of their job. N-COUNT

**in|ves|ti|ga|tory** /ɪnvestɪgətri, AM -tɔːri/ **Investigatory** means the same as **investigative**. ❑ *At no time did I make an attempt to impede any investigatory effort.* ADJ: ADJ n

**in|ves|ti|ture** /ɪnvestɪtʃəʳ/ **(investitures)** An **investiture** is a ceremony in which someone is given an official title. ❑ *...Edward VIII's investiture as Prince of Wales in 1911.* N-COUNT

**in|vest|ment** /ɪnvesmənt/ **(investments)** ◆◆◇ 1 **Investment** is the activity of investing money. ❑ *He said the government must introduce tax incentives to encourage investment.* N-UNCOUNT: usu with supp, oft N *in* n 2 An **investment** is an amount of money that you invest, or the thing that you invest it in. ❑ *You'll be able to earn an average rate of return of 8% on your investments.* N-VAR: usu with supp 3 If you describe something you buy as an **investment**, you mean that it will be useful, especially because it will help you to do a task more cheaply or efficiently. ❑ *When selecting boots, fine, quality leather will be a wise investment.* N-COUNT: usu sing, usu adj N 4 **Investment** of time or effort is the spending of time or effort on something in order to make it a success. ❑ *I worry about this big investment of time and effort.* N-UNCOUNT: usu N *of* n

**in|ves|tor** /ɪnvestəʳ/ **(investors)** An **investor** is a person or organization that buys stocks or shares, or pays money into a bank in order to receive a profit. ❑ *The main investor in the project is the French bank Credit National.* ◆◆◇ N-COUNT

**in|vet|er|ate** /ɪnvetərət/ If you describe someone as, for example, an **inveterate** liar or smoker, you mean that they have lied or smoked for a long time and are not likely to stop doing it. ❑ *...an inveterate gambler.* ADJ: ADJ n

**in|vidi|ous** /ɪnvɪdiəs/ 1 If you describe a task or job as **invidious**, you mean that it is unpleasant because it is likely to make you unpopular. ❑ *The local authority could find itself in the invidious position of having to refuse.* ADJ 2 An **invidious** comparison or choice between two things is an unfair one because the two things are very different or are equally good or bad. ❑ *Police officers fear invidious comparisons.* ADJ: oft *it* v-link ADJ to-inf

**in|vigi|late** /ɪnvɪdʒɪleɪt/ **(invigilates, invigilating, invigilated)** Someone who **invigilates** an examination supervises the people who are taking it in order to ensure that it starts and finishes at the correct time, and that there is no cheating. [BRIT] ❑ *I've taught sixth formers and invigilated exams.* ♦ **in|vigi|la|tor** **(invigilators)** *...an exam invigilator.* VERB V n Also V N-COUNT

**in|vig|or|ate** /ɪnvɪgəreɪt/ **(invigorates, invigorating, invigorated)** 1 If something **invigorates** you, it makes you feel more energetic. ❑ *Take a deep breath in to invigorate you.* ♦ **in|vig|or|at|ed** *She seemed invigorated, full of life and energy.* VERB V n ADJ: usu v-link ADJ 2 To **invigorate** a situation or a process means to make it more efficient or more effective. ❑ *...the promise that they would invigorate the economy.* VERB = stimulate V n

**in|vig|or|at|ing** /ɪnvɪgəreɪtɪŋ/ If you describe something as **invigorating**, you mean that it makes you feel more energetic. ❑ *...the bright Finnish sun and invigorating northern air.* ADJ

**in|vin|cible** /ɪnvɪnsɪbᵊl/ 1 If you describe an army or sports team as **invincible**, you believe that they cannot be defeated. ❑ *When Sotomayor is on form he is virtually invincible.* ♦ **in|vin|cibil|ity** /ɪnvɪnsɪbɪlɪti/ *...symbols of the invincibility of the Roman army.* ADJ = unbeatable N-UNCOUNT 2 If someone has an **invincible** belief or attitude, it cannot be changed. ❑ *He also had an invincible faith in the medicinal virtues of garlic.* ADJ: usu ADJ n

**in|vio|lable** /ɪnvaɪələbᵊl/ 1 If a law or principle is **inviolable**, you must not break it. [FORMAL] ❑ *The game had a single inviolable rule: obstacles were to be overcome, not circumvented.* ADJ 2 If a country says its borders are **inviolable**, it means they must not be changed or crossed without permission. [FORMAL] ❑ *Yesterday's resolution says the present Polish border is 'inviolable'.* ♦ **in|vio|labil|ity** /ɪnvaɪələbɪlɪti/ *Parliament has recognised the inviolability of the current border.* ADJ N-UNCOUNT

**in|vio|late** /ɪnvaɪələt/ If something is **inviolate**, it has not been or cannot be harmed or affected by anything. [FORMAL] ❑ *We believed our love was inviolate.* ADJ

**in|vis|ible** /ɪnvɪzɪbᵊl/ [1] If you describe something as **invisible**, you mean that it cannot be seen, for example because it is transparent, hidden, or very small. ❑ *The lines were so finely etched as to be invisible from a distance.* ♦ **in|vis|ibly** /ɪnvɪzɪbli/ *A thin coil of smoke rose almost invisibly into the sharp, bright sky.* [2] You can use **invisible** when you are talking about something that cannot be seen but has a definite effect. In this sense, **invisible** is often used before a noun which refers to something that can usually be seen. ❑ *Parents fear they might overstep these invisible boundaries.* ♦ **in|vis|ibly** *...the tradition that invisibly shapes things in the present.* [3] If you say that you feel **invisible**, you are complaining that you are being ignored by other people. If you say that a particular problem or situation is **invisible**, you are complaining that it is not being considered or dealt with. ❑ *The problems of the poor are largely invisible.* ♦ **in|vis|ibil|ity** /ɪnvɪzɪbɪlɪti/ *...the invisibility of women's concerns in society.* [4] In stories, **invisible** people or things have a magic quality which makes people unable to see them. ❑ *...The Invisible Man.* [5] In economics, **invisible** earnings are the money that a country makes as a result of services such as banking and tourism, rather than by producing goods. [BUSINESS] ❑ *Tourism is Britain's single biggest invisible export.* ADJ: usu v-link ADJ ≠ visible; ADV: ADV with v; ADJ: ADJ n; ADV: ADV with v; ADJ; N-UNCOUNT; ADJ; ADJ: ADJ n ≠ visible

**in|vi|ta|tion** /ɪnvɪteɪʃᵊn/ **(invitations)** [1] An **invitation** is a written or spoken request to come to an event such as a party, a meal, or a meeting. ❑ *...an invitation to lunch... He's understood to be there at the personal invitation of President Daniel Arap Moi.* [2] An **invitation** is the card or paper on which an invitation is written or printed. ❑ *Hundreds of invitations are being sent out this week.* [3] If you believe that someone's action is likely to have a particular result, especially a bad one, you can refer to the action as an **invitation to** that result. ❑ *Don't leave your shopping on the back seat of your car – it's an open invitation to a thief.* ♦◇◇ N-COUNT: oft N to-inf, N *to* n; N-COUNT; N-SING: N *to* n

**in|vite** **(invites, inviting, invited)** ♦♦◇

> The verb is pronounced /ɪnvaɪt/. The noun is pronounced /ɪnvaɪt/.

[1] If you **invite** someone to something such as a party or a meal, you ask them to come to it. ❑ *She invited him to her 26th birthday party in New Jersey... Barron invited her to accompany him to the races... I haven't been invited. ...an invited audience of children from inner-city schools.* [2] If you **are invited to** do something, you are formally asked or given permission to do it. ❑ *At a future date, managers will be invited to apply for a management buy-out... If a new leader emerged, it would then be for the Queen to invite him to form a government... The Department is inviting applications from groups within the Borough.* [3] If something you say or do **invites** trouble or criticism, it makes trouble or criticism more likely. ❑ *Their refusal to compromise will inevitably invite more criticism from the UN.* [4] An **invite** is an invitation to something such as a party or a meal. [INFORMAL] ❑ *They haven't got an invite to the wedding.* VERB; V n prep/adv; V n to-inf; *be* V-ed; V-ed; VERB; *be* V-ed to-inf; V n to-inf; V n; VERB; V n; N-COUNT

**in|vit|ing** /ɪnvaɪtɪŋ/ If you say that something is **inviting**, you mean that it has good qualities that attract you or make you want to experience it. ❑ *The February air was soft, cool, and inviting.* ♦ **in|vit|ing|ly** *The waters of the tropics are invitingly clear.* → See also **invite**. ADJ; ADV: ADV adj, ADV with v

**in vi|tro** /ɪn viːtroʊ/ **In vitro** fertilization is a method of helping a woman to have a baby in which an egg is removed from one of her ovaries, fertilized outside her body, and then replaced in her womb. ADJ: ADJ n

**in|vo|ca|tion** /ɪnvəkeɪʃᵊn/ **(invocations)** [1] An **invocation** is a request for help or forgiveness made to a god. [FORMAL] ❑ *...an invocation for divine guidance.* [2] An **invocation** is a prayer at a public meeting, usually at the beginning. [AM] N-VAR: oft N prep; N-COUNT

**in|voice** /ɪnvɔɪs/ **(invoices, invoicing, invoiced)** [1] An **invoice** is a document that lists goods that have been supplied or services that have been done, and says how much money you owe for them. ❑ *We will then send you an invoice for the total course fees.* [2] If you **invoice** someone, you send them a bill for goods or services you have provided them with. ❑ *The agency invoices the client.* N-COUNT: oft N *for* n = bill; VERB = bill; V n

**in|voke** /ɪnvoʊk/ **(invokes, invoking, invoked)** [1] If you **invoke** a law, you state that you are taking a particular action because that law allows or tells you to. ❑ *The judge invoked an international law that protects refugees.* [2] If you **invoke** something such as a principle, a saying, or a famous person, you refer to them in order to support your argument. ❑ *He invoked memories of Britain's near-disastrous disarmament in the 1930s.* [3] If something such as a piece of music **invokes** a feeling or an image, it causes someone to have the feeling or to see the image. Many people consider this use to be incorrect. ❑ *The music invoked the wide open spaces of the prairies.* VERB; V n; VERB; V n; VERB = evoke; V n

**in|vol|un|tary** /ɪnvɒləntri, AM -teri/ [1] If you make an **involuntary** movement or exclamation, you make it suddenly and without intending to because you are unable to control yourself. ❑ *Another surge of pain in my ankle caused me to give an involuntary shudder.* ♦ **in|vol|un|tari|ly** /ɪnvɒləntrəli, AM -teərɪli/ *His left eyelid twitched involuntarily.* [2] You use **involuntary** to describe an action or situation which is forced on someone. ❑ *...insurance policies that cover involuntary unemployment.* ADJ; ADV: ADV with v; ADJ = forced

**in|volve** /ɪnvɒlv/ **(involves, involving, involved)** [1] If a situation or activity **involves** something, that thing is a necessary part or consequence of it. ❑ *Running a kitchen involves a great deal of discipline and speed... Nicky's job as a public relations director involves spending quite a lot of time with other people.* [2] If a situation or activity **involves** someone, they are taking part in it. ❑ *If there was a cover-up, it involved people at the very highest levels of government.* [3] If you say that someone **involves** themselves **in** something, you mean that they take part in it, often in a way that is unnecessary or unwanted. ❑ *I seem to have involved myself in something I don't understand.* [4] If you **involve** someone else **in** something, you get them to take part in it. ❑ *Noel and I do everything together, he involves me in everything.* [5] If one thing **involves** you **in** another thing, especially something unpleasant or inconvenient, the first thing causes you to do or deal with the second. ❑ *A late booking may involve you in extra cost.* ♦♦◇ VERB = entail; V n/-ing; V n/-ing; VERB; V n; VERB; V pron-refl *in* n; VERB; V n *in* n/-ing; VERB; V n *in* n

**in|volved** /ɪnvɒlvd/ [1] If you are **involved in** a situation or activity, you are taking part in it or have a strong connection with it. ❑ *If she were involved in business, she would make a strong chief executive.* [2] If you are **involved in** something, you give a lot of time, effort, or attention to it. ❑ *The family were deeply involved in Jewish culture.* [3] The things **involved in** something such as a job or system are the necessary parts or consequences of it. ❑ *We believe the time and hard work involved in completing such an assignment are worthwhile.* [4] If a situation or activity is **involved**, it has a lot of different parts or aspects, often making it difficult to understand, explain, or do. ❑ *The operations can be quite involved, requiring many procedures.* [5] If one person is **involved with** another, especially someone they are not married to, they are having a sexual or romantic relationship. ❑ *He became romantically involved with a married woman.* ♦♦◇ ADJ: v-link ADJ, usu ADJ *in/with* n; ADJ: v-link ADJ, usu ADJ *in* n; ADJ: v-link ADJ, oft ADJ *in* n; ADJ = complex, complicated; ADJ: oft v-link ADJ *with* n

**in|volve|ment** /ɪnvɒlvmənt/ **(involvements)** [1] Your **involvement in** something is the fact that you are taking part in it. ❑ *She disliked his involvement with the group and disliked his friends.* [2] **Involvement** is the enthusiasm that you feel when you care deeply about something. ❑ *Ben has* ♦◇◇ N-UNCOUNT: oft N *in/with* n; N-UNCOUNT *always felt a deep involvement with animals.* [3] An **involvement** is a close relationship between two people, especially if they are not married to each other. ❑ *There was no romantic involvement.* N-VAR

**in|vul|ner|able** /ɪnvʌlnərəbᵊl/ If someone or something is **invulnerable**, they cannot be harmed or damaged. ❑ *Many daughters assume that their mothers are invulnerable.* ADJ: oft ADJ *to* n ≠ vulnerable
♦ **in|vul|ner|abil|ity** /ɪnvʌlnərəbɪlɪti/ *They have a sense of invulnerability to disease.* N-UNCOUNT

**in|ward** /ɪnwəʳd/ [1] Your **inward** thoughts or feelings are the ones that you do not express or show to other people. ❑ *I sighed with inward relief.* ADJ: ADJ n = inner
♦ **in|ward|ly** *Sara, while remaining outwardly amiable toward all concerned, was inwardly furious.* ADV: ADV with v, ADV adj
[2] An **inward** movement is one towards the inside or centre of something. ❑ *...a sharp, inward breath like a gasp.* ADJ: ADJ n [3] ➔ See also **inwards**.

**in|ward in|vest|ment** **Inward investment** is the investment of money in a country by companies from outside that country. [BUSINESS] N-UNCOUNT

**inward-looking** If you describe a people or society as **inward-looking**, you mean that they are more interested in themselves than in other people or societies. ❑ *...an insular and inward-looking community.* ADJ [disapproval]

**in|wards** /ɪnwəʳdz/ also **inward.** If something moves or faces **inwards**, it moves or faces towards the inside or centre of something. ❑ *She pressed back against the door until it swung inwards.* ADV: ADV after v ≠ outwards

**in-your-face** also **in-yer-face.** Someone who has an **in-your-face** attitude seems determined to behave in a way that is unusual or shocking, and does not care what people think of them. [INFORMAL] ❑ *It's in-your-face feminism.* ADJ: usu ADJ n

**iodine** /aɪədiːn, AM -daɪn/ **Iodine** is a dark-coloured substance used in medicine and photography. N-UNCOUNT

**ion** /aɪən/ **(ions)** **Ions** are electrically charged atoms. [TECHNICAL] N-COUNT: usu pl

**-ion** ➔ see **-ation**.

**ion|iz|er** /aɪənaɪzəʳ/ **(ionizers)**

✔ in BRIT, also use **ioniser**

An **ionizer** is a device which is meant to make the air in a room more healthy by removing positive ions. N-COUNT

**iota** /aɪoʊtə/ [1] If you say that there is not **an iota** or not **one iota** of something, you are emphasizing that there is not even a very small amount of it. ❑ *He's never shown an iota of interest in any kind of work.* QUANT: with brd-neg, QUANT *of* n-uncount [emphasis] = jot
[2] You can use **an iota** or **one iota** to emphasize a negative statement. **Not an iota** or **not one iota** means not even to a small extent or degree. ❑ *Our credit standards haven't changed one iota.* PHRASE: with brd-neg, PHR after v [emphasis] = jot

**IOU** /aɪ oʊ juː/ **(IOUs)** An **IOU** is a written promise that you will pay back some money that you have borrowed. **IOU** is an abbreviation for 'I owe you'. N-COUNT

**IP ad|dress** /aɪ piː ədres, AM ædres/ **(IP addresses)** An **IP address** is a series of numbers that identifies which particular computer or network is connected to the Internet. **IP** is an abbreviation for 'Internet Protocol'. [COMPUTING] ❑ *Every connection that you make to the network is stamped with your IP address.* N-COUNT

**ipso fac|to** /ɪpsoʊ fæktoʊ/ If something is **ipso facto** true, it must be true, because of a fact that has been mentioned. ❑ *If a crime occurs then there is, ipso facto, a guilty party.* ADV: ADV with cl/group

**IQ** /aɪ kjuː/ **(IQs)** Your **IQ** is your level of intelligence, as indicated by a special test that you do. **IQ** is an abbreviation for 'intelligence quotient'. Compare **EQ**. ❑ *His IQ is above average.* N-VAR: usu with supp

**ir-**

✔ Usually pronounced /ɪr-/ before an unstressed syllable, and /ɪr-/ before a stressed syllable.

**Ir-** is added to words that begin with the letter 'r' to form words with the opposite meaning. ❑ *His behaviour was becoming increasingly irrational. ...its mixture of satirical wit, irreverence and spontaneity.* PREFIX

**Ira|nian** /ɪreɪniən/ **(Iranians)** [1] **Iranian** means belonging or relating to Iran, or to its people or culture. ADJ [2] An **Iranian** is an Iranian citizen, or a person of Iranian origin. N-COUNT

**Ira|qi** /ɪrɑːki:, ɪræki/ **(Iraqis)** [1] **Iraqi** means belonging or relating to Iraq, or to its people or culture. ADJ [2] An **Iraqi** is an Iraqi citizen, or a person of Iraqi origin. N-COUNT

**iras|cible** /ɪræsɪbᵊl/ If you describe someone as **irascible**, you mean that they become angry very easily. [WRITTEN] ❑ *He had an irascible temper.* ADJ = fiery

**irate** /aɪreɪt/ If someone is **irate**, they are very angry about something. ❑ *The owner was so irate he almost threw me out of the place.* ADJ = furious

**IRC** /aɪ ɑːʳ siː/ **IRC** is a way of having conversations with people who are using the Internet, especially people you do not know. **IRC** is an abbreviation for 'Internet Relay Chat'. N-UNCOUNT

**ire** /aɪəʳ/ **Ire** is anger. [FORMAL] ❑ *Their ire was directed mainly at the government.* N-UNCOUNT = wrath, fury

**iri|des|cent** /ɪrɪdesᵊnt/ Something that is **iridescent** has many bright colours that seem to keep changing. [LITERARY] ❑ *...iridescent bubbles.* ADJ

**iris** /aɪərɪs/ **(irises)** [1] The **iris** is the round coloured part of a person's eye. N-COUNT [2] An **iris** is a tall plant with long leaves and large purple, yellow, or white flowers. N-COUNT

**Irish** /aɪərɪʃ/ [1] **Irish** means belonging or relating to Ireland, or to its people, language, or culture. **Irish** sometimes refers to the whole of Ireland, and sometimes only to the Republic of Ireland. ADJ [2] **The Irish** are the people of Ireland, or of the Republic of Ireland. N-PLURAL: usu *the* N [3] **Irish** is a Celtic language spoken by people who live in Ireland, especially in the Republic of Ireland. N-UNCOUNT

**Irish|man** /aɪərɪʃmən/ **(Irishmen)** An **Irishman** is a man who is an Irish citizen or is of Irish origin. N-COUNT

**Irish|woman** /aɪərɪʃwʊmən/ **(Irishwomen)** An **Irishwoman** is a woman who is an Irish citizen or is of Irish origin. N-COUNT

**irk** /ɜːʳk/ **(irks, irking, irked)** If something **irks** you, it irritates or annoys you. [FORMAL] ❑ *The rehearsal process also irked him increasingly... I must admit it irks me to see this guy get all this free publicity... It irks them that some people have more of a chance than others for their voices to be heard.* VERB V n *it* V n to-inf *it* V n that
♦ **irked** *Claire had seemed a little irked when he left.* ADJ: v-link ADJ

**irk|some** /ɜːʳksəm/ If something is **irksome**, it irritates or annoys you. [FORMAL] ❑ *...the irksome regulations.* ADJ = tiresome

**iron** /aɪəʳn/ **(irons, ironing, ironed)** ◆◇◇ [1] **Iron** is an element which usually takes the form of a hard, dark grey metal. It is used to make steel, and also forms part of many tools, buildings, and vehicles. Very small amounts of iron occur in your blood and in food. ❑ *The huge, iron gate was locked. ...the highest grade iron ore deposits in the world.* ➔ See also **cast-iron**. N-UNCOUNT: oft N n
[2] An **iron** is an electrical device with a flat metal base. You heat it until the base is hot, then rub it over clothes to remove creases. N-COUNT
[3] If you **iron** clothes, you remove the creases from them using an iron. ❑ *She used to iron his shirts. ...a freshly ironed shirt.* VERB V n V-ed
♦ **iron|ing** *I managed to get all the ironing done this morning.* N-UNCOUNT
[4] You can use **iron** to describe the character or behaviour of someone who is very firm in their decisions and actions, or who can control their feelings well. ❑ *...a man of icy nerve and iron will.* ADJ: ADJ n
[5] **Iron** is used in expressions such as **an iron hand** and **iron discipline** to describe strong, harsh, or unfair methods of control which do not allow people much freedom. ❑ *He died in* ADJ: ADJ n

*1985 after ruling Albania with an iron fist for 40 years.*
6 If someone has a lot of **irons in the fire**, they are involved in several different activities or have several different plans. PHRASE

♦ **iron out** If you **iron out** difficulties, you resolve them and bring them to an end. ❑ *It was in the beginning, when we were still ironing out problems.* PHRASAL VERB V P n (not pron)

**Iron Age The Iron Age** was a period of time which began when people started making things from iron about three thousand years ago. ❑ *...the remains of an Iron Age fort.* N-PROPER: the N

**iron|clad** /aɪəʳnklæd/ also **iron-clad.** If you describe a guarantee or plan as **ironclad**, you are emphasizing that it has been carefully put together, and that you think it is absolutely certain to work or be successful. ❑ *...ironclad guarantees of safe passage.* ADJ [emphasis]

**Iron Cur|tain** People referred to the border that separated the Soviet Union and the communist countries of Eastern Europe from the Western European countries as **the Iron Curtain**. N-PROPER: the N

**iron|ic** /aɪrɒnɪk/ or **ironical** /aɪrɒnɪkəl/
1 When you make an **ironic** remark, you say something that you do not mean, as a joke. ❑ *People used to call me Mr Popularity at high school, but they were being ironic.* ADJ 2 If you say that it is **ironic** that something should happen, you mean that it is odd or amusing because it involves a contrast. ❑ *Does he not find it ironic that the sort of people his movie celebrates hardly ever watch this kind of movie?* ADJ: oft it v-link ADJ that

**ironi|cal|ly** /aɪrɒnɪkli/ 1 You use **ironically** to draw attention to a situation which is odd or amusing because it involves a contrast. ❑ *Ironically, for a man who hated war, he would have made a superb war cameraman.* ADV: ADV with cl 2 If you say something **ironically**, you do not mean it and are saying it as a joke. ❑ *Classmates at West Point had ironically dubbed him Beauty.* ADV: ADV with v

**iron|ing board (ironing boards)** An **ironing board** is a long narrow board covered with cloth on which you iron clothes. N-COUNT

**iron|monger** /aɪəʳnmʌŋgəʳ/ **(ironmongers)**
1 An **ironmonger** is a shopkeeper who sells articles for the house and garden such as tools, nails, and pans. [BRIT] N-COUNT

✔ in AM, usually use **hardware dealer**

2 An **ironmonger** or an **ironmonger's** is a shop where articles for the house and garden such as tools, nails, and pans are sold. [BRIT] N-COUNT: oft the N

✔ in AM, usually use **hardware store**

**iron|mongery** /aɪəʳnmʌŋgəri/ **Ironmongery** is articles for the house and garden such as tools, nails, and pans which are sold in an ironmonger's shop. [BRIT] N-UNCOUNT = hardware

✔ in AM, usually use **hardware**

**iron|work** /aɪəʳnwɜːʳk/ Iron objects or structures are referred to as **ironwork**. ❑ *...the ironwork on the doors.* N-UNCOUNT

**iro|ny** /aɪrəni/ **(ironies)** 1 **Irony** is a subtle form of humour which involves saying things that you do not mean. ❑ *Sinclair examined the closed, clever face for any hint of irony, but found none.* N-UNCOUNT 2 If you talk about the **irony** of a situation, you mean that it is odd or amusing because it involves a contrast. ❑ *The irony is that many officials agree in private that their policy is inconsistent.* N-VAR: oft N of/in n

**ir|ra|di|ate** /ɪreɪdieɪt/ **(irradiates, irradiating, irradiated)** If someone or something **is irradiated**, they are exposed to a large amount of radioactivity. [TECHNICAL] ❑ *...the Chernobyl disaster, which irradiated large parts of Europe.* VERB V n ♦ **ir|ra|dia|tion** /ɪreɪdieɪʃən/ *...the harmful effects of irradiation and pollution.* N-UNCOUNT

**ir|ra|tion|al** /ɪræʃənəl/ If you describe someone's feelings and behaviour as **irrational**, you mean they are not based on logical reasons or clear thinking. ❑ *...an irrational fear of science.* ADJ = unreasonable ≠rational ♦ **ir|ra|tion|al|ly** *The market is behaving irrationally... My husband is irrationally jealous over my past loves.* ADV: ADV with v, ADV adj, ADV with cl ♦ **ir|ra|tion|al|ity** /ɪræʃənælɪti/ *...the irrationality of his behaviour.* N-UNCOUNT

**ir|rec|on|cil|able** /ɪrekənsaɪləbəl/ 1 If two things such as opinions or proposals are **irreconcilable**, they are so different from each other that it is not possible to believe or have both of them. [FORMAL] ❑ *These old concepts are irreconcilable with modern life.* ADJ: oft ADJ with n = incompatible 2 An **irreconcilable** disagreement or conflict is so serious that it cannot be settled. [FORMAL] ❑ *...an irreconcilable clash of personalities.* ADJ

**ir|re|deem|able** /ɪrɪdiːməbəl/ If someone or something has an **irredeemable** fault, it cannot be corrected. [FORMAL] ❑ *He is still, in the eyes of some, an irredeemable misogynist.* ADJ = incurable ♦ **ir|re|deem|ably** /ɪrɪdiːməbli/ *The applicant was irredeemably incompetent.* ADV: ADV adj/-ed

**ir|re|duc|ible** /ɪrɪdjuːsɪbəl/ **Irreducible** things cannot be made simpler or smaller. [FORMAL] ❑ *...the irreducible complexity of human life.* ADJ: usu ADJ n ≠reducible

**ir|refu|table** /ɪrɪfjuːtəbəl/ **Irrefutable** evidence, statements, or arguments cannot be shown to be incorrect or unsatisfactory. [FORMAL] ❑ *The pictures provide irrefutable evidence of the incident.* ADJ = indisputable

**ir|regu|lar** /ɪregjʊləʳ/ 1 If events or actions occur at **irregular** intervals, the periods of time between them are of different lengths. ❑ *Cars passed at irregular intervals... He worked irregular hours.* ADJ ≠regular ♦ **ir|regu|lar|ly** *He was eating irregularly, steadily losing weight.* ADV: ADV with v ♦ **ir|regu|lar|ity** /ɪregjʊlærɪti/ **(irregularities)** *...a dangerous irregularity in her heartbeat.* N-VAR 2 Something that is **irregular** is not smooth or straight, or does not form a regular pattern. ❑ *He had bad teeth, irregular and discolored.* ADJ = uneven ≠regular ♦ **ir|regu|lar|ly** *Located off-center in the irregularly shaped lake was a fountain.* ADV: usu ADV -ed ♦ **ir|regu|lar|ity** *...treatment of abnormalities or irregularities of the teeth.* N-VAR 3 **Irregular** behaviour is dishonest or not in accordance with the normal rules. ❑ *...the minister accused of irregular business practices.* ADJ ♦ **ir|regu|lar|ity** *...charges arising from alleged financial irregularities.* N-VAR 4 An **irregular** verb, noun, or adjective has different forms from most other verbs, nouns, or adjectives in the language. For example, 'break' is an irregular verb because its past form is 'broke', not 'breaked'. ADJ ≠regular

**ir|rel|evance** /ɪrelɪvəns/ **(irrelevances)** 1 If you talk about **the irrelevance of** something, you mean that it is irrelevant. ❑ *...the utter irrelevance of the debate.* N-UNCOUNT: oft N of n ≠relevance 2 If you describe something as an **irrelevance**, you have a low opinion of it because it is not important in a situation. ❑ *The Patriotic Front has been a political irrelevance.* N-COUNT

**ir|rel|evan|cy** /ɪrelɪvənsi/ **(irrelevancies)** If you describe something as an **irrelevancy**, you have a low opinion of it because it is not important in a situation. ❑ *Why was he wasting her time with these irrelevancies?* N-COUNT = irrelevance

**ir|rel|evant** /ɪrelɪvənt/ 1 If you describe something such as a fact or remark as **irrelevant**, you mean that it is not connected with what you are discussing or dealing with. ❑ *The government decided that their testimony would be irrelevant to the case.* ADJ: oft ADJ to n ≠relevant ♦ **ir|rel|evant|ly** *She would have hated the suit, I thought irrelevantly.* ADV: ADV with v, ADV with cl 2 If you say that something is **irrelevant**, you mean that it is not important in a situation. ❑ *The choice of subject matter is irrelevant.* ADJ: oft ADJ to n

**ir|re|li|gious** /ɪrɪlɪdʒəs/ An **irreligious** person does not accept the beliefs of any religion or opposes all religions. ADJ = atheistic

**ir|re|medi|able** /ɪrɪmiːdiəbəl/ If a bad situation or change is **irremediable**, the situation cannot be improved. [FORMAL] ❑ *His memory suffered irremediable damage.* ADJ = irreparable

**ir|repa|rable** /ɪreprəbəl/ **Irreparable** damage or harm is so bad that it cannot be repaired or put right. [FORMAL] ❑ *The move would cause irrepa-* ADJ = irreversible

*rable harm to the organization.* ♦ **ir|repa|rably** /ɪreprəbli/ *Her heart was irreparably damaged by a virus.*
ADV: ADV with v, ADV -ed

**ir|re|place|able** /ɪrɪpleɪsəbᵊl/ **Irreplaceable** things are so special that they cannot be replaced if they are lost or destroyed. ❑ *...a rare and irreplaceable jewel.*
ADJ ≠ replaceable

**ir|re|press|ible** /ɪrɪpresɪbᵊl/ An **irrepressible** person is lively and energetic and never seems to be depressed. ❑ *Jon's exuberance was irrepressible.* ♦ **ir|re|press|ibly** /ɪrɪpresɪbli/ *Gavin was irrepressibly rebellious.*
ADJ; ADV: usu ADV adj/-ed

**ir|re|proach|able** /ɪrɪproutʃəbᵊl/ If you say that someone's character or behaviour is **irreproachable**, you mean that they behave so well that they cannot be criticized.
ADJ = impeccable

**ir|re|sist|ible** /ɪrɪzɪstɪbᵊl/ **1** If you describe something such as a desire or force as **irresistible**, you mean that it is so powerful that it makes you act in a certain way, and there is nothing you can do to prevent this. ❑ *It proved an irresistible temptation to Hall to go back.* ♦ **ir|re|sist|ibly** /ɪrɪzɪstɪbli/ *I found myself irresistibly drawn to Steve's world.* **2** If you describe something or someone as **irresistible**, you mean that they are so good or attractive that you cannot stop yourself from liking them or wanting them. [INFORMAL] ❑ *The music is irresistible.* ♦ **ir|re|sist|ibly** *She had a gamine charm which men found irresistibly attractive.*
ADJ = overwhelming; ADV: ADV with v; ADJ; ADV: ADV adj

**ir|reso|lute** /ɪrezəluːt/ Someone who is **irresolute** cannot decide what to do. [FORMAL] ❑ *The worst reason to launch an attack would be a fear of seeming irresolute.*
ADJ = indecisive

**ir|re|spec|tive** /ɪrɪspektɪv/ If you say that something happens or should happen **irrespective of** a particular thing, you mean that it is not affected or should not be affected by that thing. [FORMAL] ❑ *...their commitment to a society based on equality for all citizens irrespective of ethnic origin.*
PREP-PHRASE = regardless of

**ir|re|spon|sible** /ɪrɪspɒnsɪbᵊl/ If you describe someone as **irresponsible**, you are criticizing them because they do things without properly considering their possible consequences. ❑ *I felt that it was irresponsible to advocate the legalisation of drugs.* ♦ **ir|re|spon|sibly** /ɪrɪspɒnsɪbli/ *They have behaved irresponsibly.* ♦ **ir|re|spon|sibil|ity** /ɪrɪspɒnsɪbɪlɪti/ *...the irresponsibility of people who advocate such destruction to our environment.*
ADJ: oft *it* v-link ADJ to-inf, disapproval, ≠ responsible; ADV: usu ADV with v; N-UNCOUNT

**ir|re|triev|able** /ɪrɪtriːvəbᵊl/ If you talk about **irretrievable** damage or an **irretrievable** situation, you mean that the damage or situation is so bad that there is no possibility of putting it right. [FORMAL] ❑ *...a country in irretrievable decline.* ♦ **ir|re|triev|ably** /ɪrɪtriːvəbli/ *Eventually her marriage broke down irretrievably.*
ADJ = irreparable; ADV: usu ADV with v

**ir|rev|er|ent** /ɪrevərənt/ If you describe someone as **irreverent**, you mean that they do not show respect for people or things that are generally respected. ❑ *Taylor combined great knowledge with an irreverent attitude to history.* ♦ **ir|rev|er|ence** *His irreverence for authority marks him out as a troublemaker.* ♦ **ir|rev|er|ent|ly** *'Jobs for the boys,' said Crosby irreverently.*
ADJ approval; N-UNCOUNT; ADV: ADV with v, ADV adj

**ir|re|vers|ible** /ɪrɪvɜːʳsɪbᵊl/ If a change is **irreversible**, things cannot be changed back to the way they were before. ❑ *She could suffer irreversible brain damage if she is not treated within seven days.* ♦ **ir|re|vers|ibly** *Television has irreversibly changed our perception of the Royal Family.*
ADJ; ADV: ADV with v

**ir|revo|cable** /ɪrevəkəbᵊl/ If a decision, action, or change is **irrevocable**, it cannot be changed or reversed. [FORMAL] ❑ *He said the decision was irrevocable.* ♦ **ir|revo|cably** /ɪrevəkəbli/ *My relationships with friends have been irrevocably altered by my illness.*
ADJ; ADV: usu ADV with v, also ADV adj

**ir|ri|gate** /ɪrɪgeɪt/ **(irrigates, irrigating, irrigated)** To **irrigate** land means to supply it with water in order to help crops grow. ❑ *None of the water from Lake Powell is used to irrigate the area.* ♦ **ir|ri|ga|tion** /ɪrɪgeɪʃᵊn/ *The agricultural land is hilly and the irrigation poor.*
VERB V n; N-UNCOUNT: oft N n

**ir|ri|table** /ɪrɪtəbᵊl/ If you are **irritable**, you are easily annoyed. ❑ *He had been waiting for over an hour and was beginning to feel irritable.* ♦ **ir|ri|tably** /ɪrɪtəbli/ *'Why are you whispering?' he asked irritably.* ♦ **ir|ri|tabil|ity** /ɪrɪtəbɪlɪti/ *Patients usually suffer from increased irritability.*
ADJ; ADV: ADV with v; N-UNCOUNT

**ir|ri|tant** /ɪrɪtənt/ **(irritants)** **1** If you describe something as an **irritant**, you mean that it keeps annoying you. [FORMAL] ❑ *He said the issue was not a major irritant.* **2** An **irritant** is a substance which causes a part of your body to itch or become sore. [FORMAL] ❑ *Many pesticides are irritants.*
N-COUNT = annoyance; N-COUNT

**ir|ri|tate** /ɪrɪteɪt/ **(irritates, irritating, irritated)** **1** If something **irritates** you, it keeps annoying you. ❑ *Their attitude irritates me... Perhaps they were irritated by the sound of crying.* ♦ **ir|ri|tat|ed** *Not surprisingly, her teacher is getting irritated with her.* **2** If something **irritates** a part of your body, it causes it to itch or become sore. ❑ *Wear rubber gloves while chopping chillies as they can irritate the skin.*
VERB = annoy V n; ADJ; VERB V n

**ir|ri|tat|ing** /ɪrɪteɪtɪŋ/ **1** Something that is **irritating** keeps annoying you. ❑ *They also have the irritating habit of interrupting.* ♦ **ir|ri|tat|ing|ly** *They can be irritatingly indecisive at times.* **2** An **irritating** substance can cause your body to itch or become sore. ❑ *In heavy concentrations, ozone is irritating to the eyes, nose and throat.*
ADJ = annoying; ADV: usu ADV adj; ADJ: oft ADJ *to* n

**ir|ri|ta|tion** /ɪrɪteɪʃᵊn/ **(irritations)** **1** **Irritation** is a feeling of annoyance, especially when something is happening that you cannot easily stop or control. ❑ *He tried not to let his irritation show as he blinked in the glare of the television lights.* **2** An **irritation** is something that keeps annoying you. ❑ *Don't allow a minor irritation in the workplace to mar your ambitions.* **3** **Irritation** in a part of your body is a feeling of slight pain and discomfort there. ❑ *These oils may cause irritation to sensitive skins.*
N-UNCOUNT = annoyance; N-COUNT = annoyance; N-VAR

**IRS** /aɪ ɑːr es/ In the United States, **the IRS** is the government authority which collects taxes. **IRS** is an abbreviation for 'Inland Revenue Service'.
N-PROPER: *the* N

**is** /ɪz/ **Is** is the third person singular of the present tense of **be**. **Is** is often added to other words and shortened to **-'s**.

**ISDN** /aɪ es diː en/ **ISDN** is a telephone network that can send voice and computer messages. **ISDN** is an abbreviation for 'Integrated Service Digital Network'. ❑ *...an ISDN phone line.*
N-UNCOUNT: oft N n

**-ise** /-aɪz/ → see **-ize**.

**-ish** /-ɪʃ/ **1** **-ish** is added to adjectives to form adjectives which indicate that someone or something has a quality to a small extent. For example, something that is largish is fairly large. ❑ *She is tallish, brown-haired, and clear-skinned... With her was a youngish man in a dinner jacket.* **2** **-ish** is added to nouns and names to form adjectives which indicate that someone or something is like a particular kind of person or thing. For example, 'childish' means like a child, or typical of a child. ❑ *She had entirely lost her girlish chubbiness. ...a man of monkish appearance.* **3** **-ish** is added to words referring to times, dates, or ages to form words which indicate that the time or age mentioned is approximate. ❑ *I'll call you guys tomorrow. Noonish... The nurse was fiftyish.*
SUFFIX; SUFFIX; SUFFIX

**Is|lam** /ɪzlɑːm, AM ɪslɑːm/ **1** **Islam** is the religion of the Muslims, which was started by Mohammed. **2** Some people use **Islam** to refer to all the countries where Islam is the main religion. ❑ *...relations between Islam and the West.*
N-UNCOUNT; N-UNCOUNT

**Is|lam|ic** /ɪzlæmɪk/ **Islamic** means belonging or relating to Islam. ❑ *...Islamic law. ...Islamic fundamentalists.*
ADJ: ADJ n

**Is|lam|ist** /ɪzləmɪst/ **(Islamists)** An **Islamist** is someone who believes strongly in Islamic ideas
N-COUNT: oft N n

and laws. ❑ *It was clear that there was significant support for the Islamists.*

**is|land** /aɪlənd/ **(islands)** An **island** is a piece of land that is completely surrounded by water. ❑ *...the Canary Islands.* ◆◆◇ N-COUNT; N-IN-NAMES

**is|land|er** /aɪləndəʳ/ **(islanders)** **Islanders** are people who live on an island. ❑ *The islanders endured centuries of exploitation.* N-COUNT: usu pl

**isle** /aɪl/ **(isles)** An **isle** is an island; often used as part of an island's name, or in literary English. ❑ *...the Isle of Man.* N-COUNT; N-IN-NAMES

**is|let** /aɪlət/ **(islets)** An **islet** is a small island. [LITERARY] N-COUNT

**-ism** /-ɪzəm/ **(-isms)** 1 **-ism** is used to form uncount nouns that refer to political or religious movements and beliefs. ❑ *Gere became interested in Buddhism in the 1970s. ...a time of growing Slovak nationalism.* SUFFIX 2 **-ism** is used to form uncount nouns that refer to attitudes and behaviour. ❑ *...an act of heroism... He didn't hide his pacifism.* SUFFIX 3 **-ism** is used to form uncount nouns that refer to unfair or hostile treatment of a particular group of people. ❑ *...discrimination based on racism, sexism and disability.* SUFFIX

**isn't** /ɪzᵊnt/ **Isn't** is the usual spoken form of 'is not'.

**iso|late** /aɪsəleɪt/ **(isolates, isolating, isolated)**
1 To **isolate** a person or organization means to cause them to lose their friends or supporters. ❑ *This policy could isolate the country from the other permanent members of the United Nations Security Council... Political influence is being used to shape public opinion and isolate critics.* ♦ **iso|lat|ed** *They are finding themselves increasingly isolated within the teaching profession.* ♦ **iso|la|tion** /aɪsəleɪʃᵊn/ *Diplomatic isolation could lead to economic disaster.* VERB; V n from n; V n; ADJ: usu v-link ADJ; N-UNCOUNT: usu with supp
2 If you **isolate yourself**, or if something **isolates** you, you become physically or socially separated from other people. ❑ *When he was thinking out a problem Tweed's habit was never to isolate himself in his room... His radicalism and refusal to compromise isolated him... Police officers had a siege mentality that isolated them from the people they served... But of course no one lives totally alone, isolated from the society around them.* VERB = cut off; V pron-refl; V n; V n from n; V-ed
3 If you **isolate** something such as an idea or a problem, you separate it from others that it is connected with, so that you can concentrate on it or consider it on its own. ❑ *Our anxieties can also be controlled by isolating thoughts, feelings and memories... Gandhi said that those who isolate religion from politics don't understand the nature of either.* VERB; V n; V n from n
4 To **isolate** a substance means to obtain it by separating it from other substances using scientific processes. [TECHNICAL] ❑ *We can use genetic engineering techniques to isolate the gene that is responsible... Researchers have isolated a new protein from the seeds of poppies.* VERB; V n; V n from n
5 To **isolate** a sick person or animal means to keep them apart from other people or animals, so that their illness does not spread. ❑ *You don't have to isolate them from the community.* VERB; V n from n

**iso|lat|ed** /aɪsəleɪtɪd/ 1 An **isolated** place is a long way away from large towns and is difficult to reach. ❑ *Many of the refugee villages are in isolated areas.* ADJ = remote 2 If you feel **isolated**, you feel lonely and without friends or help. ❑ *Some patients may become very isolated and depressed.* ADJ: usu v-link ADJ = cut off 3 An **isolated** example is an example of something that is not very common. ❑ *They said the allegations related to an isolated case of cheating.* ADJ: ADJ n = rare

**iso|la|tion** /aɪsəleɪʃᵊn/ 1 **Isolation** is the state of feeling alone and without friends or help. ❑ *Many deaf people have feelings of isolation and loneliness.* → See also **isolate**. N-UNCOUNT
**PHRASES** 2 If something is considered **in isolation from** other things that it is connected with, it is considered separately, and those other things are not considered. ❑ *Punishment cannot be discussed in isolation from social theory.* PHRASE: oft with brd-neg, PHR after v, oft PHR from n = separately 3 If someone does something **in isolation**, they do it without other people being present or without their help. ❑ *Malcolm works in isolation but I have no doubts about his abilities.* PHRASE: PHR after v = alone

**iso|la|tion|ism** /aɪsəleɪʃənɪzəm/ If you refer to **isolationism**, you are referring to a country's policy of avoiding close relationships with other countries and of not taking sides in disputes between other countries. ❑ *...the perils of isolationism.* N-UNCOUNT
♦ **iso|la|tion|ist** **(isolationists)** *The government had to overcome isolationist opposition to the plan.* N-COUNT: oft N n

**iso|met|rics** /aɪsəmetrɪks/

> ✔ The form **isometric** is used as a modifier.

**Isometrics** or **isometric** exercises are exercises in which you make your muscles work against each other or against something else, for example by pressing your hands together. N-PLURAL

**iso|tope** /aɪsətoʊp/ **(isotopes)** **Isotopes** are atoms that have the same number of protons and electrons but different numbers of neutrons and therefore have different physical properties. [TECHNICAL] ❑ *...tritium, a radioactive isotope of hydrogen.* N-COUNT

**ISP** /aɪ es piː/ **(ISPs)** An **ISP** is a company that provides Internet and e-mail services. **ISP** is an abbreviation for 'Internet Service Provider'. N-COUNT

**Is|rae|li** /ɪzreɪli/ **(Israelis)** 1 **Israeli** means belonging or relating to Israel, or to its people or culture. ADJ 2 An **Israeli** is an Israeli citizen, or a person of Israeli origin. N-COUNT

**is|sue** /ɪsjuː, ɪʃuː/ **(issues, issuing, issued)** ◆◆◆
1 An **issue** is an important subject that people are arguing about or discussing. ❑ *Agents will raise the issue of prize-money for next year's championships... Is it right for the Church to express a view on political issues?* → See also **side issue**. N-COUNT: usu with supp = subject, matter
2 If something is **the issue**, it is the thing you consider to be the most important part of a situation or discussion. ❑ *I was earning a lot of money, but that was not the issue... The real issue was never addressed.* N-SING: the N
3 An **issue** of something such as a magazine or newspaper is the version of it that is published, for example, in a particular month or on a particular day. ❑ *The growing problem is underlined in the latest issue of the Lancet.* N-COUNT = edition
4 If you **issue** a statement or a warning, you make it known formally or publicly. ❑ *Last night he issued a statement denying the allegations... Yesterday his kidnappers issued a second threat to kill him.* VERB = put out; V n; V n
5 If you **are issued with** something, it is officially given to you. ❑ *On your appointment you will be issued with a written statement of particulars of employment.* ♦ **Issue** is also a noun. ❑ *...a standard army issue rifle.* VERB: usu passive be V-ed with n; N-UNCOUNT: oft N n
6 When something such as a liquid, sound, or smell **issues from** something, it comes out of that thing. [FORMAL] ❑ *A tinny voice issued from a speaker.* VERB; V from n
**PHRASES** 7 The question or point **at issue** is the question or point that is being argued about or discussed. ❑ *The problems of immigration were not the question at issue.* PHRASE: usu v-link PHR
8 If you **make an issue of** something, you try to make other people think about it or discuss it, because you are concerned or annoyed about it. ❑ *It seemed the Colonel had no desire to make an issue of the affair.* PHRASE: V inflects
9 If you **take issue with** someone or something they said, you disagree with them, and start arguing about it. ❑ *I will not take issue with the fact that we have a recession.* PHRASE: V inflects, PHR n = argue

**is|sue price** **(issue prices)** The **issue price** of shares is the price at which they are offered for sale when they first become available to the public. [BUSINESS] ❑ *Shares in the company slipped below their issue price on their first day of trading.* N-COUNT

**-ist** /-ɪst/ **(-ists)** 1 **-ist** is used in place of -ism to form count nouns and adjectives. The nouns refer to people who have particular beliefs. The adjectives describe something related to or based on particular beliefs. ❑ *Later he was to become famous as a pacifist. ...fascist organisations.* SUFFIX 2 **-ist** is used to form count nouns referring to people who do a particular kind of work. ❑ *Susi Arnott is a biologist.* SUFFIX 3 **-ist** is added to nouns referring to mu- SUFFIX sical instruments, in order to form nouns that refer to people who play these instruments. ❑ *...Hungarian pianist Christina Kiss.*

**isth|mus** /ɪsməs/ **(isthmuses)** An **isthmus** is a narrow piece of land connecting two very large areas of land. ❑ *...the Isthmus of Panama.* — N-COUNT: oft in names

**it** /ɪt/ ◆◆◆

> ✔ **It** is a third person singular pronoun. **It** is used as the subject or object of a verb, or as the object of a preposition.

1 You use **it** to refer to an object, animal, or other thing that has already been mentioned. ❑ *It's a wonderful city, really. I'll show it to you if you want... My wife has become crippled by arthritis. She is embarrassed to ask the doctor about it.* — PRON
2 You use **it** to refer to a child or baby whose sex you do not know or whose sex is not relevant to what you are saying. ❑ *She could, if she wanted, compel him, through a court of law, to support the child after it was born.* — PRON
3 You use **it** to refer in a general way to a situation that you have just described. ❑ *He was through with sports, not because he had to be but because he wanted it that way.* — PRON
4 You use **it** before certain nouns, adjectives, and verbs to introduce your feelings or point of view about a situation. ❑ *It was nice to see Steve again... It seems that you are letting things get you down.* — PRON
5 You use **it** in passive clauses which report a situation or event. ❑ *It has been said that stress causes cancer.* — PRON
6 You use **it** with some verbs that need a subject or object, although there is no noun that it refers to. ❑ *Of course, as it turned out, three-fourths of the people in the group were psychiatrists.* — PRON
7 You use **it** as the subject of 'be', to say what the time, day, or date is. ❑ *It's three o'clock in the morning... It was a Monday, so she was at home.* — PRON
8 You use **it** as the subject of a link verb to describe the weather, the light, or the temperature. ❑ *It was very wet and windy the day I drove over the hill to Milland... It's getting dark. Let's go inside.* — PRON
9 You use **it** when you are telling someone who you are, or asking them who they are, especially at the beginning of a phone call. You also use **it** in statements and questions about the identity of other people. ❑ *'Who is it?' he called. — 'It's your neighbor.'... Hello Freddy, it's only me, Maxine.* — PRON
10 When you are emphasizing or drawing attention to something, you can put that thing immediately after **it** and a form of the verb 'be'. ❑ *It was the country's rulers who devised this system.* — PRON emphasis
11 You use **it** in expressions such as **it's not that** or **it's not simply that** when you are giving a reason for something and are suggesting that there are several other reasons. ❑ *It's not that I didn't want to be with my family.* — PHRASE
12 **if it wasn't for** → see **be**.

**IT** /aɪ tiː/ **IT** is an abbreviation for **information technology**.

**Ital|ian** /ɪtæliən/ **(Italians)** 1 **Italian** means belonging or relating to Italy, or to its people, language, or culture. — ADJ
2 An **Italian** is an Italian citizen, or a person of Italian origin. — N-COUNT
3 **Italian** is the language spoken in Italy, and in parts of Switzerland. — N-UNCOUNT

**ital|ic** /ɪtælɪk/ **(italics)** 1 **Italics** are letters which slope to the right. Italics are often used to emphasize a particular word or sentence. The examples in this dictionary are printed in italics. — N-PLURAL
2 **Italic** letters slope to the right. ❑ *She addressed them by hand in her beautiful italic script.* — ADJ: ADJ n

**itch** /ɪtʃ/ **(itches, itching, itched)** 1 When a part of your body **itches**, you have an unpleasant feeling on your skin that makes you want to scratch. ❑ *When someone has hayfever, the eyes and nose will stream and itch. ...dry, itching skin.* ♦ **Itch** is also a noun. ❑ *Scratch my back – I've got an itch.* ♦ **itch|ing** *It may be that the itching is caused by contact with irritant material.* — VERB; V; V-ing; N-COUNT; N-UNCOUNT
2 If you **are itching** to do something, you are very eager or impatient to do it. [INFORMAL] ❑ *I was itching to get involved and to bring my own theories into practice... The general was itching for a fight.* ♦ **Itch** is also a noun. ❑ *...viewers with an insatiable itch to switch channels.* — VERB: usu cont; V to-inf; V for n; N-SING: usu N to-inf

**itchy** /ɪtʃi/ 1 If a part of your body or something you are wearing is **itchy**, you have an unpleasant feeling on your skin that makes you want to scratch. [INFORMAL] ❑ *...itchy, sore eyes.* — ADJ
2 If you have **itchy feet**, you have a strong desire to leave a place and to travel. [INFORMAL] ❑ *The trip gave me itchy feet and I wanted to travel more.* — PHRASE: usu PHR after v

**it'd** /ɪtəd/ 1 **It'd** is a spoken form of 'it would'. ❑ *It'd be better for a place like this to remain closed.* 2 **It'd** is a spoken form of 'it had', especially when 'had' is an auxiliary verb. ❑ *Marcie was watching the news. It'd just started.*

**item** /aɪtəm/ **(items)** ◆◆◇ 1 An **item** is one of a collection or list of objects. ❑ *The most valuable item on show will be a Picasso drawing.* → See also **collector's item**. — N-COUNT
2 An **item** is one of a list of things for someone to do, deal with, or talk about. ❑ *The other item on the agenda is the tour.* — N-COUNT = matter, topic
3 An **item** is a report or article in a newspaper or magazine, or on television or radio. ❑ *There was an item in the paper about him.* — N-COUNT
4 If you say that two people are an **item**, you mean that they are having a romantic or sexual relationship. [INFORMAL] ❑ *She and Gino were an item.* — N-SING: a N

**item|ize** /aɪtəmaɪz/ **(itemizes, itemizing, itemized)**

> ✔ in BRIT, also use **itemise**

If you **itemize** a number of things, you make a list of them. ❑ *Itemise your gear and mark major items with your name and post code. ...a fully itemised bill.* — VERB; V n; V-ed

**It-girl** **(It-girls)** also **It girl.** Journalists sometimes use **It-girl** to describe a young woman who is well-known because she goes to the most fashionable places and events and knows famous people. [INFORMAL, JOURNALISM] ❑ *It-girl Tamara Beckwith was livid at being turned away from the party.* — N-COUNT

**itin|er|ant** /aɪtɪnərənt/ **(itinerants)** 1 An **itinerant** worker travels around a region, working for short periods in different places. [FORMAL] ❑ *...the author's experiences as an itinerant musician.* — ADJ: ADJ n = travelling
2 An **itinerant** is someone whose way of life involves travelling around, usually someone who is poor and homeless. [FORMAL] — N-COUNT

**itin|er|ary** /aɪtɪnərəri, AM -eri/ **(itineraries)** An **itinerary** is a plan of a journey, including the route and the places that you will visit. ❑ *The next place on our itinerary was Silistra.* — N-COUNT

**it'll** /ɪtᵊl/ **It'll** is a spoken form of 'it will'. ❑ *It's ages since I've seen her so it'll be nice to meet her in town on Thursday.*

**its** /ɪts/ ◆◆◆

> ✔ **Its** is a third person singular possessive determiner.

You use **its** to indicate that something belongs or relates to a thing, place, or animal that has just been mentioned or whose identity is known. You can use **its** to indicate that something belongs or relates to a child or baby. ❑ *The British Labor Party concludes its annual conference today in Brighton. ...Japan, with its extreme housing shortage.* — DET

**it's** /ɪts/ 1 **It's** is the usual spoken form of 'it is'. ❑ *It's the best news I've heard in a long time.* 2 **It's** is the usual spoken form of 'it has', especially when 'has' is an auxiliary verb. ❑ *It's been such a long time since I played.*

**it|self** /ɪtself/ ◆◆◆ 1 **Itself** is used as the object of a verb or preposition when it refers to something that is the same thing as the subject of the verb. ❑ *Scientists have discovered remarkable new evidence showing how the body rebuilds itself while we sleep... Unemployment does not correct itself.* — PRON: v PRON, prep PRON
2 You use **itself** to emphasize the thing you are referring to. ❑ *I think life itself is a learning process... The involvement of the foreign ministers was itself a sign of progress.* — PRON emphasis
3 If you say that someone is, for exam- — PRON:

ple, politeness **itself** or kindness **itself**, you are emphasizing they are extremely polite or extremely kind. ❑ *I was never really happy there, although the people were kindness itself.* [4] **an end in itself** → see **end**. n PRON [emphasis]

**ITV** /aɪ tiː viː/ [1] **ITV** refers to the group of British commercial television companies that broadcasts programmes on one channel. **ITV** is an abbreviation for 'Independent Television'. [BRIT] ❑ *ITV has set its sights on winning a younger and more upmarket audience.* [2] **ITV** is the television channel that is run by ITV. ❑ *The first episode will be shown tomorrow at 10.40pm on ITV.* ◆◇◇ N-PROPER-COLL; N-PROPER

**-ity** /-ɪti/ **(-ities)** **-ity** is added to adjectives, sometimes in place of '-ious', to form nouns referring to the state, quality, or behaviour described by the adjective. ❑ *He enjoyed the tranquillity of village life. ...life with all its contradictions and complexities.* SUFFIX

**IUD** /aɪ juː diː/ **(IUDs)** An **IUD** is a piece of plastic or metal which is put inside a woman's womb in order to prevent her from becoming pregnant. **IUD** is an abbreviation for 'intra-uterine device'. N-COUNT = *coil*

**I've** /aɪv/ **I've** is the usual spoken form of 'I have', especially when 'have' is an auxiliary verb. ❑ *I've been invited to meet with the American Ambassador... I've no other appointments.*

**IVF** /aɪ viː ef/ **IVF** is a method of helping a woman to have a baby in which an egg is removed from one of her ovaries, fertilized outside her body, and then replaced in her womb. **IVF** is an abbreviation for 'in vitro fertilization'. N-UNCOUNT

**ivo|ry** /aɪvəri/ [1] **Ivory** is a hard cream-coloured substance which forms the tusks of elephants. It is valuable and can be used for making carved ornaments. ❑ *...the international ban on the sale of ivory.* [2] **Ivory** is a creamy-white colour. N-UNCOUNT; COLOUR

**ivo|ry tow|er** **(ivory towers)** If you describe someone as living in an **ivory tower**, you mean that they have no knowledge or experience of the practical problems of everyday life. ❑ *They don't really, in their ivory towers, understand how pernicious drug crime is.* N-COUNT: usu prep N, N n [disapproval]

**ivy** /aɪvi/ **(ivies)** **Ivy** is an evergreen plant that grows up walls or along the ground. N-VAR

**Ivy League** **The Ivy League** is a group of eight universities in the north-eastern part of the United States, which have high academic and social status. ❑ *...an Ivy League college.* N-PROPER: *the* N; oft N n

**-ize** /-aɪz/ **(-izes, -izing, -ized)**

✔ in BRIT, also use **-ise**

Verbs that can end in either '-ize' or '-ise' are dealt with in this dictionary at the '-ize' spelling. Many verbs ending in **-ize** describe processes by which things or people are brought into a new state. ❑ *The dispute could jeopardize the negotiations. ...a way of trying to regularize and standardize practice.* SUFFIX

# J j

**J, j** /dʒeɪ/ **(J's, j's) J** is the tenth letter of the English alphabet. N-VAR

**jab** /dʒæb/ **(jabs, jabbing, jabbed)** 1 If you **jab** one thing into another, you push it there with a quick, sudden movement and with a lot of force. VERB = stab ❑ *He saw her jab her thumb on a red button – a panic button... A needle was jabbed into the baby's arm... Stern jabbed at me with his glasses.* V n prep; be V-ed *into* n; V *at* n 2 A **jab** is a sudden, sharp punch. N-COUNT ❑ *He was simply too powerful for his opponent, rocking him with a steady supply of left jabs.* 3 A **jab** is an injection of something into your blood to prevent illness. [BRIT, INFORMAL] N-COUNT ❑ *...painful anti malaria jabs.*

**jab|ber** /dʒæbəʳ/ **(jabbers, jabbering, jabbered)** If you say that someone **is jabbering**, you mean that they are talking very quickly and excitedly, and you cannot understand them. VERB [disapproval] ❑ *The girl jabbered incomprehensibly... After a minute or two I left them there jabbering away.* V; V *away*

**jack** /dʒæk/ **(jacks)** 1 A **jack** is a device for lifting a heavy object off the ground, for example a car. N-COUNT 2 A **jack** is a playing card whose value is between a ten and a queen. A jack is usually represented by a picture of a young man. N-COUNT: oft N *of* n 3 → See also **jack-of-all-trades, Union Jack.**

♦ **jack up** If you **jack up** a heavy object such as a car, you raise it off the ground using a jack. PHRASAL VERB ❑ *They jacked up the car... All I had to do was jack the car up and put on the spare.* V P n; V n P

**jack|al** /dʒækɔːl/ **(jackals)** A **jackal** is a wild animal that looks like a dog, has long legs and pointed ears, and lives in Africa and Southern Asia. N-COUNT

**jack|boot** /dʒækbuːt/ **(jackboots)** 1 **Jackboots** are heavy boots that come up to the knee, such as the ones worn by some soldiers. N-COUNT: usu pl 2 If a country or group of people is **under the jackboot**, they are suffering because the government is cruel and undemocratic. PHRASE [disapproval]

**jack|daw** /dʒækdɔː/ **(jackdaws)** A **jackdaw** is a large black and grey bird that is similar to a crow, and lives in Europe and Asia. N-COUNT

**jack|et** /dʒækɪt/ **(jackets)** ◆◇◇ 1 A **jacket** is a short coat with long sleeves. N-COUNT ❑ *...a black leather jacket.* 2 Potatoes baked in their **jackets** are baked with their skin on. N-COUNT: usu pl 3 The **jacket** of a book is the paper cover that protects the book. [mainly AM] N-COUNT 4 A record **jacket** is the cover in which a record is kept. [AM] N-COUNT

✔ in BRIT, use **sleeve**

5 → See also **bomber jacket, dinner jacket, flak jacket, hacking jacket, life jacket, sports jacket, straitjacket.**

**jack|et po|ta|to** **(jacket potatoes)** A **jacket potato** is a large potato that has been baked with its skin on. [BRIT] N-COUNT = baked potato

✔ in AM, use **baked potato**

**jack-in-the-box** **(jack-in-the-boxes)** A **jack-in-the-box** is a child's toy that consists of a box with a doll inside it that jumps out when the lid is opened. N-COUNT

**jack-knife** **(jack-knifes, jack-knifing, jack-knifed)** also **jackknife.** If a truck that is in two parts **jack-knifes**, the back part swings around at a sharp angle to the front part in an uncontrolled way as the truck is moving. VERB ❑ *His vehicle jack-knifed, and crashed across all three lanes of the opposite carriageway.* V

**jack-of-all-trades** **(jacks-of-all-trades)** also **jack of all trades.** If you refer to someone as a **jack-of-all-trades**, you mean that they are able to do a variety of different jobs. You are also often suggesting that they are not very good at any of these jobs. N-COUNT

**jack|pot** /dʒækpɒt/ **(jackpots)** 1 A **jackpot** is the most valuable prize in a game or lottery, especially when the game involves increasing the value of the prize until someone wins it. N-COUNT: usu sing ❑ *A nurse won the £5 million jackpot.* 2 If you **hit the jackpot**, you have a great success, for example by winning a lot of money or having a piece of good luck. [INFORMAL] PHRASE: V inflects

**Jaco|bean** /dʒækəbiːən/ A **Jacobean** building, piece of furniture, or work of art was built or produced in Britain in the style of the period between 1603 and 1625. ADJ: usu ADJ n

**Ja|cuz|zi** /dʒəkuːzi/ **(Jacuzzis)** A **Jacuzzi** is a large circular bath which is fitted with a device that makes the water move around. [TRADEMARK] N-COUNT

**jade** /dʒeɪd/ **Jade** is a hard stone, usually green in colour, that is used for making jewellery and ornaments. N-UNCOUNT

**jad|ed** /dʒeɪdɪd/ If you are **jaded**, you feel bored, tired, and not enthusiastic, for example because you have had too much of the same thing. ADJ = bored ❑ *We had both become jaded, disinterested, and disillusioned.*

**jag|ged** /dʒægɪd/ Something that is **jagged** has a rough, uneven shape or edge with lots of sharp points. ADJ ❑ *...jagged black cliffs... A jagged scar runs through his lower lip.*

**jagu|ar** /dʒægjuəʳ, AM -gwɑːr/ **(jaguars)** A **jaguar** is a large animal of the cat family with dark spots on its back. N-COUNT

**jail** /dʒeɪl/ **(jails, jailing, jailed)** ◆◇◇

✔ in BRIT, also use **gaol**

1 A **jail** is a place where criminals are kept in order to punish them, or where people waiting to be tried are kept. N-VAR = prison ❑ *Three prisoners escaped from a jail.* 2 If someone **is jailed**, they are put into jail. VERB: usu passive ❑ *He was jailed for twenty years.* be V-ed

**jail|bird** /dʒeɪlbɜːʳd/ **(jailbirds)** If you refer to someone as a **jailbird**, you mean that they are in prison, or have been in prison. [INFORMAL, OLD-FASHIONED] N-COUNT = convict

**jail|break** /dʒeɪlbreɪk/ **(jailbreaks)** A **jailbreak** is an escape from jail. N-COUNT

**jail|er** /dʒeɪləʳ/ **(jailers)**

✔ in BRIT, also use **gaoler**

A **jailer** is a person who is in charge of a jail and the prisoners in it. [OLD-FASHIONED] N-COUNT = warder

**jail|house** /dʒeɪlhaʊs/ **(jailhouses)** A **jailhouse** is a small prison. [AM] N-COUNT

**jala|peño** /hæləpeɪnjoʊ/ **(jalapeños)** **Jalapeños** are small hot peppers which can be green or red when they are ripe. They are often used in Mexican cooking. N-COUNT

**jam** /dʒæm/ **(jams, jamming, jammed)** 1 **Jam** is a thick sweet food that is made by cooking fruit N-MASS with a large amount of sugar, and that is usually spread on bread. [mainly BRIT] ❑ *...home-made jam.*

in AM, usually use **jelly**

2 If you **jam** something somewhere, you push or put it there roughly. ❑ *He picked his cap up off the ground and jammed it on his head... Pete jammed his hands into his pockets.* 3 If something such as a part of a machine **jams**, or if something **jams** it, the part becomes fixed in position and is unable to move freely or work properly. ❑ *The second time he fired his gun jammed... A rope jammed the boat's propeller... Cracks appeared in the wall and a door jammed shut... The intake valve was jammed open... Every few minutes the motor cut out as the machinery became jammed.* 4 If vehicles **jam** a road, there are so many of them that they cannot move. ❑ *Hundreds of departing motorists jammed the roads.* ♦ **Jam** is also a noun. ❑ *Trucks sat in a jam for ten hours waiting to cross the bridge.* ♦ **jammed** *Nearby roads and the dirt track to the beach were jammed with cars.* 5 If a lot of people **jam** a place, or **jam into** a place, they are pressed tightly together so that they can hardly move. ❑ *Hundreds of people jammed the boardwalk to watch... They jammed into buses provided by the Red Cross and headed for safety.* ♦ **jammed** *The stadium was jammed and they had to turn away hundreds of disappointed fans.* 6 To **jam** a radio or electronic signal means to interfere with it and prevent it from being received or heard clearly. ❑ *They will try to jam the transmissions electronically.* ♦ **jam|ming** *The plane is used for electronic jamming and radar detection.* 7 If callers **are jamming** telephone lines, there are so many callers that the people answering the telephones find it difficult to deal with them all. ❑ *Hundreds of callers jammed the BBC switchboard for more than an hour.* 8 When jazz or rock musicians **are jamming**, they are informally playing music that has not been written down or planned in advance. [INFORMAL] ❑ *He was jamming with his saxophone.* ♦ **Jam** is also a noun. ❑ *...a jam session.* 9 → See also **traffic jam**.

VERB; V n prep; V n prep; VERB; V; V n; V adj; *be* V-ed adj; V-ed; Also V n adj; VERB; V n; N-COUNT; ADJ: oft ADJ *with* n; VERB = cram; V n; V *into* n; ADJ = packed; VERB; V n; N-UNCOUNT: usu with supp; VERB; V n; VERB; V; N-COUNT

**Ja|mai|can** /dʒəmeɪkən/ **(Jamaicans)** 1 **Jamaican** means belonging or relating to Jamaica or to its people or culture. 2 A **Jamaican** is a person who comes from Jamaica. ADJ; N-COUNT

**jamb** /dʒæm/ **(jambs)** A **jamb** is a post that forms the side part or upright of a door frame or window frame. N-COUNT: usu n N

**jam|bo|ree** /dʒæmbəriː/ **(jamborees)** A **jamboree** is a party, celebration, or other gathering where there is a large number of people and a lot of excitement, fun, and enjoyment. N-COUNT: usu sing

**jam|my** /dʒæmi/ **(jammier, jammiest)** If you describe someone as **jammy**, you mean that they are very lucky because something good has happened to them, without their making much effort or deserving such luck. [BRIT, INFORMAL] ADJ: usu ADJ n

**jam-packed** If somewhere is **jam-packed**, it is so full of people or things that there is no room for any more. [INFORMAL] ❑ *His room was jam-packed with fruit, flowers, gifts etc.* ADJ: oft ADJ *with* n = packed

**Jan.** Jan. is a written abbreviation for **January**.

**jan|gle** /dʒæŋgəl/ **(jangles, jangling, jangled)** 1 When objects strike against each other and make an unpleasant ringing noise, you can say that they **jangle** or **are jangled**. ❑ *Her bead necklaces and bracelets jangled as she walked... Jane took out her keys and jangled them.* 2 If your nerves **are jangling** or if something **jangles** them, you are very anxious. ❑ *Behind that quietness his nerves are jangling, he's in a terrible state... The caffeine in coffee can jangle the nerves.* VERB; V; V n; VERB; V; V n

**jani|tor** /dʒænɪtəʳ/ **(janitors)** A **janitor** is a person whose job is to look after a building. [mainly AM] N-COUNT = caretaker

**Janu|ary** /dʒænjəri, AM -jueri/ **(Januaries)** **January** is the first month of the year in the Western calendar. ❑ *We always have snow in January... She was born on January 6, 1946.* N-VAR

**Japa|nese** /dʒæpəniːz/ **(Japanese)** 1 **Japanese** means belonging or relating to Japan, or to its people, language, or culture. 2 The **Japanese** are the people of Japan. 3 **Japanese** is the language spoken in Japan. ADJ; N-PLURAL; N-UNCOUNT

**jape** /dʒeɪp/ **(japes)** A **jape** is a silly trick that you play on someone which is quite funny and which does not really involve upsetting them. [OLD-FASHIONED] N-COUNT = prank

**jar** /dʒɑːʳ/ **(jars, jarring, jarred)** 1 A **jar** is a glass container with a lid that is used for storing food. ❑ *...yellow cucumbers in great glass jars.* 2 You can use **jar** to refer to a jar and its contents, or to the contents only. ❑ *She opened up a glass jar of plums. ...two jars of filter coffee.* 3 If something **jars on** you, you find it unpleasant, disturbing, or shocking. ❑ *Sometimes a light remark jarred on her father. ...televised congressional hearings that jarred the nation's faith in the presidency... You shouldn't have too many colours in a small space as the effect can jar.* ♦ **jar|ring** *In the context of this chapter, Dore's comments strike a jarring note.* 4 If an object **jars**, or if something **jars** it, the object moves with a fairly hard shaking movement. ❑ *The ship jarred a little... The impact jarred his arm.* N-COUNT; N-COUNT: oft N *of* n; VERB; V *on* n; V n; V; ADJ; VERB; V, V n

**jar|gon** /dʒɑːʳgən/ You use **jargon** to refer to words and expressions that are used in special or technical ways by particular groups of people, often making the language difficult to understand. ❑ *The manual is full of the jargon and slang of self-improvement courses.* N-UNCOUNT

**jas|mine** /dʒæzmɪn/ **(jasmines)** **Jasmine** is a climbing plant which has small white or yellow flowers with a pleasant smell. N-VAR

**jaun|dice** /dʒɔːndɪs/ **Jaundice** is an illness that makes your skin and eyes become yellow. N-UNCOUNT

**jaun|diced** /dʒɔːndɪst/ If someone has a **jaundiced** view of something, they can see only the bad aspects of it. ❑ *The financial markets are taking a jaundiced view of the Government's motives.* ADJ: usu ADJ n

**jaunt** /dʒɔːnt/ **(jaunts)** A **jaunt** is a short journey which you go on for pleasure or excitement. N-COUNT = trip

**jaun|ty** /dʒɔːnti/ **(jauntier, jauntiest)** If you describe someone or something as **jaunty**, you mean that they are full of confidence and energy. ❑ *...a jaunty little man.* ♦ **jaun|ti|ly** /dʒɔːntɪli/ *He walked jauntily into the cafe.* ADJ: usu ADJ n; ADV: ADV with v, ADV adj

**Java** /dʒɑːvə/ **Java** is a computer programming language. It is used especially in creating websites. [TRADEMARK] N-UNCOUNT

**jave|lin** /dʒævlɪn/ **(javelins)** 1 A **javelin** is a long spear that is used in sports competitions. Competitors try to throw the javelin as far as possible. 2 You can refer to the competition in which the javelin is thrown as **the javelin**. ❑ *...Steve Backley who won the javelin.* N-COUNT; N-SING: *the* N

**jaw** /dʒɔː/ **(jaws)** 1 Your **jaw** is the lower part of your face below your mouth. The movement of your jaw is sometimes considered to express a particular emotion. For example, if your **jaw drops**, you are very surprised. ❑ *He thought for a moment, stroking his well-defined jaw.* 2 A person's or animal's **jaws** are the two bones in their head which their teeth are attached to. ❑ *...a forest rodent with powerful jaws.* 3 If you talk about the **jaws of** something unpleasant such as death or hell, you are referring to a dangerous or unpleasant situation. ❑ *A family dog rescued a newborn boy from the jaws of death.* N-COUNT: usu sing, poss N; N-COUNT; N-PLURAL: N *of* n

**jaw|bone** /dʒɔːboʊn/ **(jawbones)** also **jaw bone.** A **jawbone** is the bone in the lower jaw of a person or animal. N-COUNT

**jaw-dropping** Something that is **jaw-dropping** is extremely surprising, impressive, or shocking. [mainly BRIT, INFORMAL, JOURNALISM] ❑ *One insider who has seen the report said it was pretty jaw-dropping stuff.* ADJ = amazing

**jaw|line** /dʒɔːlaɪn/ **(jawlines)** also **jaw line.** Your **jawline** is the part of your lower jaw which N-COUNT: usu sing forms the outline of the bottom of your face. ❑ *...high cheekbones and strong jawline.*

**jay** /dʒeɪ/ **(jays)** [1] In Europe and Asia, a **jay** is a brownish-pink bird with blue and black wings. N-COUNT [2] In North America, a **jay** is a bird with bright blue feathers. N-COUNT

**jay|walk|ing** /dʒeɪwɔːkɪŋ/ **Jaywalking** is the act of walking across a street in a careless and dangerous way, or not at the proper place. N-UNCOUNT

**jazz** /dʒæz/ **(jazzes, jazzing, jazzed) Jazz** is a style of music that was invented by African American musicians in the early part of the twentieth century. Jazz music has very strong rhythms and often involves improvisation. ❑ *The pub has live jazz on Sundays.* ◆◇◇ N-UNCOUNT: oft N n

♦ **jazz up** [1] If you **jazz** something **up**, you make it look more interesting, colourful, or exciting. [INFORMAL] ❑ *Mary Ann had made an effort at jazzing up the chilly modern interiors... I don't think they're just jazzing it up for the media.* PHRASAL VERB V P n (not pron) V n P [2] If someone **jazzes up** a piece of music, they change it in order to make it sound more like popular music or jazz. ❑ *Instead of playing it in the traditional style, she jazzed it up... Stephen and I are going to jazz up the love songs.* PHRASAL VERB V n P V P n (not pron)

**jazzy** /dʒæzi/ **(jazzier, jazziest)** If you describe something as **jazzy**, you mean that it is colourful and modern. ❑ *...a jazzy tie.* ADJ: usu ADJ n

**jeal|ous** /dʒeləs/ [1] If someone is **jealous**, they feel angry or bitter because they think that another person is trying to take a lover or friend, or a possession, away from them. ❑ *She got insanely jealous and there was a terrible fight.* ADJ ♦ **jeal|ous|ly** *The formula is jealously guarded.* ADV: ADV with v [2] If you are **jealous of** another person's possessions or qualities, you feel angry or bitter because you do not have them. ❑ *She was jealous of his wealth... You're jealous because the record company rejected your idea.* ADJ: oft ADJ *of* n ♦ **jeal|ous|ly** *Gloria eyed them jealously.* ADV: ADV after v

**jeal|ousy** /dʒeləsi/ **(jealousies)** [1] **Jealousy** is the feeling of anger or bitterness which someone has when they think that another person is trying to take a lover or friend, or a possession, away from them. ❑ *At first his jealousy only showed in small ways – he didn't mind me talking to other guys.* N-UNCOUNT: also N in pl [2] **Jealousy** is the feeling of anger or bitterness which someone has when they wish that they could have the qualities or possessions that another person has. ❑ *Her beauty causes envy and jealousy.* N-UNCOUNT: also N in pl

**jeans** /dʒiːnz/ **Jeans** are casual trousers that are usually made of strong blue cotton cloth called denim. N-PLURAL: also *a pair of* N

**Jeep** /dʒiːp/ **(Jeeps)** A **Jeep** is a type of car that can travel over rough ground. [TRADEMARK] ❑ *...a U.S. Army Jeep.* N-COUNT

**jeer** /dʒɪəʳ/ **(jeers, jeering, jeered)** [1] To **jeer at** someone means to say or shout rude and insulting things to them to show that you do not like or respect them. ❑ *Marchers jeered at white passers-by, but there was no violence, nor any arrests... Demonstrators have jeered the mayor as he arrived for a week long visit... I didn't come here today to jeer: I want to give advice. ...mobs of jeering bystanders.* VERB V *at* n V n V V-ing ♦ **jeer|ing** *There was constant jeering and interruption from the floor.* N-UNCOUNT [2] **Jeers** are rude and insulting things that people shout to show they do not like or respect someone. ❑ *...the heckling and jeers of his audience.* N-COUNT: usu pl

**Jeez** /dʒiːz/ also **Jees.** Some people say **Jeez** when they are shocked or surprised about something, or to introduce a remark or response. **Jeez** is short for 'Jesus'. This use could cause offence. [INFORMAL] ❑ *Jeez, I wish they'd tell us what the hell is going on.* EXCLAM

**Je|ho|vah** /dʒɪhoʊvə/ **Jehovah** is the name given to God in the Old Testament. N-PROPER

**Je|ho|vah's Wit|ness (Jehovah's Witnesses)** A **Jehovah's Witness** is a member of a religious organization which accepts some Christian ideas and believes that the world is going to end very soon. N-COUNT

**je|june** /dʒɪdʒuːn/ [1] If you describe something or someone as **jejune**, you are criticizing them for being very simple and unsophisticated. [FORMAL] ❑ *They were of great service in correcting my jejune generalizations.* ADJ [disapproval] [2] If you describe something or someone as **jejune**, you mean they are dull and boring. [OLD-FASHIONED] ❑ *We knew we were in for a pretty long, jejune evening.* ADJ

**jell** /dʒel/ → see **gel**.

**jel|lied** /dʒelid/ **Jellied** food is prepared and eaten in a jelly. ❑ *...jellied eels.* ADJ: ADJ n

**Jell-O Jell-O** is a transparent, usually coloured food that is eaten as a dessert. It is made from gelatine, fruit juice, and sugar. [AM, TRADEMARK] N-UNCOUNT

☑ in BRIT, use **jelly**

**jel|ly** /dʒeli/ **(jellies)** [1] **Jelly** is a transparent, usually coloured food that is eaten as a dessert. It is made from gelatine, fruit juice, and sugar. [BRIT] ❑ *...a large bowl of jelly.* N-MASS

☑ in AM, use **Jell-O**

[2] **Jelly** is a thick sweet food that is made by cooking fruit with a large amount of sugar, and that is usually spread on bread. [AM] ❑ *I had two peanut butter and jelly sandwiches.* N-MASS

☑ in BRIT, use **jam**

[3] A **jelly** is a transparent substance that is not completely solid. ❑ *...meat in jelly.* N-VAR [4] → See also **royal jelly**.

**jel|ly bean (jelly beans)** also **jellybean. Jelly beans** are small coloured sweets that are hard on the outside and soft inside. N-COUNT: usu pl

**jelly|fish** /dʒelifɪʃ/ **(jellyfish)** A **jellyfish** is a sea creature that has a clear soft body and can sting you. N-COUNT

**jel|ly roll (jelly rolls) Jelly roll** is a cylindrical cake made from a thin, flat cake which is covered with jam or cream on one side, then rolled up. [AM] N-VAR

☑ in BRIT, use **swiss roll**

**jeop|ard|ize** /dʒepəʳdaɪz/ **(jeopardizes, jeopardizing, jeopardized)**

☑ in BRIT, also use **jeopardise**

To **jeopardize** a situation or activity means to do something that may destroy it or cause it to fail. ❑ *He has jeopardised the future of his government.* VERB = *threaten, endanger* V n

**jeop|ardy** /dʒepəʳdi/ If someone or something is **in jeopardy**, they are in a dangerous situation where they might fail, be lost, or be destroyed. ❑ *A series of setbacks have put the whole project in jeopardy.* PHRASE: PHR after v, v-link PHR

**jerk** /dʒɜːʳk/ **(jerks, jerking, jerked)** [1] If you **jerk** something or someone in a particular direction, or they **jerk** in a particular direction, they move a short distance very suddenly and quickly. ❑ *Mr Griffin jerked forward in his chair... 'This is Brady Coyne,' said Sam, jerking his head in my direction... Eleanor jerked her wrist free.* VERB V adv/prep V n adv/prep V n adj ♦ **Jerk** is also a noun. ❑ *He indicated the bedroom with a jerk of his head.* N-COUNT [2] If you call someone a **jerk**, you are insulting them because you think they are stupid or you do not like them. [INFORMAL, OFFENSIVE] N-COUNT [disapproval] [3] → See also **knee-jerk**.

**jer|kin** /dʒɜːʳkɪn/ **(jerkins)** A **jerkin** is a sleeveless jacket worn by men or women. [OLD-FASHIONED] N-COUNT

**jerky** /dʒɜːʳki/ **(jerkier, jerkiest) Jerky** movements are very sudden and quick, and do not flow smoothly. ❑ *Mr Griffin made a jerky gesture.* ADJ: usu ADJ n ≠ *smooth* ♦ **jerki|ly** /dʒɜːʳkɪli/ *Using his stick heavily, he moved jerkily towards the car.* ADV: ADV with v

**jerry-built** /dʒeri bɪlt/ If you describe houses or blocks of flats as **jerry-built**, you are critical of the fact that they have been built very quickly and cheaply, without much care for safety or ADJ [disapproval] quality. ❑ *...jerry-built equipment... The place is a bit jerry-built.*

**jer|sey** /dʒɜːʳzi/ **(jerseys)** 1 A **jersey** is a knitted piece of clothing that covers the upper part of your body and your arms and does not open at the front. Jerseys are usually worn over a shirt or blouse. [OLD-FASHIONED] ❑ *His grey jersey and trousers were sodden with the rain.* 2 **Jersey** is a knitted, slightly stretchy fabric used especially to make women's clothing. ❑ *Sheila had come to dinner in a black jersey top.* ◆◇◇ N-COUNT = jumper, sweater, pullover; N-VAR: oft N n

**Jer|sey (Jerseys)** A **Jersey cow** or a **Jersey** is a light brown cow that produces very creamy milk. N-COUNT: oft N n

**Je|ru|sa|lem ar|ti|choke** /dʒəruːsələm ɑːʳtɪtʃoʊk/ **(Jerusalem artichokes)** **Jerusalem artichokes** are small, yellowish-white vegetables that grow underground and look like potatoes. N-VAR

**jest** /dʒest/ **(jests, jesting, jested)** 1 A **jest** is something that you say that is intended to be amusing. [FORMAL] ❑ *It was a jest rather than a reproach.* ● If you say something **in jest**, you do not mean it seriously, but want to be amusing. ❑ *Don't say that, even in jest.* 2 If you **jest**, you tell jokes or say amusing things. [FORMAL] ❑ *He enjoyed drinking and jesting with his cronies.* N-COUNT = joke; PHRASE: PHR after v ≠ seriously; VERB = joke; V

**jest|er** /dʒestəʳ/ **(jesters)** In the courts of kings and queens in medieval Europe, the **jester** was the person whose job was to do silly things in order to make people laugh. N-COUNT = fool

**Jesu|it** /dʒezjuɪt, AM dʒeʒuɪt/ **(Jesuits)** A **Jesuit** is a Catholic priest who belongs to the Society of Jesus. N-COUNT

**Jesus** /dʒiːzəs/ 1 **Jesus** or **Jesus Christ** is the name of the man who Christians believe was the son of God, and whose teachings are the basis of Christianity. 2 **Jesus** is used by some people to express surprise, shock, or annoyance. This use could cause offence. ◆◇◇ N-PROPER; EXCLAM [feelings]

**jet** /dʒet/ **(jets, jetting, jetted)** 1 A **jet** is an aircraft that is powered by jet engines. ❑ *Her private jet landed in the republic on the way to Japan... He had arrived from Jersey by jet.* → See also **jump jet**. 2 If you **jet** somewhere, you travel there in a fast plane. ❑ *He and his wife, Val, will be jetting off on a two-week holiday in America.* 3 A **jet** of liquid or gas is a strong, fast, thin stream of it. ❑ *A jet of water poured through the windows.* 4 **Jet** is a hard black stone that is used in jewellery. ◆◇◇ N-COUNT: also by N; VERB: V adv/prep; N-COUNT: oft N of n; N-UNCOUNT

**jet air|craft (jet aircraft)** A **jet aircraft** is an aircraft that is powered by one or more jet engines. N-COUNT

**jet black** also **jet-black.** Something that is **jet black** is a very intense black. ❑ *...jet-black hair.* ADJ

**jet en|gine (jet engines)** A **jet engine** is an engine in which hot air and gases are forced out at the back. Jet engines are used for most modern aircraft. N-COUNT

**jet lag**

✔ in BRIT, also use **jetlag**

If you are suffering from **jet lag**, you feel tired and slightly confused after a long journey by aeroplane, especially after travelling between places that have a time difference of several hours. N-UNCOUNT

**jet-lagged** Someone who is **jet-lagged** is suffering from jet lag. ❑ *I'm still a little jet-lagged.* ADJ: usu v-link ADJ

**jet|liner** /dʒetlaɪnəʳ/ **(jetliners)** A **jetliner** is a large aircraft, especially one which carries passengers. [AM] N-COUNT

**jet|sam** /dʒetsəm/ → see **flotsam**.

**jet set** also **jet-set.** You can refer to rich and successful people who live in a luxurious way as **the jet set**. ❑ *The winter sports bring the jet set from England.* N-SING: usu the N

**jet-setting** You use **jet-setting** to describe people who are rich and successful and who have a luxurious lifestyle. ❑ *...the international jet-setting elite.* ADJ: ADJ n

**jet ski (jet skis)** A **jet ski** is a small machine like a motorcycle that is powered by a jet engine and can travel on the surface of water. [TRADEMARK] N-COUNT

**jet stream (jet streams)** The **jet stream** is a very strong wind that blows high in the earth's atmosphere and has an important influence on the weather. N-COUNT

**jet|ti|son** /dʒetɪsən/ **(jettisons, jettisoning, jettisoned)** 1 If you **jettison** something, for example an idea or a plan, you deliberately reject it or decide not to use it. ❑ *The Government seems to have jettisoned the plan.* 2 To **jettison** something that is not needed or wanted means to throw it away or get rid of it. ❑ *The crew jettisoned excess fuel and made an emergency landing.* VERB = abandon; V n; VERB = discard; V n

**jet|ty** /dʒeti/ **(jetties)** A **jetty** is a wide stone wall or wooden platform where boats stop to let people get on or off, or to load or unload goods. N-COUNT: usu the N in sing

**Jew** /dʒuː/ **(Jews)** A **Jew** is a person who believes in and practises the religion of Judaism. ◆◇◇ N-COUNT

**jew|el** /dʒuːəl/ **(jewels)** 1 A **jewel** is a precious stone used to decorate valuable things that you wear, such as rings or necklaces. ❑ *...a golden box containing precious jewels.* → See also **crown jewels**. 2 If you describe something or someone as a **jewel**, you mean that they are better, more beautiful, or more special than other similar things or than other people. ❑ *Walk down Castle Street and admire our little jewel of a cathedral.* 3 If you refer to an achievement or thing as the **jewel in** someone's **crown**, you mean that it is considered to be their greatest achievement or the thing they can be most proud of. ❑ *His achievement is astonishing and this book is the jewel in his crown.* N-COUNT; N-COUNT: oft N of n = gem; PHRASE: usu v-link PHR

**jew|el case (jewel cases)** 1 A **jewel case** is a box for keeping jewels in. 2 A **jewel case** is the plastic box in which a compact disc is kept. N-COUNT; N-COUNT

**jew|elled** /dʒuːəld/

✔ in AM, use **jeweled**

**Jewelled** items and ornaments are decorated with precious stones. ADJ

**jew|el|ler** /dʒuːələʳ/ **(jewellers)**

✔ in AM, use **jeweler**

1 A **jeweller** is a person who makes, sells, and repairs jewellery and watches. 2 A **jeweller** or a **jeweller's** is a shop where jewellery and watches are made, sold, and repaired. N-COUNT; N-COUNT

**jew|el|lery** /dʒuːəlri/

✔ in AM, use **jewelry**

**Jewellery** is ornaments that people wear, for example rings, bracelets, and necklaces. It is often made of a valuable metal such as gold, and sometimes decorated with precious stones. N-UNCOUNT

**Jew|ish** /dʒuːɪʃ/ **Jewish** means belonging or relating to the religion of Judaism or to Jews. ❑ *...the Jewish festival of the Passover.* ◆◇◇ ADJ

**Jew|ish|ness** /dʒuːɪʃnəs/ Someone's **Jewishness** is the fact that they are a Jew. N-UNCOUNT: oft with poss

**Jew|ry** /dʒʊəri, AM dʒuːri/ **Jewry** is all the people, or all the people in a particular place, who believe in and practise the religion of Judaism. [FORMAL] ❑ *There could be no better way to strengthen the unity of world Jewry.* N-UNCOUNT: usu adj N

**jib** /dʒɪb/ **(jibs, jibbing, jibbed)** 1 **The jib** is the small triangular sail that is sometimes used at the front of a sailing boat. 2 If you **jib at** something, you are unwilling to do it or to accept it. [OLD-FASHIONED] ❑ *...those who jib at the idea of selling their land.* N-COUNT: usu the N in sing; VERB = balk; V at n/-ing; Also V

**jibe** /dʒaɪb/ **(jibes, jibing, jibed)**

✔ The spelling **gibe** is also used for meanings 1 and 2.

1 A **jibe** is a rude or insulting remark about someone that is intended to make them look foolish. ❑ *...a cheap jibe about his loss of hair.* 2 To **jibe** means to say something rude or insulting which is intended to make another person look N-COUNT; VERB

foolish. [WRITTEN] ❑ *'No doubt he'll give me the chance to fight him again,' he jibed, tongue in cheek.* V with quote
[3] If numbers, statements, or events **jibe**, they are exactly the same as each other or they are consistent with each other. [mainly AM] ❑ *The numbers don't jibe... How did your expectations jibe with the reality?* V-RECIP = tally; pl-n V; V with n

**jif|fy** /dʒɪfi/ If you say that you will do something **in a jiffy**, you mean that you will do it very quickly or very soon. [INFORMAL] PHRASE: PHR after v

**jig** /dʒɪg/ **(jigs, jigging, jigged)** [1] A **jig** is a lively dance. ❑ *She danced an Irish jig.* N-COUNT [2] To **jig** means to dance or move energetically, especially bouncing up and down. ❑ *You didn't just jig about by yourself, I mean you danced properly.* VERB; V adv/prep; Also V

**jig|ger** /dʒɪgəʳ/ **(jiggers)** A **jigger of** a drink such as whisky or gin is the amount of it you are given when you order it in a bar. [mainly AM] ❑ *...a jigger of brandy.* N-COUNT: oft N *of* n

**jiggery-pokery** /dʒɪgəri poʊkəri/ If you describe behaviour as **jiggery-pokery**, you mean that it involves tricking people or being dishonest. [BRIT, INFORMAL, OLD-FASHIONED] ❑ *It seems astonishing that Bond got away with so much jiggery-pokery for as long as he did.* N-UNCOUNT

**jig|gle** /dʒɪgəl/ **(jiggles, jiggling, jiggled)** [1] If you **jiggle** something, you move it quickly up and down or from side to side. [INFORMAL] ❑ *He jiggled the doorknob noisily.* VERB; V n [2] To **jiggle** around means to move quickly up and down or from side to side. [INFORMAL] ❑ *He tapped his feet, hummed tunes and jiggled about.* VERB; V adv

**jig|saw** /dʒɪgsɔː/ **(jigsaws)** [1] A **jigsaw** or **jigsaw puzzle** is a picture on cardboard or wood that has been cut up into odd shapes. You have to make the picture again by putting the pieces together correctly. N-COUNT = puzzle [2] You can describe a complicated situation as a **jigsaw**. ❑ *...the jigsaw of high-level diplomacy.* N-COUNT: usu sing, with supp

**ji|had** /dʒihæd, AM -hɑːd/ A **jihad** is a holy war which Islam allows Muslims to fight against those who reject its teachings. N-SING

**jilt** /dʒɪlt/ **(jilts, jilting, jilted)** If someone **is jilted**, the person they are having a romantic relationship with suddenly ends the relationship in a surprising and upsetting way. [INFORMAL] ❑ *She was jilted by her first fiancé... Driven to distraction, he murdered the woman who jilted him.* VERB; *be* V-ed; V n

**jin|gle** /dʒɪŋgəl/ **(jingles, jingling, jingled)** [1] When something **jingles** or when you **jingle** it, it makes a gentle ringing noise, like small bells. ❑ *Brian put his hands in his pockets and jingled some change... Her bracelets jingled like bells.* ♦ **Jingle** is also a noun. ❑ *...the jingle of money in a man's pocket.* VERB; V n; V; N-SING: oft N *of* n [2] A **jingle** is a short, simple tune, often with words, which is used to advertise a product or programme on radio or television. ❑ *...advertising jingles.* N-COUNT

**jin|go|ism** /dʒɪŋgoʊɪzəm/ **Jingoism** is a strong and unreasonable belief in the superiority of your own country. N-UNCOUNT [disapproval]

**jin|go|is|tic** /dʒɪŋgoʊɪstɪk/ **Jingoistic** behaviour shows a strong and unreasonable belief in the superiority of your own country. ❑ *The press continued its jingoistic display.* ADJ: usu ADJ n [disapproval]

**jink** /dʒɪŋk/ **(jinks, jinking, jinked)** To **jink** somewhere means to move there quickly in an irregular way, rather than by moving in a straight line. [BRIT, INFORMAL] ❑ *As they reached the start-finish line Prost jinked right and drew abreast.* → See also **high jinks**. VERB; V adv/prep; Also V

**jinx** /dʒɪŋks/ **(jinxes)** You can call something or someone that is considered to be unlucky or to bring bad luck a **jinx**. ❑ *He was beginning to think he was a jinx.* N-COUNT: usu sing

**jinxed** /dʒɪŋkst/ If something is **jinxed**, it is considered to be unlucky or to bring bad luck. ADJ

**jit|ters** /dʒɪtəʳz/ If you have the **jitters**, you feel extremely nervous, for example because you have to do something important or because you are expecting important news. [INFORMAL] ❑ *Officials feared that any public announcements would only increase market jitters.* N-PLURAL: oft *the* N

**jit|tery** /dʒɪtəri/ If someone is **jittery**, they feel nervous or are behaving nervously. [INFORMAL] ❑ *International investors have become jittery about the country's economy.* ADJ

**jive** /dʒaɪv/ **(jives, jiving, jived)** [1] If you **jive**, you dance energetically, especially to rock and roll or swing music. [INFORMAL] ❑ *I learnt to jive there when they got the jukebox.* VERB; V [2] **Jive** is rock and roll or swing music that you jive to. N-UNCOUNT

**Jnr**

☑ in AM, use **Jr.**

**Jnr** is a written abbreviation for **Junior**. It is used after a man's name to distinguish him from an older member of his family with the same name. [BRIT] = Jr

**job** /dʒɒb/ **(jobs)** [1] A **job** is the work that someone does to earn money. ❑ *Once I'm in America I can get a job... Thousands have lost their jobs... I felt the pressure of being the first woman in the job. ...overseas job vacancies.* ◆◆◆ N-COUNT [2] A **job** is a particular task. ❑ *He said he hoped that the job of putting together a coalition wouldn't take too much time.* N-COUNT: usu with supp, oft N *of* n, n N [3] The **job** of a particular person or thing is their duty or function. ❑ *Their main job is to preserve health rather than treat illness... Drinking a lot helps the kidneys do their job.* N-COUNT: usu with poss [4] If you say that someone is doing a good **job**, you mean that they are doing something well. In British English, you can also say that they are making a good **job** of something. ❑ *We could do a far better job of managing it than they have.* N-SING: usu adj N, oft N *of* -ing/n [5] If you say that you have **a job** doing something, you are emphasizing how difficult it is. ❑ *He may have a hard job selling that argument to investors.* N-SING: usu N -ing, N to-inf [emphasis] [6] → See also **jobbing**, **day job**, **hatchet job**, **on-the-job**.

PHRASES [7] If you refer to work as **jobs for the boys**, you mean that the work is unfairly given to someone's friends, supporters, or relations, even though they may not be the best qualified people to do it. [BRIT] PHRASE [disapproval] [8] If you say that something is **just the job**, you mean that it is exactly what you wanted or needed. [BRIT, INFORMAL] ❑ *Not only is it just the job for travelling, but it's handy for groceries too.* PHRASE: usu v-link PHR [9] If someone is **on the job**, they are actually doing a particular job or task. ❑ *The top pay scale after five years on the job would reach $5.00 an hour.* PHRASE [10] **it's a good job** → see **good**. **the job in hand** → see **hand**.

**job|bing** /dʒɒbɪŋ/ A **jobbing** worker does not work for someone on a regular basis, but does particular jobs when they are asked to. [BRIT] ❑ *...a jobbing builder.* ADJ: ADJ n

**job cen|tre** **(job centres)** also **Jobcentre.** In Britain, a **job centre** is a place where people who are looking for work can go to get advice on finding a job, and to look at advertisements placed by people who are looking for new employees. N-COUNT

**job de|scrip|tion** **(job descriptions)** A **job description** is a written account of all the duties and responsibilities involved in a particular job or position. N-COUNT: usu sing

**job|less** /dʒɒbləs/ Someone who is **jobless** does not have a job, although they would like one. ♦ **The jobless** are people who are jobless. ❑ *They joined the ranks of the jobless.* ♦ **job|less|ness** *Concern over the rising level of joblessness was a feature of yesterday's debate.* ADJ = unemployed; N-PLURAL: *the* N; N-UNCOUNT = unemployment

**job lot** **(job lots)** A **job lot** is a number of cheap things of low quality which are sold together, for example in auctions or second-hand shops. N-COUNT

**job sat|is|fac|tion** **Job satisfaction** is the pleasure that you get from doing your job. ❑ *I doubt I'll ever get rich, but I get job satisfaction.* N-UNCOUNT

**job seek|er** **(job seekers)** A **job seeker** is an unemployed person who is trying to get a job. N-COUNT

**job share** **(job shares, job sharing, job shared)** If two people **job share**, they share the same job by working part-time, for example one person working in the mornings and the other in the afternoons. ❑ *They both want to job share.* ♦ **Job share** is also a noun. ❑ *She works in a bank job share.* ♦ **job shar|ing** *Part-time work and job sharing will become commonplace.* — VERB; V; N-COUNT; N-UNCOUNT

**jobs|worth** /dʒɒbzwɜːʳθ/ **(jobsworths)** If you refer to someone as a **jobsworth**, you are criticizing them for using the rules connected to their job as an excuse not to be helpful. [BRIT] ❑ *A surly jobsworth alerted security.* — N-COUNT; disapproval

**jock** /dʒɒk/ **(jocks)** A **jock** is a young man who is enthusiastic about a particular sport and spends a lot of time playing it. [INFORMAL] ❑ *...an all-American football jock.* — N-COUNT

**jock|ey** /dʒɒki/ **(jockeys, jockeying, jockeyed)** 1 A **jockey** is someone who rides a horse in a race. 2 If you say that someone **is jockeying for** something, you mean that they are using whatever methods they can in order to get it or do it before their competitors can get it or do it. ❑ *The rival political parties are already jockeying for power... Already, both sides are jockeying to belittle the other side.* ● If someone **is jockeying for position**, they are using whatever methods they can in order to get into a better position than their rivals. — N-COUNT; VERB; V *for* n; V to-inf; PHRASE: V inflects

**jock|ey shorts** **Jockey shorts** are a type of men's underpants. [TRADEMARK] — N-PLURAL: also *a pair of* N

**jock|strap** /dʒɒkstræp/ **(jockstraps)** A **jockstrap** is a piece of underwear worn by sportsmen to support their genitals. — N-COUNT

**jocu|lar** /dʒɒkjʊləʳ/ If you say that someone has a **jocular** manner, you mean that they are cheerful and often make jokes or try to make people laugh. [FORMAL] ❑ *He was in a less jocular mood than usual.* — ADJ; = *jovial*

**jodh|purs** /dʒɒdpəʳz/

✔ The form **jodhpur** is used as a modifier.

**Jodhpurs** are trousers that people wear when they ride a horse. Jodhpurs are usually loose above the knee and tight below the knee. — N-PLURAL: also *a pair of* N

**jog** /dʒɒg/ **(jogs, jogging, jogged)** 1 If you **jog**, you run slowly, often as a form of exercise. ❑ *I got up early the next morning to jog.* ♦ **Jog** is also a noun. ❑ *He went for another early morning jog.* ♦ **jog|ging** *It isn't the walking and jogging that got his weight down.* 2 If you **jog** something, you push or bump it slightly so that it moves. ❑ *Avoid jogging the camera.* 3 If something or someone **jogs** your **memory**, they cause you to suddenly remember something that you had forgotten. ❑ *Police have planned a reconstruction of the crime tomorrow in the hope this will jog the memory of passers-by.* — VERB; V; N-COUNT; N-UNCOUNT; VERB; V n; PHRASE: V inflects

**jog|ger** /dʒɒgəʳ/ **(joggers)** A **jogger** is a person who jogs as a form of exercise. — N-COUNT

**joie de vi|vre** /ʒwɑː də viːvrə/ **Joie de vivre** is a feeling of happiness and enjoyment of life. [LITERARY] ❑ *He has plenty of joie de vivre.* — N-UNCOUNT

**join** /dʒɔɪn/ **(joins, joining, joined)** ◆◆◆ 1 If one person or vehicle **joins** another, they move or go to the same place, for example so that both of them can do something together. ❑ *His wife and children moved to join him in their new home.* 2 If you **join** an organization, you become a member of it or start work as an employee of it. ❑ *He joined the Army five years ago.* 3 If you **join** an activity that other people are doing, you take part in it or become involved with it. ❑ *Telephone operators joined the strike and four million engineering workers are also planning action... The pastor requested the women present to join him in prayer... Private contractors joined in condemning the Government's stance.* 4 If you **join** a queue, you stand at the end of it so that you are part of it. ❑ *Make sure you join the queue inside the bank.* 5 To **join** two things means to fix or fasten them together. ❑ *The opened link is used to join the two ends of the chain. ...the conjunctiva, the skin which joins the eye to the lid.* 6 If something such as a line or path **joins** two things, it connects them. ❑ *It has a dormer roof joining both gable ends. ...a global highway of cables joining all the continents together.* 7 If two roads or rivers **join**, they meet or come together at a particular point. ❑ *Do you know the highway to Tulsa? The airport road joins it. ...Allahabad, where the Ganges and the Yamuna rivers join.* 8 A **join** is a place where two things are fastened or fixed together. 9 **join forces** → see **force**. to **join the ranks** → see **rank**. — VERB; V n; VERB; V n; VERB; V n; V n *in* n/-ing; V *in* -ing; VERB; V n; VERB; V pl-n; V n prep/adv; VERB; V pl-n; V-ing; V-RECIP; V n; pl-n V; N-COUNT

♦ **join in** If you **join in** an activity, you take part in it or become involved in it. ❑ *I hope that everyone will be able to join in the fun... He started to sing and I joined in.* — PHRASAL VERB; V P n; V P

♦ **join up** 1 If someone **joins up**, they become a member of the army, the navy, or the air force. ❑ *When hostilities broke out he returned to England and joined up.* 2 If one person or organization **joins up with** another, they start doing something together. ❑ *Councils are joining up with their European counterparts... They began to join up in communities.* — PHRASAL VERB = *enlist*; V P; PHRASAL VERB = *get together, link up*; V P *with* n; pl-n V P

**joined-up** 1 In **joined-up** writing, you join all the letters in each word together, without taking your pen off the paper. This sort of writing is used by older children and adults. 2 Journalists sometimes use **joined-up** to describe plans, ideas, or organizations which seem sensible, sophisticated, and mature, especially when they think that they have been unsophisticated or immature in the past. ❑ *...another step towards joined-up government.* — ADJ: ADJ n; ADJ: ADJ n; approval

**join|er** /dʒɔɪnəʳ/ **(joiners)** A **joiner** is a person who makes wooden window frames, door frames, doors, and cupboards. [mainly BRIT] — N-COUNT

**join|ery** /dʒɔɪnəri/ **Joinery** is the skill and work of a joiner. [mainly BRIT] — N-UNCOUNT

**joint** /dʒɔɪnt/ **(joints)** ◆◆◇ 1 **Joint** means shared by or belonging to two or more people. ❑ *She and Frank had never gotten around to opening a joint account.* ♦ **joint|ly** *The Port Authority is an agency jointly run by New York and New Jersey.* 2 A **joint** is a part of your body such as your elbow or knee where two bones meet and are able to move together. ❑ *Her joints ache if she exercises.* 3 A **joint** is the place where two things are fastened or fixed together. → See also **dovetail joint**. 4 A **joint** is a fairly large piece of meat which is suitable for roasting. [BRIT] ❑ *He carved the joint of beef.* — ADJ: ADJ n; ADV: ADV with v; N-COUNT; N-COUNT; N-COUNT

✔ in AM, use **roast**

5 You can refer to a cheap place where people go for some form of entertainment as a **joint**. [INFORMAL] ❑ *...a hamburger joint.* 6 A **joint** is a cigarette which contains cannabis or marijuana. 7 If something puts someone's **nose out of joint**, it upsets or offends them because it makes them feel less important or less valued. [INFORMAL] ❑ *Barry had his nose put out of joint by Lucy's aloof sophistication.* — N-COUNT: usu supp N; N-COUNT; PHRASE: PHR after v, v-link PHR

**joint|ed** /dʒɔɪntɪd/ 1 Something that is **jointed** has joints that move. ❑ *The glass cover for this is cleverly jointed in the middle.* 2 A **jointed** chicken or other bird has been cut into pieces so that it is ready to cook. [BRIT] — ADJ; ADJ

**joint-stock company** **(joint-stock companies)** A **joint-stock company** is a company that is owned by the people who have bought shares in that company. [BUSINESS] — N-COUNT

**joint ven|ture** **(joint ventures)** A **joint venture** is a business or project in which two or more companies or individuals have invested, with the intention of working together. [BUSINESS] ❑ *It will be sold to a joint venture created by Dow Jones and Westinghouse Broadcasting.* — N-COUNT

**joist** /dʒɔɪst/ **(joists)** **Joists** are long thick pieces of metal, wood, or concrete that form part — N-COUNT = *beam* of the structure of a building, usually to support a floor or ceiling.

**jo|jo|ba** /hoʊhoʊbə/ **Jojoba** or **jojoba oil** is made from the seeds of the jojoba plant. It is used in many cosmetics such as shampoos. N-UNCOUNT

**joke** /dʒoʊk/ **(jokes, joking, joked)** 1 A **joke** is something that is said or done to make you laugh, for example a funny story. ❑ *He debated whether to make a joke about shooting rabbits, but decided against it... No one told worse jokes than Claus.* ◆◇◇ N-COUNT: oft N *about* n
2 If you **joke**, you tell funny stories or say amusing things. ❑ *She would joke about her appearance... Lorna was laughing and joking with Trevor... The project was taking so long that Stephen joked that it would never be finished... 'Well, a beautiful spring Thursday would probably be a nice day to be buried on,' Nancy joked.* VERB; V *about* n; V *with* n; V that; V with quote
3 A **joke** is something untrue that you tell another person in order to amuse yourself. ❑ *It was probably just a joke to them, but it wasn't funny to me.* N-COUNT
4 If you **joke**, you tell someone something that is not true in order to amuse yourself. ❑ *Don't get defensive, Charlie. I was only joking... 'I wish you made as much fuss of me,' Vera joked.* VERB; V; V with quote
5 If you say that something or someone is **a joke**, you think they are ridiculous and do not deserve respect. [INFORMAL] ❑ *It's ridiculous, it's pathetic, it's a joke.* N-SING: *a* N; disapproval

**PHRASES** 6 If you say that an annoying or worrying situation is **beyond a joke**, you are emphasizing that it is worse than you think is fair or reasonable. [BRIT] ❑ *I'm not afraid of a fair fight but this is beginning to get beyond a joke.* PHRASE: v-link PHR, PHR after v; emphasis
7 If you **make a joke of** something, you laugh at it even though it is in fact rather serious or sad. ❑ *I wish I had your courage, Michael, to make a joke of it like that.* PHRASE: V inflects, PHR n
8 If you describe a situation as **no joke**, you are emphasizing that it is very difficult or unpleasant. [INFORMAL] ❑ *Two hours on a bus is no joke, is it.* PHRASE: v-link PHR; emphasis
9 If you say that **the joke is on** a particular person, you mean that they have been made to look very foolish by something. ❑ *'For once,' he said, 'the joke's on me. And it's not very funny.'* PHRASE: V inflects, PHR n
10 If you say that someone **cannot take a joke**, you are criticizing them for getting upset or angry at something you think is funny. ❑ *'What's the matter with you, Simon?' Curly said. 'Can't you take a joke?'* PHRASE: V inflects; disapproval
11 You say **you're joking** or **you must be joking** to someone when they have just told you something that is so surprising or unreasonable that you find it difficult to believe. [SPOKEN] ❑ *One hundred and forty quid for a pair of headphones, you've got to be joking!* CONVENTION; feelings

**jok|er** /dʒoʊkəʳ/ **(jokers)** 1 Someone who is a **joker** likes making jokes or doing amusing things. ❑ *He is, by nature, a joker, a witty man with a sense of fun.* N-COUNT
2 The **joker** in a pack of playing cards is the card which does not belong to any of the four suits. N-COUNT
3 You can call someone a **joker** if you think they are behaving in a stupid or dangerous way. [INFORMAL] ❑ *Keep your eye on these jokers, you never know what they will come up with.* N-COUNT; disapproval; = idiot
4 If you describe someone or something as **the joker in the pack**, you mean that they are different from the other people or things in their group, and can be unpredictable. PHRASE

**jok|ey** /dʒoʊki/ If someone behaves in a **jokey** way, they do things in a way that is intended to be amusing, rather than serious. [INFORMAL] ❑ *Bruno has not got his younger brother's jokey manner.* ADJ: usu ADJ n; ≠ serious

**jok|ing|ly** /dʒoʊkɪŋli/ If you say or do something **jokingly**, you say or do it with the intention of amusing someone, rather than with any serious meaning or intention. ❑ *Sarah jokingly called her 'my monster'.* ADV: ADV with v

**jol|lity** /dʒɒlɪti/ **Jollity** is cheerful behaviour. [OLD-FASHIONED] ❑ *...the singing and jollity of the celebration.* N-UNCOUNT

**jol|ly** /dʒɒli/ **(jollier, jolliest)** 1 Someone who is **jolly** is happy and cheerful in their appearance or behaviour. ❑ *She was a jolly, kindhearted woman.* ADJ
2 A **jolly** event is lively and enjoyable. ❑ *She had a very jolly time in Korea.* ADJ: usu ADJ n
3 **Jolly** is sometimes used to emphasize an adjective or adverb. [BRIT, INFORMAL, OLD-FASHIONED] ❑ *It was jolly hard work, but I loved it.* ADV: ADV adj/adv; emphasis; = very, extremely

**jolt** /dʒoʊlt/ **(jolts, jolting, jolted)** 1 If something **jolts** or if something **jolts** it, it moves suddenly and quite violently. ❑ *The wagon jolted again... The train jolted into motion... They were working frantically in the fear that an aftershock would jolt the house again.* VERB; V; V prep; V n
♦ **Jolt** is also a noun. ❑ *We were worried that one tiny jolt could worsen her injuries.* N-COUNT
2 If something **jolts** someone, it gives them an unpleasant surprise or shock. ❑ *A stinging slap across the face jolted her.* VERB; V n
♦ **Jolt** is also a noun. ❑ *The campaign came at a time when America needed such a jolt.* N-COUNT

**Joneses** /dʒoʊnzɪz/ also **Jones.** If you say that someone is **keeping up with the Joneses**, you mean that they are doing something in order to show that they have as much money as other people, rather than because they really want to do it. ❑ *Many people were holding down three jobs just to keep up with the Joneses.* PHRASE: V inflects

**Jor|da|nian** /dʒɔːʳdeɪniən/ **(Jordanians)**
1 **Jordanian** means belonging or relating to the country of Jordan, or to its people or culture. ADJ
2 A **Jordanian** is a Jordanian citizen, or a person of Jordanian origin. N-COUNT

**joss stick** /dʒɒs stɪk/ **(joss sticks)** A **joss stick** is a thin stick covered with a substance that burns very slowly and smells pleasant. N-COUNT

**jos|tle** /dʒɒsəl/ **(jostles, jostling, jostled)** 1 If people **jostle** you, they bump against you or push you in a way that annoys you, usually because you are in a crowd and they are trying to get past you. ❑ *You get 2,000 people jostling each other and bumping into furniture... We spent an hour jostling with the crowds as we did our shopping... She was cheered and clapped by tourists who jostled to see her.* VERB; V n; V prep/adv; V to-inf; Also V n prep/adv
2 If people or things **are jostling for** something such as attention or a reward, they are competing with other people or things in order to get it. ❑ *...the contenders who have been jostling for the top job.* VERB; = compete; V *for* n

**jot** /dʒɒt/ **(jots, jotting, jotted)** 1 If you **jot** something short such as an address somewhere, you write it down so that you will remember it. ❑ *Could you just jot his name on there for me please.* VERB; = write; V n prep/adv
♦ **Jot down** means the same as **jot**. ❑ *Keep a pad handy to jot down queries as they occur... Listen carefully to the instructions and jot them down.* PHRASAL VERB; V P n (not pron); V n P
2 If you say that there is not **a jot** or not **one jot** of something, you are emphasizing that there is not even a very small amount of it. [OLD-FASHIONED] ❑ *There is not a jot of evidence to say it does them any good... It makes not one jot of difference.* QUANT: with brd-neg, QUANT *of* n-uncount; emphasis; = bit

**jot|ting** /dʒɒtɪŋ/ **(jottings) Jottings** are brief, informal notes that you write down. N-COUNT: usu pl; = note

**joule** /dʒuːl/ **(joules)** In physics, a **joule** is a unit of energy or work. [TECHNICAL] N-COUNT

**jour|nal** /dʒɜːʳnəl/ **(journals)** 1 A **journal** is a magazine, especially one that deals with a specialized subject. ❑ *All our results are published in scientific journals.* ◆◆◇ N-COUNT
2 A **journal** is a daily or weekly newspaper. The word journal is often used in the name of the paper. ❑ *He was a newspaperman for The New York Times and some other journals.* N-COUNT
3 A **journal** is an account which you write of your daily activities. ❑ *Sara confided to her journal.* N-COUNT; = diary

**jour|nal|ism** /dʒɜːʳnəlɪzəm/ **Journalism** is the job of collecting news and writing about it for newspapers, magazines, television, or radio. ❑ *He began a career in journalism, working for the North London Press Group.* → See also **chequebook journalism**. N-UNCOUNT

**jour|nal|ist** /dʒɜːʳnəlɪst/ **(journalists)** A **journalist** is a person whose job is to collect news and write about it for newspapers, magazines, television, or radio. ◆◆◇ N-COUNT; = reporter

**jour|nal|is|tic** /dʒɜːʳnəlɪstɪk/ **Journalistic** means relating to journalism, or produced by or typical of a journalist. ❑ *He began his journalistic career in the early eighties in Australia.* — ADJ: ADJ n

**jour|ney** /dʒɜːʳni/ **(journeys, journeying, journeyed)** ◆◇◇ 1 When you make a **journey**, you travel from one place to another. ❑ *There is an express service from Paris which completes the journey to Bordeaux in under 4 hours.* — N-COUNT: oft supp N, N prep 2 You can refer to a person's experience of changing or developing from one state of mind to another as a **journey**. ❑ *My films try to describe a journey of discovery, both for myself and the watcher.* — N-COUNT: with supp 3 If you **journey** somewhere, you travel there. [FORMAL] ❑ *In February 1935, Naomi journeyed to the United States for the first time... She has journeyed on horseback through Africa and Turkey.* — VERB = travel; V to n; V prep/adv

**journey|man** /dʒɜːʳnimən/ **(journeymen)** If you refer to someone as a **journeyman**, you mean that they have the basic skill which their job requires, but are not very talented or original. [JOURNALISM] ❑ *Douglas was a 29-year-old journeyman fighter, erratic in his previous fights.* — N-COUNT: oft N n

**joust** /dʒaʊst/ **(jousts, jousting, jousted)** 1 When two or more people or organizations **joust**, they compete to see who is better. [LITERARY] ❑ *...lawyers joust in the courtroom... The oil company jousts with Esso for lead position in UK sales.* — V-RECIP = dispute; pl-n V; V with n 2 In medieval times, when two knights on horseback **jousted**, they fought against each other using long spears called lances. ❑ *Knights joust and frolic.* ♦ **joust|ing** *...medieval jousting tournaments.* — V-RECIP; pl-n V; Also V with n; N-UNCOUNT

**jo|vial** /dʒoʊviəl/ If you describe a person as **jovial**, you mean that they are happy and behave in a cheerful way. [WRITTEN] ❑ *Father Whittaker appeared to be in a jovial mood.* ♦ **jo|vi|al|ity** /dʒoʊviælɪti/ *...his old expansive joviality.* ♦ **jo|vi|al|ly** *'No problem,' he said jovially.* — ADJ; N-UNCOUNT; ADV: ADV with v

**jowl** /dʒaʊl/ **(jowls)** 1 You can refer to someone's lower cheeks as their **jowls**, especially when they hang down towards their jaw. [LITERARY] — N-COUNT: usu pl 2 If you say that people or things are **cheek by jowl** with each other, you are indicating that they are very close to each other. ❑ *She and her family have to live cheek by jowl with these people.* — PHRASE: usu v PHR, v-link PHR, PHR n, oft PHR with n

**jowly** /dʒaʊli/ Someone who is **jowly** has fat cheeks which hang down towards their jaw. — ADJ

**joy** /dʒɔɪ/ **(joys)** ◆◇◇ 1 **Joy** is a feeling of great happiness. ❑ *Salter shouted with joy. ...tears of joy.* — N-UNCOUNT 2 A **joy** is something or someone that makes you feel happy or gives you great pleasure. ❑ *One can never learn all there is to know about cooking, and that is one of the joys of being a chef.* — N-COUNT: with supp = delight 3 If you get no **joy**, you do not have success or luck in achieving what you are trying to do. [BRIT, INFORMAL] ❑ *They expect no joy from the vote itself.* — N-UNCOUNT: with brd-neg 4 If you say that someone **is jumping for joy**, you mean that they are very pleased or happy about something. ❑ *He jumped for joy on being told the news.* — PHRASE: V inflects 5 one's **pride and joy** → see **pride**.

**joy|ful** /dʒɔɪfʊl/ 1 Something that is **joyful** causes happiness and pleasure. [FORMAL] ❑ *A wedding is a joyful celebration of love.* — ADJ 2 Someone who is **joyful** is extremely happy. [FORMAL] ❑ *We're a very joyful people; we're very musical people and we love music.* ♦ **joy|ful|ly** *They greeted him joyfully.* — ADJ; ADV

**joy|less** /dʒɔɪləs/ Something that is **joyless** produces no happiness or pleasure. [FORMAL] ❑ *Life seemed joyless... Eating in East Berlin used to be a hazardous and joyless experience.* — ADJ = cheerless ≠ joyous

**joy|ous** /dʒɔɪəs/ **Joyous** means extremely happy. [LITERARY] ❑ *She had made their childhood so joyous and carefree.* ♦ **joy|ous|ly** *Sarah accepted joyously.* — ADJ = joyful; ADV

**joy|ride** /dʒɔɪraɪd/ **(joyrides)** also **joy ride.** If someone goes on a **joyride**, they steal a car and drive around in it at high speed. — N-COUNT

**joy|rider** /dʒɔɪraɪdəʳ/ **(joyriders)** also **joy rider.** A **joyrider** is someone who steals cars in order to drive around in them at high speed. — N-COUNT

**joy|rid|ing** /dʒɔɪraɪdɪŋ/ also **joy riding. Joyriding** is the crime of stealing a car and driving around in it at high speed. — N-UNCOUNT

**joy|stick** /dʒɔɪstɪk/ **(joysticks)** 1 In some computer games, the **joystick** is the lever which the player uses in order to control the direction of the things on the screen. — N-COUNT: usu sing 2 In an aircraft, **the joystick** is the lever which the pilot uses to control the direction and height of the aeroplane. — N-COUNT: usu sing

**JP** /dʒeɪ piː/ **(JPs)** A **JP** is a **Justice of the Peace.** — N-COUNT = magistrate

**JPEG** /dʒeɪpeg/ **(JPEGs)** also **Jpeg. JPEG** is a standard file format for compressing pictures so they can be stored or sent by e-mail more easily. **JPEG** is an abbreviation for 'Joint Photographic Experts Group'. [COMPUTING] ❑ *...JPEG images.* ♦ A **JPEG** is a JPEG file or picture. *... downloaded JPEGs.* — N-UNCOUNT: oft N n; N-COUNT

**Jr**

in AM, use **Jr.**

**Jr** is a written abbreviation for **Junior**. It is used after a man's name to distinguish him from an older member of his family with the same name. ❑ *...Harry Connick Jr.* — = Jnr

**ju|bi|lant** /dʒuːbɪlənt/ If you are **jubilant**, you feel extremely happy because of a success. ❑ *Ferdinand was jubilant after making an impressive comeback from a month on the injured list.* — ADJ = ecstatic

**ju|bi|la|tion** /dʒuːbɪleɪʃən/ **Jubilation** is a feeling of great happiness and pleasure, because of a success. [FORMAL] ❑ *His resignation was greeted by jubilation on the streets of Sofia.* — N-UNCOUNT

**ju|bi|lee** /dʒuːbɪliː/ **(jubilees)** A **jubilee** is a special anniversary of an event, especially the 25th or 50th anniversary. ❑ *...Queen Victoria's jubilee.* → See also **golden jubilee, silver jubilee.** — N-COUNT

**Ju|da|ic** /dʒuːdeɪɪk/ **Judaic** means belonging or relating to Judaism. [FORMAL] — ADJ: ADJ n

**Ju|da|ism** /dʒuːdeɪɪzəm/ **Judaism** is the religion of the Jewish people. It is based on the Old Testament of the Bible and the Talmud. — N-UNCOUNT

**Judas** /dʒuːdəs/ **(Judases)** If you accuse someone of being a **Judas**, you are accusing them of being deceitful and betraying their friends or country. — N-COUNT disapproval = traitor

**jud|der** /dʒʌdəʳ/ **(judders, juddering, juddered)** If something **judders**, it shakes or vibrates violently. [BRIT] ❑ *The lift started off, juddered, and went out of action.* — VERB; V

**judge** /dʒʌdʒ/ **(judges, judging, judged)** ◆◆◇ 1 A **judge** is the person in a court of law who decides how the law should be applied, for example how criminals should be punished. ❑ *The judge adjourned the hearing until next Tuesday... Judge Mr Justice Schiemann jailed him for life.* — N-COUNT; N-TITLE 2 A **judge** is a person who decides who will be the winner of a competition. ❑ *A panel of judges is now selecting the finalists.* — N-COUNT 3 If you **judge** something such as a competition, you decide who or what is the winner. ❑ *Colin Mitchell will judge the entries each week... A grade B judge could only be allowed to judge alongside a qualified grade A judge.* ♦ **judg|ing** *The judging was difficult as always.* — VERB; V n; V; N-UNCOUNT 4 If you **judge** something or someone, you form an opinion about them after you have examined the evidence or thought carefully about them. ❑ *It will take a few more years to judge the impact of these ideas... I am ready to judge any book on its merits... It's for other people to judge how much I have improved... The UN withdrew its relief personnel because it judged the situation too dangerous... I judged it to be one of the worst programmes ever screened... The doctor judged that the man's health had, up to the time of the wound, been good.* — VERB; V n; V n on n; V wh; V n adj; V n to-inf; V that 5 If you **judge** something, you guess its amount, size, or value or you guess what it is. ❑ *It is important to judge the weight of your washing load correctly... I judged him to be about for-* — VERB = estimate; V n; V n to-inf *ty... Though the shoreline could be dimly seen, it was impossible to judge how far away it was.* V wh 6 If someone is a good **judge of** something, they understand it and can make sensible decisions about it. If someone is a bad **judge of** something, they cannot do this. ❑ *I'm a pretty good judge of character.* N-COUNT: usu sing, usu N *of* n

PHRASES 7 You use **judging by, judging from,** or **to judge from** to introduce the reasons why you believe or think something. ❑ *Judging by the opinion polls, he seems to be succeeding... Judging from the way he laughed as he told it, it was meant to be humorous.* PREP-PHRASE 8 If you say that something is true **as far as** you **can judge** or **so far as** you **can judge**, you are assuming that it is true, although you do not know all the facts about it. ❑ *The book, so far as I can judge, is remarkably accurate.* PHRASE: PHR with cl

**judg|ment** /dʒʌdʒmənt/ **(judgments)** ◆◇◇

✔ in BRIT, also use **judgement**

1 A **judgment** is an opinion that you have or express after thinking carefully about something. ❑ *In your judgment, what has changed over the past few years?... I don't really want to make any judgments on the decisions they made.* N-VAR 2 **Judgment** is the ability to make sensible guesses about a situation or sensible decisions about what to do. ❑ *I respect his judgement and I'll follow any advice he gives me.* N-UNCOUNT: oft with poss 3 A **judgment** is a decision made by a judge or by a court of law. ❑ *The industry was awaiting a judgment from the European Court.* N-VAR = verdict, ruling

PHRASES 4 If something is **against** your **better judgment**, you believe that it would be more sensible or better not to do it. ❑ *Against my better judgement I agreed.* PHRASE: PHR with cl, PHR after v, v-link PHR 5 If you **pass judgment** on someone or something, you give your opinion about it, especially if you are making a criticism. ❑ *It's not for me to pass judgement, it's a personal matter between the two of you.* PHRASE: V inflects 6 If you **reserve judgment on** something, you refuse to give an opinion about it until you know more about it. ❑ *Doctors are reserving judgement on his ability to travel until later in the week.* PHRASE: V inflects, usu PHR *on* n 7 To **sit in judgment** means to decide whether or not someone is guilty of doing something wrong. ❑ *He argues very strongly that none of us has the right to sit in judgement.* PHRASE: V inflects

**judg|men|tal** /dʒʌdʒmentᵊl/

✔ in BRIT, also use **judgemental**

If you say that someone is **judgmental**, you are critical of them because they form opinions of people and situations very quickly, when it would be better for them to wait until they know more about the person or situation. ❑ *We tried not to seem critical or judgmental while giving advice that would protect him from ridicule.* ADJ [disapproval]

**judg|ment call** **(judgment calls)**

✔ in BRIT, also use **judgement call**

If you refer to a decision as a **judgment call**, you mean that there are no firm rules or principles that can help you make it, so you simply have to rely on your own judgement and instinct. ❑ *Well, physicians make judgment calls every day.* N-COUNT

**ju|di|cial** /dʒuːdɪʃᵊl/ **Judicial** means relating to the legal system and to judgments made in a court of law. ❑ *...an independent judicial inquiry. ...judicial decisions.* ADJ: ADJ n ♦ **ju|di|cial|ly** *Even if the amendment is passed it can be defeated judicially.* ADV: ADV with v

**ju|di|ci|ary** /dʒuːdɪʃəri, AM -ʃieri/ **The judiciary** is the branch of authority in a country which is concerned with law and the legal system. [FORMAL] ❑ *The judiciary must think very hard before jailing non-violent offenders.* N-SING: *the* N

**ju|di|cious** /dʒuːdɪʃəs/ If you describe an action or decision as **judicious**, you approve of it because you think that it shows good judgment and sense. [FORMAL] ❑ *The President authorizes the judicious use of military force to protect our citizens.* ADJ [approval] = wise ♦ **ju|di|cious|ly** *Modern fertilisers should be used judiciously.* ADV: ADV with v

**judo** /dʒuːdoʊ/ **Judo** is a sport in which two people fight and try to throw each other to the ground. N-UNCOUNT

**jug** /dʒʌg/ **(jugs)** A **jug** is a cylindrical container with a handle and is used for holding and pouring liquids. N-COUNT ♦ A **jug** of liquid is the amount that the jug contains. ❑ *...a jug of water.* N-COUNT

**jug|ger|naut** /dʒʌgəʳnɔːt/ **(juggernauts)** 1 A **juggernaut** is a very large truck. [mainly BRIT] N-COUNT 2 If you describe an organization or group as a **juggernaut**, you are critical of them because they are large and extremely powerful, and you think they are not being controlled properly. ❑ *The group became a sales juggernaut in the commodity options business.* N-COUNT [disapproval]

**jug|gle** /dʒʌgᵊl/ **(juggles, juggling, juggled)** 1 If you **juggle** lots of different things, for example your work and your family, you try to give enough time or attention to all of them. ❑ *The management team meets several times a week to juggle budgets and resources... Mike juggled the demands of a family of 11 with a career as a TV reporter.* VERB V n V n *with* n Also V *with* n 2 If you **juggle**, you entertain people by throwing things into the air, catching each one and throwing it up again so that there are several of them in the air at the same time. ❑ *Soon she was juggling five eggs... I can't juggle.* VERB V n V ♦ **jug|gl|ing** *He can perform an astonishing variety of acts, including mime and juggling.* N-UNCOUNT

**jug|gler** /dʒʌglәʳ/ **(jugglers)** A **juggler** is someone who juggles in order to entertain people. N-COUNT

**jug|gl|ing act** **(juggling acts)** If you say that a situation is a **juggling act**, you mean that someone is trying to do two or more things at once, and that they are finding it difficult to do those things properly. ❑ *Trying to continue with a demanding career and manage a child or two is an impossible juggling act.* N-COUNT

**jugu|lar** /dʒʌgjʊləʳ/ **(jugulars)** 1 A **jugular** or **jugular** vein is one of the three important veins in your neck that carry blood from your head back to your heart. N-COUNT 2 If you say that someone **went for the jugular**, you mean that they strongly attacked another person's weakest points in order to harm them. [INFORMAL] ❑ *Mr Black went for the jugular, asking intimate sexual questions.* PHRASE: V inflects

**juice** /dʒuːs/ **(juices)** ◆◇◇ 1 **Juice** is the liquid that can be obtained from a fruit. ❑ *...fresh orange juice.* N-MASS: usu with supp 2 The **juices** of a piece of meat are the liquid that comes out of it when you cook it. ❑ *When cooked, drain off the juices and put the meat in a processor or mincer.* N-PLURAL

**juicy** /dʒuːsi/ **(juicier, juiciest)** 1 If food is **juicy**, it has a lot of juice in it and is very enjoyable to eat. ❑ *...a thick, juicy steak.* ADJ 2 **Juicy** gossip or stories contain details about people's lives, especially details which are normally kept private. [INFORMAL] ❑ *It provided some juicy gossip for a few days.* ADJ: usu ADJ n

**juke|box** /dʒuːkbɒks/ **(jukeboxes)** also **juke-box.** A **jukebox** is a machine that plays CDs in a place such as a pub or bar. You put money in and choose the song you want to hear. ❑ *My favorite song is on the jukebox.* N-COUNT

**Jul.** **Jul.** is a written abbreviation for **July**.

**July** /dʒʊlaɪ/ **(Julys)** **July** is the seventh month of the year in the Western calendar. ❑ *In late July 1914, he and Violet spent a few days with friends near Berwick-upon-Tweed... I expect you to report for work on July the twenty-eighth.* N-VAR

**jum|ble** /dʒʌmbᵊl/ **(jumbles, jumbling, jumbled)** 1 **A jumble** of things is a lot of different things that are all mixed together in a disorganized or confused way. ❑ *The shoreline was made up of a jumble of huge boulders.* N-COUNT: usu sing, usu N *of* n 2 If you **jumble** things or if things **jumble**, they become mixed together so that they are untidy or are not in the correct order. ❑ *He's making a new film by jumbling together bits of his other movies... His thoughts jumbled and raced like children fighting.* VERB V n with *together* V ♦ To **jumble up** PHRASAL VERB means the same as to **jumble**. ❑ *They had jumbled it all up into a heap... The bank scrambles all that money together, jumbles it all up and lends it out to hundreds and thousands of borrowers... The watch parts fell apart and jumbled up... There were six wires jumbled up, tied together, all painted black.* V n P prep/adv V n P V P V-ed P Also V P n (not pron) [3] **Jumble** is old or unwanted things that people give away to charity. [BRIT] ❑ *She expects me to drive round collecting jumble for the church.* N-UNCOUNT

in AM, use **rummage**

**jum|bled** /dʒʌmbəld/ If you describe things or ideas as **jumbled**, you mean that they are mixed up and not in order. ❑ *These jumbled priorities should be no cause for surprise.* ADJ

**jum|ble sale** **(jumble sales)** A **jumble sale** is a sale of cheap second-hand goods, usually held to raise money for charity. [BRIT] N-COUNT

in AM, use **rummage sale**

**jum|bo** /dʒʌmboʊ/ **(jumbos)** [1] **Jumbo** means very large; used mainly in advertising and in the names of products. ❑ *...a jumbo box of tissues.* ADJ: ADJ n = giant [2] A **jumbo** or a **jumbo jet** is a very large jet aircraft that can carry several hundred passengers. ❑ *...a British Airways jumbo.* N-COUNT

**jump** /dʒʌmp/ **(jumps, jumping, jumped)** ◆◆◇ [1] If you **jump**, you bend your knees, push against the ground with your feet, and move quickly upwards into the air. ❑ *I jumped over the fence... I'd jumped seventeen feet six in the long jump, which was a school record... Whoever heard of a basketball player who doesn't need to jump?* VERB V prep/adv V n V ♦ **Jump** is also a noun. ❑ *She was taking tiny jumps in her excitement.* N-COUNT [2] If you **jump** from something above the ground, you deliberately push yourself into the air so that you drop towards the ground. ❑ *He jumped out of a third-floor window... I jumped the last six feet down to the deck.* VERB = leap V prep/adv V n Also V [3] If you **jump** something such as a fence, you move quickly up and through the air over or across it. ❑ *He jumped the first fence beautifully.* VERB V n [4] If you **jump** somewhere, you move there quickly and suddenly. ❑ *Adam jumped from his seat at the girl's cry.* VERB V prep/adv [5] If something **makes** you **jump**, it makes you make a sudden movement because you are frightened or surprised. ❑ *The phone shrilled, making her jump.* VERB V [6] If an amount or level **jumps**, it suddenly increases or rises by a large amount in a short time. ❑ *Sales jumped from $94 million to over $101 million... The number of crimes jumped by ten per cent last year... Shares in EuroDisney jumped 17p.* VERB V *to/from* amount V *by* amount V amount ♦ **Jump** is also a noun. ❑ *...a big jump in energy conservation.* N-COUNT: usu N *in* n [7] If someone **jumps** a queue, they move to the front of it and are served or dealt with before it is their turn. [BRIT] ❑ *The prince refused to jump the queue for treatment at the local hospital.* VERB V n [8] If you **jump at** an offer or opportunity, you accept it quickly and eagerly. ❑ *Members of the public would jump at the chance to become part owners of the corporation.* VERB: no cont V *at* n [9] If someone **jumps on** you, they quickly criticize you if you do something that they do not approve of. ❑ *A lot of people jumped on me about that, you know.* VERB V *on* n [10] → See also **bungee jumping**, **high jump**, **long jump**, **queue-jumping**, **show jumping**, **triple jump**. [11] If you **get a jump on** something or someone or **get the jump on** them, you gain an advantage over them. [AM] ❑ *Helicopters helped fire crews get a jump on the blaze.* PHRASE: V inflects, PHR n [12] to **jump on the bandwagon** → see **bandwagon**. to **jump bail** → see **bail**. to **jump to a conclusion** → see **conclusion**. to **jump the gun** → see **gun**. to **jump for joy** → see **joy**.

♦ **jump in** If you **jump in**, you act quickly, often without thinking much about what you are doing. ❑ *The Government had to jump in and purchase millions of dollars worth of supplies.* PHRASAL VERB V P

♦ **jump out** If you say that something **jumps out at** you, you mean that it is easy to notice it because it is different from other things of its type. ❑ *A phrase jumped out at me in a piece about copyright.* PHRASAL VERB V P *at* n Also V P

**jumped-up** If you describe someone as **jumped-up**, you disapprove of them because they consider themselves to be more important than they really are. [BRIT, INFORMAL] ❑ *He's nothing better than a jumped-up bank clerk!* ADJ: usu ADJ n disapproval

**jump|er** /dʒʌmpəʳ/ **(jumpers)** [1] A **jumper** is a warm knitted piece of clothing which covers the upper part of your body and your arms. [BRIT] ❑ *Isabel had on a simple jumper and skirt.* N-COUNT = sweater, pullover

in AM, use **sweater**

[2] A **jumper** is a sleeveless dress that is worn over a blouse or sweater. [AM] ❑ *She wore a checkered jumper and had ribbons in her hair.* N-COUNT

in BRIT, use **pinafore**

[3] If you refer to a person or a horse as a particular kind of **jumper**, you are describing how good they are at jumping or the way that they jump. ❑ *He is a terrific athlete and a brilliant jumper.* N-COUNT: usu adj N

**jump|er ca|bles** **Jumper cables** are the same as **jump leads**. [AM] N-PLURAL

**jumping-off point** A **jumping-off point** or a **jumping-off place** is a place, situation, or occasion which you use as the starting point for something. ❑ *Lectoure is a bustling market town and the best jumping-off point for a first visit to Le Gers.* N-SING

**jump jet** **(jump jets)** A **jump jet** is a jet aircraft that can take off and land vertically. N-COUNT

**jump jock|ey** **(jump jockeys)** A **jump jockey** is someone who rides horses in races such as steeplechases, where the horses have to jump over obstacles. N-COUNT

**jump leads** /dʒʌmp liːdz/ **Jump leads** are two thick wires that can be used to start a car when its battery does not have enough power. The jump leads are used to connect the battery to the battery of another car that is working properly. [BRIT] N-PLURAL

in AM, use **jumper cables**

**jump rope** **(jump ropes)** A **jump rope** is a piece of rope, usually with handles at each end. You exercise with it by turning it round and round and jumping over it. [AM] N-COUNT

in BRIT, use **skipping rope**

**jump-start** **(jump-starts, jump-starting, jump-started)** also **jump start**. [1] To **jump-start** a vehicle which has a flat battery means to make the engine start by getting power from the battery of another vehicle, using special cables called jump leads. ❑ *He was huddled with John trying to jump-start his car.* VERB V n ♦ **Jump-start** is also a noun. ❑ *I drove out to give him a jump start because his battery was dead.* N-COUNT [2] To **jump-start** a system or process that has stopped working or progressing means to do something that will make it start working quickly or effectively. ❑ *The EU is trying to jump start the peace process.* VERB V n ♦ **Jump-start** is also a noun. ❑ *...attempts to give the industry a jump-start.* N-COUNT: usu sing

**jump|suit** /dʒʌmpsuːt/ **(jumpsuits)** A **jumpsuit** is a piece of clothing in the form of a top and trousers in one continuous piece. N-COUNT

**jumpy** /dʒʌmpi/ If you are **jumpy**, you are nervous or worried about something. [INFORMAL] ❑ *I told myself not to be so jumpy... When he spoke his voice was jumpy.* ADJ: usu v-link ADJ = jittery, edgy

**Jun.** **Jun.** is a written abbreviation for **June**.

**junc|tion** /dʒʌŋkʃən/ **(junctions)** A **junction** is a place where roads or railway lines join. [BRIT] ❑ *Follow the road to a junction and turn left.* N-COUNT; N-IN-NAMES

in AM, usually use **intersection**

**junc|ture** /dʒʌŋktʃəʳ/ **(junctures)** At a particular **juncture** means at a particular point in time, especially when it is a very important time in a process or series of events. ❑ *What's important at this juncture is the ability of the three republics to work together.* N-COUNT: usu with supp, usu *at* N

**June** /dʒuːn/ **(Junes)** **June** is the sixth month of the year in the Western calendar. ❑ *He spent two and a half weeks with us in June 1986... I am moving out on June 5.* N-VAR

**jun|gle** /dʒʌŋgᵊl/ **(jungles)** 1 A **jungle** is a forest in a tropical country where large numbers of tall trees and plants grow very close together. ❑ *...the mountains and jungles of Papua New Guinea... The mountain area is covered entirely in dense jungle.* N-VAR 2 If you describe a place as **a jungle**, you are emphasizing that it is full of lots of things and very untidy. ❑ *...a jungle of stuffed birds, knick-knacks, potted plants.* N-SING: with supp [emphasis] 3 If you describe a situation as **a jungle**, you dislike it because it is complicated and difficult to get what you want from it. ❑ *Social security law and procedure remain a jungle of complex rules.* N-SING: with supp [disapproval] 4 If you refer to **the law of the jungle**, you are referring to a situation in which there are no laws or rules to govern the way that people behave and people use force to get what they want. ❑ *If you make aggression pay, this becomes the law of the jungle.* PHRASE [disapproval]

**jun|ior** /dʒuːniəʳ/ **(juniors)** ◆◇◇ 1 A **junior** official or employee holds a low-ranking position in an organization or profession. ❑ *Junior and middle-ranking civil servants have pledged to join the indefinite strike. ...a junior minister attached to the prime minister's office.* ADJ: usu ADJ n ≠ *senior* ♦ **Junior** is also a noun. ❑ *The Lord Chancellor has said legal aid work is for juniors when they start out in the law.* N-COUNT 2 If you are someone's **junior**, you are younger than they are. ❑ *She now lives with actor Denis Lawson, 10 years her junior.* N-SING: poss N 3 **Junior** is sometimes used after the name of the younger of two men in a family who have the same name, sometimes in order to prevent confusion. The abbreviation **Jr** is also used. [AM] ❑ *His son, Arthur Ochs Junior, is expected to succeed him as publisher.* N-IN-NAMES 4 In the United States, a student in the third year of a high school or university course is called a **junior**. N-COUNT

**jun|ior high** **(junior highs)** In the United States, **junior high** is the school that young people attend between the ages of 11 or 12 and 14 or 15. ❑ *...Benjamin Franklin Junior High.* N-COUNT; N-IN-NAMES

**jun|ior school** **(junior schools)** In England and Wales, a **junior school** is a school for children between the ages of about seven and eleven. ❑ *...Middleton Road Junior School.* N-VAR; N-IN-NAMES oft in names after n

**ju|ni|per** /dʒuːnɪpəʳ/ **(junipers)** A **juniper** is an evergreen bush with purple berries which can be used in cooking and medicine. N-VAR

**junk** /dʒʌŋk/ **(junks, junking, junked)** 1 **Junk** is old and used goods that have little value and that you do not want any more. ❑ *What are you going to do with all that junk, Larry?* N-UNCOUNT: oft N n 2 If you **junk** something, you get rid of it or stop using it. [INFORMAL] ❑ *Consumers will not have to junk their old cassettes to use the new format.* VERB = *ditch, jettison* V n

**junk bond** **(junk bonds)** If a company issues **junk bonds**, it borrows money from investors, usually at a high rate of interest, in order to finance a particular deal, for example the setting up or the taking over of another company. [BUSINESS] N-COUNT: usu pl

**jun|ket** /dʒʌŋkɪt/ **(junkets)** If you describe a trip or visit by an official or businessman as a **junket**, you disapprove of it because it is expensive, unnecessary, and often has been paid for with public money. [INFORMAL] N-COUNT [disapproval]

**junk food** **(junk foods)** If you refer to food as **junk food**, you mean that it is quick and easy to prepare but is not good for your health. N-MASS

**junkie** /dʒʌŋki/ **(junkies)** 1 A **junkie** is a drug addict. [INFORMAL] N-COUNT 2 You can use **junkie** to refer to someone who is very interested in a particular activity, especially when they spend a lot of time on it. [INFORMAL] ❑ *...a computer junkie.* N-COUNT: n N

**junk mail** **Junk mail** is advertisements and publicity materials that you receive through the post which you have not asked for and which you do not want. N-UNCOUNT

**junk|yard** /dʒʌŋkjɑːʳd/ **(junkyards)** A **junkyard** is the same as a **scrapyard**. N-COUNT

**jun|ta** /dʒʌntə, hʊntə/ **(juntas)** A **junta** is a military government that has taken power by force, and not through elections. N-COUNT-COLL

**ju|ris|dic|tion** /dʒʊərɪsdɪkʃᵊn/ **(jurisdictions)** 1 **Jurisdiction** is the power that a court of law or an official has to carry out legal judgments or to enforce laws. [FORMAL] ❑ *The British police have no jurisdiction over foreign bank accounts.* N-UNCOUNT = *authority* 2 A **jurisdiction** is a state or other area in which a particular court and system of laws has authority. [LEGAL] N-COUNT

**ju|ris|pru|dence** /dʒʊərɪspruːdᵊns/ **Jurisprudence** is the study of law and the principles on which laws are based. [FORMAL] N-UNCOUNT

**ju|rist** /dʒʊərɪst/ **(jurists)** A **jurist** is a person who is an expert on law. [FORMAL] N-COUNT

**ju|ror** /dʒʊərəʳ/ **(jurors)** A **juror** is a member of a jury. N-COUNT

**jury** /dʒʊəri/ **(juries)** ◆◇◇ 1 In a court of law, the **jury** is the group of people who have been chosen from the general public to listen to the facts about a crime and to decide whether the person accused is guilty or not. ❑ *The jury convicted Mr Hampson of all offences. ...the tradition of trial by jury.* N-COUNT-COLL: also *by* N 2 A **jury** is a group of people who choose the winner of a competition. ❑ *I am not surprised that the Booker Prize jury included it on their shortlist.* N-COUNT-COLL = *panel* 3 If you say that **the jury is out** or that **the jury is still out** on a particular subject, you mean that people in general have still not made a decision or formed an opinion about that subject. ❑ *The jury is out on whether or not this is true.* PHRASE: oft PHR *on* wh/n

| just |
|---|
| ① ADVERB USES |
| ② ADJECTIVE USE |

**① just** /dʒʌst/ ◆◆◆

⇒ Please look at category 20 to see if the expression you are looking for is shown under another headword. 1 You use **just** to say that something happened a very short time ago, or is starting to happen at the present time. For example, if you say that someone **has just arrived**, you mean that they arrived a very short time ago. ❑ *I've just bought a new house... The two had only just met... I just had the most awful dream... I'm only just beginning to take it in that he's still missing.* ADV: ADV before v 2 If you say that you are **just** doing something, you mean that you are doing it now and will finish it very soon. If you say that you are **just about to** do something, or **just going to** do it, you mean that you will do it very soon. ❑ *I'm just making the sauce for the cauliflower... I'm just going to walk down the lane now and post some letters... The Vietnam War was just about to end.* ADV: ADV before v, ADV *about/going* to-inf 3 You can use **just** to emphasize that something is happening at exactly the moment of speaking or at exactly the moment that you are talking about. ❑ *Randall would just now be getting the Sunday paper... Just then the phone rang... Just as she prepared to set off to the next village, two friends arrived in a taxi.* ADV: ADV adv/prep, ADV *as/when* cl [emphasis] 4 You use **just** to indicate that something is no more important, interesting, or difficult, for example, than you say it is, especially when you want to correct a wrong idea that someone may get or has already got. ❑ *It's just a suggestion... It's not just a financial matter... You can tell just by looking at me that I am all right.* ADV: ADV group/cl [emphasis] = *simply* 5 You use **just** to emphasize that you are talking about a small part, not the whole of an amount. ❑ *That's just one example of the kind of experiments you can do.* ADV: ADV n [emphasis] = *only, merely* 6 You use **just** to emphasize how small an amount is or how short a length of time is. ❑ *Stephanie and David redecorated a room in just three days.* ADV: ADV amount [emphasis] = *only* 7 You can use **just** in front of a verb to indicate that the result of something is unfortunate or undesirable and is likely to make the situation worse rather than better. ADV: ADV before v = *only*

❑ *Leaving like I did just made it worse.* [8] You use **just** to indicate that what you are saying is the case, but only by a very small degree or amount. ❑ *Her hand was just visible by the light from the sitting room... I arrived just in time for my flight to London.* ADV: ADV adj/adv/prep, ADV before v

[9] You use **just** with 'might,' 'may,' and 'could', when you mean that there is a small chance of something happening, even though it is not very likely. ❑ *It's an old trick but it just might work.* ADV: ADV with modal

[10] You use **just** to emphasize the following word or phrase, in order to express feelings such as annoyance, admiration, or certainty. ❑ *She just won't relax... I knew you'd be here. I just knew.* ADV: ADV before v, ADV adj/n [emphasis]

[11] You use **just** in expressions such as **just a minute** and **just a moment** to ask someone to wait for a short time. [SPOKEN] ❑ *'Let me in, Di.' — 'Okay. Just a minute.'* ADV: ADV n = hold on

[12] You can use **just** in expressions such as **just a minute** and **just a moment** to interrupt someone, for example in order to disagree with them, explain something, or calm them down. [SPOKEN] ❑ *Well, now just a second, I don't altogether agree with the premise.* ADV: ADV n

[13] You can use **just** with negative question tags, for example **'isn't he just?'** and **'don't they just!'**, to say that you agree completely with what has been said. [BRIT, SPOKEN] ❑ *'That's crazy,' I said. 'Isn't it just?' he said... 'The manager's going to have some tough decisions to make.' — 'Won't he just.'* ADV: with neg, cl ADV [emphasis]

[14] If you say that you can **just** see or hear something, you mean that it is easy for you to imagine seeing or hearing it. ❑ *I can just hear her telling her friends, 'Well, I blame his mother!'* ADV: ADV before v = almost

[15] You use **just** to mean exactly, when you are specifying something precisely or asking for precise information. ❑ *There are no statistics about just how many people won't vote... My arm hurts too, just here.* ADV: ADV cl/prep/adv

[16] You use **just** to emphasize that a particular thing is exactly what is needed or fits a particular description exactly. ❑ *Kiwi fruit are just the thing for a healthy snack... 'Let's get a coffee somewhere.' — 'I know just the place.'* ADV: ADV n [emphasis]

[17] You use **just** in expressions such as **just like**, **just as...as**, and **just the same** when you are emphasizing the similarity between two things or two people. ❑ *Behind the facade they are just like the rest of us... He worked just as hard as anyone.* ADV: ADV *like* n, ADV *as* adj/adv, ADV n [emphasis]

**PHRASES** [18] You use **just about** to indicate that what you are talking about is so close to being the case that it can be regarded as being the case. ❑ *What does she read? Just about everything.* PHRASE: PHR n/adj/adv = practically

[19] You use **just about** to indicate that what you are talking about is in fact the case, but only by a very small degree or amount. ❑ *We've got just about enough time to get there.* PHRASE: PHR before v, PHR n/adj

[20] **just my luck** → see **luck**. **not just** → see **not**. **just now** → see **now**. **only just** → see **only**. **it just goes to show** → see **show**.

**②just** /dʒʌst/ [1] If you describe a situation, action, or idea as **just**, you mean that it is right or acceptable according to particular moral principles, such as respect for all human beings. [FORMAL] ❑ *In a just society there must be a system whereby people can seek redress through the courts.* ADJ = fair ≠ unjust

♦ **just|ly** *No government can justly claim authority unless it is based on the will of the people.* ADV: ADV with v = fairly ≠ unjustly

[2] to **get** your **just deserts** → see **desert**.

**jus|tice** /dʒʌstɪs/ **(justices)** ◆◆◇ [1] **Justice** is fairness in the way that people are treated. ❑ *He has a good overall sense of justice and fairness... There is no justice in this world!* N-UNCOUNT

[2] The **justice of** a cause, claim, or argument is its quality of being reasonable, fair, or right. ❑ *We are a minority and must win people round to the justice of our cause.* N-UNCOUNT = legitimacy

[3] **Justice** is the legal system that a country uses in order to deal with people who break the law. ❑ *Many in Toronto's black community feel that the justice system does not treat them fairly.* N-UNCOUNT: oft N n

[4] A **justice** is a judge. [AM] ❑ *Thomas will be sworn in today as a justice on the Supreme Court.* N-COUNT

[5] **Justice** is used before the names of judges. ❑ *A preliminary hearing was due to start today before Mr Justice Hutchison, but was adjourned.* N-TITLE

[6] → See also **miscarriage of justice**.

**PHRASES** [7] If a criminal is **brought to justice**, he or she is punished for a crime by being arrested and tried in a court of law. ❑ *They demanded that those responsible be brought to justice.* PHRASE: V inflects

[8] To **do justice** to a person or thing means to reproduce them accurately and show how good they are. ❑ *The photograph I had seen didn't do her justice.* PHRASE: V inflects

[9] If you **do justice to** someone or something, you deal with them properly and completely. ❑ *No one article can ever do justice to the topic of fraud.* PHRASE: V inflects, usu PHR *to* n

[10] If you **do yourself justice**, you do something as well as you are capable of doing it. ❑ *I don't think he could do himself justice playing for England.* PHRASE: V inflects

[11] If you describe someone's treatment or punishment as **rough justice**, you mean that it is not given according to the law. [BRIT] ❑ *Trial by television makes for very rough justice indeed.* PHRASE

**Jus|tice of the Peace** **(Justices of the Peace)** [1] In Britain, a **Justice of the Peace** is a person who is not a lawyer but who can act as a judge in a local criminal law court. The abbreviation **JP** is also used. N-COUNT = magistrate

[2] In some states in the United States, a **Justice of the Peace** is an official who can carry out some legal tasks, such as settling minor cases in court or performing marriages. The abbreviation **JP** is also used. N-COUNT = magistrate

**jus|ti|fi|able** /dʒʌstɪfaɪəbəl/ An action, situation, emotion, or idea that is **justifiable** is acceptable or correct because there is a good reason for it. ❑ *The violence of the revolutionary years was justifiable on the grounds of political necessity.* ADJ: oft *it* v-link ADJ to-inf = legitimate

♦ **jus|ti|fi|ably** /dʒʌstɪfaɪəbli/ *He was justifiably proud of his achievements.* ADV

**jus|ti|fi|ca|tion** /dʒʌstɪfɪkeɪʃən/ **(justifications)** A **justification for** something is an acceptable reason or explanation for it. ❑ *To me the only justification for a zoo is educational.* N-VAR

**jus|ti|fied** /dʒʌstɪfaɪd/ [1] If you describe a decision, action, or idea as **justified**, you think it is reasonable and acceptable. ❑ *In my opinion, the decision was wholly justified.* ADJ

[2] If you think that someone is **justified in** doing something, you think that their reasons for doing it are good and valid. ❑ *He's absolutely justified in resigning. He was treated shamefully.* ADJ: v-link ADJ *in* -ing

**jus|ti|fy** /dʒʌstɪfaɪ/ **(justifies, justifying, justified)** ◆◇◇ [1] To **justify** a decision, action, or idea means to show or prove that it is reasonable or necessary. ❑ *No argument can justify a war... Ministers agreed that this decision was fully justified by economic conditions.* VERB V n V n

[2] To **justify** printed text means to adjust the spaces between the words so that each line of type is exactly the same length. [COMPUTING] ❑ *Click on this icon to align or justify text.* VERB V n

→ See also **left-justify**, **right-justify**.

**just|ly** /dʒʌstli/ You use **justly** to show that you approve of someone's attitude towards something, because it seems to be based on truth or reality. ❑ *Australians are justly proud of their native wildlife.* → See also **just**. ADV: usu ADV adj, also ADV with v [approval] = justifiably

**jut** /dʒʌt/ **(juts, jutting, jutted)** [1] If something **juts out**, it sticks out above or beyond a surface. ❑ *The northern end of the island juts out like a long, thin finger into the sea.* VERB = protrude V adv/prep

[2] If you **jut** a part of your body, especially your chin, or if it **juts**, you push it forward in an aggressive or determined way. ❑ *His jaw jutted stubbornly forward; he would not be denied... Gwen jutted her chin forward and did not answer the teacher... Ken's jaw jutted with determination.* VERB V adv/prep V n adv/prep V, Also V n

**jute** /dʒuːt/ **Jute** is a substance that is used to make cloth and rope. It comes from a plant which grows mainly in South-East Asia. N-UNCOUNT

**ju|venile** /dʒuːvənaɪl/ **(juveniles)** [1] A **juvenile** is a child or young person who is not yet old enough to be regarded as an adult. [FORMAL] ❑ *The number of juveniles in the general population has fallen by a fifth in the past 10 years.* N-COUNT

[2] **Juvenile** activity or behaviour involves young people who ADJ: ADJ n

are not yet adults. ❑ *Juvenile crime is increasing at a terrifying rate.* [3] If you describe someone's behaviour as **juvenile**, you are critical of it because you think that it is silly or childish. ❑ *He's a typical male, as he gets older he becomes more juvenile.* ADJ [disapproval] = *childish*

**ju|venile court (juvenile courts)** A **juvenile court** is a court which deals with crimes committed by young people who are not yet old enough to be considered as adults. N-VAR

**ju|venile de|lin|quen|cy** **Juvenile delinquency** is destruction of property and other criminal behaviour that is committed by young people who are not old enough to be legally considered as adults. N-UNCOUNT

**ju|venile de|lin|quent (juvenile delinquents)** A **juvenile delinquent** is a young person who is guilty of committing crimes, especially destruction of property or violence. N-COUNT

**jux|ta|pose** /dʒʌkstəpoʊz/ **(juxtaposes, juxtaposing, juxtaposed)** If you **juxtapose** two contrasting objects, images, or ideas, you place them together or describe them together, so that the differences between them are emphasized. [FORMAL] ❑ *The technique Mr Wilson uses most often is to juxtapose things for dramatic effect... Contemporary photographs are juxtaposed with a sixteenth century, copper Portuguese mirror. ...art's oldest theme: the celebration of life juxtaposed with the terror of mortality.* VERB V pl-n *be* V-ed *with* n V-ed Also V n *with* n

**jux|ta|po|si|tion** /dʒʌkstəpəzɪʃən/ **(juxtapositions)** The **juxtaposition of** two contrasting objects, images, or ideas is the fact that they are placed together or described together, so that the differences between them are emphasized. [FORMAL] ❑ *This juxtaposition of brutal reality and lyrical beauty runs through Park's stories.* N-VAR: usu N *of* n

# K k

**K, k** /keɪ/ **(K's, k's)** [1] **K** is the eleventh letter of the English alphabet. N-VAR [2] **K** or **k** is used as an abbreviation for words beginning with k, such as 'kilometre', 'kilobyte', or 'king'. [3] **K** or **k** is sometimes used to represent the number 1000, especially when referring to sums of money. [INFORMAL] NUM: usu num NUM ❑ *I used to make over 40k.*

**ka|bob** /kəbɒb/ **(kabobs)** → see **kebab**.

**kaf|tan** /kæftæn/ **(kaftans)** → see **caftan**.

**Kal|ash|ni|kov** /kəlæʃnɪkɒf/ **(Kalashnikovs)** N-COUNT A **Kalashnikov** is a type of rifle that is made in Russia.

**kale** /keɪl/ **Kale** is a vegetable that is similar to a cabbage. N-UNCOUNT

**ka|lei|do|scope** /kəlaɪdəskoʊp/ **(kaleidoscopes)** [1] A **kaleidoscope** is a toy in the shape of a tube with a small hole at one end. If you look through the hole and turn the other end of the tube, you can see a pattern of colours which changes as you turn the tube round. N-COUNT [2] You can describe something that is made up of a lot of different and frequently changing colours or elements as a **kaleidoscope**. N-SING: usu with supp, oft N *of* n ❑ *...the vivid kaleidoscope of colours displayed in the plumage of the peacock.*

**ka|lei|do|scop|ic** /kəlaɪdəskɒpɪk/ If you describe something as **kaleidoscopic**, you mean that it consists of a lot of very different parts, such as different colours, patterns, or shapes. ADJ: ADJ n ❑ *...a kaleidoscopic study of the shifting ideas and symbols of French nationhood.*

**ka|mi|ka|ze** /kæmɪkɑːzi/ If someone such as a soldier or terrorist performs a **kamikaze** act, they attack the enemy knowing that they will be killed doing it. ADJ: ADJ n ❑ *...kamikaze pilots ready to bomb nuclear installations.*

**kan|ga|roo** /kæŋgəruː/ **(kangaroos)** A **kangaroo** is a large Australian animal which moves by jumping on its back legs. Female kangaroos carry their babies in a pouch on their stomach. N-COUNT

**kan|ga|roo court** **(kangaroo courts)** If you refer to a court or a meeting as a **kangaroo court**, you disapprove of it because it is unofficial or unfair, and is intended to find someone guilty. N-COUNT [disapproval]

**ka|put** /kəpʊt/ If you say that something is **kaput**, you mean that it is completely broken, useless, or finished. [INFORMAL] ADJ: usu v-link ADJ ❑ *'What's happened to your car?' — 'It's kaput.'... He finally admitted that his film career was kaput.*

**kara|oke** /kærioʊki/ **Karaoke** is a form of entertainment in which a machine plays the tunes of songs, and people take it in turns to sing the words. N-UNCOUNT

**ka|ra|te** /kərɑːti/ **Karate** is a Japanese sport or way of fighting in which people fight using their hands, elbows, feet, and legs. N-UNCOUNT

**kar|ma** /kɑːʳmə/ In religions such as Hinduism and Buddhism, **karma** is the belief that your actions in this life affect all your future lives. N-UNCOUNT

**kart** /kɑːʳt/ **(karts)** A **kart** is the same as a **go-kart**. N-COUNT

**kay|ak** /kaɪæk/ **(kayaks)** A **kayak** is a narrow boat like a canoe, used by the Inuit people and in the sport of canoeing. N-COUNT

**ka|zoo** /kəzuː/ **(kazoos)** A **kazoo** is a small musical instrument that consists of a pipe with a hole in the top. You play the kazoo by blowing into it while making sounds. N-COUNT

**ke|bab** /kəbæb, AM -bɑːb/ **(kebabs)**

✔ in AM, also use **kabob**

A **kebab** is pieces of meat or vegetables grilled on a long thin stick, or slices of grilled meat served in pitta bread. N-VAR

**ked|geree** /kedʒəriː/ **Kedgeree** is a cooked dish consisting of rice, fish, and eggs. N-UNCOUNT

**keel** /kiːl/ **(keels, keeling, keeled)** [1] The **keel** of a boat is the long, specially shaped piece of wood or steel along the bottom of it. N-COUNT [2] If you say that someone or something is **on an even keel**, you mean that they are working or progressing smoothly and steadily, without any sudden changes. PHRASE: PHR after v, v-link PHR ❑ *Jason had helped him out with a series of loans, until he could get back on an even keel.*

♦ **keel over** If someone **keels over**, they collapse because they are tired or ill. [INFORMAL] PHRASAL VERB V P ❑ *He then keeled over and fell flat on his back.*

**keen** /kiːn/ **(keener, keenest)** ◆◇◇ [1] If you are **keen on** doing something, you very much want to do it. If you are **keen that** something should happen, you very much want it to happen. [mainly BRIT] ADJ: v-link ADJ, ADJ *on* -ing/n, ADJ that, ADJ to-inf ❑ *You're not keen on going, are you?... I'm very keen that the European Union should be as open as possible to trade from Russia... She's still keen to keep in touch... I am not keen for her to have a bicycle.* ♦ **keen|ness** *...Doyle's keenness to please. ...a keenness for the idea of a co-ordinated approach to development.* N-UNCOUNT: oft N to-inf = *enthusiasm* [2] If you are **keen on** something, you like it a lot and are very enthusiastic about it. [mainly BRIT] ADJ: v-link ADJ *on* n ❑ *I got quite keen on the idea.* ♦ **keen|ness** *...his keenness for the arts.* N-UNCOUNT [3] You use **keen** to indicate that someone has a lot of enthusiasm for a particular activity and spends a lot of time doing it. ADJ: ADJ n, v-link ADJ *on* n/-ing ❑ *She was a keen amateur photographer.* [4] If you describe someone as **keen**, you mean that they have an enthusiastic nature and are interested in everything that they do. ADJ = *enthusiastic* ❑ *He's a very keen student and works very hard.* ♦ **keen|ness** *...the keenness of the students.* N-UNCOUNT [5] A **keen** interest or emotion is one that is very intense. ADJ: usu ADJ n ❑ *He had retained a keen interest in the progress of the work.* ♦ **keen|ly** *She remained keenly interested in international affairs... This is a keenly awaited project.* ADV: ADV adj, ADV with v [6] If you are a **keen** supporter of a cause, movement, or idea, you support it enthusiastically. ADJ: ADJ n ❑ *He's been a keen supporter of the Labour Party all his life.* [7] If you say that someone has a **keen** mind, you mean that they are very clever and aware of what is happening around them. ADJ: ADJ n ❑ *They described him as a man of keen intellect.* ♦ **keen|ly** *They're keenly aware that whatever they decide will set a precedent.* ADV: ADV adj, ADV with v [8] If you have a **keen** eye or ear, you are able to notice things that are difficult to detect. ADJ: usu ADJ n = *sharp* ❑ *...an amateur artist with a keen eye for detail.* ♦ **keen|ly** *Charles listened keenly.* ADV: ADV with v [9] A **keen** fight or competition is one in which the competitors are all trying very hard to win, and it is not easy to predict who will win. ADJ ❑ *There is expected to be a keen fight in the local elections.* ♦ **keen|ly** *The contest should be very keenly fought.* ADV [10] **Keen** prices are low and competitive. [mainly ADJ

BRIT] ❑ *The company negotiates very keen prices with their suppliers.* ♦ **keen|ly** *The shops also offer a keenly priced curtain-making service.* ADV: ADV -ed [11] If you say that someone is **mad keen on** something, you are emphasizing that they are very enthusiastic about it. [BRIT, INFORMAL] ❑ *So you're not mad keen on science then?* PHRASE: v-link PHR, PHR n emphasis

**keep** /kiːp/ **(keeps, keeping, kept)** ♦♦♦ [1] If someone **keeps** or **is kept** in a particular state, they remain in it. ❑ *The noise kept him awake... To keep warm they burnt wood in a rusty oil barrel... For several years I kept in touch with her.* V-LINK V n adj/prep V adj/prep V adj/prep [2] If you **keep** or you **are kept** in a particular position or place, you remain in it. ❑ *Keep away from the doors while the train is moving... He kept his head down, hiding his features... Doctors will keep her in hospital for at least another week.* VERB V adv/prep V n with adv V n prep [3] If you **keep off** something or **keep away from** it, you avoid it. If you **keep out of** something, you avoid getting involved in it. You can also say that you **keep** someone **off**, **away from** or **out of** something. ❑ *I managed to stick to the diet and keep off sweet foods... The best way to keep babies off sugar is to go back to the natural diet and eat lots of fresh fruit.* VERB V prep/adv V n prep/adv [4] If someone or something **keeps** you **from** a particular action, they prevent you from doing it. ❑ *Embarrassment has kept me from doing all sorts of things.* VERB = stop V n *from* -ing [5] If you try to **keep from** doing something, you try to stop yourself from doing it. ❑ *She bit her lip to keep from crying.* VERB V *from* -ing [6] If you **keep** something **from** someone, you do not tell them about it. ❑ *She knew that Gabriel was keeping something from her.* VERB V n *from* n [7] If you **keep** doing something, you do it repeatedly or continue to do it. ❑ *I keep forgetting it's December... I turned back after a while, but he kept walking.* ♦ **Keep on** means the same as **keep**. ❑ *Did he give up or keep on trying?* VERB V -ing V -ing PHRASAL VERB V P -ing [8] **Keep** is used with some nouns to indicate that someone does something for a period of time or continues to do it. For example, if you **keep a grip on** something, you continue to hold or control it. ❑ *Until last year, the regime kept a tight grip on the country... One of them would keep a look-out on the road behind to warn us of approaching vehicles.* VERB V n V n [9] If you **keep** something, you continue to have it in your possession and do not throw it away, give it away, or sell it. ❑ *Lathan had to choose between marrying her and keeping his job.* VERB V n [10] If you **keep** something in a particular place, you always have it or store it in that place so that you can use it whenever you need it. ❑ *She kept her money under the mattress... To make it easier to contact us, keep this card handy.* VERB V n prep/adv V n adj [11] When you **keep** something such as a promise or an appointment, you do what you said you would do. ❑ *I'm hoping you'll keep your promise to come for a long visit.* VERB V n [12] If you **keep** a record of a series of events, you write down details of it so that they can be referred to later. ❑ *Eleanor began to keep a diary.* VERB V n [13] If you **keep** yourself or **keep** someone else, you support yourself or the other person by earning enough money to provide food, clothing, money, and other necessary things. ❑ *She could just about afford to keep her five kids... I just cannot afford to keep myself... The pay was enough to keep him in whisky for a day or two.* VERB V n V pron-refl V n *in* n [14] Someone's **keep** is the cost of food and other things that they need in their daily life. ❑ *Ray will earn his keep on local farms while studying.* N-SING: poss N [15] If you **keep** animals, you own them and take care of them. ❑ *I've brought you some eggs. We keep chickens.* VERB V n [16] If someone or something **keeps** you, they delay you and make you late. ❑ *'What kept you?' — 'I went in the wrong direction.'* VERB V n [17] If food **keeps** for a certain length of time, it stays fresh and suitable to eat for that time. ❑ *Whatever is left over may be put into the refrigerator, where it will keep for 2-3 weeks.* VERB V [18] You can say or ask how someone **is keeping** as a way of saying or asking whether they are well. ❑ *She hasn't been keeping too well lately.* VERB: only cont V adv [19] A **keep** is the main tower of a medieval castle, in which people lived. N-COUNT

**PHRASES** [20] If you **keep at it**, you continue doing something that you have started, even if you are tired and would prefer to stop. ❑ *It may take a number of attempts, but it is worth keeping at it.* PHRASE: V inflects [21] If you **keep going**, you continue moving along or doing something that you have started, even if you are tired and would prefer to stop. ❑ *She forced herself to keep going.* PHRASE: *keep* inflects [22] If one thing is **in keeping with** another, it is suitable in relation to that thing. If one thing is **out of keeping with** another, it is not suitable in relation to that thing. ❑ *His office was in keeping with his station and experience.* PHRASE: v-link PHR, PHR with cl, oft PHR *with* n [23] If you **keep it up**, you continue working or trying as hard as you have been in the past. ❑ *You're doing a great job! Keep it up!* PHRASE: V inflects [24] If you **keep** something **to yourself**, you do not tell anyone else about it. ❑ *I have to tell someone. I can't keep it to myself.* PHRASE: V inflects [25] If you **keep yourself to yourself** or **keep to yourself**, you stay on your own most of the time and do not mix socially with other people. ❑ *He was a quiet man who kept himself to himself.* PHRASE: V inflects ≠ *socialize* [26] to **keep** someone **company** → see **company**. to **keep a straight face** → see **face**. to **keep** your **head** → see **head**. to **keep pace** → see **pace**. to **keep the peace** → see **peace**. to **keep a secret** → see **secret**. to **keep time** → see **time**. to **keep track** → see **track**.

♦ **keep back** [1] If you **keep back** part of something, you do not use or give away all of it, so that you still have some to use at a later time. ❑ *Roughly chop the vegetables, and keep back a little to chop finely and serve as a garnish.* PHRASAL VERB = *set aside, hold back* V P n, Also V n P [2] If you **keep** some information **back**, you do not tell all that you know about something. ❑ *Neither of them is telling the whole truth. Invariably, they keep something back.* PHRASAL VERB V n P Also V P n (not pron)

♦ **keep down** [1] If you **keep** the number, size, or amount of something **down**, you do not let it get bigger or go higher. ❑ *The prime aim is to keep inflation down... Administration costs were kept down to just £460.* PHRASAL VERB V n P V P n (not pron) [2] If someone **keeps** a group of people **down**, they prevent them from getting power and status and being completely free. ❑ *No matter what a woman tries to do to improve her situation, there is some barrier or attitude to keep her down.* PHRASAL VERB = *hold back* V n P Also V P n (not pron) [3] If you **keep** food or drink **down**, you manage to swallow it properly and not vomit, even though you feel sick. ❑ *I tried to give her something to drink but she couldn't keep it down.* PHRASAL VERB V n P

♦ **keep on** [1] → see **keep 7**. [2] If you **keep** someone **on**, you continue to employ them, for example after they are old enough to retire or after other employees have lost their jobs. ❑ *Sometimes they keep you on a bit longer if there's no one quite ready to step into your shoes.* PHRASAL VERB V n P

♦ **keep on about** If you say that someone **keeps on about** something, you mean that they keep talking about it in a boring way. [BRIT, INFORMAL] ❑ *He kept on about me being 'defensive'.* PHRASAL VERB = *go on about* V P P n

♦ **keep on at** If you **keep on at** someone, you repeatedly ask or tell them something in a way that annoys them. [BRIT, INFORMAL] ❑ *You've constantly got to keep on at people about that... She kept on at him to get some qualifications.* PHRASAL VERB = *nag* V P P n V P P n to-inf

♦ **keep to** [1] If you **keep to** a rule, plan, or agreement, you do exactly what you are expected or supposed to do. ❑ *You've got to keep to the speed limit.* PHRASAL VERB = *stick to* V P n [2] If you **keep to** something such as a path or river, you do not move away from it as you go somewhere. ❑ *Please keep to the paths.* PHRASAL VERB = *stick to* V P n [3] If you **keep to** a particular subject, you talk only about that subject, and do not talk about anything else. ❑ *Let's keep to the subject, or you'll get me too confused.* PHRASAL VERB = *stick to* V P n [4] If you **keep** something **to** a particular number or quantity, you limit it to that number or quantity. ❑ *Keep costs to a minimum.* PHRASAL VERB V n P n

♦ **keep up** [1] If you **keep up with** someone or something that is moving near you, you move at the same speed. ❑ *She shook her head and started to walk on. He kept up with her.* PHRASAL VERB V P *with* n Also V P [2] To **keep up** PHRASAL VERB

**with** something that is changing means to be able to cope with the change, usually by changing at the same rate. ❑ *...wage increases which keep up with inflation... Things are changing so fast, it's hard to keep up.* [V P with n; V P] [3] If you **keep up with** your work or **with** other people, you manage to do or understand all your work, or to do or understand it as well as other people. ❑ *Penny tended to work through her lunch hour in an effort to keep up with her work... Life is tough for kids who aren't keeping up in school.* [PHRASAL VERB; V P with n; V P] [4] If you **keep up with** what is happening, you make sure that you know about it. ❑ *She did not bother to keep up with the news.* [PHRASAL VERB; V P with n; Also V P] [5] If you **keep** something **up**, you continue to do it or provide it. ❑ *I was so hungry all the time that I could not keep the diet up for longer than a month... They risk losing their homes because they can no longer keep up the repayments.* [PHRASAL VERB; V n P; V P n (not pron)] [6] If you **keep** something **up**, you prevent it from growing less in amount, level, or degree. ❑ *There will be a major incentive among TV channels to keep standards up... Opposition forces are keeping up the pressure against the government.* [PHRASAL VERB; V n P; V P n (not pron)] [7] → See also **keep 23**.

**keep|er** /kiːpəʳ/ **(keepers)** [1] In football, the **keeper** is the same as the **goalkeeper**. [BRIT, INFORMAL] [N-COUNT] [2] In American football, a **keeper** is a play in which the quarterback keeps the ball. [AM] [N-COUNT] [3] A **keeper** at a zoo is a person who takes care of the animals. [N-COUNT] [4] If you say that you **are not** someone**'s keeper**, you mean that you are not responsible for what they do or for what happens to them. [PHRASE: V inflects] [5] → See also **keep**.

**keep-fit** also **keep fit**. **Keep-fit** is the activity of keeping your body in good condition by doing special exercises. [mainly BRIT] [N-UNCOUNT: oft N n]

**keep|sake** /kiːpseɪk/ **(keepsakes)** A **keepsake** is a small present that someone gives you so that you will not forget them. [N-COUNT = memento]

**keg** /keg/ **(kegs)** A **keg** is a small barrel used for storing something such as beer or other alcoholic drinks. [N-COUNT: oft n N]

**kelp** /kelp/ **Kelp** is a type of flat brown seaweed. [N-UNCOUNT]

**ken** /ken/ If something is **beyond** your **ken**, you do not have enough knowledge to be able to understand it. ❑ *The subject matter was so technical as to be beyond the ken of the average layman.* [PHRASE: usu v-link PHR]

**ken|nel** /kenəl/ **(kennels)** [1] A **kennel** is a small building made especially for a dog to sleep in. [mainly BRIT] [N-COUNT]

✔ in AM, use **doghouse**

[2] **Kennels** or **a kennels** or **a kennel** is a place where dogs are bred and trained, or looked after when their owners are away. ❑ *The guard dog was now in kennels as it was not aggressive.* [N-COUNT: oft in N in pl]

**Ken|yan** /kenjən/ **(Kenyans)** [1] **Kenyan** means belonging or relating to Kenya, or to its people or culture. [ADJ] [2] A **Kenyan** is a Kenyan citizen, or a person of Kenyan origin. [N-COUNT]

**kept** /kept/ **Kept** is the past tense and past participle of **keep**.

**kerb** /kɜːʳb/ **(kerbs)**

✔ in AM, use **curb**

**The kerb** is the raised edge of a pavement or sidewalk which separates it from the road. ❑ *Stewart stepped off the kerb.* [N-COUNT: usu the N]

**kerb-crawling** **Kerb-crawling** is the activity of driving slowly along the side of a road in order to find and hire a prostitute. [BRIT] [N-UNCOUNT]

**ker|chief** /kɜːʳtʃɪf/ **(kerchiefs)** A **kerchief** is a piece of cloth that you can wear on your head or round your neck. [OLD-FASHIONED] [N-COUNT]

**ker|fuf|fle** /kəʳfʌfəl/ A **kerfuffle** is a lot of argument, noisy activity, or fuss. [BRIT, INFORMAL] ❑ *There was a bit of a kerfuffle during the race when a dog impeded the leading runners.* [N-SING = commotion]

**ker|nel** /kɜːʳnəl/ **(kernels)** [1] The **kernel** of a nut is the part that is inside the shell. [N-COUNT] [2] The **kernel of** something is the central and most important part of it. ❑ *The kernel of that message was that peace must not be a source of advantage or disadvantage for anyone.* [N-COUNT: usu sing, usu N of n = core, crux] [3] A **kernel of** something is a small element of it. ❑ *For all I know, there may be a kernel of truth in what he says.* [N-COUNT: usu sing, usu N of n = grain]

**kero|sene** /kerəsiːn/ **Kerosene** is a clear, strong-smelling liquid which is used as a fuel, for example in heaters and lamps. [mainly AM] [N-UNCOUNT = paraffin]

✔ in BRIT, use **paraffin**

**kes|trel** /kestrəl/ **(kestrels)** A **kestrel** is a small bird of prey. [N-COUNT]

**ketch** /ketʃ/ **(ketches)** A **ketch** is a type of sailing ship that has two masts. [N-COUNT]

**ketch|up** /ketʃʌp/

✔ in AM, also use **catsup**

**Ketchup** is a thick, cold sauce, usually made from tomatoes, that is sold in bottles. [N-UNCOUNT]

**ket|tle** /ketəl/ **(kettles)** [1] A **kettle** is a covered container that you use for boiling water. It has a handle, and a spout for the water to come out of. [mainly BRIT] ❑ *I'll put the kettle on and make us some tea.* [N-COUNT] ♦ A **kettle of** water is the amount of water contained in a kettle. ❑ *Pour a kettle of boiling water over the onions.* [N-COUNT: usu N of n]

✔ in AM, use **teakettle**

[2] A **kettle** is a metal pot for boiling or cooking things in. [mainly AM] ❑ *Put the meat into a small kettle.* [N-COUNT]

✔ in BRIT, use **pan**

[3] If you say that something is **a different kettle of fish**, you mean that it is very different from another related thing that you are talking about. [INFORMAL] ❑ *Playing for the reserve team is a totally different kettle of fish.* [PHRASE: v-link PHR]

**kettle|drum** /ketəldrʌm/ **(kettledrums)** A **kettledrum** is a large bowl-shaped drum which can be tuned to play a particular note. [N-COUNT = timpani]

**key** /kiː/ **(keys, keying, keyed)** [1] A **key** is a specially shaped piece of metal that you place in a lock and turn in order to open or lock a door, or to start or stop the engine of a vehicle. ❑ *They put the key in the door and entered.* [◆◆◇ N-COUNT] [2] The **keys** on a computer keyboard or typewriter are the buttons that you press in order to operate it. [N-COUNT: usu pl] [3] The **keys** of a piano or organ are the long narrow pieces of wood or plastic that you press in order to play it. [N-COUNT: usu pl] [4] In music, a **key** is a scale of musical notes that starts on one specific note. ❑ *...the key of A minor.* [N-VAR] [5] The **key** on a map or diagram or in a technical book is a list of the symbols or abbreviations used and their meanings. ❑ *You will find a key at the front of the book.* [N-COUNT] [6] The **key** person or thing in a group is the most important one. ❑ *He is expected to be the key witness at the trial.* [ADJ: ADJ n] [7] The **key to** a desirable situation or result is the way in which it can be achieved. ❑ *The key to success is to be ready from the start.* [N-COUNT: usu N to n] [8] → See also **master key**.

♦ **key in** If you **key** something **in**, you put information into a computer or you give the computer a particular instruction by typing the information or instruction on the keyboard. ❑ *Brian keyed in his personal code.* [PHRASAL VERB = type in; V P n (not pron); Also V n P]

**key|board** /kiːbɔːʳd/ **(keyboards)** [1] The **keyboard** of a typewriter or computer is the set of keys that you press in order to operate it. [N-COUNT] [2] The **keyboard** of a piano or organ is the set of black and white keys that you press in order to play it. ❑ *Tanya's hands rippled over the keyboard.* [N-COUNT] [3] People sometimes refer to musical instruments that have a keyboard as **keyboards**. ❑ *...Sean O'Hagan on keyboards.* [N-COUNT: usu pl]

**key|board|er** /kiːbɔːʳdəʳ/ **(keyboarders)** A **keyboarder** is a person whose job is typing information into a computer or word processor. [N-COUNT]

**key|board|ing** /kiːbɔːʳdɪŋ/ **Keyboarding** is the activity of typing information into a computer or word processor. N-UNCOUNT

**key|board|ist** /kiːbɔːʳdɪst/ **(keyboardists)** A **keyboardist** is someone who plays keyboard instruments, especially in popular music. N-COUNT

**key card** **(key cards)** A **key card** is a small plastic card which you can use instead of a key to open a door or barrier, for example in some hotels and car parks. N-COUNT

**keyed up** If you are **keyed up**, you are very excited or nervous before an important or dangerous event. ❑ *I wasn't able to sleep that night, I was so keyed up.* ADJ: v-link ADJ = tense

**key|hole** /kiːhoʊl/ **(keyholes)** A **keyhole** is the hole in a lock that you put a key in. ❑ *I looked through the keyhole.* N-COUNT

**key|hole sur|gery** **Keyhole surgery** is a surgical technique in which the surgeon inserts the instruments through small cuts in the patient's body, using as a guide an image provided by equipment inserted into the patient's body. [MEDICAL] N-UNCOUNT

**key|note** /kiːnoʊt/ **(keynotes)** The **keynote of** a policy, speech, or idea is the main theme of it or the part of it that is emphasized the most. ❑ *He would be setting out his plans for the party in a keynote speech.* N-COUNT: usu sing, oft N n, N *of* n

**key|pad** /kiːpæd/ **(keypads)** The **keypad** on a modern telephone is the set of buttons that you press in order to operate it. Some other machines, such as cash dispensers, also have a keypad. N-COUNT

**key play|er** **(key players)** The **key players** in a particular organization, event, or situation are the most important people or things involved in it. ❑ *The former chairman was a key player in the deals that pushed the bank to the top.* N-COUNT

**key ring** **(key rings)** also **keyring.** A **key ring** is a metal ring which you use to keep your keys together. You pass the ring through the holes in your keys. N-COUNT

**key|stone** /kiːstoʊn/ **(keystones)** A **keystone of** a policy, system, or process is an important part of it, which is the basis for later developments. ❑ *Keeping inflation low is the keystone of their economic policy.* N-COUNT: usu sing, oft N *of/in* n

**key|stroke** /kiːstroʊk/ **(keystrokes)** A **keystroke** is one touch of one of the keys on a computer or typewriter keyboard. N-COUNT

**key|worker** /kiːwɜːʳkəʳ/ **(keyworkers)** The **keyworker** for a particular group of clients or patients is the person who works with them most closely and has most responsibility for them. N-COUNT

**kg** **kg** is an abbreviation for **kilogram** or **kilograms**.

**kha|ki** /kɑːki, AM kæki/ 1 **Khaki** is a strong material of a greenish brown colour, used especially to make uniforms for soldiers. ❑ *On each side of me was a figure in khaki.* N-UNCOUNT 2 Something that is **khaki** is greenish brown in colour. ❑ *He was dressed in khaki trousers.* COLOUR

**kHz** **kHz** is a written abbreviation for **kilohertz**. It is often written on radios beside a range of numbers to help you find a particular radio station. = kilohertz

**kib|butz** /kɪbʊts/ **(kibbutzim** /kɪbʊtsiːm/**)** A **kibbutz** is a place of work in Israel, for example a farm or factory, where the workers live together and share all the duties and income. N-COUNT

**kick** /kɪk/ **(kicks, kicking, kicked)** ◆◆◇ 1 If you **kick** someone or something, you hit them forcefully with your foot. VERB ❑ *He kicked the door hard...* V n *He threw me to the ground and started to kick...* V *He escaped by kicking open the window...* V n with adj *The fiery actress kicked him in the shins...* V n *in* n *An ostrich can kick a man to death.* V n *to* n ♦ **Kick** is also a noun. N-COUNT ❑ *He suffered a kick to the knee.* 2 When you **kick** a ball or other object, you hit it with your foot so that it moves through the air. VERB ❑ *I went to kick the ball and I completely missed it...* V n *He kicked the ball away...* V n with adv *A furious player kicked his racket into the grandstand.* V n prep ♦ **Kick** is also a noun. N-COUNT ❑ *Schmeichel swooped to save the first kick from Borisov.* 3 If you **kick** or if you **kick** your legs, you move your legs with very quick, small, and forceful movements, once or repeatedly. VERB ❑ *They were dragged away struggling and kicking...* V *First he kicked the left leg, then he kicked the right...* V n *He kicked his feet away from the window.* V n adv/prep ♦ **Kick out** means the same as **kick**. PHRASAL VERB ❑ *As its rider tried to free it, the horse kicked out.* V P 4 If you **kick** your legs, you lift your legs up very high one after the other, for example when you are dancing. VERB ❑ *He was kicking his legs like a Can Can dancer...* V n *She begins dancing, kicking her legs high in the air.* V n adj 5 If you **kick** a habit, you stop doing something that is bad for you and that you find difficult to stop doing. [INFORMAL] VERB ❑ *She's kicked her drug habit and learned that her life has value.* V n 6 If something gives you **a kick**, it makes you feel very excited or very happy for a short period of time. [INFORMAL] N-SING: *a* N ❑ *I got a kick out of seeing my name in print.*

**PHRASES** 7 If you say that someone **kicks** you **when** you **are down**, you think they are behaving unfairly because they are attacking you when you are in a weak position. PHRASE: V inflects ❑ *In the end I just couldn't kick Jimmy when he was down.* 8 If you say that someone does something **for kicks**, you mean that they do it because they think it will be exciting. [INFORMAL] PHRASE: PHR after v ❑ *They made a few small bets for kicks.* 9 If you say that someone is dragged **kicking and screaming into** a particular course of action, you are emphasizing that they are very unwilling to do what they are being made to do. PHRASE: PHR after v, oft PHR *into* n/-ing emphasis ❑ *He had to be dragged kicking and screaming into action.* 10 If you describe an event as **a kick in the teeth**, you are emphasizing that it is very disappointing and upsetting. [INFORMAL] PHRASE: usu v-link PHR, PHR after v emphasis = setback ❑ *We've been struggling for years and it's a real kick in the teeth to see a new band make it ahead of us.* 11 You use **kick yourself** in expressions such as **I could have kicked myself** and **you're going to kick yourself** to indicate that you were annoyed or are going to be annoyed that you got something wrong. PHRASE: V inflects feelings ❑ *I was still kicking myself for not paying attention.* 12 **alive and kicking** → see **alive**. to **kick up a fuss** → see **fuss**.

♦ **kick around** If you **kick around** ideas or suggestions, you discuss them informally. [INFORMAL] PHRASAL VERB ❑ *We kicked a few ideas around...* V n P *They started to kick around the idea of an electric scraper.* V P n (not pron)

♦ **kick back** If you **kick back**, you relax. [mainly AM, INFORMAL] PHRASAL VERB ❑ *As soon as they've finished up, they kick back and wait for the next show.* V P

♦ **kick down** or **kick in** If someone **kicks** something **down** or if they **kick** it **in**, they hit it violently with their foot so that it breaks or falls over. PHRASAL VERB = break down, smash down ❑ *She was forced to kick down the front door.* V P n, Also V n P

♦ **kick in** 1 If something **kicks in**, it begins to take effect. PHRASAL VERB ❑ *As discounts kicked in, bookings for immediate travel rose by 15%.* V P 2 If someone **kicks in** a particular amount of money, they provide that amount of money to help pay for something. [AM] PHRASAL VERB = contribute ❑ *Kansas City area churches kicked in $35,000 to support the event.* V P n (not pron) → See also **kick down**.

♦ **kick off** 1 In football, when the players **kick off**, they start a game by kicking the ball from the centre of the pitch. PHRASAL VERB ❑ *Liverpool kicked off an hour ago.* V P 2 If an event, game, series, or discussion **kicks off**, or **is kicked off**, it begins. PHRASAL VERB ❑ *The shows kick off on October 24th...* V P *The Mayor kicked off the party...* V P n *We kicked off with a slap-up dinner.* V P *with* n Also V n P 3 If you **kick off** your shoes, you shake your feet so that your shoes come off. PHRASAL VERB ❑ *She stretched out on the sofa and kicked off her shoes.* V P n 4 To **kick** someone **off** an area of land means to force them to leave it. [INFORMAL] PHRASAL VERB ❑ *We can't kick them off the island.* V n P n

♦ **kick out** To **kick** someone **out of** a place means to force them to leave it. [INFORMAL] PHRASAL VERB = throw out ❑ *The country's leaders kicked five foreign journalists out of* V n P *of* n the country... Her family kicked her out. → See also kick 3. V n P Also V P n (not pron)

♦ **kick up** [1] If you **kick up** a fuss about something, you make it very obvious that you are annoyed or dissatisfied. ❑ *Those customers who have kicked up a fuss have received refunds.* PHRASAL VERB V P n (not pron) [2] If you **kick up** dust or dirt, you create a cloud of dust or dirt as you move along a dusty road. ❑ *She shuffled along, kicking up clouds of dust.* PHRASAL VERB = stir up V P n (not pron)

**kick|back** /kɪkbæk/ **(kickbacks)** A **kickback** is a sum of money that is paid to someone illegally, for example money which a company pays someone to arrange for the company to be chosen to do an important job. ❑ *...alleged kickbacks and illegal party financing.* N-COUNT

**kick box|ing** also **kickboxing. Kick boxing** is a type of boxing in which the opponents are allowed to kick as well as punch each other. N-UNCOUNT

**kick-off (kick-offs)**

in AM, use **kickoff**

[1] In football, the **kick-off** is the time at which a particular game starts. [BRIT] ❑ *The kick-off is at 1.30.* N-VAR [2] In American football, a **kickoff** is the kick that begins a play, for example at the beginning of a half or after a touchdown or field goal. [AM] N-COUNT [3] The **kick-off** of an event or activity is its beginning. [INFORMAL] ❑ *People stood waiting for the kick-off of the parade.* N-SING

**kick-start (kick-starts, kick-starting, kick-started)** also **kickstart.** [1] To **kick-start** a process that has stopped working or progressing is to take a course of action that will quickly start it going again. ❑ *The President has chosen to kick-start the economy by slashing interest rates.* VERB V n ♦ **Kick-start** is also a noun. ❑ *The housing market needs a kick-start.* N-COUNT [2] If you **kick-start** a motorcycle, you press the lever that starts it with your foot. ❑ *He lifted the bike off its stand and kick-started it.* VERB V n

**kid** /kɪd/ **(kids, kidding, kidded)** [1] You can refer to a child as a **kid**. [INFORMAL] ❑ *They've got three kids... All the kids in my class could read.* ◆◆◇ N-COUNT [2] You can refer to your younger brother as your **kid** brother and your younger sister as your **kid** sister. [INFORMAL] ADJ: ADJ n [3] A **kid** is a young goat. N-COUNT [4] If you **are kidding**, you are saying something that is not really true, as a joke. [INFORMAL] ❑ *I'm not kidding, Frank. There's a cow out there, just standing around... Are you sure you're not kidding me?* VERB: usu cont V V n [5] If you **kid** someone, you tease them. ❑ *He liked to kid Ingrid a lot... He used to kid me about being chubby.* VERB V n V n about -ing/n [6] If people **kid themselves**, they allow themselves to believe something that is not true because they wish that it was true. ❑ *We're kidding ourselves, Bill. We're not winning, we're not even doing well... I could kid myself that you did this for me, but it would be a lie.* VERB = fool V pron-refl V pron-refl that [7] You can say **'No kidding?'** to show that you are interested or surprised when someone tells you something. [INFORMAL] ❑ *'We won.' — 'No kidding?'* CONVENTION [feelings]

PHRASES [8] You can say **'you've got to be kidding'** or **'you must be kidding'** to someone if they have said something that you think is ridiculous or completely untrue. [INFORMAL] ❑ *You've got to be kidding! I can't live here!.* PHRASE: V inflects [feelings] [9] You can say **'who is she kidding?'** or **'who is he trying to kid?'** if you think it is obvious that someone is not being sincere and does not mean what they say. [INFORMAL] ❑ *She played the role of a meek, innocent, shy girl. I don't know who she was trying to kid.* PHRASE: V inflects

**kid|die** /kɪdi/ **(kiddies)** also **kiddy.** A **kiddie** is a very young child. [INFORMAL] N-COUNT

**kiddo** /kɪdoʊ/ **(kiddos)** You can call someone **kiddo**, especially someone who is younger than you, as a sign of affection. [mainly AM, INFORMAL] ❑ *I'll miss you kiddo.* N-VOC

**kid gloves** If you treat someone or something **with kid gloves**, or if you give them the **kid glove** treatment, you are very careful in the way you deal with them. ❑ *In presidential campaigns, foreign policy is treated with kid gloves.* N-PLURAL: oft with N

**kid|nap** /kɪdnæp/ **(kidnaps, kidnapping, kidnapped)**

in AM, also use **kidnaped, kidnaping**

[1] To **kidnap** someone is to take them away illegally and by force, and usually to hold them prisoner in order to demand something from their family, employer, or government. ❑ *Police in Brazil uncovered a plot to kidnap him... They were intelligent and educated, yet they chose to kidnap and kill... The kidnapped man was said to have been seized by five people.* VERB V n V V-ed ♦ **kid|nap|per (kidnappers)** *His kidnappers have threatened that they will kill him unless three militants are released from prison.* N-COUNT ♦ **kid|nap|ping (kidnappings)** *Two youngsters have been arrested and charged with kidnapping.* N-VAR [2] **Kidnap** or a **kidnap** is the crime of taking someone away by force. ❑ *He was charged with the kidnap of a 25 year-old woman.* N-VAR = abduction

**kid|ney** /kɪdni/ **(kidneys)** [1] Your **kidneys** are the organs in your body that take waste matter from your blood and send it out of your body as urine. N-COUNT [2] **Kidneys** are the kidneys of an animal, for example a lamb, calf, or pig, that are eaten as meat. ❑ *...steak and kidney pie.* N-VAR

**kid|ney bean (kidney beans)** [1] **Kidney beans** are small, reddish-brown beans that are eaten as a vegetable. They are the seeds of a bean plant. → See picture on page 1712. N-COUNT: usu pl [2] **Kidney beans** are long, very narrow beans that are green in colour and are eaten as a vegetable. They grow on a tall climbing plant and are the cases that contain the seeds of the plant. [AM] N-COUNT: usu pl

in BRIT, use **French beans**

**kill** /kɪl/ **(kills, killing, killed)** [1] If a person, animal, or other living thing **is killed**, something or someone causes them to die. ❑ *More than 1,000 people have been killed by the armed forces... He had attempted to kill himself on several occasions... The earthquake killed 62 people... Heroin can kill.* ◆◆◆ VERB be V-ed V pron-refl V n V ♦ **kill|ing** *There is tension in the region following the killing of seven civilians.* N-UNCOUNT: usu N of n [2] The act of killing an animal after hunting it is referred to as **the kill**. ❑ *After the kill the men and old women collect in an open space and eat a meal of whale meat.* N-COUNT: usu sing [3] If someone or something **kills** a project, activity, or idea, they completely destroy or end it. ❑ *His objective was to kill the space station project altogether.* VERB V n ♦ **Kill off** means the same as **kill**. ❑ *He would soon launch a second offensive, killing off the peace process... The Government's financial squeeze had killed the scheme off.* PHRASAL VERB V P n (not pron) V n P [4] If something **kills** pain, it weakens it so that it is no longer as strong as it was. ❑ *He was forced to take opium to kill the pain.* VERB V n [5] If you say that something **is killing** you, you mean that it is causing you physical or emotional pain. [INFORMAL] ❑ *My feet are killing me.* VERB: only cont V pron [6] If you say that you **kill yourself to** do something, you are emphasizing that you make a great effort to do it, even though it causes you a lot of trouble or suffering. [INFORMAL] ❑ *You shouldn't always have to kill yourself to do well.* VERB [emphasis] V pron-refl [7] If you say that you will **kill** someone for something they have done, you are emphasizing that you are extremely angry with them. ❑ *Tell Richard I'm going to kill him when I get hold of him.* VERB [emphasis] V n [8] If you say that something will not **kill** you, you mean that it is not really as difficult or unpleasant as it might seem. [INFORMAL] ❑ *Three or four more weeks won't kill me!* VERB V pron [9] If you **are killing** time, you are doing something because you have some time available, not because you really want to do it. ❑ *I'm just killing time until I can talk to the other witnesses... To kill the hours while she waited, Ann worked in the garden.* VERB V n V n Also V n -ing

PHRASES [10] If you say that you will do something **if it kills** you, you are emphasizing that you are determined to do it even though it is extremely difficult or painful. ❑ *I'll make this marriage work if it kills me.* PHRASE: V inflects, PHR with cl [emphasis] [11] If you say that you **killed yourself laughing**, you are emphasizing that you laughed a lot because you thought something was PHRASE: V inflects [emphasis] extremely funny. [INFORMAL] 12 If you **move in for the kill** or if you **close in for the kill**, you take advantage of a changed situation in order to do something that you have been preparing to do. ❑ *Seeing his chance, Dennis moved in for the kill.* 13 to **kill two birds with one stone** → see **bird**. **dressed to kill** → see **dressed**. to **be killed outright** → see **outright**.

PHRASE: V inflects

♦ **kill off** 1 → see **kill** 3. 2 If you say that a group or an amount of something **has been killed off**, you mean that all of them or all of it have been killed or destroyed. ❑ *Their natural predators have been killed off... It is an effective treatment for the bacteria and does kill it off... All blood products are now heat treated to kill off any infection.*

PHRASAL VERB; be V-ed P; V n P; V P n (not pron)

**kill|er** /kɪləʳ/ **(killers)** 1 A **killer** is a person who has killed someone, or who intends to kill someone. ❑ *The police are searching for his killers.* 2 You can refer to something that causes death or is likely to cause death as a **killer**. ❑ *Heart disease is the biggest killer of men in most developed countries.*

◆◇◇ N-COUNT = murderer; N-COUNT

**kill|er bee** **(killer bees)** A **killer bee** is a type of bee which is very aggressive and likely to attack and sting people.

N-COUNT

**kill|er in|stinct** **(killer instincts)** If you say that a sports player or politician has **the killer instinct**, you admire them for their toughness and determination to succeed. ❑ *He quit the sport when he realised he didn't have the killer instinct.*

N-VAR approval

**kill|er whale** **(killer whales)** A **killer whale** is a type of black and white whale.

N-COUNT

**kill|ing** /kɪlɪŋ/ **(killings)** 1 A **killing** is an act of deliberately killing a person. ❑ *This is a brutal killing.* 2 If you **make a killing**, you make a large profit very quickly and easily. [INFORMAL] ❑ *They have made a killing on the deal.*

◆◇◇ N-COUNT = murder; PHRASE: V and N inflect

**kill|joy** /kɪldʒɔɪ/ **(killjoys)** If you call someone a **killjoy**, you are critical of them because they stop other people from enjoying themselves, often by reminding them of something unpleasant. ❑ *Don't be such a killjoy!.*

N-COUNT disapproval = spoilsport

**kiln** /kɪln/ **(kilns)** A **kiln** is an oven that is used to bake pottery and bricks in order to make them hard.

N-COUNT

**kilo** /kiːloʊ/ **(kilos)** A **kilo** is the same as a **kilogram**. ❑ *He'd lost ten kilos in weight. ...a kilo of rice.*

N-COUNT: num N

**kilo-** /kɪloʊ-/ **Kilo-** is added to some nouns that refer to units of measurement in order to form other nouns referring to units a thousand times bigger. ❑ *...100 kilojoules of energy. ...an explosion of around 20 kilotons.*

PREFIX

**kilo|byte** /kɪləbaɪt/ **(kilobytes)** In computing, a **kilobyte** is one thousand bytes of data.

N-COUNT

**kilo|gram** /kɪləgræm/ **(kilograms)** also **kilogramme.** A **kilogram** is a metric unit of weight. One kilogram is a thousand grams, or a thousandth of a metric ton, and is equal to 2.2 pounds. ❑ *...a parcel weighing around 4.5 kilograms.*

N-COUNT: num N, oft N of n = kilo

**kilo|hertz** /kɪləhɜːʳts/ **(kilohertz)** A **kilohertz** is a unit of measurement of radio waves. One kilohertz is a thousand hertz.

N-COUNT: num N

**kilo|metre** /kɪləmiːtəʳ, kɪlɒmɪtəʳ/ **(kilometres)**

◆◇◇

☑ in AM, use **kilometer**

A **kilometre** is a metric unit of distance or length. One kilometre is a thousand metres and is equal to 0.62 miles. ❑ *...about twenty kilometres from the border... The fire destroyed some 40,000 square kilometres of forest.*

N-COUNT: num N

**kilo|watt** /kɪləwɒt/ **(kilowatts)** A **kilowatt** is a unit of power. One kilowatt is a thousand watts.

N-COUNT: num N, oft N of n

**kilowatt-hour** **(kilowatt-hours)** A **kilowatt-hour** is a unit of energy that is equal to the energy provided by a thousand watts in one hour.

N-COUNT

**kilt** /kɪlt/ **(kilts)** A **kilt** is a skirt with a lot of vertical folds, traditionally worn by Scottish men. Kilts can also be worn by women and girls.

N-COUNT

**kil|ter** /kɪltəʳ/ 1 If one thing is **out of kilter with** another, the first thing does not agree with or fit in with the second. ❑ *Her lifestyle was out of kilter with her politics.* 2 If something or someone is **out of kilter** or **off kilter**, they are not completely right. ❑ *Ignoring feelings of tiredness knocks our body clocks out of kilter.*

PHRASE: oft v-link PHR with n; PHRASE: oft v-link PHR

**ki|mo|no** /kɪmoʊnoʊ, AM -nə/ **(kimonos)** A **kimono** is an item of Japanese clothing. It is long, shaped like a coat, and has wide sleeves.

N-COUNT

**kin** /kɪn/ Your **kin** are your relatives. [DIALECT or OLD-FASHIONED] ❑ *She has gone to live with her husband's kin.* → See also **kith and kin**, **next of kin**.

N-PLURAL

| kind |
|---|
| ① NOUN USES AND PHRASES |
| ② ADJECTIVE USES |

① **kind** /kaɪnd/ **(kinds)** 1 If you talk about a particular **kind of** thing, you are talking about one of the types or sorts of that thing. ❑ *The party needs a different kind of leadership... Had Jamie ever been in any kind of trouble?... This book prize is the biggest of its kind in the world.* 2 If you refer to someone's **kind**, you are referring to all the other people that are like them or that belong to the same class or set. ❑ *I can take care of your kind.*

◆◆◆ N-COUNT: usu N of n = sort, type; N-COUNT: poss N disapproval = sort, type

PHRASES 3 You can use **all kinds of** to emphasize that there are a great number and variety of particular things or people. ❑ *Adoption can fail for all kinds of reasons.* 4 You use **kind of** when you want to say that something or someone can be roughly described in a particular way. [SPOKEN] ❑ *It was kind of sad, really.* 5 You can use **of a kind** to indicate that something is not as good as it might be expected to be, but that it seems to be the best that is possible or available. ❑ *She finds solace of a kind in alcohol.* 6 If you refer to someone or something as **one of a kind**, you mean that there is nobody or nothing else like them. ❑ *She's a very unusual woman, one of a kind.* 7 If you refer, for example, to **two, three,** or **four of a kind**, you mean two, three, or four similar people or things that seem to go well or belong together. ❑ *They were two of a kind, from the same sort of background.* 8 If you respond **in kind**, you react to something that someone has done to you by doing the same thing to them. ❑ *They hurled defiant taunts at the riot police, who responded in kind.* 9 If you pay a debt **in kind**, you pay it in the form of goods or services and not money. ❑ *...benefits in kind.*

PHRASE: PHR n emphasis; PHRASE: PHR adj/adv/n, PHR before v vagueness; PHRASE: n PHR; PHRASE approval; PHRASE; PHRASE: PHR after v; PHRASE: PHR after v, n PHR

② **kind** /kaɪnd/ **(kinder, kindest)** 1 Someone who is **kind** behaves in a gentle, caring, and helpful way towards other people. ❑ *I must thank you for being so kind to me... It was very kind of you to come.* ♦ **kind|ly** *'You seem tired this morning, Jenny,' she said kindly.* 2 You can use **kind** in expressions such as **please be so kind as to** and **would you be kind enough to** in order to ask someone to do something in a firm but polite way. ❑ *I wonder if you'd be kind enough to call him.* 3 → See also **kindly**, **kindness**.

ADJ: oft ADJ to n, it v-link ADJ of n to-inf; ADV: ADV after v; ADJ: v-link ADJ politeness

**kinda** /kaɪndə/ **Kinda** is used in written English to represent the words 'kind of' when they are pronounced informally. ❑ *I'd kinda like to have a sheep farm in New Mexico.*

**kin|der|gar|ten** /kɪndəʳgɑːʳtᵊn/ **(kindergartens)** A **kindergarten** is an informal kind of school for very young children, where they learn things by playing. ❑ *She's in kindergarten now.*

N-COUNT: also in/to/at N = nursery

**kind-hearted** If you describe someone as **kind-hearted**, you mean that they are kind, caring, and generous. ❑ *He was a warm, generous and kind-hearted man.*

ADJ = kind

**kin|dle** /kɪndᵊl/ **(kindles, kindling, kindled)** 1 If something **kindles** a particular emotion in someone, it makes them start to feel it. ❑ *The second world war kindled his enthusiasm for politics.* 2 If you **kindle** a fire, you light paper or wood in

VERB: V n; VERB

order to start it. ❑ *I came in and kindled a fire in the stove.* V n

**kin|dling** /kɪndlɪŋ/ **Kindling** is small pieces of dry wood and other materials that you use to start a fire. N-UNCOUNT

**kind|ly** /kaɪndli/ 1 A **kindly** person is kind, caring, and sympathetic. ❑ *He was a stern critic but an extremely kindly man.* ADJ: usu ADJ n 2 If someone **kindly** does something for you, they act in a thoughtful and helpful way. ❑ *He kindly carried our picnic in a rucksack.* ADV: ADV before v 3 If someone asks you to **kindly** do something, they are asking you in a way which shows that they have authority over you, or that they are angry with you. [FORMAL] ❑ *Will you kindly obey the instructions I am about to give?* ADV: ADV before v 4 → See also **kind**.

PHRASES 5 If you **look kindly on** or **look kindly upon** someone or something, you support them or approve of what they are doing. ❑ *Recent historical work looks kindly on the regime.* PHRASE: V inflects, PHR n 6 If someone **does not take kindly to** something, they do not like it. ❑ *She did not take kindly to being offered advice.* PHRASE: V inflects, PHR n/-ing

**kind|ness** /kaɪndnəs/ **Kindness** is the quality of being gentle, caring, and helpful. ❑ *We have been treated with such kindness by everybody.* N-UNCOUNT

**kin|dred** /kɪndrɪd/ 1 Your **kindred** are your family, and all the people who are related to you. [DIALECT or OLD-FASHIONED] N-UNCOUNT: with poss = relatives 2 **Kindred** things are similar to each other. [FORMAL] ❑ *I recall many discussions with her on these and kindred topics.* ADJ: usu ADJ n = similar

**kin|dred spir|it** (**kindred spirits**) A **kindred spirit** is a person who has the same view of life or the same interests as you. N-COUNT

**ki|net|ic** /kɪnetɪk/ In physics, **kinetic** is used to describe something that is concerned with movement. [TECHNICAL] ADJ: usu ADJ n

**ki|net|ic en|er|gy** In physics, **kinetic energy** is the energy that is produced when something moves. [TECHNICAL] N-UNCOUNT

**king** /kɪŋ/ (**kings**) ◆◆◇ 1 A **king** is a man who is the most important member of the royal family of his country, and who is considered to be the Head of State of that country. ❑ *...the king and queen of Spain... In 1154, Henry II became King of England.* N-TITLE; N-COUNT: oft *the* N *of* n 2 If you describe a man as **the king of** something, you mean that he is the most important person doing that thing or he is the best at doing it. ❑ *He's the king of unlicensed boxing.* N-COUNT: *the* N *of* n 3 A **king** is a playing card with a picture of a king on it. ❑ *...the king of diamonds.* N-COUNT: oft N *of* n 4 In chess, the **king** is the most important piece. When you are in a position to capture your opponent's king, you win the game. N-COUNT

**king|dom** /kɪŋdəm/ (**kingdoms**) 1 A **kingdom** is a country or region that is ruled by a king or queen. ❑ *The kingdom's power declined. ...the United Kingdom.* N-COUNT: usu sing, oft in names 2 All the animals, birds, and insects in the world can be referred to together as the animal **kingdom**. All the plants can be referred to as the plant **kingdom**. N-SING: usu n N

**king|fisher** /kɪŋfɪʃəʳ/ (**kingfishers**) A **kingfisher** is a brightly-coloured bird which lives near rivers and lakes and catches fish. N-COUNT

**king|ly** /kɪŋli/ **Kingly** means like a king, or related to the duties of a king. [LITERARY] ❑ *...a noble man, kingly in stature... They thought that he should resume his kingly duties.* ADJ: usu ADJ n

**king|pin** /kɪŋpɪn/ (**kingpins**) If you describe someone as the **kingpin of** an organization, you mean that they are the most important person involved in it. [JOURNALISM] ❑ *...one of the alleged kingpins of Colombia's largest drugs ring.* N-COUNT: oft N *of* n, n N = linchpin

**king|ship** /kɪŋʃɪp/ **Kingship** is the fact or position of being a king. ❑ *...the duties of kingship.* N-UNCOUNT

**king-size** also **king-sized.** A **king-size** or **king-sized** version of something is a larger size than the standard version, and may be the largest size available. ❑ *...a king-size bed. ...king-size cigarettes.* ADJ: usu ADJ n

**kink** /kɪŋk/ (**kinks, kinking, kinked**) 1 A **kink** is a curve or twist in something which is otherwise normally straight. ❑ *...a tiny black kitten with tufted ears and a kink in her tail.* N-COUNT: oft N *in* n 2 If something **kinks** or **is kinked**, it has, or it develops a curve or twist in it. ❑ *...her wet hair kinking in the breeze... Care is needed when loading the roll to prevent twisting or kinking the film.* VERB V V n

**kinky** /kɪŋki/ (**kinkier, kinkiest**) If you describe something, usually a sexual practice or preference, as **kinky**, you mean that it is unusual and would be considered strange by most people. [INFORMAL] ❑ *He had been engaging in some kind of kinky sexual activity.* ADJ

**kins|folk** /kɪnzfoʊk/

> ✓ The spellings **kinfolk**, and sometimes in American English **kinfolks** are also used.

Your **kinsfolk** or **kinfolk** are the people who are related to you. [LITERARY] ❑ *Poor Emily. Her kinsfolk should come to her... I sent my other son to the country to stay with kinfolk.* N-PLURAL: oft poss N = family, relations

**kin|ship** /kɪnʃɪp/ 1 **Kinship** is the relationship between members of the same family. ❑ *The ties of kinship may have helped the young man find his way in life.* N-UNCOUNT 2 If you feel **kinship with** someone, you feel close to them, because you have a similar background or similar feelings or ideas. ❑ *She evidently felt a sense of kinship with the woman.* N-UNCOUNT

**kins|man** /kɪnzmən/ (**kinsmen**) Someone's **kinsman** is their male relative. [LITERARY or WRITTEN] N-COUNT: oft with poss

**kins|woman** /kɪnzwʊmən/ (**kinswomen**) Someone's **kinswoman** is their female relative. [LITERARY or WRITTEN] N-COUNT: oft poss N

**ki|osk** /kiːɒsk/ (**kiosks**) 1 A **kiosk** is a small building or structure from which people can buy things such as sandwiches or newspapers through an open window. ❑ *I was getting cigarettes at the kiosk.* N-COUNT 2 A **kiosk** or a **telephone kiosk** is a public telephone box. [BRIT] ❑ *He phoned me from a kiosk.* N-COUNT

**kip** /kɪp/ (**kips, kipping, kipped**) 1 **Kip** is sleep. [BRIT, INFORMAL] ❑ *Mason went home for a couple of hours' kip.* N-SING: also no det = sleep 2 If you **kip** somewhere, usually somewhere that is not your own home or bed, you sleep there. [BRIT, INFORMAL] ❑ *He moved from one friend's flat to another, first kipping on the floor of Theodore's studio.* VERB = sleep V prep/adv Also V

**kip|per** /kɪpəʳ/ (**kippers**) A **kipper** is a fish, usually a herring, which has been preserved by being hung in smoke. N-COUNT

**kirk** /kɜːʳk/ (**kirks**) 1 A **kirk** is a church. [SCOTTISH] N-COUNT 2 **The Kirk** is the Church of Scotland, the main Protestant church in Scotland. [SCOTTISH] ❑ *...ministers of the Kirk.* N-PROPER: *the* N

**kirsch** /kɪəʳʃ/ also **Kirsch. Kirsch** is a strong, colourless, alcoholic drink made from cherries which is usually drunk after a meal. N-UNCOUNT

**kiss** /kɪs/ (**kisses, kissing, kissed**) ◆◇◇ 1 If you **kiss** someone, you touch them with your lips to show affection or sexual desire, or to greet them or say goodbye. ❑ *She leaned up and kissed him on the cheek... Her parents kissed her goodbye as she set off from their home... They kissed for almost half a minute... We kissed goodbye.* ♦ **Kiss** is also a noun. ❑ *I put my arms around her and gave her a kiss.* V-RECIP NON-RECIP: V n V n n RECIP: pl-n V pl-n V n N-COUNT 2 If you say that something **kisses** another thing, you mean that it touches that thing very gently. ❑ *The wheels of the aircraft kissed the runway.* VERB V n

PHRASES 3 If you **blow** someone **a kiss** or **blow a kiss**, you touch the palm of your hand lightly with your lips, and then blow across your hand towards the person, in order to show them your affection. ❑ *Maria blew him a kiss.* PHRASE: V inflects 4 If you say that you **kiss** something **goodbye** or **kiss goodbye to** something, you accept the fact that you are going to lose it, although you do not want to. [INFORMAL] ❑ *I felt sure I'd have to kiss my dancing career goodbye.* PHRASE: V inflects

**kiss-and-tell** If someone who has had a love affair with a famous person tells the story of that affair in public, for example in a newspaper or book, you can refer to this as a **kiss-and-tell** story. ❑ *...intimate photographs and kiss-and-tell revelations.* ADJ: ADJ n

**kiss of death** If you say that a particular event is **the kiss of death for** something, you mean that it is certain to make them fail or be a disaster. ❑ *Trying to please an audience is the kiss of death for an artist.* N-SING: usu *the* N, oft N *for/to* n

**kiss of life** If you give someone who has stopped breathing **the kiss of life**, you put your mouth onto their mouth and breathe into their lungs to make them start breathing again. [BRIT] ❑ *Julia was given the kiss of life but she could not be revived.* N-SING: *the* N

✔ in AM, use **mouth-to-mouth resuscitation**

**kit** /kɪt/ **(kits, kitting, kitted)** 1 A **kit** is a group of items that are kept together, often in the same container, because they are all used for similar purposes. ❑ *...a well-stocked first aid kit.* N-COUNT: oft n N 2 **Kit** is special clothing and equipment that you use when you take part in a particular activity, especially a sport. [mainly BRIT] ❑ *I forgot my gym kit.* N-UNCOUNT: usu supp N 3 A **kit** is a set of parts that can be put together in order to make something. ❑ *Her popular pot holder is also available in do-it-yourself kits.* N-COUNT 4 If someone **gets** their **kit off** or **takes** their **kit off**, they take off all their clothes. If they **keep** their **kit on**, they do not take off all their clothes, even though people may be expecting them to. [BRIT, INFORMAL] ❑ *I don't like taking my kit off on screen.* PHRASE: V inflects
♦ **kit out** If someone or something **is kitted out**, they have everything they need at a particular time, such as clothing, equipment, or furniture. [BRIT, INFORMAL] ❑ *She was kitted out with winter coat, skirts, jumpers... The place is kitted out in upmarket Italian cafe style.* PHRASAL VERB: usu passive = fit out; *be* V-ed P *with* n; *be* V-ed P *in* n

**kit|bag** /kɪtbæg/ **(kitbags)** A **kitbag** is a long narrow bag, usually made of canvas, in which soldiers or sailors keep their clothing and personal possessions. [mainly BRIT] N-COUNT

**kitch|en** /kɪtʃɪn/ **(kitchens)** A **kitchen** is a room that is used for cooking and for household jobs such as washing dishes. → See picture on page 1706. → See also **soup kitchen**. ◆◆◇ N-COUNT

**kitch|en cabi|net** **(kitchen cabinets)** Journalists sometimes refer to the unofficial advisers of a prime minister or president as that person's **kitchen cabinet**, especially if they disapprove of the influence that the advisers seem to have. N-COUNT: usu singular [disapproval]

**kitch|en|ette** /kɪtʃɪnet/ **(kitchenettes)** A **kitchenette** is a small kitchen, or a part of a larger room that is used for cooking. N-COUNT

**kitch|en gar|den** **(kitchen gardens)** A **kitchen garden** is a garden, or part of a garden, in which vegetables, herbs, and fruit are grown. N-COUNT

**kite** /kaɪt/ **(kites)** 1 A **kite** is an object, usually used as a toy, which is flown in the air. It consists of a light frame covered with paper or cloth and has a long string attached which you hold while the kite is flying. N-COUNT 2 If you say that someone is **as high as a kite**, you mean that they are very excited or that they are greatly affected by alcohol or drugs. PHRASE: v-link PHR

**Kite|mark** /kaɪtmɑːʳk/ In Britain, the **Kitemark** is a symbol which is put on products that have met certain standards of safety and quality. [BRIT] N-SING

**kith and kin** /kɪθ ən kɪn/ You can refer to your friends and family as your **kith and kin**. N-PLURAL

**kitsch** /kɪtʃ/ You can refer to a work of art or an object as **kitsch** if it is showy and thought by some people to be in bad taste. ❑ *...a hideous ballgown verging on the kitsch.* N-UNCOUNT ♦ **Kitsch** is also an adjective. ❑ *Blue and green eyeshadow has long been considered kitsch.* ADJ

**kit|ten** /kɪtᵊn/ **(kittens)** A **kitten** is a very young cat. N-COUNT

**kit|ty** /kɪti/ **(kitties)** 1 A **kitty** is an amount of money gathered from several people, which is meant to be spent on things that these people will share or use together. ❑ *You haven't put any money in the kitty for three weeks.* N-COUNT: usu sing 2 A **kitty** is the total amount of money which is bet in a gambling game, and which is taken by the winner or winners. ❑ *Each month the total prize kitty is £13.5 million.* N-COUNT: usu sing

**kiwi** /kiːwiː/ **(kiwis)** 1 A **kiwi** is the same as a **kiwi fruit**. N-COUNT 2 A **kiwi** is a type of bird that lives in New Zealand. Kiwis cannot fly. N-COUNT 3 People who come from New Zealand are sometimes referred to as **Kiwis**. This use could cause offence. [BRIT, AUSTRALIAN] N-COUNT

**kiwi fruit** **(kiwi fruit** or **kiwi fruits)** A **kiwi fruit** is a fruit with a brown hairy skin and green flesh. → See picture on page 1711. N-VAR

**KKK** /keɪ keɪ keɪ/ **KKK** is an abbreviation for Ku Klux Klan. N-PROPER-COLL

**Klans|man** /klænzmən/ **(Klansmen)** A **Klansman** is a man who is a member of the **Ku Klux Klan**. N-COUNT

**Kleen|ex** /kliːneks/ **(Kleenex)** A **Kleenex** is a piece of soft tissue paper that is used as a handkerchief. [TRADEMARK] ❑ *...a box of Kleenex.* N-COUNT = tissue

**klep|to|ma|ni|ac** /kleptəmeɪniæk/ **(kleptomaniacs)** A **kleptomaniac** is a person who cannot control their desire to steal things, usually because of a medical condition. N-COUNT

**kludge** /klʌdʒ/ **(kludges)** You can refer to an unsophisticated but fairly effective solution to a problem as a **kludge**. Kludge is used especially to talk about solutions to computing problems. N-COUNT

**klutz** /klʌts/ **(klutzes)** You can refer to someone who is very clumsy or who seems stupid as a **klutz**. [mainly AM, INFORMAL] N-COUNT [disapproval]

**km** **(kms** or **km)** also **km.** **km** is a written abbreviation for **kilometre**.

**knack** /næk/ **(knacks)** A **knack** is a particularly clever or skilful way of doing something successfully, especially something which most people find difficult. ❑ *He's got the knack of getting people to listen.* N-COUNT: usu sing, oft N *of/for* n/-ing

**knack|er** /nækəʳ/ **(knackers)** A **knacker** is someone who buys up old horses and then kills them for their meat, bones, or leather. [BRIT, INFORMAL] ❑ *Her horse was a show jumper whom the family rescued from the knacker's yard.* N-COUNT

**knack|ered** /nækəʳd/ 1 If you say that you are **knackered**, you are emphasizing that you are extremely tired. [BRIT, INFORMAL] ❑ *I was absolutely knackered at the end of the match.* ADJ: usu v-link ADJ 2 If you say that something is **knackered**, you mean that it is completely broken or worn out. [BRIT, INFORMAL] ❑ *My tape player's knackered.* ADJ

**knap|sack** /næpsæk/ **(knapsacks)** A **knapsack** is a canvas or leather bag that you carry on your back or over your shoulder, for example when you are walking in the countryside. N-COUNT

**knave** /neɪv/ **(knaves)** 1 If someone calls a man a **knave**, they mean that he is dishonest and should not be trusted. [OLD-FASHIONED] N-COUNT [disapproval] = rogue, scoundrel 2 In card games, **knave** is another word for **jack**. [mainly BRIT] N-COUNT

✔ in AM, use **jack**

**knead** /niːd/ **(kneads, kneading, kneaded)** 1 When you **knead** dough or other food, you press and squeeze it with your hands so that it becomes smooth and ready to cook. ❑ *Lightly knead the mixture on a floured surface.* VERB: V n 2 If you **knead** a part of someone's body, you press or squeeze it with your fingers. ❑ *She felt him knead the aching muscles.* VERB: V n

**knee** /niː/ **(knees, kneeing, kneed)** 1 Your **knee** is the place where your leg bends. ❑ *He will receive physiotherapy on his damaged left knee. ...a* ◆◇◇ N-COUNT: oft poss N *knee injury.* [2] If something or someone is **on** your **knee** or **on** your **knees**, they are resting or sitting on the upper part of your legs when you are sitting down. ❑ *He sat with the package on his knees.* N-COUNT: poss N, oft *on* N = *lap* [3] If you are **on** your **knees**, your legs are bent and your knees are on the ground. ❑ *She fell to the ground on her knees and prayed.* N-PLURAL: poss N, usu *on/to* N [4] If you **knee** someone, you hit them using your knee. ❑ *Ian kneed him in the groin.* VERB V n [5] If a country or organization **is brought to its knees**, it is almost completely destroyed by someone or something. ❑ *The country was being brought to its knees by the loss of 2.4 million manufacturing jobs.* PHRASE: V inflects

**knee|cap** /niːkæp/ **(kneecaps)** also **knee-cap.** Your **kneecaps** are the bones at the front of your knees. N-COUNT

**knee-capping** **(knee-cappings)** also **kneecapping. Knee-capping** is the act of shooting someone in the knee and is carried out by some terrorist organizations as a form of punishment. N-VAR

**knee-deep** [1] Something that is **knee-deep** is as high as your knees. ❑ *The water was only knee-deep.* ADJ [2] If a person or a place is **knee-deep in** something such as water, the level of the water comes up to a person's knees. ❑ *They spent much of their time knee-deep in mud.* ADJ: v-link ADJ *in* n, ADJ after v

**knee-high** Something that is **knee-high** is as tall or high as an adult's knees. ADJ

**knee-jerk** If you call someone's response to a question or situation a **knee-jerk** reaction, you mean that they react in a very predictable way, without thinking. ❑ *The knee-jerk reaction to this is to call for proper security in all hospitals.* ADJ: ADJ n [disapproval]

**kneel** /niːl/ **(kneels, kneeling, kneeled, knelt)**

> The forms **kneeled** and **knelt** can both be used for the past tense and past participle.

When you **kneel**, you bend your legs so that your knees are touching the ground. ❑ *She knelt by the bed and prayed... Other people were kneeling, but she just sat. ...a kneeling position.* ♦ **Kneel down** means the same as **kneel**. ❑ *She kneeled down beside him.* VERB V prep/adv V V-ing PHRASAL VERB V P

**knees-up** **(knees-ups)** A **knees-up** is a party or celebration. [BRIT, INFORMAL] N-COUNT = *shindig*

**knelt** /nelt/ **Knelt** is a past tense and past participle of **kneel**.

**knew** /njuː, AM nuː/ **Knew** is the past tense of **know**.

**knick|ers** /nɪkəʳz/

> The form **knicker** is used as a modifier.

[1] **Knickers** are a piece of underwear worn by women and girls which have holes for the legs and elastic around the waist to hold them up. [BRIT] ❑ *She bought Ann two bras and six pairs of knickers.* N-PLURAL: also *a pair of* N

> in AM, use **panties**

[2] If someone **is getting** their **knickers in a twist** about something, they are getting annoyed or upset about it without good reason. [BRIT, HUMOROUS, INFORMAL] PHRASE: V inflects

**knick-knacks** /nɪk næks/

> in AM, usually use **knickknacks**

**Knick-knacks** are small objects which people keep as ornaments or toys, rather than for a particular use. N-PLURAL

**knife** /naɪf/ **(knives, knifes, knifing, knifed)** ◆◇◇

> **knives** is the plural form of the noun and **knifes** is the third person singular of the present tense of the verb.

[1] A **knife** is a tool for cutting or a weapon and consists of a flat piece of metal with a sharp edge on the end of a handle. ❑ *...a knife and fork... Two robbers broke into her home, held a knife to her throat and stole her savings.* N-COUNT [2] To **knife** someone means to attack and injure them with a knife. ❑ *Dawson takes revenge on the man by knifing him to death.* VERB V n prep [3] A surgeon's **knife** is a piece of equipment used to cut flesh and organs during operations. It is made of metal and has a very thin sharp edge. N-COUNT = *scalpel* ● If you go **under the knife**, you have an operation in a hospital. ❑ *Kelly was about to go under the knife when her surgeon stopped everything.* PHRASE: PHR after v [4] → See also **carving knife, fish knife, flick knife, palette knife, paper knife, pocket knife, Stanley knife.**

PHRASES [5] If someone does something **like a knife through butter** or **like a hot knife through butter**, they do it very easily. ❑ *Spending by Japanese companies has left them more competitive than companies in other countries. They will be cutting through the competition like a hot knife through butter.* PHRASE: *knife* inflects, PHR after V [6] If you have been in a place where there was a very tense atmosphere, you can say that you **could have cut** the atmosphere **with a knife**. [mainly BRIT] PHRASE [7] If a lot of people want something unpleasant to happen to someone, for example if they want them to lose their job, you can say that **the knives are out for** that person. [mainly BRIT] ❑ *The Party knives are out for the leader.* PHRASE: V inflects, usu PHR *for* n [8] If you **twist the knife** or if you **turn the knife in** someone's **wound**, you do or say something to make an unpleasant situation they are in even more unpleasant. ❑ *Travis twisted the knife by laughing at her.* PHRASE: V inflects

**knife-edge** also **knife edge.** [1] To be **on a knife-edge** means to be in a situation in which nobody knows what is going to happen next, or in which one thing is just as likely to happen as another. [mainly BRIT] ❑ *The game is poised on a knife-edge. One mistake or one piece of good luck could decide it.* PHRASE: oft v-link PHR [2] You can use **knife-edge** to refer to something that is very exciting or tense because you do not know what is going to happen next. [mainly BRIT] ❑ *Tonight's knife-edge vote could be uncomfortably close.* ADJ: ADJ n

**knife|man** /naɪfmən/ **(knifemen)** A **knifeman** is someone who has attacked or killed someone with a knife. [BRIT, mainly JOURNALISM] ❑ *A crazed knifeman attacked three policewomen.* N-COUNT: usu sing

**knife|point** /naɪfpɔɪnt/ also **knife-point.** If you are attacked or robbed **at knifepoint**, someone threatens you with a knife while they attack or steal from you. [JOURNALISM] ❑ *A 15-year-old girl was attacked at knifepoint in a subway.* PHRASE: PHR after v

**knif|ing** /naɪfɪŋ/ **(knifings)** A **knifing** is an incident in which someone is attacked and injured with a knife. → See also **knife**. N-COUNT = *stabbing*

**knight** /naɪt/ **(knights, knighting, knighted)** [1] In medieval times, a **knight** was a man of noble birth, who served his king or lord in battle. N-COUNT [2] If someone **is knighted**, they are given a knighthood. ❑ *He was knighted in the Queen's birthday honours list in June 1988.* VERB: usu passive *be* V-ed [3] A **knight** is a man who has been knighted. N-COUNT [4] In chess, a **knight** is a piece which is shaped like a horse's head. N-COUNT [5] If you refer to someone as a **knight in shining armour**, you mean that they are kind and brave, and likely to rescue you from a difficult situation. ❑ *Love songs trick us into believing in knights in shining armor.* PHRASE: *knight* inflects

**knight|hood** /naɪthʊd/ **(knighthoods)** A **knighthood** is a title that is given to a man by a British king or queen for his achievements or his service to his country. A man who has been given a knighthood can put 'Sir' in front of his name instead of 'Mr'. N-COUNT

**knit** /nɪt/ **(knits, knitting, knitted)** [1] If you **knit** something, especially an article of clothing, you make it from wool or a similar thread by using two knitting needles or a machine. ❑ *I had endless hours to knit and sew... I have already started knitting baby clothes... She knitted him 10 pairs of socks to take with him... During the war, Joan helped her mother knit scarves for soldiers... She pushed up the sleeves of her grey knitted cardigan and got to work.* ♦ **Knit** is also a combining form. ❑ *Ferris wore a heavy knit sweater.* VERB V V n V n n V n *for* n V-ed Also V n *into* n COMB in ADJ: ADJ n [2] If someone or something **knits** things or people **together**, they make them fit or work together closely and suc- VERB

cessfully. ❑ *The best thing about sport is that it knits the whole family close together... Ordinary people have some reservations about their president's drive to knit them so closely to their neighbors.* ♦ **Knit** is also a combining form. ❑ *...a tightly knit society.* (V n with *together*; V n *to/into* n; Also V n; COMB in ADJ: usu ADJ n)
3 When broken bones **knit**, the broken pieces grow together again. ❑ *The bone hasn't knitted together properly. ...broken bones that have failed to knit.* (VERB; V *together*; V) 4 If you **knit** your **brows** or **knit** your **eyebrows**, you frown because you are angry or worried. [LITERARY] ❑ *They knitted their brows and started to grumble... Billy's eyebrows knitted together in a little frown.* (PHRASE: V inflects)

**knit|ting** /nɪtɪŋ/ 1 **Knitting** is something, such as an article of clothing, that is being knitted. ❑ *She had been sitting with her knitting at her fourth-floor window.* (N-UNCOUNT: usu poss N) 2 **Knitting** is the action or process of knitting. ❑ *Take up a relaxing hobby, such as knitting.* (N-UNCOUNT: oft N n)

**knit|ting nee|dle** **(knitting needles)** **Knitting needles** are thin plastic or metal rods which you use when you are knitting. (N-COUNT)

**knit|wear** /nɪtweəʳ/ **Knitwear** is clothing that has been knitted. ❑ *...expensive Italian knitwear.* (N-UNCOUNT)

**knives** /naɪvz/ **Knives** is the plural of **knife**.

**knob** /nɒb/ **(knobs)** 1 A **knob** is a round handle on a door or drawer which you use in order to open or close it. ❑ *He turned the knob and pushed against the door.* (N-COUNT) 2 A **knob** is a round switch on a piece of machinery or equipment. ❑ *...the volume knob.* (N-COUNT) 3 A **knob of** butter is a small amount of it. [mainly BRIT] ❑ *Top the steaming hot potatoes with a knob of butter and serve immediately.* (N-COUNT: N *of* n)

**knob|bly** /nɒbli/ or **knobby** /nɒbi/ Something that is **knobbly** or **knobby** has lumps on it which stick out and make the surface uneven. ❑ *...knobbly knees.* (ADJ)

**knock** /nɒk/ **(knocks, knocking, knocked)** ◆◇◇
1 If you **knock on** something such as a door or window, you hit it, usually several times, to attract someone's attention. ❑ *She went directly to Simon's apartment and knocked on the door... He knocked before going in.* (VERB; V *on/at* n; V) ♦ **Knock** is also a noun. ❑ *They heard a knock at the front door.* (N-COUNT) ♦ **knock|ing** *They were wakened by a loud knocking at the door.* (N-SING: also no det) 2 If you **knock** something, you touch or hit it roughly, especially so that it falls or moves. ❑ *She accidentally knocked the tea tin off the shelf... Isabel rose so abruptly that she knocked down her chair.* (VERB; V n prep; V n with adv) ♦ **Knock** is also a noun. ❑ *The bags have tough exterior materials to protect against knocks, rain and dust.* (N-COUNT) 3 If someone **knocks** two rooms or buildings **into** one, or **knocks** them **together**, they make them form one room or building by removing a wall. ❑ *They decided to knock the two rooms into one... The spacious kitchen was achieved by knocking together three small rooms.* (VERB; V pl-n *into* n; V pl-n with *together*) 4 To **knock** someone into a particular position or condition means to hit them very hard so that they fall over or become unconscious. ❑ *The third wave was so strong it knocked me backwards... Someone had knocked him unconscious.* (VERB; V n prep/adv; V n adj) 5 To **knock** a particular quality or characteristic **out of** someone means to make them lose it. ❑ *The stories of his links with the actress had knocked the fun out of him... Those people hurt me and knocked my confidence.* (VERB: no cont; V n *out of* n; V n) 6 If you **knock** something or someone, you criticize them and say unpleasant things about them. [INFORMAL] ❑ *I'm not knocking them: if they want to do it, it's up to them.* (VERB; V n) 7 If someone receives a **knock**, they have an unpleasant experience which prevents them from achieving something or which causes them to change their attitudes or plans. ❑ *What they said was a real knock to my self-confidence.* (N-COUNT = *blow*)
8 to **knock** something **on the head** → see **head**. to **knock** someone or something **into shape** → see **shape**.

♦ **knock about** → see **knock around**.

♦ **knock around**
✔ in BRIT, also use **knock about**

1 If someone **knocks** you **around** or **knocks** you **about**, they hit or kick you several times. [mainly BRIT, INFORMAL] ❑ *He lied to me constantly and started knocking me around.* (PHRASAL VERB; V n P) 2 If someone **knocks around** or **knocks about** somewhere, they spend time there, experiencing different situations or just passing time. ❑ *...reporters who knock around in troubled parts of the world... I know nothing about him except that he knocked about South Africa for a while.* (PHRASAL VERB; V P prep/adv; V P n) 3 If someone or something **is knocking around** or **knocking about**, they are present in a particular place. [mainly BRIT] ❑ *There were a couple of decent kits knocking around, but this wasn't one of them!.* (PHRASAL VERB: only cont; V P) 4 If you **knock around** or **knock about with** someone, you spend your spare time with them, either because you are one of their friends or because you are their boyfriend or girlfriend. [mainly BRIT] ❑ *I used to knock about with all the lads from round where Mum lives... They were knocking around together for about a year.* (PHRASAL VERB = *hang around*; V P *with* n; pl-n V P *together*)

♦ **knock back** 1 If you **knock back** a drink, especially an alcoholic one, you drink it quickly, and often in large amounts. [INFORMAL] ❑ *He was knocking back his 10th gin and tonic of the day... She poured some vodka into a glass and knocked it back in two swallows.* (PHRASAL VERB; V P n (not pron); V n P) 2 If an event, situation, or person **knocks** you **back**, they prevent you from progressing or achieving something. [mainly BRIT] ❑ *It seemed as though every time we got rolling something came along to knock us back... That really knocked back any hope for further peace negotiations.* (PHRASAL VERB = *set back*; V n P; V P n (not pron))

♦ **knock down** 1 If someone **is knocked down** or **is knocked over** by a vehicle or its driver, they are hit by a car and fall to the ground, and are often injured or killed. ❑ *He died in hospital after being knocked down by a car... A drunk driver knocked down and killed two girls... A car knocked him over.* (PHRASAL VERB = *run over*; *be* V-ed P; V P n (not pron); V n P) 2 To **knock down** a building or part of a building means to demolish it. ❑ *Why doesn't he just knock the wall down?... They have since knocked down the shack.* (PHRASAL VERB = *pull down*; V n P; V P n (not pron)) 3 To **knock down** a price or amount means to decrease it. [mainly AM] ❑ *The market might abandon the stock, and knock down its price... It manages to knock rents down considerably.* (PHRASAL VERB; V P n (not pron); V n P)
✔ in BRIT, usually use **bring down**

♦ **knock off** 1 To **knock off** an amount from a price, time, or level means to reduce it by that amount. ❑ *Udinese have knocked 10% off admission prices... When pressed they knock off 10 per cent.* (PHRASAL VERB; V amount P n; V P amount) 2 If you **knock** something **off** a list or document, you remove it. ❑ *Tighter rules for benefit entitlement have knocked many people off the unemployment register.* (PHRASAL VERB; V n P n; Also V n P) 3 When you **knock off**, you finish work at the end of the day or before a break. [INFORMAL] ❑ *If I get this report finished I'll knock off early.* (PHRASAL VERB; V P)

♦ **knock out** 1 To **knock** someone **out** means to cause them to become unconscious or to go to sleep. ❑ *The three drinks knocked him out... He had never been knocked out in a professional fight.* (PHRASAL VERB; V n P; Also V P n (not pron)) 2 If a person or team **is knocked out** of a competition, they are defeated in a game, so that they take no more part in the competition. ❑ *Henri Leconte has been knocked out in the quarter-finals of the Geneva Open... The Irish came so close to knocking England out of the European Championships.* → See also **knockout**. (PHRASAL VERB; *be* V-ed P; V n P *of* n; Also V P n) 3 If something **is knocked out** by enemy action or bad weather, it is destroyed or stops functioning because of it. ❑ *Our bombers have knocked out the mobile launchers.* (PHRASAL VERB; V P n (not pron))

♦ **knock over** → see **knock down 1**.

**knock|about** /nɒkəbaʊt/ **Knockabout** comedy is lively and often involves people doing funny things, rather than saying them. [mainly BRIT] ❑ *He gave one of his best knockabout performances in a long time.* (ADJ: usu ADJ n)

**knock|back** /nɒkbæk/ **(knockbacks)** also **knock-back**. A **knockback** is a problem or a (N-COUNT) rejection which delays your progress or which reverses some of the progress you have made. ❑ *The schedule has suffered a knockback.*

**knock|down** /nɒkdaʊn/ also **knock-down.** ADJ: ADJ n A **knockdown** price is much lower than it would be normally. [INFORMAL] ❑ *...the chance to buy it now at a knockdown price.*

**knock|er** /nɒkəʳ/ **(knockers)** N-COUNT A **knocker** is a piece of metal on the front door of a building, which you use to hit the door in order to attract the attention of the people inside. ➔ See also **knock**.

**knock-kneed** ADJ Someone who is **knock-kneed** has legs which turn inwards at the knees.

**knock|off** /nɒkɒf/ **(knockoffs)** N-COUNT: oft N n A **knockoff** is a cheap copy of a well-known product. [INFORMAL] ❑ *Frilly dresses are out; Chanel knockoffs are in... You can buy a nice knockoff watch from them.*

**knock-on** ADJ: ADJ n If there is a **knock-on** effect, one action or event causes several other events to happen one after the other. [BRIT] ❑ *The cut in new car prices has had a knock-on effect on the price of used cars.*

**knock|out** /nɒkaʊt/ **(knockouts)** also **knock-out.** 1 N-COUNT: also *by* N In boxing, a **knockout** is a situation in which a boxer wins the fight by making his opponent fall to the ground and be unable to stand up before the referee has counted to ten. 2 ADJ: ADJ n A **knockout** blow is an action or event that completely defeats an opponent. ❑ *He delivered a knockout blow to all of his rivals.* 3 ADJ: ADJ n A **knockout** competition is one in which the players or teams that win continue playing until there is only one winner left. [mainly BRIT] ❑ *...the European Cup, a knockout competition between the top teams in Europe.*

✔ in AM, use **elimination**

4 N-SING: *a* N [approval] If you describe someone or something as **a knockout**, you think that they are extremely attractive or impressive. [INFORMAL] ❑ *She was a knockout in navy and scarlet.*

**knoll** /noʊl/ **(knolls)** N-COUNT; N-IN-NAMES A **knoll** is a low hill with gentle slopes and a rounded top. [LITERARY] ❑ *...a grassy knoll. ...on Nibley Knoll.*

**knot** /nɒt/ **(knots, knotting, knotted)** 1 N-COUNT If you tie a **knot** in a piece of string, rope, cloth, or other material, you pass one end or part of it through a loop and pull it tight. ❑ *One lace had broken and been tied in a knot.* 2 VERB If you **knot** a piece of string, rope, cloth, or other material, you pass one end or part of it through a loop and pull it tight. ❑ *He knotted the laces securely together...* (V n with *together*) *He knotted the bandanna around his neck.* (V n) *...a knotted rope.* (V-ed) 3 N-COUNT: oft N *of* n If you feel a **knot** in your stomach, you get an uncomfortable tight feeling in your stomach, usually because you are afraid or excited. ❑ *There was a knot of tension in his stomach.* 4 VERB If your stomach **knots** or if something **knots** it, it feels tight because you are afraid or excited. ❑ *I felt my stomach knot with apprehension...* (V) *The old dread knotted her stomach.* (V n) 5 VERB If part of your face or your muscles **knot**, they become tense, usually because you are worried or angry. ❑ *His forehead knotted in a frown.* (V) *...his knotted muscles.* (V-ed) 6 N-COUNT A **knot** in a piece of wood is a small hard area where a branch grew. 7 N-COUNT: usu num N A **knot** is a unit of speed. The speed of ships, aircraft, and winds is measured in knots. ❑ *They travel at speeds of up to 30 knots.*

PHRASES 8 PHRASE: V inflects If you **tie yourself in knots**, you get very confused and anxious. [INFORMAL] ❑ *The press agent tied himself in knots trying to apologise.* 9 PHRASE: V inflects If you say that two people **tie the knot**, you mean that they get married. [INFORMAL] ❑ *Len tied the knot with Kate five years ago.*

**knot|ty** /nɒti/ **(knottier, knottiest)** 1 ADJ: usu ADJ n = thorny A **knotty** problem is complicated and difficult to solve. ❑ *The new management team faces some knotty problems.* 2 ADJ: usu ADJ n **Knotty** wood has a lot of small hard areas on it where branches once grew.

**know** /noʊ/ **(knows, knowing, knew, known)** ◆◆◆ 1 VERB: no cont If you **know** a fact, a piece of information, or an answer, you have it correctly in your mind. ❑ *I don't know the name of the place...* (V n) *'People like doing things for nothing.' — 'I know they do.'...* (V that) *I don't know what happened to her husband...* (V wh) *'How did he meet your mother?' — 'I don't know.'...* (V) *We all know about his early experiments in flying...* (V *about* n/-ing) *They looked younger than I knew them to be...* (V n to-inf) *It is not known whether the bomb was originally intended for the capital itself...* (*it be* V-ed wh) *It's always been known that key figures in the government do very well for themselves.* (*it be* V-ed that) 2 VERB: no cont If you **know** someone, you are familiar with them because you have met them and talked to them before. ❑ *Gifford was a friend. I'd known him for nine years...* (V n) *Do you two know each other?* (V n) 3 VERB: no cont If you say that you **know of** something, you mean that you have heard about it but you do not necessarily have a lot of information about it. ❑ *We know of the incident but have no further details...* (V *of* n) *I know of no one who would want to murder Albert.* (V *of* n) 4 VERB: no cont If you **know about** a subject, you have studied it or taken an interest in it, and understand part or all of it. ❑ *Hire someone with experience, someone who knows about real estate...* (V *about* n) *She didn't know anything about music but she liked to sing.* (V amount *about* n) 5 VERB: no cont If you **know** a language, you have learned it and can understand it. ❑ *It helps to know French and Creole if you want to understand some of the lyrics.* (V n) 6 VERB: no cont If you **know** something such as a place, a work of art, or an idea, you have visited it, seen it, read it, or heard about it, and so you are familiar with it. ❑ *No matter how well you know Paris, it is easy to get lost.* (V n) 7 VERB: no cont If you **know how to** do something, you have the necessary skills and knowledge to do it. ❑ *The health authorities now know how to deal with the disease...* (V wh-to-inf) *We know what to do to make it work.* (V wh-to-inf) 8 VERB: no cont You can say that someone **knows that** something is happening when they become aware of it. ❑ *Then I saw a gun under the hall table so I knew that something was wrong...* (V that) *The first I knew about it was when I woke up in the ambulance.* (V *about* n) 9 VERB: no cont If you **know** something or someone, you recognize them when you see them or hear them. ❑ *Would she know you if she saw you on the street?* (V n) 10 VERB: no cont If someone or something **is known as** a particular name, they are called by that name. ❑ *The disease is more commonly known as Mad Cow Disease...* (*be* V-ed *as* n) *He was born as John Birks Gillespie, but everyone knew him as Dizzy...* (V n *as* n) *He was the only boy in the school who was known by his Christian name and not his surname.* (V n *by* n) *...British Nuclear Fuels, otherwise known as BNFL.* (V-ed) 11 VERB If you **know** someone or something **as** a person or thing that has particular qualities, you consider that they have those qualities. ❑ *Lots of people know her as a very kind woman.* (V n *as* n) 12 ➔ See also **knowing**, **known**.

PHRASES 13 PHRASE: n PHR If you talk about a thing or system **as we know it**, you are referring to the form in which it exists now and which is familiar to most people. ❑ *He planned to end the welfare system as we know it.* 14 PHRASE: *get* inflects, PHR n If you **get to know** someone, you find out what they are like by spending time with them. ❑ *The new neighbours were getting to know each other.* 15 PHRASE: PHR as reply, PHR wh People use expressions such as **goodness knows**, **Heaven knows**, and **God knows** when they do not know something and want to suggest that nobody could possibly know it. [INFORMAL] ❑ *'Who's he?' — 'God knows.'* 16 CONVENTION You say **'I know'** to show that you agree with what has just been said. ❑ *'This country is so awful.' — 'I know, I know.'* 17 CONVENTION You say **'I know'** to show that you accept that something is true, but think that it is not very important or relevant. ❑ *'There are trains straight from Cambridge.' — 'I know, but it's no quicker.'* 18 PHRASE: PHR wh/that You use **'I know'** to express sympathy and understanding towards someone. ❑ *I know what you're going through.* 19 PHRASE: usu PHR *about* n, PHR that You can use **I don't know** to indicate that you do not completely agree with something or do not really think that it is true. ❑ *'He should quite simply resign.' — 'I don't know about that.'* 20 PHRASE: PHR *but* cl You can say **'I don't know about you'** to indicate that you are going to give your own opinion about something and you want to find out if someone else feels the same. ❑ *I don't know about the rest of you, but I'm hungry.* 21 You use **I don't know** in expressions which indicate criticism of someone's behaviour. For example, if you say that you **do not know how** someone can do something, you mean that you cannot understand or accept them doing it. ❑ *I don't know how he could do this to his own daughter.* PHRASE: PHR wh [disapproval]

22 People sometimes use expressions such as **I'm blessed if I know** or **damned if I know** to emphasize the fact that they do not know something. [INFORMAL] ❑ *'What was that all about?' — 'Darned if I know.'* PHRASE: oft PHR as reply, PHR wh [emphasis]

23 If you are **in the know** about something, especially something that is not known about or understood by many people, you have information about it. ❑ *It was gratifying to be in the know about important people.* PHRASE: usu v-link PHR

24 You can use expressions such as **you know what I mean** and **if you know what I mean** to suggest that the person listening to you understands what you are trying to say, and so you do not have to explain any more. [SPOKEN] ❑ *None of us stayed long. I mean, the atmosphere wasn't – well, you know what I mean.* CONVENTION

25 You say **'You never know'** or **'One never knows'** to indicate that it is not definite or certain what will happen in the future, and to suggest that there is some hope that things will turn out well. ❑ *You never know, I might get lucky.* CONVENTION [vagueness]

26 You say **'Not that I know of'** when someone has asked you whether or not something is true and you think the answer is 'no' but you cannot be sure because you do not know all the facts. ❑ *'Is he married?' — 'Not that I know of.'* CONVENTION [vagueness]

27 You can use expressions such as **What does she know?** and **What do they know?** when you think that someone has no right to comment on a situation because they do not understand it. ❑ *Don't listen to him, what does he know?* PHRASE: oft PHR *about* n [disapproval]

28 You use **you know** to emphasize or to draw attention to what you are saying. [SPOKEN] ❑ *The conditions in there are awful, you know... You know, it does worry me.* CONVENTION [emphasis]

29 You use **you know** when you are trying to explain more clearly what you mean, by referring to something that the person you are talking to knows about. [SPOKEN] ❑ *Wear the white dress, you know, the one with all the black embroidery.* CONVENTION

30 You can say **'You don't know'** in order to emphasize how strongly you feel about the remark you are going to make. [SPOKEN] ❑ *You don't know how good it is to speak to somebody from home.* PHRASE: PHR wh [emphasis]

31 to **know best** → see **best**. to **know better** → see **better**. to **know no bounds** → see **bound**. to **know** something **for a fact** → see **fact**. **as far as I know** → see **far**. **not to know the first thing about** something → see **first**. to **know full well** → see **full**. to **let** someone **know** → see **let**. **not to know the meaning of the word** → see **meaning**. to **know** your **own mind** → see **mind**. to **know the ropes** → see **rope**.

**know-all** **(know-alls)** If you say that someone is a **know-all**, you are critical of them because they think that they know a lot more than other people. [BRIT, INFORMAL] N-COUNT [disapproval]

☑ in AM, use **know-it-all**

**know-how** ◆◇◇

☑ in AM, use **knowhow**

**Know-how** is knowledge of the methods or techniques of doing something, especially something technical or practical. [INFORMAL] ❑ *He hasn't got the know-how to run a farm.* N-UNCOUNT: usu with supp = *expertise*

**know|ing** /noʊɪŋ/ A **knowing** gesture or remark is one that shows that you understand something, for example the way that someone is feeling or what they really mean, even though it has not been mentioned directly. ❑ *Ron gave her a knowing smile... Dan exchanged a knowing look with Harry.* ♦ **know|ing|ly** *He smiled knowingly.* ADJ: usu ADJ n; ADV

**know|ing|ly** /noʊɪŋli/ If you **knowingly** do something wrong, you do it even though you know it is wrong. ❑ *He repeated that he had never knowingly taken illegal drugs.* ADV: ADV before v

**know-it-all** **(know-it-alls)** If you say that someone is a **know-it-all**, you are critical of them because they think that they know a lot more than other people. [AM, INFORMAL] N-COUNT [disapproval]

☑ in BRIT, use **know-all**

**knowl|edge** /nɒlɪdʒ/ ◆◆◇ 1 **Knowledge** is information and understanding about a subject which a person has, or which all people have. ❑ *She told Parliament she had no knowledge of the affair. ...the quest for scientific knowledge.* N-UNCOUNT: usu with supp

PHRASES 2 If you say that something is true **to** your **knowledge** or **to the best of** your **knowledge**, you mean that you believe it to be true but it is possible that you do not know all the facts. ❑ *Alec never carried a gun to my knowledge.* PHRASE: PHR with cl/group

3 If you do something **safe in the knowledge that** something else is the case, you do the first thing confidently because you are sure of the second thing. [WRITTEN] ❑ *You can let your kids play here, safe in the knowledge that they won't get sunburn.* PHRASE: PHR after v, usu PHR that

**knowl|edge|able** /nɒlɪdʒəbᵊl/ Someone who is **knowledgeable** has or shows a clear understanding of many different facts about the world or about a particular subject. ❑ *We employ friendly and knowledgeable staff.* ADJ = *well-informed*
♦ **knowl|edge|ably** *Kaspar had spoken knowledgeably about the state of agriculture in Europe.* ADV: ADV after v

**known** /noʊn/ 1 **Known** is the past participle of **know**. 2 You use **known** to describe someone or something that is clearly recognized by or familiar to all people or to a particular group of people. ❑ *...He was a known drug dealer... He became one of the best known actors of his day.* ADJ: ADJ n, v-link ADJ prep, v-link adv ADJ

3 If someone or something is **known for** a particular achievement or feature, they are familiar to many people because of that achievement or feature. ❑ *He is better known for his film and TV work.* ADJ: v-link ADJ *for* n/-ing

4 If you **let it be known that** something is the case, or you **let** something **be known**, you make sure that people know it or can find out about it. ❑ *The Prime Minister has let it be known that he is against it.* PHRASE

**knuck|le** /nʌkᵊl/ **(knuckles, knuckling, knuckled)** Your **knuckles** are the rounded pieces of bone that form lumps on your hands where your fingers join your hands, and where your fingers bend. ❑ *Brenda's knuckles were white as she gripped the arms of the chair.* a **rap on the knuckles** → see **rap**. N-COUNT: usu pl, oft poss N

♦ **knuckle down** If someone **knuckles down**, they begin to work or study very hard, especially after a period when they have done very little work. [INFORMAL] ❑ *The only thing to do was knuckle down and get on with some serious hard work... He managed to knuckle down to his lessons long enough to pass his examination.* PHRASAL VERB = *buckle down*; V P; V P *to* n/-ing

♦ **knuckle under** If you **knuckle under**, you do what someone else tells you to do or what a situation forces you to do, because you realize that you have no choice. [INFORMAL] ❑ *It is arguable whether the rebels will knuckle under... The United States, he said, did not knuckle under to demands.* PHRASAL VERB = *give in, buckle under*; V P; V P *to* n

**knuckle-duster** **(knuckle-dusters)** also **knuckleduster.** A **knuckle-duster** is a piece of metal that is designed to be worn on the back of a person's hand as a weapon, so that if they hit someone they will hurt them badly. [mainly BRIT] N-COUNT

☑ in AM, use **brass knuckles**

**KO** /keɪ oʊ/ **(KO's)** **KO** is an abbreviation for **knockout**. ❑ *34 of his wins were KO's.* N-COUNT

**koa|la** /koʊɑːlə/ **(koalas)** A **koala** or a **koala bear** is an Australian animal which looks like a small bear with grey fur and lives in trees. N-COUNT

**kohl** /koʊl/ **Kohl** is a cosmetic used to make a dark line along the edges of someone's eyelids. N-UNCOUNT

**kohl|ra|bi** /koʊlrɑːbi/ **(kohlrabi)** **Kohlrabi** is a green vegetable that has a round ball of leaves like N-VAR a cabbage. It has a thick stem that you boil in water before eating.

**kook** /kuːk/ **(kooks)** You can refer to someone who you think is slightly strange or eccentric as a **kook**. [mainly AM, INFORMAL] N-COUNT

**kooky** /kuːki/ Someone who is **kooky** is slightly strange or eccentric, but often in a way which makes you like them. [INFORMAL] ❑ *It's slightly kooky, but I love it... She's been mocked for her kooky ways.* ADJ

**Ko|ran** /kɔːrɑːn/ **The Koran** is the sacred book on which the religion of Islam is based. N-PROPER: *the* N

**Ko|ran|ic** /kɔːrænɪk/ **Koranic** is used to describe something which belongs or relates to the Koran. ❑ *...Koranic schools.* ADJ: ADJ n

**Ko|rean** /kɔːriːən/ **(Koreans)** 1 **Korean** means belonging or relating to North or South Korea, or to their people, language, or culture. ADJ
2 A **Korean** is a North or South Korean citizen, or a person of North or South Korean origin. N-COUNT
3 **Korean** is the language spoken by people who live in North and South Korea. N-UNCOUNT

**ko|sher** /koʊʃəʳ/ 1 Something, especially food, that is **kosher** is approved of or allowed by the laws of Judaism. ❑ *...a kosher butcher.* ADJ
2 Something that is **kosher** is generally approved of or considered to be correct. [INFORMAL] ❑ *Acting was not a kosher trade for an upper-class girl.* ADJ

**kow|tow** /kaʊtaʊ/ **(kowtows, kowtowing, kowtowed)** also **kow-tow**. If you say that someone **kowtows to** someone else, you are criticizing them because they are too eager to obey or be polite to someone in authority. [INFORMAL] ❑ *See how stupidly they kow-tow to persons higher in the hierarchy.* VERB disapproval V *to* n Also V

**kph** /keɪ piː eɪtʃ/ **kph** is written after a number to indicate the speed of something such as a vehicle. **kph** is an abbreviation for 'kilometres per hour'.

**Krem|lin** /kremlɪn/ **The Kremlin** is the building in Moscow where Russian government business takes place. ❑ *...a two hour meeting in the Kremlin.* ◆◇◇ N-PROPER: *the* N
♦ **The Kremlin** is also used to refer to the central government of Russia and of the former Soviet Union. ❑ *The Kremlin is still insisting on a diplomatic solution to the crisis.* N-PROPER: *the* N

**kryp|ton** /krɪptɒn/ **Krypton** is an element that is found in the air in the form of a gas. It is used in fluorescent lights and lasers. N-UNCOUNT

**ku|dos** /kjuːdɒs, AM kuːdoʊz/ **Kudos** is admiration or recognition that someone or something gets as a result of a particular action or achievement. ❑ *...a new hotel chain that has won kudos for the way it treats guests.* N-UNCOUNT

**Ku Klux Klan** /kuː klʌks klæn/ **The Ku Klux Klan** is a secret organization of white Protestant men in the United States which promotes violence against black people, Jews, and other minorities. N-PROPER-COLL: oft *the* N

**kung fu** /kʌŋ fuː/ **Kung fu** is a Chinese way of fighting in which people use only their bare hands and feet. N-UNCOUNT

**Ku|wai|ti** /kʊweɪti/ **(Kuwaitis)** 1 **Kuwaiti** means belonging or relating to Kuwait, or to its people or culture. ADJ
2 A **Kuwaiti** is a Kuwaiti citizen, or a person of Kuwaiti origin. N-COUNT

**KW** also **kW**. **KW** is a written abbreviation for **kilowatt**.

# L l

**L, l** /el/ **(L's, l's)** 1 **L** is the twelfth letter of the English alphabet. 2 **L** is the symbol for 'learner driver' in Britain. A large red 'L' on a white background is attached to cars in which people are learning to drive. N-VAR N-VAR

**L8R** **L8R** is the written abbreviation for 'later', mainly used in text messages and e-mails. [COMPUTING]

**La.** **La.** is a written abbreviation for **lane**, and is used especially in addresses and on maps or signs. [BRIT] ❑ *Andy's Records, 14-16 Lower Goat La., Norwich.*

**lab** /læb/ **(labs)** 1 A **lab** is the same as a **laboratory**. 2 In Britain, **Lab** is the written abbreviation for **Labour**. ❑ *...David Blunkett, MP for Sheffield (Lab).* N-COUNT

**la|bel** /leɪbəl/ **(labels, labelling, labelled)** ◆◇◇

✔ in AM, use **labeling, labeled**

1 A **label** is a piece of paper or plastic that is attached to an object in order to give information about it. ❑ *He peered at the label on the bottle.* 2 If something **is labelled**, a label is attached to it giving information about it. ❑ *The stuff has never been properly logged and labelled... Meat labelled 'Scotch Beef' sells for a premium in supermarkets... All the products are labelled with comprehensive instructions.* 3 If you say that someone or something **is labelled as** a particular thing, you mean that people generally describe them that way and you think that this is unfair. ❑ *Too often the press are labelled as bad boys... Certain estates are labelled as undesirable... They are afraid to contact the social services in case they are labelled a problem family... If you venture from 'feminine' standards, you are labelled aggressive and hostile.* 4 If you say that someone gets a particular **label**, you mean that people show disapproval of them by describing them with a critical word or phrase. ❑ *Her treatment of her husband earned her the label of the most hated woman in America.* N-COUNT; VERB: usu passive; be V-ed; V-ed quote; V-ed *with* n; VERB: usu passive; disapproval = brand; be V-ed *as* n; be V-ed *as* adj; be V-ed n; be V-ed adj; N-COUNT: usu with supp

**la|bor** /leɪbər/ → see **labour**.

**la|bora|tory** /ləbɒrətri, AM læbrətɔːri/ **(laboratories)** 1 A **laboratory** is a building or a room where scientific experiments, analyses, and research are carried out. 2 A **laboratory** in a school, college, or university is a room containing scientific equipment where students are taught science subjects such as chemistry. 3 → See also **language laboratory**. ◆◇◇ N-COUNT N-COUNT

**La|bor Day** In the United States, **Labor Day** is a public holiday in honour of working people. It is the first Monday in September. N-UNCOUNT

**la|bor|er** /leɪbərər/ → see **labourer**.

**la|bo|ri|ous** /ləbɔːriəs/ If you describe a task or job as **laborious**, you mean that it takes a lot of time and effort. ❑ *Keeping the garden tidy all year round can be a laborious task.* ♦ **la|bo|ri|ous|ly** *...the embroidery she'd worked on so laboriously during the long winter nights.* ADJ; ADV: ADV with v

**la|bor un|ion** **(labor unions)** A **labor union** is an organization that represents the rights and interests of workers to their employers, for example in order to improve working conditions or wages. [AM] N-COUNT

✔ in BRIT, use **trade union**

**la|bour** /leɪbər/ **(labours, labouring, laboured)** ◆◆◆

✔ in AM, use **labor**

1 **Labour** is very hard work, usually physical work. ❑ *...the labour of seeding, planting and harvesting... The chef at the barbecue looked up from his labours; he was sweating.* → See also **hard labour**. 2 Someone who **labours** works hard using their hands. ❑ *...peasants labouring in the fields... Her husband laboured at the plant for 17 years.* 3 If you **labour to** do something, you do it with difficulty. ❑ *For twenty-five years now he has laboured to build a religious community. ...a young man who's labouring under all kinds of other difficulties.* 4 **Labour** is used to refer to the workers of a country or industry, considered as a group. ❑ *Latin America lacked skilled labour... They were cheap labour.* 5 The work done by a group of workers or by a particular worker is referred to as their **labour**. ❑ *The unemployed cannot withdraw their labour – they have no power.* 6 In Britain, people use **Labour** to refer to the **Labour Party**. ❑ *They all vote Labour.* 7 A **Labour** politician or voter is a member of a Labour Party or votes for a Labour Party. ❑ *...a Labour MP... Millions of Labour voters went unrepresented.* 8 If you **labour under** a delusion or misapprehension, you continue to believe something which is not true. ❑ *She laboured under the illusion that I knew what I was doing... You seem to be labouring under considerable misapprehensions.* 9 If you **labour** a point or an argument, you keep making the same point or saying the same thing, although it is unnecessary. ❑ *I don't want to labour the point but there it is.* 10 **Labour** is the last stage of pregnancy, in which the baby is gradually pushed out of the womb by the mother. ❑ *I thought the pains meant I was going into labour.* N-UNCOUNT: also N in pl, oft supp N; VERB; V; V; VERB = struggle; V to-inf; V *under* n; N-UNCOUNT: oft supp N; N-UNCOUNT: oft poss N; N-PROPER-COLL; ADJ; VERB; V *under* n; V *under* n; VERB; V n; N-UNCOUNT

**la|bour camp** **(labour camps)**

✔ in AM, use **labor camp**

A **labour camp** is a kind of prison, where the prisoners are forced to do hard, physical work, usually outdoors. N-COUNT

**la|boured** /leɪbərd/ 1 If someone's breathing is **laboured**, it is slow and seems to take a lot of effort. ❑ *From his slow walk and laboured breathing, Ginny realized he was far from well.* 2 If something such as someone's writing or speech is **laboured**, they have put too much effort into it so it seems awkward and unnatural. ❑ *Daniel's few encounters with Gold had been characterized by a laboured politeness.* ADJ ADJ

**la|bour|er** /leɪbərər/ **(labourers)**

✔ in AM, use **laborer**

A **labourer** is a person who does a job which involves a lot of hard physical work. ❑ *Her husband had been a farm labourer.* N-COUNT: oft supp N

**la|bour force** **(labour forces)** **The labour force** consists of all the people who are able to work in a country or area, or all the people who work for a particular company. [BUSINESS] N-COUNT: usu sing

**labour-intensive** **Labour-intensive** industries or methods of making things involve a lot of workers. Compare **capital-intensive**. [BUSINESS] ❑ *Construction remains a relatively labour-intensive industry.* ADJ

**la|bour mar|ket** **(labour markets)** When you talk about **the labour market**, you are referring to all the people who are able to work and want jobs in a country or area, in relation to the number of jobs there are available in that country or area. [BUSINESS] ❑ *The longer people have been unemployed, the harder it is for them to compete in the labour market.* N-COUNT: usu sing

**La|bour Par|ty** In Britain, **the Labour Party** is the main left-of-centre party. It believes that wealth and power should be shared fairly and public services should be free for everyone. ❑ *The Labour Party and the teaching unions condemned the idea.* N-PROPER: the N

**la|bour re|la|tions**

☑ in AM use **labor relations**

**Labour relations** refers to the relationship between employers and employees in industry, and the political decisions and laws that affect it. ❑ *We have to balance good labor relations against the need to cut costs.* N-PLURAL

**labour-saving** A **labour-saving** device or idea makes it possible for you to do something with less effort than usual. ❑ *...labour-saving devices such as washing machines.* ADJ: usu ADJ n

**lab|ra|dor** /læbrədɔːʳ/ **(labradors)** or **labrador retriever** or **Labrador retriever** A **labrador** or **labrador retriever** is a type of large dog with short, thick black or gold hair. N-COUNT

**la|bur|num** /ləbɜːʳnəm/ **(laburnums)** A **laburnum** or a **laburnum tree** is a small tree which has long stems of yellow flowers. N-VAR

**laby|rinth** /læbɪrɪnθ/ **(labyrinths)** [1] If you describe a place as a **labyrinth**, you mean that it is made up of a complicated series of paths or passages, through which it is difficult to find your way. [LITERARY] ❑ *...the labyrinth of corridors.* N-COUNT: oft N of n = maze [2] If you describe a situation, process, or area of knowledge as a **labyrinth**, you mean that it is very complicated. [FORMAL] ❑ *...a labyrinth of conflicting political and sociological interpretations.* N-COUNT: usu N of n = maze

**laby|rin|thine** /læbɪrɪnθaɪn/ [1] If you describe a place as **labyrinthine**, you mean that it is like a labyrinth. [FORMAL] ❑ *The streets of the Old City are narrow and labyrinthine.* ADJ: usu ADJ n [2] If you describe a situation, process, or field of knowledge as **labyrinthine**, you mean that it is very complicated and difficult to understand. [FORMAL] ❑ *...his failure to understand the labyrinthine complexities of the situation.* ADJ: usu ADJ n

**lace** /leɪs/ **(laces, lacing, laced)** [1] **Lace** is a very delicate cloth which is made with a lot of holes in it. It is made by twisting together very fine threads of cotton to form patterns. ❑ *...a plain white lace bedspread.* N-UNCOUNT [2] **Laces** are thin pieces of material that are put through special holes in some types of clothing, especially shoes. The laces are tied together in order to tighten the clothing. ❑ *Barry was sitting on the bed, tying the laces of an old pair of running shoes.* N-COUNT: usu pl [3] If you **lace** something such as a pair of shoes, you tighten the shoes by pulling the laces through the holes, and usually tying them together. ❑ *I have a good pair of skates, but no matter how tightly I lace them, my ankles wobble.* VERB = tie; V n ♦ **Lace up** means the same as **lace**. ❑ *He sat on the steps, and laced up his boots... Nancy was lacing her shoe up when the doorbell rang.* PHRASAL VERB V P n (not pron), V n P [4] To **lace** food or drink with a substance such as alcohol or a drug means to put a small amount of the substance into the food or drink. ❑ *She laced his food with sleeping pills.* VERB V n with n

♦ **lace up** → see **lace 3**.

**lac|er|ate** /læsəreɪt/ **(lacerates, lacerating, lacerated)** If something **lacerates** your skin, it cuts it badly and deeply. ❑ *Its claws lacerated his thighs.* VERB V n, Also V

♦ **lac|er|ated** *She was suffering from a badly lacerated hand.* ADJ

**lac|era|tion** /læsəreɪʃᵊn/ **(lacerations)** **Lacerations** are deep cuts on your skin. ❑ *He had lacerations on his back and thighs.* N-COUNT: usu pl, oft N prep

**lace-ups**

☑ The form **lace-up** is used as a modifier.

**Lace-ups** are shoes which are fastened with laces. [BRIT] ❑ *Slip-on shoes are easier to put on than lace-ups... He was wearing black lace-up shoes.* N-PLURAL

**lach|ry|mose** /lækrɪmous, -mouz/ Someone who is **lachrymose** cries very easily and very often. [LITERARY] ❑ *...the tears of lachrymose mourners.* ADJ

**lack** /læk/ **(lacks, lacking, lacked)** ◆◆◇ [1] If there is a **lack of** something, there is not enough of it or it does not exist at all. ❑ *Despite his lack of experience, he got the job... The charges were dropped for lack of evidence... There is a lack of people wanting to start up new businesses.* N-UNCOUNT: also a N, usu N of n [2] If you say that someone or something **lacks** a particular quality or that a particular quality **is lacking** in them, you mean that they do not have any or enough of it. ❑ *He lacked the judgment and political acumen for the post of chairman... Certain vital information is lacking in the report.* VERB V n V [3] → See also **lacking**. [4] If you say there is **no lack of** something, you are emphasizing that there is a great deal of it. ❑ *He said there was no lack of things for them to talk about.* PHRASE: PHR n, usu v-link PHR, v PHR [emphasis]

**lacka|dai|si|cal** /lækədeɪzɪkᵊl/ If you say that someone is **lackadaisical**, you mean that they are rather lazy and do not show much interest or enthusiasm in what they do. ❑ *Dr. Jonsen seemed a little lackadaisical at times. ...the lackadaisical attitude of a number of the principal players.* ADJ

**lack|ey** /læki/ **(lackeys)** If you describe someone as a **lackey**, you are critical of them because they follow someone's orders completely, without ever questioning them. N-COUNT [disapproval]

**lack|ing** /lakɪŋ/ If something or someone **is lacking in** a particular quality, they do not have any of it or enough of it. ❑ *She felt nervous, increasingly lacking in confidence about herself... Why was military intelligence so lacking?* → See also **lack**. ADJ: v-link ADJ, usu ADJ in n

**lack|lustre** /læklʌstəʳ/

☑ in AM, use **lackluster**

If you describe something or someone as **lacklustre**, you mean that they are not exciting or energetic. ❑ *He has already been blamed for his party's lackluster performance during the election campaign.* ADJ

**la|con|ic** /ləkɒnɪk/ If you describe someone as **laconic**, you mean that they use very few words to say something, so that they seem casual or unfriendly. ❑ *Usually so laconic in the office, Dr. Lahey seemed less guarded, more relaxed.* ADJ

**lac|quer** /lækəʳ/ **(lacquers)** **Lacquer** is a special liquid which is painted on wood or metal in order to protect it and to make it shiny. ❑ *We put on the second coating of lacquer... Only the finest lacquers are used for finishes.* N-MASS

**lac|quered** /lækəʳd/ **Lacquered** is used to describe things that have been coated or sprayed with lacquer. ❑ *...17th-century lacquered cabinets. ...perfectly lacquered hair and face powder.* ADJ: ADJ n

**la|crosse** /ləkrɒs, AM -krɔːs/ **Lacrosse** is an outdoor game in which players use long sticks with nets at the end to catch and throw a small ball, in order to try and score goals. N-UNCOUNT

**lac|ta|tion** /lækteɪʃᵊn/ **Lactation** is the production of milk by women and female mammals during the period after they give birth. [FORMAL] N-UNCOUNT

**lac|tic acid** /læktɪk æsɪd/ **Lactic acid** is a type of acid which is found in sour milk and is also produced by your muscles when you have been exercising a lot. N-UNCOUNT

**lac|tose** /læktous/ **Lactose** is a type of sugar which is found in milk and which is sometimes added to food. N-UNCOUNT

**la|cu|na** /ləkjuːnə/ **(lacunae)** If you say that there is a **lacuna** in something such as a document or a person's argument, you mean that it does not deal with an important issue and is therefore not effective or convincing. [FORMAL] N-COUNT

**lacy** /leɪsi/ **(lacier, laciest)** 1 **Lacy** things are made from lace or have pieces of lace attached to them. ❑ *...lacy nightgowns.* 2 **Lacy** is used to describe something that looks like lace, especially because it is very delicate. ❑ *...lacy ferns.* ADJ: usu ADJ n / ADJ: usu ADJ n

**lad** /læd/ **(lads)** 1 A **lad** is a young man or boy. [INFORMAL] ❑ *When I was a lad his age I would laugh at the strangest things... Come along, lad. Time for you to get home.* 2 Some men refer to their male friends or colleagues as **the lads**. [BRIT, INFORMAL] ❑ *...a drink with the lads.* ◆◇◇ N-COUNT; N-VOC / N-PLURAL: the N

**lad|der** /lædəʳ/ **(ladders)** 1 A **ladder** is a piece of equipment used for climbing up something or down from something. It consists of two long pieces of wood, metal, or rope with steps fixed between them. 2 You can use **the ladder** to refer to something such as a society, organization, or system which has different levels that people can progress up or drop down. ❑ *If they want to climb the ladder of success they should be given that opportunity.* 3 A **ladder** is a hole or torn part in a woman's stocking or tights, where some of the vertical threads have broken, leaving only the horizontal threads. [mainly BRIT] N-COUNT / N-SING: the N, usu with supp / N-COUNT

☑ in AM, use **run**

**lad|die** /lædi/ **(laddies)** A **laddie** is a young man or boy. [mainly SCOTTISH, INFORMAL] ❑ *...this little laddie, aged about four... Now then, laddie, what's the trouble?* N-COUNT; N-VOC

**lad|dish** /lædɪʃ/ If you describe someone as **laddish**, you mean that they behave in a way that people think is typical of young men, for example by being rough and noisy, drinking a lot of alcohol, and having a bad attitude towards women. ❑ *Their manager is unconcerned at the laddish image and the drinking that goes with it.* ADJ [disapproval]

**lad|en** /leɪdᵊn/ 1 If someone or something is **laden with** a lot of heavy things, they are holding or carrying them. [LITERARY] ❑ *I came home laden with cardboard boxes. ...heavily-laden mules.* 2 If you describe a person or thing as **laden with** something, particularly something bad, you mean that they have a lot of it. ❑ *Many of their heavy industries are laden with debt.* ADJ: oft ADJ with n / ADJ: v-link ADJ with n

**-laden** /-leɪdᵊn/ **-laden** combines with nouns to form adjectives which indicate that something has a lot of a particular thing or quality. ❑ *...a fat-laden meal. ...smoke-laden air. ...a technology-laden military.* COMB in ADJ usu ADJ n

**lad|ette** /lædet/ **(ladettes)** A **ladette** is a young woman whose behaviour is regarded as typical of young men, for example because she drinks a lot of alcohol, swears, and behaves badly in public. [BRIT, JOURNALISM] N-COUNT [disapproval]

**la-di-da** /lɑː di dɑː/ also **lah-di-dah.** If you describe someone as **la-di-da**, you mean that they have an upper-class way of behaving, which you think seems unnatural and is only done to impress people. [OLD-FASHIONED] ❑ *I wouldn't trust them in spite of all their la-di-da manners.* ADJ [disapproval]

**ladies' man** If you say that a man is a **ladies' man**, you mean that he enjoys spending time socially with women and that women find him attractive. [OLD-FASHIONED] N-SING: usu a N

**ladies' room** Some people refer to a public toilet for women as **the ladies' room**. N-SING: usu the N = ladies

**la|dle** /leɪdᵊl/ **(ladles, ladling, ladled)** 1 A **ladle** is a large, round, deep spoon with a long handle, used for serving soup, stew, or sauce. ➔ See picture on page 1710. 2 If you **ladle** food such as soup or stew, you serve it, especially with a ladle. ❑ *Barry held the bowls while Liz ladled soup into them... Mrs King went to the big black stove and ladled out steaming soup.* N-COUNT / VERB / V n prep / V n with adv / Also V n

**lady** /leɪdi/ **(ladies)** 1 You can use **lady** when you are referring to a woman, especially when you are showing politeness or respect. ❑ *She's a very sweet old lady. ...a lady doctor. ...a cream-coloured lady's shoe.* ➔ See also **old lady**. 2 You can say '**ladies**' when you are addressing a group of women in a formal and respectful way. ❑ *Your table is ready, ladies, if you'd care to come through... Good afternoon, ladies and gentlemen.* 3 A **lady** is a woman from the upper classes, especially in former times. ❑ *Our governess was told to make sure we knew how to talk like English ladies.* 4 In Britain, **Lady** is a title used in front of the names of some female members of the nobility, or the wives of knights. ❑ *My dear Lady Mary, how very good to see you.* 5 If you say that a woman is a **lady**, you mean that she behaves in a polite, dignified, and graceful way. ❑ *His wife was great as well, beautiful-looking and a real lady.* 6 People sometimes refer to a public toilet for women as **the ladies**. [BRIT, INFORMAL] ❑ *At Temple station, Charlotte rushed into the Ladies.* 7 '**Lady**' is sometimes used by men as a form of address when they are talking to a woman that they do not know, especially in shops and in the street. [AM, INFORMAL] ❑ *What seems to be the trouble, lady?* 8 ➔ See also **First Lady**, **Our Lady**. ◆◆◇ N-COUNT / N-VOC [politeness] / N-COUNT / N-TITLE / N-COUNT / N-SING: usu the N / N-VOC [politeness]

**lady|bird** /leɪdibɜːʳd/ **(ladybirds)** A **ladybird** is a small round beetle that is red with black spots. [BRIT] N-COUNT

☑ in AM, use **ladybug**

**lady|bug** /leɪdibʌg/ **(ladybugs)** ➔ see **ladybird**.

**lady friend** **(lady friends)** A man's **lady friend** is the woman with whom he is having a romantic or sexual relationship. [BRIT, OLD-FASHIONED] N-COUNT: usu poss N

**lady-in-waiting** **(ladies-in-waiting)** A **lady-in-waiting** is a woman whose job is to help a queen or princess. N-COUNT

**lady-killer** **(lady-killers)** If you refer to a man as a **lady-killer**, you mean that you think he is very successful at attracting women but quickly leaves them. [OLD-FASHIONED] N-COUNT

**lady|like** /leɪdilaɪk/ If you say that a woman or girl is **ladylike**, you mean that she behaves in a polite, dignified, and graceful way. ❑ *I hate to be blunt, Frankie, but she just didn't strike me as being very ladylike... She crossed the room with quick, ladylike steps.* ADJ

**Lady|ship** /leɪdiʃɪp/ **(Ladyships)** In Britain, you use the expressions **Your Ladyship**, **Her Ladyship**, or **Their Ladyships** when you are addressing or referring to female members of the nobility or the wives of knights. ❑ *Her Ladyship's expecting you, sir.* N-VOC; N-PROPER: det-poss N [politeness]

**lag** /læg/ **(lags, lagging, lagged)** 1 If one thing or person **lags behind** another thing or person, their progress is slower than that of the other. ❑ *Britain still lags behind most of Europe in its provisions for women who want time off to have babies... The restructuring of the pattern of consumption in Britain also lagged behind... He now lags 10 points behind the champion... A poll for the Observer showed Labour on 39 per cent with the Tories lagging a point behind... Hague was lagging badly in the polls.* 2 A time **lag** or a **lag** of a particular length of time is a period of time between one event and another related event. ❑ *There's a time lag between infection with HIV and developing AIDS... Price rises have matched rises in the money supply with a lag of two or three months.* 3 If you **lag** the inside of a roof, a pipe, or a water tank, you cover it with a special material in order to prevent heat escaping from it or to prevent it from freezing. [mainly BRIT] ❑ *If you have to take the floorboards up, take the opportunity to lag any pipes at the same time... Water tanks should be well lagged and the roof well insulated.* ➔ See also **lagging**. VERB / V behind n / V behind / V amount behind n / V amount behind / V / N-COUNT: with supp / VERB / V n / V n

**la|ger** /lɑːgəʳ/ **(lagers)** **Lager** is a type of light beer. [BRIT] ❑ *...a pint of lager... He claims to sell the widest range of beers and lagers in the world.* ♦ A glass of lager can be referred to as a **lager**. ❑ *Hewitt ordered a lager.* N-MASS / N-COUNT

**lag|gard** /lægəʳd/ **(laggards)** If you describe a country, company, or product as a **laggard**, you mean that it is not performing as well as its com- N-COUNT petitors. ❑ *The company has developed a reputation as a technological laggard in the personal-computer arena.*

**lag|ging** /lægɪŋ/ **Lagging** is special material which is used to cover pipes, water tanks, or the inside of a roof so that heat does not escape from them or so they do not freeze. [mainly BRIT] N-UNCOUNT

**la|goon** /ləguːn/ **(lagoons)** A **lagoon** is an area of calm sea water that is separated from the ocean by a line of rock or sand. N-COUNT

**lah-di-dah** /lɑː di dɑː/ → see **la-di-da**.

**laid** /leɪd/ **Laid** is the past tense and past participle of **lay**.

**laid-back** If you describe someone as **laid-back**, you mean that they behave in a calm relaxed way as if nothing will ever worry them. [INFORMAL] ❑ *Nothing worried him, he was really laid back.* ADJ

**lain** /leɪn/ **Lain** is the past participle of **lie**.

**lair** /leəʳ/ **(lairs)** 1 A **lair** is a place where a wild animal lives, usually a place which is underground or well-hidden. ❑ *...a fox's lair.* N-COUNT: usu with poss 2 Someone's **lair** is the particular room or hiding place that they go to, especially when they want to get away from other people. [INFORMAL] ❑ *The village was once a pirates' lair.* N-COUNT: usu with poss

**laird** /leəʳd/ **(lairds)** A **laird** is someone who owns a large area of land in Scotland. N-COUNT

**laissez-faire** /leɪseɪ feəʳ, les-/ **Laissez-faire** is the policy which is based on the idea that governments and the law should not interfere with business, finance, or the conditions of people's working lives. [BUSINESS] ❑ *...a policy of laissez faire.* N-UNCOUNT

**la|ity** /leɪɪti/ **The laity** are all the people involved in the work of a church who are not clergymen, monks, or nuns. ❑ *The Church and the laity were increasingly active in charity work... Clergy and laity alike are divided in their views.* N-SING-COLL: also no det

**lake** /leɪk/ **(lakes)** A **lake** is a large area of fresh water, surrounded by land. ❑ *They can go fishing in the lake... The Nile flows from Lake Victoria in East Africa north to the Mediterranean Sea.* ◆◇◇ N-COUNT: oft in names

**lake|side** /leɪksaɪd/ **The lakeside** is the area of land around the edge of a lake. ❑ *They were out by the lakeside a lot. ...the picturesque Italian lakeside town of Lugano.* N-SING

**La-La land** /lɑːlɑː lænd/ also **La La land, la-la land.** 1 People sometimes refer to Los Angeles, in particular the Hollywood district of Los Angeles, as **La-La land**. [HUMOROUS, INFORMAL] ❑ *...her position as La-La land's premiere hairdresser.* N-UNCOUNT 2 People sometimes use **La-La land** to mean an imaginary place. [INFORMAL] ❑ *For much of the time he was in hospital, he was under sedation. 'I was in La La Land,' he said.* N-UNCOUNT = cloud-cuckoo land

**lam** /læm/ If someone is **on the lam** or if they go **on the lam**, they are trying to escape or hide from someone such as the police or an enemy. [mainly AM, INFORMAL] ❑ *He was on the lam for seven years.* PHRASE: v-link PHR, PHR after v

**lama** /lɑːmə/ **(lamas)** A **lama** is a Buddhist priest or monk in Tibet or Mongolia. ◆◇◇ N-COUNT; N-TITLE

**lamb** /læm/ **(lambs)** 1 A **lamb** is a young sheep. N-COUNT ♦ **Lamb** is the flesh of a lamb eaten as food. ❑ *Laura was basting the leg of lamb.* N-UNCOUNT 2 People sometimes use **lamb** when they are addressing or referring to someone who they are fond of and who is young, gentle, or unfortunate. ❑ *She came and put her arms around me. 'You poor lamb. What's wrong?'* N-COUNT feelings 3 **mutton dressed as lamb** → see **mutton**.

**lam|bast** /læmbæst/ **(lambasts, lambasting, lambasted)**

✔ in AM, usually use **lambaste** /læmbeɪst/

If you **lambast** someone, you criticize them severely, usually in public. [FORMAL] ❑ *Grey took every opportunity to lambast Thompson and his organization.* VERB V n

**lamb|ing** /læmɪŋ/ **Lambing** is the time in the spring when female sheep give birth to lambs. ❑ *...the lambing season.* N-UNCOUNT: oft N n

**lame** /leɪm/ **(lamer, lamest)** 1 If someone is **lame**, they are unable to walk properly because of damage to one or both of their legs. ❑ *He was aware that she was lame in one leg... David had to pull out of the Championships when his horse went lame.* ADJ ♦ **The lame** are people who are lame. ❑ *...the wounded and the lame of the last war.* N-PLURAL: the N 2 If you describe something, for example an excuse, argument, or remark, as **lame**, you mean that it is poor or weak. ❑ *He mumbled some lame excuse about having gone to sleep... All our theories sound pretty lame.* ADJ = weak, feeble ♦ **lame|ly** *'Lovely house,' I said lamely.* ADV: ADV with v

**lamé** /lɑːmeɪ, AM læmeɪ/ **Lamé** is cloth that has threads of gold or silver woven into it, which make it reflect light. ❑ *...a silver lamé dress.* N-UNCOUNT: usu supp N

**lame duck** **(lame ducks)** 1 If you describe someone or something as a **lame duck**, you are critical of them because they are not successful and need to be helped a lot. ❑ *...lame-duck industries.* N-COUNT: oft N n disapproval 2 If you refer to a politician or a government as a **lame duck**, you mean that they have little real power, for example because their period of office is coming to an end. ❑ *...a lame duck government.* N-COUNT: usu N n

**la|ment** /ləment/ **(laments, lamenting, lamented)** 1 If you **lament** something, you express your sadness, regret, or disappointment about it. [mainly FORMAL or WRITTEN] ❑ *Ken began to lament the death of his only son... He laments that people in Villa El Salvador are suspicious of the police... 'Prices are down 40 per cent since Christmas,' he lamented.* VERB V n V that V with quote Also V 2 Someone's **lament** is an expression of their sadness, regret, or disappointment about something. [mainly FORMAL or WRITTEN] ❑ *She spoke of the professional woman's lament that a woman's judgment is questioned more than a man's.* N-COUNT: oft with poss 3 A **lament** is a poem, song, or piece of music which expresses sorrow that someone has died. N-COUNT

**lam|en|table** /læməntəbᵊl, ləment-/ If you describe something as **lamentable**, you mean that it is very unfortunate or disappointing. [LITERARY] ❑ *This lamentable state of affairs lasted until 1947... His command of English was lamentable.* ADJ feelings ♦ **lam|en|tably** /læməntəbli/ *There are still lamentably few women surgeons... They have failed lamentably.* ADV: usu ADV adj, also ADV with v, ADV with cl

**la|men|ta|tion** /læmenteɪʃᵊn/ **(lamentations)** A **lamentation** is an expression of great sorrow. [FORMAL] ❑ *It was a time for mourning and lamentation. ...special prayers and lamentations.* N-VAR

**lami|nate** /læmɪneɪt/ **(laminates)** A **laminate** is a tough material that is made by sticking together two or more layers of a particular substance. N-MASS

**lami|nat|ed** /læmɪneɪtɪd/ 1 Material such as wood or plastic that is **laminated** consists of several thin sheets or layers that are stuck together. ❑ *Modern windscreens are made from laminated glass.* ADJ: usu ADJ n 2 A product that is **laminated** is covered with a thin sheet of something, especially clear or coloured plastic, in order to protect it. ❑ *The photographs were mounted on laminated cards. ...laminated work surfaces.* ADJ: usu ADJ n

**lamp** /læmp/ **(lamps)** 1 A **lamp** is a light that works by using electricity or by burning oil or gas. ❑ *She switched on the bedside lamp... In the evenings we eat by the light of an oil lamp.* N-COUNT 2 A **lamp** is an electrical device which produces a special type of light or heat, used especially in medical or beauty treatment. ❑ *...a sun lamp. ...the use of infra-red lamps.* N-COUNT: usu supp N

**lamp|light** /læmplaɪt/ **Lamplight** is the light produced by a lamp. ❑ *Her cheeks glowed red in the lamplight.* N-UNCOUNT

**lam|poon** /læmpuːn/ **(lampoons, lampooning, lampooned)** 1 If you **lampoon** someone or something, you criticize them very strongly, using VERB humorous means. ❑ *He was lampooned for his short stature and political views.* V n [2] A **lampoon** is a piece of writing or speech which criticizes someone or something very strongly, using humorous means. N-VAR ❑ *...his scathing lampoons of consumer culture... The style Shelley is using here is that of popular lampoon.*

**lamp-post** **(lamp-posts)** also **lamppost.** A **lamp-post** is a tall metal or concrete pole that is fixed beside a road and has a light at the top. [mainly BRIT] N-COUNT

☑ in AM, usually use **street lamp, street light**

**lamp|shade** /læmpʃeɪd/ **(lampshades)** A **lampshade** is a covering that is fitted round or over an electric light bulb in order to protect it or decorate it, or to make the light less harsh. N-COUNT = *shade*

**LAN** /læn/ **(LANs)** A **LAN** is a group of personal computers and associated equipment that are linked by cable, for example in an office building, and that share a communications line. **LAN** is an abbreviation for 'local area network'. [COMPUTING] N-COUNT ❑ *You can take part in multiplayer games either on a LAN network or via the internet.*

**lance** /lɑːns, læns/ **(lances, lancing, lanced)** [1] If a boil on someone's body **is lanced**, a small cut is made in it so that the liquid inside comes out. [MEDICAL] VERB: usu passive ❑ *It is a painful experience having the boil lanced.* have n V-ed Also be V-ed [2] A **lance** is a long spear used in former times by soldiers on horseback. N-COUNT ❑ *...the clang of lances striking armour.*

**land** /lænd/ **(lands, landing, landed)** ◆◆◆ [1] **Land** is an area of ground, especially one that is used for a particular purpose such as farming or building. N-UNCOUNT ❑ *Good agricultural land is in short supply. ...160 acres of land. ...a small piece of grazing land.* [2] You can refer to an area of land which someone owns as their **land** or their **lands**. N-COUNT: poss N ❑ *Their home is on his father's land... His lands were poorly farmed.* [3] If you talk about **the land**, you mean farming and the way of life in farming areas, in contrast to life in the cities. N-SING: the N ❑ *Living off the land was hard enough at the best of times.* [4] **Land** is the part of the world that consists of ground, rather than sea or air. N-UNCOUNT: also the N ❑ *It isn't clear whether the plane went down over land or sea. ...a stretch of sandy beach that was almost inaccessible from the land.* [5] You can use **land** to refer to a country in a poetic or emotional way. [LITERARY] N-COUNT: with supp ❑ *...America, land of opportunity.* [6] When someone or something **lands**, they come down to the ground after moving through the air or falling. VERB ❑ *Three mortar shells had landed close to a crowd of people.* V [7] When someone **lands** a plane, ship, or spacecraft, or when it **lands**, it arrives somewhere after a journey. VERB ❑ *The jet landed after a flight of just under three hours...* V *The crew finally landed the plane on its belly on the soft part of the runway.* V n [8] To **land** goods somewhere means to unload them there at the end of a journey, especially by ship. [mainly BRIT] VERB ❑ *The vessels will have to land their catch at designated ports.* V n [9] If you **land in** an unpleasant situation or place or if something **lands** you **in** it, something causes you to be in it. [INFORMAL] VERB ❑ *He landed in a psychiatric ward...* V in n *This is not the first time his exploits have landed him in trouble.* V n in n [10] If someone or something **lands** you **with** a difficult situation, they cause you to have to deal with the difficulties involved. [mainly BRIT, INFORMAL] VERB = *saddle, lumber with* ❑ *The other options simply complicate the situation and could land him with more expense.* V n with n [11] If something **lands** somewhere, it arrives there unexpectedly, often causing problems. [INFORMAL] VERB = *arrive* ❑ *Two days later the book had already landed on his desk.* V prep/adv [12] If you **land** something that is difficult to get and that many people want, you are successful in getting it. [INFORMAL] VERB ❑ *He landed a place on the graduate training scheme...* V n *His flair with hair soon landed him a part-time job at his local barbers.* V n n [13] to **land on** your **feet** → see **foot**.

♦ **land up** If you say that you **land up** in a place or situation, you mean that you arrive there after a long journey or at the end of a long series of events. [mainly BRIT, INFORMAL] PHRASAL VERB = *end up, wind up* ❑ *Half of those who went east seem to have landed up in southern India...* V P prep/adv *We landed up at the Las Vegas at about 6.30.* V P prep/adv

**land|ed** /lændɪd/ **Landed** means owning or including a large amount of land, especially land that has belonged to the same family for several generations. ADJ: ADJ n ❑ *Most of them were the nobility and the landed gentry.*

**land|fall** /lændfɔːl/ **(landfalls)** **Landfall** is the act of arriving somewhere after a journey at sea, or the land that you arrive at. N-VAR ❑ *By the time we had made landfall the boat looked ten years older!*

**land|fill** /lændfɪl/ **(landfills)** [1] **Landfill** is a method of getting rid of very large amounts of rubbish by burying it in a large deep hole. N-UNCOUNT ❑ *...the environmental costs of landfill.* [2] A **landfill** is a large deep hole in which very large amounts of rubbish are buried. N-COUNT: oft N n ❑ *The rubbish in modern landfills does not rot. ...the cost of disposing of refuse in landfill sites.*

**land|ing** /lændɪŋ/ **(landings)** [1] In a house or other building, the **landing** is the area at the top of the staircase which has rooms leading off it. N-COUNT: usu the N in sing ❑ *I ran out onto the landing.* [2] A **landing** is an act of bringing an aircraft or spacecraft down to the ground. N-VAR ❑ *I had to make a controlled landing into the sea... The plane had been cleared for landing at Brunswick's Glynco Airport.* [3] When a **landing** takes place, troops are unloaded from boats or aircraft at the beginning of a military invasion or other operation. N-COUNT ❑ *American forces have begun a big landing.* [4] A **landing** is the same as a **landing stage**. N-COUNT

**land|ing craft** **(landing craft)** A **landing craft** is a small boat designed for the landing of troops and equipment on the shore. N-COUNT

**land|ing gear** The **landing gear** of an aircraft is its wheels and the structures that support the wheels. N-UNCOUNT

**land|ing stage** **(landing stages)** also **landing-stage.** A **landing stage** is a platform built over water where boats stop to let people get off, or to load or unload goods. [mainly BRIT] N-COUNT = *jetty, landing*

**land|ing strip** **(landing strips)** A **landing strip** is a long flat piece of land from which aircraft can take off and land, especially one used only by private or military aircraft. N-COUNT

**land|lady** /lændleɪdi/ **(landladies)** [1] Someone's **landlady** is the woman who allows them to live or work in a building which she owns, in return for rent. N-COUNT ❑ *We had been made homeless by our landlady.* [2] The **landlady** of a pub is the woman who owns or runs it, or the wife of the man who owns or runs it. [BRIT] N-COUNT ❑ *...Bet, the landlady of the Rovers Return.*

**land|less** /lændləs/ Someone who is **landless** is prevented from owning the land that they farm. ADJ ❑ *...landless peasants.* ♦ **The landless** are people who are landless. N-PLURAL: the N ❑ *We are giving an equal area of land to the landless.*

**land|locked** /lændlɒkt/ also **land-locked.** A **landlocked** country is surrounded by other countries and does not have its own ports. ADJ: usu ADJ n ❑ *...the landlocked West African nation of Mali.*

**land|lord** /lændlɔːʳd/ **(landlords)** [1] Someone's **landlord** is the man who allows them to live or work in a building which he owns, in return for rent. N-COUNT ❑ *His landlord doubled the rent.* [2] The **landlord** of a pub is the man who owns or runs it, or the husband of the woman who owns or runs it. [mainly BRIT] N-COUNT ❑ *The landlord refused to serve him because he considered him too drunk.*

**land|lubber** /lændlʌbəʳ/ **(landlubbers)** A **landlubber** is someone who is not used to or does not like travelling by boat, and has little knowledge of boats and the sea. [OLD-FASHIONED] N-COUNT

**land|mark** /lændmɑːʳk/ **(landmarks)** [1] A **landmark** is a building or feature which is easily noticed and can be used to judge your position or N-COUNT the position of other buildings or features. ❑ *The Ambassador Hotel is a Los Angeles landmark.* [2] You can refer to an important stage in the development of something as a **landmark**. ❑ *...a landmark arms control treaty... The baby was one of the big landmarks in our relationship.* N-COUNT: oft N n, N *in* n

**land mass** **(land masses)** also **landmass.** A **land mass** is a very large area of land such as a continent. ❑ *...the Antarctic landmass. ...the country's large land mass of 768 million hectares.* N-COUNT

**land|mine** /lændmaɪn/ **(landmines)** also **land mine.** A **landmine** is an explosive device which is placed on or under the ground and explodes when a person or vehicle touches it. N-COUNT = mine

**land|owner** /lændoʊnəʳ/ **(landowners)** A **landowner** is a person who owns land, especially a large amount of land. ❑ *...rural communities involved in conflicts with large landowners.* N-COUNT

**land|owning** /lændoʊnɪŋ/ **Landowning** is used to describe people who own a lot of land, especially when they are considered as a group within society. ❑ *...the Anglo-Irish landowning class.* ADJ: ADJ n

**land re|form** **(land reforms)** **Land reform** is a change in the system of land ownership, especially when it involves giving land to the people who actually farm it and taking it away from people who own large areas for profit. ❑ *...the new land reform policy under which thousands of peasant families are to be resettled.* N-VAR

**land reg|is|try** **(land registries)** In Britain, a **land registry** is a government office where records are kept about each area of land in a country or region, including information about who owns it. N-COUNT

**land|scape** /lændskeɪp/ **(landscapes, landscaping, landscaped)** ◆◇◇ [1] The **landscape** is everything you can see when you look across an area of land, including hills, rivers, buildings, trees, and plants. ❑ *...Arizona's desert landscape... We moved to Northamptonshire and a new landscape of hedges and fields.* N-VAR: oft supp N [2] A **landscape** is all the features that are important in a particular situation. ❑ *June's events completely altered the political landscape.* N-COUNT: with supp [3] A **landscape** is a painting which shows a scene in the countryside. N-COUNT [4] If an area of land **is landscaped**, it is changed to make it more attractive, for example by adding streams or ponds and planting trees and bushes. ❑ *The gravel pits have been landscaped and planted to make them attractive to wildfowl... They had landscaped their property with trees, shrubs, and lawns. ...a smart suburb of landscaped gardens and wide streets.* VERB *be* V-ed V n *with* n V-ed Also V n ♦ **land|scap|ing** *The landowner insisted on a high standard of landscaping.* N-UNCOUNT

**land|scape archi|tect** **(landscape architects)** A **landscape architect** is the same as a **landscape gardener**. N-COUNT

**land|scape gar|den|er** **(landscape gardeners)** A **landscape gardener** is a person who designs gardens or parks so that they look attractive. N-COUNT

**land|slide** /lændslaɪd/ **(landslides)** [1] A **landslide** is a victory in an election in which a person or political party gets far more votes or seats than their opponents. ❑ *He won last month's presidential election by a landslide... The NLD won a landslide victory in the elections five months ago.* N-COUNT [2] A **landslide** is a large amount of earth and rocks falling down a cliff or the side of a mountain. ❑ *The storm caused landslides and flooding in Savona.* N-COUNT

**land|slip** /lændslɪp/ **(landslips)** A **landslip** is a small movement of soil and rocks down a slope. [mainly BRIT] ❑ *Roads were flooded or blocked by landslips.* N-COUNT

✔ in AM, use **slide, mudslide**

**land|ward** /lændwəʳd/ The **landward** side of something is the side nearest to the land or facing the land, rather than the sea. ❑ *Rebels surrounded the city's landward sides.* ADJ: ADJ n

**lane** /leɪn/ **(lanes)** ◆◇◇ [1] A **lane** is a narrow road, especially in the country. ❑ *...a quiet country lane... Follow the lane to the river.* N-COUNT [2] **Lane** is also used in the names of roads, either in cities or in the country. ❑ *...The Dorchester Hotel, Park Lane.* N-IN-NAMES [3] A **lane** is a part of a main road which is marked by the edge of the road and a painted line, or by two painted lines. ❑ *The lorry was travelling at 20mph in the slow lane... I pulled out into the eastbound lane of Route 2.* N-COUNT: usu adj N [4] At a swimming pool or athletics track, a **lane** is a long narrow section which is marked by lines or ropes. N-COUNT [5] A **lane** is a route that is frequently used by aircraft or ships. ❑ *The collision took place in the busiest shipping lanes in the world.* N-COUNT: usu n N

**lan|guage** /læŋgwɪdʒ/ **(languages)** ◆◆◇ [1] A **language** is a system of communication which consists of a set of sounds and written symbols which are used by the people of a particular country or region for talking or writing. ❑ *...the English language... Students are expected to master a second language.* N-COUNT [2] **Language** is the use of a system of communication which consists of a set of sounds or written symbols. ❑ *Students examined how children acquire language.* N-UNCOUNT [3] You can refer to the words used in connection with a particular subject as **the language of** that subject. ❑ *...the language of business.* N-UNCOUNT: *the* N *of* n, supp N [4] You can refer to someone's use of rude words or swearing as **bad language** when you find it offensive. ❑ *Television companies tend to censor bad language in feature films... There's a girl gonna be in the club, so you guys watch your language.* N-UNCOUNT: adj N, poss N [5] The **language** of a piece of writing or speech is the style in which it is written or spoken. ❑ *...a booklet summarising it in plain language... The tone of his language was diplomatic and polite.* N-UNCOUNT: with supp [6] You can use **language** to refer to various means of communication involving recognizable symbols, non-verbal sounds, or actions. ❑ *Some sign languages are very sophisticated means of communication. ...the digital language of computers.* N-VAR: supp N, N *of* n

**lan|guage la|bora|tory** **(language laboratories)** A **language laboratory** is a classroom equipped with tape recorders or computers where people can practise listening to and talking foreign languages. N-COUNT

**lan|guid** /læŋgwɪd/ If you describe someone as **languid**, you mean that they show little energy or interest and are very slow and casual in their movements. [LITERARY] ❑ *To his delight a familiar, tall, languid figure lowered itself down the steps of a club.* ADJ ♦ **lan|guid|ly** *We sat about languidly after dinner.* ADV: usu ADV with v, also ADV adj

**lan|guish** /læŋgwɪʃ/ **(languishes, languishing, languished)** [1] If someone **languishes** somewhere, they are forced to remain and suffer in an unpleasant situation. ❑ *Pollard continues to languish in prison.* VERB V prep/adv [2] If something **languishes**, it is not successful, often because of a lack of effort or because of a lot of difficulties. ❑ *Without the founder's drive and direction, the company gradually languished.* VERB V

**lan|guor** /læŋgəʳ/ **Languor** is a pleasant feeling of being relaxed and not having any energy or interest in anything. [LITERARY] ❑ *She, in her languor, had not troubled to eat much.* N-UNCOUNT

**lan|guor|ous** /læŋgərəs/ If you describe an activity as **languorous**, you mean that it is lazy, relaxed, and not energetic, usually in a pleasant way. [LITERARY] ❑ *...languorous morning coffees on the terrace.* ADJ: usu ADJ n

**lank** /læŋk/ If someone's hair is **lank**, it is long and perhaps greasy and hangs in a dull and unattractive way. ADJ

**lanky** /læŋki/ **(lankier, lankiest)** If you describe someone as **lanky**, you mean that they are tall and thin and move rather awkwardly. ❑ *He was six feet four, all lanky and leggy.* ADJ

**lan|tern** /læntəʳn/ **(lanterns)** A **lantern** is a lamp in a metal frame with glass sides and with a handle on top so you can carry it. N-COUNT

**Lao|tian** /leɪoʊʃᵊn/ **(Laotians)** [1] **Laotian** means belonging or relating to Laos, or its people, language, or culture. ADJ [2] A **Laotian** is a Laotian N-COUNT citizen, or a person of Laotian origin. [3] **Laotian** is the language spoken by people who live in Laos. N-UNCOUNT

**lap** /læp/ **(laps, lapping, lapped)** [1] If you have something on your **lap** when you are sitting down, it is on top of your legs and near to your body. ❑ *She waited quietly with her hands in her lap... Hugh glanced at the child on her mother's lap.* ◆◇◇ N-COUNT: poss N [2] In a race, a competitor completes a **lap** when they have gone round a course once. ❑ *...that last lap of the race... On lap two, Baker edged forward.* N-COUNT: usu ord/ adj N, N num [3] In a race, if you **lap** another competitor, you go past them while they are still on the previous lap. ❑ *He was caught out while lapping a slower rider.* VERB V n [4] A **lap** of a long journey is one part of it, between two points where you stop. ❑ *I had thought we might travel as far as Oak Valley, but we only managed the first lap of the journey.* N-COUNT: N *of* n, ord/ adj N = *leg* [5] When water **laps** against something such as the shore or the side of a boat, it touches it gently and makes a soft sound. [WRITTEN] ❑ *...the water that lapped against the pillars of the boathouse... The building was right on the river and the water lapped the walls.* VERB V prep/adv V n ♦ **lap|ping** *The only sound was the lapping of the waves.* N-UNCOUNT: *the* N *of* n [6] When an animal **laps** a drink, it uses short quick movements of its tongue to take liquid up into its mouth. ❑ *The cat lapped milk from a dish.* VERB V n ♦ **Lap up** means the same as **lap**. ❑ *She poured some water into a plastic bowl. Faust, her Great Dane, lapped it up with relish.* PHRASAL VERB V n P [7] If you say that a situation is **in the lap of the gods**, you mean that its success or failure depends entirely on luck or on things that are outside your control. ❑ *They had to stop the operation, so at that stage my life was in the lap of the gods.* PHRASE: v-link PHR

♦ **lap up** If you say that someone **laps up** something such as information or attention, you mean that they accept it eagerly, usually when you think they are being foolish for believing that it is sincere. ❑ *Their audience will lap up whatever they throw at them... They just haven't been to school before. They're so eager to learn, they lap it up.* → see **lap 6**. PHRASAL VERB V P n (not pron) V n P

**lap danc|ing Lap dancing** is a type of entertainment in a bar or club in which a woman who is wearing very few clothes dances in a sexy way close to customers or sitting on their laps. N-UNCOUNT ♦ **lap danc|er (lap dancers)** ❑ *...a club full of lap dancers.* N-COUNT

**la|pel** /ləpel/ **(lapels)** The **lapels** of a jacket or coat are the two top parts at the front that are folded back on each side and join on to the collar. N-COUNT

**la|pis lazu|li** /læpɪs læzjʊlaɪ, AM -liː/ **Lapis lazuli** is a bright blue stone, used especially in making jewellery. N-UNCOUNT

**lap of hon|our (laps of honour)** If the winner of a race or game does a **lap of honour**, they run or drive slowly around a race track or sports field in order to receive the applause of the crowd. [BRIT] N-COUNT

**lapse** /læps/ **(lapses, lapsing, lapsed)** [1] A **lapse** is a moment or instance of bad behaviour by someone who usually behaves well. ❑ *On Friday he showed neither decency nor dignity. It was an uncommon lapse.* N-COUNT: usu adj N, N *in* n [2] A **lapse of** something such as concentration or judgment is a temporary lack of that thing, which can often cause you to make a mistake. ❑ *I had a little lapse of concentration in the middle of the race... The incident was being seen as a serious security lapse.* N-COUNT: N *of* n, supp N [3] If you **lapse into** a quiet or inactive state, you stop talking or being active. ❑ *She muttered something unintelligible and lapsed into silence.* VERB V *into* n [4] If someone **lapses into** a particular way of speaking, or behaving, they start speaking or behaving in that way, usually for a short period. ❑ *Teenagers occasionally find it all too much to cope with and lapse into bad behaviour.* VERB = *slip* V *into* n ♦ **Lapse** is also a noun. ❑ *Her lapse into German didn't seem peculiar. After all, it was her native tongue.* N-COUNT: usu N *into* n [5] A **lapse of** time is a period that is long enough for a situation to change or for people to have a different opinion about it. ❑ *...the restoration of diplomatic relations after a lapse of 24 years... There is usually a time lapse between receipt of new information and its publication.* N-SING: usu N *of* n, supp N [6] If a period of time **lapses**, it passes. ❑ *New products and production processes are transferred to the developing countries only after a substantial amount of time has lapsed.* VERB V [7] If a situation or legal contract **lapses**, it is allowed to end rather than being continued, renewed, or extended. ❑ *Her membership of the Labour Party has lapsed... Ford allowed the name and trademark to lapse during the Eighties.* VERB V V [8] If a member of a particular religion **lapses**, they stop believing in it or stop following its rules and practices. ❑ *She calls herself a lapsed Catholic.* VERB V-ed

**lap|top** /læptɒp/ **(laptops)** A **laptop** or a **laptop computer** is a small portable computer. ❑ *She used to work at her laptop until four in the morning.* N-COUNT

**lap|wing** /læpwɪŋ/ **(lapwings)** A **lapwing** is a small dark green bird which has a white breast and feathers sticking up on its head. N-COUNT

**lar|ceny** /lɑːʳsəni/ **Larceny** is the crime of stealing. [LEGAL] ❑ *Haggerman now faces two to 20 years in prison on grand larceny charges.* N-UNCOUNT = *theft*

**larch** /lɑːʳtʃ/ **(larches)** A **larch** is a tree with needle-shaped leaves. N-VAR

**lard** /lɑːʳd/ **(lards, larding, larded) Lard** is soft white fat obtained from pigs. It is used in cooking. N-UNCOUNT

**lar|der** /lɑːʳdəʳ/ **(larders)** A **larder** is a room or large cupboard in a house, usually near the kitchen, in which food is kept. [mainly BRIT] N-COUNT = *pantry*

☑ in AM, use **pantry**

**large** /lɑːʳdʒ/ **(larger, largest)** [1] A **large** thing or person is greater in size than usual or average. ❑ *The Pike lives mainly in large rivers and lakes... In the largest room about a dozen children and seven adults are sitting on the carpet... He was a large man with thick dark hair.* ◆◆◆ ADJ = *big* ≠ *small* [2] A **large** amount or number of people or things is more than the average amount or number. ❑ *The gang finally fled with a large amount of cash and jewellery... There are a large number of centres where you can take full-time courses... The figures involved are truly very large.* ADJ ≠ *small* [3] A **large** organization or business does a lot of work or commercial activity and employs a lot of people. ❑ *...a large company in Chicago... Many large organizations run courses for their employees.* ADJ = *big* ≠ *small* [4] **Large** is used to indicate that a problem or issue which is being discussed is very important or serious. ❑ *...the already large problem of under-age drinking... There's a very large question about the viability of the newspaper.* ADJ: usu ADJ n = *serious*

PHRASES [5] You use **at large** to indicate that you are talking in a general way about most of the people mentioned. ❑ *I think the chances of getting reforms accepted by the community at large remain extremely remote.* PHRASE: n PHR = *in general* [6] If you say that a dangerous person, thing, or animal is **at large**, you mean that they have not been captured or made safe. ❑ *The man who tried to have her killed is still at large.* PHRASE: v-link PHR = *free* [7] You use **by and large** to indicate that a statement is mostly but not completely true. ❑ *By and large, the papers greet the government's new policy document with a certain amount of scepticism.* PHRASE: PHR with cl = *on the whole* [8] **to a large extent** → see **extent**. **larger than life** → see **life**. **in large measure** → see **measure**.

**large|ly** /lɑːʳdʒli/ [1] You use **largely** to say that a statement is not completely true but is mostly true. ❑ *The fund is largely financed through government borrowing... I largely work with people who already are motivated... Their weapons have been largely stones.* ◆◆◇ ADV: ADV with v, ADV with cl/ group = *mainly* [2] **Largely** is used to introduce the main reason for a particular event or situation. ❑ *Retail sales dipped 6/10ths of a percent last month, largely because Americans were buying fewer cars.* ADV: ADV prep = *mainly*

**large-scale** also **large scale.** [1] A **large-scale** action or event happens over a very wide area or involves a lot of people or things. ❑ *...a large scale military operation.* ADJ: ADJ n ≠ *small-scale* [2] A **large-scale** map ADJ: ADJ n or diagram represents a small area of land or a building or machine on a scale that is large enough for small details to be shown. ❑ *...a large-scale map of the county.* ≠small-scale

**lar|gesse** /lɑːʳʒes/

✓ in AM, use **largess**

**Largesse** is a generous gift of money or a generous act of kindness. [FORMAL] ❑ *...grateful recipients of their largesse. ...his most recent act of largesse.* N-UNCOUNT

**larg|ish** /lɑːʳdʒɪʃ/ **Largish** means fairly large. ❑ *...a largish modern city.* ADJ: usu ADJ n = biggish

**lar|go** /lɑːʳgoʊ/ **(largos)** 1 **Largo** written above a piece of music means that it should be played slowly. ADV: ADV after v 2 A **largo** is a piece of music, especially part of a longer piece, that is played slowly. N-COUNT

**lark** /lɑːʳk/ **(larks)** 1 A **lark** is a small brown bird which makes a pleasant sound. N-COUNT 2 If you say that doing something is a **lark**, you mean that it is fun, although perhaps naughty or dangerous. ❑ *The children thought it was a great lark.* N-COUNT

**lar|va** /lɑːʳvə/ **(larvae** /lɑːʳviː/**)** A **larva** is an insect at the stage of its life after it has developed from an egg and before it changes into its adult form. ❑ *The eggs quickly hatch into larvae.* N-COUNT

**lar|val** /lɑːʳvᵊl/ **Larval** means concerning insect larvae or in the state of being an insect larva. ADJ: ADJ n

**lar|yn|gi|tis** /lærɪndʒaɪtɪs/ **Laryngitis** is an infection of the throat in which your larynx becomes swollen and painful, making it difficult to speak. N-UNCOUNT

**lar|ynx** /lærɪŋks/ **(larynxes)** Your **larynx** is the top part of the passage that leads from your throat to your lungs and contains your vocal cords. [MEDICAL] N-COUNT = voice box

**la|sa|gne** /ləsænjə/ **(lasagnes)** also **lasagna. Lasagne** is a food dish that consists of layers of pasta, sauce, and a filling such as meat or cheese, baked in an oven. N-VAR

**las|civ|ious** /ləsɪviəs/ If you describe someone as **lascivious**, you disapprove of them because they show a very strong interest in sex. ❑ *The man was lascivious, sexually perverted and insatiable. ...their lewd and lascivious talk.* ADJ [disapproval]

**la|ser** /leɪzəʳ/ **(lasers)** 1 A **laser** is a narrow beam of concentrated light produced by a special machine. It is used for cutting very hard materials, and in many technical fields such as surgery and telecommunications. ❑ *...new laser technology.* N-COUNT 2 A **laser** is a machine that produces a laser beam. ❑ *...the first-ever laser, built in 1960.* N-COUNT

**la|ser disc (laser discs)** also **laser disk.** A **laser disc** is a shiny flat disc which can be played on a machine which uses lasers to convert signals on the disc into television pictures and sound of a very high quality. N-COUNT: oft N n, also *on* N

**la|ser print|er (laser printers)** A **laser printer** is a computer printer that produces clear words and pictures by using laser beams. N-COUNT

**lash** /læʃ/ **(lashes, lashing, lashed)** 1 Your **lashes** are the hairs that grow on the edge of your upper and lower eyelids. ❑ *...sombre grey eyes, with unusually long lashes... Joanna studied him through her lashes.* N-COUNT: usu pl = eyelash 2 If you **lash** two or more things together, you tie one of them firmly to the other. ❑ *Secure the anchor by lashing it to the rail... The shelter is built by lashing poles together to form a small dome... We were worried about the lifeboat which was not lashed down.* VERB = tie; V n *to* n; V pl-n with *together*; V n with adv; Also V n 3 If wind, rain, or water **lashes** someone or something, it hits them violently. [WRITTEN] ❑ *The worst winter storms of the century lashed the east coast of North America... Suddenly rain lashed against the windows.* VERB; V n; V prep/adv 4 If someone **lashes** you or **lashes into** you, they speak very angrily to you, criticizing you or saying you have done something wrong. ❑ *She went quiet for a moment while she summoned up the words to lash him... The report lashes into police commanders for failing to act on intelligence information.* VERB; V n; V *into* n 5 A **lash** is a thin strip of leather at the end of a whip. N-COUNT 6 A **lash** is a blow with a whip, especially a blow on someone's back as a punishment. ❑ *The villagers sentenced one man to five lashes for stealing a ham from his neighbor.* N-COUNT

♦ **lash out** 1 If you **lash out**, you attempt to hit someone quickly and violently with a weapon or with your hands or feet. ❑ *Riot police fired in the air and lashed out with clubs to disperse hundreds of demonstrators... Her husband has a terrible temper and lashes out at her when he's angry.* PHRASAL VERB; V P; V P *at* n 2 If you **lash out at** someone or something, you speak to them or about them very angrily or critically. ❑ *As a politician Jefferson frequently lashed out at the press.* PHRASAL VERB; V P *at/against* n

**lash|ing** /læʃɪŋ/ **(lashings)** 1 **Lashings of** something means a large quantity or amount of it. [mainly BRIT, INFORMAL] ❑ *Serve by cutting the scones in half and spreading with jam and lashings of clotted cream.* QUANT: QUANT *of* n-uncount 2 **Lashings** are ropes or cables that are used to tie one thing to another. ❑ *We made a tour of the yacht, checking lashings and emergency gear.* N-COUNT: usu pl 3 If you refer to someone's comments as a **lashing**, you mean that they are very critical and angry. ❑ *He never grew used to the lashings he got from the critics.* N-COUNT 4 A **lashing** is a punishment in which a person is hit with a whip. N-COUNT

**lass** /læs/ **(lasses)** A **lass** is a young woman or girl. [mainly SCOTTISH or NORTHERN ENGLISH] ❑ *Anne is a Lancashire lass from Longton, near Preston... 'What is it, lass?' Finlay cried.* N-COUNT; N-VOC

**las|sie** /læsi/ **(lassies)** A **lassie** is a young woman or girl. [mainly SCOTTISH, INFORMAL] N-COUNT; N-VOC

**las|si|tude** /læsɪtjuːd, AM -tuːd/ **Lassitude** is a state of tiredness, laziness, or lack of interest. [FORMAL] ❑ *Symptoms of anaemia include general fatigue and lassitude.* N-UNCOUNT

**las|so** /læsuː, AM læsoʊ/ **(lassoes, lassoing, lassoed)** 1 A **lasso** is a long rope with a loop at one end, used especially by cowboys for catching cattle. N-COUNT 2 If you **lasso** an animal, you catch it by throwing a lasso round its neck and pulling it tight. ❑ *Cowboys drove covered wagons and rode horses, lassoing cattle.* VERB; V n

**last** /lɑːst, læst/ **(lasts, lasting, lasted)** ◆◆◆ 1 You use **last** in expressions such as **last Friday, last night,** and **last year** to refer, for example, to the most recent Friday, night, or year. ❑ *I got married last July... He never made it home at all last night... It is not surprising they did so badly in last year's elections.* DET 2 The **last** event, person, thing, or period of time is the most recent one. ❑ *Much has changed since my last visit... At the last count inflation was 10.9 per cent... I split up with my last boyfriend three years ago... The last few weeks have been hectic.* ADJ: det ADJ ♦ **Last** is also a pronoun. ❑ *The next tide, it was announced, would be even higher than the last.* PRON 3 If something **last** happened on a particular occasion, that is the most recent occasion on which it happened. ❑ *When were you there last?... The house is a little more dilapidated than when I last saw it... Hunting on the trust's 625,000 acres was last debated two years ago.* ADV: ADV with v 4 The **last** thing, person, event, or period of time is the one that happens or comes after all the others of the same kind. ❑ *This is his last chance as prime minister. ...the last three pages of the chapter... She said it was the very last house on the road... They didn't come last in their league.* ORD ≠first ♦ **Last** is also a pronoun. ❑ *It wasn't the first time that this particular difference had divided them and it wouldn't be the last... The trickiest bits are the last on the list.* PRON 5 If you do something **last**, you do it after everyone else does, or after you do everything else. ❑ *I testified last... I was always picked last for the football team at school... The foreground, nearest the viewer, is painted last.* ADV: ADV after v 6 If you are **the last to** do or know something, everyone else does or knows it before you. ❑ *She was the last to go to bed... Riccardo and I are always the last to know what's going on.* PRON: PRON to-inf 7 **Last** is used to refer to the only thing, person, or part of something that remains. ❑ *Jed nodded, finishing off the last piece of pizza.* ADJ: det ADJ

*...the freeing of the last hostage.* ♦ **Last** is also a noun. ❑ *He finished off the last of the wine... The last of the ten inmates gave themselves up after twenty eight hours on the roof of the prison.* N-SING: *the* N *of* n [8] You use **last** before numbers to refer to a position that someone has reached in a competition after other competitors have been knocked out. ❑ *Sampras reached the last four at Wimbledon. ...the only woman among the authors making it through to the last six.* ADJ: det ADJ

[9] You can use **last** to indicate that something is extremely undesirable or unlikely. ❑ *The last thing I wanted to do was teach... He would be the last person who would do such a thing.* ADJ: det ADJ emphasis ♦ **Last** is also a pronoun. ❑ *I would be the last to say that science has explained everything.* PRON: PRON to-inf [10] **The last** you see of someone or **the last** you hear of them is the final time that you see them or talk to them. ❑ *She disappeared shouting, 'To the river, to the river!' And that was the last we saw of her... I had a feeling it would be the last I heard of him.* PRON: *the* PRON that ≠ first [11] If an event, situation, or problem **lasts** for a particular length of time, it continues to exist or happen for that length of time. ❑ *The marriage had lasted for less than two years... The games lasted only half the normal time... Enjoy it because it won't last.* VERB V *for* n V n V, Also V adv [12] If something **lasts** for a particular length of time, it continues to be able to be used for that time, for example because there is some of it left or because it is in good enough condition. ❑ *You only need a very small blob of glue, so one tube lasts for ages... The repaired sail lasted less than 24 hours... The implication is that this battery lasts twice as long as other batteries.* VERB V *for* n V n V adv Also V [13] → See also **lasting**.

**PHRASES** [14] If you say that something has happened **at last** or **at long last** you mean it has happened after you have been hoping for it for a long time. ❑ *I'm so glad that we've found you at last!... Here, at long last, was the moment he had waited for... At last the train arrived in the station.* PHRASE: PHR with cl = finally [15] You use expressions such as **the night before last**, **the election before last** and **the leader before last** to refer to the period of time, event, or person that came immediately before the most recent one in a series. ❑ *It was the dog he'd heard the night before last... In the budget before last a tax penalty on the mobile phone was introduced.* PHRASE [16] You can use phrases such as the **last but one**, the **last but two**, or the **last but three**, to refer to the thing or person that is, for example, one, two, or three before the final person or thing in a group or series. ❑ *It's the last but one day in the athletics programme... The British team finished last but one.* PHRASE: PHR n, PHR after v [17] You can use expressions such as **the last I heard** and **the last she heard** to introduce a piece of information that is the most recent that you have on a particular subject. ❑ *The last I heard, Joe and Irene were still happily married.* PHRASE: PHR with cl [18] If you **leave** something or someone **until last**, you delay using, choosing, or dealing with them until you have used, chosen, or dealt with all the others. ❑ *I have left my best wine until last... I picked first all the people who usually were left till last.* PHRASE: V inflects [19] to **have the last laugh** → see **laugh**. **last-minute** → see **minute**. **the last straw** → see **straw**. **last thing** → see **thing**.

**last-ditch** A **last-ditch** action is done only because there are no other ways left to achieve something or to prevent something happening. It is often done without much hope that it will succeed. ❑ *...a last-ditch attempt to prevent civil war.* ADJ: ADJ n

**last hur|rah** Someone's **last hurrah** is the last occasion on which they do something, especially at the end of their career. ❑ *I haven't even begun to think about quitting, or having a last hurrah, or allowing my career to wind down.* N-COUNT: usu sing

**last|ing** /lɑːstɪŋ, læst-/ You can use **lasting** to describe a situation, result, or agreement that continues to exist or have an effect for a very long time. ❑ *We are well on our way to a lasting peace... She left a lasting impression on him.* → See also **last**. ADJ: usu ADJ n

**Last Judge|ment** also **Last Judgment.** In the Christian religion, **the Last Judgement** is the last day of the world when God will judge everyone who has died and decide whether they will go to Heaven or Hell. N-PROPER: *the* N

**last|ly** /lɑːstli, læst-/ [1] You use **lastly** when you want to make a final point, ask a final question, or mention a final item that is connected with the other ones you have already asked or mentioned. ❑ *Lastly, I would like to ask about your future plans.* ADV: ADV with cl/group = finally [2] You use **lastly** when you are saying what happens after everything else in a series of actions or events. ❑ *They wash their hands, arms and faces, and lastly, they wash their feet.* ADV: ADV cl = finally

**last-minute** → see **minute**.

**last rites** **The last rites** are a religious ceremony performed by a Christian priest for a dying person. ❑ *Father Stephen Lea administered the last rites to the dead men.* N-PLURAL: *the* N

**latch** /lætʃ/ **(latches, latching, latched)** [1] A **latch** is a fastening on a door or gate. It consists of a metal bar which you lift in order to open the door. ❑ *You left the latch off the gate and the dog escaped.* N-COUNT [2] A **latch** is a lock on a door which locks automatically when you shut the door, so that you need a key in order to open it from the outside. ❑ *...a key clicked in the latch of the front door.* N-COUNT [3] If you **latch** a door or gate, you fasten it by means of a latch. ❑ *He latched the door, tested it, and turned around to speak to Frank.* VERB V n

♦ **latch onto** or **latch on** [1] If someone **latches onto** a person or an idea or **latches on**, they become very interested in the person or idea, often finding them so useful that they do not want to leave them. [INFORMAL] ❑ *Rob had latched onto me. He followed me around, sat beside me at lunch, and usually ended up working with me... Other trades have been quick to latch on.* PHRASAL VERB V P n V P [2] If one thing **latches onto** another, or if it **latches on**, it attaches itself to it and becomes part of it. ❑ *These are substances which specifically latch onto the protein on the cell membrane.* PHRASAL VERB V P n Also V P

**latch|key** /lætʃkiː/ also **latch-key.** If you refer to a child as a **latchkey** kid, you disapprove of the fact that they have to let themselves into their home when returning from school because their parents are out at work. ADJ: ADJ n disapproval

**late** /leɪt/ **(later, latest)** [1] **Late** means near the end of a day, week, year, or other period of time. ❑ *It was late in the afternoon... She had to work late at night... His autobiography was written late in life... The case is expected to end late next week.* ♦♦♦ ADV: ADV with cl, ADV prep/n ≠ early ♦ **Late** is also an adjective. ❑ *The talks eventually broke down in late spring... He was in his late 20s. ...the late 1960s.* ADJ: ADJ n [2] If it is **late**, it is near the end of the day or it is past the time that you feel something should have been done. ❑ *It was very late and the streets were deserted... We've got to go now. It's getting late.* ADJ: v-link ADJ ♦ **late|ness** *A large crowd had gathered despite the lateness of the hour.* N-UNCOUNT [3] **Late** means after the time that was arranged or expected. ❑ *Steve arrived late... The talks began some fifteen minutes late... We got up late.* ADV: ADV after v, oft amount ADV ♦ **Late** is also an adjective. ❑ *His campaign got off to a late start... We were a little late... The train was 40 minutes late... He's a half hour late.* ADJ: oft amount ADJ ♦ **late|ness** *He apologised for his lateness.* N-UNCOUNT [4] **Late** means after the usual time that a particular event or activity happens. ❑ *We went to bed very late... He married late.* ADV: ADV after v ♦ **Late** is also an adjective. ❑ *They had a late lunch in a cafe... He was a very late developer.* ADJ: ADJ n [5] You use **late** when you are talking about someone who is dead, especially someone who has died recently. ❑ *...my late husband. ...the late Mr Parkin.* ADJ: det ADJ [6] Someone who is **late of** a particular place or institution lived or worked there until recently. [FORMAL] ❑ *...Cousin Zachary, late of Bellevue Avenue. ...Strobe Talbott, late of Time magazine.* ADJ: v-link ADJ *of* n [7] → See also **later**, **latest**.

[8] If you say **better late than never** when someone has done something, you think they CONVENTION

should have done it earlier. ❑ *It's been a long time coming but better late than never.*

**PHRASES** 9 If you say that someone is doing something **late in the day**, you mean that their action or behaviour may not be fully effective because they have waited too long before doing it. ❑ *I'd left it all too late in the day to get anywhere with these strategies.* 10 If an action or event is **too late**, it is useless or ineffective because it occurs after the best time for it. ❑ *It was too late to turn back... We realized too late that we were caught like rats in a trap.* 11 **a late night** → see **night**. PHRASE: PHR after v, PHR with cl; PHRASE: v-link PHR, PHR with v

**late|comer** /leɪtkʌməʳ/ **(latecomers)** A **latecomer** is someone who arrives after the time that they should have done, or later than others. ❑ *The latecomers stood just outside at door and window.* N-COUNT

**late|ly** /leɪtli/ 1 You use **lately** to describe events in the recent past, or situations that started a short time ago. ❑ *Dad's health hasn't been too good lately... Lord Tomas had lately been appointed Chairman of the Centre for Policy Studies... 'Have you talked to her lately?'* ADV: ADV with v, ADV with cl = recently 2 You can use **lately** to refer to the job a person has been doing until recently. [FORMAL] ❑ *...Timothy Jean Geoffrey Pratt, lately deputy treasury solicitor.* ADV: ADV n/-ed

**late-night** 1 **Late-night** is used to describe events, especially entertainments, that happen late in the evening or late at night. ❑ *...John Peel's late-night show on BBC Radio One. ...late-night drinking parties.* ADJ: ADJ n 2 **Late-night** is used to describe services that are available late at night and do not shut when most commercial activities finish. ❑ *Saturday night was a late-night shopping night. ...late-night trains.* ADJ: ADJ n

**la|tent** /leɪtᵊnt/ **Latent** is used to describe something which is hidden and not obvious at the moment, but which may develop further in the future. ❑ *Advertisements attempt to project a latent meaning behind an overt message.* ADJ: usu ADJ n ≠ overt

**lat|er** /leɪtəʳ/ ◆◆◆ 1 **Later** is the comparative of **late**. 2 You use **later** to refer to a time or situation that is after the one that you have been talking about or after the present one. ❑ *He resigned ten years later... I'll join you later... Burke later admitted he had lied.* ● You use **later on** to refer to a time or situation that is after the one that you have been talking about or after the present one. ❑ *Later on I'll be speaking to Patty Davis... This is only going to cause me more problems later on.* ADV: ADV with cl, oft amount ADV; PHRASE: PHR with cl 3 You use **later** to refer to an event, period of time, or other thing which comes after the one that you have been talking about or after the present one. ❑ *At a later news conference, he said differences should not be dramatized... The competition should have been re-scheduled for a later date.* ADJ: ADJ n, *the* ADJ, *the* ADJ *of* n 4 You use **later** to refer to the last part of someone's life or career or the last part of a period of history. ❑ *He found happiness in later life... In his later years he wrote very little. ...the later part of the 20th century.* ADJ: ADJ n 5 → See also **late**. 6 **sooner or later** → see **sooner**.

**lat|er|al** /lætərəl/ **Lateral** means relating to the sides of something, or moving in a sideways direction. ❑ *McKinnon estimated the lateral movement of the bridge to be between four and six inches.* ADJ: usu ADJ n ♦ **lat|er|al|ly** *Shafts were sunk, with tunnels dug laterally.* ADV: usu ADV after v

**lat|er|al think|ing** **Lateral thinking** is a method of solving problems by using your imagination to help you think of solutions that are not obvious at first. [mainly BRIT] N-UNCOUNT

**lat|est** /leɪtɪst/ ◆◆◇ 1 **Latest** is the superlative of **late**. 2 You use **latest** to describe something that is the most recent thing of its kind. ❑ *...her latest book... Latest reports say another five people have been killed.* ADJ: oft v-link ADJ *in/of* n 3 You can use **latest** to describe something that is very new and modern and is better than older things of a similar kind. ❑ *Crooks are using the latest laser photocopiers to produce millions of fake banknotes... I got to drive the latest model... Computers have always represented the latest in technology.* ADJ: oft v-link ADJ *in/of* n 4 → See also **late**. 5 You use **at the latest** in order to indicate that something must happen at or before a particular time and not after that time. ❑ *She should be back by ten o'clock at the latest.* PHRASE: amount PHR [emphasis]

**la|tex** /leɪteks/ **Latex** is a substance obtained from some kinds of trees, which is used to make products like rubber and glue. N-UNCOUNT

**lathe** /leɪð/ **(lathes)** A **lathe** is a machine which is used for shaping wood or metal. N-COUNT

**lath|er** /lɑːðəʳ, læðəʳ/ **(lathers, lathering, lathered)** 1 A **lather** is a white mass of bubbles which is produced by mixing a substance such as soap or washing powder with water. ❑ *...the sort of water that easily makes a lather with soap... He wiped off the remains of the lather with a towel.* N-SING 2 When a substance such as soap or washing powder **lathers**, it produces a white mass of bubbles because it has been mixed with water. ❑ *The shampoo lathers and foams so much it's very hard to rinse it all out.* VERB V 3 If you **lather** something, you rub a substance such as soap or washing powder on it until a lather is produced, in order to clean it. ❑ *Lather your hair as normal... For super-soft skin, lather on a light body lotion before you bathe.* VERB V n, V n with adv, Also V n prep

**Lat|in** /lætɪn/ **(Latins)** ◆◇◇ 1 **Latin** is the language which the ancient Romans used to speak. N-UNCOUNT 2 **Latin** countries are countries where Spanish, or perhaps Portuguese, Italian, or French, is spoken. You can also use **Latin** to refer to things and people that come from these countries. ❑ *Cuba was one of the least Catholic of the Latin countries... The enthusiasm for Latin music is worldwide.* ADJ: usu ADJ n 3 **Latins** are people who come from countries where Spanish, or perhaps Portuguese, Italian, or French, are spoken or whose families come from one of these countries. ❑ *They are role models for thousands of young Latins.* N-COUNT: usu pl

**Lat|in Ameri|can** **(Latin Americans)** 1 **Latin American** means belonging or relating to the countries of South America, Central America, and Mexico. **Latin American** also means belonging or relating to the people of culture of these countries. ADJ: usu ADJ n 2 A **Latin American** is someone who lives in or comes from South America, Central America, or Mexico. N-COUNT

**La|ti|no** /lætiːnoʊ/ **(Latinos)** also **latino**. 1 A **Latino** is a citizen of the United States who originally came from Latin America, or whose family originally came from Latin America. [mainly AM] ❑ *He was a champion for Latinos and blacks within the educational system. ...the city's office of Latino Affairs.* N-COUNT: oft N n 2 **Latino** means belonging or relating to Latino people or their culture. ADJ

**lati|tude** /lætɪtjuːd, AM -tuːd/ **(latitudes)** 1 The **latitude** of a place is its distance from the equator. Compare **longitude**. ❑ *In the middle to high latitudes rainfall has risen steadily over the last 20-30 years.* N-VAR ♦ **Latitude** is also an adjective. ❑ *The army must cease military operations above 36 degrees latitude north.* ADJ: usu amount ADJ 2 **Latitude** is freedom to choose the way in which you do something. [FORMAL] ❑ *He would be given every latitude in forming a new government.* N-UNCOUNT

**la|trine** /lətriːn/ **(latrines)** A **latrine** is a structure, usually consisting of a hole in the ground, that is used as a toilet, for example in a military camp. N-COUNT

**lat|te** /læteɪ, AM lɑːteɪ/ **(lattes)** **Latte** is strong coffee made with hot milk. ♦ A **latte** is a cup of latte. N-UNCOUNT; N-COUNT

**lat|ter** /lætəʳ/ ◆◇◇ 1 When two people, things, or groups have just been mentioned, you can refer to the second of them as **the latter**. ❑ *He tracked down his cousin and uncle. The latter was sick.* PRON: *the* PRON ♦ **Latter** is also an adjective. ❑ *There are the people who speak after they think and the people who think while they're speaking. Mike definitely belongs in the latter category.* ADJ: ADJ n 2 You use **latter** to describe the later ADJ: ADJ n part of a period of time or event. ❑ *The latter part of the debate concentrated on abortion.* = later

**lat|ter-day** **Latter-day** is used to describe someone or something that is a modern equivalent of a person or thing in the past. ❑ *He holds the belief that he is a latter-day prophet.* ADJ: ADJ n

**lat|ter|ly** /lætəʳli/ You can use **latterly** to indicate that a situation or event is the most recent one. [WRITTEN] ❑ *He was to remain active in the association, latterly as vice president, for the rest of his life.* ADV: ADV with cl/group

**lat|tice** /lætɪs/ **(lattices)** A **lattice** is a pattern or structure made of strips of wood or another material which cross over each other diagonally leaving holes in between. ❑ *We were crawling along the narrow steel lattice of the bridge.* N-COUNT: usu sing

**lat|ticed** /lætɪst/ Something that is **latticed** is decorated with or is in the form of a lattice. ❑ *...latticed doors... The surface of the brain is pinky-grey and latticed with tiny blood vessels.* ADJ: usu ADJ n, also v-link ADJ with n

**lat|tice|work** /lætɪswɜːʳk/ **Latticework** is any structure that is made in the form of a lattice. ❑ *...latticework chairs.* N-UNCOUNT

**laud** /lɔːd/ **(lauds, lauding, lauded)** If people **laud** someone, they praise and admire them. [JOURNALISM] ❑ *He lauded the work of the UN High Commissioner for Refugees... They lauded the former president as a hero... Dickens was lauded for his social and moral sensitivity.* ♦ **laud|ed** *...the most lauded actress in New York.* VERB; V n; V n as n; V n for n; ADJ

**laud|able** /lɔːdəbᵊl/ Something that is **laudable** deserves to be praised or admired. [FORMAL] ❑ *One of Emma's less laudable characteristics was her jealousy.* ADJ = admirable

**lauda|tory** /lɔːdətri, AM -tɔːri/ A **laudatory** piece of writing or speech expresses praise or admiration for someone. [FORMAL] ❑ *The New York Times has this very laudatory article about your retirement... Beth spoke of Dr. Hammer in laudatory terms.* ADJ: usu ADJ n = complimentary

**laugh** /lɑːf, læf/ **(laughs, laughing, laughed)** ◆◆◆

1 When you **laugh**, you make a sound with your throat while smiling and show that you are happy or amused. People also sometimes laugh when they feel nervous or are being unfriendly. ❑ *He was about to offer an explanation, but she was beginning to laugh... He laughed with pleasure when people said he looked like his dad... The British don't laugh at the same jokes as the French... 'I'll be astonished if I win on Sunday,' laughed Lyle.* ♦ **Laugh** is also a noun. ❑ *Lysenko gave a deep rumbling laugh at his own joke.* VERB; V; V with n; V at n; V with quote; N-COUNT

2 If people **laugh at** someone or something, they mock them or make jokes about them. ❑ *I thought they were laughing at me because I was ugly.* VERB; V at n

PHRASES 3 If you do something **for a laugh** or **for laughs**, you do it as a joke or for fun. ❑ *They were persuaded onstage for a laugh by their mates... It's a project she's doing for laughs.* PHRASE: PHR with v

4 If a person or their comment **gets a laugh** or **raises a laugh**, they make the people listening to them laugh. [mainly BRIT] ❑ *The joke got a big laugh, which encouraged me to continue.* PHRASE: V inflects

5 If you describe a situation as **a laugh**, **a good laugh**, or **a bit of a laugh**, you think that it is fun and do not take it too seriously. [mainly BRIT, INFORMAL] ❑ *Working there's great. It's quite a good laugh actually.* PHRASE: v-link PHR

6 If you describe someone as **a laugh** or **a good laugh**, you like them because they are amusing and fun to be with. [mainly BRIT] ❑ *Mickey was a good laugh and great to have in the dressing room.* PHRASE: v-link PHR

7 If you say that you **have the last laugh**, you mean that you become successful at something so that people who criticize or oppose you look foolish. ❑ *Des O'Connor is expecting to have the last laugh on his critics by soaring to the top of the Christmas hit parade.* PHRASE: V inflects

8 **to laugh your head off** → see **head**. **no laughing matter** → see **matter**.

♦ **laugh off** If you **laugh off** a difficult or serious situation, you try to suggest that it is amusing and unimportant, for example by making a joke about it. ❑ *The couple laughed off rumours that their marriage was in trouble... Whilst I used to laugh it off, I'm now getting irritated by it.* PHRASAL VERB; V P n (not pron); V n P

**laugh|able** /lɑːfəbᵊl, læf-/ If you say that something such as an idea or suggestion is **laughable**, you mean that it is so stupid as to be funny and not worth serious consideration. ❑ *The idea that TV shows like 'Dallas' or 'Dynasty' represent typical American life is laughable.* ♦ **laugh|ably** *To an outsider, the issues that we fight about would seem almost laughably petty.* ADJ: usu v-link ADJ = ludicrous; ADV: usu ADV adj

**laugh|ing gas** **Laughing gas** is a type of anaesthetic gas which sometimes has the effect of making people laugh uncontrollably. N-UNCOUNT = nitrous oxide

**laugh|ing|ly** /lɑːfɪŋli, læf-/ If you **laughingly** refer to something with a particular name or description, the description is not appropriate and you think that this is either amusing or annoying. ❑ *I spent much of what I laughingly call 'the holidays' working through 621 pages of typescript.* ADV: ADV with v

**laugh|ing stock** **(laughing stocks)** also **laughing-stock.** If you say that a person or an organization has become **a laughing stock**, you mean that they are supposed to be important or serious but have been made to seem ridiculous. ❑ *The truth must never get out. If it did she would be a laughing-stock. ...his policies became the laughing stock of the financial community.* N-COUNT

**laugh|ter** /lɑːftəʳ, læf-/ ◆◇◇

1 **Laughter** is the sound of people laughing, for example because they are amused or happy. ❑ *Their laughter filled the corridor... He delivered the line perfectly, and everybody roared with laughter. ...hysterical laughter.* N-UNCOUNT

2 **Laughter** is the fact of laughing, or the feeling of fun and amusement that you have when you are laughing. ❑ *Pantomime is about bringing laughter to thousands.* N-UNCOUNT

**launch** /lɔːntʃ/ **(launches, launching, launched)** ◆◆◇

1 To **launch** a rocket, missile, or satellite means to send it into the air or into space. ❑ *NASA plans to launch a satellite to study cosmic rays... A Delta II rocket was launched from Cape Canaveral early this morning.* ♦ **Launch** is also a noun. ❑ *This morning's launch of the space shuttle Columbia has been delayed.* VERB; V n; V n; N-VAR

2 To **launch** a ship or a boat means to put it into water, often for the first time after it has been built. ❑ *There was no time to launch the lifeboats because the ferry capsized with such alarming speed.* ♦ **Launch** is also a noun. ❑ *The launch of a ship was a big occasion.* VERB; V n; N-COUNT: usu with poss

3 To **launch** a large and important activity, for example a military attack, means to start it. ❑ *Heavy fighting has been going on after the guerrillas had launched their offensive... The police have launched an investigation into the incident.* ♦ **Launch** is also a noun. ❑ *...the launch of a campaign to restore law and order.* VERB; V n; V n; N-COUNT: oft N of n

4 If a company **launches** a new product, it makes it available to the public. ❑ *Crabtree & Evelyn has just launched a new jam, Worcesterberry Preserve... Marks & Spencer recently hired model Linda Evangelista to launch its new range.* ♦ **Launch** is also a noun. ❑ *The company's spending has also risen following the launch of a new Sunday magazine.* VERB; V n; V n; N-COUNT: oft N of n

5 A **launch** is a large motorboat that is used for carrying people on rivers and lakes and in harbours. ❑ *The captain was on the deck of the launch, steadying the boat for the pilot.* N-COUNT: also by N

♦ **launch into** If you **launch into** something such as a speech, task, or fight, you enthusiastically start it. ❑ *Horrigan launched into a speech about the importance of new projects... Geoff has launched himself into fatherhood with great enthusiasm.* PHRASAL VERB; V P n; V pron-refl P n

**launch|ing pad** **(launching pads)** A **launching pad** is the same as a **launch pad**. N-COUNT

**launch pad** **(launch pads)**

1 A **launch pad** or **launching pad** is a platform from which rockets, missiles, or satellites are launched. N-COUNT

2 A **launch pad** or **launching pad** is a situation, for example a job, which you can use in order to go forward to something better or more important. N-COUNT = stepping stone

❑ *Wimbledon has been a launch pad for so many players.*

**laun|der** /lɔːndəʳ/ **(launders, laundering, laundered)** 1 When you **launder** clothes, sheets, and towels, you wash and iron them. [OLD-FASHIONED] ❑ *How many guests who expect clean towels every day in an hotel launder their own every day at home?* — VERB; V n

2 To **launder** money that has been obtained illegally means to process it through a legitimate business or to send it abroad to a foreign bank, so that when it comes back nobody knows that it was illegally obtained. ❑ *The House voted today to crack down on banks that launder drug money.* — VERB; V n

♦ **laun|der|er (launderers)** *...a businessman and self-described money launderer.* — N-COUNT

**Laun|der|ette** /lɔːndret/ **(Launderettes)**

☑ in BRIT, also use **laundrette**

A **Launderette** is a place where people can pay to use machines to wash and dry their clothes. [mainly BRIT, TRADEMARK] — N-COUNT

☑ in AM, usually use **Laundromat**

**Laun|dro|mat** /lɔːndrəmæt/ **(Laundromats)** A **Laundromat** is the same as a **Launderette**. [AM, TRADEMARK] — N-COUNT

**laun|dry** /lɔːndri/ **(laundries)** 1 **Laundry** is used to refer to clothes, sheets, and towels that are about to be washed, are being washed, or have just been washed. ❑ *I'll do your laundry... He'd put his dirty laundry in the clothes basket.* — N-UNCOUNT = washing

2 A **laundry** is a firm that washes and irons clothes, sheets, and towels for people. ❑ *We had to have the washing done at the laundry.* — N-COUNT

3 A **laundry** or a **laundry room** is a room in a house, hotel, or institution where clothes, sheets, and towels are washed. ❑ *He worked in the laundry at Oxford prison.* — N-COUNT: usu sing

4 to **wash** your **dirty laundry in public** → see **dirty**.

**laun|dry list (laundry lists)** If you describe something as a **laundry list of** things, you mean that it is a long list of them. ❑ *...a laundry list of reasons why shareholders should reject the bid.* — N-COUNT: usu N of n

**lau|rel** /lɒrəl, AM lɔːr-/ **(laurels)** 1 A **laurel** or a **laurel tree** is a small evergreen tree with shiny leaves. The leaves are sometimes used to make decorations such as wreaths. — N-VAR

2 If someone is **resting on** their **laurels**, they appear to be satisfied with the things they have achieved and have stopped putting effort into what they are doing. ❑ *The government can't rest on its laurels and must press ahead with major policy changes.* — PHRASE: V inflects [disapproval]

**lava** /lɑːvə/ **(lavas)** **Lava** is the very hot liquid rock that comes out of a volcano. — N-MASS

**lava|to|rial** /lævətɔːriəl/ **Lavatorial** jokes or stories involve childish references to urine or faeces. [mainly BRIT] — ADJ: usu ADJ n

**lava|tory** /lævətri, AM -tɔːri/ **(lavatories)** A **lavatory** is the same as a **toilet**. [mainly BRIT] ❑ *...the ladies' lavatory at the University of London. ...a public lavatory.* — N-COUNT = toilet

**lava|tory pa|per** **Lavatory paper** is paper that you use to clean yourself after you have got rid of urine or faeces from your body. [BRIT, FORMAL] — N-UNCOUNT = toilet paper

☑ in AM, use **toilet paper**

**lav|en|der** /lævɪndəʳ/ **(lavenders)** 1 **Lavender** is a garden plant with sweet-smelling, bluish-purple flowers. — N-UNCOUNT: also N in pl

2 **Lavender** is used to describe things that are pale bluish-purple in colour. — COLOUR

**lav|ish** /lævɪʃ/ **(lavishes, lavishing, lavished)** 1 If you describe something as **lavish**, you mean that it is very elaborate and impressive and a lot of money has been spent on it. ❑ *...a lavish party to celebrate Bryan's fiftieth birthday... He staged the most lavish productions of Mozart.* — ADJ

♦ **lav|ish|ly** *...the train's lavishly furnished carriages.* — ADV: ADV with v

2 If you say that spending, praise, or the use of something is **lavish**, you mean that someone spends a lot or that something is praised or used a lot. ❑ *Critics attack his lavish spending and flamboyant style... The book drew lavish praise from literary critics.* — ADJ = extravagant

3 If you say that someone is **lavish** in the way they behave, you mean that they give, spend, or use a lot of something. ❑ *American reviewers are lavish in their praise of this book... He was always a lavish spender.* — ADJ: oft ADJ in/with n

♦ **lav|ish|ly** *Entertaining in style needn't mean spending lavishly.* — ADV: ADV with v VERB

4 If you **lavish** money, affection, or praise **on** someone or something, you spend a lot of money on them or give them a lot of affection or praise. ❑ *Prince Sadruddin lavished praise on Britain's contributions to world diplomacy...* — V n on/upon n
*The emperor promoted the general and lavished him with gifts.* — V n with n

**law** /lɔː/ **(laws)** ◆◆◆ 1 **The law** is a system of rules that a society or government develops in order to deal with crime, business agreements, and social relationships. You can also use the **law** to refer to the people who work in this system. ❑ *Obscene and threatening phone calls are against the law... They are seeking permission to begin criminal proceedings against him for breaking the law on financing political parties... There must be changes in the law quickly to stop this sort of thing ever happening to anyone else... The book analyses why women kill and how the law treats them.* — N-SING: the N

2 **Law** is used to refer to a particular branch of the law, such as **criminal law** or **company law**. ❑ *He was a professor of criminal law at Harvard University law school... Important questions of constitutional law were involved.* — N-UNCOUNT: usu adj N

3 A **law** is one of the rules in a system of law which deals with a particular type of agreement, relationship, or crime. ❑ *...the country's liberal political asylum law... The law was passed on a second vote.* — N-COUNT: oft n N

4 **The laws of** an organization or activity are its rules, which are used to organize and control it. ❑ *...the laws of the Church of England... Match officials should not tolerate such behaviour but instead enforce the laws of the game.* — N-PLURAL: the N of n, supp N = rule

5 A **law** is a rule or set of rules for good behaviour which is considered right and important by the majority of people for moral, religious, or emotional reasons. ❑ *...inflexible moral laws.* — N-COUNT = code

6 A **law** is a natural process in which a particular event or thing always leads to a particular result. ❑ *The laws of nature are absolute.* — N-COUNT: with supp

7 A **law** is a scientific rule that someone has invented to explain a particular natural process. ❑ *...the law of gravity.* — N-COUNT: with supp

8 **Law** or **the law** is all the professions which deal with advising people about the law, representing people in court, or giving decisions and punishments. ❑ *A career in law is becoming increasingly attractive to young people... Nearly 100 law firms are being referred to the Solicitors' Disciplinary Tribunal.* — N-UNCOUNT

9 **Law** is the study of systems of law and how laws work. ❑ *He came to Oxford and studied law... He holds a law degree from Bristol University.* — N-UNCOUNT

10 → See also **court of law**, **rule of law**.

**PHRASES** 11 If you accuse someone of thinking they are **above the law**, you criticize them for thinking that they are so clever or important that they do not need to obey the law. ❑ *One opposition member of parliament accuses the government of wanting to be above the law.* — PHRASE: v-link PHR [disapproval]

12 **The law of averages** is the idea that something is sure to happen at some time, because of the number of times it generally happens or is expected to happen. ❑ *On the law of averages we just can't go on losing.* — PHRASE

13 If you have to do something **by law** or if you are not allowed to do something **by law**, the law states that you have to do it or that you are not allowed to do it. ❑ *By law all restaurants must display their prices outside.* — PHRASE: PHR with cl

14 If you say that someone **lays down the law**, you are critical of them because they give other people orders and they think that they are always right. ❑ *...traditional parents, who believed in laying down the law for their offspring.* — PHRASE: V inflects [disapproval]

15 If someone **takes the law into** their **own hands**, they punish someone or do something to put a situation right, instead of waiting for the police or the legal system to take action. ❑ *The speeding motorist was pinned to the* — PHRASE: V inflects

*ground by angry locals who took the law into their own hands until police arrived.* 16 If you say that someone is **a law unto** himself or herself, you mean that they behave in an independent way, ignoring laws, rules, or conventional ways of doing things. ❑ *Some of the landowners were a law unto themselves. There was nobody to check their excesses and they exploited the people.* 17 **Sod's law** → see **sod**. PHRASE: v-link PHR

**law-abiding** A **law-abiding** person always obeys the law and is considered to be good and honest because of this. ❑ *The Prime Minister said: 'I am anxious that the law should protect decent law-abiding citizens and their property'.* ADJ: usu ADJ n

**law and or|der** When there is **law and order** in a country, the laws are generally accepted and obeyed, so that society there functions normally. ❑ *If there were a breakdown of law and order, the army might be tempted to intervene.* N-UNCOUNT

**law-breaker** **(law-breakers)** also **law-breaker.** A **law-breaker** is someone who breaks the law. N-COUNT

**law-breaking** also **law breaking.** **Law-breaking** is any kind of illegal activity. ❑ *Civil disobedience, violent or non-violent, is intentional law breaking.* N-UNCOUNT

**law court** **(law courts)** A **law court** is a place where legal matters are decided by a judge and jury or by a magistrate. ❑ *She would never resort to the law courts to resolve her marital problems.* N-COUNT

**law-enforcement** **Law-enforcement** agencies or officials are responsible for catching people who break the law. [mainly AM] ❑ *We need to restore respect for the law-enforcement agencies.* N-UNCOUNT: usu N n

**law|ful** /lɔːfʊl/ If an activity, organization, or product is **lawful**, it is allowed by law. [FORMAL] ❑ *It was lawful for the doctors to treat her in whatever way they considered was in her best interests... Hunting is a lawful activity.* ♦ **law|ful|ly** *Amnesty International is trying to establish whether the police acted lawfully in shooting him.* ADJ = legal ≠ unlawful, illegal; ADV: ADV with v ≠ unlawfully

**law|less** /lɔːləs/ 1 **Lawless** actions break the law, especially in a wild and violent way. ❑ *The government recognised there were problems in urban areas but these could never be an excuse for lawless behaviour.* ♦ **law|less|ness** *Lawlessness is a major problem.* 2 A **lawless** place or time is one where people do not respect the law. ❑ *...lawless inner-city streets plagued by muggings, thefts, assaults and even murder.* ADJ: usu ADJ n; N-UNCOUNT; ADJ: usu ADJ n

**law|maker** /lɔːmeɪkəʳ/ **(lawmakers)** A **lawmaker** is someone such as a politician who is responsible for proposing and passing new laws. [AM] N-COUNT

**law|man** /lɔːmæn/ **(lawmen)** 1 **Lawmen** are men such as policemen or lawyers, whose work involves the law. [JOURNALISM] ❑ *...the 61-year-old lawman who headed the enquiry.* 2 In former times in western North America, a **lawman** was a sheriff or deputy sheriff. [AM] N-COUNT; N-COUNT

**lawn** /lɔːn/ **(lawns)** A **lawn** is an area of grass that is kept cut short and is usually part of someone's garden or backyard, or part of a park. → See picture on page 1705. N-VAR

**lawn|mow|er** /lɔːnmoʊəʳ/ **(lawnmowers)** also **lawn mower.** A **lawnmower** is a machine for cutting grass on lawns. N-COUNT

**lawn ten|nis** **Lawn tennis** is the same as **tennis**. N-UNCOUNT

**law|suit** /lɔːsuːt/ **(lawsuits)** A **lawsuit** is a case in a court of law which concerns a dispute between two people or organizations. [FORMAL] ❑ *The dispute culminated last week in a lawsuit against the government.* N-COUNT

**law|yer** /lɔɪəʳ/ **(lawyers)** A **lawyer** is a person who is qualified to advise people about the law and represent them in court. ❑ *Prosecution and defense lawyers are expected to deliver closing arguments next week.* ◆◆◇ N-COUNT

**lax** /læks/ **(laxer, laxest)** If you say that a person's behaviour or a system is **lax**, you mean they are not careful or strict about maintaining high standards. ❑ *One of the problem areas is lax security for airport personnel... There have been allegations from survivors that safety standards had been lax.* ♦ **lax|ity** *The laxity of export control authorities has made a significant contribution to the problem.* ADJ; N-UNCOUNT

**laxa|tive** /læksətɪv/ **(laxatives)** 1 A **laxative** is food or medicine that you take to make you go to the toilet. ❑ *Foods that ferment quickly in the stomach are excellent natural laxatives.* 2 A **laxative** food or medicine is one that you take to make you go to the toilet. ❑ *The artificial sweetener sorbitol has a laxative effect... Molasses are mildly laxative and something of a general tonic.* N-MASS; ADJ

| **lay** |
|---|
| ① VERB AND NOUN USES |
| ② ADJECTIVE USES |

**① lay** /leɪ/ **(lays, laying, laid)** ◆◆◇

> In standard English, the form **lay** is also the past tense of the verb **lie** in some meanings. In informal English, people sometimes use the word **lay** instead of **lie** in those meanings.

⇛ Please look at category 9 to see if the expression you are looking for is shown under another headword. 1 If you **lay** something somewhere, you put it there in a careful, gentle, or neat way. ❑ *Lay a sheet of newspaper on the floor... My father's work-ing bench was covered with a cloth and his coffin was laid there... Mothers routinely lay babies on their backs to sleep.* 2 If you **lay** the table or **lay** the places at a table, you arrange the knives, forks, and other things that people need on the table before a meal. [mainly BRIT] ❑ *The butler always laid the table.* VERB; V n prep/adv; V n prep/adv; V n prep/adv; VERB; V n

✓ in AM, use **set**

3 If you **lay** something such as carpets, cables, or foundations, you put them into their permanent position. ❑ *A man came to lay the saloon carpet... Public utilities dig up roads to lay pipes.* 4 To **lay** a trap means to prepare it in order to catch someone or something. ❑ *They were laying a trap for the kidnapper.* 5 When a female bird **lays** an egg, it produces an egg by pushing it out of its body. ❑ *My canary has laid an egg... Freezing weather in spring hampered the hens' ability to lay.* 6 **Lay** is used with some nouns to talk about making official preparations for something. For example, if you **lay the basis** for something or **lay plans** for it, you prepare it carefully. ❑ *Diplomats meeting in Chile have laid the groundwork for far-reaching environmental regulations... The organisers meet in March to lay plans.* 7 **Lay** is used with some nouns in expressions about accusing or blaming someone. For example, if you **lay the blame** for a mistake on someone, you say it is their fault, or if the police **lay charges** against someone, they officially accuse that person of a crime. ❑ *She refused to lay the blame on any one party... Police have decided not to lay charges over allegations of a telephone tapping operation.* 8 If you **lay** yourself **open to** criticism or attack, or if something **lays** you **open to** it, something you do makes it possible or likely that other people will criticize or attack you. ❑ *The party thereby lays itself open to charges of conflict of interest... Such a statement could lay her open to ridicule.* 9 to **lay** something **bare** → see **bare**. to **lay claim to** something → see **claim**. to **lay** something **at** someone's **door** → see **door**. to **lay eyes on** something → see **eye**. to **lay a finger on** someone → see **finger**. to **lay** your **hands on** something → see **hand**. to **lay down the law** → see **law**. to **lay down** your **life** → see **life**. to **lay** something **to rest** → see **rest**. to **lay siege to** something → see **siege**. VERB; V n; V n; VERB; V n; VERB; V n; V; VERB; V n; V n; VERB; V n prep; V n; PHRASE: V inflects, PHR n

♦ **lay aside** 1 If you **lay** something **aside**, you put it down, usually because you have finished using it or want to save it to use later. ❑ *He* PHRASAL VERB; V n P

*finished the tea and laid the cup aside... This allowed Ms. Kelley to lay aside money to start her business.* V P n (not pron)
[2] If you **lay aside** a feeling or belief, you reject it or give it up in order to progress with something. ❑ *Perhaps the opposed parties will lay aside their sectional interests and rise to this challenge.* PHRASAL VERB = *put aside* V P n (not pron)

♦ **lay down** [1] If you **lay** something **down**, you put it down, usually because you have finished using it. ❑ *Daniel finished the article and laid the newspaper down on his desk... She laid down her knife and fork and pushed her plate away.* PHRASAL VERB V n P V P n (not pron) [2] If rules or people in authority **lay down** what people should do or must do, they officially state what they should or must do. ❑ *Taxis must conform to the rigorous standards laid down by the police.* PHRASAL VERB = *set down* V P n (not pron) [3] If someone **lays down** their weapons, they stop fighting a battle or war and make peace. ❑ *The drug-traffickers have offered to lay down their arms.* PHRASAL VERB V P n (not pron)

♦ **lay in** If you **lay in** an amount of something, you buy it and store it to be used later. ❑ *They began to lay in extensive stores of food supplies.* PHRASAL VERB V P n (not pron)

♦ **lay off** If workers **are laid off**, they are told by their employers to leave their job, usually because there is no more work for them to do. [BUSINESS] ❑ *100,000 federal workers will be laid off to reduce the deficit... They did not sell a single car for a month and had to lay off workers.* ➔ See also **layoff**. PHRASAL VERB be V-ed P V P n (not pron) Also V n P

♦ **lay on** If you **lay on** something such as food, entertainment, or a service, you provide or supply it, especially in a generous or grand way. [mainly BRIT] ❑ *They laid on a superb evening.* PHRASAL VERB V P n, Also V n P

♦ **lay out** [1] If you **lay out** a group of things, you spread them out and arrange them neatly, for example so that they can all be seen clearly. ❑ *Grace laid out the knives and forks at the lunch-table... She took a deck of cards and began to lay them out.* PHRASAL VERB V P n (not pron) V n P [2] To **lay out** ideas, principles, or plans means to explain or present them clearly, for example in a document or a meeting. ❑ *Maxwell listened closely as Johnson laid out his plan... Cuomo laid it out in simple language.* PHRASAL VERB V P n (not pron) V n P [3] To **lay out** an area of land or a building means to plan and design how its different parts should be arranged. ❑ *When we laid out the car parks, we reckoned on one car per four families... Only people that use a kitchen all the time understand the best way to lay it out.* PHRASAL VERB V P n (not pron) V n P [4] If you **lay out** money on something, you spend a large amount of money on it. [INFORMAL] ❑ *You won't have to lay out a fortune for this dining table.* PHRASAL VERB = *fork out, shell out* V P n (not pron) [5] ➔ See also **layout**.

♦ **lay up** If someone **is laid up with** an illness, the illness makes it necessary for them to stay in bed. [INFORMAL] ❑ *I was laid up in bed with acute rheumatism... Powell ruptured a disc in his back and was laid up for a year.* PHRASAL VERB: usu passive be V-ed P with n be V-ed P

② **lay** /leɪ/ [1] You use **lay** to describe people who are involved with a Christian church but are not members of the clergy or are not monks or nuns. ❑ *Edwards is a Methodist lay preacher and social worker.* ADJ: ADJ n [2] You use **lay** to describe people who are not experts or professionals in a particular subject or activity. ❑ *It is difficult for a lay person to gain access to medical libraries.* ADJ: ADJ n

**lay|about** /leɪəbaʊt/ **(layabouts)** If you say that someone is a **layabout**, you disapprove of them because they do not work and you think they are lazy. [mainly BRIT] N-COUNT [disapproval]

**lay-by** **(lay-bys)** A **lay-by** is a short strip of road by the side of a main road, where cars can stop for a while. [BRIT] ❑ *I left my car in a lay-by and set off on foot.* N-COUNT

✔ in AM, use **pull-off**, **turn-out**

**lay|er** /leɪəʳ/ **(layers, layering, layered)** [1] A **layer** of a material or substance is a quantity or piece of it that covers a surface or that is between two other things. ❑ *A fresh layer of snow covered the street... Arrange all the vegetables except the potatoes in layers.* ◆◇◇ N-COUNT: usu with supp, oft N *of* n [2] If something such as a system or an idea has many **layers**, it has many different levels or parts. ❑ *...an astounding ten layers of staff between the factory worker and the chief executive... Critics and the public puzzle out the layers of meaning in his photos.* N-COUNT [3] If you **layer** something, you arrange it in layers. ❑ *Layer the potatoes, asparagus and salmon in the tin.* VERB V n

**lay|ered** /leɪəʳd/ Something that is **layered** is made or exists in layers. ❑ *Maria wore a layered white dress that rustled when she moved.* ADJ

**lay|man** /leɪmən/ **(laymen)** [1] A **layman** is a person who is not trained, qualified, or experienced in a particular subject or activity. ❑ *The mere mention of the words 'heart failure', can conjure up, to the layman, the prospect of imminent death.* N-COUNT ≠*expert* [2] A **layman** is a man who is involved with the Christian church but is not a member of the clergy or a monk. ❑ *In 1932, one Boston layman wrote to Archbishop William O'Connell in support of Father Coughlin.* N-COUNT

**lay|off** /leɪɒf, AM -ɔːf/ **(layoffs)** [1] When there are **layoffs** in a company, workers are told by their employers to leave their job, usually because there is no more work for them in the company. [BUSINESS] ❑ *It will close more than 200 stores nationwide resulting in the layoffs of an estimated 2,000 employees.* N-COUNT: usu pl [2] A **layoff** is a period of time in which people do not work or take part in their normal activities, often because they are resting or are injured. ❑ *They both made full recoveries after lengthy injury layoffs.* N-COUNT

**lay|out** /leɪaʊt/ **(layouts)** The **layout** of a garden, building, or piece of writing is the way in which the parts of it are arranged. ❑ *He tried to recall the layout of the farmhouse... This boat has a good deck layout making everything easy to operate.* N-COUNT: usu with supp, oft the N *of* n

**lay per|son** **(lay persons** or **lay people)** also **layperson.** A **lay person** is a person who is not trained, qualified, or experienced in a particular subject or activity. N-COUNT ≠*expert*

**laze** /leɪz/ **(lazes, lazing, lazed)** If you **laze** somewhere for a period of time, you relax and enjoy yourself, not doing any work or anything else that requires effort. ❑ *Fred lazed in an easy chair... They used the swimming-pool, rode, lazed in the deep shade of the oaks in the heat of the day.* VERB V V prep ♦ **Laze around** or **laze about** means the same as **laze**. ❑ *He went to Spain for nine months, to laze around and visit relations... I was happy enough to laze about on the beach.* PHRASAL VERB = *lie around, lounge around* V P V P

**lazy** /leɪzi/ **(lazier, laziest)** [1] If someone is **lazy**, they do not want to work or make any effort to do anything. ❑ *Lazy and incompetent police officers are letting the public down... I was too lazy to learn how to read music.* ADJ = *idle* ♦ **la|zi|ness** *Current employment laws will be changed to reward effort and punish laziness.* N-UNCOUNT [2] You can use **lazy** to describe an activity or event in which you are very relaxed and which you do or take part in without making much effort. ❑ *Her latest novel is perfect for a lazy summer's afternoon reading... We would have a lazy lunch and then lie on the beach in the sun.* ADJ: ADJ n = *relaxed* ♦ **la|zi|ly** /leɪzɪli/ *Liz went back into the kitchen, stretching lazily.* ADV: ADV with v

**lb** **lb** is a written abbreviation for **pound**, when it refers to weight. ❑ *The baby was born three months early weighing only 3 lb 5oz.* = *pound*

**LCD** /el siː diː/ **(LCDs)** An **LCD** is a display of information on a screen, which uses liquid crystals that become visible when electricity is passed through them. **LCD** is an abbreviation for 'liquid crystal display'. N-COUNT

**lead**
① BEING AHEAD OR TAKING SOMEONE SOMEWHERE
② SUBSTANCES

① **lead** /liːd/ **(leads, leading, led)** ◆◆◆
⇛ Please look at category 21 to see if the expression you are looking for is shown under another headword. [1] If you **lead** a group of people, you walk or ride in front of them. ❑ *John Major and the* VERB V n

*Duke of Edinburgh led the mourners... He walks with a stick but still leads his soldiers into battle... Tom was leading, a rifle slung over his back.* V n prep/adv V

2 VERB If you **lead** someone to a particular place or thing, you take them there. ❑ *He took Dickon by the hand to lead him into the house... Leading the horse, Evandar walked to the door.* V n prep/adv V n

3 VERB If a road, gate, or door **leads** somewhere, you can get there by following the road or going through the gate or door. ❑ *...the doors that led to the yard. ...a short roadway leading to the car park.* V prep/adv V prep/adv

4 VERB If you **are leading** at a particular point in a race or competition, you are winning at that point. ❑ *He's leading in the presidential race... So far Fischer leads by five wins to two... Aston Villa last led the League in March 1990.* V V *by* amount V n

5 N-SING: *the* N, oft *in/into the* N If you have **the lead** or are **in the lead** in a race or competition, you are winning. ❑ *England took the lead after 31 minutes with a goal by Peter Nail... Labour are still in the lead in the opinion polls.*

6 N-SING: with supp, oft N *over* n Someone's **lead over** a competitor at a particular point in a race or competition is the distance, amount of time, or number of points by which they are ahead of them. ❑ *...a commanding lead for the opposition is clearly emerging throughout the country... His goal gave Forest a two-goal lead against Southampton... Sainz now has a lead of 28 points.*

7 VERB If one company or country **leads** others in a particular activity such as scientific research or business, it is more successful or advanced than they are in that activity. ❑ *When it comes to pop music we not only lead Europe, we lead the world. ...foodstores such as Marks & Spencer, which led the market in microwaveable meals.* V n V n *in* n

8 VERB If you **lead** a group of people, an organization, or an activity, you are in control or in charge of the people or the activity. ❑ *Mr Mendes was leading a campaign to save Brazil's rainforest from exploitation.* V n

9 N-COUNT: usu supp N If you give a **lead**, you do something new or develop new ideas or methods that other people consider to be a good example or model to follow. ❑ *The American and Japanese navies took the lead in the development of naval aviation... Over the next 150 years, many others followed his lead.*

10 VERB You can use **lead** when you are saying what kind of life someone has. For example, if you **lead** a busy life, your life is busy. ❑ *She led a normal, happy life with her sister and brother.* V n

11 VERB If something **leads to** a situation or event, usually an unpleasant one, it begins a process which causes that situation or event to happen. ❑ *Ethnic tensions among the republics could lead to civil war... He warned yesterday that a pay rise for teachers would lead to job cuts.* V *to* n V *to* n

12 VERB If something **leads** you **to** do something, it influences or affects you in such a way that you do it. ❑ *His abhorrence of racism led him to write The Algiers Motel Incident... What was it ultimately that led you to leave Sarajevo for Zagreb?* V n to-inf V n to-inf

13 VERB If you say that someone or something **led** you **to** think something, you mean that they caused you to think it, although it was not true or did not happen. ❑ *Mother had led me to believe the new baby was a kind of present for me... It was not as straightforward as we were led to believe.* V n to-inf V n to-inf

14 VERB If you **lead** a conversation or discussion, you control the way that it develops so that you can introduce a particular subject. ❑ *After a while I led the conversation around to her job... He planned to lead the conversation and keep Matt from changing the subject.* V n adv/prep V n

15 VERB = bring You can say that one point or topic in a discussion or piece of writing **leads** you **to** another in order to introduce a new point or topic that is linked with the previous one. ❑ *Well, I think that leads me to the real point.* V n *to* n

16 N-COUNT A **lead** is a piece of information or an idea which may help people to discover the facts in a situation where many facts are not known, for example in the investigation of a crime or in a scientific experiment. ❑ *The inquiry team is also following up possible leads after receiving 400 calls from the public.*

17 N-COUNT **The lead** in a play, film, or show is the most important part in it. The person who plays this part can also be called the **lead**. ❑ *Nina Ananiashvili and Alexei Fadeyechev from the Bolshoi Ballet dance the leads... The leads are Jack Hawkins and Glynis Johns.*

18 N-COUNT A dog's **lead** is a long, thin chain or piece of leather which you attach to the dog's collar so that you can control the dog. [mainly BRIT] ❑ *An older man came out with a little dog on a lead.*

☑ in AM, use **leash**

19 N-COUNT A **lead** in a piece of equipment is a piece of wire covered in plastic which supplies electricity to the equipment or carries it from one part of the equipment to another.

20 N-SING: oft N n The **lead story** or **lead** in a newspaper or on the television or radio news is the most important story. ❑ *The Turkish situation makes the lead in tomorrow's Guardian... Cossiga's reaction is the lead story in the Italian press.*

21 → See also **leading, -led**. to **lead** someone **astray** → see **astray**. **one thing led to another** → see **thing**. to **lead the way** → see **way**.

♦ **lead off** 1 PHRASAL VERB If a door, room, or path **leads off** a place or **leads off from** a place, you can go directly from that place through that door, into that room, or along that path. ❑ *There were two doors leading off the central room... The treatment rooms lead off from the swimming pool... A corridor led off to the left.* V P n V P *from* n V P prep

2 PHRASAL VERB = start off If someone **leads off** in an activity, meeting, or conversation, they start it. ❑ *Whenever there was a dance he and I led off... Boren surprisingly led off the most intensive line of questioning today.* V P V P n (not pron)

♦ **lead on** PHRASAL VERB If someone **leads** you **on**, they encourage you to do something, especially by pretending that something is true. ❑ *I bet she led him on – but how could he be so weak?* V n P

♦ **lead up to** 1 PHRASAL VERB The events that **led up to** a particular event happened one after the other until that event occurred. ❑ *Alan Tomlinson has reconstructed the events that led up to the deaths... They had a series of arguments, leading up to a decision to separate.* V P P n V P P n → See also **lead-up**.

2 PHRASAL VERB: usu cont The period of time **leading up to** an event is the period of time immediately before it happens. ❑ *...the weeks leading up to Christmas.* V P P n

3 PHRASAL VERB If someone **leads up to** a particular subject, they gradually guide a conversation to a point where they can introduce it. ❑ *I'm leading up to something quite important.* V P P n

②**lead** /led/ **(leads)** 1 N-UNCOUNT **Lead** is a soft, grey, heavy metal. ❑ *...drinking water supplied by old-fashioned lead pipes.* 2 N-COUNT The **lead** in a pencil is the centre part of it which makes a mark on paper.

**lead|ed** /ledɪd/ 1 ADJ: ADJ n ≠unleaded **Leaded** petrol has had lead added to it. ❑ *Japanese refiners stopped producing leaded petrol in December 1987.* 2 ADJ: ADJ n **Leaded** windows are made of small pieces of glass held together by strips of lead.

**lead|en** /ledᵊn/ 1 ADJ A **leaden** sky or sea is dark grey and has no movement of clouds or waves. [LITERARY] ❑ *The weather was at its worst; bitterly cold, with leaden skies that gave minimum visibility.* 2 ADJ = dull A **leaden** conversation or piece of writing is not very interesting. ❑ *...a leaden English translation from the Latin.* 3 ADJ = heavy If your movements are **leaden**, you move slowly and heavily, usually because you are tired. [LITERARY] ❑ *He heard the father's leaden footsteps move down the stairs.*

**lead|er** /liːdəʳ/ **(leaders)** ♦♦♦ 1 N-COUNT: usu N *of* n, n N The **leader** of a group of people or an organization is the person who is in control of it or in charge of it. ❑ *We now need a new leader of the party and a new style of leadership... We are going to hold a rally next month to elect a new leader.* 2 N-COUNT The **leader** at a particular point in a race or competition is the person who is winning at that point. ❑ *The world drivers' championship leader crossed the line ahead of the Swede.* 3 N-COUNT The **leader** among a range of products or companies is the one that is most successful. ❑ *Procter & Gamble is the leader in the mass market cosmetics industry.* 4 N-COUNT A **leader** in a newspaper is a piece of writing which gives the editor's opinion on an important news item. [BRIT]

☑ in AM, use **editorial**

5 A **leader** in a newspaper is the most important story in it. [AM] N-COUNT

in BRIT, use **lead, lead story**

**lead|er|board** /liːdəʳbɔʳd/ **The leaderboard** is a board that shows the names and positions of the leading competitors in a competition, especially a golf tournament. N-SING: usu *the* N

**lead|er|ship** /liːdəʳʃɪp/ **(leaderships)** 1 You refer to people who are in control of a group or organization as the **leadership**. ❑ *He is expected to hold talks with both the Croatian and Slovenian leaderships. ...the Labour leadership of Haringey council in north London.* ◆◆◇ N-COUNT 2 Someone's **leadership** is their position or state of being in control of a group of people. ❑ *He praised her leadership during the crisis.* N-UNCOUNT: oft with poss 3 **Leadership** refers to the qualities that make someone a good leader, or the methods a leader uses to do his or her job. ❑ *What most people want to see is determined, decisive action and firm leadership.* N-UNCOUNT

**lead-free** /led friː/ Something such as petrol or paint which is **lead-free**, is made without lead, or has no lead added to it. ADJ

**lead-in** /liːd ɪn/ **(lead-ins)** A **lead-in** is something that is said or done as an introduction before the main subject or event, especially before a radio or television programme. N-COUNT

**lead|ing** /liːdɪŋ/ 1 The **leading** person or thing in a particular area is the one which is most important or successful. ❑ *...a leading member of Bristol's Sikh community.* ◆◆◇ ADJ: ADJ n 2 The **leading** role in a play or film is the main role. A **leading** lady or man is an actor who plays this role. ADJ: ADJ n 3 The **leading** group, vehicle, or person in a race or procession is the one that is at the front. ADJ: ADJ n

**lead|ing ar|ti|cle** **(leading articles)** 1 A **leading article** in a newspaper is a piece of writing which gives the editor's opinion on an important news item. [BRIT] N-COUNT

in AM, use **editorial**

2 A **leading article** in a newspaper is the most important story in it. [AM] N-COUNT

in BRIT, use **lead**

**lead|ing edge** **The leading edge of** a particular area of research or development is the area of it that seems most advanced or sophisticated. ❑ *I think Israel tends to be at the leading edge of technological development.* ♦ **leading-edge** *...leading-edge technology.* N-SING: usu *the* N *of* n = cutting edge; ADJ

**lead|ing light** **(leading lights)** If you say that someone is a **leading light** in an organization, campaign, or community, you mean that they are one of the most important, active, enthusiastic, and successful people in it. N-COUNT

**lead|ing ques|tion** **(leading questions)** A **leading question** is expressed in such a way that it suggests what the answer should be. N-COUNT

**lead sing|er** /liːd sɪŋəʳ/ **(lead singers)** The **lead singer** of a pop group is the person who sings most of the songs. N-COUNT

**lead time** **(lead times)** 1 **Lead time** is the time between the original design or idea for a particular product and its actual production. [BUSINESS] ❑ *They aim to cut production lead times to under 18 months.* N-COUNT 2 **Lead time** is the period of time that it takes for goods to be delivered after someone has ordered them. [BUSINESS] ❑ *Lead times on new equipment orders can run as long as three years.* N-COUNT

**lead-up** /liːd ʌp/ The **lead-up to** an event is the things connected to that event that happen before it. [mainly BRIT] ❑ *The lead-up to the wedding was extremely interesting.* N-SING: usu *the* N *to* n

in AM, usually use **run-up**

**leaf** /liːf/ **(leaves, leafs, leafing, leafed)** 1 The **leaves** of a tree or plant are the parts that are flat, thin, and usually green. Many trees and plants lose their leaves in the winter and grow new leaves in the spring. ❑ *In the garden, the leaves of the horse chestnut had already fallen... The Japanese maple that stands across the drive had just come into leaf.* → See also **-leaved**. ◆◇◇ N-COUNT: usu pl, also *in/into* N 2 A **leaf** is one of the pieces of paper of which a book is made. ❑ *He flattened the wrappers and put them between the leaves of his book.* N-COUNT = page

**PHRASES** 3 If you **take a leaf from** someone's **book** you behave in the same way as them because you want to be like that person or as successful as they are. ❑ *Maybe we should take a leaf out of Branson's book. It's easy to see how he became a billionaire.* PHRASE: V inflects 4 If you say that you are going to **turn over a new leaf**, you mean that you are going to start to behave in a better or more acceptable way. ❑ *He realized he was in the wrong and promised to turn over a new leaf.* PHRASE: V inflects

♦ **leaf through** If you **leaf through** something such as a book or magazine, you turn the pages without reading or looking at them very carefully. ❑ *Most patients derive enjoyment from leafing through old picture albums.* PHRASAL VERB; V P n

**leaf|less** /liːfləs/ If a tree or plant is **leafless**, it has no leaves. ADJ = bare

**leaf|let** /liːflət/ **(leaflets, leafleting, leafleted)** 1 A **leaflet** is a little book or a piece of paper containing information about a particular subject. ❑ *Campaigners handed out leaflets on passive smoking.* N-COUNT 2 If you **leaflet** a place, you distribute leaflets there, for example by handing them to people, or by putting them through letter boxes. ❑ *We've leafleted the university today to try to drum up some support... The only reason we leafleted on the Jewish New Year was because more people than usual go to the synagogue on that day.* VERB; V n; V

**leaf mould**

in AM, use **leaf mold**

**Leaf mould** is a substance consisting of decayed leaves that is used to improve the soil. N-UNCOUNT

**leafy** /liːfi/ 1 **Leafy** trees and plants have lots of leaves on them. ❑ *His two-story brick home was graced with a patio and surrounded by tall, leafy trees.* ADJ 2 You say that a place is **leafy** when there are lots of trees and plants there. ❑ *...semi-detached homes with gardens in leafy suburban areas.* ADJ

**league** /liːg/ **(leagues)** 1 A **league** is a group of people, clubs, or countries that have joined together for a particular purpose, or because they share a common interest. ❑ *...the League of Nations. ...the World Muslim League.* ◆◆◇ N-COUNT: oft in names 2 A **league** is a group of teams that play the same sport or activity against each other. ❑ *...the American League series between the Boston Red Sox and World Champion Oakland Athletics... The club are on the brink of promotion to the Premier League.* N-COUNT 3 You use the word **league** to make comparisons between different people or things, especially in terms of their quality. ❑ *Her success has taken her out of my league... Their record sales would put them in the same league as The Rolling Stones.* N-COUNT: with supp 4 If you say that someone is **in league with** another person to do something bad, you mean that they are working together to do that thing. ❑ *There is no evidence that the broker was in league with the fraudulent vendor.* PHRASE: usu v-link PHR, oft PHR *with* n

**league ta|ble** **(league tables)** A **league table** is a list that shows how successful an organization such as a sports team or a business is when it is compared to other similar organizations. [mainly BRIT] ❑ *...a league table of British schools ranked by exam results.* N-COUNT

**leak** /liːk/ **(leaks, leaking, leaked)** 1 If a container **leaks**, there is a hole or crack in it which lets a substance such as liquid or gas escape. You can also say that a container **leaks** a substance such as liquid or gas. ❑ *The roof leaked... The pool's fiberglass sides had cracked and the water had leaked out... A large diesel tank mysteriously leaked its contents into the river.* ♦ **Leak** is also a noun. ❑ *It's thought a gas leak may have caused the blast.* ◆◇◇ VERB; V; V prep/adv; V n *into* n; Also V n; N-COUNT 2 A **leak** is a crack, hole, or other gap that a substance N-COUNT: oft N *in* n such as a liquid or gas can pass through. ❑ *...a leak in the radiator... In May engineers found a leak in a hydrogen fuel line.* 3 If a secret document or piece of information **leaks** or **is leaked**, someone lets the public know about it. ❑ *Last year, a civil servant was imprisoned for leaking a document to the press... He revealed who leaked a confidential police report... We don't know how the transcript leaked. ...a leaked report.* ♦ **Leak** is also a noun. ❑ *More serious leaks, possibly involving national security, are likely to be investigated by the police.* ♦ **Leak out** means the same as **leak**. ❑ *More details are now beginning to leak out... He said it would leak out to the newspapers and cause a scandal.* VERB V n to n V n V V-ed N-COUNT PHRASAL VERB V P V P to n

**leak|age** /liːkɪdʒ/ **(leakages)** A **leakage** is an amount of liquid or gas that is escaping from a pipe or container by means of a crack, hole, or other fault. ❑ *A leakage of kerosene has polluted water supplies... It should be possible to reduce leakage from pipes.* N-VAR

**leak|er** /liːkəʳ/ **(leakers)** A **leaker** is someone who lets people know secret information. [JOURNALISM] ❑ *He found no direct evidence to identify a leaker.* N-COUNT

**leaky** /liːki/ **(leakiest)** Something that is **leaky** has holes, cracks, or other faults which allow liquids and gases to pass through. ❑ *...the cost of repairing the leaky roof.* ADJ

**lean** /liːn/ **(leans, leaning, leaned, leant, leaner, leanest)** ◆◇◇

> American English uses the form **leaned** as the past tense and past participle. British English uses either **leaned** or **leant**.

1 When you **lean** in a particular direction, you bend your body in that direction. ❑ *Eileen leaned across and opened the passenger door... They stopped to lean over a gate.* 2 If you **lean on** or **against** someone or something, you rest against them so that they partly support your weight. If you **lean** an object **on** or **against** something, you place the object so that it is partly supported by that thing. ❑ *She was feeling tired and was glad to lean against him... Lean the plants against a wall and cover the roots with peat.* 3 If you describe someone as **lean**, you mean that they are thin but look strong and healthy. ❑ *Like most athletes, she was lean and muscular... She watched the tall, lean figure step into the car.* 4 If meat is **lean**, it does not have very much fat. ❑ *It is a beautiful meat, very lean and tender.* 5 If you describe an organization as **lean**, you mean that it has become more efficient and less wasteful by getting rid of staff, or by dropping projects which were unprofitable. ❑ *The value of the pound will force British companies to be leaner and fitter.* 6 If you describe periods of time as **lean**, you mean that people have less of something such as money or are less successful than they used to be. ❑ *...the lean years of the 1930s... With fewer tourists in town, the taxi trade is going through its leanest patch for 30 years.* VERB V adv/prep V adv/prep VERB V adv V n adv/prep ADJ [approval] ADJ ≠ fatty ADJ ADJ: usu ADJ n

♦ **lean on** or **lean upon** If you **lean on** someone or **lean upon** them, you depend on them for support and encouragement. ❑ *She leaned on him to help her to solve her problems.* PHRASAL VERB V P n

♦ **lean towards** If you **lean towards** or **lean toward** a particular idea, belief, or type of behaviour, you have a tendency to think or act in a particular way. ❑ *Most scientists would probably lean toward this viewpoint.* PHRASAL VERB V P n

**lean|ing** /liːnɪŋ/ **(leanings)** Your particular **leanings** are the beliefs, ideas, or aims you hold or a tendency you have towards them. ❑ *Many companies are wary of their socialist leanings... I always had a leaning towards sport.* N-COUNT: usu pl, with supp, oft N *towards* n = tendency

**lean manu|fac|tur|ing** **Lean manufacturing** is a manufacturing method which aims to reduce wastage, for example by keeping stocks low and by working more flexibly. [BUSINESS] ❑ *...efficiency-raising techniques such as lean manufacturing.* N-UNCOUNT

**lean pro|duc|tion** **Lean production** is the same as **lean manufacturing**. [BUSINESS] ❑ *...Japanese-style lean production techniques.* N-UNCOUNT

**leant** /lent/ **Leant** is one of the forms of the past tense and past participle of **lean**. [BRIT]

**lean-to** **(lean-tos)** A **lean-to** is a building such as a shed or garage which is attached to one wall of a larger building, and which usually has a sloping roof. N-COUNT

**leap** /liːp/ **(leaps, leaping, leaped** or **leapt)** ◆◇◇

> British English usually uses the form **leapt** as the past tense and past participle. American English usually uses **leaped**.

1 If you **leap**, you jump high in the air or jump a long distance. ❑ *He had leapt from a window in the building and escaped... The man threw his arms out as he leapt.* ♦ **Leap** is also a noun. ❑ *Smith took Britain's fifth medal of the championships with a leap of 2.37 metres.* 2 If you **leap** somewhere, you move there suddenly and quickly. ❑ *The two men leaped into the jeep and roared off... With a terrible howl, he leapt forward and threw himself into the water.* 3 If a vehicle **leaps** somewhere, it moves there in a short sudden movement. ❑ *The car leapt forward.* 4 A **leap** is a large and important change, increase, or advance. [JOURNALISM] ❑ *The result has been a giant leap in productivity. ...the leap in the unemployed from 35,000 to 75,000... Contemporary art has taken a huge leap forward in the last five or six years.* 5 If you **leap to** a particular place or position, you make a large and important change, increase, or advance. ❑ *Warwicks leap to third in the table, 31 points behind leaders Essex.* 6 If you **leap at** a chance or opportunity, you accept it quickly and eagerly. ❑ *The post of principal of the theatre school became vacant and he leapt at the chance.* 7 You can use **in leaps and bounds** or **by leaps and bounds** to emphasize that someone or something is improving or increasing quickly and greatly. ❑ *He's improved in leaps and bounds this season... The total number of species on the planet appears to be growing by leaps and bounds.* VERB = jump V prep/adv V N-COUNT VERB V prep/adv V prep/adv VERB V adv/prep N-COUNT: oft N *in* n VERB V prep VERB = jump V *at* n PHRASE: usu PHR after v [emphasis]

**leap|frog** /liːpfrɒg, AM -frɔːg/ **(leapfrogs, leapfrogging, leapfrogged)** 1 **Leapfrog** is a game which children play, in which a child bends over, while others jump over their back. 2 If one group of people **leapfrogs** into a particular position or **leapfrogs** someone else, they use the achievements of another person or group in order to make advances of their own. ❑ *It is already obvious that all four American systems have leapfrogged over the European versions... American researchers have now leapfrogged the Japanese and are going to produce a digital system within a year or two.* N-UNCOUNT VERB V prep V n

**leap of faith** **(leaps of faith)** If you take **a leap of faith**, you do something even though you are not sure it is right or will succeed. ❑ *Take a leap of faith and trust them.* N-COUNT: a N in sing

**leapt** /lept/ **Leapt** is a past tense and past participle of **leap**.

**leap year** **(leap years)** A **leap year** is a year which has 366 days. The extra day is the 29th February. There is a leap year every four years. N-COUNT

**learn** /lɜːʳn/ **(learns, learning, learned, learnt)** ◆◆◆

> American English uses the form **learned** as the past tense and past participle. British English uses either **learned** or **learnt**.

1 If you **learn** something, you obtain knowledge or a skill through studying or training. ❑ *Their children were going to learn English... He is learning to play the piano. ...learning how to use new computer systems... Experienced teachers help you learn quickly.* ♦ **learn|ing** *...a bilingual approach to the learning of English.* 2 If you **learn** of something, you find out about it. ❑ *It was only after his death that she learned of his affair with Betty... It didn't come as a shock to learn that the fuel and cooling systems are the most common causes of breakdown. ...the Admiral,* VERB V n V to-inf V wh V N-UNCOUNT VERB = find out V *of* n V that V wh

who, on learning who I was, wanted to meet me. [3] If people **learn to** behave or react in a particular way, they gradually start to behave in that way as a result of a change in attitudes. ❑ *You have to learn to face your problem... We are learning how to confront death instead of avoiding its reality.* VERB; V to-inf; V wh-to-inf [4] If you **learn from** an unpleasant experience, you change the way you behave so that it does not happen again or so that, if it happens again, you can deal with it better. ❑ *I am convinced that he has learned from his mistakes... The company failed to learn any lessons from this experience.* VERB; V from n; V n from n [5] If you **learn** something such as a poem or a role in a play, you study or repeat the words so that you can remember them. ❑ *He learned this song as an inmate at a Texas prison.* VERB; V n [6] → See also **learned, learning**. [7] to **learn** something **the hard way** → see **hard**. to **learn the ropes** → see **rope**.

**learn|ed** /lɜːʳnɪd/ [1] A **learned** person has gained a lot of knowledge by studying. ❑ *He is a serious scholar, a genuinely learned man.* ADJ: usu ADJ n [2] **Learned** books or papers have been written by someone who has gained a lot of knowledge by studying. ❑ *This learned book should start a debate on policy towards the Baltics.* ADJ: usu ADJ n [3] → See also **learn**.

**learn|er** /lɜːʳnəʳ/ **(learners)** A **learner** is someone who is learning about a particular subject or how to do something. ❑ *...a new aid for younger children or slow learners.* N-COUNT

**learn|ing** /lɜːʳnɪŋ/ **Learning** is the process of gaining knowledge through studying. ❑ *The brochure described the library as the focal point of learning on the campus.* → See also **learn, seat of learning**. N-UNCOUNT

**learn|ing curve** **(learning curves)** A **learning curve** is a process where people develop a skill by learning from their mistakes. A steep learning curve involves learning very quickly. ❑ *Both he and the crew are on a steep learning curve.* N-COUNT: usu sing

**learnt** /lɜːʳnt/ **Learnt** is a past tense and past participle of **learn**. [BRIT]

**lease** /liːs/ **(leases, leasing, leased)** ◆◇◇ [1] A **lease** is a legal agreement by which the owner of a building, a piece of land, or something such as a car allows someone else to use it for a period of time in return for money. ❑ *He took up a 10 year lease on the house at Rossie Priory.* N-COUNT [2] If you **lease** property or something such as a car from someone or if they **lease** it **to** you, they allow you to use it in return for regular payments of money. ❑ *He went to Toronto, where he leased an apartment... She hopes to lease the building to students... He will need more grazing land and perhaps La Prade could lease him a few acres.* VERB; V n; V n to n; V n n [3] If you say that someone or something has been given **a new lease of life**, you are emphasizing that they are much more lively or successful than they have been in the past. ❑ *The operation has given me a new lease of life.* PHRASE: PHR after v

**lease|hold** /liːshoʊld/ [1] If a building or land is described as **leasehold**, it is allowed to be used in return for payment according to the terms of a lease. [mainly BRIT] ❑ *I went into a leasehold property at £450 rent per year.* ADJ [2] If you have the **leasehold** of a building or piece of land, you have the legal right to use it for a period of time as arranged according to a lease. [mainly BRIT] N-COUNT

**lease|holder** /liːshoʊldəʳ/ **(leaseholders)** A **leaseholder** is a person who is allowed to use a property according to the terms of a lease. [mainly BRIT] N-COUNT

**leash** /liːʃ/ **(leashes)** A dog's **leash** is a long thin piece of leather or a chain, which you attach to the dog's collar so that you can keep the dog under control. ❑ *All dogs in public places should be on a leash.* N-COUNT = lead

**least** /liːst/ ◆◆◆

> **Least** is often considered to be the superlative form of **little**.

[1] You use **at least** to say that a number or amount is the smallest that is possible or likely and that the actual number or amount may be greater. The forms **at the least** and **at the very least** are also used. ❑ *Aim to have at least half a pint of milk each day... Normally it has only had eleven or twelve members in all. Now it will have seventeen at the very least.* PHRASE: PHR amount, amount PHR [2] You use **at least** to say that something is the minimum that is true or possible. The forms **at the least** and **at the very least** are also used. ❑ *She could take a nice holiday at least... At the least, I needed some sleep... His possession of classified documents in his home was, at the very least, a violation of Navy security regulations.* PHRASE: PHR with cl/group [3] You use **at least** to indicate an advantage that exists in spite of the disadvantage or bad situation that has just been mentioned. ❑ *We've no idea what his state of health is but at least we know he is still alive... If something awful happens to you at least you can write about it.* PHRASE: PHR with cl [4] You use **at least** to indicate that you are correcting or changing something that you have just said. ❑ *It's not difficult to get money for research or at least it's not always difficult.* PHRASE: PHR with cl/group [5] You use **the least** to mean a smaller amount than anyone or anything else, or the smallest amount possible. ❑ *I try to offend the least amount of people possible... If you like cheese, go for the ones with the least fat.* ADJ: the ADJ n ≠ most ♦ **Least** is also a pronoun. ❑ *On education funding, Japan performs best but spends the least per student.* PRON: the PRON ♦ **Least** is also an adverb. ❑ *Damming the river may end up benefitting those who need it the least.* ADV: the ADV after v [6] You use **least** to indicate that someone or something has less of a particular quality than most other things of its kind. ❑ *The least experienced athletes had caused a great many false-starts through the day's proceedings.* ADV: ADV adj/adv ≠ most [7] You use **the least** to emphasize the smallness of something, especially when it hardly exists at all. ❑ *I don't have the least idea of what you're talking about... They neglect their duty at the least hint of fun elsewhere.* ADJ: the ADJ n [emphasis] [8] You use **least** to indicate that something is true or happens to a smaller degree or extent than anything else or at any other time. ❑ *He had a way of throwing her off guard with his charm when she least expected it.* ADV: ADV with v ≠ most [9] You use **least** in structures where you are emphasizing that a particular situation or event is much less important or serious than other possible or actual ones. ❑ *Having to get up at three o'clock every morning was the least of her worries... At that moment, they were among the least of the concerns of the government.* ADJ: ADJ of def-n [emphasis] [10] You use **the least** in structures where you are stating the minimum that should be done in a situation, and suggesting that more should really be done. ❑ *Well, the least you can do, if you won't help me yourself, is to tell me where to go instead... The least his hotel could do is provide a little privacy.* PRON: the PRON cl

PHRASES [11] You can use **in the least** and **the least bit** to emphasize a negative. ❑ *I'm not like that at all. Not in the least... I'm not in the least bit touched by the Marilyn Monroe kind of beauty... Alice wasn't the least bit frightened.* PHRASE: with brd-neg, PHR with cl, PHR adj [emphasis] [12] You use **last but not least** to say that the last person or thing to be mentioned is as important as all the others. ❑ *...her four sons, Christopher, twins Daniel and Nicholas, and last but not least 2-year-old Jack.* PHRASE: PHR with cl/group [13] You can use **least of all** after a negative statement to emphasize that it applies especially to the person or thing mentioned. ❑ *No one ever reads these articles, least of all me... Such a speech should never have been made, least of all by a so called responsible politician.* PHRASE: with brd-neg, PHR cl/group [emphasis] [14] You can use **not least** to emphasize a particularly important example or reason. ❑ *Dieting can be bad for you, not least because it is a cause of stress... Everyone is more reluctant to travel these days, not least the Americans.* PHRASE: PHR cl/group [emphasis] [15] You can use **to say the least** to suggest that a situation is actually much more extreme or serious than you say it is. ❑ *Accommodation was basic to say the least... Some members of the public can be a bit abusive to say the least.* PHRASE: PHR with cl [emphasis]

**leath|er** /le̱ðəʳ/ **(leathers) Leather** is treated animal skin which is used for making shoes, clothes, bags, and furniture. ❑ *He wore a leather jacket and dark trousers. ...an impressive range of upholstered furniture, in a choice of fabrics and leathers.* ◆◇◇ N-MASS

**leath|ery** /le̱ðəri/ If the texture of something, for example someone's skin, is **leathery**, it is tough and hard, like leather. ADJ

**leave** /li̱ːv/ **(leaves, leaving, left)** [1] If you **leave** a place or person, you go away from that place or person. ❑ *He would not be allowed to leave the country... I simply couldn't bear to leave my little girl... My flight leaves in less than an hour... The last of the older children had left for school.* ◆◆◆ VERB V n V n V V *for* n [2] If you **leave** an institution, group, or job, you permanently stop attending that institution, being a member of that group, or doing that job. ❑ *He left school with no qualifications... I am leaving to concentrate on writing fiction. ...a leaving present.* VERB V n V V-ing [3] If you **leave** your husband, wife, or some other person with whom you have had a close relationship, you stop living with them or you finish the relationship. ❑ *He'll never leave you. You need have no worry... I would be insanely jealous if Bill left me for another woman.* VERB V n V n *for* n Also V [4] If you **leave** something or someone in a particular place, you let them remain there when you go away. If you **leave** something or someone with a person, you let them remain with that person so they are safe while you are away. ❑ *From the moment that Philippe had left her in the bedroom at the hotel, she had heard nothing of him... Leave your key with a neighbour in case you lock yourself out one day.* VERB V n prep/adv V n *with* n [5] If you **leave** a message or an answer, you write it, record it, or give it to someone so that it can be found or passed on. ❑ *You can leave a message on our answering machine... Decide whether the ball is in square A, B, C, or D, then call and leave your answer... I left my phone number with several people.* VERB V n prep/adv V n V n *with* n [6] If you **leave** someone doing something, they are doing that thing when you go away from them. ❑ *Salter drove off, leaving Callendar surveying the scene.* VERB V n -ing [7] If you **leave** someone **to** do something, you go away from them so that they do it on their own. If you **leave** someone **to** himself or herself, you go away from them and allow them to be alone. ❑ *I'd better leave you to get on with it, then... Diana took the hint and left them to it... One of the advantages of a department store is that you are left to yourself to try things on.* VERB V n to-inf V n *to it* *be* V-ed *to* pron-refl [8] To **leave** an amount of something means to keep it available after the rest has been used or taken away. ❑ *He always left a little food for the next day... Double rooms at any of the following hotels should leave you some change from £150.* VERB V n *for* n V n n [9] If you take one number away from another, you can say that it **leaves** the number that remains. For example, five take away two leaves three. VERB = *equal* [10] To **leave** someone **with** something, especially when that thing is unpleasant or difficult to deal with, means to make them have it or make them responsible for it. ❑ *...a crash which left him with a broken collar-bone.* VERB V n *with* n [11] If an event **leaves** people or things in a particular state, they are in that state when the event has finished. ❑ *...violent disturbances which have left at least ten people dead... The documentary left me in a state of shock.* VERB V n adj V n prep/adv [12] If you **leave** food or drink, you do not eat or drink it, often because you do not like it. ❑ *If you don't like the cocktail you ordered, just leave it and try a different one.* VERB V n [13] If something **leaves** a mark, effect, or sign, it causes that mark, effect, or sign to remain as a result. ❑ *A muscle tear will leave a scar after healing.* VERB V n [14] If you **leave** something in a particular state, position, or condition, you let it remain in that state, position, or condition. ❑ *He left the album open on the table... I've left the car lights on... I left the engine running.* VERB V n adj V n adv/prep V n -ing [15] If you **leave** a space or gap in something, you deliberately make that space or gap. ❑ *Leave a gap at the top and bottom so air can circulate.* VERB V n [16] If you **leave** a job, decision, or choice **to** someone, you give them the responsibility for dealing with it or making it. ❑ *Affix the blue airmail label and leave the rest to us... The judge should not have left it to the jury to decide... For the moment, I leave you to take all decisions.* VERB V n *to* n V *it to* n to-inf V n to-inf [17] If you say that something such as an arrangement or an agreement **leaves** a lot **to** another thing or person, you are critical of it because it is not adequate and its success depends on the other thing or person. ❑ *The ceasefire leaves a lot to the goodwill of the forces involved.* VERB [disapproval] V amount *to* n [18] To **leave** someone **with** a particular course of action or the opportunity to do something means to let it be available to them, while restricting them in other ways. ❑ *This left me only one possible course of action... He was left with no option but to resign.* VERB V n n *be* V-ed *with* n [19] If you **leave** something **until** a particular time, you delay doing it or dealing with it until then. ❑ *Don't leave it all until the last minute.* ● If you **leave** something **too late**, you delay doing it so that when you eventually do it, it is useless or ineffective. ❑ *I hope I haven't left it too late.* VERB V n *until/to* n PHRASE: V inflects [20] If you **leave** a particular subject, you stop talking about it and start discussing something else. ❑ *I think we'd better leave the subject of Nationalism... He suggested we get together for a drink sometime. I said I'd like that, and we left it there.* VERB V n V n prep/adv [21] If you **leave** property or money **to** someone, you arrange for it to be given to them after you have died. ❑ *He died two and a half years later, leaving everything to his wife.* VERB V n *to* n [22] **Leave** is a period of time when you are not working at your job, because you are on holiday or vacation, or for some other reason. If you are **on leave**, you are not working at your job. ❑ *Why don't you take a few days' leave? ...Jennifer is still on maternity leave... He is home on leave from the Navy.* N-UNCOUNT: oft *on* N [23] ➔ See also **left**.

PHRASES [24] If you **leave** someone or something **alone**, or if you **leave** them **be**, you do not pay them any attention or bother them. ❑ *Some people need to confront a traumatic past; others find it better to leave it alone... Why can't you leave him be?* PHRASE: V inflects [25] If something continues **from where** it **left off**, it starts happening again at the point where it had previously stopped. ❑ *As soon as the police disappear the violence will take up from where it left off.* PHRASE: PHR after v, oft *from* PHR [26] to **leave a lot to be desired** ➔ see **desire**. to **leave** someone **to** their **own devices** ➔ see **device**. to **take leave of** your **senses** ➔ see **sense**. **take it or leave it** ➔ see **take**.

♦ **leave behind** [1] If you **leave** someone or something **behind**, you go away permanently from them. ❑ *Many of the women had left their husbands behind and they told of their fears that they may never see them again... We hear of women who run away, leaving behind their homes and families.* PHRASAL VERB V n P V P n (not pron) [2] If you **leave behind** an object or a situation, it remains after you have left a place. ❑ *I don't want to leave anything behind... A misty rain in the morning had left behind a coolness that would stay for hours.* PHRASAL VERB V n P V P n (not pron) [3] If a person, country, or organization **is left behind**, they remain at a lower level than others because they are not as quick at understanding things or developing. ❑ *We're going to be left behind by the rest of the world... I got left behind at school with the maths... Inflation has left them way behind.* PHRASAL VERB *be* V-ed P *get* V-ed P V n P

♦ **leave off** [1] If someone or something **is left off** a list, they are not included on that list. ❑ *She has been deliberately left off the guest list... The judge left Walsh's name off the list of those he wanted arrested.* PHRASAL VERB *be* V-ed P n V n P n Also V n P [2] If someone **leaves off** doing something, they stop doing it. ❑ *We all left off eating and stood about with bowed heads... Some of the patients left off treatment.* PHRASAL VERB = *stop* V P -ing V P n (not pron)

♦ **leave out** If you **leave** someone or something **out** of an activity, collection, discussion, or group, you do not include them in it. ❑ *Some would question the wisdom of leaving her out of the* PHRASAL VERB V n P *of* n

*team... If you prefer mild flavours reduce or leave out the chilli... Now have we left any country out?* V P n (not pron) V n P
● If someone **feels left out**, they feel sad because they are not included in a group or activity. PHRASE: V inflects

**-leaved** /-liːvd/ also **-leafed**. **-leaved** or **-leafed** combines with adjectives to form other adjectives which describe the type of leaves a tree or plant has. ❑ *...broad-leaved trees. ...very dense and small-leafed maples.* COMB in ADJ

**leav|en** /levᵊn/ **(leavens, leavening, leavened)** If a situation or activity **is leavened by** or **with** something, it is made more interesting or cheerful. ❑ *His mood of deep pessimism cannot have been leavened by his mode of transport – a black cab... He found congenial officers who knew how to leaven war's rigours with riotous enjoyment.* VERB be V-ed by/with n; V n by/with n; Also V n

**leave of ab|sence (leaves of absence)** If you have **leave of absence** you have permission to be away from work for a certain period. N-VAR

**leaves** /liːvz/ **Leaves** is the plural form of **leaf**, and the third person singular form of **leave**.

**Leba|nese** /lebəniːz/ **(Lebanese)** 1 **Lebanese** means belonging or relating to Lebanon, or to its people or culture. ADJ 2 A **Lebanese** is a Lebanese citizen, or a person of Lebanese origin. N-COUNT

**lech|er** /letʃəʳ/ **(lechers)** If you describe a man as a **lecher**, you disapprove of him because you think he behaves towards women in a way which shows he is only interested in them sexually. [INFORMAL] N-COUNT disapproval

**lech|er|ous** /letʃərəs/ If you describe a man as **lecherous**, you disapprove of him because he behaves towards women in a way which shows he is only interested in them sexually. ADJ: usu ADJ n disapproval

**lech|ery** /letʃəri/ **Lechery** is the behaviour of men who are only interested in women sexually. ❑ *His lechery made him the enemy of every self-respecting husband and father in the county.* N-UNCOUNT disapproval

**lec|tern** /lektəʳn/ **(lecterns)** A **lectern** is a high sloping desk on which someone puts their notes when they are standing up and giving a lecture. N-COUNT

**lec|ture** /lektʃəʳ/ **(lectures, lecturing, lectured)** ◆◇◇ 1 A **lecture** is a talk someone gives in order to teach people about a particular subject, usually at a university or college. ❑ *...a series of lectures by Professor Eric Robinson.* N-COUNT 2 If you **lecture on** a particular subject, you give a lecture or a series of lectures about it. ❑ *She then invited him to Atlanta to lecture on the history of art... She has danced, choreographed, lectured and taught all over the world.* VERB V on/in n; V 3 If someone **lectures** you about something, they criticize you or tell you how they think you should behave. ❑ *He used to lecture me about getting too much sun... Chuck would lecture me, telling me to get a haircut... She was no longer interrogating but lecturing.* VERB V n about/on n; V n; V ♦ **Lecture** is also a noun. ❑ *Our captain gave us a stern lecture on safety.* N-COUNT

**lec|tur|er** /lektʃərəʳ/ **(lecturers)** A **lecturer** is a teacher at a university or college. ❑ *...a lecturer in law at Southampton University.* N-COUNT

**lec|ture|ship** /lektʃəʳʃɪp/ **(lectureships)** A **lectureship** is the position of lecturer at a university or college. N-COUNT

**led** /led/ **Led** is the past tense and past participle of **lead**.

**-led** /-led/ 1 **-led** combines with nouns to form adjectives which indicate that something is organized, directed, or controlled by a particular person or group. ❑ *...the student-led democracy movement. ...a German-led European consortium.* COMB in ADJ: usu ADJ n 2 **-led** combines with nouns to form adjectives which indicate that something is mainly caused or influenced by a particular factor. ❑ *Their prosperity depends on export-led growth. ...a market-led economy.* COMB in ADJ

**ledge** /ledʒ/ **(ledges)** 1 A **ledge** is a piece of rock on the side of a cliff or mountain, which is in the shape of a narrow shelf. N-COUNT 2 A **ledge** is a narrow shelf along the bottom edge of a window. ❑ *She had climbed onto the ledge outside his window.* N-COUNT

**ledg|er** /ledʒəʳ/ **(ledgers)** A **ledger** is a book in which a company or organization writes down the amounts of money it spends and receives. [BUSINESS] N-COUNT

**lee** /liː/ **(lees)** ◆◇◇ 1 **The lee** of a place is the shelter that it gives from the wind or bad weather. [LITERARY] ❑ *...the cathedral, which nestles in the lee of a hill beneath the town.* N-SING: with poss 2 In sailing, the **lee** side of a ship is the one that is away from the wind. [TECHNICAL] ADJ: ADJ n

**leech** /liːtʃ/ **(leeches)** 1 A **leech** is a small animal which looks like a worm and lives in water. Leeches feed by attaching themselves to other animals and sucking their blood. N-COUNT 2 If you describe someone as a **leech**, you disapprove of them because they deliberately depend on other people, often making money out of them. ❑ *They're just a bunch of leeches cadging off others!* N-COUNT disapproval

**leek** /liːk/ **(leeks) Leeks** are long thin vegetables which smell similar to onions. They are white at one end, have long light green leaves, and are eaten cooked. ➔ See picture on page 1712. N-VAR

**leer** /lɪəʳ/ **(leers, leering, leered)** If someone **leers** at you, they smile in an unpleasant way, usually because they are sexually interested in you. ❑ *Men were standing around, swilling beer and occasionally leering at passing females... He looked back at Kenworthy and leered.* VERB disapproval V prep/adv; V ♦ **Leer** is also a noun. ❑ *When I asked the clerk for my room key, he gave it to me with a leer.* N-COUNT

**leery** /lɪəri/ 1 If you are **leery of** something, you are cautious and suspicious about it and try to avoid it. [INFORMAL] ❑ *Executives say they are leery of the proposed system... They were leery about investing in a company controlled by a single individual.* ADJ: usu v-link ADJ, oft ADJ of/about n = wary 2 If someone looks or smiles at you in a **leery** way, they look or smile at you in an unpleasant way, usually because they are sexually interested in you. ❑ *...a leery grin.* ADJ disapproval

**lee|way** /liːweɪ/ **Leeway** is the freedom that someone has to take the action they want to or to change their plans. ❑ *Rarely do schoolteachers have leeway to teach classes the way they want.* N-UNCOUNT

**left**
① REMAINING
② DIRECTION AND POLITICAL GROUPINGS

① **left** /left/ ◆◇◇ 1 **Left** is the past tense and past participle of **leave**. 2 If there is a certain amount of something **left**, or if you have a certain amount of it **left**, it remains when the rest has gone or been used. ❑ *Is there any gin left?... He's got plenty of money left... They still have six games left to play.* ADJ: v-link ADJ, v n ADJ ● If there is a certain amount of something **left over**, or if you have it **left over**, it remains when the rest has gone or been used. ❑ *So much income is devoted to monthly mortgage payments that nothing is left over. ...a large bucket of cut flowers left over from the wedding.* PHRASE: usu v-link PHR

② **left** /left/ ◆◆◆

> The spelling **Left** is also used for meanings 3 and 4.

1 The **left** is one of two opposite directions, sides, or positions. If you are facing north and you turn to the left, you will be facing west. In the word 'to', the 't' is to the left of the 'o'. ❑ *In Britain cars drive on the left. ...the brick wall to the left of the conservatory... Beaufort Castle is on your left.* N-SING: usu the N ≠ right ♦ **Left** is also an adverb. ❑ *Turn left at the crossroads into Clay Lane.* ADV: ADV after v 2 Your **left** arm, leg, or ear, for example, is the one which is on the left side of your body. Your **left** shoe or glove is the one which is intended to be worn on your left foot or hand. ADJ: ADJ n ≠ right 3 You can refer to people who support the political ideals of socialism as **the left**. They are often contrasted with **the right**, who support the political ideals of capitalism and conservatism. N-SING-COLL: the N ≠ right

❑ *...the traditional parties of the Left.* 4 If you say that a person or political party has moved **to the left**, you mean that their political beliefs have become more left-wing. ❑ *After Mrs Thatcher's first election victory in 1979, Labour moved sharply to the left.* N-SING: *the* N, usu *to the* N ≠ right

**left-click** **(left-clicks, left-clicking, left-clicked)** To **left-click** or to **left-click on** something means to press the left-hand button on a computer mouse. [COMPUTING] ❑ *When the menu has popped up you should left-click on one of the choices to make it operate.* VERB ≠ right-click; V *on* n

**left field** 1 If you say that someone or something has come **out of left field** or is **out in left field**, you mean that they are untypical, unusual, or strange in some way. ❑ *The question came out of left field, but Mary Ann wasn't really surprised... He is, like most theorists, out there in left field, ignoring the experimental evidence.* 2 **Left-field** means slightly odd or unusual. [mainly BRIT, INFORMAL] ❑ *...a left-field cabaret act... Her parents were creative and left-field and wanted Polly to become a singer or a truck driver.* N-SING: usu prep N; ADJ: usu ADJ n = unconventional

**left-hand** If something is on the **left-hand** side of something, it is positioned on the left of it. ❑ *The keys are in the back left-hand corner of the drawer.* ADJ: ADJ n ≠ right-hand

**left-hand drive** A **left-hand drive** vehicle has the steering wheel on the left side, and is designed to be used in countries where people drive on the right-hand side of the road. ADJ: usu ADJ n

**left-handed** Someone who is **left-handed** uses their left hand rather than their right hand for activities such as writing and sports and for picking things up. ❑ *There is a place in London that supplies practically everything for left-handed people.* ♦ **Left-handed** is also an adverb. ❑ *My father thought that I'd be at a disadvantage if I wrote left-handed.* ADJ ≠ right-handed; ADV: ADV after v

**left-hander** **(left-handers)** You can describe someone as a **left-hander** if they use their left hand rather than their right hand for activities such as writing and sports and for picking things up. N-COUNT ≠ right-hander

**left|ism** /leftɪzəm/ **Leftism** refers to the beliefs and behaviour of people who support socialist ideals. ❑ *...changes which would move the party away from the dreamy leftism that alienated so many people.* N-UNCOUNT

**left|ist** /leftɪst/ **(leftists)** 1 Socialists and Communists are sometimes referred to as **leftists**. ❑ *Two of the men were leftists and two were centrists. ...Chilean leftists.* 2 If you describe someone, their ideals or their activities as **leftist**, you mean that they support the ideas of socialism or communism. ❑ *...an alliance of seven leftist parties. ...extreme leftist ideas.* N-COUNT; ADJ: ADJ n

**left-justify** **(left-justifies, left-justifying, left-justified)** If printed text is **left-justified**, each line begins at the same distance from the left-hand edge of the page or column. ❑ *The data in the cells should be left-justified.* VERB ≠ right-justify; *be* V-ed; Also V, V n

**left lug|gage** **Left luggage** is used to refer to luggage that people leave at a special place in a railway station or an airport, and which they collect later. [BRIT] ❑ *...a left luggage locker at Victoria Station.* N-UNCOUNT: usu N n

**left-of-centre**

✔ in AM, use **left of center**

**Left-of-centre** people or political parties support political ideas which are closer to socialism than to capitalism. ADJ: usu ADJ n

**left|over** /leftoʊvəʳ/ **(leftovers)** also **left-over.** 1 You can refer to food that has not been eaten after a meal as **leftovers**. ❑ *Refrigerate any leftovers.* 2 You use **leftover** to describe an amount of something that remains after the rest of it has been used or eaten. ❑ *Leftover chicken makes a wonderful salad.* N-PLURAL; ADJ: ADJ n

**left|ward** /leftwəʳd/ also **leftwards. Leftward** or **leftwards** means on or towards a political position that is closer to socialism than to capitalism. ❑ *Their success does not necessarily reflect a leftward shift in politics.* ♦ **Leftward** is also an adverb. ❑ *He seemed to move leftwards as he grew older.* ADJ: ADJ n ≠ rightward; ADV: ADV after v

**left-wing** also **left wing.** 1 **Left-wing** people have political ideas that are based on socialism. ❑ *They said they would not be voting for him because he was too left-wing.* 2 **The left wing** of a group of people, especially a political party, consists of the members of it whose beliefs are closer to socialism than are those of its other members. ❑ *The left-wing of the party is confident that the motion will be carried.* ADJ ≠ right-wing; N-SING: usu *the* N

**left-winger** **(left-wingers)** A **left-winger** is a person whose political beliefs are close to socialism, or closer to them than most of the other people in the same group or party. ❑ *We were accused of being militant left-wingers.* N-COUNT ≠ right-winger

**lefty** /lefti/ **(lefties)** also **leftie.** 1 If you refer to someone as a **lefty**, you mean that they have socialist beliefs. [mainly BRIT, INFORMAL] ❑ *...a large group of students and trendy lefties.* 2 A **lefty** is someone, especially a sports player, who is left-handed. [mainly AM, INFORMAL] N-COUNT: oft N n disapproval; N-COUNT

**leg** /leg/ **(legs)** 1 A person or animal's **legs** are the long parts of their body that they use to stand on. ❑ *He was tapping his walking stick against his leg.* ♦ **-legged** /-legɪd/ *Her name was Sheila, a long-legged blonde. ...a large four-legged animal.* 2 The **legs** of a pair of trousers are the parts that cover your legs. ❑ *He moved on through wet grass that soaked his trouser legs.* 3 A **leg** of lamb, pork, chicken, or other meat is a piece of meat that consists of the animal's or bird's leg, especially the thigh. ❑ *...a chicken leg. ...a leg of mutton.* 4 The **legs** of a table, chair, or other piece of furniture are the parts that rest on the floor and support the furniture's weight. ❑ *His ankles were tied to the legs of the chair.* ♦ **-legged** *...a three-legged stool.* 5 A **leg** of a long journey is one part of it, usually between two points where you stop. ❑ *The first leg of the journey was by boat to Lake Naivasha in Kenya.* 6 A **leg** of a sports competition is one of a series of games that are played to find an overall winner. [mainly BRIT] ❑ *They will televise both legs of Leeds' European Cup clash with Rangers.* ◆◆◇ N-COUNT: usu poss N; COMB in ADJ; N-COUNT: usu pl; N-COUNT: n N, N *of* n; N-COUNT: usu with supp, oft n N, N *of* n; COMB in ADJ; N-COUNT: usu ord N, N *of* n; N-COUNT

PHRASES 7 If you say that something or someone is **on** their **last legs**, you mean that the period of time when they were successful or strong is ending. [INFORMAL] ❑ *This relationship is on its last legs.* 8 If you **are pulling** someone's **leg**, you are teasing them by telling them something shocking or worrying as a joke. [INFORMAL] ❑ *Of course I won't tell them; I was only pulling your leg.* 9 If you say that someone does not **have a leg to stand on**, or **hasn't got a leg to stand on**, you mean that a statement or claim they have made cannot be justified or proved. [INFORMAL] ❑ *It's only my word against his, I know. So I don't have a leg to stand on.* 10 **an arm and a leg** → see **arm. with** your **tail between** your **legs** → see **tail**. PHRASE: usu v-link PHR; PHRASE: V inflects; PHRASE: with brd-neg

**lega|cy** /legəsi/ **(legacies)** 1 A **legacy** is money or property which someone leaves to you when they die. ❑ *You could make a real difference to someone's life by leaving them a generous legacy.* 2 A **legacy of** an event or period of history is something which is a direct result of it and which continues to exist after it is over. ❑ *...a programme to overcome the legacy of inequality and injustice created by Apartheid.* N-COUNT; N-COUNT: with supp, usu N *of* n, n N

**le|gal** /liːgəl/ 1 **Legal** is used to describe things that relate to the law. ❑ *He vowed to take legal action. ...the British legal system... I sought legal advice on this.* ♦ **le|gal|ly** *There are reasons to doubt that a second trial is morally, legally or politically justified... It could be a bit problematic, legally speaking.* 2 An action or situation that is **legal** is allowed ◆◆◇ ADJ: ADJ n; ADV: ADV with v, ADV adj, ADV with cl; ADJ or required by law. ❑ *What I did was perfectly legal. ...drivers who have more than the legal limit of alcohol.* ≠ *illegal*

**le|gal aid** **Legal aid** is money given by the government or another organization to people who cannot afford to pay for a lawyer. N-UNCOUNT

**le|gal|ise** /liːgəlaɪz/ → see **legalize**.

**le|gal|is|tic** /liːgəlɪstɪk/ If you say that someone's language or ideas are **legalistic**, you are criticizing them for paying too much attention to legal details. ❑ *...complicated legalistic language. ...his fussily legalistic mind.* ADJ: usu ADJ n [disapproval]

**le|gal|ity** /ligælɪti/ If you talk about **the legality of** an action or situation, you are talking about whether it is legal or not. ❑ *The auditor has questioned the legality of the contracts.* N-UNCOUNT: usu *the* N *of* n

**le|gal|ize** /liːgəlaɪz/ **(legalizes, legalizing, legalized)**

☑ in BRIT, also use **legalise**

If something **is legalized**, a law is passed that makes it legal. ❑ *Divorce was legalized in 1981. ...the decision of the Georgian government to legalise multi-party elections.* ♦ **le|gali|za|tion** /liːgəlaɪzeɪʃᵊn/ *She ruled out the legalisation of drugs.* VERB *be* V-ed V n N-UNCOUNT: usu *the* N *of* n

**le|gal ten|der** **Legal tender** is money, especially a particular coin or banknote, which is officially part of a country's currency at a particular time. N-UNCOUNT

**leg|ate** /legɪt/ **(legates)** A **legate** is a person who is the official representative of another person, especially the Pope's official representative in a particular country. [FORMAL] N-COUNT = *representative*

**le|ga|tion** /lɪgeɪʃᵊn/ **(legations)** [1] A **legation** is a group of government officials and diplomats who work in a foreign country and represent their government in that country. ❑ *...a member of the US legation.* [2] A **legation** is the building in which a legation works. N-COUNT: usu supp N N-COUNT

**leg|end** /ledʒᵊnd/ **(legends)** [1] A **legend** is a very old and popular story that may be true. ❑ *...the legends of ancient Greece... The play was based on Irish legend.* [2] If you refer to someone as a **legend**, you mean that they are very famous and admired by a lot of people. ❑ *...blues legends John Lee Hooker and B.B. King.* [3] A **legend** is a story that people talk about, concerning people, places, or events that exist or are famous at the present time. ❑ *The incident has since become a family legend... His frequent brushes with death are the stuff of legend among the press.* N-VAR N-COUNT [approval] N-VAR

**leg|end|ary** /ledʒᵊndri, AM -deri/ [1] If you describe someone or something as **legendary**, you mean that they are very famous and that many stories are told about them. ❑ *...the legendary Jazz singer Adelaide Hall... His political skill is legendary.* [2] A **legendary** person, place, or event is mentioned or described in an old legend. ❑ *The hill is supposed to be the resting place of the legendary King Lud.* ADJ ADJ: usu ADJ n

**-legged** /-legɪd/ → see **leg**.

**leg|gings** /legɪŋz/ [1] **Leggings** are close-fitting trousers, usually made out of a stretchy fabric, that are worn by women and girls. [2] **Leggings** are an outer covering of leather or other strong material, often in the form of trousers, that you wear over your normal trousers in order to protect them. ❑ *...a pair of leggings to slip on over your other clothes.* N-PLURAL: also *a pair of* N N-PLURAL: also *a pair of* N

**leg|gy** /legi/ If you describe someone, usually a woman, as **leggy**, you mean that they have very long legs and usually that you find this attractive. ❑ *The leggy beauty was none other than our own Naomi Campbell.* ADJ

**leg|ible** /ledʒɪbᵊl/ **Legible** writing is clear enough to read. ❑ *My handwriting isn't very legible. ...a barely legible sign.* ADJ ≠ *illegible*

**le|gion** /liːdʒᵊn/ **(legions)** [1] A **legion** is a large group of soldiers who form one section of an army. ❑ *...the Sudan-based troops of the Libyan Islamic Legion.* [2] A **legion of** people or things is a great number of them. [WRITTEN] ❑ *His delightful sense of humour won him a legion of friends.* [3] If you say that things of a particular kind are **legion**, you mean that there are a great number of them. [FORMAL] ❑ *Ellie's problems are legion.* N-COUNT: oft in names after n N-COUNT: usu N *of* n ADJ: v-link ADJ

**leg|is|late** /ledʒɪsleɪt/ **(legislates, legislating, legislated)** When a government or state **legislates**, it passes a new law. [FORMAL] ❑ *Most member countries have already legislated against excessive overtime... You cannot legislate to change attitudes. ...attempts to legislate a national energy strategy.* VERB V *against/for/on* n V to-inf V n

**leg|is|la|tion** /ledʒɪsleɪʃᵊn/ ◆◇◇ **Legislation** consists of a law or laws passed by a government. [FORMAL] ❑ *...a letter calling for legislation to protect women's rights.* N-UNCOUNT

**leg|is|la|tive** /ledʒɪslətɪv, AM -leɪ-/ **Legislative** means involving or relating to the process of making and passing laws. [FORMAL] ❑ *Today's hearing was just the first step in the legislative process. ...the country's highest legislative body.* ADJ: ADJ n

**leg|is|la|tor** /ledʒɪsleɪtəʳ/ **(legislators)** A **legislator** is a person who is involved in making or passing laws. [FORMAL] ❑ *...an attempt to get US legislators to change the system.* N-COUNT

**leg|is|la|ture** /ledʒɪslətʃəʳ, AM -leɪ-/ **(legislatures)** The **legislature** of a particular state or country is the group of people in it who have the power to make and pass laws. [FORMAL] ❑ *The proposals before the legislature include the creation of two special courts to deal exclusively with violent crimes.* N-COUNT: usu *the* N in sing

**le|git** /lədʒɪt/ If you describe a person or thing as **legit**, you mean that they are in accordance with the law or with a particular set of rules and regulations. [INFORMAL] ❑ *I checked him out, he's legit... What is the point of going legit and getting married?* ADJ: usu v-link ADJ

**le|giti|mate** /lɪdʒɪtɪmət/ [1] Something that is **legitimate** is acceptable according to the law. ❑ *The government will not seek to disrupt the legitimate business activities of the defendant.* ♦ **le|giti|ma|cy** /lɪdʒɪtɪmɪsi/ *The opposition parties do not recognise the political legitimacy of his government.* ♦ **le|giti|mate|ly** *The government has been legitimately elected by the people.* [2] If you say that something such as a feeling or claim is **legitimate**, you think that it is reasonable and justified. ❑ *That's a perfectly legitimate fear... The New York Times has a legitimate claim to be a national newspaper.* ♦ **le|giti|ma|cy** *As if to prove the legitimacy of these fears, the Cabinet of Franz von Papen collapsed on December 2.* ♦ **le|giti|mate|ly** *They could quarrel quite legitimately with some of my choices.* [3] A **legitimate** child is one whose parents were married before he or she was born. ❑ *We only married in order that the child should be legitimate.* ADJ N-UNCOUNT: usu with supp ADV: ADV with v ADJ N-UNCOUNT: usu with supp ADV: ADV with v ADJ ≠ *illegitimate*

**le|giti|mize** /lɪdʒɪtɪmaɪz/ **(legitimizes, legitimizing, legitimized)**

☑ The spellings **legitimise** in British English, and **legitimatize** in American English are also used.

To **legitimize** something, especially something bad, means to officially allow it, approve it, or make it seem acceptable. [FORMAL] ❑ *They will accept no agreement that legitimizes the ethnic division of the country.* VERB = *sanction* V n

**leg|less** /legləs/ [1] A **legless** person or animal has no legs. [2] If you say that someone is **legless**, you mean that they are extremely drunk. [BRIT, INFORMAL] ❑ *They found the locals getting legless on tequila.* ADJ: ADJ n ADJ: usu v-link ADJ

**leg room** **Leg room** is the amount of space, especially in a car or other vehicle, that is available in front of your legs. ❑ *Tall drivers won't have enough leg room.* N-UNCOUNT

**leg|ume** /legjuːm/ **(legumes)** People sometimes use **legumes** to refer to peas, beans, and other related vegetables. [TECHNICAL] N-COUNT = *pulse*

**lei|sure** /leʒəʳ, AM liːʒ-/ [1] **Leisure** is the time when you are not working and you can relax and do things that you enjoy. ❑ *...a relaxing way to fill my leisure time. ...one of Britain's most popular leisure activities.* N-UNCOUNT: usu N n
[2] If someone does something **at leisure** or **at** their **leisure**, they enjoy themselves by doing it when they want to, without hurrying. ❑ *You will be able to stroll at leisure through the gardens... He could read all the national papers at his leisure.* PHRASE: PHR after v

**lei|sure cen|tre** **(leisure centres)** A **leisure centre** is a large public building containing different facilities for leisure activities, such as a sports hall, a swimming pool, and rooms for meetings. [BRIT] N-COUNT: oft in names

**lei|sured** /leʒəʳd, AM liːʒ-/ [1] **Leisured** people are people who do not work, usually because they are rich. ❑ *...the leisured classes.* ADJ: ADJ n [2] **Leisured** activities are done in a relaxed way or do not involve work. ❑ *...this leisured life of reading and writing.* ADJ

**lei|sure|ly** /leʒəʳli, AM liːʒ-/ A **leisurely** action is done in a relaxed and unhurried way. ❑ *Lunch was a leisurely affair... Tweed walked at a leisurely pace.* ADJ: usu ADJ n ♦ **Leisurely** is also an adverb. ❑ *We walked leisurely into the hotel.* ADV: ADV with v

**leisure|wear** /leʒəʳweəʳ, AM liːʒ-/ **Leisurewear** is informal clothing which you wear when you are not working, for example at weekends or on holiday. [BRIT, WRITTEN] ❑ *Their range of leisurewear is aimed at fashion-conscious 13 to 25 year-olds.* N-UNCOUNT

**leit|mo|tif** /laɪtmoʊtiːf/ **(leitmotifs)** also **leitmotiv.** A **leitmotif** in something such as a book or film or in a person's life is an idea or an object which occurs again and again. [FORMAL] ❑ *The title of one of Dietrich's best-known songs could serve as the leitmotif for her life.* N-COUNT

**lem|ming** /lemɪŋ/ **(lemmings)** [1] A **lemming** is an animal that looks like a large rat with thick fur. Lemmings live in cold northern regions and sometimes travel in very large numbers. N-COUNT [2] If you say that a large group of people are acting like **lemmings**, you are critical of them because they all follow each other into an action without thinking about it. ❑ *The French crowds pour like lemmings down the motorway to Paris.* N-COUNT: usu pl [disapproval]

**lem|on** /lemən/ **(lemons)** [1] A **lemon** is a bright yellow fruit with very sour juice. Lemons grow on trees in warm countries. ➔ See picture on page 1711. ❑ *...a slice of lemon. ...oranges, lemons and other citrus fruits. ...lemon juice.* N-VAR [2] **Lemon** is a drink that tastes of lemons. N-UNCOUNT

**lem|on|ade** /lemənеɪd/ **(lemonades)** **Lemonade** is a colourless sweet fizzy drink. A drink that is made from lemons, sugar, and water and is not fizzy can also be referred to as **lemonade**. ❑ *He was pouring ice and lemonade into tall glasses.* N-UNCOUNT ♦ A glass of lemonade can be referred to as a **lemonade**. ❑ *I'm going to get you a lemonade.* N-COUNT

**lem|on curd** **Lemon curd** is a thick yellow food made from lemons. You spread it on bread or use it to fill cakes or pastries. [mainly BRIT] N-UNCOUNT

**lem|on|grass** /leməngrɑːs, -græs/ also **lemon grass. Lemongrass** is a type of grass that grows in warm countries. It is used as a flavouring in food. N-UNCOUNT

**lem|on squeez|er** **(lemon squeezers)** A **lemon squeezer** is an object used for squeezing juice out of lemons and oranges. N-COUNT

**lem|ony** /leməni/ Something that smells or tastes of lemons can be described as **lemony**. ADJ

**lem|on yel|low** also **lemon-yellow. Lemon yellow** or **lemon** is used to describe things that are pale yellow in colour. COLOUR

**le|mur** /liːməʳ/ **(lemurs)** A **lemur** is an animal that looks like a small monkey and has a long tail and a face similar to that of a fox. N-COUNT

**lend** /lend/ **(lends, lending, lent)** [1] When people or organizations such as banks **lend** you money, they give it to you and you agree to pay it back at a future date, often with an extra amount as interest. ❑ *The bank is reassessing its criteria for lending money... I had to lend him ten pounds to take his children to the pictures. ...financial de-regulation that led to institutions being more willing to lend.* ◆◇◇ VERB; V n; V n n; V; Also V n to n, V to n ♦ **lend|ing** *...a financial institution that specializes in the lending of money. ...a slump in bank lending.* N-UNCOUNT: usu with supp
[2] If you **lend** something that you own, you allow someone to have it or use it for a period of time. ❑ *Will you lend me your jacket for a little while?... He had lent the bungalow to the Conrads for a couple of weeks.* VERB; V n n; V n to n [3] If you **lend** your support **to** someone or something, you help them with what they are doing or with a problem that they have. ❑ *He was approached by the organisers to lend support to a benefit concert... Stipe attended yesterday's news conference to lend his support.* VERB = give; V n to n; V n; Also V n n [4] If something **lends itself to** a particular activity or result, it is easy for it to be used for that activity or to achieve that result. ❑ *The room lends itself well to summer eating with its light, airy atmosphere.* VERB; V pron-refl to n [5] If something **lends** a particular quality **to** something else, it adds that quality to it. ❑ *Enthusiastic applause lent a sense of occasion to the proceedings... A more relaxed regime and regular work lends the inmates a dignity not seen in other prisons.* VERB; V n to n; V n n; Also V n [6] ➔ See also **lent**. [7] to **lend an ear** ➔ see **ear**. to **lend a hand** ➔ see **hand**.

**lend|er** /lendəʳ/ **(lenders)** A **lender** is a person or an institution that lends money to people. [BUSINESS] ❑ *...the six leading mortgage lenders.* N-COUNT

**lend|ing li|brary** **(lending libraries)** A **lending library** is a library from which the public are allowed to borrow books. N-COUNT

**lend|ing rate** **(lending rates)** The **lending rate** is the rate of interest that you have to pay when you are repaying a loan. [BUSINESS] ❑ *The bank left its lending rates unchanged.* N-COUNT

**length** /leŋθ/ **(lengths)** [1] The **length** of something is the amount that it measures from one end to the other along the longest side. ❑ *It is about a metre in length. ...the length of the fish... The plane had a wing span of 34ft and a length of 22ft.* ◆◆◇ N-VAR: oft with poss, oft amount in N, N of amount
[2] The **length** of something such as a piece of writing is the amount of writing that is contained in it. ❑ *...a book of at least 100 pages in length... The length of a paragraph depends on the information it conveys.* N-VAR: oft with poss, oft amount in N
[3] The **length** of an event, activity, or situation is the period of time from beginning to end for which something lasts or during which something happens. ❑ *The exact length of each period may vary... His film, over two hours in length, is a subtle study of family life.* N-VAR: oft with poss, oft amount in N
[4] A **length of** rope, cloth, wood, or other material is a piece of it that is intended to be used for a particular purpose or that exists in a particular situation. ❑ *...a 30ft length of rope... You can hang lengths of fabric behind the glass.* N-COUNT: with supp, oft N of n
[5] The **length of** something is its quality of being long. ❑ *Many have been surprised at the length of time it has taken him to make up his mind... I noticed, too, the length of her fingers.* N-UNCOUNT: usu with supp, oft N of n
[6] If you swim a **length** in a swimming pool, you swim the distance from one end to the other. ❑ *I swim 40 lengths a day.* N-COUNT: usu num N
[7] In boat racing or horse racing, a **length** is the distance from the front to the back of the boat or horse. You can talk about one boat or horse being one or more **lengths** in front of or behind another. ❑ *Harvard won by four lengths.* N-COUNT: usu num N
[8] If something happens or exists along **the length of** something, it happens or exists for the whole way along it. ❑ *I looked along the length of the building... The inspiration stemming from his travels lasted the length of his career.* N-SING: the N of n
[9] ➔ See also **full-length**.

PHRASES [10] If someone does something **at length**, they do it after a long period of time. [LITERARY] ❑ *At length my father went into the house.* PHRASE: PHR cl
[11] If someone does something **at length**, they do it for a long time or in great detail. ❑ *They spoke at length, reviewing the entire incident.* PHRASE: PHR after v

12 If you say that someone **goes to great lengths** to achieve something, you mean that they try very hard and perhaps do extreme things in order to achieve it. ❑ *Greta Garbo went to great lengths to hide from reporters and photographers.* PHRASE: V inflects
13 **at arm's length** → see **arm**. **the length and breadth of** → see **breadth**.

**-length** /-leŋθ/ **-length** combines with nouns to form adjectives that describe something that is of a certain length, or long enough to reach the point indicated by the noun. ❑ *...shoulder-length hair. ...knee-length boots. ...a feature-length film.* → See also **full-length**. COMB in ADJ

**length|en** /leŋθən/ **(lengthens, lengthening, lengthened)** 1 When something **lengthens** or when you **lengthen** it, it increases in length. ❑ *The evening shadows were lengthening... She began to walk faster, but he lengthened his stride to keep up with her.* VERB ≠ shorten; V; V n
2 When something **lengthens** or when you **lengthen** it, it lasts for a longer time than it did previously. ❑ *Vacations have lengthened and the work week has shortened... The council does not support lengthening the school day to fit in other activities.* VERB ≠ shorten; V; V n

**length|ways** /leŋθweɪz/ or **lengthwise** /leŋθwaɪz/ **Lengthways** or **lengthwise** means in a direction or position along the length of something. ❑ *Cut the aubergines in half lengthways.* ADV: ADV after v

**length|wise** /leŋθwaɪz/ **Lengthwise** means the same as **lengthways**. ❑ *Peel the onion and cut it in half lengthwise.* ADV: ADV after v

**lengthy** /leŋθi/ **(lengthier, lengthiest)** 1 You use **lengthy** to describe an event or process which lasts for a long time. ❑ *...a lengthy meeting. ...the lengthy process of filling out passport application forms.* ADJ: usu ADJ n
2 A **lengthy** report, article, book, or document contains a lot of speech, writing, or other material. ❑ *...a lengthy report from the Council of Ministers.* ADJ: usu ADJ n

**le|ni|en|cy** /liːniənsi/ **Leniency** is a lenient attitude or lenient behaviour. ❑ *The judge rejected pleas for leniency and sentenced him to six months in prison.* N-UNCOUNT: oft N *to/towards* n

**le|ni|ent** /liːniənt/ When someone in authority is **lenient**, they are not as strict or severe as expected. ❑ *He believes the government already is lenient with drug traffickers... Professor Oswald takes a sightly more lenient view.* ADJ: oft ADJ *with* n ♦ **le|ni|ent|ly** *Many people believe reckless drivers are treated too leniently.* ADV: ADV after v

**lens** /lenz/ **(lenses)** ◆◇◇ 1 A **lens** is a thin curved piece of glass or plastic used in things such as cameras, telescopes, and pairs of glasses. You look through a lens in order to make things look larger, smaller, or clearer. ❑ *...a camera lens... I packed your sunglasses with the green lenses.* N-COUNT
2 In your eye, the **lens** is the part behind the pupil that focuses light and helps you to see clearly. N-COUNT: usu sing
3 → See also **contact lens**, **telephoto lens**, **wide-angle lens**, **zoom lens**.

**lent** /lent/ **Lent** is the past tense and past participle of **lend**.

**Lent** **Lent** is the period of forty days before Easter, during which some Christians give up something that they enjoy. N-UNCOUNT

**len|til** /lentɪl/ **(lentils) Lentils** are the seeds of a lentil plant. They are usually dried and are used to make soups and stews. N-COUNT: usu pl

**Leo** /liːoʊ/ **(Leos)** 1 **Leo** is one of the twelve signs of the zodiac. Its symbol is a lion. People who are born approximately between the 23rd of July and the 22nd of August come under this sign. N-UNCOUNT
2 A **Leo** is a person whose sign of the zodiac is Leo. N-COUNT

**leo|nine** /liːənaɪn/ **Leonine** means like a lion, and is used especially to describe men with a lot of hair on their head, or with big beards. [LITERARY] ❑ *...a tall leonine grey-haired man.* ADJ: usu ADJ n

**leop|ard** /lepəʳd/ **(leopards)** A **leopard** is a type of large, wild cat. Leopards have yellow fur and black spots, and live in Africa and Asia. N-COUNT

**leo|tard** /liːətɑːʳd/ **(leotards)** A **leotard** is a tight-fitting piece of clothing, covering the body but not the legs, that some people wear when they practise dancing or do exercise. N-COUNT

**lep|er** /lepəʳ/ **(lepers)** 1 A **leper** is a person who has leprosy. N-COUNT
2 If you refer to someone as a **leper**, you mean that people in their community avoid them because they have done something that has shocked or offended people. ❑ *The newspaper article had branded her a social leper not fit to be seen in company.* N-COUNT

**lep|ro|sy** /leprəsi/ **Leprosy** is an infectious disease that damages people's flesh. N-UNCOUNT

**les|bian** /lezbiən/ **(lesbians)** ◆◇◇ 1 **Lesbian** is used to describe homosexual women. ❑ *Many of her best friends were lesbian.* ADJ ♦ A **lesbian** is a woman who is lesbian. ❑ *...a youth group for lesbians, gays and bisexuals.* N-COUNT
2 **Lesbian** is used to describe the relationships and activities of homosexual women, and the organizations or publications intended for them or created by them. ❑ *...a long-term lesbian relationship.* ADJ

**les|bi|an|ism** /lezbiənɪzəm/ **Lesbianism** refers to homosexual relationships between women or the preference that a woman shows for sexual relationships with women. ❑ *...today's increased public awareness of lesbianism.* N-UNCOUNT

**le|sion** /liːʒᵊn/ **(lesions)** A **lesion** is an injury or wound to someone's body. [MEDICAL] ❑ *...skin lesions. ...a lesion of the spinal cord.* N-COUNT

**less** /les/ ◆◆◆

> **Less** is often considered to be the comparative form of **little**.

1 You use **less** to indicate that there is a smaller amount of something than before or than average. You can use 'a little', 'a lot', 'a bit', 'far', and 'much' in front of **less**. ❑ *People should eat less fat to reduce the risk of heart disease. ...a dishwasher that uses less water and electricity than older machines.* DET: DET n-uncount ≠ more ♦ **Less** is also a pronoun. ❑ *Borrowers are striving to ease their financial position by spending less and saving more.* PRON ≠ more ♦ **Less** is also a quantifier. ❑ *Last year less of the money went into high-technology companies.* QUANT: QUANT *of* def-n-uncount/sing
2 You use **less than** before a number or amount to say that the actual number or amount is smaller than this. ❑ *Motorways actually cover less than 0.1 percent of the countryside... Less than a half hour later he returned upstairs.* PREP-PHRASE: PREP amount
3 You use **less** to indicate that something or someone has a smaller amount of a quality than they used to or than is average or usual. ❑ *Other amenities, less commonly available, include a library and exercise room... Poverty is less of a problem now than it used to be.* ADV: ADV adj/adv, ADV *of a* n ≠ more
4 If you say that something is **less** one thing **than** another, you mean that it is like the second thing rather than the first. ❑ *At first sight it looked less like a capital city than a mining camp.* ADV: ADV group *than* group/cl
5 If you do something **less** than before or **less** than someone else, you do it to a smaller extent or not as often. ❑ *We are eating more and exercising less... I see less of any of my friends than I used to.* ADV: ADV with v ≠ more
6 You use the expressions **still less**, **much less**, and **even less** after a negative statement in order to introduce and emphasize a further statement, and to make it negative too. [FORMAL] ❑ *I never talked about it, still less about her... The boy didn't have a girlfriend, much less a wife.* PHRASE [emphasis]
7 When you are referring to amounts, you use **less** in front of a number or quantity to indicate that it is to be subtracted from another number or quantity already mentioned. ❑ *...Boyton Financial Services Fees: £750, less £400... Company car drivers will pay between ten and twenty five percent, less tax.* PREP = minus ≠ plus

PHRASES 8 You use **less than** to say that something does not have a particular quality. For example, if you describe something as **less than** perfect, you mean that it is not perfect at all. ❑ *Her greeting was less than enthusiastic... Her advice has frequently been less than wholly helpful.* PHRASE: PHR adj/adv [emphasis]
9 You use **no less than** before an amount to indicate PHRASE: PHR amount [emphasis]

that the amount is larger than you expected. ❑ *No less than 35 per cent of the country is protected in the form of parks and nature sanctuaries... He is lined up for no less than four US television interviews.* 10 **couldn't care less** → see **care**. **more or less** → see **more**.

**-less** /-ləs/ SUFFIX **-less** is added to nouns in order to form adjectives that indicate that someone or something does not have the thing that the noun refers to. ❑ *...drink and talk and meaningless laughter... He is not as friendless as he appeared to be.*

**les|see** /lesiː/ **(lessees)** N-COUNT A **lessee** is a person who has taken out a lease on something such as a house or piece of land. [LEGAL]

**less|en** /lesᵊn/ **(lessens, lessening, lessened)** VERB ≠ *increase* If something **lessens** or you **lessen** it, it becomes smaller in size, amount, degree, or importance. ❑ V *He is used to a lot of attention from his wife, which will inevitably lessen when the baby is born...* V n *Make sure that your immunisations are up to date to lessen the risk of serious illness.* ♦ **less|en|ing** N-UNCOUNT: usu N *of/in* n *...increased trade and a lessening of tension on the border.*

**less|er** /lesəʳ/ 1 ADJ: ADJ n, *the* ADJ *of* n You use **lesser** in order to indicate that something is smaller in extent, degree, or amount than another thing that has been mentioned. ❑ *No medication works in isolation but is affected to a greater or lesser extent by many other factors... The more obvious potential allies are Ireland, Denmark and, to a lesser degree, the Netherlands.* ♦ **Lesser** is also an adverb. ADV: ADV -ed ❑ *...lesser known works by famous artists.* 2 ADJ: ADJ n, *the* ADJ *of* n You can use **lesser** to refer to something or someone that is less important than other things or people of the same type. ❑ *They pleaded guilty to lesser charges of criminal damage... He was feared by other, lesser, men.* 3 **the lesser of two evils** → see **evil**.

**les|son** /lesᵊn/ **(lessons)** ◆◇◇ 1 N-COUNT A **lesson** is a fixed period of time when people are taught about a particular subject or taught how to do something. ❑ *It would be his last French lesson for months... Johanna took piano lessons.* 2 N-COUNT: usu sing You use **lesson** to refer to an experience which acts as a warning to you or an example from which you should learn. ❑ *There's still one lesson to be learned from the crisis – we all need to better understand the thinking of the other side.* ● PHRASE: V inflects If you say that you are going to **teach** someone **a lesson**, you mean that you are going to punish them for something that they have done so that they do not do it again.

**les|sor** /lesɔːʳ/ **(lessors)** N-COUNT A **lessor** is a person who owns something such as a house or piece of land and leases it to someone else. [LEGAL]

**lest** /lest/ CONJ = *in case* If you do something **lest** something unpleasant should happen, you do it to try to prevent the unpleasant thing from happening. [FORMAL] ❑ *I was afraid to open the door lest he should follow me... And, lest we forget, Einstein wrote his most influential papers while working as a clerk.*

**let** /let/ **(lets, letting)** ◆◆◆

> ✔ The form **let** is used in the present tense and is the past tense and past participle.

1 VERB If you **let** something happen, you allow it to happen without doing anything to stop or prevent it. ❑ V n inf *Thorne let him talk...* V n inf *She let the door slam...* V pron-refl inf *I can't let myself be distracted by those things.* 2 VERB If you **let** someone do something, you give them your permission to do it. ❑ V n inf *I love sweets but Mum doesn't let me have them very often...* V n prep/adv *Visa or no visa, they won't let you into the country.* 3 VERB If you **let** someone into, out of, or through a place, you allow them to enter, leave, or go through it, for example by opening a door or making room for them. ❑ V n prep/adv *I had to get up at seven o'clock this morning to let them into the building because they had lost their keys... I'd better go and let the dog out.* 4 VERB: only imper You use **let me** when you are introducing something you want to say. ❑ V *me* inf *Let me tell you what I saw last night... Let me explain why.* 5 VERB: only imper politeness You use **let me** when you are offering politely to do something. ❑ V *me* inf *Let me take your coat... Let me get you something to drink.*

6 VERB: only imper You say **let's** or, in more formal English, **let us**, to direct the attention of the people you are talking to towards the subject that you want to consider next. ❑ V *us* inf *Let's consider ways of making it easier...* V *us* inf *Let us look at these views in more detail.* 7 VERB: only imper You say **let's** or, in formal English, **let us**, when you are making a suggestion that involves both you and the person you are talking to, or when you are agreeing to a suggestion of this kind. ❑ V *us* inf *I'm bored. Let's go home...* V *'s* *'Shall we go in and have some supper?' — 'Yes, let's.'* 8 VERB: only imper politeness Someone in authority, such as a teacher, can use **let's** or, in more formal English, **let us**, in order to give a polite instruction to another person or group of people. ❑ V *us* inf *Let's have some hush, please...* V *us* inf *'Let us pray,' said the Methodist chaplain.* 9 VERB vagueness People often use **let** in expressions such as **let me see** or **let me think** when they are hesitating or thinking of what to say next. ❑ V pron inf *Now, let's see. Where did I leave my bag?...* V pron inf *'How long you been living together then?' — 'Erm, let me think. It's about four years now.'* 10 VERB: only imper You can use **let** to say that you do not care if someone does something, although you think it is unpleasant or wrong. ❑ V n inf *If he wants to do that, let him do it...* V n inf *Let them talk about me; I'll be dead, anyway.* 11 VERB: only imper You can use **let** when you are saying what you think someone should do, usually when they are behaving in a way that you think is unreasonable or wrong. ❑ V n inf *Let him get his own cup of tea.* 12 VERB: only imper You can use **let** when you are praying or hoping very much that something will happen. ❑ V n inf *Please God, let him telephone me.* 13 VERB: only imper You can use **let** to introduce an assumption on which you are going to base a theory, calculation, or story. ❑ V n inf *Let x equal 5 and y equal 3.* 14 VERB = *rent* If you **let** your house or land **to** someone, you allow them to use it in exchange for money that they pay you regularly. [mainly BRIT] ❑ V n *to* n *She is thinking of letting her house to an American serviceman...* V n *The reasons for letting a house, or part of one, are varied.* ♦ **Let out** PHRASAL VERB means the same as **let**. ❑ V n P *I couldn't sell the London flat, so I let it out to pay the mortgage...* V P n (not pron) *Home owners who have extra space available may want to let out a room.*

> ✔ in AM, use **rent**

**PHRASES** 15 PHRASE emphasis **Let alone** is used after a statement, usually a negative one, to indicate that the statement is even more true of the person, thing, or situation that you are going to mention next. ❑ *It is incredible that the 12-year-old managed to even reach the pedals, let alone drive the car.* 16 PHRASE: *let* inflects, oft PHR *of* n If you **let go of** someone or something, you stop holding them. ❑ *She let go of Mona's hand and took a sip of her drink.* 17 PHRASE: *let* inflects If you **let** someone or something **go**, you allow them to leave or escape. ❑ *They held him for three hours and they let him go.* 18 PHRASE: *let* inflects When someone leaves a job, either because they are told to or because they want to, the employer sometimes says that they are **letting** that person **go**. [BUSINESS] ❑ *I've assured him I have no plans to let him go... Peterson was let go after less than two years.* 19 PHRASE: V inflects, usu with brd-neg, PHR n If you say that you did not know what you were **letting yourself in for** when you decided to do something, you mean you did not realize how difficult, unpleasant, or expensive it was going to be. ❑ *He got the impression that Miss Hawes had no idea of what she was letting herself in for.* 20 PHRASE: *let* inflects, oft PHR that/wh, PHR n, PHR *about* n If you **let** someone **know** something, you tell them about it or make sure that they know about it. ❑ *They want to let them know they are safe... If you do want to go, please let me know.* 21 to **let fly** → see **fly**. to **let** your **hair down** → see **hair**. to **let** someone **off the hook** → see **hook**. to **let it be known** → see **known**. to **let the side down** → see **side**. to **let off steam** → see **steam**.

♦ **let down** PHRASAL VERB 1 If you **let** someone **down**, you disappoint them, by not doing something that you have said you will do or that they expected you to do. ❑ V n P *Don't worry, Xiao, I won't let you down...* V P n (not pron) *When such advisers fail in their duty, they* *let down the whole system.* ♦ **let down** *The company now has a large number of workers who feel badly let down.* ADJ: v-link ADJ [2] If something **lets** you **down**, it is the reason you are not as successful as you could have been. PHRASAL VERB ❑ *Many believe it was his shyness and insecurity which let him down... Sadly, the film is let down by an excessively simple plot.* V n P; Also V P n (not pron) [3] If you **let down** something such as a tyre, you allow air to escape from it. [mainly BRIT] PHRASAL VERB = deflate ❑ *I let the tyres down on his car... Remove wheelnuts, let down tyre, put on spare.* V n P; V P n

♦ **let in** If an object **lets in** something such as air, light, or water, it allows air, light, or water to get into it, for example because the object has a hole in it. PHRASAL VERB ❑ *...balconies shaded with lattice-work which lets in air but not light.* V P n (not pron); Also V n P

♦ **let in on** If you **let** someone **in on** something that is a secret from most people, you allow them to know about it. PHRASAL VERB ❑ *I'm going to let you in on a little secret.* V n P P n

♦ **let into** If you **let** someone **into** a secret, you allow them to know it. PHRASAL VERB ❑ *I'll let you into a little showbiz secret.* V n P n

♦ **let off** [1] If someone in authority **lets** you **off** a task or duty, they give you permission not to do it. [mainly BRIT] PHRASAL VERB ❑ *In those days they didn't let you off work to go home very often.* V n P n/-ing [2] If you **let** someone **off**, you give them a lighter punishment than they expect or no punishment at all. PHRASAL VERB ❑ *Because he was a Christian, the judge let him off... When police realised who he was, they asked for an autograph and let him off with a warning.* V n P; V n P prep/adv [3] If you **let off** an explosive or a gun, you explode or fire it. PHRASAL VERB ❑ *A resident of his neighbourhood had let off fireworks to celebrate the Revolution.* V P n (not pron); Also V n P

♦ **let on** If you do not **let on** that something is true, you do not tell anyone that it is true, and you keep it a secret. [INFORMAL] PHRASAL VERB: usu with brd-neg ❑ *She never let on that anything was wrong... I didn't let on to the staff what my conversation was... He knows the culprit but is not letting on.* V P that/wh; V P *to* n that/wh; V P

♦ **let out** [1] If something or someone **lets** water, air, or breath **out**, they allow it to flow out or escape. PHRASAL VERB ❑ *It lets sunlight in but doesn't let heat out... Meer let out his breath in a long sigh.* V n P; V P n [2] If you **let out** a particular sound, you make that sound. [WRITTEN] PHRASAL VERB = give out ❑ *When she saw him, she let out a cry of horror.* V P n; Also V n P [3] ➔ See also **let 14**.

♦ **let up** If an unpleasant, continuous process **lets up**, it stops or becomes less intense. PHRASAL VERB: oft with brd-neg ❑ *The rain had let up.* V P ➔ See also **let-up**.

**let-down** **(let-downs)** also **letdown**. A **let-down** is a disappointment that you suffer, usually because something has not happened in the way in which you expected it to happen. N-VAR = disappointment ❑ *The flat was really very nice, but compared with what we'd been used to, it was a terrible let-down... The sense of let-down today is all the greater because in the past doctors have been over-confident about these treatments.*

**le|thal** /liːθəl/ [1] A substance that is **lethal** can kill people or animals. ADJ ❑ *...a lethal dose of sleeping pills.* [2] If you describe something as **lethal**, you mean that it is capable of causing a lot of damage. ADJ ❑ *Frost and wet are the lethal combination for plants.*

**le|thar|gic** /lɪθɑːʳdʒɪk/ If you are **lethargic**, you do not have much energy or enthusiasm. ADJ ≠ energetic ❑ *He felt too miserable and lethargic to get dressed.*

**leth|ar|gy** /leθəʳdʒi/ **Lethargy** is the condition or state of being lethargic. N-UNCOUNT ❑ *Symptoms include tiredness, paleness, and lethargy.*

**let's** /lets/ **Let's** is the usual spoken form of 'let us'. ◆◆◇

**let|ter** /letəʳ/ **(letters, lettering, lettered)** ◆◆◆ [1] If you write a **letter** to someone, you write a message on paper and send it to them, usually by post. N-COUNT: also *by* N ❑ *I had received a letter from a very close friend. ...a letter of resignation... Our long courtship had been conducted mostly by letter.* [2] **Letters** are written symbols which represent one of the sounds in a language. N-COUNT ❑ *...the letters of the alphabet. ...the letter E.* [3] If a student earns a **letter** in sports or athletics by being part of the university or college team, they are entitled to wear on their jacket the initial letter of the name of their university or college. [AM] N-COUNT ❑ *Valerie earned letters in three sports: volleyball, basketball, and field hockey.* [4] If a student **letters** in sports or athletics by being part of the university or college team, they are entitled to wear on their jacket the initial letter of the name of their university or college. [AM] VERB ❑ *Burkoth lettered in soccer.* V prep [5] ➔ See also **capital letter**, **covering letter**, **dead letter**, **love letter**, **newsletter**, **poison-pen letter**. [6] If you say that someone carries out instructions **to the letter**, you mean that they do exactly what they are told to do, paying great attention to every detail. PHRASE: PHR after v ❑ *She obeyed his instructions to the letter.*

**let|ter bomb** **(letter bombs)** A **letter bomb** is a small bomb which is disguised as a letter or parcel and sent to someone through the post. It is designed to explode when it is opened. N-COUNT

**let|ter|box** /letəʳbɒks/ **(letterboxes)** also **letter box**. [1] A **letterbox** is a rectangular hole in a door or a small box at the entrance to a building into which letters and small parcels are delivered. Compare **post box**. [mainly BRIT] N-COUNT ➔ See picture on page 1705.

☑ in AM, usually use **mailbox**

[2] If something is displayed on a television or computer screen in **letterbox** format, it is displayed across the middle of the screen with dark bands at the top and bottom of the screen. ADJ

**let|tered** /letəʳd/ Something that is **lettered** is covered or decorated with letters or words. ADJ ❑ *...a crudely lettered cardboard sign.*

**letter|head** /letəʳhed/ **(letterheads)** A **letterhead** is the name and address of a person, company, or organization which is printed at the top of their writing paper. N-COUNT ❑ *Colleagues at work enjoy having a letterhead with their name at the top.*

**let|ter|ing** /letərɪŋ/ **Lettering** is writing, especially when you are describing the type of letters used. N-UNCOUNT: usu supp N ❑ *...a small blue sign with white lettering.*

**let|ter of cred|it** **(letters of credit)** [1] A **letter of credit** is a letter written by a bank authorizing another bank to pay someone a sum of money. Letters of credit are often used by importers and exporters. [BUSINESS] N-COUNT [2] A **letter of credit** is a written promise from a bank stating that they will repay bonds to lenders if the borrowers is unable to pay them. [BUSINESS] N-COUNT ❑ *The project is being backed by a letter of credit from Lasalle Bank.*

**let|tuce** /letɪs/ **(lettuces)** A **lettuce** is a plant with large green leaves that is the basic ingredient of many salads. N-VAR ➔ See picture on page 1712.

**let-up** If there is **no let-up in** something, usually something unpleasant, there is no reduction in the intensity of it. N-UNCOUNT: also *a* N, usu with brd-neg ❑ *There was no let-up in the battle on the money markets yesterday.*

**leu|kae|mia** /lukiːmiə/

☑ in AM, use **leukemia**

**Leukaemia** is a disease of the blood in which the body produces too many white blood cells. N-UNCOUNT

**lev|el** /levəl/ **(levels, levelling, levelled)** ◆◆◆

☑ in AM, use **leveling, leveled**

[1] A **level** is a point on a scale, for example a scale of amount, quality, or difficulty. N-COUNT: with supp ❑ *If you don't know your cholesterol level, it's a good idea to have it checked... We do have the lowest level of inflation for some years... The exercises are marked according to their level of difficulty.* [2] The **level** of a river, lake, or ocean or the **level** of liquid in a container is the height of its surface. N-SING: the N ❑ *The water level of the Mississippi River is already 6.5 feet below normal... The gauge relies upon a sensor in the tank to relay the fuel level.* ➔ See also **sea level**. [3] In cookery, a **level** spoonful of a substance such as flour or sugar is ADJ: ADJ n ≠ heaped

an amount that fills the spoon exactly, without going above the top edge. ❑ *Stir in 1 level teaspoon of yeast.* [4] If something is at a particular **level**, it is at that height. ❑ *Liz sank down until the water came up to her chin and the bubbles were at eye level.* N-SING: usu supp N [5] If one thing is **level with** another thing, it is at the same height as it. ❑ *He leaned over the counter so his face was almost level with the boy's... Amy knelt down so that their eyes were level.* ADJ: v-link ADJ, oft ADJ *with* n [6] When something is **level**, it is completely flat with no part higher than any other. ❑ *The floor was level, but the ceiling sloped toward his head. ...a plateau of fairly level ground.* ADJ [7] If you draw **level** with someone or something, you get closer to them until you are by their side. [mainly BRIT] ❑ *Just before we drew level with the gates, he slipped out of the jeep and disappeared into the crowd.* ADV: ADV after v ♦ **Level** is also an adjective. ❑ *He waited until they were level with the door before he turned around sharply and punched Graham.* ADJ: v-link ADJ, oft ADJ *with* n [8] If someone or something such as a violent storm **levels** a building or area of land, they destroy it completely or make it completely flat. ❑ *The storm was the most powerful to hit Hawaii this century. It leveled sugar plantations and destroyed homes.* VERB V n [9] If an accusation or criticism **is levelled at** someone, they are accused of doing wrong or they are criticized for something they have done. ❑ *Allegations of corruption were levelled at him and his family... He leveled bitter criticism against the US.* VERB *be* V-ed *at/against* n V n *at/against* n [10] If you **level** an object at someone or something, you lift it and point it in their direction. ❑ *He said thousands of Koreans still levelled guns at one another along the demilitarised zone between them.* VERB V n *at* n Also V n [11] If you **level with** someone, you tell them the truth and do not keep anything secret. [INFORMAL] ❑ *I'll level with you. I'm no great detective. I've no training or anything.* VERB V *with* n [12] ➔ See also **A level**. [13] If you say that you will **do** your **level best** to do something, you are emphasizing that you will try as hard as you can to do it, even if the situation makes it very difficult. ❑ *The President told American troops that he would do his level best to bring them home soon.* PHRASE: V inflects, usu PHR to-inf [emphasis] [14] a **level playing field** ➔ see **playing field**.

♦ **level off** or **level out** [1] If a changing number or amount **levels off** or **levels out**, it stops increasing or decreasing at such a fast speed. ❑ *The figures show evidence that murders in the nation's capital are beginning to level off... Inflation is finally levelling out at around 11% a month.* PHRASAL VERB V P V P prep [2] If an aircraft **levels off** or **levels out**, it travels horizontally after having been travelling in an upwards or downwards direction. ❑ *The aircraft levelled out at about 30,000 feet.* PHRASAL VERB V P

♦ **level out** ➔ see **level off**.

**lev|el cross|ing** (**level crossings**) A **level crossing** is a place where a railway line crosses a road. [BRIT] N-COUNT

> in AM, use **grade crossing, railroad crossing**

**level-headed** If you describe a person as **level-headed**, you mean that they are calm and sensible even in difficult situations. ❑ *Simon is level-headed and practical... His level-headed approach suggests he will do what is necessary.* ADJ = sensible

**lev|el|ler** /levələʳ/ (**levellers**)

> in AM, use **leveler**

If you describe something as a **leveller**, you mean that it makes all people seem the same, in spite of their differences in, for example, age or social status. ❑ *The computer is a leveller, making information available to everyone.* N-COUNT: usu sing, oft adj N

**lev|el peg|ging** also **level-pegging.** If two opponents in a competition or contest are **level pegging**, they are equal with each other. [BRIT] ❑ *An opinion poll published in May showed Mrs Yardley was level-pegging with Mr Simpson.* ADJ: v-link ADJ, oft ADJ *with* n

**lev|er** /liːvəʳ, AM also lev-/ (**levers, levering, levered**) [1] A **lever** is a handle or bar that is attached to a piece of machinery and which you push or pull in order to operate the machinery. ❑ *Push the tiny lever on the lock... The taps have a lever to control the mix of hot and cold water.* ➔ See also **gear lever**. N-COUNT [2] A **lever** is a long bar, one end of which is placed under a heavy object so that when you press down on the other end you can move the object. N-COUNT [3] If you **lever** something in a particular direction, you move it there, especially by using a lot of effort. ❑ *Neighbours eventually levered open the door with a crowbar... Insert the fork about 6in. from the root and simultaneously lever it backwards.* VERB V n with adj V n adv/prep [4] A **lever** is an idea or action that you can use to make people do what you want them to do, rather than what they want to do. ❑ *Radical, militant factions want to continue using the hostages as a lever to gain concessions from the west.* N-COUNT

**lev|er|age** /liːvərɪdʒ, AM lev-/ (**leverages, leveraging, leveraged**) [1] **Leverage** is the ability to influence situations or people so that you can control what happens. ❑ *His function as a Mayor affords him the leverage to get things done through attending committee meetings.* N-UNCOUNT [2] **Leverage** is the force that is applied to an object when something such as a lever is used. ❑ *The spade and fork have longer shafts, providing better leverage.* N-UNCOUNT [3] To **leverage** a company or investment means to use borrowed money in order to buy it or pay for it. [BUSINESS] ❑ *He might feel that leveraging the company at a time when he sees tremendous growth opportunities would be a mistake.* VERB V n ♦ **lev|er|aged** *The committee voted to limit tax refunds for corporations involved in leveraged buyouts.* ADJ: usu ADJ n

**le|via|than** /lɪvaɪəθən/ (**leviathans**) A **leviathan** is something which is extremely large and difficult to control, and which you find rather frightening. [LITERARY] ❑ *Democracy survived the Civil War and the developing industrial leviathan and struggled on into the twentieth century.* N-COUNT: usu sing

**Levi's** /liːvaɪz/ also **Levis. Levi's** are jeans. [TRADEMARK] N-PLURAL: also *a pair of* N

**levi|tate** /levɪteɪt/ (**levitates, levitating, levitated**) If someone or something **levitates**, they appear to rise and float in the air without any support from other people or objects. ❑ *He has claimed he can levitate... Nina can, apparently, levitate a small ball between her hands.* VERB V V n ♦ **levi|ta|tion** /levɪteɪʃᵊn/ *...such magical powers as levitation, prophecy, and healing.* N-UNCOUNT

**lev|ity** /levɪti/ **Levity** is behaviour that shows a tendency to treat serious matters in a non-serious way. [LITERARY] ❑ *At the time, Arnold had disapproved of such levity.* N-UNCOUNT = frivolity

**levy** /levi/ (**levies, levying, levied**) [1] A **levy** is a sum of money that you have to pay, for example as a tax to the government. ❑ *...an annual motorway levy on all drivers.* N-COUNT [2] If a government or organization **levies** a tax or other sum of money, it demands it from people or organizations. ❑ *They levied religious taxes on Christian commercial transactions... Taxes should not be levied without the authority of Parliament.* VERB V n *on* n V n

**lewd** /ljuːd, AM luːd/ If you describe someone's behaviour as **lewd**, you are critical of it because it is sexual in a rude and unpleasant way. ❑ *Drew spends all day eyeing up the women and making lewd comments.* ADJ [disapproval] ♦ **lewd|ness** *The critics condemned the play for lewdness.* N-UNCOUNT

**lexi|cal** /leksɪkᵊl/ **Lexical** means relating to the words of a language. ❑ *We chose a few of the commonest lexical items in the languages.* ADJ: usu ADJ n

**lexi|cog|ra|phy** /leksɪkɒgrəfi/ **Lexicography** is the activity or profession of writing dictionaries. N-UNCOUNT ♦ **lexi|cog|ra|pher** (**lexicographers**) ❑ *A lexicographer's job is to describe the language.* N-COUNT

**lexi|con** /leksɪkən/ (**lexicons**) [1] The **lexicon** of a particular subject is all the terms associated with it. The **lexicon** of a person or group is all the words they commonly use. ❑ *...the lexicon of management... Chocolate equals sin in most people's lexicon.* N-SING: with supp [2] A **lexicon** is an alphabetical list of the N-COUNT words in a language or the words associated with a particular subject.

**lex|is** /leksɪs/ In linguistics, the words of a language can be referred to as the **lexis** of that language. [TECHNICAL] N-UNCOUNT = *vocabulary*

**lia|bil|ity** /laɪəbɪlɪti/ **(liabilities)** [1] If you say that someone or something is **a liability**, you mean that they cause a lot of problems or embarrassment. ❑ *As the president's prestige continues to fall, they're clearly beginning to consider him a liability. ...what was once a vote catching policy, is now a political liability.* N-COUNT: usu sing [2] A company's or organization's **liabilities** are the sums of money which it owes. [BUSINESS or LEGAL] ❑ *The company had assets of $138 million and liabilities of $120.5 million.* N-COUNT: usu pl ≠ *asset* [3] → See also **liable**.

**lia|ble** /laɪəbᵊl/ [1] When something **is liable to** happen, it is very likely to happen. ❑ *Only a small minority of the mentally ill are liable to harm themselves or others.* PHRASE [2] If people or things are **liable to** something unpleasant, they are likely to experience it or do it. ❑ *She will grow into a woman particularly liable to depression... Steroids are used to reduce the inflammation, which makes the muscles of the airways liable to constriction.* ADJ: v-link ADJ *to* n = *prone* [3] If you are **liable for** something such as a debt, you are legally responsible for it. ❑ *The airline's insurer is liable for damages to the victims' families... As the killings took place outside British jurisdiction, the Ministry of Defence could not be held liable.* ADJ: v-link ADJ, usu ADJ *for* n ♦ **lia|bil|ity** /laɪəbɪlɪti/ *He is claiming damages from London Underground, which has admitted liability but disputes the amount of his claim.* N-UNCOUNT

**li|aise** /lieɪz/ **(liaises, liaising, liaised)** When organizations or people **liaise**, or when one organization **liaises with** another, they work together and keep each other informed about what is happening. ❑ *Detectives are liaising with Derbyshire police following the bomb explosion early today... The three groups will all liaise with each other to help the child... Social services and health workers liaise closely.* V-RECIP; V *with* n; pl-n V *with* pron-recip; pl-n V

**liai|son** /lieɪzɒn, AM liːeɪz-/ [1] **Liaison** is co-operation and the exchange of information between different organizations or between different sections of an organization. ❑ *Liaison between police forces and the art world is vital to combat art crime. ...those who work in close liaison with alcoholics.* N-UNCOUNT [2] If someone acts as **liaison** with a particular group, or **between** two or more groups, their job is to encourage co-operation and the exchange of information. ❑ *I have a professor on my staff here as liaison with our higher education institutions... She acts as a liaison between patients and staff.* N-UNCOUNT: also *a* N, oft N *with* n [3] You can refer to a sexual or romantic relationship between two people as a **liaison**. ❑ *She embarked on a series of sexual liaisons with society figures.* N-COUNT = *affair*

**liar** /laɪəʳ/ **(liars)** If you say that someone is a **liar**, you mean that they tell lies. ❑ *He was a liar and a cheat... 'She seems at times an accomplished liar,' he said.* N-COUNT

**lib** /lɪb/ **Lib** is used in the names of some movements that are concerned with achieving social and legal freedom for particular groups in society. **Lib** is an abbreviation for 'liberation'. ❑ *...Women's Lib.* → See also **ad-lib**. N-UNCOUNT

**li|ba|tion** /laɪbeɪʃᵊn/ **(libations)** In ancient Greece and Rome, a **libation** was an alcoholic drink that was offered to the gods. [LITERARY] N-COUNT

**Lib Dem** /lɪb dem/ **(Lib Dems)** In Britain, you can refer to the Liberal Democrat Party or its members as **the Lib Dems**. ❑ *Three published polls all revealed the Lib Dems gaining ground at the Tories' expense. ...Lib-Dem councillors.* N-PROPER: *the* N, N n

**li|bel** /laɪbᵊl/ **(libels, libelling, libelled)**

☑ in AM, use **libeling, libeled**

[1] **Libel** is a written statement which wrongly accuses someone of something, and which is therefore against the law. Compare **slander**. [LEGAL] ❑ *Warren sued him for libel over the remarks. ...a libel action against the paper.* N-VAR [2] To **libel** someone means to write or print something in a book, newspaper, or magazine which wrongly damages that person's reputation and is therefore against the law. [LEGAL] ❑ *The newspaper which libelled him had already offered compensation.* VERB; V n

**li|bel|lous** /laɪbələs/

☑ in AM, use **libelous**

If a statement in a book, newspaper, or magazine is **libellous**, it wrongly accuses someone of something, and is therefore against the law. ❑ *He claimed the articles were libellous and damaging to the interests of the team.* ADJ

**lib|er|al** /lɪbərəl/ **(liberals)** ◆◆◇ [1] Someone who has **liberal** views believes people should have a lot of freedom in deciding how to behave and think. ❑ *She is known to have liberal views on divorce and contraception.* ADJ: usu ADJ n ♦ **Liberal** is also a noun. ❑ *...a nation of free-thinking liberals.* N-COUNT [2] A **liberal** system allows people or organizations a lot of political or economic freedom. ❑ *...a liberal democracy with a multiparty political system... They favour liberal free-market policies.* ADJ: usu ADJ n ♦ **Liberal** is also a noun. ❑ *These kinds of price controls go against all the financial principles of the free market liberals.* N-COUNT [3] A **Liberal** politician or voter is a member of a Liberal Party or votes for a Liberal Party. ❑ *The Liberal leader has announced his party's withdrawal from the ruling coalition.* ADJ: ADJ n ♦ **Liberal** is also a noun. ❑ *The Liberals hold twenty-three seats in parliament.* N-COUNT [4] **Liberal** means giving, using, or taking a lot of something, or existing in large quantities. ❑ *As always he is liberal with his jokes... She made liberal use of her elder sister's make-up and clothes.* ADJ: oft ADJ *with* n ♦ **lib|er|al|ly** *Chemical products were used liberally over agricultural land.* ADV: ADV with v

**lib|er|al arts** At a university or college, **liberal arts** courses are on subjects such as history or literature rather than science, law, medicine, or business. [AM] N-PLURAL

**Lib|er|al Demo|crat (Liberal Democrats)** In Britain, a **Liberal Democrat** is a member of the Liberal Democrat Party. N-PROPER

**Lib|er|al Demo|crat Par|ty The Liberal Democrat Party** is the third largest political party in Britain and the main centre party. It believes in improving the constitution and the voting system and in providing good welfare services. N-PROPER: *the* N, N n

**lib|er|al|ism** /lɪbərəlɪzəm/ [1] **Liberalism** is a belief in gradual social progress by changing laws, rather than by revolution. ❑ *...a democrat who has decided that economic liberalism is the best way to secure change. ...the tradition of nineteenth-century liberalism.* N-UNCOUNT [2] **Liberalism** is the belief that people should have a lot of political and individual freedom. ❑ *He was concerned over growing liberalism in the Church.* N-UNCOUNT

**lib|er|al|ize** /lɪbrəlaɪz/ **(liberalizes, liberalizing, liberalized)**

☑ in BRIT, also use **liberalise**

When a country or government **liberalizes**, or **liberalizes** its laws or its attitudes, it becomes less strict and allows people more freedom in their actions. ❑ *...authoritarian states that have only now begun to liberalise. ...the decision to liberalize travel restrictions.* VERB; V; V n ♦ **lib|er|ali|za|tion** /lɪbrəlaɪzeɪʃᵊn/ *...the liberalization of divorce laws in the late 1960s.* N-UNCOUNT: oft N *of* n = *relaxation*

**Lib|er|al Par|ty** In Britain, **the Liberal Party** was a political party which believed in limited controls on industry, the providing of welfare services, and more local government and individual freedom. **Liberal Party** is also used to refer to similar parties in some other countries. N-PROPER: *the* N, N n

**lib|er|ate** /lɪbəreɪt/ **(liberates, liberating, liberated)** ◆◇◇ [1] To **liberate** a place or the people in it means to free them from the political or military control of another country, area, or group of people. ❑ *They planned to march on and liberate the city.* VERB; V n ♦ **lib|era|tion** /lɪbəreɪʃᵊn/ *...a mass liberation movement.* N-UNCOUNT [2] To **liberate** someone **from** something means to help them escape from it or over- VERB = *free*

come it, and lead a better way of life. ❑ *He asked how committed the leadership was to liberating its people from poverty.* ♦ **lib|er|at|ing** *If you have the chance to spill your problems out to a therapist it can be a very liberating experience.* ♦ **lib|era|tion** *...the women's liberation movement.* [3] To **liberate** a prisoner means to set them free. ❑ *The government is devising a plan to liberate prisoners held in detention camps.*
V n *from* n; Also V n; ADJ; N-UNCOUNT; VERB; V n

**lib|er|at|ed** /lɪbəreɪtɪd/ If you describe someone as **liberated**, you mean that they do not accept their society's traditional values or restrictions on behaviour. ❑ *She was determined that she would become a liberated businesswoman.*
ADJ; approval; = *emancipated*

**lib|era|tion the|ol|ogy** **Liberation theology** is the belief that the Christian Church should be actively involved in politics in order to bring about social change.
N-UNCOUNT

**lib|era|tor** /lɪbəreɪtəʳ/ **(liberators)** A **liberator** is someone who sets people free from a system, situation, or set of ideas that restricts them in some way. [FORMAL] ❑ *We were the people's liberators from the Bolsheviks.*
N-COUNT

**Li|berian** /laɪbɪəriən/ **(Liberians)** [1] **Liberian** means belonging or relating to Liberia, its people, or its culture. [2] A **Liberian** is a person who comes from Liberia, or a person of Liberian origin.
ADJ; N-COUNT

**lib|er|tar|ian** /lɪbəʳteəriən/ **(libertarians)** If someone is **libertarian** or has **libertarian** attitudes, they believe in or support the idea that people should be free to think and behave in the way that they want. [FORMAL] ❑ *...the libertarian argument that people should be allowed to choose.* ♦ A **libertarian** is someone who with libertarian views. ❑ *Libertarians argue that nothing should be censored.*
ADJ; = *liberal*; N-COUNT; = *liberal*

**lib|er|tine** /lɪbəʳtiːn/ **(libertines)** If you refer to someone as a **libertine**, you mean that they are sexually immoral and do not care about the effect their behaviour has on other people. [LITERARY]
N-COUNT; disapproval

**lib|er|ty** /lɪbəʳti/ **(liberties)** [1] **Liberty** is the freedom to live your life in the way that you want, without interference from other people or the authorities. ❑ *Wit Wolzek claimed the legislation could impinge on privacy, self determination and respect for religious liberty... Such a system would be a fundamental blow to the rights and liberties of the English people.* → See also **civil liberties**. [2] **Liberty** is the freedom to go wherever you want, which you lose when you are a prisoner. ❑ *Why not say that three convictions before court for stealing cars means three months' loss of liberty.*
◆◇◇; N-VAR; = *freedom*; N-UNCOUNT: oft *at* N

**PHRASES** [3] If someone is **at liberty to** do something, they have been given permission to do it. ❑ *The island's in the Pacific Ocean; I'm not at liberty to say exactly where, because we're still negotiating for its purchase.* [4] If you say that you have **taken the liberty of** doing something, you are saying that you have done it without asking permission. People say this when they do not think that anyone will mind what they have done. ❑ *I took the liberty of going into Assunta's wardrobe, as it was open; I was looking for a towel.* [5] If you **take liberties** or **take a liberty** with someone or something, you act in a way that is too free and does not show enough respect. ❑ *Try and retain the excitement of the event in your writing, without taking liberties with the truth... She knew she was taking a big liberty in developing Mick's photos without his knowledge.*
PHRASE: PHR to-inf, usu v-link PHR; = *able*; PHRASE: V inflects, PHR -ing; politeness; PHRASE: V and N inflect, oft PHR *with* n

**li|bidi|nous** /lɪbɪdɪnəs/ People who are **libidinous** have strong sexual feelings and express them in their behaviour. [LITERARY] ❑ *Powell let his libidinous imagination run away with him.*
ADJ

**li|bi|do** /lɪbiːdoʊ/ **(libidos)** A person's **libido** is the part of their personality that is considered to cause their emotional, especially sexual, desires. ❑ *Lack of sleep is a major factor in loss of libido.*
N-VAR

**Li|bra** /liːbrə/ **(Libras)** [1] **Libra** is one of the twelve signs of the zodiac. Its symbol is a pair of scales. People who are born approximately between the 23rd of September and the 22nd of October come under this sign. [2] A **Libra** is a person whose sign of the zodiac is Libra.
N-UNCOUNT; N-COUNT

**li|brar|ian** /laɪbreəriən/ **(librarians)** A **librarian** is a person who is in charge of a library or who has been specially trained to work in a library.
N-COUNT

**li|brary** /laɪbrəri, AM -breri/ **(libraries)** [1] A public **library** is a building where things such as books, newspapers, videos, and music are kept for people to read, use, or borrow. ❑ *...the local library... She issued them library cards.* [2] A private **library** is a collection of things such as books or music, that is normally only used with the permission of the owner. ❑ *My thanks go to the British School of Osteopathy, for the use of their library.*
◆◇◇; N-COUNT; N-COUNT

**li|bret|tist** /lɪbretɪst/ **(librettists)** A **librettist** is a person who writes the words that are used in an opera or musical play.
N-COUNT

**li|bret|to** /lɪbretoʊ/ **(librettos** or **libretti)** The **libretto** of an opera is the words that are sung in it. ❑ *...the author of one or two opera librettos.*
N-COUNT

**Liby|an** /lɪbiən/ **(Libyans)** [1] **Libyan** means belonging or relating to Libya, or to its people or culture. [2] A **Libyan** is a Libyan citizen, or a person of Libyan origin.
ADJ; N-COUNT

**lice** /laɪs/ **Lice** is the plural of **louse**.

**li|cence** /laɪsəns/ **(licences)** ◆◇◇

✔ in AM, use **license**

[1] A **licence** is an official document which gives you permission to do, use, or own something. ❑ *Payne lost his driving licence a year ago for drink-driving... The painting was returned to Spain on a temporary import licence... It gained a licence to operate as a bank from the Bank of England in 1981.* [2] If you say that something gives someone **licence** or **a licence to** act in a particular way, you mean that it gives them an excuse to behave in an irresponsible or excessive way. ❑ *'Dropping the charges has given racists a licence to kill,' said Jim's aunt.* [3] → See also **poetic licence**. [4] If someone does something **under licence**, they do it by special permission from a government or other authority. ❑ *...a company which made the Mig-21 jet fighter under licence from Russia.*
N-COUNT; N-UNCOUNT: also *a* N, N to-inf; disapproval; PHRASE: PHR after v

**li|cense** /laɪsəns/ **(licenses, licensing, licensed)** To **license** a person or activity means to give official permission for the person to do something or for the activity to take place. ❑ *...a proposal that would require the state to license guns... Under the agreement, the council can license a U.S. company to produce the drug.*
VERB; V n; V n to-inf; Also V n *to* n

**li|censed** /laɪsənst/ [1] If you are **licensed to** do something, you have official permission from the government or from the authorities to do it. ❑ *There were about 250 people on board, about 100 more than the ferry was licensed to carry. ...a licensed doctor.* [2] If something that you own or use is **licensed**, you have official permission to own it or use it. ❑ *While searching the house they discovered an unlicensed shotgun and a licensed rifle.* [3] If a place such as a restaurant or hotel is **licensed**, it has been given a licence to sell alcoholic drinks. [BRIT] ❑ *...licensed premises.*
ADJ: oft ADJ to-inf; ADJ; ADJ

**li|cen|see** /laɪsənsiː/ **(licensees)** [1] A **licensee** is a person or organization that has been given a licence. [FORMAL] [2] A **licensee** is someone who has been given a licence to sell alcoholic drinks, for example in a pub. [BRIT]
N-COUNT; N-COUNT

**li|cense num|ber** **(license numbers)** The **license number** of a car or other road vehicle is the series of letters and numbers that are shown at the front and back of it. [AM]
N-COUNT

✔ in BRIT, use **registration number**

**li|cense plate (license plates)** A **license plate** is a sign on the front and back of a vehicle that shows its license number. [AM] ➔ See picture on page 1707. N-COUNT

in BRIT, use **number plate**

**li|cens|ing laws** In Britain, the **licensing laws** are the laws which control the selling of alcoholic drinks. N-PLURAL

**li|cen|tious** /laɪse̲ntʃəs/ If you describe a person as **licentious**, you mean that they are very immoral, especially in their sexual behaviour. [FORMAL] ❑ *...alarming stories of licentious behaviour.* ADJ disapproval
♦ **li|cen|tious|ness** *...moral licentiousness.* N-UNCOUNT

**li|chen** /la̲ɪkən/ **(lichens) Lichen** is a group of tiny plants that looks like moss and grows on the surface of things such as rocks, trees, and walls. N-MASS

**lick** /lɪ̲k/ **(licks, licking, licked)** [1] When people or animals **lick** something, they move their tongue across its surface. ❑ *The dog rose awkwardly to his feet and licked the man's hand excitedly.* VERB V n ♦ **Lick** is also a noun. ❑ *Kevin wanted a lick of Sarah's lollipop.* N-COUNT: usu sing [2] to **lick** your **lips** ➔ see **lip**. to **lick into shape** ➔ see **shape**.

**lick|ing** /lɪ̲kɪŋ/ **(lickings)** A **licking** is a severe defeat by someone in a fight, battle, or competition. ❑ *They gave us a hell of a licking.* N-COUNT: usu sing = thrashing

**lico|rice** /lɪ̲kərɪʃ, -ɪs/

in BRIT, also use **liquorice**

**Licorice** is a firm black substance with a strong taste. It is used for making sweets. N-UNCOUNT

**lid** /lɪ̲d/ **(lids)** [1] A **lid** is the top of a box or other container which can be removed or raised when you want to open the container. ➔ See picture on page 1710. N-COUNT = top [2] Your **lids** are the pieces of skin which cover your eyes when you close them. ❑ *A dull pain began to throb behind his lids.* N-COUNT: usu pl = eyelid [3] If you say that someone is **keeping the lid on** an activity or a piece of information, you mean that they are restricting the activity or are keeping the information secret. [INFORMAL] ❑ *The soldiers' presence seemed to keep a lid on the violence... Their finance ministry is still trying to put a lid on the long-simmering securities scandal.* N-SING

**lid|ded** /lɪ̲dɪd/ [1] **Lidded** is used to describe a container that has a lid. ❑ *...a lidded saucepan.* ADJ: ADJ n [2] When someone has **lidded** eyes, their eyelids are partly or fully closed. [LITERARY] ❑ *Julie squinted at her through lidded eyes.* ADJ

**lido** /li̲ːdoʊ/ **(lidos)** A **lido** is an outdoor swimming pool or a part of a beach which is used by the public for swimming or water sports. [mainly BRIT] N-COUNT

**lie**
① POSITION OR SITUATION
② THINGS THAT ARE NOT TRUE

**① lie** /la̲ɪ/ **(lies, lying, lay, lain)** ♦♦◇
⇛ Please look at category 8 to see if the expression you are looking for is shown under another headword. [1] If you **are lying** somewhere, you are in a horizontal position and are not standing or sitting. ❑ *There was a child lying on the ground... He lay awake watching her for a long time.* VERB V prep/adv V adj [2] If an object **lies** in a particular place, it is in a flat position in that place. ❑ *...a newspaper lying on a nearby couch... Broken glass lay scattered on the carpet.* VERB V prep/adv V adj [3] If you say that a place **lies** in a particular position or direction, you mean that it is situated there. ❑ *The islands lie at the southern end of the Kurile chain.* VERB = sit V prep/adv [4] You can use **lie** to say that something is or remains in a particular state or condition. For example, if something **lies forgotten**, it has been and remains forgotten. ❑ *The picture lay hidden in the archives for over 40 years... His country's economy lies in ruins.* V-LINK V adj V prep [5] You can use **lie** to say what position a competitor or team is in during a competition. [mainly BRIT] ❑ *I was going well and was lying fourth... Blyth Tait is lying in second place.* VERB V ord V *in* n [6] You can talk about where something such as a problem, solution, or fault **lies** to say what you think it consists of, involves, or is caused by. ❑ *The problem lay in the large amounts spent on defence.* VERB V prep/adv [7] You use **lie** in expressions such as **lie ahead**, **lie in store**, and **lie in wait** when you are talking about what someone is going to experience in the future, especially when it is something unpleasant or difficult. ❑ *She'd need all her strength and bravery to cope with what lay in store... The President's most serious challenges lie ahead.* VERB V prep/adv V prep/adv [8] to **lie in state** ➔ see **state**. to **take** something **lying down** ➔ see **take**.

♦ **lie around**

in BRIT, also use **lie about**

If things are left **lying around** or **lying about**, they are not tidied away but left casually somewhere where they can be seen. ❑ *People should be careful about their possessions and not leave them lying around.* PHRASAL VERB V P

♦ **lie behind** If you refer to what **lies behind** a situation or event, you are referring to the reason the situation exists or the event happened. ❑ *It seems that what lay behind the clashes was disagreement over the list of candidates.* PHRASAL VERB V P n

♦ **lie down** When you **lie down**, you move into a horizontal position, usually in order to rest or sleep. ❑ *Why don't you go upstairs and lie down for a bit?* PHRASAL VERB V P

**② lie** /la̲ɪ/ **(lies, lying, lied)** [1] A **lie** is something that someone says or writes which they know is untrue. ❑ *'Who else do you work for?' — 'No one.' — 'That's a lie.'... I've had enough of your lies... All the boys told lies about their adventures.* ➔ See also **white lie**. ♦◇◇ N-COUNT [2] If someone **is lying**, they are saying something which they know is not true. ❑ *I know he's lying... If asked, he lies about his age... She lied to her husband so she could meet her lover... He reportedly called her 'a lying little twit'.* VERB V V *about* n V *to* n V-ing ♦ **ly|ing** *Lying is something that I will not tolerate.* N-UNCOUNT [3] If you say that something **lies**, you mean that it does not express or represent something accurately. ❑ *The camera can sometimes lie.* VERB [4] ➔ See also **lying**. V

**lie de|tec|tor (lie detectors)** A **lie detector** is an electronic machine used mainly by the police to find out whether a suspect is telling the truth. ❑ *...the results of a lie detector test.* N-COUNT: oft N n = polygraph

**lie-down** If you have **a lie-down**, you have a short rest, usually in bed. [BRIT, INFORMAL] ❑ *She had departed upstairs for a lie-down.* N-SING

**lie-in (lie-ins)** If you have **a lie-in**, you rest by staying in bed later than usual in the morning. [BRIT, INFORMAL] ❑ *I have a lie-in on Sundays.* N-COUNT: usu sing

**lieu** /lju̲ː, AM lu̲ː/ [1] If you do, get, or give one thing **in lieu of** another, you do, get, or give it instead of the other thing, because the two things are considered to have the same value or importance. [FORMAL] ❑ *He left what little furniture he owned to his landlord in lieu of rent.* PREP-PHRASE [2] If you do, get, or give something **in lieu**, you do, get, or give it instead of something else, because the two things are considered to have the same value or importance. [mainly BRIT, FORMAL] ❑ *...an increased salary or time off in lieu.* PHRASE

**Lieut. Lieut.** is a written abbreviation for **lieutenant** when it is a person's title. ❑ *...Lieut. J. J. Doughty.* = Lt

**lieu|ten|ant** /lefte̲nənt, AM luː-/ **(lieutenants)** [1] A **lieutenant** is a person who holds a junior officer's rank in the army, navy, marines, or air force, or in the American police force. ❑ *Lieutenant Campbell ordered the man at the wheel to steer for the gunboat.* N-COUNT; N-TITLE ♦ **Lieutenant** is also a combining form. ❑ *...Lieutenant Colonel Gale Carter.* COMB in N-TITLE [2] If you refer to someone as a person's **lieutenant**, you mean they are that person's assistant, especially their main assistant, in an organization or activity. ❑ *He was my right-hand man, my lieutenant on the field, a cool, calculated footballer.* N-COUNT: usu poss N = second-in-command

**lieu|ten|ant gov|er|nor (lieutenant governors)** [1] A **lieutenant governor** is an elected official who acts as the deputy of a state governor in the United States. [AM] N-COUNT [2] A **lieutenant governor** is an official elected by the Canadian government to act as a representative of the British king or queen in a province of Canada. N-COUNT

**life** /laɪf/ **(lives** /laɪvz/**)** ◆◆◆ [1] **Life** is the quality which people, animals, and plants have when they are not dead, and which objects and substances do not have. N-UNCOUNT ❑ *...a baby's first minutes of life... Amnesty International opposes the death penalty as a violation of the right to life. ...the earth's supply of life-giving oxygen.* [2] You can use **life** to refer to things or groups of things which are alive. N-UNCOUNT: with supp ❑ *Is there life on Mars?... The book includes some useful facts about animal and plant life.* [3] If you refer to someone's **life**, you mean their state of being alive, especially when there is a risk or danger of them dying. N-COUNT: usu poss N ❑ *Your life is in danger... A nurse began to try to save his life... The intense fighting is reported to have claimed many lives.* [4] Someone's **life** is the period of time during which they are alive. N-COUNT: poss N ❑ *He spent the last fourteen years of his life in retirement... For the first time in his life he regretted that he had no faith.* [5] You can use **life** to refer to a period of someone's life when they are in a particular situation or job. N-COUNT: with supp, usu poss N ❑ *Interior designers spend their working lives keeping up to date with the latest trends... That was the beginning of my life in the television business.* [6] You can use **life** to refer to particular activities which people regularly do during their lives. N-COUNT: supp N ❑ *My personal life has had to take second place to my career... Most diabetics have a normal sex life.* [7] You can use **life** to refer to the events and experiences that happen to people while they are alive. N-UNCOUNT ❑ *Life won't be dull!... It's the people with insecurities who make life difficult.* [8] If you know a lot about **life**, you have gained many varied experiences, for example by travelling a lot and meeting different kinds of people. N-UNCOUNT ❑ *I was 19 and too young to know much about life... I needed some time off from education to experience life.* [9] You can use **life** to refer to the things that people do and experience that are characteristic of a particular place, group, or activity. N-UNCOUNT: usu supp N ❑ *How did you adjust to college life? ...the culture and life of north Africa.* [10] A person, place, book, or film that is full of **life** gives an impression of excitement, energy, or cheerfulness. N-UNCOUNT approval ❑ *The town itself was full of life and character.* [11] If someone is sentenced to **life**, they are sentenced to stay in prison for the rest of their life or for a very long time. [INFORMAL] N-UNCOUNT ❑ *He could get life in prison, if convicted.* [12] The **life** of something such as a machine, organization, or project is the period of time that it lasts for. N-COUNT: with poss ❑ *The repairs did not increase the value or the life of the equipment.*

**PHRASES** [13] If you **bring** something **to life** or if it **comes to life**, it becomes interesting or exciting. PHRASE: V inflects ❑ *The cold, hard cruelty of two young men is vividly brought to life in this true story... Poems which had seemed dull and boring suddenly came to life.* [14] If something or someone **comes to life**, they become active. PHRASE: V inflects ❑ *The volcano came to life a week ago.* [15] If you say that someone **is fighting for** their **life**, you mean that they are in a very serious condition and may die as a result of an accident or illness. [JOURNALISM] PHRASE: V inflects ❑ *He was in a critical condition, fighting for his life in hospital.* [16] **For life** means for the rest of a person's life. PHRASE: PHR after v, n PHR ❑ *He was jailed for life in 1966 for the murder of three policemen... She may have been scarred for life.* [17] If you say that someone does something **for dear life** or **for** their **life**, you mean that they do it using all their strength and effort because they are in a dangerous or urgent situation. [INFORMAL] PHRASE: PHR after v emphasis ❑ *I made for the life raft and hung on for dear life.* [18] If you tell someone to **get a life**, you are expressing frustration with them because their life seems boring or they seem to care too much about unimportant things. [INFORMAL] PHRASE disapproval [19] You can use **in all my life** or **in my life** to emphasize that you have never previously experienced something to such a degree. PHRASE: usu with brd-neg, usu PHR after v emphasis ❑ *I have never been so scared in all my life.* [20] If you say that someone or something is **larger than life**, you mean that they appear or behave in a way that seems more exaggerated or important than usual. PHRASE: v-link PHR, PHR n ❑ *...not that we should expect all good publishers to be larger than life... Throughout his career he's always been a larger than life character.* [21] If someone **lays down** their **life** for another person, they die so that the other person can live. [LITERARY] PHRASE: V inflects, usu PHR *for* n ❑ *Man can have no greater love than to lay down his life for his friends.* [22] If someone **risks life and limb**, they do something very dangerous that may cause them to die or be seriously injured. PHRASE: V inflects ❑ *Viewers will remember the dashing hero, Dirk, risking life and limb to rescue Daphne from the dragons.* [23] If you refer to someone as **the life and soul of the party**, you mean that they are very lively and entertaining on social occasions, and are good at mixing with people. In American English, you usually say that they are **the life of the party**. PHRASE: usu v-link PHR approval [24] If something **starts life** or **begins life** as a particular thing, it is that thing when it first starts to exist. PHRASE: V inflects, usu PHR *as* n ❑ *Herr's book started life as a dramatic screenplay.* [25] If someone **takes** another person's **life**, they kill them. If someone **takes** their own **life**, they kill themselves. [FORMAL] PHRASE: V and N inflect ❑ *Before execution, he admitted to taking the lives of at least 35 more women... He helped his first wife take her life when she was dying of cancer.* [26] You can use expressions such as **to come to life**, **to spring to life**, and **to roar into life** to indicate that a machine or vehicle suddenly starts working or moving. [LITERARY] PHRASE: V inflects ❑ *To his great relief the engine came to life... In the garden of the Savoy Hotel the sprinklers suddenly burst into life.* [27] → See also **fact of life**, **kiss of life**. a matter of **life and death** → see **death**. **a new lease of life** → see **lease**. to **have the time of** your **life** → see **time**. **true to life** → see **true**.

**life-affirming** A **life-affirming** activity or attitude emphasizes the positive aspects of life. ADJ: usu ADJ n approval ❑ *The exhibition is an enjoyable and, ultimately, life-affirming experience.*

**life-and-death** → see **death**.

**life as|sur|ance** **Life assurance** is the same as **life insurance**. [BRIT] N-UNCOUNT ❑ *...a life assurance policy.*

**life|belt** /laɪfbelt/ **(lifebelts)** A **lifebelt** is a large ring, usually made of a light substance such as cork, which someone who has fallen into deep water can use to float. N-COUNT

**life|blood** /laɪfblʌd/ also **life-blood**. The **lifeblood** of an organization, area, or person is the most important thing that they need in order to exist, develop, or be successful. N-SING: usu with poss ❑ *Small businesses are the lifeblood of the economy... Coal and steel were the region's lifeblood.*

**life|boat** /laɪfboʊt/ **(lifeboats)** [1] A **lifeboat** is a medium-sized boat that is sent out from a port or harbour in order to rescue people who are in danger at sea. N-COUNT [2] A **lifeboat** is a small boat that is carried on a ship, which people on the ship use to escape when the ship is in danger of sinking. N-COUNT

**life coach (life coaches)** A **life coach** is someone whose job involves helping people to improve their lives by doing challenging or worthwhile things. N-COUNT ♦ **life coach|ing** N-UNCOUNT ❑ *...life-coaching workshops.*

**life cy|cle (life cycles)** [1] The **life cycle** of an animal or plant is the series of changes and developments that it passes through from the beginning of its life until its death. N-COUNT: usu with poss ❑ *The dormant period is another stage in the life cycle of the plant.* [2] The **life cycle** of something such as an idea, product, or organization is the series of developments that take place in it from its beginning until the end of its usefulness. N-COUNT ❑ *Each new product would have a relatively long life cycle.*

**life-enhancing** If you describe something as **life-enhancing**, you mean that it makes you feel happier and more content. ❑ *...a life-enhancing and exciting trip... His letters, like his poetry, are life-enhancing and a delight.* ADJ

**life ex|pec|tan|cy** (**life expectancies**) The **life expectancy** of a person, animal, or plant is the length of time that they are normally likely to live. ❑ *The average life expectancy was 40... They had longer life expectancies than their parents.* N-UNCOUNT: also N in pl

**life force** also **life-force. Life force** is energy that some people believe exists in all living things and keeps them alive. N-UNCOUNT

**life form** (**life forms**) A **life form** is any living thing such as an animal or plant. N-COUNT: with supp

**life|guard** /laɪfgɑːʳd/ (**lifeguards**) A **lifeguard** is a person who works at a beach or swimming pool and rescues people when they are in danger of drowning. N-COUNT

**life his|to|ry** (**life histories**) The **life history** of a person is all the things that happen to them during their life. ❑ *Some people give you their life history without much prompting.* N-COUNT

**life im|pris|on|ment** If someone is sentenced to **life imprisonment**, they are sentenced to stay in prison for the rest of their life, or for a very long period of time. N-UNCOUNT = *life*

**life in|sur|ance Life insurance** is a form of insurance in which a person makes regular payments to an insurance company, in return for a sum of money to be paid to them after a period of time, or to their family if they die. ❑ *I have also taken out a life insurance policy on him just in case.* N-UNCOUNT = *life assurance*

**life jack|et** (**life jackets**) also **lifejacket.** A **life jacket** is a sleeveless jacket which helps you to float when you have fallen into deep water. N-COUNT

**life|less** /laɪfləs/ [1] If a person or animal is **lifeless**, they are dead, or are so still that they appear to be dead. ❑ *Their cold-blooded killers had then dragged their lifeless bodies upstairs to the bathroom.* ADJ [2] If you describe an object or a machine as **lifeless**, you mean that they are not living things, even though they may resemble living things. ❑ *It was made of plaster, hard and white and lifeless, bearing no resemblance to human flesh.* ADJ [3] A **lifeless** place or area does not have anything living or growing there at all. ❑ *Dry stone walls may appear stark and lifeless, but they provide a valuable habitat for plants and animals.* ADJ [4] If you describe a person, or something such as an artistic performance or a town as **lifeless**, you mean they lack any lively or exciting qualities. ❑ *...a lifeless portrait of an elderly woman.* ADJ [disapproval]

**life|like** /laɪflaɪk/ Something that is **lifelike** has the appearance of being alive. ❑ *...a lifelike doll.* ADJ

**life|line** /laɪflaɪn/ (**lifelines**) A **lifeline** is something that enables an organization or group to survive or to continue with an activity. ❑ *Information about the job market can be a lifeline for those who are out of work.* N-COUNT: oft N *for/to* n

**life|long** /laɪflɒŋ, AM -lɔːŋ/ **Lifelong** means existing or happening for the whole of a person's life. ❑ *...her lifelong friendship with Naomi.* ADJ: ADJ n

**life mem|ber** (**life members**) If you are a **life member** of a club or organization, you have paid or been chosen to be a member for the rest of your life. N-COUNT: oft N *of* n

**life peer** (**life peers**) In Britain, a **life peer** is a person who is given a title such as 'Lord' or 'Lady' which they can use for the rest of their life but which they cannot pass on when they die. ❑ *He was made a life peer in 1991.* N-COUNT

**life pre|serv|er** (**life preservers**) A **life preserver** is something such as a life jacket, which helps you to float when you have fallen into deep water. [AM] N-COUNT

**lif|er** /laɪfəʳ/ (**lifers**) A **lifer** is a criminal who has been given a life sentence. [INFORMAL] N-COUNT

**life raft** (**life rafts**) also **life-raft.** A **life raft** is a small rubber boat carried on an aircraft or large boat which can be filled with air and used in an emergency. N-COUNT

**life|sav|er** /laɪfseɪvəʳ/ (**lifesavers**) If you say that something is a **lifesaver**, you mean that it helps people in a very important way, often in a way that is important to their health. ❑ *The cervical smear test is a lifesaver.* N-COUNT

**life-saving** [1] A **life-saving** drug, operation, or action is one that saves someone's life or is likely to save their life. ❑ *...life-saving drugs such as antibiotics... She decided her child should go to America for life-saving treatment.* ADJ: usu ADJ n [2] You use **life-saving** to refer to the skills and activities connected with rescuing people, especially people who are drowning. N-UNCOUNT

**life sci|ence** (**life sciences**) The **life sciences** are sciences such as zoology, botany, and anthropology which are concerned with human beings, animals, and plants. N-COUNT: usu pl

**life sen|tence** (**life sentences**) If someone receives a **life sentence**, they are sentenced to stay in prison for the rest of their life, or for a very long period of time. ❑ *Some were serving life sentences for murder.* N-COUNT

**life-size** A **life-size** representation of someone or something, for example a painting or sculpture, is the same size as the person or thing that they represent. ❑ *...a life-size statue of an Indian boy.* ADJ

**life-sized Life-sized** means the same as **life-size**. ADJ

**life|span** /laɪfspæn/ (**lifespans**) also **life span.** [1] The **lifespan** of a person, animal, or plant is the period of time for which they live or are normally expected to live. ❑ *A 15-year lifespan is not uncommon for a dog.* N-VAR: oft with poss [2] The **lifespan** of a product, organization, or idea is the period of time for which it is expected to work properly or to last. ❑ *Most boilers have a lifespan of 15 to 20 years.* N-COUNT: oft with poss

**life|style** /laɪfstaɪl/ (**lifestyles**) also **life style, life-style.** [1] The **lifestyle** of a particular person or group of people is the living conditions, behaviour, and habits that are typical of them or are chosen by them. ❑ *They enjoyed an income and lifestyle that many people would envy.* N-VAR: usu with supp [2] **Lifestyle** magazines, television programmes, and products are aimed at people who wish to be associated with glamorous and successful lifestyles. ❑ *Her dream is to present a lifestyle show on television.* ADJ: ADJ n [3] **Lifestyle** drugs are drugs that are intended to improve people's quality of life rather than to treat particular medical disorders. ❑ *'I see anti-depressants as a lifestyle drug,' says Dr Charlton.* ADJ: ADJ n

**life-support ma|chine** (**life-support machines**) A **life-support machine** is the equipment that is used to keep a person alive when they are very ill and cannot breathe without help. [mainly BRIT] ❑ *He is in a coma and on a life-support machine.* N-COUNT

☑ in AM, use **respirator**

**life-support sys|tem** (**life-support systems**) A **life-support system** is the same as a **life-support machine**. N-COUNT

**life's work** Someone's **life's work** or **life work** is the main activity that they have been involved in during their life, or their most important achievement. ❑ *An exhibition of his life's work is being shown in the garden of his home... My father's life work was devoted to the conservation of the Longleat estate.* N-SING: usu poss N

**life-threatening** If someone has a **life-threatening** illness or is in a **life-threatening** situation, there is a strong possibility that the illness or the situation will kill them. ❑ *Caitlin was born with a life-threatening heart abnormality.* ADJ: oft adv ADJ

**life|time** /laɪftaɪm/ (**lifetimes**) [1] A **lifetime** is the length of time that someone is alive. ❑ *Dur-* N-COUNT: usu sing, oft poss N *ing my lifetime I haven't got around to much travelling. ...an extraordinary lifetime of achievement.* 2 N-SING: with poss — The **lifetime** of a particular thing is the period of time that it lasts. ❑ *...the lifetime of a parliament. ...a satellite's lifetime.* 3 PHRASE: n PHR [emphasis] — If you describe something as the chance or experience **of a lifetime**, you are emphasizing that it is the best or most important chance or experience that you are ever likely to have. ❑ *This could be not just the trip of a lifetime but the experience of a lifetime.*

**lift** /lɪft/ **(lifts, lifting, lifted)** ◆◆◇ 1 VERB — If you **lift** something, you move it to another position, especially upwards. ❑ V n *The Colonel lifted the phone and dialed his superior...* V n prep/adv *She lifted the last of her drink to her lips.* ♦ PHRASAL VERB **Lift up** means the same as **lift**. ❑ V n P *She put her arms around him and lifted him up...* V P n (not pron) *Curious shoppers lifted up their children to take a closer look at the parade.* 2 VERB = raise — If you **lift** a part of your body, you move it to a higher position. ❑ V n *Amy lifted her arm to wave. 'Goodbye,' she called...* V n *She lifted her foot and squashed the wasp into the ground.* ♦ PHRASAL VERB **Lift up** means the same as **lift**. ❑ V n P *Tom took his seat again and lifted his feet up on to the railing...* V P n (not pron) *The boys lifted up their legs, indicating they wanted to climb in.* 3 VERB = raise — If you **lift** your eyes or your head, you look up, for example when you have been reading and someone comes into the room. ❑ V n *When he finished he lifted his eyes and looked out the window.* 4 VERB — If people in authority **lift** a law or rule that prevents people from doing something, they end it. ❑ V n *The European Commission has urged France to lift its ban on imports of British beef.* 5 VERB — If something **lifts** your spirits or your mood, or if they **lift**, you start feeling more cheerful. ❑ V n *He used his incredible sense of humour to lift my spirits...* V *As soon as she heard the telephone ring her spirits lifted.* 6 N-SING: usu *a* N = boost — If something gives you a **lift**, it gives you a feeling of greater confidence, energy, or enthusiasm. [INFORMAL] ❑ *My selection for the team has given me a tremendous lift.* 7 N-COUNT — A **lift** is a device that carries people or goods up and down inside tall buildings. [BRIT] ❑ *They took the lift to the fourth floor.*

> ✔ in AM, use **elevator**

8 N-COUNT = ride — If you give someone a **lift** somewhere, you take them there in your car as a favour to them. ❑ *He had a car and often gave me a lift home.* 9 VERB = fly — If a government or organization **lifts** people or goods in or out of an area, it transports them there by aircraft, especially when there is a war. ❑ V n prep/adv *The army lifted people off rooftops where they had climbed to escape the flooding.* 10 VERB = increase — To **lift** something means to increase its amount or to increase the level or the rate at which it happens. ❑ V n *to/from/by* amount *The bank lifted its basic home loans rate to 10.99% from 10.75%...* V n *A barrage would halt the flow upstream and lift the water level.* 11 VERB — If fog, cloud, or mist **lifts**, it reduces, for example by moving upwards or by becoming less thick. ❑ V *The fog had lifted and revealed a warm, sunny day.* 12 to **lift a finger** → see **finger**.

♦ **lift off** PHRASAL VERB = take off — When an aircraft or rocket **lifts off**, it leaves the ground and rises into the air. ❑ V P *The plane lifted off and climbed steeply into the sky.*

♦ **lift up** → see **lift 1, 2**.

**lift-off** **(lift-offs)** N-VAR — **Lift-off** is the beginning of a rocket's flight into space, when it leaves the ground. ❑ *The lift-off was delayed about seven minutes... The rocket tumbled out of control shortly after lift-off.*

**liga|ment** /lɪgəmənt/ **(ligaments)** N-COUNT — A **ligament** is a band of strong tissue in a person's body which connects bones. ❑ *He suffered torn ligaments in his knee.*

> **light**
> ① BRIGHTNESS OR ILLUMINATION
> ② NOT GREAT IN WEIGHT, AMOUNT, OR INTENSITY
> ③ UNIMPORTANT OR NOT SERIOUS

① **light** /laɪt/ **(lights, lighting, lit, lighted, lighter, lightest)** ◆◆◇

> ✔ The form **lit** is the usual past tense and past participle, but the form **lighted** is also used.

⇒ Please look at category 19 to see if the expression you are looking for is shown under another headword. 1 N-UNCOUNT: also *the* N ≠ darkness — **Light** is the brightness that lets you see things. Light comes from sources such as the sun, moon, lamps, and fire. ❑ *Cracks of light filtered through the shutters... It was difficult to see in the dim light. ...ultraviolet light.* 2 N-COUNT — A **light** is something such as an electric lamp which produces light. ❑ *The janitor comes round to turn the lights out. ...street lights.* 3 N-PLURAL — You can use **lights** to refer to a set of traffic lights. ❑ *...the heavy city traffic with its endless delays at lights and crossings.* 4 VERB — If a place or object **is lit** by something, it has light shining on it. ❑ V n *It was dark and a giant moon lit the road so brightly you could see the landscape clearly...* V n *The room was lit by only the one light...* V n *with* n *The low sun lit the fortress walls with yellow light.* 5 ADJ ≠ dark — If it is **light**, the sun is providing light at the beginning or end of the day. ❑ *It was still light when we arrived at Lalong Creek. ...light summer evenings.* 6 ADJ = bright ≠ dark — If a room or building is **light**, it has a lot of natural light in it, for example because it has large windows. ❑ *It is a light room with tall windows.* ♦ **light|ness** N-UNCOUNT: usu with supp — *The dark green spare bedroom is in total contrast to the lightness of the large main bedroom.* 7 VERB — If you **light** something such as a cigarette or fire, or if it **lights**, it starts burning. ❑ V n *Stephen hunched down to light a cigarette...* V *If the charcoal does fail to light, use a special liquid spray and light it with a long taper.* V-ed *...a lighted candle.* 8 N-SING: *a* N — If someone asks you for **a light**, they want a match or cigarette lighter so they can start smoking. [INFORMAL] ❑ *Have you got a light anybody?* 9 N-COUNT: with supp — If something is presented in a particular **light**, it is presented so that you think about it in a particular way or so that it appears to be of a particular nature. ❑ *He has worked hard in recent months to portray New York in a better light.* 10 → See also **lighter**, **lighting**, **bright lights**, **night light**, **pilot light**, **red light**.

PHRASES 11 PHRASE: V inflects — If something **comes to light** or **is brought to light**, it becomes obvious or is made known to a lot of people. ❑ *The truth is unlikely to be brought to light by the promised enquiry.* 12 PHRASE: V inflects — If **light dawns on** you, you begin to understand something after a period of not being able to understand it. ❑ *At last the light dawned. He was going to marry Phylis!* 13 PHRASE: PHR after v, v-link PHR — If someone in authority gives you **a green light**, they give you permission to do something. ❑ *The food industry was given a green light to extend the use of these chemicals.* 14 PREP-PHRASE — If something is possible **in the light of** particular information, it is only possible because you have this information. ❑ *In the light of this information it is now possible to identify a number of key issues.* 15 PHRASE: V inflects — If someone **sees the light**, they finally realise something or change their attitude or way of behaving to a better one. ❑ *I saw the light and ditched him.* 16 PHRASE: V inflects: PHR n — If you **set light to** something, you make it start burning. [mainly BRIT] ❑ *They had poured fuel through the door of the flat and had then set light to it.*

> ✔ in AM, use **set fire to**

17 PHRASE: V inflects, PHR n = clarify — To **shed light on**, **throw light on**, or **cast light on** something means to make it easier to understand, because more information is known about it. ❑ *A new approach offers an answer, and may shed light on an even bigger question.* 18 PHRASE — When you talk about **the light at the end of the tunnel**, you are referring to the end of the difficult or unpleasant situation that you are in at the moment. ❑ *All I can do is tell her to hold on, that there's light at the end of the tunnel.* 19 **all sweetness and light** → see **sweetness**.

♦ **light up** PHRASAL VERB 1 — If you **light** something **up** or if it **lights up**, it becomes bright, usually when you shine light on it. ❑ V P *...a keypad that lights up when you pick up the handset...* V P n (not pron) Also V n P *On September 5, at the end of the festival, a massive display of fireworks will light* *up the sky around Broadlands.* [2] If your face or your eyes **light up** you suddenly look very surprised or happy. ❑ *Sue's face lit up with surprise... You should see his eyes light up when he talks about home.* [3] If you **light up**, you make a cigarette, cigar, or pipe start burning and you start smoking it. [INFORMAL] ❑ *He held a match while she lit up... He took his time lighting up a cigarette.* PHRASAL VERB V P with n V P PHRASAL VERB V P V P n (not pron) Also V n P

**③light** /laɪt/ **(lighter, lightest)** [1] Something that is **light** does not weigh very much, or weighs less than you would expect it to. ❑ *Modern tennis rackets are now apparently 20 per cent lighter. ...weight training with light weights... Try to wear light, loose clothes.* ♦ **light|ness** *The toughness, lightness, strength, and elasticity of whalebone gave it a wide variety of uses.* [2] Something that is **light** is not very great in amount, degree, or intensity. ❑ *It's a Sunday like any other with the usual light traffic in the city. ...a light breeze.* ♦ **light|ly** *Put the onions in the pan and cook until lightly browned.* [3] **Light** equipment and machines are small and easily moved, especially because they are not heavy. ❑ *...a convoy of light armoured vehicles... They used light machine guns and AK forty-sevens.* [4] Something that is **light** is very pale in colour. ❑ *The walls are light in colour and covered in paper... He is light haired with gray eyes.* ♦ **Light** is also a combining form. ❑ *We know he has a light green van. ...a light blue box.* [5] A **light** sleep is one that is easily disturbed and in which you are often aware of the things around you. If you are a **light** sleeper, you are easily woken when you are asleep. ❑ *She had drifted into a light sleep... She was usually a light sleeper.* ♦ **light|ly** *He was dozing lightly in his chair.* [6] A **light** sound, for example someone's voice, is pleasantly quiet. ❑ *The voice was sweet and light.* [7] A **light** meal consists of a small amount of food, or of food that is easy to digest. ❑ *...a light, healthy lunch.* ♦ **light|ly** *She found it impossible to eat lightly.* [8] **Light** work does not involve much physical effort. ❑ *He was on the training field for some light work yesterday.* [9] If you describe the result of an action or a punishment as **light**, you mean that it is less serious or severe than you expected. ❑ *She confessed her astonishment at her light sentence when her father visited her at the jail.* ♦ **light|ly** *One of the accused got off lightly in exchange for pleading guilty to withholding information from Congress.* [10] Movements and actions that are **light** are graceful or gentle and are done with very little force or effort. ❑ *Use a light touch when applying cream or make-up... There was a light knock at the door.* ♦ **light|ly** *He kissed her lightly on the mouth... Knead the dough very lightly.* ♦ **light|ness** *She danced with a grace and lightness that were breathtaking.* [11] → See also **lighter**.

◆◇◇ ADJ ≠ heavy N-UNCOUNT: usu with supp ADJ ADV: usu ADV -ed, also ADV after v ADJ: ADJ n ADJ ≠ dark COMB in COLOUR ADJ: ADJ n ≠ deep ADV: ADV after v ADJ ADJ ≠ heavy ADV: ADV after v ADJ: usu ADJ n ADJ = lenient ADV: ADV after v ADJ = gentle ADV: ADV with v N-UNCOUNT

**③light** /laɪt/ **(lighter, lightest)** ◆◇◇

⇛ Please look at category 5 to see if the expression you are looking for is shown under another headword. [1] If you describe things such as books, music, and films as **light**, you mean that they entertain you without making you think very deeply. ❑ *...light classical music. ...a light entertainment programme.* [2] If you say something in a **light** way, you sound as if you think that something is not important or serious. ❑ *Talk to him in a friendly, light way about the relationship... Let's finish on a lighter note.* ♦ **light|ly** *'Once a detective, always a detective,' he said lightly.* ♦ **light|ness** *'I'm not an authority on them,' Jessica said with forced lightness.* [3] If you say that something is not a **light** matter, you mean that it should be treated or considered as being important and serious. ❑ *It can be no light matter for the Home Office that so many young prisoners should have wanted to kill or injure themselves.* ♦ **light|ly** *His allegations cannot be lightly dismissed.* [4] If you **make light of** something, you treat it as though it is not serious or important, when in fact it is. ❑ *Roberts attempted to make light of his discomfort.* [5] → See also **lighter**. to **make light work of** → see **work**.

ADJ: usu ADJ n ADJ: usu ADJ n ≠ serious ADV: ADV after v N-UNCOUNT ADJ: usu with brd-neg ADV: ADV with v PHRASE: V inflects = play down

**light air|craft** **(light aircraft)** A **light aircraft** is a small aeroplane that is designed to carry a small number of passengers or a small amount of goods. N-COUNT

**light bulb** **(light bulbs)** A **light bulb** or **bulb** is the round glass part of an electric light or lamp which light shines from. N-COUNT = bulb

**light cream** **Light cream** is thin cream that does not have a lot of fat in it. [AM] N-UNCOUNT

✓ in BRIT, use **single cream**

**light|en** /laɪtᵊn/ **(lightens, lightening, lightened)** [1] When something **lightens** or when you **lighten** it, it becomes less dark in colour. ❑ *The sky began to lighten... Leslie lightens her hair and has now had it cut into a short, feathered style.* [2] If someone **lightens** a situation, they make it less serious or less boring. ❑ *Anthony felt the need to lighten the atmosphere.* [3] If your attitude, or mood **lightens**, or if someone or something **lightens** it, they make you feel more cheerful, happy, and relaxed. ❑ *As they approached the outskirts of the city, Ella's mood visibly lightened... The sun was streaming in through the window, yet it did nothing to lighten his mood.* [4] If you **lighten** something, you make it less heavy. ❑ *It is a good idea to blend it in a food processor as this lightens the mixture... He pulled the lightened sled with all his strength.*

VERB ≠ darken V V n VERB V n VERB V V n VERB V n V-ed

**light|er** /laɪtəʳ/ **(lighters)** A **lighter** is a small device that produces a flame which you can use to light cigarettes, cigars, and pipes. N-COUNT

**light-fingered** If you say that someone is **light-fingered**, you mean that they steal things. [INFORMAL] ADJ

**light-headed** If you feel **light-headed**, you feel rather unsteady and strange, for example because you are ill or because you have drunk too much alcohol. ADJ: usu v-link ADJ

**light-hearted** [1] Someone who is **light-hearted** is cheerful and happy. ❑ *They were light-hearted and prepared to enjoy life.* [2] Something that is **light-hearted** is intended to be entertaining or amusing, and not at all serious. ❑ *There have been many attempts, both light-hearted and serious, to locate the Loch Ness Monster.* ADJ ADJ

**light heavy|weight** **(light heavyweights)** A **light heavyweight** is a professional boxer who weighs between 160 and 175 pounds, or an amateur boxer who weighs between 165 and 179 pounds. N-COUNT = cruiserweight

**light|house** /laɪthaus/ **(lighthouses)** A **lighthouse** is a tower containing a powerful flashing lamp that is built on the coast or on a small island. Lighthouses are used to guide ships or to warn them of danger. N-COUNT

**light in|dus|try** **(light industries)** **Light industry** is industry in which only small items are made, for example household goods and clothes. N-VAR

**light|ing** /laɪtɪŋ/ [1] The **lighting** in a place is the way that it is lit, for example by electric lights, by candles, or by windows, or the quality of the light in it. ❑ *...the bright fluorescent lighting of the laboratory... The whole room is bathed in soft lighting. ...street lighting.* [2] The **lighting** in a film or play is the use of different electric lights to give a particular effect. ❑ *Peter Mumford's lighting and David Freeman's direction make a crucial contribution to the success of the staging.* N-UNCOUNT N-UNCOUNT

**light|ning** /laɪtnɪŋ/ [1] **Lightning** is the very bright flashes of light in the sky that happen during thunderstorms. ❑ *One man died when he was struck by lightning... Another flash of lightning lit up the cave. ...thunder and lightning.* → See also **forked lightning**. [2] **Lightning** describes things that happen very quickly or last for only a short time. ❑ *Driving today demands lightning reflexes.* N-UNCOUNT ADJ: ADJ n

**light|ning bug** **(lightning bugs)** A **lightning bug** is a type of beetle that produces light from its body. [AM] N-COUNT = firefly

**light|ning con|duc|tor** **(lightning conductors)** A **lightning conductor** is a long thin piece of metal on top of a building that attracts lightning and allows it to reach the ground safely. [BRIT] N-COUNT

in AM, use **lightning rod**

**light|ning rod** **(lightning rods)** 1 A **lightning rod** is the same as a **lightning conductor**. [AM] N-COUNT 2 If you say that someone **is a lightning rod for** something, you mean that they attract that thing to themselves. [AM] ❑ *He is a lightning rod for controversy.* PHRASE: PHR n

**light|ning strike** **(lightning strikes)** A **lightning strike** is a strike in which workers stop work suddenly and without any warning, in order to protest about something. [BRIT] ❑ *Bank staff are to stage a series of lightning strikes in a dispute over staffing.* N-COUNT

**light|ship** /laɪtʃɪp/ **(lightships)** A **lightship** is a small ship that stays in one place and has a powerful flashing lamp. Lightships are used to guide ships or to warn them of danger. N-COUNT

**light|weight** /laɪtweɪt/ **(lightweights)** also **light-weight**. 1 Something that is **lightweight** weighs less than most other things of the same type. ❑ *...lightweight denim... The company manufactures a range of innovative light-weight cycles.* ADJ: usu ADJ n 2 **Lightweight** is a category in some sports, such as boxing, judo, or rowing, based on the weight of the athlete. ❑ *By the age of sixteen he was the junior lightweight champion of Poland.* ♦ A **lightweight** is a person who is in the lightweight category in a particular sport. N-UNCOUNT: usu N n; N-COUNT 3 If you describe someone as a **lightweight**, you are critical of them because you think that they are not very important or skilful in a particular area of activity. ❑ *Hill considered Sam a lightweight, a real amateur.* ♦ **Lightweight** is also an adjective. ❑ *Some of the discussion in the book is lightweight and unconvincing.* N-COUNT disapproval ≠ heavyweight; ADJ

**light year** **(light years)** 1 A **light year** is the distance that light travels in a year. ❑ *...a star system millions of light years away.* N-COUNT 2 You can say that two things are **light years** apart to emphasize a very great difference or a very long distance or period of time between them. [INFORMAL] ❑ *She says the French education system is light years ahead of the English one.* N-COUNT: usu pl, N prep/adv emphasis

**lik|able** /laɪkəbᵊl/ → see **likeable**.

**like**
1. PREPOSITION AND CONJUNCTION USES
2. VERB USES
3. NOUN USES AND PHRASES

**①like** /laɪk, laɪk/ **(likes)** 1 If you say that one person or thing is **like** another, you mean that they share some of the same qualities or features. ❑ *He looks like Father Christmas... Kathy is a great mate, we are like sisters... It's nothing like what happened in the mid-Seventies... This is just like old times. ...a mountain shaped like a reclining woman.* ◆◆◆ PREP 2 If you talk about what something or someone is **like**, you are talking about their qualities or features. ❑ *What was Bulgaria like?... What did she look like?... What was it like growing up in Hillsborough?* PREP 3 You can use **like** to introduce an example of the set of things or people that you have just mentioned. ❑ *The neglect that large cities like New York have received over the past 12 years is tremendous... He could say things like, 'Let's go to the car' or 'Let us go for a walk' in French.* PREP: n PREP n/-ing = such as 4 You can use **like** to say that someone or something is in the same situation as another person or thing. ❑ *It also moved those who, like me, are too young to have lived through the war.* PREP 5 If you say that someone is behaving **like** something or someone else, you mean that they are behaving in a way that is typical of that kind of thing or person. **Like** is used in this way in many fixed expressions, for example **to cry like a baby** and **to watch someone like a hawk**. ❑ *I was shaking all over, trembling like a leaf... Greenfield was behaving like an irresponsible idiot.* PREP: v PREP n 6 You can use **like** in expressions such as **that's just like her** and **it wasn't like him** to indicate that the person's behaviour is or is not typical of their character. ❑ *You should have told us. But it's just like you not to share.* PREP: v-link PREP n 7 **Like** is sometimes used as a conjunction in order to say that something appears to be the case when it is not. Some people consider this use to be incorrect. ❑ *On the train up to Waterloo, I felt like I was going on an adventure.* CONJ = as if 8 **Like** is sometimes used as a conjunction in order to indicate that something happens or is done in the same way as something else. Some people consider this use to be incorrect. ❑ *People are strolling, buying ice cream for their children, just like they do every Sunday... He spoke exactly like I did... We really were afraid, not like in the cinema.* CONJ = as 9 You can use **like** in negative expressions such as **nothing like it** and **no place like it** to emphasize that there is nothing as good as the situation, thing, or person mentioned. ❑ *There's nothing like candlelight for creating a romantic mood... There was no feeling like it in the world.* PREP: with neg emphasis 10 You can use **like** in expressions such as **nothing like** to make an emphatic negative statement. ❑ *Three hundred million dollars will be nothing like enough... It's really not anything like as bad as it looks.* PREP: with neg emphasis

**②like** /laɪk/ **(likes, liking, liked)** 1 If you **like** something or someone, you think they are interesting, enjoyable, or attractive. ❑ *He likes baseball... I can't think why Grace doesn't like me... What music do you like best?... I just didn't like being in crowds... Do you like to go swimming?... I like my whisky neat... That's one of the things I like about you. You're strong.* ◆◆◆ VERB: no cont; V n; V -ing; V to-inf; V n adj/prep; V n *about* n/-ing 2 If you ask someone how they **like** something, you are asking them for their opinion of it and whether they enjoy it or find it pleasant. ❑ *How do you like America?... How did you like the trip?* VERB: no cont, no passive; V n/-ing 3 If you **like** something such as a particular course of action or way of behaving, you approve of it. ❑ *I've been looking at the cookery book. I like the way it is set out... The US administration would like to see a negotiated settlement to the war... Opal, his wife, didn't really like him drinking so much... I don't like relying on the judges' decisions.* VERB: no cont; V n; V to-inf; V n -ing; V -ing 4 If you say that you **like to** do something or that you **like** something to be done, you mean that you prefer to do it or prefer it to be done as part of your normal life or routine. ❑ *I like to get to airports in good time... I hear Mary's husband likes her to be home no later than six o'clock.* VERB: no cont, no passive; V to-inf; V n to-inf 5 If you say that you **would like** something or **would like** to do something, you are indicating a wish or desire that you have. ❑ *I'd like a bath... If you don't mind, I think I'd like to go home.* VERB: no cont, no passive; V n; V to-inf 6 You can say that you **would like** to say something to indicate that you are about to say it. ❑ *I'd like to apologize... I would like to take this opportunity of telling you about a new service which we are offering.* VERB: no cont, no passive; V to-inf; V to-inf 7 If you ask someone if they **would like** something or **would like** to do something, you are making a polite offer or invitation. ❑ *Here's your change. Would you like a bag?... Perhaps while you wait you would like a drink at the bar... Would you like to come back for coffee?* VERB: no cont, no passive politeness; V n; V n; V to-inf 8 If you say to someone that you **would like** something or you **would like** them to do something, or ask them if they **would like** to do it, you are politely telling them what you want or what you want them to do. ❑ *I'd like an explanation... We'd like you to look around and tell us if anything is missing... Would you like to tell me what happened?* VERB: no cont, no passive politeness; V n; V n to-inf; V to-inf

**③like** /laɪk/ **(likes)** 1 You can use **like** in expressions such as **like attracts like**, when you are referring to two or more people or things that have the same or similar characteristics. ❑ *You have to make sure you're comparing like with like... Homeopathic treatment is based on the 'like cures like' principle.* ◆◆◆ N-UNCOUNT 2 Someone's **likes** are the things that they enjoy or find pleasant. ❑ *I thought that I knew* N-PLURAL: usu poss N ≠ dislikes *everything about Jemma: her likes and dislikes, her political viewpoints.* [3] → See also **liking**.

**PHRASES** [4] You say **if you like** when you are making or agreeing to an offer or suggestion in a casual way. ❑ *You can stay here if you like... 'Shall we stop talking about her?' — 'If you like.'* [5] You say **if you like** when you are expressing something in a different way, or in a way that you think some people might disagree with or find strange. ❑ *This is more like a downpayment, or a deposit, if you like.* [6] You can use the expressions **like anything**, **like crazy**, or **like mad** to emphasize that someone is doing something or something is happening in a very energetic or noticeable way. [INFORMAL] ❑ *He's working like mad at the moment.* [7] You say **like this**, **like that**, or **like so** when you are showing someone how something is done. ❑ *It opens and closes, like this.* [8] You use **like this** or **like that** when you are drawing attention to something that you are doing or that someone else is doing. ❑ *I'm sorry to intrude on you like this... Stop pacing like that.* [9] You use the expression **something like** with an amount, number, or description to indicate that it is approximately accurate. ❑ *They can get something like £3,000 a year... 'When roughly would this be? Monday?' — 'Something like that.'* [10] If you refer to something **the like of which** or **the likes of which** has never been seen before, you are emphasizing how important, great, or noticeable the thing is. ❑ *...technological advances the like of which the world had previously only dreamed of... We are dealing with an epidemic the likes of which we have never seen in this century.*

PHRASE: PHR with cl
PHRASE: PHR with cl/group = *let's say*
PHRASE: PHR after v [emphasis]
PHRASE: usu PHR with cl
PHRASE: PHR after v
PHRASE: PHR n = *about*
PHRASE: n PHR cl [emphasis] = *such as*

**-like** /-laɪk/ **-like** combines with nouns to form adjectives which describe something as being similar to the thing referred to by the noun. ❑ *...beautiful purple-red petunia-like flowers. ...a tiny worm-like creature.* COMB in ADJ: usu ADJ n

**like|able** /laɪkəbᵊl/ also **likable.** Someone or something that is **likeable** is pleasant and easy to like. ❑ *He was an immensely likeable chap.* ADJ = *pleasant*

**like|li|hood** /laɪklihʊd/ [1] The **likelihood of** something happening is how likely it is to happen. ❑ *The likelihood of infection is minimal.* [2] If something is a **likelihood**, it is likely to happen. ❑ *But the likelihood is that people would be willing to pay if they were certain that their money was going to a good cause.* [3] If you say that something will happen **in all likelihood**, you mean that it will probably happen. ❑ *In all likelihood, the committee will have to interview every woman who's worked with Thomas.*

N-UNCOUNT: usu N *of* n/-ing, N that = *probability*
N-SING = *probability*
PHRASE: PHR with cl = *in all probability*

**like|ly** /laɪkli/ **(likelier, likeliest)** [1] You use **likely** to indicate that something is probably the case or will probably happen in a particular situation. ❑ *Experts say a 'yes' vote is still the likely outcome... If this is your first baby, it's far more likely that you'll get to the hospital too early... Francis thought it likely John still loved her.* ♦ **Likely** is also an adverb. ❑ *Profit will most likely have risen by about £25 million... Very likely he'd told them he had American business interests.* [2] If someone or something is **likely to** do a particular thing, they will very probably do it. ❑ *In the meantime the war of nerves seems likely to continue... Once people have seen that something actually works, they are much more likely to accept change.* [3] A **likely** person, place, or thing is one that will probably be suitable for a particular purpose. ❑ *At one point he had seemed a likely candidate to become Prime Minister... We aimed the microscope at a likely looking target.* [4] You can say **not likely** as an emphatic way of saying 'no', especially when someone asks you whether you are going to do something. [INFORMAL] ❑ *'How about having a phone out here?' — 'Not likely!'*

◆◆◆
ADJ: oft *it* v-link ADJ that = *probable* ≠ *unlikely*
ADV: ADV with cl/group = *probably*
ADJ: v-link ADJ to-inf ≠ *unlikely*
ADJ: ADJ n
CONVENTION [emphasis] = *no way*

**like-minded** **Like-minded** people have similar opinions, ideas, attitudes, or interests. ❑ *...the opportunity to mix with hundreds of like-minded people.* ADJ: usu ADJ n

**lik|en** /laɪkən/ **(likens, likening, likened)** If you **liken** one thing or person **to** another thing or person, you say that they are similar. ❑ *The pain is often likened to being drilled through the side of the head.* VERB = *compare* V n *to* n/-ing

**like|ness** /laɪknəs/ **(likenesses)** [1] If two things or people have a **likeness to** each other, they are similar to each other. ❑ *These myths have a startling likeness to one another... There might be a likeness between their features, but their eyes were totally dissimilar.* [2] A **likeness of** someone is a picture or sculpture of them. ❑ *The museum displays wax likenesses of every US president.* [3] If you say that a picture of someone is a good **likeness**, you mean that it looks just like them. ❑ *She says the artist's impression is an excellent likeness of her abductor.*

N-SING: oft N *to*/*between* n = *similarity*
N-COUNT: with poss
N-COUNT: usu sing, usu adj N

**like|wise** /laɪkwaɪz/ [1] You use **likewise** when you are comparing two methods, states, or situations and saying that they are similar. ❑ *All attempts by the Socialists to woo him back were spurned. Similar overtures from the right have likewise been rejected.* [2] If you do something and someone else does **likewise**, they do the same or a similar thing. ❑ *He lent money, made donations and encouraged others to do likewise.*

ADV: ADV with v, ADV with cl/group = *similarly*
ADV: ADV after v

**lik|ing** /laɪkɪŋ/ [1] If you have **a liking for** something or someone, you like them. ❑ *She had a liking for good clothes... Mrs Jermyn took a great liking to him.* N-SING: with supp, oft N *for* n

**PHRASES** [2] If something is, for example, too fast **for** your **liking**, you would prefer it to be slower. If it is not fast enough **for** your **liking**, you would prefer it to be faster. ❑ *She's asking far too many personal questions for my liking.* [3] If something is **to** your **liking**, it suits your interests, tastes, or wishes. ❑ *London was more to his liking than Rome.*

PHRASE: with *too*/*not enough*, usu group PHR
PHRASE: v-link PHR, PHR after v

**li|lac** /laɪlək/ **(lilacs** or **lilac)** [1] A **lilac** or a **lilac tree** is a small tree which has sweet-smelling purple, pink, or white flowers in large, cone-shaped groups. ❑ *Lilacs grew against the side wall. ...a twig of lilac.* ♦ **Lilacs** are the flowers which grow on this tree. ❑ *...a vase of tulips, lilies, lilacs and primroses... Her hair smelt of lilac.* [2] Something that is **lilac** is pale pinkish-purple in colour. ❑ *All shades of mauve, lilac, lavender and purple were fashionable.*

N-VAR
N-VAR
COLOUR

**lilt** /lɪlt/ If someone's voice has a **lilt** in it, the pitch of their voice rises and falls in a pleasant way, as if they were singing. ❑ *Her voice is child-like, with a West Country lilt.* N-SING

**lilt|ing** /lɪltɪŋ/ A **lilting** voice or song rises and falls in pitch in a pleasant way. ❑ *He had a pleasant, lilting northern accent.* ADJ: usu ADJ n

**lily** /lɪli/ **(lilies)** A **lily** is a plant with large flowers. Lily flowers are often white. N-VAR

**lily of the val|ley** **(lilies of the valley** or **lily of the valley)** **Lily of the valley** are small plants with large leaves and small, white, bell-shaped flowers. N-VAR

**lima bean** /liːmə biːn/ **(lima beans)** **Lima beans** are flat round beans that are light green in colour and are eaten as a vegetable. They are the seeds of a plant that grows in tropical parts of America. N-COUNT: usu pl

**limb** /lɪm/ **(limbs)** [1] Your **limbs** are your arms and legs. ❑ *She would be able to stretch out her cramped limbs and rest for a few hours.* [2] The **limbs** of a tree are its branches. [LITERARY] ❑ *This entire rickety structure was hanging from the limb of an enormous leafy tree.* [3] If someone goes **out on a limb**, they do something they strongly believe in even though it is risky or extreme, and is likely to fail or be criticized by other people. ❑ *They can see themselves going out on a limb, voting for a very controversial energy bill.* [4] to **risk life and limb** → see **life**.

N-COUNT: usu pl
N-COUNT
PHRASE: PHR after v, v-link PHR

**-limbed** /-lɪmd/ **-limbed** combines with adjectives to form other adjectives which indicate that a person or animal has limbs of a particular COMB in ADJ type or appearance. ❑ *He was long-limbed and dark-eyed.*

**lim|ber** /lɪmbəʳ/ **(limbers, limbering, limbered)**

♦ **limber up** If you **limber up**, you prepare for an energetic physical activity such as a sport by moving and stretching your body. ❑ *Next door, 200 girls are limbering up for their ballet exams... A short walk will limber up the legs.*

PHRASAL VERB = *warm up*; V P; V P n (not pron)

**lim|bo** /lɪmboʊ/ If you say that someone or something is **in limbo**, you mean that they are in a situation where they seem to be caught between two stages and it is unclear what will happen next. ❑ *The negotiations have been in limbo since mid-December.*

N-UNCOUNT: usu *in/into* N

**lime** /laɪm/ **(limes)** 1 A **lime** is a green fruit that tastes like a lemon. Limes grow on trees in tropical countries. ❑ *...peeled slices of lime... Add a few drops of lime juice.* 2 A **lime** is a large tree with pale green leaves. It is often planted in parks in towns and cities. ❑ *...dilapidated avenues of limes.* 3 **Lime** is a substance containing calcium. It is found in soil and water. ❑ *If your soil is very acid, add lime.* ♦ **Lime** is also a combining form. ❑ *...lime-rich sand. ...old lime-stained baths.*

N-VAR; N-COUNT; N-UNCOUNT; COMB in ADJ

**lime green** also **lime-green.** Something that is **lime green** is light yellowish-green in colour.

COLOUR

**lime|light** /laɪmlaɪt/ If someone is in the **limelight**, a lot of attention is being paid to them, because they are famous or because they have done something very unusual or exciting. ❑ *Tony has now been thrust into the limelight, with a high-profile job.*

N-UNCOUNT: usu prep *the* N

**lim|er|ick** /lɪmərɪk/ **(limericks)** A **limerick** is a humorous poem which has five lines.

N-COUNT

**lime|stone** /laɪmstoʊn/ **(limestones)** **Limestone** is a whitish-coloured rock which is used for building and for making cement. ❑ *...high limestone cliffs... The local limestone is very porous.*

N-MASS: oft N n

**lim|ey** /laɪmi/ **(limeys)** Some Americans refer to British people as **limeys**. Some people consider this use offensive. [INFORMAL]

N-COUNT

**lim|it** /lɪmɪt/ **(limits, limiting, limited)** 1 A **limit** is the greatest amount, extent, or degree of something that is possible. ❑ *Her love for him was being tested to its limits... There is no limit to how much fresh fruit you can eat in a day.* 2 A **limit** of a particular kind is the largest or smallest amount of something such as time or money that is allowed because of a rule, law, or decision. ❑ *The three month time limit will be up in mid-June... The economic affairs minister announced limits on petrol sales.*

◆◆◇ N-COUNT: usu sing, usu with supp; N-COUNT: usu with supp

3 The **limit** of an area is its boundary or edge. ❑ *...the city limits of Baghdad.* 4 **The limits of** a situation are the facts involved in it which make only some actions or results possible. ❑ *She has to work within the limits of a fairly tight budget... He outlined the limits of British power.* 5 If you **limit** something, you prevent it from becoming greater than a particular amount or degree. ❑ *He limited payments on the country's foreign debt... The view was that the economy would grow by 2.25 per cent. This would limit unemployment to around 2.5 million.* 6 If you **limit yourself** to something, or if someone or something **limits** you, the number of things that you have or do is reduced. ❑ *It is now accepted that men should limit themselves to 20 units of alcohol a week... Voters cut councillors' pay and limited them to one staff member each.* ♦ **lim|it|ing** *The conditions laid down to me were not too limiting.* 7 If something **is limited to** a particular place or group of people, it exists only in that place, or is had or done only by that group. ❑ *The protests were not limited to New York... Entry to this prize draw is limited to UK residents.* 8 → See also **age limit**, **limited**.

N-COUNT: with supp; N-PLURAL: usu N *of* n; VERB = *restrict*; V n; V n *to* n; VERB; V pron-refl *to* n/-ing; V n *to* n/-ing; ADJ; VERB: usu passive; *be* V-ed *to* n/-ing; *be* V-ed *to* n/-ing

**PHRASES** 9 If an area or a place is **off limits**, you are not allowed to go there. ❑ *A one-mile area around the wreck is still off limits... These establishments are off limits to ordinary citizens.* 10 If someone **is over the limit**, they have drunk more alcohol than they are legally allowed to when driving a vehicle. [BRIT] ❑ *If police breathalyse me and find I am over the limit I face a long ban.* 11 If you say **the sky is the limit**, you mean that there is nothing to prevent someone or something from being very successful. ❑ *They have found that, in terms of both salary and career success, the sky is the limit.* 12 If you add **within limits** to a statement, you mean that it is true or applies only when talking about reasonable or normal situations. ❑ *In the circumstances we'll tell you what we can, within limits, of course, and in confidence.*

PHRASE: v-link PHR, oft PHR *to* n; PHRASE: usu v-link PHR; PHRASE: V inflects; PHRASE: PHR with cl = *within reason*

**limi|ta|tion** /lɪmɪteɪʃən/ **(limitations)** 1 The **limitation** of something is the act or process of controlling or reducing it. ❑ *All the talk had been about the limitation of nuclear weapons. ...damage limitation.* 2 A **limitation on** something is a rule or decision which prevents that thing from growing or extending beyond certain limits. ❑ *...a limitation on the tax deductions for people who make more than $100,000 a year... There is to be no limitation on the number of opposition parties.* 3 If you talk about the **limitations** of someone or something, you mean that they can only do some things and not others, or cannot do something very well. ❑ *Parents are too likely to blame schools for the educational limitations of their children.* 4 A **limitation** is a fact or situation that allows only some actions and makes others impossible. ❑ *This drug has one important limitation. Its effects only last six hours.*

N-UNCOUNT: usu with supp, oft N *of* n; N-VAR: usu N *on* n; N-PLURAL: usu with poss; N-VAR: usu with supp

**lim|it|ed** /lɪmɪtɪd/ 1 Something that is **limited** is not very great in amount, range, or degree. ❑ *They may only have a limited amount of time to get their points across.* 2 A **limited** company is one whose owners are legally responsible for only a part of any money that it may owe if it goes bankrupt. [mainly BRIT, BUSINESS] ❑ *They had plans to turn the club into a limited company... He is the founder of International Sports Management Limited.*

◆◇◇ ADJ: usu ADJ n = *small*; ADJ: ADJ n, n ADJ

☑ in AM, use **incorporated**

**lim|it|ed edi|tion** **(limited editions)** A **limited edition** is a work of art, such as a book which is only produced in very small numbers, so that each one will be valuable in the future.

N-COUNT

**lim|it|less** /lɪmɪtləs/ If you describe something as **limitless**, you mean that there is or appears to be so much of it that it will never be exhausted. ❑ *...a cheap and potentially limitless supply of energy... The opportunities are limitless.*

ADJ = *endless*

**limo** /lɪmoʊ/ **(limos)** A **limo** is a **limousine**. [INFORMAL]

N-COUNT: also *by* N

**lim|ou|sine** /lɪməziːn/ **(limousines)** A **limousine** is a large and very comfortable car. Limousines are usually driven by a chauffeur and are used by very rich or important people.

N-COUNT

**limp** /lɪmp/ **(limps, limping, limped, limper, limpest)** 1 If a person or animal **limps**, they walk with difficulty or in an uneven way because one of their legs or feet is hurt. ❑ *I wasn't badly hurt, but I injured my thigh and had to limp... He had to limp off with a leg injury.* ♦ **Limp** is also a noun. ❑ *A stiff knee following surgery forced her to walk with a limp.* 2 If you say that something such as an organization, process, or vehicle **limps along**, you mean that it continues slowly or with difficulty, for example because it has been weakened or damaged. ❑ *In recent years the newspaper had been limping along on limited resources... A British battleship, which had been damaged severely in the battle of Crete, came limping into Pearl Harbor.* 3 If you describe something as **limp**, you mean that it is soft or weak when it should be firm or strong. ❑ *A residue can build up on the hair shaft, leaving the hair limp and dull looking.* ♦ **limp|ly** *Flags and bunting hung limply in the still, warm air.* 4 If someone is **limp**, their body has no strength and is not moving, for example because they are asleep or un-

VERB; V; V adv/prep; N-COUNT: usu *a* N in sing; VERB; V adv/prep; V adv/prep; ADJ; ADV: ADV with v; ADJ

conscious. ❑ *He carried her limp body into the room and laid her on the bed.*

**lim|pet** /lɪ̲mpɪt/ **(limpets)** A **limpet** is a small sea animal with a cone-shaped shell which attaches itself tightly to rocks. N-COUNT

**lim|pid** /lɪ̲mpɪd/ [1] If you say that something is **limpid**, you mean that it is very clear and transparent. [LITERARY] ❑ *...limpid blue eyes. ...limpid rock-pools.* ADJ = *translucent* [2] If you describe speech, writing, or music as **limpid**, you like it because it is clear, simple and flowing. [LITERARY] ❑ *He thought the speech a model of its kind, limpid and unaffected.* ADJ [approval]

**linch|pin** /lɪ̲ntʃpɪn/ **(linchpins)** also **lynchpin.** If you refer to a person or thing as the **linchpin** of something, you mean that they are the most important person or thing involved in it. ❑ *He's the lynchpin of our team and crucial to my long-term plans.* N-COUNT: with supp, usu N *of* n

**lin|den** /lɪ̲ndᵊn/ **(lindens)** A **linden** or a **linden tree** is a large tree with pale green leaves which is often planted in parks in towns and cities. N-VAR = *lime*

**line** /la̲ɪn/ **(lines, lining, lined)** ◆◆◆ [1] A **line** is a long thin mark which is drawn or painted on a surface. ❑ *Draw a line down that page's center. ...a dotted line... The ball had clearly crossed the line.* N-COUNT [2] The **lines** on someone's skin, especially on their face, are long thin marks that appear there as they grow older. ❑ *He has a large, generous face with deep lines.* N-COUNT: usu pl = *wrinkle* [3] A **line** of people or things is a number of them arranged one behind the other or side by side. ❑ *The sparse line of spectators noticed nothing unusual.* N-COUNT: oft N *of* n = *row* [4] A **line** of people or vehicles is a number of them that are waiting one behind another, for example in order to buy something or to go in a particular direction. ❑ *Children clutching empty bowls form a line.* N-COUNT = *queue* [5] A **line** of a piece of writing is one of the rows of words, numbers, or other symbols in it. ❑ *The next line should read: Five days, 23.5 hours... Tina wouldn't have read more than three lines.* N-COUNT [6] A **line** of a poem, song, or play is a group of words that are spoken or sung together. If an actor **learns** his or her **lines** for a play or film, they learn what they have to say. ❑ *...a line from Shakespeare's Othello: 'one that loved not wisely but too well'... Learning lines is very easy. Acting is very difficult.* N-COUNT [7] You can refer to a long piece of wire, string, or cable as a **line** when it is used for a particular purpose. ❑ *She put her washing on the line. ...a piece of fishing-line... The winds downed power lines.* N-VAR: usu with supp [8] A **line** is a connection which makes it possible for two people to speak to each other on the telephone. ❑ *The telephone lines went dead... It's not a very good line. Shall we call you back Susan?... She's on the line from her home in Boston.* N-COUNT: oft *on the* N [9] You can use **line** to refer to a telephone number which you can ring in order to get information or advice. ❑ *...the 24-hours information line.* N-COUNT: oft in names after n [10] A **line** is a route, especially a dangerous or secret one, along which people move or send messages or supplies. ❑ *Negotiators say they're keeping communication lines open. ...the guerrillas' main supply lines.* N-COUNT: usu pl, usu with supp [11] The **line** in which something or someone moves is the particular route that they take, especially when they keep moving straight ahead. ❑ *Walk in a straight line... The wings were at right angles to the line of flight.* N-COUNT [12] A **line** is a particular route, involving the same stations, roads, or stops along which a train or bus service regularly operates. ❑ *They've got to ride all the way to the end of the line... I would be able to stay on the Piccadilly Line and get off the tube at South Kensington.* N-COUNT: usu with supp, oft in names after n [13] A railway **line** consists of the pieces of metal and wood which form the track that the trains travel along. N-COUNT = *track* [14] A shipping, air, or bus **line** is a company which provides services for transporting people or goods by sea, air, or bus. [BUSINESS] ❑ *The Foreign Office offered to pay the shipping line all the costs of diverting the ship to Bermuda.* N-COUNT: usu supp N = *company* [15] A state or county **line** is a boundary between two states or counties. [AM] ❑ *...the California state line.* N-COUNT: usu sing, with supp = *border* [16] You can use **lines** to refer to the set of physical defences or the soldiers that have been established along the boundary of an area occupied by an army. ❑ *Their unit was shelling the German lines only seven miles away.* N-COUNT [17] The particular **line** that a person has towards a problem is the attitude that they have towards it. For example, if someone takes a **hard line** on something, they have a firm strict policy which they refuse to change. ❑ *Forty members of the governing Conservative party rebelled, voting against the government line.* N-COUNT: usu sing, with supp [18] You can use **line** to refer to the way in which someone's thoughts or activities develop, particularly if it is logical. ❑ *What are some of the practical benefits likely to be of this line of research?* N-COUNT: usu N *of* n/-ing [19] If you say that something happens **along** particular **lines**, or **on** particular **lines**, you are giving a general summary or approximate account of what happens, which may not be correct in every detail. ❑ *He'd said something along those lines already... Our forecast for 1990 was on the right lines.* N-PLURAL: usu *along/on* N with supp [20] If something is organized **on** particular **lines**, or **along** particular **lines**, it is organized according to that method or principle. ❑ *...so-called autonomous republics based on ethnic lines. ...reorganising old factories to work along Japanese lines.* N-PLURAL: *on/along* N with supp [21] Your **line of** business or work is the kind of work that you do. [BUSINESS] ❑ *So what was your father's line of business?... In my line of work I often get home too late for dinner.* N-COUNT: usu N *of* n [22] A **line** is a particular type of product that a company makes or sells. ❑ *His best selling line is the cheapest lager at £1.99.* N-COUNT [23] In a factory, a **line** is an arrangement of workers or machines where a product passes from one worker to another until it is finished. ❑ *...a production line capable of producing three different products.* N-COUNT [24] You can use **line** when you are referring to a number of people who are ranked according to status. ❑ *Nicholas Paul Patrick was seventh in the line of succession to the throne. ...the man who stands next in line for the presidency.* N-COUNT: usu sing, oft N *of* n, ord *in* N [25] A particular **line of** people or things is a series of them that has existed over a period of time, when they have all been similar in some way, or done similar things. ❑ *We were part of a long line of artists... It's the latest in a long line of tragedies.* N-COUNT: usu sing, usu N *of* n [26] If people or things **line** a road, room, or other place, they are present in large numbers along its edges or sides. ❑ *Thousands of local people lined the streets and clapped as the procession went by.* V n *...a square lined with pubs and clubs.* V-ed ♦ **-lined** *...a long tree-lined drive.* COMB in ADJ [27] If you **line** a wall, container, or other object, you put a layer of something such as leaves or paper on the inside surface of it in order to make it stronger, warmer, or cleaner. ❑ *Scoop the blanket weed out and use it to line hanging baskets...* V n *Female bears tend to line their dens with leaves or grass.* V n *with* n ♦ **-lined** *...a dark, suede-lined case.* VERB; COMB in ADJ [28] If something **lines** a container or area, especially an area inside a person, animal, or plant, it forms a layer on the inside surface. ❑ *...the muscles that line the intestines.* VERB; V n [29] → See also **lined, lining, bottom line, branch line, dividing line, front line, party line, picket line, yellow line.**

**PHRASES** [30] If you **draw the line at** a particular activity, you refuse to do it, because you disapprove of it or because it is more extreme than what you normally do. ❑ *Letters have come from prisoners, declaring that they would draw the line at hitting an old lady.* PHRASE: V inflects, oft PHR *at* n/-ing [31] If you **draw a line between** two things, you make a distinction between them. ❑ *It is, however, not possible to draw a distinct line between the two categories.* PHRASE: V inflects = *distinguish* [32] If you do something or if it happens to you **in the line of duty**, you do it or it happens as part of your regular work or as a result of it. ❑ *More than 3,000 police officers were wounded in the line of duty last year.* PHRASE: PHR after v, v-link PHR [33] If you refer to a method as **the first line of**, for example, defence or treatment, you mean that it is the first or most important method to be used in dealing with a problem. ❑ *Pass-* PHRASE: PHR n

*port checks will remain the first line of defence against terrorists.* **34** If you are **in line for** something, it is likely to happen to you or you are likely to obtain it. If something is **in line to** happen, it is likely to happen. ❑ *He must be in line for a place in the Guinness Book of Records... Public sector pay is also in line to be hit hard.* PHRASE: PHR *for* n, PHR to-inf = *due*
**35** If one object is **in line with** others, or moves **into line with** others, they are arranged in a line. You can also say that a number of objects are **in line** or move **into line**. ❑ *The device itself was right under the vehicle, almost in line with the gear lever... Venus, the Sun and Earth all moved into line.* PHRASE: v-link PHR, PHR after v, oft PHR *with* n
**36** If one thing is **in line with** another, or is brought **into line with** it, the first thing is, or becomes, similar to the second, especially in a way that has been planned or expected. ❑ *The structure of our schools is now broadly in line with the major countries of the world... This brings the law into line with most medical opinion.* PHRASE: usu PHR after v, v-link PHR, oft PHR *with* n
**37** When people **stand in line** or **wait in line**, they stand one behind the other in a line, waiting their turn for something. [AM] ❑ *I had been standing in line for three hours.* PHRASE: V inflects

✔ in BRIT, use **queue**

**38** If you **keep** someone **in line** or **bring** them **into line**, you make them obey you, or you make them behave in the way you want them to. ❑ *All this was just designed to frighten me and keep me in line. ...if the Prime Minister fails to bring rebellious Tories into line.* PHRASE: PHR after v
**39** If a machine or piece of equipment comes **on line**, it starts operating. If it is **off line**, it is not operating. ❑ *The new machine will go on line in June 2006... Every second her equipment was off line cost the company money.* PHRASE: usu PHR after v
**40** If you do something **on line**, you do it using a computer or a computer network. ❑ *They can order their requirements on line. ...on-line transaction processing.* PHRASE: PHR after v, v-link PHR, PHR n
**41** If something such as your job, career, or reputation is **on the line**, you may lose or harm it as a result of what you are doing or of the situation you are in. [INFORMAL] ❑ *He wouldn't put his career on the line to help a friend.* PHRASE: usu PHR after v, v-link PHR
**42** If one thing is **out of line** with another, the first thing is different from the second in a way that was not agreed, planned, or expected. ❑ *...if one set of figures is sharply out of line with a trend.* PHRASE: usu v-link PHR, oft PHR *with* n
**43** If someone steps **out of line**, they disobey someone or behave in an unacceptable way. ❑ *Any one of my players who steps out of line will be in trouble with me as well... You're way out of line, lady.* PHRASE: v PHR, v-link PHR
**44** If you **read between the lines**, you understand what someone really means, or what is really happening in a situation, even though it is not said openly. ❑ *Reading between the lines, it seems neither Cole nor Ledley King will be going to Japan.* PHRASE: V inflects
**45** to **sign on the dotted line** → see **dotted**. to **line** your **pockets** → see **pocket**. **the line of least resistance** → see **resistance**. to **toe the line** → see **toe**.

♦ **line up** **1** If people **line up** or if you **line** them **up**, they move so that they are standing in a line. ❑ *The senior leaders lined up behind him in orderly rows... The gym teachers lined us up against the cement walls... When he came back the sergeant had lined up the terrorists.* PHRASAL VERB V P, V n P, V P n (not pron)
**2** If you **line** things **up**, you move them into a straight row. ❑ *I would line up my toys on this windowsill and play... He finished polishing the cocktail glasses and lined them up behind the bar.* PHRASAL VERB V P n (not pron), V n P
**3** If you **line** one thing **up with** another, or one thing **lines up with** another, the first thing is moved into its correct position in relation to the second. You can also say that two things **line up**, or **are lined up**. ❑ *You have to line the car up with the ones beside you... Gas cookers are adjustable in height to line up with your kitchen work top... Mahoney had lined up two of the crates... When the images line up exactly, the projectors should be fixed in place... All we have to do is to get the two pieces lined up properly.* PHRASAL VERB = *align* V n P *with* n, V P *with* n, V P pl-n, pl-n V P, V-ed P
**4** If you **line up** an event or activity, you arrange for it to happen. If you **line** someone **up** for an event or activity, you arrange for them to be available for that event or activity. ❑ *She lined up executives, politicians and educators to serve on the board of directors... Bob Dylan is lining up a two-week UK tour for the New Year.* PHRASAL VERB V P n to-inf, V P n (not pron), Also V n P, V n P to-inf
**5** → See also **line-up**.

**lin|eage** /lɪniɪdʒ/ (**lineages**) Someone's **lineage** is the series of families from which they are directly descended. [FORMAL] ❑ *They can trace their lineage directly back to the 18th century.* N-VAR

**lin|eal** /lɪniəl/ A **lineal** descendant of a particular person or family is someone in a later generation who is directly related to them. [FORMAL] ADJ: ADJ n = *direct*

**lin|ear** /lɪniəʳ/ **1** A **linear** process or development is one in which something changes or progresses straight from one stage to another, and has a starting point and an ending point. ❑ *...the linear view of time, with the idea that the past is moving into the present and the present into the future.* ADJ: usu ADJ n
**2** A **linear** shape or form consists of straight lines. ❑ *...the sharp, linear designs of the Seventies and Eighties.* ADJ: usu ADJ n
**3** **Linear** movement or force occurs in a straight line rather than in a curve. ADJ: usu ADJ n

**line|back|er** /laɪnbækəʳ/ (**linebackers**) In American football, a **linebacker** is a player who tries to stop members of the other team from scoring by tackling them. N-COUNT

**lined** /laɪnd/ **1** If someone's face or skin is **lined**, it has lines on it as a result of old age, tiredness, worry, or illness. ❑ *His lined face was that of an old man.* ADJ
**2** **Lined** paper has lines printed across it to help you write neatly. ADJ
**3** → See also **line**.

**line danc|ing** **Line dancing** is a style of dancing in which people move across the floor in a line, accompanied by country and western music. N-UNCOUNT

**line draw|ing** (**line drawings**) A **line drawing** is a drawing which consists only of lines. N-COUNT

**line man|ag|er** (**line managers**) Your **line manager** is the person at work who is in charge of your department, group, or project. [BRIT, BUSINESS] N-COUNT

**lin|en** /lɪnɪn/ (**linens**) **1** **Linen** is a kind of cloth that is made from a plant called flax. It is used for making clothes and things such as tablecloths and sheets. ❑ *...a white linen suit. ...cottons, woolens, silks and linens.* N-MASS
**2** **Linen** is tablecloths, sheets, pillowcases, and similar things made of cloth that are used in the home. ❑ *...embroidered bed linen.* N-UNCOUNT: also N in pl
**3** to **wash** your **dirty linen in public** → see **dirty**.

**line of sight** (**lines of sight**) Your **line of sight** is an imaginary line that stretches between your eye and the object that you are looking at. ❑ *He was trying to keep out of the bird's line of sight.* N-COUNT: usu sing, oft with poss

**line of vi|sion** Your **line of vision** is the same as your **line of sight**. ❑ *Any crack in a car windscreen always seems to be right in the driver's line of vision.* N-SING: usu with poss

**lin|er** /laɪnəʳ/ (**liners**) A **liner** is a large ship in which people travel long distances, especially on holiday. ❑ *...luxury ocean liners.* → See also **bin liner**. N-COUNT: oft n N

**lin|er note** (**liner notes**) The **liner notes** on record jackets are short pieces of writing that tell you something about the record or the musicians playing on the record. [AM] N-COUNT: usu pl

✔ in BRIT, use **sleeve notes**

**lines|man** /laɪnzmən/ (**linesmen**) A **linesman** is an official who assists the referee or umpire in games such as football and tennis by indicating when the ball goes over the lines around the edge of the field or court. N-COUNT

**line-up** (**line-ups**) **1** A **line-up** is a group of people or a series of things that have been gathered together to be part of a particular event. ❑ *The programme is back for a new series with a great line-up of musicians and comedy acts.* N-COUNT
**2** At a **line-up**, a witness to a crime tries to identify the crimi- N-COUNT = *identity parade*

nal from among a line of people. ❑ *He failed to identify Graham from photographs, but later picked him out of a police line-up.*

**lin|ger** /lɪŋgəʳ/ **(lingers, lingering, lingered)** 1 When something such as an idea, feeling, or illness **lingers**, it continues to exist for a long time, often much longer than expected. ❑ *The scent of her perfume lingered on in the room... He was ashamed. That feeling lingered, and he was never comfortable in church after that... He would rather be killed in a race than die a lingering death in hospital.* VERB V adv/prep V V-ing 2 If you **linger** somewhere, you stay there for a longer time than is necessary, for example because you are enjoying yourself. ❑ *Customers are welcome to linger over coffee until around midnight... It is a dreary little town where few would choose to linger.* VERB V adv/prep V

**lin|gerie** /lænʒəri, AM -reɪ/ **Lingerie** is women's underwear and nightclothes. N-UNCOUNT

**lin|go** /lɪŋgoʊ/ **(lingos)** 1 People sometimes refer to a foreign language, especially one that they do not speak or understand, as a **lingo**. [INFORMAL] ❑ *I don't speak the lingo.* N-COUNT: usu sing 2 A **lingo** is a range of words or a style of language which is used in a particular situation or by a particular group of people. [INFORMAL] ❑ *In record-business lingo, that means he wanted to buy the rights to the song and market it. ...an author who writes in a lurid lingo, freely punctuated with crude expletives.* N-UNCOUNT: also *a* N, usu with supp

**lin|gua fran|ca** /lɪŋgwə fræŋkə/ A **lingua franca** is a language or way of communicating which is used between people who do not speak one another's native language. [FORMAL] ❑ *English is rapidly becoming the lingua franca of Asia.* N-SING

**lin|guist** /lɪŋgwɪst/ **(linguists)** 1 A **linguist** is someone who is good at speaking or learning foreign languages. ❑ *Her brother was an accomplished linguist.* N-COUNT 2 A **linguist** is someone who studies or teaches linguistics. N-COUNT

**lin|guis|tic** /lɪŋgwɪstɪks/ **(linguistics)**
1 **Linguistic** abilities or ideas relate to language or linguistics. ❑ *...linguistic skills. ...linguistic theory.* ADJ: usu ADJ n ♦ **lin|guis|ti|cal|ly** /lɪŋgwɪstɪkli/ *Somalia is an ethnically and linguistically homogeneous nation.* ADV: usu ADV adj/-ed 2 **Linguistics** is the study of the way in which language works. ❑ *...applied linguistics.* N-UNCOUNT

**lini|ment** /lɪnɪmənt/ **(liniments) Liniment** is a liquid that you rub into your skin in order to reduce pain or stiffness. N-MASS

**lin|ing** /laɪnɪŋ/ **(linings)** 1 The **lining** of something such as a piece of clothing or a curtain is a layer of cloth attached to the inside of it in order to make it thicker or warmer, or in order to make it hang better. ❑ *...a padded satin jacket with quilted lining.* N-VAR 2 You can use **lining** to refer to a layer of paper, plastic, metal, or another substance that is attached to the inside of something, for example in order to protect it. ❑ *...brake linings... Moss makes an attractive lining to wire baskets.* N-VAR
3 The **lining** of your stomach or other organ is a layer of tissue on the inside of it. ❑ *...a bacterium that attacks the lining of the stomach. ...the uterine lining.* N-COUNT: usu with supp 4 → See also **line**.

**link** /lɪŋk/ **(links, linking, linked)** 1 If there is a **link between** two things or situations, there is a relationship between them, for example because one thing causes or affects the other. ❑ *...the link between smoking and lung cancer.* ◆◆◇ N-COUNT: usu N *between/with* n = connection 2 If someone or something **links** two things or situations, there is a relationship between them, for example because one thing causes or affects the other. ❑ *The UN Security Council has linked any lifting of sanctions to compliance with the ceasefire terms... Liver cancer is linked to the hepatitis B virus... The detention raised two distinct but closely linked questions.* → See also **index-linked**. VERB V n to/with n V n to/with n V-ed 3 A **link between** two things or places is a physical connection between them. ❑ *...the high-speed rail link between London and the Channel Tunnel... Stalin insisted that the radio link with the German Foreign Ministry should remain open.* N-COUNT: oft supp N, usu N *between/with* n
4 If two places or objects **are linked** or something **links** them, there is a physical connection between them. ❑ *...the Rama Road, which links the capital, Managua, with the Caribbean coast... The campus is linked by regular bus services to Coventry. ...the Channel Tunnel linking Britain and France.* VERB V n *with/to* n V n *with/to* n V pl-n 5 A **link** between two people, organizations, or places is a friendly or business connection between them. ❑ *Kiev hopes to cement close links with Bonn... In 1984 the long link between AC Cars and the Hurlock family was severed... A cabinet minister came under investigation for links to the Mafia.* N-COUNT: usu N *with/between/to* n 6 A **link** to another person or organization is something that allows you to communicate with them or have contact with them. ❑ *She was my only link with the past... These projects will provide vital links between companies and universities.* N-COUNT: N *with/between/to* n 7 If you **link** one person or thing to another, you claim that there is a relationship or connection between them. ❑ *Criminologist Dr Ann Jones has linked the crime to social circumstances... They've linked her with various men, including magnate Donald Trump.* VERB V n *to/with* n V n *to/with* n Also V pl-n 8 In computing, a **link** is a connection between different documents, or between different parts of the same document, using hypertext. ♦ **Link** is also a verb. ❑ *Certainly, Andreessen didn't think up using hypertext to link Internet documents.* N-COUNT VERB V n 9 A **link** is one of the rings in a chain. N-COUNT 10 If you **link** one thing with another, you join them by putting one thing through the other. ❑ *She linked her arm through his... He linked the fingers of his hands together on his stomach.* VERB V n prep/adv V n prep/adv Also V n ● If two or more people **link arms**, or if one person **links arms** with another, they stand next to each other, and each person puts their arm round the arm of the person next to them. ❑ *She stayed with them, linking arms with the two girls, joking with the boys.* PHRASE: pl-n PHR, PHR *with* n 11 → See also **link-up**.

♦ **link up** 1 If you **link up with** someone, you join them for a particular purpose. ❑ *They linked up with a series of local anti-nuclear and anti-apartheid groups... The Russian and American armies linked up for the first time on the banks of the river Elbe.* PHRASAL VERB = join up V P *with* n pl-n V P 2 If one thing **is linked up to** another, the two things are connected to each other. ❑ *The television screens of the next century will be linked up to an emerging world telecommunications grid.* PHRASAL VERB: usu passive = connect *be* V-ed P *to* n Also *be* V-ed P

**link|age** /lɪŋkɪdʒ/ **(linkages)** 1 A **linkage between** two things is a link or connection between them. The **linkage of** two things is the act of linking or connecting them. ❑ *No one disputes the direct linkage between the unemployment rate and crime... We're trying to establish linkages between these groups and financial institutions. ...the creation of new research materials by the linkage of previously existing sources.* N-VAR: oft N *between/with/of* n 2 **Linkage** is an arrangement where one country agrees to do something only if another country agrees to do something in return. ❑ *There is no formal linkage between the two agreements... He insisted that there could be no linkage with other Mideast problems.* N-UNCOUNT: oft N *between/with* n

**link|ing verb (linking verbs)**

☑ in BRIT, also use **link verb**

A **linking verb** is a verb which links the subject of a clause and a complement. 'Be', 'seem', and 'become' are linking verbs. N-COUNT = *copula*

**link|ing word (linking words)**

☑ in BRIT, also use **link word**

A **linking word** is a word which shows a connection between clauses or sentences. 'However' and 'so' are linking words. N-COUNT

**link-up (link-ups)** 1 A **link-up** is a connection between two machines or communication systems. ❑ *...a live satellite link-up with Bonn. ...computer link-ups with banks in Spain, Portugal, and France.* N-COUNT: oft N *with/between* n
2 A **link-up** is a relationship or partnership between two organizations. ❑ *...new link-ups between school and commerce.* N-COUNT: oft N *with/between* n

**lino** /laɪnoʊ/ **Lino** is the same as **linoleum**. [BRIT] ❑ *...lino floors.* N-UNCOUNT: oft N n

**li|no|leum** /lɪnoʊliəm/ **Linoleum** is a floor covering which is made of cloth covered with a hard shiny substance. ❑ *...a gray linoleum floor. ...black-and-white squares of linoleum.* N-UNCOUNT: oft N n

**lin|seed oil** /lɪnsiːd ɔɪl/ **Linseed oil** is an oil made from seeds of the flax plant. It is used to make paints and inks, or to rub into wooden surfaces to protect them. N-UNCOUNT

**lint** /lɪnt/ [1] **Lint** is cotton or linen fabric which you can put on your skin if you have a cut. N-UNCOUNT [2] **Lint** is small unwanted threads or fibres that collect on clothes. [mainly AM] N-UNCOUNT = fluff

**lin|tel** /lɪntəl/ **(lintels)** A **lintel** is a piece of stone or wood over a door or window which supports the bricks above the door or window. → See picture on page 1705. N-COUNT

**lion** /laɪən/ **(lions)** A **lion** is a large wild member of the cat family that is found in Africa. Lions have yellowish fur, and male lions have long hair on their head and neck. N-COUNT

**li|on|ess** /laɪənɪs/ **(lionesses)** A **lioness** is a female lion. N-COUNT

**li|on|ize** /laɪənaɪz/ **(lionizes, lionizing, lionized)**

✔ in BRIT, also use **lionise**

If someone **is lionized**, they are treated as if they are very important or special by a particular group of people, often when they do not really deserve to be. [FORMAL] ❑ *By the 1920's, he was lionised by literary London... The press began to lionize him enthusiastically... In 1936, Max Schmeling had been lionised as boxing's great hope.* VERB *be* V-ed; V n; *be* V-ed *as* n

**lion's share** If a person, group, or project gets **the lion's share of** something, they get the largest part of it, leaving very little for other people. ❑ *Military and nuclear research have received the lion's share of public funding.* N-SING: usu *the* N *of* n

**lip** /lɪp/ **(lips)** ◆◇◇ [1] Your **lips** are the two outer parts of the edge of your mouth. ❑ *Wade stuck the cigarette between his lips.* N-COUNT: usu pl, oft poss N [2] The **lip** of something such as a container or a high area of land is its edge. ❑ *...the lip of the jug. ...the lip of Mount Etna's smouldering crater.* N-COUNT: usu with supp, oft N *of* n = rim [3] If you **lick** your **lips**, you move your tongue across your lips as you think about or taste something pleasant. ❑ *They licked their lips in anticipation... We swallowed the chocolates in one gulp, licking our lips.* PHRASE: V inflects

**lip gloss (lip glosses) Lip gloss** is a clear or very slightly coloured substance that some women put on their lips to make them shiny. N-MASS

**lipo|suc|tion** /lɪpoʊsʌkʃən/ **Liposuction** is a form of cosmetic surgery where fat is removed from a particular area of the body by dissolving it with special chemicals and then sucking it out with a tube. N-UNCOUNT

**-lipped** /-lɪpt/ **-lipped** combines with adjectives to form other adjectives which describe the sort of lips that someone has. ❑ *A thin-lipped smile spread over the captain's face. ...his full-lipped mouth.* → See also **tight-lipped**. COMB in ADJ

**lip|py** /lɪpi/ **(lippies)** [1] If someone is **lippy**, they speak to other people in a way that shows no respect. [BRIT, INFORMAL] ❑ *Bruce Willis plays a lippy cop battling it out with a female partner.* ADJ [2] **Lippy** is short for **lipstick**. [BRIT, INFORMAL] N-MASS

**lip-read (lip-reads, lip-reading)**

✔ The form **lip-read** is pronounced /lɪpriːd/ when it is the present tense, and /lɪpred/ when it is the past tense and past participle.

If someone can **lip-read**, they are able to understand what someone else is saying by looking at the way the other person's lips move as they speak, without actually hearing any of the words. ❑ *They are not given hearing aids or taught to lip-read.* ♦ **lip read|ing** *The teacher should not move around too much as this makes lip reading more difficult.* VERB; V; N-UNCOUNT

**lip ser|vice** If you say that someone pays **lip service** to an idea, you are critical of them because they say they are in favour of it, but they do not do anything to support it. ❑ *Unhappily, he had done no more than pay lip service to their views.* N-UNCOUNT: usu N *to* n/-ing [disapproval]

**lip|stick** /lɪpstɪk/ **(lipsticks) Lipstick** is a coloured substance in the form of a stick which women put on their lips. ❑ *She was wearing red lipstick.* ♦ A **lipstick** is a small tube containing this substance. N-MASS; N-COUNT

**liq|ue|fy** /lɪkwɪfaɪ/ **(liquefies, liquefying, liquefied)** When a gas or solid substance **liquefies** or **is liquefied**, it changes its form and becomes liquid. ❑ *Heat the jam until it liquefies... You can liquefy the carbon dioxide to separate it from the other constituents. ...a truck carrying liquefied petroleum gas.* VERB; V; V n; V-ed

**li|queur** /lɪkjʊəʳ, AM -kɜːr/ **(liqueurs)** A **liqueur** is a strong alcoholic drink with a sweet taste. You drink it after a meal. ❑ *...liqueurs such as Grand Marnier and Kirsch. ...small glasses of liqueur.* ♦ A **liqueur** is a glass of liqueur. ❑ *'What about a liqueur with your coffee?' suggested the waitress.* N-MASS; N-COUNT

**liq|uid** /lɪkwɪd/ **(liquids)** [1] A **liquid** is a substance which is not solid but which flows and can be poured, for example water. ❑ *Drink plenty of liquid... Boil for 20 minutes until the liquid has reduced by half... Solids turn to liquids at certain temperatures.* N-MASS [2] A **liquid** substance is in the form of a liquid rather than being solid or a gas. ❑ *Wash in warm water with liquid detergent. ...liquid nitrogen... Fats are solid at room temperature, and oil is liquid at room temperature.* ADJ [3] **Liquid** assets are the things that a person or company owns which can be quickly turned into cash if necessary. [BUSINESS] ❑ *The bank had sufficient liquid assets to continue operations.* ADJ

**liq|ui|date** /lɪkwɪdeɪt/ **(liquidates, liquidating, liquidated)** [1] To **liquidate** a company is to close it down and sell all its assets, usually because it is in debt. [BUSINESS] ❑ *A unanimous vote was taken to liquidate the company.* ♦ **liq|ui|da|tion** /lɪkwɪdeɪʃən/ **(liquidations)** *The company went into liquidation... The number of company liquidations rose 11 per cent.* VERB; V n; N-VAR [2] If a company **liquidates** its assets, its property such as buildings or machinery is sold in order to get money. [BUSINESS] ❑ *The company closed down operations and began liquidating its assets in January.* VERB; V n [3] If someone in a position of power **liquidates** people who are causing problems, they get rid of them, usually by killing them. ❑ *They have not hesitated in the past to liquidate their rivals.* VERB = eliminate; V n

**liq|ui|da|tor** /lɪkwɪdeɪtəʳ/ **(liquidators)** A **liquidator** is a person who is responsible for settling the affairs of a company that is being liquidated. [BUSINESS] N-COUNT

**liq|uid crys|tal (liquid crystals)** A **liquid crystal** is a liquid that has some of the qualities of crystals, for example reflecting light from different directions in different ways. N-COUNT

**liq|uid crys|tal dis|play (liquid crystal displays)** also **liquid-crystal display**. A **liquid crystal display** is a display of information on a screen, which uses liquid crystals that become visible when electricity is passed through them. N-COUNT = LCD

**li|quid|ity** /lɪkwɪdɪti/ In finance, a company's **liquidity** is the amount of cash or liquid assets it has easily available. [BUSINESS] ❑ *The company maintains a high degree of liquidity.* N-UNCOUNT: oft N n

**liq|uid|ize** /lɪkwɪdaɪz/ **(liquidizes, liquidizing, liquidized)**

✔ in BRIT, also use **liquidise**

If you **liquidize** food, you process it using an electrical appliance in order to make it liquid. VERB

**liq|uid|iz|er** /lɪkwɪdaɪzəʳ/ **(liquidizers)**

✔ in BRIT, also use **liquidiser**

A **liquidizer** is an electric machine that you use to liquidize food. [mainly BRIT] N-COUNT

✔ in AM, use **blender**

**liq|uor** /lɪkəʳ/ **(liquors)** Strong alcoholic drinks such as whisky, vodka, and gin can be referred to N-MASS as **liquor**. [AM] ❑ *The room was filled with cases of liquor. ...intoxicating liquors.*

✓ in BRIT, use **spirits**

**liquo|rice** /lɪkərɪʃ, -ɪs/ → see **licorice**.

**liq|uor store** **(liquor stores)** A **liquor store** is a store which sells beer, wine, and other alcoholic drinks. [AM] N-COUNT

✓ in BRIT, use **off-licence**

**lira** /lɪərə/ **(lire** /lɪərə/**)** The **lira** was the unit of money that is used in Italy. Turkey and Syria also have a unit of money called a **lira**. In 2002 it was replaced by the euro in Italy. ❑ *It only cost me 400,000 lire... Coin-operated telephones took 100, 200 and 500 lire coins.* N-COUNT: usu num N ♦ **The lira** was also used to refer to the Italian currency system, and it also sometimes refers to the currency system of other countries which use the lira. ❑ *The franc had been under no pressure compared with the lira and the pound.* N-SING: the N

**lisp** /lɪsp/ **(lisps, lisping, lisped)** [1] If someone has **a lisp**, they pronounce the sounds 's' and 'z' as if they were 'th'. For example, they say 'thing' instead of 'sing'. ❑ *He has a slight lisp.* N-COUNT: usu sing [2] If someone **lisps**, they say something with a lisp or speak with a lisp. ❑ *The little man, upset, was lisping badly... Bochmann lisped his congratulations. ...her low, lisping voice.* VERB V V n V-ing

**list** /lɪst/ **(lists, listing, listed)** ◆◆◆ [1] A **list** of things such as names or addresses is a set of them which all belong to a particular category, written down one below the other. ❑ *We are making a list of the top ten men we would not want to be married to... There were six names on the list. ...fine wine from the hotel's exhaustive wine list.* → See also **Civil List, hit list, honours list, laundry list, mailing list, shopping list, waiting list**. N-COUNT: oft N of n [2] A **list** of things is a set of them that you think of as being in a particular order. ❑ *High on the list of public demands is to end military control of broadcasting... I would have thought if they were looking for redundancies I would be last on the list... 'First City' joined a long list of failed banks.* N-COUNT: oft N of n [3] To **list** several things such as reasons or names means to write or say them one after another, usually in a particular order. ❑ *Manufacturers must list ingredients in order of the amount used.* VERB V n [4] To **list** something in a particular way means to include it in that way in a list or report. ❑ *A medical examiner has listed the deaths as homicides... He was not listed under his real name on the residents panel.* VERB V n prep V-ed [5] If a company **is listed**, or if it **lists**, on a stock exchange, it obtains an official quotation for its shares so that people can buy and sell them. [BUSINESS] ❑ *It will list on the London Stock Exchange next week with a value of 130 million pounds.* VERB V Also V n [6] → See also **listed, listing**.

**list|ed** /lɪstɪd/ In Britain, a **listed** building is protected by law against being destroyed or altered because it is historically or architecturally important. ADJ: usu ADJ n

**list|ed com|pa|ny** **(listed companies)** A **listed company** is a company whose shares are quoted on a stock exchange. [BUSINESS] N-COUNT

**lis|ten** /lɪsᵊn/ **(listens, listening, listened)** ◆◆◇ [1] If you **listen to** someone who is talking or **to** a sound, you give your attention to them or it. ❑ *He spent his time listening to the radio... Sonia was not listening.* VERB V to n V ♦ **lis|ten|er** **(listeners)** *One or two listeners had fallen asleep while the President was speaking.* N-COUNT [2] If you **listen for** a sound, you keep alert and are ready to hear it if it occurs. ❑ *We listen for footsteps approaching... They're both asleep upstairs, but you don't mind listening just in case, do you?* VERB V for n V ♦ **Listen out** means the same as **listen**. [BRIT] ❑ *I didn't really listen out for the lyrics.* PHRASAL VERB V P for n Also V P [3] If you **listen to** someone, you do what they advise you to do, or you believe them. ❑ *Anne, you need to listen to me this time... When I asked him to stop, he would not listen.* VERB V to n V [4] You say **listen** when you want someone to pay attention to you because you are going to say something important. ❑ *Listen, I finish at one.* CONVENTION = look

♦ **listen in** If you **listen in** to a private conversation, you secretly listen to it. ❑ *He assigned federal agents to listen in on Martin Luther King's phone calls.* PHRASAL VERB = eavesdrop V P to/on n Also V P

**lis|ten|able** /lɪsᵊnəbᵊl/ If something is **listenable**, it is very pleasant to listen to. ❑ *It's an eminently listenable CD.* ADJ

**lis|ten|er** /lɪsnəʳ/ **(listeners)** [1] A **listener** is a person who listens to the radio or to a particular radio programme. ❑ *I'm a regular listener to her show.* N-COUNT [2] If you describe someone as a good **listener**, you mean that they listen carefully and sympathetically to you when you talk, for example about your problems. ❑ *Dr Brian was a good listener... If you can be a sympathetic listener, it may put your own problems in perspective.* N-COUNT: adj N [3] → See also **listen**.

**list|ing** /lɪstɪŋ/ **(listings)** A **listing** is a published list, or an item in a published list. ❑ *A full listing of the companies will be published quarterly.* N-COUNT

**list|less** /lɪstləs/ Someone who is **listless** has no energy or enthusiasm. ❑ *He was listless and pale and wouldn't eat much.* ADJ ♦ **list|less|ly** *Usually, you would just sit listlessly, too hot to do anything else.* ADV: ADV with v ♦ **list|less|ness** *Amy was distressed by Helen's listlessness.* N-UNCOUNT

**list price** **(list prices)** The **list price** of an item is the price which the manufacturer suggests that a shopkeeper should charge for it. N-COUNT

**lit** /lɪt/ **Lit** is a past tense and past participle of **light**.

**lita|ny** /lɪtəni/ **(litanies)** [1] If you describe what someone says as a **litany of** things, you mean that you have heard it many times before, and you think it is boring or insincere. ❑ *She remained in the doorway, listening to his litany of complaints against her client.* N-COUNT: usu with supp, oft N of n [disapproval] [2] A **litany** is part of a church service in which the priest says a set group of words and the people reply, also using a set group of words. N-COUNT

**lite** /laɪt/ **Lite** is used to describe foods or drinks that contain few calories or low amounts of sugar, fat, or alcohol. ❑ *...lite beer. ...lite yogurt.* ADJ

**li|ter** /liːtəʳ/ → see **litre**.

**lit|era|cy** /lɪtərəsi/ **Literacy** is the ability to read and write. ❑ *Many adults have some problems with literacy and numeracy... The literacy rate there is the highest in Central America.* N-UNCOUNT

**lit|er|al** /lɪtərəl/ [1] The **literal** sense of a word or phrase is its most basic sense. ❑ *In many cases, the people there are fighting, in a literal sense, for their homes.* ADJ: usu ADJ n [2] A **literal** translation is one in which you translate each word of the original work rather than giving the meaning of each expression or sentence using words that sound natural. ❑ *A literal translation of the name Tapies is 'walls.'* ADJ: usu ADJ n [3] You use **literal** to describe someone who uses or understands words in a plain and simple way. ❑ *Dennis is a very literal person.* ADJ [4] If you describe something as the **literal** truth or a **literal** fact, you are emphasizing that it is true. ❑ *He was saying no more than the literal truth.* ADJ: usu ADJ n [emphasis]

**lit|er|al|ly** /lɪtərəli/ [1] You can use **literally** to emphasize a statement. Some careful speakers of English think that this use is incorrect. ❑ *We've got to get the economy under control or it will literally eat us up... The views are literally breath-taking.* ADV: ADV with cl/group (not last in cl), ADV before v [emphasis] [2] You use **literally** to emphasize that what you are saying is true, even though it seems exaggerated or surprising. ❑ *Putting on an opera is a tremendous enterprise involving literally hundreds of people... I literally crawled to the car.* ADV: ADV with cl/group (not last in cl), ADV before v [emphasis] [3] If a word or expression is translated **literally**, its most simple or basic meaning is translated. ❑ *The word 'volk' translates literally as 'folk'... A stanza is, literally, a room.* ADV: ADV with v, ADV with cl [4] If you **take** something **literally**, you think that a word or expression is being used with its most simple or basic meaning. ❑ *If you tell a person to 'step on it' or 'throw on your coat,' they may take you literally, with disastrous consequences.* PHRASE: V inflects

**lit|er|ary** /lɪtərəri, AM -reri/ ◆◇◇ 1 **Literary** means concerned with or connected with the writing, study, or appreciation of literature. ❑ *She's the literary editor of the 'Sunday Review'. ...a literary masterpiece.* ADJ: usu ADJ n 2 **Literary** words and expressions are often unusual in some way and are used to create a special effect in a piece of writing such as a poem, speech, or novel. ADJ

**lit|er|ary criti|cism** **Literary criticism** is the academic study of the techniques used in the creation of literature. N-UNCOUNT

**lit|er|ate** /lɪtərət/ 1 Someone who is **literate** is able to read and write. ❑ *Over one-quarter of the adult population are not fully literate.* ADJ ≠ illiterate 2 If you describe someone as **literate**, you mean that they are intelligent and well-educated, especially about literature and the arts. ❑ *Scientists should be literate and articulate as well as able to handle figures.* ADJ approval 3 If you describe someone as **literate** in a particular subject, especially one that many people do not know anything about, you mean that they have a good knowledge and understanding of that subject. ❑ *Head teachers need to be financially literate.* ADJ: usu adv ADJ
→ See also **computer-literate**.

**lit|era|ti** /lɪtərɑːti/ **Literati** are well-educated people who are interested in literature. ❑ *...the Australian storyteller who was loved by readers but disdained by the literati.* N-PLURAL

**lit|era|ture** /lɪtrətʃəʳ, AM -tərətʃʊr/ ◆◇◇ **(literatures)** 1 Novels, plays, and poetry are referred to as **literature**, especially when they are considered to be good or important. ❑ *...classic works of literature. ...a Professor of English Literature... It may not be great literature but it certainly had me riveted!... The book explores the connection between American ethnic and regional literatures.* N-VAR 2 **The literature** on a particular subject of study is all the books and articles that have been published about it. ❑ *The literature on immigration policy is almost unrelievedly critical of the state... This work is documented in the scientific literature.* N-UNCOUNT: usu with supp 3 **Literature** is written information produced by people who want to sell you something or give you advice. ❑ *I am sending you literature from two other companies that provide a similar service.* N-UNCOUNT: usu with supp

**lithe** /laɪð/ A **lithe** person is able to move and bend their body easily and gracefully. ❑ *...a lithe young gymnast... His walk was lithe and graceful.* ADJ

**litho|graph** /lɪθəgrɑːf, -græf/ **(lithographs)** A **lithograph** is a printed picture made by the method of lithography. N-COUNT

**li|thog|ra|phy** /lɪθɒgrəfi/ **Lithography** is a method of printing in which a piece of stone or metal is specially treated so that ink sticks to some parts of it and not to others. N-UNCOUNT
♦ **litho|graph|ic** ❑ *The book's 85 colour lithographic plates look staggeringly fresh and bold.* ADJ: ADJ n

**Lithua|nian** /lɪθjueɪniən/ **(Lithuanians)** 1 **Lithuanian** means belonging or relating to Lithuania, or to its people, language, or culture. ADJ 2 A **Lithuanian** is a Lithuanian citizen, or a person of Lithuanian origin. N-COUNT 3 **Lithuanian** is the language spoken by people who live in Lithuania. N-UNCOUNT

**liti|gant** /lɪtɪgənt/ **(litigants)** A **litigant** is a person who is involved in a civil legal case, either because they are making a formal complaint about someone, or because a complaint is being made about them. [LEGAL] N-COUNT

**liti|gate** /lɪtɪgeɪt/ **(litigates, litigating, litigated)** To **litigate** means to take legal action. [LEGAL] ❑ *...the cost of litigating personal injury claims in the county court... If we have to litigate, we will.* VERB V n V

**liti|ga|tion** /lɪtɪgeɪʃən/ **Litigation** is the process of fighting or defending a case in a civil court of law. ❑ *The settlement ends more than four years of litigation on behalf of the residents.* N-UNCOUNT

**liti|ga|tor** /lɪtɪgeɪtəʳ/ **(litigators)** A **litigator** is a lawyer who helps someone take legal action. [LEGAL] N-COUNT

**li|ti|gious** /lɪtɪdʒəs/ Someone who is **litigious** often makes formal complaints about people to a civil court of law. [FORMAL] ADJ

**lit|mus test** /lɪtməs test/ **(litmus tests)** If you say that something is a **litmus test of** something, you mean that it is an effective and definite way of proving it or measuring it. ❑ *Ending the fighting must be the absolute priority, the litmus test of the agreements' validity... The success of wind power represents a litmus test for renewable energy.* N-COUNT: usu sing, usu N of/for n

**li|tre** /liːtəʳ/ **(litres)**

☑ in AM, use **liter**

A **litre** is a metric unit of volume that is a thousand cubic centimetres. It is equal to 1.76 British pints or 2.11 American pints. ❑ *...15 litres of water... This tax would raise petrol prices by about 3.5p per litre. ...a Ford Escort with a 1.9-litre engine.* N-COUNT: num N, oft N of n

**lit|ter** /lɪtəʳ/ **(litters, littering, littered)** 1 **Litter** is rubbish that is left lying around outside. ❑ *If you see litter in the corridor, pick it up... On Wednesday we cleared a beach and woodland of litter.* N-UNCOUNT = rubbish 2 A **litter of** things is a quantity of them that are lying around in a disorganized way. ❑ *He pushed aside the litter of books and papers and laid two places at the table.* N-UNCOUNT: usu N of n 3 If a number of things **litter** a place, they are scattered untidily around it or over it. ❑ *Glass from broken bottles litters the pavement.* VERB V n
♦ **lit|tered** *The entrance hall is littered with toys and wellington boots... Concrete purpose-built resorts are littered across the mountainsides.* ADJ: v-link ADJ prep 4 If something is **littered with** things, it contains many examples of it. ❑ *History is littered with men and women spurred into achievement by a father's disregard... Charles' speech is littered with lots of marketing buzzwords like 'package' and 'product'.* ADJ: v-link ADJ with n 5 A **litter** is a group of animals born to the same mother at the same time. ❑ *...a litter of pups.* N-COUNT 6 **Litter** is a dry substance that you put in the container where you want your cat to go to the toilet. N-UNCOUNT

**lit|ter bin** **(litter bins)** A **litter bin** is a container, usually in a street, park, or public building, into which people can put rubbish. [BRIT] N-COUNT = rubbish bin

☑ in AM, use **trash can**

| **little** |
| --- |
| ① DETERMINER, QUANTIFIER, AND ADVERB USES |
| ② ADJECTIVE USES |

① **lit|tle** /lɪtəl/ ◆◆◆ 1 You use **little** to indicate that there is only a very small amount of something. You can use 'so', 'too', and 'very' in front of **little**. ❑ *I had little money and little free time... I find that I need very little sleep these days... There is little doubt that a diet high in fibre is more satisfying... So far little progress has been made towards ending the fighting.* DET: DET n-uncount ♦ **Little** is also a quantifier. ❑ *Little of the existing housing is of good enough quality.* QUANT: QUANT of def-n ≠ much ♦ **Little** is also a pronoun. ❑ *In general, employers do little to help the single working mother... Little is known about his childhood.* PRON 2 **Little** means not very often or to only a small extent. ❑ *On their way back to Marseille they spoke very little.* ADV: ADV with v 3 **A little** of something is a small amount of it, but not very much. You can also say **a very little**. ❑ *Mrs Caan needs a little help getting her groceries home... A little food would do us all some good... I shall be only a very little time.* DET: DET n-uncount ♦ **Little** is also a pronoun. ❑ *They get paid for it. Not much. Just a little.* PRON ♦ **Little** is also a quantifier. ❑ *Pour a little of the sauce over the chicken... I'm sure she won't mind sparing us a little of her time.* QUANT: QUANT of def-n-uncount/sing 4 If you do something **a little**, you do it for a short time. ❑ *He walked a little by himself in the garden.* ADV: ADV after v 5 **A little** or **a little bit** means to a small extent or degree. ❑ *He complained a little of a nagging pain between his shoulder blades... He was a little bit afraid of his father's reaction... If you have to drive when you are tired, go a little more slowly than you would normally.* ADV: ADV after v, ADV adj/adv 6 If something happens **little by little**, it happens very gradually. ❑ *In the begin-* PHRASE: PHR with cl = gradually *ning he had felt well, but little by little he was becoming weaker.*

**② lit|tle** /lɪtəl/ **(littler, littlest)** ◆◆◆

> The comparative **littler** and the superlative **littlest** are sometimes used in spoken English for meanings 1, 3, and 4, but otherwise the comparative and superlative forms of the adjective **little** are not used.

[1] **Little** things are small in size. **Little** is slightly more informal than **small**. ❑ *We sat around a little table, eating and drinking wine. ...the little group of art students.* ADJ: usu ADJ n = small ≠ big [2] You use **little** to indicate that someone or something is small, in a pleasant and attractive way. ❑ *She's got the nicest little house not far from the library. ...a little old lady... James usually drives a little hatchback.* ADJ: ADJ n [3] A **little** child is young. ❑ *I have a little boy of 8... When I was little I was very hyper-active.* ADJ [4] Your **little** sister or brother is younger than you are. ❑ *Whenever Daniel's little sister was asked to do something she always had a naughty reply.* ADJ: ADJ n ≠ big [5] A **little** distance, period of time, or event is short in length. ❑ *Just go down the road a little way, turn left, and cross the bridge... Why don't we just wait a little while and see what happens... I've been wanting to have a little talk with you.* ADJ: ADJ n ≠ long [6] A **little** sound or gesture is quick. ❑ *I had a little laugh to myself... She stood up quickly, giving a little cry of astonishment... He turned with a little nod and I watched him walk away.* ADJ: ADJ n [7] You use **little** to indicate that something is not serious or important. ❑ *...irritating little habits... Harry found himself getting angry over little things that had never bothered him before.* ADJ: ADJ n

**lit|tle fin|ger (little fingers)** Your **little finger** is the smallest finger on your hand. N-COUNT

**Lit|tle League** The **Little League** is an organization of children's baseball teams that compete against each other in the United States. N-PROPER

**lit|to|ral** /lɪtərəl/ **(littorals)** In geography, the **littoral** means the coast. [TECHNICAL] ❑ *...the countries of the north African littoral. ...the littoral countries of the Persian Gulf.* N-COUNT: usu sing, usu *the* N, N n

**li|tur|gi|cal** /lɪtɜːrdʒɪkəl/ **Liturgical** things are used in or relate to church services. [FORMAL] ADJ: usu ADJ n

**lit|ur|gy** /lɪtərdʒi/ **(liturgies)** A **liturgy** is a particular form of religious service, usually one that is set and approved by a branch of the Christian Church. ❑ *A clergyman read the liturgy from the prayer-book. ...the many similarities in ministry, liturgy and style between the two churches.* N-VAR

> **live**
> ① VERB USES
> ② ADJECTIVE USES

**① live** /lɪv/ **(lives, living, lived)** ◆◆◆

⇒ Please look at category 8 to see if the expression you are looking for is shown under another headword. [1] If someone **lives** in a particular place or with a particular person, their home is in that place or with that person. ❑ *She has lived here for 10 years... She always said I ought to live alone... Where do you live?... He still lives with his parents.* VERB V adv/prep V adv/prep V adv/prep V adv/prep [2] If you say that someone **lives** in particular circumstances or that they **live** a particular kind of life, you mean that they are in those circumstances or that they have that kind of life. ❑ *We lived quite grandly... Compared to people living only a few generations ago, we have greater opportunities to have a good time... We can start living a normal life again now.* VERB V adv/prep V adv/prep V n [3] If you say that someone **lives for** a particular thing, you mean that it is the most important thing in their life. ❑ *He lived for his work.* VERB V *for* n [4] To **live** means to be alive. If someone **lives to** a particular age, they stay alive until they are that age. ❑ *He's got a terrible disease and will not live long... He lived to be 103... Matilda was born in northern Italy in 1046 and apparently lived to a ripe old age... The blue whale is the largest living thing on the planet.* VERB V adv V to-inf V *to* n V-ing [5] If people **live by** doing a particular activity, they get the money, food, or clothing they need by doing that activity. ❑ *...the last indigenous people to live by hunting... These crimes were committed largely by professional criminals who lived by crime.* VERB: no cont V *by* -ing/n V *by* -ing/n [6] If you **live by** a particular rule, belief, or ideal, you behave in the way in which it says you should behave. ❑ *They live by the principle that we are here to add what we can to life, not to get what we want from it.* VERB V *by* n [7] ➔ See also **living**. [8] **to live hand to mouth** ➔ see **hand**. **to live beyond your means** ➔ see **means**. **to live in sin** ➔ see **sin**.

♦ **live down** If you are unable to **live down** a mistake, failure, or bad reputation, you are unable to make people forget about it. ❑ *Labour was also unable to live down its reputation as the party of high taxes... I thought I'd never live it down.* PHRASAL VERB V P n (not pron) V n P

♦ **live off** If you **live off** another person, you rely on them to provide you with money. ❑ *...a man who all his life had lived off his father.* PHRASAL VERB V P n

♦ **live on** or **live off** [1] If you **live on** or **live off** a particular amount of money, you have that amount of money to buy things. ❑ *Even with efficient budgeting, most students are unable to live on £4000 per year... You'll have enough to live on.* PHRASAL VERB V P amount V P amount [2] If you **live on** or **live off** a particular source of income, that is where you get the money that you need. ❑ *The proportion of Americans living on welfare rose... He's been living off state benefits.* PHRASAL VERB V P n V P n [3] If an animal **lives on** or **lives off** a particular food, this is the kind of food that it eats. ❑ *The fish live on the plankton... Most species live off aquatic snails.* PHRASAL VERB V P n V P n [4] If you say that a person **lives on** or **lives off** a particular kind of food, you mean that it seems to be the only thing that they eat, for example because they like it a lot or because they do not have other foods. ❑ *The children live on chips... Their room was bare of furniture and they lived off porridge.* PHRASAL VERB V P n V P n

♦ **live on** If someone **lives on**, they continue to be alive for a long time after a particular point in time or after a particular event. ❑ *I know my life has been cut short by this terrible virus but Daniel will live on after me.* PHRASAL VERB V P

♦ **live out** [1] If you **live out** your life in a particular place or in particular circumstances, you stay in that place or in those circumstances until the end of your life or until the end of a particular period of your life. ❑ *Gein did not stand trial but lived out his days in a mental asylum... I couldn't live my life out on tour like he does.* PHRASAL VERB V P n (not pron) V n P [2] If you **live out** a dream or idea, you do the things that you have thought about. ❑ *He began living out his rock 'n' roll fantasy during his last year in law school... I suppose some people create an idea of who they want to be, and then they live it out.* PHRASAL VERB V P n (not pron) V n P

♦ **live through** If you **live through** an unpleasant event or change, you experience it and survive. ❑ *We are too young to have lived through the war.* PHRASAL VERB V P n

♦ **live together** If two people are not married but live in the same house and have a sexual relationship, you can say that they **live together**. ❑ *The couple had been living together for 16 years.* PHRASAL VERB V P

♦ **live up to** If someone or something **lives up to** what they were expected to be, they are as good as they were expected to be. ❑ *Sales have not lived up to expectations this year.* PHRASAL VERB V P P n

**② live** /laɪv/ ◆◇◇ [1] **Live** animals or plants are alive, rather than being dead or artificial. ❑ *...a protest against the company's tests on live animals. ...baskets of live chickens.* ADJ: ADJ n ≠ dead [2] A **live** television or radio programme is one in which an event or performance is broadcast at exactly the same time as it happens, rather than being recorded first. ❑ *Murray was a guest on a live radio show. ...we were laughing and gossiping, oblivious to the fact that we were on live TV... A broadcast of the speech was heard in San Francisco, but it is not known if this was live.* ADJ ♦ **Live** is also an adverb. ❑ *It was broadcast live in 50 countries... We'll be going live to Nottingham later* ADV: ADV after v *in this bulletin.* 3 A **live** performance is given in front of an audience, rather than being recorded and then broadcast or shown in a film. ❑ *The Rainbow has not hosted live music since the end of 1981... A live audience will pose the questions... The band was forced to cancel a string of live dates.* ♦ **Live** is also an adverb. ❑ *Kat Bjelland has been playing live with her new band.* 4 A **live** recording is a recording of a band playing at a concert, rather than in a studio. ❑ *This is my favourite live album of all time.* 5 A **live** wire or piece of electrical equipment is directly connected to a source of electricity. ❑ *The plug broke, exposing live wires... He warned others about the live electric cables as they climbed to safety.* 6 **Live** bullets are made of metal, rather than rubber or plastic, and are intended to kill people rather than injure them. ❑ *They trained in the jungle using live ammunition.* 7 A **live** bomb or missile is one which has not yet exploded. ❑ *A live bomb had earlier been defused.*

ADJ: usu ADJ n | ADV: ADV after v | ADJ: usu ADJ n | ADJ: usu ADJ n | ADJ: usu ADJ n | ADJ: usu ADJ n

**live-in** /lɪv ɪn/ 1 A **live-in** partner is someone who lives in the same house as the person they are having a sexual relationship with, but is not married to them. ❑ *She shared the apartment with her live-in partner.* 2 A **live-in** servant or other domestic worker sleeps and eats in the house where they work. ❑ *I have a live-in nanny for my youngest daughter.*

◆◇◇ ADJ: ADJ n | ADJ: ADJ n

**live|li|hood** /laɪvlihʊd/ **(livelihoods)** Your **livelihood** is the job or other source of income that gives you the money to buy the things you need. ❑ *...fishermen who depend on the seas for their livelihood... As a result of this conflict he lost both his home and his means of livelihood.* N-VAR

**live|ly** /laɪvli/ **(livelier, liveliest)** 1 You can describe someone as **lively** when they behave in an enthusiastic and cheerful way. ❑ *Josephine was bright, lively and cheerful.* ♦ **live|li|ness** *Amy could sense his liveliness even from where she stood.* 2 A **lively** event or a **lively** discussion, for example, has lots of interesting and exciting things happening or being said in it. ❑ *It turned out to be a very interesting session with a lively debate... Their 4-1 win in Honduras was a particularly lively affair.* ♦ **live|li|ness** *Some may enjoy the liveliness of such a restaurant for a few hours a day or week.* 3 Someone who has a **lively** mind is intelligent and interested in a lot of different things. ❑ *She was a very well educated girl with a lively mind, a girl with ambition. ...her very lively imagination.*

ADJ | N-UNCOUNT | ADJ: usu ADJ n | N-UNCOUNT | ADJ: usu ADJ n

**liv|en** /laɪvᵊn/ **(livens, livening, livened)**

♦ **liven up** 1 If a place or event **livens up**, or if something **livens** it **up**, it becomes more interesting and exciting. ❑ *How could we decorate the room to liven it up?... The multicoloured rag rug was chosen to liven up the grey carpet... The arena livens up only on Saturdays and Sundays when a flea market is open there.* 2 If people **liven up**, or if something **livens** them **up**, they become more cheerful and energetic. ❑ *Talking about her daughters livens her up... George livens up after midnight, relaxing a little.*

PHRASAL VERB | V n P | V P n (not pron) | V P | PHRASAL VERB = perk up | V n P | V P

**liv|er** /lɪvəʳ/ **(livers)** 1 Your **liver** is a large organ in your body which processes your blood and helps to clean unwanted substances out of it. 2 **Liver** is the liver of some animals, especially lambs, pigs, and cows, which is cooked and eaten. ❑ *...grilled calves' liver.*

N-COUNT | N-VAR

**liv|eried** /lɪvərid/ A **liveried** servant is one who wears a special uniform. ❑ *The tea was served to guests by liveried footmen.* ADJ: ADJ n

**liv|ery** /lɪvəri/ **(liveries)** 1 A servant's **livery** is the special uniform that he or she wears. 2 The **livery** of a particular company is the special design or set of colours associated with it that is put on its products and possessions. ❑ *...buffet cars in the railway company's bright red and yellow livery.*

N-VAR | N-COUNT: usu with poss

**lives** 1 **Lives** is the plural of **life**. 2 **Lives** is the third person singular form of **live**.

**live|stock** /laɪvstɒk/ Animals such as cattle and sheep which are kept on a farm are referred to as **livestock**. ❑ *The heavy rains and flooding killed scores of livestock.* N-UNCOUNT-COLL

**live wire** /laɪv waɪəʳ/ **(live wires)** If you describe someone as a **live wire**, you mean that they are lively and energetic. [INFORMAL] N-COUNT

**liv|id** /lɪvɪd/ 1 Someone who is **livid** is extremely angry. [INFORMAL] ❑ *I am absolutely livid about it... She is livid that I have invited Dick.* 2 Something that is **livid** is an unpleasant dark purple or red colour. ❑ *The scarred side of his face was a livid red.*

ADJ: usu v-link ADJ = furious | ADJ

**liv|ing** /lɪvɪŋ/ **(livings)** 1 The work that you do for a **living** is the work that you do in order to earn the money that you need. ❑ *Father never talked about what he did for a living... He earns his living doing all kinds of things.* 2 You use **living** when you are talking about the quality of people's daily lives. ❑ *Olivia has always been a model of healthy living. ...the stresses of urban living.* 3 You use **living** to talk about the places where people relax when they are not working. ❑ *The spacious living quarters were on the second floor... The study links the main living area to the kitchen.* 4 **The living** are people who are alive, rather than people who have died. ❑ *The young man is dead. We have only to consider the living.* 5 **in living memory** → see **memory**.

◆◇◇ N-COUNT: usu sing | N-UNCOUNT: with supp | ADJ: ADJ n | N-PLURAL: the N ≠ dead

**liv|ing room** **(living rooms)** also **living-room.** The **living room** in a house is the room where people sit and relax. → See picture on page 1706. ❑ *We were sitting on the couch in the living room watching TV.* N-COUNT = sitting room, lounge

**liv|ing stand|ard** **(living standards)** **Living standards** or **living standard** is used to refer to the level of comfort in which people live, which usually depends on how much money they have. ❑ *Cheaper housing would vastly improve the living standards of ordinary people... Critics say his reforms have caused the fall in living standards.* N-COUNT: usu pl

**liv|ing wage** A **living wage** is a wage which is just enough to enable you to buy food, clothing, and other necessary things. ❑ *Many farmers have to depend on subsidies to make a living wage.* N-SING: usu a N

**liv|ing will** **(living wills)** A **living will** is a document in which you say what medical or legal decisions you want people to make for you if you become too ill to make these decisions yourself. N-COUNT

**liz|ard** /lɪzəʳd/ **(lizards)** A **lizard** is a reptile with short legs and a long tail. N-COUNT

**-'ll** /-ᵊl/ **-'ll** is the usual spoken form of 'will'. It is added to the end of the pronoun which is the subject of the verb. For example, 'you will' can be shortened to 'you'll'.

**lla|ma** /lɑːmə/ **(llamas)** A **llama** is a South American animal with thick hair, which looks like a small camel without a hump. N-COUNT

**lo** /loʊ/ **Lo and behold** or **lo** is used to emphasize a surprising event that is about to be mentioned, or to emphasize in a humorous way that something is not surprising at all. [HUMOROUS or LITERARY] ❑ *He called the minister of the interior and, lo and behold, within about an hour, the prisoners were released... I looked and lo! every one of the fifteen men who had been standing with me had disappeared.* CONVENTION emphasis

**load** /loʊd/ **(loads, loading, loaded)** 1 If you **load** a vehicle or a container, you put a large quantity of things into it. ❑ *The three men seemed to have finished loading the truck... Mr. Dambar had loaded his plate with lasagne... They load all their equipment into backpacks... She deposited the loaded tray.* ♦ **Load up** means the same as **load**. ❑ *I've just loaded my truck up... The giggling couple loaded up their red sports car and drove off... We loaded up carts with all the blankets, bandages, medication, water we could spare... She loaded up his valuable collection of vintage wines into crates.* ♦ **load|ing** *...the loading of baggage onto international flights.*

◆◇◇ VERB | V n | V n with n | V n into/onto n | V-ed | PHRASAL VERB | V n P | V P n (not pron) | V P n with n | V P n into/onto n | N-SING: usu the N of n

[2] A **load** is something, usually a large quantity or heavy object, which is being carried. ❑ *He drove by with a big load of hay... He was carrying a very heavy load.* N-COUNT [3] If you refer to **a load of** people or things or **loads of** them, you are emphasizing that there are a lot of them. [INFORMAL] ❑ *I've got loads of money... His people came up with a load of embarrassing information. ...a load of kids.* QUANT: QUANT *of* n-uncount/ pl-n [emphasis] [4] When someone **loads** a weapon such as a gun, they put a bullet or missile in it so that it is ready to use. ❑ *I knew how to load and handle a gun... He carried a loaded gun.* VERB V n V-ed [5] To **load** a camera or other piece of equipment means to put film, tape, or data into it so that it is ready to use. ❑ *A photographer from the newspaper was loading his camera with film... The data can subsequently be loaded on a computer for processing.* VERB V n *with* n V n *into/onto/on* n [6] You can refer to the amount of work you have to do as a **load**. ❑ *She's taking some of the load off the secretaries.* N-COUNT [7] The **load** of a system or piece of equipment, especially a system supplying electricity or a computer, is the extent to which it is being used at a particular time. ❑ *An efficient bulb may lighten the load of power stations... Several processors can share the load of handling data in a single program.* N-COUNT [8] The **load on** something is the amount of weight that is pressing down on it or the amount of strain that it is under. ❑ *Some of these chairs have flattened feet which spread the load on the ground... High blood pressure imposes an extra load on the heart.* N-SING [9] → See also **loaded**. **a load off** your **mind** → see **mind**.

♦ **load up** → see **load 1**.

**-load** /-loʊd/ **(-loads) -load** combines with nouns referring to a vehicle or container to form nouns that refer to the total amount of something that the vehicle or container mentioned can hold or carry. ❑ *The first plane-loads of food, children's clothing and medical supplies began arriving. ...a lorry-load of sheep on their way across Europe.* COMB in N-COUNT

**load|ed** /loʊdɪd/ [1] A **loaded** question or word has more meaning or purpose than it appears to have, because the person who uses it hopes it will cause people to respond in a particular way. ❑ *That's a loaded question. ...the loaded word 'sexist'.* ADJ [2] If something is **loaded with** a particular characteristic, it has that characteristic to a very great degree. ❑ *The President's visit is loaded with symbolic significance... The phrase is loaded with irony.* ADJ: usu v-link ADJ, usu ADJ *with* n [3] If you say that something is **loaded in favour of** someone, you mean it works unfairly to their advantage. If you say it is **loaded against** them, you mean it works unfairly to their disadvantage. ❑ *The press is loaded in favour of this present government... The article was heavily loaded against Morrissey.* ADJ: usu v-link ADJ *in favour of/against* n [disapproval] = biased

**loaf** /loʊf/ **(loaves)** A **loaf** of bread is bread which has been shaped and baked in one piece. It is usually large enough for more than one person and can be cut into slices. ❑ *...a loaf of crusty bread. ...freshly baked loaves.* N-COUNT: oft N *of* n

**loaf|er** /loʊfəʳ/ **(loafers) Loafers** are flat leather shoes with no straps or laces. [mainly AM] N-COUNT

**loam** /loʊm/ **Loam** is soil that is good for growing crops and plants in because it contains a lot of decayed vegetable matter and does not contain too much sand or clay. N-UNCOUNT

**loan** /loʊn/ **(loans, loaning, loaned)** ◆◆◇ [1] A **loan** is a sum of money that you borrow. ❑ *The president wants to make it easier for small businesses to get bank loans. ...loan repayments.* → See also **bridging loan, soft loan.** N-COUNT [2] If someone gives you a **loan of** something, you borrow it from them. ❑ *He had offered the loan of his small villa at Cap Ferrat.* N-SING: N *of* n [3] If you **loan** something to someone, you lend it to them. ❑ *He had kindly offered to loan us all the plants required for the exhibit... We were approached by the Royal Yachting Association to see if we would loan our boat to them.* VERB = lend V n n V n *to* n Also V n ♦ **Loan out** means the same as **loan**. ❑ *It is common practice for clubs to loan out players to sides in the lower divisions... The ground was loaned out for numerous events including pop concerts.* PHRASAL VERB V P n (not pron) *to* n *be* V-ed *out* Also V n P, V P n [4] If something is **on loan**, it has been borrowed. ❑ *...impressionist paintings on loan from the National Gallery.* PHRASE: v-link PHR, PHR after v

**loan shark (loan sharks)** If you describe someone as a **loan shark**, you disapprove of them because they lend money to people and charge them very high rates of interest on the loan. [INFORMAL] N-COUNT [disapproval]

**loath** /loʊθ/ also **loth.** If you are **loath to** do something, you do not want to do it. ❑ *The new finance minister seems loth to cut income tax.* ADJ: v-link ADJ to-inf = reluctant

**loathe** /loʊð/ **(loathes, loathing, loathed)** If you **loathe** something or someone, you dislike them very much. ❑ *The two men loathe each other... She loathed being the child of impoverished labourers.* VERB = detest V n V -ing

**loath|ing** /loʊðɪŋ/ **Loathing** is a feeling of great dislike and disgust. ❑ *She looked at him with loathing.* N-UNCOUNT = hatred

**loath|some** /loʊðsəm/ If you describe someone or something as **loathsome**, you are indicating how much you dislike them or how much they disgust you. ❑ *...the loathsome spectacle we were obliged to witness.* ADJ = repulsive

**loaves** /loʊvz/ **Loaves** is the plural of **loaf**.

**lob** /lɒb/ **(lobs, lobbing, lobbed)** If you **lob** something, you throw it so that it goes quite high in the air. ❑ *Enemy forces lobbed a series of artillery shells onto the city... A group of protesters gathered outside, chanting and lobbing firebombs.* VERB V n prep/adv V n

**lob|by** /lɒbi/ **(lobbies, lobbying, lobbied)** ◆◇◇ [1] If you **lobby** someone such as a member of a government or council, you try to persuade them that a particular law should be changed or that a particular thing should be done. ❑ *Carers from all over the UK lobbied Parliament last week to demand a better financial deal... Gun control advocates are lobbying hard for new laws.* VERB V n V *for/against* n ♦ **lob|by|ing** *The aid was frozen in June after intense lobbying by conservative Republicans.* N-UNCOUNT [2] A **lobby** is a group of people who represent a particular organization or campaign, and try to persuade a government or council to help or support them. ❑ *He set up this lobby of independent producers.* N-COUNT: usu with supp, oft supp N, N *of* n [3] In a hotel or other large building, the **lobby** is the area near the entrance that usually has corridors and staircases leading off it. ❑ *I met her in the lobby of the museum.* N-COUNT

**lob|by|ist** /lɒbiɪst/ **(lobbyists)** A **lobbyist** is someone who tries actively to persuade a government or council that a particular law should be changed or that a particular thing should be done. N-COUNT

**lobe** /loʊb/ **(lobes)** [1] The **lobe** of your ear is the soft, fleshy part at the bottom. N-COUNT = earlobe [2] A **lobe** is a rounded part of something, for example one of the sections of your brain or lungs, or one of the rounded sections along the edges of some leaves. ❑ *...damage to the temporal lobe of the brain.* N-COUNT: usu with supp

**lo|boto|my** /ləbɒtəmi/ **(lobotomies)** A **lobotomy** is a surgical operation in which some of the nerves in the brain are cut in order to treat severe mental illness. [MEDICAL] N-VAR

**lob|ster** /lɒbstəʳ/ **(lobsters)** A **lobster** is a sea creature that has a hard shell, two large claws, and eight legs. ❑ *She sold me a couple of live lobsters.* N-VAR ♦ **Lobster** is the flesh of a lobster eaten as food. ❑ *...lobster on a bed of fresh vegetables.* N-UNCOUNT

**lob|ster pot (lobster pots)** A **lobster pot** is a trap used for catching lobsters. It is in the shape of a basket. N-COUNT

**lo|cal** /loʊkəl/ **(locals)** ◆◆◆ [1] **Local** means existing in or belonging to the area where you live, or to the area that you are talking about. ❑ *We'd better check on the match in the local paper... Some local residents joined the students' protest... I was going to pop up to the local library.* ADJ: ADJ n ♦ The **locals** are local people. ❑ *That's what the locals call the place.* N-COUNT: usu pl, oft *the* N ♦ **lo|cal|ly** *We've got cards which are drawn and printed and designed by someone locally.* ADV: ADV -ed, ADV after v [2] **Local** government is elected by people in one area of a country and controls aspects such as education, ADJ: usu ADJ n ≠ national housing, and transport within that area. ❑ *Education comprises two-thirds of all local council spending.* [3] Your **local** is a pub which is near where you live and where you often go for a drink. [BRIT, INFORMAL] ❑ *The Black Horse is my local.* [4] A **local** anaesthetic or condition affects only a small area of your body. [MEDICAL]

N-COUNT: usu sing, usu poss N · ADJ

**lo|cal area net|work (local area networks)** A **local area network** is a group of personal computers and associated equipment that are linked by cable, for example in an office building, and that share a communications line. The abbreviation **LAN** is also used. [COMPUTING] ❑ *Users can easily move files between PCs connected by local area networks or the internet.*

N-COUNT

**lo|cal author|ity (local authorities)** A **local authority** is an organization that is officially responsible for all the public services and facilities in a particular area. [BRIT]

◆◇◇ N-COUNT

☑ in AM, use **local government**

**lo|cal col|our**

☑ in AM, use **local color**

**Local colour** is used to refer to customs, traditions, dress, and other things which give a place or period of history its own particular character. ❑ *The fishing boat harbour was usually bustling with lots of local colour.*

N-UNCOUNT

**lo|cale** /loʊkɑːl/ **(locales)** A **locale** is a small area, for example the place where something happens or where the action of a book or film is set. [FORMAL] ❑ *An amusement park is the perfect locale for a bunch of irrepressible youngsters to have all sorts of adventures.*

N-COUNT = setting

**lo|cal gov|ern|ment (local governments)** [1] **Local government** is the system of electing representatives to be responsible for the administration of public services and facilities in a particular area. [2] A **local government** is the same as a **local authority**. [AM]

N-UNCOUNT · N-COUNT

**lo|cal|ity** /loʊkælɪti/ **(localities)** A **locality** is a small area of a country or city. [FORMAL] ❑ *Following the discovery of the explosives the president cancelled his visit to the locality.*

N-COUNT = area

**lo|cal|ize** /loʊkəlaɪz/ **(localizes, localizing, localized)**

☑ in BRIT, also use **localise**

[1] If you **localize** something, you identify precisely where it is. ❑ *Examine the painful area carefully in an effort to localize the most tender point.* [2] If you **localize** something, you limit the size of the area that it affects and prevent it from spreading. ❑ *Few officers thought that a German-Czech war could be localized.*

VERB = identify V n · VERB = limit V n

**lo|cal|ized** /loʊkəlaɪzd/

☑ in BRIT, also use **localised**

Something that is **localized** remains within a small area and does not spread. ❑ *She had localized breast cancer and both of her doctors had advised surgery.*

ADJ

**lo|cal time** **Local time** is the official time in a particular region or country. ❑ *It was around 10.15 pm local time, 3.15 am at home.*

N-UNCOUNT

**lo|cate** /loʊkeɪt, AM loʊkeɪt/ **(locates, locating, located)** [1] If you **locate** something or someone, you find out where they are. [FORMAL] ❑ *The scientists want to locate the position of the gene on a chromosome... We've simply been unable to locate him.* [2] If you **locate** something in a particular place, you put it there or build it there. [FORMAL] ❑ *Atlanta was voted the best city in which to locate a business by more than 400 chief executives... Tudor Court represents your opportunity to locate at the heart of the new Birmingham.* [3] If you **locate** in a particular place, you move there or open a business there. [mainly AM, BUSINESS] ❑ *...tax breaks for businesses that locate in run-down neighborhoods.*

VERB = find V n · V n · VERB V n prep/adv · V prep/adv · VERB V

**lo|cat|ed** /loʊkeɪtɪd, AM loʊkeɪt-/ If something is **located** in a particular place, it is present or has been built there. [FORMAL] ❑ *A boutique and beauty salon are conveniently located within the grounds.*

ADJ: v-link ADJ prep, adv ADJ = situated

**lo|ca|tion** /loʊkeɪʃᵊn/ **(locations)** [1] A **location** is the place where something happens or is situated. ❑ *The first thing he looked at was his office's location... Macau's newest small luxury hotel has a beautiful location.* [2] The **location** of someone or something is their exact position. ❑ *She knew the exact location of The Eagle's headquarters.* [3] A **location** is a place away from a studio where a film or part of a film is made. ❑ *...an art movie with dozens of exotic locations... We're shooting on location.*

◆◇◇ N-COUNT: usu with supp = setting · N-COUNT: with poss = position · N-VAR: oft *on* N

**loch** /lɒx, lɒk/ **(lochs)** A **loch** is a large area of water in Scotland that is completely or almost completely surrounded by land. ❑ *...twenty miles north of Loch Ness.*

N-COUNT: oft in names before n

**loci** /loʊsaɪ, loʊkaɪ/ **Loci** is the plural of **locus**.

**lock** /lɒk/ **(locks, locking, locked)** [1] When you **lock** something such as a door, drawer, or case, you fasten it, usually with a key, so that other people cannot open it. ❑ *Are you sure you locked the front door?... Wolfgang moved along the corridor towards the locked door at the end.* [2] The **lock** on something such as a door or a drawer is the device which is used to keep it shut and prevent other people from opening it. Locks are opened with a key. ❑ *At that moment he heard Gill's key turning in the lock of the door... An intruder forced open a lock on French windows at the house.* [3] If you **lock** something or someone in a place, room, or container, you put them there and fasten the lock. ❑ *Her maid locked the case in the safe... They beat them up and locked them in a cell.* [4] If you **lock** something in a particular position or if it **lock** there, it is held or fitted firmly in that position. ❑ *He leaned back in the swivel chair and locked his fingers behind his head... There was a whine of hydraulics as the undercarriage locked into position.* [5] On a canal or river, a **lock** is a place where walls have been built with gates at each end so that boats can move to a higher or lower section of the canal or river, by gradually changing the water level inside the gates. [6] A **lock of** hair is a small bunch of hairs on your head that grow together and curl or curve in the same direction. ❑ *She brushed a lock of hair off his forehead.* [7] **lock, stock, and barrel** → see **barrel**.

◆◇◇ VERB V n · V-ed · N-COUNT · VERB V n *in/into* n · V n *in/into* n · VERB V n prep/adv · V prep/adv · N-COUNT · N-COUNT: usu N *of* n

♦ **lock away** [1] If you **lock** something **away** in a place or container, you put or hide it there and fasten the lock. ❑ *She meticulously cleaned the gun and locked it away in its case... He had even locked away all the videos of his previous exploits.* [2] To **lock** someone **away** means to put them in prison or a secure mental hospital. ❑ *Locking them away is not sufficient, you have to give them treatment.* [3] If you **lock** yourself **away**, you go somewhere where you can be alone, and do not come out or see anyone for some time. ❑ *I locked myself away with books and magazines.*

PHRASAL VERB V n P · V P n (not pron) · PHRASAL VERB V n P Also V P n · PHRASAL VERB = hide away, shut away V pron-refl P

♦ **lock in** If you **lock** someone **in**, you put them in a room and lock the door so that they cannot get out. ❑ *Manda cried out that Mr Hoelt had no right to lock her in.*

PHRASAL VERB V n P

♦ **lock out** [1] If someone **locks** you **out** of a place, they prevent you entering it by locking the doors. ❑ *They had had a row, and she had locked him out of the apartment... My husband's locked me out.* [2] If you **lock** yourself **out** of a place, such as your house, you cannot get in because the door is locked and you do not have your keys. ❑ *The new tenants locked themselves out of their apartment and had to break in... There had been a knock at the door and when she opened it she locked herself out... The wind had made the door swing closed, and she was now locked out.* [3] In an industrial dispute, if a company **locks** its workers **out**, it closes the factory or office in order to prevent the employees coming to work. [BUSINESS] ❑ *The company locked out the workers, and then the rest of the work force went on strike.*

PHRASAL VERB V n P *of* n · V n P · PHRASAL VERB V pron-refl P *of* n · V pron-refl P · V-ed P · PHRASAL VERB V P n (not pron) Also V n P

♦ **lock up** [1] If you **lock** something **up** in a place or container, you put or hide it there and fasten the lock. ❑ *Give away any food you have on hand, or lock it up and give the key to the neighbours... Control of materials could be maintained by locking up bombs.* [2] To **lock** someone **up** means to put them in prison or a secure psychiatric hospital. ❑ *Mr Milner persuaded the federal prosecutors not to lock up his client.* [3] When you **lock up** a building or car or **lock up**, you make sure that all the doors and windows are locked so that nobody can get in. ❑ *Don't forget to lock up... Leave your car here and lock it up.* PHRASAL VERB V n P V P n (not pron) PHRASAL VERB V P n Also V n P PHRASAL VERB V P V n P

**locked** /lɒkt/ If you say that people are **locked in** conflict or in battle, you mean they are arguing or fighting in a fierce or determined way, and neither side seems likely to stop. ◆◇◇ ADJ: v-link ADJ *in* n

**lock|er** /lɒkəʳ/ **(lockers)** A **locker** is a small metal or wooden cupboard with a lock, where you can put your personal possessions, for example in a school, place of work, or sports club. N-COUNT

**lock|er room (locker rooms)** A **locker room** is a room in which there are a lot of lockers. N-COUNT

**lock|et** /lɒkɪt/ **(lockets)** A **locket** is a piece of jewellery containing something such as a picture, which a woman wears on a chain around her neck. N-COUNT

**lock-keeper (lock-keepers)** A **lock-keeper** is a person whose job is to be in charge of and maintain a lock or group of locks on a canal. N-COUNT

**lock-out (lock-outs)**

☑ in AM, use **lockout**

A **lock-out** is a situation in which employers close a place of work and prevent workers from entering it until the workers accept the employer's new proposals on pay or conditions of work. [BUSINESS] N-COUNT

**lock-up (lock-ups)** also **lockup.** [1] A **lock-up** is the same as a **jail**. [AM, INFORMAL] [2] A **lock-up** is a garage that is used by someone, but is not next to their house. [BRIT] ♦ **Lock-up** is also an adjective. ❑ *...a lock-up garage.* N-COUNT N-COUNT ADJ: ADJ n

**lo|co|mo|tion** /loʊkəmoʊʃᵊn/ **Locomotion** is the ability to move and the act of moving from one place to another. [FORMAL] ❑ *Flight is the form of locomotion that puts the greatest demands on muscles.* N-UNCOUNT

**lo|co|mo|tive** /loʊkəmoʊtɪv/ **(locomotives)** A **locomotive** is a large vehicle that pulls a railway train. [FORMAL] N-COUNT

**lo|cum** /loʊkəm/ **(locums)** A **locum** is a doctor or priest who does the work for another doctor or priest who is ill or on holiday. [mainly BRIT] N-COUNT

**lo|cus** /loʊkəs/ **(loci)** The **locus of** something is the place where it happens or the most important area or point with which it is associated. [FORMAL] ❑ *Barcelona is the locus of Spanish industry.* N-COUNT: usu sing, N *of* n

**lo|cust** /loʊkəst/ **(locusts) Locusts** are large insects that live mainly in hot countries. They fly in large groups and eat crops. N-COUNT

**lodge** /lɒdʒ/ **(lodges, lodging, lodged)** [1] A **lodge** is a house or hut in the country or in the mountains where people stay on holiday, especially when they want to shoot or fish. ❑ *...a Victorian hunting lodge. ...a ski lodge.* [2] A **lodge** is a small house at the entrance to the grounds of a large house. ❑ *I drove out of the gates, past the keeper's lodge.* [3] In some organizations, a **lodge** is a local branch or meeting place of the organization. ❑ *My father would occasionally go to his Masonic lodge.* [4] If you **lodge** a complaint, protest, accusation, or claim, you officially make it. ❑ *He has four weeks in which to lodge an appeal.* [5] If you **lodge** somewhere, such as in someone else's house or if you **are lodged** there, you live there, usually paying rent. ❑ *...the story of the farming family she lodged with as a young teacher... The building he was lodged in turned out to be a church.* [6] If someone **lodges** you somewhere, they give you a place to stay, for example because they are responsible for your safety or comfort. ❑ *They lodged the delegates in different hotels.* [7] If an object **lodges** somewhere, it becomes stuck there. ❑ *The bullet lodged in the sergeant's leg, shattering his thigh bone... His car has a bullet lodged in the passenger door.* [8] → See also **lodging**. N-COUNT: usu supp N N-COUNT N-COUNT: usu supp N VERB = make V n VERB V prep/adv *be* V-ed prep/adv VERB V n prep/adv VERB V prep/adv V-ed

**lodg|er** /lɒdʒəʳ/ **(lodgers)** A **lodger** is a person who pays money to live in someone else's house. ❑ *Jennie took in a lodger to help with the mortgage.* N-COUNT

**lodg|ing** /lɒdʒɪŋ/ **(lodgings)** [1] If you are provided with **lodging** or **lodgings**, you are provided with a place to stay for a period of time. You can use **lodgings** to refer to one or more of these places. ❑ *He was given free lodging in a three-room flat. ...travel expenses including meals and lodgings while traveling away from home.* [2] If you live in **lodgings**, you live in a room or rooms in someone's house and you pay them for this. ❑ *David had changed his lodgings, leaving no address behind.* [3] → See also **board and lodging**. N-UNCOUNT: also N in pl N-COUNT: usu pl

**lodg|ing house (lodging houses)** A **lodging house** is a house where people can rent rooms to live in or stay in. [mainly BRIT] N-COUNT

☑ in AM, usually use **rooming house**

**loft** /lɒft, AM lɔːft/ **(lofts)** [1] A **loft** is the space inside the sloping roof of a house or other building, where things are sometimes stored. ❑ *A loft conversion can add considerably to the value of a house.* [2] A **loft** is an apartment in the upper part of a building, especially a building such as a warehouse or factory that has been converted for people to live in. Lofts are usually large and not divided into separate rooms. N-COUNT = attic N-COUNT

**lofty** /lɒfti, AM lɔːf-/ **(loftier, loftiest)** [1] A **lofty** ideal or ambition is noble, important, and admirable. ❑ *It was a bank that started out with grand ideas and lofty ideals.* [2] A **lofty** building or room is very high. [FORMAL] ❑ *...a light, lofty apartment in the suburbs of Salzburg.* [3] If you say that someone behaves in a **lofty** way, you are critical of them for behaving in a proud and rather unpleasant way, as if they think they are very important. ❑ *...the lofty disdain he often expresses for his profession. ...lofty contempt.* ADJ: usu ADJ n ADJ: usu ADJ n ADJ: usu ADJ n [disapproval]

**log** /lɒg, AM lɔːg/ **(logs, logging, logged)** [1] A **log** is a piece of a thick branch or of the trunk of a tree that has been cut so that it can be used for fuel or for making things. ❑ *He dumped the logs on the big stone hearth. ...the original log cabin where Lincoln was born.* [2] A **log** is an official written account of what happens each day, for example on board a ship. ❑ *The family made an official complaint to a ship's officer, which was recorded in the log.* [3] If you **log** an event or fact, you record it officially in writing or on a computer. ❑ *Details of the crime are then logged in the computer.* [4] → See also **logging**. N-COUNT: oft N n N-COUNT VERB = record V n

♦ **log in** or **log on** When someone **logs in** or **logs on**, or **logs into** a computer system, they start using the system, usually by typing their name or identity code and a password. ❑ *Customers pay to log on and gossip with other users... They would log into their account and take a look at prices and decide what they'd like to do.* PHRASAL VERB V P V P n

♦ **log out** or **log off** When someone who is using a computer system **logs out** or **logs off**, they finish using the system by typing a particular command. ❑ *If a computer user fails to log off, the system is accessible to all.* PHRASAL VERB V P

**logan|berry** /loʊgənbəri, AM -beri/ **(loganberries)** A **loganberry** is a purplish red fruit that is similar to a raspberry. N-COUNT

**loga|rithm** /lɒgərɪðəm, AM lɔːg-/ **(logarithms)** In mathematics, the **logarithm** of a number is a number that it can be represented by in order to make a difficult multiplication or division sum simpler. N-COUNT

**log book (log books)** A **log book** is a book in which someone records details and events relating N-COUNT to something, for example a journey or period of their life, or a vehicle.

**log|ger** /lɒgəʳ, AM lɔːg-/ **(loggers)** A **logger** is a man whose job is to cut down trees. [AM] N-COUNT

in BRIT, use **lumberjack**

**log|ger|heads** /lɒgəʳhed, AM lɔːg-/ If two or more people or groups are **at loggerheads**, they disagree very strongly with each other. ❑ *For months dentists and the health department have been at loggerheads over fees... France was left isolated and at loggerheads with other EU member countries over its refusal to fall into line with demands to cut state borrowing.* PHRASE: usu v-link PHR, oft PHR *with* n

**log|gia** /lɒdʒə/ **(loggias)** A **loggia** is a roofed area attached to a house. [FORMAL] N-COUNT

**log|ging** /lɒgɪŋ, AM lɔːg-/ **Logging** is the activity of cutting down trees in order to sell the wood. ❑ *Logging companies would have to leave a central area of the forest before the end of the year.* N-UNCOUNT: oft N n

**log|ic** /lɒdʒɪk/ 1 **Logic** is a method of reasoning that involves a series of statements, each of which must be true if the statement before it is true. ❑ *Apart from criminal investigation techniques, students learn forensic medicine, philosophy and logic.* N-UNCOUNT 2 The **logic** of a conclusion or an argument is its quality of being correct and reasonable. ❑ *I don't follow the logic of your argument... There would be no logic in upsetting the agreements.* N-UNCOUNT: oft N *of* n 3 A particular kind of **logic** is the way of thinking and reasoning about things that is characteristic of a particular type of person or particular field of activity. ❑ *The plan was based on sound commercial logic.* N-UNCOUNT: with supp, oft adj N

**logi|cal** /lɒdʒɪkəl/ 1 In a **logical** argument or method of reasoning, each step must be true if the step before it is true. ❑ *Only when each logical step has been checked by other mathematicians will the proof be accepted.* ♦ **logi|cal|ly** /lɒdʒɪkli/ *My professional training has taught me to look at things logically.* ADJ: usu ADJ n; ADV: usu ADV with v 2 The **logical** conclusion or result of a series of facts or events is the only one which can come from it, according to the rules of logic. ❑ *If the climate gets drier, then the logical conclusion is that even more drought will occur. ...a society that dismisses God as a logical impossibility.* ♦ **logi|cal|ly** *From that it followed logically that he would not be meeting Hildegarde.* ADJ: usu ADJ n; ADV: ADV with v 3 Something that is **logical** seems reasonable or sensible in the circumstances. ❑ *Connie suddenly struck her as a logical candidate... There was a logical explanation... It is logical to take precautions.* ♦ **logi|cal|ly** *This was the one possibility I hadn't taken into consideration, though logically I should have done.* ADJ: oft *it* v-link ADJ to-inf/that = reasonable; ADV: ADV with cl, ADV with v

**-logical** → see **-ological**.

**log|ic bomb** **(logic bombs)** A **logic bomb** is an unauthorized program that is inserted into a computer system so that when it is started it affects the operation of the computer. [COMPUTING] N-COUNT

**lo|gi|cian** /lədʒɪʃən/ **(logicians)** A **logician** is a person who is a specialist in logic. N-COUNT

**-logist** → see **-ologist**.

**lo|gis|tic** /lədʒɪstɪk/ or **logistical** /lədʒɪstɪkəl/ **Logistic** or **logistical** means relating to the organization of something complicated. ❑ *Logistical problems may be causing the delay... She described the distribution of food and medical supplies as a logistical nightmare.* ♦ **lo|gis|ti|cal|ly** /lədʒɪstɪkli/ *Organised junior football was either restricted or logistically impossible to operate... It is about time that the UN considers logistically deploying additional military resources... Logistically it is very difficult to value unit-linked policies.* ADJ: ADJ n; ADV: ADV adj, ADV with v, ADV with cl

**lo|gis|tics** /lədʒɪstɪks/ If you refer to the **logistics** of doing something complicated that involves a lot of people or equipment, you are referring to the skilful organization of it so that it can be done successfully and efficiently. ❑ *The skills and logistics of getting such a big show on the road pose enormous practical problems.* N-UNCOUNT-COLL

**log|jam** /lɒgdʒæm/ **(logjams)** To break the **logjam** means to change or deal with a difficult situation which has existed for a long time. [JOURNALISM] ❑ *A new initiative was needed to break the logjam.* N-COUNT: usu sing

**logo** /loʊgoʊ/ **(logos)** The **logo** of a company or organization is the special design or way of writing its name that it puts on all its products, notepaper, or advertisements. N-COUNT

**-logy** → see **-ology**.

**loin** /lɔɪn/ **(loins)** 1 Someone's **loins** are the front part of their body between their waist and legs, especially their sexual parts. [LITERARY, OLD-FASHIONED] N-PLURAL 2 **Loin** or a **loin** is a piece of meat which comes from the back or sides of an animal, quite near the tail end. ❑ *Heat the honey and brush it on to the outside of the loin. ...roast loin of venison.* N-VAR

**loin|cloth** /lɔɪnklɒθ, AM -klɔːθ/ **(loincloths)** A **loincloth** is a piece of cloth sometimes worn by men in order to cover their sexual parts, especially in countries when it is too hot to wear anything else. N-COUNT

**loi|ter** /lɔɪtəʳ/ **(loiters, loitering, loitered)** If you **loiter** somewhere, you remain there or walk up and down without any real purpose. ❑ *Unemployed young men loiter at the entrance of the factory.* VERB; V

**loll** /lɒl/ **(lolls, lolling, lolled)** 1 If you **loll** somewhere, you sit or lie in a very relaxed position. ❑ *He was lolling on the sofa in the shadows near the fire... He lolled back in his comfortable chair.* VERB = lounge, sprawl; V prep/adv; V prep/adv 2 If something fairly heavy, especially someone's head or tongue, **lolls**, it hangs down in a loose, uncontrolled way. ❑ *When he let go the head lolled sideways... Tongue lolling, the dog came lolloping back from the forest.* VERB; V adv/prep; V

**lol|li|pop** /lɒlipɒp/ **(lollipops)** A **lollipop** is a sweet consisting of a hard disc or ball of a sugary substance on the end of a stick. N-COUNT = lolly

**lol|lop** /lɒləp/ **(lollops, lolloping, lolloped)** When an animal or a person **lollops** along, they run along awkwardly and not very fast. [mainly BRIT, LITERARY] ❑ *A herd of elephants lolloped across the plains towards a watering hole.* VERB; V prep/adv

**lol|ly** /lɒli/ **(lollies)** A **lolly** is the same as a **lollipop**. [mainly BRIT] → See also **ice lolly**. N-COUNT

**lone** /loʊn/ 1 If you talk about a **lone** person or thing, you mean that they are alone. ❑ *He was shot by a lone gunman.* ADJ: ADJ n 2 A **lone** parent is a parent who is looking after her or his child or children and who is not married or living with a partner. [mainly BRIT] ❑ *Ninety per cent of lone parent families are headed by mothers.* ADJ: ADJ n = single

**lone|li|ness** /loʊnlinəs/ **Loneliness** is the unhappiness that is felt by someone because they do not have any friends or do not have anyone to talk to. ❑ *I have so many friends, but deep down, underneath, I have a fear of loneliness.* N-UNCOUNT

**lone|ly** /loʊnli/ **(lonelier, loneliest)** 1 Someone who is **lonely** is unhappy because they are alone or do not have anyone they can talk to. ❑ *...lonely people who just want to talk... I feel lonelier in the middle of London than I do on my boat in the middle of nowhere.* ♦ **The lonely** are people who are lonely. ❑ *He looks for the lonely, the lost, the unloved.* ADJ; N-PLURAL: the N 2 A **lonely** situation or period of time is one in which you feel unhappy because you are alone or do not have anyone to talk to. ❑ *I desperately needed something to occupy me during those long, lonely nights. ...her lonely childhood.* ADJ 3 A **lonely** place is one where very few people come. ❑ *It felt like the loneliest place in the world. ...dark, lonely streets.* ADJ

**lone|ly hearts** A **lonely hearts** section in a newspaper or a **lonely hearts** club is used by people who are trying to find a lover or friend. ADJ: ADJ n

**lon|er** /loʊnəʳ/ **(loners)** If you describe someone as a **loner**, you mean they prefer to be alone rather than with a group of people. ❑ *I'm very much a loner – I never go out.* N-COUNT

**lone|some** /loʊnsəm/ [1] Someone who is **lonesome** is unhappy because they do not have any friends or do not have anyone to talk to. [mainly AM] ❑ *I've grown so lonesome, thinking of you.* ADJ: usu v-link ADJ = *lonely*
[2] A **lonesome** place is one which very few people come to and which is a long way from places where people live. [AM] ❑ *He was finding the river lonesome.* ADJ = *lonely*

| **long** |
|---|
| ① TIME |
| ② DISTANCE AND SIZE |
| ③ PHRASES |
| ④ VERB USES |

①**long** /lɒŋ, AM lɔːŋ/ **(longer** /lɒŋgəʳ, AM lɔːŋgər/, **longest** /lɒŋgɪst, AM lɔːŋgɪst/**)** ◆◆◆ [1] **Long** means a great amount of time or for a great amount of time. ❑ *Repairs to the cable did not take too long... Have you known her parents long?... I learned long ago to avoid these invitations... The railway had obviously been built long after the house. ...long-established social traditions.* ADV: ADV with v, oft ADV adv/prep ● The expression **for long** is used to mean 'for a great amount of time'. ❑ *'Did you live there?' — 'Not for long.'... Developing countries won't put up with the situation for much longer... For too long there was a huge gap in the market.* PHRASE: PHR after v [2] A **long** event or period of time lasts for a great amount of time or takes a great amount of time. ❑ *We had a long meeting with the attorney general... They sat looking at each other for a long while... He must have started writing his book a long time ago.* ADJ: usu ADJ n ≠ *short* [3] You use **long** to ask or talk about amounts of time. ❑ *How long have you lived around here?... He has been on a diet for as long as any of his friends can remember... She reflected no longer than a second before she decisively slit the envelope.* ADV: *how* ADV, *as* ADV *as*, ADV-compar *than* ♦ **Long** is also an adjective. ❑ *How long is the usual stay in hospital?... The average commuter journey there is five hours long.* ADJ: *how* ADJ, amount ADJ [4] A **long** speech, book, film, or list contains a lot of information or a lot of items and takes a lot of time to listen to, read, watch, or deal with. ❑ *He was making quite a long speech... This is a long film, three hours and seven minutes.* ADJ: usu ADJ n ≠ *short* [5] If you describe a period of time or work as **long**, you mean it lasts for more hours or days than is usual, or seems to last for more time than it actually does. ❑ *Go to sleep. I've got a long day tomorrow... She was a TV reporter and worked long hours... This has been the longest week of my life.* ADJ: usu ADJ n ≠ *short* [6] If someone has a **long** memory, they are able to remember things that happened far back in the past. ADJ: usu ADJ n ≠ *short* [7] **Long** is used in expressions such as **all year long, the whole day long**, and **your whole life long** to say and emphasize that something happens for the whole of a particular period of time. ❑ *We played that record all night long... Snow is sometimes found all summer long upon the highest peaks.* ADV: n ADV [emphasis]

②**long** /lɒŋ, AM lɔːŋ/ **(longer** /lɒŋgəʳ, AM lɔːŋgər/, **longest** /lɒŋgɪst, AM lɔːŋgɪst/**)** ◆◆◆ [1] Something that is **long** measures a great distance from one end to the other. ❑ *...a long table... A long line of people formed outside the doctor's office... Her hair was long and dark.* ADJ ≠ *short* [2] A **long** distance is a great distance. A **long** journey or route covers a great distance. ❑ *His destination was Chobham Common, a long way from his Cotswold home... The long journey tired him... I went for a long walk.* ADJ: usu ADJ n ≠ *short* [3] A **long** piece of clothing covers the whole of someone's legs or more of their legs than usual. Clothes with **long** sleeves cover the whole of someone's arms. ❑ *She is wearing a long black dress. ...a long-sleeved blouse.* ADJ: ADJ n ≠ *short* [4] You use **long** to talk or ask about the distance something measures from one end to the other. ❑ *An eight-week-old embryo is only an inch long... How long is the tunnel?... In the roots of the olives, you could find centipedes as long as a pencil.* ADJ: amount ADJ, *how* ADJ, *as* ADJ *as*, ADJ-compar *than* ♦ **Long** is also a combining form. ❑ *...a three-foot-long gash in the tanker's side.* COMB in ADJ

③**long** /lɒŋ, AM lɔːŋ/ **(longer** /lɒŋgəʳ, AM lɔːŋgər/**)** ◆◆◆
⇒ Please look at category 6 to see if the expression you are looking for is shown under another headword. [1] If you say that something is the case **as long as** or **so long as** something else is the case, you mean that it is only the case if the second thing is the case. ❑ *The interior minister said he would still support them, as long as they didn't break the rules... The president need not step down so long as the elections are held under international supervision.* PHRASE [2] If you say that someone **won't be long**, you mean that you think they will arrive or be back soon. If you say that it **won't be long** before something happens, you mean that you think it will happen soon. ❑ *'What's happened to her?' — 'I'm sure she won't be long.'... If every tune from Radiohead is as good as this one it, it can't be long before they are household names.* PHRASE: oft *it* PHR *before* cl [3] If you say that something will happen or happened **before long**, you mean that it will happen or happened soon. ❑ *German interest rates will come down before long... Before long he took over the editing of the magazine.* PHRASE: PHR after v, PHR with cl [4] Something that is **no longer** the case used to be the case but is not the case now. You can also say that something is not the case **any longer**. ❑ *Food shortages are no longer a problem... I noticed that he wasn't sitting by the door any longer.* PHRASE: PHR group/cl, PHR with v [5] You can say **so long** as an informal way of saying goodbye. ❑ *Well, so long, pal, see you around.* CONVENTION [formulae] = *bye* [6] **a long face** → see **face**. **at long last** → see **last**. **in the long run** → see **run**. **a long shot** → see **shot**. **in the long term** → see **term**. **long in the tooth** → see **tooth**. **to take the long view** → see **view**. **to go a long way** → see **way**.

④**long** /lɒŋ, AM lɔːŋ/ **(longs, longing, longed)** If you **long for** something, you want it very much. ❑ *Steve longed for the good old days... I'm longing to meet her... He longed for the winter to be over.* → See also **longing**. VERB V *for* n V to-inf V *for* n to-inf

**long-awaited** A **long-awaited** event or thing is one that someone has been waiting for for a long time. ❑ *...the long-awaited signing of a peace agreement.* ADJ: ADJ n

**long-distance** [1] **Long-distance** is used to describe travel between places that are far apart. ❑ *Trains are reliable, cheap and best for long-distance journeys.* ADJ: ADJ n [2] **Long-distance** is used to describe communication that takes place between people who are far apart. ❑ *He received a long-distance phone call from his girlfriend in Colorado.* ADJ: usu ADJ n ≠ *local* ♦ **Long-distance** is also an adverb. ❑ *I phoned Nicola long distance to suggest it.* ADV: ADV after v

**long drawn out** also **long-drawn-out.** A **long drawn out** process or conflict lasts an unnecessarily long time or an unpleasantly long time. ❑ *...a long drawn out election campaign.* ADJ: usu ADJ n

**longed-for** A **longed-for** thing or event is one that someone wants very much. ❑ *...the wet weather that prevents your longed-for picnic.* ADJ: ADJ n

**lon|gev|ity** /lɒndʒevɪti/ **Longevity** is long life. [FORMAL] ❑ *Human longevity runs in families... The main characteristic of the strike has been its longevity.* N-UNCOUNT

**long|hand** /lɒŋhænd, AM lɔːŋ-/ If you write something down in **longhand**, you write it by hand using complete words and normal letters rather than typing it or using shortened forms or special symbols. N-UNCOUNT: usu *in* N

**long-haul** **Long-haul** is used to describe things that involve transporting passengers or goods over long distances. Compare **short-haul**. ❑ *...learning how to avoid the unpleasant side-effects of long-haul flights.* ADJ: ADJ n ≠ *short-haul*

**long-hours cul|ture** The **long-hours culture** is the way in which some workers feel that they are expected to work much longer hours than they are paid to do. [BUSINESS] N-SING

**long|ing** /lɒŋɪŋ, AM lɔːŋ-/ **(longings)** If you feel **longing** or a **longing for** something, you have a rather sad feeling because you want it very much. N-VAR: oft N *for* n, N to-inf

❑ *He felt a longing for the familiar... Imelda spoke of her longing to return home.*

**long|ing|ly** /lɒŋɪŋli, AM lɔːŋ-/ If you look **longingly** at something you want, or think **longingly** about it, you look at it or think about it with a feeling of desire. ❑ *Claire looked longingly at the sunlit gardens outside the window.* ADV: ADV with v

**long|ish** /lɒŋɪʃ, AM lɔːŋ-/ **Longish** means fairly long. ❑ *She's about my age, with longish hair.* ADJ: usu ADJ n

**lon|gi|tude** /lɒndʒɪtjuːd, AM -tuːd/ **(longitudes)** The **longitude** of a place is its distance to the west or east of a line passing through Greenwich. Compare **latitude.** ❑ *He noted the latitude and longitude, then made a mark on the admiralty chart.* N-VAR ♦ **Longitude** is also an adjective. ❑ *A similar feature is found at 13 degrees North between 230 degrees and 250 degrees longitude.* ADJ: usu amount ADJ

**lon|gi|tu|di|nal** /lɒndʒɪtjuːdɪnᵊl, AM -tuː-/ A **longitudinal** line or structure goes from one end of an object to the other rather than across it from side to side. ADJ: ADJ n

**long johns** **Long johns** are warm underpants with long legs. N-PLURAL: also *a pair of* N

**long jump** **The long jump** is an athletics contest which involves jumping as far as you can from a marker which you run up to. N-SING: *the* N

**long-lasting** **(longer-lasting)** also **long lasting.** Something that is **long-lasting** lasts for a long time. ❑ *One of the long-lasting effects of the infection is damage to a valve in the heart.* ADJ

**long-life** **Long-life** light bulbs and batteries are manufactured so that they last longer than ordinary ones. **Long-life** fruit juice and milk have been specially treated so that they last a long time. ADJ: ADJ n

**long-list** **(long-lists, long-listing, long-listed)** also **longlist.** [1] A **long-list** for something such as a job or a prize is a large group that has been chosen from all the people who applied for the job, or all the people or things that are competing for the prize. The successful ones from this group are chosen to go on the **shortlist.** ❑ *There are 27 riders on the long-list.* N-COUNT [2] If someone or something **is long-listed** for a job or a prize, they are put on a long-list of those to be considered for that job or prize. ❑ *She was long-listed for the senior team last year.* VERB *be* V-ed *for* n

**long-lived** also **long lived.** Something that is **long-lived** lives or lasts for a long time. ❑ *The flowers may only last a day but the plants are long-lived. ...huge piles of long-lived radioactive material.* ADJ ≠short-lived

**long-lost** You use **long-lost** to describe someone or something that you have not seen for a long time. ❑ *...finding a long-lost sixth century manuscript.* ADJ: ADJ n

**long-range** [1] A **long-range** piece of military equipment or vehicle is able to hit or detect a target a long way away or to travel a long way in order to do something. ❑ *He is very keen to reach agreement with the US on reducing long-range nuclear missiles. ...the growing use on the North Atlantic routes of long-range twin-engined aircraft.* ADJ: usu ADJ n ≠short-range [2] A **long-range** plan or prediction relates to a period extending a long time into the future. ❑ *Eisenhower was intensely aware of the need for long-range planning.* ADJ: usu ADJ n

**long-running** **(longest-running)** Something that is **long-running** has been in existence, or has been performed, for a long time. ❑ *...a long-running trade dispute.* ADJ: ADJ n

**long|shore|man** /lɒŋʃɔːmən, AM lɔːŋ-/ **(longshoremen)** A **longshoreman** is a person who works in the docks, loading and unloading ships. [AM] N-COUNT

✔ in BRIT, use **docker**

**long-sighted** **Long-sighted** people cannot see things clearly that are close to them, and therefore need to wear glasses. [BRIT] ADJ ≠short-sighted

✔ in AM, use **far-sighted**

**long-standing** A **long-standing** situation has existed for a long time. ❑ *They are on the brink of resolving their long-standing dispute over money. ...long-standing economic links between Europe and much of Africa.* ADJ: usu ADJ n

**long-suffering** Someone who is **long-suffering** patiently puts up with a lot of trouble or unhappiness, especially when it is caused by someone else. ❑ *He went back to Yorkshire to join his loyal, long-suffering wife.* ADJ: usu ADJ n

**long-term** **(longer-term)** ◆◆◇ [1] Something that is **long-term** has continued for a long time or will continue for a long time in the future. ❑ *A new training scheme to help the long-term unemployed is expected... The association believes new technology will provide a long-term solution to credit card fraud.* ADJ: usu ADJ n ≠short-term [2] When you talk about what happens in **the long term**, you are talking about what happens over a long period of time, either in the future or after a particular event. ❑ *In the long term the company hopes to open in Moscow and other major cities... Over the long term, such measures may only make the underlying situation worse.* N-SING: *the* N

**long-time** ◆◇◇ You use **long-time** to describe something that has existed or been a particular thing for a long time. ❑ *She married her long-time boyfriend.* ADJ: ADJ n

**long wave** **Long wave** is a range of radio waves which are used for broadcasting. ❑ *...broadcasting on long wave. ...1500m on long wave.* N-UNCOUNT

**long-wearing** also **long wearing.** Something that is **long-wearing** is strong and well made so that it lasts for a long time and stays in good condition even though it is used a lot. [AM] ❑ *...luxurious, long-wearing, real-leather slippers.* ADJ

✔ in BRIT, use **hard-wearing**

**long-winded** If you describe something that is written or said as **long-winded**, you are critical of it because it is longer than necessary. ❑ *The manifesto is long-winded, repetitious and often ambiguous or poorly drafted... I hope I'm not being too long-winded.* ADJ: usu v-link ADJ [disapproval]

**loo** /luː/ **(loos)** A **loo** is a toilet. [BRIT, INFORMAL] ❑ *I asked if I could go to the loo.* N-COUNT: usu *the* N in sing

**loo|fah** /luːfə/ **(loofahs)** A **loofah** is a long rough sponge-like piece of plant fibre which you use to scrub your body. N-COUNT

| **look** |
|---|
| ① USING YOUR EYES OR YOUR MIND |
| ② APPEARANCE |

**①look** /lʊk/ **(looks, looking, looked)** ◆◆◆

⇒ Please look at category 14 to see if the expression you are looking for is shown under another headword. [1] If you **look** in a particular direction, you direct your eyes in that direction, especially so that you can see what is there or see what something is like. ❑ *I looked down the hallway to room number nine... She turned to look at him... He looked away, apparently enraged... If you look, you'll see what was a lake.* VERB V prep/adv V prep/adv V prep/adv V ♦ **Look** is also a noun. ❑ *Lucille took a last look in the mirror... Assisi has a couple of churches that are worth a look if you have time.* N-SING [2] If you **look at** a book, newspaper, or magazine, you read it fairly quickly or read part of it. ❑ *You've just got to look at the last bit of Act Three.* VERB V *at* n ♦ **Look** is also a noun. ❑ *A quick look at Monday's British newspapers shows that there's plenty of interest in foreign news.* N-SING: oft N *at* n [3] If someone, especially an expert, **looks** at something, they examine it, and then deal with it or say how it should be dealt with. ❑ *Can you look at my back? I think something's wrong.* VERB V *at* n Also V ♦ **Look** is also a noun. ❑ *The car has not been running very well and a mechanic had to come over to have a look at it.* N-SING: usu N *at* n [4] If you **look at** someone in a particular way, you look at them with your expression showing what you are feeling or thinking. ❑ *She looked at him earnestly. 'You don't mind?'* VERB V *at* n adv/prep ♦ **Look** is also a noun. ❑ *He gave her a blank look, as if he had* N-COUNT: usu with supp, *no idea who she was... Sally spun round, a feigned look of surprise on her face.* [oft adj N, N *of* n] [5] If you **look for** something, for example something that you have lost, you try to find it. [VERB] ❑ *I'm looking for a child. I believe your husband can help me find her... I had gone to Maine looking for a place to work... I looked everywhere for ideas... Have you looked on the piano?* [V *for* n] [V *for* n] [V prep/adv] [*for* n] [V prep/adv] ♦ **Look** is also a noun. ❑ *Go and have another look.* [N-SING] [6] If you **are looking for** something such as the solution to a problem or a new method, you want it and are trying to obtain it or think of it. [VERB = seek] ❑ *The working group will be looking for practical solutions to the problems faced by doctors.* [V *for* n] [7] If you **look at** a subject, problem, or situation, you think about it or study it, so that you know all about it and can perhaps consider what should be done in relation to it. [VERB = examine, consider] ❑ *Next term we'll be looking at the Second World War period... He visited Florida a few years ago looking at the potential of the area to stage a big match.* [V *at* n] [V *at* n] ♦ **Look** is also a noun. ❑ *A close look at the statistics reveals a troubling picture.* [N-SING: oft N *at* n] [8] If you **look at** a person, situation, or subject from a particular point of view, you judge them or consider them from that point of view. [VERB] ❑ *Brian had learned to look at her with new respect... It depends how you look at it.* [V *at* n prep/adv] [9] You say **look** when you want someone to pay attention to you because you are going to say something important. [CONVENTION] ❑ *Look, I'm sorry. I didn't mean it... Now, look, here is how things stand.* [10] You can use **look** to draw attention to a particular situation, person, or thing, for example because you find it very surprising, significant, or annoying. [VERB: only imper] ❑ *Hey, look at the time! We'll talk about it tonight. All right?... Look what a mess you've made of your life.* [V *at* n] [V wh] [11] If something such as a building or window **looks** somewhere, it has a view of a particular place. [VERB] ❑ *The castle looks over private parkland.* [V prep] ♦ **Look out** means the same as **look**. [PHRASAL VERB] ❑ *We sit on the terrace, which looks out on the sea.* [V P prep] [12] If you **are looking** to do something, you are aiming to do it. [VERB] ❑ *We're not looking to make a fortune.* [V to-inf] [13] If you say or shout '**look out!**' to someone, you are warning them that they are in danger. [EXCLAM] ❑ *'Look out!' somebody shouted, as the truck started to roll toward the sea.* [14] to **look down** your **nose at** someone → see **nose**.

♦ **look after** [1] If you **look after** someone or something, you do what is necessary to keep them healthy, safe, or in good condition. [PHRASAL VERB] ❑ *I love looking after the children... People don't look after other people's property in the same way as they look after their own.* [V P n] [V P n] [2] If you **look after** something, you are responsible for it and deal with it or make sure it is all right, especially because it is your job to do so. [PHRASAL VERB] ❑ *...the farm manager who looks after the day-to-day organization... We'll help you look after your finances.* [V P n] [V P n]

♦ **look ahead** If you **look ahead**, you think about what is going to happen in the future and perhaps make plans for the future. [PHRASAL VERB] ❑ *I'm trying to look ahead at what might happen and be ready to handle it.* [V P]

♦ **look around**

☑ in BRIT, also use **look round**

If you **look around** or **look round** a building or place, you walk round it and look at the different parts of it. [PHRASAL VERB] ❑ *We went to look round the show homes... I'm going to look around and see what I can find.* [V P n] [V P]

♦ **look back** If you **look back**, you think about things that happened in the past. [PHRASAL VERB] ❑ *Looking back, I am staggered how easily it was all arranged.* [V P]

♦ **look down on** To **look down on** someone means to consider that person to be inferior or unimportant, usually when this is not true. [PHRASAL VERB] ❑ *I wasn't successful, so they looked down on me.* [V P P n]

♦ **look forward to** [1] If you **look forward to** something that is going to happen, you want it to happen because you think you will enjoy it. [PHRASAL VERB] ❑ *He was looking forward to working with the new Prime Minister.* [V P P -ing/n] [2] If you say that someone **is looking forward** to something useful or positive, you mean they expect it to happen. [PHRASAL VERB] ❑ *Motor traders are looking forward to a further increase in vehicle sales.* [V P P n]

♦ **look into** If a person or organization **is looking into** a possible course of action, a problem, or a situation, they are finding out about it and examining the facts relating to it. [PHRASAL VERB = investigate] ❑ *He had once looked into buying his own island off Nova Scotia.* [V P -ing/n]

♦ **look on** If you **look on** while something happens, you watch it happening without taking part yourself. [PHRASAL VERB = watch] ❑ *About 150 local people looked on in silence as the two coffins were taken into the church.* [V P]

♦ **look on** or **look upon** If you **look on** or **look upon** someone or something in a particular way, you think of them in that way. [PHRASAL VERB = consider] ❑ *A lot of people looked on him as a healer... A lot of people look on it like that... Employers look favourably on applicants who have work experience.* [V P n *as* n] [V P n prep/adv] [V adv P n]

♦ **look out** → see **look 11**.

♦ **look out for** If you **look out for** something, you pay attention to things so that you notice it if or when it occurs. [PHRASAL VERB = watch for] ❑ *Look out for special deals.* [V P P n]

♦ **look over** If you **look** something **over**, you examine it quite quickly in order to get a general idea of what it is like. [PHRASAL VERB] ❑ *They presented their draft to the president, who looked it over, nodded and signed it... He could have looked over the papers in less than ten minutes.* [V n P] [V P n (not pron)]

♦ **look round** → see **look around**.

♦ **look through** [1] If you **look through** a group of things, you examine each one so that you can find or choose the one that you want. [PHRASAL VERB = go through] ❑ *Peter starts looking through the mail as soon as the door shuts.* [V P n] [2] If you **look through** something that has been written or printed, you read it. [PHRASAL VERB] ❑ *He happened to be looking through the medical book 'Gray's Anatomy' at the time.* [V P n]

♦ **look to** [1] If you **look to** someone or something for a particular thing that you want, you expect or hope that they will provide it. [PHRASAL VERB] ❑ *The difficulties women encounter with their doctors partly explain why so many of us are looking to alternative therapies.* [V P n] [2] If you **look to** something that will happen in the future, you think about it. [PHRASAL VERB] ❑ *Looking to the future, though, we asked him what the prospects are for a vaccine to prevent infection in the first place.* [V P n]

♦ **look up** [1] If you **look up** a fact or a piece of information, you find it out by looking in something such as a reference book or a list. [PHRASAL VERB] ❑ *I looked your address up in the personnel file... Many people have to look up the meaning of this word in the dictionary.* [V n P] [V P n (not pron)] [2] If you **look** someone **up**, you visit them after not having seen them for a long time. [PHRASAL VERB = visit] ❑ *I'll try to look him up, ask him a few questions... She looked up some friends of bygone years.* [V n P] [V P n] [3] If a situation **is looking up**, it is improving. [INFORMAL] [PHRASAL VERB: usu cont = improve] ❑ *Things could be looking up in the computer industry.* [V P]

♦ **look upon** → see **look on**.

♦ **look up to** If you **look up to** someone, especially someone older than you, you respect and admire them. [PHRASAL VERB = admire] ❑ *You're a popular girl, Grace, and a lot of the younger ones look up to you.* [V P P n]

② **look** /lʊk/ **(looks, looking, looked)** ♦♦♦ [1] You use **look** when describing the appearance of a person or thing or the impression that they give. [V-LINK] ❑ *Sheila was looking miserable... He does not look the most reliable of animals... They look like stars to the naked eye... He looked as if he was going to smile... Everybody in the club looked to be fourteen years old.* [V adj] [V n] [V *like* n] [V like/as if] [V to-inf] ♦ **-looking** *She was a very peculiar-looking woman.* [COMB in ADJ] [2] If someone or something has a particular **look**, they have a particular appearance or expression. [N-SING: with supp] ❑ *She had the look of someone deserted and betrayed... When he came to decorate the kitchen, Kenneth opted for a friendly rustic look.* [3] When you refer to someone's **looks**, you are referring to how [N-PLURAL] beautiful or ugly they are, especially how beautiful they are. ❑ *I never chose people just because of their looks. ...a young woman with wholesome good looks.* 4 You use **look** when indicating what you think will happen in the future or how a situation seems to you. ❑ *He had lots of time to think about the future, and it didn't look good... Britain looks set to send a major force of over 100 tanks and supporting equipment... So far it looks like Warner Brothers' gamble is paying off... The Europeans had hoped to win, and, indeed, had looked like winning... The team had stormed into a two-goal lead and looked to be cruising to a third round place.* 5 You use expressions such as **by the look of him** and **by the looks of it** when you want to indicate that you are giving an opinion based on the appearance of someone or something. ❑ *He was not a well man by the look of him... By the look of things, Mr Stone and company will stay busy.*

V-LINK; V adj; V adj; *it* V like/as if; V *like* -ing/n; V to-inf; PHRASE

**PHRASES** 6 If you **don't like the look of** something or someone, you feel that they may be dangerous or cause problems. ❑ *I don't like the look of those clouds.* 7 If you ask **what** someone or something **looks like**, you are asking for a description of them.

PHRASE: V inflects, PHR n; PHRASE: V inflects

**look|alike** /lʊkəlaɪk/ **(lookalikes)** also **look-alike.** A **lookalike** is someone who has a very similar appearance to another person, especially a famous person. ❑ *...a Marilyn Monroe look-alike.*

N-COUNT: usu n-proper N

**look|er** /lʊkəʳ/ **(lookers)** You can refer to an attractive man or woman as a **looker** or a **good looker.** [INFORMAL] ❑ *She was quite a looker before this happened.*

N-COUNT

**look-in** If you are trying to take part in an activity and you do not get a **look-in**, you do not get the chance to take part because too many other people are doing it. [BRIT, INFORMAL] ❑ *They want to make sure the newcomers don't get a look-in.*

N-SING: usu with brd-neg, *a* N

**look|ing glass** **(looking glasses)** also **looking-glass.** A **looking glass** is a mirror. [OLD-FASHIONED]

N-COUNT

**look|out** /lʊkaʊt/ **(lookouts)** 1 A **lookout** is a place from which you can see clearly in all directions. ❑ *Troops tried to set up a lookout post inside a refugee camp.* 2 A **lookout** is someone who is watching for danger in order to warn other people about it. 3 If someone **keeps a lookout**, especially on a boat, they look around all the time in order to make sure there is no danger. ❑ *He denied that he'd failed to keep a proper lookout that night.*

N-COUNT; N-COUNT; PHRASE: V inflects

**loom** /luːm/ **(looms, looming, loomed)** 1 If something **looms over** you, it appears as a large or unclear shape, often in a frightening way. ❑ *...the bleak mountains that loomed out of the blackness and towered around us.* 2 If a worrying or threatening situation or event **is looming**, it seems likely to happen soon. [JOURNALISM] ❑ *Another government spending crisis is looming in the United States... The threat of renewed civil war looms ahead. ...the looming threat of recession.* 3 A **loom** is a machine that is used for weaving thread into cloth.

VERB; V prep/adv; Also V; VERB; V; V adv/prep; V-ing; N-COUNT

**loony** /luːni/ **(loonies, loonier, looniest)** 1 If you describe someone's behaviour or ideas as **loony**, you mean that they seem mad, strange, or eccentric. Some people consider this use offensive. [INFORMAL] ❑ *What's she up to? She's as loony as her brother!* 2 If you refer to someone as a **loony**, you mean that they behave in a way that seems mad, strange, or eccentric. Some people consider this use offensive. [INFORMAL] ❑ *At first they all thought I was a loony.*

ADJ [disapproval]; N-COUNT [disapproval]

**loop** /luːp/ **(loops, looping, looped)** 1 A **loop** is a curved or circular shape in something long, for example in a piece of string. ❑ *Mrs. Morrell reached for a loop of garden hose.* 2 If you **loop** something such as a piece of rope around an object, you tie a length of it in a loop around the object, for example in order to fasten it to the object. ❑ *He looped the rope over the wood... He wore the watch and chain looped round his neck like a medallion.* 3 If something **loops** somewhere, it goes there in a circular direction that makes the shape of a loop. ❑ *The helicopter took off and headed north. Then it looped west, heading for the hills.* 4 If someone is **in the loop**, they are part of a group of people who make decisions about important things, or they know about these decisions. If they are **out of the loop**, they do not make or know about important decisions. [mainly AM, INFORMAL] ❑ *I think that the vice president was in the loop... These activists don't want to feel out of the loop.*

N-COUNT: usu with supp; VERB; V n prep; V-ed; VERB; V prep/adv; PHRASE: usu v-link PHR

**loop|hole** /luːphoʊl/ **(loopholes)** A **loophole** in the law is a small mistake which allows people to do something that would otherwise be illegal. ❑ *It is estimated that 60,000 shops open every Sunday and trade by exploiting some loophole in the law to avoid prosecution.*

N-COUNT: oft N *in* n

**loose** /luːs/ **(looser, loosest, looses, loosing, loosed)** ◆◇◇ 1 Something that is **loose** is not firmly held or fixed in place. ❑ *If a tooth feels very loose, your dentist may recommend that it's taken out... Two wooden beams had come loose from the ceiling... She idly pulled at a loose thread on her skirt.* ♦ **loose|ly** *Tim clasped his hands together and held them loosely in front of his belly.* 2 Something that is **loose** is not attached to anything, or held or contained in anything. ❑ *Frank emptied a handful of loose change on the table... A page came loose and floated onto the tiles.* 3 If people or animals break **loose** or are set **loose**, they are no longer held, tied, or kept somewhere and can move around freely. ❑ *She broke loose from his embrace and crossed to the window... Why didn't you tell me she'd been set loose?* 4 Clothes that are **loose** are rather large and do not fit closely. ❑ *Wear loose clothes as they're more comfortable.* ♦ **loose|ly** *His shirt hung loosely over his thin shoulders.* 5 If your hair is **loose**, it hangs freely round your shoulders and is not tied back. ❑ *She was still in her nightdress, with her hair hanging loose over her shoulders.* 6 If something is **loose** in texture, there is space between the different particles or threads it consists of. ❑ *She gathered loose soil and let it filter slowly through her fingers.* 7 A **loose** grouping, arrangement, or organization is flexible rather than strictly controlled or organized. ❑ *Murray and Alison came to some sort of loose arrangement before he went home... He wants a loose coalition of leftwing forces.* ♦ **loose|ly** *The investigation had aimed at a loosely organised group of criminals.* 8 If a person or an animal is **on the loose**, they are free because they have escaped from a person or place. ❑ *Up to a thousand prisoners may be on the loose inside the jail.* 9 a **loose cannon** → see **cannon**. **all hell breaks loose** → see **hell**.

ADJ; ADV: ADV with v; ADJ: usu ADJ n; ADJ: ADJ after v, ADJ n, v-link ADJ = free; ADJ = baggy ≠ tight; ADV: ADV after v, ADV -ed; ADJ; ADJ; ADJ: usu ADJ n; ADV: ADV with v; PHRASE: v-link PHR

**loose end** **(loose ends)** 1 A **loose end** is part of a story, situation, or crime that has not yet been explained. ❑ *There are some annoying loose ends in the plot.* 2 If you are **at a loose end**, you are bored because you do not have anything to do and cannot think of anything that you want to do. In American English, you usually say that you are **at loose ends.** [INFORMAL] ❑ *Adolescents are most likely to get into trouble when they're at a loose end.*

N-COUNT; PHRASE: v-link PHR

**loose-fitting** also **loose fitting.** **Loose-fitting** clothes are rather large and do not fit tightly on your body.

ADJ: usu ADJ n

**loos|en** /luːsᵊn/ **(loosens, loosening, loosened)** 1 If someone **loosens** restrictions or laws, for example, they make them less strict or severe. ❑ *Drilling regulations, too, have been loosened to speed the development of the fields.* ♦ **loos|en|ing** *Domestic conditions did not justify a loosening of monetary policy.* 2 If someone or something **loosens** the ties between people or groups of people, or if the ties **loosen**, they become weaker. ❑ *The Federal Republic must loosen its ties with the United States... The deputy leader is cautious about loosening the links with the unions... The ties that bind them together are loosening.* 3 If you **loosen** your clothing or

VERB ≠ tighten; V n; N-SING: usu N *of* n; VERB; V n; V n; V; VERB something that is tied or fastened or if it **loosens**, you undo it slightly so that it is less tight or less firmly held in place. ❑ *Loosen the bolt so the bars can be turned... Her hair had loosened and was tangled around her shoulders.* [4] If you **loosen** something that is stretched across something else, you make it less stretched or tight. ❑ *Insert a small knife into the top of the chicken breast to loosen the skin.* [5] If you **loosen** your grip on something, or if your grip **loosens**, you hold it less tightly. ❑ *Harry loosened his grip momentarily and Anna wriggled free... When his grip loosened she eased herself away.* [6] If a government or organization **loosens** its grip on a group of people or an activity, or if its grip **loosens**, it begins to have less control over it. ❑ *There is no sign that the Party will loosen its tight grip on the country... The Soviet Union's grip on Eastern Europe loosened.*

≠ tighten; V n; V; VERB; V n; VERB = relax ≠ tighten; V n; V; VERB = relax; V n; V

♦ **loosen up** [1] If a person or situation **loosens up**, they become more relaxed and less tense. ❑ *Young people often loosen up on the dance floor... I think people have loosened up their standards.* [2] If you **loosen up** your body, or if it **loosens up**, you do simple exercises to get your muscles ready for a difficult physical activity, such as running or playing football. ❑ *Squeeze the foot with both hands, again to loosen up tight muscles... Close your eyes. Relax. Let your body loosen up.*

PHRASAL VERB; V P; V P n; PHRASAL VERB; V P n (not pron); V P; Also V n P

**loot** /luːt/ **(loots, looting, looted)** [1] If people **loot** shops or houses, they steal things from them, for example during a war or riot. ❑ *The trouble began when gangs began breaking windows and looting shops... There have been reports of youths taking advantage of the general confusion to loot and steal.* ♦ **loot|ing** *In the country's largest cities there has been rioting and looting.* [2] If someone **loots** things, they steal them, for example during a war or riot. ❑ *The town has been plagued by armed thugs who have looted food supplies and terrorized the population.* [3] **Loot** is stolen money or goods. [INFORMAL] ❑ *Most criminals steal in order to sell their loot for cash on the black market.*

VERB; V n; V; N-UNCOUNT; VERB; V n; N-UNCOUNT = plunder, spoils

**loot|er** /luːtəʳ/ **(looters)** A **looter** is a person who steals things from shops or houses, for example during a war or riot.

N-COUNT

**lop** /lɒp/ **(lops, lopping, lopped)**

♦ **lop off** [1] If you **lop** something **off**, you cut it away from what it was attached to, usually with a quick, strong stroke. ❑ *Somebody lopped the heads off our tulips. ...men with axes, lopping off branches... His ponytail had been lopped off.* [2] If you **lop** an amount of money or time **off** something such as a budget or a schedule, you reduce the budget or schedule by that amount. [INFORMAL] ❑ *The Air France plane lopped over four hours off the previous best time... More than 100 million pounds will be lopped off the prison building programme.*

PHRASAL VERB = chop; V n P; V P n (not pron); PHRASAL VERB; V n P n; Also V P n, V n P

**lope** /loʊp/ **(lopes, loping, loped)** If a person or animal **lopes** somewhere, they run in an easy and relaxed way, taking long steps. ❑ *He was loping across the sand toward Nancy... Matty saw him go loping off, running low.* ♦ **lop|ing** *She turned and walked away with long, loping steps.*

VERB; V prep/adv; Also V; ADJ: ADJ n

**lop|sided** /lɒpsaɪdɪd/ also **lop-sided.** Something that is **lopsided** is uneven because one side is lower or heavier than the other. ❑ *His suit had shoulders that made him look lopsided. ...a friendly, lopsided grin.*

ADJ

**lo|qua|cious** /ləkweɪʃəs/ If you describe someone as **loquacious**, you mean that they talk a lot. [FORMAL] ❑ *The normally loquacious Mr O'Reilly has said little.*

ADJ = talkative, garrulous

**lord** /lɔːʳd/ **(lords)** [1] In Britain, a **lord** is a man who has a high rank in the nobility, for example an earl, a viscount, or a marquis. ❑ *She married a lord and lives in this huge house in the Cotswolds... A few days earlier he had received a telegram from Lord Lloyd.* [2] In Britain, judges, bishops, and some male members of the nobility are addressed as '**my Lord**'. ❑ *My lord, I am instructed by my client to claim that the evidence has been tampered with.* [3] In Britain, **Lord** is used in the titles of some officials of very high rank. ❑ *He was Lord Chancellor from 1970 until 1974. ...Sir Brian Hutton, the Lord Chief Justice for Northern Ireland.* [4] **The Lords** is the same as **the House of Lords**. ❑ *It's very likely the bill will be defeated in the Lords.* [5] In the Christian church, people refer to God and to Jesus Christ as the **Lord**. ❑ *I know the Lord will look after him... She prayed now. 'Lord, help me to find courage.' ...the birth of the Lord Jesus Christ.* → See also **Our Lord**. [6] **Lord** is used in exclamations such as '**good Lord!**' and '**oh Lord!**' to express surprise, shock, frustration, or annoyance about something. ❑ *'Good lord, that's what he is: he's a policeman.'... 'They didn't fire you for drinking, did they?' — 'Lord, no! I only drink beer, nowadays.'*

◆◆◇ N-COUNT; N-TITLE; N-VOC: *my* N [politeness]; N-PROPER-COLL: *the* N; N-PROPER: usu *the* N; N-VOC; EXCLAM [feelings]

**lord|ly** /lɔːʳdli/ [1] If you say that someone's behaviour is **lordly**, you are critical of them because they treat other people in a proud and arrogant way. ❑ *...their usual lordly indifference to patients.* [2] **Lordly** means impressive and suitable for a lord. ❑ *...the site of a lordly mansion.*

ADJ: usu ADJ n [disapproval]; ADJ: ADJ n

**Lord|ship** /lɔːʳdʃɪp/ **(Lordships)** You use the expressions **Your Lordship**, **His Lordship**, or **Their Lordships** when you are addressing or referring to a judge, bishop, or male member of the nobility. ❑ *My name is Richard Savage, your Lordship... His Lordship expressed the hope that the Law Commission might look at the subject.*

N-VOC; N-PROPER: det-poss N [politeness]

**Lord's Prayer** **The Lord's Prayer** is a Christian prayer that was originally taught by Jesus Christ to his followers.

N-PROPER: *the* N

**lore** /lɔːʳ/ The **lore** of a particular country or culture is its traditional stories and history. ❑ *...the Book of the Sea, which was stuffed with sailors' lore. ...ancient Catalan lore.*

N-UNCOUNT: with supp

**lor|ry** /lɒri, AM lɔːri/ **(lorries)** A **lorry** is a large vehicle that is used to transport goods by road. [BRIT] ❑ *...a seven-ton lorry.*

N-COUNT

✔ in AM, use **truck**

**lose** /luːz/ **(loses, losing, lost)** [1] If you **lose** a contest, a fight, or an argument, you do not succeed because someone does better than you and defeats you. ❑ *A C Milan lost the Italian Cup Final... The government lost the argument over the pace of reform... No one likes to be on the losing side.* [2] If you **lose** something, you do not know where it is, for example because you have forgotten where you put it. ❑ *I lost my keys... I had to go back for my checkup; they'd lost my X-rays.* [3] You say that you **lose** something when you no longer have it because it has been taken away from you or destroyed. ❑ *I lost my job when the company moved to another state... She was terrified they'd lose their home.* [4] If someone **loses** a quality, characteristic, attitude, or belief, they no longer have it. ❑ *He lost all sense of reason... He had lost his desire to live.* [5] If you **lose** an ability, you stop having that ability because of something such as an accident. ❑ *They lost their ability to hear... He had lost the use of his legs.* [6] If someone or something **loses** heat, their temperature becomes lower. ❑ *Babies lose heat much faster than adults.* [7] If you **lose** blood or fluid from your body, it leaves your body so that you have less of it. ❑ *During fever a large quantity of fluid is lost in perspiration.* [8] If you **lose** weight, you become less heavy, and usually look thinner. ❑ *I have lost a lot of weight... Martha was able to lose 25 pounds.* [9] If you **lose** a part of your body, it is cut off in an operation or in an accident. ❑ *He lost a foot when he was struck by a train.* [10] If someone **loses** their life, they die. ❑ *...the ferry disaster in 1987, in which 192 people lost their lives... Hundreds of lives were lost in fighting.* [11] If you **lose** a close relative or friend, they die. ❑ *My Grandma lost her brother in the war.* [12] If things **are lost**, they are destroyed in a disaster. ❑ *...the famous Nankin pottery that was lost in a shipwreck off the coast of China.* [13] If you **lose** time,

◆◆◆ VERB; V n; V n; V-ing; VERB; V n; V n; VERB; V n; V n; VERB; V n; V n; VERB; V n; V n; VERB; V n; VERB; V n; VERB; V n; V n; VERB; V n; VERB; V n; V n; VERB; V n; VERB: usu passive *be* V-ed; VERB

something slows you down so that you do not make as much progress as you hoped. ❑ *They claim that police lost valuable time in the early part of the investigation... Six hours were lost in all.* [V n] **14** If you **lose** an opportunity, you do not take advantage of it. [V n; VERB] ❑ *If you don't do it soon you're going to lose the opportunity... They did not lose the opportunity to say what they thought of events. ...a lost opportunity.* [V n; V n to-inf; V-ed] **15** If you **lose yourself in** something or if you **are lost in** it, you give a lot of attention to it and do not think about anything else. [VERB = absorb] ❑ *Michael held on to her arm, losing himself in the music... He was lost in the contemplation of the landscape.* [V pron-refl *in* n; *be* V-ed *in* n] **16** If a business **loses** money, it earns less money than it spends, and is therefore in debt. [BUSINESS] [VERB] ❑ *His shops stand to lose millions of pounds.* [V n] **17** If something **loses** you a contest or **loses** you something that you had, it causes you to fail or to no longer have what you had. [VERB] ❑ *My own stupidity lost me the match... His economic mismanagement has lost him the support of the general public.* [V n n; V n n] **18** → See also **lost**.

**PHRASES** **19** If someone **loses it**, they become extremely angry or upset. [INFORMAL] [PHRASE: V inflects] ❑ *I completely lost it. I went mad, berserk.* **20** If you **lose** your **way**, you become lost when you are trying to go somewhere. [PHRASE: V inflects] ❑ *The men lost their way in a sandstorm.* **21** to **lose** your **balance** → see **balance**. to **lose the battle but win the war** → see **battle**. to **lose contact** → see **contact**. to **lose** your **cool** → see **cool**. to **lose face** → see **face**. to **lose** your **grip** → see **grip**. to **lose** your **head** → see **head**. to **lose heart** → see **heart**. to **lose** your **mind** → see **mind**. to **lose** your **nerve** → see **nerve**. to **lose the plot** → see **plot**. to **lose sight of** → see **sight**. to **lose** your **temper** → see **temper**. to **lose touch** → see **touch**. to **lose track of** → see **track**.

♦ **lose out** If you **lose out**, you suffer a loss or disadvantage because you have not succeeded in what you were doing. [PHRASAL VERB = miss out] ❑ *We both lost out... Laura lost out to Tom... Women have lost out in this new pay flexibility... Egypt has lost out on revenues from the Suez Canal.* [V P; V P *to* n; V P *in* n; V P *on* n]

**los|er** /luːzəʳ/ **(losers)** **1** The **losers** of a game, contest, or struggle are the people who are defeated or beaten. [N-COUNT: usu pl ≠ winner] ❑ *...the Dallas Cowboys and Buffalo Bills, the winners and losers of this year's Super Bowl.* ● If someone is a **good loser**, they accept that they have lost a game or contest without complaining. If someone is a **bad loser**, they hate losing and complain about it. [PHRASE: usu v-link PHR] ❑ *I'm sure the prime minister will turn out to be a good loser... You are a very bad loser Lou, aren't you?* **2** If you refer to someone as a **loser**, you have a low opinion of them because you think they are always unsuccessful. [INFORMAL] [N-COUNT disapproval = failure] ❑ *They've only been trained to compete with other men, so a successful woman can make them feel like a real loser.* **3** People who are **losers** as the result of an action or event, are in a worse situation because of it or do not benefit from it. [N-COUNT: usu pl ≠ winner] ❑ *Some of Britain's top business leaders of the 1980s became the country's greatest losers in the recession.*

**loss** /lɒs, AM lɔːs/ **(losses)** ♦♦◇ **1** **Loss** is the fact of no longer having something or having less of it than before. [N-VAR: usu with supp] ❑ *...loss of sight... The loss of income for the government is about $250 million a month. ...hair loss... The job losses will reduce the total workforce to 7,000.* **2** **Loss** of life occurs when people die. [N-VAR: usu with supp] ❑ *...a terrible loss of human life... The allies suffered less than 20 casualties while enemy losses were said to be high.* **3** The **loss** of a relative or friend is their death. [N-UNCOUNT: with supp, usu *the* N *of* n] ❑ *They took the time to talk about the loss of Thomas and how their grief was affecting them. ...the loss of his mother.* **4** If a business makes a **loss**, it earns less than it spends. [N-VAR ≠ profit] ❑ *In 1986 Rover made a loss of nine hundred million pounds... The company said it will stop producing fertilizer in 1990 because of continued losses. ...profit and loss.* **5** **Loss** is the feeling of sadness you experience when someone or something you like is taken away from you. [N-UNCOUNT] ❑ *Talk to others about your feelings of loss and grief.* **6** A **loss** is the disadvantage you suffer when a valuable and useful person or thing leaves or is taken away. [N-COUNT: usu sing] ❑ *She said his death was a great loss to herself.* **7** The **loss** of something such as heat, blood, or fluid is the gradual reduction of it or of its level in a system or in someone's body. [N-UNCOUNT: with supp] ❑ *...blood loss. ...weight loss. ...a rapid loss of heat from the body.*

**PHRASES** **8** If a business produces something **at a loss**, they sell it at a price which is less than it cost them to produce it or buy it. [BUSINESS] [PHRASE: PHR after v ≠ at a profit] ❑ *New fashion designs have to be sold off at a loss if sales are poor.* **9** If you say that you are **at a loss**, you mean that you do not know what to do in a particular situation. [PHRASE: usu v-link PHR, usu PHR *for* n, PHR to-inf] ❑ *The government is at a loss to know how to tackle the violence.* **10** If you **cut** your **losses**, you stop doing what you were doing in order to prevent the bad situation that you are in becoming worse. [PHRASE: V inflects] ❑ *Directors are right to cut their losses, admit they chose the wrong man and make a change.* **11** If you say that someone or something is **a dead loss**, you have a low opinion of them because you think they are completely useless or unsuccessful. [BRIT, INFORMAL] [PHRASE: usu v-link PHR disapproval] ❑ *I'd had no experience of organizing anything of that sort. I think I was largely a dead loss.*

**loss ad|just|er** **(loss adjusters)** also **loss adjustor.** A **loss adjuster** is someone who is employed by an insurance company to decide how much money should be paid to a person making a claim. [BRIT, BUSINESS] [N-COUNT]

> ✔ in AM, use **insurance adjuster, claims adjuster**

**loss lead|er** **(loss leaders)** also **loss-leader.** A **loss leader** is an item that is sold at such a low price that it makes a loss in the hope that customers will be attracted by it and buy other goods at the same shop. [BUSINESS] [N-COUNT]

**lost** /lɒst, AM lɔːst/ ♦◇◇ **1** **Lost** is the past tense and past participle of **lose**. **2** If you are **lost** or if you get **lost**, you do not know where you are or are unable to find your way. [ADJ: usu v-link ADJ] ❑ *Barely had I set foot in the street when I realised I was lost... I took a wrong turn and we got lost in the mountains.* **3** If something is **lost**, or gets **lost**, you cannot find it, for example because you have forgotten where you put it. [ADJ] ❑ *...a lost book... My paper got lost... He was scrabbling for his pen, which had got lost somewhere under the sheets of paper.* **4** If you feel **lost**, you feel very uncomfortable because you are in an unfamiliar situation. [ADJ: usu v-link ADJ] ❑ *Of the funeral he remembered only the cold, the waiting, and feeling very lost... I feel lost and lonely in a strange town alone.* **5** If you describe a person or group of people as **lost**, you think that they do not have a clear idea of what they want to do or achieve. [ADJ] ❑ *They are a lost generation in search of an identity.* **6** If you describe something as **lost**, you mean that you no longer have it or it no longer exists. [ADJ] ❑ *...a lost job or promotion... The sense of community is lost... The riots will also mean lost income for Los Angeles County.* **7** You use **lost** to refer to a period or state of affairs that existed in the past and no longer exists. [ADJ: ADJ n] ❑ *He seemed to pine for his lost youth. ...the relics of a lost civilisation.* **8** If something is **lost**, it is not used properly and is considered wasted. [ADJ: usu v-link ADJ] ❑ *Fox is not bitter about the lost opportunity to compete in the Games... The advantage is lost.* **9** If advice or a comment **is lost on** someone, they do not understand it or they pay no attention to it. [PHRASE: V inflects, PHR n] ❑ *The meaning of that was lost on me.*

**lost and found** **1** **Lost and found** is the place where lost property is kept. [AM] [N-SING]

> ✔ in BRIT, use **lost property**

**2** **Lost and found** things are things which someone has lost and which someone else has found. [ADJ] ❑ *...the shelf where they stored lost-and-found articles. ...the local paper's lost-and-found column.*

**lost cause** **(lost causes)** N-COUNT If you refer to something or someone as **a lost cause**, you mean that people's attempts to change or influence them have no chance of succeeding. ❑ *They do not want to expend energy in what, to them, is a lost cause.*

**lost prop|er|ty** 1 N-UNCOUNT **Lost property** consists of things that people have lost or accidentally left in a public place, for example on a train or in a school. ❑ *Lost property should be handed to the driver.* 2 N-UNCOUNT **Lost property** is a place where lost property is kept. [BRIT] ❑ *I was enquiring in Lost Property at Derby.*

in AM, use **lost and found**

**lost soul** **(lost souls)** N-COUNT If you call someone a **lost soul**, you mean that they seem unhappy, and unable to fit in with any particular group of people in society. ❑ *They just clung to each other like two lost souls.*

**lot** /lɒt/ **(lots)** ◆◆◆ 1 QUANT: QUANT *of* n **A lot of** something or **lots of** it is a large amount of it. **A lot of** people or things, or **lots of** them, is a large number of them. ❑ *A lot of our land is used to grow crops for export... I remember a lot of things... 'You'll find that everybody will try and help their colleague.' — 'Yeah. There's a lot of that.'... He drank lots of milk... A lot of the play is very funny.* ♦ PRON **Lot** is also a pronoun. ❑ *There's lots going on at Selfridges this month... I learned a lot from him about how to run a band... I know a lot has been said about my sister's role in my career.* 2 ADV: ADV after v, oft ADV compar **A lot** means to a great extent or degree. ❑ *Matthew's out quite a lot doing his research... I like you, a lot... If I went out and accepted a job at a lot less money, I'd jeopardize a good career.* 3 ADV: ADV after v If you do something **a lot**, you do it often or for a long time. ❑ *They went out a lot, to the Cafe Royal or the The Ivy... He talks a lot about his own children.* 4 N-COUNT: num N, oft N *of* n You can use **lot** to refer to a set or group of things or people. ❑ *He bought two lots of 1,000 shares in the company during August and September... We've just sacked one lot of builders.* 5 N-SING: adj N = *bunch* You can refer to a specific group of people as a particular **lot**. [INFORMAL] ❑ *Future generations are going to think that we were a pretty boring lot.* 6 N-SING: *the* N You can use **the lot** to refer to the whole of an amount that you have just mentioned. [INFORMAL] ❑ *Instead of using the money to pay his rent, he went to a betting shop and lost the lot in half an hour.* 7 N-SING: usu with poss Your **lot** is the kind of life you have or the things that you have or experience. ❑ *She tried to accept her marriage as her lot in life but could not.* 8 N-COUNT A **lot** is a small area of land that belongs to a person or company. [AM] ❑ *If oil or gold are discovered under your lot, you can sell the mineral rights.* → See also **parking lot**. 9 N-COUNT A **lot** in an auction is one of the objects or groups of objects that are being sold. ❑ *The receivers are keen to sell the stores as one lot.*

PHRASES 10 PHRASE: V inflects If people **draw lots** to decide who will do something, they each take a piece of paper from a container. One or more pieces of paper is marked, and the people who take marked pieces are chosen. ❑ *For the first time in a World Cup finals, lots had to be drawn to decide who would finish second and third.* 11 PHRASE: V inflects, PHR n = *join forces with* If you **throw in** your **lot with** a particular person or group, you decide to work with them and support them from then on, whatever happens. ❑ *He has decided to throw in his lot with the far-right groups in parliament.*

**loth** /ləʊθ/ → see **loath**.

**lo|tion** /ləʊʃən/ **(lotions)** N-MASS: usu n N = *cream* A **lotion** is a liquid that you use to clean, improve, or protect your skin or hair. ❑ *...suntan lotion. ...cleansing lotions.*

**lot|tery** /lɒtəri/ **(lotteries)** 1 N-COUNT A **lottery** is a type of gambling game in which people buy numbered tickets. Several numbers are then chosen, and the people who have those numbers on their tickets win a prize. ❑ *...the national lottery.* 2 N-SING: *a* N If you describe something as **a lottery**, you mean that what happens depends entirely on luck or chance. ❑ *Which judges are assigned to a case is always a bit of a lottery.*

**lo|tus** /ləʊtəs/ **(lotuses)** N-COUNT A **lotus** or a **lotus flower** is a type of water lily that grows in Africa and Asia.

**lo|tus po|si|tion** N-SING: usu *the* N If someone doing meditation or yoga is in **the lotus position**, they are sitting with their legs crossed and each foot resting on top of the opposite thigh.

**louche** /luːʃ/ ADJ = *disreputable* If you describe a person or place as **louche**, you mean that they are unconventional and not respectable, but often in a way that people find rather attractive. [WRITTEN] ❑ *...that section of London society which somehow managed to be louche and fashionable at the same time.*

**loud** /laʊd/ **(louder, loudest)** ◆◇◇ 1 ADJ ≠ *quiet* If a noise is **loud**, the level of sound is very high and it can be easily heard. Someone or something that is **loud** produces a lot of noise. ❑ *Suddenly there was a loud bang... His voice became harsh and loud... The band was starting to play a fast, loud number. ...amazingly loud discos.* ♦ ADV: ADV after v **Loud** is also an adverb. ❑ *She wonders whether Paul's hearing is OK because he turns the television up very loud.* ♦ ADV: ADV with v **loud|ly** *His footsteps echoed loudly in the tiled hall.* ♦ N-UNCOUNT **loud|ness** *The students began to enter the classroom and Anna was startled at their loudness.* 2 ADJ: oft ADJ *in* n/-ing If someone is **loud** in their support for or criticism of something, they express their opinion very often and in a very strong way. ❑ *Mr Adams' speech yesterday was very loud in condemnation of the media... Mr Jones received loud support from his local community.* ♦ ADV: ADV with v **loud|ly** *Mac talked loudly in favour of the good works done by the Church.* 3 ADJ disapproval = *garish* If you describe something, especially a piece of clothing, as **loud**, you dislike it because it has very bright colours or very large, bold patterns which look unpleasant. ❑ *He liked to shock with his gold chains and loud clothes.*

PHRASES 4 PHRASE: usu PHR after v If you tell someone something **loud and clear**, you are very easily understood, either because your voice is very clear or because you express yourself very clearly. ❑ *Lisa's voice comes through loud and clear... The message is a powerful one, and I hope it will be heard loud and clear by the tobacco industry.* 5 PHRASE: usu PHR after v If you say or read something **out loud**, you say it or read it so that it can be heard, rather than just thinking it. ❑ *Even Ford, who seldom smiled, laughed out loud a few times... He began to read out loud.* 6 **for crying out loud** → see **cry**.

**loud|hail|er** /laʊdheɪlər/ **(loudhailers)** also **loud-hailer.** N-COUNT = *megaphone* A **loudhailer** is a portable device with a microphone at one end and a cone-shaped speaker at the other end, used to make your voice heard more easily outdoors. [BRIT]

in AM, use **bullhorn**

**loud|mouth** /laʊdmaʊθ/ **(loudmouths** /laʊdmaʊðz/**)** N-COUNT disapproval If you describe someone as a **loudmouth**, you are critical of them because they talk a lot, especially in an unpleasant, offensive, or stupid way.

**loud-mouthed** ADJ: usu ADJ n disapproval If you describe someone as **loud-mouthed**, you are critical of them because they talk a lot, especially in an unpleasant, offensive, or stupid way. ❑ *...a loud-mouthed oaf with very little respect for women.*

**loud|speaker** /laʊdspiːkər/ **(loudspeakers)** also **loud speaker.** N-COUNT = *speaker* A **loudspeaker** is a piece of equipment, for example part of a radio or hi-fi system, through which sound comes out.

**lounge** /laʊndʒ/ **(lounges, lounging, lounged)** 1 N-COUNT = *living room* In a house, a **lounge** is a room where people sit and relax. [mainly BRIT] → See picture on page 1706. ❑ *The Holmbergs were sitting before a roaring fire in the lounge, sipping their cocoa.* 2 N-COUNT In a hotel, club, or other public place, a **lounge** is a room where people can sit and relax. ❑ *I spoke to her in the lounge of a big Johannesburg hotel where she was attending a union meeting.* 3 N-COUNT: usu supp N In an airport, a **lounge** is a very large room where people can sit and wait for aircraft to arrive or leave. ❑ *Instead of taking me to the departure lounge they took me right* to my seat on the plane. [4] If you **lounge** somewhere, you sit or lie there in a relaxed or lazy way. ❑ *They ate and drank and lounged in the shade.* VERB V prep

**louse** /laʊs/ **(lice)** **Lice** are small insects that live on the bodies of people or animals and bite them in order to feed off their blood. N-COUNT: usu pl

**lousy** /laʊzi/ **(lousier, lousiest)** [1] If you describe something as **lousy**, you mean that it is of very bad quality or that you do not like it. [INFORMAL] ❑ *He blamed Fiona for a lousy weekend... It's lousy to be the new kid.* ADJ = rotten [2] If you describe someone as **lousy**, you mean that they are very bad at something they do. [INFORMAL] ❑ *I was a lousy secretary... There can be no argument about how lousy he is at public relations.* ADJ: oft ADJ *at* n = awful, terrible [3] If you describe the number or amount of something as **lousy**, you mean it is smaller than you think it should be. [INFORMAL] ❑ *The pay is lousy.* ADJ [4] If you feel **lousy**, you feel very ill. [INFORMAL] ❑ *I wasn't actually sick but I felt lousy.* ADJ: feel/look ADJ

**lout** /laʊt/ **(louts)** If you describe a man or boy as a **lout**, you are critical of them because they behave in an impolite or aggressive way. ❑ *...a drunken lout.* N-COUNT disapproval

**lout|ish** /laʊtɪʃ/ If you describe a man or a boy as **loutish**, you are critical of them because their behaviour is impolite and aggressive. ❑ *I was appalled by the loutish behaviour.* ADJ: usu ADJ n disapproval

**lou|vre** /luːvəʳ/ **(louvres)**

in AM, use **louver**

A **louvre** is a door or window with narrow, flat, sloping pieces of wood or glass across its frame. N-COUNT: oft N n

**lov|able** /lʌvəbᵊl/ If you describe someone as **lovable**, you mean that they have attractive qualities, and are easy to like. ❑ *His vulnerability makes him even more lovable.* ADJ = endearing

**love** /lʌv/ **(loves, loving, loved)** [1] If you **love** someone, you feel romantically or sexually attracted to them, and they are very important to you. ❑ *Oh, Amy, I love you... We love each other. We want to spend our lives together.* ◆◆◆ VERB V n V n [2] **Love** is a very strong feeling of affection towards someone who you are romantically or sexually attracted to. ❑ *Our love for each other has been increased by what we've been through together. ...a old fashioned love story. ...an album of love songs.* N-UNCOUNT [3] You say that you **love** someone when their happiness is very important to you, so that you behave in a kind and caring way towards them. ❑ *You'll never love anyone the way you love your baby.* VERB V n [4] **Love** is the feeling that a person's happiness is very important to you, and the way you show this feeling in your behaviour towards them. ❑ *My love for all my children is unconditional... She's got a great capacity for love.* N-UNCOUNT [5] If you **love** something, you like it very much. ❑ *We loved the food so much, especially the fish dishes... I loved reading. ...one of these people that loves to be in the outdoors... I love it when I hear you laugh.* VERB V n/-ing V n/-ing V to-inf V *it* wh [6] You can say that you **love** something when you consider that it is important and want to protect or support it. ❑ *I love my country as you love yours.* VERB V n [7] **Love** is a strong liking for something, or a belief that it is important. ❑ *The French are known for their love of their language.* N-UNCOUNT: oft N *of* n [8] Your **love** is someone or something that you love. ❑ *'She is the love of my life,' he said... Music's one of my great loves.* N-COUNT: usu with poss [9] If you **would love to** have or do something, you very much want to have it or do it. ❑ *I would love to play for England again... I would love a hot bath and clean clothes... His wife would love him to give up his job.* VERB V to-inf V n V n to-inf [10] Some people use **love** as an affectionate way of addressing someone. [BRIT, INFORMAL] ❑ *Well, I'll take your word for it then, love... Don't cry, my love.* N-VOC feelings = dear, darling [11] In tennis, **love** is a score of zero. ❑ *He beat Thomas Muster of Austria three sets to love.* NUM [12] You can use expressions such as **'love'**, **'love from'**, and **'all my love'**, followed by your name, as an informal way of ending a letter to a friend or relation. ❑ *...with love from Grandma and Grandpa.* CONVENTION [13] If you send someone your **love**, you ask another person, who will soon be speaking or writing to them, to tell them that you are thinking about them with affection. ❑ *Please give her my love.* N-UNCOUNT: poss N [14] → See also **-loved**, **loving**, **free love**, **peace-loving**, **tug-of-love**.

PHRASES [15] If you **fall in love with** someone, you start to be in love with them. ❑ *I fell in love with him because of his kind nature... We fell madly in love.* PHRASE: V inflects, oft PHR *with* n [16] If you **fall in love with** something, you start to like it very much. ❑ *Working with Ford closely, I fell in love with the cinema.* PHRASE: V inflects, usu PHR *with* n [17] If you **are in love with** someone, you feel romantically or sexually attracted to them, and they are very important to you. ❑ *Laura had never before been in love... I've never really been in love with anyone... We were madly in love for about two years.* PHRASE: V inflects, oft PHR *with* n [18] If you are **in love with** something, you like it very much. ❑ *He had always been in love with the enchanted landscape of the West.* PHRASE: V inflects, usu PHR *with* n [19] When two people **make love**, they have sex. ❑ *Have you ever made love to a girl before?* PHRASE: V inflects, oft pl-n PHR, PHR *to/with* n

**love af|fair** **(love affairs)** [1] A **love affair** is a romantic and usually sexual relationship between two people who love each other but who are not married or living together. ❑ *...a stressful love affair with a married man.* N-COUNT: oft N *with/between* n = relationship [2] If you refer to someone's **love affair with** something, you mean that they like it a lot and are very enthusiastic about it. ❑ *...the American love affair with firearms.* N-SING: with supp, usu N *with* n

**love|birds** /lʌvbɜːʳdz/ You can refer to two people as **lovebirds** when they are obviously very much in love. [HUMOROUS] N-PLURAL

**love bite** **(love bites)** also **lovebite.** A **love bite** is a mark which someone has on their body as a result of being bitten by their partner when they were kissing or making love. N-COUNT

**love child** **(love children)** also **love-child.** If journalists refer to someone as a **love child**, they mean that the person was born as a result of a love affair between two people who have never been married to each other. ❑ *Eric has a secret love child.* N-COUNT

**-loved** /-lʌvd/ **-loved** combines with adverbs to form adjectives that describe how much someone or something is loved. ❑ *The similarities between the much-loved father and his son are remarkable. ...two of Mendelssohn's best-loved works.* COMB in ADJ: usu ADJ n

**love-hate re|la|tion|ship** **(love-hate relationships)** If you have a **love-hate relationship** with someone or something, your feelings towards them change suddenly and often from love to hate. ❑ *...a book about the close love-hate relationship between two boys.* N-COUNT: usu sing

**love|less** /lʌvləs/ A **loveless** relationship or situation is one where there is no love. ❑ *She is in a loveless relationship.* ADJ: usu ADJ n

**love let|ter** **(love letters)** A **love letter** is a letter that you write to someone in order to tell them that you love them. N-COUNT

**love life** **(love lives)** Someone's **love life** is the part of their life that consists of their romantic and sexual relationships. ❑ *His love life was complicated, and involved intense relationships.* N-COUNT

**love|lorn** /lʌvlɔːʳn/ **Lovelorn** means the same as **lovesick**. ❑ *He was acting like a lovelorn teenager.* ADJ: usu ADJ n

**love|ly** /lʌvli/ **(lovelier, loveliest)** [1] If you describe someone or something as **lovely**, you mean that they are very beautiful and therefore pleasing to look at or listen to. [mainly BRIT] ❑ *You look lovely, Marcia... He had a lovely voice... It was just one of those lovely old English gardens.* ♦ **love|li|ness** *You are a vision of loveliness.* ◆◇◇ ADJ = beautiful N-UNCOUNT = beauty [2] If you describe something as **lovely**, you mean that it gives you pleasure. [mainly BRIT, mainly SPOKEN] ❑ *Mary! How lovely to see you!... It's a lovely day... What a lovely surprise!* ADJ = marvellous, wonderful [3] If you describe someone as **lovely**, you mean that they are friendly, kind, or generous. [mainly ADJ = delightful

BRIT] ❑ *Laura is a lovely young woman... She's a lovely child.*

**love|making** /lʌvmeɪkɪŋ/ also **love-making. Lovemaking** refers to sexual activities that take place between two people who love each other. ❑ *Their love-making became less and less frequent.* N-UNCOUNT

**love nest** **(love nests)** also **love-nest.** A **love nest** is a house or flat where two people who are having a love affair live or meet. [JOURNALISM] N-COUNT: usu sing

**lov|er** /lʌvəʳ/ **(lovers)** ◆◇◇ [1] Someone's **lover** is someone who they are having a sexual relationship with but are not married to. ❑ *He and Liz became lovers soon after they first met.* N-COUNT: oft poss N [2] If you are a **lover** of something such as animals or the arts, you enjoy them very much and take great pleasure in them. ❑ *She is a great lover of horses and horse racing... Are you an opera lover?* N-COUNT: with supp

**love rat** **(love rats)** Journalists sometimes use **love rat** to refer to a man who treats his wife or girlfriend in a cruel way, especially by having sexual relationships with other women. [JOURNALISM] ❑ *...the womanising of royal love rat James Hewitt.* N-COUNT [disapproval]

**love|sick** /lʌvsɪk/ If you describe someone as **lovesick**, you mean that they are so in love with someone who does not love them, that they are behaving in a strange and foolish way. ❑ *...a lovesick boy consumed with self-pity.* ADJ: usu ADJ n = lovelorn

**love sto|ry** **(love stories)** A **love story** is something such as a novel or film about a love affair. N-COUNT

**love-stricken** also **lovestruck.** If you describe someone as **love-stricken**, you mean that they are so much in love that they are behaving in a strange and foolish way. ADJ

**love tri|an|gle** **(love triangles)** A **love triangle** is a relationship in which three people are each in love with at least one other person in the relationship. [JOURNALISM] N-COUNT: usu sing

**lovey-dovey** /lʌvi dʌvi/ You can use **lovey-dovey** to describe, in a humorous or slightly disapproving way, lovers who show their affection for each other very openly. [INFORMAL] ❑ *All my friends were either lovey-dovey couples or wild, single girls.* ADJ [disapproval]

**lov|ing** /lʌvɪŋ/ [1] Someone who is **loving** feels or shows love to other people. ❑ *Jim was a most loving husband and father... The children there were very loving to me.* ADJ = affectionate ♦ **lov|ing|ly** *Brian gazed lovingly at Mary Ann.* ADV [2] **Loving** actions are done with great enjoyment and care. ❑ *The house has been restored with loving care.* ADJ: usu ADJ n ♦ **lov|ing|ly** *I lifted the box and ran my fingers lovingly over the top.* ADV: ADV after v, ADV -ed [3] ➔ See also **peace-loving**.

**low** /loʊ/ **(lower, lowest, lows)** ◆◆◆ [1] Something that is **low** measures only a short distance from the bottom to the top, or from the ground to the top. ❑ *...the low garden wall that separated the front garden from next door... She put it down on the low table... The Leisure Center is a long and low modern building.* ADJ [2] If something is **low**, it is close to the ground, to sea level, or to the bottom of something. ❑ *He bumped his head on the low beams... It was late afternoon and the sun was low in the sky... They saw a government war plane make a series of low-level bombing raids.* ADJ [3] When a river is **low**, it contains less water than usual. ❑ *...pumps that guarantee a constant depth of water even when the supplying river is low.* ADJ: usu v-link ADJ ≠ high [4] You can use **low** to indicate that something is small in amount or that it is at the bottom of a particular scale. You can use phrases such as **in the low 80s** to indicate that a number or level is less than 85 but not as little as 80. ❑ *British casualties remained remarkably low... They are still having to live on very low incomes... The temperature's in the low 40s.* ADJ ≠ high [5] **Low** is used to describe people who are not considered to be very important because they are near the bottom of a particular scale or system. ❑ *She refused to promote Colin above the low rank of 'legal adviser'.* ADJ: usu ADJ n ≠ high [6] If something reaches a **low** of a particular amount or degree, that is the smallest it has ever been. ❑ *Eventually my weight stabilised at seven and a half stone after dropping to a low of five and a half stone... The dollar fell to a new low.* N-COUNT: usu sing, oft N *of* amount ≠ high [7] If you drive or ride a bicycle in a **low** gear, you use a gear, usually first or second, which gives you the most control over your car or bicycle when travelling slowly. ❑ *She selected a low gear and started down the track carefully.* ADJ ≠ high [8] If the quality or standard of something is **low**, it is very poor. ❑ *A school would not accept low-quality work from any student. ...low-grade coal.* ADJ = poor ≠ high [9] If a food or other substance is **low in** a particular ingredient, it contains only a small amount of that ingredient. ❑ *They look for foods that are low in calories.* ADJ: v-link ADJ *in* n ≠ high ♦ **Low** is also a combining form. ❑ *...low-sodium tomato sauce... Low-odour paints help make decorating so much easier.* COMB in ADJ: usu ADJ n [10] If you describe someone such as a student or a worker as a **low** achiever, you mean that they are not very good at their work, and do not achieve or produce as much as others. ❑ *Low achievers in schools will receive priority.* ADJ: ADJ n ≠ high [11] If you have a **low** opinion of someone or something, you disapprove of them or dislike them. ❑ *I have an extremely low opinion of the British tabloid newspapers.* ADJ ≠ high [12] You can use **low** to describe negative feelings and attitudes. ❑ *We are all very tired and morale is low... People had very low expectations.* ADJ [13] If a sound or noise is **low**, it is deep. ❑ *Then suddenly she gave a low, choking moan and began to tremble violently... My voice has got so low now I was mistaken for a man the other day on the phone.* ADJ = deep ≠ high [14] If someone's voice is **low**, it is quiet or soft. ❑ *Her voice was so low he had to strain to catch it.* ADJ [15] A light that is **low** is not bright or strong. ❑ *Their eyesight is poor in low light.* ADJ = dim [16] If a radio, oven, or light is on **low**, it has been adjusted so that only a small amount of sound, heat, or light is produced. ❑ *She turned her little kitchen radio on low... Buy a dimmer switch and keep the light on low, or switch it off altogether... Cook the sauce over a low heat until it boils and thickens.* ADJ [17] If you are **low on** something or if a supply of it is **low**, there is not much of it left. ❑ *We're a bit low on bed linen... World stocks of wheat were getting very low.* ADJ: v-link ADJ, usu ADJ *on* n [18] If you are **low**, you are depressed. [INFORMAL] ❑ *'I didn't ask for this job, you know,' he tells friends when he is low.* ADJ = down [19] ➔ See also **lower**. [20] If you **are lying low**, you are hiding or not drawing attention to yourself. [INFORMAL] ❑ *Far from lying low, Kuti became more outspoken than ever.* PHRASE: V inflects [21] to look **high and low** ➔ see **high**. **low profile** ➔ see **profile**. to **be running low** ➔ see **run**.

**low|brow** /loʊbraʊ/ also **low-brow.** If you say that something is **lowbrow**, you mean that it is easy to understand or appreciate rather than intellectual and is therefore perhaps inferior. ❑ *His choice of subject matter has been regarded as low-brow. ...low-brow novels.* ADJ ≠ highbrow

**low-cal** **Low-cal** food is food that contains only a few calories. People who are trying to lose weight eat low-cal food. ADJ: usu ADJ n

**low-cut** **Low-cut** dresses and blouses do not cover the top part of a woman's chest. ADJ: usu ADJ n

**low-down** also **lowdown.** [1] If someone gives you **the low-down on** a person or thing, they tell you all the important information about them. [INFORMAL] ❑ *We want you to give us the low-down on your team-mates.* N-SING: *the* N, oft N *on* n = gen [2] You can use **low-down** to emphasize how bad, dishonest, or unfair you consider a particular person or their behaviour to be. [INFORMAL] ❑ *...a lowdown, evil drunkard... They will stoop to every low-down trick.* ADJ: ADJ n [emphasis] = despicable

**low|er** /loʊəʳ/ **(lowers, lowering, lowered)** ◆◇◇ [1] You can use **lower** to refer to the bottom one of a pair of things. ❑ *She bit her lower lip. ...the lower deck of the bus... The upper layer of felt should overlap the lower. ...the lower of the two holes.* ADJ: ADJ n, *the* ADJ, *the* ADJ *of* n ≠ upper [2] You can use **lower** to refer to the bottom part of something. ❑ *Use a small cushion to help give sup-* ADJ: ADJ n ≠ upper port to the lower back. *...fires which started in the lower part of a tower block.* 3 You can use **lower** to refer to people or things that are less important than similar people or things. ❑ *Already the awards are causing resentment in the lower ranks of council officers... The nation's highest court reversed the lower court's decision... The higher orders of society must rule the lower.* 4 If you **lower** something, you move it slowly downwards. ❑ *Two reporters had to help lower the coffin into the grave... Sokolowski lowered himself into the black leather chair... 'No movies of me getting out of the pool, boys.' They dutifully lowered their cameras.* ♦ **low\|er\|ing** *...the extinguishing of the Olympic flame and the lowering of the flag.* 5 If you **lower** something, you make it less in amount, degree, value, or quality. ❑ *The Central Bank has lowered interest rates by 2 percent.* ♦ **low\|er\|ing** *...a package of social measures which included the lowering of the retirement age.* 6 If someone **lowers** their head or eyes, they look downwards, for example because they are sad or embarrassed. ❑ *She lowered her head and brushed past photographers as she went back inside... She lowered her gaze to the hands in her lap.* 7 If you say that you would not **lower yourself** by doing something, you mean that you would not behave in a way that would make you or other people respect you less. ❑ *Don't lower yourself, don't be the way they are... I've got no qualms about lowering myself to Lemmer's level to get what I want.* 8 If you **lower** your voice or if your voice **lowers**, you speak more quietly. ❑ *The man moved closer, lowering his voice... His voice lowers confidentially.* 9 → See also **low**.

ADJ: ADJ n, *the* ADJ ≠ *higher* / VERB / V n prep/adv / V pron-refl prep/adv / V n / N-UNCOUNT: usu N *of* n / VERB / V n / N-UNCOUNT: usu N *of* n / VERB ≠ *raise* / V n / V n / VERB: oft with brd-neg / V pron-refl / V pron-refl *to* n / VERB / V n / V

**low\|er case** also **lower-case.** **Lower-case** letters are small letters, not capital letters. ❑ *It was printed in lower case... We did the logo in lower-case letters instead of capitals.* — N-UNCOUNT: oft N n ≠ *upper case*

**low\|er class** **(lower classes)** also **lower-class.** Some people use **the lower class** or **the lower classes** to refer to the division of society that they consider to have the lowest social status. ❑ *Education now offers the lower classes access to job opportunities.* ♦ **Lower class** is also an adjective. ❑ *...lower-class families.* — N-COUNT-COLL: usu pl / ADJ

**low\|est com\|mon de\|nomi\|na\|tor** **(lowest common denominators)** 1 If you describe a plan or policy as **the lowest common denominator**, you are critical of it because it has been deliberately made too simple so that nobody will disagree. ❑ *Although the plan received unanimous approval, this does not mean that it represents the lowest common denominator.* 2 If you say that something is designed to appeal to **the lowest common denominator**, you are critical of it because it is designed to be liked by the majority of people. ❑ *Tabloid newspapers pander to the lowest common denominator.* 3 In mathematics, **the lowest common denominator** is the smallest number that all the numbers on the bottom of a particular group of fractions can be divided into. [TECHNICAL] — N-COUNT: usu sing [disapproval] / N-COUNT: usu sing [disapproval] / N-COUNT

**low-flying** **Low-flying** aircraft or birds are flying very close to the ground, or lower than normal. — ADJ: ADJ n

**low-impact** 1 **Low-impact** exercise does not put a lot of stress on your body. 2 **Low-impact** projects, developments, and activities such as holidays are designed to cause minimum harm to the environment. ❑ *...sensitive, enlightened, low-impact ecotourism.* — ADJ: usu ADJ n ≠ *high-impact* / ADJ: usu ADJ n

**low-key** If you say that something is **low-key**, you mean that it is on a small scale rather than involving a lot of activity or being made to seem impressive or important. ❑ *The wedding will be a very low-key affair... He wanted to keep the meetings low-key.* — ADJ

**low\|lands** /loʊləndz/ also **lowland.**

✔ The form **lowland** is also used as a modifier.

**Lowlands** are an area of low, flat land. ❑ *...wherever you travel in the lowlands of the United Kingdom. ...the fever-haunted old town on the lowland across the lake. ...lowland areas.* — N-PLURAL: usu *the* N ≠ *uplands*

**low life** also **low-life, lowlife.** People sometimes use **low life** to refer in a disapproving way to people who are involved in criminal, dishonest, or immoral activities, or to these activities. ❑ *...the sort of low-life characters who populate this film.* — N-UNCOUNT: oft N n [disapproval]

**low\|ly** /loʊli/ **(lowlier, lowliest)** If you describe someone or something as **lowly**, you mean that they are low in rank, status, or importance. ❑ *...lowly bureaucrats pretending to be senators.* — ADJ

**low-lying** **Low-lying** land is at, near, or below sea level. ❑ *Sea walls collapsed, and low-lying areas were flooded.* — ADJ: usu ADJ n

**low-paid** If you describe someone or their job as **low-paid**, you mean that their work earns them very little money. ❑ *...low-paid workers... The majority of working women are in low-paid jobs.* ♦ **The low-paid** are people who are low-paid. — ADJ / N-PLURAL: *the* N

**low-pitched** 1 A sound that is **low-pitched** is deep. ❑ *With a low-pitched rumbling noise, the propeller began to rotate.* 2 A voice that is **low-pitched** is very soft and quiet. ❑ *He kept his voice low-pitched in case someone was listening.* — ADJ / ADJ

**low-rent** 1 If someone lives in a **low-rent** house, they only have to pay a small amount of money to live there. ❑ *...a low-rent housing development.* 2 You can use **low-rent** to describe something that is of poor quality, especially when it is compared with something else. ❑ *...a low-rent horror movie.* — ADJ / ADJ [disapproval]

**low sea\|son** **The low season** is the time of year when a place receives the fewest visitors, and fares and holiday accommodation are often cheaper. [BRIT] ❑ *Prices drop to £315 in the low season.* — N-SING: *the* N

✔ in AM, use **off-season**

**low-slung** **Low-slung** chairs or cars are very low, so that you are close to the ground when you are sitting in them. — ADJ: usu ADJ n

**low-tech** **Low-tech** machines or systems are ones that do not use modern or sophisticated technology. ❑ *...a simple form of low-tech electric propulsion.* — ADJ: usu ADJ n ≠ *hi-tech*

**low tide** **(low tides)** At the coast, **low tide** is the time when the sea is at its lowest level because the tide is out. ❑ *The causeway to the island is only accessible at low tide.* — N-VAR: oft *at* N ≠ *high tide*

**low wa\|ter** **Low water** is the same as **low tide**. — N-UNCOUNT

**lox** /lɒks/ **Lox** is salmon that has been smoked and is eaten raw. [mainly AM] — N-UNCOUNT

**loy\|al** /lɔɪəl/ Someone who is **loyal** remains firm in their friendship or support for a person or thing. ❑ *They had remained loyal to the president... He'd always been such a loyal friend to us all.* ♦ **loy\|al\|ly** *They have loyally supported their party and their leader.* — ADJ: oft ADJ *to* n [approval] = *faithful* ≠ *disloyal* / ADV: ADV with v

**loy\|al\|ist** /lɔɪəlɪst/ **(loyalists)** A **loyalist** is a person who remains firm in their support for a government or ruler. ❑ *Party loyalists responded as they always do, waving flags and carrying placards.* — N-COUNT

**loy\|al\|ty** /lɔɪəlti/ **(loyalties)** 1 **Loyalty** is the quality of staying firm in your friendship or support for someone or something. ❑ *I have sworn an oath of loyalty to the monarchy... This is seen as a reward for the army's loyalty during a barracks revolt earlier this month.* 2 **Loyalties** are feelings of friendship, support, or duty towards someone or something. ❑ *She had developed strong loyalties to the Manet family.* — N-UNCOUNT: oft N *to* n / N-COUNT: usu pl, oft N *to* n

**loy\|al\|ty card** **(loyalty cards)** A **loyalty card** is a plastic card that some shops give to regular customers. Each time the customer buys something from the shop, points are electronically stored on their card and can be exchanged later for goods or services. — N-COUNT

**loz|enge** /lɒzɪndʒ/ **(lozenges)** 1 **Lozenges** are sweets which you can suck to make a cough or sore throat better. ❑ *...throat lozenges.* [N-COUNT] 2 A **lozenge** is a shape with four corners. The two corners that point up and down are further away than the two pointing sideways. [N-COUNT = diamond]

**LP** /el piː/ **(LPs)** An **LP** is a record which usually has about 25 minutes of music or speech on each side. **LP** is an abbreviation for 'long-playing record'. ❑ *...his first LP since 1986.* [N-COUNT]

**LPG** /el piː dʒiː/ **LPG** is a type of fuel consisting of hydrocarbon gases in liquid form. **LPG** is an abbreviation for 'liquefied petroleum gas'. [N-UNCOUNT]

**L-plate** **(L-plates)** In Britain, **L-plates** are signs with a red 'L' on them which you attach to a car to warn other drivers that you are a learner. [N-COUNT: usu pl]

**LSD** /el es diː/ **LSD** is a very powerful illegal drug which makes the user see things that only exist in their mind. [N-UNCOUNT]

**Lt** **Lt** is a written abbreviation for **lieutenant**. ❑ *He was replaced by Lt Frank Fraser.*

**Ltd** **Ltd** is a written abbreviation for **limited** when it is used after the name of a company. Compare **plc**. [BRIT, BUSINESS] [◆◇◇]

**lub|ri|cant** /luːbrɪkənt/ **(lubricants)** 1 A **lubricant** is a substance which you put on the surfaces or parts of something, especially something mechanical, to make the parts move smoothly. ❑ *Its nozzle was smeared with some kind of lubricant. ...industrial lubricants.* [N-MASS] 2 If you refer to something as a **lubricant** in a particular situation, you mean that it helps to make things happen without any problems. ❑ *I think humor is a great lubricant for life.* [N-COUNT: usu supp N]

**lu|bri|cate** /luːbrɪkeɪt/ **(lubricates, lubricating, lubricated)** 1 If you **lubricate** something such as a part of a machine, you put a substance such as oil on it so that it moves smoothly. [FORMAL] ❑ *Mineral oils are used to lubricate machinery.* [VERB, V n] *...lubricating oil.* [V-ing] ♦ **lu|bri|ca|tion** /luːbrɪkeɪʃᵊn/ *Use a touch of linseed oil for lubrication.* [N-UNCOUNT] 2 If you say that something **lubricates** a particular situation, you mean that it helps things to happen without any problems. ❑ *Franklin's task was to lubricate the discussions with the French.* [VERB, V n]

**lu|cerne** /luːsɜːʳn/ **Lucerne** is a plant that is grown for animals to eat and in order to improve the soil. [BRIT] [N-UNCOUNT = alfalfa]

☑ in AM, use **alfalfa**

**lu|cid** /luːsɪd/ 1 **Lucid** writing or speech is clear and easy to understand. ❑ *...a lucid account of the history of mankind... His prose as always lucid and compelling.* [ADJ = clear] ♦ **lu|cid|ly** *Both of them had the ability to present complex matters lucidly.* [ADV: ADV with v] ♦ **lu|cid|ity** /luːsɪdɪti/ *His writings were marked by an extraordinary lucidity.* [N-UNCOUNT] 2 If someone is **lucid**, they are thinking clearly again after a period of illness or confusion. [FORMAL] ❑ *He wasn't very lucid, he didn't quite know where he was.* [ADJ] ♦ **lu|cid|ity** *The pain had lessened in the night, but so had his lucidity.* [N-UNCOUNT]

**luck** /lʌk/ 1 **Luck** or **good luck** is success or good things that happen to you, that do not come from your own abilities or efforts. ❑ *I knew I needed a bit of luck to win... The Sri Lankans have been having no luck with the weather... The goal, when it came, owed more to good luck than good planning.* [◆◇◇ N-UNCOUNT] 2 **Bad luck** is lack of success or bad things that happen to you, that have not been caused by yourself or other people. ❑ *I had a lot of bad luck during the first half of this season... Randall's illness was only bad luck.* [N-UNCOUNT] 3 → See also **hard luck**. 4 If you ask someone the question **'Any luck?'** or **'No luck?'**, you want to know if they have been successful in something they were trying to do. [INFORMAL] ❑ *'Any luck?' — 'No.'* [CONVENTION] 5 You can say **'Bad luck'**, or **'Hard luck'**, to someone when you want to express sympathy to them. [INFORMAL] ❑ *Well, hard luck, mate.* [CONVENTION formulae]

**PHRASES** 6 If you describe someone as **down on their luck**, you mean that they have had bad experiences, often because they do not have enough money. [PHRASE: usu v-link PHR] 7 If you say **'Good luck'** or **'Best of luck'** to someone, you are telling them that you hope they will be successful in something they are trying to do. [INFORMAL] ❑ *He kissed her on the cheek. 'Best of luck!'* [CONVENTION formulae] 8 You can say someone **is in luck** when they are in a situation where they can have what they want or need. ❑ *You're in luck. The doctor's still in.* [PHRASE: V inflects] 9 If you say that someone **is out of luck**, you mean that they cannot have something which they can normally have. ❑ *'What do you want, Roy? If it's money, you're out of luck.'* [PHRASE: V inflects] 10 If you say that someone **is pushing** their **luck**, you think they are taking a bigger risk than is sensible, and may get into trouble. ❑ *I didn't dare push my luck too far and did not ask them to sign statements.* [PHRASE: V inflects] 11 If someone **tries their luck at** something, they try to succeed at it, often when it is very difficult or there is little chance of success. ❑ *She was going to try her luck at the Las Vegas casinos.* [PHRASE: V inflects] 12 **pot luck** → see **pot**.

**lucki|ly** /lʌkɪli/ You add **luckily** to a statement to indicate that it is good that a particular thing happened or is the case because otherwise the situation would have been difficult or unpleasant. ❑ *Luckily, we both love football... Luckily for me, he spoke very good English.* [ADV: ADV with cl = fortunately]

**luck|less** /lʌkləs/ If you describe someone or something as **luckless**, you mean that they are unsuccessful or unfortunate. [WRITTEN] ❑ *...the luckless parent of an extremely difficult child.* [ADJ: usu ADJ n]

**lucky** /lʌki/ **(luckier, luckiest)** 1 You say that someone is **lucky** when they have something that is very desirable or when they are in a very desirable situation. ❑ *I am luckier than most. I have a job... He is incredibly lucky to be alive... Those who are lucky enough to be wealthy have a duty to give to the hungry.* [◆◇◇ ADJ: oft ADJ to-inf = fortunate] 2 Someone who is **lucky** seems to always have good luck. ❑ *Some people are born lucky aren't they?... He had always been lucky at cards.* [ADJ] 3 If you describe an action or experience as **lucky**, you mean that it was good or successful, and that it happened by chance and not as a result of planning or preparation. ❑ *They admit they are now desperate for a lucky break... He was lucky that it was only a can of beer that knocked him on the head.* [ADJ] 4 A **lucky** object is something that people believe helps them to be successful. ❑ *He did not have on his other lucky charm, a pair of green socks.* [ADJ: usu ADJ n] 5 → See also **happy-go-lucky**.

**PHRASES** 6 If you say that someone **will be lucky to** do or get something, you mean that they are very unlikely to do or get it, and will definitely not do or get any more than that. ❑ *You'll be lucky if you get any breakfast... Those remaining in work will be lucky to get the smallest of pay increases.* [PHRASE: V inflects, usu PHR if, PHR to-inf] 7 If you **strike lucky** or **strike it lucky**, you have some good luck. [mainly BRIT, INFORMAL] ❑ *You may strike lucky and find a sympathetic and helpful clerk, but, there again, you might not.* [PHRASE: V inflects]

**lucky dip** **(lucky dips)** a **lucky dip** is a game in which you take a prize out of a container full of hidden prizes and then find out what you have chosen. [BRIT] [N-COUNT]

☑ in AM, use **grab bag**

**lu|cra|tive** /luːkrətɪv/ A **lucrative** activity, job, or business deal is very profitable. ❑ *Thousands of ex-army officers have found lucrative jobs in private security firms.* [ADJ]

**lu|cre** /luːkəʳ/ People sometimes refer to money or profit as **lucre**, especially when they think that it has been obtained by dishonest means. [HUMOROUS or OLD-FASHIONED] ❑ *...so they can feel less guilty about their piles of filthy lucre.* [N-UNCOUNT disapproval]

**Lud|dite** /lʌdaɪt/ **(Luddites)** If you refer to someone as a **Luddite**, you are criticizing them for opposing changes in industrial methods, especially the introduction of new machines and [N-COUNT: oft N n disapproval] modern methods. ❑ *The majority have a built-in Luddite mentality; they are resistant to change.*

**lu|di|crous** /luːdɪkrəs/ If you describe something as **ludicrous**, you are emphasizing that you think it is foolish, unreasonable, or unsuitable. ❑ *It was ludicrous to suggest that the visit could be kept secret... It's a completely ludicrous idea.*
ADJ: oft *it* v-link ADJ to-inf
emphasis
= ridiculous

♦ **lu|di|crous|ly** *By Western standards the prices are ludicrously low.*
ADV

**lug** /lʌg/ **(lugs, lugging, lugged)** If you **lug** a heavy or awkward object somewhere, you carry it there with difficulty. [INFORMAL] ❑ *Nobody wants to lug around huge suitcases full of clothes... I hastily packed the hamper and lugged it to the car.*
VERB
V n with adv
V n prep
Also V n

**luge** /luːʒ/ **(luges)** A **luge** is an object that is designed to be used for racing downhill over snow or ice. Riders lie on their backs and travel with their feet pointing towards the front of the luge.
N-COUNT

**lug|gage** /lʌgɪdʒ/ **Luggage** is the suitcases and bags that you take with you when travel. ❑ *Leave your luggage in the hotel... Each passenger was allowed two 30-kg pieces of luggage.* → See also **left luggage**.
N-UNCOUNT

**lug|gage rack (luggage racks)** 1 A **luggage rack** is a shelf for putting luggage on, on a vehicle such as a train or bus.
N-COUNT

2 A **luggage rack** is a metal frame that is fixed on top of a car and used for carrying large objects. [AM]
N-COUNT

☑ in BRIT, use **roof rack**

**lu|gu|bri|ous** /luːguːbriəs/ If you say that someone or something is **lugubrious**, you mean that they are sad rather than lively or cheerful. [LITERARY] ❑ *...a tall, thin man with a long and lugubrious face... He plays some passages so slowly that they become lugubrious.*
ADJ
= melancholy

♦ **lu|gu|bri|ous|ly** *The dog gazed at us lugubriously for a few minutes.*
ADV: ADV with v, ADV adj

**luke|warm** /luːkwɔːm/ 1 Something, especially a liquid, that is **lukewarm** is only slightly warm. ❑ *Wash your face with lukewarm water... The coffee was weak and lukewarm.*
ADJ
= tepid

2 If you describe a person or their attitude as **lukewarm**, you mean that they are not showing much enthusiasm or interest. ❑ *The study received a lukewarm response from the Home Secretary.*
ADJ: oft ADJ *towards* n

**lull** /lʌl/ **(lulls, lulling, lulled)** 1 A **lull** is a period of quiet or calm in a longer period of activity or excitement. ❑ *There was a lull in political violence after the election of the current president. ...a lull in the conversation.*
N-COUNT: oft N *in* n

2 If you **are lulled into** feeling safe, someone or something causes you to feel safe at a time when you are not safe. ❑ *It is easy to be lulled into a false sense of security... Lulled by almost uninterrupted economic growth, too many European firms assumed that this would last for ever.*
VERB
*be* V-ed *into* n/-ing
V-ed
Also V n *into* n/-ing

3 If someone or something **lulls** you, they cause you to feel calm or sleepy. ❑ *With the shutters half-closed and the calm airy height of the room to lull me, I soon fell into a doze... Before he knew it, the heat and hum of the forest had lulled him to sleep.*
VERB
V n
V n *into/to* n

4 If you describe a situation as **the lull before the storm**, you mean that although it is calm now, there is going to be trouble in the future.
PHRASE: v-link PHR

**lulla|by** /lʌləbaɪ/ **(lullabies)** A **lullaby** is a quiet song which is intended to be sung to babies and young children to help them go to sleep.
N-COUNT

**lum|ba|go** /lʌmbeɪgoʊ/ If someone has **lumbago**, they have pains in the lower part of their back.
N-UNCOUNT

**lum|bar** /lʌmbəʳ/ **Lumbar** means relating to the lower part of your back. [MEDICAL] ❑ *Lumbar support is very important if you're driving a long way.*
ADJ: ADJ n

**lum|ber** /lʌmbəʳ/ **(lumbers, lumbering, lumbered)** 1 **Lumber** consists of trees and large pieces of wood that have been roughly cut up. [mainly AM] ❑ *It was made of soft lumber, spruce by the look of it... He was going to have to purchase all his lumber at full retail price.*
N-UNCOUNT

2 If someone or something **lumbers** from one place to another, they move there very slowly and clumsily. ❑ *He turned and lumbered back to his chair... He looked straight ahead and overtook a lumbering lorry.*
VERB
V adv/prep
V-ing

♦ **lumber with** If you **are lumbered with** someone or something, you have to deal with them or take care of them even though you do not want to and this annoys you. [BRIT, INFORMAL] ❑ *I was lumbered with the job of taking charge of all the money... She was lumbered with a bill for about ninety pounds.*
PHRASAL VERB: usu passive
disapproval
*be* V-ed P n
*be* V-ed P n

**lumber|jack** /lʌmbəʳdʒæk/ **(lumberjacks)** A **lumberjack** is a person whose job is to cut down trees.
N-COUNT

**lumber|man** /lʌmbəʳmən/ **(lumbermen)** A **lumberman** is a man who sells timber. [AM]
N-COUNT

**lumber|yard** /lʌmbəʳjɑːʳd/ **(lumberyards)** also **lumber yard.** A **lumberyard** is a place where wood is stored and sold. [AM]
N-COUNT

☑ in BRIT, use **timber yard**

**lu|mi|nary** /luːmɪnəri, AM -neri/ **(luminaries)** If you refer to someone as a **luminary**, you mean that they are an expert in a particular subject or activity. [LITERARY] ❑ *...the political opinions of such luminaries as Sartre or de Beauvoir.*
N-COUNT
= expert

**lu|mi|nes|cence** /luːmɪnesᵊns/ **Luminescence** is a soft, glowing light. [LITERARY] ❑ *Lights reflected off dust-covered walls creating a ghostly luminescence.*
N-UNCOUNT

**lu|mi|nos|ity** /luːmɪnɒsɪti/ 1 The **luminosity** of a star or sun is how bright it is. [TECHNICAL] ❑ *For a few years its luminosity flared up to about 10,000 times the present-day luminosity of the Sun.*
N-UNCOUNT

2 You can talk about the **luminosity** of someone's skin when it has a healthy glow. ❑ *Ultrafine powder with a rosy tinge gives the skin warmth and luminosity.*
N-UNCOUNT

**lu|mi|nous** /luːmɪnəs/ Something that is **luminous** shines or glows in the dark. ❑ *The luminous dial on the clock showed five minutes to seven.*
ADJ: usu ADJ n

**lump** /lʌmp/ **(lumps, lumping, lumped)** 1 A **lump of** something is a solid piece of it. ❑ *The potter shaped and squeezed the lump of clay into a graceful shape. ...a lump of wood... They used to buy ten kilos of beef in one lump.*
N-COUNT: oft N *of* n

2 A **lump** on or in someone's body is a small, hard swelling that has been caused by an injury or an illness. ❑ *I've got a lump on my shoulder... Howard had to have cancer surgery for a lump in his chest.*
N-COUNT

3 A **lump of** sugar is a small cube of it. ❑ *'No sugar,' I said, and Jim asked for two lumps.* → See also **sugar lump**.
N-COUNT: oft N *of* n

4 → See also **lump sum**.

5 If you say that you have a **lump in** your **throat**, you mean that you have a tight feeling in your throat because of a strong emotion such as sorrow or gratitude. ❑ *I stood there with a lump in my throat and tried to fight back tears.*
PHRASE: Ns inflect, usu PHR after v

♦ **lump together** If a number of different people or things **are lumped together**, they are considered as a group rather than separately. ❑ *Policemen, bankers and butchers are all lumped together in the service sector... Because she was lumped together with alcoholics and hard-drug users, Claire felt out of place.*
PHRASAL VERB: usu passive
*be* V-ed P
*be* V-ed P *with* n

**lum|pec|to|my** /lʌmpektəmi/ **(lumpectomies)** A **lumpectomy** is an operation in which a woman has a lump such as a tumour removed from one of her breasts, rather than having the whole breast removed.
N-COUNT

**lump|en** /lʌmpən/ 1 A **lumpen** object is large, heavy, and lumpy. [mainly BRIT, LITERARY] ❑ *She was kneading a lumpen mass of dough... Lumpen shapes began to appear out of the shadows.*
ADJ: usu ADJ n

2 If you describe people as **lumpen**, you think they are dull and clumsy. [mainly BRIT, LITERARY] ❑ *The people seemed lumpen and boring.*
ADJ: usu ADJ n
disapproval

**lump sum (lump sums)** A **lump sum** is an amount of money that is paid as a large amount on a single occasion rather than as smaller amounts on several separate occasions. ❑ *...a tax-free lump sum of £50,000 at retirement age.*
N-COUNT

**lumpy** /lʌmpi/ **(lumpier, lumpiest)** Something that is **lumpy** contains lumps or is covered with lumps. ❑ *When the rice isn't cooked properly it goes lumpy and gooey.* ADJ

**lu|na|cy** /luːnəsi/ [1] If you describe someone's behaviour as **lunacy**, you mean that it seems very strange or foolish. ❑ *...the lunacy of the tax system... It remains lunacy to produce yet more coal to add to power stations' stockpiles.* N-UNCOUNT disapproval [2] **Lunacy** is severe mental illness. [OLD-FASHIONED] N-UNCOUNT

**lu|nar** /luːnəʳ/ **Lunar** means relating to the moon. ❑ *The vast volcanic slope was eerily reminiscent of a lunar landscape. ...a magazine article celebrating the anniversary of man's first lunar landing.* ADJ: ADJ n

**lu|na|tic** /luːnətɪk/ **(lunatics)** [1] If you describe someone as a **lunatic**, you think they behave in a dangerous, stupid, or annoying way. [INFORMAL] ❑ *Her son thinks she's an absolute raving lunatic.* N-COUNT disapproval [2] If you describe someone's behaviour or ideas as **lunatic**, you think they are very foolish and possibly dangerous. ❑ *...the operation of the market taken to lunatic extremes. ...a country spurned until now by all except the more lunatic of journalists and adventurers.* ADJ disapproval = mad, insane [3] If you describe a place or situation as **lunatic**, you mean that it is confused and seems out of control. ❑ *He pleads for sanity in a lunatic world.* ADJ: ADJ n [4] People who were mentally ill used to be called **lunatics**. [OLD-FASHIONED] N-COUNT

**lu|na|tic asy|lum** **(lunatic asylums)** A **lunatic asylum** was a place where mentally disturbed people used to be locked up. [OLD-FASHIONED] N-COUNT

**lu|na|tic fringe** If you refer to a group of people as the **lunatic fringe**, you mean that they are very extreme in their opinions or behaviour. ❑ *Demands for a separate Siberia are confined for now to the lunatic fringe.* N-SING: usu the N

**lunch** /lʌntʃ/ **(lunches, lunching, lunched)** ◆◆◇ [1] **Lunch** is the meal that you have in the middle of the day. ❑ *Shall we meet somewhere for lunch?... He did not enjoy business lunches... If anyone wants me, I'm at lunch with a client.* N-VAR [2] When you **lunch**, you have lunch, especially at a restaurant. [FORMAL] ❑ *Only the extremely rich could afford to lunch at the Mirabelle... Having not yet lunched, we went to the refreshment bar for ham sandwiches.* VERB V adv/prep V

**lunch box** **(lunch boxes)** also **lunchbox.** A **lunch box** is a small container with a lid. You put food such as sandwiches in it to eat for lunch at work or at school. N-COUNT

**lunch break** **(lunch breaks)** also **lunchbreak.** Your **lunch break** is the period in the middle of the day when you stop work in order to have a meal. N-COUNT: usu poss N

**lunch coun|ter** **(lunch counters)** A **lunch counter** is an informal café or a counter in a shop where people can buy and eat meals. [AM] N-COUNT

**lunch|eon** /lʌntʃən/ **(luncheons)** A **luncheon** is a formal lunch, for example to celebrate an important event or to raise money for charity. ❑ *Earlier this month, a luncheon for former UN staff was held in Vienna.* N-COUNT

**lunch|eon|ette** /lʌntʃənet/ **(luncheonettes)** A **luncheonette** is a small restaurant that serves light meals. [AM] N-COUNT

**lunch|eon meat** **(luncheon meats)** [1] **Luncheon meat** is meat that you eat in a sandwich or salad, and that is usually cold and either sliced or formed into rolls. [AM] N-VAR [2] **Luncheon meat** is a type of cooked meat that is often sold in tins. It is a mixture of pork and cereal. [BRIT] N-MASS

**lunch hour** **(lunch hours)** Your **lunch hour** is the period in the middle of the day when you stop working, usually for one hour, in order to have a meal. N-COUNT: usu poss N

**lunch|room** /lʌntʃruːm/ **(lunchrooms)** also **lunch room.** A **lunchroom** is the room in a school or company where you buy and eat your lunch. [AM] N-COUNT

**lunch|time** /lʌntʃtaɪm/ **(lunchtimes)** also **lunch time. Lunchtime** is the period of the day when people have their lunch. ❑ *Could we meet at lunchtime? ...a lunchtime meeting.* N-VAR

**lung** /lʌŋ/ **(lungs)** Your **lungs** are the two organs inside your chest which fill with air when you breathe in. N-COUNT: usu pl

**lunge** /lʌndʒ/ **(lunges, lunging, lunged)** If you **lunge** in a particular direction, you move in that direction suddenly and clumsily. ❑ *He lunged at me, grabbing me violently... I lunged forward to try to hit him.* ♦ **Lunge** is also a noun. ❑ *The attacker knocked on their door and made a lunge for Wendy when she answered.* VERB V prep/adv V prep/adv N-COUNT: usu sing

**lung|ful** /lʌŋfʊl/ **(lungfuls)** If someone takes a **lungful** of something such as fresh air or smoke, they breathe in deeply so that their lungs feel as if they are full of that thing. [WRITTEN] ❑ *I bobbed to the surface and gasped a lungful of air.* N-COUNT: usu N of n

**lurch** /lɜːʳtʃ/ **(lurches, lurching, lurched)** [1] To **lurch** means to make a sudden movement, especially forwards, in an uncontrolled way. ❑ *As the car sped over a pothole she lurched forward... Henry looked, stared, and lurched to his feet.* ♦ **Lurch** is also a noun. ❑ *The car took a lurch forward but grounded in a deep rut.* VERB V adv/prep V adv/prep Also V N-COUNT [2] If you say that a person or organization **lurches from** one thing **to** another, you mean they move suddenly from one course of action or attitude to another in an uncontrolled way. ❑ *The state government has lurched from one budget crisis to another... The first round of multilateral trade talks has lurched between hope and despair.* ♦ **Lurch** is also a noun. ❑ *The property sector was another casualty of the lurch towards higher interest rates.* VERB disapproval V from n to n V prep/adv N-COUNT: usu N prep [3] If someone **leaves** you **in the lurch**, they go away or stop helping you at a very difficult time. [INFORMAL] ❑ *You wouldn't leave an old friend in the lurch, surely?* PHRASE: V inflects

**lure** /ljʊəʳ, AM lʊr/ **(lures, luring, lured)** [1] To **lure** someone means to trick them into a particular place or to trick them into doing something that they should not do. ❑ *He lured her to his home and shot her with his father's gun... The company aims to lure smokers back to cigarettes.* VERB = entice V n prep/adv V n prep/adv [2] A **lure** is an object which is used to attract animals so that they can be caught. N-COUNT [3] A **lure** is an attractive quality that something has, or something that you find attractive. ❑ *The excitement of hunting big game in Africa has been a lure to Europeans for 200 years... The lure of rural life is proving as strong as ever.* N-COUNT: usu sing

**lu|rid** /ljʊərɪd, AM lʊrɪd/ [1] If you say that something is **lurid**, you are critical of it because it involves a lot of violence, sex, or shocking detail. ❑ *...lurid accounts of Claire's sexual exploits... Some reports have contained lurid accounts of deaths and mutilations.* ♦ **lu|rid|ly** *His cousin was soon cursing luridly.* ADJ: usu ADJ n disapproval = sensational ADV: ADV with v [2] If you describe something as **lurid**, you do not like it because it is very brightly coloured. ❑ *She took care to paint her toe nails a lurid red or orange.* ♦ **lu|rid|ly** *It had a high ceiling and a luridly coloured square of carpet on the floor.* ADJ: usu ADJ n disapproval ADV: usu ADV adj/-ed

**lurk** /lɜːʳk/ **(lurks, lurking, lurked)** [1] If someone **lurks** somewhere, they wait there secretly so that they cannot be seen, usually because they intend to do something bad. ❑ *He thought he saw someone lurking above the chamber during the address.* VERB V [2] If something such as a danger, doubt, or fear **lurks** somewhere, it exists but is not obvious or easily recognized. ❑ *Hidden dangers lurk in every family saloon car... Around every corner lurked doubt and uncertainty.* VERB V V

**lus|cious** /lʌʃəs/ [1] If you describe a woman or something about her as **luscious**, you mean that you find her or this thing sexually attractive. ❑ *...a luscious young blonde... What I like most about Gabby is her luscious lips!* ADJ: usu ADJ n [2] **Luscious** food is juicy and very good to eat. ❑ *...a small apricot tree which bore luscious fruit.* ADJ

**lush** /lʌʃ/ **(lusher, lushest)** [1] **Lush** fields or gardens have a lot of very healthy grass or plants. ❑ *...the lush green meadows bordering the river... The beautifully landscaped gardens sprawl with lush vegetation.* ♦ **lush|ness** *...a tropical lushness.* N-UNCOUNT [2] If you describe a place or thing as **lush**, you mean that it is very luxurious. ❑ *...a mirrored bathroom done in soft pink tiles with a lush, plush carpet... The fabrics were lush.* ADJ; ADJ: v-link ADJ

**lust** /lʌst/ [1] **Lust** is a feeling of strong sexual desire for someone. ❑ *His relationship with Angie was the first which combined lust with friendship... His lust for her grew until it was overpowering.* N-UNCOUNT [2] A **lust** for something is a very strong and eager desire to have it. ❑ *It was Fred's lust for glitz and glamour that was driving them apart.* N-UNCOUNT: oft N *for* n = passion

♦ **lust after** or **lust for** [1] If you **lust after** someone or **lust for** them, you feel a very strong sexual desire for them. ❑ *From what I hear, half the campus is lusting after her.* PHRASAL VERB; V P n [2] If you **lust after** or **lust for** something, you have a very strong desire to possess it. ❑ *Sheard lusted after the Directorship.* PHRASAL VERB; V P n

**lust|ful** /lʌstfʊl/ **Lustful** means feeling or expressing strong sexual desire. ❑ *...lustful thoughts.* ADJ: usu ADJ n

**lus|tre** /lʌstəʳ/

✓ in AM, use **luster**

[1] **Lustre** is gentle shining light that is reflected from a surface, for example from polished metal. ❑ *Gold retains its lustre for far longer than other metals... It is softer than cotton and nylon and has a similar lustre to silk.* N-UNCOUNT [2] **Lustre** is the qualities that something has that make it interesting and exciting. ❑ *What do you do if your relationship is beginning to lose its lustre?* N-UNCOUNT

**lus|trous** /lʌstrəs/ Something that is **lustrous** shines brightly and gently, because it has a smooth or shiny surface. ❑ *...a head of thick, lustrous, wavy brown hair.* ADJ

**lusty** /lʌsti/ **(lustier, lustiest)** If you say that something is **lusty**, you mean that it is healthy and full of strength and energy. ❑ *...plants with large, lusty roots. ...remembering his lusty singing in the open park.* ♦ **lusti|ly** *Bob ate lustily.* ADJ: usu ADJ n; ADV: ADV with v

**lute** /luːt/ **(lutes)** A **lute** is a stringed instrument with a rounded body that is quite like a guitar and is played with the fingers. N-VAR: oft *the* N

**luv** /lʌv/ **Luv** is a written form of the word 'love', when it is being used as an informal way of addressing someone. [BRIT] ❑ *'Don't worry, luv.'* N-VOC

**luv|vie** /lʌvi/ **(luvvies)** People sometimes refer to actors as **luvvies** as a humorous way of criticizing their emotional behaviour and their feeling that they are important. [BRIT, HUMOROUS, INFORMAL] N-COUNT [disapproval]

**luxu|ri|ant** /lʌgʒʊəriənt/ [1] **Luxuriant** plants, trees, and gardens are large, healthy, and growing well. ❑ *There were two very large oak trees in front of our house with wide spreading branches and luxuriant foliage.* ADJ: usu ADJ n [2] If you describe someone's hair as **luxuriant**, you mean that it is very thick and healthy. ❑ *Hair that's thick and luxuriant needs regular trimming.* ADJ

**luxu|ri|ate** /lʌgʒʊərieɪt/ **(luxuriates, luxuriating, luxuriated)** If you **luxuriate in** something, you relax in it and enjoy it very much, especially because you find it comfortable and luxurious. ❑ *Lie back and luxuriate in the scented oil... Ralph was luxuriating in the first real holiday he'd had in years.* VERB; V *in* n; V *in* n

**luxu|ri|ous** /lʌgʒʊəriəs/ [1] If you describe something as **luxurious**, you mean that it is very comfortable and expensive. ❑ *She had come to enjoy Roberto's luxurious life-style.* ♦ **luxu|ri|ous|ly** *The dining-room is luxuriously furnished and carpeted.* ADJ; ADV [2] **Luxurious** means feeling or expressing great pleasure and comfort. ❑ *Amy tilted her wine in her glass with a luxurious sigh.* ♦ **luxu|ri|ous|ly** *Liz laughed, stretching luxuriously.* ADJ; ADV: ADV after v

**luxu|ry** /lʌkʃəri/ **(luxuries)** [1] **Luxury** is very great comfort, especially among beautiful and expensive surroundings. ❑ *By all accounts he leads a life of considerable luxury... She was brought up in an atmosphere of luxury and wealth.* ◆◇◇ N-UNCOUNT = extravagance [2] A **luxury** is something expensive which is not necessary but which gives you pleasure. ❑ *A week by the sea is a luxury they can no longer afford... Telephones are still a luxury in some parts of Spain, Portugal, and Greece.* N-COUNT = extravagance [3] A **luxury** item is something expensive which is not necessary but which gives you pleasure. ❑ *He could not afford luxury food on his pay... He rode on the president's luxury train through his own state.* ADJ: ADJ n [4] A **luxury** is a pleasure which you do not often have the opportunity to enjoy. ❑ *Hot baths are my favourite luxury... We were going to have the luxury of a free weekend, to rest and do whatever we pleased.* N-SING: with supp

**luxu|ry goods** **Luxury goods** are things which are not necessary, but which give you pleasure or make your life more comfortable. ❑ *...increased taxes on luxury goods, such as boats, fur coats and expensive cars.* N-PLURAL

**LW** **LW** is an abbreviation for **long wave**.

**-ly** /-li/ **(-lier, -liest)** [1] **-ly** is added to adjectives to form adverbs that indicate the manner or nature of something. ❑ *I saw Louise walking slowly to the bus stop... They were badly injured... Sarah has typically British fair skin.* SUFFIX [2] **-ly** is added to nouns to form adjectives that describe someone or something as being like or typical of a particular kind of person or thing. ❑ *The staff are very friendly... This was a cowardly thing to do.* SUFFIX [3] **-ly** is added to nouns referring to periods of time to form adjectives or adverbs that say how often something happens or is done. ❑ *...a weekly newspaper. ...monthly payments. ...the language that we use daily.* SUFFIX

**ly|chee** /laɪtʃiː, AM liːtsiː/ **(lychees)** **Lychees** are Chinese fruit which have white flesh and large stones inside and a pinkish-brown skin. N-VAR

**Ly|cra** /laɪkrə/ **Lycra** is a type of stretchy fabric, similar to elastic, which is used to make tight-fitting garments such as tights and swimming costumes. [TRADEMARK] N-UNCOUNT

**ly|ing** /laɪɪŋ/ **Lying** is the present participle of **lie**.

**lymph node** /lɪmf noʊd/ **(lymph nodes)** **Lymph nodes** or **lymph glands** are small masses of tissue in your body where white blood cells are formed. N-COUNT: usu pl

**lynch** /lɪntʃ/ **(lynches, lynching, lynched)** If an angry crowd of people **lynch** someone, they kill that person by hanging them, without letting them have a trial, because they believe that that person has committed a crime. ❑ *They were about to lynch him when reinforcements from the army burst into the room and rescued him.* ♦ **lynch|ing** **(lynchings)** *Some towns found that lynching was the only way to drive away bands of outlaws.* VERB; V n; N-VAR

**lynch mob** **(lynch mobs)** [1] A **lynch mob** is an angry crowd of people who want to kill someone without a trial, because they believe that person has committed a crime. N-COUNT [2] You can refer to a group of people as a **lynch mob** if they are very angry with someone because they believe that person has done something bad or wrong. ❑ *Something approaching a lynch mob has been gathering against the Chancellor for even daring to consider higher interest rates.* N-COUNT

**lynch|pin** /lɪntʃpɪn/ → see **linchpin**.

**lynx** /lɪŋks/ **(lynxes)** A **lynx** is a wild animal similar to a large cat. N-COUNT

**lyre** /laɪəʳ/ **(lyres)** A **lyre** is a stringed instrument that looks like a small harp. N-COUNT

**lyr|ic** /lɪrɪk/ **(lyrics)** [1] The **lyrics** of a song are its words. ❑ *...Kurt Weill's Broadway opera with lyrics by Langston Hughes.* N-COUNT: usu pl [2] **Lyric** poetry is written in a simple and direct style, and usually expresses personal emotions such as love. ❑ *...Lawrence's splendid short stories and lyric poetry.* ADJ: ADJ n

**lyri|cal** /lɪrɪkəl/ Something that is **lyrical** is poetic and romantic. ❑ *His paintings became more lyrical. ...its remarkable free-flowing and often lyrical style.* to **wax lyrical** → see **wax**. ADJ

**lyri|cism** /lɪrɪsɪzəm/ **Lyricism** is gentle and romantic emotion, often expressed in writing, poetry, or music. ❑ *...a natural lyricism which can be expressed through dance and music.* N-UNCOUNT

**lyri|cist** /lɪrɪsɪst/ **(lyricists)** A **lyricist** is someone who writes the words for modern songs or for musicals. N-COUNT

# M m

**M, m** /em/ **(M's, m's)** 1 **M** is the thirteenth letter of the English alphabet. 2 **m** is a written abbreviation for **metres** or **metre**. ❑ *The island is only 200m wide at its narrowest point.* 3 **m** is a written abbreviation for the number **million**. ❑ *Last year exports reached $150m in value. ...500m tonnes of coal.* N-VAR

**-'m** /-m/ **'m** is the usual spoken form of 'am', used after 'I' in 'I'm'.

**ma** /mɑː/ **(mas)** Some people refer to or address their mother as **ma**. [INFORMAL] ❑ *Ma was still at work when I got back.* N-FAMILY = *mum*

**MA** /em eɪ/ **(MAs)** also **M.A.** An **MA** is a master's degree in an arts or social science subject. **MA** is an abbreviation for 'Master of Arts'. ❑ *She then went on to university where she got a BA and then an MA.* N-COUNT

**ma'am** /mæm, mɑːm/ People sometimes say **ma'am** as a very formal and polite way of addressing a woman whose name they do not know or a woman of superior rank. [mainly AM] ❑ *Would you repeat that please, ma'am?* N-VOC [politeness] = *madam*

**mac** /mæk/ **(macs)** A **mac** is a raincoat, especially one made from a particular kind of waterproof cloth. [BRIT] N-COUNT

**ma|ca|bre** /məkɑːbrə/ You describe something such as an event or story as **macabre** when it is strange and horrible or upsetting, usually because it involves death or injury. ❑ *Police have made a macabre discovery.* ADJ: usu ADJ n = *chilling*

**maca|ro|ni** /mækərouni/ **Macaroni** is a kind of pasta made in the shape of short hollow tubes. N-UNCOUNT

**maca|ro|ni cheese**

✔ in AM, use **macaroni and cheese**

**Macaroni cheese** is a dish made from macaroni and cheese sauce. N-UNCOUNT

**maca|roon** /mækəruːn/ **(macaroons) Macaroons** are sweet cake-like biscuits that are flavoured with coconut or almond. N-COUNT

**mace** /meɪs/ **(maces)** 1 A **mace** is an ornamental stick carried by an official or placed somewhere as a symbol of authority. N-COUNT 2 **Mace** is a substance that causes tears and sickness, and that is used in sprays as a defence against rioters or attackers. [TRADEMARK] N-UNCOUNT

**mac|er|ate** /mæsəreɪt/ **(macerates, macerating, macerated)** If you **macerate** food, or if it **macerates**, you soak it in a liquid for a period of time so that it absorbs the liquid. ❑ *I like to macerate the food in liqueur for a few minutes before serving... Cognac is also used to macerate and flavour ingredients and casseroles... Seal tightly then leave for four to five days to macerate.* VERB = *marinate* V n *in* n; V n; V

**Mach** /mɑːk/ **Mach** is used as a unit of measurement in stating the speed of a moving object in relation to the speed of sound. For example, if an aircraft is travelling at Mach 1, it is travelling at exactly the speed of sound. [TECHNICAL] N-UNCOUNT: N n/num

**ma|chete** /məʃeti/ **(machetes)** A **machete** is a large knife with a broad blade. N-COUNT

**Machia|vel|lian** /mækiəveliən/ If you describe someone as **Machiavellian**, you are critical of them because they often make clever and secret plans to achieve their aims and are not honest with people. ❑ *...Machiavellian republicans plotting to destabilise the throne... A Machiavellian plot was suspected.* ADJ: usu ADJ n [disapproval] = *devious*

**machi|na|tions** /mækɪneɪʃənz, mæʃ-/ You use **machinations** to describe secret and complicated plans, especially to gain power. ❑ *...the political machinations that brought him to power.* N-PLURAL: usu with supp [disapproval]

**ma|chine** /məʃiːn/ **(machines, machining, machined)** ◆◆◇ 1 A **machine** is a piece of equipment which uses electricity or an engine in order to do a particular kind of work. ❑ *I put the coin in the machine and pulled the lever. ...a color photograph of the sort taken by machine to be pasted in passports.* N-COUNT: also *by* N 2 If you **machine** something, you make it or work on it using a machine. ❑ *The material is machined in a factory... All parts are machined from top grade, high tensile aluminium. ...machined brass zinc alloy gears.* VERB: usu passive *be* V-ed; *be* V-ed *from* n; V-ed ♦ **ma|chin|ing** *...our machining, fabrication and finishing processes.* N-UNCOUNT 3 You can use **machine** to refer to a large and well-controlled system or organization. ❑ *...Nazi Germany's military machine... He has put the party publicity machine behind another candidate.* N-COUNT: usu supp N 4 → See also **fruit machine, sewing machine, slot machine, vending machine**.

**ma|chine code** **Machine code** is a way of expressing instructions and information in the form of numbers which can be understood by a computer or microchip. [COMPUTING] N-UNCOUNT

**ma|chine gun** **(machine guns)** also **machine-gun.** A **machine gun** is a gun which fires a lot of bullets one after the other very quickly. ❑ *...a burst of machine-gun fire.* → See also **sub-machine gun**. N-COUNT

**ma|chin|ery** /məʃiːnəri/ 1 You can use **machinery** to refer to machines in general, or machines that are used in a factory or on a farm. ❑ *...quality tools and machinery. ...your local garden machinery specialist.* N-UNCOUNT 2 **The machinery** of a government or organization is the system and all the procedures that it uses to deal with things. ❑ *The machinery of democracy could be created quickly.* N-SING: *the* N, oft N *of* n

**ma|chine tool** **(machine tools)** A **machine tool** is a machine driven by power that cuts, shapes, or finishes metal or other materials. N-COUNT

**ma|chin|ist** /məʃiːnɪst/ **(machinists)** A **machinist** is a person whose job is to operate a machine, especially in a factory. N-COUNT

**ma|chis|mo** /mætʃɪzmoʊ, AM mɑːtʃiːz-/ You use **machismo** to refer to men's behaviour or attitudes when they are very conscious and proud of their masculinity. ❑ *Hooky, naturally, has to prove his machismo by going on the scariest rides twice.* N-UNCOUNT

**macho** /mætʃoʊ, AM mɑː-/ You use **macho** to describe men who are very conscious and proud of their masculinity. [INFORMAL] ❑ *...displays of macho bravado.* ADJ

**mac|in|tosh** /mækɪntɒʃ/ → see **mackintosh**.

**macke|rel** /mækərəl/ **(mackerel)** A **mackerel** is a sea fish with a dark, patterned back. ❑ *They'd gone out to fish for mackerel.* N-VAR ♦ **Mackerel** is this fish eaten as food. N-UNCOUNT

**mack|in|tosh** /mækɪntɒʃ/ **(mackintoshes)** A **mackintosh** is a raincoat, especially one made N-COUNT from a particular kind of waterproof cloth. [mainly BRIT]

**macro** /mækroʊ/ **(macros)** 1 You use **macro** to indicate that something relates to a general area, rather than being detailed or specific. [TECHNICAL] ❑ *...coordinated programmes of regulation of the economy both at the macro level and at the micro level.* ADJ: usu ADJ n = global ≠ micro 2 A **macro** is a shortened version of a computer command which makes the computer carry out a set of actions. [COMPUTING] N-COUNT

**macro-** /mækroʊ-/ **Macro-** is added to words in order to form new words that are technical and that refer to things which are large or involve the whole of something. ❑ *...the cornerstone of macro-economic policy. ...the macro-relationship between unemployment and imprisonment.* PREFIX ≠ micro-

**macro|bi|ot|ic** /mækroʊbaɪɒtɪk/ **Macrobiotic** food consists of whole grains and vegetables that are grown without chemicals. [TECHNICAL] ❑ *...a strict macrobiotic diet.* ADJ: usu ADJ n = wholefood

**macro|bi|ot|ics** /mækroʊbaɪɒtɪks/ **Macrobiotics** is the practice of eating macrobiotic food. [TECHNICAL] N-UNCOUNT

**macro|cosm** /mækroʊkɒzəm/ A **macrocosm** is a complex organized system such as the universe or a society, considered as a single unit. [FORMAL] ❑ *The macrocosm of the universe is mirrored in the microcosm of the mind.* N-SING: usu *the* N ≠ microcosm

**macro|eco|nom|ic** /mækroʊiːkənɒmɪk, -ek-/ also **macro-economic. Macroeconomic** means relating to the major, general features of a country's economy, such as the level of inflation, unemployment, or interest rates. [BUSINESS] ❑ *...the attempt to substitute low inflation for full employment as a goal of macro-economic policy.* ADJ: usu ADJ n

**mad** /mæd/ **(madder, maddest)** 1 Someone who is **mad** has a mind that does not work in a normal way, with the result that their behaviour is very strange. ❑ *She was afraid of going mad.* ◆◇◇ ADJ = insane ♦ **mad|ness** *He was driven to the brink of madness.* N-UNCOUNT 2 You use **mad** to describe people or things that you think are very foolish. ❑ *You'd be mad to work with him again... Isn't that a rather mad idea?* ADJ [disapproval] = crazy ♦ **mad|ness** *It is political madness.* N-UNCOUNT 3 If you say that someone is **mad**, you mean that they are very angry. [INFORMAL] ❑ *You're just mad at me because I don't want to go.* ADJ: usu v-link ADJ, oft ADJ *at/about* n 4 If you are **mad about** or **mad on** something or someone, you like them very much indeed. [INFORMAL] ❑ *She's not as mad about sport as I am... He's mad about you... He's mad on trains.* ADJ: v-link ADJ *about/on* n ♦ **Mad** is also a combining form. ❑ *...his football-mad son... He's not power-mad.* COMB in ADJ 5 **Mad** behaviour is wild and uncontrolled. ❑ *You only have an hour to complete the game so it's a mad dash against the clock... The audience went mad.* ADJ ♦ **mad|ly** *Down in the streets people were waving madly.* ADV: ADV with v

PHRASES 6 If you say that someone or something **drives** you **mad**, you mean that you find them extremely annoying. [INFORMAL] ❑ *There are certain things he does that drive me mad... This itching is driving me mad.* PHRASE: V inflects 7 If you do something **like mad**, you do it very energetically or enthusiastically. [INFORMAL] ❑ *He was weight training like mad.* PHRASE: PHR after v 8 → See also **madly. mad keen** → see **keen**.

**mad|am** /mædəm/ also **Madam.** People sometimes say **Madam** as a very formal and polite way of addressing a woman whose name they do not know or a woman of superior rank. For example, a shop assistant might address a woman customer as **Madam**. ❑ *Try them on, madam.* N-VOC [politeness]

**mad|cap** /mædkæp/ A **madcap** plan or scheme is very foolish and not likely to succeed. [INFORMAL] ❑ *The politicians simply flitted from one madcap scheme to another.* ADJ: usu ADJ n

**mad cow dis|ease** **Mad cow disease** is a disease which affects the nervous system of cattle and causes death. [mainly BRIT] N-UNCOUNT = BSE

**mad|den** /mædᵊn/ **(maddens, maddening, maddened)** To **madden** a person or animal means to make them very angry. ❑ *He knew that what he was saying did not reach her. And the knowledge of it maddened him.* VERB = infuriate V n

**mad|den|ing** /mædənɪŋ/ If you describe something as **maddening**, you mean that it makes you feel angry, irritated, or frustrated. ❑ *Shopping in the January sales can be maddening.* ADJ = infuriating ♦ **mad|den|ing|ly** *The service here is maddeningly slow.* ADV: ADV adj, ADV after v, ADV with cl

**made** /meɪd/ 1 **Made** is the past tense and past participle of **make**. 2 If something is **made of** or **made out of** a particular substance, that substance was used to build it. ❑ *The top of the table is made of glass... What is the statue made out of?* ADJ: v-link ADJ *of/out of* n 3 If you say that someone **has it made** or **has got it made**, you mean that they are certain to be rich or successful. [INFORMAL] ❑ *When I was at school, I thought I had it made.* PHRASE: V inflects

**-made** /-meɪd/ **-made** combines with words such as 'factory' to make adjectives that indicate that something has been made or produced in a particular place or in a particular way. ❑ *...a British-made car. ...specially-made footwear.* COMB in ADJ: usu ADJ n

**made-to-measure** A **made-to-measure** suit, shirt, or other item of clothing is one that is made by a tailor to fit you exactly, rather than one that you buy already made in a shop. ADJ: usu ADJ n

**made-up** also **made up.** 1 If you are **made-up**, you are wearing make-up such as powder or eye shadow. ❑ *She was beautifully made-up, beautifully groomed.* ◆◇◇ ADJ: v-link ADJ, adv ADJ n 2 A **made-up** word, name, or story is invented, rather than really existing or being true. ❑ *It looks like a made-up word.* ADJ: usu ADJ n ≠ real

**mad|house** /mædhaʊs/ **(madhouses)** If you describe a place or situation as a **madhouse**, you mean that it is full of confusion and noise. ❑ *That place is a madhouse.* N-COUNT: usu sing

**mad|ly** /mædli/ 1 You can use **madly** to indicate that one person loves another a great deal. ❑ *She has fallen madly in love with a young officer.* ADV: ADV prep, ADV after v = completely 2 You can use **madly** in front of an adjective in order to emphasize the quality expressed by the adjective. [mainly BRIT] ❑ *Inside it is madly busy.* ADV: ADV adj [emphasis] = insanely

**mad|man** /mædmən/ **(madmen)** A **madman** is a man who is insane. ❑ *He wanted to jump up and run outside, screaming like a madman.* N-COUNT

**Ma|don|na** /mədɒnə/ Catholics and other Christians sometimes call Mary, the mother of Jesus Christ, **the Madonna**. N-PROPER: *the* N

**mad|ras** /mədræs, -drɑːs/ A **madras** curry is a rather hot spicy curry. ADJ: ADJ n

**mad|ri|gal** /mædrɪgᵊl/ **(madrigals)** A **madrigal** is a song sung by several singers without any musical instruments. Madrigals were popular in England in the sixteenth century. N-COUNT

**mad|woman** /mædwʊmən/ **(madwomen)** A **madwoman** is a woman who is insane. [INFORMAL] N-COUNT

**mael|strom** /meɪlstrɒm/ **(maelstroms)** If you describe a situation as a **maelstrom**, you mean that it is very confused or violent. [LITERARY] ❑ *...the maelstrom of ethnic hatreds and vendetta politics... Inside, she was a maelstrom of churning emotions.* N-COUNT: usu sing, usu with supp, oft N *of* n

**maes|tro** /maɪstroʊ/ **(maestros)** A **maestro** is a skilled and well-known musician or conductor. ❑ *...the urbane maestro's delightful first show.* N-COUNT; N-VOC

**ma|fia** /mæfiə, AM mɑːf-/ **(mafias)** 1 **The Mafia** is a criminal organization that makes money illegally, especially by threatening people and dealing in drugs. ❑ *The Mafia is by no means ignored by Italian television.* N-COUNT-COLL: *the* N 2 You can use **mafia** to refer to an organized group of people who you disapprove of because they use unfair or illegal means in order to get what they want. ❑ *They are well-connected with the south-based education-reform mafia.* N-COUNT: usu with supp [disapproval]

**mag** /mæg/ **(mags)** A **mag** is the same as a magazine. [INFORMAL] ❑ *...a well-known glossy mag.* N-COUNT

**maga|zine** /mægəziːn, AM -ziːn/ **(magazines)** ◆◆◇ 1 N-COUNT A **magazine** is a publication with a paper cover which is issued regularly, usually every week or every month, and which contains articles, stories, photographs, and advertisements. ❑ *Her face is on the cover of a dozen or more magazines.* 2 N-COUNT In an automatic gun, the **magazine** is the part that contains the bullets.

**ma|gen|ta** /mədʒentə/ **(magentas)** COLOUR **Magenta** is used to describe things that are dark reddish-purple in colour.

**mag|got** /mægət/ **(maggots)** N-COUNT **Maggots** are creatures that look like very small worms and turn into flies.

**mag|ic** /mædʒɪk/ ◆◇◇ 1 N-UNCOUNT **Magic** is the power to use supernatural forces to make impossible things happen, such as making people disappear or controlling events in nature. ❑ *They believe in magic... Older legends say that Merlin raised the stones by magic.* 2 N-UNCOUNT You can use **magic** when you are referring to an event that is so wonderful, strange, or unexpected that it seems as if supernatural powers have caused it. You can also say that something happens **as if by magic** or **like magic**. ❑ *All this was supposed to work magic... The picture will now appear, as if by magic!* 3 ADJ: ADJ n You use **magic** to describe something that does things, or appears to do things, by magic. ❑ *So it's a magic potion? ...the magic ingredient that helps to keep skin looking smooth.* 4 N-UNCOUNT: oft N n **Magic** is the art and skill of performing mysterious tricks to entertain people, for example by making things appear and disappear. ❑ *His secret hobby: performing magic tricks.* 5 N-UNCOUNT: usu with supp If you refer to **the magic of** something, you mean that it has a special mysterious quality which makes it seem wonderful and exciting to you and which makes you feel happy. ❑ *It infected them with some of the magic of a lost age.* ♦ ADJ **Magic** is also an adjective. ❑ *Then came those magic moments in the rose-garden.* 6 N-UNCOUNT: usu with poss If you refer to a person's **magic**, you mean a special talent or ability that they have, which you admire or consider very impressive. ❑ *The fighter believes he can still regain some of his old magic.* 7 ADJ: the ADJ n You can use expressions such as **the magic number** and **the magic word** to indicate that a number or word is the one which is significant or desirable in a particular situation. ❑ *...their quest to gain the magic number of 270 electoral votes on Election Day.* 8 ADJ: ADJ n, with neg **Magic** is used in expressions such as **there is no magic formula** and **there is no magic solution** to say that someone will have to make an effort to solve a problem, because it will not solve itself. ❑ *There is no magic formula for producing winning products.* 9 ADJ [approval] = brilliant If you say that something is **magic**, you think it is very good or enjoyable. [mainly BRIT, INFORMAL] ❑ *It was magic – one of the best days of my life.*

**magi|cal** /mædʒɪkəl/ 1 ADJ Something that is **magical** seems to use magic or to be able to produce magic. ❑ *...the story of Sin-Sin, a little boy who has magical powers.* ♦ **magi|cal|ly** /mædʒɪkli/ ADV: ADV with v *...the story of a young boy's adventures after he is magically transported through the cinema screen.* 2 ADJ You can say that a place or object is **magical** when it has a special mysterious quality that makes it seem wonderful and exciting. ❑ *The beautiful island of Cyprus is a magical place to get married.*

**mag|ic bul|let** **(magic bullets)** 1 N-COUNT In medicine, a **magic bullet** is a drug or treatment that can cure a disease quickly and completely. 2 N-COUNT A **magic bullet** is an easy solution to a difficult problem. [INFORMAL] ❑ *A lot of people are looking for some sort of magic bullet that will solve this problem.*

**mag|ic car|pet** **(magic carpets)** N-COUNT In stories, a **magic carpet** is a special carpet that can carry people through the air.

**ma|gi|cian** /mədʒɪʃən/ **(magicians)** N-COUNT A **magician** is a person who entertains people by doing magic tricks.

**mag|ic mush|room** **(magic mushrooms)** N-COUNT: usu pl **Magic mushrooms** are a type of mushroom which contain a drug and may make the person who eats them believe they are seeing things which are not real.

**mag|ic re|al|ism** also **magical realism.** N-UNCOUNT **Magic realism** is a style of writing or painting which sometimes describes dreams as though they were real, and real events as though they were dreams.

**mag|ic wand** **(magic wands)** 1 N-COUNT = wand A **magic wand** or a **wand** is a long thin rod that magicians and fairies wave when they are performing tricks and magic. 2 N-COUNT: usu with brd-neg You use **magic wand**, especially in the expression **there is no magic wand**, to indicate that someone is dealing with a difficult problem which cannot be solved quickly and easily. ❑ *There is no magic wand to secure a just peace.*

**mag|is|te|rial** /mædʒɪstɪəriəl/ ADJ: usu ADJ n If you describe someone's behaviour or work as **magisterial**, you mean that they show great authority or ability. [FORMAL] ❑ *...his magisterial voice and bearing... The Cambridge World History of Human Disease is a magisterial work.*

**mag|is|trate** /mædʒɪstreɪt/ **(magistrates)** N-COUNT A **magistrate** is an official who acts as a judge in law courts which deal with minor crimes or disputes.

**mag|na|nim|ity** /mægnənɪmɪti/ N-UNCOUNT = generosity **Magnanimity** is kindness and generosity towards someone, especially after defeating them or being treated badly by them. [FORMAL] ❑ *The father of one victim spoke with remarkable magnanimity.*

**mag|nani|mous** /mægnænɪməs/ ADJ = generous ≠ vindictive If you are **magnanimous**, you behave kindly and generously towards someone, especially after defeating them or being treated badly by them. ❑ *I was prepared to be magnanimous, prepared to feel compassion for him.* ♦ **mag|nani|mous|ly** ADV: usu ADV with v *'You were right, and we were wrong,' he said magnanimously.*

**mag|nate** /mægneɪt/ **(magnates)** N-COUNT: usu supp N = tycoon A **magnate** is someone who has earned a lot of money from a particular business or industry. ❑ *...a multimillionaire shipping magnate.*

**mag|ne|sium** /mægniːziəm/ N-UNCOUNT **Magnesium** is a light silvery-white metal which burns with a bright white flame.

**mag|net** /mægnɪt/ **(magnets)** 1 N-COUNT: usu a N in sing, oft N for n If you say that something is a **magnet** or is like a **magnet**, you mean that people are very attracted by it and want to go to it or look at it. ❑ *Prospect Park, with its vast lake, is a magnet for all health freaks.* 2 N-COUNT A **magnet** is a piece of iron or other material which attracts iron towards it. ❑ *...a fridge magnet.*

**mag|net|ic** /mægnetɪk/ 1 ADJ: usu ADJ n If something metal is **magnetic**, it acts like a magnet. ❑ *...magnetic particles.* 2 ADJ You use **magnetic** to describe something that is caused by or relates to the force of magnetism. ❑ *The electrically charged gas particles are affected by magnetic forces.* ♦ **mag|neti|cal|ly** /mægnetɪkli/ ADV: ADV after v *...metal fragments held together magnetically.* 3 ADJ: usu ADJ n You use **magnetic** to describe tapes and other objects which have a coating of a magnetic substance and contain coded information that can be read by computers or other machines. ❑ *...her magnetic strip ID card.* 4 ADJ: usu ADJ n If you describe something as **magnetic**, you mean that it is very attractive to people because it has unusual, powerful, and exciting qualities. ❑ *...the magnetic effect of the prosperous German economy on would-be immigrants.*

**mag|net|ic field** **(magnetic fields)** N-COUNT A **magnetic field** is an area around a magnet, or something functioning as a magnet, in which the magnet's power to attract things is felt.

**mag|net|ic tape** **(magnetic tapes)** N-VAR = tape **Magnetic tape** is plastic tape covered with iron oxide or a similar magnetic substance. It is used for recording sounds, film, or computer information.

**mag|net|ism** /mæɡnɪtɪzəm/ 1 Someone or something that has **magnetism** has unusual, powerful, and exciting qualities which attract people to them. ❑ *There was no doubting the animal magnetism of the man.* 2 **Magnetism** is the natural power of some objects and substances, especially iron, to attract other objects towards them.
N-UNCOUNT: usu with supp
N-UNCOUNT

**mag|net|ize** /mæɡnɪtaɪz/ **(magnetizes, magnetizing, magnetized)**

in BRIT, also use **magnetise**

If you **magnetize** something, you make it magnetic. ❑ *Make a Mobius strip out of a ribbon of mild steel and magnetise it. ...a small metal chessboard with magnetized playing pieces.*
VERB
V n
V-ed

**mag|net school** **(magnet schools)** A **magnet school** is a state-funded school, usually in a poor area, which is given extra resources in order to attract new pupils from other areas and help improve the school's performance. [JOURNALISM]
N-COUNT

**mag|ni|fi|ca|tion** /mæɡnɪfɪkeɪʃən/ **(magnifications)** 1 **Magnification** is the act or process of magnifying something. ❑ *Pores are visible without magnification.* 2 **Magnification** is the degree to which a lens, mirror, or other device can magnify an object, or the degree to which the object is magnified. ❑ *The electron microscope uses a beam of electrons to produce images at high magnifications.*
N-UNCOUNT
N-VAR

**mag|nifi|cent** /mæɡnɪfɪsənt/ If you say that something or someone is **magnificent**, you mean that you think they are extremely good, beautiful, or impressive. ❑ *...a magnificent country house in wooded grounds. ...magnificent views over the San Fernando Valley.* ♦ **mag|nifi|cence** *...the magnificence of the Swiss mountains.* ♦ **mag|nifi|cent|ly** *The team played magnificently throughout the competition.*
ADJ = *splendid*
N-UNCOUNT: oft N *of* n
ADV: ADV after v, ADV adj/-ed

**mag|ni|fy** /mæɡnɪfaɪ/ **(magnifies, magnifying, magnified)** 1 To **magnify** an object means to make it appear larger than it really is, by means of a special lens or mirror. ❑ *This version of the Digges telescope magnifies images 11 times... A lens would magnify the picture so it would be like looking at a large TV screen. ...magnifying lenses.* 2 To **magnify** something means to increase its effect, size, loudness, or intensity. ❑ *Their noises were magnified in the still, wet air.* 3 If you **magnify** something, you make it seem more important or serious than it really is. ❑ *They do not grasp the broad situation and spend their time magnifying ridiculous details.*
VERB = *enlarge* ≠ *reduce*
V n n
V n
V-ing
VERB
V n
VERB = *exaggerate*
V n

**mag|ni|fy|ing glass** **(magnifying glasses)** A **magnifying glass** is a piece of glass which makes objects appear bigger than they actually are.
N-COUNT

**mag|ni|tude** /mæɡnɪtjuːd, AM -tuːd/ 1 If you talk about the **magnitude** of something, you are talking about its great size, scale, or importance. ❑ *An operation of this magnitude is going to be difficult.* 2 You can use **order of magnitude** when you are giving an approximate idea of the amount or importance of something. ❑ *America and Russia do not face a problem of the same order of magnitude as Japan.*
N-UNCOUNT: usu with supp
PHRASE: *order* inflects = *scale*

**mag|no|lia** /mæɡnoʊliə/ **(magnolias)** A **magnolia** is a kind of tree with white, pink, yellow, or purple flowers.
N-COUNT

**mag|num** /mæɡnəm/ **(magnums)** A **magnum** is a wine bottle holding the equivalent of two normal bottles, approximately 1.5 litres. ❑ *...a magnum of champagne.*
N-COUNT: oft N *of* n

**mag|num opus** A **magnum opus** is the greatest or most important work produced by a writer, artist, musician, or academic. ❑ *...Gadamer's magnum opus 'Truth and Method'.*
N-SING: oft poss N

**mag|pie** /mæɡpaɪ/ **(magpies)** A **magpie** is a large black and white bird with a long tail.
N-COUNT

**ma|ha|ra|ja** /mɑːhərɑːdʒə/ **(maharajas)** also **maharajah.** A **maharaja** is the head of one of the royal families that used to rule parts of India.
N-COUNT

**ma|hoga|ny** /məhɒɡəni/ **Mahogany** is a dark reddish-brown wood that is used to make furniture. ❑ *...mahogany tables and chairs.*
N-UNCOUNT: oft N n

**maid** /meɪd/ **(maids)** A **maid** is a woman who works as a servant in a hotel or private house. ❑ *A maid brought me breakfast at half past eight.* ➔ See also **old maid**.
N-COUNT

**maid|en** /meɪdən/ **(maidens)** 1 A **maiden** is a young girl or woman. [LITERARY] ❑ *...stories of noble princes and their brave deeds on behalf of beautiful maidens.* 2 The **maiden** voyage or flight of a ship or aircraft is the first official journey that it makes. ❑ *In 1912, the Titanic sank on her maiden voyage.*
N-COUNT
ADJ: ADJ n

**maid|en aunt** **(maiden aunts)** A **maiden aunt** is an aunt who is not married. [OLD-FASHIONED]
N-COUNT

**maid|en name** **(maiden names)** A married woman's **maiden name** is her parents' surname, which she used before she got married and started using her husband's surname.
N-COUNT: usu poss N ≠ *married name*

**maid|en speech** **(maiden speeches)** A politician's **maiden speech** is the first speech that he or she makes in parliament after becoming a member of it. [BRIT]
N-COUNT

**maid of hon|our** **(maids of honour)** A **maid of honour** is the chief bridesmaid at a wedding. [AM]
N-COUNT

**mail** /meɪl/ **(mails, mailing, mailed)** 1 **The mail** is the public service or system by which letters and parcels are collected and delivered. ❑ *Your check is in the mail... The firm has offices in several large cities, but does most of its business by mail.* 2 You can refer to letters and parcels that are delivered to you as **mail**. ❑ *There was no mail except the usual junk addressed to the occupier.* 3 If you **mail** a letter or parcel to someone, you send it to them by putting it in a post box or taking it to a post office. [mainly AM] ❑ *Last year, he mailed the documents to French journalists... He mailed me the contract... The Government has already mailed some 18 million households with details of the public offer.*
◆◇◇
N-SING: *the* N, also *by* N = *post*
N-UNCOUNT: also *the* N = *post*
VERB
V n *to* n
V n n
V n *with* n
Also V n

in BRIT, usually use **post**

4 To **mail** a message to someone means to send it to them by means of e-mail or a computer network. ❑ *...if a report must be electronically mailed to an office by 9 am the next day.* ♦ **Mail** is also a noun. ❑ *If you have any problems then send me some mail.* 5 ➔ See also **mailing**, **chain mail**, **e-mail**, **electronic mail**, **hate mail**, **junk mail**, **surface mail**.
VERB
*be* V-ed prep
Also V n
N-UNCOUNT

♦ **mail out** If someone **mails out** things such as letters, leaflets, or bills, they send them to a large number of people at the same time. [mainly AM] ❑ *This week, the company mailed out its annual report.*
PHRASAL VERB = *send out*
V P n (not pron)
Also V n P

in BRIT, use **send out**

**mail|bag** /meɪlbæɡ/ **(mailbags)** also **mail bag.** A **mailbag** is a large bag that is used by postal workers for carrying mail.
N-COUNT

**mail|box** /meɪlbɒks/ **(mailboxes)** 1 A **mailbox** is a box outside your house where your letters are delivered. [AM] 2 A **mailbox** is a metal box in a public place, where you put letters and packets to be collected. They are then sorted and delivered. [mainly AM]
N-COUNT
N-COUNT

in BRIT, use **post box**

3 On a computer, your **mailbox** is the file where your e-mail is stored.
N-COUNT: usu sing

**mail|ing** /meɪlɪŋ/ **(mailings)** 1 **Mailing** is the activity of sending things to people through the postal service. ❑ *The newsletter was printed towards the end of June in readiness for mailing... The owners of the store have stepped up customer mailings.* 2 A **mailing** is something that is sent to people through the postal service. ❑ *The seniors organizations sent out mailings to their constituencies.*
N-UNCOUNT: also N in pl
N-COUNT

**mail|ing list** **(mailing lists)** A **mailing list** is a list of names and addresses that a company or organization keeps, so that they can send people information or advertisements. N-COUNT

**mail|man** /meɪlmæn/ **(mailmen)** A **mailman** is a man whose job is to collect and deliver letters and parcels that are sent by post. [AM] N-COUNT

✔ in BRIT, usually use **postman**

**mail merge** **Mail merge** is a word processing procedure which enables you to combine a document with a data file, for example a list of names and addresses, so that copies of the document are different for each person it is sent to. [COMPUTING] ❑ *He sent every member of staff a mail-merge letter wishing them a merry Christmas!* N-UNCOUNT

**mail or|der** **(mail orders)** 1 **Mail order** is a system of buying and selling goods. You choose the goods you want from a company by looking at their catalogue, and the company sends them to you by post. ❑ *The toys are available by mail order from Opi Toys.* N-UNCOUNT: oft *by* N, N n 2 **Mail orders** are goods that have been ordered by mail order. [mainly AM] ❑ *I supervise the packing of all mail orders.* N-COUNT: usu pl

**mail|shot** /meɪlʃɒt/ **(mailshots)** A **mailshot** is a letter advertising something or appealing for money for a particular charity. Mailshots are sent out to a large number of people at once. [BRIT] N-COUNT

**maim** /meɪm/ **(maims, maiming, maimed)** To **maim** someone means to injure them so badly that part of their body is permanently damaged. VERB ❑ *Mines have been scattered in rice paddies and jungles, maiming and killing civilians.* V n

**main** /meɪn/ **(mains)** ◆◆◆ 1 The **main** thing is the most important one of several similar things in a particular situation. ❑ *...one of the main tourist areas of Amsterdam... My main concern now is to protect the children... What are the main differences and similarities between them?* ADJ: det ADJ = chief 2 If you say that something is true **in the main**, you mean that it is generally true, although there may be exceptions. ❑ *Tourists are, in the main, sympathetic people.* PHRASE: PHR with cl = on the whole 3 The **mains** are the pipes which supply gas or water to buildings, or which take sewage away from them. ❑ *...the water supply from the mains... The capital has been without mains water since Wednesday night.* N-COUNT: usu pl, usu with supp 4 **The mains** are the wires which supply electricity to buildings, or the place where the wires end inside the building. [mainly BRIT] ❑ *...amplifiers which plug into the mains.* N-PLURAL: usu *the* N

**main clause** **(main clauses)** A **main clause** is a clause that can stand alone as a complete sentence. Compare **subordinate clause**. N-COUNT

**main drag** **The main drag** in a town or city is its main street. [mainly AM, INFORMAL] N-SING: the N

**main|frame** /meɪnfreɪm/ **(mainframes)** A **mainframe** or **mainframe computer** is a large powerful computer which can be used by many people at the same time and which can do very large or complicated tasks. N-COUNT

**main|land** /meɪnlænd/ You can refer to the largest part of a country or continent as **the mainland** when contrasting it with the islands around it. ❑ *She was going to Nanaimo to catch the ferry to the mainland. ...the islands that lie off the coast of mainland Britain.* N-SING: *the* N, N n

**main|line** /meɪnlaɪn/ 1 A **mainline** railway is a major railway between two important places. ❑ *...the first mainline railway to be built in Britain for almost a hundred years. ...London's mainline stations.* ADJ: ADJ n 2 You can use **mainline** to describe people, ideas, and activities that belong to the most central, conventional, and normal part of a tradition, institution, or business. ❑ *We observe a striking shift away from a labor theory among all mainline economists.* ADJ: ADJ n = mainstream

**main|ly** /meɪnli/ ◆◆◇ 1 You use **mainly** when mentioning the main reason or thing involved in something. ❑ *The stockmarket scandal is refusing to go away, mainly because there's still no consensus over how it should be dealt with... The birds live mainly on nectar.* ADV: ADV with cl/group, ADV with v = primarily 2 You use **mainly** when you are referring to a group and stating something that is true of most of it. ❑ *The African half of the audience was mainly from Senegal or Mali... The spacious main bedroom is mainly blue.* ADV: ADV with group = mostly

**main road** **(main roads)** A **main road** is an important road that leads from one town or city to another. ❑ *Webb turned off the main road and drove round to the car park.* N-COUNT

**main|spring** /meɪnsprɪŋ/ **(mainsprings)** If you say that an idea, emotion, or other factor is **the mainspring of** something, you mean that it is the most important reason or motive for that thing. [WRITTEN] ❑ *My life has been music, and a constant search for it has been the mainspring of my life... You begin to understand what actions were the mainspring of the story.* N-COUNT: usu sing, usu *the* N *of* n

**main|stay** /meɪnsteɪ/ **(mainstays)** If you describe something as **the mainstay of** a particular thing, you mean that it is the most basic part of it. ❑ *Fish and rice were the mainstays of the country's diet... This principle of collective bargaining has been a mainstay in labor relations in this country.* N-COUNT: usu *the* N *of* n

**main|stream** /meɪnstriːm/ **(mainstreams)** People, activities, or ideas that are part of the **mainstream** are regarded as the most typical, normal, and conventional because they belong to the same group or system as most others of their kind. ❑ *...people outside the economic mainstream... The show wanted to attract a mainstream audience.* N-COUNT: usu sing, usu with supp

**Main Street** 1 In small towns in the United States, the street where most of the shops are is often called **Main Street**. N-PROPER 2 **Main Street** is used by journalists to refer to the ordinary people of America who live in small towns rather than big cities or are not very rich. [AM] ❑ *This financial crisis had a much greater impact on Main Street.* N-UNCOUNT

**main|tain** /meɪnteɪn/ **(maintains, maintaining, maintained)** ◆◆◇ 1 If you **maintain** something, you continue to have it, and do not let it stop or grow weaker. ❑ *The Department maintains many close contacts with the chemical industry.* VERB V n 2 If you say that someone **maintains that** something is true, you mean that they have stated their opinion strongly but not everyone agrees with them or believes them. ❑ *He has maintained that the money was donated for international purposes... 'Not all feminism has to be like this,' Jo maintains... He had always maintained his innocence.* VERB = claim V that V with quote V n 3 If you **maintain** something **at** a particular rate or level, you keep it at that rate or level. ❑ *The government was right to maintain interest rates at a high level.* VERB V n *at* n 4 If you **maintain** a road, building, vehicle, or machine, you keep it in good condition by regularly checking it and repairing it when necessary. ❑ *The house costs a fortune to maintain... The cars are getting older and less well-maintained.* VERB = look after V n V-ed 5 If you **maintain** someone, you provide them with money and other things that they need. ❑ *...the basic costs of maintaining a child.* VERB = provide for, support V n

**main|te|nance** /meɪntɪnəns/ 1 The **maintenance** of a building, vehicle, road, or machine is the process of keeping it in good condition by regularly checking it and repairing it when necessary. ❑ *...maintenance work on government buildings... The window had been replaced last week during routine maintenance.* N-UNCOUNT 2 **Maintenance** is money that someone gives regularly to another person to pay for the things that the person needs. ❑ *...the government's plan to make absent fathers pay maintenance for their children.* N-UNCOUNT 3 If you ensure the **maintenance of** a state or process, you make sure that it continues. ❑ *...the maintenance of peace and stability in Asia.* N-UNCOUNT: usu N *of* n

**mai|son|ette** /meɪzənet/ **(maisonettes)** A **maisonette** is a flat that usually has a separate door to the outside from other flats in the same building. Many maisonettes are on two floors. [BRIT] N-COUNT

**maize** /meɪz/ **Maize** is a tall plant which produces long objects covered with yellow seeds called sweetcorn. It is often grown as a food crop. [mainly BRIT] ❑ *...vast fields of maize.* N-UNCOUNT

✓ in AM, usually use **corn**

**Maj** **Maj** is a written abbreviation for **Major** when it is used as a title. ❑ *...Maj D B Lee.* N-TITLE

**ma|jes|tic** /mədʒestɪk/ If you describe something or someone as **majestic**, you think they are very beautiful, dignified, and impressive. ❑ *...a majestic country home that once belonged to the Astor family.* ♦ **ma|jes|ti|cal|ly** /mədʒestɪkli/ *Fuji is a majestically beautiful mountain.* ADJ = grand; ADV: usu ADV with v, also ADV adj

**maj|es|ty** /mædʒɪsti/ **(majesties)** [1] You use majesty in expressions such as **Your Majesty** or **Her Majesty** when you are addressing or referring to a King or Queen. ❑ *His Majesty requests your presence in the royal chambers.* [2] **Majesty** is the quality of being beautiful, dignified, and impressive. ❑ *...the majesty of the mainland mountains.* N-VOC: poss N; PRON; poss PRON [politeness]; N-UNCOUNT

**ma|jor** /meɪdʒəʳ/ **(majors, majoring, majored)** ◆◆◆
[1] You use **major** when you want to describe something that is more important, serious, or significant than other things in a group or situation. ❑ *The major factor in the decision to stay or to leave was usually professional... Drug abuse has long been a major problem for the authorities there... Exercise has a major part to play in preventing and combating disease.* [2] A **major** is an officer who is one rank above captain in the British army or the United States army, air force, or marines. ❑ *...Major Alan Bulman.* [3] At a university or college in the United States, a student's **major** is the main subject that they are studying. ❑ *English majors would be asked to explore the roots of language.* [4] At a university or college in the United States, if a student is, for example, a geology **major**, geology is the main subject they are studying. ❑ *She was named the outstanding undergraduate history major at the University of Oklahoma.* [5] If a student at a university or college in the United States **majors in** a particular subject, that subject is the main one they study. ❑ *He majored in finance at Claremont Men's College in California.* [6] In music, a **major** scale is one in which the third note is two tones higher than the first. ❑ *...Mozart's Symphony No 35 in D Major.* [7] A **major** is a large or important company. [BUSINESS] ❑ *Oil majors need not fear being unable to sell their crude.* [8] **The majors** are groups of professional sports teams that compete against each other, especially in American baseball. [mainly AM] ❑ *I knew what I could do in the minor leagues, I just wanted a chance to prove myself in the majors.* [9] A **major** is an important sporting competition, especially in golf or tennis. ❑ *Sarazen became the first golfer to win all four majors.*
ADJ: ADJ n = key, crucial; N-COUNT; N-TITLE; N-VOC; N-COUNT: oft poss N; N-COUNT: n N; VERB; V in n; ADJ: n ADJ, ADJ n ≠ minor; N-COUNT: oft n N; N-PLURAL: the N; N-COUNT

**ma|jor|ette** /meɪdʒəret/ **(majorettes)** A **majorette** is one of a group of girls or young women who march at the front of a musical band in a procession. N-COUNT

**ma|jor gen|er|al** **(major generals)** also **major-general.** In Britain, a **major general** is a senior officer in the army, one rank above a brigadier. In the United States, a **major general** is a senior officer in the army, air force, or marines, one rank above brigadier general. N-COUNT; N-TITLE; N-VOC

**ma|jor|ity** /mədʒɒrɪti, AM -dʒɔːr-/ **(majorities)** ◆◆◇ [1] The **majority** of people or things in a group is more than half of them. ❑ *The vast majority of our cheeses are made with pasteurised milk... Still, a majority continue to support the treaty.* ● If a group is **in a majority** or **in the majority**, they form more than half of a larger group. ❑ *Surveys indicate that supporters of the treaty are still in the majority.* [2] A **majority** is the difference between the number of votes or seats in parliament or legislature that the winner gets in an election, and the number of votes or seats that the next person or party gets. ❑ *Members of parliament approved the move by a majority of ninety-nine... According to most opinion polls, he is set to win a clear majority.* [3] **Majority** is used to describe opinions, decisions, and systems of government that are supported by more than half the people involved. ❑ *...her continuing disagreement with the majority view... A majority vote of 75% is required from shareholders for the plan to go ahead.* [4] **Majority** is the state of legally being an adult. In Britain and most states in the United States, people reach their majority at the age of eighteen. ❑ *The age of majority in Romania is eighteen.* [5] → See also **absolute majority**, **moral majority**.
N-SING-COLL: usu sing, usu N of n ≠ minority; PHRASE: v-link PHR; N-COUNT: usu with supp; ADJ: ADJ n; N-UNCOUNT: oft with poss

**ma|jor league** **(major leagues)** [1] **The major leagues** are groups of professional sports teams that compete against each other, especially in American baseball. ❑ *Chandler was instrumental in making Jackie Robinson the first black player in the major leagues.* [2] **Major league** means connected with the major leagues in baseball. ❑ *...a town with no major league baseball.* [3] **Major league** people or institutions are important or successful. ❑ *James Hawes's first film boasts major-league stars.* [4] If someone **moves into the major league** or **makes it into the major league**, they become very successful in their career. [JOURNALISM] ❑ *Once a girl has made it into the major league every detail is mapped out by her agency.*
N-PLURAL: the N; ADJ: usu ADJ n; ADJ; PHRASE: Vs inflect

**make**

① CARRYING OUT AN ACTION
② CAUSING OR CHANGING
③ CREATING OR PRODUCING
④ LINK VERB USES
⑤ ACHIEVING OR REACHING
⑥ STATING AN AMOUNT OR TIME
⑦ PHRASAL VERBS

**①make** /meɪk/ **(makes, making, made)** ◆◆◆

> **Make** is used in a large number of expressions which are explained under other words in this dictionary. For example, the expression 'to make sense' is explained at 'sense'.

[1] You can use **make** with a wide range of nouns to indicate that someone performs an action or says something. For example, if you **make** a suggestion, you suggest something. ❑ *I'd just like to make a comment... I made a few phone calls... I think you're making a serious mistake.* [2] You can use **make** with certain nouns to indicate that someone does something well or badly. For example, if you **make** a success of something, you do it successfully, and if you **make** a mess of something, you do it very badly. ❑ *Apparently he made a mess of his audition... Are you really going to make a better job of it this time?* [3] If you **make as if to** do something or **make to** do something, you behave in a way that makes it seem that you are just about to do it. [WRITTEN] ❑ *Mary made as if to protest, then hesitated... He made to chase Davey, who ran back laughing.* [4] In cricket, if a player **makes** a particular number of runs, they score that number of runs. In baseball or American football, if a player **makes** a particular score, they achieve that score. ❑ *He made 1,972 runs for the county.*
VERB; V n; V n; V n; VERB; V n of n; V n of n; VERB; V as if to-inf; V to-inf; VERB = score; V amount

PHRASES [5] If you **make do with** something, you use or have it instead of something else that you do not have, although it is not as good. ❑ *Why make do with a copy if you can afford the genuine article?* [6] If you **make like** you are doing something, you act as if you are doing it, and if you **make like** someone, you act as if you are that person. [INFORMAL] ❑ *Bob makes like he's a fish blowing bubbles.*
PHRASE: make inflects, oft PHR with n; PHRASE: V inflects, PHR cl, PHR n

**②make** /meɪk/ **(makes, making, made)** ◆◆◆
⇒ Please look at category 11 to see if the expression you are looking for is shown under another headword. [1] If something **makes** you do something, it causes you to do it. ❑ *Grit from the highway made him cough... I was made to feel guilty and*
VERB; V n inf; be V-ed to-inf

*irresponsible.* 2 If you **make** someone do something, you force them to do it. ❑ *You can't make me do anything... They were made to pay $8.8 million in taxes.* VERB V n inf *be* V-ed to-inf

3 You use **make** to talk about causing someone or something to be a particular thing or to have a particular quality. For example, to **make** someone a star means to cause them to become a star, and to **make** someone angry means to cause them to become angry. ❑ *...James Bond, the role that made him a star... She made life very difficult for me... She's made it obvious that she's appalled by me... Rationing has made it easier to find some products like eggs, butter and meat... Does your film make a hero of Jim Garrison?* VERB V n n V n adj V *it* adj that V *it* adj to-inf V n *of* n

4 If you say that one thing or person **makes** another seem, for example, small, stupid, or good, you mean that they cause them to seem small, stupid, or good in comparison, even though they are not. ❑ *They live in fantasy worlds which make Euro Disney seem uninventive.* VERB V n inf adj/prep/n

5 If you **make yourself** understood, heard, or known, you succeed in getting people to understand you, hear you, or know that you are there. ❑ *Aron couldn't speak Polish. I made myself understood with difficulty.* VERB V pron-refl -ed

6 If you **make** someone something, you appoint them to a particular job, role, or position. ❑ *Mr Blair made him transport minister.* VERB V n n

7 If you **make** something **into** something else, you change it in some way so that it becomes that other thing. ❑ *We made it into a beautiful home.* VERB V n *into* n

8 To **make** a total or score a particular amount means to increase it to that amount. ❑ *This makes the total cost of the bulb and energy £27.* VERB V n amount

9 When someone **makes** a friend or an enemy, someone becomes their friend or their enemy, often because of a particular thing they have done. ❑ *Lorenzo was a natural leader who made friends easily... He was unruly in class and made an enemy of most of his teachers.* VERB V n V n *of* n

10 If someone **makes something of** themselves or **makes something of** their **life**, they become successful. ❑ *My father lived long enough to see that I'd made something of myself... The nuns who taught him urged him to make something of his life and he did.* PHRASE: V inflects

11 to **make friends** → see **friend**.

③ **make** /meɪk/ **(makes, making, made)** ◆◆◆

1 To **make** something means to produce, construct, or create it. ❑ *She made her own bread... Having curtains made professionally can be costly... They make compost out of all kinds of waste.* VERB V n *have* n V-ed V n *from/out of* n

2 If you **make** a note or list, you write something down in that form. ❑ *Mr Perry made a note in his book... Make a list of your questions beforehand.* VERB = write V n V n

3 If you **make** rules or laws, you decide what these should be. ❑ *The police don't make the laws, they merely enforce them.* VERB V n

4 If you **make** money, you get it by working for it, by selling something, or by winning it. ❑ *I think every business's goal is to make money... Can it be moral to make so much money out of a commodity which is essential to life?* VERB V n V n *out of/from* n

5 If something **makes** something else, it is responsible for the success of that thing. ❑ *What really makes the book are the beautiful designs.* VERB V n

6 The **make** of something such as a car or radio is the name of the company that made it. ❑ *...a certain make of wristwatch.* N-COUNT: supp N, N *of* n = brand

7 If you say that someone is **on the make**, you disapprove of them because they are trying to get a lot of money or power, possibly by illegal or immoral methods. PHRASE: v-link PHR [disapproval]

④ **make** /meɪk/ **(makes, making, made)** ◆◆◆

1 You can use **make** to say that someone or something has the right qualities for a particular task or role. For example, if you say that someone will **make** a good politician, you mean that they have the right qualities to be a good politician. ❑ *You've a very good idea there. It will make a good book... I'm very fond of Maurice and I'd make him a good wife.* V-LINK V n V n n

2 If people **make** a particular pattern such as a line or a circle, they arrange themselves in this way. ❑ *A group of people made a circle around the Pentagon.* V-LINK = form V n

3 You can use **make** to say what two numbers add up to. ❑ *Four twos make eight.* V-LINK V amount

⑤ **make** /meɪk/ **(makes, making, made)** ◆◆◆

1 If someone **makes** a particular team or **makes** a particular high position, they do so well that they are put in that team or get that position. ❑ *The athletes are just happy to make the British team... He knew he was never going to make director.* VERB V n V n

2 If you **make** a place in or by a particular time, you get there in or by that time, often with some difficulty. ❑ *They were trying to make New Orleans by nightfall.* VERB V n prep

**PHRASES** 3 If you **make it** somewhere, you succeed in getting there, especially in time to do something. ❑ *...the hostages who never made it home... I just made it!* PHRASE: V inflects, oft PHR prep/adv

4 If you **make it**, you are successful in achieving something difficult, or in surviving through a very difficult period. ❑ *I believe I have the talent to make it.* PHRASE: V inflects

5 If you cannot **make it**, you are unable to attend an event that you have been invited to. ❑ *He hadn't been able to make it to our dinner.* PHRASE: V inflects, usu with brd-neg, oft PHR *to* n

⑥ **make** /meɪk/ **(makes, making, made)** ◆◆◆

1 You use **make it** when saying what you calculate or guess an amount to be. ❑ *All I want to know is how many T-shirts Jim Martin has got. I make it three.* VERB V *it* amount

2 You use **make it** when saying what time your watch says it is. ❑ *I make it nearly 9.30... 'What time d'you make it?' — 'Thirteen past.'* VERB V *it* n Also V n n

⑦ **make** /meɪk/ **(makes, making, made)** ◆◆◆

♦ **make for** 1 If you **make for** a place, you move towards it. ❑ *He rose from his seat and made for the door.* PHRASAL VERB V P n

2 If something **makes for** another thing, it causes or helps to cause that thing to happen or exist. [INFORMAL] ❑ *A happy parent makes for a happy child.* PHRASAL VERB V P n

♦ **make of** If you ask a person what they **make of** something, you want to know what their impression, opinion, or understanding of it is. ❑ *Nancy wasn't sure what to make of Mick's apology.* PHRASAL VERB V P n

♦ **make off** If you **make off**, you leave somewhere as quickly as possible, often in order to escape. ❑ *They broke free and made off in a stolen car.* PHRASAL VERB V P

♦ **make off with** If you **make off with** something, you steal it and take it away with you. ❑ *Masked robbers broke in and made off with $8,000.* PHRASAL VERB V P P n

♦ **make out** 1 If you **make** something **out**, you manage with difficulty to see or hear it. ❑ *I could just make out a tall, pale, shadowy figure tramping through the undergrowth... She thought she heard a name. She couldn't make it out, though... I heard the voices, but couldn't make out what they were saying.* PHRASAL VERB V P n (not pron) V n P V P wh

2 If you try to **make** something **out**, you try to understand it or decide whether or not it is true. ❑ *I couldn't make it out at all... It is hard to make out what criteria are used... At first I thought it was an accident, but as far as I can make out, the police consider that's unlikely.* PHRASAL VERB = understand V n P V P wh V P

3 If you **make out that** something is the case or **make** something **out to** be the case, you try to cause people to believe that it is the case. ❑ *They were trying to make out that I'd actually done it... I don't think it was as glorious as everybody made it out to be... He was never half as bad as his teachers made out.* PHRASAL VERB V P that V n P to-inf V P

4 If you **make out** a case **for** something, you try to establish or prove that it is the best thing to do. ❑ *You could certainly make out a case for this point of view.* PHRASAL VERB V P n (not pron) *for/against* n Also V n P

5 When you **make out** a cheque, receipt, or order form, you write all the necessary information on it. ❑ *If you would like to send a donation, you can make a cheque out to Feed the Children... I'm going to make out a receipt for you.* PHRASAL VERB V n P *to* n V P n (not pron)

6 If two people **are making out**, they are engaged in sexual activity. [mainly AM, INFORMAL] ❑ *...pictures of the couple making out in their underwear on the beach.* PHRASAL VERB pl-n V P Also V P *with* n

♦ **make up** 1 The people or things that **make up** something are the members or parts that form that thing. ❑ *North Africans make up the largest and poorest immigrant group in the country... Insects are made up of tens of thousands of proteins.* PHRASAL VERB = form, constitute V P n (not pron) *be* V-ed P *of* n Also V n P

2 If you **make up** something such as a story or excuse, you invent it, sometimes in order to de- PHRASAL VERB

ceive people. ❑ *I think it's very unkind of you to make up stories about him... I'm not making it up. The character exists in real life.* [3] If you **make** yourself **up** or if someone else **makes** you **up**, make-up such as powder or lipstick is put on your face. ❑ *She spent too much time making herself up... She chose Maggie to make her up for her engagement photographs... I can't be bothered to make up my face.* [4] If you **make up** an amount, you add something to it so that it is as large as it should be. ❑ *Less than half of the money that students receive is in the form of grants, and loans have made up the difference... The team had six professionals and made the number up with five amateurs... For every £100 you invest into a pension plan the Inland Revenue makes it up to £125.* [5] If you **make up** time or hours, you work some extra hours because you have previously taken some time off work. ❑ *They'll have to make up time lost during the strike.* [6] If two people **make up** or **make it up** after a quarrel or disagreement, they become friends again. ❑ *She came back and they made up... They never made up the quarrel... They should make up with their ex-enemy in the West... I'll make it up with him again sometime soon.* [7] If you **make up** something such as food or medicine, you prepare it by mixing or putting different things together. ❑ *Prepare the souffle dish before making up the souffle mixture.* [8] If you **make up** a bed, you put sheets and blankets on it so that someone can sleep there. ❑ *Her mother made up a bed in her old room.*

V P n (not pron) / V n P / PHRASAL VERB / V n P / V n P / V P n (not pron) / PHRASAL VERB / V P n (not pron) / V n P / V n P to amount / PHRASAL VERB / V P n / Also V n P / PHRASAL VERB / pl-n V P / pl-n V P n / V P with n / V it P with n / PHRASAL VERB / V P n / Also V n P / PHRASAL VERB / V P n (not pron)

♦ **make up for** To **make up for** a bad experience or the loss of something means to make the situation better or make the person involved happier. ❑ *Ask for an extra compensation payment to make up for the stress you have been caused.*

PHRASAL VERB = compensate for / V P P n

♦ **make up to** If you say that you will **make it up to** someone, you are promising that you will do something good for them after they have been upset or disappointed, especially by you. ❑ *I'll make it up to you, I promise... I must make it up to him for the awful intrusion of last night.*

PHRASAL VERB / V it P P n / V it P P n for n/-ing

**make-believe** [1] If someone is living in a **make-believe** world, they are pretending that things are better, different, or more exciting than they really are instead of facing up to reality. ❑ *...the glamorous make-believe world of show business.* [2] You use **make-believe** to refer to the activity involved when a child plays a game in which they pretend something, for example that they are someone else. ❑ *She used to play games of make-believe with her elder sister. ...his make-believe playmate.* [3] You use **make-believe** to describe things, for example in a play or film, that imitate or copy something real, but which are not what they appear to be. ❑ *The violence in those films was too unreal, it was make-believe.*

N-UNCOUNT disapproval / N-UNCOUNT / ADJ

**make|over** /meɪkoʊvəʳ/ **(makeovers)** [1] If a person or room is given a **makeover**, their appearance is improved, usually by an expert. ❑ *She received a cosmetic makeover at a beauty salon as a birthday gift.* [2] If an organization or system is given a **makeover**, important changes are made in order to improve it. ❑ *The biggest makeover has been in TV drama.*

N-COUNT / N-COUNT

**mak|er** /meɪkəʳ/ **(makers)** [1] The **maker** of a product is the firm that manufactures it. ❑ *...Japan's two largest car makers.* [2] You can refer to the person who makes something as its **maker**. ❑ *...the makers of news and current affairs programmes.* [3] → See also **peacemaker**.

◆◆◇ N-COUNT: usu with supp / N-COUNT: usu with supp

**make|shift** /meɪkʃɪft/ **Makeshift** things are temporary and usually of poor quality, but they are used because there is nothing better available. ❑ *...the cardboard boxes and makeshift shelters of the homeless.*

ADJ: usu ADJ n

**make-up** also **makeup.** [1] **Make-up** consists of things such as lipstick, eye shadow, and powder which some women put on their faces to make themselves look more attractive or which actors use to change or improve their appearance. ❑ *Normally she wore little make-up.* [2] Someone's **make-up** is their nature and the various qualities in their character. ❑ *There was some fatal flaw in his makeup, and as time went on he lapsed into long silences or became off-hand.* [3] The **make-up** of something consists of its different parts and the way these parts are arranged. ❑ *The ideological make-up of the unions is now radically different from what it had been.*

◆◇◇ N-UNCOUNT / N-UNCOUNT: with supp, usu poss N = personality / N-UNCOUNT: with supp

**make|weight** /meɪkweɪt/ **(makeweights)** If you describe someone or something as a **makeweight**, you think that they are not good or valuable and that they have been included in an activity in order to fill up a gap. ❑ *He has not been signed to the club as a makeweight to fill out the numbers.*

N-COUNT disapproval

**mak|ing** /meɪkɪŋ/ **(makings)** [1] The **making** of something is the act or process of producing or creating it. ❑ *...Salamon's book about the making of this movie.*

N-UNCOUNT: the N of n, n N

**PHRASES** [2] If you describe a person or thing as something **in the making**, you mean that they are going to become known or recognized as that thing. ❑ *Her drama teacher is confident Julie is a star in the making.* [3] If something **is the making of** a person or thing, it is the reason that they become successful or become very much better than they used to be. ❑ *This discovery may yet be the making of him.* [4] If you say that a person or thing **has the makings of** something, you mean it seems possible or likely that they will become that thing, as they have the necessary qualities. ❑ *Godfrey had the makings of a successful journalist.* [5] If you say that something such as a problem you have is **of** your **own making**, you mean you have caused or created it yourself. ❑ *Some of the university's financial troubles are of its own making.*

PHRASE: usu n PHR / PHRASE: V inflects, PHR n / PHRASE: V inflects, PHR n / PHRASE: v-link PHR

**mal-** /mæl-/ **Mal-** is added to words in order to form new words which describe things that are bad or unpleasant, or that are unsuccessful or imperfect. ❑ *Forty per cent of the population is suffering from malnutrition... The animals were seriously maltreated.*

PREFIX

**mal|ad|just|ed** /mælədʒʌstɪd/ If you describe a child as **maladjusted**, you mean that they have psychological problems and behave in a way which is not acceptable to society. ❑ *...a school for maladjusted children.*

ADJ

**mal|ad|min|is|tra|tion** /mælædmɪnɪstreɪʃᵊn/ **Maladministration** is the act or process of running a system or organization incorrectly. [FORMAL] ❑ *...a request to investigate a claim about maladministration.*

N-UNCOUNT

**mala|droit** /mælədrɔɪt/ If you describe someone as **maladroit**, you mean that they are clumsy or handle situations badly. [FORMAL] ❑ *Some of his first interviews with the press were rather maladroit.*

ADJ

**mala|dy** /mælədi/ **(maladies)** [1] A **malady** is an illness or disease. [OLD-FASHIONED] ❑ *He was stricken at twenty-one with a crippling malady.* [2] In written English, people sometimes use **maladies** to refer to serious problems in a society or situation. ❑ *When apartheid is over the maladies will linger on.*

N-COUNT / N-COUNT

**ma|laise** /mæleɪz/ [1] **Malaise** is a state in which there is something wrong with a society or group, for which there does not seem to be a quick or easy solution. [FORMAL] ❑ *There is no easy short-term solution to Britain's chronic economic malaise.* [2] **Malaise** is a state in which people feel dissatisfied or unhappy but feel unable to change, usually because they do not know what is wrong. [FORMAL] ❑ *He complained of depression, headaches and malaise.*

N-UNCOUNT / N-UNCOUNT

**ma|laria** /məleəriə/ **Malaria** is a serious disease carried by mosquitoes which causes periods of fever.

N-UNCOUNT

**ma|lar|ial** /məleəriəl/ You can use **malarial** to refer to things connected with malaria or areas

ADJ: usu ADJ n

which are affected by malaria. ❑ *...malarial parasites.*

**Ma|lay** /məleɪ/ **(Malays)** 1 **Malay** means belonging or relating to the people, language, or culture of the largest racial group in Malaysia. ADJ: usu ADJ n 2 A **Malay** is a member of the largest racial group in Malaysia. N-COUNT 3 **Malay** is a language that is spoken in Malaysia and in parts of Indonesia. N-UNCOUNT

**Ma|lay|sian** /məleɪʒən/ **(Malaysians)** Something that is **Malaysian** belongs or relates to Malaysia or to its people. ADJ ♦ **Malaysians** are people who are Malaysian. N-COUNT

**mal|con|tent** /mælkəntent/ **(malcontents)** N-COUNT: usu pl [disapproval] You can describe people as **malcontents** when you disapprove of the fact that they are dissatisfied with a situation and want to change. [FORMAL] ❑ *Five years ago a band of malcontents, mainly half-educated radicals, seized power.*

**male** /meɪl/ **(males)** ◆◆◇ 1 Someone who is **male** is a man or a boy. ADJ ≠female ❑ *Many women achievers appear to pose a threat to their male colleagues... Most of the demonstrators were white and male.* ♦ **male|ness** N-UNCOUNT *...the solidarity among men which is part of maleness.* 2 Men and boys are sometimes referred to as **males** when they are being considered as a type. N-COUNT = man ≠female ❑ *A high proportion of crime is perpetrated by young males in their teens and twenties.* 3 **Male** means relating, belonging, or affecting men rather than women. ADJ: ADJ n ≠female ❑ *The rate of male unemployment in Britain is now the third worst in Europe. ...a deep male voice.* 4 You can refer to any creature that belongs to the sex that cannot lay eggs or have babies as a **male**. N-COUNT ≠female ❑ *Males and females take turns brooding the eggs.* ♦ **Male** is also an adjective. ADJ ≠female ❑ *After mating the male wasps tunnel through the sides of their nursery.*

**male chau|vin|ism** If you accuse a man of **male chauvinism**, you disapprove of him because his beliefs and behaviour show that he thinks men are naturally superior to women. N-UNCOUNT [disapproval]

**male chau|vin|ist** **(male chauvinists)** If you describe an attitude or remark as **male chauvinist**, you are critical of it because you think it is based on the belief that men are naturally superior to women. ADJ: usu ADJ n [disapproval] ❑ *The male chauvinist attitude of some people in the company could get you down.* ♦ A **male chauvinist** is a man who has male chauvinist views. N-COUNT ❑ *I'm not a male chauvinist.*

**male-dominated** A **male-dominated** society, organization, or area of activity is one in which men have most of the power and influence. ADJ: usu ADJ n ❑ *...the male-dominated world of journalism.*

**mal|efac|tor** /mælɪfæktəʳ/ **(malefactors)** A **malefactor** is someone who has done something bad or illegal. N-COUNT = wrong-doer [FORMAL] ❑ *...a well-known criminal lawyer who had saved many a malefactor from going to jail.*

**ma|levo|lent** /məlevələnt/ A **malevolent** person deliberately tries to cause harm or evil. ADJ ≠benevolent [FORMAL] ❑ *Her stare was malevolent, her mouth a thin line.* ♦ **ma|levo|lence** N-UNCOUNT *...a rare streak of malevolence.* ♦ **ma|levo|lent|ly** ADV *Mark watched him malevolently.*

**mal|for|ma|tion** /mælfɔːʳmeɪʃən/ **(malformations)** A **malformation** in a person's body is a part which does not have the proper shape or form, especially when it has been like this since birth. N-COUNT = deformity [WRITTEN] ❑ *...babies with a high incidence of congenital malformations.*

**mal|formed** /mælfɔːʳmd/ If people or parts of their body are **malformed**, they do not have the shape or form that they are supposed to, especially when they have been like this since birth. ADJ = deformed [FORMAL] ❑ *...malformed babies... More rarely, the tubes have been malformed from birth.*

**mal|func|tion** /mælfʌŋkʃən/ **(malfunctions, malfunctioning, malfunctioned)** If a machine or part of the body **malfunctions**, it fails to work properly. VERB [FORMAL] ❑ *The radiation can damage microprocessors and computer memories, causing them to malfunction.* V ♦ **Malfunction** is also a noun. N-COUNT ❑ *There must have been a computer malfunction.*

**mal|ice** /mælɪs/ **Malice** is behaviour that is intended to harm people or their reputations, or cause them embarrassment and upset. N-UNCOUNT ❑ *There was a strong current of malice in many of his portraits.*

**ma|li|cious** /məlɪʃəs/ If you describe someone's words or actions as **malicious**, you mean that they are intended to harm people or their reputation, or cause them embarrassment and upset. ADJ ❑ *That might merely have been malicious gossip.* ♦ **ma|li|cious|ly** ADV: usu ADV with v, also ADV adj *...his maliciously accurate imitation of Hubert de Burgh.*

**ma|lign** /məlaɪn/ **(maligns, maligning, maligned)** 1 If you **malign** someone, you say unpleasant and untrue things about them. VERB [FORMAL] ❑ *We maligned him dreadfully when you come to think of it.* V n 2 If something is **malign**, it causes harm. ADJ: ADJ n = harmful ≠benign [FORMAL] ❑ *...the malign influence jealousy had on their lives.* 3 → See also **much-maligned**.

**ma|lig|nan|cy** /məlɪgnənsi/ **(malignancies)** A tumour or disease in a state of **malignancy** is out of control and is likely to cause death. N-VAR [MEDICAL] ❑ *Tissue that is removed during the operation is checked for signs of malignancy.*

**ma|lig|nant** /məlɪgnənt/ 1 A **malignant** tumour or disease is out of control and likely to cause death. ADJ: usu ADJ n ≠benign [MEDICAL] ❑ *She developed a malignant breast tumour.* 2 If you say that someone is **malignant**, you think they are cruel and like to cause harm. ADJ ❑ *He said that we were evil, malignant and mean.*

**ma|lin|ger** /məlɪŋgəʳ/ **(malingers, malingering, malingered)** If someone **is malingering**, they pretend to be ill in order to avoid working. VERB: usu cont [disapproval] V ❑ *She was told by her doctor that she was malingering.*

**mall** /mɔːl, mæl/ **(malls)** A **mall** is a very large enclosed shopping area. N-COUNT

**mal|lard** /mælɑːʳd/ **(mallards)** A **mallard** is a kind of wild duck which is very common. N-COUNT

**mal|le|able** /mæliəbəl/ 1 If you say that someone is **malleable**, you mean that they are easily influenced or controlled by other people. ADJ [WRITTEN] ❑ *She was young enough to be malleable.* 2 A substance that is **malleable** is soft and can easily be made into different shapes. ADJ ≠rigid ❑ *Silver is the most malleable of all metals.*

**mal|let** /mælɪt/ **(mallets)** A **mallet** is a wooden hammer with a square head. N-COUNT → See picture on page 1709.

**mall rat** **(mall rats)** **Mall rats** are young people who spend a lot of time hanging around in shopping malls with their friends. N-COUNT [disapproval] [AM]

**mal|nour|ished** /mælnʌrɪʃt/ If someone is **malnourished**, they are physically weak because they do not eat enough food or do not eat the right kind of food. ADJ: usu v-link ADJ = undernourished ❑ *About thirty per-cent of the country's children were malnourished.*

**mal|nu|tri|tion** /mælnjuːtrɪʃən, AM -nuːt-/ If someone is suffering from **malnutrition**, they are physically weak and extremely thin because they have not eaten enough food. N-UNCOUNT ❑ *Infections are more likely in those suffering from malnutrition.*

**mal|odor|ous** /mæloʊdərəs/ Something that is **malodorous** has an unpleasant smell. ADJ: usu ADJ n = smelly [LITERARY] ❑ *...tons of malodorous garbage bags.*

**mal|prac|tice** /mælpræktɪs/ **(malpractices)** If you accuse someone of **malpractice**, you are accusing them of breaking the law or the rules of their profession in order to gain some advantage for themselves. N-VAR: oft N n [FORMAL] ❑ *There were only one or two serious allegations of malpractice. ...alleged financial malpractices.*

**malt** /mɔːlt/ **(malts)** 1 **Malt** is a substance made from grain that has been soaked in water and then dried in a hot oven. Malt is used in the production of whisky, beer, and other alcoholic drinks. N-UNCOUNT ❑ *German beer has traditionally been made from just four ingredients – hops, malt, yeast and wa-*

ter. [2] A **malt** is a drink made from malted milk and sometimes other flavourings. [AM] N-COUNT

**malt|ed** /mɔːltɪd/ **Malted** barley has been soaked in water and then dried in a hot oven. It is used in the production of whisky, beer, and other alcoholic drinks. ADJ: ADJ n

**Mal|tese** /mɒltiːz/ **(Maltese)** [1] **Maltese** means belonging or relating to Malta, or to its people, language, or culture. ADJ: usu ADJ n [2] A **Maltese** is a Maltese citizen, or a person of Maltese origin. N-COUNT [3] **Maltese** is a language spoken by people who live in Malta. N-UNCOUNT

**mal|treat** /mælt̲riːt/ **(maltreats, maltreating, maltreated)** If a person or animal **is maltreated**, they are treated badly, especially by being hurt. ❑ *He said that he was not tortured or maltreated during his detention.* VERB: usu passive = mistreat *be* V-ed

**mal|treat|ment** /mælt̲riːtmənt/ **Maltreatment** is cruel behaviour, especially involving hurting a person or animal. ❑ *2,000 prisoners died as a result of torture and maltreatment.* N-UNCOUNT: oft N *of* n = mistreatment

**malt whis|ky** **(malt whiskies)** **Malt whisky** or **malt** is whisky that is made from malt. N-MASS

**mam** /mæm/ **(mams)** **Mam** is used to mean mother. [BRIT, DIALECT] ❑ *You sit here and rest, Mam.* N-FAMILY = mum

**mama** /məmɑː/ **(mamas)** **Mama** means the same as **mother**. [BRIT, OLD-FASHIONED] N-FAMILY

**mam|ma** /mɑːmə/ **(mammas)** also **mama.** **Mamma** means the same as **mother**. [AM, INFORMAL] N-FAMILY = mommy

**mam|mal** /mæməl/ **(mammals)** **Mammals** are animals such as humans, dogs, lions, and whales. In general, female mammals give birth to babies rather than laying eggs, and feed their young with milk. N-COUNT

**mam|ma|lian** /mæme̲ɪliən/ In zoology, **mammalian** means relating to mammals. [TECHNICAL] ❑ *The disease can spread from one mammalian species to another.* ADJ: ADJ n

**mam|ma|ry** /mæməri/ **Mammary** means relating to the breasts. [TECHNICAL] ❑ *...the mammary glands.* ADJ: ADJ n

**mam|mo|gram** /mæməgræm/ **(mammograms)** A **mammogram** is a test used to check whether women have breast cancer, using x-rays. N-COUNT

**Mam|mon** /mæmən/ You can use **Mammon** to refer to money and business activities if you want to show your disapproval of people who think that becoming rich is the most important thing in life. ❑ *It is not every day that one meets a business-person who is not obsessed with Mammon.* N-UNCOUNT [disapproval]

**mam|moth** /mæməθ/ **(mammoths)** [1] You can use **mammoth** to emphasize that a task or change is very large and needs a lot of effort to achieve. ❑ *...the mammoth task of relocating the library.* ADJ: usu ADJ n [emphasis] = massive [2] A **mammoth** was an animal like an elephant, with very long tusks and long hair, that lived a long time ago but no longer exists. N-COUNT

**mam|my** /mæmi/ **(mammies)** In some dialects of English, **mammy** is used to mean mother. [INFORMAL] N-FAMILY

**man** /mæn/ **(men, mans, manning, manned)** ◆◆◆
[1] A **man** is an adult male human being. ❑ *He had not expected the young man to reappear before evening... I have always regarded him as a man of integrity. ...the thousands of men, women and children who are facing starvation.* N-COUNT [2] **Man** and **men** are sometimes used to refer to all human beings, including both males and females. Some people dislike this use. ❑ *The chick initially has no fear of man.* N-VAR [3] If you say that a man is, for example, **a gambling man** or **an outdoors man**, you mean that he likes gambling or outdoor activities. ❑ *Are you a gambling man, Mr Graham?* N-COUNT: supp N [4] If you say that a man is, for example, **a London man** or **an Oxford man**, you mean that he comes from London or Oxford, or went to university there. ❑ *...as the Stockport man collected his winnings.* N-COUNT: n-proper N [5] If you refer to a particular company's or organization's **man**, you mean a man who works for or represents that company or organization. [JOURNALISM] ❑ *...the Daily Telegraph's man in Abu Dhabi.* N-COUNT: poss N [6] Some people refer to a woman's husband, lover, or boyfriend as her **man**. [INFORMAL] ❑ *...if they see your man cuddle you in the kitchen or living room.* N-SING: poss N [7] In very informal social situations, **man** is sometimes used as a greeting or form of address to a man. ❑ *Hey wow, man! Where d'you get those boots?* N-VOC [formulae] [8] If you **man** something such as a place or machine, you operate it or are in charge of it. ❑ *...the person manning the phone at the complaints department...* V n *The station is seldom manned in the evening.* V n VERB [9] → See also **manned, ladies' man, no-man's land.**

PHRASES [10] If you say that a man is **man enough** to do something, you mean that he has the necessary courage or ability to do it. ❑ *I told him that he should be man enough to admit he had done wrong.* PHRASE: v-link PHR [11] If you describe a man as **a man's man**, you mean that he has qualities which make him popular with other men rather than with women. PHRASE: v-link PHR [12] If you say that a man **is** his **own man**, you approve of the fact that he makes his decisions and his plans himself, and does not depend on other people. ❑ *Be your own man. Make up your own mind.* PHRASE: V inflects [approval] [13] If you say that a group of men are, do, or think something **to a man**, you are emphasizing that every one of them is, does, or thinks that thing. ❑ *To a man, the surveyors blamed the government.* PHRASE: PHR with v [emphasis] [14] A **man-to-man** conversation or meeting takes place between two men, especially two men who meet to discuss a serious personal matter. ❑ *He called me to his office for a man-to-man talk... Me and Ben should sort this out man to man.* PHRASE: PHR n, PHR after v [15] **the man in the street** → see **street.** **man of the world** → see **world.**

**-man** /-mæn/ **-man** combines with numbers to make adjectives which indicate that something involves or is intended for that number of people. ❑ *The four-man crew on board the fishing trawler. ...a two-man tent.* COMB in ADJ: ADJ n = -person

**mana|cle** /mænəkəl/ **(manacles, manacling, manacled)** [1] **Manacles** are metal devices attached to a prisoner's wrists or legs in order to prevent him or her from moving or escaping. N-COUNT: usu pl [2] If a prisoner **is manacled**, their wrists or legs are put in manacles in order to prevent them from moving or escaping. ❑ *His hands were manacled behind his back... He was manacled by the police.* VERB: usu passive *be* V-ed prep/adv *be* V-ed

**man|age** /mænɪdʒ/ **(manages, managing, managed)** ◆◆◇ [1] If you **manage** an organization, business, or system, or the people who work in it, you are responsible for controlling them. ❑ *Within two years he was managing the store...* V n *Most factories in the area are obsolete and badly managed...* V n *There is a lack of confidence in the government's ability to manage the economy.* V n VERB = run, organize [2] If you **manage** time, money, or other resources, you deal with them carefully and do not waste them. ❑ *In a busy world, managing your time is increasingly important...* V n *Josh expects me to manage all the household expenses on very little.* V n VERB [3] If you **manage to** do something, especially something difficult, you succeed in doing it. ❑ *Somehow, he'd managed to persuade Kay to buy one for him...* V to-inf *Over the past 12 months the company has managed a 10 per cent improvement.* V n VERB [4] If you **manage**, you succeed in coping with a difficult situation. ❑ *She had managed perfectly well without medication for three years...* V *I am managing, but I could not possibly give up work.* V VERB = cope [5] If you say that you can **manage** an amount of time or money for something, you mean that you can afford to spend that time or money on it. ❑ *'All right, I can manage a fiver,' McMinn said with reluctance.* V n VERB = spare [6] If you say that someone **managed** a particular response, such as a laugh or a greeting, you mean that it was difficult for them to do it because they were feeling sad or upset. ❑ *He looked dazed as he spoke to reporters, managing only a weak smile.* V n VERB [7] You say **'I can manage'** or **'I'll manage'** as a way of refusing someone's offer of help CONVENTION and insisting on doing something by yourself. ❑ *I know you mean well, but I can manage by myself.*

**man|age|able** /mænɪdʒəbᵊl/ Something that is **manageable** is of a size, quantity, or level of difficulty that people are able to deal with. ❑ *He will now try to cut down the task to a manageable size... The present flow of refugees was manageable.* ADJ

**man|age|ment** /mænɪdʒmənt/ **(managements)** ◆◆◇ [1] **Management** is the control and organizing of a business or other organization. ❑ *The zoo needed better management rather than more money... The dispute is about wages, working conditions and the management of the mining industry. ...the responsibility for its day to day management.* N-UNCOUNT [2] You can refer to the people who control and organize a business or other organization as the **management**. [BUSINESS] ❑ *The management is doing its best to improve the situation... We need to get more women into top management.* N-VAR-COLL [3] **Management** is the way people control different parts of their lives. ❑ *...her management of her professional life. ...intelligent money management, for example paying big bills monthly where possible.* N-UNCOUNT: usu with supp

**man|age|ment buy|out** **(management buyouts)** A **management buyout** is the buying of a company by its managers. The abbreviation **MBO** is also used. [BUSINESS] ❑ *Of the first three franchises to be awarded, two went to management buyouts led by former BR executives.* N-COUNT

**man|age|ment con|sult|ant** **(management consultants)** A **management consultant** is someone whose job is to advise companies on the most efficient ways to run their business. [BUSINESS] ❑ *...a leading firm of management consultants.* N-COUNT

**man|ag|er** /mænɪdʒəʳ/ **(managers)** ◆◆◇ [1] A **manager** is a person who is responsible for running part of or the whole of a business organization. ❑ *The chef, staff and managers are all Chinese. ...a retired bank manager.* N-COUNT [2] The **manager** of a pop star or other entertainer is the person who looks after their business interests. N-COUNT [3] The **manager** of a sports team is the person responsible for training the players and organizing the way they play. In American English, **manager** is only used for baseball; in other sports, **coach** is used instead. N-COUNT

**man|ag|er|ess** /mænɪdʒəres/ **(manageresses)** The **manageress** of a shop, restaurant, or other small business is the woman who is responsible for running it. Some women object to this word and prefer to be called a 'manager'. ❑ *...the manageress of a betting shop.* N-COUNT

**mana|gerial** /mænɪdʒɪəriᵊl/ **Managerial** means relating to the work of a manager. ❑ *...his managerial skills. ...a managerial career... Some see themselves as the provider of ideas, while others view their role as essentially managerial.* ADJ: usu ADJ n

**man|ag|ing di|rec|tor** **(managing directors)** The **managing director** of a company is the most important working director, and is in charge of the way the company is managed. The abbreviation **MD** is also used. [mainly BRIT, BUSINESS] N-COUNT

☑ in AM, usually use **chief executive officer**

**man|da|rin** /mændərɪn/ **(mandarins)** [1] Journalists sometimes use **mandarin** to refer to someone who has an important job in the Civil Service. [BRIT] ❑ *...Foreign Office mandarins.* N-COUNT: usu supp N [2] **Mandarin** is the official language of China. N-UNCOUNT [3] A **mandarin** or a **mandarin orange** is a small orange whose skin comes off easily. N-COUNT [4] A **mandarin** was, in former times, an important government official in China. N-COUNT

**man|date** /mændeɪt/ **(mandates, mandating, mandated)** [1] If a government or other elected body has a **mandate** to carry out a particular policy or task, they have the authority to carry it out as a result of winning an election or vote. ❑ *The President and his supporters are almost certain to read this vote as a mandate for continued economic reform.* N-COUNT: oft N *for* n, N to-inf [2] If someone is given a **mandate** to carry out a particular policy or task, they are given the official authority to do it. ❑ *How much longer does the independent prosecutor have a mandate to pursue this investigation?* N-COUNT: oft N to-inf [3] You can refer to the fixed length of time that a country's leader or government remains in office as their **mandate**. [FORMAL] ❑ *...his intention to leave politics once his mandate ends.* N-COUNT: usu with poss [4] When someone **is mandated to** carry out a particular policy or task, they are given the official authority to do it. [FORMAL] ❑ *He'd been mandated by the West African Economic Community to go in and to enforce a ceasefire... The elections are mandated by a peace accord signed by the government last May.* VERB: usu passive; *be* V-ed to-inf; *be* V-ed [5] To **mandate** something means to make it mandatory. [AM] ❑ *The proposed initiative would mandate a reduction of carbon dioxide of 40%... Quebec mandated that all immigrants send their children to French schools. ...constitutionally mandated civil rights.* VERB; V n; V that; V-ed

**man|da|tory** /mændətri ɑm -tɔːri/ [1] If an action or procedure is **mandatory**, people have to do it, because it is a rule or a law. [FORMAL] ❑ *...the mandatory retirement age of 65... Attendance is mandatory.* ADJ = *compulsory* [2] If a crime carries a **mandatory** punishment, that punishment is fixed by law for all cases, in contrast to crimes for which the judge or magistrate has to decide the punishment for each particular case. [FORMAL] ❑ *...the mandatory life sentence for murder.* ADJ ≠ *discretionary*

**man|di|ble** /mændɪbᵊl/ **(mandibles)** [1] A **mandible** is the bone in the lower jaw of a person or animal. [TECHNICAL] N-COUNT = *jawbone* [2] An insect's **mandibles** are the two parts of its mouth which it uses for biting, similar to an animal's jaws. [TECHNICAL] N-COUNT: usu pl

**man|do|lin** /mændəlɪn, -lɪn/ **(mandolins)** A **mandolin** is a musical instrument that looks like a small guitar and has four pairs of strings. N-VAR: oft *the* N

**mane** /meɪn/ **(manes)** The **mane** on a horse or lion is the long thick hair that grows from its neck. N-COUNT

**man-eating** A **man-eating** animal is one that has killed and eaten human beings, or that people think might do so. ❑ *...man-eating lions.* ADJ: ADJ n

**ma|neu|ver** /mənuːvəʳ/ → see **manoeuvre**.

**ma|neu|ver|able** /mənuːvərəbᵊl/ → see **manoeuvrable**.

**man|ful|ly** /mænfᵊli/ If you say that someone, especially a man, does something **manfully**, you mean that they do it in a very determined or brave way. ❑ *They stuck to their task manfully.* ADV: ADV with v

**man|ga|nese** /mæŋgəniːz/ **Manganese** is a greyish-white metal that is used in making steel. N-UNCOUNT

**man|ger** /meɪndʒəʳ/ **(mangers)** A **manger** is a low open container which cows, horses, and other animals feed from when indoors. [OLD-FASHIONED] N-COUNT

**mange|tout** /mɒ̃ʒtuː/ **(mangetout** or **mangetouts)** also **mange-tout**. **Mangetout** are a type of pea whose pods are eaten as well as the peas inside them. [BRIT] N-COUNT: usu pl

☑ in AM, use **snow pea**

**man|gle** /mæŋgᵊl/ **(mangles, mangling, mangled)** [1] If a physical object **is mangled**, it is crushed or twisted very forcefully, so that it is difficult to see what its original shape was. ❑ *His body was crushed and mangled beyond recognition. ...the mangled wreckage.* VERB: usu passive; *be* V-ed; V-ed [2] If you say that someone **mangles** words or information, you are criticizing them for not speaking or writing clearly or correctly. ❑ *They don't know what they're talking about and mangle scientific information.* VERB [disapproval] V n

**man|go** /mæŋgoʊ/ **(mangoes** or **mangos)** A **mango** is a large sweet yellowish fruit which grows on a tree in hot countries. ❑ *Peel, stone and dice the mango. ...mango chutney.* N-VAR ♦ A **mango** is the tree that this fruit grows on. ❑ *...orchards of lime and mango trees.* N-COUNT: oft N n

**man|grove** /mæŋgroʊv/ **(mangroves)** A **mangrove** or **mangrove tree** is a tree with roots which are above the ground and that grows along coasts or on the banks of large rivers in hot countries. ❑ *...mangrove swamps.* N-COUNT: oft N n

**man|gy** /meɪndʒi/ **(mangier, mangiest)** A **mangy** animal looks dirty, uncared for or ill. ❑ *...mangy old dogs.* ADJ: usu ADJ n

**man|handle** /mænhændᵊl/ **(manhandles, manhandling, manhandled)** 1 If someone **is manhandled**, they are physically held or pushed, for example when they are being taken somewhere. ❑ *Foreign journalists were manhandled by armed police, and told to leave... They manhandled the old man along the corridor.* 2 If you **manhandle** something big or heavy somewhere, you move it there by hand. ❑ *The three of us manhandled the uncovered dinghy out of the shed.* VERB; *be* V-ed; V n prep/adv; Also V n; VERB; V n prep/adv

**man|hole** /mænhoʊl/ **(manholes)** A **manhole** is a large hole in a road or path, covered by a metal plate that can be removed. Workers climb down through manholes when they want to examine or clean the drains. N-COUNT

**man|hood** /mænhʊd/ **Manhood** is the state of being a man rather than a boy. ❑ *They were failing lamentably to help their sons grow from boyhood to manhood.* N-UNCOUNT

**man-hour** **(man-hours)** A **man-hour** is the average amount of work that one person can do in an hour. **Man-hours** are used to estimate how long jobs take, or how many people are needed to do a job in a particular time. ❑ *The restoration took almost 4,000 man-hours over four years.* N-COUNT: usu pl

**man|hunt** /mænhʌnt/ **(manhunts)** A **manhunt** is a major search for someone who has escaped or disappeared. N-COUNT: oft N *for* n

**ma|nia** /meɪniə/ **(manias)** 1 If you say that a person or group has a **mania for** something, you mean that they enjoy it very much or spend a lot of time on it. ❑ *It seemed to some observers that the English had a mania for travelling. ...Mozart mania.* 2 **Mania** is a mental illness which causes the sufferer to become very worried or concerned about something. ❑ *...the treatment of mania.* N-COUNT: usu sing, oft N *for* n/-ing, n N; N-UNCOUNT: also N in pl

**ma|ni|ac** /meɪniæk/ **(maniacs)** 1 A **maniac** is a mad person who is violent and dangerous. ❑ *...a drug-crazed maniac.* 2 If you describe someone's behaviour as **maniac**, you are emphasizing that it is extremely foolish and uncontrolled. ❑ *A maniac driver sped 35 miles along the wrong side of a motorway at 110 mph.* 3 If you call someone, for example, a religious **maniac** or a sports **maniac**, you are critical of them because they have such a strong interest in religion or sport. ❑ *My mum is turning into a religious maniac. ...football maniacs.* N-COUNT; ADJ: ADJ n [emphasis] = *lunatic*; N-COUNT: supp N [disapproval] = *fanatic*

**ma|nia|cal** /mənaɪəkᵊl/ If you describe someone's behaviour as **maniacal**, you mean that it is extreme, violent, or very determined, as if the person were insane. ❑ *He was almost maniacal in his pursuit of sporting records... She is hunched forward over the wheel with a maniacal expression.* ♦ **ma|nia|cal|ly** /mənaɪəkli/ *He was last seen striding maniacally to the hotel reception.* ADJ [disapproval]; ADV: usu ADV with v, also ADV adj

**man|ic** /mænɪk/ 1 If you describe someone as **manic**, you mean that they do things extremely quickly or energetically, often because they are very excited or anxious about something. ❑ *He was really manic... He seemed to have an almost manic energy.* ♦ **man|ic|al|ly** /mænɪkli/ *We cleaned the house manically over the weekend.* 2 If you describe someone's smile, laughter, or sense of humour as **manic**, you mean that it seems excessive or strange, as if they were insane. ❑ *...a manic grin.* ADJ; ADV: usu ADV with v, also ADV adj; ADJ

**manic-depressive** **(manic-depressives)** also **manic depressive.** If someone is **manic-depressive**, they have a medical condition in which they sometimes feel excited and confident and at other times very depressed. ❑ *She told them that her daughter-in-law was manic-depressive.* ♦ A **manic-depressive** is someone who is manic-depressive. ❑ *Her mother is a manic depressive.* ADJ; N-COUNT

**mani|cure** /mænɪkjʊəʳ/ **(manicures, manicuring, manicured)** If you **manicure** your hands or nails, you care for them by softening your skin and cutting and polishing your nails. ❑ *He was surprised to see how carefully she had manicured her broad hands.* ♦ **Manicure** is also a noun. ❑ *I have a manicure occasionally.* VERB; V n; N-COUNT

**mani|cured** /mænɪkjʊəʳd/ A **manicured** lawn, park, or garden has very short neatly cut grass. [WRITTEN] ❑ *...the manicured lawns of Government House.* ADJ: oft adv ADJ

**mani|cur|ist** /mænɪkjʊərɪst/ **(manicurists)** A **manicurist** is a person whose job is manicuring people's hands and nails. N-COUNT

**mani|fest** /mænɪfest/ **(manifests, manifesting, manifested)** 1 If you say that something is **manifest**, you mean that it is clearly true and that nobody would disagree with it if they saw it or considered it. [FORMAL] ❑ *...the manifest failure of this government's policies... There may be unrecognised cases of manifest injustice of which we are unaware.* ♦ **mani|fest|ly** *She manifestly failed to last the mile and a half of the race.* 2 If you **manifest** a particular quality, feeling, or illness, or if it **manifests itself**, it becomes visible or obvious. [FORMAL] ❑ *He manifested a pleasing personality on stage... Their frustration and anger will manifest itself in crying and screaming.* ♦ **Manifest** is also an adjective. ❑ *The same alarm is manifest everywhere.* ADJ: usu ADJ n = *patent*; ADV: ADV with v, ADV with cl/group; VERB = *show*; V n; V pron-refl *in* n/-ing; ADJ: usu v-link ADJ

**mani|fes|ta|tion** /mænɪfesteɪʃᵊn/ **(manifestations)** A **manifestation of** something is one of the different ways in which it can appear. [FORMAL] ❑ *Different animals in the colony had different manifestations of the disease.* N-COUNT: with supp, oft N *of* n

**mani|fes|to** /mænɪfestoʊ/ **(manifestos** or **manifestoes)** A **manifesto** is a statement published by a person or group of people, especially a political party, or a government, in which they say what their aims and policies are. ❑ *The Tories are currently drawing up their election manifesto.* N-COUNT: usu sing, usu with poss

**mani|fold** /mænɪfoʊld/ Things that are **manifold** are of many different kinds. [LITERARY] ❑ *Gaelic can be heard here in manifold forms.* ADJ

**ma|nila** /mənɪlə/ also **manilla.** A **manila** envelope or folder is made from a strong paper that is usually light brown. ADJ: ADJ n

**ma|nipu|late** /mənɪpjʊleɪt/ **(manipulates, manipulating, manipulated)** 1 If you say that someone **manipulates** people, you disapprove of them because they skilfully force or persuade people to do what they want. ❑ *He is a very difficult character. He manipulates people... She's always borrowing my clothes and manipulating me to give her vast sums of money... They'll have kids who are two, three, who are manipulating them into buying toys.* ♦ **ma|nipu|la|tion** /mənɪpjʊleɪʃᵊn/ **(manipulations)** *...repeated criticism or manipulation of our mind.* 2 If you say that someone **manipulates** an event or situation, you disapprove of them because they use or control it for their own benefit, or cause it to develop in the way they want. ❑ *She was unable, for once, to control and manipulate events.* ♦ **ma|nipu|la|tion** *...accusations of political manipulation.* 3 If you **manipulate** something that requires skill, such as a complicated piece of equipment or a difficult idea, you operate it or process it. ❑ *The puppets are expertly manipulated by Liz Walker.* ♦ **ma|nipu|la|tion** *...science that requires only the simplest of mathematical manipulations.* 4 If someone **manipulates** your bones or muscles, they skilfully move and press them with their hands in order to push the bones into their correct position or make the muscles less stiff. ❑ *The way he can manipulate my leg has helped my arthritis so much.* ♦ **ma|nipu|la|tion** *A permanent* VERB [disapproval]; V n; V n to-inf; V n *into* -ing; N-VAR; VERB [disapproval]; V n; N-VAR; VERB; V n; N-VAR; VERB; V n; N-VAR

*cure will only be effected by acupuncture, chiropractic or manipulation.*

**ma|nipu|la|tive** /mənɪpjʊlətɪv/ If you describe someone as **manipulative**, you disapprove of them because they skilfully force or persuade people to act in the way that they want. ❑ *He described Mr Long as cold, calculating and manipulative.* ADJ [disapproval]

**ma|nipu|la|tor** /mənɪpjʊleɪtəʳ/ **(manipulators)** If you describe someone as a **manipulator**, you mean that they skilfully control events, situations, or people, often in a way that other people disapprove of. ❑ *Jean Brodie is a manipulator. She cons everybody.* N-COUNT

**man|kind** /mænkaɪnd/ You can refer to all human beings as **mankind** when considering them as a group. Some people dislike this use. ❑ *...the evolution of mankind.* N-UNCOUNT

**man|ly** /mænli/ **(manlier, manliest)** If you describe a man's behaviour or appearance as **manly**, you approve of it because it shows qualities that are considered typical of a man, such as strength or courage. ❑ *He was the ideal of manly beauty.* ♦ **man|li|ness** *He has no doubts about his manliness.* ADJ: usu ADJ n [approval] N-UNCOUNT: poss N

**man-made** **Man-made** things are created or caused by people, rather than occurring naturally. ❑ *Man-made and natural disasters have disrupted the Government's economic plans. ...a variety of materials, both natural and man-made.* ADJ ≠ natural

**man man|age|ment** **Man management** involves controlling and organizing the people who work in a business or organization. [BUSINESS] ❑ *Team captains need to have effective man-management skills.* N-UNCOUNT

**man|na** /mænə/ If you say that something unexpected is **manna from heaven**, you mean that it is good and happened just at the time that it was needed. ❑ *Ex-forces personnel could be the manna from heaven employers are seeking...* PHRASE: oft v-link PHR

**manned** /mænd/ A **manned** vehicle such as a spacecraft has people in it who are operating its controls. ❑ *In thirty years from now the United States should have a manned spacecraft on Mars.* → See also **man**. ADJ ≠ unmanned

**man|ne|quin** /mænɪkɪn/ **(mannequins)** A **mannequin** is a life-sized model of a person which is used to display clothes, especially in shop windows. [OLD-FASHIONED] N-COUNT

**man|ner** /mænəʳ/ **(manners)** [1] The **manner** in which you do something is the way that you do it. ❑ *She smiled again in a friendly manner... I'm a professional and I have to conduct myself in a professional manner... The manner in which young children are spoken to varies depending on who is present.* ◆◇◇ N-SING: with supp
[2] Someone's **manner** is the way in which they behave and talk when they are with other people, for example whether they are polite, confident, or bad-tempered. ❑ *His manner was self-assured and brusque.* ♦ **-mannered** *Forrest was normally mild-mannered, affable, and untalkative... The British are considered ill-mannered, badly dressed and unsophisticated.* N-SING: usu poss N; COMB in ADJ
[3] If someone has **good manners**, they are polite and observe social customs. If someone has **bad manners**, they are impolite and do not observe these customs. ❑ *He dressed well and had impeccable manners... They taught him his manners.* N-PLURAL
[4] → See also **bedside manner**, **table manners**.
PHRASES [5] If you refer to **all manner of** objects or people, you are talking about objects or people of many different kinds. ❑ *Mr Winchester is impressively knowledgeable about all manner of things.* PHRASE: PHR n
[6] You say **in a manner of speaking** to indicate that what you have just said is true, but not absolutely or exactly true. ❑ *An attorney is your employee, in a manner of speaking.* PHRASE: PHR with cl [vagueness] = in a way

**man|nered** /mænəʳd/ [1] If you describe someone's behaviour or a work of art as **mannered**, you dislike it because it is elaborate or formal, and therefore seems false or artificial. ❑ *...Naomi's mannered voice... If you arrange your picture too systematically the results can look very mannered and artificial.* ADJ: usu ADJ n [disapproval] [2] **Mannered** behaviour is polite and observes social customs. ❑ *Its intention is to restore pride in the past and create a more mannered society.* ADJ = well-mannered

**man|ner|ism** /mænərɪzəm/ **(mannerisms)** Someone's **mannerisms** are the gestures or ways of speaking which are very characteristic of them, and which they often use. ❑ *His mannerisms are more those of a preoccupied math professor.* N-COUNT

**man|nish** /mænɪʃ/ If you describe a woman's appearance or behaviour as **mannish**, you mean it is more like a man's appearance or behaviour than a woman's. ❑ *She shook hands in a mannish way, her grip dry and firm. ...a mannish trouser suit.* ADJ: usu ADJ n

**ma|noeu|vrable** /mənuːvərəbᵊl/

✔ in AM, use **maneuverable**

Something that is **manoeuvrable** can be easily moved into different positions. ❑ *Ferries are very powerful and manoeuvrable compared to cargo ships. ...the light, manoeuvrable cart.* ADJ

**ma|noeu|vre** /mənuːvəʳ/ **(manoeuvres, manoeuvring, manoeuvred)**

✔ in AM, use **maneuver**

[1] If you **manoeuvre** something into or out of an awkward position, you skilfully move it there. ❑ *We attempted to manoeuvre the canoe closer to him... I manoeuvred my way among the tables to the back corner of the place... The pilot instinctively maneuvered to avoid them.* ♦ **Manoeuvre** is also a noun. ❑ *...a ship capable of high speed and rapid manoeuvre.* VERB V n adv/prep V way prep/adv V N-VAR
[2] If you **manoeuvre** a situation, you change it in a clever and skilful way so that you can benefit from it. ❑ *The authorities have to manoeuvre the markets into demanding a cut in interest rates... He manoeuvres to foster recovery.* ♦ **Manoeuvre** is also a noun. ❑ *...manoeuvres to block the electoral process.* ♦ **man|oeuv|ring** **(manoeuvrings)** *...his unrivalled skill in political manoeuvring. ...his manoeuvrings on the matter of free trade.* VERB = manipulate V n prep/adv V N-COUNT N-VAR
[3] Military **manoeuvres** are training exercises which involve the movement of soldiers and equipment over a large area. ❑ *Allied troops begin maneuvers tomorrow to show how quickly forces could be mobilized in case of a new invasion.* N-PLURAL
[4] **room for manoeuvre** → see **room**.

**man|or** /mænəʳ/ **(manors)** A **manor** is a large private house in the country, usually built in the Middle Ages, and also includes the land and smaller buildings around it. [BRIT] ❑ *Thieves broke into the manor at night.* N-COUNT: oft in names after n

**man|or house** **(manor houses)** A **manor house** is the main house that is or was on a medieval manor. [BRIT] N-COUNT

**man|power** /mænpaʊəʳ/ Workers are sometimes referred to as **manpower** when they are being considered as a part of the process of producing goods or providing services. ❑ *...the shortage of skilled manpower in the industry... These people do not have the equipment or the manpower to cut down the trees.* N-UNCOUNT

**man|qué** /mɒŋkeɪ, AM -keɪ/ You use **manqué** to describe someone who has never had the type of job indicated, although they had the ability for it or wanted it. ❑ *...his inescapable feeling that he is a great actor manqué.* ADJ: n ADJ

**manse** /mæns/ **(manses)** In some Christian churches, a **manse** is the house provided for a clergyman to live in. [mainly BRIT] N-COUNT

**man|servant** /mænsɜːʳvᵊnt/ **(manservants)** A **manservant** is a man who works as a servant in a private house. [BRIT, OLD-FASHIONED] N-COUNT

✔ in AM, use **houseman**

**man|sion** /mænʃᵊn/ **(mansions)** A **mansion** is a very large house. ❑ *...an eighteenth century mansion in Hampshire.* N-COUNT

**man|slaughter** /mænslɔːtəʳ/ **Manslaughter** is the illegal killing of a person by N-UNCOUNT someone who did not intend to kill them. [LEGAL] ❑ *A judge accepted her plea that she was guilty of manslaughter, not murder.*

**man|tel** /mæntəl/ **(mantels)** A **mantel** is a mantelpiece. [OLD-FASHIONED] N-COUNT

**mantel|piece** /mæntəlpiːs/ **(mantelpieces)** also **mantlepiece.** A **mantelpiece** is a wood or stone shelf which is the top part of a border round a fireplace. ❑ *On the mantelpiece are a pair of bronze Ming vases.* N-COUNT: usu sing

**mantel|shelf** /mæntəlʃelf/ **(mantelshelves)** also **mantleshelf.** A **mantelshelf** is a mantelpiece. [OLD-FASHIONED] N-COUNT: usu sing

**man|tle** /mæntəl/ **(mantles)** 1 If you take on **the mantle of** something such as a profession or an important job, you take on the responsibilities and duties which must be fulfilled by anyone who has this profession or job. [WRITTEN] ❑ *Glasgow has broadened its appeal since taking on the mantle of European City of Culture in 1990.* N-SING: the N of n 2 A **mantle** of something is a layer of it covering a surface, for example a layer of snow on the ground. [WRITTEN] ❑ *The parks and squares looked grim under a mantle of soot and ash.* N-COUNT: with supp = blanket 3 → See also **mantel**.

**mantle|piece** /mæntəlpiːs/ → see **mantelpiece**.

**man-to-man** → see **man**.

**man|tra** /mæntrə/ **(mantras)** 1 A **mantra** is a word or phrase repeated by Buddhists and Hindus when they meditate, or to help them feel calm. N-COUNT 2 You can use **mantra** to refer to a statement or a principle that people repeat very often because they think it is true, especially when you think that it not true or is only part of the truth. ❑ *Listening to customers is now part of the mantra of new management in public services.* N-COUNT

**manu|al** /mænjuəl/ **(manuals)** 1 **Manual** work is work in which you use your hands or your physical strength rather than your mind. ❑ *...skilled manual workers... They have no reservations about taking factory or manual jobs.* ADJ: usu ADJ n = blue-collar ≠ clerical 2 **Manual** is used to talk about movements which are made by someone's hands. [FORMAL] ❑ *...toys designed to help develop manual dexterity.* ADJ: ADJ n 3 **Manual** means operated by hand, rather than by electricity or a motor. ❑ *There is a manual pump to get rid of the water.* ADJ: ADJ n ♦ **manu|al|ly** *The device is manually operated, using a simple handle.* ADV: ADV with v 4 A **manual** is a book which tells you how to do something or how a piece of machinery works. ❑ *...the instruction manual.* N-COUNT

**manu|fac|ture** /mænjʊfæktʃəʳ/ **(manufactures, manufacturing, manufactured)** ◆◇◇ 1 To **manufacture** something means to make it in a factory, usually in large quantities. [BUSINESS] ❑ *They manufacture the class of plastics known as thermoplastic materials... We import foreign manufactured goods.* VERB = produce V n V-ed ♦ **Manufacture** is also a noun. ❑ *...the manufacture of nuclear weapons. ...celebrating 90 years of car manufacture.* N-UNCOUNT: with supp ♦ **manu|fac|tur|ing** *...management headquarters for manufacturing.* N-UNCOUNT 2 **Manufactures** are goods or products which have been made in a factory. [BUSINESS] ❑ *...a long-term rise in the share of manufactures in non-oil exports.* N-COUNT: usu pl 3 If you say that someone **manufactures** information, you are criticizing them because they invent information that is not true. ❑ *According to the prosecution, the officers manufactured an elaborate story.* VERB disapproval = fabricate V n

**manu|fac|tur|er** /mænjʊfæktʃərəʳ/ **(manufacturers)** ◆◇◇ A **manufacturer** is a business or company which makes goods in large quantities to sell. [BUSINESS] ❑ *...the world's largest doll manufacturer.* N-COUNT: oft supp N

**ma|nure** /mənjʊəʳ, AM -nʊr/ **(manures) Manure** is animal faeces, sometimes mixed with chemicals, that is spread on the ground in order to make plants grow healthy and strong. ❑ *...bags of manure.* N-MASS

**manu|script** /mænjʊskrɪpt/ **(manuscripts)** A **manuscript** is a handwritten or typed document, especially a writer's first version of a book before it is published. ❑ *He had seen a manuscript of the book... I am grateful to him for letting me read his early chapters in manuscript.* N-COUNT: also in N

**Manx** /mæŋks/ **Manx** is used to describe people or things that belong to or concern the Isle of Man and the people who live there. ADJ

**many** /meni/ ◆◆◆ 1 You use **many** to indicate that you are talking about a large number of people or things. ❑ *I don't think many people would argue with that... Not many films are made in Finland... Many holidaymakers had avoided the worst of the delays by consulting tourist offices... Acting is definitely a young person's profession in many ways.* DET: DET pl-n, oft with brd-neg ≠ few ♦ **Many** is also a pronoun. ❑ *We stood up, thinking through the possibilities. There weren't many.* PRON ≠ few, some ♦ **Many** is also a quantifier. ❑ *So, once we have cohabited, why do many of us feel the need to get married?... It seems there are not very many of them left in the sea.* QUANT: QUANT of def-pl-n ♦ **Many** is also an adjective. ❑ *Among his many hobbies was the breeding of fine horses... The possibilities are many.* ADJ: det ADJ, v-link ADJ 2 You use **many** in expressions such as 'not many', 'not very many', and 'too many' when replying to questions about numbers of things or people. ❑ *'How many of the songs that dealt with this theme became hit songs?' — 'Not very many.'... How many years is it since we've seen each other? Too many, anyway.* ADV: ADV as reply 3 You use **many** followed by 'a' and a noun to emphasize that there are a lot of people or things involved in something. ❑ *Many a mother tries to act out her unrealized dreams through her daughter.* PREDET emphasis 4 You use **many** after 'how' to ask questions about numbers or quantities. You use **many** after 'how' in reported clauses to talk about numbers or quantities. ❑ *How many years have you been here?... No-one knows how many people have been killed since the war began.* DET: how DET pl-n ♦ **Many** is also a pronoun. ❑ *How many do you smoke a day?* PRON: how PRON 5 You use **many** with 'as' when you are comparing numbers of things or people. ❑ *I've always entered as many photo competitions as I can... We produced ten times as many tractors as the United States.* DET: as DET pl-n, usu as DET pl-n as cl/group ♦ **Many** is also a pronoun. ❑ *Let the child try on as many as she likes.* PRON: as PRON 6 You use **many** to mean 'many people'. ❑ *Iris Murdoch was regarded by many as a supremely good and serious writer.* PRON 7 **The many** means a large group of people, especially the ordinary people in society, considered as separate from a particular small group. ❑ *The printing press gave power to a few to change the world for the many.* N-SING: the N

**PHRASES** 8 You use **as many as** before a number to suggest that it is surprisingly large. ❑ *As many as four and a half million people watched today's parade.* PHRASE: PHR num emphasis 9 You use **a good many** or **a great many** to emphasize that you are referring to a large number of things or people. ❑ *We've both had a good many beers... For a great many men and women, romance can be a most important part of marriage.* PHRASE: PHR pl-n emphasis 10 **many happy returns** → see **return**. **in so many words** → see **word**.

**Mao|ri** /maʊri/ **(Maoris)** 1 **Maori** means belonging to or relating to the race of people who have lived in New Zealand and the Cook Islands since before Europeans arrived. ADJ 2 The **Maori** or the **Maoris** are people who are Maori. N-COUNT

**map** /mæp/ **(maps, mapping, mapped)** ◆◇◇ 1 A **map** is a drawing of a particular area such as a city, a country, or a continent, showing its main features as they would appear if you looked at them from above. ❑ *He unfolded the map and set it on the floor... Have you got a map of the city centre?* N-COUNT: oft N of n 2 To **map** an area means to make a map of it. ❑ *...a spacecraft which is using radar to map the surface of Venus.* VERB V n 3 If you say that someone or something **put** a person, thing, or place **on the map**, you approve of the fact that they made it become well-known and important. ❑ *...the attempts of the* PHRASE: V inflects approval

*Edinburgh Festival's organisers to put C.P. Taylor firmly on the map.*

♦ **map out** If you **map out** something that you are intending to do, you work out in detail how you will do it. ❑ *I went home and mapped out my strategy... I cannot conceive of anybody writing a play by sitting down and mapping it out... This whole plan has been most carefully mapped out.* PHRASAL VERB V P n (not pron) V n P *be* V-ed P

**ma|ple** /meɪpəl/ **(maples)** A **maple** or a **maple tree** is a tree with five-pointed leaves which turn bright red or gold in autumn. N-VAR ♦ **Maple** is the wood of this tree. ❑ *...a solid maple worktop.* N-UNCOUNT

**ma|ple syr|up** **Maple syrup** is a sweet, sticky, brown liquid made from the sap of maple trees, that can be eaten with pancakes or used to make desserts. N-UNCOUNT

**mar** /mɑːʳ/ **(mars, marring, marred)** To **mar** something means to spoil or damage it. ❑ *A number of problems marred the smooth running of this event.* VERB V n

**Mar.** **Mar.** is a written abbreviation for **March**.

**mara|thon** /mærəθən, AM -θɒn/ **(marathons)** 1 A **marathon** is a race in which people run a distance of 26 miles, which is about 42 km. ❑ *...running in his first marathon... Rodgers can also claim four victories in the New York Marathon.* N-COUNT 2 If you use **marathon** to describe an event or task, you are emphasizing that it takes a long time and is very tiring. ❑ *People make marathon journeys to buy glass here. ...a marathon session of talks with government representatives.* ADJ: ADJ n [emphasis]

**ma|raud|er** /mərɔːdəʳ/ **(marauders)** If you describe a group of people or animals as **marauders**, you mean they are unpleasant and dangerous, because they wander around looking for opportunities to steal or kill. [LITERARY] ❑ *They were raided by roaming bands of marauders.* N-COUNT

**ma|raud|ing** /mərɔːdɪŋ/ If you talk about **marauding** groups of people or animals, you mean they are unpleasant and dangerous, because they wander around looking for opportunities to steal or kill. [LITERARY] ❑ *Marauding gangs of armed men have been looting food relief supplies.* ADJ: ADJ n

**mar|ble** /mɑːʳbəl/ **(marbles)** 1 **Marble** is a type of very hard rock which feels cold when you touch it and which shines when it is cut and polished. Statues and parts of buildings are sometimes made of marble. ❑ *The house has a superb staircase made from oak and marble.* N-UNCOUNT: oft N n 2 **Marbles** are sculptures made of marble. ❑ *...marbles and bronzes from the Golden Age of Athens.* N-COUNT: usu pl 3 **Marbles** is a children's game played with small balls, usually made of coloured glass. You roll a ball along the ground and try to hit an opponent's ball with it. ❑ *On the far side of the street, two boys were playing marbles.* N-UNCOUNT 4 A **marble** is one of the small balls used in the game of marbles. N-COUNT

**mar|bled** /mɑːʳbəld/ Something that is **marbled** has a pattern or colouring like that of marble. ❑ *...green marbled soap.* ADJ: usu ADJ n, also v-link ADJ *with/in* n

**march** /mɑːʳtʃ/ **(marches, marching, marched)** ◆◇◇ 1 When soldiers **march** somewhere, or when a commanding officer **marches** them somewhere, they walk there with very regular steps, as a group. ❑ *A Scottish battalion was marching down the street... Captain Ramirez called them to attention and marched them off to the main camp... We marched fifteen miles to Yadkin River.* VERB V prep/adv V n adv/prep V amount/n ♦ **March** is also a noun. ❑ *After a short march, the column entered the village.* Also V N-COUNT 2 When a large group of people **march** for a cause, they walk somewhere together in order to express their ideas or to protest about something. ❑ *The demonstrators then marched through the capital chanting slogans and demanding free elections.* VERB V prep/adv ♦ **March** is also a noun. ❑ *Organisers expect up to 300,000 protesters to join the march.* N-COUNT ♦ **march|er** **(marchers)** *Fights between police and marchers lasted for three hours.* N-COUNT 3 If you say that someone **marches** somewhere, you mean that they walk there quickly and in a determined way, for example because they are angry. ❑ *He marched into the kitchen without knocking.* VERB V prep/adv 4 If you **march** someone somewhere, you force them to walk there with you, for example by holding their arm tightly. ❑ *I marched him across the room, down the hall and out onto the doorstep.* VERB V n prep/adv 5 **The march of** something is its steady development or progress. ❑ *It is easy to feel trampled by the relentless march of technology.* N-SING: usu *the* N *of* n 6 A **march** is a piece of music with a regular rhythm that you can march to. ❑ *A military band played Russian marches and folk tunes.* N-COUNT: usu with supp

PHRASES 7 If you give someone their **marching orders**, you tell them that you no longer want or need them, for example as your employee or as your lover. [BRIT] ❑ *What does it take for a woman to say 'that's enough' and give her man his marching orders?* PHRASE: PHR after v

✔ in AM, use **walking papers**

8 If you **steal a march on** someone, you start doing something before they do it in order to gain an advantage over them. ❑ *If its strategy succeeds, Mexico could even steal a march on its northern neighbour.* PHRASE: V inflects, oft PHR *on* n

**March** **(Marches)** **March** is the third month of the year in the Western calendar. ❑ *I flew to Milan in early March... She was born in Austria on March 6, 1920... The election could be held as early as next March.* N-VAR

**march|ing band** **(marching bands)** A **marching band** is a group of musicians who play music as they march along the street or march as part of a ceremony. N-COUNT

**mar|chion|ess** /mɑːʳʃənes/ **(marchionesses)** A **marchioness** is the wife of a marquis, or a woman with the same rank as a marquis. N-COUNT; N-TITLE

**march-past** **(march-pasts)** also **march past.** When soldiers take part in a **march-past**, they march past an important person as part of a ceremonial occasion. N-COUNT

**Mar|di Gras** /mɑːʳdi grɑː/ **Mardi Gras** is the Christian festival of Shrove Tuesday, the day before Lent, which people in some places celebrate by wearing colourful costumes and dancing through the streets. N-UNCOUNT

**mare** /meəʳ/ **(mares)** A **mare** is an adult female horse. N-COUNT

**mar|ga|rine** /mɑːʳdʒəriːn, AM -rɪn/ **(margarines)** **Margarine** is a yellow substance made from vegetable oil and animal fats that is similar to butter. You spread it on bread or use it for cooking. N-MASS

**marge** /mɑːʳdʒ/ also **marg.** **Marge** is the same as **margarine**. [BRIT, INFORMAL] N-UNCOUNT

**mar|gin** /mɑːʳdʒɪn/ **(margins)** ◆◇◇ 1 A **margin** is the difference between two amounts, especially the difference in the number of votes or points between the winner and the loser in an election or other contest. ❑ *They could end up with a 50-point winning margin... The Sunday Times remains the brand leader by a huge margin.* N-COUNT: with supp 2 The **margin** of a written or printed page is the empty space at the side of the page. ❑ *She added her comments in the margin.* N-COUNT 3 If there is a **margin** for something in a situation, there is some freedom to choose what to do or decide how to do it. ❑ *The money is collected in a straightforward way with little margin for error.* N-VAR: with supp 4 The **margin** of a place or area is the extreme edge of it. ❑ *...the low coastal plain along the western margin.* N-COUNT: with supp 5 To be **on the margins** of a society, group, or activity means to be among the least typical or least important parts of it. ❑ *Students have played an important role in the past, but for the moment, they're on the margins.* N-PLURAL: with supp 6 → See also **profit margin**.

**mar|gin|al** /mɑːʳdʒɪnəl/ **(marginals)** 1 If you describe something as **marginal**, you mean that it is small or not very important. ❑ *This is a marginal improvement on October... The role of the opposition party proved marginal.* ADJ 2 If you describe people as **marginal**, you mean that they are not in- ADJ ≠ *mainstream* volved in the main events or developments in society because they are poor or have no power. ❑ *The tribunals were established for the well-integrated members of society and not for marginal individuals.* [3] In political elections, a **marginal** seat or constituency is one which is usually won or lost by only a few votes, and is therefore of great interest to politicians and journalists. [BRIT] ❑ *...the views of voters in five marginal seats.* [ADJ: usu ADJ n] ♦ A **marginal** is a marginal seat. [BRIT] ❑ *The votes in the marginals are those that really count.* [N-COUNT] [4] **Marginal** activities, costs, or taxes are not the main part of a business or an economic system, but often make the difference between its success or failure, and are therefore important to control. [BUSINESS] ❑ *The analysts applaud the cuts in marginal businesses, but insist the company must make deeper sacrifices.* [ADJ: usu ADJ n]

**mar|gin|al|ize** /mɑːʳdʒɪnəlaɪz/ **(marginalizes, marginalizing, marginalized)**

✓ in BRIT, also use **marginalise**

To **marginalize** a group of people means to make them feel isolated and unimportant. ❑ *We've always been marginalized, exploited, and constantly threatened.* [VERB] [V n]

**mar|gin|al|ly** /mɑːʳdʒɪnəli/ **Marginally** means to only a small extent. ❑ *Sales last year were marginally higher than in 1991... These cameras have increased only marginally in value over the past decade.* [ADV: ADV adv/adj/prep, ADV with v = slightly]

**mari|gold** /mærɪgoʊld/ **(marigolds)** A **marigold** is a type of yellow or orange flower. [N-VAR]

**ma|ri|jua|na** /mærɪwɑːnə/ **Marijuana** is a drug which is made from the dried leaves and flowers of the hemp plant, and which can be smoked. [N-UNCOUNT]

**ma|ri|na** /məriːnə/ **(marinas)** A **marina** is a small harbour for small boats that are used for leisure. [N-COUNT]

**mari|nade** /mærɪneɪd/ **(marinades, marinading, marinaded)** [1] A **marinade** is a sauce of oil, vinegar, spices, and herbs, which you pour over meat or fish before you cook it, in order to add flavour, or to make the meat or fish softer. [N-COUNT] [2] To **marinade** means the same as to **marinate**. ❑ *Marinade the chicken breasts in the tandoori paste... Leave to marinade for 24 hours.* [VERB] [V n] [V]

**mari|nate** /mærɪneɪt/ **(marinates, marinating, marinated)** If you **marinate** meat or fish, or if it **marinates**, you keep it in a mixture of oil, vinegar, spices, and herbs, before cooking it, so that it can develop a special flavour. ❑ *Marinate the chicken for at least 4 hours... Put it in a screw-top jar with French dressing and leave to marinate.* [VERB] [V n] [V]

**ma|rine** /məriːn/ **(marines)** [1] A **marine** is a member of an armed force, for example the US Marine Corps or the Royal Marines, who is specially trained for military duties at sea as well as on land. [◆◇◇ N-COUNT] [2] **Marine** is used to describe things relating to the sea or to the animals and plants that live in the sea. ❑ *...breeding grounds for marine life. ...research in marine biology.* [ADJ: ADJ n] [3] **Marine** is used to describe things relating to ships and their movement at sea. ❑ *...a solicitor specialising in marine law. ...marine insurance claims.* [ADJ: ADJ n = maritime]

**mari|ner** /mærɪnəʳ/ **(mariners)** A **mariner** is a sailor. [LITERARY] [N-COUNT = seafarer]

**mari|on|ette** /mæriənet/ **(marionettes)** A **marionette** is a puppet whose different parts you can move using strings or wires. [N-COUNT]

**mari|tal** /mærɪtᵊl/ **Marital** is used to describe things relating to marriage. ❑ *Caroline was keen to make her marital home in London... Her son had no marital problems.* [ADJ: ADJ n]

**mari|tal sta|tus** Your **marital status** is whether you are married, single, or divorced. [FORMAL] ❑ *How well off you are in old age is largely determined by race, sex, and marital status.* [N-UNCOUNT]

**mari|time** /mærɪtaɪm/ **Maritime** is used to describe things relating to the sea and to ships. ❑ *...the largest maritime museum of its kind.* [ADJ: ADJ n]

**mar|jo|ram** /mɑːʳdʒərəm/ **Marjoram** is a kind of herb. [N-UNCOUNT]

**mark** /mɑːʳk/ **(marks, marking, marked)** [1] A **mark** is a small area of something such as dirt that has accidentally got onto a surface or piece of clothing. ❑ *The dogs are always rubbing against the wall and making dirty marks... A properly fitting bra should never leave red marks.* [◆◆◇ N-COUNT] [2] If something **marks** a surface, or if the surface **marks**, the surface is damaged by marks or a mark. ❑ *Leather overshoes were put on the horses' hooves to stop them marking the turf... I have to be more careful with the work tops, as wood marks easily.* [VERB] [V n] [V] [3] A **mark** is a written or printed symbol, for example a letter of the alphabet. ❑ *He made marks with a pencil.* [N-COUNT] [4] If you **mark** something with a particular word or symbol, you write that word or symbol on it. ❑ *The bank marks the check 'certified'... Mark the frame with your postcode... For more details about these products, send a postcard marked HB/FF.* [VERB] [V n quote] [V n *with* n] [V-ed] [5] A **mark** is a point that is given for a correct answer or for doing something well in an exam or competition. A **mark** can also be a written symbol such as a letter that indicates how good a student's or competitor's work or performance is. ❑ *...a simple scoring device of marks out of 10, where '1' equates to 'Very poor performance'... He did well to get such a good mark.* [N-COUNT: oft supp N] [6] If someone gets good or high **marks** for doing something, they have done it well. If they get poor or low **marks**, they have done it badly. ❑ *You have to give her top marks for moral guts... His administration has earned low marks for its economic policies.* [N-PLURAL: supp N] [7] When a teacher **marks** a student's work, the teacher decides how good it is and writes a number or letter on it to indicate this opinion. ❑ *He was marking essays in his small study.* [VERB] [V n] ♦ **mark|ing** *For the rest of the lunchbreak I do my marking.* [N-UNCOUNT] [8] A particular **mark** is a particular number, point, or stage which has been reached or might be reached, especially a significant one. ❑ *Unemployment is rapidly approaching the one million mark.* [N-COUNT: usu *the* supp N] [9] The **mark of** something is the characteristic feature that enables you to recognize it. ❑ *The mark of a civilized society is that it looks after its weakest members.* [N-COUNT: N *of* n/-ing = sign] [10] If you say that a type of behaviour or an event is **a mark of** a particular quality, feeling, or situation, you mean it shows that that quality, feeling, or situation exists. ❑ *It was a mark of his unfamiliarity with Hollywood that he didn't understand that an agent was paid out of his client's share.* [N-SING: *a* N *of* n = indication, sign] [11] If something **marks** a place or position, it shows where something else is or where it used to be. ❑ *A huge crater marks the spot where the explosion happened.* [VERB] [V n] [12] An event that **marks** a particular stage or point is a sign that something different is about to happen. ❑ *The announcement marks the end of an extraordinary period in European history.* [VERB] [V n] [13] If you do something to **mark** an event or occasion, you do it to show that you are aware of the importance of the event or occasion. ❑ *Hundreds of thousands of people took to the streets to mark the occasion.* [VERB] [V n] [14] Something that **marks** someone **as** a particular type of person indicates that they are that type of person. ❑ *Her opposition to abortion and feminism mark her as a convinced traditionalist.* [VERB] [V n *as* n] [15] In a team game, when a defender **is marking** an attacker, they are trying to stay close to the attacker and prevent them from getting the ball. [mainly BRIT] ❑ *...Manchester United defender Rio Ferdinand, who so effectively marked Michael Owen.* [VERB] [V n]

✓ in AM, use **guard**, **cover**

♦ **mark|ing** *They had stopped Ecuador from building up attacks with good marking.* [N-UNCOUNT] [16] The **mark** was the unit of money that was used in Germany. In 2002 it was replaced by the euro. ❑ *The government gave 30 million marks for new school books.* [N-COUNT: usu num N] ♦ **The mark** was also used to refer to the German [N-SING: *the* N]

currency system. ❑ *The mark appreciated 12 per cent against the dollar.* [17] **Mark** is used before a number to indicate a particular temperature level in a gas oven. [BRIT] ❑ *Set the oven at gas mark 4.* (N-UNCOUNT: N num)
[18] **Mark** is used before a number to indicate a particular version or model of a vehicle, machine, or device. ❑ *...his Mark II Ford Cortina.* [19] → See also **marked, marking, black mark, check mark, exclamation mark, full marks, high-water mark, punctuation mark, question mark, scuff mark, stretch marks.** (N-UNCOUNT: N num)

**PHRASES** [20] If someone or something **leaves** their **mark** or **leaves a mark**, they have a lasting effect on another person or thing. ❑ *Years of conditioning had left their mark on her, and she never felt inclined to talk to strange men.* (PHRASE: V inflects, oft PHR *on* n) [21] If you **make** your **mark** or **make a mark**, you become noticed or famous by doing something impressive or unusual. ❑ *She made her mark in the film industry in the 1960s.* (PHRASE: V inflects, oft PHR *on/in* n) [22] If you are **quick off the mark**, you are quick to understand or respond to something. If you are **slow off the mark**, you are slow to understand or respond to something. (PHRASE: usu v-link PHR) [23] **On your marks** in British English, or **on your mark** in American English, is a command given to runners at the beginning of a race in order to get them into the correct position to start. ❑ *On your marks – get set – go!* (CONVENTION) [24] If something is **off the mark**, it is inaccurate or incorrect. If it is **on the mark**, it is accurate or correct. ❑ *Robinson didn't think the story was so far off the mark.* (PHRASE: usu v-link PHR) [25] If something such as a claim or estimate is **wide of the mark**, it is incorrect or inaccurate. ❑ *That comparison isn't as wide of the mark as it seems.* (PHRASE: usu v-link PHR) [26] to **overstep the mark** → see **overstep**.

♦ **mark down** [1] If you **mark** something **down**, you write it down. ❑ *I tend to forget things unless I mark them down... As he marks down the prices, he stops now and then to pack things into a large bag.* (PHRASAL VERB; V n P; V P n (not pron)) [2] If you **mark** someone **down as** a particular type of person, especially a type that you do not like, you consider that they have the qualities which make them that type of person. ❑ *If he'd taken that five pounds, I would have marked him down as a greedy fool.* (PHRASAL VERB; V n P *as* n) [3] To **mark** an item **down** or **mark** its price **down** means to reduce its price. ❑ *A toy store has marked down the Sonic Hedgehog computer game... Clothes are the best bargain, with many items marked down.* (PHRASAL VERB = reduce ≠ mark up; V P n; V-ed P; Also V n P) [4] If a teacher **marks** a student **down**, the teacher puts a lower grade on the student's work because of a mistake that has been made. ❑ *If you mark each other's work, they don't mark you down because then you can mark them down.* (PHRASAL VERB; V n P)

♦ **mark off** [1] If you **mark off** a piece or length of something, you make it separate, for example by putting a line on it or around it. ❑ *He used a rope to mark off the circle.* (PHRASAL VERB; V P n (not pron)) [2] If a particular quality or feature **marks** someone or something **off** from other people or things, it is unusual and makes them obviously different. ❑ *Her clothes, of course, marked her off from a great number of the delegates at the conference... The traditionalist influences within the navy marked it off as a rather old-fashioned institution.* (PHRASAL VERB; V n P *from* n; V n P *as* n)

♦ **mark out** [1] To **mark out** an area or shape means to show where it begins and ends. ❑ *When planting seedlings I prefer to mark out the rows in advance.* (PHRASAL VERB; V P n; Also V n P) [2] If a particular quality or feature **marks** someone or something **out**, it makes them obviously different from other people or things. ❑ *There were several things about that evening that marked it out as very unusual... Her independence of spirit marked her out from her male fellow officers.* (PHRASAL VERB; V n P *as* adj/n; V n P *from* n; Also V P n (not pron))

♦ **mark up** If you **mark** something **up**, you increase its price. ❑ *You can sell it to them at a set wholesale price, allowing them to mark it up for retail... A typical warehouse club marks up its goods by only 10 to 15 percent.* → See also **mark-up**. (PHRASAL VERB = increase ≠ mark down; V n P; V P n (not pron))

**mark|down** /mɑːʳkdaʊn/ **(markdowns)** A **markdown** is a reduction in the price of something. ❑ *Customers know that our stocktake sales offer genuine markdowns across the store.* (N-COUNT)

**marked** /mɑːʳkt/ ◆◇◇ [1] A **marked** change or difference is very obvious and easily noticed. ❑ *There has been a marked increase in crimes against property... He was a man of austere habits, in marked contrast to his more flamboyant wife.* ♦ **mark|ed|ly** /mɑːʳkɪdli/ *America's current economic downturn is markedly different from previous recessions.* (ADJ; ADV: ADV adj, ADV with v) [2] If you describe someone as a **marked** man or woman, you mean that they are in danger from someone who wants to harm or kill them. ❑ *All he needs to do is make one phone call and I'm a marked man.* (ADJ: ADJ n)

**mark|er** /mɑːʳkəʳ/ **(markers)** [1] A **marker** is an object which is used to show the position of something, or is used to help someone remember something. ❑ *He put a marker in his book and followed her out.* (N-COUNT) [2] If you refer to something as a **marker for** a particular quality or feature, you mean that it demonstrates the existence or presence of that quality or feature. ❑ *Vitamin C is a good marker for the presence of other vitamins and nutrients in frozen food.* (N-COUNT: oft N *for* n) [3] A **marker** or a **marker pen** is a pen with a thick tip made of felt, which is used for drawing and for colouring things. ❑ *Draw your child's outline with a heavy black marker.* (N-COUNT)

**mar|ket** /mɑːʳkɪt/ **(markets, marketing, marketed)** ◆◆◆ [1] A **market** is a place where goods are bought and sold, usually outdoors. ❑ *He sold boots on a market stall.* (N-COUNT) [2] The **market** for a particular type of thing is the number of people who want to buy it, or the area of the world in which it is sold. [BUSINESS] ❑ *The foreign market was increasingly crucial. ...the Russian market for personal computers.* (N-COUNT: usu sing, with supp, oft N *for/in* n)
[3] The **market** refers to the total amount of a product that is sold each year, especially when you are talking about the competition between the companies who sell that product. [BUSINESS] ❑ *The two big companies control 72% of the market.* (N-SING: *the* N)
[4] If you talk about a **market** economy, or the **market** price of something, you are referring to an economic system in which the prices of things depend on how many are available and how many people want to buy them, rather than prices being fixed by governments. [BUSINESS] ❑ *Their ultimate aim was a market economy for Hungary... He must sell the house for the current market value. ...the market price of cocoa.* (ADJ: ADJ n) [5] To **market** a product means to organize its sale, by deciding on its price, where it should be sold, and how it should be advertised. [BUSINESS] ❑ *...if you marketed our music the way you market pop music. ...if a soap is marketed as an anti-acne product.* (VERB; V n; *be* V-ed *as* n) [6] **The job market** or **the labour market** refers to the people who are looking for work and the jobs available for them to do. [BUSINESS] ❑ *Every year, 250,000 people enter the job market. ...the changes in the labour market during the 1980s.* (N-SING: *the* n N) [7] The stock market is sometimes referred to as **the market**. [BUSINESS] ❑ *The market collapsed last October.* (N-SING: *the* N) [8] → See also **black market, market forces, open market.**

**PHRASES** [9] If you say that it is **a buyer's market**, you mean that it is a good time to buy a particular thing, because there is a lot of it available, so its price is low. If you say that it is **a seller's market**, you mean that very little of it is available, so its price is high. [BUSINESS] ❑ *Don't be afraid to haggle: for the moment, it's a buyer's market.* (PHRASE: v-link PHR)
[10] If you are **in the market for** something, you are interested in buying it. ❑ *If you're in the market for a new radio, you'll see that the latest models are very different.* (PHRASE: v-link PHR, PHR n) [11] If something is **on the market**, it is available for people to buy. If it comes **onto the market**, it becomes available for people to buy. [BUSINESS] ❑ *...putting more empty offices on the market. ...new medicines that have just come onto the market.* (PHRASE: v-link PHR, PHR after v) [12] If you **price** yourself **out of the market**, you try to sell goods or services at a higher price than other people, with the result (PHRASE: V inflects)

that no one buys them from you. [BUSINESS] ❑ *At £150,000 for a season, he really is pricing himself out of the market.*

**mar|ket|able** /mɑːʳkɪtəbᵊl/ Something that is **marketable** is able to be sold because people want to buy it. [BUSINESS] ❑ *...telling them how to turn their prize research projects into marketable products.* ADJ

**mar|ket|eer** /mɑːʳkɪtɪəʳ/ **(marketeers)** A **marketeer** is the same as a **marketer**. [BUSINESS] ➔ See also **black marketeer, free-marketeer.** N-COUNT

**mar|ket|er** /mɑːʳkɪtəʳ/ **(marketers)** A **marketer** is someone whose job involves marketing. [BUSINESS] N-COUNT

**mar|ket forces** When politicians and economists talk about **market forces**, they mean the economic factors that affect the availability of goods and the demand for them, without any help or control by governments. [BUSINESS] ❑ *...opening the economy to market forces and increasing the role of private enterprise.* N-PLURAL

**mar|ket gar|den** **(market gardens)** A **market garden** is a small farm where vegetables and fruit are grown for sale. [mainly BRIT] N-COUNT

in AM, use **truck farm**

**mar|ket|ing** /mɑːʳkɪtɪŋ/ **Marketing** is the organization of the sale of a product, for example, deciding on its price, the areas it should be supplied to, and how it should be advertised. [BUSINESS] ❑ *...expert advice on production and marketing. ...a marketing campaign.* ◆◇◇ N-UNCOUNT: oft N n

**mar|ket|ing mix** A company's **marketing mix** is the combination of marketing activities it uses in order to promote a particular product or service. [BUSINESS] ❑ *The key focus of the marketing mix will be on price and distribution.* N-SING

**mar|ket lead|er** **(market leaders)** A **market leader** is a company that sells more of a particular product or service than most of its competitors do. [BUSINESS] ❑ *We are becoming one of the market leaders in the fashion industry.* N-COUNT

**market|place** /mɑːʳkɪtpleɪs/ **(marketplaces)** also **market place.** 1 The **marketplace** refers to the activity of buying and selling products. [BUSINESS] ❑ *It's our hope that we will play an increasingly greater role in the marketplace and, therefore, supply more jobs.* N-COUNT: usu *the* N in sing 2 A **marketplace** is a small area in a town or city where goods are bought and sold, often outdoors. ❑ *The marketplace was jammed with a noisy crowd of buyers and sellers.* N-COUNT

**mar|ket re|search** **Market research** is the activity of collecting and studying information about what people want, need, and buy. [BUSINESS] ❑ *A new all-woman market research company has been set up to find out what women think about major news and issues.* N-UNCOUNT

**mar|ket share** **(market shares)** A company's **market share** in a product is the proportion of the total sales of that product that is produced by that company. [BUSINESS] ❑ *Ford has been gaining market share this year at the expense of GM.* N-VAR: oft with poss

**mar|ket test** **(market tests, market testing, market tested)** 1 If a company carries out a **market test**, it asks a group of people to try a new product or service and give their opinions on it. [BUSINESS] ❑ *Results from market tests in the US and Europe show little enthusiasm for the product.* N-COUNT 2 If a new product or service **is market tested**, a group of people are asked to try it and then asked for their opinions on it. [BUSINESS] ❑ *The company uses the simulator to market test new designs.* VERB V n ♦ **mar|ket test|ing** *They learnt a lot from the initial market testing exercise.* N-UNCOUNT

**mar|ket town** **(market towns)** A **market town** is a town, especially in a country area, that has or used to have a market in it. N-COUNT

**mark|ing** /mɑːʳkɪŋ/ **(markings)** **Markings** are coloured lines, shapes, or patterns on the surface of something, which help to identify it. ❑ *A plane with Danish markings was over-flying his vessel.* ➔ See also **mark**. N-COUNT: usu pl

**marks|man** /mɑːʳksmən/ **(marksmen)** A **marksman** is a person who can shoot very accurately. ❑ *Police marksmen opened fire.* N-COUNT

**marks|man|ship** /mɑːʳksmənʃɪp/ **Marksmanship** is the ability to shoot accurately. N-UNCOUNT

**mark-up** **(mark-ups)**

in AM, also use **markup**

A **mark-up** is an increase in the price of something, for example the difference between its cost and the price that it is sold for. N-COUNT

**mar|ma|lade** /mɑːʳməleɪd/ **(marmalades)** **Marmalade** is a food made from oranges, lemons, or grapefruit that is similar to jam. It is eaten on bread or toast at breakfast. N-MASS

**mar|mo|set** /mɑːʳməzet/ **(marmosets)** A **marmoset** is a type of small monkey. N-COUNT

**ma|roon** /mərуːn/ **(maroons, marooning, marooned)** 1 Something that is **maroon** is dark reddish-purple in colour. ❑ *...maroon velvet curtains.* COLOUR 2 If someone **is marooned** somewhere, they are left in a place that is difficult for them to escape from. ❑ *Five couples were marooned in their caravans when the River Avon broke its banks.* VERB: usu passive *be* V-ed prep/adv

**ma|rooned** /məruːnd/ If you say that you are **marooned**, you mean that you feel alone and helpless and you cannot escape from the place or situation you are in. ❑ *...families marooned in decaying inner-city areas.* ADJ: usu v-link ADJ, oft ADJ prep = stuck

**marque** /mɑːʳk/ **(marques)** A **marque** is the name of a famous company that makes motor vehicles, or the vehicles it produces. ❑ *...a marque long-associated with motor racing success, Alfa Romeo.* N-COUNT

**mar|quee** /mɑːʳkiː/ **(marquees)** 1 A **marquee** is a large tent which is used at a fair, garden party, or other outdoor event, usually for eating and drinking in. N-COUNT 2 A **marquee** is a cover over the entrance of a building, for example a hotel or a theatre. [AM] N-COUNT

**mar|quis** /mɑːʳkwɪs/ **(marquises)** also **marquess.** A **marquis** is a male member of the nobility who has a rank between duke and earl. N-COUNT; N-TITLE

**mar|riage** /mærɪdʒ/ **(marriages)** 1 A **marriage** is the relationship between a husband and wife. ❑ *When I was 35 my marriage broke up... His son by his second marriage lives in Paris.* ◆◆◇ N-COUNT 2 A **marriage** is the act of marrying someone, or the ceremony at which this is done. ❑ *I opposed her marriage to Darryl.* N-VAR 3 **Marriage** is the state of being married. ❑ *Marriage might not suit you.* N-UNCOUNT 4 ➔ See also **arranged marriage.**

**mar|riage|able** /mærɪdʒəbᵊl/ If you describe someone as **marriageable**, you mean that they are suitable for marriage, especially that they are the right age to marry. [OLD-FASHIONED] ❑ *...girls of marriageable age. ...a marriageable daughter.* ADJ: usu ADJ n

**mar|riage guid|ance** **Marriage guidance** is advice given to couples who are having problems in their relationship. [BRIT] N-UNCOUNT: usu N n

**mar|ried** /mærid/ 1 If you are **married**, you have a husband or wife. ❑ *We have been married for 14 years... She is married to an Englishman. ...a married man with two children.* ◆◇◇ ADJ: oft ADJ *to* n 2 **Married** means relating to marriage or to people who are married. ❑ *For the first ten years of our married life we lived in a farmhouse.* ADJ: ADJ n 3 If you say that someone is **married to** their work or another activity, you mean that they are very involved with it and have little interest in anything else. ❑ *She was a very strict Christian who was married to her job.* ADJ: v-link ADJ *to* n

**mar|row** /mærəʊ/ **(marrows)** 1 A **marrow** is a long, thick, green vegetable with soft white flesh that is eaten cooked. [BRIT] N-VAR

in AM, use **squash**

2 **The marrow of** something is the most important and basic part of it. ❑ *We're getting into the marrow of the film.* N-SING: *the* N, usu N *of* n = crux

**mar|row bone** **(marrow bones)** also **marrowbone.** **Marrow bones** are the bones of certain animals, especially cows, that contain a lot of bone marrow. They are used in cooking and in dog food. ❑ *...marrowbone jelly.* N-VAR

**mar|ry** /mæri/ **(marries, marrying, married)** ◆◆◇
1 When two people **get married** or **marry**, they legally become husband and wife in a special ceremony. **Get married** is less formal and more commonly used than **marry**. ❑ *I thought he would change after we got married... They married a month after they met... He wants to marry her... He got married to wife Beryl when he was 19... I am getting married on Monday... She ought to marry again, don't you think?* V-RECIP; pl-n *get* V-ed; pl-n V; V n; *get* V-ed *to* n; *get* V-ed (non-recip); V (non-recip)
2 When a priest or official **marries** two people, he or she conducts the ceremony in which the two people legally become husband and wife. ❑ *The local vicar has agreed to marry us in the chapel on the estate.* VERB; V n

**marsh** /mɑːʳʃ/ **(marshes)** A **marsh** is a wet, muddy area of land. N-VAR = bog

**mar|shal** /mɑːʳʃᵊl/ **(marshals, marshalling, marshalled)**

☑ in AM, use **marshaling, marshaled**

1 If you **marshal** people or things, you gather them together and arrange them for a particular purpose. ❑ *Richard was marshalling the doctors and nurses, showing them where to go. ...the way in which Britain marshalled its economic and political resources to protect its security interests.* VERB = organize; V n; V n
2 A **marshal** is an official who helps to supervise a public event, especially a sports event. ❑ *The grand prix is controlled by well-trained marshals.* N-COUNT
3 In the United States and some other countries, a **marshal** is a police officer, often one who is responsible for a particular area. ❑ *A federal marshal was killed in a shoot-out.* N-COUNT
4 A **marshal** is an officer in a fire department. [AM] ❑ *...a Cleveland county fire marshal.* N-COUNT
5 In Britain and some other countries, a **marshal** is an officer who has the highest rank in an army or air force. ❑ *...Air Chief Marshal Sir Kenneth Cross.* N-COUNT; N-TITLE

**marsh|land** /mɑːʳʃlænd/ **(marshlands)** **Marshland** is land with a lot of wet, muddy areas. N-UNCOUNT: also N in pl

**marsh|mal|low** /mɑːʳʃmælou, AM -mel-/ **(marshmallows)**
1 **Marshmallow** is a soft, sweet food that is used in some cakes, puddings, and sweets. N-UNCOUNT
2 **Marshmallows** are sweets made from marshmallow. N-COUNT

**marshy** /mɑːʳʃi/ **Marshy** land is always wet and muddy. ❑ *...the broad, marshy plain of the River Spey.* ADJ: usu ADJ n

**mar|su|pial** /mɑːʳsuːpiəl/ **(marsupials)** A **marsupial** is an animal such as a kangaroo or an opossum. Female marsupials carry their babies in a pouch on their stomach. N-COUNT

**mart** /mɑːʳt/ **(marts)** A **mart** is a place such as a market where things are bought and sold. [AM] ❑ *...the flower mart.* N-COUNT: oft n N

**mar|tial** /mɑːʳʃᵊl/ **Martial** is used to describe things relating to soldiers or war. [FORMAL] ❑ *The paper was actually twice banned under the martial regime.* → See also **court martial**. ADJ: usu ADJ n

**mar|tial art** **(martial arts)** A **martial art** is one of the methods of fighting, often without weapons, that come from the Far East, for example kung fu, karate, or judo. N-COUNT

**mar|tial law** **Martial law** is control of an area by soldiers, not the police. ❑ *The military leadership have lifted martial law in several more towns.* N-UNCOUNT

**Mar|tian** /mɑːʳʃᵊn/ **(Martians)**
1 A **Martian** is an imaginary creature from the planet Mars. ❑ *Orson Welles managed to convince many Americans that they were being invaded by Martians.* N-COUNT
2 Something that is **Martian** exists on or relates to the planet Mars. ❑ *The Martian atmosphere contains only tiny amounts of water.* ADJ: usu ADJ n

**mar|tin** /mɑːʳtɪn/ **(martins)** A **martin** is a small bird with a forked tail. N-COUNT

**mar|ti|net** /mɑːʳtɪnet/ **(martinets)** If you say that someone is a **martinet**, you are criticizing them because they are very strict and demand that people obey their rules and orders. [FORMAL] ❑ *He's a retired Lieutenant Colonel and a bit of a martinet.* N-COUNT [disapproval]

**mar|tyr** /mɑːʳtəʳ/ **(martyrs, martyring, martyred)**
1 A **martyr** is someone who is killed or made to suffer greatly because of their religious or political beliefs, and is admired and respected by people who share those beliefs. ❑ *...a glorious martyr to the cause of liberty. ...a Christian martyr.* N-COUNT: oft N *to* n
2 If someone **is martyred**, they are killed or made to suffer greatly because of their religious or political beliefs. ❑ *St Pancras was martyred in 304 AD. ...whether its martyred leader is released or not.* VERB: usu passive; *be* V-ed; V-ed
3 If you refer to someone as a **martyr**, you disapprove of the fact that they pretend to suffer, or exaggerate their suffering, in order to get sympathy or praise from other people. ❑ *When are you going to quit acting like a martyr?* N-COUNT [disapproval]
4 If you say that someone is a **martyr to** something, you mean that they suffer as a result of it. ❑ *Ellsworth was a martyr to his sense of honour and responsibility.* N-COUNT: usu N *to* n
5 → See also **martyred**.

**mar|tyr|dom** /mɑːʳtəʳdəm/
1 If someone suffers **martyrdom**, they are killed or made to suffer greatly because of their religious or political beliefs. ❑ *...the martyrdom of Bishop Feliciano... He suffered martyrdom by stoning.* N-UNCOUNT
2 If you describe someone's behaviour as **martyrdom**, you are critical of them because they are exaggerating their suffering in order to gain sympathy or praise. ❑ *She sat picking at her small plate of rice salad with an air of martyrdom.* N-UNCOUNT [disapproval]

**mar|tyred** /mɑːʳtəʳd/ If you describe a person or their behaviour as **martyred**, you mean that they often exaggerate their suffering in order to gain sympathy or praise. [LITERARY] ❑ *'As usual,' muttered his martyred wife. ...with a lot of sighs, moans and a martyred air.* ADJ: ADJ n [disapproval]

**mar|vel** /mɑːʳvᵊl/ **(marvels, marvelling, marvelled)**

☑ in AM, use **marveling, marveled**

1 If you **marvel** at something, you express your great surprise, wonder, or admiration. ❑ *Her fellow members marveled at her seemingly infinite energy... Sara and I read the story and marveled... 'That's the weirdest thing I've ever seen,' marveled Carl... He marvelled that a man in such intense pain could be so coherent.* VERB; V *at* n; V; V with quote; V that
2 You can describe something or someone as a **marvel** to indicate that you think that they are wonderful. ❑ *The whale, like the dolphin, has become a symbol of the marvels of creation.* N-COUNT: oft N *of* n = wonder
3 **Marvels** are things that people have done, or that have happened, which are very unexpected or surprising. ❑ *He's done marvels with the team.* N-COUNT: usu pl = wonders

**mar|vel|lous** /mɑːʳvələs/

☑ in AM, use **marvelous**

If you describe someone or something as **marvellous**, you are emphasizing that they are very good. ❑ *He certainly is a marvellous actor... He looked marvellous.* ADJ = wonderful ♦ **mar|vel|lous|ly** *He always painted marvellously.* ADV: ADV with v, ADV adj/adv

**Marx|ism** /mɑːʳksɪzəm/ **Marxism** is a political philosophy based on the writings of Karl Marx which stresses the importance of the struggle between different social classes. N-UNCOUNT

**Marx|ist** /mɑːʳksɪst/ **(Marxists)**
1 **Marxist** means based on Marxism or relating to Marxism. ❑ *...a Marxist state. ...Marxist ideology.* ADJ
2 A **Marxist** is a person who believes in Marxism or who is a member of a Marxist party. N-COUNT

**mar|zi|pan** /mɑːʳzɪpæn/ **Marzipan** is a paste made of almonds, sugar, and egg which is sometimes put on top of cakes. N-UNCOUNT

**masc.** **Masc.** is a written abbreviation of **masculine**.

**mas|cara** /mæskɑːrə, AM -kær-/ **(mascaras)** [N-MASS] **Mascara** is a substance used as make-up to make eyelashes darker. ❑ *...water-resistant mascaras.*

**mas|car|pone** /mæskəʳpoʊni/ [N-UNCOUNT] **Mascarpone** is a soft white cheese traditionally made in Italy. It is used to make desserts.

**mas|cot** /mæskɒt/ **(mascots)** [N-COUNT: usu with supp] A **mascot** is an animal, toy, or symbol which is associated with a particular organization or event, and which is thought to bring good luck. ❑ *...the official mascot of the Barcelona Games.*

**mas|cu|line** /mæskjʊlɪn/ 1 [ADJ: usu ADJ n = male ≠ female] **Masculine** qualities and things relate to or are considered typical of men, in contrast to women. ❑ *...masculine characteristics like a husky voice and facial hair. ...masculine pride.* 2 [ADJ ≠ feminine] If you say that someone or something is **masculine**, you mean that they have qualities such as strength or confidence which are considered typical of men. ❑ *...her aggressive, masculine image... The Duke's study was very masculine, with deep red wall-covering and dark oak shelving.* 3 [ADJ] In some languages, a **masculine** noun, pronoun, or adjective has a different form from a feminine or neuter one, or behaves in a different way.

**mas|cu|lin|ity** /mæskjʊlɪnɪti/ 1 [N-UNCOUNT] A man's **masculinity** is the fact that he is a man. ❑ *...a project on the link between masculinity and violence.* 2 [N-UNCOUNT = manhood ≠ femininity] **Masculinity** means the qualities, especially sexual qualities, which are considered to be typical of men. ❑ *The old ideas of masculinity do not work for most men.*

**mas|cu|lin|ize** /mæskjʊlɪnaɪz/ **(masculinizes, masculinizing, masculinized)**

☑ in BRIT, also use **masculinise**

[VERB: usu passive] To **masculinize** something means to make it into something that involves mainly men or is thought suitable for or typical of men. [FORMAL] ❑ *Not all plantation work has been masculinized.* [be V-ed]

**mash** /mæʃ/ **(mashes, mashing, mashed)** 1 [VERB] If you **mash** food that is solid but soft, you crush it so that it forms a soft mass. ❑ *Mash the bananas* [V n] *with a fork. ...mashed potatoes.* [V-ed] 2 [N-UNCOUNT] **Mash** is mashed potato. [BRIT, INFORMAL]

**mask** /mɑːsk, mæsk/ **(masks, masking, masked)** ◆◇◇ 1 [N-COUNT] A **mask** is a piece of cloth or other material, which you wear over your face so that people cannot see who you are, or so that you look like someone or something else. ❑ *The gunman, whose mask had slipped, fled. ...actors wearing masks.* 2 [N-COUNT: oft supp N] A **mask** is a piece of cloth or other material that you wear over all or part of your face to protect you from germs or harmful substances. ❑ *You must wear goggles and a mask that will protect you against the fumes.* 3 [N-COUNT: oft N of n] If you describe someone's behaviour as a **mask**, you mean that they do not show their real feelings or character. ❑ *His mask of detachment cracked, and she saw for an instant an angry and violent man.* 4 [N-COUNT] A **mask** is a thick cream or paste made of various substances, which you spread over your face and leave for some time in order to improve your skin. ❑ *This mask leaves your complexion feeling soft and supple.* 5 [VERB = conceal, hide] If you **mask** your feelings, you deliberately do not show them in your behaviour, so that people cannot know what you really feel. ❑ *Dena lit a* [V n] *cigarette, trying to mask her agitation.* 6 [VERB] If one thing **masks** another, it prevents people from noticing or recognizing the other thing. ❑ *Too much* [V n] *salt masks the true flavour of the food.* 7 → See also **death mask**, **gas mask**, **oxygen mask**.

**masked** /mɑːskt, mæskt/ [ADJ] If someone is **masked**, they are wearing a mask. ❑ *Masked youths threw stones and fire-bombs.*

**mask|ing tape** [N-UNCOUNT] **Masking tape** is plastic or paper tape which is sticky on one side and is used, for example, to protect part of a surface that you are painting.

**maso|chism** /mæsəkɪzəm/ 1 [N-UNCOUNT ≠ sadism] **Masochism** is behaviour in which someone gets sexual pleasure from their own pain or suffering. ❑ *The tendency towards masochism is however always linked with elements of sadism.* ♦ **maso|chist** **(masochists)** [N-COUNT] *...consensual sexual masochists.* 2 [N-UNCOUNT ≠ sadism] If you describe someone's behaviour as **masochism**, you mean that they seem to be trying to get into a situation which causes them suffering or great difficulty. ❑ *Once you have tasted life in southern California, it takes a peculiar kind of masochism to return to a British winter.* ♦ **maso|chist** [N-COUNT] *Anybody who enjoys this is a masochist.* 3 → See also **sado-masochism**.

**maso|chis|tic** /mæsəkɪstɪk/ 1 [ADJ ≠ sadistic] **Masochistic** behaviour involves a person getting sexual pleasure from their own pain or suffering. ❑ *...his masochistic tendencies.* 2 [ADJ ≠ sadistic] If you describe someone's behaviour as **masochistic**, you mean that they seem to be trying to get into a situation which causes them suffering or great difficulty. ❑ *It seems masochistic, somehow.* 3 → See also **sado-masochistic**.

**ma|son** /meɪsᵊn/ **(masons)** 1 [N-COUNT] A **mason** is a person who is skilled at making things or building things with stone. In American English, **masons** are people who work with stone or bricks. 2 [N-COUNT] A **Mason** is the same as a **Freemason**.

**Ma|son|ic** /məsɒnɪk/ [ADJ: ADJ n] **Masonic** is used to describe things relating to the organization of Freemasons. ❑ *...a Masonic lodge on Broughton Street.*

**ma|son|ry** /meɪsənri/ [N-UNCOUNT] **Masonry** is bricks or pieces of stone which have been stuck together with cement as part of a wall or building.

**mas|quer|ade** /mæskəreɪd/ **(masquerades, masquerading, masqueraded)** 1 [VERB] To **masquerade as** someone or something means to pretend to be that person or thing, particularly in order to deceive other people. ❑ *He masqueraded as a doctor* [V as n] *and fooled everyone.* 2 [N-COUNT = sham] A **masquerade** is an attempt to deceive people about the true nature or identity of something. ❑ *He told a news conference that the elections would be a masquerade.* 3 [N-COUNT] A **masquerade** is an event such as a party or dance where people dress up in disguise and wear masks. ❑ *...a masquerade ball.*

**mass** /mæs/ **(masses, massing, massed)** ◆◆◇ 1 [N-SING: N of n] A **mass of** things is a large number of them grouped together. ❑ *On his desk is a mass of books and papers.* 2 [N-SING: N of n] A **mass of** something is a large amount of it. ❑ *She had a mass of auburn hair.* 3 [QUANT: QUANT of n-uncount/pl-n] **Masses of** something means a great deal of it. [INFORMAL] ❑ *There's masses of work for her to do... It has masses of flowers each year.* 4 [ADJ: ADJ n] **Mass** is used to describe something which involves or affects a very large number of people. ❑ *...ideas on combating mass unemployment. ...weapons of mass destruction.* 5 [N-COUNT: oft N of n] A **mass of** a solid substance, a liquid, or a gas is an amount of it, especially a large amount which has no definite shape. ❑ *...before it cools and sets into a solid mass... The fourteenth century cathedral was reduced to a mass of rubble.* 6 [N-PLURAL: the N] If you talk about **the masses**, you mean the ordinary people in society, in contrast to the leaders or the highly educated people. ❑ *His music is commercial. It is aimed at the masses.* 7 [N-SING: the N of n = bulk, majority] **The mass of** people are most of the people in a country, society, or group. ❑ *The 1939-45 world war involved the mass of the population.* 8 [VERB = gather] When people or things **mass**, or when you **mass** them, they gather together into a large crowd or group. ❑ *Shortly after the* [V] *workers went on strike, police began to mass at the shipyard... The General was massing his troops for a* [V n] *counterattack.* 9 [N-SING: N of n] If you say that something is **a mass of** things, you mean that it is covered with them or full of them. ❑ *In the spring, the meadow is a mass of daffodils.* 10 [N-VAR] In physics, the **mass** of an object is the amount of physical matter that it has. [TECHNICAL] ❑ *Astronomers know that Pluto and Triton have nearly the same size, mass, and density.* 11 [N-VAR] **Mass** is a Christian church ceremony, especially in a Roman Catholic or Orthodox church, during which people eat bread and drink wine in order to remember the last meal of Jesus Christ. ❑ *She attended a convent school and went to Mass each day.* 12 → See also **massed**, **critical mass**, **land mass**.

**mas|sa|cre** /mæsəkəʳ/ **(massacres, massacring, massacred)** 1 A **massacre** is the killing of a large number of people at the same time in a violent and cruel way. [N-VAR] ❑ *Maria lost her 62-year-old mother in the massacre. ...reports of massacre, torture and starvation.* 2 If people **are massacred**, a large number of them are attacked and killed in a violent and cruel way. [VERB] ❑ *300 civilians are believed to have been massacred by the rebels...* [be V-ed] *Troops indiscriminately massacred the defenceless population.* [V n]

**mas|sage** /mæsɑːʒ, AM məsɑːʒ/ **(massages, massaging, massaged)** 1 **Massage** is the action of squeezing and rubbing someone's body, as a way of making them relax or reducing their pain. [N-VAR] ❑ *Alex asked me if I wanted a massage.* 2 If you **massage** someone or a part of their body, you squeeze and rub their body, in order to make them relax or reduce their pain. [VERB] ❑ *She continued massaging her right foot, which was bruised and aching.* [V n] 3 If you say that someone **massages** statistics, figures, or evidence, you are criticizing them for changing or presenting the facts in a way that misleads people. [VERB] [disapproval] ❑ *Their governments have no reason to 'massage' the statistics.* [V n]

**mas|sage par|lour** **(massage parlours)**

✓ in AM, use **massage parlor**

A **massage parlour** is a place where people go and pay for a massage. Some places that are called **massage parlours** are in fact places where people pay to have sex. [N-COUNT]

**masse** → see **en masse**.

**massed** /mæst/ **Massed** is used to describe a large number of people who have been brought together for a particular purpose. [ADJ: ADJ n] ❑ *He could not escape the massed ranks of newsmen.*

**mas|seur** /mæsɜːʳ, AM -sʊəʳ/ **(masseurs)** A **masseur** is a person whose job is to give massages. [N-COUNT]

**mas|seuse** /mæsɜːz, AM -suːs/ **(masseuses)** A **masseuse** is a woman whose job is to give massages. [N-COUNT]

**mas|sif** /mæsiːf/ **(massifs)** A **massif** is a group of mountains that form part of a mountain range. [N-COUNT: oft in names]

**mas|sive** /mæsɪv/ 1 Something that is **massive** is very large in size, quantity, or extent. [◆◇◇] [ADJ] [emphasis] [= huge] ❑ *There was evidence of massive fraud. ...massive air attacks... The scale of the problem is massive.* ♦ **mas|sive|ly** *...a massively popular board game.* [ADV] 2 If you describe a medical condition as **massive**, you mean that it is extremely serious. [ADJ: ADJ n] ❑ *He died six weeks later of a massive heart attack.*

**mass mar|ket** **(mass markets)** 1 **Mass market** is used to refer to the large numbers of people who want to buy a particular product. [N-COUNT] [BUSINESS] ❑ *They now have access to the mass markets of Japan and the UK.* 2 **Mass-market** products are designed and produced for selling to large numbers of people. [ADJ: ADJ n] [BUSINESS] ❑ *...mass-market paperbacks.*

**mass me|dia** You can use the **mass media** to refer to the various ways, especially television, radio, newspapers, and magazines, by which information and news are given to large numbers of people. [N-SING-COLL: usu *the* N] ❑ *...mass media coverage of the issue.*

**mass mur|der** **(mass murders)** **Mass murder** is the deliberate illegal killing of a large number of people by a person or an organization. [N-VAR]

**mass mur|der|er** **(mass murderers)** A **mass murderer** is someone who deliberately kills a large number of people illegally. [N-COUNT]

**mass noun** **(mass nouns)** 1 A **mass noun** is a noun such as 'wine' which is usually uncount but is used with 'a' or 'an' or used in the plural when it refers to types of that substance, as in 'a range of Australian wines'. [N-COUNT] 2 In some descriptions of grammar, a **mass noun** is the same as an **uncount noun**. [N-COUNT]

**mass-produce** **(mass-produces, mass-producing, mass-produced)** If someone **mass-produces** something, they make it in large quantities, usually by machine. This means that the product can be sold cheaply. [VERB] [BUSINESS] ❑ *...the invention of machinery to mass-produce footwear.* [V n] ♦ **mass-produced** *...the first mass-produced mountain bike.* [ADJ: ADJ n]

**mass pro|duc|tion** also **mass-production**. **Mass production** is the production of something in large quantities, especially by machine. [N-UNCOUNT: oft N *of* n] [BUSINESS] ❑ *...equipment that would allow the mass production of baby food.*

**mast** /mɑːst, mæst/ **(masts)** 1 The **masts** of a boat are the tall upright poles that support its sails. [N-COUNT] 2 A radio **mast** is a tall upright structure that is used to transmit radio or television signals. [N-COUNT]

**mas|tec|to|my** /mæstektəmi/ **(mastectomies)** A **mastectomy** is a surgical operation to remove a woman's breast. [N-VAR]

**mas|ter** /mɑːstəʳ, mæs-/ **(masters, mastering, mastered)** [◆◆◇] 1 A servant's **master** is the man that he or she works for. [N-COUNT] ❑ *My master ordered me not to deliver the message except in private.* 2 A dog's **master** is the man or boy who owns it. [N-COUNT: usu poss N] ❑ *The dog yelped excitedly when his master opened a desk drawer and produced his leash.* 3 If you say that someone is a **master** of a particular activity, you mean that they are extremely skilled at it. [N-COUNT: usu N *of/at/in* n/-ing] ❑ *They appear masters in the art of making regulations work their way.* → See also **past master**. ♦ **Master** is also an adjective. [ADJ: ADJ n] ❑ *...a master craftsman. ...a master criminal.* 4 If you are **master** of a situation, you have complete control over it. [N-VAR: usu N *of* n] ❑ *Jackson remained calm and always master of his passions.* 5 If you **master** something, you learn how to do it properly or you succeed in understanding it completely. [VERB] ❑ *Duff soon mastered the skills of radio production...* [V n] *Students are expected to master a second language.* [V n] 6 If you **master** a difficult situation, you succeed in controlling it. [VERB] ❑ *When you have mastered one situation you have to go on to the next.* [V n] 7 A famous male painter of the past is often called a **master**. [N-COUNT] ❑ *...a portrait by the Dutch master, Vincent Van Gogh.* → See also **old master**. 8 A **master** copy of something such as a film or a tape recording is an original copy that can be used to produce other copies. [ADJ: ADJ n] ❑ *Keep one as a master copy for your own reference and circulate the others.* 9 A **master's degree** can be referred to as a **master's**. [N-SING] ❑ *I've a master's in economics.*

**mas|ter bed|room** **(master bedrooms)** The **master bedroom** in a large house is the largest bedroom. [N-COUNT]

**mas|ter|class** /mɑːstəʳklɑːs, mæstəʳklæs/ **(masterclasses)** A **masterclass** is a lesson where someone who is an expert at something such as dancing or music gives advice to a group of good students. Masterclasses usually take place in public or are broadcast on television. [N-COUNT]

**mas|ter|ful** /mɑːstəʳfʊl, mæs-/ 1 If you describe a man as **masterful**, you approve of him because he behaves in a way which shows that he is in control of a situation and can tell other people what to do. [ADJ] [approval] ❑ *Big, successful moves need bold, masterful managers.* 2 If you describe someone's behaviour or actions as **masterful**, you mean that they show great skill. [ADJ] [= virtuoso] ❑ *...a masterful performance of boxing and punching skills.*

**mas|ter key** **(master keys)** A **master key** is a key which will open all the locks in a set, even though each lock has its own different key. [N-COUNT]

**mas|ter|ly** /mɑːstəʳli, mæs-/ If you describe something as **masterly**, you admire it because it has been done extremely well or shows the highest level of ability and skill. [ADJ] [approval] ❑ *Malcolm Hebden gives a masterly performance.*

**master|mind** /mɑːstəʳmaɪnd, mæs-/ **(masterminds, masterminding, masterminded)** 1 If you **mastermind** a difficult or complicated activity, you plan it in detail and then make sure that it happens successfully. ❑ *The finance minister will continue to mastermind Poland's economic reform.* 2 The **mastermind behind** a difficult or complicated plan, often a criminal one, is the person who is responsible for planning and organizing it. ❑ *He was the mastermind behind the plan to acquire the explosives.* VERB; V n; N-COUNT: usu sing, usu with supp, oft N *behind/of* n

**Mas|ter of Arts** A **Master of Arts** degree is the same as an **MA** degree. N-SING

**mas|ter of cer|emo|nies (masters of ceremonies)** At events such as formal dinners, award ceremonies, and variety shows, the **master of ceremonies** is the person who introduces the speakers or performers, and who announces what is going to happen next. N-COUNT

**Mas|ter of Sci|ence** A **Master of Science** degree is the same as an **MSc** or **MS** degree. N-SING

**master|piece** /mɑːstəʳpiːs, mæs-/ **(masterpieces)** 1 A **masterpiece** is an extremely good painting, novel, film, or other work of art. ❑ *His book, I must add, is a masterpiece.* 2 An artist's, writer's, or composer's **masterpiece** is the best work that they have ever produced. ❑ *'Man's Fate,' translated into sixteen languages, is probably his masterpiece.* 3 A **masterpiece** is an extremely clever or skilful example of something. ❑ *The whole thing was a masterpiece of crowd management.* N-COUNT; N-COUNT: with poss; N-COUNT: oft N *of* n

**mas|ter plan (master plans)** A **master plan** is a clever plan that is intended to help someone succeed in a very difficult or important task. ❑ *...the master plan for the reform of the economy.* N-COUNT

**mas|ter's de|gree (master's degrees)** also **Master's degree.** A **master's degree** is a university degree such as an MA or an MSc which is of a higher level than a first degree and usually takes one or two years to complete. N-COUNT

**master|stroke** /mɑːstəʳstroʊk, mæs-/ **(masterstrokes)** A **masterstroke** is something you do which is unexpected but very clever and which helps you to achieve something. ❑ *Graham pulled a masterstroke by playing Paul Merson in the centre of midfield.* N-COUNT: usu sing

**master|work** /mɑːstəʳwɜːʳk, mæs-/ **(masterworks)** If you describe something such as a book or a painting as a **masterwork**, you think it is extremely good or the best that someone has produced. ❑ *They endure as masterworks of American musical theatre.* N-COUNT: oft poss N, N *of* n = masterpiece

**mas|tery** /mɑːstəri, mæs-/ If you show **mastery of** a particular skill or language, you show that you have learned or understood it completely and have no difficulty using it. ❑ *He doesn't have mastery of the basic rules of grammar.* N-UNCOUNT: oft N *of* n

**mast|head** /mɑːsthed, mæst-/ **(mastheads)** 1 A ship's **masthead** is the highest part of its mast. 2 A newspaper's **masthead** is the part at the top of the front page where its name appears in big letters. N-COUNT; N-COUNT: usu sing, usu with poss

**mas|ti|cate** /mæstɪkeɪt/ **(masticates, masticating, masticated)** When you **masticate** food, you chew it. [FORMAL] ❑ *Her mouth was working, as if she was masticating some tasty titbit... Don't gulp everything down without masticating.* ♦ **mas|ti|ca|tion** /mæstɪkeɪʃən/ *Poor digestion can be caused by defective mastication of the food in the mouth.* VERB; V n; V; N-UNCOUNT

**mas|tiff** /mæstɪf/ **(mastiffs)** A **mastiff** is a large, powerful, short-haired dog. N-COUNT

**mas|tur|bate** /mæstəʳbeɪt/ **(masturbates, masturbating, masturbated)** If someone **masturbates**, they stroke or rub their own genitals in order to get sexual pleasure. ♦ **mas|tur|ba|tion** /mæstəʳbeɪʃən/ ❑ *The sperm sample is produced by masturbation.* VERB; N-UNCOUNT

**mat** /mæt/ **(mats)** 1 A **mat** is a small piece of something such as cloth, card, or plastic which you put on a table to protect it from plates or cups. ❑ *The food is served on polished tables with mats.* 2 A **mat** is a small piece of carpet or other thick material which is put on the floor for protection, decoration, or comfort. ❑ *There was a letter on the mat.* 3 ➔ See also **matt**, **place mat**. N-COUNT; N-COUNT

**mata|dor** /mætədɔːʳ/ **(matadors)** A **matador** is the person in a bullfight who is supposed to kill the bull. N-COUNT = bullfighter

**match** /mætʃ/ **(matches, matching, matched)** ◆◆◆ 1 A **match** is an organized game of football, tennis, cricket, or some other sport. [mainly BRIT] ❑ *He was watching a football match... France won the match 28-19.* 2 A **match** is a small wooden stick with a substance on one end that produces a flame when you rub it along the rough side of a matchbox. ❑ *...a packet of cigarettes and a box of matches.* 3 If something of a particular colour or design **matches** another thing, they have the same colour or design, or have a pleasing appearance when they are used together. ❑ *Her nails were painted bright red to match her dress... All the chairs matched... You don't have to match your lipstick exactly to your outfit... Mix and match your tableware and textiles from the new Design House collection.* ♦ **Match up** means the same as **match**. ❑ *The pillow cover can match up with the sheets... Because false eyelashes come in various lengths and shades, it's so easy to match them up with your own.* 4 If something such as an amount or a quality **matches with** another amount or quality, they are both the same or equal. If you **match** two things, you make them the same or equal. ❑ *Their strengths in memory and spatial skills matched... Our value system does not match with their value system. ...efforts to match demand with supply by building new schools.* 5 If one thing **matches** another, they are connected or suit each other in some way. ❑ *The students are asked to match the books with the authors... It can take time and effort to match buyers and sellers... The sale would only go ahead if the name and number matched... Pictures of road signs are matched with their Highway Code meanings.* ♦ **Match up** means the same as **match**. ❑ *The consultant seeks to match up jobless professionals with small companies in need of expertise... They compared the fat intake of groups of vegetarians and meat eaters, and matched their diets up with levels of harmful blood fats... My sister and I never really matched up... I'm sure that yellow lead matched up to that yellow socket.* 6 If a combination of things or people is a good **match**, they have a pleasing effect when placed or used together. ❑ *Helen's choice of lipstick was a good match for her skin-tone... Moira was a perfect match for him.* 7 If you **match** something, you are as good as it or equal to it, for example in speed, size, or quality. ❑ *They played some fine attacking football, but I think we matched them in every respect.* 8 In a sport or other contest, if you **match** one person or team against another, in sports or other contests, you make them compete with each other to see which one is better. ❑ *The finals of the Championship begin today, matching the United States against France.* 9 ➔ See also **matched**, **matching**.
N-COUNT = game; N-COUNT; V-RECIP; V n; pl-n V; V n *to/with* n; V pl-n; PHRASAL VERB; V P *with/to* n; V n P *with/to* n; V-RECIP; pl-n V; V *with* n; V n *with* n; Also V pl-n; V-RECIP; V n *with/to* n; V pl-n; pl-n V; *be* V-ed *with* n; PHRASAL VERB; V P n (not pron) *with* n; V n P *with* n; pl-n V P; V P *to/with* n; Also V P pl-n; N-SING: adj N; VERB; V n; VERB; V n *with/against* n

**PHRASES** 10 If you **meet** your **match**, you find that you are competing or fighting against someone who you cannot beat because they are as good as you, or better than you. ❑ *I had finally met my match in power and intellect.* 11 If one person or thing is **no match for** another, they are unable to compete successfully with the other person or thing. ❑ *I was no match for a man with such power.* PHRASE: V inflects; PHRASE: v-link PHR, PHR n

♦ **match up** ➔ see **match 3, 5.**

♦ **match up to** If someone or something does not **match up to** what was expected, they are smaller, less impressive, or of poorer quality. ❑ *Her career never quite matched up to its promise.* PHRASAL VERB; V P P n

**match|box** /mætʃbɒks/ **(matchboxes)** A **matchbox** is a small box that you buy with matches in it. N-COUNT

**matched** /mætʃt/ [1] If you say that two people are well **matched**, you mean that they have qualities that will enable them to have a good relationship. ❑ *My parents were not very well matched.* ADJ: adv ADJ [2] In sports and other competitions, if the two opponents or teams are well **matched**, they are both of the same standard in strength or ability. ❑ *Two well-matched sides conjured up an entertaining game.* ADJ: adv ADJ

**match|ing** /mætʃɪŋ/ **Matching** is used to describe things which are of the same colour or design. ❑ *...a coat and a matching handbag.* ADJ: ADJ n

**match|less** /mætʃləs/ You can use **matchless** to emphasize that you think something is extremely good. ❑ *A timeless comic actor – his simplicity and his apparent ease are matchless... The Savoy provides a matchless hotel experience.* ADJ: usu ADJ n [emphasis] *= unparalleled*

**match|maker** /mætʃmeɪkə^r/ **(matchmakers)** A **matchmaker** is someone who tries to encourage people they know to form a romantic relationship or to get married. ❑ *Some friends played matchmaker and had us both over to dinner.* N-COUNT

**match|making** /mætʃmeɪkɪŋ/ **Matchmaking** is the activity of encouraging people you know to form relationships or get married. N-UNCOUNT

**match play** **Match play** is a form of golf where the game is scored by the number of holes someone wins rather than the number of strokes it takes them to complete the course. N-UNCOUNT: usu N n

**match point** **(match points)** In a game of tennis, **match point** is the situation when the player who is in the lead can win the whole match if they win the next point. N-VAR

**match|stick** /mætʃstɪk/ **(matchsticks)** A **matchstick** is the wooden part of a match. N-COUNT

**mate** /meɪt/ **(mates, mating, mated)** ◆◇◇ [1] You can refer to someone's friends as their **mates**, especially when you are talking about a man and his male friends. [BRIT, INFORMAL] ❑ *He's off drinking with his mates.* N-COUNT: usu with poss *= pal* [2] Some men use **mate** as a way of addressing other men when they are talking to them. [BRIT, INFORMAL] ❑ *Come on mate, things aren't that bad.* N-VOC *= pal* [3] Someone's wife, husband, or sexual partner can be referred to as their **mate**. ❑ *He has found his ideal mate.* N-COUNT: usu sing, oft poss N [4] An animal's **mate** is its sexual partner. ❑ *The males guard their mates zealously.* N-COUNT: usu poss N [5] When animals **mate**, a male and a female have sex in order to produce young. ❑ *This allows the pair to mate properly and stops the hen staying in the nest-box... They want the males to mate with wild females... It is easy to tell when a female is ready to mate. ...the mating season.* V-RECIP; pl-n V; V *with* n; V (non-recip); V-ing [6] On a commercial ship, **the mate** or **the first mate** is the most important officer except for the captain. Officers of lower rank are also called **mates**. ❑ *...the mate of a fishing trawler.* N-COUNT [7] In chess, **mate** is the same as **checkmate**. N-UNCOUNT [8] ➔ See also **cellmate**, **classmate**, **flatmate**, **playmate**, **roommate**, **running mate**, **schoolmate**, **shipmate**, **soul mate**.

**ma|terial** /mətɪəriəl/ **(materials)** ◆◆◇ [1] A **material** is a solid substance. ❑ *...electrons in a conducting material such as a metal. ...the design of new absorbent materials.* N-VAR [2] **Material** is cloth. ❑ *...the thick material of her skirt... The materials are soft and comfortable to wear.* N-MASS [3] **Materials** are the things that you need for a particular activity. ❑ *The builders ran out of materials. ...sewing materials.* N-PLURAL: usu supp N [4] Ideas or information that are used as a basis for a book, play, or film can be referred to as **material**. ❑ *In my version of the story, I added some new material.* N-UNCOUNT [5] **Material** things are related to possessions or money, rather than to more abstract things such as ideas or values. ❑ *Every room must have been stuffed with material things. ...the material world.* ADJ: usu ADJ n ≠ *spiritual* ♦ **ma|teri|al|ly** *He has tried to help this child materially and spiritually.* ADV: ADV with v, ADV adj/-ed, ADV with cl [6] If you say that someone is a particular kind of **material**, you mean that they have the qualities or abilities to do a particular job or task. ❑ *She was not university material... His message has changed little since he became presidential material.* N-UNCOUNT: supp N [7] **Material** evidence or information is directly relevant and important in a legal or academic argument. [FORMAL] ❑ *The nature and availability of material evidence was not to be discussed.* ADJ: ADJ n

**ma|teri|al|ise** /mətɪəriəlaɪz/ ➔ see **materialize**.

**ma|teri|al|ism** /mətɪəriəlɪzəm/ [1] **Materialism** is the attitude of someone who attaches a lot of importance to money and wants to possess a lot of material things. ❑ *...the rising consumer materialism in society at large.* N-UNCOUNT ♦ **ma|teri|al|ist** **(materialists)** *Leo is a materialist, living for life's little luxuries.* N-COUNT [2] **Materialism** is the belief that only physical matter exists, and that there is no spiritual world. N-UNCOUNT

**ma|teri|al|ist** /mətɪəriəlɪst/ **Materialist** is used to describe things relating to the philosophy of materialism. ❑ *...the materialist view of nature and society.* ADJ: usu ADJ n

**ma|teri|al|is|tic** /mətɪəriəlɪstɪk/ If you describe a person or society as **materialistic**, you are critical of them because they attach too much importance to money and material possessions. ❑ *In the 1980s Britain was a very materialistic society.* ADJ [disapproval]

**ma|teri|al|ize** /mətɪəriəlaɪz/ **(materializes, materializing, materialized)**

☑ in BRIT, also use **materialise**

[1] If a possible or expected event does not **materialize**, it does not happen. ❑ *A rebellion by radicals failed to materialize.* VERB: usu with brd-neg V [2] If a person or thing **materializes**, they suddenly appear, after they have been invisible or in another place. ❑ *Tamsin materialized at her side, notebook at the ready.* VERB = *appear* V

**ma|ter|nal** /mətɜːʳnəl/ [1] **Maternal** is used to describe feelings or actions which are typical of those of a kind mother towards her child. ❑ *She had little maternal instinct... Her feelings towards him were almost maternal.* ADJ: usu ADJ n [2] **Maternal** is used to describe things that relate to the mother of a baby. ❑ *Maternal smoking can damage the unborn child.* ADJ: ADJ n [3] A **maternal** relative is one who is related through a person's mother rather than their father. ❑ *Her maternal grandfather was Mayor of Karachi.* ADJ: ADJ n

**ma|ter|nity** /mətɜːʳnɪti/ **Maternity** is used to describe things relating to the help and medical care given to a woman when she is pregnant and when she gives birth. ❑ *Your job will be kept open for your return after maternity leave. ...maternity clothes.* ADJ: ADJ n

**matey** /meɪti/ [1] If someone is **matey**, they behave in a very friendly way, usually without sincerity. [BRIT, INFORMAL] ❑ *...her irritatingly matey tone.* ADJ [2] You can address someone as **matey** when you are being friendly towards them. People sometimes also use **matey** when they are annoyed with someone. [BRIT, INFORMAL] ❑ *No problem, matey.* N-VOC [feelings]

**math** /mæθ/ **Math** is the same as **mathematics**. [AM] ❑ *He studied math in college.* N-UNCOUNT

☑ in BRIT, use **maths**

**math|emati|cal** /mæθəmætɪkəl/ [1] Something that is **mathematical** involves numbers and calculations. ❑ *...mathematical calculations.* ADJ: ADJ n ♦ **math|emati|cal|ly** /mæθəmætɪkli/ *...a mathematically complicated formula... Mathematically, it made sense.* ADV: ADV with v, ADV adj, ADV with cl [2] If you have **mathematical** abilities or a **mathematical** mind, you are clever at doing calculations or understanding problems that involve numbers. ❑ *...a mathematical genius.* ADJ: usu ADJ n ♦ **math|emati|cal|ly** *Anyone can be an astrologer as long as they are mathematically minded.* ADV: ADV -ed/adj

**math|ema|ti|cian** /mæθəmətɪʃən/ **(mathematicians)** [1] A **mathematician** is a person N-COUNT who is trained in the study of numbers and calculations. ❑ *The risks can be so complex that banks hire mathematicians to puzzle them out.* [2] A **mathematician** is a person who is good at doing calculations and using numbers. ❑ *I'm not a very good mathematician.* N-COUNT

**math|emat|ics** /mæθəmætɪks/ [1] **Mathematics** is the study of numbers, quantities, or shapes. ❑ *...a professor of mathematics at Boston College.* N-UNCOUNT [2] **The mathematics of** a problem is the calculations that are involved in it. ❑ *Once you understand the mathematics of debt you can work your way out of it.* N-UNCOUNT

**maths** /mæθs/ **Maths** is the same as **mathematics.** [BRIT] ❑ *He taught science and maths.* N-UNCOUNT

✔ in AM, use **math**

**mati|nee** /mætɪneɪ, AM -neɪ/ **(matinees)** A **matinee** is a performance of a play or a showing of a film which takes place in the afternoon. N-COUNT

**ma|tri|arch** /meɪtriɑːʳk/ **(matriarchs)** [1] A **matriarch** is a woman who rules in a society in which power passes from mother to daughter. N-COUNT [2] A **matriarch** is an old and powerful female member of a family, for example a grandmother. N-COUNT

**ma|tri|ar|chal** /meɪtriɑːʳkəl/ [1] A **matriarchal** society, family, or system is one in which the rulers are female and power or property is passed from mother to daughter. ❑ *...the 3,000 years of the matriarchal Sumerian society.* ADJ ≠patriarchal [2] If you describe a woman as **matriarchal**, you mean that she has authority and power within her family or group. ❑ *...the matriarchal figure of his grandmother.* ADJ: usu ADJ n

**ma|tri|ar|chy** /meɪtriɑːʳki/ **(matriarchies)** A **matriarchy** is a system in which power or property is passed from mother to daughter. N-VAR ≠patriarchy

**ma|tri|ces** /meɪtrɪsiːz/ **Matrices** is the plural of **matrix.**

**ma|tricu|late** /mətrɪkjʊleɪt/ **(matriculates, matriculating, matriculated)** In some countries, if you **matriculate**, you register formally as a student at a university, or you satisfy the academic requirements necessary for registration for a course. ❑ *I had to matriculate if I wanted to do a degree.* VERB V ♦ **ma|tricu|la|tion** /mətrɪkjʊleɪʃən/ *The head decided I should have another go at matriculation.* N-UNCOUNT

**mat|ri|mo|nial** /mætrɪmoʊniəl/ **Matrimonial** means concerning marriage or married people. [FORMAL] ❑ *...the matrimonial home.* ADJ: usu ADJ n

**mat|ri|mo|ny** /mætrɪməni, AM -moʊni/ **Matrimony** is marriage. [FORMAL] ❑ *...the bonds of matrimony.* N-UNCOUNT

**ma|trix** /meɪtrɪks/ **(matrices)** [1] A **matrix** is the environment or context in which something such as a society develops and grows. [FORMAL] ❑ *...the matrix of their culture.* N-COUNT: with supp [2] In mathematics, a **matrix** is an arrangement of numbers, symbols, or letters in rows and columns which is used in solving mathematical problems. N-COUNT

**ma|tron** /meɪtrən/ **(matrons)** The **matron** in a nursing home is the woman who is in charge of all the nurses. In the past, the woman in charge of the nurses in a hospital was also called a **matron.** [BRIT] ❑ *The Matron at the nursing home expressed a wish to attend.* N-COUNT; N-TITLE

**ma|tron|ly** /meɪtrənli/ You can use **matronly** to describe a woman who is fairly fat and looks middle-aged, especially if you think the clothes she is wearing are not fashionable or attractive. ❑ *...a matronly woman with an air of authority.* ADJ

**matt** /mæt/

✔ The spellings **matte** in British English, and **matte** or **mat** in American English are also used.

A **matt** colour, paint, or surface is dull rather than shiny. ❑ *...a creamy white matt emulsion. ...matt black.* ADJ

**mat|ted** /mætɪd/ If you describe someone's hair as **matted**, you mean that it has become a thick untidy mass, often because it is wet or dirty. ❑ *She had matted hair and torn dusty clothes.* ADJ

**mat|ter** /mætəʳ/ **(matters, mattering, mattered)** ◆◆◆ [1] A **matter** is a task, situation, or event which you have to deal with or think about, especially one that involves problems. ❑ *It was clear that she wanted to discuss some private matter... Until the matter is resolved the athletes will be ineligible to compete... Don't you think this is now a matter for the police?... Business matters drew him to Paris.* N-COUNT: usu with supp = affair [2] You use **matters** to refer to the situation you are talking about, especially when something is affecting the situation in some way. ❑ *If your ordinary life is out of control, then retreating into a cosy ritual will not improve matters... If it would facilitate matters, I would be happy to come to New York... Matters took an unexpected turn.* N-PLURAL: no det [3] If you say that a situation is **a matter of** a particular thing, you mean that that is the most important thing to be done or considered when you are involved in the situation or explaining it. ❑ *History is always a matter of interpretation... Jack had attended these meetings as a matter of routine for years.* N-SING: *a* N *of* n/-ing = question [4] Printed **matter** consists of books, newspapers, and other texts that are printed. Reading **matter** consists of things that are suitable for reading, such as books and newspapers. ❑ *...the Government's plans to levy VAT on printed matter. ...a rich variety of reading matter.* N-UNCOUNT: supp N [5] **Matter** is the physical part of the universe consisting of solids, liquids, and gases. ❑ *A proton is an elementary particle of matter.* N-UNCOUNT [6] You use **matter** to refer to a particular type of substance. ❑ *...waste matter from industries.* N-UNCOUNT: with supp [7] You use **matter** in expressions such as **'What's the matter?'** or **'Is anything the matter?'** when you think that someone has a problem and you want to know what it is. ❑ *Carole, what's the matter? You don't seem happy... She told him there was nothing the matter.* N-SING: *the* N, oft N *with* n [8] You use **matter** in expressions such as **'a matter of weeks'** when you are emphasizing how small an amount is or how short a period of time is. ❑ *Within a matter of days she was back at work.* N-SING: *a* N *of* pl-n emphasis [9] If you say that something does not **matter**, you mean that it is not important to you because it does not have an effect on you or on a particular situation. ❑ *A lot of the food goes on the floor but that doesn't matter... As long as staff are smart, it does not matter how long their hair is... Does it matter that people don't know this?... Money is the only thing that matters to them.* VERB: no cont, usu with brd-neg V *it* V wh *it* V that V *to* n Also *it* V [10] → See also **grey matter, subject matter.**

PHRASES [11] If you say that something is **another matter** or **a different matter**, you mean that it is very different from the situation that you have just discussed. ❑ *Being responsible for one's own health is one thing, but being responsible for another person's health is quite a different matter.* PHRASE: v-link PHR [12] If you are going to do something **as a matter of** urgency or priority, you are going to do it as soon as possible, because it is important. ❑ *Your doctor and health visitor can help a great deal and you need to talk about it with them as a matter of urgency.* PHRASE: PHR n [13] If something is **no easy matter**, it is difficult to do it. ❑ *Choosing the colour for the drawing-room walls was no easy matter.* PHRASE: v-link PHR [14] If someone says **that's the end of the matter** or **that's an end to the matter**, they mean that a decision that has been taken must not be changed or discussed any more. ❑ *'He's moving in here,' Maria said. 'So that's the end of the matter.'* PHRASE [15] You use **the fact of the matter is** or **the truth of the matter is** to introduce a fact which supports what you are saying or which is not widely known, for example because it is a secret. ❑ *The fact of the matter is that most people consume far more protein than they actually need.* PHRASE: V inflects, PHR that [16] You can use **for that matter** to emphasize that the remark you are making is true in the same way as your previous, similar remark. ❑ *The irony was that Shawn had not seen her. Nor for that matter had anyone else.* PHRASE: PHR with cl emphasis = come to that [17] You say **'it doesn't matter'** to tell someone who is apologiz- CONVENTION ing to you that you are not angry or upset, and that they should not worry. ❑ *'Did I wake you?' — 'Yes, but it doesn't matter.'* 18 If you say that something is **no laughing matter**, you mean that it is very serious and not something that you should laugh or joke about. ❑ *Their behaviour is an offence. It's no laughing matter.* 19 If you say that something **makes matters worse**, you mean that it makes a difficult situation even more difficult. ❑ *Don't let yourself despair; this will only make matters worse.* 20 You use **no matter** in expressions such as '**no matter how**' and '**no matter what**' to say that something is true or happens in all circumstances. ❑ *No matter what your age, you can lose weight by following this program.* 21 If you say that you are going to do something **no matter what**, you are emphasizing that you are definitely going to do it, even if there are obstacles or difficulties. ❑ *He had decided to publish the manuscript no matter what.* 22 If you say that a statement is **a matter of opinion**, you mean that it is not a fact, and that other people, including yourself, do not agree with it. ❑ *'We're not that contrived. We're not that theatrical.' — 'That's a matter of opinion.'* 23 If you say that something is just **a matter of time**, you mean that it is certain to happen at some time in the future. ❑ *It would be only a matter of time before he went through with it.* 24 a matter of **life and death** → see **death**. **as a matter of course** → see **course**. **as a matter of fact** → see **fact**. **mind over matter** → see **mind**.

PHRASE: v-link PHR = *no joke*

PHRASE: V inflects, oft PHR with cl

PHRASE: PHR wh

PHRASE: PHR with cl [emphasis] = *come what may*

PHRASE: v-link PHR

PHRASE: v-link PHR

**matter-of-fact** If you describe a person as **matter-of-fact**, you mean that they show no emotions such as enthusiasm, anger, or surprise, especially in a situation where you would expect them to be emotional. ❑ *John was doing his best to give Francis the news in a matter-of-fact way.* ♦ **matter-of-factly** *'She thinks you're a spy,' Scott said matter-of-factly.* ADJ; ADV: ADV after v

**mat|ting** /mætɪŋ/ **Matting** is strong thick material, usually made from a material like rope, straw, or rushes, which is used as a floor covering. N-UNCOUNT

**mat|tress** /mætrəs/ **(mattresses)** A **mattress** is the large, flat object which is put on a bed to make it comfortable to sleep on. N-COUNT

**matu|ra|tion** /mætjʊreɪʃən/ 1 The **maturation** of something such as wine or cheese is the process of its being left for a time to become mature. [FORMAL] ❑ *The period of maturation is determined by the cellar master.* 2 The **maturation** of a young person's body is the process of it becoming like an adult's. [FORMAL] N-UNCOUNT; N-UNCOUNT

**ma|ture** /mətjʊəʳ/ **(matures, maturing, matured, maturer, maturest)** 1 When a child or young animal **matures**, it becomes an adult. ❑ *You will learn what to expect as your child matures physically.* 2 When something **matures**, it reaches a state of complete development. ❑ *When the trees matured they were cut in certain areas.* 3 If someone **matures**, they become more fully developed in their personality and emotional behaviour. ❑ *Hopefully after three years at university I will have matured.* 4 If you describe someone as **mature**, you think that they are fully developed and balanced in their personality and emotional behaviour. ❑ *They are emotionally mature and should behave responsibly.* 5 If something such as wine or cheese **matures** or **is matured**, it is left for a time to allow its full flavour or strength to develop. ❑ *Unlike wine, brandy matures only in wood, not glass. ...the cellars where the cheeses are matured.* 6 **Mature** cheese or wine has been left for a time to allow its full flavour or strength to develop. ❑ *Grate some mature cheddar cheese.* 7 When an investment such as a savings policy or pension plan **matures**, it reaches the stage when you stop paying money and the company pays you back the money you have saved, and the interest your money has earned. [BUSINESS] ❑ *These bonuses will be paid when your savings plan matures in ten years' time.* 8 If you say that someone is **mature** or of **mature** years, you are saying politely that they are middle-aged or old. ❑ *...a man of mature years who had been in the job for longer than most of the members could remember.*

VERB = *grow up*; V; VERB; V; VERB; V; ADJ [approval]; VERB; V; *be* V-ed; ADJ: usu ADJ n; VERB; V; ADJ [politeness]

**ma|ture stu|dent** **(mature students)** A **mature student** is a person who begins their studies at university or college a number of years after leaving school, so that they are older than most of the people they are studying with. [BRIT] N-COUNT

☑ in AM, use **adult student**

**ma|tur|ity** /mətjʊərɪti/ **(maturities)** 1 **Maturity** is the state of being fully developed or adult. ❑ *Humans experience a delayed maturity; we arrive at all stages of life later than other mammals.* 2 Someone's **maturity** is their quality of being fully developed in their personality and emotional behaviour. ❑ *Her speech showed great maturity and humanity.* 3 When an investment such as a savings policy or pension plan reaches **maturity**, it reaches the stage when you stop paying money and the company pays you back the money you have saved, and the interest your money has earned. [BUSINESS] ❑ *Customers are told what their policies will be worth on maturity.* N-UNCOUNT; N-UNCOUNT; N-VAR

**maud|lin** /mɔːdlɪn/ 1 If you describe someone as **maudlin**, you mean that they are being sad and sentimental in a foolish way, perhaps because of drinking alcohol. ❑ *Jimmy turned maudlin after three drinks. ...maudlin self-pity.* 2 If you describe a song, book, or film as **maudlin**, you are criticizing it for being very sentimental. ❑ *...the most maudlin song of all time. ...a hugely entertaining (if over-long and maudlin) movie.* ADJ; ADJ [disapproval]

**maul** /mɔːl/ **(mauls, mauling, mauled)** If you **are mauled** by an animal, you are violently attacked by it and badly injured. ❑ *He had been mauled by a bear... The dog went berserk and mauled one of the girls.* VERB = *savage*; *be* V-ed *by* n; V n

**Maun|dy Thurs|day** /mɔːndi θɜːʳzdeɪ/ **Maundy Thursday** is the Thursday before Easter Sunday. N-UNCOUNT

**Mau|ri|tian** /mərɪʃən, AM mɔːr-/ **(Mauritians)** 1 **Mauritian** means belonging or relating to Mauritius, or to its people or culture. 2 A **Mauritian** is a Mauritian citizen, or a person of Mauritian origin. ADJ; N-COUNT

**mau|so|leum** /mɔːzəliːəm/ **(mausoleums)** A **mausoleum** is a building which contains the grave of a famous person or the graves of a rich family. N-COUNT

**mauve** /moʊv/ **(mauves)** Something that is **mauve** is of a pale purple colour. ❑ *It bears clusters of mauve flowers in early summer.* COLOUR

**mav|er|ick** /mævərɪk/ **(mavericks)** If you describe someone as a **maverick**, you mean that they are unconventional and independent, and do not think or behave in the same way as other people. ❑ *He was too much of a maverick ever to hold high office.* ♦ **Maverick** is also an adjective. ❑ *...a maverick group of scientists, who oppose the prevailing medical opinion on the disease.* N-COUNT; ADJ: ADJ n

**maw** /mɔː/ **(maws)** If you describe something as a **maw**, you mean that it is like a big open mouth which swallows everything near it. [LITERARY] ❑ *...helping to chop wood to feed the red maw of the stove.* N-COUNT: usu sing, usu with supp

**mawk|ish** /mɔːkɪʃ/ You can describe something as **mawkish** when you think it is sentimental and silly. ❑ *A sordid, sentimental plot unwinds, with an inevitable mawkish ending.* ADJ [disapproval] = *soppy*

**max.** /mæks/ **Max.** is an abbreviation for **maximum**, and is often used after numbers or amounts. ❑ *I'll give him eight out of 10, max.* ADJ: num ADJ, ADJ n

**max|im** /mæksɪm/ **(maxims)** A **maxim** is a rule for good or sensible behaviour, especially one in the form of a saying. ❑ *I believe in the maxim 'if it ain't broke, don't fix it'.* N-COUNT

**max|im|ize** /mæksımaız/ **(maximizes, maximizing, maximized)**

in BRIT, also use **maximise**

1 If you **maximize** something, you make it as great in amount or importance as you can. ❑ *In order to maximize profit the firm would seek to maximize output.* ♦ **maxi|mi|za|tion** /mæksımaızeıʃᵊn/ *...a pricing policy that was aimed at profit maximisation.* 2 If you **maximize** a window on a computer screen, you make it as large as possible. ❑ *Click on the square icon to maximize the window.* — VERB ≠ minimize; V n; N-UNCOUNT: usu N of n; VERB ≠ minimize; V n

**maxi|mum** /mæksıməm/ ◆◇◇ 1 You use **maximum** to describe an amount which is the largest that is possible, allowed, or required. ❑ *Under planning law the maximum height for a fence or hedge is 2 metres... China headed the table with maximum points.* ♦ **Maximum** is also a noun. ❑ *The law provides for a maximum of two years in prison.* 2 You use **maximum** to indicate how great an amount is. ❑ *...the maximum amount of information... It was achieved with minimum fuss and maximum efficiency. ...a maximum security prison.* 3 If you say that something is a particular amount **maximum**, you mean that this is the greatest amount it should be or could possibly be, although a smaller amount is acceptable or very possible. ❑ *We need an extra 6g a day maximum.* 4 If you say that someone does something **to the maximum**, you are emphasizing that they do it to the greatest degree possible. ❑ *You have to develop your capabilities to the maximum.* — ADJ: ADJ n ≠ minimum; N-SING: oft a N of amount; ADJ: ADJ n ≠ minimum; ADV: amount ADV ≠ minimum; PHRASE: PHR after v [emphasis] = to the full

**may** /meı/ ◆◆◆

**May** is a modal verb. It is used with the base form of a verb.

1 You use **may** to indicate that something will possibly happen or be true in the future, but you cannot be certain. ❑ *We may have some rain today... I may be back next year... I don't know if they'll publish it or not. They may... Scientists know that cancer may not show up for many years.* 2 You use **may** to indicate that there is a possibility that something is true, but you cannot be certain. ❑ *Civil rights officials say there may be hundreds of other cases of racial violence.* 3 You use **may** to indicate that something is sometimes true or is true in some circumstances. ❑ *A vegetarian diet may not provide enough calories for a child's normal growth... Up to five inches of snow may cover the mountains.* 4 You use **may have** with a past participle when suggesting that it is possible that something happened or was true, or when giving a possible explanation for something. ❑ *He may have been to some of those places... The chaos may have contributed to the deaths of up to 20 people.* 5 You use **may** in statements where you are accepting the truth of a situation, but contrasting it with something that is more important. ❑ *I may be almost 50, but there's not a lot of things I've forgotten.* 6 You use **may** when you are mentioning a quality or fact about something that people can make use of if they want to. ❑ *The bag has narrow straps, so it may be worn over the shoulder or carried in the hand.* 7 You use **may** to indicate that someone is allowed to do something, usually because of a rule or law. You use **may not** to indicate that someone is not allowed to do something. ❑ *Any two persons may marry in Scotland provided that both persons are at least 16 years of age on the day of their marriage... Adolescents under the age of 18 may not work in jobs that require them to drive.* 8 You use **may** when you are giving permission to someone to do something, or when asking for permission. [FORMAL] ❑ *Mr Hobbs? May we come in?... If you wish, you may now have a glass of milk.* 9 You use **may** when you are making polite requests. [FORMAL] ❑ *I'd like the use of your living room, if I may... May I come with you to Southampton?* 10 You use **may** when you are mentioning the reaction or attitude that you think someone is likely to have to something you are about to say. ❑ *You know, Brian, whatever you may think, I work hard for a living.* 11 You use **may** in expressions such as **I may add** and **I may say** in order to emphasize a statement that you are making. ❑ *They spent their afternoons playing golf – extremely badly, I may add – around Loch Lomond... Both of them, I may say, are thoroughly reliable men.* 12 If you do something so that a particular thing **may** happen, you do it so that there is an opportunity for that thing to happen. ❑ *...the need for an increase in the numbers of surgeons so that patients may be treated as soon as possible.* 13 People sometimes use **may** to express hopes and wishes. [FORMAL] ❑ *Courage seems now to have deserted him. May it quickly reappear.* 14 **be that as it may** → see **be**. **may as well** → see **well**. — MODAL [vagueness] = might; MODAL [vagueness] = might; MODAL = might; MODAL [vagueness]; MODAL; MODAL = can; MODAL; MODAL = can; MODAL [politeness] = can; MODAL; MODAL [emphasis]; MODAL = can; MODAL: MODAL n v

**May** /meı/ **(Mays)** **May** is the fifth month of the year in the Western calendar. — N-VAR

**may|be** /meıbi/ ◆◆◇ 1 You use **maybe** to express uncertainty, for example when you do not know that something is definitely true, or when you are mentioning something that may possibly happen in the future in the way you describe. ❑ *Maybe she is in love... I do think about having children, maybe when I'm 40.* 2 You use **maybe** when you are making suggestions or giving advice. **Maybe** is also used to introduce polite requests. ❑ *Maybe we can go to the movies or something... Wait a while, maybe a few days.* 3 You use **maybe** to indicate that, although a comment is partly true, there is also another point of view that should be considered. ❑ *Maybe there is jealousy, but I think the envy is more powerful.* 4 You can say **maybe** as a response to a question or remark, when you do not want to agree or disagree. ❑ *'Is she coming back?' — 'Maybe. No one hears from her.'* 5 You use **maybe** when you are making a rough guess at a number, quantity, or value, rather than stating it exactly. ❑ *The men were maybe a hundred feet away and coming closer.* 6 People use **maybe** to mean 'sometimes', particularly in a series of general statements about what someone does, or about something that regularly happens. ❑ *They'll come to the bar for a year, or maybe even two, then they'll find another favourite spot.* — ADV: ADV with cl/group [vagueness] = perhaps; ADV: ADV with cl/group [politeness] = perhaps; ADV: ADV cl = perhaps; ADV: ADV as reply = perhaps; ADV: ADV amount [vagueness] = about; ADV: ADV with cl/group

**May|day** /meıdeı/ **(Maydays)** If someone in a plane or ship sends out a **Mayday** or a **Mayday** message, they send out a radio message calling for help because they are in serious difficulty. ❑ *He raced to pick up the lifejackets while his stepmother sent out a Mayday call.* — N-COUNT

**May Day** **May Day** is the 1st of May, which in many countries is celebrated as a public holiday, especially as one in honour of working people. — N-UNCOUNT

**may|fly** /meıflaı/ **(mayflies)** A **mayfly** is an insect which lives near water and only lives for a very short time as an adult. — N-COUNT

**may|hem** /meıhem/ You use **mayhem** to refer to a situation that is not controlled or ordered, when people are behaving in a disorganized, confused, and often violent way. ❑ *Their arrival caused mayhem as crowds of refugees rushed towards them.* — N-UNCOUNT = chaos

**mayn't** /meıənt/ **Mayn't** is a spoken form of 'may not'.

**mayo** /meıoʊ/ **Mayo** is the same as **mayonnaise**. [INFORMAL] — N-UNCOUNT

**may|on|naise** /meıəneız/ **Mayonnaise** is a thick pale sauce made from egg yolks and oil. It is put on salad. — N-UNCOUNT

**mayor** /meəʳ, meıəʳ/ ◆◇◇ **(mayors)** The **mayor** of a town or city is the person who has been elected to represent it for a fixed period of time or, in some places, to run its government. — N-COUNT: oft the N of n

**mayor|ess** /meəres, meıəres/ **(mayoresses)** 1 A woman who holds the office of mayor is sometimes referred to as a **mayoress**. [BRIT] 2 A **mayoress** is the wife of a mayor. [BRIT] — N-COUNT; N-COUNT

**may've** /meɪəv/ **May've** is a spoken form of 'may have', especially when 'have' is an auxiliary verb.

**maze** /meɪz/ **(mazes)** [1] A **maze** is a complex system of passages or paths between walls or hedges and is designed to confuse people who try to find their way through it, often as a form of amusement. ❑ *The palace has extensive gardens, a maze, and tennis courts.* N-COUNT [2] A **maze of** streets, rooms, or tunnels is a large number of them that are connected in a complicated way, so that it is difficult to find your way through them. ❑ *The children lead me through the maze of alleys to the edge of the city.* N-COUNT: usu N *of* n = *labyrinth* [3] You can refer to a set of ideas, topics, or rules as a **maze** when a large number of them are related to each other in a complicated way that makes them difficult to understand. ❑ *The book tries to steer you through the maze of alternative therapies.* N-COUNT: usu N *of* n

**MBA** /em biː eɪ/ **(MBAs)**

☑ in AM, also use **M.B.A.**

An **MBA** is a master's degree in business administration. You can also refer to a person who has this degree as an **MBA**. **MBA** is an abbreviation for 'Master of Business Administration'. N-COUNT

**MBE** /em biː iː/ **(MBEs)** An **MBE** is a British honour that is awarded to a person by the King or Queen for a particular achievement. **MBE** is an abbreviation for 'Member of the Order of the British Empire'. ❑ *He had to go to Buckingham Palace to accept an MBE from the Queen.* N-COUNT: usu sing

**MBO** /em biː oʊ/ An **MBO** is the buying of a company by its managers. **MBO** is an abbreviation for 'management buyout'. [BUSINESS] N-COUNT

**MC** /em siː/ **(MCs)** An **MC** is the same as a **master of ceremonies**. N-COUNT; N-TITLE

**McCoy** /məkɔɪ/ If you describe someone or something as **the real McCoy**, you mean that they really are what they claim to be and are not an imitation. [INFORMAL] PHRASE: v-link PHR, PHR after v = *the genuine article*

**MD** /em diː/ **(MDs)**

☑ in AM, also use **M.D.**

[1] **MD** is written after someone's name to indicate that they have been awarded a degree in medicine and are qualified to practise as a doctor. [2] **MD** is an abbreviation for **managing director**. [mainly BRIT, BUSINESS] ❑ *He's going to be the MD of the Park Lane company.* N-COUNT

**me** /mi, STRONG miː/ ◆◆◆ A speaker or writer uses **me** to refer to himself or herself. **Me** is a first person singular pronoun. **Me** is used as the object of a verb or a preposition. ❑ *He asked me to go to Cambridge with him... She looked up at me, smiling.* PRON: v PRON, prep PRON

**ME** /em iː/ **ME** is a long-lasting illness that is thought to be caused by a virus. Its symptoms include feeling tired all the time and muscle pain. **ME** is an abbreviation for 'myalgic encephalomyelitis'. N-UNCOUNT = *chronic fatigue syndrome, CFS*

**mead** /miːd/ In former times, **mead** was an alcoholic drink made of honey, spices, and water. N-UNCOUNT

**mead|ow** /medoʊ/ **(meadows)** A **meadow** is a field which has grass and flowers growing in it. N-COUNT

**mea|gre** /miːgə^r^/

☑ in AM, use **meager**

If you describe an amount or quantity of something as **meagre**, you are critical of it because it is very small or not enough. ❑ *The bank's staff were already angered by a meagre 3.1% pay rise.* ADJ [disapproval]

**meal** /miːl/ **(meals)** ◆◇◇ [1] A **meal** is an occasion when people sit down and eat, usually at a regular time. ❑ *She sat next to him throughout the meal... It's rare that I have an evening meal with my children.* N-COUNT [2] A **meal** is the food you eat during a meal. ❑ *The waiter offered him red wine or white wine with his meal.* N-COUNT [3] → See also **bone meal**.

PHRASES [4] If you think someone is taking more time and energy to do something than is necessary, you can say that they are **making a meal of it**. [BRIT, INFORMAL] ❑ *Lawyers always make such a meal of the simplest little thing.* PHRASE: V inflects [disapproval] [5] If you have a **square meal**, you have a large healthy meal. PHRASE: N inflects

**meals on wheels** also **Meals on Wheels**. In Britain, **meals on wheels** is a service provided by the local authority that delivers hot meals to people who are too old or too sick to cook for themselves. N-UNCOUNT

**meal tick|et** also **meal-ticket**. If you say that something or someone is **a meal ticket**, you mean that they provide a person with money or a lifestyle which they would not otherwise have. ❑ *His chosen field was unlikely to be a meal ticket for life... I don't intend to be a meal-ticket for anyone.* N-SING: usu *a* N

**meal|time** /miːltaɪm/ **(mealtimes)** also **meal time**. **Mealtimes** are occasions when you eat breakfast, lunch, or dinner. ❑ *At mealtimes he would watch her eat.* N-VAR: usu pl

**mealy** /miːli/ Food that is dry and powdery can be described as **mealy**. ❑ *...the mealy stodge of pulse, grain and potato dishes.* ADJ

**mealy-mouthed** /miːlimaʊðd/ If you say that someone is being **mealy-mouthed**, you are critical of them for being unwilling to speak in a simple or open way because they want to avoid talking directly about something unpleasant. ❑ *He repeated that he did not intend to be mealy-mouthed with the country's leaders.* ADJ [disapproval]

| **mean** |
|---|
| ① VERB USES |
| ② ADJECTIVE USES |
| ③ NOUN USE |

**① mean** /miːn/ **(means, meaning, meant)** ◆◆◆ ⇛ Please look at category 19 to see if the expression you are looking for is shown under another headword. [1] If you want to know what a word, code, signal, or gesture **means**, you want to know what it refers to or what its message is. ❑ *In modern Welsh, 'glas' means 'blue'... The red signal means you can shoot.* VERB: no cont V n V that [2] If you ask someone what they **mean**, you are asking them to explain exactly what or who they are referring to or what they are intending to say. ❑ *Do you mean me?... I think he means that he does not want this marriage to turn out like his friend's.* VERB: no cont V n V that [3] If something **means** something **to** you, it is important to you in some way. ❑ *The idea that she witnessed this shameful incident meant nothing to him... It would mean a lot to them to win.* VERB: no cont V amount *to* n *it* V amount to-inf Also V amount [4] If one thing **means** another, it shows that the second thing exists or is true. ❑ *An enlarged prostate does not necessarily mean cancer... Just because he has a beard doesn't necessarily mean he's a hippy.* VERB: no cont V n V that [5] If one thing **means** another, the first thing leads to the second thing happening. ❑ *It would almost certainly mean the end of NATO... The change will mean that the country no longer has full diplomatic relations with other states.* VERB: no cont V n V that [6] If doing one thing **means** doing another, it involves doing the second thing. ❑ *Managing well means communicating well.* VERB V -ing [7] If you say that you **mean** what you are saying, you are telling someone that you are serious about it and are not joking, exaggerating, or just being polite. ❑ *He says you're fired if you're not back at work on Friday. And I think he meant it.* VERB: no cont V n [8] If you say that someone **meant to** do something, you are saying that they did it deliberately. ❑ *I didn't mean to hurt you... I can see why you believed my letters were threatening but I never meant them to be.* VERB: no cont = *intend* V to-inf V n to-inf [9] If you say that someone **did not mean any** harm, offence, or disrespect, you are saying that they did not intend to upset or offend people or to cause problems, even though they may in fact have done so. ❑ *I'm sure he didn't mean any harm.* VERB: no cont, with brd-neg = *intend* V n [10] If you **mean to** do something, you intend or plan to do it. ❑ *Summer is the perfect time to catch up on the new books you meant to read.* VERB: no cont = *intend* V to-inf [11] If you say that something **was meant to** happen, you believe that it was made to happen by God or fate, and did not just happen by VERB: usu passive, no cont chance. ❑ *John was constantly reassuring me that we were meant to be together.* be V-ed to-inf

**PHRASES** [12] You say '**I mean**' when making clearer something that you have just said. [SPOKEN] ❑ *It was his idea. Gordon's, I mean.* PHRASE: PHR with cl [13] You can use '**I mean**' to introduce a statement, especially one that justifies something that you have just said. [SPOKEN] ❑ *I'm sure he wouldn't mind. I mean, I was the one who asked him.* PHRASE: PHR with cl [14] You say **I mean** when correcting something that you have just said. [SPOKEN] ❑ *It was law or classics – I mean English or classics.* PHRASE: PHR with cl [15] If you **know what it means** to do something, you know everything that is involved in a particular activity or experience, especially the effect that it has on you. ❑ *I know what it means to lose a child under such tragic circumstances.* PHRASE: Vs inflect, oft PHR to-inf

[16] If a name, word, or phrase **means something to** you, you have heard it before and you know what it refers to. ❑ *'Oh, Gairdner,' he said, as if that meant something to him.* PHRASE: V inflects, PHR n [17] If you say that someone **means well**, you mean they are trying to be kind and helpful, even though they might be causing someone problems or upsetting them. ❑ *I know you mean well, but I can manage by myself.* PHRASE: V inflects

[18] You use '**you mean**' in a question to check that you have understood what someone has said. ❑ *What accident? You mean Christina's?... 'What if I had said no?' 'About the apartment, you mean?'* PHRASE: PHR with cl

[19] → See also **meaning**, **means**, **meant**. **to mean business** → see **business**. **if you know what I mean** → see **know**.

**②mean** /miːn/ **(meaner, meanest)** [1] If you describe someone as **mean**, you are being critical of them because they are unwilling to spend much money or to use very much of a particular thing. [mainly BRIT] ❑ *Don't be mean with fabric, otherwise curtains will end up looking skimpy.* ADJ [disapproval] = stingy

✔ in AM, use **cheap, stingy**

♦ **mean|ness** *This very careful attitude to money can sometimes border on meanness.* N-UNCOUNT [2] If you describe an amount as **mean**, you are saying that it is very small. [BRIT] ❑ *...the meanest grant possible from the local council.* ADJ [disapproval] [3] If someone is being **mean**, they are being unkind to another person, for example by not allowing them to do something. ❑ *The little girls had locked themselves in upstairs because Mack had been mean to them... I'd feel mean saying no.* ADJ: usu v-link ADJ, oft ADJ to n ♦ **mean|ly** *He had been behaving very meanly to his girlfriend.* ADV: usu ADV with v, also ADV adj

[4] If you describe a person or animal as **mean**, you are saying that they are very bad-tempered and cruel. [mainly AM] ❑ *...the meanest fighter in the world.* ADJ [5] If you describe a place as **mean**, you think that it looks poor and dirty. ❑ *He was raised on the mean streets of the central market district of Panama City.* ADJ: usu ADJ n

**PHRASES** [6] You can use **no mean** in expressions such as '**no mean writer**' and '**no mean golfer**' to indicate that someone does something well. [INFORMAL] ❑ *She was no mean performer on a variety of other instruments.* PHRASE: PHR n [approval] [7] You can use **no mean** in expressions such as '**no mean achievement**' and '**no mean task**' to indicate that someone has done something they deserve to be proud of. ❑ *To destroy 121 enemy aircraft is no mean record.* PHRASE: PHR n

**③mean** /miːn/ **The mean** is a number that is the average of a set of numbers. ❑ *Take a hundred and twenty values and calculate the mean. ...the mean score for 26-year-olds.* → See also **means**. N-SING: the N, oft N n = average

**me|ander** /miændəʳ/ **(meanders, meandering, meandered)** [1] If a river or road **meanders**, it has a lot of bends, rather than going in a straight line from one place to another. ❑ *...roads that meandered round the edges of the fields... We crossed a small iron bridge over a meandering stream.* VERB V prep/adv V-ing Also V [2] A **meander** is a large bend in a river. N-COUNT [3] If you **meander** somewhere, you move slowly and not in a straight line. ❑ *We meandered through a landscape of mountains, rivers, and vineyards.* VERB V prep/adv [4] If a speech, account, or piece of writing **meanders**, it seems to move from one topic to another without any order or purpose. ❑ *His talk appears to meander but by the end focuses attention on the true state of affairs. ...a rich and meandering novel.* VERB V V-ing

**mean|ing** /miːnɪŋ/ **(meanings)** [1] The **meaning** of a word, expression, or gesture is the thing or idea that it refers to or represents and which can be explained using other words. ❑ *I hadn't a clue to the meaning of 'activism'... I became more aware of the symbols and their meanings.* ◆◇◇ N-VAR

[2] The **meaning** of what someone says or of something such as a book or film is the thoughts or ideas that are intended to be expressed by it. ❑ *Unsure of the meaning of this remark, Ryle chose to remain silent.* N-VAR = significance [3] If an activity or action has **meaning**, it has a purpose and is worthwhile. ❑ *Art has real meaning when it helps people to understand themselves. ...a challenge that gives meaning to life.* N-UNCOUNT [4] If you mention something and say that someone **doesn't know the meaning of the word**, you are emphasizing that they have never experienced the thing mentioned or do not have the quality mentioned. ❑ *Don't mention failure when Kevin is around. He doesn't know the meaning of the word.* PHRASE: V inflects [emphasis]

**mean|ing|ful** /miːnɪŋfʊl/ [1] If you describe something as **meaningful**, you mean that it is serious, important, or useful in some way. ❑ *She believes these talks will be the start of a constructive and meaningful dialogue... He asked people to tell him about a meaningful event or period in their lives.* ADJ [2] A **meaningful** look or gesture is one that is intended to express something, usually to a particular person, without anything being said. ❑ *Upon the utterance of this word, Dan and Harry exchanged a quick, meaningful look.* ADJ: ADJ n ♦ **mean|ing|ful|ly** *He glanced meaningfully at the other policeman, then he went up the stairs.* ADV: usu ADV after v, also ADV -ed [3] → See also **meaningfully**.

**mean|ing|ful|ly** /miːnɪŋfʊli/ You use **meaningfully** to indicate that someone has deliberately chosen their words in order to express something in a way which is not obvious but which is understood by the person they are talking to. ❑ *'I have a knack for making friends, you know,' Patricia added meaningfully.* → See also **meaningful**. ADV: ADV after v

**mean|ing|less** /miːnɪŋləs/ [1] If something that someone says or writes is **meaningless**, it has no meaning, or appears to have no meaning. ❑ *She is fascinated by algebra while he considers it meaningless nonsense.* ADJ [2] Something that is **meaningless** in a particular situation is not important or relevant. ❑ *Fines are meaningless to guys earning millions.* ADJ [3] If something that you do is **meaningless**, it has no purpose and is not at all worthwhile. ❑ *They seek strong sensations to dull their sense of a meaningless existence.* ADJ = futile

**means** /miːnz/ [1] A **means** of doing something is a method, instrument, or process which can be used to do it. **Means** is both the singular and the plural form for this use. ❑ *The move is a means to fight crime... The army had perfected the use of terror as a means of controlling the population... Business managers are focused on increasing their personal wealth by any available means.* ◆◆◇ N-COUNT: with supp [2] You can refer to the money that someone has as their **means**. [FORMAL] ❑ *...a person of means... He did not have the means to compensate her.* N-PLURAL

**PHRASES** [3] If someone is living **beyond** their **means**, they are spending more money than they can afford. If someone is living **within** their **means**, they are not spending more money than they can afford. ❑ *The more gifts she received, the more she craved, until he was living beyond his means.* PHRASE: v PHR, v-link PHR

[4] If you do something **by means of** a particular method, instrument, or process, you do it using that method, instrument, or process. ❑ *This is a two year course taught by means of lectures and seminars.* PREP-PHRASE [5] You can say '**by all means**' to tell someone that you are very willing to allow them to do something. ❑ *'Can I come and have a look at your house?' — 'Yes by all means'.* CONVENTION [formulae] [6] You use expres- PHRASE:

sions such as **'by no means'**, **'not by any means'**, and **'by no manner of means'** to emphasize that something is not true. ❑ *This is by no means out of the ordinary... They were not finished, however, not by any means.* PHR with cl/group, PHR before v [emphasis] 7 If you say that something is **a means to an end**, you mean that it helps you to achieve what you want, although it may not be enjoyable or important itself. ❑ *We seem to have lost sight of the fact that marketing is only a means to an end.* PHRASE: usu v-link PHR

**means test** **(means tests)** A **means test** is a test in which your income is calculated in order to decide whether you qualify for a grant or benefit from the state. N-COUNT: usu sing

**means-tested** A grant or benefit that is **means-tested** varies in amount depending on a means test. ❑ *...means-tested benefits.* ADJ

**meant** /ment/ 1 **Meant** is the past tense and past participle of **mean**. 2 You use **meant to** to say that something or someone was intended to be or do a particular thing, especially when they have failed to be or do it. ❑ *I can't say any more, it's meant to be a big secret... I'm meant to be on holiday.* ADJ: v-link ADJ to-inf 3 If something **is meant for** particular people or for a particular situation, it is intended for those people or for that situation. ❑ *Fairy tales weren't just meant for children... The seeds were not meant for human consumption.* ADJ: v-link ADJ *for* n

**PHRASES** 4 If you say that something **is meant to** happen, you mean that it is expected to happen or that it ought to happen. ❑ *Parties are meant to be fun.* PHRASE 5 If you say that something **is meant to** have a particular quality or characteristic, you mean that it has a reputation for being like that. ❑ *Beaujolais is meant to be a really good wine.* PHRASE

**mean|time** /miːntaɪm/ 1 **In the meantime** or **meantime** means in the period of time between two events. ❑ *Eventually your child will leave home to lead her own life as a fully independent adult, but in the meantime she relies on your support... It now hopes to hold elections in February. Meantime, the state will continue to be run from Delhi.* PHRASE: PHR with cl = *meanwhile* 2 **For the meantime** means for a period of time from now until something else happens. ❑ *The Prime Minister has, for the meantime, seen off the challenge of the opposition.* PHRASE: PHR with cl

**mean|while** /miːnʰwaɪl/ ◆◆◇ 1 **Meanwhile** means while a particular thing is happening. ❑ *Brush the aubergines with oil, add salt and pepper, and bake till soft. Meanwhile, heat the remaining oil in a heavy pan... Kate turned to beckon Peter across from the car, but Bill waved him back, meanwhile pushing Kate inside.* ADV: ADV with cl 2 **Meanwhile** means in the period of time between two events. ❑ *You needn't worry; I'll be ready to greet them. Meanwhile I'm off to discuss the Fowler's party with Felix.* ADV: ADV with cl 3 You use **meanwhile** to introduce a different aspect of a particular situation, especially one that is completely opposite to the one previously mentioned. ❑ *He had always found his wife's mother a bit annoying. The mother-daughter relationship, meanwhile, was close.* ADV: ADV with cl

**mea|sles** /miːzᵊlz/ **Measles** is an infectious illness that gives you a high temperature and red spots on your skin. N-UNCOUNT: also *the* N

**mea|sly** /miːzli/ If you describe an amount, quantity, or size as **measly**, you are critical of it because it is very small or inadequate. [INFORMAL] ❑ *The average British bathroom measures a measly 3.5 square metres. ...a measly twelve-year-old like me.* ADJ: usu ADJ n, oft *a* ADJ amount [disapproval]

**meas|ur|able** /meʒərəbᵊl/ 1 If you describe something as **measurable**, you mean that it is large enough to be noticed or to be significant. [FORMAL] ❑ *Both leaders seemed to expect measurable progress.* ADJ: usu ADJ n ♦ **meas|ur|ably** *The old man's voice was measurably weaker than the last time they'd talked.* ADV: ADV adj/adv, ADV with v 2 Something that is **measurable** can be measured. ❑ *Economists emphasize measurable quantities – the number of jobs, the per capita income.* ADJ

**meas|ure** /meʒəʳ/ **(measures, measuring, measured)** ◆◆◇ 1 If you **measure** the quality, value, or effect of something, you discover or judge how great it is. ❑ *I continued to measure his progress against the charts in the doctor's office... It was difficult to measure the precise impact of the labor action.* VERB; V n prep; V n 2 If you **measure** a quantity that can be expressed in numbers, such as the length of something, you discover it using a particular instrument or device, for example a ruler. ❑ *Measure the length and width of the gap.* VERB; V n 3 If something **measures** a particular length, width, or amount, that is its size or intensity, expressed in numbers. ❑ *The house is more than twenty metres long and measures six metres in width.* VERB: no cont = *be*; V amount 4 A **measure of** a particular quality, feeling, or activity is a fairly large amount of it. [FORMAL] ❑ *The colonies were claiming a larger measure of self-government.* N-SING: N *of* n 5 If you say that one aspect of a situation is **a measure of** that situation, you mean that it shows that the situation is very serious or has developed to a very great extent. ❑ *That is a measure of how bad things have become at the bank.* N-SING: N *of* n/wh 6 When someone, usually a government or other authority, takes **measures** to do something, they carry out particular actions in order to achieve a particular result. [FORMAL] ❑ *The government warned that police would take tougher measures to contain the trouble.* N-COUNT: oft N to-inf, N *against* n 7 A **measure of** a strong alcoholic drink such as brandy or whisky is an amount of it in a glass. In pubs and bars, a **measure** is an official standard amount. ❑ *He poured himself another generous measure of malt.* N-COUNT: usu N *of* n 8 In music, a **measure** is one of the several short parts of the same length into which a piece of music is divided. [AM] N-COUNT

✔ in BRIT, use **bar**

9 → See also **measured**, **measuring**, **countermeasure**, **half measure**, **tape measure**.

**PHRASES** 10 If you say that something has changed or that it has affected you **beyond measure**, you are emphasizing that it has done this to a great extent. ❑ *Mankind's knowledge of the universe has increased beyond measure.* PHRASE: PHR after v [emphasis] 11 If you say that something is done **for good measure**, you mean that it is done in addition to a number of other things. ❑ *I repeated my question for good measure.* PHRASE: PHR after v, PHR with cl 12 If you **get** or **take the measure of** someone or something, you discover what they are like, so that you are able to control them or deal with them. If you **have the measure of** someone or something, you have succeeded in doing this. *The governments of the industrialized world had failed to get the measure of the crisis... Lili was the only person I knew who had the measure of her brother.* PHRASE: V inflects, PHR n 13 If something is true **in some measure** or **in large measure**, it is partly or mostly true. [FORMAL] ❑ *Power is in some measure an act of will.* PHRASE: PHR with cl

♦ **measure out** If you **measure out** a certain amount of something, you measure that amount and take it or mark it because it is the amount that you want or need. ❑ *I'd already measured out the ingredients.* PHRASAL VERB; V P n (not pron)

♦ **measure up** If you do not **measure up to** a standard or to someone's expectations, you are not good enough to achieve the standard or fulfil the person's expectations. ❑ *It was fatiguing sometimes to try to measure up to her standard of perfection... She's always comparing me to other people, and somehow I never measure up.* PHRASAL VERB: usu with brd-neg; V P *to* n; V P

**meas|ured** /meʒəʳd/ You use **measured** to describe something that is careful and deliberate. ❑ *The men spoke in soft, measured tones... Her more measured response will appeal to voters.* ADJ: usu ADJ n

**meas|ure|ment** /meʒəʳmənt/ **(measurements)** 1 A **measurement** is a result, usually expressed in numbers, that you obtain by measuring something. ❑ *We took lots of measurements.* N-COUNT 2 **Measurement** of something is the process of measuring it in order to obtain a result expressed in numbers. ❑ *Measurement of blood pressure can be undertaken by practice nurses.* N-VAR: oft N *of* n 3 The **measure-** N-VAR:

**ment** of the quality, value, or effect of something is the activity of deciding how great it is. ❑ *...the measurement of output in the non-market sector.* — oft N *of* n

4 Your **measurements** are the size of your waist, chest, hips, and other parts of your body, which you need to know when you are buying clothes. — N-PLURAL: with poss

**meas|ur|ing** /meʒərɪŋ/ A **measuring** jug, cup, or spoon is specially designed for measuring quantities, especially in cooking. — ADJ: ADJ n

**meat** /miːt/ **(meats)** 1 **Meat** is flesh taken from a dead animal that people cook and eat. ❑ *Meat and fish are relatively expensive. ...imported meat products. ...a buffet of cold meats and salads.* — ◆◇◇ N-MASS

2 → See also **luncheon meat**, **red meat**, **white meat**.

**meat|ball** /miːtbɔːl/ **(meatballs) Meatballs** are small balls of chopped meat. They are usually eaten with a sauce. — N-COUNT: usu pl

**meat grind|er** **(meat grinders)** A **meat grinder** is a machine which cuts meat into very small pieces by forcing it through very small holes. [AM] — N-COUNT

✓ in BRIT, use **mincer**

**meat loaf** **(meat loaves)** also **meatloaf. Meat loaf** is chopped meat made into the shape of a loaf of bread. — N-VAR

**meaty** /miːti/ **(meatier, meatiest)** 1 Food that is **meaty** contains a lot of meat. ❑ *...a pleasant lasagne with a meaty sauce.* — ADJ

2 You can describe something such as a piece of writing or a part in a film as **meaty** if it contains a lot of interesting or important material. ❑ *The short, meaty reports are those he likes best.* — ADJ: usu ADJ n

3 You can describe a part of someone's body as **meaty** if it is big and strong. ❑ *He looked up and down the corridor, meaty hands resting on his thighs.* — ADJ: usu ADJ n

**mec|ca** /mekə/ **(meccas)** 1 **Mecca** is a city in Saudi Arabia, which is the holiest city in Islam because the Prophet Mohammed was born there. All Muslims face towards Mecca when they pray. — N-PROPER

2 If you describe a place as a **mecca** or **Mecca** for a particular thing or activity, you mean that many people who are interested in it go there. ❑ *Thailand has become the tourist mecca of Asia.* — N-COUNT: usu sing, with supp

**me|chan|ic** /mɪkænɪk/ **(mechanics)** 1 A **mechanic** is someone whose job is to repair and maintain machines and engines, especially car engines. ❑ *If you smell gas fumes or burning, take the car to your mechanic.* — N-COUNT

2 **The mechanics of** a process, system, or activity are the way in which it works or the way in which it is done. ❑ *What are the mechanics of this new process?* — N-PLURAL: usu *the* N *of* n

3 **Mechanics** is the part of physics that deals with the natural forces that act on moving or stationary objects. ❑ *He has not studied mechanics or engineering.* — N-UNCOUNT

**me|chani|cal** /mɪkænɪkəl/ 1 A **mechanical** device has parts that move when it is working, often using power from an engine or from electricity. ❑ *...a small mechanical device that taps out the numbers. ...the oldest working mechanical clock in the world.* — ADJ: usu ADJ n

♦ **me|chani|cal|ly** /mɪkænɪkli/ *The air was circulated mechanically.* — ADV: ADV with v

2 **Mechanical** means relating to machines and engines and the way they work. ❑ *...mechanical engineering... The train had stopped due to a mechanical problem.* — ADJ: ADJ n

♦ **me|chani|cal|ly** *The car was mechanically sound, he decided.* — ADV: ADV adj/-ed

3 If you describe a person as **mechanical**, you mean they are naturally good at understanding how machines work. ❑ *He was a very mechanical person, who knew a lot about sound.* — ADJ

♦ **me|chani|cal|ly** *I'm not mechanically minded.* — ADV: ADV -ed

4 If you describe someone's action as **mechanical**, you mean that they do it automatically, without thinking about it. ❑ *It is real prayer, and not mechanical repetition.* — ADJ

♦ **me|chani|cal|ly** *He nodded mechanically, his eyes fixed on the girl.* — ADV: ADV with v

**mecha|nise** /mekənaɪz/ → see **mechanize**.

**mecha|nism** /mekənɪzəm/ **(mechanisms)** 1 In a machine or piece of equipment, a **mechanism** is a part, often consisting of a set of smaller parts, which performs a particular function. ❑ *...the locking mechanism... A bomb has been detonated by a special mechanism.* — ◆◇◇ N-COUNT: usu sing, with supp

2 A **mechanism** is a special way of getting something done within a particular system. ❑ *There's no mechanism for punishing arms exporters who break the rules.* — N-COUNT: with supp

3 A **mechanism** is a part of your behaviour that is automatic and that helps you to survive or to cope with a difficult situation. ❑ *...a survival mechanism, a means of coping with intolerable stress.* — N-COUNT: with supp

4 → See also **defence mechanism**.

**mecha|nis|tic** /mekənɪstɪk/ If you describe a view or explanation of something as **mechanistic**, you are criticizing it because it describes a natural or social process as if it were a machine. ❑ *...a mechanistic view of things that ignores the emotional realities in people's lives... Most of my colleagues in biology are still very mechanistic in their thinking.* — ADJ [disapproval]

**mecha|nize** /mekənaɪz/ **(mechanizes, mechanizing, mechanized)**

✓ in BRIT, also use **mechanise**

If someone **mechanizes** a process, they cause it to be done by a machine or machines, when it was previously done by people. ❑ *Only gradually are technologies being developed to mechanize the task.* — VERB; V n

♦ **mecha|nized** *...highly mechanised production methods.* — ADJ

♦ **mecha|ni|za|tion** /mekənaɪzeɪʃən/ *Mechanization happened years ago on the farms of Islay.* — N-UNCOUNT

**med|al** /medəl/ **(medals)** A **medal** is a small metal disc which is given as an award for bravery or as a prize in a sporting event. — ◆◇◇ N-COUNT

**me|dal|lion** /mɪdæliən/ **(medallions)** A **medallion** is a round metal disc which some people wear as an ornament, especially on a chain round their neck. — N-COUNT

**med|al|list** /medəlɪst/ **(medallists)** A **medallist** is a person who has won a medal in sport. [JOURNALISM] ❑ *...the Olympic gold medallists.* — N-COUNT: usu supp N

**med|dle** /medəl/ **(meddles, meddling, meddled)** If you say that someone **meddles** in something, you are criticizing the fact that they try to influence or change it without being asked. ❑ *Already some people are asking whether scientists have any right to meddle in such matters... If only you hadn't felt compelled to meddle. ...the inept and meddling bureaucrats.* — VERB [disapproval] = interfere; V *in/with* n; V; V-ing

♦ **med|dler** **(meddlers)** *They view activists as little more than meddlers.* — N-COUNT

**med|dle|some** /medəlsəm/ If you describe a person as **meddlesome**, you are criticizing them because they try to influence or change things that do not concern them. ❑ *...a meddlesome member of the public.* — ADJ [disapproval] = interfering

**me|dia** /miːdiə/ 1 You can refer to television, radio, newspapers, and magazines as **the media**. ❑ *It is hard work and not a glamorous job as portrayed by the media. ...bias in the news media... Media coverage of cycling in July was pretty impressive.* → See also **mass media**, **multimedia**. — ◆◆◇ N-SING-COLL: *the* N

2 **Media** is a plural of **medium**.

**me|dia cir|cus** **(media circuses)** If an event is described as a **media circus**, a large group of people from the media is there to report on it and take photographs. ❑ *The couple married in the Caribbean to avoid a media circus.* — N-COUNT [disapproval]

**me|di|aeval** /mediiːvəl, AM miːd-/ → see **medieval**.

**me|dian** /miːdiən/ **(medians)** 1 The **median** value of a set of values is the middle one when they are arranged in order. For example, if a group of five students take a test and their marks are 5, 7, 7, 8, and 10, the median mark is 7. [TECHNICAL] — ADJ: ADJ n

2 A **median** is the same as a **median strip**. [AM] — N-COUNT

**me|dian strip** **(median strips)** The **median strip** is the strip of ground, often covered with grass, that separates the two sides of a major road. [AM] — N-COUNT

✓ in BRIT, use **central reservation**

**me|di|ate** /miːdieɪt/ **(mediates, mediating, mediated)** 1 If someone **mediates between** two groups of people, or **mediates** an agreement **between** them, they try to settle an argument between them by talking to both groups and trying to find things that they can both agree to. ❑ *My mom was the one who mediated between Zelda and her mom... United Nations officials have mediated a series of peace meetings between the two sides... The Vatican successfully mediated in a territorial dispute between Argentina and Chile in 1984... UN peacekeepers mediated a new cease-fire.* ♦ **me|dia|tion** /miːdieɪʃᵊn/ *The agreement provides for United Nations mediation between the two sides.* ♦ **me|dia|tor (mediators)** *An archbishop has been acting as mediator between the rebels and the authorities.* 2 If something **mediates** a particular process or event, it allows that process or event to happen and influences the way in which it happens. [FORMAL] ❑ *...the thymus, the organ which mediates the response of the white blood cells.* ♦ **me|dia|tion** *This works through the mediation of the central nervous system.*

VERB; V between pl-n; V n between pl-n; V; V n; N-UNCOUNT; N-COUNT; VERB; V n; N-UNCOUNT

**med|ic** /medɪk/ **(medics)** 1 A **medic** is a doctor or medical student. [INFORMAL] 2 A **medic** is a doctor who works with the armed forces, as part of a medical corps. [AM] ❑ *A Navy medic was wounded by sniper fire.*

N-COUNT; N-COUNT

**medi|cal** /medɪkᵊl/ **(medicals)** 1 **Medical** means relating to illness and injuries and to their treatment or prevention. ❑ *Several police officers received medical treatment for cuts and bruises. ...the medical profession.* ♦ **medi|cal|ly** /medɪkli/ *Therapists cannot prescribe drugs as they are not necessarily medically qualified.* 2 A **medical** is a thorough examination of your body by a doctor, for example before you start a new job.

◆◆◇ ADJ: ADJ n; ADV: ADV with v, ADV adj, ADV with cl; N-COUNT

**medi|cal ex|am|in|er (medical examiners)** 1 A **medical examiner** is a medical expert who is responsible for investigating the deaths of people who have died in a sudden, violent, or unusual way. [AM] 2 A **medical examiner** is a doctor whose job is to examine people, for example when they apply for a job or for health insurance. [AM]

N-COUNT; N-COUNT

**medi|cat|ed** /medɪkeɪtɪd/ A **medicated** soap or shampoo contains substances which are intended to kill bacteria and therefore make your skin or hair healthier.

ADJ: usu ADJ n

**medi|ca|tion** /medɪkeɪʃᵊn/ **(medications)** **Medication** is medicine that is used to treat and cure illness. ❑ *Are you on any medication?*

N-VAR

**me|dici|nal** /medɪsənᵊl/ **Medicinal** substances or substances with **medicinal** effects can be used to treat and cure illnesses. ❑ *...medicinal plants.* ♦ **me|dici|nal|ly** *Root ginger has been used medicinally for centuries.*

ADJ; ADV: ADV after v

**medi|cine** /medsᵊn, AM medɪsɪn/ **(medicines)** 1 **Medicine** is the treatment of illness and injuries by doctors and nurses. ❑ *He pursued a career in medicine... I was interested in alternative medicine and becoming an aromatherapist... Psychiatry is an accepted branch of medicine.* 2 **Medicine** is a substance that you drink or swallow in order to cure an illness. ❑ *People in hospitals are dying because of shortage of medicine. ...herbal medicines.*

◆◇◇ N-UNCOUNT; N-MASS

**me|di|eval** /mediiːvᵊl, AM miːd-/

> in BRIT, also use **mediaeval**

Something that is **medieval** relates to or was made in the period of European history between the end of the Roman Empire in 476 AD and about 1500 AD. ❑ *...a medieval castle. ...the medieval chroniclers.*

ADJ: usu ADJ n

**me|dio|cre** /miːdioʊkəʳ/ If you describe something as **mediocre**, you mean that it is of average quality but you think it should be better. ❑ *His school record was mediocre. ...mediocre music.*

ADJ [disapproval]

**me|di|oc|rity** /miːdiɒkrɪti, med-/ If you refer to the **mediocrity** of something, you mean that it is of average quality but you think it should be better. ❑ *...the mediocrity of most contemporary literature.*

N-UNCOUNT [disapproval]

**medi|tate** /medɪteɪt/ **(meditates, meditating, meditated)** 1 If you **meditate on** something, you think about it very carefully and deeply for a long time. ❑ *On the day her son began school, she meditated on the uncertainties of his future.* 2 If you **meditate** you remain in a silent and calm state for a period of time, as part of a religious training or so that you are more able to deal with the problems and difficulties of everyday life. ❑ *I was meditating, and reached a higher state of consciousness.*

VERB; V on n; VERB; V

**medi|ta|tion** /medɪteɪʃᵊn/ **(meditations)** 1 **Meditation** is the act of remaining in a silent and calm state for a period of time, as part of a religious training, or so that you are more able to deal with the problems of everyday life. ❑ *Many busy executives have begun to practice yoga and meditation.* ➔ See also **transcendental meditation**. 2 **Meditation** is the act of thinking about something very carefully and deeply for a long time. ❑ *...the man, lost in meditation, walking with slow steps along the shore... In his lonely meditations Antony had been forced to the conclusion that there had been rumours.*

N-UNCOUNT; N-UNCOUNT: also N in pl = contemplation

**medi|ta|tive** /medɪtətɪv, AM -teɪt-/ **Meditative** describes things that are related to the act of meditating or the act of thinking very deeply about something. ❑ *Music can induce a meditative state in the listener. ...moments of meditative silence.* ♦ **medi|ta|tive|ly** *Martin rubbed his chin meditatively.*

ADJ: ADJ n; ADV: ADV after v

**Medi|ter|ra|nean** /medɪtəreɪniən/ 1 **The Mediterranean** is the sea between southern Europe and North Africa. 2 **The Mediterranean** refers to the southern part of Europe, which is next to the Mediterranean Sea. ❑ *...one of the most dynamic and prosperous cities in the Mediterranean.* 3 Something that is **Mediterranean** is characteristic of or belongs to the people or region around the Mediterranean Sea. ❑ *...the classic Mediterranean diet.*

N-PROPER: the N; N-PROPER: the N; ADJ

**me|dium** /miːdiəm/ **(mediums, media)** ◆◇◇

> The plural of the noun can be either **mediums** or **media** for meanings 4 and 5. The form **mediums** is the plural for meaning 6.

1 If something is of **medium** size, it is neither large nor small, but approximately half way between the two. ❑ *A medium dose produces severe nausea within hours... He was of medium height with blond hair and light blue eyes.* 2 You use **medium** to describe something which is average in degree or amount, or approximately half way along a scale between two extremes. ❑ *Foods that contain only medium levels of sodium are bread, cakes, milk, butter and margarine. ...a sweetish, medium-strength beer.* ♦ **Medium** is also an adverb. ❑ *Cook under a medium-hot grill.* 3 If something is of a **medium** colour, it is neither light nor dark, but approximately half way between the two. ❑ *Andrea has medium brown hair, grey eyes and very pale skin.* 4 A **medium** is a way or means of expressing your ideas or of communicating with people. ❑ *In Sierra Leone, English is used as the medium of instruction for all primary education... But Artaud was increasingly dissatisfied with film as a medium.* 5 A **medium** is a substance or material which is used for a particular purpose or in order to produce a particular effect. ❑ *Blood is the medium in which oxygen is carried to all parts of the body... Hyatt has found a way of creating these qualities using the more permanent medium of oil paint.* 6 A **medium** is a person who claims to be able to contact and speak to people who are dead, and to pass messages between them and people who are still alive. 7 ➔ See also **media**. 8 If you strike or find a **happy medium** between two extreme and opposite courses of action, you find a sensible way of behaving that is somewhere between the two ex-

ADJ: usu ADJ n; ADJ: usu ADJ n; ADV: ADV adj COMB in COLOUR; N-COUNT; N-COUNT; N-COUNT; PHRASE: PHR after v

tremes. ❑ *I still aim to strike a happy medium between producing football that's worth watching and getting results.*

**medium-dry** also **medium dry.** **Medium-dry** wine or sherry is not very sweet. ADJ

**medium-sized** also **medium size.** **Medium-sized** means neither large nor small, but approximately half way between the two. ❑ *...a medium-sized saucepan. ...medium-sized accountancy firms.* ADJ: usu ADJ n

**medium-term** **The medium-term** is the period of time which lasts a few months or years beyond the present time, in contrast with the short term or the long term. ❑ *The medium-term economic prospects remained poor... If a woman gives up her job to look after her baby, she will risk losing her salary in the medium-term and may seriously damage her long-term career prospects.* N-SING: usu N n

**me|dium wave** **Medium wave** is a range of radio waves which are used for broadcasting. [mainly BRIT] ❑ *...a station broadcasting pop music on medium wave.* N-UNCOUNT: usu *on* N

**med|ley** /medli/ **(medleys)** 1 In music, a **medley** is a collection of different tunes or songs that are played one after the other as a single piece of music. ❑ *...a medley of traditional songs.* N-COUNT: oft N *of* n
2 In sport, a **medley** is a swimming race in which the four main strokes are used one after the other. ❑ *Japan won the Men's 200 metres Individual Medley.* N-COUNT: oft supp N

**meek** /miːk/ **(meeker, meekest)** If you describe a person as **meek**, you think that they are gentle and quiet, and likely to do what other people say. ❑ *He was a meek, mild-mannered fellow.* ♦ **meek|ly** *Most have meekly accepted such advice.* ADJ; ADV: ADV with v

**meet** /miːt/ **(meets, meeting, met)** ◆◆◆ 1 If you **meet** someone, you happen to be in the same place as them and start talking to them. You may know the other person, but be surprised to see them, or you may not know them at all. ❑ *I have just met the man I want to spend the rest of my life with... He's the kindest and sincerest person I've ever met... We met by chance.* ♦ **Meet up** means the same as **meet**. ❑ *When he was in the supermarket, he met up with a buddy he was at Oxford... They met up in 1956, when they were both young schoolboys.* V-RECIP; V n; V n; pl-n V; PHRASAL VERB; V P *with* n; pl-n V P
2 If two or more people **meet**, they go to the same place, which they have earlier arranged to do, so that they can talk or do something together. ❑ *We could meet for a drink after work... Meet me down at the beach tomorrow, at 6am sharp.* ♦ **Meet up** means the same as **meet**. ❑ *We tend to meet up for lunch once a week... My intention was to have a holiday and meet up with old friends.* V-RECIP; pl-n V; V n; PHRASAL VERB; pl-n V P; V P *with* n
3 If you **meet** someone, you are introduced to them and begin talking to them and getting to know them. ❑ *Hey, Terry, come and meet my Dad.* VERB; V n
4 You use **meet** in expressions such as **'Pleased to meet you'** and **'Nice to have met you'** when you want to politely say hello or goodbye to someone you have just met for the first time. ❑ *'Jennifer,' Miss Mallory said, 'this is Leigh Van-Vooren.' — 'Pleased to meet you,' Jennifer said... I have to leave. Nice to have met you.* VERB; formulae; V n; V n
5 If you **meet** someone off their train, plane, or bus, you go to the station, airport, or bus stop in order to be there when they arrive. ❑ *Mama met me at the station... Lili and my father met me off the boat... Kurt's parents weren't able to meet our plane so we took a taxi.* VERB; V n prep/adv; V n *off* n; V n
6 When a group of people such as a committee **meet**, they gather together for a particular purpose. ❑ *Officials from the two countries will meet again soon to resume negotiations... The commission met 14 times between 1988 and 1991.* VERB; V; V
7 If you **meet with** someone, you have a meeting with them. [mainly AM] ❑ *Most of the lawmakers who met with the president yesterday said they backed the mission.* VERB; V *with* n
8 If something such as a suggestion, proposal, or new book **meets with** or **is met with** a particular reaction, it gets that reaction from people. ❑ *The idea met with a cool response from various quarters... Reagan's speech was met with incredulity in the US.* VERB; V *with* n; V n *with* n
9 If something **meets** a need, requirement, or condition, it is good enough to do what is required. ❑ *The current arrangements for the care of severely mentally ill people are inadequate to meet their needs... Out of the original 23,000 applications, 16,000 candidates meet the entry requirements.* VERB = satisfy; V n; V n
10 If you **meet** something such as a problem or challenge, you deal with it satisfactorily or do what is required. ❑ *They had worked heroically to meet the deadline.* VERB; V n
11 If you **meet** the cost of something, you provide the money that is needed for it. ❑ *The government said it will help meet some of the cost of the damage... As your income increases you will find less difficulty in finding the money to meet your monthly repayments.* VERB; V n; V n
12 If you **meet** a situation, attitude, or problem, you experience it or become aware of it. ❑ *I honestly don't know how I will react the next time I meet a potentially dangerous situation.* VERB = come across, encounter; V n
13 You can say that someone **meets with** success or failure when they are successful or unsuccessful. ❑ *Attempts to find civilian volunteers have met with embarrassing failure.* VERB; V *with* n
14 When a moving object **meets** another object, it hits or touches it. ❑ *You sense the stresses in the hull each time the keel meets the ground... Nick's head bent slowly over hers until their mouths met.* V-RECIP; V n; pl-n V
15 If your eyes **meet** someone else's, you both look at each other at the same time. [WRITTEN] ❑ *Nina's eyes met her sisters' across the table... I found myself smiling back instinctively when our eyes met.* V-RECIP; V n; pl-n V
16 If two areas **meet**, especially two areas of land or sea, they are next to one another. ❑ *It is one of the rare places in the world where the desert meets the sea. ...the southernmost point of South America where the Pacific and Atlantic oceans meet.* V-RECIP; V n; pl-n V
17 The place where two lines **meet** is the place where they join together. ❑ *Parallel lines will never meet no matter how far extended... The track widened as it met the road.* V-RECIP; pl-n V; V n
18 If two sportsmen, teams, or armies **meet**, they compete or fight against one another. ❑ *The two women will meet tomorrow in the final. ...when England last met the Aussies in a cricket Test match.* V-RECIP; pl-n V; V n
19 A **meet** is an event in which athletes come to a particular place in order to take part in a race or races. ❑ *John Pennel became the first person to pole-vault 17 ft., at a meet in Miami, Florida.* N-COUNT
PHRASES 20 If you do not **meet** someone's **eyes** or **meet** someone's **gaze**, you do not look at them although they are looking at you, for example because you are ashamed. ❑ *He hesitated, then shook his head, refusing to meet her eyes.* PHRASE: V inflects
21 If someone **meets** their **death** or **meets** their **end**, they die, especially in a violent or suspicious way. [WRITTEN] ❑ *Jacob Sinclair met his death at the hands of a soldier.* PHRASE: V inflects
22 to **make ends meet** → see **end**. **there's more to** this **than meets the eye** → see **eye**. to **meet** someone's **eyes** → see **eye**. to **meet** someone **halfway** → see **halfway**. to **meet** your **match** → see **match**.
♦ **meet up** → see **meet 1, 2**.

**meet|ing** /miːtɪŋ/ **(meetings)** ◆◆◆ 1 A **meeting** is an event in which a group of people come together to discuss things or make decisions. ❑ *Can we have a meeting to discuss that? ...business meetings.* ♦ You can also refer to the people at a meeting as **the meeting**. ❑ *The meeting decided that further efforts were needed.* N-COUNT; N-SING: *the* N
2 When you meet someone, either by chance or by arrangement, you can refer to this event as a **meeting**. ❑ *In January, 37 years after our first meeting, I was back in the studio with Denis.* N-COUNT: oft with poss = encounter

**meet|ing house** **(meeting houses)** A **meeting house** is a building in which certain groups of Christians, for example Quakers, meet in order to worship together. N-COUNT

**meet|ing place** **(meeting places)** A **meeting place** is a place where people meet. N-COUNT

**mega** /megə/ 1 Young people sometimes use **mega** in front of adjectives or adverbs in order to emphasize them. [INFORMAL] ❑ *He has be-* ADV: usu ADV adj/adv; emphasis = really *come mega rich.* [2] Young people sometimes use **mega** in front of nouns in order to emphasize that the thing they are talking about is very good, very large, or very impressive. [INFORMAL] ❑ *...the mega superstar Madonna.* ADJ: ADJ n emphasis

**mega-** /megə-/ [1] **Mega-** is added to nouns that refer to units of measurement in order to form other nouns referring to units that are a million times bigger. ❑ *...a 100 megaton explosion. ...a two thousand megawatt surge in electricity.* PREFIX
[2] **Mega-** combines with nouns and adjectives in order to emphasize the size, quality, or importance of something. [INFORMAL] ❑ *Now he can begin to earn the sort of mega-bucks he has always dreamed about.* PREFIX emphasis

**mega|byte** /megəbaɪt/ **(megabytes)** In computing, a **megabyte** is one million bytes of data. N-COUNT

**mega|hertz** /megəhɜːʳts/ **(megahertz)** A **megahertz** is a unit of frequency, used especially for radio frequencies. One megahertz equals one million cycles per second. ❑ *...UHF frequencies of around 900 megahertz.* N-COUNT: num N

**mega|lo|ma|nia** /megələmeɪniə/ **Megalomania** is the belief that you are more powerful and important than you really are. Megalomania is sometimes a mental illness. N-UNCOUNT

**mega|lo|ma|ni|ac** /megələmeɪniæk/ **(megalomaniacs)** If you describe someone as a **megalomaniac**, you are criticizing them because they enjoy being powerful, or because they believe that they are more powerful or important than they really are. N-COUNT: oft N n disapproval

**mega|mall** /megəmɔːl, -mæl/ **(megamalls)** also **mega-mall.** A **megamall** is a very large shopping area containing very many shops, cinemas, and restaurants. N-COUNT

**mega|phone** /megəfoʊn/ **(megaphones)** A **megaphone** is a cone-shaped device for making your voice sound louder in the open air. N-COUNT

**mega|ton** /megətʌn/ **(megatons)** You can use **megaton** to refer to the power of a nuclear weapon. A one megaton bomb has the same power as one million tons of TNT. N-COUNT: num N

**mega|watt** /megəwɒt/ **(megawatts)** A **megawatt** is a unit of power. One megawatt is a million watts. ❑ *The project is designed to generate around 30 megawatts of power for the national grid.* N-COUNT: num N, oft N *of* n

**-meister** /-maɪstəʳ/ **(-meisters)** **-meister** combines with nouns to form nouns which refer to someone who is extremely good at a particular activity. ❑ *The film – tautly directed by horror-meister Sam Raimi – is almost assured an Oscar nomination.* COMB in N-COUNT

**mel|an|cho|lia** /melənkoʊliə/ **Melancholia** is a feeling of great sadness, especially one that lasts a long time. [LITERARY] ❑ *He sank into deep melancholia.* N-UNCOUNT

**mel|an|chol|ic** /melənkɒlɪk/ **(melancholics)** If you describe someone or something as **melancholic**, you mean that they are very sad. [LITERARY] ❑ *...his gentle, melancholic songs.* ADJ

**mel|an|choly** /melənkɒli/ [1] You describe something that you see or hear as **melancholy** when it gives you an intense feeling of sadness. ❑ *The only sounds were the distant, melancholy cries of the sheep.* ADJ [2] **Melancholy** is an intense feeling of sadness which lasts for a long time and which strongly affects your behaviour and attitudes. [LITERARY] ❑ *I was deeply aware of his melancholy as he stood among the mourners.* N-UNCOUNT [3] If someone feels or looks **melancholy**, they feel or look very sad. [LITERARY] ❑ *It was in these hours of the late afternoon that Tom Mulligan felt most melancholy... He fixed me with those luminous, empty eyes and his melancholy smile.* ADJ

**me|lange** /meɪlɒndʒ/ **(melanges)** also **mélange.** A **melange of** things is a mixture of them, especially when this is attractive or exciting. [WRITTEN] ❑ *...a successful melange of music styles, from soul and rhythm and blues to rap. ...a wonderful melange of flavours.* N-COUNT: with supp, oft N *of* n

**mela|nin** /melənɪn/ **Melanin** is a dark substance in the skin, eyes, and hair of people and animals, which gives them colour and can protect them against strong sunlight. N-UNCOUNT

**mela|no|ma** /melənoʊmə/ **(melanomas)** A **melanoma** is an area of cancer cells in the skin which is caused by very strong sunlight. N-VAR

**me|lee** /meleɪ, AM meɪ-/ **(melees)** also **mêlée.** [1] A **melee** is a noisy confusing fight between the people in a crowd. [WRITTEN] ❑ *A policeman was killed and scores of people were injured in the melee.* N-COUNT: usu sing [2] A **melee** of things is a large, confusing, disorganized group of them. [WRITTEN] ❑ *...the melee of streets around the waterfront.* N-SING: usu N *of* n

**mel|lif|lu|ous** /mɪlɪfluəs/ A **mellifluous** voice or piece of music is smooth and gentle and very pleasant to listen to. [FORMAL] ❑ *I grew up around people who had wonderful, mellifluous voices.* ADJ: usu ADJ n

**mel|low** /meloʊ/ **(mellower, mellowest, mellows, mellowing, mellowed)** [1] **Mellow** is used to describe things that have a pleasant, soft, rich colour, usually red, orange, yellow, or brown. ❑ *...the softer, mellower light of evening.* ADJ: usu ADJ n/colour [2] A **mellow** sound or flavour is pleasant, smooth, and rich. ❑ *His voice was deep and mellow and his speech had a soothing and comforting quality. ...a delightfully mellow, soft and balanced wine.* ADJ [3] If someone **mellows** or if something **mellows** them, they become kinder or less extreme in their behaviour, especially as a result of growing older. ❑ *When the children married and had children of their own, he mellowed a little... Marriage had not mellowed him.* VERB V V n ♦ **Mellow** is also an adjective. ❑ *Is she more mellow and tolerant?* ADJ [4] If someone is **mellow**, they feel very relaxed and cheerful, especially as the result of alcohol or good food. [INFORMAL] ❑ *He'd had a few glasses of champagne himself and was fairly mellow.* ADJ

**me|lod|ic** /mɪlɒdɪk/ [1] **Melodic** means relating to melody. ❑ *...Schubert's effortless gift for melodic invention.* ADJ: usu ADJ n ♦ **me|lodi|cal|ly** /mɪlɒdɪkli/ *...the third of Tchaikovsky's ten operas, and melodically one of his richest scores.* ADV [2] Music that is **melodic** has beautiful tunes in it. ❑ *Wonderfully melodic and tuneful, his songs have made me weep.* ADJ ♦ **me|lodi|cal|ly** *The leader has also learned to play more melodically.* ADV: ADV after v

**me|lo|dious** /mɪloʊdiəs/ A **melodious** sound is pleasant to listen to. [LITERARY] ❑ *She spoke in a quietly melodious voice.* ADJ = musical

**melo|dra|ma** /melədrɑːmə/ **(melodramas)** A **melodrama** is a story or play in which there are a lot of exciting or sad events and in which people's emotions are very exaggerated. N-VAR

**melo|dra|mat|ic** /melədrəmætɪk/ **Melodramatic** behaviour is behaviour in which someone treats a situation as much more serious than it really is. ❑ *'Don't you think you're being rather melodramatic?' Jane asked.* ADJ ♦ **melo|dra|mati|cal|ly** /melədrəmætɪkli/ *'For God's sake,' Michael said melodramatically, 'Whatever you do, don't look down.'* ADV: ADV with v

**melo|dy** /melədi/ **(melodies)** A **melody** is a tune. [FORMAL] N-COUNT

**mel|on** /melən/ **(melons)** A **melon** is a large fruit which is sweet and juicy inside and has a hard green or yellow skin. → See picture on page 1711. N-VAR

**melt** /melt/ **(melts, melting, melted)** [1] When a solid substance **melts** or when you **melt** it, it changes to a liquid, usually because it has been heated. ❑ *The snow had melted, but the lake was still frozen solid... Meanwhile, melt the white chocolate in a bowl suspended over simmering water... Add the melted butter, molasses, salt, and flour.* VERB V V n V-ed [2] If something such as your feelings **melt**, they suddenly disappear and you no longer feel them. [LITERARY] ❑ *His anxiety about the outcome melted, to return later but not yet.* VERB = dissolve V ♦ **Melt away** means the same as **melt**. ❑ *When he heard these words, Shinran felt his* PHRASAL VERB V P *inner doubts melt away.* [3] If a person or thing **melts into** something such as darkness or a crowd of people, they become difficult to see, for example because they are moving away from you or are the same colour as the background. [LITERARY] ❑ *The youths dispersed and melted into the darkness.* [4] If someone or something **melts** your heart, or if your heart **melts**, you start to feel love or sympathy towards them. ❑ *When his lips break into a smile, it is enough to melt any woman's heart... When a bride walks down the aisle to a stirring tune, even the iciest of hearts melt.* VERB = disappear; V *into* n; VERB; V n; V

♦ **melt away** If a crowd of people **melts away**, members of the crowd gradually leave until there is no-one left. ❑ *The crowd around the bench began to melt away.* ➔ See also **melt 2**. PHRASAL VERB; V P

♦ **melt down** If an object **is melted down**, it is heated until it melts, so that the material can be used to make something else. ❑ *Some of the guns were melted down and used to help build a statue... When Jefferson didn't like a pair of goblets given to him as a gift, he asked a local smith to melt them down... Some thieves do not even bother to melt down stolen silver for its scrap value.* PHRASAL VERB; *be* V-ed P; V n P; V P n (not pron)

**melt|down** /meltdaʊn/ **(meltdowns)** [1] If there is **meltdown** in a nuclear reactor, the fuel rods start melting because of a failure in the system, and radiation starts to escape. ❑ *Emergency cooling systems could fail and a reactor meltdown could occur.* [2] The **meltdown** of a company, organization, or system is its sudden and complete failure. [JOURNALISM] ❑ *Urgent talks are going on to prevent the market going into financial meltdown during the summer.* N-VAR; N-UNCOUNT: with supp

**melt|ing point** **(melting points)** The **melting point** of a substance is the temperature at which it melts when you heat it. N-COUNT: oft with poss

**melt|ing pot** **(melting pots)** [1] A **melting pot** is a place or situation in which people or ideas of different kinds gradually get mixed together. ❑ *The republic is a melting pot of different nationalities.* [2] If something is **in the melting pot**, you do not know what is going to happen to it. [mainly BRIT] ❑ *Their fate is still in the melting-pot.* N-COUNT: usu sing; PHRASE: v-link PHR, PHR after v

**mem|ber** /membəʳ/ **(members)** [1] A **member** of a group is one of the people, animals, or things belonging to that group. ❑ *He refused to name the members of staff involved... Their lack of training could put members of the public at risk.* [2] A **member** of an organization such as a club or a political party is a person who has officially joined the organization. ❑ *The support of our members is of great importance to the Association... Britain is a full member of NATO.* [3] A **member country** or **member state** is one of the countries that has joined an international organization or group. ❑ *...the member countries of the European Free Trade Association.* [4] A **member** or **Member** is a person who has been elected to a parliament or legislature. ❑ *He was elected to Parliament as the Member for Leeds.* ◆◆◆ N-COUNT: with supp, oft N *of* n; N-COUNT: usu with supp, oft N *of* n; ADJ: ADJ n; N-COUNT: usu N *for* n

**Mem|ber of Con|gress** **(Members of Congress)** A **Member of Congress** is a person who has been elected to the United States Congress. N-COUNT

**Mem|ber of Par|lia|ment** **(Members of Parliament)** A **Member of Parliament** is a person who has been elected by the people in a particular area to represent them in a country's parliament. The abbreviation **MP** is often used. N-COUNT = MP

**mem|ber|ship** /membəʳʃɪp/ **(memberships)** [1] **Membership** of an organization is the state of being a member of it. ❑ *The country has also been granted membership of the World Trade Organisation... He sent me a membership form.* [2] The **membership** of an organization is the people who belong to it, or the number of people who belong to it. ❑ *The European Builders Confederation has a membership of over 350,000 building companies. ...the recent fall in party membership.* ◆◇◇ N-UNCOUNT: also N in pl; N-VAR-COLL

**mem|brane** /membreɪn/ **(membranes)** A **membrane** is a thin piece of skin which connects or covers parts of a person's or animal's body. N-COUNT

**me|men|to** /mɪmentoʊ/ **(mementos** or **mementoes)** A **memento** is an object which you keep because it reminds you of a person or a special occasion. ❑ *More anglers are taking cameras when they go fishing to provide a memento of catches.* N-COUNT: oft N *of* n = souvenir

**memo** /memoʊ/ **(memos)** A **memo** is a short official note that is sent by one person to another within the same company or organization. N-COUNT

**mem|oirs** /memwɑːʳz/ A person's **memoirs** are a written account of the people who they have known and events that they remember. ❑ *In his memoirs, De Gaulle wrote that he had come to London determined to save the French nation.* N-PLURAL: usu with poss

**memo|ra|bilia** /memərəbɪliə/ **Memorabilia** are things that you collect because they are connected with a person or organization in which you are interested. N-PLURAL

**memo|rable** /memərəbᵊl/ Something that is **memorable** is worth remembering or likely to be remembered, because it is special or very enjoyable. ❑ *...the perfect setting for a nostalgic memorable day... Annette's performance as Eliza Doolittle in 'Pygmalion' was truly memorable.* ♦ **memo|rably** *The National Theatre's production is memorably staged.* ADJ; ADV: usu ADV with v, also ADV adj

**memo|ran|dum** /memərændəm/ **(memoranda** or **memorandums)** [1] A **memorandum** is a written report that is prepared for a person or committee in order to provide them with information about a particular matter. ❑ *The delegation submitted a memorandum to the Commons on the blatant violations of basic human rights.* [2] A **memorandum** is a short official note that is sent by one person to another within the same company or organization. [FORMAL] N-COUNT; N-COUNT = memo

**me|mo|rial** /mɪmɔːriəl/ **(memorials)** [1] A **memorial** is a structure built in order to remind people of a famous person or event. ❑ *Every village had its war memorial.* [2] A **memorial** event, object, or prize is in honour of someone who has died, so that they will be remembered. ❑ *A memorial service is being held for her at St Paul's Church.* [3] If you say that something will be a **memorial to** someone who has died, you mean that it will continue to exist and remind people of them. ❑ *The museum will serve as a memorial to the millions who passed through Ellis Island.* N-COUNT: usu with supp; ADJ: ADJ n; N-COUNT: usu sing, N *to* n

**Me|mo|rial Day** In the United States, **Memorial Day** is a public holiday when people honour the memory of Americans who have died in wars. Memorial Day is celebrated in most states on the last Monday in May. N-UNCOUNT

**me|mo|ri|al|ize** /mɪmɔːriəlaɪz/ **(memorializes, memorializing, memorialized)**

☑ in BRIT, also use **memorialise**

If a person or event **is memorialized**, something is produced that will continue to exist and remind people of them. ❑ *He was praised in print and memorialized in stone throughout the South... When she died in 1946, her friends wanted to memorialize her in some significant way.* VERB; *be* V-ed; V n

**memo|rize** /meməraɪz/ **(memorizes, memorizing, memorized)**

☑ in BRIT, also use **memorise**

If you **memorize** something, you learn it so that you can remember it exactly. ❑ *He studied his map, trying to memorize the way to Rose's street.* VERB; V n

**memo|ry** /meməri/ **(memories)** [1] Your **memory** is your ability to remember things. ❑ *All the details of the meeting are fresh in my memory... He'd a good memory for faces, and he was sure he hadn't seen her before... But locals with long memories thought this was fair revenge for the injustice of 1961.* [2] A **memory** is something that you remember from the past. ❑ *She cannot bear to watch the film* ◆◆◇ N-VAR: oft poss N; N-COUNT: usu with supp, oft N *of* n *because of the bad memories it brings back... Her earliest memory is of singing at the age of four to wounded soldiers... He had happy memories of his father.* 3 A computer's **memory** is the part of the computer where information is stored, especially for a short time before it is transferred to disks or magnetic tapes. [COMPUTING] ❑ *The data are stored in the computer's memory.* N-COUNT 4 If you talk about the **memory** of someone who has died, especially someone who was loved or respected, you are referring to the thoughts, actions, and ceremonies by which they are remembered. ❑ *She remained devoted to his memory... The congress opened with a minute's silence in memory of those who died in the struggle.* N-SING: usu with poss, also *in* N *of* n

PHRASES 5 If you do something **from memory**, for example speak the words of a poem or play a piece of music, you do it without looking at it, because you know it very well. ❑ *Many members of the church sang from memory.* PHRASE: PHR after v 6 If you say that something is, for example, the best, worst, or first thing of its kind **in living memory**, you are emphasizing that it is the only thing of that kind that people can remember. ❑ *The floods are the worst in living memory.* PHRASE: n/adj PHR, usu with adj-superl/brd-neg [emphasis] 7 If you **lose your memory**, you forget things that you used to know. ❑ *He lost his memory.* PHRASE: V inflects 8 to **commit** something **to memory** → see **commit**.

**memo|ry chip** **(memory chips)** In a computer, the **memory chip** is the microchip in which information is stored. N-COUNT

**mem|sa|hib** /memsɑːb/ **(memsahibs)** **Memsahib** was used to refer to or address white women in India, especially during the period of British rule, or sometimes to refer to or address upper-class Indian women. [OLD-FASHIONED] N-COUNT; N-TITLE; N-VOC

**men** /men/ **Men** is the plural of **man**.

**men|ace** /menɪs/ **(menaces, menacing, menaced)** 1 If you say that someone or something is a **menace** to other people or things, you mean that person or thing is likely to cause serious harm. ❑ *In my view you are a menace to the public. ...the menace of fascism.* N-COUNT: usu sing, oft N *to* n, N *of* n = threat 2 You can refer to someone or something as a **menace** when you want to say that they cause you trouble or annoyance. [INFORMAL] ❑ *You're a menace to my privacy, Kenworthy.* N-COUNT: usu sing = nuisance 3 **Menace** is a quality or atmosphere that gives you the feeling that you are in danger or that someone wants to harm you. ❑ *...a voice full of menace.* N-UNCOUNT 4 If you say that one thing **menaces** another, you mean that the first thing is likely to cause the second thing serious harm. ❑ *The European states retained a latent capability to menace Britain's own security.* VERB = threaten V n 5 If you **are menaced** by someone, they threaten to harm you. ❑ *She's being menaced by her sister's latest boyfriend.* VERB = threaten *be* V-ed Also V n

**men|ac|ing** /menɪsɪŋ/ If someone or something looks **menacing**, they give you a feeling that they are likely to cause you harm or put you in danger. ❑ *The strong dark eyebrows give his face an oddly menacing look.* ADJ = threatening ♦ **men|ac|ing|ly** *A group of men suddenly emerged from a doorway and moved menacingly forward to block her way.* ADV: usu ADV after v, also ADV adj/-ed

**me|nage** /meɪnɑːʒ/ also **ménage.** A **menage** is a group of people living together in one house. [FORMAL] N-SING: usu with supp

**me|nage a trois** /meɪnɑːʒ ɑː twɑː/ **(menages a trois)** also **ménage à trois.** A **menage a trois** is a situation where three people live together, especially when one of them is having a sexual relationship with both of the others. N-COUNT: usu sing

**me|nag|erie** /mənædʒəri/ **(menageries)** A **menagerie** is a collection of wild animals. N-COUNT

**mend** /mend/ **(mends, mending, mended)** 1 If you **mend** something that is broken or not working, you repair it, so that it works properly or can be used. ❑ *They took a long time to mend the roof... I should have had the catch mended, but never got round to it.* VERB = repair, fix V n *have* n V-ed 2 If a person or a part of their body **mends** or **is mended**, they get better after they have been ill or have had an injury. ❑ *I'm feeling a good bit better. The cut aches, but it's mending... He must have a major operation on his knee to mend severed ligaments.* VERB = heal V V n 3 If you try to **mend** divisions between people, you try to end the disagreements or quarrels between them. ❑ *He sent Evans as his personal envoy to discuss ways to mend relations between the two countries.* V n

PHRASES 4 If a relationship or situation is **on the mend** after a difficult or unsuccessful period, it is improving. [INFORMAL] ❑ *More evidence that the economy was on the mend was needed.* PHRASE: v-link PHR 5 If you are **on the mend** after an illness or injury, you are recovering from it. [INFORMAL] ❑ *The baby had been poorly but seemed on the mend.* PHRASE: v-link PHR 6 If someone who has been behaving badly **mends** their **ways**, they begin to behave well. ❑ *He has promised drastic disciplinary action if they do not mend their ways.* PHRASE: V inflects 7 to **mend fences** → see **fence**.

**men|da|cious** /mendeɪʃəs/ A **mendacious** person is someone who tells lies. A **mendacious** statement is one that is a lie. [FORMAL] ADJ

**men|dac|ity** /mendæsɪti/ **Mendacity** is lying, rather than telling the truth. [FORMAL] ❑ *...an astonishing display of cowardice and mendacity.* N-UNCOUNT

**mend|ing** /mendɪŋ/ **Mending** is the sewing and repairing of clothes that have got holes in them. [OLD-FASHIONED] ❑ *Who will then do the cooking, the washing, the mending?* → See also **mend**. N-UNCOUNT

**men|folk** /menfoʊk/ When women refer to their **menfolk**, they mean the men in their family or society. N-PLURAL: usu poss N

**me|nial** /miːniəl/ **Menial** work is very boring, and the people who do it have a low status and are usually badly paid. ❑ *...low paid menial jobs, such as cleaning and domestic work.* ADJ

**men|in|gi|tis** /menɪndʒaɪtɪs/ **Meningitis** is a serious infectious illness which affects your brain and spinal cord. N-UNCOUNT

**meno|pause** /menəpɔːz/ **The menopause** is the time during which a woman gradually stops menstruating, usually when she is about fifty years old. ♦ **meno|pau|sal** ❑ *...a menopausal woman.* N-SING: also no det ADJ

**men's room** **(men's rooms)** **The men's room** is a toilet for men in a public building. [mainly AM] N-COUNT: usu *the* N in sing

**men|strual** /menstruəl/ **Menstrual** means relating to menstruation. ❑ *...the menstrual cycle.* ADJ: ADJ n

**men|stru|ate** /menstrueɪt/ **(menstruates, menstruating, menstruated)** When a woman **menstruates**, a flow of blood comes from her womb. Women menstruate once a month unless they are pregnant or have reached the menopause. [FORMAL] ❑ *Lean hard-training women athletes may menstruate less frequently or not at all.* VERB V ♦ **men|strua|tion** /menstrueɪʃən/ *Menstruation may cease when a woman is anywhere between forty-five and fifty years of age.* N-UNCOUNT

**mens|wear** /menzweəʳ/ **Menswear** is clothing for men. ❑ *...the menswear industry.* N-UNCOUNT

**-ment** **-ment** is added to some verbs to form nouns that refer to actions, processes, or states. ❑ *...shortly after the commencement of the service. ...the enrichment of uranium.* SUFFIX

**men|tal** /mentəl/ ◆◇◇ 1 **Mental** means relating to the process of thinking. ❑ *...the mental development of children. ...intensive mental effort.* ADJ: ADJ n ♦ **men|tal|ly** *I think you are mentally tired... Physically I might not have been overseas but mentally and spiritually I was with them.* ADV: ADV adj/adv, ADV with v, ADV with cl 2 **Mental** means relating to the state or the health of a person's mind. ❑ *The mental state that had created her psychosis was no longer present. ...mental health problems.* ADJ: ADJ n ♦ **men|tal|ly** *...an inmate who is mentally disturbed. ...the needs of the mentally ill and the mentally handicapped.* ADV: usu ADV with cl/group, also ADV after v 3 A **mental** act is one that involves only thinking and not physical action. ❑ *Practise mental arithmetic when you go out shopping.* ADJ: ADJ n ♦ **men|tal|ly** *This technique will help people mentally organize information.* ADV: ADV with v 4 If you say that someone ADJ is **mental**, you mean that you think they are mad. [BRIT, INFORMAL] ❑ *I just said to him 'you must be mental'.* 5 If you **make a mental note of** something, you make an effort to store it in your memory so that you will not forget it. ❑ *She made a mental note to have his prescription refilled.* disapproval = crazy, mad PHRASE: V inflects, PHR *of* n, PHR to-inf

**men|tal age** **(mental ages)** A person's **mental age** is the age which they are considered to have reached in their ability to think or reason. N-COUNT: usu sing

**men|tal hos|pi|tal** **(mental hospitals)** A **mental hospital** is a hospital for people who are suffering from mental illness. N-COUNT

**men|tal|ity** /mentælɪti/ **(mentalities)** Your **mentality** is your attitudes and your way of thinking. ❑ *...a criminal mentality... Running a business requires a very different mentality from being a salaried employee.* N-COUNT: usu sing, with supp

**men|thol** /menθɒl, AM -θɔːl/ **Menthol** is a substance that smells a bit like peppermint and is used to flavour things such as cigarettes and toothpaste. It is also used in some medicines, especially for curing colds. N-UNCOUNT

**men|tion** /menʃᵊn/ **(mentions, mentioning, mentioned)** ◆◆◇ 1 If you **mention** something, you say something about it, usually briefly. ❑ *She did not mention her mother's absence... I may not have mentioned it to her... I had mentioned that I didn't really like contemporary music... She shouldn't have mentioned how heavy the dress was... I felt as though I should mention it as an option.* VERB V n/-ing V n *to* n V that V wh V n *as* n 2 A **mention** is a reference to something or someone. ❑ *The statement made no mention of government casualties.* N-VAR: oft N *of* n 3 If someone **is mentioned** in writing, a reference is made to them by name, often to criticize or praise something that they have done. ❑ *I was absolutely outraged that I could be even mentioned in an article of this kind. ...Brigadier Ferguson was mentioned in the report as being directly responsible.* VERB: usu passive *be* V-ed *be* V-ed *as* n/adj 4 If someone **is mentioned as** a candidate for something such as a job, it is suggested that they might become a candidate. ❑ *Her name has been mentioned as a favoured leadership candidate.* VERB: usu passive *be* V-ed *as* n 5 A special or honourable **mention** is formal praise that is given for an achievement that is very good, although not usually the best of its kind. ❑ *So many people have helped me with this book that it is hard to pick out the few for special mention.* N-VAR: with supp = commendation 6 People sometimes say **'don't mention it'** as a polite reply to someone who has just thanked them for doing something. ❑ *'Thank you very much.' — 'Don't mention it.'* CONVENTION formulae 7 You use **not to mention** when you want to add extra information which emphasizes the point that you are making. ❑ *The audience, not to mention the bewildered cast, were not amused.* PHRASE: PHR group emphasis

**men|tor** /mentɔːʳ/ **(mentors, mentoring, mentored)** 1 A person's **mentor** is someone who gives them help and advice over a period of time, especially help and advice related to their job. N-COUNT: usu poss N 2 To **mentor** someone means to give them help and advice over a period of time, especially help and advice related to their job. ❑ *He had mentored scores of younger doctors.* VERB V n ♦ **men|tor|ing** *...the company's mentoring programme.* N-UNCOUNT

**menu** /menjuː/ **(menus)** 1 In a restaurant or café, or at a formal meal, the **menu** is a list of the food and drinks that are available. ❑ *A waiter offered him the menu... Even the most elaborate dishes on the menu were quite low on calories.* N-COUNT: usu sing 2 A **menu** is the food that you serve at a meal. ❑ *Try out the menu on a few friends.* N-COUNT 3 On a computer screen, a **menu** is a list of choices. Each choice represents something that you can do using the computer. N-COUNT

**meow** /miaʊ/ → see **miaow**.

**MEP** /em iː piː/ **(MEPs)** An **MEP** is a person who has been elected to the European Parliament. **MEP** is an abbreviation for 'Member of the European Parliament'. N-COUNT

**mer|can|tile** /mɜːʳkəntaɪl/ **Mercantile** means relating to or involved in trade. [FORMAL] ❑ *...the emergence of a new mercantile class.* ADJ: ADJ n

**mer|ce|nary** /mɜːʳsənri, AM -neri/ **(mercenaries)** 1 A **mercenary** is a soldier who is paid to fight by a country or group that they do not belong to. N-COUNT 2 If you describe someone as **mercenary**, you are criticizing them because you think that they are only interested in the money that they can get from a particular person or situation. ADJ disapproval

**mer|chan|dise** /mɜːʳtʃəndaɪz, -daɪs/ **Merchandise** is goods that are bought, sold, or traded. [FORMAL] N-UNCOUNT

**mer|chan|dis|er** /mɜːʳtʃəndaɪzəʳ/ **(merchandisers)** A **merchandiser** is a person or company that sells goods to the public. [AM, BUSINESS] ❑ *In 1979, Liquor Barn thrived as a discount merchandiser.* N-COUNT: usu supp N

✔ in BRIT, use **retailer**

**mer|chan|dis|ing** /mɜːʳtʃəndaɪzɪŋ/ 1 **Merchandising** consists of goods such as toys and clothes that are linked with something such as a film, sports team, or pop group. ❑ *We are selling the full range of World Cup merchandising... The club says it will make increasing amounts from merchandising.* N-UNCOUNT 2 **Merchandising** is used to refer to the way shops and businesses organize the sale of their products, for example the way they are displayed and the prices that are chosen. [mainly AM, BUSINESS] ❑ *Company executives say revamped merchandising should help Macy's earnings to grow.* N-UNCOUNT

**mer|chant** /mɜːʳtʃənt/ **(merchants)** ◆◇◇ 1 A **merchant** is a person who buys or sells goods in large quantities, especially one who imports and exports them. ❑ *Any knowledgeable wine merchant would be able to advise you.* N-COUNT 2 A **merchant** is a person who owns or runs a shop, store, or other business. [AM] ❑ *The family was forced to live on credit from local merchants.* N-COUNT

✔ in BRIT, usually use **retailer, shopkeeper**

3 **Merchant** seamen or ships are involved in carrying goods for trade. ❑ *There's been a big reduction in the size of the British merchant fleet in recent years.* ADJ: ADJ n

**mer|chant bank** **(merchant banks)** A **merchant bank** is a bank that deals mainly with firms, investment, and foreign trade, rather than with the public. [BUSINESS] N-COUNT

**mer|chant bank|er** **(merchant bankers)** A **merchant banker** is someone who works for a merchant bank. [BUSINESS] N-COUNT

**mer|ci|ful** /mɜːʳsɪfʊl/ 1 If you describe God or a person in a position of authority as **merciful**, you mean that they show kindness and forgiveness to people. ❑ *We can only hope the court is merciful.* ADJ 2 If you describe an event or situation as **merciful**, you mean that it is a good thing, especially because it stops someone's suffering or discomfort. ❑ *Eventually the session came to a merciful end.* ADJ

**mer|ci|ful|ly** /mɜːʳsɪfʊli/ You can use **mercifully** to show that you are glad that something good has happened, or that something bad has not happened or has stopped. ❑ *Mercifully, a friend came to the rescue.* ADV: ADV with cl, ADV adj, ADV with v feelings

**mer|ci|less** /mɜːʳsɪləs/ If you describe someone as **merciless**, you mean that they are very cruel or determined and do not show any concern for the effect their actions have on other people. ❑ *...the merciless efficiency of a modern police state.* ADJ = ruthless ♦ **mer|ci|less|ly** *We teased him mercilessly... The sun beat down mercilessly* ADV: usu ADV with v, also ADV adj, ADV with cl

**mer|cu|rial** /mɜːʳkjʊəriəl/ If you describe someone as **mercurial**, you mean that they frequently change their mind or mood without warning. [LITERARY] ❑ *...his mercurial temperament.* ADJ = volatile

**mer|cu|ry** /mɜːʳkjʊri/ **Mercury** is a silver-coloured liquid metal that is used especially in thermometers and barometers. N-UNCOUNT

**mer|cy** /mɜːʳsi/ **(mercies)** 1 If someone in authority shows **mercy**, they choose not to harm someone they have power over, or they forgive someone they have the right to punish. ❑ *Neither side took prisoners or showed any mercy... They cried for mercy but their pleas were met with abuse and laughter.* *N-UNCOUNT* 2 **Mercy** is used to describe a special journey to help someone in great need, such as people who are sick or made homeless by war. [JOURNALISM] ❑ *She vanished nine months ago while on a mercy mission to West Africa.* *ADJ: ADJ n* 3 If you refer to an event or situation as **a mercy**, you mean that it makes you feel happy or relieved, usually because it stops something unpleasant happening. ❑ *It really was a mercy that he'd died so rapidly at the end.* *N-COUNT: usu a N*

**PHRASES** 4 If one person or thing is **at the mercy of** another, the first person or thing is in a situation where they cannot prevent themselves being harmed or affected by the second. ❑ *Buildings are left to decay at the mercy of vandals and the weather.* *PHRASE: with poss, usu PHR after v, v-link PHR* 5 If you tell someone who is in an unpleasant situation that they should be **grateful** or **thankful for small mercies**, you mean that although their situation is bad, it could be even worse, and so they should be happy. ❑ *But so low has morale sunk that the team and the fans would have been grateful for small mercies.* *PHRASE: usu v-link PHR*

**mer|cy kill|ing** **(mercy killings)** A **mercy killing** is an act of killing someone who is very ill, in order to stop them suffering any more pain. *N-VAR*

**mere** /mɪəʳ/ **(merest)** ◆◇◇

> **Mere** does not have a comparative form. The superlative form **merest** is used to emphasize how small something is, rather than in comparisons.

1 You use **mere** to emphasize how unimportant or inadequate something is, in comparison to the general situation you are describing. ❑ *...successful exhibitions which go beyond mere success... There is more to good health than the mere absence of disease... She'd never received the merest hint of any communication from him.* *ADJ: ADJ n* [emphasis] 2 You use **mere** to indicate that a quality or action that is usually unimportant has a very important or strong effect. ❑ *The mere mention of food had triggered off hunger pangs... The team manager has been quick to clamp down on the merest hint of complacency.* *ADJ: ADJ n* 3 You use **mere** to emphasize how small a particular amount or number is. ❑ *Sixty per cent of teachers are women, but a mere 5 percent of women are heads and deputies.* *ADJ: a ADJ amount* [emphasis]

**mere|ly** /mɪəʳli/ ◆◇◇ 1 You use **merely** to emphasize that something is only what you say and not better, more important, or more exciting. ❑ *Michael is now merely a good friend... They are offering merely technical assistance.* *ADV: ADV with cl/group, ADV before v* [emphasis] *= just, simply* 2 You use **merely** to emphasize that a particular amount or quantity is very small. ❑ *The brain accounts for merely three per cent of body weight.* *ADV: ADV amount* [emphasis] *= only* 3 You use **not merely** before the less important of two contrasting statements, as a way of emphasizing the more important statement. ❑ *The team needs players who want to play cricket for England, not merely any country that will have them.* *PHRASE: PHR with cl/group, PHR before v* [emphasis]

**mer|etri|cious** /merɪtrɪʃəs/ If you describe something as **meretricious**, you disapprove of it because although it looks attractive it is actually of little value. [FORMAL] ❑ *...vulgar, meretricious and shabby souvenirs.* *ADJ* [disapproval]

**merge** /mɜːʳdʒ/ **(merges, merging, merged)** 1 If one thing **merges with** another, or **is merged with** another, they combine or come together to make one whole thing. You can also say that two things **merge**, or **are merged**. ❑ *Bank of America merged with a rival bank... The rivers merge just north of a vital irrigation system... The two countries merged into one... He sees sense in merging the two agencies while both are new... Then he showed me how to merge the graphic with text on the same screen.* *V-RECIP* *V with n* *pl-n V* *pl-n V into n* *V pl-n* *V n with n* 2 If one sound, colour, or object **merges** into another, the first changes so gradually into the second that you do not notice the change. ❑ *Like a chameleon, he could merge unobtrusively into the background... His features merged with the darkness... Night and day begin to merge.* *V-RECIP* *V into n* *V with n* *pl-n V*

**mer|ger** /mɜːʳdʒəʳ/ **(mergers)** A **merger** is the joining together of two separate companies or organizations so that they become one. [BUSINESS] ❑ *...a merger between two of Britain's biggest trades unions.* ◆◇◇ *N-COUNT*

**me|rid|ian** /mərɪdiən/ **(meridians)** A **meridian** is an imaginary line from the North Pole to the South Pole. Meridians are drawn on maps to help you describe the position of a place. *N-COUNT*

**me|ringue** /məræŋ/ **(meringues)** **Meringue** is a mixture of beaten egg whites and sugar which is baked in the oven. *N-VAR*

**mer|it** /merɪt/ **(merits, meriting, merited)** 1 If something has **merit**, it has good or worthwhile qualities. ❑ *The argument seemed to have considerable merit... Box-office success mattered more than artistic merit.* *N-UNCOUNT: usu with supp* 2 The **merits** of something are its advantages or other good points. ❑ *...the technical merits of a film.* *N-PLURAL: usu with poss* 3 If someone or something **merits** a particular action or treatment, they deserve it. [FORMAL] ❑ *He said he had done nothing wrong to merit a criminal investigation.* *VERB = deserve* *V n* 4 If you judge something or someone **on merit** or **on** their **merits**, your judgment is based on what you notice when you consider them, rather than on things that you know about them from other sources. ❑ *Everybody is selected on merit... Each case is judged on its merits.* *PHRASE: PHR after v*

**meri|toc|ra|cy** /merɪtɒkrəsi/ **(meritocracies)** A **meritocracy** is a society or social system in which people get status or rewards because of what they achieve, rather than because of their wealth or social status. *N-VAR*

**meri|to|crat|ic** /merɪtəkrætɪk/ A **meritocratic** society or social system gives people status or rewards because of what they achieve, rather than because of their wealth or social position. *ADJ: usu ADJ n*

**meri|to|ri|ous** /merɪtɔːriəs/ If you describe something as **meritorious**, you approve of it for its good or worthwhile qualities. [FORMAL] ❑ *I had been promoted for what was called gallant and meritorious service.* *ADJ* [approval]

**mer|maid** /mɜːʳmeɪd/ **(mermaids)** In fairy stories and legends, a **mermaid** is a woman with a fish's tail instead of legs, who lives in the sea. *N-COUNT*

**mer|ri|ly** /merɪli/ 1 If you say that someone **merrily** does something, you are critical of the fact that they do it without realizing that there are a lot of problems which they have not thought about. ❑ *There they were, merrily describing their 16-hour working days while simultaneously claiming to be happily married.* *ADV: ADV with v* [disapproval] *= blithely* 2 If you say that something is happening **merrily**, you mean that it is happening fairly quickly, and in a pleasant or satisfactory way. ❑ *The ferry cut merrily through the water.* *ADV: ADV with v* 3 → See also **merry**.

**mer|ri|ment** /merɪmənt/ **Merriment** means laughter. [OLD-FASHIONED] *N-UNCOUNT*

**mer|ry** /meri/ **(merrier, merriest)** 1 If you describe someone's character or behaviour as **merry**, you mean that they are happy and cheerful. [OLD-FASHIONED] ❑ *From the house come the bursts of merry laughter.* *ADJ = jolly* ♦ **mer|ri|ly** *Chris threw back his head and laughed merrily.* *ADV: ADV after v* 2 If you get **merry**, you get slightly drunk. [BRIT, INFORMAL] ❑ *They went off to Glengarriff to get merry.* *ADJ: v-link ADJ* 3 Some people use **merry** to emphasize something that they are saying, often when they want to express disapproval or humour. ❑ *It hasn't stopped the British Navy proceeding on its merry way.* *ADJ: ADJ n* [emphasis] 4 → See also **merrily**. 5 Just before Christmas and on Christmas Day, people say '**Merry Christmas**' to other people to express the hope that they will have a happy *CONVENTION* [formulae] time. ❑ *Merry Christmas, everyone... I just wanted to wish you a merry Christmas.* [6] to **play merry hell** → see **hell**.

**merry-go-round** (**merry-go-rounds**) [1] A **merry-go-round** is a large circular platform at a fairground on which there are model animals or vehicles for people to sit on or in as it turns round. N-COUNT [2] You can refer to a continuous series of activities as a **merry-go-round**. ❑ *...a merry-go-round of teas, fetes, musical events and the like.* N-COUNT: usu sing, oft N *of* n

**merry-making** **Merry-making** is the activities of people who are enjoying themselves together in a lively way, for example by eating, drinking, or dancing. ❑ *...a time of merry-making, feasting and visiting friends.* N-UNCOUNT

**me|sa** /meɪsə/ (**mesas**) A **mesa** is a large hill with a flat top and steep sides; used mainly of hills in the south-western United States. [AM] N-COUNT

**mesh** /meʃ/ (**meshes, meshing, meshed**) [1] **Mesh** is material like a net made from wire, thread, or plastic. ❑ *The ground-floor windows are obscured by wire mesh.* N-VAR [2] If two things or ideas **mesh** or **are meshed**, they go together well or fit together closely. ❑ *Their senses of humor meshed perfectly... This of course meshes with the economic philosophy of those on the right... Meshing the research and marketing operations will be Mr. Furlaud's job.* V-RECIP; pl-n V; V *with* n; V n-pl; Also V n *with* n

**mes|mer|ize** /mezməraɪz/ (**mesmerizes, mesmerizing, mesmerized**)

> in BRIT, also use **mesmerise**

If you **are mesmerized** by something, you are so interested in it or so attracted to it that you cannot think about anything else. ❑ *He was absolutely mesmerised by Pavarotti on television... There was something about Pearl that mesmerised her.* VERB; *be* V-ed; V n ♦ **mes|mer|ized** *I sat mesmerized long after the fairground closed.* ADJ: usu v-link ADJ ♦ **mes|mer|iz|ing** *She has a mesmerising smile.* ADJ: ADJ n

**mess** /mes/ (**messes, messing, messed**) ◆◇◇ [1] If you say that something is **a mess** or **in a mess**, you think that it is in an untidy state. ❑ *The house is a mess... Linda can't stand mess.* N-SING: also no det [2] If you say that a situation is **a mess**, you mean that it is full of trouble or problems. You can also say that something is **in a mess**. ❑ *I've made such a mess of my life. ...the many reasons why the economy is in such a mess.* N-VAR [3] **A mess** is something liquid or sticky that has been accidentally dropped on something. ❑ *I'll clear up the mess later.* N-VAR [4] The **mess** at a military base or military barracks is the building in which members of the armed forces can eat or relax. ❑ *...a party at the officers' mess.* N-COUNT: usu sing

♦ **mess around**

> in BRIT, also use **mess about**

[1] If you **mess around** or **mess about**, you spend time doing things without any particular purpose or without achieving anything. ❑ *We were just messing around playing with paint... Boys and girls will enjoy messing about with any kind of machine.* PHRASAL VERB; V P; V P *with* n [2] If you say that someone **is messing around with** or **messing about with** something, you mean that they are interfering with it in a harmful way. ❑ *I'd like to know who's been messing about with the pram.* PHRASAL VERB; V P *with* n [3] If someone **is messing around** or **messing about**, they are behaving in a joking or silly way. ❑ *I thought she was messing about.* PHRASAL VERB = *fool around*; V P [4] If you **mess** someone **around** or **mess** them **about**, you treat them badly, for example by not being honest with them, or by continually changing plans which affect them. [mainly BRIT] ❑ *I think they've been messed around far too much.* PHRASAL VERB; V n P

♦ **mess up** [1] If you **mess** something **up** or if you **mess up**, you cause something to fail or be spoiled. [INFORMAL] ❑ *When politicians mess things up, it is the people who pay the price... He had messed up one career... If I messed up, I would probably be fired.* PHRASAL VERB; V n P; V P n (not pron); V P [2] If you **mess up** a place or a thing, you make it untidy or dirty. [INFORMAL] ❑ *I hope they haven't messed up your video tapes.* PHRASAL VERB; V P n; Also V n P [3] If something **messes** someone **up**, it causes them to be very confused or worried, or to have psychological problems. [INFORMAL] ❑ *That really messed them up, especially the boys.* PHRASAL VERB; V n P; Also V P n (not pron)

♦ **mess with** If you tell someone not to **mess with** a person or thing, you are warning them not to get involved with that person or thing. ❑ *You are messing with people's religion and they don't like that... Do you know who you're messing with – do you know who I am?* PHRASAL VERB; V P n; V P n

**mes|sage** /mesɪdʒ/ (**messages, messaging, messaged**) ◆◆◇ [1] A **message** is a piece of information or a request that you send to someone or leave for them when you cannot speak to them directly. ❑ *I got a message you were trying to reach me... Would you like to leave a message?* N-COUNT [2] The **message** that someone is trying to communicate, for example in a book or play, is the idea or point that they are trying to communicate. ❑ *The report's message was unequivocal... I think they got the message that this is wrong.* N-COUNT: usu sing, usu with supp [3] If you **message** someone, you send them a message electronically using a computer or another device such as a mobile phone. ❑ *People who message a lot feel unpopular if they don't get many back... She messaged him saying she wished they were together.* VERB; V; V n

**mes|sag|ing** /mesɪdʒɪŋ/ **Messaging** is the sending of written or spoken messages using a computer or another electronic device such as a mobile phone. ❑ *Messaging allows real-time communication by keyboard with up to five people at any one time.* N-UNCOUNT

**mes|sen|ger** /mesɪndʒəʳ/ (**messengers**) A **messenger** takes a message to someone, or takes messages regularly as their job. ❑ *There will be a messenger at the Airport to collect the photographs from our courier.* N-COUNT: also *by* N

**mes|sen|ger boy** (**messenger boys**) A **messenger boy** is a boy who is employed to take messages to people. N-COUNT

**mess hall** (**mess halls**) A **mess hall** is a large room where a particular group of people, especially members of the armed forces, eat meals together. N-COUNT

**mes|si|ah** /mɪsaɪə/ (**messiahs**) [1] For Jews, **the Messiah** is the King of the Jews, who will be sent to them by God. N-PROPER [2] For Christians, **the Messiah** is Jesus Christ. N-PROPER [3] If you refer to someone as a **messiah**, you mean that they are expected to do wonderful things, especially to rescue people from a very difficult or dangerous situation, or that they are thought to have done these things. ❑ *People saw Mandela as their messiah.* N-COUNT: usu with supp

**mes|si|an|ic** /mesiænɪk/ also **Messianic**. [1] **Messianic** means relating to the belief that a divine being has been born, or will be born, who will change the world. ❑ *The cult leader saw himself as a Messianic figure.* ADJ: ADJ n [2] **Messianic** means relating to the belief that there will be a complete change in the social order in a country or in the world. ❑ *The defeated radicals of the French Revolution were the first to have this messianic vision in 1794.* ADJ: usu ADJ n

**Messrs** /mesəʳz/

> in AM, use **Messrs.**

**Messrs** is used before the names of two or more men as part of the name of a business. [BRIT] ❑ *The repairs were to be done by Messrs Clegg & Sons of Balham.* N-TITLE

**messy** /mesi/ (**messier, messiest**) [1] A **messy** person or activity makes things dirty or untidy. ❑ *She was a good, if messy, cook... As the work tends to be a bit messy, wear old clothes.* ADJ ♦ **messi|ly** *She wrote it hastily and messily on a scrap of paper.* ADV: usu ADV with v, also ADV adj [2] Something that is **messy** is dirty or untidy. ❑ *Don't worry if this first coat of paint looks messy.* ADJ [3] If you describe a situation as **messy**, you are emphasizing that it is confused or complicated, ADJ and therefore unsatisfactory. ❑ *John had been through a messy divorce himself.*

**met** /met/ **Met** is the past tense and past participle of **meet**.

**meta|bol|ic** /metəbɒlɪk/ **Metabolic** means relating to a person's or animal's metabolism. ❑ *...people who have inherited a low metabolic rate.* ADJ: ADJ n

**me|tabo|lism** /mɪtæbəlɪzəm/ **(metabolisms)** Your **metabolism** is the way that chemical processes in your body cause food to be used in an efficient way, for example to make new cells and to give you energy. N-VAR: oft with poss

**me|tabo|lize** /mɪtæbəlaɪz/ **(metabolizes, metabolizing, metabolized)**

✓ in BRIT, also use **metabolise**

When you **metabolize** a substance, it is affected by chemical processes in your body so that, for example, it is broken down, absorbed, and used. [TECHNICAL] ❑ *Diabetics cannot metabolise glucose properly.* VERB V n

**met|al** /metᵊl/ **(metals) Metal** is a hard substance such as iron, steel, gold, or lead. ❑ *...pieces of furniture in wood, metal and glass... He hit his head against a metal bar.* ➔ See also **base metal**. ◆◇◇ N-MASS

**meta|lan|guage** /metəlæŋgwɪdʒ/ **(metalanguages)** also **meta-language**. In linguistics, the words and expressions that people use to describe or refer to language can be called **metalanguage**. [TECHNICAL] N-VAR

**met|alled** /metᵊld/ A **metalled** road has a level surface made of small pieces of stone; used especially of country roads and tracks. [mainly BRIT] ADJ: ADJ n

**me|tal|lic** /mətælɪk/ 1 A **metallic** sound is like the sound of one piece of metal hitting another. ❑ *There was a metallic click and the gates swung open.* 2 **Metallic** paint or colours shine like metal. ❑ *He had painted all the wood with metallic silver paint.* 3 Something that tastes **metallic** has a bitter unpleasant taste. ❑ *There was a metallic taste at the back of his throat.* 4 **Metallic** means consisting entirely or partly of metal. ❑ *Even the smallest metallic object, whether a nail file or cigarette lighter, is immediately confiscated.* ADJ: usu ADJ n; ADJ: usu ADJ n; ADJ; ADJ: usu ADJ n = metal

**met|al|lur|gist** /metælərdʒɪst, AM metəlɜːrdʒɪst/ **(metallurgists)** A **metallurgist** is an expert in metallurgy. N-COUNT

**met|al|lur|gy** /metælərdʒi, AM metəlɜːrdʒi/ **Metallurgy** is the scientific study of the properties and uses of metals. N-UNCOUNT

**metal|work** /metᵊlwɜːrk/ 1 **Metalwork** is the activity of making objects out of metal in a skilful way. ❑ *He was a craftsman in metalwork from Dresden.* 2 **The metalwork** is the metal part of something. ❑ *Rust and flaking paint mean the metalwork is in poor condition.* N-UNCOUNT; N-UNCOUNT

**meta|mor|phose** /metəmɔːrfoʊz/ **(metamorphoses, metamorphosing, metamorphosed)** To **metamorphose** or **be metamorphosed** means to develop and change into something completely different. [FORMAL] ❑ *...hysterical laughter which gradually metamorphoses into convulsive sobs... The tadpoles metamorphose and emerge onto land... She had been metamorphosed by the war.* ➔ See also **metamorphosis**. VERB V into/from n; V; be V-ed; Also V n

**meta|mor|pho|sis** /metəmɔːrfəsɪs/ **(metamorphoses)** When a **metamorphosis** occurs, a person or thing develops and changes into something completely different. [FORMAL] ❑ *...his metamorphosis from a republican to a democrat.* N-VAR = transformation

**meta|phor** /metəfɔːr/ **(metaphors)** 1 A **metaphor** is an imaginative way of describing something by referring to something else which is the same in a particular way. For example, if you want to say that someone is very shy and frightened of things, you might say that they are a mouse. ❑ *...the avoidance of 'violent expressions and metaphors' like 'kill two birds with one stone'. ...the writer's use of metaphor.* 2 If one thing is a **metaphor for** another, it is intended or regarded as a symbol of it. ❑ *The divided family remains a powerful metaphor for a society that continued to tear itself apart.* 3 If you **mix** your **metaphors**, you use two conflicting metaphors. People do this accidentally, or sometimes deliberately as a joke. ❑ *To mix yet more metaphors, you were trying to run before you could walk, and I've clipped your wings.* N-VAR; N-VAR: oft N for n; PHRASE: V inflects

**meta|phori|cal** /metəfɒrɪkᵊl, AM -fɔːr-/ You use the word **metaphorical** to indicate that you are not using words with their ordinary meaning, but are describing something by means of an image or symbol. ❑ *It turns out Levy is talking in metaphorical terms.* ♦ **meta|phori|cal|ly** *You're speaking metaphorically, I hope.* ADJ; ADV: usu ADV with cl, ADV with v

**meta|physi|cal** /metəfɪzɪkᵊl/ **Metaphysical** means relating to metaphysics. ❑ *...metaphysical questions like personal responsibility for violence.* ADJ: usu ADJ n

**meta|phys|ics** /metəfɪzɪks/ **Metaphysics** is a part of philosophy which is concerned with understanding reality and developing theories about what exists and how we know that it exists. N-UNCOUNT

**mete** /miːt/ **(metes, meting, meted)**

♦ **mete out** To **mete out** a punishment means to order that someone should be punished in a certain way. [FORMAL] ❑ *His father meted out punishment with a slipper.* PHRASAL VERB V P n (not pron)

**me|teor** /miːtiər/ **(meteors)** A **meteor** is a piece of rock or metal that burns very brightly when it enters the earth's atmosphere from space. N-COUNT

**me|teor|ic** /miːtiɒrɪk, AM -ɔːr-/ If you use **meteoric** when you are describing someone's career, you mean that they achieved success very quickly. ❑ *...his meteoric rise to fame.* ADJ

**me|teor|ite** /miːtiəraɪt/ **(meteorites)** A **meteorite** is a large piece of rock or metal from space that has landed on Earth. N-COUNT

**me|teoro|logi|cal** /miːtiərəlɒdʒɪkᵊl/ **Meteorological** means relating to meteorology. ❑ *...adverse meteorological conditions.* ADJ: ADJ n

**me|teor|ol|ogy** /miːtiərɒlədʒi/ **Meteorology** is the study of the processes in the Earth's atmosphere that cause particular weather conditions, especially in order to predict the weather. ♦ **me|teor|olo|gist** /miːtiərɒlədʒɪst/ **(meteorologists)** ❑ *Meteorologists have predicted mild rains for the next few days.* N-UNCOUNT; N-COUNT

**me|ter** /miːtər/ **(meters, metering, metered)** 1 A **meter** is a device that measures and records something such as the amount of gas or electricity that you have used. ❑ *He was there to read the electricity meter.* 2 To **meter** something such as gas or electricity means to use a meter to measure how much of it people use, usually in order to calculate how much they have to pay. ❑ *Only a third of these households thought it reasonable to meter water... Metered taxis are relatively inexpensive.* 3 A **meter** is the same as a **parking meter**. 4 ➔ See also **metre**. N-COUNT; VERB V n; V-ed; N-COUNT

**me|thane** /miːθeɪn, AM meθ-/ **Methane** is a colourless gas that has no smell. Natural gas consists mostly of methane. N-UNCOUNT

**meth|od** /meθəd/ **(methods)** A **method** is a particular way of doing something. ❑ *The pill is the most efficient method of birth control. ...new teaching methods.* ◆◆◇ N-COUNT: oft N of n/-ing

**me|thodi|cal** /məθɒdɪkᵊl/ If you describe someone as **methodical**, you mean that they do things carefully, thoroughly, and in order. ❑ *Da Vinci was methodical in his research, carefully recording his observations and theories.* ♦ **me|thodi|cal|ly** /məθɒdɪkli/ *She methodically put the things into her suitcase.* ADJ; ADV: ADV with v

**Meth|od|ism** /meθədɪzəm/ **Methodism** is the beliefs and practices of Methodists. N-UNCOUNT

**Meth|od|ist** /meθədɪst/ **(Methodists) Methodists** are Christians who follow the teachings of John Wesley and who have their own branch of the Christian church and their own form of worship. N-COUNT

**meth|od|ol|ogy** /meθədɒlədʒi/ **(methodologies)** A **methodology** is a system of methods and principles for doing something, for example for teaching or for carrying out research. [FORMAL] ❑ *Teaching methodologies vary according to the topic.* N-VAR
♦ **meth|odo|logi|cal** /meθədəlɒdʒɪkəl/ *...theoretical and methodological issues raised by the study of literary texts.* ADJ: usu ADJ n

**meths** /meθs/ **Meths** is the same as **methylated spirits.** [BRIT] N-UNCOUNT

**meth|yl|at|ed spir|its** /meθəleɪtɪd spɪrɪts/ **Methylated spirits** is a liquid made from alcohol and other chemicals. It is used for removing stains and as a fuel in small lamps and heaters. [BRIT] N-UNCOUNT

**me|ticu|lous** /mətɪkjʊləs/ If you describe someone as **meticulous**, you mean that they do things very carefully and with great attention to detail. ❑ *He was so meticulous about everything... The painting had been executed with meticulous attention to detail.* ♦ **me|ticu|lous|ly** *The flat had been meticulously cleaned.* ADJ; ADV: usu ADV with v, also ADV adj

**me|ti|er** /metieɪ, AM metjeɪ/ **(metiers)** also **métier.** Your **metier** is the type of work that you have a natural talent for and do well. [FORMAL] ❑ *It was as the magazine's business manager that he found his true metier.* N-COUNT: usu with poss

**me|tre** /miːtəʳ/ **(metres)** ◆◇◇

in AM, use **meter**

1 A **metre** is a metric unit of length equal to 100 centimetres. ❑ *Chris Boardman won the Olympic 4,000 metres pursuit... The tunnel is 10 metres wide and 600 metres long.* N-COUNT: num N, oft N *of* n
2 In the study of poetry, **metre** is the regular and rhythmic arrangement of syllables according to particular patterns. [TECHNICAL] ❑ *They must each compose a poem in strict alliterative metre... All of the poems are written in traditional metres and rhyme schemes.* N-VAR

**met|ric** /metrɪk/ **Metric** means relating to the metric system. ❑ *Converting metric measurements to U.S. equivalents is easy.* ADJ: usu num ADJ n

**met|ric sys|tem** **The metric system** is the system of measurement that uses metres, grams, and litres. N-SING: *the* N

**met|ric ton** **(metric tons)** A **metric ton** is 1,000 kilograms. ❑ *The Wall Street Journal uses 220,000 metric tons of newsprint each year.* N-COUNT: num N, oft N *of* n

**met|ro** /metroʊ/ **(metros)** also **Metro. The metro** is the underground railway system in some cities, for example in Paris. N-COUNT: usu *the* N in sing

**met|ro|nome** /metrənoʊm/ **(metronomes)** A **metronome** is a device which is used to indicate how quickly a piece of music should be played. It can be adjusted to make regular sounds at different speeds. N-COUNT

**me|tropo|lis** /mətrɒpəlɪs/ **(metropolises)** A **metropolis** is the largest, busiest, and most important city in a country or region. ❑ *...the bustling metropolis of Chengdu.* N-COUNT: usu sing

**met|ro|poli|tan** /metrəpɒlɪtən/ **Metropolitan** means belonging to or typical of a large busy city. ❑ *...the metropolitan district of Miami. ...a dozen major metropolitan hospitals. ...metropolitan sophistication and rustic naivety.* ADJ: ADJ n

**met|tle** /metəl/ Someone's **mettle** is their ability to do something well in difficult circumstances. ❑ *His first important chance to show his mettle came when he opened the new session of the Legislature.* N-UNCOUNT: usu poss N

**mew** /mjuː/ **(mews, mewing, mewed)** When a cat **mews**, it makes a soft high-pitched noise. ❑ *From somewhere, the kitten mewed.* VERB V

**mews** /mjuːz/ **(mews)** A **mews** is a street or small area surrounded by houses that were originally built as stables. [BRIT] ❑ *The house is in a secluded mews.* N-COUNT: oft in names

**Mexi|can** /meksɪkən/ **(Mexicans)** 1 **Mexican** means belonging or relating to Mexico, or to its people or culture. ADJ
2 A **Mexican** is a Mexican citizen, or a person of Mexican origin. N-COUNT

**Mexi|can stand-off** **(Mexican stand-offs)** A **Mexican stand-off** is a situation in which neither of the people or groups in a conflict or dispute can win and neither wants to give in first. [AM] N-COUNT: usu sing

**Mexi|can wave** **(Mexican waves)** If a crowd of people do a **Mexican wave**, each person in the crowd stands up and puts their arms in the air after the person to one side of them, creating a continuous wave-like motion through the crowd. [BRIT] N-COUNT

in AM, use **wave**

**mez|za|nine** /mezəniːn/ **(mezzanines)** 1 A **mezzanine** is a small floor which is built between two main floors of a building. ❑ *...the dining room on the mezzanine.* N-COUNT
2 The **mezzanine** is the lowest balcony in a theatre, or the front rows in the lowest balcony. [AM] N-COUNT: oft *the* N

in BRIT, usually use **dress circle**

**mez|zo** /metsoʊ/ **(mezzos)** A **mezzo** is the same as a **mezzo-soprano.** N-COUNT

**mezzo-soprano** **(mezzo-sopranos)** A **mezzo-soprano** is a female singer who sings with a higher range than a contralto but a lower range than a soprano. ❑ *She became a professional mezzo-soprano. ...her remarkable mezzo soprano voice.* N-COUNT

**mg** **mg** is a written abbreviation for **milligram** or **milligrams.** ❑ *...300 mg of calcium.*

**Mgr** **Mgr** is a written abbreviation for **Monsignor.**

**MHz** **MHz** is a written abbreviation for **megahertz.**

**MIA** /em aɪ eɪ/ **MIA** is used to describe members of the armed forces who do not return from a military operation but who are not known to have been killed or captured. **MIA** is an abbreviation for 'missing in action'. [mainly AM] ❑ *He was listed as MIA.* ADJ

**miaow** /miaʊ/ **(miaows, miaowing, miaowed)** or **meow** **Miaow** is used to represent the noise that a cat makes. ❑ *He made a frightened noise a little like the miaow of a cat.* ♦ **Miaow** is also a verb. ❑ *Cats miaow when they are unhappy, purr when they are happy.* N-COUNT; SOUND; VERB V

**mi|as|ma** /miæzmə/ **(miasmas)** You can describe something bad or confused that seems to be in the air all around you as a **miasma.** [LITERARY] ❑ *As time went on, his ambition to be part of the US Supreme Court faded in a miasma of alcohol and despair.* N-VAR

**mic.** /maɪk/ **(mics)** A **mic.** is the same as a **microphone.** [INFORMAL] N-COUNT

**mica** /maɪkə/ **(micas)** **Mica** is a hard mineral which is found as small flat crystals in rocks. It has a great resistance to heat and electricity. N-MASS

**mice** /maɪs/ **Mice** is the plural of **mouse.**

**mick|ey** /mɪki/ If you **take the mickey** out of someone or something, you make fun of them, usually in an unkind way. [BRIT, INFORMAL] ❑ *He started taking the mickey out of this poor man just because he is bald.* PHRASE: V inflects, oft PHR *out of* n = mock, tease

**Mickey Mouse** You use **Mickey Mouse** to show that you think something is silly, childish, easy, or worthless. ❑ *This is not a Mickey Mouse course where every player has a chance.* ADJ [disapproval]

**mi|cro** /maɪkroʊ/ You use **micro** to indicate that something relates to a specific area, rather than a general one [mainly TECHNICAL] ❑ *The vital task was to allow the economy to operate freely at a micro level.* ADJ: usu ADJ n ≠ macro

**micro-** /maɪkroʊ-/ **Micro-** is used to form nouns that refer to something that is a very small example or fraction of a particular type of thing. ❑ *These are the cells that directly attack and kill* PREFIX *micro-organisms... The pulse is usually timed in microseconds.*

**mi|crobe** /maɪkroʊb/ **(microbes)** A **microbe** is a very small living thing, which you can only see if you use a microscope. N-COUNT = *micro-organism*

**micro|bio|logi|cal** /maɪkroʊbaɪəlɒdʒɪkəl/ **Microbiological** refers to studies or tests relating to very small living things such as bacteria and their effects on people. ❑ *...microbiological testing.* ADJ: ADJ n

**micro|bi|ol|ogy** /maɪkroʊbaiɒlədʒi/ **Microbiology** is the branch of biology which is concerned with very small living things such as bacteria and their effects on people. ❑ *...a professor of microbiology.* N-UNCOUNT ♦ **micro|bi|olo|gist** **(microbiologists)** *...a microbiologist at Liverpool University.* N-COUNT

**micro-brewery** **(micro-breweries)** A **micro-brewery** is a type of small brewery where beer is produced using traditional methods. N-COUNT

**micro|chip** /maɪkroʊtʃɪp/ **(microchips)** A **microchip** is a very small piece of silicon inside a computer. It has electronic circuits on it and can hold large quantities of information or perform mathematical and logical operations. N-COUNT

**micro|com|put|er** /maɪkroʊkəmpjuːtəʳ/ **(microcomputers)** also **micro-computer.** A **microcomputer** is a small computer, especially one used for writing documents. N-COUNT

**micro|cosm** /maɪkroʊkɒzəm/ **(microcosms)** A **microcosm** is a small society, place, or activity which has all the typical features of a much larger one and so seems like a smaller version of it. [FORMAL] ❑ *Kitchell says the city was a microcosm of all American culture during the '60s.* N-COUNT: oft N *of* n, also *in* N

**micro|cred|it** /maɪkroʊkredɪt/ **Microcredit** is credit in the form of small loans offered to local businesses, especially in developing countries. [BUSINESS] ❑ *...a microcredit scheme which provides credit to small businesses.* N-UNCOUNT

**micro|elec|tron|ics** /maɪkroʊelektrɒnɪks/

☑ The form **microelectronic** is used as a modifier.

**Microelectronics** is the branch of electronics that deals with miniature electronic circuits. N-UNCOUNT

**micro|fibre** /maɪkroʊfaɪbəʳ/ **(microfibres)**

☑ in AM, use **microfiber**

**Microbfibres** are extremely light artificial fibres that are used to make cloth. ❑ *Microfibre fabrics are three times finer than cotton.* N-VAR: oft N n

**micro|fiche** /maɪkroʊfiːʃ/ **(microfiches)** A **microfiche** is a small sheet of film on which writing or other information is stored, greatly reduced in size. N-VAR

**micro|film** /maɪkroʊfɪlm/ **(microfilms)** **Microfilm** is film that is used for photographing information and storing it in a reduced form. N-VAR

**micro-organism** **(micro-organisms)** also **microorganism.** A **micro-organism** is a very small living thing which you can only see if you use a microscope. N-COUNT = *microbe*

**micro|phone** /maɪkrəfoʊn/ **(microphones)** A **microphone** is a device that is used to make sounds louder or to record them on a tape recorder. N-COUNT

**micro|pro|ces|sor** /maɪkroʊproʊsesəʳ/ **(microprocessors)** In a computer, the **microprocessor** is the main microchip, which controls its most important functions. [COMPUTING] N-COUNT

**micro|scope** /maɪkrəskoʊp/ **(microscopes)** [1] A **microscope** is a scientific instrument which makes very small objects look bigger so that more detail can be seen. N-COUNT [2] If you say that something is **under the microscope**, you mean that it is being studied very closely, usually because it is believed that something is wrong with it. ❑ *The media put their every decision under the microscope.* PHRASE: PHR after v, v-link PHR

**micro|scop|ic** /maɪkrəskɒpɪk/ [1] **Microscopic** objects are extremely small, and usually can be seen only through a microscope. ❑ *...microscopic fibres of protein.* ADJ: usu ADJ n [2] A **microscopic** examination is done using a microscope. ❑ *Microscopic examination of a cell's chromosomes can reveal the sex of the fetus.* ADJ: ADJ n ♦ **micro|scopi|cal|ly** *The tissue is examined microscopically to rule out or confirm cancer.* ADV: ADV with v [3] If you say that something is done in **microscopic** detail, you are emphasizing that it is done in a very thorough, detailed way. ❑ *He carefully recounts the tale, the microscopic details of those crucial minutes.* ADJ: usu ADJ n [emphasis]

**micro|sec|ond** /maɪkroʊsekənd/ **(microseconds)** A **microsecond** is one millionth of a second. N-COUNT

**micro|sur|gery** /maɪkroʊsɜːʳdʒəri/ **Microsurgery** is a form of surgery where doctors repair or remove parts of the body that are so small that they can only be seen clearly using a microscope. N-UNCOUNT

**micro|wave** /maɪkroʊweɪv/ **(microwaves, microwaving, microwaved)** [1] A **microwave** or a **microwave oven** is an oven which cooks food very quickly by electromagnetic radiation rather than by heat. N-COUNT [2] To **microwave** food or drink means to cook or heat it in a microwave oven. ❑ *Steam or microwave the vegetables until tender.* VERB V n

**micro|wave|able** /maɪkroʊweɪvəbəl/ also **microwavable. Microwaveable** food can be cooked in a microwave. ADJ

**mid-** /mɪd-/ **Mid-** is used to form nouns or adjectives that refer to the middle part of a particular period of time, or the middle point of a particular place. ❑ *...the mid-eighteenth century... Davis is in her mid-thirties. ...the mid-west of America.* PREFIX

**mid-air** If something happens in **mid-air**, it happens in the air, rather than on the ground. ❑ *The bird stopped and hovered in mid-air. ...a mid-air collision.* N-UNCOUNT

**mid|day** /mɪddeɪ/ [1] **Midday** is twelve o'clock in the middle of the day. ❑ *At midday everyone would go down to Reg's Cafe... It's eight minutes after midday.* N-UNCOUNT: oft prep N [2] **Midday** is the middle part of the day, from late morning to early afternoon. ❑ *People were beginning to tire in the midday heat.* N-UNCOUNT: usu N n

**mid|dle** /mɪdəl/ **(middles)** ◆◆◆ [1] **The middle of** something is the part of it that is furthest from its edges, ends, or outside surface. ❑ *Howard stood in the middle of the room sipping a cup of coffee... Hyde accelerated away from the kerb, swerving out into the middle of the street... Make sure the roast potatoes aren't raw in the middle.* **the middle of nowhere** → see **nowhere.** N-COUNT: usu *the* N in sing, oft N *of* n = *centre* [2] The **middle** object in a row of objects is the one that has an equal number of objects on each side. ❑ *The middle button of his uniform jacket was strained over his belly. ...the middle finger of her left hand.* ADJ: ADJ n [3] **The middle of** an event or period of time is the part that comes after the first part and before the last part. ❑ *I woke up in the middle of the night and could hear a tapping on the window... It was now the middle of November, cold and often foggy.* N-SING: *the* N *of* n ♦ **Middle** is also an adjective. ❑ *The month began and ended quite dry, but the middle fortnight saw nearly 100mm of rain fall nationwide.* ADJ: ADJ n [4] The **middle** course or way is a moderate course of action that lies between two opposite and extreme courses. ❑ *He favoured a middle course between free enterprise and state intervention.* ADJ: ADJ n

PHRASES [5] If you divide or split something **down the middle**, you divide or split it into two equal halves or groups. ❑ *They agreed to split the bill down the middle.* PHRASE: PHR after v = *in half* [6] If you are **in the middle of** doing something, you are busy doing it. ❑ *It's a bit hectic. I'm in the middle of cooking for nine people.* PHRASE: v-link PHR -ing/n

**mid|dle age** **Middle age** is the period in your life when you are no longer young but have not yet become old. Middle age is usually considered to take place between the ages of 40 and 60. ❑ *Men tend to put on weight in middle age.* N-UNCOUNT

**middle-aged** [1] If you describe someone as **middle-aged**, you mean that they are neither young nor old. People between the ages of 40 and ADJ

60 are usually considered to be middle-aged. ❑ *...middle-aged, married businessmen.* [2] If you describe someone's activities or interests as **middle-aged**, you are critical of them because you think they are typical of a middle-aged person, for example by being conventional or old-fashioned. ❑ *Her novels are middle-aged and boring.* ADJ disapproval

**Mid|dle Ages** In European history, **the Middle Ages** was the period between the end of the Roman Empire in 476 AD and about 1500 AD, especially the later part of this period. N-PLURAL: the N

**Mid|dle Ameri|ca** [1] Journalists use **Middle America** to refer to middle class people in America who are believed not to like change. ❑ *People in the United States want the president to pay attention to Middle America.* [2] **Middle America** is the same as the **Midwest**. [3] **Middle America** is used to refer to the area consisting of Mexico and Central America, sometimes including the West Indies. N-UNCOUNT; N-PROPER; N-PROPER

**middle|brow** /mɪdᵊlbraʊ/ also **middle-brow.** If you describe a piece of entertainment such as a book or film as **middlebrow**, you mean that although it may be interesting and enjoyable, it does not require much thought. ❑ *...such middle-brow fare as Poirot, Sherlock Holmes and Jeeves and Wooster.* ADJ: usu ADJ n

**mid|dle class** **(middle classes)** **The middle class** or **middle classes** are the people in a society who are not working class or upper class. Business people, managers, doctors, lawyers, and teachers are usually regarded as middle class. ❑ *...the expansion of the middle class in the late 19th century... The President may have secured some support from the middle classes.* ♦ **Middle class** is also an adjective. ❑ *He is rapidly losing the support of blue-collar voters and of middle-class conservatives.* ◆◇◇ N-COUNT-COLL: usu the N; ADJ

**mid|dle dis|tance** [1] If you are looking **into the middle distance**, you are looking at a place that is neither near nor far away. ❑ *He stares detachedly into the middle distance, towards nothing in particular.* [2] A **middle-distance** runner is someone who takes part in races of medium length, for example 800 metres. N-SING: the N, usu into/in the N; ADJ: ADJ n

**Mid|dle East** **The Middle East** is the area around the eastern Mediterranean that includes Iran and all the countries in Asia to the west and south-west of Iran. ❑ *The two great rivers of the Middle East rise in the mountains of Turkey.* ◆◆◇ N-PROPER: the N

**Mid|dle East|ern** **Middle Eastern** means relating to the Middle East. ❑ *Most Middle Eastern countries have extremely high rates of population growth.* ADJ: ADJ n

**Mid|dle Eng|land** Journalists use **Middle England** to refer to middle class people in England who are believed not to like change. ❑ *This shows that the people of Middle England no longer trust the Tories.* N-UNCOUNT

**middle|man** /mɪdᵊlmæn/ **(middlemen)** [1] A **middleman** is a person or company which buys things from the people who produce them and sells them to the people who want to buy them. [BUSINESS] ❑ *Why don't they cut out the middleman and let us do it ourselves?* [2] A **middleman** is a person who helps in negotiations between people who are unwilling to meet each other directly. ❑ *The two sides would only meet indirectly, through middlemen.* N-COUNT; N-COUNT = go-between

**mid|dle man|age|ment** **Middle management** refers to managers who are below the top level of management, and who are responsible for controlling and running an organization rather than making decisions about how it operates. [BUSINESS] ❑ *The proportion of women in middle management has risen to 40%. ...middle-management jobs.* N-UNCOUNT

**mid|dle name** **(middle names)** [1] Your **middle name** is the name that comes between your first name and your surname. ❑ *His middle name is Justin.* [2] You can use **middle name** in expressions such as '**discretion was her middle name**' and '**his middle name is loyalty**' to indicate that someone always behaves with a great deal of a particular quality. [HUMOROUS] ❑ *Geniality is my middle name. I rarely write a fierce word about any restaurant.* N-COUNT: usu poss N; N-COUNT: usu poss N

**middle-of-the-road** [1] If you describe someone's opinions or policies as **middle-of-the-road**, you mean that they are neither left-wing nor right-wing, and not at all extreme. ❑ *Consensus need not be weak, nor need it result in middle-of-the-road policies.* [2] If you describe something or someone as **middle-of-the-road**, you mean that they are ordinary or unexciting. ❑ *I actually don't want to be a middle-of-the-road person, married with a mortgage.* [3] **Middle-of-the-road** music is pop music which a large number of people like because it is pleasant and does not sound extreme or unusual. The abbreviation **MOR** is also used. ❑ *I like cheerful, uplifting middle-of-the-road pop.* ADJ; ADJ; ADJ

**middle-ranking** A **middle-ranking** person has a fairly important or responsible position in a particular organization, but is not one of the most important people in it. ❑ *...middle-ranking army officers.* ADJ: ADJ n

**mid|dle school** **(middle schools)** [1] In the United States, a **middle school** is a school for children in the fifth to eighth grades, between the ages of 10 and 13 or 14. ❑ *...Harlem Park Middle School.* [2] In Britain, a **middle school** is a state school that children go to between the ages of 8 or 9 and 12 or 13. N-VAR: oft in names after n; N-VAR: oft in names after n

**Mid|dle West** **The Middle West** is the central part of the United States. N-PROPER: the N = Midwest

**mid|dling** /mɪdəlɪŋ/ If you describe a quality such as the size of something as **middling**, you mean that it is average. ❑ *The Beatles enjoyed only middling success until 1963. ...a man of middling height.* ADJ: usu ADJ n = average

**midge** /mɪdʒ/ **(midges)** **Midges** are very small insects which bite. N-COUNT

**midg|et** /mɪdʒɪt/ **(midgets)** People who are very short are sometimes referred to as **midgets**. [OFFENSIVE] N-COUNT

**Mid|lands** /mɪdləndz/ **The Midlands** is the region or area in the central part of a country, in particular the central part of England. ❑ *...an engineering company in the Midlands.* N-PROPER-COLL: the N

**mid|life cri|sis** /mɪdlaɪf kraɪsɪs/ **(midlife crises)** A **midlife crisis** is a period of doubt and anxiety that some people experience in middle age, when they think about whether their life is the kind of life that they want. ❑ *I went through my midlife crisis about four or five years ago, when I was forty.* N-COUNT: usu sing

**mid|night** /mɪdnaɪt/ [1] **Midnight** is twelve o'clock in the middle of the night. ❑ *It was well after midnight by the time Anne returned to her apartment.* [2] **Midnight** is used to describe something which happens or appears at midnight or in the middle of the night. ❑ *It is totally out of the question to postpone the midnight deadline.* [3] If someone **is burning the midnight oil**, they are staying up very late in order to study or do some other work. ❑ *Chris is asleep after burning the midnight oil trying to finish his article.* ◆◇◇ N-UNCOUNT: usu prep N; ADJ: ADJ n; PHRASE: V inflects

**mid|night blue** Something that is **midnight blue** is a very dark blue colour, almost black. COLOUR

**mid|point** /mɪdpɔɪnt/ also **mid-point.** [1] **The midpoint between** two things is the point that is the same distance from both things. ❑ *...the midpoint between Paris and Warsaw.* [2] **The midpoint of** an event is the time halfway between the beginning and the end of it. ❑ *She has not yet reached the midpoint of her life.* N-SING: oft N between/of n; N-SING: oft N of n = middle

**mid-range** You can use **mid-range** to describe products or services which are neither the ADJ: ADJ n most expensive nor the cheapest of their type. ❑ *...the price of a mid-range family car.*

**mid|riff** /mɪdrɪf/ **(midriffs)** Someone's **midriff** is the middle part of their body, between their waist and their chest. ❑ *...the girl with the bare midriff.* N-COUNT: usu sing

**mid|sized** /mɪdsaɪzd/ also **mid-sized, midsize.** You use **midsized** or **midsize** to describe products, cities, companies, and other things that are neither large nor small. ❑ *...a low-cost midsized car. ...a mid-size city.* ADJ: ADJ n = medium-sized

**midst** /mɪdst/ 1 If you are **in the midst of** doing something, you are doing it at the moment. ❑ *We are in the midst of one of the worst recessions for many, many years.* PREP-PHRASE: usu v-link PREP -ing/n 2 If something happens **in the midst of** an event, it happens during it. ❑ *Eleanor arrived in the midst of a blizzard.* PREP-PHRASE 3 If someone or something is **in the midst of** a group of people or things, they are among them or surrounded by them. ❑ *Many were surprised to see him exposed like this in the midst of a large crowd.* PREP-PHRASE = amid, among 4 You say that someone is **in** your **midst** when you are drawing attention to the fact that they are in your group. [FORMAL] ❑ *We're lucky to have such a man in our midst.* PHRASE: v-link PHR

**mid|stream** /mɪdstriːm/ also **mid-stream.** 1 Someone or something that is **in midstream** is in the middle of a river, where the current is strongest. ❑ *Their boat had capsized in midstream.* N-UNCOUNT: oft *in* N ♦ **Midstream** is also an adverb. ❑ *Some of them got caught midstream by the tide.* ADV: usu ADV after v, also n ADV 2 If someone who has been doing something such as talking stops or pauses **in midstream,** they stop doing it, often before continuing. ❑ *I was cut off in midstream.* N-UNCOUNT: oft *in* N ♦ **Midstream** is also an adverb. ❑ *The most difficult thing in a fast game of rugby is to change course midstream.* ADV: ADV after v

**mid|sum|mer** /mɪdsʌməʳ/ **Midsummer** is the period in the middle of the summer. ❑ *In midsummer every town is impossibly crowded... It was a lovely midsummer morning.* N-UNCOUNT

**Mid|sum|mer's Day** **Midsummer's Day** or **Midsummer Day** is the 24th of June. N-PROPER

**mid|way** /mɪdweɪ/ also **mid-way.** 1 If something is **midway between** two places, it is between them and the same distance from each of them. ❑ *The studio is midway between his aunt's old home and his cottage.* ADV: ADV prep = halfway ♦ **Midway** is also an adjective. ❑ *...the midway point between Gloucester, Hereford and Worcester.* ADJ: ADJ n = halfway 2 If something happens **midway through** a period of time, it happens during the middle part of it. ❑ *He crashed midway through the race.* ADV: ADV after v, usu ADV *through* n ♦ **Midway** is also an adjective. ❑ *They were denied an obvious penalty before the midway point of the first half.* ADJ: ADJ n

**mid|week** /mɪdwiːk/ **Midweek** describes something that happens in the middle of the week. ❑ *The package includes midweek flights from Gatwick.* ADJ: ADJ n ♦ **Midweek** is also an adverb. ❑ *They'll be able to go up to London midweek.* ADV: ADV after v, prep ADV

**Mid|west** /mɪdwest/ **The Midwest** is the region in the north of the central part of the United States. ❑ *...farmers in the Midwest. ...the Midwest states.* N-PROPER: usu *the* N

**Mid|west|ern** /mɪdwestəʳn/ **Midwestern** means belonging or relating to the Midwest. ❑ *...the Midwestern plains. ...traditional Midwestern values. ...the midwestern plains.* ADJ: usu ADJ n

**mid|wife** /mɪdwaɪf/ **(midwives)** A **midwife** is a nurse who is trained to deliver babies and to advise pregnant women. N-COUNT

**mid|wife|ry** /mɪdwɪfəri/ **Midwifery** is the work of delivering babies and advising pregnant women. N-UNCOUNT

**mid|win|ter** /mɪdwɪntəʳ/ also **mid-winter. Midwinter** is the period in the middle of winter. ❑ *...the bleak midwinter. ...the cold midwinter weather.* N-UNCOUNT

**mien** /miːn/ Someone's **mien** is their general appearance and manner, especially the expression on their face, which shows what they are feeling or thinking. [LITERARY] ❑ *It was impossible to tell from his mien whether he was offended. ...his mild manner and aristocratic mien.* N-SING: usu poss N

**miffed** /mɪft/ If you are **miffed,** you are slightly annoyed and hurt because of something which someone has said or done to you. [INFORMAL] ❑ *I was a bit miffed about that.* ADJ: usu v-link ADJ

| might |
| --- |
| ① MODAL USES |
| ② NOUN USES |

**① might** /maɪt/ ◆◆◆

> **Might** is a modal verb. It is used with the base form of a verb.

⇛ Please look at category 13 to see if the expression you are looking for is shown under another headword. 1 You use **might** to indicate that something will possibly happen or be true in the future, but you cannot be certain. ❑ *Smoking might be banned totally in most buildings... I might well regret it later... He said he might not be back until tonight.* MODAL [vagueness] = may 2 You use **might** to indicate that there is a possibility that something is true, but you cannot be certain. ❑ *She and Simon's father had not given up hope that he might be alive... You might be right.* MODAL [vagueness] = may 3 You use **might** to indicate that something could happen or be true in particular circumstances. ❑ *America might sell more cars to the islands if they were made with the steering wheel on the right. ...the type of person who might appear in a fashion magazine.* MODAL [vagueness] = could 4 You use **might have** with a past participle to indicate that it is possible that something happened or was true, or when giving a possible explanation for something. ❑ *I heard what might have been an explosion... She thought the shooting might have been an accident.* MODAL = could have 5 You use **might have** with a past participle to indicate that something was a possibility in the past, although it did not actually happen. ❑ *Had the bomb dropped over a populated area of the city, there might have been a great deal of damage.* MODAL 6 You use **might** in statements where you are accepting the truth of a situation, but contrasting it with something that is more important. ❑ *They might not have two cents to rub together, but at least they have a kind of lifestyle that is different.* MODAL = may 7 You use **might** when you are saying emphatically that someone ought to do the thing mentioned, especially when you are annoyed because they have not done it. ❑ *You might have told me that before!* MODAL [emphasis] = could 8 You use **might** to make a suggestion or to give advice in a very polite way. ❑ *They might be wise to stop advertising on television... You might try the gas station down the street.* MODAL [politeness] 9 You use **might** as a polite way of interrupting someone, asking a question, making a request, or introducing what you are going to say next. [FORMAL, SPOKEN] ❑ *Might I make a suggestion?... Might I draw your readers' attention to the dangers in the Government's proposal.* MODAL [politeness] = could 10 You use **might** in expressions such as **as you might expect** and **as you might imagine** in order to indicate that the statement you are making is not surprising. ❑ *'How's Jan?' she asked. — 'Bad. As you might expect.'... The drivers, as you might imagine, didn't care much for that.* MODAL = would 11 You use **might** in expressions such as **I might add** and **I might say** in order to emphasize a statement that you are making. ❑ *It didn't come as a great surprise to me, I might say.* MODAL [emphasis] 12 You use **might** in expressions such as **I might have known** and **I might have guessed** to indicate that you are not surprised at a disappointing event or fact. ❑ *'I detest clutter, you know.' — 'I didn't know, but I might have guessed.'* MODAL = should 13 **might as well** → see **well**.

**② might** /maɪt/ 1 **Might** is power or strength. [FORMAL] ❑ *The might of the army could prove a decisive factor.* N-UNCOUNT: usu with supp = strength 2 If you do something **with all** your **might,** you do it using all your PHRASE: PHR with v strength and energy. ❑ *She swung the hammer at his head with all her might.*

**mighti|ly** /maɪtɪli/ **Mightily** means to a great extent or degree. [OLD-FASHIONED] ❑ *He had given a mightily impressive performance... She strove mightily to put Mike from her thoughts.* ADV: ADV adj/adv, ADV after v [emphasis]

**mightn't** /maɪtᵊnt/ **Mightn't** is a spoken form of 'might not'.

**might've** /maɪtəv/ **Might've** is the usual spoken form of 'might have', especially when 'have' is an auxiliary verb.

**mighty** /maɪti/ **(mightier, mightiest)** 1 **Mighty** is used to describe something that is very large or powerful. [LITERARY] ❑ *There was a flash and a mighty bang.* ADJ: usu ADJ n 2 **Mighty** is used in front of adjectives and adverbs to emphasize the quality that they are describing. [mainly AM, INFORMAL] ❑ *It's something you'll be mighty proud of.* ADV: ADV adj/adv [emphasis] 3 → See also **high and mighty**.

**mi|graine** /miːgreɪn, AM maɪ-/ **(migraines)** A **migraine** is an extremely painful headache that makes you feel very ill. ❑ *Her mother suffered from migraines.* N-VAR

**mi|grant** /maɪgrənt/ **(migrants)** 1 A **migrant** is a person who moves from one place to another, especially in order to find work. ❑ *The government divides asylum-seekers into economic migrants and genuine refugees. ...migrant workers following harvests northward.* N-COUNT 2 **Migrants** are birds, fish, or animals that migrate from one part of the world to another. ❑ *Migrant birds shelter in the reeds.* N-COUNT: oft N n

**mi|grate** /maɪgreɪt, AM maɪgreɪt/ **(migrates, migrating, migrated)** 1 If people **migrate**, they move from one place to another, especially in order to find work or to live somewhere for a short time. ❑ *People migrate to cities like Jakarta in search of work... Farmers have learned that they have to migrate if they want to survive.* VERB V prep/adv V ♦ **mi|gra|tion** /maɪgreɪʃᵊn/ **(migrations)** *...the migration of Soviet Jews to Israel.* N-VAR 2 When birds, fish, or animals **migrate**, they move at a particular season from one part of the world or from one part of a country to another, usually in order to breed or to find new feeding grounds. ❑ *Most birds have to fly long distances to migrate. ...a dam system that kills the fish as they migrate from streams to the ocean.* VERB V V prep/adv ♦ **mi|gra|tion** *...the migration of animals in the Serengeti.* N-VAR

**mi|gra|tory** /maɪgrətəri, AM -tɔːri/ 1 A **migratory** bird, fish, or animal is one that migrates every year. ADJ: usu ADJ n 2 **Migratory** means relating to the migration of people, birds, fish, or animals. ❑ *...migratory farm labour.* ADJ: ADJ n

**mike** /maɪk/ **(mikes)** A **mike** is the same as a **microphone**. [INFORMAL] N-COUNT

**mil** /mɪl/ **Mil** means the same as **million**. [INFORMAL] ❑ *Zhamnov, 22, signed for $1.25 mil over three years.* NUM

**mild** /maɪld/ **(milder, mildest)** 1 **Mild** is used to describe something such as a feeling, attitude, or illness that is not very strong or severe. ❑ *Teddy turned to Mona with a look of mild confusion... Anna put up a mild protest.* ◆◇◇ ADJ: usu ADJ n ≠ extreme ♦ **mild|ly** *Josephine must have had the disease very mildly as she showed no symptoms.* ADV: usu ADV adj/adv, also ADV after v 2 A **mild** person is gentle and does not get angry easily. ❑ *He is a mild man, who is reasonable almost to the point of blandness.* ADJ: usu ADJ n ≠ aggressive ♦ **mild|ly** *'I'm not meddling,' Kenworthy said mildly, 'I'm just curious.'* ADV: ADV after v 3 **Mild** weather is pleasant because it is neither extremely hot nor extremely cold. ❑ *The area is famous for its very mild winter climate.* ADJ ≠ severe, harsh 4 You describe food as **mild** when it does not taste or smell strong, sharp, or bitter, especially when you like it because of this. ❑ *This cheese has a soft, mild flavour. ...a mild curry powder.* ADJ ≠ strong 5 → See also **mildly**.

**mil|dew** /mɪldjuː, AM -duː/ **Mildew** is a soft white fungus that grows in damp places. ❑ *The room smelled of mildew.* N-UNCOUNT

**mil|dewed** /mɪldjuːd, AM -duːd/ Something that is **mildewed** has mildew growing on it. ADJ

**mild|ly** /maɪldli/ 1 → see **mild**. 2 You use **to put it mildly** to indicate that you are describing something in language that is much less strong, direct, or critical than what you really think. ❑ *But not all the money, to put it mildly, has been used wisely.* PHRASE: V inflects

**mild-mannered** If you describe someone as **mild-mannered**, you approve of them because they are gentle, kind, and polite. ADJ [approval]

**mile** /maɪl/ **(miles)** 1 A **mile** is a unit of distance equal to 1760 yards or approximately 1.6 kilometres. ❑ *They drove 600 miles across the desert... The hurricane is moving to the west at about 18 miles per hour... She lives just half a mile away. ...a 50-mile bike ride.* ◆◆◇ N-COUNT: num N 2 **Miles** is used, especially in the expression **miles away**, to refer to a long distance. ❑ *If you enrol at a gym that's miles away, you won't be visiting it as often as you should... I was miles and miles from anywhere.* N-PLURAL 3 **Miles** or **a mile** is used with the meaning 'very much' in order to emphasize the difference between two things or qualities, or the difference between what you aimed to do and what you actually achieved. [INFORMAL] ❑ *You're miles better than most of the performers we see nowadays... With a Labour candidate in place they won by a mile... The rehearsals were miles too slow and no work was getting done.* N-COUNT: usu pl [emphasis]

PHRASES 4 If you say that someone is **miles away**, you mean that they are unaware of what is happening around them because they are thinking about something else. [INFORMAL] ❑ *What were you thinking about? You were miles away.* PHRASE: v-link PHR 5 If you say that someone is willing to **go the extra mile**, you mean that they are willing to make a special effort to do or achieve something. ❑ *The President is determined 'to go the extra mile for peace'.* PHRASE: V inflects 6 If you say that you can see or recognize something **a mile off**, you are emphasizing that it is very obvious and easy to recognize. [INFORMAL] ❑ *You can spot undercover cops a mile off.* PHRASE: PHR after v [emphasis] 7 If you say that someone would **run a mile** when faced with a particular situation, you mean that they would be very frightened or unwilling to deal with it. [INFORMAL] ❑ *If anybody had told me when I first got married that I was going to have seven children, I would have run a mile.* PHRASE: V inflects 8 If you say that something or someone **sticks out a mile** or **stands out a mile**, you are emphasizing that they are very obvious and easy to recognize. [INFORMAL] ❑ *'How do you know he's Irish?' — 'Sticks out a mile.'.* PHRASE: V inflects [emphasis]

**mile|age** /maɪlɪdʒ/ **(mileages)** 1 **Mileage** refers to the distance that you have travelled, measured in miles. ❑ *Most of their mileage is in and around town.* N-UNCOUNT: also N in pl 2 The **mileage** of a vehicle is the number of miles that it can travel using one gallon or litre of fuel. ❑ *They are willing to pay up to $500 more for cars that get better mileage.* N-UNCOUNT: also N in pl 3 The **mileage** in a particular course of action is its usefulness in getting you what you want. ❑ *It's obviously important to get as much mileage out of the convention as possible.* N-UNCOUNT: usu N *out of*/*in* n/-ing

**mile|stone** /maɪlstoʊn/ **(milestones)** A **milestone** is an important event in the history or development of something or someone. ❑ *He said the launch of the party represented a milestone in Zambian history.* N-COUNT

**mi|lieu** /miːljɜː, AM mɪljuː/ **(milieux** or **milieus)** Your **milieu** is the group of people or activities that you live among or are familiar with. [FORMAL] ❑ *They stayed, safe and happy, within their own social milieu.* N-COUNT: usu supp N

**mili|tant** /mɪlɪtənt/ **(militants)** You use **militant** to describe people who believe in something very strongly and are active in trying to bring about political or social change, often in extreme ways that other people find unacceptable. ❑ *Militant mineworkers in the Ukraine have voted for a one-day stoppage next month.* ◆◇◇ ADJ ♦ **Militant** is also a N-COUNT: usu pl noun. ❑ *The militants might still find some new excuse to call a strike.* ♦ **mili|tan|cy** *...the rise of trade union militancy.* N-UNCOUNT ♦ **mili|tant|ly** *Their army is militantly nationalist.* ADV: usu ADV adj

**mili|ta|rism** /mɪlɪtərɪzəm/ **Militarism** is a country's desire to strengthen their armed forces in order to make themselves more powerful. ❑ *The country slipped into a dangerous mixture of nationalism and militarism.* N-UNCOUNT [disapproval]

**mili|ta|rist** /mɪlɪtərɪst/ **(militarists)** 1 If you describe someone as a **militarist**, you mean that they want their country's armed forces to be strengthened in order to make it more powerful. N-COUNT: oft N n [disapproval] 2 **Militarist** means the same as **militaristic**. ❑ *...militarist policies.* ADJ: usu ADJ n [disapproval]

**mili|ta|ris|tic** /mɪlɪtərɪstɪk/ **Militaristic** is used to describe groups, ideas, or policies which support the strengthening of the armed forces of their country in order to make it more powerful. ❑ *...aggressive militaristic governments.* ADJ [disapproval]

**mili|ta|rized** /mɪlɪtəraɪzd/

✔ in BRIT, also use **militarised**

1 A **militarized** area or region has members of the armed forces and military equipment in it. ❑ *...the militarized zone that separates the faction leaders' areas of control.* ADJ: usu ADJ n 2 You can use **militarized** to show disapproval of something that has many military characteristics, for example the quality of being aggressive or strict. ❑ *...a militarized and confrontationist style of politics.* ADJ [disapproval]

**mili|tary** /mɪlɪtri, AM -teri/ **(militaries)** ♦♦♦
1 **Military** means relating to the armed forces of a country. ❑ *Military action may become necessary... The president is sending in almost 20,000 military personnel to help with the relief efforts. ...last year's military coup.* ADJ: usu ADJ n ♦ **mili|tari|ly** /mɪlteərɪli/ *They remain unwilling to intervene militarily in what could be an unending war.* ADV: ADV with v, ADV adj 2 **The military** are the armed forces of a country, especially officers of high rank. ❑ *The bombing has been far more widespread than the military will admit.* N-COUNT-COLL: usu sing, the N 3 **Military** means well-organized, controlled, or neat, in a way that is typical of a soldier. ❑ *Your working day will need to be organized with military precision.* ADJ

**mili|tary po|lice** 1 **The military police** are the part of an army, navy, or air force that act as its police force. ❑ *The government has said it will reform the military police.* N-SING-COLL 2 **Military police** are men and women who are members of the part of an army, navy, or air force that act as its police force. ❑ *The camp is surrounded by razor-wire fences and guarded by military police.* N-PLURAL

**mili|tary police|man** **(military policemen)** A **military policeman** is a member of the military police. N-COUNT

**mili|tary ser|vice** **Military service** is a period of service in the armed forces that every man in certain countries has to do. ❑ *Many conscripts resent having to do their military service.* N-UNCOUNT: oft with poss

**mili|tate** /mɪlɪteɪt/ **(militates, militating, militated)** To **militate against** something means to make it less possible or likely. To **militate against** someone means to prevent them from achieving something. [FORMAL] ❑ *Her background militates against her... We can never promise to sail anywhere in particular, because the weather might militate against it.* VERB V *against* n V *against* n

**mi|li|tia** /mɪlɪʃə/ **(militias)** A **militia** is an organization that operates like an army but whose members are not professional soldiers. ❑ *The troops will not attempt to disarm the warring militias.* N-COUNT

**mi|li|tia|man** /mɪlɪʃəmən/ **(militiamen)** A **militiaman** is a member of a militia. N-COUNT

**milk** /mɪlk/ **(milks, milking, milked)** 1 **Milk** is the white liquid produced by cows, goats, and some other animals, which people drink and use to make butter, cheese, and yoghurt. ❑ *He popped out to buy a pint of milk. ...basic foods such as meat, bread and milk.* ♦◇◇ N-UNCOUNT 2 If someone **milks** a cow or goat, they get milk from it, using either their hands or a machine. ❑ *Farm-workers milked cows by hand.* VERB V n 3 **Milk** is the white liquid produced by women to feed their babies. ❑ *Milk from the mother's breast is a perfect food for the human baby.* N-UNCOUNT 4 Liquid products for cleaning your skin or making it softer are sometimes referred to as **milks**. ❑ *...sales of cleansing milks, creams and gels.* N-MASS = lotion 5 If you say that someone **milks** something, you mean that they get as much benefit or profit as they can from it, without caring about the effects this has on other people. ❑ *A few people tried to milk the insurance companies... The callous couple milked money from a hospital charity to fund a lavish lifestyle.* VERB [disapproval] V n V n *from* n 6 → See also **coconut milk**, **condensed milk**, **evaporated milk**, **skimmed milk**.

**milk choco|late** **Milk chocolate** is chocolate that has been made with milk. It is lighter in colour and has a creamier taste than plain chocolate. N-UNCOUNT

**milk float** **(milk floats)** A **milk float** is a small electric van with a roof and no sides which is used to deliver milk to people's houses. [BRIT] N-COUNT

**milk|maid** /mɪlkmeɪd/ **(milkmaids)** In former times, a **milkmaid** was a woman who milked cows and made butter and cheese on a farm. N-COUNT

**milk|man** /mɪlkmən, AM -mæn/ **(milkmen)** A **milkman** is a person who delivers milk to people's homes. N-COUNT

**milk prod|uct** **(milk products)** **Milk products** are foods made from milk, for example butter, cheese, and yoghurt. N-COUNT: usu pl = dairy products

**milk round** **(milk rounds)** 1 If someone has a **milk round**, they work as a milkman, going from house to house delivering milk. [BRIT] ❑ *Milk rounds are threatened as customers switch to buying from supermarkets.* N-COUNT 2 **The milk round** is an event that happens once a year when people from large companies visit colleges and universities and interview students who are interested in working for them. [BRIT] ❑ *He obtained his first job through the milk round.* N-SING: the N

**milk|shake** /mɪlkʃeɪk/ **(milkshakes)** also **milk shake.** A **milkshake** is a cold drink made by mixing milk with a flavouring or fruit, and sometimes ice cream. ❑ *...a strawberry milkshake.* N-COUNT

**milk tooth** **(milk teeth)** Your **milk teeth** are the first teeth that grow in your mouth, which later fall out and are replaced by a second set. N-COUNT: usu pl

**milk white** You can use **milk white** to describe things that are a milky white colour. [LITERARY] ❑ *Mist was rising, and trees and shrubs began to disappear in a milk-white haze.* COLOUR

**milky** /mɪlki/ **(milkier, milkiest)** 1 If you describe something as **milky**, you mean that it is pale white in colour. You can describe other colours as **milky** when they are very pale. ❑ *A milky mist filled the valley.* ADJ 2 Drinks or food that are **milky** contain a lot of milk. ❑ *...a large bowl of milky coffee.* ADJ

**Milky Way** **The Milky Way** is the pale strip of light consisting of many stars that you can see stretched across the sky at night. N-PROPER: the N

**mill** /mɪl/ **(mills, milling, milled)** 1 A **mill** is a building in which grain is crushed to make flour. ♦◇◇ N-COUNT 2 A **mill** is a small device used for grinding something such as coffee beans or pepper into powder. ❑ *...a pepper mill.* N-COUNT: supp N = grinder 3 A **mill** is a factory used for making and processing materials such as steel, wool, or cotton. ❑ *...a steel mill. ...a textile mill.* N-COUNT: usu supp N 4 To **mill** something such as wheat or pepper means to grind it in a mill. ❑ *They mill 1000 tonnes of flour a day in every Australian state. ...freshly milled black pepper.* VERB V n V-ed 5 → See also **milling**, **rolling mill**, **run-of-the-mill**, **watermill**. **grist to the mill** → see **grist**.

♦ **mill around**

✔ in BRIT, also use **mill about**

When a crowd of people **mill around** or **mill** PHRASAL VERB

**about**, they move around within a particular place or area, so that the movement of the whole crowd looks very confused. ❑ *Quite a few people were milling about, but nothing was happening... Dozens of people milled around Charing Cross Road and Denmark Street.* V P / V P n

**mil|len|nium** /mɪleniəm/ **(millenniums** or **millennia)** 1 A **millennium** is a period of one thousand years, especially one which begins and ends with a year ending in '000', for example the period from the year 1000 to the year 2000. [FORMAL] N-COUNT 2 Many people refer to the year 2000 as **the Millennium**. ❑ *...the eve of the Millennium.* N-SING: usu *the* N, N n

**mil|ler** /mɪləʳ/ **(millers)** A **miller** is a person who owns or operates a mill in which grain is crushed to make flour. N-COUNT

**mil|let** /mɪlɪt/ **(millets) Millet** is a cereal crop that is grown for its seeds or for hay. N-MASS

**milli-** /mɪlɪ-/ **Milli-** is added to some nouns that refer to units of measurement in order to form other nouns referring to units a thousand times smaller. ❑ *...a small current, around 5 milliamps.* PREFIX

**mil|li|gram** /mɪlɪgræm/ **(milligrams)**

> in BRIT, also use **milligramme**

A **milligram** is a unit of weight that is equal to a thousandth of a gramme. ❑ *...0.5 milligrams of mercury.* N-COUNT: num N, oft N *of* n

**mil|li|li|tre** /mɪlɪli:təʳ/ **(millilitres)**

> in AM, use **milliliter**

A **millilitre** is a unit of volume for liquids and gases that is equal to a thousandth of a litre. ❑ *...100 millilitres of blood.* N-COUNT: num N, oft N *of* n

**mil|li|metre** /mɪlɪmi:təʳ/ **(millimetres)**

> in AM, use **millimeter**

A **millimetre** is a metric unit of length that is equal to a tenth of a centimetre or a thousandth of a metre. ❑ *...a tiny little transparent pill, about 20 millimetres long.* N-COUNT: num N, oft N *of* n

**mil|li|ner** /mɪlɪnəʳ/ **(milliners)** A **milliner** is a person whose job is making or selling women's hats. N-COUNT

**mil|li|nery** /mɪlɪnəri, AM -neri/ **Millinery** is used to refer to women's hats. [FORMAL] ❑ *...her aunt's modest millinery shop.* N-UNCOUNT: oft N n

**mill|ing** /mɪlɪŋ/ The people in a **milling** crowd move around within a particular place or area, so that the movement of the whole crowd looks very confused. ❑ *They moved purposefully through the milling crowd.* ADJ: ADJ n

**mil|lion** /mɪliən/ **(millions)** ◆◆◆

> The plural form is **million** after a number, or after a word or expression referring to a number, such as 'several' or 'a few'.

1 A **million** or one **million** is the number 1,000,000. ❑ *Up to five million people a year visit the county... Profits for 1999 topped £100 million.* NUM 2 If you talk about **millions of** people or things, you mean that there is a very large number of them but you do not know or do not want to say exactly how many. ❑ *The programme was viewed on television in millions of homes.* QUANT-PLURAL: QUANT *of* pl-n

**mil|lion|aire** /mɪliəneəʳ/ **(millionaires)** A **millionaire** is a very rich person who has money or property worth at least a million pounds or dollars. ❑ *By the time he died, he was a millionaire.* N-COUNT

**mil|lion|air|ess** /mɪliəneəres/ **(millionairesses)** A **millionairess** is a woman who has money or property worth at least a million pounds or dollars. N-COUNT

**mil|lionth** /mɪliənθ/ **(millionths)** ◆◆◇ 1 The **millionth** item in a series is the one you count as number one million. ❑ *Last year the millionth truck rolled off the assembly line.* ORD 2 A **millionth of** something is one of a million equal parts of it. ❑ *The bomb must explode within less than a millionth of a second.* FRACTION

**mil|li|pede** /mɪlɪpi:d/ **(millipedes)** A **millipede** is a small creature with a long narrow body and a lot of legs. N-COUNT

**mil|li|sec|ond** /mɪlisekənd/ **(milliseconds)** A **millisecond** is a unit of time equal to one thousandth of a second. N-COUNT

**mill|stone** /mɪlstoun/ **(millstones)** 1 A **millstone** is a large, flat, round stone which is one of a pair of stones used to grind grain into flour. N-COUNT 2 If you describe something as **a millstone** or **a millstone around** your **neck**, you mean that it is a very unpleasant problem or responsibility that you cannot escape from. ❑ *For today's politicians, the treaty is becoming a millstone... That contract proved to be a millstone around his neck.* PHRASE: usu v-link PHR [disapproval]

**mime** /maɪm/ **(mimes, miming, mimed)** 1 **Mime** is the use of movements and gestures in order to express something or tell a story without using speech. ❑ *Music, mime and strong visual imagery play a strong part in the productions. ...a mime artist.* N-VAR 2 If you **mime** something, you describe or express it using mime rather than speech. ❑ *It featured a solo dance in which a woman in a short overall mimed a lot of dainty housework... I remember asking her to mime getting up in the morning.* VERB V n/-ing V n/-ing Also V 3 If you **mime**, you pretend to be singing or playing an instrument, although the music is in fact coming from a CD or cassette. ❑ *Richey's not miming, he's playing very quiet guitar... In concerts, the group mime their songs... The waiters mime to records playing on the jukebox.* VERB V V n V *to* n

**mi|met|ic** /mɪmetɪk/ **Mimetic** movements or activities are ones in which you imitate something. [FORMAL] ❑ *Both realism and naturalism are mimetic systems or practices of representation.* ADJ: usu ADJ n

**mim|ic** /mɪmɪk/ **(mimics, mimicking, mimicked)** 1 If you **mimic** the actions or voice of a person or animal, you imitate them, usually in a way that is meant to be amusing or entertaining. ❑ *He could mimic anybody.* VERB = imitate V n 2 If someone or something **mimics** another person or thing, they try to be like them. ❑ *The computer doesn't mimic human thought; it reaches the same ends by different means.* VERB = imitate V n 3 A **mimic** is a person who is able to mimic people or animals. N-COUNT

**mim|ic|ry** /mɪmɪkri/ **Mimicry** is the action of mimicking someone or something. ❑ *One of his few strengths was his skill at mimicry.* N-UNCOUNT

**min.** **Min.** is a written abbreviation for **minimum**, or for **minutes** or **minute**.

**mina|ret** /mɪnəret/ **(minarets)** A **minaret** is a tall thin tower which is part of a mosque. N-COUNT

**mince** /mɪns/ **(minces, mincing, minced)** 1 **Mince** is meat which has been cut into very small pieces using a machine. [mainly BRIT] ❑ *Brown the mince in a frying pan.* N-UNCOUNT

> in AM, use **ground beef**, **hamburger meat**

2 If you **mince** food such as meat, you put it into a machine which cuts it into very small pieces. [mainly BRIT] ❑ *Perhaps I'll buy lean meat and mince it myself. ...minced beef.* VERB V n V-ed

> in AM, usually use **grind**

3 If you say that someone, especially a homosexual man, **minces** somewhere, you mean that they walk there with quick small steps. ❑ *They minced in, in beach costumes and make-up.* VERB [disapproval] V prep/adv 4 If you say that someone does not **mince** their **words**, you mean that they speak in a forceful and direct way, especially when saying something unpleasant to someone. ❑ *The doctors didn't mince their words, and predicted the worst.* PHRASE: V inflects, with brd-neg

**mince|meat** /mɪnsmi:t/ 1 **Mincemeat** is a sticky mixture of small pieces of dried fruit. It is usually cooked in pastry to make mince pies. N-UNCOUNT 2 **Mincemeat** is the same as **mince**. [mainly BRIT] N-UNCOUNT = mince

> in AM, use **ground beef**, **hamburger meat**

3 If you **make mincemeat of** someone or **make mincemeat out of** them, you defeat them completely in an argument, fight, or competition. ❑ *I can imagine a defence lawyer making mincemeat of him if we ever put him up in court.*
PHRASE: V inflects

**mince pie** **(mince pies)** **Mince pies** are small pies containing a sticky mixture of small pieces of dried fruit. Mince pies are usually eaten at Christmas.
N-COUNT

**minc|er** /mɪnsəʳ/ **(mincers)** A **mincer** is a machine which cuts meat into very small pieces by forcing it through very small holes. [BRIT]
N-COUNT

✔ in AM, use **meat grinder**

**mind**
① NOUN USES
② VERB USES

## ① mind /maɪnd/ (minds) ◆◆◆

⇛ Please look at category 45 to see if the expression you are looking for is shown under another headword.

1 You refer to someone's **mind** when talking about their thoughts. For example, if you say that something is **in your mind**, you mean that you are thinking about it, and if you say that something is **at the back of your mind**, you mean that you are aware of it, although you are not thinking about it very much. ❑ *I'm trying to clear my mind of all this... There was no doubt in his mind that the man was serious... I put what happened during that game to the back of my mind... He spent the next hour going over the trial in his mind.*
N-COUNT: with poss = *head*

2 Your **mind** is your ability to think and reason. ❑ *You have a good mind... Studying stretched my mind and got me thinking about things.*
N-COUNT: supp N = *intellect*

3 If you have a particular type of **mind**, you have a particular way of thinking which is part of your character, or a result of your education or professional training. ❑ *Andrew, you have a very suspicious mind... The key to his success is his logical mind. ...an American writer who has researched the criminal mind.*
N-COUNT: usu sing, with supp

4 You can refer to someone as a particular kind of **mind** as a way of saying that they are clever, intelligent, or imaginative. ❑ *She moved to London, meeting some of the best minds of her time.*
N-COUNT: with supp = *intellect*

5 → See also **minded**, **-minded**, **frame of mind**, **state of mind**.

PHRASES

6 If you tell someone to **bear** something **in mind** or to **keep** something **in mind**, you are reminding or warning them about something important which they should remember. ❑ *Bear in mind that petrol stations are scarce in the more remote areas... I should not be surprised about some of her comments, bearing in mind the party she belongs to.*
PHRASE: V inflects, oft PHR that, PHR n

7 If something **brings** another thing **to mind** or **calls** another thing **to mind**, it makes you think of that other thing, usually because it is similar in some way. ❑ *That brings to mind a wonderful poem by Riokin.*
PHRASE: V inflects, usu PHR n

8 If you **cast** your **mind back to** a time in the past, you think about what happened then. ❑ *Cast your mind back to 1978, when Forest won the title.*
PHRASE: V and N inflect, oft PHR *to* n

9 If you **close** your **mind to** something, you deliberately do not think about it or pay attention to it. ❑ *She has closed her mind to last year's traumas.*
PHRASE: V and N inflect, usu PHR *to* n

10 If you **change** your **mind**, or if someone or something **changes** your **mind**, you change a decision you have made or an opinion that you had. ❑ *I was going to vote for him, but I changed my mind and voted for Reagan... It would be impossible to change his mind.*
PHRASE: V and N inflect

11 If something **comes to mind** or **springs to mind**, you think of it without making any effort. ❑ *Integrity and honesty are words that spring to mind when talking of the man.*
PHRASE: V inflects

12 If you say that an idea or possibility never **crossed** your **mind**, you mean that you did not think of it. ❑ *It had never crossed his mind that there might be a problem.*
PHRASE: V and N inflect, oft with brd-neg, oft *it* PHR that

13 If you see something **in** your **mind's eye**, you imagine it and have a clear picture of it in your mind. ❑ *In his mind's eye, he can imagine the effect he's having.*
PHRASE: PHR after v, PHR with cl

14 If you **have a mind to** do something, you want, intend, or choose to do it. ❑ *The captain of the guard looked as if he had a mind to challenge them.*
PHRASE: V inflects, oft PHR inf

15 If you say that you **have a good mind to** do something or **have half a mind to** do it, you are threatening or announcing that you have a strong desire to do it, although you probably will not do it. ❑ *He raged on about how he had a good mind to resign.*
PHRASE: V inflects, usu PHR inf

16 If you ask someone what they **have in mind**, you want to know in more detail about an idea or wish they have. ❑ *'Maybe we could celebrate tonight.' — 'What did you have in mind?'*
PHRASE: V inflects

17 If you **have it in mind to** do something, you intend or want to do it. ❑ *Collins Harvill had it in mind to publish a short volume about Pasternak.*
PHRASE: V inflects, usu PHR inf

18 If you do something **with** a particular thing **in mind**, you do it with that thing as your aim or as the reason or basis for your action. ❑ *These families need support. With this in mind a group of 35 specialists met last weekend.*
PHRASE: PHR after v, PHR with cl

19 If you say that something such as an illness is **all in the mind**, you mean that it relates to someone's feelings or attitude, rather than having any physical cause. ❑ *It could be a virus, or it could be all in the mind.*
PHRASE: v-link PHR

20 If you **know** your **own mind**, you are sure about your opinions, and are not easily influenced by other people.
PHRASE: V and N inflect

21 If you say that someone **is losing** their **mind**, you mean that they are becoming mad. ❑ *Sometimes I feel I'm losing my mind.*
PHRASE: V and N inflect

22 If you **make up** your **mind** or **make** your **mind up**, you decide which of a number of possible things you will have or do. ❑ *Once he made up his mind to do something, there was no stopping him... She said her mind was made up.*
PHRASE: V and N inflect, oft PHR to-inf = *decide*

23 You can use the expression **mind over matter** to describe situations in which a person seems to be able to control events, physical objects, or the condition of their own body using their mind. ❑ *Good health is simply a case of mind over matter.*
PHRASE: oft n prep PHR

24 If a number of people are **of one mind**, **of like mind**, or **of the same mind**, they all agree about something. ❑ *Contact with other disabled yachtsmen of like mind would be helpful... The food companies are not of one mind about these new regulations.*
PHRASE: v-link PHR

25 If you say that something that happens is **a load off** your **mind** or **a weight off** your **mind**, you mean that it causes you to stop worrying, for example because it solves a problem that you had.
PHRASE: *mind* inflects, v-link PHR

26 If something is **on** your **mind**, you are worried or concerned about it and think about it a lot. ❑ *This game has been on my mind all week... I just forgot. I've had a lot on my mind.*
PHRASE: N inflects, v-link PHR, PHR after v

27 If your **mind is on** something or you **have** your **mind on** something, you are thinking about that thing. ❑ *At school I was always in trouble – my mind was never on my work.*
PHRASE: V and N inflect, PHR n/-ing

28 If you have **an open mind**, you avoid forming an opinion or making a decision until you know all the facts. ❑ *It's hard to see it any other way, though I'm trying to keep an open mind.*
PHRASE: N inflects, PHR after v

29 If something **opens** your **mind to** new ideas or experiences, it makes you more willing to accept them or try them. ❑ *She also stimulated his curiosity and opened his mind to other cultures.*
PHRASE: V and N inflect, usu PHR *to* n

30 If you say that someone is **out of their mind**, you mean that they are mad or very foolish. [INFORMAL] ❑ *What are you doing? Are you out of your mind?*
PHRASE: N inflects, v-link PHR, disapproval = *crazy*

31 If you say that someone is **out of their mind with** a feeling such as worry or fear, you are emphasizing that they are extremely worried or afraid. [INFORMAL]
PHRASE: N inflects, v-link PHR, usu PHR *with* n, emphasis

32 If you say that someone is, for example, **bored out of** their **mind**, **scared out of** their **mind**, or **stoned out of** their **mind**, you are emphasizing that they are extremely bored, scared, or affected by drugs. [INFORMAL]
PHRASE: N inflects, v-link PHR, emphasis

33 If you **put** your **mind to** something, you start making an effort to do it. ❑ *You could do fine in the world if you put your mind to it.*
PHRASE: V and N inflect, PHR n

34 If something **puts** you **in mind of** something else, it reminds you of it because it is similar to it or is associated with it. ❑ *This put me in mind of something Patrick said many years ago.*
PHRASE: V inflects, PHR n = *remind*

35 If you can **read** someone's **mind**, you know what they are thinking without them saying anything. ❑ *Don't*
PHRASE: V and N inflect

*expect others to read your mind.* 36 To **put** someone's **mind at rest** or **set** their **mind at rest** means to stop them worrying about something. ❑ *It may be advisable to have a blood test to put your mind at rest.*
PHRASE: V and N inflect

37 If you say that nobody **in** their **right mind** would do a particular thing, you are emphasizing that it is an irrational thing to do and you would be surprised if anyone did it. ❑ *No one in her right mind would make such a major purchase without asking questions.*
PHRASE: with brd-neg, n PHR [emphasis]

38 If you **set** your **mind on** something or **have** your **mind set on** it, you are determined to do it or obtain it. ❑ *When my wife sets her mind on something, she invariably finds a way to achieve it.*
PHRASE: V and N inflect, PHR n

39 If something **slips** your **mind**, you forget it. ❑ *I was going to mention it, but it slipped my mind.*
PHRASE: V and N inflect

40 If you **speak** your **mind**, you say firmly and honestly what you think about a situation, even if this may offend or upset people. ❑ *Martina Navratilova has never been afraid to speak her mind.*
PHRASE: V and N inflect

41 If something **sticks in** your **mind**, it remains firmly in your memory. ❑ *I've always been fond of poetry and one piece has always stuck in my mind.*
PHRASE: V and N inflect

42 If something **takes** your **mind off** a problem or unpleasant situation, it helps you to forget about it for a while. ❑ *'How about a game of tennis?' suggested Alan. 'That'll take your mind off things.'*
PHRASE: V and N inflect, PHR n

43 You say or write **to my mind** to indicate that the statement you are making is your own opinion. ❑ *There are scenes in this play which to my mind are incredibly violent.*
PHRASE: PHR with cl

44 If you are **in two minds**, you are uncertain about what to do, especially when you have to choose between two courses of action. The expression **of two minds** is also used, especially in American English. ❑ *Like many parents, I am in two minds about school uniforms.*
PHRASE: usu v-link PHR, oft PHR *about* n, PHR whether *= unsure, undecided*

45 to **give** someone **a piece of** your **mind** → see **piece**.

## ② **mind** /maɪnd/ **(minds, minding, minded)** ◆◇◇

⇛ Please look at category 18 to see if the expression you are looking for is shown under another headword.

1 If you do not **mind** something, you are not annoyed or bothered by it. ❑ *I don't mind the noise during the day... Do you mind being alone?... I hope you don't mind me calling in like this, without an appointment... It involved a little extra work, but nobody seemed to mind.*
VERB: usu with brd-neg; V n/-ing; V n/-ing; V n -ing; V

2 You use **mind** in the expressions **'do you mind?'** and **'would you mind?'** as a polite way of asking permission or asking someone to do something. ❑ *Do you mind if I ask you one more thing?... Would you mind waiting outside for a moment?... 'Would you like me to read that for you?' — 'If you wouldn't mind, please.'*
VERB [politeness]; V if; V -ing; V

3 If someone does not **mind** what happens or what something is like, they do not have a strong preference for any particular thing. ❑ *I don't mind what we play, really.*
VERB: with brd-neg; V wh

4 If you tell someone to **mind** something, you are warning them to be careful not to hurt themselves or other people, or damage something. [BRIT] ❑ *Mind that bike!*
VERB: usu imper *= watch*; V n

✔ in AM, usually use **watch**

5 You use **mind** when you are reminding someone to do something or telling them to be careful not to do something. [BRIT] ❑ *Mind you don't burn those sausages.*
VERB: only imper *= watch*; V that

✔ in AM, usually use **make sure, take care**

6 If you **mind** a child or something such as a shop or luggage, you look after it, usually while the person who owns it or is usually responsible for it is somewhere else. [BRIT] ❑ *Jim Coulters will mind the store while I'm away.*
VERB; V n

✔ in AM, usually use **take care of, watch**

7 If you are offered something or offered a choice and you say **'I don't mind'**, you are saying politely that you will be happy with any of the things offered. [BRIT] ❑ *'Which one of these do you want?' — 'I don't mind.'*
CONVENTION [formulae]

8 You say **'Don't mind me'** to apologize for your presence when you think that it might embarrass someone, and to tell them to carry on with what they were doing or about to do.
CONVENTION

**PHRASES** 9 You use **don't mind** in expressions such as **don't mind him** or **don't mind them** to apologize for someone else's behaviour when you think it might have offended the person you are speaking to. ❑ *Don't mind the old lady. She's getting senile.*
PHRASE: PHR n

10 Some people say **'Mind how you go'** when they are saying goodbye to someone who is leaving. [BRIT, INFORMAL]
CONVENTION [formulae] *= take care*

11 People use the expression **if you don't mind** when they are rejecting an offer or saying that they do not want to do something, especially when they are annoyed. ❑ *'Sit down.' — 'I prefer standing for a while, if you don't mind.'.*
PHRASE: PHR with cl [feelings]

12 You use **mind you** to emphasize a piece of information that you are adding, especially when the new information explains what you have said or contrasts with it. Some people use **mind** in a similar way. ❑ *They pay full rates. Mind you, they can afford it... You need a bit of cold water in there to make it comfortable. Not too cold, mind.*
PHRASE: PHR with cl [emphasis]

13 You say **never mind** when you are emphasizing that something is not serious or important, especially when someone is upset about it or is saying sorry to you.
CONVENTION [emphasis]

14 You use **never mind** to tell someone that they need not do something or worry about something, because it is not important or because you will do it yourself. ❑ *'Was his name David?' — 'No I don't think it was, but never mind, go on.'... Dorothy, come on. Never mind your shoes. They'll soon dry off... 'Fewter didn't seem to think so.' — 'Never mind what Fewter said.'*
PHRASE: oft PHR n/wh

15 You use **never mind** after a statement, often a negative one, to indicate that the statement is even more true of the person, thing, or situation that you are going to mention next. ❑ *I'm not going to believe it myself, never mind convince anyone else.*
PHRASE [emphasis]

16 You use **never you mind** to tell someone not to ask about something because it is not their concern or they should not know about it. [SPOKEN] ❑ *'Where is it?' — 'Never you mind.'*
CONVENTION

17 If you say that you **wouldn't mind** something, you mean that you would quite like it. ❑ *I wouldn't mind a coffee.*
PHRASE: PHR n/-ing

18 to **mind** your **own business** → see **business**.

## **mind-altering**
A **mind-altering** drug is one that produces mood changes in the person who has taken it.
ADJ: usu ADJ n

## **mind-bending**
1 If you describe something as **mind-bending**, you mean that it is difficult to understand or think about. ❑ *...mind-bending debates about the nature of life.*
ADJ: usu ADJ n

2 **Mind-bending** means the same as **mind-altering**. ❑ *...mind-bending drugs.*
ADJ: usu ADJ n

## **mind-blowing** also **mind blowing.**
If you describe something as **mind-blowing**, you mean that it is extremely impressive or surprising. [INFORMAL] ❑ *...a mind-blowing array of treatments.*
ADJ *= incredible*

## **mind-boggling** also **mind boggling.**
If you say that something is **mind-boggling**, you mean that it is so large, complicated, or extreme that it is very hard to imagine. [INFORMAL] ❑ *The amount of paperwork involved is mind-boggling.*
ADJ *= unbelievable*

## **mind|ed** /maɪndɪd/
If someone is **minded to** do something, they want or intend to do it. [FORMAL] ❑ *The Home Office said at that time that it was minded to reject his application for political asylum.*
ADJ: v-link ADJ, ADJ to-inf, *so* ADJ *= inclined*

## **-minded** /-maɪndɪd/
1 **-minded** combines with adjectives to form words that describe someone's character, attitude, opinions, or intelligence. ❑ *These are evil-minded people... He is famous for his tough-minded professionalism.*
COMB in ADJ

2 **-minded** combines with adverbs to form adjectives that indicate that someone is interested in a particular subject or is able to think in a particular way. ❑ *I am not an academically-minded person.*
COMB in ADJ

3 **-minded** combines with nouns to form adjectives that indicate that someone thinks a particular thing is important or cares a lot about it. ❑ *He is seen as more business-minded than his predecessor... We weren't career-minded like girls are today.*
COMB in ADJ *= -oriented*

**mind|er** /maɪndəʳ/ **(minders)** 1 A **minder** is a person whose job is to protect someone, especially someone famous. [mainly BRIT, INFORMAL] N-COUNT = bodyguard
2 A **minder** is the same as a **childminder**. [BRIT] N-COUNT

**mind|ful** /maɪndfʊl/ If you are **mindful of** something, you think about it and consider it when taking action. [FORMAL] ❑ *We must be mindful of the consequences of selfishness.* ADJ: v-link ADJ, usu ADJ *of* n = aware

**mind|less** /maɪndləs/ 1 If you describe a violent action as **mindless**, you mean that it is done without thought and will achieve nothing. [mainly BRIT] ❑ *...a plot that mixes blackmail, extortion and mindless violence.* ADJ: usu ADJ n [disapproval] = senseless 2 If you describe a person or group as **mindless**, you mean that they are stupid or do not think about what they are doing. ❑ *She wasn't at all the mindless little wife so many people perceived her to be.* ADJ [disapproval] ♦ **mind|less|ly** *I was annoyed with myself for having so quickly and mindlessly lost thirty dollars.* ADV: ADV with v 3 If you describe an activity as **mindless**, you mean that it is so dull that people do it or take part in it without thinking. ❑ *...the mindless repetitiveness of some tasks.* ADJ [disapproval] ♦ **mind|less|ly** *I spent many hours mindlessly banging a tennis ball against the wall.* ADV: ADV with v

**mind-numbing** If you describe an event or experience as **mind-numbing**, you mean that it is so bad, boring, or great in extent that you are unable to think about it clearly. ❑ *It was another day of mind-numbing tedium.* ADJ ♦ **mind-numbingly** *...a mind-numbingly boring sport.* ADV: ADV adj

**mind-set** **(mind-sets)** also **mindset.** If you refer to someone's **mind-set**, you mean their general attitudes and the way they typically think about things. ❑ *The greatest challenge for the Americans is understanding the mindset of Eastern Europeans.* N-COUNT: oft with poss, adj N

**mine**
① PRONOUN USE
② NOUN AND VERB USES

① **mine** /maɪn/ **Mine** is the first person singular possessive pronoun. A speaker or writer uses **mine** to refer to something that belongs or relates to himself or herself. ❑ *Her right hand is inches from mine... I'm looking for a friend of mine who lives here.* ◆◆◆ PRON: oft n *of* PRON

② **mine** /maɪn/ **(mines, mining, mined)** 1 A **mine** is a place where deep holes and tunnels are dug under the ground in order to obtain a mineral such as coal, diamonds, or gold. ❑ *...coal mines.* N-COUNT: oft n N
2 When a mineral such as coal, diamonds, or gold **is mined**, it is obtained from the ground by digging deep holes and tunnels. ❑ *The pit is being shut down because it no longer has enough coal that can be mined economically.* VERB: usu passive *be* V-ed 3 A **mine** is a bomb which is hidden in the ground or in water and which explodes when people or things touch it. N-COUNT
4 If an area of land or water **is mined**, mines are placed there which will explode when people or things touch them. ❑ *The approaches to the garrison have been heavily mined.* VERB *be* V-ed Also V n 5 If you say that someone is a **mine of information**, you mean that they know a great deal about something. PHRASE: *mine* inflects, usu v-link PHR
6 → See also **mining**.

**mine|field** /maɪnfiːld/ **(minefields)** 1 A **minefield** is an area of land or water where explosive mines have been hidden. N-COUNT 2 If you describe a situation as a **minefield**, you are emphasizing that there are a lot of hidden dangers or problems, and where people need to behave with care because things could easily go wrong. ❑ *The whole subject is a political minefield.* N-COUNT: oft adj N, N *of* n [emphasis]

**min|er** /maɪnəʳ/ **(miners)** A **miner** is a person who works underground in mines in order to obtain minerals such as coal, diamonds, or gold. ◆◇◇ N-COUNT

**min|er|al** /mɪnərəl/ **(minerals)** A **mineral** is a substance such as tin, salt, or sulphur that is formed naturally in rocks and in the earth. Minerals are also found in small quantities in food and drink. N-COUNT

**min|er|al wa|ter** **(mineral waters)** **Mineral water** is water that comes out of the ground naturally and is considered healthy to drink. N-MASS

**min|estro|ne** /mɪnɪstroʊni/ **Minestrone** soup is a type of soup made from meat stock that contains small pieces of vegetable and pasta. N-UNCOUNT

**mine|sweeper** /maɪnswiːpəʳ/ **(minesweepers)** also **mine sweeper.** A **minesweeper** is a ship that is used to clear away explosive mines in the sea. N-COUNT

**min|gle** /mɪŋgəl/ **(mingles, mingling, mingled)**
1 If things such as sounds, smells, or feelings **mingle**, they become mixed together but are usually still recognizable. ❑ *Now the cheers and applause mingled in a single sustained roar... Foreboding mingled with his excitement.* V-RECIP pl-n V V *with* n 2 At a party, if you **mingle with** the other people there, you move around and talk to them. ❑ *Go out of your way to mingle with others at the wedding... Guests ate and mingled... Alison mingled for a while and then went to where Douglas stood with John.* V-RECIP V *with* pl-n pl-n V V (non-recip)

**mini** /mɪni/ **(minis)** A **mini** is the same as a **mini-skirt**. N-COUNT

**mini-** /mɪni-/ **Mini-** is used before nouns to form nouns which refer to something which is a smaller version of something else. ❑ *Provisions may be purchased from the mini-market... We were playing mini-golf.* PREFIX

**minia|ture** /mɪnɪtʃəʳ, AM mɪniətʃʊr/ **(miniatures)** 1 **Miniature** is used to describe something which is very small, especially a smaller version of something which is normally much bigger. ❑ *...miniature roses... He looked like a miniature version of his handsome and elegant big brother.* ADJ: ADJ n 2 If you describe one thing as another thing **in miniature**, you mean that it is much smaller in size or scale than the other thing, but is otherwise exactly the same. ❑ *Ecuador provides a perfect introduction to South America; it's a continent in miniature.* PHRASE: usu n PHR, PHR after v
3 A **miniature** is a very small detailed painting, often of a person. N-COUNT 4 A **miniature** is a very small bottle of strong alcohol such as whisky or brandy, and usually contains enough for one or two drinks. N-COUNT

**minia|tur|ize** /mɪnɪtʃəraɪz/ **(miniaturizes, miniaturizing, miniaturized)**

☑ in BRIT, also use **miniaturise**

If you **miniaturize** something such as a machine, you produce a very small version of it. ❑ *...the problems of further miniaturizing the available technologies. ...miniaturized amplifiers and receivers.* VERB V n V-ed ♦ **minia|turi|za|tion** /mɪnɪtʃəraɪzeɪʃən/ *...increasing miniaturization in the computer industry.* N-UNCOUNT

**mini|bar** /mɪnibɑːʳ/ **(minibars)** In a hotel room, a **minibar** is a small fridge containing alcoholic drinks. N-COUNT

**mini-break** **(mini-breaks)** A **mini-break** is a short holiday. [BRIT, JOURNALISM] N-COUNT

**mini|bus** /mɪnibʌs/ **(minibuses)** also **mini-bus.** A **minibus** is a large van which has seats in the back for passengers, and windows along its sides. N-COUNT: also *by* N

**mini|cab** /mɪnikæb/ **(minicabs)** also **mini-cab.** A **minicab** is a taxi which you have to arrange to pick you up by telephone. [BRIT] ❑ *If you want a cheap ride, take a minicab.* N-COUNT ≠ hackney cab

**mini|cam** /mɪnikæm/ **(minicams)** A **minicam** is a very small television camera. N-COUNT

**mini|disc** /mɪnidɪsk/ **(minidiscs)** A **minidisc** is a small compact disc which you can record music or data on. [TRADEMARK] N-COUNT

**mini|dish** /mɪnidɪʃ/ **(minidishes)** A **minidish** is a small satellite dish that can receive signals from communications satellites for media such as television programmes and the Internet. N-COUNT

**min|im** /mɪnɪm/ **(minims)** A **minim** is a musical note that has a time value equal to two crotchets or two quarter notes. [BRIT] N-COUNT

☑ in AM, use **half note**

**mini|mal** /mɪnɪməl/ Something that is **minimal** is very small in quantity, value, or degree. ❑ *The co-operation between the two is minimal... One aim of these reforms is effective defence with minimal expenditure.* ADJ

**mini|mal|ism** /mɪnɪməlɪzəm/ **Minimalism** is a style in which a small number of very simple things are used to create a particular effect. ❑ *In her own home, she replaced austere minimalism with cosy warmth and colour.* N-UNCOUNT

**mini|mal|ist** /mɪnɪməlɪst/ **(minimalists)** 1 A **minimalist** is an artist or designer who uses minimalism. ❑ *He was influenced by the minimalists in the 1970s.* N-COUNT 2 **Minimalist** is used to describe ideas, artists, or designers that are influenced by minimalism. ❑ *The two designers settled upon a minimalist approach.* ADJ

**mini|mize** /mɪnɪmaɪz/ **(minimizes, minimizing, minimized)**

in BRIT, also use **minimise**

1 If you **minimize** a risk, problem, or unpleasant situation, you reduce it to the lowest possible level, or prevent it increasing beyond that level. ❑ *Many of these problems can be minimised by sensible planning.* VERB ≠ *maximize* V n 2 If you **minimize** something, you make it seem smaller or less significant than it really is. ❑ *Some have minimized the importance of ideological factors.* VERB = *play down* ≠ *maximize* V n 3 If you **minimize** a window on a computer screen, you make it very small, because you do not want to use it. ❑ *Click the square icon again to minimize the window.* VERB ≠ *maximize* V n

**mini|mum** /mɪnɪməm/ ◆◇◇ 1 You use **minimum** to describe an amount which is the smallest that is possible, allowed, or required. ❑ *He was only five feet nine, the minimum height for a policeman. ...a rise in the minimum wage.* ADJ: ADJ n ≠ *maximum* ♦ **Minimum** is also a noun. ❑ *This will take a minimum of one hour... Four foot should be seen as an absolute minimum.* N-SING: oft *a* N *of* amount 2 You use **minimum** to state how small an amount is. ❑ *The basic needs of life are available with minimum effort... Neil and Chris try to spend the minimum amount of time on the garden.* ADJ: ADJ n ♦ **Minimum** is also a noun. ❑ *With a minimum of fuss, she produced the grandson he had so desperately wished for.* N-SING: *a* N *of* n 3 If you say that something is a particular amount **minimum**, you mean that this is the smallest amount it should be or could possibly be, although a larger amount is acceptable or very possible. ❑ *You're talking over a thousand pounds minimum for one course.* ADV: amount ADV ≠ *maximum*

PHRASES 4 You use **at a minimum**, or **at the minimum**, when you want to indicate that something is the very least which could or should happen. ❑ *This would take three months at a minimum.* PHRASE: amount PHR, PHR with cl, PHR after v ≠ *at the maximum* 5 If you say that someone keeps something **to a minimum**, or **to the minimum**, you mean that they keep the amount of it as small as possible. ❑ *Office machinery is kept to a minimum.* PHRASE: PHR after v

**mini|mum se|cu|rity pris|on** **(minimum security prisons)** A **minimum security prison** is a prison where there are fewer restrictions on prisoners than in a normal prison. [mainly AM] N-COUNT

in BRIT, use **open prison**

**mini|mum wage** **The minimum wage** is the lowest wage that an employer is allowed to pay an employee, according to a law or agreement. N-SING

**min|ing** /maɪnɪŋ/ **Mining** is the industry and activities connected with getting valuable or useful minerals from the ground, for example coal, diamonds, or gold. ❑ *...traditional industries such as coal mining and steel making.* N-UNCOUNT

**min|ion** /mɪnjən/ **(minions)** If you refer to someone's **minions**, you are referring to people who have to do what that person tells them to do, especially unimportant or boring tasks. [LITERARY] ❑ *She delegated the job to one of her minions.* N-COUNT: usu pl, usu poss N disapproval = *underling*

**mini-series** **(mini-series)** A **mini-series** is a drama shown on television in two or three parts, usually in one week. N-COUNT

**mini-skirt** **(mini-skirts)** also **miniskirt.** A **mini-skirt** is a very short skirt. N-COUNT

**min|is|ter** /mɪnɪstər/ **(ministers, ministering, ministered)** ◆◆◆ 1 In Britain and some other countries, a **minister** is a person who is in charge of a particular government department. ❑ *When the government had come to power, he had been named minister of culture... The new Defence Minister is Senator Robert Ray.* N-COUNT: oft N *of* n, n N 2 A **minister** is a person who officially represents their government in a foreign country and has a lower rank than an ambassador. ❑ *He concluded a deal with the Danish minister in Washington.* N-COUNT: usu supp N 3 A **minister** is a member of the clergy, especially in Protestant churches. ❑ *His father was a Baptist minister.* N-COUNT 4 If you **minister to** people or **to** their needs, you serve them or help them, for example by making sure that they have everything they need or want. [FORMAL] ❑ *For 44 years he had ministered to the poor, the sick, the neglected and the deprived.* VERB V *to* n

**min|is|terial** /mɪnɪstɪəriəl/ You use **ministerial** to refer to people, events, or jobs that are connected with government ministers. ❑ *The prime minister's initial ministerial appointments haven't pleased all his supporters.* ADJ: ADJ n

**mini|stra|tions** /mɪnɪstreɪʃənz/ A person's **ministrations** are the things they do to help or care for someone in a particular situation, especially someone who is weak or ill. [HUMOROUS or LITERARY] ❑ *...the tender ministrations of the buxom woman who cut his hair.* N-PLURAL: usu with poss

**min|is|try** /mɪnɪstri/ **(ministries)** ◆◆◇ 1 In Britain and some other countries, a **ministry** is a government department which deals with a particular thing or area of activity, for example trade, defence, or transport. ❑ *...the Ministry of Justice. ...a spokesman for the Agriculture Ministry.* N-COUNT: oft N *of* n, n N 2 The **ministry** of a religious person is the work that they do that is based on or inspired by their religious beliefs. ❑ *His ministry is among the poor.* N-COUNT: usu sing, usu with poss

**mink** /mɪŋk/ **(minks** or **mink)** 1 A **mink** is a small animal with highly valued fur. ❑ *...a proposal for a ban on the hunting of foxes, mink and hares.* N-COUNT ♦ **Mink** is the fur of a mink. ❑ *...a mink coat.* N-UNCOUNT: oft N n 2 A **mink** is a coat or other garment made from the fur of a mink. ❑ *Some people like to dress up in minks and diamonds.* N-COUNT

**min|now** /mɪnoʊ/ **(minnows)** A **minnow** is a very small fish that lives in lakes and rivers. N-COUNT

**mi|nor** /maɪnər/ **(minors, minoring, minored)** ◆◇◇ 1 You use **minor** when you want to describe something that is less important, serious, or significant than other things in a group or situation. ❑ *She is known in Italy for a number of minor roles in films... Western officials say the problem is minor, and should be quickly overcome.* ADJ ≠ *major* 2 A **minor** illness or operation is not likely to be dangerous to someone's life or health. ❑ *Sarah had been plagued continually by a series of minor illnesses... His mother had to go to the hospital for minor surgery.* ADJ: usu ADJ n ≠ *major* 3 In European music, a **minor** scale is one in which the third note is three semitones higher than the first. ❑ *...the unfinished sonata movement in F minor.* ADJ: n ADJ, ADJ n ≠ *major* 4 A **minor** is a person who is still legally a child. In Britain and most states in the United States, people are minors until they reach the age of eighteen. ❑ *The approach has virtually ended cigarette sales to minors.* N-COUNT 5 At a university or college in the United States, a student's **minor** is a subject that they are studying in addition to their main subject, or major. N-COUNT: oft poss N ≠ *major* 6 At a university or college in the United States, if a student is, for example, a geology **minor**, they are studying geology as well as their main subject. N-COUNT: n N ≠ *major* 7 If a student at a university or college in the United States **minors in** a particular subject, they study it in addition to their main subject. ❑ *I'm minoring in computer science.* VERB ≠ *major* V *in* n

**mi|nor|ity** /maɪnɒrɪti, AM -nɔːr-/ **(minorities)** ◆◆◇ 1 If you talk about a **minority** of people or things in a larger group, you are referring to a number of them that forms less than half of the larger group, usually much less than half. ❑ *Local authority nursery provision covers only a tiny minority of working mothers. ...minority shareholders.* ● If people are **in a minority** or **in the minority**, they belong to a group of people or things that form less than half of a larger group. ❑ *Even in the 1960s, politically active students and academics were in a minority... In the past conservatives have been in the minority.* 2 A **minority** is a group of people of the same race, culture, or religion who live in a place where most of the people around them are of a different race, culture, or religion. ❑ *...the region's ethnic minorities.*

N-SING: oft N *of* n ≠ *majority* / PHRASE: usu v-link PHR / N-COUNT

**min|strel** /mɪnstrəl/ **(minstrels)** In medieval times, a **minstrel** was a singer and musician who travelled around and entertained noble families. N-COUNT

**mint** /mɪnt/ **(mints, minting, minted)** 1 **Mint** is a herb with fresh-tasting leaves. ❑ *Garnish with mint sprigs.* 2 A **mint** is a sweet with a peppermint flavour. Some people suck mints in order to make their breath smell fresher. 3 **The mint** is the place where the official coins of a country are made. ❑ *In 1965 the mint stopped putting silver in dimes.* 4 To **mint** coins or medals means to make them in a mint. ❑ *...the right to mint coins.* 5 If you say that someone makes **a mint**, you mean that they make a very large amount of money. [INFORMAL] ❑ *Everybody thinks I'm making a mint.* 6 If you say that something is **in mint condition**, you mean that it is in perfect condition.

N-UNCOUNT / N-COUNT / N-COUNT: usu sing, usu *the* N / VERB / V n / N-SING: usu *a* N = *loads* / PHRASE: usu v-link PHR

**mint|ed** /mɪntɪd/ If you describe something as **newly minted** or **freshly minted**, you mean that it is very new, and that it has only just been produced or completed. ❑ *He seemed to be pleased by this newly minted vehicle. ...the movie's freshly minted script.* ADJ: usu ADJ n, adv ADJ

**mint sauce** **Mint sauce** is a sauce made from mint leaves, vinegar, and sugar, which is often eaten with lamb. N-UNCOUNT

**minu|et** /mɪnjuet/ **(minuets)** 1 In the music of the seventeenth and eighteenth centuries, a **minuet** is a piece of music with three beats in a bar which is played at moderate speed. 2 A **minuet** is a fairly slow and formal dance which was popular in the seventeenth and eighteenth centuries.

N-COUNT / N-COUNT

**mi|nus** /maɪnəs/ **(minuses)** 1 You use **minus** to show that one number or quantity is being subtracted from another. ❑ *One minus one is zero... They've been promised their full July salary minus the hardship payment.* 2 **Minus** before a number or quantity means that the number or quantity is less than zero. ❑ *The aircraft was subjected to temperatures of minus 65 degrees and plus 120 degrees.* 3 Teachers use **minus** in grading work in schools and colleges. 'B minus' is not as good as 'B', but is a better grade than 'C'. ❑ *I'm giving him a B minus.* 4 To be **minus** something means not to have that thing. ❑ *The film company collapsed, leaving Chris jobless and minus his life savings.* 5 A **minus** is a disadvantage. [INFORMAL] ❑ *The minuses far outweigh that possible gain.* 6 You use **plus or minus** to give the amount by which a particular number may vary. ❑ *The poll has a margin of error of plus or minus 5 per cent.*

CONJ = *less* ≠ *plus* / ADJ: ADJ amount / ≠ *plus* / PREP = *without* / N-COUNT = *drawback* ≠ *plus* / PHRASE: PHR amount

**mi|nus|cule** /mɪnɪskjuːl/ If you describe something as **minuscule**, you mean that it is very small. ❑ *The film was shot in 17 days, a minuscule amount of time.* ADJ = *minute*

**mi|nus sign** **(minus signs)** A **minus sign** is the sign - which is put between two numbers in order to show that the second number is being subtracted from the first one. It is also put before a number to show that the number is less than zero. N-COUNT

**minute**
① NOUN AND VERB USES
② ADJECTIVE USE

**① min|ute** /mɪnɪt/ **(minutes, minuting, minuted)** ◆◆◆ 1 A **minute** is one of the sixty parts that an hour is divided into. People often say **'a minute'** or **'minutes'** when they mean a short length of time. ❑ *The pizza will then take about twenty minutes to cook... Bye Mum, see you in a minute... Within minutes we realized our mistake.* 2 The **minutes** of a meeting are the written records of the things that are discussed or decided at it. ❑ *He'd been reading the minutes of the last meeting.* 3 When someone **minutes** something that is discussed or decided at a meeting, they make a written record of it. ❑ *You don't need to minute that.* 4 → See also **up-to-the-minute**. 5 People often use expressions such as **wait a minute** or **just a minute** when they want to stop you doing or saying something. ❑ *Wait a minute, folks, something is wrong here... Hey, just a minute!*

N-COUNT: oft num N / N-PLURAL: oft N *of* n / VERB / V n / CONVENTION = *hang on*

**PHRASES** 6 If you say that something will or may happen **at any minute** or **any minute now**, you are emphasizing that it is likely to happen very soon. ❑ *It looked as though it might rain at any minute... Any minute now, that phone is going to ring.* 7 If you say that you do **not** believe **for a minute** or **for one minute** that something is true, you are emphasizing that you do not believe that it is true. ❑ *I don't believe for one minute she would have been scared.* 8 A **last-minute** action is one that is done at the latest time possible. ❑ *She was doing some last-minute revision for her exams... He will probably wait until the last minute.* 9 You use the expression **the next minute** or expressions such as **'one minute** he was there, **the next** he was gone' to emphasize that something happens suddenly. ❑ *The next minute my father came in... Jobs are there one minute, gone the next.* 10 If you say that something happens **the minute** something else happens, you are emphasizing that it happens immediately after the other thing. ❑ *The minute you do this, you'll lose control.* 11 If you say that something must be done **this minute**, you are emphasizing that it must be done immediately. ❑ *Anna, stop that. Sit down this minute.*

PHRASE [emphasis] / PHRASE: with brd-neg, PHR with v [emphasis] = *for a moment* / PHRASE: PHR n, prep PHR / PHRASE [emphasis] = *the next moment* / PHRASE: PHR that [emphasis] / PHRASE [emphasis] = *now, immediately*

**② mi|nute** /maɪnjuːt, AM -nuːt-/ **(minutest)** If you say that something is **minute**, you mean that it is very small. ❑ *Only a minute amount is needed... The party was planned in the minutest detail.* ADJ = *tiny*

**mi|nute|ly** /maɪnjuːtli, AM -nuːt-/ 1 You use **minutely** to indicate that something is done in great detail. ❑ *The metal is then minutely examined to ensure there are no cracks.* 2 You use **minutely** to indicate that the size or extent of something is very small. ❑ *The benefit of an x-ray far outweighs the minutely increased risk of cancer.*

ADV: ADV with v / ADV: usu ADV adj/-ed

**mi|nu|tiae** /maɪnjuːʃiiː, AM mɪnuːʃ-/ **The minutiae of** something such as someone's job or life are the very small details of it. [FORMAL] ❑ *Much of his early work is concerned with the minutiae of rural life.* N-PLURAL: usu *the* N *of* n

**mira|cle** /mɪrəkəl/ **(miracles)** 1 If you say that a good event is a **miracle**, you mean that it is very surprising and unexpected. ❑ *It is a miracle no one was killed.* 2 A **miracle** drug or product does something that was thought almost impossible. [JOURNALISM] ❑ *...a miracle drug that is said to be a cure for Aids and cancer.* 3 A **miracle** is a wonderful and surprising event that is believed to be caused by God. ❑ *...Jesus's ability to perform miracles.*

N-COUNT / ADJ: ADJ n / N-COUNT

**mira|cle work|er** **(miracle workers)** If you describe someone as a **miracle worker**, you mean that they have achieved or are able to achieve success in something that other people have found very difficult. ❑ *At work he was regarded as a miracle worker, the man who took risks and could not lose.* N-COUNT [approval]

**mi|racu|lous** /mɪrækjʊləs/ ADJ 1 If you describe a good event as **miraculous**, you mean that it is very surprising and unexpected. ❑ *The horse made a miraculous recovery to finish a close third. ...a miraculous escape.* ♦ **mi|racu|lous|ly** ADV: usu ADV with cl, ADV with v, also ADV adj *Miraculously, the guards escaped death or serious injury.* 2 ADJ If someone describes a wonderful event as **miraculous**, they believe that the event was caused by God. ❑ *...miraculous healing. ...miraculous powers.*

**mi|rage** /mɪrɑːʒ/ **(mirages)** 1 N-COUNT A **mirage** is something which you see when it is extremely hot, for example in the desert, and which appears to be quite near but is actually a long way away or does not really exist. ❑ *It hovered before his eyes like the mirage of an oasis.* 2 N-COUNT: usu sing = illusion If you describe something as a **mirage**, you mean that it is not real or true, although it may seem to be. ❑ *The girl was a mirage, cast up by his troubled mind.*

**mire** /maɪəʳ/ 1 N-SING: oft N *of* n You can refer to an unpleasant or difficult situation as a **mire** of some kind. [LITERARY] ❑ *...a mire of poverty and ignorance.* 2 N-UNCOUNT **Mire** is dirt or mud. [LITERARY] ❑ *...the muck and mire of sewers and farmyards.*

**mir|ror** /mɪrəʳ/ **(mirrors, mirroring, mirrored)** ◆◇◇ 1 N-COUNT A **mirror** is a flat piece of glass which reflects light, so that when you look at it you can see yourself reflected in it. ❑ *He absent-mindedly looked at himself in the mirror.* ♦ **mir|rored** ADJ *...a mirrored ceiling.* 2 VERB = reflect If something **mirrors** something else, it has similar features to it, and therefore seems like a copy or representation of it. ❑ V n *The book inevitably mirrors my own interests and experiences.* 3 VERB = reflect If you see something reflected in water, you can say that the water **mirrors** it. [LITERARY] ❑ V n *...the sudden glitter where a newly-flooded field mirrors the sky.*

**mir|ror im|age (mirror images)** also **mirror-image.** N-COUNT: oft N *of* n If something is a **mirror image** of something else, it is like a reflection of it, either because it is exactly the same or because it is the same but reversed. ❑ *I saw in him a mirror image of my younger self.*

**mir|ror site (mirror sites)** N-COUNT A **mirror site** is a website which is the same as another website operated by the same person or organization but has a slightly different address. Mirror sites are designed to make it easier for more people to visit a popular website.

**mirth** /mɜːʳθ/ N-UNCOUNT = hilarity **Mirth** is amusement which you express by laughing. [LITERARY] ❑ *That caused considerable mirth amongst pupils and sports masters alike.*

**mirth|less** /mɜːʳθləs/ ADJ: usu ADJ n If someone gives a **mirthless** laugh or smile, it is obvious that they are not really amused. [WRITTEN]

**mis-** /mɪs-/ PREFIX **Mis-** is added to some verbs and nouns to form new verbs and nouns which indicate that something is done badly or wrongly. ❑ *The local newspaper misreported the story by claiming the premises were rented... He was eventually convicted for the misuse of official funds.*

**mis|ad|ven|ture** /mɪsədventʃəʳ/ **(misadventures)** N-VAR A **misadventure** is an unfortunate incident. [FORMAL] ❑ *...a series of misadventures... A verdict of death by misadventure was recorded.*

**mis|an|thrope** /mɪzənθroʊp/ **(misanthropes)** N-COUNT A **misanthrope** is a person who does not like other people. [FORMAL]

**mis|an|throp|ic** /mɪzənθrɒpɪk/ ADJ If you describe a person or their feelings as **misanthropic**, you mean that they do not like other people. [FORMAL]

**mis|an|thro|py** /mɪzænθrəpi/ N-UNCOUNT **Misanthropy** is a general dislike of people. [FORMAL]

**mis|ap|pli|ca|tion** /mɪsæplɪkeɪʃən/ **(misapplications)** N-VAR: usu N *of* n = misuse If you talk about the **misapplication of** something, you mean it is used for a purpose it was not intended for. ❑ *He's charged with conspiracy, misapplication of funds and other crimes. ...a common misapplication of the law.*

**mis|ap|ply** /mɪsəplaɪ/ **(misapplies, misapplying, misapplied)** VERB: usu passive = misused If something **is misapplied**, it is used for a purpose for which it is not intended or not suitable. ❑ be V-ed *Many lines from Shakespeare's plays are misquoted and misapplied...* be V-ed *The law had been misapplied.*

**mis|ap|pre|hen|sion** /mɪsæprɪhenʃən/ **(misapprehensions)** N-VAR: oft N that, under N = misunderstanding A **misapprehension** is a wrong idea or impression that you have about something. ❑ *Men still appear to be labouring under the misapprehension that women want hairy, muscular men.*

**mis|ap|pro|pri|ate** /mɪsəproʊprieɪt/ **(misappropriates, misappropriating, misappropriated)** VERB If someone **misappropriates** money which does not belong to them, they take it without permission and use it for their own purposes. ❑ V n *I took no money for personal use and have not misappropriated any funds whatsoever.* ♦ **mis|ap|pro|pria|tion** N-UNCOUNT: usu N *of* n /mɪsəproʊprieɪʃən/ *He pleaded guilty to charges of misappropriation of bank funds.*

**mis|be|have** /mɪsbɪheɪv/ **(misbehaves, misbehaving, misbehaved)** VERB If someone, especially a child, **misbehaves**, they behave in a way that is not acceptable to other people. ❑ V *When the children misbehaved she was unable to cope.*

**mis|be|hav|iour** /mɪsbɪheɪvjəʳ/

☑ in AM, use **misbehavior**

N-UNCOUNT **Misbehaviour** is behaviour that is not acceptable to other people. [FORMAL] ❑ *If the toddler had been dealt with properly at first, the rest of his misbehaviour would have been avoided.*

**mis|cal|cu|late** /mɪskælkjʊleɪt/ **(miscalculates, miscalculating, miscalculated)** VERB If you **miscalculate**, you make a mistake in judging a situation or in making a calculation. ❑ V n *It's clear that he has badly miscalculated the mood of the people...* V *The government appears to have miscalculated and bills are higher as a result.* ♦ **mis|cal|cu|la|tion** N-VAR /mɪskælkjʊleɪʃən/ **(miscalculations)** *The coup failed because of miscalculations by the plotters.*

**mis|car|riage** /mɪskærɪdʒ, -kær-/ **(miscarriages)** N-VAR If a pregnant woman has a **miscarriage**, her baby dies and she gives birth to it before it is properly formed.

**mis|car|riage of jus|tice (miscarriages of justice)** N-VAR A **miscarriage of justice** is a wrong decision made by a court, as a result of which an innocent person is punished. ❑ *I can imagine no greater miscarriage of justice than the execution of an innocent man.*

**mis|car|ry** /mɪskæri, -kæri/ **(miscarries, miscarrying, miscarried)** VERB If a woman **miscarries**, she has a miscarriage. ❑ V *Many women who miscarry eventually have healthy babies.* Also V n

**mis|cast** /mɪskɑːst, -kæst/ ADJ: usu v-link ADJ If someone who is acting in a play or film is **miscast**, the role that they have is not suitable for them, so that they appear silly or unconvincing to the audience.

**mis|cel|la|neous** /mɪsəleɪniəs/ ADJ: ADJ n A **miscellaneous** group consists of many different kinds of things or people that are difficult to put into a particular category. ❑ *...a hoard of miscellaneous junk.*

**mis|cel|la|ny** /mɪseləni, AM mɪsəleɪni/ **(miscellanies)** N-COUNT: oft N *of* n = assortment A **miscellany** of things is a collection or group of many different kinds of things. [WRITTEN] ❑ *...glass cases filled with a miscellany of objects.*

**mis|chief** /mɪstʃɪf/ 1 N-UNCOUNT **Mischief** is playing harmless tricks on people or doing things you are not supposed to do. It can also refer to the desire to do this. ❑ *The little lad was a real handful. He was always up to mischief... His eyes were full of mischief.* 2 N-UNCOUNT **Mischief** is behaviour that is intended to cause trouble for people. It can also refer to the trouble that is caused. ❑ *The more sinister explana-*

*tion is that he is about to make mischief in the Middle East again.*

**mischief-maker** **(mischief-makers)** If you say that someone is a **mischief-maker**, you are criticizing them for saying or doing things which are intended to cause trouble between people. ❑ *The letter had come from an unknown mischief-maker.* N-COUNT [disapproval]

**mis|chie|vous** /mɪstʃɪvəs/ [1] A **mischievous** person likes to have fun by playing harmless tricks on people or doing things they are not supposed to do. ❑ *She rocks back and forth on her chair like a mischievous child.* ♦ **mis|chie|vous|ly** *Kathryn winked mischievously.* [2] A **mischievous** act or suggestion is intended to cause trouble. ❑ *...a mischievous campaign by the press to divide the ANC.* ♦ **mis|chie|vous|ly** *That does not require 'massive' military intervention, as some have mischievously claimed.* ADJ; ADV: usu ADV with v; ADJ = malicious; ADV: usu ADV with v

**mis|con|ceived** /mɪskənsiːvd/ If you describe a plan or method as **misconceived**, you mean it is not the right one for dealing with a particular problem or situation. ❑ *The teachers say the tests for 14-year-olds are misconceived. ...Lawrence's worthy but misconceived idea.* ADJ = misguided

**mis|con|cep|tion** /mɪskənsepʃᵊn/ **(misconceptions)** A **misconception** is an idea that is not correct. ❑ *There are many fears and misconceptions about cancer.* N-COUNT

**mis|con|duct** /mɪskɒndʌkt/ **Misconduct** is bad or unacceptable behaviour, especially by a professional person. ❑ *Dr Lee was cleared of serious professional misconduct.* N-UNCOUNT

**mis|con|strue** /mɪskənstruː/ **(misconstrues, misconstruing, misconstrued)** If you **misconstrue** something that has been said or something that happens, you interpret it wrongly. [FORMAL] ❑ *An outsider might misconstrue the nature of the relationship.* VERB = misinterpret; V n

**mis|cre|ant** /mɪskriənt/ **(miscreants)** A **miscreant** is someone who has done something illegal or behaved badly. [LITERARY] ❑ *Local people demanded that the District Magistrate apprehend the miscreants.* N-COUNT

**mis|deed** /mɪsdiːd/ **(misdeeds)** A **misdeed** is a bad or evil act. [FORMAL] ❑ *...the alleged financial misdeeds of his government.* N-COUNT

**mis|de|mean|our** /mɪsdɪmiːnəʳ/ **(misdemeanours)**

✔ in AM, use **misdemeanor**

[1] A **misdemeanour** is an act that some people consider to be wrong or unacceptable. [FORMAL] ❑ *Emily knew nothing about her husband's misdemeanours.* [2] In the United States and other countries where the legal system distinguishes between very serious crimes and less serious ones, a **misdemeanour** is a less serious crime. [LEGAL] ❑ *She was charged with a misdemeanour, that of carrying a concealed weapon.* N-COUNT; N-COUNT

**mis|di|rect** /mɪsdɪrekt, -daɪr-/ **(misdirects, misdirecting, misdirected)** [1] If resources or efforts **are misdirected**, they are used in the wrong way or for the wrong purposes. ❑ *Many of the aid projects in the developing world have been misdirected in the past.* ♦ **mis|di|rect|ed** *...a misdirected effort to mollify the bishop.* [2] If you **misdirect** someone, you send them in the wrong direction. ❑ *He had deliberately misdirected the reporters.* VERB: usu passive; *be* V-ed; ADJ; VERB; V n

**mi|ser** /maɪzəʳ/ **(misers)** If you say that someone is a **miser**, you disapprove of them because they seem to hate spending money, and to spend as little as possible. ❑ *I'm married to a miser.* N-COUNT [disapproval] = skinflint

**mis|er|able** /mɪzərəbᵊl/ [1] If you are **miserable**, you are very unhappy. ❑ *I took a series of badly paid secretarial jobs which made me really miserable.* ♦ **mis|er|ably** /mɪzərəbli/ *He looked miserably down at his plate.* [2] If you describe a place or situation as **miserable**, you mean that it makes you feel unhappy or depressed. ❑ *There was nothing at all in this miserable place to distract him.* [3] If you describe the weather as **miserable**, you mean that it makes you feel depressed, because it is raining or dull. ❑ *It was a grey, wet, miserable day.* [4] If you describe someone as **miserable**, you mean that you do not like them because they are bad-tempered or unfriendly. ❑ *He always was a miserable man. He never spoke to me nor anybody else.* [5] You can describe a quantity or quality as **miserable** when you think that it is much smaller or worse than it ought to be. ❑ *Our speed over the ground was a miserable 2.2 knots.* ♦ **mis|er|ably** *...the miserably inadequate supply of books now provided for schools.* [6] A **miserable** failure is a very great one. ❑ *The film was a miserable commercial failure both in Italy and in the United States.* ♦ **mis|er|ably** *Some manage it. Some fail miserably.* ADJ: usu v-link ADJ; ADV: usu ADV after v; ADJ: usu ADJ n = depressing; ADJ; ADJ: ADJ n; ADJ: usu *a* ADJ amount [emphasis]; ADV: ADV adj; ADJ: ADJ n [emphasis]; ADV: ADV with v

**mi|ser|ly** /maɪzəʳli/ [1] If you describe someone as **miserly**, you disapprove of them because they seem to hate spending money, and to spend as little as possible. ❑ *He is miserly with both his time and his money.* [2] If you describe an amount of something as **miserly**, you are critical of it because it is very small. ❑ *Being a student today with miserly grants and limited career prospects is difficult.* ADJ [disapproval] = mean; ADJ: usu ADJ n [disapproval] = measly

**mis|ery** /mɪzəri/ **(miseries)** [1] **Misery** is great unhappiness. ❑ *All that money brought nothing but sadness and misery and tragedy. ...the miseries of his youth.* [2] **Misery** is the way of life and unpleasant living conditions of people who are very poor. ❑ *A tiny, educated elite profited from the misery of their two million fellow countrymen.* N-VAR; N-UNCOUNT

**PHRASES** [3] If someone **makes** your **life a misery**, they behave in an unpleasant way towards you over a period of time and make you very unhappy. ❑ *...the gangs of kids who make our lives a misery.* [4] If you **put** someone **out of** their **misery**, you tell them something that they are very anxious to know. [INFORMAL] ❑ *Please put me out of my misery. How do you do it?* [5] If you **put** an animal **out of** its **misery**, you kill it because it is sick or injured and cannot be cured or healed. PHRASE: V and *life* inflect; PHRASE: V inflects; PHRASE: V inflects = put down

**mis|fire** /mɪsfaɪəʳ/ **(misfires, misfiring, misfired)** [1] If a plan **misfires**, it goes wrong and does not have the results that you intend it to have. ❑ *Some of their policies had misfired.* [2] If an engine **misfires**, the fuel fails to start burning when it should. ❑ *The boat's engine misfired after he tried to start it up.* [3] If a gun **misfires**, the bullet is not sent out as it should be when the gun is fired. ❑ *The gun misfired after one shot and jammed.* VERB; V; VERB; V; VERB; V

**mis|fit** /mɪsfɪt/ **(misfits)** A **misfit** is a person who is not easily accepted by other people, often because their behaviour is very different from that of everyone else. ❑ *I have been made to feel a social and psychological misfit for not wanting children.* N-COUNT

**mis|for|tune** /mɪsfɔːʳtʃuːn/ **(misfortunes)** A **misfortune** is something unpleasant or unlucky that happens to someone. ❑ *She seemed to enjoy the misfortunes of others... He had his full share of misfortune.* N-VAR

**mis|giv|ing** /mɪsgɪvɪŋ/ **(misgivings)** If you have **misgivings** about something that is being suggested or done, you feel that it is not quite right, and are worried that it may have unwanted results. ❑ *She had some misgivings about what she was about to do.* N-VAR

**mis|guid|ed** /mɪsgaɪdɪd/ If you describe an opinion or plan as **misguided**, you are critical of it because you think it is based on an incorrect idea. You can also describe people as misguided. ❑ *In a misguided attempt to be funny, he manages only offensiveness.* ADJ [disapproval]

**mis|han|dle** /mɪshændᵊl/ **(mishandles, mishandling, mishandled)** If you say that someone **has mishandled** something, you are critical of them because you think they have dealt with it badly. ❑ *The judge said the police had mishandled the siege.* ♦ **mis|han|dling** *...the Government's mishandling of the economy.* VERB [disapproval] = mismanage; V n; N-UNCOUNT: usu poss N *of* n

**mis|hap** /mɪshæp/ **(mishaps)** A **mishap** is an unfortunate but not very serious event that happens to someone. ❑ *After a number of mishaps she did manage to get back to Germany... The plot passed off without mishap.* N-VAR

**mis|hear** /mɪshɪəʳ/ **(mishears, mishearing, misheard)** If you **mishear** what someone says, you hear it incorrectly, and think they said something different. ❑ *You misheard me, Frank... She must have misheard.* VERB; V n; V

**mish|mash** /mɪʃmæʃ/ also **mish-mash.** If you say that something is a **mishmash**, you are criticizing it because it is a confused mixture of different types of things. ❑ *The letter was a mishmash of ill-fitting proposals taken from two different reform plans.* N-SING: usu *a* N *of* n; [disapproval]; = hotch-potch, hodgepodge

**mis|in|form** /mɪsɪnfɔːʳm/ **(misinforms, misinforming, misinformed)** If you **are misinformed**, you are told something that is wrong or inaccurate. ❑ *He has been misinformed by members of his own party... The president defended the news blackout, accusing the media of misinforming the people.* VERB; *be* V-ed; V n

**mis|in|for|ma|tion** /mɪsɪnfəʳmeɪʃᵊn/ **Misinformation** is wrong information which is given to someone, often in a deliberate attempt to make them believe something which is not true. ❑ *This was a deliberate piece of misinformation.* N-UNCOUNT

**mis|in|ter|pret** /mɪsɪntɜːʳprɪt/ **(misinterprets, misinterpreting, misinterpreted)** If you **misinterpret** something, you understand it wrongly. ❑ *He was amazed that he'd misinterpreted the situation so completely.* ♦ **mis|in|ter|pre|ta|tion** /mɪsɪntɜːʳprɪteɪʃᵊn/ **(misinterpretations)** *...a misinterpretation of the aims and ends of socialism.* VERB; = misread; V n; N-VAR

**mis|judge** /mɪsdʒʌdʒ/ **(misjudges, misjudging, misjudged)** If you say that someone **has misjudged** a person or situation, you mean that they have formed an incorrect idea or opinion about them, and often that they have made a wrong decision as a result of this. ❑ *Perhaps I had misjudged him, and he was not so predictable after all.* VERB; V n

**mis|judg|ment** /mɪsdʒʌdʒmənt/ **(misjudgments)**

> ✓ in BRIT, also use **misjudgement**

A **misjudgment** is an incorrect idea or opinion that is formed about someone or something, especially when a wrong decision is made as a result of this. ❑ *...a misjudgment in British foreign policy which had far-reaching consequences... Many accidents were due to pilot misjudgement.* N-VAR

**mis|kick** **(miskicks, miskicking, miskicked)**

> ✓ The verb is pronounced /mɪskɪk/. The noun is pronounced /mɪskɪk/.

To **miskick** the ball in a game such as football means to kick it badly so that it does not go in the direction you want it to. [JOURNALISM] ❑ *He miskicked the ball twice at the edge of the penalty box... He miskicked completely as he lost his footing.* ♦ **Miskick** is also a noun. ❑ *A miskick gave Mark Leonard a clear shot at goal.* VERB; V n; V; N-COUNT

**mis|lay** /mɪsleɪ/ **(mislays, mislaying, mislaid)** If you **mislay** something, you put it somewhere and then forget where you have put it. ❑ *I appear to have mislaid my jumper.* VERB; = misplace; V n

**mis|lead** /mɪsliːd/ **(misleads, misleading, misled)** If you say that someone **has misled** you, you mean that they have made you believe something which is not true, either by telling you a lie or by giving you a wrong idea or impression. ❑ *Jack was furious with his London doctors for having misled him.* VERB; V n

**mis|lead|ing** /mɪsliːdɪŋ/ If you describe something as **misleading**, you mean that it gives you a wrong idea or impression. ❑ *It would be misleading to say that we were friends... The article contains several misleading statements.* ♦ **mis|lead|ing|ly** *The data had been presented misleadingly.* ADJ: oft *it* v-link ADJ to-inf; ADV: usu ADV with v, also ADV adj

**mis|led** /mɪsled/ **Misled** is the past tense and past participle of **mislead**.

**mis|man|age** /mɪsmænɪdʒ/ **(mismanages, mismanaging, mismanaged)** To **mismanage** something means to manage it badly. ❑ *75% of voters think the President has mismanaged the economy.* VERB; = mishandle; V n

**mis|man|age|ment** /mɪsmænɪdʒmənt/ Someone's **mismanagement** of a system or organization is the bad way they have dealt with it or organized it. ❑ *His gross mismanagement left the company desperately in need of restructuring.* N-UNCOUNT: oft poss N, N *of* n; = mishandling

**mis|match** **(mismatches, mismatching, mismatched)**

> ✓ The noun is pronounced /mɪsmætʃ/. The verb is pronounced /mɪsmætʃ/.

1 If there is a **mismatch between** two or more things or people, they do not go together well or are not suitable for each other. ❑ *There is a mismatch between the skills offered by people and the skills needed by industry. ...an unfortunate mismatch of styles.* N-COUNT: oft N *between*/*of* pl-n, N *of* pl-n

2 To **mismatch** things or people means to put them together although they do not go together well or are not suitable for each other. ❑ *She was deliberately mismatching articles of clothing.* ♦ **mis|matched** *The two opponents are mismatched.* VERB; V pl-n; ADJ

**mis|named** /mɪsneɪmd/ If you say that something or someone **is misnamed**, you mean that they have a name that describes them incorrectly. ❑ *...a high school teacher who was misnamed Mr. Witty. ...the misnamed Grand Hotel... The truth is that junk bonds were misnamed, and therefore misunderstood.* V-PASSIVE; *be* V-ed n; V-ed; *be* V-ed

**mis|no|mer** /mɪsnoʊməʳ/ **(misnomers)** If you say that a word or name is a **misnomer**, you mean that it describes something incorrectly. ❑ *Herbal 'tea' is something of a misnomer because these drinks contain no tea at all.* N-COUNT: usu *a* N in sing

**mi|sogy|nist** /mɪsɒdʒɪnɪst/ **(misogynists)** 1 A **misogynist** is a man who dislikes women. N-COUNT 2 **Misogynist** attitudes or actions are ones that involve or show a strong dislike of women. ADJ: usu ADJ n

**miso|gyn|is|tic** /mɪsɒdʒɪnɪstɪk/ **Misogynistic** means the same as **misogynist**. ADJ

**mi|sogy|ny** /mɪsɒdʒɪni/ **Misogyny** is a strong dislike of women. N-UNCOUNT

**mis|place** /mɪspleɪs/ **(misplaces, misplacing, misplaced)** If you **misplace** something, you lose it, usually only temporarily. ❑ *Somehow the suitcase with my clothes was misplaced.* VERB; = mislay; *be* V-ed

**mis|placed** /mɪspleɪst/ If you describe a feeling or action as **misplaced**, you are critical of it because you think it is inappropriate, or directed towards the wrong thing or person. ❑ *Lenders rely on the misplaced loyalty of existing borrowers to make their profit.* ADJ; [disapproval]

**mis|print** /mɪsprɪnt/ **(misprints)** A **misprint** is a mistake in the way something is printed, for example a spelling mistake. N-COUNT

**mis|pro|nounce** /mɪsprənaʊns/ **(mispronounces, mispronouncing, mispronounced)** If you **mispronounce** a word, you pronounce it wrongly. ❑ *He repeatedly mispronounced words and slurred his speech.* VERB; V n

**mis|quote** /mɪskwoʊt/ **(misquotes, misquoting, misquoted)** If someone **is misquoted**, something that they have said or written is repeated incorrectly. ❑ *He claimed that he had been misquoted and he threatened to sue the magazine for libel.* VERB; *be* V-ed

**mis|read** /mɪsriːd/ **(misreads, misreading)**

> ✓ The form **misread** is used in the present tense, and is the past tense and past participle, when it is pronounced /mɪsred/.

1 If you **misread** a situation or someone's behaviour, you do not understand it properly. ❑ *The government largely misread the mood of the electorate... Mothers may also misread signals and think the baby is crying because he is hungry.* ♦ **mis|read|ing** **(misreadings)** *...a misreading of opinion in France.* VERB; = misinterpret; V n; V n; N-COUNT

2 If you **misread** something that has been written or printed, you look at it VERB

and think that it says something that it does not say. ❑ *His chauffeur misread his route and took a wrong turning.* V n

**mis|re|mem|ber** /mɪsrɪme̱mbəʳ/ **(misremembers, misremembering, misremembered)** VERB If you **misremember** something, you remember it incorrectly. [mainly AM, FORMAL] ❑ *He proved overconfident on the witness stand, misremembering a key piece of evidence.* V n

**mis|rep|re|sent** /mɪsreprɪze̱nt/ **(misrepresents, misrepresenting, misrepresented)** VERB If someone **misrepresents** a person or situation, they give a wrong or inaccurate account of what the person or situation is like. ❑ *He said that the press had misrepresented him as arrogant and bullying...* V n *as* adj *Hollywood films misrepresented us as drunks, maniacs and murderers...* V n *as* n *Keynes deliberately misrepresented the views of his opponents.* V n ♦ **mis|rep|re|sen|ta|tion** N-VAR /mɪsreprɪzenteɪ̱ʃᵊn/ **(misrepresentations)** *I wish to point out your misrepresentation of the facts.*

**mis|rule** /mɪsru̱ːl/ N-UNCOUNT [disapproval] If you refer to someone's government of a country as **misrule**, you are critical of them for governing their country badly or unfairly. ❑ *He was arrested last December, accused of corruption and misrule.*

| **miss** |
|---|
| ① USED AS A TITLE OR A FORM OF ADDRESS |
| ② VERB AND NOUN USES |

**①Miss** /mɪs/ **(Misses)** ◆◆◆ [1] N-TITLE You use **Miss** in front of the name of a girl or unmarried woman when you are speaking to her or referring to her. ❑ *It was nice talking to you, Miss Giroux.* [2] N-VOC In some schools, children address their women teachers as **Miss.** [mainly BRIT] ❑ *'Chivers!' — 'Yes, Miss?'*

**②miss** /mɪs/ **(misses, missing, missed)** ◆◆◇

⇛ Please look at category 11 to see if the expression you are looking for is shown under another headword. [1] VERB ≠ hit If you **miss** something, you fail to hit it, for example when you have thrown something at it or you have shot a bullet at it. ❑ *She hurled the ashtray across the room, narrowly missing my head...* V n *When I'd missed a few times, he suggested I rest the rifle on a rock to steady it.* V ♦ **Miss** is also a noun. N-COUNT ❑ *After more misses, they finally put two arrows into the lion's chest.* [2] VERB In sport, if you **miss** a shot, you fail to get the ball in the goal, net, or hole. ❑ *He scored four of the goals but missed a penalty.* V n Also V ♦ **Miss** is also a noun. N-COUNT ❑ *Striker Alan Smith was guilty of two glaring misses.* [3] VERB ≠ notice If you **miss** something, you fail to notice it. ❑ *From this vantage point he watched, his searching eye never missing a detail...* V n *It's the first thing you see as you come round the corner. You can't miss it.* V n [4] VERB ≠ get If you **miss** the meaning or importance of something, you fail to understand or appreciate it. ❑ *Tambov had slightly missed the point.* V n [5] VERB ≠ seize If you **miss** a chance or opportunity, you fail to take advantage of it. ❑ *Williams knew that she had missed her chance of victory...* V n *It was too good an opportunity to miss.* V n [6] VERB If you **miss** someone who is no longer with you or who has died, you feel sad and wish that they were still with you. ❑ *Your mama and I are gonna miss you at Christmas.* V n [7] VERB If you **miss** something, you feel sad because you no longer have it or are no longer doing or experiencing it. ❑ *I could happily move back into a flat if it wasn't for the fact that I'd miss my garden...* V n/-ing *He missed having good friends.* V n/-ing [8] VERB ≠ catch If you **miss** something such as a plane or train, you arrive too late to catch it. ❑ *He just missed the last bus home.* V n [9] VERB If you **miss** something such as a meeting or an activity, you do not go to it or take part in it. ❑ *It's a pity Makku and I had to miss our lesson last week...* V n *'Are you coming to the show?' — 'I wouldn't miss it for the world.'* V n [10] PHRASE: V inflects If you **give** something **a miss**, you decide not to do it or not to go to it. [BRIT, INFORMAL] ❑ *Do you mind if I give it a miss?* [11] ➔ See also **missing**, **hit and miss**, **near miss**. **to miss the boat** ➔ see **boat**. **not to miss a trick** ➔ see **trick**.

♦ **miss out** [1] PHRASAL VERB = lose out If you **miss out on** something that would be enjoyable or useful to you, you are not involved in it or do not take part in it. ❑ *We're missing out on a tremendous opportunity...* V P *on* n *Well, I'm glad you could make it. I didn't want you to miss out.* V P [2] PHRASAL VERB = leave out If you **miss out** something or someone, you fail to include them. [BRIT] ❑ *There should be an apostrophe here, and look, you've missed out the word 'men' altogether!...* V P n (not pron) *What about Sally? You've missed her out.* V n P

| ✔ in AM, use **leave out** |
|---|

**mis-sell** **(mis-sells, mis-selling, mis-sold)** VERB To **mis-sell** something such as a pension or an insurance policy means to sell it to someone even though you know that it is not suitable for them. [BUSINESS] ❑ *The company has been accused of mis-selling products to thousands of elderly investors.* V n

**mis|shap|en** /mɪsʃe̱ɪpən/ ADJ If you describe something as **misshapen**, you think that it does not have a normal or natural shape. ❑ *...misshapen vegetables... Her hands were misshapen by arthritis.*

**mis|sile** /mɪ̱saɪl, AM -sᵊl/ **(missiles)** ◆◇◇ [1] N-COUNT A **missile** is a tube-shaped weapon that travels long distances through the air and explodes when it reaches its target. ❑ *The authorities offered to stop firing missiles if the rebels agreed to stop attacking civilian targets. ...nuclear missiles.* [2] N-COUNT Anything that is thrown as a weapon can be called a **missile**. ❑ *The football supporters began throwing missiles, one of which hit the referee.* [3] ➔ See also **cruise missile**, **guided missile**.

**miss|ing** /mɪ̱sɪŋ/ ◆◇◇ [1] ADJ: usu v-link ADJ If something is **missing**, it is not in its usual place, and you cannot find it. ❑ *It was only an hour or so later that I discovered that my gun was missing... The playing cards had gone missing.* [2] ADJ If a part of something is **missing**, it has been removed or has come off, and has not been replaced. ❑ *Three buttons were missing from his shirt.* [3] ADJ: usu v-link ADJ, oft ADJ *from* n If you say that something is **missing**, you mean that it has not been included, and you think that it should have been. ❑ *She had given me an incomplete list. One name was missing from it.* [4] ADJ Someone who is **missing** cannot be found, and it is not known whether they are alive or dead. ❑ *Five people died in the explosion and more than one thousand were injured. One person is still missing.* ● PHRASE: usu v-link PHR If a member of the armed forces is **missing in action**, they have not returned from a battle, their body has not been found, and they are not thought to have been captured.

**miss|ing link** **(missing links)** N-COUNT: usu sing The **missing link** in a situation is the piece of information or evidence that you need in order to make your knowledge or understanding of something complete. ❑ *We're dealing with probably the biggest missing link in what we know about human evolution.*

**miss|ing per|son** **(missing persons)** N-COUNT A **missing person** has suddenly left their home without telling their family where they are going, and it is not known whether they are alive or dead.

**mis|sion** /mɪ̱ʃᵊn/ **(missions)** ◆◆◇ [1] N-COUNT: usu with supp A **mission** is an important task that people are given to do, especially one that involves travelling to another country. ❑ *Salisbury sent him on a diplomatic mission to North America. ...the most crucial stage of his latest peace mission.* [2] N-COUNT: usu with supp = delegation A **mission** is a group of people who have been sent to a foreign country to carry out an official task. ❑ *...a senior member of a diplomatic mission.* [3] N-COUNT: usu supp N A **mission** is a special journey made by a military aeroplane or space rocket. ❑ *...a bomber that crashed during a training mission in the west Texas mountains. ...the first shuttle mission.* [4] N-SING: usu poss N, also n *of* N = vocation If you say that you have a **mission**, you mean that you have a strong commitment and sense of duty to do or achieve something. ❑ *He viewed his mission in life as protecting the weak from the evil.* [5] N-COUNT A **mission** is the activities of a group of Christians who have been sent to a place to teach people about Christianity. ❑ *They say God spoke to* *them and told them to go on a mission to the poorest country in the Western Hemisphere.*

**mis|sion|ary** /mɪʃənri, -neri/ **(missionaries)** [1] A **missionary** is a Christian who has been sent to a foreign country to teach people about Christianity. N-COUNT [2] **Missionary** is used to describe the activities of missionaries. ❑ *You should be in missionary work.* ADJ: ADJ n [3] If you refer to someone's enthusiasm for an activity or belief as **missionary** zeal, you are emphasizing that they are very enthusiastic about it. ❑ *She had a kind of missionary zeal about bringing culture to the masses.* ADJ: ADJ n [emphasis]

**mis|sion|ary po|si|tion** The **missionary position** is a position for sexual intercourse in which the man lies on top of the woman and they are facing each other. N-SING: usu *the* N

**mis|sion con|trol** **Mission control** is the group of people on Earth who are in charge of a flight by a spacecraft, or the place where these people work. N-UNCOUNT

**mis|sion state|ment** **(mission statements)** A company's or organization's **mission statement** is a document which states what they aim to achieve and the kind of service they intend to provide. [BUSINESS] N-COUNT

**mis|sive** /mɪsɪv/ **(missives)** A **missive** is a letter or other message that someone sends. [HUMOROUS or LITERARY] ❑ *...the customary missive from your dear mother.* N-COUNT = epistle

**mis|spell** /mɪsspel/ **(misspells, misspelling, misspelled** or **misspelt)** If someone **misspells** a word, they spell it wrongly. ❑ *Sorry I misspelled your last name.* VERB V n ♦ **mis|spell|ing (misspellings)** *...a misspelling of the writer's name.* N-COUNT

**mis|spend** /mɪsspend/ **(misspends, misspending, misspent)** If you say that time or money **has been misspent**, you disapprove of the way in which it has been spent. ❑ *Much of the money was grossly misspent.* VERB [disapproval] = waste *be* V-ed

**mis|state** /mɪssteɪt/ **(misstates, misstating, misstated)** If you **misstate** something, you state it incorrectly or give false information about it. [mainly AM] ❑ *Look at the false police reports that omitted or misstated crucial facts... The amount was misstated in the table because of an error by regulators.* VERB V n *be* V-ed

**mis|state|ment** /mɪssteɪtmənt/ **(misstatements)** A **misstatement** is an incorrect statement, or the giving of false information. [mainly AM] ❑ *He finally corrected his misstatement and offered to reduce the fee... While this booklet has become an official source of information, it is filled with misstatements of fact.* N-COUNT

**mis|sus** /mɪsɪz/ also **missis.** [1] Some people refer to a man's wife as his **missus**. [INFORMAL] ❑ *That's what bugs my missus more than anything... I do a bit of shopping for the missus.* N-SING: poss/*the* N = old lady [2] In some parts of Britain, people use **missus** as a very informal way of addressing a woman who they do not know. ❑ *Thanks, missus.* N-VOC

**mist** /mɪst/ **(mists, misting, misted)** [1] **Mist** consists of a large number of tiny drops of water in the air, which make it difficult to see very far. ❑ *Thick mist made flying impossible... Mists and fog swirled about the road.* N-VAR [2] If a piece of glass **mists** or **is misted**, it becomes covered with tiny drops of moisture, so that you cannot see through it easily. ❑ *The windows misted, blurring the stark streetlight... The temperature in the car was misting the window.* VERB V V n ♦ **Mist over** and **mist up** mean the same as **mist**. ❑ *The front windshield was misting over... She stood in front of the misted-up mirror.* PHRASAL VERB V P V-ed P

♦ **mist over** → see **mist 2**.

♦ **mist up** → see **mist 2**.

**mis|take** /mɪsteɪk/ **(mistakes, mistaking, mistook, mistaken)** ◆◆◇ [1] If you make a **mistake**, you do something which you did not intend to do, or which produces a result that you do not want. ❑ *They made the big mistake of thinking they could seize its border with a relatively small force... I think it's a serious mistake to confuse books with life... There must be some mistake... He has been arrested by mistake.* N-COUNT: oft N *of* -ing, also *by* N [2] A **mistake** is something or part of something which is incorrect or not right. ❑ *Her mother sighed and rubbed out another mistake in the crossword puzzle. ...spelling mistakes.* N-COUNT = error [3] If you **mistake** one person or thing **for** another, you wrongly think that they are the other person or thing. ❑ *I mistook you for Carlos.* VERB V n *for* n [4] If you **mistake** something, you fail to recognize or understand it. ❑ *The government completely mistook the feeling of the country... No one should mistake how serious the issue is.* VERB = misjudge V n V wh [5] You can say **there is no mistaking** something when you are emphasizing that you cannot fail to recognize or understand it. ❑ *There's no mistaking the eastern flavour of the food.* PHRASE: V inflects, PHR n [emphasis]

**mis|tak|en** /mɪsteɪkən/ [1] If you are **mistaken about** something, you are wrong about it. ❑ *I see I was mistaken about you... You couldn't be more mistaken, Alex. You've utterly misread the situation.* ADJ: v-link ADJ, oft ADJ *about* n = wrong ● You use expressions such as **if I'm not mistaken** and **unless I'm very much mistaken** as a polite way of emphasizing the statement you are making, especially when you are confident that it is correct. ❑ *I think he wanted to marry her, if I am not mistaken... Unless I'm mistaken, he didn't specify what time.* PHRASE: PHR with cl [emphasis] [2] A **mistaken** belief or opinion is incorrect. ❑ *...a limited understanding of addiction and mistaken beliefs about how it can be overcome.* ADJ: ADJ n ♦ **mis|tak|en|ly** *He says they mistakenly believed the standard licenses they held were sufficient.* ADV: ADV with v

**mis|tak|en iden|tity** When someone incorrectly thinks that they have found or recognized a particular person, you refer to this as a case of **mistaken identity**. ❑ *The dead men could have been the victims of mistaken identity. Their attackers may have wrongly believed them to be soldiers.* N-UNCOUNT

**mis|ter** /mɪstəʳ/ Men are sometimes addressed as **mister**, especially by children and especially when the person talking to them does not know their name. [INFORMAL] ❑ *Look, Mister, we know our job, so don't try to tell us what to do.* N-VOC

**mis|time** /mɪstaɪm/ **(mistimes, mistiming, mistimed)** If you **mistime** something, you do it at the wrong time, so that it is not successful. ❑ *You're bound to mistime a tackle every so often. ...a certain mistimed comment.* VERB V n V-ed

**mis|tle|toe** /mɪsəltoʊ/ **Mistletoe** is a plant with pale berries that grows on the branches of some trees. Mistletoe is used in Britain and the United States as a Christmas decoration, and people often kiss under it. N-UNCOUNT

**mis|took** /mɪstʊk/ **Mistook** is the past tense and past participle of **mistake**.

**mis|treat** /mɪstriːt/ **(mistreats, mistreating, mistreated)** If someone **mistreats** a person or an animal, they treat them badly, especially by making them suffer physically. ❑ *She has been mistreated by men in the past.* VERB = ill-treat *be* V-ed

**mis|treat|ment** /mɪstriːtmənt/ **Mistreatment** of a person or animal is cruel behaviour towards them, especially by making them suffer physically. ❑ *...issues like police brutality and mistreatment of people in prisons.* N-UNCOUNT = maltreatment

**mis|tress** /mɪstrəs/ **(mistresses)** [1] A married man's **mistress** is a woman who is not his wife and with whom he is having a sexual relationship. [OLD-FASHIONED] ❑ *She was his mistress for three years.* N-COUNT: usu with poss [2] A dog's **mistress** is the woman or girl who owns it. ❑ *The huge wolfhound danced in circles around his mistress.* N-COUNT: usu poss N

**mis|tri|al** /mɪstraɪəl, AM -traɪ-/ **(mistrials)** [1] A **mistrial** is a legal trial that is conducted unfairly, for example because not all the evidence is considered, so that there must be a new trial. ❑ *The past has been scarred by countless mistrials and perversions of justice.* N-COUNT [2] A **mistrial** is a legal trial which ends without a verdict, for example because the jury cannot agree on one. [AM] ❑ *The judge said he would declare a mistrial if the jury did not reach its verdict today.* N-COUNT

**mis|trust** /mɪstrʌst/ **(mistrusts, mistrusting, mistrusted)** [1] **Mistrust** is the feeling that you have towards someone who you do not trust. ❑ *There was mutual mistrust between the two men. ...a deep mistrust of state banks.* [2] If you **mistrust** someone or something, you do not trust them. ❑ *It appears that Bell mistrusts all journalists.*
N-UNCOUNT = *distrust*; VERB = *distrust*; V n

**mis|trust|ful** /mɪstrʌstfʊl/ If you are **mistrustful** of someone, you do not trust them. ❑ *He had always been mistrustful of women.*
ADJ: oft ADJ *of* n = *distrustful*

**misty** /mɪsti/ On a **misty** day, there is a lot of mist in the air. ❑ *The air was cold and misty.*
ADJ: oft *it* v-link ADJ

**misty-eyed** If you say that something makes you **misty-eyed**, you mean that it makes you feel so happy or sentimental, especially about the past, that you feel as if you are going to cry. ❑ *They got misty-eyed listening to records of Ruby Murray singing 'Danny Boy'.*
ADJ: usu v-link ADJ

**mis|under|stand** /mɪsʌndəʳstænd/ **(misunderstands, misunderstanding, misunderstood)** If you **misunderstand** someone or something, you do not understand them properly. ❑ *They have simply misunderstood what rock and roll is... Maybe I misunderstood you.* ➔ See also **misunderstood**.
VERB; V wh; V n
● You can say **don't misunderstand me** when you want to correct a wrong impression that you think someone may have got about what you are saying. ❑ *I'm not saying what he did was good, don't misunderstand me.*
CONVENTION

**mis|under|stand|ing** /mɪsʌndəʳstændɪŋ/ **(misunderstandings)** [1] A **misunderstanding** is a failure to understand something properly, for example a situation or a person's remarks. ❑ *Tell your midwife what you want to so she can make a note of it and avoid misunderstandings.* [2] You can refer to a disagreement or slight quarrel as a **misunderstanding**. [FORMAL] ❑ *...a little misunderstanding with the police.*
N-VAR; N-COUNT

**mis|under|stood** /mɪsʌndəʳstʊd/ [1] **Misunderstood** is the past tense and past participle of **misunderstand**. [2] If you describe someone or something as **misunderstood**, you mean that people do not understand them and have a wrong impression or idea of them. ❑ *Eric is very badly misunderstood... The cost of capital is widely misunderstood.*
ADJ

**mis|use** **(misuses, misusing, misused)**

> The noun is pronounced /mɪsjuːs/. The verb is pronounced /mɪsjuːz/.

[1] The **misuse** of something is incorrect, careless, or dishonest use of it. ❑ *...the misuse of power and privilege... The effectiveness of this class of drug has, however, led to their misuse.* [2] If someone **misuses** something, they use it incorrectly, carelessly, or dishonestly. ❑ *You are protected instantly if a thief misuses your credit card.*
N-VAR: usu with supp, oft N *of* n; VERB; V n

**mite** /maɪt/ **(mites)** [1] **A mite** means to a small extent or degree. It is sometimes used to make a statement less extreme. ❑ *I can't help feeling just a mite uneasy about it.* [2] **Mites** are very tiny creatures that live on plants, for example, or in animals' fur. *...an itching skin disorder caused by parasitic mites.*
PHRASE: PHR adj/adv = *a bit, a touch*; N-COUNT: usu pl

**miti|gate** /mɪtɪgeɪt/ **(mitigates, mitigating, mitigated)** To **mitigate** something means to make it less unpleasant, serious, or painful. [FORMAL] ❑ *...ways of mitigating the effects of an explosion.*
VERB = *alleviate*; V n

**miti|gat|ing** /mɪtɪgeɪtɪŋ/ **Mitigating** circumstances or factors make a bad action, especially a crime, easier to understand and excuse, and may result in the person responsible being punished less severely. [LEGAL or FORMAL] ❑ *The judge found that in her case there were mitigating circumstances... There are various mitigating factors.*
ADJ: ADJ n

**miti|ga|tion** /mɪtɪgeɪʃᵊn/ [1] If someone, especially in a court, is told something **in mitigation**, they are told something that makes a crime or fault easier to understand and excuse. [FORMAL] ❑ *Kieran Coonan QC told the judge in mitigation that the offences had been at the lower end of the scale.* [2] **Mitigation** is a reduction in the unpleasantness, seriousness, or painfulness of something. [FORMAL] ❑ *...the mitigation or cure of a physical or mental condition.*
PHRASE: PHR with cl; N-UNCOUNT = *alleviation*

**mitt** /mɪt/ **(mitts)** [1] You can refer to a person's hands as their **mitts**. [INFORMAL] ❑ *I pressed a dime into his grubby mitt.* [2] A baseball **mitt** is a large glove worn by a player whose job involves catching the ball.
N-COUNT = *paw*; N-COUNT: usu supp N

**mit|ten** /mɪtᵊn/ **(mittens)** **Mittens** are gloves which have one section that covers your thumb and another section that covers your four fingers together.
N-COUNT: usu pl

**mix** /mɪks/ **(mixes, mixing, mixed)** [1] If two substances **mix** or if you **mix** one substance **with** another, you stir or shake them together, or combine them in some other way, so that they become a single substance. ❑ *Oil and water don't mix... It mixes easily with cold or hot water to make a tasty, filling drink... A quick stir will mix them thoroughly... Mix the cinnamon with the rest of the sugar... Mix the ingredients together slowly.* ♦ **mix|ing** *This final part of the mixing is done slowly and delicately.* [2] If you **mix** something, you prepare it by mixing other things together. ❑ *He had spent several hours mixing cement... Are you sure I can't mix you a drink?* [3] A **mix** is a powder containing all the substances that you need in order to make something such as a cake or a sauce. When you want to use it, you add liquid. ❑ *For speed we used packets of pizza dough mix.* [4] A **mix of** different things or people is two or more of them together. ❑ *The story is a magical mix of fantasy and reality... We get a very representative mix of people.* [5] If two things or activities do not **mix** or if one thing does not **mix with** another, it is not a good idea to have them or do them together, because the result would be unpleasant or dangerous. ❑ *Politics and sport don't mix. ...some of these pills that don't mix with drink... Ted managed to mix business with pleasure... The military has accused the clergy of mixing religion and politics.* [6] If you **mix with** other people, you meet them and talk to them. You can also say that people **mix**. ❑ *I ventured the idea that the secret of staying young was to mix with older people... People are supposed to mix, do you understand?... When you came away you made a definite effort to mix.* [7] When a record producer **mixes** a piece of music, he or she puts together the various sounds that have been recorded in order to make the finished record. ❑ *They've been mixing tracks for a new album due out later this year.* ♦ **mix|ing** *Final mixing should be completed by the end of this week.* [8] ➔ See also **mixed**, **cake mix**. to **mix** your **metaphors** ➔ see **metaphor**.
◆◆◇ V-RECIP; pl-n V; V *with* n; V pl-n; V n *with* n; V n with adv; N-UNCOUNT; VERB; V n; V n n; N-VAR: usu supp N; N-COUNT: usu sing, with supp; V-RECIP: usu with brd-neg; pl-n V; V *with* n; V n *with* n; V pl-n; V-RECIP = *socialize*; V *with* n; pl-n V; V (non-recip); VERB; V n; N-UNCOUNT

♦ **mix up** [1] If you **mix up** two things or people, you confuse them, so that you think that one of them is the other one. ❑ *People often mix me up with other actors... Depressed people may mix up their words... Any time you told one of them something, they'd swear you'd mixed them up and told the other.* [2] If you **mix up** a number of things, you put things of different kinds together or place things so that they are not in order. ❑ *I like to mix up designer clothes... Part of the plan was that the town should not fall into office, industrial and residential zones, but mix the three up together... This is music from a different era. I've taken those sounds from childhood and mixed them up with other things.* [3] ➔ See also **mixed up**, **mix-up**.
PHRASAL VERB; V n P *with* n; V P pl-n (not pron); V pl-n P; PHRASAL VERB; V P pl-n (not pron); V pl-n P; V n P *with* n

**mixed** /mɪkst/ [1] If you have **mixed** feelings about something or someone, you feel uncertain about them because you can see both good and bad points about them. ❑ *I came home from the meeting with mixed feelings... There has been a very mixed reaction to the decision.* [2] A **mixed** group of people consists of people of many different types. ❑ *I found a very mixed group of individuals some of whom I could relate to and others with whom I had very little in common.* [3] **Mixed** is used to describe something that involves people from two
◆◇◇ ADJ: usu ADJ n; ADJ; ADJ: usu ADJ n

or more different races. ❑ *...a woman of mixed race... She had attended a racially mixed school.* 4 **Mixed** education or accommodation is intended for both males and females. ❑ *Girls who have always been at a mixed school know how to stand up for themselves.* 5 **Mixed** is used to describe something which includes or consists of different things of the same general kind. ❑ *...a small mixed salad. ...a teaspoon of mixed herbs.* 6 **a mixed blessing** → see **blessing**. ADJ: usu ADJ n / ADJ: ADJ n

**mixed abil|ity** A **mixed ability** class or teaching system is one in which pupils are taught together in the same class, even though their abilities are different. [BRIT] ADJ: usu ADJ n

**mixed bag** If you describe a situation or a group of things or people as **a mixed bag**, you mean that it contains some good items, features, or people and some bad ones. ❑ *Research on athletes has yielded a mixed bag of results... This autumn's collections are a very mixed bag.* N-SING: usu *a* N, oft N *of* n

**mixed dou|bles** In some sports, such as tennis and badminton, **mixed doubles** is a match in which a man and a woman play as partners against another man and woman. N-UNCOUNT: also *the* N

**mixed econo|my** **(mixed economies)** A **mixed economy** is an economic system in which some companies are owned by the state and some are not. [BUSINESS] N-COUNT

**mixed mar|riage** **(mixed marriages)** A **mixed marriage** is a marriage between two people who are not of the same race or religion. N-COUNT

**mixed up** 1 If you are **mixed up**, you are confused, often because of emotional or social problems. ❑ *I think he's a rather mixed up kid.* ADJ
2 To be **mixed up in** something bad, or **with** someone you disapprove of, means to be involved in it or with them. ❑ *Why did I ever get mixed up with you?* ADJ: v-link ADJ *in/with* n

**mix|er** /mɪksəʳ/ **(mixers)** 1 A **mixer** is a machine used for mixing things together. ❑ *...an electric mixer.* → See also **cement mixer**, **food mixer**. N-COUNT: usu supp N
2 A **mixer** is a non-alcoholic drink such as fruit juice that you mix with strong alcohol such as gin. N-COUNT 3 If you say that someone is a good **mixer**, you mean that they are good at talking to people and making friends. ❑ *Cooper was a good mixer, he was popular.* N-COUNT: adj N 4 A **mixer** is a piece of equipment that is used to make changes to recorded music or film. ❑ *...a three channel audio mixer.* N-COUNT: usu with supp

**mix|ing bowl** **(mixing bowls)** A **mixing bowl** is a large bowl used for mixing ingredients. N-COUNT

**mix|ture** /mɪkstʃəʳ/ **(mixtures)** 1 A **mixture of** things consists of several different things together. ❑ *They looked at him with a mixture of horror, envy, and awe. ...a mixture of spiced, grilled vegetables served cold.* 2 A **mixture** is a substance that consists of other substances which have been stirred or shaken together. ❑ *Prepare the gravy mixture. ...a mixture of water and sugar and salt.* → See also **cough mixture**. ◆◇◇ N-SING: usu N *of* pl-n / N-COUNT: oft supp N, N *of* n

**mix-up** **(mix-ups)** A **mix-up** is a mistake or a failure in the way that something has been planned. [INFORMAL] ❑ *...a mix-up over travel arrangements.* N-COUNT

**Mk** **Mk** is a written abbreviation for **mark**. **Mk** is used to refer to a particular model or design of a car or machine. ❑ *...a 1974 white MG Midget Mk 3.*

**ml** **ml** is a written abbreviation for **millilitre** or **millilitres**. ❑ *Boil the sugar and 100 ml of water.*

**MLA** /em el eɪ/ **(MLAs)** In Australia and some other countries, an **MLA** is a person who has been elected as a member of parliament. **MLA** is an abbreviation for 'member of the legislative assembly'. N-COUNT

**mm** **mm** is an abbreviation for **millimetre** or **millimetres**. ❑ *...a 135mm lens. ...0.25mm of rain.* ◆◇◇

**mne|mon|ic** /nɪmɒnɪk/ **(mnemonics)** A **mnemonic** is a word, short poem, or sentence that is intended to help you remember things such as scientific rules or spelling rules. For example, 'i before e, except after c' is a mnemonic to help people remember how to spell words like 'believe' and 'receive'. ❑ *...mnemonic devices.* N-COUNT: oft N n

**mo** /moʊ/ A **mo** is a very short length of time. It is short for **moment**. [BRIT, INFORMAL, SPOKEN] ❑ *Hang on a mo.* N-SING: *a* N = sec, tick

**moan** /moʊn/ **(moans, moaning, moaned)** 1 If you **moan**, you make a low sound, usually because you are unhappy or in pain. ❑ *Tony moaned in his sleep and then turned over on his side... 'My head, my head,' he moaned. 'I can't see.'* ♦ **Moan** is also a noun. ❑ *Suddenly she gave a low, choking moan and began to tremble violently.* 2 To **moan** means to complain or speak in a way which shows that you are very unhappy. ❑ *I used to moan if I didn't get at least six hours' sleep at night. ...moaning about the weather... Meg moans, 'I hated it!'... The gardener was moaning that he had another garden to do later that morning.* 3 A **moan** is a complaint. [INFORMAL] ❑ *They have been listening to people's gripes, moans and praise.* 4 If you **have a moan**, you complain about something. [INFORMAL] ❑ *You can go see him and have a good old moan.* 5 A **moan** is a low noise. [LITERARY] ❑ *...the occasional moan of the wind round the house.* VERB = groan / V / V with quote / N-COUNT / VERB disapproval / V / V prep/adv / V with quote / V that / N-COUNT / PHRASE: V inflects / N-COUNT: usu with supp

**moan|er** /moʊnəʳ/ **(moaners)** If you refer to someone as a **moaner**, you are critical of them because they often complain about things. [INFORMAL] ❑ *Film critics are dreadful moaners.* N-COUNT disapproval

**moat** /moʊt/ **(moats)** A **moat** is a deep, wide channel dug round a place such as a castle and filled with water, in order to protect the place from attack. N-COUNT

**mob** /mɒb/ **(mobs, mobbing, mobbed)** 1 A **mob** is a large, disorganized, and often violent crowd of people. ❑ *The inspectors watched a growing mob of demonstrators gathering.* 2 People sometimes use **the mob** to refer in a disapproving way to the majority of people in a country or place, especially when these people are behaving in a violent or uncontrolled way. ❑ *If they continue like this there is a danger of the mob taking over.* 3 You can refer to the people involved in organized crime as **the Mob**. [INFORMAL] ❑ *...casinos that the Mob had operated.* 4 If you say that someone **is being mobbed by** a crowd of people, you mean that the people are trying to talk to them or get near them in an enthusiastic or threatening way. ❑ *They found themselves being mobbed in the street for autographs.* N-COUNT / N-SING: *the* N, N n disapproval / N-SING: usu *the* N, N n / VERB: usu passive / *be* V-ed

**mo|bile** /moʊbaɪl, AM -bəl/ **(mobiles)** 1 You use **mobile** to describe something large that can be moved easily from place to place. ❑ *...the four hundred seat mobile theatre.* 2 If you are **mobile**, you can move or travel easily from place to place, for example because you are not physically disabled or because you have your own transport. ❑ *I'm still very mobile.* ♦ **mo|bil|ity** /moʊbɪlɪti/ ❑ *Two cars gave them the freedom and mobility to go their separate ways.* 3 In a **mobile** society, people move easily from one job, home, or social class to another. ❑ *We're a very mobile society, and people move after they get divorced. ...young, mobile professionals.* ♦ **mo|bil|ity** *Prior to the nineteenth century, there were almost no channels of social mobility.* 4 A **mobile** is a decoration which you hang from a ceiling. It usually consists of several small objects which move as the air around them moves. 5 A **mobile** is the same as a **mobile phone**. 6 → See also **upwardly mobile**. ◆◇◇ ADJ: usu ADJ n / ADJ: usu v-link ADJ / N-UNCOUNT / ADJ / N-UNCOUNT / N-COUNT / N-COUNT

**mo|bile home** **(mobile homes)** A **mobile home** is a large caravan that people live in and that usually remains in the same place, but which can be pulled to another place using a car or van. N-COUNT

**mo|bile phone** **(mobile phones)** A **mobile phone** is a telephone that you can carry with you and use to make or receive calls wherever you are. [BRIT] N-COUNT

✔ in AM, use **cellular phone**, **cellphone**

**mo|bi|lize** /moʊbɪlaɪz/ **(mobilizes, mobilizing, mobilized)**

☑ in BRIT, also use **mobilise**

1 If you **mobilize** support or **mobilize** people to do something, you succeed in encouraging people to take action, especially political action. If people **mobilize**, they prepare to take action. ❑ *The best hope is that we will mobilize international support and get down to action... Faced with crisis, people mobilized.* ♦ **mo|bi|li|za|tion** /moʊbɪlaɪzeɪʃᵊn/ *...the rapid mobilization of international opinion in support of the revolution.* VERB V n V N-UNCOUNT: oft N *of* n
2 If you **mobilize** resources, you start to use them or make them available for use. ❑ *If you could mobilize the resources, you could get it done.* ♦ **mo|bi|li|za|tion** *...the mobilisation of resources for education.* VERB V n N-UNCOUNT: oft N *of* n
3 If a country **mobilizes**, or **mobilizes** its armed forces, or if its armed forces **mobilize**, they are given orders to prepare for a conflict. [JOURNALISM or MILITARY] ❑ *Sudan even threatened to mobilize in response to the ultimatums... India is now in a better position to mobilise its forces.* ♦ **mo|bi|li|za|tion** *...a demand for full-scale mobilisation to defend the republic.* VERB V V n N-UNCOUNT

**mob|ster** /mɒbstəʳ/ **(mobsters)** A **mobster** is someone who is a member of an organized group of violent criminals. N-COUNT = *gangster*

**moc|ca|sin** /mɒkəsɪn/ **(moccasins) Moccasins** are soft leather shoes which have a low heel and a raised join round the top of the front part. N-COUNT

**mock** /mɒk/ **(mocks, mocking, mocked)** 1 If someone **mocks** you, they show or pretend that they think you are foolish or inferior, for example by saying something funny about you, or by imitating your behaviour. ❑ *I thought you were mocking me... 'I'm astonished, Benjamin,' she mocked.* VERB V n V with quote
2 You use **mock** to describe something which is not real or genuine, but which is intended to be very similar to the real thing. ❑ *'It's tragic!' swoons Jeffrey in mock horror.* ADJ: ADJ n
3 **Mocks** are practice exams that you take as part of your preparation for real exams. [BRIT, INFORMAL] ❑ *She went from a D in her mocks to a B in the real thing.* N-COUNT: usu pl

**mock|ery** /mɒkəri/ 1 If someone mocks you, you can refer to their behaviour or attitude as **mockery**. ❑ *Was there a glint of mockery in his eyes?* N-UNCOUNT
2 If something makes **a mockery of** something, it makes it appear worthless and foolish. ❑ *This action makes a mockery of the Government's continuing protestations of concern.* N-SING

**mock|ing** /mɒkɪŋ/ A **mocking** expression or **mocking** behaviour indicates that you think someone or something is stupid or inferior. ❑ *She gave a mocking smile... Behind the mocking laughter lurks a growing sense of unease.* ADJ

**mocking|bird** /mɒkɪŋbɜːʳd/ **(mockingbirds)** A **mockingbird** is a grey bird with a long tail which is found in North America. Mockingbirds are able to copy the songs of other birds. N-COUNT

**mock-up (mock-ups)** A **mock-up of** something such as a machine or building is a model of it which is used in tests or to show people what it will look like. ❑ *There's a mock-up of the high street where the Goodwins go shopping.* N-COUNT: oft N *of* n

**mod** /mɒd/ **(mods) Mods** are young people in Britain who wear a special kind of neat clothes, ride motor scooters, and like soul music. Many young people were mods in the early 1960s. N-COUNT

**mod|al** /moʊdᵊl/ **(modals)** In grammar, a **modal** or a **modal auxiliary** is a word such as 'can' or 'would' which is used with a main verb to express ideas such as possibility, intention, or necessity. [TECHNICAL] N-COUNT

**mod cons Mod cons** are the modern facilities in a house that make it easy and pleasant to live in. [BRIT, INFORMAL] ❑ *The house is spacious with all mod cons, handy for the station and has a garden.* N-PLURAL

**mode** /moʊd/ **(modes)** 1 A **mode** of life or behaviour is a particular way of living or behaving. [FORMAL] ❑ *He switched automatically into interview mode.* N-COUNT: usu N *of* n
2 A **mode** is a particular style in art, literature, or dress. ❑ *...a slightly more elegant and formal mode of dress.* N-COUNT: usu with supp
3 On some cameras or electronic devices, the different **modes** available are the different programs or settings that you can choose when you use them. ❑ *...when the camera is in manual mode.* N-COUNT: usu supp N

**mod|el** /mɒdᵊl/ **(models, modelling, modelled)** ◆◆◇

☑ in AM, use **modeling, modeled**

1 A **model** of an object is a physical representation that shows what it looks like or how it works. The model is often smaller than the object it represents. ❑ *...an architect's model of a wooden house. ...a working scale model of the whole Bay Area... I made a model out of paper and glue.* ♦ **Model** is also an adjective. ❑ *I had made a model aeroplane. ...a model railway.* N-COUNT: oft N *of* n ADJ: ADJ n
2 A **model** is a system that is being used and that people might want to copy in order to achieve similar results. [FORMAL] ❑ *He wants companies to follow the European model of social responsibility.* N-COUNT: with supp
3 A **model** of a system or process is a theoretical description that can help you understand how the system or process works, or how it might work. [TECHNICAL or FORMAL] ❑ *Darwin eventually put forward a model of biological evolution.* N-COUNT: usu with supp
4 If someone such as a scientist **models** a system or process, they make an accurate theoretical description of it in order to understand or explain how it works. [TECHNICAL or FORMAL] ❑ *...the mathematics needed to model a nonlinear system like an atmosphere.* VERB V n
5 If you say that someone or something is **a model of** a particular quality, you are showing approval of them because they have that quality to a large degree. ❑ *A model of good manners, he has conquered any inward fury.* N-COUNT: N *of* n [approval]
6 You use **model** to express approval of someone when you think that they perform their role or duties extremely well. ❑ *As a girl she had been a model pupil.* ADJ: ADJ n [approval] = *exemplary*
7 If one thing **is modelled on** another, the first thing is made so that it is like the second thing in some way. ❑ *The quota system was modelled on those operated in America and continental Europe... She asked the author if she had modelled her hero on anybody in particular.* VERB *be* V-ed *on/after* n V n *on/after* n
8 If you **model** yourself **on** someone, you copy the way that they do things, because you admire them and want to be like them. ❑ *There's absolutely nothing wrong in modelling yourself on an older woman... They will tend to model their behaviour on the teacher's behaviour.* VERB V pron-refl *on/after* n V n *on/after* n
9 A particular **model** of a machine is a particular version of it. ❑ *To keep the cost down, opt for a basic model... The model number is 1870/285.* N-COUNT: usu supp N
10 An artist's **model** is a person who stays still in a particular position so that the artist can make a picture or sculpture of them. N-COUNT
11 If someone **models** for an artist, they stay still in a particular position so that the artist can make a picture or sculpture of them. ❑ *Tullio has been modelling for Sandra for eleven years.* VERB V *for* n Also V
12 A fashion **model** is a person whose job is to display clothes by wearing them. ❑ *...Paris's top photographic fashion model.* N-COUNT
13 If someone **models** clothes, they display them by wearing them. ❑ *I wasn't here to model clothes... She began modelling in Paris aged 15.* ♦ **mod|el|ling** *She was being offered a 12 month modelling contract.* VERB V n V N-UNCOUNT: oft N n
14 If you **model** shapes or figures, you make them out of a substance such as clay or wood. ❑ *There she began to model in clay... Sometimes she carved wood and sometimes stone; sometimes she modelled clay.* VERB V V n
15 → See also **role model**.

**mod|el|ler** /mɒdələʳ/ **(modellers)**

☑ in AM, use **modeler**

1 A **modeller** is someone who makes shapes or figures out of substances such as wood or clay. N-COUNT
2 A **modeller** is someone who makes theoretical descriptions of systems or processes in order to N-COUNT: usu supp N

understand them and be able to predict how they will develop. ❑ *...climate modellers.*

**mo|dem** /moʊdem/ **(modems)** A **modem** is a device which uses a telephone line to connect computers or computer systems. [COMPUTING] ❑ *He sent his work to his publishers by modem.* N-COUNT: also *by* N

**mod|er|ate** **(moderates, moderating, moderated)** ◆◇◇

> The adjective and noun are pronounced /mɒdərət/. The verb is pronounced /mɒdəreɪt/.

1 **Moderate** political opinions or policies are not extreme. ❑ *He was an easygoing man of very moderate views... Both countries have called for a moderate approach to the use of force.* ADJ ≠ extreme 2 You use **moderate** to describe people or groups who have moderate political opinions or policies. ❑ *...a moderate Democrat. ...the moderate wing of the army.* ADJ ♦ A **moderate** is someone with moderate political opinions. ❑ *If he presents himself as a radical he risks scaring off the moderates.* N-COUNT 3 You use **moderate** to describe something that is neither large nor small in amount or degree. ❑ *While a moderate amount of stress can be beneficial, too much stress can exhaust you. ...moderate exercise.* ADJ: usu ADJ n = reasonable ≠ excessive ♦ **mod|er|ate|ly** *Both are moderately large insects... I don't smoke and I drink only moderately.* ADV: usu ADV adj/-ed, also ADV after v 4 A **moderate** change in something is a change that is not great. ❑ *Most drugs offer either no real improvement or, at best, only moderate improvements.* ADJ ♦ **mod|er|ate|ly** *Share prices on the Tokyo Exchange declined moderately.* ADV: ADV after v 5 If you **moderate** something or if it **moderates**, it becomes less extreme or violent and easier to deal with or accept. ❑ *They are hoping that once in office he can be persuaded to moderate his views...* VERB V n *Amongst relief workers, the immediate sense of crisis has moderated somewhat.* V ♦ **mod|era|tion** /mɒdəreɪʃᵊn/ *A moderation in food prices helped to offset the first increase in energy prices.* N-UNCOUNT: oft N *of/in* n

**mod|era|tion** /mɒdəreɪʃᵊn/ 1 If you say that someone's behaviour shows **moderation**, you approve of them because they act in a way that you think is reasonable and not extreme. ❑ *The United Nations Secretary General called on all parties to show moderation.* N-UNCOUNT approval = restraint ● If you say that someone does something such as eat, drink, or smoke **in moderation**, you mean that they do not eat, smoke, or drink too much or more than is reasonable. ❑ *Many adults are able to drink in moderation, but others become dependent on alcohol.* PHRASE: PHR after v 2 ➔ See also **moderate**.

**mod|era|tor** /mɒdəreɪtəʳ/ **(moderators)** 1 In some Protestant churches, a **moderator** is a senior member of the clergy who is in charge at large and important meetings. ❑ *...a former moderator of the General Assembly of the Church of Scotland.* N-COUNT 2 In debates and negotiations, the **moderator** is the person who is in charge of the discussion and makes sure that it is conducted in a fair and organized way. [FORMAL] N-COUNT = chair

**mod|ern** /mɒdəʳn/ 1 **Modern** means relating to the present time, for example the present decade or present century. ❑ *...the problem of materialism in modern society. ...the risks facing every modern marriage.* ◆◆◇ ADJ: ADJ n = contemporary 2 Something that is **modern** is new and involves the latest ideas or equipment. ❑ *Modern technology has opened our eyes to many things... In many ways, it was a very modern school for its time.* ADJ ♦ **mo|der|nity** /mɒdɜːʳnɪti/ *...an office block that astonished the city with its modernity.* N-UNCOUNT 3 People are sometimes described as **modern** when they have opinions or ways of behaviour that have not yet been accepted by most people in a society. ❑ *She is very modern in outlook.* ADJ = progressive ≠ traditional 4 **Modern** is used to describe styles of art, dance, music, and architecture that have developed in recent times, in contrast to classical styles. ❑ *...a modern dance company. ...the Museum of Modern Art.* ADJ: ADJ n

**modern-day** **Modern-day** is used to refer to the new or modern aspects of a place, an activity, or a society. ❑ *...modern-day America. ...the by-products of modern-day living.* ADJ: ADJ n = contemporary

**mod|ern|ise** /mɒdəʳnaɪz/ ➔ see **modernize**.

**mod|ern|ism** /mɒdəʳnɪzəm/ **Modernism** was a movement in the arts in the first half of the twentieth century that rejected traditional values and techniques, and emphasized the importance of individual experience. ➔ See also **post-modernism**. N-UNCOUNT

**mod|ern|ist** /mɒdəʳnɪst/ **(modernists)** **Modernist** means relating to the ideas and methods of modern art. ❑ *...modernist architecture. ...modernist art.* ➔ See also **post-modernist**. ADJ: usu ADJ n

**mod|ern|is|tic** /mɒdəʳnɪstɪk/ A **modernistic** building or piece of furniture looks very modern. ADJ ≠ old-fashioned

**mod|ern|ize** /mɒdəʳnaɪz/ **(modernizes, modernizing, modernized)**

> in BRIT, also use **modernise**

To **modernize** something such as a system or a factory means to change it by replacing old equipment or methods with new ones. ❑ *...plans to modernize the refinery.* VERB V n ♦ **mod|ern|iz|ing** *In effect, modernizing societies are portrayed as battlegrounds.* ADJ ♦ **mod|erni|za|tion** /mɒdəʳnaɪzeɪʃᵊn/ *...a five-year modernization programme.* N-UNCOUNT

**mod|ern|iz|er** /mɒdəʳnaɪzəʳ/ **(modernizers)**

> in BRIT, also use **moderniser**

A **modernizer** is someone who replaces old equipment or methods with new ones. N-COUNT

**mod|ern lan|guages** **Modern languages** refers to the modern European languages, for example French, German, and Russian, which are studied at school or university. ❑ *...head of modern languages at a London grammar school.* N-PLURAL

**mod|est** /mɒdɪst/ 1 A **modest** house or other building is not large or expensive. ❑ *...the modest home of a family who lived off the land... A one-night stay in a modest hotel costs around £35, including breakfast.* ◆◇◇ ADJ 2 You use **modest** to describe something such as an amount, rate, or improvement which is fairly small. ❑ *Swiss unemployment rose to the still modest rate of 0.7%... The democratic reforms have been modest.* ADJ ♦ **mod|est|ly** *Britain's balance of payments improved modestly last month.* ADV: ADV after v, ADV adj/-ed/adv 3 If you say that someone is **modest**, you approve of them because they do not talk much about their abilities or achievements. ❑ *He's modest, as well as being a great player.* ADJ approval ♦ **mod|est|ly** *'You really must be very good at what you do.' — 'I suppose I am,' Kate said modestly.* ADV: ADV with v 4 You can describe a woman as **modest** when she avoids doing or wearing anything that might cause men to have sexual feelings towards her. You can also describe her clothes or behaviour as **modest**. ❑ *Asian women are more modest and shy, yet they tend to have an inner force.* ADJ ♦ **mod|est|ly** *She sat down cautiously on the red canvas cushions, knees modestly together.* ADV: ADV with v, ADV adj/adv

**mod|es|ty** /mɒdɪsti/ 1 Someone who shows **modesty** does not talk much about their abilities or achievements. ❑ *His modesty does him credit, for the food he produces speaks for itself.* N-UNCOUNT approval 2 You can refer to the **modesty** of something such as a place or amount when it is fairly small. ❑ *The modesty of the town itself comes as something of a surprise.* N-UNCOUNT: usu N *of* n 3 If someone, especially a woman, shows **modesty**, they are cautious about the way they dress and behave because they are aware that other people may view them in a sexual way. ❑ *There were shrieks of embarrassment as the girls struggled to protect their modesty.* N-UNCOUNT: usu with supp

**modi|cum** /mɒdɪkəm/ A **modicum** of something, especially something that is good or desirable, is a reasonable but not large amount of QUANT: QUANT *of* n-uncount it. [FORMAL] ❑ *I'd like to think I've had a modicum of success. ...a modicum of privacy.*

**modi|fi|er** /mɒdɪfaɪəʳ/ **(modifiers)** A **modifier** is a word or group of words that modifies another word or group. In some descriptions of grammar, only words that are used before a noun are called **modifiers**. N-COUNT

**modi|fy** /mɒdɪfaɪ/ **(modifies, modifying, modified)** [1] If you **modify** something, you change it slightly, usually in order to improve it. ❑ *The club members did agree to modify their recruitment policy... The plane was a modified version of the C-130.* VERB V n V-ed

♦ **modi|fi|ca|tion** /mɒdɪfɪkeɪʃᵊn/ **(modifications)** *Relatively minor modifications were required.* N-VAR

[2] A word or group of words that **modifies** another word describes or classifies something, or restricts the meaning of the word. [TECHNICAL] ❑ *It is a rule of English that adjectives generally precede the noun they modify: we say 'a good cry', not 'a cry good'.* VERB V n

**mod|ish** /moʊdɪʃ/ Something that is **modish** is fashionable. [LITERARY] ❑ *...a short checklist of much that is modish at the moment. ...modish young women from London society.* ADJ

**modu|lar** /mɒdʒʊləʳ/ [1] In building, **modular** means relating to the construction of buildings in parts called modules. ❑ *They ended up buying a prebuilt modular home on a two-acre lot.* ADJ [2] **Modular** means relating to the teaching of courses at college or university in units called modules. [BRIT] ❑ *The course is modular in structure.* ADJ

**modu|late** /mɒdʒʊleɪt/ **(modulates, modulating, modulated)** [1] If you **modulate** your voice or a sound, you change or vary its loudness, pitch, or tone in order to create a particular effect. [WRITTEN] ❑ *He carefully modulated his voice.* VERB V n Also V [2] To **modulate** an activity or process means to alter it so that it is more suitable for a particular situation. [FORMAL] ❑ *These chemicals modulate the effect of potassium.* VERB V n ♦ **modu|la|tion** /mɒdʒʊleɪʃᵊn/ **(modulations)** *The famine turned the normal modulation of climate into disaster.* N-VAR

**mod|ule** /mɒdʒuːl/ **(modules)** [1] A **module** is one of the separate parts of a course taught at a college or university. [BRIT] ❑ *These courses cover a twelve-week period and are organised into three four-week modules.* N-COUNT = unit [2] A **module** is a part of a spacecraft which can operate by itself, often away from the rest of the spacecraft. ❑ *A rescue plan could be achieved by sending an unmanned module to the space station.* N-COUNT

**mo|dus op|eran|di** /moʊdəs ɒpərændiː, -daɪ/ A **modus operandi** is a particular way of doing something. [FORMAL] ❑ *An example of her modus operandi was provided during a terse exchange with the defendant.* N-SING

**mo|dus vi|ven|di** /moʊdəs vɪvendiː, -daɪ/ A **modus vivendi** is an arrangement which allows people who have different attitudes to live or work together. [FORMAL] ❑ *After 1940, a modus vivendi between church and state was achieved.* N-SING

**mog|gy** /mɒgi/ **(moggies)** also **moggie.** A **moggy** is a cat. [BRIT, INFORMAL] N-COUNT

**mo|gul** /moʊgᵊl/ **(moguls)** [1] A **Mogul** was a Muslim ruler in India in the sixteenth to eighteenth centuries. N-COUNT [2] A **mogul** is an important, rich, and powerful businessman, especially one in the news, film, or television industry. ❑ *...an international media mogul. ...Hollywood movie moguls.* N-COUNT: usu supp N

**mo|hair** /moʊheəʳ/ **Mohair** is a type of very soft wool. ❑ *...a brown mohair dress.* N-UNCOUNT: oft N n

**moist** /mɔɪst/ **(moister, moistest)** Something that is **moist** is slightly wet. ❑ *Wipe off any excess make-up with a clean, moist cotton flannel.* ADJ ≠ dry

**mois|ten** /mɔɪsᵊn/ **(moistens, moistening, moistened)** To **moisten** something means to make it slightly wet. ❑ *She took a sip of water to moisten her dry throat.* VERB V n

**mois|ture** /mɔɪstʃəʳ/ **Moisture** is tiny drops of water in the air, on a surface, or in the ground. ❑ *When the soil is dry, more moisture is lost from the plant.* N-UNCOUNT

**mois|tur|ize** /mɔɪstʃəraɪz/ **(moisturizes, moisturizing, moisturized)**

| ✓ in BRIT, also use **moisturise** |
|---|

If you **moisturize** your skin, you rub cream into it to make it softer. If a cream **moisturizes** your skin, it makes it softer. ❑ *...products to moisturise, protect and firm your skin... The lotion moisturizes while it cleanses.* VERB V n V

**moist|ur|iz|er** /mɔɪstʃəraɪzəʳ/ **(moisturizers)** also **moisturiser.** A **moisturizer** is a cream that you put on your skin to make it feel softer and smoother. N-MASS

**mo|lar** /moʊləʳ/ **(molars)** Your **molars** are the large, flat teeth towards the back of your mouth that you use for chewing food. N-COUNT

**mo|las|ses** /məlæsɪz/ **Molasses** is a thick, dark brown syrup which is produced when sugar is processed. It is used in cooking. N-UNCOUNT

**mold** /moʊld/ → see **mould**.

**mold|ing** /moʊldɪŋ/ → see **moulding**.

**moldy** /moʊldi/ → see **mouldy**.

**mole** /moʊl/ **(moles)** [1] A **mole** is a natural dark spot or small dark lump on someone's skin. N-COUNT [2] A **mole** is a small animal with black fur that lives underground. N-COUNT [3] A **mole** is a member of a government or other organization who gives secret information to the press or to a rival organization. ❑ *He had been recruited by the Russians as a mole and trained in Moscow.* N-COUNT

**mo|lecu|lar** /məlekjʊləʳ/ **Molecular** means relating to or involving molecules. ❑ *...the molecular structure of fuel.* ADJ: ADJ n

**mo|lecu|lar bi|ol|ogy** **Molecular biology** is the study of the structure and function of the complex chemicals that are found in living things. N-UNCOUNT ♦ **mo|lecu|lar bi|olo|gist** **(molecular biologists)** ❑ *This substance has now been cloned by molecular biologists.* N-COUNT

**mol|ecule** /mɒlɪkjuːl/ **(molecules)** A **molecule** is the smallest amount of a chemical substance which can exist by itself. ❑ *...the hydrogen bonds between water molecules.* N-COUNT: usu with supp, oft supp N

**mole|hill** /moʊlhɪl/ **(molehills)** [1] A **molehill** is a small pile of earth made by a mole digging a tunnel. N-COUNT [2] If you say that someone is **making a mountain out of a molehill**, you are critical of them for making an unimportant fact or difficulty seem like a serious one. ❑ *The British press, making a mountain out of a molehill, precipitated an unnecessary economic crisis.* PHRASE: V and Ns inflect [disapproval]

**mo|lest** /məlest/ **(molests, molesting, molested)** A person who **molests** someone, especially a woman or a child, interferes with them in a sexual way against their will. ❑ *He was accused of sexually molesting a female colleague.* VERB V n ♦ **mo|les|ta|tion** /mɒlesteɪʃᵊn, AM moʊl-/ *Any case of sexual molestation of a child should be reported to the police.* N-UNCOUNT ♦ **mo|lest|er** **(molesters)** *He'd been publicly labeled a child molester.* N-COUNT

**mol|li|fy** /mɒlɪfaɪ/ **(mollifies, mollifying, mollified)** If you **mollify** someone, you do or say something to make them less upset or angry. [FORMAL] ❑ *The investigation was undertaken primarily to mollify pressure groups.* VERB = placate V n

**mol|lusc** /mɒləsk/ **(molluscs)**

| ✓ in AM, use **mollusk** |
|---|

A **mollusc** is an animal such as a snail, clam, or octopus which has a soft body. Many types of mollusc have hard shells to protect them. N-COUNT

**molly|coddle** /mɒlikɒdᵊl/ **(mollycoddles, mollycoddling, mollycoddled)** If you accuse someone of **mollycoddling** someone else, you are critical of them for doing too many things for the other person and protecting them too much from unpleasant experiences. ❑ *Christopher accused me of mollycoddling Andrew.* VERB [disapproval] V n

**Molotov cock|tail** /mɒlətɒv kɒkteɪl/ **(Molotov cocktails)** A **Molotov cocktail** is a simple bomb made by putting petrol and cloth into a bottle. It is exploded by setting fire to the cloth. N-COUNT

**molt** /oʊlt/ → see **moult**.

**mol|ten** /moʊltᵊn/ **Molten** rock, metal, or glass has been heated to a very high temperature and has become a hot thick liquid. ❑ *The molten metal is poured into the mould.* ADJ: usu ADJ n

**mom** /mɒm/ **(moms)** Your **mom** is your mother. [AM, INFORMAL] ❑ *We waited for Mom and Dad to get home.* N-FAMILY

✔ in BRIT, use **mum**

**mo|ment** /moʊmənt/ **(moments)** ◆◆◆ 1 You can refer to a very short period of time, for example a few seconds, as a **moment** or **moments**. ❑ *In a moment he was gone... She stared at him a moment, then turned away... Stop for one moment and think about it!... In moments, I was asleep once more.* N-COUNT = minute, second 2 A particular **moment** is the point in time at which something happens. ❑ *At this moment a car stopped at the house... Many people still remember the moment when they heard that President Kennedy had been assassinated.* N-COUNT: with supp

**PHRASES** 3 If you say that something will or may happen **at any moment** or **any moment now**, you are emphasizing that it is likely to happen very soon. ❑ *They ran the risk of being shot at any moment... He'll be here to see you any moment now.* PHRASE emphasis

4 You use expressions such as **at the moment**, **at this moment**, and **at the present moment** to indicate that a particular situation exists at the time when you are speaking. ❑ *At the moment, no one is talking to me... This is being planned at the present moment.* PHRASE = now, currently 5 If you say that you do not believe **for a moment** or **for one moment** that something is true, you are emphasizing that you do not believe that it could possibly be true. ❑ *I don't for a moment think there'll be a divorce.* PHRASE: with brd-neg, PHR with v emphasis = for a minute 6 You use **for the moment** to indicate that something is true now, even if it will not be true in the future. ❑ *For the moment, however, the government is happy to live with it.* PHRASE: PHR with cl 7 If you say that someone or something **has** their **moments**, you are indicating that there are times when they are successful or interesting, but that this does not happen very often. ❑ *The film has its moments.* PHRASE: V inflects 8 If someone does something at **the last moment**, they do it at the latest time possible. ❑ *They changed their minds at the last moment and refused to go.* PHRASE: prep PHR 9 You use the expression **the next moment**, or expressions such as '**one moment** he was there, **the next** he was gone', to emphasize that something happens suddenly, especially when it is very different from what was happening before. ❑ *The next moment there was an almighty crash... He is unpredictable, weeping one moment, laughing the next.* PHRASE emphasis 10 You use **of the moment** to describe someone or something that is or was especially popular at a particular time, especially when you want to suggest that their popularity is unlikely to last long or did not last long. ❑ *He's the man of the moment, isn't he?* PHRASE: n PHR 11 If you say that something happens **the moment** something else happens, you are emphasizing that it happens immediately after the other thing. ❑ *The moment I closed my eyes, I fell asleep.* PHRASE: PHR that emphasis 12 **spur of the moment** → see **spur**.

**mo|men|tari|ly** /moʊmənteərɪli/ 1 **Momentarily** means for a short time. [mainly BRIT or WRITTEN] ❑ *She paused momentarily when she saw them.* ADV: usu ADV with v = briefly 2 **Momentarily** means very soon. [AM] ❑ *The Senate Judiciary Committee is expected to vote momentarily on his nomination to the Supreme Court.* ADV: usu ADV after v

**mo|men|tary** /moʊməntəri, AM -teri/ Something that is **momentary** lasts for a very short period of time, for example for a few seconds or less. ❑ *...a momentary lapse of concentration.* ADJ = brief

**mo|ment of truth** **(moments of truth)** If you refer to a time or event as **the moment of truth**, you mean that it is an important time when you must make a decision quickly, and whatever you decide will have important consequences in the future. ❑ *Both men knew the moment of truth had arrived.* N-COUNT = crunch

**mo|men|tous** /moʊmentəs/ If you refer to a decision, event, or change as **momentous**, you mean that it is very important, often because of the effects that it will have in the future. ❑ *...the momentous decision to send in the troops.* ADJ

**mo|men|tum** /moʊmentəm/ 1 If a process or movement gains **momentum**, it keeps developing or happening more quickly and keeps becoming less likely to stop. ❑ *This campaign is really gaining momentum.* N-UNCOUNT = impetus 2 In physics, **momentum** is the mass of a moving object multiplied by its speed in a particular direction. [TECHNICAL] N-UNCOUNT

**mom|ma** /mɒmə/ **(mommas)** **Momma** means the same as **mommy**. [AM, INFORMAL] N-FAMILY

**mom|my** /mɒmi/ **(mommies)** Some people, especially young children, call their mother **mommy**. [AM, INFORMAL] ❑ *Mommy and I went in an aeroplane.* N-FAMILY

✔ in BRIT, use **mummy**

**Mon.** **Mon.** is a written abbreviation for **Monday**. ❑ *...Mon Oct 19.*

**mon|arch** /mɒnəʳk/ **(monarchs)** The **monarch** of a country is the king, queen, emperor, or empress. N-COUNT

**mo|nar|chi|cal** /mɒnɑːʳkɪkᵊl/ **Monarchical** means relating to a monarch or monarchs. ❑ *...a monarchical system of government.* ADJ: usu ADJ n

**mon|ar|chist** /mɒnəʳkɪst/ **(monarchists)** If someone has **monarchist** views, they believe that their country should have a monarch, such as a king or queen. ❑ *...the tiny monarchist party.* ♦ A **monarchist** is someone with monarchist views. ADJ = royalist ≠ republican N-COUNT

**mon|ar|chy** /mɒnəʳki/ **(monarchies)** 1 A **monarchy** is a system in which a country has a monarch. ❑ *...a serious debate on the future of the monarchy.* N-VAR ≠ republic 2 A **monarchy** is a country that has a monarch. N-COUNT ≠ republic 3 The **monarchy** is used to refer to the monarch and his or her family. ❑ *The monarchy has to create a balance between its public and private lives.* N-COUNT: usu the N

**mon|as|tery** /mɒnəstri, AM -teri/ **(monasteries)** A **monastery** is a building or collection of buildings in which monks live. N-COUNT

**mo|nas|tic** /mənæstɪk/ **Monastic** means relating to monks or to a monastery. ❑ *He was drawn to the monastic life.* ADJ: usu ADJ n

**Mon|day** /mʌndeɪ, -di/ **(Mondays)** **Monday** is the day after Sunday and before Tuesday. ❑ *I went back to work on Monday... The attack took place last Monday... I'm usually here on Mondays and Fridays.* N-VAR

**mon|etar|ism** /mʌnɪtərɪzəm, AM mɑːn-/ **Monetarism** is an economic policy that involves controlling the amount of money that is available and in use in a country at any one time. [BUSINESS] N-UNCOUNT

**mon|etar|ist** /mʌnɪtərɪst, AM mɑːn-/ **(monetarists)** **Monetarist** policies or views are based on the theory that the amount of money that is available and in use in a country at any one time should be controlled. [BUSINESS] ❑ *...tough monetarist policies.* ♦ A **monetarist** is someone with monetarist views. ADJ N-COUNT

**mon|etary** /mʌnɪtri, AM mɑːnɪteri/ ◆◇◇ **Monetary** means relating to money, especially the total amount of money in a country. [BUSINESS] ❑ *Some countries tighten monetary policy to avoid inflation.* ADJ: ADJ n

**mon|ey** /mʌni/ **(monies** or **moneys)** ◆◆◆ 1 **Money** is the coins or bank notes that you use to buy things, or the sum that you have in a bank account. ❑ *A lot of the money that you pay at the cinema goes back to the film distributors... Players should be allowed to earn money from advertising. ...discounts and money saving offers.* N-UNCOUNT 2 **Monies** is used to refer to several separate sums of money that form N-PLURAL part of a larger amount that is received or spent. [FORMAL] ❑ *We drew up a schedule of payments for the rest of the monies owed.* 3 → See also **blood money**, **pocket money**.

**PHRASES** 4 If you say that someone **has money to burn**, you mean that they have more money than they need or that they spend their money on things that you think are unnecessary. ❑ *He was a high-earning broker with money to burn.* PHRASE: V inflects 5 If you are **in the money**, you have a lot of money to spend. [INFORMAL] ❑ *If you are one of the lucky callers chosen to play, you could be in the money.* PHRASE: usu v-link PHR 6 If you **make money**, you obtain money by earning it or by making a profit. ❑ *...the only bit of the firm that consistently made money.* PHRASE: V inflects 7 If you say that you want someone to **put** their **money where their mouth is**, you want them to spend money to improve a bad situation, instead of just talking about improving it. ❑ *The government might be obliged to put its money where its mouth is to prove its commitment.* PHRASE: V inflects 8 If you say that **the smart money** is on a particular person or thing, you mean that people who know a lot about it think that this person will be successful, or this thing will happen. [JOURNALISM] ❑ *With England not playing, the smart money was on the Germans.* PHRASE 9 If you say that **money talks**, you mean that if someone has a lot of money, they also have a lot of power. ❑ *The formula in Hollywood is simple – money talks.* PHRASE 10 If you say that someone is **throwing money at** a problem, you are critical of them for trying to improve it by spending money on it, instead of doing more thoughtful and practical things to improve it. ❑ *The Australian government's answer to the problem has been to throw money at it.* PHRASE: V inflects, PHR n [disapproval] 11 If you say that someone is **throwing good money after bad**, you are critical of them for trying to improve a bad situation by spending more money on it, instead of doing more thoughtful or practical things to improve it. ❑ *Further heavy intervention would be throwing good money after bad.* PHRASE: V inflects [disapproval] 12 If you **get** your **money's worth**, you get something which is worth the money that it costs or the effort you have put in. ❑ *The fans get their money's worth.* PHRASE: PHR after v 13 to **be rolling in money** → see **rolling**. **money for old rope** → see **rope**. to **give** someone **a run for** their **money** → see **run**.

**mon|ey box** **(money boxes)** A **money box** is a small box with an opening at the top, into which a child puts coins as a way of saving money. [mainly BRIT] N-COUNT

**mon|eyed** /mʌnid/ also **monied**. A **moneyed** person has a lot of money. [FORMAL] ❑ *Fear of crime among Japan's new monied classes is rising rapidly.* ADJ = affluent

**mon|ey laun|der|ing** **Money laundering** is the crime of processing stolen money through a legitimate business or sending it abroad to a foreign bank, to hide the fact that the money was illegally obtained. ❑ *...the largest money-laundering scandal in history.* N-UNCOUNT

**money|lender** /mʌnilendəʳ/ **(moneylenders)** also **money-lender**. A **moneylender** is a person who lends money which has to be paid back at a high rate of interest. [OLD-FASHIONED] N-COUNT

**money-maker** **(money-makers)** also **moneymaker**. If you say that a business, product, or investment is a **money-maker**, you mean that it makes a big profit. [BUSINESS] N-COUNT = money-spinner

**mon|ey mar|ket** **(money markets)** A country's **money market** consists of all the banks and other organizations that deal with short-term loans, capital, and foreign exchange. [BUSINESS] ❑ *On the money markets the dollar was weaker against European currencies.* N-COUNT

**mon|ey or|der** **(money orders)** A **money order** is a piece of paper representing a sum of money which you can buy at a post office and send to someone as a way of sending them money by post. [AM] N-COUNT

☑ in BRIT, use **postal order**

**money-spinner** **(money-spinners)** also **moneyspinner**. If you say that something is a **money-spinner**, you mean that it earns a lot of money for someone. [INFORMAL] ❑ *The films have been fantastic money-spinners.* N-COUNT: usu adj N = money-maker

**mon|ey sup|ply** **The money supply** is the total amount of money in a country's economy at any one time. [BUSINESS] ❑ *They believed that controlling the money supply would reduce inflation.* N-UNCOUNT: usu *the* N

**Mon|gol** /mɒŋgəl/ **(Mongols)** 1 The **Mongols** were an Asian people who, led by Genghis Khan and Kublai Khan, took control of large areas of China and Central Asia in the 12th and 13th centuries A.D. N-COUNT 2 **Mongol** means belonging or relating to the Mongols. ❑ *...the Mongol invasions of the 13th century.* ADJ: ADJ n

**Mon|go|lian** /mɒŋgoʊliən/ **(Mongolians)** 1 **Mongolian** means belonging or relating to Mongolia, or to its people, language, or culture. ADJ 2 A **Mongolian** is a Mongolian citizen, or a person of Mongolian origin. N-COUNT 3 **Mongolian** is the language that is spoken in Mongolia. N-UNCOUNT

**mon|grel** /mʌŋgrəl/ **(mongrels)** A **mongrel** is a dog which is a mixture of different breeds. N-COUNT

**mon|ied** /mʌnid/ → see **moneyed**.

**moni|ker** /mɒnɪkəʳ/ **(monikers)** The **moniker** of a person or thing is their name, especially when they have changed it. [INFORMAL] ❑ *She's the author of three detective novels under the moniker of Janet Neel.* N-COUNT

**moni|tor** /mɒnɪtəʳ/ **(monitors, monitoring, monitored)** ◆◇◇ 1 If you **monitor** something, you regularly check its development or progress, and sometimes comment on it. ❑ *Officials had not been allowed to monitor the voting... You need feedback to monitor progress.* ♦ **moni|tor|ing** *...analysis and monitoring of the global environment.* VERB; V n; V n; N-UNCOUNT 2 If someone **monitors** radio broadcasts from other countries, they record them or listen carefully to them in order to obtain information. ❑ *Peter Murray is in London and has been monitoring reports out of Monrovia.* VERB; V n 3 A **monitor** is a machine that is used to check or record things, for example processes or substances inside a person's body. ❑ *The heart monitor shows low levels of consciousness.* N-COUNT: usu n N 4 A **monitor** is a screen which is used to display certain kinds of information, for example in airports or television studios. ❑ *He was watching a game of tennis on a television monitor.* N-COUNT: oft N n = screen 5 You can refer to a person who checks that something is done correctly, or that it is fair, as a **monitor**. ❑ *Government monitors will continue to accompany reporters.* N-COUNT: usu supp N

**monk** /mʌŋk/ **(monks)** A **monk** is a member of a male religious community that is usually separated from the outside world. ❑ *...saffron-robed Buddhist monks.* N-COUNT

**mon|key** /mʌŋki/ **(monkeys)** 1 A **monkey** is an animal with a long tail which lives in hot countries and climbs trees. N-COUNT 2 If you refer to a child as a **monkey**, you are saying in an affectionate way that he or she is very lively and naughty. ❑ *She's such a little monkey.* N-COUNT: usu adj N [feelings]

**mon|key bars** **Monkey bars** are metal or wooden bars that are joined together to form a structure for children to climb and play on. [AM] N-PLURAL

☑ in BRIT, use **climbing frame**

**mon|key wrench** **(monkey wrenches)** → see **wrench**.

**mono** /mɒnoʊ/ 1 **Mono** is used to describe a system of playing music in which all the sound is directed through one speaker only. Compare **stereo**. ❑ *This model has a mono soundtrack.* ADJ 2 **Mono** is the same as **mononucleosis**. [AM, INFORMAL] N-UNCOUNT

**mono-** /mɒnoʊ-/ **Mono-** is used at the beginning of nouns and adjectives that have 'one' or PREFIX 'single' as part of their meanings. ❑ *...high in mono-unsaturated fats. ...interaction between bilingual parents and monolingual teachers.*

**mono|chrome** /mɒnəkroʊm/ 1 A **monochrome** film, photograph, or television shows black, white, and shades of grey, but no other colours. ❑ *...color and monochrome monitors.* 2 A **monochrome** picture uses only one colour in various shades. ❑ *...an old monochrome etching of a brewery.* — ADJ: usu ADJ n = black and white; ADJ: usu ADJ n

**mono|cle** /mɒnəkᵊl/ **(monocles)** A **monocle** is a glass lens which people wore in former times in front of one of their eyes to improve their ability to see with that eye. — N-COUNT

**mo|noga|mous** /mənɒgəməs/ 1 Someone who is **monogamous** or who has a **monogamous** relationship has a sexual relationship with only one partner. ❑ *Do you believe that men are not naturally monogamous?* 2 **Monogamous** animals have only one sexual partner during their lives or during each mating season. — ADJ; ADJ

**mo|noga|my** /mənɒgəmi/ 1 **Monogamy** is used to refer to the state or custom of having a sexual relationship with only one partner. ❑ *People still opt for monogamy and marriage.* 2 **Monogamy** is the state or custom of being married to only one person at a particular time. ❑ *In many non-Western societies, however, monogamy has never dominated.* — N-UNCOUNT; N-UNCOUNT

**mono|gram** /mɒnəgræm/ **(monograms)** A **monogram** is a design based on the first letters of a person's names, which is put on things they own, such as their clothes. — N-COUNT

**mono|grammed** /mɒnəgræmd/ **Monogrammed** means marked with a design based on the first letters of a person's names. ❑ *...a monogrammed handkerchief.* — ADJ

**mono|graph** /mɒnəgrɑːf, -græf/ **(monographs)** A **monograph** is a book which is a detailed study of only one subject. [FORMAL] ❑ *...a monograph on her favourite author, John Masefield.* — N-COUNT: oft N *on* n

**mono|lin|gual** /mɒnoʊlɪŋgwəl/ **Monolingual** means involving, using, or speaking one language. ❑ *...a largely monolingual country such as Great Britain.* — ADJ: usu ADJ n

**mono|lith** /mɒnəlɪθ/ **(monoliths)** 1 A **monolith** is a very large, upright piece of stone, especially one that was put in place in ancient times. 2 If you refer to an organization or system as a **monolith**, you are critical of it because it is very large and very slow to change, and it does not seem to have different parts with different characters. ❑ *A deal between the two powerful institutions would have created a banking monolith.* — N-COUNT; N-COUNT disapproval

**mono|lith|ic** /mɒnəlɪθɪk/ 1 If you refer to an organization or system as **monolithic**, you are critical of it because it is very large and very slow to change, and does not seem to have different parts with different characters. ❑ *...an authoritarian and monolithic system.* 2 If you describe something such as a building as **monolithic**, you do not like it because it is very large and plain with no character. ❑ *...a huge monolithic concrete building.* — ADJ disapproval; ADJ: usu ADJ n disapproval

**mono|logue** /mɒnəlɒg, AM -lɔːg/ **(monologues)** 1 If you refer to a long speech by one person during a conversation as a **monologue**, you mean it prevents other people from talking or expressing their opinions. ❑ *Morris ignored the question and continued his monologue.* 2 A **monologue** is a long speech which is spoken by one person as an entertainment, or as part of an entertainment such as a play. ❑ *...a monologue based on the writing of Quentin Crisp.* — N-COUNT; N-VAR

**mono|nu|cleo|sis** /mɒnoʊnjuːklioʊsɪs/ **Mononucleosis** is a disease which causes swollen glands, fever, and a sore throat. [mainly AM] — N-UNCOUNT

✔ in BRIT, usually use **glandular fever**

**mo|nopo|lis|tic** /mənɒpəlɪstɪk/ If you refer to a business or its practices as **monopolistic**, you mean that it tries to control as much of an industry as it can and does not allow fair competition. — ADJ: usu ADJ n

**mo|nopo|lize** /mənɒpəlaɪz/ **(monopolizes, monopolizing, monopolized)**

✔ in BRIT, also use **monopolise**

1 If you say that someone **monopolizes** something, you mean that they have a very large share of it and prevent other people from having a share. ❑ *They are controlling so much cocoa that they are virtually monopolizing the market... Johnson, as usual, monopolized the conversation.* ♦ **mo|nopo|li|za|tion** /mənɒpəlaɪzeɪʃᵊn/ *...the monopolization of a market by a single supplier.* 2 If something or someone **monopolizes** you, they demand a lot of your time and attention, so that there is very little time left for anything or anyone else. ❑ *He would monopolize her totally, to the exclusion of her brothers and sisters.* — VERB; V n; V n; N-UNCOUNT: oft N *of* n; VERB; V n

**mo|nopo|ly** /mənɒpəli/ **(monopolies)** 1 If a company, person, or state has a **monopoly on** something such as an industry, they have complete control over it, so that it is impossible for others to become involved in it. [BUSINESS] ❑ *...Russian moves to end a state monopoly on land ownership. ...the governing party's monopoly over the media.* 2 A **monopoly** is a company which is the only one providing a particular product or service. [BUSINESS] ❑ *...a state-owned monopoly.* 3 If you say that someone does not have a **monopoly on** something, you mean that they are not the only person who has that thing. ❑ *Women do not have a monopoly on feelings of betrayal.* — N-VAR: oft with poss, oft N *on/over* n/-ing; N-COUNT; N-SING: with brd-neg, usu N *on* n

**mono|rail** /mɒnoʊreɪl/ **(monorails)** A **monorail** is a system of transport in which small trains travel along a single rail which is usually high above the ground. — N-COUNT: also *by* N

**mono|so|dium glu|ta|mate** /mɒnəsoʊdiəm gluːtəmeɪt/ **Monosodium glutamate** is a substance which is sometimes added to savoury food to make it taste better. The abbreviation **MSG** is also used. — N-UNCOUNT

**mono|syl|lab|ic** /mɒnoʊsɪlæbɪk/ If you refer to someone or the way they speak as **monosyllabic**, you mean that they say very little, usually because they do not want to have a conversation. ❑ *He could be gruff and monosyllabic.* — ADJ

**mono|syl|la|ble** /mɒnoʊsɪləbᵊl/ **(monosyllables)** If you say that someone speaks in **monosyllables** you mean that they speak very little, usually because they do not want to have a conversation. ❑ *A taciturn man, he replied to my questions in monosyllables.* — N-COUNT: usu *in* N in pl

**mono|tone** /mɒnətoʊn/ **(monotones)** 1 If someone speaks in a **monotone**, their voice does not vary at all in tone or loudness and so it is not interesting to listen to. ❑ *The evidence was read out to the court in a dull monotone.* 2 A **monotone** sound or surface does not have any variation in its tone or colour. ❑ *He was seen on TV delivering platitudes about the crisis in a monotone voice.* — N-COUNT: usu sing, also *in* N; ADJ: usu ADJ n

**mo|noto|nous** /mənɒtənəs/ Something that is **monotonous** is very boring because it has a regular, repeated pattern which never changes. ❑ *It's monotonous work, like most factory jobs.* ♦ **mo|noto|nous|ly** *The rain dripped monotonously from the trees.* — ADJ = repetitive ≠ varied; ADV

**mo|noto|ny** /mənɒtəni/ The **monotony** of something is the fact that it never changes and is boring. ❑ *A night on the town may help to break the monotony of the week.* — N-UNCOUNT: oft N *of* n

**mon|ox|ide** /mənɒksaɪd/ → see **carbon monoxide**.

**Mon|sig|nor** /mɒnsiːnjɔːʳ/ **(Monsignors)** **Monsignor** is the title of a priest of high rank in the Catholic Church. ❑ *Monsignor Jaime Goncalves was also there.* — N-TITLE; N-COUNT: usu sing

**mon|soon** /mɒnsuːn/ **(monsoons)** 1 [N-COUNT: oft *the* N] The **monsoon** is the season in Southern Asia when there is a lot of very heavy rain. ❑ *...the end of the monsoon.* 2 [N-PLURAL: oft *the* N] Monsoon rains are sometimes referred to as **the monsoons**. ❑ *In Bangladesh, the monsoons have started.*

**mon|ster** /mɒnstəʳ/ **(monsters)** 1 [N-COUNT] A **monster** is a large imaginary creature that looks very ugly and frightening. 2 [N-COUNT] A **monster** is something which is extremely large, especially something which is difficult to manage or which is unpleasant. ❑ *...the monster which is now the London marathon.* 3 [ADJ: ADJ n] [emphasis] [= giant] **Monster** means extremely and surprisingly large. [INFORMAL] ❑ *The film will be a monster hit.* 4 [N-COUNT] If you describe someone as a **monster**, you mean that they are cruel, frightening, or evil.

**mon|stros|ity** /mɒnstrɒsɪti/ **(monstrosities)** [N-COUNT] [disapproval] If you describe something, especially something large, as a **monstrosity**, you mean that you think it is extremely ugly. ❑ *Most of the older buildings have been torn down and replaced by modern monstrosities.*

**mon|strous** /mɒnstrəs/ 1 [ADJ: usu ADJ n] [= atrocious] If you describe a situation or event as **monstrous**, you mean that it is extremely shocking or unfair. ❑ *She endured the monstrous behaviour for years.* ♦ **mon|strous|ly** [ADV: ADV after v] *Your husband's family has behaved monstrously.* 2 [ADJ: usu ADJ n] [emphasis] If you describe an unpleasant thing as **monstrous**, you mean that it is extremely large in size or extent. ❑ *...a monstrous copper edifice.* ♦ **mon|strous|ly** [ADV: ADV adj/-ed] *It would be monstrously unfair.* 3 [ADJ: usu ADJ n] [= hideous] If you describe something as **monstrous**, you mean that it is extremely frightening because it appears unnatural or ugly. ❑ *...the film's monstrous fantasy figure.*

**mon|tage** /mɒntɑːʒ, mɒntɑːʒ/ **(montages)** [N-COUNT] A **montage** is a picture, film, or piece of music which consists of several different items that are put together, often in an unusual combination or sequence. ❑ *...a photo montage of some of Italy's top television stars.*

**month** /mʌnθ/ **(months)** ◆◆◆ 1 [N-COUNT] A **month** is one of the twelve periods of time that a year is divided into, for example January or February. ❑ *The trial is due to begin next month. ...an exhibition which opens this month at London's Design Museum... I send him fifteen dollars a month.* 2 [N-COUNT] A **month** is a period of about four weeks. ❑ *She was here for a month... Over the next several months I met most of her family. ...a month's unlimited train travel.*

**month|ly** /mʌnθli/ **(monthlies)** ◆◇◇ 1 [ADJ: ADJ n] A **monthly** event or publication happens or appears every month. ❑ *Many people are now having trouble making their monthly house payments. ...Young Guard, a monthly journal founded in 1922.* ♦ **Monthly** is also an adverb. [ADV: ADV after v] ❑ *In some areas the property price can rise monthly.* 2 [N-COUNT: oft in names] You can refer to a publication that is published monthly as a **monthly**. ❑ *...Scallywag, a London satirical monthly.* 3 [ADJ: ADJ n] **Monthly** quantities or rates relate to a period of one month. ❑ *The monthly rent for a two-bedroom flat would be £953.33.*

**monu|ment** /mɒnjʊmənt/ **(monuments)** 1 [N-COUNT] A **monument** is a large structure, usually made of stone, which is built to remind people of an event in history or of a famous person. 2 [N-COUNT] A **monument** is something such as a castle or bridge which was built a very long time ago and is regarded as an important part of a country's history. ❑ *...the ancient monuments of England, Scotland and Wales.* 3 [N-COUNT: N *to* n] If you describe something as a **monument to** someone's qualities, you mean that it is a very good example of the results or effects of those qualities. ❑ *By his international achievements he leaves a fitting monument to his beliefs.*

**monu|men|tal** /mɒnjʊmentəl/ 1 [ADJ: usu ADJ n] [emphasis] [= huge, massive] You can use **monumental** to emphasize the size or extent of something. ❑ *...a series of monumental disappointments.* ♦ **monu|men|tal|ly** [ADV: usu ADV adj/-ed, also ADV after v] *Suddenly it was monumentally successful. ...the most monumentally hideous night of my life.* 2 [ADJ: usu ADJ n] [emphasis] If you describe a book or musical work as **monumental**, you are emphasizing that it is very large and impressive, and is likely to be important for a long time. ❑ *...his monumental work on Chinese astronomy.* 3 [ADJ: ADJ n] A **monumental** building or sculpture is very large and impressive. ❑ *I take no real interest in monumental sculpture.*

**moo** /muː/ **(moos, mooing, mooed)** [VERB] When cattle, especially cows, **moo**, they make the long low sound that cattle typically make. ❑ [V] *...a sound like a cow mooing.* ♦ **Moo** is also a noun. [N-COUNT; SOUND] ❑ *The cow says 'moo-moo'.*

**mooch** /muːtʃ/ **(mooches, mooching, mooched)**

♦ **mooch around**

☑ in BRIT, also use **mooch about**

[PHRASAL VERB] [= wander around] If you **mooch around** or **mooch about** a place, you move around there slowly with no particular purpose. ❑ [V P n] *Andrew was left to mooch around the house on his own...* [V P] *He was awake at 3am, mooching about in the darkness.*

**mood** /muːd/ **(moods)** ◆◇◇ 1 [N-COUNT: with supp, oft adj N, oft *in* N] Your **mood** is the way you are feeling at a particular time. If you are **in** a good **mood**, you feel cheerful. If you are **in** a bad **mood**, you feel angry and impatient. ❑ *He is clearly in a good mood today... When he came back, he was in a foul mood... His moods swing alarmingly.* ● [PHRASE: v-link PHR, PHR after v, oft PHR *for* n/-ing, PHR to-inf] If you say that you are **in the mood for** something, you mean that you want to do it or have it. If you say that you are **in no mood to** do something, you mean that you do not want to do it or have it. ❑ *After a day of air and activity, you should be in the mood for a good meal... He was in no mood to celebrate.* 2 [N-COUNT: oft *in a* N] [= temper] If someone is **in a mood**, the way they are behaving shows that they are feeling angry and impatient. ❑ *She was obviously in a mood.* 3 [N-SING: usu with supp, oft with poss] **The mood** of a group of people is the way that they think and feel about an idea, event, or question at a particular time. ❑ *They largely misread the mood of the electorate.* 4 [N-COUNT] [= atmosphere] The **mood** of a place is the general impression that you get of it. ❑ *First set the mood with music.* 5 [N-VAR] In grammar, the **mood** of a clause is the way in which the verb forms are used to show whether the clause is, for example, a statement, a question, or an instruction.

**moody** /muːdi/ **(moodier, moodiest)** 1 [ADJ] If you describe someone as **moody**, you mean that their feelings and behaviour change frequently, and in particular that they often become depressed or angry without any warning. ❑ *David's mother was unstable and moody.* ♦ **moodi|ly** /muːdɪli/ [ADV: usu ADV with v] *He sat and stared moodily out the window.* ♦ **moodi|ness** [N-UNCOUNT] *His moodiness may have been caused by his poor health.* 2 [ADJ: usu ADJ n] [= atmospheric] If you describe a picture, film, or piece of music as **moody**, you mean that it suggests particular emotions, especially sad ones. ❑ *...moody black and white photographs.*

**moon** /muːn/ **(moons)** ◆◇◇ 1 [N-SING: usu *the* N, also *full/new* N] **The moon** is the object that you can often see in the sky at night. It goes round the Earth once every four weeks, and as it does so its appearance changes from a circle to part of a circle. ❑ *...the first man on the moon. ...the light of a full moon.* → See also **new moon**. 2 [N-COUNT: usu poss N] A **moon** is an object similar to a small planet that travels around a planet. ❑ *...Neptune's large moon.*

PHRASES 3 [PHRASE: PHR with cl] [emphasis] If you say that something happens **once in a blue moon**, you are emphasizing that it does not happen very often at all. ❑ *Once in a blue moon you get some problems.* 4 [PHRASE: v-link PHR] [= overjoyed] If you say that you are **over the moon**, you mean that you are very pleased about something. [BRIT, INFORMAL]

**moon|beam** /muːnbiːm/ **(moonbeams)** [N-COUNT] A **moonbeam** is a ray of light from the moon.

**moon|less** /muːnləs/ [ADJ] A **moonless** sky or night is dark because there is no moon.

**moon|light** /muːnlaɪt/ **(moonlights, moonlighting, moonlighted)** 1 [N-UNCOUNT] **Moonlight** is the light that comes from the moon at night. ❑ *They walked along the road in the moonlight... We went to the temple of Atlantis and saw it by moonlight.* [2] If someone **moonlights**, they have a second job in addition to their main job, often without informing their main employers or the tax office. ❑ *...an engineer who was moonlighting as a taxi driver... Workers in state enterprises were permitted to moonlight.* VERB; V *as* n; V

**moon|lit** /muːnlɪt/ Something that is **moonlit** is lit by moonlight. ❑ *...a beautiful moonlit night.* ADJ: usu ADJ n

**moon|shine** /muːnʃaɪn/ [1] **Moonshine** is whisky that is made illegally. [mainly AM] [2] If you say that someone's thoughts, ideas, or comments are **moonshine**, you think they are foolish and not based on reality. ❑ *As Morison remarks, the story is pure moonshine.* N-UNCOUNT; N-UNCOUNT; disapproval; = nonsense

**moor** /mʊəʳ/ **(moors, mooring, moored)** [1] A **moor** is an area of open and usually high land with poor soil that is covered mainly with grass and heather. [mainly BRIT] ❑ *Colliford is higher, right up on the moors... Exmoor National Park stretches over 265 square miles of moor.* [2] If you **moor** a boat somewhere, you stop and tie it to the land with a rope or chain so that it cannot move away. ❑ *She had moored her barge on the right bank of the river... I decided to moor near some tourist boats.* [3] The **Moors** were a Muslim people who established a civilization in North Africa and Spain between the 8th and the 15th century A.D. [4] → See also **mooring**. N-VAR; VERB = tie up; V n; V; N-COUNT: usu pl

**moor|ing** /mʊərɪŋ/ **(moorings)** [1] A **mooring** is a place where a boat can be tied so that it cannot move away, or the object it is tied to. ❑ *Free moorings will be available.* [2] **Moorings** are the ropes, chains, and other objects used to moor a boat. ❑ *Emergency workers fear that the burning ship could slip its moorings.* N-COUNT; N-PLURAL

**Moor|ish** /mʊərɪʃ/ Something that is **Moorish** belongs to or is characteristic of the Muslim civilization in North Africa and Spain between the 8th and the 15th century A.D. ❑ *...a medieval Moorish palace.* ADJ: usu ADJ n

**moor|land** /mʊəʳlænd/ **(moorlands)** **Moorland** is land which consists of moors. ❑ *...rugged Yorkshire moorland.* N-UNCOUNT: also N in pl

**moose** /muːs/ **(moose)** A **moose** is a large type of deer. Moose have big flat horns called antlers and are found in Northern Europe, Asia, and North America. Some British speakers use **moose** to refer to the North American variety of this animal, and **elk** to refer to the European and Asian varieties. N-COUNT

**moot** /muːt/ **(moots, mooting, mooted)** [1] If a plan, idea, or subject **is mooted**, it is suggested or introduced for discussion. [FORMAL] ❑ *Plans have been mooted for a 450,000-strong Ukrainian army.* [2] If something is a **moot** point or question, people cannot agree about it. ❑ *How long he'll be able to do so is a moot point.* VERB: usu passive = propose, put forward; *be* V-ed; ADJ

**mop** /mɒp/ **(mops, mopping, mopped)** [1] A **mop** is a piece of equipment for washing floors. It consists of a sponge or many pieces of string attached to a long handle. [2] If you **mop** a surface such as a floor, you clean it with a mop. ❑ *There was a woman mopping the stairs.* [3] If you **mop** sweat from your forehead or **mop** your forehead, you wipe it with a piece of cloth. ❑ *He mopped perspiration from his forehead... The Inspector took out a handkerchief and mopped his brow.* [4] If someone has a **mop of** hair, they have a lot of hair and it looks rather untidy. ❑ *He was long-limbed and dark-eyed, with a mop of tight, dark curls.* N-COUNT; VERB; V n; VERB = wipe; V n *from* n; V n; N-COUNT: usu N *of* n

♦ **mop up** [1] If you **mop up** a liquid, you clean it with a cloth so that the liquid is absorbed. ❑ *A waiter mopped up the mess as best he could... When the washing machine spurts out water at least we can mop it up... Michael mopped up quickly with his napkin.* [2] If you **mop up** something that you think is undesirable or dangerous, you remove it or deal with it so that it is no longer a problem. ❑ *The infantry divisions mopped up remaining centres of resistance.* PHRASAL VERB; V P n (not pron); V n P; V P; PHRASAL VERB; V P n (not pron)

**mope** /moʊp/ **(mopes, moping, moped)** If you **mope**, you feel miserable and do not feel interested in doing anything. ❑ *Get on with life and don't sit back and mope.* VERB; V

♦ **mope around**

☑ in BRIT, also use **mope about**

If you **mope around** or **mope about** a place, you wander around there not doing anything, looking and feeling unhappy. ❑ *He moped around the office for a while, feeling bored... He mopes about all day.* PHRASAL VERB; V P n; V P

**mo|ped** /moʊped/ **(mopeds)** A **moped** is a small motorcycle which you can also pedal like a bicycle. [mainly BRIT] N-COUNT

**MOR** /em oʊ ɑːʳ/ **MOR** is a type of pop music which is pleasant and not extreme or unusual. **MOR** is an abbreviation of 'middle-of-the-road'. ❑ *...MOR singer Daniel O'Donnell.* N-UNCOUNT: oft N n

**mor|al** /mɒrᵊl, AM mɔːr-/ **(morals)** [1] **Morals** are principles and beliefs concerning right and wrong behaviour. ❑ *...Western ideas and morals... They have no morals.* [2] **Moral** means relating to beliefs about what is right or wrong. ❑ *She describes her own moral dilemma in making the film. ...matters of moral teaching.* ♦ **mor|al|ly** *When, if ever, is it morally justifiable to allow a patient to die?* [3] **Moral** courage or duty is based on what you believe is right or acceptable, rather than on what the law says should be done. ❑ *The Government had a moral, if not a legal duty to pay compensation.* [4] A **moral** person behaves in a way that is believed by most people to be good and right. ❑ *The people who will be on the committee are moral, cultured, competent people.* ♦ **mor|al|ly** *Art is not there to improve you morally.* [5] If you give someone **moral** support, you encourage them in what they are doing by expressing approval. ❑ *Moral as well as financial support was what the West should provide.* [6] **The moral** of a story or event is what you learn from it about how you should or should not behave. ❑ *I think the moral of the story is let the buyer beware.* [7] **moral victory** → see **victory**. ◆◇◇ N-PLURAL; ADJ: ADJ n = ethical; ADV: ADV adj/adv, ADV after v, ADV with cl; ADJ: ADJ n; ADJ: usu ADJ n = ethical; ADV: ADV with v; ADJ: ADJ n; N-COUNT: usu *the* N in sing = message

**mo|rale** /mərɑːl, -ræl/ **Morale** is the amount of confidence and cheerfulness that a group of people have. ❑ *Many pilots are suffering from low morale.* N-UNCOUNT: oft with poss

**mo|rale boost|er** **(morale boosters)** You can refer to something that makes people feel more confident and cheerful as a **morale booster**. ❑ *This win has been a great morale booster.* N-COUNT: usu sing

**morale-boosting** A **morale-boosting** action or event makes people feel more confident and cheerful. ❑ *...the President's morale-boosting visit to the troops.* ADJ: usu ADJ n

**mor|al fi|bre**

☑ in AM, use **moral fiber**

**Moral fibre** is the quality of being determined to do what you think is right. ❑ *...a man of stern moral fibre.* N-UNCOUNT

**mor|al|ise** /mɒrəlaɪz, AM mɔːr-/ → see **moralize**.

**mor|al|ist** /mɒrəlɪst, AM mɔːr-/ **(moralists)** A **moralist** is someone who has strong ideas about right and wrong behaviour, and who tries to make other people behave according to these ideas. N-COUNT

**mor|al|is|tic** /mɒrəlɪstɪk, AM mɔːr-/ If you describe someone or something as **moralistic**, you are critical of them for making harsh judgments of other people on the basis of their own ideas about what is right and wrong. ❑ *He has become more moralistic.* ADJ; disapproval; = judgmental

**mo|ral|ity** /məræləti/ **(moralities)** [1] **Morality** is the belief that some behaviour is right and acceptable and that other behaviour is wrong. ❑ *...standards of morality and justice in society.* [2] A **morality** is a system of principles and values con- N-UNCOUNT; N-COUNT = ethic cerning people's behaviour, which is generally accepted by a society or by a particular group of people. ❑ *...a morality that is sexist.* [3] **The morality of** something is how right or acceptable it is. ❑ *...the arguments about the morality of blood sports.* N-UNCOUNT: usu *the* N *of* n

**mor|al|ize** /mɒrəlaɪz, AM mɔːr-/ **(moralizes, moralizing, moralized)**

✓ in BRIT, also use **moralise**

If you say that someone **is moralizing**, you are critical of them for telling people what they think is right or wrong, especially when they have not been asked their opinion. ❑ *As a dramatist I hate to moralize.* VERB [disapproval] = preach V ♦ **mor|al|iz|ing** *We have tried to avoid any moralising.* N-UNCOUNT

**mor|al ma|jor|ity** If there is a large group in society that holds strong, conservative opinions on matters of morality and religion, you can refer to these people as **the moral majority**. In the United States, there is an organized group called **the Moral Majority**. ❑ *...unless the writers begin to write decent comedy and stop pandering to the moral majority.* N-SING-COLL; N-PROPER-COLL: *the* N

**mo|rass** /məræs/ **(morasses)** If you describe an unpleasant or confused situation as a **morass**, you mean that it seems impossible to escape from or resolve, because it has become so serious or so complicated. ❑ *I tried to drag myself out of the morass of despair. ...the economic morass.* N-COUNT: usu sing, with supp, oft N *of* n = quagmire

**mora|to|rium** /mɒrətɔːriəm, AM mɔːr-/ **(moratoriums** or **moratoria)** A **moratorium on** a particular activity or process is the stopping of it for a fixed period of time, usually as a result of an official agreement. ❑ *The House voted to impose a one-year moratorium on nuclear testing.* N-COUNT: usu sing, oft N *on* n

**mor|bid** /mɔːʳbɪd/ If you describe a person or their interest in something as **morbid**, you mean that they are very interested in unpleasant things, especially death, and you think this is strange. ❑ *Some people have a morbid fascination with crime.* ADJ [disapproval] ♦ **mor|bid|ly** *There's something morbidly fascinating about the thought.* ADV: usu ADV adj

**mor|dant** /mɔːʳdᵊnt/ **Mordant** humour is very critical and often mocks someone or something. [FORMAL] ❑ *A wicked, mordant sense of humour has come to the fore in Blur's world.* ADJ: usu ADJ n = caustic

**more** /mɔːʳ/ ♦♦♦

**More** is often considered to be the comparative form of **much** and **many**.

[1] You use **more** to indicate that there is a greater amount of something than before or than average, or than something else. You can use 'a little', 'a lot', 'a bit', 'far', and 'much' in front of **more**. ❑ *More and more people are surviving heart attacks... He spent more time perfecting his dance moves instead of gym work. ...teaching more children foreign languages other than English.* DET: DET pl-n/n-uncount ≠ less ♦ **More** is also a pronoun. ❑ *As the level of work increased from light to heavy, workers ate more... He had four hundred dollars in his pocket. Billy had more.* PRON ♦ **More** is also a quantifier. ❑ *Employees may face increasing pressure to take on more of their own medical costs in retirement.* QUANT: QUANT *of* def-n

[2] You use **more than** before a number or amount to say that the actual number or amount is even greater. ❑ *The Afghan authorities say the airport had been closed for more than a year. ...classy leather and silk jackets at more than £250.* PREP-PHRASE: PREP amount = over

[3] You use **more** to indicate that something or someone has a greater amount of a quality than they used to or than is average or usual. ❑ *Prison conditions have become more brutal... We can satisfy our basic wants more easily than in the past.* ADV: ADV adj/adv ≠ less

[4] If you say that something is **more** one thing **than** another, you mean that it is like the first thing rather than the second. ❑ *The exhibition at Boston's Museum of Fine Arts is more a production than it is a museum display... He's more like a film star than a life-guard, really... She looked more sad than in pain... Sue screamed, not loudly, more in surprise than terror... She's more of a social animal than me.* ADV: ADV group *than* group/cl, ADV *of a* n ≠ less

[5] If you do something **more** than before or **more** than someone else, you do it to a greater extent or more often. ❑ *When we are tired, tense, depressed or unwell, we feel pain much more... What impressed me more was that she knew Tennessee Williams.* ADV: ADV with v ≠ less

[6] You can use **more** to indicate that something continues to happen for a further period of time. ❑ *Things might have been different if I'd talked a bit more.* ADV: ADV after v ● You can use **some more** to indicate that something continues to happen for a further period of time. ❑ *We walked some more.* PHRASE: PHR after v

[7] You use **more** to indicate that something is repeated. For example, if you do something 'once more', you do it again once. ❑ *This train would stop twice more in the suburbs before rolling southeast toward Munich... The breathing exercises should be repeated several times more.* ADV: adv ADV, n ADV

[8] You use **more** to refer to an additional thing or amount. You can use 'a little', 'a lot', 'a bit', 'far' and 'much' in front of **more**. ❑ *They needed more time to consider whether to hold an inquiry.* DET: DET pl-n/n-uncount ♦ **More** is also an adjective. ❑ *We stayed in Danville two more days... Are you sure you wouldn't like some more wine?* ADJ: ADJ n ♦ **More** is also a pronoun. ❑ *Oxfam has appealed to western nations to do more to help the refugees... 'None of them are very nice folks.' — 'Tell me more.'* PRON

[9] You use **more** in conversations when you want to draw someone's attention to something interesting or important that you are about to say. ❑ *Europe's economies have converged in several areas. More interestingly, there has been convergence in economic growth rates... More seriously for him, there are members who say he is wrong on this issue.* ADV: ADV adv/adj ≠ less

PHRASES [10] You can use **more and more** to indicate that something is becoming greater in amount, extent, or degree all the time. ❑ *Her life was heading more and more where she wanted it to go.* PHRASE: usu PHR with v, PHR group/cl

[11] If something is **more or less** true, it is true in a general way, but is not completely true. ❑ *The Conference is more or less over... He more or less started the firm.* PHRASE: PHR with group/cl, PHR before v [vagueness]

[12] If something is **more than** a particular thing, it has greater value or importance than this thing. ❑ *He's more than a coach, he's a friend.* PHRASE: v-link PHR n

[13] You use **more than** to say that something is true to a greater degree than is necessary or than average. ❑ *Lithuania produces more than enough food to feed itself.* PHRASE: PHR n, PHR adj

[14] You use **no more than** or **not more than** when you want to emphasize how small a number or amount is. ❑ *He was a kid really, not more than eighteen or nineteen.* PHRASE: PHR amount [emphasis] ≠ no less than

[15] If you say that someone or something is **nothing more than** a particular thing, you are emphasizing that they are only that thing, and nothing more interesting or important. ❑ *The newly discovered notes are nothing more than Lang's personal journal.* PHRASE: v-link PHR n [emphasis]

[16] You can use **what is more** or **what's more** to introduce an extra piece of information which supports or emphasizes the point you are making. ❑ *You should remember it, and what's more, you should get it right.* PHRASE: V inflects, PHR cl [emphasis] = moreover, furthermore

[17] **all the more** → see **all**. **any more** → see **any**.

**more|ish** /mɔːrɪʃ/ If you describe food as **moreish**, you mean that it is so nice that you want to keep eating more of it once you have started. [INFORMAL] ❑ *Thai food's very moreish, isn't it?* ADJ

**more|over** /mɔːrouvəʳ/ You use **moreover** to introduce a piece of information that adds to or supports the previous statement. [FORMAL] ❑ *She saw that there was indeed a man immediately behind her. Moreover, he was observing her strangely.* ♦◇◇ ADV: ADV with cl (not last in cl)

**mo|res** /mɔːreɪz/ The **mores** of a particular place or group of people are the customs and behaviour that are typically found in that place or group. [FORMAL] ❑ *...the accepted mores of British society.* N-PLURAL: usu with supp

**morgue** /mɔːʳg/ **(morgues)** A **morgue** is a building or a room in a hospital where dead bodies are kept before they are buried or cremated, or before they are identified or examined. N-COUNT = mortuary

**mori|bund** /mɒrɪbʌnd, AM mɔːr-/ ADJ If you describe something as **moribund**, you mean that it is in a very bad condition. [FORMAL] ❑ *...the moribund economy.*

**Mor|mon** /mɔːʳmən/ ADJ **(Mormons)** **Mormon** means relating to the religion started by Joseph Smith in the United States. ❑ *...the Mormon church.* N-COUNT ♦ **Mormons** are people who are Mormon.

**morn** /mɔːʳn/ N-SING: also no det **Morn** means the same as morning. [LITERARY] ❑ *...one cold February morn.*

**morn|ing** /mɔːʳnɪŋ/ ◆◆◆ **(mornings)** N-VAR [1] The **morning** is the part of each day between the time that people usually wake up and 12 o'clock noon or lunchtime. ❑ *During the morning your guide will take you around the city... On Sunday morning Bill was woken by the telephone... He read about it in his morning paper.* N-SING: the N [2] If you refer to a particular time in **the morning**, you mean a time between 12 o'clock midnight and 12 o'clock noon. ❑ *I often stayed up until two or three in the morning.*

**PHRASES** PHRASE [3] If you say that something will happen **in the morning**, you mean that it will happen during the morning of the following day. ❑ *I'll fly it to London in the morning.* PHRASE: PHR after v [4] If you say that something happens **morning, noon and night**, you mean that it happens all the time. ❑ *You get fit by playing the game, day in, day out, morning, noon and night.*

**morning-after pill** N-COUNT: usu the N in sing **(morning-after pills)** The **morning-after pill** is a pill that a woman can take some hours after having sex to prevent herself from becoming pregnant.

**morn|ing dress** N-UNCOUNT **Morning dress** is a suit that is worn by men for very formal occasions such as weddings. It consists of a grey or black coat that is longer at the back than the front, grey trousers, a white shirt, a grey tie, and often a top hat.

**morn|ing room** **(morning rooms)** also **morning-room.** N-COUNT In some large, old houses, the **morning room** is a living room which gets the sun in the morning. [OLD-FASHIONED]

**morn|ing sick|ness** N-UNCOUNT **Morning sickness** is a feeling of sickness that some women have, often in the morning, when they are pregnant.

**morn|ing star** N-SING: the N **The morning star** is the planet Venus, which can be seen shining in the sky just after the sun rises.

**Mo|roc|can** /mərɒkən/ **(Moroccans)** ADJ [1] **Moroccan** means belonging or relating to Morocco or to its people or culture. N-COUNT [2] A **Moroccan** is a Moroccan citizen, or a person of Moroccan origin.

**mor|on** /mɔːrɒn/ **(morons)** N-COUNT disapproval = idiot If you refer to someone as a **moron**, you think that they are very stupid. [OFFENSIVE] ❑ *I used to think that Gordon was a moron.*

**mo|ron|ic** /mɔːrɒnɪk/ ADJ disapproval = mindless If you say that a person or their behaviour is **moronic**, you think that they are very stupid. [OFFENSIVE] ❑ *It was wanton, moronic vandalism.*

**mo|rose** /mərous/ ADJ Someone who is **morose** is miserable, bad-tempered, and not willing to talk very much to other people. ❑ *She was morose, pale, and reticent.* ADV: usu ADV with v ♦ **mo|rose|ly** *One elderly man sat morosely at the bar.*

**morph** /mɔːʳf/ VERB **(morphs, morphing, morphed)** If one thing **morphs into** another thing, especially something very different, the first thing changes into the second. [INFORMAL] V into n ❑ *Mild-mannered Stanley morphs into a confident, grinning hero.*

**mor|pheme** /mɔːʳfiːm/ N-COUNT **(morphemes)** A **morpheme** is the smallest unit of meaning in a language. The words 'the', 'in', and 'girl' consist of one morpheme. The word 'girls' consists of two morphemes: 'girl' and 's'.

**mor|phine** /mɔːʳfiːn/ N-UNCOUNT **Morphine** is a drug used to relieve pain.

**morph|ing** /mɔːʳfɪŋ/ N-UNCOUNT **Morphing** is a technique which involves using a computer to make an image on film or television appear to change shape or change into something else.

**mor|phol|ogy** /mɔːʳfɒlədʒi/ N-UNCOUNT The **morphology** of something is its form and structure. In linguistics, **morphology** refers to the way words are constructed with stems, prefixes, and suffixes. [TECHNICAL]

**mor|ris danc|er** /mɒrɪs dɑːnsəʳ, - dæns-/ N-COUNT **(morris dancers)** A **morris dancer** is a person who takes part in morris dancing.

**mor|ris danc|ing** /mɒrɪs dɑːnsɪŋ, - dæns-/ N-UNCOUNT **Morris dancing** is a type of old English country dancing which is performed by people wearing special costumes.

**mor|row** /mɒrou, AM mɔːr-/ N-SING: the N, oft on the N [1] **The morrow** means the next day or tomorrow. [LITERARY or OLD-FASHIONED] ❑ *We do depart for Wales on the morrow.* CONVENTION [2] **Good morrow** means the same as 'good morning'. [LITERARY or OLD-FASHIONED] ❑ *Good morrow to you, my lord.*

**morse code** /mɔːʳs koud/ also **Morse code.** N-UNCOUNT **Morse code** or **morse** is a code used for sending messages. It represents each letter of the alphabet using short and long sounds or flashes of light, which can be written down as dots and dashes.

**mor|sel** /mɔːʳsəl/ N-COUNT: usu with supp, oft N of n **(morsels)** A **morsel** is a very small amount of something, especially a very small piece of food. ❑ *...a delicious little morsel of meat.*

**mor|tal** /mɔːʳtəl/ **(mortals)** ADJ ≠ immortal [1] If you refer to the fact that people are **mortal**, you mean that they have to die and cannot live for ever. ❑ *A man is deliberately designed to be mortal. He grows, he ages, and he dies.* N-UNCOUNT: usu poss N ♦ **mor|tal|ity** /mɔːʳtælɪti/ *She has suddenly come face to face with her own mortality.* N-COUNT = human [2] You can describe someone as a **mortal** when you want to say that they are an ordinary person. ❑ *Tickets seem unobtainable to the ordinary mortal.* ADJ: ADJ n [3] You can use **mortal** to show that something is very serious or may cause death. ❑ *The police were defending themselves and others against mortal danger.* ADV: usu ADV -ed/adj/adv ♦ **mor|tal|ly** *He falls, mortally wounded.* ADJ: ADJ n emphasis [4] You can use **mortal** to emphasize that a feeling is extremely great or severe. ❑ *When self-esteem is high, we lose our mortal fear of jealousy.* ADV: ADV -ed/adj/adv ♦ **mor|tal|ly** *Candida admits to having been 'mortally embarrassed'.*

**mor|tal|ity** /mɔːʳtælɪti/ N-UNCOUNT: oft N n = death rate The **mortality** in a particular place or situation is the number of people who die. ❑ *The nation's infant mortality rate has reached a record low.*

**mor|tal sin** N-VAR **(mortal sins)** In the Roman Catholic Church, a **mortal sin** is an extremely serious sin and the person who has committed it will be punished after death unless they are forgiven by the Church.

**mor|tar** /mɔːʳtəʳ/ **(mortars)** N-COUNT [1] A **mortar** is a big gun which fires missiles high into the air over a short distance. ❑ *He was killed in a mortar attack.* N-UNCOUNT [2] **Mortar** is a mixture of sand, water, and cement or lime which is put between bricks to hold them together. N-COUNT [3] A **mortar** is a bowl in which you can crush things such as herbs, spices, or grain using a rod called a pestle. [4] **bricks and mortar** → see **brick**.

**mor|tar board** **(mortar boards)** also **mortarboard.** N-COUNT A **mortar board** is a stiff black cap which has a flat square top with a bunch of threads attached to it. In Britain, mortar boards are sometimes worn on formal occasions by university students and teachers. In the United States, mortar boards are worn by students at graduation ceremonies at high schools, colleges, and universities.

**mort|gage** /mɔːʳgɪdʒ/ ◆◆◇ **(mortgages, mortgaging, mortgaged)** N-COUNT: oft N n [1] A **mortgage** is a loan of money which you get from a bank or building society in order to buy a house. ❑ *...an increase in mortgage rates.* VERB [2] If you **mortgage** your house or land, you use it as a guarantee to a company in order to borrow money from them. ❑ *They had to mortgage their home to pay the bills.* V n

**mor|tice lock** /mɔːʳtɪs lɒk/ **(mortice locks)** also **mortise lock.** A **mortice lock** is a type of lock which fits into a hole cut into the edge of a door rather than being fixed to one side of it. N-COUNT

**mor|ti|cian** /mɔːʳtɪʃᵊn/ **(morticians)** A **mortician** is a person whose job is to deal with the bodies of people who have died and to arrange funerals. [mainly AM] N-COUNT = *undertaker*

**mor|ti|fi|ca|tion** /mɔːʳtɪfɪkeɪʃᵊn/ **Mortification** is a strong feeling of shame and embarrassment. ❑ *The chairman tried to disguise his mortification.* N-UNCOUNT: oft poss N

**mor|ti|fied** /mɔːʳtɪfaɪd/ If you say that someone is **mortified**, you mean that they feel extremely offended, ashamed, or embarrassed. ❑ *If I reduced somebody to tears I'd be mortified.* ADJ: usu v-link ADJ

**mor|ti|fy** /mɔːʳtɪfaɪ/ **(mortifies, mortifying, mortified)** If you say that something **mortifies** you, you mean that it offends or embarrasses you a great deal. ❑ *Jane mortified her family by leaving her husband.* VERB: no cont; V n

**mor|ti|fy|ing** /mɔːʳtɪfaɪɪŋ/ If you say that something is **mortifying**, you mean that it makes you feel extremely ashamed or embarrassed. ❑ *She felt it would be utterly mortifying to be seen in such company as his by anyone.* ADJ

**mor|tise lock** /mɔːʳtɪs lɒk/ → see **mortice lock.**

**mor|tu|ary** /mɔːʳtʃuəri, AM -eri/ **(mortuaries)** A **mortuary** is a building or a room in a hospital where dead bodies are kept before they are buried or cremated, or before they are identified or examined. N-COUNT = *morgue*

**mo|sa|ic** /moʊzeɪɪk/ **(mosaics)** A **mosaic** is a design which consists of small pieces of coloured glass, pottery, or stone set in concrete or plaster. ❑ *...a Roman villa which once housed a fine collection of mosaics.* N-VAR

**mo|sey** /moʊzi/ **(moseys, moseying, moseyed)** If you **mosey** somewhere, you go there slowly, often without any particular purpose. [INFORMAL] ❑ *He usually moseys into town for no special reason.* VERB = *wander, stroll*; V adv/prep

**mosh** /mɒʃ/ **(moshes, moshing, moshed)** If people at a rock concert **mosh**, they jump up and down together in front of the stage, often pushing each other. ❑ *Moshing down the front, crushed against the stage in a sweat-drenched T-shirt is all part of the gig experience.* VERB; V

**mosh|pit** /mɒʃpɪt/ **(moshpits)** also **mosh pit.** The **moshpit** at a rock concert is the area in front of the stage where people jump up and down. [mainly BRIT] N-COUNT

**Mos|lem** /mɒzləm, mʊzlɪm/ → see **Muslim.**

**mosque** /mɒsk/ **(mosques)** A **mosque** is a building where Muslims go to worship. N-COUNT

**mos|qui|to** /mɒskiːtoʊ/ **(mosquitoes** or **mosquitos) Mosquitos** are small flying insects which bite people and animals in order to suck their blood. N-COUNT

**mos|qui|to net (mosquito nets)** A **mosquito net** is a curtain made of very fine cloth which is hung round a bed in order to keep mosquitoes and other insects away from a person while they are sleeping. N-COUNT

**moss** /mɒs, AM mɔːs/ **(mosses) Moss** is a very small soft green plant which grows on damp soil, or on wood or stone. ❑ *...ground covered over with moss.* N-MASS

**mossy** /mɒsi, AM mɔːsi/ A **mossy** surface is covered with moss. ❑ *...a mossy wall.* ADJ

**most** /moʊst/ ◆◆◆

> **Most** is often considered to be the superlative form of **much** and **many**.

[1] You use **most** to refer to the majority of a group of things or people or the largest part of something. ❑ *By stopping smoking you are undoing most of the damage smoking has caused... Sadly, most of the house was destroyed by fire in 1828.* ♦ **Most** is also a determiner. ❑ *Most people think the Queen has done a good job over the last 50 years.* ♦ **Most** is also a pronoun. ❑ *Seventeen civilians were hurt. Most are students who had been attending a twenty-first birthday party.* QUANT: QUANT *of* def-n; DET: DET pl-n; PRON

[2] You use **the most** to mean a larger amount than anyone or anything else, or the largest amount possible. ❑ *The President himself won the most votes.* ♦ **Most** is also a pronoun. ❑ *The most they earn in a day is ten roubles.* ADJ: *the* ADJ n; PRON

[3] You use **most** to indicate that something is true or happens to a greater degree or extent than anything else. ❑ *What she feared most was becoming like her mother. ...Professor Morris, the person he most hated.* ● You use **most of all** to indicate that something happens or is true to a greater extent than anything else. ❑ *She said she wanted most of all to be fair.* ADV: ADV with v ≠ *least*; PHRASE: PHR with v

[4] You use **most** to indicate that someone or something has a greater amount of a particular quality than most other things of its kind. ❑ *He was one of the most influential performers of modern jazz... If anything, swimming will appeal to her most strongly.* ADV: ADV adj/adv ≠ *least*

[5] If you do something **the most**, you do it to the greatest extent possible or with the greatest frequency. ❑ *What question are you asked the most?* ADV: *the* ADV after v

[6] You use **most** in conversations when you want to draw someone's attention to something very interesting or important that you are about to say. ❑ *Most surprisingly, quite a few said they don't intend to vote at all.* ADV: ADV adv/adj

[7] You use **most** to emphasize an adjective or adverb. [FORMAL] ❑ *I'll be most pleased to speak to them.* ADV: ADV adj/adv [emphasis]

**PHRASES** [8] You use **at most** or **at the most** to say that a number or amount is the maximum that is possible and that the actual number or amount may be smaller. ❑ *Poach the pears in apple juice for perhaps ten minutes at most. ...staying on at school for two extra years to study only three, or at the most four subjects.* PHRASE: amount PHR, PHR with cl

[9] If you **make the most of** something, you get the maximum use or advantage from it. ❑ *Happiness is the ability to make the most of what you have.* PHRASE: V inflects

[10] **for the most part** → see **part.**

**-most** /-moʊst/ **-most** is added to adjectives in order to form other adjectives that describe something as being further in a particular direction than other things of the same kind. ❑ *...the topmost branches of the trees... Many patients have told me their innermost thoughts. ...the northernmost suburbs of Chicago.* SUFFIX

**most|ly** /moʊstli/ You use **mostly** to indicate that a statement is generally true, for example true about the majority of a group of things or people, true most of the time, or true in most respects. ❑ *I am working with mostly highly motivated people... Cars are mostly metal. ...men and women, mostly in their 30s.* ◆◇◇ ADV: ADV with cl/group = *mainly*

**MOT** /em oʊ tiː/ **(MOTs)** In Britain, an **MOT** is a test which, by law, must be made each year on all road vehicles that are more than 3 years old, in order to check that they are safe to drive. ❑ *My car is due for its MOT in two days' time.* N-COUNT

**mo|tel** /moʊtel/ **(motels)** A **motel** is a hotel intended for people who are travelling by car. N-COUNT

**moth** /mɒθ, AM mɔːθ/ **(moths)** A **moth** is an insect like a butterfly which usually flies about at night. N-COUNT

**moth|ball** /mɒθbɔːl, AM mɔːθ-/ **(mothballs, mothballing, mothballed)** [1] A **mothball** is a small ball made of a special chemical, which you can put among clothes or blankets in order to keep moths away. N-COUNT [2] If someone in authority **mothballs** a plan, factory, or piece of equipment, they decide to stop developing or using it, perhaps temporarily. [JOURNALISM] ❑ *...the decision to mothball the Bataan Nuclear Power Plant, for safety and political reasons.* VERB; V n

**moth-eaten** 1 **Moth-eaten** clothes look very old and have holes in them. 2 If you describe something as **moth-eaten**, you mean that it seems unattractive or useless because it is old or has been used too much. ❑ *We drove through a somewhat moth-eaten deer park... This strategy looks increasingly moth-eaten.* ADJ ADJ [disapproval]

**moth|er** /mʌðəʳ/ **(mothers, mothering, mothered)** ◆◆◆ 1 Your **mother** is the woman who gave birth to you. You can also call someone your **mother** if she brings you up as if she was this woman. ❑ *She sat on the edge of her mother's bed... She's an English teacher and a mother of two children... I'm here, Mother.* N-FAMILY 2 If a woman **mothers** a child, she looks after it and brings it up, usually because she is its mother. ❑ *Colleen had dreamed of mothering a large family.* ♦ **moth|er|ing** *The reality of mothering is frequently very different from the romantic ideal.* VERB V n N-UNCOUNT 3 If you **mother** someone, you treat them with great care and affection, as if they were a small child. ❑ *Stop mothering me.* VERB V n

**mother|board** /mʌðəʳbɔːʳd/ **(motherboards)** In a computer, the **motherboard** is the main electronic circuit board to which the microchips that perform important functions are attached. N-COUNT

**moth|er coun|try** **(mother countries)** also **Mother Country.** 1 Someone's **mother country** is the country in which they or their ancestors were born and to which they still feel emotionally linked, even if they live somewhere else. ❑ *Dr Kengerli looks to Turkey as his mother country.* N-COUNT: oft with poss = motherland 2 If you refer to **the mother country** of a particular state or country, you are referring to the very powerful country that used to control its affairs. ❑ *Australia, New Zealand, and Canada, had no colonial conflict with the mother country.* N-SING: usu the N

**moth|er fig|ure** **(mother figures)** also **mother-figure.** If you regard someone as a **mother figure**, you think of them as having the role of a mother and being the person you can turn to for help, advice, or support. N-COUNT

**mother|fucker** /mʌðəʳfʌkəʳ/ **(motherfuckers)** If someone calls a person, usually a man, a **motherfucker**, they are insulting him in a very unpleasant way. [mainly AM, ⚠ VERY RUDE] N-COUNT [disapproval]

**moth|er|hood** /mʌðəʳhʊd/ **Motherhood** is the state of being a mother. ❑ *...women who try to combine work and motherhood.* N-UNCOUNT

**Moth|er|ing Sun|day** **Mothering Sunday** is the fourth Sunday in Lent, when children give cards and presents to their mothers as a sign of their love for them. [BRIT, OLD-FASHIONED] N-UNCOUNT = Mother's Day

**mother-in-law** **(mothers-in-law)** Someone's **mother-in-law** is the mother of their husband or wife. N-COUNT: oft poss N

**mother|land** /mʌðəʳlænd/ also **Motherland.** **The motherland** is the country in which you or your ancestors were born and to which you still feel emotionally linked, even if you live somewhere else. ❑ *...love for the motherland.* N-SING: usu the N = mother country

**moth|er|less** /mʌðəʳləs/ You describe children as **motherless** if their mother has died or does not live with them. ❑ *...Michael's seven motherless children.* ADJ

**moth|er|ly** /mʌðəʳli/ **Motherly** feelings or actions are like those of a kind mother. ❑ *It was an incredible display of motherly love and forgiveness.* ADJ: usu ADJ n = maternal

**Moth|er Na|ture** **Mother Nature** is sometimes used to refer to nature, especially when it is being considered as a force that affects human beings. ❑ *...when Mother Nature created Iceland out of volcanic lava and glaciers.* N-UNCOUNT

**Moth|er of God** In Christianity, **the Mother of God** is another name for the Virgin Mary, the mother of Jesus Christ. N-PROPER

**mother-of-pearl** also **mother of pearl.** **Mother-of-pearl** is the shiny layer on the inside of some shells. It is used to make buttons or to decorate things. N-UNCOUNT

**Moth|er's Day** **Mother's Day** is a special day on which children give cards and presents to their mothers as a sign of their love for them. In Britain, Mother's Day is the fourth Sunday in Lent. In the United States, it is the second Sunday in May. N-UNCOUNT

**Moth|er Su|peri|or** **(Mother Superiors)** A **Mother Superior** is a nun who is in charge of the other nuns in a convent. N-COUNT

**mother-to-be** **(mothers-to-be)** A **mother-to-be** is a woman who is pregnant, especially for the first time. N-COUNT

**moth|er tongue** **(mother tongues)** also **mother-tongue.** Your **mother tongue** is the language that you learn from your parents when you are a baby. N-COUNT: oft poss N = native tongue

**mo|tif** /moʊtiːf/ **(motifs)** A **motif** is a design which is used as a decoration or as part of an artistic pattern. ❑ *...a rose motif.* N-COUNT: usu with supp

**mo|tion** /moʊʃən/ **(motions, motioning, motioned)** ◆◇◇ 1 **Motion** is the activity or process of continually changing position or moving from one place to another. ❑ *...the laws governing light, sound, and motion... One group of muscles sets the next group in motion... The wind from the car's motion whipped her hair around her head.* N-UNCOUNT = movement 2 A **motion** is an action, gesture, or movement. ❑ *He made a neat chopping motion with his hand.* N-COUNT: usu with supp = movement 3 A **motion** is a formal proposal or statement in a meeting, debate, or trial, which is discussed and then voted on or decided on. ❑ *The conference is now debating the motion and will vote on it shortly... Opposition parties are likely to bring a no-confidence motion against the government.* N-COUNT 4 If you **motion** to someone, you move your hand or head as a way of telling them to do something or telling them where to go. ❑ *She motioned for the locked front doors to be opened... He stood aside and motioned Don to the door... I motioned him to join us... He motioned to her to go behind the screen.* VERB = signal, gesture V for n to-inf V n prep/adv V n to-inf V to n to-inf 5 → See also **slow motion, time and motion.**

PHRASES 6 If you say that someone **is going through the motions**, you think they are only saying or doing something because it is expected of them without being interested, enthusiastic, or sympathetic. ❑ *'You really don't care, do you?' she said quietly. 'You're just going through the motions.'* PHRASE: V inflects 7 If a process or event is **in motion**, it is happening. If it is set **in motion**, it is happening or beginning to happen. ❑ *His job as England manager begins in earnest now his World Cup campaign is in motion... Her sharp, aggressive tone set in motion the events that led to her downfall.* PHRASE: usu v-link PHR, PHR after v 8 If someone **sets the wheels in motion**, they take the necessary action to make something start happening. ❑ *I have set the wheels in motion to sell Endsleigh Court.* PHRASE: V inflects

**mo|tion|less** /moʊʃənləs/ Someone or something that is **motionless** is not moving at all. ❑ *He stood there motionless.* ADJ: usu v-link ADJ = still

**mo|tion pic|ture** **(motion pictures)** A **motion picture** is a film made for cinema. [mainly AM] ❑ *It was there that I saw my first motion picture.* N-COUNT = movie

**mo|ti|vate** /moʊtɪveɪt/ **(motivates, motivating, motivated)** ◆◇◇ 1 If you **are motivated** by something, especially an emotion, it causes you to behave in a particular way. ❑ *They are motivated by a need to achieve... I don't want to be missing out. And that motivates me to get up and do something every day.* ♦ **mo|ti|vat|ed** *...highly motivated employees.* ♦ **mo|ti|va|tion** /moʊtɪveɪʃən/ *His poor performance may be attributed to lack of motivation rather than to reading difficulties.* VERB be V-ed V n to-inf Also V n ADJ N-UNCOUNT 2 If someone **motivates** you to do something, they make you feel determined to do it. ❑ *How do you motivate people to work hard and efficiently?... Never let it be said that the manager doesn't know how to motivate his players.* ♦ **mo|ti|va|tion** *Gross's skill in motivation looked in doubt when his side began the second half badly.* VERB = inspire V n to-inf V n N-UNCOUNT

**mo|ti|va|tion** /moʊtɪveɪʃᵊn/ **(motivations)** N-COUNT: usu with poss Your **motivation** for doing something is what causes you to want to do it. ❑ *Money is my motivation... The timing of the attack, and its motivations, are unknown.*

**mo|tive** /moʊtɪv/ **(motives)** N-COUNT: oft N prep Your **motive** for doing something is your reason for doing it. ❑ *Police have ruled out robbery as a motive for the killing. ...the motives and objectives of British foreign policy.*

**mot|ley** /mɒtli/ ADJ: ADJ n You can describe a group of things as a **motley** collection if you think they seem strange together because they are all very different. ❑ *...a motley collection of vans, old buses, cattle-trucks, and even a fire engine.*

**mo|tor** /moʊtəʳ/ **(motors)** ◆◆◇ 1 N-COUNT = engine The **motor** in a machine, vehicle, or boat is the part that uses electricity or fuel to produce movement, so that the machine, vehicle, or boat can work. ❑ *She got in and started the motor.* 2 ADJ: ADJ n **Motor** vehicles and boats have a petrol or diesel engine. ❑ *Theft of motor vehicles is up by 15.9%.* 3 ADJ: ADJ n **Motor** is used to describe activities relating to vehicles such as cars and buses. [mainly BRIT] ❑ *...the future of the British motor industry... He worked as a motor mechanic.*

☑ in AM, usually use **automotive**, **automobile**

4 N-COUNT Some people refer to a car as a **motor**. [BRIT, INFORMAL] 5 ➔ See also **motoring**, **outboard motor**.

**motor|bike** /moʊtəʳbaɪk/ **(motorbikes)** also **motor-bike.** 1 N-COUNT A **motorbike** is the same as a **motorcycle**. [BRIT] 2 N-COUNT A **motorbike** is a lighter, less powerful motorcycle. [AM]

**motor|boat** /moʊtəʳboʊt/ **(motorboats)** also **motor boat.** N-COUNT A **motorboat** is a boat that is driven by an engine.

**motor|cade** /moʊtəʳkeɪd/ **(motorcades)** N-COUNT A **motorcade** is a line of slow-moving cars carrying important people, usually as part of a public ceremony. ❑ *At times the president's motorcade slowed to a crawl.*

**mo|tor car** **(motor cars)** also **motorcar.** N-COUNT A **motor car** is the same as a **car**. [OLD-FASHIONED]

**motor|cycle** /moʊtəʳsaɪkᵊl/ **(motorcycles)** N-COUNT = motorbike A **motorcycle** is a vehicle with two wheels and an engine.

**motor|cyclist** /moʊtəʳsaɪklɪst/ **(motorcyclists)** N-COUNT A **motorcyclist** is a person who rides a motorcycle.

**mo|tor home** **(motor homes)** N-COUNT A **motor home** is a large vehicle containing beds and equipment for cooking and washing. Motor homes can be used for holidays or very long journeys.

**mo|tor|ing** /moʊtərɪŋ/ ADJ: ADJ n **Motoring** means relating to cars and driving. [mainly BRIT] ❑ *...a three-month sentence for motoring offences... Police and motoring organizations said the roads were slightly busier than normal.*

☑ in AM, usually use **driving**, **automobile**

**mo|tor|ised** /moʊtəraɪzd/ ➔ see **motorized**.

**mo|tor|ist** /moʊtərɪst/ **(motorists)** N-COUNT = driver A **motorist** is a person who drives a car. [mainly BRIT]

☑ in AM, use **driver**

**mo|tor|ized** /moʊtəraɪzd/

☑ in BRIT, also use **motorised**

1 ADJ: usu ADJ n A **motorized** vehicle has an engine. ❑ *Around 1910 motorized carriages were beginning to replace horse-drawn cabs.* 2 ADJ: usu ADJ n A **motorized** group of soldiers is equipped with motor vehicles. ❑ *...motorized infantry and artillery.*

**motor|mouth** /moʊtəʳmaʊθ/ N-SING disapproval If you describe someone as a **motormouth**, you mean that they talk a lot, especially in a loud or aggressive way. [INFORMAL]

**mo|tor neu|rone dis|ease** N-UNCOUNT **Motor neurone disease** is a disease which destroys the part of a person's nervous system that controls movement.

**motor|way** /moʊtəʳweɪ/ **(motorways)** N-VAR A **motorway** is a major road that has been specially built for fast travel over long distances. Motorways have several lanes and special places where traffic gets on and leaves. [BRIT] ❑ *...the M1 motorway. ...the national motorway network.*

☑ in AM, usually use **freeway**

**mott|led** /mɒtᵊld/ ADJ Something that is **mottled** is covered with patches of different colours which do not form a regular pattern. ❑ *...mottled green and yellow leaves.*

**mot|to** /mɒtoʊ/ **(mottoes** or **mottos)** N-COUNT: oft with poss A **motto** is a short sentence or phrase that expresses a rule for sensible behaviour, especially a way of behaving in a particular situation. ❑ *Our motto is 'Plan for the worst and hope for the best'.*

**mould** /moʊld/ **(moulds, moulding, moulded)**

☑ in AM, use **mold**

1 N-COUNT A **mould** is a hollow container that you pour liquid into. When the liquid becomes solid, it takes the same shape as the mould. ❑ *Spoon the mixture carefully into the mould. ...jelly moulds.* 2 N-COUNT: usu with supp If a person fits into or is cast in a **mould** of a particular kind, they have the characteristics, attitudes, behaviour, or lifestyle that are typical of that type of person. ❑ *He was from the same mould as the men she had gazed at worshipfully when a child: rich, handsome, of impeccable social standing.* ● PHRASE: V inflects If you say that someone **breaks the mould**, you mean that they do completely different things from what has been done before or from what is usually done. ❑ *Memorial services have become tedious and expected. I would like to help break the mould.* 3 VERB If you **mould** a soft substance such as plastic or clay, you make it into a particular shape or into an object. ❑ V n *into* n *Using 2 spoons, mould the cheese mixture into small balls or ovals.* 4 VERB = form, shape To **mould** someone or something means to change or influence them over a period of time so that they develop in a particular way. ❑ V n *She was only 17 at the time and the experience moulded her personality...* V n *into* n *Too often we try to mold our children into something they do not wish to be.* 5 VERB When something **moulds** to an object or when you **mould** it there, it fits round the object tightly so that the shape of the object can still be seen. ❑ V *to/around/round* n *You need a malleable pillow that will mould to the curves of your neck...* V n *around/round/to* n *She stood there, the wind moulding the dress around her.* 6 N-MASS **Mould** is a soft grey, green, or blue substance that sometimes forms in spots on old food or on damp walls or clothes. ➔ See also **leaf mould**.

**mould|er** /moʊldəʳ/ **(moulders, mouldering, mouldered)**

☑ in AM, use **molder**

VERB: usu cont If something **is mouldering**, it is decaying slowly where it has been left. ❑ V *...one of your scripts that's been mouldering under the bed for ages...* V *It is clear that such ideas will be left to moulder.* V-ing *...the empty, mouldering old house.*

**mould|ing** /moʊldɪŋ/ **(mouldings)**

☑ in AM, use **molding**

N-COUNT A **moulding** is a strip of plaster or wood along the top of a wall or round a door, which has been made into an ornamental shape or decorated with a pattern.

**mouldy** /moʊldi/

☑ in AM, use **moldy**

ADJ Something that is **mouldy** is covered with mould. ❑ *...mouldy bread... Oranges can be kept for a long time without going mouldy.*

**moult** /moʊlt/ **(moults, moulting, moulted)**

☑ in AM, use **molt**

VERB When an animal or bird **moults**, it gradually loses its coat or feathers so that a new coat or feathers can grow. ❑ *Finches start to moult at around twelve weeks of age.* V

**mound** /maʊnd/ **(mounds)** 1 A **mound** of something is a large rounded pile of it. ❑ *The bulldozers piled up huge mounds of dirt.* N-COUNT: usu N *of* n 2 In baseball, the **mound** is the raised area where the pitcher stands when he or she throws the ball. N-COUNT: usu *the* N in sing

**mount** /maʊnt/ **(mounts, mounting, mounted)** ◆◇◇ 1 If you **mount** a campaign or event, you organize it and make it take place. ❑ *...a security operation mounted by the army.* VERB = organize V n 2 If something **mounts**, it increases in intensity. ❑ *For several hours, tension mounted... There was mounting concern in her voice.* VERB = rise V V-ing 3 If something **mounts**, it increases in quantity. ❑ *The uncollected garbage mounts in city streets... He ignored his mounting debts.* VERB V V-ing ♦ To **mount up** means the same as to **mount**. ❑ *Her medical bills mounted up.* PHRASAL VERB V P 4 If you **mount** the stairs or a platform, you go up the stairs or go up onto the platform. [FORMAL] ❑ *Llewelyn was mounting the stairs up into the keep.* VERB V n 5 If you **mount** a horse or cycle, you climb on to it so that you can ride it. ❑ *A man in a crash helmet was mounting a motorbike... He went to the small stable where his horse was, harnessed it, mounted, and rode out to the beach.* VERB = get on V n V 6 If you **mount** an object **on** something, you fix it there firmly. ❑ *Her husband mounts the work on velour paper and makes the frame. ...a specially mounted horse shoe.* ♦ **-mounted** *...a wall-mounted electric fan.* VERB V n *on* n V-ed Also V n COMB in ADJ 7 If you **mount** an exhibition or display, you organize and present it. ❑ *The gallery has mounted an exhibition of art by Irish women painters.* VERB = put on, stage V n 8 **Mount** is used as part of the name of a mountain. ❑ *...Mount Everest.* N-IN-NAMES 9 → See also **mounted**.
♦ **mount up** → see **mount 3**.

**moun|tain** /maʊntɪn, AM -tᵊn/ **(mountains)** ◆◆◇ 1 A **mountain** is a very high area of land with steep sides. ❑ *Ben Nevis, in Scotland, is Britain's highest mountain.* N-COUNT 2 If you talk about a **mountain of** something, or **mountains of** something, you are emphasizing that there is a large amount of it. [INFORMAL] ❑ *They are faced with a mountain of bureaucracy.* QUANT: QUANT *of* pl-n/n-uncount [emphasis] 3 If you say that someone has **a mountain to climb**, you mean that it will be difficult for them to achieve what they want to achieve. [JOURNALISM] ❑ *'We had a mountain to climb after the second goal went in,' said Crosby.* PHRASE: usu v PHR 4 to **make a mountain out of a molehill** → see **molehill**.

**moun|tain bike** **(mountain bikes)** A **mountain bike** is a type of bicycle that is suitable for riding over rough ground. It has a strong frame and thick tyres. N-COUNT

**moun|tain|eer** /maʊntɪnɪəʳ/ **(mountaineers)** A **mountaineer** is a person who is skilful at climbing the steep sides of mountains. N-COUNT

**moun|tain|eer|ing** /maʊntɪnɪərɪŋ/ **Mountaineering** is the activity of climbing the steep sides of mountains as a hobby or sport. N-UNCOUNT

**moun|tain lion** **(mountain lions)** A **mountain lion** is a wild animal that is a member of the cat family. Mountain lions have brownish-grey fur and live in mountain regions of North and South America. [mainly AM] N-COUNT = cougar

✓ in BRIT, use **puma**

**moun|tain|ous** /maʊntɪnəs/ 1 A **mountainous** place has a lot of mountains. ❑ *...the mountainous region of Campania.* ADJ 2 You use **mountainous** to emphasize that something is great in size, quantity, or degree. ❑ *The plan is designed to reduce some of the company's mountainous debt.* ADJ: ADJ n [emphasis] = huge

**moun|tain|side** /maʊntɪnsaɪd/ **(mountainsides)** A **mountainside** is one of the steep sides of a mountain. ❑ *The couple trudged up the dark mountainside.* N-COUNT

**mount|ed** /maʊntɪd/ **Mounted** police or soldiers ride horses when they are on duty. ❑ *A dozen mounted police rode into the square.* → See also **mount**. ADJ: ADJ n

**mourn** /mɔːʳn/ **(mourns, mourning, mourned)** 1 If you **mourn** someone who has died or **mourn for** them, you are very sad that they have died and show your sorrow in the way that you behave. ❑ *Joan still mourns her father... He mourned for his valiant men... As the nation continued to mourn, the new President of South Africa paid his own tribute.* VERB V n V *for* n V 2 If you **mourn** something or **mourn for** it, you regret that you no longer have it and show your regret in the way that you behave. ❑ *We mourned the loss of our cities... She mourned for the beloved past.* VERB V n V *for* n 3 → See also **mourning**.

**mourn|er** /mɔːʳnəʳ/ **(mourners)** A **mourner** is a person who attends a funeral, especially as a relative or friend of the dead person. N-COUNT

**mourn|ful** /mɔːʳnfʊl/ 1 If you are **mournful**, you are very sad. ❑ *He looked mournful, even near to tears.* ♦ **mourn|ful|ly** *He stood mournfully at the gate waving bye bye.* ADJ ADV: usu ADV with v 2 A **mournful** sound seems very sad. ❑ *...the mournful wail of bagpipes.* ADJ

**mourn|ing** /mɔːʳnɪŋ/ 1 **Mourning** is behaviour in which you show sadness about a person's death. ❑ *Expect to feel angry, depressed and confused. It's all part of the mourning process.* N-UNCOUNT 2 If you are **in mourning**, you are dressed or behaving in a particular way because someone you love or respect has died. ❑ *Yesterday the whole of Greece was in mourning.* PHRASE: usu v-link PHR

**mouse** /maʊs/ **(mice)**

✓ The plural **mouses** can be used for meaning 2.

1 A **mouse** is a small furry animal with a long tail. ❑ *...a mouse running in a wheel in its cage.* N-COUNT 2 A **mouse** is a device that is connected to a computer. By moving it over a flat surface and pressing its buttons, you can move the cursor around the screen and do things without using the keyboard. N-COUNT 3 **game of cat and mouse** → see **cat**.

**mouse mat** **(mouse mats)** also **mousemat.** A **mouse mat** is a flat piece of plastic or some other material that you rest the mouse on while using a computer. [BRIT] N-COUNT

**mouse pad** **(mouse pads)** also **mousepad.** A **mouse pad** is the same as a **mouse mat**. [mainly AM] N-COUNT

**mouse|trap** /maʊstræp/ **(mousetraps)** A **mousetrap** is a small device that catches or kills mice. N-COUNT

**mous|ey** /maʊsi/ → see **mousy**.

**mous|sa|ka** /mʊsɑːkə/ **(moussakas)** **Moussaka** is a Greek dish consisting of layers of meat and aubergine. N-VAR

**mousse** /muːs/ **(mousses)** 1 **Mousse** is a sweet light food made from eggs and cream. It is often flavoured with fruit or chocolate. N-VAR 2 **Mousse** is a soft substance containing a lot of tiny bubbles, for example one that you can put in your hair to make it easier to shape into a particular style. N-MASS

**mous|tache** /məstɑːʃ, AM mʊstæʃ/ **(moustaches)** also **mustache.** A man's **moustache** is the hair that grows on his upper lip. If it is very long, it is sometimes referred to as his **moustaches**. ❑ *He was short and bald and had a moustache.* ♦ **mous|tached** *...three burly, moustached middle-aged men.* N-COUNT ADJ

**mous|ta|chi|oed** /məstæʃioʊd, AM -tæʃoʊd/ also **mustachioed.** A **moustachioed** man has a moustache. [HUMOROUS or WRITTEN] ADJ

**mousy** /maʊsi/ also **mousey.** 1 **Mousy** hair is a dull light brown colour. ❑ *He was aged between 25 and 30, with a medium build and collar-length mousy hair.* ADJ: usu ADJ n 2 If you describe someone as **mousy**, you mean that they are quiet and shy and that people do not notice them. ❑ *The Inspector remembered her as a small, mousy woman, invariably worried.* ADJ: usu ADJ n

**mouth** **(mouths, mouthing, mouthed)** ◆◆◇

> Pronounced /maʊθ/ for the noun, and /maʊð/ for the verb. The form **mouths** is pronounced /maʊðz/.

[1] Your **mouth** is the area of your face where your lips are or the space behind your lips where your teeth and tongue are. ❑ *She clamped her hand against her mouth... His mouth was full of peas.* N-COUNT: oft poss N ♦ **-mouthed** /-maʊðd/ *He straightened up and looked at me, open-mouthed.* COMB in ADJ [2] You can say that someone has a particular kind of **mouth** to indicate that they speak in a particular kind of way or that they say particular kinds of things. ❑ *You've got such a crude mouth!* N-COUNT: with supp, oft adj N ♦ **-mouthed** *...Simon, their smart-mouthed teenage son.* COMB in ADJ [3] The **mouth** of a cave, hole, or bottle is its entrance or opening. ❑ *By the mouth of the tunnel he bent to retie his lace.* N-COUNT: usu with supp, oft N *of* n ♦ **-mouthed** *He put the flowers in a wide-mouthed blue vase.* COMB in ADJ [4] The **mouth** of a river is the place where it flows into the sea. ❑ *...the town at the mouth of the River Dart.* N-COUNT: usu with supp [5] If you **mouth** something, you form words with your lips without making any sound. ❑ *I mouthed a goodbye and hurried in behind Momma... 'It's for you,' he mouthed.* VERB V n V with quote [6] If you **mouth** something, you say it, especially without believing it or without understanding it. ❑ *I mouthed some sympathetic platitudes.* VERB V n

**PHRASES** [7] If you have a number of **mouths to feed**, you have the responsibility of earning enough money to feed and look after that number of people. ❑ *He had to feed his family on the equivalent of four hundred pounds a month and, with five mouths to feed, he found this very hard.* PHRASE: N inflects [8] If you say that someone does not **open** their **mouth**, you are emphasizing that they never say anything at all. ❑ *Sometimes I hardly dare open my mouth.* PHRASE: V and N inflect, with brd-neg emphasis [9] If you **keep** your **mouth shut** about something, you do not talk about it, especially because it is a secret. ❑ *You wouldn't be here now if she'd kept her mouth shut.* PHRASE: V and N inflect [10] to **live hand to mouth** → see **heart**. **heart in** your **mouth** → see **hand**. **from the horse's mouth** → see **horse**. to **put** your **money where** your **mouth is** → see **money**. **shut** your **mouth** → see **shut**. to be **born with a silver spoon in** your **mouth** → see **spoon**. **word of mouth** → see **word**.

**mouth|ful** /maʊθfʊl/ **(mouthfuls)** [1] A **mouthful of** drink or food is the amount that you put or have in your mouth. ❑ *She gulped down a mouthful of coffee.* N-COUNT: oft N *of* n [2] If you describe a long word or phrase as **a mouthful**, you mean that it is difficult to say. [INFORMAL] ❑ *It's called the Pan-Caribbean Disaster Preparedness and Prevention Project, which is quite a mouthful.* N-SING: *a* N

**mouth or|gan** **(mouth organs)** A **mouth organ** is the same as a **harmonica**. [mainly BRIT] N-COUNT

**mouth|piece** /maʊθpiːs/ **(mouthpieces)** [1] The **mouthpiece** of a telephone is the part that you speak into. ❑ *He shouted into the mouthpiece.* N-COUNT [2] The **mouthpiece** of a musical instrument or other device is the part that you put into your mouth. ❑ *He showed him how to blow into the ivory mouthpiece.* N-COUNT [3] The **mouthpiece** of an organization or person is someone who informs other people of the opinions and policies of that organization or person. ❑ *Their mouthpiece is the vice-president.* N-COUNT: usu with poss

**mouth-to-mouth re|sus|ci|ta|tion** or **mouth-to-mouth** If you give someone who has stopped breathing **mouth-to-mouth resuscitation**, you breathe into their mouth to make them start breathing again. N-UNCOUNT

**mouth|wash** /maʊθwɒʃ/ **(mouthwashes)** **Mouthwash** is a liquid that you put in your mouth and then spit out in order to clean your mouth and make your breath smell pleasant. N-MASS

**mouth-watering** also **mouthwatering.** [1] **Mouth-watering** food looks or smells extremely nice. ❑ *...hundreds of cheeses, in a mouth-watering variety of shapes, textures and tastes.* ADJ [2] If you describe something as **mouth-watering**, you are emphasizing that it is very attractive. [JOURNALISM] ❑ *...prizes worth a mouth-watering £9.6 million.* ADJ emphasis

**mov|able** /muːvəbᵊl/ also **moveable.** Something that is **movable** can be moved from one place or position to another. ❑ *It's a vinyl doll with movable arms and legs.* ADJ

**move** /muːv/ **(moves, moving, moved)** ◆◆◆

[1] When you **move** something or when it **moves**, its position changes and it does not remain still. ❑ *She moved the sheaf of papers into position... A traffic warden asked him to move his car... I could see the branches of the trees moving back and forth... The train began to move.* VERB V n prep/adv V n V prep/adv V [2] When you **move**, you change your position or go to a different place. ❑ *She waited for him to get up, but he didn't move... He moved around the room, putting his possessions together.* VERB V V prep/adv ♦ **Move** is also a noun. ❑ *The doctor made a move towards the door... Daniel's eyes followed her every move.* N-COUNT: usu sing = movement [3] If you **move**, you act or you begin to do something. ❑ *Industrialists must move fast to take advantage of new opportunities in Eastern Europe.* VERB = act V [4] A **move** is an action that you take in order to achieve something. ❑ *The one point cut in interest rates was a wise move... The thirty-five member nations agreed to the move.* N-COUNT: usu sing [5] If a person or company **moves**, they leave the building where they have been living or working, and they go to live or work in a different place, taking their possessions with them. ❑ *My family home is in Yorkshire and they don't want to move... She had often considered moving to London... They move house fairly frequently.* VERB V V *to* n V n ♦ **Move** is also a noun. ❑ *Modigliani announced his move to Montparnasse in 1909.* N-COUNT [6] If people in authority **move** someone, they make that person go from one place or job to another one. ❑ *His superiors moved him to another parish... Ms Clark is still in position and there are no plans to move her.* VERB = transfer V n prep/adv V n [7] If you **move from** one job or interest **to** another, you change to it. ❑ *He moved from being an extramural tutor to being a lecturer in social history... In the early days Christina moved jobs to get experience.* VERB V *from/to* n/-ing V n ♦ **Move** is also a noun. ❑ *His move to the chairmanship means he will take a less active role in day-to-day management.* N-COUNT [8] If you **move to** a new topic in a conversation, you start talking about something different. ❑ *Let's move to another subject, Dan.* VERB V *from/to* n/-ing [9] If you **move** an event or the date of an event, you change the time at which it happens. ❑ *The club has moved its meeting to Saturday, January 22nd... The band have moved forward their Leeds date to October 27.* VERB V n *to* n V n with adv Also V n [10] If you **move** towards a particular state, activity, or opinion, you start to be in that state, do that activity, or have that opinion. ❑ *Since the Convention was drawn up international opinion has begun to move against it.* VERB V prep/adv ♦ **Move** is also a noun. ❑ *His move to the left was not a sudden leap but a natural working out of ideas.* N-COUNT = shift [11] If a situation or process **is moving**, it is developing or progressing, rather than staying still. ❑ *Events are moving fast... Someone has got to get things moving.* VERB: usu cont V V n -ing [12] If you say that you will not **be moved**, you mean that you have come to a decision and nothing will change your mind. ❑ *Everyone thought I was mad to go back, but I wouldn't be moved.* VERB: usu passive, with neg = budge *be* V-ed [13] If something **moves** you **to** do something, it influences you and causes you to do it. ❑ *It was punk that first moved him to join a band seriously.* VERB V n to-inf [14] If something **moves** you, it has an effect on your emotions and causes you to feel sadness or sympathy for another person. ❑ *These stories surprised and moved me... His prayer moved me to tears.* VERB V n V n *to* n ♦ **moved** *Those who listened to him were deeply moved.* ADJ: v-link ADJ [15] If you say that someone **moves in** a particular society, circle, or world, you mean that they know people in a particular social class or group and spend most of their time with them. ❑ *She moves in high-society circles in London.* VERB V *in* n [16] At a meeting, if you **move** a motion, you formally suggest it so that everyone present can vote on it. ❑ *Labour quickly moved a closure motion to end* VERB = put forward, propose V n

*the debate... I move that the case be dismissed.* V that
17 A **move** is an act of putting a chess piece or other counter in a different position on a board when it is your turn to do so in a game. ❑ *With no idea of what to do for my next move, my hand hovered over the board.* N-COUNT

PHRASES 18 If you say that one **false move** will cause a disaster, you mean that you or someone else must not make any mistakes because the situation is so difficult or dangerous. ❑ *He knew one false move would end in death.* PHRASE 19 If you tell someone to **get a move on**, you are telling them to hurry. [INFORMAL] PHRASE = hurry up 20 If you **make a move**, you prepare or begin to leave one place and go somewhere else. ❑ *He glanced at his wristwatch. 'I suppose we'd better make a move.'* PHRASE: V inflects, oft PHR to-inf 21 If you **make a move**, you take a course of action. ❑ *The week before the deal was supposed to close, fifteen Japanese banks made a move to pull out.* PHRASE: V inflects, oft PHR to-inf 22 If you are **on the move**, you are going from one place to another. ❑ *Jack never wanted to stay in one place for very long, so they were always on the move.* PHRASE: usu PHR after v, v-link PHR 23 to **move the goalposts** → see **goalpost**. to **move a muscle** → see **muscle**.

♦ **move about** → see **move around**.

♦ **move along** 1 If someone, especially a police officer, tells you to **move along**, or if they **move** you **along**, they tell you to stop standing in a particular place and to go somewhere else. PHRASAL VERB ❑ *Curious pedestrians were ordered to move along...* V P *Our officers are moving them along and not allowing them to gather in large groups.* V n P Also V P n 2 If a process **moves along** or if something **moves** it **along**, it progresses. PHRASAL VERB ❑ *Research tends to move along at a slow but orderly pace...* V P *Delay is part of the normal process, but I hope we can move things along.* V n P

♦ **move around**

✔ in BRIT, also use **move about**

If you **move around** or **move about**, you keep changing your job or keep changing the place where you live. PHRASAL VERB ❑ *I was born in Fort Worth but we moved around a lot and I was reared in east Texas...* V P *He moved around the country working in orange groves.* V P n

♦ **move away** If you **move away**, you go and live in a different town or area of a country. PHRASAL VERB ❑ *He moved away and broke off relations with the family.* V P

♦ **move down** If someone or something **moves down**, they go to a lower level, grade, or class. PHRASAL VERB ❑ *Gold prices moved down.* V P, Also V P n

♦ **move in** 1 When you **move in** somewhere, you begin to live there as your home. PHRASAL VERB ≠ move out ❑ *Her house was in perfect order when she moved in...* V P *Her husband had moved in with a younger woman...* V P with n *We'd been seeing each other for a year when he suggested we should move in together.* V P together 2 If police, soldiers, or attackers **move in**, they go towards a place or person in order to deal with or attack them. PHRASAL VERB ❑ *Police moved in to disperse the crowd...* V P *Forces were moving in on the town of Knin.* V P on n 3 If someone **moves in on** an area of activity which was previously only done by a particular group of people, they start becoming involved with it for the first time. PHRASAL VERB ❑ *These black models are moving in on what was previously white territory: the lucrative cosmetic contracts.* V P on n Also V P

♦ **move into** If you **move into** a new house, you start living there. PHRASAL VERB ❑ *I want you to move into my apartment. We've a spare room.* V P n

♦ **move off** When you **move off**, you start moving away from a place. PHRASAL VERB = set off ❑ *Gil waved his hand and the car moved off.* V P

♦ **move on** 1 When you **move on** somewhere, you leave the place where you have been staying or waiting and go there. PHRASAL VERB ❑ *Mr Brooke moved on from Paris to Belgrade...* V P prep/adv *What's wrong with his wanting to sell his land and move on?* V P 2 If someone such as a policeman **moves** you **on**, they order you to stop standing in a particular place and to go somewhere else. PHRASAL VERB ❑ *Eventually the police were called to move them on.* V n P Also V P n 3 If you **move on**, you finish or stop one activity and start doing something different. PHRASAL VERB ❑ *She ran this shop for ten years before deciding to move on to fresh challenges...* V P to n *Now, can we move on and discuss the business of the day.* V P

♦ **move out** If you **move out**, you stop living in a particular house or place and go to live somewhere else. PHRASAL VERB ≠ move in ❑ *The harassment had become too much to tolerate and he decided to move out...* V P *They had a huge row and Sally moved out of the house.* V P of n

♦ **move over** 1 If you **move over to** a new system or way of doing something, you change to it. PHRASAL VERB = change ❑ *The government is having to introduce some difficult changes, particularly in moving over to a market economy.* V P to n Also V P 2 If someone **moves over**, they leave their job or position in order to let someone else have it. PHRASAL VERB ❑ *They said Mr Jenkins should make balanced programmes about the Black community or move over and let someone else who can.* V P 3 If you **move over**, you change your position in order to make room for someone else. PHRASAL VERB ❑ *Move over and let me drive.* V P

♦ **move up** 1 If you **move up**, you change your position, especially in order to be nearer someone or to make room for someone else. PHRASAL VERB ❑ *Move up, John, and let the lady sit down.* V P 2 If someone or something **moves up**, they go to a higher level, grade, or class. PHRASAL VERB = go up ❑ *Share prices moved up...* V P *Children learn in mixed ability classes and move up a class each year.* V P n

**move|able** /muːvəbᵊl/ → see **movable**.

**move|ment** /muːvmənt/ **(movements)** ◆◆◇ 1 A **movement** is a group of people who share the same beliefs, ideas, or aims. N-COUNT: usu supp N ❑ *It's part of a broader Hindu nationalist movement that's gaining strength throughout the country.* 2 **Movement** involves changing position or going from one place to another. N-VAR ❑ *There was movement behind the window in the back door... A tall, thin man was waving his arms in an effort to direct the movements of a large removal van.* 3 A **movement** is a planned change in position that an army makes during a battle or military exercise. N-VAR ❑ *There are reports of fresh troop movements across the border.* 4 **Movement** is a gradual development or change of an attitude, opinion, or policy. N-VAR: with supp, usu N towards/away from n ❑ *...the movement towards democracy in Latin America.* 5 Your **movements** are everything which you do or plan to do during a period of time. N-PLURAL: poss N ❑ *I want a full account of your movements the night Mr Gower was killed.* 6 A **movement** of a piece of classical music is one of its main sections. N-COUNT: usu with supp ❑ *...the first movement of Beethoven's 7th symphony.*

**mov|er** /muːvəʳ/ **(movers)** 1 If you describe a person or animal as a particular kind of **mover**, you mean that they move at that speed or in that way. N-COUNT: adj N ❑ *We found him a nice horse – a good mover who could gallop.* → See also **prime mover**. 2 **Movers** are people whose job is to move furniture or equipment from one building to another. [mainly AM] N-COUNT: usu pl

✔ in BRIT, usually use **removal men**

3 The **movers and shakers** in a place or area of activity are the people who have most power or influence. PHRASE: usu with supp ❑ *It is the movers and shakers of the record industry who will decide which bands make it.*

**movie** /muːvi/ **(movies)** ◆◆◇ 1 A **movie** is a film. [AM; also BRIT, INFORMAL] N-COUNT ❑ *In the first movie Tony Curtis ever made he played a grocery clerk.* 2 You can talk about **the movies** when you are talking about seeing a movie in a movie theater. [mainly AM] N-PLURAL: the N ❑ *He took her to the movies.*

✔ in BRIT, usually use **the cinema**

**movie|goer** /muːvigouəʳ/ **(moviegoers)** also **movie-goer**. A **moviegoer** is a person who often goes to the cinema. [AM] N-COUNT

✔ in BRIT, usually use **cinema-goer**, **film-goer**

**movie house** **(movie houses)** A **movie house** is the same as a **movie theater**. [AM] N-COUNT

**movie star** **(movie stars)** A **movie star** is a famous actor or actress who appears in films. [mainly AM] N-COUNT

in BRIT, usually use **film star**

**movie thea|ter** **(movie theaters)** A **movie theater** is a place where people go to watch films for entertainment. [AM] N-COUNT

in BRIT, use **cinema**

**mov|ing** /muːvɪŋ/ 1 If something is **moving**, it makes you feel strongly an emotion such as sadness, pity, or sympathy. ❑ *It is very moving to see how much strangers can care for each other.* ♦ **mov|ing|ly** *You write very movingly of your sister Amy's suicide.* 2 A **moving** model or part of a machine moves or is able to move. 3 The **moving spirit** or **moving force** behind something is the person or thing that caused it to start and to keep going, or that influenced people to take part in it. ❑ *She alone must have been the moving spirit behind the lawsuit that lost me my position.* ADJ = touching; ADV: ADV with v; ADJ: ADJ n; PHRASE: oft PHR *behind/in* n

**mov|ing pic|ture** **(moving pictures)** A **moving picture** is a film. [OLD-FASHIONED] N-COUNT

**mow** /moʊ/ **(mows, mowing, mowed, mowed** or **mown)** If you **mow** an area of grass, you cut it using a machine called a lawn mower. ❑ *He continued to mow the lawn and do other routine chores.* VERB V n Also V

♦ **mow down** If someone **is mown down**, they are killed violently by a vehicle or gunfire. ❑ *She was mown down on a pedestrian crossing... Gunmen mowed down 10 people in one attack.* PHRASAL VERB *be* V-ed P; V P n; Also V n P

**mow|er** /moʊəʳ/ **(mowers)** 1 A **mower** is the same as a **lawnmower**. 2 A **mower** is a machine that has sharp blades for cutting something such as corn or wheat. N-COUNT; N-COUNT

**MP** /em piː/ **(MPs)** In Britain, an **MP** is a person who has been elected to represent the people from a particular area in the House of Commons. **MP** is an abbreviation for 'Member of Parliament'. ❑ *Several Conservative MPs have voted against the government.* ◆◆◇ N-COUNT

**MP3** /em piː θriː/ **MP3** is a kind of technology which enables you to record and play music from the Internet. N-UNCOUNT

**MPEG** /empeg/ **MPEG** is a standard file format for compressing video images so that they can be stored or sent by e-mail more easily. **MPEG** is an abbreviation for 'Motion Picture Experts Group'. [COMPUTING] N-UNCOUNT: oft N n

**mpg** /em piː dʒiː/ **mpg** is written after a number to indicate how many miles a vehicle can travel using one gallon of fuel. **mpg** is an abbreviation for 'miles per gallon'. ❑ *Fuel consumption is 38 mpg around town, 55 mpg on the open road.*

**mph** **mph** is written after a number to indicate the speed of something such as a vehicle. **mph** is an abbreviation for 'miles per hour'. ❑ *Inside these zones, traffic speeds are restricted to 20 mph.*

**MPV** /em piː viː/ **(MPVs)** An **MPV** is a large, tall car whose seats can be moved or removed, for example so that it can carry large loads. **MPV** is an abbreviation for 'multi-purpose vehicle'. N-COUNT

**Mr** /mɪstəʳ/

in AM, use **Mr.**

1 **Mr** is used before a man's name when you are speaking or referring to him. ❑ *...Mr Grant. ...Mr Bob Price. ...Mr and Mrs Daniels.* 2 **Mr** is sometimes used in front of words such as 'President' and 'Chairman' to address the man who holds the position mentioned. ❑ *Mr. President, you're aware of the system.* 3 → See also **Messrs**. N-TITLE; N-VOC: N n

**MRI** /em ɑːr aɪ/ **MRI** is a method by which medical staff can get a picture of soft parts inside a patient's body, using a powerful magnetic field. **MRI** is an abbreviation for 'magnetic resonance imaging'. N-UNCOUNT

**Mrs** /mɪsɪz/

in AM, use **Mrs.**

**Mrs** is used before the name of a married woman when you are speaking or referring to her. ❑ *Hello, Mrs Miles. ...Mrs Anne Penn. ...Mr and Mrs D H Alder.* N-TITLE

**Ms** /məz, mɪz/

in AM, use **Ms.**

**Ms** is used, especially in written English, before a woman's name when you are speaking to her or referring to her. If you use **Ms**, you are not specifying if the woman is married or not. ❑ *...Ms Brown. ...Ms Elizabeth Harman.* N-TITLE

**ms.** **(mss)** **ms.** is a written abbreviation for **manuscript**.

**MS** /em es/ 1 **MS** is a serious disease of the nervous system, which gradually makes a person weaker, and sometimes affects their sight or speech. **MS** is an abbreviation for 'multiple sclerosis'. 2 An **MS** or **M.S.** is the same as an **MSc**. [AM] N-UNCOUNT

**MSc** /em es siː/ **(MScs)** also **M.Sc.** An **MSc** is a master's degree in a science subject. **MSc** is an abbreviation for 'Master of Science'. N-COUNT

**MSG** /em es dʒiː/ **MSG** is an abbreviation for **monosodium glutamate**. N-UNCOUNT

**Msgr** also **Msgr.** **Msgr** is a written abbreviation for **Monsignor**.

**MSP** /em es piː/ **(MSPs)** An **MSP** is someone who has been elected as a member of the Scottish Parliament. **MSP** is an abbreviation for 'Member of the Scottish Parliament'. N-COUNT

**Mt** **(Mts)** also **Mt.** **Mt** is a written abbreviation for **Mount** or **Mountain**. ❑ *...Mt Everest. ...the Rocky Mts.*

**much** /mʌtʃ/ 1 You use **much** to indicate the great intensity, extent, or degree of something such as an action, feeling, or change. **Much** is usually used with 'so', 'too', and 'very', and in negative clauses with this meaning. ❑ *She laughs too much... Thank you very much... My hairstyle hasn't changed much since I was five.* 2 If something does not happen **much**, it does not happen very often. ❑ *He said that his father never talked much about the war... Gwen had not seen her Daddy all that much, because mostly he worked on the ships... Do you get back East much?* 3 You use **much** in front of 'too' or comparative adjectives and adverbs in order to emphasize that there is a large amount of a particular quality. ❑ *The skin is much too delicate... You'd be so much happier if you could see yourself the way I see you.* 4 If one thing is **much** the same as another thing, it is very similar to it. ❑ *The day ended much as it began... Sheep's milk is produced in much the same way as goat's milk.* 5 You use **much** to indicate that you are referring to a large amount of a substance or thing. ❑ *They are grown on the hillsides in full sun, without much water... The Home Office acknowledges that much crime goes unreported.* ♦ **Much** is also a pronoun. ❑ *...eating too much and drinking too much... There was so much to talk about.* ♦ **Much** is also a quantifier. ❑ *Much of the time we do not notice that we are solving problems... She does much of her work abroad.* 6 You use **much** in expressions such as **not much**, **not very much**, and **too much** when replying to questions about amounts. ❑ *'Can you hear it where you live?' He shook his head. 'Not much.'... 'Do you care very much about what other people think?' — 'Too much.'* 7 If you do not see **much of** someone, you do not see them very often. ❑ *I don't see much of Tony nowadays.* 8 You use **much** in the expression **how much** to ask questions about amounts or degrees, and also in reported clauses and statements to give information about the amount or degree of something. ❑ *How much money can I afford?... See just how much fat and cholesterol you're eating.* ♦ **Much** is also an adverb. ❑ *She knows how much this upsets me but she persists in doing it.* ♦ **Much** is also a pronoun. ◆◆◆ ADV: ADV after v; ADV: oft with brd-neg, ADV after v = often; ADV: ADV compar, ADV *too* [emphasis] = far; ADV: ADV *as/like* cl, ADV *like* n, ADV n *as* n, ADV n; DET: DET n-uncount, oft with brd-neg; PRON ≠ little; QUANT: QUANT *of* def-n-uncount/def-sing-n; ADV: ADV as reply; QUANT: with brd-neg, QUANT *of* n-proper/pron; DET: *how* DET; ADV: *how* ADV, ADV with cl, ADV compar; PRON: *how* PRON

❑ *How much do you earn?* 9 You use **much** in the expression **as much** when you are comparing amounts. ❑ *Their aim will be to produce as much milk as possible.* DET: *as* DET n, usu *as* DET n *as* cl/group

PHRASES 10 You use **much as** to introduce a fact which makes something else you have just said or will say rather surprising. ❑ *Much as they hope to go home tomorrow, they're resigned to staying on until the end of the year.* PHRASE 11 You use **as much** in expressions such as '**I thought as much**' and '**I guessed as much**' after you have just been told something and you want to say that you already believed or expected it to be true. ❑ *You're waiting for a woman – I thought as much.* PHRASE: v PHR 12 You use **as much as** before an amount to suggest that it is surprisingly large. ❑ *The organisers hope to raise as much as £6m for charity.* PHRASE: PHR amount [emphasis] 13 You use **much less** after a statement, often a negative one, to indicate that the statement is more true of the person, thing, or situation that you are going to mention next. ❑ *They are always short of water to drink, much less to bathe in.* PHRASE: PHR cl/group, PHR before v 14 You say **nothing much** to refer to something that is not very interesting or important. ❑ *'What was stolen?' — 'Oh, nothing much.'.* PHRASE 15 If you describe something as **not much of a** particular type of thing, you mean that it is small or of poor quality. ❑ *It hasn't been much of a holiday.* PHRASE: PHR n 16 **So much for** is used to indicate that you have finished talking about a subject. [SPOKEN] ❑ *Well, so much for the producers. But what of the consumers?* PHRASE: PHR n 17 If you say **so much for** a particular thing, you mean that it has not been successful or helpful. [INFORMAL] ❑ *He has spent 19 million pounds, lost three cup finals and been relegated. So much for money.* PHRASE: PHR n 18 If you say that something is not **so much** one thing **as** another, you mean that it is more like the second thing than the first. ❑ *I don't really think of her as a daughter so much as a very good friend.* PHRASE: with brd-neg, PHR group, PHR before v 19 If you say that someone did not do **so much as** perform a particular action, you are emphasizing that they did not even do that, when you were expecting them to do more. ❑ *I didn't so much as catch sight of him all day long.* PHRASE: with brd-neg, PHR before v [emphasis] 20 You use **so much so** to indicate that your previous statement is true to a very great extent, and therefore it has the result mentioned. ❑ *He himself believed in freedom, so much so that he would rather die than live without it.* PHRASE: PHR that

21 If a situation or action is **too much for** you, it is so difficult, tiring, or upsetting that you cannot cope with it. ❑ *His inability to stay at one job for long had finally proved too much for her.* PHRASE: v-link PHR, oft PHR *for* n 22 You use **very much** to emphasize that someone or something has a lot of a particular quality, or that the description you are about to give is particularly accurate. ❑ *...a man very much in charge of himself.* PHRASE: oft PHR n [emphasis] 23 **a bit much** → see **bit**. **not up to much** → see **up**.

**much-** /mʌtʃ-/ **Much-** combines with past participles to form adjectives which emphasize the intensity of the specified state or action. ❑ *I'm having a much-needed rest. ...a much-improved version of last season's model.* COMB in ADJ [emphasis]

**much-maligned** If you describe someone or something as **much-maligned**, you mean that they are often criticized by people, but you think the criticism is unfair or exaggerated because they have good qualities too. ❑ *I'm happy for James. He's a much-maligned player but has tremendous spirit.* ADJ: usu ADJ n

**much-travelled**

✔ in AM, use **much-traveled**

A **much-travelled** person has travelled a lot in foreign countries. ADJ = well-travelled

**muck** /mʌk/ **(mucks, mucking, mucked) Muck** is dirt or some other unpleasant substance. [INFORMAL] ❑ *This muck was interfering with the filter.* N-UNCOUNT

♦ **muck around**

✔ in BRIT, also use **muck about**

1 If you **muck around** or **muck about**, you behave in a childish or silly way, often so that you waste your time and fail to achieve anything. [mainly BRIT, INFORMAL] ❑ *We do not want people of his age mucking around risking people's lives... He'd spent his boyhood summers mucking about in boats.* PHRASAL VERB = mess about; V P; V P prep/adv 2 If you **muck around with** or **muck about with** something, you alter it, often making it worse than it was. [mainly BRIT, INFORMAL] ❑ *The president's wife doesn't muck around with policy or sit in on Cabinet meetings.* PHRASAL VERB = mess around; V P *with* n 3 If you **muck** someone **around** or **muck** them **about**, you treat them badly, for example by not being honest with them or by continually changing plans which affect them. [mainly BRIT, INFORMAL] ❑ *He does not tolerate anyone who mucks him about.* PHRASAL VERB = mess about; V n P

♦ **muck in** If someone **mucks in**, they join in with an activity or help other people with a job and do not consider themselves to be too important to do it. [mainly BRIT, INFORMAL] ❑ *Course residents are expected to muck in and be prepared to share rooms... She mucked in with the chores and did her own washing and ironing.* PHRASAL VERB; V P; V P *with* n

♦ **muck up** If you **muck up** or **muck** something **up**, you do something very badly so that you fail to achieve what you wanted to. [mainly BRIT, INFORMAL] ❑ *I mucked up at the 13th hole and told myself that this was getting stupid... Scientists should figure out how to keep the natural world from mucking up the affairs of people.* PHRASAL VERB = mess up; V P; V P n (not pron); Also V n P

**muck-raking** also **muckraking**. If you accuse someone of **muck-raking**, you are criticizing them for finding and spreading unpleasant or embarrassing information about someone, especially a public figure. ❑ *The Prime Minister accused opposition leaders of muck-raking.* N-UNCOUNT [disapproval]

**mucky** /mʌki/ **(muckier, muckiest)** Something that is **mucky** is very dirty. [INFORMAL] ADJ

**mu|cous mem|brane** /mjuːkəs membreɪn/ **(mucous membranes)** A **mucous membrane** is skin that produces mucus to prevent itself from becoming dry. It covers delicate parts of the body such as the inside of your nose. [TECHNICAL] N-COUNT

**mu|cus** /mjuːkəs/ **Mucus** is a thick liquid that is produced in some parts of your body, for example the inside of your nose. N-UNCOUNT

**mud** /mʌd/ **Mud** is a sticky mixture of earth and water. ❑ *His uniform was crumpled, untidy, splashed with mud.* N-UNCOUNT

**mud|dle** /mʌdᵊl/ **(muddles, muddling, muddled)** 1 If people or things are **in a muddle**, they are in a state of confusion or disorder. ❑ *My thoughts are all in a muddle. ...a general muddle of pencils and boxes.* N-VAR: oft *in/into a* N = mess 2 If you **muddle** things or people, you get them mixed up, so that you do not know which is which. ❑ *Already, one or two critics have begun to muddle the two names.* VERB = mix up, confuse; V n ♦ **Muddle up** means the same as **muddle**. ❑ *The question muddles up three separate issues... He sometimes muddles me up with other patients.* PHRASAL VERB; V P pl-n; V n P *with* n; Also V pl-n P ♦ **mud|dled up** *I know that I am getting my words muddled up.* ADJ

♦ **muddle through** If you **muddle through**, you manage to do something even though you do not have the proper equipment or do not really know how to do it. ❑ *We will muddle through and just play it day by day... The BBC may be able to muddle through the next five years like this... Somehow or other, we muddled our way through.* PHRASAL VERB; V P; V P n; V *way* P

♦ **muddle up** → see **muddle 2**.

**mud|dled** /mʌdᵊld/ If someone is **muddled**, they are confused about something. ❑ *I'm afraid I'm a little muddled. I'm not exactly sure where to begin.* ADJ

**mud|dy** /mʌdi/ **(muddier, muddiest, muddies, muddying, muddied)** 1 Something that is **muddy** contains mud or is covered in mud. ❑ *...a muddy track... The ground was still very muddy.* ADJ 2 If you **muddy** something, you cause it to be muddy. ❑ *The ground still smelled of rain and they muddied their shoes.* VERB; V n 3 If someone or something **muddies** a situation or issue, they cause it to seem less clear VERB

and less easy to understand. ❑ *It's difficult enough without muddying the issue with religion.* V n
♦ **mud|died** *Overseas the legal issues are more muddied.* ADJ
● If someone or something **muddies the waters**, they cause a situation or issue to seem less clear and less easy to understand. ❑ *They keep on muddying the waters by raising other political issues.* PHRASE: V inflects

**mud|flats** /mʌdflæts/ **Mudflats** are areas of flat empty land at the coast which are covered by the sea only when the tide is in. N-PLURAL

**mud|guard** /mʌdgɑːʳd/ **(mudguards)** The **mudguards** of a bicycle or other vehicle are curved pieces of metal or plastic above the tyres, which stop mud getting on the rider or vehicle. [mainly BRIT] ➔ See picture on page 1708. N-COUNT: usu pl

☑ in AM, usually use **fender, splashguard**

**mud|slide** /mʌdslaɪd/ **(mudslides)** A **mudslide** is a large amount of mud sliding down a mountain, usually causing damage or destruction. N-COUNT

**mud-slinging** If you accuse someone of **mud-slinging**, you are accusing them of making insulting, unfair, and damaging remarks about their opponents. ❑ *Voters are disillusioned with the mud-slinging campaigns run by many candidates in recent years.* N-UNCOUNT [disapproval]

**mues|li** /mjuːzli/ **(mueslis)** **Muesli** is a breakfast cereal made from chopped nuts, dried fruit, and grains. N-MASS

**mu|ez|zin** /muezɪn/ **(muezzins)** A **muezzin** is an official who calls from the tower of a mosque when it is time for Muslims to pray. N-COUNT

**muff** /mʌf/ **(muffs, muffing, muffed)** [1] If you **muff** something, you do it badly or you make a mistake while you are doing it, so that it is not successful. [INFORMAL] ❑ *He muffed his opening speech.* VERB; V n
[2] A **muff** is a piece of fur or thick cloth shaped like a short hollow cylinder. You wear a muff on your hands to keep them warm in cold weather. N-COUNT

**muf|fin** /mʌfɪn/ **(muffins)** [1] **Muffins** are small, round, sweet cakes, usually with fruit or bran inside. They are often eaten with butter for breakfast. [AM] ❑ *...breakfasts of pancakes, blueberry muffins, eggs, and bacon.* N-COUNT
[2] **Muffins** are small, flat, sweet bread rolls that you eat hot with butter. [BRIT] N-COUNT

☑ in AM, use **English muffins**

**muf|fle** /mʌfᵊl/ **(muffles, muffling, muffled)** If something **muffles** a sound, it makes it quieter and more difficult to hear. ❑ *Blake held his handkerchief over the mouthpiece to muffle his voice... She heard a muffled cough behind her.* VERB; V n; V-ed

**muf|fled** /mʌfᵊld/ If you are **muffled**, you are wearing a lot of heavy clothes so that very little of your body or face is visible. ❑ *...children muffled in scarves and woolly hats.* ADJ: usu v-link ADJ

**muf|fler** /mʌfləʳ/ **(mufflers)** [1] A **muffler** is the same as a **scarf**. [OLD-FASHIONED] N-COUNT
[2] A **muffler** is a device on a car exhaust that makes it quieter. [AM] N-COUNT

☑ in BRIT, use **silencer**

**mug** /mʌg/ **(mugs, mugging, mugged)** [1] A **mug** is a large deep cup with straight sides and a handle, used for hot drinks. ❑ *He spooned instant coffee into two of the mugs.* N-COUNT
♦ A **mug** of something is the amount of it contained in a mug. ❑ *He had been drinking mugs of coffee to keep himself awake.* N-COUNT: usu N *of* n
[2] If someone **mugs** you, they attack you in order to steal your money. ❑ *I was walking out to my car when this guy tried to mug me.* VERB; V n
♦ **mug|ging** **(muggings)** *Bank robberies, burglaries and muggings are reported almost daily in the press.* N-VAR
[3] If you say that someone is a **mug**, you mean that they are stupid and easily deceived by other people. [BRIT, INFORMAL] ❑ *He's a mug as far as women are concerned.* N-COUNT [disapproval]
[4] If you say that an activity is **a mug's game**, you mean that it is not worth doing because it does not give the person who is doing it any benefit or satisfaction. [BRIT, INFORMAL] ❑ *I used to be a very heavy gambler, but not any more. It's a mug's game.* PHRASE: v-link PHR [disapproval]
[5] Someone's **mug** is their face. [INFORMAL] ❑ *He managed to get his ugly mug on the telly.* N-COUNT: usu poss N

**mug|ger** /mʌgəʳ/ **(muggers)** A **mugger** is a person who attacks someone violently in a street in order to steal money from them. N-COUNT

**mug|gy** /mʌgi/ **Muggy** weather is unpleasantly warm and damp. ❑ *It was muggy and overcast.* ADJ: oft *it* v-link ADJ = *humid*

**mug shot** **(mug shots)** A **mug shot** is a photograph of someone, especially a photograph of a criminal which has been taken by the police. [INFORMAL] N-COUNT

**mul|berry** /mʌlbəri, AM -beri/ **(mulberries)** A **mulberry** or a **mulberry tree** is a tree which has small purple berries which you can eat. N-VAR
♦ **Mulberries** are the fruit of a mulberry tree. N-COUNT

**mulch** /mʌltʃ/ **(mulches, mulching, mulched)** [1] A **mulch** is a layer of something such as old leaves, small pieces of wood, or manure which you put on the soil round plants in order to protect them and help them to grow. N-MASS
[2] To **mulch** plants means to put a mulch round them to protect them and help them to grow. ❑ *In May, mulch the bed with garden compost.* VERB; V n *with* n; Also V n

**mule** /mjuːl/ **(mules)** [1] A **mule** is an animal whose parents are a horse and a donkey. N-COUNT
[2] A **mule** is a shoe or slipper which is open around the heel. N-COUNT: usu pl

**mull** /mʌl/ **(mulls, mulling, mulled)** If you **mull** something, you think about it for a long time before deciding what to do. [AM] ❑ *Last month, a federal grand jury began mulling evidence in the case... Do you know why he was mulling and hesitating?* VERB; V n; V
♦ **mull over** If you **mull** something **over**, you think about it for a long time before deciding what to do. ❑ *McLaren had been mulling over an idea to make a movie... I'll leave you alone here so you can mull it over.* PHRASAL VERB = *consider*; V P n (not pron); V n P

**mul|lah** /mʊlə, mʌlə/ **(mullahs)** A **mullah** is a Muslim who is a religious teacher or leader. N-COUNT; N-TITLE

**mulled** /mʌld/ **Mulled** wine has sugar and spice added to it and is then heated. ADJ: ADJ n

**mul|let** /mʌlɪt/ **(mullets** or **mullet)** A **mullet** is a small sea fish that people cook and eat. N-VAR
♦ **Mullet** is this fish eaten as food. N-UNCOUNT

**multi-** /mʌlti-/ **Multi-** is used to form adjectives indicating that something consists of many things of a particular kind. ❑ *...the introduction of multi-party democracy. ...a multi-million-dollar outfit.* PREFIX

**multi|col|oured** /mʌltikʌləʳd/ also **multi-coloured.**

☑ in AM, use **multicolored** or **multi-colored**

A **multicoloured** object has many different colours. ❑ *...a sea of multicoloured umbrellas.* ADJ: usu ADJ n

**multi|cul|tur|al** /mʌltikʌltʃərəl/ also **multi-cultural. Multicultural** means consisting of or relating to people of many different nationalities and cultures. ❑ *...children growing up in a multicultural society.* ADJ: usu ADJ n

**multi|cul|tur|al|ism** /mʌltikʌltʃərəlɪzəm/ **Multiculturalism** is a situation in which all the different cultural or racial groups in a society have equal rights and opportunities, and none is ignored or regarded as unimportant. N-UNCOUNT

**multi-faceted** also **multifaceted. Multi-faceted** means having a variety of different and important features or elements. ❑ *Webb is a multi-faceted performer... Her job is multi-faceted.* ADJ: usu ADJ n

**multi|fari|ous** /mʌltɪfeəriəs/ If you describe things as **multifarious**, you mean that they are many in number and of many different kinds. [LITERARY] ❑ *Spain is a composite of multifarious traditions and people... The reasons for closure are multifarious.* ADJ

**multi|lat|er|al** /mʌltilætərᵊl/ **Multilateral** means involving at least three different groups of people or nations. ❑ *Many want to abandon the multilateral trade talks in Geneva.* ADJ: usu ADJ n

**multi-level mar|ket|ing** **Multi-level marketing** is a marketing technique which involves people buying a product, then earning a commission by selling it to their friends. The abbreviation **MLM** is also used. ❑ *...multi-level marketing schemes.* N-UNCOUNT

**multi|lin|gual** /mʌltilɪŋgwᵊl/ also **multilingual.** [1] **Multilingual** means involving several different languages. ❑ *...a multilingual country. ...multilingual dictionaries.* ADJ: usu ADJ n [2] A **multilingual** person is able to speak more than two languages very well. ❑ *He recruited two multilingual engineers.* ADJ

**multi|media** /mʌltimiːdiə/ [1] You use **multimedia** to refer to computer programs and products which involve sound, pictures, and film, as well as text. ❑ *...the next generation of computers, which will be 'multimedia machines' that allow users to control and manipulate sound, video, text and graphics.* N-UNCOUNT: usu N n [2] In education, **multimedia** is the use of television and other different media in a lesson, as well as books. N-UNCOUNT

**multi-millionaire** (**multi-millionaires**) also **multimillionaire.** A **multi-millionaire** is a very rich person who has money or property worth several million pounds or dollars. N-COUNT

**multi|na|tion|al** /mʌltinæʃənᵊl/ (**multinationals**) also **multi-national.** [1] A **multinational** company has branches or owns companies in many different countries. ADJ: usu ADJ n ♦ **Multinational** is also a noun. ❑ *...multinationals such as Ford and IBM.* N-COUNT [2] **Multinational** armies, organizations, or other groups involve people from several different countries. ❑ *The US troops would be part of a multinational force.* ADJ: usu ADJ n [3] **Multinational** countries or regions have a population that is made up of people of several different nationalities. ADJ: usu ADJ n

**multi|ple** /mʌltɪpᵊl/ (**multiples**) [1] You use **multiple** to describe things that consist of many parts, involve many people, or have many uses. ❑ *He died of multiple injuries... The most common multiple births are twins, two babies born at the same time.* ADJ: usu ADJ n [2] If one number is a **multiple of** a smaller number, it can be exactly divided by that smaller number. ❑ *Their numerical system, derived from the Babylonians, was based on multiples of the number six.* N-COUNT: N *of* n [3] A **multiple** or a **multiple store** is a shop with a lot of branches in different towns. [BRIT] ❑ *It made it almost impossible for the smaller retailer to compete against the multiples.* N-COUNT

**multi|ple choice** also **multiple-choice.** In a **multiple choice** test or question, you have to choose the answer that you think is right from several possible answers that are listed on the question paper. ADJ: usu ADJ n

**multi|ple scle|ro|sis** /mʌltɪpᵊl skləroʊsɪs/ **Multiple sclerosis** is a serious disease of the nervous system, which gradually makes a person weaker, and sometimes affects their sight or speech. The abbreviation **MS** is also used. N-UNCOUNT

**multi|plex** (**multiplexes** /mʌltipleks/) A **multiplex** is a cinema complex with six or more screens. N-COUNT

**multi|pli|ca|tion** /mʌltɪplɪkeɪʃᵊn/ [1] **Multiplication** is the process of calculating the total of one number multiplied by another. ❑ *There will be simple tests in addition, subtraction, multiplication and division.* N-UNCOUNT [2] The **multiplication** of things of a particular kind is the process or fact of them increasing in number or amount. ❑ *Increasing gravity is known to speed up the multiplication of cells.* N-UNCOUNT: usu N *of* n

**multi|pli|ca|tion sign** (**multiplication signs**) A **multiplication sign** is the sign x which is put between two numbers to show that they are being multiplied. N-COUNT

**multi|pli|ca|tion ta|ble** (**multiplication tables**) A **multiplication table** is a list of the multiplications of numbers between one and twelve. Children often have to learn multiplication tables at school. N-COUNT = table

**multi|plic|ity** /mʌltɪplɪsɪti/ A **multiplicity of** things is a large number or a large variety of them. [FORMAL] ❑ *...a writer who uses a multiplicity of styles.* QUANT: QUANT *of* pl-n = many

**multi|ply** /mʌltɪplaɪ/ (**multiplies, multiplying, multiplied**) [1] When something **multiplies** or when you **multiply** it, it increases greatly in number or amount. ❑ *Such disputes multiplied in the eighteenth and nineteenth centuries... Her husband multiplied his demands on her time.* VERB V V n [2] When animals and insects **multiply**, they increase in number by giving birth to large numbers of young. ❑ *These creatures can multiply quickly.* VERB V [3] If you **multiply** one number by another, you add the first number to itself as many times as is indicated by the second number. For example 2 multiplied by 3 is equal to 6. ❑ *What do you get if you multiply six by nine? ...the remarkable ability to multiply huge numbers correctly without pen or paper.* VERB V n *by* n V pl-n

**multi|ra|cial** /mʌltireɪʃᵊl/ also **multiracial.** **Multiracial** means consisting of or involving people of many different nationalities and cultures. ❑ *We live in a multiracial society.* ADJ: usu ADJ n = multicultural

**multi-skilled** **Multi-skilled** employees have a number of different skills, enabling them to do more than one kind of work. ❑ *...the development of a more adaptable, multi-skilled workforce, capable of moving with the times.* ADJ

**multi-skilling** **Multi-skilling** is the practice of training employees to do a number of different tasks. ❑ *He said restructuring at the station would lead to increased multi-skilling among staff.* N-UNCOUNT

**multi-storey** also **multistorey, multistoreyed.**

> in AM, use **multi-story**, **multistory** or **multi-storied** are also used.

A **multi-storey** building has several floors at different levels above the ground. ❑ *...the Moskovski Department Store, a vast multi-story complex near the city's center. ...a multi-storey car park.* ADJ: usu ADJ n

**multi-tasking** **Multi-tasking** is a situation in which a computer or person does more than one thing at the same time. ❑ *The big advantage of multi-tasking is that all equipment is used most of the time.* N-UNCOUNT

**multi|tude** /mʌltɪtjuːd, AM -tuːd/ (**multitudes**) [1] A **multitude of** things or people is a very large number of them. ❑ *There are a multitude of small quiet roads to cycle along... Addiction to drugs can bring a multitude of other problems.* QUANT: QUANT *of* pl-n ● If you say that something covers or hides **a multitude of sins**, you mean that it hides something unattractive or does not reveal the true nature of something. ❑ *'Strong, centralized government' is a term that can cover a multitude of sins.* PHRASE: PHR after v [2] You can refer to a very large number of people as a **multitude**. [WRITTEN] ❑ *...surrounded by a noisy multitude.* N-COUNT = crowd [3] You can refer to the great majority of people in a particular country or situation as **the multitude** or **the multitudes**. ❑ *The hideous truth was hidden from the multitude.* N-COUNT-COLL: *the* N

**mum** /mʌm/ (**mums**) [1] Your **mum** is your mother. [mainly BRIT, INFORMAL] ❑ *He misses his mum... Mum and Dad are coming for lunch... Don't worry, Mum.* ◆◇◇ N-FAMILY

> in AM, usually use **mom**

[2] If you **keep mum** or **stay mum** about something, you do not tell anyone about it. [INFORMAL] ❑ *He is keeping mum about his feelings on the matter.* PHRASE: V inflects = keep quiet

**mum|ble** /mʌmbᵊl/ (**mumbles, mumbling, mumbled**) If you **mumble**, you speak very quietly and not at all clearly with the result that the words are difficult to understand. ❑ *Her grandmother mumbled in her sleep... He mumbled a few words of thanks... 'Today of all days,' she mumbled.* VERB V V n V with quote

♦ **Mumble** is also a noun. ❑ *He could hear the low mumble of Navarro's voice.* N-COUNT

**mum|bo jum|bo** /mʌmbou dʒʌmbou/ also **mumbo-jumbo.** If you describe ideas or words, especially religious or technical ones, as **mumbo jumbo**, you mean that they are nonsense. [INFORMAL] ❑ *It's all full of psychoanalytic mumbo-jumbo.* N-UNCOUNT disapproval

**mum|mi|fy** /mʌmɪfaɪ/ **(mummifies, mummifying, mummified)** If a dead body **is mummified**, it is preserved, for example by rubbing it with special oils and wrapping it in cloth. ❑ *In America, people are paying up to $150,000 to be mummified after death. ...the mummified pharaoh.* VERB: usu passive = embalm *be* V-ed V-ed

**mum|my** /mʌmi/ **(mummies)** 1 Some people, especially young children, call their mother **mummy**. [BRIT, INFORMAL] ❑ *I want my mummy... Mummy says I can play out in the garden.* N-FAMILY

✔ in AM, use **mommy**

2 A **mummy** is a dead body which was preserved long ago by being rubbed with special oils and wrapped in cloth. ❑ *...an Egyptian mummy.* N-COUNT

**mumps** /mʌmps/ **Mumps** is a disease usually caught by children. It causes a mild fever and painful swelling of the glands in the neck. N-UNCOUNT

**munch** /mʌntʃ/ **(munches, munching, munched)** If you **munch** food, you eat it by chewing it slowly, thoroughly, and rather noisily. ❑ *Luke munched the chicken sandwiches... Across the table, his son Benjie munched appreciatively... Sheep were munching their way through a yellow carpet of leaves.* VERB V n V V *way through* n Also V *away at/on* n

**mun|chies** /mʌntʃiz/ If someone gets **the munchies**, they suddenly feel a strong desire to eat a snack or something sweet, especially when they have been taking drugs. [INFORMAL] ❑ *...an attack of the munchies.* N-PLURAL: *the* N

**mun|dane** /mʌndeɪn/ Something that is **mundane** is very ordinary and not at all interesting or unusual. ❑ *Be willing to do even mundane tasks. ...the mundane realities of life.* ♦ You can refer to mundane things as **the mundane**. ❑ *It's an attitude that turns the mundane into something rather more interesting and exciting.* ADJ = boring N-SING: *the* N

**mu|nici|pal** /mjuːnɪsɪpᵊl/ **Municipal** means associated with or belonging to a city or town that has its own local government. ❑ *The municipal authorities gave the go-ahead for the march. ...next month's municipal elections. ...the municipal library.* ADJ: ADJ n

**mu|nici|pal|ity** /mjuːnɪsɪpælɪti/ **(municipalities)** 1 In Britain, a **municipality** is a city or town which is governed by its own locally-appointed officials. You can also refer to a city's or town's local government as a **municipality**. N-COUNT 2 In the United States, a **municipality** is a city or town that is incorporated and can elect its own government, which is also called a **municipality**. N-COUNT

**mu|nifi|cent** /mjuːnɪfɪsənt/ A **munificent** person is very generous. [FORMAL] ❑ *...one of the country's most munificent artistic benefactors. ...a munificent donation.* ADJ

**mu|ni|tions** /mjuːnɪʃᵊnz/ **Munitions** are military equipment and supplies, especially bombs, shells, and guns. ❑ *...the shortage of men and munitions. ...a munitions factory.* N-PLURAL

**mu|ral** /mjʊərəl/ **(murals)** A **mural** is a picture painted on a wall. ❑ *...a mural of Tangier bay.* N-COUNT

**mur|der** /mɜːʳdəʳ/ **(murders, murdering, murdered)** 1 **Murder** is the deliberate and illegal killing of a person. ❑ *The three accused, aged between 19 and 20, are charged with attempted murder... She refused to testify, unless the murder charge against her was dropped. ...brutal murders.* 2 To **murder** someone means to commit the crime of killing them deliberately. ❑ *...a thriller about two men who murder a third to see if they can get away with it. ...the body of a murdered religious and political leader.* 3 If you say that someone **gets away with murder**, you are complaining that they can do whatever they like without anyone trying to control them or punish them. [INFORMAL] ❑ *His charm and the fact that he is so likeable often allows him to get away with murder.* ◆◆◇ N-VAR VERB V n V-ed Also V PHRASE: V inflects disapproval

**mur|der|er** /mɜːʳdərəʳ/ **(murderers)** A **murderer** is a person who has murdered someone. ❑ *One of these men may have been the murderer.* N-COUNT

**mur|der|ess** /mɜːʳdərɪs/ **(murderesses)** A **murderess** is a woman who has murdered someone. N-COUNT = murderer

**mur|der|ous** /mɜːʳdərəs/ 1 Someone who is **murderous** is likely to murder someone and may already have murdered someone. ❑ *This murderous lunatic could kill them both without a second thought.* 2 A **murderous** attack or other action is very violent and intended to result in someone's death. ❑ *He made a murderous attack on his wife that evening.* ADJ: usu ADJ n ADJ: usu ADJ n

**mur|der|ous|ly** /mɜːʳdərəsli/ You use **murderously** to indicate that something is extremely unpleasant or threatening. ❑ *Beauchamp glared at her murderously.* ADV: ADV adj, ADV with v

**murk** /mɜːʳk/ **The murk** is darkness, dark water, or thick mist that is very difficult to see through. ❑ *All of a sudden a tall old man in a black cloak loomed out of the murk.* N-SING: usu *the* N

**murky** /mɜːʳki/ **(murkier, murkiest)** 1 A **murky** place or time of day is dark and rather unpleasant because there is not enough light. ❑ *The large lamplit room was murky with woodsmoke.* ADJ 2 **Murky** water or fog is so dark and dirty that you cannot see through it. ❑ *...the deep, murky waters of Loch Ness.* ADJ 3 If you describe an activity or situation as **murky**, you suspect that it is dishonest or morally wrong. [BRIT] ❑ *There has been a murky conspiracy to keep them out of power.* ADJ disapproval = shady 4 If you describe something as **murky**, you mean that the details of it are not clear or that it is difficult to understand. ❑ *The law here is a little bit murky.* ADJ = obscure

**mur|mur** /mɜːʳməʳ/ **(murmurs, murmuring, murmured)** 1 If you **murmur** something, you say it very quietly, so that not many people can hear what you are saying. ❑ *He turned and murmured something to the professor... She murmured a few words of support... 'How lovely,' she murmured... Murmuring softly that they must go somewhere to talk, he led her from the garden.* VERB V n *to* n V n V with quote V that 2 A **murmur** is something that is said which can hardly be heard. ❑ *They spoke in low murmurs.* N-COUNT: usu adj N 3 A **murmur** is a continuous low sound, like the noise of a river or of voices far away. ❑ *The piano music mixes with the murmur of conversation... The clamor of traffic has receded to a distant murmur.* N-SING: with supp = hum 4 A **murmur of** a particular emotion is a quiet expression of it. ❑ *The promise of some basic working rights draws murmurs of approval.* N-COUNT: with supp 5 A **murmur** is an abnormal sound which is made by the heart and which shows that there is probably something wrong with it. ❑ *The doctor said James had now developed a heart murmur.* N-COUNT: usu sing 6 If someone does something **without a murmur**, they do it without complaining. PHRASE: PHR after v

**mur|mur|ings** /mɜːʳmərɪŋz/ If there are **murmurings of**, for example, approval or disapproval, people are expressing their approval or disapproval of something in a quiet way. ❑ *For some time there have been murmurings of discontent over the government policy on inflation... At this point there were murmurings of approval from the experts.* N-PLURAL: usu N *of* n

**Murphy's Law** /mɜːʳfiz lɔː/ **Murphy's Law** is the idea that whatever can go wrong in a situation will go wrong. N-PROPER = Sod's Law

**mus|cle** /mʌsᵊl/ **(muscles, muscling, muscled)** 1 A **muscle** is a piece of tissue inside your body which connects two bones and which you use when you make a movement. ❑ *Keeping your muscles strong and in tone helps you to avoid back problems... He is suffering from a strained thigh muscle.* 2 If you say that someone has **muscle**, you mean that they have power and influence, which enables them to do difficult things. ❑ *Eisenhower* ◆◇◇ N-VAR N-UNCOUNT = clout *used his muscle to persuade Congress to change the law.*

**PHRASES** [3] If a group, organization, or country **flexes** its **muscles**, it does something to impress or frighten people, in order to show them that it has power and is considering using it. ❑ *The Fair Trade Commission has of late been flexing its muscles, cracking down on cases of corruption.* [4] If you say that someone did not **move a muscle**, you mean that they stayed absolutely still. ❑ *He stood without moving a muscle, unable to believe what his eyes saw so plainly.* PHRASE: V inflects PHRASE: V inflects, with brd-neg

♦ **muscle in** If someone **muscles in on** something, they force their way into a situation where they have no right to be and where they are not welcome, in order to gain some advantage for themselves. ❑ *Cohen complained that Kravis was muscling in on his deal... It would be surprising were the Mafia not to have muscled in.* PHRASAL VERB [disapproval] V P *on* n V P

**muscle-bound** If you describe someone as **muscle-bound**, you mean that their muscles are well developed, usually in an unattractive way. ❑ *...a cartoon of a muscle-bound woman standing victorious astride a prone male.* ADJ

**mus|cu|lar** /mʌskjʊləʳ/ [1] **Muscular** means involving or affecting your muscles. ❑ *As a general rule, all muscular effort is enhanced by breathing in as the effort is made... Early symptoms include anorexia, muscular weakness and fatigue.* [2] If a person or their body is **muscular**, they are very fit and strong, and have firm muscles which are not covered with a lot of fat. ❑ *Like most female athletes, she was lean and muscular.* ADJ: ADJ n ADJ

**mus|cu|lar dys|tro|phy** /mʌskjʊləʳ dɪstrəfi/ **Muscular dystrophy** is a serious disease in which your muscles gradually weaken. N-UNCOUNT

**mus|cu|la|ture** /mʌskjʊlətʃəʳ/ **Musculature** is used to refer to all the muscles in your body, or to a system of muscles that you use to perform a particular type of action. [FORMAL] N-UNCOUNT: oft with poss

**muse** /mjuːz/ **(muses, musing, mused)** [1] If you **muse** on something, you think about it, usually saying or writing what you are thinking at the same time. [WRITTEN] ❑ *Many of the papers muse on the fate of the President... 'As a whole,' she muses, 'the 'organized church' turns me off'... He once mused that he would have voted Labour in 1964 had he been old enough.* ♦ **mus|ing** **(musings)** *His musings were interrupted by Montagu who came and sat down next to him.* [2] A **muse** is a person, usually a woman, who gives someone, usually a man, a desire to create art, poetry, or music, and gives them ideas for it. ❑ *Once she was a nude model and muse to French artist Henri Matisse.* VERB V *on/about/over* n V with quote V that N-COUNT N-COUNT

**mu|seum** /mjuːziːəm/ **(museums)** A **museum** is a building where a large number of interesting and valuable objects, such as works of art or historical items, are kept, studied, and displayed to the public. ❑ *For months Malcolm had wanted to visit the Parisian art museums. ...the American Museum of Natural History.* ◆◆◇ N-COUNT

**mu|seum piece** **(museum pieces)** If you describe an object or building as a **museum piece**, you mean that it is old and unusual. ❑ *One day these are multi-million dollar war machines and the next they are museum pieces.* N-COUNT

**mush** /mʌʃ/ **(mushes, mushing, mushed)** [1] **Mush** is a thick, soft paste. ❑ *The brown mush in the fridge is some veg soup left over.* [2] If you describe something such as a film or book as **mush**, you mean that it is very sentimental. ❑ *Whenever famous actresses get together to make a 'woman's film' you can bet on an overload of sentimental mush.* [3] If you **mush** something, you make it into a mush. ❑ *...mushed-up potato and cauliflower.* N-VAR: also *a* N N-UNCOUNT [disapproval] VERB V-ed *up* Also V n, V-ed

**mush|room** /mʌʃruːm/ **(mushrooms, mushrooming, mushroomed)** [1] **Mushrooms** are fungi that you can eat. → See picture on page 1712. ❑ *There are many types of wild mushrooms. ...mushroom omelette.* → See also **button mushroom**. [2] If something such as an industry or a place **mushrooms**, it grows or comes into existence very quickly. ❑ *The media training industry has mushroomed over the past decade... A sleepy capital of a few hundred thousand people has mushroomed to a crowded city of 2 million.* N-VAR VERB V V *to/into* n

**mush|room cloud** **(mushroom clouds)** A **mushroom cloud** is an extremely large cloud caused by a nuclear explosion. N-COUNT

**mushy** /mʌʃi/ [1] Vegetables and fruit that are **mushy** are soft and have lost most of their shape. ❑ *When the fruit is mushy and cooked, remove from the heat.* [2] If you describe someone or something as **mushy**, you mean that they are very sentimental. ❑ *Don't go getting all mushy and sentimental.* ADJ ADJ [disapproval]

**mu|sic** /mjuːzɪk/ [1] **Music** is the pattern of sounds produced by people singing or playing instruments. ❑ *...classical music. ...the music of George Gershwin.* [2] **Music** is the art of creating or performing music. ❑ *He went on to study music, specialising in the clarinet. ...a music lesson.* [3] **Music** is the symbols written on paper which represent musical sounds. ❑ *He's never been able to read music.* → See also **sheet music**. ◆◆◆ N-UNCOUNT N-UNCOUNT N-UNCOUNT

**PHRASES** [4] If something that you hear is **music to** your **ears**, it makes you feel very happy. ❑ *Popular support – it's music to the ears of any politician.* [5] If you **face the music**, you put yourself in a position where you will be criticized or punished for something you have done. ❑ *Sooner or later, I'm going to have to face the music.* PHRASE: v-link PHR [feelings] PHRASE: V inflects

**mu|si|cal** /mjuːzɪkᵊl/ **(musicals)** [1] You use **musical** to indicate that something is connected with playing or studying music. ❑ *We have a wealth of musical talent in this region... Stan Getz's musical career spanned five decades.* ♦ **mu|si|cal|ly** /mjuːzɪkli/ *Musically there is a lot to enjoy tonight.* [2] A **musical** is a play or film that uses singing and dancing in the story. ❑ *...London's smash hit musical Miss Saigon.* [3] Someone who is **musical** has a natural ability and interest in music. ❑ *I came from a musical family.* [4] Sounds that are **musical** are light and pleasant to hear. ❑ *He had a soft, almost musical voice.* ◆◇◇ ADJ: ADJ n ADV: ADV with cl/group, ADV after v N-COUNT ADJ ADJ

**mu|si|cal box** **(musical boxes)** A **musical box** is the same as a **music box**. [BRIT] N-COUNT

**mu|si|cal chairs** [1] **Musical chairs** is a game that children play at parties. They run round a row of chairs while music plays and try to sit down on one when the music stops. [2] If you describe the situation within a particular organization or area of activity as **musical chairs**, you are critical of the fact that people in that organization or area exchange jobs or positions very often. ❑ *It was musical chairs. Creative people would switch jobs just to get more money.* N-UNCOUNT N-UNCOUNT [disapproval]

**mu|si|cal com|edy** **(musical comedies)** **Musical comedy** is a type of play or film that has singing and dancing as part of the story and that is humorous and entertaining, especially one written before the middle of the twentieth century. N-VAR

**mu|si|cal di|rec|tor** **(musical directors)** A **musical director** is the same as a **music director**. N-COUNT

**mu|si|cal in|stru|ment** **(musical instruments)** A **musical instrument** is an object such as a piano, guitar, or violin which you play in order to produce music. ❑ *The drum is one of the oldest musical instruments.* N-COUNT = instrument

**mu|sic box** **(music boxes)** A **music box** is a box that plays a tune when you open the lid. N-COUNT = musical box

**mu|sic di|rec|tor** **(music directors)** The **music director** of an orchestra or other group of musicians is the person who decides what they will play and where, and usually conducts them as well. N-COUNT = musical director

**mu|sic hall** **(music halls)** also **music-hall**. [1] **Music hall** was a popular form of entertainment in the theatre in the nineteenth and early N-UNCOUNT: oft N n twentieth century. It consisted of a series of performances by comedians, singers, and dancers. [mainly BRIT] ❑ *...an old music hall song.*

☑ in AM, usually use **vaudeville**

2 A **music hall** was a theatre that presented popular entertainment. [mainly BRIT] N-COUNT

☑ in AM, usually use **vaudeville theater**

**mu|si|cian** /mjuːzɪʃᵊn/ **(musicians)** A **musician** is a person who plays a musical instrument as their job or hobby. ❑ *...one of Britain's best known rock musicians.* ◆◇◇ N-COUNT

**mu|si|cian|ship** /mjuːzɪʃᵊnʃɪp/ **Musicianship** is the skill involved in performing music. ❑ *Her musicianship is excellent.* N-UNCOUNT

**mu|sic stand** **(music stands)** A **music stand** is a device that holds pages of music in position while you play a musical instrument. N-COUNT

**musk** /mʌsk/ **Musk** is a substance with a strong smell which is used in making perfume. N-UNCOUNT

**mus|ket** /mʌskɪt/ **(muskets)** A **musket** was an early type of gun with a long barrel, which was used before rifles were invented. N-COUNT

**musky** /mʌski/ A **musky** smell is strong, warm, and sweet. ❑ *She dabbed a drop of the musky perfume behind each ear.* ADJ

**Mus|lim** /mʊzlɪm, mʊːs-, AM mʌz-/ **(Muslims)** 1 A **Muslim** is someone who believes in Islam and lives according to its rules. 2 **Muslim** means relating to Islam or Muslims. ❑ *...Iran and other Muslim countries.* ◆◆◇ N-COUNT ADJ

**mus|lin** /mʌzlɪn/ **(muslins)** **Muslin** is very thin cotton cloth. ❑ *...white muslin curtains.* N-MASS

**muso** /mjuːzoʊ/ **(musos)** 1 A **muso** is a musician. [INFORMAL] ❑ *...country muso Shania Twain.* N-COUNT
2 **Muso** means the same as **musical**. [INFORMAL] ❑ *Bruce Springsteen has re-hired his muso collective, the E Street Band.* ADJ

**muss** /mʌs/ **(musses, mussing, mussed)** To **muss** something, especially someone's hair, or to **muss** it **up**, means to make it untidy. [mainly AM] ❑ *He reached out and mussed my hair... His clothes were all mussed up.* VERB V n *be* V-ed *up*

**mus|sel** /mʌsᵊl/ **(mussels)** **Mussels** are a kind of shellfish that you can eat from their shells. N-COUNT

**must** /məst, STRONG mʌst/ **(musts)** ◆◆◆

☑ The noun is pronounced /mʌst/.

> **Must** is a modal verb. It is followed by the base form of a verb.

1 You use **must** to indicate that you think it is very important or necessary for something to happen. You use **must not** or **mustn't** to indicate that you think it is very important or necessary for something not to happen. ❑ *What you wear should be stylish and clean, and must definitely fit well... The doctor must not allow the patient to be put at risk.* MODAL
2 You use **must** to indicate that it is necessary for something to happen, usually because of a rule or law. ❑ *Candidates must satisfy the general conditions for admission... Equipment must be supervised if children are in the house.* MODAL
3 You use **must** to indicate that you are fairly sure that something is the case. ❑ *At 29 Russell must be one of the youngest ever Wembley referees... I'm sure he must feel he has lost a close family friend, because I know I do... I must have been a bore.* MODAL
4 You use **must**, or **must have** with a past participle, to indicate that you believe that something is the case, because of the available evidence. ❑ *'You must be Emma,' said the visitor... Miss Holloway had a weak heart. She must have had a heart attack.* MODAL
5 If you say that one thing **must have** happened in order for something else to happen, you mean that it is necessary for the first thing to have happened before the second thing can happen. ❑ *In order to take that job, you must have left another job.* MODAL
6 You use **must** to express your intention to do something. ❑ *I must be getting back... I must telephone my parents... He told the Prime Minister that he felt he must now leave.* MODAL
7 You use **must** to make suggestions or invitations very forcefully. ❑ *You must see a doctor, Frederick... You must see the painting Paul has given me as a wedding present.* MODAL
8 You use **must** in remarks and comments where you are expressing sympathy. ❑ *This must be a very difficult job for you.* MODAL
9 You use **must** in conversation in expressions such as **'I must say'** and **'I must admit'** in order to emphasize a point that you are making. ❑ *This came as a surprise, I must say... I must admit I like looking feminine.* MODAL [emphasis]
10 You use **must** in expressions such as **'it must be noted'** and **'it must be remembered'** in order to draw the reader's or listener's attention to what you are about to say. ❑ *It must be noted, however, that not all British and American officers carried out orders... It must be stated that this illness is one of the most complex conditions known to man.* MODAL
11 You use **must** in questions to express your anger or irritation about something that someone has done, usually because you do not understand their behaviour. ❑ *Why must she interrupt?... Must you always run when the pressure gets too much?* MODAL [feelings]
12 You use **must** in exclamations to express surprise or shock. ❑ *'Go! Please go.' — 'You must be joking!'... I really must be quite mad!.* MODAL [emphasis]
13 If you refer to something as **a must**, you mean that it is absolutely necessary. [INFORMAL] ❑ *The new 37th issue of National Savings Certificates is a must for any taxpayer.* N-COUNT: usu *a* N in sing

**PHRASES** 14 You say **'if you must'** when you know that you cannot stop someone doing something that you think is wrong or stupid. ❑ *If you must be in the sunlight, use the strongest filter cream you can get... 'Could I have a word?' — 'Oh dear, if you must.'.* PHRASE: usu PHR inf
15 You say **'if you must know'** when you tell someone something that you did not want them to know and you want to suggest that you think they were wrong to ask you about it. ❑ *'Why don't you wear your jogging shorts Mum?' — 'Well, my legs are too skinny, if you must know.'* PHRASE: PHR with cl

**must-** /mʌst-/ **Must-** is added to verbs such as 'see', 'have', or 'read' to form adjectives and nouns which describe things that you think people should see, have, or read. For example, a **must-have** is something which you think people should get, and a **must-win** game is one which a team needs to win. [JOURNALISM or INFORMAL] ❑ *...a list of must-see movies.* COMB in ADJ and N-COUNT

**mus|tache** /məstɑːʃ, AM mʊstæʃ/ → see **moustache**.

**mus|tang** /mʌstæŋ/ **(mustangs)** A **mustang** is a small wild horse which lives on the plains of North America. N-COUNT

**mus|tard** /mʌstᵊrd/ **(mustards)** 1 **Mustard** is a yellow or brown paste usually eaten with meat. It tastes hot and spicy. ❑ *...a pot of mustard.* N-MASS
2 **Mustard** is used to describe things that are brownish yellow in colour. ❑ *...a mustard coloured jumper.* COLOUR
3 If someone does not **cut the mustard**, their work or their performance is not as good as it should be or as good as it is expected to be. [INFORMAL] PHRASE: V inflects, usu with neg

**mus|tard and cress** **Mustard and cress** is very young mustard plants and cress plants grown together and eaten in salad. N-UNCOUNT

**mus|tard gas** **Mustard gas** is a gas which burns the skin and was used in war as a weapon. N-UNCOUNT

**mus|tard pow|der** **Mustard powder** is a yellow powder. You add hot water to it in order to make mustard. N-UNCOUNT

**mus|ter** /mʌstəʳ/ **(musters, mustering, mustered)** 1 If you **muster** something such as support, strength, or energy, you gather as much of it as you can in order to do something. ❑ *He travelled around West Africa trying to muster support for his movement.* VERB V n
2 When soldiers **muster** or **are mustered**, they gather together in one place in order to take part in a military action. ❑ *The men mustered before their clan chiefs... The general had* VERB = gather V V n

*mustered his troops north of the Hindu Kush.* 3 If someone or something **passes muster**, they are good enough for the thing they are needed for. PHRASE: V inflects ❑ *I could not pass muster in his language... If it doesn't pass muster, a radio station could have its license challenged.*

**mustn't** /mʌsᵊnt/ **Mustn't** is the usual spoken form of 'must not'.

**must've** /mʌstəv/ **Must've** is the usual spoken form of 'must have', especially when 'have' is an auxiliary verb.

**mus|ty** /mʌsti/ Something that is **musty** smells old and damp. ❑ *...that terrible musty smell.* ADJ = fusty

**mu|tant** /mjuːtᵊnt/ **(mutants)** A **mutant** is an animal or plant that is physically different from others of the same species because of a change in its genes. N-COUNT = mutation

**mu|tate** /mjuːteɪt, AM mjuːteɪt/ **(mutates, mutating, mutated)** 1 If an animal or plant **mutates**, or something **mutates** it, it develops different characteristics as the result of a change in its genes. VERB ❑ *The virus mutates in the carrier's body...* V *A newer anti-HIV drug called pyridinone caused HIV to mutate into a form which could not reproduce or infect new cells...* V into n *The technique has been to mutate the genes by irradiation or chemicals.* V n, Also V n into n ♦ **mu|ta|tion** /mjuːteɪʃᵊn/ **(mutations)** *Scientists have found a genetic mutation that appears to be the cause of Huntington's disease.* N-VAR 2 If something **mutates into** something different, it changes into that thing. VERB ❑ *Overnight, the gossip begins to mutate into headlines.* V into n

**mute** /mjuːt/ **(mutes, muting, muted)** 1 Someone who is **mute** is silent for a particular reason and does not speak. ADJ ❑ *He was mute, distant, and indifferent.* ♦ **Mute** is also an adverb. ADV: ADV after v ❑ *He could watch her standing mute by the phone.* ♦ **mute|ly** *I crouched by him and grasped his hand, mutely offering what comfort I could.* ADV: ADV with v 2 Someone who is **mute** is unable to speak. ADJ [OLD-FASHIONED] ❑ *Marianna, the duke's daughter, became mute after a shock.* 3 If someone **mutes** something such as their feelings or their activities, they reduce the strength or intensity of them. VERB ❑ *The corruption does not seem to have muted the country's prolonged economic boom.* V n ♦ **mut|ed** *The threat contrasted starkly with his administration's previous muted criticism.* ADJ 4 If you **mute** a noise or sound, you lower its volume or make it less distinct. VERB ❑ *They begin to mute their voices, not be as assertive.* V n ♦ **mut|ed** *'Yes,' he muttered, his voice so muted I hardly heard his reply.* ADJ

**mut|ed** /mjuːtɪd/ **Muted** colours are soft and gentle, not bright and strong. ADJ: usu ADJ n ❑ *He likes sombre, muted colours – she likes bright colours.*

**mu|ti|late** /mjuːtɪleɪt/ **(mutilates, mutilating, mutilated)** 1 If a person or animal **is mutilated**, their body is severely damaged, usually by someone who physically attacks them. VERB ❑ *More than 30 horses have been mutilated in the last nine months...* be V-ed *He tortured and mutilated six young men...* V n *The mutilated bodies of seven men have been found beside a railway line.* V-ed ♦ **mu|ti|la|tion** /mjuːtɪleɪʃᵊn/ **(mutilations)** *Amnesty International chronicles cases of torture and mutilation.* N-VAR 2 If something **is mutilated**, it is deliberately damaged or spoiled. VERB ❑ *Brecht's verdict was that his screenplay had been mutilated.* be V-ed, Also V n

**mu|ti|neer** /mjuːtɪnɪəʳ/ **(mutineers)** A **mutineer** is a person who takes part in a mutiny. N-COUNT

**mu|ti|nous** /mjuːtɪnəs/ If someone is **mutinous**, they are strongly dissatisfied with a person in authority and are likely to stop obeying them. ADJ ❑ *His own army, stung by defeats, is mutinous.*

**mu|ti|ny** /mjuːtɪni/ **(mutinies, mutinying, mutinied)** 1 A **mutiny** is a refusal by people, usually soldiers or sailors, to continue obeying a person in authority. N-VAR ❑ *A series of coup attempts and mutinies within the armed forces destabilized the regime.* 2 If a group of people, usually soldiers or sailors, **mutiny**, they refuse to continue obeying a person in authority. VERB ❑ *Units stationed around the capital mutinied because they had received no pay for nine months...* V *Sailors at a naval base had mutinied against their officers.* V against n

**mutt** /mʌt/ **(mutts)** A **mutt** is the same as a **mongrel**. N-COUNT [INFORMAL]

**mut|ter** /mʌtəʳ/ **(mutters, muttering, muttered)** VERB If you **mutter**, you speak very quietly so that you cannot easily be heard, often because you are complaining about something. ❑ *'God knows what's happening in that madman's mind,' she muttered...* V with quote *She can hear the old woman muttering about consideration...* V about n *He sat there shaking his head, muttering to himself...* V to n *She was staring into the fire muttering.* V ♦ **Mutter** is also a noun. N-COUNT ❑ *They make no more than a mutter of protest.* ♦ **mut|ter|ing (mutterings)** *He heard muttering from the front of the crowd.* N-VAR

**mut|ton** /mʌtᵊn/ 1 **Mutton** is meat from an adult sheep that is eaten as food. N-UNCOUNT ❑ *...a leg of mutton. ...mutton stew.* 2 If you describe a woman as **mutton dressed as lamb**, you are criticizing her for trying to look younger than she really is, in a way that you consider unattractive. PHRASE: usu v-link PHR, disapproval [BRIT, INFORMAL]

**mu|tu|al** /mjuːtʃuəl/ ◆◇◇ 1 You use **mutual** to describe a situation, feeling, or action that is experienced, felt, or done by both of two people mentioned. ADJ ❑ *The East and the West can work together for their mutual benefit and progress... It's plain that he adores his daughter, and the feeling is mutual.* ♦ **mu|tu|al|ly** *Attempts to reach a mutually agreed solution had been fruitless.* ADV: ADV adj/adv, ADV before v → see **exclusive**. 2 You use **mutual** to describe something such as an interest which two or more people share. ADJ: usu ADJ n ❑ *They do, however, share a mutual interest in design... We were introduced by a mutual friend.* 3 If a building society or an insurance company has **mutual** status, it is not owned by shareholders but by its customers, who receive a share of the profits. ADJ: ADJ n [BRIT, BUSINESS] ❑ *Britain's third largest building society abandoned its mutual status and became a bank.*

**mu|tu|al fund (mutual funds)** A **mutual fund** is an organization which invests money in many different kinds of business and which offers units for sale to the public as an investment. N-COUNT [AM, BUSINESS]

✔ in BRIT, use **unit trust**

**Mu|zak** /mjuːzæk/ also **muzak**. 1 **Muzak** is recorded music that is played as background music in shops or restaurants. N-UNCOUNT [TRADEMARK] 2 If you describe music as **muzak**, you dislike it because you think it is dull or unnecessary. N-UNCOUNT, disapproval

**muz|zle** /mʌzᵊl/ **(muzzles, muzzling, muzzled)** 1 The **muzzle** of an animal such as a dog is its nose and mouth. N-COUNT 2 A **muzzle** is an object that is put over a dog's nose and mouth so that it cannot bite people or make a noise. N-COUNT ❑ *...dogs like pit bulls which have to wear a muzzle.* 3 If you **muzzle** a dog or other animal, you put a muzzle over its nose and mouth. VERB ❑ *He was convicted of failing to muzzle a pit bull.* V n 4 If you say that someone **is muzzled**, you are complaining that they are prevented from expressing their views freely. VERB, disapproval = gag ❑ *He complained of being muzzled by the chairman...* be V-ed *She was opposed to new laws to muzzle the press.* V n 5 The **muzzle** of a gun is the end where the bullets come out when it is fired. N-COUNT: usu N of n

**muz|zy** /mʌzi/ 1 If someone feels **muzzy**, they are confused and unable to think clearly, usually because they are ill or have drunk too much alcohol. ADJ = groggy [mainly BRIT, INFORMAL] 2 If a photograph or television picture is **muzzy**, it is unclear. ADJ = fuzzy [mainly BRIT, INFORMAL]

**MVP** /em viː piː/ **(MVPs)** Journalists sometimes use **MVP** to talk about the player in a sports team who has performed best in a particular match or series of matches. N-COUNT: oft N n **MVP** is an abbreviation for 'most valuable player'. [AM] ❑ *Brondello secured the MVP award by scoring 357 points.*

**MW** [1] **MW** is a written abbreviation for **medium wave.** [2] **MW** is a written abbreviation for **megawatt.**

**my** /maɪ/ ◆◆◆

**My** is the first person singular possessive determiner.

[1] A speaker or writer uses **my** to indicate that something belongs or relates to himself or herself. ❑ *I invited him back to my flat for a coffee... John's my best friend.* DET [2] In conversations or in letters, **my** is used in front of a word like 'dear' or 'darling' to show affection. ❑ *Yes, of course, my darling.* DET feelings [3] **My** is used in phrases such as '**My God**' and '**My goodness**' to express surprise or shock. [SPOKEN] ❑ *My God, I've never seen you so nervous... My goodness, Tim, you have changed!* DET feelings

**myo|pia** /maɪoupiə/ **Myopia** is the inability to see things properly when they are far away, because there is something wrong with your eyes. [FORMAL] N-UNCOUNT = short-sightedness

**my|op|ic** /maɪɒpɪk/ [1] If you describe someone as **myopic**, you are critical of them because they seem unable to realize that their actions might have negative consequences. ❑ *The Government still has a myopic attitude to spending.* ADJ disapproval = short-sighted [2] If someone is **myopic**, they are unable to see things which are far away from them. [FORMAL] ADJ = short-sighted

**myri|ad** /mɪriəd/ [1] **A myriad** or **myriads of** people or things is a very large number or great variety of them. ❑ *They face a myriad of problems bringing up children... These myriads of fish would be enough to keep any swimmer entranced for hours.* QUANT: QUANT *of* pl-n [2] **Myriad** means having a large number or great variety. ❑ *...British pop and culture in all its myriad forms.* ADJ: ADJ n = many

**my|self** /maɪself/ ◆◆◇

**Myself** is the first person singular reflexive pronoun.

[1] A speaker or writer uses **myself** to refer to himself or herself. **Myself** is used as the object of a verb or preposition when the subject refers to the same person. ❑ *I asked myself what I would have done in such a situation... I looked at myself in the mirror.* PRON: v PRON, prep PRON [2] You use **myself** to emphasize a first person singular subject. In more formal English, **myself** is sometimes used instead of 'me' as the object of a verb or preposition, for emphasis. ❑ *I myself enjoy cinema, poetry, eating out and long walks... I'm fond of cake myself.* PRON emphasis [3] If you say something such as 'I did it **myself**', you are emphasizing that you did it, rather than anyone else. ❑ *'Where did you get that embroidery?' — 'I made it myself.'* PRON emphasis

**mys|teri|ous** /mɪstɪəriəs/ [1] Someone or something that is **mysterious** is strange and is not known about or understood. ❑ *He died in mysterious circumstances... A mysterious illness confined him to bed for over a month... The whole thing seems very mysterious.* ADJ ♦ **mys|teri|ous|ly** *A couple of messages had mysteriously disappeared.* ADV: usu ADV with v [2] If someone is **mysterious** about something, they deliberately do not talk much about it, sometimes because they want to make people more interested in it. ❑ *As for his job – well, he was very mysterious about it.* ADJ: v-link ADJ, oft ADJ *about* n ♦ **mys|teri|ous|ly** *Asked what she meant, she said mysteriously: 'Work it out for yourself'.* ADV: ADV after v

**mys|tery** /mɪstəri/ **(mysteries)** [1] A **mystery** is something that is not understood or known about. ❑ *The source of the gunshots still remains a mystery. ...the mysteries of mental breakdown.* ◆◇◇ N-COUNT [2] If you talk about the **mystery** of someone or something, you are talking about how difficult they are to understand or know about, especially when this gives them a rather strange or magical quality. ❑ *She's a lady of mystery... It is an elaborate ceremony, shrouded in mystery.* N-UNCOUNT [3] A **mystery** person or thing is one whose identity or nature is not known. ❑ *The mystery hero immediately alerted police after spotting a bomb. ...a mystery prize of up to £1,000.* ADJ: ADJ n [4] A **mystery** is a story in which strange things happen that are not explained until the end. ❑ *His fourth novel is a murder mystery set in London.* N-COUNT

**mys|tic** /mɪstɪk/ **(mystics)** [1] A **mystic** is a person who practises or believes in religious mysticism. ❑ *...an Indian mystic known as Bhagwan Shree Rajneesh.* N-COUNT [2] **Mystic** means the same as **mystical.** ❑ *...mystic union with God.* ADJ: ADJ n

**mys|ti|cal** /mɪstɪkəl/ Something that is **mystical** involves spiritual powers and influences that most people do not understand. ❑ *That was clearly a deep mystical experience.* ADJ: usu ADJ n = mystic

**mys|ti|cism** /mɪstɪsɪzəm/ **Mysticism** is a religious practice in which people search for truth, knowledge, and closeness to God through meditation and prayer. N-UNCOUNT

**mys|ti|fy** /mɪstɪfaɪ/ **(mystifies, mystifying, mystified)** If you **are mystified** by something, you find it impossible to explain or understand. ❑ *The audience must have been totally mystified by the plot... There was something strange in her attitude which mystified me.* VERB = baffle *be* V-ed V n ♦ **mys|ti|fy|ing** *I find your attitude a little mystifying, Moira.* ADJ = puzzling

**mys|tique** /mɪstiːk/ If there is a **mystique** about someone or something, they are thought to be special and people do not know much about them. ❑ *His book destroyed the mystique of monarchy.* N-SING: also N-UNCOUNT

**myth** /mɪθ/ **(myths)** [1] A **myth** is a well-known story which was made up in the past to explain natural events or to justify religious beliefs or social customs. ❑ *There is a famous Greek myth in which Icarus flew too near to the Sun.* ◆◇◇ N-VAR [2] If you describe a belief or explanation as a **myth**, you mean that many people believe it but it is actually untrue. ❑ *Contrary to the popular myth, women are not reckless spendthrifts.* N-VAR = fallacy

**myth|ic** /mɪθɪk/ [1] Someone or something that is **mythic** exists only in myths and is therefore imaginary. [LITERARY] ❑ *...the mythic figure of King Arthur.* ADJ: usu ADJ n = mythical [2] If you describe someone or something as **mythic**, you mean that they have become very famous or important. ❑ *...a team whose reputation has achieved mythic proportions.* ADJ: usu ADJ n

**mythi|cal** /mɪθɪkəl/ [1] Something or someone that is **mythical** exists only in myths and is therefore imaginary. ❑ *...the Hydra, the mythical beast that had seven or more heads.* ADJ: usu ADJ n [2] If you describe something as **mythical**, you mean that it is untrue or does not exist. ❑ *...the American West, not the mythical, romanticized West of cowboys and gunslingers, but the real West.* ADJ: usu ADJ n

**my|thol|ogy** /mɪθɒlədʒi/ **(mythologies)** [1] **Mythology** is a group of myths, especially all the myths from a particular country, religion, or culture. ❑ *In Greek mythology, the god Zeus took the form of a swan to seduce Leda... This is well illustrated in the mythologies of many cultures.* N-VAR ♦ **mytho|logi|cal** /mɪθəlɒdʒɪkəl/ *...the mythological beast that was part lion and part goat.* ADJ: usu ADJ n [2] You can use **mythology** to refer to the beliefs or opinions that people have about something, when you think that they are false or untrue. ❑ *Altman strips away the pretence and mythology to expose the film industry as a business like any other.* N-VAR

# N n

**N, n** /en/ **(N's, n's)** [1] **N** is the fourteenth letter of the English alphabet. N-VAR [2] **N** or **n** is used as an abbreviation for words beginning with N or n, such as 'north', 'northern', or 'noun'.

**'n'** /ən/ The word 'and' is sometimes written as **'n'** between certain pairs of words, as in 'rock **'n'** roll'. [INFORMAL] CONJ = and ❑ *...a country 'n' western song. ...a fish 'n' chips restaurant.*

**N.A.** also **n/a. N.A.** is a written abbreviation for **not applicable** or **not available**. CONVENTION

**naan** /nɑːn/ **(naans)** also **nan. Naan** or **naan bread** is a type of bread that comes in a large, round, flat piece and is usually eaten with Indian food. N-VAR

**nab** /næb/ **(nabs, nabbing, nabbed)** If people in authority such as the police **nab** someone who they think has done something wrong, they catch them or arrest them. [INFORMAL] VERB = collar ❑ *He killed 12 people before the authorities finally nabbed him...* V n *Soon he was back in the armed robbery business. Again, he got nabbed.* get V-ed

**na|dir** /neɪdɪəʳ, AM -dər/ [1] The **nadir** of something such as someone's career or the history of an organization is its worst time. [LITERARY] N-SING: usu with poss ≠ zenith ❑ *1945 to 1946 was the nadir of Truman's presidency.* [2] In astronomy, **the nadir** is the point at which the sun or moon is directly below you, on the other side of the earth. Compare **zenith**. [TECHNICAL] N-SING: the N

**naff** /næf/ **(naffer, naffest)** If you say that something is **naff**, you mean it is very unfashionable or unsophisticated. [BRIT, INFORMAL] ADJ ❑ *The music's really naff. ...naff 'his and hers' matching outfits.*

**nag** /næg/ **(nags, nagging, nagged)** [1] If someone **nags** you, they keep asking you to do something you have not done yet or do not want to do. VERB [disapproval] ❑ *The more Sarah nagged her, the more stubborn Cissie became...* V n *My girlfriend nagged me to cut my hair...* V n to-inf *She had stopped nagging him about never being home.* V n about n *...children nagging their parents into buying things.* V n into -ing Also V ♦ A **nag** is someone who nags. N-COUNT ❑ *Aunt Molly is a nag about regular meals.* ♦ **nag|ging** N-UNCOUNT *Her endless nagging drove him away from home.* [2] If something such as a doubt or worry **nags at** you, or **nags** you, it keeps worrying you. VERB = niggle ❑ *He could be wrong about her. The feeling nagged at him.* V at n *...the anxiety that had nagged Amy all through lunch...* V n *Something was nagging in the back of his mind.* V

**nag|ging** /nægɪŋ/ A **nagging** pain is not very severe but is difficult to cure. ADJ: ADJ n ❑ *He complained of a nagging pain between his shoulder blades.* ➔ See also **nag**.

**nail** /neɪl/ **(nails, nailing, nailed)** [1] A **nail** is a thin piece of metal with one pointed end and one flat end. You hit the flat end with a hammer in order to push the nail into something such as a wall. N-COUNT ➔ See picture on page 1709. ❑ *A mirror hung on a nail above the washstand.* [2] If you **nail** something somewhere, you fix it there using one or more nails. VERB ❑ *Frank put the first plank down and nailed it in place...* V n prep/adv *They nail shut the front door.* V n with adj [3] Your **nails** are the thin hard parts that grow at the ends of your fingers and toes. N-COUNT: usu poss N in pl ❑ *Keep your nails short and your hands clean.* [4] To **nail** someone means to catch them and prove that they have been breaking the law. [INFORMAL] VERB ❑ *The prosecution still managed to nail him for robberies at the homes of leading industrialists.* V n

**PHRASES** [5] If you say that someone is **as hard as nails**, you mean that they are extremely tough and aggressive, either physically or in their attitude towards other people or other situations. PHRASE: v-link PHR ❑ *He's a shrewd businessman and hard as nails.* [6] If you say that someone **has hit the nail on the head**, you think they are exactly right about something. PHRASE: V inflects ❑ *'I think it would civilize people a bit more if they had decent conditions.' — 'I think you've hit the nail on the head.'* [7] **a nail in the coffin** ➔ see **coffin**. to **fight tooth and nail** ➔ see **tooth**.

♦ **nail down** [1] If you **nail down** something unknown or uncertain, you find out exactly what it is. PHRASAL VERB = pin down ❑ *It would be useful if you could nail down the source of this tension.* V P n Also V n P [2] If you **nail down** an agreement, you manage to reach a firm agreement with a definite result. PHRASAL VERB ❑ *The Secretary of State and his Russian counterpart met to try to nail down the elusive accord.* V P n (not pron) Also V n P

**nail-biting** If you describe something such as a story or a sports match as **nail-biting**, you mean that it makes you feel very excited or nervous because you do not know how it is going to end. ADJ ❑ *...the nail-biting legal thriller, 'The Pelican Brief'.*

**nail bomb (nail bombs)** A **nail bomb** is a bomb which contains nails that are intended to cause a lot of damage and injury when the bomb goes off. N-COUNT

**nail brush (nail brushes)** also **nailbrush.** A **nail brush** is a small brush that you use to clean your nails when washing your hands. N-COUNT

**nail file (nail files)** also **nailfile.** A **nail file** is a small strip of rough metal or card that you rub across the ends of your nails to shorten them or shape them. N-COUNT

**nail pol|ish (nail polishes** /neɪl pɒlɪʃ/**) Nail polish** is a thick liquid that women paint on their nails. N-MASS = nail varnish

**nail scis|sors** also **nail-scissors. Nail scissors** are small scissors that you use for cutting your nails. N-PLURAL: also a pair of N ❑ *Mishka got some nail scissors and started carefully trimming his fingernails.*

**nail var|nish (nail varnishes) Nail varnish** is the same as **nail polish**. [BRIT] N-MASS

☑ in AM, use **nail polish**

**na|ive** /naɪiːv, AM nɑː-/ also **naïve.** If you describe someone as **naive**, you think they lack experience and so expect things to be easy or people to be honest or kind. ADJ: oft it v-link ADJ to-inf, ADJ to-inf = unrealistic ❑ *It's naive to think that teachers are always tolerant. ...naive idealists... Their view was that he had been politically naive.* ♦ **na|ive|ly** ADV: usu ADV with v *...naively applying Western solutions to Eastern problems... I thought, naively, that this would be a nine-to-five job.* ♦ **na|ive|ty** /naɪiːvɪti/ N-UNCOUNT *I was alarmed by his naivety and ignorance of international affairs.*

**na|ked** /neɪkɪd/ [1] Someone who is **naked** is not wearing any clothes. ADJ: ADJ n, ADJ after v, v-link ADJ ❑ *Her naked body was found wrapped in a sheet in a field... The hot paving stones scorched my naked feet... They stripped me naked... He stood naked in front of me.*

♦ **na|ked|ness** *He had pulled the blanket over his body to hide his nakedness.* → See also **stark naked.** N-UNCOUNT: oft poss N

2 If an animal or part of an animal is **naked**, it has no fur or feathers on it. ❑ *The nest contained eight little mice that were naked and blind.* ADJ

3 You can describe an object as **naked** when it does not have its normal covering. ❑ *...a naked bulb dangling in a bare room.* ADJ: usu ADJ n

4 You can use **naked** to describe unpleasant or violent actions and behaviour which are not disguised or hidden in any way. [JOURNALISM] ❑ *Naked aggression and an attempt to change frontiers by force could not go unchallenged.* ADJ: ADJ n = *blatant*

5 If you say that something cannot be seen **by the naked eye**, you mean that it cannot be seen without the help of equipment such as a telescope or microscope. ❑ *There's so much going on that you can't see with the naked eye.* PHRASE: usu *to/with/by* PHR

**name** /neɪm/ **(names, naming, named)** ◆◆◆ 1 The **name** of a person, place, or thing is the word or group of words that is used to identify them. ❑ *'What's his name?' — 'Peter.'... I don't even know if Sullivan's his real name... They changed the name of the street.* N-COUNT: usu with poss

2 When you **name** someone or something, you give them a name, usually at the beginning of their life. ❑ *My mother insisted on naming me Horace. ...a man named John T. Benson.* VERB V n n V-ed

3 If you **name** someone or something **after** another person or thing, you give them the same name as that person or thing. ❑ *Why have you not named any of your sons after yourself?* VERB V n *after* n Also V n *for* n

4 If you **name** someone, you identify them by stating their name. ❑ *It's nearly thirty years since a journalist was jailed for refusing to name a source... One of the victims of the weekend's snowstorm has been named as twenty-year-old John Barr.* VERB V n V n *as* n

5 If you **name** something such as a price, time, or place, you say what you want it to be. ❑ *Call Marty, tell him to name his price.* VERB = *state* V n

6 If you **name** the person for a particular job, you say who you want to have the job. ❑ *The England manager will be naming a new captain, to replace the injured David Beckham... When the chairman of Campbell's retired, McGovern was named as his successor... Early in 1941 he was named commander of the Afrika Korps.* VERB V n *be* V-ed *as* n *be* V-ed n

7 You can refer to the reputation of a person or thing as their **name**. ❑ *He had a name for good judgement... She's never had any drug problems or done anything to give jazz a bad name.* N-COUNT: usu sing = *reputation*

8 You can refer to someone as, for example, a famous **name** or a great **name** when they are well-known. [JOURNALISM] ❑ *...some of the most famous names in modelling and show business.* N-COUNT: usu with supp, oft adj N = *star*

9 → See also **assumed name, big name, brand name, Christian name, code name, first name, given name, maiden name, middle name, pet name.**

**PHRASES** 10 If something is **in** someone's **name**, it officially belongs to them or is reserved for them. ❑ *The house is in my husband's name... A double room had been reserved for him in the name of Muller.* PHRASE: v-link PHR, PHR after v

11 If someone does something **in the name of** a group of people, they do it as the representative of that group. ❑ *In the United States the majority governs in the name of the people.* PHRASE: PHR n, usu PHR after v

12 If you do something **in the name of** an ideal or an abstract thing, you do it in order to preserve or promote that thing. ❑ *...one of those rare occasions in history when a political leader risked his own power in the name of the greater public good.* PHRASE: PHR n/-ing, usu PHR after v

13 People sometimes use expressions such as **'in the name of** heaven' or **'in the name of** humanity' to add emphasis to a question or request. ❑ *What in the name of heaven's going on?... In the name of humanity I ask the government to reappraise this important issue.* PHRASE: PHR n, PHR with cl [emphasis]

14 When you mention someone or something **by name**, or address someone **by name**, you use their name. ❑ *He greets customers by name and enquires about their health.* PHRASE: PHR after v

15 You can use **by name** or **by the name of** when you are saying what someone is called. [FORMAL] ❑ *...a young Australian, Harry Busteed by name... This guy, Jack Smith, does he go by the name of Jackal?* PHRASE

16 If someone **calls** you **names**, they insult you by saying unpleasant things to you or about you. ❑ *At my last school they called me names because I was so slow... They had called her rude names.* PHRASE: V inflects

17 If you say that something is **the name of the game**, you mean that it is the most important aspect of a situation. [INFORMAL] ❑ *The name of the game is survival.* PHRASE

18 If you **make a name for yourself** or **make** your **name as** something, you become well-known for that thing. ❑ *She was beginning to make a name for herself as a portrait photographer... He made his name with several collections of short stories.* PHRASE: V inflects, oft PHR *as* n

19 If you **name names**, you identify the people who have done something, often something wrong. ❑ *Nobody was prepared to risk prosecution by actually naming names.* PHRASE: V inflects

20 If something such as a newspaper or an official body **names and shames** people who have performed badly or who have done something wrong, it identifies those people by name. ❑ *The government will also name and shame the worst performing airlines.* PHRASE: Vs inflect

21 You say **you name it**, usually after or before a list, to indicate that you are talking about a very wide range of things. ❑ *I also enjoy windsurfing, tennis, racquetball, swimming, you name it.* PHRASE

**name|check** /neɪmtʃek/ **(namechecks, namechecking, namechecked)** also **name-check.** If someone gets a **namecheck** in something such as an article or interview, their name is mentioned in it. ❑ *She has had many credits and name-checks in American Vogue.* ♦ **Namecheck** is also a verb. ❑ *Several bands have namechecked Lee Hazelwood in interviews.* N-COUNT; VERB V n

**name-drop** **(name-drops, name-dropping, name-dropped)** If you say that someone **name-drops**, you disapprove of them referring to famous people they have met in order to impress people. ❑ *The assistant carried on talking to his mate, name-dropping all the famous riders he knew... I must stop saying everyone famous is a good friend. It sounds as if I'm name-dropping.* ♦ **name-dropping** *One can do a lot of name-dropping with names of the school's parents. President Nixon sent his daughters there.* VERB [disapproval] V n V; N-UNCOUNT

**name|less** /neɪmləs/ 1 You describe people or things as **nameless** when you do not know their name or when they do not have a name. ❑ *They can have their cases rejected, without reasons being given, by nameless officials.* ADJ: usu ADJ n

2 If you say that someone or something **will remain nameless**, you mean that you will not mention their name, often because you do not want to embarrass them. ❑ *A local friend who shall be nameless warned me that I was in for trouble soon.* ADJ: v-link ADJ = *anonymous*

**name|ly** /neɪmli/ You use **namely** to introduce detailed information about the subject you are discussing, or a particular aspect of it. ❑ *One group of people seems to be forgotten, namely pensioners... They were hardly aware of the challenge facing them, namely, to re-establish prosperity.* ADV: ADV n, ADV cl

**name|plate** /neɪmpleɪt/ **(nameplates)** also **name-plate.** A **nameplate** is a sign on a door, wall, or desk which shows the name of the person or organization that occupies a particular place. N-COUNT

**name|sake** /neɪmseɪk/ **(namesakes)** Someone's or something's **namesake** has the same name as they do. [WRITTEN] ❑ *He is putting together a four-man team, including his son and namesake Tony O'Reilly Jnr... Notre-Dame Cathedral in Senlis is less famous than its namesake in Paris.* N-COUNT: usu poss N

**nan** /næn/ **(nans)** 1 Some people refer to their grandmother as their **nan.** [BRIT, INFORMAL] ❑ *I was brought up by my nan.* N-COUNT; N-VOC = *gran* 2 → See also **naan.**

**nan|dro|lone** /nændrəloʊn/ **Nandrolone** is type of drug that can improve performance in sports and is used illegally by some sportspeople. N-UNCOUNT

**nan|ny** /næni/ **(nannies)** A **nanny** is a woman who is paid by parents to look after their child or children. N-COUNT

**nan|ny|ing** /nænɪɪŋ/ [1] **Nannying** is the job of being a nanny. [mainly BRIT] ❑ *...low-paid jobs such as nannying.* [2] If you refer to activities such as helping and advising people as **nannying**, you disapprove of these activities because you think that they are protecting people too much. [mainly BRIT] ❑ *...governmental nannying and interference in markets.* N-UNCOUNT; N-UNCOUNT disapproval

**nan|ny state** If you refer to the government as **the nanny state**, you disapprove of it because you think it tries to protect its citizens too much and makes them rely on the state too much. [mainly BRIT] ❑ *The tussle to free the individual from the nanny state is still far from won.* N-SING: usu *the* N disapproval

**nano|tech|nol|ogy** /nænoʊteknɒlədʒi/ **Nanotechnology** is the science of making or working with things that are so small that they can only be seen using a powerful microscope. N-UNCOUNT

**nap** /næp/ **(naps, napping, napped)** [1] If you have a **nap**, you have a short sleep, usually during the day. ❑ *Use your lunch hour to have a nap in your chair... I might take a little nap.* [2] If you **nap**, you sleep for a short period of time, usually during the day. ❑ *An elderly person may nap during the day and then sleep only five hours a night.* [3] The **nap** of a carpet or of a cloth such as velvet is the top layer of short threads, which usually lie smoothly in one direction. [4] If someone **is caught napping**, something happens when they are not prepared for it, although they should have been. [INFORMAL] ❑ *The security services were clearly caught napping.* N-COUNT = snooze, doze; VERB = doze; V; N-SING; PHRASE: V inflects

**na|palm** /neɪpɑːm/ **(napalms, napalming, napalmed)** [1] **Napalm** is a substance containing petrol which is used to make bombs that burn people, buildings, and plants. ❑ *The government has consistently denied using napalm.* [2] If people **napalm** other people or places, they attack and burn them using napalm. ❑ *Why napalm a village now?* N-UNCOUNT; VERB; V n

**nape** /neɪp/ **(napes)** The **nape** of your neck is the back of it. ❑ *...the way that his hair grew at the nape of his neck.* N-COUNT: usu sing, usu *the* N *of* n

**nap|kin** /næpkɪn/ **(napkins)** A **napkin** is a square of cloth or paper that you use when you are eating to protect your clothes, or to wipe your mouth or hands. ❑ *She was taking tiny bites of a hot dog and daintily wiping her lips with a napkin.* N-COUNT

**nap|kin ring** **(napkin rings)** A **napkin ring** is a ring-shaped object which is used to hold a rolled-up napkin. N-COUNT

**nap|py** /næpi/ **(nappies)** A **nappy** is a piece of soft thick cloth or paper which is fastened round a baby's bottom in order to soak up its urine and faeces. [BRIT] N-COUNT

✔ in AM, use **diaper**

**nap|py rash** If a baby has **nappy rash**, the skin under its nappy is red and sore. [BRIT] N-UNCOUNT

✔ in AM, use **diaper rash**

**nar|cis|si** /nɑːʳsɪsaɪ/ **narcissi** is a plural form of **narcissus**.

**nar|cis|sism** /nɑːʳsɪsɪzəm/ **Narcissism** is the habit of always thinking about yourself and admiring yourself. [FORMAL] ❑ *Those who suffer from narcissism become self-absorbed or chronic show-offs.* N-UNCOUNT disapproval

**nar|cis|sis|tic** /nɑːʳsɪsɪstɪk/ If you describe someone as **narcissistic**, you disapprove of them because they think about themselves a lot and admire themselves too much. [FORMAL] ❑ *He was insufferable at times – self-centred and narcissistic.* ADJ disapproval

**nar|cis|sus** /nɑːʳsɪsəs/ **(narcissi** or **narcissus)** **Narcissi** are plants which have yellow or white flowers with cone-shaped centres that appear in the spring. N-COUNT: usu pl

**narco-** /nærkoʊ-/ **Narco-** is added to words to form new words that relate to illegal narcotics. ❑ *...efforts to curb illicit and illegal narco-trafficking.* PREFIX

**nar|co|lep|sy** /nɑːʳkəlepsi/ **Narcolepsy** is a rare medical condition. It causes people who suffer from it to fall into a deep sleep at any time without any warning. N-UNCOUNT

**nar|cot|ic** /nɑːʳkɒtɪk/ **(narcotics)** [1] **Narcotics** are drugs such as opium or heroin which make you sleepy and stop you feeling pain. You can also use **narcotics**, especially in American English, to mean any kind of illegal drug. ❑ *He was indicted for dealing in narcotics.* [2] If something, especially a drug, has a **narcotic** effect, it makes the person who uses it feel sleepy. ❑ *...hormones that have a narcotic effect on the immune system.* N-COUNT; ADJ

**narked** /nɑːʳkt/ Someone who is **narked** is annoyed about something. [BRIT, INFORMAL] ❑ *He's probably narked because he didn't see the ad himself.* ADJ: v-link ADJ = annoyed

**nar|rate** /nəreɪt, AM næreɪt/ **(narrates, narrating, narrated)** [1] If you **narrate** a story, you tell it from your own point of view. [FORMAL] ❑ *The book is narrated by Richard Papen, a Californian boy.* ♦ **nar|ra|tion** /nəreɪʃᵊn/ *Its story-within-a-story method of narration is confusing.* ♦ **nar|ra|tor** /nəreɪtəʳ, AM næreɪt-/ **(narrators)** *Jules, the story's narrator, is an actress in her late thirties.* [2] The person who **narrates** a film or programme speaks the words which accompany the pictures, but does not appear in it. ❑ *She also narrated a documentary about the Kirov Ballet School.* ♦ **nar|ra|tion** *As the crew gets back from lunch, we can put your narration on it right away.* ♦ **nar|ra|tor** **(narrators)** *...the narrator of the documentary.* VERB; V n; N-UNCOUNT; N-COUNT; VERB; V n; Also V; N-UNCOUNT; N-COUNT

**nar|ra|tive** /nærətɪv/ **(narratives)** [1] A **narrative** is a story or an account of a series of events. ❑ *...a fast-moving narrative... Sloan began his narrative with the day of the murder.* [2] **Narrative** is the description of a series of events, usually in a novel. ❑ *Neither author was very strong on narrative. ...Nye's simple narrative style.* N-COUNT; N-UNCOUNT

**nar|row** /næroʊ/ **(narrower, narrowest, narrows, narrowing, narrowed)** ◆◆◇ [1] Something that is **narrow** measures a very small distance from one side to the other, especially compared to its length or height. ❑ *...through the town's narrow streets... She had long, narrow feet. ...the narrow strip of land joining the peninsula to the rest of the island.* ♦ **nar|row|ness** *...the narrowness of the river mouth.* [2] If something **narrows**, it becomes less wide. ❑ *The wide track narrows before crossing another stream.* [3] If your eyes **narrow** or if you **narrow** your eyes, you almost close them, for example because you are angry or because you are trying to concentrate on something. [WRITTEN] ❑ *Coggins' eyes narrowed angrily. 'You think I'd tell you?'... He paused and narrowed his eyes in concentration.* [4] If you describe someone's ideas, attitudes, or beliefs as **narrow**, you disapprove of them because they are restricted in some way, and often ignore the more important aspects of an argument or situation. ❑ *...a narrow and outdated view of family life.* ♦ **nar|row|ly** *They're making judgments based on a narrowly focused vision of the world.* ♦ **nar|row|ness** *...the narrowness of their mental and spiritual outlook.* [5] If something **narrows** or if you **narrow** it, its extent or range becomes smaller. ❑ *Most recent opinion polls suggest that the gap between the two main parties has narrowed... Senate negotiators further narrowed their differences over the level of federal spending for anti-drug programs.* ♦ **nar|row|ing** *...a narrowing of the gap between rich members and poor.* [6] If you have a **narrow** victory, you succeed in winning but only by a small amount. ❑ *Delegates have voted by a narrow majority in favour of considering electoral reform.* ♦ **nar|row|ly** *She narrowly failed to win enough votes.* ♦ **nar|row|ness** *The narrowness of the government's victory reflected deep division within the Party.* [7] If you have a **narrow** escape, something unpleasant nearly happens to you. ❑ *Two police officers had a narrow escape when separatists attacked their vehicles.* ♦ **nar|row|ly** *Five firemen narrowly escaped death when a staircase collapsed beneath their* ADJ ≠ wide; N-UNCOUNT: usu N *of* n; VERB; V; VERB ≠ widen; V; V n; ADJ disapproval = limited ≠ broad; ADV: ADV after v, ADV -ed/adj; N-UNCOUNT: usu N *of* n; VERB ≠ widen; V; V n; N-SING; ADJ: usu ADJ n; ADV; N-UNCOUNT: usu N *of* n; ADJ: ADJ n; ADV: ADV with v

feet. [8] **on the straight and narrow** → see **straight**.

♦ **narrow down** If you **narrow down** a range of things, you reduce the number of things included in it. ❑ *What's happened is that the new results narrow down the possibilities... I've managed to narrow the list down to twenty-three.* — PHRASAL VERB; V P n (not pron); V n P *to* n; Also V n P

**nar|row boat** **(narrow boats)** also **narrowboat.** A **narrow boat** is a long, low boat used on canals. [BRIT] — N-COUNT; = barge

**nar|row|ly** /nærouli/ If you look at someone **narrowly**, you look at them in a concentrated way, often because you think they are not giving you full information about something. ❑ *He grimaced and looked narrowly at his colleague.* → See also **narrow**. — ADV: ADV after v; = closely

**narrow-minded** If you describe someone as **narrow-minded**, you are criticizing them because they are unwilling to consider new ideas or other people's opinions. ❑ *...a narrow-minded bigot.* — ADJ; disapproval; ≠ broad-minded

♦ **narrow-mindedness** *It is unbelievable that as a result of this narrow-mindedness a group of people should suffer.* — N-UNCOUNT

**NASA** /næsə/ **NASA** is the American government organization concerned with spacecraft and space travel. **NASA** is an abbreviation for 'National Aeronautics and Space Administration'. — N-PROPER

**na|sal** /neɪzᵊl/ [1] **Nasal** is used to describe things relating to the nose and the functions it performs. ❑ *...inflamed nasal passages. ...nasal decongestant sprays.* — ADJ: ADJ n [2] If someone's voice is **nasal**, it sounds as if air is passing through their nose as well as their mouth while they are speaking. ❑ *She talked in a deep nasal monotone.* — ADJ

**nas|cent** /næsᵊnt/ **Nascent** things or processes are just beginning, and are expected to become stronger or to grow bigger. [FORMAL] ❑ *...Kenya's nascent democracy. ...the still nascent science of psychology.* — ADJ: ADJ n; = budding

**na|stur|tium** /næstɜːʳʃəm/ **(nasturtiums)** **Nasturtiums** are low plants with large round leaves and orange, red, and yellow flowers. — N-COUNT

**nas|ty** /nɑːsti, næsti/ **(nastier, nastiest)** [1] Something that is **nasty** is very unpleasant to see, experience, or feel. ❑ *...an extremely nasty murder... This divorce could turn nasty.* — ADJ; = horrible ♦ **nas|ti|ness** *...the nastiness of war.* — N-UNCOUNT [2] If you describe a person or their behaviour as **nasty**, you mean that they behave in an unkind and unpleasant way. ❑ *What nasty little snobs you all are... The guards looked really nasty... Mummy is so nasty to me when Daddy isn't here.* — ADJ; = horrid; ≠ nice ♦ **nas|ti|ly** *She took the money and eyed me nastily... Nikki laughed nastily.* — ADV: ADV after v ♦ **nas|ti|ness** *As the years went by his nastiness began to annoy his readers.* — N-UNCOUNT [3] If you describe something as **nasty**, you mean it is unattractive, undesirable, or in bad taste. ❑ *...Emily's nasty little house in Balham... That damned Farrel made some nasty jokes here about Mr. Lane.* — ADJ; = horrid; ≠ nice [4] A **nasty** problem or situation is very worrying and difficult to deal with. ❑ *A spokesman said this firm action had defused a very nasty situation.* — ADJ: usu ADJ n [5] If you describe an injury or a disease as **nasty**, you mean that it is serious or looks unpleasant. ❑ *Lili had a nasty chest infection.* — ADJ [6] → See also **video nasty**.

**natch** /nætʃ/ **Natch** is used to indicate that a particular fact or event is what you would expect and not at all surprising. [mainly JOURNALISM, INFORMAL] ❑ *Ina is a bad girl so, natch, ends up in prison.* — ADV: ADV with cl/group; = naturally

**na|tion** /neɪʃᵊn/ **(nations)** ◆◆◆ [1] A **nation** is an individual country considered together with its social and political structures. ❑ *Such policies would require unprecedented cooperation between nations... The Arab nations agreed to meet in Baghdad.* — N-COUNT [2] **The nation** is sometimes used to refer to all the people who live in a particular country. [JOURNALISM] ❑ *It was a story that touched the nation's heart.* — N-SING

**na|tion|al** /næʃənᵊl/ **(nationals)** ◆◆◆ [1] **National** means relating to the whole of a country or nation rather than to part of it or to other nations. ❑ *Ruling parties have lost ground in national and local elections. ...major national and international issues.* — ADJ: usu ADJ n ♦ **na|tion|al|ly** *...a nationally televised speech... Duncan Campbell is nationally known for his investigative work.* — ADV: ADV with v, ADV adj [2] **National** means typical of the people or customs of a particular country or nation. ❑ *...the national characteristics and history of the country... Baseball is the national pastime.* — ADJ: ADJ n [3] You can refer to someone who is legally a citizen of a country as a **national** of that country. ❑ *...a Sri-Lankan-born British national.* — N-COUNT: usu adj N; = citizen

**na|tion|al an|them** **(national anthems)** A **national anthem** is a nation's official song which is played or sung on public occasions. — N-COUNT: usu sing

**Na|tion|al Cur|ricu|lum** The **National Curriculum** is the course of study that most school pupils in England and Wales are meant to follow between the ages of 5 and 16. — N-PROPER: *the* N

**na|tion|al gov|ern|ment** **(national governments)** A **national government** is a government with members from more than one political party, especially one that is formed during a crisis. [mainly BRIT] — N-COUNT: usu sing

**Na|tion|al Guard** **(National Guards)** In the United States, **the National Guard** is a military force within an individual state, which can become part of the national army if there is a war or emergency. ❑ *...the leader of the Arkansas National Guard.* — N-COUNT: usu *the* N

**Na|tion|al Guards|man** **(National Guardsmen)** A **National Guardsman** is a member of the National Guard in the United States. — N-COUNT

**Na|tion|al Health Ser|vice** In Britain, **the National Health Service** is the state system for providing medical care. It is paid for by taxes. ❑ *An increasing number of these treatments are now available on the National Health Service.* — N-PROPER: *the* N; = NHS

**na|tion|al in|sur|ance** In Britain, **national insurance** is the state system of paying money to people who are ill, unemployed, or retired. It is financed by money that the government collects from people who work, or from their employers. [BUSINESS] — N-UNCOUNT

**na|tion|al|ise** /næʃənəlaɪz/ → see **nationalize**.

**na|tion|al|ism** /næʃənəlɪzəm/ [1] **Nationalism** is the desire for political independence of people who feel they are historically or culturally a separate group within a country. ❑ *...the rising tide of Slovak nationalism.* — N-UNCOUNT: oft supp N [2] You can refer to a person's great love for their nation as **nationalism**. It is often associated with the belief that a particular nation is better than any other nation, and in this case is often used showing disapproval. ❑ *This kind of fierce nationalism is a powerful and potentially volatile force.* — N-UNCOUNT: oft supp N

**na|tion|al|ist** /næʃənəlɪst/ **(nationalists)** ◆◇◇ [1] **Nationalist** means connected with the desire of a group of people within a country for political independence. ❑ *The crisis has set off a wave of nationalist feelings in Quebec.* — ADJ: ADJ n ♦ A **nationalist** is someone with nationalist views. ❑ *...demands by Slovak nationalists for an independent state.* — N-COUNT [2] **Nationalist** means connected with a person's great love for their nation. It is often associated with the belief that their nation is better than any other nation, and in this case is often used showing disapproval. ❑ *Political life has been infected by growing nationalist sentiment.* — ADJ: ADJ n ♦ A **nationalist** is someone with nationalist views. ❑ *Some nationalists would like to depict the British monarchy as a purely English institution.* — N-COUNT

**na|tion|al|is|tic** /næʃənəlɪstɪk/ If you describe someone as **nationalistic**, you mean they are very proud of their nation. They also often believe that their nation is better than any other nation, and in this case it is often used showing disapproval. ❑ *...the nationalistic pride of the Catalan people.* — ADJ

**na|tion|al|ity** /næʃənælɪti/ **(nationalities)** N-VAR
1 If you have the **nationality** of a particular country, you were born there or have the legal right to be a citizen. ❑ *The crew are of different nationalities and have no common language.* N-COUNT 2 You can refer to people who have the same racial origins as a **nationality**, especially when they do not have their own independent country. ❑ *...the many nationalities that comprise Ethiopia.*

**na|tion|al|ize** /næʃənəlaɪz/ **(nationalizes, nationalizing, nationalized)**

in BRIT, also use **nationalise**

VERB ≠ privatize
If a government **nationalizes** a private company or industry, that company or industry becomes owned by the state and controlled by the government. [BUSINESS] ❑ V n *In 1987, Garcia introduced legislation to nationalize Peru's banking and financial systems.* ♦ **na|tion|ali|za|tion** /næʃənəlaɪzeɪʃən/ **(nationalizations)** N-UNCOUNT: also N in pl ≠ privatization *...the campaign for the nationalization of the coal mines... The steel workers were relatively indifferent to the issue of nationalization.*

**na|tion|al park** **(national parks)** N-COUNT; N-IN-NAMES: oft in names after n
A **national park** is a large area of land which is protected by the government because of its natural beauty, plants, or animals, and which the public can usually visit. ❑ *...the Masai Mara game reserve and Amboseli national park.*

**na|tion|al ser|vice** N-UNCOUNT = military service
**National service** is service in the armed forces, which young people in certain countries have to do by law. [mainly BRIT] ❑ *Banks spent his national service in the Royal Navy.*

in AM, use **selective service**

**nation-building** N-UNCOUNT: oft N n
Journalists sometimes use **nation-building** to refer to government policies that are designed to create a strong sense of national identity. [JOURNALISM] ❑ *...calling for reconciliation and nation building after the bitter election campaign... This revolutionary expansion required energetic nation-building policies.*

**na|tion|hood** /neɪʃənhʊd/ N-UNCOUNT
A country's **nationhood** is its status as a nation. ❑ *To them, the monarchy is the special symbol of nationhood.*

**nation-state** **(nation-states)** also **nation state.** N-COUNT
A **nation-state** is an independent state which consists of people from one particular national group. ❑ *Albania is a small nation state of around 3 million people.*

**nation|wide** /neɪʃənwaɪd/ ADJ: usu ADJ n = national
**Nationwide** activities or situations happen or exist in all parts of a country. ❑ *The rising number of car crimes is a nationwide problem. ...the strike by teachers which is nationwide.* ♦ **Nationwide** is also an adverb. ADV = nationally ❑ *The figures show unemployment falling nationwide last month.*

**na|tive** /neɪtɪv/ **(natives)** ◆◇◇ ADJ: ADJ n
1 Your **native** country or area is the country or area where you were born and brought up. ❑ *It was his first visit to his native country since 1948... Mother Teresa visited her native Albania.* N-COUNT: N of n 2 A **native of** a particular country or region is someone who was born in that country or region. ❑ *Dr Aubin is a native of St Blaise.* ♦ **Native** is also an adjective. ADJ: ADJ n, v-link ADJ to n ❑ *Joshua Halpern is a native Northern Californian. ...men and women native to countries such as Japan.* N-COUNT 3 Some European people use **native** to refer to a person living in a non-Western country who belongs to the race or tribe that the majority of people there belong to. This use could cause offence. ❑ *They used force to banish the natives from the more fertile land.* ♦ **Native** is also an adjective. ADJ: ADJ n = indigenous ❑ *Native people were allowed to retain some sense of their traditional culture and religion.* ADJ: ADJ n 4 Your **native** language or tongue is the first language that you learned to speak when you were a child. ❑ *She spoke not only her native language, Swedish, but also English and French... French is not my native tongue.* ADJ: ADJ n, v-link ADJ to n = indigenous 5 Plants or animals that are **native to** a particular region live or grow there naturally and were not brought there. ❑ *...a project to create a 50 acre forest of native Caledonian pines... Many of the plants are native to Brazil.* ♦ **Native** is also a noun. N-COUNT: N of n ❑ *The coconut palm is a native of Malaysia.* ADJ: ADJ n = innate 6 A **native** ability or quality is one that you possess naturally without having to learn it. ❑ *We have our native inborn talent, yet we hardly use it.*

**Na|tive Ameri|can** **(Native Americans)** N-COUNT = American Indian
**Native Americans** are people from any of the many groups who were already living in North America before Europeans arrived. ❑ *The eagle is the animal most sacred to the Native Americans.* ♦ **Native American** is also an adjective. ADJ: ADJ n ❑ *...a gathering of Native American elders.*

**na|tive speak|er** **(native speakers)** N-COUNT
A **native speaker** of a language is someone who speaks that language as their first language rather than having learned it as a foreign language. ❑ *Our programme ensures daily opportunities to practice your study language with native speakers.*

**Na|tiv|ity** /nətɪvɪti/ N-SING: the N
**The Nativity** is the birth of Jesus, which is celebrated by Christians at Christmas. ❑ *They admired the tableau of the Nativity. ...the Nativity story.*

**na|tiv|ity play** **(nativity plays)** N-COUNT
A **nativity play** is a play about the birth of Jesus, usually one performed by children at Christmas time.

**NATO** /neɪtoʊ/ ◆◇◇ N-PROPER
**NATO** is an international organization which consists of the USA, Canada, Britain, and other European countries, all of whom have agreed to support one another if they are attacked. **NATO** is an abbreviation for 'North Atlantic Treaty Organization'. ❑ *NATO says it will keep a reduced number of modern nuclear weapons to guarantee peace.*

**nat|ter** /nætəʳ/ **(natters, nattering, nattered)** V-RECIP = chat
When people **natter**, they talk casually for a long time about unimportant things. [mainly BRIT, INFORMAL] ❑ pl-n V *If something dramatic has happened during the day, we'll sit and natter about it...* pl-n V away/on *Susan and the girl were still nattering away in German...* V with n *Ahead of you is a day of nattering with fellow farmers at the local market...* NON-RECIP: V V to n *You natter all day long at the hospital... His mother would natter to anyone.* ♦ **Natter** is also a noun. N-SING: a N = chinwag, chat ❑ *What's the topic of conversation when a group of new mums get together for a natter?*

**nat|ty** /næti/ **(nattier, nattiest)** ADJ: usu ADJ n [approval]
1 If you describe clothes, especially men's clothes, as **natty**, you mean that they are smart and neat. [INFORMAL] ❑ *...a natty pin stripe suit... Cliff was a natty dresser.* ADJ: usu ADJ n [approval] = nifty 2 If you describe something as **natty**, you think it is smart and cleverly designed. [INFORMAL] ❑ *...natty little houses.*

**natu|ral** /nætʃərəl/ **(naturals)** ◆◆◇ ADJ: oft it v-link ADJ to-inf/that = normal ≠ unnatural, unusual
1 If you say that it is **natural** for someone to act in a particular way or for something to happen in that way, you mean that it is reasonable in the circumstances. ❑ *It is only natural for youngsters to crave the excitement of driving a fast car... A period of depression can be a perfectly natural response to certain aspects of life.* ADJ 2 **Natural** behaviour is shared by all people or all animals of a particular type and has not been learned. ❑ *...the insect's natural instinct to feed... Anger is the natural reaction we experience when we feel threatened or frustrated.* ADJ: usu ADJ n = instinctive 3 Someone with a **natural** ability or skill was born with that ability and did not have to learn it. ❑ *She has a natural ability to understand the motives of others... He had a natural flair for business.* N-COUNT: usu a N in sing 4 If you say that someone is **a natural**, you mean that they do something very well and very easily. ❑ *He's a natural with any kind of engine... She proved to be a natural on camera.* ADJ ≠ forced 5 If someone's behaviour is **natural**, they appear to be relaxed and are not trying to hide anything. ❑ *Bethan's sister was as friendly and natural as the rest of the family.* ♦ **natu|ral|ly** ADV: ADV after v *For pictures of people behaving naturally, not posing for the camera, it is essential to shoot unnoticed... She is magnificent at making you feel you can talk quite naturally to her.* ♦ **natu|ral|ness** N-UNCOUNT *The critics praised the reality of the scenery and the naturalness of the acting.* ADJ: ADJ n 6 **Natural** things exist or oc-

cur in nature and are not made or caused by people. ❑ *It has called the typhoon the worst natural disaster in South Korea in many years... The gigantic natural harbour of Poole is a haven for boats.* ≠ *artificial, man-made*
♦ **natu|ral|ly** *Nitrates are chemicals that occur naturally in water and the soil.* ADV: ADV with v, ADV adj [7] If someone dies **of** or **from natural causes**, they die because they are ill or old rather than because of an accident or violence. ❑ *According to the Home Office, your brother died of natural causes.* PHRASE: usu prep PHR

**natu|ral child|birth** If a woman gives birth by **natural childbirth**, she is not given any drugs to relieve her pain or to send her to sleep. N-UNCOUNT

**natu|ral gas** **Natural gas** is gas which is found underground or under the sea. It is collected and stored, and piped into people's homes to be used for cooking and heating. N-UNCOUNT

**natu|ral his|to|ry** **Natural history** is the study of animals and plants and other living things. ❑ *Schools regularly bring children to the beach for natural history lessons.* N-UNCOUNT: usu N n

**natu|ral|ise** /nætʃərəlaɪz/ → see **naturalize**.

**natu|ral|ism** /nætʃərəlɪzəm/ **Naturalism** is a theory in art and literature which states that people and things should be shown in a realistic way. N-UNCOUNT

**natu|ral|ist** /nætʃərəlɪst/ **(naturalists)** A **naturalist** is a person who studies plants, animals, insects, and other living things. N-COUNT

**natu|ral|is|tic** /nætʃərəlɪstɪk/ [1] **Naturalistic** art or writing tries to show people and things in a realistic way. ❑ *These drawings are among his most naturalistic.* ADJ [2] **Naturalistic** means resembling something that exists or occurs in nature. ❑ *Further research is needed under rather more naturalistic conditions.* ADJ

**natu|ral|ize** /nætʃərəlaɪz/ **(naturalizes, naturalizing, naturalized)**

✔ in BRIT, also use **naturalise**

[1] To **naturalize** a species of plant means to start it growing in an area where it is not usually found. If a plant **naturalizes** in an area where it was not found before, it starts to grow there naturally. ❑ *A friend sent me a root from Mexico, and I hope to naturalize it... The plant naturalises well in grass.* VERB; V n; V [2] If the government of a country **naturalizes** someone, they allow a person who was not born in that country to become a citizen of it. ❑ *No one expects the Baltic states to naturalise young Russian soldiers, but army pensioners can be given citizenship.* → See also **naturalized**. VERB; V n
♦ **natu|rali|za|tion** /nætʃərəlaɪzeɪʃən/ *They swore their allegiance to the USA and received their naturalization papers.* N-UNCOUNT

**natu|ral|ized** /nætʃərəlaɪzd/

✔ in BRIT, also use **naturalised**

A **naturalized** citizen of a particular country is someone who has legally become a citizen of that country, although they were not born there. ADJ: ADJ n

**natu|ral|ly** /nætʃərəli/ ♦◇◇ [1] You use **naturally** to indicate that you think something is very obvious and not at all surprising in the circumstances. ❑ *When things go wrong, all of us naturally feel disappointed and frustrated... Naturally these comings and goings excited some curiosity... He had been stunned and, naturally, deeply upset.* ADV: ADV before v, ADV with cl, ADV adj [2] If one thing develops **naturally** from another, it develops as a normal consequence or result of it. ❑ *A study of yoga leads naturally to meditation.* ADV: ADV after v = *logically* [3] You can use **naturally** to talk about a characteristic of someone's personality when it is the way that they normally act. ❑ *He has a lively sense of humour and appears naturally confident.* ADV: ADV adj [4] If someone is **naturally** good at something, they learn it easily and quickly and do it very well. ❑ *Some individuals are naturally good communicators.* ADV: ADV adj [5] If something **comes naturally to** you, you find it easy to do and quickly become good at it. ❑ *With football, it was just something that came naturally to me.* PHRASE: V inflects, usu PHR *to* n

**natu|ral re|sources** **Natural resources** are all the land, forests, energy sources and minerals existing naturally in a place that can be used by people. ❑ *Angola was a country rich in natural resources.* N-PLURAL

**natu|ral se|lec|tion** **Natural selection** is a process by which species of animals and plants that are best adapted to their environment survive and reproduce, while those that are less well adapted die out. ❑ *Natural selection ensures only the fittest survive to pass their genes on to the next generation.* N-UNCOUNT

**natu|ral wast|age** **Natural wastage** is the process of employees leaving their jobs because they want to retire or move to other jobs, rather than because their employer makes them leave. [mainly BRIT, BUSINESS] ❑ *The company hopes the job cuts will be made through natural wastage and voluntary redundancy.* N-UNCOUNT

✔ in AM, usually use **attrition**

**na|ture** /neɪtʃəʳ/ **(natures)** [1] **Nature** is all the animals, plants, and other things in the world that are not made by people, and all the events and processes that are not caused by people. ❑ *...grasses that grow wild in nature. ...the ecological balance of nature.* → See also **Mother Nature**. ♦♦◇ N-UNCOUNT
[2] The **nature** of something is its basic quality or character. ❑ *Mr Sharp would not comment on the nature of the issues being investigated. ...the ambitious nature of the programme... The rise of a major power is both economic and military in nature.* N-SING: with supp, oft n N, also *by/in* N
[3] Someone's **nature** is their character, which they show by the way they behave. ❑ *Jeya feels that her ambitious nature made her unsuitable for an arranged marriage... She trusted people. That was her nature... He was by nature affectionate.* → See also **human nature**. N-SING: with poss, also *by* N
PHRASES [4] If you want to get **back to nature**, you want to return to a simpler way of living. ❑ *She was very anxious to get away from cities and back to nature.* PHRASE: PHR after v [5] If you say that something has a particular characteristic **by** its **nature** or **by** its **very nature**, you mean that things of that type always have that characteristic. ❑ *Peacekeeping, by its nature, makes pre-planning difficult... One could argue that smoking, by its very nature, is addictive.* PHRASE: N inflects, PHR with cl
[6] Some people talk about **a call of nature** when referring politely to the need to go to the toilet. ❑ *I'm afraid I have to answer a call of nature.* PHRASE: PHR after v, politeness
[7] If you say that something is **in the nature of things**, you mean that you would expect it to happen in the circumstances mentioned. ❑ *Many have already died, and in the nature of things many more will die.* PHRASE: PHR with cl [8] If you say that one thing is **in the nature of** another, you mean that it is like the other thing. ❑ *It was in the nature of a debate rather than an argument.* PHRASE: PHR n, usu v-link PHR [9] If a way of behaving is **second nature to** you, you do it almost without thinking because it is easy for you or obvious to you. ❑ *Planning ahead had always come as second nature to her... It's not easy at first, but it soon becomes second nature.* PHRASE: v-link PHR, oft PHR *to* n

**na|ture study** **Nature study** is the study of animals and plants by looking at them directly, for example when it is taught to young children. N-UNCOUNT

**na|ture trail** **(nature trails)** A **nature trail** is a route through an area of countryside which has signs drawing attention to interesting animals, plants, or rocks. N-COUNT

**na|tur|ism** /neɪtʃərɪzəm/ **Naturism** is the same as **nudism**. [mainly BRIT] N-UNCOUNT ♦ **na|tur|ist** **(naturists)** ❑ *...a naturist beach.* N-COUNT: oft N n

**naught** /nɔːt/ → see **nought**.

**naugh|ty** /nɔːti/ **(naughtier, naughtiest)** [1] If you say that a child is **naughty**, you mean that they behave badly or do not do what they are told. ❑ *Girls, you're being very naughty... You naughty boy, you gave me such a fright.* ADJ = *bad* ≠ *good* [2] You can describe books, pictures, or words, as **naughty** when they are slightly rude or related to sex. ❑ *You know what* ADJ *little boys are like with naughty words. ...saucy TV shows, crammed full of naughty innuendo.*

**nau|sea** /nɔːziə/ **Nausea** is the condition of feeling sick and the feeling that you are going to vomit. ❑ *I was overcome with a feeling of nausea.* N-UNCOUNT

**nau|seam** /nɔːziæm/ → see **ad nauseam**.

**nau|seate** /nɔːzieɪt/ **(nauseates, nauseating, nauseated)** If something **nauseates** you, it makes you feel as if you are going to vomit. ❑ *The smell of frying nauseated her... She could not eat anything without feeling nauseated.* VERB V n V-ed

**nau|seat|ing** /nɔːzieɪtɪŋ/ If you describe someone's attitude or their behaviour as **nauseating**, you mean that you find it extremely unpleasant and feel disgusted by it. ❑ *The judge described the offences as nauseating and unspeakable... For them to attack the Liberals for racism is nauseating hypocrisy.* ADJ [disapproval] = *sickening*

**nau|seous** /nɔːziəs, AM -ʃəs/ If you feel **nauseous**, you feel as if you want to vomit. ❑ *If the patient is poorly nourished, the drugs make them feel nauseous... A nauseous wave of pain broke over her.* ADJ

**nau|ti|cal** /nɔːtɪkəl/ **Nautical** means relating to ships and sailing. ❑ *...a nautical chart of the region you sail.* ADJ: usu ADJ n

**nau|ti|cal mile** **(nautical miles)** A **nautical mile** is a unit of measurement used at sea. It is equal to 1852 metres. N-COUNT

**na|val** /neɪvəl/ **Naval** means belonging to, relating to, or involving a country's navy. ❑ *He was the senior serving naval officer. ...the US naval base at Guantanamo Bay.* ◆◇◇ ADJ: ADJ n

**nave** /neɪv/ **(naves)** The **nave** of a church is the long central part where people gather to worship. N-COUNT

**na|vel** /neɪvəl/ **(navels)** Your **navel** is the small hollow just below your waist at the front of your body. N-COUNT

**navel-gazing** If you refer to an activity as **navel-gazing**, you are critical of it because people are thinking about something for a long time but take no action on it. ❑ *She dismisses the reform process as an exercise in collective navel gazing.* N-UNCOUNT [disapproval]

**navi|gable** /nævɪgəbəl/ A **navigable** river is wide and deep enough for a boat to travel along safely. [FORMAL] ❑ *...the navigable portion of the Nile.* ADJ

**navi|gate** /nævɪgeɪt/ **(navigates, navigating, navigated)** [1] When someone **navigates** a ship or an aircraft somewhere, they decide which course to follow and steer it there. You can also say that a ship or an aircraft **navigates** somewhere. ❑ *Captain Cook safely navigated his ship without accident for 100 voyages... The purpose of the visit was to navigate into an ice-filled fiord. ...the new navigation system which will enable aircraft to navigate with total pinpoint accuracy.* ♦ **navi|ga|tion** /nævɪgeɪʃən/ **(navigations)** *The expedition was wrecked by bad planning and poor navigation. ...the boat's navigation system.* [2] When a ship or boat **navigates** an area of water, it sails on or across it. ❑ *...a lock system to allow sea-going craft to navigate the upper reaches of the river... Such boats can navigate on the Nile.* [3] When someone in a car **navigates**, they decide what roads the car should be driven along in order to get somewhere. ❑ *When travelling on fast roads at night it is impossible to drive and navigate at the same time. ...the relief at successfully navigating across the Golden Gate Bridge to arrive here... They had just navigated their way through Maidstone on their way to the coast.* [4] When fish, animals, or insects **navigate** somewhere, they find the right direction to go and travel there. ❑ *In tests, the bees navigate back home after being placed in a field a mile away.* [5] If you **navigate** an obstacle, you move carefully in order to avoid hitting the obstacle or hurting yourself. ❑ *He was not able to walk without a cane and could only navigate steps backwards... In the corridors he let her navigate her own way round the trolleys and other obstacles... If guests wished to use the sofa, they had first to navigate around chairs in the middle of the room.*

VERB; V n; V prep/adv; V; N-VAR; VERB = *sail*; V n; V prep; VERB; V; V prep/adv; V *way* prep; Also V n; VERB; V adv/prep; Also V; VERB = *negotiate*; V n; V *way* prep; V prep/adv

**navi|ga|tion** /nævɪgeɪʃən/ You can refer to the movement of ships as **navigation**. ❑ *Pack ice around Iceland was becoming a threat to navigation.* → See also **navigate**. N-UNCOUNT

**navi|ga|tion|al** /nævɪgeɪʃənəl/ **Navigational** means relating to the act of navigating a ship or an aircraft. ❑ *The crash was a direct result of inadequate navigational aids.* ADJ: usu ADJ n

**navi|ga|tor** /nævɪgeɪtəʳ/ **(navigators)** The **navigator** on an aircraft or ship is the person whose job is to work out the direction in which the aircraft or ship should be travelling. ❑ *He became an RAF navigator during the war.* N-COUNT

**nav|vy** /nævi/ **(navvies)** A **navvy** is a person who is employed to do hard physical work, for example building roads or canals. [BRIT, OLD-FASHIONED] N-COUNT

**navy** /neɪvi/ **(navies)** [1] A country's **navy** consists of the people it employs to fight at sea, and the ships they use. ❑ *Her own son was also in the Navy. ...a United States navy ship.* [2] Something that is **navy** or **navy-blue** is very dark blue. ❑ *I mostly wore black or navy trousers. ...a navy-blue blazer.* ◆◆◇ N-COUNT: usu *the* N; COLOUR

**nay** /neɪ/ [1] You use **nay** in front of a stronger word or phrase which you feel is more correct than the one you have just used and helps to emphasize the point you are making. [FORMAL] ❑ *Long essays, nay, whole books have been written on this.* [2] **Nay** is sometimes used to mean 'no' when talking about people voting against something or refusing to give consent for something. ❑ *The House of Commons can merely say yea or nay to the executive judgment.* [3] **Nay** is an old-fashioned, literary, or dialect word for 'no'. ADV: ADV with cl/group [emphasis] = *indeed*; CONVENTION; CONVENTION [formulae]

**Nazi** /nɑːtsi/ **(Nazis)** [1] **The Nazis** were members of the right-wing political party, led by Adolf Hitler, which held power in Germany from 1933 to 1945. [2] You use **Nazi** to say that something relates to the Nazis. ❑ *...the rise of the Nazi Party. ...the Nazi occupation of the Channel Islands.* ◆◇◇ N-COUNT; ADJ

**Na|zism** /nɑːtsɪzəm/ **Nazism** was the political ideas and activities of the German Nazi Party. N-UNCOUNT

**NB** /en biː/ You write **NB** to draw someone's attention to what you are about to say or write. ❑ *NB The opinions stated in this essay do not necessarily represent those of the Church of God Missionary Society.*

**NCO** /en siː oʊ/ **(NCOs)** An **NCO** is a soldier who has a fairly low rank such as sergeant or corporal. **NCO** is an abbreviation for 'non-commissioned officer'. ❑ *Food for the ordinary Soviet troops and NCOs was very poor.* N-COUNT

**-nd** **-nd** is added to written numbers ending in 2, except for numbers ending in 12, in order to form ordinal numbers. ❑ *...22nd February. ...2nd edition.* SUFFIX

**NE** **NE** is a written abbreviation for **north-east**. ❑ *...on the NE outskirts of Bath.*

**ne|an|der|thal** /niændəʳtɑːl, -θɔːl/ **(neanderthals)** [1] **Neanderthal** people lived in Europe between 35,000 and 70,000 years ago. ❑ *Neanderthal man was able to kill woolly mammoths and bears.* ♦ You can refer to people from the Neanderthal period as **Neanderthals**. [2] If you describe people's, especially men's, ideas or ways of behaving as **Neanderthal**, you disapprove of them because they are very old-fashioned and uncivilized. ❑ *Let us deal with the question of his notoriously Neanderthal attitude to women.* [3] If you call a man a **neanderthal**, you disapprove of him because you think he behaves in a very uncivilized way. ❑ *...drunken neanderthals.* ADJ: ADJ n; N-COUNT: usu pl; ADJ: usu ADJ n [disapproval]; N-COUNT [disapproval]

**near** /nɪəʳ/ **(nearer, nearest, nears, nearing, neared)** [1] If something is **near** a place, thing, or person, it is a short distance from them. ❑ *Don't come near me... Her children went back every year to stay in a farmhouse near the cottage... He drew his* ◆◆◆ PREP *chair nearer the fire... Some of the houses nearest the bridge were on fire.* ♦ **Near** is also an adverb. ❑ *He crouched as near to the door as he could... She took a step nearer to the barrier... As we drew near, I saw that the boot lid was up.* (ADV: ADV after v, *be* ADV, oft ADV *to* n) ♦ **Near** is also an adjective. ❑ *He collapsed into the nearest chair... Where's the nearest telephone?... The nearer of the two barges was perhaps a mile away.* (ADJ: ADJ n, *the* ADJ *of* n) ♦ **near|ness** *He was suddenly aware of his nearness.* (N-UNCOUNT: usu with poss) [2] If someone or something is **near to** a particular state, they have almost reached it. ❑ *After the war, The House of Hardie came near to bankruptcy... The repairs to the Hafner machine were near to completion... Apart from anything else, he comes near to contradicting himself.* (PREP-PHRASE: PREP n/-ing = close) ♦ **Near** means the same as **near to.** ❑ *He was near tears... We are no nearer agreement now than in the past.* (PREP)

[3] If something is similar to something else, you can say that it is **near to** it. ❑ *...a sickening sensation that was near to nausea.* (PREP-PHRASE) ♦ **Near** means the same as **near to.** ❑ *Often her feelings were nearer hatred than love.* (PREP) [4] You describe the thing most similar to something as **the nearest** thing **to** it when there is no example of the thing itself. ❑ *It would appear that the legal profession is the nearest thing to a recession-proof industry.* (ADJ: *the* ADJ n *to* n, *the* ADJ *to* n) [5] If a time or event draws **near**, it will happen soon. [WRITTEN] ❑ *The time for my departure from Japan was drawing nearer every day.* (ADV: ADV after v, *be* ADV) [6] If something happens **near** a particular time, it happens just before or just after that time. ❑ *Performance is lowest between 3 a.m. and 5 a.m, and reaches a peak near midday... I'll tell you nearer the day.* (PREP) [7] You use **near** to say that something is a little more or less than an amount or number stated. ❑ *...to increase manufacturing from about 2.5 million cars a year to nearer 4.75 million.* (PREP) [8] You can say that someone will **not go near** a person or thing when you are emphasizing that they refuse to see them or go there. ❑ *He will absolutely not go near a hospital... I'm so annoyed with her that I haven't been near her for a week.* (PREP: with brd-neg [emphasis])

[9] **The near** one of two things is the one that is closer. ❑ *...a mighty beech tree on the near side of the little clearing... Jane put one foot in the near stirrup and turned to look at the stranger.* (ADJ: det ADJ n ≠far) [10] You use **near** to indicate that something is almost the thing mentioned. ❑ *She was believed to have died in near poverty on the French Riviera. ...the 48-year-old who was brought in to rescue the bank from near collapse.* (ADJ: ADJ n) ♦ **Near** is also an adverb. ❑ *...his near fatal accident two years ago.* (ADV: ADV adj) [11] In a contest, your **nearest** rival or challenger is the person or team that is most likely to defeat you. ❑ *That victory put the Ukrainians beyond the reach of their nearest challengers, Dynamo Moscow.* (ADJ: ADJ n) [12] When you **near** a place, you get quite near to it. [LITERARY] ❑ *As he neared the stable, he slowed the horse and patted it on the neck.* (VERB: no passive V n) [13] When someone or something **nears** a particular stage or point, they will soon reach that stage or point. ❑ *His age was hard to guess – he must have been nearing fifty... The project is taking a long time but is now nearing completion.* (VERB: no passive = approach V n V n) [14] You say that an important time or event **nears** when it is going to occur quite soon. [LITERARY] ❑ *As half time neared, Hardyman almost scored twice.* (VERB = approach V)

PHRASES [15] People sometimes refer to their close relatives and friends as their **nearest and dearest.** ❑ *...that English convention of not showing your feelings, even to your nearest and dearest.* (PHRASE = kith and kin) [16] You use **near and far** to indicate that you are referring to a very large area or distance. ❑ *People would gather from near and far.* (PHRASE) [17] If you say that something will happen **in the near future**, you mean that it will happen quite soon. ❑ *The controversy regarding vitamin C is unlikely to be resolved in the near future.* (PHRASE) [18] You use **nowhere near** and **not anywhere near** to emphasize that something is not the case. ❑ *They are nowhere near good enough... It was nowhere near as painful as David had expected.* (PHRASE: usu PHR adj, PHR n [emphasis])

**near|by** /nɪəʳbaɪ/ also **near by, near-by.** ♦◇◇ If something is **nearby,** it is only a short distance away. ❑ *He might easily have been seen by someone who lived nearby... There is less expensive accommodation nearby... There were one or two suspicious looks from nearby.* (ADV: ADV after v, n ADV, *from* ADV) ♦ **Nearby** is also an adjective. ❑ *At a nearby table a man was complaining in a loud voice. ...the nearby village of Crowthorne.* (ADJ: ADJ n ≠distant)

**near-death ex|peri|ence (near-death experiences)** A **near-death experience** is a strange experience that some people who have nearly died say they had when they were unconscious. (N-COUNT)

**Near East** The **Near East** is the same as **the Middle East.** (N-PROPER: *the* N)

**near|ly** /nɪəʳli/ ♦♦◇ [1] **Nearly** is used to indicate that something is not quite the case, or not completely the case. ❑ *Goldsworth stared at me in silence for nearly twenty seconds... Hunter knew nearly all of this already... Several times Thorne nearly fell... I nearly had a heart attack when she told me... The beach was nearly empty... They nearly always ate outside.* (ADV: ADV group, ADV before v = almost, practically) [2] **Nearly** is used to indicate that something will soon be the case. ❑ *It was already nearly eight o'clock... I was nearly asleep... The voyage is nearly over... You're nearly there... I've nearly finished the words for your song.* (ADV: ADV group, ADV before v = almost) [3] You use **not nearly** to emphasize that something is not the case. ❑ *Father's flat in Paris wasn't nearly as grand as this... Minerals in general are not nearly so well absorbed as other nutrients... British car workers did not earn nearly enough money to buy the products they were turning out.* (PHRASE: PHR adj/adv, PHR n [emphasis] = nowhere near)

**near|ly new** **Nearly new** items are items for sale that have belonged to another person but have not been used much and are still in very good condition. A **nearly new** shop sells nearly new items. (ADJ: usu ADJ n)

**near miss (near misses)** also **near-miss.** [1] You can say that there is a **near miss** when something is nearly hit by another thing, for example by a vehicle or a bomb. ❑ *Details have been given of a near miss between two airliners over southern England earlier this week... We've had a few near misses in the raids, as I expect you've noticed.* (N-COUNT = narrow escape) [2] A **near miss** is an attempt to do something which fails by a very small amount. ❑ *...Milan's successful defence of the European Cup and near-miss in the Italian championship last season.* (N-COUNT)

**near|side** /nɪəʳsaɪd/ [1] The **nearside** wheels, lights, or doors of a vehicle are those nearest the edge of the road when the vehicle is being driven on the correct side of the road. In Britain, the nearside is on the left. [BRIT] ❑ *The nearside front tyre had been slashed.* (ADJ: ADJ n ≠offside) [2] **The nearside** of a vehicle is the side that is nearest the edge of the road when the vehicle is being driven on the correct side of the road. [BRIT] ❑ *It hit the kerb on the nearside and seemed to ricochet across the road on two wheels.* (N-SING: *the* N ≠offside)

**near-sighted** also **nearsighted.** Someone who is **near-sighted** cannot see distant things clearly. [AM; also BRIT, OLD-FASHIONED] ❑ *The girl squinted at the photograph. She seemed to be nearsighted.* (ADJ = short-sighted ≠long-sighted)

**neat** /niːt/ **(neater, neatest)** ♦◇◇ [1] A **neat** place, thing, or person is tidy and smart, and has everything in the correct place. ❑ *She undressed and put her wet clothes in a neat pile in the corner. ...a girl in a neat grey flannel suit... Everything was neat and tidy and gleamingly clean.* (ADJ: usu ADJ n) ♦ **neat|ly** *He folded his paper neatly and sipped his coffee... At the door was a neatly dressed, dignified man.* (ADV: ADV with v = tidily) ♦ **neat|ness** *The grounds were a perfect balance between neatness and natural wildness.* (N-UNCOUNT = tidiness) [2] Someone who is **neat** keeps their home or possessions tidy, with everything in the correct place. ❑ *'That's not like Alf,' he said, 'leaving papers muddled like that. He's always so neat.'* (ADJ = tidy ≠untidy) ♦ **neat|ly** *He had maybe a thousand tapes, all neatly labelled and catalogued.* (ADV: ADV with v) ♦ **neat|ness** *...a paragon of neatness, efficiency and reliability.* (N-UNCOUNT) [3] A **neat** object, part of the body, or shape is quite small and has a smooth outline. ❑ *...a faded woman with neat features. ...neat handwriting.* (ADJ: usu ADJ n) ♦ **neat|ly** *She was a small woman, slender and neatly made.* (ADV: ADV -ed) [4] A **neat** (ADJ:)

movement or action is done accurately and skilfully, with no unnecessary movements. ❑ *A neat move between Black and Keane left Nigel Clough in the clear, but his shot skimmed wide of the far post.* ♦ **neat|ly** *He watched her peel and dissect a pear neatly, no mess, no sticky fingers.* [5] A **neat** way of organizing, achieving, explaining, or expressing something is clever and convenient. ❑ *It had been such a neat, clever plan... Neat solutions are not easily found to these issues.* ♦ **neat|ly** *Real people do not fit neatly into these categories.* ♦ **neat|ness** *He knew full well he had been outflanked, and he appreciated the neatness of it.* [6] If you say that something is **neat**, you mean that it is very good. [AM, INFORMAL] ❑ *'Oh, those new apartments are really neat,' the girl babbled on... It'll be neat to have a father and son playing on the same team.* [7] When someone drinks strong alcohol **neat**, they do not add a weaker liquid such as water to it. [mainly BRIT] ❑ *He poured himself a brandy and swallowed it neat... He took a mouthful of neat whisky, and coughed.*

usu ADJ n ≠ clumsy · ADV: ADV with v · ADJ = nice · ADV: ADV with v · N-UNCOUNT · ADJ approval = great, cool · ADJ: v n ADJ, ADJ n

✓ in AM, use **straight**

**nebu|la** /nebjələ/ **(nebulae)** A **nebula** is a cloud of dust and gas in space. New stars are produced from nebulae.
N-COUNT: oft in names

**nebu|lous** /nebjələs/ If you describe something as **nebulous**, you mean that it is vague and not clearly defined or not easy to describe. ❑ *The notions we children were able to form of the great world beyond were exceedingly nebulous... Music is such a nebulous thing.*
ADJ = vague

**nec|es|sari|ly** /nesɪserɪli, -srɪli/ [1] If you say that something is **not necessarily** the case, you mean that it may not be the case or is not always the case. ❑ *Anger is not necessarily the most useful or acceptable reaction to such events... A higher fee does not necessarily mean a better course.* ● If you reply '**Not necessarily**', you mean that what has just been said or suggested may not be true. ❑ *'He was lying, of course.' — 'Not necessarily.'* [2] If you say that something **necessarily** happens or is the case, you mean that it has to happen or be the case and cannot be any different. ❑ *The most desirable properties necessarily command astonishingly high prices... Tourism is an industry that has a necessarily close connection with governments.*
◆◇◇ ADV: with neg, ADV group, ADV before v vagueness · CONVENTION · ADV: ADV before v, ADV group = inevitably

**nec|es|sary** /nesɪsəri/ [1] Something that is **necessary** is needed in order for something else to happen. ❑ *I kept the engine running because it might be necessary to leave fast... We will do whatever is necessary to stop them... Is that really necessary?... Make the necessary arrangements.* [2] A **necessary** consequence or connection must happen or exist, because of the nature of the things or events involved. ❑ *Wastage was no doubt a necessary consequence of war... Scientific work is differentiated from art by its necessary connection with the idea of progress.* [3] If you say that something will happen **if necessary**, **when necessary**, or **where necessary**, you mean that it will happen if it is necessary, when it is necessary, or where it is necessary. ❑ *If necessary, the airship can stay up there for days to keep out of danger... The army needs men who are willing to fight, when necessary... All the rigging had been examined, and renewed where necessary.*
◆◆◇ ADJ: oft it v-link ADJ to-inf ≠ unnecessary · ADJ: ADJ n · PHRASE: PHR with cl

**ne|ces|si|tate** /nɪsesɪteɪt/ **(necessitates, necessitating, necessitated)** If something **necessitates** an event, action, or situation, it makes it necessary. [FORMAL] ❑ *A prolonged drought had necessitated the introduction of water rationing.*
VERB = require · V n/-ing

**ne|ces|sity** /nɪsesɪti/ **(necessities)** [1] The **necessity** of something is the fact that it must happen or exist. ❑ *There is agreement on the necessity of reforms... Most women, like men, work from economic necessity... Some people have to lead stressful lifestyles out of necessity.* ● If you say that something is **of necessity** the case, you mean that it is the case because nothing else is possible or practical in the circumstances. [FORMAL] ❑ *Negotiations between the enemies are of necessity indirect.* [2] A **necessity** is something that you must have in order to live properly or do something. ❑ *Water is a basic necessity of life. ...food, fuel and other daily necessities.* [3] A situation or action that is a **necessity** is necessary and cannot be avoided. ❑ *The President pleaded that strong rule from the centre was a regrettable, but temporary necessity.*
N-UNCOUNT: usu with supp · PHRASE: usu PHR before v, PHR n/adj/adv · N-COUNT = essential ≠ luxury · N-COUNT: usu sing

**neck** /nek/ **(necks, necking, necked)** [1] Your **neck** is the part of your body which joins your head to the rest of your body. ❑ *She threw her arms round his neck and hugged him warmly... He was short and stocky, and had a thick neck.* [2] The **neck** of an article of clothing such as a shirt, dress, or sweater is the part which surrounds your neck. ❑ *...the low, ruffled neck of her blouse... He wore a blue shirt open at the neck.* [3] The **neck** of something such as a bottle or a guitar is the long narrow part at one end of it. ❑ *Catherine gripped the broken neck of the bottle.* [4] If two people **are necking**, they are kissing each other in a sexual way. [INFORMAL] ❑ *They sat talking and necking in the car for another ten minutes... I found myself behind a curtain, necking with my best friend's wife.*
◆◇◇ N-COUNT: usu poss N · N-COUNT: usu sing · N-COUNT: usu *the* N *of* n · V-RECIP: usu cont = snog pl-n V V *with* n Also V n (non-recip)

PHRASES [5] If you say that someone **is breathing down** your **neck**, you mean that they are watching you very closely and checking everything you do. ❑ *Most farmers have bank managers breathing down their necks.* [6] In a competition, especially an election, if two or more competitors are **neck and neck**, they are level with each other and have an equal chance of winning. ❑ *The latest polls indicate that the two main parties are neck and neck... The party is running neck-and-neck with Labour.* [7] If you say that someone **is risking** their **neck**, you mean they are doing something very dangerous, often in order to achieve something. ❑ *I won't have him risking his neck on that motorcycle.* [8] If you **stick** your **neck out**, you bravely say or do something that might be criticized or might turn out to be wrong. [INFORMAL] ❑ *During my political life I've earned myself a reputation as someone who'll stick his neck out, a bit of a rebel.* [9] If you say that someone is in some sort of trouble or criminal activity **up to** their **neck**, you mean that they are deeply involved in it. [INFORMAL] ❑ *He is probably up to his neck in debt.* [10] Someone or something that is from your **neck of the woods** is from the same part of the country as you are. [INFORMAL] ❑ *It's so good to see you. What brings you to this neck of the woods?* [11] to **have a millstone round** your **neck** → see **millstone**. **the scruff of** your **neck** → see **scruff**.
PHRASE: V and N inflect · PHRASE: usu v-link PHR, oft PHR *with* n · PHRASE: V and N inflect · PHRASE: V and N inflect · PHRASE: N inflects · PHRASE: usu *in* PHR

**neck|er|chief** /nekərtʃiːf, -tʃif/ **(neckerchiefs)** A **neckerchief** is a piece of cloth which is folded to form a triangle and worn round your neck.
N-COUNT

**neck|lace** /neklɪs/ **(necklaces)** A **necklace** is a piece of jewellery such as a chain or a string of beads which someone, usually a woman, wears round their neck. ❑ *...a diamond necklace and matching earrings.*
N-COUNT

**neck|line** /neklaɪn/ **(necklines)** The **neckline** of a dress, blouse, or other piece of clothing is the edge that goes around your neck, especially the front part of it. ❑ *...a dress with pale pink roses around the neckline.*
N-COUNT: oft supp N = neck

**neck|tie** /nektaɪ/ **(neckties)** A **necktie** is a narrow piece of cloth that someone, usually a man, puts under his shirt collar and ties so that the ends hang down in front.
N-COUNT = tie

**nec|ro|man|cy** /nekrəmænsi/ **Necromancy** is magic that some people believe brings a dead person back to this world so that you can talk to them. [FORMAL]
N-UNCOUNT

**nec|ro|philia** /nekrəfɪliə/ **Necrophilia** is the act of having sexual intercourse with a dead body, or the desire to do this.
N-UNCOUNT

**ne|cropo|lis** /nekrɒpəlɪs/ **(necropolises)** A **necropolis** is a place where dead people are buried. [FORMAL]
N-COUNT

**ne|cro|sis** /nekrəʊsɪs/ **Necrosis** is the death of part of someone's body, for example because it is not getting enough blood. [MEDICAL] ❑ *...liver necrosis.* N-UNCOUNT: usu supp N

**nec|tar** /nektəʳ/ **(nectars) Nectar** is a sweet liquid produced by flowers, which bees and other insects collect. N-UNCOUNT: also N in pl

**nec|tar|ine** /nektəriːn, -rɪn/ **(nectarines)** A **nectarine** is a round, juicy fruit which is similar to a peach but has a smooth skin. ➔ See picture on page 1711. N-COUNT

**née** /neɪ/ also **nee.** You use **née** after a married woman's name and before you mention the surname she had before she got married. [FORMAL] ❑ *...Lady Helen Taylor (née Windsor).* = born

**need** /niːd/ **(needs, needing, needed)** ◆◆◆

> **Need** sometimes behaves like an ordinary verb, for example 'She needs to know' and 'She doesn't need to know' and sometimes like a modal, for example 'She need know', 'She needn't know', or, in more formal English, 'She need not know.'

1 If you **need** something, or **need to** do something, you cannot successfully achieve what you want or live properly without it. ❑ *He desperately needed money... I need to make a phone call... I need you to do something for me... I need you here tomorrow afternoon, Wally... I need you sane and sober.* VERB: no cont; V n; V to-inf; V n to-inf; V n adv/prep; V n adj ◆ **Need** is also a noun. ❑ *Charles has never felt the need to compete with anyone. ...the child who never had his need for attention and importance satisfied. ...the special nutritional needs of the elderly.* N-COUNT: usu with supp, oft N to-inf, N *for* n

2 If an object or place **needs** something doing to it, that action should be done to improve the object or place. If a task **needs** doing, it should be done to improve a particular situation. ❑ *The building needs quite a few repairs. ...a garden that needs tidying... The taste of vitamins is not too nice so the flavour sometimes needs to be disguised.* VERB: no cont; V n/-ing; V n/-ing; V to-inf

3 If there is a **need for** something, that thing would improve a situation or something cannot happen without it. ❑ *Mr Forrest believes there is a need for other similar schools throughout Britain... 'I think we should see a specialist.' — 'I don't think there's any need for that.'... There's no need for you to stay.* N-SING: usu with supp, oft N *for* n, N to-inf

4 If you say that someone **needn't** do something, you are telling them not to do it, or advising or suggesting that they should not do it. ❑ *Look, you needn't shout... She need not know I'm here.* MODAL: with neg ◆ **Need** is also a verb. ❑ *Come along, Mother, we don't need to take up any more of Mr Kemp's time.* VERB: no cont, with neg; V to-inf

5 If you tell someone that they **needn't** do something, or that something **needn't** happen, you are telling them that that thing is not necessary, in order to make them feel better. ❑ *You needn't worry... Buying budget-priced furniture needn't mean compromising on quality or style... Loneliness can be horrible, but it need not remain that way.* MODAL: with brd-neg ◆ **Need** is also a verb. ❑ *He replied, with a reassuring smile, 'Oh, you don't need to worry about them.'... You don't need to be a millionaire to consider having a bank account in Switzerland.* VERB: no cont, with neg; V to-inf; V to-inf

6 You use **needn't** when you are giving someone permission not to do something. ❑ *You needn't come again, if you don't want to.* MODAL: with neg ◆ **Need** is also a verb. ❑ *You don't need to wait for me.* VERB: no cont; V to-inf

7 If something **need not** be true, it is not necessarily true or not always true. [FORMAL] ❑ *What is right for us need not be right for others... Freedom need not mean independence.* MODAL: with neg

8 If someone **needn't have** done something, it was not necessary or useful for them to do it, although they did it. ❑ *I was a little nervous when I announced my engagement to Grace, but I needn't have worried... We spent a hell of a lot of money that we needn't have spent.* MODAL: with neg ◆ If someone **didn't need to** do something, they needn't have done it. ❑ *You didn't need to give me any more money you know, but thank you.* VERB: no cont, with neg; V to-inf

9 You use **need** in expressions such as **I need hardly say** and **I needn't add** to emphasize that the person you are talking to already knows what you are going to say. ❑ *I needn't add that if you fail to do as I ask, you will suffer the consequences.* MODAL: oft with brd-neg; emphasis ◆ **Need** is also a verb. ❑ *I hardly need to say that I have never lost contact with him.* VERB: no cont; V to-inf

10 You can use **need** in expressions such as **'Need I say more'** and **'Need I go on'** when you want to avoid stating an obvious consequence of something you have just said. ❑ *Mid-fifties, short black hair, grey moustache, distinctive Russian accent. Need I go on?* MODAL

**PHRASES** 11 People **in need** do not have enough of essential things such as money, food, or good health. ❑ *The education authorities have to provide for children in need... Remember that when both of you were in need, I was the one who loaned you money.* PHRASE: usu v-link PHR

12 If you are **in need of** something, you need it or ought to have it. ❑ *I was all right but in need of rest... He was badly in need of a shave... The house was in need of modernisation when they bought it.* PHRASE: PHR n

13 If you say that you will do something, especially an extreme action, **if need be**, you mean that you will do if it is necessary. In British English, you can also say **if needs be**. ❑ *They will now seek permission to take their case to the House of Lords, and, if need be, to the European Court of Human Rights.* PHRASE: PHR with cl

14 You can tell someone that **there's no need** for them to do something as a way of telling them not to do it or of telling them to stop doing it, for example because it is unnecessary. [SPOKEN] ❑ *There's no need to call a doctor... 'I'm going to come with you.' — 'Now look, Sue, there's no need.'* PHRASE: oft PHR to-inf, PHR *for* n

15 You can say **'Who needs** something?' as a way of emphasizing that you think that this thing is unnecessary or not useful. [INFORMAL] ❑ *With apologies to my old history teacher, who needs history lessons?... Cigarettes, who needs them?* PHRASE: PHR n

**need|ful** /niːdfʊl/ **Needful** means necessary. [OLD-FASHIONED] ❑ *The section of society most needful of such guidance is the young male. ...stoppages for needful rest and recreation.* ADJ

**nee|dle** /niːdəl/ **(needles, needling, needled)**

1 A **needle** is a small, very thin piece of polished metal which is used for sewing. It has a sharp point at one end and a hole in the other for a thread to go through. N-COUNT

2 Knitting **needles** are thin sticks that are used for knitting. They are usually made of plastic or metal and have a point at one end. N-COUNT: usu supp N

3 A **needle** is a thin hollow metal rod with a sharp point, which is part of a medical instrument called a syringe. It is used to put a drug into someone's body, or to take blood out. N-COUNT

4 A **needle** is a thin metal rod with a point which is put into a patient's body during acupuncture. N-COUNT

5 On an instrument which measures something such as speed or weight, the **needle** is the long strip of metal or plastic on the dial that moves backwards and forwards, showing the measurement. ❑ *She kept looking at the dial on the boiler. The needle had reached 250 degrees.* N-COUNT

6 The **needles** of a fir or pine tree are its thin, hard, pointed leaves. ❑ *The carpet of pine needles was soft underfoot.* N-COUNT: usu pl

7 If someone **needles** you, they annoy you continually, especially by criticizing you. ❑ *Blake could see he had needled Jerrold, which might be unwise.* VERB; V n

8 ➔ See also **pins and needles. like looking for a needle in a haystack** ➔ see **haystack.**

**nee|dle ex|change (needle exchanges)** also **needle-exchange.** A **needle exchange** is a place where drug addicts are able to obtain new syringes in exchange for used ones. ❑ *...needle exchange schemes.* N-COUNT

**need|less** /niːdləs/ 1 Something that is **needless** is completely unnecessary. ❑ *But his death was so needless... 'I have never knowingly exposed any patient to needless risks,' he said.* ADJ ◆ **need|less|ly** *Half a million women die needlessly each year during childbirth.* ADV: ADV with v, ADV adj

2 You use **needless to say** when you want to emphasize that what you are about to say is obvious and to be expected in PHRASE: PHR with cl; emphasis

the circumstances. ❑ *Our budgie got out of its cage while our cat was in the room. Needless to say, the cat moved quicker than me and caught it.* = of course

**needle|work** /niːdəlwɜːʳk/ [1] **Needlework** is sewing or stitching that is done by hand. ❑ *She did beautiful needlework and she embroidered table napkins.* [2] **Needlework** is the activity of sewing or stitching. ❑ *...watching my mother and grandmothers doing needlework.* N-UNCOUNT; N-UNCOUNT = sewing

**needn't** /niːdənt/ **Needn't** is the usual spoken form of 'need not'.

**needy** /niːdi/ **(needier, neediest)** **Needy** people do not have enough food, medicine, or clothing, or adequate houses. ❑ *...a multinational force aimed at ensuring that food and medicine get to needy Somalis.* ♦ **The needy** are people who are needy. ❑ *There will be efforts to get larger amounts of food to the needy.* ADJ: usu ADJ n; N-PLURAL: the N

**ne|fari|ous** /nɪfeəriəs/ If you describe an activity as **nefarious**, you mean that it is wicked and immoral. [LITERARY] ❑ *Why make a whole village prisoner if it was not to some nefarious purpose?* ADJ: usu ADJ n

**neg.** **Neg.** is a written abbreviation for **negative**.

**ne|gate** /nɪgeɪt/ **(negates, negating, negated)** [1] If one thing **negates** another, it causes that other thing to lose the effect or value that it had. [FORMAL] ❑ *These weaknesses negated his otherwise progressive attitude towards the staff.* [2] If someone **negates** something, they say that it does not exist. [FORMAL] ❑ *He warned that to negate the results of elections would only make things worse.* VERB ≠ confirm, V n; VERB ≠ affirm, V n

**ne|ga|tion** /nɪgeɪʃən/ [1] The **negation of** something is its complete opposite or something which destroys it or makes it lose its effect. [FORMAL] ❑ *Unintelligible legislation is the negation of the rule of law and of parliamentary democracy.* [2] **Negation** is disagreement, refusal, or denial. [FORMAL] ❑ *Irena shook her head, but in bewilderment, not negation.* N-SING: N of n; N-UNCOUNT ≠ affirmation

**nega|tive** /negətɪv/ **(negatives)** [1] A fact, situation, or experience that is **negative** is unpleasant, depressing, or harmful. ❑ *The news from overseas is overwhelmingly negative... All this had an extremely negative effect on the criminal justice system.* ♦ **nega|tive|ly** *This will negatively affect the result over the first half of the year.* [2] If someone is **negative** or has a **negative** attitude, they consider only the bad aspects of a situation, rather than the good ones. ❑ *When asked for your views about your current job, on no account must you be negative about it... Why does the media present such a negative view of this splendid city?* ♦ **nega|tive|ly** *A few weeks later he said that maybe he viewed all his relationships rather negatively.* ♦ **nega|tiv|ity** /negətɪvɪti/ *I loathe negativity. I can't stand people who moan.* [3] A **negative** reply or decision indicates the answer 'no'. ❑ *Dr Velayati gave a vague but negative response... Upon a negative decision, the applicant loses the protection offered by Belgian law.* ♦ **nega|tive|ly** *60 percent of the sample answered negatively.* [4] A **negative** is a word, expression, or gesture that means 'no' or 'not'. ❑ *In the past we have heard only negatives when it came to following a healthy diet.* [5] In grammar, a **negative** clause contains a word such as 'not', 'never', or 'no-one'. [6] If a medical test or scientific test is **negative**, it shows no evidence of the medical condition or substance that you are looking for. ❑ *So far 57 have taken the test and all have been negative. ...negative test results.* [7] **HIV negative** → see **HIV**. [8] In photography, a **negative** is an image that shows dark areas as light and light areas as dark. Negatives are made from a camera film, and are used to print photographs. [9] A **negative** charge or current has the same electrical charge as an electron. ❑ *Stimulate the site of greatest pain with a small negative current.* ♦ **nega|tive|ly** *As these electrons are negatively charged they will attempt to repel each other.* [10] A **negative** number, quantity, or measurement is less than zero. ❑ *The weakest students can end up with a negative score.* [11] If an answer is **in the negative**, it is 'no' or means 'no'. ❑ *Seventy-nine voted in the affirmative, and none in the negative.* ◆◇◇ ADJ ≠ positive; ADV: ADV with v; ADJ ≠ positive; ADV: usu ADV after v; N-UNCOUNT; ADJ ≠ affirmative; ADV: ADV after v; N-COUNT; ADJ; ADJ ≠ positive; N-COUNT; ADJ ≠ positive; ADV: ADV -ed; ADJ: usu ADJ n = minus; PHRASE: PHR after v

**nega|tive equi|ty** If someone who has borrowed money to buy a house or flat has **negative equity**, the amount of money they owe is greater than the present value of their home. [BRIT, BUSINESS] N-UNCOUNT

**ne|glect** /nɪglekt/ **(neglects, neglecting, neglected)** [1] If you **neglect** someone or something, you fail to look after them properly. ❑ *The woman denied that she had neglected her child... Feed plants and they grow, neglect them and they suffer. ...an ancient and neglected church.* ♦ **Neglect** is also a noun. ❑ *The town's old quayside is collapsing after years of neglect.* [2] If you **neglect** someone or something, you fail to give them the amount of attention that they deserve. ❑ *He'd given too much to his career, worked long hours, neglected her... If you are not careful, children tend to neglect their homework.* ♦ **ne|glect|ed** *The fact that she is not coming today makes her grandmother feel lonely and neglected. ... a neglected aspect of London's forgotten history... The journal she had begun lay neglected on her bedside table.* [3] If you **neglect to** do something that you ought to do or **neglect** your duty, you fail to do it. ❑ *We often neglect to make proper use of our bodies... They never neglect their duties.* VERB; V n; V n; V-ed; N-UNCOUNT; VERB; V n; V n; ADJ: v-link ADJ, ADJ n, ADJ after v = forgotten; VERB; V to-inf; V n

**ne|glect|ful** /nɪglektfʊl/ [1] If you describe someone as **neglectful**, you think they fail to do everything they should do to look after someone or something properly. ❑ *...neglectful parents.* [2] If someone is **neglectful of** something, they do not give it the attention or consideration that it should be given. ❑ *Have I been neglectful of my friend, taking him for granted?* ADJ = negligent; ADJ: oft v-link ADJ of n

**neg|li|gee** /neglɪʒeɪ, AM -ʒeɪ/ **(negligees)** also **négligée.** A **negligee** is a very thin garment which a woman wears over her nightclothes. ❑ *...a pink satin negligee.* N-COUNT

**neg|li|gence** /neglɪdʒəns/ If someone is guilty of **negligence**, they have failed to do something which they ought to do. [FORMAL] ❑ *The soldiers were ordered to appear before a disciplinary council on charges of negligence.* N-UNCOUNT

**neg|li|gent** /neglɪdʒənt/ If someone in a position of responsibility is **negligent**, they do not do something which they ought to do. ❑ *The jury determined that the airline was negligent in training and supervising the crew... The Council had acted in a negligent manner.* ♦ **neg|li|gent|ly** *A manufacturer negligently made and marketed a car with defective brakes.* ADJ; ADV: ADV with v

**neg|li|gible** /neglɪdʒɪbəl/ An amount or effect that is **negligible** is so small that it is not worth considering or worrying about. ❑ *The pay that the soldiers received was negligible... Senior managers are convinced that the strike will have a negligible impact.* ADJ = minimal ≠ significant

**ne|go|tiable** /nɪgoʊʃəbəl/ [1] Something that is **negotiable** can be changed or agreed when people discuss it. ❑ *He warned that his economic programme for the country was not negotiable... The Manor is for sale at a negotiable price.* [2] Contracts or assets that are **negotiable** can be transferred to another person in exchange for money. ❑ *The bonds may no longer be negotiable. ...negotiable bearer bonds.* ADJ ≠ fixed; ADJ

**ne|go|ti|ate** /nɪgoʊʃieɪt/ **(negotiates, negotiating, negotiated)** [1] If people **negotiate with** each other or **negotiate** an agreement, they talk about a problem or a situation such as a business arrangement in order to solve the problem or complete the arrangement. ❑ *It is not clear whether the president is willing to negotiate with the democrats... When you have two adversaries negotiating, you need to be on neutral territory... The local government and the army negotiated a truce... Western governments have this week urged him to negotiate and* ◆◆◇ V-RECIP; V with n; pl-n V; pl-n V n; NON-RECIP: V avoid force... The South African president has negotiated an end to white-minority rule... His publishing house had just begun negotiating for her next books... There were reports that three companies were negotiating to market the drug. *V n / V for n / V to-inf / Also V n with n* 2 If you **negotiate** an area of land, a place, or an obstacle, you successfully travel across it or around it. ❑ *Frank Mariano negotiates the desert terrain in his battered pickup... I negotiated my way out of the airport and joined the flow of cars.* VERB = navigate / V n / V way prep/adv

**ne|go|ti|at|ing ta|ble** If you say that people are at **the negotiating table**, you mean that they are having discussions in order to settle a dispute or reach an agreement. ❑ *'We want to settle all matters at the negotiating table,' he said.* N-SING: usu the N

**ne|go|tia|tion** /nɪgoʊʃieɪʃən/ **(negotiations)** ◆◆◇ **Negotiations** are formal discussions between people who have different aims or intentions, especially in business or politics, during which they try to reach an agreement. ❑ *We have had meaningful negotiations and I believe we are very close to a deal... After 10 years of negotiation, the Senate ratified the strategic arms reduction treaty.* N-VAR

**ne|go|tia|tor** /nɪgoʊʃieɪtər/ **(negotiators)** **Negotiators** are people who take part in political or financial negotiations. ❑ *...the rebels' chief negotiator at the peace talks... The two American negotiators are calling for substantial cuts in external subsidies.* N-COUNT

**Ne|gro** /niːgroʊ/ **(Negroes)** A **Negro** is someone with dark skin who comes from Africa or whose ancestors came from Africa. [OFFENSIVE, OLD-FASHIONED] N-COUNT

**neigh** /neɪ/ **(neighs, neighing, neighed)** When a horse **neighs**, it makes a loud sound with its mouth. ❑ *The mare neighed once more, turned and disappeared amongst the trees.* ♦ **Neigh** is also a noun. ❑ *The horse gave a loud neigh.* VERB = whinny / V / N-COUNT = whinny

**neigh|bour** /neɪbər/ **(neighbours)** ◆◇◇

✔ in AM, use **neighbor**

1 Your **neighbour** is someone who lives near you. ❑ *I got chatting with my neighbour in the garden.* N-COUNT: oft poss N 2 You can refer to the person who is standing or sitting next to you as your **neighbour**. ❑ *The woman prodded her neighbour and whispered urgently in his ear.* N-COUNT: oft poss N 3 You can refer to something which stands next to something else of the same kind as its **neighbour**. ❑ *Each house was packed close behind its neighbour.* N-COUNT: usu poss N

**neigh|bour|hood** /neɪbərhʊd/ **(neighbourhoods)**

✔ in AM, use **neighborhood**

1 A **neighbourhood** is one of the parts of a town where people live. ❑ *It seemed like a good neighbourhood to raise my children.* N-COUNT = area 2 The **neighbourhood** of a place or person is the area or the people around them. ❑ *He was born and grew up in the Flatbush neighbourhood of Brooklyn.* N-COUNT

PHRASES 3 **In the neighbourhood of** a number means approximately that number. ❑ *He's won in the neighbourhood of four million dollars.* PREP-PHRASE: PREP amount = roughly, about 4 A place **in the neighbourhood of** another place is near it. ❑ *...the loss of woodlands in the neighbourhood of large towns.* PHRASE: PHR n

**neigh|bour|ing** /neɪbərɪŋ/

✔ in AM, use **neighboring**

**Neighbouring** places or things are near other things of the same kind. ❑ *Rwanda is to hold talks with leaders of neighbouring countries next week. ...the hotel's boutique and neighboring shops.* ADJ: ADJ n

**neigh|bour|ly** /neɪbərli/

✔ in AM, use **neighborly**

If the people who live near you are **neighbourly**, they are friendly and helpful. If you live in a **neighbourly** place, it has a friendly atmosphere. ❑ *The noise would have provoked alarm and neighbourly concern... The older people had stopped being neighbourly to each other.* ADJ

**nei|ther** /naɪðər, niːðər/ ◆◆◇ 1 You use **neither** in front of the first of two or more words or expressions when you are linking two or more things which are not true or do not happen. The other thing is introduced by 'nor'. ❑ *Professor Hisamatsu spoke neither English nor German... The play is neither as funny nor as disturbing as Tabori thinks it is.* CONJ 2 You use **neither** to refer to each of two things or people, when you are making a negative statement that includes both of them. ❑ *At first, neither man could speak.* DET ♦ **Neither** is also a quantifier. ❑ *Neither of us felt like going out.* QUANT ♦ **Neither** is also a pronoun. ❑ *They both smiled; neither seemed likely to be aware of my absence for long.* PRON 3 If you say that one person or thing does not do something and **neither** does another, what you say is true of all the people or things that you are mentioning. ❑ *I never learned to swim and neither did they... Britain does not agree and neither do Denmark, Portugal and Ireland.* CONJ = nor 4 You use **neither** after a negative statement to emphasize that you are introducing another negative statement. [FORMAL] ❑ *I can't ever recall Dad hugging me. Neither did I sit on his knee.* CONJ = nor 5 If you say that something is **neither here nor there**, you mean that it does not matter because it is not a relevant point. ❑ *'I'd never heard of her before I came here.' — 'That is neither here nor there.'* PHRASE: v-link PHR

**nem|esis** /neməsɪs/ The **nemesis** of a person or thing is a situation, event, or person which causes them to be seriously harmed, especially as a punishment. ❑ *Yet the imminent crisis in its balance of payments may be the President's nemesis.* N-UNCOUNT: oft with poss

**neo-** /niːoʊ-/ **Neo-** is used with nouns to form adjectives and nouns that refer to modern versions of styles and political groups that existed in the past. ❑ *...10ft high neo-Victorian gates... The neo-Socialists were a small right wing group.* PREFIX

**neo|clas|si|cal** /niːoʊklæsɪkəl/ also **neo-classical. Neoclassical** architecture or art is from the late 18th century and uses designs from Roman and Greek architecture and art. ❑ *The building was erected between 1798 and 1802 in the neoclassical style of the time.* ADJ

**Neo|lith|ic** /niːəlɪθɪk/ also **neolithic. Neolithic** is used to describe things relating to the period when people had started farming but still used stone for making weapons and tools. ❑ *...neolithic culture. ...the monument was Stone Age or Neolithic.* ADJ

**ne|olo|gism** /niːɒlədʒɪzəm, niɒl-/ **(neologisms)** A **neologism** is a new word or expression in a language, or a new meaning for an existing word or expression. [TECHNICAL] ❑ *The newspaper used the neologism 'dinks', Double Income No Kids.* N-COUNT

**neon** /niːɒn/ 1 **Neon** lights or signs are made from glass tubes filled with neon gas which produce a bright electric light. ❑ *In the city squares the neon lights flashed in turn.* ADJ: ADJ n = fluorescent 2 **Neon** is a gas which occurs in very small amounts in the atmosphere. ❑ *...inert gases like neon and argon.* N-UNCOUNT

**neo|na|tal** /niːoʊneɪtəl/ **Neonatal** means relating to the first few days of life of a new born baby. ❑ *...the neonatal intensive care unit.* ADJ: ADJ n

**neo-Nazi** **(neo-Nazis)** **Neo-Nazis** are people who admire Adolf Hitler and the beliefs of the right-wing party which he led in Germany from 1933 to 1945. N-COUNT: oft N n

**neo|phyte** /niːəfaɪt/ **(neophytes)** A **neophyte** is someone who is new to a particular activity. [FORMAL] ❑ *...the self-proclaimed political neophyte Ross Perot.* N-COUNT = novice

**neph|ew** /nefjuː, nev-/ **(nephews)** Someone's **nephew** is the son of their sister or brother. ❑ *I am planning a 25th birthday party for my nephew.* N-COUNT: oft poss N

**nepo|tism** /nepətɪzəm/ **Nepotism** is the unfair use of power in order to get jobs or other benefits for your family or friends. ❑ *Many will regard his appointment as the kind of nepotism British banking ought to avoid.* N-UNCOUNT disapproval

**nerd** /nɜːrd/ **(nerds)** If you say that someone is a **nerd**, you mean that they are stupid or ridicu- N-COUNT disapproval lous, especially because they wear unfashionable clothes or show too much interest in computers or science. [INFORMAL, OFFENSIVE] ❑ *Mark claimed he was made to look a nerd. ...the notion that users of the Internet are all sad computer nerds.*

**nerdy** /nɜːʳdi/ **(nerdier, nerdiest)** ADJ disapproval If you describe someone as **nerdy**, you think that they are a nerd or look like a nerd. [INFORMAL] ❑ *...nerdy types who never exercise. ...the Prince's nerdy hairstyle.*

**nerve** /nɜːʳv/ **(nerves)** ◆◇◇ 1 N-COUNT **Nerves** are long thin fibres that transmit messages between your brain and other parts of your body. ❑ *...spinal nerves. ...in cases where the nerve fibres are severed.* 2 N-PLURAL: usu poss N If you refer to someone's **nerves**, you mean their ability to cope with problems such as stress, worry, and danger. ❑ *Jill's nerves are stretched to breaking point... I can be very patient, and then I can burst if my nerves are worn out.* 3 N-PLURAL = nervousness You can refer to someone's feelings of anxiety or tension as **nerves**. ❑ *I just played badly. It wasn't nerves.* 4 N-UNCOUNT = courage **Nerve** is the courage that you need in order to do something difficult or dangerous. ❑ *The brandy made him choke, but it restored his nerve... He never got up enough nerve to meet me.*

PHRASES 5 PHRASE: V inflects If someone or something **gets on** your **nerves**, they annoy or irritate you. [INFORMAL] ❑ *Lately he's not done a bloody thing and it's getting on my nerves.* 6 PHRASE: V inflects disapproval If you say that someone **has a nerve** or **has the nerve** to do something, you are criticizing them for doing something which you feel they had no right to do. [INFORMAL] ❑ *They've got a nerve, complaining about our behaviour... He had the nerve to ask me to prove who I was.* 7 PHRASE: V inflects = keep your cool If you **hold** your **nerve** or **keep** your **nerve**, you remain calm and determined in a difficult situation. ❑ *He held his nerve to beat Andre Agassi in a five-set thriller on Court One... We need to keep our nerve now.* 8 PHRASE: V inflects If you **lose** your **nerve**, you suddenly panic and become too afraid to do something that you were about to do. ❑ *The bomber had lost his nerve and fled.* 9 PHRASE: V inflects If you say that you have **touched a nerve** or **touched a raw nerve**, you mean that you have accidentally upset someone by talking about something that they feel strongly about or are very sensitive about. ❑ *Alistair saw Henry shrink, as if the words had touched a nerve... The mere mention of John had touched a very raw nerve indeed.*

**nerve agent** **(nerve agents)** N-MASS A **nerve agent** is a chemical weapon that affects people's nervous systems.

**nerve cen|tre** **(nerve centres)**

in AM, use **nerve center**

N-COUNT: usu with poss The **nerve centre** of an organization is the place from where its activities are controlled and where its leaders meet. ❑ *My office is the nerve centre of the operation.*

**nerve end|ing** **(nerve endings)** N-COUNT: usu pl Your **nerve endings** are the millions of points on the surface of your body and inside it which send messages to your brain when you feel sensations such as heat, cold, and pain.

**nerve gas** **(nerve gases)** N-MASS **Nerve gas** is a poisonous gas used in war as a weapon.

**nerve-racking** also **nerve-wracking.** ADJ A **nerve-racking** situation or experience makes you feel very tense and worried. ❑ *The women and children spent a nerve-racking day outside waiting while fighting continued around them... It was more nerve-wracking than taking a World Cup penalty.*

**ner|vo|sa** /nɜːʳvoʊsə/ → see **anorexia, bulimia.**

**nerv|ous** /nɜːʳvəs/ ◆◇◇ 1 ADJ: usu v-link ADJ, oft ADJ *about/of* n = anxious If someone is **nervous**, they are frightened or worried about something that is happening or might happen, and show this in their behaviour. ❑ *The party has become deeply nervous about its prospects of winning the next election... She described Mr Hutchinson as nervous and jumpy after his wife's disappearance.* ♦ **nerv|ous|ly** ADV: ADV with v *Brunhilde stood up nervously as the men came into the room.* ♦ **nerv|ous|ness** N-UNCOUNT *I smiled warmly so he wouldn't see my nervousness.* 2 ADJ: usu ADJ n A **nervous** person is very tense and easily upset. ❑ *She was apparently a very nervous woman, and that affected her career.* 3 ADJ: ADJ n A **nervous** illness or condition is one that affects your emotions and your mental state. ❑ *The number of nervous disorders was rising in the region... He developed nervous problems after people began repeatedly correcting him.*

**nerv|ous break|down** **(nervous breakdowns)** N-COUNT If someone has a **nervous breakdown**, they become extremely depressed and cannot cope with their normal life. ❑ *His wife would not be able to cope and might suffer a nervous breakdown.*

**nerv|ous sys|tem** **(nervous systems)** N-COUNT Your **nervous system** consists of all the nerves in your body together with your brain and spinal cord.

**nerv|ous wreck** **(nervous wrecks)** N-COUNT If you say that someone is **a nervous wreck**, you mean that they are extremely nervous or worried about something. ❑ *She was a nervous wreck, crying when anyone asked her about her experience.*

**nervy** /nɜːʳvi/ 1 ADJ = jumpy If someone is **nervy**, their behaviour shows that they are very tense or anxious, or they are the type of person who is easily upset. [mainly BRIT] ❑ *Alan was irritable, and very evidently in a nervy state.* 2 ADJ If you say that someone is **nervy**, you mean that their behaviour is bold or daring. [AM] ❑ *John liked him because he was a nervy guy and would go out and shoot anybody who John wanted him to shoot.*

**-ness** /-nəs/ SUFFIX **-ness** is added to adjectives to form nouns which often refer to a state or quality. For example, 'sadness' is the state of being sad and 'kindness' is the quality of being kind. ❑ *'This is not good,' he said with great seriousness.*

**nest** /nest/ **(nests, nesting, nested)** 1 N-COUNT: oft poss N A bird's **nest** is the home that it makes to lay its eggs in. ❑ *I can see an eagle's nest on the rocks.* 2 VERB When a bird **nests** somewhere, it builds a nest and settles there to lay its eggs. ❑ V *Some species may nest in close proximity to each other.* V-ing *...nesting sites.* 3 N-COUNT: usu poss N A **nest** is a home that a group of insects or other creatures make in order to live in and give birth to their young in. ❑ *Some solitary bees make their nests in burrows in the soil. ...a rat's nest.* 4 → See also **crow's nest, love nest.** 5 PHRASE: V inflects = leave home When children **fly the nest**, they leave their parents' home to live on their own. ❑ *When their children had flown the nest, he and his wife moved to a thatched cottage in Dorset.* 6 **a hornet's nest** → see **hornet.**

**nest egg** **(nest eggs)** also **nest-egg.** N-COUNT: usu sing A **nest egg** is a sum of money that you are saving for a particular purpose. [INFORMAL] ❑ *They have a little nest egg tucked away somewhere for a rainy day.*

**nes|tle** /nesəl/ **(nestles, nestling, nestled)** 1 VERB = snuggle If you **nestle** or **are nestled** somewhere, you move into a comfortable position, usually by pressing against someone or against something soft. ❑ V prep *John took one child into the crook of each arm and let them nestle against him...* V n prep *Jade nestled her first child in her arms.* 2 VERB If something such as a building **nestles** somewhere or if it **is nestled** somewhere, it is in that place and seems safe or sheltered. ❑ V prep *Nearby, nestling in the hills, was the children's home...* V n prep *She nestled the eggs safely in the straw in Jim's basket.*

**nest|ling** /nestlɪŋ/ **(nestlings)** N-COUNT = fledgling A **nestling** is a young bird that has not yet learned to fly.

**net**
① NOUN AND VERB USES
② ADJECTIVE AND ADVERB USES

①**net** /net/ **(nets, netting, netted)** ◆◇◇ 1 N-UNCOUNT **Net** is a kind of cloth that you can see through. It is made of very fine threads woven together so that there are small equal spaces between them. 2 N-COUNT A **net** is a piece of netting which is used as a protective covering for something, for example to protect vegetables from birds. ❑ *I threw aside my mosquito* *net and jumped out of bed.* [3] A **net** is a piece of netting which is used for catching fish, insects, or animals. ❑ *Several fishermen sat on wooden barrels, tending their nets.* N-COUNT [4] **The Net** is the same as the **Internet**. N-SING: *the* N [5] If you **net** a fish or other animal, you catch it in a net. ❑ *I'm quite happy to net a fish and then let it go.* VERB = land V n [6] In games such as tennis, **the net** is the piece of netting across the centre of the court which the ball has to go over. N-COUNT: usu *the* N in sing [7] **The net** on a football or hockey field is the framework with netting over it which is attached to the back of the goal. ❑ *He let the ball slip through his grasp and into the net.* N-COUNT: usu *the* N in sing = goal [8] In basketball, **the net** is the netting which hangs from the metal hoop. You score goals by throwing the ball through the hoop and netting. N-COUNT [9] If you **net** something, you manage to get it, especially by using skill. ❑ *They took to the water intent on netting the £250,000 reward offered for conclusive proof of the monster's existence.* VERB V n [10] If you **net** a particular amount of money, you gain it as profit after all expenses have been paid. ❑ *Last year he netted a cool 3 million pounds by selling his holdings.* VERB = make V n [11] ➔ See also **netting**, **safety net**.

PHRASES [12] If you **cast** your **net wider**, you look for or consider a greater variety of things. ❑ *The security forces are casting their net wider.* PHRASE: V and N inflect [13] If criminals **slip through the net**, they avoid being caught by the system or trap that was meant to catch them. ❑ *Officials fear some of the thugs identified by British police may have slipped through the net.* PHRASE: V inflects [14] You use **slip through the net** or **fall through the net** to describe a situation where people are not properly cared for by the system that is intended to help them. ❑ *The existence of more than one agency with power to intervene can lead to children falling through the net.* PHRASE: V inflects

**②net** /net/ ◆◇◇

✓ in BRIT, also use **nett**

[1] A **net** amount is one which remains when everything that should be subtracted from it has been subtracted. ❑ *...a rise in sales and net profit... At the year end, net assets were £18 million... What you actually receive is net of deductions for the airfare and administration.* ADJ: ADJ n, v-link ADJ *of* n ≠gross ♦ **Net** is also an adverb. ❑ *Balances of £5,000 and above will earn 11 per cent gross, 8.25 per cent net... All bank and building society interest is paid net.* ADV: amount ADV, ADV after v [2] The **net** weight of something is its weight without its container or the material that has been used to wrap it. ❑ *...350 mg net weight.* ADJ: ADJ n [3] A **net** result is a final result after all the details have been considered or included. ❑ *We have a net gain of nearly 50 seats, the biggest for any party in Scotland... We will be a net exporter of motor cars in just a few years' time.* ADJ: ADJ n = overall

**net|ball** /netbɔːl/ In Britain and some other countries, **netball** is a game played by two teams of seven players, usually women. Each team tries to score goals by throwing a ball through a net on the top of a pole at each end of the court. N-UNCOUNT

**net cur|tain** **(net curtains)** **Net curtains** are curtains made of thin cloth that people hang across their windows to stop people outside seeing into their houses in the daytime. [BRIT] N-COUNT: usu pl

✓ in AM, use **sheers**

**net|head** /nethed/ **(netheads)** If you call someone a **nethead**, you mean that they spend a lot of time using the Internet. [INFORMAL] N-COUNT

**neth|er** /neðəʳ/ **Nether** means the lower part of a thing or place. [OLD-FASHIONED] ❑ *He was escorted back to the nether regions of Main Street.* ADJ: ADJ n

**nether|world** /neðəʳwɜːʳld/ also **nether world.** If you refer to a place as a **netherworld**, you mean that it is dangerous and full of poor people and criminals. ❑ *Waits sang about the boozy netherworld of urban America.* N-SING: usu with supp

**neti|quette** /netɪket/ **Netiquette** is the set of rules and customs that it is considered polite to follow when you are communicating by means of e-mail or the Internet. N-UNCOUNT

**net|surf|ing** /netsɜːʳfɪŋ/ **Netsurfing** is the activity of looking at different sites on the Internet, especially when you are not looking for anything in particular. [COMPUTING] N-UNCOUNT ♦ **net|surfer** **(netsurfers)** ❑ *Seen from a netsurfer's screen, there are plenty of stores to 'visit'.* N-COUNT

**nett** /net/ ➔ see **net**.

**net|ting** /netɪŋ/ **Netting** is a kind of material made of pieces of thread or metal wires. These are woven together so that there are equal spaces between them. ❑ *...mosquito netting. ...wire netting.* N-UNCOUNT: oft supp N

**net|tle** /netᵊl/ **(nettles, nettling, nettled)**

[1] **Nettles** are wild plants which have leaves covered with fine hairs that sting you when you touch them. ❑ *The nettles stung their legs.* N-COUNT [2] If you **are nettled** by something, you are annoyed or offended by it. ❑ *He was nettled by her manner... It was the suggestion that he might alter course to win an election that really nettled him.* VERB *be* V-ed V n

**net|work** /netwɜːʳk/ **(networks, networking, networked)** ◆◆◇ [1] A **network of** lines, roads, veins, or other long thin things is a large number of them which cross each other or meet at many points. ❑ *...Strasbourg, with its rambling network of medieval streets... The uterus is supplied with a rich network of blood vessels and nerves.* N-COUNT: usu N *of* n [2] A **network of** people or institutions is a large number of them that have a connection with each other and work together as a system. ❑ *Distribution of the food is going ahead using a network of local church people and other volunteers... He is keen to point out the benefits which the family network can provide.* ➔ See also **old-boy network**. N-COUNT: usu supp N, N *of* n [3] A particular **network** is a system of things which are connected and which operate together. For example, a **computer network** consists of a number of computers that are part of the same system. ❑ *...a computer network with 154 terminals... Huge sections of the rail network are out of action.* ➔ See also **neural network**. N-COUNT: oft n N [4] A radio or television **network** is a company or group of companies that broadcasts radio or television programmes throughout an area. ❑ *An American network says it has obtained the recordings.* N-COUNT: usu supp N [5] When a television or radio programme **is networked**, it is broadcast at the same time by several different television companies. ❑ *Lumsdon would like to see his programme sold and networked... He had once had his own networked chat show.* VERB: usu passive *be* V-ed V-ed [6] If you **network**, you try to meet new people who might be useful to you in your job. [BUSINESS] ❑ *In business, it is important to network with as many people as possible on a face to face basis.* VERB V *with* n Also V

**net|work card** **(network cards)** or **network interface card** A **network card** or a **network interface card** is a card that connects a computer to a network. [COMPUTING] N-COUNT

**net|work|ing** /netwɜːʳkɪŋ/ [1] **Networking** is the process of trying to meet new people who might be useful to you in your job, often through social activities. [BUSINESS] ❑ *If executives fail to exploit the opportunities of networking they risk being left behind.* N-UNCOUNT [2] You can refer to the things associated with a computer system or the process of establishing such a system as **networking**. ❑ *Managers have learned to grapple with networking, artificial intelligence, computer-aided engineering and manufacturing. ...computer and networking equipment.* N-UNCOUNT

**neu|ral** /njʊərəl, AM nʊr-/ **Neural** means relating to a nerve or to the nervous system. [MEDICAL] ❑ *...neural pathways in the brain.* ADJ

**neu|ral|gia** /njʊəræld͡ʒə, AM nʊr-/ **Neuralgia** is very severe pain along the whole length of a nerve caused when the nerve is damaged or not working properly. [MEDICAL] N-UNCOUNT

**neu|ral net|work** **(neural networks)** In computing, a **neural network** is a program or system which is modelled on the human brain and is designed to imitate the brain's method of functioning, particularly the process of learning. N-COUNT

**neuro-** /njʊərou-, AM nʊrou-/ **Neuro-** is used to form words that refer or relate to a nerve or the nervous system. ❑ *...Karl Pribram, the well-known neuro-scientist. ...disorders of the neuromuscular system.* PREFIX

**neu|ro|logi|cal** /njʊərəlɒdʒɪkəl, AM nʊr-/ **Neurological** means related to the nervous system. [MEDICAL] ❑ *...neurological disorders such as Parkinson's disease.* ADJ: ADJ n = *nervous*

**neu|rol|ogy** /njʊərɒlədʒi, AM nʊr-/ **Neurology** is the study of the structure, function, and diseases of the nervous system. [MEDICAL] ❑ *He trained in neurology at the National Hospital for Nervous Diseases.* N-UNCOUNT ♦ **neu|rolo|gist** **(neurologists)** *...Dr Simon Shorvon, consultant neurologist of the Chalfont Centre for Epilepsy.* N-COUNT

**neu|ron** /njʊərɒn, AM nʊr-/ **(neurons)** also **neurone.** A **neuron** is a cell which is part of the nervous system. Neurons send messages to and from the brain. [TECHNICAL] ❑ *Information is transferred along each neuron by means of an electrical impulse.* → See also **motor neurone disease**. N-COUNT

**neu|ro|sis** /njʊəroʊsɪs, AM nʊr-/ **(neuroses** /njʊəroʊsiːz,AM nʊr-/ **)** **Neurosis** is a mental condition which causes people to have unreasonable fears and worries over a long period of time. ❑ *He was anxious to the point of neurosis... She got a neurosis about chemicals and imagined them everywhere doing her harm.* N-VAR

**neu|rot|ic** /njʊərɒtɪk, AM nʊr-/ **(neurotics)** If you say that someone is **neurotic**, you mean that they are always frightened or worried about things that you consider unimportant. ❑ *He was almost neurotic about being followed.* ADJ [disapproval] ♦ A **neurotic** is someone who is neurotic. ❑ *These patients are not neurotics.* N-COUNT

**neu|ter** /njuːtəʳ, AM nuːt-/ **(neuters, neutering, neutered)** 1 When an animal **is neutered**, its reproductive organs are removed so that it cannot create babies. ❑ *We ask the public to have their dogs neutered and keep them under close supervision.* VERB: usu passive *have* n V-ed
2 To **neuter** an organization, group, or person means to make them powerless and ineffective. [mainly BRIT, JOURNALISM] ❑ *...the Government's 'hidden agenda' to neuter local authorities... Their air force had been neutered before the work began.* VERB V n *be* V-ed 3 In some languages, a **neuter** noun, pronoun, or adjective has a different form from a masculine or feminine one, or behaves in a different way. ADJ

**neu|tral** /njuːtrəl, AM nuːt-/ **(neutrals)** 1 If a person or country adopts a **neutral** position or remains **neutral**, they do not support anyone in a disagreement, war, or contest. ❑ *Let's meet on neutral territory... Those who had decided to remain neutral in the struggle now found themselves required to take sides.* ADJ ♦ A **neutral** is someone who is neutral. ❑ *It was a good game to watch for the neutrals.* N-COUNT ♦ **neu|tral|ity** /njuːtrælɪti, AM nuːt-/ *...a reputation for political neutrality and impartiality.* N-UNCOUNT 2 If someone speaks in a **neutral** voice or if the expression on their face is **neutral**, they do not show what they are thinking or feeling. ❑ *Isabel put her magazine down and said in a neutral voice, 'You're very late, darling.'... He told her about the death, describing the events in as neutral a manner as he could.* ADJ: usu ADJ n ♦ **neu|tral|ity** *I noticed, behind the neutrality of his gaze, a deep weariness.* N-UNCOUNT 3 If you say that something is **neutral**, you mean that it does not have any effect on other things because it lacks any significant qualities of its own, or it is an equal balance of two or more different qualities, amounts, or ideas. ❑ *Three in every five interviewed felt that the Budget was neutral and they would be no better off.* ADJ 4 **Neutral** is the position between the gears of a vehicle such as a car, in which the gears are not connected to the engine. ❑ *Graham put the van in neutral and jumped out into the road.* N-UNCOUNT: oft *into/in* N 5 In an electrical device or system, the **neutral** wire is one of the three wires needed to complete the circuit so that the current can flow. The other two wires are called the earth wire and the live or positive wire. ADJ 6 **Neutral** is used to describe things that have a pale colour such as cream or grey, or that have no colour at all. ❑ *At the horizon the land mass becomes a continuous pale neutral grey.* COLOUR 7 In chemistry, **neutral** is used to describe things that are neither acid nor alkaline. ❑ *Pure water is neutral with a pH of 7.* ADJ

**neu|tral|ize** /njuːtrəlaɪz, AM nuːt-/ **(neutralizes, neutralizing, neutralized)**

in BRIT, also use **neutralise**

1 To **neutralize** something means to prevent it from having any effect or from working properly. ❑ *The US is trying to neutralize the resolution in the UN Security Council... The intruder smashed a window to get in and then neutralized the alarm system.* VERB V n V n ♦ **neu|trali|za|tion** /njuːtrəlaɪzeɪʃən, AM nuːt-/ *...the sale or neutralization of the suspected nuclear site.* N-UNCOUNT: usu N *of* n 2 When a chemical substance **neutralizes** an acid, it makes it less acid. ❑ *Antacids are alkaline and they relieve pain by neutralizing acid in the contents of the stomach.* VERB V n

**neu|tron** /njuːtrɒn, AM nuːt-/ **(neutrons)** A **neutron** is an atomic particle that has no electrical charge. ❑ *Each atomic cluster is made up of neutrons and protons.* N-COUNT

**neu|tron bomb** **(neutron bombs)** A **neutron bomb** is a nuclear weapon that is designed to kill people and animals without a large explosion and without destroying buildings or causing serious radioactive pollution. N-COUNT

**neu|tron star** **(neutron stars)** A **neutron star** is a star that has collapsed under the weight of its own gravity. N-COUNT

**nev|er** /nevəʳ/ ◆◆◆ 1 **Never** means at no time in the past or at no time in the future. ❑ *I have never lost the weight I put on in my teens... Never had he been so free of worry... That was a mistake. We'll never do it again... Never say that. Never, do you hear?... He was never really healthy... This is never to happen again.* ADV: ADV before v, ADV group/ to-inf 2 **Never** means 'not in any circumstances at all'. ❑ *I would never do anything to hurt him... Even if you are desperate to get married, never let it show... Divorce is never easy for children... The golden rule is never to clean a valuable coin.* ADV: ADV before v, ADV group/ to-inf
3 **Never ever** is an emphatic way of saying 'never'. ❑ *I never, ever sit around thinking, 'What shall I do next?'... He's vowed never ever to talk about anything personal in public, ever again.* PHRASE: PHR before v, *be* PHR group [emphasis] 4 **Never** is used to refer to the past and means 'not'. ❑ *He never achieved anything... He waited until all the luggage was cleared, but Paula's never appeared... I never knew the lad... I'd never have dreamt of doing such a thing.* ADV 5 You say **'never!'** to indicate how surprised or shocked you are by something that someone has just said. [SPOKEN] EXCLAM [feelings] 6 You say **'Well, I never'** to indicate that you are very surprised about something that you have just seen or found out. [OLD-FASHIONED, SPOKEN] ❑ *'What were you up to there?' — 'I was head of the information department.' — 'Well I never!'* EXCLAM [feelings] 7 If you say that something **will never do** or **would never do**, you are saying, often humorously, that you think it is not appropriate or not suitable in some way. ❑ *It would never do to have Henry there in her apartment... I don't think it is an example of bad writing myself, otherwise I'd be agreeing with Leavis, and that would never do.* PHRASE: oft *it* PHR to-inf
8 **never mind** → see **mind**.

**never-ending** If you describe something bad or unpleasant as **never-ending**, you are emphasizing that it seems to last a very long time. ❑ *...a never-ending series of scandals.* ADJ [emphasis] = *interminable*

**never-never land** **Never-never land** is an imaginary place where everything is perfect and no-one has any problems. [INFORMAL] ❑ *We became suspended in some stately never-never land of pleasure, luxury and idleness.* N-UNCOUNT: also *a* N

**never|the|less** /nevəʳðəles/ ◆◇◇ You use **nevertheless** when saying something that contrasts with what has just been said. [FORMAL] ADV: ADV with cl = *nonetheless*

❑ *Most marriages fail after between five and nine years. Nevertheless, people continue to get married.*

**new** /njuː, AM nuː/ **(newer, newest)** ◆◆◆ 1 Something that is **new** has been recently created, built, or invented or is in the process of being created, built, or invented. ❑ *They've just opened a new hotel in the Stoke area... The new invention ensures the beer keeps a full, frothy head. ...the introduction of new drugs to suppress the immune system... Their epic fight is the subject of a new film... These ideas are nothing new in America.* ♦ **new|ness** *The board acknowledges problems which arise from the newness of the approach.* 2 Something that is **new** has not been used or owned by anyone. ❑ *That afternoon she went out and bought a new dress... There are many boats, new and used, for sale... They cost nine pounds new, three pounds secondhand.* 3 You use **new** to describe something which has replaced another thing, for example because you no longer have the old one, or it no longer exists, or it is no longer useful. ❑ *Under the new rules, some factories will cut emissions by as much as 90 percent... I had been in my new job only a few days... I had to find somewhere new to live... Rachel has a new boyfriend... They told me I needed a new battery.* 4 **New** is used to describe something that has only recently been discovered or noticed. ❑ *The new planet is about ten times the size of the earth.* 5 A **new** day or year is the beginning of the next day or year. ❑ *The start of a new year is a good time to reflect on the many achievements of the past.* 6 **New** is used to describe someone or something that has recently acquired a particular status or position. ❑ *...the usual exhaustion of a new mother... The Association gives a free handbook to all new members.* 7 If you are **new to** a situation or place, or if the situation or place is **new to** you, you have not previously seen it or had any experience of it. ❑ *She wasn't new to the company... His name was new to me then and it stayed in my mind... I'm new here and all I did was follow orders.* 8 **New** potatoes, carrots, or peas are produced early in the season for such vegetables and are usually small with a sweet flavour. 9 ➔ See also **brand-new**. **as good as new** ➔ see **good**. to **turn over a new leaf** ➔ see **leaf**. **a new lease of life** ➔ see **lease**. **pastures new** ➔ see **pasture**.

ADJ | N-UNCOUNT | ADJ | ADJ | ADJ: usu ADJ n | ADJ: ADJ n | ADJ: ADJ n | ADJ: v-link ADJ, oft ADJ *to* n | ADJ: ADJ n

**new-** /njuː-, AM nuː-/ **New-** combines with the past participle of some verbs to form adjectives which indicate that an action has been done or completed very recently. ❑ *He loved the smell of new-mown grass... Gerald treasures his new-won independence.* — COMB in ADJ: usu ADJ n

**New Age** **New Age** is used to describe spiritual or non-scientific activities such as meditation, astrology, and alternative medicine, or people who are connected with such activities. ❑ *She was involved in many New Age activities such as yoga and healing.* — ADJ: usu ADJ n

**New Age trav|el|ler** **(New Age travellers)** **New Age travellers** are people who live in tents and vehicles and travel from place to place, and who reject many of the values of modern society. [BRIT] — N-COUNT: usu pl

**new|bie** /njuːbi, AM nuːbi/ **(newbies)** A **newbie** is someone who is new to an activity, especially in computing or on the Internet. ❑ *All newbies are offered an individually tailored training and development programme.* — N-COUNT

**new blood** If people talk about bringing **new blood** into an organization or sports team, they are referring to new people who are likely to improve the organization or team. ❑ *That's what we need, some new blood in the team.* — N-UNCOUNT

**new|born** /njuːbɔːʳn, AM nuː-/ **(newborns)** also **new-born, new born.** A **newborn** baby or animal is one that has just been born. ❑ *This equipment has saved the lives of a number of new born children. ...new born lambs.* ♦ **The newborn** are babies or animals who are newborn. ❑ *Mild jaundice in the newborn is common and often clears without treatment.* — ADJ: usu ADJ n | N-PLURAL: *the* N

**new broom** **(new brooms)** Someone who has just started a new job and who is expected to make a lot of changes can be referred to as a **new broom**. [JOURNALISM] ❑ *The company seemed set to make a fresh start under a new broom.* — N-COUNT: usu sing

**new|comer** /njuːkʌməʳ, AM nuː-/ **(newcomers)** A **newcomer** is a person who has recently arrived in a place, joined an organization, or started a new activity. ❑ *He must be a newcomer to town and he obviously didn't understand our local customs... The candidates are both relative newcomers to politics.* — N-COUNT

**new face** **(new faces)** Someone who is new in a particular public role can be referred to as a **new face**. [JOURNALISM] ❑ *All together there are six new faces in the cabinet.* — N-COUNT

**new-fangled** /njuː fæŋgᵊld, AM nuː -/ also **newfangled.** If someone describes a new idea or a new piece of equipment as **new-fangled**, they mean that it is too complicated or is unnecessary. [OLD-FASHIONED] ❑ *Mr Goss does not believe in any of this 'new-fangled nonsense' about lean meat. ...a newfangled tax structure.* — ADJ: ADJ n | disapproval

**new-found** also **newfound.** A **new-found** quality or ability is one that you have got recently. ❑ *Juliana was brimming over with new-found confidence... The fall of the Ceausescu government brought newfound freedom to millions in Romania.* — ADJ: ADJ n

**new|ly** /njuːli, AM nuːli/ **Newly** is used before a past participle or an adjective to indicate that a particular action is very recent, or that a particular state of affairs has very recently begun to exist. ❑ *She was young at the time, and newly married. ...the newly independent countries of Africa and Asia.* — ◆◇◇ ADV: ADV -ed/adj = *recently*

**newly|wed** /njuːliwed, AM nuː-/ **(newlyweds)** also **newly-wed. Newlyweds** are a man and woman who have very recently got married to each other. ❑ *Lavalais raised his glass to propose a toast to the newlyweds.* — N-COUNT: usu pl

**new man** **(new men)** A **new man** is a man who has modern ideas about the relations between men and women, and believes that men should share the work of looking after the home and caring for the children. [mainly BRIT] ❑ *Sarah says I only change nappies when we have visitors. It is easy to be a new man in public; in private it's hard work.* — N-COUNT

**new moon** **(new moons)** A **new moon** is the moon when it first appears as a thin curved shape at the start of its four-week cycle. **The new moon** is also the time of the month when the moon appears in this way. ❑ *...the pale crescent of a new moon... The new moon was the occasion of festivals of rejoicing in Egypt.* — N-COUNT: usu sing

**news** /njuːz, AM nuːz/ 1 **News** is information about a recently changed situation or a recent event. ❑ *We waited and waited for news of him... They still haven't had any news about when they'll be able to go home... I wish I had better news for you... He's thrilled to bits at the news.* 2 **News** is information that is published in newspapers and broadcast on radio and television about recent events in the country or world or in a particular area of activity. ❑ *Foreign News is on Page 16... We'll also have the latest sports news... The announcement was made at a news conference... Those are some of the top stories in the news.* 3 **The news** is a television or radio broadcast which consists of information about recent events in the country or the world. ❑ *I heard all about the bombs on the news. ...the six o'clock news.* 4 If you say that someone or something is **news**, you mean that they are considered to be interesting and important at the moment, and that people want to hear about them on the radio and television and in newspapers. [INFORMAL] ❑ *A murder was big news... If you are a celebrity, you are headline news.*

◆◆◆ N-UNCOUNT: oft N prep | N-UNCOUNT: also *the* N | N-SING: *the* N | N-UNCOUNT: usu supp N

**PHRASES** [5] If you say that something is **bad news**, you mean that it will cause you trouble or problems. If you say that something is **good news**, you mean that it will be useful or helpful to you. ❑ *The drop in travel is bad news for the airline industry... This new attitude is good news to AIDS activists.* PHRASE: usu v-link PHR, usu PHR *for/to* n [6] If you say that something **is news to** you, you mean that you did not previously know what you have just been told, especially when you are surprised or annoyed about it. ❑ *I'd certainly tell you if I knew anything, but I don't. What you're saying is news to me.* PHRASE: V inflects, PHR n

**news agen|cy** **(news agencies)** A **news agency** is an organization that gathers news stories from a particular country or from all over the world and supplies them to journalists. ❑ *A correspondent for Reuters news agency says he saw a number of demonstrators being beaten.* ◆◇◇ N-COUNT

**news|agent** /njuːzeɪdʒᵊnt, AM nuːz-/ **(newsagents)** [1] A **newsagent** or a **newsagent's** is a shop that sells newspapers and magazines, and things such as cigarettes and sweets. [BRIT] N-COUNT: oft *the* N [2] A **newsagent** is a shopkeeper who sells newspapers and magazines, and things such as cigarettes and sweets. [BRIT] N-COUNT

**news|cast** /njuːzkɑːst, AM nuːzkæst/ **(newscasts)** A **newscast** is a news programme that is broadcast on the radio or on television. [mainly AM] N-COUNT

**news|caster** /njuːzkɑːstəʳ, AM nuːzkæstəʳ/ **(newscasters)** A **newscaster** is a person who reads the news on the radio or on television. N-COUNT = newsreader

**news con|fer|ence** **(news conferences)** A **news conference** is a meeting held by a famous or important person in which they answer journalists' questions. N-COUNT = press conference

**news|flash** /njuːzflæʃ, AM nuːz-/ **(newsflashes)** also **news flash.** A **newsflash** is an important item of news that television or radio companies broadcast as soon as they receive it, often interrupting other programmes to do so. ❑ *We interrupt our programmes for a newsflash.* N-COUNT

**news|group** /njuːzgruːp, AM nuːz-/ **(newsgroups)** A **newsgroup** is an Internet site where people can put information and opinions about a particular subject so they can be read by everyone who looks at the site. N-COUNT

**news|letter** /njuːzletəʳ, AM nuːz-/ **(newsletters)** also **news letter.** A **newsletter** is one or more printed sheets of paper containing information about an organization that is sent regularly to its members. ❑ *The organization now has around 18,000 members who receive a quarterly newsletter.* N-COUNT = bulletin

**news|man** /njuːzmən, AM nuːz-/ **(newsmen)** A **newsman** is a journalist for a newspaper or for a television or radio news programme. [JOURNALISM] N-COUNT

**news|paper** /njuːspeɪpəʳ, AM nuːz-/ **(newspapers)** [1] A **newspaper** is a publication consisting of a number of large sheets of folded paper, on which news, advertisements, and other information is printed. ❑ *He was carrying a newspaper... They read their daughter's allegations in the newspaper. ...a Sunday newspaper feature about AIDS in America.* ◆◆◇ N-COUNT [2] A **newspaper** is an organization that produces a newspaper. ❑ *It is Britain's fastest growing national daily newspaper... Alexander Lazarus is a food critic for the newspaper.* N-COUNT [3] **Newspaper** consists of pieces of old newspapers, especially when they are being used for another purpose such as wrapping things up. ❑ *He found two pots, each wrapped in newspaper.* N-UNCOUNT

**news|paper|man** /njuːspeɪpəʳmæn, AM nuːz-/ **(newspapermen)** A **newspaperman** is a journalist, especially a man, who works for a newspaper. [JOURNALISM] N-COUNT = newsman

**news|print** /njuːzprɪnt, AM nuːz-/ [1] **Newsprint** is the cheap, fairly rough paper on which newspapers are printed. N-UNCOUNT [2] **Newsprint** is the text that is printed in newspapers. ❑ *...the acres of newsprint devoted to celebrities' personal lives.* N-UNCOUNT [3] **Newsprint** is the ink which is used to print newspapers and magazines. ❑ *They get their hands covered in newsprint.* N-UNCOUNT

**news|read|er** /njuːzriːdəʳ, AM nuːz-/ **(newsreaders)** A **newsreader** is a person who reads the news on the radio or on television. [BRIT] N-COUNT

☑ in AM, use **newscaster**

**news|reel** /njuːzriːl, AM nuːz-/ **(newsreels)** A **newsreel** is a short film of national or international news events. In the past newsreels were made for showing in cinemas. N-COUNT: oft N n

**news re|lease** **(news releases)** A **news release** is a written statement about a matter of public interest which is given to the press by an organization concerned with the matter. [mainly AM] ❑ *In a news release, the company said it had experienced severe financial problems.* N-COUNT

☑ in BRIT, use **press release**

**news|room** /njuːzruːm, AM nuːz-/ **(newsrooms)** A **newsroom** is an office in a newspaper, radio, or television organization where news reports are prepared before they are printed or broadcast. N-COUNT

**news-sheet** **(news-sheets)** A **news-sheet** is a small newspaper that is usually printed and distributed in small quantities by a local political or social organization. N-COUNT

**news|stand** /njuːzstænd, AM nuːz-/ **(newsstands)** also **news-stand.** A **newsstand** is a stall in the street or a public place, which sells newspapers and magazines. ❑ *Eight new national newspapers have appeared on the newsstands since 1981.* N-COUNT

**news|worthy** /njuːzwɜːʳði, AM nuːz-/ An event, fact, or person that is **newsworthy**, is considered to be interesting enough to be reported in newspapers or on the radio or television. ❑ *The number of deaths makes the story newsworthy.* ADJ

**newt** /njuːt, AM nuːt/ **(newts)** A **newt** is a small creature that has four legs and a long tail and can live on land and in water. N-COUNT

**New Tes|ta|ment** **The New Testament** is the part of the Bible that deals with the life and teachings of Jesus Christ and with Christianity in the early Church. N-PROPER: *the* N

**new town** **(new towns)** A **new town** is a town that has been planned and built as a single project, including houses, shops, and factories, rather than one that has developed gradually. [mainly BRIT] ❑ *...Basildon New Town.* N-COUNT: oft in names

**new wave** **(new waves)** In the arts or in politics, a **new wave** is a group or movement that deliberately introduces new or unconventional ideas instead of using traditional ones. ❑ *...the new wave of satirical comedy. ...New Wave music.* N-COUNT

**New World** **The New World** is used to refer to the continents of North and South America. ❑ *...the massive growth in imports of good wines from the New World and Australasia.* N-PROPER: *the* N

**New Year** [1] **New Year** or **the New Year** is the time when people celebrate the start of a year. ❑ *Happy New Year, everyone... The restaurant was closed over the New Year... He returned home each year to celebrate Christmas and New Year with his family.* N-UNCOUNT: also *the* N [2] **The New Year** is the first few weeks of a year. ❑ *Isabel was expecting their baby in the New Year... The oil shortages could lead the government to raise prices before the New Year.* N-SING: *the* N

**New Year's** **New Year's** is another name for **New Year's Day** or **New Year's Eve**. [AM] N-UNCOUNT

**New Year's Day** **New Year's Day** is the first day of the year. In Western countries this is the 1st of January. ❑ *On New Year's Day in 1974, I started keeping a journal.* N-UNCOUNT

**New Year's Eve** **New Year's Eve** is the last day of the year, the day before New Year's Day. ❑ *On New Year's Eve I usually give a party, which is always chaotic.* N-UNCOUNT

**New Year's reso|lu|tion (New Year's resolutions)** also **New Year resolution.** If you make a **New Year's resolution**, you make a decision at the beginning of a year to start doing something or to stop doing something. ❑ *She made a New Year's resolution to get fit.* N-COUNT

**New Zea|land|er** /njuː ziːləndəʳ, AM nuː -/ **(New Zealanders)** A **New Zealander** is a citizen of New Zealand, or a person of New Zealand origin. N-COUNT

**next** /nekst/ ◆◆◆ [1] The **next** period of time, event, person, or thing is the one that comes immediately after the present one or after the previous one. ❑ *I got up early the next morning. ...the next available flight... Who will be the next prime minister?... I want my next child born at home... Many senior citizens have very few visitors from one week to the next.* ORD [2] You use **next** in expressions such as **next Friday**, **next day** and **next year** to refer, for example, to the first Friday, day, or year that comes after the present or previous one. ❑ *Let's plan a big night next week... He retires next January... Next day the EU summit strengthened their ultimatum.* DET ♦ **Next** is also an adjective. ❑ *I shall be 26 years old on Friday next.* ADJ: n ADJ ♦ **Next** is also a pronoun. ❑ *He predicted that the region's economy would grow by about six per cent both this year and next.* PRON [3] **The next** place or person is the one that is nearest to you or that is the first one that you come to. ❑ *Grace sighed so heavily that Trish could hear it in the next room... The man in the next chair was asleep... Stop at the next corner. I'm getting out.* ADJ: det ADJ [4] The thing that happens **next** is the thing that happens immediately after something else. ❑ *Next, close your eyes then screw them up tight... I don't know what to do next... The news is next.* ADV: ADV with cl, ADV after v, *be* ADV [5] When you **next** do something, you do it for the first time since you last did it. ❑ *I next saw him at his house in Berkshire... When we next met, he was much more jovial.* ADV: ADV before v [6] You use **next** to say that something has more of a particular quality than all other things except one. For example, the thing that is **next** best is the one that is the best except for one other thing. ❑ *The one thing he didn't have was a son. I think he's felt that a grandson is the next best thing... At least three times more daffodils are grown than in Holland, the next largest grower.* ADV: ADV adj-superl = *second*

**PHRASES** [7] You use **after next** in expressions such as **the week after next** to refer to a period of time after the next one. For example, when it is May, the month after next is July. ❑ *...the party's annual conference, to be held in Bournemouth the week after next.* PHRASE: n PHR [8] If you say that you do something or experience something as much **as the next** person, you mean that you are no different from anyone else in the respect mentioned. ❑ *I'm as ambitious as the next man. I'd like to manage at the very highest level.* PHRASE: *as* group PHR [emphasis] [9] If one thing is **next to** another thing, it is at the other side of it. ❑ *She sat down next to him on the sofa. ...at the southern end of the Gaza Strip next to the Egyptian border... The car was parked in the small weedy lot next to the hotel.* PREP-PHRASE = *beside* [10] You use **next to** in order to give the most important aspect of something when comparing it with another aspect. ❑ *Her children were the number two priority in her life next to her career.* PREP-PHRASE = *after* [11] You use **next to** before a negative, or a word that suggests something negative, to mean almost, but not completely. ❑ *Johnson still knew next to nothing about tobacco... Most pre-prepared weight loss products are next to useless.* PHRASE: PHR after v, v-link PHR, PHR *nothing*/adj = *virtually*

**next door**

✔ The adjective is also spelled **next-door**.

[1] If a room or building is **next door**, it is the next one to the right or left. ❑ *I went next door to the bathroom... She was next door at the time. ...the old lady who lived next door... The flat next door was empty.* ADV: ADV after v, *be* ADV, n ADV ♦ **Next door** is also an adjective. ❑ *She wandered back into the next door room... The wires trailed through other parts of the HQ into a next door building.* ADJ: ADJ n ♦ If a room or building is **next door to** another one, it is the next one to the left or right. PREP-PHRASE ❑ *The kitchen is right next door to the dining room.* [2] The people **next door** are the people who live in the house or flat to the right or left of yours. ❑ *The neighbors thought the family next door had moved.* ADV: n ADV ♦ **Next door** is also an adjective. ❑ *Our next door neighbour knocked on the door to say that our car had been stolen.* ADJ: ADJ n [3] If you refer to someone as **the boy next door** or **the girl next door**, you mean that they are pleasant and respectable but rather dull. ❑ *She was the girl-next-door type.* PHRASE

**next door's** You can use **next door's** to indicate that something belongs to the person or people who live in the house to the right or left of your own. ❑ *...next door's dog.* DET

**next of kin** **Next of kin** is sometimes used to refer to the person who is your closest relative, especially in official or legal documents. [FORMAL] ❑ *We have notified the next of kin.* N-UNCOUNT-COLL

**nex|us** /neksəs/ **(nexus)** A **nexus** is a connection or series of connections within a particular situation or system. [FORMAL] ❑ *...the nexus between the dominant class and the State.* N-COUNT: usu with supp

**NGO** /en dʒiː oʊ/ **(NGOs)** An **NGO** is an organization which is not run by the government. **NGO** is an abbreviation for 'non-governmental organization'. N-COUNT

**NHS** /en eɪt ʃes/ ◆◇◇ **NHS** is an abbreviation for **National Health Service.** ❑ *This vaccine is not normally provided free under the NHS. ...NHS patients.* N-SING: *the* N, N n

**nia|cin** /naɪəsɪn/ **Niacin** is a vitamin that occurs in milk, liver, yeast, and some other foods. N-UNCOUNT

**nib** /nɪb/ **(nibs)** A **nib** is a pointed piece of metal at the end of some pens, which controls the flow of ink as you write. N-COUNT

**nib|ble** /nɪbᵊl/ **(nibbles, nibbling, nibbled)** [1] If you **nibble** food, you eat it by biting very small pieces of it, for example because you are not very hungry. ❑ *Michael started to nibble his biscuit... She nibbled at the corner of a piece of dry toast.* VERB V n V *at/on* n Also V ♦ **Nibble** is also a noun. ❑ *We each took a nibble.* N-COUNT [2] If you **nibble** something, you bite it very gently. ❑ *John found he was kissing and nibbling her ear... Daniel Winter nibbled on his pen.* VERB V n V *on/at* n [3] When an animal **nibbles** something, it takes small bites of it quickly and repeatedly. ❑ *A herd of goats was nibbling the turf around the base of the tower... The birds cling to the wall and nibble at the brickwork.* VERB V n V *at/on* n Also V ♦ **Nibble away** means the same as **nibble.** ❑ *The rabbits nibbled away on the herbaceous plants.* PHRASAL VERB V P *on/at* n [4] If one thing **nibbles at** another, it gradually affects, harms, or destroys it. ❑ *...how best to compete with the overseas nations nibbling at our traditional markets.* VERB V *at* n ♦ **Nibble away** means the same as **nibble.** ❑ *Several manufacturers are also nibbling away at Ford's traditional customer base.* PHRASAL VERB V P *at* n [5] **Nibbles** are small snacks such as biscuits, crisps, and nuts that are often offered to you at parties. [mainly BRIT] ❑ *...crisps, nuts, and other nibbles.* N-COUNT: usu pl

**ni|cad** /naɪkæd/ also **ni-cad.** A **nicad** battery is a battery made from a combination of nickel and cadmium. ADJ

**nice** /naɪs/ ◆◆◇ **(nicer, nicest)** [1] If you say that something is **nice**, you mean that you find it attractive, pleasant, or enjoyable. ❑ *I think silk ties can be quite nice... It's nice to be here together again... We had a nice meal with a bottle of champagne.* ADJ: oft *it* v-link ADJ to-inf ♦ **nice|ly** *He's just written a book, nicely illustrated and not too technical.* ADV: ADV after v, ADV -ed/adj [2] If you say that it is **nice of** someone to say or do something, you are saying that they are being kind and thoughtful. This is often used as a way of thanking someone. ❑ *It's awfully nice of you to come all this way to see me... 'How are your boys?' — 'How nice of you to ask.'.* ADJ: *it* v-link ADJ *of* n to-inf, v-link ADJ *of* n = *kind* [3] If you say that someone is **nice**, you mean that you like them because they are friendly and pleasant. ❑ *He was a nice fellow, very quiet and courteous.* ADJ ≠ *unpleasant* ♦ **nice|ness** *Mr Pearce was rather bowled over by his niceness, his concern and his ordinariness.* N-UNCOUNT [4] If you are **nice to** people, you are friendly, pleasant, or polite towards them. ❑ *She met Mr and Mrs* ADJ: v-link ADJ, oft ADJ *to* n

*Ricciardi, who were very nice to her.* ♦ **nice|ly** *He treated you very nicely and acted like a decent guy.* ADV: ADV after v [5] When the weather is **nice**, it is warm and pleasant. ❑ *He nodded to us and said, 'Nice weather we're having.'* ADJ [6] You can use **nice** to emphasize a particular quality that you like. ❑ *With a nice dark colour, the wine is medium to full bodied... Add the oats to thicken the mixture and stir until it is nice and creamy.* ADJ: ADJ adj n, v-link ADJ *and* adj, ADJ *and* adv after v [emphasis] [7] A **nice** point or distinction is very clear, precise, and based on good reasoning. [FORMAL] ❑ *Those are nice academic arguments, but what about the immediate future?* ♦ **nice|ly** *I think this puts the problem very nicely.* ADJ; ADV: ADV after v [8] You can use **nice** when you are greeting people. For example, you can say **'Nice to meet you'**, **'Nice to have met you'**, or **'Nice to see you'**. ❑ *Good morning. Nice to meet you and thanks for being with us this weekend... 'It's so nice to see you,' said Charles.* ADJ: *it* v-link ADJ to-inf [formulae] [9] ➔ See also **nicely**.

**nice-looking** Someone who is **nice-looking** is physically attractive. ❑ *I saw this nice-looking man in a gray suit... We got on very well and she was very nice-looking.* ADJ = good-looking

**nice|ly** /naɪsli/ [1] If something is happening or working **nicely**, it is happening or working in a satisfactory way or in the way that you want it to. ❑ *She has a bit of private money, so they manage quite nicely... The crowds had been soaked and were now nicely drying out.* ➔ See also **nice**. ADV: ADV with v

PHRASES [2] If someone or something **is doing nicely**, they are being successful. ❑ *...another hotel owner who is doing very nicely.* PHRASE: V inflects, usu cont [3] If you say that something will **do nicely**, you mean that it is good enough for the situation. ❑ *A shirt and jersey and an ordinary pair of trousers will do nicely, thank you.* PHRASE: V inflects

**ni|cety** /naɪsɪti/ **(niceties) The niceties of** a situation are its details, especially with regard to good manners or the appropriate behaviour for that situation. ❑ *By the end of term, girls will have learnt the niceties of dinner party conversation... He wasted no time with social niceties.* N-COUNT: usu pl, oft *the* N *of* n, adj N

**niche** /niːʃ, AM nɪtʃ/ **(niches)** [1] A **niche** in the market is a specific area of marketing which has its own particular requirements, customers, and products. [BUSINESS] ❑ *I think we have found a niche in the toy market.* N-COUNT: usu with supp [2] **Niche** marketing is the practice of dividing the market into specialized areas for which particular products are made. A **niche** market is one of these specialized areas. [BUSINESS] ❑ *Many media experts see such all-news channels as part of a general move towards niche marketing... The Japanese are able to supply niche markets because of their flexible production methods.* ADJ: ADJ n [3] A **niche** is a hollow area in a wall which has been made to hold a statue, or a natural hollow part in a hill or cliff. ❑ *Above him, in a niche on the wall, sat a tiny veiled Ganesh, the elephant god... There was a niche in the rock where the path ended.* N-COUNT [4] Your **niche** is the job or activity which is exactly suitable for you. ❑ *Simon Lane quickly found his niche as a busy freelance model maker.* N-COUNT: usu poss N

**nick** /nɪk/ **(nicks, nicking, nicked)** [1] If someone **nicks** something, they steal it. [BRIT, INFORMAL] ❑ *He smashed a window to get in and nicked a load of silver cups.* VERB = pinch V n [2] If the police **nick** someone, they arrest them. [BRIT, INFORMAL] ❑ *The police nicked me for carrying an offensive weapon... Keep quiet or we'll all get nicked.* VERB V n *get/be* V-ed [3] If you **nick** something or **nick** yourself, you accidentally make a small cut in the surface of the object or your skin. ❑ *When I pulled out of the space, I nicked the rear bumper of the car in front of me... He dropped a bottle in the kitchen and nicked himself on broken glass.* VERB V n V pron-refl [4] A **nick** is a small cut made in the surface of something, usually in someone's skin. ❑ *The barbed wire had left only the tiniest nick just below my right eye.* N-COUNT [5] If you **are nicked** by someone, they cheat you, for example by charging you too much money. [AM, INFORMAL] ❑ *College students already are being nicked, but probably don't realize it.* VERB = rip off *be* V-ed

PHRASES [6] **Nick** is used in expressions such as **'in good nick'** or **'in bad nick'** to describe the physical condition of someone or something. [BRIT, INFORMAL] ❑ *His ribs were damaged, but other than that he's in good nick... Tom's house is actually in better nick than mine.* PHRASE: v-link PHR [7] If you say that something happens **in the nick of time**, you are emphasizing that it happens at the last possible moment. ❑ *Seems we got here just in the nick of time.* PHRASE: usu PHR after v [emphasis] = just in time

**nick|el** /nɪkᵊl/ **(nickels)** [1] **Nickel** is a silver-coloured metal that is used in making steel. N-UNCOUNT [2] In the United States and Canada, a **nickel** is a coin worth five cents. N-COUNT

**nick|name** /nɪkneɪm/ **(nicknames, nicknaming, nicknamed)** [1] A **nickname** is an informal name for someone or something. ❑ *Red got his nickname for his red hair.* N-COUNT [2] If you **nickname** someone or something, you give them an informal name. ❑ *When he got older I nicknamed him Little Alf... Which newspaper was once nicknamed The Thunderer?* VERB V n n *be* V-ed n

**nico|tine** /nɪkətiːn/ **Nicotine** is the substance in tobacco that people can become addicted to. ❑ *Nicotine marks stained his chin and fingers.* N-UNCOUNT

**niece** /niːs/ **(nieces)** Someone's **niece** is the daughter of their sister or brother. ❑ *...his niece from America, the daughter of his eldest sister.* N-COUNT: oft poss N

**nif|ty** /nɪfti/ **(niftier, niftiest)** If you describe something as **nifty**, you think it is neat and pleasing or cleverly done. [INFORMAL] ❑ *Bridgeport was a pretty nifty place... It was a nifty arrangement, a perfect partnership.* ADJ: usu ADJ n [approval]

**Ni|gerian** /naɪdʒɪəriən/ **(Nigerians)** [1] **Nigerian** means belonging or relating to Nigeria, its people, or its culture. ADJ [2] A **Nigerian** is a Nigerian citizen, or a person of Nigerian origin. N-COUNT

**nig|gard|ly** /nɪgəʳdli/ If you describe someone as **niggardly**, you are criticizing them because they do not give or provide much of something. ❑ *Officials say the EU, which is supposed to provide most of the food needs, is being particularly niggardly. ...a niggardly supply of hot water.* ADJ [disapproval] ≠ generous

**nig|ger** /nɪgəʳ/ **(niggers) Nigger** is an extremely offensive word for a black person. [⚠ VERY OFFENSIVE] N-COUNT

**nig|gle** /nɪgᵊl/ **(niggles, niggling, niggled)** [1] If something **niggles** you, it causes you to worry slightly over a long period of time. [mainly BRIT] ❑ *I realise now that the things which used to niggle and annoy me just don't really matter... It's been niggling at my mind ever since I met Neville in Nice... The puzzle niggled away in Arnold's mind.* ♦ **Niggle** is also a noun. ❑ *So why is there a little niggle at the back of my mind?* VERB V n V *at* n V *away* Also V N-COUNT [2] If someone **niggles** you, they annoy you by continually criticizing you for what you think are small or unimportant things. [mainly BRIT] ❑ *I don't react anymore when opponents try to niggle me... You tend to niggle at your partner, and get hurt when he doesn't hug you.* ♦ **Niggle** is also a noun. ❑ *The life we have built together is more important than any minor niggle either of us might have.* VERB V n V *at* n N-COUNT

**nig|gling** /nɪgəlɪŋ/ A **niggling** injury or worry is small but bothers you over a long period of time. ❑ *Both players have been suffering from niggling injuries. ...a niggling worry that the cheap car is also the one that will cause endless trouble.* ADJ: usu ADJ n

**nigh** /naɪ/ [1] If an event **is nigh**, it will happen very soon. [OLD-FASHIONED] ❑ *The end of the world may be nigh, but do we really care?* ➔ See also **well-nigh**. ADV: *be* ADV [2] **Nigh on** an amount, number, or age means almost that amount, number, or age. [OLD-FASHIONED] ❑ *I had to pay nigh on forty pounds for it.* PHRASE: PHR amount = nearly

**night** /naɪt/ **(nights)** [1] The **night** is the part of each day when the sun has set and it is dark outside, especially the time when people are sleeping. ❑ *He didn't sleep a wink all night... The fighting began in the late afternoon and continued all night... Our reporter spent the night crossing the border from Austria into Slovenia... Finally night fell.* ◆◆◆ N-VAR

[2] The **night** is the period of time between the end of the afternoon and the time that you go to bed, especially the time when you relax before going to bed. ❑ *So whose party was it last night?... Demiris took Catherine to dinner the following night.* N-COUNT

[3] A particular **night** is a particular evening when a special event takes place, such as a show or a play. ❑ *The first night crowd packed the building. ...election night.* N-COUNT: supp N

PHRASES [4] If it is a particular time **at night**, it is during the time when it is dark and is before midnight. ❑ *It's eleven o'clock at night in Moscow... He works obsessively from 7.15 am to 9 or 10 at night.* PHRASE: num PHR

[5] If something happens **at night**, it happens regularly during the evening or night. ❑ *He was going to college at night, in order to become an accountant... The veranda was equipped with heavy wooden rain doors that were kept closed at night.* PHRASE: PHR after v

[6] If something happens **day and night** or **night and day**, it happens all the time without stopping. ❑ *Dozens of doctors and nurses have been working day and night for weeks... He was at my door night and day, demanding my attention.* PHRASE: usu PHR after v

[7] If you have **an early night**, you go to bed early. If you have **a late night**, you go to bed late. ❑ *I've had a hell of a day, and all I want is an early night... In spite of the travelling and the late night, she did not feel tired.* PHRASE: N inflects

[8] **morning, noon and night** → see **morning**.

**night|cap** /naɪtkæp/ **(nightcaps)** A **nightcap** is a drink that you have just before you go to bed, usually an alcoholic drink. ❑ *Perhaps you would join me for a nightcap?* N-COUNT

**night|clothes** /naɪtkloʊðz/ **Nightclothes** are clothes that you wear in bed. N-PLURAL

**night|club** /naɪtklʌb/ **(nightclubs)** also **night club.** A **nightclub** is a place where people go late in the evening to drink and dance. N-COUNT

**night|club|bing** /naɪtklʌbɪŋ/ **Nightclubbing** is the activity of going to nightclubs. N-UNCOUNT

**night|dress** /naɪtdres/ **(nightdresses)** A **nightdress** is a sort of loose dress that a woman or girl wears in bed. [BRIT] N-COUNT

☑ in AM, use **nightgown**

**night|fall** /naɪtfɔːl/ **Nightfall** is the time of day when it starts to get dark. ❑ *I need to get to Lyon by nightfall.* N-UNCOUNT = dusk

**night|gown** /naɪtgaʊn/ **(nightgowns)** A **nightgown** is the same as a **nightdress.** [AM] N-COUNT

**nightie** /naɪti/ **(nighties)** A **nightie** is the same as a nightdress or nightgown. [INFORMAL] N-COUNT

**night|in|gale** /naɪtɪŋgeɪl, AM -tᵊn-/ **(nightingales)** A **nightingale** is a small brown bird. The male, which can be heard at night, sings beautifully. N-COUNT

**night|life** /naɪtlaɪf/ also **night-life. Nightlife** is all the entertainment and social activities that are available at night in towns and cities, such as nightclubs and theatres. ❑ *...Hamburg's energetic nightlife... There are free buses around the resort and plenty of nightlife.* N-UNCOUNT

**night light (night lights)** A **night light** is a light that is not bright and is kept on during the night, especially in a child's room. N-COUNT

**night|ly** /naɪtli/ A **nightly** event happens every night. ❑ *I'm sure we watched the nightly news, and then we turned on the movie... For months at a time, air raids were a nightly occurrence.* ♦ **Nightly** is also an adverb. ❑ *She appears nightly on the television news.* ADJ: ADJ n / ADV: usu ADV after v

**night|mare** /naɪtmeəʳ/ **(nightmares)** [1] A **nightmare** is a very frightening dream. ❑ *All the victims still suffered nightmares... Jane did not eat cheese because it gives her nightmares.* ◆◇◇ N-COUNT

[2] If you refer to a situation as a **nightmare**, you mean that it is very frightening and unpleasant. ❑ *The years in prison were a nightmare.* N-COUNT

[3] If you refer to a situation as a **nightmare**, you are saying in a very emphatic way that it is irritating because it causes you a lot of trouble. ❑ *Taking my son Peter to a restaurant was a nightmare... In practice a graduate tax is an administrative nightmare.* N-COUNT emphasis

**night|mare sce|nario (nightmare scenarios)** If you describe a situation or event as **a nightmare scenario**, you mean that it is the worst possible thing that could happen. ❑ *Discovering your child takes drugs is a nightmare scenario for most parents.* N-COUNT: usu sing

**night|mar|ish** /naɪtmeərɪʃ/ If you describe something as **nightmarish**, you mean that it is extremely frightening and unpleasant. ❑ *She described a nightmarish scene of dead bodies lying in the streets.* ADJ

**night owl (night owls)** A **night owl** is someone who regularly stays up late at night, or who prefers to work at night. [INFORMAL] N-COUNT

**night por|ter (night porters)** A **night porter** is a person whose job is to be on duty at the main reception desk of a hotel throughout the night. [mainly BRIT] N-COUNT

**night school (night schools)** Someone who goes to **night school** does an educational course in the evenings. ❑ *People can go out to work in the daylight hours and then come to night school in the evening.* N-VAR = evening classes

**night|shirt** /naɪtʃɜːʳt/ **(nightshirts)** A **nightshirt** is a long, loose shirt worn in bed. N-COUNT

**night|spot** /naɪtspɒt/ **(nightspots)** A **nightspot** is a nightclub. [INFORMAL] ❑ *...Harlem's most famous nightspot, the Cotton Club.* N-COUNT

**night stand (night stands)** A **night stand** is a small table or cupboard that you have next to your bed. [AM] N-COUNT

☑ in BRIT, use **bedside table**

**night|stick** /naɪtstɪk/ **(nightsticks)** A **nightstick** is a short thick club that is carried by policemen in the United States. [AM] N-COUNT

☑ in BRIT, use **truncheon**

**night-time** also **night time. Night-time** is the period of time between when it gets dark and when the sun rises. ❑ *They wanted someone responsible to look after the place at night-time... A twelve hour night time curfew is in force.* N-UNCOUNT: oft N n = night ≠ daytime

**night vi|sion Night vision** equipment enables people, for example soldiers or pilots, to see better at night. ❑ *...night vision goggles.* N-UNCOUNT: usu N n

**night|watch|man** /naɪtwɒtʃmən/ **(nightwatchmen)** also **night watchman.** A **nightwatchman** is a person whose job is to guard buildings at night. N-COUNT

**night|wear** /naɪtweəʳ/ **Nightwear** is clothing that you wear in bed. N-UNCOUNT

**ni|hil|ism** /naɪɪlɪzəm/ **Nihilism** is a belief which rejects all political and religious authority and current ideas in favour of the individual. ♦ **ni|hil|ist (nihilists)** ❑ *Why wasn't Weber a nihilist?* N-UNCOUNT / N-COUNT

**ni|hil|is|tic** /naɪɪlɪstɪk/ If you describe someone as **nihilistic**, you mean they do not trust political and religious authority and place their faith in the individual. ❑ *She exhibited none of the narcissistic and nihilistic tendencies of her peers.* ADJ

**nil** /nɪl/ [1] **Nil** means the same as zero. It is usually used to say what the score is in sports such as rugby or football. [BRIT] ❑ *They beat Argentina one-nil in the final.* NUM

[2] If you say that something **is nil**, you mean that it does not exist at all. ❑ *Their legal rights are virtually nil.* N-UNCOUNT = non-existent

**nim|ble** /nɪmbᵊl/ **(nimbler, nimblest)** [1] Someone who is **nimble** is able to move their fingers, hands, or legs quickly and easily. ❑ *Everything had been stitched by Molly's nimble fingers... Val, who was light and nimble on her feet, learnt to dance the tango.* ♦ **nim|bly** *Sabrina jumped nimbly out of the van.* ADJ / ADV: ADV with v

[2] If you say that someone has a **nimble** mind, you mean they are clever and can think ADJ

very quickly. ❑ *A nimble mind backed by a degree in economics gave him a firm grasp of financial matters.*

**nim|bus** /nɪmbəs/ A **nimbus** is a large grey cloud that brings rain or snow. [TECHNICAL] ❑ *...layers of cold nimbus clouds.* N-SING: usu N n

**nim|by** /nɪmbi/ also **Nimby, NIMBY.** If you say that someone has a **nimby** attitude, you are criticizing them because they do not want something such as a new road, housing estate, or prison built near to where they live. **Nimby** is an abbreviation for 'not in my backyard'. [INFORMAL] ❑ *...the usual nimby protests from local residents.* ADJ: usu ADJ n [disapproval]

**nine** /naɪn/ **(nines) Nine** is the number 9. ❑ *We still sighted nine yachts. ...nine hundred pounds.* ◆◆◆ NUM

**nine times out of ten** → see **time.**

**911** /naɪn wʌn wʌn/ **911** is the number that you call in the United States in order to contact the emergency services. ❑ *The women made their first 911 call about a prowler at 12:46 a.m.* NUM

**999** /naɪn naɪn naɪn/ **999** is the number that you call in Britain in order to contact the emergency services. ❑ *...a fire engine answering a 999 call... She dialled 999 on her mobile.* NUM

**nine|pins** /naɪnpɪnz/ If you say that people or things are going down **like ninepins**, you mean that large numbers of them are suddenly becoming ill, collapsing, or doing very badly. [mainly BRIT] ❑ *There was a time when Liverpool players never seemed to get injured, but now they are going down like ninepins.* PHRASE: PHR after v

**nine|teen** /naɪntiːn/ **(nineteens) Nineteen** is the number 19. ❑ *They have nineteen days to make up their minds.* ◆◆◆ NUM

**nine|teenth** /naɪntiːnθ/ The **nineteenth** item in a series is the one that you count as number nineteen. ❑ *...my nineteenth birthday. ...the nineteenth century.* ◆◆◇ ORD

**nine|ti|eth** /naɪntiəθ/ The **ninetieth** item in a series is the one that you count as number ninety. ❑ *He celebrates his ninetieth birthday on Friday.* ◆◆◇ ORD

**nine|ty** /naɪnti/ **(nineties)** 1 **Ninety** is the number 90. ❑ *It was decided she had to stay another ninety days.* ◆◆◆ NUM 2 When you talk about the **nineties**, you are referring to numbers between 90 and 99. For example, if you are **in** your **nineties**, you are aged between 90 and 99. If the temperature is **in the nineties**, the temperature is between 90 and 99 degrees. ❑ *By this time she was in her nineties and needed help more and more frequently.* N-PLURAL 3 **The nineties** is the decade between 1990 and 1999. ❑ *These trends only got worse as we moved into the nineties.* N-PLURAL: the N

**nin|ny** /nɪni/ **(ninnies)** If you refer to someone as a **ninny**, you think that they are foolish or silly. [INFORMAL, OLD-FASHIONED] N-COUNT [disapproval]

**ninth** /naɪnθ/ **(ninths)** 1 The **ninth** item in a series is the one that you count as number nine. ❑ *...January the ninth. ...students in the ninth grade. ...ninth century illustrated manuscripts.* ◆◆◇ ORD 2 **A ninth** is one of nine equal parts of something. ❑ *In Brussels the dollar rose by a ninth of a cent.* FRACTION

**nip** /nɪp/ **(nips, nipping, nipped)** 1 If you **nip** somewhere, usually somewhere nearby, you go there quickly or for a short time. [BRIT, INFORMAL] ❑ *Should I nip out and get some groceries?* VERB: no passive = pop V adv/prep 2 If an animal or person **nips** you, they bite you lightly or squeeze a piece of your skin between their finger and thumb. ❑ *I have known cases where dogs have nipped babies.* VERB V n ♦ **Nip** is also a noun. ❑ *Some ants can give you a nasty nip.* N-COUNT 3 A **nip** is a small amount of a strong alcoholic drink. ❑ *She had a habit of taking an occasional nip from a flask of cognac.* N-COUNT 4 to **nip** something **in the bud** → see **bud.**

**nip|per** /nɪpəʳ/ **(nippers)** A **nipper** is a child. [BRIT, INFORMAL] ❑ *I'm not ever going to forget what you've done for the nippers.* N-COUNT

**nip|ple** /nɪpᵊl/ **(nipples)** 1 The **nipples** on someone's body are the two small pieces of slightly hard flesh on their chest. Babies suck milk from their mothers' breasts through their mothers' nipples. ❑ *Sore nipples can inhibit the milk supply.* N-COUNT 2 A **nipple** is a piece of rubber or plastic which is fitted to the top of a baby's bottle. ❑ *...a white plastic bottle with a rubber nipple.* N-COUNT

**nip|py** /nɪpi/ 1 If the weather is **nippy**, it is rather cold. [INFORMAL] ❑ *It could get suddenly nippy in the evenings.* ADJ: usu v-link ADJ = chilly 2 If you describe something or someone as **nippy**, you mean that they can move very quickly over short distances. [BRIT, INFORMAL] ❑ *This nippy new car has fold down rear seats.* ADJ

**nir|va|na** /nɪəʳvɑːnə, nɜːʳ-/ 1 In the Hindu and Buddhist religions, **Nirvana** is the highest spiritual state that can possibly be achieved. ❑ *Entering the realm of Nirvana is only possible for those who have become pure.* N-UNCOUNT 2 People sometimes refer to a state of complete happiness and peace as **nirvana.** ❑ *Many businessmen think that a world where relative prices never varied would be nirvana.* N-UNCOUNT = paradise

**Nissen hut** /nɪsᵊn hʌt/ **(Nissen huts)** A **Nissen hut** is a military hut made of metal. The walls and roof form the shape of a semi-circle. [BRIT] N-COUNT

in AM, use **Quonset hut**

**nit** /nɪt/ **(nits)** 1 **Nits** are the eggs of insects called lice which live in people's hair. N-PLURAL 2 If you refer to someone as a **nit**, you think they are stupid or silly. [BRIT, INFORMAL] ❑ *I'd rather leave the business than work with such a nit.* N-COUNT [disapproval] = nitwit, twit

**nit|pick|ing** /nɪtpɪkɪŋ/ also **nit-picking.** If you refer to someone's opinion as **nitpicking**, you disapprove of the fact that it concentrates on small and unimportant details, especially to try and find fault with something. ❑ *A lot of nit-picking was going on about irrelevant things... I can get down to nitpicking detail, I am pretty fussy about certain things.* N-UNCOUNT [disapproval] = quibbling

**ni|trate** /naɪtreɪt/ **(nitrates) Nitrate** is a chemical compound that includes nitrogen and oxygen. Nitrates are used as fertilizers in agriculture. ❑ *High levels of nitrate occur in Eastern England because of the heavy use of fertilizers.* N-MASS

**ni|tric** /naɪtrɪk/ **Nitric** means relating to or containing nitrogen. ❑ *...nitric oxide.* ADJ: ADJ n

**ni|tric acid** **Nitric acid** is a strong colourless acid containing nitrogen, hydrogen, and oxygen. N-UNCOUNT

**nitro-** /naɪtroʊ-/ **Nitro-** combines with nouns to form other nouns referring to things which contain nitrogen and oxygen. ❑ *...highly corrosive substances such as nitro-phosphates.* COMB in N

**ni|tro|gen** /naɪtrədʒən/ **Nitrogen** is a colourless element that has no smell and is usually found as a gas. It forms about 78% of the earth's atmosphere, and is found in all living things. N-UNCOUNT

**ni|tro|glyc|er|in** /naɪtroʊglɪsərɪn/ also **nitroglycerine. Nitroglycerin** is a liquid that is used to make explosives and also in some medicines. N-UNCOUNT

**ni|trous** /naɪtrəs/ **Nitrous** means coming from, relating to, or containing nitrogen. ❑ *...nitrous oxides.* ADJ: ADJ n

**nitty-gritty** /nɪti grɪti/ also **nitty gritty.** If people get down to **the nitty-gritty** of a matter, situation, or activity, they discuss the most important, basic parts of it or facts about it. [INFORMAL] ❑ *...the nitty gritty of everyday politics.* N-SING: usu the N

**nit|wit** /nɪtwɪt/ **(nitwits)** If you refer to someone as a **nitwit**, you think they are stupid or silly. [INFORMAL] ❑ *You great nitwit!* N-COUNT [disapproval] = nit, twit

**no** /noʊ/ **(noes** or **no's)** 1 You use **no** to give a negative response to a question. ❑ *'Any problems?' — 'No, I'm O.K.'... 'Haven't you got your driver's licence?' — 'No.'* ◆◆◆ CONVENTION ≠ yes 2 You use **no** to say that something that someone has just said is not true. ❑ *'We thought you'd emigrated.' — 'No, no.'... 'You're getting worse than me.' — 'No I'm not.'* CONVENTION ≠ yes 3 You use **no** to refuse an offer or a request, or to refuse permission. ❑ *'Here, have mine.' — 'No, this is fine.'... 'Can you just get the message through to Pete for me?'* CONVENTION

— *'No, no I can't.'... After all, the worst the boss can do is say no if you ask him.* [4] You use **no** to indicate that you do not want someone to do something. ❑ *No. I forbid it. You cannot... She put up a hand to stop him. 'No. It's not right. We mustn't.'* [5] You use **no** to acknowledge a negative statement or to show that you accept and understand it. ❑ *'We're not on the main campus.' — 'No.'... 'It's not one of my favourite forms of music.' — 'No.'* [6] You use **no** before correcting what you have just said. ❑ *I was twenty-two – no, twenty-one.* [7] You use **no** to express shock or disappointment at something you have just been told. ❑ *'John phoned to say that his computer wasn't working.' — 'Oh God no.'* [8] You use **no** to mean not any or not one person or thing. ❑ *He had no intention of paying the cash... No job has more influence on the future of the world... No letters survive from this early period.* [9] You use **no** to emphasize that someone or something is not the type of thing mentioned. ❑ *He is no singer... I make it no secret that our worst consultants earn nothing.* [10] You can use **no** to make the negative form of a comparative. ❑ *It is to start broadcasting no later than the end of next year... Yesterday no fewer than thirty climbers reached the summit.* [11] You use **no** in front of an adjective and noun to make the noun group mean its opposite. ❑ *Sometimes a bit of selfishness, if it leads to greater self-knowledge, is no bad thing... Today's elections are of no great importance in themselves.* [12] **No** is used in notices or instructions to say that a particular activity or thing is forbidden. ❑ *The captain turned out the 'no smoking' signs. ...a notice saying 'No Dogs'.* [13] A **no** is a person who has answered 'no' to a question or who has voted against something. **No** is also used to refer to their answer or vote. ❑ *According to the latest opinion polls, the noes have 50 percent, the yeses 35 percent.* [14] If you say **there is no** doing a particular thing, you mean that it is very difficult or impossible to do that thing. ❑ *There is no going back to the life she had.* [15] not to **take no for an answer** → see **answer**. **no doubt** → see **doubt**. **no less than** → see **less**. **no longer** → see **long**. **in no way** → see **way**. **there's no way** → see **way**. **no way** → see **way**.

EXCLAM | CONVENTION = right | CONVENTION | EXCLAM [feelings] | DET | DET: DET n-sing [emphasis] | ADV: ADV compar = not | DET: DET adj n | DET | N-COUNT ≠ yes | PHRASE: PHR -ing [emphasis]

**No.** **(Nos)** **No.** is a written abbreviation for **number**. ❑ *That year he was named the nation's No. 1 college football star... Columbia Law Review, vol. no. 698 p1317.*

**no-account** A **no-account** person or thing is one that you consider worthless. [AM, INFORMAL] ❑ *...a mongrelized, no-account place.* — ADJ: usu ADJ n [disapproval]

**nob** /nɒb/ **(nobs)** If you refer to a group of people as **the nobs**, you mean they are rich or come from a much higher social class than you do. [BRIT, INFORMAL, OLD-FASHIONED] ❑ *...the nobs who live in the Big House.* — N-COUNT: usu pl

**no-ball** **(no-balls)** In cricket, a **no-ball** is a ball that is bowled in a way that is not allowed by the rules. It results in an extra run being given to the side that is batting. — N-COUNT

**nob|ble** /nɒbᵊl/ **(nobbles, nobbling, nobbled)** [1] If someone **nobbles** an important group of people such as a committee, they offer them money or threaten them in order to make them do something. [BRIT, INFORMAL] ❑ *The trial was stopped before Christmas after allegations of attempts to nobble the jury.* [2] If someone **nobbles** a racehorse, they deliberately harm it, often using drugs, in order to prevent it from winning a race. [BRIT, INFORMAL] ❑ *...the drug used to nobble two horses at Doncaster.* [3] If someone **nobbles** your plans or chances of succeeding, they prevent you from achieving what you want. [BRIT, INFORMAL] ❑ *His opportunity to re-establish himself had been nobbled by the manager's tactics.*

VERB | V n | VERB | V n | VERB | V n

**Nobel Prize** /noʊbel praɪz/ **(Nobel Prizes)** A **Nobel Prize** is one of a set of prizes that are awarded each year to people who have done important work in science, literature, or economics, or for world peace. ❑ *...the Nobel Prize for literature.* — N-COUNT: oft N *for* n

**no|bil|ity** /noʊbɪlɪti/ [1] **The nobility** of a society are all the people who have titles and belong to a high social class. ❑ *They married into the nobility and entered the highest ranks of state administration.* [2] A person's **nobility** is their noble character and behaviour. [FORMAL] ❑ *...his nobility of character, and his devotion to his country.*

N-SING-COLL: *the* N = aristocracy | N-UNCOUNT: usu with supp

**no|ble** /noʊbᵊl/ **(nobles, nobler, noblest)** [1] If you say that someone is a **noble** person, you admire and respect them because they are unselfish and morally good. ❑ *He was an upright and noble man who was always willing to help in any way he could... I wanted so much to believe he was pure and noble.* ♦ **no|bly** *Eric's sister had nobly volunteered to help with the gardening.* [2] If you say that something is a **noble** idea, goal, or action, you admire it because it is based on high moral principles. ❑ *He had implicit faith in the noble intentions of the Emperor... We'll always justify our actions with noble sounding theories.* [3] If you describe something as **noble**, you think that its appearance or quality is very impressive, making it superior to other things of its type. ❑ *...the great parks with their noble trees.* [4] **Noble** means belonging to a high social class and having a title. ❑ *Although he was of noble birth he lived as a poor man.*

ADJ [approval] | ADV: ADV with v | ADJ [approval] | ADJ = fine | ADJ: usu ADJ n = aristocratic

**noble|man** /noʊbᵊlmən/ **(noblemen)** In former times, a **nobleman** was a man who was a member of the nobility. ❑ *It had once been the home of a wealthy nobleman.* — N-COUNT = aristocrat

**no|blesse oblige** /noʊbles əbliːʒ/ **Noblesse oblige** is the idea that people with advantages, for example those of a high social class, should help and do things for other people. [FORMAL] ❑ *They did so without hope of further profit and out of a sense of noblesse oblige.* — N-UNCOUNT

**noble|woman** /noʊbᵊlwʊmən/ **(noblewomen)** In former times, a **noblewoman** was a woman who was a member of the nobility. — N-COUNT = aristocrat

**no|body** /noʊbɒdi/ **(nobodies)** ◆◆◇ [1] **Nobody** means not a single person, or not a single member of a particular group or set. ❑ *They were shut away in a little room where nobody could overhear... Nobody realizes how bad things are... Nobody else in the neighbourhood can help.* [2] If someone says that a person is a **nobody**, they are saying in an unkind way that the person is not at all important. ❑ *A man in my position has nothing to fear from a nobody like you.*

PRON: usu PRON v = no one | N-COUNT: usu *a* N in sing [disapproval]

**no-brainer** /noʊ breɪnəʳ/ **(no-brainers)** [1] If you describe a question or decision as **a no-brainer**, you mean that it is a very easy one to answer or make. [AM, INFORMAL] ❑ *If it's illegal for someone under 21 to drive, it should be illegal for them to drink and drive. That's a no-brainer.* [2] If you describe a person or action as a **no-brainer**, you mean that they are stupid. [AM, INFORMAL]

N-COUNT | N-COUNT [disapproval]

**no claims** also **no-claims**. A **no claims** discount or bonus is a reduction in the money that you have to pay for an insurance policy, which you get when you have not made any claims in the previous year. ❑ *Motorists could lose their no-claims discount, even if they are not at fault in an accident.* — ADJ: ADJ n

**no-confidence** [1] If members of an organization pass a vote or motion of **no-confidence** in someone, they take a vote which shows that they no longer support that person or their ideas. ❑ *A call for a vote of no-confidence in the president was rejected. ...a no-confidence motion.* [2] You can refer to something people say or do as **a vote of no-confidence** when it shows that they no longer support a particular person or organization. ❑ *Many police officers view this action as a vote of no-confidence in their service.*

N-UNCOUNT: usu n *of* N, N n ≠ confidence | N-UNCOUNT: usu n *of* N ≠ confidence

**noc|tur|nal** /nɒktɜːʳnᵊl/ [1] **Nocturnal** means occurring at night. ❑ *...long nocturnal walks.* [2] **Nocturnal** creatures are active mainly at

ADJ: usu ADJ n | ADJ

night. ❑ *When there is a full moon, this nocturnal rodent is careful to stay in its burrow.*

**noc|turne** /nɒktɜːʳn/ **(nocturnes)** A **nocturne** is a short gentle piece of music, often one written to be played on the piano. N-COUNT: usu with supp

**nod** /nɒd/ **(nods, nodding, nodded)** [1] If you **nod**, you move your head downwards and upwards to show that you are answering 'yes' to a question, or to show agreement, understanding, or approval. ◆◇◇ VERB: no passive ❑ *'Are you okay?' I asked. She nodded* V *and smiled... Jacques tasted one and nodded his approval...* V n *'Oh, yes,' she nodded. 'I understand you very well.'* V with quote ♦ **Nod** is also a noun. N-COUNT: usu *a* N ❑ *She gave a nod and said, 'I see'... He gave Sabrina a quick nod of acknowledgement.* [2] If you **nod** in a particular direction, you bend your head once in that direction in order to indicate something or to give someone a signal. VERB: no passive ❑ *'Does it work?' he asked, nodding at the piano...* V prep *He lifted the end of the canoe, nodding to me to take up mine.* V *to* n to-inf [3] If you **nod**, you bend your head once, as a way of saying hello or goodbye. VERB: no passive ❑ *All the girls nodded and said 'Hi'...* V *Tom nodded a greeting* V n *but didn't say anything... Both of them smiled and nodded at friends...* V *at/to* n *They nodded goodnight to the security man.* V n *to* n [4] In football, if a player **nods** the ball in a particular direction, they hit the ball there with their head. VERB = head [BRIT, INFORMAL] ❑ *Taylor leapt up to nod the ball home.* V n adv/prep

♦ **nod off** If you **nod off**, you fall asleep, especially when you had not intended to. PHRASAL VERB = doze off [INFORMAL] ❑ *The judge appeared to nod off yesterday while a witness was being cross-examined...* V P *He was nodding off to sleep in an armchair.* V P *to* n

**node** /noʊd/ **(nodes)** A **node** is a point, especially in the form of lump or swelling, where one thing joins another. N-COUNT ❑ *Cut them off cleanly through the stem just below the node. ...nerve nodes.*

**nod|ule** /nɒdjuːl, AM -dʒuːl/ **(nodules)** [1] A **nodule** is a small round lump that can appear on your body and is a sign of an illness. N-COUNT [MEDICAL] [2] A **nodule** is a small round lump which is found on the roots of certain plants. N-COUNT: oft n N

**Noel** /noʊel/ **Noel** is sometimes printed on Christmas cards and Christmas wrapping paper to mean 'Christmas'. N-PROPER

**no-fly zone** **(no-fly zones)** A **no-fly zone** is an area of sky where military and other aircraft are not allowed to fly, especially because of a war. N-COUNT

**no-go area** **(no-go areas)** [1] If you refer to a place as a **no-go area**, you mean that it has a reputation for violence and crime which makes people frightened to go there. N-COUNT [mainly BRIT] ❑ *...a subway system whose reputation for violence and lawlessness makes it a no-go area for many natives of the city.* [2] A **no-go area** is a place which is controlled by a group of people who use force to prevent other people from entering it. N-COUNT [mainly BRIT] ❑ *The area of the President's residence is a no-go area after six p.m.*

**noise** /nɔɪz/ **(noises)** [1] **Noise** is a loud or unpleasant sound. ◆◇◇ N-UNCOUNT ❑ *There was too much noise in the room and he needed peace... The noise of bombs and guns was incessant... The baby was filled with alarm at the darkness and the noise.* [2] A **noise** is a sound that someone or something makes. N-COUNT ❑ *Sir Gerald made a small noise in his throat. ...birdsong and other animal noises.* [3] If someone **makes noises** of a particular kind about something, they say things that indicate their attitude to it in a rather indirect or vague way. N-PLURAL: usu with supp ❑ *The President took care to make encouraging noises about the future... His mother had also started making noises about it being time for him to leave home.* [4] If you say that someone **makes the right noises** or **makes all the right noises**, you think that they are showing concern or enthusiasm about something because they feel they ought to rather than because they really want to. PHRASE: V inflects ❑ *He was making all the right noises about multi-party democracy and human rights.* [5] → See also **big noise**.

**noise|less** /nɔɪzləs/ Something or someone that is **noiseless** does not make any sound. ADJ = silent ≠noisy ❑ *The snow was light and noiseless as it floated down.* ♦ **noise|less|ly** *I shut the door noiselessly behind me.* ADV: ADV with v

**noi|some** /nɔɪsəm/ If you describe something or someone as **noisome**, you mean that you find them extremely unpleasant. ADJ: usu ADJ n = noxious [LITERARY] ❑ *Noisome vapours arise from the mud left in the docks... His noisome reputation for corruption had already begun to spread.*

**noisy** /nɔɪzi/ **(noisier, noisiest)** [1] A **noisy** person or thing makes a lot of loud or unpleasant noise. ADJ ≠quiet ❑ *...my noisy old typewriter... His daughter was very active and noisy in the mornings.* ♦ **noisi|ly** *The students on the grass bank cheered noisily... She sat by the window, noisily gulping her morning coffee.* ADV: usu ADV with v, also ADV adj [2] A **noisy** place is full of a lot of loud or unpleasant noise. ADJ ≠quiet, peaceful ❑ *It's a noisy place with film clips showing constantly on one of the cafe's giant screens... The baggage hall was crowded and noisy.* [3] If you describe someone as **noisy**, you are critical of them for trying to attract attention to their views by frequently and forcefully discussing them. ADJ [disapproval] = strident ❑ *...the noisy and unpopular fringe groups that are attempting to change the culture of their society.*

**no|mad** /noʊmæd/ **(nomads)** A **nomad** is a member of a group of people who travel from place to place rather than living in one place all the time. N-COUNT ❑ *...a country of nomads who raise cattle and camels.*

**no|mad|ic** /noʊmædɪk/ [1] **Nomadic** people travel from place to place rather than living in one place all the time. ADJ ❑ *...the great nomadic tribes of the Western Sahara.* [2] If someone has a **nomadic** way of life, they travel from place to place and do not have a settled home. ADJ ❑ *The daughter of a railway engineer, she at first had a somewhat nomadic childhood.*

**no-man's land** [1] **No-man's land** is an area of land that is not owned or controlled by anyone, for example the area of land between two opposing armies. N-UNCOUNT: also *a* N ❑ *In Tobruk, leading a patrol in no-man's land, he was blown up by a mortar bomb. ...the no-man's land between the Jordanian and Iraqi frontier posts.* [2] If you refer to a situation as a **no-man's land** between different things, you mean that it seems unclear because it does not fit into any of the categories. N-SING ❑ *The play is set in the dangerous no-man's land between youth and adolescence.*

**nom de guerre** /nɒm də geəʳ/ **(noms de guerre)** A **nom de guerre** is a false name which is sometimes used by people who belong to an unofficial military organization. N-COUNT [FORMAL] ❑ *...a Serb militia leader who goes by the nom de guerre Arkan.*

**nom de plume** /nɒm də pluːm/ **(noms de plume)** An author's **nom de plume** is a name that he or she uses instead of their real name. N-COUNT = pen name, pseudonym [FORMAL] ❑ *She writes under the nom de plume of Alison Cooper.*

**no|men|cla|ture** /nəmeŋklətʃəʳ, AM noʊmənkleɪtʃər/ **(nomenclatures)** The **nomenclature** of a particular set of things is the system of naming those things. N-UNCOUNT: also N in pl, usu supp N [FORMAL] ❑ *...mistakes arising from ignorance of the nomenclature of woody plants.*

**no|men|kla|tu|ra** /noʊmenklɑtʊərə/ In former communist countries, **the nomenklatura** were the people the communist party approved of and appointed to positions of authority. N-SING: *the* N

**nomi|nal** /nɒmɪnəl/ [1] You use **nominal** to indicate that someone or something is supposed to have a particular identity or status, but in reality does not have it. ADJ: usu ADJ n ❑ *As he was still not allowed to run a company, his wife became its nominal head... I was brought up a nominal Christian.* ♦ **nomi|nal|ly** *The Sultan was still nominally the Chief of Staff.* ADV: ADV with cl/group, ADV before v [2] A **nominal** price or sum of money is very ADJ: ADJ n

small in comparison with the real cost or value of the thing that is being bought or sold. ❑ *All the ferries carry bicycles free or for a nominal charge.* [3] In economics, the **nominal** value, rate, or level of something is the one expressed in terms of current prices or figures, without taking into account general changes in prices that take place over time. ❑ *Inflation would be lower and so nominal rates would be rather more attractive in real terms.*
ADJ: ADJ n ≠ real

**nomi|nal group** **(nominal groups)** A **nominal group** is the same as a **noun group**.
N-COUNT

**nomi|nate** /nɒmɪneɪt/ **(nominates, nominating, nominated)** [1] If someone **is nominated** for a job or position, their name is formally suggested as a candidate for it. ❑ *Under party rules each candidate has to be nominated by 55 Labour MPs... The public will be able to nominate candidates for awards such as the MBE. ...a presidential decree nominating him as sports ambassador.*
VERB = propose; *be* V-ed; V n *for* n; V n *as* n

[2] If you **nominate** someone to a job or position, you formally choose them to hold that job or position. ❑ *Voters will choose fifty of the seventy five deputies. The Emir will nominate the rest... The EU would nominate two members to the committee... He was nominated by the African National Congress as one of its team at the Groote Sehuur talks... It is legally possible for an elderly person to nominate someone to act for them, should they become incapable of looking after themselves.*
VERB = appoint; V n; V n *to* n; *be* V-ed *as* n; V n to-inf; Also V n *as* n, V n n

[3] If someone or something such as an actor or a film **is nominated** for an award, someone formally suggests that they should be given that award. ❑ *Practically every movie he made was nominated for an Oscar. ...a campaign to nominate the twice World Champion as Sports Personality of the Year.*
VERB = put forward; *be* V-ed *for* n; V n *as* n; Also V n *for* n

**nomi|na|tion** /nɒmɪneɪʃᵊn/ **(nominations)** [1] A **nomination** is an official suggestion of someone as a candidate in an election or for a job. ❑ *...his candidacy for the Republican presidential nomination. ...a list of nominations for senior lectureships.*
N-COUNT: oft N *for* n

[2] A **nomination for** an award is an official suggestion that someone or something should be given that award. ❑ *They say he's certain to get a nomination for best supporting actor... Alan Parker's film 'The Commitments' has six nominations.*
N-COUNT: usu N *for* n

[3] The **nomination** of someone to a particular job or position is their appointment to that job or position. ❑ *They opposed the nomination of a junior officer to the position of Inspector General of Police.*
N-VAR: usu with supp

**nomi|na|tive** /nɒmɪnətɪv/ In the grammar of some languages, **the nominative** or **the nominative case** is the case used for a noun when it is the subject of a verb. Compare **accusative**.
N-SING: *the* N

**nomi|nee** /nɒmɪniː/ **(nominees)** A **nominee** is someone who is nominated for a job, position, or award. ❑ *I was delighted to be a nominee and to receive such a prestigious award in recognition of our company's achievements.*
N-COUNT: oft N *for* n

**non-** /nɒn-/ [1] **Non-** is used in front of adjectives and nouns to form adjectives that describe something as not having a particular quality or feature. ❑ *...non-nuclear weapons. ...non-verbal communication.*
PREFIX

[2] **Non-** is used in front of nouns to form nouns which refer to situations where a particular action has not or will not take place. ❑ *He was disqualified from the council for non-attendance... Both countries agreed that normal relations would be based on non-interference in each other's internal affairs.*
PREFIX

[3] **Non-** is used in front of nouns to form nouns which refer to people who do not belong to a particular group or category. ❑ *Children of smokers are more likely to start smoking than are children of non-smokers.*
PREFIX

**non-aggression**

✓ in AM, also use **nonaggression**

If a country adopts a policy of **non-aggression**, it declares that it will not attack or try to harm a particular country in any way. ❑ *A non-aggression pact will be signed between the two countries.*
N-UNCOUNT: usu with supp

**non-alcoholic**

✓ in AM, also use **nonalcoholic**

A **non-alcoholic** drink does not contain alcohol. ❑ *...bottles of non-alcoholic beer.*
ADJ: usu ADJ n ≠ alcoholic

**non-aligned**

✓ in AM, also use **nonaligned**

**Non-aligned** countries did not support or were in no way linked to groups of countries headed by the United States or the former Soviet Union. ❑ *...foreign ministers from non-aligned countries.*
ADJ: usu ADJ n

**non-alignment**

✓ in AM, also use **nonalignment**

**Non-alignment** is the state or policy of being non-aligned. ❑ *The Afro-Asian nations had approved the basic general principles of non-alignment.*
N-UNCOUNT

**non|cha|lant** /nɒnʃələnt, AM -lɑːnt/ If you describe someone as **nonchalant**, you mean that they appear not to worry or care about things and that they seem very calm. ❑ *Clark's mother is nonchalant about her role in her son's latest work... It merely underlines our rather more nonchalant attitude to life.*
ADJ = casual

♦ **non|cha|lance** /nɒnʃələns, AM -lɑːns/ *Affecting nonchalance, I handed her two hundred dollar bills.*
N-UNCOUNT

♦ **non|cha|lant|ly** *'Does Will intend to return?' Joanna asked as nonchalantly as she could.*
ADV: usu ADV with v, also ADV adj

**non-combatant** **(non-combatants)**

✓ in AM, usually use **noncombatant**

[1] **Non-combatant** troops are members of the armed forces whose duties do not include fighting. ❑ *The General does not like non-combatant personnel near a scene of action.*
N-COUNT: usu N n ≠ combatant

[2] In a war, **non-combatants** are people who are not members of the armed forces. ❑ *The Red Cross has arranged two local ceasefires, allowing non-combatants to receive medical help.*
N-COUNT: usu pl = civilian ≠ combatant

**non-commissioned**

✓ in AM, use **noncommissioned**

A **non-commissioned** officer in the armed forces is someone with a rank such as corporal or sergeant who used to have a lower rank, rather than an officer of higher rank who has been given a commission.
ADJ: ADJ n

**non|com|mit|tal** /nɒnkəmɪtᵊl/ also **non-committal.** You can describe someone as **non-committal** when they deliberately do not express their opinion or intentions clearly. ❑ *Mr Hall is non-committal about the number of jobs that the development corporation has created... Sylvia's face was noncommittal. ...a very bland non-committal answer.*
ADJ: usu v-link ADJ

♦ **non|com|mit|tal|ly** *'I like some of his novels better than others,' I said noncommittally.*
ADV: ADV after v

**non|con|form|ist** /nɒnkənfɔːʳmɪst/ **(nonconformists)** also **non-conformist.** [1] If you say that someone's way of life or opinions are **nonconformist**, you mean that they are different from those of most people. ❑ *Their views are nonconformist and their political opinions are extreme. ...a nonconformist lifestyle.*
ADJ = unconventional ≠ conventional

♦ A **nonconformist** is someone who is nonconformist. ❑ *Victoria stood out as a dazzling non-conformist.*
N-COUNT

[2] In Britain, **nonconformist** churches are Protestant churches which are not part of the Church of England. ❑ *His father was a Nonconformist minister.*
ADJ: ADJ n

♦ A **nonconformist** is a member of a nonconformist church. ❑ *Although he seems to be an old-fashioned non-conformist, he is in fact a very devout Catholic.*
N-COUNT

**non|con|form|ity** /nɒnkənfɔːʳmɪti/ also **non-conformity. Nonconformity** is behaviour or thinking which is different from that of most people. ❑ *You're deliberately unconventional. Even your choice of clothes is a statement of your nonconformity... Lovelock's principled nonconformity can be traced to his childhood.*
N-UNCOUNT

**non-custodial** [1] If someone who has been found guilty of a crime or offence is given a **non-custodial** sentence, their punishment does not involve going to prison. [FORMAL] ❑ *...non-custodial*
ADJ: usu ADJ n ≠ custodial

*punishments for minor criminals.* 2 The **non-custodial** parent in a couple who are separated or divorced is the parent who does not live with the children. ❑ *More than half the children of divorce did not see the non-custodial parent on a regular basis.* [ADJ: ADJ n]

**non|de|script** /nɒndɪskrɪpt/ If you describe something or someone as **nondescript**, you mean that their appearance is rather dull, and not at all interesting or attractive. ❑ *Europa House is one of those hundreds of nondescript buildings along the Bath Road. ...a nondescript woman of uncertain age.* [ADJ: usu ADJ n]

**none** /nʌn/ 1 **None of** something means not even a small amount of it. **None of** a group of people or things means not even one of them. ❑ *She did none of the maintenance on the vehicle itself... None of us knew how to treat her.* [◆◆◇ QUANT: QUANT *of* def-n] ♦ **None** is also a pronoun. ❑ *I turned to bookshops and libraries seeking information and found none... No one could imagine a great woman painter. None had existed yet... Only two cars produced by Austin-Morris could reach 100 mph and none could pass the 10-second acceleration test.* [PRON]

PHRASES 2 If you say that someone **will have none of** something, or **is having none of** something, you mean that they refuse to accept it. [INFORMAL] ❑ *He knew his own mind and was having none of their attempts to keep him at home.* [PHRASE: *be* inflects, PHR n] 3 You use **none too** in front of an adjective or adverb in order to emphasize that the quality mentioned is not present. [FORMAL] ❑ *He was none too thrilled to hear from me at that hour... Her hand grasped my shoulder, none too gently.* [PHRASE: PHR adj/adv, emphasis] 4 You use **none the** to say that someone or something does not have any more of a particular quality than they did before. ❑ *You could end up committed to yet another savings scheme and none the wiser about managing your finances... He became convinced that his illness was purely imaginary: that made it none the better.* [PHRASE: PHR compar = no] 5 **none of your business** → see **business**. **none other than** → see **other**. **second to none** → see **second**.

**non|en|tity** /nɒnentɪti/ **(nonentities)** If you refer to someone as a **nonentity**, you mean that they are not special or important in any way. ❑ *Amidst the current bunch of nonentities, he is a towering figure... She was written off then as a political nonentity.* [N-COUNT, disapproval = nobody]

**non-essential (non-essentials)**

☑ in AM, also use **nonessential**

1 **Non-essential** means not absolutely necessary. ❑ *The crisis has led to the closure of a number of non-essential government services. ...non-essential goods.* [ADJ: usu ADJ n ≠ essential] 2 **Non-essentials** are things that are not absolutely necessary. ❑ *In a recession, consumers could be expected to cut down on non-essentials like toys.* [N-PLURAL ≠ necessities]

**none|the|less** /nʌnðəles/ **Nonetheless** means the same as **nevertheless**. [FORMAL] ❑ *There was still a long way to go. Nonetheless, some progress had been made... His face is serious but nonetheless very friendly.* [ADV: ADV with cl = nevertheless]

**non-event (non-events)**

☑ in AM, also use **nonevent**

If you say that something was a **non-event**, you mean that it was disappointing or dull, especially when this was not what you had expected. ❑ *Unfortunately, the entire evening was a total non-event.* [N-COUNT = anticlimax]

**non-executive (non-executives)** 1 Someone who has a **non-executive** position in a company or organization gives advice but is not responsible for making decisions or ensuring that decisions are carried out. [BUSINESS] ❑ *...non-executive directors.* [ADJ: ADJ n ≠ executive] 2 A **non-executive** is someone who has a non-executive position in a company or organization. [BUSINESS] [N-COUNT]

**non-existence** also **nonexistence. Non-existence** is the fact of not existing. ❑ *I was left with puzzlement as to the existence or non-existence of God.* [N-UNCOUNT ≠ existence]

**non-existent** also **nonexistent.** If you say that something is **non-existent**, you mean that it does not exist when you feel that it should. ❑ *Hygiene was non-existent: no running water, no bathroom.* [ADJ]

**non-fat** also **nonfat. Non-fat** foods have very low amounts of fat in them. ❑ *...plain non-fat yogurt.* [ADJ = fat-free]

**non-fiction** also **nonfiction. Non-fiction** is writing that gives information or describes real events, rather than telling a story. ❑ *The series will include both fiction and non-fiction... Lewis is the author of thirteen novels and ten non-fiction books.* [N-UNCOUNT: oft N n ≠ fiction]

**non-finite** also **nonfinite.** A **non-finite** clause is a clause which is based on an infinitive or a participle and has no tense. Compare **finite**. [ADJ: usu ADJ n]

**non-governmental or|gani|za|tion (non-governmental organizations)** A **non-governmental organization** is the same as an **NGO**. [N-COUNT]

**non-human** also **nonhuman. Non-human** means not human or not produced by humans. ❑ *Hostility towards outsiders is characteristic of both human and non-human animals.* [ADJ ≠ human]

**non-intervention**

☑ in AM, also use **nonintervention**

**Non-intervention** is the practice or policy of not becoming involved in a dispute or disagreement between other people and of not helping either side. ❑ *Generally, I think the policy of non-intervention is the correct one.* [N-UNCOUNT ≠ intervention]

**non-linear** also **nonlinear.** If you describe something as **non-linear**, you mean that it does not progress or develop smoothly from one stage to the next in a logical way. Instead, it makes sudden changes, or seems to develop in different directions at the same time. ❑ *...a non-linear narrative structure.* [ADJ ≠ linear]

**non-member (non-members)**

☑ in AM, also use **nonmember**

**Non-members** of a club or organization are people who are not members of it. ❑ *The scheme is also open to non-members... Spain imposed levies on farm imports from non-member states.* [N-COUNT: usu pl ≠ member]

**non-nuclear**

☑ in AM, also use **nonnuclear**

**Non-nuclear** means not using or involving nuclear weapons or nuclear power. ❑ *The agreement is the first postwar treaty to reduce non-nuclear weapons in Europe.* [ADJ ≠ nuclear]

**no-no** If you say that something is **a no-no**, you think it is undesirable or unacceptable. [INFORMAL] ❑ *We all know that cheating on our taxes is a no-no.* [N-SING: *a* N]

**no-nonsense** 1 If you describe someone as a **no-nonsense** person, you approve of the fact that they are efficient, direct, and quite tough. ❑ *She saw herself as a direct, no-nonsense modern woman.* [ADJ: usu ADJ n, approval] 2 If you describe something as a **no-nonsense** thing, you approve of the fact that it is plain and does not have unnecessary parts. ❑ *You'll need no-nonsense boots for the jungle.* [ADJ: usu ADJ n, approval ≠ fancy]

**non-partisan**

☑ in AM, use **nonpartisan**

A person or group that is **non-partisan** does not support or help a particular political party or group. ❑ *...a non-partisan organization that does economic research for business and labor groups. ...the president's Thanksgiving Day call for a non-partisan approach to the problem.* [ADJ = neutral]

**non-payment** also **nonpayment. Non-payment** is a failure to pay a sum of money that you owe. ❑ *She has received an eviction order from the council for non-payment of rent.* [N-UNCOUNT: usu N *of* n ≠ payment]

**non|plussed** /nɒnplʌst/ If you are **nonplussed**, you feel confused and unsure how to react. ❑ *She expected him to ask for a scotch and was rather nonplussed when he asked her to mix him a martini and lemonade.* ADJ: usu v-link ADJ = at a loss

**non-profit** also **nonprofit.** A **non-profit** organization is one which is not run with the aim of making a profit. [BUSINESS] ❑ *Her center is typical of many across the country – a non-profit organization that cares for about 50 children.* ADJ: usu ADJ n

**non-profit-making** also **nonprofit-making.** A **non-profit-making** organization or charity is not run with the intention of making a profit. [mainly BRIT, BUSINESS] ❑ *...the Film Theatre Foundation, a non-profit-making company which raises money for the arts.* ADJ: usu ADJ n

**non-proliferation** also **nonproliferation. Non-proliferation** is the limiting of the production and spread of something such as nuclear or chemical weapons. ❑ *...the Nuclear Non-Proliferation Treaty.* N-UNCOUNT: usu N n

**non-resident** **(non-residents)**

✓ in AM, also use **nonresident**

A **non-resident** person is someone who is visiting a particular place but who does not live or stay there permanently. ❑ *The paper said that 100,000 non-resident workers would have to be sent back to their home villages.* ADJ ≠ resident ♦ A **non-resident** is someone who is non-resident. ❑ *Both hotels have gardens and restaurants open to non-residents.* N-COUNT ≠ resident

**non|sense** /nɒnsəns/ [1] If you say that something spoken or written is **nonsense**, you mean that you consider it to be untrue or silly. ❑ *Most orthodox doctors however dismiss this as complete nonsense. ...all that poetic nonsense about love... 'I'm putting on weight.' — 'Nonsense my dear.'* N-UNCOUNT [disapproval] = rubbish [2] You can use **nonsense** to refer to something that you think is foolish or that you disapprove of. ❑ *Surely it is an economic nonsense to deplete the world of natural resources... I think there is a limit to how much of this nonsense people are going to put up with.* N-UNCOUNT: also *a* N, usu supp N [disapproval] [3] You can refer to spoken or written words that do not mean anything because they do not make sense as **nonsense**. ❑ *...a children's nonsense poem by Charles E Carryl.* N-UNCOUNT [4] → See also **no-nonsense.** [5] To **make a nonsense of** something or to **make nonsense of** it means to make it seem ridiculous or pointless. ❑ *The fighting made a nonsense of peace pledges made in London last week.* PHRASE: V inflects, PHR n

**non|sen|si|cal** /nɒnsensɪkᵊl/ If you say that something is **nonsensical**, you think it is stupid, ridiculous, or untrue. ❑ *It seemed to me that Sir Robert's arguments were nonsensical... There were no nonsensical promises about reviving the economy.* ADJ: usu v-link ADJ [disapproval] = absurd

**non se|qui|tur** /nɒn sekwɪtəʳ/ **(non sequiturs)** A **non sequitur** is a statement, remark, or conclusion that does not follow naturally or logically from what has just been said. [FORMAL] ❑ *Had she missed something important, or was this just a non sequitur?* N-VAR

**non-smoker** **(non-smokers)** also **nonsmoker.** A **non-smoker** is someone who does not smoke. ❑ *Nobody will be allowed to smoke in an office if there are non-smokers present.* N-COUNT ≠ smoker

**non-smoking** also **nonsmoking.** [1] A **non-smoking** area in a public place is an area in which people are not allowed to smoke. ❑ *More and more restaurants are providing non-smoking areas.* ADJ ≠ smoking [2] A **non-smoking** person is a person who does not smoke. ❑ *The fertility of women who smoke is half that of non-smoking women.* ADJ

**non-specific** also **nonspecific.** [1] **Non-specific** medical conditions or symptoms have more than one possible cause. ❑ *...non-specific headaches.* ADJ: usu ADJ n [2] Something that is **non-specific** is general rather than precise or exact. ❑ *I intend to use these terms in a deliberately non-specific and all-embracing way.* ADJ: usu ADJ n

**non-standard** also **nonstandard. Non-standard** things are different from the usual version or type of that thing. ❑ *The shop is completely out of non-standard sizes.* ADJ: usu ADJ n ≠ standard

**non-starter** **(non-starters)** also **nonstarter.** If you describe a plan or idea as a **non-starter**, you mean that it has no chance of success. [INFORMAL] ❑ *The United States is certain to reject the proposal as a non-starter.* N-COUNT

**non-stick** also **nonstick. Non-stick** saucepans, frying pans, or baking tins have a special coating on the inside which prevents food from sticking to them. ADJ: usu ADJ n

**non-stop** also **nonstop.** Something that is **non-stop** continues without any pauses or interruptions. ❑ *Many US cities now have non-stop flights to Aspen. ...80 minutes of non-stop music... The training was non-stop and continued for three days.* ADJ ♦ **Non-stop** is also an adverb. ❑ *Amy and her group had driven non-stop through Spain... The snow fell non-stop for 24 hours.* ADV: ADV after v

**non-union**

✓ in AM, use **nonunion**

**Non-union** workers do not belong to a trade union or labor union. A **non-union** company or organization does not employ workers who belong to a trade union or labor union. [BUSINESS] ❑ *The company originally intended to reopen the factory with non-union workers.* ADJ: usu ADJ n

**non-verbal** also **nonverbal. Non-verbal** communication consists of things such as the expression on your face, your arm movements, or your tone of voice, which show how you feel about something without using words. ADJ: usu ADJ n ≠ verbal

**non-violent** also **nonviolent.** [1] **Non-violent** methods of bringing about change do not involve hurting people or causing damage. ❑ *King was a worldwide symbol of non-violent protest against racial injustice... I would only belong to an environmental movement if it was explicitly non-violent.* ADJ ≠ violent ♦ **non-violence** *His commitment to non-violence led to a Nobel peace prize in 1989.* N-UNCOUNT [2] You can refer to someone or something such as a crime as **non-violent** when that person or thing does not hurt or injure people. ❑ *...non-violent offenders.* ADJ ≠ violent

**non-white** **(non-whites)**

✓ in AM, also use **nonwhite**

A **non-white** person is a member of a race of people who are not of European origin. ❑ *Non-white people are effectively excluded from certain jobs... 60 percent of the population is non-white.* ADJ ≠ white ♦ **Non-white** is also a noun. ❑ *Not one non-white has ever been selected to play for the team.* N-COUNT

**noo|dle** /nuːdᵊl/ **(noodles) Noodles** are long, thin, curly strips of pasta. They are used especially in Chinese and Italian cooking. N-COUNT: usu pl

**nook** /nʊk/ **(nooks)** A **nook** is a small and sheltered place. ❑ *We found a seat in a little nook, and had some lunch.* N-COUNT ● If you talk about every **nook and cranny** of a place or situation, you mean every part or every aspect of it. ❑ *Boxes are stacked in every nook and cranny at the factory. ...Cole's vast knowledge of the nooks and crannies of British politics.* PHRASE: Ns inflect [emphasis] = corner

**nookie** /nʊki/ also **nooky.** You can refer to sexual intercourse as **nookie**. Some people consider this word offensive. [INFORMAL] ❑ *...the fearful Hollywood sin of pre-marital nookie.* N-UNCOUNT

**noon** /nuːn/ [1] **Noon** is twelve o'clock in the middle of the day. ❑ *The long day of meetings started at noon... Our branches are open from 9am to 5pm during the week and until 12 noon on Saturdays.* N-UNCOUNT: oft prep N = midday → See also **high noon.** [2] **Noon** means happening or appearing in the middle part of the day. ❑ *The noon sun was fierce... He expected the transfer to go through by today's noon deadline.* ADJ: ADJ n = midday [3] **morning, noon, and night** → see **morning.**

**noon|day** /nuːndeɪ/ **Noonday** means happening or appearing in the middle part of the day. ❑ *It was hot, nearly 90 degrees in the noonday sun.* ADJ: ADJ n = midday

**no one** also **no-one. No one** means not a single person, or not a single member of a particular group or set. ❑ *Everyone wants to be a hero, but no one wants to die... No one can open mail except the person to whom it has been addressed.* ◆◆◇ PRON: usu PRON v = nobody

**noose** /nuːs/ **(nooses)** A **noose** is a circular loop at the end of a piece of rope or wire. A noose is tied with a knot that allows it to be tightened, and it is usually used to trap animals or hang people. N-COUNT

**nope** /noʊp/ **Nope** is sometimes used instead of 'no' as a negative response. [INFORMAL, SPOKEN] ❑ *'Is she supposed to work today?' — 'Nope, tomorrow.'* CONVENTION

**nor** /nɔːʳ/ [1] You use **nor** after 'neither' in order to introduce the second alternative or the last of a number of alternatives in a negative statement. ❑ *Neither Mr Rose nor Mr Woodhead was available for comment yesterday... I can give you neither an opinion nor any advice... They can neither read nor write, nor can they comprehend such concepts.* ◆◆◇ CONJ [2] You use **nor** after a negative statement in order to indicate that the negative statement also applies to you or to someone or something else. ❑ *'None of us has any idea how long we're going to be here.' — 'Nor do I.'... 'If my husband has no future,' she said, 'then nor do my children.'... He doesn't want to live in the country when he grows up, nor does he want to live in the city.* CONJ = neither [3] You use **nor** after a negative statement in order to introduce another negative statement which adds information to the previous one. ❑ *Cooking up a quick dish doesn't mean you have to sacrifice flavour. Nor does fast food have to be junk food.* CONJ = neither

**Nor|dic** /nɔːʳdɪk/ **Nordic** means relating to the Scandinavian countries of northern Europe. ❑ *The Nordic countries have been quick to assert their interest in the development of the Baltic States.* ADJ: ADJ n

**norm** /nɔːʳm/ **(norms)** [1] **Norms** are ways of behaving that are considered normal in a particular society. ❑ *...the commonly accepted norms of democracy. ...a social norm that says drunkenness is inappropriate behaviour.* N-COUNT: usu pl, usu with supp [2] If you say that a situation is **the norm**, you mean that it is usual and expected. ❑ *Families of six or seven are the norm in Borough Park... The changes will lead to more flexible leases, and leases nearer to 15 years than the present norm of 25 years.* N-SING: the N, oft N for/of/in n [3] A **norm** is an official standard or level that organizations are expected to reach. ❑ *...an agency which would establish European norms and co-ordinate national policies to halt pollution.* N-COUNT: usu with supp

**nor|mal** /nɔːʳməl/ [1] Something that is **normal** is usual and ordinary, and is what people expect. ❑ *He has occasional injections to maintain his good health but otherwise he lives a normal life... The two countries resumed normal diplomatic relations... Some of the shops were closed but that's quite normal for a Thursday afternoon... Life in Israel will continue as normal.* ◆◆◇ ADJ [2] A **normal** person has no serious physical or mental health problems. ❑ *Statistics indicate that depressed patients are more likely to become ill than are normal people... Will the baby be normal?* ADJ = healthy

**nor|mal|cy** /nɔːʳməlsi/ **Normalcy** is a situation in which everything is normal. ❑ *Underneath this image of normalcy, addiction threatened to rip this family apart.* N-UNCOUNT = normality

**nor|mal|ity** /nɔːʳmælɪti/ **Normality** is a situation in which everything is normal. ❑ *A semblance of normality has returned with people going to work and shops re-opening.* N-UNCOUNT: oft N of n

**nor|mal|ize** /nɔːʳməlaɪz/ **(normalizes, normalizing, normalized)**

✔ in BRIT, also use **normalise**

[1] When you **normalize** a situation or when it **normalizes**, it becomes normal. ❑ *Meditation tends to lower or normalize blood pressure... There may be some deep-seated emotional reason which has to be dealt with before your eating habits normalize.* VERB V n V [2] If people, groups, or governments **normalize** relations, or when relations **normalize**, they become normal or return to normal. ❑ *The two governments were close to normalizing relations... The United States says they are not prepared to join in normalizing ties with their former enemy... If relations between Hanoi and Washington begin to normalise, anything is possible.* V-RECIP pl-n V n V n with n V ♦ **nor|mali|za|tion** /nɔːʳməlaɪzeɪʃən/ *The two sides would like to see the normalisation of diplomatic relations.* N-UNCOUNT

**nor|mal|ly** /nɔːʳməli/ [1] If you say that something **normally** happens or that you **normally** do a particular thing, you mean that it is what usually happens or what you usually do. ❑ *All airports in the country are working normally today... Social progress is normally a matter of struggles and conflicts... Normally, the transportation system in Paris carries 950,000 passengers a day.* ◆◇◇ ADV: ADV with v, ADV with cl/group [2] If you do something **normally**, you do it in the usual or conventional way. ❑ *She would apparently eat normally and then make herself sick. ...failure of the blood to clot normally.* ADV: ADV after v

**Nor|man** /nɔːʳmən/ **(Normans)** [1] **The Normans** were the people who came from northern France and took control of England in 1066, or their descendants. N-COUNT [2] **Norman** is used to refer to the period of history in Britain from 1066 until around 1300, and in particular to the style of architecture of that period. ❑ *In Norman England, the greyhound was a symbol of nobility. ...a Norman castle.* ADJ

**nor|ma|tive** /nɔːʳmətɪv/ **Normative** means creating or stating particular rules of behaviour. [FORMAL] ❑ *Normative sexual behaviour in our society remains heterosexual. ...a normative model of teaching.* ADJ: usu ADJ n

**Norse** /nɔːʳs/ [1] **Norse** means belonging or relating to Scandinavian countries in medieval times. ❑ *In Norse mythology the moon is personified as male.* ADJ [2] **Norse** is the language that was spoken in Scandinavian countries in medieval times. N-UNCOUNT

**Norse|man** /nɔːʳsmən/ **(Norsemen)** **The Norsemen** were people who lived in Scandinavian countries in medieval times. N-COUNT

**north** /nɔːʳθ/ also **North.** [1] The **north** is the direction which is on your left when you are looking towards the direction where the sun rises. ❑ *In the north the ground becomes very cold as the winter snow and ice covers the ground... Birds usually migrate from north to south.* ◆◆◆ N-UNCOUNT: also the N [2] **The north** of a place, country, or region is the part which is in the north. ❑ *The scheme mostly benefits people in the North and Midlands. ...a tiny house in a village in the north of France.* N-SING: usu the N, oft N of n [3] If you go **north**, you travel towards the north. ❑ *Anita drove north up Pacific Highway.* ADV: ADV after v [4] Something that is **north** of a place is positioned to the north of it. ❑ *...a little village a few miles north of Portsmouth.* ADV: usu ADV of n [5] The **north** edge, corner, or part of a place or country is the part which is towards the north. ❑ *...the north side of the mountain... They were coming in to land on the north coast of Crete.* ADJ: ADJ n [6] **'North'** is used in the names of some countries, states, and regions in the north of a larger area. ❑ *There were demonstrations this weekend in cities throughout North America, Asia and Europe.* ADJ: ADJ n [7] A **north** wind is a wind that blows from the north. ❑ *...a bitterly cold north wind.* ADJ: ADJ n [8] **The North** is used to refer to the richer, more developed countries of the world. ❑ *Malaysia has emerged as the toughest critic of the North's environmental attitudes.* N-SING: the N

**north|bound** /nɔːʳθbaʊnd/ **Northbound** roads or vehicles lead or are travelling towards the north. ❑ *A 25 mile traffic jam clogged the northbound carriageway of the M6... Traffic was already very congested by six thirty this morning, particularly on the M1 northbound.* ADJ: ADJ n, n ADJ

**north-east** also **northeast.** [1] The **north-east** is the direction which is halfway be- ◆◆◇ N-UNCOUNT: also the N tween north and east. ❑ *The land to the north-east fell away into meadows.* [2] **The north-east** of a place, country, or region is the part which is in the north-east. ❑ *The north-east, with 60 million people, is the most densely populated part of the United States... They're all from Newcastle in the North East of England.* (N-SING: *the* N, oft N *of* n) [3] If you go **north-east**, you travel towards the north-east. ❑ *The streets were jammed with slow moving traffic, army convoys moving north-east.* (ADV: ADV after v) [4] Something that is **north-east of** a place is positioned to the north-east of it. ❑ *This latest attack was at Careysburg, twenty miles north-east of the capital, Monrovia.* (ADV: ADV *of* n) [5] The **north-east** edge, corner, or part of a place is the part which is towards the north-east. ❑ *...Waltham Abbey on the north-east outskirts of London.* (ADJ: ADJ n = *north-eastern*) [6] A **north-east** wind is a wind that blows from the north-east. ❑ *By 9.15 a bitter north-east wind was blowing.* (ADJ: ADJ n)

**north-easterly** also **northeasterly.** A **north-easterly** point, area, or direction is to the north-east or towards the north-east. (ADJ: usu ADJ n)

**north-eastern** also **north eastern.** **North-eastern** means in or from the north-east of a region or country. ❑ *...the north-eastern coast of the United States.* (ADJ: usu ADJ n)

**nor|ther|ly** /nɔːʳðəʳli/ [1] A **northerly** point, area, or direction is to the north or towards the north. ❑ *Unst is the most northerly island in the British Isles... I wanted to go a more northerly route across Montana.* (ADJ: usu ADJ n = *northern*) [2] A **northerly** wind is a wind that blows from the north. (ADJ)

**north|ern** /nɔːʳðəʳn/ also **Northern.** ◆◆◇ **Northern** means in or from the north of a region, state, or country. ❑ *Prices at three-star hotels fell furthest in several northern cities.* (ADJ: ADJ n)

**north|ern|er** /nɔːʳðəʳnəʳ/ **(northerners)** A **northerner** is a person who was born in or who lives in the north of a place or country. ❑ *I like the openness and directness of northerners.* (N-COUNT)

**north|ern|most** /nɔːʳðəʳnmoʊst/ The **northernmost** part of an area or the **northernmost** place is the one that is farthest towards the north. ❑ *...the northernmost tip of the British Isles... The Chablis vineyard is the northernmost in Burgundy.* (ADJ: usu ADJ n)

**North Pole** **The North Pole** is the place on the surface of the earth which is farthest towards the north. (N-PROPER: usu *the* N)

**north|ward** /nɔːʳθwəʳd/ also **northwards.** **Northward** or **northwards** means towards the north. ❑ *Tropical storm Marco is pushing northward up Florida's coast. ...the flow of immigrants northward.* (ADV: usu ADV after v, also n ADV) ♦ **Northward** is also an adjective. ❑ *The northward journey from Jalalabad was no more than 120 miles.* (ADJ: ADJ n)

**north-west** also **northwest.** ◆◆◇ [1] The **north-west** is the direction which is halfway between north and west. ❑ *...Ushant, five miles out to the north-west.* (N-UNCOUNT: also *the* N) [2] **The north-west** of a place, country, or region is the part which is towards the north-west. ❑ *Labour took its pre-election campaign to the North-West. ...the extreme north-west of South America.* (N-SING: *the* N, oft N *of* n) [3] If you go **north-west**, you travel towards the north-west. ❑ *Take the narrow lane going north-west parallel with the railway line.* (ADV: ADV after v) [4] Something that is **north-west of** a place is positioned to the north-west of it. ❑ *This was situated to the north-west of the town, a short walk from the railway station.* (ADV: ADV *of* n) [5] The **north-west** part of a place, country, or region is the part which is towards the north-west. ❑ *...the north-west coast of the United States. ...Sydney's north-west suburbs.* (ADJ: ADJ n = *north-western*) [6] A **north-west** wind is a wind that blows from the north-west. ❑ *A brisk north-west wind swept across the region.* (ADJ: ADJ n)

**north-westerly** also **northwesterly.** A **north-westerly** point, area, or direction is to the north-west or towards the north-west. (ADJ: usu ADJ n)

**north-western** also **north western.** **North-western** means in or from the north-west of a region or country. ❑ *He was from north-western Russia.* (ADJ: usu ADJ n)

**Nor|we|gian** /nɔːʳwiːdʒəⁿ/ **(Norwegians)** [1] **Norwegian** means belonging or relating to Norway, or to its people, language, or culture. (ADJ) ♦ A **Norwegian** is a person who comes from Norway. (N-COUNT) [2] **Norwegian** is the language spoken by people who live in Norway. (N-UNCOUNT)

**no-score draw** **(no-score draws)** A **no-score draw** is the result of a football match in which neither team scores any goals. (N-COUNT)

**nose** /noʊz/ **(noses, nosing, nosed)** ◆◇◇ [1] Your **nose** is the part of your face which sticks out above your mouth. You use it for smelling and breathing. ❑ *She wiped her nose with a tissue... She's got funny eyes and a big nose.* (N-COUNT: oft poss N) [2] The **nose** of a vehicle such as a car or aeroplane is the front part of it. ❑ *Sue parked off the main street, with the van's nose pointing away from the street.* (N-COUNT: oft poss N) [3] You can refer to your sense of smell as your **nose**. ❑ *The river that runs through Middlesbrough became ugly on the eye and hard on the nose.* (N-COUNT) [4] If a vehicle **noses** in a certain direction or if you **nose** it there, you move it slowly and carefully in that direction. ❑ *He could not see the driver as the car nosed forward... Ben drove past them, nosing his car into the garage.* (VERB; V adv/prep; V n prep/adv) [5] → See also **hard-nosed**, **toffee-nosed**.

**PHRASES** [6] If you **keep** your **nose clean**, you behave well and stay out of trouble. [INFORMAL] ❑ *If you kept your nose clean, you had a job for life.* (PHRASE: V and N inflect) [7] If you **follow** your **nose** to get to a place, you go straight ahead or follow the most obvious route. ❑ *Just follow your nose and in about five minutes you're at the old railway.* (PHRASE: V and N inflect) [8] If you **follow** your **nose**, you do something in a particular way because you feel it should be done like that, rather than because you are following any plan or rules. ❑ *You won't have to think, just follow your nose.* (PHRASE: V and N inflect) [9] If you say that someone **has a nose for** something, you mean that they have a natural ability to find it or recognize it. ❑ *He had a nose for trouble and a brilliant tactical mind.* (PHRASE: V inflects, PHR n) [10] If you say that someone or something **gets up** your **nose**, you mean that they annoy you. [BRIT, INFORMAL] ❑ *He's just getting up my nose so much at the moment.* (PHRASE: V and N inflect) [11] If you say that someone **looks down** their **nose** at something or someone, you mean that they believe they are superior to that person or thing and treat them with disrespect. ❑ *They rather looked down their noses at anyone who couldn't speak French.* (PHRASE: V and N inflect, usu PHR *at* n; disapproval) [12] If you say that you **paid through the nose** for something, you are emphasizing that you had to pay what you consider too high a price for it. [INFORMAL] ❑ *We don't like paying through the nose for our wine when eating out.* (PHRASE: V inflects, oft PHR *for* n; emphasis) [13] If someone **pokes** their **nose into** something or **sticks** their **nose into** something, they try to interfere with it even though it does not concern them. [INFORMAL] ❑ *We don't like strangers who poke their noses into our affairs... Why did you have to stick your nose in?* (PHRASE: V and N inflect, PHR n; disapproval = *meddle*) [14] To **rub** someone's **nose in** something that they do not want to think about, such as a failing or a mistake they have made, means to remind them repeatedly about it. [INFORMAL] ❑ *His enemies will attempt to rub his nose in past policy statements.* (PHRASE: V and N inflect, PHR n) [15] If you say that someone **is cutting off** their **nose to spite** their **face**, you mean they do something that they think will hurt someone, without realizing or caring that it will hurt themselves as well. ❑ *There is evidence that the industry's greed means that it is cutting off its nose to spite its face.* (PHRASE: V inflects; disapproval) [16] If vehicles are **nose to tail**, the front of one vehicle is close behind the back of another. [mainly BRIT] ❑ *...a line of about twenty fast-moving trucks driving nose to tail.* (PHRASE: v-link PHR, PHR after v)

☑ in AM, use **bumper-to-bumper**

[17] If you **thumb** your **nose at** someone, you behave in a way that shows that you do not care what they think. ❑ *He has always thumbed his nose at the media.* (PHRASE: V and N inflect, usu PHR *at* n) [18] If you **turn up** your **nose at** (PHRASE:)

something, you reject it because you think that it is not good enough for you. ❑ *I'm not in a financial position to turn up my nose at several hundred thousand pounds.* 19 If you do something **under** someone's **nose**, you do it right in front of them, without trying to hide it from them. ❑ *Okay so have an affair, but not right under my nose.* 20 to put someone's **nose out of joint** → see **joint**. V and N inflect, usu PHR *at* n PHRASE: N inflects

**nose|bleed** /nəʊzbliːd/ **(nosebleeds)** also **nose bleed.** If someone has a **nosebleed**, blood comes out from inside their nose. ❑ *Whenever I have a cold I get a nosebleed.* N-COUNT

**nose|dive** /nəʊzdaɪv/ **(nosedives, nosediving, nosedived)** also **nose-dive.** 1 If prices, profits, or exchange rates **nosedive**, they suddenly fall by a large amount. [JOURNALISM] ❑ *The value of other shares nosedived by £2.6 billion.* ♦ **Nosedive** is also a noun. ❑ *The bank yesterday revealed a 30 per cent nosedive in profits.* 2 If something such as someone's reputation or career **nosedives**, it suddenly gets much worse. [JOURNALISM] ❑ *Since the US invasion the president's reputation has nosedived.* ♦ **Nosedive** is also a noun. ❑ *He told the tribunal his career had 'taken a nosedive' since his dismissal last year.* VERB = plummet V N-SING VERB V N-SING

**nose job** **(nose jobs)** A **nose job** is a surgical operation that some people have to improve the shape of their nose. [INFORMAL] ❑ *I've never had plastic surgery, though people always think I've had a nose job.* N-COUNT

**nos|ey** /nəʊzi/ → see **nosy**.

**nosh** /nɒʃ/ **(noshes, noshing, noshed)** 1 Food can be referred to as **nosh**. [BRIT, INFORMAL] ❑ *Fancy some nosh?* 2 A **nosh** is a snack or light meal. [AM, INFORMAL] 3 If you **nosh**, you eat. [INFORMAL] ❑ *She sprinkled pepper on my grub, watching me nosh. ...a big-bellied bird noshing some heather.* N-UNCOUNT = grub N-SING VERB V V n

**nos|tal|gia** /nɒstældʒə/ **Nostalgia** is an affectionate feeling you have for the past, especially for a particularly happy time. ❑ *He might be influenced by nostalgia for his happy youth... He discerned in the novel an air of Sixties nostalgia.* N-UNCOUNT: oft N *for* n

**nos|tal|gic** /nɒstældʒɪk/ 1 **Nostalgic** things cause you to think affectionately about the past. ❑ *Although we still depict nostalgic snow scenes on Christmas cards, winters are now very much warmer... Somehow the place even smelt wonderfully nostalgic.* 2 If you feel **nostalgic**, you think affectionately about experiences you had in the past. ❑ *Many people were nostalgic for the good old days.* ♦ **nos|tal|gi|cal|ly** /nɒstældʒɪkli/ *People look back nostalgically on the war period, simply because everyone pulled together.* ADJ ADJ: usu v-link ADJ, oft ADJ *for/about* n ADV: ADV with v, ADV adj

**nos|tril** /nɒstrɪl/ **(nostrils)** Your **nostrils** are the two openings at the end of your nose. N-COUNT

**nos|trum** /nɒstrəm/ **(nostrums)** 1 You can refer to ideas or theories about how something should be done as **nostrums**, especially when you think they are old-fashioned or wrong in some way. [FORMAL] ❑ *...yesterday's failed socialist nostrums.* 2 If you refer to a medicine as a **nostrum**, you mean that it is not effective or has not been tested in a proper scientific way. ❑ *...pills and other nostrums claiming to be magic potions.* N-COUNT: usu pl, oft N *of* n N-COUNT

**nosy** /nəʊzi/ **(nosier, nosiest)** also **nosey.** If you describe someone as **nosy**, you mean that they are interested in things which do not concern them. [INFORMAL] ❑ *He was having to whisper in order to avoid being overheard by their nosy neighbours... I agree that the press is often too nosy about a candidate's personal history.* ADJ disapproval

**not** /nɒt/ ♦♦♦

> **Not** is often shortened to **n't** in spoken English, and added to the auxiliary or modal verb. For example, 'did not' is often shortened to 'didn't'.

1 You use **not** with verbs to form negative statements. ❑ *The sanctions are not working the way they were intended... I was not in Britain at the time... There are many things you won't understand here... I don't trust my father anymore.* 2 You use **not** to form questions to which you expect the answer 'yes'. ❑ *Haven't they got enough problems there already?... Didn't I see you at the party last week?... Didn't you just love the Waltons?* 3 You use **not**, usually in the form **n't**, in questions which imply that someone should have done something, or to express surprise that something is not the case. ❑ *Why didn't you do it months ago?... Hasn't anyone ever kissed you before?... Shouldn't you have gone further?* 4 You use **not**, usually in the form **n't**, in question tags after a positive statement. ❑ *'It's a nice piece of jewellery though, isn't it?'... I've been a great husband, haven't I?* 5 You use **not**, usually in the form **n't**, in polite suggestions. ❑ *Actually we do have a position in mind. Why don't you fill out our application?... Couldn't they send it by train?* 6 You use **not** to represent the negative of a word, group, or clause that has just been used. ❑ *'Have you found Paula?' — 'I'm afraid not, Kate.'... At first I really didn't care whether he came or not.* 7 You can use **not** in front of 'all' or 'every' when you want to say something that applies only to some members of the group that you are talking about. ❑ *Not all the money, to put it mildly, has been used wisely... Not every applicant had a degree.* 8 If something is **not** always the case, you mean that sometimes it is the case and sometimes it is not. ❑ *She couldn't always afford a babysitter... The life of an FBI agent wasn't always as glamorous as people thought.* 9 You can use **not** or **not even** in front of 'a' or 'one' to emphasize that there is none at all of what is being mentioned. ❑ *The houses are beautiful, but there's no shop, not even a pub to go into... I sent report after report. But not one word was published.* 10 You can use **not** in front of a word referring to a distance, length of time, or other amount to say that the actual distance, time, or amount is less than the one mentioned. ❑ *The tug crossed our stern not fifty yards away... They were here not five minutes ago!* 11 You use **not** when you are contrasting something that is true with something that is untrue. You use this especially to indicate that people might think that the untrue statement is true. ❑ *He has his place in the Asian team not because he is white but because he is good... Training is an investment not a cost.* 12 You use **not** in expressions such as 'not only', 'not just', and 'not simply' to emphasize that something is true, but it is not the whole truth. ❑ *These movies were not only making money; they were also perceived to be original... There is always a 'black market' not just in Britain but in Europe as a whole.* 13 You use **not that** to introduce a negative clause that contradicts something that the previous statement implies. ❑ *His death took me a year to get over; not that you're ever really over it.* 14 **Not at all** is an emphatic way of saying 'No' or of agreeing that the answer to a question is 'No'. ❑ *'Sorry. I sound like Abby, don't I?' — 'No. Not at all.'... 'You don't think that you've betrayed your country.' — 'No I don't. No, not at all.'* 15 **Not at all** is a polite way of acknowledging a person's thanks. ❑ *'Thank you very much for speaking with us.' — 'Not at all.'* 16 **not half** → see **half**. **if not** → see **if**. **not least** → see **least**. **not to mention** → see **mention**. **nothing if not** → see **nothing**. **more often than not** → see **often**. NEG NEG NEG NEG NEG politeness NEG NEG NEG NEG emphasis NEG: NEG amount NEG NEG emphasis PHRASE CONVENTION emphasis CONVENTION formulae

**no|table** /nəʊtəbᵊl/ Someone or something that is **notable** is important or interesting. ❑ *The proposed new structure is notable not only for its height, but for its shape... With a few notable exceptions, doctors are a pretty sensible lot.* ADJ: oft ADJ *for* n

**no|tably** /nəʊtəbli/ 1 You use **notably** to specify an important or typical example of something that you are talking about. ❑ *The divorce would be granted when more important problems, notably the fate of the children, had been decided... It* ADV: ADV group/cl = particularly *was a question of making sure certain needs were addressed, notably in the pensions area.* 2 ADV: ADV adj/adv [emphasis] You can use **notably** to emphasize a particular quality that someone or something has. ❑ *Old established friends are notably absent, so it's a good opportunity to make new contacts.*

**no|ta|ry** /noutəri/ **(notaries)** N-COUNT A **notary** or a **notary public** is a person, usually a lawyer, who has legal authority to witness the signing of documents in order to make them legally valid.

**no|ta|tion** /nouteɪʃᵊn/ **(notations)** N-VAR: usu supp N A system of **notation** is a set of written symbols that are used to represent something such as music or mathematics. ❑ *Musical notation was conceived for the C major scale and each line and space represents a note in this scale. ...some other abstract notation system like a computer language.*

**notch** /nɒtʃ/ **(notches, notching, notched)** 1 N-COUNT You can refer to a level on a scale of measurement or achievement as a **notch**. [JOURNALISM] ❑ *Average earnings in the economy moved up another notch in August... In this country the good players are pulled down a notch or two.* 2 VERB If you **notch** a success, especially in a sporting contest, you achieve it. [JOURNALISM] ❑ V n *The President is keen to notch a political triumph that would foster freer world trade and faster economic growth.* 3 N-COUNT = nick A **notch** is a small V-shaped or circular cut in the surface or edge of something. ❑ *They cut notches in the handle of their pistol for each man they shot.* 4 ➔ See also **top-notch**.

♦ **notch up** PHRASAL VERB If you **notch up** something such as a score or total, you achieve it. [JOURNALISM] ❑ V P n (not pron) *He had notched up more than 25 victories worldwide.*

**note** /nout/ **(notes, noting, noted)** ◆◆◇ 1 N-COUNT = message A **note** is a short letter. ❑ *Stevens wrote him a note asking him to come to his apartment... I'll have to leave a note for Karen.* 2 N-COUNT A **note** is something that you write down to remind yourself of something. ❑ *I knew that if I didn't make a note I would lose the thought so I asked to borrow a pen or pencil... Take notes during the consultation as the final written report is very concise.* 3 N-COUNT In a book or article, a **note** is a short piece of additional information. ❑ *See Note 16 on page p. 223.* 4 N-COUNT: with supp A **note** is a short document that has to be signed by someone and that gives official information about something. ❑ *Since Mr Bennett was going to need some time off work, he asked for a sick note... I've got half a ton of gravel in the lorry but he won't sign my delivery note.* 5 N-COUNT You can refer to a banknote as a **note**. [BRIT] ❑ *They exchange travellers cheques at a different rate from notes. ...a five pound note.*

☑ in AM, use **bill**

6 N-COUNT: usu with supp In music, a **note** is the sound of a particular pitch, or a written symbol representing this sound. ❑ *She has a deep voice and doesn't even try for the high notes.* 7 N-SING: with supp, usu N *of* n = tone You can use **note** to refer to a particular quality in someone's voice that shows how they are feeling. ❑ *There is an unmistakable note of nostalgia in his voice when he looks back on the early years of the family business... It was not difficult for him to catch the note of bitterness in my voice.* 8 N-SING: with supp You can use **note** to refer to a particular feeling, impression, or atmosphere. ❑ *Yesterday's testimony began on a note of passionate but civilized disagreement... Somehow he tells these stories without a note of horror... The furniture strikes a traditional note which is appropriate to its Edwardian setting.* 9 VERB If you **note** a fact, you become aware of it. ❑ V n *The White House has noted his promise to support any attack that was designed to enforce the UN resolutions...* V that *Suddenly, I noted that the rain had stopped...* V wh *Haig noted how he 'looked pinched and rather tired'.* 10 VERB If you tell someone to **note** something, you are drawing their attention to it. ❑ V n *Note the statue to Sallustio Bandini, a prominent Sienese...* V that *Please note that there are a limited number of tickets.* 11 VERB = observe If you **note** something, you mention it in order to draw people's attention to it. ❑ V that *The report notes that export and import volumes picked up in leading economies...* V n *The yearbook also noted a sharp drop in reported cases of sexually transmitted disease.* 12 VERB When you **note** something, you write it down as a record of what has happened. ❑ V with quote *'He has had his tonsils out and has been ill, too,' she noted in her diary...* V n *One policeman was clearly visible noting the number plates of passing cars...* V wh *A guard came and took our names and noted where each of us was sitting.* Also V that 13 ➔ See also **noted**, **promissory note**, **sleeve note**.

PHRASES 14 PHRASE: V inflects, oft PHR *on* n, PHR *with* n = discuss If you **compare notes** with someone on a particular subject, you talk to them and find out whether their opinion, information, or experience is the same as yours. ❑ *The women were busily comparing notes on the queen's outfit.* 15 PHRASE: n PHR Someone or something that is **of note** is important, worth mentioning, or well-known. ❑ *...politicians of note... He has published nothing of note in the last ten years.* 16 PHRASE: V inflects If someone or something **strikes** a particular **note** or **sounds** a particular **note**, they create a particular feeling, impression, or atmosphere. ❑ *Before his first round of discussions, Mr Baker sounded an optimistic note... Plants growing out of cracks in paving strike the right note up a cottage-garden path.* 17 PHRASE: V inflects, oft PHR *of* n, PHR that If you **take note of** something, you pay attention to it because you think that it is important or significant. ❑ *Take note of the weather conditions... They took note that she showed no surprise at the news of the murder.* 18 to **make a mental note** ➔ see **mental**.

♦ **note down** PHRASAL VERB If you **note down** something, you write it down quickly, so that you have a record of it. ❑ V P n (not pron) *She had noted down the names and she told me the story simply and factually...* V n P *If you find a name that's on the list I've given you, note it down...* V P wh *Please note down what I'm about to say.*

**note|book** /noutbʊk/ **(notebooks)** 1 N-COUNT A **notebook** is a small book for writing notes in. ❑ *He brought out a notebook and pen from his pocket. ...her reporter's notebook.* 2 N-COUNT: usu N n A **notebook** computer is a small personal computer. ❑ *...a range of notebook computers which allows all your important information to travel safely with you.*

**not|ed** /noutɪd/ ◆◇◇ ADJ: oft ADJ *for* n/-ing = renowned To be **noted for** something you do or have means to be well-known and admired for it. ❑ *...a television programme noted for its attacks on organised crime... Lawyers are not noted for rushing into change.*

**note|pad** /noutpæd/ **(notepads)** N-COUNT A **notepad** is a pad of paper that you use for writing notes or letters on.

**note|paper** /noutpeɪpəʳ/ N-UNCOUNT: oft supp N **Notepaper** is paper that you use for writing letters on. ❑ *He had written letters on official notepaper to promote a relative's company.*

**note|worthy** /noutwɜːʳði/ ADJ: oft *it* v-link ADJ that = notable A fact or event that is **noteworthy** is interesting, remarkable, or significant in some way. [FORMAL] ❑ *It is noteworthy that the programme has been shifted from its original August slot to July... I found nothing particularly noteworthy to report... The most noteworthy feature of the list is that there are no women on it.*

**noth|ing** /nʌθɪŋ/ **(nothings)** ◆◆◆ 1 PRON **Nothing** means not a single thing, or not a single part of something. ❑ *I've done nothing much since coffee time... Mr Pearson said he knew nothing of his wife's daytime habits... He was dressed in jeans and nothing else... There is nothing wrong with the car.* 2 PRON You use **nothing** to indicate that something or someone is not important or significant. ❑ *Because he had always had money it meant nothing to him... While the increase in homicides is alarming, it is nothing compared to what is to come in the rest of the decade... She kept bursting into tears over nothing at work... Do our years together mean nothing?* ♦ N-COUNT: usu sing **Nothing** is also a noun. ❑ *It is the picture itself that is the problem; so small, so dull. It's a nothing, really.* 3 PRON If you say that something cost **nothing** or is worth **nothing**, you are indicating that it cost or is worth a surprisingly small amount of money. ❑ *The furniture was threadbare; he'd obviously picked it up for nothing... Homes in this corner of Mantua that once went for $350,000 are now worth nothing.*

PRON: PRON adj, PRON to-inf
[4] You use **nothing** before an adjective or 'to'-infinitive to say that something or someone does not have the quality indicated. ❑ *Around the lake the countryside generally is nothing special... There was nothing remarkable about him... All kids her age do silly things; it's nothing to worry about.*

PRON: PRON *so* adj/adv, PRON compar [emphasis]
[5] You can use **nothing** before 'so' and an adjective or adverb, or before a comparative, to emphasize how strong or great a particular quality is. ❑ *Youngsters learn nothing so fast as how to beat the system... I consider nothing more important in my life than songwriting... There's nothing better than a good cup of hot coffee.*

**PHRASES**

PHRASE: v-link PHR
[6] You can use **all or nothing** to say that either something must be done fully and completely or else it cannot be done at all. ❑ *Either he went through with this thing or he did not; it was all or nothing.*

PHRASE: v-link PHR
[7] If you say that something is **better than nothing**, you mean that it is not what is required, but that it is better to have that thing than to have nothing at all. ❑ *After all, 15 minutes of exercise is better than nothing.*

PHRASE: PHR n/inf/-ing
[8] You use **nothing but** in front of a noun, an infinitive without 'to', or an '-ing' form to mean 'only'. ❑ *All that money brought nothing but sadness and misery and tragedy... It did nothing but make us ridiculous... They care for nothing but fighting.*

PHRASE: V inflects, PHR *but* to-inf, PHR *but* n
[9] If you say that **there is nothing for it** but to take a particular action, you mean that it is the only possible course of action that you can take, even though it might be unpleasant. [BRIT] ❑ *Much depends on which individual ingredients you choose. There is nothing for it but to taste and to experiment for yourself.*

PHRASE: v-link PHR adj [emphasis]
[10] You use **nothing if not** in front of an adjective to indicate that someone or something clearly has a lot of the particular quality mentioned. ❑ *Professor Fish has been nothing if not professional.*

CONVENTION [formulae] = *don't mention it*
[11] People sometimes say **'It's nothing'** as a polite response after someone has thanked them for something they have done. ❑ *'Thank you for the wonderful dinner.' — 'It's nothing,' Sarah said... 'I'll be on my way. I can't thank you enough, Alan.' — 'It was nothing, but take care.'*

PHRASE: *there* v-link PHR
[12] If you say about a story or report that there is **nothing in it** or **nothing to it**, you mean that it is untrue. ❑ *It's all rubbish and superstition, and there's nothing in it.*

PHRASE: *there* v-link PHR
[13] If you say about an activity that there is **nothing to it** or **nothing in it**, you mean that it is extremely easy. ❑ *This device has a gripper that electrically twists off the jar top. Nothing to it... If you've shied away from making pancakes in the past, don't be put off – there's really nothing in it!*

PHRASE: *there* v-link PHR
[14] If you say about a contest or competition that there is **nothing in it**, you mean that two or more of the competitors are level and have an equal chance of winning.

PHRASE: PHR after v, v-link PHR [emphasis]
[15] **Nothing of the sort** is used when strongly contradicting something that has just been said. ❑ *'We're going to talk this over in my office.' — 'We're going to do nothing of the sort.'... Mrs Adamson said that she was extremely sorry, in tones that made it clear that she was nothing of the sort.*

[16] → See also **sweet nothings**. **nothing to write home about** → see **home**. to **say nothing of** → see **say**. **nothing short of** → see **short**. to **stop at nothing** → see **stop**. to **think nothing of** → see **think**.

**noth|ing|ness** /nʌθɪŋnəs/

N-UNCOUNT
[1] **Nothingness** is the fact of not existing. ❑ *There might be something beyond the grave, you know, and not nothingness.*

N-UNCOUNT
[2] **Nothingness** means complete emptiness. ❑ *Her eyes, glazed with the drug, stared with half closed lids at nothingness.*

**no|tice** /noʊtɪs/ **(notices, noticing, noticed)** ◆◆◇

VERB: V n, V that, V wh, V n -ing, V, Also V n inf
[1] If you **notice** something or someone, you become aware of them. ❑ *People should not hesitate to contact the police if they've noticed anyone acting suspiciously... I noticed that most academics were writing papers during the summer... Luckily, I'd noticed where you left the car... Mrs Shedden noticed a bird sitting on the garage roof... She needn't worry that he'll think she looks a mess. He won't notice.*

N-COUNT
[2] A **notice** is a written announcement in a place where everyone can read it. ❑ *A few guest houses had 'No Vacancies' notices in their windows. ...a notice which said 'Beware Flooding'.*

N-UNCOUNT: usu with supp
[3] If you give **notice** about something that is going to happen, you give a warning in advance that it is going to happen. ❑ *Interest is paid monthly. Three months' notice is required for withdrawals... She was transferred without notice.*

N-COUNT = *announcement*
[4] A **notice** is a formal announcement in a newspaper or magazine about something that has happened or is going to happen. ❑ *I rang The Globe with news of Blake's death, and put notices in the personal column of The Times.*

N-COUNT: usu supp N
[5] A **notice** is one of a number of letters that are similar or exactly the same which an organization sends to people in order to give them information or ask them to do something. ❑ *Bonus notices were issued each year from head office to local agents.*

N-COUNT = *review*
[6] A **notice** is a written article in a newspaper or magazine in which someone gives their opinion of a play, film, or concert. ❑ *Nevertheless, it's good to know you've had good notices, even if you don't read them.*

**PHRASES**

PHRASE: usu PHR after v
[7] **Notice** is used in expressions such as **'at short notice'**, **'at a moment's notice'** or **'at twenty-four hours' notice'**, to indicate that something can or must be done within a short period of time. ❑ *There's no one available at such short notice to take her class... All our things stayed in our suitcase, as if we had to leave at a moment's notice.*

PHRASE: V inflects
[8] If you **bring** something **to** someone's **notice**, you make them aware of it. ❑ *I am so glad that you have brought this to my notice.*

PHRASE: V inflects
[9] If something **comes to** your **notice**, you become aware of it. ❑ *Her work also came to the notice of the French actor-producer Louis Jouvet.*

PHRASE: V inflects, oft PHR that
[10] If something **escapes** your **notice**, you fail to recognize it or realize it. ❑ *It hasn't escaped our notice that the hospital has come out of all the proposed changes really quite nicely.*

PHRASE: PHR after v
[11] If a situation is said to exist **until further notice**, it will continue for an uncertain length of time until someone changes it. ❑ *All flights to Lanchow had been cancelled until further notice.*

PHRASE: V inflects
[12] If an employer **gives** an employee **notice**, the employer tells the employee that he or she must leave his or her job within a fixed period of time. [BUSINESS] ❑ *The next morning I telephoned him and gave him his notice.*

PHRASE: V inflects = *quit*
[13] If you **hand in** your **notice** or **give in** your **notice**, you tell your employer that you intend to leave your job soon within a set period of time. [BUSINESS] ❑ *He handed in his notice at the bank and ruined his promising career.*

PHRASE: V inflects, oft PHR *of* n
[14] If you **take notice of** a particular fact or situation, you behave in a way that shows that you are aware of it. ❑ *We want the government to take notice of what we think they should do for single parents... This should make people sit up and take notice.*

PHRASE: V inflects, usu PHR *of* n = *ignore*
[15] If you **take no notice of** someone or something, you do not consider them to be important enough to affect what you think or what you do. ❑ *They took no notice of him, he did not stand out, he was in no way remarkable... I tried not to take any notice at first but then I was offended by it.*

**no|tice|able** /noʊtɪsəbəl/

ADJ: oft *it* v-link ADJ that
Something that is **noticeable** is very obvious, so that it is easy to see, hear, or recognize. ❑ *It is noticeable that women do not have the rivalry that men have... The most noticeable effect of these changes is in the way people are now working together.*

ADV: ADV with v, ADV group
♦ **no|tice|ably** *Standards of living were deteriorating rather noticeably... There are also many physical signs, most noticeably a change in facial features.*

**no|tice|board** /noʊtɪsbɔːʳd/ **(noticeboards)**

N-COUNT
A **noticeboard** is a board which is usually attached to a wall in order to display notices giving information about something. [BRIT] ❑ *She added her name to the list on the noticeboard.*

✔ in AM, use **bulletin board**

**no|ti|fi|able** /noʊtɪfaɪəbᵊl/ A **notifiable** disease or crime is one that must be reported to the authorities whenever it occurs, because it is considered to be dangerous to the community. ❑ *Many doctors fail to report cases, even though food poisoning is a notifiable disease.* ADJ

**no|ti|fi|ca|tion** /noʊtɪfɪkeɪʃᵊn/ **(notifications)** If you are given **notification of** something, you are officially informed of it. ❑ *Names of the dead and injured are being withheld pending notification of relatives... Payments should be sent with the written notification.* N-VAR: oft N *of* n

**no|ti|fy** /noʊtɪfaɪ/ **(notifies, notifying, notified)** If you **notify** someone of something, you officially inform them about it. [FORMAL] ❑ *The skipper notified the coastguard of the tragedy... Earlier this year they were notified that their homes were to be cleared away... She confirmed that she would notify the police and the hospital.* VERB = *inform*; V n *of/about* n; *be* V-ed that; V n; Also V n that

**no|tion** /noʊʃᵊn/ **(notions)** A **notion** is an idea or belief about something. ❑ *We each have a notion of just what kind of person we'd like to be... I reject absolutely the notion that privatisation of our industry is now inevitable.* ◆◇◇ N-COUNT: oft N *of* n/-ing/wh, N that = *idea*

**no|tion|al** /noʊʃənᵊl/ Something that is **notional** exists only in theory or as a suggestion or idea, but not in reality. [FORMAL] ❑ *...the notional value of state assets.* ADJ = *theoretical* ♦ **no|tion|al|ly** *...those who notionally supported the republic but did nothing in terms of action... That meant that he, notionally at least, outranked them all.* ADV: ADV with cl/group, ADV with v

**no|to|ri|ety** /noʊtəraɪɪti/ To achieve **notoriety** means to become well-known for something bad. ❑ *He achieved notoriety as chief counsel to President Nixon in the Watergate break-in.* N-UNCOUNT

**no|to|ri|ous** /noʊtɔːriəs/ To be **notorious** means to be well-known for something bad. ❑ *...an area notorious for drugs, crime and violence... She told us the story of one of Britain's most notorious country house murders.* ADJ: oft ADJ *for* n/-ing = *infamous* ♦ **no|to|ri|ous|ly** *The train company is overstaffed and notoriously inefficient... Doctors notoriously neglect their own health and fail to seek help when they should.* ADV: usu ADV group, also ADV before v

**not|with|stand|ing** /nɒtwɪðstændɪŋ/ If something is true **notwithstanding** something else, it is true in spite of that other thing. [FORMAL] ❑ *He despised William Pitt, notwithstanding the similar views they both held.* PREP ♦ **Notwithstanding** is also an adverb. ❑ *His relations with colleagues, differences of opinion notwithstanding, were unfailingly friendly.* ADV: n ADV

**nou|gat** /nuːgɑː, AM -gət/ **Nougat** is a kind of firm sweet, containing nuts and sometimes fruit. N-UNCOUNT

**nought** /nɔːt/ **(noughts)**

> ☑ The spelling **naught** is also used for meaning 2.

1 **Nought** is the number 0. [mainly BRIT] ❑ *Sales rose by nought point four per cent last month... Houses are graded from nought to ten for energy efficiency.* NUM = *zero*

> ☑ in AM, use **zero**

2 If you try to do something but your efforts are not successful, you can say that your efforts **come to nought**. [FORMAL] ❑ *Numerous attempts to persuade him to write his memoirs came to nought.* PHRASE: V inflects

**noun** /naʊn/ **(nouns)** A **noun** is a word such as 'car', 'love', or 'Anne' which is used to refer to a person or thing. → See also **collective noun, count noun, mass noun, proper noun, singular noun, uncount noun.** N-COUNT

**noun group (noun groups)** A **noun group** is a noun or pronoun, or a group of words based on a noun or pronoun. In the sentence, 'He put the bottle of wine on the kitchen table', 'He', 'the bottle of wine', and 'the kitchen table' are all noun groups. N-COUNT = *noun phrase*

**noun phrase (noun phrases)** A **noun phrase** is the same as a **noun group**. N-COUNT

**nour|ish** /nʌrɪʃ, AM nɜːrɪʃ/ **(nourishes, nourishing, nourished)** 1 To **nourish** a person, animal, or plant means to provide them with the food that is necessary for life, growth, and good health. ❑ *The food she eats nourishes both her and the baby. ...microbes in the soil which nourish the plant.* VERB; V n; V n ♦ **nour|ish|ing** *Most of these nourishing substances are in the yolk of the egg. ...sensible, nourishing food.* ADJ 2 To **nourish** something such as a feeling or belief means to allow or encourage it to grow. ❑ *Journalists on the whole don't create public opinion. They can help to nourish it.* VERB; V n 3 → See also **-nourished**.

**-nourished** /-nʌrɪʃt, AM -nɜːr-/ **-nourished** is used with adverbs such as 'well' or 'under' to indicate how much food someone eats or whether it is the right kind of food. ❑ *To make sure the children are well-nourished, vitamin drops are usually recommended. ...under-nourished and poorly dressed orphans.* COMB in ADJ

**nour|ish|ment** /nʌrɪʃmənt, AM nɜːr-/ 1 If something provides a person, animal, or plant with **nourishment**, it provides them with the food that is necessary for life, growth, and good health. ❑ *He was unable to take nourishment for several days.* N-UNCOUNT 2 The action of nourishing someone or something, or the experience of being nourished, can be referred to as **nourishment**. ❑ *Sugar gives quick relief to hunger but provides no lasting nourishment.* N-UNCOUNT

**nous** /naʊs/ **Nous** is intelligence or common sense. [BRIT] ❑ *Few ministers have the nous or the instinct required to understand the ramifications... He is a man of extraordinary vitality, driving ambition and political nous.* N-UNCOUNT: usu with supp

**nou|veau riche** /nuːvoʊ riːʃ/ **(nouveau riche** or **nouveaux riches)** also **nouveau-riche.** 1 **The nouveaux riches** are people who have only recently become rich and who have tastes and manners that some people consider vulgar. ❑ *The nouveau riche have to find a way to be accepted.* N-PLURAL: usu *the* N [disapproval] 2 **Nouveau-riche** means belonging or relating to the nouveaux riches. ❑ *...critics who did not appreciate his nouveau-riche taste.* ADJ [disapproval]

**nou|velle cui|sine** /nuːvel kwɪziːn/ **Nouvelle cuisine** is a style of cooking in which very fresh foods are lightly cooked and served in unusual combinations. You can also refer to food that has been cooked in this way as **nouvelle cuisine.** ❑ *...dining out is easy with everything from a hamburger to hyper expensive nouvelle cuisine on your doorstep.* N-UNCOUNT

**Nov.** **Nov.** is a written abbreviation for **November**. ❑ *The first ballot is on Tuesday Nov 20.*

**nov|el** /nɒvᵊl/ **(novels)** 1 A **novel** is a long written story about imaginary people and events. ❑ *...a novel by Herman Hesse. ...historical novels set in the time of the Pharaohs.* ◆◆◇ N-COUNT 2 **Novel** things are new and different from anything that has been done, experienced, or made before. ❑ *Protesters found a novel way of demonstrating against steeply rising oil prices... The very idea of a sixth form college was novel in 1962.* ADJ

**nov|el|ist** /nɒvəlɪst/ **(novelists)** A **novelist** is a person who writes novels. ❑ *...a romantic novelist.* N-COUNT

**no|vel|la** /noʊvelə/ **(novellas)** A **novella** is a short novel or a long short story. ❑ *...an autobiographical novella from French writer Marguerite Duras.* N-COUNT

**nov|el|ty** /nɒvᵊlti/ **(novelties)** 1 **Novelty** is the quality of being different, new, and unusual. ❑ *In the contemporary western world, rapidly changing styles cater to a desire for novelty and individualism.* N-UNCOUNT: oft *the* N *of* n 2 A **novelty** is something that is new and therefore interesting. ❑ *It came from the days when a motor car was a novelty.* N-COUNT 3 **Novelties** are cheap toys, ornaments, or other objects that are sold as presents or souvenirs. ❑ *At Easter, we give them plastic eggs filled with small toys, novelties and coins.* N-COUNT

**No|vem|ber** /noʊvembəʳ/ **(Novembers)** **November** is the eleventh month of the year in the Western calendar. ❑ *He arrived in London in Novem-* N-VAR *ber 1939... There's no telling what the voters will do next November.*

**nov|ice** /nɒvɪs/ **(novices)** 1 [N-COUNT: oft N *at* n, N n] A **novice** is someone who has been doing a job or other activity for only a short time and so is not experienced at it. ❑ *I'm a novice at these things, Lieutenant. You're the professional... As a novice writer, this is something I'm interested in.* 2 [N-COUNT] In a monastery or convent, a **novice** is a person who is preparing to become a monk or nun.

**now** /naʊ/ ◆◆◆ 1 [ADV: ADV with cl, oft prep ADV] You use **now** to refer to the present time, often in contrast to a time in the past or the future. ❑ *She's a widow now... But we are now a much more fragmented society... Beef now costs well over 30 roubles a pound... She should know that by now.* ♦ [PRON] **Now** is also a pronoun. ❑ *Now is the time when we must all live as economically as possible.* 2 [ADV: ADV after v] If you do something **now**, you do it immediately. ❑ *I'm sorry, but I must go now... I fear that if I don't write now I shall never have another opportunity to do so.* ♦ [PRON] **Now** is also a pronoun. ❑ *Now is your chance to talk to him.* 3 [CONJ] You use **now** or **now that** to indicate that an event has occurred and as a result something else may or will happen. ❑ *Now you're settled, why don't you take up some serious study?... Now that she was retired she lived with her sister.* 4 [ADV: ADV with cl, ADV before v] You use **now** to indicate that a particular situation is the result of something that has recently happened. ❑ *She told me not to repeat it, but now I don't suppose it matters... Diplomats now expect the mission to be much less ambitious.* 5 [ADV: ADV with cl, oft prep ADV] In stories and accounts of past events, **now** is used to refer to the particular time that is being written or spoken about. ❑ *She felt a little better now... It was too late now for Blake to lock his room door... By now it was completely dark outside.* 6 [ADV: ADV with v, n ADV] You use **now** in statements which specify the length of time up to the present that something has lasted. ❑ *They've been married now for 30 years... They have been missing for a long time now... It's some days now since I heard anything.* 7 [ADV: ADV cl] You say '**Now**' or '**Now then**' to indicate to the person or people you are with that you want their attention, or that you are about to change the subject. [SPOKEN] ❑ *'Now then,' Max said, 'to get back to the point.'... Now, can we move on and discuss the vital business of the day, please.* 8 [ADV: ADV with cl] You use **now** to give a slight emphasis to a request or command. [SPOKEN] ❑ *Come on now. You know you must be hungry... Come and sit down here, now... Now don't talk so loud and bother him, honey.* 9 [ADV: ADV cl] You can say '**Now**' to introduce information which is relevant to the part of a story or account that you have reached, and which needs to be known before you can continue. [SPOKEN] ❑ *My son went to Almeria in Southern Spain. Now he and his wife are people who love a quiet holiday... Now, I hadn't told him these details, so he must have done some research on his own.* 10 [ADV: ADV cl] You say '**Now**' to introduce something which contrasts with what you have just said. [SPOKEN] ❑ *Now, if it was me, I'd want to do more than just change the locks.*
**PHRASES** 11 [PHRASE: PHR with cl] If you say that something happens **now and then** or **every now and again**, you mean that it happens sometimes but not very often or regularly. ❑ *My father has a collection of magazines to which I return every now and then... Now and again he'd join in when we were playing video games.* 12 [PHRASE: PHR with cl] If you say that something will happen **any day now**, **any moment now**, or **any time now**, you mean that it will happen very soon. ❑ *Jim expects to be sent to Europe any day now... Any moment now the silence will be broken.* 13 [PHRASE: PHR n] People such as television presenters sometimes use **now for** when they are going to start talking about a different subject or presenting a new activity. [SPOKEN] ❑ *And now for something completely different... Now for a quick look at some of the other stories in the news.* 14 [PHRASE: PHR with cl] **Just now** means a very short time ago. [SPOKEN] ❑ *You looked pretty upset just now... I spoke just now of being in love.* 15 [PHRASE: cl PHR] You use **just now** when you want to say that a particular situation exists at the time when you are speaking, although it may change in the future. [SPOKEN] ❑ *I'm pretty busy just now... Mr Goldsworth is not available just now.* 16 [PHRASE: V inflects] If you say '**It's now or never**', you mean that something must be done immediately, because if it is not done immediately there will not be another chance to do it. [SPOKEN] ❑ *It's now or never, so make up your mind.* 17 [CONVENTION = there there] You can say '**now, now**' as a friendly way of trying to comfort someone who is upset or distressed. [SPOKEN] ❑ *'I figure it's all over.' — 'Now, now. You did just fine.'* 18 [CONVENTION] You can say '**Now, then**' or '**Now, now**' when you want to give someone you know well a friendly warning not to behave in a particular way. [SPOKEN] ❑ *Now then, no unpleasantness, please... Now, now Roger, I'm sure you didn't mean it but that remark was in very poor taste.*

**nowa|days** /naʊədeɪz/ [ADV: ADV with cl] **Nowadays** means at the present time, in contrast with the past. ❑ *Nowadays it's acceptable for women to be ambitious. But it wasn't then... I don't see much of Tony nowadays.*

**no|where** /nəʊ$^{h}$weə$^{r}$/ ◆◇◇ 1 [ADV: ADV with *be*, ADV after v, oft ADV cl/group, emphasis] You use **nowhere** to emphasize that a place has more of a particular quality than any other places, or that it is the only place where something happens or exists. ❑ *Nowhere is language a more serious issue than in Hawaii... This kind of forest exists nowhere else in the world... If you are extremely rich, you could stay nowhere better than the Ruislip Court Hotel.* 2 [ADV: *be* ADV, ADV after v, usu ADV to-inf, ADV adj/-ed to-inf] You use **nowhere** when making negative statements to say that a suitable place of the specified kind does not exist. ❑ *There was nowhere to hide and nowhere to run... I have nowhere else to go, nowhere in the world... He had nowhere to call home.* 3 [ADV: *be* ADV, oft ADV to-inf, ADV adv/prep] You use **nowhere** to indicate that something or someone cannot be seen or found. ❑ *Michael glanced anxiously down the corridor, but Wilfred was nowhere to be seen... The escaped prisoner was nowhere in sight.* 4 [ADV: ADV after v, *from/to* ADV] You can use **nowhere** to refer in a general way to small, unimportant, or uninteresting places. ❑ *...endless paths that led nowhere in particular. ...country roads that go from nowhere to nowhere.* 5 [ADV: *from/out of* ADV] If you say that something or someone appears **from nowhere** or **out of nowhere**, you mean that they appear suddenly and unexpectedly. ❑ *A car came from nowhere, and I had to jump back into the hedge just in time... Houses had sprung up out of nowhere on the hills.* 6 [ADV: ADV before v, *be* ADV, oft ADV prep, emphasis] You use **nowhere** to mean not in any part of a text, speech, or argument. ❑ *He nowhere offers concrete historical background to support his arguments... Point taken, but nowhere did we suggest that this yacht's features were unique... The most important issue for most ordinary people was nowhere on the proposed agenda.*
**PHRASES** 7 [PHRASE: usu PHR after v, v-link PHR] If you say that a place is **in the middle of nowhere**, you mean that it is a long way from other places. ❑ *At dusk we pitched camp in the middle of nowhere.* 8 [PHRASE: V inflects] If you say that you **are getting nowhere**, or **getting nowhere fast**, or that something **is getting** you **nowhere**, you mean that you are not achieving anything or having any success. ❑ *My mind won't stop going round and round on the same subject and I seem to be getting nowhere... 'Getting nowhere fast,' pronounced Crosby, 'that's what we're doing.'... Oh, stop it! This is getting us nowhere.* 9 [PHRASE, emphasis] If you use **nowhere near** in front of a word or expression, you are emphasizing that the real situation is very different from, or has not yet reached, the state which that word or expression suggests. ❑ *He's nowhere near recovered yet from his experiences... The chair he sat in was nowhere near as comfortable as the custom-designed one behind his desk.*

**no-win** [ADJ: ADJ n] If you are in a **no-win** situation, any action you take will fail to benefit you in any way. ❑ *It was a no-win situation. Either she pretended she hated Ned and felt awful or admitted she loved him and felt even worse!*

**nowt** /naʊt/ **Nowt** is sometimes used to mean the same as 'nothing'. [BRIT, DIALECT] ❑ *I'd got nowt to worry about.* PRON

**nox|ious** /nɒkʃəs/ [1] A **noxious** gas or substance is poisonous or very harmful. ❑ *Many household products give off noxious fumes.* ADJ: usu ADJ n [2] If you refer to someone or something as **noxious**, you mean that they are extremely unpleasant. [FORMAL] ❑ *...the heavy, noxious smell of burning sugar, butter, fats, and flour... Their behaviour was noxious.* ADJ: usu ADJ n

**noz|zle** /nɒzᵊl/ **(nozzles)** The **nozzle** of a hose or pipe is a narrow piece fitted to the end to control the flow of liquid or gas. ❑ *If he put his finger over the nozzle he could produce a forceful spray.* N-COUNT

**nr** In addresses, **nr** is used as a written abbreviation for **near**. [BRIT] ❑ *Brackhurst Agricultural College, nr Southwell, Notts.*

**-n't** /-ᵊnt/ → see **not**.

**nth** /enθ/ If you refer to the most recent item in a series of things as the **nth** item, you are emphasizing the number of times something has happened. ❑ *The story was raised with me for the nth time two days before the article appeared.* ADJ: ADJ n [emphasis] = umpteenth

**nu|ance** /njuːɑːns, AM nuː-/ **(nuances)** A **nuance** is a small difference in sound, feeling, appearance, or meaning. ❑ *We can use our eyes and facial expressions to communicate virtually every subtle nuance of emotion there is.* N-VAR

**nub** /nʌb/ **The nub** of a situation, problem, or argument is the central and most basic part of it. ❑ *That, I think, is the nub of the problem... Here we reach the nub of the argument.* N-SING: the N, usu N *of* n = crux

**nu|bile** /njuːbaɪl, AM nuːbɪl/ A **nubile** woman is young, physically mature, and sexually attractive. ❑ *What is this current television obsession with older men and nubile young women?* ADJ: usu ADJ n

**nu|clear** /njuːkliəʳ, AM nuːk-/ ◆◆◇ [1] **Nuclear** means relating to the nuclei of atoms, or to the energy released when these nuclei are split or combined. ❑ *...a nuclear power station. ...nuclear energy. ...nuclear physics.* ADJ: ADJ n [2] **Nuclear** means relating to weapons that explode by using the energy released when the nuclei of atoms are split or combined. ❑ *They rejected a demand for the removal of all nuclear weapons from UK soil. ...nuclear testing.* ADJ: ADJ n = atomic

**nu|clear ca|pa|bil|ity** **(nuclear capabilities)** If a country has **nuclear capability**, it is able to produce nuclear power and usually nuclear weapons. N-VAR

**nu|clear fami|ly** **(nuclear families)** A **nuclear family** is a family unit that consists of father, mother, and children. N-COUNT

**nuclear-free** A **nuclear-free** place is a place where nuclear energy or nuclear weapons are forbidden. ❑ *Strathclyde council has declared itself a nuclear-free zone.* ADJ: usu ADJ n

**nu|clear fuel** **(nuclear fuels)** **Nuclear fuel** is fuel that provides nuclear energy, for example in power stations. N-VAR

**nu|clear re|ac|tor** **(nuclear reactors)** A **nuclear reactor** is a machine which is used to produce nuclear energy or the place where this machine and other related machinery and equipment is kept. ❑ *They shut down the nuclear reactor for safety reasons.* N-COUNT

**nu|clear win|ter** **Nuclear winter** refers to the possible effects on the environment of a war in which large numbers of nuclear weapons are used. It is thought that there would be very low temperatures and very little light during a nuclear winter. N-UNCOUNT: also *a* N

**nu|cleic acid** /njuːkleɪɪk æsɪd, AM nuː-/ **(nucleic acids)** **Nucleic acids** are complex chemical substances, such as DNA, which are found in living cells. [TECHNICAL] N-MASS

**nu|cleus** /njuːkliəs, AM nuː-/ **(nuclei** /njuːkliaɪ, AM nuː-/ **)** [1] The **nucleus** of an atom or cell is the central part of it. ❑ *Neutrons and protons are bound together in the nucleus of an atom.* N-COUNT: usu with supp [2] **The nucleus of** a group of people or things is the small number of members which form the most important part of the group. ❑ *The Civic Movement could be the nucleus of a centrist party of the future.* N-COUNT: usu *the* N *of* n = core

**nude** /njuːd, AM nuːd/ **(nudes)** [1] A **nude** person is not wearing any clothes. ❑ *The occasional nude bather comes here... She turned down £1.2 million to pose nude in Playboy.* ADJ: ADJ n, ADJ after v, v-link ADJ ● If you do something **in the nude**, you are not wearing any clothes. If you paint or draw someone **in the nude**, they are not wearing any clothes. ❑ *Sleeping in the nude, if it suits you, is not a bad idea.* PHRASE: usu PHR after v = naked [2] A **nude** is a picture or statue of a person who is not wearing any clothes. A **nude** is also a person in a picture who is not wearing any clothes. ❑ *He was one of Australia's most distinguished artists, renowned for his portraits, landscapes and nudes.* N-COUNT

**nudge** /nʌdʒ/ **(nudges, nudging, nudged)** [1] If you **nudge** someone, you push them gently, usually with your elbow, in order to draw their attention to something. ❑ *I nudged Stan and pointed again.* VERB V n ♦ **Nudge** is also a noun. ❑ *She slipped her arm under his and gave him a nudge.* N-COUNT: usu sing [2] If you **nudge** someone or something into a place or position, you gently push them there. ❑ *Edna Swinson nudged him into the sitting room.* VERB V n prep/adv ♦ **Nudge** is also a noun. ❑ *McKinnon gave the wheel another slight nudge.* N-COUNT: usu sing [3] If you **nudge** someone into doing something, you gently persuade them to do it. ❑ *Bit by bit Bob had nudged Fritz into selling his controlling interest... Foreigners must use their power to nudge the country towards greater tolerance... British tour companies are nudging clients to travel further afield.* VERB V n *into* -ing/n, V n *towards* n, V n to-inf ♦ **Nudge** is also a noun. ❑ *I had a feeling that the challenge appealed to him. All he needed was a nudge.* N-COUNT: usu sing [4] If someone or something **is nudging** a particular amount, level, or state, they have almost reached it. ❑ *The temperature when we were there was nudging 80°F.* VERB: usu cont = approaching V n

**nud|ism** /njuːdɪzəm, AM nuː-/ **Nudism** is the practice of not wearing any clothes on beaches and other areas specially set aside for this purpose. ❑ *Nudism, the council decided, was doing the resort more harm than good.* N-UNCOUNT = naturism ♦ **nud|ist** **(nudists)** *There are no nudist areas and topless sunbathing is only allowed on a few beaches.* N-COUNT: oft N n = naturist

**nu|dity** /njuːdɪti, AM nuː-/ **Nudity** is the state of wearing no clothes. ❑ *...constant nudity and bad language on TV.* N-UNCOUNT

**nug|get** /nʌgɪt/ **(nuggets)** A **nugget** is a small lump of something, especially gold. ❑ *...pure high-grade gold nuggets. ...a small nugget of butter.* N-COUNT: oft n N, N *of* n

**nui|sance** /njuːsᵊns, AM nuː-/ **(nuisances)** If you say that someone or something is a **nuisance**, you mean that they annoy you or cause you a lot of problems. ❑ *He could be a bit of a nuisance when he was drunk... Sorry to be a nuisance.* N-COUNT: usu sing = pain ● If someone **makes a nuisance of** themselves, they behave in a way that annoys other people. ❑ *He spent three days making an absolute nuisance of himself.* PHRASE: V and N inflect

**nuke** /njuːk, AM nuːk/ **(nukes, nuking, nuked)** [1] A **nuke** is a nuclear weapon. [INFORMAL] ❑ *They have nukes, and if they're sufficiently pushed, they'll use them.* N-COUNT [2] If one country **nukes** another, it attacks it using nuclear weapons. [INFORMAL] ❑ *He wanted to nuke the area.* VERB V n

**null** /nʌl/ If an agreement, a declaration, or the result of an election is **null and void**, it is not legally valid. ❑ *A spokeswoman said the agreement had been declared null and void.* PHRASE: PHR after v

**nul|li|fy** /nʌlɪfaɪ/ **(nullifies, nullifying, nullified)** [1] To **nullify** a legal decision or procedure means to declare that it is not legally valid. [FORMAL] ❑ *He used his broad executive powers to nullify decisions by local governments... It is worth remembering that previous wills are nullified automatically upon marriage.* VERB = invalidate V n, V n [2] To **nullify** something means to make it have VERB no effect. [FORMAL] ❑ *He may be able to nullify that disadvantage by offering a wider variety of produce.* = negate V n

**numb** /nʌm/ **(numbs, numbing, numbed)** [1] If a part of your body is **numb**, you cannot feel anything there. ❑ *He could feel his fingers growing numb at their tips... My legs felt numb and my toes ached.* ADJ: usu v-link ADJ ♦ **numb|ness** *I have recently been suffering from pain and numbness in my hands.* N-UNCOUNT: oft N *in* n [2] If you are **numb with** shock, fear, or grief, you are so shocked, frightened, or upset that you cannot think clearly or feel any emotion. ❑ *The mother, numb with grief, has trouble speaking... I was so shocked I went numb.* ADJ: usu v-link ADJ, oft ADJ *with* n ♦ **numb|ness** *Many men become more aware of emotional numbness in their 40s.* N-UNCOUNT: oft adj N ♦ **numb|ly** /nʌmli/ *He walked numbly into the cemetery.* ADV: ADV with v [3] If an event or experience **numbs** you, you can no longer think clearly or feel any emotion. ❑ *For a while the shock of Philippe's letter numbed her... The horror of my experience has numbed my senses.* ➔ See also **mind-numbing**. VERB V n V n ♦ **numbed** *I'm so numbed with shock that I can hardly think. ...the sort of numbed hush which usually follows an automobile accident.* ADJ: usu v-link ADJ [4] If cold weather, a drug, or a blow **numbs** a part of your body, you can no longer feel anything in it. ❑ *An injection of local anaesthetic is usually given first to numb the area... She awoke with a numbed feeling in her left leg.* VERB V n V-ed

**num|ber** /nʌmbəʳ/ **(numbers, numbering, numbered)** ◆◆◆ [1] A **number** is a word such as 'two', 'nine', or 'twelve', or a symbol such as 1, 3, or 47. You use numbers to say how many things you are referring to or where something comes in a series. ❑ *No, I don't know the room number... Stan Laurel was born at number 3, Argyll Street... The number 47 bus leaves in 10 minutes.* N-COUNT: usu with supp [2] You use **number** with words such as 'large' or 'small' to say approximately how many things or people there are. ❑ *Quite a considerable number of interviews are going on... I have had an enormous number of letters from single parents... Growing numbers of people in the rural areas are too frightened to vote.* N-COUNT: adj N, usu N *of* n [3] If there are **a number of** things or people, there are several of them. If there are **any number of** things or people, there is a large quantity of them. ❑ *I seem to remember that Sam told a number of lies... There must be any number of people in my position.* N-SING: *a/any* N, usu N *of* n [4] You can refer to someone's or something's position in a list of the most successful or most popular of a particular type of thing as, for example, **number** one or **number** two. ❑ *...the world number one, Tiger Woods... Before you knew it, the single was at Number 90 in the US singles charts.* N-UNCOUNT: N num [5] If a group of people or things **numbers** a particular total, that is how many there are. ❑ *They told me that their village numbered 100... This time the dead were numbered in hundreds, not dozens.* VERB V num *be* V-ed *in* num [6] A **number** is the series of numbers that you dial when you are making a telephone call. ❑ *Sarah sat down and dialled a number. ...a list of names and telephone numbers... My number is 414-3925... 'You must have a wrong number,' she said. 'There's no one of that name here.'* N-COUNT [7] You can refer to a short piece of music, a song, or a dance as a **number**. ❑ *...'Unforgettable', a number that was written and performed in 1951... Responsibility for the dance numbers was split between Robert Alton and the young George Balanchine.* N-COUNT [8] If someone or something **is numbered among** a particular group, they are believed to belong in that group. [FORMAL] ❑ *The Leicester Swannington Railway is numbered among Britain's railway pioneers... He numbered several Americans among his friends.* VERB *be* V-ed *among* n V n *among* n [9] If you **number** something, you mark it with a number, usually starting at 1. ❑ *He cut his paper up into tiny squares, and he numbered each one.* VERB V n [10] ➔ See also **opposite number**, **prime number**, **serial number**.

**PHRASES** [11] If you say that someone's or something's **days are numbered**, you mean that they will not survive or be successful for much longer. ❑ *Critics believe his days are numbered because audiences are tired of watching him.* PHRASE: V inflects, with poss [12] If you refer to **the numbers game**, **the numbers racket**, or **the numbers**, you are referring to an illegal lottery or illegal betting. [AM] ➔ See also **numbers game**. PHRASE [13] **safety in numbers** ➔ see **safety**.

**num|ber crunch|er** **(number crunchers)** If you refer to **number crunchers**, you mean people whose jobs involve dealing with numbers or mathematical calculations, for example in finance or statistics. [INFORMAL] ❑ *Even if the recovery is under way, it may be some time before the official number crunchers confirm it.* N-COUNT: usu pl

**num|ber crunch|ing** If you refer to **number crunching**, you mean activities or processes concerned with numbers or mathematical calculation, for example in finance, statistics, or computing. [INFORMAL] ❑ *The computer does most of the number crunching.* N-UNCOUNT: oft N n

**num|ber|less** /nʌmbəʳləs/ If there are **numberless** things, there are too many to be counted. [LITERARY] ❑ *...numberless acts of personal bravery by firefighters and rescue workers.* ADJ: usu ADJ n = countless

**num|ber one** **(number ones)** [1] **Number one** means better, more important, or more popular than anything else of its kind. [INFORMAL] ❑ *The economy is the number one issue by far... By the way, I'm your number-one fan.* ADJ: ADJ n [2] In popular music, the **number one** is the best selling CD in any one week, or the group or person who has made that CD. [INFORMAL] ❑ *Paula is the only artist to achieve four number ones from a debut album.* N-COUNT

**num|ber plate** **(number plates)** also **numberplate.** A **number plate** is a sign on the front and back of a vehicle that shows its registration number. [BRIT] ➔ See picture on page 1707. ❑ *He drove a Rolls-Royce with a personalised number plate.* N-COUNT

in AM, use **license plate**

**num|bers game** [1] If you say that someone is playing **the numbers game**, you think that they are concentrating on the aspects of something which can be expressed in statistics, usually in order to mislead people. ❑ *Regrettably, he resorts to the familiar numbers game when he boasts that fewer than 300 state enterprises currently remain in the public sector.* N-SING disapproval [2] ➔ See also **number**.

**Num|ber Ten** **Number Ten** is often used to refer to 10 Downing Street, London, which is the official home of the British Prime Minister. ❑ *He called senior Unionist politicians to a meeting at Number Ten.* N-PROPER

**numb|skull** /nʌmskʌl/ **(numbskulls)** If you refer to someone as a **numbskull**, you mean that they are very stupid. [INFORMAL, OLD-FASHIONED] ❑ *How were we to know that he was a numbskull?* N-COUNT disapproval

**nu|mera|cy** /njuːmərəsi, AM nuː-/ **Numeracy** is the ability to do arithmetic. ❑ *Six months later John had developed literacy and numeracy skills, plus confidence.* N-UNCOUNT: oft N n

**nu|mer|al** /njuːmərəl, AM nuː-/ **(numerals)** **Numerals** are written symbols used to represent numbers. ❑ *...a flat, square wristwatch with classic Roman numerals. ...the numeral six.* N-COUNT

**nu|mer|ate** /njuːmərət, AM nuː-/ Someone who is **numerate** is able to do arithmetic. ❑ *Your children should be literate and numerate.* ADJ

**nu|meri|cal** /njuːmerɪkəl, AM nuː-/ **Numerical** means expressed in numbers or relating to numbers. ❑ *Your job is to group them by letter and put them in numerical order.* ADJ: usu ADJ n ♦ **nu|meri|cal|ly** *...a numerically coded colour chart... Numerically, there are a lot of young people involved in crime.* ADV

**nu|mer|ol|ogy** /njuːmərɒlədʒi, AM nuː-/ **Numerology** is the study of particular numbers, such as a person's date of birth, in the belief that they may have special significance in a person's life. N-UNCOUNT

**nu|mer|ous** /njuːmərəs, AM nuːm-/ If people or things are **numerous**, they exist or are ◆◇◇ ADJ present in large numbers. ❑ *Sex crimes were just as numerous as they are today... Despite numerous attempts to diet, her weight soared.*

**nu|mi|nous** /njuːmɪnəs, AM nuːm-/ Things that are **numinous** seem holy or spiritual and mysterious. [LITERARY] ❑ *The account of spiritual struggle that follows has a humbling and numinous power.* — ADJ

**nun** /nʌn/ **(nuns)** A **nun** is a member of a female religious community. ❑ *Mr Thomas was taught by the Catholic nuns whose school he attended.* — N-COUNT

**nun|cio** /nʌnsioʊ/ **(nuncios)** In the Roman Catholic church, a **nuncio** is an official who represents the Pope in a foreign country. ❑ *...the papal nuncio.* — N-COUNT

**nun|nery** /nʌnəri/ **(nunneries)** A **nunnery** is a group of buildings in which a community of nuns live together. [OLD-FASHIONED] — N-COUNT = *convent*

**nup|tial** /nʌpʃəl/ **(nuptials)** 1 **Nuptial** is used to refer to things relating to a wedding or to marriage. [OLD-FASHIONED] ❑ *I went to the room which he had called the nuptial chamber.* — ADJ: usu ADJ n
2 Someone's **nuptials** are their wedding celebrations. [OLD-FASHIONED] ❑ *She became immersed in planning her nuptials.* — N-PLURAL: usu with poss = *wedding*

**nurse** /nɜːʳs/ **(nurses, nursing, nursed)** ◆◇◇ 1 A **nurse** is a person whose job is to care for people who are ill. ❑ *She had spent 29 years as a nurse... Patients were dying because of an acute shortage of nurses.* — N-COUNT; N-TITLE; N-VOC
2 If you **nurse** someone, you care for them when they are ill. ❑ *All the years he was sick my mother had nursed him... She rushed home to nurse her daughter back to health.* — VERB; V n; V n back to n
3 If you **nurse** an illness or injury, you allow it to get better by resting as much as possible. ❑ *We're going to go home and nurse our colds.* — VERB; V n
4 If you **nurse** an emotion or desire, you feel it strongly for a long time. ❑ *Jane still nurses the pain of rejection... He had nursed an ambition to lead his own big orchestra.* — VERB = *harbour*; V n; V n
5 When a baby **nurses** or when its mother **nurses** it, it feeds by sucking milk from its mother's breast. [OLD-FASHIONED] ❑ *Most authorities recommend letting the baby nurse whenever it wants. ...young women nursing babies... Young people and nursing mothers are exempted from charges.* — VERB = *suckle*; V; V n; V-ing
6 → See also **nursery nurse**, **nursing**, **wet nurse**.

**nurse|maid** /nɜːʳsmeɪd/ **(nursemaids)** A **nursemaid** is a woman or girl who is paid to look after young children. [AM; also BRIT, OLD-FASHIONED] — N-COUNT = *nurse, nanny*

**nurse|ry** /nɜːʳsəri/ **(nurseries)** 1 A **nursery** is a place where children who are not old enough to go to school are looked after. ❑ *This nursery will be able to cater for 29 children... Her company ran its own workplace nursery.* → See also **day nursery**. — N-COUNT: also *at/from/to* N
2 **Nursery** is a school for very young children. ❑ *An affordable nursery education service is an essential basic amenity. ...a nursery teacher.* — N-VAR: oft N n
3 A **nursery** is a room in a family home in which the young children of the family sleep or play. ❑ *He has painted murals in his children's nursery.* — N-COUNT
4 A **nursery** is a place where plants are grown in order to be sold. ❑ *The garden, developed over the past 35 years, includes a nursery.* — N-COUNT

**nursery|man** /nɜːʳsərimən/ **(nurserymen)** A **nurseryman** is a man who works in a place where young plants are grown in order to be sold. — N-COUNT

**nurse|ry nurse** **(nursery nurses)** A **nursery nurse** is a person who has been trained to look after very young children. [BRIT] — N-COUNT

**nurse|ry rhyme** **(nursery rhymes)** A **nursery rhyme** is a poem or song for young children, especially one that is old or well known. — N-COUNT

**nurse|ry school** **(nursery schools)** A **nursery school** or a **nursery** is a school for very young children. ❑ *The availability of nursery school places varies widely across London.* — N-VAR = *kindergarten*

**nurs|ing** /nɜːʳsɪŋ/ **Nursing** is the profession of looking after people who are ill. ❑ *She had no aptitude for nursing... Does the nursing staff seem to care?* — N-UNCOUNT

**nurs|ing bot|tle** **(nursing bottles)** A **nursing bottle** is a plastic bottle with a special rubber top through which a baby can suck milk or another liquid. [AM] — N-COUNT

☑ in BRIT, use **feeding bottle**

**nurs|ing home** **(nursing homes)** A **nursing home** is a private hospital, especially one for old people. ❑ *He died in a nursing home at the age of 87.* — N-COUNT

**nur|ture** /nɜːʳtʃəʳ/ **(nurtures, nurturing, nurtured)** 1 If you **nurture** something such as a young child or a young plant, you care for it while it is growing and developing. [FORMAL] ❑ *Parents want to know the best way to nurture and raise their child to adulthood... The modern conservatory is not an environment for nurturing plants.* ♦ **nur|tur|ing** *She was not receiving warm nurturing care.* ♦ **nur|tur|ing** *Which adult in these children's lives will provide the nurturing they need?* — VERB; V n; V n; ADJ; N-UNCOUNT
2 If you **nurture** plans, ideas, or people, you encourage them or help them to develop. [FORMAL] ❑ *She had always nurtured great ambitions for her son. ...parents whose political views were nurtured in the sixties.* ♦ **nur|tur|ing** *The decision to cut back on film-making had a catastrophic effect on the nurturing of new talent.* — VERB; V n; V n; N-UNCOUNT
3 **Nurture** is care that is given to someone while they are growing and developing. ❑ *The human organism learns partly by nature, partly by nurture.* — N-UNCOUNT

**nut** /nʌt/ **(nuts)** 1 The firm shelled fruit of some trees and bushes are called **nuts**. Some nuts can be eaten. ❑ *Nuts and seeds are good sources of vitamin E.* → See also **groundnut**, **hazelnut**, **peanut**. — N-COUNT
2 A **nut** is a thick metal ring which you screw onto a metal rod called a bolt. Nuts and bolts are used to hold things such as pieces of machinery together. → See picture on page 1709. ❑ *If you want to repair the wheels you just undo the four nuts. ...nuts and bolts that haven't been tightened up.* — N-COUNT
3 If you describe someone as, for example, a football **nut** or a health **nut**, you mean that they are extremely enthusiastic about the thing mentioned. [INFORMAL] ❑ *...a football nut who spends thousands of pounds travelling to watch games.* — N-COUNT: usu with supp = *fanatic*
4 If you are **nuts about** something or someone, you like them very much. [INFORMAL] ❑ *She's nuts about you.* — ADJ: v-link ADJ *about* n [feelings]
5 If you refer to someone as a **nut**, you mean that they are mad. [INFORMAL] ❑ *There's some nut out there with a gun.* — N-COUNT [disapproval]
6 If you say that someone goes **nuts** or is **nuts**, you mean that they go crazy or are very foolish. [INFORMAL] ❑ *You guys are nuts... A number of the French players went nuts, completely out of control.* — ADJ: v-link ADJ

PHRASES 7 If someone **goes nuts**, or in British English **does** their **nut**, they become extremely angry. [INFORMAL] ❑ *My father would go nuts if he saw bruises on me... We heard your sister doing her nut.* — PHRASE: V inflects
8 If you talk about **the nuts and bolts of** a subject or an activity, you are referring to the detailed practical aspects of it rather than abstract ideas about it. ❑ *He's more concerned about the nuts and bolts of location work.* — PHRASE: usu *the* PHR *of* n

**nut-brown** **Nut-brown** is used to describe things that are dark reddish brown in colour. — COLOUR

**nut|case** /nʌtkeɪs/ **(nutcases)** also **nut case.** If you refer to someone as a **nutcase**, you mean that they are mad or that their behaviour is very strange. [INFORMAL] ❑ *The woman's a nutcase. She needs locking up.* — N-COUNT [disapproval]

**nut|cracker** /nʌtkrækəʳ/ **(nutcrackers)** A **nutcracker** is a device used to crack the shell of a nut. **Nutcrackers** can be used to refer to one or more of these devices. — N-COUNT

**nut|meg** /nʌtmeg/ **Nutmeg** is a spice made from the seed of a tree that grows in hot countries. Nutmeg is usually used to flavour sweet food. — N-UNCOUNT

**nu|tri|ent** /njuːtriənt, AM nuː-/ **(nutrients)** **Nutrients** are substances that help plants and — N-COUNT: usu pl animals to grow. ❑ *...the role of vegetable fibres, vitamins, minerals and other essential nutrients.*

**nu|tri|tion** /njuːtrɪʃ^ən, AM nuː-/ **Nutrition** is the process of taking food into the body and absorbing the nutrients in those foods. ❑ *There are alternative sources of nutrition to animal meat.* N-UNCOUNT

**nu|tri|tion|al** /njuːtrɪʃən^əl, AM nuː-/ The **nutritional** content of food is all the substances that are in it which help you to remain healthy. ❑ *It does sometimes help to know the nutritional content of foods... Cooking vegetables reduces their nutritional value.* ♦ **nu|tri|tion|al|ly** *...a nutritionally balanced diet.* ADJ: usu ADJ n; ADV

**nu|tri|tion|ist** /njuːtrɪʃənɪst, AM nuː-/ **(nutritionists)** A **nutritionist** is a person whose job is to give advice on what you should eat to remain healthy. ❑ *Nutritionists say only 33% of our calorie intake should be from fat.* N-COUNT

**nu|tri|tious** /njuːtrɪʃəs, AM nuː-/ **Nutritious** food contains substances which help your body to be healthy. ❑ *It is always important to choose enjoyable, nutritious foods... Some ready made meals are nutritious and very easy to prepare.* ADJ = *nourishing*

**nu|tri|tive** /njuːtrɪtɪv, AM nuː-/ The **nutritive** content of food is all the substances that are in it which help you to remain healthy. ❑ *Coconut milk has little nutritive value.* ADJ: ADJ n = *nutritional*

**nut|shell** /nʌtʃel/ You can use **in a nutshell** to indicate that you are saying something in a very brief way, using few words. ❑ *In a nutshell, the owners thought they knew best.* PHRASE: usu PHR with cl

**nut|ter** /nʌtə^r/ **(nutters)** If you refer to someone as a **nutter**, you mean that they are mad or that their behaviour is very strange. [BRIT, INFORMAL] ❑ *He was a bit of a nutter.* N-COUNT disapproval = *nut, nutcase*

**nut|ty** /nʌti/ **(nuttier, nuttiest)** 1 If you describe food as **nutty**, you mean that it tastes of nuts, has the texture of nuts, or is made with nuts. ❑ *...nutty butter cookies... Chick peas have a distinctive, delicious and nutty flavour.* 2 If you describe someone as **nutty**, you mean that their behaviour is very strange or foolish. [INFORMAL] ❑ *He looked like a nutty professor... That's a nutty idea.* ADJ; ADJ disapproval

**nuz|zle** /nʌz^əl/ **(nuzzles, nuzzling, nuzzled)** If you **nuzzle** someone or something, you gently rub your nose and mouth against them to show affection. ❑ *She nuzzled me and I cuddled her... The dog came and nuzzled up against me.* VERB V n V adv/prep

**NW** **NW** is a written abbreviation for **north-west**. ❑ *...Ivor Place, London NW 1.*

**ny|lon** /naɪlɒn/ **(nylons)** 1 **Nylon** is a strong, flexible artificial fibre. ❑ *I put on a new pair of nylon socks.* 2 **Nylons** are stockings made of nylon. [OLD-FASHIONED] ❑ *This woman wore seamed nylons and kept smoothing her skirt.* N-UNCOUNT: oft N n; N-PLURAL

**nymph** /nɪmf/ **(nymphs)** 1 In Greek and Roman mythology, **nymphs** were spirits of nature who appeared as young women. 2 A **nymph** is the larva, or young form, of an insect such as a dragonfly. N-COUNT; N-COUNT

**nym|pho|ma|ni|ac** /nɪmfəmeɪniæk/ **(nymphomaniacs)** If someone refers to a woman as a **nymphomaniac**, they mean that she has sex or wants to have sex much more often than they consider normal or acceptable. N-COUNT disapproval

# O o

**O, o** /oʊ/ **(O's, o's)** 1 **O** is the fifteenth letter of the English alphabet. N-VAR 2 **O** is used to mean zero, for example when you are telling someone a telephone number, or mentioning a year such as 1908. [SPOKEN] NUM 3 **O** is used in exclamations, especially when you are expressing strong feelings. [LITERARY] ❑ *O how mistaken you are!... O God, I want to go home.* ➔ See also **oh**. EXCLAM [feelings]

**o'** /ə/ **O'** is used in written English to represent the word 'of' pronounced in a particular way. ❑ *I lost a lot o' blood... Can we have a cup o' coffee, please?* ➔ See also **o'clock**. PREP

**oaf** /oʊf/ **(oafs)** If you refer to someone, especially a man or boy, as an **oaf**, you think that they are impolite, clumsy, or aggressive. ❑ *Leave the lady alone, you drunken oaf.* N-COUNT: oft adj N [disapproval] = lout

**oaf|ish** /oʊfɪʃ/ If you describe someone, especially a man or a boy, as **oafish**, you disapprove of their behaviour because you think that it is impolite, clumsy, or aggressive. ❑ *The bodyguards, as usual, were brave but oafish. ...oafish humour.* ADJ [disapproval] = loutish

**oak** /oʊk/ **(oaks)** An **oak** or an **oak tree** is a large tree that often grows in woods and forests and has strong, hard wood. ❑ *Many large oaks were felled during the war. ...forests of beech, chestnut, and oak.* N-VAR ♦ **Oak** is the wood of this tree. ❑ *The cabinet was made of oak.* N-UNCOUNT

**OAP** /oʊ eɪ piː/ **(OAPs)** An **OAP** is a person who is old enough to receive an old age pension from the government. **OAP** is an abbreviation for 'old age pensioner'. [BRIT] ❑ *...tickets only £6 each and half that for OAPs and kids.* N-COUNT = senior citizen

**oar** /ɔːʳ/ **(oars) Oars** are long poles with a wide, flat blade at one end which are used for rowing a boat. N-COUNT

**oar|lock** /ɔːʳlɒk/ **(oarlocks)** The **oarlocks** on a rowing boat are the U-shaped pieces of metal that keep the oars in position while you move them backwards and forwards. [AM] N-COUNT

✔ in BRIT, use **rowlock**

**oasis** /oʊeɪsɪs/ **(oases** /oʊeɪsiːz/**)** 1 An **oasis** is a small area in a desert where water and plants are found. N-COUNT 2 You can refer to a pleasant place or situation as an **oasis** when it is surrounded by unpleasant ones. ❑ *The immaculately tended gardens are an oasis in the midst of Cairo's urban sprawl.* N-COUNT

**oath** /oʊθ/ **(oaths)** 1 An **oath** is a formal promise, especially a promise to be loyal to a person or country. ❑ *He took an oath of loyalty to the government.* ➔ See also **Hippocratic oath**. N-COUNT: oft N *of* n = pledge 2 In a court of law, when someone takes **the oath**, they make a formal promise to tell the truth. You can say that someone is **on oath** or **under oath** when they have made this promise. ❑ *His girlfriend had gone into the witness box and taken the oath... Under oath, Aston finally admitted that he had lied... Three officers gave evidence on oath against him.* N-SING: *the* N, also *on/under* N 3 An **oath** is an offensive or emphatic word or expression which you use when you are angry or shocked. [WRITTEN] ❑ *Wellor let out a foul oath and hurled himself upon him.* N-COUNT = curse

**oat|meal** /oʊtmiːl/ 1 **Oatmeal** is a kind of flour made by crushing oats. ❑ *...oatmeal biscuits.* N-UNCOUNT: oft N n 2 **Oatmeal** is a thick sticky food made from oats cooked in water or milk and eaten hot, especially for breakfast. [mainly AM] N-UNCOUNT = porridge

✔ in BRIT, usually use **porridge**

**oats** /oʊts/

✔ The form **oat** is used as a modifier.

1 **Oats** are a cereal crop or its grains, used for making biscuits or a food called porridge, or for feeding animals. ❑ *Oats provide good, nutritious food for horses. ...oat bran.* N-PLURAL 2 If a young person **sows** their **wild oats**, they behave in a rather uncontrolled way, especially by having a lot of sexual relationships. ❑ *The kids need to sow a few wild oats.* PHRASE: V inflects

**ob|du|ra|cy** /ɒbdjʊrəsi, AM -dʊr-/ If you accuse someone of **obduracy**, you think their refusal to change their decision or opinion is unreasonable. [FORMAL] ❑ *MPs have accused the government of obduracy.* N-UNCOUNT [disapproval] = obstinacy

**ob|du|rate** /ɒbdjʊrət, AM -dʊr-/ If you describe someone as **obdurate**, you think that they are being unreasonable in their refusal to change their decision or opinion. [FORMAL] ❑ *Parts of the administration may be changing but others have been obdurate defenders of the status quo.* ADJ [disapproval] = obstinate

**obedi|ent** /oʊbiːdiənt/ A person or animal who is **obedient** does what they are told to do. ❑ *He was very respectful at home and obedient to his parents.* ADJ ♦ **obedi|ence** *...unquestioning obedience to the law.* N-UNCOUNT: oft N *to* n ♦ **obedi|ent|ly** *He was looking obediently at Keith, waiting for orders.* ADV: ADV with v

**obei|sance** /oʊbeɪsəns/ **(obeisances)** 1 **Obeisance to** someone or something is great respect shown for them. [FORMAL] ❑ *While he was still young and strong all paid obeisance to him.* N-UNCOUNT: usu N *to* n 2 An **obeisance** is a physical gesture, especially a bow, that you make in order to show your respect for someone or something. [FORMAL] ❑ *One by one they came forward, mumbled grudging words of welcome, made awkward obeisances.* N-VAR

**ob|elisk** /ɒbəlɪsk/ **(obelisks)** An **obelisk** is a tall stone pillar that has been built in honour of a person or an important event. N-COUNT

**obese** /oʊbiːs/ If someone is **obese**, they are extremely fat. ❑ *Obese people tend to have higher blood pressure than lean people.* ADJ ♦ **obesity** /oʊbiːsɪti/ *...the excessive consumption of sugar that leads to problems of obesity.* N-UNCOUNT

**obey** /oʊbeɪ/ **(obeys, obeying, obeyed)** If you **obey** a person, a command, or an instruction, you do what you are told to do. ❑ *Cissie obeyed her mother without question... Most people obey the law... It was still Baker's duty to obey.* VERB V n V n V

**ob|fus|cate** /ɒbfʌskeɪt/ **(obfuscates, obfuscating, obfuscated)** To **obfuscate** something means to deliberately make it seem confusing and difficult to understand. [FORMAL] ❑ *They are obfuscating the issue, as only insurance companies can... Macdonald accepted that such information could be used to manipulate, to obfuscate, and to mislead.* VERB ≠ elucidate V n V

**obi|tu|ary** /oʊbɪtʃuəri, AM -ʃueri/ **(obituaries)** Someone's **obituary** is an account of their life and character which is printed in a newspaper or broadcast soon after they die. ❑ *I read your brother's obituary in the Times.* N-COUNT: oft poss N

**ob|ject** **(objects, objecting, objected)** ◆◆◇

✔ The noun is pronounced /ɒbdʒɪkt/. The verb is pronounced /əbdʒekt/.

[1] An **object** is anything that has a fixed shape or form, that you can touch or see, and that is not alive. ❑ *...an object the shape of a coconut... In the cosy consulting room the children are surrounded by familiar objects.* — N-COUNT
[2] The **object** of what someone is doing is their aim or purpose. ❑ *The object of the exercise is to raise money for the charity... My object was to publish a scholarly work on Peter Mourne.* — N-COUNT: usu with poss
[3] The **object of** a particular feeling or reaction is the person or thing it is directed towards or that causes it. ❑ *The object of her hatred was 24-year-old model Ros French... The object of great interest at the Temple was a large marble tower built in memory of Buddha.* ➔ See also **sex object**. — N-COUNT: N *of* n
[4] In grammar, the **object** of a verb or a preposition is the word or phrase which completes the structure begun by the verb or preposition. ➔ See also **direct object**, **indirect object**. — N-COUNT
[5] If you **object** to something, you express your dislike or disapproval of it. ❑ *A lot of people will object to the book...* (V *to* n) *Cullen objected that his small staff would be unable to handle the added work...* (V that) *We objected strongly but were outvoted...* (V) *'Hey, I don't know what you're talking about,' Russo objected.* (V with quote) — VERB
[6] If you say that **money is no object** or **distance is no object**, you are emphasizing that you are willing or able to spend as much money as necessary or travel whatever distance is required. ❑ *Hugh Johnson's shop in London has a range of superb Swedish crystal glasses that I would have if money were no object... Although he was based in Wales, distance was no object.* — PHRASE: V inflects [emphasis]

**ob|jec|tion** /əbdʒekʃᵊn/ **(objections)** [1] If you make or raise an **objection to** something, you say that you do not like it or agree with it. ❑ *Some managers have recently raised objection to the PFA handling these negotiations... Despite objections by the White House, the Senate voted today to cut off aid.* — N-VAR ≠ *approval*
[2] If you say that you have **no objection to** something, you mean that you are not annoyed or bothered by it. ❑ *I have no objection to banks making money... I no longer have any objection to your going to see her.* — N-UNCOUNT: with brd-neg

**ob|jec|tion|able** /əbdʒekʃənəbᵊl/ If you describe someone or something as **objectionable**, you consider them to be extremely offensive and unacceptable. [FORMAL] ❑ *I don't like your tone young woman, in fact I find it highly objectionable.* — ADJ

**ob|jec|tive** /əbdʒektɪv/ **(objectives)** [1] Your **objective** is what you are trying to achieve. ❑ *Our main objective was the recovery of the child safe and well... His objective was to play golf and win.* — ◆◇◇ N-COUNT: usu with poss = *aim, goal*
[2] **Objective** information is based on facts. ❑ *He had no objective evidence that anything extraordinary was happening.* — ADJ: ADJ n
♦ **ob|jec|tive|ly** *We simply want to inform people objectively about events.* — ADV: usu ADV with v
♦ **ob|jec|tiv|ity** /ɒbdʒektɪvɪti/ *The poll, whose objectivity is open to question, gave the party a 39% share of the vote.* — N-UNCOUNT
[3] If someone is **objective**, they base their opinions on facts rather than on their personal feelings. ❑ *I believe that a journalist should be completely objective... I would really like to have your objective opinion on this.* — ADJ = *impartial* ≠ *subjective*
♦ **ob|jec|tive|ly** *Try to view situations more objectively, especially with regard to work.* — ADV: usu ADV with v
♦ **ob|jec|tiv|ity** *The psychiatrist must learn to maintain an unusual degree of objectivity.* — N-UNCOUNT

**ob|ject les|son** **(object lessons)** If you describe an action, event, or situation as an **object lesson**, you think that it demonstrates the correct way to do something, or that it demonstrates the truth of a particular principle. ❑ *It was an object lesson in how to use television as a means of persuasion.* — N-COUNT: oft N *on/in* n = *example*

**ob|ject|or** /əbdʒektəʳ/ **(objectors)** An **objector** is someone who states or shows that they oppose or disapprove of something. ❑ *The district council agreed with the objectors and turned down the application.* ➔ See also **conscientious objector**. — N-COUNT ≠ *supporter*

**object-oriented** In computing, **object-oriented** programming involves dealing with code and data in blocks so that it is easier to change or do things with. ❑ *...object-oriented software.* — ADJ: usu ADJ n

**ob|jet d'art** /ɒbʒeɪ dɑːʳ/ **(objets d'art)** **Objets d'art** are small ornaments that are considered to be attractive and of quite good quality. [FORMAL] — N-COUNT: usu pl

**ob|li|gate** /ɒblɪgeɪt/ **(obligates, obligating, obligated)** If something **obligates** you to do a particular thing, it creates a situation where you have to do it. [FORMAL] ❑ *The ruling obligates airlines to release information about their flight delays.* — VERB; V n to-inf

**ob|li|gat|ed** /ɒblɪgeɪtɪd/ If you feel **obligated** to do something, you feel that it is your duty to do it. If you are **obligated to** someone, you feel that it is your duty to look after them. [FORMAL] ❑ *I felt obligated to let him read the letter... He had got a girl pregnant and felt obligated to her and the child.* — ADJ: v-link ADJ, oft ADJ to-inf, ADJ *to* n

**ob|li|ga|tion** /ɒblɪgeɪʃᵊn/ **(obligations)** [1] If you have an **obligation to** do something, it is your duty to do that thing. ❑ *When teachers assign homework, students usually feel an obligation to do it... Ministers are under no obligation to follow the committee's recommendations.* — N-VAR: usu N to-inf
[2] If you have an **obligation to** a person, it is your duty to look after them or protect their interests. ❑ *The United States will do that which is necessary to meet its obligations to its own citizens... I have an ethical and a moral obligation to my client.* — N-VAR: usu N *to* n = *responsibility*
[3] In advertisements, if a product or a service is available **without obligation**, you do not have to pay for that product or service until you have tried it and are satisfied with it. ❑ *If you are selling your property, why not call us for a free valuation without obligation?* — PHRASE

**ob|liga|tory** /əblɪgətri, AM -tɔːri/ [1] If something is **obligatory**, you must do it because of a rule or a law. ❑ *Most women will be offered an ultrasound scan during pregnancy, although it's not obligatory... These rates do not include the charge for obligatory medical consultations.* — ADJ = *compulsory* ≠ *optional*
[2] If you describe something as **obligatory**, you mean that it is done from habit or custom and not because the person involved has thought carefully about it or really means it. ❑ *She was wearing the obligatory sweater and pearl necklace.* — ADJ: ADJ n = *customary*

**oblige** /əblaɪdʒ/ **(obliges, obliging, obliged)** [1] If you **are obliged to** do something, a situation, rule, or law makes it necessary for you to do that thing. ❑ *The storm got worse and worse. Finally, I was obliged to abandon the car and continue on foot...* (*be* V-ed to-inf) *This decree obliges unions to delay strikes.* (V n to-inf) — VERB = *compel*
[2] To **oblige** someone means to be helpful to them by doing what they have asked you to do. ❑ *If you ever need help with the babysitting, I'd be glad to oblige...* (V) *We called up three economists to ask how to eliminate the deficit and they obliged with very straightforward answers...* (V *with* n) *Mr Oakley always has been ready to oblige journalists with information.* (V n *with* n; Also V n) — VERB
[3] People sometimes use **obliged** in expressions such as '**much obliged**' or '**I am obliged to you**' when they want to indicate that they are very grateful for something. [FORMAL or OLD-FASHIONED] ❑ *Much obliged for your assistance... Thank you very much indeed, Doctor, I am extremely obliged to you.* — CONVENTION [formulae]
[4] If you tell someone that you **would be obliged** or **should be obliged** if they would do something, you are telling them in a polite but firm way that you want them to do it. [FORMAL] ❑ *I would be obliged if you could read it to us.* — CONVENTION [politeness]

**oblig|ing** /əblaɪdʒɪŋ/ If you describe someone as **obliging**, you think that they are willing and eager to be helpful. [OLD-FASHIONED or WRITTEN] ❑ *He is an extremely pleasant and obliging man.* — ADJ [approval] = *accommodating*
♦ **oblig|ing|ly** *He swung round and strode towards the door. Benedict obligingly held it open.* — ADV: ADV with v

**oblique** /oʊbliːk/ [1] If you describe a statement as **oblique**, you mean that is not expressed directly or openly, making it difficult to understand. ❑ *Mr Golding delivered an oblique warning, talking of the danger of sudden action.* — ADJ = *indirect*
♦ **oblique|ly** *He obliquely referred to the US, Britain and Saudi Ara-* — ADV: ADV with v = *indirectly*

*bia.* [2] An **oblique** line is a straight line that is not horizontal or vertical. An **oblique** angle is any angle other than a right angle. ❑ *It lies between the plain and the sea at an oblique angle to the coastline.* ♦ **oblique|ly** *This muscle runs obliquely downwards inside the abdominal cavity.*
ADJ: usu ADJ n
ADV: ADV after v

**oblit|erate** /əblɪtəreɪt/ **(obliterates, obliterating, obliterated)** [1] If something **obliterates** an object or place, it destroys it completely. ❑ *Their warheads are enough to obliterate the world several times over.* ♦ **oblit|era|tion** /əblɪtəreɪʃən/ *...the obliteration of three isolated rainforests.* [2] If you **obliterate** something such as a memory, emotion, or thought, you remove it completely from your mind. [LITERARY] ❑ *There was time enough to obliterate memories of how things once were for him.*
VERB; V n
N-UNCOUNT: oft N *of* n
VERB = eradicate; V n

**oblivi|on** /əblɪviən/ [1] **Oblivion** is the state of not being aware of what is happening around you, for example because you are asleep or unconscious. ❑ *He just drank himself into oblivion.* [2] **Oblivion** is the state of having been forgotten or of no longer being considered important. ❑ *It seems that the so-called new theory is likely to sink into oblivion.* [3] If you say that something is bombed or blasted **into oblivion**, you are emphasizing that it is completely destroyed. ❑ *An entire poor section of town was bombed into oblivion.*
N-UNCOUNT: usu *into* N
N-UNCOUNT: usu *into* N = obscurity
N-UNCOUNT: *into* N [emphasis]

**oblivi|ous** /əblɪviəs/ If you are **oblivious** to something or oblivious of it, you are not aware of it. ❑ *She lay motionless where she was, oblivious to pain.* ♦ **ob|livi|ous|ly** *Burke was asleep, sprawled obliviously against the window.* ♦ **ob|livi|ous|ness** *Her obliviousness of what was happening in Germany seems extraordinary.*
ADJ: usu v-link ADJ, oft ADJ *to/of* n
ADV: ADV with v
N-UNCOUNT

**ob|long** /ɒblɒŋ, AM -lɔːŋ/ **(oblongs)** An **oblong** is a shape which has two long sides and two short sides and in which all the angles are right angles. ❑ *...an oblong table.*
N-COUNT: oft N n = rectangle

**ob|nox|ious** /ɒbnɒkʃəs/ If you describe someone as **obnoxious**, you think that they are very unpleasant. ❑ *One of the parents was a most obnoxious character. No-one liked him.*
ADJ [disapproval]

**oboe** /oʊboʊ/ **(oboes)** An **oboe** is a musical instrument shaped like a tube which you play by blowing through a double reed in the top end.
N-VAR: oft *the* N

**obo|ist** /oʊboʊɪst/ **(oboists)** An **oboist** is someone who plays the oboe.
N-COUNT

**ob|scene** /ɒbsiːn/ [1] If you describe something as **obscene**, you mean it offends you because it relates to sex or violence in a way that you think is unpleasant and shocking. ❑ *I'm not prudish but I think these photographs are obscene... He continued to use obscene language and also to make threats.* [2] In legal contexts, books, pictures, or films which are judged **obscene** are illegal because they deal with sex or violence in a way that is considered offensive to the general public. ❑ *A city magistrate ruled that the novel was obscene and copies should be destroyed.* [3] If you describe something as **obscene**, you disapprove of it very strongly and consider it to be offensive or immoral. ❑ *It was obscene to spend millions producing unwanted food.*
ADJ
ADJ
ADJ: oft *it* v-link ADJ to-inf/that [disapproval] = offensive

**ob|scen|ity** /ɒbsenɪti/ **(obscenities)** [1] **Obscenity** is behaviour, art, or language that is sexual and offends or shocks people. ❑ *He insisted these photographs were not art but obscenity.* [2] An **obscenity** is a very offensive word or expression. ❑ *They shouted obscenities at us and smashed bottles on the floor.*
N-UNCOUNT
N-VAR

**ob|scu|rant|ism** /ɒbskjʊræntɪzəm, AM ɒbskjʊrənt-/ **Obscurantism** is the practice or policy of deliberately making something vague and difficult to understand, especially in order to prevent people from finding out the truth. [FORMAL or WRITTEN] ❑ *...legalistic obscurantism.*
N-UNCOUNT

**ob|scu|rant|ist** /ɒbskjʊræntɪst, AM ɒbskjʊrənt-/ If you describe something as **obscurantist**, you mean that it is deliberately vague and difficult to understand, so that it prevents people from finding out the truth about it. [FORMAL or WRITTEN] ❑ *I think that a lot of poetry published today is obscurantist nonsense.*
ADJ

**ob|scure** /ɒbskjʊəʳ/ **(obscurer, obscurest, obscures, obscuring, obscured)** [1] If something or someone is **obscure**, they are unknown, or are known by only a few people. ❑ *The origin of the custom is obscure... The hymn was written by an obscure Greek composer for the 1896 Athens Olympics.* [2] Something that is **obscure** is difficult to understand or deal with, usually because it involves so many parts or details. ❑ *The contracts are written in obscure language.* [3] If one thing **obscures** another, it prevents it from being seen or heard properly. ❑ *One wall of the parliament building is now almost completely obscured by a huge banner.* [4] To **obscure** something means to make it difficult to understand. ❑ *...the jargon that frequently obscures educational writing... This issue has been obscured by recent events.*
ADJ
ADJ ≠ straightforward
VERB; V n
VERB; V n; V n

**ob|scu|rity** /ɒbskjʊərɪti/ **(obscurities)** [1] **Obscurity** is the state of being known by only a few people. ❑ *For the lucky few, there's the chance of being plucked from obscurity and thrown into the glamorous world of modelling.* [2] **Obscurity** is the quality of being difficult to understand. An **obscurity** is something that is difficult to understand. ❑ *'How can that be?' asked Hunt, irritated by the obscurity of Henry's reply.*
N-UNCOUNT ≠ fame
N-VAR

**ob|se|qui|ous** /ɒbsiːkwiəs/ If you describe someone as **obsequious**, you are criticizing them because they are too eager to help or agree with someone more important than them. ❑ *Barrow was positively obsequious to me until he learnt that I too was the son of a labouring man.* ♦ **ob|se|qui|ous|ly** *He smiled and bowed obsequiously to Winger.* ♦ **ob|se|qui|ous|ness** *I told him to get lost and leave me alone and his tone quickly changed from obsequiousness to outright anger.*
ADJ [disapproval] = servile
ADV: ADV with v
N-UNCOUNT

**ob|serv|able** /əbzɜːʳvəbəl/ Something that is **observable** can be seen. ❑ *Mars is too faint and too low in the sky to be observable.*
ADJ

**ob|ser|vance** /əbzɜːʳvəns/ **(observances)** The **observance** of something such as a law or custom is the practice of obeying or following it. ❑ *Local councils should use their powers to ensure strict observance of laws.*
N-VAR

**ob|ser|vant** /əbzɜːʳvənt/ Someone who is **observant** pays a lot of attention to things and notices more about them than most people do. ❑ *That's a marvellous description, Mrs Drummond. You're unusually observant... An observant doctor can often detect depression from expression, posture, and movement.*
ADJ

**ob|ser|va|tion** /ɒbzəʳveɪʃən/ **(observations)** [1] **Observation** is the action or process of carefully watching someone or something. ❑ *...careful observation of the movement of the planets... In hospital she'll be under observation all the time.* [2] An **observation** is something that you have learned by seeing or watching something and thinking about it. ❑ *This book contains observations about the causes of addictions.* [3] If a person makes an **observation**, they make a comment about something or someone, usually as a result of watching how they behave. ❑ *'You're an obstinate man,' she said. 'Is that a criticism,' I said, 'or just an observation?'.* [4] **Observation** is the ability to pay a lot of attention to things and to notice more about them than most people do. ❑ *She has good powers of observation.*
N-UNCOUNT
N-COUNT
N-COUNT
N-UNCOUNT

**ob|ser|va|tion|al** /ɒbzəʳveɪʃənəl/ **Observational** means relating to the watching of people or things, especially in order to learn something new. [FORMAL] ❑ *...observational humour... The observational work is carried out on a range of telescopes.*
ADJ

**ob|ser|va|tory** /əbzɜːʳvətri, AM -tɔːri/ **(observatories)** An **observatory** is a building with a large telescope from which scientists study things such as the planets by watching them.
N-COUNT

**ob|serve** /əbzɜːʳv/ **(observes, observing, observed)** ◆◇◇ **1** If you **observe** a person or thing, you watch them carefully, especially in order to learn something about them. VERB ❑ *Stern also studies and observes the behaviour of babies...* V n *Our sniper teams observed them manning an anti-aircraft gun.* V n -ing Also V, V n inf **2** If you **observe** someone or something, you see or notice them. VERB [FORMAL] ❑ *In 1664 Hooke observed a reddish spot on the surface of the planet.* V n **3** If you **observe** that something is the case, you make a remark or comment about it, especially when it is something you have noticed and thought about a lot. VERB [FORMAL] ❑ *We observe that the first calls for radical transformation did not begin until the period of the industrial revolution...* V that *'He is a fine young man,' observed Stephen.* V with quote **4** If you **observe** something such as a law or custom, you obey it or follow it. VERB ❑ *Imposing speed restrictions is easy, but forcing motorists to observe them is trickier...* V n *The army was observing a ceasefire.* V n

**ob|serv|er** /əbzɜːʳvəʳ/ **(observers)** ◆◇◇ **1** You can refer to someone who sees or notices something as an **observer**. N-COUNT = witness ❑ *A casual observer would have taken them to be three men out for an evening stroll... Observers say the woman pulled a knife out of the bunch of flowers and stabbed him in the neck.* **2** An **observer** is someone who studies current events and situations, especially in order to comment on them and predict what will happen next. N-COUNT: oft supp N [JOURNALISM] ❑ *Political observers believe that a new cabinet may be formed shortly.* **3** An **observer** is a person who is sent to observe an important event or situation, especially in order to make sure it happens as it should, or so that they can tell other people about it. N-COUNT: oft supp N ❑ *The president suggested that a UN observer should attend the conference.*

**ob|sess** /əbses/ **(obsesses, obsessing, obsessed)** If something **obsesses** you or if you **obsess about** something, you keep thinking about it and find it difficult to think about anything else. VERB ❑ *A string of scandals is obsessing America...* V n *She stopped drinking but began obsessing about her weight...* V about/over n *I started obsessing that Trish might die.* V that

**ob|sessed** /əbsest/ If someone is **obsessed with** a person or thing, they keep thinking about them and find it difficult to think about anything else. ADJ: oft ADJ with/by n ❑ *He was obsessed with American gangster movies... She wasn't in love with Steve, she was obsessed by him physically.*

**ob|ses|sion** /əbseʃən/ **(obsessions)** If you say that someone has an **obsession** with a person or thing, you think they are spending too much time thinking about them. N-VAR: oft N with n ❑ *She would try to forget her obsession with Christopher... 95% of patients know their obsessions are irrational.*

**ob|ses|sion|al** /əbseʃənəl/ **Obsessional** means the same as **obsessive**. ADJ = obsessive ❑ *She became almost obsessional about the way she looked.*

**ob|ses|sive** /əbsesɪv/ **(obsessives)** **1** If someone's behaviour is **obsessive**, they cannot stop doing a particular thing or behaving in a particular way. ADJ: oft ADJ about n ❑ *Williams is obsessive about motor racing.* ♦ **ob|ses|sive|ly** *He couldn't help worrying obsessively about what would happen... The Ministry is being obsessively secretive about the issue.* ADV: ADV with v, ADV adj **2** An **obsessive** is someone who is obsessive about something or who behaves in an obsessive way. N-COUNT ❑ *I am not an obsessive. Not at all.*

**obsessive-compulsive dis|or|der** If someone suffers from **obsessive-compulsive disorder**, they cannot stop doing a particular thing, for example washing their hands. N-UNCOUNT

**ob|so|les|cence** /ɒbsəlesəns/ **Obsolescence** is the state of being no longer needed because something newer or more efficient has been invented. N-UNCOUNT ❑ *The aircraft was nearing obsolescence by early 1942.*

**ob|so|les|cent** /ɒbsəlesənt/ If something is **obsolescent**, it is no longer needed because something better has been invented. ADJ = obsolete ❑ *...outmoded, obsolescent equipment.*

**ob|so|lete** /ɒbsəliːt/ Something that is **obsolete** is no longer needed because something better has been invented. ADJ ❑ *So much equipment becomes obsolete almost as soon as it's made.*

**ob|sta|cle** /ɒbstəkəl/ **(obstacles)** **1** An **obstacle** is an object that makes it difficult for you to go where you want to go, because it is in your way. N-COUNT ❑ *Most competition cars will only roll over if they hit an obstacle... He left her to navigate her own way round the trolleys and other obstacles.* **2** You can refer to anything that makes it difficult for you to do something as an **obstacle**. N-COUNT: oft N to n/-ing = hindrance ❑ *Overcrowding remains a large obstacle to improving conditions... To succeed, you must learn to overcome obstacles.*

**ob|sta|cle course** **(obstacle courses)** In a race, an **obstacle course** is a series of obstacles that people have to go over or round in order to complete the race. N-COUNT

**ob|ste|tri|cian** /ɒbstətrɪʃən/ **(obstetricians)** An **obstetrician** is a doctor who is specially trained to deal with pregnant women and with women who are giving birth. N-COUNT [MEDICAL]

**ob|stet|rics** /ɒbstetrɪks/ **1** **Obstetrics** is the branch of medicine that is concerned with pregnancy and giving birth. N-UNCOUNT [MEDICAL] **2** **Obstetric** medicine and care is concerned with pregnancy and giving birth. ADJ: ADJ n [MEDICAL] ❑ *For a child to be born with this disability indicates a defect in obstetric care.*

**ob|sti|nate** /ɒbstɪnət/ **1** If you describe someone as **obstinate**, you are being critical of them because they are very determined to do what they want, and refuse to change their mind or be persuaded to do something else. ADJ [disapproval] = stubborn ❑ *He is obstinate and will not give up.* ♦ **ob|sti|nate|ly** *I stayed obstinately in my room, sitting by the telephone.* ADV: ADV with v = stubbornly ♦ **ob|sti|na|cy** *I might have become a dangerous man with all that stubbornness and obstinacy built into me.* N-UNCOUNT = stubbornness **2** You can describe things as **obstinate** when they are difficult to move, change, or destroy. ADJ ❑ *...rusted farm equipment strewn among the obstinate weeds.* ♦ **ob|sti|nate|ly** *...the door of the shop which obstinately stayed closed when he tried to push it open.* ADV: ADV with v

**ob|strep|er|ous** /ɒbstrepərəs/ If you say that someone is **obstreperous**, you think that they are noisy and difficult to control. ADJ [disapproval] ❑ *You know I have no intention of being awkward and obstreperous.*

**ob|struct** /ɒbstrʌkt/ **(obstructs, obstructing, obstructed)** **1** If something **obstructs** a road or path, it blocks it, stopping people or vehicles getting past. VERB = block ❑ *Tractors and container lorries have completely obstructed the road.* V n **2** To **obstruct** someone or something means to make it difficult for them to move forward by blocking their path. VERB = block ❑ *A number of local people have been arrested for trying to obstruct lorries loaded with logs.* V n **3** To **obstruct** progress or a process means to prevent it from happening properly. VERB ❑ *The authorities are obstructing a United Nations investigation.* V n **4** If someone or something **obstructs** your view, they are positioned between you and the thing you are trying to look at, stopping you from seeing it properly. VERB = block ❑ *Claire positioned herself so as not to obstruct David's line of sight.* V n

**ob|struc|tion** /ɒbstrʌkʃən/ **(obstructions)** **1** An **obstruction** is something that blocks a road or path. N-COUNT ❑ *John was irritated by drivers parking near his house and causing an obstruction.* **2** An **obstruction** is something that blocks a passage in your body. N-VAR ❑ *The boy was suffering from a bowel obstruction and he died.* **3** **Obstruction** is the act of deliberately delaying something or preventing something from happening, usually in business, law, or government. N-UNCOUNT ❑ *Mr Guest refused to let them in and now faces a criminal charge of obstruction.*

**ob|struc|tion|ism** /ɒbstrʌkʃənɪzəm/ N-UNCOUNT **Obstructionism** is the practice of deliberately delaying or preventing a process or change, especially in politics. ❑ *Obstructionism is generally most evident at the stage of implementing a law.*

**ob|struc|tive** /ɒbstrʌktɪv/ ADJ If you say that someone is being **obstructive**, you think that they are deliberately causing difficulties for other people. ❑ *Mr Smith was obstructive and refused to follow correct procedure.*

**ob|tain** /ɒbteɪn/ ◆◇◇ **(obtains, obtaining, obtained)** VERB To **obtain** something means to get it or achieve it. [FORMAL] V n ❑ *Evans was trying to obtain a false passport and other documents.*

**ob|tain|able** /ɒbteɪnəbᵊl/ ADJ: usu v-link ADJ, oft ADJ prep If something is **obtainable**, it is possible to get or achieve it. ❑ *The dried herb is obtainable from health shops.*

**ob|trude** /ɒbtruːd/ **(obtrudes, obtruding, obtruded)** VERB When something **obtrudes** or when you **obtrude** it, it becomes noticeable in an undesirable way. [LITERARY] V ❑ *A 40 watt bulb would be quite sufficient and would not obtrude...* V n *Gertrude now clearly felt that she had obtruded her sorrow...* V *on* n *He didn't want to obtrude on her privacy.*

**ob|tru|sive** /ɒbtruːsɪv/ ADJ If you say that someone or something is **obtrusive**, you think they are noticeable in an unpleasant way. ❑ *These heaters are less obtrusive and are easy to store away in the summer.* ♦ **ob|tru|sive|ly** ADV: ADV with v *Hawke got up and walked obtrusively out of the building.*

**ob|tuse** /əbtjuːs, AM -tuːs/ 1 ADJ Someone who is **obtuse** has difficulty understanding things, or makes no effort to understand them. [FORMAL] ❑ *I've really been very obtuse and stupid.* ♦ **ob|tuse|ness** N-UNCOUNT *Naivety bordering on obtuseness helped sustain his faith.* 2 ADJ An **obtuse** angle is between 90° and 180°. Compare **acute** angle. [TECHNICAL]

**ob|verse** /ɒbvɜːʳs/ N-SING: *the* N, oft N *of* n The **obverse** of an opinion, situation, or argument is its opposite. [FORMAL] ❑ *The obverse of rising unemployment is continued gains in productivity.*

**ob|vi|ate** /ɒbvieɪt/ **(obviates, obviating, obviated)** VERB To **obviate** something such as a problem or a need means to remove it or make it unnecessary. [FORMAL] V n ❑ *The use of a solicitor trained as a mediator would obviate the need for independent legal advice.*

**ob|vi|ous** /ɒbviəs/ ◆◆◇ 1 ADJ = clear If something is **obvious**, it is easy to see or understand. ❑ *...the need to rectify what is an obvious injustice... Determining how the Democratic challenger would conduct his presidency isn't quite so obvious.* 2 ADJ [disapproval] If you describe something that someone says as **obvious**, you are being critical of it because you think it is unnecessary or shows lack of imagination. ❑ *There are some very obvious phrases that we all know or certainly should know better than to use.* ♦ **ob|vi|ous|ness** N-UNCOUNT *Francis smiled agreement, irritated by the obviousness of his answer.* ● PHRASE: V inflects If you say that someone **is stating the obvious**, you mean that they are saying something that everyone already knows and understands. ❑ *It may be stating the obvious, but most teleworking at present is connected with computers.*

**ob|vi|ous|ly** /ɒbviəsli/ ◆◆◇ 1 ADV: ADV with cl [emphasis] = clearly You use **obviously** when you are stating something that you expect the person who is listening to know already. ❑ *Obviously, they've had sponsorship from some big companies... There are obviously exceptions to this.* 2 ADV: ADV with cl/group You use **obviously** to indicate that something is easily noticed, seen, or recognized. ❑ *They obviously appreciate you very much.*

**oc|ca|sion** /əkeɪʒᵊn/ ◆◆◇ **(occasions)** 1 N-COUNT An **occasion** is a time when something happens, or a case of it happening. ❑ *I often think fondly of an occasion some years ago at Covent Garden... Mr Davis has been asked on a number of occasions.* 2 N-COUNT: usu supp N An **occasion** is an important event, ceremony, or celebration. ❑ *Taking her with me on official occasions has been a challenge... It will be a unique family occasion.* 3 N-COUNT: N *for* n/-ing An **occasion for** doing something is an opportunity for doing it. [FORMAL] ❑ *It is an occasion for all the family to celebrate... It is always an important occasion for setting out government policy.* 4 VERB To **occasion** something means to cause it. [FORMAL] V n ❑ *He argued that the release of hostages should not occasion a change in policy.* 5 → See also **sense of occasion**.

PHRASES 6 PHRASE: V inflects, PHR to-inf If you **have occasion to** do something, it is necessary for you to do it. ❑ *We have had occasion to deal with members of the group on a variety of charges.* 7 PHRASE: N inflects, PHR with cl = occasionally If something happens **on occasion**, it happens sometimes, but not very often. ❑ *He translated not only from the French but also, on occasion, from the Polish.* 8 PHRASE: V inflects If you say that someone **rose to the occasion**, you mean that they did what was necessary to successfully overcome a difficult situation. ❑ *Inverness, however, rose to the occasion in the second half, producing some of the best football they have played for some time.*

**oc|ca|sion|al** /əkeɪʒənᵊl/ ◆◇◇ ADJ: usu ADJ n **Occasional** means happening sometimes, but not regularly or often. ❑ *I've had occasional mild headaches all my life... Esther used to visit him for the occasional days and weekends.* ♦ **oc|ca|sion|al|ly** ADV: ADV with cl/group, ADV with v *He still misbehaves occasionally.*

**oc|ci|den|tal** /ɒksɪdentᵊl/ ADJ: ADJ n = western ≠ eastern, Oriental **Occidental** means relating to the countries of Europe and America. [FORMAL] ❑ *In some respects the African mind works rather differently from the occidental one.*

**oc|cult** /ɒkʌlt, ɒkʌlt/ N-SING: *the* N **The occult** is the knowledge and study of supernatural or magical forces. ❑ *...sinister experiments with the occult.* ♦ ADJ: ADJ n **Occult** is also an adjective. ❑ *...organisations which campaign against paganism and occult practice.*

**oc|cult|ist** /ɒkʌltɪst/ **(occultists)** N-COUNT An **occultist** is a person who believes in the supernatural and the power of magic.

**oc|cu|pan|cy** /ɒkjʊpənsi/ N-UNCOUNT: usu with supp = occupation **Occupancy** is the act of using a room, building, or area of land, usually for a fixed period of time. [FORMAL] ❑ *Hotel occupancy has been as low as 40%.*

**oc|cu|pant** /ɒkjʊpənt/ **(occupants)** 1 N-COUNT = occupier The **occupants** of a building or room are the people who live or work there. ❑ *Most of the occupants had left before the fire broke out.* 2 N-PLURAL You can refer to the people who are in a place such as a room, vehicle, or bed at a particular time as the **occupants**. ❑ *The lifeboat capsized, throwing the occupants into the water.*

**oc|cu|pa|tion** /ɒkjʊpeɪʃᵊn/ ◆◇◇ **(occupations)** 1 N-COUNT Your **occupation** is your job or profession. ❑ *I suppose I was looking for an occupation which was going to be an adventure... Occupation: administrative assistant.* 2 N-COUNT An **occupation** is something that you spend time doing, either for pleasure or because it needs to be done. ❑ *Parachuting is a dangerous occupation.* 3 N-UNCOUNT The **occupation** of a country happens when it is entered and controlled by a foreign army. ❑ *...the deportation of Jews from Paris during the German occupation.*

**oc|cu|pa|tion|al** /ɒkjʊpeɪʃənᵊl/ ADJ: usu ADJ n **Occupational** means relating to a person's job or profession. ❑ *Some received substantial occupational assistance in the form of low-interest loans.* ♦ **oc|cu|pa|tion|al|ly** ADV: usu ADV adj/-ed *You might be having an occupationally related skin problem.*

**oc|cu|pa|tion|al haz|ard** **(occupational hazards)** N-COUNT An **occupational hazard** is something unpleasant that you may suffer or experience as a result of doing your job or hobby. ❑ *Catching colds is unfortunately an occupational hazard in this profession.*

**oc|cu|pa|tion|al health** N-UNCOUNT **Occupational health** is the branch of medicine that deals with the health of people in their workplace or in relation to their job. ❑ *For many years, experts in occupational health have puzzled over symptoms reported by office workers, including headache, nausea and fatigue.*

**oc|cu|pa|tion|al ther|a|pist (occupational therapists)** An **occupational therapist** is someone whose job involves helping people by means of occupational therapy. N-COUNT

**oc|cu|pa|tion|al ther|a|py** **Occupational therapy** is a method of helping people who have been ill or injured to develop skills or get skills back by giving them certain activities to do. ❑ *She will now begin occupational therapy to regain the use of her hands.* N-UNCOUNT

**oc|cu|pi|er** /ɒkjʊpaɪəʳ/ **(occupiers)** The **occupier** of a house, flat, or piece of land is the person who lives or works there. [FORMAL] ➔ See also **owner-occupier**.. N-COUNT = occupant

**oc|cu|py** /ɒkjʊpaɪ/ **(occupies, occupying, occupied)** ◆◆◇ 1 The people who **occupy** a building or a place are the people who live or work there. ❑ *There were over 40 tenants, all occupying one wing of the hospital... Land is, in most instances, purchased by those who occupy it.* VERB V n V n 2 If a room or something such as a seat **is occupied**, someone is using it, so that it is not available for anyone else. ❑ *The hospital bed is no longer occupied by his wife... I saw three camp beds, two of which were occupied.* V-PASSIVE ≠ vacant, free be V-ed be V-ed 3 If a group of people or an army **occupies** a place or country, they move into it, using force in order to gain control of it. ❑ *U.S. forces now occupy a part of the country. ...the occupied territories.* VERB V n V-ed 4 If someone or something **occupies** a particular place in a system, process, or plan, they have that place. ❑ *Men still occupy more positions of power than women.* VERB = hold V n 5 If something **occupies** you, or if you **occupy** yourself, your time, or your mind with it, you are busy doing that thing or thinking about it. ❑ *Her parliamentary career has occupied all of her time... He hurried to take the suitcases and occupy himself with packing the car... I would deserve to be pitied if I couldn't occupy myself.* VERB V n V pron-refl with n V pron-refl ♦ **oc|cu|pied** *Keep the brain occupied... I had forgotten all about it because I had been so occupied with other things.* ADJ: v-link ADJ, oft ADJ with n 6 If something **occupies** you, it requires your efforts, attention, or time. ❑ *I had other matters to occupy me, during the day at least... This challenge will occupy Europe for a generation or more.* VERB V n V n 7 If something **occupies** a particular area or place, it fills or covers it, or exists there. ❑ *Even quite small aircraft occupy a lot of space... Bookshelves occupied most of the living room walls.* VERB = take up V n V n

**oc|cur** /əkɜːʳ/ **(occurs, occurring, occurred)** ◆◆◇ 1 When something **occurs**, it happens. ❑ *If headaches only occur at night, lack of fresh air and oxygen is often the cause... The crash occurred when the crew shut down the wrong engine... In March 1770, there occurred what became known as the Boston Massacre.* VERB V V there V n 2 When something **occurs** in a particular place, it exists or is present there. ❑ *The cattle disease occurs more or less anywhere in Africa where the fly occurs... These snails do not occur on low-lying coral islands or atolls.* VERB = exist V adv/prep V adv/prep 3 If a thought or idea **occurs to** you, you suddenly think of it or realize it. ❑ *It did not occur to me to check my insurance policy... The same idea had occurred to Elizabeth.* VERB: no passive, no cont it V to n to-inf V to n

**oc|cur|rence** /əkʌrəns, AM -kɜːr-/ **(occurrences)** 1 An **occurrence** is something that happens. [FORMAL] ❑ *Complaints seemed to be an everyday occurrence... The food queues have become a daily occurrence across the country.* N-COUNT 2 **The occurrence of** something is the fact that it happens or is present. ❑ *The greatest occurrence of coronary heart disease is in those over 65.* N-COUNT: the N of n = instance

**ocean** /oʊʃən/ **(oceans)** ◆◇◇ 1 **The ocean** is the sea. ❑ *There were few sights as beautiful as the calm ocean on a warm night.* N-SING: the N 2 An **ocean** is one of the five very large areas of sea on the Earth's surface. ❑ *They spent many days cruising the northern Pacific Ocean. ...the Indian Ocean.* N-COUNT; N-IN-NAMES 3 If you say that there is an **ocean of** something, you are emphasizing that there is a very large amount of it. [INFORMAL] ❑ *I had cried oceans of tears... APEC seems be drowning in an ocean of jargon.* N-COUNT: N of n emphasis 4 If you say that something is **a drop in the ocean**, you mean that it is a very small amount which is unimportant compared to the cost of other things or is so small that it has very little effect on something. ❑ *His fee is a drop in the ocean compared with the real cost of broadcasting.* PHRASE: usu v-link PHR emphasis

**ocean-going** **Ocean-going** ships are designed for travelling on the sea rather than on rivers, canals, or lakes. ❑ *At the height of his shipping career he owned about 60 ocean-going vessels.* ADJ: usu ADJ n

**ocean|ic** /oʊʃiænɪk/ **Oceanic** means belonging or relating to an ocean or to the sea. ❑ *Many oceanic islands are volcanic.* ADJ: ADJ n

**ocean|og|ra|phy** /oʊʃənɒgrəfi/ **Oceanography** is the scientific study of sea currents, the sea bed, and the fish and animals that live in the sea. N-UNCOUNT ♦ **ocean|og|ra|pher (oceanographers)** ❑ *...an oceanographer working on an environmental protection programme.* N-COUNT ♦ **oceano|graph|ic** /oʊʃənəgræfɪk/ *...oceanographic research.* ADJ: ADJ n

**och** /ɒx/ **Och** is used to express surprise at something, or to emphasize agreement or disagreement with what has just been said. [IRISH, SCOTTISH] ❑ *'Och be quiet then,' Shawn said... Och aye. I always liked him.* CONVENTION = O, Oh

**ochre** /oʊkəʳ/ also **ocher.** Something that is **ochre** is a yellowish orange colour. ❑ *For our dining room I have chosen ochre yellow walls.* COLOUR

**o'clock** /əklɒk/ ◆◇◇ You use **o'clock** after numbers from one to twelve to say what time it is. For example, if you say that it is 9 o'clock, you mean that it is nine hours after midnight or nine hours after midday. ❑ *The trouble began just after ten o'clock last night... I went to sleep, and at two o'clock in the morning I woke up.* ADV: num ADV

**Oct.** **Oct.** is a written abbreviation for **October**. ❑ *...Tuesday Oct. 25th.*

**oc|ta|gon** /ɒktəgən/ **(octagons)** An **octagon** is a shape that has eight straight sides. N-COUNT

**oc|tago|nal** /ɒktægənəl/ Something that is **octagonal** has eight straight sides. ❑ *...a white octagonal box.* ADJ

**oc|tane** /ɒkteɪn/ **Octane** is a chemical substance that exists in petrol or gasoline and that is used to measure the quality of the fuel. ❑ *...high octane fuel for cars.* ➔ See also **high-octane**. N-UNCOUNT: usu with supp

**oc|tave** /ɒktɪv/ **(octaves)** An **octave** is a series of eight notes in a musical scale. It is also used to talk about the difference in pitch between the first and last notes in a musical scale. N-COUNT

**oc|tet** /ɒktet/ **(octets)** An **octet** is a group of eight singers or musicians. ❑ *...the Stan Tracey Octet.* N-COUNT: oft in names

**Oc|to|ber** /ɒktoʊbəʳ/ **(Octobers)** **October** is the tenth month of the year in the Western calendar. ❑ *Most seasonal hiring is done in early October... The first plane is due to leave on October 2... My grandson has been away since last October.* N-VAR

**oc|to|genar|ian** /ɒktoʊdʒɪneəriən/ **(octogenarians)** An **octogenarian** is a person who is between eighty and eighty-nine years old. N-COUNT

**oc|to|pus** /ɒktəpəs/ **(octopuses)** An **octopus** is a soft sea creature with eight long arms called tentacles which it uses to catch food. N-VAR ♦ **Octopus** is this creature eaten as food. N-UNCOUNT

**ocu|lar** /ɒkjələʳ/ **Ocular** means relating to the eyes or the ability to see. [MEDICAL] ❑ *Other ocular signs include involuntary rhythmic movement of the eyeball.* ADJ: ADJ n

**OD** /oʊ diː/ **(OD's, OD'ing, OD'd)** To **OD** means the same as to **overdose**. [INFORMAL] ❑ *His son was a junkie, the kid OD'd a year ago.* VERB V ♦ **OD** is also a noun. ❑ *'I had a friend died of an OD,' she said.* N-COUNT

**odd** /ɒd/ **(odder, oddest)** ◆◆◇ 1 If you describe someone or something as **odd**, you think that they are strange or unusual. ❑ *He'd always been odd, but not to this extent... What an odd coincidence that he should have known your family... Something odd began to happen.* ➔ See also **odd-looking**. ADJ = peculiar ♦ **odd|ly** *...an oddly shaped hill... His own boss was* ADV: ADV with v *behaving rather oddly.* 2 You use **odd** before a noun to indicate that you are not mentioning the type, size, or quality of something because it is not important. ❑ *...moving from place to place where she could find the odd bit of work... I knew that Alan liked the odd drink.* 3 You use **odd** after a number to indicate that it is only approximate. [INFORMAL] ❑ *He has now appeared in sixty odd films... 'How long have you lived here?' — 'Twenty odd years.'* 4 **Odd** numbers, such as 3 and 17, are those which cannot be divided exactly by the number two. ❑ *The odd numbers are on the left as you walk up the street... There's an odd number of candidates.* 5 You say that two things are **odd** when they do not belong to the same set or pair. ❑ *I'm wearing odd socks today by the way.* 6 **The odd man out, the odd woman out**, or **the odd one out** in a particular situation is a person who is different from the other people in it. ❑ *Azerbaijan has been the odd man out, the one republic not to hold democratic elections... Mark and Rick were the odd ones out in claiming to like this cherry beer.* 7 → See also **odds, odds and ends**.

ADJ: det ADJ = occasional
ADV: num ADV
ADJ: usu ADJ n ≠ even
ADJ ≠ matching
PHRASE: N inflects, usu v-link PHR

**odd|ball** /ɒdbɔːl/ **(oddballs)** If you refer to someone as an **oddball**, you think they behave in a strange way. [INFORMAL] ❑ *His mother and father thought Jim was a bit of an oddball too.* ♦ **Oddball** is also an adjective. ❑ *I came from a family that was decidedly oddball you know.*

N-COUNT = eccentric
ADJ = eccentric, peculiar

**odd|ity** /ɒdɪti/ **(oddities)** 1 An **oddity** is someone or something that is very strange. ❑ *Carlson noticed another oddity; his plant had bloomed twice.* 2 The **oddity of** something is the fact that it is very strange. ❑ *...the oddities of the Welsh legal system.*

N-COUNT
N-COUNT: usu *the* N *of* n = peculiarity

**odd-job man** **(odd-job men)** An **odd-job man** is a man who is paid to do various jobs such as cleaning or repairing things, usually in someone's home.

N-COUNT

**odd-looking** If you describe someone or something as **odd-looking**, you think that they look strange or unusual. ❑ *They were an odd-looking couple.*

ADJ

**odd|ly** /ɒdli/ You use **oddly** to indicate that what you are saying is true, but that it is not what you expected. ❑ *He said no and seemed oddly reluctant to talk about it... Oddly, Emma says she never considered her face was attractive.* → See also **odd**.

ADV: ADV adj, ADV with cl = strangely

**odd|ment** /ɒdmənt/ **(oddments)** **Oddments** are unimportant objects of any kind, usually ones that are old or left over from a larger group of things. ❑ *...searching street markets for interesting jewellery and oddments.*

N-COUNT

**odds** /ɒdz/ 1 You refer to how likely something is to happen as the **odds** that it will happen. ❑ *What are the odds of finding a parking space right outside the door?... The odds are that you are going to fail.* → See also **odds-on**. 2 In betting, **odds** are expressions with numbers such as '10 to 1' and '7 to 2' that show how likely something is thought to be, for example how likely a particular horse is to lose or win a race. ❑ *Gavin Jones, who put £25 on Eugene, at odds of 50 to 1, has won £1,250.*

N-PLURAL: usu *the* N
N-PLURAL

**PHRASES** 3 If someone is **at odds** with someone else, or if two people are **at odds**, they are disagreeing or quarrelling with each other. ❑ *He was at odds with his Prime Minister... An adviser said there was no reason why the two countries should remain at odds.* 4 If you say that **the odds are against** something or someone, you mean that they are unlikely to succeed. ❑ *He reckoned the odds are against the scheme going ahead.* 5 If something happens **against** all **odds**, it happens or succeeds although it seemed impossible or very unlikely. ❑ *Some women do manage to achieve business success against all odds.* 6 If you say that **the odds are in** someone's **favour**, you mean that they are likely to succeed in what they are doing. ❑ *His troops will only engage in a ground battle when all the odds are in their favour.* 7 To **shorten the odds** on something happening means to make it more likely to happen. To **lengthen the odds** means to make it less likely to happen. You can also say that the **odds shorten** or **lengthen**. ❑ *His reception there shortened the odds that he might be the next Tory leader.*

PHRASE: v-link PHR, oft PHR *with* n
PHRASE: V inflects, PHR n
PHRASE: PHR with cl
PHRASE: V inflects
PHRASE: V inflects

**odds and ends** You can refer to a disorganized group of things of various kinds as **odds and ends**. [INFORMAL] ❑ *She put in some clothes, odds and ends, and make-up.*

N-PLURAL = bits and pieces

**odds-on** also **odds on.** If there is an **odds-on** chance that something will happen, it is very likely that it will happen. [INFORMAL] ❑ *Gerald was no longer the odds-on favourite to win the contest... It was odds-on that there was no killer.*

ADJ

**ode** /oʊd/ **(odes)** An **ode** is a poem, especially one that is written in praise of a particular person, thing, or event. ❑ *...Keats' Ode to a Nightingale.*

N-COUNT

**odi|ous** /oʊdiəs/ If you describe people or things as **odious**, you think that they are extremely unpleasant. ❑ *Herr Schmidt is certainly the most odious man I have ever met.*

ADJ = obnoxious

**odium** /oʊdiəm/ **Odium** is the dislike, disapproval, or hatred that people feel for a particular person, usually because of something that the person has done. [FORMAL] ❑ *The complainant has been exposed to public odium, scandal and contempt.*

N-UNCOUNT

**odom|eter** /ɒdɒmɪtəʳ/ **(odometers)** An **odometer** is a device in a vehicle which shows how far the vehicle has travelled. [mainly AM]

N-COUNT

**odor** /oʊdəʳ/ → see **odour**.

**odour** /oʊdəʳ/ **(odours)**

✔ in AM, use **odor**

An **odour** is a particular and distinctive smell. ❑ *The whole herb has a characteristic taste and odour... The taste is only slightly bitter, and there is little odour.* → See also **body odour**.

N-VAR

**odour|less** /oʊdəʳləs/

✔ in AM, use **odorless**

An **odourless** substance has no smell. ❑ *...a completely odourless, colourless, transparent liquid... The gases are odourless.*

ADJ

**od|ys|sey** /ɒdɪsi/ **(odysseys)** An **odyssey** is a long exciting journey on which a lot of things happen. [LITERARY] ❑ *The march to Travnik was the final stretch of a 16-hour odyssey.*

N-COUNT

**Oedipus com|plex** /iːdɪpəs kɒmpleks/ If a boy or man has an **Oedipus complex**, he feels sexual desire for his mother and has hostile feelings towards his father.

N-SING

**o'er** /ɔːʳ/ **O'er** means the same as 'over'. [LITERARY, OLD-FASHIONED] ❑ *As long as mist hangs o'er the mountains, the deeds of the brave will be remembered.*

PREP

**oesopha|gus** /iːsɒfəgəs/ **(oesophaguses)**

✔ in AM, use **esophagus**

Your **oesophagus** is the part of your body that carries the food from the throat to the stomach.

N-COUNT

**oes|tro|gen** /iːstrədʒᵊn, AM e-/ also **estrogen. Oestrogen** is a hormone produced in the ovaries of female animals. Oestrogen controls the reproductive cycle and prepares the body for pregnancy. ❑ *As ovulation gets nearer, oestrogen levels rise.*

N-UNCOUNT

**of** /əv, STRONG ɒv, AM ʌv/ ♦♦♦

> In addition to the uses shown below, **of** is used after some verbs, nouns, and adjectives in order to introduce extra information. **Of** is also used in phrasal prepositions such as 'because of', 'instead of' and 'in spite of', and in phrasal verbs such as 'make of' and 'dispose of'.

1 You use **of** to combine two nouns when the first noun identifies the feature of the second noun that you want to talk about. ❑ *The average age of the women interviewed was only 21.5. ...the population of this town... The aim of the course is to*

PREP: n PREP n

*help students to comprehend the structure of contemporary political and social systems.* [2] You use **of** to combine two nouns, or a noun and a present participle, when the second noun or present participle defines or gives more information about the first noun. ❑ *She let out a little cry of pain. ...the problem of a national shortage of teachers. ...an idealized but hazy notion of world socialism. ...the recession of 1974-75.*
PREP: n PREP n/-ing

[3] You use **of** after nouns referring to actions to specify the person or thing that is affected by the action or that performs the action. For example, 'the kidnapping of the child' refers to an action affecting a child; 'the arrival of the next train' refers to an action performed by a train. ❑ *...the reduction of trade union power inside the party. ...the assessment of future senior managers. ...the death of their father.*
PREP: n PREP n

[4] You use **of** after words and phrases referring to quantities or groups of things to indicate the substance or thing that is being measured. ❑ *...7.6 litres of pure alcohol. ...dozens of people. ...billions of dollars. ...a collection of short stories.*
PREP: quant PREP n, n PREP n

[5] You use **of** after the name of someone or something to introduce the institution or place they belong to or are connected with. ❑ *...the Prince of Wales. ...the Finance Minister of Bangladesh.*
PREP: n PREP n

[6] You use **of** after a noun referring to a container to form an expression referring to the container and its contents. ❑ *Conder opened another bottle of wine. ...a box of tissues. ...a packet of cigarettes. ...a roomful of people.*
PREP: n PREP n

[7] You use **of** after a count noun and before an uncount noun when you want to talk about an individual piece or item. ❑ *...a blade of grass... Marina ate only one slice of bread... With a stick of chalk he wrote her order on a blackboard.*
PREP: n PREP n

[8] You use **of** to indicate the materials or things that form something. ❑ *...local decorations of wood and straw. ...loose-fitting garments of linen. ...a mixture of paint-thinner and petrol.*
PREP: n PREP n

[9] You use **of** after a noun which specifies a particular part of something, to introduce the thing that it is a part of. ❑ *...the other side of the square... We had almost reached the end of the street. ...the beginning of the year... Edward disappeared around 9.30pm on the 23rd of July. ...the core of the problem.*
PREP: n PREP n

[10] You use **of** after some verbs to indicate someone or something else involved in the action. ❑ *He'd been dreaming of her... Listen, I shall be thinking of you always... Her parents did not approve of her decision.*
PREP: v PREP n/-ing, v n PREP n/-ing

[11] You use **of** after some adjectives to indicate the thing that a feeling or quality relates to. ❑ *I have grown very fond of Alec... His father was quite naturally very proud of him... I think everyone was scared of her.*
PREP: adj PREP n/-ing

[12] You use **of** before a word referring to the person who performed an action when saying what you think about the action. ❑ *This has been so nice, so terribly kind of you... That's certainly very generous of you Tony.*
PREP: adj PREP pron/n-proper

[13] You use **of** after a noun which describes someone or something, to introduce the person or thing you are talking about. ❑ *...an awkward, slow-moving giant of a man.*
PREP: *a* n PREP *a* n

[14] If something is **more of** or **less of** a particular thing, it is that thing to a greater or smaller degree. ❑ *Your extra fat may be more of a health risk than you realize... As time goes by, sleeping becomes less of a problem.*
PREP: *more/less* PREP *a* n

[15] You use **of** to indicate a characteristic or quality that someone or something has. ❑ *She is a woman of enviable beauty. ...a matter of overwhelming importance.*
PREP: n PREP n, adj-superl PREP n

[16] You use **of** to specify an amount, value, or age. ❑ *Last Thursday, Nick announced record revenues of $3.4 billion... He has been sentenced to a total of 21 years in prison since 1973. ...young people under the age of 16 years.*
PREP: n PREP amount

[17] You use **of** after a noun such as 'month' or 'year' to indicate the length of time that some state or activity continues. ❑ *...eight bruising years of war... The project has gone through nearly a dozen years of planning.*
PREP: n PREP n/-ing

[18] You can use **of** to say what time it is by indicating how many minutes there are before the hour mentioned. [AM] ❑ *At about a quarter of eight in the evening Joe Urber calls... We got to the beach at five of one in the afternoon.*
PREP

## of course

◆◆◆

[1] You say **of course** to suggest that something is normal, obvious, or well-known, and should therefore not surprise the person you are talking to. [SPOKEN] ❑ *Of course there were lots of other interesting things at the exhibition... 'I have read about you in the newspapers of course,' Charlie said... The only honest answer is, of course, yes.*
ADV: ADV with cl = *naturally*

[2] You use **of course** as a polite way of giving permission. [SPOKEN] ❑ *'Can I just say something about the cup game on Saturday?' — 'Yes of course you can.'... 'Could I see these documents?' — 'Of course.'*
CONVENTION [formulae]

[3] You use **of course** in order to emphasize a statement that you are making, especially when you are agreeing or disagreeing with someone. [SPOKEN] ❑ *'I expect you're right.' — 'Of course I'm right.'... 'You will strictly observe your diet: no wine or spirits, very little meat.' — 'Of course.'*
ADV: ADV with cl, ADV as reply [emphasis]

[4] **Of course not** is an emphatic way of saying no. [SPOKEN] ❑ *'You're not really seriously considering this thing, are you?' — 'No, of course not.'*
CONVENTION [emphasis]

## off

◆◆◆

The preposition is pronounced /ɒf, AM ɔːf/. The adverb is pronounced /ɒf, AM ɔːf/

> In addition to the uses shown below, **off** is used after some verbs and nouns in order to introduce extra information. **Off** is also used in phrasal verbs such as 'get off', 'pair off', and 'sleep off'.

[1] If something is taken **off** something else or moves **off** it, it is no longer touching that thing. ❑ *He took his feet off the desk... I took the key for the room off a rack above her head... Hugh wiped the rest of the blood off his face with his handkerchief.*
PREP = *from*

♦ **Off** is also an adverb. ❑ *Lee broke off a small piece of orange and held it out to him... His exhaust fell off six laps from the finish.*
ADV: ADV after v

[2] When you get **off** a bus, train, or plane, you come out of it or leave it after you have been travelling on it. ❑ *Don't try to get on or off a moving train!... As he stepped off the aeroplane, he was shot dead.*
PREP ≠ *on*

♦ **Off** is also an adverb. ❑ *At the next stop the man got off too and introduced himself.*
ADV: ADV after v

[3] If you keep **off** a street or piece of land, you do not step on it or go there. ❑ *Locking up men does nothing more than keep them off the streets... The local police had warned visitors to keep off the beach at night.*
PREP

♦ **Off** is also an adverb. ❑ *...a sign saying 'Keep Off'.*
ADV

[4] If something is situated **off** a place such as a coast, room, or road, it is near to it or next to it, but not exactly in it. ❑ *The boat was anchored off the northern coast of the peninsula... Lily lives in a penthouse just off Park Avenue.*
PREP

[5] If you go **off**, you leave a place. ❑ *He was just about to drive off when the secretary came running out... She gave a hurried wave and set off across the grass... She was off again. Last year she had been to Kenya. This year it was Goa... When his master's off traveling, Caleb stays with Pierre's parents.*
ADV: ADV after v, *be* ADV, oft ADV -ing

[6] When you take **off** clothing or jewellery that you are wearing, you remove it from your body. ❑ *He took off his spectacles and rubbed frantically at the lens... He hastily stripped off his old uniform and began pulling on the new one.*
ADV: ADV after v

[7] If you have time **off** or a particular day **off**, you do not go to work or school, for example because you are ill or it is a day when you do not usually work. ❑ *The rest of the men had the day off... She was sacked for demanding Saturdays off... I'm off tomorrow... The average Swede was off sick 27 days last year.*
ADV: usu n ADV, also *be* ADV

♦ **Off** is also a preposition. ❑ *He could not get time off work to go on holiday.*
PREP

[8] If you keep **off** a subject, you deliberately avoid talking about it. ❑ *Keep off the subject of politics... Keep the conversation off linguistic matters.*
PREP

[9] If something such as an agreement or a sporting event is **off**, it is cancelled. ❑ *Until Pointon is completely happy, however, the deal's off... Greenpeace refused to call off the event.*
ADV: *be* ADV, ADV after v ≠ *on*

[10] If someone is **off** something harmful such as a drug, they have stopped taking or using it. ❑ *She felt better and the*
PREP

*psychiatrist took her off drug therapy.* 11 If you are **off** something, you have stopped liking it. ❑ *I'm off coffee at the moment... Diarrhoea can make you feel weak, as well as putting you off your food.* PREP

12 When something such as a machine or electric light is **off**, it is not functioning or in use. When you switch it **off**, you stop it functioning. ❑ *As he pulled into the driveway, he saw her bedroom light was off... We used sail power and turned the engine off to save our fuel... The microphones had been switched off.* ADV: *be* ADV, ADV after v ≠ *on*

13 If there is money **off** something, its price is reduced by the amount specified. ❑ *...Simons Leatherwear, 37 Old Christchurch Road. 20 per cent off all jackets this Saturday. ...discounts offering thousands of pounds off the normal price of a car.* ♦ **Off** is also an adverb. ❑ *I'm prepared to knock five hundred pounds off but nothing more.* PREP: amount PREP n; ADV: ADV after v, v-link ADV, amount ADV

14 If something is a long way **off**, it is a long distance away from you. ❑ *Florida was a long way off... Below you, though still 50 miles off, is the most treeless stretch of land imaginable.* ADV: n/amount ADV = *away*

15 If something is a long time **off**, it will not happen for a long time. ❑ *An end to the crisis seems a long way off... The required technology is probably still two years off.* ADV: n/amount ADV

16 If you get something **off** someone, you obtain it from them. [SPOKEN] ❑ *I don't really get a lot of information, and if I do I get it off Mark... 'Telmex' was bought off the government by a group of investors.* PREP = *from*

17 If food has gone **off**, it tastes and smells bad because it is no longer fresh enough to be eaten. [mainly BRIT] ❑ *Don't eat that! It's mouldy. It's gone off!* ADJ: v-link ADJ = *bad*

☑ in AM, usually use **spoiled, bad**

18 If you live **off** a particular kind of food, you eat it in order to live. If you live **off** a particular source of money, you use it to live. ❑ *Her husband's memories are of living off roast chicken and drinking whisky... Antony had been living off the sale of his own paintings.* PREP: v PREP n = *on*

19 If a machine runs **off** a particular kind of fuel or power, it uses that power in order to function. ❑ *The Auto Compact Disc Cleaner can run off batteries or mains.* PREP: v PREP n

20 If something happens **on and off**, or **off and on**, it happens occasionally, or only for part of a period of time, not in a regular or continuous way. ❑ *I was still working on and off as a waitress to support myself... We lived together, off and on, for two years.* PHRASE: PHR after v, PHR with cl

**off-air** also **off air.** In radio or television, when a programme goes **off-air** or when something happens **off-air**, it is not broadcast. ❑ *The argument continued off air.* ♦ **Off-air** is also an adjective. ❑ *...a special off-air advice line.* ADV: ADV after v, *be* ADV; ADJ: ADJ n

**of|fal** /ɒfəl, AM ɔːfəl/ **Offal** is the internal organs of animals, for example their hearts and livers, when they are cooked and eaten. N-UNCOUNT

**off-balance** also **off balance.** 1 If someone or something is **off-balance**, they can easily fall or be knocked over because they are not standing firmly. ❑ *He tried to use his own weight to push his attacker off but he was off balance.* ADJ: v n ADJ, v-link ADJ

2 If someone is caught **off-balance**, they are extremely surprised or upset by a particular event or piece of news they are not expecting. ❑ *Mullins knocked me off-balance with his abrupt change of subject... The government was thrown off-balance by the attempted coup.* ADJ: usu v n ADJ

**off-beam** also **off beam.** If you describe something or someone as **off-beam**, you mean that they are wrong or inaccurate. [INFORMAL] ❑ *Everything she says is a little off beam.* ADJ: usu v-link ADJ

**off|beat** /ɒfbiːt, AM ɔːf-/ also **off-beat.** If you describe something or someone as **offbeat**, you think that they are different from normal. ❑ *...a wickedly offbeat imagination.* ADJ: usu ADJ n = *unconventional*

**off-Broadway** /ɒf brɔːdweɪ, AM ɔːf -/

1 An **off-Broadway** theatre is located close to Broadway, the main theatre district in New York. ADJ: ADJ n

2 An **off-Broadway** play is less commercial and often more unusual than those usually staged on Broadway. ADJ: ADJ n

**off-centre**

☑ in AM, use **off-center**

1 If something is **off-centre**, it is not exactly in the middle of a space or surface. ❑ *If the blocks are placed off-centre, they will fall down.* ADJ: usu v-link ADJ

2 If you describe someone or something as **off-centre**, you mean that they are less conventional than other people or things. ❑ *Davies's writing is far too off-centre to be commercial.* ADJ: usu v-link ADJ = *unorthodox*

**off-chance** also **off chance.** If you do something **on the off-chance**, you do it because you hope that it will succeed, although you think that this is unlikely. ❑ *He had taken a flight to Paris on the off-chance that he might be able to meet Francesca.* PHRASE: PHR after v, oft PHR that, PHR *of* n/-ing

**off-colour**

☑ in AM, use **off-color**

1 If you say that you are feeling **off-colour**, you mean that you are slightly ill. [BRIT] ❑ *For three weeks Maurice felt off-colour but did not have any dramatic symptoms.* ADJ: v-link ADJ = *out of sorts*

2 If you say that someone's performance is **off-colour**, you mean that they are not performing as well as they usually do. [BRIT, JOURNALISM] ❑ *Milan looked off-colour but eventually took the lead in the 82nd minute.* ADJ

**off day** (**off days**) also **off-day.** If someone **has an off day**, they do not perform as well as usual. [INFORMAL] ❑ *Whittingham, the League's top scorer, had an off day, missing three good chances.* N-COUNT

**off-duty** When someone such as a soldier or policeman is **off-duty**, they are not working. ❑ *The place is the haunt of off-duty policemen.* ADJ

**of|fence** /əfens/ (**offences**) ◆◇◇

☑ The spelling **offense** is used in American English.

1 An **offence** is a crime that breaks a particular law and requires a particular punishment. ❑ *Thirteen people have been charged with treason – an offence which can carry the death penalty... In Britain the Consumer Protection Act makes it a criminal offence to sell goods that are unsafe.* N-COUNT

2 **Offence** or an **offence** is behaviour which causes people to be upset or embarrassed. ❑ *The book might be published without creating offense... Privilege determined by birth is an offence to any modern sense of justice.* N-VAR

3 Some people say '**no offence**' to make it clear that they do not want to upset you, although what they are saying may seem rather rude. ❑ *Dad, you need a bath. No offence.* CONVENTION formulae

4 If someone **takes offence at** something you say or do, they feel upset, often unnecessarily, because they think you are being rude to them. ❑ *She never takes offence at anything... Never had she seen him so tense, so quick to take offence as he had been in recent weeks.* PHRASE: V inflects

**of|fend** /əfend/ (**offends, offending, offended**)

1 If you **offend** someone, you say or do something rude which upsets or embarrasses them. ❑ *He apologizes for his comments and says he had no intention of offending the community... The survey found almost 90 percent of people were offended by strong swearwords... Television censors are cutting out scenes which they claim may offend.* ♦ **of|fend|ed** *She is terribly offended, angered and hurt by this.* VERB: V n; V n; V; ADJ: v-link ADJ

2 To **offend against** a law, rule, or principle means to break it. [FORMAL] ❑ *This bill offends against good sense and against justice... In showing contempt for the heavyweight championship Douglas offended a stern code.* VERB: V *against* n; V n

3 If someone **offends**, they commit a crime. [FORMAL] ❑ *In Western countries girls are far less likely to offend than boys.* VERB: no cont; V

**of|fend|er** /əfendəʳ/ (**offenders**) 1 An **offender** is a person who has committed a crime. ❑ *The authorities often know that sex offenders will attack again when they are released.* N-COUNT: oft supp N

2 You can refer to someone or something which you think is causing a problem as an **offender**. ❑ *The contraceptive pill is the worst offender, but it is not the only drug to deplete the body's vitamin levels.* N-COUNT = *culprit*

**of|fend|ing** /əfendɪŋ/ [1] You can use **offending** to describe something that is causing a problem that needs to be dealt with. ❑ *The book was withdrawn for the offending passages to be deleted.* ADJ: *the* ADJ n
[2] **Offending** is the act of committing a crime. ❑ *Ms Mann is working with young offenders and trying to break cycles of offending.* N-UNCOUNT

**of|fense** /əfens, ɒfens/ → see **offence**.

**of|fen|sive** /əfensɪv/ **(offensives)** ◆◇◇
[1] Something that is **offensive** upsets or embarrasses people because it is rude or insulting. ❑ *Some friends of his found the play horribly offensive. ...offensive remarks which called into question the integrity of my firm.* ADJ
♦ **of|fen|sive|ly** *The group who had been shouting offensively opened to let her through.* ADV: ADV after v, ADV adj
[2] A military **offensive** is a carefully planned attack made by a large group of soldiers. ❑ *Its latest military offensive against rebel forces is aimed at re-opening important trade routes.* N-COUNT: oft supp N
[3] If you conduct an **offensive**, you take strong action to show how angry you are about something or how much you disapprove of something. ❑ *Republicans acknowledged that they had little choice but to mount an all-out offensive on the Democratic nominee.* → See also **charm offensive**. N-COUNT: usu supp N
[4] If you **go on the offensive**, **go over to the offensive**, or **take the offensive**, you begin to take strong action against people who have been attacking you. ❑ *The West African forces went on the offensive in response to attacks on them... The Foreign Secretary has decided to take the offensive in the discussion on the future of the community.* PHRASE: V inflects

**of|fer** /ɒfəʳ, AM ɔːfər/ **(offers, offering, offered)** ◆◆◆
[1] If you **offer** something to someone, you ask them if they would like to have it or use it. ❑ *He has offered seats at the conference table to the Russian leader and the president of Kazakhstan... The number of companies offering them work increased... Western governments have offered aid.* VERB V n *to* n, V n n, V n
[2] If you **offer to** do something, you say that you are willing to do it. ❑ *Peter offered to teach them water-skiing... 'Can I get you a drink,' she offered.* VERB V to-inf, V with quote
[3] An **offer** is something that someone says they will give you or do for you. ❑ *The offer of talks with Moscow marks a significant change from the previous western position... 'I ought to reconsider her offer to move in,' he mused... He had refused several excellent job offers.* N-COUNT
[4] If you **offer** someone information, advice, or praise, you give it to them, usually because you feel that they need it or deserve it. ❑ *They manage a company offering advice on mergers and acquisitions... They are offered very little counselling or support.* VERB V n, V n n, Also V n *to* n
[5] If you **offer** someone something such as love or friendship, you show them that you feel that way towards them. ❑ *The President has offered his sympathy to the Georgian people... It must be better to be able to offer them love and security... John's mother and sister rallied round offering comfort.* VERB V n *to* n, V n n, V n
[6] If people **offer** prayers, praise, or a sacrifice to God or a god, they speak to or give something to their god. ❑ *Church leaders offered prayers and condemned the bloodshed... He will offer the first harvest of rice to the sun goddess.* VERB V n, V n *to* n, Also V n n
♦ **Offer up** means the same as **offer**. ❑ *He should consider offering up a prayer to St Lambert.* PHRASAL VERB V P n (not pron)
[7] If an organization **offers** something such as a service or product, it provides it. ❑ *We have been successful because we are offering a quality service... Sainsbury's is offering customers 1p for each shopping bag re-used... Eagle Star offers a 10% discount to the over-55s.* VERB V n, V n n, V n *to* n
[8] An **offer** in a shop is a specially low price for a specific product or something extra that you get if you buy a certain product. ❑ *This month's offers include a shirt, trousers and bed covers... Today's special offer gives you a choice of three destinations... Over 40 new books are on offer at 25 per cent off their normal retail price.* N-COUNT: oft supp N, also *on* N
[9] If you **offer** a particular amount of money for something, you say that you will pay that much to buy it. ❑ *Whitney has offered $21.50 a share in cash for 49.5 million Prime shares... They are offering farmers $2.15 a bushel for corn... He will write Rachel a note and offer her a fair price for the land... It was his custom in buying real estate to offer a rather low price.* VERB V amount, V n amount, V n n, V n, Also V n *to* n
[10] An **offer** is the amount of money that someone says they will pay to buy something or give to someone because they have harmed them in some way. ❑ *He has dismissed an offer of compensation.* N-COUNT

PHRASES
[11] If you **have something to offer**, you have a quality or ability that makes you important, attractive, or useful. ❑ *In your free time, explore all that this incredible city has to offer.* PHRASE: V inflects
[12] If there is something **on offer**, it is available to be used or bought. ❑ *Savings schemes are the best retail investment products on offer. ...country cottages on offer at bargain prices.* PHRASE: v-link PHR
[13] If you are **open to offers**, you are willing to do something if someone will pay you an amount of money that you think is reasonable. ❑ *It seems that while the Kiwis are keen to have him, he is still open to offers.* PHRASE: v-link PHR
♦ **offer up** → see **offer 6**.

**of|fer|ing** /ɒfərɪŋ, AM ɔːf-/ **(offerings)** ◆◇◇
[1] An **offering** is something that is specially produced to be sold. ❑ *It was very, very good, far better than vegetarian offerings in many a posh restaurant.* N-COUNT
[2] An **offering** is a gift that people offer to their God or gods as a form of worship. ❑ *...the holiest of the Shinto rituals, where offerings are made at night to the great Sun.* N-COUNT

**of|fer price** **(offer prices)** The **offer price** for a particular stock or share is the price that the person selling it says that they want for it. [BUSINESS] ❑ *BET shares closed just above the offer price, up 1.5p at 207p.* → See also **asking price**, **bid price**. N-COUNT

**off-guard** If someone is **caught off-guard**, they are not expecting a surprise or danger that suddenly occurs. ❑ *The question caught her completely off-guard.* ADJ: v n ADJ, v-link ADJ = *unawares*

**off|hand** /ɒfhænd/ also **off-hand.**
[1] If you say that someone is being **offhand**, you are critical of them for being unfriendly or impolite, and not showing any interest in what other people are doing or saying. ❑ *Consumers found the attitude of its staff offhand and generally offensive to the paying customer.* ADJ: usu v-link ADJ [disapproval]
[2] If you say something **offhand**, you say it without checking the details or facts of it. ❑ *'Have you done the repairs?' — 'Can't say off-hand, but I doubt it.'.* ADV: ADV after v

**of|fice** /ɒfɪs, AM ɔːf-/ **(offices)** ◆◆◆
[1] An **office** is a room or a part of a building where people work sitting at desks. ❑ *He had an office big enough for his desk and chair, plus his VDU... At about 4.30 p.m. Audrey arrived at the office... Telephone their head office for more details. ...an office block.* N-COUNT
[2] An **office** is a department of an organization, especially the government, where people deal with a particular kind of administrative work. ❑ *Thousands have registered with unemployment offices. ...Downing Street's press office. ...the Congressional Budget Office.* N-COUNT; N-IN-NAMES
[3] An **office** is a small building or room where people can go for information, tickets, or a service of some kind. ❑ *The tourist office operates a useful room-finding service. ...the airline ticket offices.* N-COUNT: usu supp N
[4] A doctor's or dentist's **office** is a place where a doctor or dentist sees their patients. [AM] N-COUNT

in BRIT, use **surgery**

[5] If someone holds **office** in a government, they have an important job or position of authority. ❑ *The events to mark the President's ten years in office went ahead as planned... They are fed up with the politicians and want to vote them out of office... The president shall hold office for five years... He ran for office.* N-UNCOUNT: oft *in/out of* N
[6] → See also **booking office**, **box office**, **post office**, **register office**, **registry office**.

**of|fice boy** **(office boys)** An **office boy** is a young man, especially one who has just left school, who is employed in an office to do simple tasks. [OLD-FASHIONED] N-COUNT

**office-holder** **(office-holders)** also **office holder.** An **office-holder** is a person who has an important official position in an organization N-COUNT or government. ❑ *They appear to be in a mood to vote against office-holders in the elections.*

**of|fice hours** **Office hours** are the times when an office or similar place is open for business. For example, office hours in Britain are usually between 9 o'clock and 5 o'clock from Monday to Friday. ❑ *If you have any queries, please call Anne Fisher during office hours.*
N-PLURAL: usu prep N

**of|fic|er** /ɒfɪsə$^r$, AM ɔːf-/ **(officers)** [1] In the armed forces, an **officer** is a person in a position of authority. ❑ *...a retired British army officer... Her husband served during the Civil War as an officer in the White Army.* [2] An **officer** is a person who has a responsible position in an organization, especially a government organization. ❑ *...a local authority education officer.* [3] Members of the police force can be referred to as **officers**. ❑ *...senior officers in the West Midlands police force... Thank you, Officer.* [4] → See also **commanding officer**, **petty officer**, **pilot officer**, **police officer**, **probation officer**, **returning officer**, **warrant officer**.
◆◆◆ N-COUNT; N-COUNT: usu supp N; N-COUNT: usu with supp; N-VOC

**of|fi|cial** /əfɪʃəl/ **(officials)** [1] **Official** means approved by the government or by someone in authority. ❑ *According to the official figures, over one thousand people died during the revolution... A report in the official police newspaper gave no reason for the move.* ♦ **of|fi|cial|ly** *The nine-year civil war is officially over.* [2] **Official** activities are carried out by a person in authority as part of their job. ❑ *The President is in Brazil for an official two-day visit.* [3] **Official** things are used by a person in authority as part of their job. ❑ *...the official residence of the Head of State.* [4] If you describe someone's explanation or reason for something as the **official** explanation, you are suggesting that it is probably not true, but is used because the real explanation is embarrassing. ❑ *The official reason given for the President's absence was sickness.* ♦ **of|fi|cial|ly** *Officially, the guard was to protect us. In fact, they were there to report on our movements.* [5] An **official** is a person who holds a position of authority in an organization. ❑ *A senior UN official hopes to visit Baghdad this month.* [6] An **official** at a sports event is a referee, umpire, or other person who checks that the players follow the rules.
◆◆◆ ADJ: usu ADJ n ≠ unofficial; ADV; ADJ: ADJ n ≠ private; ADJ: ADJ n; ADJ: ADJ n; ADV: ADV with cl/group; N-COUNT: oft n N; N-COUNT

**of|fi|cial|dom** /əfɪʃəldəm/ **Officialdom** is used to refer to officials who work for the government or in other organizations, especially when you think that their rules are unhelpful. ❑ *Officialdom has been against us from the start.*
N-UNCOUNT [disapproval]

**of|fi|ci|ate** /əfɪʃieɪt/ **(officiates, officiating, officiated)** [1] When someone **officiates at** a ceremony or formal occasion, they are in charge and perform the official part of it. ❑ *Bishop Silvester officiated at the funeral... A memorial service was held yesterday at Wadhurst Parish Church. The Rev Michael Inch officiated.* [2] When someone **officiates at** a sports match or competition, they are in charge and make sure the players do not break the rules. ❑ *Mr Ellis was selected to officiate at a cup game between Grimsby and Rotherham... Frik Burger will officiate when the Pumas play Scotland.*
VERB; V *at* n; V; VERB; V *at* n; V; Also V *in* n

**of|fi|cious** /əfɪʃəs/ If you describe someone as **officious**, you are critical of them because they are eager to tell people what to do when you think they should not. ❑ *When people put on uniforms, their attitude becomes more confident and their manner more officious.* ♦ **of|fi|cious|ly** *Lance Corporal Williams officiously ordered them out.*
ADJ [disapproval] = bossy; ADV: ADV with v

**of|fing** /ɒfɪŋ, AM ɔːf-/ If you say that something is **in the offing**, you mean that it is likely to happen soon. ❑ *A general amnesty for political prisoners may be in the offing.*
PHRASE: v-link PHR = imminent

**off-key** When music is **off-key**, it is not in tune. ❑ *...wailing, off-key vocals and strangled guitars.* ♦ **Off-key** is also an adverb. ❑ *Moe was having fun banging the drums and singing off-key.*
ADJ = out of tune; ADV: ADV after v = out of tune

**off-licence** **(off-licences)** An **off-licence** is a shop which sells beer, wine, and other alcoholic drinks. [BRIT]
N-COUNT: oft *the* N

☑ in AM, use **liquor store**

**off lim|its** also **off-limits**. [1] If a place is **off limits** to someone, they are not allowed to go there. ❑ *Downing Street has been off limits to the general public since 1982... Certain areas have been declared off limits to servicemen.* [2] If you say that an activity or a substance is **off limits** for someone, you mean that they are not allowed to do it or have it. ❑ *Fraternizing with the customers is off-limits.*
ADJ: usu v-link ADJ, oft ADJ *to* n; ADJ: v-link ADJ, oft ADJ *for* n

**off|line** /ɒflaɪn/ If a computer is **offline**, it is not connected to the Internet. Compare **online**. [COMPUTING] ♦ **Offline** is also an adverb. ❑ *Most software programs allow you to compose emails offline.*
ADJ; ADV: ADV with v

**off line** → see **line**.

**off|load** /ɒfloʊd, AM ɔːf-/ **(offloads, offloading, offloaded)** [1] If you **offload** something that you do not want, you get rid of it by giving it or selling it to someone else. [mainly BRIT] ❑ *Prices have been cut by developers anxious to offload unsold apartments... Already in financial difficulties, Turner offloaded the painting on to the Getty Museum.*
VERB; V n; V n *onto* n

☑ in AM, usually use **unload**

[2] When goods **are offloaded**, they are removed from a container or vehicle and put somewhere else. [mainly BRIT] ❑ *The cargo was due to be offloaded in Singapore three days later.*
VERB = unload ≠ load; *be* V-ed; Also V n

☑ in AM, usually use **unload**

**off-message** If a politician is **off-message**, they say something that does not follow the official policy of their party.
ADJ: usu v-link ADJ

**off-peak** You use **off-peak** to describe something that happens or that is used at times when there is least demand for it. Prices at off-peak times are often lower than at other times. ❑ *The price for indoor courts is £10 per hour at peak times and £7 per hour at off-peak times. ...off-peak electricity.* ♦ **Off-peak** is also an adverb. ❑ *Each tape lasts three minutes and costs 36p per minute off-peak and 48p at all other times.*
ADJ: ADJ n ≠ peak; ADV: ADV after v

**off-putting** If you describe a quality or feature of something as **off-putting**, you mean that it makes you dislike that thing or not want to get involved with it. [mainly BRIT] ❑ *Many customers found the smell of this product distinctly off-putting.*
ADJ

**off-roader** **(off-roaders)** An **off-roader** is the same as an **off-road vehicle**. [INFORMAL]
N-COUNT

**off-roading** **Off-roading** is the activity of driving off-road vehicles over rough ground. ❑ *...training sessions for anyone who wants to go off-roading.*
N-UNCOUNT

**off-road vehicle** **(off-road vehicles)** An **off-road vehicle** is a vehicle that is designed to travel over rough ground.
N-COUNT

**off-screen** also **offscreen**. You use **off-screen** to refer to the real lives of film or television actors, in contrast with the lives of the characters they play. ❑ *He was immensely attractive to women, onscreen and offscreen... Off-screen, Kathy is under the watchful eye of her father Terry.* ♦ **Off-screen** is also an adjective. ❑ *They were quick to dismiss rumours of an off-screen romance.*
ADV: ADV with cl ≠ on-screen; ADJ: ADJ n ≠ on-screen

**off sea|son** also **off-season**. [1] The **off season** is the time of the year when not many people go on holiday and when things such as hotels and plane tickets are often cheaper. ❑ *It is possible to vacation at some of the more expensive resorts if you go in the off-season... Although it was off-season, the hotel was fully occupied. ...off-season prices.* ♦ **Off season** is also an adverb. ❑ *Times become more flexible off-season, especially in the smaller provincial museums.* [2] The **off season** is the time of the year when a particular sport is not played. ❑ *He has coached and played in Italy during the Australian off-season. ...intensive off-season training.* ♦ **Off season** is also an adverb. ❑ *To stay fit off season, I play tennis or football.*
N-SING: also no det, oft N n = low season ≠ high season; ADV: usu ADV with cl, also ADV after v; N-SING: oft N n ≠ season; ADV: usu ADV with cl, also ADV after v

**off|set** /ɒfset, AM ɔːf-/ **(offsets, offsetting)**

> The form **offset** is used in the present tense and is the past tense and past participle of the verb.

If one thing **is offset** by another, the effect of the first thing is reduced by the second, so that any advantage or disadvantage is cancelled out. ❑ *The increase in pay costs was more than offset by higher productivity... The move is designed to help offset the shortfall in oil supplies caused by the UN embargo.* VERB = balance; be V-ed; V n

**off|shoot** /ɒfʃuːt, AM ɔːf-/ **(offshoots)** If one thing is an **offshoot** of another, it has developed from that other thing. ❑ *Psychology began as a purely academic offshoot of natural philosophy.* N-COUNT: usu with poss

**off|shore** /ɒfʃɔːʳ, AM ɔːf-/ [1] **Offshore** means situated or happening in the sea, near to the coast. ❑ *...Britain's offshore oil industry. ...offshore islands.* ♦ **Offshore** is also an adverb. ❑ *One day a larger ship anchored offshore... When they hit the rocks, they were just 500 yards offshore.* [2] An **offshore** wind blows from the land towards the sea. [3] **Offshore** investments or companies are located in a place, usually an island, which has fewer tax regulations than most other countries. [BUSINESS] ❑ *The island offers a wide range of offshore banking facilities.* ADJ: ADJ n; ADV: ADV after v, be ADV, oft amount ADV; ADJ: ADJ n; ADJ: ADJ n

**off|side** /ɒfsaɪd, AM ɔːf-/ also **off-side.** [1] In games such as football or hockey, when an attacking player is **offside**, they have broken the rules by being nearer to the goal than a defending player when the ball is passed to them. ❑ *The goal was disallowed because Wark was offside.* ♦ **Offside** is also an adverb. ❑ *Wise was standing at least ten yards offside.* ♦ **Offside** is also a noun. ❑ *Rush had a 45th-minute goal disallowed for offside.* [2] In American football, a player is **offside** if they cross the line of scrimmage before a play begins. [AM] [3] The **offside** of a vehicle is the side that is farthest from the edge of the road when the vehicle is being driven normally. [BRIT] ❑ *The driver of the car lowered his offside front window.* ADJ: usu v-link ADJ; ADV: ADV after v; N-UNCOUNT; ADJ: usu v-link ADJ; N-SING: usu N n ≠ nearside

**off-site** → see **site**.

**off|spring** /ɒfsprɪŋ, AM ɔːf-/ **(offspring)** You can refer to a person's children or to an animal's young as their **offspring**. [FORMAL] ❑ *Eleanor was now less anxious about her offspring than she had once been.* N-COUNT: oft with poss

**off|stage** /ɒfsteɪdʒ, AM ɔːf-/ also **off-stage.** [1] When an actor or entertainer goes **offstage**, they go into the area behind or to the side of the stage, so that the audience no longer sees them. ❑ *She ran offstage in tears... There was a lot of noise offstage.* [2] **Offstage** is used to describe the behaviour of actors or entertainers in real life, when they are not performing. ❑ *...the tragedies of their off-stage lives.* ♦ **Offstage** is also an adverb. ❑ *Despite their screen rivalry, off-stage they are friends.* ADV: ADV after v, n ADV ≠ onstage; ADJ: ADJ n ≠ onstage; ADV: ADV with cl ≠ onstage

**off-the-cuff** → see **cuff**.

**off-the-peg** → see **peg**.

**off-the-record** → see **record**.

**off-the-shelf** → see **shelf**.

**off-the-wall** [1] If you describe something as **off-the-wall**, you mean that it is unusual and rather strange but in an amusing or interesting way. [INFORMAL] ❑ *...surreal off-the-wall humor.* [2] If you say that a person, their ideas, or their ways of doing something are **off-the-wall**, you are critical of them because you think they are mad or very foolish. ❑ *It can be done without following some absurd, off-the-wall investment strategy.* ADJ: usu ADJ n; ADJ [disapproval]

**off top|ic** also **off-topic.** If you describe something that someone says or writes as **off topic**, you mean that it is not relevant to the current discussion; used especially of discussions on the Internet. ❑ *In addition to the 81 positive comments, 26 students had neutral, mixed, negative or off topic views.* ADJ

**off-white** Something that is **off-white** is not pure white, but slightly grey or yellow. COLOUR

**off-year** **(off-years)** An **off-year** is a year when no major political elections are held. [AM] ❑ *Election officials predict they'll set a new turnout record for an off-year election in Washington state.* N-COUNT: oft N n

**oft-** /ɒft-, AM ɔːft-/ **Oft** combines with past participles to form adjectives that mean that something happens or is done often. [LITERARY] ❑ *The Foreign Secretary's views on the treaty are well-documented and oft-repeated.* COMB in ADJ

**of|ten** /ɒfᵊn, AM ɔːf-/ ♦♦♦

> **Often** is usually used before the verb, but it may be used after the verb when it has a word like 'less' or 'more' before it, or when the clause is negative.

[1] If something **often** happens, it happens many times or much of the time. ❑ *They often spent Christmas at Prescott Hill... It was often hard to work and do the course at the same time... That doesn't happen very often.* [2] You use **how often** to ask questions about frequency. You also use **often** in reported clauses and other statements to give information about the frequency of something. ❑ *How often do you brush your teeth?... Unemployed Queenslanders were victims of personal crime twice as often as employed people.* ADV: ADV before v, ADV with cl/group ≠ rarely; ADV: how ADV, as ADV as n/cl

PHRASES [3] If something happens **every so often**, it happens regularly, but with fairly long intervals between each occasion. ❑ *She's going to come back every so often... Every so often he would turn and look at her.* [4] If you say that something happens **as often as not,** or **more often than not**, you mean that it happens fairly frequently, and that this can be considered as typical of the kind of situation you are talking about. ❑ *Yet, as often as not, they find themselves the target of persecution rather than praise.* PHRASE: PHR with cl = occasionally; PHRASE: PHR with cl

**often|times** /ɒfᵊntaɪmz, AM ɔːf-/ If something **oftentimes** happens, it happens many times or much of the time. [AM] ❑ *Oftentimes, I wouldn't even return the calls.* ADV: ADV with cl, ADV with v, be ADV group = often

**ogle** /oʊgᵊl/ **(ogles, ogling, ogled)** If you say that one person is **ogling** another, you disapprove of them continually staring at that person in a way that indicates a strong sexual interest. ❑ *All she did was hang around ogling the men in the factory... Paula is not used to everyone ogling at her while she undresses backstage.* VERB [disapproval]; V n; V at n; Also V

**ogre** /oʊgəʳ/ **(ogres)** If you refer to someone as an **ogre**, you are saying in a humorous way that they are very frightening. ❑ *Bank managers – like tax inspectors – do not really like being thought of as ogres.* N-COUNT

**oh** /oʊ/ ♦♦◇ [1] You use **oh** to introduce a response or a comment on something that has just been said. [SPOKEN] ❑ *'Had you seen the car before?' — 'Oh yes, it was always in the drive.'... 'You don't understand!' — 'Oh, I think I do, Grace.'* [2] You use **oh** to express a feeling such as surprise, pain, annoyance, or happiness. [SPOKEN] ❑ *'Oh!' Kenny blinked. 'Has everyone gone?'... Oh, I'm so glad you're here.* [3] You use **oh** when you are hesitating while speaking, for example because you are trying to estimate something, or because you are searching for the right word. [SPOKEN] ❑ *I've been here, oh, since the end of June.* CONVENTION; EXCLAM [feelings]; CONVENTION

**ohm** /oʊm/ **(ohms)** An **ohm** is a unit which is used to measure electrical resistance. [TECHNICAL] N-COUNT

**OHMS** /oʊ eɪtʃ em es/ **OHMS** is used on official letters from British or Commonwealth government offices. **OHMS** is the abbreviation for 'On Her Majesty's Service' or 'On His Majesty's Service'.

**OHP** /oʊ eɪtʃ piː/ **(OHPs)** An **OHP** is the same as an **overhead projector**. N-COUNT

**oi** /ɔɪ/ In informal situations, people say or shout '**oi**' to attract someone's attention, especially if they are angry. [BRIT] ❑ *Oi! You lot! Shut up!* EXCLAM

**oik** /ɔɪk/ **(oiks)** If you refer to someone as an **oik**, you think that they behave in a rude or unacceptable way, especially in a way that you believe to be typical of a low social class. [BRIT, INFORMAL] ❑ *She has to live cheek by jowl with oiks, people with tattoos and stolen videos.* N-COUNT disapproval

**oil** /ɔɪl/ **(oils, oiling, oiled)** 1 **Oil** is a smooth, thick liquid that is used as a fuel and for making the parts of machines move smoothly. Oil is found underground. ❑ *The company buys and sells about 600,000 barrels of oil a day. ...the rapid rise in prices for oil and petrol. ...a small oil lamp.* ◆◆◆ N-MASS 2 If you **oil** something, you put oil onto or into it, for example to make it work smoothly or to protect it. ❑ *A crew of assistants oiled and adjusted the release mechanism until it worked perfectly.* VERB V n 3 **Oil** is a smooth, thick liquid made from plants and is often used for cooking. ❑ *Combine the beans, chopped mint and olive oil in a large bowl.* N-MASS: usu n N 4 **Oil** is a smooth, thick liquid, often with a pleasant smell, that you rub into your skin or add to your bath. ❑ *Try a hot bath with some relaxing bath oil.* N-MASS: usu supp N 5 **Oils** are **oil paintings**. ❑ *Her colourful oils and works on paper have a naive, dreamlike quality.* N-COUNT: usu pl 6 When an artist paints in **oils**, he or she uses oil paints. ❑ *When she paints in oils she always uses the same range of colours.* N-PLURAL 7 → See also **castor oil**, **crude oil**, **olive oil**. 8 If someone or something **oils the wheels** of a process or system, they help things to run smoothly and successfully. ❑ *On all such occasions, the king stands in the wings, oiling the wheels of diplomacy.* PHRASE: V inflects 9 to **burn the midnight oil** → see **midnight**.

**oil|cloth** /ɔɪlklɒθ, AM -klɔːθ/ **(oilcloths)** 1 **Oilcloth** is a cotton fabric with a shiny waterproof surface. N-UNCOUNT 2 An **oilcloth** is a covering made from oilcloth, such as a tablecloth. N-COUNT

**oiled** /ɔɪld/ Something that is **oiled** has had oil put into or onto it, for example to make it work smoothly or to protect it. ❑ *Oiled wood is water-resistant and won't flake.* → See also **well-oiled**. ADJ: usu ADJ n

**oil|field** /ɔɪlfiːld/ **(oilfields)** also **oil field.** An **oilfield** is an area of land or sea under which there is oil. N-COUNT

**oil-fired** **Oil-fired** heating systems and power stations use oil as a fuel. ❑ *...an oil-fired furnace.* ADJ: ADJ n

**oil|man** /ɔɪlmæn/ **(oilmen)** also **oil man.** An **oilman** is a man who owns an oil company or who works in the oil business. [JOURNALISM] N-COUNT

**oil paint** **(oil paints)** **Oil paint** is a thick paint used by artists. It is made from coloured powder and linseed oil. N-UNCOUNT: also N in pl

**oil paint|ing** **(oil paintings)** An **oil painting** is a picture which has been painted using oil paints. ❑ *Several magnificent oil paintings adorn the walls.* N-COUNT

**oil pan** **(oil pans)** An **oil pan** is the place under an engine which holds the engine oil. [mainly AM] N-COUNT

✔ in BRIT, usually use **sump**

**oil plat|form** **(oil platforms)** An **oil platform** is a structure that is used when getting oil from the ground under the sea. N-COUNT

**oil rig** **(oil rigs)** An **oil rig** is a structure on land or in the sea that is used when getting oil from the ground. N-COUNT

**oil|seed rape** /ɔɪlsiːd reɪp/ also **oil-seed rape.** **Oilseed rape** is a plant with yellow flowers which is grown as a crop. Its seeds are crushed to make cooking oil. [BRIT] N-UNCOUNT

✔ in AM, use **rape**

**oil|skins** /ɔɪlskɪnz/ **Oilskins** are a coat and a pair of trousers made from thick waterproof cotton cloth. N-PLURAL

**oil slick** **(oil slicks)** An **oil slick** is a layer of oil that is floating on the sea or on a lake because it has accidentally come out of a ship or container. ❑ *The oil slick is now 35 miles long.* N-COUNT

**oil tank|er** **(oil tankers)** An **oil tanker** is a ship that is used for transporting oil. N-COUNT

**oil well** **(oil wells)** An **oil well** is a deep hole which is made in order to get oil out of the ground. N-COUNT

**oily** /ɔɪli/ **(oilier, oiliest)** 1 Something that is **oily** is covered with oil or contains oil. ❑ *He was wiping his hands on an oily rag... When she was younger, she had very oily skin.* ADJ 2 **Oily** means looking, feeling, tasting, or smelling like oil. ❑ *...traces of an oily substance.* ADJ: usu ADJ n 3 If you describe someone as **oily**, you dislike them because you think they are too polite or say exaggeratedly nice things, and are insincere. ❑ *He had behaved with undue and oily familiarity.* ADJ disapproval = smarmy

**oint|ment** /ɔɪntmənt/ **(ointments)** 1 An **ointment** is a smooth thick substance that is put on sore skin or a wound to help it heal. ❑ *A range of ointments and creams is available for the treatment of eczema... He received ointment for his flaking skin.* N-MASS 2 If you describe someone or something as a **fly in the ointment**, you think they spoil a situation and prevent it being as successful as you had hoped. ❑ *Rachel seems to be the one fly in the ointment of Caroline's smooth life.* PHRASE: v-link PHR

**OK** /oʊ keɪ/ → see **okay**.

**okay** /oʊkeɪ/ **(okays, okaying, okayed)** also **OK, O.K., ok** 1 If you say that something is **okay**, you find it satisfactory or acceptable. [INFORMAL] ❑ *...a shooting range where it's OK to use weapons... Is it okay if I come by myself?... I guess for a fashionable restaurant like this the prices are OK.* ◆◆◇ ADJ: usu v-link ADJ, oft *it* v-link ADJ to-inf, *it* v-link ADJ if = all right ♦ **Okay** is also an adverb. ❑ *We seemed to manage okay for the first year or so after David was born.* ADV: ADV after v = all right 2 If you say that someone is **okay**, you mean that they are safe and well. [INFORMAL] ❑ *Check that the baby's okay... 'Don't worry about me,' I said. 'I'll be okay.'* ADJ: v-link ADJ = all right 3 You can say **'Okay'** to show that you agree to something. [INFORMAL] ❑ *'Just tell him Sir Kenneth would like to talk to him.' — 'OK.'... 'Shall I give you a ring on Friday?' — 'Yeah okay.'* CONVENTION formulae = all right 4 You can say **'Okay?'** to check whether the person you are talking to understands what you have said and accepts it. [INFORMAL] ❑ *We'll get together next week, OK?* CONVENTION = all right 5 You can use **okay** to indicate that you want to start talking about something else or doing something else. [INFORMAL] ❑ *OK. Now, let's talk some business... Tim jumped to his feet. 'Okay, let's go.'* CONVENTION = right 6 You can use **okay** to stop someone arguing with you by showing that you accept the point they are making, though you do not necessarily regard it as very important. [INFORMAL] ❑ *Okay, there is a slight difference... Okay, so I'm forty-two.* CONVENTION 7 If someone in authority **okays** something, they officially agree to it or allow it to happen. [INFORMAL] ❑ *His doctor wouldn't OK the trip.* VERB V n ♦ **Okay** is also a noun. ❑ *He gave the okay to issue a new press release.* N-SING: the N

**okey doke** /oʊkeɪ doʊk/ or **okey dokey** **Okey doke** is used in the same way as 'OK' to show that you agree to something, or that you want to start talking about something else or doing something else. [INFORMAL, SPOKEN] ❑ *Okey doke. I'll give you a ring.* CONVENTION = alright

**okra** /oʊkrə/ **Okra** is a vegetable that consists of long green parts containing seeds. N-UNCOUNT

**old** /oʊld/ **(older, oldest)** 1 Someone who is **old** has lived for many years and is no longer young. ❑ *...a white-haired old man... He was considered too old for the job.* ◆◆◆ ADJ = elderly ≠ young ♦ **The old** are people who are old. ❑ *...providing a caring response for the needs of the old and the handicapped.* N-PLURAL: the N 2 You use **old** to talk about how many days, weeks, months, or years someone or something has lived or existed. ❑ *He was abandoned by his father when he was three months old... The paintings in the chapel were perhaps a thousand years old... How old are you now?... Bill was six years older than David.* ADJ: amount ADJ, *how* ADJ, *as* ADJ *as*, ADJ-compar *than* 3 Something that is **old** has existed for a long time. ❑ *She loved the big old house... These books must be very old. ...an old Arab proverb.* ADJ ≠ new 4 Something that is **old** is no longer in good condition because of its age or because it has been used a lot. ❑ *He took a bunch of* ADJ: usu ADJ n ≠ new keys from the pocket of his old corduroy trousers. ...an old toothbrush. 5 You use **old** to refer to something that is no longer used, that no longer exists, or that has been replaced by something else. ❑ *The old road had disappeared under grass and heather... Although the old secret police have been abolished, the military police still exist.* 6 You use **old** to refer to something that used to belong to you, or to a person or thing that used to have a particular role in your life. ❑ *I'll make up the bed in your old room... Mark was heartbroken when Jane returned to her old boyfriend.* 7 An **old** friend, enemy, or rival is someone who has been your friend, enemy, or rival for a long time. ❑ *I called my old friend John Horner... The French and English are old rivals.* 8 You can use **old** to express affection when talking to or about someone you know. [INFORMAL] ❑ *Are you all right, old chap?... Good old Bergen would do him the favor.* — ADJ: ADJ n / ADJ: poss ADJ n / ADJ: ADJ n / ADJ: ADJ n [feelings]

**PHRASES** 9 You use **any old** to emphasize that the quality or type of something is not important. If you say that a particular thing is **not any old** thing, you are emphasizing how special or famous it is. [INFORMAL] ❑ *The portraits and sumptuous ornaments, and the gold clock, show that this is not just any old front room.* 10 **In the old days** means in the past, before things changed. ❑ *In the old days we got a visit from the vet maybe once a year.* 11 When people refer to **the good old days**, they are referring to a time in the past when they think that life was better than it is now. ❑ *He remembers the good old days when everyone in his village knew him and you could leave your door open at night.* 12 **good old** → see **good**. to **settle an old score** → see **score**. **up to** one's **old tricks** → see **trick**. — PHRASE: PHR n [emphasis] / PHRASE: PHR with cl / PHRASE

**old age** Your **old age** is the period of years towards the end of your life. ❑ *They worry about how they will support themselves in their old age.* — N-UNCOUNT: oft poss N ≠ youth

**old age pen|sion** (old age pensions) also **old-age pension.** An **old age pension** is a regular amount of money that people receive from the government when they have retired from work. [BRIT] — N-COUNT

> in AM, use **social security benefit**, **social security payment**

**old age pen|sion|er** (old age pensioners) also **old-age pensioner.** An **old age pensioner** is a person who is old enough to receive an pension from their employer or the government. [BRIT] — N-COUNT = OAP, senior citizen

> in AM, use **senior citizen, retiree**

**old bat** (old bats) If someone refers to an old person, especially an old woman, as an **old bat**, they think that person is silly, annoying, or unpleasant. [INFORMAL, OFFENSIVE] — N-COUNT: usu sing [disapproval]

**old boy** (old boys) You can refer to a man who used to be a pupil at a particular school or university as an **old boy**. [BRIT] ❑ *...Eton College, with all its traditions and long list of famous old boys.* — N-COUNT

**old-boy net|work** (old-boy networks) also **old boy network.** When people talk about the **old-boy network**, they are referring to a situation in which people who went to the same public school or university use their positions of influence to help each other. [BRIT] ❑ *The majority obtained their positions through the old boy network.* — N-COUNT: usu *the* N in sing [disapproval]

**olde** /oʊld/ **Olde** is used in names of places and in advertising to make people think that something is very old and interesting. ❑ *I always feel at home at Ye Olde Starre Inn.* — ADJ: ADJ n

**old|en** /oʊldən/ If you refer to a period in the past as **the olden days**, you feel affection for it. [LITERARY] ❑ *We had a delightful time talking about the olden days on his farm. ...the nicely painted railways of olden times.* ● **In the olden days** or **in olden days** means in the past. ❑ *In the olden days the girls were married young.* — ADJ: ADJ n / PHRASE: PHR with cl

**olde worlde** /oʊldi wɜːldi/ **Olde worlde** is used to describe places and things that are or seem to be from an earlier period of history, and that look interesting or attractive. [BRIT] ❑ *...the quaint olde worlde part of town... There is an olde worlde look about the clothes for summer.* — ADJ

**old-fashioned** 1 Something such as a style, method, or device that is **old-fashioned** is no longer used, done, or admired by most people, because it has been replaced by something that is more modern. ❑ *The house was dull, old-fashioned and in bad condition... There are some traditional farmers left who still make cheese the old-fashioned way.* 2 **Old-fashioned** ideas, customs, or values are the ideas, customs, and values of the past. ❑ *She has some old-fashioned values and can be a strict disciplinarian. ...good old-fashioned English cooking.* — ADJ ≠ modern / ADJ = traditional

**old flame** (old flames) An **old flame** is someone with whom you once had a romantic relationship. ❑ *Sue was seen dating an old flame.* — N-COUNT

**old girl** (old girls) You can refer to a woman who used to be a pupil at a particular school or university as an **old girl**. [BRIT] ❑ *...the St Mary's Ascot Old Girls' Reunion Lunch.* — N-COUNT

**Old Glo|ry** People sometimes refer to the flag of the United States as **Old Glory**. [AM] — N-UNCOUNT

**old guard** If you refer to a group of people as the **old guard**, you mean that they have worked in a particular organization for a very long time and are unwilling to accept new ideas or practices. ❑ *The old guard did not like the changes that Brewer introduced.* — N-SING-COLL: usu *the*/poss N [disapproval]

**old hand** (old hands) If someone is an **old hand** at something, they are very skilled at it because they have been doing it for a long time. ❑ *An old hand at photography, Tim has been shooting wildlife as a hobby for the last 13 years.* — N-COUNT: oft N *at* n = veteran ≠ novice

**old hat** → see **hat**.

**oldie** /oʊldi/ (oldies) 1 You can refer to something such as an old song or film as an **oldie**, especially when you think it is still good. [INFORMAL] ❑ *Radio Aire only plays Top 40 stuff and oldies.* ♦ **Oldie** is also an adjective. ❑ *During the festival, we'll be showing 13 classic oldie films.* 2 You can use **oldies** to refer to fairly old people. [BRIT, HUMOROUS, INFORMAL] ❑ *...a lush English fairy tale that many oldies will remember from their youth.* — N-COUNT / ADJ: ADJ n / N-COUNT

**old lady** Some men refer to their wife, girlfriend, or mother as their **old lady**. [INFORMAL] ❑ *He had met his old lady when he was a house painter and she was a waitress.* — N-SING: usu poss N

**old maid** (old maids) People sometimes refer to an old or middle-aged woman as an **old maid** when she has never married and they think that it is unlikely that she ever will marry. This use could cause offence. ❑ *Alex is too young to be already thinking of herself as an old maid.* — N-COUNT [disapproval] = spinster

**old man** Some people refer to their father, husband, or boyfriend as their **old man**. [INFORMAL] ❑ *Her old man left her a few millions when he died.* — N-SING: *the*/poss N

**old mas|ter** (old masters) An **old master** is a painting by one of the famous European painters of the 16th, 17th, and 18th centuries. These painters can also be referred to as the **Old Masters**. ❑ *...his collection of old masters and modern art. ...portraits by Gainsborough, Rubens and other Old Masters.* — N-COUNT

**old peo|ple's home** (old people's homes) An **old people's home** is a place where old people live and are cared for when they are too old to look after themselves. [mainly BRIT] — N-COUNT

**old school tie** When people talk about **the old school tie**, they are referring to the situation in which people who attended the same public school use their positions of influence to help each other. [BRIT] ❑ *Of course, the old school tie has been a help.* — N-SING: *the* N

**old-style** You use **old-style** to describe something or someone of a type that was common or popular in the past but is not common or popular now. ❑ *...a proper barber shop with real old-style barber chairs.* — ADJ: ADJ n = *old-fashioned*

**Old Tes|ta|ment** **The Old Testament** is the first part of the Bible. It deals especially with the relationship between God and the Jewish people. — N-PROPER: *the* N

**old-time** If you describe something as **old-time**, you mean that it was common or popular in the past but is not common or popular now. ❑ *...an old-time dance hall which still has a tea dance on Monday afternoons.* — ADJ: ADJ n = *old-fashioned*

**old-timer** **(old-timers)** 1 If you refer to someone as an **old-timer**, you mean that he or she has been living in a particular place or doing a particular job for a long time. [INFORMAL] ❑ *The old-timers and established families clutched the reins of power.* — N-COUNT ≠ *newcomer* 2 An old man is sometimes referred to as an **old-timer**. [AM, INFORMAL] — N-COUNT

**old wives' tale** **(old wives' tales)** An **old wives' tale** is a traditional belief, especially one which is incorrect. ❑ *Ann Bradley dispels the old wives' tales and gives the medical facts.* — N-COUNT

**old wom|an** **(old women)** If you refer to someone, especially a man, as an **old woman**, you are critical of them because you think they are too anxious about things. [INFORMAL] — N-COUNT [disapproval]

**ole** /oʊl/ **Ole** is used in written English to represent the word 'old' pronounced in a particular way. ❑ *'I started fixin' up ole bicycles fer poor kids.'* — ADJ: ADJ n

**olean|der** /oʊliændəʳ/ **(oleanders)** An **oleander** is an evergreen tree or shrub that has white, pink, or purple flowers. Oleanders grow in Mediterranean countries and in some parts of Asia and Australia. — N-VAR

**ol|fac|tory** /ɒlfæktəri/ **Olfactory** means concerned with the sense of smell. [FORMAL] ❑ *This olfactory sense develops in the womb.* — ADJ: ADJ n

**oli|gar|chy** /ɒlɪgɑːʳki/ **(oligarchies)** 1 An **oligarchy** is a small group of people who control and run a particular country or organization. You can also refer to a country which is governed in this way as an **oligarchy**. — N-COUNT 2 **Oligarchy** is a situation in which a country or organization is run by an oligarchy. ❑ *...a protest against imperialism and oligarchy in the region.* — N-UNCOUNT

**ol|ive** /ɒlɪv/ **(olives)** 1 **Olives** are small green or black fruit with a bitter taste. Olives are often pressed to make olive oil. — N-VAR 2 An **olive tree** or an **olive** is a tree on which olives grow. ❑ *...an olive grove.* — N-COUNT 3 Something that is **olive** is yellowish-green in colour. ❑ *...glowing colours such as deep red, olive, saffron and ochre.* — COLOUR ♦ **Olive** is also a combining form. ❑ *She wore an olive-green T-shirt.* — COMB in COLOUR 4 If someone has **olive** skin, the colour of their skin is light brown. ❑ *They are handsome with dark, shining hair, olive skin and fine brown eyes.* — ADJ: usu ADJ n

**ol|ive branch** **(olive branches)** also **olive-branch**. If you offer an **olive branch** to someone, you say or do something in order to show that you want to end a disagreement or quarrel. ❑ *Clarke also offered an olive branch to critics in his party.* — N-COUNT: usu sing

**ol|ive oil** **(olive oils)** **Olive oil** is oil that is obtained by pressing olives. It is used for putting on salads or in cooking. — N-MASS

**-ological** /-əlɒdʒɪkᵊl/ **-ological** is used to replace '-ology' at the end of nouns in order to form adjectives that describe something as relating to a particular science or subject. For example, 'biological' means relating to biology. — SUFFIX

**-ologist** /-ɒlədʒɪst/ **-ologist** is used to replace '-ology' at the end of nouns that refer to people who are concerned with a particular science or subject. For example, a 'biologist' is concerned with biology. — SUFFIX

**-ology** /-ɒlədʒi/ **-ology** is used at the end of some nouns that refer to a particular science or subject, for example 'geology' or 'sociology'. — SUFFIX

**Olym|pian** /əlɪmpiən/ **(Olympians)** 1 **Olympian** means very powerful, large, or impressive. [FORMAL] ❑ *Getting his book into print has been an Olympian task in itself.* — ADJ: usu ADJ n 2 An **Olympian** is a competitor in the Olympic Games. ❑ *The importance of being an Olympian will vary from athlete to athlete.* — N-COUNT

**Olym|pic** /əlɪmpɪk/ **(Olympics)** 1 **Olympic** means relating to the Olympic Games. ❑ *...the reigning Olympic champion.* — ADJ: ADJ n 2 **The Olympics** are the Olympic Games. ❑ *She won the individual gold medal at the Winter Olympics.* — N-PROPER: *the* N

**Olym|pic Games** **The Olympic Games** are a set of international sports competitions which take place every four years, each time in a different country. ❑ *At the 1968 Olympic Games she had won gold medals in races at 200, 400, and 800m.* — N-PROPER-COLL: *the* N

**om|buds|man** /ɒmbʊdzmən/ **(ombudsmen)** **The ombudsman** is an independent official who has been appointed to investigate complaints that people make against the government or public organizations. ❑ *The leaflet explains how to complain to the banking ombudsman.* — N-COUNT: usu *the* N, supp N

**ome|lette** /ɒmlət/ **(omelettes)**

✔ in AM, use **omelet**

An **omelette** is a type of food made by beating eggs and cooking them in a flat pan. ❑ *...a cheese omelette.* — N-COUNT

**omen** /oʊmen/ **(omens)** If you say that something is an **omen**, you think it indicates what is likely to happen in the future and whether it will be good or bad. ❑ *Could this at last be a good omen for peace?* — N-COUNT

**omi|nous** /ɒmɪnəs/ If you describe something as **ominous**, you mean that it worries you because it makes you think that something unpleasant is going to happen. ❑ *There was an ominous silence at the other end of the phone.* — ADJ ♦ **omi|nous|ly** *The bar seemed ominously quiet... Ominously, car sales slumped in August.* — ADV: ADV adj, ADV with cl, ADV with v

**omis|sion** /oʊmɪʃᵊn/ **(omissions)** 1 An **omission** is something that has not been included or has not been done, either deliberately or accidentally. ❑ *The duke was surprised by his wife's omission from the guest list.* — N-COUNT ≠ *inclusion* 2 **Omission** is the act of not including a particular person or thing or of not doing something. ❑ *...the prosecution's seemingly malicious omission of recorded evidence.* — N-VAR

**omit** /oʊmɪt/ **(omits, omitting, omitted)** 1 If you **omit** something, you do not include it in an activity or piece of work, deliberately or accidentally. ❑ *Omit the salt in this recipe... Our apologies to David Pannick for omitting his name from last week's article.* — VERB = *leave out* ≠ *include*; V n; V n *from* n 2 If you **omit to** do something, you do not do it. [FORMAL] ❑ *His new girlfriend had omitted to tell him she was married.* — VERB = *fail*; V to-inf

**om|ni|bus** /ɒmnɪbʌs/ **(omnibuses)** 1 An **omnibus** edition of a radio or television programme contains two or more similar programmes that were originally broadcast separately. [BRIT] ❑ *I enjoy the omnibus edition of Eastenders on Sunday.* — N-COUNT: usu N n 2 An **omnibus** is a book which contains a large collection of stories or articles, often by a particular person or about a particular subject. ❑ *...a new omnibus edition of three Ruth Rendell chillers.* — N-COUNT

**om|nipo|tence** /ɒmnɪpətəns/ **Omnipotence** is the state of having total authority or power. [FORMAL] ❑ *...the omnipotence of God.* — N-UNCOUNT

**om|nipo|tent** /ɒmnɪpətənt/ Someone or something that is **omnipotent** has complete power over things or people. [FORMAL] ❑ *Doug lived in the shadow of his seemingly omnipotent father.* — ADJ = *all-powerful*

**om|ni|pres|ent** /ɒmniprezᵊnt/ Something that is **omnipresent** is present everywhere or seems to be always present. [FORMAL] ❑ *The sound* — ADJ *of sirens was an omnipresent background noise in New York.*

**om|nis|ci|ent** /ɒmnɪsiənt, AM -nɪʃənt/ ADJ If you describe someone as **omniscient**, you mean they know or seem to know everything. [FORMAL] ❑ *...a benevolent and omniscient deity. ...the Financial Times's omniscient data-gathering network.* ♦ **om|nis|ci|ence** N-UNCOUNT *...the divine attributes of omnipotence, benevolence and omniscience.*

**om|niv|or|ous** /ɒmnɪvərəs/ [1] ADJ An **omnivorous** person or animal eats all kinds of food, including both meat and plants. [TECHNICAL or FORMAL] ❑ *Brown bears are omnivorous, eating anything that they can get their paws on.* [2] ADJ **Omnivorous** means liking a wide variety of things of a particular type. [FORMAL] ❑ *As a child, Coleridge developed omnivorous reading habits.*

**on** ♦♦♦

> The preposition is pronounced /ɒn/. The adverb and the adjective are pronounced /ɒn/.

> In addition to the uses shown below, **on** is used after some verbs, nouns, and adjectives in order to introduce extra information. **On** is also used in phrasal verbs such as 'keep on', 'cotton on', and 'sign on'.

[1] PREP If someone or something is **on** a surface or object, the surface or object is immediately below them and is supporting their weight. ❑ *He is sitting beside her on the sofa... On top of the cupboards are vast straw baskets which Pat uses for dried flower arrangements... On the table were dishes piled high with sweets.* [2] PREP If something is **on** a surface or object, it is stuck to it or attached to it. ❑ *I admired the peeling paint on the ceiling... The clock on the wall showed one minute to twelve... There was a smear of gravy on his chin.* ♦ **On** is also an adverb. ADV: ADV after v ❑ *I know how to darn, and how to sew a button on.* [3] PREP = *onto* If you put, throw, or drop something **on** a surface, you move it or drop it so that it is then supported by the surface. ❑ *He got his winter jacket from the closet and dropped it on the sofa... He threw a folded dollar on the counter.* [4] PREP You use **on** to say what part of your body is supporting your weight. ❑ *He continued to lie on his back and look at clouds... He raised himself on his elbows, squinting into the sun... She was on her hands and knees in the bathroom.* [5] PREP You use **on** to say that someone or something touches a part of a person's body. ❑ *He leaned down and kissed her lightly on the mouth... His jaw was broken after he was hit on the head.* [6] PREP: n PREP n If someone has a particular expression **on** their face, their face has that expression. ❑ *The maid looked at him, a nervous smile on her face... She looked at him with a hurt expression on her face.* [7] ADV: ADV after v When you put a piece of clothing **on**, you place it over part of your body in order to wear it. If you have it **on**, you are wearing it. ❑ *He put his coat on while she opened the front door... I had a hat on.* [8] PREP: PREP pron You can say that you have something **on** you if you are carrying it in your pocket or in a bag. ❑ *I didn't have any money on me.* [9] PREP If someone's eyes are **on** you, they are looking or staring at you. ❑ *Everyone's eyes were fixed on him... It's as if all eyes are focused on me.* [10] PREP If you hurt yourself **on** something, you accidentally hit a part of your body against it and that thing causes damage to you. ❑ *Mr Pendle hit his head on a wall as he fell.* [11] PREP If you are **on** an area of land, you are there. ❑ *You lived on the farm until you came back to America? ...a tall tree on a mountain.* [12] PREP If something is situated **on** a place such as a road or coast, it forms part of it or is by the side of it. ❑ *Bergdorf Goodman has opened a men's store on Fifth Avenue... The hotel is on the coast... He visited relatives at their summer house on the river.* [13] PREP If you get **on** a bus, train, or plane, you go into it in order to travel somewhere. If you are **on** it, you are travelling in it. ❑ *We waited till twelve and we finally got on the plane... I never go on the bus into the town.* ♦ **On** is also an adverb. ADV: ADV after v ❑ *He showed his ticket to the conductor and got on.* [14] PREP If there is something **on** a piece of paper, it has been written or printed there. ❑ *The writing on the back of the card was cramped but scrupulously neat... The numbers she put on the chart were 98.4, 64, and 105.* [15] PREP If something is **on** a list, it is included in it. ❑ *The Queen now doesn't even appear on the list of the 40 richest people in Britain. ...the range of topics on the agenda for their talks.* [16] PREP Books, discussions, or ideas **on** a particular subject are concerned with that subject. ❑ *They offer a free counselling service which can offer help and advice on legal matters... He declined to give any information on the Presidential election.* [17] PREP You use **on** to introduce the method, principle, or system which is used to do something. ❑ *...a television that we bought on credit two months ago. ...a levelling system which acts on the same principle as a spirit level... They want all groups to be treated on an equal basis.* [18] PREP If something is done **on** an instrument or a machine, it is done using that instrument or machine. ❑ *...songs that I could just sit down and play on the piano... I could do all my work on the computer.* [19] PREP If information is, for example, **on** tape or **on** computer, that is the way that it is stored. ❑ *'I thought it was a load of rubbish.' — 'Right we've got that on tape.'... Descriptions of the pieces have been logged on computer by the Art Loss Register.* [20] PREP If something is being broadcast, you can say that it is **on** the radio or television. ❑ *Every sporting event on television and satellite over the next seven days is listed... Here, listen, they're talking about it on Radio-Paris right now.* ♦ **On** is also an adjective. ADJ: v-link ADJ ❑ *...teenagers complaining there's nothing good on.* [21] ADJ: v-link ADJ When an activity is taking place, you can say that it is **on**. ❑ *There's a marvellous match on at Wimbledon at the moment... We in Berlin hardly knew a war was on during the early part of 1941.* [22] ADV: ADV after v, amount ADV You use **on** in expressions such as '**have a lot on**' and '**not have very much on**' to indicate how busy someone is. [SPOKEN] ❑ *I have a lot on in the next week.* [23] PREP You use **on** to introduce an activity that someone is doing, particularly travelling. ❑ *I've always wanted to go on a cruise... Students on the full-time course of study are usually sponsored.* [24] ADV: *be* ADV, ADV after v ≠ *off* When something such as a machine or an electric light is **on**, it is functioning or in use. When you switch it **on**, it starts functioning. ❑ *The central heating's been turned off. I've turned it on again... The light had been left on... He didn't bother to switch on the light.* [25] PREP If you are **on** a committee or council, you are a member of it. ❑ *Claire and Beryl were on the organizing committee... He was on the Council of Foreign Relations.* [26] PREP You can indicate when something happens by saying that it happens **on** a particular day or date. ❑ *This year's event will take place on June 19th, a week earlier than usual... She travels to Korea on Monday... I was born on Christmas day... Dr. Keen arrived about seven on Sunday morning.* [27] PREP: PREP n/-ing You use **on** when mentioning an event that was followed by another one. ❑ *She waited in her hotel to welcome her children on their arrival from London... On reaching Dubai the evacuees are taken straight to Dubai international airport.* [28] ADV: ADV after v You use **on** to say that someone is continuing to do something. ❑ *They walked on in silence for a while... If the examination shows your company enjoys basically good health, read on... He happened to be in England when the war broke out and he just stayed on.* [29] ADV: *be* ADV, ADV after v, usu ADV *at* n If you say that someone goes **on at** you, you mean that they continually criticize you, complain to you, or ask you to do something. ❑ *She's been on at me for weeks to show her round the stables... He used to keep on at me about the need to win.* [30] ADV: *from* n ADV You use **on** in expressions such as **from now on** and **from then on** to indicate that something starts to happen at the time mentioned and continues to happen afterwards. ❑ *Perhaps it would be best not to see much of you from now on... We can expect trouble from this moment on.* [31] ADV: adv ADV You often use **on** after the adverbs 'early', 'late', 'far', and their compara-

tive forms, especially at the beginning or end of a sentence, or before a preposition. ❑ *The market square is a riot of colour and animation from early on in the morning... Later on I learned how to read music... The pub where I had arranged to meet Nobby was a good five minutes walk further on.*

32 Someone who is **on** a drug takes it regularly. ❑ *She was on antibiotics for an eye infection that wouldn't go away... Many of the elderly are on medication.* — PREP

33 If you live **on** a particular kind of food, you eat it. If a machine runs **on** a particular kind of power or fuel, it uses it in order to function. ❑ *The caterpillars feed on a wide range of trees, shrubs and plants... He lived on a diet of water and tinned fish. ...making and selling vehicles that run on batteries or fuel-cells.* — PREP: v PREP n = off

34 If you are **on** a particular income, that is the income that you have. ❑ *He's on three hundred a week... You won't be rich as an MP, but you'll have enough to live on.* — PREP

35 Taxes or profits that are obtained from something are referred to as taxes or profits **on** it. ❑ *...a general strike to protest a tax on food and medicine last week... The Church was to receive a cut of the profits on every record sold.* — PREP: n PREP n

36 When you buy something or pay for something, you spend money **on** it. ❑ *I resolved not to waste money on a hotel... He spent more on feeding the dog than he spent on feeding himself... More money should be spent on education and housing.* — PREP: PREP n/-ing

37 When you spend time or energy **on** a particular activity, you spend time or energy doing it. ❑ *People complain about how children spend so much time on computer games. ...the opportunity to concentrate more time and energy on America's domestic agenda.* — PREP: PREP n/-ing

PHRASES 38 If you say that something is **not on** or is **just not on**, you mean that it is unacceptable or impossible. [mainly BRIT, INFORMAL] ❑ *We shouldn't use the police in that way. It's just not on.* — PHRASE: v-link PHR

39 If you say that something happens **on and on**, you mean that it continues to happen for a very long time. ❑ *...designers, builders, fitters – the list goes on and on... Lobell drove on and on through the dense and blowing snow. ...a desert of ice stretching on and on.* — PHRASE: usu PHR after v

40 If you ask someone **what** they **are on about** or **what** they **are going on about**, you are puzzled because you cannot understand what they are talking about. [BRIT, INFORMAL] ❑ *What on earth are you going on about?... Honest, Kate, I don't know what you're on about.* — PHRASE: V inflects

41 If you say that someone **knows what** they **are on about**, you are confident that what they are saying is true or makes sense, for example because they are an expert. [BRIT, INFORMAL] ❑ *It looks like he knows what he's on about.* — PHRASE: Vs inflect

42 If someone **has** something **on** you, they have evidence that you have done something wrong or bad. If they **have** nothing **on** you, they cannot prove that you have done anything wrong or bad. [INFORMAL] ❑ *He may have something on her. He may have supplied her with drugs, and then threatened to tell if she didn't do this... You've got nothing on me and you know it. Your theory would never stand up in a court of law.* — PHRASE: V inflects

43 **on behalf of** → see **behalf**. **on and off** → see **off**. **and so on** → see **so**. **on top of** → see **top**.

**once** /wʌns/ ◆◆◆ 1 If something happens **once**, it happens one time only. ❑ *I met Wilma once, briefly... Since that evening I haven't once slept through the night... Mary had only been to Manchester once before.* ♦ **Once** is also a pronoun. ❑ *'Have they been to visit you yet?' — 'Just the once, yeah.'... Listen to us, if only this once.* — ADV: ADV with v; PRON: *the/this* PRON

2 You use **once** with 'a' and words like 'day', 'week', and 'month' to indicate that something happens regularly, one time in each day, week, or month. ❑ *Lung cells die and are replaced about once a week... We arranged a special social event once a year to which we invited our major customers.* — ADV: ADV *a* n

3 If something was **once** true, it was true at some time in the past, but is no longer true. ❑ *The culture minister once ran a theatre... I lived there once myself, before I got married... The house where she lives was once the village post office... My memory isn't as good as it once was.* — ADV: ADV with v, ADV with *be*, ADV with group/cl

4 If someone **once** did something, they did it at some time in the past. ❑ *I once went camping at Lake Darling with a friend... We once walked across London at two in the morning... Diana had taken that path once.* — ADV: ADV with v

5 If something happens **once** another thing has happened, it happens immediately afterwards. ❑ *The decision had taken about 10 seconds once he'd read a market research study... Once customers come to rely on these systems they almost never take their business elsewhere.* — CONJ

PHRASES 6 If something happens **all at once**, it happens suddenly, often when you are not expecting it to happen. ❑ *All at once there was someone knocking on the door.* — PHRASE: PHR with cl = *all of a sudden*

7 If you do something **at once**, you do it immediately. ❑ *I have to go, I really must, at once... Remove from the heat, add the parsley, toss and serve at once... The audience at once greeted him warmly.* — PHRASE: PHR with v = *immediately*

8 If a number of different things happen **at once** or **all at once**, they all happen at the same time. ❑ *You can't be doing two things at once... No bank could ever pay off its creditors if they all demanded their money at once.* — PHRASE: PHR after v, PHR adj/n *and* adj/n

9 **For once** is used to emphasize that something happens on this particular occasion, especially if it has never happened before, and may never happen again. ❑ *For once, dad is not complaining... His smile, for once, was genuine.* — PHRASE: PHR with cl [emphasis]

10 If something happens **once again** or **once more**, it happens again. ❑ *Amy picked up the hairbrush and smoothed her hair once more... Once again an official inquiry has spoken of weak management and ill-trained workers.* — PHRASE: PHR with v, PHR with cl

11 If something happens **once and for all**, it happens completely or finally. ❑ *We have to resolve this matter once and for all... If we act fast, we can once and for all prevent wild animals in Britain from suffering terrible cruelty.* — PHRASE: PHR with v [emphasis]

12 If something happens **once in a while**, it happens sometimes, but not very often. ❑ *Earrings need to be taken out and cleaned once in a while.* — PHRASE: PHR with cl = *occasionally*

13 If you have done something **once or twice**, you have done it a few times, but not very often. ❑ *I popped my head round the door once or twice... Once or twice she had caught a flash of interest in William's eyes.* — PHRASE: PHR with cl, PHR with v

14 **Once upon a time** is used to indicate that something happened or existed a long time ago or in an imaginary world. It is often used at the beginning of children's stories. ❑ *'Once upon a time,' he began, 'there was a man who had everything.'... Once upon a time, asking a woman if she has a job was quite a straightforward question.* — PHRASE: PHR with cl

15 **once in a blue moon** → see **moon**.

**once-over** If you **give** something or someone **the once-over**, you quickly look at or examine them. [INFORMAL] ❑ *She gave the apartment a once-over.* — PHRASE: V inflects, PHR after v

**on|coming** /ɒnkʌmɪŋ/ **Oncoming** means moving towards you. ❑ *She was thrown from his car after it skidded into the path of an oncoming car.* — ADJ: ADJ n

**one** /wʌn/ **(ones)** ◆◆◆ 1 **One** is the number 1. ❑ *They had three sons and one daughter. ...one thousand years ago... Scotland beat England one-nil at Wembley. ...one of the children killed in the crash.* — NUM

2 If you say that someone or something is the **one** person or thing of a particular kind, you are emphasizing that they are the only person or thing of that kind. ❑ *They had alienated the one man who knew the business... His one regret is that he has never learned a language.* — ADJ: det ADJ [emphasis] = *only*

3 **One** can be used instead of 'a' to emphasize the following noun. ❑ *There is one thing I would like to know – What is it about Tim that you find so irresistible?... One person I hate is Russ.* — DET: DET sing-n [emphasis]

4 You can use **one** instead of 'a' to emphasize the following adjective or expression. [INFORMAL] ❑ *If we ever get married we'll have one terrific wedding... It's like one enormous street carnival here.* — DET: DET adj sing-n [emphasis]

5 You can use **one** to refer to the first of two or more things that you are comparing. ❑ *Prices vary from one shop to another... The road hugs the coast for hundreds of miles, the South China* — DET: DET sing-n

*Sea on one side, jungle on the other.* ♦ **One** is also an adjective. ❑ *We ask why peace should have an apparent chance in the one territory and not the other.* ♦ **One** is also a pronoun. ❑ *The twins were dressed differently and one was thinner than the other.* ADJ: det ADJ / PRON

6 You can use **one** or **ones** instead of a noun when it is clear what type of thing or person you are referring to and you are describing them or giving more information about them. ❑ *They are selling their house to move to a smaller one... We test each one to see that it flies well.* PRON

7 You use **ones** to refer to people in general. ❑ *We are the only ones who know.* PRON

8 You can use **one** instead of a noun group when you have just mentioned something and you want to describe it or give more information about it. ❑ *His response is one of anger and frustration... The issue of land reform was one that dominated Hungary's parliamentary elections.* PRON: PRON *of* n, PRON that

9 You can use **one** when you have been talking or writing about a group of people or things and you want to say something about a particular member of the group. ❑ *'A college degree isn't enough', said one honors student.* ♦ **One** is also a pronoun. ❑ *Some of them couldn't eat a thing. One couldn't even drink.* DET: DET sing-n / PRON

10 You use **one** in expressions such as **'one of the biggest airports'** or **'one of the most experienced players'** to indicate that something or someone is bigger or more experienced than most other things or people of the same kind. ❑ *Subaru is one of the smallest Japanese car makers.* QUANT: QUANT *of* adj-superl

11 You can use **one** when referring to a time in the past or in the future. For example, if you say that you did something **one day**, you mean that you did it on a day in the past. ❑ *How would you like to have dinner one night, just you and me?... Then one evening Harry phoned, asking me to come to their flat as soon as possible.* **one day** → see **day**. DET: DET sing-n

12 You use **one** to make statements about people in general which also apply to themselves. **One** can be used as the subject or object of a sentence. [FORMAL] ❑ *If one looks at the longer run, a lot of positive things are happening... Shares and bonds can bring one quite a considerable additional income.* PRON

**PHRASES** 13 If you say that someone is **one for** or is **a one for** something, you mean that they like or approve of it or enjoy doing it. ❑ *I'm not one for political discussions... She was a real one for flirting with the boys.* PHRASE: oft with brd-neg, v-link PHR n/-ing

14 You can use **for one** to emphasize that a particular person is definitely reacting or behaving in a particular way, even if other people are not. ❑ *I, for one, hope you don't get the job.* PHRASE: PHR before v [emphasis]

15 You can use expressions such as **a hundred and one**, **a thousand and one**, and **a million and one** to emphasize that you are talking about a large number of things or people. ❑ *There are a hundred and one ways in which you can raise money.* PHRASE: usu PHR pl-n [emphasis]

16 You can use **in one** to indicate that something is a single unit, but is made up of several different parts or has several different functions. ❑ *...a love story and an adventure all in one... This cream moisturises and repairs in one.* PHRASE: pl-n PHR, PHR after v

17 You use **one after the other** or **one after another** to say that actions or events happen with very little time between them. ❑ *My three guitars broke one after the other... One after another, people described how hard it is for them to get medical care.* PHRASE: PHR with cl

18 **The one and only** can be used in front of the name of an actor, singer, or other famous person when they are being introduced on a show. ❑ *...one of the greatest ever rock performers, the one and only Tina Turner.* PHRASE: PHR n-proper

19 You can use **one by one** to indicate that people do things or that things happen in sequence, not all at the same time. ❑ *We went into the room one by one... One by one the houses burst into flames.* PHRASE: PHR with cl

20 You use **one or other** to refer to one or more things or people in a group, when it does not matter which particular one or ones are thought of or chosen. ❑ *One or other of the two women was wrong.* PHRASE: usu PHR *of* pl-n

21 **One or two** means a few. ❑ *We may make one or two changes... I asked one or two of the stallholders about it.* PHRASE: oft PHR pl-n, PHR *of* pl-n

22 If you say that someone is **not one to** do something, you think that it is very unlikely that they would do it because it is not their normal behaviour. ❑ *I'm not one to waste time on just anyone.* PHRASE: PHR to-inf, usu v-link PHR

23 If you try to get **one up on** someone, you try to gain an advantage over them. ❑ *...the competitive kind who will see this as the opportunity to be one up on you.* PHRASE: PHR n, usu v-link PHR, PHR after v

24 **one another** → see **another**. **one** thing **after another** → see **another**. **of one mind** → see **mind**. **in one piece** → see **piece**.

**one-armed bandit** (**one-armed bandits**) A **one-armed bandit** is the same as a **fruit machine**. N-COUNT

**one-horse** 1 If someone describes a town as a **one-horse** town, they mean it is very small, dull, and old-fashioned. ❑ *Would you want to live in a small, one-horse town for your whole life?* ADJ: ADJ n [disapproval]

2 If a contest is described as a **one-horse** race, it is thought that one person or thing will obviously win it. ❑ *He described the referendum as a one-horse race.* ADJ: ADJ n

**one-liner** (**one-liners**) A **one-liner** is a funny remark or a joke told in one sentence, for example in a play or comedy programme. [INFORMAL] ❑ *The book is witty and peppered with good one-liners.* N-COUNT

**one-man** 1 A **one-man** performance is given by only one man rather than by several people. ❑ *I saw him do his one-man show in London, which I loved.* ADJ: ADJ n

2 A **one-man** organization, such as a business or type of government is controlled by one person, rather than by several people. ❑ *It has grown from a one-man business to a multi-million dollar business with close to $10 million in assets... He established one-man rule in his country seven months ago.* ADJ: ADJ n

**one-man band** (**one-man bands**) A **one-man band** is a street entertainer who wears and plays a lot of different instruments at the same time. N-COUNT

**one-night stand** (**one-night stands**) A **one-night stand** is a very brief sexual relationship, usually one that is casual and perhaps only lasts one night. [INFORMAL] N-COUNT

**one-of-a-kind** You use **one-of-a-kind** to describe something that is special because there is nothing else exactly like it. [mainly AM] ❑ *...a small one-of-a-kind publishing house.* ADJ: ADJ n = *unique*

**one-off** (**one-offs**) 1 You can refer to something as a **one-off** when it is made or happens only once. [mainly BRIT] ❑ *Our survey revealed that these allergies were mainly one-offs.* N-COUNT

2 A **one-off** thing is made or happens only once. [mainly BRIT] ❑ *...one-off cash benefits.* ADJ: ADJ n

**one-on-one** A **one-on-one** situation, meeting, or contest involves only two people. ❑ *...a one-on-one therapy session.* ♦ **One-on-one** is also an adverb. ❑ *Talking one-on-one with people is not his idea of fun.* ♦ **One-on-one** is also a noun. ❑ *Holloway was beaten in a one-on-one with Miklosko just before half-time.* ADJ: usu ADJ n = *one-to-one* / ADV: ADV after v / N-SING: oft N *with* n

**one-parent fam|ily** (**one-parent families**) A **one-parent family** is a family that consists of one parent and his or her children living together. ❑ *Many children are now born into or raised in one-parent families.* N-COUNT

**one-piece** (**one-pieces**) 1 A **one-piece** article of clothing consists of one piece only, rather than two or more separate parts. ❑ *...a blue one-piece bathing suit.* ADJ: ADJ n

2 A **one-piece** is a type of woman's swimming costume that consists of one piece of material and which covers her chest. ❑ *A one-piece is more flattering than a bikini.* N-COUNT

**on|er|ous** /oʊnərəs, AM ɑːn-/ If you describe a task as **onerous**, you dislike having to do it because you find it difficult or unpleasant. [FORMAL] ❑ *...parents who have had the onerous task of bringing up a very difficult child.* ADJ

**one's** /wʌnz/ 1 Speakers and writers use **one's** to indicate that something belongs or relates to people in general, or to themselves in par- ♦◇◇ DET = *your*

ticular. [FORMAL] ❑ *...a feeling of responsibility for the welfare of others in one's community.* [2] **One's** can be used as a spoken form of 'one is' or 'one has', especially when 'has' is an auxiliary verb. ❑ *No one's going to hurt you. No one. Not any more... I think one's got to consider all the possibilities.* → see **one**.

**one|self** /wʌnse̲lf/

☑ **Oneself** is a third person singular reflexive pronoun.

[1] A speaker or writer uses **oneself** as the object of a verb or preposition in a clause where 'oneself' meaning 'me' or 'any person in general' refers to the same person as the subject of the verb. [FORMAL] ❑ *To work one must have time to oneself.* PRON
[2] **Oneself** can be used as the object of a verb or preposition, when 'one' is not present but is understood to be the subject of the verb. [FORMAL] ❑ *The historic feeling of the town makes it a pleasant place to base oneself for summer vacations... It's so easy to feel sorry for oneself.* PRON

**one-sided** [1] If you say that an activity or relationship is **one-sided**, you think that one of the people or groups involved does much more than the other or is much stronger than the other. ❑ *The negotiating was completely one-sided.* ADJ [2] If you describe someone as **one-sided**, you are critical of what they say or do because you think it shows that they have considered only one side of an issue or event. ❑ *There has been a very one-sided account of her problems with Ted.* ADJ disapproval = biased

**one-stop** A **one-stop** shop is a place where you can buy everything you need for a particular purpose. ❑ *A marvellous discovery for every bride-to-be, The Wedding Centre is the ultimate one-stop shop.* ADJ: ADJ n

**one-time** also **onetime**. **One-time** is used to describe something such as a job, position, or role which someone used to have, or something which happened in the past. [JOURNALISM] ❑ *The legislative body had voted to oust the country's onetime rulers.* ADJ: ADJ n = former

**one-to-one** [1] In a **one-to-one** relationship, one person deals directly with only one other person. ❑ *...one-to-one training. ...negotiating on a one-to-one basis.* ♦ **One-to-one** is also an adverb. ❑ *She would like to talk to people one to one.* ADJ: ADJ n; ADV: ADV after v [2] If there is a **one-to-one** match between two sets of things, each member of one set matches a member of the other set. ❑ *In English, there is not a consistent one-to-one match between each written symbol and each distinct spoken sound.* ADJ: ADJ n

**one-upmanship** /wʌn ʌpmənʃɪp/ If you refer to someone's behaviour as **one-upmanship**, you disapprove of them trying to make other people feel inferior in order to make themselves appear more important. ❑ *...political one-upmanship.* N-UNCOUNT: oft supp N disapproval

**one-way** [1] In **one-way** streets or traffic systems, vehicles can only travel along in one direction. ❑ *He zoomed through junctions without stopping and sped the wrong way down a one-way street.* ADJ: ADJ n
[2] **One-way** describes journeys which go to just one place, rather than to that place and then back again. ❑ *The trailers will be rented for one-way trips.* ADJ: usu ADJ n
[3] A **one-way** ticket or fare is for a journey from one place to another, but not back again. [mainly AM] ❑ *...a one-way ticket from New York to Los Angeles.* ♦ **One-way** is also an adverb. ❑ *Unrestricted fares will be increased as much as $80 one-way.* ADJ: usu ADJ n = single ≠ return; ADV: ADV after v

☑ in BRIT, usually use **single**

[4] If you say that a course of action is a **one-way** ticket to a place or situation, or is a **one-way** journey there, you are sure that it will lead to the place or situation mentioned. ❑ *It seemed like a one-way ticket to riches, but then it all went wrong.* ADJ: ADJ n
[5] **One-way** glass or a **one-way** mirror is a piece of glass which acts as a mirror when looked at from one side, but acts as a window when looked through from the other side. They are used for watching people without their knowledge. ADJ: usu ADJ n [6] If you describe an agreement or a relationship as a **one-way street**, you mean that only one of the sides in the agreement or relationship is offering something or is benefitting from it. ❑ *The experience of the last 10 years has shown that, for the Eurosceptics, loyalty is a one-way street; something you demand but do not give... So trade between the two nations has been something of a one-way street, with Cuba deriving the benefit.* PHRASE

**one-woman** A **one-woman** performance or business is done by only one woman, rather than by several people. ❑ *She has already presented a one-woman show of her paintings.* ADJ: ADJ n

**on|going** /ɒngoʊɪŋ/ An **ongoing** situation has been happening for quite a long time and seems likely to continue for some time in the future. ❑ *There is an ongoing debate on the issue... That research is ongoing.* ADJ = continuing

**on|ion** /ʌnjən/ (**onions**) An **onion** is a round vegetable with a brown skin that grows underground. It has many white layers on its inside which have a strong, sharp smell and taste. → See picture on page 1712. ❑ *It is made with fresh minced meat, cooked with onion and a rich tomato sauce.* N-VAR

**on|line** /ɒnlaɪn/ also **on-line**. [1] If a company goes **online**, its services become available on the Internet. [BUSINESS, COMPUTING] ❑ *...the first bank to go online. ...an online shopping centre. ...an online catalogue.* ADJ [2] If you are **online**, your computer is connected to the Internet. Compare **offline**. [COMPUTING] ❑ *You can chat to other people who are online.* ♦ **Online** is also an adverb. ❑ *...the cool stuff you find online.* **on line** → see **line**. ADJ; ADV: ADV after v

**on|looker** /ɒnlʊkəʳ/ (**onlookers**) An **onlooker** is someone who watches an event take place but does not take part in it. ❑ *A handful of onlookers stand in the field watching.* N-COUNT

**only** /oʊnli/ ♦♦♦

☑ In written English, **only** is usually placed immediately before the word it qualifies. In spoken English, however, you can use stress to indicate what **only** qualifies, so its position is not so important.

[1] You use **only** to indicate the one thing that is true, appropriate, or necessary in a particular situation, in contrast to all the other things that are not true, appropriate, or necessary. ❑ *Only the President could authorize the use of the atomic bomb... Only here were the police visible in any strength at all... 44-year-old woman seeks caring, honest male of similar age for friendship and fun. Genuine replies only... A business can only be built and expanded on a sound financial base.* ADV: ADV with group, ADV before v [2] You use **only** to introduce the thing which must happen before the thing mentioned in the main part of the sentence can happen. ❑ *The lawyer is paid only if he wins... The Bank of England insists that it will cut interest rates only when it is ready.* ADV: ADV cl/prep [3] If you talk about **the only** person or thing involved in a particular situation, you mean there are no others involved in it. ❑ *She was the only woman in Shell's legal department... My cat Gustaf was the only thing I had - the only company.* ADJ: det ADJ [4] An **only** child is a child who has no brothers or sisters. ADJ: ADJ n [5] You use **only** to indicate that something is no more important, interesting, or difficult, for example, than you say it is, especially when you want to correct a wrong idea that someone may get or has already got. ❑ *At the moment it is only a theory... 'I'm only a sergeant,' said Clements... Don't get defensive, Charlie. I was only joking.* ADV: ADV group, ADV before v = just [6] You use **only** to emphasize how small an amount is or how short a length of time is. ❑ *Child car seats only cost about £10 a week to hire. ...spacecraft guidance systems weighing only a few grams... I've only recently met him.* ADV: ADV n/adv emphasis [7] You use **only** to emphasize that you are talking about a small part of an amount or group, not the whole of it. ❑ *These are only a few of the possibilities... Only a minority of the people supported the Revolution.* ADV: ADV n emphasis
[8] **Only** is used after 'can' or 'could' to emphasize ADV:

that it is impossible to do anything except the rather inadequate or limited action that is mentioned. ❑ *For a moment I could say nothing. I could only stand and look... The police can only guess at the scale of the problem.*
modal ADV inf | emphasis

9 You can use **only** in the expressions **I only wish** or **I only hope** in order to emphasize what you are hoping or wishing. ❑ *I only wish he were here now that things are getting better for me.*
ADV: ADV before v | emphasis | = just

10 **Only** can be used to add a comment which slightly changes or limits what you have just said. [INFORMAL] ❑ *It's just as dramatic as a film, only it's real... Drop in and see me when you're ready. Only don't take too long about it.*
CONJ = but, except

11 **Only** can be used after a clause with 'would' to indicate why something is not done. [SPOKEN] ❑ *I'd invite you to come with me, only it's such a long way... I'd be quite happy to go. Only I don't know what my kids would say about living there.*
CONJ = but

12 You can use **only** before an infinitive to introduce an event which happens immediately after one you have just mentioned, and which is rather surprising or unfortunate. ❑ *Ryle tried the Embassy, only to be told that Hugh was in a meeting... He raced through the living room, only to find the front door closed.*
ADV: ADV to-inf

13 You can use **only** to emphasize how appropriate a certain course of action or type of behaviour is. ❑ *It's only fair to let her know that you intend to apply... She appeared to have changed considerably, which was only to be expected.*
ADV: usu ADV adj, also ADV to-inf | emphasis

14 You can use **only** in front of a verb to indicate that the result of something is unfortunate or undesirable and is likely to make the situation worse rather than better. ❑ *The embargo would only hurt innocent civilians... She says that legalising prostitution will only cause problems.*
ADV: ADV before v = just

**PHRASES** 15 If you say you **only have to** or **have only to** do one thing in order to achieve or prove a second thing, you are emphasizing how easily the second thing can be achieved or proved. ❑ *Any time you want a babysitter, dear, you only have to ask... We have only to read the labels to know what ingredients are in foods.*
PHRASE: V inflects, PHR inf | emphasis

16 You can say that something has **only just** happened when you want to emphasize that it happened a very short time ago. ❑ *I've only just arrived... The signs of an economic revival are only just beginning.*
PHRASE: PHR before v, PHR adv | emphasis

17 You use **only just** to emphasize that something is true, but by such a small degree that it is almost not true at all. ❑ *For centuries farmers there have only just managed to survive... I am old enough to remember the Blitz, but only just.*
PHRASE: usu PHR before v, PHR with cl/group | emphasis

18 You can use **only too** to emphasize that something is true or exists to a much greater extent than you would expect or like. ❑ *I know only too well that plans can easily go wrong... When the new baby comes along it is only too easy to shut out the others.*
PHRASE: PHR adv/adj | emphasis

19 You can say that you are **only too** happy to do something to emphasize how willing you are to do it. ❑ *I'll be only too pleased to help them out with any queries.*
PHRASE: PHR adj | emphasis

20 **if only** → see **if**. **not only** → see **not**. **the one and only** → see **one**.

**on-message** If a politician is **on-message**, they say something that follows the official policy of their party.
ADJ: usu v-link ADJ

**o.n.o.** In advertisements, **o.n.o.** is used after a price to indicate that the person who is selling something is willing to accept slightly less money than the sum they have mentioned. **o.n.o.** is a written abbreviation for 'or near offer'. [BRIT]

**ono|mato|poeia** /ɒnəmætəpiːə/ **Onomatopoeia** refers to the use of words which sound like the noise they refer to. 'Hiss', 'buzz', and 'rat-a-tat-tat' are examples of onomatopoeia. [TECHNICAL]
N-UNCOUNT

**ono|mato|poe|ic** /ɒnəmætəpiːɪk/ **Onomatopoeic** words sound like the noise they refer to. 'Hiss', 'buzz', and 'rat-a-tat-tat' are examples of onomatopoeic words. [TECHNICAL]
ADJ

**on|rush** /ɒnrʌʃ/ The **onrush** of something is its sudden development, which happens so quickly and forcefully that you are unable to control it. ❑ *The onrush of tears took me by surprise... She was screwing up her eyes against the onrush of air.*
N-SING: usu N of n = surge

**on|rush|ing** /ɒnrʌʃɪŋ/ **Onrushing** describes something such as a vehicle that is moving forward so quickly or forcefully that it would be very difficult to stop. ❑ *He was killed by an onrushing locomotive. ...the roar of the onrushing water.*
ADJ: ADJ n

**on-screen** also **onscreen**. 1 **On-screen** means appearing on the screen of a television, cinema, or computer. ❑ *...a clear and easy-to-follow menu-driven on-screen display... Read the on-screen lyrics and sing along.*
ADJ: ADJ n

2 **On-screen** means relating to the roles played by film or television actors, in contrast with their real lives. ❑ *...her first onscreen kiss.* ♦ **On-screen** is also an adverb. ❑ *He was immensely attractive to women, onscreen and offscreen.*
ADJ: ADJ n | ADV: ADV with cl

**on|set** /ɒnset/ **The onset of** something is the beginning of it, used especially to refer to something unpleasant. ❑ *Most of the passes have been closed with the onset of winter.*
N-SING: usu the N of n, also no det = start

**on|shore** /ɒnʃɔːʳ/ 1 **Onshore** means happening on or near land, rather than at sea. ❑ *...Western Europe's biggest onshore oilfield.* ♦ **Onshore** is also an adverb. ❑ *They missed the ferry and remained onshore.*
ADJ: usu ADJ n ≠ offshore | ADV: ADV after v

2 **Onshore** means happening or moving towards the land. ❑ *The onshore wind blew steadily past him.* ♦ **Onshore** is also an adverb. ❑ *There was a bit of a wind and it was blowing onshore.*
ADJ: usu ADJ n | ADV: ADV after v

**on|side** /ɒnsaɪd/ 1 In games such as football and hockey, when an attacking player is **onside**, they have not broken the rules because at least two players from the opposing team are between them and the goal when the ball is passed to them.
ADJ

2 If a person or group of people is **onside**, they support you and agree with what you are doing. ❑ *Granada and Forte are continuing to telephone shareholders in an attempt to bring them onside.*
ADJ: v-link ADJ

**on-site** → see **site**.

**on|slaught** /ɒnslɔːt/ **(onslaughts)** 1 An **onslaught** on someone or something is a very violent, forceful attack against them. ❑ *The rebels responded to a military onslaught against them by launching a major assault on an army camp.*
N-COUNT: usu with supp, oft N on/against n, N by n = assault

2 If you refer to an **onslaught of** something, you mean that there is a large amount of it, often so that it is very difficult to deal with. ❑ *...the constant onslaught of ads on American TV.*
N-COUNT: usu N of n = barrage

**on|stage** /ɒnsteɪdʒ/ When someone such as an actor or musician goes **onstage**, they go onto the stage in a theatre to give a performance. ❑ *When she walked onstage she was given a standing ovation.*
ADV: ADV after v, be ADV, ADV with cl ≠ off-stage

**on-the-job** → see **job**.

**on-the-spot** **On-the-spot** things are done at the place that you are in at the time that you are there. ❑ *Rail travellers who try to avoid paying their fares could face on-the-spot fines.*
ADJ: ADJ n

**onto** /ɒntu/ also **on to**. ◆◇◇

> In addition to the uses shown below, **onto** is used in phrasal verbs such as 'hold onto' and 'latch onto'.

1 If something moves or is put **onto** an object or surface, it is then on that object or surface. ❑ *I took my bags inside, lowered myself onto the bed and switched on the TV... Smear Vaseline on to your baby's skin to prevent soreness.*
PREP

2 You can sometimes use **onto** to mention the place or area that someone moves into. ❑ *The players emerged onto the field... Alex turned his car on to the Albert Quay and drove along until he found a parking place.*
PREP

3 You can use **onto** to introduce the place towards which a light or someone's look is directed. ❑ *...the metal part of the door onto which the sun had been shining. ...the house with its leafy garden and its view on to Regent's Park.*
PREP

4 You can use **onto** to introduce a place that you would immediately come to after leaving
PREP: v PREP n

another place that you have just mentioned, because they are next to each other. ❑ *...windows opening onto carved black-wood balconies... The door opened onto a lighted hallway.* 5 When you change the position of your body, you use **onto** to introduce the part your body which is now supporting you. PREP ❑ *As he stepped backwards she fell onto her knees, then onto her face... I willed my eyes to open and heaved myself over on to my back.* 6 When you get **onto** a bus, train, or plane, you enter it in order to travel somewhere. PREP ≠off ❑ *As he got on to the plane, he asked me how I was feeling... 'I'll see you onto the train.' — 'Thank you.'* 7 **Onto** is used after verbs such as 'hold', 'hang', and 'cling' to indicate what someone is holding firmly or where something is being held firmly. PREP ❑ *The reflector is held onto the sides of the spacecraft with a frame... She was conscious of a second man hanging on to the rail.* 8 If people who are talking get **onto** a different subject, they begin talking about it. PREP ❑ *Let's get on to more important matters... So, if we could just move onto something else?* 9 You can sometimes use **onto** to indicate that something or someone becomes included as a part of a list or system. PREP ❑ *The Macedonian question had failed to get on to the agenda... The pill itself has changed a lot since it first came onto the market... Twelve thousand workers will go onto a four-day week at their factory in Birmingham.* 10 If someone **is onto** something, they are about to discover something important. [INFORMAL] PREP: *be* PREP n ❑ *He leaned across the table and whispered to me, 'I'm really onto something.'... Archaeologists knew they were onto something big when they started digging.* 11 If someone **is onto** you, they have discovered that you are doing something illegal or wrong. [INFORMAL] PREP: *be* PREP n ❑ *I had told people what he had been doing, so now the police were onto him.*

**on|tol|ogy** /ɒntɒlədʒi/ **Ontology** is the branch of philosophy that deals with the nature of existence. [TECHNICAL] N-UNCOUNT ♦ **on|to|logi|cal** /ɒntəlɒdʒɪkəl/ ADJ: usu ADJ n ❑ *...the ontological question of the relationship between mind and body.*

**onus** /oʊnəs/ If you say that **the onus** is **on** someone **to** do something, you mean it is their duty or responsibility to do it. [FORMAL] N-SING: usu *the* N, oft N *of* n/-ing ❑ *The onus is on the shopkeeper to provide goods which live up to the quality of their description.*

**on|ward** /ɒnwərd/ also **onwards.**

> ✓ In British English, **onwards** is an adverb and **onward** is an adjective. In American English and sometimes in formal British English, **onward** may also be an adverb.

1 **Onward** means moving forward or continuing a journey. ADJ: usu ADJ n ❑ *British Airways have two flights a day to Bangkok, and there are onward flights to Phnom Penh.* ♦ **Onward** is also an adverb. ADV: ADV after v = on ❑ *The bus continued onward... He measured the distance to the nearest Antarctic coast, and onwards to the South Pole.* 2 **Onward** means developing, progressing, or becoming more important over a period of time. ADJ: usu ADJ n ❑ *...the onward march of progress in the British aircraft industry.* ♦ **Onward** is also an adverb. ADV: ADV after v ❑ *I can see things just going onwards and upwards for us now.* 3 If something happens from a particular time **onwards** or **onward**, it begins to happen at that time and continues to happen afterwards. ADV: *from* n ADV ❑ *From the turn of the century onward, she shared the life of the aborigines.*

**onyx** /ɒnɪks/ **Onyx** is a stone which can be various colours. It is used for making ornaments, jewellery, or furniture. N-UNCOUNT

**oo** /uː/ → see **ooh.**

**oodles** /uːdəlz/ If you say that there is **oodles of** something, you are emphasizing that there is a very large quantity of it. [INFORMAL] QUANT: QUANT *of* n-uncount/pl-n [emphasis] ❑ *The recipe calls for oodles of melted chocolate.*

**ooh** /uː/ also **oo.** People say **'ooh'** when they are surprised, looking forward to something, or find something pleasant or unpleasant. [INFORMAL] EXCLAM [feelings] ❑ *'Ooh dear me, that's a bit of a racist comment isn't it.'... 'Red? Ooh how nice.'*

**oomph** /ʊmf/ If you say that someone or something has **oomph**, you mean that they are energetic and exciting. [INFORMAL] N-UNCOUNT [approval] ❑ *'There's no buzz, there's no oomph about the place,' he complained.*

**oops** /ʊps, uːps/ You say **'oops'** to indicate that there has been a slight accident or mistake, or to apologize to someone for it. [INFORMAL] EXCLAM [feelings] ❑ *Today they're saying, 'Oops, we made a mistake.'*

**ooze** /uːz/ **(oozes, oozing, oozed)** 1 When a thick or sticky liquid **oozes** from something or when something **oozes** it, the liquid flows slowly and in small quantities. VERB ❑ *He saw there was a big hole in the back of the man's head, blood was still oozing from it...* V *The lava will just ooze gently out of the crater...* V adv *The wounds may heal cleanly or they may ooze a clear liquid.* V n 2 If you say that someone or something **oozes** a quality or characteristic, or **oozes** with it, you mean that they show it very strongly. VERB ❑ *The Elizabethan house oozes charm...* V n *Manchester United were by now oozing with confidence.* V *with* n

**op** /ɒp/ **(ops)** 1 An **op** is a medical operation. [mainly BRIT, INFORMAL] N-COUNT ❑ *...breast cancer ops.* 2 **Ops** are military operations. N-COUNT: usu pl ❑ *Flt Lt Beamont had completed a 200 hour tour of ops in December 1941.*

**op.** In music, **op.** is a written abbreviation for **opus.** ❑ *...Beethoven's Op. 101 and 111 sonatas.*

**opac|ity** /oʊpæsɪti/ 1 **Opacity** is the quality of being difficult to see through. [FORMAL] N-UNCOUNT ❑ *Opacity of the eye lens can be induced by deficiency of certain vitamins.* 2 If you refer to something's **opacity**, you mean that it is difficult to understand. [FORMAL] N-UNCOUNT = obscurity ≠transparency ❑ *Its dramatic nuances were often generalised to the point of opacity.*

**opal** /oʊpəl/ **(opals)** An **opal** is a precious stone. Opals are colourless or white, but other colours are reflected in them. N-VAR

**opal|es|cent** /oʊpəlesənt/ **Opalescent** means colourless or white like an opal, or changing colour like an opal. [LITERARY] ADJ ❑ *Elaine turned her opalescent eyes on him. ...a sky which was still faintly opalescent.* ♦ **opal|es|cence** N-UNCOUNT *The sunset was making great splashes of fiery opalescence across the sky.*

**opaque** /oʊpeɪk/ 1 If an object or substance is **opaque**, you cannot see through it. ADJ ≠transparent ❑ *You can always use opaque glass if you need to block a street view.* 2 If you say that something is **opaque**, you mean that it is difficult to understand. ADJ ❑ *...the opaque language of the inspector's reports.*

**op. cit.** /ɒp sɪt/ In reference books, **op. cit.** is used after an author's name to refer to a book of theirs which has already been mentioned. [FORMAL] ❑ *...quoted in Iyer, op. cit., p. 332.*

**OPEC** /oʊpek/ **OPEC** is an organization of countries that produce oil. It tries to develop a common policy and system of prices. **OPEC** is an abbreviation for 'Organization of Petroleum-Exporting Countries'. N-PROPER ❑ *Each member of OPEC would seek to maximize its own production.*

**op-ed** In a newspaper, the **op-ed** page is a page containing articles in which people express their opinions about things. [AM, INFORMAL] ADJ: ADJ n

**open** /oʊpən/ **(opens, opening, opened)** ◆◆◆ 1 If you **open** something such as a door, window, or lid, or if it **opens**, its position is changed so that it no longer covers a hole or gap. VERB ≠close, shut ❑ *He opened the window and looked out...* V n *The church doors would open and the crowd would surge out.* V ♦ **Open** is also an adjective. ADJ ❑ *...an open window... A door had been forced open.* 2 If you **open** something such as a bottle, box, parcel, or envelope, you move, remove, or cut part of it so you can take out what is inside. VERB ❑ *The Inspector opened the packet of cigarettes...* V n *The capsules are fiddly to open.* V n ♦ **Open** is also an adjective. ADJ ❑ *...an open bottle of milk... I tore*

*the letter open.* ♦ **Open up** means the same as **open**. PHRASAL VERB ❑ *He opened up a cage and lifted out a 6ft python.* V P n (not pron) Also V n P
**3** If you **open** something such as a book, an umbrella, or your hand, or if it **opens**, the different parts of it move away from each other so that the inside of it can be seen. VERB ❑ *He opened the heavy Bible...* V n *The officer's mouth opened, showing white, even teeth.* V ♦ **Open** is also an adjective. ADJ ❑ *Without warning, Bardo smacked his fist into his open hand... His mouth was a little open, as if he'd started to scream.* ♦ **Open out** means the same as **open**. PHRASAL VERB ❑ *Keith took a map from the dashboard and opened it out on his knees.* V n P *...oval tables which open out to become circular.* V P Also V P n
**4** If you **open** a computer file, you give the computer an instruction to display it on the screen. VERB [COMPUTING] ❑ *Double click on the icon to open the file.* V n
**5** When you **open** your eyes or your eyes **open**, you move your eyelids upwards, for example when you wake up, so that you can see. VERB ❑ *When I opened my eyes I saw a man with an axe standing at the end of my bed...* V n *His eyes were opening wide.* V ♦ **Open** is also an adjective. ADJ ❑ *As soon as he saw that her eyes were open he sat up.*
**6** If you **open** your arms, you stretch them wide apart in front of you, usually in order to put them round someone. VERB ❑ *She opened her arms and gave me a big hug.* V n
**7** If you describe a person or their character as **open**, you mean they are honest and do not want or try to hide anything or to deceive anyone. ADJ ❑ *He had always been open with her and she always felt she would know if he lied... She has an open, trusting nature.* ♦ **open|ness** N-UNCOUNT *...a relationship based on honesty and openness.*
**8** If you describe a situation, attitude, or way of behaving as **open**, you mean it is not kept hidden or secret. ADJ: ADJ n ❑ *The action is an open violation of the Vienna Convention... Hearing the case in open court is only one part of the judicial process.* ♦ **open|ness** N-UNCOUNT *...the new climate of political openness.*
**9** If you are **open to** suggestions or ideas, you are ready and willing to consider or accept them. ADJ: v-link ADJ *to* n = receptive ❑ *They are open to suggestions on how working conditions might be improved.*
**10** If you say that a system, person, or idea is **open to** something such as abuse or criticism, you mean they might receive abuse or criticism because of their qualities, effects, or actions. ADJ: v-link ADJ *to* n = susceptible ❑ *The system, though well-meaning, is open to abuse.*
**11** If you say that a fact or question is **open to** debate, interpretation, or discussion, you mean that people are uncertain whether it is true, what it means, or what the answer is. ADJ: oft v-link ADJ *to* n ❑ *It is an open question how long that commitment can last.*
**12** If people **open** something such as a blocked road or a border, or if it **opens**, people can then pass along it or through it. VERB ≠ close ❑ *The rebels have opened the road from Monrovia to the Ivory Coast...* V n *The solid rank of police officers lining the courtroom opened to let them pass.* V ♦ **Open** is also an adjective. ADJ ❑ *We were part of an entire regiment that had nothing else to do but to keep that highway open.* ♦ **Open up** means the same as **open**. PHRASAL VERB ❑ *As rescue workers opened up roads today, it became apparent that some small towns were totally devastated...* V P n (not pron) *When the Berlin Wall came down it wasn't just the roads that opened up but the waterways too.* V P Also V n P
**13** If a place **opens into** another, larger place, you can move from one directly into the other. VERB ❑ *The corridor opened into a low smoky room.* V *into/onto/to* n ♦ **Open out** means the same as **open**. PHRASAL VERB ❑ *...narrow streets opening out into charming squares.* V P *into/onto/to* n
**14** An **open** area is a large area that does not have many buildings or trees in it. ADJ: usu ADJ n ❑ *Officers will also continue their search of nearby open ground.*
**15** An **open** structure or object is not covered or enclosed. ADJ: ADJ n ❑ *Don't leave a child alone in a room with an open fire. ...open sandwiches.*
**16** An **open** wound is one from which a liquid such as blood is coming. ADJ: usu ADJ n
**17** If you **open** your shirt or coat, you undo the buttons or pull down the zip. VERB ❑ *I opened my coat and let him see the belt.* V n ♦ **Open** is also an adjective. ADJ: ADJ n, v-link ADJ ❑ *The top can be worn buttoned up or open over a T-shirt.*
**18** When a shop, office, or public building **opens** or **is opened**, its doors are unlocked and the public can go in. VERB ❑ *Banks closed on Friday afternoon and did not open again until Monday morning.* V *...a gang of three who'd apparently been lying in wait for him to open the shop.* V n *...opening and closing times.* V-ing ♦ **Open** is also an adjective. ADJ ❑ *His shop is open Monday through Friday, 9am to 6pm.*
**19** When a public building, factory, or company **opens** or when someone **opens** it, it starts operating for the first time. VERB ≠ close, shut ❑ *The original station opened in 1754...* V *The complex opens to the public tomorrow...* V *to* n *They are planning to open a factory in Eastern Europe.* V n ♦ **Open** is also an adjective. ADJ: v-link ADJ ❑ *...any operating subsidy required to keep the pits open.* ♦ **open|ing (openings)** N-COUNT: usu sing *He was there, though, for the official opening.*
**20** If something such as a meeting or series of talks **opens**, or if someone **opens** it, it begins. VERB ❑ *...an emergency session of the Russian Parliament due to open later this morning...* V *They are now ready to open negotiations.* V n ♦ **open|ing** N-SING: *the* N *of* n *...a communique issued at the opening of the talks.*
**21** If an event such as a meeting or discussion **opens with** a particular activity or if a particular activity **opens** an event, that activity is the first thing that happens or is dealt with. VERB = begin ≠ end You can also say that someone such as a speaker or singer **opens by** doing a particular thing. ❑ *The service opened with a hymn...* V *with* n *I opened by saying, 'Honey, you look sensational.'...* V *by* -ing *Pollard opened the conversation with some small talk.* V n *with* n
**22** On the stock exchange, the price at which currencies, shares, or commodities **open** is their value at the start of that day's trading. VERB ≠ close [BUSINESS] ❑ *Gold declined $2 in Zurich to open at 385.50...* V prep/adv *In Paris and Milan, the dollar opened almost unchanged.* V adj
**23** When a film, play, or other public event **opens**, it begins to be shown, be performed, or take place for a limited period of time. VERB ❑ *A photographic exhibition opens at the Royal College of Art on Wednesday.* V ♦ **open|ing** N-SING: *the* N *of* n *He is due to attend the opening of the Asian Games on Saturday.*
**24** If you **open** an account with a bank or a commercial organization, you begin to use their services. VERB ❑ *He tried to open an account at the branch of his bank nearest to his workplace.* V n
**25** If an opportunity or choice **is open to** you, you are able to do a particular thing if you choose to. ADJ: v-link ADJ *to* n ❑ *There are a wide range of career opportunities open to young people.*
**26** To **open** opportunities or possibilities means the same as to **open** them **up**. VERB ❑ *The chief of naval operations wants to open opportunities for women in the Navy...* V n *A series of fortunate opportunities opened to him.* V
**27** You can use **open** to describe something that anyone is allowed to take part in or accept. ADJ ❑ *A recent open meeting of College members revealed widespread dissatisfaction... A portfolio approach would keep entry into the managerial profession open and flexible. ...an open invitation.*
**28** If something such as an offer or job is **open**, it is available for someone to accept or apply for. ADJ: v-link ADJ ❑ *The offer will remain open until further notice.* → See also **opening 6**.

**PHRASES** **29** If you do something **in the open**, you do it out of doors rather than in a house or other building. PHRASE: PHR after v ❑ *Many are sleeping in the open because they have no shelter.*
**30** If an attitude or situation is **in the open** or **out in the open**, people know about it and it is no longer kept secret. PHRASE: usu v-link PHR ❑ *The medical service had advised us to keep it a secret, but we wanted it in the open.*
**31** If something is **wide open**, it is open to its full extent. PHRASE: PHR after v, v-link PHR ❑ *The child had left the inner door wide open.*
**32** If you say that a competition, race, or election is **wide open**, you mean that anyone could win it, because there is no competitor who seems to be much better than the others. PHRASE: v-link PHR, PHR after v ❑ *The competition has been thrown wide open by the absence of the world champion.*
**33** **with open arms** → see **arm**. to **open the door** → see **door**. to **keep** your **eyes open** → see **eye**. **with** your **eyes open** → see **eye**. to **open** your **eyes** → see **eye**. to **open fire** → see **fire**. to **open** your **heart** → see **heart**. **the heavens open** → see **heaven**. **an**

**open mind** → see **mind**. to **open** your **mind** → see **mind**. to **keep** your **options open** → see **option**.

♦ **open out** → see **open 3, 13**.

♦ **open up** [1] → see **open 2, 12**. [2] If a place, economy, or area of interest **opens up**, or if someone **opens** it **up**, more people can go there or become involved in it. ❑ *As the market opens up, I think people are going to be able to spend more money on consumer goods... He said he wanted to see how Albania was opening up to the world... These programmes will open up markets for farmers.* [3] If something **opens up** opportunities or possibilities, or if they **open up**, they are created. ❑ *It was also felt that the collapse of the system opened up new possibilities... New opportunities are opening up for investors who want a more direct stake in overseas companies.* [4] If you **open up** a lead in a race or competition, you get yourself into a position where you are leading, usually by quite a long way. ❑ *The Chinese team had opened up a lead of more than two minutes.* [5] When you **open up** a building, you unlock and open the door so that people can get in. ❑ *Three armed men were waiting when the postmaster and his wife arrived to open up the shop.* [6] If someone **opens up**, they start to say exactly what they think or feel. ❑ *Lorna found that people were willing to open up to her.*
PHRASAL VERB; V P; V P *to* n; V P n; PHRASAL VERB; V P n (not pron); V P; Also V n P; PHRASAL VERB; V P n (not pron); PHRASAL VERB; V P n (not pron); PHRASAL VERB; V P *to* n

**open-air** also **open air.** [1] An **open-air** place or event is outside rather than in a building. ❑ *...the Open Air Theatre in Regents Park. ...an open air concert in brilliant sunshine.* [2] If you are **in the open air**, you are outside rather than in a building. ❑ *We sleep out under the stars, and eat our meals in the open air.*
ADJ: usu ADJ n = outdoor; N-SING: *the* N, usu *in the* N

**open-and-shut** If you describe a dispute or a legal case as **open-and-shut**, you mean that is easily decided or solved because the facts are very clear. ❑ *It's an open and shut case. The hospital is at fault.*
ADJ: usu ADJ n

**open|cast** /oʊpənkɑːst, -kæst/ also **open-cast.** At an **opencast** mine, the coal, metal, or minerals are near the surface and underground passages are not needed. [BRIT]
ADJ: ADJ n

☑ in AM, use **strip mine, open pit**

**open day** **(open days)** An **open day** is a day on which members of the public are encouraged to visit a particular school, university, or other institution to see what it is like. [BRIT]
N-COUNT

☑ in AM, use **open house**

**open-door** also **open door.** If a country or organization has an **open-door** policy towards people or goods, it allows them to come there freely, without any restrictions. ❑ *...reformers who have advocated an open door economic policy.*
♦ **Open door** is also a noun. ❑ *...an open door to further foreign investment.*
ADJ: ADJ n; N-SING

**open-ended** When people begin an **open-ended** discussion or activity, they do not have a particular result, decision, or timespan in mind. ❑ *Girls do better on open-ended tasks that require them to think for themselves. ...open-ended questions about what passengers expect of an airline.*
ADJ: usu ADJ n

**open|er** /oʊpənəʳ/ **(openers)** An **opener** is a tool which is used to open containers such as tins or bottles. ❑ *...a tin opener.* → See also **eye-opener**.
N-COUNT: usu n N

**open house** [1] If you say that someone keeps **open house**, you mean that they welcome friends or visitors to their house whenever they arrive and allow them to stay for as long as they want to. ❑ *Father Illtyd kept open house and the boys would congregate in his study during their recreation time, playing cards or games.* [2] An **open house** is a day on which members of the public are encouraged to visit a particular institution or place to see what it is like. [AM] ❑ *A week later, Sara and I attended open house at Ted's school.*
N-UNCOUNT; N-VAR: also N n

☑ in BRIT, use **open day**

**open|ing** /oʊpənɪŋ/ **(openings)** [1] The **opening** event, item, day, or week in a series is the first one. ❑ *They returned to take part in the season's opening game. ...the opening day of the fifth General Synod.* [2] **The opening of** something such as a book, play, or concert is the first part of it. ❑ *The opening of the scene depicts Akhnaten and his family in a moment of intimacy.* [3] An **opening** is a hole or empty space through which things or people can pass. ❑ *He squeezed through a narrow opening in the fence.* [4] An **opening** in a forest is a small area where there are no trees or bushes. [mainly AM] ❑ *I glanced down at the beach as we passed an opening in the trees.*
◆◇◇ ADJ: ADJ n; N-COUNT: usu N *of* n = beginning; N-COUNT; N-COUNT

☑ in BRIT, usually use **clearing**

[5] An **opening** is a good opportunity to do something, for example to show people how good you are. ❑ *Her capabilities were always there; all she needed was an opening to show them.* [6] An **opening** is a job that is available. ❑ *We don't have any openings now, but we'll call you if something comes up.* [7] → See also **open**.
N-COUNT; N-COUNT

**open|ing hours** **Opening hours** are the times during which a shop, bank, library, or bar is open for business. ❑ *Opening hours are 9.30am-5.45pm, Mon-Fri.*
N-PLURAL

**open|ing night** **(opening nights)** The **opening night** of a play or an opera is the first night on which a particular production is performed.
N-COUNT = premier, first night

**open|ing time** **(opening times)** [1] You can refer to the time that a shop, bank, library, or bar opens for business as its **opening time**. ❑ *Shoppers began arriving long before the 10am opening time.* [2] The **opening times** of a place such as a shop, a restaurant, or a museum is the period during which it is open. ❑ *Ask the local tourist office about opening times.*
N-UNCOUNT: also *the* N; N-PLURAL = opening hours

**open let|ter** **(open letters)** An **open letter** is a letter that is published in a newspaper or magazine. It is addressed to a particular person but is intended for the general reader, usually in order to protest or give an opinion about something. ❑ *The Lithuanian parliament also sent an open letter to the United Nations.*
N-COUNT

**open|ly** /oʊpənli/ If you do something **openly**, you do it without hiding any facts or hiding your feelings. ❑ *The Bundesbank has openly criticised the German Government.*
ADV: ADV with v, ADV adj ≠ secretly

**open mar|ket** Goods that are bought and sold on **the open market** are advertised and sold to anyone who wants to buy them. [BUSINESS] ❑ *The Central Bank is authorized to sell government bonds on the open market.*
N-SING: *the* N

**open-minded** If you describe someone as **open-minded**, you approve of them because they are willing to listen to and consider other people's ideas and suggestions. ❑ *He was very open-minded about other people's work.* ♦ **open-mindedness** *He was praised for his enthusiasm and his open-mindedness.*
ADJ: oft ADJ *about* n [approval]; N-UNCOUNT

**open-mouthed** If someone is looking **open-mouthed**, they are staring at something with their mouth wide open because it has shocked, frightened, or excited them. ❑ *They watched almost open-mouthed as the two men came towards them... The finale had 50,000 adults standing in open-mouthed wonderment.*
ADJ: usu ADJ after v, ADJ n

**open-necked** also **open-neck.** If you are wearing an **open-necked** shirt or blouse, you are wearing a shirt or blouse which has no buttons at the top or on which the top button is not done up.
ADJ: ADJ n

**open pit** **(open pits)** An **open pit** is a mine where the coal, metal, or minerals are near the surface and underground passages are not needed. [AM]
N-COUNT = strip mine

☑ in BRIT, use **opencast mine**

**open-plan** An **open-plan** building, office, or room has no internal walls dividing it into small-
ADJ

er areas. ❑ *The firm's top managers share the same open-plan office.*

**open pris|on** **(open prisons)** An **open prison** is a prison where there are fewer restrictions on prisoners than in a normal prison. [BRIT] N-COUNT: oft in names

☑ in AM, use **minimum security prison**

**open ques|tion** **(open questions)** If something is **an open question**, people have different opinions about it and nobody can say which opinion is correct. ❑ *A British official said he thought it was an open question whether sanctions would do any good.* N-COUNT

**open se|cret** **(open secrets)** If you refer to something as **an open secret**, you mean that it is supposed to be a secret, but many people know about it. ❑ *It's an open secret that the security service bugged telephones.* N-COUNT

**open-top** also **open-topped.** An **open-top** bus has no roof, so that the people sitting on the top level can see or be seen more easily. An **open-top** car has no roof or has a roof that can be removed. ❑ *The team drove through the streets of Leeds city centre in an open-top bus.* ADJ: ADJ n

**Open Uni|ver|sity** In Britain, **the Open University** is a university that runs degree courses using the radio and television, for students who want to study part-time or mainly at home. N-PROPER: *the* N

**op|era** /ɒpərə/ **(operas)** An **opera** is a play with music in which all the words are sung. ❑ *...a one-act opera about contemporary women in America. ...an opera singer... He was also learned in classical music with a great love of opera.* ➔ See also **soap opera**. ◆◇◇ N-VAR

**op|era house** **(opera houses)** An **opera house** is a theatre that is specially designed for the performance of operas. ❑ *...Sydney Opera House.* N-COUNT; N-IN-NAMES

**op|eran|di** /ɒpərændaɪ/ ➔ see **modus operandi**.

**op|er|ate** /ɒpəreɪt/ **(operates, operating, operated)** ◆◆◆
1 If you **operate** a business or organization, you work to keep it running properly. If a business or organization **operates**, it carries out its work. ❑ *Until his death in 1986 Greenwood owned and operated an enormous pear orchard. ...allowing commercial banks to operate in the country... Operating costs jumped from £85.3m to £95m.* VERB V n V V-ing
♦ **op|era|tion** /ɒpəreɪʃən/ *Company finance is to provide funds for the everyday operation of the business.* N-UNCOUNT
2 The way that something **operates** is the way that it works or has a particular effect. ❑ *Ceiling and wall lights can operate independently... The world of work doesn't operate that way.* VERB V adv/prep V n
♦ **op|era|tion** *Why is it the case that taking part-time work is made so difficult by the operation of the benefit system?* N-UNCOUNT: oft N *of* n
3 When you **operate** a machine or device, or when it **operates**, you make it work. ❑ *A massive rock fall trapped the men as they operated a tunnelling machine... The number of fax machines operating around the world has now reached ten million.* VERB V n V
♦ **op|era|tion** *...over 1,000 dials monitoring every aspect of the operation of the aeroplane.* N-UNCOUNT
4 When surgeons **operate on** a patient in a hospital, they cut open a patient's body in order to remove, replace, or repair a diseased or damaged part. ❑ *The surgeon who operated on the King released new details of his injuries... You examine a patient and then you decide whether or not to operate.* VERB V *on* n V
5 If military forces **are operating in** a particular region, they are in that place in order to carry out their orders. ❑ *Up to ten thousand Zimbabwean soldiers are operating in Mozambique.* VERB V prep

**op|er|at|ic** /ɒpərætɪk/ **Operatic** means relating to opera. ❑ *...the local amateur operatic society.* ADJ: usu ADJ n

**op|er|at|ing** /ɒpəreɪtɪŋ/ **Operating** profits and costs are the money that a company earns and spends in carrying out its ordinary trading activities, in contrast to such things as interest and investment. [BUSINESS] ❑ *The group made operating profits of £80m before interest.* ADJ: ADJ n

**op|er|at|ing room** **(operating rooms)** An **operating room** is the same as an **operating theatre**. [AM] N-COUNT

**op|er|at|ing sys|tem** **(operating systems)** The **operating system** of a computer is its most basic program, which it needs in order to function and run other programs. [COMPUTING] N-COUNT

**op|er|at|ing ta|ble** **(operating tables)** An **operating table** is a table which a patient in a hospital lies on during a surgical operation. N-COUNT

**op|er|at|ing thea|tre** **(operating theatres)** An **operating theatre** is a special room in a hospital where surgeons carry out medical operations. [BRIT] N-COUNT = theatre

☑ in AM, use **operating room**

**op|era|tion** /ɒpəreɪʃən/ **(operations)** ◆◆◆
1 An **operation** is a highly organized activity that involves many people doing different things. ❑ *The rescue operation began on Friday afternoon... The soldiers were engaged in a military operation close to the Ugandan border. ...a big operation against the drugs trade.* N-COUNT: usu supp N
2 A business or company can be referred to as an **operation**. [BUSINESS] ❑ *Thorn's electronics operation employs around 5,000 people... The two parent groups now run their business as a single combined operation.* N-COUNT
3 When a patient has an **operation**, a surgeon cuts open their body in order to remove, replace, or repair a diseased or damaged part. ❑ *Charles was at the clinic recovering from an operation on his arm.* N-COUNT
4 If a system is **in operation**, it is being used. ❑ *Until the rail links are in operation, passengers can only travel through the tunnel by coach.* N-UNCOUNT: *in/out of* N
5 If a machine or device is **in operation**, it is working. ❑ *There are three ski lifts in operation.* N-UNCOUNT: *in/out of* N
6 When a rule, system, or plan **comes into operation** or you **put** it **into operation**, you begin to use it. ❑ *The Financial Services Act came into operation four years ago... Cheaper energy conservation techniques have been put into operation in the developed world.* PHRASE: V inflects

**op|era|tion|al** /ɒpəreɪʃənəl/
1 A machine or piece of equipment that is **operational** is in use or is ready for use. ❑ *The whole system will be fully operational by December 1995.* ADJ: usu v-link ADJ
2 **Operational** factors or problems relate to the working of a system, device, or plan. ❑ *The nuclear industry was required to prove that every operational and safety aspect had been fully researched.* ADJ: usu ADJ n
♦ **op|era|tion|al|ly** *The device had been used operationally some months previously.* ADV: ADV adj, ADV after v

**op|era|tive** /ɒpərətɪv/ **(operatives)**
1 A system or service that is **operative** is working or having an effect. [FORMAL] ❑ *The commercial telephone service was no longer operative.* ADJ: usu v-link ADJ
2 An **operative** is a worker, especially one who does work with their hands. [FORMAL] ❑ *In an automated car plant there is not a human operative to be seen.* N-COUNT
3 An **operative** is someone who works for a government agency such as the intelligence service. [mainly AM] ❑ *Naturally the CIA wants to protect its operatives.* N-COUNT
4 If you describe a word as **the operative word**, you want to draw attention to it because you think it is important or exactly true in a particular situation. ❑ *As long as the operative word is 'greed', you can't count on people keeping the costs down.* PHRASE: N inflects

**op|era|tor** /ɒpəreɪtəʳ/ **(operators)** ◆◇◇
1 An **operator** is a person who connects telephone calls at a telephone exchange or in a place such as an office or hotel. ❑ *He dialled the operator and put in a call for Rome.* N-COUNT
2 An **operator** is a person who is employed to operate or control a machine. ❑ *...computer operators.* N-COUNT: usu n N
3 An **operator** is a person or a company that runs a business. [BUSINESS] ❑ *...'Tele-Communications', the nation's largest cable TV operator.* N-COUNT: usu with supp
4 If you call someone a good **operator**, you mean that they are skilful at achieving what they want, often in a slightly dishonest way. N-COUNT: usu adj N

[INFORMAL] ❑ *...one of the shrewdest political operators in the Arab World.* [5] → See also **tour operator**.

**op|er|et|ta** /ɒpəretə/ **(operettas)** An **operetta** is a light-hearted opera which has some of the words spoken rather than sung. N-VAR

**oph|thal|mic** /ɒfθælmɪk/ **Ophthalmic** means relating to or concerned with the medical care of people's eyes. [FORMAL] ❑ *Ophthalmic surgeons are now performing laser surgery to correct myopia.* ADJ: ADJ n

**oph|thal|molo|gist** /ɒfθælmɒlədʒɪst/ **(ophthalmologists)** An **ophthalmologist** is a medical doctor who specializes in diseases and problems affecting people's eyes. N-COUNT

**oph|thal|mol|ogy** /ɒfθælmɒlədʒi/ **Ophthalmology** is branch of medicine concerned with people's eyes and the problems that affect them. N-UNCOUNT

**opi|ate** /oʊpiət/ **(opiates)** An **opiate** is a drug that contains opium. Opiates are used to reduce pain or to help people to sleep. N-COUNT

**opine** /oʊpaɪn/ **(opines, opining, opined)** To **opine** means to express your opinion. [FORMAL] ❑ *'She's probably had a row with her boyfriend,' Charles opined... He opined that the navy would have to start again from the beginning.* VERB; V with quote; V that; Also V *on/about* n

**opin|ion** /əpɪnjən/ **(opinions)** ◆◆◇ [1] Your **opinion** about something is what you think or believe about it. ❑ *I wasn't asking for your opinion, Dick... He held the opinion that a government should think before introducing a tax... Most who expressed an opinion spoke favorably of Thomas.* N-COUNT: oft poss N, N that [2] Your **opinion of** someone is your judgment of their character or ability. ❑ *That improved Mrs Goole's already favourable opinion of him.* N-SING: usu supp N, N *of* n = estimation [3] You can refer to the beliefs or views that people have as **opinion**. ❑ *Some, I suppose, might even be in positions to influence opinion... There is a broad consensus of opinion about the policies which should be pursued.* N-UNCOUNT [4] An **opinion** from an expert is the advice or judgment that they give you in the subject that they know a lot about. ❑ *Even if you have had a regular physical check-up recently, you should still seek a medical opinion.* N-COUNT: usu sing [5] → See also **public opinion**, **second opinion**.

PHRASES [6] You add expressions such as **'in my opinion'** or **'in their opinion'** to a statement in order to indicate that it is what you or someone else thinks, and is not necessarily a fact. ❑ *Well he's not making a very good job of it in my opinion.* PHRASE: PHR with cl [7] If someone is **of the opinion that** something is the case, that is what they believe. [FORMAL] ❑ *Frank is of the opinion that the 1934 yacht should have won.* PHRASE: v-link PHR that [8] **a matter of opinion** → see **matter**.

**opin|ion|at|ed** /əpɪnjəneɪtɪd/ If you describe someone as **opinionated**, you mean that they have very strong opinions and refuse to accept that they may be wrong. ❑ *Sue is the extrovert in the family; opinionated, talkative and passionate about politics.* ADJ

**opin|ion for|mer** **(opinion formers)** also **opinion maker**. **Opinion formers** are people who have a lot of influence over what the public thinks about things. N-COUNT

**opin|ion poll** **(opinion polls)** An **opinion poll** involves asking people's opinions on a particular subject, especially one concerning politics. ❑ *Nearly three-quarters of people questioned in an opinion poll agreed with the government's decision.* N-COUNT = poll

**opium** /oʊpiəm/ **Opium** is a powerful drug made from the seeds of a type of poppy. Opium is used in medicines that relieve pain or help someone sleep. N-UNCOUNT

**opos|sum** /əpɒsəm/ **(opossums)** An **opossum** is a small animal that lives in America. It carries its young in a pouch on its body, and has thick fur and a long tail. N-VAR

**op|po|nent** /əpoʊnənt/ **(opponents)** ◆◇◇ [1] A politician's **opponents** are other politicians who belong to a different party or who have different aims or policies. ❑ *...Mr Kennedy's opponent in the leadership contest... He described the detention without trial of political opponents as a cowardly act.* N-COUNT: usu with poss = adversary [2] In a sporting contest, your **opponent** is the person who is playing against you. ❑ *Norris twice knocked down his opponent in the early rounds of the fight.* N-COUNT: usu poss N [3] The **opponents of** an idea or policy do not agree with it and do not want it to be carried out. ❑ *...opponents of the spread of nuclear weapons.* N-COUNT: usu N *of* n ≠ supporter

**op|por|tune** /ɒpəʳtjuːn, AM -tuːn/ If something happens at an **opportune** time or is **opportune**, it happens at the time that is most convenient for someone or most likely to lead to success. [FORMAL] ❑ *I believe that I have arrived at a very opportune moment... The timing of the meetings was opportune.* ADJ

**op|por|tun|ism** /ɒpəʳtjuːnɪzəm, AM -tuːn-/ If you refer to someone's behaviour as **opportunism**, you are criticizing them for taking advantage of any opportunity that occurs in order to gain money or power, without thinking about whether their actions are right or wrong. ❑ *The Energy Minister responded by saying that the opposition's concern for the environment was political opportunism.* N-UNCOUNT [disapproval]

**op|por|tun|ist** /ɒpəʳtjuːnɪst, AM -tuːn-/ **(opportunists)** [1] If you describe someone as **opportunist**, you are critical of them because they take advantage of any situation in order to gain money or power, without considering whether their actions are right or wrong. ❑ *...corrupt and opportunist politicians.* ADJ: usu ADJ n [disapproval] ♦ An **opportunist** is someone who is opportunist. ❑ *Like most successful politicians, Sinclair was an opportunist... Car thieves are opportunists.* N-COUNT [2] **Opportunist** actions are not planned, but are carried out in order to take advantage of a situation that has just occurred. ❑ *Eric Cantona made the game safe with a brilliant opportunist goal.* ADJ: usu ADJ n

**op|por|tun|is|tic** /ɒpəʳtjuːnɪstɪk, AM -tuːn-/ If you describe someone's behaviour as **opportunistic**, you are critical of them because they take advantage of situations in order to gain money or power, without thinking about whether their actions are right or wrong. ❑ *Many of the party's members joined only for opportunistic reasons.* ADJ [disapproval] ♦ **op|por|tun|is|ti|cal|ly** *This nationalist feeling has been exploited opportunistically by several important politicians.* ADV: ADV with v

**op|por|tu|nity** /ɒpəʳtjuːnɪti, AM -tuːn-/ **(opportunities)** ◆◆◇ An **opportunity** is a situation in which it is possible for you to do something that you want to do. ❑ *I had an opportunity to go to New York and study... I want to see more opportunities for young people. ...equal opportunities in employment.* → See also **photo opportunity**. N-VAR = chance; oft N to-inf, N *for n/-ing*

**op|pose** /əpoʊz/ **(opposes, opposing, opposed)** ◆◇◇ If you **oppose** someone or **oppose** their plans or ideas, you disagree with what they want to do and try to prevent them from doing it. ❑ *Mr Taylor was not bitter towards those who had opposed him... Many parents oppose bilingual education in schools.* VERB ≠ support; V n; V n

**op|posed** /əpoʊzd/ ◆◇◇ [1] If you **are opposed to** something, you disagree with it or disapprove of it. ❑ *I am utterly opposed to any form of terrorism.* ADJ: v-link ADJ *to* n/-ing = against [2] You say that two ideas or systems are **opposed** when they are opposite to each other or very different from each other. ❑ *...people with policies almost diametrically opposed to his own... This was a straight conflict of directly opposed aims.* ADJ: oft ADJ *to* n = opposite [3] You use **as opposed to** when you want to make it clear that you are talking about one particular thing and not something else. ❑ *We ate in the restaurant, as opposed to the bistro.* PHRASE: PHR group

**op|pos|ing** /əpoʊzɪŋ/ [1] **Opposing** ideas or tendencies are totally different from each other. ❑ *I have a friend who has the opposing view and felt that the war was immoral.* ADJ: ADJ n = opposite [2] **Opposing** groups of people disagree about something or are in competition with one another. ❑ *The Georgian leader said in a radio address that he still favoured dialogue* ADJ: ADJ n *between the opposing sides... The opposing team must in turn try to keep the ball in the air before hitting it back over the net.*

**op|po|site** /ɒpəzɪt/ **(opposites)** [◆◇◇] 1 If one thing is **opposite** another, it is on the other side of a space from it. ❑ *Jennie had sat opposite her at breakfast.* [PREP] ♦ **Opposite** is also an adverb. ❑ *He looked up at the buildings opposite, but could see no open window.* [ADV: usu n ADV, ADV after v] 2 The **opposite** side or part of something is the side or part that is furthest away from you. ❑ *...the opposite corner of the room.* [ADJ: ADJ n = far] 3 **Opposite** is used to describe things of the same kind which are completely different in a particular way. For example, north and south are opposite directions, and winning and losing are opposite results in a game. ❑ *All the cars driving in the opposite direction had their headlights on... I should have written the notes in the opposite order.* [ADJ: usu ADJ n, also v-link ADJ to n, v-link ADJ] 4 **The opposite of** someone or something is the person or thing that is most different from them. ❑ *Ritter was a very complex man but Marius was the opposite, a simple farmer... Well, whatever he says you can bet he's thinking the opposite.* [N-COUNT: usu *the* N, oft *the* N *of* n]

**op|po|site num|ber** **(opposite numbers)** Your **opposite number** is a person who has the same job or rank as you, but works in a different department, firm, or organization. [JOURNALISM] ❑ *The French Defence Minister is to visit Japan later this month for talks with his Japanese opposite number.* [N-COUNT: usu poss N = counterpart]

**op|po|site sex** If you are talking about men and refer to **the opposite sex**, you mean women. If you are talking about women and refer to **the opposite sex**, you mean men. ❑ *Body language can also be used to attract members of the opposite sex.* [N-SING: *the* N]

**op|po|si|tion** /ɒpəzɪʃᵊn/ **(oppositions)** [◆◆◇] 1 **Opposition** is strong, angry, or violent disagreement and disapproval. ❑ *The government is facing a new wave of opposition in the form of a student strike... Much of the opposition to this plan has come from the media.* [N-UNCOUNT: oft N *to* n ≠ support] 2 **The opposition** is the political parties or groups that are opposed to a government. ❑ *The main opposition parties boycotted the election, saying it would not be conducted fairly.* [N-COUNT-COLL: usu sing, oft N n] 3 In a country's parliament or legislature, **the opposition** refers to the politicians or political parties that form part of the parliament or legislature, but are not the government. ❑ *...the Leader of the Opposition.* [N-COUNT-COLL: usu sing, oft *the* N] 4 **The opposition** is the person or team you are competing against in a sports event. ❑ *Poland provide the opposition for the Scots' last warm-up match at home.* [N-SING-COLL]

**op|press** /əpres/ **(oppresses, oppressing, oppressed)** 1 To **oppress** people means to treat them cruelly, or to prevent them from having the same opportunities, freedom, and benefits as others. ❑ *These people often are oppressed by the governments of the countries they find themselves in... We are not normal like everybody else. If we were they wouldn't be oppressing us.* [VERB: *be* V-ed, V n, Also V, V n *with* n] 2 If something **oppresses** you, it makes you feel depressed, anxious, and uncomfortable. [LITERARY] ❑ *It was not just the weather which oppressed her.* [VERB: V n]

**op|pressed** /əprest/ People who are **oppressed** are treated cruelly or are prevented from having the same opportunities, freedom, and benefits as others. ❑ *Before they took power, they felt oppressed by the white English speakers who controlled things.* [ADJ] ♦ **The oppressed** are people who are oppressed. ❑ *...a sense of community with the poor and oppressed.* [N-PLURAL: *the* N]

**op|pres|sion** /əpreʃᵊn/ **Oppression** is the cruel or unfair treatment of a group of people. ❑ *...an attempt to escape political oppression.* [N-UNCOUNT: also N in pl, oft N *of* n]

**op|pres|sive** /əpresɪv/ 1 If you describe a society, its laws, or customs as **oppressive**, you think they treat people cruelly and unfairly. ❑ *The new laws will be just as oppressive as those they replace. ...refugees from the oppressive regime.* [ADJ = repressive] 2 If you describe the weather or the atmosphere in a room as **oppressive**, you mean that it is unpleasantly hot and damp. ❑ *The oppressive afternoon heat had quite tired him out.* [ADJ = stifling] 3 An **oppressive** situation makes you feel depressed and uncomfortable. ❑ *...the oppressive sadness that weighed upon him like a physical pain.* [ADJ: usu ADJ n]

**op|pres|sor** /əpresəʳ/ **(oppressors)** An **oppressor** is a person or group of people that is treating another person or group of people cruelly or unfairly. ❑ *Lacking sovereignty, they could organise no defence against their oppressors.* [N-COUNT: oft with poss]

**op|pro|brium** /əproʊbriəm/ **Opprobrium** is open criticism or disapproval of something that someone has done. [FORMAL] ❑ *His political opinions have attracted the opprobrium of the Left.* [N-UNCOUNT = censure]

**opt** /ɒpt/ **(opts, opting, opted)** [◆◇◇] If you **opt for** something, or **opt to** do something, you choose it or decide to do it in preference to anything else. ❑ *Depending on your circumstances you may wish to opt for one method or the other... Our students can also opt to stay in residence.* [VERB: V *for* n, V to-inf]

♦ **opt in** If you can **opt in to** something, you are able to choose to be part of an agreement or system. ❑ *He proposed that only those countries which were willing and able should opt in to phase three... He didn't exactly opt out because he never opted in.* [PHRASAL VERB: V P *to* n, V P]

♦ **opt out** If you **opt out of** something, you choose to be no longer involved in it. ❑ *... powers for hospitals to opt out of health authority control... Under the agreement the Vietnamese can opt out at any time.* [PHRASAL VERB: V P *of* n, V P]

**op|tic** /ɒptɪk/ **Optic** means relating to the eyes or to sight. ❑ *The reason for this is that the optic nerve is a part of the brain.* → See also **optics**. [ADJ: ADJ n]

**op|ti|cal** /ɒptɪkᵊl/ **Optical** devices, processes, and effects involve or relate to vision, light, or images. ❑ *...optical telescopes. ...the optical effects of volcanic dust in the stratosphere.* [ADJ: usu ADJ n]

**op|ti|cal fi|bre** **(optical fibres)**

☑ in AM, use **optical fiber**

An **optical fibre** is a very thin thread of glass inside a protective coating. Optical fibres are used to carry information in the form of light. [N-VAR]

**op|ti|cal il|lu|sion** **(optical illusions)** An **optical illusion** is something that tricks your eyes so that what you think you see is different from what is really there. ❑ *Sloping walls on the bulk of the building create an optical illusion.* [N-COUNT]

**op|ti|cian** /ɒptɪʃᵊn/ **(opticians)** 1 An **optician** is someone whose job involves testing people's sight, and making or selling glasses and contact lenses. [N-COUNT] 2 An **optician** or an **optician's** is a shop where you can have your eyes tested and buy glasses and contact lenses. ❑ *Some may need specialist treatment at the optician's.* [N-COUNT: oft *the* N]

**op|tics** /ɒptɪks/ **Optics** is the branch of science concerned with vision, sight, and light. → See also **fibre optics**. [N-UNCOUNT]

**op|ti|mal** /ɒptɪmᵊl/ → see **optimum**.

**op|ti|mism** /ɒptɪmɪzəm/ **Optimism** is the feeling of being hopeful about the future or about the success of something in particular. ❑ *The Indian Prime Minister has expressed optimism about India's future relations with the USA. ...a mood of cautious optimism.* [N-UNCOUNT ≠ pessimism]

**op|ti|mist** /ɒptɪmɪst/ **(optimists)** An **optimist** is someone who is hopeful about the future. ❑ *Optimists reckon house prices will move up with inflation this year.* [N-COUNT ≠ pessimist]

**op|ti|mis|tic** /ɒptɪmɪstɪk/ [◆◇◇] Someone who is **optimistic** is hopeful about the future or the success of something in particular. ❑ *The President says she is optimistic that an agreement can be worked out soon... Michael was in a jovial and optimistic mood.* [ADJ: oft ADJ *about* n, ADJ that ≠ pessimistic] ♦ **op|ti|mis|ti|cal|ly** *Both sides have spoken optimistically about the talks.* [ADV: ADV with v]

**op|ti|mize** /ɒptɪmaɪz/ **(optimizes, optimizing, optimized)**

☑ in BRIT, also use **optimise**

[1] To **optimize** a plan, system, or machine means to arrange or design it so that it operates as smoothly and efficiently as possible. [FORMAL] ❑ *The new systems have been optimised for running Microsoft Windows.* [2] To **optimize** a situation or opportunity means to get as much advantage or benefit from it as you can. [FORMAL] ❑ *What can you do to optimize your family situation?* VERB V n VERB V n

**op|ti|mum** /ɒptɪməm/ or **optimal** The **optimum** or **optimal** level or state of something is the best level or state that it could achieve. [FORMAL] ❑ *Aim to do some physical activity three times a week for optimum health. ...regions in which optimal conditions for farming can be created.* ADJ: usu ADJ n

**op|tion** /ɒpʃᵊn/ **(options)** ◆◆◇ [1] An **option** is something that you can choose to do in preference to one or more alternatives. ❑ *He's argued from the start that America and its allies are putting too much emphasis on the military option... What other options do you have?* N-COUNT = *alternative* [2] If you have the **option** of doing something, you can choose whether to do it or not. ❑ *Criminals are given the option of going to jail or facing public humiliation... We had no option but to abandon the meeting.* N-SING: oft N *of* n/-ing, N to-inf = *choice* [3] In business, an **option** is an agreement or contract that gives someone the right to buy or sell something such as property or shares at a future date. [BUSINESS] ❑ *Each bank has granted the other an option on 19.9% of its shares.* N-COUNT [4] An **option** is one of a number of subjects which a student can choose to study as a part of his or her course. ❑ *Several options are offered for the student's senior year.* N-COUNT

PHRASES [5] If you **keep** your **options open** or **leave** your **options open**, you delay making a decision about something. ❑ *I am keeping my options open. I have not made a decision on either matter.* PHRASE: V inflects [6] If you take the **soft option**, you do the thing that is easiest or least likely to cause trouble in a particular situation. [mainly BRIT] ❑ *The job of chairman can no longer be regarded as a convenient soft option.* PHRASE: N inflects

**op|tion|al** /ɒpʃənᵊl/ If something is **optional**, you can choose whether or not you do it or have it. ❑ *Sex education is a sensitive area for some parents, and thus it should remain optional.* ADJ ≠*compulsory*

**op|tom|etrist** /ɒptɒmətrɪst/ **(optometrists)** An **optometrist** is the same as an **optician**. [mainly AM] N-COUNT

✔ in BRIT, usually use **optician**

**opt-out** **(opt-outs)** [1] An **opt-out** school or hospital has chosen to leave local government control and manage itself using national government money. [BRIT] ❑ *...teachers at opt-out schools.* ADJ: ADJ n [2] You can refer to the action taken by a school or hospital in which they choose not to be controlled by a local government authority as an **opt-out**. [BRIT] ❑ *More freedom and choice will be given to parents, and the school opt-outs will be stepped up.* N-COUNT [3] An **opt-out** clause in an agreement gives people the choice not to be involved in one part of that agreement. [mainly BRIT] ❑ *...an opt-out clause.* ADJ: ADJ n [4] You can refer to the action of choosing not to be involved in a particular part of an agreement as an **opt-out**. ❑ *...a list of demands, such as opt-outs from some parts of the treaty.* N-COUNT

**opu|lent** /ɒpjʊlənt/ [1] **Opulent** things or places look grand and expensive. [FORMAL] ❑ *...an opulent office on Wimpole Street in London's West End.* ADJ = *sumptuous* ♦ **opu|lence** *...the elegant opulence of the German embassy.* N-UNCOUNT: oft N *of* n [2] **Opulent** people are very wealthy and spend a lot of money. [FORMAL] ❑ *Most of the cash went on supporting his opulent lifestyle.* ADJ: usu ADJ n = *affluent*

**opus** /oʊpəs, ɒpəs/ **(opuses** or **opera)** [1] An **opus** is a piece of classical music by a particular composer. **Opus** is usually followed by a number which indicates at what point the piece was written. The abbreviation **op.** is also used. ❑ *...Beethoven's Piano Sonata in E minor, Opus 90.* N-COUNT: usu N num [2] You can refer to an artistic work such as a piece of music or writing or a painting as an **opus**. ❑ *...the new opus from Peter Gabriel.* ➔ See also **magnum opus**. N-COUNT = *work*

**or** /əʳ, STRONG ɔːʳ/ ◆◆◆ [1] You use **or** to link two or more alternatives. ❑ *'Tea or coffee?' John asked... He said he would try to write or call as soon as he reached the Canary Islands... Students are asked to take another course in English, or science, or mathematics.* CONJ [2] You use **or** to give another alternative, when the first alternative is introduced by 'either' or 'whether'. ❑ *Items like bread, milk and meat were either unavailable or could be obtained only on the black market... Either you can talk to him, or I will... I don't know whether people will buy it or not.* CONJ [3] You use **or** between two numbers to indicate that you are giving an approximate amount. ❑ *Everyone benefited from limiting their intake of tea to just three or four cups a day... Normally he asked questions, and had a humorous remark or two.* CONJ [4] You use **or** to introduce a comment which corrects or modifies what you have just said. ❑ *The man was a fool, he thought, or at least incompetent... There was nothing more he wanted, or so he thought.* CONJ [5] If you say that someone should do something **or** something unpleasant will happen, you are warning them that if they do not do it, the unpleasant thing will happen. ❑ *She had to have the operation, or she would die.* CONJ = *otherwise* [6] You use **or** to introduce something which is evidence for the truth of a statement you have just made. ❑ *He must have thought Jane was worth it or he wouldn't have wasted time on her, I suppose.* CONJ = *otherwise*

PHRASES [7] You use **or no** or **or not** to emphasize that a particular thing makes no difference to what is going to happen. ❑ *Chairman or no, if I want to stop the project, I can... The first difficulty is that, old-fashioned or not, it is very good.* PHRASE: group PHR [emphasis] [8] You use **or no** between two occurrences of the same noun in order to say that whether something is true or not makes no difference to a situation. ❑ *The next day, rain or no rain, it was business as usual.* PHRASE: n PHR n [9] **or else** ➔ see **else**. **or other** ➔ see **other**. **or so** ➔ see **so**. **or something** ➔ see **something**.

**-or** /-əʳ/ **-or** is used at the end of nouns that refer to people or things which perform a particular action. ❑ *...a major investor. ...the translator. ...an electric generator.* SUFFIX

**ora|cle** /ɒrəkᵊl, AM ɔːr-/ **(oracles)** In ancient Greece, an **oracle** was a priest or priestess who made statements about future events or about the truth. N-COUNT

**oral** /ɔːrəl/ **(orals)** [1] **Oral** communication is spoken rather than written. ❑ *...the written and oral traditions of ancient cultures. ...an oral agreement.* ADJ: usu ADJ n ♦ **oral|ly** *...their ability to present ideas orally and in writing.* ADV: ADV after v [2] An **oral** is an examination, especially in a foreign language, that is spoken rather than written. ❑ *I spoke privately to the candidate after the oral.* N-COUNT [3] You use **oral** to indicate that something is done with a person's mouth or relates to a person's mouth. ❑ *...good oral hygiene.* ADJ: usu ADJ n ♦ **oral|ly** *...antibiotic tablets taken orally.* ADV: usu ADV after v

**oral his|to|ry** **(oral histories)** **Oral history** consists of spoken memories, stories, and songs, and the study of these, as a way of communicating and discovering information about the past. N-VAR

**oral sex** **Oral sex** is sexual activity involving contact between a person's mouth and their partner's genitals. N-UNCOUNT

**or|ange** /ɒrɪndʒ, AM ɔːr-/ **(oranges)** ◆◆◇ [1] Something that is **orange** is of a colour between red and yellow. ❑ *...men in bright orange uniforms.* COLOUR [2] An **orange** is a round juicy fruit with a thick, orange coloured skin. ➔ See picture on page 1711. ❑ *...orange trees. ...fresh orange juice.* N-VAR: oft N n [3] **Orange** is a drink that is made from or tastes of oranges. ❑ *...vodka and orange.* N-UNCOUNT

**or|ange blos|som** The flowers of the orange tree are called **orange blossom**. Orange blossom is white and is traditionally associated with weddings in Europe and America. N-UNCOUNT

**or|ang|ery** /ɒrɪndʒri, AM ɔːr-/ **(orangeries)** An **orangery** is a building with glass walls and roof which is used for growing orange trees and other plants which need to be kept warm. N-COUNT

**or|angey** /ɒrɪndʒi, AM ɔːr-/ **Orangey** means slightly orange in colour. ♦ **Orangey** is also a combining form. ❑ *The hall is decorated in bright orangey-red with black and gold woodwork.* ADJ; COMB in COLOUR

**orang-utan** /ɔːræŋuːtæn/ **(orang-utans)** also **orang-utang, orangutan, orang-outan.** An **orang-utan** is an ape with long reddish hair that comes from Borneo and Sumatra. N-COUNT

**ora|tion** /əreɪʃən, AM ɔːr-/ **(orations)** An **oration** is a formal speech made in public. [FORMAL] ❑ *...a brief funeral oration.* N-COUNT: oft supp N = address

**ora|tor** /ɒrətəʳ, AM ɔːr-/ **(orators)** An **orator** is someone who is skilled at making formal speeches, especially ones which affect people's feelings and beliefs. ❑ *Lenin was the great orator of the Russian Revolution.* N-COUNT: oft adj N = public speaker

**ora|tori|cal** /ɒrətɒrɪkəl, AM ɔːrətɔːr-/ **Oratorical** means relating to or using oratory. [FORMAL] ❑ *He reached oratorical heights which left him and some of his players in tears.* ADJ: ADJ n

**ora|to|rio** /ɒrətɔːriou, AM ɔːr-/ **(oratorios)** An **oratorio** is a long piece of music with a religious theme which is written for singers and an orchestra. N-COUNT

**ora|tory** /ɒrətəri, AM ɔːrətɔːri/ **(oratories)**
1 **Oratory** is the art of making formal speeches which strongly affect people's feelings and beliefs. [FORMAL] ❑ *He displayed determination as well as powerful oratory.* N-UNCOUNT = rhetoric
2 An **oratory** is a room or building where Christians go to pray. ❑ *The wedding will be at the Brompton Oratory next month.* N-COUNT: oft in names

**orb** /ɔːʳb/ **(orbs)** 1 An **orb** is something that is shaped like a ball, for example the sun or moon. [LITERARY] ❑ *The moon's round orb would shine high in the sky, casting its velvety light on everything.* N-COUNT = sphere
2 An **orb** is a small, ornamental ball with a cross on top that is carried by some kings or queens at important ceremonies. N-COUNT

**or|bit** /ɔːʳbɪt/ **(orbits, orbiting, orbited)** 1 An **orbit** is the curved path in space that is followed by an object going round and round a planet, moon, or star. ❑ *Mars and Earth have orbits which change with time... The planet is probably in orbit around a small star.* N-COUNT: also *in/into* N
2 If something such as a satellite **orbits** a planet, moon, or sun, it moves around it in a continuous, curving path. ❑ *In 1957 the Soviet Union launched the first satellite to orbit the earth.* VERB = circle; V n

**or|bit|al** /ɔːʳbɪtəl/ 1 An **orbital** road goes all the way round a large city. [mainly BRIT] ❑ *...a new orbital road round Paris.* ADJ: ADJ n

✓ in AM, use **beltway**

2 **Orbital** describes things relating to the orbit of an object in space. ❑ *The newly discovered world followed an orbital path unlike that of any other planet.* ADJ: ADJ n

**or|chard** /ɔːʳtʃəʳd/ **(orchards)** An **orchard** is an area of land on which fruit trees are grown. N-COUNT

**or|ches|tra** /ɔːʳkɪstrə/ **(orchestras)** 1 An **orchestra** is a large group of musicians who play a variety of different instruments together. Orchestras usually play classical music. ❑ *...the Royal Liverpool Philharmonic Orchestra.* ➔ See also **chamber orchestra, symphony orchestra.** N-COUNT: oft in names
2 **The orchestra** or **the orchestra seats** in a theatre or concert hall are the seats on the ground floor directly in front of the stage. [mainly AM] N-SING: usu *the* N, N n

✓ in BRIT, usually use **stalls**

**or|ches|tral** /ɔːʳkestrəl/ **Orchestral** means relating to an orchestra and the music it plays. ❑ *...an orchestral concert.* ADJ: ADJ n

**or|ches|tra pit** In a theatre, **the orchestra pit** is the space reserved for the musicians playing the music for an opera, musical, or ballet, immediately in front of or below the stage. N-SING

**or|ches|trate** /ɔːʳkɪstreɪt/ **(orchestrates, orchestrating, orchestrated)** If you say that someone **orchestrates** an event or situation, you mean that they carefully organize it in a way that will produce the result that they want. ❑ *The colonel was able to orchestrate a rebellion from inside an army jail. ...a carefully orchestrated campaign.* VERB; V n; V-ed
♦ **or|ches|tra|tion** *...his skilful orchestration of latent nationalist feeling.* N-UNCOUNT

**or|ches|tra|tion** /ɔːʳkɪstreɪʃən/ **(orchestrations)** An **orchestration** is a piece of music that has been rewritten so that it can be played by an orchestra. ❑ *Mahler's own imaginative orchestration was heard in the same concert.* N-COUNT = arrangement

**or|chid** /ɔːʳkɪd/ **(orchids) Orchids** are plants with brightly coloured, unusually shaped flowers. N-COUNT

**or|dain** /ɔːʳdeɪn/ **(ordains, ordaining, ordained)**
1 When someone **is ordained**, they are made a member of the clergy in a religious ceremony. ❑ *He was ordained a Catholic priest in 1982... Women have been ordained for many years in the Church of Scotland... He ordained his own priests, and threatened to ordain bishops.* VERB; *be* V-ed n; *be* V-ed; V n
2 If some authority or power **ordains** something, they decide that it should happen or be in existence. [FORMAL] ❑ *Nehru ordained that socialism should rule... His rule was ordained by heaven... The recession may already be severe enough to ordain structural change.* VERB = decree; V that; *be* V-ed; V n

**or|deal** /ɔːʳdiːl/ **(ordeals)** If you describe an experience or situation as an **ordeal**, you think it is difficult and unpleasant. ❑ *She described her agonising ordeal.* N-COUNT: usu sing, oft with poss

**order**
① SUBORDINATING CONJUNCTION USES
② COMMANDS AND REQUESTS
③ ARRANGEMENTS, SITUATIONS, AND GROUPINGS

① **or|der** /ɔːʳdəʳ/ ◆◆◇ 1 If you do something **in order to** achieve a particular thing or **in order that** something can happen, you do it because you want to achieve that thing. ❑ *Most schools are extremely unwilling to cut down on staff in order to cut costs.* PHRASE
2 If someone must be in a particular situation **in order to** achieve something they want, they cannot achieve that thing if they are not in that situation. ❑ *They need hostages in order to bargain with the government.* PHRASE
3 If something must happen **in order for** something else to happen, the second thing cannot happen if the first thing does not happen. ❑ *In order for their computers to trace a person's records, they need both the name and address of the individual.* PHRASE: CONJ n to-inf

② **or|der** /ɔːʳdəʳ/ **(orders, ordering, ordered)** ◆◆◆
⇛ Please look at category 12 to see if the expression you are looking for is shown under another headword.
1 If a person in authority **orders** someone **to** do something, they tell them to do it. ❑ *Williams ordered him to leave... He ordered the women out of the car... 'Let him go!' he ordered... 'Go up to your room. Now,' he ordered him.* VERB = command; V n to-inf; V n prep/adv; V with quote; V n with quote
2 If someone in authority **orders** something, they give instructions that it should be done. ❑ *The President has ordered a full investigation... The radio said that the prime minister had ordered price controls to be introduced... He ordered that all party property be confiscated... The President ordered him moved because of fears that his comrades would try to free him.* VERB; V n; V n to-inf; V that; V n -ed
3 If someone in authority gives you an **order**, they tell you to do something. ❑ *The activists were shot when they refused to obey an order to halt... As darkness fell, Clinton gave orders for his men to rest... They were later arrested and executed on the orders of Stalin.* N-COUNT = command, instruction
4 A court **order** is a legal instruction stating that something must be done. ❑ *She has decided not to appeal against a court order banning her from keeping animals... He was placed under a two-year supervision order.* N-COUNT: usu supp N
5 When you **order** something that you are going to pay for, you ask for it to be brought to you, sent to you, or ob- VERB

tained for you. ❑ *Atanas ordered a shrimp cocktail and a salad... The waitress appeared. 'Are you ready to order?'... We ordered him a beer.* [6] An **order** is a request for something to be brought, made, or obtained for you in return for money. ❑ *British Rail are going to place an order for a hundred and eighty-eight trains.* [7] Someone's **order** is what they have asked to be brought, made, or obtained for them in return for money. ❑ *The waiter returned with their order and Graham signed the bill... They can't supply our order.* [8] → See also **holy orders, mail order, postal order, standing order.**

V n
V
V n n
N-COUNT: oft N *for* n
N-COUNT: poss N

**PHRASES** [9] Something that is **on order** at a shop or factory has been asked for but has not yet been supplied. ❑ *The airlines still have 2,500 new aeroplanes on order.* [10] If you do something **to order**, you do it whenever you are asked to do it. ❑ *She now makes wonderful dried flower arrangements to order.* [11] If you are **under orders to** do something, you have been told to do it by someone in authority. ❑ *I am under orders not to discuss his mission or his location with anyone.* [12] your **marching orders** → see **march**. **a tall order** → see **tall**.

PHRASE: PHR after v, v-link PHR
PHRASE: PHR after v
PHRASE: v-link PHR to-inf

♦ **order around**

✔ in BRIT, also use **order about**

If you say that someone **is ordering** you **around** or **is ordering** you **about**, you mean they are telling you what to do as if they have authority over you, and you dislike this. ❑ *Grandmother felt free to order her about just as she wished.*

PHRASAL VERB
V n P
Also V P n (not pron)

③**or|der** /ɔːʳdəʳ/ **(orders, ordering, ordered)** ◆◆◇

⇛ Please look at category 17 to see if the expression you are looking for is shown under another headword. [1] If a set of things are arranged or done **in** a particular **order**, they are arranged or done so one thing follows another, often according to a particular factor such as importance. ❑ *Write down (in order of priority) the qualities you'd like to have... Music shops should arrange their recordings in simple alphabetical order, rather than by category.* [2] **Order** is the situation that exists when everything is in the correct or expected place, or happens at the correct or expected time. ❑ *The wish to impose order upon confusion is a kind of intellectual instinct... Making lists can create order and control.* [3] **Order** is the situation that exists when people obey the law and do not fight or riot. ❑ *Troops were sent to the islands to restore order last November... He has the power to use force to maintain public order.* [4] When people talk about a particular **order**, they mean the way society is organized at a particular time. ❑ *The end of the Cold War has produced the prospect of a new world order based on international co-operation.* [5] The way that something **is ordered** is the way that it is organized and structured. ❑ *...a society which is ordered by hierarchy... We know the French order things differently. ...a carefully ordered system in which everyone has his place.* [6] If you refer to something **of** a particular **order**, you mean something of a particular kind. [FORMAL] ❑ *Another unexpected event, though of quite a different order, occurred one evening in 1973.* [7] A religious **order** is a group of monks or nuns who live according to a particular set of rules. ❑ *...the Benedictine order of monks.* [8] → See also **ordered, law and order, pecking order, point of order.**

N-UNCOUNT: also *a* N, usu with supp, oft *in/into* N
N-UNCOUNT ≠confusion, chaos
N-UNCOUNT
N-SING: with supp
VERB
*be* V-ed
V n
V-ed
N-COUNT: with supp, usu *of* supp N
N-COUNT

**PHRASES** [9] If you put or keep something **in order**, you make sure that it is tidy or properly organized. ❑ *Now he has a chance to put his life back in order... Someone comes in every day to check all is in order.* [10] If you think something is **in order**, you think it should happen or be provided. ❑ *Reforms are clearly in order.* [11] You use **in the order of** or **of the order of** when mentioning an approximate figure. ❑ *They borrowed something in the order of £10 million.* [12] If something is **in good order**, it is in good condition. ❑ *The vessel's safety equipment was not in good order.* [13] A machine or device that is **in working order** is functioning properly and is not broken. ❑ *Only half of the spacecraft's six science instruments are still in working order.* [14] If a particular way of behaving or doing something is **the order of the day**, it is very common. ❑ *These are strange times in which we live, and strange arrangements appear to be the order of the day.* [15] A machine or device that is **out of order** is broken and does not work. ❑ *Their phone's out of order.* [16] If you say that someone or their behaviour is **out of order**, you mean that their behaviour is unacceptable or unfair. [INFORMAL] ❑ *You don't think the paper's a bit out of order in publishing it?* [17] to **put** your **house in order** → see **house**. **order of magnitude** → see **magnitude.**

PHRASE: PHR after v, v-link PHR
PHRASE: v-link PHR
PREP-PHRASE: PREP amount
PHRASE: v-link PHR
PHRASE: v-link PHR
PHRASE: v-link PHR
PHRASE: v-link PHR
PHRASE: v-link PHR

**or|der book** **(order books)** When you talk about the state of a company's **order book** or **order books**, you are talking about how many orders for their goods the company has. [mainly BRIT, BUSINESS] ❑ *He has a full order book for his boat-building yard on the Thames.*

N-COUNT

**or|dered** /ɔːʳdəʳd/ An **ordered** society or system is well-organized and has a clear structure. ❑ *An objective set of rules which we all agree to accept is necessary for any ordered society.*

ADJ: usu ADJ n ≠chaotic

**or|der|ly** /ɔːʳdəʳli/ **(orderlies)** [1] If something is done in an **orderly** fashion or manner, it is done in a well-organized and controlled way. ❑ *The organizers guided them in orderly fashion out of the building... Despite the violence that preceded the elections, reports say that polling was orderly and peaceful.* [2] Something that is **orderly** is neat or arranged in a neat way. ❑ *Their vehicles were parked in orderly rows.* ♦ **or|der|li|ness** *A balance is achieved in the painting between orderliness and unpredictability.* [3] An **orderly** is a person who works in a hospital and does jobs that do not require special medical training.

ADJ ≠chaotic
ADJ
N-UNCOUNT
N-COUNT: oft supp N

**or|di|nal num|ber** /ɔːʳdɪnəl nʌmbəʳ/ **(ordinal numbers)** An **ordinal number** or an **ordinal** is a word such as 'first', 'third', and 'tenth' that tells you where a particular thing occurs in a sequence of things. Compare **cardinal number.**

N-COUNT

**or|di|nance** /ɔːʳdɪnəns/ **(ordinances)** An **ordinance** is an official rule or order. [FORMAL] ❑ *...ordinances that restrict building development.*

N-COUNT = regulation

**or|di|nari|ly** /ɔːʳdɪnərəli, AM -nerɪli/ If you say what is **ordinarily** the case, you are saying what is normally the case. ❑ *The streets would ordinarily have been full of people. There was no one. ...places where the patient does not ordinarily go.*

ADV: usu ADV with cl, also ADV adj, ADV before v = normally

**or|di|nary** /ɔːʳdɪnri, AM -neri/ [1] **Ordinary** people or things are normal and not special or different in any way. ❑ *I strongly suspect that most ordinary people would agree with me... It has 25 calories less than ordinary ice cream... It was just an ordinary weekend for us.* [2] Something that is **out of the ordinary** is unusual or different. ❑ *The boy's knowledge was out of the ordinary... I've noticed nothing out of the ordinary.*

◆◇◇
ADJ: usu ADJ n = normal
PHRASE: usu v-link PHR = unusual

**or|di|nary shares** **Ordinary shares** are shares in a company that are owned by people who have a right to vote at the company's meetings and to receive part of the company's profits after the holders of preference shares have been paid. Compare **preference shares.** [BRIT, BUSINESS]

N-PLURAL = equities

✔ in AM use **common stock**

**or|di|na|tion** /ɔːʳdɪneɪʃən/ **(ordinations)** When someone's **ordination** takes place, they are made a member of the clergy. ❑ *...supporters of the ordination of women.*

N-VAR

**ord|nance** /ɔːʳdnəns/ **Ordnance** refers to military supplies, especially weapons. [FORMAL] ❑ *...a team clearing an area littered with unexploded ordnance.*

N-UNCOUNT

**Ord|nance Sur|vey map** **(Ordnance Survey maps)** An **Ordnance Survey map** is a detailed map produced by the British or Irish government map-making organization.

N-COUNT

**ore** /ɔːʳ/ **(ores) Ore** is rock or earth from which metal can be obtained. ❑ *...a huge iron ore mine.* N-MASS

**orega|no** /ɒrɪgɑːnoʊ, AM əre̲gənoʊ/ **Oregano** is a herb that is used in cooking. N-UNCOUNT

**or|gan** /ɔ̲ːʳgən/ **(organs)** 1 An **organ** is a part of your body that has a particular purpose or function, for example your heart or lungs. ❑ *...damage to the muscles and internal organs. ...the reproductive organs. ...organ transplants.* → See also **sense organ**. N-COUNT 2 An **organ** is a large musical instrument with pipes of different lengths through which air is forced. It has keys and pedals rather like a piano. → See also **barrel organ**, **mouth organ**. N-COUNT 3 You refer to a newspaper or organization as **the organ of** the government or another group when it is used by them as a means of giving information or getting things done. ❑ *The Security Service is an important organ of the State.* N-COUNT: usu with supp = *mouthpiece*

**or|gan|die** /ɔ̲ːʳgəndi/ also **organdy. Organdie** is a thin, slightly stiff cotton fabric. N-UNCOUNT: oft N n

**or̲gan grind|er** **(organ grinders)** also **or̲gan-grinder.** An **organ grinder** was an entertainer who played a barrel organ in the streets. N-COUNT

**or|gan|ic** /ɔːʳgæ̲nɪk/ 1 **Organic** methods of farming and gardening use only natural animal and plant products to help the plants or animals grow and be healthy, rather than using chemicals. ❑ *Organic farming is expanding everywhere. ...organic fruit and vegetables.* ADJ: usu ADJ n ♦ **or|gani|cal|ly** *...organically grown vegetables.* ADV 2 **Organic** substances are of the sort produced by or found in living things. ❑ *Incorporating organic material into chalky soils will reduce the alkalinity.* ADJ: usu ADJ n ≠ *inorganic* 3 **Organic** change or development happens gradually and naturally rather than suddenly. [FORMAL] ❑ *...to manage the company and supervise its organic growth.* ADJ: usu ADJ n 4 If a community or structure is an **organic** whole, each part of it is necessary and fits well with the other parts. [FORMAL] ❑ *City planning treats the city as a unit, as an organic whole.* ADJ: ADJ n

**or|gani|sa|tion** /ɔ̲ːʳgənaɪze̲ɪʃᵊn/ → see **organization**.

**or|gani|sa|tion|al** /ɔ̲ːʳgənaɪze̲ɪʃənᵊl/ → see **organizational**.

**or|gan|ise** /ɔ̲ːʳgənaɪz/ → see **organize**.

**or|gan|is|er** /ɔ̲ːʳgənaɪzəʳ/ → see **organizer**.

**or|gan|ism** /ɔ̲ːʳgənɪzəm/ **(organisms)** An **organism** is an animal or plant, especially one that is so small that you cannot see it without using a microscope. ❑ *...the insect-borne organisms that cause sleeping sickness.* N-COUNT

**or|gan|ist** /ɔ̲ːʳgənɪst/ **(organists)** An **organist** is someone who plays the organ. N-COUNT

**or|gani|za|tion** /ɔ̲ːʳgənaɪze̲ɪʃᵊn/ **(organizations)** ◆◆◇

✔ in BRIT, also use **organisation**

1 An **organization** is an official group of people, for example a political party, a business, a charity, or a club. ❑ *Most of these specialized schools are provided by voluntary organizations. ...a report by the International Labour Organisation.* N-COUNT: oft in names 2 The **organization** of an event or activity involves making all the necessary arrangements for it. ❑ *...the exceptional attention to detail that goes into the organisation of this event... Several projects have been delayed by poor organisation.* N-UNCOUNT 3 The **organization of** something is the way in which its different parts are arranged or relate to each other. ❑ *I am aware that the organization of the book leaves something to be desired.* N-UNCOUNT: usu with supp, oft N *of* n

**or|gani|za|tion|al** /ɔ̲ːʳgənaɪze̲ɪʃənᵊl/

✔ in BRIT, also use **organisational**

1 **Organizational** abilities and methods relate to the way that work, activities, or events are planned and arranged. ❑ *Evelyn's excellent organisational skills were soon spotted by her employers... Because we took the whole class for a complete afternoon session, organisational problems were minimal.* ADJ: ADJ n 2 **Organizational** means relating to the structure of an organization. ❑ *The police now recognise that big organisational changes are needed.* ADJ: ADJ n 3 **Organizational** means relating to organizations, rather than individuals. ❑ *This problem needs to be dealt with at an organizational level.* ADJ: ADJ n

**or|gan|ize** /ɔ̲ːʳgənaɪz/ **(organizes, organizing, organized)** ◆◆◇

✔ in BRIT, also use **organise**

1 If you **organize** an event or activity, you make sure that the necessary arrangements are made. ❑ *In the end, we all decided to organize a concert for Easter. ...a two-day meeting organised by the United Nations... The initial mobilisation was well organised.* VERB V n V n V n 2 If you **organize** something that someone wants or needs, you make sure that it is provided. ❑ *I will organize transport... He rang his wife and asked her to organize coffee and sandwiches.* VERB V n V n 3 If you **organize** a set of things, you arrange them in an ordered way or give them a structure. ❑ *He began to organize his materials. ...the way in which the Army is organised.* VERB V n V n 4 If you **organize** yourself, you plan your work and activities in an ordered, efficient way. ❑ *...changing the way you organize yourself... Go right ahead, I'm sure you don't need me to organize you... Get organised and get going.* VERB V pron-refl V n V-ed 5 If someone **organizes** workers or if workers **organize**, they form a group or society such as a trade union in order to have more power. ❑ *...helping to organize women working abroad... It's the first time farmers have decided to organize. ...organised labour.* VERB V n V V-ed

**or|ga|nized** /ɔ̲ːʳgənaɪzd/ ◆◇◇

✔ in BRIT, also use **organised**

1 An **organized** activity or group involves a number of people doing something together in a structured way, rather than doing it by themselves. ❑ *...organised groups of art thieves. ...organised religion. ...years of steadfast, organized resistance.* ADJ: ADJ n 2 Someone who is **organized** plans their work and activities efficiently. ❑ *These people are very efficient, very organized and excellent time managers.* ADJ ≠ *disorganized*

**-organized** /-ɔːʳgənaɪzd/

✔ in BRIT, also use **-organised**

**-organized** is added to nouns to form adjectives which indicate who organizes something. ❑ *...student-organized seminars.* COMB in ADJ: ADJ n

**or̲|ga|nized cri̲me**

✔ in BRIT, also use **organised crime**

**Organized crime** refers to criminal activities which involve large numbers of people and are organized and controlled by a small group. N-UNCOUNT

**or|gan|iz|er** /ɔ̲ːʳgənaɪzəʳ/ **(organizers)** ◆◇◇

✔ in BRIT, also use **organiser**

The **organizer** of an event or activity is the person who makes sure that the necessary arrangements are made. ❑ *The organisers of the demonstration concede that they hadn't sought permission for it... She was a good organiser.* → See also **personal organizer**. N-COUNT

**or|gano|phos|phate** /ɔːgæ̲noʊfɒ̲sfeɪt/ **(organophosphates) Organophosphates** are chemical substances that are used to make crops grow or protect them from insects. N-COUNT

**or|gan|za** /ɔːʳgæ̲nzə/ **Organza** is a thin, stiff fabric made of silk, cotton, or an artificial fibre. N-UNCOUNT: oft N n

**or|gasm** /ɔ̲ːʳgæzəm/ **(orgasms)** An **orgasm** is the moment of greatest pleasure and excitement in sexual activity. N-VAR

**or|gas|mic** /ɔːʳgæ̲zmɪk/ 1 **Orgasmic** means relating to a sexual orgasm. ❑ *Testosterone does not increase their erectile or orgasmic ability.* ADJ: usu ADJ n 2 Some people refer to things they find extremely enjoyable or exciting as **orgasmic**. [mainly JOURNALISM] ❑ *...jerking the neck of his guitar in orgasmic fits of ecstasy.* ADJ: usu ADJ n

**or|gi|as|tic** /ɔːʳdʒiæstɪk/ An **orgiastic** event is one in which people enjoy themselves in an extreme, uncontrolled way. ❑ *...an orgiastic party.* ADJ: ADJ n

**orgy** /ɔːʳdʒi/ **(orgies)** 1 An **orgy** is a party in which people behave in a very uncontrolled way, especially one involving sexual activity. ❑ *...a drunken orgy.* N-COUNT 2 You can refer to an activity as an **orgy** of that activity to emphasize that it is done to an excessive extent. ❑ *One eye-witness said the rioters were engaged in an orgy of destruction.* N-COUNT: with supp, usu N *of* n [emphasis]

**ori|ent** /ɔːrient/ **(orients, orienting, oriented)** or **orientate** 1 When you **orient yourself to** a new situation or course of action, you learn about it and prepare to deal with it. [FORMAL] ❑ *You will need the time to orient yourself to your new way of eating.* VERB = accustom; V pron-refl *towards/to* n/-ing 2 → See also **oriented**.

**Ori|ent** /ɔːriənt/ The eastern part of Asia is sometimes referred to as **the Orient**. [LITERARY, OLD-FASHIONED] N-PROPER: *the* N = East

**ori|en|tal** /ɔːrientᵊl/ **(orientals)** 1 **Oriental** means coming from or associated with eastern Asia, especially China and Japan. ❑ *There were Oriental carpets on the floors. ...oriental food.* ADJ: usu ADJ n = eastern 2 Some people refer to people from eastern Asia, especially China or Japan as **Orientals**. This use could cause offence. N-COUNT

**Ori|en|tal|ist** /ɔːrientəlɪst/ **(Orientalists)** also **orientalist**. An **Orientalist** is someone from the West who studies the language, culture, history, or customs of countries in eastern Asia. N-COUNT

**ori|en|tate** /ɔːriənteɪt/ → see **orient**.

**ori|en|tat|ed** /ɔːriənteɪtɪd/ → see **oriented**.

**-orientated** /-ɔːriənteɪtɪd/ → see **-oriented**.

**ori|en|ta|tion** /ɔːrienteɪʃᵊn/ **(orientations)** 1 If you talk about the **orientation** of an organization or country, you are talking about the kinds of aims and interests it has. ❑ *...a marketing orientation... To a society which has lost its orientation he has much to offer... The movement is liberal and social democratic in orientation.* N-VAR: with supp = inclination 2 Someone's **orientation** is their basic beliefs or preferences. ❑ *...legislation that would have made discrimination on the basis of sexual orientation illegal.* N-VAR: supp N = inclination 3 **Orientation** is basic information or training that is given to people starting a new job, school, or course. ❑ *...a one-day orientation session.* N-UNCOUNT: oft N n = induction 4 The **orientation** of a structure or object is the direction it faces. ❑ *Farnese had the orientation of the church changed so that the front would face a square.* N-COUNT: usu with poss

**ori|ent|ed** /ɔːrientɪd/ or **orientated** If someone **is oriented towards** or **oriented to** a particular thing or person, they are mainly concerned with that thing or person. ❑ *It seems almost inevitable that North African economies will still be primarily oriented towards Europe... Most students here are oriented to computers.* ADJ: v-link ADJ *towards/to* n

**-oriented** /-ɔːrientɪd/ or **-orientated**. **-oriented** is added to nouns and adverbs to form adjectives which describe what someone or something is mainly interested in or concerned with. ❑ *...a market-oriented economy. ...family oriented holidays.* COMB in ADJ

**ori|ent|eer|ing** /ɔːrientɪərɪŋ/ **Orienteering** is a sport in which people run from one place to another, using a compass and a map to guide them between points that are marked along the route. N-UNCOUNT

**ori|fice** /ɒrɪfɪs, AM ɔːr-/ **(orifices)** An **orifice** is an opening or hole, especially one in your body such as your mouth. [FORMAL] ❑ *After a massive heart attack, he was strapped to a bed, with tubes in every orifice.* N-COUNT

**ori|ga|mi** /ɒrɪgɑːmi, AM ɔːr-/ **Origami** is the craft of folding paper to make models of animals, people, and objects. N-UNCOUNT

**ori|gin** /ɒrɪdʒɪn, AM ɔːr-/ **(origins)** ◆◇◇ 1 You can refer to the beginning, cause, or source of something as its **origin** or **origins**. ❑ *...theories about the origin of life... The disorder in military policy had its origins in Truman's first term... Their medical problems are basically physical in origin... Most of the thickeners are of plant origin.* N-COUNT: usu with poss, also *in/of* N 2 When you talk about a person's **origin** or **origins**, you are referring to the country, race, or social class of their parents or ancestors. ❑ *Thomas has not forgotten his humble origins. ...people of Asian origin... They are forced to return to their country of origin.* N-COUNT: usu poss N, also *of/in* N

**origi|nal** /ərɪdʒɪnᵊl/ **(originals)** ◆◆◇ 1 You use **original** when referring to something that existed at the beginning of a process or activity, or the characteristics that something had when it began or was made. ❑ *The inhabitants have voted overwhelmingly to restore the city's original name of Chemnitz.* ADJ: det ADJ 2 If something such as a document, a work of art, or a piece of writing is an **original**, it is not a copy or a later version. ❑ *When you have filled in the questionnaire, copy it and send the original to your employer... For once the sequel is as good as the original.* N-COUNT 3 An **original** document or work of art is not a copy. ❑ *...an original movie poster.* ADJ: usu ADJ n 4 An **original** piece of writing or music was written recently and has not been published or performed before. ❑ *...its policy of commissioning original work. ...with catchy original songs by Richard Warner.* ADJ: usu ADJ n 5 If you describe someone or their work as **original**, you mean that they are very imaginative and have new ideas. ❑ *It is one of the most original works of imagination in the language. ...an original writer.* ADJ [approval] = innovative ♦ **origi|nal|ity** /ərɪdʒɪnælɪti/ *He was capable of writing things of startling originality.* N-UNCOUNT 6 If you read or sing something **in the original** or, for example, **in the original French**, you read or sing it in the language it was written in, rather than a translation. ❑ *He read every book or author it deals with, often in the original... The texts were sung in the original Italian.* PHRASE: PHR after v

**origi|nal|ly** /ərɪdʒɪnəli/ ◆◇◇ When you say what happened or was the case **originally**, you are saying what happened or was the case when something began or came into existence, often to contrast it with what happened later. ❑ *The plane has been kept in service far longer than originally intended... France originally refused to sign the treaty.* ADV: ADV with v, ADV with cl/group = initially

**origi|nal sin** According to some Christians, **original sin** is the wickedness that all human beings are born with, because the first human beings, Adam and Eve, disobeyed God. N-UNCOUNT

**origi|nate** /ərɪdʒɪneɪt/ **(originates, originating, originated)** When something **originates** or when someone **originates** it, it begins to happen or exist. [FORMAL] ❑ *The disease originated in Africa... I suppose no one has any idea who originated the story?* VERB V prep/adv; V n

**origi|na|tor** /ərɪdʒɪneɪtəʳ/ **(originators)** The **originator** of something such as an idea or scheme is the person who first thought of it or began it. [FORMAL] ❑ *...the originator of the theory of relativity.* N-COUNT: usu with poss

**or|na|ment** /ɔːʳnəmənt/ **(ornaments)** 1 An **ornament** is an attractive object that you display in your home or in your garden. ❑ *...a shelf containing a few photographs and ornaments. ...Christmas tree ornaments.* N-COUNT 2 Decorations and patterns on a building or a piece of furniture can be referred to as **ornament**. [FORMAL] ❑ *...walls of glass overlaid with ornament.* N-UNCOUNT

**or|na|men|tal** /ɔːʳnəmentᵊl/ 1 **Ornamental** things have no practical function but are put in a place because they look attractive. ❑ *...ornamental trees.* ADJ: usu ADJ n = decorative 2 Something that is **ornamental** is attractive and decorative. ❑ *...ornamental plaster mouldings.* ADJ

**or|na|men|ta|tion** /ɔːʳnəmenteɪʃᵊn/ Decorations and patterns can be referred to as **ornamentation**. [FORMAL] ❑ *The chairs were comfortable, functional and free of ornamentation.* N-UNCOUNT = decoration

**or|na|ment|ed** /ɔːʳnəmentɪd/ If something is **ornamented with** attractive objects or patterns, it is decorated with them. ❑ *It had a high ceiling, ornamented with plaster fruits and flowers.* ADJ: oft ADJ *with* n

**or|nate** /ɔːʳneɪt/ An **ornate** building, piece of furniture, or object is decorated with complicated patterns or shapes. ❑ *...an ornate iron staircase.* ♦ **or|nate|ly** *Eventually they reached a pair of ornately carved doors.*
ADJ = *elaborate* ≠ *plain, simple*
ADV: usu ADV -ed = *elaborately*

**or|nery** /ɔːʳnəri/ If you describe someone as **ornery**, you mean that they are bad-tempered, difficult, and often do things that are mean. [AM, INFORMAL] ❑ *The old lady was still being ornery, but at least she had consented to this visit.*
ADJ [disapproval] = *mean*

**or|ni|thol|ogy** /ɔːʳnɪθɒlədʒi/ **Ornithology** is the study of birds. [FORMAL]
N-UNCOUNT
♦ **or|ni|tho|logi|cal** /ɔːʳnɪθəlɒdʒɪkəl/ ❑ *...a member of the Hampshire Ornithological Society.*
ADJ: ADJ n
♦ **or|ni|tholo|gist** **(ornithologists)** *That area is an ornithologist's paradise.*
N-COUNT

**or|phan** /ɔːʳfən/ **(orphans, orphaned)** [1] An **orphan** is a child whose parents are dead. ❑ *...a young orphan girl brought up by peasants.*
N-COUNT
[2] If a child **is orphaned**, their parents die, or their remaining parent dies. ❑ *...a fifteen-year-old boy left orphaned by the recent disaster.*
V-PASSIVE: no cont
V-ed

**or|phan|age** /ɔːʳfənɪdʒ/ **(orphanages)** An **orphanage** is a place where orphans live and are looked after.
N-COUNT

**ortho|don|tist** /ɔːʳθədɒntɪst/ **(orthodontists)** An **orthodontist** is a dentist who corrects the position of people's teeth.
N-COUNT

**ortho|dox** /ɔːʳθədɒks/

> ✔ The spelling **Orthodox** is also used for meaning 3.

[1] **Orthodox** beliefs, methods, or systems are ones which are accepted or used by most people. ❑ *Many of these ideas are now being incorporated into orthodox medical treatment.*
ADJ = *conventional* ≠ *unorthodox*
[2] If you describe someone as **orthodox**, you mean that they hold the older and more traditional ideas of their religion or party. ❑ *...orthodox Jews. ...orthodox communists.*
ADJ: usu ADJ n = *conservative, traditional*
[3] The **Orthodox** churches are Christian churches in Eastern Europe which separated from the western church in the eleventh century. ❑ *...the Greek Orthodox Church.*
ADJ

**ortho|doxy** /ɔːʳθədɒksi/ **(orthodoxies)** [1] An **orthodoxy** is an accepted view about something. ❑ *These ideas rapidly became the new orthodoxy in linguistics... What was once a novel approach had become orthodoxy.*
N-VAR
[2] The old, traditional beliefs of a religion, political party, or philosophy can be referred to as **orthodoxy**. ❑ *...a conflict between Nat's religious orthodoxy and Rube's belief that his mission is to make money.*
N-UNCOUNT: also N in pl

**ortho|paedic** /ɔːʳθəpiːdɪk/ also **ortho-pedic. Orthopaedic** means relating to problems affecting people's joints and spines. [MEDICAL] ❑ *...an orthopaedic surgeon. ...orthopedic shoes.*
ADJ: ADJ n

**os|cil|late** /ɒsɪleɪt/ **(oscillates, oscillating, oscillated)** [1] If an object **oscillates**, it moves repeatedly from one position to another and back again, or keeps getting bigger and smaller. [FORMAL] ❑ *I checked to see if the needle indicating volume was oscillating.*
VERB
V
♦ **os|cil|la|tion** /ɒsɪleɪʃən/ **(oscillations)** *Some oscillation of the fuselage had been noticed on early flights.*
N-VAR
[2] If the level or value of something **oscillates between** one amount and another, it keeps going up and down between the two amounts. [FORMAL] ❑ *Oil markets oscillated on the day's reports from Geneva. ...an oscillating signal of microwave frequency.*
VERB: no passive = *fluctuate*
V
V-ing
♦ **os|cil|la|tion** **(oscillations)** *There have always been slight oscillations in world temperature.*
N-VAR
[3] If you **oscillate between** two moods, attitudes, or types of behaviour, you keep changing from one to the other and back again. [FORMAL] ❑ *The president of the Republic oscillated between a certain audacity and a prudent realism.*
VERB: no passive
V *between* n *and* n
♦ **os|cil|la|tion** *...that perpetual oscillation between despair and distracted joy.*
N-UNCOUNT

**os|mo|sis** /ɒsmoʊsɪs/ [1] **Osmosis** is the process by which a liquid passes through a thin piece of solid substance such as the roots of a plant. [TECHNICAL] ❑ *...the processes of diffusion and osmosis.*
N-UNCOUNT
[2] If you say that people influence each other **by osmosis**, or that skills are gained **by osmosis**, you mean that this is done gradually and without any obvious effort. [FORMAL] ❑ *She allowed her life to be absorbed by his, taking on as if by osmosis his likes and dislikes.*
N-UNCOUNT: usu *by/through* N

**os|si|fy** /ɒsɪfaɪ/ **(ossifies, ossifying, ossified)** If an idea, system, or organization **ossifies** or if something **ossifies** it, it becomes fixed and difficult to change. [FORMAL] ❑ *It reckons that rationing would ossify the farm industry... British society tended to ossify and close ranks as the 1930s drew to their close.*
VERB [disapproval] = *fossilize*
V n
V

**os|ten|sible** /ɒstensɪbəl/ **Ostensible** is used to describe something that seems to be true or is officially stated to be true, but about which you or other people have doubts. [FORMAL] ❑ *The ostensible purpose of these meetings was to gather information on financial strategies.*
ADJ: ADJ n = *alleged*
♦ **os|ten|sibly** /ɒstensɪbli/ *...ostensibly independent organisations.*
ADV: usu ADV with cl/group

**os|ten|ta|tion** /ɒstenteɪʃən/ If you describe someone's behaviour as **ostentation**, you are criticizing them for doing or buying things in order to impress people. [FORMAL] ❑ *On the whole she had lived modestly, with a notable lack of ostentation.*
N-UNCOUNT [disapproval]

**os|ten|ta|tious** /ɒstenteɪʃəs/ [1] If you describe something as **ostentatious**, you disapprove of it because it is expensive and is intended to impress people. [FORMAL] ❑ *...an ostentatious wedding reception.*
ADJ [disapproval]
[2] If you describe someone as **ostentatious**, you disapprove of them because they want to impress people with their wealth or importance. [FORMAL] ❑ *Obviously he had plenty of money and was generous in its use without being ostentatious.*
ADJ [disapproval]
♦ **os|ten|ta|tious|ly** *Her servants were similarly, if less ostentatiously attired.*
ADV
[3] You can describe an action or behaviour as **ostentatious** when it is done in an exaggerated way to attract people's attention. ❑ *His wife was fairly quiet but she is not an ostentatious person anyway.*
ADJ: usu ADJ n
♦ **os|ten|ta|tious|ly** *Harry stopped under a street lamp and ostentatiously began inspecting the contents of his bag.*
ADV: usu ADV with v

**os|teo|path** /ɒstiəpæθ/ **(osteopaths)** An **osteopath** is a person who treats painful conditions or illnesses by pressing and moving parts of the patient's body.
N-COUNT

**os|teo|po|ro|sis** /ɒstioʊpəroʊsɪs/ **Osteoporosis** is a condition in which your bones lose calcium and become more likely to break. [MEDICAL]
N-UNCOUNT

**os|tra|cism** /ɒstrəsɪzəm/ **Ostracism** is the state of being ostracized or the act of ostracizing someone. [FORMAL] ❑ *...those who have decided to risk social ostracism and stay on the wrong side of town. ...denunciation, tougher sanctions and ostracism from the civilised world.*
N-UNCOUNT

**os|tra|cize** /ɒstrəsaɪz/ **(ostracizes, ostracizing, ostracized)**

> ✔ in BRIT, also use **ostracise**

If someone **is ostracized**, people deliberately behave in an unfriendly way towards them and do not allow them to take part in any of their social activities. [FORMAL] ❑ *She claims she's being ostracized by some members of her local community.*
VERB: usu passive
*be* V-ed

**os|trich** /ɒstrɪtʃ, AM ɔːst-/ **(ostriches)** An **ostrich** is a very large African bird that cannot fly.
N-COUNT

**OTC** /oʊ tiː siː/ **OTC** is an abbreviation for **over-the-counter**. ❑ *...the first OTC heartburn drug. ...head of OTC trading at PaineWebber Inc.*
ADJ: ADJ n

**oth|er** /ʌðəʳ/ **(others)** ♦♦♦

> When **other** follows the determiner **an**, it is written as one word: see **another**.

[1] You use **other** to refer to an additional thing or person of the same type as one that has been mentioned or is known about. ❑ *They were just like any other young couple... The communique gave no other details.*
ADJ: det ADJ, ADJ n
♦ **Other** is also a pronoun. ❑ *Four*
PRON

*crewmen were killed, one other was injured... In 1914 he (like so many others) lied about his age so that he could join the war effort.* [2] You use **other** to indicate that a thing or person is not the one already mentioned, but a different one. ❑ *Calls cost 36p per minute cheap rate and 48p per minute at all other times... He would have to accept it; there was no other way.* ♦ **Other** is also a pronoun. ❑ *This issue, more than any other, has divided her cabinet... Some of these methods will work. Others will not.* [3] You use **the other** to refer to the second of two things or people when the identity of the first is already known or understood, or has already been mentioned. ❑ *The Captain was at the other end of the room... Half of PML's scientists have first degrees, the other half have PhDs.* ♦ **The other** is also a pronoun. ❑ *Almost everybody had a cigarette in one hand and a martini in the other.* [4] You use **other** at the end of a list or a group of examples, to refer generally to people or things like the ones just mentioned. ❑ *Queensway Quay will incorporate shops, restaurants and other amenities... Place them in a jam jar, porcelain bowl, or other similar container.* ♦ **Other** is also a pronoun. ❑ *Descartes received his stimulus from the new physics and astronomy of Copernicus, Galileo, and others.* [5] You use **the other** to refer to the rest of the people or things in a group, when you are talking about one particular person or thing. ❑ *When the other pupils were taken to an exhibition, he was left behind.* ♦ **The others** is also a pronoun. ❑ *Aubrey's on his way here, with the others.* [6] **Other** people are people in general, as opposed to yourself or a person you have already mentioned. ❑ *The suffering of other people appals me... She likes to be with other people.* ♦ **Others** means the same as **other people**. ❑ *His humour depended on contempt for others.* [7] You use **other** in informal expressions of time such as **the other day**, **the other evening**, or **the other week** to refer to a day, evening, or week in the recent past. ❑ *I rang her the other day and she said she'd like to come round.*

ADJ: det ADJ, ADJ n
PRON
ADJ: det ADJ
PRON: *the* PRON
ADJ: det ADJ, ADJ n
PRON
ADJ: det ADJ
PRON: *the* PRON
ADJ: ADJ n
PRON
ADJ: *the* ADJ n

**PHRASES** [8] You use expressions like **among other** things or **among others** to indicate that there are several more facts, things, or people like the one or ones mentioned, but that you do not intend to mention them all. ❑ *He moved to England in 1980 where, among other things, he worked as a journalist... His travels took him to Dublin, among other places... He is expected to be supported at the meeting by Dennis Skinner and Tony Benn among others.* [9] If something happens, for example, **every other day** or **every other month**, there is a day or month when it does not happen between each day or month when it happens. ❑ *Their food is adequate. It includes meat at least every other day, vegetables and fruit... Now that their children have grown up she joins Paddy in London every other week.* [10] You use **every other** to emphasize that you are referring to all the rest of the people or things in a group. ❑ *The same will apply in every other country.* [11] You use **none other than** and **no other than** to emphasize the name of a person or thing when something about that person or thing is surprising in a particular situation. ❑ *He called together all his employees and announced that the manager was none other than his son.* [12] You use **nothing other than** and **no other than** when you are going to mention a course of action, decision, or description and emphasize that it is the only one possible in the situation. ❑ *Nothing other than an immediate custodial sentence could be justified... The rebels would not be happy with anything other than the complete removal of the current regime... They have left us with no other choice than to take formal action.* [13] You use **or other** in expressions like **somehow or other** and **someone or other** to indicate that you cannot or do not want to be more precise about the information that you are giving. ❑ *The Foundation is holding a dinner in honour of something or other... Somehow or other he's involved.* [14] You use **other than** after a negative statement to say that the person, item, or thing that follows is the only exception to the statement. ❑ *She makes no reference to any feminist work other than her own.* [15] **each other** → see **each**. **one after the other** → see **one**. **one or other** → see **one**. **this, that and the other** → see **this**. **in other words** → see **word**.

PHRASE: PHR with cl, oft PHR n [vagueness]
PHRASE: usu PHR after v
PHRASE: PHR n [emphasis]
PHRASE: PHR n [emphasis]
PHRASE: PHR n [emphasis]
PHRASE: n/adv PHR [vagueness]
PHRASE: with brd-neg, PHR n/-ing

**oth|er|ness** /ʌðə^r nəs/ **Otherness** is the quality that someone or something has which is different from yourself or from the things that you have experienced. ❑ *I like the otherness of men's minds and bodies.* N-UNCOUNT

**other|wise** /ʌðə^r waɪz/ ◆◆◇ [1] You use **otherwise** after stating a situation or fact, in order to say what the result or consequence would be if this situation or fact was not the case. ❑ *Make a note of the questions you want to ask. You will invariably forget some of them otherwise... I'm lucky that I'm interested in school work, otherwise I'd go mad.* ADV: ADV with cl [2] You use **otherwise** before stating the general condition or quality of something, when you are also mentioning an exception to this general condition or quality. ❑ *The decorations for the games have lent a splash of colour to an otherwise drab city. ...a blue and gold caravan, slightly travel-stained but otherwise in good condition.* ADV: ADV group [3] You use **otherwise** to refer in a general way to actions or situations that are very different from, or the opposite to, your main statement. [WRITTEN] ❑ *Take approximately 60mg up to four times a day, unless advised otherwise by a doctor... All photographs are by the author unless otherwise stated.* ADV: ADV with v [4] You use **otherwise** to indicate that other ways of doing something are possible in addition to the way already mentioned. ❑ *The studio could punish its players by keeping them out of work, and otherwise controlling their lives.* ADV: ADV before v [5] You use **or otherwise** or **and otherwise** to mention something that is not the thing just referred to or is the opposite of that thing. ❑ *It was for the police to assess the validity or otherwise of the evidence... I was feeling really ill, mentally and otherwise.* PHRASE: n/adj PHR

**other|wordly** /ʌðə^r wɜː^r ldli/ also **other-worldly**. **Otherworldly** people, things, and places seem strange or spiritual, and not much connected with ordinary things. ❑ *They encourage an image of the region as an otherworldly sort of place. ...a strange, other-worldly smile.* ADJ: usu ADJ n ≠ *worldly*

**OTT** /oʊ tiː tiː/ If you describe something as **OTT**, you mean that it is exaggerated and extreme. **OTT** is an abbreviation for 'over the top'. [BRIT, INFORMAL] ❑ *...an OTT comedy cabaret revue.* ADJ ≠ *subtle, understated*

**ot|ter** /ɒtə^r/ **(otters)** An **otter** is a small animal with brown fur, short legs, and a long tail. Otters swim well and eat fish. N-COUNT

**ouch** /aʊtʃ/ **'Ouch!'** is used in writing to represent the noise that people make when they suddenly feel pain. ❑ *She was barefoot and stones dug into her feet. 'Ouch, ouch,' she cried.* EXCLAM

**ought** /ɔːt/ ◆◇◇

> ✔ **Ought to** is a phrasal modal verb. It is used with the base form of a verb. The negative form of **ought to** is **ought not to**, which is sometimes shortened to **oughtn't to** in spoken English.

[1] You use **ought to** to mean that it is morally right to do a particular thing or that it is morally right for a particular situation to exist, especially when giving or asking for advice or opinions. ❑ *Mark, you've got a good wife. You ought to take care of her... You ought to be ashamed of yourselves. You've created this problem.* PHRASE = *should* [2] You use **ought to** when saying that you think it is a good idea and important for you or someone else to do a particular thing, especially when giving or asking for advice or opinions. ❑ *You don't have to be alone with him and I don't think you ought to be... You ought to ask a lawyer's advice... We ought not to be* PHRASE = *should*

*quarrelling now.* [3] You use **ought to** to indicate that you expect something to be true or to happen. You use **ought to have** to indicate that you expect something to have happened already. ❑ *'This ought to be fun,' he told Alex, eyes gleaming.* PHRASE = should
[4] You use **ought to** to indicate that you think that something should be the case, but might not be. ❑ *By rights the Social Democrats ought to be the favourites in the election. But nothing looks less certain... Though this gives them a nice feeling, it really ought to worry them.* PHRASE = should
[5] You use **ought to** to indicate that you think that something has happened because of what you know about the situation, but you are not certain. ❑ *He ought to have reached the house some time ago.* PHRASE vagueness = should
[6] You use **ought to have** with a past participle to indicate that something was expected to happen or be the case, but it did not happen or was not the case. ❑ *Basically the system ought to have worked... The money to build the power station ought to have been sufficient.* PHRASE
[7] You use **ought to have** with a past participle to indicate that although it was best or correct for someone to do something in the past, they did not actually do it. ❑ *I realize I ought to have told you about it... Perhaps we ought to have trusted people more... I ought not to have asked you a thing like that. I'm sorry... I'm beginning to feel now we oughtn't to have let her go away like that.* PHRASE
[8] You use **ought to** when politely telling someone that you must do something, for example that you must leave. ❑ *I really ought to be getting back now... I think I ought to go.* PHRASE politeness = should

**oughtn't** /ɔːtᵊnt/ **Oughtn't** is a spoken form of 'ought not'. = shouldn't

**oui|ja board** /wiːdʒə bɔːʳd/ **(ouija boards)** A **ouija board** is a board with the letters of the alphabet written on it. It is used to ask questions which are thought to be answered by the spirits of dead people. N-COUNT

**ounce** /aʊns/ **(ounces)** [1] An **ounce** is a unit of weight used in Britain and the USA. There are sixteen ounces in a pound and one ounce is equal to 28.35 grams. ❑ *...four ounces of sugar.* N-COUNT: num N, oft N *of* n
[2] You can refer to a very small amount of something, such as a quality or characteristic, as an **ounce**. ❑ *If only my father had possessed an ounce of business sense... I spent every ounce of energy trying to hide.* N-SING: usu N *of* n
[3] → See also **fluid ounce**.

**our** /aʊəʳ/ ◆◆◆

> **Our** is the first person plural possessive determiner.

[1] You use **our** to indicate that something belongs or relates both to yourself and to one or more other people. ❑ *We're expecting our first baby... I locked myself out of our apartment and had to break in.* DET
[2] A speaker or writer sometimes uses **our** to indicate that something belongs or relates to people in general. ❑ *We are all entirely responsible for our actions, and for our reactions.* DET

**Our Lady** Some Christians, especially Catholics, refer to Mary, the mother of Jesus Christ, as **Our Lady**. ❑ *Will you pray to Our Lady for me?* N-PROPER

**Our Lord** Christians refer to Jesus Christ as **Our Lord**. ❑ *Let us remember the words of Our Lord from the gospel of Mark.* N-PROPER

**ours** /aʊəʳz/

> **Ours** is the first person plural possessive pronoun.

You use **ours** to refer to something that belongs or relates both to yourself and to one or more other people. ❑ *There are few strangers in a town like ours... Half the houses had been fitted with alarms and ours hadn't.* PRON

**our|self** /aʊəʳself/ **Ourself** is sometimes used instead of 'ourselves' when it clearly refers to a singular subject. Some people consider this use to be incorrect. ❑ *...the way we think of ourself and others.* PRON: v PRON, prep PRON

**our|selves** /aʊəʳselvz/ ◆◇◇

> **Ourselves** is the first person plural reflexive pronoun.

[1] You use **ourselves** to refer to yourself and one or more other people as a group. ❑ *We sat round the fire to keep ourselves warm... It was the first time we admitted to ourselves that we were tired.* PRON: v PRON, prep PRON
[2] A speaker or writer sometimes uses **ourselves** to refer to people in general. **Ourselves** is used as the object of a verb or preposition when the subject refers to the same people. ❑ *We all know that when we exert ourselves our heart rate increases.* PRON: v PRON, prep PRON
[3] You use **ourselves** to emphasize a first person plural subject. In more formal English, **ourselves** is sometimes used instead of 'us' as the object of a verb or preposition, for emphasis. ❑ *Others are feeling just the way we ourselves would feel in the same situation... The people who will suffer won't be people like ourselves.* PRON emphasis
[4] If you say something such as 'We did it **ourselves**', you are indicating that something was done by you and a particular group of other people, rather than anyone else. ❑ *We built that ourselves, we had no help from anyone.* PRON

**oust** /aʊst/ **(ousts, ousting, ousted)** If someone **is ousted** from a position of power, job, or place, they are forced to leave it. [JOURNALISM] ❑ *The leaders have been ousted from power by nationalists... Last week they tried to oust him in a parliamentary vote of no confidence. ...the ousted government.* VERB *be* V-ed V n V-ed
♦ **oust|ing** *The ousting of his predecessor was one of the most dramatic coups the business world had seen in years.* N-UNCOUNT = removal

> **out**
> ① ADVERB USES
> ② ADJECTIVE AND ADVERB USES
> ③ VERB USE
> ④ PREPOSITION USES

**① out** /aʊt/ ◆◆◆

> **Out** is often used with verbs of movement, such as 'walk' and 'pull', and also in phrasal verbs such as 'give out' and 'run out'.

[1] When something is in a particular place and you take it **out**, you remove it from that place. ❑ *Carefully pull out the centre pages... He took out his notebook and flipped the pages... They paid in that cheque a couple of days ago, and drew out around two thousand in cash.* ADV: ADV after v
[2] You can use **out** to indicate that you are talking about the situation outside, rather than inside buildings. ❑ *It's hot out – very hot, very humid.* ADV: ADV after v = outside
[3] If you are **out**, you are not at home or not at your usual place of work. ❑ *I tried to get in touch with you yesterday evening, but I think you were out... She had to go out.* ADV: *be* ADV, ADV after v
[4] If you say that someone is **out** in a particular place, you mean that they are in a different place, usually one far away. ❑ *The police tell me they've finished their investigations out there... Rosie's husband was now out East.* ADV: ADV adv/prep
[5] When the sea or tide goes **out**, the sea moves away from the shore. ❑ *The tide was out and they walked among the rock pools.* ADV: *be* ADV, ADV after v ≠ in
[6] If you are **out** a particular amount of money, you have that amount less than you should or than you did. [mainly AM] ❑ *Me and my friends are out ten thousand dollars, with nothing to show for it!* ADV: ADV n

**② out** /aʊt/ ◆◆◆ [1] If a light or fire is **out** or goes **out**, it is no longer shining or burning. ❑ *All the lights were out in the house... Several of the lights went out, one after another.* ADJ: v-link ADJ
[2] If flowers are **out**, their petals have opened. ❑ *Well, the daffodils are out in the gardens and they're always a beautiful show.* ADJ: v-link ADJ
♦ **Out** is also an adverb. ❑ *I usually put it in my diary when I see the wild flowers coming out.* ADV: ADV after v
[3] If something such as a book or CD is **out**, it is available for people to buy. ❑ *...cover versions of 40 British Number Ones – out now.* ADJ: v-link ADJ
♦ **Out** is also an adverb. ❑ *The French edition came out in early 1992.* ADV: ADV after v
[4] If workers are **out**, they are on strike. [INFORMAL] ❑ *We've been out for two and a half months and* ADJ: v-link ADJ = on strike

*we're not going back until we get what we're asking for.* ♦ **Out** is also an adverb. ❑ *In June last year, 26 people came out on strike protesting against a compulsory 65-hour week.* ADV: ADV after v [5] In a game or sport, if someone is **out**, they can no longer take part either because they are unable to or because they have been defeated. ADJ: v-link ADJ [6] In baseball, a player is **out** if they do not reach a base safely. When three players in a team are out in an inning, then the team is **out**. ADJ: usu v-link ADJ [7] If you say that a proposal or suggestion is **out**, you mean that it is unacceptable. ❑ *That's right out, I'm afraid.* ADJ: v-link ADJ [8] If you say that a particular thing is **out**, you mean that it is no longer fashionable at the present time. ❑ *Romance is making a comeback. Reality is out.* ADJ: v-link ADJ ≠ in [9] If you say that a calculation or measurement is **out**, you mean that it is incorrect. ❑ *When the two ends of the tunnel met in the middle they were only a few inches out.* ADJ: v-link ADJ, oft amount ADJ [10] If someone is **out** to do something, they intend to do it. [INFORMAL] ❑ *Most companies these days are just out to make a quick profit.* ADJ: v-link ADJ to-inf

③ **out** /aʊt/ **(outs, outing, outed)** If a group of people **out** a public figure or famous person, they reveal that person's homosexuality against their wishes. VERB ❑ *The New York gay action group 'Queer Nation' recently outed an American Congressman.* V n ♦ **out|ing** *The gay and lesbian rights group, Stonewall, sees outing as completely unhelpful.* N-UNCOUNT

④ **out** ♦♦♦

> **Out of** is used with verbs of movement, such as 'walk' and 'pull', and also in phrasal verbs such as 'do out of' and 'grow out of'. In American English and informal British English, **out** is often used instead of **out of**.

[1] If you go **out of** a place, you leave it. ❑ *She let him out of the house.* PREP-PHRASE ≠ into [2] If you take something **out of** the container or place where it has been, you remove it so that it is no longer there. ❑ *I always took my key out of my bag and put it in my pocket.* PREP-PHRASE [3] If you look or shout **out of** a window, you look or shout away from the room where you are towards the outside. ❑ *He went on staring out of the window... He looked out the window at the car on the street below.* PREP-PHRASE [4] If you are **out of** the sun, the rain, or the wind, you are sheltered from it. ❑ *People can keep out of the sun to avoid skin cancer.* PREP-PHRASE [5] If someone or something gets **out of** a situation, especially an unpleasant one, they are then no longer in it. If they keep **out of** it, they do not start being in it. ❑ *In the past army troops have relied heavily on air support to get them out of trouble... The economy is starting to climb out of recession.* PREP-PHRASE [6] You can use **out of** to say that someone leaves an institution. ❑ *You come out of university and find there are no jobs available... Doctors should be able to decide who they can safely let out of hospital early.* PREP-PHRASE [7] If you are **out of** range of something, you are beyond the limits of that range. ❑ *Shaun was in the bedroom, out of earshot, watching television... He turned to look back, but by then she was out of sight.* PREP-PHRASE [8] You use **out of** to say what feeling or reason causes someone to do something. For example, if you do something **out of** pity, you do it because you pity someone. ❑ *He took up office out of a sense of duty.* PREP-PHRASE [9] If you get something such as information or work **out of** someone, you manage to make them give it to you, usually when they are unwilling to give it. ❑ *'Where is she being held prisoner?' I asked. 'Did you get it out of him?'... We knew we could get better work out of them.* PREP-PHRASE [10] If you get pleasure or an advantage **out of** something, you get it as a result of being involved with that thing or making use of it. ❑ *We all had a lot of fun out of him... To get the most out of your money, you have to invest.* PREP-PHRASE = from [11] If you are **out of** something, you no longer have any of it. ❑ *I can't find the sugar – and we're out of milk.* PREP-PHRASE [12] If something is made **out of** a particular material, it consists of that material because it has been formed or constructed from it. ❑ *Would you advise people to make a building out of wood or stone?* PREP-PHRASE = from [13] You use **out of** to indicate what proportion of a group of things something is true of. For example, if something is true of one **out of** five things, it is true of one fifth of all things of that kind. ❑ *Two out of five thought the business would be sold privately on their retirement.* PREP-PHRASE: num PREP num = in

**out-** /aʊt-/ You can use **out-** to form verbs that describe an action as being done better by one person than by another. For example, if you can outswim someone, you can swim further or faster than they can. ❑ *European investors may outspend the Japanese this year. ...a younger brother who always outperformed him.* PREFIX

**out|age** /aʊtɪdʒ/ **(outages)** An **outage** is a period of time when the electricity supply to a building or area is interrupted, for example because of damage to the cables. [AM] ❑ *A windstorm in Washington is causing power outages throughout the region.* N-COUNT

> ☑ in BRIT, use **power cut**

**out-and-out** You use **out-and-out** to emphasize that someone or something has all the characteristics of a particular type of person or thing. ❑ *Much of what has been written about us is out-and-out lies.* ADJ: ADJ n [emphasis] = complete, utter

**out|back** /aʊtbæk/ The parts of Australia that are far away from towns are referred to as **the outback**. N-SING: the N

**out|bid** /aʊtbɪd/ **(outbids, outbidding)**

> ☑ The form **outbid** is used in the present tense and is the past tense and past participle.

If you **outbid** someone, you offer more money than they do for something that you both want to buy. VERB ❑ *The Museum has antagonised rivals by outbidding them for the world's greatest art treasures.* V n

**out|board** /aʊtbɔːʳd/ An **outboard** motor is one that you can fix to the back of a small boat. ADJ: ADJ n

**out|bound** /aʊtbaʊnd/ An **outbound** flight is one that is leaving or about to leave a particular place. ADJ: usu ADJ n

**out|break** /aʊtbreɪk/ **(outbreaks)** If there is an **outbreak of** something unpleasant, such as violence or a disease, it suddenly starts to happen. ❑ *...the outbreak of war in the Middle East... In Peru, a cholera outbreak continues to spread.* N-COUNT: usu sing, usu with supp

**out|build|ing** /aʊtbɪldɪŋ/ **(outbuildings)** **Outbuildings** are small buildings for keeping things in or working in which are near a house, on the land belonging to it. N-COUNT: usu pl

**out|burst** /aʊtbɜːʳst/ **(outbursts)** [1] An **outburst** of an emotion, especially anger, is a sudden strong expression of that emotion. ❑ *...a spontaneous outburst of cheers and applause... There has been another angry outburst against the new local tax introduced today.* N-COUNT: usu with supp, oft N *of* n [2] An **outburst of** violent activity is a sudden period of this activity. ❑ *Five people were reported killed today in a fresh outburst of violence. ...this first great outburst of nationalist student protest.* N-COUNT: usu N *of* n = eruption

**out|cast** /aʊtkɑːst, -kæst/ **(outcasts)** An **outcast** is someone who is not accepted by a group of people or by society. ❑ *He had always been an outcast, unwanted and alone.* N-COUNT

**out|class** /aʊtklɑːs, -klæs/ **(outclasses, outclassing, outclassed)** [1] If you **are outclassed** by someone, they are a lot better than you are at a particular activity. VERB ❑ *Mason was outclassed by Lennox Lewis in his tragic last fight at Wembley...* *be* V-ed *Few city hotels can outclass the Hotel de Crillon.* V n [2] If one thing **outclasses** another thing, the first thing is of a much higher quality than the second thing. VERB ❑ *These planes are outclassed by the most recent designs from the former Soviet Union...* *be* V-ed *The story outclasses anything written by Frederick Forsyth.* V n

**out|come** /aʊtkʌm/ **(outcomes)** The **outcome** of an activity, process, or situation is the situation that exists at the end of it. ❑ *Mr. Singh* ♦◇◇ N-COUNT: usu sing, oft *the* N *of* n *said he was pleased with the outcome... It's too early to know the outcome of her illness.*

**out|crop** /aʊtkrɒp/ **(outcrops)** or **outcropping** An **outcrop** is a large area of rock sticking out of the ground. ❑ *...an outcrop of rugged granite.* N-COUNT: usu with supp, oft N *of* n

**out|cry** /aʊtkraɪ/ **(outcries)** An **outcry** is a reaction of strong disapproval and anger shown by the public or media about a recent event. ❑ *The killing caused an international outcry.* N-VAR: usu with supp

**out|dat|ed** /aʊtdeɪtɪd/ If you describe something as **outdated**, you mean that you think it is old-fashioned and no longer useful or relevant to modern life. ❑ *...outdated and inefficient factories... Caryl Churchill's play about Romania is already outdated.* ADJ

**out|did** /aʊtdɪd/ **Outdid** is the past tense of **outdo**.

**out|dis|tance** /aʊtdɪstəns/ **(outdistances, outdistancing, outdistanced)** [1] If you **outdistance** someone, you are a lot better and more successful than they are at a particular activity over a period of time. ❑ *It didn't matter that Ingrid had outdistanced them as a movie star.* VERB = outdo; V n [2] If you **outdistance** your opponents in a contest of some kind, you beat them easily. ❑ *...a millionaire businessman who easily outdistanced his major rivals for the nomination.* VERB = outstrip; V n

**out|do** /aʊtduː/ **(outdoes, outdoing, outdid, outdone)** [1] If you **outdo** someone, you are a lot more successful than they are at a particular activity. ❑ *Both sides have tried to outdo each other to show how tough they can be.* VERB; V n [2] You use **not to be outdone** to introduce an action which someone takes in response to a previous action. ❑ *She wore a lovely tiara but the groom, not to be outdone, had on a very smart embroidered waistcoat.* PHRASE: PHR with cl

**out|door** /aʊtdɔːʳ/ **Outdoor** activities or things happen or are used outside and not in a building. ❑ *If you enjoy outdoor activities, this is the trip for you... There were outdoor cafes on almost every block.* ADJ: ADJ n ≠ indoor

**out|doors** /aʊtdɔːʳz/ [1] If something happens **outdoors**, it happens outside in the fresh air rather than in a building. ❑ *It was warm enough to be outdoors all afternoon... The ceremony was being held outdoors.* ADV: *be* ADV, ADV after v ≠ indoors [2] You refer to **the outdoors** when talking about work or leisure activities which take place outside away from buildings. ❑ *I'm a lover of the outdoors... Life in the great outdoors isn't supposed to be luxurious.* N-SING: *the* N

**out|er** /aʊtəʳ/ The **outer** parts of something are the parts which contain or enclose the other parts, and which are furthest from the centre. ❑ *He heard a voice in the outer room. ...the outer suburbs of the city.* ADJ: ADJ n ≠ inner

**outer|most** /aʊtəʳmoʊst/ The **outermost** thing in a group is the one that is furthest from the centre. ❑ *...Pluto, the outermost known planet.* ADJ: ADJ n ≠ innermost

**out|er space** **Outer space** is the area outside the earth's atmosphere where the other planets and stars are situated. ❑ *In 1957, the Soviets launched Sputnik 1 into outer space.* N-UNCOUNT

**outer|wear** /aʊtəʳweəʳ/ **Outerwear** is clothing that is not worn underneath other clothing. ❑ *The latest in sports bras are colorful tops designed as outerwear.* N-UNCOUNT

**out|fall** /aʊtfɔːl/ **(outfalls)** An **outfall** is a place where water or waste flows out of a drain, often into the sea. ❑ *During the winter months, great flocks of gulls gather at rubbish tips and sewage outfalls.* N-COUNT

**out|field** /aʊtfiːld/ In baseball and cricket, **the outfield** is the part of the field that is furthest from the batting area. N-SING: *the* N

**out|field|er** /aʊtfiːldəʳ/ **(outfielders)** In baseball and cricket, the **outfielders** are the players in the part of the field that is furthest from the batting area. N-COUNT

**out|fit** /aʊtfɪt/ **(outfits, outfitting, outfitted)** [1] An **outfit** is a set of clothes. ❑ *She was wearing an outfit she'd bought the previous day.* N-COUNT [2] You can refer to an organization as an **outfit**. ❑ *He works for a private security outfit.* N-COUNT: oft supp N [3] To **outfit** someone or something means to provide them with equipment for a particular purpose. [mainly AM] ❑ *They outfitted him with artificial legs.* VERB = fit out; V n *with/as* n

**out|fit|ter** /aʊtfɪtəʳ/ **(outfitters)** also **outfitters.** An **outfitter** or an **outfitters** is a shop that sells clothes and equipment for a specific purpose. [mainly BRIT] ❑ *...J. Hepworth, the men's outfitter. ...a sports outfitters.* N-COUNT: oft supp N

**out|flank** /aʊtflæŋk/ **(outflanks, outflanking, outflanked)** [1] In a battle, when one group of soldiers **outflanks** another, it succeeds in moving past the other group in order to be able to attack it from the side. ❑ *...plans designed by General Schwarzkopf to outflank them from the west.* VERB; V n [2] If you **outflank** someone, you succeed in getting into a position where you can defeat them, for example in an argument. ❑ *He had tried to outflank them.* VERB; V n

**out|flow** /aʊtfloʊ/ **(outflows)** When there is an **outflow of** money or people, a large amount of money or people move from one place to another. ❑ *There was a net outflow of about £650m in short-term capital. ...an increasing outflow of refugees.* N-COUNT: usu N *of* n

**out|fox** /aʊtfɒks/ **(outfoxes, outfoxing, outfoxed)** If you **outfox** someone, you defeat them in some way because you are cleverer than they are. ❑ *There is no greater thrill than to bluff a man, trap him and outfox him.* VERB = outwit, outsmart; V n

**out|going** /aʊtgoʊɪŋ/ [1] You use **outgoing** to describe a person in charge of something who is soon going to leave that position. ❑ *...the outgoing director of the Edinburgh International Festival.* ADJ: ADJ n [2] **Outgoing** things such as planes, mail, and passengers are leaving or being sent somewhere. ❑ *All outgoing flights were grounded.* ADJ: ADJ n ≠ incoming [3] Someone who is **outgoing** is very friendly and likes meeting and talking to people. ADJ = extrovert

**out|go|ings** /aʊtgoʊɪŋz/ Your **outgoings** are the regular amounts of money which you have to spend every week or every month, for example in order to pay your rent or bills. [BRIT] ❑ *She suggests you first assess your income and outgoings. ...monthly outgoings.* N-PLURAL

✔ in AM, usually use **outlay, expenses**

**out|grow** /aʊtgroʊ/ **(outgrows, outgrowing, outgrew, outgrown)** [1] If a child **outgrows** a piece of clothing, they grow bigger, so that it no longer fits them. ❑ *She outgrew her clothes so rapidly that Patsy was always having to buy new ones.* VERB = grow out of; V n [2] If you **outgrow** a particular way of behaving or thinking, you change and become more mature, so that you no longer behave or think in that way. ❑ *The girl may or may not outgrow her interest in fashion.* VERB = grow out of; V n

**out|growth** /aʊtgroʊθ/ **(outgrowths)** Something that is an **outgrowth of** another thing has developed naturally as a result of it. ❑ *Her first book is an outgrowth of an art project she began in 1988.* N-COUNT: usu N *of* n

**out|guess** /aʊtges/ **(outguesses, outguessing, outguessed)** If you **outguess** someone, you try to predict what they are going to do in order to gain some advantage. ❑ *Only by being him can you hope to out-guess him... A very good investor will outguess the market.* VERB; V n; V n

**out|gun** /aʊtgʌn/ **(outguns, outgunning, outgunned)** [1] In a battle, if one army **is outgunned**, they are in a very weak position because the opposing army has more or better weapons. ❑ *First Airborne Division was heavily outgunned by German forces.* VERB: usu passive; *be* V-ed [2] If you **are outgunned** in a contest, you are beaten because your rival is stronger or better than you. ❑ *Clearly, the BBC is being outgunned by ITV's original drama... He soon hit top speed to outgun all his rivals in the opening qualifying session.* VERB; *be* V-ed; V n

**out|house** /aʊthaʊs/ **(outhouses)** 1 An **outhouse** is a small building attached to a house or very close to the house, used, for example, for storing things in. N-COUNT 2 An **outhouse** is an outside toilet. [AM] N-COUNT

**out|ing** /aʊtɪŋ/ **(outings)** 1 An **outing** is a short enjoyable trip, usually with a group of people, away from your home, school, or place of work. ❑ *One evening, she made a rare outing to the local discotheque. ...families on a Sunday afternoon outing.* N-COUNT 2 In sport, an **outing** is an occasion when a player competes in a particular contest or competition. ❑ *Playing against Zebre in England's first outing, he suffered a whiplash injury to his neck.* N-COUNT 3 ➔ See also **out 3**.

**out|land|ish** /aʊtlændɪʃ/ If you describe something as **outlandish**, you disapprove of it because you think it is very unusual, strange, or unreasonable. ❑ *This idea is not as outlandish as it sounds.* ADJ disapproval = bizarre

**out|last** /aʊtlɑːst, -læst/ **(outlasts, outlasting, outlasted)** If one thing **outlasts** another thing, the first thing lives or exists longer than the second. ❑ *These naturally dried flowers will outlast a bouquet of fresh blooms.* VERB: no passive V n

**out|law** /aʊtlɔː/ **(outlaws, outlawing, outlawed)** 1 When something **is outlawed**, it is made illegal. ❑ *In 1975 gambling was outlawed... The German government has outlawed some fascist groups. ...the outlawed political parties.* VERB = ban be V-ed V n V-ed 2 An **outlaw** is a criminal who is hiding from the authorities. [OLD-FASHIONED] N-COUNT

**out|lay** /aʊtleɪ/ **(outlays)** **Outlay** is the amount of money that you have to spend in order to buy something or start a project. ❑ *Apart from the capital outlay of buying the machine, dishwashers can actually save you money.* N-VAR: usu with supp

**out|let** /aʊtlet/ **(outlets)** 1 An **outlet** is a shop or organization which sells the goods made by a particular manufacturer. ❑ *...the largest retail outlet in the city.* N-COUNT: usu supp N 2 An **outlet** or an **outlet store** is a place which sells slightly damaged or outdated goods from a particular manufacturer, or goods that it made in greater quantities than needed. ❑ *...the factory outlet store in Belmont.* N-COUNT: also N n 3 If someone has an **outlet for** their feelings or ideas, they have a means of expressing and releasing them. ❑ *Her father had found an outlet for his ambition in his work.* N-COUNT: oft N *for* n = channel 4 An **outlet** is a hole or pipe through which liquid or air can flow away. ❑ *...a warm air outlet.* N-COUNT 5 An **outlet** is a place, usually in a wall, where you can connect electrical devices to the electricity supply. [mainly AM] N-COUNT

✔ in BRIT, usually use **socket**

**out|line** /aʊtlaɪn/ **(outlines, outlining, outlined)** ◆◇◇ 1 If you **outline** an idea or a plan, you explain it in a general way. ❑ *The mayor outlined his plan to clean up the town's image.* VERB V n 2 An **outline** is a general explanation or description of something. ❑ *Following is an outline of the survey findings... The proposals were given in outline by the Secretary of State.* N-COUNT: also *in* N 3 You say that an object **is outlined** when you can see its general shape because there is light behind it. ❑ *The Ritz was outlined against the lights up there.* V-PASSIVE be V-ed 4 The **outline** of something is its general shape, especially when it cannot be clearly seen. ❑ *He could see only the hazy outline of the goalposts.* N-COUNT: usu N *of* n

**out|live** /aʊtlɪv/ **(outlives, outliving, outlived)** If one person **outlives** another, they are still alive after the second person has died. If one thing **outlives** another thing, the first thing continues to exist after the second has disappeared or been replaced. ❑ *I'm sure Rose will outlive many of us... The UN is an organisation which has long since outlived its usefulness.* VERB V n V n

**out|look** /aʊtlʊk/ **(outlooks)** 1 Your **outlook** is your general attitude towards life. ❑ *I adopted a positive outlook on life... We were quite different in outlook, Philip and I.* N-COUNT: usu sing, with supp, also *in* N 2 The **outlook** for something is what people think will happen in relation to it. ❑ *The economic outlook is one of rising unemployment.* N-SING: oft supp N = prospect

**out|ly|ing** /aʊtlaɪɪŋ/ **Outlying** places are far away from the main cities of a country. ❑ *Tourists can visit outlying areas like the Napa Valley Wine Country.* ADJ: ADJ n = remote

**out|ma|noeu|vre** /aʊtmənuːvəʳ/ **(outmanoeuvres, outmanoeuvring, outmanoeuvred)**

✔ in AM, use **outmaneuver**

If you **outmanoeuvre** someone, you gain an advantage over them in a particular situation by behaving in a clever and skilful way. ❑ *He has shown once again that he's able to outmanoeuvre the military.* VERB V n

**out|mod|ed** /aʊtmoʊdɪd/ If you describe something as **outmoded**, you mean that you think it is old-fashioned and no longer useful or relevant to modern life. ❑ *Romania badly needs aid to modernise its outmoded industries... The political system has become thoroughly outmoded.* ADJ = outdated

**out|num|ber** /aʊtnʌmbəʳ/ **(outnumbers, outnumbering, outnumbered)** If one group of people or things **outnumbers** another, the first group has more people or things in it than the second group. ❑ *...a town where men outnumber women four to one.* VERB V n

**out of** ➔ see **out 4**.

**out-of-body** An **out-of-body** experience is one in which you feel as if you are outside your own body, watching it and what is going on around it. ADJ: ADJ n

**out of date** also **out-of-date.** Something that is **out of date** is old-fashioned and no longer useful. ❑ *Think how rapidly medical knowledge has gone out of date in recent years.* ADJ

**out of doors** also **out-of-doors.** If you are **out of doors**, you are outside a building rather than inside it. ❑ *Sometimes we eat out of doors.* ADV: *be* ADV, ADV after v = outdoors ≠ indoors

**out-of-pocket** **Out-of-pocket** expenses are those which you pay out of your own money on behalf of someone else, and which are often paid back to you later. ➔ See also **pocket**. ADJ: ADJ n

**out-of-the-way** also **out of the way.** **Out-of-the-way** places are difficult to reach and are therefore not often visited. ❑ *...an out-of-the-way spot.* ADJ = remote

**out of touch** 1 Someone who is **out of touch with** a situation is not aware of recent changes in it. ❑ *Washington politicians are out of touch with the American people.* ADJ: v-link ADJ, oft ADJ *with* n 2 If you are **out of touch** with someone, you have not been in contact with them recently and are not familiar with their present situation. ❑ *James wasn't invited. We've been out of touch for years.* ADJ: v-link ADJ, oft ADJ *with* n

**out-of-town** 1 **Out-of-town** shops or facilities are situated away from the centre of a town or city. ❑ *...shopping at cheaper, out-of-town supermarkets.* ADJ: ADJ n 2 **Out-of-town** is used to describe people who do not live in a particular town or city, but have travelled there for a particular purpose. ❑ *...a deluxe hotel for out-of-town visitors.* ADJ: ADJ n

**out of work** Someone who is **out of work** does not have a job. ❑ *...a town where half the men are usually out of work. ...an out of work actor.* ADJ = unemployed

**out|pace** /aʊtpeɪs/ **(outpaces, outpacing, outpaced)** To **outpace** someone or something means to perform a particular action faster or better than they can. ❑ *These hovercraft can easily outpace most boats... The Japanese economy will continue to outpace its foreign rivals for years to come.* VERB V n V n

**out|pa|tient** /aʊtpeɪʃənt/ **(outpatients)** also **out-patient.** An **outpatient** is someone who receives treatment at a hospital but does not spend the night there. ❑ *...the outpatient clinic... She received psychiatric care as an outpatient.* N-COUNT: oft N n

**out|per|form** /aʊtpəʳfɔːʳm/ **(outperforms, outperforming, outperformed)** If one thing **outperforms** another, the first is more successful or efficient than the second. [JOURNALISM] ❑ *In recent* VERB V n *years the Austrian economy has outperformed most other industrial economies.*

**out|place|ment** /aʊtpleɪsmənt/ An **outplacement** agency gives advice to managers and other professional people who have recently become unemployed, and helps them find new jobs. [BUSINESS] — N-UNCOUNT: usu N n

**out|play** /aʊtpleɪ/ **(outplays, outplaying, outplayed)** In sports, if one person or team **outplays** an opposing person or team, they play much better than their opponents. ❑ *He was outplayed by the Swedish 21-year-old.* — VERB; V n

**out|point** /aʊtpɔɪnt/ **(outpoints, outpointing, outpointed)** In boxing, if one boxer **outpoints** another, they win the match by getting more points then their opponent. ❑ *Kane won the world title in 1938 when he outpointed Jackie Durich.* — VERB; V n

**out|post** /aʊtpoʊst/ **(outposts)** An **outpost** is a small group of buildings used for trading or military purposes, either in a distant part of your own country or in a foreign country. ❑ *...a remote mountain outpost, linked to the outside world by the poorest of roads.* — N-COUNT: usu with supp, oft supp N, N *of* n

**out|pour|ing** /aʊtpɔːrɪŋ/ **(outpourings)** An **outpouring of** something such as an emotion or a reaction is the expression of it in an uncontrolled way. ❑ *The news of his death produced an instant outpouring of grief.* — N-COUNT: usu sing, usu N *of* n

**out|put** /aʊtpʊt/ **(outputs)** ◆◇◇ 1 **Output** is used to refer to the amount of something that a person or thing produces. ❑ *Government statistics show the largest drop in industrial output for ten years.* — N-VAR: usu supp N 2 The **output** of a computer or word processor is the information that it displays on a screen or prints on paper as a result of a particular program. ❑ *You run the software, you look at the output, you make modifications.* — N-VAR

**out|rage** **(outrages, outraging, outraged)**

> ✔ The verb is pronounced /aʊtreɪdʒ/. The noun is pronounced /aʊtreɪdʒ/.

1 If you **are outraged** by something, it makes you extremely shocked and angry. ❑ *Many people have been outraged by some of the things that have been said... Reports of torture and mass executions in Serbia's detention camps have outraged the world's religious leaders.* — VERB: *be* V-ed, V n ♦ **out|raged** *He is truly outraged about what's happened to him.* — ADJ: oft ADJ *at/about* n 2 **Outrage** is an intense feeling of anger and shock. ❑ *The decision provoked outrage from women and human rights groups.* — N-UNCOUNT: usu with supp 3 You can refer to an act or event which you find very shocking as an **outrage**. ❑ *The latest outrage was to have been a co-ordinated gun and bomb attack on the station.* — N-COUNT

**out|ra|geous** /aʊtreɪdʒəs/ If you describe something as **outrageous**, you are emphasizing that it is unacceptable or very shocking. ❑ *I must apologise for my outrageous behaviour... Charges for local telephone calls are particularly outrageous.* — ADJ [emphasis] ♦ **out|ra|geous|ly** *Car-parks are few, crammed, and outrageously expensive.* — ADV: usu ADV adj

**out|ran** /aʊtræn/ **Outran** is the past tense of **outrun**.

**out|rank** /aʊtræŋk/ **(outranks, outranking, outranked)** If one person **outranks** another person, he or she has a higher position or grade within an organization than the other person. ❑ *The most junior executive officer outranked the senior engineer officer aboard ship.* — VERB; V n

**outré** /uːtreɪ, AM uːtreɪ/ Something that is **outré** is very unusual and strange. [FORMAL] ❑ *...outré outfits designed by students at the Royal College of Art.* — ADJ

**out|reach** /aʊtriːtʃ/ **Outreach** programmes and schemes try to find people who need help or advice rather than waiting for those people to come and ask for help. ❑ *Their brief is to undertake outreach work aimed at young African Caribbeans on the estate.* — N-UNCOUNT: usu N n

**out|rid|er** /aʊtraɪdəʳ/ **(outriders) Outriders** are people such as policemen who ride on motorcycles or horses beside or in front of an official vehicle, in order to protect the people in the vehicle. ❑ *...a black Mercedes with motorcycle outriders provided by the city's police.* — N-COUNT: usu n N

**out|right**

> ✔ The adjective is pronounced /aʊtraɪt/. The adverb is pronounced /aʊtraɪt/.

1 You use **outright** to describe behaviour and actions that are open and direct, rather than indirect. ❑ *Kawaguchi finally resorted to an outright lie. ...outright condemnation.* — ADJ: ADJ n ♦ **Outright** is also an adverb. ❑ *Why are you so mysterious? Why don't you tell me outright?* — ADV: ADV after v 2 **Outright** means complete and total. ❑ *She had failed to win an outright victory... The response of the audience varied from outright rejection to warm hospitality.* — ADJ: ADJ n = absolute ♦ **Outright** is also an adverb. ❑ *The peace plan wasn't rejected outright.* — ADV: ADV after v ● If someone **is killed outright**, they die immediately, for example in an accident. ❑ *My driver was killed outright.* — PHRASE: V inflects

**out|run** /aʊtrʌn/ **(outruns, outrunning, outran)**

> ✔ The form **outrun** is used in the present tense and is also the past participle of the verb.

1 If you **outrun** someone, you run faster than they do, and therefore are able to escape from them or to arrive somewhere before they do. ❑ *There are not many players who can outrun me.* — VERB; V n 2 If one thing **outruns** another thing, the first thing develops faster than the second thing. ❑ *Spending could outrun the capacity of businesses to produce the goods.* — VERB = exceed, outstrip; V n

**out|sell** /aʊtsel/ **(outsells, outselling, outsold)** If one product **outsells** another product, the first product is sold more quickly or in larger quantities than the second. [BUSINESS] ❑ *Armani consistently outsells all other European designers.* — VERB; V n

**out|set** /aʊtset/ If something happens **at the outset** of an event, process, or period of time, it happens at the beginning of it. If something happens **from the outset** it happens from the beginning and continues to happen. ❑ *Decide at the outset what kind of learning programme you want to follow... From the outset he had put his trust in me, the son of his old friend.* — PHRASE: PHR after v, PHR cl

**out|shine** /aʊtʃaɪn/ **(outshines, outshining, outshone)** If you **outshine** someone at a particular activity, you are much better at it than they are. ❑ *Jesse has begun to outshine me in sports.* — VERB; V n

**out|side** /aʊtsaɪd/ **(outsides)** ◆◆◆

> ✔ The form **outside of** can also be used as a preposition. This form is more usual in American English.

1 The **outside** of something is the part which surrounds or encloses the rest of it. ❑ *...the outside of the building... Cook over a fairly high heat until the outsides are browned.* — N-COUNT: usu *the* N, oft N *of* n ≠ inside ♦ **Outside** is also an adjective. ❑ *...high up on the outside wall.* — ADJ: ADJ n 2 If you are **outside**, you are not inside a building but are quite close to it. ❑ *'Was the car inside the garage?' — 'No, it was still outside.'... Outside, the light was fading rapidly... The shouting outside grew louder.* — ADV: *be* ADV, ADV after v, n ADV, ADV with cl ≠ inside ♦ **Outside** is also a preposition. ❑ *The victim was outside a shop when he was attacked.* — PREP ≠ inside ♦ **Outside** is also an adjective. ❑ *...the outside temperature. ...an outside toilet.* — ADJ: ADJ n 3 If you are **outside** a room, you are not in it but are in the passage or area next to it. ❑ *She'd sent him outside the classroom... He stood in the narrow hallway just outside the door.* — PREP ≠ inside ♦ **Outside** is also an adverb. ❑ *They heard voices coming from outside in the corridor.* — ADV: n ADV, ADV after v ≠ inside 4 When you talk about the **outside** world, you are referring to things that happen or exist in places other than your own home or community. ❑ *...a side of Morris's character she hid carefully from the outside world... It's important to have outside interests.* — ADJ: ADJ n ♦ **Outside** is also an adverb. ❑ *The scheme was good for the prisoners because it brought them outside* — ADV: ADV after v

*into the community.* [5] People or things **outside** a country, town, or region are not in it. ❑ *...an old castle outside Budapest... The number of warships stationed outside European waters roughly doubled.* PREP: n/-ed PREP n ≠in
♦ **Outside** is also a noun. ❑ *Peace cannot be imposed from the outside by the United States or anyone else.* N-SING: the N
[6] On a road with two separate carriageways, the **outside** lanes are the ones which are closest to its centre. ❑ *It was travelling in the outside lane at 78mph.* ADJ: ADJ n ≠inside
[7] **Outside** people or organizations are not part of a particular organization or group. ❑ *The company now makes much greater use of outside consultants.* ADJ: ADJ n
♦ **Outside** is also a preposition. ❑ *He is hoping to recruit a chairman from outside the company.* PREP
[8] **Outside** a particular institution or field of activity means in other fields of activity or in general life. ❑ *...the largest merger ever to take place outside the oil industry.* PREP
[9] Something that is **outside** a particular range of things is not included within it. ❑ *She is a beautiful boat, but way, way outside my price range.* PREP = beyond ≠within
[10] Something that happens **outside** a particular period of time happens at a different time from the one mentioned. ❑ *They are open outside normal daily banking hours.* PREP
[11] You use **at the outside** to say that you think that a particular amount is the largest possible in a particular situation, or that a particular time is the latest possible time for something to happen. ❑ *Give yourself forty minutes at the outside.* PHRASE: PHR with cl, amount PHR

**out|side broad|cast** **(outside broadcasts)** N-COUNT
An **outside broadcast** is a radio or television programme that is not recorded or filmed in a studio, but in another building or in the open air. [BRIT]

✔ in AM, use **remote broadcast**

**out|sid|er** /aʊtsaɪdəʳ/ **(outsiders)** [1] An **outsider** is someone who does not belong to a particular group or organization. ❑ *The most likely outcome may be to subcontract much of the work to an outsider.* N-COUNT
[2] An **outsider** is someone who is not accepted by a particular group, or who feels that they do not belong in it. ❑ *Malone, a cop, felt as much an outsider as any of them.* N-COUNT
[3] In a competition, an **outsider** is a competitor who is unlikely to win. ❑ *He was an outsider in the race to be the new UN Secretary-General.* N-COUNT

**out|size** /aʊtsaɪz/ also **outsized. Outsize** or **outsized** things are much larger than usual or much larger than you would expect. [BRIT] ❑ *...an outsize pair of scissors.* ADJ: usu ADJ n

**out|skirts** /aʊtskɜːʳts/ **The outskirts of** a city or town are the parts of it that are farthest away from its centre. ❑ *Hours later we reached the outskirts of New York.* N-PLURAL: the N, oft N of n

**out|smart** /aʊtsmɑːʳt/ **(outsmarts, outsmarting, outsmarted)** If you **outsmart** someone, you defeat them or gain an advantage over them in a clever and sometimes dishonest way. ❑ *Troy was very clever for his age and had already figured out ways to outsmart her.* VERB = outwit; V n

**out|sold** /aʊtsoʊld/ **Outsold** is the past tense and past participle of **outsell**.

**out|source** /aʊtsɔːʳs/ **(outsources, outsourcing, outsourced)** If a company **outsources** work or things, it pays workers from outside the company to do the work or supply the things. [BUSINESS] ❑ *Increasingly, corporate clients are seeking to outsource the management of their facilities.* VERB; V n; Also V
♦ **out|sourc|ing** *The difficulties of outsourcing have been compounded by the increasing resistance of trade unions.* N-UNCOUNT

**out|spo|ken** /aʊtspoʊkən/ Someone who is **outspoken** gives their opinions about things openly and honestly, even if they are likely to shock or offend people. ❑ *Some church leaders have been outspoken in their support for political reform in Kenya.* ADJ = forthright
♦ **out|spo|ken|ness** *His outspokenness has ensured that he has at least one senior enemy within the BBC hierarchy.* N-UNCOUNT

**out|stand|ing** /aʊtstændɪŋ/ [1] If you describe someone or something as **outstanding**, you think that they are very remarkable and impressive. ❑ *Derartu is an outstanding athlete and deserved to win. ...an area of outstanding natural beauty.* ◆◇◇ ADJ = exceptional
[2] Money that is **outstanding** has not yet been paid and is still owed to someone. ❑ *You have to pay your outstanding bill before joining the scheme.* ADJ
[3] **Outstanding** issues or problems have not yet been resolved. ❑ *We still have some outstanding issues to resolve before we'll have a treaty that is ready to sign.* ADJ: usu ADJ n
[4] **Outstanding** means very important or obvious. ❑ *The company is an outstanding example of a small business that grew into a big one.* ADJ

**out|stand|ing|ly** /aʊtstændɪŋli/ You use **outstandingly** to emphasize how good, or occasionally how bad, something is. ❑ *Salzburg is an outstandingly beautiful place to visit.* ADV: ADV adj/adv [emphasis] = exceedingly, exceptionally

**out|stay** /aʊtsteɪ/ **(outstays, outstaying, outstayed) to outstay** your **welcome** → see **welcome**.

**out|stretched** /aʊtstretʃt/ If a part of the body of a person or animal is **outstretched**, it is stretched out as far as possible. ❑ *She came to Anna her arms outstretched.* ADJ

**out|strip** /aʊtstrɪp/ **(outstrips, outstripping, outstripped)** If one thing **outstrips** another, the first thing becomes larger in amount, or more successful or important, than the second thing. ❑ *In 1989 and 1990 demand outstripped supply, and prices went up by more than a third.* VERB

**out-take** **(out-takes)** also **outtake.** An **out-take** is a piece of film or a song that is not in the final version of a programme, film, or record, for example because it contains a mistake. N-COUNT

**out-there** Someone or something that is **out-there** is very extreme or unusual. [INFORMAL] ❑ *...various artists with out-there names like Furry Green Lamppost.* ADJ = way-out

**out tray** **(out trays)** also **out-tray.** An **out tray** is a shallow container used in offices to put letters and documents in when they have been dealt with and are ready to be sent somewhere else. Compare **in tray**. N-COUNT ≠in tray

**out|vote** /aʊtvoʊt/ **(outvotes, outvoting, outvoted)** If you **are outvoted**, more people vote against what you are suggesting than vote for it, so that your suggestion is defeated. ❑ *They walked out in protest after being outvoted by the National Salvation Front majority... Twice his colleagues have outvoted him.* VERB; be V-ed; V n

**out|ward** /aʊtwəʳd/ [1] An **outward** journey is a journey that you make away from a place that you are intending to return to later. ❑ *Tickets must be bought seven days in advance, with outward and return journey dates specified.* ADJ: ADJ n ≠return
[2] The **outward** feelings, qualities, or attitudes of someone or something are the ones they appear to have rather than the ones that they actually have. ❑ *In spite of my outward calm I was very shaken... What the military rulers have done is to restore the outward appearance of order.* ADJ: ADJ n
[3] The **outward** features of something are the ones that you can see from the outside. ❑ *Mark was lying unconscious but with no outward sign of injury.* ADJ: ADJ n
[4] → See also **outwards**.

**out|ward|ly** /aʊtwəʳdli/ You use **outwardly** to indicate the feelings or qualities that a person or situation may appear to have, rather than the ones that they actually have. ❑ *They may feel tired and though outwardly calm, can be irritable... Outwardly this looked like the beginning of a terrific programme but the stage was actually set for a major disaster.* ADV: ADV adj/adv, ADV with cl

**out|wards** /aʊtwəʳdz/ also **outward.** [1] If something moves or faces **outwards**, it moves or faces away from the place you are in or the place you are talking about. ❑ *The top door opened outwards.* ADV: ADV after v ≠inwards
[2] If you say that a person or a group of people, such as a government, looks **outwards**, you mean that they turn their attention to anoth- ADV: ADV after v

er group that they are interested in or would like greater involvement with. ❑ *Other poor countries looked outward, strengthening their ties to the economic superpowers.*

**out|weigh** /aʊtweɪ/ **(outweighs, outweighing, outweighed)** If one thing **outweighs** another, the first thing is of greater importance, benefit, or significance than the second thing. [FORMAL] ❑ *The advantages of this deal largely outweigh the disadvantages.* VERB V n

**out|wit** /aʊtwɪt/ **(outwits, outwitting, outwitted)** If you **outwit** someone, you use your intelligence or a clever trick to defeat them or to gain an advantage over them. ❑ *To win the presidency he had first to outwit his rivals within the Socialist Party.* VERB V n

**out|with** /aʊtwɪθ/ In Scottish English, **outwith** means outside. ❑ *It is, however, necessary on occasion to work outwith these hours.* PREP

**out|worn** /aʊtwɔːʳn/ If you describe a belief or custom as **outworn**, you mean that it is old-fashioned and no longer has any meaning or usefulness. ❑ *...an ancient nation irretrievably sunk in an outworn culture.* ADJ

**ouzo** /uːzoʊ/ **(ouzos) Ouzo** is a strong aniseed-flavoured alcoholic drink that is made in Greece. ♦ A glass of ouzo can be referred to as an **ouzo**. N-UNCOUNT N-COUNT

**ova** /oʊvə/ **Ova** is the plural of **ovum**.

**oval** /oʊvᵊl/ **(ovals) Oval** things have a shape that is like a circle but is wider in one direction than the other. ❑ *...the small oval framed picture of a little boy.* ♦ **Oval** is also a noun. ❑ *Using 2 spoons, mould the cheese into small balls or ovals.* ADJ: usu ADJ n N-COUNT: usu sing

**ovar|ian** /oʊveəriən/ **Ovarian** means in or relating to the ovaries. ❑ *...a new treatment for ovarian cancer.* ADJ: ADJ n

**ova|ry** /oʊvəri/ **(ovaries)** A woman's **ovaries** are the two organs in her body that produce eggs. N-COUNT

**ova|tion** /oʊveɪʃᵊn/ **(ovations)** An **ovation** is a large amount of applause from an audience for a particular performer or speaker. [FORMAL] ❑ *They had lost by a wide margin, but their supporters gave them a defiant, loyal ovation.* → See also **standing ovation**. N-COUNT

**oven** /ʌvᵊn/ **(ovens)** An **oven** is a device for cooking that is like a box with a door. You heat it and cook food inside it. N-COUNT

**oven|proof** /ʌvᵊnpruːf/ An **ovenproof** dish is one that has been specially made to be used in an oven without being damaged by the heat. ADJ: usu ADJ n

| **over** |
|---|
| ① POSITION AND MOVEMENT |
| ② AMOUNTS AND OCCURRENCES |
| ③ OTHER USES |

**① over** /oʊvəʳ/ ◆◆◆

> In addition to the uses shown below, **over** is used after some verbs, nouns, and adjectives in order to introduce extra information. **Over** is also used in phrasal verbs such as 'hand over' and 'glaze over'.

1 If one thing is **over** another thing or is moving **over** it, the first thing is directly above the second, either resting on it, or with a space between them. ❑ *He looked at himself in the mirror over the table... ...a bridge over the river Danube.* ♦ **Over** is also an adverb. ❑ *...planes flying over every 10 or 15 minutes.* PREP ≠ under ADV: ADV after v

2 If one thing is **over** another thing, it is supported by it and its ends are hanging down on each side of it. ❑ *A grey mackintosh was folded over her arm... Joe's clothing was flung over the back of a chair.* PREP: usu -ed PREP n

3 If one thing is **over** another thing, it covers part or all of it. ❑ *Mix the ingredients and pour over the mushrooms... He was wearing a light-grey suit over a shirt... He pulled the cap halfway over his ears.* ♦ **Over** is also an adverb. ❑ *Heat this syrup and pour it over.* PREP ADV: ADV after v

4 If you lean **over** an object, you bend your body so that the top part of it is above the object. ❑ *They stopped to lean over a gate... Everyone in the room was bent over her desk.* ♦ **Over** is also an adverb. ❑ *Sam leant over to open the door of the car.* PREP: v PREP n ADV: ADV after v

5 If you look or talk **over** an object, you look or talk across the top of it. ❑ *I went and stood beside him, looking over his shoulder. ...conversing over the fence with your friend.* PREP: usu v PREP n

6 If a window has a view **over** an area of land or water, you can see the land or water through the window. ❑ *...a light and airy bar with a wonderful view over the River Amstel.* PREP: n PREP n, v PREP n = onto

7 If someone or something goes **over** a barrier, obstacle, or boundary, they get to the other side of it by going across it, or across the top of it. ❑ *I stepped over a broken piece of wood... He'd just come over the border.* ♦ **Over** is also an adverb. ❑ *I climbed over into the back seat.* PREP: v PREP n ADV: ADV after v

8 If someone or something moves **over** an area or surface, they move across it, from one side to the other. ❑ *She ran swiftly over the lawn to the gate... Joe passed his hand over his face and looked puzzled.* PREP = across

9 If something is on the opposite side of a road or river, you can say that it is **over** the road or river. ❑ *...a fashionable neighbourhood, just over the river from Manhattan.* PREP = across

10 If you go **over** to a place, you go to that place. ❑ *I got out the car and drove over to Dervaig... I thought you might have invited her over.* ADV: ADV after v, oft ADV to n

11 You can use **over** to indicate a particular position or place a short distance away from someone or something. ❑ *He noticed Rolfe standing silently over by the window... John reached over and took Joanna's hand.* ADV: ADV after v, oft ADV prep

12 You use **over** to say that someone or something falls towards or onto the ground, often suddenly or violently. ❑ *He was knocked over by a bus and broke his leg... The truck had gone off the road and toppled over.* ADV: ADV after v

13 If something rolls **over** or is turned **over**, its position changes so that the part that was facing upwards is now facing downwards. ❑ *His car rolled over after a tyre was punctured... The alarm did go off but all I did was yawn, turn over and go back to sleep.* ADV: ADV after v

**PHRASES** 14 **All over** a place means in every part of it. ❑ *...the letters she received from people all over the world.* PREP-PHRASE

15 **Over here** means near you, or in the country you are in. ❑ *Why don't you come over here tomorrow evening.* PHRASE: usu PHR after v, v-link PHR

16 **Over there** means in a place a short distance away from you, or in another country. ❑ *The cafe is just across the road over there... She'd married some American and settled down over there.* PHRASE: usu PHR after v, v-link PHR

**② over** /oʊvəʳ/ ◆◆◆ 1 If something is **over** a particular amount, measurement, or age, it is more than that amount, measurement, or age. ❑ *Cigarettes kill over a hundred thousand Britons every year... I met George well over a year ago.* ♦ **Over** is also an adverb. ❑ *...people aged 65 and over.* PREP: PREP amount ADV: amount *and* ADV

2 **Over and above** an amount, especially a normal amount, means more than that amount or in addition to it. ❑ *Expenditure on education has gone up by seven point eight per cent over and above inflation.* PREP-PHRASE

3 If you say that you have some food or money **over**, you mean that it remains after you have used all that you need. ❑ *Larsons pay me well enough, but there's not much over for luxuries when there's two of you to live on it... Primrose was given an apple, left over from our picnic lunch.* ADV: *be* ADV, n ADV, ADV after v

4 If you do something **over**, you do it again or start doing it again from the beginning. [AM] ❑ *She said if she had the chance to do it over, she would have hired a press secretary.* ADV: ADV after v = again

**PHRASES** 5 If you say that something happened **twice over**, **three times over** and so on, you are stating the number of times that it happened and emphasizing that it happened more than once. ❑ *He had to have everything spelled out twice over for him.* PHRASE: PHR after v [emphasis]

6 If you do something **over again**, you do it again or start doing it again from the beginning. [BRIT] ❑ *If I was living my life over again I wouldn't have attended so many committee meetings.* PHRASE: PHR after v

7 If you say that something is happening **all over again**, you are emphasizing that it is happening again, and you are suggesting that it is tir- PHRASE: PHR after v [emphasis]

ing, boring, or unpleasant. ❑ *The whole process started all over again... He had to prove himself all over again.* [8] If you say that something happened **over and over** or **over and over again**, you are emphasizing that it happened many times. ❑ *He plays the same songs over and over... 'I don't understand it,' he said, over and over again.* PHRASE: PHR after v [emphasis]

③ **over** /oʊvəʳ/ ◆◆◆ [1] If an activity is **over** or **all over**, it is completely finished. ❑ *Warplanes that have landed there will be kept until the war is over... I am glad it's all over.* ADJ: v-link ADJ [2] If you are **over** an illness or an experience, it has finished and you have recovered from its effects. ❑ *I'm glad that you're over the flu... She was still getting over the shock of what she had been told.* PREP [3] If you have control or influence **over** someone or something, you are able to control them or influence them. ❑ *He's never had any influence over her... The oil companies have lost their power over oil price and oil production.* PREP: n PREP n [4] You use **over** to indicate what a disagreement or feeling relates to or is caused by. ❑ *...concern over recent events in Burma... Staff at some air and sea ports are beginning to protest over pay.* PREP: n PREP n, v PREP n = about [5] If something happens **over** a particular period of time or **over** something such as a meal, it happens during that time or during the meal. ❑ *Many strikes over the last few years have not ended successfully... Over breakfast we discussed plans for the day. ...discussing the problem over a glass of wine.* PREP [6] You use **over** to indicate that you give or receive information using a telephone, radio, or other piece of electrical equipment. ❑ *I'm not prepared to discuss this over the telephone... The head of state addressed the nation over the radio.* PREP = on [7] The presenter of a radio or television programme says '**over to** someone' to indicate the person who will speak next. ❑ *With the rest of the sports news, over to Colin Maitland.* PREP-PHRASE [8] When people such as the police or the army are using a radio to communicate, they say '**Over**' to indicate that they have finished speaking and are waiting for a reply. CONVENTION [formulae] [9] In cricket, an **over** consists of six correctly bowled balls. ❑ *At the start of the last over, bowled by Chris Lewis, the Welsh county were favourites.* N-COUNT

**over-** /oʊvəʳ-/ You can add **over-** to an adjective or verb to indicate that a quality exists or an action is done to too great an extent. For example, if you say that someone is being over-cautious, you mean that they are being too cautious. ❑ *Tony looked tired and over-anxious... When depressed, they dramatically overindulge in chocolate and sweets.* PREFIX

**over|achieve** /oʊvərətʃiːv/ **(overachieves, overachieving, overachieved)** If someone **overachieves** in something such as school work or a job, they work very hard, especially in a way that makes them tired or unhappy. They want to be successful because it is very important to them to do well and not because they enjoy what they are doing. ❑ *...emotions such as guilt, compulsion to please or overachieve, or depression.* VERB, V ♦ **over|achiev|er (overachievers)** *He comes from a family of overachievers.* N-COUNT

**over|act** /oʊvərækt/ **(overacts, overacting, overacted)** If you say that someone **overacts**, you mean they exaggerate their emotions and movements, usually when acting in a play. ❑ *Sometimes he had overacted in his role as Prince.* VERB, V

**over-age** [1] If you are **over-age**, you are officially too old to do something. ❑ *He was a couple of months over-age for the youth team.* ADJ [2] You use **over-age** to describe someone who is doing something that is usually done by much younger people, and which therefore seems inappropriate or silly. ❑ *...an over-age nightclub singer.* ADJ: ADJ n [disapproval]

**over|all (overalls)** ◆◆◇

> ✔ The adjective and adverb are pronounced /oʊvərɔːl/. The noun is pronounced /oʊvərɔːl/.

[1] You use **overall** to indicate that you are talking about a situation in general or about the whole of something. ❑ *...the overall rise in unemployment... Cut down your overall amount of physical activity.* ADJ: ADJ n ♦ **Overall** is also an adverb. ❑ *Overall I was disappointed... The college has few ways to assess the quality of education overall.* ADV: ADV with cl [2] **Overalls** consist of a single piece of clothing that combines trousers and a jacket. You wear overalls over your clothes in order to protect them while you are working. ❑ *...workers in blue overalls.* N-PLURAL: also *a pair of* N [3] **Overalls** are trousers that are attached to a piece of cloth which covers your chest and which has straps going over your shoulders. [AM] ❑ *An elderly man dressed in faded overalls took the witness stand.* N-PLURAL: also *a pair of* N

> ✔ in BRIT, use **dungarees**

[4] An **overall** is a piece of clothing shaped like a coat that you wear over your clothes in order to protect them while you are working. [BRIT] N-COUNT

**over|all ma|jor|ity (overall majorities)** If a political party wins **an overall majority** in an election or vote, they get more votes than the total number of votes or seats won by all their opponents. N-COUNT: usu sing

**over|arch|ing** /oʊvərɑːʳtʃɪŋ/ You use **overarching** to indicate that you are talking about something that includes or affects everything or everyone. [FORMAL] ❑ *The overarching question seems to be what happens when the US pulls out?* ADJ: ADJ n

**over|arm** /oʊvərɑːʳm/ You use **overarm** to describe actions, such as throwing a ball, in which you stretch your arm over your shoulder. ❑ *...a single overarm stroke.* ADJ: ADJ n ≠ underarm

**over|awe** /oʊvərɔː/ **(overawes, overawing, overawed)** If you **are overawed by** something or someone, you are very impressed by them and a little afraid of them. ❑ *Don't be overawed by people in authority, however important they are.* VERB: usu passive, be V-ed ♦ **over|awed** *Benjamin said that he had been rather overawed to meet one of the Billington family.* ADJ: usu v-link ADJ

**over|bal|ance** /oʊvəʳbæləns/ **(overbalances, overbalancing, overbalanced)** If you **overbalance**, you fall over or nearly fall over, because you are not standing properly. ❑ *He overbalanced and fell head first.* VERB, V

**over|bear|ing** /oʊvəʳbeərɪŋ/ An **overbearing** person tries to make other people do what he or she wants in an unpleasant and forceful way. ❑ *My husband can be quite overbearing with our son.* ADJ [disapproval] = domineering

**over|blown** /oʊvəʳbloʊn/ Something that is **overblown** makes something seem larger, more important, or more significant than it really is. ❑ *Warnings of disaster may be overblown... The reporting of the hostage story was fair, if sometimes overblown.* ADJ = exaggerated

**over|board** /oʊvəʳbɔːʳd/ [1] If you fall **overboard**, you fall over the side of a boat into the water. ❑ *His sailing instructor fell overboard and drowned during a lesson.* ADV: ADV after v

**PHRASES** [2] If you say that someone **goes overboard**, you mean that they do something to a greater extent than is necessary or reasonable. [INFORMAL] ❑ *Women sometimes damage their skin by going overboard with abrasive cleansers.* PHRASE: V inflects [3] If you **throw** something **overboard**, for example an idea or suggestion, you reject it completely. ❑ *They had thrown their neutrality overboard in the crisis.* PHRASE: V inflects

**over|book** /oʊvəʳbʊk/ **(overbooks, overbooking, overbooked)** If an organization such as an airline or a theatre company **overbooks**, they sell more tickets than they have places for. ❑ *Planes are crowded, airlines overbook, and departures are almost never on time.* VERB, V, Also V n

**over|booked** /oʊvəʳbʊkt/ If something such as a hotel, bus, or aircraft is **overbooked**, more people have booked than the number of places that are available. ❑ *Sorry, the plane is overbooked.* ADJ: usu v-link ADJ

**over|bur|dened** /oʊvəʳbɜːʳdᵊnd/ [1] If a system or organization is **overburdened**, it has ADJ: oft ADJ *with/by* n too many people or things to deal with and so does not function properly. ❑ *The city's hospitals are overburdened by casualties. ...an overburdened air traffic control system.* [2] If you are **overburdened with** something such as work or problems, you have more of it than you can cope with. ❑ *The Chief Inspector disliked being overburdened with insignificant detail. ...overburdened teachers.* — ADJ: oft ADJ *with/by* n

**over|came** /oʊvərkeɪm/ **Overcame** is the past tense of **overcome**.

**over|ca|pac|ity** /oʊvərkəpæsɪti/ — N-UNCOUNT = surplus. If there is **overcapacity** in a particular industry or area, more goods have been produced than are needed, and the industry is therefore less profitable than it could be. [BUSINESS] ❑ *There is huge overcapacity in the world car industry.*

**over|cast** /oʊvərkɑːst, -kæst/ — ADJ. If it is **overcast**, or if the sky or the day is **overcast**, the sky is completely covered with cloud and there is not much light. ❑ *For three days it was overcast... The weather forecast is for showers and overcast skies.*

**over|charge** /oʊvərtʃɑːrdʒ/ **(overcharges, overcharging, overcharged)** — VERB. If someone **overcharges** you, they charge you too much for their goods or services. ❑ *If you feel a taxi driver has overcharged you, say so.* (V n) ♦ **over|charg|ing** (N-UNCOUNT) *...protests of overcharging and harsh treatment of small businesses.*

**over|coat** /oʊvərkoʊt/ **(overcoats)** — N-COUNT. An **overcoat** is a thick warm coat that you wear in winter.

**over|come** /oʊvərkʌm/ **(overcomes, overcoming, overcame)** ◆◇◇

> The form **overcome** is used in the present tense and is also the past participle.

[1] VERB. If you **overcome** a problem or a feeling, you successfully deal with it and control it. ❑ *Molly had fought and overcome her fear of flying.* (V n) [2] VERB = overwhelm. If you **are overcome by** a feeling or event, it is so strong or has such a strong effect that you cannot think clearly. ❑ *The night before the test I was overcome by fear and despair...* (*be* V-ed) *A dizziness overcame him, blurring his vision.* (V n) [3] VERB: usu passive. If you **are overcome by** smoke or a poisonous gas, you become very ill or die from breathing it in. ❑ *The residents were trying to escape from the fire but were overcome by smoke.* (*be* V-ed)

**over|crowd|ed** /oʊvərkraʊdɪd/ — ADJ: usu ADJ n. An **overcrowded** place has too many things or people in it. ❑ *...a windswept, overcrowded, unattractive beach.*

**over|crowd|ing** /oʊvərkraʊdɪŋ/ — N-UNCOUNT. If there is a problem of **overcrowding**, there are more people living in a place than it was designed for. ❑ *Students were protesting at overcrowding in the university hostels.*

**over|do** /oʊvərduː/ **(overdoes, overdoing, overdid, overdone)** [1] VERB. If someone **overdoes** something, they behave in an exaggerated or extreme way. ❑ *...a recognition by the US central bank that it may have overdone its tightening when it pushed rates up to 6 per cent...* (V n) *He wants to give up working and stay home to look after the children. She feels, however, that this is overdoing it a bit.* (V *it*) [2] VERB. If you **overdo** an activity, you try to do more than you can physically manage. ❑ *It is important never to overdo new exercises...* (V n) *The taxi drivers' association is urging its members, who can work as many hours as they want, not to overdo it.* (V *it*)

**over|done** /oʊvərdʌn/ [1] ADJ = overcooked. If food is **overdone**, it has been spoiled by being cooked for too long. ❑ *The meat was overdone and the vegetables disappointing.* [2] ADJ: usu v-link ADJ. If you say that something is **overdone**, you mean that you think it is excessive or exaggerated. ❑ *In fact, the panic is overdone. As the map shows, the drought has been confined to the south and east of Britain.*

**over|dose** /oʊvərdoʊs/ **(overdoses, overdosing, overdosed)** [1] N-COUNT: usu sing. If someone takes an **overdose** of a drug, they take more of it than is safe. ❑ *Each year, one in 100 girls aged 15-19 takes an overdose.* [2] VERB. If someone **overdoses on** a drug, they take more of it than is safe. ❑ *He'd overdosed on heroin...* (V *on* n) *Medical opinion varies on how many tablets it takes to overdose.* (V) [3] N-COUNT: usu sing, oft N *of* n. You can refer to too much of something, especially something harmful, as an **overdose**. ❑ *An overdose of sun, sea, sand and chlorine can give lighter hair a green tinge.* [4] VERB. You can say that someone **overdoses on** something if they have or do too much of it. ❑ *The city, he concluded, had overdosed on design.* (V *on* n)

**over|draft** /oʊvərdrɑːft, -dræft/ **(overdrafts)** — N-COUNT. If you have an **overdraft**, you have spent more money than you have in your bank account, and so you are in debt to the bank.

**over|drawn** /oʊvərdrɔːn/ — ADJ: usu v-link ADJ. If you are **overdrawn** or if your bank account is **overdrawn**, you have spent more money than you have in your account, and so you are in debt to the bank. ❑ *Nick's bank sent him a letter saying he was £100 overdrawn.*

**over|dressed** /oʊvərdrest/ — ADJ. If you say that someone is **overdressed**, you are criticizing them for wearing clothes that are not appropriate for the occasion because they are too formal or too smart.

**over|drive** /oʊvərdraɪv/ **(overdrives)** [1] N-COUNT: usu sing, oft N n. The **overdrive** in a vehicle is a very high gear that is used when you are driving at high speeds. [2] PHRASE: PHR after v. If you go **into overdrive**, you begin to work very hard or perform a particular activity in a very intense way. ❑ *In the courtroom everybody went into overdrive, assuming that there might well be a verdict soon.*

**over|due** /oʊvərdjuː, -duː/ [1] ADJ: usu v-link ADJ. If you say that a change or an event is **overdue**, you mean that you think it should have happened before now. ❑ *This debate is long overdue.* [2] ADJ. **Overdue** sums of money have not been paid, even though it is later than the date on which they should have been paid. ❑ *Teachers have joined a strike aimed at forcing the government to pay overdue salaries and allowances.* [3] ADJ. An **overdue** library book has not been returned to the library, even though the date on which it should have been returned has passed.

**over|eat** /oʊvəriːt/ **(overeats, overeating, overate, overeaten)** — VERB. If you say that someone **overeats**, you mean they eat more than they need to or more than is healthy. ❑ *If you tend to overeat because of depression, first take steps to recognize the source of your sadness.* (V) *...people who overeat spicy foods.* (V n) ♦ **over|eater** **(overeaters)** (N-COUNT) *She eats in secret like most compulsive overeaters.* ♦ **over|eat|ing** (N-UNCOUNT) *If you have a serious problem with overeating you should get together with others who share this problem.*

**over|em|pha|sis** /oʊvəremfəsɪs/ — N-SING: also no det, usu N *on* n. If you say that there is **an overemphasis on** a particular thing, you mean that more importance or attention is given to it than is necessary. ❑ *He attributed the party's lack of success to an overemphasis on ideology and ideas.*

**over|em|pha|size** /oʊvəremfəsaɪz/ **(overemphasizes, overemphasizing, overemphasized)**

> in BRIT, also use **overemphasise**

[1] VERB. If you say that someone **overemphasizes** something, you mean that they give it more importance than it deserves or than you consider appropriate. ❑ *Democrats will complain he overemphasizes punishment at the expense of prevention and treatment.* (V n) [2] VERB: with brd-neg [emphasis]. If you say that something **cannot be overemphasized**, you are emphasizing that you think it is very important. ❑ *The importance of education cannot be overemphasised...* (*be* V-ed) *I can't overemphasize the cleanliness of this place.* (V n)

**over|es|ti|mate** **(overestimates, overestimating, overestimated)**

> The verb is pronounced /oʊvərestɪmeɪt/. The noun is pronounced /oʊvərestɪmət/.

[1] VERB ≠ underestimate. If you say that someone **overestimates** something, you mean that they think it is greater in

amount or importance than it really is. ❑ *With hindsight, he was overestimating their desire for peace.* V n Also V
♦ **Overestimate** is also a noun. ❑ *Average earnings in the South East were about £59,000, although that may be an overestimate.* N-COUNT
♦ **over|es|ti|ma|tion** /oʊvəʳestɪmeɪʃᵊn/ *...excessive overestimation of one's own importance.* N-SING: also no det, usu N *of* n ≠*underestimation*
[2] If you say that something **cannot be overestimated**, you are emphasizing that you think it is very important. ❑ *The importance of participating in the life of the country cannot be overestimated... It is hard to overestimate the potential gains from this process.* VERB: with brd-neg [emphasis] *be* V-ed, V n
[3] If you **overestimate** someone, you think that they have more of a skill or quality than they really have. ❑ *I think you overestimate me, Fred.* VERB ≠*underestimate* V n

**over-excited** also **overexcited.** If you say that someone is **over-excited**, you mean that they are more excited than you think is desirable. ❑ *You'll need to provide continuous, organised entertainment or children may get over-excited.* ADJ: usu v-link ADJ

**over|ex|posed** /oʊvərɪkspoʊzd/ An **overexposed** photograph is of poor quality because the film has been exposed to too much light, either when the photograph was taken or during the developing process. ADJ

**over|ex|tend|ed** /oʊvərɪkstendɪd/ If a person or organization is **overextended**, they have become involved in more activities than they can financially or physically manage. ❑ *The British East India Tea Company was overextended and faced bankruptcy.* ADJ

**over|flight** /oʊvəʳflaɪt/ **(overflights)** An **overflight** is the passage of an aircraft from one country over another country's territory. ❑ *Nations react strongly to unauthorized overflights.* N-VAR

**over|flow (overflows, overflowing, overflowed)**

✔ The verb is pronounced /oʊvəʳfloʊ/. The noun is pronounced /oʊvəʳfloʊ/.

[1] If a liquid or a river **overflows**, it flows over the edges of the container or place it is in. ❑ *Pour in some of the syrup, but not all of it, as it will probably overflow... Rivers and streams have overflowed their banks in countless places.* VERB: no passive V, V n
[2] If a place or container **is overflowing with** people or things, it is too full of them. ❑ *The great hall was overflowing with people... Jails and temporary detention camps are overflowing.* VERB: usu cont V *with* n, V
[3] The **overflow** is the extra people or things that something cannot contain or deal with because it is not large enough. ❑ *Tents have been set up next to hospitals to handle the overflow.* N-COUNT: usu *the* N in sing
[4] An **overflow** is a hole or pipe through which liquid can flow out of a container when it gets too full. N-COUNT
[5] If a place or container is filled **to overflowing**, it is so full of people or things that no more can fit in. ❑ *The kitchen garden was full to overflowing with fresh vegetables.* PHRASE: adj PHR, PHR after v

**over|fly** /oʊvəʳflaɪ/ **(overflies, overflying, overflew, overflown)** When an aircraft **overflies** an area, it flies over it. [FORMAL] ❑ *Permission has not yet been granted for the airline to overfly Tanzania.* VERB V n

**over|ground** /oʊvəʳgraʊnd/

✔ The adjective is pronounced /oʊvəʳgraʊnd/. The adverb is pronounced /oʊvəʳgraʊnd/.

In an **overground** transport system, vehicles run on the surface of the ground, rather than below it. [BRIT] ❑ *Bus routes and railways, both overground and underground, converged on the station.* ADJ: ADJ n ≠*underground*
♦ **Overground** is also an adverb. ❑ *There are plans to run the line overground close to the village of Boxley.* ADV

**over|grown** /oʊvəʳgroʊn/ [1] If a garden or other place is **overgrown**, it is covered with a lot of untidy plants because it has not been looked after. ❑ *We hurried on until we reached a courtyard overgrown with weeds.* ADJ
[2] If you describe an adult as an **overgrown** child, you mean that their behaviour and attitudes are like those of a child, and that you dislike this. ❑ *...a bunch of overgrown kids.* ADJ: ADJ n [disapproval]

**over|hang (overhangs, overhanging, overhung)**

✔ The verb is pronounced /oʊvəʳhæŋ/. The noun is pronounced /oʊvəʳhæŋ/.

[1] If one thing **overhangs** another, it sticks out over and above it. ❑ *Part of the rock wall overhung the path.* VERB V n
[2] An **overhang** is the part of something that sticks out over and above something else. ❑ *A sharp overhang of rock gave them cover.* N-COUNT

**over|haul (overhauls, overhauling, overhauled)**

✔ The verb is pronounced /oʊvəʳhɔːl/. The noun is pronounced /oʊvəʳhɔːl/.

[1] If a piece of equipment **is overhauled**, it is cleaned, checked thoroughly, and repaired if necessary. ❑ *They had ensured the plumbing was overhauled a year ago... Our car was towed away to have its suspension overhauled.* VERB: usu passive = *service* *be* V-ed, *have* n V-ed
♦ **Overhaul** is also a noun. ❑ *...the overhaul of aero engines.* N-COUNT
[2] If you **overhaul** a system or method, you examine it carefully and make many changes in it in order to improve it. ❑ *The government said it wanted to overhaul the training scheme to make it cost effective.* VERB V n
♦ **Overhaul** is also a noun. ❑ *There must be a complete overhaul of air traffic control systems.* N-COUNT: usu N *of* n

**over|head**

✔ The adjective is pronounced /oʊvəʳhed/. The adverb is pronounced /oʊvəʳhed/.

You use **overhead** to indicate that something is above you or above the place that you are talking about. ❑ *She turned on the overhead light and looked around the little room.* ADJ: ADJ n
♦ **Overhead** is also an adverb. ❑ *...planes passing overhead.* ADV: ADV after v, *be* ADV

**over|head pro|jec|tor (overhead projectors)** An **overhead projector** is a machine that has a light inside it and makes the writing or pictures on a sheet of plastic appear on a screen or wall. The abbreviation **OHP** is also used. N-COUNT

**over|heads** /oʊvəʳhedz/ The **overheads** of a business are its regular and essential expenses, such as salaries, rent, electricity, and telephone bills. [BUSINESS] ❑ *We are having to cut our costs to reduce overheads and remain competitive.* N-PLURAL

**over|hear** /oʊvəʳhɪəʳ/ **(overhears, overhearing, overheard)** If you **overhear** someone, you hear what they are saying when they are not talking to you and they do not know that you are listening. ❑ *I overheard two doctors discussing my case.* VERB V n

**over|heat** /oʊvəʳhiːt/ **(overheats, overheating, overheated)** [1] If something **overheats** or if you **overheat** it, it becomes hotter than is necessary or desirable. ❑ *The engine was overheating and the car was not handling well... Why do we pay to overheat pubs and hotels?* VERB V, V n
♦ **over|heat|ed** *...that stuffy, overheated apartment.* ADJ
[2] If a country's economy **overheats** or if conditions **overheat** it, it grows so rapidly that inflation and interest rates rise very quickly. [BUSINESS] ❑ *The private sector is increasing its spending so sharply that the economy is overheating... Their prime consideration has been not to overheat the economy.* VERB V, V n
♦ **over|heat|ed** *...the disastrous consequences of an overheated market.* ADJ

**over|heat|ed** /oʊvəʳhiːtɪd/ Someone who is **overheated** is very angry about something. ❑ *I think the reaction has been a little overheated.* ADJ

**over|hung** /oʊvəʳhʌŋ/ **Overhung** is the past tense and past participle of **overhang**.

**over|in|dulge** /oʊvərɪndʌldʒ/ **(overindulges, overindulging, overindulged)** If you **overindulge**, or **overindulge in** something that you like very much, usually food or drink, you allow yourself to have more of it than is good for you. ❑ *We all overindulge occasionally... Don't abuse your body by overindulging in alcohol.* VERB V, V *in* n

**over|joyed** /oʊvəʳdʒɔɪd/ If you are **overjoyed**, you are extremely pleased about something. ❑ *Shelley was overjoyed to see me... He was overjoyed at his son's return.* ADJ: v-link ADJ, oft ADJ to-inf, ADJ *at* n = *delighted*

**over|kill** /oʊvəʳkɪl/ You can say that something is **overkill** when you think that there is N-UNCOUNT more of it than is necessary or appropriate. ❑ *Such security measures may well be overkill.*

**over|land** /oʊvəʳlænd/ An **overland** journey is made across land rather than by ship or aeroplane. ❑ *...an overland journey through Iraq, Turkey, Iran and Pakistan... The overland route is across some really tough mountains.* ♦ **Overland** is also an adverb. ❑ *They're travelling to Baghdad overland.*
ADJ: ADJ n
ADV: ADV after v

**over|lap** **(overlaps, overlapping, overlapped)**

> ✔ The verb is pronounced /oʊvəʳlæp/. The noun is pronounced /oʊvəʳlæp/.

1 If one thing **overlaps** another, or if you **overlap** them, a part of the first thing occupies the same area as a part of the other thing. You can also say that two things **overlap**. ❑ *When the bag is folded flat, the bag bottom overlaps one side of the bag... Overlap the slices carefully so there are no gaps... Use vinyl seam adhesive where vinyls overlap... The edges must overlap each other or weeds will push through the gaps.* 2 If one idea or activity **overlaps** another, or **overlaps** with another, they involve some of the same subjects, people, or periods of time. ❑ *Elizabeth met other Oxford intellectuals some of whom overlapped Naomi's world... Christian holy week overlaps with the beginning of the Jewish holiday of Passover... The needs of patients invariably overlap.* ♦ **Overlap** is also a noun. ❑ *...the overlap between civil and military technology.*
V-RECIP
V n
V pl-n
pl-n V
pl-n V n
V-RECIP
V n
V *with* n
pl-n V
N-VAR: oft N *between* pl-n

**over|lay** /oʊvəʳleɪ/ **(overlays, overlaying, overlaid)** 1 If something **is overlaid with** something else, it is covered by it. ❑ *The floor was overlaid with rugs of oriental design.* 2 If something **is overlaid with** a feeling or quality, that feeling or quality is the most noticeable one, but there may be deeper and more important ones involved. [WRITTEN] ❑ *The party had been overlaid with a certain nervousness. ...a surge of feeling which at this moment overlaid all others.*
VERB: usu passive *be* V-ed *with* n
VERB
*be* V-ed *with* n
V n

**over|leaf** /oʊvəʳliːf/ **Overleaf** is used in books and magazines to say that something is on the other side of the page you are reading. ❑ *Answer the questionnaire overleaf.*
ADV: n ADV, ADV after v, ADV with cl

**over|load** **(overloads, overloading, overloaded)**

> ✔ The verb is pronounced /oʊvəʳloʊd/. The noun is pronounced /oʊvəʳloʊd/.

1 If you **overload** something such as a vehicle, you put more things or people into it than it was designed to carry. ❑ *Don't overload the boat or it will sink... Large meals overload the digestive system.* ♦ **over|load|ed** *Some trains were so overloaded that their suspension collapsed.* 2 To **overload** someone **with** work, problems, or information means to give them more work, problems, or information than they can cope with. ❑ *...an effective method that will not overload staff with yet more paperwork.* ♦ **Overload** is also a noun. ❑ *57 per cent complained of work overload... The greatest danger is that we simply create information overload for our executives.* ♦ **over|load|ed** *The bar waiter was already overloaded with orders.* 3 If you **overload** an electrical system, you cause too much electricity to flow through it, and so damage it. ❑ *Never overload an electrical socket.*
VERB
V n
V n
ADJ
VERB
V n *with* n
N-UNCOUNT: usu supp N
ADJ
VERB
V n

**over|look** /oʊvəʳlʊk/ **(overlooks, overlooking, overlooked)** 1 If a building or window **overlooks** a place, you can see the place clearly from the building or window. ❑ *Pretty and comfortable rooms overlook a flower-filled garden.* 2 If you **overlook** a fact or problem, you do not notice it, or do not realize how important it is. ❑ *We overlook all sorts of warning signals about our own health.* 3 If you **overlook** someone's faults or bad behaviour, you forgive them and take no action. ❑ *...satisfying relationships that enable them to overlook each other's faults.*
VERB
V n
VERB
V n
VERB
V n

**over|lord** /oʊvəʳlɔːʳd/ **(overlords)** 1 If you refer to someone as an **overlord**, you mean that they have great power and are likely to use it in a bad way. [WRITTEN] ❑ *We really don't want to be the overlords of the Palestinian population... The running of Welsh rugby was left in chaos yesterday after a vote of no confidence in the game's overlords.* 2 In former times, an **overlord** was someone who had power over many people. ❑ *Henry II was the first king to be recognized as overlord of Ireland.*
N-COUNT: usu with supp
N-COUNT

**over|ly** /oʊvəʳli/ **Overly** means more than is normal, necessary, or reasonable. ❑ *Employers may become overly cautious about taking on new staff.*
ADV: ADV adj/adv/-ed = excessively

**over|manned** /oʊvəʳmænd/ If you say that a place or an industry is **overmanned**, you mean that you think there are more people working there or doing the work than is necessary. ❑ *Many factories were chronically overmanned.*
ADJ = overstaffed ≠ undermanned

**over|man|ning** /oʊvəʳmænɪŋ/ If there is a problem of **overmanning** in an industry, there are more people working there or doing the work than is necessary.
N-UNCOUNT

**over|much** /oʊvəʳmʌtʃ/ If something happens **overmuch**, it happens too much or very much. [FORMAL] ❑ *He was not a man who thought overmuch about clothes.*
ADV: usu ADV after v, also ADV -ed

**over|night** /oʊvəʳnaɪt/ **(overnights, overnighting, overnighted)** ◆◇◇ 1 If something happens **overnight**, it happens throughout the night or at some point during the night. ❑ *The decision was reached overnight.* ♦ **Overnight** is also an adjective. ❑ *Travel and overnight accommodation are included.* 2 You can say that something happens **overnight** when it happens very quickly and unexpectedly. ❑ *The rules are not going to change overnight... Almost overnight, she had aged ten years and become fat.* ♦ **Overnight** is also an adjective. ❑ *In 1970 he became an overnight success in America.* 3 **Overnight** bags or clothes are ones that you take when you go and stay somewhere for one or two nights. ❑ *He realized he'd left his overnight bag at Mary's house.* 4 If you **overnight** somewhere, you spend the night there. ❑ *They had told her she would be overnighting in Sydney.* ♦ **Overnight** is also a noun. ❑ *Overnights can be arranged.*
ADV: ADV after v
ADJ: ADJ n
ADV: ADV after v
ADJ: ADJ n
ADJ: ADJ n
VERB
V prep/adv
N-COUNT

**over|paid** /oʊvəʳpeɪd/ If you say that someone is **overpaid**, you mean that you think they are paid more than they deserve for the work they do. ❑ *...grossly overpaid corporate lawyers.* → See also **overpay**.
ADJ ≠ underpaid

**over|pass** /oʊvəʳpɑːs, -pæs/ **(overpasses)** An **overpass** is a structure which carries one road over the top of another one. [mainly AM] ❑ *...a $16 million highway overpass over Route 1.*
N-COUNT

> ✔ in BRIT, usually use **flyover**

**over|pay** /oʊvəʳpeɪ/ **(overpays, overpaying, overpaid)** If you **overpay** someone, or if you **overpay** for something, you pay more than is necessary or reasonable. ❑ *Management has to make sure it does not overpay its staff... The council is said to have been overpaying for repairs made by its housing department... The scheme will overpay some lawyers and underpay others.* → See also **overpaid**.
VERB
V n to-inf
V *for* n
V n
Also V

**over|play** /oʊvəʳpleɪ/ **(overplays, overplaying, overplayed)** 1 If you say that someone **is overplaying** something such as a problem, you mean that they are making it seem more important than it really is. ❑ *I think the historical factor is overplayed, that it really doesn't mean much.* 2 If someone **overplays** their **hand**, they act more confidently than they should because they believe that they are in a stronger position than they actually are. ❑ *The United States has to be careful it doesn't overplay its hand.*
VERB = exaggerate
V n
PHRASE: V inflects

**over|popu|lat|ed** /oʊvəʳpɒpjʊleɪtɪd/ If an area is **overpopulated**, there are problems because it has too many people living there. ❑ *Environmentalists say Australia is already overpopulated.*
ADJ

**over|popu|la|tion** /oʊvəʳpɒpjʊleɪʃᵊn/ If there is a problem of **overpopulation** in an area, there are more people living there than can be supported properly. ❑ *...young persons who are concerned about overpopulation in the world.*
N-UNCOUNT

**over|pow|er** /oʊvəʳpaʊəʳ/ **(overpowers, overpowering, overpowered)** 1 If you **overpower** someone, you manage to take hold of and keep hold of them, although they struggle a lot. ❑ *It took ten guardsmen to overpower him.* VERB; V n 2 If a feeling **overpowers** you, it suddenly affects you very strongly. ❑ *A sudden dizziness overpowered him.* VERB = overwhelm; V n 3 In a sports match, when one team or player **overpowers** the other, they play much better than them and beat them easily. ❑ *Britain's tennis No 1 yesterday overpowered American Brian Garrow 7-6, 6-3.* VERB; V n 4 If something such as a colour or flavour **overpowers** another colour or flavour, it is so strong that it makes the second one less noticeable. ❑ *On fair skin, pale shades are delicate enough not to overpower your colouring.* VERB = overwhelm; V n

**over|pow|er|ing** /oʊvəʳpaʊərɪŋ/ 1 An **overpowering** feeling is so strong that you cannot resist it. ❑ *...hard, cold, overpowering anger... The desire for revenge can be overpowering.* ADJ = overwhelming 2 An **overpowering** smell or sound is so strong that you cannot smell or hear anything else. ❑ *There was an overpowering smell of alcohol.* ADJ 3 An **overpowering** person makes other people feel uncomfortable because they have such a strong personality. ❑ *Mrs Winter was large and somewhat overpowering.* ADJ = overwhelming

**over|priced** /oʊvəʳpraɪst/ If you say that something is **overpriced**, you mean that you think it costs much more than it should. ❑ *Any property which does not sell within six weeks is overpriced.* ADJ

**over|ran** /oʊvəʳræn/ **Overran** is the past tense of **overrun**.

**over|rate** /oʊvəʳreɪt/ **(overrates, overrating, overrated)** also **over-rate.** If you say that something or someone **is overrated**, you mean that people have a higher opinion of them than they deserve. ❑ *More men are finding out that the joys of work have been overrated... If you consider him a miracle man, you're overrating him.* VERB ≠ underrate; be V-ed; V n ♦ **over|rat|ed** *Life in the wild is vastly overrated.* ADJ ≠ underrated

**over|reach** /oʊvəʳriːtʃ/ **(overreaches, overreaching, overreached)** also **over-reach.** If you say that someone **overreaches themselves**, you mean that they fail at something because they are trying to do more than they are able to. ❑ *The company had overreached itself and made unwise investments.* VERB; V pron-refl

**over|react** /oʊvəʳriækt/ **(overreacts, overreacting, overreacted)** also **over-react.** If you say that someone **overreacts to** something, you mean that they have and show more of an emotion than is necessary or appropriate. ❑ *Is the council right to be concerned, or is it overreacting?... I overreact to anything sad.* VERB; V; V to n ♦ **over|reac|tion** /oʊvəʳriækʃən/ **(overreactions)** *This is actually an outrageous overreaction.* N-VAR

**over|ride** **(overrides, overriding, overrode, overridden)** also **over-ride.**

> The verb is pronounced /oʊvəʳraɪd/. The noun is pronounced /oʊvəʳraɪd/.

1 If one thing in a situation **overrides** other things, it is more important than them. ❑ *The welfare of a child should always override the wishes of its parents.* VERB; V n 2 If someone in authority **overrides** a person or their decisions, they cancel their decisions. ❑ *The president vetoed the bill, and the Senate failed by a single vote to override his veto.* VERB = overrule; V n 3 An **override** is an attempt to cancel someone's decisions by using your authority over them or by gaining more votes than them in an election or contest. [AM] ❑ *The bill now goes to the House where an override vote is expected to fail.* N-COUNT

**over|rid|ing** /oʊvəʳraɪdɪŋ/ In a particular situation, the **overriding** factor is the one that is the most important. ❑ *My overriding concern is to raise the standards of state education.* ADJ: usu ADJ n

**over|rule** /oʊvəʳruːl/ **(overrules, overruling, overruled)** If someone in authority **overrules** a person or their decision, they officially decide that the decision is incorrect or not valid. ❑ *In 1991, the Court of Appeal overruled this decision... I told them it was a lousy idea, but I was overruled.* VERB = override; V n; V n

**over|run** /oʊvəʳrʌn/ **(overruns, overrunning, overran)** 1 If an army or an armed force **overruns** a place, area, or country, it succeeds in occupying it very quickly. ❑ *A group of rebels overran the port area and most of the northern suburbs.* VERB; V n 2 If you say that a place is **overrun with** things that you consider undesirable, you mean that there are a large number of them there. ❑ *The Hotel has been ordered to close because it is overrun by mice and rats... Padua and Vicenza are prosperous, well-preserved cities, not overrun by tourists.* ADJ: v-link ADJ, usu ADJ *with/by* n 3 If an event or meeting **overruns** by, for example, ten minutes, it continues for ten minutes longer than it was intended to. ❑ *Tuesday's lunch overran by three-quarters of an hour... The talks overran their allotted time.* VERB; V by n; V n; Also V 4 If costs **overrun**, they are higher than was planned or expected. [BUSINESS] ❑ *We should stop the nonsense of taxpayers trying to finance new weapons whose costs always overrun hugely... Costs overran the budget by about 30%.* VERB; V; V n ♦ **Overrun** is also a noun. ❑ *He was stunned to discover cost overruns of at least $1 billion.* N-COUNT: usu n N

**over|seas** /oʊvəʳsiːz/ ◆◇◇ 1 You use **overseas** to describe things that involve or are in foreign countries, usually across a sea or an ocean. ❑ *He has returned to South Africa from his long overseas trip. ...overseas trade figures.* ADJ: ADJ n = foreign ♦ **Overseas** is also an adverb. ❑ *If you're staying for more than three months or working overseas, a full 10-year passport is required.* ADV: ADV after v, be ADV = abroad 2 An **overseas** student or visitor comes from a foreign country, usually across a sea or an ocean. ❑ *Every year nine million overseas visitors come to London.* ADJ: ADJ n = foreign

**over|see** /oʊvəʳsiː/ **(oversees, overseeing, oversaw, overseen)** If someone in authority **oversees** a job or an activity, they make sure that it is done properly. ❑ *Use a surveyor or architect to oversee and inspect the different stages of the work.* VERB = supervise; V n

**over|seer** /oʊvəʳsiːəʳ/ **(overseers)** 1 An **overseer** is someone whose job is to make sure that employees are working properly. ❑ *I was put in the tailor shop, and I loved it. I was promoted to overseer.* N-COUNT = supervisor 2 If a person or organization is the **overseer** of a particular system or activity, they are responsible for making sure that the system or activity works properly and is successful. ❑ *...the department's role as overseer of oil production.* N-COUNT: usu with poss

**over|sell** /oʊvəʳsel/ **(oversells, overselling, oversold)** If you say that something or someone **is oversold**, you mean that people say they are better or more useful than they really are. ❑ *The couple idea is oversold. There's so much pressure to become a couple that people feel failure if they don't conform.* VERB ≠ undersell; be V-ed

**over|sexed** /oʊvəʳsekst/ If you describe someone as **oversexed**, you mean that they are more interested in sex or more involved in sexual activities than you think they should be. ADJ [disapproval]

**over|shad|ow** /oʊvəʳʃædoʊ/ **(overshadows, overshadowing, overshadowed)** 1 If an unpleasant event or feeling **overshadows** something, it makes it less happy or enjoyable. ❑ *Fears for the President's safety could overshadow his peace-making mission.* VERB = cloud; V n 2 If you **are overshadowed by** a person or thing, you are less successful, important, or impressive than they are. ❑ *Hester is overshadowed by her younger and more attractive sister.* VERB: usu passive = eclipse; be V-ed 3 If one building, tree, or large structure **overshadows** another, it stands near it, is much taller than it, and casts a shadow over it. ❑ *She said stations should be in the open, near housing, not overshadowed by trees or walls.* VERB; V-ed

**over|shoot** **(overshoots, overshooting, overshot)**

> The verb is pronounced /oʊvəʳʃuːt/. The noun is pronounced /oʊvəʳʃuːt/.

1 If you **overshoot** a place that you want to get to, you go past it by mistake. ❑ *The plane apparently overshot the runway after landing.* [VERB; V n] 2 If a government or organization **overshoots** its budget, it spends more than it had planned to. ❑ *The government usually overshot its original spending target.* [VERB; V n] ♦ **Overshoot** is also a noun. ❑ *...the 100 million pounds overshoot in the cost of building the hospital.* [N-COUNT: usu supp N]

**over|sight** /oʊvəʳsaɪt/ **(oversights)** 1 If there has been an **oversight**, someone has forgotten to do something which they should have done. ❑ *By an unfortunate oversight, full instructions do not come with the product.* [N-COUNT] 2 If someone has **oversight of** a process or system, they are responsible for making sure that it works efficiently and correctly. ❑ *...a new system, where there'll be greater oversight of doctors.* [N-UNCOUNT: oft N *of* n = supervision]

**over|sim|pli|fy** /oʊvəʳsɪmplɪfaɪ/ **(oversimplifies, oversimplifying, oversimplified)** If you say that someone is **oversimplifying** something, you mean that they are describing or explaining it so simply that what they say is no longer true or reasonable. ❑ *One should not oversimplify the situation.* [VERB; V n] ♦ **over|sim|pli|fied** *...an oversimplified view of mathematics and the social sciences.* [ADJ: usu ADJ n] ♦ **over|sim|pli|fi|ca|tion** /oʊvəʳsɪmplɪfɪkeɪʃᵊn/ **(oversimplifications)** *There is an old saying that 'we are what we eat'. Obviously this is an oversimplification.* [N-VAR]

**over|size** /oʊvəʳsaɪz/ also **oversized**. **Oversize** or **oversized** things are too big, or much bigger than usual. ❑ *...the oversize white sweater she had worn at school. ...an oversized bed.* [ADJ: usu ADJ n]

**over|sleep** /oʊvəʳsliːp/ **(oversleeps, oversleeping, overslept)** If you **oversleep**, you sleep longer than you should have done. ❑ *I'm really sorry I'm late, Andrew. I forgot to set my alarm and I overslept.* [VERB; V]

**over|spend** **(overspends, overspending, overspent)**

> ✓ The verb is pronounced /oʊvəʳspend/. The noun is pronounced /oʊvəʳspend/.

1 If you **overspend**, you spend more money than you can afford to. ❑ *Don't overspend on your home and expect to get the money back when you sell... I overspent by £1 on your shopping so I'm afraid you owe me... He argued that local councils which overspend should be forced to face fresh elections.* [VERB; V *on* n; V *by* amount; V] 2 If an organization or business has an **overspend**, it spends more money than was planned or allowed in its budget. [BRIT, BUSINESS] ❑ *Efforts are under way to avoid a £800,000 overspend.* [N-COUNT: usu sing]

> ✓ in AM, use **overrun**

**over|spill** /oʊvəʳspɪl/ 1 **Overspill** is used to refer to people who live near a city because there is no room in the city itself. [BRIT] ❑ *...new towns built to absorb overspill from nearby cities.* [N-UNCOUNT: also *a* N, oft N n] 2 You can use **overspill** to refer to things or people which there is no room for in the usual place because it is full. ❑ *With the best seats taken, it was ruled that the overspill could stand at the back of the court.* [N-UNCOUNT: also *a* N]

**over|staffed** /oʊvəʳstɑːft, -stæft/ If you say that a place is **overstaffed**, you think there are more people working there than is necessary. ❑ *Many workers believe that the factory is overstaffed.* [ADJ]

**over|state** /oʊvəʳsteɪt/ **(overstates, overstating, overstated)** If you say that someone **is overstating** something, you mean they are describing it in a way that makes it seem more important or serious than it really is. ❑ *The authors no doubt overstated their case with a view to catching the public's attention.* [VERB = exaggerate; V n]

**over|state|ment** /oʊvəʳsteɪtmənt/ **(overstatements)** If you refer to the way something is described is **an overstatement**, you mean it is described in a way that makes it seem more important or serious than it really is. ❑ *This may have been an improvement, but 'breakthrough' was an overstatement.* [N-VAR = exaggeration ≠ understatement]

**over|stay** /oʊvəʳsteɪ/ **(overstays, overstaying, overstayed)** If you **overstay** your time, you stay somewhere for longer than you should. ❑ *Up to forty per cent of the students had overstayed their visas.* to **overstay** your **welcome** → see **welcome**. [VERB: no passive = outstay; V n; Also V]

**over|step** /oʊvəʳstep/ **(oversteps, overstepping, overstepped)** If you say that someone **oversteps** the limits of a system or situation, you mean that they do something that is not allowed or is not acceptable. ❑ *The Commission is sensitive to accusations that it is overstepping its authority.* [VERB = go beyond; V n] ● If someone **oversteps the mark**, they behave in a way that is considered unacceptable. ❑ *He overstepped the mark and we had no option but to suspend him.* [PHRASE: V inflects = go too far]

**over|stretch** /oʊvəʳstretʃ/ **(overstretches, overstretching, overstretched)** If you **overstretch** something or someone or if they **overstretch**, you force them to do something they are not really capable of, and they may be harmed as a result. ❑ *Dr Boutros Ghali said the operation would overstretch resources... Do what you know you can do well and don't overstretch yourself... Never force your legs to overstretch, or you can cause injuries.* [VERB; V n; V pron-refl; V]

**over|stretched** /oʊvəʳstretʃt/ If a system or organization is **overstretched**, it is being forced to work more than it is supposed to. ❑ *Analysts fear the overstretched air traffic control system could reach breaking point.* [ADJ]

**over|sub|scribed** /oʊvəʳsəbskraɪbd/ If something such as an event or a service is **oversubscribed**, too many people apply to attend the event or use the service. ❑ *The popular schools – the sort you really might drive across town for – tend to be heavily oversubscribed.* [ADJ: usu v-link ADJ]

**overt** /oʊvɜːʳt/ An **overt** action or attitude is done or shown in an open and obvious way. ❑ *Although there is no overt hostility, black and white students do not mix much.* [ADJ: usu ADJ n = open] ♦ **overt|ly** *He's written a few overtly political lyrics over the years.* [ADV: usu ADV adj = openly]

**over|take** /oʊvəʳteɪk/ **(overtakes, overtaking, overtook, overtaken)** 1 If you **overtake** a vehicle or a person that is ahead of you and moving in the same direction, you pass them. [mainly BRIT] ❑ *When he eventually overtook the last truck he pulled over to the inside lane... The red car was pulling out ready to overtake.* [VERB; V n; V]

> ✓ in AM, usually use **pass**

2 If someone or something **overtakes** a competitor, they become more successful than them. ❑ *Sales are booming in Japan, which has overtaken Britain as the Mini's biggest market.* [VERB; V n] 3 If an event **overtakes** you, it happens unexpectedly or suddenly. ❑ *Tragedy was shortly to overtake him, however.* [VERB = befall; V n] 4 If a feeling **overtakes** you, it affects you very strongly. [LITERARY] ❑ *Something like panic overtook me.* [VERB = overwhelm; V n]

**over|tax** /oʊvəʳtæks/ **(overtaxes, overtaxing, overtaxed)** 1 If you **overtax** someone or something, you force them to work harder than they can really manage, and may do them harm as a result. ❑ *...a contralto who has overtaxed her voice.* [VERB; V n] 2 If you say that a government **is overtaxing** its people, you mean that it is making them pay more tax than you think they should pay. ❑ *You can't help Britain by overtaxing its people.* [VERB; V n]

**over-the-counter** → see **counter**.

**over-the-top** → see **top**.

**over|throw** **(overthrows, overthrowing, overthrew, overthrown)**

> ✓ The verb is pronounced /oʊvəʳθroʊ/. The noun is pronounced /oʊvəʳθroʊ/.

When a government or leader **is overthrown**, they are removed from power by force. ❑ *That government was overthrown in a military coup three years ago. ...an attempt to overthrow the president.* [VERB; *be* V-ed; V n]

♦ **Overthrow** is also a noun. ❑ *They were charged with plotting the overthrow of the state.* [N-SING: oft N *of* n]

**over|time** /oʊvəʳtaɪm/ [1] **Overtime** is time that you spend doing your job in addition to your normal working hours. ❑ *He would work overtime, without pay, to finish a job.* [N-UNCOUNT] [2] If you say that someone **is working overtime** to do something, you mean that they are using a lot of energy, effort, or enthusiasm trying to do it. [INFORMAL] ❑ *We had to battle very hard and our defence worked overtime to keep us in the game.* [PHRASE: V inflects, usu PHR to-inf] [3] **Overtime** is an additional period of time that is added to the end of a sports match in which the two teams are level, as a way of allowing one of the teams to win. [AM] ❑ *Denver had won the championship by defeating the Cleveland Browns 23-20 in overtime.* [N-UNCOUNT]

✔ in BRIT, use **extra time**

**over|tired** /oʊvəʳtaɪəʳd/ If you are **overtired**, you are so tired that you feel unhappy or bad-tempered, or feel that you cannot do things properly. [ADJ: usu v-link ADJ]

**over|tone** /oʊvəʳtoʊn/ **(overtones)** If something has **overtones of** a particular thing or quality, it suggests that thing or quality but does not openly express it. ❑ *It's a quite profound story, with powerful religious overtones.* [N-COUNT: usu pl, with supp]

**over|took** /oʊvəʳtʊk/ **Overtook** is the past tense of **overtake**.

**over|ture** /oʊvəʳtʃʊəʳ/ **(overtures)** [1] An **overture** is a piece of music, often one that is the introduction to an opera or play. ❑ *The programme opened with the overture to Wagner's Flying Dutchman.* [N-COUNT; N-IN-NAMES] [2] If you make **overtures to** someone, you behave in a friendly or romantic way towards them. ❑ *He had lately begun to make clumsy yet endearing overtures of friendship.* [N-COUNT: usu pl]

**over|turn** /oʊvəʳtɜːʳn/ **(overturns, overturning, overturned)** [1] If something **overturns** or if you **overturn** it, it turns upside down or on its side. ❑ *The lorry veered out of control, overturned and smashed into a wall... Alex jumped up so violently that he overturned his glass of sherry. ...a battered overturned boat.* [VERB; V; V n; V-ed] [2] If someone in authority **overturns** a legal decision, they officially decide that that decision is incorrect or not valid. ❑ *His nine-month sentence was overturned by Appeal Court judge Lord Justice Watkins.* [VERB = overrule; V n] [3] To **overturn** a government or system means to remove it or destroy it. ❑ *He accused his opponents of wanting to overturn the government.* [VERB; V n]

**over|use** **(overuses, overusing, overused)**

✔ The verb is pronounced /oʊvəʳjuːz/. The noun is pronounced /oʊvəʳjuːs/.

[1] If someone **overuses** something, they use more of it than necessary, or use it more often than necessary. ❑ *Don't overuse heated appliances on you hair.* [VERB; V n] ♦ **Overuse** is also a noun. ❑ *Supplies are under increasing threat from overuse and pollution.* [N-UNCOUNT] [2] If you say that people **overuse** a word or idea, you mean that they use it so often that it no longer has any real meaning or effect. ❑ *Which words or phrases do you most overuse?* [VERB; V n] ♦ **over|used** *'Just Do It' has become one of the most overused catch phrases in recent memory.* [ADJ = overworked]

**over|value** /oʊvəʳvæljuː/ **(overvalues, overvaluing, overvalued)** To **overvalue** something, often a cost or rate of exchange, means to fix its value at too high a level compared with other similar things. ❑ *...a rate which does not overvalue the pound... Many, perhaps all, Internet stocks are hugely overvalued.* [VERB ≠ undervalue; V n; *be* V-ed] ♦ **over|valu|ation** /oʊvəʳvæljueɪʃᵊn/ *These problems were aggravated by the overvaluation of the pound.* [N-UNCOUNT: oft N *of* n] ♦ **over|valued** *It still can be argued that Japanese shares are overvalued in terms of the return they offer.* [ADJ ≠ undervalued]

**over|view** /oʊvəʳvjuː/ **(overviews)** An **overview of** a situation is a general understanding or description of it as a whole. ❑ *The central section of the book is a historical overview of drug use.* [N-COUNT: usu sing, oft N *of* n]

**over|ween|ing** /oʊvəʳwiːnɪŋ/ If you want to emphasize your disapproval of someone's great ambition or pride, you can refer to their **overweening** ambition or pride. [FORMAL] ❑ *'Your modesty is a cover for your overweening conceit,' she said.* [ADJ: usu ADJ n] [disapproval]

**over|weight** /oʊvəʳweɪt/ Someone who is **overweight** weighs more than is considered healthy or attractive. ❑ *Being even moderately overweight increases your risk of developing high blood pressure.* [ADJ]

**over|whelm** /oʊvəʳʰwelm/ **(overwhelms, overwhelming, overwhelmed)** [1] If you **are overwhelmed by** a feeling or event, it affects you very strongly, and you do not know how to deal with it. ❑ *He was overwhelmed by a longing for times past... The need to talk to someone, anyone, overwhelmed her.* [VERB = overpower; *be* V-ed; V n] ♦ **over|whelmed** *Sightseers may be a little overwhelmed by the crowds and noise.* [ADJ: usu v-link ADJ] [2] If a group of people **overwhelm** a place or another group, they gain complete control or victory over them. ❑ *It was clear that one massive Allied offensive would overwhelm the weakened enemy.* [VERB = overpower; V n]

**over|whelm|ing** /oʊvəʳʰwelmɪŋ/ [1] If something is **overwhelming**, it affects you very strongly, and you do not know how to deal with it. ❑ *The task won't feel so overwhelming if you break it down into small, easy-to-accomplish steps... She felt an overwhelming desire to have another child.* [◆◇◇ ADJ = overpowering] ♦ **over|whelm|ing|ly** *...the overwhelmingly strange medieval city of Fès.* [ADV: ADV adj] [2] You can use **overwhelming** to emphasize that an amount or quantity is much greater than other amounts or quantities. ❑ *The overwhelming majority of small businesses go broke within the first twenty-four months... The vote was overwhelming – 283 in favour, and only twenty-nine against.* [ADJ: usu ADJ n] [emphasis] ♦ **over|whelm|ing|ly** *The House of Commons has overwhelmingly rejected calls to bring back the death penalty for murder.* [ADV: usu ADV with v, also ADV adj]

**over|work** /oʊvəʳwɜːʳk/ **(overworks, overworking, overworked)** If you **overwork** or if someone **overworks** you, you work too hard, and are likely to become very tired or ill. ❑ *He's overworking and has got a lot on his mind... He overworks and underpays the poor clerk whom he employs.* [VERB; V; V n] ♦ **Overwork** is also a noun. ❑ *He died of a heart attack brought on by overwork.* [N-UNCOUNT] ♦ **over|worked** *...an overworked doctor.* [ADJ]

**over|worked** /oʊvəʳwɜːʳkt/ If you describe a word, expression, or idea as **overworked**, you mean it has been used so often that it no longer has much effect or meaning. ❑ *'Ecological' has become one of the most overworked adjectives among manufacturers of garden supplies.* [ADJ: usu ADJ n]

**over|wrought** /oʊvəʳrɔːt/ Someone who is **overwrought** is very upset and is behaving in an uncontrolled way. ❑ *One overwrought member had to be restrained by friends.* [ADJ]

**ovu|late** /ɒvjʊleɪt/ **(ovulates, ovulating, ovulated)** When a woman or female animal **ovulates**, an egg is produced from one of her ovaries. ❑ *Some girls may first ovulate even before they menstruate.* [VERB; V] ♦ **ovu|la|tion** /ɒvjʊleɪʃᵊn/ *By noticing these changes, the woman can tell when ovulation is about to occur.* [N-UNCOUNT]

**ovum** /oʊvəm/ **(ova)** An **ovum** is one of the eggs of a woman or female animal. [TECHNICAL] [N-COUNT]

**ow** /aʊ/ **'Ow!'** is used in writing to represent the noise that people make when they suddenly feel pain. ❑ *Ow! Don't do that!* [EXCLAM = ouch]

**owe** /oʊ/ **(owes, owing, owed)** [1] If you **owe** money **to** someone, they have lent it to you and you have not yet paid it back. You can also say that the money **is owing**. ❑ *The company owes money to more than 60 banks... Blake already owed him nearly £50... I'm broke, Livy, and I owe a couple of million dollars... He could take what was owing for the rent.* [◆◇◇ VERB; V n *to* n; V n n; V n; V] [2] If someone or something **owes** a particular quality or their success **to** a person or thing, [VERB: no passive] they only have it because of that person or thing. ❑ *He owed his survival to his strength as a swimmer... I owe him my life.* V n *to* n V n n 3 If you say that you **owe** a great deal **to** someone or something, you mean that they have helped you or influenced you a lot, and you feel very grateful to them. ❑ *As a professional composer I owe much to Radio 3... He's been fantastic. I owe him a lot.* VERB V amount *to* n V n amount 4 If you say that something **owes** a great deal to a person or thing, you mean that it exists, is successful, or has its particular form mainly because of them. ❑ *The island's present economy owes a good deal to whisky distilling.* VERB V amount *to* n 5 If you say that you **owe** someone gratitude, respect, or loyalty, you mean that they deserve it from you. [FORMAL] ❑ *Perhaps we owe these people more respect... I owe you an apology. You must have found my attitude very annoying... I owe a big debt of gratitude to her.* VERB V n n V n n V n *to* n 6 If you say that you **owe it to** someone to do something, you mean that you should do that thing because they deserve it. ❑ *I can't go. I owe it to him to stay... You owe it to yourself to get some professional help... Of course she would have to send a letter; she owed it to the family.* VERB: no passive V *it to* n to-inf V *it to* pron-refl to-inf V *it to* n 7 You use **owing to** when you are introducing the reason for something. ❑ *Owing to staff shortages, there was no restaurant car on the train.* PREP-PHRASE: PREP n

**owl** /aʊl/ **(owls)** An **owl** is a bird with a flat face, large eyes, and a small sharp beak. Most owls obtain their food by hunting small animals at night. ➔ See also **night owl**. N-COUNT

**owl|ish** /aʊlɪʃ/ An **owlish** person looks rather like an owl, especially because they wear glasses, and seems to be very serious and clever. ❑ *With his owlish face, it is easy to understand why he was called 'The Professor'.* ADJ: usu ADJ n

**own** /oʊn/ **(owns, owning, owned)** ◆◆◆ 1 You use **own** to indicate that something belongs to a particular person or thing. ❑ *My wife decided I should have my own shop... He could no longer trust his own judgement... His office had its own private entrance.* ADJ: poss ADJ ♦ **Own** is also a pronoun. ❑ *He saw the Major's face a few inches from his own.* PRON: poss PRON 2 You use **own** to indicate that something is used by, or is characteristic of, only one person, thing, or group. ❑ *Jennifer insisted on her own room... I let her tell me about it in her own way... Each nation has its own peculiarities when it comes to doing business.* ADJ: poss ADJ ♦ **Own** is also a pronoun. ❑ *This young lady has a sense of style that is very much her own.* PRON: poss PRON 3 You use **own** to indicate that someone does something without any help from other people. ❑ *They enjoy making their own decisions... He'll have to make his own arrangements.* ADJ: poss ADJ ♦ **Own** is also a pronoun. ❑ *There's no career structure, you have to create your own.* PRON: poss PRON 4 If you **own** something, it is your property. ❑ *His father owns a local pub.* VERB V n

**PHRASES** 5 If you have something you can **call** your **own**, it belongs only to you, rather than being controlled by or shared with someone else. ❑ *I would like a place I could call my own.* PHRASE 6 If someone or something **comes into** their **own**, they become very successful or start to perform very well because the circumstances are right. ❑ *The goalkeeper came into his own with a series of brilliant saves.* PHRASE: V inflects 7 If you **get** your **own back** on someone, you have your revenge on them because of something bad that they have done to you. [mainly BRIT, INFORMAL] ❑ *Renshaw reveals 20 bizarre ways in which women have got their own back on former loved ones.* PHRASE: V inflects, oft PHR *on* n 8 If you say that someone has a particular thing **of** their **own**, you mean that that thing belongs or relates to them, rather than to other people. ❑ *He set out in search of ideas for starting a company of his own.* PHRASE: n PHR 9 If someone or something has a particular quality or characteristic **of** their **own**, that quality or characteristic is especially theirs, rather than being shared by other things or people of that type. ❑ *The cries of the seagulls gave this part of the harbour a fascinating character all of its own.* PHRASE: n PHR 10 When you are **on** your **own**, you are alone. ❑ *He lives on his own... I told him how scared I was of being on my own.* PHRASE: PHR after v, v-link PHR = alone 11 If you do something **on** your **own**, you do it without any help from other people. ❑ *I work best on my own. ...the jobs your child can do on her own.* PHRASE: PHR after v 12 to **hold** your **own** ➔ see **hold**.

♦ **own up** If you **own up** to something wrong that you have done, you admit that you did it. ❑ *The headmaster is waiting for someone to own up... Last year my husband owned up to a secret affair with his secretary.* PHRASAL VERB = admit V P V P *to* n/-ing

**own brand** **(own brands)** **Own brands** are products which have the trademark or label of the shop which sells them, especially a supermarket chain. They are normally cheaper than other popular brands. [BUSINESS] ❑ *This range is substantially cheaper than any of the other own brands available. ...own-brand cola.* N-COUNT

**-owned** /-oʊnd/ **-owned** combines with nouns, adjectives, and adverbs to form adjectives that indicate who owns something. ❑ *More than 50 state-owned companies have been sold since the early 1980s. ...the Japanese-owned Bel Air Hotel in Los Angeles.* COMB in ADJ

**own|er** /oʊnəʳ/ **(owners)** The **owner** of something is the person to whom it belongs. ❑ *The owner of the store was sweeping his floor when I walked in... New owners will have to wait until September before moving in.* ➔ See also **home owner**, **landowner**. ◆◆◇ N-COUNT: usu with supp

**owner-occupier** **(owner-occupiers)** An **owner-occupier** is a person who owns the house or flat that they live in. [BRIT] N-COUNT

**own|er|ship** /oʊnəʳʃɪp/ **Ownership** of something is the state of owning it. ❑ *On January 23rd, America decided to relax its rules on the foreign ownership of its airlines. ...the growth of home ownership in Britain.* ◆◇◇ N-UNCOUNT: usu with supp

**own goal** **(own goals)** 1 In sport, if someone scores **an own goal**, they accidentally score a goal for the team they are playing against. [BRIT] N-COUNT: usu sing 2 If a course of action that someone takes harms their own interests, you can refer to it as **an own goal**. [BRIT] ❑ *Because of the legislation I could not employ a woman. Women have made themselves unemployable. They have scored an own goal.* N-COUNT: usu sing

**own la|bel** **(own labels)** **Own label** is the same as **own brand**. [BUSINESS] ❑ *People will trade down to own labels which are cheaper.* N-COUNT

**ox** /ɒks/ **(oxen** /ɒksən/**)** An **ox** is a bull that has been castrated. Oxen are used in some countries for pulling vehicles or carrying things. N-COUNT

**Ox|bridge** /ɒksbrɪdʒ/ **Oxbridge** is used to refer to the British universities of Oxford and Cambridge together. [BRIT] ❑ *...an offer of a place at Oxbridge.* N-PROPER

**oxi|da|tion** /ɒksɪdeɪʃᵊn/ **Oxidation** is a process in which a chemical substance changes because of the addition of oxygen. [TECHNICAL] N-UNCOUNT

**ox|ide** /ɒksaɪd/ **(oxides)** An **oxide** is a compound of oxygen and another chemical element. N-MASS: usu supp N

**oxi|dize** /ɒksɪdaɪz/ **(oxidizes, oxidizing, oxidized)**

✔ in BRIT, also use **oxidise**

When a substance **is oxidized** or when it **oxidizes**, it changes chemically because of the effect of oxygen on it. ❑ *Aluminium is rapidly oxidized in air... The original white lead pigments have oxidized and turned black.* VERB *be* V-ed V

**ox|tail** /ɒksteɪl/ **(oxtails)** **Oxtail** is meat from the tail of a cow. It is used for making soups and stews. ❑ *...oxtail soup.* N-VAR

**oxy|gen** /ɒksɪdʒən/ **Oxygen** is a colourless gas that exists in large quantities in the air. All plants and animals need oxygen in order to live. ❑ *The human brain needs to be without oxygen for only four minutes before permanent damage occurs.* N-UNCOUNT

**oxy|gen|ate** /ɒksɪdʒɪneɪt/ **(oxygenates, oxygenating, oxygenated)** To **oxygenate** something VERB means to mix or dissolve oxygen into it. ❑ *Previous attempts at filtering and oxygenating aquarium water had failed. ...freshly oxygenated blood.* V n V-ed

**oxy|gen mask** **(oxygen masks)** An **oxygen mask** is a device that is connected to a cylinder of oxygen by means of a tube. It is placed over the nose and mouth of someone who is having difficulty in breathing in order to help them breath more easily. N-COUNT

**oxy|mo|ron** /ɒksimɔːrɒn/ **(oxymorons)** If you describe a phrase as an **oxymoron**, you mean that what it refers to combines two opposite qualities or ideas and therefore seems impossible. [TECHNICAL] ❑ *This has made many Americans conclude that business ethics is an oxymoron.* N-COUNT

**oys|ter** /ɔɪstəʳ/ **(oysters)** 1 An **oyster** is a large flat shellfish. Some oysters can be eaten and others produce valuable objects called pearls. N-COUNT
2 If you say that **the world is** someone's **oyster**, you mean that they can do anything or go anywhere that they want to. ❑ *You're young, you've got a lot of opportunity. The world is your oyster.* PHRASE: V inflects

**oys|ter bed** **(oyster beds)** An **oyster bed** is a place where oysters breed and grow naturally or are kept for food or pearls. N-COUNT

**oyster|catcher** /ɔɪstəʳkætʃəʳ/ **(oystercatchers)** An **oystercatcher** is a black and white bird with a long red beak. It lives near the sea and eats small shellfish. N-COUNT

**oz** **Oz** is a written abbreviation for **ounce**. ❑ *Whisk 25g (1 oz) of butter into the sauce.*

**ozone** /oʊzoʊn/ **Ozone** is a colourless gas which is a form of oxygen. There is a layer of ozone high above the earth's surface. ❑ *What they find could provide clues to what might happen worldwide if ozone depletion continues.* N-UNCOUNT: oft N n

**ozone-friendly** **Ozone-friendly** chemicals, products, or technology do not cause harm to the ozone layer. ❑ *...ozone-friendly chemicals for fridges and air conditioners.* ADJ

**ozone lay|er** **The ozone layer** is the part of the Earth's atmosphere that has the most ozone in it. The ozone layer protects living things from the harmful radiation of the sun. N-SING

# P p

**P, p** /piː/ **(P's, p's)** 1 **P** is the sixteenth letter of the English alphabet. (N-VAR) 2 **p** is an abbreviation for **pence** or **penny**. ❑ *They cost 5p each. ...plans to increase income tax by 1p.* 3 You write **p.** before a number as an abbreviation for 'page'. The plural form is 'pp.'. ❑ *See p. 246 for Thom Bean's response. ...see Chapter 4 (pp. 109-13).*

**pa** /pɑː/ **(pas)** Some people address or refer to their father as **pa**. [INFORMAL] ❑ *Pa used to be in the army.* (N-FAMILY = dad)

**PA** /piː eɪ/ **(PAs)** ◆◇◇ 1 A **PA** is the same as a **personal assistant**. [BUSINESS] (N-COUNT) 2 If you refer to the **PA** or the **PA system** in a place, you are referring to the public address system. ❑ *A voice came booming over the PA.* (N-COUNT: usu *the* N in sing)

**p.a.** **p.a.** is a written abbreviation for **per annum**. ❑ *...dentists with an average net income of £48,000 p.a.*

**pace** /peɪs/ **(paces, pacing, paced)** ◆◇◇ 1 The **pace** of something is the speed at which it happens or is done. ❑ *Many people were not satisfied with the pace of change. ...people who prefer to live at a slower pace... Interest rates would come down as the recovery gathered pace.* (N-SING: usu with supp = speed) 2 Your **pace** is the speed at which you walk. ❑ *He moved at a brisk pace down the rue St Antoine.* (N-SING: usu with supp) 3 A **pace** is the distance that you move when you take one step. ❑ *He'd only gone a few paces before he stopped again.* (N-COUNT: usu with supp) 4 If you **pace** a small area, you keep walking up and down it, because you are anxious or impatient. (VERB) ❑ *As they waited, Kravis paced the room nervously...* (V n) *He found John pacing around the flat, unable to sleep...* (V prep/adv) *She stared as he paced and yelled.* (V) 5 If you **pace yourself** when doing something, you do it at a steady rate. (VERB) ❑ *It was a tough race and I had to pace myself.* (V pron-refl)

PHRASES 6 If something **keeps pace with** something else that is changing, it changes quickly in response to it. ❑ *Farmers are angry because the rise fails to keep pace with inflation.* (PHRASE: V inflects, oft PHR *with* n = keep up) 7 If you **keep pace with** someone who is walking or running, you succeed in going as fast as them, so that you remain close to them. ❑ *With four laps to go, he kept pace with the leaders.* (PHRASE: V inflects, oft PHR *with* n = keep up) 8 If you do something **at** your **own pace**, you do it at a speed that is comfortable for you. ❑ *The computer will give students the opportunity to learn at their own pace.* (PHRASE: PHR after v) 9 If you **put** someone **through** their **paces** or make them **go through** their **paces**, you get them to show you how well they can do something. ❑ *The British coach is putting the boxers through their paces.* (PHRASE: V inflects) 10 **at a snail's pace** → see **snail**.

**paced** /peɪst/ If you talk about the way that something such as a film or book is **paced**, you are referring to the speed at which the story is told. ❑ *This excellent thriller is fast paced and believable.* (ADJ: adv ADJ)

**pace|maker** /peɪsmeɪkəʳ/ **(pacemakers)** 1 A **pacemaker** is a device that is placed inside someone's body in order to help their heart beat in the right way. ❑ *She was fitted with a pacemaker after suffering serious heart trouble.* (N-COUNT) 2 A **pacemaker** is a competitor in a race whose task is to start the race very quickly in order to help the other runners achieve a very fast time. Pacemakers usually stop before the race is finished. (N-COUNT)

**pace|setter** /peɪssetəʳ/ **(pacesetters)** also **pace-setter.** 1 A **pacesetter** is someone who is in the lead during part of a race or competition and therefore decides the speed or standard of the race or competition for that time. ❑ *Real's victory keeps them five points behind the pacesetters, Barcelona... Hammond was the early pace-setter.* (N-COUNT) 2 A **pacesetter** is a person or a company that is considered to be the leader in a particular field or activity. ❑ *Mongolia seemed an unlikely candidate as the pacesetter for political change in Asia.* (N-COUNT)

**pacey** /peɪsi/ → see **pacy**.

**pa|cif|ic** /pəsɪfɪk/ A **pacific** person, country, or course of action is peaceful or has the aim of bringing about peace. [FORMAL] ❑ *The Liberals were traditionally seen as the more pacific party.* (ADJ: usu ADJ n ≠ belligerent)

**Pa|cif|ic** 1 **The Pacific** or **the Pacific Ocean** is a very large sea to the west of North and South America, and to the east of Asia and Australia. ❑ *...an island in the Pacific.* (N-PROPER: *the* N) 2 **Pacific** is used to describe things that are in or that relate to the Pacific Ocean. ❑ *...the tiny Pacific island of Pohnpei.* (ADJ: ADJ n)

**paci|fi|er** /pæsɪfaɪəʳ/ **(pacifiers)** A **pacifier** is a rubber or plastic object that you give to a baby to suck so that he or she feels comforted. [AM] (N-COUNT)

✓ in BRIT, use **dummy**

**paci|fism** /pæsɪfɪzəm/ **Pacifism** is the belief that war and violence are always wrong. (N-UNCOUNT)

**paci|fist** /pæsɪfɪst/ **(pacifists)** 1 A **pacifist** is someone who believes that violence is wrong and refuses to take part in wars. (N-COUNT) 2 If someone has **pacifist** views, they believe that war and violence are always wrong. (ADJ: usu ADJ n)

**paci|fy** /pæsɪfaɪ/ **(pacifies, pacifying, pacified)** 1 If you **pacify** someone who is angry, upset, or not pleased, you succeed in making them calm or pleased. (VERB = placate) ❑ *Is this a serious step, or is this just something to pacify the critics?* (V n) 2 If the army or the police **pacify** a group of people, they use force to overcome their resistance or protests. (VERB) ❑ *Government forces have found it difficult to pacify the rebels.* (V n) ♦ **paci|fi|ca|tion** /pæsɪfɪkeɪʃᵊn/ *...the pacification of the country.* (N-UNCOUNT)

**pack** /pæk/ **(packs, packing, packed)** ◆◆◇ 1 When you **pack** a bag, you put clothes and other things into it, because you are leaving a place or going on holiday. (VERB) ❑ *When I was 17, I packed my bags and left home...* (V n) *I packed and said goodbye to Charlie.* (V) ♦ **pack|ing** *She left Frances to finish her packing.* (N-UNCOUNT) 2 When people **pack** things, for example in a factory, they put them into containers or parcels so that they can be transported and sold. (VERB) ❑ *They offered me a job packing goods in a warehouse...* (V n) *Machines now exist to pack olives in jars.* (V n *in* n) *...sardines packed in oil.* (V-ed) ♦ **pack|ing** *His onions cost 9p a lb wholesale; packing and transport costs 10p.* (N-UNCOUNT) 3 If people or things **pack into** a place or if they **pack** a place, there are so many of them that the place is full. (VERB = cram) ❑ *Hundreds of thousands of people packed into the mosque...* (V *into* n) *Seventy thousand people will pack the stadium.* (V n) 4 A **pack of** things is a collection of them that is sold or given together in a box or bag. ❑ *The club will send a free information pack. ...a pack of cigarettes.* (N-COUNT: oft N *of* n) 5 A **pack** is a bag containing your possessions that you carry on your (N-COUNT = rucksack, backpack) back when you are travelling. ❑ *I hid the money in my pack.* 6 You can refer to a group of people who go around together as a **pack**, especially when it is a large group that you feel threatened by. ❑ *...a pack of journalists eager to question him.* N-COUNT: usu N *of* n

7 A **pack of** wolves or dogs is a group of them that hunt together. N-COUNT: oft N *of* n 8 A **pack of** playing cards is a complete set of playing cards. [mainly BRIT] N-COUNT: oft N *of* n

> in AM, usually use **deck**

**PHRASES** 9 → See also **packed**, **packing**. 10 If you say that an account is **a pack of lies**, you mean that it is completely untrue. ❑ *You told me a pack of lies.* PHRASE: PHR after v, v-link PHR 11 If you **send** someone **packing**, you make them go away. [INFORMAL] ❑ *I decided I wanted to live alone and I sent him packing.* PHRASE: V inflects

♦ **pack in** 1 If you **pack** something **in**, you stop doing it. [mainly BRIT, INFORMAL] ❑ *I'd just packed in a job the day before... Pack it in. Stop being spiteful.* PHRASAL VERB V P n (not pron) V n P 2 If someone **packs in** things or people, they fit a lot of them into a limited space or time. ❑ *Prisons are having to pack in as many inmates as possible... It's kind of a referendum, though a lot of issues are packed in.* PHRASAL VERB V P n (not pron) Also V n P ● If a play, film or event **packs them in**, lots of people go to see it. [INFORMAL] ❑ *'Blow your head!' is still packing them in at Camden's Jazz Café every Friday night.* PHRASE: V inflects

♦ **pack into** 1 If someone **packs** a lot of something **into** a limited space or time, they fit a lot into it. ❑ *I have tried to pack a good deal into a few words.* PHRASAL VERB = cram into V n P n 2 If people or things **are packed into** a place, so many of them are put in there that the place becomes very full. ❑ *Some 700 people were packed into a hotel room.* PHRASAL VERB: usu passive = cram into *be* V-ed P n

♦ **pack off** If you **pack** someone **off** somewhere, you send them there to stay for a period of time. [INFORMAL] ❑ *He packed off his wife and children to stay in a caravan in Wales... I finally succeeded in packing her off to bed.* PHRASAL VERB V P n (not pron) to-inf V n P *to* n Also V n P

♦ **pack up** 1 If you **pack up** or if you **pack up** your things, you put your possessions or the things you have been using in a case or bag, because you are leaving. ❑ *They packed up and went home... He quickly began packing up his things.* PHRASAL VERB V P V P n Also V n P 2 If a machine or a part of the body **packs up**, it stops working. [BRIT, INFORMAL] ❑ *In the end it was his stomach and lungs that packed up.* PHRASAL VERB V P

**pack|age** /pækɪdʒ/ **(packages, packaging, packaged)** ◆◆◇ 1 A **package** is a small parcel. ❑ *I tore open the package. ...a package addressed to Miss Claire Montgomery.* N-COUNT 2 A **package** is a small container in which a quantity of something is sold. Packages are either small boxes made of thin cardboard, or bags or envelopes made of paper or plastic. [mainly AM] ❑ *...a package of doughnuts... It is listed among the ingredients on the package.* N-COUNT

> in BRIT, usually use **packet**

3 A **package** is a set of proposals that are made by a government or organization and which must be accepted or rejected as a group. ❑ *The government has announced a package of measures to help the British film industry.* N-COUNT 4 When a product **is packaged**, it is put into containers to be sold. ❑ *The beans are then ground and packaged for sale as ground coffee... Packaged foods have to show a list of ingredients.* VERB: usu passive *be* V-ed V-ed 5 If something **is packaged** in a particular way, it is presented or advertised in that way in order to make it seem attractive or interesting. ❑ *A city has to be packaged properly to be attractive to tourists. ...entertainment packaged as information.* VERB: usu passive *be* V-ed *be* V-ed *as* n 6 A **package** tour, or in British English a **package** holiday, is a holiday arranged by a travel company in which your travel and your accommodation are booked for you. N-COUNT: usu N n

**pack|age deal (package deals)** A **package deal** is a set of offers or proposals which is made by a government or an organization, and which must be accepted or rejected as a whole. N-COUNT: usu sing

**pack|ag|ing** /pækɪdʒɪŋ/ **Packaging** is the container or covering that something is sold in. ❑ *It is selling very well, in part because the packaging is so attractive.* N-UNCOUNT

**pack ani|mal (pack animals)** A **pack animal** is an animal such as a horse or donkey that is used to carry things on journeys. N-COUNT

**packed** /pækt/ 1 A place that is **packed** is very crowded. ❑ *From 3.30 until 7pm, the shop is packed... The streets were packed with men, women and children.* ADJ 2 Something that is **packed with** things contains a very large number of them. ❑ *The Encyclopedia is packed with clear illustrations and over 250 recipes.* ADJ: v-link ADJ *with* n

**packed lunch (packed lunches)** A **packed lunch** is food, for example sandwiches, which you take to work, to school, or on a trip and eat as your lunch. [BRIT] N-COUNT

> in AM, use **box lunch**

**packed out** If a place is **packed out**, it is very full of people. [BRIT, INFORMAL] ❑ *There are 350 cinemas in Paris and most are packed out.* ADJ: usu v-link ADJ

> in AM, use **packed**

**pack|er** /pækəʳ/ **(packers)** A **packer** is a worker whose job is to pack things into containers. ❑ *Norma Jones worked as a packer in a local chemical factory.* N-COUNT

**pack|et** /pækɪt/ **(packets)** 1 A **packet** is a small container in which a quantity of something is sold. Packets are either small boxes made of thin cardboard, or bags or envelopes made of paper or plastic. [mainly BRIT] ❑ *Cook the rice according to instructions on the packet. ...a cigarette packet.* N-COUNT = pack ♦ A **packet of** something is an amount of it contained in a packet. ❑ *He had smoked half a packet of cigarettes.* N-COUNT: usu N *of* n = pack

> in AM, usually use **pack**, **package**

2 A **packet** is a small flat parcel. [mainly BRIT] ❑ *...a packet of photographs.* N-COUNT 3 You can refer to a lot of money as **a packet**. [BRIT, INFORMAL] ❑ *It'll cost you a packet.* N-SING: *a* N = fortune

> in AM, use **bundle**

4 → See also **pay packet**, **wage packet**.

**pack|et switch|ing** also **packet-switching**. **Packet-switching** is a method of sending computer data on telephone lines which automatically divides the data into short pieces in order to send it and puts it together again when it is received. [COMPUTING] N-UNCOUNT

**pack ice** **Pack ice** is an area of ice that is floating on the sea. It is made up of pieces of ice that have been pushed together. N-UNCOUNT

**pack|ing** /pækɪŋ/ **Packing** is the paper, plastic, or other material which is put round things that are being sent somewhere. → See also **pack**. N-UNCOUNT

**pack|ing box (packing boxes)** A **packing box** is the same as a **packing case**. [mainly AM] N-COUNT

**pack|ing case (packing cases)** A **packing case** is a large wooden box in which things are put so that they can be stored or taken somewhere. [mainly BRIT] N-COUNT

> in AM, usually use **packing box**

**pack|ing house (packing houses)** A **packing house** is a company that processes and packs food, especially meat, to be sold. [AM] N-COUNT

**pact** /pækt/ **(pacts)** A **pact** is a formal agreement between two or more people, organizations, or governments to do a particular thing or to help each other. ❑ *Last month he signed a new non-aggression pact with Germany.* ◆◇◇ N-COUNT: oft supp N

**pacy** /peɪsi/ **(pacier, paciest)** also **pacey**. 1 You use **pacy** to describe someone, especially a sports player, who has the ability to move very quickly. [BRIT] ❑ *...United's pacey new striker.* ADJ 2 If you describe a story or a film as **pacy**, you mean that it is exciting because the events happen very quickly one after another. [BRIT] ❑ *Set in contemporary Dublin, this pacy thriller features kidnapping, mayhem and murder.* ADJ

**pad** /pæd/ **(pads, padding, padded)** 1 A **pad** is a fairly thick, flat piece of a material such as cloth or rubber. Pads are used, for example, to clean things, to protect things, or to change their shape. ❑ *He withdrew the needle and placed a pad of cotton-wool over the spot. ...a scouring pad.* N-COUNT 2 A **pad of** paper is a number of pieces of paper which are fixed together along the top or the side, so that each piece can be torn off when it has been used. ❑ *She wrote on a pad of paper... Have a pad and pencil ready and jot down some of your thoughts.* N-COUNT 3 When someone **pads** somewhere, they walk there with steps that are fairly quick, light, and quiet. ❑ *Freddy speaks very quietly and pads around in soft velvet slippers... I often bumped into him as he padded the corridors.* VERB V prep/adv V n 4 A **pad** is a platform or an area of flat, hard ground where helicopters take off and land or rockets are launched. ❑ *...a little round helicopter pad. ...a landing pad on the back of the ship.* → See also **launch pad**. N-COUNT 5 The **pads of** a person's fingers and toes or of an animal's feet are the soft, fleshy parts of them. ❑ *Tap your cheeks all over with the pads of your fingers.* N-COUNT: usu pl, usu N *of* n 6 If you **pad** something, you put something soft in it or over it in order to make it less hard, to protect it, or to give it a different shape. ❑ *Pad the back of a car seat with a pillow... I can tell you I always padded my bras.* VERB V n *with* n V n ♦ **pad|ded** *...a padded jacket. ...back-rests padded with camel's wool.* ADJ 7 → See also **padding**.

♦ **pad out** If you **pad out** a piece of writing or a speech **with** unnecessary words or pieces of information, you include them in it to make it longer and hide the fact that you have not got very much to say. ❑ *The reviewer padded out his review with a lengthy biography of the author.* PHRASAL VERB V P n *with* n Also V n P, V n P *with* n

**pad|ded cell** **(padded cells)** A **padded cell** is a small room with padded walls in a mental hospital or prison, where a person who may behave violently can be put so that they do not hurt themselves. N-COUNT

**pad|ding** /pædɪŋ/ 1 **Padding** is soft material which is put on something or inside it in order to make it less hard, to protect it, or to give it a different shape. ❑ *...the foam rubber padding on the headphones... Players must wear padding to protect them from injury.* N-UNCOUNT 2 **Padding** is unnecessary words or information used to make a piece of writing or a speech longer. ❑ *...the kind of subject that politicians put in their speeches for a bit of padding.* N-UNCOUNT

**pad|dle** /pædᵊl/ **(paddles, paddling, paddled)** 1 A **paddle** is a short pole with a wide flat part at one end or at both ends. You hold it in your hands and use it as an oar to move a small boat through water. ❑ *We might be able to push ourselves across with the paddle.* N-COUNT 2 If you **paddle** a boat, you move it through water using a paddle. ❑ *...the skills you will use to paddle the canoe. ...paddling around the South Pacific in a kayak.* VERB V n V prep/adv 3 If you **paddle**, you walk or stand in shallow water, for example at the edge of the sea, for pleasure. ❑ *Wear sandals when you paddle. ...a lovely little stream that you can paddle in.* VERB V V prep ♦ **Paddle** is also a noun. ❑ *Ruth enjoyed her paddle.* N-SING

**pad|dle boat** **(paddle boats)** A **paddle boat** or a **paddle steamer** is a large boat that is pushed through the water by the movement of large wheels that are attached to its sides. N-COUNT

**pad|dling pool** **(paddling pools)** A **paddling pool** is a shallow artificial pool for children to paddle in. [BRIT] N-COUNT

✔ in AM, use **wading pool**

**pad|dock** /pædək/ **(paddocks)** 1 A **paddock** is a small field where horses are kept. ❑ *The family kept horses in the paddock in front of the house.* N-COUNT 2 In horse racing or motor racing, the **paddock** is the place where the horses or cars are kept just before each race. N-COUNT

**pad|dy** /pædi/ **(paddies)** A **paddy** or a **paddy field** is a field that is kept flooded with water and is used for growing rice. ❑ *...the paddy fields of China.* N-COUNT

**pad|lock** /pædlɒk/ **(padlocks, padlocking, padlocked)** 1 A **padlock** is a lock which is used for fastening two things together. It consists of a block of metal with a U-shaped bar attached to it. One end of the bar is released by turning a key in the lock. ❑ *They had put a padlock on the door of his flat.* N-COUNT 2 If you **padlock** something, you lock it or fasten it to something else using a padlock. ❑ *Eddie parked his cycle against a lamp post and padlocked it.* VERB V n Also V n *to* n

**pa|dre** /pɑːdreɪ/ **(padres)** A **padre** is a Christian priest, especially one who works with the armed forces. [INFORMAL] ❑ *Could I speak to you in private a moment, padre.* N-COUNT; N-VOC

**paean** /piːən/ **(paeans)** A **paean** is a piece of music, writing, or film that expresses praise, admiration, or happiness. [LITERARY] ❑ *...a paean to deep, passionate love.* N-COUNT: usu N *to* n = *eulogy*

**pae|dia|tri|cian** /piːdiətrɪʃᵊn/ **(paediatricians)**

✔ in AM, use **pediatrician**

A **paediatrician** is a doctor who specializes in treating sick children. N-COUNT

**pae|di|at|rics** /piːdiætrɪks/

✔ The spelling **pediatrics** is used in American English. The form **paediatric** is used as a modifier.

**Paediatrics** is the area of medicine that is concerned with the treatment of children's illnesses. N-UNCOUNT

**pae|do|phile** /piːdəfaɪl/ **(paedophiles)**

✔ in AM, use **pedophile**

A **paedophile** is a person, usually a man, who is sexually attracted to children. N-COUNT

**pae|do|philia** /piːdəfɪliə/

✔ in AM, use **pedophilia**

**Paedophilia** is sexual activity with children or the condition of being sexually attracted to children. N-UNCOUNT

**pa|el|la** /paɪelə/ **(paellas)** **Paella** is a dish cooked especially in Spain, which consists of rice mixed with small pieces of vegetables, fish, and chicken. N-VAR

**paeo|ny** /piːəni/ → see **peony**.

**pa|gan** /peɪgən/ **(pagans)** 1 **Pagan** beliefs and activities do not belong to any of the main religions of the world and take nature and a belief in many gods as a basis. They are older, or are believed to be older, than other religions. ADJ: usu ADJ n 2 In former times, **pagans** were people who did not believe in Christianity and who many Christians considered to be inferior people. ❑ *The new religion was eager to convert the pagan world.* N-COUNT: oft N n ≠ *Christian*

**pa|gan|ism** /peɪgənɪzəm/ **Paganism** is pagan beliefs and activities. ❑ *The country swayed precariously between Christianity and paganism.* N-UNCOUNT

**page** /peɪdʒ/ **(pages, paging, paged)** ◆◆◆ 1 A **page** is one side of one of the pieces of paper in a book, magazine, or newspaper. Each page usually has a number printed at the top or bottom. ❑ *Where's your book? Take it out and turn to page 4. ...the front page of the Guardian. ...1,400 pages of top-secret information.* N-COUNT: oft N num 2 The **pages** of a book, magazine, or newspaper are the pieces of paper it consists of. ❑ *He turned the pages of his notebook... Over the page you can read all about the six great books on offer.* N-COUNT 3 You can refer to an important event or period of time as a **page** of history. [LITERARY] ❑ *...a new page in the country's political history.* N-COUNT: with supp 4 If someone who is in a public place **is paged**, they receive a message, often over a speaker, telling them that someone is trying to contact them. ❑ *He was paged repeatedly as the flight was boarding... I'll have them paged and tell them you're here.* VERB *be* V-ed *have* n V-ed 5 A **page** is a young person N-COUNT who takes messages or does small jobs for members of the United States Congress or state legislatures. [AM]

**pag|eant** /pædʒənt/ **(pageants)** 1 A **pageant** is a colourful public procession, show, or ceremony. Pageants are usually held out of doors and often celebrate events or people from history. [N-COUNT] 2 A **pageant** or a **beauty pageant** is a competition in which young women are judged to decide which one is the most beautiful. [N-COUNT]

**pag|eant|ry** /pædʒəntri/ People use **pageantry** to refer to the colourful and formal things that are done for special official or royal occasions, for example the wearing of special clothes and the playing of special music. ❑ *...all the pageantry of an official state visit.* [N-UNCOUNT]

**page|boy** /peɪdʒbɔɪ/ **(pageboys)** also **page-boy.** A **pageboy** is a small boy who accompanies the bride at a wedding. [mainly BRIT] [N-COUNT]

☑ in AM, usually use **page**

**pag|er** /peɪdʒəʳ/ **(pagers)** A **pager** is a small electronic device which you can carry around with you and which gives you a number or a message when someone is trying to contact you. [mainly BRIT] [N-COUNT]

☑ in AM, usually use **beeper**

**pa|go|da** /pəgoʊdə/ **(pagodas)** A **pagoda** is a tall building which is used for religious purposes, especially by Buddhists, in China, Japan, and South-East Asia. Pagodas are usually very highly decorated. [N-COUNT]

**pah** /pæ/ **Pah** is used in writing to represent the sound someone makes when showing disgust or contempt. [EXCLAM]

**paid** /peɪd/ 1 **Paid** is the past tense and past participle of **pay**. 2 **Paid** workers, or people who do **paid** work, receive money for the work that they do. ❑ *Apart from a small team of paid staff, the organisation consists of unpaid volunteers.* [ADJ: ADJ n ≠unpaid] 3 If you are given **paid** holiday, you get your wages or salary even though you are not at work. ❑ *...10 days' paid holiday for house hunting.* [ADJ: ADJ n] 4 If you are well **paid**, you receive a lot of money for the work that you do. If you are badly **paid**, you do not receive much money. ❑ *...a well-paid accountant... Fruit-picking is boring, badly paid and very hard work.* [ADJ: adv ADJ] 5 If an unexpected event **puts paid to** someone's hopes, chances, or plans, it completely ends or destroys them. [mainly BRIT] ❑ *...a series of airforce strikes that put paid to the General's hopes of fighting on.* [PHRASE: V inflects, PHR n]

**paid-up** also **paid up.** 1 If a person or country is a **paid-up** member of a group, they are an enthusiastic member or are recognized by most people as being a member of it. ❑ *...our future as an independent nation lies as a fully paid-up member of Europe.* [ADJ: ADJ n] 2 If someone is a **paid-up** member of a political party or other organization, they have paid the money needed to become an official member. ❑ *...a fully paid-up member of the Labour Party.* [ADJ: ADJ n]

**pail** /peɪl/ **(pails)** A **pail** is a bucket, usually made of metal or wood. [mainly AM; also BRIT, OLD-FASHIONED] [N-COUNT]

**pain** /peɪn/ **(pains, pained)** 1 **Pain** is the feeling of great discomfort you have, for example when you have been hurt or when you are ill. ❑ *...back pain. ...a bone disease that caused excruciating pain... I felt a sharp pain in my lower back. ...chest pains.* [◆◆◇ N-VAR] ● If you are **in pain**, you feel pain in a part of your body, because you are injured or ill. ❑ *She was writhing in pain, bathed in perspiration.* [PHRASE: PHR after v] 2 **Pain** is the feeling of unhappiness that you have when something unpleasant or upsetting happens. ❑ *...grey eyes that seemed filled with pain.* [N-UNCOUNT = anguish] 3 If a fact or idea **pains** you, it makes you feel upset and disappointed. ❑ *This public acknowledgment of Ted's disability pained my mother... It pains me to think of you struggling all alone.* [VERB: no cont; V n; it V n to-inf; Also it V n that]

PHRASES 4 In informal English, if you call someone or something **a pain** or **a pain in the neck**, you mean that they are very annoying or irritating. Expressions such as **a pain in the arse** and **a pain in the backside** in British English, or **a pain in the ass** and **a pain in the butt** in American English, are also used, but most people consider them offensive. [INFORMAL] [PHRASE: *pain* inflects, v-link PHR, PHR to-inf; disapproval] 5 If someone **is at pains to** do something, they are very eager and anxious to do it, especially because they want to avoid a difficult situation. ❑ *Mobil is at pains to point out that the chances of an explosion at the site are remote.* [PHRASE: V inflects, usu PHR to-inf = anxious] 6 If someone is ordered not to do something **on pain of** or **under pain of** death, imprisonment, or arrest, they will be killed, put in prison, or arrested if they do it. ❑ *We were forbidden, under pain of imprisonment, to use our native language.* [PREP-PHRASE] 7 If you **take pains to** do something or **go to great pains to** do something, you try hard to do it, because you think it is important to do it. ❑ *Social workers went to great pains to acknowledge men's domestic rights... I had taken great pains with my appearance.* [PHRASE: V inflects, usu PHR to-inf]

**pain bar|ri|er** If you say that a sports player has gone through **the pain barrier**, you mean that he or she is continuing to make a great effort in spite of being injured or exhausted. [BRIT, JOURNALISM] ❑ *England's World Cup hero is determined to play through the pain barrier.* [N-SING: *the* N]

**pained** /peɪnd/ If you have a **pained** expression or look, you look upset, worried, or slightly annoyed. [ADJ]

**pain|ful** /peɪnfʊl/ 1 If a part of your body is **painful**, it hurts because it is injured or because there is something wrong with it. ❑ *Her glands were swollen and painful.* [◆◇◇ ADJ: oft ADJ to-inf] ♦ **pain|ful|ly** *His tooth had started to throb painfully again.* [ADV: ADV with v] 2 If something such as an illness, injury, or operation is **painful**, it causes you a lot of physical pain. ❑ *...a painful back injury.* [ADJ] ♦ **pain|ful|ly** *He cracked his head painfully against the cupboard.* [ADV: ADV with v] 3 Situations, memories, or experiences that are **painful** are difficult and unpleasant to deal with, and often make you feel sad and upset. ❑ *Remarks like that brought back painful memories... She finds it too painful to return there without him.* [ADJ: oft ADJ to-inf] ♦ **pain|ful|ly** *...their old relationship, which he had painfully broken off.* [ADV: ADV with v] 4 If a performance or interview is **painful**, it is so bad that it makes you feel embarrassed for the people taking part in it. [INFORMAL] ❑ *The interview was painful to watch.* [ADJ: oft ADJ to-inf]

**pain|ful|ly** /peɪnfʊli/ You use **painfully** to emphasize a quality or situation that is undesirable. ❑ *Things are moving painfully slowly. ...a painfully shy young man.* ➔ See also **painful.** [ADV: ADV adv/adj; emphasis]

**pain|killer** /peɪnkɪləʳ/ **(painkillers)** A **painkiller** is a drug which reduces or stops physical pain. [N-COUNT]

**pain|less** /peɪnləs/ 1 Something such as a treatment that is **painless** causes no physical pain. ❑ *Acupuncture treatment is gentle, painless, and, invariably, most relaxing. ...a quick and painless death.* [ADJ ≠painful] ♦ **pain|less|ly** *...a technique to eliminate unwanted facial hair quickly and painlessly.* [ADV: ADV with v] 2 If a process or activity is **painless**, there are no difficulties involved, and you do not have to make a great effort or suffer in any way. ❑ *House-hunting is in fact relatively painless in this region.* [ADJ] ♦ **pain|less|ly** *...a game for children which painlessly teaches essential pre-reading skills.* [ADV: ADV with v]

**pains|taking** /peɪnsteɪkɪŋ/ A **painstaking** search, examination, or investigation is done extremely carefully and thoroughly. ❑ *Forensic experts carried out a painstaking search of the debris.* [ADJ: usu ADJ n = thorough] ♦ **pains|taking|ly** *Broken bones were painstakingly pieced together and reshaped.* [ADV: usu ADV before v]

**paint** /peɪnt/ **(paints, painting, painted)** 1 **Paint** is a coloured liquid that you put onto a surface with a brush in order to protect the surface or to make it look nice, or that you use to produce a picture. ❑ *...a pot of red paint... They saw* [◆◆◇ N-MASS] *some large letters in white paint. ...water-based artist's paints.* [2] On a wall or object, **the paint** is the covering of dried paint on it. ❑ *The paint was peeling on the window frames.* (N-SING: *the* N) [3] If you **paint** a wall or an object, you cover it with paint. ❑ *They started to mend the woodwork and paint the walls... I made a guitar and painted it red. ...painted furniture.* (VERB; V n; V n colour; V-ed) [4] If you **paint** something or **paint** a picture of it, you produce a picture of it using paint. ❑ *He is painting a huge volcano... Why do people paint pictures?... I had come here to paint.* (VERB; V n; V n; V) [5] When you **paint** a design or message on a surface, you put it on the surface using paint. ❑ *...a machine for painting white lines down roads... The recesses are decorated with gold stars, with smaller stars painted along the edges.* (VERB; V n prep; V-ed) [6] If a woman **paints** her lips or nails, she puts a coloured cosmetic on them. ❑ *She propped the mirror against her handbag and began to paint her lips... She painted her fingernails bright red.* (VERB; V n; V n colour) [7] If you **paint** a grim or vivid picture of something, you give a description of it that is grim or vivid. ❑ *The report paints a grim picture of life there.* (VERB; V n) [8] → See also **painting**, **gloss paint**, **oil paint**, **poster paint**, **war paint**.

**paint|box** /peɪntbɒks/ **(paintboxes)** A **paintbox** is a small flat plastic or metal container with a number of little blocks of paint inside which can be made wet and used to paint a picture. (N-COUNT)

**paint|brush** /peɪntbrʌʃ/ **(paintbrushes)** also **paint brush, paint-brush.** A **paintbrush** is a brush which you use for painting. → See picture on page 1709. (N-COUNT)

**paint|er** /peɪntəʳ/ **(painters)** [1] A **painter** is an artist who paints pictures. (N-COUNT) [2] A **painter** is someone who paints walls, doors, and some other parts of buildings as their job. (N-COUNT)

**paint|er|ly** /peɪntəʳli/ **Painterly** means relating to or characteristic of painting or painters. ❑ *...his painterly talents... The film has a painterly eye.* (ADJ: usu ADJ n)

**paint|ing** /peɪntɪŋ/ **(paintings)** ◆◆◇ [1] A **painting** is a picture which someone has painted. ❑ *...a large oil-painting of Queen Victoria.* (N-COUNT) [2] **Painting** is the activity of painting pictures. ❑ *...two hobbies she really enjoyed, painting and gardening.* (N-UNCOUNT) [3] **Painting** is the activity of painting doors, walls, and some other parts of buildings. ❑ *...painting and decorating.* (N-UNCOUNT)

**paint strip|per** **(paint strippers)** **Paint stripper** is a liquid which you use in order to remove old paint from things such as doors or pieces of furniture. (N-MASS)

**paint|work** /peɪntwɜːʳk/ The **paintwork** of a building, room, or vehicle is the covering of paint on it, or the parts of it that are painted. ❑ *The paintwork, the wardrobes and the bedside cupboards were coffee-cream.* (N-UNCOUNT)

**pair** /peəʳ/ **(pairs, pairing, paired)** ◆◆◇ [1] A **pair of** things are two things of the same size and shape that are used together or are both part of something, for example shoes, earrings, or parts of the body. ❑ *...a pair of socks. ...trainers that cost up to 90 pounds a pair... 72,000 pairs of hands clapped in unison to the song.* (N-COUNT: usu with supp) [2] Some objects that have two main parts of the same size and shape are referred to as a **pair**, for example **a pair of trousers** or **a pair of scissors.** ❑ *...a pair of faded jeans. ...a pair of binoculars.* (N-COUNT: usu with supp) [3] You can refer to two people as a **pair** when they are standing or walking together or when they have some kind of relationship with each other. ❑ *A pair of teenage boys were smoking cigarettes.* (N-SING) [4] If one thing **is paired with** another, it is put with it or considered with it. ❑ *The trainees will then be paired with experienced managers.* (VERB: usu passive; *be* V-ed *with* n) ♦ **pair|ing** *...the pairing of these two fine musicians.* (N-UNCOUNT: usu *the* N *of* n) [5] → See also **au pair**. [6] If you say that someone is or has **a safe pair of hands**, you mean that they are reliable and will not make any serious mistakes. [BRIT, JOURNALISM] ❑ *He has now held five cabinet posts and remains a safe pair of hands.* (PHRASE: PHR after v)

♦ **pair off** When people **pair off** or **are paired off**, they form a pair, often in order to become girlfriend and boyfriend. ❑ *I knew she wouldn't be able to resist pairing me off with someone... The squad members paired off to find places to eat and sleep.* (PHRASAL VERB; V n P *with* n; pl-n V P; Also V P *with* n)

♦ **pair up** If people **pair up** or **are paired up**, they form a pair, especially in order to do something together. ❑ *They asked us to pair up with the person next to us and form teams... Men and teenage girls pair up to dance... Smokers and nonsmokers are paired up as roommates.* (PHRASAL VERB; V P *with* n; pl-n V P; pl-n *be* V-ed; Also V n P *with* n)

**pair|ing** /peərɪŋ/ **(pairings)** Two people, especially sports players, actors, or musicians, who are working together as a pair can be referred to as a **pairing.** ❑ *In first place we now find the Belgian pairing of Nancy Feber and Laurence Courtois.* (N-COUNT = pair)

**pais|ley** /peɪzli/ **(paisleys)** **Paisley** is a special pattern of curving shapes and colours, used especially on fabric. ❑ *He was elegantly dressed in a grey suit, blue shirt and paisley tie.* (N-VAR)

**pa|jam|as** /pədʒɑːməz/ → see **pyjamas.**

**Pa|ki|stani** /pɑːkɪstɑːni/ **(Pakistanis)** [1] **Pakistani** means belonging or relating to Pakistan, or to its people or culture. (ADJ) [2] A **Pakistani** is a Pakistani citizen, or a person of Pakistani origin. (N-COUNT: usu pl)

**pal** /pæl/ **(pals)** Your **pals** are your friends. [INFORMAL, OLD-FASHIONED] (N-COUNT: usu with poss)

**pal|ace** /pælɪs/ **(palaces)** ◆◇◇ [1] A **palace** is a very large impressive house, especially one which is the official home of a king, queen, or president. ❑ *...Buckingham Palace... They entered the palace courtyard.* (N-COUNT: oft in names after n, N n) [2] When the members of a royal palace make an announcement through an official spokesperson, they can be referred to as **the Palace.** ❑ *The palace will not comment on questions about the family's private life.* (N-SING: *the* N)

**palae|on|tol|ogy** /pæliɒntɒlədʒi, AM peɪl-/ also **paleontology. Palaeontology** is the study of fossils as a guide to the history of life on earth. (N-UNCOUNT) ♦ **palae|on|tolo|gist** **(palaeontologists)** ❑ *...just as a palaeontologist can reconstruct a dinosaur from one of its toes.* (N-COUNT)

**pal|at|able** /pælətəbᵊl/ [1] If you describe food or drink as **palatable**, you mean that it tastes pleasant. [FORMAL] ❑ *...flavourings and preservatives, designed to make the food look more palatable.* (ADJ ≠unpalatable) [2] If you describe something such as an idea or method as **palatable**, you mean that people are willing to accept it. ❑ *...a palatable way of sacking staff.* (ADJ = acceptable ≠unpalatable)

**pal|ate** /pælɪt/ **(palates)** [1] Your **palate** is the top part of the inside of your mouth. (N-COUNT: usu poss N) [2] You can refer to someone's **palate** as a way of talking about their ability to judge good food or drink. ❑ *...fresh pasta sauces to tempt more demanding palates.* (N-COUNT: usu with supp)

**pa|la|tial** /pəleɪʃᵊl/ A **palatial** house, hotel, or office building is very large and impressive. ❑ *...a palatial Hollywood mansion.* (ADJ: usu ADJ n)

**pa|la|ver** /pəlɑːvəʳ, -læv-/ **Palaver** is unnecessary fuss and bother about the way something is done. [INFORMAL] ❑ *We don't want all that palaver, do we?* (N-UNCOUNT)

**pale** /peɪl/ **(paler, palest, pales, paling, paled)** ◆◇◇ [1] If something is **pale**, it is very light in colour or almost white. ❑ *Migrating birds filled the pale sky... As we age, our skin becomes paler.* (ADJ ≠dark) ♦ **Pale** is also a combining form. ❑ *...a pale blue sailor dress.* (COMB in COLOUR) [2] If someone looks **pale**, their face looks lighter colour than usual, usually because they are ill, frightened, or shocked. ❑ *She looked pale and tired.* (ADJ: usu v-link ADJ) ♦ **pale|ness** *...his paleness when he realized that he was bleeding.* (N-UNCOUNT: oft with poss) [3] If one thing **pales** in comparison with another, it is made to seem much less important, serious, or good by it. ❑ *When someone you love has a life-threatening illness, everything else pales in comparison. ...a soap opera against which other soaps pale into insignificance.* (VERB; V; V prep) [4] If you think that someone's actions or behaviour are not accept- (PHRASE: PHR after v, oft PHR *of* n)

able, you can say that they are **beyond the pale**. = *unacceptable*
❑ *This sort of thing really is quite beyond the pale.*

**pale|on|tol|ogy** /pæliɒntɒlədʒi, AM peɪl-/ → see **palaeontology**.

**Pal|es|tin|ian** /pælɪstɪniən/ **(Palestinians)** [1] **Palestinian** means belonging or relating to the region between the River Jordan and the Mediterranean Sea which used to be called Palestine, or to the Arabs who come from this region. ADJ [2] A **Palestinian** is an Arab who comes from the region that used to be called Palestine. N-COUNT: usu pl

**pal|ette** /pælɪt/ **(palettes)** [1] A **palette** is a flat piece of wood or plastic on which an artist mixes paints. N-COUNT [2] You can refer to the range of colours that are used by a particular artist or group of artists as their **palette**. ❑ *David Fincher paints from a palette consisting almost exclusively of grey and mud brown.* N-COUNT: usu sing

**pal|ette knife** **(palette knives)** A **palette knife** is a knife with a broad, flat, flexible blade, used in cookery and in oil painting. N-COUNT

**pali|mo|ny** /pælɪmouni/ **Palimony** is money that a person pays to a partner they have lived with for a long time and are now separated from. Compare **alimony**. N-UNCOUNT

**pal|in|drome** /pælɪndroum/ **(palindromes)** A **palindrome** is a word or a phrase that is the same whether you read it backwards or forwards, for example the word 'refer'. N-COUNT

**pali|sade** /pælɪseɪd/ **(palisades)** A **palisade** is a fence of wooden posts which are driven into the ground in order to protect people from attack. N-COUNT

**pall** /pɔːl/ **(palls, palled)** [1] If something **palls**, it becomes less interesting or less enjoyable after a period of time. ❑ *Already the allure of meals in restaurants had begun to pall.* VERB: no cont, V [2] If a **pall of** smoke hangs over a place, there is a thick cloud of smoke above it. ❑ *A pall of oily black smoke drifted over the cliff-top.* N-COUNT: usu N *of* n [3] If something unpleasant **casts a pall over** an event or occasion, it makes it less enjoyable than it should be. ❑ *The unrest has cast a pall over what is usually a day of national rejoicing.* PHRASE: V inflects, PHR n

**pall|bearer** /pɔːlbeərəʳ/ **(pallbearers)** At a funeral, a **pallbearer** is a person who helps to carry the coffin or who walks beside it. N-COUNT

**pal|let** /pælɪt/ **(pallets)** [1] A **pallet** is a narrow mattress filled with straw which is put on the floor for someone to sleep on. N-COUNT [2] A **pallet** is a hard, narrow bed. ❑ *He was given only a wooden pallet with a blanket.* N-COUNT [3] A **pallet** is a flat wooden or metal platform on which goods are stored so that they can be lifted and moved using a forklift truck. ❑ *The warehouse will hold more than 90,000 pallets storing 30 million Easter eggs.* N-COUNT

**pal|lia|tive** /pæliətɪv, AM -eɪt-/ **(palliatives)** [1] A **palliative** is a drug or medical treatment that relieves suffering without treating the cause of the suffering. N-COUNT [2] A **palliative** is an action that is intended to make the effects of a problem less severe but does not actually solve the problem. [FORMAL] ❑ *The loan was a palliative, not a cure, for ever-increasing financial troubles.* N-COUNT

**pal|lid** /pælɪd/ [1] Someone or something that is **pallid** is pale in an unattractive or unnatural way. ❑ *...helpless grief on pallid faces.* ADJ [2] You can describe something such as a performance or book as **pallid** if it is weak or not at all exciting. ❑ *...a pallid account of the future of transport.* ADJ

**pal|lor** /pæləʳ/ If you refer to the **pallor** of someone's face or skin, you mean that it is pale and unhealthy. ❑ *The deathly pallor of her skin had been replaced by the faintest flush of color.* N-SING: usu with supp

**pal|ly** /pæli/ If you are **pally with** someone, you are friendly with them. [INFORMAL] ADJ: oft ADJ *with* n

**palm** /pɑːm/ **(palms, palming, palmed)** [1] A **palm** or a **palm tree** is a tree that grows in hot countries. It has long leaves growing at the top, and no branches. N-COUNT [2] The **palm of** your hand is the inside part. ❑ *Dornberg slapped the table with the palm of his hand... He wiped his sweaty palm.* N-COUNT: usu poss N, N *of* n [3] If you have someone or something **in the palm of** your **hand**, you have control over them. ❑ *Johnson thought he had the board of directors in the palm of his hand.* PHRASE: Ns inflect

♦ **palm off** If you say that someone **has palmed** something **off on** you, you feel annoyed because they have made you accept it although it is not valuable or is not your responsibility. ❑ *I couldn't keep palming her off on friends... Joseph made sure that he was never palmed off with inferior stuff.* PHRASAL VERB [disapproval] V n P *on* n, *be* V-ed P *with* n

♦ **palm off with** If you say that you **are palmed off with** a lie or an excuse, you are annoyed because you are told something in order to stop you asking any more questions. [mainly BRIT] ❑ *Mark was palmed off with a series of excuses.* PHRASAL VERB: usu passive [disapproval] *be* V-ed P *with* n

**palm|cord|er** /pɑːmkɔːʳdəʳ/ **(palmcorders)** A **palmcorder** is a small video camera that you can hold in the palm of your hand. N-COUNT

**palm|is|try** /pɑːmɪstri/ **Palmistry** is the practice and art of trying to find out what people are like and what will happen in their future life by examining the lines on the palms of their hands. N-UNCOUNT

**palm oil** **Palm oil** is a yellow oil which comes from the fruit of certain palm trees and is used in making soap and sometimes as a fat in cooking. N-UNCOUNT

**Palm Sun|day** **Palm Sunday** is the Sunday before Easter. It is the day when Christians remember Jesus Christ's arrival in Jerusalem a few days before he was killed. N-UNCOUNT

**palm|top** /pɑːmtɒp/ **(palmtops)** A **palmtop** is a small computer that you can hold in your hand. [COMPUTING] N-COUNT

**palo|mi|no** /pæləmiːnou/ **(palominos)** A **palomino** is a horse which is yellowish or cream in colour and has a white tail. N-COUNT

**pal|pable** /pælpəbᵊl/ You describe something as **palpable** when it is obvious or intense and easily noticed. ❑ *The tension between Amy and Jim is palpable.* ADJ ♦ **pal|pably** /pælpəbli/ *The scene was palpably intense to watch.* ADV: ADV with cl/group

**pal|pi|tate** /pælpɪteɪt/ **(palpitates, palpitating, palpitated)** [1] If someone's heart **palpitates**, it beats very fast in an irregular way, because they are frightened or anxious. ❑ *He felt suddenly faint, and his heart began to palpitate.* VERB, V [2] If something **palpitates**, it shakes or seems to shake. [LITERARY] ❑ *She lay on the bed, her eyes closed and her bosom palpitating.* VERB, V-ing, Also V

**pal|pi|ta|tion** /pælpɪteɪʃᵊn/ **(palpitations)** When someone has **palpitations**, their heart beats very fast in an irregular way. ❑ *Caffeine can cause palpitations and headaches.* N-VAR

**pal|sy** /pɔːlzi/ **Palsy** is a loss of feeling in part of your body. → See also **cerebral palsy**. N-UNCOUNT

**pal|try** /pɔːltri/ A **paltry** amount of money or of something else is one that you consider to be very small. ❑ *...a paltry fine of £150.* ADJ: usu ADJ n, oft *a* ADJ amount

**pam|pas** /pæmpəs, -əz/ **The pampas** is the large area of flat, grassy land in South America. N-SING: *the* N

**pam|per** /pæmpəʳ/ **(pampers, pampering, pampered)** If you **pamper** someone, you make them feel comfortable by doing things for them or giving them expensive or luxurious things, sometimes in a way which has a bad effect on their character. ❑ *Why don't you let your mother pamper you for a while?... Pamper yourself with our luxury gifts.* VERB, V n, V pron-refl ♦ **pam|pered** *...today's pampered superstars.* ADJ

**pam|phlet** /pæmflət/ **(pamphlets)** A **pamphlet** is a very thin book, with a paper cover, which gives information about something. N-COUNT = *booklet*

**pam|phlet|eer** /pæmflətɪəʳ/ **(pamphleteers)** A **pamphleteer** is a person who writes pamphlets, especially about political subjects. N-COUNT

**pan** /pæn/ **(pans, panning, panned)** [1] A **pan** is a round metal container with a long handle, which is used for cooking things in, usually on top of a cooker or stove. ❑ *Heat the butter and oil in a large pan.* ◆◇◇ N-COUNT = *saucepan* [2] If something such as a film or a VERB:

book **is panned** by journalists, they say it is very bad. [INFORMAL] ❑ *His first high-budget movie, called 'Brain Donors', was panned by the critics.* usu passive = slate be V-ed [3] If you **pan** a film or television camera or if it **pans** somewhere, it moves slowly round so that a wide area is filmed. ❑ *The camera panned along the line of players... A television camera panned the stadium.* VERB V prep/adv V n [4] If someone **pans for** gold, they use a shallow metal container to try to find small pieces of gold from a river. ❑ *People came westward in the 1800s to pan for gold... Every year they panned about a ton and a half of gold.* VERB V for n V n

♦ **pan out** If something, for example a project or some information, **pans out**, it produces something useful or valuable. [INFORMAL] ❑ *None of Morgan's proposed financings panned out.* PHRASAL VERB V P

**pan-** /pæn-/ **pan-** is added to the beginning of adjectives and nouns to form other adjectives and nouns that describe something as being connected with all places or people of a particular kind. ❑ *...a pan-European defence system. ...the ideology of pan-Arabism.* PREFIX

**pana|cea** /pænəsiːə/ **(panaceas)** If you say that something is not a **panacea for** a particular set of problems, you mean that it will not solve all those problems. ❑ *Membership of the ERM is not a panacea for Britain's economic problems.* N-COUNT: usu with brd-neg

**pa|nache** /pənæʃ/ If you do something with **panache**, you do it in a confident, stylish, and elegant way. ❑ *The BBC Symphony Orchestra played with great panache.* N-UNCOUNT = flair

**pana|ma hat** /pænəmɑː hæt/ **(panama hats)** A **panama hat** or a **panama** is a hat, worn especially by men, that is woven from the leaves of a palm-like plant and worn when it is sunny. N-COUNT

**pan|cake** /pænkeɪk/ **(pancakes)** A **pancake** is a thin, flat, circular piece of cooked batter made from milk, flour, and eggs. Pancakes are often rolled up or folded and eaten hot with a sweet or savoury filling inside. In America, pancakes are usually eaten for breakfast, with butter and maple syrup. **flat as a pancake** → see **flat**. N-COUNT

**Pan|cake Day** **Pancake Day** is the popular name for **Shrove Tuesday**. [BRIT] N-UNCOUNT

**pan|cake roll** **(pancake rolls)** A **pancake roll** is an item of Chinese food consisting of a small roll of thin crisp pastry filled with vegetables and sometimes meat. N-COUNT = spring roll

**pan|cre|as** /pæŋkriəs/ **(pancreases)** Your **pancreas** is an organ in your body that is situated behind your stomach. It produces insulin and substances that help your body digest food. N-COUNT

**pan|cre|at|ic** /pæŋkriætɪk/ **Pancreatic** means relating to or involving the pancreas. ❑ *...pancreatic juices.* ADJ: ADJ n

**pan|da** /pændə/ **(pandas)** A **panda** or a **giant panda** is a large animal rather like a bear, which has black and white fur and lives in the bamboo forests of China. N-COUNT

**pan|da car** **(panda cars)** A **panda car** is a police car. [BRIT, INFORMAL] N-COUNT

**pan|dem|ic** /pændemɪk/ **(pandemics)** A **pandemic** is an occurrence of a disease that affects many people over a very wide area. [FORMAL] ❑ *They feared a new cholera pandemic.* N-COUNT

**pan|de|mo|nium** /pændɪmoʊniəm/ If there is **pandemonium** in a place, the people there are behaving in a very noisy and uncontrolled way. ❑ *There was pandemonium in court as the judge gave his summing up.* N-UNCOUNT

**pan|der** /pændəʳ/ **(panders, pandering, pandered)** If you **pander to** someone or **to** their wishes, you do everything that they want, often to get some advantage for yourself. ❑ *He has offended the party's traditional base by pandering to the rich and the middle classes.* VERB [disapproval] V to n

**Pandora** /pændɔːrə/ If someone or something **opens Pandora's box** or **opens a Pandora's box**, they do something that causes a lot of problems to appear that did not exist or were not known about before. PHRASE: V inflects

**p & p** also **p and p.** You use **p & p** as a written abbreviation for 'postage and packing', when stating the cost of packing goods in a parcel and sending them through the post to a customer. [BRIT, BUSINESS] ❑ *The guide costs £9.95 (inc. p & p).*

**pane** /peɪn/ **(panes)** A **pane** of glass is a flat sheet of glass in a window or door. N-COUNT: oft N of n

**pan|egyr|ic** /pænɪdʒɪrɪk/ **(panegyrics)** A **panegyric** is a speech or piece of writing that praises someone or something. [FORMAL] ❑ *...Prince Charles's panegyric on rural living.* N-COUNT = eulogy

**pan|el** /pænᵊl/ **(panels)** [1] A **panel** is a small group of people who are chosen to do something, for example to discuss something in public or to make a decision. ❑ *He assembled a panel of scholars to advise him... The advisory panel disagreed with the decision.* ◆◇◇ N-COUNT-COLL [2] A **panel** is a flat rectangular piece of wood or other material that forms part of a larger object such as a door. ❑ *...the frosted glass panel set in the centre of the door.* N-COUNT [3] A control **panel** or instrument **panel** is a board or surface which contains switches and controls to operate a machine or piece of equipment. ❑ *The equipment was extremely sophisticated and was monitored from a central control-panel.* N-COUNT: n N

**pan|elled** /pænᵊld/

✔ in AM, use **paneled**

[1] A **panelled** room has decorative wooden panels covering its walls. ❑ *...a large, comfortable, panelled room... The cheerful room was panelled in pine.* ADJ: usu ADJ n ♦ **-panelled** combines with nouns to form adjectives that describe the way a room or wall is decorated or the way a door or window is made. ❑ *...a wood-panelled dining room.* COMB in ADJ [2] A **panelled** wall, door, or window does not have a flat surface but has square or rectangular areas set into its surface. ❑ *The panelled walls were covered with portraits.* ADJ: usu ADJ n

**pan|el|ling** /pænəlɪŋ/

✔ in AM, use **paneling**

**Panelling** consists of boards or strips of wood covering a wall inside a building. ❑ *...an apartment with oak beams and rosewood panelling.* N-UNCOUNT

**pan|el|list** /pænəlɪst/ **(panellists)**

✔ in AM, use **panelist**

A **panellist** is a person who is a member of a panel and speaks in public, especially on a radio or television programme. N-COUNT

**pan-fried** **Pan-fried** food is is food that has been cooked in hot fat or oil in a frying pan. ADJ

**pang** /pæŋ/ **(pangs)** A **pang** is a sudden strong feeling or emotion, for example of sadness or pain. ❑ *For a moment she felt a pang of guilt about the way she was treating him.* N-COUNT: oft N of n, n N

**pan|han|dle** /pænhændᵊl/ **(panhandles, panhandling, panhandled)** [1] A **panhandle** is a narrow strip of land joined to a larger area of land. [AM] ❑ *...the Texas panhandle.* N-COUNT [2] If someone **panhandles**, they stop people in the street and ask them for food or money. [mainly AM, INFORMAL] ❑ *Many of these street people seemed to support themselves by panhandling and doing odd jobs... There was also a guy panhandling for quarters.* VERB V V for n Also V n

✔ in BRIT, usually use **beg**

♦ **pan|han|dling** *Sergeant Rivero says arrests for panhandling take place every day.* N-UNCOUNT

**pan|han|dler** /pænhændləʳ/ **(panhandlers)** A **panhandler** is a person who stops people in the street and asks them for food or money. [mainly AM, INFORMAL] N-COUNT

✔ in BRIT, usually use **beggar**

**pan|ic** /pænɪk/ **(panics, panicking, panicked)** ◆◇◇ [1] **Panic** is a very strong feeling of anxiety or fear, which makes you act without thinking carefully. ❑ *An earthquake hit the capital, causing panic among the population... I phoned the doctor in a pan-* N-VAR *ic, crying that I'd lost the baby.* [2] **Panic** or **a panic** is a situation in which people are affected by a strong feeling of anxiety. ❑ *There was a moment of panic in Britain as it became clear just how vulnerable the nation was... I'm in a panic about getting everything done in time... The policy announcement caused panic buying of petrol.* [3] If you **panic** or if someone **panics** you, you suddenly feel anxious or afraid, and act quickly and without thinking carefully. ❑ *Guests panicked and screamed when the bomb exploded... The unexpected and sudden memory briefly panicked her... She refused to be panicked into a hasty marriage.* N-UNCOUNT: also a N; VERB; V; V n; be V-ed *into* n

**pan|icky** /pænɪki/ A **panicky** feeling or **panicky** behaviour is characterized by panic. ❑ *Many women feel panicky travelling home at night alone.* ADJ

**panic-stricken** If someone is **panic-stricken** or is behaving in a **panic-stricken** way, they are so anxious or afraid that they may act without thinking carefully. ❑ *Panic-stricken travellers fled for the borders.* ADJ

**pan|ni|er** /pæniəʳ/ **(panniers)** [1] A **pannier** is one of two bags or boxes for carrying things in, which are fixed on each side of the back wheel of a bicycle or motorbike. N-COUNT [2] A **pannier** is a large basket or bag, usually one of two that are put over an animal and used for carrying loads. N-COUNT

**pano|ply** /pænəpli/ A **panoply of** things is a wide range of them, especially one that is considered impressive. [FORMAL] ❑ *He was attended, as are all heads of state, by a full panoply of experts.* N-SING: usu N *of* n = array

**pano|ra|ma** /pænərɑːmə, -ræmə/ **(panoramas)** [1] A **panorama** is a view in which you can see a long way over a wide area of land, usually because you are on high ground. ❑ *Horton looked out over a panorama of fertile valleys and gentle hills.* N-COUNT: oft N *of* n = vista [2] A **panorama** is a broad view of a state of affairs or of a constantly changing series of events. ❑ *The play presents a panorama of the history of communism.* N-COUNT: usu N *of* n

**pano|ram|ic** /pænəræmɪk/ If you have a **panoramic** view, you can see a long way over a wide area. ❑ *The terrain's high points provide a panoramic view of Los Angeles.* ADJ: usu ADJ n

**pan|sy** /pænzi/ **(pansies)** [1] A **pansy** is a small brightly coloured garden flower with large round petals. N-COUNT [2] If someone describes a man as a **pansy**, they mean that he is a homosexual. [INFORMAL, OFFENSIVE, OLD-FASHIONED] N-COUNT

**pant** /pænt/ **(pants, panting, panted)** If you **pant**, you breathe quickly and loudly with your mouth open, because you have been doing something energetic. ❑ *She climbed rapidly until she was panting with the effort.* → See also **pants**. VERB; V

**pan|ta|loons** /pæntəluːnz/ **Pantaloons** are long trousers with very wide legs, gathered at the ankle. N-PLURAL

**pan|theism** /pænθiːɪzəm/ [1] **Pantheism** is the religious belief that God is in everything in nature and the universe. N-UNCOUNT [2] **Pantheism** is a willingness to worship and believe in all gods. N-UNCOUNT

**pan|theis|tic** /pænθiɪstɪk/ **Pantheistic** religions involve believing that God is in everything in nature and the universe. ADJ: usu ADJ n

**pan|the|on** /pænθiɒn/ **(pantheons)** You can refer to a group of gods or a group of important people as a **pantheon**. [WRITTEN] ❑ *...the birthplace of Krishna, another god of the Hindu pantheon.* N-COUNT: oft N *of* n

**pan|ther** /pænθəʳ/ **(panthers)** A **panther** is a large wild animal that belongs to the cat family. Panthers are usually black. N-COUNT

**panties** /pæntiz/ **Panties** are short, close-fitting underpants worn by women or girls. [mainly AM] N-PLURAL: also *a pair of* N

✔ in BRIT, usually use **pants, knickers**

**pan|to** /pæntoʊ/ **(pantos)** A **panto** is the same as a **pantomime**. [BRIT, INFORMAL] ❑ *...a Christmas panto.* N-VAR

**pan|to|mime** /pæntəmaɪm/ **(pantomimes)** [1] A **pantomime** is a funny musical play for children. Pantomimes are usually based on fairy stories and are performed at Christmas. [BRIT] N-COUNT [2] If you say that a situation or a person's behaviour is a **pantomime**, you mean that it is silly or exaggerated and that there is something false about it. [mainly BRIT] ❑ *They were made welcome with the usual pantomime of exaggerated smiles and gestures.* N-SING = farce

**pan|try** /pæntri/ **(pantries)** A **pantry** is a small room or large cupboard in a house, usually near the kitchen, where food is kept. N-COUNT = larder

**pants** /pænts/ [1] **Pants** are a piece of underwear which have two holes to put your legs through and elastic around the top to hold them up round your waist or hips. [BRIT] ❑ *I put on my bra and pants.* N-PLURAL: also *a pair of* N = knickers

✔ in AM, usually use **underpants**

[2] **Pants** are a piece of clothing that covers the lower part of your body and each leg. [AM] ❑ *He wore brown corduroy pants and a white cotton shirt.* N-PLURAL: also *a pair of* N

✔ in BRIT, use **trousers**

[3] If you say that something is **pants**, you mean that it is very poor in quality. [BRIT, INFORMAL] ❑ *The place is pants, yet so popular.* N-UNCOUNT

PHRASES [4] If someone bores, charms, or scares **the pants off** you, for example, they bore, charm, or scare you a lot. [INFORMAL] ❑ *You'll bore the pants off your grandchildren.* PHRASE: V PHR emphasis [5] If you **fly by the seat of** your **pants** or do something **by the seat of** your **pants**, you use your instincts to tell you what to do in a new or difficult situation rather than following a plan or relying on equipment. PHRASE: V inflects [6] to **wear the pants** → see **wear**.

**pan|ty|hose** /pæntihoʊz/ also **panty hose. Pantyhose** are nylon tights worn by women. [mainly AM] N-PLURAL: also *a pair of* N

✔ in BRIT, usually use **tights**

**pap** /pæp/ If you describe something such as information, writing, or entertainment as **pap**, you mean that you consider it to be of no worth, value, or serious interest. N-UNCOUNT disapproval = drivel

**papa** /pəpɑː, AM pɑːpə/ **(papas)** Some people refer to or address their father as **papa**. [OLD-FASHIONED] ❑ *He was so much older than me, older even than my papa.* N-FAMILY

**pa|pa|cy** /peɪpəsi/ also **Papacy. The papacy** is the position, power, and authority of the Pope, including the period of time that a particular person holds this position. ❑ *Throughout his papacy, John Paul has called for a second evangelization of Europe.* N-SING: usu *the* N

**pa|pal** /peɪpəl/ **Papal** is used to describe things relating to the Pope. ❑ *...the doctrine of papal infallibility.* ADJ: ADJ n

**pa|pa|raz|zo** /pæpərætsoʊ/ **(paparazzi** /pæpərætsi/**) The paparazzi** are photographers who follow famous people around, hoping to take interesting or shocking photographs of them that they can sell to a newspaper. ❑ *The paparazzi pursue Armani wherever he travels.* N-COUNT: usu pl

**pa|pa|ya** /pəpaɪə/ **(papayas)** A **papaya** is a fruit with a green skin, sweet yellow flesh, and small black seeds. Papayas grow on trees in hot countries such as the West Indies. N-COUNT = pawpaw

**pa|per** /peɪpəʳ/ **(papers, papering, papered)** ◆◆◆ [1] **Paper** is a material that you write on or wrap things with. The pages of this book are made of paper. ❑ *He wrote his name down on a piece of paper for me... She sat at the table with pen and paper. ...a sheet of pretty wrapping paper. ...a paper bag.* N-UNCOUNT [2] A **paper** is a newspaper. ❑ *I'll cook and you read the paper.* N-COUNT [3] You can refer to newspapers in general as **the paper** or **the papers**. ❑ *You can't believe everything you read in the paper.* N-COUNT: *the* N [4] Your **papers** are sheets of paper with writing or information on them, which you might keep in a safe place at home. ❑ *Her papers included unpublished articles and correspondence.* N-PLURAL: usu with poss [5] Your **papers** are official docu- N-PLURAL:

ments, for example your passport or identity card, which prove who you are or which give you official permission to do something. ❑ *They have arrested four people who were trying to leave the country with forged papers.* [6] A **paper** is a long, formal piece of writing about an academic subject. ❑ *He just published a paper in the journal Nature analyzing the fires.* [7] A **paper** is an essay written by a student. [mainly AM] ❑ *...the ten common errors that appear most frequently in student papers.* → See also **term paper**. [8] A **paper** is a part of a written examination in which you answer a number of questions in a particular period of time. ❑ *We sat each paper in the Hall.* [9] A **paper** prepared by a government or a committee is a report on a question they have been considering or a set of proposals for changes in the law. ❑ *...a new government paper on European policy.* → See also **Green Paper**, **White Paper**. [10] **Paper** agreements, qualifications, or profits are ones that are stated by official documents to exist, although they may not really be effective or useful. ❑ *We're looking for people who have experience rather than paper qualifications.* [11] If you **paper** a wall, you put wallpaper on it. ❑ *We papered all four bedrooms... The room was strange, the walls half papered, half painted.*

usu poss N = identification; N-COUNT; N-COUNT; N-COUNT; N-COUNT; ADJ: ADJ n; VERB V n V-ed

PHRASES [12] If you put your thoughts down **on paper**, you write them down. ❑ *It is important to get something down on paper.* [13] If something seems to be the case **on paper**, it seems to be the case from what you read or hear about it, but it may not really be the case. ❑ *On paper, their country is a multi-party democracy.* [14] If you say that a promise, an agreement, or a guarantee **is not worth the paper it's written on**, you mean that although it has been written down and seems to be official, it is in fact worthless because what has been promised will not be done.

PHRASE: PHR after v; PHRASE; PHRASE: Vs inflect [disapproval]

♦ **paper over** If people **paper over** a disagreement between them, they find a temporary solution to it in order to give the impression that things are going well. ❑ *...his determination to paper over the cracks in his party and avoid confrontation.* PHRASAL VERB V P n

**paper|back** /peɪpəʳbæk/ **(paperbacks)** A **paperback** is a book with a thin cardboard or paper cover. Compare **hardback**. ❑ *She said she would buy the book when it comes out in paperback.* N-COUNT: also *in* N

**paper|boy** /peɪpəʳbɔɪ/ **(paperboys)** also **paper boy.** A **paperboy** is a boy who delivers newspapers to people's homes. N-COUNT

**pa|per clip** **(paper clips)** also **paper-clip, paperclip.** A **paper clip** is a small piece of bent wire that is used to fasten papers together. N-COUNT

**paper|girl** /peɪpəʳgɜːʳl/ **(papergirls)** also **paper girl.** A **papergirl** is a girl who delivers newspapers to people's homes. N-COUNT

**pa|per knife** **(paper knives)** also **paper-knife.** A **paper knife** is a tool shaped like a knife, which is used for opening envelopes. N-COUNT

**paper|less** /peɪpəʳləs/ **Paperless** is used to describe business or office work which is done by computer or telephone, rather than by writing things down. ❑ *Paperless trading can save time and money. ...the paperless office.* ADJ: ADJ n

**pa|per mon|ey** **Paper money** is money which is made of paper. Paper money is usually worth more than coins. N-UNCOUNT

**pa|per round** **(paper rounds)** A **paper round** is a job of delivering newspapers to houses along a particular route. Paper rounds are usually done by children before or after school. [BRIT] N-COUNT

✔ in AM, use **paper route**

**pa|per route** **(paper routes)** A **paper route** is the same as a **paper round**. [AM] N-COUNT

**pa|per shop** **(paper shops)** A **paper shop** is a shop that sells newspapers and magazines, and also things such as tobacco, sweets, and cards. [BRIT] N-COUNT = newsagent

**paper-thin** also **paper thin.** If something is **paper-thin**, it is very thin. ❑ *Cut the onion into paper-thin slices.* ADJ

**pa|per ti|ger** **(paper tigers)** If you say that an institution, a country, or a person is a **paper tiger**, you mean that although they seem powerful they do not really have any power. N-COUNT

**pa|per trail** Documents which provide evidence of someone's activities can be referred to as a **paper trail**. [mainly AM] ❑ *Criminals are very reluctant to leave a paper trail.* N-SING

**paper|weight** /peɪpəʳweɪt/ **(paperweights)** A **paperweight** is a small heavy object which you place on papers to prevent them from being disturbed or blown away. N-COUNT

**paper|work** /peɪpəʳwɜːʳk/ **Paperwork** is the routine part of a job which involves writing or dealing with letters, reports, and records. ❑ *At every stage in the production there will be paperwork – forms to fill in, permissions to obtain, letters to write.* N-UNCOUNT

**pa|pery** /peɪpəri/ Something that is **papery** is thin and dry like paper. ❑ *Leave each garlic clove in its papery skin.* ADJ

**papier-mâché** /pæpieɪ mæʃeɪ, AM peɪpəʳ məʃeɪ/ **Papier-mâché** is a mixture of pieces of paper and glue. It can be made, while still damp, into objects such as bowls, ornaments, and models. ❑ *...papier-mâché bowls.* N-UNCOUNT: oft N n

**pa|pist** /peɪpɪst/ **(papists)** also **Papist.** Some Protestants refer to Catholics as **Papists**. [OFFENSIVE] N-COUNT

**pap|ri|ka** /pəpriːkə, pæprɪkə/ **Paprika** is a red powder used for flavouring meat and other food. N-UNCOUNT

**pap smear** **(pap smears)** also **pap test.** A **pap smear** is a medical test in which cells are taken from a woman's cervix and analysed to see if any cancer cells are present. [AM] N-COUNT

✔ in BRIT, use **smear**

**pa|py|rus** /pəpaɪrəs/ **(papyri)** [1] **Papyrus** is a tall water plant that grows in Africa. [2] **Papyrus** is a type of paper made from papyrus stems that was used in ancient Egypt, Rome, and Greece. [3] A **papyrus** is an ancient document that is written on papyrus. N-UNCOUNT; N-UNCOUNT; N-COUNT

**par** /pɑːʳ/ [1] If you say that two people or things are **on a par with** each other, you mean that they are equally good or bad, or equally important. ❑ *Parts of Glasgow are on a par with the worst areas of London and Liverpool for burglaries.* [2] In golf, **par** is the number of strokes that a good player should take to get the ball into a hole or into all the holes on a particular golf course. ❑ *He was five under par after the first round.*

PHRASE: PHR n/-ing, usu v-link PHR, PHR after v; N-UNCOUNT: N with num, *under/over* N

PHRASES [3] If you say that someone or something is **below par** or **under par**, you are disappointed in them because they are below the standard you expected. ❑ *Duffy's primitive guitar playing is well below par.* [4] If you say that someone or something is not **up to par**, you are disappointed in them because they are below the standard you expected. ❑ *His performance was not up to par.* [5] If you **feel below par** or **under par**, you feel tired and unable to perform as well as you normally do. [6] If you say that something that happens is **par for the course**, you mean that you are not pleased with it but it is what you expected to happen. ❑ *He said long hours are par for the course.*

PHRASE: v-link PHR, PHR after v, PHR n; PHRASE: usu with neg, v-link PHR, PHR after v; PHRASE: usu v-link PHR; PHRASE: v-link PHR

**para** /pærə/ **(paras)** A **para** is a **paratrooper**. [BRIT, INFORMAL] ❑ *...some guys just out of the paras.* N-COUNT: usu pl, usu *the* N

**para.** /pærə/ **(paras)** **Para.** is a written abbreviation for **paragraph**. ❑ *See Chapter 9, para. 1.2.*

**para|ble** /pærəbᵊl/ **(parables)** A **parable** is a short story, which is told in order to make a moral or religious point, like those in the Bible. ❑ *... the parable of the Good Samaritan.* N-COUNT: oft N *of* n

**pa|rabo|la** /pəræbələ/ **(parabolas)** A **parabola** is a type of curve such as the path of some- N-COUNT = arc thing that is thrown up into the air and comes down in a different place. [TECHNICAL]

**para|bol|ic** /pærəbɒlɪk/ A **parabolic** object or curve is shaped like a parabola. ❑ *...a parabolic mirror.* ADJ: usu ADJ n

**pa|ra|ceta|mol** /pærəsiːtəmɒl/ **(paracetamol)** **Paracetamol** is a mild drug which reduces pain and fever. [BRIT] ❑ *I often take paracetamol at work if I get a bad headache.* N-VAR

**para|chute** /pærəʃuːt/ **(parachutes, parachuting, parachuted)** 1 A **parachute** is a device which enables a person to jump from an aircraft and float safely to the ground. It consists of a large piece of thin cloth attached to your body by strings. ❑ *They fell 41,000 ft. before opening their parachutes.* N-COUNT: also *by* N 2 If a person **parachutes** or someone **parachutes** them somewhere, they jump from an aircraft using a parachute. ❑ *He was a courier and parachuted into Warsaw... He was parachuted in.* VERB V prep/adv *be* V-ed prep/adv 3 To **parachute** something somewhere means to drop it somewhere by parachute. ❑ *Supplies were parachuted into the mountains.* VERB = drop V n prep/adv

**para|chut|ing** /pærəʃuːtɪŋ/ **Parachuting** is the activity or sport of jumping from an aircraft with a parachute. ❑ *His hobby is freefall parachuting.* N-UNCOUNT

**para|chut|ist** /pærəʃuːtɪst/ **(parachutists)** A **parachutist** is a person who jumps from an aircraft using a parachute. ❑ *He was an experienced parachutist who had done over 150 jumps.* N-COUNT

**pa|rade** /pəreɪd/ **(parades, parading, paraded)** 1 A **parade** is a procession of people or vehicles moving through a public place in order to celebrate an important day or event. ❑ *A military parade marched slowly and solemnly down Pennsylvania Avenue.* N-COUNT 2 When people **parade** somewhere, they walk together in a formal group or a line, usually with other people watching them. ❑ *More than four thousand soldiers, sailors and airmen paraded down the Champs Elysee.* VERB V prep/adv 3 **Parade** is a formal occasion when soldiers stand in lines to be seen by an officer or important person, or march in a group. ❑ *He had them on parade at six o'clock in the morning.* N-VAR: oft *on* N 4 If prisoners **are paraded** through the streets of a town or on television, they are shown to the public, usually in order to make the people who are holding them seem more powerful or important. ❑ *Five leading fighter pilots have been captured and paraded before the media.* VERB: usu passive *be* V-ed prep 5 If you say that someone **parades** a person, you mean that they show that person to others only in order to gain some advantage for themselves. ❑ *Children are paraded on television alongside the party leaders to win votes.* VERB: usu passive *be* V-ed 6 If people **parade** something, they show it in public so that it can be admired. ❑ *Valentino is keen to see celebrities parading his clothes at big occasions.* VERB = show off V n 7 If someone **parades**, they walk about somewhere in order to be seen and admired. ❑ *I love to put on a bathing suit and parade on the beach... They danced and paraded around.* VERB V prep/adv V prep/adv 8 If you say that something **parades as** or **is paraded as** a good or important thing, you mean that some people say that it is good or important but you think it probably is not. ❑ *The Chancellor will be able to parade his cut in interest rates as a small victory. ...all the fashions that parade as modern movements in art.* VERB V n *as* n V *as* n 9 If you talk about a **parade of** people or things, you mean that there is a series of them that seems never to end. ❑ *When I ask Nick about his childhood, he remembers a parade of baby-sitters. ...an endless parade of advertisements.* N-COUNT: N *of* n 10 A **parade** is a short row of shops, usually set back from the main street. [BRIT] N-COUNT 11 **Parade** is used as part of the name of a street. ❑ *...Queens Hotel, Clarence Parade, Southsea.* N-IN-NAMES 12 → See also **hit parade**, **identity parade**.

**pa|rade ground** **(parade grounds)** A **parade ground** is an area of ground where soldiers practise marching and have parades. N-COUNT

**para|digm** /pærədaɪm/ **(paradigms)** 1 A **paradigm** is a model for something which explains it or shows how it can be produced. [FORMAL] ❑ *...a new paradigm of production.* N-VAR: usu with supp 2 A **paradigm** is a clear and typical example of something. [FORMAL] ❑ *He had become the paradigm of the successful man.* N-COUNT: usu with supp

**para|dig|mat|ic** /pærədɪgmætɪk/ You can describe something as **paradigmatic** if it acts as a model or example for something. [FORMAL] ❑ *Their great academic success was paraded as paradigmatic.* ADJ

**para|dise** /pærədaɪs/ **(paradises)** 1 According to some religions, **paradise** is a wonderful place where people go after they die, if they have led good lives. ❑ *The Koran describes paradise as a place containing a garden of delight.* N-PROPER = heaven 2 You can refer to a place or situation that seems beautiful or perfect as **paradise** or **a paradise**. ❑ *...one of the world's great natural paradises.* N-VAR 3 You can use **paradise** to say that a place is very attractive to a particular kind of person and has everything they need for a particular activity. ❑ *The Algarve is a golfer's paradise.* → See also **fool's paradise**. N-COUNT: supp N

**para|dox** /pærədɒks/ **(paradoxes)** 1 You describe a situation as a **paradox** when it involves two or more facts or qualities which seem to contradict each other. ❑ *The paradox is that the region's most dynamic economies have the most primitive financial systems.* N-COUNT 2 A **paradox** is a statement in which it seems that if one part of it is true, the other part of it cannot be true. ❑ *Although I'm so successful I'm really rather a failure. That's a paradox, isn't it?* N-VAR

**para|doxi|cal** /pærədɒksɪkəl/ If something is **paradoxical**, it involves two facts or qualities which seem to contradict each other. ❑ *Some sedatives produce the paradoxical effect of making the person more anxious.* ADJ ♦ **para|doxi|cal|ly** /pærədɒksɪkli/ *Paradoxically, the less you have to do the more you may resent the work that does come your way.* ADV: usu ADV with cl/group, ADV with v

**par|af|fin** /pærəfɪn/ 1 **Paraffin** is a strong-smelling liquid which is used as a fuel in heaters, lamps, and engines. [mainly BRIT] ❑ *...a paraffin lamp.* N-UNCOUNT

✔ in AM, use **kerosene**

2 **Paraffin** wax, or in American English **paraffin**, is a white wax obtained from petrol or coal. It is used to make candles and in beauty treatments. N-UNCOUNT

**para|glide** /pærəglaɪd/ **(paraglides, paragliding, paraglided)** If a person **paraglides**, they jump from an aircraft or off a hill or tall building while wearing a special parachute which allows them to control the way they float to the ground. ❑ *They planned to paraglide from Long Mountain.* VERB V prep Also V ♦ **para|glid|ing** *Hang gliding and paragliding are allowed from the top of Windy Hill.* N-UNCOUNT

**para|glid|er** /pærəglaɪdəʳ/ **(paragliders)** 1 A **paraglider** is a special type of parachute that you use for paragliding. N-COUNT 2 A **paraglider** is a person who paraglides. N-COUNT

**para|gon** /pærəgɒn/ **(paragons)** If you refer to someone as a **paragon**, you mean that they are perfect or have a lot of a good quality. ❑ *We don't expect candidates to be paragons of virtue.* N-COUNT: oft N *of* n

**para|graph** /pærəgrɑːf, -græf/ **(paragraphs)** A **paragraph** is a section of a piece of writing. A paragraph always begins on a new line and contains at least one sentence. ❑ *The length of a paragraph depends on the information it conveys.* N-COUNT

**para|keet** /pærəkiːt/ **(parakeets)** also **parrakeet**. A **parakeet** is a type of small parrot which is brightly coloured and has a long tail. N-COUNT

**para|le|gal** /pærəliːgəl/ **(paralegals)** A **paralegal** is someone who helps lawyers with their work but is not yet completely qualified as a lawyer. [AM] N-COUNT

**par|al|lax** /pærəlæks/ **(parallaxes)** **Parallax** is when an object appears to change its position be- N-VAR cause the person or instrument observing it has changed their position. [TECHNICAL]

**par|al|lel** /pærəlel/ **(parallels, parallelling, parallelled)**

✔ in AM, use **paralleling**, **paralleled**

[1] If something has a **parallel**, it is similar to something else, but exists or happens in a different place or at a different time. If it has **no parallel** or is **without parallel**, it is not similar to anything else. ❑ *Readers familiar with English history will find a vague parallel to the suppression of the monasteries... It's an ecological disaster with no parallel anywhere else in the world.* N-COUNT [2] If there are **parallels** between two things, they are similar in some ways. ❑ *Detailed study of folk music from a variety of countries reveals many close parallels... Friends of the dead lawyer were quick to draw a parallel between the two murders.* N-COUNT: oft N *between/to/with* n [3] If one thing **parallels** another, they happen at the same time or are similar, and often seem to be connected. ❑ *Often there are emotional reasons paralleling the financial ones... His remarks paralleled those of the president.* VERB = echo; V n; V n [4] **Parallel** events or situations happen at the same time as one another, or are similar to one another. ❑ *...parallel talks between the two countries' Foreign Ministers... Their instincts do not always run parallel with ours.* ADJ: oft ADJ *with/to* n [5] If two lines, two objects, or two lines of movement are **parallel**, they are the same distance apart along their whole length. ❑ *...seventy-two ships, drawn up in two parallel lines... Farthing Lane's just above the High Street and parallel with it.* ADJ: oft ADJ *to/with* n [6] A **parallel** is an imaginary line round the earth that is parallel to the equator. Parallels are shown on maps. ❑ *...the area south of the 38th parallel.* N-COUNT: usu *the* ord N [7] Something that occurs **in parallel with** something else occurs at the same time as it. ❑ *Davies has managed to pursue his diverse interests in parallel with his fast-moving career.* PHRASE: PHR after v, usu PHR *with/to* n

**par|al|lel bars** **Parallel bars** consist of a pair of horizontal bars on posts, which are used for doing physical exercises. N-PLURAL

**par|al|lel|ism** /pærəlelɪzəm/ When there is **parallelism between** two things, there are similarities between them. [FORMAL] ❑ *The last thing we should do is make any parallelism between the murderers and their victims.* N-UNCOUNT

**par|al|lelo|gram** /pærəleləgræm/ **(parallelograms)** A **parallelogram** is a four-sided shape in which each side is parallel to the side opposite it. N-COUNT

**par|al|lel pro|cess|ing** In computing, **parallel processing** is a system in which several instructions are carried out at the same time instead of one after the other. [COMPUTING] N-UNCOUNT

**para|lyse** /pærəlaɪz/ **(paralyses, paralysing, paralysed)**

✔ in AM, use **paralyze**

[1] If someone **is paralysed** by an accident or an illness, they have no feeling in their body, or in part of their body, and are unable to move. ❑ *Her married sister had been paralysed in a road accident. ...a virus which paralysed his legs.* ♦ **para|lysed** *The disease left him with a paralysed right arm.* VERB; *be* V-ed; V n; ADJ [2] If a person, place, or organization **is paralysed by** something, they become unable to act or function properly. ❑ *For weeks now the government has been paralysed by indecision... The strike has virtually paralysed the island.* ♦ **para|lysed** *He was absolutely paralysed with shock.* ♦ **para|lys|ing** *...paralysing shyness.* VERB; *be* V-ed; V n; ADJ; ADJ: ADJ n

**pa|raly|sis** /pəræləsɪs/ [1] **Paralysis** is the loss of the ability to move and feel in all or part of your body. ❑ *...paralysis of the leg.* N-UNCOUNT [2] **Paralysis** is the state of being unable to act or function properly. ❑ *The paralysis of the leadership leaves the army without its supreme command.* N-UNCOUNT

**para|lyt|ic** /pærəlɪtɪk/ [1] **Paralytic** means suffering from or related to paralysis. ❑ *...paralytic disease.* ADJ: usu ADJ n [2] Someone who is **paralytic** is very drunk. [BRIT, INFORMAL] ❑ *By the end of the evening they were all absolutely paralytic.* ADJ: usu v-link ADJ

**para|med|ic** /pærəmedɪk, AM -medɪk/ **(paramedics)** A **paramedic** is a person whose training is similar to that of a nurse and who helps to do medical work. ❑ *We intend to have a paramedic on every ambulance within the next three years.* N-COUNT

**para|medi|cal** /pærəmedɪkəl/ **Paramedical** workers and services help doctors and nurses in medical work. ❑ *...doctors and paramedical staff.* ADJ: ADJ n

**pa|ram|eter** /pəræmɪtəʳ/ **(parameters)** **Parameters** are factors or limits which affect the way that something can be done or made. [FORMAL] ❑ *That would be enough to make sure we fell within the parameters of our loan agreement.* N-COUNT: usu pl

**para|mili|tary** /pærəmɪlɪtri, AM -teri/ **(paramilitaries)** [1] A **paramilitary** organization is organized like an army and performs either civil or military functions in a country. ❑ *Searches by the army and paramilitary forces have continued today.* ADJ: ADJ n ♦ **Paramilitaries** are members of a paramilitary organization. ❑ *Paramilitaries and army recruits patrolled the village.* N-COUNT: usu pl [2] A **paramilitary** organization is an illegal group that is organized like an army. ❑ *...a law which said that all paramilitary groups must be disarmed.* ADJ: ADJ n ♦ **Paramilitaries** are members of an illegal paramilitary organization. ❑ *Loyalist paramilitaries were blamed for the shooting.* N-COUNT: usu pl

**para|mount** /pærəmaʊnt/ Something that is **paramount** or of **paramount** importance is more important than anything else. ❑ *The child's welfare must be seen as paramount.* ADJ

**par|amour** /pærəmʊəʳ/ **(paramours)** Someone's **paramour** is their lover. [OLD-FASHIONED] N-COUNT: oft poss N

**para|noia** /pærənɔɪə/ [1] If you say that someone suffers from **paranoia**, you think that they are too suspicious and afraid of other people. ❑ *The mood is one of paranoia and expectation of war.* N-UNCOUNT [2] In psychology, if someone suffers from **paranoia**, they wrongly believe that other people are trying to harm them, or believe themselves to be much more important than they really are. N-UNCOUNT

**para|noi|ac** /pærənɔɪæk/ **Paranoiac** means the same as **paranoid**. [FORMAL] ADJ

**para|noid** /pærənɔɪd/ **(paranoids)** [1] If you say that someone is **paranoid**, you mean that they are extremely suspicious and afraid of other people. ❑ *I'm not going to get paranoid about it. ...a paranoid politician who saw enemies all around him.* ADJ [2] Someone who is **paranoid** suffers from the mental illness of paranoia. ❑ *...paranoid delusions. ...a paranoid schizophrenic.* ADJ ♦ A **paranoid** is someone who is paranoid. N-COUNT

**para|nor|mal** /pærənɔːʳməl/ A **paranormal** event or power, for example the appearance of a ghost, cannot be explained by scientific laws and is thought to involve strange, unknown forces. ❑ *Science may be able to provide some explanations of paranormal phenomena.* ADJ: usu ADJ n ♦ You can refer to paranormal events and matters as **the paranormal**. ❑ *We have been looking at the shadowy world of the paranormal.* N-SING: *the* N

**para|pet** /pærəpɪt/ **(parapets)** [1] A **parapet** is a low wall along the edge of something high such as a bridge or roof. N-COUNT [2] If you say that someone **puts** their **head above the parapet**, you mean they take a risk. If you say they **keep** their **head below the parapet**, you mean they avoid taking a risk. [BRIT] PHRASE: V and *head* inflect

**para|pher|na|lia** /pærəfəʳneɪliə/ [1] You can refer to a large number of objects that someone has with them or that are connected with a particular activity as **paraphernalia**. ❑ *...a large courtyard full of builders' paraphernalia.* N-UNCOUNT [2] If you disapprove of the things and events that are involved in a particular system or activity, and you think they are unnecessary, you can refer to them as **paraphernalia**. ❑ *The public don't necessarily want the paraphernalia of a full hearing.* N-UNCOUNT: usu with supp, oft N *of* n [disapproval]

**para|phrase** /pærəfreɪz/ **(paraphrases, paraphrasing, paraphrased)** 1 If you **paraphrase** someone or **paraphrase** something that they have said or written, you express what they have said or written in a different way. ❑ *Parents, to paraphrase Philip Larkin, can seriously damage your health... I'm paraphrasing but this is honestly what he said.* 2 A **paraphrase** of something written or spoken is the same thing expressed in a different way.
VERB; V n; V; N-COUNT: oft N *of* n

**para|plegia** /pærəpliːdʒə/ **Paraplegia** is the condition of being unable to move the lower half of your body. [MEDICAL]
N-UNCOUNT

**para|plegic** /pærəpliːdʒɪk/ **(paraplegics)** A **paraplegic** is someone who cannot move the lower half of their body, for example because of an injury to their spine. ♦ **Paraplegic** is also an adjective. ❑ *A passenger was injured so badly he will be paraplegic for the rest of his life.*
N-COUNT; ADJ

**para|psy|chol|ogy** /pærəsaɪkɒlədʒi/ **Parapsychology** is the study of strange mental abilities that seem to exist but cannot be explained by accepted scientific theories.
N-UNCOUNT

**para|quat** /pærəkwæt/ **Paraquat** is a very poisonous substance that is used to kill weeds. [TRADEMARK]
N-UNCOUNT

**para|site** /pærəsaɪt/ **(parasites)** 1 A **parasite** is a small animal or plant that lives on or inside a larger animal or plant, and gets its food from it. 2 If you disapprove of someone because you think that they get money or other things from other people but do not do anything in return, you can call them a **parasite**.
N-COUNT; N-COUNT [disapproval]

**para|sit|ic** /pærəsɪtɪk/ also **parasitical.**
1 **Parasitic** diseases are caused by parasites. ❑ *Will global warming mean the spread of tropical parasitic diseases?* 2 **Parasitic** animals and plants live on or inside larger animals or plants and get their food from them. ❑ *...tiny parasitic insects.*
3 If you describe a person or organization as **parasitic**, you mean that they get money or other things from people without doing anything in return.
ADJ: usu ADJ n; ADJ: usu ADJ n; ADJ [disapproval]

**para|sol** /pærəsɒl, AM -sɔːl/ **(parasols)** A **parasol** is an object like an umbrella that provides shade from the sun.
N-COUNT = *sunshade*

**para|troop|er** /pærətruːpəʳ/ **(paratroopers)** **Paratroopers** are soldiers who are trained to be dropped by parachute into battle or into enemy territory.
N-COUNT: usu pl

**para|troops** /pærətruːps/

✔ The form **paratroop** is used as a modifier.

**Paratroops** are soldiers who are trained to be dropped by parachute into battle or into enemy territory. ❑ *The airport is in the hands of French paratroops.*
N-PLURAL

**par|boil** /pɑːʳbɔɪl/ **(parboils, parboiling, parboiled)** If you **parboil** food, especially vegetables, you boil it until it is partly cooked. ❑ *Roughly chop and parboil the potatoes.*
VERB; V n

**par|cel** /pɑːʳsəl/ **(parcels)** 1 A **parcel** is something wrapped in paper, usually so that it can be sent to someone by post. [mainly BRIT] ❑ *...parcels of food and clothing... He had a large brown paper parcel under his left arm.*
N-COUNT

✔ in AM, usually use **package**

2 A **parcel of** land is a piece of land. ❑ *These small parcels of land were purchased for the most part by local people.* 3 If you say that something is **part and parcel of** something else, you are emphasizing that it is involved or included in it. ❑ *Payment was part and parcel of carrying on insurance business within the UK.*
N-COUNT: N *of* n; PHRASE: v-link PHR, usu PHR *of* n [emphasis]

**par|cel bomb** **(parcel bombs)** A **parcel bomb** is a small bomb which is sent in a parcel through the post and which is designed to explode when the parcel is opened. [BRIT]
N-COUNT

**parched** /pɑːʳtʃt/ 1 If something, especially the ground or a plant, is **parched**, it is very dry, because there has been no rain. ❑ *...a hill of parched brown grass.* 2 If your mouth, throat, or lips are **parched**, they are unpleasantly dry. 3 If you say that you are **parched**, you mean that you are very thirsty. [INFORMAL]
ADJ; ADJ; ADJ: v-link ADJ

**parch|ment** /pɑːʳtʃmənt/ **(parchments)** 1 In former times, **parchment** was the skin of a sheep or goat that was used for writing on. ❑ *...old manuscripts written on parchment.* 2 **Parchment** is a kind of thick yellowish paper. ❑ *...an old lamp with a parchment shade... Cover with a sheet of non-stick baking parchment.*
N-UNCOUNT; N-UNCOUNT

**par|don** /pɑːʳdən/ **(pardons, pardoning, pardoned)** 1 You say **'Pardon?'** or **'I beg your pardon?'** or, in American English, **'Pardon me?'** when you want someone to repeat what they have just said because you have not heard or understood it. [SPOKEN] ❑ *'Will you let me open it?' — 'Pardon?' — 'Can I open it?'.* 2 People say **'I beg your pardon?'** when they are surprised or offended by something that someone has just said. [SPOKEN] ❑ *'Would you get undressed, please?' — 'I beg your pardon?' — 'Will you get undressed?'*
3 You say **'I beg your pardon'** or **'I do beg your pardon'** as a way of apologizing for accidentally doing something wrong, such as disturbing someone or making a mistake. [SPOKEN] ❑ *I was impolite and I do beg your pardon.* 4 Some people say **'Pardon me'** instead of 'Excuse me' when they want to politely get someone's attention or interrupt them. [mainly BRIT, SPOKEN] ❑ *Pardon me, are you finished, madam?*
CONVENTION [formulae]; CONVENTION [feelings]; CONVENTION [formulae]; CONVENTION [formulae]

✔ in AM, use **excuse me**

5 You can say things like **'Pardon me for asking'** or **'Pardon my frankness'** as a way of showing you understand that what you are going to say may sound rude. [SPOKEN] ❑ *That, if you'll pardon my saying so, is neither here nor there.*
6 Some people say things like **'If you'll pardon the expression'** or **'Pardon my French'** just before or after saying something which they think might offend people. [SPOKEN] ❑ *It's enough to make you wet yourself, if you'll pardon the expression.*
7 If someone who has been found guilty of a crime **is pardoned**, they are officially allowed to go free and are not punished. ❑ *Hundreds of political prisoners were pardoned and released.* ♦ **Pardon** is also a noun. ❑ *He was granted a presidential pardon.*
CONVENTION [politeness]; CONVENTION [formulae]; VERB: usu passive; *be* V-ed; N-COUNT

**par|don|able** /pɑːʳdənəbəl/ You describe someone's action or attitude as **pardonable** if you think it is wrong but you understand why they did that action or have that attitude. ❑ *'I have', he remarked with pardonable pride, 'done what I set out to do.'*
ADJ

**pare** /peəʳ/ **(pares, paring, pared)** 1 When you **pare** something, or **pare** part of it **off** or **away**, you cut off its skin or its outer layer. ❑ *Pare the brown skin from the meat with a very sharp knife... He took out a slab of cheese, pared off a slice and ate it hastily. ...thinly pared lemon rind.* ➔ See also **paring.** 2 If you **pare** something **down** or **back**, or if you **pare** it, you reduce it. ❑ *The number of Ministries has been pared down by a third... The luxury tax won't really do much to pare down the budget deficit... Local authorities must pare their budgets.*
VERB; V n *from* n; V n with adv; V-ed; VERB; *be* V-ed adv; V n with adv; V n

**pared-down** If you describe something as **pared-down**, you mean that it has no unnecessary features, and has been reduced to a very simple form. ❑ *Her style is pared-down and simple.*
ADJ ≠ *elaborate*

**par|ent** /peərənt/ **(parents)** 1 Your **parents** are your mother and father. ❑ *Children need their parents... When you become a parent the things you once cared about seem to have less value.* ➔ See also **foster parent, one-parent family, single parent.** 2 An organization's **parent** organization is the organization that created it and usually still controls it. ❑ *Each unit including the parent company has its own, local management.*
◆◆◆ N-COUNT: usu pl; ADJ: ADJ n

**par|ent|age** /peərəntɪdʒ/ Your **parentage** is the identity and origins of your parents. For example, if you are of Greek **parentage**, your parents are Greek. ❑ *She's a Londoner of mixed parentage (English and Jamaican).* N-UNCOUNT: oft *of* adj N

**pa|ren|tal** /pərentᵊl/ **Parental** is used to describe something that relates to parents in general, or to one or both of the parents of a particular child. ❑ *Medical treatment was sometimes given to children without parental consent.* ADJ: usu ADJ n

**pa|ren|tal leave** **Parental leave** is time away from work, usually without pay, that parents are allowed in order to look after their children. [BUSINESS] ❑ *Parents are entitled to 13 weeks' parental leave.* N-UNCOUNT

**pa|ren|thesis** /pərenθəsɪs/ **(parentheses** /pərenθəsiːz/**)** 1 **Parentheses** are a pair of curved marks that you put around words or numbers to indicate that they are additional, separate, or less important. (This sentence is in parentheses.) N-COUNT: usu pl = *bracket* 2 A **parenthesis** is a remark that is made in the middle of a piece of speech or writing, and which gives a little more information about the subject being discussed. N-COUNT 3 You say **'in parenthesis'** to indicate that you are about to add something before going back to the main topic. PHRASE: PHR cl

**par|en|the|ti|cal** /pærənθetɪkᵊl/ A **parenthetical** remark or section is put into something written or spoken but is not essential to it. ❑ *Fox was making a long parenthetical remark about his travels on the border of the country.* ADJ: usu ADJ n ♦ **par|en|the|ti|cal|ly** *Well, parenthetically, I was trying to quit smoking at the time... And what, we may ask parenthetically, does it mean?* ADV: ADV with cl, ADV with v, ADV adj

**par|ent|hood** /peərənthʊd/ **Parenthood** is the state of being a parent. ❑ *She may feel unready for the responsibilities of parenthood.* N-UNCOUNT

**par|ent|ing** /peərəntɪŋ/ **Parenting** is the activity of bringing up and looking after your child. ❑ *Parenting is not fully valued by society. ...parenting classes.* N-UNCOUNT: oft N n

**parent-teacher as|so|cia|tion** **(parent-teacher associations)** A **parent-teacher association** is the same as a **PTA**. N-COUNT

**par ex|cel|lence** /pɑːʳ eksəlɑːns, AM -lɑːns/ You say that something is a particular kind of thing **par excellence** in order to emphasize that it is a very good example of that kind of thing. ❑ *He has been a meticulous manager, a manager par excellence.* ADJ: n ADJ [emphasis] ♦ **Par excellence** is also an adverb. ❑ *Bresson is par excellence the Catholic filmmaker.* ADV: ADV after v

**pa|ri|ah** /pəraɪə/ **(pariahs)** If you describe someone as a **pariah**, you mean that other people dislike them so much that they refuse to associate with them. ❑ *His landlady had treated him like a dangerous criminal, a pariah.* N-COUNT [disapproval] = *outcast*

**par|ing** /peərɪŋ/ **(parings)** **Parings** are thin pieces that have been cut off things such as a fingernails, fruit, or vegetables. ❑ *...nail parings. ...vegetable parings.* N-COUNT: usu pl

**par|ish** /pærɪʃ/ **(parishes)** 1 A **parish** is a village or part of a town which has its own church and priest. ❑ *...the parish of St Mark's, Lakenham. ...a 13th century parish church.* N-COUNT: oft N n 2 A **parish** is a small country area in England which has its own elected council. ❑ *...elected representatives, such as County and Parish Councillors.* N-COUNT: usu N n

**pa|rish|ion|er** /pərɪʃənəʳ/ **(parishioners)** A priest's **parishioners** are the people who live in his or her parish, especially the ones who go to his or her church. N-COUNT: usu pl

**Pa|ris|ian** /pærɪziən/ **(Parisians)** 1 **Parisian** means belonging or relating to Paris. ❑ *...Parisian fashion.* ADJ: usu ADJ n 2 A **Parisian** is a person who comes from Paris. N-COUNT

**par|ity** /pærɪti/ 1 If there is **parity** between two things, they are equal. [FORMAL] ❑ *Women have yet to achieve wage or occupational parity in many fields.* N-UNCOUNT 2 If there is **parity** between the units of currency of two countries, the exchange rate is such that the units are equal to each other. [TECHNICAL] ❑ *The government was ready to let the pound sink to parity with the dollar if necessary.* N-VAR

**park** /pɑːʳk/ **(parks, parking, parked)** ◆◆◇ 1 A **park** is a public area of land with grass and trees, usually in a town, where people go in order to relax and enjoy themselves. ❑ *...Regent's Park... They stopped and sat on a park bench.* N-COUNT 2 When you **park** a vehicle or **park** somewhere, you drive the vehicle into a position where it can stay for a period of time, and leave it there. ❑ *Greenfield turned into the next side street and parked... He found a place to park the car... Ben parked across the street. ...rows of parked cars.* ➔ See also **double-park**. VERB V V n V prep/adv V-ed 3 You can refer to a place where a particular activity is carried out as a **park**. ❑ *...a science and technology park. ...a business park.* N-COUNT: supp N 4 A private area of grass and trees around a large country house is referred to as a **park**. [BRIT] ❑ *...a 19th century manor house in six acres of park and woodland.* N-VAR 5 ➔ See also **parked**, **amusement park**, **ballpark**, **car park**, **national park**, **safari park**, **theme park**.

**par|ka** /pɑːʳkə/ **(parkas)** A **parka** is a jacket or coat which has a thick lining and a hood with fur round the edge. N-COUNT

**parked** /pɑːʳkt/ If you are **parked** somewhere, you have parked your car there. ❑ *My sister was parked down the road... We're parked out front.* ADJ: v-link ADJ

**park|ing** /pɑːʳkɪŋ/ 1 **Parking** is the action of moving a vehicle into a place in a car park or by the side of the road where it can be left. ❑ *In many towns parking is allowed only on one side of the street... I knew I'd never find a parking space in the Square.* N-UNCOUNT 2 **Parking** is space for parking a vehicle in. ❑ *Cars allowed, but parking is limited.* N-UNCOUNT

**park|ing gar|age** **(parking garages)** A **parking garage** is a building where people can leave their cars. [AM] ❑ *...a multi-level parking garage.* N-COUNT

> in BRIT, use **car park**, **multi-storey car park**

**park|ing light** **(parking lights)** The **parking lights** on a vehicle are the small lights at the front that help other drivers to notice the vehicle and to judge its width. [AM] N-COUNT

> in BRIT, use **sidelights**

**park|ing lot** **(parking lots)** A **parking lot** is an area of ground where people can leave their cars. [AM] ❑ *A block up the street I found a parking lot.* N-COUNT

> in BRIT, use **car park**

**park|ing me|ter** **(parking meters)** A **parking meter** is a device which you have to put money into when you park in a parking space. N-COUNT = *meter*

**park|ing tick|et** **(parking tickets)** A **parking ticket** is a piece of paper with instructions to pay a fine, and is put on your car when you have parked it somewhere illegally. N-COUNT

**park-keeper** **(park-keepers)** also **park keeper.** A **park-keeper** is a person whose job is to look after a park. [mainly BRIT] N-COUNT

**park|land** /pɑːʳklænd/ **(parklands)** **Parkland** is land with grass and trees on it. ❑ *Its beautiful gardens and parkland are also open to the public.* N-UNCOUNT: also N in pl

**park|way** /pɑːʳkweɪ/ **(parkways)** A **parkway** is a wide road with trees and grass on both sides. [mainly AM] N-COUNT

**par|lance** /pɑːʳləns/ You use **parlance** when indicating that the expression you are using is normally used by a particular group of people. [FORMAL] ❑ *The phrase is common diplomatic parlance for spying.* N-UNCOUNT: supp N, usu *in* N

**par|ley** /pɑːʳli/ **(parleys, parleying, parleyed)** 1 **A parley** is a discussion between two opposing people or groups in which both sides try to come to an agreement. [OLD-FASHIONED] N-VAR 2 When two opposing people or groups **parley**, they meet to discuss something in order to come to an agreement. [HUMOROUS or INFORMAL] ❑ *...a place where we* V-RECIP V *meet and parley... I don't think you've ever tried parleying with Gleed, have you?* V with n

**par|lia|ment** /pɑːʳləmənt/ **(parliaments)** ◆◆◇ also **Parliament.** [1] The **parliament** of some countries, for example Britain, is the group of people who make or change its laws, and decide what policies the country should follow. ❑ *Parliament today approved the policy, but it has not yet become law.* ➔ See also **Houses of Parliament, Member of Parliament.** N-COUNT; N-PROPER [2] A particular **parliament** is a particular period of time in which a parliament is doing its work, between two elections or between two periods of holiday. ❑ *The legislation is expected to be passed in the next parliament.* N-COUNT

**par|lia|men|tar|ian** /pɑːʳləmenteəriən/ **(parliamentarians)** [1] **Parliamentarians** are Members of a Parliament; used especially to refer to a group of Members of Parliament who are dealing with a particular task. ❑ *He's been meeting with British parliamentarians and government officials.* N-COUNT [2] A **parliamentarian** is a Member of Parliament who is an expert on the rules and procedures of Parliament and takes an active part in debates. ❑ *He is a veteran parliamentarian whose views enjoy widespread respect.* N-COUNT

**par|lia|men|ta|ry** /pɑːʳləmentəri/ **Parliamentary** is used to describe things that are connected with a parliament or with Members of Parliament. ❑ *He used his influence to make sure she was not selected as a parliamentary candidate.* ◆◇◇ ADJ: ADJ n

**par|lour** /pɑːʳləʳ/ **(parlours)**

✔ in AM, use **parlor**

**Parlour** is used in the names of some types of shops which provide a service, rather than selling things. ❑ *...a funeral parlour. ...a notorious massage parlour.* N-COUNT: n N

**par|lour game** **(parlour games)**

✔ in AM, use **parlor game**

A **parlour game** is a game that is played indoors by families or at parties, for example a guessing game or word game. N-COUNT

**par|lour|maid** /pɑːʳləʳmeɪd/ **(parlourmaids)**

✔ in AM, use **parlormaid**

In former times, a **parlourmaid** was a female servant in a private house whose job involved serving people at table. N-COUNT

**par|lous** /pɑːʳləs/ If something is in a **parlous** state, it is in a bad or dangerous condition. [FORMAL] ❑ *...the parlous state of our economy.* ADJ: usu ADJ n = dire

**Par|me|san** /pɑːʳmɪzæn/ also **parmesan. Parmesan** or **Parmesan cheese** is a hard cheese with a strong flavour which is often used in Italian cooking. N-UNCOUNT

**pa|ro|chial** /pəroʊkiəl/ If you describe someone as **parochial**, you are critical of them because you think they are too concerned with their own affairs and should be thinking about more important things. ADJ [disapproval] = insular

**pa|ro|chi|al|ism** /pəroʊkiəlɪzəm/ **Parochialism** is the quality of being parochial in your attitude. ❑ *We have been guilty of parochialism, of resistance to change.* N-UNCOUNT [disapproval]

**paro|dy** /pærədi/ **(parodies, parodying, parodied)** [1] A **parody** is a humorous piece of writing, drama, or music which imitates the style of a well-known person or represents a familiar situation in an exaggerated way. ❑ *'The Scarlet Capsule' was a parody of the popular 1959 TV series 'The Quatermass Experiment'.* N-VAR: oft N *of* n [2] When someone **parodies** a particular work, thing, or person, they imitate it in an amusing or exaggerated way. ❑ *...a sketch parodying the views of Jean-Marie Le Pen.* VERB V n [3] When you say that something is a **parody of** a particular thing, you are criticizing it because you think it is a very poor example or bad imitation of that thing. ❑ *The first trial was a parody of justice.* N-COUNT: usu N *of* n [disapproval] = travesty

**pa|role** /pəroʊl/ **(paroles, paroling, paroled)** [1] If a prisoner is given **parole**, he or she is released before the official end of their prison sentence and has to promise to behave well. ❑ *Although sentenced to life, he will become eligible for parole after serving 10 years.* N-UNCOUNT ● If a prisoner is **on parole**, he or she is released before the official end of their prison sentence and will not be sent back to prison if their behaviour is good. ❑ *If released, he will continue to be on parole for eight more years.* PHRASE: usu v-link PHR [2] If a prisoner **is paroled**, he or she is given parole. ❑ *He faces at most 12 years in prison and could be paroled after eight years.* VERB: usu passive *be* V-ed

**par|ox|ysm** /pærəksɪzəm/ **(paroxysms)** [1] A **paroxysm of** emotion is a sudden, very strong occurrence of it. ❑ *He exploded in a paroxysm of rage.* N-COUNT: usu N *of* n = fit [2] A **paroxysm** is a series of sudden, violent, uncontrollable movements that your body makes because you are coughing, laughing, or in great pain. ❑ *He broke into a paroxysm of coughing.* N-COUNT: usu N *of* n/-ing = spasm

**par|quet** /pɑːʳkeɪ, AM -keɪ/ **Parquet** is a floor covering made of small rectangular blocks of wood fitted together in a pattern. ❑ *...the polished parquet floors.* N-UNCOUNT: usu N n

**par|ra|keet** ➔ see **parakeet.**

**par|rot** /pærət/ **(parrots, parroting, parroted)** [1] A **parrot** is a tropical bird with a curved beak and brightly-coloured or grey feathers. Parrots can be kept as pets. Some parrots are able to copy what people say. N-COUNT [2] If you disapprove of the fact that someone is just repeating what someone else has said, often without really understanding it, you can say that they **are parroting** it. ❑ *Generations of students have learnt to parrot the standard explanations.* VERB [disapproval] = repeat V n

**parrot-fashion** also **parrot fashion.** If you learn or repeat something **parrot-fashion**, you do it accurately but without really understanding what it means. [BRIT] ❑ *Under the old system pupils often had to stand to attention and repeat lessons parrot fashion.* ADV: ADV after v = by rote

**par|ry** /pæri/ **(parries, parrying, parried)** [1] If you **parry** a question or argument, you cleverly avoid answering it or dealing with it. ❑ *In an awkward press conference, Mr King parried questions on the allegations.* VERB = counter V n [2] If you **parry** a blow from someone who is attacking you, you push aside their arm or weapon so that you are not hurt. ❑ *I did not want to wound him, but to restrict myself to defence, to parry his attacks... I parried, and that's when my sword broke.* VERB = deflect V n V

**parse** /pɑːʳz/ **(parses, parsing, parsed)** In grammar, if you **parse** a sentence, you examine each word and clause in order to work out what grammatical type each one is. [TECHNICAL] VERB: V n

**par|si|mo|ni|ous** /pɑːʳsɪmoʊniəs/ Someone who is **parsimonious** is very unwilling to spend money. [FORMAL] ADJ: usu ADJ n [disapproval]

**par|si|mo|ny** /pɑːʳsɪməni, AM -moʊni/ **Parsimony** is extreme unwillingness to spend money. [FORMAL] ❑ *Due to official parsimony only the one machine was built.* N-UNCOUNT [disapproval]

**pars|ley** /pɑːʳsli, AM -zli/ **Parsley** is a small plant with curly leaves that are used for flavouring or decorating savoury food. ❑ *...parsley sauce.* N-UNCOUNT

**pars|nip** /pɑːʳsnɪp/ **(parsnips)** A **parsnip** is a long cream-coloured root vegetable. ➔ See picture on page 1712. N-COUNT

**par|son** /pɑːʳsən/ **(parsons)** A **parson** is a priest in the Church of England with responsibility for a small local area, or can be used to refer to any clergyman in some other churches. [OLD-FASHIONED] N-COUNT

**par|son|age** /pɑːʳsənɪdʒ/ **(parsonages)** A **parsonage** is the house where a parson lives. [OLD-FASHIONED] N-COUNT

**part**
① NOUN USES, QUANTIFIER USES, AND PHRASES
② VERB USES

**① part** /pɑːʳt/ **(parts)** ◆◆◆
⇛ Please look at category 18 to see if the expression you are looking for is shown under another headword. [1] A **part of** something is one of the pieces, sections, or elements that it consists of. ❑ *I like that part of Cape Town... Respect is a very important part of any relationship.* N-COUNT: usu N *of* n
[2] A **part** for a machine or vehicle is one of the smaller pieces that is used to make it. ❑ *...spare parts for military equipment.* N-COUNT = *component*
[3] **Part of** something is some of it. ❑ *It was a very severe accident and he lost part of his foot... Mum and he were able to walk part of the way together.* QUANT: QUANT *of* sing-n/n-uncount
[4] If you say that something is **part** one thing, **part** another, you mean that it is to some extent the first thing and to some extent the second thing. ❑ *The television producer today has to be part news person, part educator.* ADV: ADV n, ADV adj = *half*
[5] You can use **part** when you are talking about the proportions of substances in a mixture. For example, if you are told to use five **parts** water to one **part** paint, the mixture should contain five times as much water as paint. ❑ *Use turpentine and linseed oil, three parts to two.* N-COUNT
[6] A **part** in a play or film is one of the roles in it which an actor or actress can perform. ❑ *Alf Sjoberg offered her a large part in the play he was directing... He was just right for the part.* N-COUNT = *role*
[7] Your **part in** something that happens is your involvement in it. ❑ *If only he could conceal his part in the accident.* N-SING: poss N *in* n = *involvement*
[8] If something or someone is **part of** a group or organization, they belong to it or are included in it. ❑ *I was a part of the team and wanted to remain a part of the team.* N-UNCOUNT: also *a* N, N *of* n
[9] The **part** in someone's hair is the line running from the front to the back of their head where their hair lies in different directions. [AM] N-COUNT
✔ in BRIT, use **parting**

**PHRASES** [10] → See also **private parts**.
[11] If something or someone **plays** a large or important **part in** an event or situation, they are very involved in it and have an important effect on what happens. ❑ *These days work plays an important part in a single woman's life.* PHRASE: V inflects, oft PHR *in* n/-ing
[12] If you **take part in** an activity, you do it together with other people. ❑ *Thousands of students have taken part in demonstrations.* PHRASE: V inflects, usu PHR *in* n/-ing
[13] When you are describing people's thoughts or actions, you can say **for** her **part** or **for** my **part**, for example, to introduce what a particular person thinks or does. [FORMAL] ❑ *For my part, I feel elated and close to tears.* PHRASE: PHR with cl
[14] If you talk about a feeling or action **on** someone's **part**, you are referring to something that they feel or do. ❑ *There is no need for any further instructions on my part.* PHRASE: PHR with cl/group
[15] **For the most part** means mostly or usually. ❑ *Professors, for the most part, are committed to teaching, not research.* PHRASE: PHR with cl = *by and large*
[16] You use **in part** to indicate that something exists or happens to some extent but not completely. [FORMAL] ❑ *Blood glucose levels depend in part on what and when you eat.* PHRASE: PHR with cl/group = *partly*
[17] If you say that something happened for **the best part** or **the better part of** a period of time, you mean that it happened for most of that time. ❑ *He had been in Israel for the best part of twenty-four hours.* PHRASE: PHR n = *most of*
[18] **part and parcel** → see **parcel**.

**② part** /pɑːʳt/ **(parts, parting, parted)** ◆◇◇
⇛ Please look at category 5 to see if the expression you are looking for is shown under another headword. [1] If things that are next to each other **part** or if you **part** them, they move in opposite directions, so that there is a space between them. ❑ *Her lips parted as if she were about to take a deep breath... He crossed to the window of the sitting-room and parted the curtains.* VERB = *open*; V; V n
[2] If you **part** your hair in the middle or at one side, you make it lie in two different directions so that there is a straight line running from the front of your head to the back. ❑ *Picking up a brush, Joanna parted her hair... His hair was slicked back and neatly parted.* VERB; V n; V-ed
[3] When two people **part**, or if one person **parts from** another, they leave each other. [FORMAL] ❑ *He gave me the envelope and we parted... He has confirmed he is parting from his Swedish-born wife Eva.* V-RECIP; pl-n V; V *from* n
[4] If you **are parted from** someone you love, you are prevented from being with them. ❑ *I don't believe we will ever be parted... A stay in hospital may be the first time a child is ever parted from its parents.* V-RECIP = *separated*; pl-n *be* V-ed; *be* V-ed *from* n
[5] → See also **parting**. to **part company** → see **company**.
♦ **part with** If you **part with** something that is valuable or that you would prefer to keep, you give it or sell it to someone else. ❑ *Buyers might require further assurances before parting with their cash.* PHRASAL VERB; V P n

**part-** /pɑːʳt-/ **Part-** combines with adjectives, nouns, and verbs to mean partly but not completely. [BRIT] ❑ *...part-baked breads and rolls... Some associations provide homes to buy or part-buy.* PREFIX

**par|take** /pɑːʳteɪk/ **(partakes, partaking, partook, partaken)** [1] If you **partake of** food or drink, you eat or drink some of it. [FORMAL] ❑ *They were happy to partake of our feast, but not to share our company.* VERB; V *of* n
[2] If you **partake in** an activity, you take part in it. [FORMAL] ❑ *You will probably be asked about whether you partake in vigorous sports.* VERB = *participate*; V *in* n

**part ex|change** also **part-exchange.** If you give an old item **in part exchange** for something you are buying, the seller accepts the old item as part of the payment, so you do not have to give them as much money. [BRIT] ❑ *Electrical retailers will often take away old appliances if you buy a new one, sometimes in part-exchange.* N-UNCOUNT: oft *in* N

**par|tial** /pɑːʳʃəl/ [1] You use **partial** to refer to something that is not complete or whole. ❑ *...a partial ban on the use of cars in the city. ...partial blindness.* ADJ: usu ADJ n
[2] If you are **partial to** something, you like it. ❑ *He's partial to sporty women with blue eyes.* ADJ: v-link ADJ *to* n/-ing
♦ **par|tial|ity** /pɑːʳʃiælɪti/ *He has a great partiality for chocolate biscuits.* N-UNCOUNT: oft N *for* n
[3] Someone who is **partial** supports a particular person or thing, for example in a competition or dispute, instead of being completely fair. ❑ *I might be accused of being partial.* ADJ: v-link ADJ = *biased* ≠ *impartial*
♦ **par|tial|ity** *She is criticized by some others for her one-sidedness and partiality.* N-UNCOUNT = *bias* ≠ *impartiality*

**par|tial|ly** /pɑːʳʃəli/ If something happens or exists **partially**, it happens or exists to some extent, but not completely. ❑ *Lisa is partially blind.* ADV: ADV with cl/group = *partly*

**par|tici|pant** /pɑːʳtɪsɪpənt/ **(participants)** The **participants** in an activity are the people who take part in it. ❑ *40 of the course participants are offered employment with the company.* N-COUNT

**par|tici|pate** /pɑːʳtɪsɪpeɪt/ **(participates, participating, participated)** ◆◇◇ If you **participate in** an activity, you take part in it. ❑ *They expected him to participate in the ceremony. ...special contracts at lower rates for participating corporations.* VERB; V *in* n; V-ing
♦ **par|tici|pa|tion** /pɑːʳtɪsɪpeɪʃən/ *...participation in religious activities.* N-UNCOUNT

**par|tici|pa|tive** /pɑːʳtɪsɪpətɪv/ **Participative** management or decision-making involves the participation of all the people engaged in an activity or affected by certain decisions. [FORMAL] ❑ *...a participative management style.* ADJ: usu ADJ n

**par|tici|pa|tory** /pɑːʳtɪsɪpeɪtəri, AM -tɔːri/ A **participatory** system, activity, or role involves a particular person or group of people taking part in it. ❑ *Fishing is said to be the most popular participatory sport in the U.K.* ADJ: usu ADJ n

**par|ti|cipi|al** /pɑːʳtɪsɪpiəl/ In grammar, **participial** means relating to a participle. ADJ

**par|ti|ci|ple** /pɑːʳtɪsɪpəl/ **(participles)** In grammar, a **participle** is a form of a verb that can be used in compound tenses of the verb. There are two participles in English: the past participle, which usually ends in '-ed', and the present participle, which ends in '-ing'. N-COUNT

**par|ti|cle** /pɑːʳtɪkəl/ **(particles)** [1] A **particle of** something is a very small piece or amount of it. ❑ *There is a particle of truth in his statement. ...food particles.* N-COUNT: oft N *of* n
[2] In physics, a **particle** is a N-COUNT

piece of matter smaller than an atom, for example an electron or a proton. [TECHNICAL] [3] In grammar, a **particle** is a preposition such as 'into' or an adverb such as 'out' which can combine with a verb to form a phrasal verb. N-COUNT

**par|ti|cle ac|cel|era|tor (particle accelerators)** A **particle accelerator** is a machine used for research in nuclear physics which can make particles that are smaller than atoms move very fast. N-COUNT

**par|ti|cle phys|ics** **Particle physics** is the study of the qualities of atoms and molecules and the way they behave and react. N-UNCOUNT

**par|ticu|lar** /pəʳtɪkjʊləʳ/ ◆◆◇ [1] You use **particular** to emphasize that you are talking about one thing or one kind of thing rather than other similar ones. ❑ *I remembered a particular story about a postman who was a murderer... I have to know exactly why it is I'm doing a particular job.* ADJ: ADJ n emphasis [2] If a person or thing has a **particular** quality or possession, it is distinct and belongs only to them. ❑ *I have a particular responsibility to ensure I make the right decision.* ADJ: ADJ n [3] You can use **particular** to emphasize that something is greater or more intense than usual. ❑ *Particular emphasis will be placed on oral language training.* ADJ: ADJ n emphasis [4] If you say that someone is **particular**, you mean that they choose things and do things very carefully, and are not easily satisfied. ❑ *Ted was very particular about the colors he used.* ADJ: usu v-link ADJ, oft ADJ *about* n [5] → See also **particulars**.

PHRASES [6] You use **in particular** to indicate that what you are saying applies especially to one thing or person. ❑ *The situation in Ethiopia in particular is worrying... Why should he notice her car in particular?* PHRASE: PHR with cl/group = particularly [7] You use **nothing in particular** or **nobody in particular** to mean nothing or nobody important or special. ❑ *Drew made some remarks to nobody in particular and said goodbye.* PHRASE

**par|ticu|lar|ity** /pəʳtɪkjʊlærɪti/ **(particularities)** [1] The **particularity of** something is its quality of being different from other things. The **particularities of** something are the features that make it different. [FORMAL] ❑ *What is lacking is an insight into the particularity of our societal system... Time inevitably glosses over the particularities of each situation.* N-UNCOUNT: also N in pl [2] **Particularity** is the giving or showing of details. [FORMAL] N-UNCOUNT

**par|ticu|lar|ize** /pəʳtɪkjʊləraɪz/ **(particularizes, particularizing, particularized)**

✓ in BRIT, also use **particularise**

If you **particularize** something that you have been talking about in a general way, you give details or specific examples of it. [FORMAL] ❑ *Mr Johnson particularizes the general points he wants to make... A farmer is entitled to a certain particularized tax treatment.* VERB V n V-ed Also V

**par|ticu|lar|ly** /pəʳtɪkjʊləʳli/ ◆◆◇ [1] You use **particularly** to indicate that what you are saying applies especially to one thing or situation. ❑ *Keep your office space looking good, particularly your desk... I often do absent-minded things, particularly when I'm worried.* ADV: ADV with cl/group = especially [2] **Particularly** means more than usual or more than other things. ❑ *Progress has been particularly disappointing... I particularly liked the wooden chests and chairs.* ADV: ADV with cl/group emphasis = especially

**par|ticu|lars** /pəʳtɪkjʊləz/ The **particulars** of something or someone are facts or details about them which are written down and kept as a record. ❑ *The nurses at the admission desk asked her for particulars.* N-PLURAL

**par|ticu|late** /pɑːʳtɪkjʊlət/ **(particulates)** **Particulates** are very small particles of a substance, especially those that are produced when fuel is burned. [TECHNICAL] ❑ *...the particulate pollution in our atmosphere.* N-COUNT: oft N n

**part|ing** /pɑːʳtɪŋ/ **(partings)** [1] **Parting** is the act of leaving a particular person or place. A **parting** is an occasion when this happens. ❑ *It was a dreadfully emotional parting.* N-VAR [2] Your **parting** words or actions are the things that you say or do as you are leaving a place or person. ❑ *Her parting words left him feeling empty and alone.* ADJ: ADJ n [3] The **parting** in someone's hair is the line running from the front to the back of their head where their hair lies in different directions. [BRIT] N-COUNT

✓ in AM, use **part**

[4] When there is **a parting of the ways**, two or more people or groups of people stop working together or travelling together. ❑ *...a negotiated parting of the ways for the three Baltic republics.* PHRASE

**part|ing shot (parting shots)** If someone makes a **parting shot**, they make an unpleasant or forceful remark at the end of a conversation, and then leave so that no-one has the chance to reply. ❑ *He turned to face her for his parting shot. 'You're one coldhearted woman, you know that?'* N-COUNT

**par|ti|san** /pɑːʳtɪzæn, AM -zən/ **(partisans)** [1] Someone who is **partisan** strongly supports a particular person or cause, often without thinking carefully about the matter. ❑ *He is clearly too partisan to be a referee.* ADJ: usu v-link ADJ [2] **Partisans** are ordinary people, rather than soldiers, who join together to fight enemy soldiers who are occupying their country. ❑ *He was rescued by some Italian partisans.* N-COUNT

**par|ti|san|ship** /pɑːʳtɪzænʃɪp, AM -zən-/ **Partisanship** is support for a person or group without fair consideration of the facts and circumstances. ❑ *His politics were based on loyal partisanship.* N-UNCOUNT = prejudice

**par|ti|tion** /pɑːʳtɪʃᵊn/ **(partitions, partitioning, partitioned)** [1] A **partition** is a wall or screen that separates one part of a room or vehicle from another. ❑ *...new offices divided only by glass partitions.* N-COUNT [2] If you **partition** a room, you separate one part of it from another by means of a partition. ❑ *Bedrooms have again been created by partitioning a single larger room... He sat on the two-seater sofa in the partitioned office.* VERB V n V-ed [3] If a country **is partitioned**, it is divided into two or more independent countries. ❑ *Korea was partitioned in 1945... Britain was accused of trying to partition the country 'because of historic enmity'... The island has been partitioned since the mid-seventies.* ♦ **Partition** is also a noun. ❑ *...fighting which followed the partition of India.* VERB be V-ed V n V-ed N-UNCOUNT: oft N *of* n

**part|ly** /pɑːʳtli/ ◆◇◇ You use **partly** to indicate that something happens or exists to some extent, but not completely. ❑ *It's partly my fault... He let out a long sigh, mainly of relief, partly of sadness... I feel partly responsible for the problems we're in.* ADV: ADV with cl/group = partially

**part|ner** /pɑːʳtnəʳ/ **(partners, partnering, partnered)** ◆◆◇ [1] Your **partner** is the person you are married to or are having a romantic or sexual relationship with. ❑ *Wanting other friends doesn't mean you don't love your partner. ...his choice of marriage partner.* N-COUNT: oft poss N [2] Your **partner** is the person you are doing something with, for example dancing with or playing with in a game against two other people. ❑ *My partner for the event was the marvellous American player. ...a partner in crime.* N-COUNT [3] The **partners** in a firm or business are the people who share the ownership of it. [BUSINESS] ❑ *He's a partner in a Chicago law firm.* N-COUNT [4] The **partner** of a country or organization is another country or organization with which they work or do business. ❑ *Spain has been one of Cuba's major trading partners.* N-COUNT: usu with supp [5] If you **partner** someone, you are their partner in a game or in a dance. ❑ *He had partnered the famous Russian ballerina... He will be partnered by Ian Baker, the defending champion... He partnered Andre Agassi to victory.* VERB V n be V-ed by/with n V n *to* n

**part|ner|ship** /pɑːʳtnəʳʃɪp/ **(partnerships)** ◆◇◇ **Partnership** or a **partnership** is a relationship in which two or more people, organizations, or countries work together as partners. ❑ *...the partnership between Germany's banks and its businesses.* N-VAR

**part of speech (parts of speech)** A **part of speech** is a particular grammatical class of word, for example noun, adjective, or verb. N-COUNT

**par|took** /pɑːʳtʊk/ **Partook** is the past tense of **partake**.

**par|tridge** /pɑːʳtrɪdʒ/ **(partridges)** N-COUNT A **partridge** is a wild bird with brown feathers, a round body, and a short tail. ♦ N-UNCOUNT **Partridge** is the flesh of this bird eaten as food. ❑ *...a main course of partridge.*

**part-time**

☑ The adverb is also spelled **part time**.

ADJ ≠ full-time If someone is a **part-time** worker or has a **part-time** job, they work for only part of each day or week. ❑ *Many businesses are cutting back by employing lower-paid part-time workers... I'm part-time. I work three days a week.* ♦ ADV: ADV after v **Part-time** is also an adverb. ❑ *I want to work part-time.*

**part-timer** **(part-timers)** N-COUNT A **part-timer** is a person who works part-time. ❑ *Customer service departments are often staffed by part-timers.*

**part way** also **part-way.** ADV: ADV after v, ADV prep/adv **Part way** means part of the way or partly. ❑ *Local authorities will run out of money part way through the financial year... She was on the hillside, part way up... It might go part way to repaying the debt.*

**par|ty** /pɑːʳti/ **(parties, partying, partied)** ♦♦♦ 1 N-COUNT A **party** is a political organization whose members have similar aims and beliefs. Usually the organization tries to get its members elected to the government of a country. ❑ *...a member of the Labour party. ...India's ruling party. ...opposition parties. ...her resignation as party leader.* 2 N-COUNT A **party** is a social event, often in someone's home, at which people enjoy themselves doing things such as eating, drinking, dancing, talking, or playing games. ❑ *The couple met at a party... We threw a huge birthday party... Most teenagers like to go to parties.* → See also **dinner party**, **garden party**, **hen party**, **stag party**. 3 VERB If you **party**, you enjoy yourself doing things such as going out to parties, drinking, dancing, and talking to people. ❑ V *They come to eat and drink, to swim, to party. Sometimes they never go to bed.* 4 N-COUNT: usu with supp A **party of** people is a group of people who are doing something together, for example travelling together. ❑ *They became separated from their party. ...a party of sightseers.* → See also **search party**, **working party**. 5 N-COUNT: usu supp N One of the people involved in a legal agreement or dispute can be referred to as a particular **party**. [LEGAL] ❑ *It has to be proved that they are the guilty party.* → See also **third party**. 6 PHRASE: V inflects, PHR n Someone who **is a party to** or **is party to** an action or agreement is involved in it, and therefore partly responsible for it. ❑ *Crook had resigned his post rather than be party to such treachery.*

**party-goer** /pɑːʳtigoʊəʳ/ **(party-goers)** also **partygoer.** N-COUNT A **party-goer** is someone who likes going to parties or someone who is at a particular party. ❑ *At least half the partygoers were under 15.*

**par|ty line** N-SING The **party line** on a particular issue is the official view taken by a political party, which its members are expected to support. ❑ *They ignored the official party line.*

**par|ty piece** **(party pieces)** N-COUNT: oft poss N Someone's **party piece** is something that they often do to entertain people, especially at parties, for example singing a particular song or saying a particular poem. [INFORMAL]

**par|ty po|liti|cal** ADJ: ADJ n **Party political** matters relate to political parties. [BRIT] ❑ *The debate is being conducted almost exclusively on party political lines.*

**par|ty po|liti|cal broad|cast** **(party political broadcasts)** N-COUNT A **party political broadcast** is a short broadcast on radio or television made by a political party, especially before an election. It explains their views and often criticizes other political parties. [BRIT]

**par|ty poli|tics** 1 N-UNCOUNT **Party politics** is political activity involving political parties. ❑ *He thinks the Archbishop has identified himself too closely with party politics.* 2 N-UNCOUNT disapproval If politicians are accused of playing **party politics**, they are being accused of saying or doing something in order to make their party seem good or another party seem bad, rather than for a better reason. ❑ *Usually when Opposition MPs question Ministers they are just playing party politics.*

**par|ty poop|er** /pɑːʳti puːpəʳ/ **(party poopers)** N-COUNT disapproval You describe someone as a **party pooper** when you think that they spoil other people's fun and their enjoyment of something. [INFORMAL] ❑ *I hate to be a party pooper, but I am really tired.*

**par|ty spir|it** N-UNCOUNT = party mood If you talk about someone being **in** the **party spirit**, you mean that they are in the mood to enjoy a party or to have fun. ❑ *Sparkling wine can also put you in the party spirit.*

**par|venu** /pɑːʳvənjuː, AM -nuː/ **(parvenus)** N-COUNT disapproval If you describe someone as a **parvenu**, you think that although they have acquired wealth or high status they are not very cultured or well-educated. [FORMAL]

**pas de deux**

☑ **pas de deux** is both the singular and the plural form; both forms are pronounced /pɑː də dɜː/ and the plural form can also be pronounced /pɑː də dɜːz/.

N-COUNT In ballet, a **pas de deux** is a dance sequence for two dancers.

**pash|mi|na** /pæʃmiːnə/ **(pashminas)** 1 N-UNCOUNT **Pashmina** is very fine, soft wool made from the hair of goats. ❑ *...pashmina scarves.* 2 N-COUNT A **pashmina** is a type of shawl made from pashmina.

**pass** /pɑːs, pæs/ **(passes, passing, passed)** ♦♦♦ 1 VERB To **pass** someone or something means to go past them without stopping. ❑ V n *As she passed the library door, the telephone began to ring...* V *Jane stood aside to let her pass...* V-ing *I sat in the garden and watched the passing cars.* 2 VERB = go When someone or something **passes** in a particular direction, they move in that direction. ❑ V prep/adv *He passed through the doorway into Ward B...* V prep/adv *The car passed over the body twice, once backward and then forward.* 3 VERB If something such as a road or pipe **passes** along a particular route, it goes along that route. ❑ V prep/adv *After going over the Col de Vars, the route passes through St-Paul-sur-Ubaye...* V n *The road passes a farmyard.* 4 VERB If you **pass** something through, over, or round something else, you move or push it through, over, or round that thing. ❑ V n prep/adv *'I don't understand,' the Inspector mumbled, passing a hand through his hair.* 5 VERB = hand If you **pass** something **to** someone, you take it in your hand and give it to them. ❑ V n *to* n *Ken passed the books to Sergeant Parrott...* V n n *Pass me that bottle.* 6 VERB If something **passes** or **is passed from** one person **to** another, the second person then has it instead of the first. ❑ V *to* n *His mother's small estate had passed to him after her death...* be V-ed *to* n *These powers were eventually passed to municipalities.* be V-ed *from* n *to* n *...a genetic trait, which can be passed from one generation to the next.* 7 VERB If you **pass** information **to** someone, you give it to them because it concerns them. ❑ V n *to* n *Officials failed to pass vital information to their superiors.* ♦ PHRASAL VERB **Pass on** means the same as **pass**. ❑ V n P *I do not know what to do with the information if I cannot pass it on...* V P n (not pron) *to* n *From time to time he passed on confidential information to him...* V P n (not pron), also V n P *to* n *He has written a note asking me to pass on his thanks.* 8 VERB If you **pass** the ball **to** someone in your team in a game such as football, basketball, hockey, or rugby, you kick, hit, or throw it to them. ❑ V n adv/prep *Your partner should then pass the ball back to you...* V prep/adv *Dodd passed back to Flowers.* ♦ N-COUNT **Pass** is also a noun. ❑ *Hirst rolled a short pass to Merson.* 9 VERB = go by When a period of time **passes**, it happens and finishes. ❑ V *He couldn't imagine why he had let so much time pass without contacting her...* V *Several minutes passed before the girls were noticed.* 10 VERB If you **pass** a period of time in a particular way, you spend it in that way. ❑ V n -ing/adv *The children passed the time playing in the streets...* V n *To pass the time they sang songs and played cards.* 11 VERB = go If you **pass through** a stage of development or a period of time, you experience it. ❑ V *through* n *The country was passing through a grave crisis.* 12 VERB If an

amount **passes** a particular total or level, it becomes greater than that total or level. ❑ *They became the first company in their field to pass the £2 billion turn-over mark.*
= exceed
V n

13 If someone or something **passes** a test, they are considered to be of an acceptable standard. ❑ *Kevin has just passed his driving test... I didn't pass.*
VERB ≠ fail
V n
V

14 A **pass** in an examination, test, or course is a successful result in it. ❑ *An A-level pass in Biology is preferred for all courses.*
N-COUNT ≠ fail

15 If someone in authority **passes** a person or thing, they declare that they are of an acceptable standard or have reached an acceptable standard. ❑ *Several popular beaches were found unfit for bathing although the government passed them last year... The medical board would not pass him fit for General Service.*
VERB
V n
V n adj

16 When people in authority **pass** a new law or a proposal, they formally agree to it or approve it. ❑ *The Estonian parliament has passed a resolution declaring the republic fully independent.*
VERB
V n

17 When a judge **passes** sentence on someone, he or she says what their punishment will be. ❑ *Passing sentence, the judge said it all had the appearance of a con trick.*
VERB
V n

18 If you **pass** comment or **pass** a comment, you say something. ❑ *I don't really know so I could not pass comment on that.*
VERB
V n

19 If someone or something **passes for** or **passes as** something that they are not, they are accepted as that thing or mistaken for that thing. ❑ *Children's toy guns now look so realistic that they can often pass for the real thing. ...a woman passing as a man.*
VERB
V for/as n
V for/as n

20 If someone **passes** water or **passes** urine, they urinate. ❑ *A sensitive bladder can make you feel the need to pass water frequently.*
VERB
V n

21 A **pass** is a document that allows you to do something. ❑ *I got myself a pass into the barracks.*
N-COUNT

22 A **pass** is a narrow path or route between mountains. ❑ *The monastery is in a remote mountain pass.*
N-COUNT; N-IN-NAMES

23 → See also **passing**.

24 If someone **makes a pass at** you, they try to begin a romantic or sexual relationship with you. [INFORMAL] ❑ *Nancy wasn't sure if Dirk was making a pass at her.*
PHRASE: V inflects, usu PHR *at* n

25 to **pass the buck** → see **buck**. to **pass judgment** → see **judgment**.

♦ **pass away** You can say that someone **passed away** to mean that they died, if you want to avoid using the word 'die' because you think it might upset or offend people. ❑ *He unfortunately passed away last year.*
PHRASAL VERB
V P

♦ **pass by** If you **pass by** something, you go past it or near it on your way to another place. ❑ *I see them pass by my house every day... They were injured when a parked car exploded as their convoy passed by.*
PHRASAL VERB
V P n
V P

♦ **pass off** If an event **passes off** without any trouble, it happens and ends without any trouble. ❑ *The main demonstration passed off peacefully.*
PHRASAL VERB
V P adv/prep

♦ **pass off as** If you **pass** something **off as** another thing, you convince people that it is that other thing. ❑ *He passed himself off as a senior psychologist... I've tried to pass off my accent as a convent school accent. ...horse meat being passed off as ground beef.*
PHRASAL VERB
V n P P n
V P n (not pron) P n
*be* V-ed P P n (not pron)

♦ **pass on** 1 If you **pass** something **on to** someone, you give it to them so that they have it instead of you. ❑ *The Queen is passing the money on to a selection of her favourite charities... There is a risk of passing the virus on... The late Earl passed on much of his fortune to his daughter... Tenants remain liable if they pass on their lease.*
PHRASAL VERB
V n P *to* n
V n P
V P n (not pron) *to* n
V P n (not pron)

2 If you **pass on** costs or savings **to** someone else, you make them pay for your costs or allow them to benefit from your savings. ❑ *They pass on their cost of borrowing and add to it their profit margin... I found we could make some saving and it is right to pass the savings on to the customer.*
PHRASAL VERB
V P n (not pron)
V n P *to* n

3 You can say that someone **passed on** to mean that they died, if you want to avoid using the word 'die' because you think it might upset or offend people. ❑ *He passed on at the age of 72.*
PHRASAL VERB = pass away
V P

4 → See also **pass 7**.

♦ **pass out** 1 If you **pass out**, you faint or collapse. ❑ *He felt sick and dizzy and then passed out.*
PHRASAL VERB
V P

2 When a police, army, navy, or air force cadet **passes out**, he or she completes his or her training. [BRIT] ❑ *He passed out in November 1924 and was posted to No 24 Squadron.*
PHRASAL VERB
V P

♦ **pass over** 1 If someone **is passed over for** a job or position, they do not get the job or position and someone younger or less experienced is chosen instead. ❑ *She claimed she was repeatedly passed over for promotion... They've been rejected, disappointed, ignored, passed over.*
PHRASAL VERB: usu passive
*be* V-ed P *for* n
*be* V-ed P

2 If you **pass over** a topic in a conversation or speech, you do not talk about it. ❑ *He largely passed over the government's record... They seem to think her crimes should be passed over in silence.*
PHRASAL VERB
V P n
*be* V-ed P

♦ **pass up** If you **pass up** a chance or an opportunity, you do not take advantage of it. ❑ *The official urged the government not to pass up the opportunity that has now presented itself... 'I can't pass this up.' She waved the invitation.*
PHRASAL VERB
V P n (not pron)
V n P

**pass|able** /pɑːsəbəl, pæs-/ 1 If something is a **passable** effort or of **passable** quality, it is satisfactory or quite good. ❑ *Stan puffed out his thin cheeks in a passable imitation of his dad.*
ADJ: usu ADJ n

♦ **pass|ably** /pɑːsəbli, pæs-/ *She has always been quick to pick things up, doing passably well in school without really trying.*
ADV: usu ADV adj/adv, also ADV after v

2 If a road is **passable**, it is not completely blocked, and people can still use it. ❑ *The airport road is passable today for the first time in a week.*
ADJ: usu v-link ADJ ≠ impassable

**pas|sage** /pæsɪdʒ/ **(passages)** 1 A **passage** is a long narrow space with walls or fences on both sides, which connects one place or room with another. ❑ *Harry stepped into the passage and closed the door behind him.*
◆◇◇ N-COUNT = passage-way, corridor

2 A **passage** in a book, speech, or piece of music is a section of it that you are considering separately from the rest. ❑ *He reads a passage from Milton. ...the passage in which Blake spoke of the world of imagination.*
N-COUNT: usu with supp = excerpt, extract

3 A **passage** is a long narrow hole or tube in your body, which air or liquid can pass along. ❑ *...blocked nasal passages.*
N-COUNT: usu supp N

4 A **passage through** a crowd of people or things is an empty space that allows you to move through them. ❑ *He cleared a passage for himself through the crammed streets.*
N-COUNT: oft N *through* n = way

5 The **passage** of someone or something is their movement from one place to another. ❑ *Germany had not requested Franco's consent for the passage of troops through Spain.*
N-UNCOUNT: usu with poss

6 The **passage** of someone or something is their progress from one situation or one stage in their development to another. ❑ *...the passage from school to college.*
N-UNCOUNT: usu N *from/to* n, oft with poss = transition

7 **The passage of** a period of time is its passing. ❑ *An asset that increases in value with the passage of time.*
N-SING: the N *of* n = passing

8 A **passage** is a journey by ship. ❑ *We'd arrived the day before after a 10-hour passage from Swansea.*
N-COUNT = crossing

9 If you are granted **passage** through a country or area of land, you are given permission to go through it. ❑ *Mr Thomas would be given safe passage to and from Jaffna.*
N-UNCOUNT: oft N prep

**passage|way** /pæsɪdʒweɪ/ **(passageways)** A **passageway** is a long narrow space with walls or fences on both sides, which connects one place or room with another. ❑ *Outside, in the passageway, I could hear people moving about.*
N-COUNT = passage

**pass|book** /pɑːsbʊk, pæs-/ **(passbooks)** A **passbook** is a small book recording the amount of money you pay in or take out of a savings account at a bank or building society. [BRIT]
N-COUNT

**pas|sé** /pæseɪ/ If someone describes something as **passé**, they think that it is no longer fashionable or that it is no longer effective. ❑ *Punk is passé.*
ADJ: usu v-link ADJ disapproval = old hat

**pas|sen|ger** /pæsɪndʒə$^r$/ **(passengers)** 1 A **passenger** in a vehicle such as a bus, boat, or plane is a person who is travelling in it, but who is not driving it or working on it. ❑ *Mr Fullemann was a passenger in the car when it crashed. ...a flight from Milan with more than forty passengers on board.*
◆◇◇ N-COUNT

2 **Passenger** is used to describe something that is designed for passengers, rather than for drivers
ADJ: ADJ n

or goods. ❑ *I sat in the passenger seat. ...a passenger train.*

**passer-by** **(passers-by)** also **passerby.** A **passer-by** is a person who is walking past someone or something. ❑ *A passer-by described what he saw moments after the car bomb had exploded.* N-COUNT

**pas|sim** /pæsɪm/ In indexes and notes, **passim** indicates that a particular name or subject occurs frequently throughout a particular piece of writing or section of a book. ❑ *...The Theories of their Relation (London, 1873), p. 8 and passim.*

**pass|ing** /pɑːsɪŋ, pæs-/ 1 A **passing** fashion, activity, or feeling lasts for only a short period of time and is not worth taking very seriously. ❑ *Hamnett does not believe environmental concern is a passing fad.* ADJ: ADJ n ≠lasting 2 The **passing** of something such as a time or system is the fact of its coming to an end. ❑ *It was an historic day, yet its passing was not marked by the slightest excitement.* N-SING: with poss 3 You can refer to someone's death as their **passing**, if you want to avoid using the word 'death' because you think it might upset or offend people. ❑ *His passing will be mourned by many people.* N-SING: with poss 4 **The passing of** a period of time is the fact or process of its going by. ❑ *The passing of time brought a sense of emptiness.* N-SING: the N of n = passage 5 A **passing** mention or reference is brief and is made while you are talking or writing about something else. ❑ *It was just a passing comment, he didn't go on about it.* ADJ: ADJ n = casual 6 → See also **pass**. 7 If you mention something **in passing**, you mention it briefly while you are talking or writing about something else. ❑ *The army is only mentioned in passing.* PHRASE: PHR with cl, PHR after v = incidentally

**pas|sion** /pæʃᵊn/ **(passions)** ◆◇◇ 1 **Passion** is strong sexual feelings towards someone. ❑ *...my passion for a dark-haired, slender boy named James. ...the expression of love and passion.* N-UNCOUNT: also N in pl 2 **Passion** is a very strong feeling about something or a strong belief in something. ❑ *He spoke with great passion.* N-UNCOUNT: also N in pl 3 If you have a **passion for** something, you have a very strong interest in it and like it very much. ❑ *She had a passion for gardening.* N-COUNT: usu with supp

**pas|sion|ate** /pæʃənət/ 1 A **passionate** person has very strong feelings about something or a strong belief in something. ❑ *...his passionate commitment to peace... I'm a passionate believer in public art... He is very passionate about the project.* ADJ ♦ **pas|sion|ate|ly** *I am passionately opposed to the death penalty.* ADV 2 A **passionate** person has strong romantic or sexual feelings and expresses them in their behaviour. ❑ *...a beautiful, passionate woman of twenty-six.* ADJ ♦ **pas|sion|ate|ly** *He was passionately in love with her.* ADV

**pas|sion fruit** **(passion fruit)** A **passion fruit** is a small, round, brown fruit that is produced by certain types of tropical flower. N-VAR

**pas|sion|less** /pæʃᵊnləs/ If you describe someone or something as **passionless**, you mean that they do not have or show strong feelings. ❑ *...a passionless academic. ...their late and apparently passionless marriage.* ADJ ≠passionate

**pas|sive** /pæsɪv/ 1 If you describe someone as **passive**, you mean that they do not take action but instead let things happen to them. ❑ *His passive attitude made things easier for me.* ADJ [disapproval] ≠active ♦ **pas|sive|ly** *He sat there passively, content to wait for his father to make the opening move.* ADV: usu ADV with v ♦ **pas|sivi|ty** /pæsɪvɪti/ *...the passivity of the public under the military occupation.* N-UNCOUNT 2 A **passive** activity involves watching, looking at, or listening to things rather than doing things. ❑ *They want less passive ways of filling their time.* ADJ: ADJ n ≠active 3 **Passive** resistance involves showing opposition to the people in power in your country by not co-operating with them and protesting in non-violent ways. ❑ *They made it clear that they would only exercise passive resistance in the event of a military takeover.* ADJ: ADJ n ≠active 4 In grammar, **the passive** or **the passive voice** is formed using 'be' and the past participle of a verb. The subject of a passive clause does not perform the action expressed by the verb but is affected by it. For example, in 'He's been murdered', the verb is in the passive. Compare **active**. N-SING: the N

**pas|sive smok|ing** **Passive smoking** involves breathing in the smoke from other people's cigarettes because you happen to be near them. ❑ *...the dangers of passive smoking.* N-UNCOUNT

**Pass|over** /pɑːsouvəʳ, pæs-/ **Passover** is a Jewish festival that begins in March or April and lasts for seven or eight days. Passover begins with a special meal that reminds Jewish people of how God helped their ancestors escape from Egypt. N-UNCOUNT: also *the* N

**pass|port** /pɑːspɔːʳt, pæs-/ **(passports)** 1 Your **passport** is an official document containing your name, photograph, and personal details, which you need to show when you enter or leave a country. ❑ *You should take your passport with you when changing money. ...a South African businessman travelling on a British passport.* N-COUNT 2 If you say that a thing is a **passport to** success or happiness, you mean that this thing makes success or happiness possible. ❑ *Victory would give him a passport to the riches he craves.* N-COUNT: N *to* n

**pass|word** /pɑːswɜːʳd, pæs-/ **(passwords)** A **password** is a secret word or phrase that you must know in order to be allowed to enter a place such as a military base, or to be allowed to use a computer system. ❑ *No-one could use the computer unless they had a password.* N-COUNT

**past** /pɑːst, pæst/ **(pasts)** ◆◆◆

> In addition to the uses shown below, **past** is used in the phrasal verb 'run past'.

1 **The past** is the time before the present, and the things that have happened. ❑ *In the past, about a third of the babies born to women with diabetes were lost... He should learn from the mistakes of the past. We have been here before.* N-SING: the N ≠future, present ● If you accuse someone of **living in the past**, you mean that they think too much about the past or believe that things are the same as they were in the past. ❑ *What was the point in living in the past, thinking about what had or had not happened?* PHRASE: V inflects [disapproval] 2 Your **past** consists of all the things that you have done or that have happened to you. ❑ *...revelations about his past. ...Germany's recent past.* N-COUNT: usu sing, usu with supp 3 **Past** events and things happened or existed before the present time. ❑ *I knew from past experience that alternative therapies could help... The list of past champions includes many British internationals.* ADJ: ADJ n = previous 4 You use **past** to talk about a period of time that has just finished. For example, if you talk about the **past five years**, you mean the period of five years that has just finished. ❑ *Most shops have remained closed for the past three days.* ADJ: det ADJ n = last ≠next 5 If a situation is **past**, it has ended and no longer exists. [LITERARY] ❑ *Many economists believe the worst of the economic downturn is past. ...images from years long past.* ADJ: v-link ADJ = gone 6 In grammar, the **past tenses** of a verb are the ones used to talk about things that happened at some time before the present. The simple past tense uses the past form of a verb, which for regular verbs ends in '-ed', as in 'They walked back to the car'. → See also **past perfect**. ADJ: ADJ n 7 You use **past** when you are stating a time which is thirty minutes or less after a particular hour. For example, if it is **twenty past** six, it is twenty minutes after six o'clock. ❑ *It's ten past eleven... I arrived at half past ten.* PREP: num PREP num ≠to ♦ **Past** is also an adverb. ❑ *I have my lunch at half past.* ADV: num ADV 8 If it is **past** a particular time, it is later than that time. ❑ *It was past midnight... It's past your bedtime.* PREP = after 9 If you go **past** someone or something, you go near them and keep moving, so that they are then behind you. ❑ *I dashed past him and out of the door... A steady procession of people filed past the coffin.* PREP = by ♦ **Past** is also an adverb. ❑ *An ambulance drove past.* ADV = by 10 If you look or point **past** a person or thing, you look or point at something behind them. ❑ *She stared past Christine at the bed.* PREP: v PREP n 11 If something is **past** a place, it is PREP: v-link PREP n

on the other side of it. ❑ *Go north on I-15 to the exit just past Barstow.* ≠before [12] If someone or something is **past** a particular point or stage, they are no longer at that point or stage. ❑ *He was well past retirement age.* PREP: usu v-link PREP n [13] If you are **past** doing something, you are no longer able to do it. For example, if you are **past caring**, you do not care about something any more because so many bad things have happened to you. ❑ *She was past caring about anything by then and just wanted the pain to end... Often by the time they do accept the truth they are past being able to put words to feelings.* PREP: v-link PREP -ing = beyond ● If you say that someone or something is **past it**, they are no longer able to do what they used to do. [INFORMAL] ❑ *We could do with a new car. The one we've got is a bit past it.* PHRASE: v-link PHR [disapproval] [14] If you say that you **would not put it past** someone **to** do something bad, you mean that you would not be surprised if they did it because you think their character is bad. ❑ *You know what she's like. I wouldn't put it past her to call the police and say I stole them.* PHRASE: oft PHR to-inf

**pas|ta** /pǽstə, AM pɑ́ːstə/ **(pastas)** **Pasta** is a type of food made from a mixture of flour, eggs, and water that is formed into different shapes and then boiled. Spaghetti, macaroni, and noodles are types of pasta. N-MASS

**paste** /peɪst/ **(pastes, pasting, pasted)** [1] **Paste** is a soft, wet, sticky mixture of a substance and a liquid, which can be spread easily. Some types of paste are used to stick things together. ❑ *Blend a little milk with the custard powder to form a paste. ...wallpaper paste.* N-MASS [2] **Paste** is a soft smooth mixture made of crushed meat, fruit, or vegetables. You can, for example, spread it onto bread or use it in cooking. ❑ *...tomato paste. ...fish paste sandwiches.* N-MASS [3] If you **paste** something on a surface, you put glue or paste on it and stick it on the surface. ❑ *...pasting labels on bottles... Activists pasted up posters criticizing the leftist leaders.* VERB V n prep V n with adv [4] **Paste** is a hard shiny glass that is used for making imitation jewellery. ❑ *...paste emeralds.* N-UNCOUNT: oft N n [5] → See also **pasting**.

**pas|tel** /pǽstəl, AM pæstél/ **(pastels)** [1] **Pastel** colours are pale rather than dark or bright. ❑ *...delicate pastel shades. ...pastel pink, blue, peach and green.* ADJ: ADJ n, ADJ colour ♦ **Pastel** is also a noun. ❑ *The lobby is decorated in pastels.* N-COUNT [2] **Pastels** are also small sticks of different coloured chalks that are used for drawing pictures. ❑ *...pastels and charcoal. ...the portrait in pastels.* N-COUNT: usu pl [3] A **pastel** is a picture that has been done using pastels. ❑ *...Degas's paintings, pastels, and prints.* N-COUNT

**pas|teur|ized** /pɑ́ːstʃəraɪzd, pǽs-/

✓ in BRIT, also use **pasteurised**

**Pasteurized** milk, cream, or cheese has had bacteria removed from it by a special heating process to make it safer to eat or drink. ADJ: usu ADJ n

**pas|tiche** /pæstíːʃ/ **(pastiches)** A **pastiche** is something such as a piece of writing or music in which the style is copied from somewhere else, or which contains a mixture of different styles. [FORMAL] ❑ *Peter Baker's bathroom is a brilliant pastiche of expensive interior design.* N-VAR

**pas|tille** /pǽstəl, AM pæstíːl/ **(pastilles)** A **pastille** is a small, round sweet or piece of candy that has a fruit flavour. Some pastilles contain medicine and you can suck them if you have a sore throat or a cough. N-COUNT

**pas|time** /pɑ́ːstaɪm, pǽs-/ **(pastimes)** A **pastime** is something that you do in your spare time because you enjoy it or are interested in it. ❑ *His favourite pastime is golf.* N-COUNT = hobby

**past|ing** /péɪstɪŋ/ [1] If something or someone takes a **pasting**, they are severely criticized. [mainly BRIT, INFORMAL] ❑ *The people who run Lloyd's of London took a pasting yesterday. ...the critical pasting that the film received.* N-SING [2] If a sports team or political party is given a **pasting**, they are heavily defeated. [mainly BRIT, INFORMAL] N-SING = thrashing

**past mas|ter** **(past masters)** If you are a **past master at** something, you are very skilful at it because you have had a lot of experience doing it. ❑ *He was a past-master at manipulating the media for his own ends... She is an adept rock-climber and a past master of the assault course.* N-COUNT: usu N *at/in/of* n = expert

**pas|tor** /pɑ́ːstəʳ, pǽstəʳ/ **(pastors)** A **pastor** is a member of the Christian clergy in some Protestant churches. N-COUNT

**pas|to|ral** /pɑ́ːstərəl, pǽst-/ [1] The **pastoral** duties of a priest or other religious leader involve looking after the people he or she has responsibility for, especially by helping them with their personal problems. ❑ *Many churches provide excellent pastoral counselling.* ADJ: ADJ n [2] If a school offers **pastoral** care, it is concerned with the personal needs and problems of its pupils, not just with their schoolwork. [mainly BRIT] ❑ *A few schools now offer counselling sessions; all have some system of pastoral care.* ADJ: ADJ n [3] A **pastoral** place, atmosphere, or idea is characteristic of peaceful country life and scenery. ❑ *...a tranquil pastoral scene.* ADJ: ADJ n = rustic

**past par|ti|ci|ple** **(past participles)** In grammar, the **past participle** of a verb is a form that is usually the same as the past form and so ends in '-ed'. A number of verbs have irregular past participles, for example 'break' - past participle 'broken', and 'come' - past participle 'come'. Past participles are used to form perfect tenses and the passive voice, and many of them can be used like an adjective in front of a noun. N-COUNT

**past per|fect** In grammar, the **past perfect** tenses of a verb are the ones used to talk about things that happened before a specific time. The simple past perfect tense uses 'had' and the past participle of the verb, as in 'She had seen him before'. It is sometimes called the **pluperfect**. ADJ: ADJ n

**pas|tra|mi** /pæstrɑ́ːmi/ **Pastrami** is strongly seasoned smoked beef. N-UNCOUNT

**pas|try** /péɪstri/ **(pastries)** [1] **Pastry** is a food made from flour, fat, and water that is mixed together, rolled flat, and baked in the oven. It is used, for example, for making pies. N-UNCOUNT [2] A **pastry** is a small cake made with sweet pastry. N-COUNT

**pas|ture** /pɑ́ːstʃəʳ, pǽs-/ **(pastures)** [1] **Pasture** is land with grass growing on it for farm animals to eat. ❑ *The cows are out now, grazing in the pasture.* N-VAR

PHRASES [2] If someone leaves for **greener pastures**, or in British English **pastures new**, they leave their job, their home, or the situation they are in for something they think will be much better. ❑ *Michael decided he wanted to move on to pastures new for financial reasons.* PHRASE: prep PHR, v PHR [3] If you **put** animals **out to pasture**, you move them out into the fields so they can eat the grass. PHRASE: V inflects

**pasty** **(pasties)**

✓ The adjective is pronounced /péɪsti/. The noun is pronounced /pǽsti/.

[1] If you are **pasty** or if you have a **pasty** face, you look pale and unhealthy. ❑ *My complexion remained pale and pasty.* ADJ [2] In Britain, a **pasty** is a small pie which consists of pastry folded around meat, vegetables, or cheese. → See also **Cornish pasty**. N-COUNT

**pat** /pæt/ **(pats, patting, patted)** [1] If you **pat** something or someone, you tap them lightly, usually with your hand held flat. ❑ *'Don't you worry about any of this,' she said patting me on the knee... The landlady patted her hair nervously... Wash the lettuce and pat it dry.* VERB V n *on* n V n V n adj ♦ **Pat** is also a noun. ❑ *He gave her an encouraging pat on the shoulder.* N-COUNT [2] A **pat of** butter or something else that is soft is a small lump of it. N-COUNT: usu N *of* n [3] If you say that an answer or explanation is **pat**, you disapprove of it because it is too simple and sounds as if it has been prepared in advance. ❑ *There's no pat answer to that.* ADJ [disapproval]

PHRASES [4] If you give someone **a pat on the back** or if you **pat** them **on the back**, you show them that you think they have done well and de- PHRASE: V inflects [approval] serve to be praised. ❑ *The players deserve a pat on the back.* [5] If you **have** an answer or explanation **down pat** or **off pat**, you have prepared and learned it so you are ready to say it at any time. ❑ *I have my story down pat.* PHRASE: V inflects

**patch** /pætʃ/ **(patches, patching, patched)** [1] A **patch** on a surface is a part of it which is different in appearance from the area around it. ❑ *...the bald patch on the top of his head... There was a small patch of blue in the grey clouds.* N-COUNT: usu with supp [2] A **patch of** land is a small area of land where a particular plant or crop grows. ❑ *...a patch of land covered in forest. ...the little vegetable patch in her backyard.* N-COUNT: with supp, oft N of n [3] A **patch** is a piece of material which you use to cover a hole in something. ❑ *...jackets with patches on the elbows.* N-COUNT [4] A **patch** is a small piece of material which you wear to cover an injured eye. ❑ *She went to the hospital and found him lying down with a patch over his eye.* → See also **eye patch**. N-COUNT [5] If you **patch** something that has a hole in it, you mend it by fastening a patch over the hole. ❑ *He and Walker patched the barn roof. ...their patched clothes.* VERB V n V-ed [6] A **patch** is a piece of computer program code written as a temporary solution for dealing with a virus in computer software and distributed by the makers of the original program. [COMPUTING] ❑ *Older machines will need a software patch to be loaded to correct the date.* N-COUNT

**PHRASES** [7] If you have or go through **a bad patch** or **a rough patch**, you have a lot of problems for a time. [mainly BRIT] ❑ *His marriage was going through a bad patch.* PHRASE: N inflects [8] If you say that someone or something is **not a patch on** another person or thing, you mean that they are not as good as that person or thing. [BRIT, INFORMAL] ❑ *Handsome, she thought, but not a patch on Alex.* PHRASE: v-link PHR, PHR n

♦ **patch up** [1] If you **patch up** a quarrel or relationship, you try to be friendly again and not to quarrel any more. ❑ *She has gone on holiday with her husband to try to patch up their marriage... He has now patched up his differences with the Minister... France patched things up with New Zealand... They managed to patch it up.* PHRASAL VERB V P n (not pron) V P n (not pron) *with* n V n P *with* n V n P [2] If you **patch up** something which is damaged, you mend it or patch it. ❑ *We can patch up those holes.* PHRASAL VERB V P n Also V n P [3] If doctors **patch** someone **up** or **patch** their wounds **up**, they treat their injuries. ❑ *...the medical staff who patched her up after the accident... Emergency surgery patched up his face.* PHRASAL VERB V n P V P n (not pron)

**patch|work** /pætʃwɜːʳk/ [1] A **patchwork** quilt, cushion, or piece of clothing is made by sewing together small pieces of material of different colours or patterns. ❑ *...beds covered in patchwork quilts.* ADJ: ADJ n ♦ **Patchwork** is also a noun. ❑ *For centuries, quilting and patchwork have been popular needlecrafts.* N-UNCOUNT [2] If you refer to something as a **patchwork**, you mean that it is made up of many different parts, pieces or colours. ❑ *The low mountains were a patchwork of green and brown. ...this complex republic, a patchwork of cultures, religions and nationalities.* N-SING: oft N *of* n

**patchy** /pætʃi/ [1] A **patchy** substance or colour exists in some places but not in others, or is thick in some places and thin in others. ❑ *Thick patchy fog and irresponsible driving were to blame. ...the brown, patchy grass.* ADJ [2] If something is **patchy**, it is not completely reliable or satisfactory because it is not always good. ❑ *The evidence is patchy.* ADJ

**pate** /peɪt/ **(pates)** Your **pate** is the top of your head. [OLD-FASHIONED] ❑ *...Bryan's bald pate.* N-COUNT

**pâté** /pæteɪ, AM pɑːteɪ/ **(pâtés) Pâté** is a soft mixture of meat, fish, or vegetables with various flavourings, and is eaten cold. N-MASS

**pa|tent** /peɪtᵊnt, AM pæt-/ **(patents, patenting, patented)**

> ✔ The pronunciation /pætᵊnt/ is also used for meanings 1 and 2 in British English.

[1] A **patent** is an official right to be the only person or company allowed to make or sell a new product for a certain period of time. ❑ *P&G applied for a patent on its cookies... He held a number of patents for his many innovations.* N-COUNT [2] If you **patent** something, you obtain a patent for it. ❑ *He patented the idea that the atom could be split. ...a patented machine called the VCR II.* VERB V n V-ed [3] You use **patent** to describe something, especially something bad, in order to indicate in an emphatic way that you think its nature or existence is clear and obvious. ❑ *This was patent nonsense. ...a patent lie.* ADJ emphasis = obvious ♦ **pa|tent|ly** *He made his displeasure patently obvious.* ADV = clearly

**pa|tent leath|er Patent leather** is leather which has a shiny surface. It is used to make shoes, bags, and belts. ❑ *He wore patent leather shoes.* N-UNCOUNT: oft N n

**pa|ter|nal** /pətɜːʳnᵊl/ [1] **Paternal** is used to describe feelings or actions which are typical of those of a kind father towards his child. ❑ *He put his hand under her chin in an almost paternal gesture.* ADJ: usu ADJ n [2] A **paternal** relative is one that is related through a person's father rather than their mother. ❑ *...my paternal grandparents.* ADJ: ADJ n

**pa|ter|nal|ism** /pətɜːʳnəlɪzəm/ **Paternalism** means taking all the decisions for the people you govern, employ, or are responsible for, so that they cannot or do not have to make their own decisions. ❑ *...the company's reputation for paternalism.* N-UNCOUNT

**pa|ter|nal|ist** /pətɜːʳnəlɪst/ **(paternalists)** [1] A **paternalist** is a person who acts in a paternalistic way. ❑ *Primo de Rivera himself was a benevolent and sincere paternalist.* N-COUNT [2] **Paternalist** means the same as **paternalistic**. ❑ *...a paternalist policy of state welfare for the deserving poor.* ADJ: usu ADJ n

**pa|ter|nal|is|tic** /pətɜːʳnəlɪstɪk/ Someone who is **paternalistic** takes all the decisions for the people they govern, employ, or are responsible for. ❑ *The doctor is being paternalistic. He's deciding what information the patient needs to know.* ADJ

**pa|ter|nity** /pətɜːʳnɪti/ **Paternity** is the state or fact of being the father of a particular child. [FORMAL] ❑ *He was tricked into marriage by a false accusation of paternity.* N-UNCOUNT

**pa|ter|nity leave** If a man has **paternity leave**, his employer allows him some time off work because his child has just been born. [BUSINESS] N-UNCOUNT

**pa|ter|nity suit (paternity suits)** If a woman starts or takes out a **paternity suit**, she asks a court of law to help her to prove that a particular man is the father of her child, often in order to claim financial support from him. N-COUNT

**path** /pɑːθ, pæθ/ **(paths)** [1] A **path** is a long strip of ground which people walk along to get from one place to another. → See picture on page 1705. ❑ *We followed the path along the clifftops... Feet had worn a path in the rock... He went up the garden path to knock on the door.* ◆◇◇ N-COUNT [2] Your **path** is the space ahead of you as you move along. ❑ *A group of reporters blocked his path.* N-COUNT: usu poss N [3] The **path** of something is the line which it moves along in a particular direction. ❑ *He stepped without looking into the path of a reversing car.* N-COUNT: with poss [4] A **path** that you take is a particular course of action or way of achieving something. ❑ *The opposition appear to have chosen the path of cooperation rather than confrontation.* N-COUNT: oft N *of/to* n = road, route [5] You can say that something is in your **path** or blocking your **path** to mean that it is preventing you from doing or achieving what you want. ❑ *The Church of England put a serious obstacle in the path of women who want to become priests.* N-COUNT: usu with poss = way [6] If you **cross** someone's **path** or if your **paths cross**, you meet them by chance. ❑ *It was highly unlikely that their paths would cross again.* PHRASE: V inflects

**pa|thet|ic** /pəθetɪk/ [1] If you describe a person or animal as **pathetic**, you mean that they are sad and weak or helpless, and they make you feel very sorry for them. ❑ *The small group of onlookers presented a pathetic sight... She now looked small, shrunken and pathetic.* ADJ ♦ **pa|theti|cal|ly** ADV

/pəθetɪkli/ *She was pathetically thin.* 2 If you describe someone or something as **pathetic**, you mean that they make you feel impatient or angry, often because they are weak or not very good. ❑ *What pathetic excuses... It's a pound for a small glass of wine, which is pathetic.* ♦ **pa|theti|cal|ly** *Five women in a group of 18 people is a pathetically small number.* ADJ disapproval ADV: ADV adj

**path|finder** /pɑːθfaɪndəʳ, pæθ-/ **(pathfinders)** A **pathfinder** is someone whose job is to find routes across areas. N-COUNT

**patho|gen** /pæθədʒen/ **(pathogens)** A **pathogen** is any organism which can cause disease in a person, animal, or plant. [TECHNICAL] N-COUNT

**patho|gen|ic** /pæθədʒenɪk/ A **pathogenic** organism can cause disease in a person, animal, or plant. [TECHNICAL] ADJ: usu ADJ n

**patho|logi|cal** /pæθəlɒdʒɪkəl/ 1 You describe a person or their behaviour as **pathological** when they behave in an extreme and unacceptable way, and have very powerful feelings which they cannot control. ❑ *He's a pathological liar. ...a pathological fear of snakes.* ADJ: usu ADJ n 2 **Pathological** means relating to pathology or illness. [MEDICAL] ❑ *...pathological conditions in animals.* ADJ

**pa|tholo|gist** /pəθɒlədʒɪst/ **(pathologists)** A **pathologist** is someone who studies or investigates diseases and illnesses, and examines dead bodies in order to find out the cause of death. N-COUNT

**pa|thol|ogy** /pəθɒlədʒi/ **Pathology** is the study of the way diseases and illnesses develop. [MEDICAL] N-UNCOUNT

**pa|thos** /peɪθɒs/ **Pathos** is a quality in a situation, film, or play that makes people feel sadness and pity. ❑ *...the pathos of man's isolation.* N-UNCOUNT

**path|way** /pɑːθweɪ, pæθ-/ **(pathways)** 1 A **pathway** is a path which you can walk along or a route which you can take. ❑ *Richard was coming up the pathway. ...a pathway leading towards the nearby river.* N-COUNT 2 A **pathway** is a particular course of action or a way of achieving something. ❑ *Diplomacy will smooth your pathway to success.* N-COUNT: oft N *to* n = path

**pa|tience** /peɪʃəns/ 1 If you have **patience**, you are able to stay calm and not get annoyed, for example when something takes a long time, or when someone is not doing what you want them to do. ❑ *He doesn't have the patience to wait... It was exacting work and required all his patience.* N-UNCOUNT ≠ impatience 2 If someone **tries** your **patience** or **tests** your **patience**, they annoy you so much that it is very difficult for you to stay calm. ❑ *He tended to stutter, which tried her patience.* PHRASE: V inflects

**pa|tient** /peɪʃənt/ **(patients)** 1 A **patient** is a person who is receiving medical treatment from a doctor or hospital. A **patient** is also someone who is registered with a particular doctor. ❑ *The earlier the treatment is given, the better the patient's chances... He specialized in treatment of cancer patients.* ◆◆◇ N-COUNT 2 If you are **patient**, you stay calm and do not get annoyed, for example when something takes a long time, or when someone is not doing what you want them to do. ❑ *Please be patient – your cheque will arrive... He was endlessly kind and patient with children.* ♦ **pa|tient|ly** *She waited patiently for Frances to finish.* ADJ ≠ impatient ADV: ADV with v

**pati|na** /pætɪnə/ 1 A **patina** is a thin layer of something that has formed on the surface of something. ❑ *He allowed a fine patina of old coffee to develop around the inside of the mug.* N-SING: with supp 2 The **patina** on an old object is an attractive soft shine that has developed on its surface, usually because it has been used a lot. ❑ *...a mahogany door that is golden brown with the patina of age.* N-SING: with supp 3 If you say that someone has a **patina of** a quality or characteristic, you mean that they have a small but impressive amount of this quality or characteristic. ❑ *...a superficial patina of knowledge.* N-SING: with supp, oft N *of* n

**pa|tio** /pætioʊ/ **(patios)** A **patio** is an area of flat blocks or concrete next to a house, where people can sit and relax or eat. N-COUNT

**pa|tio door** **(patio doors)** **Patio doors** are glass doors that lead onto a patio. N-COUNT

**pa|tis|serie** /pətiːsəri, AM -tɪs-/ **(patisseries)** 1 A **patisserie** is a shop where cakes and pastries are sold. N-COUNT 2 **Patisserie** is cakes and pastries. ❑ *Blois is famous for patisserie.* N-UNCOUNT: also N in pl

**pat|ois**

> **patois** is both the singular and the plural form; the singular form is pronounced /pætwɑː/, and the plural form is pronounced /pætwɑːz/.

1 A **patois** is a form of a language, especially French, that is spoken in a particular area of a country. ❑ *In France patois was spoken in rural, less developed regions.* N-VAR = dialect 2 A **patois** is a language that has developed from a mixture of other languages. ❑ *A substantial proportion of the population speak a French-based patois.* N-VAR = creole

**pa|tri|arch** /peɪtriɑːʳk/ **(patriarchs)** 1 A **patriarch** is the male head of a family or tribe. ❑ *The patriarch of the house, Mr Jawad, rules it with a ferocity renowned throughout the neighbourhood.* N-COUNT 2 A **patriarch** is the head of one of a number of Eastern Christian Churches. N-COUNT; N-TITLE

**pa|tri|ar|chal** /peɪtriɑːʳkəl/ A **patriarchal** society, family, or system is one in which the men have all or most of the power and importance. ❑ *To feminists she is a classic victim of the patriarchal society.* ADJ: usu ADJ n

**pa|tri|ar|chy** /peɪtriɑːʳki/ **(patriarchies)** 1 **Patriarchy** is a system in which men have all or most of the power and importance in a society or group. ❑ *The main cause of women's and children's oppression is patriarchy.* N-UNCOUNT 2 A **patriarchy** is a patriarchal society. N-COUNT

**pa|tri|cian** /pətrɪʃən/ **(patricians)** 1 A **patrician** is a person who comes from a family of high social rank. [FORMAL] ❑ *...the patrician banker Sir Charles Villiers.* N-COUNT ≠ plebeian 2 If you describe someone as **patrician**, you mean that they behave in a sophisticated way, and look as though they are from a high social rank. ❑ *He was a lean, patrician gent in his early sixties.* ADJ

**pat|ri|mo|ny** /pætrɪməni, AM -moʊni/ 1 Someone's **patrimony** is the possessions that they have inherited from their father or ancestors. [FORMAL] ❑ *I left my parents' house, relinquished my estate and my patrimony.* N-SING 2 A country's **patrimony** is its land, buildings, and works of art. [FORMAL] ❑ *In the 1930's, The National Trust began its campaign to save Britain's patrimony of threatened country houses.* N-SING = heritage

**pa|tri|ot** /pætriət, peɪt-/ **(patriots)** Someone who is a **patriot** loves their country and feels very loyal towards it. ❑ *They were staunch British patriots and had portraits of the Queen in their flat.* N-COUNT: oft supp N

**pat|ri|ot|ic** /pætriɒtɪk, peɪt-/ Someone who is **patriotic** loves their country and feels very loyal towards it. ❑ *Woosnam is fiercely patriotic... The crowd sang 'Land of Hope and Glory' and other patriotic songs.* ADJ

**pat|ri|ot|ism** /pætriətɪzəm, peɪt-/ **Patriotism** is love for your country and loyalty towards it. ❑ *He was a country boy who had joined the army out of a sense of patriotism and adventure.* N-UNCOUNT

**pa|trol** /pətroʊl/ **(patrols, patrolling, patrolled)** 1 When soldiers, police, or guards **patrol** an area or building, they move around it in order to make sure that there is no trouble there. ❑ *Prison officers continued to patrol the grounds within the jail.* ♦ **Patrol** is also a noun. ❑ *He failed to return from a patrol.* VERB V n N-COUNT 2 Soldiers, police, or guards who are **on patrol** are patrolling an area. ❑ *The army is now on patrol in Srinagar and a curfew has been imposed.* PHRASE: usu v-link PHR 3 A **patrol** is a group of soldiers or vehicles that N-COUNT are patrolling an area. ❑ *Guerrillas attacked a patrol with hand grenades.*

**pa|trol car** **(patrol cars)** A **patrol car** is a police car used for patrolling streets and roads. [N-COUNT = *squad car*]

**patrol|man** /pətroulmən/ **(patrolmen)** 1 A **patrolman** is a policeman who patrols a particular area. [AM] [N-COUNT] 2 A **patrolman** is a person employed by a motoring organization to help members of the organization when their cars break down. [BRIT] [N-COUNT]

**pa|trol wag|on** **(patrol wagons)** A **patrol wagon** is a van or truck which the police use for transporting prisoners. [AM] [N-COUNT]

**pa|tron** /peɪtrən/ **(patrons)** 1 A **patron** is a person who supports and gives money to artists, writers, or musicians. ❑ *Catherine the Great was a patron of the arts and sciences.* [N-COUNT: with supp, oft N *of* n = *sponsor*] 2 The **patron** of a charity, group, or campaign is an important person who allows his or her name to be used for publicity. ❑ *Fiona and Alastair have become patrons of the National Missing Person's Helpline.* [N-COUNT: with supp, oft N *of* n] 3 The **patrons** of a place such as a pub, bar, or hotel are its customers. [FORMAL] [N-COUNT]

**pat|ron|age** /pætrənɪdʒ, peɪt-/ **Patronage** is the support and money given by someone to a person or a group such as a charity. ❑ *...government patronage of the arts in Europe.* [N-UNCOUNT: oft with poss = *sponsorship*]

**pa|tron|ess** /peɪtrənes/ **(patronesses)** A woman who is a patron of something can be described as a **patroness**. [N-COUNT: usu with supp = *sponsor*]

**pat|ron|ize** /pætrənaɪz, AM peɪt-/ **(patronizes, patronizing, patronized)**

in BRIT, also use **patronise**

1 If someone **patronizes** you, they speak or behave towards you in a way which seems friendly, but which shows that they think they are superior to you in some way. ❑ *Don't you patronize me!...* [V n] *Cornelia often felt patronised by her tutors.* [V-ed] [VERB, disapproval] 2 Someone who **patronizes** artists, writers, or musicians supports them and gives them money. [FORMAL] ❑ *The Japanese Imperial family patronises the Japanese Art Association.* [V n] [VERB] 3 If someone **patronizes** a place such as a pub, bar, or hotel, they are one of its customers. [FORMAL] ❑ *The ladies of Berne liked to patronize the Palace for tea and little cakes.* [V n] [VERB = *frequent*]

**pat|ron|iz|ing** /pætrənaɪzɪŋ, AM peɪt-/

in BRIT, also use **patronising**

If someone is **patronizing**, they speak or behave towards you in a way that seems friendly, but which shows that they think they are superior to you. ❑ *The tone of the interview was unnecessarily patronizing .* [ADJ, disapproval]

**pat|ron saint** **(patron saints)** The **patron saint of** a place, an activity, or a group of people is a saint who is believed to give them special help and protection. ❑ *Chiswick church is dedicated to St Nicholas, patron saint of sailors.* [N-COUNT: usu with poss]

**pat|sy** /pætsi/ **(patsies)** If you describe someone as a **patsy**, you mean that they are rather stupid and are easily tricked by other people, or can be made to take the blame for other people's actions. [AM, INFORMAL] ❑ *Davis was nobody's patsy.* [N-COUNT, disapproval = *mug*]

**pat|ter** /pætər/ **(patters, pattering, pattered)** 1 If something **patters** on a surface, it hits it quickly several times, making quiet, tapping sounds. ❑ *Rain pattered gently outside, dripping on to the roof from the pines.* [VERB, V adv/prep] 2 A **patter** is a series of quick, quiet, tapping sounds. ❑ *...the patter of the driving rain on the roof.* [N-SING: oft *the* N *of* n] 3 Someone's **patter** is a series of things that they say quickly and easily, usually in order to entertain people or to persuade them to buy or do something. ❑ *Fran began her automatic patter about how Jon had been unavoidably detained.* [N-SING: usu poss N]

**pat|tern** /pætərn/ **(patterns)** ◆◆◇ 1 A **pattern** is the repeated or regular way in which something happens or is done. ❑ *All three attacks followed the same pattern... A change in the pattern of his breathing became apparent.* [N-COUNT: oft *the* N *of* n] 2 A **pattern** is an arrangement of lines or shapes, especially a design in which the same shape is repeated at regular intervals over a surface. ❑ *...a golden robe embroidered with red and purple thread stitched into a pattern of flames.* [N-COUNT] 3 A **pattern** is a diagram or shape that you can use as a guide when you are making something such as a model or a piece of clothing. ❑ *...cutting out a pattern for trousers.* [N-COUNT]

**pat|terned** /pætərnd/ 1 Something that is **patterned** is covered with a pattern or design. ❑ *...a plain carpet with a patterned border. ...bone china patterned with flowers.* [ADJ: oft ADJ *with* n] 2 If something new **is patterned on** something else that already exists, it is deliberately made so that it has similar features. [mainly AM] ❑ *New York City announced a 10-point policy patterned on the federal bill of rights for taxpayers...* [*be* V-ed *on* n] *He says this contract should not be patterned after the Deere pact.* [*be* V-ed *after* n] [V-PASSIVE]

**pat|tern|ing** /pætərnɪŋ/ 1 **Patterning** is the forming of fixed ways of behaving or of doing things by constantly repeating something or copying other people. [FORMAL] ❑ *...social patterning. ...the patterning of behaviour.* [N-UNCOUNT: usu with supp] 2 You can refer to lines, spots, or other patterns as **patterning**. ❑ *...geometric patterning. ...a jazzy patterning of lights.* [N-UNCOUNT: usu with supp]

**pat|ty** /pæti/ **(patties)** 1 A **patty** is a small, round meat pie. [mainly AM] [N-COUNT] 2 A **patty** is an amount of minced beef formed into a flat, round shape. [N-COUNT]

**pau|city** /pɔːsɪti/ If you say that there is a **paucity of** something, you mean that there is not enough of it. [FORMAL] ❑ *Even the film's impressive finale can't hide the first hour's paucity of imagination. ...the paucity of good British women sprinters.* [N-SING: N *of* n]

**paunch** /pɔːntʃ/ **(paunches)** If a man has a **paunch**, he has a fat stomach. ❑ *He finished his dessert and patted his paunch.* [N-COUNT = *pot-belly*]

**paunchy** /pɔːntʃi/ **(paunchier, paunchiest)** A man who is **paunchy** has a fat stomach. [ADJ: usu v-link ADJ = *pot-bellied*]

**pau|per** /pɔːpər/ **(paupers)** A **pauper** is a very poor person. [FORMAL] ❑ *He did die a pauper and is buried in an unmarked grave.* [N-COUNT]

**pause** /pɔːz/ **(pauses, pausing, paused)** ◆◇◇ 1 If you **pause** while you are doing something, you stop for a short period and then continue. ❑ *'It's rather embarrassing,' he began, and paused...* [V] *On leaving, she paused for a moment at the door...* [V] *He talked for two hours without pausing for breath.* [V *for* n] [VERB] 2 A **pause** is a short period when you stop doing something before continuing. ❑ *After a pause Alex said sharply: 'I'm sorry if I've upset you'.* [N-COUNT]

**pave** /peɪv/ **(paves, paving, paved)** 1 If a road or an area of ground **has been paved**, it has been covered with flat blocks of stone or concrete, so that it is suitable for walking or driving on. ❑ *The avenue had never been paved, and deep mud made it impassable in winter.* [*be* V-ed] [VERB: usu passive] ♦ **paved** *...a small paved courtyard.* [ADJ: oft ADJ *with* n] 2 If one thing **paves the way for** another, it creates a situation in which it is possible or more likely that the other thing will happen. [JOURNALISM] ❑ *The discussions are aimed at paving the way for formal negotiations between the two countries.* [PHRASE: V inflects]

**pave|ment** /peɪvmənt/ **(pavements)** 1 A **pavement** is a path with a hard surface, usually by the side of a road. [BRIT] ❑ *He was hurrying along the pavement.* [N-COUNT: oft supp N]

in AM, use **sidewalk**

2 The **pavement** is the hard surface of a road. [AM] [N-COUNT]

**pa|vil|ion** /pəvɪliən/ **(pavilions)** 1 A **pavilion** is a building on the edge of a sports field where players can change their clothes and wash. [BRIT] ❑ *...the cricket pavilion.* [N-COUNT: oft supp N] 2 A **pavilion** is a large temporary structure such as a tent, which is used at outdoor public events. ❑ *...the United States pavilion at the Expo '70 exhibition in Japan.* [N-COUNT: oft supp N]

**pav|ing** /peɪvɪŋ/ *N-UNCOUNT: oft supp N* **Paving** is flat blocks of stone or concrete covering an area. ❑ *In the centre of the paving stood a statue. ...concrete paving.*

**pav|ing stone** **(paving stones)** *N-COUNT* **Paving stones** are flat pieces of stone or concrete, usually square in shape, that are put on the ground, for example to make a path. [mainly BRIT]

**pav|lo|va** /pævloʊvə/ **(pavlovas)** *N-VAR* A **pavlova** is a dessert which consists of a hard base made of egg whites and sugar with fruit and cream on top.

**paw** /pɔː/ **(paws, pawing, pawed)** 1 *N-COUNT: oft with poss* The **paws** of an animal such as a cat, dog, or bear are its feet, which have claws for gripping things and soft pads for walking on. ❑ *The kitten was black with white front paws and a white splotch on her chest.* 2 *N-COUNT: oft poss N, adj N* You can describe someone's hand as their **paw**, especially if it is very large or if they are very clumsy. [mainly HUMOROUS, INFORMAL] ❑ *He shook Keaton's hand with his big paw.* 3 *VERB* If an animal **paws** something, it draws its foot over it or down it. ❑ *Madigan's horse pawed the ground...* (V n) *The dogs continued to paw and claw frantically at the chain mesh.* (V at n) 4 *VERB* [disapproval] If one person **paws** another, they touch or stroke them in a way that the other person finds offensive. ❑ *Stop pawing me, Giles!...* (V n) *He pawed at my jacket with his free hand.* (V at n)

**pawn** /pɔːn/ **(pawns, pawning, pawned)** 1 *VERB* If you **pawn** something that you own, you leave it with a pawnbroker, who gives you money for it and who can sell it if you do not pay back the money before a certain time. ❑ *He is contemplating pawning his watch.* (V n) 2 *N-COUNT* In chess, a **pawn** is the smallest and least valuable playing piece. Each player has eight pawns at the start of the game. 3 *N-COUNT: usu with supp, oft N in n* If you say that someone is using you as a **pawn**, you mean that they are using you for their own advantage. ❑ *It looks as though he is being used as a political pawn by the President.*

**pawn|broker** /pɔːnbroʊkəʳ/ **(pawnbrokers)** *N-COUNT* A **pawnbroker** is a person who lends people money. People give the pawnbroker something they own, which can be sold if they do not pay back the money before a certain time.

**pawn shop** **(pawn shops)** also **pawnshop.** *N-COUNT* A **pawn shop** is a pawnbroker's shop.

**paw|paw** /pɔːpɔː/ **(pawpaws)** also **paw-paw.** *N-VAR = papaya* A **pawpaw** is a fruit with green skin, sweet yellow flesh, and black seeds and grows in hot countries such as the West Indies. [BRIT]

✔ in AM, use **papaya**

**pay** /peɪ/ **(pays, paying, paid)** ◆◆◆ 1 *VERB* When you **pay** an amount of money **to** someone, you give it to them because you are buying something from them or because you owe it to them. When you **pay** something such as a bill or a debt, you pay the amount that you owe. ❑ *Accommodation is free – all you pay for is breakfast and dinner...* (V for n) *We paid £35 for each ticket...* (V n for n) *The wealthier may have to pay a little more in taxes...* (V n) *He proposes that businesses should pay taxes to the federal government...* (V n to n) *You can pay by credit card.* (V adv/prep) 2 *VERB* When you **are paid**, you get your wages or salary from your employer. ❑ *The lawyer was paid a huge salary...* (be/get V-ed n) *I get paid monthly...* (get/be V-ed adv) *They could wander where they wished and take jobs from who paid best.* (V adv) 3 *N-UNCOUNT* Your **pay** is the money that you get from your employer as wages or salary. ❑ *...their complaints about their pay and conditions. ...the workers' demand for a twenty per cent pay rise.* 4 *VERB* If you **are paid to** do something, someone gives you some money so that you will help them or perform some service for them. ❑ *Students were paid substantial sums of money to do nothing all day but lie in bed...* (be V-ed to-inf) *If you help me, I'll pay you anything.* (V n n) 5 *VERB* If a government or organization makes someone **pay for** something, it makes them responsible for providing the money for it, for example by increasing prices or taxes. ❑ *...a legally binding international treaty that establishes who must pay for environmental damage...* (V for n) *If you don't subsidize ballet and opera, seat prices will have to go up to pay for it.* (V for n, Also V) 6 *VERB* If a job, deal, or investment **pays** a particular amount, it brings you that amount of money. ❑ *We're stuck in jobs that don't pay very well...* (V adv) *The account does not pay interest on a credit balance.* (V n) 7 *VERB* If a job, deal, or investment **pays**, it brings you a profit or earns you some money. ❑ *They owned land; they made it pay.* (V) 8 *VERB* When you **pay** money **into** a bank account, you put the money in the account. ❑ *He paid £20 into his savings account...* (V n into n) *There is nothing more annoying than queueing when you only want to pay in a few cheques.* (V n with adv) 9 *VERB* If a course of action **pays**, it results in some advantage or benefit for you. ❑ *It pays to invest in protective clothing...* (it V to-inf) *He talked of defending small nations, of ensuring that aggression does not pay.* (V) 10 *VERB* If you **pay for** something that you do or have, you suffer as a result of it. ❑ *Britain was to pay dearly for its lack of resolve...* (V for n) *Why should I pay the penalty for somebody else's mistake?...* (V n for n) *She feels it's a small price to pay for the pleasure of living in this delightful house.* (V n for n, Also V) 11 *VERB* You use **pay** with some nouns, for example in the expressions **pay a visit** and **pay attention**, to indicate that something is given or done. ❑ *Do pay us a visit next time you're in Birmingham...* (V n n) *He felt a heavy bump, but paid no attention to it...* (V n to n) *He had nothing to do with arranging the funeral, but came along to pay his last respects.* (V n) 12 *ADJ: ADJ n* **Pay** television consists of programmes and channels which are not part of a public broadcasting system, and for which people have to pay. ❑ *The company has set up joint-venture pay-TV channels in Belgium, Spain, and Germany.* 13 → See also **paid**, **sick pay**.

**PHRASES** 14 *PHRASE: V inflects* If something that you buy or invest in **pays for itself** after a period of time, the money you gain from it, or save because you have it, is greater than the amount you originally spent or invested. ❑ *...investments in energy efficiency that would pay for themselves within five years.* 15 *PHRASE: V inflects* If you **pay** your **way**, you have or earn enough money to pay for what you need, without needing other people to give or lend you money. ❑ *I went to college anyway, as a part-time student, paying my own way... The British film industry could not pay its way without a substantial export market.* 16 **to pay dividends** → see **dividend**. **to pay through the nose** → see **nose**. **he who pays the piper calls the tune** → see **piper**.

◆ **pay back** 1 *PHRASAL VERB* If you **pay back** some money that you have borrowed or taken from someone, you give them an equal sum of money at a later time. ❑ *He burst into tears, begging her to forgive him and swearing to pay back what he had stolen...* (V P n) *I'll pay you back that two quid tomorrow.* (V n P n, Also V n P) 2 *PHRASAL VERB* If you **pay** someone **back for** doing something unpleasant to you, you take your revenge on them or make them suffer for what they did. ❑ *Some day I'll pay you back for this!* (V n P for n, Also V n P)

◆ **pay off** 1 *PHRASAL VERB* If you **pay off** a debt, you give someone all the money that you owe them. ❑ *It would take him the rest of his life to pay off that loan.* (V P n (not pron), Also V n P) 2 *PHRASAL VERB* If you **pay off** someone, you give them the amount of money that you owe them or that they are asking for, so that they will not take action against you or cause you any trouble. ❑ *...his bid to raise funds to pay off his creditors.* (V P n, Also V n P) 3 *PHRASAL VERB* If an action **pays off**, it is successful or profitable after a period of time. ❑ *Sandra was determined to become a doctor and her persistence paid off.* (V P) 4 → See also **payoff**.

◆ **pay out** 1 *PHRASAL VERB* If you **pay out** money, usually a large amount, you spend it on something. ❑ *...football clubs who pay out millions of pounds for players.* (V P n for/to n, Also V P n) 2 *PHRASAL VERB* When an insurance policy **pays out**, the person who has the policy receives the money that they are entitled to receive. ❑ *Many policies pay out only after a period of weeks or months.* (V P) 3 → See also **payout**.

◆ **pay up** *PHRASAL VERB* If you **pay up**, you give someone the money that you owe them or that they are entitled to, even though you would prefer not to give it. ❑ *We claimed a refund from the association, but they would not pay up.* V P

**pay|able** /peɪəbəl/ 1 If an amount of money is **payable**, it has to be paid or it can be paid. ❑ *Purchase tax was not payable on goods for export.* ADJ: v-link ADJ, oft ADJ *on/to* n
2 If a cheque or postal order is made **payable to** you, it has your name written on it to indicate that you are the person who will receive the money. ❑ *Write, enclosing a cheque made payable to Cobuild Limited.* ADJ: v n ADJ, n ADJ, ADJ *to* n

**pay-as-you-go** also **pay as you go. Pay-as-you-go** is a system in which a person or organization pays for the costs of something when they occur rather than before or afterwards. ❑ *Pensions are paid by the state on a pay-as-you-go basis.* ADJ

**pay|back** /peɪbæk/ **(paybacks)** also **pay-back.** 1 You can use **payback** to refer to the profit or benefit that you obtain from some- thing that you have spent money, time, or effort on. [mainly AM] ❑ *There is a substantial payback in terms of employee and union relations.* N-COUNT: usu sing 2 The **payback** period of a loan is the time in which you are required or allowed to pay it back. ADJ: ADJ n
3 **Payback time** is when someone has to take the consequences of what they have done in the past. You can use this expression to talk about good or bad consequences. ❑ *This was payback time. I've proved once and for all I can become champion.* PHRASE: v-link PHR

**pay cheque (pay cheques)**

☑ in AM, use **paycheck**

Your **pay cheque** is a piece of paper that your employer gives you as your wages or salary, and which you can then cash at a bank. You can also use **pay cheque** as a way of referring to your wages or salary. ❑ *They've worked for about two weeks without a paycheck.* N-COUNT: oft poss N

**pay day (pay days)** also **payday.** 1 **Pay day** is the day of the week or month on which you receive your wages or salary. ❑ *Until next payday, I was literally without any money.* N-UNCOUNT: also N in pl 2 If a sports player has a big **pay day**, he or she earns a lot of money from winning or taking part in a game or contest. [JOURNALISM] N-COUNT: oft adj N

**pay|dirt** /peɪdɜːʳt/ also **pay dirt.** If you say that someone **has struck paydirt** or **has hit paydirt**, you mean that they have achieved sudden success or gained a lot of money very quickly. [mainly AM, INFORMAL] ❑ *Howard Hawks hit paydirt with 'Rio Bravo'.* PHRASE: V inflects

**PAYE** /piː eɪ waɪ iː/ In Britain, **PAYE** is a system of paying income tax in which your employer pays your tax directly to the government, and then takes this amount from your salary or wages. **PAYE** is an abbreviation for 'pay as you earn'. [BUSINESS] N-UNCOUNT

**payee** /peɪiː/ **(payees)** The **payee** of a cheque or similar document is the person who should receive the money. [FORMAL] N-COUNT: usu sing

**pay en|velope (pay envelopes)** Your **pay envelope** is the envelope containing your wages, which your employer gives you at the end of every week. [AM] N-COUNT: oft poss N

☑ in BRIT, use **pay packet**

**pay|er** /peɪəʳ/ **(payers)** 1 You can refer to someone as a **payer** if they pay a particular kind of bill or fee. For example, a mortgage **payer** is someone who pays a mortgage. ❑ *Lower interest rates pleased millions of mortgage payers.* ➔ See also **ratepayer, taxpayer.** N-COUNT: usu with supp, oft n N 2 A good **payer** pays you quickly or pays you a lot of money. A bad **payer** takes a long time to pay you, or does not pay you very much. ❑ *I have always been a good payer and have never gone into debt.* N-COUNT: adj N

**pay|ing guest (paying guests)** A **paying guest** is a person who pays to stay with someone in their home, usually for a short time. ❑ *At that time my mother took in paying guests.* N-COUNT

**pay|load** /peɪloʊd/ **(payloads)** 1 The **payload** of an aircraft or spacecraft is the amount or weight of things or people that it is carrying. [TECHNICAL] ❑ *With these very large passenger payloads one question looms above all others – safety.* N-VAR = cargo
2 The **payload** of a missile or similar weapon is the quantity of explosives it contains. [MILITARY] ❑ *...a hypervelocity gun capable of delivering substantial payloads to extreme ranges.* N-VAR

**pay|master** /peɪmɑːstəʳ, -mæst-/ **(paymasters)** 1 A **paymaster** is a person or organization that pays and therefore controls another person or organization. ❑ *...the ruling party's paymasters in business and banking.* N-COUNT: oft with poss 2 A **paymaster** is an official in the armed forces who is responsible for the payment of wages and salaries. [MILITARY] N-COUNT

**pay|ment** /peɪmənt/ **(payments)** ◆◆◇ 1 A **payment** is an amount of money that is paid to someone, or the act of paying this money. ❑ *Thousands of its customers are in arrears with loans and mortgage payments... The fund will make payments of just over £1 billion next year.* N-COUNT: oft n N, N *to/of/on* n 2 **Payment** is the act of paying money to someone or of being paid. ❑ *He had sought to obtain payment of a sum which he had claimed was owed to him.* N-UNCOUNT: oft N *of/for* n
3 ➔ See also **balance of payments, down payment.**

**pay|ment card (payment cards)** A **payment card** is a plastic card which you use like a credit card in order to pay for things, but which takes the money directly from your bank account. N-COUNT = debit card

**pay|off** /peɪɒf/ **(payoffs)** also **pay-off.**
1 The **payoff from** an action is the advantage or benefit that you get from it. ❑ *If such materials became generally available to the optics industry the payoffs from such a breakthrough would be enormous.* N-COUNT: oft N *from* n
2 A **payoff** is a payment which is made to someone, often secretly or illegally, so that they will not cause trouble. ❑ *Soldiers in both countries supplement their incomes with payoffs from drugs exporters.* N-COUNT: oft N *from* n 3 A **payoff** is a large payment made to someone by their employer when the person has been forced to leave their job. ❑ *The ousted chairman received a £1.5 million payoff from the loss-making oil company.* N-COUNT

**pay|ola** /peɪoʊlə/ **Payola** is the illegal practice of paying radio broadcasters to play certain CDs, so that the CDs will become more popular and therefore make more profits for the record company. [AM] N-UNCOUNT

**pay|out** /peɪaʊt/ **(payouts)** also **pay-out.** A **payout** is a sum of money, especially a large one, that is paid to someone, for example by an insurance company or as a prize. ❑ *...long delays in receiving insurance payouts.* N-COUNT

**pay pack|et (pay packets)** 1 Your **pay packet** is the envelope containing your wages, which your employer gives you at the end of every week. [BRIT] N-COUNT: oft poss N

☑ in AM, use **pay envelope**

2 You can refer to someone's wages or salary as their **pay packet.** [BRIT] N-COUNT: oft poss N

☑ in AM, use **paycheck, pay**

**pay-per-view Pay-per-view** is a cable or satellite television system in which you have to pay a fee if you want to watch a particular programme. ❑ *The match appeared on pay-per-view television.* N-UNCOUNT: oft N n

**pay|phone** /peɪfoʊn/ **(payphones)** also **pay phone.** A **payphone** is a telephone which you need to put coins or a card in before you can make a call. Payphones are usually in public places. N-COUNT

**pay|roll** /peɪroʊl/ **(payrolls)** The people **on** the **payroll** of a company or an organization are the people who work for it and are paid by it. [BUSINESS] ❑ *They had 87,000 employees on the payroll.* N-COUNT: oft *on* N

**pay|slip** /peɪslɪp/ **(payslips)** also **pay slip.** N-COUNT A **payslip** is a piece of paper given to an employee at the end of each week or month, which states how much money he or she has earned and how much has been taken from that sum for things such as tax and national insurance. [BRIT]

**PC** /piː siː/ **(PCs)** ◆◇◇ 1 N-COUNT; N-TITLE In Britain, a **PC** is a male police officer of the lowest rank. **PC** is an abbreviation for 'police constable'. ❑ *The PCs took her to the local station... PC Keith Gate helped arrest the men.* 2 N-COUNT A **PC** is a computer that is used by one person at a time in a business, a school, or at home. **PC** is an abbreviation for 'personal computer'. ❑ *The price of a PC has fallen by an average of 25% a year since 1982.* 3 ADJ If you say that someone is **PC**, you mean that they are extremely careful not to offend or upset any group of people in society who have a disadvantage. **PC** is an abbreviation for 'politically correct'.

**pcm** **pcm** is used in advertisements for housing, when indicating how much the rent will be. **pcm** is a written abbreviation for 'per calendar month'. [BRIT]

**pd** **pd** is a written abbreviation for **paid**. It is written on a bill to indicate that it has been paid.

**PDA** /piː diː eɪ/ **(PDAs)** N-COUNT A **PDA** is a hand-held computer, used mainly for storing and accessing personal information such as addresses, telephone numbers, and memos. **PDA** is an abbreviation for 'personal digital assistant'. ❑ *A typical PDA can function as a mobile phone, fax sender, and personal organizer.*

**PE** /piː iː/ N-UNCOUNT In schools, **PE** is a lesson in which pupils do physical exercises or sport. **PE** is an abbreviation for 'physical education'.

**pea** /piː/ **(peas)** N-COUNT: usu pl **Peas** are round green seeds which grow in long thin cases and are eaten as a vegetable. → See picture on page 1712.

**peace** /piːs/ ◆◆◆ 1 N-UNCOUNT: usu N n If countries or groups involved in a war or violent conflict are discussing **peace**, they are talking to each other in order to try to end the conflict. ❑ *Leaders of some rival factions signed a peace agreement last week... They hope the treaty will bring peace and stability to Southeast Asia.* 2 N-UNCOUNT: oft *at* N ≠war If there is **peace** in a country or in the world, there are no wars or violent conflicts going on. ❑ *The President spoke of a shared commitment to world peace and economic development. ...the Nobel Peace Prize.* 3 N-UNCOUNT: usu N n If you disapprove of weapons, especially nuclear weapons, you can use **peace** to refer to campaigns and other activities intended to reduce their numbers or stop their use. ❑ *...two peace campaigners accused of causing damage to an F1-11 nuclear bomber.* 4 N-UNCOUNT: oft *in* N If you have **peace**, you are not being disturbed, and you are in calm, quiet surroundings. ❑ *All I want is to have some peace and quiet and spend a couple of nice days with my grandchildren... One more question and I'll leave you in peace.* 5 N-UNCOUNT: oft *at* N If you have a feeling of **peace**, you feel contented and calm and not at all worried. You can also say that you are **at peace**. ❑ *I had a wonderful feeling of peace and serenity when I saw my husband.* 6 N-UNCOUNT: oft *in* N If there is **peace** among a group of people, they live or work together in a friendly way and do not quarrel. You can also say that people live or work **in peace with** each other. ❑ *...a period of relative peace in the country's industrial relations.* 7 N-IN-NAMES: the N *of* n **The Peace of** a particular place is a treaty or an agreement that was signed there, bringing an end to a war. [OLD-FASHIONED] ❑ *The Peace of Ryswick was signed in September 1697.* 8 → See also **breach of the peace**, **Justice of the Peace**.

PHRASES 9 PHRASE: V inflects = keep quiet If you **hold** or **keep** your **peace**, you do not speak, even though there is something you want or ought to say. [FORMAL] ❑ *...people who knew about this evil man but held their peace.* 10 PHRASE: V inflects If someone in authority, such as the army or the police, **keeps the peace**, they make sure that people behave and do not fight or quarrel with each other. ❑ *...the first UN contingent assigned to help keep the peace in Cambodia.* 11 PHRASE: PHR after v, *for* PHR If something gives you **peace of mind**, it stops you from worrying about a particular problem or difficulty. ❑ *He began to insist upon a bullet-proof limousine, just for peace of mind.* 12 PHRASE: usu PHR after modal If you express the wish that a dead person may **rest in peace**, you are showing respect and sympathy for him or her. **'Rest in peace'** is also sometimes written on gravestones. [FORMAL]

**peace|able** /piːsəbəl/ ADJ Someone who is **peaceable** tries to avoid quarrelling or fighting with other people. [WRITTEN] ❑ *...an attempt by ruthless people to impose their will on a peaceable majority.*

**peace|ably** /piːsəbli/ ADV: ADV with v If you do something **peaceably**, you do it quietly or peacefully, without violence or anger. [WRITTEN] ❑ *The rival guerrilla groups had agreed to stop fighting and settle their differences peaceably.*

**Peace Corps** also **peace corps.** N-PROPER: *the* N **The Peace Corps** is an American organization that sends young people to help with projects in developing countries.

**peace divi|dend** **(peace dividends)** N-COUNT: usu sing The **peace dividend** is the economic benefit that was expected in the world after the end of the Cold War, as a result of money previously spent on defence and arms becoming available for other purposes. ❑ *The peace dividend has not materialised despite military spending going down in most countries.*

**peace|ful** /piːsful/ ◆◇◇ 1 ADJ: usu ADJ n **Peaceful** activities and situations do not involve war. ❑ *He has attempted to find a peaceful solution to the Ossetian conflict... They emphasised that their equipment was for peaceful and not military purposes.* ♦ **peace|ful|ly** ADV: ADV with v *The US military expects the matter to be resolved peacefully.* 2 ADJ ≠violent **Peaceful** occasions happen without violence or serious disorder. ❑ *The farmers staged a noisy but peaceful protest outside the headquarters of the organization.* ♦ **peace|ful|ly** ADV: ADV with v *Ten thousand people are reported to have taken part in the protest which passed off peacefully.* 3 ADJ **Peaceful** people are not violent and try to avoid quarrelling or fighting with other people. ❑ *...warriors who killed or enslaved the peaceful farmers.* ♦ **peace|ful|ly** ADV: ADV with v *They've been living and working peacefully with members of various ethnic groups.* 4 ADJ A **peaceful** place or time is quiet, calm, and free from disturbance. ❑ *...a peaceful Georgian house in the heart of Dorset.* ♦ **peace|ful|ly** ADV: ADV after v *Except for traffic noise the night passed peacefully.*

**peace|ful|ly** /piːsfuli/ ADV: ADV after v If you say that someone died **peacefully**, you mean that they suffered no pain or violence when they died. ❑ *He died peacefully on 10th December after a short illness.* → See also **peaceful**.

**peace|keep|er** /piːskiːpəʳ/ **(peacekeepers)** also **peace-keeper.** 1 N-COUNT: usu pl, oft supp N **Peacekeepers** are soldiers who are members of a peacekeeping force. ❑ *There's been much fear that the United Nations peacekeepers would be under attack in a situation like that.* 2 N-COUNT: usu sing If you describe a country or an organization as a **peacekeeper**, you mean that it often uses its influence or armed forces to try to prevent wars or violent conflicts in the world. ❑ *They want the United Nations to play a bigger role as the world's peacekeeper.*

**peace|keep|ing** /piːskiːpɪŋ/ also **peace-keeping.** N-UNCOUNT: usu N n A **peacekeeping** force is a group of soldiers that is sent to a country where there is war or fighting, in order to try to prevent more violence. Peacekeeping forces are usually made up of troops from several different countries. ❑ *...the possibilities of a UN peacekeeping force monitoring the ceasefire in the country.*

**peace-loving** ADJ: usu ADJ n If you describe someone as **peace-loving**, you mean that they try to avoid quarrelling or fighting with other people. ❑ *By and large, these people are peace-loving, law-abiding citizens.*

**peace|maker** /piːsmeɪkəʳ/ **(peacemakers)** also **peace-maker, peace maker.** N-COUNT You can describe an organization, a country or a person as a **peacemaker** when they try to persuade countries or people to stop fighting or quarrelling. ❑ *...the Labour government's vision of acting as a peacemaker and mediator.*

**peace|making** /piːsmeɪkɪŋ/ also **peace-making. Peacemaking** N-UNCOUNT: usu N n efforts are attempts to persuade countries or groups to stop fighting with each other. ❑ *...the failure of international peace-making efforts... The United States is more than ever the prime mover in Middle East peace-making.*

**peace|nik** /piːsnɪk/ **(peaceniks)** N-COUNT If you describe someone as a **peacenik**, you mean that they are strongly opposed to war. [INFORMAL]

**peace of|fer|ing** **(peace offerings)** N-COUNT: usu sing You can use **peace offering** to refer to something that you give someone to show that you want to end the quarrel between you. ❑ *'A peace offering,' Roberts said as he handed the box of cigars to Cohen.*

**peace pro|cess** **(peace processes)** N-COUNT: usu sing, oft *the* N A **peace process** consists of all the meetings, agreements, and negotiations in which people such as politicians are involved when they are trying to arrange peace between countries or groups that are fighting with each other.

**peace|time** /piːstaɪm/ also **peace-time.** N-UNCOUNT: oft *in* N **Peacetime** is a period of time during which a country is not at war. ❑ *The British could afford to reduce defence spending in peacetime without excessive risk.*

**peach** /piːtʃ/ **(peaches)** 1 N-COUNT: oft N n A **peach** is a soft, round, slightly furry fruit with sweet yellow flesh and pinky-orange skin. Peaches grow in warm countries. ➔ See picture on page 1711. 2 COLOUR Something that is **peach** is pale pinky-orange in colour. ❑ *...a peach silk blouse.*

**peaches and cream** ADJ: usu ADJ n [approval] If you say that a woman or a girl has a **peaches and cream complexion**, you mean that she has very clear, smooth, pale skin.

**peachy** /piːtʃi/ 1 ADJ: usu ADJ n, ADJ colour If you describe something as **peachy**, you mean that it tastes or smells like a peach or is similar in colour to a peach. ❑ *...a rich, peachy dessert wine. ...peachy pink.* 2 ADJ If you say that something is **peachy** or **peachy keen**, you mean that it is very nice. [AM, INFORMAL] ❑ *Everything in her life is just peachy.*

**pea|cock** /piːkɒk/ **(peacocks)** N-COUNT A **peacock** is a large bird. The male has a very large tail covered with blue and green spots, which it can spread out like a fan. ❑ *...peacocks strutting slowly across the garden. ...peacock feathers.*

**pea|cock blue** COLOUR Something that is **peacock blue** is a deep, bright, greeny-blue in colour.

**peak** /piːk/ **(peaks, peaking, peaked)** ◆◇◇ 1 N-COUNT: usu sing, usu with supp The **peak** of a process or an activity is the point at which it is at its strongest, most successful, or most fully developed. ❑ *The party's membership has fallen from a peak of fifty-thousand after the Second World War... The bomb went off in a concrete dustbin at the peak of the morning rush hour. ...a flourishing career that was at its peak at the time of his death.* 2 VERB When something **peaks**, it reaches its highest value or its highest level. ❑ V *at* n *Temperatures have peaked at over thirty degrees Celsius...* V *His career peaked during the 1970's.* 3 ADJ: ADJ n The **peak** level or value of something is its highest level or value. ❑ *Calls cost 36p (cheap rate) and 48p (peak rate) per minute.* 4 ADJ: ADJ n ≠ *off-peak* **Peak** times are the times when there is most demand for something or most use of something. ❑ *It's always crowded at peak times.* ➔ See also **peak time**. 5 N-COUNT A **peak** is a mountain or the top of a mountain. ❑ *...the snow-covered peaks.* 6 N-COUNT The **peak** of a cap is the part at the front that sticks out above your eyes.

**peaked** /piːkt/ ADJ: ADJ n A **peaked** cap has a pointed or rounded part that sticks out above your eyes. ❑ *...a man in a blue-grey uniform and peaked cap.*

**peak time** N-UNCOUNT: oft *at/in* N, N n Programmes which are broadcast at **peak time** are broadcast when the greatest number of people are watching television or listening to the radio. [mainly BRIT] ❑ *The news programme goes out four times a week at peak time.*

☑ in AM, usually use **prime time**

**peal** /piːl/ **(peals, pealing, pealed)** 1 VERB When bells **peal**, they ring one after another, making a musical sound. ❑ V *Church bells pealed at the stroke of midnight.* ♦ N-COUNT **Peal** is also a noun. ❑ *...the great peal of the Abbey bells.* 2 N-COUNT: oft N *of* n A **peal of** laughter or thunder consists of a long, loud series of sounds. ❑ *I heard a peal of merry laughter.*

**pea|nut** /piːnʌt/ **(peanuts)** 1 N-COUNT: usu pl, oft N n **Peanuts** are small nuts that grow under the ground. Peanuts are often eaten as a snack, especially roasted and salted. ❑ *...a packet of peanuts... Add 2 tablespoons of peanut oil.* 2 N-PLURAL [disapproval] If you say that a sum of money is **peanuts**, you mean that it is very small. [INFORMAL] ❑ *The cost was peanuts compared to a new kitchen.*

**pea|nut but|ter** N-UNCOUNT **Peanut butter** is a brown paste made out of crushed peanuts which you can spread on bread and eat.

**pear** /peəʳ/ **(pears)** N-COUNT A **pear** is a sweet, juicy fruit which is narrow near its stalk, and wider and rounded at the bottom. Pears have white flesh and thin green or yellow skin. ➔ See picture on page 1711.

**pearl** /pɜːʳl/ **(pearls)** 1 N-COUNT A **pearl** is a hard round object which is shiny and creamy white in colour. Pearls grow inside the shell of an oyster and are used for making expensive jewellery. ❑ *She wore a string of pearls at her throat.* ➔ See also **mother-of-pearl**. 2 ADJ: usu ADJ n **Pearl** is used to describe something which looks like a pearl. ❑ *...tiny pearl buttons.*

**pearly** /pɜːʳli/ ADJ: usu ADJ n Something that is **pearly** is pale and shines softly, like a pearl. ❑ *...the pearly light of early morning.* ♦ COMB in COLOUR **Pearly** is also a combining form. ❑ *...pearly pink lipstick.*

**pear-shaped** 1 ADJ Something that is **pear-shaped** has a shape like a pear. ❑ *...her pear-shaped diamond earrings.* 2 ADJ If someone, especially a woman, is **pear-shaped**, they are wider around their hips than around the top half of their body. 3 PHRASE: V inflects If a situation **goes pear-shaped**, bad things start happening. [INFORMAL] ❑ *He feared his career had gone a bit pear-shaped.*

**peas|ant** /pezᵊnt/ **(peasants)** N-COUNT: oft supp N, N n A **peasant** is a poor person of low social status who works on the land; used of people who live in countries where farming is still a common way of life. ❑ *...the peasants in the Peruvian highlands.*

**peas|ant|ry** /pezᵊntri/ N-SING-COLL: also no det, usu *the* N You can refer to all the peasants in a particular country as **the peasantry**. ❑ *The Russian peasantry stood on the brink of disappearance.*

**peat** /piːt/ N-UNCOUNT: oft N n **Peat** is decaying plant material which is found under the ground in some cool, wet regions. Peat can be added to soil to help plants grow, or can be burnt on fires instead of coal.

**peaty** /piːti/ ADJ: usu ADJ n **Peaty** soil or land contains a large quantity of peat.

**peb|ble** /pebᵊl/ **(pebbles)** N-COUNT A **pebble** is a small, smooth, round stone which is found on beaches and at the bottom of rivers.

**peb|bly** /pebəli/ ADJ: usu ADJ n A **pebbly** beach is covered in pebbles.

**pe|can** /piːkən, AM pɪkɑːn/ **(pecans)** N-COUNT **Pecans** or **pecan nuts** are nuts with a thin, smooth shell that grow on trees in the southern United States and central America and that you can eat.

**pec|ca|dil|lo** /pekədɪloʊ/ **(peccadilloes** or **peccadillos)** N-COUNT: usu pl **Peccadilloes** are small, unimportant sins or faults. [WRITTEN] ❑ *People are prepared to be tolerant of extra-marital peccadilloes by public figures.*

**peck** /pek/ **(pecks, pecking, pecked)** 1 If a bird **pecks at** something or **pecks** something, it moves its beak forward quickly and bites at it. ❑ *It was winter and the sparrows were pecking at whatever they could find... Chickens pecked in the dust... It pecked his leg... They turn on their own kind and peck each other to death... These birds peck off all the red flowers.* [VERB; V at n; V prep/adv; V n; V n prep; V n with adv] 2 If you **peck** someone **on** the cheek, you give them a quick, light kiss. ❑ *Elizabeth walked up to him and pecked him on the cheek... She pecked his cheek.* [VERB; V n on n; V n] ♦ **Peck** is also a noun. ❑ *He gave me a little peck on the cheek.* [N-COUNT: usu a N]

**peck|er** /pekəʳ/ **(peckers)** 1 If you tell someone to **keep** their **pecker up**, you are encouraging them to be cheerful in a difficult situation. [BRIT, INFORMAL] [PHRASE = keep one's chin up] 2 A man's **pecker** is his penis. [AM, INFORMAL, RUDE] [N-COUNT]

**peck|ing or|der (pecking orders)** The **pecking order** of a group is the way that the positions people have are arranged according to their status or power within the group. ❑ *He knew his place in the pecking order.* [N-COUNT: usu sing]

**peck|ish** /pekɪʃ/ If you say that you are feeling **peckish**, you mean that you are slightly hungry. [BRIT, INFORMAL] [ADJ: usu v-link ADJ]

**pecs** /peks/ **Pecs** are the same as **pectorals**. [INFORMAL] [N-PLURAL]

**pec|tin** /pektɪn/ **(pectins) Pectin** is a substance that is found in fruit. It is used when making jam to help it become firm. [N-MASS]

**pec|to|ral** /pektərəl/ **(pectorals)** Your **pectorals** are the large chest muscles that help you to move your shoulders and your arms. [N-COUNT: usu pl]

**pe|cu|liar** /pɪkjuːliəʳ/ 1 If you describe someone or something as **peculiar**, you think that they are strange or unusual, sometimes in an unpleasant way. ❑ *Mr Kennet has a rather peculiar sense of humour... Rachel thought it tasted peculiar.* [ADJ = odd, strange] ♦ **pe|cu|liar|ly** *His face had become peculiarly expressionless.* [ADV] 2 If something is **peculiar to** a particular thing, person, or situation, it belongs or relates only to that thing, person, or situation. ❑ *The problem is by no means peculiar to America.* [ADJ: oft ADJ to n = unique] ♦ **pe|cu|liar|ly** *Cricket is so peculiarly English.* [ADV]

**pe|cu|li|ar|ity** /pɪkjuːliærɪti/ **(peculiarities)** 1 A **peculiarity** that someone or something has is a strange or unusual characteristic or habit. ❑ *Joe's other peculiarity was that he was constantly munching hard candy.* [N-COUNT: with supp, oft N of n] 2 A **peculiarity** is a characteristic or quality which belongs or relates only to one person or thing. ❑ *...a strange peculiarity of the Soviet system.* [N-COUNT: with supp, oft N of n]

**pe|cu|ni|ary** /pɪkjuːniəri, AM -eri/ **Pecuniary** means concerning or involving money. [FORMAL] ❑ *She denies obtaining a pecuniary advantage by deception.* [ADJ: usu ADJ n = monetary]

**peda|gog|ic** /pedəgɒdʒɪk/ **Pedagogic** means the same as **pedagogical**. [ADJ: ADJ n]

**peda|gogi|cal** /pedəgɒdʒɪkəl/ **Pedagogical** means concerning the methods and theory of teaching. [FORMAL] ❑ *...the pedagogical methods used in the classroom.* [ADJ: ADJ n]

**peda|gogue** /pedəgɒg/ **(pedagogues)** If you describe someone as a **pedagogue**, you mean that they like to teach people things in a firm way as if they know more than anyone else. [FORMAL] ❑ *De Gaulle was a born pedagogue who used the public platform and the television screen to great effect.* [N-COUNT]

**peda|go|gy** /pedəgɒdʒi, AM -goʊdʒi/ **Pedagogy** is the study and theory of the methods and principles of teaching. [FORMAL] [N-UNCOUNT]

**ped|al** /pedəl/ **(pedals, pedalling, pedalled)**

✓ in AM, use **pedaling, pedaled**

1 The **pedals** on a bicycle are the two parts that you push with your feet in order to make the bicycle move. → See picture on page 1708. [N-COUNT] 2 When you **pedal** a bicycle, you push the pedals around with your feet to make it move. ❑ *She climbed on her bike with a feeling of pride and pedalled the five miles home... She was too tired to pedal back.* → See also **back-pedal, soft-pedal.** [VERB; V n; V adv/prep] 3 A **pedal** in a car or on a machine is a lever that you press with your foot in order to control the car or machine. ❑ *...the brake or accelerator pedals.* [N-COUNT]

**ped|al bin (pedal bins)** A **pedal bin** is a container for waste, usually in a kitchen or bathroom. It has a lid which is controlled by a pedal that you press with your foot. [BRIT] [N-COUNT]

**ped|ant** /pedənt/ **(pedants)** If you say that someone is a **pedant**, you mean that they are too concerned with unimportant details or traditional rules, especially in connection with academic subjects. ❑ *I am no pedant and avoid being dogmatic concerning English grammar and expression.* [N-COUNT; disapproval]

**pe|dan|tic** /pɪdæntɪk/ If you think someone is **pedantic**, you mean that they are too concerned with unimportant details or traditional rules, especially in connection with academic subjects. ❑ *His lecture was so pedantic and uninteresting.* [ADJ; disapproval]

**ped|ant|ry** /pedəntri/ If you accuse someone of **pedantry**, you mean that you disapprove of them because they pay excessive attention to unimportant details or traditional rules, especially in connection with academic subjects. [N-UNCOUNT; disapproval]

**ped|dle** /pedəl/ **(peddles, peddling, peddled)** 1 Someone who **peddles** things goes from place to place trying to sell them. [OLD-FASHIONED] ❑ *His attempts to peddle his paintings around London's tiny gallery scene proved unsuccessful.* [VERB; V n] 2 Someone who **peddles** drugs sells illegal drugs. ❑ *When a drug pusher offered the Los Angeles youngster $100 to peddle drugs, Jack refused.* [VERB = push; V n] ♦ **ped|dling** *The war against drug peddling is all about cash.* [N-UNCOUNT] 3 If someone **peddles** an idea or a piece of information, they try very hard to get people to accept it. ❑ *They even set up their own news agency to peddle anti-isolationist propaganda.* [VERB; disapproval; V n]

**ped|dler** /pedləʳ/ **(peddlers)**

✓ The spelling **pedlar** is also used in British English for meanings 1 and 3.

1 A **peddler** is someone who goes from place to place in order to sell something. [AM; also BRIT, OLD-FASHIONED] [N-COUNT] 2 A **drug peddler** is a person who sells illegal drugs. [N-COUNT] 3 A **peddler of** information or ideas is someone who frequently expresses such ideas to other people. ❑ *...the peddlers of fear.* [N-COUNT: usu N of n; disapproval]

**ped|es|tal** /pedɪstəl/ **(pedestals)** 1 A **pedestal** is the base on which something such as a statue stands. ❑ *...a larger than life sized bronze statue on a granite pedestal.* [N-COUNT] 2 If you put someone **on a pedestal**, you admire them very much and think that they cannot be criticized. If someone is knocked **off** a **pedestal** they are no longer admired. ❑ *Since childhood, I put my own parents on a pedestal. I felt they could do no wrong.* [N-COUNT]

**pe|des|trian** /pɪdestriən/ **(pedestrians)** 1 A **pedestrian** is a person who is walking, especially in a town or city, rather than travelling in a vehicle. ❑ *In Los Angeles a pedestrian is a rare spectacle.* [N-COUNT: oft N n] 2 If you describe something as **pedestrian**, you mean that it is ordinary and not at all interesting. ❑ *His style is so pedestrian that the book becomes a real bore.* [ADJ; disapproval]

**pe|des|trian cross|ing (pedestrian crossings)** A **pedestrian crossing** is a place where pedestrians can cross a street and where motorists must stop to let them cross. [BRIT] [N-COUNT]

✓ in AM, use **crosswalk**

**pe|des|tri|an|ized** /pɪdestriənaɪzd/

✓ in BRIT, also use **pedestrianised**

A **pedestrianized** area has been made into an area that is intended for pedestrians, not vehicles. ❑ *...pedestrianized streets... There's plans to make Birmingham city centre pedestrianized.* [ADJ: usu ADJ n]

**pe|des|trian mall (pedestrian malls)** A **pedestrian mall** is the same as a **pedestrian precinct**. [AM] [N-COUNT]

**pe|des|trian pre|cinct** **(pedestrian precincts)** A **pedestrian precinct** is a street or part of a town where vehicles are not allowed. [BRIT] N-COUNT

in AM, usually use **pedestrian mall**

**pe|dia|tri|cian** /piːdiətrɪʃᵊn/ → see **paediatrician**.

**pe|di|at|rics** /piːdiætrɪks/ → see **paediatrics**.

**pedi|cure** /pedɪkjʊəʳ/ **(pedicures)** If you have a **pedicure**, you have your toenails cut and the skin on your feet softened. N-COUNT

**pedi|gree** /pedɪgriː/ **(pedigrees)** [1] If a dog, cat, or other animal has a **pedigree**, its ancestors are known and recorded. An animal is considered to have a good pedigree when all its known ancestors are of the same type. ❑ *60 per cent of dogs and ten per cent of cats have pedigrees.* N-COUNT [2] A **pedigree** animal is descended from animals which have all been of a particular type, and is therefore considered to be of good quality. ❑ *...a pedigree dog.* ADJ: usu ADJ n [3] Someone's **pedigree** is their background or their ancestors. ❑ *Hammer's business pedigree almost guaranteed him the acquaintance of U.S. presidents.* N-COUNT: oft poss N

**pedi|ment** /pedɪmənt/ **(pediments)** A **pediment** is a large triangular structure built over a door or window as a decoration. N-COUNT

**ped|lar** /pedləʳ/ **(pedlars)** → see **peddler**.

**pe|do|phile** /piːdəfaɪl/ **(pedophiles)** → see **paedophile**.

**pe|do|philia** /piːdəfɪliə/ → see **paedophilia**.

**pee** /piː/ **(pees, peeing, peed)** When someone **pees**, they urinate. [INFORMAL] ❑ *He needed to pee.* VERB, V ♦ **Pee** is also a noun. ❑ *The driver was probably having a pee.* N-SING: *a* N

**peek** /piːk/ **(peeks, peeking, peeked)** If you **peek at** something or someone, you have a quick look at them, often secretly. ❑ *On two occasions she had peeked at him through a crack in the wall.* VERB = peep, V *at* n ♦ **Peek** is also a noun. ❑ *American firms have been paying outrageous fees for a peek at the technical data.* N-COUNT: usu *a* N, oft N *at/into* n = peep

**peeka|boo** /piːkəbuː/ also **peek-a-boo**. **Peekaboo** is a game you play with babies in which you cover your face with your hands or hide behind something and then suddenly show your face, saying 'peekaboo!' N-UNCOUNT, also EXCLAM

**peel** /piːl/ **(peels, peeling, peeled)** [1] The **peel** of a fruit such as a lemon or an apple is its skin. ❑ *...grated lemon peel.* N-UNCOUNT ♦ You can also refer to a **peel**. [AM] ❑ *...a banana peel.* N-COUNT [2] When you **peel** fruit or vegetables, you remove their skins. ❑ *She sat down in the kitchen and began peeling potatoes.* VERB, V n [3] If you **peel off** something that has been sticking to a surface or if it **peels off**, it comes away from the surface. ❑ *One of the kids was peeling plaster off the wall... It took me two days to peel off the labels... Paint was peeling off the walls... The wallpaper was peeling away close to the ceiling. ...an unrenovated bungalow with slightly peeling blue paint.* VERB, V n *off/from* n, V n with *off/away*, V *off/from* n, V *off/away*, V-ing [4] If a surface **is peeling**, the paint on it is coming away. ❑ *Its once-elegant white pillars are peeling.* VERB: usu cont, V [5] If you **are peeling** or if your skin **is peeling**, small pieces of skin are coming off, usually because you have been burned by the sun. ❑ *His face, at the moment, was peeling from sunburn.* VERB: usu cont, V

♦ **peel off** If you **peel off** a tight piece of clothing, you take it off, especially by turning it inside out. ❑ *She peeled off her gloves.* PHRASAL VERB, V P n, Also V n P

**peel|er** /piːləʳ/ **(peelers)** A **peeler** is a special tool used for removing the skin from fruit and vegetables. → See picture on page 1710. ❑ *...a potato peeler.* N-COUNT

**peel|ings** /piːlɪŋz/ **Peelings** are pieces of skin removed from vegetables and fruit. ❑ *...potato peelings.* N-PLURAL: usu supp N

**peep** /piːp/ **(peeps, peeping, peeped)** [1] If you **peep**, or **peep at** something, you have a quick look at it, often secretly and quietly. ❑ *Children came to peep at him round the doorway... Now and then she peeped to see if he was noticing her.* VERB = peek, V *at* n, V ♦ **Peep** is also a noun. ❑ *'Fourteen minutes,' Chris said, taking a peep at his watch.* N-SING: *a* N = peek [2] If something **peeps** out from behind or under something, a small part of it is visible or becomes visible. ❑ *Purple and yellow flowers peeped up between rocks.* VERB, V prep/adv

**peep|hole** /piːphoʊl/ **(peepholes)** A **peephole** is small hole in a door or wall through which you can look secretly at what is happening on the other side. N-COUNT = spyhole

**Peep|ing Tom** **(Peeping Toms)** If you refer to someone as a **Peeping Tom**, you mean that they secretly watch other people, especially when those people are taking their clothes off. N-COUNT, disapproval = voyeur

**peep|show** /piːpʃoʊ/ **(peepshows)** A **peepshow** is box containing moving pictures which you can look at through a small hole. Peepshows used to be a form of entertainment at fairs. N-COUNT

**peer** /pɪəʳ/ **(peers, peering, peered)** ◆◇◇ [1] If you **peer at** something, you look at it very hard, usually because it is difficult to see clearly. ❑ *I had been peering at a computer print-out that made no sense at all... He watched the Customs official peer into the driver's window.* VERB, V prep, V prep [2] In Britain, a **peer** is a member of the nobility who has or had the right to vote in the House of Lords. ❑ *Lord Swan was made a life peer in 1981.* N-COUNT [3] Your **peers** are the people who are the same age as you or who have the same status as you. ❑ *His engaging personality made him popular with his peers.* N-COUNT: usu pl, poss N

**peer|age** /pɪərɪdʒ/ **(peerages)** [1] If someone has a **peerage**, they have the rank of a peer. ❑ *The Prime Minister offered him a peerage.* N-COUNT [2] The peers of a particular country are referred to as **the peerage**. N-SING: *the* N

**peer|ess** /pɪəres/ **(peeresses)** In Britain, a **peeress** is a female peer or a peer's wife. N-COUNT

**peer group** **(peer groups)** Your **peer group** is the group of people you know who are the same age as you or who have the same social status as you. ❑ *It is important for a manager to be able to get the support of his peer group.* N-COUNT

**peer|less** /pɪəʳləs/ Something that is **peerless** is so beautiful or wonderful that you feel that nothing can equal it. [FORMAL] ❑ *...two days of clear sunshine under peerless blue skies.* ADJ: usu ADJ n = matchless

**peer of the realm** **(peers of the realm)** In Britain, a **peer of the realm** is a member of the nobility who has the right to sit in the House of Lords. N-COUNT

**peeved** /piːvd/ If you are **peeved** about something, you are annoyed about it. [INFORMAL] ❑ *Susan couldn't help feeling a little peeved. ...complaints from peeved citizens who pay taxes.* ADJ: usu v-link ADJ

**peev|ish** /piːvɪʃ/ Someone who is **peevish** is bad-tempered. ❑ *Aubrey had slept little and that always made him peevish... She glared down at me with a peevish expression on her face.* ADJ ♦ **peev|ish|ly** *Brian sighed peevishly... She had grown ever more peevishly dependent on him.* ADV: ADV with v, ADV adj ♦ **peev|ish|ness** *He complained with characteristic peevishness.* N-UNCOUNT

**peg** /peg/ **(pegs, pegging, pegged)** ◆◇◇ [1] A **peg** is a small hook or knob that is attached to a wall or door and is used for hanging things on. ❑ *His work jacket hung on the peg in the kitchen.* N-COUNT [2] A **peg** is a small device which you use to fasten clothes to a washing line. [mainly BRIT] N-COUNT

in AM, usually use **clothespin**

[3] A **peg** is a small piece of wood or metal that is used for fastening something to something else. ❑ *He builds furniture using wooden pegs instead of nails.* N-COUNT [4] If you **peg** something somewhere or **peg** it **down**, you fix it there with pegs. ❑ *...trying to peg a double sheet on a washing line on a blustery day... Peg down netting over the top to keep out leaves. ...a tent pegged to the ground nearby for the kids.* VERB, V n prep/adv, V n with adv, V-ed prep [5] If a price or amount of something **is** VERB

**pegged at** a particular level, it is fixed at that level. ❑ *Its currency is pegged to the dollar... UK trading profits were pegged at £40 million... The Bank wants to peg rates at 9%. ...a pegged European currency.* → See also **level-pegging**. [6] **Off-the-peg** clothes are made in large numbers and sent to shops, not made specially for a particular person. [BRIT] ❑ *...an off-the-peg two-piece suit.*
*be V-ed to n / be V-ed at n / V n at amount / V-ed / PHRASE: PHR n, PHR after v ≠ made-to-measure*

☑ in AM, use **off-the-rack**

**pe|jo|ra|tive** /pədʒɒrətɪv, AM -dʒɔːr-/ A **pejorative** word or expression is one that expresses criticism of someone or something. [FORMAL] ❑ *I agree I am ambitious, and I don't see that as a pejorative term.* *ADJ = derogatory, disparaging*

**pe|kin|ese** /piːkɪniːz/ **(pekineses)** also **pekingese.** A **pekinese** is a type of small dog with long hair, short legs, and a short, flat nose. *N-COUNT*

**peli|can** /pelɪkən/ **(pelicans)** A **pelican** is a type of large water bird. It catches fish and keeps them in the bottom part of its beak which is shaped like a large bag. *N-COUNT*

**peli|can cross|ing** **(pelican crossings)** A **pelican crossing** is a place where people who are walking can cross a busy road. They press a button at the side of the road, which operates traffic lights to stop the traffic. [BRIT] *N-COUNT*

**pel|let** /pelɪt/ **(pellets)** A **pellet** is a small ball of paper, mud, lead, or other material. ❑ *He was shot in the head by an air gun pellet.* *N-COUNT: usu with supp*

**pell-mell** /pel mel/ If you move **pell-mell** somewhere, you move there in a hurried, uncontrolled way. ❑ *All three of us rushed pell-mell into the kitchen.* *ADV: ADV after v*

**pel|lu|cid** /peluːsɪd/ Something that is **pellucid** is extremely clear. [LITERARY] ❑ *...her pellucid blue eyes. ...the warm pellucid water.* *ADJ = limpid*

**pel|met** /pelmɪt/ **(pelmets)** A **pelmet** is a long, narrow piece of wood or fabric which is fitted at the top of a window for decoration and to hide the curtain rail. [BRIT] *N-COUNT*

☑ in AM, use **valance**

**pe|lo|ta** /pelɒutɑ/ **Pelota** is a game that is played in Spain, America, and the Philippines, in which the players hit a ball against a wall using a long basket tied to their wrist. *N-UNCOUNT*

**pelt** /pelt/ **(pelts, pelting, pelted)** [1] The **pelt** of an animal is its skin, which can be used to make clothing or rugs. ❑ *...a bed covered with beaver pelts.* *N-COUNT: usu pl = hide* [2] If you **pelt** someone **with** things, you throw things at them. ❑ *Some of the younger men began to pelt one another with snowballs.* *VERB / V n with n* [3] If the rain **is pelting down**, or if **it is pelting with** rain, it is raining very hard. [INFORMAL] ❑ *The rain now was pelting down... It's pelting with rain... We drove through pelting rain.* *VERB: usu cont / V adv / it V with n / V-ing* [4] If you **pelt** somewhere, you run there very fast. [INFORMAL] ❑ *Without thinking, she pelted down the stairs in her nightgown.* *VERB = dash / V prep* [5] If you do something **full pelt** or **at full pelt**, you do it very quickly indeed. [INFORMAL] ❑ *Alice leapt from the car and ran full pelt towards the emergency room.* *PHRASE: PHR after v*

**pel|vic** /pelvɪk/ **Pelvic** means near or relating to your pelvis. *ADJ: ADJ n*

**pel|vis** /pelvɪs/ **(pelvises)** Your **pelvis** is the wide, curved group of bones at the level of your hips. *N-COUNT*

**pen** /pen/ **(pens, penning, penned)** [1] A **pen** is a long thin object which you use to write in ink. → See also **fountain pen**. **ballpoint pen** → see **ballpoint**. **felt-tip pen** → see **felt-tip**. *◆◇◇ N-COUNT* [2] If someone **pens** a letter, article, or book, they write it. [FORMAL] ❑ *She penned a short memo to his private secretary.* *VERB / V n to n / Also V n n* [3] A **pen** is also a small area with a fence round it in which farm animals are kept for a short time. ❑ *...a holding pen for sheep.* → See also **playpen**. *N-COUNT = enclosure* [4] If people or animals **are penned** somewhere or **are penned up**, they are forced to remain in a very small area. ❑ *...to drive the cattle back to the house so they could be milked and penned for the night... I don't have to stay in my room penned up like a prisoner.* *VERB: usu passive / be V-ed / V-ed up*

**pe|nal** /piːnᵊl/ [1] **Penal** means relating to the punishment of criminals. ❑ *...director-general of penal affairs at the justice ministry. ...penal and legal systems.* *ADJ: usu ADJ n* [2] A **penal** institution or colony is one where criminals are kept as punishment. ❑ *...imprisoned on an island that has served as a penal colony since Roman times.* *ADJ: ADJ n*

**pe|nal code** **(penal codes)** The **penal code** of a country consists of all the laws that are related to crime and punishment. [FORMAL] *N-COUNT*

**pe|nal|ize** /piːnəlaɪz/ **(penalizes, penalizing, penalized)**

☑ in BRIT, also use **penalise**

If a person or group **is penalized** for something, they are made to suffer in some way because of it. ❑ *Some of the players may, on occasion, break the rules and be penalized.* *VERB: usu passive = punish / be V-ed*

**pe|nal ser|vi|tude** **Penal servitude** is the punishment of being sent to prison and forced to do hard physical work. [FORMAL] *N-UNCOUNT = hard labour*

**pen|al|ty** /penᵊlti/ **(penalties)** [1] A **penalty** is a punishment that someone is given for doing something which is against a law or rule. ❑ *One of those arrested could face the death penalty... The maximum penalty is up to 7 years imprisonment or an unlimited fine.* *◆◇◇ N-COUNT: usu sing* [2] In sports such as football, rugby, and hockey, a **penalty** is an opportunity to score a goal, which is given to the attacking team if the defending team breaks a rule near their own goal. ❑ *Referee Michael Reed had no hesitation in awarding a penalty.* *N-COUNT* [3] **The penalty** that you pay for something you have done is something unpleasant that you experience as a result. ❑ *Why should I pay the penalty for somebody else's mistake?* *N-COUNT: usu the N in sing*

**pen|al|ty area** **(penalty areas)** In football, the **penalty area** is the rectangular area in front of the goal. Inside this area the goalkeeper is allowed to handle the ball, and if the defending team breaks a rule here, the opposing team gets a penalty. [mainly BRIT] *N-COUNT = penalty box*

**pen|al|ty box** **(penalty boxes)** [1] In football, the **penalty box** is the same as the **penalty area**. [mainly BRIT] *N-COUNT: usu the N in sing* [2] In ice hockey, the **penalty box** is an area in which players who have broken a rule have to sit for a period of time. *N-COUNT*

**pen|al|ty shoot-out** **(penalty shoot-outs)** In football, a **penalty shoot-out** is a way of deciding the result of a game that has ended in a draw. Players from each team try to score a goal in turn until one player fails to score and their team loses the game. [mainly BRIT] *N-COUNT*

**pen|ance** /penəns/ **(penances)** If you do **penance** for something wrong that you have done, you do something that you find unpleasant to show that you are sorry. ❑ *...a time of fasting, penance and pilgrimage.* *N-VAR*

**pen and ink** A **pen and ink** drawing is done using a pen rather than a pencil. *ADJ: usu ADJ n*

**pence** /pens/ → see **penny**.

**pen|chant** /pɒnʃɒn, pentʃənt/ If someone has a **penchant for** something, they have a special liking for it or a tendency to do it. [FORMAL] ❑ *...a stylish woman with a penchant for dark glasses.* *N-SING: N for n/-ing = fondness*

**pen|cil** /pensᵊl/ **(pencils, pencilling, pencilled)** [1] A **pencil** is an object that you write or draw with. It consists of a thin piece of wood with a rod of a black or coloured substance through the middle. If you write or draw something **in pencil**, you do it using a pencil. ❑ *I found a pencil and some blank paper in her desk... He had written her a note in pencil.* *N-COUNT: also in N* [2] If you **pencil** a letter or a note, you write it using a pencil. ❑ *He pencilled a note to Joseph Daniels.* *VERB / V n to n* ♦ **pen|cilled** *...folded notepaper with the pencilled block letters on the outside.* *ADJ*

♦ **pencil in** If an event or appointment **is pencilled in**, it has been agreed that it should take place, but it will have to be confirmed later. *PHRASAL VERB: usu passive*

❑ *He told us that the tour was pencilled in for the following March.* be V-ed P

**pen|cil push|er** **(pencil pushers)** If you call someone a **pencil pusher**, you mean that their work consists of writing or dealing with documents, and does not seem very useful or important. [AM] ❑ *...the pencil pushers who decide the course of people's lives.* N-COUNT [disapproval] = *bureaucrat*

✔ in BRIT, use **pen-pusher**

**pen|dant** /pendənt/ **(pendants)** A **pendant** is an ornament on a chain that you wear round your neck. N-COUNT

**pend|ing** /pendɪŋ/ 1 If something such as a legal procedure is **pending**, it is waiting to be dealt with or settled. [FORMAL] ❑ *In 1989, the court had 600 pending cases... She had a libel action against the magazine pending.* ADJ 2 If something is done **pending** a future event, it is done until that event happens. [FORMAL] ❑ *A judge has suspended a ban on the magazine pending a full inquiry.* PREP 3 Something that is **pending** is going to happen soon. [FORMAL] ❑ *A growing number of customers have been inquiring about the pending price rises.* ADJ = *imminent*

**pen|du|lous** /pendʒʊləs/ Something that is **pendulous** hangs downwards and moves loosely, usually in an unattractive way. [LITERARY] ❑ *...a stout, gloomy man with a pendulous lower lip. ...pendulous cheeks.* ADJ

**pen|du|lum** /pendʒʊləm/ **(pendulums)** 1 The **pendulum** of a clock is a rod with a weight at the end which swings from side to side in order to make the clock work. N-COUNT 2 You can use the idea of a **pendulum** and the way it swings regularly as a way of talking about regular changes in a situation or in people's opinions. ❑ *The political pendulum has swung in favour of the liberals.* N-SING: usu *the* N

**pen|etrate** /penɪtreɪt/ **(penetrates, penetrating, penetrated)** 1 If something or someone **penetrates** a physical object or an area, they succeed in getting into it or passing through it. ❑ *X-rays can penetrate many objects.* VERB V n ♦ **pen|etra|tion** /penɪtreɪʃən/ **(penetrations)** *The exterior walls are three to three and a half feet thick to prevent penetration by bombs.* N-UNCOUNT: also N in pl 2 If someone **penetrates** an organization, a group, or a profession, they succeed in entering it although it is difficult to do so. ❑ *...the continuing failure of women to penetrate the higher levels of engineering.* VERB V n 3 If someone **penetrates** an enemy group or a rival organization, they succeed in joining it in order to get information or cause trouble. ❑ *The CIA had requested our help to penetrate a drugs ring operating out of Munich.* VERB = *infiltrate* V n ♦ **pen|etra|tion** *...the successful penetration by the KGB of the French intelligence service.* N-UNCOUNT: with supp 4 If a company or country **penetrates** a market or area, they succeed in selling their products there. [BUSINESS] ❑ *There have been around 15 attempts from outside France to penetrate the market.* VERB V n ♦ **pen|etra|tion** *...import penetration across a broad range of heavy industries.* N-UNCOUNT: with supp

**pen|etrat|ing** /penɪtreɪtɪŋ/ 1 A **penetrating** sound is loud and usually high-pitched. ❑ *Mary heard the penetrating bell of an ambulance.* ADJ = *piercing* 2 If someone gives you a **penetrating** look, it makes you think that they know what you are thinking. ❑ *He gazed at me with a sharp, penetrating look that made my heart pound.* ADJ: usu ADJ n = *piercing* 3 Someone who has a **penetrating** mind understands and recognizes things quickly and thoroughly. ❑ *...a thoughtful, penetrating mind.* ADJ: usu ADJ n

**pene|tra|tive** /penɪtrətɪv, AM -treɪt-/ If a man has **penetrative** sex with someone, he inserts his penis into his partner's vagina or anus. ADJ: ADJ n

**pen-friend** **(pen-friends)** also **penfriend.** A **pen-friend** is someone you write friendly letters to and receive letters from, although the two of you may never have met. [BRIT] N-COUNT = *pen pal*

✔ in AM, use **pen pal**

**pen|guin** /peŋgwɪn/ **(penguins)** A **penguin** is a type of large black and white sea bird found mainly in the Antarctic. Penguins cannot fly but use their short wings for swimming. N-COUNT

**peni|cil|lin** /penɪsɪlɪn/ **Penicillin** is a drug that kills bacteria and is used to treat infections. N-UNCOUNT

**pe|nile** /piːnaɪl/ **Penile** means relating to a penis. [FORMAL] ❑ *...penile cancer.* ADJ: ADJ n

**pen|in|su|la** /pənɪnsjʊlə/ **(peninsulas)** A **peninsula** is a long narrow piece of land which sticks out from a larger piece of land and is almost completely surrounded by water. ❑ *I had walked around the entire peninsula.* N-COUNT: oft in names

**pe|nis** /piːnɪs/ **(penises)** A man's **penis** is the part of his body that he uses when urinating and when having sex. N-COUNT

**peni|tence** /penɪtəns/ **Penitence** is sincere regret for wrong or evil things that you have done. N-UNCOUNT = *repentance*

**peni|tent** /penɪtənt/ Someone who is **penitent** is very sorry for something wrong that they have done, and regrets their actions. [LITERARY] ❑ *Robert Gates sat before them, almost penitent about the past. ...penitent criminals.* ADJ: usu v-link ADJ ♦ **peni|tent|ly** *He sat penitently in his chair by the window.* ADV: ADV after v

**peni|ten|tial** /penɪtenʃəl/ **Penitential** means expressing deep sorrow and regret at having done something wrong. [FORMAL] ❑ *...penitential psalms.* ADJ: usu ADJ n

**peni|ten|tia|ry** /penɪtenʃəri/ **(penitentiaries)** A **penitentiary** is a prison. [AM, FORMAL] N-COUNT

**pen|knife** /pennaɪf/ **(penknives)** A **penknife** is a small knife with a blade that folds back into the handle. N-COUNT

**pen name** **(pen names)** also **pen-name.** A writer's **pen name** is the name that he or she uses on books and articles instead of his or her real name. ❑ *...Baroness Blixen, also known by her pen-name Isak Dinesen.* N-COUNT = *pseudonym*

**pen|nant** /penənt/ **(pennants)** 1 A **pennant** is a long, narrow, triangular flag. ❑ *The second car was flying the Ghanaian pennant.* N-COUNT 2 In baseball, a **pennant** is a flag that is given each year to the top team in a league. The championship is also called **the pennant.** [AM] ❑ *The Red Sox lost the pennant to Detroit by a single game.* N-COUNT

**pen|nies** /peniz/ **Pennies** is the plural of **penny. Pennies** is mainly used to refer only to coins, rather than to amounts.

**pen|ni|less** /penɪləs/ Someone who is **penniless** has hardly any money at all. ❑ *They'd soon be penniless and homeless if she couldn't find suitable work. ...a penniless refugee.* ADJ: usu v-link ADJ

**penn'orth** /penəθ/ During a discussion about something, if you have your **two penn'orth** or put in your **two penn'orth**, you add your own opinion. [BRIT, INFORMAL] ❑ *Please do be patient – I'm sure you want to have your two penn'orth.* PHRASE: det-poss PHR, usu PHR after v

✔ in AM, use **two cents' worth**

**pen|ny** /peni/ **(pennies, pence)** ◆◇◇

✔ The form **pence** is used for the plural of meaning 1.

1 In Britain, a **penny** is one hundredth of a pound, or a coin worth this amount of money. ❑ *Cider also goes up by a penny a pint while sparkling wine will cost another eight pence a bottle. ...a shiny newly minted penny.* N-COUNT 2 A **penny** is a British coin used before 1971 that was worth one twelfth of a shilling. N-COUNT 3 A **penny** is one cent, or a coin worth one cent. [AM, INFORMAL] ❑ *Unleaded gasoline rose more than a penny a gallon.* N-COUNT 4 If you say, for example, that you do not have **a penny**, or that something does not cost **a penny**, you are emphasizing that you do not have any money at all, or that something did not cost you any money at all. ❑ *The Brilliantons paid their rent on time and did not owe him a penny.* N-SING: *a* N [emphasis]

PHRASES [5] If you say **the penny dropped**, you mean that someone suddenly understood or realized something. [mainly BRIT, INFORMAL] [6] Things that are said to be **two a penny** or **ten a penny** are not valuable or interesting because they are very common and easy to find. [BRIT, INFORMAL] ❑ *Leggy blondes are two a penny in Hollywood.* PHRASE: V inflects / PHRASE: v-link PHR

✔ in AM, use **a dime a dozen**

**pen|ny-far|thing** **(penny-farthings)** also **pen|ny farthing.** A **penny-farthing** is an old-fashioned bicycle that had a very large front wheel and a small back wheel. [mainly BRIT] N-COUNT

**pen|ny-pinching** [1] **Penny-pinching** is the practice of trying to spend as little money as possible. ❑ *Government penny-pinching is blamed for the decline in food standards.* [2] **Penny-pinching** people spend as little money as possible. ❑ *...small-minded penny-pinching administrators.* N-UNCOUNT disapproval / ADJ disapproval

**pen|ny shares** **Penny shares** are shares that are offered for sale at a low price. [BUSINESS] N-PLURAL

**pen pal** **(pen pals)** also **pen-pal.** A **pen pal** is someone you write friendly letters to and receive letters from, although the two of you may never have met. N-COUNT = pen-friend

**pen-pusher** **(pen-pushers)** also **penpusher.** If you call someone a **pen-pusher**, you mean that their work consists of writing or dealing with documents, and does not seem very useful or important. [BRIT] ❑ *As a result, industry was overmanned and pen-pushers were everywhere.* N-COUNT disapproval = bureaucrat

✔ in AM, use **pencil pusher**

**pen|sion** /pe̲nʃ^ən/ **(pensions, pensioning, pensioned)** Someone who has a **pension** receives a regular sum of money from the state or from a former employer because they have retired or because they are widowed or disabled. ❑ *...struggling by on a pension. ...a company pension scheme.* ◆◇◇ N-COUNT

♦ **pension off** If someone **is pensioned off**, they are made to retire from work and are given a pension. ❑ *Many successful women do not want to be pensioned off at 60... When his employees were no longer of use to him, he pensioned them off.* PHRASAL VERB be V-ed P / V n P / Also V P n (not pron)

**pen|sion|able** /pe̲nʃənəb^əl/ **Pensionable** means relating to someone's right to receive a pension. ❑ *...civil servants nearing pensionable age.* ADJ: ADJ n

**pen|sion book** **(pension books)** In Britain, a **pension book** is a small book which is given to pensioners by the government. Each week, one page can be exchanged for money at a Post Office. N-COUNT

**pen|sion|er** /pe̲nʃənə^r/ **(pensioners)** A **pensioner** is someone who receives a pension, especially a pension paid by the state to retired people. N-COUNT = OAP

**pen|sion plan** **(pension plans)** A **pension plan** is an arrangement to receive a pension from an organization such as an insurance company or a former employer in return for making regular payments to them over a number of years. [BUSINESS] ❑ *I would have been much wiser to start my own pension plan when I was younger.* N-COUNT

**pen|sion scheme** **(pension schemes)** A **pension scheme** is the same as a **pension plan**. [mainly BRIT, BUSINESS] ❑ *His company has the best pension scheme in the industry.* N-COUNT

**pen|sive** /pe̲nsɪv/ If you are **pensive**, you are thinking deeply about something, especially something that worries you slightly. ❑ *He looked suddenly sombre, pensive.* ♦ **pen|sive|ly** *Angela stared pensively out of the window.* ADJ = thoughtful / ADV: ADV with v

**pen|ta|gon** /pe̲ntəgən, AM -gɑːn/ **(pentagons)** A **pentagon** is a shape with five sides. N-COUNT

**Pen|ta|gon** **The Pentagon** is the main building of the US Defense Department, in Washington. The US Defense Department is often referred to as **the Pentagon**. ❑ *...a news conference at the Pentagon.* N-PROPER: the N, N n

**pen|tam|eter** /pentæ̲mɪtə^r/ **(pentameters)** In literary criticism, a **pentameter** is a line of poetry that has five strong beats in it. [TECHNICAL] N-COUNT

**pen|tath|lon** /pentæ̲θlɒn/ **(pentathlons)** A **pentathlon** is an athletics competition in which each person must compete in five different events. N-COUNT: oft the N

**Pen|tecost** /pe̲ntɪkɒst, AM -kɔːst/ [1] **Pentecost** is a Christian festival that takes place on the seventh Sunday after Easter and celebrates the sending of the Holy Spirit to the first followers of Christ. [2] **Pentecost** is a Jewish festival that takes place 50 days after Passover and celebrates the harvest. N-UNCOUNT / N-UNCOUNT

**Pen|tecos|tal** /pe̲ntɪkɒ̲st^əl, AM -kɔ̲ːst-/ **Pentecostal** churches are Christian churches that emphasize the work of the Holy Spirit and the exact truth of the Bible. ADJ: ADJ n

**pent|house** /pe̲nthaʊs/ **(penthouses)** A **penthouse** or a **penthouse** apartment or suite is a luxurious flat or set of rooms at the top of a tall building. ❑ *...her swish Manhattan penthouse.* N-COUNT: oft N n

**pent-up** /pe̲nt ʌ̲p/ **Pent-up** emotions, energies, or forces have been held back and not expressed, used, or released. ❑ *He still had a lot of pent-up anger to release.* ADJ: usu ADJ n

**pe|nul|ti|mate** /penʌ̲ltɪmət/ The **penultimate** thing in a series of things is the last but one. [FORMAL] ❑ *...on the penultimate day of the Asian Games. ...in the penultimate chapter.* ADJ: det ADJ

**pe|num|bra** /pɪnʌ̲mbrə/ **(penumbras)** A **penumbra** is an area of light shadow. [FORMAL] N-COUNT

**penu|ry** /pe̲njʊri/ **Penury** is the state of being extremely poor. [FORMAL] ❑ *He was brought up in penury, without education.* N-UNCOUNT

**peo|ny** /piːəni/ **(peonies)** also **paeony.** A **peony** is a medium-sized garden plant which has large round flowers, usually pink, red, or white. N-COUNT

**peo|ple** /piːp^əl/ **(peoples, peopling, peopled)** ◆◆◆ [1] **People** are men, women, and children. **People** is normally used as the plural of **person**, instead of 'persons'. ❑ *Millions of people have lost their homes. ...the people of Angola. ...homeless young people... I don't think people should make promises they don't mean to keep.* [2] **The people** is sometimes used to refer to ordinary men and women, in contrast to the government or the upper classes. ❑ *...the will of the people.* [3] A **people** is all the men, women, and children of a particular country or race. ❑ *...the native peoples of Central and South America.* [4] If a place or country **is peopled by** a particular group of people, that group of people live there. ❑ *It was peopled by a fiercely independent race of peace-loving Buddhists. ...a small town peopled by lay workers and families.* N-PLURAL / N-PLURAL: the N / N-COUNT-COLL / VERB: usu passive = populate be V-ed by/with n V-ed

**peo|ple car|ri|er** **(people carriers)** A **people carrier** is a large family car which looks similar to a van and has three rows of seats for passengers. N-COUNT

**peo|ple mov|er** **(people movers)** also **people-mover.** A **people mover** is the same as a **people carrier**. N-COUNT

**pep** /pe̲p/ **(peps, pepping, pepped)** **Pep** is liveliness and energy. [INFORMAL, OLD-FASHIONED] ❑ *Many say that, given a choice, they would opt for a holiday to put the pep back in their lives.* N-UNCOUNT

♦ **pep up** If you try to **pep** something **up**, you try to make it more lively, more interesting, or stronger. [INFORMAL] ❑ *The prime minister aired some ideas about pepping up trade in the region... How about pepping up plain tiles with transfers?* PHRASAL VERB V P n (not pron) Also V n P

**pep|per** /pe̲pə^r/ **(peppers, peppering, peppered)** ◆◇◇ [1] **Pepper** is a hot-tasting spice which is used to flavour food. ❑ *Season with salt and pepper. ...freshly ground black pepper.* [2] A **pepper**, or in American English a **bell pepper**, is a hollow green, red, or yellow vegetable with seeds inside it. → See picture on page 1712. [3] If something **is peppered with** small objects, a lot of those objects hit it. ❑ *He was wounded in both legs and severely peppered with shrapnel.* [4] If something **is peppered with** things, it has a lot of those things in it or on it. ❑ *While her English was correct,* N-UNCOUNT / N-COUNT / VERB: usu passive be V-ed with n / VERB be V-ed with n *it was peppered with French phrases... Yachts peppered the tranquil waters of Botafogo Bay.* V n

**pepper|corn** /pepəʳkɔːʳn/ **(peppercorns)** **Peppercorns** are the small berries which are dried and crushed to make pepper. They are sometimes used whole in cooking. N-COUNT

**pepper|corn rent** **(peppercorn rents)** A **peppercorn rent** is an extremely low rent. [BRIT] N-COUNT

**pep|per mill** **(pepper mills)** also **peppermill.** A **pepper mill** is a container in which peppercorns are crushed to make pepper. You turn the top of the container and the pepper comes out of the bottom. N-COUNT

**pepper|mint** /pepəʳmɪnt/ **(peppermints)** 1 **Peppermint** is a strong, sharp flavouring that is obtained from the peppermint plant or that is made artificially. N-UNCOUNT 2 A **peppermint** is a peppermint-flavoured sweet or piece of candy. N-COUNT

**pep|pero|ni** /pepərouni/ **Pepperoni** is a kind of spicy sausage which is often sliced and put on pizzas. N-UNCOUNT

**pepper|pot** /pepəʳpɒt/ **(pepperpots)** also **pepper pot.** A **pepperpot** is a small container with holes in the top, used for shaking pepper onto food. [mainly BRIT] N-COUNT

> ✔ in AM, usually use **pepper shaker**

**pep|per shak|er** **(pepper shakers)** A **pepper shaker** is the same as a **pepperpot**. [mainly AM] N-COUNT

**pep|pery** /pepəri/ Food that is **peppery** has a strong, hot taste like pepper. ❑ *...a crisp green salad with a few peppery radishes.* ADJ

**pep|py** /pepi/ Someone or something that is **peppy** is lively and full of energy. [INFORMAL] ❑ *At the end of every day, jot down a brief note on how peppy or tired you felt. ...peppy dance-numbers.* ADJ

**pep ral|ly** **(pep rallies)** A **pep rally** at a school, college, or university is a gathering to support a football team or sports team. [AM] N-COUNT

**pep talk** **(pep talks)** also **pep-talk.** A **pep talk** is a speech which is intended to encourage someone to make more effort or feel more confident. [INFORMAL] ❑ *Powell spent the day giving pep talks to the troops.* N-COUNT

**pep|tic ul|cer** /peptɪk ʌlsəʳ/ **(peptic ulcers)** A **peptic ulcer** is an ulcer that occurs in the digestive system. N-COUNT

**per** /pɜːʳ/ ◆◆◇ 1 You use **per** to express rates and ratios. For example, if something costs £50 **per** year, you must pay £50 each year for it. If a vehicle is travelling at 40 miles **per** hour, it travels 40 miles each hour. ❑ *Social Security refused to pay her more than £17 per week... Buses and trains use much less fuel per person than cars.* **per head** → see **head**. PREP: amount PREP n 2 If something happens **as per** a particular plan or suggestion, it happens in the way planned or suggested. [FORMAL] ❑ *When they reach here they complain that they are not being paid as per the agreement.* PREP-PHRASE

**per|am|bu|late** /pəræmbjʊleɪt/ **(perambulates, perambulating, perambulated)** When someone **perambulates**, they walk about for pleasure. [OLD-FASHIONED] VERB ♦ **per|am|bu|la|tion** /pəræmbjʊleɪʃᵊn/ **(perambulations)** ❑ *It was time now to end our perambulation round Paris.* N-COUNT

**per an|num** /pər ænəm/ A particular amount **per annum** means that amount each year. ❑ *...a fee of £35 per annum... Kenya's population is growing at 4.1 per cent per annum.* ADV: amount ADV

**per capi|ta** /pəʳ kæpɪtə/ The **per capita** amount of something is the total amount of it in a country or area divided by the number of people in that country or area. ❑ *They have the world's largest per capita income.* ADJ: ADJ n ♦ **Per capita** is also an adverb. ❑ *Ethiopia has almost the lowest oil consumption per capita in the world.* ADV: n ADV

**per|ceive** /pəʳsiːv/ **(perceives, perceiving, perceived)** 1 If you **perceive** something, you see, notice, or realize it, especially when it is not obvious. ❑ *A key task is to get pupils to perceive for themselves the relationship between success and effort.* VERB V n 2 If you **perceive** someone or something **as** doing or being a particular thing, it is your opinion that they do this thing or that they are that thing. ❑ *Stress is widely perceived as contributing to coronary heart disease.* VERB V n *as* n/-ing

**per cent** /pəʳ sent/ **(per cent)** also **percent.** ◆◆◆ You use **per cent** to talk about amounts. For example, if an amount is 10 per cent (10%) of a larger amount, it is equal to 10 hundredths of the larger amount. ❑ *20 to 40 per cent of the voters are undecided... We aim to increase sales by 10 per cent.* N-COUNT: num N, oft N *of* n ♦ **Per cent** is also an adjective. ❑ *There has been a ten per cent increase in the number of new students arriving at polytechnics this year.* ADJ: ADJ n ♦ **Per cent** is also an adverb. ❑ *...its prediction that house prices will fall 5 per cent over the year.* ADV: ADV with v

**per|cent|age** /pəʳsentɪdʒ/ **(percentages)** ◆◇◇ A **percentage** is a fraction of an amount expressed as a particular number of hundredths of that amount. ❑ *Only a few vegetable-origin foods have such a high percentage of protein.* N-COUNT: usu N *of* n

**per|cep|tible** /pəʳseptɪbᵊl/ Something that is **perceptible** can only just be seen or noticed. ❑ *Pasternak gave him a barely perceptible smile.* ADJ = discernible ♦ **per|cep|tibly** /pəʳseptɪbli/ *The tension was mounting perceptibly.* ADV: ADV with v

**per|cep|tion** /pəʳsepʃᵊn/ **(perceptions)** 1 Your **perception of** something is the way that you think about it or the impression you have of it. ❑ *He is interested in how our perceptions of death affect the way we live.* N-COUNT: usu poss N, N *of* n 2 Someone who has **perception** realizes or notices things that are not obvious. ❑ *It did not require a great deal of perception to realise the interview was over.* N-UNCOUNT 3 **Perception** is the recognition of things using your senses, especially the sense of sight. N-COUNT: usu with supp

**per|cep|tive** /pəʳseptɪv/ If you describe a person or their remarks or thoughts as **perceptive**, you think that they are good at noticing or realizing things, especially things that are not obvious. ❑ *He was one of the most perceptive US political commentators.* ADJ [approval] ♦ **per|cep|tive|ly** *The stages in her love affair with Harry are perceptively written.* ADV: usu ADV with v, also ADV adj

**per|cep|tual** /pəʳseptʃuəl/ **Perceptual** means relating to the way people interpret and understand what they see or notice. [FORMAL] ❑ *Some children have more finely trained perceptual skills than others.* ADJ: ADJ n

**perch** /pɜːʳtʃ/ **(perches, perching, perched)**

> ✔ The form **perch** is used for both the singular and plural in meaning 6.

1 If you **perch on** something, you sit down lightly on the very edge or tip of it. ❑ *He lit a cigarette and perched on the corner of the desk... He perched himself on the side of the bed.* VERB V prep/adv V pron-refl prep/adv ♦ **perched** *She was perched on the edge of the sofa.* ADJ: v-link ADJ prep/adv 2 To **perch** somewhere means to be on the top or edge of something. ❑ *...the vast slums that perch precariously on top of the hills around which the city was built.* VERB V prep/adv ♦ **perched** *St. John's is a small college perched high up in the hills.* ADJ: v-link ADJ prep/adv 3 If you **perch** something **on** something else, you put or balance it on the top or edge of that thing. ❑ *The builders have perched a light concrete dome on eight slender columns.* VERB V n *on* n 4 When a bird **perches on** something such as a branch or a wall, it lands on it and stands there. ❑ *A blackbird flew down and perched on the parapet outside his window.* VERB V prep 5 A **perch** is a short rod for a bird to stand on. N-COUNT 6 A **perch** is an edible fish. There are several kinds of perch. N-COUNT

**per|chance** /pəʳtʃɑːns, -tʃæns/ **Perchance** means **perhaps**. [LITERARY, OLD-FASHIONED] ADV: ADV with group/cl

**per|co|late** /pɜːʳkəleɪt/ **(percolates, percolating, percolated)** 1 If an idea, feeling, or piece of information **percolates** through a group of people or a thing, it spreads slowly through the group or thing. ❑ *New fashions took a long time to percolate down. ...all of these thoughts percolated through my mind.* VERB V prep/adv V prep/adv 2 When you **percolate** coffee or when VERB

coffee **percolates**, you prepare it in a percolator. ❑ *She percolated the coffee and put croissants in the oven to warm.* V n Also V
[3] To **percolate** somewhere means to pass slowly through something that has very small holes or gaps in it. ❑ *Rain water will only percolate through slowly.* VERB V prep/adv

**per|co|la|tor** /pɜːʳkəleɪtəʳ/ **(percolators)** A **percolator** is a piece of equipment for making and serving coffee, in which steam passes through crushed coffee beans. N-COUNT

**per|cus|sion** /pəʳkʌʃᵊn/ **Percussion** instruments are musical instruments that you hit, such as drums. N-UNCOUNT: oft N n

**per|cus|sion|ist** /pəʳkʌʃᵊnɪst/ **(percussionists)** A **percussionist** is a person who plays percussion instruments such as drums. N-COUNT

**per|cus|sive** /pəʳkʌsɪv/ **Percussive** sounds are like the sound of drums. ❑ *...using all manner of percussive effects.* ADJ: usu ADJ n

**per diem** /pəʳ diːəm/ A **per diem** is an amount of money that someone is given to cover their daily expenses while they are working. [mainly AM] ❑ *He received a per diem allowance to cover his travel expenses.* N-SING: oft N n

**per|di|tion** /pɜːʳdɪʃᵊn/ If you say that someone is on the road to **perdition**, you mean that their behaviour is likely to lead them to failure and disaster. [LITERARY] N-UNCOUNT: usu prep N

**per|egrine fal|con** /perɪgrɪn fɔːlkən/ **(peregrine falcons)** A **peregrine falcon** or a **peregrine** is a bird of prey. N-COUNT

**per|emp|tory** /pərem͟ptəri/ Someone who does something in a **peremptory** way does it in a way that shows that they expect to be obeyed immediately. [FORMAL] ❑ *With a brief, almost peremptory gesture he pointed to a chair.* ADJ: usu ADJ n disapproval
♦ **per|emp|to|ri|ly** /pəremptərɪli/ *'Hello!' the voice said, more peremptorily. 'Who is it? Who do you want?'* ADV: ADV with v

**per|en|nial** /pəreniəl/ **(perennials)** [1] You use **perennial** to describe situations or states that keep occurring or which seem to exist all the time; used especially to describe problems or difficulties. ❑ *...the perennial urban problems of drugs and homelessness.* ADJ: usu ADJ n = constant
♦ **per|en|ni|al|ly** *Both services are perennially short of staff.* ADV: usu ADV adj
[2] A **perennial** plant lives for several years and has flowers each year. ❑ *...a perennial herb with greenish-yellow flowers.* ADJ: usu ADJ n
♦ **Perennial** is also a noun. ❑ *...a low-growing perennial.* N-COUNT

**pe|re|stroi|ka** /perɪstrɔɪkə/ **Perestroika** is a term which was used to describe the changing political and social structure of the former Soviet Union during the late 1980s. N-UNCOUNT

**per|fect** **(perfects, perfecting, perfected)** ◆◆◇

> The adjective is pronounced /pɜːʳfɪkt/. The verb is pronounced /pəʳfekt/.

[1] Something that is **perfect** is as good as it could possibly be. ❑ *He spoke perfect English... Hiring a nanny has turned out to be the perfect solution... Nobody is perfect.* ADJ
[2] If you say that something is **perfect for** a particular person, thing, or activity, you are emphasizing that it is very suitable for them or for that activity. ❑ *Carpet tiles are perfect for kitchens because they're easy to take up and wash... So this could be the perfect time to buy a home.* ADJ: oft ADJ *for* n emphasis = ideal
[3] If an object or surface is **perfect**, it does not have any marks on it, or does not have any lumps, hollows, or cracks in it. ❑ *Use only clean, Grade A, perfect eggs. ...their perfect white teeth.* ADJ
[4] You can use **perfect** to give emphasis to the noun following it. ❑ *She was a perfect fool... What he had said to her made perfect sense.* ADJ: ADJ n emphasis = complete
[5] If you **perfect** something, you improve it so that it becomes as good as it can possibly be. ❑ *We perfected a hand-signal system so that he could keep me informed of hazards.* VERB V n
[6] The **perfect** tenses of a verb are the ones used to talk about things that happened or began before a particular time, as in 'He's already left' and 'They had always liked her'. The present perfect tense is sometimes called the **perfect** tense. → See also **future**, **present perfect**, **past perfect**. ADJ: ADJ n

**per|fec|tion** /pəʳfekʃᵊn/ [1] **Perfection** is the quality of being as good as it is possible for something of a particular kind to be. ❑ *Physical perfection in a human being is exceedingly rare.* N-UNCOUNT
[2] If you say that something is **perfection**, you mean that you think it is as good as it could possibly be. ❑ *The house and garden were perfection.* N-UNCOUNT
[3] **The perfection of** something such as a skill, system, or product involves making it as good as it could possibly be. ❑ *Madame Clicquot is credited with the perfection of this technique.* N-UNCOUNT: usu *the* N *of* n
[4] If something is done **to perfection**, it is done so well that it could not be done any better. ❑ *...fresh fish, cooked to perfection.* PHRASE: PHR after v

**per|fec|tion|ism** /pəʳfekʃənɪzəm/ **Perfectionism** is the attitude or behaviour of a perfectionist. N-UNCOUNT

**per|fec|tion|ist** /pəʳfekʃənɪst/ **(perfectionists)** Someone who is a **perfectionist** refuses to do or accept anything that is not as good as it could possibly be. N-COUNT

**per|fect|ly** /pɜːʳfɪktli/ ◆◇◇ [1] You can use **perfectly** to emphasize an adjective or adverb, especially when you think the person you are talking to might doubt what you are saying. ❑ *There's no reason why you can't have a perfectly normal child... They made it perfectly clear that it was pointless to go on... You know perfectly well what happened.* ADV: ADV adj/adv emphasis = quite
[2] If something is done **perfectly**, it is done so well that it could not possibly be done better. ❑ *This adaptation perfectly captures the spirit of Kurt Vonnegut's novel... The system worked perfectly.* ADV: ADV with v
[3] If you describe something as **perfectly** good or acceptable, you are emphasizing that there is no reason to use or get something else, although other people may disagree. ❑ *You can buy perfectly good instruments for a lot less.* ADV: ADV adj/adv emphasis

**per|fect pitch** Someone who has **perfect pitch** is able to identify or sing musical notes correctly. N-UNCOUNT

**per|fidi|ous** /pəʳfɪdiəs/ If you describe someone as **perfidious**, you mean that they have betrayed someone or cannot be trusted. [LITERARY] ❑ *Their feet will trample on the dead bodies of their perfidious aggressors.* ADJ: usu ADJ n = treacherous

**per|fi|dy** /pɜːʳfɪdi/ **Perfidy** is the action of betraying someone or behaving very badly towards someone. [LITERARY] N-UNCOUNT = treachery

**per|fo|rate** /pɜːʳfəreɪt/ **(perforates, perforating, perforated)** To **perforate** something means to make a hole or holes in it. ❑ *I refused to wear headphones because they can perforate your eardrums.* VERB V n
♦ **per|fo|rat|ed** *Keep good apples in perforated polythene bags.* ADJ: ADJ n

**per|fo|ra|tion** /pɜːʳfəreɪʃᵊn/ **(perforations)** **Perforations** are small holes that are made in something, especially in paper. ❑ *Tear off the form along the perforations and send it to Sales.* N-COUNT: usu pl

**per|force** /pəʳfɔːʳs/ **Perforce** is used to indicate that something happens or is the case because it cannot be prevented or avoided. [OLD-FASHIONED] ❑ *The war in 1939 perforce ushered in an era of more grime and drabness.* ADV: ADV with cl, ADV with v

**per|form** /pəʳfɔːʳm/ **(performs, performing, performed)** ◆◆◇ [1] When you **perform** a task or action, especially a complicated one, you do it. ❑ *His council had had to perform miracles on a tiny budget... Several grafts may be performed at one operation.* VERB V n V n
[2] If something **performs** a particular function, it has that function. ❑ *A complex engine has many separate components, each performing a different function.* VERB V n
[3] If you **perform** a play, a piece of music, or a dance, you do it in front of an audience. ❑ *Gardiner has pursued relentlessly high standards in performing classical music... This play was first performed in 411 BC... He began performing in the early fifties, singing and playing guitar.* VERB V n V n V
[4] If some- VERB

one or something **performs well**, they work well or achieve a good result. If they **perform badly**, they work badly or achieve a poor result. ❑ *He had not performed well in his exams... 'State-owned industries will always perform poorly,' John Moore informed readers.* V adv V adv

**per|for|mance** /pəʳfɔːʳməns/ **(performances)** ◆◆◇ [1] A **performance** involves entertaining an audience by doing something such as singing, dancing, or acting. ❑ *Inside the theatre, they were giving a performance of Bizet's Carmen. ...her performance as the betrayed Medea.* N-COUNT [2] Someone's or something's **performance** is how successful they are or how well they do something. ❑ *That study looked at the performance of 18 surgeons... The job of the new director-general was to ensure that performance targets were met.* N-VAR: oft with poss [3] A car's **performance** is its ability to go fast and to increase its speed quickly. N-UNCOUNT [4] A **performance** car is one that can go very fast and can increase its speed very quickly. ➔ See also **high-performance**. ADJ: ADJ n [5] **The performance of** a task is the fact or action of doing it. ❑ *He devoted in excess of seventy hours a week to the performance of his duties.* N-SING: usu *the* N *of* n [6] You can describe something that is or looks complicated or difficult to do as **a performance**. [INFORMAL] ❑ *The whole process is quite a performance.* N-SING: usu *a* N [7] **a repeat performance** ➔ see **repeat**.

**per|for|mance art** **Performance art** is a theatrical presentation that includes various art forms such as dance, music, painting, and sculpture. N-UNCOUNT

**performance-related pay** **Performance-related pay** is a rate of pay which is based on how well someone does their job. [BUSINESS] N-UNCOUNT

**per|form|er** /pəʳfɔːʳməʳ/ **(performers)** [1] A **performer** is a person who acts, sings, or does other entertainment in front of audiences. ❑ *A performer in evening dress plays classical selections on the violin.* N-COUNT [2] You can use **performer** when describing someone or something in a way that indicates how well they do a particular thing. ❑ *Until 1987, Canada's industry had been the star performer... He is a world class performer.* N-COUNT: supp N

**per|form|ing arts** Dance, drama, music, and other forms of entertainment that are usually performed live in front of an audience are referred to as **the performing arts**. N-PLURAL: usu *the* N

**per|fume** /pɜːʳfjuːm, pəʳfjuːm/ **(perfumes, perfuming, perfumed)** [1] **Perfume** is a pleasant-smelling liquid which women put on their skin to make themselves smell nice. ❑ *The hall smelled of her mother's perfume. ...a bottle of perfume.* N-MASS = scent [2] **Perfume** is the ingredient that is added to some products to make them smell nice. ❑ *...a delicate white soap without perfume.* N-MASS [3] If something is used to **perfume** a product, it is added to the product to make it smell nice. ❑ *The oil is used to flavour and perfume soaps, foam baths, and scents. ...shower gel perfumed with the popular Paris fragrance.* VERB V n V-ed *with* n

**per|fumed** /pɜːʳfjuːmd, pəʳfjuːmd/ [1] Something such as fruit or wine that is **perfumed** has a sweet pleasant smell. ❑ *Champenois wines can be particularly fragrant and perfumed.* ADJ [2] **Perfumed** things have a sweet pleasant smell, either naturally or because perfume has been added to them. ❑ *She opened the perfumed envelope.* ADJ: usu ADJ n = scented

**per|fum|ery** /pəʳfjuːməri/ **(perfumeries)** [1] **Perfumery** is the activity or business of producing perfume. ❑ *...the perfumery trade.* N-UNCOUNT: oft N n [2] A **perfumery** is a shop or a department in a store where perfume is the main product that is sold. N-COUNT

**per|func|tory** /pəʳfʌŋktəri, AM -tɔːri/ A **perfunctory** action is done quickly and carelessly, and shows a lack of interest in what you are doing. ❑ *She gave the list only a perfunctory glance... Our interest was purely perfunctory.* ADJ: usu ADJ n

♦ **per|func|to|ri|ly** /pəʳfʌŋktərɪli, AM -tɔːr-/ *Melina was perfunctorily introduced to the men.* ADV: ADV with v

**per|go|la** /pɜːʳgələ/ **(pergolas)** In a garden, a **pergola** is an arch or a structure with a roof over which climbing plants can be grown. N-COUNT

**per|haps** /pəʳhæps, præps/ ◆◆◆ [1] You use **perhaps** to express uncertainty, for example, when you do not know that something is definitely true, or when you are mentioning something that may possibly happen in the future in the way you describe. ❑ *Millson regarded her thoughtfully. Perhaps she was right... In the end they lose millions, perhaps billions... It was bulky, perhaps three feet long and almost as high... Perhaps, in time, the message will get through... They'd come soon, perhaps when the radio broadcast was over.* ADV: ADV with cl/group [vagueness] = maybe [2] You use **perhaps** in opinions and remarks to make them appear less definite or more polite. ❑ *Perhaps the most important lesson to be learned is that you simply cannot please everyone... His last paintings are perhaps the most puzzling... Do you perhaps disapprove of Agatha Christie and her Poirot and Miss Marple?* ADV: ADV with cl/group [vagueness] [3] You use **perhaps** when you are making suggestions or giving advice. **Perhaps** is also used in formal English to introduce requests. ❑ *Perhaps I may be permitted a few suggestions... Well, perhaps you'll come and see us at our place?* ADV: ADV with cl [politeness] [4] You can say **perhaps** as a response to a question or remark, when you do not want to agree or accept, but think that it would be rude to disagree or refuse. ❑ *'I'm sure we can make it,' he says. Perhaps, but it will not be easy.* ADV: ADV as reply

**per|il** /perɪl/ **(perils)** [1] **Perils** are great dangers. [FORMAL] ❑ *...the perils of the sea... We are in the gravest peril.* N-VAR: usu with supp [2] The **perils** of a particular activity or course of action are the dangers or problems it may involve. ❑ *...the perils of starring in a television commercial.* N-PLURAL: with poss [3] If you say that someone does something **at** their **peril**, you are warning them that they will probably suffer as a result of doing it. ❑ *Anyone who breaks the law does so at their peril.* PHRASE: PHR after v

**peri|lous** /perɪləs/ Something that is **perilous** is very dangerous. [LITERARY] ❑ *...a perilous journey across the war-zone... The road grew even steeper and more perilous.* ADJ ♦ **peri|lous|ly** *The track snaked perilously upwards.* ADV: ADV after v, ADV adj

**pe|rim|eter** /pərɪmɪtəʳ/ **(perimeters)** The **perimeter** of an area of land is the whole of its outer edge or boundary. ❑ *...the perimeter of the airport... Officers dressed in riot gear are surrounding the perimeter fence.* N-COUNT

**peri|na|tal** /perineɪtᵊl/ **Perinatal** deaths, problems, or experiences happen at the time of birth or soon after the time of birth. [MEDICAL] ❑ *Premature birth is the main cause of perinatal mortality.* ADJ: ADJ n

**pe|ri|od** /pɪəriəd/ **(periods)** ◆◆◇ [1] A **period** is a length of time. ❑ *This crisis might last for a long period of time. ...a period of a few months. ...for a limited period only.* N-COUNT: usu with supp [2] A **period** in the life of a person, organization, or society is a length of time which is remembered for a particular situation or activity. ❑ *...a period of economic good health and expansion... He went through a period of wanting to be accepted... The South African years were his most creative period.* N-COUNT: with supp [3] A particular length of time in history is sometimes called a **period**. For example, you can talk about **the Victorian period** or **the Elizabethan period** in Britain. ❑ *...the Roman period... No reference to their existence appears in any literature of the period.* N-COUNT: usu with supp [4] **Period** costumes, furniture, and instruments were made at an earlier time in history, or look as if they were made then. ❑ *...dressed in full period costume.* ADJ: ADJ n [5] Exercise, training, or study **periods** are lengths of time that are set aside for exercise, training, or study. ❑ *They accompanied him during his exercise periods.* N-COUNT: usu n N [6] At a school or college, a **period** is one of the parts that the day is divided into during which lessons or other activities take place. ❑ *...periods of private study.* N-COUNT [7] When a woman has a **period**, she bleeds from her womb. This usually happens once a month, N-COUNT unless she is pregnant. [8] Some people say **period** after stating a fact or opinion when they want to emphasize that they are definite about something and do not want to discuss it further. ❑ *I don't want to do it, period.* [9] A **period** is the punctuation mark (.) which you use at the end of a sentence when it is not a question or an exclamation. [AM] ADV: cl ADV emphasis N-COUNT

✓ in BRIT, use **full stop**

**pe|ri|od|ic** /pɪəriɒdɪk/ **Periodic** events or situations happen occasionally, at fairly regular intervals. ❑ *...periodic bouts of illness.* ADJ: usu ADJ n = periodical

**pe|ri|odi|cal** /pɪəriɒdɪkəl/ **(periodicals)** [1] **Periodicals** are magazines, especially serious or academic ones, that are published at regular intervals. ❑ *The walls would be lined with books and periodicals.* [2] **Periodical** events or situations happen occasionally, at fairly regular intervals. ❑ *She made periodical visits to her dentist.* ♦ **pe|ri|odi|cal|ly** /pɪəriɒdɪkli/ *Meetings are held periodically to monitor progress on the case.* N-COUNT ADJ: usu ADJ n = periodic ADV: ADV with v

**pe|ri|od|ic ta|ble** In chemistry, **the periodic table** is a table showing the chemical elements arranged according to their atomic numbers. N-SING: the N

**perio|don|tal** /periouðɒntəl/ **Periodontal** disease is disease of the gums. [TECHNICAL] ADJ: ADJ n

**pe|ri|od pain** **(period pains)** **Period pain** is the pain that some women have when they have a monthly period. N-VAR

**pe|ri|od piece** **(period pieces)** A **period piece** is a play, book, or film that is set at a particular time in history and describes life at that time. N-COUNT

**peri|pa|tet|ic** /perɪpətetɪk/ If someone has a **peripatetic** life or career, they travel around a lot, living or working in places for short periods of time. [FORMAL] ❑ *Her father was in the army and the family led a peripatetic existence.* ADJ: usu ADJ n

**pe|riph|er|al** /pərɪfərəl/ **(peripherals)** [1] A **peripheral** activity or issue is one which is not very important compared with other activities or issues. ❑ *Companies are increasingly keen to contract out peripheral activities like training... Science is peripheral to that debate.* ♦ **pe|riph|er|al|ly** *The Marshall Plan did not include Britain, except peripherally.* [2] **Peripheral** areas of land are ones which are on the edge of a larger area. ❑ *...urban development in the outer peripheral areas of large towns.* [3] **Peripherals** are devices that can be attached to computers. [COMPUTING] ❑ *...peripherals to expand the use of our computers.* ADJ ADV ADJ: usu ADJ n N-COUNT: usu pl, oft N n

**pe|riph|ery** /pərɪfəri/ **(peripheries)** [1] If something is on the **periphery** of an area, place, or thing, it is on the edge of it. [FORMAL] ❑ *Geographically, the UK is on the periphery of Europe, while Paris is at the heart of the continent.* [2] The **periphery** of a subject or area of interest is the part of it that is not considered to be as important or basic as the main part. ❑ *The sociological study of religion moved from the centre to the periphery of sociology.* N-COUNT: usu with poss N-COUNT: usu with poss

**peri|scope** /perɪskoup/ **(periscopes)** A **periscope** is a vertical tube which people inside submarines can look through to see above the surface of the water. N-COUNT

**per|ish** /perɪʃ/ **(perishes, perishing, perished)** [1] If people or animals **perish**, they die as a result of very harsh conditions or as the result of an accident. [WRITTEN] ❑ *Most of the butterflies perish in the first frosts of autumn.* [2] If a substance or material **perishes**, it starts to fall to pieces and becomes useless. [mainly BRIT] ❑ *Their tyres are slowly perishing.* ♦ **per|ished** *...tattered pieces of ancient, perished leather.* VERB V VERB = disintegrate V ADJ: usu ADJ n

**per|ish|able** /perɪʃəbəl/ Goods such as food that are **perishable** go bad after quite a short length of time. ❑ *...perishable food like fruit, vegetables and meat.* ADJ

**per|ished** /perɪʃt/ [1] If someone is **perished**, they are extremely cold. [BRIT, INFORMAL] ❑ *I was absolutely perished.* [2] → See also **perish**. ADJ: usu v-link ADJ

**peri|to|ni|tis** /perɪtənaɪtɪs/ **Peritonitis** is a disease in which the inside wall of your abdomen becomes swollen and very painful. [MEDICAL] N-UNCOUNT

**peri|win|kle** /perɪwɪŋkəl/ **(periwinkles)** [1] **Periwinkle** is a plant that grows along the ground and has blue flowers. [2] **Periwinkles** are small sea snails that can be eaten. N-VAR N-COUNT = winkle

**per|jure** /pɜːrdʒər/ **(perjures, perjuring, perjured)** If someone **perjures themselves** in a court of law, they lie, even though they have promised to tell the truth. ❑ *Witnesses lied and perjured themselves.* VERB V pron-refl

**per|jured** /pɜːrdʒərd/ In a court of law, **perjured** evidence or **perjured** testimony is a false statement of events. ❑ *...information that was based on perjured testimony.* ADJ: usu ADJ n

**per|jury** /pɜːrdʒəri/ If someone who is giving evidence in a court of law commits **perjury**, they lie. [LEGAL] ❑ *This witness has committed perjury and no reliance can be placed on her evidence.* N-UNCOUNT

**perk** /pɜːrk/ **(perks, perking, perked)** **Perks** are special benefits that are given to people who have a particular job or belong to a particular group. ❑ *...a company car, private medical insurance and other perks... One of the perks of being a student is cheap travel.* N-COUNT: usu pl

♦ **perk up** [1] If something **perks** you **up** or if you **perk up**, you become cheerful and lively, after feeling tired, bored, or depressed. ❑ *He perks up and jokes with them. ...suggestions to make you smile and perk you up.* [2] If you **perk** something **up**, you make it more interesting. ❑ *To make the bland taste more interesting, the locals began perking it up with local produce... Psychological twists perk up an otherwise predictable story line.* [3] If sales, prices, or economies **perk up**, or if something **perks** them **up**, they begin to increase or improve. [JOURNALISM] ❑ *House prices could perk up during the autumn... Anything that could save the company money and perk up its cash flow was examined.* PHRASAL VERB V P V n P PHRASAL VERB V n P V P n PHRASAL VERB V P V P n (not pron) Also V n P

**perky** /pɜːrki/ **(perkier, perkiest)** If someone is **perky**, they are cheerful and lively. ❑ *He wasn't quite as perky as normal.* ADJ

**perm** /pɜːrm/ **(perms, perming, permed)** [1] If you have a **perm**, your hair is curled and treated with chemicals so that it stays curly for several months. [mainly BRIT] N-COUNT

✓ in AM, usually use **permanent**

[2] When a hair stylist **perms** someone's hair, they curl it and treat it with chemicals so that it stays curly for several months. ❑ *She had her hair permed.* ♦ **permed** *...dry, damaged or permed hair.* VERB *have* n V-ed ADJ

**per|ma|frost** /pɜːrməfrɒst/ **Permafrost** is land that is permanently frozen to a great depth. N-UNCOUNT

**per|ma|nent** /pɜːrmənənt/ **(permanents)** ♦◇◇ [1] Something that is **permanent** lasts for ever. ❑ *Heavy drinking can cause permanent damage to the brain... The ban is intended to be permanent.* ♦ **per|ma|nent|ly** *His reason had been permanently affected by what he had witnessed.* ♦ **per|ma|nence** *Anything which threatens the permanence of the treaty is a threat to peace.* [2] You use **permanent** to describe situations or states that keep occurring or which seem to exist all the time; used especially to describe problems or difficulties. ❑ *...a permanent state of tension... They feel under permanent threat.* ♦ **per|ma|nent|ly** *...the heavy, permanently locked gate.* [3] A **permanent** employee is one who is employed for an unlimited length of time. ❑ *...a permanent job.* ♦ **per|ma|nent|ly** *...permanently employed registered dockers.* [4] Your **permanent** home or your **permanent** address is the one at which you spend most of your time or the one that you return to after having stayed in other places. ❑ *York Cottage was as near to a permanent home as the children knew.* [5] A **permanent** is a treatment where ADJ ≠ temporary ADV: ADV with v, ADV adj N-UNCOUNT ADJ: usu ADJ n = constant ADV ADJ: ADJ n ≠ temporary ADV: ADV with v ADJ: ADJ n N-COUNT

a hair stylist curls your hair and treats it with a chemical so that it stays curly for several months. [AM]

✔ in BRIT, use **perm**

**per|ma|nent wave** **(permanent waves)** A **permanent wave** is the same as a **perm**. [OLD-FASHIONED] N-COUNT

**per|me|able** /pɜːʳmiəbᵊl/ If a substance is **permeable**, something such as water or gas can pass through it or soak into it. ❑ *A number of products have been developed which are permeable to air and water.* ADJ ≠ *impermeable*

**per|me|ate** /pɜːʳmieɪt/ **(permeates, permeating, permeated)** [1] If an idea, feeling, or attitude **permeates** a system or **permeates** society, it affects every part of it or is present throughout it. ❑ *Bias against women permeates every level of the judicial system... An obvious change of attitude at the top will permeate through the system.* [2] If something **permeates** a place, it spreads throughout it. ❑ *The smell of roast beef permeated the air... Eventually, the water will permeate through the surrounding concrete.* VERB V n V *through* n VERB V n V *through* n

**per|mis|sible** /pəʳmɪsəbᵊl/ If something is **permissible**, it is considered to be acceptable because it does not break any laws or rules. ❑ *Religious practices are permissible under the Constitution.* ADJ: usu v-link ADJ

**per|mis|sion** /pəʳmɪʃᵊn/ **(permissions)** [1] If someone who has authority over you gives you **permission to** do something, they say that they will allow you to do it. ❑ *He asked permission to leave the room... Finally his mother relented and gave permission for her youngest son to marry... They cannot leave the country without permission.* [2] A **permission** is a formal, written statement from an official group or place allowing you to do something. ❑ *...oil exploration permissions.* ➔ See also **planning permission**. ◆◇◇ N-UNCOUNT: oft N to-inf, N *for* n to-inf, N *for* n N-COUNT: usu pl

**per|mis|sive** /pəʳmɪsɪv/ A **permissive** person, society, or way of behaving allows or tolerates things which other people disapprove of. ❑ *...the permissive tolerance of the 1960s.* ♦ **per|mis|sive|ness** *Permissiveness and democracy go together.* ADJ N-UNCOUNT

**per|mit** **(permits, permitting, permitted)** ◆◇◇

✔ The verb is pronounced /pəʳmɪt/. The noun is pronounced /pɜːʳmɪt/.

[1] If someone **permits** something, they allow it to happen. If they **permit** you **to** do something, they allow you to do it. [FORMAL] ❑ *He can let the court's decision stand and permit the execution... Employees are permitted to use the golf course during their free hours... No outside journalists have been permitted into the country... If they appear to be under 12, then the doorman is not allowed to permit them entry to the film.* [2] A **permit** is an official document which says that you may do something. For example you usually need a **permit** to work in a foreign country. ❑ *The majority of foreign nationals working here have work permits.* [3] If a situation **permits** something, it makes it possible for that thing to exist, happen, or be done or it provides the opportunity for it. [FORMAL] ❑ *He sets about creating an environment that just doesn't permit experiment, it encourages it... Try to go out for a walk at lunchtime, if the weather permits... This method of cooking also permits heat to penetrate evenly from both sides.* [4] If you **permit yourself** something, you allow yourself to do something that you do not normally do or that you think you probably should not do. ❑ *Captain Bowen permitted himself one cigar a day... Only once in his life had Douglas permitted himself to lose control of his emotions.* [5] You can use **permit me** when you are about to say something or to make a suggestion. [FORMAL] ❑ *Permit me to give you some advice.* VERB V n V n to-inf *be* V-ed *into* n V n n N-COUNT VERB = *allow* V n V V n to-inf Also V *of* n VERB = *allow* V pron-refl n V pron-refl to-inf PHRASE: PHR to-inf [politeness] = *allow me*

**per|mu|ta|tion** /pɜːʳmjuːteɪʃᵊn/ **(permutations)** A **permutation** is one of the ways in which a number of things can be ordered or arranged. ❑ *Variation among humans is limited to the possible permutations of our genes.* N-COUNT: usu pl

**per|ni|cious** /pəʳnɪʃəs/ If you describe something as **pernicious**, you mean that it is very harmful. [FORMAL] ❑ *I did what I could, but her mother's influence was pernicious.* ADJ

**per|ni|cious anaemia** also **pernicious anemia. Pernicious anaemia** is a very severe blood disease. N-UNCOUNT

**per|nick|ety** /pəʳnɪkɪti/ If you describe someone as **pernickety**, you think that they pay too much attention to small, unimportant details. [BRIT, INFORMAL] ❑ *Customs officials can get extremely pernickety about things like that.* ADJ [disapproval] = *fussy*

✔ in AM, use **persnickety**

**pero|ra|tion** /perəreɪʃᵊn/ **(perorations)** [1] A **peroration** is the last part of a speech, especially the part where the speaker sums up his or her argument. [FORMAL] [2] If someone describes a speech as a **peroration**, they mean that they dislike it because they think it is very long and not worth listening to. [FORMAL] N-COUNT N-COUNT [disapproval]

**per|ox|ide** /pərɒksaɪd/ **(peroxides)** **Peroxide** is a chemical that is often used for making hair lighter in colour. It can also be used to kill germs. ➔ See also **hydrogen peroxide**. N-MASS

**per|ox|ide blonde** **(peroxide blondes)** You can refer to a woman whose hair has been artificially been made lighter in colour as a **peroxide blonde**, especially when you want to show that you disapprove of this, or that you think her hair looks unnatural or unattractive. N-COUNT

**per|pen|dicu|lar** /pɜːʳpəndɪkjʊləʳ/ [1] A **perpendicular** line or surface points straight up, rather than being sloping or horizontal. ❑ *We made two slits for the eyes and a perpendicular line for the nose... The sides of the loch are almost perpendicular.* [2] If one thing is **perpendicular to** another, it is at an angle of 90 degrees to it. [FORMAL] ❑ *The left wing dipped until it was perpendicular to the ground.* ADJ: usu ADJ n = *vertical* ADJ: usu v-link ADJ *to* n

**per|pe|trate** /pɜːʳpɪtreɪt/ **(perpetrates, perpetrating, perpetrated)** If someone **perpetrates** a crime or any other immoral or harmful act, they do it. [FORMAL] ❑ *A high proportion of crime in any country is perpetrated by young males in their teens and twenties.* ♦ **per|pe|tra|tion** /pɜːʳpɪtreɪʃᵊn/ *...a very small minority who persist in the perpetration of these crimes.* ♦ **per|pe|tra|tor** **(perpetrators)** *The perpetrator of this crime must be traced.* VERB = *commit* V n N-SING: usu N *of* n N-COUNT

**per|pet|ual** /pəʳpetʃuəl/ [1] A **perpetual** feeling, state, or quality is one that never ends or changes. ❑ *...the creation of a perpetual union.* ♦ **per|pet|ual|ly** *They were all perpetually starving.* [2] A **perpetual** act, situation, or state is one that happens again and again and so seems never to end. ❑ *I thought her perpetual complaints were going to prove too much for me.* ♦ **per|pet|ual|ly** *He perpetually interferes in political affairs.* ADJ: usu ADJ n = *permanent* ADV: ADV with v, ADV adj/prep ADJ: usu ADJ n ADV: ADV with v, ADV adj/prep

**per|pet|ual mo|tion** also **perpetual-motion.** The idea of **perpetual motion** is the idea of something continuing to move for ever without getting energy from anything else. N-UNCOUNT

**per|petu|ate** /pəʳpetʃueɪt/ **(perpetuates, perpetuating, perpetuated)** If someone or something **perpetuates** a situation, system, or belief, especially a bad one, they cause it to continue. ❑ *We must not perpetuate the religious divisions of the past... This image is a myth perpetuated by the media.* ♦ **per|petua|tion** /pəʳpetʃueɪʃᵊn/ *The perpetuation of nuclear deployments is morally unacceptable.* VERB V n V-ed N-SING: usu N *of* n

**per|pe|tu|ity** /pɜːʳpɪtjuːɪti/ If something is done **in perpetuity**, it is intended to last for ever. [FORMAL] ❑ *The US Government gave the land to the tribe in perpetuity.* PHRASE: PHR after v

**per|plex** /pəʳpleks/ **(perplexes, perplexing, perplexed)** If something **perplexes** you, it confuses and worries you because you do not understand it VERB or because it causes you difficulty. ❑ *It perplexed him because he was tackling it the wrong way.* V n

**per|plexed** /pəʳplekst/ If you are **perplexed**, you feel confused and slightly worried by something because you do not understand it. ❑ *She is perplexed about what to do for her daughter.* ADJ: usu v-link ADJ

**per|plex|ing** /pəʳpleksɪŋ/ If you find something **perplexing**, you do not understand it or do not know how to deal with it. ❑ *It took years to understand many perplexing diseases.* ADJ: usu ADJ n = puzzling

**per|plex|ity** /pəʳpleksɪti/ **(perplexities)** 1 **Perplexity** is a feeling of being confused and frustrated because you do not understand something. ❑ *He began counting them and then, with growing perplexity, counted them a second time.* N-UNCOUNT 2 The **perplexities** of something are those things about it which are difficult to understand because they are complicated. ❑ *...the perplexities of quantum mechanics.* N-COUNT: usu pl

**per|qui|site** /pɜːʳkwɪzɪt/ **(perquisites)** A **perquisite** is the same as a **perk**. [FORMAL] ❑ *...cost-free long-distance calls, a perquisite of her employment.* N-COUNT

**per se** /pɜːʳ seɪ/ **Per se** means 'by itself' or 'in itself', and is used when you are talking about the qualities of one thing considered on its own, rather than in connection with other things. ❑ *The authors' argument is not with the free market per se but with the western society in which it works.* ADV

**per|secute** /pɜːʳsɪkjuːt/ **(persecutes, persecuting, persecuted)** 1 If someone **is persecuted**, they are treated cruelly and unfairly, often because of their race or beliefs. ❑ *Mr Weaver and his family have been persecuted by the authorities for their beliefs... They began by brutally persecuting the Catholic Church. ...a persecuted minority.* VERB be V-ed V n V-ed 2 If you say that someone **is persecuting** you, you mean that they are deliberately making your life difficult. ❑ *He said his first wife persecuted him with her unreasonable demands.* VERB V n

**per|secu|tion** /pɜːʳsɪkjuːʃən/ **(persecutions)** **Persecution** is cruel and unfair treatment of a person or group, especially because of their religious or political beliefs, or their race. ❑ *...the persecution of minorities. ...victims of political persecution.* N-UNCOUNT: also N in pl

**per|secu|tor** /pɜːʳsɪkjuːtəʳ/ **(persecutors)** The **persecutors** of a person or group treat them cruelly and unfairly, especially because of their religious or political beliefs, or their race. N-COUNT: usu pl

**per|sever|ance** /pɜːʳsɪvɪərəns/ **Perseverance** is the quality of continuing with something even though it is difficult. N-UNCOUNT = persistence

**per|severe** /pɜːʳsɪvɪəʳ/ **(perseveres, persevering, persevered)** If you **persevere with** something, you keep trying to do it and do not give up, even though it is difficult. ❑ *...his ability to persevere despite obstacles and setbacks. ...a school with a reputation for persevering with difficult and disruptive children... She persevered in her idea despite obvious objections raised by friends.* ♦ **per|sever|ing** *He is a persevering, approachable family man.* VERB = persist V V with n V prep ADJ

**Per|sian** /pɜːʳʒən/ **(Persians)** 1 Something that is **Persian** belongs or relates to the ancient kingdom of Persia, or sometimes to the modern state of Iran. ADJ 2 **Persians** were the people who came from the ancient kingdom of Persia. N-COUNT 3 **Persian** carpets and rugs traditionally come from Iran. They are made by hand from silk or wool and usually have patterns in deep colours. ADJ 4 **Persian** is the language that is spoken in Iran, and was spoken in the ancient Persian empire. N-UNCOUNT

**Per|sian Gulf** **The Persian Gulf** is the area of sea between Saudi Arabia and Iran. N-PROPER: usu the N

**per|sim|mon** /pɜːʳsɪmən/ **(persimmons)** A **persimmon** is a soft, orange fruit that looks rather like a large tomato. Persimmons grow on trees in hot countries. N-COUNT

**per|sist** /pəʳsɪst/ **(persists, persisting, persisted)** 1 If something undesirable **persists**, it continues to exist. ❑ *Contact your doctor if the cough persists... These problems persisted for much of the decade.* VERB V V 2 If you **persist in** doing something, you continue to do it, even though it is difficult or other people are against it. ❑ *Why does Britain persist in running down its defence forces?... He urged the United States to persist with its efforts to bring about peace... 'You haven't answered me,' she persisted... When I set my mind to something, I persist.* VERB V in -ing V with/in n V with quote V

**per|sis|tence** /pəʳsɪstəns/ 1 If you have **persistence**, you continue to do something even though it is difficult or other people are against it. ❑ *Skill comes only with practice, patience and persistence.* N-UNCOUNT = perseverance 2 **The persistence of** something, especially something bad, is the fact of its continuing to exist for a long time. ❑ *...an expression of concern at the persistence of inflation and high interest rates.* N-UNCOUNT: usu the N of n

**per|sis|tent** /pəʳsɪstənt/ 1 Something that is **persistent** continues to exist or happen for a long time; used especially about bad or undesirable states or situations. ❑ *His cough grew more persistent until it never stopped... Shoppers picked their way through puddles caused by persistent rain.* ADJ 2 Someone who is **persistent** continues trying to do something, even though it is difficult or other people are against it. ❑ *...a persistent critic of the government's transport policies.* ADJ

**per|sis|tent|ly** /pəʳsɪstəntli/ 1 If something happens **persistently**, it happens again and again or for a long time. ❑ *The allegations have been persistently denied by ministers.* ADV: ADV with v, ADV adj 2 If someone does something **persistently**, they do it with determination even though it is difficult or other people are against it. ❑ *Rachel gently but persistently imposed her will upon Douglas.* ADV: ADV with v

**per|sis|tent veg|eta|tive state** **(persistent vegetative states)** If someone is in a **persistent vegetative state**, they are unable to think, speak, or move because they have severe brain damage, and their condition is not likely to improve. [MEDICAL] N-COUNT

**per|snick|ety** /pəʳsnɪkɪti/ If you describe someone as **persnickety**, you think that they pay too much attention to small, unimportant details. [AM, INFORMAL] ❑ *He is a very rigorous man, very persnickety.* ADJ disapproval = fussy

✔ in BRIT, use **pernickety**

**per|son** /pɜːʳsən/ **(people, persons)** ♦♦♦

✔ The usual word for 'more than one person' is **people**. The form **persons** is used as the plural in formal or legal language.

1 A **person** is a man, woman, or child. ❑ *At least one person died and several others were injured... Everyone knows he's the only person who can do the job... The amount of sleep we need varies from person to person.* N-COUNT 2 **Persons** is used as the plural of **person** in formal, legal, and technical writing. ❑ *...removal of the right of accused persons to remain silent.* N-PLURAL 3 If you talk about someone **as a person**, you are considering them from the point of view of their real nature. ❑ *Robin didn't feel good about herself as a person.* N-COUNT 4 If someone says, for example, **'I'm an outdoor person'** or **'I'm not a coffee person'**, they are saying whether or not they like that particular activity or thing. [mainly SPOKEN] ❑ *I am not a country person at all. I prefer the cities.* N-COUNT: a supp N 5 If you do something **in person**, you do it yourself rather than letting someone else do it for you. ❑ *She went to New York to receive the award in person.* PHRASE: PHR after v 6 If you meet, hear, or see someone **in person**, you are in the same place as them, rather than, for example, speaking to them on the telephone, writing to them, or seeing them on television. ❑ *It was the first time she had seen him in person.* PHRASE: PHR after v 7 Your **person** is your body. [FORMAL] ❑ *The suspect had refused to give any details of his identity and had carried no documents on his person.* N-COUNT: poss N 8 You can use **in the person of** when mentioning the name of someone you have just referred to in a more general or indirect way. [WRITTEN] ❑ *We had a knowledgeable guide in the person of George Adams.* PHRASE: PHR n 9 In grammar, we use the term **first person** N-COUNT:

when referring to 'I' and 'we', **second person** when referring to 'you', and **third person** when referring to 'he', 'she', 'it', 'they', and all other noun groups. **Person** is also used like this when referring to the verb forms that go with these pronouns and noun groups. → See also **first person**, **second person**, **third person**. usu supp N

**-person** /-pɜːʳsᵊn/ **(-people** or **-persons)** [1] **-person** is added to numbers to form adjectives which indicate how many people are involved in something or can use something. **People** is not used in this way. ❑ *...two-person households. ...the spa's 32-person staff. ...his 1971 one-person exhibition.* COMB in ADJ: ADJ n [2] **-person** is added to nouns to form nouns which refer to someone who does a particular job or is in a particular group. **-person** is used by people who do not want to use a term which indicates whether someone is a man or a woman. **-people** can also be used in this way. ❑ *...Mrs. Sahana Pradhan, chairperson of the United Leftist Front... He had a staff of six salespeople working for him.* COMB in N-COUNT

**per|so|na** /pəʳsoʊnə/ **(personas** or **personae** /pəʳsoʊnaɪ/**)** Someone's **persona** is the aspect of their character or nature that they present to other people, perhaps in contrast to their real character or nature. [FORMAL] ❑ *...the contradictions between her private life and the public persona.* → See also **persona non grata**. N-COUNT = image

**per|son|able** /pɜːʳsənəbᵊl/ Someone who is **personable** has a pleasant appearance and character. ❑ *The people I met were intelligent, mature, personable.* ADJ [approval]

**per|son|age** /pɜːʳsənɪdʒ/ **(personages)** [1] A **personage** is a famous or important person. [FORMAL] ❑ *...MPs, film stars and other important personages.* N-COUNT [2] A **personage** is a character in a play or book, or in history. [FORMAL] ❑ *There is no evidence for such a historical personage.* N-COUNT

**per|son|al** /pɜːʳsənᵊl/ ◆◆◇ [1] A **personal** opinion, quality, or thing belongs or relates to one particular person rather than to other people. ❑ *He learned this lesson the hard way – from his own personal experience... That's my personal opinion. ...books, furniture, and other personal belongings. ...an estimated personal fortune of almost seventy million dollars.* ADJ: ADJ n [2] If you give something your **personal** care or attention, you deal with it yourself rather than letting someone else deal with it. ❑ *...a business that requires a great deal of personal contact. ...a personal letter from the President's secretary.* ADJ: usu ADJ n [3] **Personal** matters relate to your feelings, relationships, and health. ❑ *...teaching young people about marriage and personal relationships... You never allow personal problems to affect your performance.* ADJ [4] **Personal** comments refer to someone's appearance or character in an offensive way. ❑ *Newspapers resorted to personal abuse.* ADJ [5] **Personal** care involves looking after your body and appearance. ❑ *...men who take as much trouble over personal hygiene as women.* ADJ: ADJ n [6] A **personal** relationship is one that is not connected with your job or public life. ❑ *He was a personal friend whom I've known for many many years.* ADJ [7] → See also **personals**.

**per|son|al as|sis|tant (personal assistants)** A **personal assistant** is a person who does office work and administrative work for someone. The abbreviation **PA** is also used. [BUSINESS] N-COUNT

**per|son|al best (personal bests)** A sports player's **personal best** is the highest score or fastest time that they have ever achieved. ❑ *She ran a personal best of 13.01 sec.* N-COUNT: usu sing

**per|son|al col|umn (personal columns)** The **personal column** in a newspaper or magazine contains messages for individual people and advertisements of a private nature. [mainly BRIT] N-COUNT

✔ in AM, usually use **personals**

**per|son|al com|put|er (personal computers)** A **personal computer** is a computer that is used by one person at a time in a business, a school, or at home. The abbreviation **PC** is also used. N-COUNT

**per|son|al dig|ital as|sis|tant (personal digital assistants)** A **personal digital assistant** is a hand-held computer, used mainly for storing and accessing personal information such as addresses, telephone numbers, and memos. The abbreviation **PDA** is also used. N-COUNT

**per|son|al|ity** /pɜːʳsənælɪti/ **(personalities)** ◆◇◇ [1] Your **personality** is your whole character and nature. ❑ *She has such a kind, friendly personality... Through sheer force of personality Hugh Trenchard had got his way... The contest was as much about personalities as it was about politics.* N-VAR: usu with supp [2] If someone has **personality** or is a **personality**, they have a strong and lively character. ❑ *...a woman of great personality... He is such a personality – he is so funny.* N-VAR: usu with supp = character [3] You can refer to a famous person, especially in entertainment, broadcasting, or sport, as a **personality**. ❑ *...the radio and television personality, Jimmy Saville.* N-COUNT

**per|son|al|ize** /pɜːʳsənᵊlaɪz/ **(personalizes, personalizing, personalized)**

✔ in BRIT, also use **personalise**

[1] If an object **is personalized**, it is marked with the name or initials of its owner. ❑ *The clock has easy-to-read numbers and is personalised with the child's name and birth date.* VERB: usu passive be V-ed ♦ **per|son|al|ized** *...a Rolls-Royce with a personalised number plate.* ADJ: ADJ n [2] If you **personalize** something, you do or design it specially according to the needs of an individual or to your own needs. ❑ *Personalising your car has never been cheaper. ...an ideal centre for professional men or women who need intensive, personalised French courses.* VERB V n V-ed [3] If you **personalize** an argument, discussion, idea, or issue, you consider it from the point of view of individual people and their characters or relationships, rather than considering the facts in a general or abstract way. ❑ *Women tend to personalise rejection more than men... The contest has become personalised, if not bitter.* VERB V n V-ed Also V

**per|son|al|ly** /pɜːʳsənəli/ ◆◇◇ [1] You use **personally** to emphasize that you are giving your own opinion. ❑ *Personally I think it's a waste of time... You can disagree about them, and I personally do, but they are great ideas that have made people think.* ADV: ADV with cl [emphasis] [2] If you do something **personally**, you do it yourself rather than letting someone else do it. ❑ *The minister is returning to Paris to answer the allegations personally... When the great man arrived, the club's manager personally escorted him upstairs.* ADV: ADV with v [3] If you meet or know someone **personally**, you meet or know them in real life, rather than knowing about them or knowing their work. ❑ *He did not know them personally, but he was familiar with their reputation.* ADV: ADV with v [4] You can use **personally** to say that something refers to an individual person rather than to other people. ❑ *He was personally responsible for all that the people had suffered under his rule... In order for me to spend three months on something it has to interest me personally.* ADV: ADV with v, ADV adj [5] You can use **personally** to show that you are talking about someone's private life rather than their professional or public life. ❑ *This has taken a great toll on me personally and professionally.* ADV: oft ADV with cl [6] If you **take** someone's remarks **personally**, you are upset because you think that they are criticizing you in particular. ❑ *Remember, stick to the issues and don't take it personally.* PHRASE: V inflects

**per|son|al or|gan|iz|er (personal organizers)**

✔ in BRIT, also use **personal organiser**

A **personal organizer** is a book containing personal or business information, which you can add pages to or remove pages from to keep the information up to date. Small computers with a similar function are also called **personal organizers**. N-COUNT

**per|son|al pro|noun (personal pronouns)** A **personal pronoun** is a pronoun such as 'I', N-COUNT 'you', 'she', or 'they' which is used to refer to the speaker or the person spoken to, or to a person or thing whose identity is clear, usually because they have already been mentioned.

**per|son|als** /pɜːʳsənᵊlz/ The section in a newspaper or magazine which contains messages for individual people and advertisements of a private nature is called **the personals**. [AM] N-PLURAL: usu *the* N

✔ in BRIT, usually use **personal column**

**per|son|al space** [1] If someone invades your **personal space**, they stand or lean too close to you, so that you feel uncomfortable. N-UNCOUNT: oft poss N [2] If you need your **personal space**, you need time on your own, with the freedom to do something that you want to do or to think about something. ❑ *Self-confidence means being relaxed enough to allow your lover their personal space.* N-UNCOUNT: oft poss N

**per|son|al ste|reo** **(personal stereos)** A **personal stereo** is a small cassette or CD player with very light headphones, which people carry round so that they can listen to music while doing something else. N-COUNT = *Walkman*

**per|so|na non gra|ta** /pəʳsoʊnə nɒn grɑːtə/ **(personae non gratae)** If someone becomes or is declared **persona non grata**, they become unwelcome or unacceptable because of something they have said or done. ❑ *The government has declared the French ambassador persona non grata and ordered him to leave the country.* PHRASE: PHR after v, v-link PHR

**per|soni|fi|ca|tion** /pəʳsɒnɪfɪkeɪʃᵊn/ **(personifications)** If you say that someone is **the personification of** a particular thing or quality, you mean that they are a perfect example of that thing or that they have a lot of that quality. ❑ *He was usually the personification of kindness.* N-SING: usu *the* N *of* n

**per|soni|fy** /pəʳsɒnɪfaɪ/ **(personifies, personifying, personified)** If you say that someone **personifies** a particular thing or quality, you mean that they seem to be a perfect example of that thing, or to have that quality to a very large degree. ❑ *She seemed to personify goodness and nobility...* V n *On other occasions she can be charm personified.* V-ed VERB

**per|son|nel** /pɜːʳsənel/ ◆◇◇ [1] The **personnel** of an organization are the people who work for it. ❑ *Since 1954 Japan has never dispatched military personnel abroad... There has been very little renewal of personnel in higher education.* N-PLURAL: oft N n = *staff* [2] **Personnel** is the department in a large company or organization that deals with employees, keeps their records, and helps with any problems they might have. [BUSINESS] ❑ *Her first job was in personnel.* N-UNCOUNT = *human resources*

**person-to-person** If you make a **person-to-person** call, you say that you want to talk to one person in particular. If that person cannot come to the telephone, you do not have to pay for the call. [FORMAL] ADJ

**per|spec|tive** /pəʳspektɪv/ **(perspectives)** ◆◇◇ [1] A particular **perspective** is a particular way of thinking about something, especially one that is influenced by your beliefs or experiences. ❑ *He says the death of his father 18 months ago has given him a new perspective on life... Most literature on the subject of immigrants in France has been written from the perspective of the French themselves... I would like to offer a historical perspective.* N-COUNT: usu with supp [2] If you get something **in perspective** or **into perspective**, you judge its real importance by considering it in relation to everything else. If you get something **out of perspective**, you fail to judge its real importance in relation to everything else. ❑ *Remember to keep things in perspective... It helps to put their personal problems into perspective... I let things get out of perspective.* PHRASE: PHR after v [3] **Perspective** is the art of making some objects or people in a picture look further away than others. N-UNCOUNT

**per|spex** /pɜːʳspeks/ also **Perspex**. **Perspex** is a strong clear plastic which is sometimes used instead of glass. [BRIT, TRADEMARK] N-UNCOUNT: usu N n

**per|spi|ca|cious** /pɜːʳspɪkeɪʃəs/ Someone who is **perspicacious** notices, realizes, and understands things quickly. [FORMAL] ❑ *...one of the most perspicacious and perceptive historians of that period.* ADJ = *perceptive* ♦ **per|spi|cac|ity** /pɜːʳspɪkæsɪti/ *Channel 4's overseas buyers have foreseen the audience demand with their usual perspicacity.* N-UNCOUNT

**per|spi|ra|tion** /pɜːʳspɪreɪʃᵊn/ **Perspiration** is the liquid which comes out on the surface of your skin when you are hot or frightened. [FORMAL] ❑ *His hands were wet with perspiration.* N-UNCOUNT = *sweat*

**per|spire** /pəʳspaɪəʳ/ **(perspires, perspiring, perspired)** When you **perspire**, a liquid comes out on the surface of your skin, because you are hot or frightened. [FORMAL] ❑ *He began to perspire heavily.* V *...mopping their perspiring brows.* V-ing VERB = *sweat*

**per|suade** /pəʳsweɪd/ **(persuades, persuading, persuaded)** ◆◇◇ [1] If you **persuade** someone **to** do something, you cause them to do it by giving them good reasons for doing it. ❑ *My husband persuaded me to come...* V n to-inf *They were eventually persuaded by the police to give themselves up.* Also V n *into* n/-ing, V n VERB ♦ **per|suad|er** **(persuaders)** *All great persuaders and salesmen are the same.* N-COUNT [2] If something **persuades** someone **to** take a particular course of action, it causes them to take that course of action because it is a good reason for doing so. ❑ *The Conservative Party's victory in April's general election persuaded him to run for President again.* V n to-inf VERB [3] If you **persuade** someone **that** something is true, you say things that eventually make them believe that it is true. ❑ *I've persuaded Mrs Tennant that it's time she retired...* V n that *Derek persuaded me of the feasibility of the idea.* V n *of* n VERB = *convince* ♦ **per|suad|ed** *He is not persuaded of the need for electoral reform.* ADJ: v-link ADJ, ADJ *of* n, ADJ that

**per|sua|sion** /pəʳsweɪʒᵊn/ **(persuasions)** [1] **Persuasion** is the act of persuading someone to do something or to believe that something is true. ❑ *She was using all her powers of persuasion to induce the Griffins to remain in Rollway.* N-UNCOUNT [2] If you are **of** a particular **persuasion**, you have a particular belief or set of beliefs. [FORMAL] ❑ *It is a national movement and has within it people of all political persuasions.* N-COUNT: usu with supp

**per|sua|sive** /pəʳsweɪsɪv/ Someone or something that is **persuasive** is likely to persuade a person to believe or do a particular thing. ❑ *What do you think were some of the more persuasive arguments on the other side?... I can be very persuasive when I want to be.* ADJ ♦ **per|sua|sive|ly** *...a trained lawyer who can present arguments persuasively.* ADV: ADV with v ♦ **per|sua|sive|ness** *He has the personality and the persuasiveness to make you change your mind.* N-UNCOUNT

**pert** /pɜːʳt/ [1] If someone describes a young woman as **pert**, they mean that they like her because she is lively and not afraid to say what she thinks. This use could cause offence. ❑ *...a pert redhead in uniform. ...pert replies by servant girls.* ADJ [2] If you say that someone has, for example, a **pert** bottom or nose, you mean that it is quite small and neat, and you think it is attractive. ADJ [approval]

**per|tain** /pəʳteɪn/ **(pertains, pertaining, pertained)** If one thing **pertains to** another, it relates, belongs, or applies to it. [FORMAL] ❑ *...matters pertaining to naval district defense.* V *to* n VERB

**per|ti|na|cious** /pɜːʳtɪneɪʃəs/ Someone who is **pertinacious** continues trying to do something difficult rather than giving up quickly. [FORMAL] ADJ

**per|ti|nent** /pɜːʳtɪnənt/ Something that is **pertinent** is relevant to a particular subject. [FORMAL] ❑ *She had asked some pertinent questions. ...knowledge and skills pertinent to classroom teaching.* ADJ: oft ADJ *to* n

**per|turb** /pəʳtɜːʳb/ **(perturbs, perturbing, perturbed)** If something **perturbs** you, it worries you quite a lot. [FORMAL] ❑ *What perturbs me is that magazine articles are so much shorter nowadays.* V n VERB → See also **perturbed**.

**per|tur|ba|tion** /pɜːʳtəʳbeɪʃᵊn/ **(perturbations)** [1] A **perturbation** is a small change in the movement, quality, or behaviour of something, especially an unusual change. [TECHNICAL] N-VAR

❑ *...perturbations in Jupiter's gravitational field.* 2 **Perturbation** is worry caused by some event. [FORMAL] ❑ *This message caused perturbation in the Middle East Headquarters.* N-UNCOUNT = *alarm*

**per|turbed** /pəʳtɜ:ʳbd/ If someone is **perturbed by** something, they are worried by it. [FORMAL] ❑ *He apparently was not perturbed by the prospect of a policeman coming to call.* ADJ: usu v-link ADJ, oft ADJ *by/at* n, ADJ that = *alarmed*

**per|tus|sis** /pəʳtʌsɪs/ **Pertussis** is the medical term for **whooping cough**. N-UNCOUNT

**pe|rus|al** /pəru:zəl/ **Perusal of** something such as a letter, article, or document is the action of reading it. [FORMAL] ❑ *Peter Cooke undertook to send each of us a sample contract for perusal.* N-UNCOUNT: also *a* N

**pe|ruse** /pəʳru:z/ **(peruses, perusing, perused)** If you **peruse** something such as a letter, article, or document, you read it. [FORMAL] ❑ *We perused the company's financial statements for the past five years.* VERB V n

**Pe|ru|vian** /pəru:viən/ **(Peruvians) Peruvian** means belonging or related to Peru, or to its people or culture. ♦ A **Peruvian** is someone who is Peruvian. ADJ N-COUNT

**per|vade** /pəʳveɪd/ **(pervades, pervading, pervaded)** If something **pervades** a place or thing, it is a noticeable feature throughout it. [FORMAL] ❑ *The smell of sawdust and glue pervaded the factory... Throughout the book there is a pervading sense of menace.* VERB V n V-ing

**per|va|sive** /pəʳveɪsɪv/ Something, especially something bad, that is **pervasive** is present or felt throughout a place or thing. [FORMAL] ❑ *...the pervasive influence of the army in national life.* ♦ **per|va|sive|ness** *...the pervasiveness of computer technology.* ADJ N-UNCOUNT

**per|verse** /pəʳvɜ:ʳs/ Someone who is **perverse** deliberately does things that are unreasonable or that result in harm for themselves. ❑ *It would be perverse to stop this healthy trend... In some perverse way the ill-matched partners do actually need each other.* ♦ **per|verse|ly** *She was perversely pleased to be causing trouble.* ADJ: oft *it* v-link ADJ to-inf [disapproval] ADV: usu ADV with v

**per|ver|sion** /pəʳvɜ:ʳʃən, -ʒən/ **(perversions)** 1 You can refer to a sexual desire or action that you consider to be abnormal and unacceptable as a **perversion**. 2 A **perversion of** something is a form of it that is bad or wrong, or the changing of it into this form. ❑ *What monstrous perversion of the human spirit leads a sniper to open fire on a bus carrying children?* N-VAR [disapproval] N-VAR: usu with supp [disapproval]

**per|vert** **(perverts, perverting, perverted)**

> The verb is pronounced /pəʳvɜ:ʳt/. The noun is pronounced /pɜ:ʳvɜ:ʳt/.

1 If you **pervert** something such as a process or society, you interfere with it so that it is not as good as it used to be or as it should be. [FORMAL] ❑ *Any reform will destroy and pervert our constitution.* 2 If someone **perverts the course of justice**, they deliberately do something that will make it difficult to discover who really committed a particular crime, for example, destroying evidence or lying to the police. [LEGAL] ❑ *He was charged with conspiring to pervert the course of justice.* 3 If you say that someone is a **pervert**, you mean that you consider their behaviour, especially their sexual behaviour, to be immoral or unacceptable. VERB [disapproval] V n PHRASE: V inflects N-COUNT [disapproval]

**per|vert|ed** /pəʳvɜ:ʳtɪd/ 1 If you say that someone is **perverted**, you mean that you consider their behaviour, especially their sexual behaviour, to be immoral or unacceptable. ❑ *You've been protecting sick and perverted men.* 2 You can use **perverted** to describe actions or ideas which you think are wrong, unnatural, or harmful. ❑ *...a perverted form of knowledge.* ADJ [disapproval] ADJ [disapproval]

**pe|seta** /pəseɪtə/ **(pesetas)** The **peseta** was the unit of money that was used in Spain before it was replaced by the euro. N-COUNT

**pesky** /peski/ **Pesky** means irritating. [INFORMAL] ❑ *...as if he were a pesky tourist asking silly questions of a busy man.* ADJ: ADJ n

**peso** /peɪsoʊ/ **(pesos)** The **peso** is the unit of money that is used in Argentina, Colombia, Cuba, the Dominican Republic, Mexico, the Philippines, and Uruguay. N-COUNT

**pes|sa|ry** /pesəri/ **(pessaries)** 1 A **pessary** is a small block of a medicine or a contraceptive chemical that a woman puts in her vagina. 2 A **pessary** is a device that is put in a woman's vagina to support her womb. N-COUNT N-COUNT

**pes|si|mism** /pesɪmɪzəm/ **Pessimism** is the belief that bad things are going to happen. ❑ *...universal pessimism about the economy... My first reaction was one of deep pessimism.* N-UNCOUNT: oft N *about/over* n ≠ *optimism*

**pes|si|mist** /pesɪmɪst/ **(pessimists)** A **pessimist** is someone who thinks that bad things are going to happen. ❑ *I'm a natural pessimist; I usually expect the worst.* N-COUNT ≠ *optimist*

**pes|si|mis|tic** /pesɪmɪstɪk/ Someone who is **pessimistic** thinks that bad things are going to happen. ❑ *Not everyone is so pessimistic about the future... Hardy has often been criticised for an excessively pessimistic view of life.* ♦ **pes|si|mis|ti|cal|ly** /pesɪmɪstɪkli/ *'But it'll not happen,' she concluded pessimistically.* ADJ: oft ADJ *about* n ≠ *optimistic* ADV: ADV with v

**pest** /pest/ **(pests)** 1 **Pests** are insects or small animals which damage crops or food supplies. ❑ *...crops which are resistant to some of the major insect pests and diseases. ...new and innovative methods of pest control.* 2 You can describe someone, especially a child, as a **pest** if they keep bothering you. [INFORMAL] ❑ *He climbed on the table, pulled my hair, and was generally a pest.* N-COUNT N-COUNT [disapproval] = *nuisance*

**pes|ter** /pestəʳ/ **(pesters, pestering, pestered)** If you say that someone **is pestering** you, you mean that they keep asking you to do something, or keep talking to you, and you find this annoying. ❑ *I thought she'd stop pestering me, but it only seemed to make her worse... I know he gets fed up with people pestering him for money. ...that creep who's been pestering you to go out with him.* VERB [disapproval] V n V n prep V n to-inf Also V

**pes|ti|cide** /pestɪsaɪd/ **(pesticides) Pesticides** are chemicals which farmers put on their crops to kill harmful insects. N-MASS

**pes|ti|lence** /pestɪləns/ **(pestilences) Pestilence** is any disease that spreads quickly and kills large numbers of people. [LITERARY] N-VAR

**pes|ti|len|tial** /pestɪlenʃəl/ 1 **Pestilential** is used to refer to things that cause disease or are caused by disease. [FORMAL] ❑ *...people who were dependent for their water supply on this pestilential stream. ...a pestilential fever.* 2 **Pestilential** animals destroy crops or exist in such large numbers that they cause harm. [FORMAL] ADJ: ADJ n ADJ: ADJ n

**pes|tle** /pesəl/ **(pestles)** A **pestle** is a short rod with a thick round end. It is used for crushing things such as herbs, spices, or grain in a bowl called a mortar. N-COUNT

**pes|to** /pestoʊ/ **Pesto** is an Italian sauce made from basil, garlic, pine nuts, cheese, and olive oil. N-UNCOUNT

**pet** /pet/ **(pets, petting, petted)** 1 A **pet** is an animal that you keep in your home to give you company and pleasure. ❑ *It is plainly cruel to keep turtles as pets. ...a bachelor living alone in a flat with his pet dog.* 2 Someone's **pet** theory, project, or subject is one that they particularly support or like. ❑ *He would not stand by and let his pet project be killed off.* 3 If you **pet** a person or animal, you touch them in an affectionate way. ❑ *The policeman reached down and petted the wolfhound.* ◆◇◇ N-COUNT ADJ VERB V n

**pet|al** /petəl/ **(petals)** The **petals** of a flower are the thin coloured or white parts which together form the flower. ❑ *...bowls of dried rose petals.* N-COUNT

**pe|tard** /petɑ:ʳd/ **(petards)** If someone who has planned to harm someone else is **hoist with** their **own petard** or **hoist by** their **own petard**, their plan in fact results in harm to themselves. ❑ *The students were hoist by their own petards, however, as Granada decided to transmit the programme anyway.* PHRASE: N inflects

**pe|ter** /piːtəʳ/ **(peters, petering, petered)**
♦ **peter out** If something **peters out**, it gradually comes to an end. ❑ *The six-month strike seemed to be petering out.* PHRASAL VERB V P

**Peter** If you say that someone **is robbing Peter to pay Paul**, you mean that they are transferring money from one group of people or place to another, rather than providing extra money. ❑ *Sometimes he was moving money from one account to another, robbing Peter to pay Paul.* PHRASE: *rob* inflects [disapproval]

**pet|it bour|geois** /peti bʊəʳʒwɑː/ also **petty bourgeois.** Someone or something that is **petit bourgeois** belongs or relates to the lower middle class. ❑ *He had a petit bourgeois mentality.* ADJ [disapproval]

**pet|it bour|geoi|sie** /peti bʊəʳʒwɑːziː/ also **petty bourgeoisie. The petit bourgeoisie** are people in the lower middle class. N-SING-COLL: *the* N [disapproval]

**pe|tite** /pətiːt/ If you describe a woman as **petite**, you are politely saying that she is small and is not fat. ADJ

**pet|it four** /peti fɔːʳ/ **(petits fours** or **petit fours) Petits fours** are very small sweet cakes. They are sometimes served with coffee at the end of a meal. N-COUNT: usu pl

**pe|ti|tion** /pətɪʃən/ **(petitions, petitioning, petitioned)** [1] A **petition** is a document signed by a lot of people which asks a government or other official group to do a particular thing. ❑ *We recently presented the government with a petition signed by 4,500 people.* N-COUNT: usu with supp [2] A **petition** is a formal request made to a court of law for some legal action to be taken. [LEGAL] ❑ *His lawyers filed a petition for all charges to be dropped.* N-COUNT [3] If you **petition** someone in authority, you make a formal request to them. [FORMAL or LEGAL] ❑ *...couples petitioning for divorce... All the attempts to petition the Congress had failed... She's petitioning to regain custody of the child.* VERB V *for* n V n V to-inf

**pe|ti|tion|er** /pətɪʃənəʳ/ **(petitioners)** [1] A **petitioner** is a person who presents or signs a petition. N-COUNT [2] A **petitioner** is a person who brings a legal case to a court of law. [LEGAL] ❑ *The judge awarded the costs of the case to the petitioners.* N-COUNT

**pet name (pet names)** A **pet name** is a special name that you use for a close friend or a member of your family instead of using their real name. N-COUNT

**pet|rel** /petrəl/ **(petrels)** A **petrel** is a type of sea bird which often flies a long way from land. There are many kinds of petrel. N-COUNT

**pet|ri|fied** /petrɪfaɪd/ [1] If you are **petrified**, you are extremely frightened, perhaps so frightened that you cannot think or move. ❑ *I've always been petrified of being alone... Most people seem to be petrified of snakes.* ADJ: oft ADJ *of* n/-ing, ADJ that = *terrified* [2] A **petrified** plant or animal has died and has gradually turned into stone. ❑ *...a block of petrified wood.* ADJ: ADJ n

**pet|ri|fy** /petrɪfaɪ/ **(petrifies, petrifying, petrified)** If something **petrifies** you, it makes you feel very frightened. ❑ *Prison petrifies me and I don't want to go there.* ♦ **pet|ri|fy|ing** *I found the climb absolutely petrifying.* VERB = *terrify* V n ADJ = *terrifying*

**pet|ro|chemi|cal** /petroʊkemɪkəl/ **(petrochemicals)** also **petro-chemical. Petrochemicals** are chemicals that are obtained from petroleum or natural gas. N-COUNT: usu pl

**pet|ro|dol|lars** /petroʊdɒləʳz/ also **petrodollars. Petrodollars** are a unit of money used to calculate how much a country has earned by exporting petroleum or natural gas. N-PLURAL

**pet|rol** /petrəl/ **Petrol** is a liquid which is used as a fuel for motor vehicles. [BRIT] N-UNCOUNT

✓ in AM, use **gas, gasoline**

**pet|rol bomb (petrol bombs)** A **petrol bomb** is a simple bomb consisting of a bottle full of petrol with a cloth in it that is lit just before the bottle is thrown. [mainly BRIT] N-COUNT

✓ in AM, use **Molotov cocktail**

**pe|tro|leum** /pətroʊliəm/ **Petroleum** is oil which is found under the surface of the earth or under the sea bed. Petrol and paraffin are obtained from petroleum. N-UNCOUNT

**pe|tro|leum jel|ly Petroleum jelly** is a soft, clear substance obtained from oil or petroleum. It is put on the skin to protect or soften it, or put on surfaces to make them move against each other easily. N-UNCOUNT

**pet|rol sta|tion (petrol stations)** A **petrol station** is a garage by the side of the road where petrol is sold and put into vehicles. [BRIT] N-COUNT

✓ in AM, use **gas station**

**pet|rol tank (petrol tanks)** The **petrol tank** in a motor vehicle is the container for petrol. [BRIT] N-COUNT

✓ in AM, use **gas tank**

**pet|ti|coat** /petikoʊt/ **(petticoats)** A **petticoat** is a piece of clothing like a thin skirt, which is worn under a skirt or dress. [OLD-FASHIONED] N-COUNT

**pet|ti|fog|ging** /petifɒgɪŋ/ You can describe an action or situation as **pettifogging** when you think that unnecessary attention is being paid to unimportant, boring details. [OLD-FASHIONED] ❑ *...pettifogging bureaucratic interference.* ADJ: ADJ n [disapproval]

**pet|ting** /petɪŋ/ [1] **Petting** is when two people kiss and touch each other in a sexual way, but without having sexual intercourse. N-UNCOUNT [2] A **petting** zoo or a **petting** farm is a place with animals which small children can safely stroke or play with. N-UNCOUNT: N n

**pet|ty** /peti/ **(pettier, pettiest)** [1] You can use **petty** to describe things such as problems, rules, or arguments which you think are unimportant or relate to unimportant things. ❑ *He was miserable all the time and rows would start over petty things. ...endless rules and petty regulations.* ADJ: usu ADJ n [disapproval] [2] If you describe someone's behaviour as **petty**, you mean that they care too much about small, unimportant things and perhaps that they are unnecessarily unkind. ❑ *I think that attitude is a bit petty.* ADJ: usu v-link ADJ [disapproval] ♦ **pet|ti|ness** *Never had she met such spite and pettiness.* N-UNCOUNT [3] **Petty** is used of people or actions that are less important, serious, or great than others. ❑ *...petty crime, such as handbag-snatching and minor break-ins.* ADJ: ADJ n

**pet|ty bour|geois** → see **petit bourgeois.**

**pet|ty bour|geoi|sie** → see **petit bourgeoisie.**

**pet|ty cash Petty cash** is money that is kept in the office of a company, for making small payments in cash when necessary. [BUSINESS] N-UNCOUNT

**pet|ty of|fic|er (petty officers)** A **petty officer** is an officer of low rank in the navy. N-COUNT; N-TITLE

**petu|lance** /petʃʊləns/ **Petulance** is unreasonable, childish bad temper over something unimportant. ❑ *His petulance made her impatient.* N-UNCOUNT

**petu|lant** /petʃʊlənt/ Someone who is **petulant** is unreasonably angry and upset in a childish way. ❑ *His critics say he's just being silly and petulant.* ♦ **petu|lant|ly** *'I don't need help,' he said petulantly.* ADJ ADV: ADV with v

**pe|tu|nia** /pɪtjuːniə, AM -tuː-/ **(petunias)** A **petunia** is a type of garden plant with pink, white, or purple flowers shaped like short, wide cones. N-COUNT

**pew** /pjuː/ **(pews)** A **pew** is a long wooden seat with a back, which people sit on in church. ❑ *Claire sat in the front pew.* N-COUNT

**pew|ter** /pjuːtəʳ/ **Pewter** is a grey metal which is made by mixing tin and lead. Pewter was often used in former times to make ornaments or containers for eating and drinking. ❑ *...pewter plates. ...the best 18th century pewter.* N-UNCOUNT: oft N n

**PG** /piː dʒiː/ In Britain, films that are labelled **PG** are not considered suitable for younger children to see without an adult being with them. **PG** is an abbreviation for 'parental guidance'.

**PG-13** /piː dʒiː θɜːʳtiːn/ In the United States, films that are labelled **PG-13** are not considered suitable for children under the age of thirteen, but parents can decide whether or not to allow their children to see the films. **PG** is an abbreviation for 'parental guidance'.

**PGCE** /piː dʒiː siː iː/ **(PGCEs)** In Britain, a **PGCE** is a teaching qualification that qualifies someone with a degree to teach in a state school. **PGCE** is an abbreviation for 'Postgraduate Certificate of Education'. Compare **BEd**. N-COUNT

**pH** /piː eɪtʃ/ The **pH of** a solution indicates how acid or alkaline the solution is. A pH of less than 7 indicates that it is an acid, and a pH of more than 7 indicates that it is an alkali. ❑ *...the pH of sea water... Skin is naturally slightly acidic and has a pH of 5.5.* N-UNCOUNT: also *a* N, oft N *of* n, N num

**phal|anx** /fælæŋks/ **(phalanxes** or **phalanges** /fəlændʒiːz/**)** 1 A **phalanx** is a group of soldiers or police who are standing or marching close together ready to fight. [FORMAL] N-COUNT 2 A **phalanx of** people is a large group who are brought together for a particular purpose. [FORMAL] ❑ *...a phalanx of waiters.* N-COUNT: usu N *of* n

**phal|lic** /fælɪk/ Something that is **phallic** is shaped like an erect penis. It can also relate to male sexual powers. ❑ *...a phallic symbol.* ADJ: usu ADJ n

**phal|lus** /fæləs/ **(phalluses** or **phalli** /fælaɪ/**)** 1 A **phallus** is a model of an erect penis, especially one used as a symbol in ancient religions. N-COUNT 2 A **phallus** is a penis. [TECHNICAL] N-COUNT

**phan|tas|ma|go|ri|cal** /fæntæzməgɒrɪkəl, AM -gɔːr-/ **Phantasmagorical** means very strange, like something in a dream. [LITERARY] ADJ: usu ADJ n

**phan|ta|sy** /fæntəzi/ **(phantasies)** → see **fantasy**.

**phan|tom** /fæntəm/ **(phantoms)** 1 A **phantom** is a ghost. ❑ *They vanished down the stairs like two phantoms.* N-COUNT 2 You use **phantom** to describe something which you think you experience but which is not real. ❑ *She was always taking days off for what her colleagues considered phantom illnesses. ...a phantom pregnancy.* ADJ: ADJ n 3 **Phantom** can refer to something that is done by an unknown person, especially something criminal. ❑ *...victims of alleged 'phantom' withdrawals from high-street cash machines.* ADJ: ADJ n 4 **Phantom** is used to describe business organizations, agreements, or goods which do not really exist, but which someone pretends do exist in order to cheat people. ❑ *...a phantom trading scheme at a Wall Street investment bank.* ADJ: ADJ n

**phar|aoh** /feərou/ **(pharaohs)** A **pharaoh** was a king of ancient Egypt. ❑ *...Rameses II, Pharaoh of All Egypt.* N-COUNT; N-PROPER

**Phari|see** /færɪsiː/ **(Pharisees)** The **Pharisees** were a group of Jews, mentioned in the New Testament of the Bible, who believed in strictly obeying the laws of Judaism. N-PROPER-PLURAL

**phar|ma|ceu|ti|cal** /fɑːʳməsuːtɪkəl/ **(pharmaceuticals)** 1 **Pharmaceutical** means connected with the industrial production of medicine. ❑ *...a Swiss pharmaceutical company.* ADJ: ADJ n 2 **Pharmaceuticals** are medicines. ❑ *Antibiotics were of no use, neither were other pharmaceuticals.* N-PLURAL

**phar|ma|cist** /fɑːʳməsɪst/ **(pharmacists)** 1 A **pharmacist** is a person who is qualified to prepare and sell medicines. N-COUNT = chemist 2 A **pharmacist** or a **pharmacist's** is a shop in which drugs and medicines are sold by a pharmacist. [mainly BRIT] N-COUNT

☑ in AM, usually use **pharmacy**

**phar|ma|col|ogy** /fɑːʳməkɒlədʒi/ **Pharmacology** is the branch of science relating to drugs and medicines. N-UNCOUNT ♦ **phar|ma|co|logi|cal** /fɑːʳməkəlɒdʒɪkəl/ ❑ *As little as 50mg of caffeine can sometimes produce pharmacological effects.* ADJ: ADJ n ♦ **phar|ma|colo|gist** **(pharmacologists)** *...a pharmacologist from the University of California.* N-COUNT

**phar|ma|co|poeia** /fɑːʳməkoupiːə/ **(pharmacopoeias)** also **pharmacopeia.** A **pharmacopoeia** is an official book that lists all the drugs that can be used to treat people in a particular country, and describes how to use them. N-COUNT

**phar|ma|cy** /fɑːʳməsi/ **(pharmacies)** 1 A **pharmacy** is a shop or a department in a shop where medicines are sold or given out. ❑ *...the pharmacy section of the drugstore.* N-COUNT 2 **Pharmacy** is the job or the science of preparing medicines. ❑ *He spent four years studying pharmacy.* N-UNCOUNT

**phase** /feɪz/ **(phases, phasing, phased)** 1 A **phase** is a particular stage in a process or in the gradual development of something. ❑ *This autumn, 6000 residents will participate in the first phase of the project... The crisis is entering a crucial, critical phase... Most kids will go through a phase of being faddy about what they eat.* ◆◇◇ N-COUNT 2 If an action or change **is phased over** a period of time, it is done in stages. ❑ *The redundancies will be phased over two years. ...a phased withdrawal of American forces from the Philippines.* VERB: usu passive *be* V-ed V-ed 3 If two things are **out of phase with** each other, they are not working or happening together as they should. If two things are **in phase**, they are working or occurring together as they should. ❑ *The Skills Programme is out of phase with the rest of the curriculum.* PHRASE: usu PHR after v, v-link PHR

♦ **phase in** If a new way of doing something **is phased in**, it is introduced gradually. ❑ *The Health Secretary told Parliament that the reforms would be phased in over three years... The change is part of the government's policy of phasing in Arabic as the official academic language.* PHRASAL VERB *be* V-ed P V P n (not pron) Also V n P

♦ **phase out** If something **is phased out**, people gradually stop using it. ❑ *They said the present system of military conscription should be phased out... They phased out my job in favor of a computer.* PHRASAL VERB *be* V-ed P V P n (not pron) Also V n P

**PhD** /piː eɪtʃ diː/ **(PhDs)** also **Ph.D.** 1 A **PhD** is a degree awarded to people who have done advanced research into a particular subject. **PhD** is an abbreviation for 'Doctor of Philosophy'. ❑ *He is more highly educated, with a PhD in Chemistry. ...an unpublished PhD thesis.* N-COUNT 2 **PhD** is written after someone's name to indicate that they have a PhD. ❑ *...R.D. Combes, PhD.*

**pheas|ant** /fezənt/ **(pheasants** or **pheasant)** A **pheasant** is a bird with a long tail. Pheasants are often shot as a sport and then eaten. N-COUNT ♦ **Pheasant** is the flesh of this bird eaten as food. ❑ *...roast pheasant.* N-UNCOUNT

**phe|nom|ena** /fɪnɒmɪnə/ **Phenomena** is the plural of **phenomenon**.

**phe|nom|enal** /fɪnɒmɪnəl/ Something that is **phenomenal** is so great or good that it is very unusual indeed. ❑ *Exports of Australian wine have been growing at a phenomenal rate... The performances have been absolutely phenomenal.* ADJ emphasis = incredible ♦ **phe|nom|enal|ly** *Scots-born Annie, 37, has recently re-launched her phenomenally successful singing career.* ADV: ADV adj/adv, ADV after v

**phe|nom|enol|ogy** /fɪnɒmɪnɒlədʒi/ **Phenomenology** is a branch of philosophy which deals with consciousness, thought, and experience. N-UNCOUNT ♦ **phe|nom|eno|logi|cal** /fɪnɒmɪnəlɒdʒɪkəl/ ❑ *...a phenomenological approach to the definition of 'reality'.* ADJ: usu ADJ n

**phe|nom|enon** /fɪnɒmɪnən, AM -nɑːn/ **(phenomena)** A **phenomenon** is something that is observed to happen or exist. [FORMAL] ❑ *...scientific explanations of natural phenomena.* N-COUNT

**phero|mone** /ferəmoun/ **(pheromones)** Some animals and insects produce chemicals called **pheromones** which affect the behaviour of other animals and insects of the same type, for example by attracting them sexually. [TECHNICAL] N-COUNT

**phew** /fjuː/ **Phew** is used in writing to represent the soft whistling sound that you make when you breathe out quickly, for example when you are relieved or shocked about something or when you are very hot. ❑ *Phew, what a relief!* EXCLAM

**phial** /faɪəl/ **(phials)** A **phial** is a small tube-shaped glass bottle used, for example, to hold medicine. [FORMAL] N-COUNT

**phi|lan|der|er** /fɪlændərəʳ/ **(philanderers)** If you say that a man is a **philanderer**, you mean N-COUNT disapproval = womanizer that he has a lot of casual sexual relationships with women.

**phi|lan|der|ing** /fɪlændərɪŋ/ **(philanderings)**
1 A **philandering** man has a lot of casual sexual relationships with women. ❑ *...her philandering husband.* 2 **Philandering** means having a lot of casual sexual relationships with women. ❑ *She intended to leave her husband because of his philandering.*
ADJ: ADJ n disapproval; N-UNCOUNT: also N in pl disapproval

**phil|an|throp|ic** /fɪlənθrɒpɪk/ A **philanthropic** person or organization freely gives money or other help to people who need it. ❑ *Some of the best services for the ageing are sponsored by philanthropic organizations.* ADJ: usu ADJ n

**phi|lan|thro|pist** /fɪlænθrəpɪst/ **(philanthropists)** A **philanthropist** is someone who freely gives money and help to people who need it. N-COUNT

**phi|lan|thro|py** /fɪlænθrəpi/ **Philanthropy** is the giving of money to people who need it, without wanting anything in return. ❑ *...a retired banker well known for his philanthropy.* N-UNCOUNT

**phi|lat|elist** /fɪlætəlɪst/ **(philatelists)** A **philatelist** is a person who collects and studies postage stamps. [FORMAL] N-COUNT

**phi|lat|ely** /fɪlætəli/ **Philately** is the hobby of collecting and learning about postage stamps. [FORMAL] N-UNCOUNT

**-phile** /-faɪl/ or **-ophile** /-əfaɪl/ **(-philes** or **-ophiles) -phile** or **-ophile** occurs in words which refer to someone who has a very strong liking for people or things of a particular kind. ❑ *...the operaphile Hirotaro Higuchi, president of the tour's chief sponsors. ...essential reading for the culture-hungry Yankophile.* SUFFIX

**phil|har|mon|ic** /fɪlɑːʳmɒnɪk/ A **philharmonic** orchestra is a large orchestra which plays classical music. ❑ *The Lithuanian Philharmonic Orchestra played Beethoven's Ninth Symphony.* ♦ **Philharmonic** is also a noun. ❑ *He will conduct the Vienna Philharmonic in the final concert of the season.* ADJ: ADJ n; N-IN-NAMES

**Phil|ip|pine** /fɪlɪpiːn/ **Philippine** means belonging or relating to the Philippines, or to their people or culture. ADJ

**phil|is|tine** /fɪlɪstaɪn, AM -stiːn/ **(philistines)**
1 If you call someone a **philistine**, you mean that they do not care about or understand good art, music, or literature, and do not think that they are important. 2 You can use **philistine** to describe people or organizations who you think do not care about or understand the value of good art, music, or literature. ❑ *...a philistine government that allowed the arts to decline.*
N-COUNT disapproval; ADJ: ADJ n disapproval

**phil|is|tin|ism** /fɪlɪstɪnɪzəm/ **Philistinism** is the attitude or quality of not caring about, understanding, or liking good art, music, or literature. N-UNCOUNT disapproval

**phi|lol|ogy** /fɪlɒlədʒi/ **Philology** is the study of words, especially the history and development of the words in a particular language or group of languages. ♦ **phi|lolo|gist (philologists)** ❑ *He is a philologist, specialising in American poetry.* N-UNCOUNT; N-COUNT

**phi|loso|pher** /fɪlɒsəfəʳ/ **(philosophers)** 1 A **philosopher** is a person who studies or writes about philosophy. ❑ *...the Greek philosopher Plato.* 2 If you refer to someone as a **philosopher**, you mean that they think deeply and seriously about life and other basic matters. N-COUNT; N-COUNT

**philo|soph|ic** /fɪləsɒfɪk/ **Philosophic** means the same as **philosophical**. ADJ

**philo|sophi|cal** /fɪləsɒfɪkᵊl/ 1 **Philosophical** means concerned with or relating to philosophy. ❑ *He was not accustomed to political or philosophical discussions.* ♦ **philo|sophi|cal|ly** /fɪləsɒfɪkli/ *Wiggins says he's not a coward, but that he's philosophically opposed to war.* 2 Someone who is **philosophical** does not get upset when disappointing or disturbing things happen. ❑ *Lewis has grown philosophical about life.* ♦ **philo|sophi|cal|ly** *She says philosophically: 'It could have been far worse.'*
ADJ; ADV: ADV with v, ADV adj, ADV with cl; ADJ approval; ADV: ADV after v

**phi|loso|phize** /fɪlɒsəfaɪz/ **(philosophizes, philosophizing, philosophized)**
✓ in BRIT, also use **philosophise**
If you say that someone **is philosophizing**, you mean that they are talking or thinking about important subjects, sometimes instead of doing something practical. ❑ *He philosophized, he admitted, not because he was certain of establishing the truth, but because it gave him pleasure. ...a tendency to philosophize about racial harmony.* ♦ **phi|loso|phiz|ing** *The General was anxious to cut short the philosophizing and get down to more urgent problems.*
VERB; V; V about/on n, also V with quote; N-UNCOUNT

**phi|loso|phy** /fɪlɒsəfi/ **(philosophies)** ◆◇◇
1 **Philosophy** is the study or creation of theories about basic things such as the nature of existence, knowledge, and thought, or about how people should live. ❑ *He studied philosophy and psychology at Cambridge. ...traditional Chinese philosophy.* 2 A **philosophy** is a particular set of ideas that a philosopher has. ❑ *...the philosophies of Socrates, Plato, and Aristotle.* 3 A **philosophy** is a particular theory that someone has about how to live or how to deal with a particular situation. ❑ *The best philosophy is to change your food habits to a low-sugar, high-fibre diet.*
N-UNCOUNT; N-COUNT: usu with supp; N-COUNT: usu with supp, oft N *of* n, N that

**phlegm** /flem/ **Phlegm** is the thick yellowish substance that develops in your throat and at the back of your nose when you have a cold. N-UNCOUNT = *mucus*

**phleg|mat|ic** /flegmætɪk/ Someone who is **phlegmatic** stays calm even when upsetting or exciting things happen. [FORMAL] ADJ

**-phobe** /-foʊb/ or **-ophobe** /-əfoʊb/ **(-phobes) -phobe** or **-ophobe** occurs in words which refer to someone who has a very strong, irrational fear or hatred of people or things of a particular kind. ❑ *Its design makes it suitable for the computerphobe who just wants to type and see something come out looking right.* SUFFIX

**pho|bia** /foʊbiə/ **(phobias)** A **phobia** is a very strong irrational fear or hatred of something. ❑ *The man had a phobia about flying.* N-COUNT: oft N *about/of* n/-ing

**-phobia** /-foʊbiə/ **-phobia** occurs in words which refer to a very strong, irrational fear or hatred of people or things of a particular kind. ❑ *The place seethed with Europhobia... Technophobia increases with age.* SUFFIX

**pho|bic** /foʊbɪk/ **(phobics)** 1 A **phobic** feeling or reaction results from or is related to a strong, irrational fear or hatred of something. ❑ *Many children acquire a phobic horror of dogs.* 2 Someone who is **phobic** has a strong, irrational fear or hatred of something. ❑ *In Victorian times people were phobic about getting on trains. They weren't used to it.* ♦ **Phobic** is also a noun. ❑ *Social phobics quake at the thought of meeting strangers.*
ADJ; ADJ; N-COUNT

**-phobic** /-foʊbɪk/ **-phobic** occurs in words which describe something relating to a strong, irrational fear or hatred of people or things of a particular kind. ❑ *I'm statistic-phobic, and hopelessly ignorant of medicine.* SUFFIX

**phoe|nix** /fiːnɪks/ **(phoenixes)** 1 A **phoenix** is an imaginary bird which, according to ancient stories, burns itself to ashes every five hundred years and is then born again. 2 If you describe someone or something as a **phoenix**, you mean that they return again after seeming to disappear or be destroyed. [LITERARY] ❑ *Out of the ashes of the economic shambles, a phoenix of recovery can arise.*
N-COUNT: usu sing; N-SING

**phone** /foʊn/ **(phones, phoning, phoned)** ◆◆◇
1 **The phone** is an electrical system that you use to talk to someone else in another place, by dialling a number on a piece of equipment and speaking into it. ❑ *You can buy insurance over the phone... She looked forward to talking to her daughter by phone... Do you have an address and phone number for him?* 2 **The phone** is the piece of equipment that you use when you dial someone's phone number and talk to them. ❑ *Two minutes*
N-SING: usu *the* N, also *by* N = *telephone*; N-COUNT: usu *the* N = *telephone*

*later the phone rang... Doug's 14-year-old son Jamie answered the phone.* → See also **cellular phone**, **mobile phone**. [3] If you say that someone picks up or puts down **the phone**, you mean that they lift or replace the receiver. ❑ *She picked up the phone, and began to dial Maurice Campbell's number.* N-SING: usu *the* N = *receiver* [4] When you **phone** someone, you dial their phone number and speak to them by phone. ❑ *He had phoned Laura to see if she was better... I got more and more angry as I waited for her to phone.* VERB = *telephone, ring* V n V [5] If you say that someone is **on the phone**, you mean that they are speaking to someone else by phone. ❑ *She's always on the phone, wanting to know what I've been up to.* PHRASE: v-link PHR, PHR after v

♦ **phone in** [1] If you **phone in** to a radio or television show, you telephone the show in order to give your opinion on a matter that the show has raised. ❑ *Listeners have been invited to phone in to pick the winner.* PHRASAL VERB V P [2] If you **phone in** to a place, you make a telephone call to that place. ❑ *He has phoned in to say he is thinking over his options.* PHRASAL VERB [3] If you **phone in** an order for something, you place the order by telephone. ❑ *Just phone in your order three or more days prior to departure.* PHRASAL VERB V P n Also V n P [4] If you **phone in sick**, you telephone your workplace to say that you will not come to work because you are ill. ❑ *On Monday I was still upset and I phoned in sick to work.* PHRASE: V inflects

♦ **phone up** When you **phone** someone **up**, you dial their phone number and speak to them by phone. ❑ *Phone him up and tell him to come and have dinner with you one night.* PHRASAL VERB V n P Also V P n (not pron)

**phone book** **(phone books)** A **phone book** is a book that contains an alphabetical list of the names, addresses, and telephone numbers of the people in a town or area. N-COUNT

**phone booth** **(phone booths)** [1] A **phone booth** is a place in a station, hotel, or other public building where there is a public telephone. N-COUNT [2] A **phone booth** is the same as a **phone box**. [AM] N-COUNT = *call box, phone box*

**phone box** **(phone boxes)** A **phone box** is a small shelter in the street in which there is a public telephone. [BRIT] N-COUNT

✓ in AM, use **phone booth**

**phone call** **(phone calls)** If you make a **phone call**, you dial someone's phone number and speak to them by phone. ❑ *Wait there for a minute. I have to make a phone call.* N-COUNT

**phone|card** /fo͟ʊnkɑːʳd/ **(phonecards)** also **phone card.** A **phonecard** is a plastic card that you can use instead of money in some public telephones. N-COUNT

**phone-in** **(phone-ins)** A **phone-in** is a programme on radio or television in which people telephone with questions or opinions and their calls are broadcast. [mainly BRIT] ❑ *She took part in a BBC radio phone-in programme.* N-COUNT

✓ in AM, usually use **call-in**

**pho|neme** /fo͟ʊniːm/ **(phonemes)** A **phoneme** is the smallest unit of sound which is significant in a language. [TECHNICAL] N-COUNT

**phone-tapping** **Phone-tapping** is the activity of listening secretly to someone's phone conversations using special electronic equipment. In most cases phone-tapping is illegal. ❑ *There have also been claims of continued phone-tapping and bugging.* → See also **tap**. N-UNCOUNT

**pho|net|ics** /fəne̱tɪks/

✓ The form **phonetic** is used as a modifier.

[1] In linguistics, **phonetics** is the study of speech sounds. N-UNCOUNT [2] **Phonetic** means relating to the sound of a word or to the sounds that are used in languages. ❑ *...the Japanese phonetic system, with its relatively few, simple sounds.* ADJ: usu ADJ n ♦ **pho|neti|cal|ly** /fəne̱tɪkli/ *It's wonderful to watch her now going through things phonetically learning how to spell things.* ADV: ADV with v

**pho|ney** /fo͟ʊni/ **(phoneys)** also **phony.** [1] If you describe something as **phoney**, you disapprove of it because it is false rather than genuine. [INFORMAL] ❑ *He'd telephoned with some phoney excuse she didn't believe for a minute.* ADJ [disapproval] [2] If you say that someone is **phoney**, you disapprove of them because they are pretending to be someone that they are not in order to deceive people. [INFORMAL] ❑ *He looks totally phoney to me.* ADJ [disapproval] ♦ **Phoney** is also a noun. ❑ *'He's false, a phoney,' Harry muttered.* N-COUNT

**pho|ney war** also **phony war.** A **phoney war** is when two opposing groups are openly hostile towards each other or are in competition with each other, as if they were at war, but there is no real fighting. [BRIT] N-SING

**phon|ic** /fɒ̱nɪk/ In linguistics, **phonic** means relating to the sounds of speech. [TECHNICAL] ❑ *...the phonic system underlying a particular language.* ADJ: usu ADJ n

**pho|no|graph** /fo͟ʊnəgrɑːf, -græf/ **(phonographs)** A **phonograph** is a record player. [AM; also BRIT, OLD-FASHIONED] N-COUNT

**pho|nol|ogy** /fənɒ̱lədʒi/ In linguistics, **phonology** is the study of speech sounds in a particular language. [TECHNICAL] N-UNCOUNT

**pho|ny** /fo͟ʊni/ → see **phoney**.

**phos|phate** /fɒ̱sfeɪt/ **(phosphates)** A **phosphate** is a chemical compound that contains phosphorus. Phosphates are often used in fertilizers. N-MASS

**phos|pho|res|cence** /fɒ̱sfəre̱səns/ **Phosphorescence** is a glow or soft light which is produced in the dark without using heat. N-UNCOUNT

**phos|pho|res|cent** /fɒ̱sfəre̱sənt/ A **phosphorescent** object or colour glows in the dark with a soft light, but gives out little or no heat. ❑ *...phosphorescent paint.* ADJ: usu ADJ n

**phos|phor|ic acid** /fɒsfɒ̱rɪk æ̱sɪd, AM -fɔ͟ːr-/ **Phosphoric acid** is a type of acid which contains phosphorus. [TECHNICAL] N-UNCOUNT

**phos|pho|rus** /fɒ̱sfərəs/ **Phosphorus** is a poisonous yellowish-white chemical element. It glows slightly, and burns when air touches it. N-UNCOUNT

**pho|to** /fo͟ʊtoʊ/ **(photos)** A **photo** is the same as a **photograph**. ❑ *We must take a photo!... I've got a photo of him on the wall.* ◆◆◆ N-COUNT

**photo-** /fo͟ʊtoʊ-/ **Photo-** is added to nouns and adjectives in order to form other nouns and adjectives which refer or relate to photography or photographic processes, or to light. ❑ *...an eight-day photo-trip to northern Greece. ...a photo-sensitive detector system.* PREFIX

**photo|copi|er** /fo͟ʊtoʊkɒpiəʳ/ **(photocopiers)** A **photocopier** is a machine which quickly copies documents onto paper by photographing them. N-COUNT

**photo|copy** /fo͟ʊtoʊkɒpi/ **(photocopies, photocopying, photocopied)** [1] A **photocopy** is a copy of a document made using a photocopier. N-COUNT [2] If you **photocopy** a document, you make a copy of it using a photocopier. ❑ *Staff photocopied the cheque before cashing it.* VERB V n

**photo-finish** **(photo-finishes)** also **photo finish.** If the end of a race is a **photo-finish**, two or more of the competitors cross the finishing line so close together that a photograph of the finish has to be examined to decide who has won. ❑ *He was just beaten in a photo-finish.* N-COUNT

**Photo|fit** /fo͟ʊtoʊfɪt/ **(Photofits)** A **Photofit** is a picture of someone wanted by the police which is made up of several photographs or drawings of different parts of the face. Compare **e-fit**, **identikit**. [BRIT, TRADEMARK] ❑ *The girl sat down with a police artist to compile a Photofit of her attacker.* N-COUNT

**photo|gen|ic** /fo͟ʊtədʒe̱nɪk/ Someone who is **photogenic** looks nice in photographs. ❑ *I've got a million photos of my boy. He's very photogenic.* ADJ

**photo|graph** /fo͟ʊtəgrɑːf, -græf/ **(photographs, photographing, photographed)** [1] A ◆◆◇ N-COUNT

**photograph** is a picture that is made using a camera. ❑ *He wants to take some photographs of the house... Her photograph appeared on the front page of The New York Times.* [2] When you **photograph** someone or something, you use a camera to obtain a picture of them. ❑ *She photographed the children... They were photographed kissing on the platform.* VERB V n *be* V-ed -ing

**pho|tog|ra|pher** /fətɒgrəfəʳ/ **(photographers)** A **photographer** is someone who takes photographs as a job or hobby. ◆◇◇ N-COUNT

**photo|graph|ic** /foʊtəgræfɪk/ [1] **Photographic** means connected with photographs or photography. ❑ *...photographic equipment... The bank is able to provide photographic evidence of who used the machine.* ADJ: usu ADJ n ♦ **photo|graphi|cal|ly** /foʊtəgræfɪkli/ *...photographically reproduced copies of his notes.* ADV [2] If you have a **photographic memory**, you are able to remember things in great detail after you have seen them. ❑ *He had a photographic memory for maps.* ADJ: usu ADJ n

**pho|tog|ra|phy** /fətɒgrəfi/ **Photography** is the skill, job, or process of producing photographs. ❑ *Photography is one of her hobbies. ...some of the top names in fashion photography.* N-UNCOUNT

**photo|jour|nal|ism** /foʊtoʊdʒɜːʳnəlɪzəm/ also **photo-journalism. Photojournalism** is a form of journalism in which stories are presented mainly through photographs rather than words. ❑ *...some of the finest photo-journalism of the Civil Rights era.* N-UNCOUNT ♦ **photo|jour|nal|ist (photojournalists)** *...the agency for many international photojournalists, Magnum Photos.* N-COUNT

**pho|ton** /foʊtɒn/ **(photons)** A **photon** is a particle of light. [TECHNICAL] N-COUNT

**pho|to op|por|tu|nity (photo opportunities)** If a politician or other public figure arranges a **photo opportunity**, they invite the newspapers and television to photograph them doing something which they think will interest or impress the public. N-COUNT

**pho|to shoot (photo shoots)** also **photo-shoot.** A **photo shoot** is an occasion when a photographer takes pictures, especially of models or famous people, to be used in a newspaper or magazine. ❑ *...a long day of interviews and photo-shoots.* N-COUNT

**pho|to|stat** /foʊtəstæt/ **(photostats)** A **photostat** is a particular type of photocopy. [TRADEMARK] ❑ *...a photostat of the actual script.* N-COUNT

**photo|syn|the|sis** /foʊθoʊsɪnθəsɪs/ **Photosynthesis** is the way that green plants make their food using sunlight. [TECHNICAL] N-UNCOUNT

**phras|al verb** /freɪzᵊl vɜːʳb/ **(phrasal verbs)** A **phrasal verb** is a combination of a verb and an adverb or preposition, for example 'shut up' or 'look after', which together have a particular meaning. N-COUNT

**phrase** /freɪz/ **(phrases, phrasing, phrased)** ◆◇◇ [1] A **phrase** is a short group of words that people often use as a way of saying something. The meaning of a phrase is often not obvious from the meaning of the individual words in it. ❑ *He used a phrase I hate: 'You have to be cruel to be kind.'* N-COUNT [2] A **phrase** is a small group of words which forms a unit, either on its own or within a sentence. ❑ *It is impossible to hypnotise someone simply by saying a particular word or phrase.* N-COUNT [3] If you **phrase** something in a particular way, you express it in words in that way. ❑ *I would have phrased it quite differently... They phrased it as a question.* VERB V n adv V n *as* n [4] If someone has a particular **turn of phrase**, they have a particular way of expressing themselves in words. ❑ *...Schwarzkopf's distinctive turn of phrase.* PHRASE: N inflects • to **coin a phrase** → see **coin**.

**phrase book (phrase books)** A **phrase book** is a book used by people travelling to a foreign country. It has lists of useful words and expressions, together with the translation of each word or expression in the language of that country. ❑ *We bought a Danish phrase book.* N-COUNT

**phra|seol|ogy** /freɪziɒlədʒi/ If something is expressed using a particular type of **phraseology**, it is expressed in words and expressions of that type. ❑ *This careful phraseology is clearly intended to appeal to various sides of the conflict.* N-UNCOUNT: usu with supp

**phras|ing** /freɪzɪŋ/ The **phrasing of** something that is said or written is the exact words that are chosen to express the ideas in it. ❑ *The phrasing of the question was vague.* N-UNCOUNT: oft N *of* n = wording

**phre|nol|ogy** /frɪnɒlədʒi/ **Phrenology** is the study of the size and shape of people's heads in the belief that you can find out about their characters and abilities from this. N-UNCOUNT ♦ **phre|nolo|gist (phrenologists)** ❑ *Queen Victoria had her own personal phrenologist.* N-COUNT

**physi|cal** /fɪzɪkᵊl/ **(physicals)** ◆◆◇ [1] **Physical** qualities, actions, or things are connected with a person's body, rather than with their mind. ❑ *...the physical and mental problems caused by the illness... The attraction between them is physical.* ADJ: usu ADJ n ♦ **physi|cal|ly** *You may be physically and mentally exhausted after a long flight. ...disabled people who cannot physically use a telephone.* ADV: ADV adj, ADV with v [2] **Physical** things are real things that can be touched and seen, rather than ideas or spoken words. ❑ *Physical and ideological barriers had come down in Eastern Europe. ...physical evidence to support the story.* ADJ: usu ADJ n ♦ **physi|cal|ly** *...physically cut off from every other country.* ADV [3] **Physical** means relating to the structure, size, or shape of something that can be touched and seen. ❑ *...the physical characteristics of the terrain.* ADJ: ADJ n [4] **Physical** means connected with physics or the laws of physics. ❑ *...the physical laws of combustion and thermodynamics.* ADJ: ADJ n [5] Someone who is **physical** touches people a lot, either in an affectionate way or in a rough way. ❑ *We decided that in the game we would be physical and aggressive.* ADJ [6] **Physical** is used in expressions such as **physical love** and **physical relationships** to refer to sexual relationships between people. ❑ *It had been years since they had shared any meaningful form of physical relationship.* ADJ: ADJ n [7] A **physical** is a medical examination, done in order to see if someone is fit and well enough to do a particular job or to join the army. ❑ *Bob failed his physical.* N-COUNT = medical

**physi|cal edu|ca|tion Physical education** is the school subject in which children do physical exercises or take part in physical games and sports. N-UNCOUNT

**physi|cal|ity** /fɪzɪkælɪti/ If you refer to the **physicality** of something such as an artist's or a musician's work, you mean that their energy and enthusiasm is obvious in the work they produce. ❑ *There's not another guitarist to rival the sheer physicality of his work.* N-UNCOUNT

**physi|cal sci|ence (physical sciences) The physical sciences** are branches of science such as physics, chemistry, and geology that are concerned with natural forces and with things that do not have life. N-COUNT: usu pl

**physi|cal thera|py Physical therapy** is the same as **physiotherapy**. N-UNCOUNT

**phy|si|cian** /fɪzɪʃᵊn/ **(physicians)** In formal American English or old-fashioned British English, a **physician** is a doctor. N-COUNT

**physi|cist** /fɪzɪsɪst/ **(physicists)** A **physicist** is a person who does research connected with physics or who studies physics. ❑ *...a nuclear physicist.* N-COUNT

**phys|ics** /fɪzɪks/ **Physics** is the scientific study of forces such as heat, light, sound, pressure, gravity, and electricity, and the way that they affect objects. ❑ *...the laws of physics. ...experiments in particle physics.* N-UNCOUNT

**physio** /fɪzioʊ/ **(physios)** [1] A **physio** is a **physiotherapist**. [mainly BRIT, INFORMAL] ❑ *The athlete is checked by their physio or doctor.* N-COUNT [2] **Physio** is **physiotherapy**. [BRIT, INFORMAL] ❑ *I have been for some physio.* N-UNCOUNT

**physi|og|no|my** /fɪziɒnəmi/ **(physiognomies)** Your **physiognomy** is your face, especially when it is considered to show your real character. [FORMAL] *N-COUNT* ❑ *He was fascinated by her physiognomy – the prominent nose, brooding eyes and thick hair.*

**physi|ol|ogy** /fɪziɒlədʒi/ [1] **Physiology** is the scientific study of how people's and animals' bodies function, and of how plants function. *N-UNCOUNT* ❑ *...the Nobel Prize for Medicine and Physiology.* ♦ **physi|olo|gist (physiologists)** *... a retired plant physiologist.* *N-COUNT* [2] The **physiology** of a human or animal's body or of a plant is the way that it functions. *N-UNCOUNT: usu with supp* ❑ *...the physiology of respiration. ...insect physiology.* ♦ **physio|logi|cal** /fɪziəlɒdʒɪkəl/ *ADJ* *...the physiological effects of stress.*

**physio|thera|pist** /fɪzioʊθerəpɪst/ **(physiotherapists)** A **physiotherapist** is a person who treats people using physiotherapy. *N-COUNT*

**physio|thera|py** /fɪzioʊθerəpi/ **Physiotherapy** is medical treatment for problems of the joints, muscles, or nerves, which involves doing exercises or having part of your body massaged or warmed. *N-UNCOUNT* ❑ *He'll need intensive physiotherapy.*

**phy|sique** /fɪziːk/ **(physiques)** Someone's **physique** is the shape and size of their body. *N-COUNT: usu sing, usu with supp = build* ❑ *He has the physique and energy of a man half his age. ...men of powerful physique.*

**pi** /paɪ/ **Pi** is a number, approximately 3.142, which is equal to the distance round a circle divided by its width. It is usually represented by the Greek letter *π*. *NUM*

**pia|nis|si|mo** /piænɪsɪmoʊ/ A piece of music that is played **pianissimo** is played very quietly. [TECHNICAL] *ADV: ADV after v ≠ fortissimo*

**pia|nist** /piːənɪst, AM piæn-/ **(pianists)** A **pianist** is a person who plays the piano. *N-COUNT*

**pi|ano (pianos)**

> Pronounced /piænoʊ/ for meaning 1, and /piɑːnoʊ/ for meaning 2.

[1] A **piano** is a large musical instrument with a row of black and white keys. When you press these keys with your fingers, little hammers hit wire strings inside the piano which vibrate to produce musical notes. *N-VAR: oft the N* ❑ *I taught myself how to play the piano... He started piano lessons at the age of 7. ...sonatas for cello and piano.* → See also **grand piano, upright piano.** [2] A piece of music that is played **piano** is played quietly. [TECHNICAL] *ADV: ADV after v*

**pi|ano|for|te** /piænoʊfɔːʳteɪ/ **(pianofortes)** A **pianoforte** is a **piano**. [OLD-FASHIONED] *N-COUNT*

**pia|no|la** /piːænoʊlə/ **(pianolas)** A **pianola** is a type of mechanical piano. When you press the pedals, air is forced through holes in a roll of paper to press the keys and play a tune. [BRIT, TRADEMARK] *N-VAR: oft the N*

> in AM, use **player piano**

**pi|az|za** /piætsə/ **(piazzas)** A **piazza** is a large open square in a town or city, especially in Italy. *N-COUNT: oft in names before n* ❑ *They were seated at a table outside a pub in a pleasant piazza close by St Paul's.*

**pic** /pɪk/ **(pics)** [1] A **pic** is a cinema film. [INFORMAL] *N-COUNT = picture* ❑ *'Angels with Dirty Faces' is a Cagney gangster pic.* [2] A **pic** is a photograph. [INFORMAL] *N-COUNT = picture* ❑ *Photographer Weegee shot to fame with his shocking pics of New York crime in the 30s.*

**pica|resque** /pɪkəresk/ A **picaresque** story is one in which a dishonest but likeable person travels around and has lots of exciting experiences. [LITERARY] *ADJ: usu ADJ n*

**pic|co|lo** /pɪkəloʊ/ **(piccolos)** A **piccolo** is a small musical instrument that is like a flute but produces higher notes. *N-VAR*

**pick** /pɪk/ **(picks, picking, picked)** ◆◆◇ [1] If you **pick** a particular person or thing, you choose that one. *VERB* ❑ *Mr Nowell had picked ten people to interview for six sales jobs in London...* *V n* *I had deliberately picked a city with a tropical climate.* *V n* [2] You can refer to the best things or people in a particular group as **the pick of** that group. *N-SING: the N, usu the N of n* ❑ *The boys here are the pick of the under-15 cricketers in the country.* [3] When you **pick** flowers, fruit, or leaves, you break them off the plant or tree and collect them. *VERB* ❑ *She used to pick flowers in the Cromwell Road.* *V n* [4] If you **pick** something from a place, you remove it from there with your fingers or your hand. *VERB* ❑ *He picked the napkin from his lap and placed it alongside his plate.* *V n prep* [5] If you **pick** your **nose** or **teeth**, you remove substances from inside your nose or between your teeth. *VERB* ❑ *Edgar, don't pick your nose, dear.* *V n* [6] If you **pick** a fight or quarrel **with** someone, you deliberately cause one. *VERB* ❑ *He picked a fight with a waiter and landed in jail.* *V n with n* [7] If someone such as a thief **picks** a lock, they open it without a key, for example by using a piece of wire. *VERB* ❑ *He picked each lock deftly, and rifled the papers within each drawer.* *V n* [8] A **pick** is the same as a **pickaxe**. *N-COUNT* [9] → See also **hand-pick, ice pick.**

**PHRASES** [10] If you **pick and choose**, you carefully choose only things that you really want and reject the others. *PHRASE: Vs inflect, usu PHR n* ❑ *We, the patients, cannot pick and choose our doctors.* [11] If you **have** your **pick of** a group of things, you are able to choose any of them that you want. *PHRASE: V inflects, PHR of n* ❑ *Here is an actress who could have her pick of any part.* [12] If you are told to **take** your **pick**, you can choose any one that you like from a group of things. *PHRASE: V inflects, oft PHR of/from n* ❑ *Accountants can take their pick of company cars.* [13] If you **pick** your **way** across an area, you walk across it very carefully in order to avoid obstacles or dangerous things. *PHRASE: V inflects, PHR prep/adv* ❑ *The girls were afraid of snakes and picked their way along with extreme caution.* [14] to **pick** someone's **brains** → see **brain**. to **pick holes in** something → see **hole**. to **pick** someone's **pocket** → see **pocket**.

♦ **pick at** If you **pick at** the food that you are eating, you eat only very small amounts of it. *PHRASAL VERB* ❑ *Sarah picked at a plate of cheese for supper, but she wasn't really hungry.* *V P n*

♦ **pick off** If someone **picks off** people or aircraft, they shoot them down one by one, aiming carefully at them from a distance. *PHRASAL VERB* ❑ *Both groups on either side are just picking off innocent bystanders...* *V P n (not pron)* *Any decent shot with telescopic sights could pick us off at random.* *V n P*

♦ **pick on** [1] If someone **picks on** you, they repeatedly criticize you unfairly or treat you unkindly. [INFORMAL] *PHRASAL VERB* ❑ *Bullies pick on younger children.* *V P n* [2] If someone **picks on** a particular person or thing, they choose them, for example for special attention or treatment. [mainly BRIT] *PHRASAL VERB = pick* ❑ *When you have made up your mind, pick on a day when you will not be under much stress.* *V P n*

♦ **pick out** [1] If you **pick out** someone or something, you recognize them when it is difficult to see them, for example because they are among a large group. *PHRASAL VERB* ❑ *The detective-constable picked out the words with difficulty...* *V P n (not pron)* *Steven describes himself as 'a regular guy – you couldn't pick me out of a crowd'.* *V n P* [2] If you **pick out** someone or something, you choose them from a group of people or things. *PHRASAL VERB = select* ❑ *I have been picked out to represent the whole team...* *V P n (not pron)* *There are so many great newscasters it's difficult to pick one out.* *V n P* [3] If part of something **is picked out in** a particular colour, it is painted in that colour so that it can be seen clearly beside the other parts. *PHRASAL VERB: usu passive = highlight* ❑ *The name is picked out in gold letters over the shop-front.* *be V-ed P*

♦ **pick over** If you **pick over** a quantity of things, you examine them carefully, for example to reject the ones you do not want. *PHRASAL VERB* ❑ *Pick over the fruit and pile on top of the cream.* *V P n (not pron)*

♦ **pick up** [1] When you **pick** something **up**, you lift it up. *PHRASAL VERB* ❑ *He picked his cap up from the floor and stuck it back on his head...* *V n P* *Ridley picked up a pencil and fiddled with it.* *V P n (not pron)* [2] When you **pick yourself up** after you have fallen or been knocked down, you stand up rather slowly. *PHRASAL VERB* ❑ *Anthony picked himself up and set off along the track.* *V pron-refl P* [3] When you **pick up** someone or something that is waiting to be collected, you go to the place where they are *PHRASAL VERB* and take them away, often in a car. ❑ *She went over to her parents' house to pick up some clean clothes... I picked her up at Covent Garden to take her to lunch with my mother.* [V P n (not pron); V n P] 4 If someone **is picked up** by the police, they are arrested and taken to a police station. ❑ *Rawlings had been picked up by police at his office... The police picked him up within the hour.* [PHRASAL VERB; be V-ed P; V n P] 5 If you **pick up** something such as a skill or an idea, you acquire it without effort over a period of time. [INFORMAL] ❑ *Where did you pick up your English?* [PHRASAL VERB; V P n (not pron)] 6 If you **pick up** someone you do not know, you talk to them and try to start a sexual relationship with them. [INFORMAL] ❑ *He had picked her up at a nightclub on Kallari Street, where she worked as a singer.* [PHRASAL VERB; V n P; Also V P n (not pron)] 7 If you **pick up** an illness, you get it from somewhere or something. ❑ *They've picked up a really nasty infection from something they've eaten.* [PHRASAL VERB = catch; V P n; Also V n P] 8 If a piece of equipment, for example a radio or a microphone, **picks up** a signal or sound, it receives it or detects it. ❑ *We can pick up Italian television.* [PHRASAL VERB; V P n (not pron)] 9 If you **pick up** something, such as a feature or a pattern, you discover or identify it. ❑ *Consumers in Europe are slow to pick up trends in the use of information technology.* [PHRASAL VERB; V P n (not pron)] 10 If someone **picks up** a point or topic that has already been mentioned, or if they **pick up on** it, they refer to it or develop it. ❑ *Can I just pick up that gentleman's point?... I'll pick up on what I said a couple of minutes ago.* [PHRASAL VERB; V P n; V P P n; Also V n P] 11 If trade or the economy of a country **picks up**, it improves. ❑ *Industrial production is beginning to pick up.* [PHRASAL VERB; V P] 12 If you **pick** someone **up on** something that they have said or done, you mention it and tell them that you think it is wrong. [mainly BRIT] ❑ *...if I may pick you up on that point.* [PHRASAL VERB; V n P P n] 13 → See also **pick-up**.

**PHRASES** 14 When you **pick up the pieces** after a disaster, you do what you can to get the situation back to normal again. ❑ *Do we try and prevent problems or do we try and pick up the pieces afterwards?* [PHRASE: V inflects] 15 When a vehicle **picks up speed**, it begins to move more quickly. ❑ *Brian pulled away slowly, but picked up speed.* [PHRASE: V inflects = accelerate]

**pick|axe** /pɪkæks/ **(pickaxes)**

> ✔ in AM, use **pickax**

A **pickaxe** is a large tool consisting of a curved, pointed piece of metal with a long handle joined to the middle. Pickaxes are used for breaking up rocks or the ground. → See picture on page 1709. [N-COUNT = pick]

**pick|er** /pɪkə$^r$/ **(pickers)** A fruit **picker** or cotton **picker**, for example, is a person who picks fruit or cotton, usually for money. [N-COUNT: usu supp N]

**pick|et** /pɪkɪt/ **(pickets, picketing, picketed)** 1 When a group of people, usually trade union members, **picket** a place of work, they stand outside it in order to protest about something, to prevent people from going in, or to persuade the workers to join a strike. ❑ *The miners went on strike and picketed the power stations... 100 union members and supporters picketed outside.* [VERB; V n; V] ♦ **Picket** is also a noun. ❑ *...forty demonstrators who have set up a twenty four hour picket.* [N-COUNT] ♦ **pick|et|ing** *There was widespread picketing of mines where work was continuing.* [N-UNCOUNT] 2 **Pickets** are people who are picketing a place of work. ❑ *The strikers agreed to remove their pickets and hold talks with the government.* [N-COUNT]

**pick|et fence** **(picket fences)** A **picket fence** is a fence made of pointed wooden sticks fixed into the ground, with pieces of wood nailed across them. [N-COUNT]

**pick|et line** **(picket lines)** A **picket line** is a group of pickets outside a place of work. ❑ *No one tried to cross the picket lines.* [N-COUNT]

**pick|ings** /pɪkɪŋz/ You can refer to the money that can be made easily in a particular place or area of activity as the **pickings**. ❑ *Traditional hiding places are easy pickings for experienced burglars.* [N-PLURAL: usu supp N]

**pick|le** /pɪkəl/ **(pickles, pickling, pickled)** 1 **Pickles** are vegetables or fruit, sometimes cut into pieces, which have been kept in vinegar or salt water for a long time so that they have a strong, sharp taste. [N-PLURAL] 2 **Pickle** is a cold spicy sauce with pieces of vegetables and fruit in it. ❑ *...jars of pickle.* [N-MASS] 3 When you **pickle** food, you keep it in vinegar or salt water so that it does not go bad and it develops a strong, sharp taste. ❑ *Select your favourite fruit or veg and pickle them while they are still fresh.* [VERB; V n] ♦ **pick|ling** *Small pickling onions can be used instead of sliced ones.* [N-UNCOUNT: oft N n]

**pick|led** /pɪkəld/ **Pickled** food, such as vegetables, fruit, and fish, has been kept in vinegar or salt water to preserve it. ❑ *...a jar of pickled fruit.* [ADJ: usu ADJ n]

**pick-me-up** **(pick-me-ups)** A **pick-me-up** is something that you have or do when you are tired or depressed in order to make you feel better. [INFORMAL] ❑ *This is an ideal New Year pick-me-up – a five day holiday in the Bahamas.* [N-COUNT]

**pick 'n' mix** also **pick and mix**. **Pick 'n' mix** is used to describe a way of getting a collection of things together by choosing a number of different ones. [BRIT] ❑ *It is, as some senior officials conceded, a pick 'n' mix approach to policy. ...a pick-and-mix selection of fabrics and wallpapers.* [ADJ: ADJ n]

**pick|pocket** /pɪkpɒkɪt/ **(pickpockets)** A **pickpocket** is a person who steals things from people's pockets or bags in public places. [N-COUNT]

**pick-up** **(pick-ups)** also **pickup**. ◆◇◇ 1 A **pick-up** or a **pick-up truck** is a small truck with low sides that can be easily loaded and unloaded. [N-COUNT] 2 A **pick-up in** trade or **in** a country's economy is an improvement in it. ❑ *...a pick-up in the housing market.* [N-SING: usu N *in* n] 3 A **pick-up** takes place when someone picks up a person or thing that is waiting to be collected. ❑ *The company had pick-up points in most cities.* [N-COUNT: usu N n] 4 When a **pick-up** takes place, someone talks to a person in a friendly way in the hope of having a casual sexual relationship with them. [INFORMAL] ❑ *They had come to the world's most famous pick-up joint.* [N-COUNT]

**picky** /pɪki/ Someone who is **picky** is difficult to please and only likes a small range of things. [INFORMAL] ❑ *Some people are very picky about who they choose to share their lives with.* [ADJ disapproval = fussy]

**pic|nic** /pɪknɪk/ **(picnics, picnicking, picnicked)** 1 When people have a **picnic**, they eat a meal out of doors, usually in a field or a forest, or at the beach. ❑ *We're going on a picnic tomorrow... We'll take a picnic lunch.* [N-COUNT] 2 When people **picnic** somewhere, they have a picnic. ❑ *Afterwards, we picnicked on the riverbank. ...such a perfect day for picnicking.* [VERB; V; V-ing] ♦ **pic|nick|er** **(picnickers)** *...fires started by careless picnickers.* [N-COUNT] 3 If you say that an experience, task, or activity **is no picnic**, you mean that it is quite difficult or unpleasant. [INFORMAL] ❑ *Emigrating is no picnic.* [PHRASE: V inflects]

**pic|to|rial** /pɪktɔːriəl/ **Pictorial** means using or relating to pictures. ❑ *...a pictorial history of the Special Air Service.* [ADJ: usu ADJ n] ♦ **pic|to|ri|al|ly** *Each section is explained pictorially.* [ADV]

**pic|ture** /pɪktʃə$^r$/ **(pictures, picturing, pictured)** ◆◆◇ 1 A **picture** consists of lines and shapes which are drawn, painted, or printed on a surface and show a person, thing, or scene. ❑ *A picture of Rory O'Moore hangs in the dining room at Kildangan.* [N-COUNT] 2 A **picture** is a photograph. ❑ *The tourists have nothing to do but take pictures of each other.* [N-COUNT] 3 Television **pictures** are the scenes which you see on a television screen. ❑ *...heartrending television pictures of human suffering.* [N-COUNT: usu pl] 4 To **be pictured** somewhere, for example in a newspaper or magazine, means to appear in a photograph or picture. ❑ *The golfer is pictured on many of the front pages, kissing his trophy as he holds it aloft. ...a woman who claimed she had been pictured dancing with a celebrity in Stringfellows nightclub... The rattan and wrought-iron chair pictured here costs £125.* [VERB: usu passive; be V-ed; be V-ed -ing; V-ed] 5 You can refer to a film as a **picture**. ❑ *...a director of epic action pictures.* [N-COUNT] 6 If you go to **the pictures**, you go to a cinema to see a film. [BRIT] ❑ *We're going to the pictures tonight.* [N-PLURAL: the N = cinema]

> ✔ in AM, use **the movies**

7 If you have a **picture** of something in your mind, you have a clear idea or memory of it in your mind as if you were actually seeing it. ❑ *We are just trying to get our picture of the whole afternoon straight.* N-COUNT: oft N *of* n = *image*

8 If you **picture** something in your mind, you think of it and have such a clear memory or idea of it that you seem to be able to see it. ❑ *He pictured her with long black braided hair... He pictured Claire sitting out in the car, waiting for him... I tried to picture the place, but could not.* VERB = *imagine* V n prep V n -ing V n

9 A **picture** of something is a description of it or an indication of what it is like. ❑ *I'll try and give you a better picture of what the boys do.* N-COUNT: usu sing, with supp

10 When you refer to the **picture** in a particular place, you are referring to the situation there. ❑ *It's a similar picture across the border in Ethiopia.* N-SING: oft *the* N = *situation*

**PHRASES** 11 If you **get the picture**, you understand the situation, especially one which someone is describing to you. ❑ *Luke never tells you the whole story, but you always get the picture.* PHRASE: V inflects = *get the idea*

12 If you say that someone is **in the picture**, you mean that they are involved in the situation that you are talking about. If you say that they are **out of the picture**, you mean that they are not involved in the situation. ❑ *Meyerson is back in the picture after disappearing in July.* PHRASE: v-link PHR, PHR after v

13 You use **picture** to describe what someone looks like. For example, if you say that someone is **a picture of health** or **the picture of misery**, you mean that they look extremely healthy or extremely miserable. ❑ *We found her standing on a chair, the picture of terror, screaming hysterically.* PHRASE: v-link PHR

14 If you **put** someone **in the picture**, you tell them about a situation which they need to know about. ❑ *Has Inspector Fayard put you in the picture?* PHRASE: V inflects

**pic|ture book (picture books)** also **picture-book.** A **picture book** is a book with a lot of pictures in and not much writing. Many picture books are intended for children. N-COUNT

**pic|ture li|brary (picture libraries)** A **picture library** is a collection of photographs that is held by a particular company or organization. Newspapers or publishers can pay to use the photographs in their publications. N-COUNT: oft in names

**pic|ture post|card (picture postcards)**

> ✔ The spelling **picture-postcard** is also used for meaning 2.

1 A **picture postcard** is a postcard with a photograph of a place on it. People often buy picture postcards of places they visit when on holiday. N-COUNT

2 You can use **picture postcard** to describe a place that is very attractive. ❑ *...picture-postcard Normandy villages.* ADJ: ADJ n = *picturesque*

**pic|ture rail (picture rails)** also **picture-rail.** A **picture rail** is a continuous narrow piece of wood which is fixed round a room just below the ceiling. Pictures can be hung from it using string and hooks. [mainly BRIT] N-COUNT

**pic|ture show (picture shows)** A **picture show** is a film or cinema. [AM, OLD-FASHIONED] N-COUNT

**pic|tur|esque** /pɪktʃəresk/ 1 A **picturesque** place is attractive and interesting, and has no ugly modern buildings. ❑ *Alte, in the hills northwest of Loule, is the Algarve's most picturesque village.* ♦ You can refer to picturesque things as **the picturesque**. ❑ *...lovers of the picturesque.* ♦ **pic|tur|esque|ly** *...the shanty-towns perched picturesquely on the hillsides.* ADJ N-SING: *the* N ADV

2 **Picturesque** words and expressions are unusual or poetic. ❑ *Every inn had a picturesque name – the Black Locust Inn, the Blueberry Inn.* ♦ **pic|tur|esque|ly** *The historian described it picturesquely as a 'mother of castles'.* ADJ ADV: ADV with v

**pic|ture win|dow (picture windows)** A **picture window** is a window containing one large sheet of glass, so that people have a good view of what is outside. N-COUNT

**pid|dle** /pɪdᵊl/ **(piddles, piddling, piddled)** To **piddle** means to urinate. [INFORMAL] VERB

**pid|dling** /pɪdəlɪŋ/ **Piddling** means small or unimportant. [INFORMAL] ❑ *...arguing over piddling amounts of money.* ADJ: usu ADJ n

**pidg|in** /pɪdʒɪn/ 1 **Pidgin** is a simple form of a language which speakers of a different language use to communicate. **Pidgin** is not anyone's first language. ❑ *He's at ease speaking pidgin with the factory workers and guys on the docks.* N-VAR

2 If someone is speaking their own language simply or another language badly and is trying to communicate, you can say that they are speaking, for example, **pidgin** English or **pidgin** Italian. ❑ *The restaurant owner could only speak pidgin English.* ADJ: ADJ n

**pie** /paɪ/ **(pies)** 1 A **pie** consists of meat, vegetables, or fruit baked in pastry. ❑ *...a pork pie. ...apple pie and custard.* → See also **cottage pie, shepherd's pie.** N-VAR

2 If you describe an idea, plan, or promise of something good as **pie in the sky**, you mean that you think that it is very unlikely to happen. ❑ *The true regeneration of devastated Docklands seemed like pie in the sky.* to **eat humble pie** → see **humble**. PHRASE: usu v-link PHR

**pie|bald** /paɪbɔːld/ A **piebald** animal has patches of black and white on it. ❑ *...a piebald pony.* ADJ

**piece** /piːs/ **(pieces, piecing, pieced)** ◆◆◇ 1 A **piece of** something is an amount of it that has been broken off, torn off, or cut off. ❑ *...a piece of cake. ...a few words scrawled on a piece of paper... Cut the ham into pieces... Do you want another piece?* N-COUNT: usu N *of* n

2 A **piece** of an object is one of the individual parts or sections which it is made of, especially a part that can be removed. ❑ *The equipment was taken down the shaft in pieces.* N-COUNT = *bit*

3 A **piece of** land is an area of land. ❑ *People struggle to get the best piece of land.* N-COUNT: usu N *of* n

4 You can use **piece of** with many uncount nouns to refer to an individual thing of a particular kind. For example, you can refer to some advice as a **piece of advice**. ❑ *When I produced this piece of work, my lecturers were very critical. ...an interesting piece of information. ...a sturdy piece of furniture.* N-COUNT: N *of* n

5 You can refer to an article in a newspaper or magazine, some music written by someone, a broadcast, or a play as a **piece**. ❑ *I disagree with Andrew Russell over his piece on British Rail.* N-COUNT

6 You can refer to a work of art as a **piece**. [FORMAL] ❑ *Each piece is unique, an exquisite painting of a real person, done on ivory.* N-COUNT

7 You can refer to specific coins as **pieces**. For example, a 10p **piece** is a coin that is worth 10p. N-COUNT: supp N

8 The **pieces** which you use when you play a board game such as chess are the specially made objects which you move around on the board. N-COUNT

9 **A piece of** something is part of it or a share of it. [AM] ❑ *They got a small piece of the net profits and a screen credit.* QUANT: QUANT *of* def-n

10 → See also **museum piece, party piece, set piece.**

**PHRASES** 11 If you **give** someone **a piece of** your **mind**, you tell them very clearly that you think they have behaved badly. [INFORMAL] ❑ *How very thoughtless. I'll give him a piece of my mind.* PHRASE: V inflects

12 If something with several different parts is **all of a piece**, each part is consistent with the others. If one thing is **of a piece with** another, it is consistent with it. ❑ *At its peak in the Thirties, Underground design and architecture was all of a piece.* PHRASE: v-link PHR, oft PHR *with* n

13 If someone or something is still **in one piece** after a dangerous journey or experience, they are safe and not damaged or hurt. ❑ *...providing that my brother gets back alive and in one piece from his mission.* PHRASE: v-link PHR, PHR after v = *intact*

14 You use **to pieces** in expressions such as 'smash to pieces', and mainly in British English 'fall to pieces' or 'take something to pieces', when you are describing how something is broken or comes apart so that it is in separate pieces. ❑ *If the shell had hit the boat, it would have blown it to pieces... Do you wear your old clothes until they fall to pieces?* PHRASE: PHR after v

15 If you **go to pieces**, you are so upset or nervous that you lose control of yourself and cannot do what you PHRASE: V inflects

should do. [INFORMAL] ❑ *She's a strong woman, but she nearly went to pieces when Arnie died.* 16 **a piece of the action** → see **action**. **bits and pieces** → see **bit**. **a piece of cake** → see **cake**. to **pick up the pieces** → see **pick up**.

♦ **piece together** 1 If you **piece together** the truth about something, you gradually discover it. ❑ *They've pieced together his movements for the last few days before his death... In the following days, Francis was able to piece together what had happened... Frank was beginning to piece things together.* 2 If you **piece** something **together**, you gradually make it by joining several things or parts together. ❑ *This process is akin to piecing together a jigsaw puzzle.*

PHRASAL VERB | V P n (not pron) | V P wh | V n P | PHRASAL VERB | V P n (not pron)

**-piece** /-piːs/ **-piece** combines with numbers to form adjectives indicating that something consists of a particular number of items. ❑ *...his well-cut three-piece suit. ...a hundred-piece dinner service.*

COMB in ADJ: ADJ n

**pièce de ré|sis|tance** /pjes də reɪzɪstɒns, AM -zɪstɑːns/ The **pièce de résistance** of a collection or series of things is the most impressive thing in it. [FORMAL] ❑ *The pièce de résistance, however, was a gold evening gown.*

N-SING

**piece|meal** /piːsmiːl/ If you describe a change or process as **piecemeal**, you disapprove of it because it happens gradually, usually at irregular intervals, and is probably not satisfactory. ❑ *...piecemeal changes to the constitution.* ♦ **Piecemeal** is also an adverb. ❑ *The government plans to sell the railways piecemeal to the private sector.*

ADJ: usu ADJ n | disapproval | ADV: ADV after v

**piece|work** /piːswɜːrk/ also **piece-work**. If you do **piecework**, you are paid according to the amount of work that you do rather than the length of time that you work. ❑ *All my men are on piece-work... The tobacco workers were paid on a piecework basis.*

N-UNCOUNT

**pie chart** (**pie charts**) A **pie chart** is a circle divided into sections to show the relative proportions of a set of things.

N-COUNT

**pied-à-terre** /pjeɪd ɑː teəʳ/ (**pieds-à-terre**) A **pied-à-terre** is a small house or flat, especially in a town, which you own or rent but only use occasionally.

N-COUNT

**pier** /pɪəʳ/ (**piers**) A **pier** is a platform sticking out into water, usually the sea, which people walk along or use when getting onto or off boats. ❑ *...Brighton Pier.*

N-COUNT: oft in names after n

**pierce** /pɪəʳs/ (**pierces, piercing, pierced**) 1 If a sharp object **pierces** something, or if you **pierce** something **with** a sharp object, the object goes into it and makes a hole in it. ❑ *One bullet pierced the left side of his chest... Pierce the skin of the potato with a fork.* 2 If you **have** your ears or some other part of your body **pierced**, you have a small hole made through them so that you can wear a piece of jewellery in them. ❑ *I'm having my ears pierced on Saturday. ...her pierced ears with their tiny gold studs.*

VERB | V n | V n | VERB | *have* n V-ed | V-ed | Also V n

**pierc|ing** /pɪəʳsɪŋ/ 1 A **piercing** sound or voice is high-pitched and very sharp and clear in an unpleasant way. ❑ *A piercing scream split the air. ...a piercing whistle.* ♦ **pierc|ing|ly** *She screamed again, piercingly.* 2 If someone has **piercing** eyes or a **piercing** stare, they seem to look at you very intensely. [WRITTEN] ❑ *...his sandy blond hair and piercing blue eyes.* ♦ **pierc|ing|ly** *Ben looked at him piercingly.* 3 A **piercing** wind makes you feel very cold.

ADJ: usu ADJ n | ADV | ADJ: usu ADJ n = penetrating | ADV | ADJ

**pi|eties** /paɪɪtiz/ You refer to statements about what is morally right as **pieties** when you think they are insincere or unrealistic. ❑ *...politicians who constantly intone pieties about respect for the rule of law.*

N-PLURAL | disapproval

**pi|ety** /paɪɪti/ **Piety** is strong religious belief, or behaviour that is religious or morally correct.

N-UNCOUNT

**pif|fle** /pɪfᵊl/ If you describe what someone says as **piffle**, you think that it is nonsense. [INFORMAL] ❑ *He talks such a load of piffle.*

N-UNCOUNT | disapproval | = rubbish

**pif|fling** /pɪfəlɪŋ/ If you describe something as **piffling**, you are critical of it because it is very small or unimportant. [INFORMAL] ❑ *...some piffling dispute regarding visiting rights.*

ADJ: usu ADJ n | disapproval | = trifling

**pig** /pɪg/ (**pigs, pigging, pigged**) 1 A **pig** is a pink or black animal with short legs and not much hair on its skin. Pigs are often kept on farms for their meat, which is called pork, ham, bacon, or gammon. ❑ *...the grunting of the pigs. ...a pig farmer.* → See also **guinea pig**. 2 If you call someone a **pig**, you think that they are unpleasant in some way, especially that they are greedy or unkind. [INFORMAL] 3 If you say that people **are pigging themselves**, you are criticizing them for eating a very large amount at one meal. [BRIT, INFORMAL] ❑ *After pigging herself on ice cream she went upstairs.*

N-COUNT = hog | N-COUNT | disapproval | VERB | disapproval | V pron-refl

PHRASES 4 If you say '**pigs might fly**' after someone has said that something might happen, you are emphasizing that you think it is very unlikely. [HUMOROUS, INFORMAL] ❑ *'There's a chance he won't get involved in this, of course.' — 'And pigs might fly.'* 5 If you say that someone **is making a pig of themselves**, you are criticizing them for eating a very large amount at one meal. [INFORMAL] ❑ *I'm afraid I made a pig of myself at dinner.*

PHRASE | emphasis | PHRASE: V and N inflect | disapproval

♦ **pig out** If you say that people **are pigging out**, you are criticizing them for eating a very large amount at one meal. [INFORMAL] ❑ *I stopped pigging out on chips and crisps.*

PHRASAL VERB | disapproval | V P

**pi|geon** /pɪdʒɪn/ (**pigeons**) A **pigeon** is a bird, usually grey in colour, which has a fat body. Pigeons often live in towns. → See also **clay pigeon, homing pigeon**. to **put the cat among the pigeons** → see **cat**.

N-COUNT

**pigeon-hole** (**pigeon-holes, pigeon-holing, pigeon-holed**) also **pigeonhole**. 1 A **pigeon-hole** is one of the sections in a frame on a wall where letters and messages can be left for someone, or one of the sections in a writing desk where you can keep documents. 2 To **pigeon-hole** someone or something means to decide that they belong to a particular class or category, often without considering all their qualities or characteristics. ❑ *He felt they had pigeonholed him... I don't want to be pigeonholed as a kids' presenter.*

N-COUNT | VERB | V n | *be* V-ed *as* n

**pigeon-toed** Someone who is **pigeon-toed** walks with their toes pointing slightly inwards.

ADJ

**pig|gery** /pɪgəri/ (**piggeries**) A **piggery** is a farm or building where pigs are kept. [mainly BRIT]

N-COUNT

**pig|gy** /pɪgi/ (**piggies**) 1 A **piggy** is a child's word for a pig or a piglet. 2 If someone has **piggy** eyes, their eyes are small and unattractive.

N-COUNT | ADJ: ADJ n

**piggy|back** /pɪgibæk/ (**piggybacks, piggybacking, piggybacked**) also **piggy-back**. 1 If you give someone a **piggyback**, you carry them high on your back, supporting them under their knees. ❑ *They give each other piggy-back rides.* ♦ **Piggyback** is also an adverb. ❑ *My father carried me up the hill, piggyback.* 2 If you **piggyback on** something that someone else has thought of or done, you use it to your advantage. ❑ *I was just piggybacking on Stokes's idea... They are piggybacking onto developed technology.*

N-COUNT | ADV: ADV after v | VERB | V *on* n | V *onto* n | Also V

**pig|gy bank** (**piggy banks**) also **piggybank**. A **piggy bank** is a small container shaped like a pig, with a narrow hole in the top through which to put coins. Children often use piggy banks to save money.

N-COUNT

**piggy-in-the-middle** also **pig-in-the-middle**. 1 **Piggy-in-the-middle** or **pig-in-the-middle** is a game in which two children throw a ball to each other and a child standing between them tries to catch it. [BRIT] 2 If someone is **piggy-in-the-middle** or **pig-in-the-middle**, they are unwillingly involved in a dispute between two people or groups. [BRIT]

N-UNCOUNT | N-SING: also no det

**pig-headed** also **pigheaded**. If you describe someone as **pig-headed**, you are critical of them because they refuse to change their

ADJ | disapproval | = stubborn, obstinate

mind about things, and you think they are unreasonable. ❑ *She, in her pig-headed way, insists that she is right and that everyone else is wrong.* ♦ **pig-headedness** *I am not sure whether this was courage or pig-headedness.* N-UNCOUNT

**pig|let** /pɪglət/ **(piglets)** A **piglet** is a young pig. N-COUNT

**pig|ment** /pɪgmənt/ **(pigments)** A **pigment** is a substance that gives something a particular colour. [FORMAL] ❑ *The Romans used natural pigments on their fabrics and walls.* N-MASS

**pig|men|ta|tion** /pɪgmenteɪʃən/ The **pigmentation** of a person's or animal's skin is its natural colouring. [FORMAL] ❑ *I have a skin disorder, it destroys the pigmentation in my skin.* N-UNCOUNT

**pig|ment|ed** /pɪgmentɪd/ **Pigmented** skin has a lot of natural colouring. [FORMAL] ADJ

**pig|my** /pɪgmi/ → see **pygmy**.

**pig|pen** /pɪgpen/ **(pigpens)** also **pig pen.** A **pigpen** is an enclosed place where pigs are kept on a farm. [mainly AM] N-COUNT = pigsty

✔ in BRIT, use **pigsty**

**pig|skin** /pɪgskɪn/ **Pigskin** is leather made from the skin of a pig. N-UNCOUNT: oft N n

**pig|sty** /pɪgstaɪ/ **(pigsties)** also **pig sty.** 1 A **pigsty** is an enclosed place where pigs are kept on a farm. [mainly BRIT] N-COUNT

✔ in AM, usually use **pigpen**

2 If you describe a room or a house as a **pigsty**, you are criticizing the fact that it is very dirty and untidy. [mainly BRIT, INFORMAL] ❑ *The office is a pigsty.* N-COUNT: usu sing [disapproval] = tip

**pig|swill** /pɪgswɪl/ 1 **Pigswill** is waste food that is fed to pigs. N-UNCOUNT 2 If you describe food as **pigswill**, you are criticizing it because it is of very poor quality. [INFORMAL] N-UNCOUNT [disapproval]

**pig|tail** /pɪgteɪl/ **(pigtails)** If someone has a **pigtail** or **pigtails**, their hair is plaited or braided into one or two lengths. ❑ *...a little girl with pigtails.* N-COUNT

**pike** /paɪk/ **(pikes)**

✔ The form **pike** is often used as the plural for meaning 1.

1 A **pike** is a large fish that lives in rivers and lakes and eats other fish. N-VAR ♦ **Pike** is this fish eaten as food. N-UNCOUNT 2 In former times, a **pike** was a weapon consisting of a pointed blade on the end of a long pole. N-COUNT 3 When something **comes down the pike**, it happens or occurs. [AM, INFORMAL] ❑ *There have been threats to veto any legislation that comes down the pike.* PHRASE: V inflects

**pil|af** /pɪlæf, AM pɪlɑːf/ **(pilafs)** also **pilaff. Pilaf** is the same as **pilau.** N-MASS

**pi|las|ter** /pɪlɑːstəʳ/ **(pilasters) Pilasters** are shallow decorative pillars attached to a wall. N-COUNT: usu pl

**pi|lau** /piːlaʊ, AM pɪloʊ/ **(pilaus) Pilau** or **pilau rice** is rice flavoured with spices, often mixed with pieces of meat or fish. N-MASS

**pil|chard** /pɪltʃəʳd/ **(pilchards) Pilchards** are small fish that live in the sea. Pilchards can be eaten as food. ❑ *...tinned pilchards.* N-COUNT

**pile** /paɪl/ **(piles, piling, piled)** 1 A **pile of** things is a mass of them that is high in the middle and has sloping sides. ❑ *...a pile of sand... The leaves had been swept into huge piles.* ◆◇◇ N-COUNT: usu N of n = heap, mound 2 A **pile of** things is a quantity of things that have been put neatly somewhere so that each thing is on top of the one below. ❑ *...a pile of boxes... The clothes were folded in a neat pile.* N-COUNT: usu N of n 3 If you **pile** things somewhere, you put them there so that they form a pile. ❑ *He was piling clothes into the suitcase... A few newspapers and magazines were piled on a table.* VERB V n adv/prep V n adv/prep 4 If something **is piled with** things, it is covered or filled with piles of things. ❑ *Tables were piled high with local produce.* VERB: usu passive, be V-ed with n 5 If you talk about a **pile of** something or **piles of** something, you mean a large amount of it. [INFORMAL] ❑ *...a whole pile of disasters.* QUANT: QUANT of pl-n/n-uncount 6 If a group of people **pile into** or **out of** a vehicle, they all get into it or out of it in a disorganized way. ❑ *They all piled into Jerrold's car... A fleet of police cars suddenly arrived. Dozens of officers piled out.* VERB V into/out of n V in/out 7 You can refer to a large impressive building as a **pile**, especially when it is the home of a rich important person. ❑ *...some stately pile in the country.* N-COUNT 8 **Piles** are wooden, concrete, or metal posts which are pushed into the ground and on which buildings or bridges are built. Piles are often used in very wet areas so that the buildings do not flood. ❑ *...settlements of wooden houses, set on piles along the shore.* N-COUNT: usu pl 9 **Piles** are painful swellings that can appear in the veins inside a person's anus. N-PLURAL 10 The **pile** of a carpet or of a fabric such as velvet is its soft surface. It consists of a lot of little threads standing on end. ❑ *...the carpet's thick pile.* N-SING 11 Someone who is **at the bottom of the pile** is low down in society or low down in an organization. Someone who is **at the top of the pile** is high up in society or high up in an organization. [INFORMAL] PHRASE: oft v-link PHR

♦ **pile up** 1 If you **pile up** a quantity of things or if they **pile up**, they gradually form a pile. ❑ *Bulldozers piled up huge mounds of dirt... Mail was still piling up at the office.* PHRASAL VERB V P n V P 2 If you **pile up** work, problems, or losses or if they **pile up**, you get more and more of them. ❑ *Problems were piling up at work... He piled up huge debts.* PHRASAL VERB V P V P n (not pron)

**pile-up (pile-ups)**

✔ in AM, use **pileup**

A **pile-up** is a road accident in which a lot of vehicles crash into each other. ❑ *...a 54-car pile-up.* N-COUNT

**pil|fer** /pɪlfəʳ/ **(pilfers, pilfering, pilfered)** If someone **pilfers**, they steal things, usually small cheap things. ❑ *Staff were pilfering behind the bar... When food stores close, they go to work, pilfering food for resale on the black market.* VERB V V n ♦ **pil|fer|ing** *Precautions had to be taken to prevent pilfering.* N-UNCOUNT

**pil|grim** /pɪlgrɪm/ **(pilgrims) Pilgrims** are people who make a journey to a holy place for a religious reason. N-COUNT

**pil|grim|age** /pɪlgrɪmɪdʒ/ **(pilgrimages)** 1 If you make a **pilgrimage** to a holy place, you go there for a religious reason. ❑ *...the pilgrimage to Mecca.* N-COUNT 2 A **pilgrimage** is a journey that someone makes to a place that is very important to them. ❑ *...a private pilgrimage to family graves.* N-COUNT: usu with supp

**pil|ing** /paɪlɪŋ/ **(pilings) Pilings** are wooden, concrete, or metal posts which are pushed into the ground and on which buildings or bridges are built. Pilings are often used in very wet areas so that the buildings do not flood. ❑ *...bridges set on stone pilings.* N-COUNT: usu pl = pile

**pill** /pɪl/ **(pills)** 1 **Pills** are small solid round masses of medicine or vitamins that you swallow without chewing. ❑ *Why do I have to take all these pills? ...sleeping pills.* ◆◇◇ N-COUNT = tablet 2 If a woman is **on the pill**, she takes a special pill that prevents her from becoming pregnant. ❑ *She had been on the pill for three years.* N-SING: the N

**PHRASES** 3 If a person or group has to accept a failure or an unpleasant piece of news, you can say that it was **a bitter pill** or **a bitter pill to swallow**. ❑ *You're too old to be given a job. That's a bitter pill to swallow.* PHRASE: N inflects 4 If someone does something to **sweeten the pill** or **sugar the pill**, they do it to make some unpleasant news or an unpleasant measure more acceptable. ❑ *He sweetened the pill by increasing wages, although by slightly less than he raised prices.* PHRASE: V inflects

**pil|lage** /pɪlɪdʒ/ **(pillages, pillaging, pillaged)** If a group of people **pillage** a place, they steal property from it using violent methods. ❑ *Soldiers went on a rampage, pillaging stores and shooting. ...the boldness to pillage and rape.* VERB = plunder V n V ♦ **Pillage** is also a noun. ❑ *There were no signs of violence or pillage.* N-UNCOUNT ♦ **pil|lag|ing** *...pillaging by people looking for something to eat.* N-UNCOUNT

**pil|lar** /pɪləʳ/ **(pillars)** 1 A **pillar** is a tall solid structure, which is usually used to support part of a building. ❑ *...the pillars supporting the roof.* N-COUNT = column

[2] If something is the **pillar of** a system or agreement, it is the most important part of it or what makes it strong and successful. ❑ *The pillar of her economic policy was keeping tight control over money supply.* [3] If you describe someone as a **pillar of** society or as a **pillar of** the community, you approve of them because they play an important and active part in society or in the community. ❑ *My father had been a pillar of the community.*
N-COUNT: usu N *of* n
N-COUNT: N *of* n [approval]

**pil|lar box** **(pillar boxes)** also **pillar-box.** In Britain, a **pillar box** is a tall red box in the street in which you put letters that you are sending by post. [BRIT]
N-COUNT

☑ in AM, use **mailbox**

**pil|lared** /pɪləʳd/ A **pillared** building is a building that is supported by pillars.
ADJ: usu ADJ n

**pill|box** /pɪlbɒks/ **(pillboxes)** also **pill box.** [1] A **pillbox** is a small tin or box in which you can keep pills. [2] A **pillbox** is a small building made of concrete and is used to defend a place. [3] A **pillbox** or a **pillbox hat** is a small round hat for a woman.
N-COUNT
N-COUNT
N-COUNT

**pil|lion** /pɪliən/ **(pillions)** [1] If someone rides **pillion** on a motorcycle or bicycle, they sit behind the person who is controlling it. ❑ *She rode pillion on her son's motor bike.* [2] On a motorcycle, the **pillion** is the seat or part behind the rider. ❑ *As a learner rider you must not carry a pillion passenger.*
ADV: ADV after v
N-COUNT: oft N n

**pil|lock** /pɪlək/ **(pillocks)** If you call someone a **pillock**, you are showing that you think they are very stupid. [BRIT, INFORMAL] ❑ *The guy you put in charge is a complete pillock.*
N-COUNT [disapproval]

**pil|lo|ry** /pɪləri/ **(pillories, pillorying, pilloried)** If someone **is pilloried**, a lot of people, especially journalists, criticize them and make them look stupid. ❑ *A man has been forced to resign as a result of being pilloried by some of the press.*
VERB: usu passive = ridicule
*be* V-ed

**pil|low** /pɪloʊ/ **(pillows)** A **pillow** is a rectangular cushion which you rest your head on when you are in bed.
N-COUNT

**pillow|case** /pɪloʊkeɪs/ **(pillowcases)** also **pillow case.** A **pillowcase** is a cover for a pillow, which can be removed and washed.
N-COUNT

**pil|low slip** **(pillow slips)** A **pillow slip** is the same as a **pillowcase**.
N-COUNT

**pil|low talk** Conversations that people have when they are in bed together can be referred to as **pillow talk**, especially when they are about secret or private subjects.
N-UNCOUNT

**pi|lot** /paɪlət/ **(pilots, piloting, piloted)** [1] A **pilot** is a person who is trained to fly an aircraft. ❑ *He spent seventeen years as an airline pilot. ...fighter pilots of the British Royal Air Force.* [2] A **pilot** is a person who steers a ship through a difficult stretch of water, for example the entrance to a harbour. [3] If someone **pilots** an aircraft or ship, they act as its pilot. ❑ *He piloted his own plane part of the way to Washington.* [4] A **pilot** scheme or a **pilot** project is one which is used to test an idea before deciding whether to introduce it on a larger scale. ❑ *The service is being expanded following the success of a pilot scheme.* [5] If a government or organization **pilots** a programme or a scheme, they test it, before deciding whether to introduce it on a larger scale. ❑ *The trust is looking for 50 schools to pilot a programme aimed at teenage pupils preparing for work.* [6] If a government minister **pilots** a new law or bill through parliament, he or she makes sure that it is introduced successfully. ❑ *We are now piloting through Parliament a new strategy to tackle youth crime.* [7] A **pilot** or a **pilot episode** is a single television programme that is shown in order to find out whether a particular series of programmes is likely to be popular. ❑ *A pilot episode of Nothing's Impossible has already been filmed.* [8] → See also **automatic pilot, test pilot**.
◆◇◇ N-COUNT
N-COUNT
VERB
V n
N-COUNT: usu N n
VERB
V n
VERB
V n *through* n
Also V n
N-COUNT: oft N n

**pi|lot light** **(pilot lights)** A **pilot light** is a small gas flame in a cooker, stove, boiler, or fire. It burns all the time and lights the main large flame when the gas is turned fully on.
N-COUNT

**pi|lot of|fic|er** **(pilot officers)** In the British Royal Air Force, a **pilot officer** is someone who has the rank below Flying Officer.
N-COUNT; N-TITLE

**pi|men|to** /pɪmentoʊ/ **(pimentos)** A **pimento** is a small red pepper.
N-VAR

**pimp** /pɪmp/ **(pimps, pimping, pimped)** [1] A **pimp** is a man who gets clients for prostitutes and takes a large part of the money the prostitutes earn. [2] Someone who **pimps** gets clients for prostitutes and takes a large part of the money the prostitutes earn. ❑ *He stole, lied, deceived and pimped his way out of poverty.* ♦ **pimp|ing** *...corruption, pimping and prostitution.*
N-COUNT
VERB
V n
N-UNCOUNT

**pim|per|nel** /pɪmpəʳnel/ **(pimpernels)** A **pimpernel** is a small wild plant that usually has red flowers.
N-VAR

**pim|ple** /pɪmpᵊl/ **(pimples)** **Pimples** are small raised spots, especially on the face. ❑ *...spots and pimples... His face was covered with pimples.*
N-COUNT

**pim|ply** /pɪmpli/ If someone is **pimply** or has a **pimply** face, they have a lot of pimples on their face. ❑ *...pimply teenagers. ...an old man with a pimply nose.*
ADJ

**pin** /pɪn/ **(pins, pinning, pinned)** [1] **Pins** are very small thin pointed pieces of metal. They are used in sewing to fasten pieces of material together until they have been sewn. ❑ *...needles and pins.* [2] If you **pin** something **on** or **to** something, you attach it with a pin, a drawing pin, or a safety pin. ❑ *They pinned a notice to the door... He had pinned up a map of Finland.* [3] If someone **pins** you to something, they press you against a surface so that you cannot move. ❑ *I pinned him against the wall... She fought at the bulk that pinned her.* [4] A **pin** is any long narrow piece of metal or wood that is not sharp, especially one that is used to fasten two things together. ❑ *...the 18-inch steel pin holding his left leg together.* [5] If someone tries to **pin** something **on** you or to **pin the blame on** you, they say, often unfairly, that you were responsible for something bad or illegal. ❑ *The trade unions are pinning the blame for the violence on the government.* [6] If you **pin** your hopes **on** something or **pin** your faith **on** something, you hope very much that it will produce the result you want. ❑ *The Democrats are pinning their hopes on the next election.* [7] If someone **pins** their **hair** up or **pins** their **hair** back, they arrange their hair away from their face using hair pins. ❑ *Cleanse your face thoroughly and pin back your hair... In an effort to look older she has pinned her fair hair into a French pleat.* [8] A **pin** is something worn on your clothing, for example as jewellery, which is fastened with a pointed piece of metal. [AM] ❑ *...necklaces, bracelets, and pins.* [9] → See also **pins and needles, drawing pin, rolling pin, safety pin**.
◆◇◇ N-COUNT
VERB
V n prep
V n with adv
VERB
V n adv/prep
V n
N-COUNT
VERB
V n *on* n
VERB
V n *on* n
VERB
V n with adv
V n prep
N-COUNT

♦ **pin down** [1] If you try to **pin** something **down**, you try to discover exactly what, where, or when it is. ❑ *It has taken until now to pin down its exact location... I can only pin it down to between 1936 and 1942... If we cannot pin down exactly what we are supposed to be managing, how can we manage it?* [2] If you **pin** someone **down**, you force them to make a decision or to tell you what their decision is, when they have been trying to avoid doing this. ❑ *She couldn't pin him down to a date... If you pin people down, they will tell you some puzzling things about stress.*
PHRASAL VERB
V P n (not pron)
V n P *to* n
V P wh
Also V n P
PHRASAL VERB
V n P *to/on* n
V n P

**PIN** /pɪn/ Someone's **PIN** or **PIN number** is a secret number which they can use, for example, with a bank card to withdraw money from a cash machine or ATM. **PIN** is an abbreviation for 'personal identification number'.
N-SING: oft N n

**pina co|la|da** /piːnə koʊlɑːdə, AM piːnjə -/ **(pina coladas)** A **pina colada** is a drink made from rum, coconut juice, and pineapple juice.
N-COUNT

**pina|fore** /pɪnəfɔːʳ/ **(pinafores)** A **pinafore** or a **pinafore dress** is a sleeveless dress. It is worn over a blouse or sweater. [mainly BRIT] N-COUNT: oft N n

☑ in AM, usually use **jumper**

**pin|ball** /pɪnbɔːl/ **Pinball** is a game in which a player presses two buttons on each side of a pinball machine in order to hit a small ball to the top of the machine. The aim of the game is to prevent the ball reaching the bottom of the machine by pressing the buttons. N-UNCOUNT

**pin|ball ma|chine (pinball machines)** A **pinball machine** is a games machine on which pinball is played. It consists of a sloping table with objects that a ball hits as it rolls down. N-COUNT

**pince-nez** /pæns neɪ/ **Pince-nez** are old-fashioned glasses that consist of two lenses that fit tightly onto the top of your nose and do not have parts that rest on your ears. N-PLURAL: also *a* N

**pin|cer** /pɪnsəʳ/ **(pincers)** 1 **Pincers** consist of two pieces of metal that are hinged in the middle. They are used as a tool for gripping things or for pulling things out. ➔ See picture on page 1709. ❑ *His surgical instruments were a knife and a pair of pincers.* N-PLURAL: also *a pair of* N 2 The **pincers** of an animal such as a crab or a lobster are its front claws. N-COUNT: usu pl

**pin|cer move|ment (pincer movements)** A **pincer movement** is an attack by an army or other group in which they attack their enemies in two places at once with the aim of surrounding them. ❑ *They are moving in a pincer movement to cut the republic in two.* N-COUNT

**pinch** /pɪntʃ/ **(pinches, pinching, pinched)** 1 If you **pinch** a part of someone's body, you take a piece of their skin between your thumb and first finger and give it a short squeeze. ❑ *She pinched his arm as hard as she could... We both kept pinching ourselves to prove that it wasn't all a dream.* ♦ **Pinch** is also a noun. ❑ *She gave him a little pinch.* VERB; V n; V pron-refl; N-COUNT 2 A **pinch of** an ingredient such as salt is the amount of it that you can hold between your thumb and your first finger. ❑ *Put all the ingredients, including a pinch of salt, into a food processor.* to **take** something **with a pinch of salt** ➔ see **salt**. N-COUNT: usu N *of* n 3 To **pinch** something, especially something of little value, means to steal it. [INFORMAL] ❑ *...pickpockets who pinched his wallet.* VERB; V n

PHRASES 4 If you say that something is possible **at a pinch**, or in American English if you say that something is possible **in a pinch**, you mean that it would be possible if it was necessary, but it might not be very comfortable or convenient. ❑ *Six people, and more at a pinch, could be seated comfortably at the table.* PHRASE: PHR with cl/group 5 If a person or company **is feeling the pinch**, they do not have as much money as they used to, and so they cannot buy the things they would like to buy. ❑ *Consumers are spending less and traders are feeling the pinch.* PHRASE: V inflects

**pinched** /pɪntʃt/ If someone's face is **pinched**, it looks thin and pale, usually because they are ill or old. ❑ *Her face was pinched and drawn.* ADJ

**pinch-hit (pinch-hits, pinch-hitting, pinch-hit)** also **pinch hit.** 1 If you **pinch-hit for** someone, you do something for them because they are unexpectedly unable to do it. [AM] ❑ *The staff here can pinch hit for each other when the hotel is busy.* VERB; V *for* n 2 In a game of baseball, if you **pinch-hit** for another player, you hit the ball instead of them. [AM] ❑ *Davalillo goes up to pinch-hit.* VERB; V ♦ **pinch-hitter (pinch-hitters)** *Pinch-hitter Francisco Cabrera lashed a single to left field.* N-COUNT

**pin|cushion** /pɪnkʊʃən/ **(pincushions)** also **pin-cushion.** A **pincushion** is a very small cushion that you stick pins and needles into so that you can get them easily when you need them. N-COUNT

**pine** /paɪn/ **(pines, pining, pined)** 1 A **pine tree** or a **pine** is a tall tree which has very thin, sharp leaves and a fresh smell. Pine trees have leaves all year round. ❑ *...high mountains covered in pine trees.* ♦ **Pine** is the wood of this tree. ❑ *...a big pine table.* N-VAR; N-UNCOUNT: oft N n 2 If you **pine for** someone who has died or gone away, you want them to be with you very much and feel sad because they are not there. ❑ *She'd be sitting at home pining for her lost husband... Make sure your pet won't pine while you're away.* VERB; V *for* n; V 3 If you **pine for** something, you want it very much, especially when it is unlikely that you will be able to have it. ❑ *I pine for the countryside.* VERB; V *for* n

**pine|apple** /paɪnæpəl/ **(pineapples)** A **pineapple** is a large oval fruit that grows in hot countries. It is sweet, juicy, and yellow inside. It has a thick brownish skin. ➔ See picture on page 1711. N-VAR

**pine cone (pine cones)** A **pine cone** is one of the brown oval seed cases produced by a pine tree. N-COUNT

**pine nee|dle (pine needles) Pine needles** are very thin, sharp leaves that grow on pine trees. N-COUNT: usu pl

**pine nut (pine nuts) Pine nuts** are small cream-coloured seeds that grow on pine trees. They can be used in salads and other dishes. N-COUNT: usu pl

**pine|wood** /paɪnwʊd/ **(pinewoods)**

☑ The spelling **pine wood** is also used for meaning 1.

1 A **pinewood** is a wood which consists mainly of pine trees. ❑ *...the hilly pinewoods of northeast Georgia.* N-COUNT 2 **Pinewood** is wood that has come from a pine tree. ❑ *...Italian pinewood furniture.* N-UNCOUNT: usu N n

**ping** /pɪŋ/ **(pings, pinging, pinged)** If a bell or a piece of metal **pings**, it makes a short, high-pitched noise. ❑ *The lift bell pinged at the fourth floor.* ♦ **Ping** is also a noun. ❑ *...a metallic ping.* VERB; V; N-COUNT

**ping-pong Ping-pong** is the game of **table tennis.** [INFORMAL] N-UNCOUNT

**pin|head** /pɪnhed/ **(pinheads)** A **pinhead** is the small metal or plastic part on the top of a pin. ❑ *It may even be possible to make computers the size of a pinhead one day.* N-COUNT

**pin|hole** /pɪnhoʊl/ **(pinholes)** A **pinhole** is a tiny hole. N-COUNT

**pin|ion** /pɪnjən/ **(pinions, pinioning, pinioned)** If you **are pinioned**, someone prevents you from moving or escaping, especially by holding or tying your arms. ❑ *At nine the next morning Bentley was pinioned, hooded and hanged.* VERB; *be* V-ed; Also V n

**pink** /pɪŋk/ **(pinker, pinkest, pinks)** 1 **Pink** is the colour between red and white. ❑ *...pink lipstick. ...white flowers edged in pink. ...sweaters in a variety of pinks and blues.* ♦ **pink|ish** *Her nostrils were pinkish, as though she had a cold.* ♦ **pink|ness** *Meat which has been cooked thoroughly shows no traces of pinkness.* ◆◆◇ COLOUR; ADJ; N-UNCOUNT 2 If you **go pink**, your face turns a slightly redder colour than usual because you are embarrassed or angry, or because you are doing something energetic. ❑ *She went pink again as she remembered her mistake.* COLOUR: usu v-link COLOUR = *flush* 3 **Pink** is used to refer to things relating to or connected with homosexuals. ❑ *Businesses are now more aware of the importance of the 'pink pound'.* ADJ 4 **Pinks** are small plants that people grow in their gardens. They have sweet-smelling pink, white, or red flowers. N-COUNT: usu pl

**pinkie** /pɪŋki/ **(pinkies)** also **pinky.** Your **pinkie** is the smallest finger on your hand. [INFORMAL] ❑ *He pushes his glasses up his nose with his pinkie.* N-COUNT

**pinko** /pɪŋkoʊ/ **(pinkos** or **pinkoes)** If you call someone a **pinko**, you mean that they have left-wing views. [INFORMAL] N-COUNT [disapproval]

**pinky** /pɪŋki/ ➔ see **pinkie**.

**pin mon|ey Pin money** is small amounts of extra money that someone earns or gets in order to buy things that they want but that they do not really need. [INFORMAL] ❑ *She'd do anything for a bit of pin money.* N-UNCOUNT

**pin|na|cle** /pɪnɪkəl/ **(pinnacles)** 1 A **pinnacle** is a pointed piece of stone or rock that is high above the ground. ❑ *A walker fell 80ft from a rocky pinnacle.* N-COUNT 2 If someone reaches **the pinnacle of** N-COUNT:

their career or **the pinnacle of** a particular area of life, they are at the highest point of it. ❑ *She was still a screen goddess at the pinnacle of her career.* usu sing, N of n

**pin|ny** /pɪni/ **(pinnies)** A **pinny** is an **apron**. [BRIT, INFORMAL] N-COUNT

**pin|point** /pɪnpɔɪnt/ **(pinpoints, pinpointing, pinpointed)** 1 If you **pinpoint** the cause of something, you discover or explain the cause exactly. ❑ *It was almost impossible to pinpoint the cause of death. ...if you can pinpoint exactly what the anger is about... The commission pinpoints inadequate housing as a basic problem threatening village life.* 2 If you **pinpoint** something or its position, you discover or show exactly where it is. ❑ *I could pinpoint his precise location on a map... Computers pinpointed where the shells were coming from.* 3 If something is placed with **pinpoint** accuracy, it is placed in exactly the right place or position. ❑ *...the pinpoint accuracy of the bombing campaigns.* VERB = identify V n V wh V n as n VERB V n V wh ADJ: ADJ n

**pin|prick** /pɪnprɪk/ **(pinpricks)** also **pinprick, pin prick.** A very small spot of something can be described as a **pinprick**. ❑ *...a pinprick of light.* N-COUNT: with supp

**pins and nee|dles** If you have **pins and needles** in part of your body, you feel small sharp pains there for a short period of time. It usually happens when that part of your body has been in an uncomfortable position. ❑ *I had pins and needles in the tips of my fingers.* N-UNCOUNT

**pin|stripe** /pɪnstraɪp/ **(pinstripes)** also **pinstripe. Pinstripes** are very narrow vertical stripes found on certain types of clothing. Businessmen's suits often have pinstripes. ❑ *He wore an expensive, dark blue pinstripe suit.* N-COUNT: usu N n

**pin|striped** /pɪnstraɪpt/ A **pinstriped** suit is made of cloth that has very narrow vertical stripes. ADJ: usu ADJ n

**pint** /paɪnt/ **(pints)** 1 A **pint** is a unit of measurement for liquids. In Britain, it is equal to 568 cubic centimetres or one eighth of an imperial gallon. In America, it is equal to 473 cubic centimetres or one eighth of an American gallon. ❑ *...a pint of milk... The military requested 6,000 pints of blood from the American Red Cross.* 2 If you go for a **pint**, you go to the pub to drink a pint of beer or more. [BRIT] N-COUNT: usu N of n N-COUNT

**pint-sized** If you describe someone or something as **pint-sized**, you think they are smaller than is normal or smaller than they should be. [INFORMAL] ❑ *Two pint-sized kids emerged from a doorway.* ADJ: usu ADJ n

**pin-up (pin-ups)** also **pinup.** A **pin-up** is an attractive man or woman who appears on posters, often wearing very few clothes. ❑ *...pin-up boys.* N-COUNT

**pio|neer** /paɪənɪəʳ/ **(pioneers, pioneering, pioneered)** 1 Someone who is referred to as a **pioneer** in a particular area of activity is one of the first people to be involved in it and develop it. ❑ *...one of the leading pioneers of British photo journalism.* 2 Someone who **pioneers** a new activity, invention, or process is one of the first people to do it. ❑ *...Professor Alec Jeffreys, who invented and pioneered DNA tests. ...the folk-tale writing style pioneered by Gabriel Garcia Marquez.* 3 **Pioneers** are people who leave their own country or the place where they were living, and go and live in a place that has not been lived in before. ❑ *...abandoned settlements of early European pioneers.* N-COUNT: oft N of/in n, N n VERB V n V-ed N-COUNT

**pio|neer|ing** /paɪənɪəʳɪŋ/ **Pioneering** work or a **pioneering** individual does something that has not been done before, for example by developing or using new methods or techniques. ❑ *The school has won awards for its pioneering work with the community.* ADJ: usu ADJ n

**pi|ous** /paɪəs/ 1 Someone who is **pious** is very religious and moral. ❑ *He was brought up by pious female relatives. ...pious acts of charity.* ♦ **pi|ous|ly** *Conti kneeled and crossed himself piously.* 2 If you describe someone's words as **pious**, you think that their words are full of good intentions but do not lead to anything useful being done. ❑ *What we need is not manifestos of pious intentions, but real action.* ♦ **pi|ous|ly** *The groups at the conference spoke piously of their fondness for democracy.* ADJ ADV: ADV with v ADJ: ADJ n [disapproval] ADV: ADV with v

**pip** /pɪp/ **(pips, pipping, pipped)** 1 **Pips** are the small hard seeds in a fruit such as an apple, orange, or pear. → See picture on page 1711. 2 If someone **is pipped to** something such as a prize or an award, they are defeated by only a small amount. [BRIT, INFORMAL] ❑ *It's still possible for the losers to be pipped by West Germany for a semi-final place... She pipped actress Meryl Streep to the part.* 3 If someone **is pipped at the post** or **pipped to the post** they are just beaten in a competition or in a race to achieve something. [BRIT, INFORMAL] ❑ *I didn't want us to be pipped to the post.* N-COUNT: usu pl VERB be V-ed prep V n prep PHRASE

**pipe** /paɪp/ **(pipes, piping, piped)** 1 A **pipe** is a long, round, hollow object, usually made of metal or plastic, through which a liquid or gas can flow. ❑ *They had accidentally damaged a gas pipe while drilling.* 2 A **pipe** is an object which is used for smoking tobacco. You put the tobacco into the cup-shaped part at the end of the pipe, light it, and breathe in the smoke through a narrow tube. 3 A **pipe** is a simple musical instrument in the shape of a tube with holes in it. You play a pipe by blowing into it while covering and uncovering the holes with your fingers. 4 An **organ pipe** is one of the long hollow tubes in which air vibrates and produces a musical note. 5 If liquid or gas **is piped** somewhere, it is transferred from one place to another through a pipe. ❑ *The heated gas is piped through a coil surrounded by water... The villagers piped in drinking water from the reservoir... Most of the houses in the capital don't have piped water.* 6 → See also **piping**, **piping hot**. ◆◇◇ N-COUNT N-COUNT N-COUNT N-COUNT VERB be V-ed prep V n with adv V-ed

**pipe bomb (pipe bombs)** A **pipe bomb** is a small bomb in a narrow tube made by someone such as a terrorist. N-COUNT

**pipe clean|er (pipe cleaners)** A **pipe cleaner** is a piece of wire covered with a soft substance which is used to clean a tobacco pipe. N-COUNT

**piped mu|sic** **Piped music** is recorded music which is played in some supermarkets, restaurants, and other public places. [BRIT] N-UNCOUNT

✔ in AM, use **Muzak**

**pipe dream (pipe dreams)** also **pipe-dream.** A **pipe dream** is a hope or plan that you have which you know will never really happen. ❑ *You could waste your whole life on a pipe-dream.* N-COUNT

**pipe|line** /paɪplaɪn/ **(pipelines)** 1 A **pipeline** is a large pipe which is used for carrying oil or gas over a long distance, often underground. ❑ *A consortium plans to build a natural-gas pipeline from Russia to supply eastern Germany.* 2 If something is **in the pipeline**, it has already been planned or begun. ❑ *Already in the pipeline is a 2.9 per cent pay increase for teachers.* N-COUNT PHRASE: v-link PHR, PHR after v

**pip|er** /paɪpəʳ/ **(pipers)** 1 A **piper** is a musician who plays the bagpipes. 2 If you say '**He who pays the piper**' or '**He who pays the piper calls the tune**', you mean that the person who provides the money for something decides what will be done, or has a right to decide what will be done. N-COUNT PHRASE

**pipe|work** /paɪpwɜːʳk/ **Pipework** consists of the pipes that are part of a machine, building, or structure. ❑ *The stainless steel pipework has been constructed and inspected to very high standards.* N-UNCOUNT

**pip|ing** /paɪpɪŋ/ **Piping** is metal, plastic, or another substance made in the shape of a pipe or tube. ❑ *...rolls of bright yellow plastic piping.* N-UNCOUNT

**pip|ing hot** also **piping-hot.** Food or water that is **piping hot** is very hot. ❑ *...large cups of piping-hot coffee.* ADJ

**pi|quant** /piːkənt, -kɑːnt/ 1 Food that is **piquant** has a pleasantly spicy taste. [WRITTEN] ❑ *...a crisp mixed salad with an unusually piquant* ADJ

*dressing.* ♦ **pi|quan|cy** /piːkənsi/ *A little mustard is served on the side to add further piquancy.* N-UNCOUNT
2 Something that is **piquant** is interesting and exciting. [WRITTEN] ❑ *There may well have been a piquant novelty about her books when they came out.* ADJ
♦ **pi|quan|cy** *Piquancy was added to the situation because Dr Porter was then on the point of marrying Hugh Miller.* N-UNCOUNT

**pique** /piːk/ **(piques, piquing, piqued)**
1 **Pique** is the feeling of annoyance you have when you think someone has not treated you properly. ❑ *Mimi had gotten over her pique at Susan's refusal to accept the job.* N-UNCOUNT
2 If something **piques** your interest or curiosity, it makes you interested or curious. ❑ *This phenomenon piqued Dr Morris' interest... Their curiosity piqued, they stopped writing.* VERB = arouse; V n; V-ed
3 If someone does something **in a fit of pique**, they do it suddenly because they are annoyed at being not treated properly. ❑ *Lawrence, in a fit of pique, left the Army and took up a career in the City.* PHRASE

**piqued** /piːkt/ If someone is **piqued**, they are offended or annoyed, often by something that is not very important. ❑ *Granny was astounded and a little piqued, I think, because it had all been arranged without her knowledge... She wrinkled her nose, piqued by his total lack of enthusiasm.* ADJ: usu v-link ADJ

**pi|ra|cy** /paɪrəsi/ 1 **Piracy** is robbery at sea carried out by pirates. ❑ *Seven of the fishermen have been formally charged with piracy.* N-UNCOUNT
2 You can refer to the illegal copying of things such as video tapes and computer programs as **piracy**. ❑ *...protection against piracy of books and films.* N-UNCOUNT

**pi|ra|nha** /pɪrɑːnə/ **(piranhas** or **piranha)** A **piranha** is a small, fierce fish which is found in South America. N-COUNT

**pi|rate** /paɪrət/ **(pirates, pirating, pirated)**
1 **Pirates** are sailors who attack other ships and steal property from them. ❑ *In the nineteenth century, pirates roamed the seas.* N-COUNT
2 Someone who **pirates** video tapes, cassettes, books, or computer programs copies and sells them when they have no right to do so. ❑ *A school technician pirated anything from video nasties to computer games.* VERB; V n
♦ **pi|rat|ed** *Pirated copies of music tapes are flooding the market.* ADJ
3 A **pirate** version of something is an illegal copy of it. ❑ *Pirate copies of the video are already said to be in Britain.* ADJ: ADJ n

**pi|rate ra|dio** **(pirate radios)** **Pirate radio** is the broadcasting of radio programmes illegally. [BRIT] ❑ *...a pirate radio station.* N-VAR

**pirou|ette** /pɪruet/ **(pirouettes, pirouetting, pirouetted)** 1 A **pirouette** is a movement in ballet dancing. The dancer stands on one foot and spins their body round fast. N-COUNT
2 If someone **pirouettes**, they perform one or more pirouettes. ❑ *She pirouetted in front of the glass.* VERB; V

**Pi|sces** /paɪsiːz/ 1 **Pisces** is one of the twelve signs of the zodiac. Its symbol is two fish. People who are born approximately between the 19th of February and the 20th of March come under this sign. N-UNCOUNT
2 **A Pisces** is a person whose sign of the zodiac is Pisces. N-SING: *a* N

**piss** /pɪs/ **(pisses, pissing, pissed)** 1 To **piss** means to urinate. [INFORMAL, RUDE] VERB: V
2 If someone has **a piss**, they urinate. [INFORMAL, RUDE] N-SING: *a* N
3 **Piss** is urine. [INFORMAL, RUDE] N-UNCOUNT
4 If **it is pissing with** rain, it is raining very hard. VERB: usu cont
♦ **Piss down** means the same as **piss**. [BRIT, INFORMAL, RUDE] ❑ *It was pissing down out there.* PHRASAL VERB; V P
5 If someone **is pissing themselves**, or **is pissing themselves** laughing, they are laughing a lot. [BRIT, INFORMAL, RUDE] ❑ *I just pissed myself with laughter.* VERB; V pron-refl
6 If you **take the piss out of** someone, you tease them and make fun of them. [BRIT, INFORMAL, RUDE] PHRASE: V inflects

♦ **piss around**

✔ in BRIT, also use **piss about**

1 If you say that someone **pisses around** or **pisses about**, you mean they waste a lot of time doing unimportant things. [mainly BRIT, INFORMAL, RUDE] ❑ *Now, let's stop pissing about, shall we?* PHRASAL VERB; disapproval; = mess about; V P
2 If you say that someone **pisses around** or **pisses about**, you mean they behave in a silly, childish way. [BRIT, INFORMAL, RUDE] ❑ *We just pissed about, laughing.* PHRASAL VERB = mess about; V P

♦ **piss down** → see **piss** 4.

♦ **piss off** 1 If someone or something **pisses** you **off**, they annoy you. [INFORMAL, RUDE] ❑ *It pisses me off when they start moaning about going to war.* PHRASAL VERB; V n P
♦ **pissed off** *I was really pissed off.* ADJ
2 If someone tells a person to **piss off**, they are telling the person in a rude way to go away. [BRIT, INFORMAL, RUDE] PHRASAL VERB: V P

**pissed** /pɪst/ 1 Someone who is **pissed** is drunk. [BRIT, INFORMAL, RUDE] ❑ *He was just lying there completely pissed.* ADJ
2 If you say that someone is **pissed**, you mean that they are annoyed. [AM, INFORMAL, RUDE] ❑ *You know Molly's pissed at you.* ADJ: v-link ADJ, oft ADJ *at* n

**piss-poor** If you describe something as **piss-poor**, you think it is of extremely poor quality. [BRIT, INFORMAL, RUDE] ❑ *...a piss-poor comedy directed by John Landis.* ADJ

**piss-take** **(piss-takes)** A **piss-take** is an act of making fun of someone or something. [BRIT, INFORMAL, RUDE] N-COUNT: usu sing

**piss-up** **(piss-ups)** If a group of people have a **piss-up**, they drink a lot of alcohol. [BRIT, INFORMAL, RUDE] N-COUNT: usu sing

**pis|ta|chio** /pɪstætʃioʊ/ **(pistachios)** **Pistachios** or **pistachio nuts** are small, green, edible nuts. N-VAR

**piste** /piːst/ **(pistes)** A **piste** is a track of firm snow for skiing on. N-COUNT

**pis|tol** /pɪstᵊl/ **(pistols)** A **pistol** is a small gun. N-COUNT

**pis|ton** /pɪstᵊn/ **(pistons)** A **piston** is a cylinder or metal disc that is part of an engine. Pistons slide up and down inside tubes and cause various parts of the engine to move. N-COUNT

**pit** /pɪt/ **(pits, pitting, pitted)** 1 A **pit** is a coal mine. ❑ *It was a better community then when all the pits were working.* ◆◇◇ N-COUNT
2 A **pit** is a large hole that is dug in the ground. ❑ *Eric lost his footing and began to slide into the pit.* N-COUNT
3 A **gravel pit** or **clay pit** is a very large hole that is left where gravel or clay has been dug from the ground. ❑ *This area of former farmland was worked as a gravel pit until 1964.* N-COUNT: supp N
4 If two opposing things or people **are pitted against** one another, they are in conflict. ❑ *You will be pitted against people who are every bit as good as you are... This was one man pitted against the universe.* VERB: usu passive; *be* V-ed *against* n; V-ed
5 In motor racing, **the pits** are the areas at the side of the track where drivers stop to get more fuel and to repair their cars during races. → See also **pit stop**. N-PLURAL: usu pl
6 If you describe something as **the pits**, you mean that it is extremely bad. [SPOKEN] ❑ *Mary Ann asked him how dinner had been. 'The pits,' he replied.* N-PLURAL: *the* N
7 A **pit** is the stone of a fruit or vegetable. [AM] → See picture on page 1711. N-COUNT
8 → See also **pitted**, **fleapit**, **orchestra pit**, **sandpit**.

**PHRASES** 9 If you **pit** your **wits against** someone, you compete with them in a test of knowledge or intelligence. ❑ *I'd like to pit my wits against the best.* PHRASE: V inflects
10 If you have a feeling **in the pit of** your **stomach**, you have a tight or sick feeling in your stomach, usually because you are afraid or anxious. ❑ *I had a feeling in the pit of my stomach.* PHRASE
11 **a bottomless pit** → see **bottomless**.

**pita** /piːtə/ **(pitas)** → see **pitta**.

**pit bull ter|ri|er** **(pit bull terriers)** A **pit bull terrier** or a **pit bull** is a very fierce kind of dog. Some people train pit bull terriers to fight other dogs. N-COUNT

**pitch** /pɪtʃ/ **(pitches, pitching, pitched)** 1 A **pitch** is an area of ground that is marked out and used for playing a game such as football, cricket, or hockey. [mainly BRIT] ❑ *There was a swimming-pool, cricket pitches, playing fields... Their conduct both on and off the pitch was excellent.* ◆◇◇ N-COUNT: oft n N

✔ in AM, usually use **field**

[2] If you **pitch** something somewhere, you throw it with quite a lot of force, usually aiming it carefully. ❑ *Simon pitched the empty bottle into the lake.* VERB V n prep
[3] To **pitch** somewhere means to fall forwards suddenly and with a lot of force. ❑ *The movement took him by surprise, and he pitched forward... I was pitched into the water and swam ashore.* VERB V adv be V-ed prep/adv
[4] If someone **is pitched into** a new situation, they are suddenly forced into it. ❑ *They were being pitched into a new adventure... This could pitch the government into confrontation with the work-force.* VERB be V-ed prep V n prep
[5] In the game of baseball or rounders, when you **pitch** the ball, you throw it to the batter for them to hit it. ❑ *We passed long, hot afternoons pitching a baseball.* VERB V n
♦ **pitch|ing** *His pitching was a legend among major league hitters.* N-UNCOUNT
[6] The **pitch** of a sound is how high or low it is. ❑ *He raised his voice to an even higher pitch.* → See also **perfect pitch**. N-UNCOUNT
[7] If a sound **is pitched at** a particular level, it is produced at the level indicated. ❑ *His cry is pitched at a level that makes it impossible to ignore... Her voice was well pitched and brisk.* → See also **high-pitched**, **low-pitched**. VERB: usu passive be V-ed prep/adv V-ed
[8] If something **is pitched at** a particular level or degree of difficulty, it is set at that level. ❑ *I think the material is pitched at too high a level for our purposes... The government has pitched High Street interest rates at a new level.* VERB be V-ed prep V n prep
[9] If something such as a feeling or a situation rises to a high **pitch**, it rises to a high level. ❑ *Tension has reached such a pitch that the armed forces say soldiers may have to use their weapons to defend themselves against local people.* → See also **fever pitch**. N-SING: usu with supp
[10] If you **pitch** your **tent**, or **pitch camp**, you put up your tent in a place where you are going to stay. ❑ *He had pitched his tent in the yard... At dusk we pitched camp in the middle of nowhere.* VERB V n V n
[11] If a boat **pitches**, it moves violently up and down with the movement of the waves when the sea is rough. ❑ *The ship is pitching and rolling in what looks like about fifteen foot seas.* VERB V
[12] → See also **pitched**.
[13] If someone **makes a pitch for** something, they try to persuade people to do or buy it. ❑ *The President speaks in New York today, making another pitch for his economic program.* → See also **sales pitch**. PHRASE: V inflects, oft PHR *for* n

♦ **pitch for** If someone **is pitching for** something, they are trying to persuade other people to give it to them. ❑ *...laws prohibiting the state's accountants from pitching for business.* PHRASAL VERB: usu cont V P n

♦ **pitch in** If you **pitch in**, you join in and help with an activity. [INFORMAL] ❑ *The agency says international relief agencies also have pitched in... The entire company pitched in to help.* PHRASAL VERB V P V P to-inf

**pitch-black** If a place or the night is **pitch-black**, it is completely dark. ❑ *...a cold pitch-black winter morning.* ADJ = pitch-dark

**pitch-dark** also **pitch dark**. **Pitch-dark** means the same as **pitch-black**. ❑ *It was pitch-dark in the room and I couldn't see a thing.* ADJ = pitch-black

**pitched** /pɪtʃt/ A **pitched** roof is one that slopes as opposed to one that is flat. ❑ *...a rather quaint lodge with a steeply-pitched roof.* → See also **high-pitched**, **low-pitched**. ADJ = slanting

**pitched bat|tle** **(pitched battles)** A **pitched battle** is a very fierce and violent fight involving a large number of people. ❑ *Pitched battles were fought with the police.* N-COUNT

**pitch|er** /pɪtʃəʳ/ **(pitchers)** [1] A **pitcher** is a jug. [mainly AM] ❑ *...a pitcher of iced water.* N-COUNT
[2] A **pitcher** is a large container made of clay. Pitchers are usually round in shape and have a narrow neck and two handles shaped like ears. N-COUNT
[3] In baseball, the **pitcher** is the person who throws the ball to the batter, who tries to hit it. N-COUNT

**pitch|fork** /pɪtʃfɔːʳk/ **(pitchforks)** A **pitchfork** is a tool with a long handle and two pointed parts that is used on a farm for lifting hay or cut grass. N-COUNT

**pitch in|va|sion** **(pitch invasions)** If there is a **pitch invasion** during or after a football, rugby, or cricket match, fans run on to the pitch. [BRIT] N-COUNT

**pit|eous** /pɪtiəs/ Something that is **piteous** is so sad that you feel great pity for the person involved. [WRITTEN] ❑ *As they pass by, a piteous wailing is heard.* ADJ = pitiful

**pit|fall** /pɪtfɔːl/ **(pitfalls)** The **pitfalls** involved in a particular activity or situation are the things that may go wrong or may cause problems. ❑ *The pitfalls of working abroad are numerous.* N-COUNT: usu pl

**pith** /pɪθ/ **The pith** of an orange, lemon, or similar fruit is the white substance between the skin and the inside of the fruit. N-UNCOUNT: usu *the* N

**pit|head** /pɪthed/ **(pitheads)** **The pithead** at a coal mine is all the buildings and machinery which are above ground. ❑ *Across the river the railway track ran up to the pithead.* N-COUNT: usu *the* N in sing

**pithy** /pɪθi/ **(pithier, pithiest)** A **pithy** comment or piece of writing is short, direct, and full of meaning. [WRITTEN] ❑ *His pithy advice to young painters was, 'Above all, keep your colours fresh.'... Many of them made a point of praising the film's pithy dialogue.* ADJ: usu ADJ n
♦ **pithi|ly** *Louis Armstrong defined jazz pithily as 'what I play for a living'.* ADV: ADV with v

**piti|able** /pɪtiəbᵊl/ Someone who is **pitiable** is in such a sad or weak state that you feel pity for them. [WRITTEN] ❑ *Her grandmother seemed to her a pitiable figure.* ADJ = pitiful
♦ **piti|ably** /pɪtiəbli/ *Their main grievance was that they had not received their pitiably low pay... She found Frances lying on the bed crying pitiably.* ADV: ADV with v, ADV adj = pitifully

**piti|ful** /pɪtɪfʊl/ [1] Someone or something that is **pitiful** is so sad, weak, or small that you feel pity for them. ❑ *It was the most pitiful sight I had ever seen.* ADJ
♦ **piti|ful|ly** *His legs were pitifully thin compared to the rest of his bulk.* ADV
[2] If you describe something as **pitiful**, you mean that it is completely inadequate. ❑ *The choice is pitiful and the quality of some of the products is very low.* ADJ [disapproval]
♦ **piti|ful|ly** *State help for the mentally handicapped is pitifully inadequate.* ADV: ADV adj, ADV with v

**piti|less** /pɪtiləs/ Someone or something that is **pitiless** shows no pity or kindness. [LITERARY] ❑ *He saw the pitiless eyes of his enemy.* ADJ = merciless
♦ **piti|less|ly** *She had scorned him pitilessly.* ADV

**pit|man** /pɪtmən/ **(pitmen)** **Pitmen** are **coal miners**. [AM; also BRIT, JOURNALISM] ❑ *Many of the older pitmen may never work again.* N-COUNT: usu pl

**pit stop** **(pit stops)** In motor racing, if a driver makes a **pit stop**, he or she stops in a special place at the side of the track to get more fuel and to make repairs. ❑ *He had to make four pit stops during the race.* N-COUNT

**pit|ta** /pɪtə/ **(pittas)**

> ✔ The spelling **pita** is used in American English, pronounced /piːtə/.

**Pitta** or **pitta bread** is a type of bread in the shape of a flat oval. It can be split open and filled with food such as meat and salad. N-VAR

**pit|tance** /pɪtᵊns/ **(pittances)** If you say that you receive a **pittance**, you are emphasizing that you get only a very small amount of money, probably not as much as you think you deserve. ❑ *Her secretaries work tirelessly for a pittance.* N-COUNT: usu sing [emphasis]

**pit|ted** /pɪtɪd/ [1] **Pitted** fruits have had their stones removed. ❑ *...green and black pitted olives.* ADJ: ADJ n
[2] If the surface of something is **pitted**, it is covered with a lot of small, shallow holes. ❑ *Everywhere building facades are pitted with shell and bullet holes. ...the pitted surface of the moon.* ADJ: oft ADJ *with* n

**pi|tui|tary gland** /pɪtjuːɪtri glænd, AM -tuːɪteri -/ **(pituitary glands)** The **pituitary gland** or the **pituitary** is a gland that is attached to the base of the brain. It produces hormones which affect growth, sexual development, and other functions of the body. [TECHNICAL] N-COUNT: usu sing

**pity** /pɪti/ **(pities, pitying, pitied)** [1] If you feel **pity for** someone, you feel very sorry for them. N-UNCOUNT: oft N *for* n

❑ *He felt a sudden tender pity for her... She knew that she was an object of pity among her friends.* ➔ See also **self-pity**. [2] If you **pity** someone, you feel very sorry for them. ❑ *I don't know whether to hate or pity him.* [3] If you say that it is **a pity** that something is the case, you mean that you feel disappointment or regret about it. ❑ *It is a great pity that all pupils in the city cannot have the same chances... It seemed a pity to let it all go to waste.* [4] If someone shows **pity**, they do not harm or punish someone they have power over. ❑ *One should avoid showing too much pity.* [5] If you **take pity on** someone, you feel sorry for them and help them. ❑ *No woman had ever felt the need to take pity on him before.*

VERB: V n / N-SING: *a* N, oft *it* v-link N that/to-inf [feelings] / N-UNCOUNT / PHRASE: V inflects

**pity|ing** /pɪtiɪŋ/ A **pitying** look shows that someone feels pity and perhaps slight contempt. ❑ *She gave him a pitying look; that was the sort of excuse her father would use.* ♦ **pity|ing|ly** *Stasik looked at him pityingly and said nothing.*

ADJ: usu ADJ n / ADV: ADV after v

**piv|ot** /pɪvət/ **(pivots, pivoting, pivoted)** [1] **The pivot** in a situation is the most important thing which everything else is based on or arranged around. ❑ *Forming the pivot of the exhibition is a large group of watercolours.* [2] If something **pivots**, it balances or turns on a central point. ❑ *The boat pivoted on its central axis and pointed straight at the harbour entrance... She pivots gracefully on the stage... He pivoted his whole body through ninety degrees.* [3] A **pivot** is the pin or the central point on which something balances or turns. ❑ *The pedal had sheared off at the pivot.*

N-COUNT: usu *the* N in sing, oft *the* N *of* n / VERB: V prep/adv, V prep/adv, V n prep / N-COUNT: usu sing

**piv|ot|al** /pɪvətᵊl/ A **pivotal** role, point or figure in something is one that is very important and affects the success of that thing. ❑ *The Court of Appeal has a pivotal role in the English legal system.*

ADJ = critical

**pix** /pɪks/ **Pix** is an informal way of spelling **pics** meaning 'photographs' or 'films'. ❑ *...splendid pix by ace photographer Mike Goldwater.*

N-PLURAL

**pix|el** /pɪksᵊl/ **(pixels)** A **pixel** is the smallest area on a computer screen which can be given a separate colour by the computer. [COMPUTING]

N-COUNT

**pixie** /pɪksi/ **(pixies)** A **pixie** is an imaginary little creature like a fairy. Pixies have pointed ears and wear pointed hats.

N-COUNT

**piz|za** /piːtsə/ **(pizzas)** A **pizza** is a flat, round piece of dough covered with tomatoes, cheese, and other savoury food, and then baked in an oven. ❑ *...the last piece of pizza... We went for a pizza together at lunch-time.*

N-VAR

**piz|zazz** /pɪzæz/ also **pzazz, pizazz.** If you say that someone or something has **pizzazz**, you mean that they are very exciting, energetic, and stylish. [INFORMAL] ❑ *...a young woman with a lot of energy and pizzazz.*

N-UNCOUNT [approval]

**piz|ze|ria** /piːtsəriːə/ **(pizzerias)** A **pizzeria** is a place where pizza is made, sold, and eaten.

N-COUNT

**piz|zi|ca|to** /pɪtsɪkɑːtoʊ/ **(pizzicatos)** If a stringed instrument is played **pizzicato**, it is played by pulling the strings with the fingers rather than by using the bow. [TECHNICAL] ♦ **Pizzicato** is also a noun. ❑ *...an extended pizzicato section.*

ADV: ADV after v / N-COUNT: oft N n

**pkt** **Pkt** is used in recipes as a written abbreviation for **packet**.

**pl** also **pl.** [1] In addresses and on maps and signs, **Pl** is often used as a written abbreviation for **Place**. ❑ *...27 Queensdale Pl, London W11, England.* [2] In grammar, **pl** is often used as a written abbreviation for **plural**. [3] **Pl.** is sometimes used as a written abbreviation for **please**.

**plac|ard** /plækɑːʳd/ **(placards)** A **placard** is a large notice that is carried in a march or displayed in a public place. ❑ *The protesters sang songs and waved placards.*

N-COUNT

**pla|cate** /pləkeɪt, AM pleɪkeɪt/ **(placates, placating, placated)** If you **placate** someone, you do or say something to make them stop feeling angry. [FORMAL] ❑ *He smiled, trying to placate me... 'I didn't mean to upset you,' Agnew said in a placating voice.*

VERB = appease / V n / V-ing

**placa|tory** /pləkeɪtəri, AM pleɪkətɔːri/ A **placatory** remark or action is intended to make someone stop feeling angry. [FORMAL] ❑ *When next he spoke he was more placatory... He raised a placatory hand. 'All right, we'll see what we can do.'*

ADJ = appeasing

**place** /pleɪs/ **(places, placing, placed)** ◆◆◆ [1] A **place** is any point, building, area, town, or country. ❑ *...Temple Mount, the place where the Temple actually stood. ...a list of museums and places of interest... We're going to a place called Mont-St-Jean. ...the opportunity to visit new places... The best place to catch fish on a canal is close to a lock... The pain is always in the same place.* [2] You can use **the place** to refer to the point, building, area, town, or country that you have already mentioned. ❑ *Except for the remarkably tidy kitchen, the place was a mess.* [3] You can refer to somewhere that provides a service, such as a hotel, restaurant, or institution, as a particular kind of **place**. ❑ *He found a bed-and-breakfast place... My wife and I discovered some superb places to eat.* [4] When something **takes place**, it happens, especially in a controlled or organized way. ❑ *The discussion took place in a famous villa on the lake's shore... Elections will now take place on November the twenty-fifth.* [5] **Place** can be used after 'any', 'no', 'some', or 'every' to mean 'anywhere', 'nowhere', 'somewhere', or 'everywhere'. [mainly AM, INFORMAL] ❑ *The poor guy obviously didn't have any place to go for Easter.* [6] If you go **places**, you visit pleasant or interesting places. [mainly AM] ❑ *I don't have money to go places.* [7] You can refer to the position where something belongs, or where it is supposed to be, as its **place**. ❑ *He returned the album to its place on the shelf... He returned to his place on the sofa.* [8] A **place** is a seat or position that is available for someone to occupy. ❑ *He walked back to the table and sat at the nearest of two empty places.* [9] Someone's or something's **place** in a society, system, or situation is their position in relation to other people or things. ❑ *...the important place of Christianity in our national culture.* [10] Your **place** in a race or competition is your position in relation to the other competitors. If you are in first place, you are ahead of all the other competitors. ❑ *Jane's goals helped Britain win third place in the Barcelona games.* [11] If you get a **place** in a team, on a committee, or on a course of study, for example, you are accepted as a member of the team or committee or as a student on the course. ❑ *I eventually got a place at York University... They should be in residential care but there are no places available.* [12] A good **place to** do something in a situation or activity is a good time or stage at which to do it. ❑ *It seemed an appropriate place to end somehow... This is not the place for a lengthy discussion.* [13] Your **place** is the house or flat where you live. [INFORMAL] ❑ *Let's all go back to my place!... He kept encouraging Rosie to find a place of her own.* [14] Your **place in** a book or speech is the point you have reached in reading the book or making the speech. ❑ *He lost his place in his notes.* [15] If you say how many decimal **places** there are in a number, you are saying how many numbers there are to the right of the decimal point. ❑ *A pocket calculator only works to eight decimal places.* [16] If you **place** something somewhere, you put it in a particular position, especially in a careful, firm, or deliberate way. ❑ *Brand folded it in his handkerchief and placed it in the inside pocket of his jacket... Chairs were hastily placed in rows for the parents.* [17] To **place** a person or thing in a particular state means to cause them to be in it. ❑ *Widespread protests have placed the President under serious pressure... The remaining 30 percent of each army will be placed under UN control.* [18] You can use **place** instead of 'put' or 'lay' in certain expressions where the meaning is carried by the following noun. For example, if you **place empha-**

N-COUNT: usu with supp / N-SING: *the* N / N-COUNT: usu with supp / PHRASE: V inflects / N-SING: det N / ADV: ADV after v / N-COUNT: poss N / N-COUNT: usu with supp / N-COUNT: with poss / N-COUNT: usu sing, usu ord N / N-COUNT: usu with supp / N-SING: with supp, oft N to-inf, N *for* n/-ing = time / N-COUNT: usu sing, usu poss N / N-COUNT: usu sing, usu poss N / N-COUNT: usu num N / VERB: V n prep/adv, V n prep/adv / VERB = put: V n prep, *be* V-ed prep / VERB = put

**sis on** something, you emphasize it, and if you **place the blame on** someone, you blame them. ❑ *He placed great emphasis on the importance of family life and ties... His government is placing its faith in international diplomacy.* (V n *on/upon* n; V n *in* n) 19 If you **place** someone or something in a particular class or group, you label or judge them in that way. (VERB = *put*) ❑ *The authorities have placed the drug in Class A, the same category as heroin and cocaine.* (V n prep) 20 If a competitor **is placed** first, second, or last, for example, that is their position at the end of a race or competition. In American English, **be placed** often means 'finish in second position'. (VERB: usu passive) ❑ *I had been placed 2nd and 3rd a few times but had never won... Second-placed Auxerre suffered a surprising 2-0 home defeat to Nantes.* (*be* V-ed ord; ord V-ed) 21 If you **place** an order **for** a product or **for** a meal, you ask for it to be sent or brought to you. (VERB) ❑ *It is a good idea to place your order well in advance... Before placing your order for a meal, study the menu.* (V n; V n *for* n) 22 If you **place** an advertisement **in** a newspaper, you arrange for the advertisement to appear in the newspaper. (VERB = *put*) ❑ *They placed an advertisement in the local paper for a secretary.* (V n *in* n; Also V n) 23 If you **place** a telephone call to a particular place, you give the telephone operator the number of the person you want to speak to and ask them to connect you. (VERB) ❑ *I'd like to place an overseas call.* (V n) 24 If you **place** a bet, you bet money on something. (VERB) ❑ *For this race, though, he had already placed a bet on one of the horses.* (V n *on* n; Also V n) 25 If an agency or organization **places** someone, it finds them a job or somewhere to live. (VERB) ❑ *In 1861, they managed to place fourteen women in paid positions in the colonies... In cases where it proves difficult to place a child, the reception centre provides long-term care.* (V n *in* n; V n) 26 If you say that you cannot **place** someone, you mean that you recognize them but cannot remember exactly who they are or where you have met them before. (VERB) ❑ *It was a voice he recognized, though he could not immediately place it.* (V n) 27 ➔ See also **meeting place**.

**PHRASES** 28 If something is happening **all over the place**, it is happening in many different places. (PHRASE: PHR after v, v-link PHR) ❑ *Businesses are closing down all over the place.* 29 If things are **all over the place**, they are spread over a very large area, usually in a disorganized way. (PHRASE: v-link PHR, PHR after v) ❑ *Our fingerprints are probably all over the place.* 30 If you say that someone is **all over the place**, you mean that they are confused or disorganized, and unable to think clearly or act properly. [mainly BRIT] (PHRASE: v-link PHR) ❑ *He was careful and diligent. I was all over the place.* 31 If you **change places with** another person, you start being in their situation or role, and they start being in yours. (PHRASE: V inflects, pl-n PHR, PHR *with* n = *swap*) ❑ *When he has tried to identify all the items, you can change places, and he can test you.* 32 If you have been trying to understand something puzzling and then everything **falls into place** or **clicks into place**, you suddenly understand how different pieces of information are connected and everything becomes clearer. (PHRASE: V inflects) ❑ *When the reasons behind the decision were explained, of course, it all fell into place.* 33 If things **fall into place**, events happen naturally to produce a situation you want. (PHRASE: V inflects) ❑ *Once the decision was made, things fell into place rapidly.* 34 If you say that someone **is going places**, you mean that they are showing a lot of talent or ability and are likely to become very successful. (PHRASE: V inflects, oft cont) ❑ *You always knew Barbara was going places, she was different.* 35 People **in high places** are people who have powerful and influential positions in a government, society, or organization. (PHRASE: usu n PHR) ❑ *He had friends in high places.* 36 If something is **in place**, it is in its correct or usual position. If it is **out of place**, it is not in its correct or usual position. (PHRASE: PHR after v, v-link PHR) ❑ *Geoff hastily pushed the drawer back into place... Not a strand of her golden hair was out of place.* 37 If something such as a law, a policy, or an administrative structure is **in place**, it is working or able to be used. (PHRASE: v-link PHR, PHR after v) ❑ *Similar legislation is already in place in Wales.* 38 If one thing or person is used or does something **in place of** another, they replace the other thing or person. (PHRASE) ❑ *Cooked kidney beans can be used in place of French beans.* 39 If something has particular characteristics or features **in places**, it has them at several points within an area. (PHRASE: PHR with cl/group) ❑ *The snow along the roadside was six feet deep in places.* 40 If you say what you would have done **in** someone else's **place**, you say what you would have done if you had been in their situation and had been experiencing what they were experiencing. (PHRASE) ❑ *In her place I wouldn't have been able to resist it... What would you have done in my place, my dear?* 41 You say **in the first place** when you are talking about the beginning of a situation or about the situation as it was before a series of events. (PHRASE: PHR after v) ❑ *What brought you to Washington in the first place?* 42 You say **in the first place** and **in the second place** to introduce the first and second in a series of points or reasons. **In the first place** can also be used to emphasize a very important point or reason. (PHRASE: PHR with cl) ❑ *In the first place you are not old and in the second place you are a very attractive man.* 43 If you say that **it is not** your **place to** do something, you mean that it is not right or appropriate for you to do it, or that it is not your responsibility to do it. (PHRASE: V inflects, usu PHR to-inf) ❑ *He says that it is not his place to comment on government commitment to further funds.* 44 If someone or something seems **out of place** in a particular situation, they do not seem to belong there or to be suitable for that situation. (PHRASE: v-link PHR) ❑ *I felt out of place in my suit and tie.* 45 If you say that someone has found their **place in the sun**, you mean that they are in a job or a situation where they will be happy and have everything that they want. (PHRASE: usu poss PHR) 46 If you **place** one thing **above**, **before**, or **over** another, you think that the first thing is more important than the second and you show this in your behaviour. (PHRASE = *put*) ❑ *He continued to place security above all other objectives.* 47 If you **put** someone **in** their **place**, you show them that they are less important or clever than they think they are. (PHRASE: V inflects) ❑ *In a few words she had put him in his place.* 48 If you say that someone should **be shown** their **place** or **be kept in** their **place**, you are saying, often in a humorous way, that they should be made aware of their low status. (PHRASE) ❑ *...an uppity publican who needs to be shown his place.* 49 If one thing **takes second place to** another, it is considered to be less important and is given less attention than the other thing. (PHRASE: V inflects, oft PHR *to* n) ❑ *My personal life has had to take second place to my career.* 50 If one thing or person **takes the place of** another or **takes** another's **place**, they replace the other thing or person. (PHRASE: V inflects) ❑ *Optimism was gradually taking the place of pessimism... He eventually took Charlie's place in a popular Latin band.* 51 **pride of place** ➔ see **pride**.

**Place** **Place** is used as part of the name of a square or short street in a town. (N-IN-NAMES) ❑ *...15 Portland Place, London W1A 4DD.*

**pla|cebo** /pləsiːboʊ/ **(placebos)** A **placebo** is a substance with no effects that a doctor gives to a patient instead of a drug. Placebos are used when testing new drugs or sometimes when a patient has imagined their illness. (N-COUNT)

**pla|cebo ef|fect** **(placebo effects)** The **placebo effect** is the fact that some patients' health improves after taking what they believe is an effective drug but which is in fact only a placebo. (N-COUNT: usu *the* N in sing)

**place card** **(place cards)** A **place card** is a small card with a person's name on it which is put on a table at a formal meal to indicate where that person is to sit. (N-COUNT)

**-placed** /-pleɪst/ 1 **-placed** combines with adverbs to form adjectives which describe how well or badly someone is able to do a particular task. (COMB in ADJ) ❑ *A member of the Royal Commission on Criminal Justice, Miss Rafferty is well-placed to comment... Fund managers are poorly placed to monitor firms.* 2 **-placed** combines with adverbs to form adjec- (COMB in ADJ) tives which indicate how good or bad the position of a building or area is considered to be. ❑ *The hotel is wonderfully placed only a minute's walk from the city centre.*

**place|man** /pleɪsmən/ **(placemen)** If you refer to a public official as a **placeman**, you disapprove of the fact that they use their position for their own personal benefit or to provide political support for those who appointed them. [BRIT] ❑ *...the party's programme to purify the Commons by the removal of placemen.* N-COUNT: usu pl [disapproval]

**place mat** **(place mats)** also **placemat. Place mats** are mats that are put on a table before a meal for people to put their plates or bowls on. N-COUNT

**place|ment** /pleɪsmənt/ **(placements)** 1 **The placement of** something or someone is the act of putting them in a particular place or position. ❑ *The treatment involves the placement of twenty-two electrodes in the inner ear.* N-UNCOUNT: with supp, usu *the* N *of* n 2 If someone who is training gets a **placement**, they get a job for a period of time which is intended to give them experience in the work they are training for. ❑ *He had a six-month work placement with the Japanese government.* N-COUNT: usu supp N 3 The **placement** of someone in a job, home, or school is the act or process of finding them a job, home, or school. ❑ *The children were waiting for placement in a foster care home.* N-UNCOUNT: with supp

**pla|cen|ta** /pləsentə/ **(placentas) The placenta** is the mass of veins and tissue inside the womb of a pregnant woman or animal, which the unborn baby is attached to. ❑ *The drug can be transferred to the baby via the placenta.* N-COUNT: usu *the* N

**place set|ting** **(place settings)** 1 A **place setting** is an arrangement of knives, forks, spoons, and glasses that has been laid out on a table for the use of one person at a meal. N-COUNT 2 A **place setting** of china or of knives, forks, and spoons is a complete set of all the things that one person might use at a meal. ❑ *A seven-piece place setting costs about £45.* N-COUNT

**plac|id** /plæsɪd/ 1 A **placid** person or animal is calm and does not easily become excited, angry, or upset. ❑ *She was a placid child who rarely cried.* ADJ ♦ **plac|id|ly** *'No matter, we will pay the difference,' Helena said placidly.* ADV: ADV with v 2 A **placid** place, area of water, or life is calm and peaceful. ❑ *...the placid waters of Lake Erie.* ADJ: usu ADJ n

**plac|ings** /pleɪsɪŋz/ **The placings** in a competition are the relative positions of the competitors at the end or at a particular stage of the competition. ❑ *Northampton were third in the League placings.* N-PLURAL: usu *the* N, oft supp N

**pla|gia|rism** /pleɪdʒərɪzəm/ **Plagiarism** is the practice of using or copying someone else's idea or work and pretending that you thought of it or created it. ❑ *Now he's in real trouble. He's accused of plagiarism.* N-UNCOUNT ♦ **pla|gia|rist** **(plagiarists)** *Colleagues call Oates an unlikely plagiarist.* N-COUNT

**pla|gia|rize** /pleɪdʒəraɪz/ **(plagiarizes, plagiarizing, plagiarized)**

✔ in BRIT, also use **plagiarise**

If someone **plagiarizes** another person's idea or work, they use it or copy it and pretend that they thought of it or created it. ❑ *Moderates are plagiarizing his ideas in hopes of wooing voters... The poem employs as its first lines a verse plagiarized from a billboard.* VERB; V n; V-ed *from* n

**plague** /pleɪg/ **(plagues, plaguing, plagued)** 1 **Plague** or **the plague** is a very infectious disease which usually results in death. The patient has a severe fever and swellings on his or her body. ❑ *...a fresh outbreak of plague.* N-UNCOUNT: also *the* N 2 A **plague of** unpleasant things is a large number of them that arrive or happen at the same time. ❑ *The city is under threat from a plague of rats.* N-COUNT: N *of* n = epidemic 3 If you **are plagued by** unpleasant things, they continually cause you a lot of trouble or suffering. ❑ *She was plagued by weakness, fatigue, and dizziness... Fears about job security plague nearly half the workforce.* VERB; *be* V-ed *by* n; V n

**plaice** /pleɪs/ **(plaice) Plaice** are a type of flat sea fish. N-VAR ♦ **Plaice** is this fish eaten as food. ❑ *...a fillet of plaice with sautéed rice and vegetables.* N-UNCOUNT

**plaid** /plæd/ **(plaids) Plaid** is material with a check design on it. **Plaid** is also the design itself. ❑ *Eddie wore blue jeans and a plaid shirt.* N-MASS: oft N n

**plain** /pleɪn/ **(plainer, plainest, plains)** ◆◇◇ 1 A **plain** object, surface, or fabric is entirely in one colour and has no pattern, design, or writing on it. ❑ *In general, a plain carpet makes a room look bigger... He wore a plain blue shirt, open at the collar.* ADJ: usu ADJ n 2 Something that is **plain** is very simple in style. ❑ *Bronwen's dress was plain but it hung well on her.* ADJ ≠fancy, elaborate ♦ **plain|ly** *He was very tall and plainly dressed.* ADV: ADV -ed 3 If a fact, situation, or statement is **plain**, it is easy to recognize or understand. ❑ *It was plain to him that I was having a nervous breakdown... He's made it plain that he loves the game and wants to be involved still.* → See also **plain-spoken**. ADJ: usu v-link ADJ, oft *it* v-link ADJ that = clear 4 If you describe someone as **plain**, you think they look ordinary and not at all beautiful. ❑ *...a shy, rather plain girl with a pale complexion.* ADJ 5 A **plain** is a large flat area of land with very few trees on it. ❑ *Once there were 70 million buffalo on the plains.* N-COUNT 6 You can use **plain** before an adjective in order to emphasize it. ❑ *The food was just plain terrible.* ADV: ADV adj [emphasis] ♦ **Plain** is also used before a noun. ❑ *Is it love of publicity or plain stupidity on her part?* ADJ: ADJ n 7 If a police officer is **in plain clothes**, he or she is wearing ordinary clothes instead of a police uniform. ❑ *Three officers in plain clothes told me to get out of the car.* PHRASE: v-link PHR, PHR after v **plain sailing** → see **sailing**.

**plain choco|late** **Plain chocolate** is dark brown chocolate that has a stronger and less sweet taste than milk chocolate. [BRIT] N-UNCOUNT

✔ in AM, use **dark chocolate**

**plain-clothes** also **plainclothes. Plain-clothes** police officers wear ordinary clothes instead of a police uniform. ❑ *He was arrested by plain-clothes detectives as he walked through the customs hall.* ADJ: ADJ n ≠uniformed **in plain clothes** → see **plain**.

**plain flour** **Plain flour** is flour that does not make cakes and biscuits rise when they are cooked because it has no chemicals added to it. [BRIT] N-UNCOUNT

✔ in AM, use **all-purpose flour**

**plain|ly** /pleɪnli/ 1 You use **plainly** to indicate that you believe something is obviously true, often when you are trying to convince someone else that it is true. ❑ *The judge's conclusion was plainly wrong... Plainly, a more objective method of description must be adopted.* ADV: ADV with cl, not last in cl [emphasis] 2 You use **plainly** to indicate that something is easily seen, noticed, or recognized. ❑ *He was plainly annoyed... I could plainly see him turning his head to the right and left.* → See also **plain**. ADV: ADV with v, ADV adj = clearly

**plain-spoken** also **plainspoken.** If you say that someone is **plain-spoken**, you mean that they say exactly what they think, even when they know that what they say may not please other people. ❑ *...a plain-spoken American full of scorn for pomp and pretense.* ADJ [approval] = frank

**plaint** /pleɪnt/ **(plaints)** A **plaint** is a complaint or a sad cry. [LITERARY] ❑ *..a forlorn, haunting plaint.* N-COUNT

**plain|tiff** /pleɪntɪf/ **(plaintiffs)** A **plaintiff** is a person who brings a legal case against someone in a court of law. N-COUNT

**plain|tive** /pleɪntɪv/ A **plaintive** sound or voice sounds sad. [LITERARY] ❑ *They lay on the firm sands, listening to the plaintive cry of the seagulls.* ADJ = mournful ♦ **plain|tive|ly** *'Why don't we do something?' Davis asked plaintively.* ADV: usu ADV with v, also ADV adj

**plait** /plæt, AM pleɪt/ **(plaits, plaiting, plaited)** 1 If you **plait** three or more lengths of hair, rope, or other material together, you twist them over and under each other to make one thick length. [mainly BRIT] ❑ *Joanna parted her hair, and then began to plait it into two thick braids. ...a plaited leather belt.* VERB; V n; V-ed

✔ in AM, usually use **braid**

[2] A **plait** is a length of hair that has been plaited [mainly BRIT] N-COUNT

☑ in AM, usually use **braid**

**plan** /plæn/ **(plans, planning, planned)** [1] A **plan** is a method of achieving something that you have worked out in detail beforehand. ❑ *The three leaders had worked out a peace plan. ...a detailed plan of action for restructuring the group... He maintains that everything is going according to plan.* ◆◆◆ N-COUNT: usu with supp, also *according to* N

[2] If you **plan** what you are going to do, you decide in detail what you are going to do, and you intend to do it. ❑ *If you plan what you're going to eat, you reduce your chances of overeating... He planned to leave Baghdad on Monday... It would be difficult for schools to plan for the future... I had been planning a trip to the West Coast... A planned demonstration has been called off by its organisers.* VERB V wh V to-inf V *for* n V n V-ed

[3] If you have **plans**, you are intending to do a particular thing. ❑ *'I'm sorry,' she said. 'I have plans for tonight.'* N-PLURAL: usu with supp, oft N *for* n/-ing, N to-inf

[4] When you **plan** something that you are going to make, build, or create, you decide what the main parts of it will be and do a drawing of how it should be made. ❑ *We are planning a new kitchen.* VERB V n

[5] A **plan of** something that is going to be built or made is a detailed diagram or drawing of it. ❑ *...when you have drawn a plan of the garden.* N-COUNT: oft N *of/for* n

[6] → See also **planning**.

♦ **plan on** If you **plan on** doing something, you intend to do it. ❑ *They were planning on getting married.* PHRASAL VERB V P -ing/n

**plane** /pleɪn/ **(planes, planing, planed)** [1] A **plane** is a vehicle with wings and one or more engines, which can fly through the air. ❑ *He had plenty of time to catch his plane... Her mother was killed in a plane crash. ...fighter planes.* ◆◆◇ N-COUNT = *aeroplane, airplane*

[2] A **plane** is a flat, level surface which may be sloping at a particular angle. ❑ *...a building with angled planes.* N-COUNT

[3] If a number of points are in the same **plane**, one line or one flat surface could pass through them all. ❑ *All the planets orbit the Sun in roughly the same plane, round its equator.* N-SING

[4] A **plane** is a tool that has a flat bottom with a sharp blade in it. You move the plane over a piece of wood in order to remove thin pieces of its surface. → See picture on page 1709. N-COUNT

[5] If you **plane** a piece of wood, you make it smaller or smoother by using a plane. ❑ *She watches him plane the surface of a walnut board... Again I planed the surface flush.* VERB V n V n adj

[6] A **plane** or a **plane tree** is a large tree with broad leaves which often grows in towns. N-COUNT

**plane|load** /pleɪnloʊd/ **(planeloads)** A **planeload of** people or goods is as many people or goods as a plane can carry. ❑ *The British Red Cross has sent four planeloads of relief supplies to the stricken areas.* N-COUNT: usu N *of* n

**plan|et** /plænɪt/ **(planets)** A **planet** is a large, round object in space that moves around a star. The Earth is a planet. ❑ *The picture shows six of the nine planets in the solar system.* ◆◇◇ N-COUNT

**plan|etar|ium** /plænɪteəriəm/ **(planetariums)** A **planetarium** is a building where lights are shone on the ceiling to represent the planets and the stars and to show how they appear to move. N-COUNT

**plan|etary** /plænɪtri, AM -teri/ **Planetary** means relating to or belonging to planets. ❑ *Within our own galaxy there are probably tens of thousands of planetary systems.* ADJ: ADJ n

**plan|gent** /plændʒənt/ A **plangent** sound is a deep, loud sound, which may be sad. [LITERARY] ❑ *...plangent violins.* ADJ

**plank** /plæŋk/ **(planks)** [1] A **plank** is a long, flat, rectangular piece of wood. ❑ *It was very strong, made of three solid planks of wood.* N-COUNT: oft N *of* n

[2] The main **plank of** a particular group or political party is the main principle on which it bases its policy, or its main aim. [JOURNALISM] ❑ *Encouraging people to shop locally is a central plank of his environment policy.* N-COUNT: with supp, usu N *of* n

**plank|ing** /plæŋkɪŋ/ **Planking** is wood that has been cut into long flat pieces. It is used especially to make floors. N-UNCOUNT

**plank|ton** /plæŋktən/ **Plankton** is a mass of tiny animals and plants that live in the surface layer of the sea. ❑ *...its usual diet of plankton and other small organisms.* N-UNCOUNT

**plan|ner** /plænəʳ/ **(planners)** **Planners** are people whose job is to make decisions about what is going to be done in the future. For example, town planners decide how land should be used and what new buildings should be built. ❑ *...a panel that includes city planners, art experts and historians.* N-COUNT: oft supp N

**plan|ning** /plænɪŋ/ [1] **Planning** is the process of deciding in detail how to do something before you actually start to do it. ❑ *The trip needs careful planning... The new system is still in the planning stages.* → See also **family planning**. ◆◇◇ N-UNCOUNT

[2] **Planning** is control by the local government of the way that land is used in an area and of what new buildings are built there. ❑ *...a masterpiece of 18th-century town planning.* N-UNCOUNT

**plan|ning ap|pli|ca|tion** **(planning applications)** In Britain, a **planning application** is a formal request to a local authority for permission to build something new or to add something to an existing building. N-COUNT

**plan|ning per|mis|sion** **(planning permissions)** In Britain, **planning permission** is official permission that you must get from the local authority before building something new or adding something to an existing building. N-COUNT

**plant** /plɑːnt, plænt/ **(plants, planting, planted)** [1] A **plant** is a living thing that grows in the earth and has a stem, leaves, and roots. ❑ *Water each plant as often as required. ...exotic plants.* → See also **bedding plant**, **pot plant**, **rubber plant**. ◆◆◆ N-COUNT

[2] When you **plant** a seed, plant, or young tree, you put it into the ground so that it will grow there. ❑ *He says he plans to plant fruit trees and vegetables.* ♦ **plant|ing** *Extensive flooding in the country has delayed planting and many crops are still under water.* VERB V n N-UNCOUNT

[3] When someone **plants** land **with** a particular type of plant or crop, they put plants, seeds, or young trees into the land to grow them there. ❑ *They plan to plant the area with grass and trees... Recently much of their energy has gone into planting a large vegetable garden. ...newly planted fields.* VERB V n *with* n V n V-ed

[4] A **plant** is a factory or a place where power is produced. ❑ *...Ford's British car assembly plants... The plant provides forty per cent of the country's electricity.* N-COUNT

[5] **Plant** is large machinery that is used in industrial processes. ❑ *...investment in plant and equipment.* N-UNCOUNT = *machinery*

[6] If you **plant** something somewhere, you put it there firmly. ❑ *She planted her feet wide and bent her knees slightly. ...with his enormous feet planted heavily apart.* VERB V n adv/prep V-ed adv/prep

[7] To **plant** something such as a bomb means to hide it somewhere so that it explodes or works there. ❑ *So far no one has admitted planting the bomb.* VERB V n

[8] If something such as a weapon or drugs **is planted** on someone, it is put among their possessions or in their house so that they will be wrongly accused of a crime. ❑ *He claimed that the drugs had been planted to incriminate him.* VERB: oft passive *be* V-ed

[9] If an organization **plants** someone somewhere, they send that person there so that they can get information or watch someone secretly. ❑ *Journalists informed police who planted an undercover detective to trap Smith.* VERB V n

♦ **plant out** When you **plant out** young plants, you plant them in the ground in the place where they are to be left to grow. ❑ *Plant out the spring cabbage whenever opportunities arise.* PHRASAL VERB V P n (not pron) Also V n P

**plan|tain** /plæntɪn/ **(plantains)** [1] A **plantain** is a type of green banana which can be cooked and eaten as a vegetable. N-VAR

[2] A **plantain** is a wild plant with broad leaves and a head of tiny green flowers on a long stem. N-VAR

**plan|ta|tion** /plɑːnteɪʃən, plæn-/ **(plantations)** 1 N-COUNT A **plantation** is a large piece of land, especially in a tropical country, where crops such as rubber, coffee, tea, or sugar are grown. ❑ *...banana plantations in Costa Rica.* 2 N-COUNT A **plantation** is a large number of trees that have been planted together. ❑ *...a plantation of almond trees.*

**plant|er** /plɑːntəʳ, plæn-/ **(planters)** 1 N-COUNT **Planters** are people who own or manage plantations in tropical countries. 2 N-COUNT A **planter** is a container for plants that people keep in their homes.

**plant pot** **(plant pots)** N-COUNT = *flowerpot* A **plant pot** is a container that is used for growing plants. [mainly BRIT]

☑ in AM, usually use **pot, planter**

**plaque** /plæk, plɑːk/ **(plaques)** 1 N-COUNT A **plaque** is a flat piece of metal or stone with writing on it which is fixed to a wall or other structure to remind people of an important person or event. ❑ *After touring the hospital, Her Majesty unveiled a commemorative plaque.* 2 N-UNCOUNT **Plaque** is a substance containing bacteria that forms on the surface of your teeth. ❑ *Deposits of plaque build up between the tooth and the gum.*

**plas|ma** /plæzmə/ N-UNCOUNT **Plasma** is the clear liquid part of blood which contains the blood cells.

**plas|ter** /plɑːstəʳ, plæs-/ **(plasters, plastering, plastered)** 1 N-UNCOUNT **Plaster** is a smooth paste made of sand, lime, and water which goes hard when it dries. Plaster is used to cover walls and ceilings and is also used to make sculptures. ❑ *There were huge cracks in the plaster, and the green shutters were faded.* 2 VERB If you **plaster** a wall or ceiling, you cover it with a layer of plaster. ❑ V n *The ceiling he had just plastered fell in and knocked him off his ladder.* 3 VERB If you **plaster** a surface or a place **with** posters or pictures, you stick a lot of them all over it. ❑ V n *with* n *They plastered the city with posters condemning her election...* be V-ed *with* n *His room is plastered with pictures of Porsches and Ferraris.* 4 VERB If you **plaster yourself in** some kind of sticky substance, you cover yourself in it. ❑ V pron-refl *in* n *She plastered herself from head to toe in high factor sun lotion.* 5 N-COUNT A **plaster** is a strip of sticky material used for covering small cuts or sores on your body. [BRIT]

☑ in AM, usually use **Band-Aid**

6 → See also **plastered**. 7 PHRASE If you have a leg or arm **in plaster**, you have a cover made of plaster of Paris around your leg or arm, in order to protect a broken bone and allow it to mend. [mainly BRIT]

☑ in AM, use **in a cast**

**plaster|board** /plɑːstəʳbɔːʳd, plæs-/ N-UNCOUNT **Plasterboard** is cardboard covered with plaster which is used for covering walls and ceilings instead of using plaster.

**plas|ter cast** **(plaster casts)** 1 N-COUNT A **plaster cast** is a cover made of plaster of Paris which is used to protect a broken bone by keeping part of the body stiff. 2 N-COUNT A **plaster cast** is a copy of a statue or other object, made from plaster of Paris. ❑ *...a plaster cast of the Venus de Milo.*

**plas|tered** /plɑːstəʳd, plæs-/ 1 ADJ: v-link ADJ prep/adv If something is **plastered to** a surface, it is sticking to the surface. ❑ *His hair was plastered down to his scalp by the rain.* 2 ADJ: v-link ADJ, usu ADJ *with/in* n If something or someone is **plastered with** a sticky substance, they are covered with it. ❑ *My hands, boots and trousers were plastered with mud.* 3 ADJ: v-link ADJ prep/adv If a story or photograph is **plastered all over** the front page of a newspaper, it is given a lot of space on the page and made very noticeable. ❑ *His picture was plastered all over the newspapers on the weekend.*

**plas|ter|er** /plɑːstərəʳ, plæs-/ **(plasterers)** N-COUNT A **plasterer** is a person whose job it is to cover walls and ceilings with plaster.

**plas|ter of Paris** /plɑːstər əv pærɪs, plæs-/ N-UNCOUNT **Plaster of Paris** is a type of plaster made from white powder and water which dries quickly. It is used to make plaster casts.

**plas|tic** /plæstɪk/ **(plastics)** ◆◇◇ 1 N-MASS: oft N n **Plastic** is a material which is produced from oil by a chemical process and which is used to make many objects. It is light in weight and does not break easily. ❑ *...a wooden crate, sheltered from wetness by sheets of plastic... A lot of the plastics that carmakers are using cannot be recycled. ...a black plastic bag.* 2 ADJ disapproval If you describe something as **plastic**, you mean that you think it looks or tastes unnatural or not real. ❑ *...plastic airline food.* 3 N-UNCOUNT If you use **plastic** or **plastic money** to pay for something, you pay for it with a credit card instead of using cash. [INFORMAL] ❑ *Using plastic to pay for an order is simplicity itself.* 4 ADJ Something that is **plastic** is soft and can easily be made into different shapes. ❑ *The mud is smooth, gray, soft, and plastic as butter.* ♦ **plas|tic|ity** /plæstɪsɪti/ N-UNCOUNT *...the plasticity of the flesh.*

**plas|tic bul|let** **(plastic bullets)** N-COUNT A **plastic bullet** is a large bullet made of plastic, which is intended to make people stop rioting, rather than to kill people.

**plas|tic ex|plo|sive** **(plastic explosives)** N-MASS **Plastic explosive** is a substance which explodes and which is used in making small bombs.

**Plas|ti|cine** /plæstɪsiːn/ N-UNCOUNT **Plasticine** is a soft coloured substance like clay which children use for making models. [BRIT, TRADEMARK]

**plas|tic sur|geon** **(plastic surgeons)** N-COUNT A **plastic surgeon** is a doctor who performs operations to repair or replace skin which has been damaged, or to improve people's appearance.

**plas|tic sur|gery** N-UNCOUNT **Plastic surgery** is the practice of performing operations to repair or replace skin which has been damaged, or to improve people's appearance. ❑ *She even had plastic surgery to change the shape of her nose.*

**plas|tic wrap** N-UNCOUNT = *Saran wrap* **Plastic wrap** is a thin, clear, stretchy plastic which you use to cover food to keep it fresh. [AM]

☑ in BRIT, use **clingfilm**

**plate** /pleɪt/ **(plates)** ◆◇◇ 1 N-COUNT A **plate** is a round or oval flat dish that is used to hold food. ❑ *Anita pushed her plate away; she had eaten virtually nothing.* ♦ N-COUNT: usu N *of* n A **plate of** food is the amount of food on the plate. ❑ *...a huge plate of bacon and eggs.* 2 N-COUNT A **plate** is a flat piece of metal, especially on machinery or a building. 3 N-COUNT A **plate** is a small, flat piece of metal with someone's name written on it, which you usually find beside the front door of an office or house. 4 N-PLURAL On a road vehicle, the **plates** are the panels at the front and back which display the license number in the United States, and the registration number in Britain. ❑ *...dusty-looking cars with New Jersey plates.* → See also **number plate, license plate**. 5 N-UNCOUNT **Plate** is dishes, bowls, and cups that are made of precious metal, especially silver or gold. ❑ *...gold and silver plate, jewellery, and roomfuls of antique furniture.* 6 N-COUNT A **plate** in a book is a picture or photograph which takes up a whole page and is usually printed on better quality paper than the rest of the book. ❑ *Fermor's book has 55 colour plates.* 7 N-COUNT In geology, a **plate** is a large piece of the earth's surface, perhaps as large as a continent, which moves very slowly. [TECHNICAL]

PHRASES 8 PHRASE: V inflects If you **have enough on** your **plate** or **have a lot on** your **plate**, you have a lot of work to do or a lot of things to deal with. ❑ *We have enough on our plate. There is plenty of work to be done on what we have.* 9 PHRASE: V inflects disapproval If you say that someone has things **handed to** them **on a plate**, you disapprove of them because they get good things easily. [mainly BRIT] ❑ *Even the presidency was handed to him on a plate.*

**plat|eau** /plætoʊ, AM plætoʊ/ **(plateaus** or **plateaux, plateaus, plateauing, plateaued)** 1 N-COUNT A **plateau** is a large area of high and fairly flat land. ❑ *A broad valley opened up leading to a high, flat plateau of cultivated land.* 2 N-COUNT If you say that an activity or process has reached a **plateau**, you mean that it has reached a stage where there is no further change or development. ❑ *The US heroin market now appears to have reached a plateau.* [3] If something such as an activity, process, or cost **plateaus** or **plateaus out**, it reaches a stage where there is no further change or development. ❑ *Evelyn's career is accelerating, and mine is plateauing out a bit... The shares plateaued at 153p.* — VERB; V *out*; V *at* n

**plat|ed** /pleɪtɪd/ If something made of metal is **plated with** a thin layer of another type of metal, it is covered with it. ❑ *...a range of jewellery, plated with 22-carat nickel-free gold.* — ADJ: v-link ADJ *with* n

**-plated** /-pleɪtɪd/ [1] Something made of metal that is **plated** is covered with a thin layer of another type of metal such as gold and silver. ❑ *...a gold-plated watch.* [2] → See also **armour-plated, gold-plated, silver-plated.** — COMB in ADJ

**plate|ful** /pleɪtfʊl/ **(platefuls)** A **plateful of** food is an amount of food that is on a plate and fills it. ❑ *...a greasy plateful of bacon and eggs.* — N-COUNT: usu N *of* n

**plate glass** also **plate-glass. Plate glass** is thick glass made in large, flat pieces, which is used especially to make large windows and doors. — N-UNCOUNT

**plate|let** /pleɪtlət/ **(platelets) Platelets** are a kind of blood cell. If you cut yourself and you are bleeding, platelets help to stop the bleeding. [TECHNICAL] — N-COUNT: usu pl

**plate tec|ton|ics Plate tectonics** is the way that large pieces of the earth's surface move slowly around. [TECHNICAL] — N-UNCOUNT

**plat|form** /plætfɔːʳm/ **(platforms)** [1] A **platform** is a flat, raised structure, usually made of wood, which people stand on when they make speeches or give a performance. ❑ *Nick finished what he was saying and jumped down from the platform.* — ◆◇◇ N-COUNT [2] A **platform** is a flat raised structure or area, usually one which something can stand on or land on. ❑ *They found a spot on a rocky platform where they could pitch their tents.* — N-COUNT [3] A **platform** is a structure built for people to work and live on when drilling for oil or gas at sea, or when extracting it. — N-COUNT [4] A **platform** in a railway station is the area beside the rails where you wait for or get off a train. ❑ *The train was about to leave and I was not even on the platform.* — N-COUNT [5] The **platform** of a political party is what they say they will do if they are elected. ❑ *...a platform of political and economic reforms.* — N-COUNT: with supp = programme [6] If someone has a **platform**, they have an opportunity to tell people what they think or want. ❑ *The demonstration provided a platform for a broad cross section of speakers.* — N-COUNT

**plat|ing** /pleɪtɪŋ/ **Plating** is a thin layer of metal on something, or a covering of metal plates. ❑ *The tanker began spilling oil the moment her outer plating ruptured.* — N-UNCOUNT

**plati|num** /plætɪnəm/ [1] **Platinum** is a very valuable, silvery-grey metal. It is often used for making jewellery. — N-UNCOUNT [2] **Platinum** hair is very fair, almost white. ❑ *...a platinum blonde with thick eye shadow and scarlet lipstick.* — COLOUR

**plati|tude** /plætɪtjuːd, AM -tuːd/ **(platitudes)** A **platitude** is a statement which is considered meaningless and boring because it has been made many times before in similar situations. ❑ *Why couldn't he say something original instead of spouting the same old platitudes?* — N-COUNT [disapproval]

**pla|ton|ic** /plətɒnɪk/

> ✔ The spelling **Platonic** is also used for meaning 2.

[1] **Platonic** relationships or feelings of affection do not involve sex. ❑ *She values the platonic friendship she has had with Chris for ten years.* — ADJ ≠ physical [2] **Platonic** means relating to the ideas of the Greek philosopher Plato. ❑ *...the Platonic tradition of Greek philosophy.* — ADJ: usu ADJ n

**pla|toon** /plətuːn/ **(platoons)** A **platoon** is a small group of soldiers, usually one which is commanded by a lieutenant. — N-COUNT

**plat|ter** /plætəʳ/ **(platters)** A **platter** is a large, flat plate used for serving food. [mainly AM] ❑ *The food was being served on silver platters.* — N-COUNT ♦ A **platter of** food is the amount of food on a platter. — N-COUNT

**plau|dits** /plɔːdɪtz/ If a person or a thing receives **plaudits** from a group of people, those people express their admiration for or approval of that person or thing. [FORMAL] ❑ *They won plaudits and prizes for their accomplished films.* — N-PLURAL = acclaim

**plau|sible** /plɔːzɪbᵊl/ [1] An explanation or statement that is **plausible** seems likely to be true or valid. ❑ *A more plausible explanation would seem to be that people are fed up with the Conservative government.* — ADJ = reasonable ♦ **plau|sibly** /plɔːzɪbli/ *Having bluffed his way in without paying, he could not plausibly demand his money back.* — ADV: ADV with v ♦ **plau|sibil|ity** /plɔːzɪbɪlɪti/ *...the plausibility of the theory.* — N-UNCOUNT = credibility [2] If you say that someone is **plausible**, you mean that they seem to be telling the truth and to be sincere and honest. ❑ *He was so plausible that he conned everybody.* — ADJ = believable

**play** /pleɪ/ **(plays, playing, played)** [1] When children, animals, or perhaps adults **play**, they spend time doing enjoyable things, such as using toys and taking part in games. ❑ *They played in the little garden... Polly was playing with her teddy bear.* — ◆◆◆ VERB; V; V *with* n ♦ **Play** is also a noun. ❑ *...a few hours of play until the baby-sitter takes them off to bed.* — N-UNCOUNT [2] When you **play** a sport, game, or match, you take part in it. ❑ *While the twins played cards, Francis sat reading... Alain was playing cards with his friends... I used to play basketball... I want to play for my country... He captained the team but he didn't actually play.* — V-RECIP; pl-n V n; V n *with* n; V n (non-recip); V *for* n (non-recip); V (non-recip) ♦ **Play** is also a noun. ❑ *Both sides adopted the Continental style of play.* — N-UNCOUNT [3] When one person or team **plays** another or **plays against** them, they compete against them in a sport or game. ❑ *Northern Ireland will play Latvia... I've played against him a few times.* — VERB; V n; V *against* n ♦ **Play** is also a noun. ❑ *Fischer won after 5 hours and 41 minutes of play.* — N-UNCOUNT [4] When you **play** the ball or **play** a shot in a game or sport, you kick or hit the ball. ❑ *Think first before playing the ball... I played the ball back slightly.* — VERB; V n; V n adv [5] If you **play** a joke or a trick **on** someone, you deceive them or give them a surprise in a way that you think is funny, but that often causes problems for them or annoys them. ❑ *Someone had played a trick on her, stretched a piece of string at the top of those steps... I thought: 'This cannot be happening, somebody must be playing a joke'.* — VERB; V n *on* n; V n [6] If you **play with** an object or with your hair, you keep moving it or touching it with your fingers, perhaps because you are bored or nervous. ❑ *She stared at the floor, idly playing with the strap of her handbag.* — VERB; V *with* n [7] A **play** is a piece of writing which is performed in a theatre, on the radio, or on television. ❑ *The company put on a play about the homeless... It's my favourite Shakespeare play.* — N-COUNT [8] If an actor **plays** a role or character in a play or film, he or she performs the part of that character. ❑ *...Dr Jekyll and Mr Hyde, in which he played Hyde... His ambition is to play the part of Dracula.* — VERB; V n; V n [9] You can use **play** to describe how someone behaves, when they are deliberately behaving in a certain way or like a certain type of person. For example, to **play the innocent**, means to pretend to be innocent, and to **play deaf** means to pretend not to hear something. ❑ *Hill tried to play the peacemaker... So you want to play nervous today?* — V-LINK = act; V n; V adj [10] You can describe how someone deals with a situation by saying that they **play it** in a certain way. For example, if someone **plays it cool**, they keep calm and do not show much emotion, and if someone **plays it straight**, they behave in an honest and direct way. ❑ *Investors are playing it cautious, and they're playing it smart.* — VERB; V *it* adj/adv [11] If you **play** a musical instrument or **play** a tune on a musical instrument, or if a musical instrument **plays**, music is produced from it. ❑ *Nina had been playing the piano... He played for me... Place your baby in her seat and play her a lullaby... The guitars played.* — VERB; V n; V *for* n; V n n, V [12] If you **play** a — VERB record, a CD, or a tape, you put it into a machine and sound is produced. If a record, CD, or tape **is playing**, sound is being produced from it. ❑ *She played her records too loudly... There is classical music playing in the background.* [13] If a musician or group of musicians **plays** or **plays** a concert, they perform music for people to listen or dance to. ❑ *A band was playing... He will play concerts in Amsterdam and Paris.*

V n · V · Also V n n · VERB · V · V n

**PHRASES** [14] If you ask **what** someone **is playing at**, you are angry because you think they are doing something stupid or wrong. [INFORMAL] ❑ *What the hell are you playing at?* [15] When something **comes into play** or **is brought into play**, it begins to be used or to have an effect. ❑ *The real existence of a military option will come into play.*

PHRASE: V inflects · feelings · PHRASE: V inflects

[16] If something or someone **plays a part** or **plays a role in** a situation, they are involved in it and have an effect on it. ❑ *The UN would play a major role in monitoring a ceasefire. ...the role played by diet in disease.* [17] **to play ball** → see **ball**. **to play** your **cards right** → see **card**. **to play it by ear** → see **ear**. **to play fair** → see **fair**. **to play second fiddle** → see **fiddle**. **to play the field** → see **field**. **to play with fire** → see **fire**. **to play the fool** → see **fool**. **to play to the gallery** → see **gallery**. **to play into** someone's **hands** → see **hand**. **to play hard to get** → see **hard**. **to play havoc** → see **havoc**. **to play host** → see **host**. **to play safe** → see **safe**. **to play for time** → see **time**. **to play truant** → see **truant**.

PHRASE: V inflects, usu PHR *in* n

♦ **play along** If you **play along with** a person, with what they say, or with their plans, you appear to agree with them and do what they want, even though you are not sure whether they are right. ❑ *My mother has learnt to play along with the bizarre conversations begun by father... He led the way to the lift. Fox played along, following him.*

PHRASAL VERB: no passive · V P with n · V P

♦ **play around** [1] If you **play around**, you behave in a silly way to amuse yourself or other people. [INFORMAL] ❑ *Stop playing around and eat!... Had he taken the keys and played around with her car?* [2] If you **play around with** a problem or an arrangement of objects, you try different ways of organizing it in order to find the best solution or arrangement. [INFORMAL] ❑ *I can play around with the pictures to make them more eye-catching.*

PHRASAL VERB · V P · V P *with* n · PHRASAL VERB · V P *with* n

♦ **play at** [1] If you say that someone **is playing at** something, you disapprove of the fact that they are doing it casually and not very seriously. ❑ *We were still playing at war – dropping leaflets instead of bombs.* [2] If someone, especially a child, **plays at** being someone or doing something, they pretend to be that person or do that thing as a game. ❑ *Ed played at being a pirate.* [3] If you do not know what someone **is playing at**, you do not understand what they are doing or what they are trying to achieve. [INFORMAL] ❑ *She began to wonder what he was playing at.*

PHRASAL VERB: no passive · disapproval · V P n/-ing · PHRASAL VERB: no passive · V P n/-ing · PHRASAL VERB · V P

♦ **play back** When you **play back** a tape or film, you listen to the sounds or watch the pictures after recording them. ❑ *He bought an answering machine that plays back his messages when he calls... Ted might benefit from hearing his own voice recorded and played back... I played the tape back.* → See also **playback**.

PHRASAL VERB · V P n (not pron) · V-ed P · V n P

♦ **play down** If you **play down** something, you try to make people believe that it is not particularly important. ❑ *Western diplomats have played down the significance of the reports... Both London and Dublin are playing the matter down.*

PHRASAL VERB ≠ *play up* · V P n (not pron) · V n P

♦ **play on** If you **play on** someone's fears, weaknesses, or faults, you deliberately use them in order to persuade that person to do something, or to achieve what you want. ❑ *...an election campaign which plays on the population's fear of change.*

PHRASAL VERB = *exploit* · V P n

♦ **play out** If a dramatic event **is played out**, it gradually takes place. ❑ *Her union reforms were played out against a background of rising unemployment.*

PHRASAL VERB: usu passive = *unfold* · *be* V-ed P · Also V P n

♦ **play up** [1] If you **play up** something, you emphasize it and try to make people believe that it is important. ❑ *The media played up the prospects for a settlement... His Japanese ancestry has been played up by some of his opponents.* [2] If something such as a machine or a part of your body **is playing up** or **is playing** you **up**, it is causing problems because it is not working properly. [BRIT, INFORMAL] ❑ *The engine had been playing up... It was his back playing him up.* [3] When children **play up**, they are naughty and difficult to control. [BRIT, INFORMAL] ❑ *Patrick often plays up when he knows I'm in a hurry.*

PHRASAL VERB ≠ *play down* · V P n (not pron) · V P n, Also V n P · PHRASAL VERB: usu cont, no passive · V P · V n P · PHRASAL VERB · V P

**play-act** (**play-acts, play-acting, play-acted**) If someone **is play-acting**, they are pretending to have attitudes or feelings that they do not really have. ❑ *The 'victim' revealed he was only play acting.*

VERB: usu cont · V

**play-acting** **Play-acting** is behaviour where someone pretends to have attitudes or feelings that they do not really have. ❑ *It was just a piece of play-acting.*

N-UNCOUNT

**play|back** /pleɪbæk/ (**playbacks**) The **playback** of a tape is the operation of playing it on a machine in order to listen to the sound or watch the pictures recorded on it. ❑ *I heard a playback of one of the tapes.*

N-COUNT: usu sing

**play|boy** /pleɪbɔɪ/ (**playboys**) You can refer to a rich man who spends most of his time enjoying himself as a **playboy**. ❑ *Father was a rich playboy. ...the playboy millionaire.*

N-COUNT

**Play-Doh** /pleɪdoʊ/ **Play-Doh** is a soft coloured substance like clay which children use for making models. [TRADEMARK]

N-UNCOUNT

**play|er** /pleɪəʳ/ (**players**) [1] A **player** in a sport or game is a person who takes part, either as a job or for fun. ❑ *...his greatness as a player... She was a good golfer and tennis player.* [2] You can use **player** to refer to a musician. For example, a **piano player** is someone who plays the piano. ❑ *...a professional trumpet player.* [3] If a person, country, or organization is a **player in** something, they are involved in it and important in it. ❑ *Big business has become a major player in the art market.* [4] A **player** is an actor. ❑ *...a company of players... Oscar nominations went to all five leading players.* [5] → See also **cassette player**, **CD player**, **record player**, **team player**.

◆◆◆ N-COUNT · N-COUNT · N-COUNT: oft supp N, N *in* n · N-COUNT

**player-manager** (**player-managers**) In football and some other sports, a **player-manager** is a person who plays for a team and also manages the team.

N-COUNT

**play|er pia|no** (**player pianos**) A **player piano** is a type of mechanical piano. When you press the pedals, air is forced through holes in a roll of paper to press the keys and play a tune. [mainly AM]

N-COUNT

✓ in BRIT, usually use **pianola**

**play|ful** /pleɪfʊl/ [1] A **playful** gesture or person is friendly or humorous. ❑ *...a playful kiss on the tip of his nose.* ♦ **play|ful|ly** *She pushed him away playfully.* ♦ **play|ful|ness** *...the child's natural playfulness.* [2] A **playful** animal is lively and cheerful. ❑ *...a playful puppy.*

ADJ · ADV · N-UNCOUNT · ADJ

**play|ground** /pleɪgraʊnd/ (**playgrounds**) [1] A **playground** is a piece of land, at school or in a public area, where children can play. → See also **adventure playground**. [2] If you describe a place as a **playground** for a certain group of people, you mean that those people like to enjoy themselves there or go on holiday there. ❑ *...St Tropez, playground of the rich and famous.*

N-COUNT · N-COUNT: usu sing, oft N supp

**play|group** /pleɪgruːp/ (**playgroups**) also **play group**. A **playgroup** is an informal school for very young children, where they learn things by playing.

N-COUNT: also prep N

**play|house** /pleɪhaʊs/ (**playhouses**) [1] A **playhouse** is a theatre. ❑ *The Theatre Royal is one of the oldest playhouses in Britain.* [2] A **playhouse** is a small house made for children to play in. ❑ *My father built me a playhouse.*

N-COUNT · N-COUNT = *Wendy house*

**play|ing card** **(playing cards)** **Playing cards** are thin pieces of cardboard with numbers or pictures printed on them, which are used to play various games. N-COUNT = card

**play|ing field** **(playing fields)** 1 A **playing field** is a large area of grass where people play sports. ❑ *...the playing fields of the girls' Grammar School.* N-COUNT 2 You talk about **a level playing field** to mean a situation that is fair, because no competitor or opponent in it has an advantage over another. ❑ *We ask for a level playing field when we compete with foreign companies.* PHRASE: N inflects

**play|list** /pleɪlɪst/ **(playlists, playlisting, playlisted)** 1 A **playlist** is a list of songs, albums, and artists that a radio station broadcasts. ❑ *Radio 1's playlist is dominated by top-selling youth-orientated groups.* N-COUNT 2 If a song, album, or artist **is playlisted**, it is put on a radio station's playlist. ❑ *We've playlisted many artists like Beth Orton who got picked up down the line by others.* VERB V n

**play|mate** /pleɪmeɪt/ **(playmates)** A child's **playmate** is another child who often plays with him or her. ❑ *The young girl loved to play with her playmates.* N-COUNT

**play-off** **(play-offs)** also **playoff.** 1 A **playoff** is an extra game which is played to decide the winner of a sports competition when two or more people have got the same score. ❑ *Nick Faldo was beaten by Peter Baker in a play-off.* N-COUNT 2 You use **playoffs** to refer to a series of games between the winners of different leagues, to decide which teams will play for a championship. ❑ *The winner will face the Oakland A's in the playoffs this weekend.* N-COUNT: usu N in pl

**play on words** **(plays on words)** A **play on words** is the same as a **pun**. N-COUNT: usu *a* N in sing

**play park** **(play parks)** A **play park** is a children's playground. N-COUNT

**play|pen** /pleɪpen/ **(playpens)** A **playpen** is a small structure which is designed for a baby or young child to play safely in. It has bars or a net round the sides and is open at the top. N-COUNT

**play|room** /pleɪruːm/ **(playrooms)** A **playroom** is a room in a house for children to play in. N-COUNT

**play|school** /pleɪskuːl/ **(playschools)** also **play school.** A **playschool** is an informal type of school for very young children where they learn things by playing. [mainly BRIT] N-COUNT: also prep N = playgroup

**play|thing** /pleɪθɪŋ/ **(playthings)** A **plaything** is a toy or other object that a child plays with. ❑ *...an untidy garden scattered with children's playthings.* N-COUNT

**play|time** /pleɪtaɪm/ In a school for young children, **playtime** is the period of time between lessons when they can play outside. ❑ *Any child who is caught will be kept in at playtime.* N-UNCOUNT = break

**play|wright** /pleɪraɪt/ **(playwrights)** A **playwright** is a person who writes plays. N-COUNT = dramatist

**pla|za** /plɑːzə, AM plæzə/ **(plazas)** 1 A **plaza** is an open square in a city. ❑ *Across the busy plaza, vendors sell hot dogs and croissant sandwiches.* N-COUNT 2 A **plaza** is a group of stores or buildings that are joined together or share common areas. [AM] N-COUNT

**plc** /piː el siː/ **(plcs)** also **PLC.** In Britain, **plc** means a company whose shares can be bought by the public and is usually used after the name of a company. **plc** is an abbreviation for 'public limited company'. Compare **Ltd.** [BUSINESS] ❑ *...British Telecommunications plc.* N-COUNT: usu sing, usu n N

**plea** /pliː/ **(pleas)** 1 A **plea** is an appeal or request for something, made in an intense or emotional way. [JOURNALISM] ❑ *Mr Nicholas made his emotional plea for help in solving the killing.* N-COUNT: oft N *for* n, N to-inf = appeal 2 In a court of law, a person's **plea** is the answer that they give when they have been charged with a crime, saying whether or not they are guilty of that crime. ❑ *The judge questioned him about his guilty plea... We will enter a plea of not guilty.* N-COUNT: usu adj N, N *of* adj 3 A **plea** is a reason which is given, to a court of law or to other people, as an excuse for doing something or for not doing something. ❑ *Phillips murdered his wife, but got off on a plea of insanity.* N-COUNT: usu N *of* n

**plea bar|gain** **(plea bargains, plea bargaining, plea bargained)** 1 In some legal systems, a **plea bargain** is an agreement that, if an accused person says they are guilty, they will be charged with a less serious crime or will receive a less severe punishment. ❑ *A plea bargain was offered by the state assuring her that she would not go to prison.* N-COUNT 2 If an accused person **plea bargains**, they accept a plea bargain. ❑ *More and more criminals will agree to plea-bargain.* VERB V ♦ **plea bar|gain|ing** *...the introduction of a system of plea bargaining.* N-UNCOUNT

**plead** /pliːd/ **(pleads, pleading, pleaded)** 1 If you **plead with** someone **to** do something, you ask them in an intense, emotional way to do it. ❑ *The lady pleaded with her daughter to come back home... He was kneeling on the floor pleading for mercy... 'Do not say that,' she pleaded... I pleaded to be allowed to go.* VERB = beg V *with* n to-inf, V *for* n, V with quote, V to-inf-passive 2 When someone charged with a crime **pleads guilty** or **not guilty** in a court of law, they officially state that they are guilty or not guilty of the crime. ❑ *Morris had pleaded guilty to robbery.* VERB V adj 3 If you **plead the case** or **cause** of someone or something, you speak out in their support or defence. ❑ *He appeared before the Committee to plead his case.* VERB V n 4 If you **plead** a particular thing as the reason for doing or not doing something, you give it as your excuse. ❑ *Mr Giles pleads ignorance as his excuse... It was no defence to plead that they were only obeying orders.* VERB V n, V that

**plead|ing** /pliːdɪŋ/ **(pleadings)** 1 A **pleading** expression or gesture shows someone that you want something very much. ❑ *...the pleading expression on her face.* ADJ: usu ADJ n ♦ **plead|ing|ly** *He looked at me pleadingly.* ADV: ADV after v 2 **Pleading** is asking someone for something you want very much, in an intense or emotional way. ❑ *He simply ignored Sid's pleading.* N-UNCOUNT: also N in pl
→ See also **special pleading**.

**pleas|ant** /plezᵊnt/ **(pleasanter, pleasantest)** ◆◇◇ 1 Something that is **pleasant** is nice, enjoyable, or attractive. ❑ *I've got a pleasant little apartment... It's always pleasant to do what you're good at doing.* ADJ: oft *it* v-link ADJ to-inf, ADJ to-inf ♦ **pleas|ant|ly** *We talked pleasantly of old times.* ADV: ADV with v, ADV adj 2 Someone who is **pleasant** is friendly and likeable. ❑ *The woman had a pleasant face.* ADJ: oft ADJ to-inf

**pleas|ant|ry** /plezᵊntri/ **(pleasantries)** **Pleasantries** are casual, friendly remarks which you make in order to be polite. ❑ *He exchanged pleasantries about his hotel and the weather.* N-COUNT: usu pl

**please** /pliːz/ **(pleases, pleasing, pleased)** ◆◆◇ 1 You say **please** when you are politely asking or inviting someone to do something. ❑ *Can you help us please?... Would you please open the door?... Please come in... 'May I sit here?' — 'Please do.'... Can we have the bill please?* ADV: ADV with cl [politeness] 2 You say **please** when you are accepting something politely. ❑ *'Tea?' — 'Yes, please.'... 'You want an apple with your cheese?' — 'Please.'* ADV: ADV with cl, ADV as reply [formulae] 3 You can say **please** to indicate that you want someone to stop doing something or stop speaking. You would say this if, for example, what they are doing or saying makes you angry or upset. ❑ *Please, Mary, this is all so unnecessary.* CONVENTION [feelings] 4 You can say **please** in order to attract someone's attention politely. Children in particular say '**please**' to attract the attention of a teacher or other adult. [mainly BRIT] ❑ *Please sir, can we have some more?* CONVENTION [politeness] 5 If someone or something **pleases** you, they make you feel happy and satisfied. ❑ *More than anything, I want to please you... Much of the food pleases rather than excites... It pleased him to talk to her.* VERB V n, V, *it* V n to-inf 6 You use **please** in expressions such as **as she pleases, whatever you please**, and **anything he pleases** to indicate that someone can do or have whatever they want. ❑ *Women should be free to dress and act as they please... Isabel can live where she pleases.* PHRASE: PHR after v 7 **If you please** is sometimes used as a very polite and formal way of attracting someone's attention or of asking them to do something. ❑ *Ladies and gentlemen, if you please. Miss Taylor's going to play for us.* CONVENTION [politeness]

8 You say **'please yourself'** to indicate in a rather rude way that you do not mind or care whether the person you are talking to does a particular thing or not. [INFORMAL] ❑ *'Do you mind if I wait?' I asked. Melanie shrugged: 'Please yourself.'* CONVENTION feelings

**pleased** /pliːzd/ ◆◇◇ 1 If you are **pleased**, you are happy about something or satisfied with something. ❑ *Felicity seemed pleased at the suggestion... I think he's going to be pleased that we identified the real problems... They're pleased to be going home... He glanced at her with a pleased smile.* ADJ: usu v-link ADJ, usu ADJ prep/that/to-inf 2 If you say you will be **pleased to** do something, you are saying in a polite way that you are willing to do it. ❑ *We will be pleased to answer any questions you may have.* ADJ: v-link ADJ to-inf politeness = happy 3 You can tell someone that you are **pleased with** something they have done in order to express your approval. ❑ *I'm pleased with the way things have been going... I am very pleased about the result... We are pleased that the problems have been resolved... We were very pleased to hear this encouraging news.* ADJ: v-link ADJ, usu ADJ prep/that/to-inf feelings = happy 4 When you are about to give someone some news which you know will please them, you can say that you are **pleased to** tell them the news or that they will be **pleased to** hear it. ❑ *I'm pleased to say that he is now doing well.* ADJ: v-link ADJ to-inf = happy 5 In official letters, people often say they will be **pleased to** do something, as a polite way of introducing what they are going to do or inviting people to do something. ❑ *We will be pleased to delete the charge from the original invoice.* ADJ: v-link ADJ to-inf politeness 6 If someone seems very satisfied with something they have done, you can say that they are **pleased with themselves**, especially if you think they are more satisfied than they should be. ❑ *He was pleased with himself for having remembered her name.* PHRASE: v-link PHR, PHR with cl 7 You can say **'Pleased to meet you'** as a polite way of greeting someone who you are meeting for the first time. CONVENTION formulae

**pleas|ing** /pliːzɪŋ/ Something that is **pleasing** gives you pleasure and satisfaction. ❑ *This area of France has a pleasing climate in August... It's pleasing to listen to.* ADJ: oft ADJ *to* n, ADJ to-inf ♦ **pleas|ing|ly** *The interior design is pleasingly simple.* ADV: usu ADV adj

**pleas|ur|able** /pleʒərəbᵊl/ **Pleasurable** experiences or sensations are pleasant and enjoyable. ❑ *The most pleasurable experience of the evening was the wonderful fireworks display.* ADJ ♦ **pleas|ur|ably** /pleʒərəbli/ *They spent six weeks pleasurably together.* ADV: ADV with v, ADV adj

**pleas|ure** /pleʒəʳ/ (**pleasures**) ◆◇◇ 1 If something gives you **pleasure**, you get a feeling of happiness, satisfaction, or enjoyment from it. ❑ *Watching sport gave him great pleasure... Everybody takes pleasure in eating.* N-UNCOUNT: oft N *from*/*in* n/-ing 2 **Pleasure** is the activity of enjoying yourself, especially rather than working or doing what you have a duty to do. ❑ *He mixed business and pleasure in a perfect and dynamic way... I read for pleasure.* N-UNCOUNT 3 A **pleasure** is an activity, experience or aspect of something that you find very enjoyable or satisfying. ❑ *Watching TV is our only pleasure. ...the pleasure of seeing a smiling face.* N-COUNT: oft N *of* n/-ing 4 If you meet someone for the first time, you can say, as a way of being polite, that it is **a pleasure to meet** them. You can also ask for **the pleasure of** someone's **company** as a polite and formal way of inviting them somewhere. ❑ *'A pleasure to meet you, sir,' he said.* CONVENTION politeness 5 You can say **'It's a pleasure'** or **'My pleasure'** as a polite way of replying to someone who has just thanked you for doing something. ❑ *'Thanks very much anyhow.' — 'It's a pleasure.'* CONVENTION formulae

**pleas|ure boat** (**pleasure boats**) A **pleasure boat** is a large boat which takes people for trips on rivers, lakes, or on the sea for pleasure. N-COUNT

**pleas|ure craft** (**pleasure craft**) A **pleasure craft** is the same as a **pleasure boat**. N-COUNT

**pleat** /pliːt/ (**pleats**) A **pleat** in a piece of clothing is a permanent fold that is made in the cloth by folding one part over the other and sewing across the top end of the fold. N-COUNT

**pleat|ed** /pliːtɪd/ A **pleated** piece of clothing has pleats in it. ❑ *...a short white pleated skirt.* ADJ: usu ADJ n

**pleb** /pleb/ (**plebs**) If someone refers to people as **plebs**, they mean they are of a low social class or do not appreciate culture. [BRIT, INFORMAL] N-COUNT: usu pl disapproval = prole

**ple|beian** /pləbiːən/ also **plebian.** 1 A person, especially one from an earlier period of history, who is **plebeian**, comes from a low social class. ADJ: usu ADJ n 2 If someone describes something as **plebeian**, they think that it is unsophisticated and connected with or typical of people from a low social class. [FORMAL] ❑ *...a philosophy professor with a cockney accent and an alarmingly plebeian manner.* ADJ: usu ADJ n disapproval = common ≠ genteel

**plebi|scite** /plebɪsaɪt, -sɪt/ (**plebiscites**) A **plebiscite** is a direct vote by the people of a country or region in which they say whether they agree or disagree with a particular policy, for example whether a region should become an independent state. N-COUNT = referendum

**pledge** /pledʒ/ (**pledges, pledging, pledged**) ◆◇◇ 1 When someone makes a **pledge**, they make a serious promise that they will do something. ❑ *The meeting ended with a pledge to step up co-operation between the six states of the region. ...a £1.1m pledge of support from the Spanish ministry of culture.* N-COUNT: usu N to-inf = promise 2 When someone **pledges to** do something, they promise in a serious way to do it. When they **pledge** something, they promise to give it. ❑ *Mr Dudley has pledged to give any award to charity... Philip pledges support and offers to help in any way that he can... I pledge that by next year we will have the problem solved.* VERB V to-inf V n V that 3 If you **pledge** a sum of money to an organization or activity, you promise to pay that amount of money to it at a particular time or over a particular period. ❑ *The French President is pledging $150 million in French aid next year.* VERB V n ♦ **Pledge** is also a noun. ❑ *...a pledge of forty two million dollars a month.* N-COUNT: oft N *of* n 4 If you **pledge yourself to** something, you commit yourself to following a particular course of action or to supporting a particular person, group, or idea. ❑ *The President pledged himself to increase taxes for the rich but not the middle classes... The treaties renounce the use of force and pledge the two countries to co-operation.* VERB = commit V pron-refl to-inf V n *to* n 5 If you **pledge** something such as a valuable possession or a sum of money, you leave it with someone as a guarantee that you will repay money that you have borrowed. ❑ *He asked her to pledge the house as security for a loan.* VERB V n

**ple|na|ry** /pliːnəri, plen-/ (**plenaries**) A **plenary session** or **plenary meeting** is one that is attended by everyone who has the right to attend. [TECHNICAL] ❑ *The programme was approved at a plenary session of the Central Committee last week.* ADJ: ADJ n ♦ **Plenary** is also a noun. ❑ *There'll be another plenary at the end of the afternoon after the workshop.* N-COUNT

**pleni|po|ten|ti|ary** /plenɪpətenʃəri, AM -ʃieri/ (**plenipotentiaries**) also **Plenipotentiary.** 1 A **plenipotentiary** is a person who has full power to make decisions or take action on behalf of their government, especially in a foreign country. [FORMAL] ❑ *...the British Plenipotentiary to the UN conference.* N-COUNT 2 An **ambassador plenipotentiary** or **minister plenipotentiary** has full power or authority to represent their country. [FORMAL] ADJ: n ADJ 3 If someone such as an ambassador has **plenipotentiary powers**, they have full power or authority to represent their country. [FORMAL] ADJ: ADJ n

**pleni|tude** /plenɪtjuːd, AM -tuːd/ 1 **Plenitude** is a feeling that an experience is satisfying because it is full or complete. [FORMAL] ❑ *The music brought him a feeling of plenitude and freedom.* N-UNCOUNT = fullness, completeness 2 If there is a **plenitude of** something, there is a great quantity of it. [FORMAL] ❑ *What is the use of a book about interior design without a plenitude of pictures in color?* N-SING: usu N *of* n = abundance

**plen|ti|ful** /plentɪful/ Things that are **plentiful** exist in such large amounts or numbers that there is enough for people's wants or needs. ❑ *Fish are plentiful in the lake. ...a plentiful supply of vegeta-* ADJ: usu v-link ADJ bles and salads and fruits. ♦ **plen|ti|ful|ly** *Nettle grows plentifully on any rich waste ground.* ADV

**plen|ty** /plenti/ ◆◇◇ QUANT: QUANT *of* n-uncount/pl-n 1 If there is **plenty of** something, there is a large amount of it. If there are **plenty of** things, there are many of them. **Plenty** is used especially to indicate that there is enough of something, or more than you need. ❑ *There was still plenty of time to take Jill out for pizza... Most businesses face plenty of competition... Are there plenty of fresh fruits and vegetables in your diet?* ♦ **Plenty** is also a pronoun. PRON ❑ *I don't believe in long interviews. Fifteen minutes is plenty.* 2 **Plenty** is a situation in which people have a lot to eat or a lot of money to live on. [FORMAL] N-UNCOUNT ❑ *You are all fortunate to be growing up in a time of peace and plenty.* 3 You use **plenty** in front of adjectives or adverbs to emphasize the degree of the quality they are describing. [INFORMAL] ADV: ADV adj/adv [emphasis] ❑ *The water looked plenty deep... The compartment is plenty big enough.*

**ple|num** /pliːnəm/ **(plenums)** A **plenum** is a meeting that is attended by all the members of a committee or conference. [TECHNICAL] N-COUNT = *plenary*

**pletho|ra** /pleθərə/ A **plethora of** something is a large amount of it, especially an amount of it that is greater than you need, want, or can cope with. [FORMAL] N-SING: N *of* n ❑ *A plethora of new operators will be allowed to enter the market.*

**pleu|ri|sy** /plʊərɪsi/ **Pleurisy** is a serious illness in which a person's lungs are sore and breathing is difficult. N-UNCOUNT

**plex|us** /pleksəs/ → see **solar plexus**.

**pli|able** /plaɪəbᵊl/ If something is **pliable**, you can bend it easily without cracking or breaking it. ADJ ≠ *rigid* ❑ *As your baby grows bigger, his bones become less pliable.*

**pli|ant** /plaɪənt/ 1 A **pliant** person can be easily influenced and controlled by other people. ADJ = *compliant, pliable* ❑ *She's proud and stubborn, you know, under that pliant exterior.* 2 If something is **pliant**, you can bend it easily without breaking it. ADJ = *pliable, supple* ❑ *...pliant young willows.*

**pli|ers** /plaɪəʳz/ **Pliers** are a tool with two handles at one end and two hard, flat, metal parts at the other. **Pliers** are used for holding or pulling out things such as nails, or for bending or cutting wire. → See picture on page 1709. N-PLURAL: also *a pair of* N

**plight** /plaɪt/ **(plights)** If you refer to someone's **plight**, you mean that they are in a difficult or distressing situation that is full of problems. N-COUNT: usu sing, with supp ❑ *...the worsening plight of Third World countries plagued by debts.*

**plim|soll** /plɪmsoul/ **(plimsolls) Plimsolls** are canvas shoes with flat rubber soles. People wear plimsolls for sports and leisure activities. [BRIT] N-COUNT: usu pl

☑ in AM, use **sneakers**

**plinth** /plɪnθ/ **(plinths)** A **plinth** is a rectangular block of stone on which a statue or pillar stands. N-COUNT

**plod** /plɒd/ **(plods, plodding, plodded)** 1 If someone **plods**, they walk slowly and heavily. VERB ❑ *Crowds of French and British families plodded around in yellow plastic macs.* V adv/prep 2 If you say that someone **plods on** or **plods along** with a job, you mean that the job is taking a long time. VERB ❑ *He is plodding on with negotiations...* V adv *Aircraft production continued to plod along at an agonizingly slow pace.* V adv

**plod|der** /plɒdəʳ/ **(plodders)** If you say that someone is a **plodder**, you have a low opinion of them because they work slowly and steadily but without showing enthusiasm or having new ideas. [INFORMAL] N-COUNT [disapproval] ❑ *He was quiet, conscientious, a bit of a plodder.*

**plonk** /plɒŋk/ **(plonks, plonking, plonked)** 1 If you **plonk** something somewhere, you put it or drop it there heavily and carelessly. [BRIT, INFORMAL] VERB ❑ *She plonked the beer on the counter.* V n prep/adv

☑ in AM, use **plunk**

2 If you **plonk yourself** somewhere, you sit down carelessly without paying attention to the people around you. [BRIT, INFORMAL] VERB ❑ *Steve plonked himself down on a seat and stayed motionless as the bus moved away.* V pron-refl adv/prep

☑ in AM, use **plunk**

3 **Plonk** is cheap or poor quality wine. [mainly BRIT, INFORMAL] N-MASS 4 A **plonk** is a heavy, hollow sound. [mainly BRIT] N-SING; SOUND ❑ *...the dry plonk of tennis balls.*

**plonk|er** /plɒŋkəʳ/ **(plonkers)** If someone calls a person, especially a man, a **plonker**, they think he is stupid. [BRIT, INFORMAL, OFFENSIVE] N-COUNT [disapproval]

**plop** /plɒp/ **(plops, plopping, plopped)** 1 A **plop** is a soft, gentle sound, like the sound made by something dropping into water without disturbing the surface much. N-COUNT; SOUND ❑ *Another drop of water fell with a soft plop.* 2 If something **plops** somewhere, it drops there with a soft, gentle sound. VERB ❑ *The ice cream plopped to the ground.* V prep

**plot** /plɒt/ **(plots, plotting, plotted)** ◆◇◇ 1 A **plot** is a secret plan by a group of people to do something that is illegal or wrong, usually against a person or a government. N-COUNT: usu N to-inf, N *against* n ❑ *Security forces have uncovered a plot to overthrow the government... He was responding to reports of an assassination plot against him.* 2 If people **plot to** do something or **plot** something that is illegal or wrong, they plan secretly to do it. VERB ❑ *Prosecutors in the trial allege the defendants plotted to overthrow the government...* V to-inf *The military were plotting a coup...* V n *They are awaiting trial on charges of plotting against the state.* V *against* n 3 When people **plot** a strategy or a course of action, they carefully plan each step of it. VERB ❑ *Yesterday's meeting was intended to plot a survival strategy for the party.* V n 4 The **plot** of a film, novel, or play is the connected series of events which make up the story. N-VAR → See also **sub-plot**. 5 A **plot of** land is a small piece of land, especially one that has been measured or marked out for a special purpose, such as building houses or growing vegetables. N-COUNT: usu with supp, oft N *of* n ❑ *The bottom of the garden was given over to vegetable plots.* 6 When someone **plots** something on a graph, they mark certain points on it and then join the points up. VERB ❑ *We plot about eight points on the graph.* V n 7 When someone **plots** the position or course of a plane or ship, they mark it on a map using instruments to obtain accurate information. VERB ❑ *We were trying to plot the course of the submarine.* V n 8 If someone **plots** the progress or development of something, they make a diagram or a plan which shows how it has developed in order to give some indication of how it will develop in the future. VERB ❑ *They used a computer to plot the movements of everyone in the building.* V n 9 If someone **loses the plot**, they become confused and do not know what they should do. [INFORMAL] PHRASE: V inflects ❑ *The Tories have lost the plot on law and order.*

**plot|ter** /plɒtəʳ/ **(plotters)** 1 A **plotter** is a person who secretly plans with others to do something that is illegal or wrong, usually against a person or government. N-COUNT: usu pl = *conspirator* ❑ *Coup plotters tried to seize power in Moscow.* 2 A **plotter** is a person or instrument that marks the position of something such as a ship on a map or chart. N-COUNT

**plough** /plaʊ/ **(ploughs, ploughing, ploughed)**

☑ in AM, use **plow**

1 A **plough** is a large farming tool with sharp blades which is pulled across the soil to turn it over, usually before seeds are planted. N-COUNT → See also **snowplough**. 2 When someone **ploughs** an area of land, they turn over the soil using a plough. VERB ❑ *They ploughed nearly 100,000 acres of virgin moorland.* V n *...a carefully ploughed field.* V-ed ♦ **plough|ing** *In Roman times November was a month of hard work in ploughing and sowing.* N-UNCOUNT 3 to **plough a furrow** → see **furrow**.

♦ **plough back** If profits **are ploughed back into** a business, they are used to increase the size of the business or to improve it. [BUSINESS] PHRASAL VERB: usu passive ❑ *About 70 per cent of its profits are being ploughed back into the investment programme.* *be* V-ed P *into* n

♦ **plough into** [1] If something, for example a car, **ploughs into** something else, it goes out of control and crashes violently into it. ❑ *A young girl and her little brother were seriously hurt when a car ploughed into them on a crossing.* [2] If you say that money **is ploughed into** something such as a business or a service, you are emphasizing that the amount of money which is invested in it or spent on it in order to improve it is very large. [BUSINESS] ❑ *Huge sums of private capital will be ploughed into the ailing industries of the east... He claimed he ploughed all his money into his antique business.*

PHRASAL VERB; V P n; PHRASAL VERB [emphasis]; be V-ed P n/-ing; V n P n/-ing

♦ **plough up** If someone **ploughs up** an area of land, they plough it, usually in order to turn it into land used for growing crops. ❑ *It would pay farmers to plough up the scrub and plant wheat.*

PHRASAL VERB; V P n

**plough|man** /plaʊmən/ **(ploughmen)** A **ploughman** is a man whose job it is to plough the land, especially with a plough pulled by horses or oxen. N-COUNT

**plough|man's lunch** **(ploughman's lunches)** A **ploughman's lunch** or a **ploughman's** is a meal consisting of bread, cheese, salad, and pickle, usually eaten in a pub. [BRIT] N-COUNT

**plough|share** /plaʊʃeəʳ/ **(ploughshares)**

✔ in AM, use **plowshare**

If you say that **swords have been turned into ploughshares** or **beaten into ploughshares**, you mean that a state of conflict between two or more groups of people has ended and a period of peace has begun. [JOURNALISM] PHRASE: V inflects

**plov|er** /plʌvəʳ/ **(plovers)** A **plover** is a bird with a rounded body, a short tail, and a short beak that is found by the sea or by lakes. N-COUNT

**plow** /plaʊ/ **(plows, plowing, plowed)** → see **plough**.

**plow|share** /plaʊʃeəʳ/ **(plowshares)** → see **ploughshare**.

**ploy** /plɔɪ/ **(ploys)** A **ploy** is a way of behaving that someone plans carefully and secretly in order to gain an advantage for themselves. ❑ *Christmas should be a time of excitement and wonder, not a cynical marketing ploy.* N-COUNT: oft adj N, N to-inf, N *of* -ing

**pls** **Pls** is a written abbreviation for **please**. ❑ *Have you moved yet? Pls advise address, phone no.*

**pluck** /plʌk/ **(plucks, plucking, plucked)** [1] If you **pluck** a fruit, flower, or leaf, you take it between your fingers and pull it in order to remove it from its stalk where it is growing. [WRITTEN] ❑ *I plucked a lemon from the tree... He plucked a stalk of dried fennel.* [2] If you **pluck** something **from** somewhere, you take it between your fingers and pull it sharply from where it is. [WRITTEN] ❑ *He plucked the cigarette from his mouth and tossed it out into the street.* [3] If you **pluck** a guitar or other musical instrument, you pull the strings with your fingers and let them go, so that they make a sound. ❑ *Nell was plucking a harp.* [4] If you **pluck** a chicken or other dead bird, you pull its feathers out to prepare it for cooking. ❑ *She looked relaxed as she plucked a chicken.* [5] If a woman **plucks** her **eyebrows**, she pulls out some of the hairs using tweezers. ❑ *You've plucked your eyebrows at last!* [6] If someone unknown is given an important job or role and quickly becomes famous because of it, you can say that they **have been plucked from** obscurity or **plucked from** an unimportant position. [WRITTEN] ❑ *She was plucked from the corps de ballet to take on Juliet... The agency plucked Naomi from obscurity and turned her into one of the world's top models.* [7] If someone is rescued from a dangerous situation, you can say that they **are plucked from** it or **are plucked to** safety. ❑ *A workman was plucked from the roof of a burning power station by a police helicopter... Ten fishermen were plucked to safety from life-rafts.*

VERB; V n *from* n; V n; VERB; V n *from/out of/off* n; VERB; V n; VERB; V n; VERB; V n; VERB: usu passive; be V-ed *from* n; V n *from* n; VERB: usu passive; be V-ed *from* n; be V-ed *to* n

PHRASES [8] If you **pluck up the courage to** do something that you feel nervous about, you make an effort to be brave enough to do it. ❑ *It took me about two hours to pluck up courage to call.* [9] If you say that someone **plucks** a figure, name, or date **out of the air**, you mean that they say it without thinking much about it before they speak. ❑ *Is this just a figure she plucked out of the air?*

PHRASE: V inflects, oft PHR to-inf; PHRASE: V inflects

♦ **pluck at** If you **pluck at** something, you take it between your fingers and pull it sharply but gently. ❑ *The boy plucked at Adam's sleeve.* PHRASAL VERB; V P n

**plucky** /plʌki/ If someone, for example a sick child, is described as **plucky**, it means that although they are weak, they face their difficulties with courage. [JOURNALISM] ❑ *The plucky schoolgirl amazed doctors by hanging on to life for nearly two months.* ADJ: usu ADJ n [approval]

**plug** /plʌg/ **(plugs, plugging, plugged)** [1] A **plug** on a piece of electrical equipment is a small plastic object with two or three metal pins which fit into the holes of an electric socket and connects the equipment to the electricity supply. [2] A **plug** is an electric socket. [INFORMAL] [3] A **plug** is a thick, circular piece of rubber or plastic that you use to block the hole in a bath or sink when it is filled with water. ❑ *She put the plug in the sink and filled it with cold water.* [4] A **plug** is a small, round piece of wood, plastic, or wax which is used to block holes. ❑ *A plug had been inserted in the drill hole.* [5] If you **plug** a hole, you block it with something. ❑ *Crews are working to plug a major oil leak.* [6] If someone **plugs** a commercial product, especially a book or a film, they praise it in order to encourage people to buy it or see it because they have an interest in it doing well. ❑ *We did not want people on the show who are purely interested in plugging a book or film.* ♦ **Plug** is also a noun. ❑ *Let's do this show tonight and it'll be a great plug, a great promotion.* [7] → See also **earplug**, **spark plug**. [8] If someone in a position of power **pulls the plug on** a project or **on** someone's activities, they use their power to stop them continuing. ❑ *The banks have the power to pull the plug on the project.*

N-COUNT; N-COUNT; N-COUNT; N-COUNT; VERB; V n; VERB = promote; V n; N-COUNT; PHRASE: V inflects, usu PHR *on* n

♦ **plug in** or **plug into** [1] If you **plug** a piece of electrical equipment **into** an electricity supply or if you **plug** it **in**, you push its plug into an electric socket so that it can work. ❑ *They plugged in their tape-recorders... I filled the kettle while she was talking and plugged it in... He took the machine from its bag and plugged it into the wall socket.* [2] If you **plug** one piece of electrical equipment **into** another or if you **plug** it **in**, you make it work by connecting the two. ❑ *They plugged their guitars into amplifiers... He plugged in his guitar.* [3] If one piece of electrical equipment **plugs in** or **plugs into** another piece of electrical equipment, it works by being connected by an electrical cord or lead to an electricity supply or to the other piece of equipment. ❑ *A CD-I deck looks like a video recorder and plugs into the home television and stereo system... They've found out where the other speaker plugs in.* [4] If you **plug** something **into** a hole, you push it into the hole. ❑ *Her instructor plugged live bullets into the gun's chamber.*

PHRASAL VERB; V P n (not pron); V n P; V n P n; PHRASAL VERB; V n P n; V P n; PHRASAL VERB; V P n; V P; PHRASAL VERB; V n P n

♦ **plug into** [1] If you **plug into** a computer system, you are able to use it or see the information stored on it. ❑ *It is possible to plug into remote databases to pick up information.* [2] → See also **plug-in**. PHRASAL VERB; V P n

**plug-and-play** **Plug-and-play** is used to describe computer equipment, for example a printer, that is ready to use immediately when you connect it to a computer. [COMPUTING] ❑ *... a plug-and-play USB camera.* ADJ: ADJ n

**plug|hole** /plʌghoʊl/ **(plugholes)** A **plughole** is a small hole in a bath or sink which allows the water to flow away and into which you can put a plug. [BRIT] N-COUNT

✔ in AM, use **drain**

**plug-in** **(plug-ins)** [1] A **plug-in** machine is a piece of electrical equipment that is operated by being connected to an electricity supply or to an- ADJ: ADJ n other piece of electrical equipment by means of a plug. ❑ *...a plug-in radio.* [2] A **plug-in** is something such as a piece of software that can be added to a computer system to give extra features or functions. [COMPUTING] ❑ *...a plug-in memory card.* N-COUNT: oft N n

**plum** /plʌm/ **(plums)** [1] A **plum** is a small, sweet fruit with a smooth red or yellow skin and a stone in the middle. → See picture on page 1711. N-COUNT [2] Something that is **plum** or **plum-coloured** is a dark reddish-purple colour. ❑ *...plum-coloured silk.* COLOUR [3] A **plum** job, contract, or role is a very good one that a lot of people would like. [JOURNALISM] ❑ *Laura landed a plum job with a smart art gallery.* ADJ: ADJ n

**plum|age** /pluːmɪdʒ/ A bird's **plumage** is all the feathers on its body. N-UNCOUNT

**plumb** /plʌm/ **(plumbs, plumbing, plumbed)** [1] If you **plumb** something mysterious or difficult to understand, you succeed in understanding it. [LITERARY] ❑ *She never abandoned her attempts to plumb my innermost emotions.* VERB = fathom; V n [2] When someone **plumbs** a building, they put in all the pipes for carrying water. ❑ *She learned to wire and plumb the house herself.* VERB; V n

**PHRASES** [3] If someone **plumbs the depths of** an unpleasant emotion or quality, they experience it or show it to an extreme degree. ❑ *They frequently plumb the depths of loneliness, humiliation and despair.* PHRASE: V inflects, oft PHR *of* n [4] If you say that something **plumbs new depths**, you mean that it is worse than all the things of its kind that have existed before, even though some of them have been very bad. ❑ *Relations between the two countries have plumbed new depths.* PHRASE: V inflects, oft PHR *of* n

**plumb|er** /plʌməʳ/ **(plumbers)** A **plumber** is a person whose job is to connect and repair things such as water and drainage pipes, baths, and toilets. N-COUNT

**plumb|ing** /plʌmɪŋ/ [1] The **plumbing** in a building consists of the water and drainage pipes, baths, and toilets in it. ❑ *The electrics and the plumbing were sound.* N-UNCOUNT [2] **Plumbing** is the work of connecting and repairing things such as water and drainage pipes, baths, and toilets. ❑ *She learned the rudiments of brick-laying, wiring and plumbing.* N-UNCOUNT

**plumb line** **(plumb lines)** A **plumb line** is a piece of string with a weight attached to the end that is used to check that something such as a wall is vertical or that it slopes at the correct angle. N-COUNT

**plume** /pluːm/ **(plumes)** [1] A **plume of** smoke, dust, fire, or water is a large quantity of it that rises into the air in a column. ❑ *The rising plume of black smoke could be seen all over Kabul.* N-COUNT: usu N *of* n [2] A **plume** is a large, soft bird's feather. ❑ *...broad straw hats decorated with ostrich plumes.* N-COUNT

**plumed** /pluːmd/ **Plumed** means decorated with a plume or plumes. ❑ *...a young man wearing a plumed hat.* ADJ: usu ADJ n

**plum|met** /plʌmɪt/ **(plummets, plummeting, plummeted)** [1] If an amount, rate, or price **plummets**, it decreases quickly by a large amount. [JOURNALISM] ❑ *In Tokyo share prices have plummeted for the sixth successive day... The Prime Minister's popularity has plummeted to an all-time low in recent weeks... The shares have plummeted from 130p to 2.25p in the past year.* VERB = plunge; V; V *to* n; V *from/to/by* n [2] If someone or something **plummets**, they fall very fast towards the ground, usually from a great height. ❑ *The jet burst into flames and plummeted to the ground.* VERB; V prep

**plum|my** /plʌmi/ If you say that someone has a **plummy** voice or accent, you mean that they sound very upper-class. You usually use **plummy** to criticize the way someone speaks. [BRIT] ❑ *...those precious, plummy-voiced radio announcers. ...a plummy accent.* ADJ [disapproval]

**plump** /plʌmp/ **(plumper, plumpest, plumps, plumping, plumped)** [1] You can describe someone or something as **plump** to indicate that they are rather fat or rounded. ❑ *Maria was small and plump with a mass of curly hair. ...red pears, ripe peaches and plump nectarines.* ♦ **plump|ness** *There was a sturdy plumpness about her hips.* ADJ; N-UNCOUNT [2] If you **plump** a pillow or cushion, you shake it and hit it gently so that it goes back into a rounded shape. ❑ *She panics when people pop in unexpectedly, rushing round plumping cushions.* ♦ **Plump up** means the same as **plump**. ❑ *'You need to rest,' she told her reassuringly as she moved to plump up her pillows.* VERB; V n; PHRASAL VERB; V P n (not pron) [3] If you **plump for** someone or something, you choose them, often after hesitating or thinking carefully. [mainly BRIT] ❑ *I think Tessa should plump for Malcolm, her long-suffering admirer.* VERB; V *for* n

**plum pud|ding** **(plum puddings)** **Plum pudding** is a special pudding eaten at Christmas which is made with dried fruit, spices, and suet. [AM; also BRIT, OLD-FASHIONED] N-COUNT = Christmas pudding

**plum to|ma|to** **(plum tomatoes)** **Plum tomatoes** are long egg-shaped tomatoes. N-VAR

**plun|der** /plʌndəʳ/ **(plunders, plundering, plundered)** [1] If someone **plunders** a place or **plunders** things **from** a place, they steal things from it. [LITERARY] ❑ *They plundered and burned the market town of Leominster... She faces charges of helping to plunder her country's treasury of billions of dollars... This has been done by plundering £4 billion from the Government reserves.* VERB = loot; V n; V n *of* n; V n *from* n ♦ **Plunder** is also a noun. ❑ *...a guerrilla group infamous for torture and plunder.* N-UNCOUNT [2] **Plunder** is property that is stolen. [LITERARY] ❑ *The thieves are often armed and in some cases have killed for their plunder.* N-UNCOUNT

**plunge** /plʌndʒ/ **(plunges, plunging, plunged)** ◆◇◇ [1] If something or someone **plunges** in a particular direction, especially into water, they fall, rush, or throw themselves in that direction. ❑ *At least 50 people died when a bus plunged into a river.* VERB; V prep/adv ♦ **Plunge** is also a noun. ❑ *...a plunge into cold water.* N-COUNT: usu sing [2] If you **plunge** an object **into** something, you push it quickly or violently into it. ❑ *A soldier plunged a bayonet into his body... I plunged in my knife and fork.* VERB; V n into n; V n with *in* [3] If a person or thing **is plunged into** a particular state or situation, or if they **plunge into** it, they are suddenly in that state or situation. ❑ *The government's political and economic reforms threaten to plunge the country into chaos... Eddy finds himself plunged into a world of brutal violence... The economy is plunging into recession.* VERB; V n *into* n; V-ed; V *into* n ♦ **Plunge** is also a noun. ❑ *That peace often looked like a brief truce before the next plunge into war.* N-COUNT: usu sing, N *into* n [4] If you **plunge into** an activity or **are plunged into** it, you suddenly get very involved in it. ❑ *The two men plunged into discussion... The prince should be plunged into work without delay... Take the opportunity to plunge yourself into your career.* VERB; V *into* n, *be* V-ed *into* n; V pron-refl *into* n ♦ **Plunge** is also a noun. ❑ *His sudden plunge into the field of international diplomacy is a major surprise.* N-COUNT: usu sing, N *into* n [5] If an amount or rate **plunges**, it decreases quickly and suddenly. ❑ *His weight began to plunge... The Pound plunged to a new low on the foreign exchange markets yesterday... Shares have plunged from £17 to £7.55... The bank's profits plunged by 87 per cent... Its net profits plunged 73% last year.* VERB = plummet; V, V *to* n; V *from/to* amount; V *by* amount; V amount ♦ **Plunge** is also a noun. ❑ *Japan's banks are in trouble because of bad loans and the stock market plunge.* N-COUNT [6] → See also **plunging**. [7] If you **take the plunge**, you decide to do something that you consider difficult or risky. ❑ *If you have been thinking about buying shares, now could be the time to take the plunge.* PHRASE: V inflects

**plung|er** /plʌndʒəʳ/ **(plungers)** A **plunger** is a device for clearing waste pipes. It consists of a rubber cup on the end of a stick which you press down several times over the end of the pipe. N-COUNT

**plung|ing** /plʌndʒɪŋ/ A dress or blouse with a **plunging** neckline is cut in a very low V-shape at the front. ADJ: ADJ n

**plunk** /plʌŋk/ **(plunks, plunking, plunked)** [1] If you **plunk** something somewhere, you put it there without great care. [AM, INFORMAL] ❑ *Melanie plunked her cosmetic case down on a chair... She swept up a hat from where it had fallen on the ground, and plunked it on her hair.* VERB; V n with *down*; V n *on* n

☑ in BRIT, use **plonk**

2 If you **plunk yourself** somewhere, or **plunk down**, you sit down heavily and clumsily. [AM, INFORMAL] ❑ *I watched them go and plunked down on one of the small metal chairs.* VERB V *down*

☑ in BRIT, use **plonk**

**plu|per|fect** /pluːpɜːʳfɪkt/ **The pluperfect** is the same as the **past perfect**. N-SING: *the* N

**plu|ral** /plʊərəl/ **(plurals)** 1 The **plural** form of a word is the form that is used when referring to more than one person or thing. ❑ *'Data' is the Latin plural form of 'datum'. ...his use of the plural pronoun 'we'.* ADJ ≠ *singular* 2 The **plural** of a noun is the form of it that is used to refer to more than one thing. ❑ *What is the plural of 'person'?* N-COUNT

**plu|ral|ism** /plʊərəlɪzəm/ If there is **pluralism** within a society, it has many different groups and political parties. [FORMAL] ❑ *...as the country shifts towards political pluralism.* N-UNCOUNT

**plu|ral|ist** /plʊərəlɪst/ A **pluralist** society is one in which many different groups and political parties are allowed to exist. [FORMAL] ❑ *...an attempt to create a pluralist democracy.* ADJ: usu ADJ n = *pluralistic*

**plu|ral|ist|ic** /plʊərəlɪstɪk/ **Pluralistic** means the same as **pluralist**. [FORMAL] ❑ *Our objective is a free, open and pluralistic society.* ADJ: usu ADJ n

**plu|ral|ity** /plʊəræləti/ **(pluralities)** 1 If there is a **plurality of** things, a number of them exist. [FORMAL] ❑ *Federalism implies a plurality of political authorities, each with its own powers.* QUANT-PLURAL 2 If a candidate, political party, or idea has the support of a **plurality of** people, they have more support than any other candidate, party, or idea. [FORMAL] ❑ *The Conservative party retained a plurality of the votes.* QUANT-PLURAL 3 A **plurality** in an election is the number of votes that the winner gets, when this is less than the total number of votes for all the other candidates. [AM] ❑ *He only got a plurality on November 3rd, just 49 percent.* N-COUNT 4 A **plurality** in an election is the difference in the number of votes between the candidate who gets the most votes and the candidate who comes second. [AM] ❑ *Franklin had won with a plurality in electoral votes of 449 to 82.* N-COUNT = *majority*

**plus** /plʌs/ **(pluses** or **plusses)** 1 You say **plus** to show that one number or quantity is being added to another. ❑ *Send a cheque for £18.99 plus £2 for postage and packing... They will pay about $673 million plus interest.* ◆◆◇ CONJ ≠ *minus* 2 **Plus** before a number or quantity means that the number or quantity is greater than zero. ❑ *The aircraft was subjected to temperatures of minus 65 degrees and plus 120 degrees.* ADJ: ADJ amount ≠ *minus* **plus or minus** → see **minus**. 3 You can use **plus** when mentioning an additional item or fact. [INFORMAL] ❑ *There's easily enough room for two adults and three children, plus a dog in the boot.* CONJ = *and* 4 You use **plus** after a number or quantity to indicate that the actual number or quantity is greater than the one mentioned. ❑ *There are only 35 staff to serve 30,000-plus customers.* ADJ: amount ADJ 5 Teachers use **plus** in grading work in schools and colleges. 'B plus' is a better grade than 'B', but it is not as good as 'A'. ≠ *minus* 6 A **plus** is an advantage or benefit. [INFORMAL] ❑ *Experience of any career in sales is a big plus.* N-COUNT ≠ *drawback*

**plus-fours** also **plus fours. Plus-fours** are short wide trousers fastened below the knees which people used to wear when hunting or playing golf. [OLD-FASHIONED] N-PLURAL: also *a pair of* N

**plush** /plʌʃ/ **(plusher, plushest)** 1 If you describe something as **plush**, you mean that it is very smart, comfortable, or expensive. ❑ *...a plush, four-storey, Georgian house in Mayfair.* ADJ: usu ADJ n 2 **Plush** is a thick soft material like velvet, used especially for carpets and to cover furniture. ❑ *All the seats were in red plush.* N-UNCOUNT

**plus sign (plus signs)** A **plus sign** is the sign + which is put between two numbers in order to show that the second number is being added to the first. It can also be put before a number to show that the number is greater than zero (+3), and after a number to indicate a number that is more than a minimum number or amount (18+). N-COUNT

**plu|toc|ra|cy** /pluːtɒkrəsi/ **(plutocracies)** A **plutocracy** is a country which is ruled by its wealthiest people, or a class of wealthy people who rule a country. [FORMAL] N-COUNT

**plu|to|crat** /pluːtəkræt/ **(plutocrats)** If you describe someone as a **plutocrat**, you disapprove of them because you believe they are powerful only because they are rich. [FORMAL] N-COUNT [disapproval]

**plu|to|nium** /pluːtoʊniəm/ **Plutonium** is a radioactive element used especially in nuclear weapons and as a fuel in nuclear power stations. N-UNCOUNT

**ply** /plaɪ/ **(plies, plying, plied)** 1 If you **ply** someone **with** food or drink, you keep giving them more of it. ❑ *Elsie, who had been told that Maria wasn't well, plied her with food.* VERB V n *with* n 2 If you **ply** someone **with** questions, you keep asking them questions. ❑ *Giovanni plied him with questions with the intention of prolonging his stay.* VERB V n *with* n 3 If you **ply** a trade, you do a particular kind of work regularly as your job, especially a kind of work that involves trying to sell goods or services to people outdoors. ❑ *...the market traders noisily plying their wares... It's illegal for unmarked mini-cabs to ply for hire.* VERB V n V *for* n

**-ply** /-plaɪ/ You use **-ply** after a number to indicate how many pieces are twisted together to make a type of wool, thread, or rope. ❑ *You need 3 balls of any 4-ply knitting wool.* COMB in ADJ: ADJ n

**ply|wood** /plaɪwʊd/ **Plywood** is wood that consists of thin layers of wood stuck together. ❑ *...a sheet of plywood.* N-UNCOUNT

**PM** /piː em/ **(PMs)** The **PM** is an abbreviation for the **Prime Minister**. [BRIT, INFORMAL] ❑ *The PM pledged to make life better for the poorest families.* ◆◇◇ N-COUNT: *the* N

**p.m.** /piː em/ also **pm. p.m.** is used after a number to show that you are referring to a particular time between 12 noon and 12 midnight. Compare **a.m.** ❑ *The spa closes at 9:00 pm.* ADV: num ADV

**PMS** /piː em es/ **PMS** is an abbreviation for **premenstrual syndrome**. N-UNCOUNT

**PMT** /piː em tiː/ **PMT** is an abbreviation for **premenstrual tension**. [BRIT] N-UNCOUNT

**pneu|mat|ic** /njuːmætɪk/ 1 A **pneumatic drill** is operated by air under pressure and is very powerful. Pneumatic drills are often used for digging up roads. ❑ *...the sound of a pneumatic drill hammering away.* ADJ: ADJ n 2 **Pneumatic** means filled with air. ❑ *...pneumatic tyres.* ADJ: ADJ n

**pneu|mo|nia** /njuːmoʊniə/ **Pneumonia** is a serious disease which affects your lungs and makes it difficult for you to breathe. ❑ *She nearly died of pneumonia.* N-UNCOUNT: also *a* N

**PO** /piː oʊ/ also **P.O. PO** is an abbreviation for **Post Office** or **postal order**.

**poach** /poʊtʃ/ **(poaches, poaching, poached)** 1 If someone **poaches** fish, animals, or birds, they illegally catch them on someone else's property. ❑ *Many wildlife parks are regularly invaded by people poaching game.* VERB V n Also V ♦ **poach|er (poachers)** *Security cameras have been installed to guard against poachers.* N-COUNT ♦ **poach|ing** *...the poaching of elephants for their tusks.* N-UNCOUNT 2 If an organization **poaches** members or customers **from** another organization, they secretly or dishonestly persuade them to join them or become their customers. ❑ *The company authorised its staff to poach customers from the opposition. ...allegations that it had poached members from other unions.* VERB = *steal* V n V n *from* n ♦ **poach|ing** *The union was accused of poaching.* N-UNCOUNT 3 If someone **poaches** an idea, they dishonestly or illegally use the idea. ❑ *The opposition parties complained that the government had poached their ideas.* VERB = *steal* V n 4 When you **poach** an egg, you cook it gently in boiling water without its shell. ❑ *Poach the eggs for 4 minutes... He had a light breakfast of poached eggs and tea.* VERB V n V-ed 5 If you **poach** food such as fish, you cook it gently in boiling water, milk, or other liquid. ❑ *Poach* VERB V n *the chicken until just cooked. ...a pear poached in red wine.* V-ed ♦ **poach|ing** *You will need a pot of broth for poaching.* N-UNCOUNT

**PO Box** /piː oʊ bɒks/ also **P.O. Box. PO Box** is used before a number as a kind of address. The Post Office keeps letters addressed to the PO Box until they are collected by the person who has paid for the service.

**pocked** /pɒkt/ ADJ: usu v-link ADJ, oft ADJ *with* n **Pocked** means the same as **pockmarked**. ❑ *...a bus pocked with bullet holes.*

**pock|et** /pɒkɪt/ **(pockets, pocketing, pocketed)** ◆◇◇ 1 N-COUNT: oft poss N, n N A **pocket** is a kind of small bag which forms part of a piece of clothing, and which is used for carrying small things such as money or a handkerchief. ❑ *He took his flashlight from his jacket pocket and switched it on... The man stood with his hands in his pockets.* 2 N-COUNT You can use **pocket** in a lot of different ways to refer to money that people have, get, or spend. For example, if someone gives or pays a lot of money, you can say that they **dig deep into** their **pocket**. If you approve of something because it is very cheap to buy, you can say that it **suits people's pockets**. ❑ *...ladies' fashions to suit all shapes, sizes and pockets.* 3 ADJ: ADJ n You use **pocket** to describe something that is small enough to fit into a pocket, often something that is a smaller version of a larger item. ❑ *...a pocket calculator. ...my pocket edition of the Oxford English Dictionary.* 4 N-COUNT: usu N *of* n A **pocket of** something is a small area where something is happening, or a small area which has a particular quality, and which is different from the other areas around it. ❑ *He survived the earthquake after spending 3 days in an air pocket... The army controls the city apart from a few pockets of resistance.* 5 VERB If someone who is in possession of something valuable such as a sum of money **pockets** it, they steal it or take it for themselves, even though it does not belong to them. ❑ *Dishonest importers would be able to pocket the VAT collected from customers.* V n 6 VERB If you say that someone **pockets** something such as a prize or sum of money, you mean that they win or obtain it, often without needing to make much effort or in a way that seems unfair. [JOURNALISM] ❑ *He pocketed more money from this tournament than in his entire three years as a professional.* V n 7 VERB If someone **pockets** something, they put it in their pocket, for example because they want to steal it or hide it. ❑ *Anthony snatched his letters and pocketed them.* V n

**PHRASES** 8 PHRASE: usu v-link PHR [disapproval] If you say that someone is **in** someone else's **pocket**, you disapprove of the fact that the first person is willing to do whatever the second person tells them, for example out of weakness or in return for money. ❑ *The board of directors must surely have been in Johnstone's pocket.* 9 PHRASE: V inflects [disapproval] If you say that someone **is lining** their own or someone else's **pockets**, you disapprove of them because they are making money dishonestly or unfairly. ❑ *It is estimated that 5,000 bank staff could be lining their own pockets from customer accounts.* 10 PHRASE: v-link PHR, PHR after v If you are **out of pocket**, you have less money than you should have or than you intended, for example because you have spent too much or because of a mistake. ❑ *They were well out of pocket – they had spent far more in Hollywood than he had earned.* → See also **out-of-pocket**. 11 PHRASE: V and N inflect If someone **picks** your **pocket**, they steal something from your pocket, usually without you noticing. ❑ *They were more in danger of having their pockets picked than being shot at.*

**pocket|book** /pɒkɪtbʊk/ **(pocketbooks)** 1 N-COUNT You can use **pocketbook** to refer to people's concerns about the money they have or hope to earn. [AM, JOURNALISM] ❑ *People feel pinched in their pocketbooks and insecure about their futures.* 2 N-COUNT A **pocketbook** is a small bag which a woman uses to carry things such as her money and keys in when she goes out. [AM]

☑ in BRIT, use **handbag, bag**

3 N-COUNT A **pocketbook** is a small flat folded case, usually made of leather or plastic, where you can keep banknotes and credit cards. [mainly AM]

☑ in BRIT, usually use **wallet**

**pock|et knife (pocket knives)** also **pocketknife.** N-COUNT = penknife A **pocket knife** is a small knife with several blades which fold into the handle so that you can carry it around with you safely.

**pock|et mon|ey** also **pocket-money.** N-UNCOUNT **Pocket money** is money which children are given by their parents, usually every week. [mainly BRIT] ❑ *Her parents agreed to give her £6 a week pocket money.*

☑ in AM, usually use **allowance**

**pocket-sized** also **pocket-size.** ADJ: usu ADJ n [approval] If you describe something as **pocket-sized**, you approve of it because it is small enough to fit in your pocket. ❑ *...a handy pocket-sized reference book.*

**pock|mark** /pɒkmɑːʳk/ **(pockmarks)** also **pock mark.** N-COUNT: usu pl **Pockmarks** are small hollows on the surface of something. ❑ *She has a poor complexion and pock marks on her forehead... The pockmarks made by her bullets are still on the wall.*

**pock|marked** /pɒkmɑːʳkt/ also **pock-marked.** ADJ: oft ADJ *with* n = pocked If the surface of something is **pockmarked**, it has small hollow marks covering it. ❑ *He had a pockmarked face... The living room is pockmarked with bullet holes.*

**pod** /pɒd/ **(pods)** N-COUNT A **pod** is a seed container that grows on plants such as peas or beans. → See picture on page 1712. ❑ *...fresh peas in the pod. ...hot red pepper pods.*

**podgy** /pɒdʒi/ ADJ If you describe someone as **podgy**, you think that they are slightly fat. [BRIT, INFORMAL]

☑ in AM, use **pudgy**

**po|dia|trist** /pədaɪətrɪst/ **(podiatrists)** N-COUNT A **podiatrist** is a person whose job is to treat and care for people's feet. **Podiatrist** is a more modern term for **chiropodist**.

**po|dia|try** /pədaɪətri/ N-UNCOUNT **Podiatry** is the professional care and treatment of people's feet. **Podiatry** is a more modern term for **chiropody** and also deals with correcting foot problems relating to the way people stand and walk.

**po|dium** /poʊdiəm/ **(podiums)** N-COUNT: usu sing A **podium** is a small platform on which someone stands in order to give a lecture or conduct an orchestra.

**poem** /poʊɪm/ **(poems)** ◆◇◇ N-COUNT A **poem** is a piece of writing in which the words are chosen for their beauty and sound and are carefully arranged, often in short lines which rhyme.

**poet** /poʊɪt/ **(poets)** ◆◇◇ N-COUNT A **poet** is a person who writes poems. ❑ *He was a painter and poet.*

**po|et|ess** /poʊɪtes/ **(poetesses)** N-COUNT A **poetess** is a female poet. Most female poets prefer to be called poets.

**po|et|ic** /poʊetɪk/ 1 ADJ Something that is **poetic** is very beautiful and expresses emotions in a sensitive or moving way. ❑ *Nikolai Demidenko gave an exciting yet poetic performance.* ♦ **po|eti|cal|ly** ADV: ADV with v, ADV adj *The speech was as poetically written as any he'd ever heard.* 2 ADJ **Poetic** means relating to poetry. ❑ *There's a very rich poetic tradition in Gaelic.*

**po|eti|cal** /poʊetɪkᵊl/ ADJ **Poetical** means the same as **poetic**. ❑ *...a work of real merit and genuine poetical feeling.*

**po|et|ic jus|tice** N-UNCOUNT If you describe something bad that happens to someone as **poetic justice**, you mean that it is exactly what they deserve because of the things that that person has done.

**po|et|ic li|cence** N-UNCOUNT If someone such as a writer or film director uses **poetic licence**, they break the usual rules of language or style, or they change the facts, in order to create a particular effect. ❑ *All that stuff about catching giant fish was just a bit of poetic licence.*

**poet lau|reate** /poʊɪt lɒriət, AM - lɔːr-/ **(poet laureates** or **poets laureate)** N-COUNT: **The poet lau-**

**reate** is the official poet of a country. In Britain the poet laureate is paid by the government for the rest of their life. In the United States they are paid for a fixed period. — usu *the* N

**po|et|ry** /poʊɪtri/ ◆◇◇ [1] Poems, considered as a form of literature, are referred to as **poetry**. ❑ *...Russian poetry... Lawrence Durrell wrote a great deal of poetry.* — N-UNCOUNT [2] You can describe something very beautiful as **poetry**. ❑ *His music is purer poetry than a poem in words.* — N-UNCOUNT

**po-faced** /poʊ feɪst/ If you describe someone as **po-faced**, you think that they are being unnecessarily serious about something. [BRIT] ❑ *Coltrane took a rather po-faced view of this.* — ADJ, disapproval

**pog|rom** /pɒgrəm, AM pəgrɑːm/ **(pogroms)** A **pogrom** is organized, official violence against a group of people for racial or religious reasons. — N-COUNT

**poign|an|cy** /pɔɪnjənsi/ **Poignancy** is the quality that something has when it affects you deeply and makes you feel very sad. ❑ *The film contains moments of almost unbearable poignancy.* — N-UNCOUNT

**poign|ant** /pɔɪnjənt/ Something that is **poignant** affects you deeply and makes you feel sadness or regret. ❑ *...a poignant combination of very beautiful surroundings and tragic history.* — ADJ ♦ **poign|ant|ly** *Naomi's mothering experiences are poignantly described in her fiction.* — ADV: ADV with v, ADV adj

**poin|set|tia** /pɔɪnsetiə/ **(poinsettias)** A **poinsettia** is a plant with groups of bright red or pink leaves that grows in Central and South America. Poinsettias are very popular in Britain and the United States, especially at Christmas. — N-COUNT

**point** /pɔɪnt/ **(points, pointing, pointed)** ◆◆◆ [1] You use **point** to refer to something that someone has said or written. ❑ *We disagree with every point Mr Blunkett makes... The following tale will clearly illustrate this point.* — N-COUNT [2] If you say that someone **has a point**, or if you **take** their **point**, you mean that you accept that what they have said is important and should be considered. ❑ *'If he'd already killed once, surely he'd have killed Sarah?' She had a point there.* — N-SING: *a* N, poss N [3] **The point** of what you are saying or discussing is the most important part that provides a reason or explanation for the rest. ❑ *'Did I ask you to talk to me?' — 'That's not the point.'... The American Congress and media mostly missed the point about all this.* — N-SING: *the* N [4] If you ask what **the point of** something is, or say that there is **no point in** it, you are indicating that a particular action has no purpose or would not be useful. ❑ *What was the point of thinking about him?... There was no point in staying any longer.* — N-SING: usu N *of/in* n/-ing [5] A **point** is a detail, aspect, or quality of something or someone. ❑ *The most interesting point about the village was its religion... Science was never my strong point at school.* — N-COUNT: usu with supp [6] A **point** is a particular place or position where something happens. ❑ *The pain originated from a point in his right thigh.* — N-COUNT [7] You use **point** to refer to a particular time, or to a particular stage in the development of something. ❑ *We're all going to die at some point... At this point Diana arrived... It got to the point where he had to leave.* — N-SING: with supp, oft *at* N [8] The **point** of something such as a pin, needle, or knife is the thin, sharp end of it. — N-COUNT: oft N *of* n [9] In spoken English, you use **point** to refer to the dot or mark in a decimal number that separates the whole numbers from the fractions. ❑ *Inflation at nine point four percent is the worst for eight years.* [10] In some sports, competitions, and games, a **point** is one of the single marks that are added together to give the total score. ❑ *They lost the 1977 World Cup final to Australia by a single point.* — N-COUNT [11] The **points of the compass** are directions such as North, South, East, and West. ❑ *Sightseers arrived from all points of the compass.* — N-COUNT: usu with supp [12] On a railway track, the **points** are the levers and rails at a place where two tracks join or separate. The points enable a train to move from one track to another. [BRIT] ❑ *...the rattle of the wheels across the points.* — N-PLURAL

✓ in AM, use **switches**

[13] A **point** is an electric socket. [BRIT] ❑ *...too far away from the nearest electrical point.* — N-COUNT: usu supp N [14] If you **point at** a person or thing, you hold out your finger towards them in order to make someone notice them. ❑ *I pointed at the boy sitting nearest me... He pointed to a chair, signalling for her to sit.* — VERB; V *at* n; V *to* n [15] If you **point** something **at** someone, you aim the tip or end of it towards them. ❑ *David Khan pointed his finger at Mary... A man pointed a gun at them and pulled the trigger.* — VERB; V n *at* n; V n *at* n [16] If something **points to** a place or **points** in a particular direction, it shows where that place is or it faces in that direction. ❑ *An arrow pointed to the toilets... You can go anywhere and still the compass points north or south.* — VERB; V prep/adv; V prep/adv [17] If something **points to** a particular situation, it suggests that the situation exists or is likely to occur. ❑ *Private polls and embassy reports pointed to a no vote.* — VERB; V *to* n [18] If you **point to** something that has happened or that is happening, you are using it as proof that a particular situation exists. ❑ *George Fodor points to other weaknesses in the way the campaign has progressed.* — VERB; V *to* n [19] When builders **point** a wall, they put a substance such as cement into the gaps between the bricks or stones in order to make the wall stronger and seal it. — VERB: V n [20] → See also **pointed**, **breaking point**, **focal point**, **point of sale**, **point of view**, **power point**, **sticking point**, **vantage point**.

PHRASES [21] If you say that something is **beside the point**, you mean that it is not relevant to the subject that you are discussing. ❑ *Brian didn't like it, but that was beside the point.* — PHRASE: v-link PHR = *irrelevant* [22] When someone **comes to the point** or **gets to the point**, they start talking about the thing that is most important to them. ❑ *Was she ever going to get to the point?* — PHRASE: V inflects [23] If you **make** your **point** or **prove** your **point**, you prove that something is true, either by arguing about it or by your actions or behaviour. ❑ *I think you've made your point, dear... The tie-break proved the point.* — PHRASE: V inflects [24] If you **make a point of** doing something, you do it in a very deliberate or obvious way. ❑ *She made a point of spending as much time as possible away from Osborne House.* — PHRASE: V inflects, PHR -ing [25] If you are **on the point of** doing something, you are about to do it. ❑ *He was on the point of saying something when the phone rang... She looked on the point of tears.* — PHRASE: v-link PHR n/-ing [26] Something that is **to the point** is relevant to the subject that you are discussing, or expressed neatly without wasting words or time. ❑ *The description which he had been given was brief and to the point.* — PHRASE: v-link PHR [27] If you say that something is true **up to a point**, you mean that it is partly but not completely true. ❑ *'Was she good?' — 'Mmm. Up to a point.'* — PHRASE: PHR with cl [28] **a case in point** → see **case**. **in point of fact** → see **fact**. **to point the finger at** someone → see **finger**. **a sore point** → see **sore**.

♦ **point out** [1] If you **point out** an object or place, you make people look at it or show them where it is. ❑ *They kept standing up to take pictures and point things out to each other... They'd already driven along the wharf so that she could point out her father's boat.* — PHRASAL VERB; V n P; V P n (not pron) [2] If you **point out** a fact or mistake, you tell someone about it or draw their attention to it. ❑ *I should point out that these estimates cover just the hospital expenditures... We all too easily point out our mothers' failings.* — PHRASAL VERB; V P that; V P n (not pron)

**point-blank** [1] If you say something **point-blank**, you say it very directly or rudely, without explaining or apologizing. ❑ *The army apparently refused point blank to do what was required of them.* — ADV: ADV after v ♦ **Point-blank** is also an adjective. ❑ *...a point-blank refusal.* — ADJ: ADJ n [2] If someone or something is shot **point-blank**, they are shot when the gun is touching them or extremely close to them. ❑ *He fired point-blank at Bernadette.* — ADV: ADV after v ♦ **Point-blank** is also an adjective. ❑ *He had been shot at point-blank range in the back of the head.* — ADJ: ADJ n

**point|ed** /pɔɪntɪd/ [1] Something that is **pointed** has a point at one end. ❑ *...a pointed* — ADJ: usu ADJ n roof. ...*pointed shoes.* [2] **Pointed** comments or behaviour express criticism in a clear and direct way. ❑ *I couldn't help but notice the pointed remarks slung in my direction.* ♦ **point|ed|ly** *They were pointedly absent from the news conference.* ADJ: usu ADJ n; ADV: usu ADV with v, also ADV adj

**point|er** /pɔɪntəʳ/ **(pointers)** [1] A **pointer** is a piece of advice or information which helps you to understand a situation or to find a way of making progress. ❑ *I hope at least my daughter was able to offer you some useful pointers.* [2] A **pointer to** something suggests that it exists or gives an idea of what it is like. [mainly BRIT] ❑ *Sunday's elections should be a pointer to the public mood.* [3] A **pointer** is a long stick that is used to point at something such as a large chart or diagram when explaining something to people. ❑ *She tapped on the world map with her pointer.* [4] The **pointer** on a measuring instrument is the long, thin piece of metal that points to the numbers. N-COUNT: with supp; N-COUNT: N *to/towards* n; N-COUNT; N-COUNT = needle

**point|ing** /pɔɪntɪŋ/ [1] **Pointing** is a way of filling in the gaps between the bricks or stones on the outside of a building so that the surface becomes sealed. ❑ *He did the pointing in the stonework himself.* [2] **Pointing** is the cement between the bricks or stones in a wall. N-UNCOUNT; N-UNCOUNT

**point|less** /pɔɪntləs/ If you say that something is **pointless**, you are criticizing it because it has no sense or purpose. ❑ *Violence is always pointless. ...pointless arguments.* ♦ **point|less|ly** *Chemicals were pointlessly poisoning the soil.* ♦ **point|less|ness** *You cannot help wondering about the pointlessness of it all.* ADJ: usu v-link ADJ [disapproval]; ADV: usu ADV with v; N-UNCOUNT

**point of or|der (points of order)** In a formal debate, a **point of order** is an official complaint that someone makes because the rules about how the debate is meant to be organized have been broken. [FORMAL] ❑ *A point of order was raised in parliament by Mr Ben Morris.* N-COUNT: usu sing

**point of ref|er|ence (points of reference)** A **point of reference** is something which you use to help you understand a situation or communicate with someone. ❑ *Do we still have any fixed point of reference in the teaching of English?* N-COUNT

**point of sale (points of sale)** [1] The **point of sale** is the place in a shop where a product is passed from the seller to the customer. The abbreviation **POS** is also used. [BUSINESS] [2] **Point of sale** is used to describe things which occur or are located or used at the place where you buy something. The abbreviation **POS** is also used. [BUSINESS] ❑ *...point-of-sale advertising.* N-COUNT; N-UNCOUNT: usu N n

**point of view (points of view)** [1] You can refer to the opinions or attitudes that you have about something as your **point of view.** ❑ *Thanks for your point of view, John... Try to look at this from my point of view.* [2] If you consider something **from** a particular **point of view**, you are using one aspect of a situation in order to judge that situation. ❑ *Do you think that, from the point of view of results, this exercise was worth the cost?* ◆◇◇ N-COUNT: oft with poss = viewpoint; N-COUNT: usu sing, usu *from* N with poss

**pointy** /pɔɪnti/ **(pointier, pointiest)** Something that is **pointy** has a point at one end. [INFORMAL] ❑ *...a pointy little beard.* ADJ: usu ADJ n = pointed

**poise** /pɔɪz/ [1] If someone has **poise**, they are calm, dignified, and self-controlled. ❑ *It took a moment for Mark to recover his poise.* [2] **Poise** is a graceful, very controlled way of standing and moving. ❑ *Ballet classes are important for poise and grace.* N-UNCOUNT: oft poss N; N-UNCOUNT

**poised** /pɔɪzd/ [1] If a part of your body is **poised**, it is completely still but ready to move at any moment. ❑ *He studied the keyboard carefully, one finger poised.* [2] If someone is **poised to** do something, they are ready to take action at any moment. ❑ *Britain was poised to fly medical staff to the country at short notice... US forces are poised for a massive air, land and sea assault.* [3] If you are **poised**, you are calm, dignified, and self-controlled. ❑ *Rachel appeared poised and calm.* ADJ; ADJ: v-link ADJ, usu ADJ to-inf, ADJ *for* n; ADJ: usu v-link ADJ

**poi|son** /pɔɪzᵊn/ **(poisons, poisoning, poisoned)** [1] **Poison** is a substance that harms or kills people or animals if they swallow it or absorb it. ❑ *Poison from the weaver fish causes paralysis, swelling, and nausea... Mercury is a known poison.* [2] If someone **poisons** another person, they kill the person or make them ill by giving them poison. ❑ *The rumours that she had poisoned him could never be proved.* ♦ **poi|son|ing** *She was sentenced to twenty years' imprisonment for poisoning and attempted murder.* [3] If you **are poisoned by** a substance, it makes you very ill and sometimes kills you. ❑ *Employees were taken to hospital yesterday after being poisoned by fumes... Toxic waste could endanger lives and poison fish.* ♦ **poi|son|ing** *His illness was initially diagnosed as food poisoning.* [4] If someone **poisons** a food, drink, or weapon, they add poison to it so that it can be used to kill someone. ❑ *If I was your wife I would poison your coffee.* ♦ **poi|soned** *He was terrified to eat, suspecting that the food was poisoned. ...an umbrella tipped with a poisoned dart.* [5] To **poison** water, air, or land means to damage it with harmful substances such as chemicals. ❑ *The land has been completely poisoned by chemicals. ...dying forests, poisoned rivers and lakes.* [6] Something that **poisons** a good situation or relationship spoils it or destroys it. ❑ *The whole atmosphere has really been poisoned. ...ill-feeling that will poison further talk of a common foreign policy.* N-MASS; VERB: V n; N-UNCOUNT; VERB: *be* V-ed *by* n, V n; N-UNCOUNT: supp N; VERB: V n; ADJ; VERB: V n, V-ed; VERB: *be* V-ed, V n

**poi|son|er** /pɔɪzənəʳ/ **(poisoners)** A **poisoner** is someone who has killed or harmed another person by using poison. ❑ *Soon they were dead, victims of a mysterious poisoner.* N-COUNT

**poi|son gas** **Poison gas** is a gas that is poisonous and is usually used to kill people in war or to execute criminals. N-UNCOUNT

**poi|son ivy** **Poison ivy** is a wild plant that grows in North America and that causes a rash or skin problems if you touch it. N-UNCOUNT

**poi|son|ous** /pɔɪzᵊnəs/ [1] Something that is **poisonous** will kill you or make you ill if you swallow or absorb it. ❑ *...a large cloud of poisonous gas.* [2] An animal that is **poisonous** produces a poison that will kill you or make you ill if the animal bites you. ❑ *There are hundreds of poisonous spiders and snakes.* [3] If you describe something as **poisonous**, you mean that it is extremely unpleasant and likely to spoil or destroy a good relationship or situation. ❑ *...poisonous comments.* ADJ; ADJ; ADJ: usu ADJ n

**poison-pen let|ter (poison-pen letters)** A **poison-pen letter** is an unpleasant unsigned letter which is sent in order to upset someone or to cause trouble. N-COUNT

**poi|son pill (poison pills)** A **poison pill** refers to what some companies do to reduce their value in order to prevent themselves being taken over by another company. [BUSINESS] N-COUNT

**poke** /poʊk/ **(pokes, poking, poked)** [1] If you **poke** someone or something, you quickly push them with your finger or with a sharp object. ❑ *Lindy poked him in the ribs.* ♦ **Poke** is also a noun. ❑ *John smiled at them and gave Richard a playful poke.* [2] If you **poke** one thing **into** another, you push the first thing into the second thing. ❑ *He poked his finger into the hole.* [3] If something **pokes out of** or **through** another thing, you can see part of it appearing from behind or underneath the other thing. ❑ *He saw the dog's twitching nose poke out of the basket... His fingers poked through the worn tips of his gloves.* [4] If you **poke** your head through an opening or if it **pokes** through an opening, you push it through, often so that you can see something more easily. ❑ *Julie tapped on my door and poked her head in... Raymond's head poked through the doorway.* [5] to **poke fun at** → see **fun**. to **poke** your **nose into** something → see **nose**. VERB = jab: V n; N-COUNT = prod; VERB: V n *into* n; VERB: V *out of* n, V *through* n; VERB: V n adv/prep, V prep/adv

**pok|er** /poʊkəʳ/ **(pokers)** [1] **Poker** is a card game that people usually play in order to win money. ❑ *Lon and I play in the same weekly poker* N-UNCOUNT *game.* [2] A **poker** is a metal bar which you use to move coal or wood in a fire in order to make it burn better. N-COUNT

**pok|er face** **(poker faces)** A **poker face** is an expression on your face that shows none of your feelings. [INFORMAL] ❑ *In business a poker face can be very useful... She managed to keep a poker face.* N-COUNT

**poker-faced** If you are **poker-faced**, you have a calm expression on your face which shows none of your thoughts or feelings. [INFORMAL] ❑ *His expressions varied from poker-faced to blank... The officer listened, poker-faced.* ADJ

**poky** /poʊki/ **(pokier, pokiest)**

> The spelling **pokey** is also used, especially for meanings 1 and 3.

[1] A room or house that is **poky** is uncomfortably small. [INFORMAL] ❑ *...pokey little offices.* ADJ disapproval
[2] If you say that someone is **poky**, you are criticizing them for moving or reacting very slowly. [AM, INFORMAL] ❑ *'Move!' she cried. 'Don't be so darn poky!'* ADJ disapproval [3] If someone is in **the pokey**, they are in prison. [mainly AM, INFORMAL] N-SING: usu *the* N

**po|lar** /poʊləʳ/ [1] **Polar** means near the North and South Poles. ❑ *Warmth melted some of the polar ice. ...polar explorers.* ADJ: ADJ n [2] **Polar** is used to describe things which are completely opposite in character, quality, or type. [FORMAL] ❑ *In many ways, Brett and Bernard are polar opposites.* ADJ: ADJ n

**po|lar bear** **(polar bears)** A **polar bear** is a large white bear which is found near the North Pole. N-COUNT

**po|lar|ise** /poʊləraɪz/ → see **polarize**.

**po|lar|ity** /poʊlærɪti/ **(polarities)** If there is a **polarity** between two people or things, they are completely different from each other in some way. [FORMAL] ❑ *...the polarities of good and evil.* N-VAR

**po|lar|ize** /poʊləraɪz/ **(polarizes, polarizing, polarized)**

> in BRIT, also use **polarise**

If something **polarizes** people or if something **polarizes**, two separate groups are formed with opposite opinions or positions. ❑ *Missile deployment did much to further polarize opinion in Britain... As the car rental industry polarizes, business will go to the bigger companies.* ♦ **po|lar|ized** *Since Independence the electorate has been polarized equally between two parties.* ♦ **po|lari|za|tion** /poʊləraɪzeɪʃən/ *There is increasing polarization between the blacks and whites in the US.* VERB V n V ADJ N-UNCOUNT

**Po|lar|oid** /poʊlərɔɪd/ **(Polaroids)** [1] A **Polaroid** camera is a small camera that can take, develop, and print a photograph in a few seconds. [TRADEMARK] ❑ *Polaroid film is very sensitive.* ADJ: ADJ n [2] A **Polaroid** is a photograph taken with a Polaroid camera. ❑ *I took a Polaroid of them so I could remember them when they were gone.* N-COUNT [3] **Polaroid** sunglasses have been treated with a special substance in order to make the sun seem less bright. ADJ: ADJ n

**pole** /poʊl/ **(poles)** [1] A **pole** is a long thin piece of wood or metal, used especially for supporting things. ❑ *The truck crashed into a telegraph pole... He reached up with a hooked pole to roll down the metal shutter.* ◆◇◇ N-COUNT [2] The earth's **poles** are the two opposite ends of its axis, its most northern and southern points. ❑ *For six months of the year, there is hardly any light at the poles.* → See also **North Pole**, **South Pole**. N-COUNT [3] The two **poles** of a range of qualities, opinions, or beliefs are the completely opposite qualities, opinions, or beliefs at either end of the range. ❑ *The two politicians represent opposite poles of the political spectrum.* N-COUNT [4] If you say that two people or things are **poles apart**, you mean that they have completely different beliefs, opinions, or qualities. PHRASE: v-link PHR emphasis

**Pole** **(Poles)** A **Pole** is a Polish citizen, or a person of Polish origin. N-COUNT

**pole-axed** also **poleaxed.** If someone is **pole-axed**, they are so surprised or shocked that they do not know what to say or do. [mainly BRIT, INFORMAL] ❑ *Sitting pole-axed on the sofa, Mahoney stared in astonishment at the spectacle before him.* ADJ: usu v-link ADJ

**pole|cat** /poʊlkæt/ **(polecats)** A **polecat** is a small, thin, fierce wild animal. Polecats have a very unpleasant smell. N-COUNT

**po|lem|ic** /pəlemɪk/ **(polemics)** A **polemic** is a very strong written or spoken attack on, or defence of, a particular belief or opinion. ❑ *...a polemic against the danger of secret societies.* N-VAR

**po|lemi|cal** /pəlemɪkəl/ **Polemical** means arguing very strongly for or against a belief or opinion. ❑ *Daniels is at his best when he's cool and direct, rather than combative and polemical. ...Kramer's biting polemical novel.* ADJ

**po|lemi|cist** /pəlemɪsɪst/ **(polemicists)** A **polemicist** is someone who is skilled at arguing very strongly for or against a belief or opinion. [FORMAL] N-COUNT

**pole po|si|tion** **(pole positions)** When a racing car is in **pole position**, it is in front of the other cars at the start of a race. N-UNCOUNT: also N in pl

**pole vault** **The pole vault** is an athletics event in which athletes jump over a high bar, using a long flexible pole to help lift themselves up. N-SING: *the* N

**pole vault|er** **(pole vaulters)** A **pole vaulter** is an athlete who performs the pole vault. N-COUNT

**po|lice** /pəliːs/ **(polices, policing, policed)** ◆◆◆
[1] The **police** are the official organization that is responsible for making sure that people obey the law. ❑ *The police are also looking for a second car... Police say they have arrested twenty people following the disturbances... I noticed a police car shadowing us.* N-SING-COLL
[2] **Police** are men and women who are members of the official organization that is responsible for making sure that people obey the law. ❑ *More than one hundred police have ringed the area.* N-PLURAL [3] If the police or military forces **police** an area or event, they make sure that law and order is preserved in that area or at that event. ❑ *...the tiny UN observer force whose job it is to police the border... The march was heavily policed.* → See also **secret police.** ♦ **po|lic|ing** *...the policing of public places.* VERB V n V-ed N-UNCOUNT
→ See also **community policing.** [4] If a person or group in authority **polices** a law or an area of public life, they make sure that what is done is fair and legal. ❑ *...Imro, the self-regulatory body that polices the investment management business.* ♦ **po|lic|ing** *Policing of business courses varies widely.* VERB V n N-UNCOUNT

**po|lice con|sta|ble** **(police constables)** A **police constable** is a policeman or policewoman of the lowest rank. [BRIT] ❑ *A police constable is handling all inquiries. ...Police Constable David Casey.* N-COUNT; N-TITLE

> in AM, use **police officer**

**po|lice dog** **(police dogs)** A **police dog** is a working dog which is owned by the police. N-COUNT

**po|lice force** **(police forces)** A **police force** is the police organization in a particular country or area. ❑ *...the South Wales police force.* N-COUNT: oft N n

**police|man** /pəliːsmən/ **(policemen)** A **policeman** is a man who is a member of the police force. ◆◇◇ N-COUNT

**po|lice of|fic|er** **(police officers)** A **police officer** is a member of the police force. ❑ *...a meeting of senior police officers.* ◆◇◇ N-COUNT

**po|lice state** **(police states)** A **police state** is a country in which the government controls people's freedom by means of the police, especially secret police. N-COUNT disapproval

**po|lice sta|tion** **(police stations)** A **police station** is the local office of a police force in a particular area. ❑ *Two police officers arrested him and took him to Kensington police station.* N-COUNT: oft in names

**police|woman** /pəliːswʊmən/ **(policewomen)** A **policewoman** is a woman who is a member of the police force. N-COUNT

**poli|cy** /pɒlɪsi/ **(policies)** [1] A **policy** is a set of ideas or plans that is used as a basis for making ◆◆◆ N-VAR decisions, especially in politics, economics, or business. ❑ *...plans which include changes in foreign policy and economic reforms. ...the UN's policy-making body.* [2] An official organization's **policy** on a particular issue or towards a country is their attitude and actions regarding that issue or country. ❑ *...the government's policy on repatriation. ...the corporation's policy of forbidding building on common land.* [3] An insurance **policy** is a document which shows the agreement that you have made with an insurance company. [BUSINESS] ❑ *You are advised to read the small print of household and motor insurance policies.* N-COUNT: usu poss N; N-COUNT: usu N n

**policy|holder** /pɒlɪsihoʊldəʳ/ **(policyholders)** also **policy-holder.** A **policyholder** is a person who has an insurance policy with an insurance company. [BUSINESS] ❑ *The first 10 per cent of legal fees will be paid by the policy-holder.* N-COUNT

**policy|maker** /pɒlɪsimeɪkəʳ/ **(policymakers)** also **policy-maker.** In politics, **policymakers** are people who are involved in making policies and policy decisions. ❑ *...top economic policymakers.* N-COUNT: usu pl

**policy-making** also **policymaking. Policy-making** is the making of policies. ❑ *He will play a key background role in government policy-making.* N-UNCOUNT: oft N n

**po|lio** /poʊlioʊ/ **Polio** is a serious infectious disease which often makes people unable to use their legs. ❑ *Gladys was crippled by polio at the age of 3.* N-UNCOUNT

**po|lio|my|eli|tis** /poʊlioʊmaɪəlaɪtɪs/ **Poliomyelitis** is the same as **polio.** [MEDICAL] N-UNCOUNT

**pol|ish** /pɒlɪʃ/ **(polishes, polishing, polished)**
[1] **Polish** is a substance that you put on the surface of an object in order to clean it, protect it, and make it shine. ❑ *The still air smelt faintly of furniture polish. ...soap powders, detergents, and polishes.* N-MASS
[2] If you **polish** something, you put polish on it or rub it with a cloth to make it shine. ❑ *Each morning he shaved and polished his shoes.* ♦ **Polish** is also a noun. ❑ *He gave his counter a polish with a soft duster.* ♦ **pol|ished** *...a highly polished floor.* VERB: V n; N-SING: *a* N; ADJ
[3] If you say that someone has **polish**, you mean that they show confidence and know how to behave socially. [4] If you say that a performance or piece of work has **polish**, you mean that it is of a very high standard. ❑ *The opera lacks the polish of his later work.* [5] If you **polish** your technique, performance, or skill at doing something, you work on improving it. ❑ *They just need to polish their technique.* ♦ **Polish up** means the same as **polish.** ❑ *Polish up your writing skills on a one-week professional course.* [6] ➔ See also **polished, French polish, nail polish.** N-UNCOUNT [approval]; N-UNCOUNT [approval]; VERB: V n; PHRASAL VERB: V P n (not pron)

♦ **polish off** If you **polish off** food or drink, you eat or drink all of it, or finish it. [INFORMAL] ❑ *No matter what he is offered to eat he polishes it off in an instant... He polished off his scotch and slammed the glass down.* PHRASAL VERB: V n P; V P n (not pron)

♦ **polish up** ➔ see **polish 5.**

**Po|lish** /poʊlɪʃ/ [1] **Polish** means belonging or relating to Poland, or to its people, language, or culture. [2] **Polish** is the language spoken in Poland. ADJ; N-UNCOUNT

**pol|ished** /pɒlɪʃt/ [1] Someone who is **polished** shows confidence and knows how to behave socially. ❑ *He is polished, charming, articulate and an excellent negotiator.* [2] If you describe a performance, ability, or skill as **polished,** you mean that it is of a very high standard. ❑ *It was simply a very polished performance.* [3] ➔ See also **polish.** ADJ: usu v-link ADJ [approval]; ADJ [approval]

**Pol|it|bu|ro** /pɒlɪtbjʊəroʊ/ **(Politburos)** In communist countries **the Politburo** is the chief committee that decides on government policy and makes decisions. N-COUNT: usu *the* N

**po|lite** /pəlaɪt/ **(politer, politest)** [1] Someone who is **polite** has good manners and behaves in a way that is socially correct and not rude to other people. ❑ *Everyone around him was trying to be polite, but you could tell they were all bored... It's not polite to point or talk about strangers in public... Gately, a quiet and very polite young man, made a favourable impression... I hate having to make polite conversation.* ♦ **po|lite|ly** *'Your home is beautiful,' I said politely.* ♦ **po|lite|ness** *She listened to him, but only out of politeness.* [2] You can refer to people who consider themselves to be socially superior and to set standards of behaviour for everyone else as **polite society** or **polite company.** ❑ *Certain words are vulgar and not acceptable in polite society.* ADJ ≠rude; ADV; N-UNCOUNT; ADJ: ADJ n

**poli|tic** /pɒlɪtɪk/ If it seems **politic to** do a particular thing, that seems to be the most sensible thing to do in the circumstances. [FORMAL] ❑ *Many towns often found it politic to change their allegiance.* ➔ See also **politics, body politic.** ADJ: usu *it* v-link ADJ to-inf

**po|liti|cal** /pəlɪtɪkəl/ ◆◆◆ [1] **Political** means relating to the way power is achieved and used in a country or society. ❑ *All other political parties there have been completely banned... The Canadian government is facing another political crisis. ...a democratic political system.* ➔ See also **party political.** ♦ **po|liti|cal|ly** /pəlɪtɪkli/ *They do not believe the killings were politically motivated... Politically and economically this is an extremely difficult question.* [2] Someone who is **political** is interested or involved in politics and holds strong beliefs about it. ❑ *This play is very political.* ADJ: usu ADJ n; ADV: ADV adj/adv, ADV with v, ADV with cl; ADJ

**po|liti|cal asy|lum Political asylum** is the right to live in a foreign country and is given by the government of that country to people who have to leave their own country for political reasons. ❑ *...a university teacher who is seeking political asylum in Britain.* N-UNCOUNT

**po|liti|cal cor|rect|ness Political correctness** is the attitude or policy of being extremely careful not to offend or upset any group of people in society who have a disadvantage, or who have been treated differently because of their sex, race, or disability. N-UNCOUNT ≠political incorrectness

**po|liti|cal econo|my Political economy** is the study of the way in which a government influences or organizes a nation's wealth. N-UNCOUNT

**po|liti|cal in|cor|rect|ness Political incorrectness** is the attitude or policy shown by someone who does not care if they offend or upset any group of people in society who have a disadvantage, or who have been treated differently because of their sex, race, or disability. N-UNCOUNT ≠political correctness

**po|liti|cal|ly cor|rect** If you say that someone is **politically correct,** you mean that they are extremely careful not to offend or upset any group of people in society who have a disadvantage, or who have been treated differently because of their sex, race, or disability. ♦ **The politically correct** are people who are politically correct. ADJ; N-PLURAL: *the* N

**po|liti|cal|ly in|cor|rect** If you say that someone is **politically incorrect,** you mean that they do not care if they offend or upset other people in society, for example with their attitudes towards sex, race, or disability. ❑ *Gershwin's lyrics would today probably be deemed politically incorrect.* ♦ **The politically incorrect** are people who are politically incorrect. ADJ ≠politically correct; N-PLURAL: *the* N

**po|liti|cal pris|on|er (political prisoners)** A **political prisoner** is someone who has been imprisoned for criticizing or disagreeing with their own government. N-COUNT

**po|liti|cal sci|ence Political science** is the study of the ways in which political power is acquired and used in a country. N-UNCOUNT

**po|liti|cal sci|en|tist (political scientists)** A **political scientist** is someone who studies, writes, or lectures about political science. N-COUNT

**poli|ti|cian** /pɒlɪtɪʃən/ **(politicians)** A **politician** is a person whose job is in politics, especially a member of parliament or congress. ❑ *They have arrested a number of leading opposition politicians.* ◆◆◇ N-COUNT

**po|liti|cize** /pəl̲ɪtɪsaɪz/ **(politicizes, politicizing, politicized)**

in BRIT, also use **politicise**

If you **politicize** someone or something, you make them more interested in politics or more involved with politics. ❑ *...ideas which might politicize the labouring classes and cause them to question the status quo... Some feminists had attempted to politicize personal life.* ♦ **po|liti|cized** *The data that's being used to fault American education is highly politicized.* ♦ **po|liti|ci|za|tion** /pəlɪtɪsaɪze̲ɪʃᵊn/ *There has been increasing politicization of the civil service.* VERB V n V n ADJ N-UNCOUNT

**poli|tick|ing** /pɒ̲lɪtɪkɪŋ/ If you describe someone's political activity as **politicking**, you think that they are engaged in it to gain votes or personal advantage for themselves. ❑ *The politicking at Westminster is extremely intense.* N-UNCOUNT disapproval

**po|liti|co** /pəl̲ɪtɪkoʊ/ **(politicos)** You can describe a politician as a **politico**, especially if you do not like them or approve of what they do. N-COUNT disapproval

**politico-** /pəl̲ɪtɪkoʊ-/ **Politico-** is added to adjectives to form other adjectives that describe something as being both political and the other thing that is mentioned. ❑ *...the capitalist politico-economic system.* COMB in ADJ: ADJ n

**poli|tics** /pɒ̲lɪtɪks/ [1] **Politics** are the actions or activities concerned with achieving and using power in a country or society. The verb that follows **politics** may be either singular or plural. ❑ *The key question in British politics was how long the prime minister could survive... The film takes no position on the politics of Northern Ireland... Politics is by no means the only arena in which women are excelling.* → See also **party politics**. [2] Your **politics** are your beliefs about how a country ought to be governed. ❑ *My politics are well to the left of centre.* [3] **Politics** is the study of the ways in which countries are governed. ❑ *He began studying politics and medieval history. ...young politics graduates.* [4] **Politics** can be used to talk about the ways that power is shared in an organization and the ways it is affected by personal relationships between people who work together. The verb that follows **politics** may be either singular or plural. ❑ *You need to understand how office politics influence the working environment.* ◆◆◇ N-PLURAL; N-PLURAL: usu with poss; N-UNCOUNT; N-PLURAL

**pol|ity** /pɒ̲lɪti/ **(polities)** A **polity** is an organized society, such as a nation, city, or church, together with its government and administration. [FORMAL] ❑ *...the role of religious belief in a democratic polity.* N-COUNT

**pol|ka** /pɒ̲lkə, AM poʊ̲lkə/ **(polkas)** A **polka** is a fast lively dance that was popular in the nineteenth century. N-COUNT

**pol|ka dots**

The spelling **polka-dot** is also used, especially as a modifier. The word **polka** is usually pronounced /poʊ̲kə/ in American English when it is part of this compound.

**Polka dots** are very small spots printed on a piece of cloth. ❑ *...a yellow bikini with polka dots. ...a tight-fitting polka dot blouse.* N-PLURAL: oft N n

**poll** /poʊ̲l/ **(polls, polling, polled)** [1] A **poll** is a survey in which people are asked their opinions about something, usually in order to find out how popular something is or what people intend to do in the future. ❑ *Polls show that the European treaty has gained support in Denmark... We are doing a weekly poll on the president, and clearly his popularity has declined.* → See also **opinion poll**, **straw poll**. [2] If you **are polled on** something, you are asked what you think about it as part of a survey. ❑ *More than 18,000 people were polled... Audiences were going to be polled on which of three pieces of contemporary music they liked best... More than 70 per cent of those polled said that they approved of his record as president.* [3] **The polls** means an election for a country's government, or the place where people go to vote in an election. ❑ *In 1945, Winston Churchill was defeated at the polls... Voters are due to go to the polls on Sunday to elect a new president.* [4] If a political party or a candidate **polls** a particular number or percentage of votes, they get that number or percentage of votes in an election. ❑ *It was a disappointing result for the Greens who polled three percent.* [5] → See also **polling**, **deed poll**. ◆◆◇ N-COUNT; VERB: usu passive be V-ed, be V-ed on wh/n, V-ed; N-PLURAL: the N; VERB V n

**pol|len** /pɒ̲lən/ **(pollens)** **Pollen** is a fine powder produced by flowers. It fertilizes other flowers of the same species so that they produce seeds. N-MASS

**pol|len count** **(pollen counts)** The **pollen count** is a measure of how much pollen is in the air at a particular place and time. Information about the pollen count is given to help people who are made ill by pollen. ❑ *Avoid trips to the country while the pollen count is high.* N-COUNT

**pol|li|nate** /pɒ̲lɪneɪt/ **(pollinates, pollinating, pollinated)** To **pollinate** a plant or tree means to fertilize it with pollen. This is often done by insects. ❑ *Many of the indigenous insects are needed to pollinate the local plants.* ♦ **pol|li|na|tion** /pɒ̲lɪne̲ɪʃᵊn/ *Without sufficient pollination, the growth of the corn is stunted.* VERB V n N-UNCOUNT

**pol|li|na|tor** /pɒ̲lɪneɪtəʳ/ **(pollinators)** A **pollinator** is something which pollinates plants, especially a type of insect. [TECHNICAL] N-COUNT

**poll|ing** /poʊ̲lɪŋ/ **Polling** is the act of voting in an election. ❑ *There has been a busy start to polling in today's local elections.* N-UNCOUNT = voting

**poll|ing booth** **(polling booths)** [1] **Polling booths** are the places where people go to vote in an election. ❑ *In Darlington, queues formed at some polling booths.* [2] A **polling booth** is one of the partly enclosed areas in a polling station, where people can vote in private. ❑ *When you are there, in the polling booth, nobody can see where you put your cross.* N-COUNT: usu pl = polling station; N-COUNT

**poll|ing day** **Polling day** is the day on which people vote in an election. [mainly BRIT] N-UNCOUNT

in AM, usually use **election day**

**poll|ing place** **(polling places)** A **polling place** is the same as a **polling station**. [AM] N-COUNT

**poll|ing sta|tion** **(polling stations)** A **polling station** is a place where people go to vote at an election. It is often a school or other public building. [BRIT] ❑ *Queues formed even before polling stations opened.* N-COUNT

in AM, use **polling place**

**poll|ster** /poʊ̲lstəʳ/ **(pollsters)** A **pollster** is a person or organization who asks large numbers of people questions to find out their opinions on particular subjects. N-COUNT

**pol|lu|tant** /pəlu̲ːtənt/ **(pollutants)** **Pollutants** are substances that pollute the environment, especially gases from vehicles and poisonous chemicals produced as waste by industrial processes. ❑ *A steady stream of California traffic clogs the air with pollutants.* N-VAR

**pol|lute** /pəlu̲ːt/ **(pollutes, polluting, polluted)** To **pollute** water, air, or land means to make it dirty and dangerous to live in or to use, especially with poisonous chemicals or sewage. ❑ *Heavy industry pollutes our rivers with noxious chemicals.* ♦ **pol|lut|ed** *The police have warned the city's inhabitants not to bathe in the polluted river.* VERB V n ADJ

**pol|lut|er** /pəlu̲ːtəʳ/ **(polluters)** A **polluter** is someone or something that pollutes the environment. N-COUNT

**pol|lu|tion** /pəlu̲ːʃᵊn/ [1] **Pollution** is the process of polluting water, air, or land, especially with poisonous chemicals. ❑ *The fine was for the company's pollution of the air near its plants... Recycling also helps control environmental pollution by reducing the need for waste dumps.* [2] **Pollution** is poisonous or dirty substances that are polluting the water, air, or land somewhere. ❑ *The level of pollution in the river was falling.* ◆◇◇ N-UNCOUNT; N-UNCOUNT

**polo** /pəʊləʊ/ **Polo** is a game played between two teams of players. The players ride horses and use wooden hammers with long handles to hit a ball. → See also **water polo**. N-UNCOUNT

**polo neck** **(polo necks)** also **polo-neck.** A **polo neck** or a **polo neck sweater** is a sweater with a high neck which folds over. [BRIT] N-COUNT

in AM, use **turtleneck**

**polo shirt** **(polo shirts)** A **polo shirt** is a soft short-sleeved piece of clothing with a collar, which you put on over your head. N-COUNT

**pol|ter|geist** /pɒltəʳgaɪst, AM poʊl-/ **(poltergeists)** A **poltergeist** is a ghost or supernatural force which is believed to move furniture or throw objects around. N-COUNT

**poly** /pɒli/ **(polys)** A **poly** is the same as a **polytechnic**. [mainly BRIT, INFORMAL] N-COUNT: oft in names after n

**poly-** /pɒli-/ **Poly-** is used to form adjectives and nouns which indicate that many things or types of something are involved in something. For example, a polysyllabic word contains many syllables. ❑ *He portrays the psyche as polycentric.* ❑ *...polyclinics that integrate primary and secondary health care.* PREFIX

**poly|es|ter** /pɒliestəʳ, AM -es-/ **(polyesters)** **Polyester** is a type of artificial cloth used especially to make clothes. ❑ *...a green polyester shirt.* N-MASS

**poly|eth|yl|ene** /pɒlieθɪliːn/ **Polyethylene** is a type of plastic made into thin sheets or bags and used especially to keep food fresh or to keep things dry. [mainly AM] N-UNCOUNT

in BRIT, usually use **polythene**

**po|lyga|mous** /pəlɪgəməs/ In a **polygamous** society, people can be legally married to more than one person at the same time. A **polygamous** person, especially a man, is married to more than one person. ❑ *Less than 1 percent of the men in any Muslim country are polygamous.* ADJ

**po|lyga|my** /pəlɪgəmi/ **Polygamy** is the custom in some societies in which someone can be legally married to more than one person at the same time. N-UNCOUNT

**poly|glot** /pɒliglɒt/ **(polyglots)** 1 **Polyglot** is used to describe something such as a book or society in which several different languages are used. [FORMAL] ❑ *...Chicago's polyglot population.* ADJ: usu ADJ n = *multilingual*
2 A **polyglot** is a person who speaks or understands many languages. N-COUNT

**poly|graph** /pɒligrɑːf, -græf/ **(polygraphs)** A **polygraph** or a **polygraph test** is a test which is used by the police to try to find out whether someone is telling the truth. ❑ *Hill's lawyers announced she had taken and passed a polygraph test.* N-COUNT = *lie detector*

**poly|mer** /pɒlɪməʳ/ **(polymers)** A **polymer** is a chemical compound with large molecules made of many smaller molecules of the same kind. Some polymers exist naturally and others are produced in laboratories and factories. N-COUNT

**pol|yp** /pɒlɪp/ **(polyps)** 1 A **polyp** is a small unhealthy growth on a surface inside your body, especially inside your nose. N-COUNT
2 A **polyp** is a small animal that lives in the sea. It has a hollow body like a tube and long parts called tentacles around its mouth. N-COUNT

**poly|pro|pyl|ene** /pɒliprɒpɪliːn/ **Polypropylene** is a strong, flexible artificial material that is used to make things such as rope, carpet, and pipes. N-UNCOUNT

**poly|sty|rene** /pɒlɪstaɪriːn/ **Polystyrene** is a very light plastic substance used to make containers or to keep things warm, cool, or protected from damage. ❑ *...polystyrene cups.* N-UNCOUNT

**poly|tech|nic** /pɒlɪteknɪk/ **(polytechnics)** 1 In Britain, a **polytechnic** was a college where you could go after leaving school in order to study academic subjects up to degree level, or to train for particular jobs. In 1992, all the polytechnics in Britain became universities. N-VAR: oft in names
2 In the United States, **polytechnic** is the former name for a school, college, or university which specialized in courses in science and technology. N-VAR: oft in names

**poly|thene** /pɒlɪθiːn/ **Polythene** is a type of plastic made into thin sheets or bags and used especially to keep food fresh or to keep things dry. [mainly BRIT] ❑ *Simply put them into a polythene bag and store them in the freezer for a day.* N-UNCOUNT

in AM, usually use **polyethylene**

**poly|un|satu|rate** /pɒliʌnsætʃʊrət/ **(polyunsaturates)** **Polyunsaturates** are types of animal or vegetable fats which are used to make cooking oil and margarine. They are thought to be less harmful to your body than other fats. N-COUNT: usu pl

**poly|un|satu|rat|ed** /pɒliʌnsætʃʊreɪtɪd/ **Polyunsaturated** oils and margarines are made mainly from vegetable fats and are considered healthier than those made from animal fats. ❑ *Use polyunsaturated spread instead of butter.* ADJ

**poly|urethane** /pɒlijʊərəθeɪn/ **(polyurethanes)** **Polyurethane** is a plastic material used especially to make paint or substances which prevent water or heat from passing through. ❑ *...polyurethane varnish.* N-MASS

**pom** /pɒm/ **(poms)** A **pom** is the same as a **pommy**. N-COUNT

**pom|egran|ate** /pɒmɪgrænɪt/ **(pomegranates)** A **pomegranate** is a round fruit with a thick reddish skin. It contains lots of small seeds with juicy flesh around them. N-VAR

**pom|mel** /pʌməl, pɒm-/ **(pommels)** A **pommel** is the part of a saddle that rises up at the front, or a knob that is fixed there. N-COUNT

**pom|my** /pɒmi/ **(pommies)** also **pommie.** A **pommy** is an English person. This use could cause offence. [mainly AUSTRALIAN, INFORMAL] N-COUNT disapproval

**pomp** /pɒmp/ **Pomp** is the use of a lot of ceremony, fine clothes, and decorations, especially on a special occasion. ❑ *...the pomp and splendour of the English aristocracy.* N-UNCOUNT

**pom-pom** **(pom-poms)** also **pompom, pom-pon.** A **pom-pom** is a ball of threads which is used to decorate things such as hats or furniture. In the United States, cheerleaders wave large pom-poms at football matches. N-COUNT

**pom|pos|ity** /pɒmpɒsɪti/ **(pomposities)** **Pomposity** means speaking or behaving in a very serious manner which shows that you think you are more important than you really are. ❑ *He hated pomposity and disliked being called a genius.* N-UNCOUNT: also N in pl disapproval

**pomp|ous** /pɒmpəs/ 1 If you describe someone as **pompous**, you mean that they behave or speak in a very serious way because they think they are more important than they really are. ❑ *He was somewhat pompous and had a high opinion of his own capabilities.* ♦ **pomp|ous|ly** *Robin said pompously that he had an important business appointment.* ADJ disapproval; ADV: usu ADV with v
2 A **pompous** building or ceremony is very grand and elaborate. ❑ *The service was grand without being pompous.* ADJ

**ponce** /pɒns/ **(ponces, poncing, ponced)** 1 A **ponce** is the same as a **pimp**. [BRIT, INFORMAL, OLD-FASHIONED] N-COUNT
2 If you call a man a **ponce**, you are insulting him because you think the way he dresses or behaves is too feminine. [BRIT, INFORMAL, RUDE] N-COUNT disapproval

♦ **ponce around**

in BRIT, also use **ponce about**

If you say that someone **is poncing around** or **poncing about**, you mean that they are not doing something properly, quickly, or seriously. [BRIT, INFORMAL, RUDE] ❑ *I spent my working life poncing around on a beach instead of doing a proper job.* PHRASAL VERB disapproval; V P

**poncey** /pɒnsi/ also **poncy.** If you say that someone or something is **poncey**, you mean you do not like them because they are too feminine or artistic. [BRIT, INFORMAL, RUDE] ❑ *...a poncy male model.* ADJ disapproval

**pon|cho** /pɒntʃoʊ/ **(ponchos)** A **poncho** is a piece of clothing that consists of a long piece of material, usually wool, with a hole cut in the middle through which you put your head. Some ponchos have a hood. N-COUNT

**pond** /pɒnd/ **(ponds)** 1 A **pond** is a small area of water that is smaller than a lake. Ponds are often made artificially. ❑ *She chose a bench beside the duck pond and sat down.* N-COUNT: oft n N 2 People sometimes refer to the Atlantic Ocean as **the pond**. [mainly JOURNALISM] ❑ *Usually, the presentation is made on the other side of the pond.* N-SING: *the* N

**pon|der** /pɒndəʳ/ **(ponders, pondering, pondered)** If you **ponder** something, you think about it carefully. ❑ *I found myself constantly pondering the question: 'How could anyone do these things?'... The Prime Minister pondered on when to go to the polls... I'm continually pondering how to improve the team.* VERB V n V *on/over* n V wh

**pon|der|ous** /pɒndərəs/ 1 **Ponderous** writing or speech is very serious, uses more words than necessary, and is rather dull. ❑ *He had a dense, ponderous style.* ♦ **pon|der|ous|ly** *...the rather ponderously titled 'Recommendation for National Reconciliation and Salvation'.* ADJ [disapproval] ADV: ADV with v 2 A movement or action that is **ponderous** is very slow or clumsy. [WRITTEN] ❑ *His steps were heavy and ponderous.* ♦ **pon|der|ous|ly** *Wilson shifted ponderously in his chair.* ADJ ADV: ADV with v

**pong** /pɒŋ, AM pɔːŋ/ **(pongs)** A **pong** is an unpleasant smell. [BRIT, INFORMAL] ❑ *...the pong of milk and sick and nappies.* N-COUNT

**pon|tiff** /pɒntɪf/ **(pontiffs)** **The Pontiff** is the Pope. [FORMAL] ❑ *The Pontiff celebrated mass in Mexico City.* N-COUNT: usu *the* N = Pope

**pon|tifi|cate** **(pontificates, pontificating, pontificated)**

> ✔ The verb is pronounced /pɒntɪfɪkeɪt/. The noun is pronounced /pɒntɪfɪkət/.

1 If someone **pontificates about** something, they state their opinions as if they are the only correct ones and nobody could possibly argue against them. [FORMAL] ❑ *Politicians like to pontificate about falling standards.* VERB V *about/on* n, Also V 2 The **pontificate** of a pope is the period of time during which he is pope. ❑ *Pope Formosus died after a pontificate of four and a half years.* N-COUNT

**pon|toon** /pɒntuːn/ **(pontoons)** A **pontoon** is a floating platform, often one used to support a bridge. ❑ *...a pontoon bridge.* N-COUNT

**pony** /poʊni/ **(ponies)** A **pony** is a type of small horse. N-COUNT

**pony|tail** /poʊniteɪl/ **(ponytails)** also **pony-tail.** A **ponytail** is a hairstyle in which someone's hair is tied up at the back of the head and hangs down like a tail. ❑ *Her long, fine hair was swept back in a ponytail.* N-COUNT

**poo** /puː/ **(poos)** **Poo** is a child's word for faeces. [INFORMAL] N-VAR

**pooch** /puːtʃ/ **(pooches)** A **pooch** is a dog. [JOURNALISM, INFORMAL] N-COUNT

**poo|dle** /puːdəl/ **(poodles)** A **poodle** is a type of dog with thick curly hair. N-COUNT

**poof** /pʊf/ **(poofs)** also **pouf.** 1 A **poof** is a homosexual man. [BRIT, INFORMAL, OFFENSIVE] N-COUNT 2 Some people say **poof** to indicate that something happened very suddenly. ❑ *They approach, embrace, and poof! they disappear in a blinding flash of light.* EXCLAM

**poof|ter** /pʊftəʳ/ **(poofters)** A **poofter** is a homosexual man. [BRIT, INFORMAL, OFFENSIVE] N-COUNT

**pooh-pooh** /puː puː/ **(pooh-poohs, pooh-poohing, pooh-poohed)** If someone **pooh-poohs** an idea or suggestion, they say or imply that it is foolish, impractical, or unnecessary. ❑ *In the past he has pooh-poohed suggestions that he might succeed Isaacs.* VERB V n

**pool** /puːl/ **(pools, pooling, pooled)** 1 A **pool** is the same as a **swimming pool**. ❑ *...a heated indoor pool... During winter, many people swim and the pool is crowded.* ◆◇◇ N-COUNT 2 A **pool** is a fairly small area of still water. ❑ *The pool had dried up and was full of bracken and reeds.* ➔ See also **rock pool**. N-COUNT 3 A **pool of** liquid or light is a small area of it on the ground or on a surface. ❑ *She was found lying in a pool of blood... The lamps on the side-tables threw warm pools of light on the polished wood.* N-COUNT: N *of* n 4 A **pool of** people, money, or things is a quantity or number of them that is available for an organization or group to use. ❑ *The new proposal would create a reserve pool of cash.* ➔ See also **car pool**. N-COUNT: with supp, usu N *of* n 5 If a group of people or organizations **pool** their money, knowledge, or equipment, they share it or put it together so that it can be used for a particular purpose. ❑ *We pooled ideas and information.* VERB V n 6 **Pool** is a game played on a large table covered with a cloth. Players use a long stick called a cue to hit a white ball across the table so that it knocks coloured balls with numbers on them into six holes around the edge of the table. N-UNCOUNT 7 If you do **the pools**, you take part in a gambling competition in which people try to win money by guessing correctly the results of football matches. [BRIT] ❑ *The odds of winning the pools are about one in 20 million.* N-PLURAL: *the* N = *football pools*

**poop** /puːp/ **(poops)** The **poop** of an old-fashioned sailing ship is the raised structure at the back end of it. ❑ *...the poop deck.* N-COUNT

**pooped** /puːpt/ If you are **pooped**, you are very tired. [AM, INFORMAL] ADJ: v-link ADJ

**poor** /pʊəʳ, pɔːʳ/ **(poorer, poorest)** 1 Someone who is **poor** has very little money and few possessions. ❑ *The reason our schools cannot afford better teachers is because people here are poor... He was one of thirteen children from a poor family.* ♦ **The poor** are people who are poor. ❑ *Even the poor have their pride.* ◆◆◇ ADJ ≠ rich N-PLURAL: *the* N 2 The people in a **poor** country or area have very little money and few possessions. ❑ *Many countries in the Third World are as poor as they have ever been. ...a settlement house for children in a poor neighborhood.* ADJ ≠ rich 3 You use **poor** to express your sympathy for someone. ❑ *I feel sorry for that poor child... Poor chap – he was killed in an air crash.* ADJ: ADJ n [feelings] 4 If you describe something as **poor**, you mean that it is of a low quality or standard or that it is in bad condition. ❑ *The flat was in a poor state of repair... The wine was poor.* ♦ **poor|ly** *Some are living in poorly built dormitories, even in tents.* ADJ ADV: ADV -ed, ADV after v 5 If you describe an amount, rate, or number as **poor**, you mean that it is less than expected or less than is considered reasonable. ❑ *...poor wages and working conditions.* ♦ **poor|ly** *During the first week, the evening meetings were poorly attended.* ADJ ADV: ADV -ed, ADV after v 6 You use **poor** to describe someone who is not very skilful in a particular activity. ❑ *He was a poor actor... Hospitals are poor at collecting information.* ♦ **poor|ly** *That is the fact of Hungarian football – they can play very well or very poorly.* ADJ: usu ADJ n, also v-link ADJ *at* -ing/n ADV: ADV after v 7 If something is **poor in** a particular quality or substance, it contains very little of the quality or substance. ❑ *...soil that is poor in zinc.* ADJ: v-link ADJ *in* n

**poor|house** /pʊəʳhaʊs, pɔːʳ-/ **(poorhouses)** also **poor-house.** In former times in Britain, a **poorhouse** was an institution in which poor people could live. It was paid for by the public. N-COUNT: usu *the* N = workhouse

**poor|ly** /pʊəʳli, pɔːʳ-/ If someone is **poorly**, they are ill. [mainly BRIT, INFORMAL] ❑ *I've just phoned Julie and she's still poorly.* ➔ See also **poor**. ADJ: usu v-link ADJ

> ✔ in AM, use **sick**

**poor re|la|tion** **(poor relations)** If you describe one thing as a **poor relation of** another, you mean that it is similar to or part of the other thing, but is considered to be inferior to it. ❑ *Watercolour still seems somehow to be the poor relation of oil painting.* N-COUNT: usu N *of* n

**pop** /pɒp/ **(pops, popping, popped)** 1 **Pop** is modern music that usually has a strong rhythm and uses electronic equipment. ❑ *...the perfect combination of Caribbean rhythms, European pop, and American soul. ...a life-size poster of a pop star... I* ◆◇◇ N-UNCOUNT: oft N n *know nothing about pop music.* [2] You can refer to fizzy drinks such as lemonade as **pop**. [mainly BRIT, INFORMAL] ❑ *He still visits the village shop for buns and fizzy pop. ...glass pop bottles.* N-UNCOUNT

☑ in AM, usually use **soda pop**

[3] **Pop** is used to represent a short sharp sound, for example the sound made by bursting a balloon or by pulling a cork out of a bottle. ❑ *His back tyre just went pop on a motorway.* N-COUNT; SOUND [4] If something **pops**, it makes a short sharp sound. ❑ *He untwisted the wire off the champagne bottle, and the cork popped and shot to the ceiling.* VERB V [5] If your eyes **pop**, you look very surprised or excited when you see something. [INFORMAL] ❑ *My eyes popped at the sight of the rich variety of food on show.* VERB V [6] If you **pop** something somewhere, you put it there quickly. [BRIT, INFORMAL] ❑ *He plucked a purple grape from the bunch and popped it in his mouth.* VERB V n prep/adv [7] If you **pop** somewhere, you go there for a short time. [BRIT, INFORMAL] ❑ *Wendy popped in for a quick bite to eat on Monday night.* VERB V adv/prep [8] Some people call their father **pop**. [mainly AM, INFORMAL] ❑ *I looked at Pop and he had big tears in his eyes.* N-FAMILY

☑ in BRIT, usually use **dad**

[9] to **pop the question** → see **question**.

♦ **pop up** If someone or something **pops up**, they appear in a place or situation unexpectedly. [INFORMAL] ❑ *She was startled when Lisa popped up at the door all smiles.* → See also **pop-up**. PHRASAL VERB = *appear* V P

**POP** /piː oʊ piː/ **(POPs)** A **POP** is equipment that gives access to the Internet. **POP** is an abbreviation for 'point of presence'. [COMPUTING] N-COUNT

**pop.** /pɒp/ **pop.** is an abbreviation for **population**. It is used before a number when indicating the total population of a city or country. ❑ *Somalia, pop. 7.9 million, income per head about £1.60 a week.*

**pop art** **Pop art** is a style of modern art which began in the 1960s. It uses bright colours and takes a lot of its techniques and subject matter from everyday, modern life. N-UNCOUNT

**pop|corn** /pɒpkɔːʳn/ **Popcorn** is a snack which consists of grains of maize or corn that have been heated until they have burst and become large and light. It can be eaten with salt or sometimes sugar. N-UNCOUNT

**pope** /poʊp/ **(popes) The Pope** is the head of the Roman Catholic Church. ❑ *...the Pope's message to the people. ...Pope John Paul II.* N-COUNT: usu *the* N; N-TITLE

**pop|lar** /pɒpləʳ/ **(poplars)** A **poplar** is a type of tall thin tree. N-VAR

**pop|lin** /pɒplɪn/ **Poplin** is a type of cotton material used to make clothes. N-UNCOUNT

**pop|pa|dom** /pɒpədɒm/ **(poppadoms)** A **poppadom** is a very thin circular crisp made from a mixture of flour and water, which is fried in oil. Poppadoms are usually eaten with Indian food. N-COUNT

**pop|per** /pɒpəʳ/ **(poppers)** A **popper** is a device for fastening clothes. It consists of two pieces of plastic or metal which you press together. [BRIT] N-COUNT

☑ in AM, use **snap fastener, snap**

**pop|py** /pɒpi/ **(poppies)** [1] A **poppy** is a plant with a large, delicate flower, usually red in colour. The drug opium is obtained from one type of poppy. ❑ *...a field of poppies.* N-COUNT [2] In Britain, on a particular day in November, people wear an artificial **poppy** in memory of the people who died in the two world wars. ❑ *...a wreath of poppies.* N-COUNT

**Pop|si|cle** /pɒpsɪkəl/ **(Popsicles)** A **Popsicle** is a piece of flavoured ice or ice cream on a stick. [AM, TRADEMARK] N-COUNT

☑ in BRIT, use **ice lolly**

**popu|lace** /pɒpjʊləs/ **The populace** of a country is its people. [FORMAL] ❑ *...a large proportion of the populace.* N-UNCOUNT: usu *the* N = *population*

**popu|lar** /pɒpjʊləʳ/ ♦♦◇ [1] Something that is **popular** is enjoyed or liked by a lot of people. ❑ *This is the most popular ball game ever devised... Chocolate sauce is always popular with youngsters.* ADJ ≠ *unpopular* ♦ **popu|lar|ity** /pɒpjʊlærɪti/ *...the growing popularity of Australian wines among consumers... Walking and golf increased in popularity during the 1980s.* N-UNCOUNT: oft with poss [2] Someone who is **popular** is liked by most people, or by most people in a particular group. ❑ *He remained the most popular politician in France.* ADJ ≠ *unpopular* ♦ **popu|lar|ity** *It is his popularity with ordinary people that sets him apart.* N-UNCOUNT: oft with poss [3] **Popular** newspapers, television programmes, or forms of art are aimed at ordinary people and not at experts or intellectuals. ❑ *Once again the popular press in Britain has been rife with stories about their marriage. ...one of the classics of modern popular music.* ADJ: ADJ n [4] **Popular** ideas, feelings, or attitudes are approved of or held by most people. ❑ *The military government has been unable to win popular support.* ADJ: usu ADJ n ♦ **popu|lar|ity** *Over time, though, Watson's views gained in popularity.* N-UNCOUNT [5] **Popular** is used to describe political activities which involve the ordinary people of a country, and not just members of political parties. ❑ *The late President Ferdinand Marcos was overthrown by a popular uprising in 1986.* ADJ: ADJ n

**popu|lar|ize** /pɒpjʊləraɪz/ **(popularizes, popularizing, popularized)**

☑ in BRIT, also use **popularise**

To **popularize** something means to make a lot of people interested in it and able to enjoy it. ❑ *Irving Brokaw popularized figure skating in the US.* VERB V n ♦ **popu|lari|za|tion** /pɒpjʊləraɪzeɪʃən/ *...the popularisation of sport through television.* N-UNCOUNT: usu N *of* n

**popu|lar|ly** /pɒpjʊləʳli/ [1] If something or someone is **popularly** known as something, most people call them that, although it is not their official name or title. ❑ *...the Mesozoic era, more popularly known as the age of dinosaurs. ...an infection popularly called mad cow disease.* ADV: ADV with -ed = *commonly* [2] If something is **popularly** believed or supposed to be the case, most people believe or suppose it to be the case, although it may not be true. ❑ *Schizophrenia is not a 'split mind' as is popularly believed.* ADV: ADV -ed = *commonly* [3] A **popularly elected** leader or government has been elected by a majority of the people in a country. ❑ *Walesa was Poland's first popularly elected President.* ADV: ADV -ed = *democratically*

**popu|late** /pɒpjʊleɪt/ **(populates, populating, populated)** [1] If an area **is populated by** certain people or animals, those people or animals live there, often in large numbers. ❑ *Before all this the island was populated by native American Arawaks. ...native Sindhis, who populate the surrounding villages.* VERB = *inhabit* *be* V-ed V n ♦ **popu|lat|ed** *The southeast is the most densely populated area.* ADJ: adv ADJ ♦ **-populated** *Shelling from federal army tanks razed half the houses in the Croat-populated part of Glina.* COMB in ADJ [2] To **populate** an area means to cause people to live there. ❑ *Successive regimes annexed the region and populated it with lowland people.* VERB V n *with* n

**popu|la|tion** /pɒpjʊleɪʃən/ **(populations)** ♦♦◇ [1] The **population** of a country or area is all the people who live in it. ❑ *Bangladesh now has a population of about 110 million. ...the annual rate of population growth.* N-COUNT [2] If you refer to a particular type of **population** in a country or area, you are referring to all the people or animals of that type there. [FORMAL] ❑ *...75.6 per cent of the male population over sixteen. ...the elephant populations of Tanzania and Kenya.* N-COUNT: usu supp N

**pop|ulism** /pɒpjʊlɪzəm/ **Populism** refers to political activities or ideas that claim to promote the interests and opinions of ordinary people. [FORMAL] ❑ *...a wave of populism.* N-UNCOUNT

**popu|list** /pɒpjʊlɪst/ **(populists)** If you describe a politician or an artist as **populist**, you mean that they claim to care about the interests and opinions of ordinary people rather than those of a small group. [FORMAL] ❑ *...Jose Sarney, the current populist president.* ADJ: usu ADJ n ≠ *elitist* ♦ A **populist** is someone who expresses populist views. N-COUNT ≠ *elitist*

**popu|lous** /pɒpjʊləs/ A **populous** country or area has a lot of people living in it. [FORMAL] ❑ *Indonesia, with 216 million people, is the fourth most populous country in the world.* — ADJ: usu ADJ n

**pop-up** [1] A **pop-up** book, usually a children's book, has pictures that stand up when you open the pages. — ADJ: ADJ n [2] A **pop-up** toaster has a mechanism that pushes slices of bread up when they are toasted. — ADJ: ADJ n

**porce|lain** /pɔːʳsəlɪn/ **(porcelains)** [1] **Porcelain** is a hard, shiny substance made by heating clay. It is used to make delicate cups, plates, and ornaments. ❑ *There were lilies everywhere in tall white porcelain vases.* — N-UNCOUNT [2] A **porcelain** is an ornament that is made of porcelain. You can refer to a number of such ornaments as **porcelain**. ❑ *...a priceless collection of English porcelain.* — N-VAR

**porch** /pɔːʳtʃ/ **(porches)** [1] A **porch** is a sheltered area at the entrance to a building. It has a roof and sometimes has walls. → See picture on page 1705. — N-COUNT [2] A **porch** is a raised platform built along the outside wall of a house and often covered with a roof. [AM] — N-COUNT

✔ in BRIT, usually use **veranda**

**por|cu|pine** /pɔːʳkjʊpaɪn/ **(porcupines)** A **porcupine** is an animal with many long, thin, sharp spikes on its back that stick out as protection when it is attacked. — N-COUNT

**pore** /pɔːʳ/ **(pores, poring, pored)** [1] Your **pores** are the tiny holes in your skin. ❑ *The size of your pores is determined by the amount of oil they produce.* — N-COUNT: usu pl [2] The **pores** of a plant are the tiny holes on its surface. ❑ *A plant's lungs are the microscopic pores in its leaves.* — N-COUNT: usu pl [3] If you **pore over** or **through** information, you look at it and study it very carefully. ❑ *We spent hours poring over travel brochures.* — VERB; V *over/through* n [4] You can say that someone has a certain quality or emotion coming from **every pore** to emphasize the strength of that quality or emotion. ❑ *She oozes sexuality from every pore.* — PHRASE [emphasis]

**pork** /pɔːʳk/ **Pork** is meat from a pig, usually fresh and not smoked or salted. ❑ *...fried pork chops. ...a packet of pork sausages.* — N-UNCOUNT

**pork bar|rel** also **pork-barrel.** If you say that someone is using **pork barrel** politics, you mean that they are spending a lot of government money on a local project in order to win the votes of the people who live in that area. [mainly AM] ❑ *Pork-barrel politicians hand out rents to win votes and influence people.* — N-SING: usu N n [disapproval]

**pork pie** **(pork pies)** A **pork pie** is a round, tall pie with cooked pork inside, which is eaten cold. [BRIT] — N-VAR

**porn** /pɔːʳn/ **Porn** is the same as **pornography**. [INFORMAL] ❑ *...a porn cinema.* → See also **soft porn, hard porn**. — N-UNCOUNT

**por|no** /pɔːʳnoʊ/ **Porno** is the same as **pornographic**. ❑ *...porno mags.* — ADJ

**por|nog|ra|pher** /pɔːʳnɒgrəfəʳ/ **(pornographers)** A **pornographer** is a person who produces or sells pornography. — N-COUNT [disapproval]

**por|no|graph|ic** /pɔːʳnəgræfɪk/ **Pornographic** materials such as films, videos, and magazines are designed to cause sexual excitement by showing naked people or referring to sexual acts. ❑ *I found out he'd been watching pornographic videos.* — ADJ: usu ADJ n [disapproval]

**por|nog|ra|phy** /pɔːʳnɒgrəfi/ **Pornography** refers to books, magazines, and films that are designed to cause sexual excitement by showing naked people or referring to sexual acts. ❑ *A nationwide campaign against pornography began in the summer.* — N-UNCOUNT [disapproval]

**po|ros|ity** /pɔːrɒsɪti/ **Porosity** is the quality of being porous. [FORMAL] ❑ *...the porosity of the coal.* — N-UNCOUNT

**po|rous** /pɔːrəs/ Something that is **porous** has many small holes in it, which water and air can pass through. ❑ *The local limestone is very porous.* — ADJ

**por|poise** /pɔːʳpəs/ **(porpoises)** A **porpoise** is a sea animal that looks like a large grey fish. Porpoises usually swim about in groups. — N-COUNT

**por|ridge** /pɒrɪdʒ, AM pɔːr-/ **Porridge** is a thick sticky food made from oats cooked in water or milk and eaten hot, especially for breakfast. [mainly BRIT] — N-UNCOUNT

✔ in AM, usually use **oatmeal**

**port** /pɔːʳt/ **(ports)** ◆◇◇ [1] A **port** is a town by the sea or on a river, which has a harbour. ❑ *Port-Louis is an attractive little fishing port. ...the Mediterranean port of Marseilles.* — N-COUNT [2] A **port** is a harbour area where ships load and unload goods or passengers. ❑ *...the bridges which link the port area to the city centre.* — N-COUNT: oft N n [3] A **port** on a computer is a place where you can attach another piece of equipment, for example a printer. [COMPUTING] — N-COUNT [4] In sailing, the **port** side of a ship is the left side when you are on it and facing towards the front. [TECHNICAL] ❑ *It is carved on the port side of the forecabin.* — ADJ ≠ *starboard* ♦ **Port** is also a noun. ❑ *USS Ogden turned slowly to port.* — N-UNCOUNT: usu *to* N ≠ *starboard* [5] **Port** is a type of strong, sweet red wine. ❑ *He asked for a glass of port after dinner.* — N-UNCOUNT

**port|able** /pɔːʳtəbᵊl/ **(portables)** [1] A **portable** machine or device is designed to be easily carried or moved. ❑ *There was a little portable television switched on behind the bar.* — ADJ: usu ADJ n ♦ **port|abil|ity** /pɔːʳtəbɪlɪti/ *When it came to choosing photographic equipment portability was as important as reliability.* — N-UNCOUNT [2] A **portable** is something such as a television, radio, or computer which can be easily carried or moved. ❑ *We bought a colour portable for the bedroom.* — N-COUNT

**Por|ta|ka|bin** /pɔːʳtəkæbɪn/ **(Portakabins)** A **Portakabin** is a small building that can be moved by truck and that can be used for a short period of time, for example as a temporary office. [TRADEMARK] — N-COUNT

**por|tal** /pɔːʳtᵊl/ **(portals)** [1] A **portal** is a large impressive doorway at the entrance to a building. [LITERARY] ❑ *I went in through the royal portal.* — N-COUNT [2] On the Internet, a **portal** is a site that consists of links to other websites. [COMPUTING] — N-COUNT

**port|cul|lis** /pɔːʳtkʌlɪs/ **(portcullises)** A **portcullis** is a strong gate above an entrance to a castle and used to be lowered to the ground in order to keep out enemies. — N-COUNT

**por|tend** /pɔːʳtend/ **(portends, portending, portended)** If something **portends** an event or occurrence, it indicates that it is likely to happen in the future. [FORMAL] ❑ *The change did not portend a basic improvement in social conditions.* — VERB; V n

**por|tent** /pɔːʳtent/ **(portents)** A **portent** is something that indicates what is likely to happen in the future. [FORMAL] ❑ *The savage civil war there could be a portent of what's to come in the rest of the region.* — N-COUNT: oft N *of* n = *indication, sign*

**por|ten|tous** /pɔːʳtentəs/ [1] If someone's way of speaking, writing, or behaving is **portentous**, they speak, write, or behave more seriously than necessary because they want to impress other people. [FORMAL] ❑ *There was nothing portentous or solemn about him. He was bubbling with humour. ...portentous prose.* — ADJ [disapproval] = *pompous* ♦ **por|ten|tous|ly** *'The difference is,' he said portentously, 'you are Anglo-Saxons, we are Latins.'* — ADV: usu ADV with v [2] Something that is **portentous** is important in indicating or affecting future events. [FORMAL] ❑ *In social politics, too, the city's contribution to 20th century thought and culture was no less portentous.* — ADJ

**por|ter** /pɔːʳtəʳ/ **(porters)** [1] A **porter** is a person whose job is to be in charge of the entrance of a building such as a hotel. [BRIT] — N-COUNT

✔ in AM, use **doorman**

[2] A **porter** is a person whose job is to carry things, for example people's luggage at a railway station or in a hotel. — N-COUNT [3] A **porter** on a train is a — N-COUNT

person whose job is to make up beds in the sleeping car and to help passengers. [AM]

in BRIT, usually use **attendant**

[4] In a hospital, a **porter** is someone whose job is to move patients from place to place. [mainly BRIT] N-COUNT

in AM, usually use **orderly**

**port|fo|lio** /pɔːʳtfoʊlioʊ/ **(portfolios)** [1] A **portfolio** is a set of pictures by someone, or photographs of examples of their work, which they use when entering competitions or applying for work. ❑ *After dinner that evening, Edith showed them a portfolio of her own political cartoons.* N-COUNT [2] In finance, a **portfolio** is the combination of shares or other investments that a particular person or company has. [BUSINESS] ❑ *Short-term securities can also be held as part of an investment portfolio. ...Roger Early, a portfolio manager at Federated Investors Corp.* N-COUNT [3] In politics, a **portfolio** is a minister's responsibility for a particular area of a government's activities. ❑ *He has held the defence portfolio since the first free elections in 1990.* N-COUNT ● A **minister without portfolio** is a politician who is given the rank of minister without being given responsibility for any particular area of a government's activities. [FORMAL] PHRASE: *minister* inflects [4] A company's **portfolio** of products or designs is their range of products or designs. [BUSINESS] N-COUNT

**port|hole** /pɔːʳthoʊl/ **(portholes)** A **porthole** is a small round window in the side of a ship or aircraft. N-COUNT

**por|ti|co** /pɔːʳtɪkoʊ/ **(porticoes** or **porticos)** A **portico** is a large covered area at the entrance to a building, with pillars supporting the roof. [FORMAL] N-COUNT

**por|tion** /pɔːʳʃᵊn/ **(portions)** [1] A **portion of** something is a part of it. ❑ *Damage was confined to a small portion of the castle... I have spent a fairly considerable portion of my life here... I had learnt a portion of the Koran.* N-COUNT: N *of* n = part [2] A **portion** is the amount of food that is given to one person at a meal. ❑ *Desserts can be substituted by a portion of fresh fruit... The portions were generous.* N-COUNT

**port|ly** /pɔːʳtli/ **(portlier, portliest)** A **portly** person, especially a man, is rather fat. [FORMAL] ADJ: usu ADJ n = stout

**port of call (ports of call)** [1] A **port of call** is a place where a ship stops during a journey. ❑ *Their first port of call will be Cape Town.* N-COUNT [2] A **port of call** is any place where you stop for a short time when you are visiting several places, shops, or people. [INFORMAL] ❑ *The local tourist office should be your first port of call in any town.* N-COUNT

**por|trait** /pɔːʳtreɪt/ **(portraits)** A **portrait** is a painting, drawing, or photograph of a particular person. ❑ *Lucian Freud has been asked to paint a portrait of the Queen.* ◆◇◇ N-COUNT

**por|trait|ist** /pɔːʳtreɪtɪst/ **(portraitists)** A **portraitist** is an artist who paints or draws people's portraits. [FORMAL] N-COUNT

**por|trai|ture** /pɔːʳtrɪtʃəʳ/ **Portraiture** is the art of painting or drawing portraits. [FORMAL] N-UNCOUNT

**por|tray** /pɔːʳtreɪ/ **(portrays, portraying, portrayed)** [1] When an actor or actress **portrays** someone, he or she plays that person in a play or film. ❑ *In 1975 he portrayed the king in a Los Angeles revival of 'Camelot'. ...the busty and rumbustious Mrs Hall, excellently portrayed by Toni Palmer.* VERB V n V-ed [2] When a writer or artist **portrays** something, he or she writes a description or produces a painting of it. ❑ *...this northern novelist, who accurately portrays provincial domestic life. ...the landscape as portrayed by painters such as Claude and Poussin.* VERB = depict V n V-ed [3] If a film, book, or television programme **portrays** someone in a certain way, it represents them in that way. ❑ *She says the programme portrayed her as a 'lady of easy virtue'. ...complaints about the way women are portrayed in adverts.* VERB V n *as* n *be* V-ed

**por|tray|al** /pɔːʳtreɪəl/ **(portrayals)** [1] An actor's **portrayal of** a character in a play or film is the way that he or she plays the character. ❑ *Mr Ying is well-known for his portrayal of a prison guard in the film 'The Last Emperor'.* N-COUNT: usu sing, usu poss N *of* n [2] An artist's **portrayal of** something is a drawing, painting, or photograph of it. ❑ *...a moving portrayal of St John the Evangelist by Simone Martini.* N-COUNT: usu N *of* n [3] The **portrayal of** something in a book or film is the act of describing it or showing it. ❑ *This is a sensitive and often funny portrayal of a friendship between two 11-year-old boys.* N-COUNT: usu sing, usu N *of* n [4] The **portrayal of** something in a book, film, or programme is the way that it is made to appear. ❑ *The media persists in its portrayal of us as muggers, dope sellers and gangsters.* N-COUNT: usu N *of* n

**Por|tu|guese** /pɔːʳtʃʊgiːz/ [1] Something that is **Portuguese** belongs or relates to Portugal, or its people, language, or culture. ADJ [2] **The Portuguese** are the people of Portugal. N-PLURAL: *the* N [3] **Portuguese** is the language spoken in Portugal, Brazil, Angola, and Mozambique. N-UNCOUNT

**POS** /piː oʊ es/ The **POS** is the place in a shop where a product is passed from the seller to the customer. **POS** is an abbreviation for 'point of sale'. [BUSINESS] ❑ *...a POS system that doubles as a stock and sales control system.*

**pos. Pos.** is the written abbreviation for **positive**.

**pose** /poʊz/ **(poses, posing, posed)** [1] If something **poses** a problem or a danger, it is the cause of that problem or danger. ❑ *This could pose a threat to jobs in the coal industry... His ill health poses serious problems for the future.* ◆◇◇ VERB V n V n [2] If you **pose** a question, you ask it. If you **pose** an issue that needs considering, you mention the issue. [FORMAL] ❑ *When I finally posed the question, 'Why?' he merely shrugged. ...the moral issues posed by new technologies.* VERB V n V-ed [3] If you **pose as** someone, you pretend to be that person in order to deceive people. ❑ *The team posed as drug dealers to trap the ringleaders.* VERB V *as* n [4] If you **pose for** a photograph or painting, you stay in a particular position so that someone can photograph you or paint you. ❑ *Before going into their meeting the six foreign ministers posed for photographs.* VERB V *for* n [5] You can say that people **are posing** when you think that they are behaving in an insincere or exaggerated way because they want to make a particular impression on other people. ❑ *He criticized them for dressing outrageously and posing pretentiously.* VERB: usu cont disapproval V [6] A **pose** is a particular way that you stand, sit, or lie, for example when you are being photographed or painted. ❑ *We have had several preliminary sittings in various poses.* N-COUNT

**pos|er** /poʊzəʳ/ **(posers)** [1] A **poser** is the same as a **poseur**. N-COUNT disapproval [2] A **poser** is a difficult problem or puzzle. [INFORMAL, OLD-FASHIONED] ❑ *Here is a little poser for you.* N-COUNT

**po|seur** /poʊzɜːʳ/ **(poseurs)** You can describe someone as a **poseur** when you think that they behave in an insincere or exaggerated way because they want to make a particular impression on other people. ❑ *I am sometimes accused of being an inveterate poseur.* N-COUNT disapproval = poser

**posh** /pɒʃ/ **(posher, poshest)** [1] If you describe something as **posh**, you mean that it is smart, fashionable, and expensive. [INFORMAL] ❑ *Celebrating a promotion, I took her to a posh hotel for a cocktail. ...a posh car.* ADJ: usu ADJ n [2] If you describe a person as **posh**, you mean that they belong to or behave as if they belong to the upper classes. [INFORMAL] ❑ *I wouldn't have thought she had such posh friends.* ADJ

**pos|it** /pɒzɪt/ **(posits, positing, posited)** If you **posit** something, you suggest or assume it as the basis for an argument or calculation. [FORMAL] ❑ *Several writers have posited the idea of a universal consciousness... Callahan posits that chemical elements radiate electromagnetic signals.* VERB = postulate V n V that

**po|si|tion** /pəzɪʃᵊn/ **(positions, positioning, positioned)** [1] The **position** of someone or something is the place where they are in relation to other things. ❑ *The ship was identified, and its name* ◆◆◆ N-COUNT

*and position were reported to the coastguard... This conservatory enjoys an enviable position overlooking a leafy expanse.* [2] When someone or something is in a particular **position**, they are sitting, lying, or arranged in that way. ❑ *Hold the upper back and neck in an erect position to give support for the head... Ensure the patient is turned into the recovery position... Mr. Dambar had raised himself to a sitting position.* N-COUNT: usu with supp
[3] If you **position** something somewhere, you put it there carefully, so that it is in the right place or position. ❑ *Place the pastry circles on to a baking sheet and position one apple on each circle.* VERB = place V n prep
[4] Your **position** in society is the role and the importance that you have in it. ❑ *...the position of older people in society.* N-COUNT: usu with supp [5] A **position** in a company or organization is a job. [FORMAL] ❑ *He left a career in teaching to take up a position with the Arts Council.* N-COUNT = post
[6] Your **position** in a race or competition is how well you did in relation to the other competitors or how well you are doing. ❑ *By the ninth hour the car was running in eighth position.* N-COUNT: usu supp N [7] You can describe your situation at a particular time by saying that you are in a particular **position**. ❑ *He's going to be in a very difficult position indeed if things go badly for him... Companies should be made to reveal more about their financial position... It was not the only time he found himself in this position.* N-COUNT: usu sing, usu with supp = situation [8] Your **position on** a particular matter is your attitude towards it or your opinion of it. [FORMAL] ❑ *He could be depended on to take a moderate position on most of the key issues.* N-COUNT: usu supp N = stance [9] If you are **in a position to** do something, you are able to do it. If you are **in no position to** do something, you are unable to do it. ❑ *The UN system will be in a position to support the extensive relief efforts needed... I am not in a position to comment.* N-SING: N to-inf [10] If someone or something is **in position**, they are in their correct or usual place or arrangement. ❑ *This second door is an extra security measure and can be locked in position during the day... Some 28,000 US troops are moving into position.* PHRASE: usu PHR after v

**po|si|tion|al** /pəzɪʃənəl/ **Positional** refers to the physical position of someone, for example in a football match. ❑ *The manager has made no positional changes for the second game.* ADJ: usu ADJ n

**po|si|tion pa|per** **(position papers)** A **position paper** is a detailed report which usually explains or recommends a particular course of action. N-COUNT

**posi|tive** /pɒzɪtɪv/ ◆◆◇ [1] If you are **positive about** things, you are hopeful and confident, and think of the good aspects of a situation rather than the bad ones. ❑ *Be positive about your future and get on with living a normal life. ...a positive frame of mind.* ADJ: usu v-link ADJ, oft ADJ about n ≠ negative ♦ **posi|tive|ly** *You really must try to start thinking positively.* ADV: ADV after v [2] A **positive** fact, situation, or experience is pleasant and helpful to you in some way. ❑ *The parting from his sister had a positive effect on John.* ADJ: usu ADJ n ≠ negative ♦ **The positive** in a situation is the good and pleasant aspects of it. ❑ *Work on the positive, creating beautiful, loving and fulfilling relationships.* N-SING: the N ≠ negative
[3] If you make a **positive** decision or take **positive** action, you do something definite in order to deal with a task or problem. ❑ *Having a good diet gives me a sense that I'm doing something positive and that I'm in control.* ADJ: usu ADJ n [4] A **positive** response to something indicates agreement, approval, or encouragement. ❑ *There's been a positive response to the UN Secretary-General's recent peace efforts.* ADJ: usu ADJ n ≠ negative ♦ **posi|tive|ly** *He responded positively and accepted the fee of £1000 I had offered.* ADV: ADV after v [5] If you are **positive** about something, you are completely sure about it. ❑ *I'm as positive as I can be about it... 'She's never late. You sure she said eight?' — 'Positive.'* ADJ: v-link ADJ
[6] **Positive** evidence gives definite proof of the truth or identity of something. ❑ *There was no positive evidence that any birth defects had arisen as a result of Vitamin A intake.* ADJ: ADJ n = conclusive ♦ **posi|tive|ly** *He has positively identified the body as that of his wife.* ADV: ADV with v [7] If a medical or scientific test is **positive**, it shows that something has happened or is present. ❑ *If the test is positive, a course of antibiotics may be prescribed... He was stripped of his Olympic Hundred Metres gold medal after testing positive for steroids.* ADJ ≠ negative **HIV positive** → see **HIV**. [8] A **positive** number is greater than zero. ❑ *It's really a simple numbers game with negative and positive numbers.* ADJ: ADJ n ≠ negative [9] If something has a **positive** electrical charge, it has the same charge as a proton and the opposite charge to an electron. [TECHNICAL] ADJ: usu ADJ n ≠ negative

**posi|tive dis|crimi|na|tion** **Positive discrimination** means making sure that people such as women, members of smaller racial groups, and disabled people get a fair share of the opportunities available. [BRIT] N-UNCOUNT

✔ in AM, use **affirmative action**

**posi|tive|ly** /pɒzɪtɪvli/ [1] You use **positively** to emphasize that you really mean what you are saying. ❑ *This is positively the worst thing that I can even imagine.* ADV: ADV adj-superl [emphasis] = absolutely [2] You use **positively** to emphasize that something really is the case, although it may sound surprising or extreme. ❑ *He's changed since he came back – he seems positively cheerful.* ADV: ADV adj, ADV before v [emphasis] [3] → See also **positive**.

**posi|tiv|ism** /pɒzɪtɪvɪsm/ **Positivism** is a philosophy which accepts only things that can be seen or proved. N-UNCOUNT ♦ **posi|tiv|ist** **(positivists)** ❑ *By far the most popular idea is the positivist one that we should keep only the facts.* N-COUNT: usu N n

**poss** /pɒs/ [1] **'If poss'** means the same as 'if possible'. [BRIT, INFORMAL] ❑ *We'll rush it round today if poss.* PHRASE: PHR with cl [2] **'As poss'** means the same as 'as possible'. [BRIT, INFORMAL] ❑ *Tell them I'll be there as soon as poss.* PHRASE: PHR with cl

**pos|se** /pɒsi/ **(posses)** [1] A **posse of** people is a group of people with the same job or purpose. [INFORMAL] ❑ *...a posse of reporters.* N-COUNT: N of n = group [2] In former times, in the United States, a **posse** was a group of men who were brought together by the local law officer to help him chase and capture a criminal. N-COUNT

**pos|sess** /pəzes/ **(possesses, possessing, possessed)** [1] If you **possess** something, you have it or own it. ❑ *He was then arrested and charged with possessing an offensive weapon... He is said to possess a fortune of more than two-and-a-half-thousand million dollars.* VERB: no passive V n V n [2] If someone or something **possesses** a particular quality, ability, or feature, they have it. [FORMAL] ❑ *...individuals who are deemed to possess the qualities of sense, loyalty and discretion.* VERB: no cont V n [3] → See also **possessed**. [4] If you ask **what possessed** someone **to** do something, you are emphasizing your great surprise that they have done something which you consider foolish or dangerous. ❑ *What on earth had possessed her to agree to marry him?* PHRASE: V inflects [feelings]

**pos|sessed** /pəzest/ [1] If someone is described as being **possessed by** an evil spirit, it is believed that their mind and body are controlled by an evil spirit. ❑ *She even claimed the couple's daughter was possessed by the devil.* ADJ: v-link ADJ, oft ADJ by n [2] → See also **possess**.

**pos|ses|sion** /pəzeʃən/ **(possessions)** [1] If you are **in possession of** something, you have it, because you have obtained it or because it belongs to you. [FORMAL] ❑ *Those documents are now in the possession of the Guardian... We should go up and take possession of the land... He was also charged with illegal possession of firearms.* N-UNCOUNT: oft in N of n [2] Your **possessions** are the things that you own or have with you at a particular time. ❑ *People had lost their homes and all their possessions... She had tidied away her possessions.* N-COUNT: usu pl, poss N = belongings [3] A country's **possessions** are countries or territories that it controls. [FORMAL] ❑ *All of them were French possessions at one time or another.* N-COUNT: usu pl, supp N = colonies

**pos|ses|sive** /pəzesɪv/ **(possessives)** [1] Someone who is **possessive about** another person wants all that person's love and attention. ❑ *Danny could be very jealous and possessive about me.* ADJ: oft ADJ about/of n = jealous ♦ **pos|ses|sive|ly** *Leaning over, he kissed her possessively on the mouth.* ADV ♦ **pos|ses|sive|ness** N-UNCOUNT

*I've ruined every relationship with my possessiveness.* = jealousy
2 Someone who is **possessive about** things that they own does not like other people to use them. ❑ *People were very possessive about their coupons.* ADJ: usu v-link ADJ, usu ADJ *about* n
3 In grammar, a **possessive determiner** or **possessive adjective** is a word such as 'my' or 'his' which shows who or what something belongs to or is connected with. The **possessive** form of a name or noun has 's added to it, as in 'Jenny's' or 'cat's'. ADJ: ADJ n
4 A **possessive** is a possessive determiner or the possessive form of a name or noun. N-COUNT

**pos|ses|sive pro|noun** (possessive pronouns) A **possessive pronoun** is a pronoun such as 'mine', 'yours', or 'theirs' which is used to refer to the thing of a particular kind that belongs to someone, as in 'Can I borrow your pen? I've lost mine.' N-COUNT

**pos|ses|sor** /pəzesəʳ/ (possessors) The **possessor of** something is the person who has it. [FORMAL] ❑ *Ms Nova is the proud possessor of a truly incredible voice.* N-COUNT: usu N *of* n

**pos|sibil|ity** /pɒsɪbɪlɪti/ (possibilities) ◆◆◇ 1 If you say there is a **possibility that** something is the case or **that** something will happen, you mean that it might be the case or it might happen. ❑ *We were not in the least worried about the possibility that sweets could rot the teeth... Tax on food has become a very real possibility.* N-COUNT: oft N that
2 A **possibility** is one of several different things that could be done. ❑ *The government now owns a lot of our land – one possibility would be to compensate us with other property... There were several possibilities open to each manufacturer.* N-COUNT = option

**pos|sible** /pɒsɪbᵊl/ (possibles) ◆◆◆ 1 If it is **possible to** do something, it can be done. ❑ *If it is possible to find out where your brother is, we shall... Everything is possible if we want it enough... This morning he had tried every way possible to contact her... It's been a beautiful evening and you have made it all possible.* ADJ: usu v-link ADJ, oft *it* v-link ADJ to-inf
2 A **possible** event is one that might happen. ❑ *He referred the matter to the Attorney General for possible action against several newspapers... Her family is discussing a possible move to America... One possible solution, if all else fails, is to take legal action.* ADJ: usu ADJ n
3 If you say that it is **possible that** something is true or correct, you mean that although you do not know whether it is true or correct, you accept that it might be. ❑ *It is possible that there's an explanation for all this.* ADJ: v-link ADJ, oft *it* v-link ADJ that [vagueness] = conceivable
4 If you do something **as** soon **as possible**, you do it as soon as you can. If you get **as** much **as possible** of something, you get as much of it as you can. ❑ *Please make your decision as soon as possible... I want to learn as much as possible about the industry so that I'm better prepared... Michael sat down as far away from her as possible.* ADJ: *as* adv/pron *as* ADJ
5 You use **possible** with superlative adjectives to emphasize that something has more or less of a quality than anything else of its kind. ❑ *They have joined the job market at the worst possible time... He is doing the best job possible.* ADJ: adj-superl ADJ n, adj-superl n ADJ [emphasis]
6 You use **possible** in expressions such as '**if possible**' and '**if at all possible**' when stating a wish or intention, to show that although this is what you really want, you may have to accept something different. ❑ *I need to see you, right away if possible. ...the moral duty to uphold peace if at all possible.* ADJ [politeness]
7 If you describe someone as, for example, a **possible** Prime Minister, you mean that they may become Prime Minister. ❑ *Bradley has been considered a possible presidential contender himself.* ADJ: ADJ n = potential
♦ **Possible** is also a noun. ❑ *Kennedy, who divorced wife Joan in 1982, was tipped as a presidential possible.* N-COUNT
8 **The possible** is everything that can be done in a situation. ❑ *He is a democrat with the skill, nerve, and ingenuity to push the limits of the possible.* N-SING: the N

**pos|sibly** /pɒsɪbli/ ◆◆◇ 1 You use **possibly** to indicate that you are not sure whether something is true or might happen. ❑ *Exercise will not only lower blood pressure but possibly protect against heart attacks... They were smartly but casually dressed; possibly students... Do you think that he could possibly be right?* ADV: ADV with cl/group, ADV with v [vagueness]
2 You use **possibly** to emphasize that you are surprised, puzzled, or shocked by something that you have seen or heard. ❑ *It was the most unexpected piece of news one could possibly imagine.* ADV: ADV before v [emphasis]
3 You use **possibly** to emphasize that someone has tried their hardest to do something, or has done it as well as they can. ❑ *They've done everything they can possibly think of.* ADV: ADV before v [emphasis]
4 You use **possibly** to emphasize that something definitely cannot happen or definitely cannot be done. ❑ *No I really can't possibly answer that!* ADV: with brd-neg, ADV before v [emphasis]

**pos|sum** /pɒsəm/ (possums) A **possum** is the same as an **opossum**. [mainly AM, INFORMAL] N-COUNT

**post**
① LETTERS, PARCELS, AND INFORMATION
② JOBS AND PLACES
③ POLES

**①post** /poʊst/ (posts, posting, posted) ◆◆◇
1 **The post** is the public service or system by which letters and packages are collected and delivered. [mainly BRIT] ❑ *You'll receive your book through the post... The winner will be notified by post... The cheque is in the post.* N-SING: the N, also *by* N

✓ in AM, usually use **mail**

2 You can use **post** to refer to letters and packages that are delivered to you. [mainly BRIT] ❑ *He flipped through the post without opening any of it... There has been no post in three weeks.* N-UNCOUNT

✓ in AM, usually use **mail**

3 **Post** is used to refer to an occasion when letters or packages are delivered. For example, **first post** on a particular day is the first time that things are delivered. [mainly BRIT] ❑ *Entries must arrive by first post next Wednesday.* N-UNCOUNT: supp N = delivery
4 If you **post** a letter or package, you send it to someone by putting it in a post box or by taking it to a post office. [mainly BRIT] ❑ *If I write a letter, would you post it for me?... I'm posting you a cheque tonight... I posted a letter to Stanley saying I was an old Army friend.* VERB V n V n n V n *to* n
♦ **Post off** means the same as **post**. ❑ *He'd left me to pack up the mail and post it off... All you do is complete and post off a form.* PHRASAL VERB V n P V P n (not pron)

✓ in AM, usually use **mail**

5 If you **post** notices, signs, or other pieces of information somewhere, you fix them to a wall or board so that everyone can see them. ❑ *Officials began posting warning notices... She has posted photographs on bulletin boards.* VERB V n V n prep/adv
♦ **Post up** means the same as **post**. ❑ *He has posted a sign up that says 'No Fishing'... We post up a set of rules for the house.* PHRASAL VERB V n P V P n
6 If you **post** information on the Internet, you make the information available to other people on the Internet. [COMPUTING] ❑ *A consultation paper has been posted on the Internet inviting input from Net users.* VERB *be* V-ed
7 If you **keep** someone **posted**, you keep giving them the latest information about a situation that they are interested in. ❑ *Keep me posted on your progress.* PHRASE: *keep* inflects, oft PHR *on/with* n

**②post** /poʊst/ (posts, posting, posted) ◆◆◇ 1 A **post** in a company or organization is a job or official position in it, usually one that involves responsibility. [FORMAL] ❑ *She had earlier resigned her post as President Menem's assistant... Sir Peter has held several senior military posts.* N-COUNT: usu with supp, oft N *of/as* n = position
2 If you **are posted** somewhere, you are sent there by the organization that you work for and usually work there for several years. ❑ *It is normal to spend two or three years working in this country before being posted overseas.* VERB: usu passive *be* V-ed prep/adv
3 You can use **post** to refer to the place where a soldier, guard, or other person has been told to remain and to do his or her job. ❑ *Quick men, back to your post!* N-COUNT: usu poss N
4 If a soldier, guard, or other person **is posted** somewhere, they are told to stand there, in order to supervise an activity or guard a place. ❑ *Police have now been posted outside* VERB *be* V-ed

*all temples... British Rail had to post a signalman at the entrance to the tunnel... We have guards posted near the windows.* [5] → See also **posting**, **staging post**. prep/adv V n prep/adv V-ed Also *be* V-ed

**③ post** /poʊst/ **(posts)**
⇛ Please look at category 4 to see if the expression you are looking for is shown under another headword. [1] A **post** is a strong upright pole made of wood or metal that is fixed into the ground. ❑ *You have to get eight wooden posts, and drive them into the ground.* N-COUNT [2] A **post** is the same as a **goalpost**. ❑ *Wimbledon were unlucky not to win after hitting the post twice.* N-COUNT [3] On a horse-racing track, **the post** is a pole which marks the finishing point. N-SING: *the* N [4] → See also **first-past-the-post**. to **pip** someone **at the post** → see **pip**.

**post-** /poʊst-/ **Post-** is used to form words that indicate that something takes place after a particular date, period, or event. ❑ *...the post-1945 era. ...post-election euphoria.* PREFIX ≠*pre-*

**post|age** /poʊstɪdʒ/ **Postage** is the money that you pay for sending letters and packages by post. N-UNCOUNT

**post|age stamp** **(postage stamps)** A **postage stamp** is a small piece of gummed paper that you buy from the post office and stick on an envelope or package before you post it. [FORMAL] N-COUNT = *stamp*

**post|al** /poʊstᵊl/ [1] **Postal** is used to describe things or people connected with the public service of carrying letters and packages from one place to another. ❑ *Compensation for lost or damaged mail will be handled by the postal service... Include your full postal address.* ADJ: ADJ n [2] **Postal** is used to describe activities that involve sending things by post. ❑ *Unions would elect their leadership by secret postal ballot.* ADJ: ADJ n

**post|al or|der** **(postal orders)** A **postal order** is a piece of paper representing a sum of money which you can buy at a post office and send to someone as a way of sending them money by post. [BRIT] N-COUNT

✓ in AM, usually use **money order**

**post|bag** /poʊstbæg/ **(postbags)** also **post-bag.** The letters that are received by an important person, a newspaper, or a television or radio company can be referred to as the **postbag**. [mainly BRIT, JOURNALISM] ❑ *Here's another selection of recent letters from our postbag... Marling's article on Northumbria attracted a large postbag.* N-COUNT: usu sing

**post|box** /poʊstbɒks/ **(postboxes)** also **post box.** A **postbox** is a metal box in a public place, where you put letters and packets to be collected. They are then sorted and delivered. Compare **letterbox**. [BRIT] N-COUNT

✓ in AM, use **mailbox**

**post|card** /poʊstkɑːʳd/ **(postcards)** also **post card.** A **postcard** is a piece of thin card, often with a picture on one side, which you can write on and send to people without using an envelope. → See also **picture postcard**. N-COUNT

**post|code** /poʊstkoʊd/ **(postcodes)** also **post code.** Your **postcode** is a short sequence of numbers and letters at the end of your address, which helps the post office to sort the mail. [BRIT] N-COUNT

✓ in AM, use **zip code**

**post-dated** On a **post-dated** cheque, the date is a later one than the date when the cheque was actually written. You write a post-dated cheque to allow a period of time before the money is taken from your account. ADJ: usu ADJ n

**post|er** /poʊstəʳ/ **(posters)** A **poster** is a large notice or picture that you stick on a wall or board, often in order to advertise something. N-COUNT

**post|er child** **(poster children)** or **poster boy** or **poster girl** [1] If someone is a **poster child for** a particular cause, characteristic, or activity, they are seen as a very good or typical example of it. [mainly AM] ❑ *Zidane has become the poster child for a whole generation of French-born youths of North African extraction.* N-COUNT: oft N *for* n [2] A **poster child** is a young man or woman who appears on an advertising poster. [mainly AM] ❑ *She went out with a Calvin Klein poster boy.* N-COUNT

**poste res|tante** /poʊst restɑːnt, AM -restɑːnt/ **Poste restante** is a service operated by post offices by which letters and packages that are sent to you are kept at a particular post office until you collect them. [mainly BRIT] N-UNCOUNT: oft N n

✓ in AM, use **general delivery**

**pos|teri|or** /pɒstɪəriəʳ/ **(posteriors)** [1] Someone's bottom can be referred to as their **posterior**. [mainly HUMOROUS] N-COUNT = *backside* [2] **Posterior** describes something that is situated at the back of something else. [MEDICAL] ❑ *...the posterior leg muscles.* ADJ: ADJ n ≠*anterior*

**pos|ter|ity** /pɒsterɪti/ You can refer to everyone who will be alive in the future as **posterity**. [FORMAL] ❑ *A photographer recorded the scene on video for posterity.* N-UNCOUNT: oft *for* N

**post|er paint** **(poster paints)** **Poster paint** is a type of brightly coloured paint which contains no oil and is used for painting pictures. [mainly BRIT] N-MASS

**post-feminist** **(post-feminists)** [1] **Post-feminist** people and attitudes accept some of the ideas of feminism, but reject others. ❑ *...the post-feminist age.* ADJ [2] A **post-feminist** is someone who accepts some of the ideas of feminism, but rejects others. N-COUNT ♦ **post-feminism** ❑ *Post-feminism does not actually exist because we are still in the phase of pre-feminism.* N-UNCOUNT

**post|grad** /poʊstgræd/ **(postgrads)** also **post-grad.** A **postgrad** is the same as a **postgraduate**. [BRIT, INFORMAL] N-COUNT

✓ in AM, use **grad student**

**post|gradu|ate** /poʊstgrædʒuət/ **(postgraduates)** also **post-graduate.** [1] A **postgraduate** or a **postgraduate student** is a student with a first degree from a university who is studying or doing research at a more advanced level. [BRIT] N-COUNT

✓ in AM, use **graduate student**

[2] **Postgraduate** study or research is done by a student who has a first degree and is studying or doing research at a more advanced level. [BRIT] ❑ *...postgraduate courses... Dr Hoffman did his postgraduate work at Leicester University.* ADJ: ADJ n

✓ in AM, use **graduate**

**post-haste** also **post haste.** If you go somewhere or do something **post-haste**, you go there or do it as quickly as you can. [FORMAL] ❑ *The pilot wisely decided to return to Farnborough post haste.* ADV: ADV after v

**post|hu|mous** /pɒstʃʊməs/ **Posthumous** is used to describe something that happens after a person's death but relates to something they did before they died. ❑ *...the posthumous publication of his first novel.* ADJ: usu ADJ n ♦ **post|hu|mous|ly** *After the war she was posthumously awarded the George Cross.* ADV: ADV with v

**postie** /poʊsti/ **(posties)** A **postie** is a **postman**. [BRIT, INFORMAL] N-COUNT

**post-industrial**

✓ in AM, usually use **postindustrial**

**Post-industrial** is used to describe many Western societies whose economies are no longer based on heavy industry. ADJ: ADJ n

**post|ing** /poʊstɪŋ/ **(postings)** [1] If you get a **posting to** a different town or country, your employers send you to work there, usually for several years. [mainly BRIT] ❑ *He was rewarded with a posting to New York.* → See also **post**. N-COUNT: with supp, oft N *to* n

✓ in AM, usually use **assignment**

[2] If a member of an armed force gets a **posting to** a particular place, they are sent to live and work there for a period. ❑ *...awaiting his posting to a field ambulance corps in early 1941.* N-COUNT: oft with supp, oft N *to* n [3] A **posting** N-COUNT

is a message that is placed on the Internet, for example on a bulletin board or website, for everyone to read. [COMPUTING] ❑ *Postings on the Internet can be accessed from anywhere in the world.*

**post|man** /poʊstmən/ **(postmen)** A **postman** is a man whose job is to collect and deliver letters and packages that are sent by post. [mainly BRIT] N-COUNT

✔ in AM, usually use **mailman**

**post|mark** /poʊstmɑːʳk/ **(postmarks)** A **postmark** is a mark which is printed on letters and packages at a post office. It shows the time and place at which something was posted. ❑ *All the letters bore an Aberdeen postmark.* N-COUNT

**post|marked** /poʊstmɑːʳkt/ If a letter is **postmarked**, it has a printed mark on the envelope showing when and where the letter was posted. ❑ *The envelope was postmarked Helsinki.* ADJ: usu v-link ADJ

**post|master** /poʊstmɑːstəʳ, -mæs-/ **(postmasters)** A **postmaster** is a man who is in charge of a local post office. [FORMAL] N-COUNT

**post|mistress** /poʊstmɪstrəs/ **(postmistresses)** A **postmistress** is a woman who is in charge of a local post office. [FORMAL] N-COUNT

**post-modern** also **postmodern. Post-modern** is used to describe something or someone that is influenced by post-modernism. ❑ *...post-modern architecture.* ADJ: usu ADJ n = *post-modernist*

**post-modernism** also **postmodernism. Post-modernism** is a late twentieth century approach in art, architecture, and literature which typically mixes styles, ideas, and references to modern society, often in an ironic way. N-UNCOUNT

**post-modernist (post-modernists)** also **postmodernist.** A **post-modernist** is a writer, artist, or architect who is influenced by post-modernism. ♦ **Post-modernist** is also an adjective. ❑ *...the post-modernist suspicion of grand ideological narratives.* N-COUNT; ADJ: usu ADJ n = *post-modern*

**post-mortem** /poʊst mɔːʳtəm/ **(post-mortems)** also **post mortem, postmortem.** [1] A **post-mortem** is a medical examination of a dead person's body in order to find out how they died. [2] A **post-mortem** is an examination of something that has recently happened, especially something that has failed or gone wrong. ❑ *The postmortem on the presidential campaign is under way.* N-COUNT = *autopsy*; N-COUNT: oft N *on* n

**post|na|tal** /poʊstneɪtᵊl/ also **post-natal. Postnatal** means happening after and relating to the birth of a baby. ❑ *...postnatal depression. ...midwives on the postnatal ward.* ADJ: ADJ n ≠ *antenatal*

**post of|fice (post offices)** [1] **The Post Office** is the national organization that is responsible for postal services. ❑ *The Post Office has confirmed that up to fifteen thousand jobs could be lost.* [2] A **post office** is a building where you can buy stamps, post letters and packages, and use other services provided by the national postal service. N-SING: usu *the* N; N-COUNT

**post of|fice box (post office boxes)** A **post office box** is a numbered box in a post office where a person's mail is kept for them until they come to collect it. N-COUNT = *PO Box*

**post|op|era|tive** /poʊstɒpərətɪv/ also **post-operative. Postoperative** means occurring after and relating to a medical operation. ❑ *...post-operative pain.* ADJ: ADJ n

**post|pone** /poʊspoʊn/ **(postpones, postponing, postponed)** If you **postpone** an event, you delay it or arrange for it to take place at a later time than was originally planned. ❑ *He decided to postpone the expedition until the following day... The visit has now been postponed indefinitely.* VERB; V n/-ing; *be* V-ed

**post|pone|ment** /poʊspoʊnmənt/ **(postponements)** The **postponement** of an event is the act of delaying it happening or arranging for it to take place at a later time than originally planned. ❑ *The postponement was due to a dispute over where the talks should be held.* N-VAR: oft N *of* n

**post-prandial** /poʊst prændiəl/ also **post-prandial.** You use **post-prandial** to refer to things you do or have after a meal. [FORMAL] ❑ *...a post-prandial nap. ...a post-prandial cigar.* ADJ: ADJ n

**post-production** also **post production.** In film and television, **post-production** is the work such as editing that takes place after the film has been shot. ❑ *The film's post-production will be completed early next year. ...a film post-production company.* N-UNCOUNT: oft N n

**post|script** /poʊstskrɪpt/ **(postscripts)** [1] A **postscript** is something written at the end of a letter after you have signed your name. You usually write 'PS' in front of it. ❑ *A brief, handwritten postscript lay beneath his signature.* [2] A **postscript** is an addition to a finished story, account, or statement, which gives further information. ❑ *I should like to add a postscript to your obituary for John Cage.* N-COUNT; N-COUNT: oft N *to* n

**post-traumatic stress dis|or|der** **Post-traumatic stress disorder** is a mental illness that can develop after someone has been involved in a very bad experience such as a war. [MEDICAL] N-UNCOUNT

**pos|tu|late** /pɒstʃʊleɪt/ **(postulates, postulating, postulated)** If you **postulate** something, you suggest it as the basis for a theory, argument, or calculation, or assume that it is the basis. [FORMAL] ❑ *...arguments postulating differing standards for human rights in different cultures... Freud postulated that we all have a death instinct as well as a life instinct.* VERB; V n; V that

**pos|tur|al** /pɒstʃərəl/ **Postural** means relating to the way a person stands or sits. [FORMAL] ❑ *Children can develop bad postural habits from quite an early age. ...postural exercises.* ADJ: ADJ n

**pos|ture** /pɒstʃəʳ/ **(postures, posturing, postured)** [1] Your **posture** is the position in which you stand or sit. ❑ *You can make your stomach look flatter instantly by improving your posture... Sit in a relaxed upright posture.* [2] A **posture** is an attitude that you have towards something. [FORMAL] ❑ *The military machine is ready to change its defensive posture to one prepared for action.* [3] You can say that someone **is posturing** when you disapprove of their behaviour because you think they are trying to give a particular impression in order to deceive people. [FORMAL] ❑ *She says the President may just be posturing.* ♦ **pos|tur|ing** *Any calls for a new UN resolution are largely political posturing.* N-VAR; N-COUNT: usu sing, usu adj N = *position, stance*; VERB: usu cont [disapproval]; V; N-UNCOUNT

**post-viral fa|tigue syn|drome** or **post-viral syndrome. Post-viral fatigue syndrome** is a long-lasting illness that is thought to be caused by a virus. Its symptoms include feeling tired all the time and muscle pain. [MEDICAL] N-UNCOUNT = *ME*

**post-war** also **postwar. Post-war** is used to describe things that happened, existed, or were made in the period immediately after a war, especially the Second World War, 1939-45. ❑ *In the post-war years her writing regularly appeared in The New Journal.* ADJ: usu ADJ n ≠ *pre-war*

**posy** /poʊzi/ **(posies)** A **posy** is a small bunch of flowers. In American English, it can also consist of a single flower. N-COUNT: oft N *of* n

**pot** /pɒt/ **(pots, potting, potted)** [1] A **pot** is a deep round container used for cooking stews, soups, and other food. ❑ *...metal cooking pots.* ♦ A **pot of** stew, soup, or other food is an amount of it contained in a pot. ❑ *He was stirring a pot of soup.* [2] You can use **pot** to refer to a teapot or coffee pot. ❑ *There's tea in the pot.* ♦ A **pot of** tea or coffee is an amount of it contained in a pot. ❑ *He spilt a pot of coffee.* [3] A **pot** is a cylindrical container for jam, paint, or some other thick liquid. ❑ *Hundreds of jam pots lined her scrubbed shelves.* ♦ A **pot of** jam, paint, or some other thick liquid is an amount of it contained in a pot. ❑ *...a pot of red paint.* [4] A **pot** is the same as a **flowerpot.** [5] If you **pot** a young plant, or part of a plant, you put it into a container filled with soil, so it can grow there. ❑ *Pot the cuttings individually.* ◆◇◇ N-COUNT; N-COUNT: usu N *of* n; N-COUNT; N-COUNT: usu N *of* n; N-COUNT: usu with supp, oft n N; N-COUNT: usu N *of* n; N-COUNT; VERB; V n

...*potted plants.* 6 **Pot** is sometimes used to refer to the drugs cannabis and marijuana. [INFORMAL] V-ed N-UNCOUNT

7 In the games of snooker and billiards, if you **pot** a ball, you succeed in hitting it into one of the pockets. ❑ *He did not pot a ball for the next two frames.* VERB = *pocket* V n

8 → See also **potted**, **chamber pot**, **chimney pot**, **coffee pot**, **lobster pot**, **melting pot**, **plant pot**. 9 If you **take pot luck**, you decide to do something even though you do not know what you will get as a result. ❑ *If you haven't made an appointment, take pot luck and knock on the door... He scorns the 'pot-luck' approach.* PHRASE: PHR after v, PHR n

**po|table** /poʊtəbᵊl/ **Potable** water is clean and safe for drinking. [mainly AM] ADJ: usu ADJ n = *drinkable*

**pot|ash** /pɒtæʃ/ **Potash** is a white powder obtained from the ashes of burnt wood and is sometimes used as a fertilizer. N-UNCOUNT

**po|tas|sium** /pətæsiəm/ **Potassium** is a soft silvery-white chemical element, which occurs mainly in compounds. These compounds are used in making such things as glass, soap, and fertilizers. N-UNCOUNT

**po|ta|to** /pəteɪtoʊ/ **(potatoes)** 1 **Potatoes** are quite round vegetables with brown or red skins and white insides. They grow under the ground. → See also **sweet potato**. → See picture on page 1712. ◆◇◇ N-VAR 2 You can refer to a difficult subject that people disagree on as a **hot potato**. ❑ *...a political hot potato such as abortion.* PHRASE: N inflects

**po|ta|to chip** **(potato chips)** 1 **Potato chips** are very thin slices of potato that have been fried until they are hard, dry, and crisp. [AM] N-COUNT: usu pl

> ✔ in BRIT, use **crisps**

2 **Potato chips** are long, thin pieces of potato fried in oil or fat and eaten hot, usually with a meal. [BRIT] N-COUNT: usu pl

> ✔ in AM, use **French fries**

**po|ta|to crisp** **(potato crisps)** **Potato crisps** are the same as **crisps**. [BRIT, FORMAL] N-COUNT: usu pl

**pot-bellied** also **potbellied**. Someone, usually a man, who is **pot-bellied** has a pot belly. ADJ

**pot bel|ly** **(pot bellies)** also **potbelly**. Someone who has a **pot belly** has a round, fat stomach which sticks out, either because they eat or drink too much, or because they have had very little to eat for some time. N-COUNT

**pot|boiler** /pɒtbɔɪləʳ/ **(potboilers)** also **pot-boiler**. If you describe a book or film as a **potboiler**, you mean that it has been created in order to earn money quickly and is of poor quality. N-COUNT [disapproval]

**po|ten|cy** /poʊtᵊnsi/ 1 **Potency** is the power and influence that a person, action, or idea has to affect or change people's lives, feelings, or beliefs. ❑ *They testify to the extraordinary potency of his personality.* N-UNCOUNT: usu with supp = *power* 2 The **potency** of a drug, poison, or other chemical is its strength. ❑ *Sunscreen can lose its potency if left over winter in the bathroom cabinet.* N-UNCOUNT: usu with poss 3 **Potency** is the ability of a man to have sex. ❑ *Alcohol abuse in men can cause loss of sex drive and reduced potency.* N-UNCOUNT

**po|tent** /poʊtᵊnt/ Something that is **potent** is very effective and powerful. ❑ *Their most potent weapon was the Exocet missile... The drug is extremely potent, but causes unpleasant side effects.* ADJ = *powerful*

**po|ten|tate** /poʊtᵊnteɪt/ **(potentates)** A **potentate** is a ruler who has complete power over his people. [FORMAL] N-COUNT

**po|ten|tial** /pətenʃᵊl/ 1 You use **potential** to say that someone or something is capable of developing into the particular kind of person or thing mentioned. ❑ *The firm has identified 60 potential customers at home and abroad... We are aware of the potential problems and have taken every precaution.* ◆◆◇ ADJ: ADJ n = *possible* ♦ **po|ten|tial|ly** *Clearly this is a potentially dangerous situation.* ADV: ADV with cl/group 2 If you say that someone or something has **potential**, you mean that they have the necessary abilities or qualities to become successful or useful in the future. ❑ *The school strives to treat pupils as individuals and to help each one to achieve their full potential... Denmark recognised the potential of wind energy early.* N-UNCOUNT: also N in pl 3 If you say that someone or something has **potential for** doing a particular thing, you mean that it is possible they may do it. If there is **the potential for** something, it may happen. ❑ *John seemed as horrified as I about his potential for violence... The meeting has the potential to be a watershed event.* N-UNCOUNT: also N in pl, with supp, oft N *for* n/-ing

**po|ten|ti|al|ity** /pətenʃiælɪti/ **(potentialities)** If something has **potentialities** or **potentiality**, it is capable of being used or developed in particular ways. [FORMAL] ❑ *The breathtaking potentialities of mechanization set the minds of manufacturers and merchants on fire... All of these are quite useful breeds whose potentiality has not been realised.* N-VAR: usu with supp = *potential*

**pot|hole** /pɒthoʊl/ **(potholes)** also **pot-hole**. 1 A **pothole** is a large hole in the surface of a road, caused by traffic and bad weather. N-COUNT 2 A **pothole** is a deep hole in the ground. Potholes often lead to underground caves and tunnels. N-COUNT

**pot-holed** also **potholed**. A **pot-holed** road has a lot of potholes in it. ADJ: usu ADJ n

**pot|hol|ing** /pɒthoʊlɪŋ/ **Potholing** is the leisure activity of going into underground caves and tunnels. [mainly BRIT] N-UNCOUNT

> ✔ in AM, use **spelunking**

**po|tion** /poʊʃᵊn/ **(potions)** A **potion** is a drink that contains medicine, poison, or something that is supposed to have magic powers. N-COUNT

**pot luck** → see **pot**.

**pot plant** **(pot plants)** A **pot plant** is a plant which is grown in a container, especially indoors. [mainly BRIT] N-COUNT

> ✔ in AM, usually use **house plant**

**pot|pour|ri** /poʊpʊəri, AM -puriː/ **(potpourris)** also **pot-pourri, pot pourri**. 1 **Potpourri** is a mixture of dried petals and leaves from different flowers. Potpourri is used to make rooms smell pleasant. N-MASS 2 A **potpourri of** things is a collection of various different items which were not originally intended to form a group. ❑ *...a potpourri of architectural styles from all over the world.* N-SING: usu N *of* n = *miscellany*

**pot roast** **(pot roasts)** A **pot roast** is a piece of meat that is cooked very slowly with a small amount of liquid in a covered pot. N-VAR

**pot shot** **(pot shots)** also **pot-shot**. 1 To **take a pot shot at** someone or something means to shoot at them without taking the time to aim carefully. [INFORMAL] N-COUNT 2 A **pot shot** is a criticism of someone which may be unexpected and unfair. [INFORMAL] ❑ *...Republican rivals taking pot shots at the president.* N-COUNT

**pot|ted** /pɒtɪd/ 1 **Potted** meat or fish is cooked meat or fish, usually in the form of a paste, which has been put into a small sealed container. ❑ *...potted shrimps.* ADJ: ADJ n 2 A **potted** history or biography contains just the main facts about someone or something. [BRIT] ❑ *The film is a potted history of the band.* ADJ: ADJ n = *condensed* 3 → See also **pot**.

**pot|ter** /pɒtəʳ/ **(potters, pottering, pottered)** A **potter** is someone who makes pottery. N-COUNT

♦ **potter around** or **potter about** If you **potter around** or **potter about**, you do pleasant but unimportant things, without hurrying. [BRIT] ❑ *I was perfectly happy just pottering around doing up my flat... At weekends he would potter around the garden.* PHRASAL VERB V P V P n

> ✔ in AM, use **putter around**

**pot|ter's wheel** **(potter's wheels)** A **potter's wheel** is a piece of equipment with a flat disc which spins round, on which a potter puts soft clay in order to shape it into a pot. N-COUNT

**pot|tery** /pɒtəri/ **(potteries)** 1 You can use **pottery** to refer to pots, dishes, and other objects which are made from clay and then baked in an oven until they are hard. N-UNCOUNT 2 You can use **pottery** to refer to the hard clay that some pots, dishes, N-UNCOUNT and other objects are made of. ❑ *Some bowls were made of pottery and wood.* 3 **Pottery** is the craft or activity of making objects out of clay. 4 A **pottery** is a factory or other place where pottery is made. N-UNCOUNT N-COUNT

**pot|ting com|post (potting composts)** **Potting compost** is soil that is specially prepared to help plants to grow, especially in containers. [BRIT] N-MASS

in AM, use **compost**

**pot|ting shed (potting sheds)** A **potting shed** is a small building in a garden, in which you can keep things such as seeds or garden tools. N-COUNT

**pot|ty** /pɒti/ **(potties)** A **potty** is a deep bowl which a small child uses instead of a toilet. N-COUNT

**pot|ty trained** also **potty-trained.** **Potty trained** means the same as **toilet trained.** [BRIT] ADJ = toilet trained

**pot|ty train|ing** also **potty-training.** **Potty training** is the same as **toilet training.** [BRIT] N-UNCOUNT = toilet training

**pouch** /paʊtʃ/ **(pouches)** 1 A **pouch** is a flexible container like a small bag. 2 The **pouch** of an animal such as a kangaroo or a koala bear is the pocket of skin on its stomach in which its baby grows. N-COUNT N-COUNT

**pouf** /pu̲f/ → see **poof.**

**poul|tice** /pou̲ltɪs/ **(poultices)** A **poultice** is a piece of cloth with a soft, often hot, substance such as clay or a mixture of herbs on it. It is put over a painful or swollen part of someone's body in order to reduce the pain or swelling. N-COUNT

**poul|try** /pou̲ltri/ You can refer to chickens, ducks, and other birds that are kept for their eggs and meat as **poultry.** ♦ Meat from these birds is also referred to as **poultry.** ❑ *The menu features roast meats and poultry.* N-PLURAL N-UNCOUNT

**pounce** /paʊns/ **(pounces, pouncing, pounced)** 1 If someone **pounces on** you, they come up towards you suddenly and take hold of you. ❑ *He pounced on the photographer, beat him up and smashed his camera... Fraud squad officers had bugged the phone and were ready to pounce.* 2 If someone **pounces on** something such as a mistake, they quickly draw attention to it, usually in order to gain an advantage for themselves or to prove that they are right. ❑ *The Democrats were ready to pounce on any Republican failings or mistakes.* 3 When an animal or bird **pounces on** something, it jumps on it and holds it, in order to kill it. ❑ *...like a tiger pouncing on its prey... Before I could get the pigeon the cat pounced.* VERB V on/upon n V VERB V on/upon n VERB V on/upon n V

**pound** /paʊnd/ **(pounds, pounding, pounded)** ◆◆◆ 1 The **pound** is the unit of money which is used in Britain. It is represented by the symbol £. One British pound is divided into a hundred pence. Some other countries, for example Egypt, also have a unit of money called a **pound.** ❑ *Beer cost three pounds a bottle... A thousand pounds worth of jewellery and silver has been stolen. ...multi-million pound profits. ...a pound coin.* 2 **The pound** is used to refer to the British currency system, and sometimes to the currency systems of other countries which use pounds. ❑ *The pound is expected to continue to increase against most other currencies.* 3 A **pound** is a unit of weight used mainly in Britain, America, and other countries where English is spoken. One pound is equal to 0.454 kilograms. A **pound of** something is a quantity of it that weighs one pound. ❑ *Her weight was under ninety pounds. ...a pound of cheese.* 4 A **pound** is a place where dogs and cats found wandering in the street are taken and kept until they are claimed by their owners. 5 A **pound** is a place where cars that have been parked illegally are taken by the police and kept until they have been claimed by their owners. 6 If you **pound** something or **pound on** it, you hit it with great force, usually loudly and repeatedly. ❑ *He pounded the table with his fist... Somebody began pounding on the front door... She came at him, pounding her fists against his chest. ...the pounding waves.* 7 If you **pound** something, you crush it into a paste or a powder or into very small pieces. ❑ *She paused as she pounded the maize grains.* 8 If your heart **is pounding**, it is beating with an unusually strong and fast rhythm, usually because you are afraid. ❑ *I'm sweating, my heart is pounding. I can't breathe.* ♦ **pound|ing** *...the fast pounding of her heart.* 9 → See also **pounding.** N-COUNT: num N N-SING: the N N-COUNT: num N, N of n N-COUNT N-COUNT VERB V n V prep/adv V n prep V-ing VERB V n VERB V N-UNCOUNT: usu N of n

**-pounder** /-paʊndəʳ/ **(-pounders)** 1 **-pounder** can be added to numbers to form nouns that refer to animals or fish that weigh a particular number of pounds. ❑ *My fish average 2 lb 8 oz and I've had two eight-pounders.* 2 **-pounder** can be added to numbers to form nouns that refer to guns that fire shells weighing a particular number of pounds. ❑ *The guns were twelve-pounders.* COMB in N-COUNT COMB in N-COUNT

**pound|ing** /paʊndɪŋ/ **(poundings)** 1 If someone or something takes a **pounding**, they are severely injured or damaged. [INFORMAL] ❑ *Sarajevo took one of its worst poundings in weeks.* 2 → See also **pound.** N-COUNT: usu sing, usu supp N

**pour** /pɔːʳ/ **(pours, pouring, poured)** ◆◇◇ 1 If you **pour** a liquid or other substance, you make it flow steadily out of a container by holding the container at an angle. ❑ *Pour a pool of sauce on two plates and arrange the meat neatly... Heat the oil in a non-stick frying-pan, then pour in the egg mixture.* 2 If you **pour** someone a drink, you put some of the drink in a cup or glass so that they can drink it. ❑ *He got up and poured himself another drink... Quietly Mark poured and served drinks for all of them.* 3 When a liquid or other substance **pours** somewhere, for example through a hole, it flows quickly and in large quantities. ❑ *Blood was pouring from his broken nose... Tears poured down both our faces... The tide poured in from the south.* 4 When it rains very heavily, you can say that **it is pouring.** ❑ *It has been pouring with rain all week... The rain was pouring down... We drove all the way through pouring rain.* 5 If people **pour** into or out of a place, they go there quickly and in large numbers. ❑ *Any day now, the Northern forces may pour across the new border... Holidaymakers continued to pour down to the coast in search of surf and sun.* 6 If something such as information **pours** into a place, a lot of it is obtained or given. ❑ *Martin, 78, died yesterday. Tributes poured in from around the globe.* 7 If someone **pours cold water on** a plan or idea, they criticize it so much that people lose their enthusiasm for it. ❑ *The education secretary poured cold water on the recommendations of a working party.* 8 to **pour scorn on** something → see **scorn.** to **pour cold water on** something → see **water.** VERB V n prep V n with adv VERB V n n V n for n VERB V prep/adv V prep/adv V prep/adv VERB: usu cont it V V down V-ing VERB = stream V prep/adv V prep/adv VERB = flood V adv/prep PHRASE: V inflects = dismiss

♦ **pour into** If you **pour** money or supplies **into** an activity or organization, or if it **pours in**, a lot of money or supplies are given in order to do the activity or help the organization. ❑ *The Government continues to pour billions of pounds into its massive road-building programme... Food donations have poured in from all over the country.* PHRASAL VERB V n P n V P

♦ **pour out** 1 If you **pour out** a drink, you put some of it in a cup or glass. ❑ *Larry was pouring out four glasses of champagne... Carefully and slowly he poured the beer out.* 2 If you **pour out** your thoughts, feelings, or experiences, you tell someone all about them. ❑ *I poured my thoughts out on paper in an attempt to rationalize my feelings.* PHRASAL VERB V P n (not pron) V n P PHRASAL VERB V n P

**pout** /paʊt/ **(pouts, pouting, pouted)** If someone **pouts**, they stick out their lips, usually in order to show that they are annoyed or to make themselves sexually attractive. ❑ *He whined and pouted when he did not get what he wanted. ...gorgeous pouting models.* ♦ **Pout** is also a noun. ❑ *She shot me a reproachful pout.* VERB V V-ing N-COUNT

**pov|er|ty** /pɒvəʳti/ ◆◇◇ 1 **Poverty** is the state of being extremely poor. ❑ *According to World Bank figures, 41 per cent of Brazilians live in absolute pover-* N-UNCOUNT ≠ wealth *ty.* [2] You can use **poverty** to refer to any situation in which there is not enough of something or its quality is poor. [FORMAL] ❑ *Britain has suffered from a poverty of ambition.* — N-SING: also no det, N *of* n ≠ *wealth*

**pov|er|ty line** If someone is on **the poverty line**, they have just enough income to buy the things they need in order to live. ❑ *Thirteen per cent of the population live below the poverty line.* — N-SING: *the* N

**poverty-stricken** **Poverty-stricken** people or places are extremely poor. ❑ *...a teacher of poverty-stricken kids.* — ADJ: usu ADJ n

**pov|er|ty trap** **(poverty traps)** If someone is in a **poverty trap**, they are very poor but cannot improve their income because the money they get from the government decreases as the money they earn increases. — N-COUNT

**POW** /piː oʊ dʌbəljuː/ **(POWs)** A **POW** is the same as a **prisoner of war**. — N-COUNT

**pow|der** /paʊdəʳ/ **(powders, powdering, powdered)** [1] **Powder** consists of many tiny particles of a solid substance. ❑ *The wood turns to powder in his fingers. ...a fine white powder. ...cocoa powder.* — N-MASS
[2] If a woman **powders** her face or some other part of her body, she puts face powder or talcum powder on it. ❑ *She powdered her face and applied her lipstick and rouge. ...the old woman's powdered face.* — VERB; V n; V-ed
[3] **Powder** is very fine snow. ❑ *...a day's powder skiing.* — N-UNCOUNT: oft N n
[4] → See also **baking powder**, **chilli powder**, **curry powder**, **talcum powder**, **washing powder**.

**pow|der blue** also **powder-blue.** Something that is **powder blue** is a pale greyish-blue colour. — COLOUR

**pow|dered** /paʊdəʳd/ A **powdered** substance is one which is in the form of a powder although it can come in a different form. ❑ *There are only two tins of powdered milk left.* — ADJ: usu ADJ n

**pow|der keg** **(powder kegs)** also **powder-keg.** If you describe a situation or a place as a **powder keg**, you mean that it could easily become very dangerous. ❑ *Unless these questions are solved, the region will remain a powder keg.* — N-COUNT

**pow|der room** **(powder rooms)** A **powder room** is a room for women in a public building such as a hotel, where they can use the toilet, have a wash, or put on make-up. [FORMAL] — N-COUNT

**pow|dery** /paʊdəri/ Something that is **powdery** looks or feels like powder. ❑ *A couple of inches of dry, powdery snow had fallen.* — ADJ

**pow|er** /paʊəʳ/ **(powers, powering, powered)** ◆◆◆
[1] If someone has **power**, they have a lot of control over people and activities. ❑ *In a democracy, power must be divided. ...a political power struggle between the Liberals and National Party.* — N-UNCOUNT
[2] Your **power to** do something is your ability to do it. ❑ *Human societies have the power to solve the problems confronting them... He was so drunk that he had lost the power of speech.* — N-UNCOUNT: usu N to-inf, N *of* n
[3] If it is **in** or **within** your **power to** do something, you are able to do it or you have the resources to deal with it. ❑ *Your debt situation is only temporary, and it is within your power to resolve it.* — N-UNCOUNT: poss N
[4] If someone in authority has the **power** to do something, they have the legal right to do it. ❑ *The police have the power of arrest.* — N-UNCOUNT: also N in pl, oft *the* N to-inf
[5] If people take **power** or come to **power**, they take charge of a country's affairs. If a group of people are **in power**, they are in charge of a country's affairs. ❑ *In 1964 Labour came into power... He first assumed power in 1970... The party has been in power since independence in 1964.* — N-UNCOUNT: oft *in* N
[6] You can use **power** to refer to a country that is very rich or important, or has strong military forces. ❑ *In Western eyes, Iraq is a major power in an area of great strategic importance.* — N-COUNT: usu supp N
[7] The **power** of something is the ability that it has to move or affect things. ❑ *The Roadrunner had better power, better tyres, and better brakes. ...massive computing power.* — N-UNCOUNT: usu supp N
[8] **Power** is energy, especially electricity, that is obtained in large quantities from a fuel source and used to operate lights, heating, and machinery. ❑ *Nuclear power is cleaner than coal... Power has been restored to most parts that were hit last night by high winds.* — N-UNCOUNT
[9] The device or fuel that **powers** a machine provides the energy that the machine needs in order to work. ❑ *The 'flywheel' battery, it is said, could power an electric car for 600 miles on a single charge.* ◆ **-powered** *...battery-powered radios. ...nuclear-powered submarines.* → See also **high-powered**. — VERB; V n; COMB in ADJ
[10] **Power** tools are operated by electricity. ❑ *...large power tools, such as chainsaws. ...a power drill.* — ADJ: ADJ n ≠ *hand*
[11] In mathematics, **power** is used in expressions such as **2 to the power of 4** or **2 to the 4th power** to indicate that 2 must be multiplied by itself 4 times. This is written in numbers as $2^4$, or 2 x 2 x 2 x 2, which equals 16. — N-SING: *to the* N *of* num, *to the* ord N
[12] You can refer to people in authority as **the powers that be**, especially when you want to say that you disagree with them or do not understand what they say or do. ❑ *The powers that be, in this case the independent Television Association, banned the advertisement altogether.* — PHRASE

♦ **power ahead** If an economy or company **powers ahead**, it becomes stronger and more successful. ❑ *The most widely held view is the market will continue to power ahead... It all leaves the way clear for Tesco to power ahead.* — PHRASAL VERB; V P; V P

♦ **power up** When you **power up** something such as a computer or a machine, you connect it to a power supply and switch it on. ❑ *Simply power up your laptop and continue work.* — PHRASAL VERB = *switch on*; V P n; Also V n P

**pow|er base** **(power bases)** also **power-base.** The **power base** of a politician or other leader is the area or the group of people from which they get most support, and which enables him or her to become powerful. ❑ *Milan was Mr Craxi's home town and his power base.* — N-COUNT: oft with poss

**power|boat** /paʊəʳboʊt/ **(powerboats)** A **powerboat** is a very fast, powerful motorboat. — N-COUNT

**pow|er bro|ker** **(power brokers)** A **power broker** is someone who has a lot of influence, especially in politics, and uses it to help other people gain power. ❑ *Jackson had been a major power-broker in the 1988 Presidential elections.* — N-COUNT

**pow|er cut** **(power cuts)** A **power cut** is a period of time when the electricity supply to a particular building or area is stopped, sometimes deliberately. [mainly BRIT] — N-COUNT

✔ in AM, use **outage**

**pow|er fail|ure** **(power failures)** A **power failure** is a period of time when the electricity supply to a particular building or area is interrupted, for example because of damage to the cables. — N-VAR = *outage*

**pow|er|ful** /paʊəʳfʊl/ ◆◆◇
[1] A **powerful** person or organization is able to control or influence people and events. ❑ *You're a powerful man – people will listen to you. ...Russia and India, two large, powerful countries.* → See also **all-powerful**. — ADJ
[2] You say that someone's body is **powerful** when it is physically strong. ❑ *Hans flexed his powerful muscles.* ♦ **pow|er|ful|ly** *He is described as a strong, powerfully-built man of 60.* — ADJ; ADV: ADV with v
[3] A **powerful** machine or substance is effective because it is very strong. ❑ *...powerful computer systems... Alcohol is also a powerful and fast-acting drug.* ♦ **pow|er|ful|ly** *Crack is a much cheaper, smokable form of cocaine which is powerfully addictive.* — ADJ: usu ADJ n; ADV: ADV adj
[4] A **powerful** smell is very strong. ❑ *There was a powerful smell of stale beer.* ♦ **pow|er|ful|ly** *The railway station smelt powerfully of cats and drains.* — ADJ: usu ADJ n; ADV: ADV after v
[5] A **powerful** voice is loud and can be heard from a long way away. ❑ *At that moment Mrs. Jones's powerful voice interrupted them, announcing a visitor.* — ADJ = *loud*
[6] You describe a piece of writing, speech, or work of art as **powerful** when it has a strong effect on people's feelings or beliefs. ❑ *...Bleasdale's powerful 11-part drama about a corrupt city leader.* ♦ **pow|er|ful|ly** *It's a play – painful, funny and powerfully acted.* — ADJ; ADV: ADV -ed, ADV after v

**pow|er game** **(power games)** You can refer to a situation in which different people or groups are — N-COUNT: oft adj N competing for power as a **power game**, especially if you disapprove of the methods they are using in order to try to win power. ❑ *...the dangerous power games in the Kremlin following Stalin's death.*

**power|house** /paʊəʳhaʊs/ **(powerhouses)** A **powerhouse** is a country or organization that has a lot of power or influence. ❑ *Nigeria is the most populous African country and an economic powerhouse for the continent.* N-COUNT

**pow|er|less** /paʊəʳləs/ [1] Someone who is **powerless** is unable to control or influence events. ❑ *If you don't have money, you're powerless.* ♦ **pow|er|less|ness** *If we can't bring our problems under control, feelings of powerlessness and despair often ensue.* [2] If you are **powerless to** do something, you are completely unable to do it. ❑ *People are being murdered every day and I am powerless to stop it.* ADJ; N-UNCOUNT = impotence; ADJ: ADJ to-inf = unable ≠ able

**pow|er line** **(power lines)** A **power line** is a cable, especially above ground, along which electricity is passed to an area or building. N-COUNT

**pow|er of at|tor|ney** Power of attorney is a legal document which allows you to appoint someone, for example a lawyer, to act on your behalf in specified matters. N-UNCOUNT

**pow|er plant** **(power plants)** A **power plant** is the same as a **power station**. N-COUNT

**pow|er play** **(power plays)** also **power-play**. [1] A **power play** is an attempt to gain an advantage by showing that you are more powerful than another person or organization, for example in a business relationship or negotiation. ❑ *Their politics consisted of unstable power-plays between rival groups.* [2] In a game of ice hockey, **power play** is a period of time when one team has more players because one or more of the other team is in the penalty box. N-COUNT; N-UNCOUNT

**pow|er point** **(power points)** A **power point** is a place in a wall where you can connect electrical equipment to the electricity supply. [BRIT] N-COUNT

☑ in AM, usually use **outlet, wall socket**

**power-sharing** also **power sharing**. **Power-sharing** is a political arrangement in which different or opposing groups all take part in government together. N-UNCOUNT

**pow|er sta|tion** **(power stations)** A **power station** is a place where electricity is produced. N-COUNT = power plant

**pow|er steer|ing** In a vehicle, **power steering** is a system for steering which uses power from the engine so that it is easier for the driver to steer the vehicle. N-UNCOUNT

**pow-wow** /paʊ waʊ/ **(pow-wows)** also **powwow**. People sometimes refer to a meeting or discussion as a **pow-wow**. [INFORMAL] ❑ *Every year my father would call a family powwow to discuss where we were going on vacation.* N-COUNT

**pox** /pɒks/ People sometimes refer to the disease syphilis as **the pox**. [INFORMAL] → See also **chickenpox, smallpox**. N-SING: the N

**poxy** /pɒksi/ If you describe something or someone as **poxy**, you think that they are insignificant, too small, or bad in some other way. [BRIT, INFORMAL, RUDE] ❑ *...some poxy band from Denver. ...a poxy one per cent of the transport budget.* ADJ: ADJ n; disapproval = crummy

**pp** [1] **pp** is written before a person's name at the bottom of a formal or business letter in order to indicate that they have signed the letter on behalf of the person whose name appears before theirs. [BUSINESS] ❑ *...J.R. Adams, pp D. Philips.* [2] **pp.** is the plural of 'p.' and means 'pages'. [WRITTEN] ❑ *See chapter 6, pp. 137-41.* ◆◇◇

**PPS** /piː piː es/ **(PPSs)** In Britain, a **PPS** is a Member of Parliament who is appointed by a more senior Member to help them with their duties. **PPS** is an abbreviation for 'parliamentary private secretary'. N-COUNT

**PPV** /piː piː viː/ **PPV** is an abbreviation for **pay-per-view**. N-UNCOUNT

**PR** /piː ɑːʳ/ [1] **PR** is an abbreviation for **public relations**. [BUSINESS] ❑ *It will be good PR. ...a PR firm.* [2] **PR** is an abbreviation for **proportional representation**. ◆◇◇ N-UNCOUNT; N-UNCOUNT

**prac|ti|cable** /præktɪkəbᵊl/ If a task, plan, or idea is **practicable**, people are able to carry it out. [FORMAL] ❑ *It is not reasonably practicable to offer her the original job back.* ♦ **prac|ti|cabil|ity** /præktɪkəbɪlɪti/ *Knotman and I discussed the practicability of the idea.* ADJ: usu v-link ADJ = feasible; N-UNCOUNT = feasibility

**prac|ti|cal** /præktɪkᵊl/ **(practicals)** [1] The **practical** aspects of something involve real situations and events, rather than just ideas and theories. ❑ *We can offer you practical suggestions on how to increase the fibre in your daily diet... This practical guidebook teaches you about relaxation, coping skills, and time management.* [2] You describe people as **practical** when they make sensible decisions and deal effectively with problems. ❑ *You were always so practical, Maria... He lacked any of the practical common sense essential in management.* [3] **Practical** ideas and methods are likely to be effective or successful in a real situation. ❑ *Although the causes of cancer are being uncovered, we do not yet have any practical way to prevent it.* [4] You can describe clothes and things in your house as **practical** when they are suitable for a particular purpose rather than just being fashionable or attractive. ❑ *Our clothes are lightweight, fashionable, practical for holidays.* [5] A **practical** is an examination or a lesson in which you make things or do experiments rather than simply writing answers to questions. [mainly BRIT] ◆◇◇ ADJ: usu ADJ n ≠ theoretical; ADJ: usu v-link ADJ approval = down-to-earth ≠ impractical; ADJ: usu ADJ n; ADJ ≠ impractical; N-COUNT

**prac|ti|cal|ity** /præktɪkælɪti/ **(practicalities)** The **practicalities of** a situation are the practical aspects of it, as opposed to its theoretical aspects. ❑ *Decisions about your children should be based on the practicalities of everyday life.* N-VAR: usu with supp, oft N of n

**prac|ti|cal joke** **(practical jokes)** A **practical joke** is a trick that is intended to embarrass someone or make them look ridiculous. N-COUNT

**prac|ti|cal|ly** /præktɪkəli/ [1] **Practically** means almost, but not completely or exactly. ❑ *He'd known the old man practically all his life... I know people who find it practically impossible to give up smoking.* [2] You use **practically** to describe something which involves real actions or events rather than ideas or theories. ❑ *The course is more practically based than the Masters degree.* ADV: ADV with group/cl = almost; ADV: ADV adj/-ed ≠ theoretically

**prac|tice** /præktɪs/ **(practices)** [1] You can refer to something that people do regularly as a **practice**. ❑ *Some firms have cut workers' pay below the level set in their contract, a practice that is illegal in Germany... Gordon Brown has demanded a public inquiry into bank practices.* [2] **Practice** means doing something regularly in order to be able to do it better. A **practice** is one of these periods of doing something. ❑ *She was taking all three of her daughters to basketball practice every day... The defending world racing champion recorded the fastest time in a final practice today.* [3] The work done by doctors and lawyers is referred to as the **practice** of medicine and law. People's religious activities are referred to as the **practice** of a religion. ❑ *...the practice of internal medicine... I eventually realized I had to change my attitude toward medical practice.* [4] A doctor's or lawyer's **practice** is his or her business, often shared with other doctors or lawyers. ❑ *The new doctor's practice was miles away from where I lived.* [5] → See also **practise**. ◆◆◇ N-COUNT; N-VAR: usu supp N; N-UNCOUNT: with supp; N-COUNT

PHRASES [6] What happens **in practice** is what actually happens, in contrast to what is supposed to happen. ❑ *...the difference between foreign policy as presented to the public and foreign policy in actual practice... In practice, workers do not work to satisfy their needs.* [7] If something such as a procedure is **normal practice** or **standard practice**, it is the usual thing that is done in a particular situation. ❑ *It is normal practice not to reveal details of a patient's condition... The transcript is full of codewords, which is standard practice in any army.* [8] If you are PHRASE: PHR with cl; PHRASE: v-link PHR; PHRASE:

**out of practice** at doing something, you have not had much experience of it recently, although you used to do it a lot or be quite good at it. ❑ *'How's your German?' — 'Not bad, but I'm out of practice.'* v-link PHR

[9] If you **put** a belief or method **into practice**, you behave or act in accordance with it. ❑ *Now that he is back, the prime minister has another chance to put his new ideas into practice.* PHRASE: V inflects

**prac|tise** /præktɪs/ **(practises, practising, practised)**

☑ in AM, use **practice**

[1] If you **practise** something, you keep doing it regularly in order to be able to do it better. ❑ *Lauren practises the piano every day... When she wanted to get something right, she would practise and practise and practise.* ➔ See also **practised**. VERB; V n; V

[2] When people **practise** something such as a custom, craft, or religion, they take part in the activities associated with it. ❑ *...countries which practise multi-party politics... Acupuncture was practised in China as long ago as the third millennium BC.* VERB; V n; V n

♦ **prac|tis|ing** *The church has broken the agreement, by insisting all employees must be practising Christians.* ADJ: ADJ n

[3] If something cruel is regularly done to people, you can say that it **is practised on** them. ❑ *There are consistent reports of electrical torture being practised on inmates.* VERB: usu passive; *be* V-ed *on* n

[4] Someone who **practises** medicine or law works as a doctor or a lawyer. ❑ *In Belgium only qualified doctors may practise alternative medicine... He was born in Hong Kong where he subsequently practised as a lawyer until his retirement... The ways in which solicitors practise are varied... An art historian and collector, he was also a practising architect.* VERB; V n; V *as* n; V; V-ing

[5] to **practise what** you **preach** ➔ see **preach**.

**prac|tised** /præktɪst/

☑ in AM, use **practiced**

Someone who is **practised at** doing something is good at it because they have had experience and have developed their skill at it. ❑ *...a practised and experienced surgeon.* ADJ: oft ADJ *at* n

**prac|ti|tion|er** /præktɪʃənəʳ/ **(practitioners)** Doctors are sometimes referred to as **practitioners** or **medical practitioners**. [FORMAL] ➔ See also **GP**. N-COUNT

**prae|to|rian guard** /prɪtɔːriən gɑːʳd/ You can use **praetorian guard** to refer to a group of people who are close associates and loyal supporters of someone important. [FORMAL] N-SING-COLL

**prag|mat|ic** /prægmætɪk/ A **pragmatic** way of dealing with something is based on practical considerations, rather than theoretical ones. A **pragmatic** person deals with things in a practical way. ❑ *...a pragmatic approach to the problems faced by Latin America.* ADJ: usu ADJ n = realistic, practical

♦ **prag|mati|cal|ly** /prægmætɪkli/ *'I can't ever see us doing anything else,' states Brian pragmatically.* ADV: usu ADV with v, also ADV with cl, ADV adj

**prag|mat|ics** /prægmætɪks/ **Pragmatics** is the branch of linguistics that deals with the meanings and effects which come from the use of language in particular situations. N-SING

**prag|ma|tism** /prægmətɪzəm/ **Pragmatism** means thinking of or dealing with problems in a practical way, rather than by using theory or abstract principles. [FORMAL] ❑ *She had a reputation for clear thinking and pragmatism.* N-UNCOUNT

♦ **prag|ma|tist** **(pragmatists)** *He is a pragmatist, not an idealist.* N-COUNT

**prai|rie** /preəri/ **(prairies)** A **prairie** is a large area of flat, grassy land in North America. Prairies have very few trees. N-VAR

**prai|rie dog** **(prairie dogs)** A **prairie dog** is a type of small furry animal that lives underground in the prairies of North America. N-COUNT

**praise** /preɪz/ **(praises, praising, praised)** [1] If you **praise** someone or something, you express approval for their achievements or qualities. ❑ *The American president praised Turkey for its courage... He praised the excellent work of the UN weapons inspectors.* ♦◇◇ VERB; V n for n/-ing; V n

[2] **Praise** is what you say or write about someone when you are praising them. ❑ *All the ladies are full of praise for the staff and service they received... That is high praise indeed.* N-UNCOUNT = commendation

[3] If you **praise** God, you express your respect, honour, and thanks to God. ❑ *She asked the church to praise God.* VERB; V n

[4] **Praise** is the expression of respect, honour, and thanks to God. ❑ *Hindus were singing hymns in praise of the god Rama.* N-UNCOUNT: also N in pl

**praise|worthy** /preɪzwɜːʳði/ If you say that something is **praiseworthy**, you mean that you approve of it and it deserves to be praised. [FORMAL] ❑ *...the government's praiseworthy efforts to improve efficiency in health and education.* ADJ [approval]

**pra|line** /prɑːliːn, preɪ-/ **Praline** is a sweet substance made from nuts cooked in boiling sugar. It is used in desserts and as a filling for chocolates. N-UNCOUNT

**pram** /præm/ **(prams)** A **pram** is a small vehicle in which a baby can lie as it is pushed along. [BRIT] N-COUNT

☑ in AM, usually use **baby carriage**

**prance** /prɑːns, præns/ **(prances, prancing, pranced)** [1] If someone **prances** around, they walk or move around with exaggerated movements, usually because they want people to look at them and admire them. ❑ *He was horrified at the thought of his son prancing about on a stage in tights.* VERB [disapproval]; V adv/prep

[2] When a horse **prances**, it moves with quick, high steps. ❑ *Their horses pranced and whinnied. ...as the carriage horses pranced through the bustling thoroughfares. ...a prancing light-footed mare named Princess.* VERB; V; V prep/adv; V-ing

**prank** /præŋk/ **(pranks)** A **prank** is a childish trick. [OLD-FASHIONED] N-COUNT

**prank|ster** /præŋkstəʳ/ **(pranksters)** A **prankster** is someone who plays tricks and practical jokes on people. [OLD-FASHIONED] N-COUNT

**prat** /præt/ **(prats)** If you describe someone as a **prat**, you are saying in an unkind way that you think that they are very stupid or foolish. [BRIT, INFORMAL] ❑ *What's that prat doing out there now?* N-COUNT [disapproval]

**prat|fall** /prætfɔːl/ **(pratfalls)** [1] If someone takes a **pratfall**, they make an embarrassing mistake. [mainly AM] ❑ *They're waiting for the poor little rich girl to take a pratfall.* N-COUNT

[2] A **pratfall** is a fall onto your bottom. [mainly AM] N-COUNT

**prat|tle** /prætəl/ **(prattles, prattling, prattled)** If you say that someone **prattles on about** something, you are criticizing them because they are talking a great deal without saying anything important. [INFORMAL] ❑ *Lou prattled on about various trivialities till I wanted to scream... She prattled on as she drove out to the Highway... Archie, shut up. You're prattling.* VERB [disapproval] = witter; V *on/away about* n; V *on/away*; V

♦ **Prattle** is also a noun. ❑ *What a bore it was to listen to the woman's prattle!* N-UNCOUNT

**prawn** /prɔːn/ **(prawns)** A **prawn** is a small shellfish with a long tail and many legs, which can be eaten. [BRIT] N-COUNT

☑ in AM, use **shrimp**

**prawn cock|tail** **(prawn cocktails)** A **prawn cocktail** is a dish that consists of prawns, salad, and a sauce. It is usually eaten at the beginning of a meal. [BRIT] N-VAR

☑ in AM, use **shrimp cocktail**

**pray** /preɪ/ **(prays, praying, prayed)** [1] When people **pray**, they speak to God in order to give thanks or to ask for his help. ❑ *He spent his time in prison praying and studying... Now all we have to do is help ourselves and to pray to God. ...all those who work and pray for peace... Kelly prayed that God would judge her with mercy.* VERB; V; V *to* n; V *for* n; V that

[2] When someone is hoping very much that something will happen, you can say that they **are praying that** it will happen. ❑ *I'm just praying that somebody in Congress will do something before it's too late... Many were secretly praying for a compromise.* VERB: usu cont = hope; V that; V *for* n

**prayer** /preəʳ/ **(prayers)** [1] **Prayer** is the activity of speaking to God. ❑ *They had joined a reli-* N-UNCOUNT gious order and dedicated their lives to prayer and good works... The night was spent in prayer.* [2] (N-COUNT) A **prayer** is the words a person says when they speak to God. ❑ *They should take a little time and say a prayer for the people on both sides.* [3] (N-COUNT: poss N) You can refer to a strong hope that you have as your **prayer**. ❑ *This drug could be the answer to our prayers.* [4] (N-PLURAL) A short religious service at which people gather to pray can be referred to as **prayers**. ❑ *He promised that the boy would be back at school in time for evening prayers.*

**prayer book** (N-COUNT) **(prayer books)** A **prayer book** is a book which contains the prayers which are used in church or at home.

**prayer meet|ing** (N-COUNT) **(prayer meetings)** A **prayer meeting** is a religious meeting where people say prayers to God.

**pre-** /priː-/ (PREFIX ≠post-) **Pre-** is used to form words that indicate that something takes place before a particular date, period, or event. ❑ *...his pre-war job. ...pre-1971 cars.*

**preach** /priːtʃ/ **(preaches, preaching, preached)** [1] (VERB) When a member of the clergy **preaches** a sermon, he or she gives a talk on a religious or moral subject during a religious service. ❑ *At High Mass the priest preached a sermon on the devil... The bishop preached to a crowd of several hundred local people... He denounced the decision to invite his fellow archbishop to preach.* (V n; V to n; V, Also V against/on n) [2] (VERB) When people **preach** a belief or a course of action, they try to persuade other people to accept the belief or to take the course of action. ❑ *The Prime Minister said he was trying to preach peace and tolerance to his people... Health experts are now preaching that even a little exercise is far better than none at all... For many years I have preached against war.* (V n; V that; V against/about n) [3] (VERB [disapproval]) If someone gives you advice in a very serious, boring way, you can say that they **are preaching at** you. ❑ *'Don't preach at me,' he shouted.* (V at n)

PHRASES [4] (PHRASE: Vs inflect) If you say that someone **practises what** they **preach**, you mean that they behave in the way that they encourage other people to behave in. ❑ *He ought to practise what he preaches.* [5] (PHRASE: V inflects) If you say that someone **is preaching to the converted**, you mean that they are wasting their time because they are trying to persuade people to think or believe in things that they already think or believe in.

**preach|er** /priːtʃəʳ/ (N-COUNT) **(preachers)** A **preacher** is a person, usually a member of the clergy, who preaches sermons as part of a church service.

**pre|am|ble** /priːæmbᵊl/ (N-VAR: oft N to/of n, without N) **(preambles)** A **preamble** is an introduction that comes before something you say or write. ❑ *The controversy has arisen over the text of the preamble to the unification treaty.*

**pre|ar|range** /priːəreɪndʒ/ (VERB) **(prearranges, prearranging, prearranged)** also **pre-arrange.** If you **prearrange** something, you plan or arrange it before the time when it actually happens. ❑ *When you prearrange your funeral, you can pick your own flowers and music.* (V n)

**pre|ar|ranged** /priːəreɪndʒd/ (ADJ: ADJ n) also **prearranged.** You use **prearranged** to indicate that something has been planned or arranged before the time when it actually happens. ❑ *Working to a prearranged plan, he rang the First Secretary and requested an appointment with the Ambassador.*

**pre|cari|ous** /prɪkeəriəs/ [1] (ADJ = uncertain ≠secure) If your situation is **precarious**, you are not in complete control of events and might fail in what you are doing at any moment. ❑ *Our financial situation had become precarious. ...the Government's precarious position.* ♦ **pre|cari|ous|ly** (ADV: ADV with v, ADV adj/adv) *The hunter-gatherer lifestyle today survives precariously in remote regions.* ♦ **pre|cari|ous|ness** (N-UNCOUNT: usu N of n) *Wells was well aware of the precariousness of human life.* [2] (ADJ) Something that is **precarious** is not securely held in place and seems likely to fall or collapse at any moment. ❑ *They looked rather comical as they crawled up precarious ladders.* ♦ **pre|cari|ous|ly** (ADV: ADV with v, ADV adj/adv) *One of my grocery bags was still precariously perched on the car bumper.*

**pre|cau|tion** /prɪkɔːʃᵊn/ (N-COUNT) **(precautions)** A **precaution** is an action that is intended to prevent something dangerous or unpleasant from happening. ❑ *Could he not, just as a precaution, move to a place of safety?... Extra safety precautions are essential in homes where older people live.*

**pre|cau|tion|ary** /prɪkɔːʃənri, AM -neri/ (ADJ: usu ADJ n) **Precautionary** actions are taken in order to prevent something dangerous or unpleasant from happening. [FORMAL] ❑ *The local administration says the curfew is a precautionary measure.*

**pre|cede** /prɪsiːd/ **(precedes, preceding, preceded)** [1] (VERB) If one event or period of time **precedes** another, it happens before it. [FORMAL] ❑ *Intensive negotiations between the main parties preceded the vote... The earthquake was preceded by a loud roar and lasted 20 seconds... Industrial orders had already fallen in the preceding months.* (V n; be V-ed by n; V-ing) [2] (VERB) If you **precede** someone somewhere, you go in front of them. [FORMAL] ❑ *He gestured to Alice to precede them from the room... They were preceded by mounted cowboys.* (V n; be V-ed by n) [3] (VERB ≠follow) A sentence, paragraph, or chapter that **precedes** another one comes just before it. ❑ *Look at the information that precedes the paragraph in question... Repeat the exercises described in the preceding section.* (V n; V-ing)

**prec|edence** /presɪdəns/ (N-UNCOUNT: usu N over n = priority) If one thing takes **precedence over** another, it is regarded as more important than the other thing. ❑ *Have as much fun as possible at college, but don't let it take precedence over work.*

**prec|edent** /presɪdənt/ (N-VAR: oft N for n) **(precedents)** If there is a **precedent for** an action or event, it has happened before, and this can be regarded as an argument for doing it again. [FORMAL] ❑ *The trial could set an important precedent for dealing with large numbers of similar cases.*

**pre|cept** /priːsept/ (N-COUNT = principle) **(precepts)** A **precept** is a general rule that helps you to decide how you should behave in particular circumstances. [FORMAL] ❑ *...an electoral process based on the precept that all men are born equal.*

**pre|cinct** /priːsɪŋkt/ **(precincts)** [1] (N-COUNT) A shopping **precinct** is an area in the centre of a town in which cars are not allowed. [BRIT] ❑ *The Centre was a pedestrian precinct with a bandstand in the middle.* [2] (N-COUNT: usu ord N) A **precinct** is a part of a city which has its own police force and fire service. [AM] ❑ *The shooting occurred in the 34th Precinct.* [3] (N-PLURAL) The **precincts** of an institution are its buildings and land. [FORMAL] ❑ *No one carrying arms is allowed within the precincts of a temple.*

**pre|cious** /preʃəs/ [1] (ADJ) If you say that something such as a resource is **precious**, you mean that it is valuable and should not be wasted or used badly. ❑ *After four months in foreign parts, every hour at home was precious... Water is becoming an increasingly precious resource.* [2] (ADJ = valuable) **Precious** objects and materials are worth a lot of money because they are rare. ❑ *...jewellery and precious objects belonging to her mother.* [3] (ADJ) If something is **precious** to you, you regard it as important and do not want to lose it. ❑ *Her family's support is particularly precious to Josie.* [4] (ADJ: ADJ n [emphasis]) People sometimes use **precious** to emphasize their dislike for things which other people think are important. [INFORMAL] ❑ *You don't care about anything but yourself and your precious face.* [5] (PHRASE [emphasis]) If you say that there is **precious little** of something, you are emphasizing that there is very little of it, and that it would be better if there were more. **Precious few** has a similar meaning. ❑ *The banks have had precious little to celebrate recently... Precious few homebuyers will notice any reduction in their monthly repayments.*

**pre|cious met|al** (N-VAR) **(precious metals)** A **precious metal** is a valuable metal such as gold or silver.

**pre|cious stone** **(precious stones)** A **precious stone** is a valuable stone, such as a diamond or a ruby, that is used for making jewellery. N-COUNT = gem

**preci|pice** /prᴇsɪpɪs/ **(precipices)** [1] A **precipice** is a very steep cliff on a mountain. N-COUNT [2] If you say that someone is on the edge of a **precipice**, you mean that they are in a dangerous situation in which they are extremely close to disaster or failure. ❑ *The King now stands on the brink of a political precipice.* N-COUNT

**pre|cipi|tate** **(precipitates, precipitating, precipitated)**

> The verb is pronounced /prɪsɪpəteɪt/. The adjective is pronounced /prɪsɪpɪtət/.

[1] If something **precipitates** an event or situation, usually a bad one, it causes it to happen suddenly or sooner than normal. [FORMAL] ❑ *The killings in Vilnius have precipitated the worst crisis yet... A slight mistake could precipitate a disaster.* VERB = bring about V n V n [2] A **precipitate** action or decision happens or is made more quickly or suddenly than most people think is sensible. [FORMAL] ❑ *I don't think we should make precipitate decisions.* ♦ **pre|cipi|tate|ly** *Somebody hired from another country is not likely to resign precipitately.* ADJ: usu ADJ n = hasty ADV: ADV with v

**pre|cipi|ta|tion** /prɪsɪpɪteɪʃ^ə^n/ [1] **Precipitation** is rain, snow, or hail. [TECHNICAL] N-UNCOUNT [2] **Precipitation** is a process in a chemical reaction which causes solid particles to become separated from a liquid. [TECHNICAL] N-UNCOUNT

**pre|cipi|tous** /prɪsɪpɪtəs/ [1] A **precipitous** slope or drop is very steep and often dangerous. ❑ *The town is perched on the edge of a steep, precipitous cliff.* ♦ **pre|cipi|tous|ly** *The ground beyond the road fell away precipitously.* ADJ: usu ADJ n ADV: usu ADV after v [2] A **precipitous** change is sudden and unpleasant. ❑ *The stock market's precipitous drop frightened foreign investors.* ♦ **pre|cipi|tous|ly** *The company has seen its profits fall precipitously over the past few years.* ADJ: usu ADJ n ADV: ADV with v [3] A **precipitous** action happens very quickly and often without being planned. ❑ *...a precipitous decision.* ♦ **pre|cipi|tous|ly** *They've got to act precipitously to make the deals.* ADJ: usu ADJ n ADV: usu ADV with v, also ADV adj

**pré|cis** /preɪsi, AM preɪsiː/

> The form **précis** is both the singular and the plural form. It is pronounced /preɪsiz/ when it is the plural.

A **précis** is a short written or spoken account of something, which gives the important points but not the details. [FORMAL] ❑ *A précis of the manuscript was sent to the magazine New Idea.* N-COUNT: oft N *of* n = summary

**pre|cise** /prɪsaɪs/ [1] You use **precise** to emphasize that you are referring to an exact thing, rather than something vague. ❑ *I can remember the precise moment when my daughter came to see me and her new baby brother in hospital... The precise location of the wreck was discovered in 1988... He was not clear on the precise nature of his mission.* ADJ: ADJ n [emphasis] = exact [2] Something that is **precise** is exact and accurate in all its details. ❑ *He does not talk too much and what he has to say is precise and to the point.* ADJ [3] You say '**to be precise**' to indicate that you are giving more detailed or accurate information than you have just given. ❑ *More than a week ago, Thursday evening to be precise, Susanne was at her evening class.* PHRASE: cl/group PHR

**pre|cise|ly** /prɪsaɪsli/ ◆◇◇ [1] **Precisely** means accurately and exactly. ❑ *Nobody knows precisely how many people are still living in the camp... The meeting began at precisely 4.00 p.m.* ADV: ADV with v, ADV with cl/group [2] You can use **precisely** to emphasize that a reason or fact is the only important one there is, or that it is obvious. ❑ *Children come to zoos precisely to see captive animals.* ADV: ADV with cl/group [emphasis] [3] You can say '**precisely**' to confirm in an emphatic way that what someone has just said is true. ❑ *'Did you find yourself wondering what went wrong?' — 'Precisely.'* ADV: as reply [emphasis] = exactly

**pre|ci|sion** /prɪsɪʒ^ə^n/ If you do something **with precision**, you do it exactly as it should be done. ❑ *The interior is planned with a precision the military would be proud of.* N-UNCOUNT: oft *with* N

**pre|clude** /prɪkluːd/ **(precludes, precluding, precluded)** [1] If something **precludes** an event or action, it prevents the event or action from happening. [FORMAL] ❑ *At 84, John feels his age precludes too much travel.* VERB V n/-ing [2] If something **precludes** you **from** doing something or going somewhere, it prevents you from doing it or going there. [FORMAL] ❑ *A constitutional amendment precludes any president from serving more than two terms.* VERB V n *from* -ing/n

**pre|co|cious** /prɪkoʊʃəs/ A **precocious** child is very clever, mature, or good at something, often in a way that you usually only expect to find in an adult. ❑ *Margaret was always a precocious child.* ♦ **pre|co|cious|ly** *He was a precociously bright school boy.* ADJ: usu ADJ n ADV: usu ADV adj, also ADV with v

**pre|coc|ity** /prɪkɒsɪti/ **Precocity** is the quality of being precocious. [FORMAL] N-UNCOUNT

**pre|con|ceived** /priːkənsiːvd/ If you have **preconceived** ideas about something, you have already formed an opinion about it before you have enough information or experience. ❑ *We all start with preconceived notions of what we want from life.* ADJ: ADJ n

**pre|con|cep|tion** /priːkənsepʃ^ə^n/ **(preconceptions)** Your **preconceptions** about something are beliefs formed about it before you have enough information or experience. ❑ *Did you have any preconceptions about the sort of people who did computing?* N-COUNT: usu with supp

**pre|con|di|tion** /priːkəndɪʃ^ə^n/ **(preconditions)** If one thing is a **precondition for** another, it must happen or be done before the second thing can happen or exist. [FORMAL] ❑ *They made multi-party democracy a precondition for giving aid.* N-COUNT: oft N *for/of/to* n/-ing

**pre-cooked** also **precooked**. **Pre-cooked** food has been prepared and cooked in advance so that it only needs to be heated quickly before you eat it. ADJ: usu ADJ n

**pre|cur|sor** /priːkɜːʳsəʳ/ **(precursors)** A **precursor** of something is a similar thing that happened or existed before it, often something which led to the existence or development of that thing. ❑ *He said that the deal should not be seen as a precursor to a merger.* N-COUNT: usu with supp, oft N *of/to* n

**pre|date** /priːdeɪt/ **(predates, predating, predated)** If you say that one thing **predated** another, you mean that the first thing happened or existed some time before the second thing. ❑ *His troubles predated the recession.* VERB V n

**preda|tor** /predətəʳ/ **(predators)** [1] A **predator** is an animal that kills and eats other animals. N-COUNT [2] People sometimes refer to predatory people or organizations as **predators**. ❑ *The company is worried about takeovers by various predators.* N-COUNT

**preda|tory** /predətri, AM -tɔːri/ [1] **Predatory** animals live by killing other animals for food. ❑ *...predatory birds like the eagle.* ADJ: usu ADJ n [2] **Predatory** people or organizations are eager to gain something out of someone else's weakness or suffering. ❑ *People who run small businesses are frightened by the predatory behaviour of the banks.* ADJ: usu ADJ n

**preda|tory pric|ing** If a company practises **predatory pricing**, it charges a much lower price for its products or services than its competitors in order to force them out of the market. [BUSINESS] ❑ *Predatory pricing by large supermarkets was threatening the livelihood of smaller businesses.* N-UNCOUNT

**pre|de|cease** /priːdɪsiːs/ **(predeceases, predeceasing, predeceased)** If one person **predeceases** another, they die before them. [FORMAL] ❑ *His wife of 63 years, Mary, predeceased him by 11 months.* VERB V n

**pre|de|ces|sor** /priːdɪsesəʳ, AM pred-/ **(predecessors)** [1] Your **predecessor** is the person who had your job before you. ❑ *He maintained that he learned everything he knew from his predecessor Kenneth Sisam.* N-COUNT: usu poss N [2] The **predecessor** of an object or machine is the object or machine that came N-COUNT: usu with poss = forerunner before it in a sequence or process of development. ❑ *The car is some 40mm shorter than its predecessor.*

**pre|des|ti|na|tion** /priːdestɪneɪʃən, AM priːdest-/ N-UNCOUNT If you believe in **predestination**, you believe that people have no control over events because everything has already been decided by a power such as God or fate.

**pre|des|tined** /priːdestɪnd/ ADJ If you say that something was **predestined**, you mean that it could not have been prevented or changed because it had already been decided by a power such as God or fate. ❑ *His was not a political career predestined from birth.*

**pre|de|ter|mined** /priːdɪtɜːʳmɪnd/ ADJ If you say that something is **predetermined**, you mean that its form or nature was decided by previous events or by people rather than by chance. ❑ *The Prince's destiny was predetermined from the moment of his birth... The capsules can be made to release the pesticides at a predetermined time.*

**pre|de|ter|min|er** /priːdɪtɜːʳmɪnəʳ/ **(predeterminers)** N-COUNT In grammar, a **predeterminer** is a word that is used before a determiner, but is still part of the noun group. For example, 'all' in 'all the time' and 'both' in 'both our children' are predeterminers.

**pre|dica|ment** /prɪdɪkəmənt/ **(predicaments)** N-COUNT: usu with supp If you are in a **predicament**, you are in an unpleasant situation that is difficult to get out of. ❑ *The decision will leave her in a peculiar predicament.*

**predi|cate (predicates, predicating, predicated)**

> ✔ The noun is pronounced /predɪkət/. The verb is pronounced /predɪkeɪt/.

1 N-COUNT In some systems of grammar, the **predicate** of a clause is the part of it that is not the subject. For example, in 'I decided what to do', 'decided what to do' is the predicate. 2 VERB: usu passive If you say that one situation **is predicated on** another, you mean that the first situation can be true or real only if the second one is true or real. [FORMAL] ❑ *Financial success is usually predicated on having money or being able to obtain it.* (be V-ed *on* n/-ing)

**pre|dict** /prɪdɪkt/ **(predicts, predicting, predicted)** ◆◇◇ VERB If you **predict** an event, you say that it will happen. ❑ *The latest opinion polls are predicting a very close contest...* (V n) *He predicted that my hair would grow back 'in no time'...* (V that) *It's hard to predict how a jury will react...* (V wh) *'The war will continue another two or three years,' he predicted.* (V with quote)

**pre|dict|able** /prɪdɪktəbəl/ ADJ ≠unpredictable If you say that an event is **predictable**, you mean that it is obvious in advance that it will happen. ❑ *This was a predictable reaction, given the bitter hostility between the two countries.* ♦ **pre|dict|ably** ADV *His article is, predictably, a scathing attack on capitalism.* ♦ **pre|dict|abil|ity** /prɪdɪktəbɪlɪti/ N-UNCOUNT *Your mother values the predictability of your Sunday calls.*

**pre|dic|tion** /prɪdɪkʃən/ **(predictions)** N-VAR If you make a **prediction** about something, you say what you think will happen. ❑ *He was unwilling to make a prediction about which books would sell in the coming year... Weather prediction has never been a perfect science.*

**pre|dic|tive** /prɪdɪktɪv/ ADJ: usu ADJ n You use **predictive** to describe something such as a test, science, or theory that is concerned with determining what will happen in the future. [FORMAL] ❑ *...the predictive branch of economics.*

**pre|dic|tor** /prɪdɪktəʳ/ **(predictors)** N-COUNT: with supp, usu N *of* n = indication You can refer to something that helps you predict something that will happen in the future as a **predictor of** that thing. ❑ *Opinion polls are an unreliable predictor of election outcomes.*

**pre|di|lec|tion** /priːdɪlekʃən, AM pred-/ **(predilections)** N-COUNT: oft N *for* n/-ing = fondness If you have a **predilection for** something, you have a strong liking for it. [FORMAL] ❑ *...his predilection for fast cars and fast horses.*

**pre|dis|pose** /priːdɪspoʊz/ **(predisposes, predisposing, predisposed)** 1 VERB If something **predisposes** you **to** think or behave in a particular way, it makes it likely that you will think or behave in that way. [FORMAL] ❑ *They hire people whose personalities predispose them to serve customers...* (V n to-inf) *There is evidence that certain factors predispose some individuals to criminal behaviour.* (V n *to* n/-ing) ♦ **pre|dis|posed** ADJ: v-link ADJ, ADJ to-inf, ADJ *to* n *...people who are predisposed to violent crime.* 2 VERB If something **predisposes** you **to** a disease or illness, it makes it likely that you will suffer from that disease or illness. [FORMAL] ❑ *...a gene that predisposes people to alcoholism.* (V n *to* n) ♦ **pre|dis|posed** ADJ: v-link ADJ, usu ADJ *to* n *Some people are genetically predisposed to diabetes.*

**pre|dis|po|si|tion** /priːdɪspəzɪʃən/ **(predispositions)** 1 N-COUNT: usu with supp, oft N to-inf, N *to/towards* n/-ing If you have a **predisposition to** behave in a particular way, you tend to behave like that because of the kind of person that you are or the attitudes that you have. [FORMAL] ❑ *There is a thin dividing line between educating the public and creating a predisposition to panic.* 2 N-COUNT: with supp, usu N *to/towards* n If you have a **predisposition to** a disease or illness, it is likely that you will suffer from that disease or illness. [FORMAL] ❑ *...a genetic predisposition to lung cancer.*

**pre|domi|nance** /prɪdɒmɪnəns/ 1 N-SING: usu N *of* n If there is a **predominance of** one type of person or thing, there are many more of that type than of any other type. [FORMAL] ❑ *Another interesting note was the predominance of London club players.* 2 N-UNCOUNT: usu with supp If someone or something has **predominance**, they have the most power or importance among a group of people or things. [FORMAL] ❑ *Eventually even their economic predominance was to suffer.*

**pre|domi|nant** /prɪdɒmɪnənt/ ADJ If something is **predominant**, it is more important or noticeable than anything else in a set of people or things. ❑ *Amanda's predominant emotion was that of confusion.*

**pre|domi|nant|ly** /prɪdɒmɪnəntli/ ADV: usu ADV group, also ADV after v = mainly, largely You use **predominantly** to indicate which feature or quality is most noticeable in a situation. ❑ *...a predominantly female profession.*

**pre|domi|nate** /prɪdɒmɪneɪt/ **(predominates, predominating, predominated)** 1 VERB If one type of person or thing **predominates** in a group, there is more of that type of person or thing in the group than of any other. [FORMAL] ❑ *In older age groups women predominate because men tend to die younger.* (V) 2 VERB When a feature or quality **predominates**, it is the most important or noticeable one in a situation. [FORMAL] ❑ *He wants to create a society where Islamic principles predominate.* (V)

**pre|domi|nate|ly** /prɪdɒmɪnətli/ ADV: usu ADV group, also ADV after v **Predominately** means the same as **predominantly**. ❑ *...a predominately white, middle-class suburb.*

**pre-eminent**

> ✔ in AM, usually use **preeminent**

ADJ If someone or something is **pre-eminent** in a group, they are more important, powerful, or capable than other people or things in the group. [FORMAL] ❑ *...his fifty years as the pre-eminent political figure in the country.* ♦ **pre-eminence** N-UNCOUNT *...London's continuing pre-eminence among European financial centres.*

**pre-eminently**

> ✔ in AM, usually use **preeminently**

ADV: ADV with v, ADV adj/adv, ADV n **Pre-eminently** means to a very great extent. ❑ *The party was pre-eminently the party of the landed interest.*

**pre-empt** /priːempt/ **(pre-empts, pre-empting, pre-empted)**

> ✔ in AM, usually use **preempt**

VERB If you **pre-empt** an action, you prevent it from happening by doing something which makes it unnecessary or impossible. ❑ *You can pre-empt pain by taking a painkiller at the first warning sign...* (V n)

*He pre-empted any decision to sack him.* V n
♦ **pre-emption** /priː empʃᵊn/ *Pre-emption was the only method of averting defeat.* N-UNCOUNT

**pre-emptive** /priːemptɪv/
☑ in AM, usually use **preemptive**

A **pre-emptive** attack or strike is intended to weaken or damage an enemy or opponent, for example by destroying their weapons before they can do any harm. ❑ *...plans for a pre-emptive strike against countries that may have biological weapons.* ADJ: usu ADJ n

**preen** /priːn/ **(preens, preening, preened)** 1 If someone **preens themselves**, they spend a lot of time making themselves look neat and attractive; used especially if you want to show that you disapprove of this behaviour or that you find it ridiculous and amusing. ❑ *50% of men under 35 spend at least 20 minutes preening themselves every morning in the bathroom... Bill preened his beard.* VERB [disapproval] V pron-refl V n 2 If someone **preens**, they think in a pleased way about how attractive, clever, or good at something they are. ❑ *She stood preening in their midst, delighted with the attention... He preened himself on the praise he had received. ...a preening prize fighter about to enter a ring.* VERB [disapproval] V V pron-refl on n V-ing 3 When birds **preen** their feathers, they clean them and arrange them neatly using their beaks. ❑ *Rare birds preen themselves right in front of your camera.* VERB V pron-refl Also V, V n

**pre-existing** also **preexisting**. A **pre-existing** situation or thing exists already or existed before something else. ❑ *...the pre-existing tensions between the two countries. ...people who have been infected in the course of their NHS treatment for a pre-existing illness.* ADJ: ADJ n

**pre|fab** /priːfæb/ **(prefabs)** 1 A **prefab** is a house built with parts which have been made in a factory and then quickly put together at the place where the house was built. [mainly BRIT] N-COUNT 2 A **prefab** building or structure is one that has been made from parts which were made in a factory and then quickly put together at the place where the structure was built . ADJ: ADJ n

**pre|fab|ri|cat|ed** /priːfæbrɪkeɪtɪd/ **Prefabricated** buildings are built with parts which have been made in a factory so that they can be easily carried and put together. ADJ

**pref|ace** /prefɪs/ **(prefaces, prefacing, prefaced)** 1 A **preface** is an introduction at the beginning of a book, which explains what the book is about or why it was written. N-COUNT = foreword 2 If you **preface** an action or speech **with** something else, you do or say this other thing first. ❑ *I will preface what I am going to say with a few lines from Shakespeare... The president prefaced his remarks by saying he has supported unemployment benefits all along.* VERB V n with n V n by -ing

**pre|fect** /priːfekt/ **(prefects)** 1 In some schools, especially in Britain, a **prefect** is an older pupil who does special duties and helps the teachers to control the younger pupils. N-COUNT 2 In some countries, a **prefect** is the head of the local government administration or of a local government department. ❑ *...the police prefect for the district of Mehedinti.* N-COUNT

**pre|fec|ture** /priːfektʃəʳ/ **(prefectures)** In some countries, administrative areas are called **prefectures**. ❑ *He was born in Yamagata prefecture, north of Tokyo.* N-COUNT: oft in names

**pre|fer** /prɪfɜːʳ/ **(prefers, preferring, preferred)** ◆◆◇ If you **prefer** someone or something, you like that person or thing better than another, and so you are more likely to choose them if there is a choice. ❑ *Does he prefer a particular sort of music?... I became a teacher because I preferred books and people to politics... I prefer to go on self-catering holidays... I would prefer him to be with us next season... Bob prefers making original pieces rather than reproductions... The woodwork's green now. I preferred it blue... Her own preferred methods of exercise are hiking and long cycle rides.* VERB: no cont V n V n to n V to-inf V n to-inf V -ing V n adj V-ed Also V that

**pref|er|able** /prefrəbᵊl/ If you say that one thing is **preferable to** another, you mean that it is more desirable or suitable. ❑ *A big earthquake a long way off is preferable to a smaller one nearby... The hazards of the theatre seemed preferable to joining the family paint business.* ADJ: usu v-link ADJ, usu ADJ to n/-ing, it v-link ADJ to-inf/that ♦ **pref|er|ably** /prefrəbli/ *Do something creative or take exercise, preferably in the fresh air.* ADV: usu ADV with cl/group

**pref|er|ence** /prefərəns/ **(preferences)** 1 If you have a **preference for** something, you would like to have or do that thing rather than something else. ❑ *Parents can express a preference for the school their child attends... Many of these products were bought in preference to their own.* N-VAR: usu N for n 2 If you **give preference to** someone with a particular qualification or feature, you choose them rather than someone else. ❑ *The Pentagon will give preference to companies which do business electronically.* N-UNCOUNT: usu N to n = priority

**pref|er|ence shares** **Preference shares** are shares in a company that are owned by people who have the right to receive part of the company's profits before the holders of ordinary shares are paid. They also have the right to have their capital repaid if the company fails and has to close. Compare **ordinary shares**. [BRIT, BUSINESS] N-PLURAL
☑ in AM use **preferred stock**

**pref|er|en|tial** /prefərenʃᵊl/ If you get **preferential** treatment, you are treated better than other people and therefore have an advantage over them. ❑ *Despite her status, the Duchess will not be given preferential treatment.* ADJ: usu ADJ n = special

**pre|fer|ment** /prɪfɜːʳmənt/ **(preferments)** **Preferment** is the act of being given a better and more important job in an organization. [FORMAL] ❑ *He was told by the governors that he could expect no further preferment.* N-VAR

**pref|erred stock** **Preferred stock** is the same as **preference shares**. [AM, BUSINESS] ➔ See also **common stock**. N-UNCOUNT

**pre|fig|ure** /priːfɪgəʳ, AM -gjər/ **(prefigures, prefiguring, prefigured)** If one thing **prefigures** another, it is a first indication which suggests or determines that the second thing will happen. [FORMAL] ❑ *The wall through Berlin was finally ruptured, prefiguring the reunification of Germany.* VERB V n

**pre|fix** /priːfɪks/ **(prefixes)** 1 A **prefix** is a letter or group of letters, for example 'un-' or 'multi-', which is added to the beginning of a word in order to form a different word. For example, the prefix 'un-' is added to 'happy' to form 'unhappy'. Compare **affix** and **suffix**. N-COUNT 2 A **prefix** is one or more numbers or letters added to the beginning of a code number to indicate, for example, what area something belongs to. ❑ *To telephone from the US use the prefix 011 33 before the numbers given here.* N-COUNT

**pre|fixed** /priːfɪkst/ A word or code number that **is prefixed by** one or more letters or numbers has them as its prefix. ❑ *Sulphur-containing compounds are often prefixed by the term 'thio'... Calls to Dublin should now be prefixed with 010 3531.* V-PASSIVE be V-ed by n be V-ed with n

**preg|nan|cy** /pregnənsi/ **(pregnancies)** ◆◇◇ **Pregnancy** is the condition of being pregnant or the period of time during which a female is pregnant. ❑ *It would be wiser to cut out all alcohol during pregnancy... She was exhausted by eight pregnancies in 13 years.* N-VAR

**preg|nan|cy test** **(pregnancy tests)** A **pregnancy test** is a medical test which women have to find out if they have become pregnant. N-COUNT

**preg|nant** /pregnənt/ 1 If a woman or female animal is **pregnant**, she has a baby or babies developing in her body. ❑ *Lena got pregnant and married... Tina was pregnant with their first daughter.* ◆◇◇ ADJ 2 A **pregnant** silence or moment has a special meaning which is not obvious but which people are aware of. ❑ *There was a long, pregnant silence.* ADJ: ADJ n, v-link ADJ with n

**pre|heat** /priːhiːt/ **(preheats, preheating, preheated)** If you **preheat** an oven, you switch it on and allow it to reach a certain temperature before VERB

you put food inside it. ❑ *Preheat the oven to 400 degrees... Bake in the preheated oven for 25 minutes or until golden brown.*
V n
V-ed

**pre|his|tor|ic** /priːhɪstɒrɪk, AM -tɔːr-/ **Prehistoric** people and things existed at a time before information was written down. ❑ *...the famous prehistoric cave paintings of Lascaux.*
ADJ

**pre|his|to|ry** /priːhɪstəri/ also **pre-history. Prehistory** is the time in history before any information was written down.
N-UNCOUNT

**pre-industrial**

✓ in AM, usually use **preindustrial**

**Pre-industrial** refers to the time before machines were introduced to produce goods on a large scale. ❑ *...the transition from pre-industrial to industrial society.*
ADJ: ADJ n

**pre|judge** /priːdʒʌdʒ/ **(prejudges, prejudging, prejudged)** If you **prejudge** a situation, you form an opinion about it before you know all the facts. [FORMAL] ❑ *They tried to prejudge the commission's findings.*
VERB
V n
Also V

**preju|dice** /predʒʊdɪs/ **(prejudices, prejudicing, prejudiced)** 1 **Prejudice** is an unreasonable dislike of a particular group of people or things, or a preference for a one group of people or things over another. ❑ *There is widespread prejudice against workers over 45... He said he hoped the Swiss authorities would investigate the case thoroughly and without prejudice.*
N-VAR: oft supp N, N *against* n

2 If you **prejudice** someone or something, you influence them so that they are unfair in some way. ❑ *I think your South American youth has prejudiced you... He claimed his case would be prejudiced if it became known he was refusing to answer questions.*
VERB
V n
V n

3 If someone **prejudices** another person's situation, they do something which makes it worse than it should be. [FORMAL] ❑ *Her study was not in any way intended to prejudice the future development of the college.*
VERB
V n

4 If you take an action **without prejudice to** an existing situation, your action does not change or harm that situation. [FORMAL] ❑ *We accept the outcome of the inquiry, without prejudice to the unsettled question of territorial waters.*
PHRASE: PHR n

**preju|diced** /predʒʊdɪst/ A person who is **prejudiced** against someone has an unreasonable dislike of them. A person who is **prejudiced** in favour of someone has an unreasonable preference for them. ❑ *Some landlords and landladies are racially prejudiced.*
ADJ: usu v-link ADJ

**preju|di|cial** /predʒʊdɪʃəl/ If an action or situation is **prejudicial to** someone or something, it is harmful to them. [FORMAL] ❑ *You could face up to eight years in jail for spreading rumours considered prejudicial to security.*
ADJ: usu v-link ADJ, oft ADJ *to* n

**prel|ate** /prelɪt/ **(prelates)** A **prelate** is a member of the clergy holding a high rank, for example a bishop or an archbishop.
N-COUNT

**pre|limi|nary** /prɪlɪmɪnri, AM -neri/ **(preliminaries)** 1 **Preliminary** activities or discussions take place at the beginning of an event, often as a form of preparation. ❑ *Preliminary results show the Republican party with 11 percent of the vote... Preliminary talks on the future of the bases began yesterday.*
ADJ: usu ADJ n

2 A **preliminary** is something that you do at the beginning of an activity, often as a form of preparation. ❑ *A background check is normally a preliminary to a presidential appointment.*
N-COUNT: oft N *to* n/-ing

3 A **preliminary** is the first part of a competition to see who will go on to the main competition. ❑ *The winner of each preliminary goes through to the final.*
N-COUNT

**prel|ude** /preljuːd, AM preɪluːd/ **(preludes)** 1 You can describe an event as a **prelude to** a more important event when it happens before it and acts as an introduction to it. ❑ *Most unions see privatisation as an inevitable prelude to job losses.*
N-COUNT: usu sing, usu N *to* n

2 A **prelude** is a short piece of music for the piano or organ. ❑ *...the famous E minor prelude of Chopin.*
N-COUNT

**pre|mari|tal** /priːmærɪtəl/ also **pre-marital. Premarital** means happening at some time before someone gets married. ❑ *I rejected the teaching that premarital sex was immoral.*
ADJ: ADJ n

**prema|ture** /premətʃʊəʳ, AM priː-/ 1 Something that is **premature** happens earlier than usual or earlier than people expect. ❑ *Accidents are still the number one cause of premature death for North Americans. ...a twenty-four-year-old man who suffered from premature baldness.*
ADJ: usu ADJ n

♦ **prema|ture|ly** *The war and the years in the harsh mountains had prematurely aged him.*
ADV: ADV adj, ADV with v

2 You can say that something is **premature** when it happens too early and is therefore inappropriate. ❑ *It now seems their optimism was premature.*
ADJ: usu v-link ADJ, oft *it* v-link ADJ to-inf

♦ **prema|ture|ly** *Holmgren is careful not to celebrate prematurely.*
ADV: ADV with v, also ADV adj

3 A **premature** baby is one that was born before the date when it was expected to be born. ❑ *When my daughter Emma was born she was two and a half months premature.*
ADJ

♦ **prema|ture|ly** *Danny was born prematurely, weighing only 3lb 3oz.*
ADV: ADV after v

**pre|medi|tat|ed** /priːmedɪteɪtɪd/ A **premeditated** crime is planned or thought about before it is done. ❑ *In a case of premeditated murder a life sentence is mandatory.*
ADJ

**pre|medi|ta|tion** /priːmedɪteɪʃən/ **Premeditation** is thinking about something or planning it before you actually do it. [FORMAL] ❑ *The judge finally concluded there was insufficient evidence of premeditation.*
N-UNCOUNT

**pre|men|stru|al** /priːmenstruəl/ **Premenstrual** is used to refer to the time immediately before menstruation and a woman's behaviour and feelings at this time. ❑ *...premenstrual symptoms.*
ADJ: ADJ n

**pre|men|stru|al syn|drome Premenstrual syndrome** is used to refer to the problems, including strain and tiredness, that many women experience before menstruation. The abbreviation **PMS** is often used. ❑ *About 70% of women suffer from premenstrual syndrome.*
N-UNCOUNT

**pre|men|stru|al ten|sion Premenstrual tension** is the same as **premenstrual syndrome**. The abbreviation **PMT** is often used. [mainly BRIT]
N-UNCOUNT

**prem|ier** /premiəʳ, AM prɪmɪr/ **(premiers)** ◆◇◇ 1 The leader of the government of a country is sometimes referred to as the country's **premier**. ❑ *...Australian premier Paul Keating.*
N-COUNT

2 **Premier** is used to describe something that is considered to be the best or most important thing of a particular type. ❑ *...the country's premier opera company.*
ADJ: ADJ n = principal, leading

**premi|ere** /premieəʳ, AM prɪmjer/ **(premieres, premiering, premiered)** 1 The **premiere** of a new play or film is the first public performance of it. ❑ *A new Czechoslovak film has had its premiere at the Karlovy Vary film festival.*
N-COUNT

2 When a film or show **premieres** or **is premiered**, it is shown to an audience for the first time. ❑ *The documentary premiered at the Jerusalem Film Festival... The opera is due to be premiered by ENO next year.*
VERB
V
*be* V-ed

**prem|ier|ship** /premiəʳʃɪp, AM prɪmɪr-/ The **premiership** of a leader of a government is the period of time during which they are the leader. ❑ *...the final years of Margaret Thatcher's premiership.*
N-SING

**prem|ise** /premɪs/ **(premises)**

✓ The spelling **premiss** is also used in British English for meaning 2.

1 The **premises** of a business or an institution are all the buildings and land that it occupies in one place. ❑ *There is a kitchen on the premises... The business moved to premises in Brompton Road.*
N-PLURAL: oft *on the* N

2 A **premise** is something that you suppose is true and that you use as a basis for developing an idea. [FORMAL] ❑ *The premise is that schools will work harder to improve if they must compete.*
N-COUNT: oft N that = assumption

**prem|ised** /premɪst/ If a theory or attitude **is premised on** an idea or belief, that idea or belief has been used as the basis for it. [FORMAL] ❑ *All our activities are premised on the basis of 'Quality with Equality'.*
V-PASSIVE
*be* V-ed *on* n

**prem|iss** /premɪs/ → see **premise**.

**pre|mium** /priːmiəm/ **(premiums)** ◆◇◇ 1 A **premium** is a sum of money that you pay regularly to an insurance company for an insurance policy. N-COUNT ❑ *It is too early to say whether insurance premiums will be affected.* 2 A **premium** is a sum of money that you have to pay for something in addition to the normal cost. N-COUNT: usu sing, oft N n ❑ *Even if customers want 'solutions', most are not willing to pay a premium for them... Callers are charged a premium rate of 48p a minute.* 3 **Premium** goods are of a higher than usual quality and are often expensive. ADJ: ADJ n = luxury ❑ *...the most popular premium ice cream in this country.*

PHRASES 4 If something is **at a premium**, it is wanted or needed, but is difficult to get or achieve. PHRASE: usu v-link PHR = scarce ❑ *If space is at a premium, choose adaptable furniture that won't fill the room.* 5 If you buy or sell something **at a premium**, you buy or sell it at a higher price than usual, for example because it is in short supply. PHRASE: PHR after v ❑ *He eventually sold the shares back to the bank at a premium.* 6 If you **place a high premium on** a quality or characteristic or **put a high premium on** it, you regard it as very important. PHRASE: V inflects, PHR n ❑ *I place a high premium on what someone is like as a person.*

**pre|mium bond** **(premium bonds)** In Britain, **premium bonds** are numbered tickets that are sold by the government. Each month, a computer selects several numbers, and the people whose tickets have those numbers win money. N-COUNT

**premo|ni|tion** /premənɪʃᵊn, AM priː-/ **(premonitions)** If you have a **premonition**, you have a feeling that something is going to happen, often something unpleasant. N-COUNT ❑ *He had an unshakable premonition that he would die.*

**pre|na|tal** /priːneɪtᵊl/ **Prenatal** is used to describe things relating to the medical care of women during pregnancy. ADJ: usu ADJ n ❑ *...a prenatal class.*

**pre|oc|cu|pa|tion** /priɒkjʊpeɪʃᵊn/ **(preoccupations)** 1 If you have a **preoccupation with** something or someone, you keep thinking about them because they are important to you. N-COUNT: oft N *with* n ❑ *In his preoccupation with Robyn, Crook had neglected everything.* 2 **Preoccupation** is a state of mind in which you think about something so much that you do not consider other things to be important. N-UNCOUNT = obsession ❑ *It was hard for him to be aware of her; he kept sinking back into black preoccupation.*

**pre|oc|cu|pied** /priɒkjʊpaɪd/ If you are **preoccupied**, you are thinking a lot about something or someone, and so you hardly notice other things. ADJ: usu v-link ADJ, oft ADJ *with/by* n ❑ *Tom Banbury was preoccupied with the missing Shepherd child and did not want to devote time to the new murder.*

**pre|oc|cu|py** /priɒkjʊpaɪ/ **(preoccupies, preoccupying, preoccupied)** If something **is preoccupying** you, you are thinking about it a lot. VERB ❑ *Crime and the fear of crime preoccupy the community.* V n

**pre|or|dained** /priːɔːʳdeɪnd/ If you say that something is **preordained**, you mean you believe it to be happening in the way that has been decided by a power such as God or fate. [FORMAL] ADJ = predestined ❑ *...the belief that our actions are the unfolding of a preordained destiny.*

**prep** /prep/ **(preps, prepping, prepped)** If you **prep** something, you prepare it. [mainly AM, INFORMAL] VERB ❑ *After prepping the boat, they sailed it down to Carloforte.* V n

**pre-packaged** also **prepackaged. Pre-packaged** foods have been prepared in advance and put in plastic or cardboard containers to be sold. ADJ

**pre-packed** also **prepacked. Pre-packed** goods are packed or wrapped before they are sent to the shop where they are sold. ADJ

**pre|paid** /priːpeɪd/ also **pre-paid. Prepaid** items are paid for in advance, before the time when you would normally pay for them. ADJ: usu ADJ n ❑ *Return the form in the prepaid envelope provided.*

**prepa|ra|tion** /prepəreɪʃᵊn/ **(preparations)** ◆◇◇ 1 **Preparation** is the process of getting something ready for use or for a particular purpose or making arrangements for something. N-UNCOUNT: usu with supp, oft N *for/of* n ❑ *Rub the surface of the wood in preparation for the varnish... Behind any successful event lay months of preparation.* 2 **Preparations** are all the arrangements that are made for a future event. N-PLURAL ❑ *The United States is making preparations for a large-scale airlift of 1,200 American citizens.* 3 A **preparation** is a mixture that has been prepared for use as food, medicine, or a cosmetic. N-COUNT ❑ *...anti-ageing creams and sensitive-skin preparations.*

**pre|para|tory** /prɪpærətri, AM -tɔːri/ 1 **Preparatory** actions are done before doing something else as a form of preparation or as an introduction. ADJ: usu ADJ n = preliminary ❑ *At least a year's preparatory work will be necessary before building can start.* 2 If one action is done **preparatory to** another, it is done before the other action, usually as preparation for it. [FORMAL] PREP-PHRASE ❑ *Sloan cleared his throat preparatory to speaking.*

**pre|para|tory school** **(preparatory schools)** A **preparatory school** is the same as a **prep school**. [BRIT] N-VAR

**pre|pare** /prɪpeəʳ/ **(prepares, preparing, prepared)** ◆◆◇ 1 If you **prepare** something, you make it ready for something that is going to happen. VERB ❑ *Two technicians were preparing a videotape recording of last week's programme... The crew of the Iowa has been preparing the ship for storage.* V n, V n *for* n 2 If you **prepare for** an event or action that will happen soon, you get yourself ready for it or make the necessary arrangements. VERB ❑ *The Party leadership is using management consultants to help prepare for the next election... He had to go back to his hotel and prepare to catch a train for New York... His doctor had told him to prepare himself for surgery.* V *for* n, V to-inf, V pron-refl *for* n 3 When you **prepare** food, you get it ready to be eaten, for example by cooking it. VERB ❑ *She made her way to the kitchen, hoping to find someone preparing dinner.* V n

**pre|pared** /prɪpeəʳd/ ◆◆◇ 1 If you are **prepared to** do something, you are willing to do it if necessary. ADJ: v-link ADJ to-inf = willing ❑ *Are you prepared to take industrial action?* 2 If you are **prepared for** something that you think is going to happen, you are ready for it. ADJ: v-link ADJ *for* n ≠ unprepared ❑ *Police are prepared for large numbers of demonstrators.* 3 You can describe something as **prepared** when it has been done or made beforehand, so that it is ready when it is needed. ADJ: ADJ n ❑ *He ended his prepared statement by thanking the police.*

**pre|par|ed|ness** /prɪpeərɪdnəs/ **Preparedness** is the state of being ready for something to happen, especially for war or a disaster. [FORMAL] N-UNCOUNT ❑ *The situation in the capital forced them to maintain military preparedness.*

**pre|pon|der|ance** /prɪpɒndərəns/ If there is a **preponderance of** one type of person or thing in a group, there is more of that type than of any other. N-SING: usu N *of* n ❑ *...a preponderance of bright, middle-class children in one group. ...Bath, with its preponderance of small businesses.*

**prepo|si|tion** /prepəzɪʃᵊn/ **(prepositions)** A **preposition** is a word such as 'by', 'for', 'into', or 'with' which usually has a noun group as its object. N-COUNT ❑ *There is nothing in the rules of grammar to suggest that ending a sentence with a preposition is wrong.*

**prepo|si|tion|al phrase** /prepəzɪʃənᵊl freɪz/ **(prepositional phrases)** A **prepositional phrase** is a structure consisting of a preposition and its object. Examples are 'on the table' and 'by the sea'. N-COUNT

**pre|pos|ter|ous** /prɪpɒstᵊrəs/ If you describe something as **preposterous**, you mean that it is extremely unreasonable and foolish. ADJ [disapproval] = ludicrous ❑ *The whole idea was preposterous.* ♦ **pre|pos|ter|ous|ly** *Some prices are preposterously high.* ADV: usu ADV adj/adv

**prep|py** /prepi/ **(preppies)** 1 **Preppies** are young people, especially in America, who have often been to an expensive private school and who are conventional and conservative in their attitudes, behaviour, and style of dress. [mainly AM] N-COUNT
2 If you describe someone or their clothes, attitudes, or behaviour as **preppy**, you mean that they are like a preppy. [mainly AM] ❑ *I couldn't believe how straight-looking he was, how preppy. ...a preppy collar and tie.* ADJ

**pre-prandial** /priː prændiəl/ also **pre-prandial.** You use **pre-prandial** to refer to things you do or have before a meal. [FORMAL] ❑ *...pre-prandial drinks.* ADJ: ADJ n ≠post-prandial

**prep school** **(prep schools)** 1 In Britain, a **prep school** is a private school where children are educated until the age of 11 or 13. N-VAR: oft prep N 2 In the United States, a **prep school** is a private school for students who intend to go to college after they leave. N-VAR

**pre|pu|bes|cent** /priːpjuːbesᵊnt/ **Prepubescent** means relating to the time just before someone's body becomes physically mature. [FORMAL] ❑ *...prepubescent boys and girls.* ADJ: usu ADJ n

**pre|quel** /priːkwəl/ **(prequels)** A **prequel** is a film that is made about an earlier stage of a story or a character's life when the later part of it has already been made into a successful film. ❑ *...'Fire Walk With Me', David Lynch's prequel to the TV series 'Twin Peaks'.* N-COUNT: oft N *to* n

**Pre-Raphaelite** /priː ræfəlaɪt/ **(Pre-Raphaelites)** 1 The **Pre-Raphaelites** were a group of British painters in the nineteenth century who painted mainly scenes from medieval history and old stories. N-COUNT 2 **Pre-Raphaelite** art was created by the Pre-Raphaelites. ADJ: ADJ n 3 If you say that a woman looks **Pre-Raphaelite**, you mean that she looks like a character in a Pre-Raphaelite painting, for example because she has long wavy hair. ADJ

**pre-recorded** also **prerecorded.** Something that is **pre-recorded** has been recorded in advance so that it can be broadcast or played later. ❑ *...a pre-recorded interview.* ADJ

**pre|requi|site** /priːrekwɪzɪt/ **(prerequisites)** If one thing is a **prerequisite for** another, it must happen or exist before the other thing is possible. ❑ *Good self-esteem is a prerequisite for a happy life.* N-COUNT: N *for/of* n

**pre|roga|tive** /prɪrɒgətɪv/ **(prerogatives)** If something is the **prerogative** of a particular person or group, it is a privilege or a power that only they have. [FORMAL] ❑ *Constitutional changes are exclusively the prerogative of the parliament.* N-COUNT: usu with poss

**pres|age** /presɪdʒ/ **(presages, presaging, presaged)** If something **presages** a situation or event, it is considered to be a warning or sign of what is about to happen. [FORMAL] ❑ *...the dawn's loud chorus that seemed to presage a bright hot summer's day.* VERB V n

**Pres|by|ter|ian** /prezbɪtɪəriən/ **(Presbyterians)** 1 **Presbyterian** means belonging or relating to a Protestant church, found especially in Scotland or the United States, which is governed by a body of official people all of equal rank. ❑ *...a Presbyterian minister.* ADJ 2 A **Presbyterian** is a member of the Presbyterian church. N-COUNT

**pres|by|tery** /prezbɪtri, AM -teri/ **(presbyteries)** A **presbytery** is the house in which a Roman Catholic priest lives. N-COUNT

**pre-school** **(pre-schools)** also **preschool.**

> ✔ Pronounced /priːskuːl/ for meaning 1, and /priːskuːl/ for meaning 2.

1 **Pre-school** is used to describe things relating to the care and education of children before they reach the age when they have to go to school. [WRITTEN] ❑ *Looking after pre-school children is very tiring... The Halsey Report emphasized the value of a pre-school education.* ADJ: ADJ n 2 In the United States, a **pre-school** is a school for children between the ages of 2 and 5 or 6. ❑ *Children graduate to the kindergarten, then pre-school, and then school.* N-VAR

**pre|schooler** /priːskuːləʳ/ **(preschoolers)** also **pre-schooler.** Children who are no longer babies but are not old enough to go to school are sometimes referred to as **preschoolers.** [WRITTEN] N-COUNT: usu pl

**pres|ci|ent** /presiənt, AM preʃ-/ If you say that someone or something was **prescient**, you mean that they were able to know or predict what was going to happen in the future. [FORMAL] ❑ *...'Bob Roberts', an eerily prescient comedy about a populist multimillionaire political candidate.* ADJ
♦ **pres|ci|ence** *Over the years he's demonstrated a certain prescience in foreign affairs.* N-UNCOUNT

**pre|scribe** /prɪskraɪb/ **(prescribes, prescribing, prescribed)** 1 If a doctor **prescribes** medicine or treatment for you, he or she tells you what medicine or treatment to have. ❑ *Our doctor diagnosed a throat infection and prescribed antibiotic and junior aspirin... She took twice the prescribed dose of sleeping tablets... The law allows doctors to prescribe contraception to the under 16s.* VERB V n V-ed V n *to* n 2 If a person or set of laws or rules **prescribes** an action or duty, they state that it must be carried out. [FORMAL] ❑ *...article II of the constitution, which prescribes the method of electing a president... Alliott told Singleton he was passing the sentence prescribed by law.* VERB V n V-ed

**pre|scrip|tion** /prɪskrɪpʃᵊn/ **(prescriptions)** 1 A **prescription** is the piece of paper on which your doctor writes an order for medicine and which you give to a chemist or pharmacist to get the medicine. ❑ *You will have to take your prescription to a chemist.* N-COUNT 2 A **prescription** is a medicine which a doctor has told you to take. ❑ *The prescription Ackerman gave me isn't doing any good.* N-COUNT ● If a medicine is available **on prescription**, you can only get it from a chemist or pharmacist if a doctor gives you a prescription for it. ❑ *The drug is available on prescription only.* PHRASE: usu PHR after v 3 A **prescription** is a proposal or a plan which gives ideas about how to solve a problem or improve a situation. ❑ *...the economic prescriptions of Ireland's political parties.* N-COUNT

**pre|scrip|tive** /prɪskrɪptɪv/ A **prescriptive** approach to something involves telling people what they should do, rather than simply giving suggestions or describing what is done. [FORMAL] ❑ *...prescriptive attitudes to language on the part of teachers... The psychologists insist, however, that they are not being prescriptive.* ADJ

**pres|ence** /prezᵊns/ **(presences)** ♦♦◇ 1 Someone's **presence** in a place is the fact that they are there. ❑ *They argued that his presence in the village could only stir up trouble... Her Majesty later honoured the Headmaster with her presence at lunch.* N-SING: with poss ≠absence 2 If you say that someone has **presence**, you mean that they impress people by their appearance and manner. ❑ *Hendrix's stage presence appealed to thousands of teenage rebels.* N-UNCOUNT: oft supp N [approval] 3 A **presence** is a person or creature that you cannot see, but that you are aware of. [LITERARY] ❑ *She started to be affected by the ghostly presence she could feel in the house.* N-COUNT 4 If a country has a military **presence** in another country, it has some of its armed forces there. ❑ *The Philippine government wants the US to maintain a military presence in Southeast Asia.* N-SING: usu supp N 5 If you refer to the **presence** of a substance in another thing, you mean that it is in that thing. ❑ *The somewhat acid flavour is caused by the presence of lactic acid.* N-UNCOUNT: with poss ≠absence 6 If you are **in** someone's **presence**, you are in the same place as that person, and are close enough to them to be seen or heard. ❑ *The talks took place in the presence of a diplomatic observer.* PHRASE: PHR after v, v-link PHR

> **present**
> ① EXISTING OR HAPPENING NOW
> ② BEING SOMEWHERE
> ③ GIFT
> ④ VERB USES

① **pres|ent** /prezᵊnt/ ♦♦◇ 1 You use **present** to describe things and people that exist now, rather than those that existed in the past or those ADJ: ADJ n = current that may exist in the future. ❑ *He has brought much of the present crisis on himself... It has been skilfully renovated by the present owners... No statement can be made at the present time.* 2 **The present** is the period of time that we are in now and the things that are happening now. ❑ *...his struggle to reconcile the past with the present. ...continuing right up to the present... Then her thoughts would switch to the present.* 3 In grammar, the **present** tenses of a verb are the ones that are used to talk about things that happen regularly or situations that exist at this time. The simple present tense uses the base form or the 's' form of a verb, as in 'I play tennis twice a week' and 'He works in a bank'. N-SING: the N; ADJ: ADJ n

**PHRASES** 4 A situation that exists **at present** exists now, although it may change. ❑ *There is no way at present of predicting which individuals will develop the disease... At present children under 14 are not permitted in bars.* 5 **The present day** is the period of history that we are in now. ❑ *...Western European art from the period of Giotto to the present day.* 6 Something that exists or will be done **for the present** exists now or will continue for a while, although the situation may change later. ❑ *The ministers had expressed the unanimous view that sanctions should remain in place for the present.* PHRASE: PHR with cl/group; PHRASE: prep PHR = today; PHRASE: PHR with cl

**②pres|ent** /prezᵊnt/ ◆◆◇ 1 If someone is **present at** an event, they are there. ❑ *The president was not present at the meeting... Nearly 85 per cent of men are present at the birth of their children... The whole family was present.* 2 If something, especially a substance or disease, is **present in** something else, it exists within that thing. ❑ *This special form of vitamin D is naturally present in breast milk.* ADJ: v-link ADJ, oft ADJ at n ≠ absent; ADJ: v-link ADJ, oft ADJ in n ≠ absent

**③pres|ent** **(presents** /prezᵊnt/) A **present** is something that you give to someone, for example at Christmas or when you visit them. ❑ *The carpet was a wedding present from the Prime Minister... I bought a birthday present for my mother... This book would make a great Christmas present.* N-COUNT = gift

**④pre|sent** /prɪzent/ **(presents, presenting, presented)** ◆◆◇ 1 If you **present** someone **with** something such as a prize or document, or if you **present** it **to** them, you formally give it to them. ❑ *The mayor presented him with a gold medal at an official city reception... Prince Michael of Kent presented the prizes... The group intended to present this petition to the parliament.* ♦ **pres|en|ta|tion** *Then came the presentation of the awards by the Queen Mother.* VERB; V n with n; V n; V n to n; N-UNCOUNT: usu N of n
2 If something **presents** a difficulty, challenge, or opportunity, it causes it or provides it. ❑ *This presents a problem for many financial consumers... Public policy on the family presents liberals with a dilemma.* 3 If an opportunity or problem **presents itself**, it occurs, often when you do not expect it. ❑ *Their colleagues insulted them whenever the opportunity presented itself.* 4 When you **present** information, you give it to people in a formal way. ❑ *We spend the time collating and presenting the information in a variety of chart forms... We presented three options to the unions for discussion... In effect, Parsons presents us with a beguilingly simple outline of social evolution.* ♦ **pres|en|ta|tion (presentations)** *...a fair presentation of the facts to a jury.* 5 If you **present** someone or something in a particular way, you describe them in that way. ❑ *The government has presented these changes as major reforms... In Europe, Aga Khan III presented himself in a completely different light.* 6 The way you **present yourself** is the way you speak and act when meeting new people. ❑ *...all those tricks which would help him to present himself in a more confident way in public.* 7 If someone or something **presents** a particular appearance or image, that is how they appear or try to appear. ❑ *The small group of onlookers presented a pathetic sight... In presenting a more professional image the party risks losing its individuality. ...presenting a calm and dignified face to the world at large.* 8 If you **present yourself** somewhere, you officially arrive there, for example for an appointment. ❑ *She was told to present herself at the Town Hall at 11.30 for the induction ceremony.* 9 If someone **presents** a programme on television or radio, they introduce each item in it. [mainly BRIT] ❑ *She presents a monthly magazine programme on the BBC.* VERB; V n; V n with n; VERB; V pron-refl; VERB; V n; V n to n; V n with n; N-VAR: oft N of n; VERB; V n as n; V n in n; VERB; V pron-refl prep/adv; VERB; V n; V n; V n to n; VERB; V pron-refl prep/adv; VERB; V n

✔ in AM, usually use **host**, **introduce**

10 When someone **presents** something such as a production of a play or an exhibition, they organize it. ❑ *The Lyric Theatre is presenting a new production of 'Over the Bridge'.* 11 If you **present** someone **to** someone else, often an important person, you formally introduce them. ❑ *Fox stepped forward, welcomed him in Malay, and presented him to Jack... Allow me to present my wife's cousin, Mr Zachary Colenso.* 12 → See also **presentation**. VERB; V n; VERB = introduce; V n to n; V n

**pre|sent|able** /prɪzentəbᵊl/ 1 If you say that someone looks **presentable**, you mean that they look fairly tidy or attractive. ❑ *She managed to make herself presentable in time for work. ...wearing his most presentable suit.* 2 If you describe something as **presentable**, you mean that it is acceptable or quite good. [mainly BRIT] ❑ *His score of 29 had helped Leicestershire reach a presentable total.* ADJ; ADJ = respectable

**pres|en|ta|tion** /prezᵊnteɪʃᵊn, AM priːzen-/ **(presentations)** 1 **Presentation** is the appearance of something, which someone has worked to create. ❑ *We serve traditional French food cooked in a lighter way, keeping the presentation simple... Check the presentation. Get it properly laid out with a title page.* 2 A **presentation** is a formal event at which someone is given a prize or award. ❑ *He received his award at a presentation in London yesterday.* 3 When someone gives a **presentation**, they give a formal talk, often in order to sell something or get support for a proposal. ❑ *James Watson, Philip Mayo and I gave a slide and video presentation.* 4 → See also **present**. N-UNCOUNT; N-COUNT; N-COUNT

**present-day** also **present day**. **Present-day** things, situations, and people exist at the time in history we are now in. ❑ *Even by present-day standards these were large aircraft. ...a huge area of northern India, stretching from present-day Afghanistan to Bengal.* ADJ: ADJ n

**pre|sent|er** /prɪzentəʳ/ **(presenters)** A radio or television **presenter** is a person who introduces the items in a particular programme. [mainly BRIT] ❑ *Most people think being a television presenter is exciting.* N-COUNT

✔ in AM, usually use **host**, **anchor**

**pre|sen|ti|ment** /prɪzentɪmənt/ **(presentiments)** A **presentiment** is a feeling that a particular event, for example someone's death, will soon take place. [FORMAL] ❑ *I had a presentiment that he represented a danger to me... He had a presentiment of disaster.* N-COUNT: usu N that, N of n

**pres|ent|ly** /prezᵊntli/ 1 If you say that something is **presently** happening, you mean that it is happening now. ❑ *She is presently developing a number of projects... The island is presently uninhabited.* 2 You use **presently** to indicate that something happened quite a short time after the time or event that you have just mentioned. [WRITTEN] ❑ *Presently, a young woman in a white coat came in.* 3 If you say that something will happen **presently**, you mean that it will happen quite soon. [FORMAL] ❑ *'Just take it easy,' David said. 'You'll feel better presently.'* ADV: ADV before v, ADV group = currently; ADV: ADV with cl; ADV: ADV after v = shortly

**pres|ent par|ti|ci|ple (present participles)** In grammar, the **present participle** of a verb is the form which ends in '-ing'. Present participles are used to form continuous tenses, as in 'She was wearing a neat blue suit'. They are often nouns, as in 'I hate cooking' and 'Cooking can be fun'. Many of them can be used like an adjective in front of a noun, as in 'their smiling faces'. N-COUNT

**pres|ent per|fect** In grammar, the **present perfect** tenses of a verb are the ones used to talk about things which happened before the time you are speaking or writing but are relevant to the present situation, or things that began in the past and are still happening. The simple present perfect tense uses 'have' or 'has' and the past participle of the verb, as in 'They have decided what to do'. ADJ: ADJ n

**pres|er|va|tion|ist** /prezəʳveɪʃənɪst/ **(preservationists)** A **preservationist** is someone who takes action to preserve something such as old buildings or an area of countryside. N-COUNT

**pres|er|va|tion or|der (preservation orders)** In Britain, a **preservation order** is an official order that makes it illegal for anyone to alter or destroy something such as an old building or an area of countryside. ❑ *The entire city is under a preservation order.* N-COUNT

**pre|serva|tive** /prɪzɜːʳvətɪv/ **(preservatives)** A **preservative** is a chemical that prevents things from decaying. Some preservatives are added to food, and others are used to treat wood or metal. ❑ *Nitrates are used as preservatives in food manufacture.* N-MASS

**pre|serve** /prɪzɜːʳv/ **(preserves, preserving, preserved)** ◆◇◇ [1] If you **preserve** a situation or condition, you make sure that it remains as it is, and does not change or end. ❑ *We will do everything to preserve peace. ...an effort to fit in more students while preserving standards.* ♦ **pres|er|va|tion** /prezəʳveɪʃən/ *...the preservation of the status quo.* VERB = maintain; V n; V n; N-UNCOUNT = maintenance [2] If you **preserve** something, you take action to save it or protect it from damage or decay. ❑ *We need to preserve the forest. ...perfectly preserved medieval houses.* ♦ **pres|er|va|tion** *...the preservation of buildings of architectural or historic interest.* VERB; V n; V-ed; N-UNCOUNT [3] If you **preserve** food, you treat it in order to prevent it from decaying so that you can store it for a long time. ❑ *I like to make puree, using only enough sugar to preserve the plums. ...preserved ginger in syrup.* VERB; V n; V-ed [4] **Preserves** are foods such as jam that are made by cooking fruit with a large amount of sugar so that they can be stored for a long time. N-PLURAL [5] If you say that a job or activity is the **preserve of** a particular person or group of people, you mean that they are the only ones who take part in it. ❑ *The conduct of foreign policy is largely the preserve of the president.* N-COUNT: usu N *of* n [6] A nature **preserve** is an area of land or water where animals are protected from hunters. [AM] ❑ *...Pantanal, one of the world's great wildlife preserves.* N-COUNT: usu supp N = reserve

**pre|set** /priːset/ **(presets, presetting)** also **pre-set.**

> The form **preset** is used in the present tense and is the past tense and past participle.

If a piece of equipment **is preset**, its controls have been set in advance of the time you want it to work. ❑ *...a computerised timer that can be preset to a variety of programs... Bake the cake in a preset oven.* VERB: usu passive; *be* V-ed; V-ed

**pre|side** /prɪzaɪd/ **(presides, presiding, presided)** If you **preside over** a meeting or an event, you are in charge. ❑ *The PM presided over a meeting of his inner Cabinet... The presiding officer ruled that the motion was out of order.* VERB; V *over/at* n; V-ing

**presi|den|cy** /prezɪdənsi/ **(presidencies)** ◆◇◇ The **presidency** of a country or organization is the position of being the president or the period of time during which someone is president. ❑ *Poverty had declined during his presidency.* N-COUNT: oft N *of* n, poss N

**presi|dent** /prezɪdənt/ **(presidents)** ◆◆◆ [1] The **president** of a country that has no king or queen is the person who is the head of state of that country. ❑ *The White House says the president would veto the bill.* N-TITLE; N-COUNT: oft *the* N; N-VOC [2] The **president** of an organization is the person who has the highest position in it. ❑ *...Alexandre de Merode, the president of the medical commission.* N-COUNT: usu N *of* n

**president-elect** The **president-elect** is the person who has been elected as the president of an organization or country, but who has not yet taken office. ❑ *...one of the president-elect's best proposals during the campaign.* N-SING

**presi|den|tial** /prezɪdenʃəl/ **Presidential** activities or things relate or belong to a president. ❑ *...Peru's presidential election... There are several presidential candidates.* ◆◆◇ ADJ: ADJ n

**press** /pres/ **(presses, pressing, pressed)** ◆◆◆ [1] If you **press** something somewhere, you push it firmly against something else. ❑ *He pressed his back against the door... They pressed the silver knife into the cake.* VERB; V n *against* n; V n prep [2] If you **press** a button or switch, you push it with your finger in order to make a machine or device work. ❑ *Drago pressed a button and the door closed.* ♦ **Press** is also a noun. ❑ *...a TV which rises from a table at the press of a button.* VERB; V n; N-COUNT: usu sing [3] If you **press** something or **press down on** it, you push hard against it with your foot or hand. ❑ *The engine stalled. He pressed the accelerator hard... She stood up and leaned forward with her hands pressing down on the desk.* VERB; V n; V adv [4] If you **press for** something, you try hard to persuade someone to give it to you or to agree to it. ❑ *Police might now press for changes in the law... They had pressed for their children to be taught French.* VERB = push; V *for* n; V *for* n to-inf [5] If you **press** someone, you try hard to persuade them to do something. ❑ *Trade unions are pressing him to stand firm... Mr King seems certain to be pressed for further details... She smiles coyly when pressed about her private life.* VERB; V n to-inf; *be* V-ed *for/about* n; *be* V-ed *for/about* n [6] If someone **presses** their claim, demand, or point, they state it in a very forceful way. ❑ *The protest campaign has used mass strikes and demonstrations to press its demands.* VERB; V n [7] If an unpleasant feeling or worry **presses on** you, it affects you very much or you are always thinking about it. ❑ *The weight of irrational guilt pressed on her.* VERB; V *on* n [8] If you **press** something **on** someone, you give it to them and insist that they take it. ❑ *All I had was money, which I pressed on her reluctant mother.* VERB; V n *on* n [9] If you **press** clothes, you iron them in order to get rid of the creases. ❑ *Vera pressed his shirt. ...clean, neatly pressed, conservative clothes.* VERB = iron; V n; V-ed [10] If you **press** fruits or vegetables, you squeeze them or crush them, usually in order to extract the juice. ❑ *The grapes are hand-picked and pressed... I pressed the juice of half a lemon into a glass of water. ...1 clove fresh garlic, pressed or diced.* VERB; *be* V-ed; V n; V-ed [11] Newspapers are referred to as **the press.** ❑ *Today the British press is full of articles on India's new prime minister... Press reports revealed that ozone levels in the upper atmosphere fell during the past month.* N-SING-COLL: *the* N [12] Journalists are referred to as **the press.** ❑ *Christie looked relaxed and calm as he faced the press afterwards.* N-SING-COLL: *the* N [13] A **press** or a **printing press** is a machine used for printing things such as books and newspapers. N-COUNT [14] → See also **pressed, pressing.**

PHRASES [15] If someone or something **gets a bad press**, they are criticized, especially in the newspapers, on television, or on radio. If they **get a good press**, they are praised. ❑ *...the bad press that career women consistently get in this country.* PHRASE: V inflects [16] If you **press charges against** someone, you make an official accusation against them which has to be decided in a court of law. ❑ *I could have pressed charges against him.* PHRASE: V inflects, oft PHR *against* n [17] When a newspaper or magazine **goes to press**, it starts being printed. ❑ *We check prices at the time of going to press.* PHRASE: V inflects

♦ **press ahead** → see **press on 1.**

♦ **press on** or **press ahead** [1] If you **press on** or **press ahead**, you continue with a task or activity in a determined way, and do not allow any problems or difficulties to delay you. ❑ *Organizers of the strike are determined to press on... Poland pressed on with economic reform.* PHRASAL VERB; V P; V P *with* n [2] If you **press on**, you continue with a journey, even though it is becoming more difficult or more dangerous. ❑ *I considered turning back, but it was getting late, so I pressed on.* PHRASAL VERB = keep going; V P

**press agen|cy** **(press agencies)** A country's **press agency** is an organization that gathers news from that country and supplies it to journalists from all over the world. N-COUNT

**press agent** **(press agents)** A **press agent** is a person who is employed by a famous person to give information about that person to the press. N-COUNT: oft with poss

**press box** **(press boxes)** **The press box** at a sports ground is a room or area which is reserved for journalists to watch sporting events. N-COUNT: usu *the* N in sing

**press con|fer|ence** **(press conferences)** A **press conference** is a meeting held by a famous or important person in which they answer journalists' questions. ❑ *She gave her reaction to his release at a press conference.* N-COUNT

**press corps** **(press corps)** **The press corps** is a group of journalists who are all working in a particular place, for different newspapers. ❑ *David McNeil is travelling with the White House press corps.* N-COUNT-COLL: usu *the* N

**pressed** /prest/ If you say that you are **pressed for** time or **pressed for** money, you mean that you do not have enough time or money at the moment. ❑ *Are you pressed for time, Mr Bayliss? If not, I suggest we have lunch.* ➔ See also **hard-pressed**. ADJ: v-link ADJ, usu ADJ *for* n

**press gal|lery** **(press galleries)** **The press gallery** is the area in a parliament, legislature, or council which is reserved for journalists who report on its activities. N-COUNT: usu *the* N in sing

**press-gang** **(press-gangs, press-ganging, press-ganged)** [1] If you **are press-ganged into** doing something, you are made or persuaded to do it, even though you do not really want to. [mainly BRIT] ❑ *I was press-ganged into working in that business... She was a volunteer, she hadn't had to be press-ganged.* [2] If people **are press-ganged**, they are captured and forced to join the army or navy. [mainly BRIT] ❑ *They left their villages to evade being press-ganged into the army... The government denies that the women were press-ganged.* ♦ **press-ganging** *...the press-ganging of young people into the country's armed forces.* [3] In former times, a **press-gang** was a group of men who used to capture boys and men and force them to join the navy. VERB: usu passive = force; *be* V-ed *into* -ing/n; *be* V-ed; VERB: usu passive; *be* V-ed *into* n; *be* V-ed; N-SING: *the* N *of* n; N-COUNT

**pres|sie** /prezi/ ➔ see **pressy**.

**press|ing** /presɪŋ/ [1] A **pressing** problem, need, or issue has to be dealt with immediately. ❑ *It is one of the most pressing problems facing this country.* [2] ➔ See also **press**. ADJ: usu ADJ n = urgent

**press|man** /presmæn/ **(pressmen)** A **pressman** is a journalist, especially a man, who works for a newspaper or magazine. [BRIT, JOURNALISM] ❑ *There were television crews and pressmen from all around the world.* N-COUNT = reporter, newspaperman

✓ in AM, use **newspaperman**

**press of|fic|er** **(press officers)** A **press officer** is a person who is employed by an organization to give information about that organization to the press. ❑ *...the Press Officer of the Bavarian Government.* N-COUNT

**press re|lease** **(press releases)** A **press release** is a written statement about a matter of public interest which is given to the press by an organization concerned with the matter. N-COUNT

**press room** **(press rooms)** also **pressroom.** A **press room** is a room for journalists to use at a special event. N-COUNT

**press sec|re|tary** **(press secretaries)** A government's or political leader's **press secretary** is someone who is employed by them to give information to the press. ❑ *...the Prime Minister's official press secretary.* N-COUNT: oft supp N

**press stud** **(press studs)** A **press stud** is a small metal object used to fasten clothes and is made up of two parts which can be pressed together. [BRIT] N-COUNT = popper

✓ in AM, use **snap fastener, snap**

**press-up** **(press-ups)** **Press-ups** are exercises to strengthen your arms and chest muscles. They are done by lying with your face towards the floor and pushing with your hands to raise your body until your arms are straight. [BRIT] ❑ *He made me do 30 press-ups.* N-COUNT: usu pl

✓ in AM, use **push-ups**

**pres|sure** /preʃəʳ/ **(pressures, pressuring, pressured)** ◆◆◆ [1] **Pressure** is force that you produce when you press hard on something. ❑ *She kicked at the door with her foot, and the pressure was enough to open it... The best way to treat such bleeding is to apply firm pressure.* [2] The **pressure** in a place or container is the force produced by the quantity of gas or liquid in that place or container. ❑ *The window in the cockpit had blown in and the pressure dropped dramatically.* [3] If there is **pressure on** a person, someone is trying to persuade or force them to do something. ❑ *He may have put pressure on her to agree... Its government is under pressure from the European Commission.* [4] If you are experiencing **pressure**, you feel that you must do a lot of tasks or make a lot of decisions in very little time, or that people expect a lot from you. ❑ *Can you work under pressure?... The pressures of modern life are great.* [5] If you **pressure** someone **to** do something, you try forcefully to persuade them to do it. ❑ *He will never pressure you to get married... The Government should not be pressured into making hasty decisions... Don't pressure me... His boss did not pressure him for results.* ♦ **pres|sured** *You're likely to feel anxious and pressured.* [6] ➔ See also **blood pressure**. N-UNCOUNT; N-UNCOUNT: also N in pl; N-UNCOUNT: also N in pl; N-UNCOUNT: also N in pl; VERB; V n to-inf; *be* V-ed *into* -ing, V n; V n *for* n; ADJ: usu v-link ADJ

**pres|sure cook|er** **(pressure cookers)** A **pressure cooker** is a large metal container with a lid that fits tightly, in which you can cook food quickly using steam at high pressure. ➔ See picture on page 1710. N-COUNT

**pres|sure group** **(pressure groups)** A **pressure group** is an organized group of people who are trying to persuade a government or other authority to do something, for example to change a law. ❑ *...the environmental pressure group Greenpeace.* N-COUNT

**pres|sur|ize** /preʃəraɪz/ **(pressurizes, pressurizing, pressurized)**

✓ in BRIT, also use **pressurise**

If you **are pressurized into** doing something, you are forcefully persuaded to do it. ❑ *Do not be pressurized into making your decision immediately... He thought she was trying to pressurize him.* ➔ See also **pressurized**. VERB = pressure; *be* V-ed *into* -ing; V n; Also V n to-inf

**pres|sur|ized** /preʃəraɪzd/

✓ in BRIT, also use **pressurised**

In a **pressurized** container or area, the pressure inside is different from the pressure outside. ❑ *Certain types of foods are also dispensed in pressurized canisters.* ADJ: usu ADJ n

**pres|sy** /prezi/ **(pressies)** also **pressie.** A **pressy** is something that you give to someone, for example at Christmas, or when you visit them. [BRIT, INFORMAL] ❑ *...Christmas pressies.* N-COUNT = present

**pres|tige** /prestiːʒ/ [1] If a person, a country, or an organization has **prestige**, they are admired and respected because of the position they hold or the things they have achieved. ❑ *It was his responsibility for foreign affairs that gained him international prestige.* [2] **Prestige** is used to describe products, places, or activities which people admire because they are associated with being rich or having a high social position. ❑ *...such prestige cars as Cadillac, Mercedes, Porsche and Jaguar.* N-UNCOUNT; ADJ: ADJ n = luxury

**pres|tig|ious** /prestɪdʒəs/ A **prestigious** institution, job, or activity is respected and admired by people. ❑ *It's one of the best equipped and most prestigious schools in the country.* ADJ: usu ADJ n

**pre|sum|ably** /prɪzjuːməbli, AM -zuːm-/ ◆◇◇ If you say that something is **presumably** the case, you mean that you think it is very likely to be the ADV: ADV with cl/group, case, although you are not certain. ❑ *He had gone to the reception desk, presumably to check out.* ADV before v [vagueness]

**pre|sume** /prɪzjuːm, AM -zuːm/ **(presumes, presuming, presumed)** [1] If you **presume that** something is the case, you think that it is the case, although you are not certain. VERB = *assume* ❑ *I presume you're here on business...* V that *Dido's told you the whole sad story, I presume?... 'Had he been home all week?' — 'I presume so.'* V that, V *so* *...areas that have been presumed to be safe... The missing person is presumed dead.* *be* V-ed to-inf, *be* V-ed adj [2] If you say that someone **presumes to** do something, you mean that they do it even though they have no right to do it. [FORMAL] VERB ❑ *They're resentful that outsiders presume to meddle in their affairs.* V to-inf [3] If an idea, theory, or plan **presumes** certain facts, it regards them as true so that they can be used as a basis for further ideas and theories. [FORMAL] VERB ❑ *The legal definition of 'know' often presumes mental control...* V n *The arrangement presumes that both lenders and borrowers are rational.* V that

**pre|sump|tion** /prɪzʌmpʃᵊn/ **(presumptions)** [1] A **presumption** is something that is accepted as true but is not certain to be true. N-COUNT = *assumption* ❑ *...the presumption that a defendant is innocent until proved guilty.* [2] If you describe someone's behaviour as **presumption**, you disapprove of it because they are doing something that they have no right to do. [FORMAL] N-UNCOUNT [disapproval] ❑ *They were angered by his presumption.*

**pre|sump|tu|ous** /prɪzʌmptʃuəs/ If you describe someone or their behaviour as **presumptuous**, you disapprove of them because they are doing something that they have no right or authority to do. ADJ: usu v-link ADJ [disapproval] ❑ *It would be presumptuous to judge what the outcome will be.*

**pre|sup|pose** /priːsəpoʊz/ **(presupposes, presupposing, presupposed)** If one thing **presupposes** another, the first thing cannot be true or exist unless the second thing is true or exists. VERB ❑ *All your arguments presuppose that he's a rational, intelligent man...* V that *The end of an era presupposes the start of another.* V n

**pre|sup|po|si|tion** /priːsʌpəzɪʃᵊn/ **(presuppositions)** A **presupposition** is something that you assume to be true, especially something which you must assume is true in order to continue with what you are saying or thinking. [FORMAL] N-COUNT ❑ *...the presupposition that human life must be sustained for as long as possible.*

**pre-tax** also **pretax. Pre-tax** profits or losses are the total profits or losses made by a company before tax has been taken away. [BUSINESS] ADJ: ADJ n ❑ *Storehouse made pre-tax profits of £3.1m.* ♦ **Pre-tax** is also an adverb. ADV: ADV after v ❑ *Last year it made £2.5m pre-tax.*

**pre-teen (pre-teens)** also **preteen.** A **preteen** is a child aged between nine and thirteen. N-COUNT: oft N n ❑ *Some preteens are able to handle a good deal of responsibility. ...pre-teen children.*

**pre|tence** /prɪtens, AM priːtens/ **(pretences)**

✔ in AM, use **pretense**

[1] A **pretence** is an action or way of behaving that is intended to make people believe something that is not true. N-VAR ❑ *Welland made a pretence of writing a note in his pad... We have to go along with the pretence that things are getting better.* [2] If you do something **under false pretences**, you do it when people do not know the truth about you and your intentions. PHRASE: usu *under* PHR ❑ *I could not go on living with a man who had married me under false pretences.*

**pre|tend** /prɪtend/ **(pretends, pretending, pretended)** [1] If you **pretend that** something is the case, you act in a way that is intended to make people believe that it is the case, although in fact it is not. VERB ❑ *I pretend that things are really okay when they're not...* V that *Sometimes the boy pretended to be asleep...* V to-inf *I had no option but to pretend ignorance.* V n [2] If children or adults **pretend that** they are doing something, they imagine that they are doing it, for example as part of a game. VERB ❑ *She can sunbathe and pretend she's in Spain...* V that *The children pretend to be different animals dancing to the music.* V to-inf [3] If you do not **pretend that** something is the case, you do not claim that it is the case. VERB: with neg V that ❑ *We do not pretend that the past six years have been without problems for us... Within this lecture I cannot pretend to deal adequately with dreams.* V to-inf

**pre|tend|er** /prɪtendəʳ/ **(pretenders)** A **pretender to** a position is someone who claims the right to that position, and whose claim is disputed by others. N-COUNT: usu N *to* n, adj N ❑ *...the Comte de Paris, pretender to the French throne.*

**pre|tense** /prɪtens, AM priːtens/ ➔ see **pretence**.

**pre|ten|sion** /prɪtenʃᵊn/ **(pretensions)** [1] If you say that someone has **pretensions**, you disapprove of them because they claim or pretend that they are more important than they really are. N-VAR [disapproval] ❑ *Her wide-eyed innocence soon exposes the pretensions of the art world... We like him for his honesty, his lack of pretension.* [2] If someone has **pretensions to** something, they claim to be or do that thing. N-UNCOUNT: also N in pl, N *to* n/-ing, N to-inf ❑ *The city has unrealistic pretensions to world-class status.*

**pre|ten|tious** /prɪtenʃəs/ If you say that someone or something is **pretentious**, you mean that they try to seem important or significant, but you do not think that they are. ADJ [disapproval] ❑ *His response was full of pretentious nonsense.* ♦ **pre|ten|tious|ness** N-UNCOUNT *He has a tendency towards pretentiousness.*

**pre|ter|natu|ral** /priːtəʳnætʃrəl/ **Preternatural** abilities, qualities, or events are very unusual in a way that might make you think that unknown forces are involved. [FORMAL] ADJ: ADJ n ❑ *Their parents had an almost preternatural ability to understand what was going on in their children's minds.* ♦ **pre|ter|natu|ral|ly** ADV: ADV adj *It was suddenly preternaturally quiet.*

**pre|text** /priːtekst/ **(pretexts)** A **pretext** is a reason which you pretend has caused you to do something. N-COUNT ❑ *They wanted a pretext for subduing the region by force.*

**pret|ti|fy** /prɪtɪfaɪ/ **(prettifies, prettifying, prettified)** To **prettify** something, especially something that is not beautiful, means to make it appear pretty. VERB [disapproval] ❑ *...just a clever effort to prettify animal slaughter...* V n *It presented an intolerably prettified view of the countryside.* V-ed

**pret|ty** /prɪti/ **(prettier, prettiest)** ◆◆◇ [1] If you describe someone, especially a girl, as **pretty**, you mean that they look nice and are attractive in a delicate way. ADJ ❑ *She's a very charming and very pretty girl.* ♦ **pret|ti|ly** /prɪtɪli/ ADV *She smiled again, prettily.* ♦ **pret|ti|ness** N-UNCOUNT *Her prettiness had been much admired.* [2] A place or a thing that is **pretty** is attractive and pleasant, in a charming but not particularly unusual way. ADJ ❑ *Whitstable is still a very pretty little town.* ♦ **pret|ti|ly** ADV *The living-room was prettily decorated.* ♦ **pret|ti|ness** N-UNCOUNT *...shells of quite unbelievable prettiness.* [3] You can use **pretty** before an adjective or adverb to mean 'quite' or 'rather'. [INFORMAL] ADV: ADV adj/adv ❑ *I had a pretty good idea what she was going to do... Pretty soon after my arrival I found lodgings.* [4] **Pretty much** or **pretty well** means 'almost'. [INFORMAL] PHRASE ❑ *His new government looks pretty much like the old one.*

**pret|zel** /pretsᵊl/ **(pretzels)** A **pretzel** is a small, crisp, shiny biscuit, which has salt on the outside. Pretzels are usually shaped like knots or sticks. N-COUNT

**pre|vail** /prɪveɪl/ **(prevails, prevailing, prevailed)** [1] If a proposal, principle, or opinion **prevails**, it gains influence or is accepted, often after a struggle or argument. VERB = *triumph* ❑ *We hope that common sense would prevail...* V *Political and personal ambitions are starting to prevail over economic interests.* V *over* n [2] If a situation, attitude, or custom **prevails** in a particular place at a particular time, it is normal or most common in that place at that time. VERB ❑ *A similar situation prevails in America...* V *How people in a certain era bury their dead says much about the prevailing attitudes toward death.* V-ing [3] If one side in a battle, VERB

contest, or dispute **prevails**, it wins. ❑ *He appears to have the votes he needs to prevail... I do hope he will prevail over the rebels.*
V
V *over/against* n
4 If you **prevail upon** someone **to** do something, you succeed in persuading them to do it. [FORMAL] ❑ *We must, each of us, prevail upon our congressman to act.*
VERB
V *upon/on* n to-inf

**pre|vail|ing** /prɪveɪlɪŋ/ The **prevailing** wind in an area is the type of wind that blows over that area most of the time. ❑ *The direction of the prevailing winds should be taken into account.*
ADJ: ADJ n

**preva|lent** /prevələnt/ A condition, practice, or belief that is **prevalent** is common. ❑ *This condition is more prevalent in women than in men... The prevalent view is that interest rates will fall.*
ADJ: usu v-link ADJ
♦ **preva|lence** *...the prevalence of asthma in Britain and western Europe.*
N-UNCOUNT

**pre|vari|cate** /prɪværɪkeɪt/ **(prevaricates, prevaricating, prevaricated)** If you **prevaricate**, you avoid giving a direct answer or making a firm decision. ❑ *British ministers continued to prevaricate.*
VERB
V
♦ **pre|vari|ca|tion** /prɪværɪkeɪʃən/ **(prevarications)** *After months of prevarication, the political decision had at last been made.*
N-UNCOUNT: also N in pl

**pre|vent** /prɪvent/ **(prevents, preventing, prevented)** ◆◆◇
1 To **prevent** something means to ensure that it does not happen. ❑ *These methods prevent pregnancy... Further treatment will prevent cancer from developing... We recognized the possibility and took steps to prevent it happening.*
VERB
V n
V n *from* -ing
V n -ing
♦ **pre|ven|tion** *...the prevention of heart disease. ...crime prevention.*
N-UNCOUNT
2 To **prevent** someone **from** doing something means to make it impossible for them to do it. ❑ *He said this would prevent companies from creating new jobs... The police have been trying to prevent them carrying weapons.*
VERB
V n *from* -ing
V n -ing

**pre|vent|able** /prɪventəbəl/ **Preventable** diseases, illnesses, or deaths could be stopped from occurring. ❑ *Forty-thousand children a day die from preventable diseases.*
ADJ

**pre|ven|ta|tive** /prɪventətɪv/ **Preventative** means the same as **preventive**.
ADJ: ADJ n

**pre|ven|tive** /prɪventɪv/ **Preventive** actions are intended to help prevent things such as disease or crime. ❑ *Too much is spent on expensive curative medicine and too little on preventive medicine.*
ADJ: usu ADJ n = *preventative*

**pre|view** /priːvjuː/ **(previews, previewing, previewed)**
1 A **preview** is an opportunity to see something such as a film, exhibition, or invention before it is open or available to the public. ❑ *He had gone to see the preview of a play. ...a sneak preview of the type of car that could be commonplace within ten years.*
N-COUNT
2 If a journalist **previews** something such as a film, exhibition, or invention, they see it and describe it to the public before the public see it for themselves. ❑ *He knew about the interview prior to its publication and had actually previewed the piece.*
VERB
V n

**pre|vi|ous** /priːviəs/ ◆◆◇
1 A **previous** event or thing is one that happened or existed before the one that you are talking about. ❑ *She has a teenage daughter from a previous marriage... He has no previous convictions.*
ADJ: ADJ n
2 You refer to the period of time or the thing immediately before the one that you are talking about as the **previous** one. ❑ *It was a surprisingly dry day after the rain of the previous week.*
ADJ: det ADJ

**pre|vi|ous|ly** /priːviəsli/ ◆◇◇
1 **Previously** means at some time before the period that you are talking about. ❑ *Guyana's railways were previously owned by private companies... Previously she had very little time to work in her own garden.*
ADV: usu ADV with v, also ADV adj, ADV with cl
2 You can use **previously** to say how much earlier one event was than another event. ❑ *He had first entered the House 12 years previously.*
ADV: n ADV = *earlier*

**pre-war** also **prewar**. **Pre-war** is used to describe things that happened, existed, or were made in the period immediately before a war, especially the Second World War, 1939-45. ❑ *...Poland's pre-war leader.*
ADJ: usu ADJ n ≠ *post-war, wartime*

**prey** /preɪ/ **(preys, preying, preyed)**
1 A creature's **prey** are the creatures that it hunts and eats in order to live. ❑ *Electric rays stun their prey with huge electrical discharges... These animals were the prey of hyenas.* → See also **bird of prey**.
N-UNCOUNT-COLL: usu with poss
2 A creature that **preys on** other creatures lives by catching and eating them. ❑ *The larvae prey upon small aphids.*
VERB = *feed*
V *on/upon* n
3 You can refer to the people who someone tries to harm or trick as their **prey**. ❑ *Police officers lie in wait for the gangs who stalk their prey at night.*
N-UNCOUNT: usu with poss
4 If someone **preys on** other people, especially people who are unable to protect themselves, they take advantage of them or harm them in some way. ❑ *The survey claims loan companies prey on weak families already in debt.*
VERB [disapproval]
V *on* n
5 If something **preys on** your mind, you cannot stop thinking and worrying about it. ❑ *He had been unwise and it preyed on his conscience.*
VERB = *weigh*
V *on* n

**price** /praɪs/ **(prices, pricing, priced)** ◆◆◆
1 The **price** of something is the amount of money that you have to pay in order to buy it. ❑ *...a sharp increase in the price of petrol... They expected house prices to rise... Computers haven't come down in price.*
N-COUNT: usu with supp, also *in* N
2 The **price** that you pay for something that you want is an unpleasant thing that you have to do or suffer in order to get it. ❑ *Slovenia will have to pay a high price for independence.*
N-SING: usu N *for* n/-ing = *penalty*
3 If something **is priced at** a particular amount, the price is set at that amount. ❑ *The shares are expected to be priced at about 330p... Digital priced the new line at less than half the cost of comparable mainframes... There is a very reasonably priced menu.*
VERB
*be* V-ed *at* n
V n *at* n
V-ed
♦ **pric|ing** *It's hard to maintain competitive pricing.*
N-UNCOUNT
4 → See also **retail price index, selling price**.

PHRASES
5 If you want something **at any price**, you are determined to get it, even if unpleasant things happen as a result. ❑ *If they wanted a deal at any price, they would have to face the consequences.*
PHRASE: PHR after v
6 If you can buy something that you want **at a price**, it is for sale, but it is extremely expensive. ❑ *Most goods are available, but at a price.*
PHRASE: PHR with cl
7 If you get something that you want **at a price**, you get it but something unpleasant happens as a result. ❑ *Fame comes at a price.*
PHRASE: usu PHR after v
8 to **price** yourself **out of the market** → see **market**.

**price|less** /praɪsləs/
1 If you say that something is **priceless**, you are emphasizing that it is worth a very large amount of money. ❑ *...the priceless treasures of the Royal Collection.*
ADJ [emphasis]
2 If you say that something is **priceless**, you approve of it because it is extremely useful. ❑ *They are a priceless record of a brief period in British history.*
ADJ [approval]

**price point** **(price points)** The **price point** of a product is the price that it sells for. [BUSINESS] ❑ *No price point exists for the machine yet... The big companies dominate the lower price points.*
N-COUNT

**price tag** **(price tags)** also **price-tag**.
1 If something **has a price tag** of a particular amount, that is the amount that you must pay in order to buy it. [WRITTEN] ❑ *The price tag on the 34-room white Regency mansion is £17.5 million.*
N-COUNT
2 In a shop, the **price tag** on an article for sale is a small piece of card or paper which is attached to the article and which has the price written on it.
N-COUNT

**price war** **(price wars)** If competing companies are involved in a **price war**, they each try to gain an advantage by lowering their prices as much as possible in order to sell more of their products and damage their competitors financially. [BUSINESS] ❑ *A vicious price war between manufacturers has cut margins to the bone.*
N-COUNT

**pricey** /praɪsi/ **(pricier, priciest)** also **pricy**. If you say that something is **pricey**, you mean that it is expensive. [INFORMAL] ❑ *Medical insurance is very pricey.*
ADJ

**prick** /prɪk/ **(pricks, pricking, pricked)**
1 If you **prick** something or **prick** holes in it, you make small holes in it with a sharp object such as a pin. ❑ *Prick the potatoes and rub the skins with salt... He pricks holes in the foil with a pin.*
VERB
V n
V n prep

2 If something sharp **pricks** you or if you **prick yourself with** something sharp, it sticks into you or presses your skin and causes you pain. ❑ *She had just pricked her finger with the needle.* 3 If something **pricks** your **conscience**, you suddenly feel guilty about it. If you **are pricked by** an emotion, you suddenly experience that emotion. ❑ *Most were sympathetic once we pricked their consciences.* 4 A **prick** is a small, sharp pain that you get when something pricks you. ❑ *At the same time she felt a prick on her neck.* 5 A man's **prick** is his penis. [INFORMAL, ⚠ VERY RUDE]
VERB; V n; VERB; V n; N-COUNT; N-COUNT: poss N

♦ **prick up** If someone **pricks up** their **ears** or if their **ears prick up**, they listen eagerly when they suddenly hear an interesting sound or an important piece of information. ❑ *She stopped talking to prick up her ears. ...ears which prick up at the mention of royalty.*
PHRASAL VERB; V P n (not pron); V P

**prick|le** /prɪkəl/ **(prickles, prickling, prickled)** 1 If your skin **prickles**, it feels as if a lot of small sharp points are being stuck into it, either because of something touching it or because you feel a strong emotion. ❑ *He paused, feeling his scalp prickling under his hat.* ♦ **Prickle** is also a noun. ❑ *I felt a prickle of disquiet.* 2 **Prickles** are small sharp points that stick out from leaves or from the stalks of plants. ❑ *...an erect stem covered at the base with a few prickles.*
VERB; V; N-COUNT; N-COUNT: usu pl

**prick|ly** /prɪkəli/ 1 Something that is **prickly** feels rough and uncomfortable, as if it has a lot of prickles. ❑ *The bunk mattress was hard, the blankets prickly and slightly damp.* 2 Someone who is **prickly** loses their temper or gets upset very easily. ❑ *You know how prickly she is.* 3 A **prickly** issue or subject is one that is rather complicated and difficult to discuss or resolve. ❑ *The issue is likely to prove a prickly one.*
ADJ; ADJ = touchy; ADJ = thorny

**prick|ly heat** **Prickly heat** is a condition caused by very hot weather, in which your skin becomes hot, uncomfortable, and covered with tiny bumps.
N-UNCOUNT

**prick|ly pear** **(prickly pears)** A **prickly pear** is a kind of cactus that has round fruit with prickles on. The fruit, which you can eat, is also called a **prickly pear**.
N-COUNT

**pricy** /praɪsi/ → see **pricey**.

**pride** /praɪd/ **(prides, priding, prided)** ◆◇◇ 1 **Pride** is a feeling of satisfaction which you have because you or people close to you have done something good or possess something good. ❑ *...the sense of pride in a job well done... We take pride in offering you the highest standards... They can look back on their endeavours with pride.* 2 **Pride** is a sense of the respect that other people have for you, and that you have for yourself. ❑ *It was a severe blow to Kendall's pride.* 3 Someone's **pride** is the feeling that they have that they are better or more important than other people. ❑ *His pride may still be his downfall.* 4 If you **pride yourself on** a quality or skill that you have, you are very proud of it. ❑ *Smith prides himself on being able to organise his own life.*
N-UNCOUNT: oft N *in* n/ing; N-UNCOUNT = self-esteem; N-UNCOUNT disapproval = arrogance; VERB; V pron-refl *on* -ing/n

**PHRASES** 5 Someone or something that is your **pride and joy** is very important to you and makes you feel very happy. ❑ *The bike soon became his pride and joy.* 6 If something takes **pride of place**, it is treated as the most important thing in a group of things. ❑ *A three-foot-high silver World Championship cup takes pride of place near a carved wooden chair.*
PHRASE: v-link PHR; PHRASE: PHR after v

**priest** /priːst/ **(priests)** ◆◇◇ 1 A **priest** is a member of the Christian clergy in the Catholic, Anglican, or Orthodox church. ❑ *He had trained to be a Catholic priest.* 2 In many non-Christian religions a **priest** is a man who has particular duties and responsibilities in a place where people worship. 3 → See also **high priest**.
N-COUNT; N-COUNT

**priest|ess** /priːstes/ **(priestesses)** A **priestess** is a woman in a non-Christian religion who has particular duties and responsibilities in a place where people worship. → See also **high priestess**.
N-COUNT

**priest|hood** /priːsthʊd/ 1 **Priesthood** is the position of being a priest or the period of time during which someone is a priest. ❑ *He spent the first twenty-five years of his priesthood as an academic.* 2 **The priesthood** is all the members of the Christian clergy, especially in a particular Church. ❑ *Should the General Synod vote women into the priesthood?*
N-UNCOUNT; N-SING: *the* N

**priest|ly** /priːstli/ **Priestly** is used to describe things that belong or relate to a priest. ❑ *Priestly robes hang on the walls. ...his priestly duties.*
ADJ: usu ADJ n

**prig** /prɪg/ **(prigs)** If you call someone a **prig**, you disapprove of them because they behave in a very moral way and disapprove of other people's behaviour as though they are superior.
N-COUNT disapproval

**prig|gish** /prɪgɪʃ/ If you describe someone as **priggish**, you think that they are a prig.
ADJ disapproval

**prim** /prɪm/ If you describe someone as **prim**, you disapprove of them because they behave too correctly and are too easily shocked by anything rude. ❑ *We tend to imagine that the Victorians were very prim and proper.* ♦ **prim|ly** *We sat primly at either end of a long settee.*
ADJ disapproval; ADV: ADV with v

**pri|ma|cy** /praɪməsi/ **The primacy of** something is the fact that it is the most important or most powerful thing in a particular situation. [FORMAL] ❑ *The political idea at the heart of this is the primacy of the individual.*
N-UNCOUNT: oft *the* N *of* n

**pri|ma don|na** /priːmə dɒnə/ **(prima donnas)** 1 A **prima donna** is the main female singer in an opera. ❑ *Her career began as prima donna with the Royal Carl Rosa Opera Company.* 2 If you describe someone as a **prima donna**, you disapprove of them because they think they can behave badly or get what they want because they have a particular talent. ❑ *Nobody who comes to this club is allowed to behave like a prima donna.*
N-COUNT; N-COUNT disapproval

**pri|mae|val** /praɪmiːvəl/ → see **primeval**.

**pri|ma fa|cie** /praɪmə feɪʃi/ **Prima facie** is used to describe something which appears to be true when you first consider it. [FORMAL] ❑ *There was a prima facie case that a contempt of court had been committed.*
ADJ: usu ADJ n

**pri|mal** /praɪməl/ **Primal** is used to describe something that relates to the origins of things or that is very basic. [FORMAL] ❑ *Jealousy is a primal emotion.*
ADJ

**pri|mari|ly** /praɪmərɪli, AM praɪmeərɪli/ You use **primarily** to say what is mainly true in a particular situation. ❑ *...a book aimed primarily at high-energy physicists... Public order is primarily an urban problem.*
ADV: ADV with v, ADV with cl/group = chiefly

**pri|ma|ry** /praɪməri, AM -meri/ **(primaries)** ◆◇◇ 1 You use **primary** to describe something that is very important. [FORMAL] ❑ *That's the primary reason the company's share price has held up so well... His misunderstanding of language was the primary cause of his other problems.* 2 **Primary** education is given to pupils between the ages of 5 and 11. [BRIT] ❑ *Britain did not introduce compulsory primary education until 1880. ...primary teachers.*
ADJ: ADJ n = main; ADJ: ADJ n

✓ in AM, use **elementary**

3 **Primary** is used to describe something that occurs first. ❑ *It is not the primary tumour that kills, but secondary growths elsewhere in the body.* 4 A **primary** or a **primary election** is an election in an American state in which people vote for someone to become a candidate for a political office. Compare **general election**. ❑ *...the 1968 New Hampshire primary.*
ADJ: ADJ n; N-COUNT

**pri|ma|ry care** **Primary care** refers to those parts of the health service, such as general practitioners and hospital casualty departments, that deal with people who are in immediate need of medical care. ❑ *...the crucial roles of primary care and of preventive work.*
N-UNCOUNT

**pri|ma|ry col|our (primary colours)**

✔ in AM, use **primary color**

**Primary colours** are basic colours that can be mixed together to produce other colours. They are usually considered to be red, yellow, blue, and sometimes green. N-COUNT: usu pl

**pri|ma|ry school (primary schools)** A **primary school** is a school for children between the ages of 5 and 11. [mainly BRIT] ❑ *...eight-to nine-year-olds in their third year at primary school... Greenside Primary School.* N-VAR: oft in names

✔ in AM, usually use **elementary school**

**pri|mate** /praɪmeɪt/ **(primates)**

✔ The pronunciation /praɪmət/ is also used for meaning 2.

1 A **primate** is a member of the group of mammals which includes humans, monkeys, and apes. ❑ *The woolly spider monkey is the largest primate in the Americas.* N-COUNT 2 **The Primate of** a particular country or region is the most important priest in that country or region. ❑ *...the Roman Catholic Primate of All Ireland.* N-COUNT: usu *the* N *of* n

**prime** /praɪm/ **(primes, priming, primed)** ◆◇◇ 1 You use **prime** to describe something that is most important in a situation. ❑ *Political stability, meanwhile, will be a prime concern... It could be a prime target for guerrilla attack... The police will see me as the prime suspect!* ADJ: ADJ n 2 You use **prime** to describe something that is of the best possible quality. ❑ *It was one of the City's prime sites, near the Stock Exchange.* ADJ: ADJ n 3 You use **prime** to describe an example of a particular kind of thing that is absolutely typical. ❑ *The prime example is Macy's, once the undisputed king of California retailers.* ADJ: ADJ n = classic 4 If someone or something is **in** their **prime**, they are at the stage in their existence when they are at their strongest, most active, or most successful. ❑ *She was in her intellectual prime... We've had a series of athletes trying to come back well past their prime. ...young persons in the prime of life.* N-UNCOUNT: usu poss N 5 If you **prime** someone **to** do something, you prepare them to do it, for example by giving them information about it beforehand. ❑ *Claire wished she'd primed Sarah beforehand... Arnold primed her for her duties... The press corps was primed to leap to the defense of the fired officials.* VERB = brief; V n; V n *for* n; *be* V-ed to-inf 6 to **prime the pump** → see **pump**.

**Prime Min|is|ter (Prime Ministers)** The leader of the government in some countries is called **the Prime Minister**. ❑ *...the former Prime Minister of Pakistan, Miss Benazir Bhutto.* ◆◆◆ N-COUNT: usu *the* N; N-TITLE; N-VOC = PM

**prime mov|er (prime movers)** The **prime mover behind** a plan, idea, or situation is someone who has an important influence in starting it. ❑ *He was the prime mover behind the coup.* N-COUNT: usu N *behind/in* n = driving force

**prime num|ber (prime numbers)** In mathematics, a **prime number** is a whole number greater than 1 that cannot be divided exactly by any whole number except itself and the number 1, for example 17. N-COUNT

**pri|mer** /praɪməʳ/ **(primers) Primer** is a type of paint that is put onto wood in order to prepare it for the main layer of paint. N-MASS

**prime rate (prime rates)** A bank's **prime rate** is the lowest rate of interest which it charges at a particular time and which is offered only to certain customers. [BUSINESS] ❑ *At least one bank cut its prime rate today.* N-COUNT

**prime time** also **primetime. Prime time** television or radio programmes are broadcast when the greatest number of people are watching television or listening to the radio, usually in the evenings. ❑ *...a prime-time television show. ...prime time viewing in mid-evening.* N-UNCOUNT: usu N n

**pri|meval** /praɪmiːvəl/

✔ in BRIT, also use **primaeval**

1 You use **primeval** to describe things that belong to a very early period in the history of the world. [FORMAL] ❑ *...the dense primeval forests that once covered inland Brittany.* ADJ: usu ADJ n = primordial 2 You use **primeval** to describe feelings and emotions that are basic and not the result of thought. ❑ *...a primeval urge to hit out at that which causes him pain.* ADJ: usu ADJ n

**primi|tive** /prɪmɪtɪv/ 1 **Primitive** means belonging to a society in which people live in a very simple way, usually without industries or a writing system. ❑ *...studies of primitive societies.* ADJ: usu ADJ n 2 **Primitive** means belonging to a very early period in the development of an animal or plant. ❑ *...primitive whales... It is a primitive instinct to flee a place of danger.* ADJ 3 If you describe something as **primitive**, you mean that it is very simple in style or very old-fashioned. ❑ *It's using some rather primitive technology.* ADJ ≠ sophisticated

**pri|mor|dial** /praɪmɔːʳdiəl/ You use **primordial** to describe things that belong to a very early time in the history of the world. [FORMAL] ❑ *Twenty million years ago, Idaho was populated by dense primordial forest.* ADJ = primeval

**prim|rose** /prɪmroʊz/ **(primroses)** A **primrose** is a wild plant which has pale yellow flowers in the spring. N-VAR

**primu|la** /prɪmjʊlə/ **(primulas)** A **primula** is a plant that has brightly coloured flowers in the spring. N-VAR

**Pri|mus** /praɪməs/ A **Primus** or a **Primus stove** is a small cooker or stove that burns paraffin and is often used in camping. [BRIT, TRADEMARK] N-SING

**prince** /prɪns/ **(princes)** 1 A **prince** is a male member of a royal family, especially the son of the king or queen of a country. ❑ *...Prince Edward and other royal guests... The Prince won warm applause for his ideas.* ◆◆◇ N-TITLE; N-COUNT 2 A **prince** is the male royal ruler of a small country or state. ❑ *He was speaking without the prince's authority.* N-TITLE; N-COUNT

**Prince Charm|ing** A woman's **Prince Charming** is a man who seems to her to be a perfect lover or boyfriend, because he is attractive, kind, and considerate. ❑ *To begin with he was Prince Charming.* N-SING: also no det [approval]

**prince|ly** /prɪnsli/ A **princely** sum of money is a large sum of money. ❑ *It'll cost them the princely sum of seventy-five pounds.* ADJ: usu ADJ n

**prin|cess** /prɪnses, AM -səs/ **(princesses)** A **princess** is a female member of a royal family, usually the daughter of a king or queen or the wife of a prince. ❑ *Princess Anne topped the guest list. ...Caroline Lindon, Princess of Monaco.* ◆◆◇ N-TITLE; N-COUNT

**prin|ci|pal** /prɪnsɪpəl/ **(principals)** 1 **Principal** means first in order of importance. ❑ *The principal reason for my change of mind is this. ...the country's principal source of foreign exchange earnings... Their principal concern is bound to be that of winning the next general election.* ◆◇◇ ADJ: ADJ n = main, chief 2 The **principal** of a school, or in Britain the **principal** of a college, is the person in charge of the school or college. ❑ *Donald King is the principal of Dartmouth High School.* N-COUNT

**prin|ci|pal|ity** /prɪnsɪpælɪti/ **(principalities)** A **principality** is a country that is ruled by a prince. ❑ *...the tiny principality of Liechtenstein.* N-COUNT

**prin|ci|pal|ly** /prɪnsɪpəli/ **Principally** means more than anything else. ❑ *This is principally because the major export markets are slowing.* ADV: ADV with cl/group = chiefly

**prin|ci|ple** /prɪnsɪpəl/ **(principles)** 1 A **principle** is a general belief that you have about the way you should behave, which influences your behaviour. ❑ *Buck never allowed himself to be bullied into doing anything that went against his principles... It's not just a matter of principle. ...a man of principle.* ◆◆◇ N-VAR: usu poss N, adj N, prep N 2 The **principles of** a particular theory or philosophy are its basic rules or laws. ❑ *...a violation of the basic principles of Marxism.* N-COUNT: usu N *of* n, adj N 3 Scientific **principles** are general scientific laws which explain how something happens or works. ❑ *These people lack all understanding of scientific principles.* N-COUNT: usu adj N, N *of* n

PHRASES 4 If you agree with something **in principle**, you agree in general terms to the idea of it, PHRASE: usu PHR after v although you do yet know the details or know if it will be possible. ❑ *I agree with it in principle but I doubt if it will happen in practice.* 5 PHRASE If something is possible **in principle**, there is no known reason why it should not happen, even though it has not happened before. ❑ *Even assuming this to be in principle possible, it will not be achieved soon.* 6 PHRASE: usu with brd-neg, PHR after v If you refuse to do something **on principle**, you refuse to do it because of a particular belief that you have. ❑ *He would vote against it on principle.*

**prin|ci|pled** /prɪnsɪpəld/ ADJ: usu ADJ n [approval] If you describe someone as **principled**, you approve of them because they have strong moral principles. ❑ *She was a strong, principled woman.*

**print** /prɪnt/ **(prints, printing, printed)** ◆◆◇ 1 VERB If someone **prints** something such as a book or newspaper, they produce it in large quantities using a machine. ❑ V n *He started to print his own posters to distribute abroad...* be V-ed prep/adv *Our brochure is printed on environmentally-friendly paper...* V-ed *We found that television and radio gave rise to far fewer complaints than did the printed media.* ♦ PHRASAL VERB In American English, **print up** means the same as **print**. ❑ V P n (not pron) *Community workers here are printing up pamphlets for peace demonstrations...* have/get n V-ed *Hey, I know what, I'll get a bumper sticker printed up.* ♦ **print|ing** N-UNCOUNT: oft N n *His brother ran a printing and publishing company. ...stocks of paper and printing ink.* 2 VERB = publish If a newspaper or magazine **prints** a piece of writing, it includes it or publishes it. ❑ V n *We can only print letters which are accompanied by the writer's name and address.* V-ed *...a questionnaire printed in the magazine recently.* 3 VERB If numbers, letters, or designs **are printed on** a surface, they are put on it in ink or dye using a machine. You can also say that a surface **is printed with** numbers, letters, or designs. ❑ V-ed *...the number printed on the receipt...* V n on n *The company has for some time printed its phone number on its products...* be V-ed with n, be V-ed prep/adv *The shirts were printed with a paisley pattern... 'Ecu' was printed in lower case rather than capital letters.* 4 N-COUNT A **print** is a piece of clothing or material with a pattern printed on it. You can also refer to the pattern itself as a **print**. ❑ *In this living room we've mixed glorious floral prints. ...multi-coloured print jackets.* 5 VERB When you **print** a photograph, you produce it from a negative. ❑ V n onto/from n *Printing a black-and-white negative on to colour paper produces a similar monochrome effect.* 6 N-COUNT A **print** is a photograph from a film that has been developed. ❑ *...black and white prints of Margaret and Jean as children. ...35mm colour print films.* 7 N-COUNT A **print** of a cinema film is a particular copy or set of copies of it. 8 N-COUNT A **print** is one of a number of copies of a particular picture. It can be either a photograph, something such as a painting, or a picture made by an artist who puts ink on a prepared surface and presses it against paper. ❑ *...William Hogarth's famous series of prints.* 9 N-UNCOUNT **Print** is used to refer to letters and numbers as they appear on the pages of a book, newspaper, or printed document. ❑ *...columns of tiny print... Laser printers give high quality print.* 10 ADJ: ADJ n The **print** media consists of newspapers and magazines, but not television or radio. ❑ *I have been convinced that the print media are more accurate and more reliable than television.* 11 VERB If you **print** words, you write in letters that are not joined together and that look like the letters in a book or newspaper. ❑ V n *Print your name and address on a postcard and send it to us.* 12 N-COUNT You can refer to a mark left by someone's foot as a **print**. ❑ *He crawled from print to print, sniffing at the earth, following the scent left in the tracks. ...boot prints.* 13 N-COUNT: usu pl = fingerprint You can refer to invisible marks left by someone's fingers as their **prints**. ❑ *Fresh prints of both girls were found in the flat.* 14 → See also **printing**.

PHRASES 15 PHRASE: PHR after v, v-link PHR If you appear **in print**, or get **into print**, what you say or write is published in a book, newspaper, or magazine. ❑ *Many of these poets appeared in print only long after their deaths.* 16 PHRASE The **small print** or the **fine print** of something such as an advertisement or a contract consists of the technical details and legal conditions, which are often printed in much smaller letters than the rest of the text. ❑ *I'm looking at the small print; I don't want to sign anything that I shouldn't sign.*

♦ **print out** PHRASAL VERB If a computer or a machine attached to a computer **prints** something **out**, it produces a copy of it on paper. ❑ V P n (not pron) *You measure yourself, enter measurements and the computer will print out the pattern...* V n P *I shall just print this out and put it in the post.* → See also **printout**.

♦ **print up** → see **print 1**.

**print|able** /prɪntəbəl/ ADJ: usu with brd-neg If you say that someone's words or remarks are not **printable**, you mean that they are likely to offend people, and are therefore not suitable to be repeated in writing or speech. [JOURNALISM] ❑ *His team-mates opened hotel windows, shouting 'Jump!' and somewhat less printable banter.*

**print|ed cir|cuit board** **(printed circuit boards)** N-COUNT A **printed circuit board** is an electronic circuit in which some of the parts and connections consist of thin metal lines and shapes on a thin board. [TECHNICAL]

**print|ed word** N-SING: the N **The printed word** is the same as **the written word**.

**print|er** /prɪntəʳ/ **(printers)** 1 N-COUNT A **printer** is a machine that can be connected to a computer in order to make copies on paper of documents or other information held by the computer. → See also **laser printer**. 2 N-COUNT A **printer** is a person or company whose job is printing things such as books. ❑ *The manuscript had already been sent off to the printers.*

**print|ing** /prɪntɪŋ/ **(printings)** N-COUNT: oft ord N If copies of a book are printed and published on a number of different occasions, you can refer to each of these occasions as a **printing**. ❑ *The American edition of 'Cloud Street' is already in its third printing.* → See also **print**.

**print|ing press** **(printing presses)** N-COUNT A **printing press** is a machine used for printing, especially one that can print books, newspapers, or documents in large numbers.

**print|mak|ing** /prɪntmeɪkɪŋ/ N-UNCOUNT **Printmaking** is an artistic technique which consists of making a series of pictures from an original, or from a specially prepared surface.

**print|out** /prɪntaʊt/ **(printouts)** also **print-out.** N-COUNT A **printout** is a piece of paper on which information from a computer or similar device has been printed. ❑ *...a computer printout of various financial projections.*

**print run** **(print runs)** N-COUNT: usu with supp, supp N, N of n In publishing, a **print run of** something such as a book or a newspaper is the number of copies of it that are printed and published at one time. ❑ *It was launched last year in paperback with an initial print run of 7,000 copies.*

**print shop** **(print shops)** N-COUNT A **print shop** is a small business which prints and copies things such as documents and cards for customers.

**pri|or** /praɪəʳ/ ◆◇◇ 1 ADJ: ADJ n You use **prior** to indicate that something has already happened, or must happen, before another event takes place. ❑ *He claimed he had no prior knowledge of the protest... The Constitution requires the president to seek the prior approval of Congress for military action.* 2 ADJ: ADJ n A **prior** claim or duty is more important than other claims or duties and needs to be dealt with first. ❑ *The firm I wanted to use had prior commitments.* 3 N-COUNT; N-TITLE A **prior** is a monk who is in charge of a priory or a monk who is the second most important person in a monastery. 4 PREP-PHRASE If something happens **prior to** a particular time or event, it happens before that time or event. [FORMAL] ❑ *Prior to his Japan trip, he went to New York.*

**pri|or|ess** /praɪəres/ **(prioresses)** N-COUNT; N-TITLE A **prioress** is a nun who is in charge of a convent.

**pri|ori|tize** /praɪɒrɪtaɪz, AM -ɔːr-/ **(prioritizes, prioritizing, prioritized)**

in BRIT, also use **prioritise**

[1] If you **prioritize** something, you treat it as more important than other things. ❑ *The government is prioritising the service sector, rather than investing in industry and production.* VERB V n [2] If you **prioritize** the tasks that you have to do, you decide which are the most important and do them first. ❑ *Make lists of what to do and prioritize your tasks.* VERB V n

**pri|or|ity** /praɪɒrɪti, AM -ɔːr-/ **(priorities)** ◆◇◇ [1] If something is a **priority**, it is the most important thing you have to do or deal with, or must be done or dealt with before everything else you have to do. ❑ *Being a parent is her first priority... The government's priority is to build more power plants.* N-COUNT

PHRASES [2] If you **give priority to** something or someone, you treat them as more important than anything or anyone else. ❑ *The school will give priority to science, maths and modern languages.* PHRASE: V inflects, usu PHR *to* n [3] If something **takes priority** or **has priority over** other things, it is regarded as being more important than them and is dealt with first. ❑ *The fight against inflation took priority over measures to combat the deepening recession.* PHRASE: V inflects, usu PHR *over* n

**pri|ory** /praɪəri/ **(priories)** A **priory** is a place where a small group of monks live and work together. N-COUNT: oft in names after n

**prise** /praɪz/ → see **prize**.

**prism** /prɪzəm/ **(prisms)** A **prism** is a block of clear glass or plastic which separates the light passing through it into different colours. N-COUNT

**pris|on** /prɪzən/ **(prisons)** ◆◆◇ A **prison** is a building where criminals are kept as punishment or where people accused of a crime are kept before their trial. ❑ *The prison's inmates are being kept in their cells... He was sentenced to life in prison.* N-VAR: oft in names after n = *jail*

**pris|on camp** **(prison camps)** [1] A **prison camp** is a guarded camp where prisoners of war or political prisoners are kept. ❑ *He was shot down over Denmark and spent three years in a prison camp.* N-COUNT [2] A **prison camp** is a prison where the prisoners are not considered dangerous and are allowed to work outside the prison. [AM] N-COUNT

**pris|on|er** /prɪzənəʳ/ **(prisoners)** ◆◆◇ [1] A **prisoner** is a person who is kept in a prison as a punishment for a crime that they have committed. ❑ *The committee is concerned about the large number of prisoners sharing cells.* N-COUNT = *inmate* [2] A **prisoner** is a person who has been captured by an enemy, for example in war. ❑ *...wartime hostages and concentration-camp prisoners... He was taken prisoner in North Africa in 1942.* N-COUNT: also *hold/take* n N [3] If you say that you are a **prisoner of** a situation, you mean that your are trapped by it. ❑ *We are all prisoners of our childhood and feel an obligation to it.* N-COUNT: N *of* n

**pris|on|er of con|science** **(prisoners of conscience)** **Prisoners of conscience** are people who have been put into prison for their political or social beliefs or for breaking the law while protesting against a political or social system. N-COUNT = *political prisoner*

**pris|on|er of war** **(prisoners of war)** **Prisoners of war** are soldiers who have been captured by their enemy during a war and kept as prisoners until the end of the war. N-COUNT = *POW*

**pris|sy** /prɪsi/ **(prissier, prissiest)** If you say that someone is **prissy**, you are critical of them because they are very easily shocked by anything rude or bad. [INFORMAL] ❑ *I dislike the people from my background – they are uptight and prissy.* ADJ [disapproval] = *prim*

**pris|tine** /prɪstiːn/ **Pristine** things are extremely clean or new. [FORMAL] ❑ *Now the house is in pristine condition.* ADJ: usu ADJ n = *immaculate*

**pri|va|cy** /prɪvəsi, AM praɪ-/ [1] If you have **privacy**, you are in a place or situation which allows you to do things without other people seeing you or disturbing you. ❑ *He saw the publication of this book as an embarrassing invasion of his privacy. ...a collection of over 60 designs to try on in the privacy of your own home.* N-UNCOUNT: oft poss N [2] If someone or something **invades** your **privacy**, they interfere in your life without your permission. ❑ *The press invade people's privacy unjustifiably every day.* PHRASE: V inflects

**pri|vate** /praɪvɪt/ **(privates)** ◆◆◇ [1] **Private** industries and services are owned or controlled by an individual person or a commercial company, rather than by the state or an official organization. [BUSINESS] ❑ *Bupa runs private hospitals in Britain... Brazil says its constitution forbids the private ownership of energy assets.* ADJ: usu ADJ n ♦ **pri|vate|ly** *No other European country had so few privately owned businesses... She was privately educated at schools in Ireland and Paris.* ADV: ADV with v [2] **Private** individuals are acting only for themselves, and are not representing any group, company, or organization. ❑ *...the law's insistence that private citizens are not permitted to have weapons... The King was on a private visit to enable him to pray at the tombs of his ancestors.* ADJ: ADJ n [3] Your **private** things belong only to you, or may only be used by you. ❑ *There are 76 individually furnished bedrooms, all with private bathrooms.* ADJ: usu ADJ n [4] **Private** places or gatherings may be attended only by a particular group of people, rather than by the general public. ❑ *673 private golf clubs took part in a recent study... The door is marked 'Private'.* ADJ: usu ADJ n ≠ *public* [5] **Private** meetings, discussions, and other activities involve only a small number of people, and very little information about them is given to other people. ❑ *Don't bug private conversations, and don't buy papers that reprint them.* ADJ: usu ADJ n ♦ **pri|vate|ly** *Few senior figures have issued any public statements but privately the resignation's been welcomed.* ADV: usu ADV with cl, also ADV after v [6] Your **private life** is that part of your life that is concerned with your personal relationships and activities, rather than with your work or business. ❑ *I've always kept my private and professional life separate.* ADJ: usu ADJ n = *personal* [7] Your **private** thoughts or feelings are ones that you do not talk about to other people. ❑ *We all felt as if we were intruding on his private grief.* ADJ: usu ADJ n ♦ **pri|vate|ly** *Privately, she worries about whether she's really good enough.* ADV: ADV with cl, ADV with v [8] You can use **private** to describe situations or activities that are understood only by the people involved in them, and not by anyone else. ❑ *Chinese waiters stood in a cluster, sharing a private joke.* ADJ: ADJ n [9] If you describe a place as **private**, or as somewhere where you can be **private**, you mean that it is a quiet place and you can be alone there without being disturbed. ❑ *It was the only reasonably private place they could find.* ADJ [10] If you describe someone as a **private** person, you mean that they are very quiet by nature and do not reveal their thoughts and feelings to other people. ❑ *Gould was an intensely private individual.* ADJ: usu ADJ n [11] You can use **private** to describe lessons that are not part of ordinary school activity, and which are given by a teacher to an individual pupil or a small group, usually in return for payment. ❑ *Martial arts: Private lessons: £8 per hour. ...Donald Tovey, who took her as his private pupil for the piano.* ADJ: usu ADJ n [12] A **private** is a soldier of the lowest rank in an army or the marines. N-COUNT; N-TITLE [13] → See also **privately**. [14] If you do something **in private**, you do it without other people being present, often because it is something that you want to keep secret. ❑ *Some of what we're talking about might better be discussed in private.* PHRASE: usu PHR after v

**pri|vate de|tec|tive** **(private detectives)** A **private detective** is someone who you can pay to find missing people or do other kinds of investigation for you. N-COUNT = *private investigator*

**pri|vate en|ter|prise** **Private enterprise** is industry and business which is owned by individual people or commercial companies, and not by the government or an official organization. [BUSINESS] ❑ *...the government's plans to sell state companies to private enterprise.* N-UNCOUNT

**pri|vate eye** **(private eyes)** You can refer to a private detective as a **private eye**, especially when he or she is a character in a film or story. [INFORMAL] N-COUNT

**pri|vate in|ves|ti|ga|tor** **(private investigators)** A **private investigator** is the same as a **private detective**. N-COUNT

**pri|vate|ly** /praɪvɪtli/ If you buy or sell something **privately**, you buy it from or sell it to another person directly, rather than in a shop or through a business. ❑ *The whole process makes buying a car privately as painless as buying from a garage... A great deal of food is distributed and sold privately without ever reaching the shops.* → See also **private**. ADV: ADV after v

**Pri|vate Mem|ber's Bill** **(Private Members' Bills)** In Britain, a **Private Member's Bill** is a law that is proposed by a Member of Parliament acting as an individual rather than as a member of his or her political party. N-COUNT

**pri|vate parts** Your **private parts** are your genitals. [INFORMAL] N-PLURAL: usu poss N = privates

**pri|vate school** **(private schools)** A **private school** is a school which is not supported financially by the government and which parents have to pay for their children to go to. ❑ *He attended Eton, the most exclusive private school in Britain.* N-VAR ≠ state school

**pri|vate sec|tor** **The private sector** is the part of a country's economy which consists of industries and commercial companies that are not owned or controlled by the government. [BUSINESS] ❑ *...small firms in the private sector.* N-SING: the N, N n ≠ public sector

**pri|vate sol|dier** **(private soldiers)** A **private soldier** is a soldier of the lowest rank in an army or the marines. [FORMAL] N-COUNT = private

**pri|va|tion** /praɪveɪʃən/ **(privations)** If you suffer **privation** or **privations**, you have to live without many of the things that are thought to be necessary in life, such as food, clothing, or comfort. [FORMAL] ❑ *They endured five years of privation during the second world war... The privations of monastery life were evident in his appearance.* N-UNCOUNT: also N in pl = hardship

**pri|vat|ize** /praɪvətaɪz/ **(privatizes, privatizing, privatized)** ◆◇◇

✓ in BRIT, also use **privatise**

If a company, industry, or service that is owned by the state **is privatized**, the government sells it and makes it a private company. [BUSINESS] ❑ *The water boards are about to be privatized. ...a pledge to privatise the rail and coal industries. ...the newly privatized FM radio stations.* ♦ **pri|vati|za|tion** /praɪvətaɪzeɪʃən/ **(privatizations)** *...the privatisation of British Rail. ...fresh rules governing the conduct of future privatizations.* VERB ≠ nationalize; be V-ed; V n; V-ed; N-VAR: oft N of n ≠ nationalization

**priv|et** /prɪvɪt/ **Privet** is a type of bush with small leaves that stay green all year round. It is often grown in gardens to form hedges. ❑ *The garden was enclosed by a privet hedge.* N-UNCOUNT

**privi|lege** /prɪvɪlɪdʒ/ **(privileges, privileging, privileged)** [1] A **privilege** is a special right or advantage that only one person or group has. ❑ *The Russian Federation has issued a decree abolishing special privileges for government officials.* [2] If you talk about **privilege**, you are talking about the power and advantage that only a small group of people have, usually because of their wealth or their high social class. ❑ *Pironi was the son of privilege and wealth, and it showed.* [3] You can use **privilege** in expressions such as **be a privilege** or **have the privilege** when you want to show your appreciation of someone or something or to show your respect. ❑ *It must be a privilege to know such a man.* [4] To **privilege** someone or something means to treat them better or differently than other people or things rather than treat them all equally. ❑ *They are privileging a tiny number to the disadvantage of the rest.* N-COUNT; N-UNCOUNT; N-SING; VERB = favour; V n

**privi|leged** /prɪvɪlɪdʒd/ [1] Someone who is **privileged** has an advantage or opportunity that most other people do not have, often because of their wealth or high social class. ❑ *They were, by and large, a very wealthy, privileged elite. ...I felt very privileged to work at the university.* ♦ **The privileged** are people who are privileged. ❑ *They are only interested in preserving the power of the privileged.* [2] **Privileged** information is known by only a small group of people, who are not legally required to give it to anyone else. ❑ *The data is privileged information, not to be shared with the general public.* ADJ; N-PLURAL: the N; ADJ: usu ADJ n = confidential

**privy** /prɪvi/ If you are **privy to** something secret, you have been allowed to know about it. [FORMAL] ❑ *Only three people, including a policeman, will be privy to the facts.* ADJ: v-link ADJ to n

**Privy Coun|cil** In Britain, **the Privy Council** is a group of people who are appointed to advise the king or queen on political affairs. N-PROPER: the N

**prize** /praɪz/ **(prizes, prizing, prized)** ◆◆◇

✓ The spelling **prise** is also used in British English for meanings 5 and 6.

[1] A **prize** is money or something valuable that is given to someone who has the best results in a competition or game, or as a reward for doing good work. ❑ *You must claim your prize by telephoning our claims line... He won first prize at the Leeds Piano Competition... They were going all out for the prize-money, £6,500 for the winning team.* [2] You use **prize** to describe things that are of such good quality that they win prizes or deserve to win prizes. ❑ *...a prize bull. ...prize blooms.* [3] You can refer to someone or something as a **prize** when people consider them to be of great value or importance. ❑ *With no lands of his own, he was no great matrimonial prize.* [4] Something that **is prized** is wanted and admired because it is considered to be very valuable or very good quality. ❑ *Military figures, made out of lead are prized by collectors... One of the gallery's most prized possessions is the portrait of Ginevra da Vinci.* [5] If you **prize** something open or **prize** it away from a surface, you force it to open or force it to come away from the surface. [mainly BRIT] ❑ *He tried to prize the dog's mouth open... I prised off the metal rim surrounding one of the dials... He held on tight but she prised it from his fingers.* N-COUNT; ADJ: ADJ n; N-COUNT; VERB: usu passive; be V-ed; V-ed; VERB; V n with adj; V n with adv; V n out of/from n

✓ in AM, usually use **pry**

[6] If you **prize** something such as information **out of** someone, you persuade them to tell you although they may be very unwilling to. [mainly BRIT] ❑ *Alison and I had to prize conversation out of him.* VERB; V n out of n; Also V n with out

✓ in AM, usually use **pry**

**prize fight** **(prize fights)** also **prizefight.** A **prize fight** is a boxing match where the boxers are paid to fight, especially one that is not official. N-COUNT

**prize fight|er** **(prize fighters)** also **prizefighter.** A **prize fighter** is a boxer who fights to win money. N-COUNT

**prize-giving** **(prize-givings)** also **prizegiving.** A **prize-giving** is a ceremony where prizes are awarded to people who have produced a very high standard of work. [BRIT] ❑ *Neil had been at a prize giving ceremony at a school in Birmingham. ...a prize-giving for cattle-breeding.* N-COUNT

**pro** /proʊ/ **(pros)** [1] A **pro** is a professional. [INFORMAL] ❑ *I have enjoyed playing with some of the top pros from Europe and America.* [2] A **pro** player is a professional sportsman or woman. You can also use **pro** to refer to sports that are played by professional sportsmen or women. [AM] ❑ *...a former college and pro basketball player.* [3] If you are **pro** a particular course of action or belief, you agree with it or support it. [mainly BRIT] ❑ *I'm one of the few that's very pro performance-related pay.* [4] The **pros and cons** of something are its advantages and disadvantages, which you consider carefully so that you can make a sensible decision. ❑ *Motherhood has both its pros and cons.* N-COUNT ≠ amateur; ADJ: ADJ n; PREP = for ≠ anti; PHRASE: PHR after v, oft PHR of -ing/n

**pro-** /proʊ-/ You can add **pro-** to adjectives and nouns in order to form adjectives that describe people who support or admire a particular person, system, or idea. ❑ *He was at the forefront of* PREFIX the pro-democracy campaign in the country... Younger voters are strongly pro-European.

**pro|ac|tive** /proʊæktɪv/ **Proactive** actions are intended to cause changes, rather than just reacting to change. ❑ *In order to survive the competition a company should be proactive not reactive.* ADJ

**pro-am** **(pro-ams)** also **pro am.** A **pro-am** is a sports competition in which professional and amateur players compete together. ❑ *...a sponsored pro-am golf tournament.* N-COUNT: oft N n

**prob|abil|is|tic** /prɒbəbɪlɪstɪk/ **Probabilistic** actions, methods, or arguments are based on the idea that you cannot be certain about results or future events but you can judge whether or not they are likely, and act on the basis of this judgment. [FORMAL] ❑ *...probabilistic exposure to risk.* ADJ: usu ADJ n

**prob|abil|ity** /prɒbəbɪlɪti/ **(probabilities)** 1 The **probability of** something happening is how likely it is to happen, sometimes expressed as a fraction or a percentage. ❑ *Without a transfusion, the victim's probability of dying was 100%... The probabilities of crime or victimization are higher with some situations than with others.* N-VAR 2 You say that there is a **probability** that something will happen when it is likely to happen. ❑ *If you've owned property for several years, the probability is that values have increased... His story-telling can push the bounds of probability a bit far at times.* N-VAR vagueness 3 If you say that something will happen **in all probability**, you mean that you think it is very likely to happen. ❑ *The Republicans had better get used to the fact that in all probability, they are going to lose.* PHRASE: PHR with cl vagueness

**prob|able** /prɒbəbᵊl/ 1 If you say that something is **probable**, you mean that it is likely to be true or likely to happen. ❑ *It is probable that the medication will suppress the symptom without treating the condition... An airline official said a bomb was the incident's most probable cause.* ADJ: oft *it* v-link ADJ that vagueness = likely ≠ unlikely 2 You can use **probable** to describe a role or function that someone or something is likely to have. ❑ *The Socialists united behind their probable presidential candidate, Michel Rocard.* ADJ: ADJ n = likely

**prob|ably** /prɒbəbli/ 1 If you say that something is **probably** the case, you think that it is likely to be the case, although you are not sure. ❑ *The White House probably won't make this plan public until July... Van Gogh is probably the best-known painter in the world.* ◆◆◆ ADV: ADV with cl/group vagueness 2 You can use **probably** when you want to make your opinion sound less forceful or definite, so that you do not offend people. ❑ *He probably thinks you're both crazy!* ADV: ADV with cl/group vagueness

**pro|bate** /proʊbeɪt/ **Probate** is the act or process of officially proving a will to be valid. ❑ *Probate cases can go on for two years or more.* N-UNCOUNT: oft N n

**pro|ba|tion** /prəbeɪʃᵊn, AM proʊ-/ 1 **Probation** is a period of time during which a person who has committed a crime has to obey the law and be supervised by a probation officer, rather than being sent to prison. ❑ *The thief was put on probation for two years.* N-UNCOUNT 2 **Probation** is a period of time during which someone is judging your character and ability while you work, in order to see if you are suitable for that type of work. ❑ *Employee appointment to the Council will be subject to a term of probation of 6 months.* N-UNCOUNT

**pro|ba|tion|ary** /prəbeɪʃənəri, AM proʊbeɪʃəneri/ A **probationary** period is a period after someone starts a job, during which their employer can decide whether the person is suitable and should be allowed to continue. [BUSINESS] ❑ *Teachers should have a probationary period of two years.* ADJ: ADJ n = trial

**pro|ba|tion|er** /prəbeɪʃənəʳ, proʊ-/ **(probationers)** 1 A **probationer** is someone who has been found guilty of committing a crime but is on probation rather than in prison. N-COUNT 2 A **probationer** is someone who is still being trained to do a job and is on trial. ❑ *...a probationer policeman.* N-COUNT

**pro|ba|tion of|fic|er** **(probation officers)** A **probation officer** is a person whose job is to supervise and help people who have committed crimes and been put on probation. N-COUNT

**probe** /proʊb/ **(probes, probing, probed)** 1 If you **probe into** something, you ask questions or try to discover facts about it. ❑ *The more they probed into his background, the more inflamed their suspicions would become... For three years, I have probed for understanding... The Office of Fair Trading has been probing banking practices... The form asks probing questions.* VERB V into n V for n V n V-ing ♦ **Probe** is also a noun. ❑ *...a federal grand-jury probe into corruption within the FDA.* N-COUNT ♦ **prob|ing** **(probings)** *If he remains here, he'll be away from the press and their probings.* N-COUNT 2 If a doctor or dentist **probes**, he or she uses a long instrument to examine part of a patient's body. ❑ *The surgeon would pick up his instruments, probe, repair and stitch up again... Dr Amid probed around the sensitive area.* VERB V V prep/adv 3 A **probe** is a long thin instrument that doctors and dentists use to examine parts of the body. ❑ *...a fibre-optic probe.* N-COUNT 4 If you **probe** a place, you search it in order to find someone or something that you are looking for. ❑ *A flashlight beam probed the underbrush only yards away from their hiding place... I probed around for some time in the bushes.* VERB V n V adv/prep 5 In a conflict such as a war, if one side **probes** another side's defences, they try to find their weaknesses, for example by attacking them in specific areas using a small number of troops. [JOURNALISM] ❑ *He probes the enemy's weak positions, ignoring his strongholds.* VERB V n ♦ **Probe** is also a noun. ❑ *Small probes would give the allied armies some combat experience before the main battle started.* N-COUNT 6 A **space probe** is a spacecraft which travels into space with no people in it, usually in order to study the planets and send information about them back to earth. N-COUNT: usu n N

**pro|bity** /proʊbɪti/ **Probity** is a high standard of correct moral behaviour. [FORMAL] ❑ *He asserted his innocence and his financial probity.* N-UNCOUNT

**prob|lem** /prɒbləm/ **(problems)** 1 A **problem** is a situation that is unsatisfactory and causes difficulties for people. ❑ *...the economic problems of the inner city... The main problem is unemployment... He told Americans that solving the energy problem was very important.* ◆◆◆ N-COUNT: usu with supp, oft N *of/with* n 2 A **problem** is a puzzle that requires logical thought or mathematics to solve it. ❑ *With mathematical problems, you can save time by approximating.* N-COUNT 3 **Problem** children or **problem** families have serious problems or cause serious problems for other people. ❑ *In some cases a problem child is placed in a special school.* ADJ: ADJ n = difficult

**prob|lem|at|ic** /prɒbləmætɪk/ Something that is **problematic** involves problems and difficulties. ❑ *Some places are more problematic than others for women traveling alone.* ADJ

**prob|lem|ati|cal** /prɒbləmætɪkᵊl/ **Problematical** means the same as **problematic**. [FORMAL] ADJ

**pro|cedur|al** /prəsiːdʒərəl/ **Procedural** means involving a formal procedure. [FORMAL] ❑ *A Spanish judge rejected the suit on procedural grounds.* ADJ: usu ADJ n

**pro|cedure** /prəsiːdʒəʳ/ **(procedures)** A **procedure** is a way of doing something, especially the usual or correct way. ❑ *A biopsy is usually a minor surgical procedure... Police insist that Michael did not follow the correct procedure in applying for a visa.* ◆◇◇ N-VAR

**pro|ceed** **(proceeds, proceeding, proceeded)** ◆◇◇

> ✓ The verb is pronounced /prəsiːd/. The plural noun in meaning 5 is pronounced /proʊsiːdz/.

1 If you **proceed to** do something, you do it, often after doing something else first. ❑ *He proceeded to tell me of my birth.* VERB V to-inf 2 If you **proceed with** a course of action, you continue with it. [FORMAL] ❑ *The group proceeded with a march they knew would lead to bloodshed... The trial has been delayed until November because the defence is not ready to proceed.* VERB V with n V 3 If an activity, process, or event **proceeds**, it goes on and does not stop. ❑ *The ideas were not new. Their development had proceeded* VERB V

*steadily since the war.* [4] If you **proceed** in a particular direction, you go in that direction. [FORMAL] ❑ *She climbed the steps and proceeded along the upstairs hallway... The freighter was allowed to proceed after satisfying them that it was not breaking sanctions.* [5] **The proceeds** of an event or activity are the money that has been obtained from it.

VERB = continue; V prep/adv; V; N-PLURAL: the N, oft the N of/from n

**pro|ceed|ing** /prəsiːdɪŋ/ **(proceedings)** [1] Legal **proceedings** are legal action taken against someone. [FORMAL] ❑ *...criminal proceedings against the former prime minister... The Council had brought proceedings to stop the store from trading on Sundays.* [2] **The proceedings** are an organized series of events that take place in a particular place. [FORMAL] ❑ *The proceedings of the enquiry will take place in private.* [3] You can refer to a written record of the discussions at a meeting or conference as **the proceedings**. ❑ *The Department of Transport is to publish the conference proceedings.*

N-COUNT: usu pl; N-COUNT: usu pl, usu the N; N-PLURAL: the N

**pro|cess** /proʊses, AM prɑːses/ **(processes, processing, processed)** ◆◆◆ [1] A **process** is a series of actions which are carried out in order to achieve a particular result. ❑ *There was total agreement to start the peace process as soon as possible... The best way to proceed is by a process of elimination.* [2] A **process** is a series of things which happen naturally and result in a biological or chemical change. ❑ *It occurs in elderly men, apparently as part of the ageing process.* [3] When raw materials or foods **are processed**, they are prepared in factories before they are used or sold. ❑ *...fish which are processed by freezing, canning or smoking... The material will be processed into plastic pellets. ...diets high in refined and processed foods.* ♦ **Process** is also a noun. ❑ *...the cost of re-engineering the production process.* ♦ **pro|cess|ing** *America sent cotton to England for processing.* [4] When people **process** information, they put it through a system or into a computer in order to deal with it. ❑ *...facilities to process the data, and the right to publish the results.* ♦ **pro|cess|ing** *...data processing.* ➔ See also **word processing**. [5] When people **are processed** by officials, their case is dealt with in stages and they pass from one stage of the process to the next. ❑ *Patients took more than two hours to be processed through the department.*

N-COUNT: oft supp N, N of n; N-COUNT; VERB; be V-ed; be V-ed into n; V-ed; N-COUNT; N-UNCOUNT: usu with supp; VERB; V n; N-UNCOUNT: supp N; VERB: usu passive; be V-ed

PHRASES [6] If you are **in the process of** doing something, you have started to do it and are still doing it. ❑ *The administration is in the process of drawing up a peace plan.* [7] If you are doing something and you do something else **in the process**, you do the second thing as part of doing the first thing. ❑ *You have to let us struggle for ourselves, even if we must die in the process.*

PHRASE: V inflects, usu v-link PHR; PHRASE: PHR with cl

**pro|cessed cheese** **(processed cheeses)** **Processed cheese** is cheese that has been specially made so that it can be sold and stored in large quantities. It is sometimes sold in the form of single wrapped slices.

N-MASS

**pro|ces|sion** /prəseʃᵊn/ **(processions)** A **procession** is a group of people who are walking, riding, or driving in a line as part of a public event. ❑ *...a funeral procession. ...religious processions.*

N-COUNT

**pro|ces|sion|al** /prəseʃənᵊl/ **Processional** means used for or taking part in a ceremonial procession. ❑ *...the processional route.*

ADJ: ADJ n

**pro|ces|sor** /proʊsesəʳ, AM prɑːs-/ **(processors)** [1] A **processor** is the part of a computer that interprets commands and performs the processes the user has requested. [COMPUTING] ➔ See also **word processor**. [2] A **processor** is someone or something which carries out a process. ❑ *...food growers and processors.*

N-COUNT = CPU; N-COUNT

**pro-choice** also **prochoice**. Someone who is **pro-choice** thinks that women have a right to choose whether or not to give birth to a child they have conceived, and to have an abortion if they do not want the child. ❑ *...the pro-choice movement... most of the electorate is pro-choice.*

ADJ ≠ pro-life

**pro|claim** /proʊkleɪm/ **(proclaims, proclaiming, proclaimed)** [1] If people **proclaim** something, they formally make it known to the public. ❑ *The Boers rebelled against British rule, proclaiming their independence on 30 December 1880... Britain proudly proclaims that it is a nation of animal lovers... He still proclaims himself a believer in the Revolution.* [2] If you **proclaim** something, you state it in an emphatic way. ❑ *'I think we have been heard today,' he proclaimed... He confidently proclaims that he is offering the best value in the market.*

VERB = declare; V n; V that; V pron-refl n; VERB; V with quote; V that

**proc|la|ma|tion** /prɒkləmeɪʃᵊn/ **(proclamations)** A **proclamation** is a public announcement about something important, often about something of national importance. ❑ *...a proclamation of independence.*

N-COUNT: oft N of n = declaration

**pro|cliv|ity** /prəklɪvɪti, AM proʊ-/ **(proclivities)** A **proclivity** is a tendency to behave in a particular way or to like a particular thing, often a bad way or thing. [FORMAL] ❑ *He was indulging his own sexual proclivities. ...a proclivity to daydream.*

N-COUNT

**pro|cras|ti|nate** /proʊkræstɪneɪt/ **(procrastinates, procrastinating, procrastinated)** If you **procrastinate**, you keep leaving things you should do until later, often because you do not want to do them. [FORMAL] ❑ *Most often we procrastinate when faced with something we do not want to do.* ♦ **pro|cras|ti|na|tion** /proʊkræstɪneɪʃᵊn/ *He hates delay and procrastination in all its forms.*

VERB; V; N-UNCOUNT

**pro|cre|ate** /proʊkrieɪt/ **(procreates, procreating, procreated)** When animals or people **procreate**, they produce young or babies. [FORMAL] ❑ *Most young women feel a biological need to procreate.* ♦ **pro|crea|tion** /proʊkrieɪʃᵊn/ *Early marriage and procreation are no longer discouraged there.*

VERB = reproduce; V; N-UNCOUNT = reproduction

**procu|ra|tor** /prɒkjʊreɪtəʳ/ **(procurators)** A **procurator** is an administrative official with legal powers, especially in the former Soviet Union, the Roman Catholic Church, or the ancient Roman Empire.

N-COUNT

**procu|ra|tor fis|cal** **(procurators fiscal)** In the Scottish legal system, **the procurator fiscal** is a public official who puts people on trial.

N-COUNT: usu the N

**pro|cure** /prəkjʊəʳ/ **(procures, procuring, procured)** [1] If you **procure** something, especially something that is difficult to get, you obtain it. [FORMAL] ❑ *It remained very difficult to procure food, fuel and other daily necessities.* [2] If someone **procures** a prostitute, they introduce the prostitute to a client. ❑ *He procured girls of 16 and 17 to be mistresses for his influential friends.*

VERB; V n; VERB; V n

**pro|cure|ment** /prəkjʊəʳmənt/ **Procurement** is the act of obtaining something such as supplies for an army or other organization. [FORMAL] ❑ *Russia was cutting procurement of new weapons 'by about 80 per cent', he said.*

N-UNCOUNT = acquisition

**prod** /prɒd/ **(prods, prodding, prodded)** [1] If you **prod** someone or something, you give them a quick push with your finger or with a pointed object. ❑ *He prodded Murray with the shotgun... Prod the windowsills to check for signs of rot... Cathy was prodding at a boiled egg.* ♦ **Prod** is also a noun. ❑ *He gave the donkey a mighty prod in the backside.* [2] If you **prod** someone **into** doing something, you remind or persuade them to do it. ❑ *The report should prod the Government into spending more on the Health Service... His remark prodded her to ask where Mora had gone.* [3] ➔ See also **cattle prod**.

VERB = poke; V n with n; V n; V at n; N-COUNT = poke; VERB; V n into n/-ing; V n to-inf

**prodi|gal** /prɒdɪgᵊl/ **(prodigals)** [1] You can describe someone as a **prodigal** son or daughter if they leave their family or friends, often after a period of behaving badly, and then return at a later time as a better person. [LITERARY] ♦ **Prodigal** is also a noun. ❑ *...the prodigal had returned.* [2] Someone who behaves in a **prodigal** way spends a lot of money carelessly without thinking about what will happen when they have none left. ❑ *Prodigal habits die hard.*

ADJ: usu ADJ n; N-COUNT; ADJ: usu ADJ n

**pro|di|gious** /prədɪdʒəs/ Something that is **prodigious** is very large or impressive. [LITERARY] ❑ *This business generates cash in prodigious amounts.* ♦ **pro|di|gious|ly** *She ate prodigiously.*

ADJ: usu ADJ n; ADV

**prodi|gy** /prɒdɪdʒi/ **(prodigies)** A **prodigy** is someone young who has a great natural ability for something such as music, mathematics, or sport. ❑ *...a Russian tennis prodigy.* N-COUNT: usu supp N

**pro|duce (produces, producing, produced)** ◆◆◆

> ✓ The verb is pronounced /prədjuːs, AM -duːs/. The noun is pronounced /prɒdjuːs, AM -duːs/ and is hyphenated prod|uce.

1 To **produce** something means to cause it to happen. VERB ❑ *The drug is known to produce side-effects in women...* V n *Talks aimed at producing a new world trade treaty have been under way for six years.* V n 2 If you **produce** something, you make or create it. VERB ❑ *The company produced circuitry for communications systems.* V n 3 When things or people **produce** something, it comes from them or slowly forms from them, especially as the result of a biological or chemical process. VERB ❑ *These plants are then pollinated and allowed to mature and produce seed.* V n *...gases produced by burning coal and oil.* V-ed 4 If you **produce** evidence or an argument, you show it or explain it to people in order to make them agree with you. VERB ❑ *They challenged him to produce evidence to support his allegations.* V n 5 If you **produce** an object from somewhere, you show it or bring it out so that it can be seen. VERB ❑ *To hire a car you must produce a passport and a current driving licence.* V n 6 If someone **produces** something such as a film, a magazine, or a CD, they organize it and decide how it should be done. VERB ❑ *He has produced his own sports magazine called Yes Sport.* V n 7 **Produce** is food or other things that are grown in large quantities to be sold. N-UNCOUNT ❑ *We manage to get most of our produce in Britain.*

**pro|duc|er** /prədjuːsəʳ, AM -duːs-/ **(producers)** ◆◆◇ 1 A **producer** is a person whose job is to produce plays, films, programmes, or CDs. N-COUNT ❑ *Vanya Kewley is a freelance film producer.* 2 A **producer** of a food or material is a company or country that grows or manufactures a large amount of it. N-COUNT ❑ *...Saudi Arabia, the world's leading oil producer.*

**prod|uct** /prɒdʌkt/ **(products)** ◆◆◆ 1 A **product** is something that is produced and sold in large quantities, often as a result of a manufacturing process. N-COUNT ❑ *Try to get the best product at the lowest price... South Korea's imports of consumer products jumped 33% in this year.* 2 If you say that someone or something is a **product of** a situation or process, you mean that the situation or process has had a significant effect in making them what they are. N-COUNT: N *of* n ❑ *We are all products of our time... The bank is the product of a 1971 merger of two Japanese banks.*

**pro|duc|tion** /prədʌkʃᵊn/ **(productions)** ◆◆◇ 1 **Production** is the process of manufacturing or growing something in large quantities. N-UNCOUNT: oft *into* N ❑ *That model won't go into production before late 1990. ...tax incentives to encourage domestic production of oil.* 2 **Production** is the amount of goods manufactured or grown by a company or country. N-UNCOUNT = output ❑ *We needed to increase the volume of production.* 3 The **production of** something is its creation as the result of a natural process. N-UNCOUNT: oft N *of* n ❑ *These proteins stimulate the production of blood cells.* 4 **Production** is the process of organizing and preparing a play, film, programme, or CD, in order to present it to the public. N-UNCOUNT: usu with supp ❑ *She is head of the production company.* 5 A **production** is a play, opera, or other show that is performed in a theatre. N-COUNT ❑ *...a critically acclaimed production of Othello.* 6 When you can do something **on production of** or **on the production of** documents, you need to show someone those documents in order to be able to do that thing. PHRASE: PHR n ❑ *Entry to the show is free to members on production of their membership cards.*

**pro|duc|tion line (production lines)** A **production line** is an arrangement of machines in a factory where the products pass from machine to machine until they are finished. N-COUNT

**pro|duc|tive** /prədʌktɪv/ 1 Someone or something that is **productive** produces or does a lot for the amount of resources used. ADJ ❑ *Training makes workers highly productive. ...fertile and productive soils.* ♦ **pro|duc|tive|ly** *The company is certain to reinvest its profits productively.* ADV: ADV with v 2 If you say that a relationship between people is **productive**, you mean that a lot of good or useful things happen as a result of it. ADJ = fruitful ❑ *He was hopeful that the next round of talks would also be productive.* ♦ **pro|duc|tive|ly** *They feel they are interacting productively with elderly patients.* ADV: ADV with v

**prod|uc|tiv|ity** /prɒdʊktɪvɪti/ **Productivity** is the rate at which goods are produced. N-UNCOUNT = output ❑ *The third-quarter results reflect continued improvements in productivity.*

**prod|uct line (product lines)** A **product line** is a group of related products produced by one manufacturer, for example products that are intended to be used for similar purposes or to be sold in similar types of shops. [BUSINESS] N-COUNT ❑ *A well-known UK supermarket launches more than 1,000 new product lines each year.*

**prod|uct place|ment (product placements)** **Product placement** is a form of advertising in which a company has its product placed where it can be clearly seen during a film or television programme. [BUSINESS] N-VAR ❑ *It was the first movie to feature onscreen product placement for its own merchandise.*

**Prof.** /prɒf/ **(Profs)** also **prof.** 1 **Prof.** is a written abbreviation for **Professor**. N-TITLE ❑ *...Prof. Richard Joyner of Liverpool University.* 2 People sometimes refer to a professor as a **prof**. [INFORMAL] N-COUNT ❑ *Write a note to my prof and tell him why I missed an exam this morning.*

**pro|fane** /prəfeɪn, AM proʊ-/ **(profanes, profaning, profaned)** 1 **Profane** behaviour shows disrespect for a religion or religious things. [FORMAL] ADJ ❑ *...profane language.* 2 Something that is **profane** is concerned with everyday life rather than religion and spiritual things. ADJ ≠ spiritual ❑ *Cardinal Daly has said that churches should not be used for profane or secular purposes.* 3 If someone **profanes** a religious belief or institution, they treat it with disrespect. [FORMAL] VERB ❑ *They have profaned the long upheld traditions of the Church.* V n

**pro|fan|ity** /prəfænɪti, AM proʊ-/ **(profanities)** 1 **Profanity** is an act that shows disrespect for a religion or religious beliefs. [FORMAL] N-UNCOUNT = sacrilege ❑ *To desecrate a holy spring is considered profanity.* 2 **Profanities** are swear words. [FORMAL] N-COUNT: usu pl = obscenity

**pro|fess** /prəfes/ **(professes, professing, professed)** 1 If you **profess to** do or have something, you claim that you do it or have it, often when you do not. [FORMAL] VERB = claim ❑ *She professed to hate her nickname...* V to-inf *Why do organisations profess that they care?...* V that *'I don't know,' Pollard replied, professing innocence.* V n *...the Republicans' professed support for traditional family values.* V-ed 2 If you **profess** a feeling, opinion, or belief, you express it. [FORMAL] VERB ❑ *He professed to be content with the arrangement...* V to-inf *Bacher professed himself pleased with the Indian tour.* V pron-refl adj *...a right to profess their faith in Islam.* V n

**pro|fes|sion** /prəfeʃᵊn/ **(professions)** ◆◇◇ 1 A **profession** is a type of job that requires advanced education or training. N-COUNT: also *by* N ❑ *Harper was a teacher by profession... Only 20 per cent of jobs in the professions are held by women.* 2 You can use **profession** to refer to all the people who have the same profession. N-COUNT-COLL: oft supp N ❑ *The attitude of the medical profession is very much more liberal now.*

**pro|fes|sion|al** /prəfeʃənᵊl/ **(professionals)** ◆◆◇ 1 **Professional** means relating to a person's work, especially work that requires special training. ADJ: ADJ n ❑ *His professional career started at Liverpool University.* ♦ **pro|fes|sion|al|ly** *...a professionally-qualified architect.* ADV 2 **Professional** people have jobs that require advanced education or training. ADJ: ADJ n ❑ *...highly qualified professional people like doctors and engineers.* ♦ **Professional** is also a noun. N-COUNT ❑ *My* *father wanted me to become a professional and have more stability.* 3 You use **professional** to describe people who do a particular thing to earn money rather than as a hobby. ❑ *This has been my worst time for injuries since I started as a professional footballer.* ♦ **Professional** is also a noun. ❑ *He had been a professional since March 1985.* ♦ **pro|fes|sion|al|ly** *By age 16 he was playing professionally with bands in Greenwich Village.* 4 **Professional** sports are played for money rather than as a hobby. ❑ *...an art student who had played professional football for a short time.* 5 If you say that something that someone does or produces is **professional**, you approve of it because you think that it is of a very high standard. ❑ *They run it with a truly professional but personal touch.* ♦ **Professional** is also a noun. ❑ *...a dedicated professional who worked harmoniously with the cast and crew.* ♦ **pro|fes|sion|al|ly** *These tickets have been produced very professionally.* 6 ➔ See also **semi-professional**.

ADJ ≠ amateur; N-COUNT; ADV: ADV after v; ADJ: ADJ n ≠ amateur; ADJ [approval] ≠ amateur; N-COUNT; ADV: ADV with v

**pro|fes|sion|al foul** **(professional fouls)** In football, if a player commits a **professional foul**, they deliberately do something which is against the rules in order to prevent another player from scoring a goal.

N-COUNT

**pro|fes|sion|al|ism** /prəfeʃənəlɪzəm/ **Professionalism** in a job is a combination of skill and high standards. ❑ *American companies pride themselves on their professionalism.*

N-UNCOUNT [approval]

**pro|fes|sion|al|ize** /prəfeʃənəlaɪz/ **(professionalizes, professionalizing, professionalized)**

in BRIT, also use **professionalise**

To **professionalize** an organization, an institution, or an activity means to make it more professional, for example by paying the people who are involved in it. ❑ *...the possibility of professionalising local government by offering salaries to senior councillors.* ♦ **pro|fes|sion|ali|za|tion** /prəfeʃənəlaɪzeɪʃən/ *The professionalization of politics is a major source of our ills.*

VERB; V n; N-UNCOUNT: oft N of n

**pro|fes|sor** /prəfesəʳ/ **(professors)** 1 A **professor** in a British university is the most senior teacher in a department. ❑ *...Professor Cameron... In 1979, only 2% of British professors were female.* 2 A **professor** in an American or Canadian university or college is a teacher of the highest rank. ❑ *Robert Dunn is a professor of economics at George Washington University.*

◆◆◇ N-TITLE; N-COUNT; N-VOC; N-COUNT; N-TITLE; N-VOC

**prof|es|so|rial** /prɒfɪsɔːriəl/ 1 If you describe someone as **professorial**, you mean that they look or behave like a professor. ❑ *His manner is not so much regal as professorial... I raised my voice to a professorial tone.* 2 **Professorial** means relating to the work of a professor. ❑ *...the cuts which have led to 36 per cent of professorial posts remaining unfilled.*

ADJ; ADJ: ADJ n

**pro|fes|sor|ship** /prəfesəʳʃɪp/ **(professorships)** A **professorship** is the post of professor in a university or college. ❑ *He has accepted a research professorship at Cambridge University.*

N-COUNT

**prof|fer** /prɒfəʳ/ **(proffers, proffering, proffered)** 1 If you **proffer** something to someone, you hold it towards them so that they can take it or touch it. [FORMAL] ❑ *He rose and proffered a silver box full of cigarettes.* 2 If you **proffer** something such as advice to someone, you offer it to them. [FORMAL] ❑ *The army has not yet proffered an explanation of how and why the accident happened.*

VERB; V n; Also V n to n; VERB = volunteer; V n; Also V n to n, V n n

**pro|fi|cien|cy** /prəfɪʃənsi/ If you show **proficiency in** something, you show ability or skill at it. ❑ *Evidence of basic proficiency in English is part of the admission requirement.*

N-UNCOUNT: oft N in n = ability

**pro|fi|cient** /prəfɪʃənt/ If you are **proficient in** something, you can do it well. ❑ *A great number of Egyptians are proficient in foreign languages.*

ADJ: oft ADJ in/at n = competent

**pro|file** /prəʊfaɪl/ **(profiles, profiling, profiled)** 1 Your **profile** is the outline of your face as it is seen when someone is looking at you from the side. ❑ *His handsome profile was turned away from us.* 2 If you see someone **in profile**, you see them from the side. ❑ *This picture shows the girl in profile.* 3 A **profile of** someone is a short article or programme in which their life and character are described. ❑ *A newspaper published profiles of the candidates' wives.* 4 To **profile** someone means to give an account of that person's life and character. [JOURNALISM] ❑ *Tamar Golan, a Paris-based journalist, profiles the rebel leader.* 5 If someone has a **high profile**, people notice them and what they do. If you keep a **low profile**, you avoid doing things that will make people notice you. ❑ *...a move that would give Egypt a much higher profile in the upcoming peace talks.* ➔ See also **high-profile**.

◆◇◇ N-COUNT; N-UNCOUNT: in N; N-COUNT: with supp, usu N of n; VERB; V n; PHRASE: PHR after v

**prof|it** /prɒfɪt/ **(profits, profiting, profited)** 1 A **profit** is an amount of money that you gain when you are paid more for something than it cost you to make, get, or do it. ❑ *The bank made pre-tax profits of £3.5 million... You can improve your chances of profit by sensible planning.* 2 If you **profit from** something, you earn a profit from it. ❑ *Footballers are accustomed to profiting handsomely from bonuses... The dealers profited shamefully at the expense of my family.* 3 If you **profit from** something, or it **profits** you, you gain some advantage or benefit from it. [FORMAL] ❑ *Jennifer wasn't yet totally convinced that she'd profit from a more relaxed lifestyle... So far the French alliance had profited the rebels little... Whom would it profit to terrify or to kill James Sinclair?* ♦ **Profit** is also a noun. ❑ *The artist found much to his profit in the Louvre.*

◆◆◇ N-VAR ≠ loss; VERB; V from/by n/-ing; V; VERB; V from/by n; V n; it V n to-inf; N-UNCOUNT

**prof|it|able** /prɒfɪtəbəl/ 1 A **profitable** organization or practice makes a profit. ❑ *Drug manufacturing is the most profitable business in America... It was profitable for them to produce large amounts of food.* ♦ **prof|it|ably** /prɒfɪtəbli/ *The 28 French stores are trading profitably.* ♦ **prof|it|abil|ity** /prɒfɪtəbɪlɪti/ *Changes were made in operating methods in an effort to increase profitability.* 2 Something that is **profitable** results in some benefit for you. ❑ *...collaboration which leads to a profitable exchange of personnel and ideas.* ♦ **prof|it|ably** *In fact he could scarcely have spent his time more profitably.*

ADJ: oft it v-link ADJ to-inf; ADV: ADV with v; N-UNCOUNT; ADJ: usu ADJ n; ADV: ADV with v

**profi|teer** /prɒfɪtɪəʳ/ **(profiteers)** If you describe someone as a **profiteer**, you are critical of them because they make large profits by charging high prices for goods that are hard to get. ❑ *...a new social class composed largely of war profiteers and gangsters.*

N-COUNT: usu pl [disapproval]

**prof|it|eer|ing** /prɒfɪtɪərɪŋ/ **Profiteering** involves making large profits by charging high prices for goods that are hard to get. [BUSINESS] ❑ *...a wave of profiteering and corruption.*

N-UNCOUNT [disapproval]

**profit-making** A **profit-making** business or organization makes a profit. [BUSINESS] ❑ *He wants to set up a profit-making company, owned mostly by the university.* ➔ See also **non-profit-making**.

ADJ: usu ADJ n

**prof|it mar|gin** **(profit margins)** A **profit margin** is the difference between the selling price of a product and the cost of producing and marketing it. [BUSINESS] ❑ *The group had a net profit margin of 30% last year.*

N-COUNT

**profit-sharing** **Profit-sharing** is a system by which all the people who work in a company have a share in its profits. [BUSINESS]

N-UNCOUNT: oft N n

**profit-taking** **Profit-taking** is the selling of stocks and shares at a profit after their value has risen or just before their value falls. [BUSINESS]

N-UNCOUNT

**prof|li|ga|cy** /prɒflɪgəsi/ **Profligacy** is the spending of too much money or the using of too much of something. [FORMAL] ❑ *...the continuing profligacy of certain states.*

N-UNCOUNT = wastefulness

**prof|li|gate** /prɒflɪgɪt/ Someone who is **profligate** spends too much money or uses too much of something. [FORMAL] ❑ *...the most profligate consumer of energy in the world.*

ADJ = wasteful

**pro for|ma** /prəʊ fɔːʳmə/ also **pro-forma**. In banking, a company's **pro forma** balance or

ADJ: usu ADJ n

earnings are their expected balance or earnings. [BUSINESS]

**pro|found** /prəfaʊnd/ **(profounder, profoundest)** 1 You use **profound** to emphasize that something is very great or intense. ❑ *...discoveries which had a profound effect on many areas of medicine. ...profound disagreement... Anna's patriotism was profound.* ♦ **pro|found|ly** *This has profoundly affected my life.* 2 A **profound** idea, work, or person shows great intellectual depth and understanding. ❑ *This is a book full of profound, original and challenging insights.*
ADJ emphasis
ADV: ADV with v, ADV adj/-ed
ADJ ≠ shallow

**pro|fun|dity** /prəfʌndɪti/ **(profundities)** 1 **Profundity** is great intellectual depth and understanding. ❑ *The profundity of this book is achieved with breathtaking lightness.* 2 If you refer to the **profundity of** a feeling, experience, or change, you mean that it is deep, powerful, or serious. ❑ *...the profundity of the structural problems besetting the country.* 3 A **profundity** is a remark that shows great intellectual depth and understanding. ❑ *His work is full of profundities and asides concerning the human condition.*
N-UNCOUNT = depth ≠ shallowness
N-UNCOUNT: usu N *of* n
N-COUNT ≠ banality

**pro|fuse** /prəfjuːs/ 1 **Profuse** sweating, bleeding, or vomiting is sweating, bleeding, or vomiting large amounts. ❑ *...a remedy that produces profuse sweating.* ♦ **pro|fuse|ly** *He was bleeding profusely.* 2 If you offer **profuse** apologies or thanks, you apologize or thank someone a lot. ❑ *Then the policeman recognised me, breaking into profuse apologies.* ♦ **pro|fuse|ly** *They were very grateful to be put right and thanked me profusely.*
ADJ: usu ADJ n
ADV: ADV after v
ADJ: usu ADJ n
ADV: ADV after v

**pro|fu|sion** /prəfjuːʒən/ If there is a **profusion of** something or if it occurs **in profusion**, there is a very large quantity or variety of it. [FORMAL] ❑ *The Dart is a delightful river with a profusion of wild flowers along its banks.*
N-SING-COLL: usu N *of* n, also *in* N = abundance

**pro|geni|tor** /proʊdʒenɪtəʳ/ **(progenitors)** 1 A **progenitor** of someone is a direct ancestor of theirs. [FORMAL] ❑ *He was also a progenitor of seven presidents of Nicaragua.* 2 The **progenitor** of an idea or invention is the person who first thought of it. [FORMAL] ❑ *...Clive Sinclair, progenitor of the C5 electric car.*
N-COUNT: usu with poss
N-COUNT: usu with poss = originator

**prog|eny** /prɒdʒəni/ You can refer to a person's children or to an animal's young as their **progeny**. [FORMAL] ❑ *Davis was never loquacious on the subject of his progeny.*
N-PLURAL: usu with poss

**pro|ges|ter|one** /proʊdʒestəroʊn/ **Progesterone** is a hormone that is produced in the ovaries of women and female animals and helps prepare the body for pregnancy. ❑ *If the egg is not fertilised oestrogen and progesterone decrease.*
N-UNCOUNT

**prog|no|sis** /prɒgnoʊsɪs/ **(prognoses** /prɒgnoʊsiːz/**)** A **prognosis** is an estimate of the future of someone or something, especially about whether a patient will recover from an illness. [FORMAL] ❑ *If the cancer is caught early the prognosis is excellent.*
N-COUNT

**prog|nos|ti|ca|tion** /prɒgnɒstɪkeɪʃən/ **(prognostications)** A **prognostication** is a statement about what you think will happen in the future. [FORMAL] ❑ *The country is currently obsessed with gloomy prognostications about its future.*
N-VAR = prediction

**pro|gram** /proʊgræm/ **(programs, programming, programmed)** ◆◆◇ 1 A **program** is a set of instructions that a computer follows in order to perform a particular task. [COMPUTING] ❑ *The chances of an error occurring in a computer program increase with the size of the program.* 2 When you **program** a computer, you give it a set of instructions to make it able to perform a particular task. [COMPUTING] ❑ *He programmed his computer to compare all the possible combinations. ...45 million people, about half of whom can program their own computers. ...a computer programmed to translate a story given to it in Chinese.* ♦ **pro|gram|ming** *...programming skills. ...the concepts of programming.* 3 → See also **programme**.
N-COUNT
VERB
V n to-inf
V n
V-ed
N-UNCOUNT: oft N n

**pro|gram|ma|ble** /proʊgræməbəl/ A **programmable** machine can be programmed, so that for example it will switch on and off automatically or do things in a particular order. ❑ *Most CD-players are programmable.*
ADJ

**pro|gram|mat|ic** /proʊgrəmætɪk/ **Programmatic** ideas or policies follow a particular programme. ❑ *He gave up on programmatic politics and turned his back on public life.*
ADJ

**pro|gramme** /proʊgræm/ **(programmes, programming, programmed)** ◆◆◆

☑ in AM, use **program**

1 A **programme** of actions or events is a series of actions or events that are planned to be done. ❑ *The general argued that the nuclear programme should still continue.* 2 A television or radio **programme** is something that is broadcast on television or radio. ❑ *...a series of TV programmes on global environment. ...local news programmes.* 3 A theatre or concert **programme** is a small book or sheet of paper which gives information about the play or concert you are attending. 4 When you **programme** a machine or system, you set its controls so that it will work in a particular way. ❑ *Parents can programme the machine not to turn on at certain times.* 5 If a living creature **is programmed to** behave in a particular way, they are likely to behave in that way because of social or biological factors that they cannot control. ❑ *We are all genetically programmed to develop certain illnesses.*
N-COUNT: usu with supp
N-COUNT: oft n N
N-COUNT
VERB
V n to-inf
VERB: usu passive
*be* V-ed to-inf
Also *be* V-ed

**pro|gramme note (programme notes)**

☑ in AM, use **program note**

A **programme note** is an article written in a programme for a play or concert, which gives information about the performance or production.
N-COUNT

**pro|gram|mer** /proʊgræməʳ/ **(programmers)** A computer **programmer** is a person whose job involves writing programs for computers. [COMPUTING]
N-COUNT

**pro|gress** **(progresses, progressing, progressed)** ◆◆◇

☑ The noun is pronounced /proʊgres, AM prɑː-/. The verb is pronounced /prəgres/.

1 **Progress** is the process of gradually improving or getting nearer to achieving or completing something. ❑ *The medical community continues to make progress in the fight against cancer... The two sides made little if any progress towards agreement.* 2 **The progress of** a situation or action is the way in which it develops. ❑ *The Chancellor is reported to have been delighted with the progress of the first day's talks.* 3 To **progress** means to move over a period of time to a stronger, more advanced, or more desirable state. ❑ *He will visit once a fortnight to see how his new staff are progressing... He started with sketching and then progressed to painting.* 4 If events **progress**, they continue to happen gradually over a period of time. ❑ *As the evening progressed, sadness turned to rage.* 5 If something is **in progress**, it has started and is still continuing. ❑ *The game was already in progress when we took our seats.*
N-UNCOUNT
N-SING: *the* N, oft N *of* n
VERB
V
V *to* n
VERB
V
PHRASE

**pro|gres|sion** /prəgreʃən/ **(progressions)** 1 A **progression** is a gradual development from one state to another. ❑ *Both drugs slow the progression of HIV, but neither cures the disease.* 2 A **progression of** things is a number of things which come one after the other. [FORMAL] ❑ *...a progression of habitats from dry meadows through marshes to open water.*
N-COUNT: usu sing, usu with supp
N-COUNT: N *of* n

**pro|gres|sive** /prəgresɪv/ **(progressives)** 1 Someone who is **progressive** or has **progressive** ideas has modern ideas about how things should be done, rather than traditional ones. ❑ *...a progressive businessman who had voted for Roosevelt in 1932 and 1936... The children go to a progressive school.* ♦ A **progressive** is someone who is progressive. ❑ *The Republicans were deeply*
ADJ ≠ conservative
N-COUNT ≠ conservative

split between progressives and conservatives. [2] A **progressive** change happens gradually over a period of time. ❑ *One prominent symptom of the disease is progressive loss of memory.* ADJ: usu ADJ n = gradual ≠ sudden
♦ **pro|gres|sive|ly** *Her symptoms became progressively worse... The amount of grant the council received from the Government was progressively reduced.* ADV: ADV compar, ADV with v = gradually
[3] In grammar, **progressive** means the same as **continuous**. ADJ: ADJ n

**pro|hib|it** /prəhɪbɪt, AM proʊ-/ **(prohibits, prohibiting, prohibited)** If a law or someone in authority **prohibits** something, they forbid it or make it illegal. [FORMAL] ❑ *...a law that prohibits tobacco advertising in newspapers and magazines... Fishing is prohibited... Federal law prohibits foreign airlines from owning more than 25% of any U.S. airline.* VERB ≠ permit; V n; V n; V n *from* -ing
♦ **pro|hi|bi|tion** *...the prohibition of women on air combat missions.* N-UNCOUNT

**pro|hi|bi|tion** /proʊɪbɪʃən/ **(prohibitions)** A **prohibition** is a law or rule forbidding something. ❑ *...a prohibition on discrimination. ...prohibitions against feeding birds at the airport.* ➔ See also **prohibit**. N-COUNT

**Pro|hi|bi|tion** In the United States, **Prohibition** was the law that prevented the manufacture, sale, and transporting of alcoholic drinks between 1919 and 1933. **Prohibition** also refers to the period when this law existed. N-UNCOUNT

**pro|hibi|tive** /prəhɪbɪtɪv, AM proʊ-/ If the cost of something is **prohibitive**, it is so high that many people cannot afford it. [FORMAL] ❑ *The cost of private treatment can be prohibitive.* ADJ
♦ **pro|hibi|tive|ly** *Meat and butter were prohibitively expensive.* ADV: ADV adj

**proj|ect** **(projects, projecting, projected)** ◆◆◇

> The noun is pronounced /prɒdʒekt/. The verb is pronounced /prədʒekt/ and is hyphenated pro|ject.

[1] A **project** is a task that requires a lot of time and effort. ❑ *Money will also go into local development projects in Vietnam... Besides film and record projects, I have continued to work in the theater.* N-COUNT: oft supp N
[2] A **project** is a detailed study of a subject by a pupil or student. ❑ *Students complete projects for a personal tutor, working at home at their own pace.* N-COUNT
[3] If something **is projected**, it is planned or expected. ❑ *Africa's mid-1993 population is projected to more than double by 2025... The government had been projecting a 5% consumer price increase for the entire year. ...a projected deficit of $1.5 million.* VERB; *be* V-ed to-inf; V n; V-ed
[4] If you **project** someone or something in a particular way, you try to make people see them in that way. If you **project** a particular feeling or quality, you show it in your behaviour. ❑ *Bradley projects a natural warmth and sincerity... He just hasn't been able to project himself as the strong leader... His first job will be to project Glasgow as a friendly city... The initial image projected was of a caring, effective president.* VERB; V n; V pron-refl *as* n; V n *as* n; V-ed
[5] If you **project** feelings or ideas **on to** other people, you imagine that they have the same ideas or feelings as you. ❑ *He projects his own thoughts and ideas onto her.* VERB; V n *on/onto/upon* n
[6] If you **project** a film or picture **onto** a screen or wall, you make it appear there. ❑ *The team tried projecting the maps with two different projectors onto the same screen.* VERB; V n
[7] If something **projects**, it sticks out above or beyond a surface or edge. [FORMAL] ❑ *...the remains of a war-time defence which projected out from the shore. ...a piece of projecting metal.* VERB; V prep/adv; V-ing
[8] ➔ See also **housing project**.

**pro|jec|tile** /prədʒektaɪl, AM -təl/ **(projectiles)** A **projectile** is an object that is fired from a gun or other weapon. [FORMAL] N-COUNT

**pro|jec|tion** /prədʒekʃən/ **(projections)** [1] A **projection** is an estimate of a future amount. ❑ *...the company's projection of 11 million visitors for the first year. ...sales projections.* N-COUNT = forecast, estimate
[2] The **projection** of a film or picture is the act of projecting it onto a screen or wall. N-UNCOUNT: usu N n

**pro|jec|tion|ist** /prədʒekʃənɪst/ **(projectionists)** A **projectionist** is someone whose job is to work a projector at a cinema. N-COUNT

**pro|jec|tor** /prədʒektəʳ/ **(projectors)** A **projector** is a machine that projects films or slides onto a screen or wall. ❑ *...a 35-millimetre slide projector.* ➔ See also **overhead projector**. N-COUNT

**pro|lapse** /proʊlæps, AM proʊlæps/ **(prolapses, prolapsing, prolapsed)**

> The verb is also pronounced /prəlæps/.

[1] A **prolapse** is when one of the organs in the body moves down from its normal position. [MEDICAL] N-VAR
[2] If an organ in someone's body **prolapses**, it moves down from its normal position. [MEDICAL] ❑ *Sometimes the original abortion was done so badly that the uterus prolapsed.* VERB; V

**prole** /proʊl/ **(proles)** A **prole** is someone in a low social class. [mainly BRIT, INFORMAL] ❑ *We had proles working alongside university types as equals.* N-COUNT disapproval = pleb

**pro|letar|ian** /proʊlɪteəriən/ **(proletarians)** [1] **Proletarian** means relating to the proletariat. ❑ *...a proletarian revolution.* ADJ
[2] A **proletarian** is a member of the proletariat. N-COUNT

**pro|letari|at** /proʊlɪteəriæt/ **The proletariat** is a term used to refer to workers without high status, especially industrial workers. ❑ *...a struggle between the bourgeoisie and the proletariat.* N-SING-COLL: *the* N = working class

**pro-life** Someone who is **pro-life** thinks that women do not have a right to choose whether or not to give birth to a child they have conceived, and that abortion is wrong in most or all circumstances. ❑ *...the pro-life movement.* ADJ: usu ADJ n ≠ pro-choice

**pro|lif|er|ate** /prəlɪfəreɪt/ **(proliferates, proliferating, proliferated)** If things **proliferate**, they increase in number very quickly. [FORMAL] ❑ *Computerized data bases are proliferating fast.* VERB; V
♦ **pro|lif|era|tion** /prəlɪfəreɪʃən/ *...the proliferation of nuclear weapons... Smoking triggers off cell proliferation.* N-UNCOUNT: oft N *of* n, n N

**pro|lif|ic** /prəlɪfɪk/ [1] A **prolific** writer, artist, or composer produces a large number of works. ❑ *She is a prolific writer of novels and short stories.* ADJ
[2] A **prolific** sports player scores a lot of goals or wins a lot of matches or races. ❑ *Another prolific scorer is Dean Saunders.* ADJ: usu ADJ n
[3] An animal, person, or plant that is **prolific** produces a large number of babies, young plants, or fruit. ❑ *They are prolific breeders, with many hens laying up to six eggs.* ADJ

**pro|logue** /proʊlɒg, AM -lɔːg/ **(prologues)** [1] A **prologue** is a speech or section of text that introduces a play or book. ❑ *The prologue to the novel is written in the form of a newspaper account.* N-COUNT
[2] If one event is a **prologue to** another event, it leads to it. [FORMAL] ❑ *This was a prologue to today's bloodless revolution.* N-COUNT: usu N *to* n

**pro|long** /prəlɒŋ, AM -lɔːŋ/ **(prolongs, prolonging, prolonged)** To **prolong** something means to make it last longer. ❑ *Mr Chesler said foreign military aid was prolonging the war.* VERB = extend; V n
♦ **pro|lon|ga|tion** /proʊlɒŋgeɪʃən, AM -lɔːŋ-/ **(prolongations)** *...the prolongation of productive human life.* N-VAR: usu N *of* n

**pro|longed** /prəlɒŋd, AM -lɔːŋd/ A **prolonged** event or situation continues for a long time, or for longer than expected. ❑ *...a prolonged period of low interest rates.* ADJ: usu ADJ n

**prom** /prɒm/ **(proms)**

> The spelling **Prom** is usually used for meaning 3.

[1] A **prom** is a formal dance at a school or college which is usually held at the end of the academic year. [AM] ❑ *I didn't want to go to the prom with Craig.* N-COUNT
[2] **The prom** is the road by the sea where people go for a walk. [BRIT] N-SING: usu *the* N
[3] **The Proms** are a series of concerts of mainly classical music that are held each year in London and some other cities. There is usually an area at these concerts where people stand, as well as seats. [mainly BRIT] N-PLURAL: also N n

**prom|enade** /prɒmənɑːd, AM -neɪd/ **(promenades, promenading, promenaded)** [1] In a seaside town, the **promenade** is the road by the sea where people go for a walk. N-COUNT = prom [2] A **promenade** is an area that is used for walking, for example a wide road or a deck on a ship. [mainly AM] N-COUNT [3] A **promenade** is a formal dance at a school or college which is usually held at the end of the academic year. [AM] N-COUNT = prom, ball

**promi|nence** /prɒmɪnəns/ If someone or something is in a position of **prominence**, they are well-known and important. ❑ *He came to prominence during the World Cup in Italy... Crime prevention had to be given more prominence.* N-UNCOUNT

**promi|nent** /prɒmɪnənt/ ◆◇◇ [1] Someone who is **prominent** is important. ❑ *...a prominent member of the Law Society.* ADJ = well-known [2] Something that is **prominent** is very noticeable or is an important part of something else. ❑ *Here the window plays a prominent part in the design.* ADJ ♦ **promi|nent|ly** *Trade will figure prominently in the second day of talks in Washington.* ADV: ADV with v

**pro|mis|cu|ous** /prəmɪskjuəs/ Someone who is **promiscuous** has sex with many different people. ❑ *She is perceived as vain, spoilt and promiscuous.* ADJ [disapproval] ♦ **promis|cu|ity** /prɒmɪskjuːɪti/ *He has recently urged more tolerance of sexual promiscuity.* N-UNCOUNT

**prom|ise** /prɒmɪs/ **(promises, promising, promised)** ◆◆◇ [1] If you **promise that** you will do something, you say to someone that you will definitely do it. VERB ❑ *The post office has promised to resume first class mail delivery to the area on Friday...* V to-inf *He had promised that the rich and privileged would no longer get preferential treatment...* V that *Promise me you will not waste your time...* V n that *'We'll be back next year,' he promised...* V with quote *'You promise?' — 'All right, I promise.'* V [2] If you **promise** someone something, you tell them that you will definitely give it to them or make sure that they have it. VERB ❑ *In 1920 the great powers promised them an independent state...* V n n *The officers promise a return to multiparty rule.* V n [3] A **promise** is a statement which you make to a person in which you say that you will definitely do something or give them something. N-COUNT: oft N to-inf, N that ❑ *If you make a promise, you should keep it.* [4] If a situation or event **promises to** have a particular quality or **to** be a particular thing, it shows signs that it will have that quality or be that thing. VERB ❑ *While it will be fun, the seminar also promises to be most instructive.* V to-inf [5] If someone or something shows **promise**, they seem likely to be very good or successful. N-UNCOUNT = potential ❑ *The boy first showed promise as an athlete in grade school.*

**prom|ised land (promised lands)** If you refer to a place or a state as a **promised land**, you mean that people desire it and expect to find happiness or success there. N-COUNT: usu sing ❑ *...the promised land of near-zero inflation.*

**prom|is|ing** /prɒmɪsɪŋ/ Someone or something that is **promising** seems likely to be very good or successful. ADJ ❑ *A school has honoured one of its brightest and most promising former pupils.*

**prom|is|ing|ly** /prɒmɪsɪŋli/ If something or someone starts **promisingly**, they begin well but often fail in the end. ADV: usu ADV with v, also ADV adj ❑ *It all started so promisingly when Speed scored a tremendous first goal.*

**prom|is|sory note** /prɒmɪsəri noʊt, AM -sɔːri/ **(promissory notes)** A **promissory note** is a written promise to pay a specific sum of money to a particular person. N-COUNT [mainly AM, BUSINESS] ❑ *...a $36.4 million, five-year promissory note.*

**pro|mo** /proʊmoʊ/ **(promos)** A **promo** is something such as a short video film which is used to promote a product. N-COUNT: oft N n [JOURNALISM, INFORMAL] ❑ *He races his cars, and hires them out for film, TV and promo videos.*

**prom|on|tory** /prɒməntri, AM -tɔːri/ **(promontories)** A **promontory** is a cliff that stretches out into the sea. N-COUNT

**pro|mote** /prəmoʊt/ **(promotes, promoting, promoted)** ◆◆◇ [1] If people **promote** something, they help or encourage it to happen, increase, or spread. VERB = encourage ≠ discourage ❑ *You don't have to sacrifice environmental protection to promote economic growth.* V n ♦ **pro|mo|tion** *The government has pledged to give the promotion of democracy higher priority.* N-UNCOUNT: with supp [2] If a firm **promotes** a product, it tries to increase the sales or popularity of that product. VERB ❑ *Paul Weller has announced a full British tour to promote his second solo album.* V n *...a special St Lucia week where the island could be promoted as a tourist destination.* be V-ed as n [3] If someone **is promoted**, they are given a more important job or rank in the organization that they work for. VERB: usu passive ❑ *I was promoted to editor and then editorial director...* be V-ed from/to n *In fact, those people have been promoted.* be V-ed [4] If a team that competes in a league **is promoted**, it starts competing in a higher division in the next season because it was one of the most successful teams in the lower division. VERB: usu passive ≠ relegate [BRIT] ❑ *Woodford Green won the Second Division title and are promoted to the First Division.* be V-ed to n ♦ **pro|mo|tion** *Fans of Leeds United have been celebrating their team's promotion to the first division.* N-UNCOUNT ≠ relegation

**pro|mot|er** /prəmoʊtəʳ/ **(promoters)** [1] A **promoter** is a person who helps organize and finance an event, especially a sports event. N-COUNT ❑ *...one of the top boxing promoters in Britain.* [2] The **promoter of** a cause or idea tries to make it become popular. N-COUNT: usu N of n ❑ *Aaron Copland was an energetic promoter of American music.*

**pro|mo|tion** /prəmoʊʃən/ **(promotions)** ◆◇◇ [1] If you are given **promotion** or a **promotion** in your job, you are given a more important job or rank in the organization that you work for. N-VAR ❑ *Consider changing jobs or trying for promotion. ...rewarding outstanding employees with promotions to higher-paid posts.* [2] A **promotion** is an attempt to make a product or event popular or successful, especially by advertising. N-VAR [BUSINESS] ❑ *During 1984, Remington spent a lot of money on advertising and promotion.* → See also **promote**.

**pro|mo|tion|al** /prəmoʊʃənəl/ **Promotional** material, events, or ideas are designed to increase the sales of a product or service. ADJ: usu ADJ n ❑ *You can use the logo in all your promotional material.*

**prompt** /prɒmpt/ **(prompts, prompting, prompted)** ◆◇◇ [1] To **prompt** someone **to** do something means to make them decide to do it. VERB ❑ *Japan's recession has prompted consumers to cut back on buying cars...* V n to-inf *The need for villagers to control their own destinies has prompted a new plan.* V n [2] If you **prompt** someone when they stop speaking, you encourage or help them to continue. If you **prompt** an actor, you tell them what their next line is when they have forgotten what comes next. VERB ❑ *'Go on,' the therapist prompted him...* V with quote *How exactly did he prompt her, Mr Markham?* V n [3] A **prompt** action is done without any delay. ADJ: usu ADJ n ❑ *It is not too late, but prompt action is needed.* [4] If you are **prompt** to do something, you do it without delay or you are not late. ADJ: v-link ADJ ❑ *You have been so prompt in carrying out all these commissions.*

**prompt|ing** /prɒmptɪŋ/ **(promptings)** If you respond to **prompting**, you do what someone encourages or reminds you to do. N-UNCOUNT: also N in pl ❑ *...the promptings of your subconscious.*

**prompt|ly** /prɒmptli/ [1] If you do something **promptly**, you do it immediately. ADV: ADV with v = immediately ❑ *Sister Francesca entered the chapel, took her seat, and promptly fell asleep.* [2] If you do something **promptly at** a particular time, you do it at exactly that time. ADV: ADV with v, ADV at/on n ❑ *Promptly at a quarter past seven, we left the hotel.*

**prom|ul|gate** /prɒməlgeɪt/ **(promulgates, promulgating, promulgated)** [1] If people **promulgate** a new law or a new idea, they make it widely known. VERB [FORMAL] ❑ *The shipping industry promulgated a voluntary code.* V n [2] If a new law **is promulgated** by a government or national leader, it is publicly approved or made official. VERB: usu passive [FORMAL] ❑ A be V-ed

*new constitution was promulgated last month.*
♦ **prom|ul|ga|tion** /prɒməlgeɪʃən/ *...the promulgation of the constitution.* N-UNCOUNT

**prone** /proʊn/ 1 To be **prone to** something, usually something bad, means to have a tendency to be affected by it or to do it. ❑ *For all her experience, she was still prone to nerves... People with fair skin who sunburn easily are very prone to develop skin cancer.* ♦ **-prone** combines with nouns to make adjectives that describe people who are frequently affected by something bad. ❑ *...the most injury-prone rider on the circuit.* ➔ See also **accident prone**. 2 If you are lying **prone**, you are lying on your front. [FORMAL] ❑ *Bob slid from his chair and lay prone on the floor.*
ADJ: v-link ADJ, ADJ *to* n, ADJ to-inf
COMB in ADJ
ADJ: ADJ after v, ADJ n ≠ *supine*

**prong** /prɒŋ, AM prɔːŋ/ **(prongs)** 1 The **prongs** of something such as a fork are the long, thin pointed parts. 2 The **prongs** of something such as a policy or plan are the separate parts of it. ❑ *The shareholder rights movement has two prongs... The second prong of the strategy is the provision of basic social services for the poor.*
N-COUNT: usu pl
N-COUNT

**-pronged** /-prɒŋd, AM -prɔːŋd/ A two-**pronged** or three-**pronged** attack, plan, or approach has two or three parts. ❑ *...a two-pronged attack on the recession.*
COMB in ADJ: ADJ n

**pro|nomi|nal** /proʊnɒmɪnəl/ **Pronominal** means relating to pronouns or like a pronoun. [TECHNICAL] ❑ *...a pronominal use.*
ADJ

**pro|noun** /proʊnaʊn/ **(pronouns)** A **pronoun** is a word that you use to refer to someone or something when you do not need to use a noun, often because the person or thing has been mentioned earlier. Examples are 'it', 'she', 'something', and 'myself'. ➔ See also **indefinite pronoun**, **personal pronoun**, **reflexive pronoun**, **relative pronoun**.
N-COUNT

**pro|nounce** /prənaʊns/ **(pronounces, pronouncing, pronounced)** 1 To **pronounce** a word means to say it using particular sounds. ❑ *Have I pronounced your name correctly?... He pronounced it Per-sha, the way the English do.* 2 If you **pronounce** something to be true, you state that it is the case. [FORMAL] ❑ *A specialist has now pronounced him fully fit... I now pronounce you man and wife.*
VERB
V n
V n n
VERB = *declare*
V n adj
V n n

**pro|nounced** /prənaʊnst/ Something that is **pronounced** is very noticeable. ❑ *Most of the art exhibitions have a pronounced Scottish theme.*
ADJ

**pro|nounce|ment** /prənaʊnsmənt/ **(pronouncements)** **Pronouncements** are public or official statements on an important subject. ❑ *...the President's latest pronouncements about the protection of minorities.*
N-COUNT: usu pl

**pron|to** /prɒntoʊ/ If you say that something must be done **pronto**, you mean that it must be done quickly and at once. [INFORMAL] ❑ *Get down to the post office pronto!*
ADV: ADV after v = *sharpish*

**pro|nun|cia|tion** /prənʌnsieɪʃən/ **(pronunciations)** The **pronunciation** of a word or language is the way in which it is pronounced. ❑ *She gave the word its French pronunciation... You're going to have to forgive my pronunciation.*
N-VAR

**proof** /pruːf/ **(proofs)** 1 **Proof** is a fact, argument, or piece of evidence which shows that something is definitely true or definitely exists. ❑ *You have to have proof of residence in the state of Texas, such as a Texas ID card... This is not necessarily proof that he is wrong.* 2 In publishing, the **proofs of** a book, magazine, or article are a first copy of it that is printed so that mistakes can be corrected before more copies are printed and published. ❑ *I'm correcting the proofs of the Spanish edition right now.* ♦ **Proof** is also an adjective. ❑ *...an uncorrected proof copy of the book.* 3 **Proof** is used after a number of degrees or a percentage, when indicating the strength of a strong alcoholic drink such as whisky. ❑ *...a glass of Wild Turkey bourbon: 101 degrees proof.* 4 **the proof of the pudding is in the eating** ➔ see **pudding**.
◆◇◇ N-VAR: oft N *of* n, N that
N-COUNT: usu pl, oft N *of* n
ADJ: ADJ n
ADJ: amount ADJ

**-proof** /-pruːf/ **(-proofs, -proofing, -proofed)** 1 **-proof** combines with nouns and verbs to form adjectives which indicate that something cannot be damaged or badly affected by the thing or action mentioned. ❑ *...a bomb-proof aircraft... In a large microwave-proof dish, melt butter for 20 seconds.* 2 **-proof** combines with nouns to form verbs which refer to protecting something against being damaged or badly affected by the thing mentioned. ❑ *...home energy efficiency grants towards the cost of draught-proofing your home. ...inflation-proofed pensions.* 3 ➔ See also **bulletproof**, **childproof**, **damp-proof course**, **fireproof**, **ovenproof**, **soundproof**, **waterproof**, **weatherproof**.
COMB in ADJ
COMB in VERB
V n
V-ed

**proof|read** /pruːfriːd/ **(proofreads, proofreading)** also **proof-read**. When someone **proofreads** something such as a book or an article, they read it before it is published in order to find and mark mistakes that need to be corrected. ❑ *I didn't even have the chance to proofread my own report.*
VERB
V n
Also V

**prop** /prɒp/ **(props, propping, propped)** 1 If you **prop** an object **on** or **against** something, you support it by putting something underneath it or by resting it somewhere. ❑ *He rocked back in the chair and propped his feet on the desk.* ♦ **Prop up** means the same as **prop**. ❑ *Sam slouched back and propped his elbows up on the bench behind him... If you have difficulty sitting like this, prop up your back against a wall.* 2 A **prop** is a stick or other object that you use to support something. 3 To be a **prop** for a system, institution, or person means to be the main thing that keeps them strong or helps them survive. ❑ *The army is one of the main props of the government.* 4 The **props** in a play or film are all the objects or pieces of furniture that are used in it. ❑ *...the backdrop and props for a stage show.*
VERB
V n *on/against* n
PHRASAL VERB
V n P prep
V P n (not pron) prep
N-COUNT
N-COUNT
N-COUNT: usu pl

♦ **prop up** 1 To **prop up** something means to support it or help it to survive. ❑ *Investments in the U.S. money market have propped up the American dollar... On the Stock Exchange, aggressive buying propped the market up.* 2 ➔ see **prop 1**.
PHRASAL VERB
V P n (not pron)
V n P

**propa|gan|da** /prɒpəgændə/ **Propaganda** is information, often inaccurate information, which a political organization publishes or broadcasts in order to influence people. ❑ *The Front adopted an aggressive propaganda campaign against its rivals.*
N-UNCOUNT: oft N n
[disapproval]

**propa|gan|dist** /prɒpəgændɪst/ **(propagandists)** A **propagandist** is a person who tries to persuade people to support a particular idea or group, often by giving inaccurate information. ❑ *He was also a brilliant propagandist for free trade.*
N-COUNT
[disapproval]

**propa|gan|dize** /prɒpəgændaɪz/ **(propagandizes, propagandizing, propagandized)**

✔ in BRIT, also use **propagandise**

If you say that a group of people **propagandize**, you think that they are dishonestly trying to persuade other people to share their views. ❑ *You can propagandize just by calling attention to something... This government shouldn't propagandize its own people.*
VERB
[disapproval]
V
V n

**propa|gate** /prɒpəgeɪt/ **(propagates, propagating, propagated)** 1 If people **propagate** an idea or piece of information, they spread it and try to make people believe it or support it. [FORMAL] ❑ *They propagated political doctrines which promised to tear apart the fabric of British society.* ♦ **propa|ga|tion** /prɒpəgeɪʃən/ *...the propagation of true Buddhism.* 2 If you **propagate** plants, you grow more of them from the original ones. [TECHNICAL] ❑ *The easiest way to propagate a vine is to take hardwood cuttings... The pasque flower can be propagated from seed.* ♦ **propa|ga|tion** *...the successful propagation of a batch of plants.*
VERB = *disseminate*
V n
N-UNCOUNT: oft N *of* n
VERB
V n
*be* V-ed *from* n
N-UNCOUNT: oft N *of* n

**pro|pane** /proʊpeɪn/ **Propane** is a gas that is used for cooking and heating. ❑ *...a propane gas cylinder.*
N-UNCOUNT: oft N n

**pro|pel** /prəpe̲l/ **(propels, propelling, propelled)** 1 To **propel** something in a particular direction means to cause it to move in that direction. ❑ *The tiny rocket is attached to the spacecraft and is designed to propel it toward Mars.* ♦ **-propelled** combines with nouns to form adjectives which indicate how something, especially a weapon, is propelled. ❑ *...rocket-propelled grenades.* 2 If something **propels** you **into** a particular activity, it causes you to do it. ❑ *It was a shooting star that propelled me into astronomy in the first place... He is propelled by both guilt and the need to avenge his father.*
VERB; V n prep; COMB in ADJ; VERB; V n prep; be V-ed

**pro|pel|lant** /prəpe̲lənt/ **(propellants)** 1 **Propellant** is a substance that causes something to move forwards. ❑ *...a propellant for nuclear rockets.* 2 **Propellant** is a gas that is used in spray cans to force the contents out of the can when you press the button. ❑ *By 1978, in the USA, the use of CFCs in aerosol propellants was banned.*
N-MASS; N-MASS

**pro|pel|ler** /prəpe̲ləʳ/ **(propellers)** A **propeller** is a device with blades which is attached to a boat or aircraft. The engine makes the propeller spin round and causes the boat or aircraft to move. ❑ *...a fixed three-bladed propeller.*
N-COUNT

**pro|pen|sity** /prəpe̲nsɪti/ **(propensities)** A **propensity to** do something or a **propensity for** something is a natural tendency that you have to behave in a particular way. [FORMAL] ❑ *Mr Bint has a propensity to put off decisions to the last minute.*
N-COUNT: oft N to-inf, N *for* n

**prop|er** /prɒ̲pəʳ/ 1 You use **proper** to describe things that you consider to be real and satisfactory rather than inadequate in some way. ❑ *Two out of five people lack a proper job... I always cook a proper evening meal.* 2 The **proper** thing is the one that is correct or most suitable. ❑ *The Supreme Court will ensure that the proper procedures have been followed... He helped to put things in their proper place.* 3 If you say that a way of behaving is **proper**, you mean that it is considered socially acceptable and right. ❑ *In those days it was not thought entirely proper for a woman to be on the stage.* 4 You can add **proper** after a word to indicate that you are referring to the central and most important part of a place, event, or object and want to distinguish it from other things which are not regarded as being important or central to it. ❑ *A distinction must be made between archaeology proper and science-based archaeology.*
♦◇◇ ADJ: ADJ n; ADJ: ADJ n = *right* ≠ *wrong*; ADJ: usu v-link ADJ = *fitting* ≠ *improper*; ADJ: n ADJ

**prop|er|ly** /prɒ̲pəʳli/ 1 If something is done **properly**, it is done in a correct and satisfactory way. ❑ *You're too thin. You're not eating properly... There needs to be a properly informed public debate.* 2 If someone behaves **properly**, they behave in a way that is considered acceptable and not rude. ❑ *He's a spoilt brat and it's about time he learnt to behave properly.*
♦◇◇ ADV: usu ADV with v, also ADV adj; ADV: ADV after v = *correctly*

**prop|er noun** **(proper nouns)** also **proper name.** A **proper noun** is the name of a particular person, place, organization, or thing. Proper nouns begin with a capital letter. Examples are 'Margaret', 'London', and 'the United Nations'. Compare **common noun.**
N-COUNT

**prop|er|tied** /prɒ̲pəʳtid/ **Propertied** people own land or property. [FORMAL] ❑ *...the propertied classes.*
ADJ: usu ADJ n

**prop|er|ty** /prɒ̲pəʳti/ **(properties)** 1 Someone's **property** is all the things that belong to them or something that belongs to them. [FORMAL] ❑ *Richard could easily destroy her personal property to punish her for walking out on him... Security forces searched thousands of homes, confiscating weapons and stolen property.* 2 A **property** is a building and the land belonging to it. [FORMAL] ❑ *This vehicle has been parked on private property.* 3 The **properties** of a substance or object are the ways in which it behaves in particular conditions. ❑ *A radio signal has both electrical and magnetic properties.*
♦♦◇ N-UNCOUNT: usu with poss; N-VAR; N-COUNT: usu pl

**proph|ecy** /prɒ̲fɪsi/ **(prophecies)** A **prophecy** is a statement in which someone says they strongly believe that a particular thing will happen. ❑ *...Biblical prophecy.*
N-VAR

**proph|esy** /prɒ̲fɪsaɪ/ **(prophesies, prophesying, prophesied)** If you **prophesy that** something will happen, you say that you strongly believe that it will happen. ❑ *He prophesied that within five years his opponent would either be dead or in prison... She prophesied a bad ending for the expedition.*
VERB = *predict*; V that; V n

**proph|et** /prɒ̲fɪt/ **(prophets)** 1 A **prophet** is a person who is believed to be chosen by God to say the things that God wants to tell people. ❑ *...the sacred name of the Holy Prophet of Islam.* 2 A **prophet** is someone who predicts that something will happen in the future. [LITERARY] ❑ *I promised myself I'd defy all the prophets of doom and battle back to fitness.*
N-COUNT; N-COUNT: with supp, usu N *of* n

**pro|phet|ic** /prəfe̲tɪk/ If something was **prophetic**, it described or suggested something that did actually happen later. ❑ *This ominous warning soon proved prophetic.*
ADJ

**prophy|lac|tic** /prɒ̲fɪlæ̲ktɪk/ **(prophylactics)** 1 **Prophylactic** means concerned with preventing disease. [MEDICAL] ❑ *Vaccination and other prophylactic measures can be carried out.* 2 A **prophylactic** is a substance or device used for preventing disease. [MEDICAL] ❑ *The region began to use quinine successfully as a prophylactic.* 3 A **prophylactic** is a condom. [FORMAL]
ADJ: usu ADJ n = *preventive*; N-COUNT; N-COUNT

**pro|pi|ti|ate** /prəpɪ̲ʃieɪt/ **(propitiates, propitiating, propitiated)** If you **propitiate** someone, you stop them being angry or impatient by doing something to please them. [FORMAL] ❑ *I've never gone out of my way to propitiate people... These ancient ceremonies propitiate the spirits of the waters.*
VERB = *appease, placate*; V n; V n

**pro|pi|tious** /prəpɪ̲ʃəs/ If something is **propitious**, it is likely to lead to success. [FORMAL] ❑ *They should wait for the most propitious moment between now and the next election... The omens for the game are still not propitious.*
ADJ = *favourable* ≠ *unfavourable*

**pro|po|nent** /prəpo̲ʊnənt/ **(proponents)** If you are a **proponent of** a particular idea or course of action, you actively support it. [FORMAL] ❑ *Halsey was identified as a leading proponent of the values of progressive education.*
N-COUNT: with poss, usu N *of* n = *advocate* ≠ *opponent*

**pro|por|tion** /prəpɔ̲ːʳʃən/ **(proportions)** 1 A **proportion of** a group or an amount is a part of it. [FORMAL] ❑ *A large proportion of the dolphins in that area will eventually die... A proportion of the rent is met by the city council.* 2 The **proportion of** one kind of person or thing in a group is the number of people or things of that kind compared to the total number of people or things in the group. ❑ *The proportion of women in the profession had risen to 17.3%.* 3 The **proportion of** one amount **to** another is the relationship between the two amounts in terms of how much there is of each thing. ❑ *Women's bodies tend to have a higher proportion of fat to water.* 4 If you refer to the **proportions** of something, you are referring to its size, usually when this is extremely large. [WRITTEN] ❑ *In the tropics plants grow to huge proportions.*
♦◇◇ N-COUNT: usu sing, usu N *of* n; N-COUNT: usu sing, usu N *of* n; N-COUNT: oft N *of* n *to* n = *ratio*; N-PLURAL: usu supp N

PHRASES 5 If one thing increases or decreases **in proportion to** another thing, it increases or decreases to the same degree as that thing. ❑ *The pressure in the cylinders would go up in proportion to the boiler pressure.* 6 If something is small or large **in proportion to** something else, it is small or large when compared with that thing. ❑ *Children tend to have relatively larger heads than adults in proportion to the rest of their body.* 7 If you say that something is **out of all proportion to** something else, you think that it is far greater or more serious than it should be. ❑ *The punishment was out of all proportion to the crime.* 8 If you get something **out of proportion**, you think it is more important or worrying than it really is. If you keep something **in proportion**, you have a realistic view of how important it is. ❑ *Everything*
PREP-PHRASE; PREP-PHRASE; PREP-PHRASE: usu v-link PREP; PHRASE: PHR after v

*just got blown out of proportion... We've got to keep this in proportion.*

**pro|por|tion|al** /prəpɔːʳʃənəl/ If one amount is **proportional to** another, the two amounts increase and decrease at the same rate so there is always the same relationship between them. [FORMAL] ❑ *Loss of weight is directly proportional to the rate at which the disease is progressing.* ADJ: usu v-link ADJ *to* n
♦ **pro|por|tion|al|ly** *You have proportionally more fat on your thighs and hips than anywhere else on your body.* ADV: ADV with v, ADV with cl/group

**pro|por|tion|al|ity** /prəpɔːʳʃənælɪti/ The principle of **proportionality** is the idea that an action should not be more severe than is necessary, especially in a war or when punishing someone for a crime. [FORMAL] ❑ *Nuclear weapons seem to violate the just war principle of proportionality... He said there was a need for proportionality in sentencing.* N-UNCOUNT

**pro|por|tion|al rep|re|sen|ta|tion** **Proportional representation** is a system of voting in which each political party is represented in a parliament or legislature in proportion to the number of people who vote for it in an election. N-UNCOUNT

**pro|por|tion|ate** /prəpɔːʳʃənət/ **Proportionate** means the same as **proportional**. ❑ *Republics will have voting rights proportionate to the size of their economies.* ADJ: oft ADJ *to* n ♦ **pro|por|tion|ate|ly** *We have significantly increased the number of people in education but the size of the classes hasn't changed proportionately.* ADV: ADV with v, ADV with cl/group

**-proportioned** /-prəpɔːʳʃənd/ **-proportioned** is added to adverbs to form adjectives that indicate that the size and shape of the different parts of something or someone are pleasing or useful. ❑ *The flat has high ceilings and well-proportioned rooms.* COMB in ADJ

**pro|po|sal** /prəpoʊzəl/ **(proposals)** ◆◆◇ 1 A **proposal** is a plan or an idea, often a formal or written one, which is suggested for people to think about and decide upon. ❑ *The President is to put forward new proposals for resolving the country's constitutional crisis... The Security Council has rejected the latest peace proposal.* N-COUNT: oft N *for* n, N to-inf 2 A **proposal** is the act of asking someone to marry you. ❑ *After a three-weekend courtship, Pamela accepted Randolph's proposal of marriage.* N-COUNT

**pro|pose** /prəpoʊz/ **(proposes, proposing, proposed)** ◆◆◇ 1 If you **propose** something such as a plan or an idea, you suggest it for people to think about and decide upon. ❑ *Britain is about to propose changes to some institutions... It was George who first proposed that we dry clothes in that locker.* VERB = suggest; V n/-ing; V that 2 If you **propose to** do something, you intend to do it. ❑ *It's still far from clear what action the government proposes to take over the affair... And where do you propose building such a huge thing?* VERB; V to-inf; V -ing 3 If you **propose** a theory or an explanation, you state that it is possibly or probably true, because it fits in with the evidence that you have considered. [FORMAL] ❑ *This highlights a problem faced by people proposing theories of ball lightning... Newton proposed that heavenly and terrestrial motion could be unified with the idea of gravity.* VERB; V n; V that 4 If you **propose** a motion for debate, or a candidate for election, you begin the debate or the election procedure by formally stating your support for that motion or candidate. ❑ *A delegate from Siberia proposed a resolution that he stand down as party chairman.* VERB; V n ♦ **pro|pos|er (proposers)** *...Mr Ian Murch, the proposer of the motion.* N-COUNT 5 If you **propose** a toast to someone or something, you ask people to drink a toast to them. ❑ *Usually the bride's father proposes a toast to the health of the bride and groom.* VERB; V n 6 If you **propose to** someone, or **propose marriage to** them, you ask them to marry you. ❑ *He had proposed to Isabel the day after taking his seat in Parliament.* VERB; V *to* n; Also V, V n, V n *to* n

**propo|si|tion** /prɒpəzɪʃən/ **(propositions, propositioning, propositioned)** 1 If you describe something such as a task or an activity as, for example, a difficult **proposition** or an attractive **proposition**, you mean that it is difficult or pleasant to do. ❑ *Making easy money has always been an attractive proposition... Even among seasoned mountaineers Pinnacle Ridge is considered quite a tough proposition.* N-COUNT: usu sing, adj N 2 A **proposition** is a statement or an idea which people can consider or discuss to decide whether it is true. [FORMAL] ❑ *The proposition that democracies do not fight each other is based on a tiny historical sample.* N-COUNT: oft N that 3 In the United States, a **proposition** is a question or statement about an issue of public policy which appears on a voting paper so that people can vote for or against it. ❑ *Vote Yes on Proposition 136, but No on Propositions 129, 133 and 134.* N-COUNT: oft N num 4 A **proposition** is an offer or a suggestion that someone makes to you, usually concerning some work or business that you might be able to do together. ❑ *You came to see me at my office the other day with a business proposition.* N-COUNT 5 If someone who you do not know very well **propositions** you, they suggest that you have sex with them. ❑ *He had allegedly tried to proposition a colleague.* VERB; V n ♦ **Proposition** is also a noun. ❑ *...unwanted sexual propositions.* N-COUNT

**pro|pound** /prəpaʊnd/ **(propounds, propounding, propounded)** If someone **propounds** an idea or point of view they have, they suggest it for people to consider. [FORMAL] ❑ *Zoologist Eugene Morton has propounded a general theory of the vocal sounds that animals make.* VERB = put forward; V n

**pro|pri|etary** /prəpraɪətri, AM -teri/ 1 **Proprietary** substances or products are sold under a trade name. [FORMAL] ❑ *...some proprietary brands of dog food... We had to take action to protect the proprietary technology.* ADJ: ADJ n ≠ generic 2 If someone has a **proprietary** attitude towards something, they act as though they own it. [FORMAL] ❑ *Directors weren't allowed any proprietary airs about the product they made.* ADJ: usu ADJ n = proprietorial

**pro|pri|eties** /prəpraɪɪtiz/ **The proprieties** are the standards of social behaviour which most people consider socially or morally acceptable. [OLD-FASHIONED] ❑ *...respectable couples who observe the proprieties but loathe each other.* N-PLURAL: usu *the* N

**pro|pri|etor** /prəpraɪətəʳ/ **(proprietors)** The **proprietor** of a hotel, shop, newspaper, or other business is the person who owns it. [FORMAL] ❑ *...the proprietor of a local restaurant.* N-COUNT = owner

**pro|pri|etorial** /prəpraɪətɔːriəl/ If your behaviour is **proprietorial**, you are behaving in a proud way because you are, or feel like you are, the owner of something. [FORMAL] ❑ *The longer I live alone the more proprietorial I become about my home.* ADJ = proprietary

**pro|pri|etress** /prəpraɪətrɪs/ **(proprietresses)** The **proprietress** of a hotel, shop, or business is the woman who owns it. [FORMAL] ❑ *The proprietress was alone in the bar.* N-COUNT = owner

**pro|pri|ety** /prəpraɪɪti/ **Propriety** is the quality of being socially or morally acceptable. [FORMAL] ❑ *Their sense of social propriety is eroded.* N-UNCOUNT ≠ impropriety

**pro|pul|sion** /prəpʌlʃən/ **Propulsion** is the power that moves something, especially a vehicle, in a forward direction. [FORMAL] ❑ *Interest in jet propulsion was now growing at the Air Ministry.* N-UNCOUNT: oft n N, N n

**pro ra|ta** /proʊ rɑːtə, AM - reɪtə/ also **pro-rata.** If something is distributed **pro rata**, it is distributed in proportion to the amount or size of something. [FORMAL] ❑ *All part-timers should be paid the same, pro rata, as full-timers doing the same job.* ADV: ADV after v ♦ **Pro rata** is also an adjective. ❑ *They are paid their salaries and are entitled to fringe benefits on a pro-rata basis.* ADJ: ADJ n

**pro|sa|ic** /proʊzeɪɪk/ Something that is **prosaic** is dull and uninteresting. [FORMAL] ❑ *His instructor offered a more prosaic explanation for the surge in interest.* ADJ = mundane ♦ **pro|sai|cal|ly** /proʊzeɪɪkli/ *Arabian jam is also known as angels' hair preserve, or more prosaically as carrot jam.* ADV: ADV with cl, ADV with v

**pro|scenium** /proʊsiːniəm/ **(prosceniums)** A **proscenium** or a **proscenium arch** is an arch N-COUNT: usu sing in a theatre which separates the stage from the audience.

**pro|scribe** /proʊskraɪb/ **(proscribes, proscribing, proscribed)** If something **is proscribed** by people in authority, the existence or the use of that thing is forbidden. [FORMAL] ❑ *In some cultures surgery is proscribed... They are proscribed by federal law from owning guns.*
VERB: usu passive = prohibit; be V-ed; be V-ed from -ing

**pro|scrip|tion** /proʊskrɪpʃᵊn/ **(proscriptions)** The **proscription of** something is the official forbidding of its existence or use. [FORMAL] ❑ *...the proscription against any religious service. ...the proscription of his records.*
N-VAR = prohibition

**prose** /proʊz/ **Prose** is ordinary written language, in contrast to poetry. ❑ *Shute's prose is stark and chillingly unsentimental.*
N-UNCOUNT: oft poss N, in N ≠ poetry, verse

**pros|ecute** /prɒsɪkjuːt/ **(prosecutes, prosecuting, prosecuted)** 1 If the authorities **prosecute** someone, they charge them with a crime and put them on trial. ❑ *The police have decided not to prosecute because the evidence is not strong enough... Photographs taken by roadside cameras will soon be enough to prosecute drivers for speeding... He is being prosecuted for two criminal offences.*
VERB; V; V n for n; V n for n; Also V n
2 When a lawyer **prosecutes** a case, he or she tries to prove that the person who is on trial is guilty. ❑ *The attorney who will prosecute the case says he cannot reveal how much money is involved. ...the prosecuting attorney.*
VERB; V n; V-ing

**pros|ecu|tion** /prɒsɪkjuːʃᵊn/ **(prosecutions)** ◆◇◇ 1 **Prosecution** is the action of charging someone with a crime and putting them on trial. ❑ *Yesterday the head of government called for the prosecution of those responsible for the deaths.*
N-VAR: usu N of n
2 The lawyers who try to prove that a person on trial is guilty are called **the prosecution**. ❑ *Colonel Pugh, for the prosecution, said that the offences occurred over a six-year period.*
N-SING: the N

**pros|ecu|tor** /prɒsɪkjuːtəʳ/ **(prosecutors)** In some countries, a **prosecutor** is a lawyer or official who brings charges against someone or tries to prove in a trial that they are guilty.
N-COUNT

**pros|elyt|ize** /prɒsɪlɪtaɪz/ **(proselytizes, proselytizing, proselytized)**

> ✓ in BRIT, also use **proselytise**

If you **proselytize**, you try to persuade someone to share your beliefs, especially religious or political beliefs. [FORMAL] ❑ *I assured him we didn't come here to proselytize... Christians were arrested for trying to convert people, to proselytise them.*
VERB; V; V n

**pros|pect** **(prospects, prospecting, prospected)** ◆◆◇

> ✓ The noun is pronounced /prɒspekt, AM prɑː-/. The verb is pronounced /prəspekt, AM prɑːspekt/ and is hyphenated pro|spect.

1 If there is some **prospect of** something happening, there is a possibility that it will happen. ❑ *Unfortunately, there is little prospect of seeing these big questions answered... The prospects for peace in the country's eight-year civil war are becoming brighter... There is a real prospect that the bill will be defeated in parliament.*
N-VAR: with supp, oft N of n/-ing
2 A particular **prospect** is something that you expect or know is going to happen. ❑ *They now face the prospect of having to wear a cycling helmet by law.*
N-SING: usu with supp, oft N of n/-ing
3 Someone's **prospects** are their chances of being successful, especially in their career. ❑ *I chose to work abroad to improve my career prospects.*
N-PLURAL: usu supp N
4 When people **prospect for** oil, gold, or some other valuable substance, they look for it in the ground or under the sea. ❑ *He had prospected for minerals everywhere from the Gobi Desert to the Transvaal... In fact, the oil companies are already prospecting not far from here.*
VERB; V for n; V
♦ **pro|spect|ing** *He was involved in oil, zinc and lead prospecting.*
N-UNCOUNT
♦ **pro|spec|tor** **(prospectors)** *The discovery of gold brought a flood of prospectors into the Territories.*
N-COUNT

**pro|spec|tive** /prəspektɪv, AM prɑː-/ 1 You use **prospective** to describe someone who wants to be the thing mentioned or who is likely to be the thing mentioned. ❑ *The story should act as a warning to other prospective buyers... When his prospective employers learned that he smoked, they said they wouldn't hire him.*
ADJ: ADJ n = would-be
2 You use **prospective** to describe something that is likely to happen soon. ❑ *...the terms of the prospective deal.*
ADJ: ADJ n

**pro|spec|tus** /prəspektəs, AM prɑː-/ **(prospectuses)** A **prospectus** is a detailed document produced by a college, school, or company, which gives details about it.
N-COUNT

**pros|per** /prɒspəʳ/ **(prospers, prospering, prospered)** If people or businesses **prosper**, they are successful and do well. [FORMAL] ❑ *The high street banks continue to prosper... His teams have always prospered in cup competitions.*
VERB; V; V

**pros|per|ity** /prɒsperɪti/ **Prosperity** is a condition in which a person or community is doing well financially. ❑ *...a new era of peace and prosperity.*
N-UNCOUNT

**pros|per|ous** /prɒspərəs/ **Prosperous** people, places, and economies are rich and successful. [FORMAL] ❑ *...the youngest son of a relatively prosperous British family.*
ADJ = wealthy

**pros|tate** /prɒsteɪt/ **(prostates)** The **prostate** or the **prostate gland** is an organ in the body of male mammals which is situated at the neck of the bladder and produces a liquid which forms part of semen.
N-COUNT

**pros|the|sis** /prɒsθiːsɪs/ **(prostheses)** A **prosthesis** is an artificial body part that is used to replace a natural part. [MEDICAL]
N-COUNT

**pros|thet|ic** /prɒsθetɪk/ **Prosthetic** parts of the body are artificial ones used to replace natural ones. [MEDICAL]
ADJ: ADJ n = artificial

**pros|ti|tute** /prɒstɪtjuːt, AM -tuːt/ **(prostitutes)** A **prostitute** is a person, usually a woman, who has sex with men in exchange for money. ❑ *He admitted last week he paid for sex with a prostitute.*
N-COUNT

**pros|ti|tu|tion** /prɒstɪtjuːʃᵊn, AM -tuː-/ **Prostitution** means having sex with people in exchange for money. ❑ *She eventually drifts into prostitution.*
N-UNCOUNT

**pros|trate** **(prostrates, prostrating, prostrated)**

> ✓ The verb is pronounced /prɒstreɪt, AM prɑːstreɪt/. The adjective is pronounced /prɒstreɪt/.

1 If you **prostrate yourself**, you lie down flat on the ground, on your front, usually to show respect for God or a person in authority. ❑ *They prostrated themselves before their king.*
VERB; V pron-refl
2 If you are lying **prostrate**, you are lying flat on the ground, on your front. ❑ *Percy was lying prostrate, his arms outstretched and his eyes closed.*
ADJ: ADJ after v
3 If someone is **prostrate**, they are so distressed or affected by a very bad experience that they are unable to do anything at all. [FORMAL] ❑ *I was prostrate with grief.*
ADJ: oft ADJ with n = devastated

**pro|tago|nist** /prətægənɪst, AM proʊ-/ **(protagonists)** 1 Someone who is a **protagonist of** an idea or movement is a supporter of it. [FORMAL] ❑ *...the main protagonists of their countries' integration into the world market.*
N-COUNT: oft N of n = proponent ≠ opponent
2 A **protagonist** in a play, novel, or real event is one of the main people in it. [FORMAL] ❑ *...the protagonist of J. D. Salinger's novel 'The Catcher in the Rye'.*
N-COUNT

**pro|tean** /proʊtiən/ If you describe someone or something as **protean**, you mean that they have the ability to continually change their nature, appearance, or behaviour. [FORMAL] ❑ *He is a protean stylist who can move from blues to ballads and grand symphony.*
ADJ: usu ADJ n

**pro|tect** /prətekt/ **(protects, protecting, protected)** ◆◆◇ 1 To **protect** someone or something means to prevent them from being harmed or damaged. ❑ *So, what can women do to protect themselves from heart disease?... The government is committed to protecting the interests of tenants.*
VERB; V n from/against n; V n
2 If an insurance policy **protects** you **against** an event
VERB

such as death, injury, fire, or theft, the insurance company will give you or your family money if that event happens. ❑ *Many manufacturers have policies to protect themselves against blackmailers.* V n *against* n, Also V *against* n

**pro|tect|ed** /prətektɪd/ **Protected** is used to describe animals, plants, and areas of land which the law does not allow to be destroyed, harmed, or damaged. ❑ *In England, thrushes are a protected species so you will not find them on any menu.* ADJ

**pro|tec|tion** /prətekʃᵊn/ **(protections)** ◆◆◇ 1 To give or be **protection** against something unpleasant means to prevent people or things from being harmed or damaged by it. ❑ *Such a diet is widely believed to offer protection against a number of cancers... It is clear that the primary duty of parents is to provide protection for our children.* N-VAR 2 If an insurance policy gives you **protection against** an event such as death, injury, fire, or theft, the insurance company will give you or your family money if that event happens. ❑ *The new policy is believed to be the first scheme to offer protection against an illness.* N-UNCOUNT: oft N *against* n 3 If a government has a policy of **protection**, it helps its own industries by putting a tax on imported goods or by restricting imports in some other way. [BUSINESS] ❑ *Over the same period trade protection has increased in the rich countries.* N-UNCOUNT

**pro|tec|tion|ism** /prətekʃənɪzəm/ **Protectionism** is the policy some countries have of helping their own industries by putting a large tax on imported goods or by restricting imports in some other way. [BUSINESS] ❑ *...talks to promote free trade and avert increasing protectionism.* N-UNCOUNT

**pro|tec|tion|ist** /prətekʃənɪst/ **(protectionists)** 1 A **protectionist** is someone who agrees with and supports protectionism. [BUSINESS] ❑ *Trade frictions between the two countries had been caused by trade protectionists.* N-COUNT 2 **Protectionist** policies, measures, and laws are meant to stop or reduce imports. [BUSINESS] ADJ

**pro|tec|tive** /prətektɪv/ 1 **Protective** means designed or intended to protect something or someone from harm. ❑ *Protective gloves reduce the absorption of chemicals through the skin... Protective measures are necessary if the city's monuments are to be preserved.* ADJ: usu ADJ n 2 If someone is **protective towards** you, they look after you and show a strong desire to keep you safe. ❑ *He is very protective towards his mother.* ADJ: oft ADJ *towards/of* n ♦ **pro|tec|tive|ly** *Simon drove me to the airport and protectively told me to look after myself.* ADV: ADV with v ♦ **pro|tec|tive|ness** *What she felt now was protectiveness towards her brothers, her sister and her new baby.* N-UNCOUNT

**pro|tec|tive cus|to|dy** If a witness in a court case is being held in **protective custody**, they are being kept in prison in order to prevent them from being harmed. ❑ *They might be doing me a good turn if they took me into protective custody.* N-UNCOUNT

**pro|tec|tor** /prətektəʳ/ **(protectors)** 1 If you refer to someone as your **protector**, you mean that they protect you from being harmed. ❑ *Many mothers see their son as a potential protector and provider.* N-COUNT 2 A **protector** is a device that protects someone or something from physical harm. ❑ *He was the only National League umpire to wear an outside chest protector.* N-COUNT: usu n N

**pro|tec|tor|ate** /prətektərət/ **(protectorates)** A **protectorate** is a country that is controlled and protected by a more powerful country. ❑ *In 1914 the country became a British protectorate.* N-COUNT

**pro|té|gé** /prɒtɪʒeɪ, AM proʊt-/ **(protégés)**

> ✔ The spelling **protégée** is often used when referring to a woman.

The **protégé** of an older and more experienced person is a young person who is helped and guided by them over a period of time. ❑ *He had been a protégé of Captain James.* N-COUNT

**pro|tein** /proʊtiːn/ **(proteins)** ◆◇◇ **Protein** is a substance found in food and drink such as meat, eggs, and milk. You need protein in order to grow and be healthy. ❑ *Fish was a major source of protein for the working man. ...a high protein diet.* N-MASS

**pro tem** /proʊ tem/ If someone has a particular position or job **pro tem**, they have it temporarily. [FORMAL] ❑ *...the president pro tem of the California State Senate.* ADV: n ADV

**pro|test** **(protests, protesting, protested)** ◆◆◇

> ✔ The verb is pronounced /prətest/. The noun is pronounced /proʊtest/.

1 If you **protest against** something or **about** something, you say or show publicly that you object to it. In American English, you usually say that you **protest** it. ❑ *Groups of women took to the streets to protest against the arrests... The students were protesting at overcrowding in the university hostels... They were protesting soaring prices... He picked up the cat before Rosa could protest.* VERB V *about/against/at* n V *about/against/at* n V n V 2 A **protest** is the act of saying or showing publicly that you object to something. ❑ *The opposition now seems too weak to stage any serious protests against the government... The unions called a two-hour strike in protest at the railway authority's announcement. ...a protest march.* N-VAR: oft N *against/at/about* n 3 If you **protest that** something is the case, you insist that it is the case, when other people think that it may not be. ❑ *When we tried to protest that Mo was beaten up they didn't believe us... 'I never said any of that to her,' he protested... He has always protested his innocence.* VERB V that V with quote V n

**Prot|es|tant** /prɒtɪstənt/ **(Protestants)** 1 A **Protestant** is a Christian who belongs to the branch of the Christian church which separated from the Catholic church in the sixteenth century. N-COUNT 2 **Protestant** means relating to Protestants or their churches. ❑ *Most Protestant churches now have women ministers.* ADJ: usu ADJ n

**Prot|es|tant|ism** /prɒtɪstəntɪzəm/ **Protestantism** is the set of Christian beliefs that are held by Protestants. ❑ *...the spread of Protestantism.* N-UNCOUNT

**pro|tes|ta|tion** /prɒtɪsteɪʃᵊn/ **(protestations)** A **protestation** is a strong declaration that something is true or not true. [FORMAL] ❑ *Despite his constant protestations of devotion and love, her doubts persisted.* N-COUNT: oft N *of* n

**pro|test|er** /prətestəʳ/ **(protesters)** also **protestor. Protesters** are people who protest publicly about an issue. ❑ *The protesters say the government is corrupt and inefficient.* N-COUNT

**pro|test vote** **(protest votes)** In an election, a **protest vote** is a vote against the party you usually support in order to show disapproval of something they are doing or planning to do. N-COUNT

**proto-** /proʊtoʊ-/ **Proto-** is used to form adjectives and nouns which indicate that something is in the early stages of its development. ❑ *...the proto-fascist tendencies of some of its supporters. ...Albion, whose own legend stretches back to the mists of proto-history.* PREFIX

**proto|col** /proʊtəkɒl, AM -kɔːl/ **(protocols)** 1 **Protocol** is a system of rules about the correct way to act in formal situations. ❑ *He has become something of a stickler for the finer observances of royal protocol. ...minor breaches of protocol.* N-VAR 2 A **protocol** is a set of rules for exchanging information between computers. [COMPUTING] N-COUNT 3 A **protocol** is a written record of a treaty or agreement that has been made by two or more countries. [FORMAL] ❑ *...the Montreal Protocol to phase out use and production of CFCs.* N-COUNT = accord 4 A **protocol** is a plan for a course of medical treatment, or a plan for a scientific experiment. [AM, FORMAL] ❑ *...the detoxification protocol.* N-COUNT

**pro|ton** /proʊtɒn/ **(protons)** A **proton** is an atomic particle that has a positive electrical charge. [TECHNICAL] N-COUNT

**proto|type** /proʊtətaɪp/ **(prototypes)** 1 A **prototype** is a new type of machine or device which is not yet ready to be made in large numbers and sold. ❑ *Chris Retzler has built a prototype of a machine called the wave rotor.* N-COUNT: oft N *of* n, N n 2 If you say that N-COUNT:

someone or something is a **prototype of** a type of person or thing, you mean that they are the first or most typical one of that type. ❑ *He was the prototype of the elder statesman.* — usu N *of* n

**proto|typi|cal** /proʊtətɪpɪkᵊl/ **Prototypical** is used to indicate that someone or something is a very typical example of a type of person or thing. [FORMAL] ❑ *Park Ridge is the prototypical American suburb. ...a prototypical socialist.* — ADJ: usu ADJ n = *archetypal*

**proto|zoan** /proʊtəzoʊən/ **(protozoa** or **protozoans) Protozoa** are very small organisms which often live inside larger animals. [TECHNICAL] — N-COUNT: usu pl

**pro|tract|ed** /prətræktɪd, AM proʊ-/ Something, usually something unpleasant, that is **protracted** lasts a long time, especially longer than usual or longer than you hoped. [FORMAL] ❑ *After protracted negotiations, Ogden got the deal he wanted... The struggle would be bitter and protracted.* — ADJ

**pro|trac|tor** /prətræktəʳ, AM proʊ-/ **(protractors)** A **protractor** is a flat, semi-circular piece of plastic or metal which is used for measuring angles. — N-COUNT

**pro|trude** /prətruːd, AM proʊ-/ **(protrudes, protruding, protruded)** If something **protrudes from** somewhere, it sticks out. [FORMAL] ❑ *...a huge round mass of smooth rock protruding from the water... The tip of her tongue was protruding slightly.* ♦ **pro|trud|ing** *...protruding ears.* — VERB; V prep; V; ADJ

**pro|tru|sion** /prətruːʒᵊn, AM proʊ-/ **(protrusions)** A **protrusion** is something that sticks out from something. [FORMAL] ❑ *He grabbed at a protrusion of rock with his right hand.* — N-COUNT

**pro|tu|ber|ance** /prətjuːbərəns, AM proʊtuːb-/ **(protuberances)** A **protuberance** is a rounded part that sticks out from the surface of something. [FORMAL] ❑ *...a protuberance on the upper jawbone.* — N-COUNT

**pro|tu|ber|ant** /prətjuːbərənt, AM proʊtuːb-/ **Protuberant** eyes, lips, noses, or teeth stick out more than usual from the face. [FORMAL] — ADJ: usu ADJ n = *protruding*

**proud** /praʊd/ **(prouder, proudest)** ◆◇◇ [1] If you feel **proud**, you feel pleased about something good that you possess or have done, or about something good that a person close to you has done. ❑ *I felt proud of his efforts... They are proud that she is doing well at school... I am proud to be a Canadian... Derek is now the proud father of a bouncing baby girl.* ♦ **proud|ly** *'That's the first part finished,' he said proudly.* [2] Your **proudest** moments or achievements are the ones that you are most proud of. ❑ *This must have been one of the proudest moments of his busy and hard working life.* [3] Someone who is **proud** has respect for themselves and does not want to lose the respect that other people have for them. ❑ *He was too proud to ask his family for help and support.* [4] Someone who is **proud** feels that they are better or more important than other people. ❑ *She was said to be proud and arrogant.* — ADJ: oft ADJ *of* n, ADJ that/to-inf ≠ *ashamed*; ADV: ADV with v; ADJ: ADJ n, usu ADJ-superl; ADJ; ADJ [disapproval] = *arrogant* ≠ *humble*

**prove** /pruːv/ **(proves, proving, proved, proved** or **proven)** ◆◆◇ [1] If something **proves to** be true or **to** have a particular quality, it becomes clear after a period of time that it is true or has that quality. ❑ *We have been accused of exaggerating before, but unfortunately all our reports proved to be true... In the past this process of transition has often proven difficult. ...an experiment which was to prove a source of inspiration for many years to come.* [2] If you **prove that** something is true, you show by means of argument or evidence that it is definitely true. ❑ *You brought this charge. You prove it!... The results prove that regulation of the salmon farming industry is inadequate. ...trying to prove how groups of animals have evolved... That made me hopping mad and determined to prove him wrong... History will prove him to have been right all along. ...a proven cause of cancer.* [3] If you **prove yourself to** have a certain good quality, you show by your actions that you have it. ❑ *Margaret proved herself to be a good mother... As a composer he proved himself adept at large dramatic forms... A man needs time to prove himself... Few would argue that this team has experience and proven ability.* [4] If you **prove** a **point**, you show other people that you know something or can do something, although your action may have no other purpose. ❑ *They made a 3,000 mile detour simply to prove a point.* — V-LINK; V to-inf; V adj; V n; VERB; V n; V that; V wh; V n adj; V n to-inf; V-ed; VERB; V pron-refl to-inf; V pron-refl adj; V pron-refl; V-ed; PHRASE: V inflects

**prov|en** /pruːvᵊn, proʊvᵊn/ **Proven** is a past participle of **prove**. **Proven** is the usual form of the past participle when you are using it as an adjective.

**prov|enance** /prɒvɪnəns/ **(provenances)** The **provenance** of something is the place that it comes from or that it originally came from. [FORMAL] ❑ *Kato was fully aware of the provenance of these treasures.* — N-VAR: usu with poss

**prov|erb** /prɒvɜːʳb/ **(proverbs)** A **proverb** is a short sentence that people often quote, which gives advice or tells you something about life. ❑ *An old Arab proverb says, 'The enemy of my enemy is my friend'.* — N-COUNT = *saying*

**pro|ver|bial** /prəvɜːʳbiəl/ You use **proverbial** to show that you know the way you are describing something is one that is often used or is part of a popular saying. ❑ *My audience certainly isn't the proverbial man in the street.* — ADJ: ADJ n

**pro|vide** /prəvaɪd/ **(provides, providing, provided)** ◆◆◆ [1] If you **provide** something that someone needs or wants, or if you **provide** them **with** it, you give it to them or make it available to them. ❑ *I'll be glad to provide a copy of this... They would not provide any details... The government was not in a position to provide them with food.* ♦ **pro|vid|er (providers)** *They remain the main providers of sports facilities.* [2] If a law or agreement **provides that** something will happen, it states that it will happen. [FORMAL] ❑ *The treaty provides that, by the end of the century, the United States must have removed its bases.* [3] → See also **provided**, **providing**. — VERB = *supply*; V n; V n; V n *with* n; N-COUNT; VERB; V that

♦ **provide for** [1] If you **provide for** someone, you support them financially and make sure that they have the things that they need. ❑ *Elaine wouldn't let him provide for her... Her father always ensured she was well provided for.* [2] If you **provide for** something that might happen or that might need to be done, you make arrangements to deal with it. ❑ *James had provided for just such an emergency.* [3] If a law or agreement **provides for** something, it makes it possible. [FORMAL] ❑ *The bill provides for the automatic review of all death sentences.* — PHRASAL VERB; V P n; *be* adv V-ed *for*; PHRASAL VERB; V P n; PHRASAL VERB; V P n

**pro|vid|ed** /prəvaɪdɪd/ If you say that something will happen **provided** or **provided that** something else happens, you mean that the first thing will happen only if the second thing also happens. ❑ *The other banks are going to be very eager to help, provided that they see that he has a specific plan... Provided they are fit I see no reason why they shouldn't go on playing for another four or five years.* — CONJ = *providing*

**provi|dence** /prɒvɪdəns/ **Providence** is God, or a force which is believed by some people to arrange the things that happen to us. [LITERARY] ❑ *These women regard his death as an act of providence.* — N-UNCOUNT = *fate*

**provi|den|tial** /prɒvɪdenʃᵊl/ A **providential** event is lucky because it happens at exactly the right time. [FORMAL] ❑ *He explained the yellow fever epidemic as a providential act to discourage urban growth... The pistols were loaded so our escape is indeed providential.* ♦ **provi|den|tial|ly** *Providentially, he had earlier made friends with a Russian Colonel.* — ADJ = *fortunate*; ADV

**pro|vid|ing** /prəvaɪdɪŋ/ If you say that something will happen **providing** or **providing that** something else happens, you mean that the first thing will happen only if the second thing also happens. ❑ *I do believe in people being able to do* — CONJ = *provided* *what they want to do, providing they're not hurting someone else.*

**prov|ince** /prɒvɪns/ **(provinces)** [1] A **province** is a large section of a country which has its own administration. ❑ *...the Algarve, Portugal's southernmost province.* [2] **The provinces** are all the parts of a country except the part where the capital is situated. ❑ *The government plans to transfer some 30,000 government jobs from Paris to the provinces.* [3] If you say that a subject or activity is a particular person's **province**, you mean that this person has a special interest in it, a special knowledge of it, or a special responsibility for it. ❑ *Industrial research is the province of the Department of Trade and Industry.* ◆◇◇ N-COUNT; N-PLURAL: usu *the* N; N-SING: with poss

**pro|vin|cial** /prəvɪnʃəl/ [1] **Provincial** means connected with the parts of a country away from the capital city. ❑ *Jeremy Styles, 34, was the house manager for a provincial theatre for ten years.* [2] If you describe someone or something as **provincial**, you disapprove of them because you think that they are old-fashioned and boring. ❑ *He decided to revamp the company's provincial image.* ADJ: ADJ n; ADJ [disapproval]

**pro|vin|cial|ism** /prəvɪnʃəlɪzəm/ **Provincialism** is the holding of old-fashioned attitudes and opinions, which some people think is typical of people in areas away from the capital city of a country. ❑ *...the stifling bourgeois provincialism of Buxton.* N-UNCOUNT [disapproval]

**prov|ing ground** **(proving grounds)** If you describe a place as a **proving ground**, you mean that new things or ideas are tried out or tested there. ❑ *New York is a proving ground today for the Democratic presidential candidates.* N-COUNT

**pro|vi|sion** /prəvɪʒən/ **(provisions)** [1] The **provision of** something is the act of giving it or making it available to people who need or want it. ❑ *The department is responsible for the provision of residential care services. ...nursery provision for children with special needs.* [2] If you make **provision for** something that might happen or that might need to be done, you make arrangements to deal with it. ❑ *Mr King asked if it had ever occurred to her to make provision for her own pension.* [3] If you make **provision for** someone, you support them financially and make sure that they have the things that they need. ❑ *Special provision should be made for children.* [4] A **provision** in a law or an agreement is an arrangement which is included in it. ❑ *He backed a provision that would allow judges to delay granting a divorce decree in some cases.* [5] **Provisions** are supplies of food. [OLD-FASHIONED] ❑ *On board were enough provisions for two weeks.* ◆◇◇ N-UNCOUNT: also *a* N, with supp, oft N *of* n; N-VAR: usu N *for* n/-ing; N-UNCOUNT: also N in pl, N *for* n; N-COUNT; N-PLURAL

**pro|vi|sion|al** /prəvɪʒənəl/ You use **provisional** to describe something that has been arranged or appointed for the present, but may be changed in the future. ❑ *...the possibility of setting up a provisional coalition government... It was announced that the times were provisional and subject to confirmation.* ♦ **pro|vi|sion|al|ly** *The seven republics had provisionally agreed to the new relationship on November 14th.* ADJ; ADV: ADV with v

**pro|vi|so** /prəvaɪzoʊ/ **(provisos)** A **proviso** is a condition in an agreement. You agree to do something if this condition is fulfilled. ❑ *I told Norman I would invest in his venture as long as he agreed to one proviso.* N-COUNT: oft N that

**pro|vo|ca|teur** /proʊvɒkətɜːʳ/ **(provocateurs)** → see **agent provocateur**.

**provo|ca|tion** /prɒvəkeɪʃən/ **(provocations)** If you describe a person's action as **provocation** or a **provocation**, you mean that it is a reason for someone else to react angrily, violently, or emotionally. ❑ *He denies murder on the grounds of provocation... The soldiers fired without provocation.* N-VAR: usu prep N

**pro|voca|tive** /prəvɒkətɪv/ [1] If you describe something as **provocative**, you mean that it is intended to make people react angrily or argue against it. ❑ *He has made a string of outspoken and sometimes provocative speeches in recent years... His behavior was called provocative and antisocial.* ♦ **pro|voca|tive|ly** *The soldiers fired into the air when the demonstrators behaved provocatively.* [2] If you describe someone's clothing or behaviour as **provocative**, you mean that it is intended to make someone feel sexual desire. ❑ *Some adolescents might be more sexually mature and provocative than others.* ♦ **pro|voca|tive|ly** *She smiled provocatively.* ADJ; ADV: usu ADV with v; ADJ; ADV: usu ADV with v, also ADV adj

**pro|voke** /prəvoʊk/ **(provokes, provoking, provoked)** [1] If you **provoke** someone, you deliberately annoy them and try to make them behave aggressively. ❑ *He started beating me when I was about fifteen but I didn't do anything to provoke him... I provoked him into doing something really stupid.* [2] If something **provokes** a reaction, it causes it. ❑ *His election success has provoked a shocked reaction.* ◆◇◇ VERB; V n; V n *into* -ing/n; VERB; V n

**prov|ost** /prɒvəst, AM proʊvoʊst/ **(provosts)** [1] In some university colleges in Britain, the **provost** is the head. [2] In some colleges and universities in the United States, a **provost** is an official who deals with matters such as the teaching staff and the courses of study. [3] A **provost** is the chief magistrate of a Scottish administrative area. [4] In the Roman Catholic and Anglican Churches, a **provost** is the person who is in charge of the administration of a cathedral. N-COUNT; N-COUNT; N-COUNT; N-COUNT

**prow** /praʊ/ **(prows)** The **prow** of a ship or boat is the front part of it. N-COUNT

**prow|ess** /praʊɪs/ Someone's **prowess** is their great skill at doing something. [FORMAL] ❑ *He's always bragging about his prowess as a cricketer.* N-UNCOUNT

**prowl** /praʊl/ **(prowls, prowling, prowled)** [1] If an animal or a person **prowls around**, they move around quietly, for example when they are hunting. ❑ *Policemen prowled around the building.* [2] If an animal is **on the prowl**, it is hunting. If a person is **on the prowl**, they are hunting for something such as a sexual partner or a business deal. ❑ *Their fellow travellers are a mix of honeymooners, single girls on the prowl and elderly couples... The new administration are on the prowl for ways to reduce spending.* VERB; V prep/adv; PHRASE: v-link PHR, oft PHR *for* n

**prowl|er** /praʊləʳ/ **(prowlers)** A **prowler** is someone who secretly follows people or hides near their houses, especially at night, in order to steal something, frighten them, or perhaps harm them. N-COUNT

**prox|im|ity** /prɒksɪmɪti/ **Proximity to** a place or person is nearness to that place or person. [FORMAL] ❑ *Part of the attraction is Darwin's proximity to Asia... Families are no longer in close proximity to each other.* N-UNCOUNT: usu N *to/of* n, *in* N

**proxy** /prɒksi/ If you do something **by proxy**, you arrange for someone else to do it for you. ❑ *Those not attending the meeting may vote by proxy.* N-UNCOUNT: usu *by* N

**Pro|zac** /proʊzæk/ **Prozac** is a drug that is used to treat people who are suffering from depression. [TRADEMARK] N-UNCOUNT

**prude** /pruːd/ **(prudes)** If you call someone a **prude**, you mean that they are too easily shocked by things relating to sex. N-COUNT [disapproval]

**pru|dence** /pruːdəns/ **Prudence** is care and good sense that someone shows when making a decision or taking action. [FORMAL] ❑ *A lack of prudence may lead to financial problems.* N-UNCOUNT

**pru|dent** /pruːdənt/ Someone who is **prudent** is sensible and careful. ❑ *It is always prudent to start any exercise programme gradually at first... Being a prudent and cautious person, you realise that the problem must be resolved.* ♦ **pru|dent|ly** *Prudently, Joanna spoke none of this aloud.* ADJ: oft *it* v-link ADJ to-inf ≠ *rash*; ADV: usu ADV with v

**prud|ery** /pruːdəri/ **Prudery** is prudish behaviour or attitudes. N-UNCOUNT [disapproval]

**prud|ish** /pruːdɪʃ/ If you describe someone as **prudish**, you mean that they are too easily ADJ [disapproval] shocked by things relating to sex. ❑ *I'm not prudish but I think these photographs are obscene.* ♦ **prud|ish|ness** *Older people will have grown up in a time of greater sexual prudishness.* N-UNCOUNT = *prudery*

**prune** /pruːn/ **(prunes, pruning, pruned)** [1] A **prune** is a dried plum. N-COUNT [2] When you **prune** a tree or bush, you cut off some of the branches so that it will grow better the next year. VERB ❑ *You have to prune a bush if you want fruit... There is no best way to prune.* V n V ♦ **Prune back** means the same as **prune**. PHRASAL VERB ❑ *Apples, pears and cherries can be pruned back when they've lost their leaves.* V P n Also V n P [3] If you **prune** something, you cut out all the parts that you do not need. VERB ❑ *Firms are cutting investment and pruning their product ranges.* V n ♦ **Prune back** means the same as **prune**. PHRASAL VERB ❑ *The company has pruned back its workforce by 20,000 since 1989.* V P n (not pron)

♦ **prune back** → see **prune 2, 3.**

**pru|ri|ence** /prʊəriəns/ **Prurience** is a strong interest that someone shows in sexual matters. [FORMAL] N-UNCOUNT [disapproval] ❑ *Nobody ever lost money by overestimating the public's prurience.*

**pru|ri|ent** /prʊəriənt/ If you describe someone as **prurient**, you mean that they show too much interest in sexual matters. [FORMAL] ADJ: usu ADJ n [disapproval] = *salacious* ❑ *We read the gossip written about them with prurient interest.*

**pry** /praɪ/ **(pries, prying, pried)** [1] If someone **pries**, they try to find out about someone else's private affairs, or look at their personal possessions. VERB ❑ *We do not want people prying into our affairs... Imelda might think she was prying... She thought she was safe from prying eyes and could do as she wished.* V *into* n V V-ing [2] If you **pry** something open or **pry** it away from a surface, you force it open or away from a surface. VERB = *prize* ❑ *They pried open a sticky can of blue paint... I pried the top off a can of chilli... Prying off the plastic lid, she took out a small scoop.* V n with adj V n prep V n with adv [3] If you **pry** something such as information **out of** someone, you persuade them to tell you although they may be very unwilling to. [mainly AM] VERB ❑ *...their attempts to pry the names from the Bureau.* V n *from/out of* n

☑ in BRIT, usually use **prize**

**PS** /piː es/ also **P.S.** You write **PS** to introduce something that you add at the end of a letter after you have signed it. ❑ *PS. Please show your friends this letter and the enclosed leaflet.*

**psalm** /sɑːm/ **(psalms)** The **Psalms** are the 150 songs, poems, and prayers which together form the Book of Psalms in the Bible. N-COUNT ❑ *He recited a verse of the twenty-third psalm.*

**pse|pholo|gist** /sɪfɒlədʒɪst, AM siː-/ **(psephologists)** A **psephologist** studies how people vote in elections. N-COUNT

**pseud** /sjuːd/ **(pseuds)** If you say that someone is a **pseud**, you mean that they are trying to appear very intellectual but you think that they appear silly. [BRIT, INFORMAL] N-COUNT [disapproval]

**pseudo-** /sjuːdoʊ-, AM suːdoʊ-/ **Pseudo-** is used to form adjectives and nouns that indicate that something is not the thing it is claimed to be. For example, if you describe a country as a pseudo-democracy, you mean that it is not really a democracy, although its government claims that it is. PREFIX ❑ *...pseudo-intellectual images.*

**pseudo|nym** /sjuːdənɪm, AM suː-/ **(pseudonyms)** A **pseudonym** is a name which someone, usually a writer, uses instead of his or her real name. N-COUNT: oft N *of/for* n ❑ *Both plays were published under the pseudonym of Philip Dayre.*

**pso|ria|sis** /səraɪəsɪs/ **Psoriasis** is a disease that causes dry red patches on the skin. N-UNCOUNT

**psst** /psst/ **Psst** is a sound that someone makes when they want to attract another person's attention secretly or quietly. ❑ *'Psst! Come over here!' one youth hissed furtively.*

**psych** /saɪk/ **(psychs, psyching, psyched)** also **psyche.**

♦ **psych out** If you **psych out** your opponent in a contest, you try to make them feel less confident by behaving in a very confident or aggressive way. [INFORMAL] PHRASAL VERB ❑ *They are like heavyweight boxers, trying to psych each other out and build themselves up.* V n P Also V P n (not pron)

♦ **psych up** If you **psych yourself up** before a contest or a difficult task, you prepare yourself for it mentally, especially by telling yourself that you can win or succeed. [INFORMAL] PHRASAL VERB ❑ *After work, it is hard to psych yourself up for an hour at the gym... Before the game everyone gets psyched up and starts shouting.* V pron-refl P *get* V-ed P

**psy|che** /saɪki/ **(psyches)** In psychology, your **psyche** is your mind and your deepest feelings and attitudes. [TECHNICAL] N-COUNT ❑ *His exploration of the myth brings insight into the American psyche.*

**psychedelia** /saɪkədiːliə/ **Psychedelia** refers to psychedelic objects, clothes, and music. N-UNCOUNT

**psychedel|ic** /saɪkədelɪk/ [1] **Psychedelic** means relating to drugs such as LSD which have a strong effect on your mind, often making you see things that are not there. ADJ: usu ADJ n ❑ *...his first real, full-blown psychedelic experience.* [2] **Psychedelic** art has bright colours and strange patterns. ADJ: usu ADJ n ❑ *...psychedelic patterns.*

**psy|chi|at|ric** /saɪkiætrɪk/ [1] **Psychiatric** means relating to psychiatry. ADJ: ADJ n ❑ *We finally insisted that he seek psychiatric help.* [2] **Psychiatric** means involving mental illness. ADJ: ADJ n ❑ *About 4% of the prison population have chronic psychiatric illnesses.*

**psy|chia|trist** /saɪkaɪətrɪst, AM sɪ-/ **(psychiatrists)** A **psychiatrist** is a doctor who treats people suffering from mental illness. N-COUNT

**psy|chia|try** /saɪkaɪətri, AM sɪ-/ **Psychiatry** is the branch of medicine concerned with the treatment of mental illness. N-UNCOUNT

**psy|chic** /saɪkɪk/ **(psychics)** [1] If you believe that someone is **psychic** or has **psychic** powers, you believe that they have strange mental powers, such as being able to read the minds of other people or to see into the future. ADJ ❑ *Trevor helped police by using his psychic powers.* ♦ A **psychic** is someone who seems to be psychic. N-COUNT [2] **Psychic** means relating to ghosts and the spirits of the dead. ADJ ❑ *He declared his total disbelief in psychic phenomena.*

**psy|chi|cal** /saɪkɪkəl/ **Psychical** means relating to ghosts and the spirits of the dead. [FORMAL] ADJ

**psy|cho** /saɪkoʊ/ **(psychos)** A **psycho** is someone who has serious mental problems and who may act in a violent way without feeling sorry for what they have done. [INFORMAL] N-COUNT = *psychopath* ❑ *Some psycho picked her up, and killed her.*

**psycho-** /saɪkoʊ-/ **Psycho-** is added to words in order to form other words which describe or refer to things connected with the mind or with mental processes. PREFIX ❑ *...the psycho-social aspects of youth unemployment.*

**psycho|ac|tive** /saɪkoʊæktɪv/ **Psychoactive** drugs are drugs that affect your mind. ADJ

**psycho|ana|lyse** /saɪkoʊænəlaɪz/ **(psychoanalyses, psychoanalysing, psychoanalysed)**

☑ in AM, use **psychoanalyze**

When a psychotherapist or psychiatrist **psychoanalyses** someone who has mental problems, he or she examines or treats them using psychoanalysis. VERB ❑ *The movie sees Burton psychoanalysing Firth to cure him of his depression.* V n

**psycho|analy|sis** /saɪkoʊənælɪsɪs/ **Psychoanalysis** is the treatment of someone who has mental problems by asking them about their feelings and their past in order to try to discover what may be causing their condition. N-UNCOUNT = *analysis*

**psycho|ana|lyst** /saɪkoʊænəlɪst/ **(psychoanalysts)** A **psychoanalyst** is someone who treats people who have mental problems using psychoanalysis. N-COUNT = *analyst*

**psycho|ana|lyt|ic** /saɪkoʊænəlɪtɪk/ **Psychoanalytic** means relating to psychoanalysis. ADJ: ADJ n ❑ *...psychoanalytic therapy.*

**psycho|ana|lyze** /saɪkoʊænəlaɪz/ → see **psychoanalyse**.

**psycho|bab|ble** /saɪkoʊbæbəl/ If you refer to language about people's feelings or behaviour as **psychobabble**, you mean that it is very complicated and perhaps meaningless. ❑ *Beneath the sentimental psychobabble, there's a likeable movie trying to get out.* N-UNCOUNT disapproval

**psycho|dra|ma** /saɪkoʊdrɑːmə/ **(psychodramas)** **Psychodrama** is a type of psychotherapy in which people express their problems by acting them out in front of other people. N-VAR

**psycho|ki|nesis** /saɪkoʊkɪniːsɪs/ **Psychokinesis** is the ability, which some people believe exists, to move objects using the power of your mind. N-UNCOUNT

**psycho|logi|cal** /saɪkəlɒdʒɪkəl/ ◆◇◇ 1 **Psychological** means concerned with a person's mind and thoughts. ❑ *John received constant physical and psychological abuse from his father... Robyn's loss of memory is a psychological problem, rather than a physical one.* ADJ: usu ADJ n = mental ♦ **psycho|logi|cal|ly** /saɪkəlɒdʒɪkli/ *It was very important psychologically for us to succeed.* ADV: ADV with cl, ADV adj/adv 2 **Psychological** means relating to psychology. ❑ *...psychological testing.* ADJ: ADJ n

**psycho|logi|cal war|fare** **Psychological warfare** consists of attempts to make your enemy lose confidence, give up hope, or feel afraid, so that you can win. N-UNCOUNT

**psy|cholo|gist** /saɪkɒlədʒɪst/ **(psychologists)** A **psychologist** is a person who studies the human mind and tries to explain why people behave in the way that they do. N-COUNT

**psy|chol|ogy** /saɪkɒlədʒi/ 1 **Psychology** is the scientific study of the human mind and the reasons for people's behaviour. ❑ *...Professor of Psychology at Bedford College.* N-UNCOUNT 2 The **psychology of** a person is the kind of mind that they have, which makes them think or behave in the way that they do. ❑ *...a fascination with the psychology of murderers.* N-UNCOUNT: usu N *of* n

**psycho|met|ric** /saɪkəmetrɪk/ **Psychometric** tests are designed to test a person's mental state, personality, and thought processes. ADJ: ADJ n

**psycho|path** /saɪkoʊpæθ/ **(psychopaths)** A **psychopath** is someone who has serious mental problems and who may act in a violent way without feeling sorry for what they have done. ❑ *She was abducted by a dangerous psychopath.* N-COUNT

**psycho|path|ic** /saɪkoʊpæθɪk/ Someone who is **psychopathic** is a psychopath. ❑ *...a report labelling him psychopathic. ...a psychopathic killer.* ADJ

**psy|cho|sis** /saɪkoʊsɪs/ **(psychoses)** **Psychosis** is mental illness of a severe kind which can make people lose contact with reality. [MEDICAL] ❑ *He may have some kind of neurosis or psychosis later in life.* N-VAR

**psycho|so|mat|ic** /saɪkoʊsoʊmætɪk/ If someone has a **psychosomatic** illness, their symptoms are caused by worry or unhappiness rather than by a physical problem. ❑ *Doctors refused to treat her, claiming that her problems were all psychosomatic.* ADJ

**psycho|thera|pist** /saɪkoʊθerəpɪst/ **(psychotherapists)** A **psychotherapist** is a person who treats people who are mentally ill using psychotherapy. N-COUNT

**psycho|thera|py** /saɪkoʊθerəpi/ **Psychotherapy** is the use of psychological methods in treating people who are mentally ill, rather than using physical methods such as drugs or surgery. ❑ *For milder depressions, certain forms of psychotherapy do work well.* N-UNCOUNT

**psy|chot|ic** /saɪkɒtɪk/ **(psychotics)** Someone who is **psychotic** has a type of severe mental illness. [MEDICAL] ADJ ♦ **Psychotic** is also a noun. ❑ *A religious psychotic in Las Vegas has killed four people.* N-COUNT

**psycho|trop|ic** /saɪkoʊtrɒpɪk/ **Psychotropic** drugs are drugs that affect your mind. ADJ

**pt (pts)** also **pt.**

✔ The plural in meaning 1 is either **pt** or **pts**.

1 **pt** is a written abbreviation for **pint**. ❑ *...1 pt single cream.* 2 **pt** is the written abbreviation for **point**. ❑ *Here's how it works – 3 pts for a correct result, 1 pt for the correct winning team.*

**PTA** /piː tiː eɪ/ **(PTAs)** A **PTA** is a school association run by some of the parents and teachers to discuss matters that affect the children and to organize events to raise money. **PTA** is an abbreviation for 'parent-teacher association'. N-COUNT

**Pte** /praɪvɪt/ **Pte** is used before a person's name as a written abbreviation for the military title **Private**. [BRIT] ❑ *...Pte Owen Butler.* N-TITLE

✔ in AM, use **Pvt.**

**PTO** /piː tiː oʊ/ also **P.T.O.** **PTO** is a written abbreviation for 'please turn over'. You write it at the bottom of a page to indicate that there is more writing on the other side.

**PTSD** /piː tiː es diː/ **PTSD** is an abbreviation for **post-traumatic stress disorder**. N-UNCOUNT

**pub** /pʌb/ ◆◇◇ **(pubs)** A **pub** is a building where people can have drinks, especially alcoholic drinks, and talk to their friends. Many pubs also serve food. [mainly BRIT] ❑ *He was in the pub until closing time... Richard used to run a pub.* N-COUNT

**pub crawl** **(pub crawls)** If people go on a **pub crawl**, they go from one pub to another having drinks in each one. [BRIT, INFORMAL] N-COUNT

**pu|ber|ty** /pjuːbərti/ **Puberty** is the stage in someone's life when their body starts to become physically mature. ❑ *Margaret had reached the age of puberty.* N-UNCOUNT

**pu|bes|cent** /pjuːbesənt/ A **pubescent** girl or boy has reached the stage in their life when their body is becoming physically like an adult's. [FORMAL] ADJ

**pu|bic** /pjuːbɪk/ **Pubic** means relating to the area just above a person's genitals. ❑ *...pubic hair.* ADJ: ADJ n

**pub|lic** /pʌblɪk/ ◆◆◆ 1 You can refer to people in general, or to all the people in a particular country or community, as **the public**. ❑ *Lauderdale House is now open to the public... Pure alcohol is not for sale to the general public... Trade unions are regarding the poll as a test of the public's confidence in the government.* N-SING-COLL: the N 2 You can refer to a set of people in a country who share a common interest, activity, or characteristic as a particular kind of **public**. ❑ *Market research showed that 93% of the viewing public wanted a hit film channel.* N-SING-COLL: supp N 3 **Public** means relating to all the people in a country or community. ❑ *The President is attempting to drum up public support for his economic program.* ADJ: ADJ n 4 **Public** means relating to the government or state, or things that are done for the people by the state. ❑ *The social services account for a substantial part of public spending.* ADJ: ADJ n = government, state ♦ **pub|lic|ly** *...publicly funded legal services.* ADV: ADV -ed 5 **Public** buildings and services are provided for everyone to use. ❑ *The new museum must be accessible by public transport. ...a public health service available to all.* ADJ: ADJ n ≠private 6 A **public** place is one where people can go about freely and where you can easily be seen and heard. ❑ *...the heavily congested public areas of international airports... I avoid working in places which are too public.* ADJ ≠private 7 If someone is a **public figure** or in **public life**, many people know who they are because they are often mentioned in newspapers and on television. ❑ *I'd like to see more women in public life, especially Parliament.* ADJ: ADJ n 8 **Public** is used to describe statements, actions, and events that are made or done in such a way that any member of the public can see them or be aware of them. ❑ *The National Heritage Committee has conducted a public inquiry to find the answer... The comments were the ministry's first detailed public statement on the subject.* ADJ: ADJ n ♦ **pub|lic|ly** *He never spoke publicly about the affair.* ADV: usu ADV with v 9 If a fact is made **public** or becomes **public**, it becomes known to everyone rather ADJ: v-link ADJ than being kept secret. ❑ *Blair wants any new evidence on IRA pub bombs made public.*

**PHRASES** [10] If someone is **in the public eye**, many people know who they are, because they are famous or because they are often mentioned on television or in the newspapers. ❑ *One expects people in the public eye to conduct their personal lives with a certain decorum.* [11] If a company **goes public**, it starts selling its shares on the stock exchange. [BUSINESS] ❑ *In 1951 AC went public, having achieved an average annual profit of more than £50,000.* [12] If you say or do something **in public**, you say or do it when a group of people are present. ❑ *By-laws are to make it illegal to smoke in public.* [13] to **wash** your **dirty linen in public** → see **dirty**. PHRASE: prep PHR / PHRASE: V inflects / PHRASE: PHR after v

**pub|lic ad|dress sys|tem** **(public address systems)** A **public address system** is a set of electrical equipment which allows someone's voice, or music, to be heard throughout a large building or area. The abbreviation **PA** is also used. N-COUNT

**pub|li|can** /pʌblɪkən/ **(publicans)** A **publican** is a person who owns or manages a pub. [BRIT, FORMAL] N-COUNT = *landlady, landlord*

**pub|li|ca|tion** /pʌblɪkeɪʃən/ **(publications)** ◆◇◇ [1] The **publication** of a book or magazine is the act of printing it and sending it to shops to be sold. ❑ *The guide is being translated into several languages for publication near Christmas... The publication of his collected poems was approaching the status of an event.* N-UNCOUNT [2] A **publication** is a book or magazine that has been published. ❑ *They have started legal proceedings against two publications which spoke of an affair.* N-COUNT [3] The **publication of** something such as information is the act of making it known to the public, for example by informing journalists or by publishing a government document. ❑ *A spokesman said: 'We have no comment regarding the publication of these photographs.'* N-UNCOUNT: usu N *of* n

**pub|lic bar** **(public bars)** In a British pub, a **public bar** is a room where the furniture is plain and the drinks are cheaper than in the pub's other bars. N-COUNT

**pub|lic com|pa|ny** **(public companies)** A **public company** is a company whose shares can be bought by the general public. [BUSINESS] N-COUNT

**pub|lic con|veni|ence** **(public conveniences)** A **public convenience** is a toilet in a public place for everyone to use. [BRIT, FORMAL] N-COUNT

**pub|lic de|fend|er** **(public defenders)** A **public defender** is a lawyer who is employed by a city or county to represent people who are accused of crimes but cannot afford to pay for a lawyer themselves. [AM] N-COUNT

**pub|lic do|main** If information is **in the public domain**, it is not secret and can be used or discussed by anyone. ❑ *It is outrageous that the figures are not in the public domain.* N-SING: usu *in the* N

**pub|lic house** **(public houses)** A **public house** is the same as a **pub**. [BRIT, FORMAL] N-COUNT

**pub|li|cise** /pʌblɪsaɪz/ → see **publicize**.

**pub|li|cist** /pʌblɪsɪst/ **(publicists)** A **publicist** is a person whose job involves getting publicity for people, events, or things such as films or books. N-COUNT

**pub|lic|ity** /pʌblɪsɪti/ ◆◇◇ [1] **Publicity** is information or actions that are intended to attract the public's attention to someone or something. ❑ *Much advance publicity was given to the talks... It was all a publicity stunt.* N-UNCOUNT [2] When the news media and the public show a lot of interest in something, you can say that it is receiving **publicity**. ❑ *The case has generated enormous publicity in Brazil. ...the renewed publicity over the Casey affair.* N-UNCOUNT

**pub|lic|ity agent** **(publicity agents)** A **publicity agent** is a person whose job is to make sure that a large number of people know about a person, show, or event so that they are successful. N-COUNT

**pub|li|cize** /pʌblɪsaɪz/ **(publicizes, publicizing, publicized)**

✔ in BRIT, also use **publicise**

If you **publicize** a fact or event, you make it widely known to the public. ❑ *The author appeared on television to publicize her latest book... He never publicized his plans. ...his highly publicized trial.* VERB / V n / V n / V-ed

**pub|lic lim|it|ed com|pa|ny** **(public limited companies)** A **public limited company** is the same as a **public company**. The abbreviation **plc** is used after such companies' names. [BUSINESS] N-COUNT

**pub|lic nui|sance** **(public nuisances)** If something or someone is, or causes, a **public nuisance**, they break the law by harming or annoying members of the public. [LEGAL] ❑ *...the 45-day jail sentence he received for causing a public nuisance after taking part in a demonstration... Back in the 1980s drug users were a public nuisance in Zurich.* N-COUNT: usu sing

**pub|lic opin|ion** **Public opinion** is the opinion or attitude of the public regarding a particular matter. ❑ *He mobilized public opinion all over the world against hydrogen-bomb tests.* N-UNCOUNT

**pub|lic prop|er|ty** [1] **Public property** is land and other assets that belong to the general public and not to a private owner. ❑ *...vandals who wrecked public property.* N-UNCOUNT ≠ *private property* [2] If you describe a person or thing as **public property**, you mean that information about them is known and discussed by everyone. ❑ *She complained that intimate aspects of her personal life had been made public property.* N-UNCOUNT

**pub|lic pros|ecu|tor** **(public prosecutors)** A **public prosecutor** is an official who puts people on trial on behalf of the government and people of a particular country. N-COUNT

**pub|lic re|la|tions** [1] **Public relations** is the part of an organization's work that is concerned with obtaining the public's approval for what it does. The abbreviation **PR** is often used. [BUSINESS] ❑ *The move was good public relations... George is a public relations officer for The John Bennett Trust.* N-UNCOUNT [2] You can refer to the opinion that the public has of an organization as **public relations**. ❑ *Limiting casualties is important for public relations.* N-PLURAL

**pub|lic school** **(public schools)** [1] In Britain, a **public school** is a private school that provides secondary education which parents have to pay for. The pupils often live at the school during the school term. ❑ *He was headmaster of a public school in the West of England.* N-VAR [2] In the United States, Australia, and many other countries, a **public school** is a school that is supported financially by the government and usually provides free education. ❑ *...Milwaukee's public school system.* N-VAR

**pub|lic sec|tor** **The public sector** is the part of a country's economy which is controlled or supported financially by the government. [BUSINESS] ❑ *60,000 public-sector jobs must be cut.* N-SING: *the* N ≠ *private sector*

**pub|lic serv|ant** **(public servants)** A **public servant** is a person who is appointed or elected to a public office, for example working for a local or state government. N-COUNT

**pub|lic ser|vice** **(public services)** [1] A **public service** is something such as health care, transport, or the removal of waste which is organized by the government or an official body in order to benefit all the people in a particular society or community. ❑ *The money is used by local authorities to pay for public services.* N-COUNT [2] You use **public service** to refer to activities and jobs which are provided or paid for by a government, especially through the civil service. ❑ *...a distinguished career in public service.* N-UNCOUNT: oft N n [3] **Public service** broadcasting consists of television and radio programmes supplied by an official or government organization, rather than by a commercial company. Such programmes often provide information or education, as well as entertainment. ADJ: ADJ n [4] **Public service** activities and types of work are concerned with helping people and providing them with what N-UNCOUNT they need, rather than making a profit. ❑ *...an egalitarian society based on cooperation and public service.*

**public-spirited** A **public-spirited** person tries to help the community that they belong to. ❑ *Thanks to a group of public-spirited citizens, the Krippendorf garden has been preserved.* — ADJ

**pub|lic util|ity** **(public utilities)** **Public utilities** are services provided by the government or state, such as the supply of electricity and gas, or the train network. ❑ *Water supplies and other public utilities were badly affected.* — N-COUNT

**pub|lic works** **Public works** are buildings, roads, and other projects that are built by the government or state for the public. — N-PLURAL

**pub|lish** /pʌblɪʃ/ **(publishes, publishing, published)** ◆◆◇ [1] When a company **publishes** a book or magazine, it prints copies of it, which are sent to shops to be sold. ❑ *They publish reference books... His latest book of poetry will be published by Faber in May.* [2] When the people in charge of a newspaper or magazine **publish** a piece of writing or a photograph, they print it in their newspaper or magazine. ❑ *The ban was imposed after the magazine published an article satirising the government... I don't encourage people to take photographs like this without permission, but by law we can publish.* [3] If someone **publishes** a book or an article that they have written, they arrange to have it published. ❑ *John Lennon found time to publish two books of his humorous prose.* [4] If you **publish** information or an opinion, you make it known to the public by having it printed in a newspaper, magazine, or official document. ❑ *The demonstrators called on the government to publish a list of registered voters.* — VERB: V n, V n; VERB: V n, V; VERB: V n; VERB: V n

**pub|lish|er** /pʌblɪʃəʳ/ **(publishers)** ◆◇◇ A **publisher** is a person or a company that publishes books, newspapers, or magazines. ❑ *The publishers planned to produce the journal on a weekly basis.* — N-COUNT

**pub|lish|ing** /pʌblɪʃɪŋ/ ◆◇◇ **Publishing** is the profession of publishing books. ❑ *I had a very high-powered job in publishing.* — N-UNCOUNT

**pub|lish|ing house** **(publishing houses)** A **publishing house** is a company which publishes books. — N-COUNT = publisher

**puce** /pjuːs/ Something that is **puce** is a dark purple colour. — COLOUR

**puck** /pʌk/ **(pucks)** In the game of ice hockey, the **puck** is the small rubber disc that is used instead of a ball. — N-COUNT

**puck|er** /pʌkəʳ/ **(puckers, puckering, puckered)** When a part of your face **puckers** or when you **pucker** it, it becomes tight or stretched, often because you are trying not to cry or are going to kiss someone. ❑ *Toby's face puckered... She puckered her lips into a rosebud and kissed him on the nose.* ♦ **puck|ered** *...puckered lips. ...a long puckered scar.* — VERB: V, V n; ADJ

**puck|ish** /pʌkɪʃ/ If you describe someone as **puckish**, you mean that they play tricks on people or tease them. [OLD-FASHIONED, WRITTEN] ❑ *He had a puckish sense of humour.* — ADJ: usu ADJ n = impish

**pud** /pʊd/ **(puds)** **Pud** is the same as **pudding**. [BRIT, INFORMAL] ❑ *...rice pud.* — N-VAR

**pud|ding** /pʊdɪŋ/ **(puddings)** [1] A **pudding** is a cooked sweet food made with flour, fat, and eggs, and usually served hot. ❑ *...a cherry sponge pudding with warm custard.* [2] Some people refer to the sweet course of a meal as the **pudding**. [BRIT] ❑ *...a menu featuring canapes, a starter, a main course and a pudding.* [3] → See also **Yorkshire pudding**. [4] If you say **the proof of the pudding** or **the proof of the pudding is in the eating**, you mean that something new can only be judged to be good or bad after it has been tried or used. — N-VAR; N-VAR = dessert, sweet; PHRASE

**pud|ding ba|sin** **(pudding basins)** A **pudding basin** is a deep round bowl that is used in the kitchen, especially for mixing or for cooking puddings. [BRIT] — N-COUNT

**pud|dle** /pʌdᵊl/ **(puddles)** A **puddle** is a small, shallow pool of liquid that has spread on the ground. ❑ *The road was shiny with puddles, but the rain was at an end. ...puddles of oil.* — N-COUNT: oft N *of* n

**pudgy** /pʌdʒi/ If you describe someone as **pudgy**, you mean that they are rather fat in an unattractive way. [AM] ❑ *He put a pudgy arm around Harry's shoulder.* — ADJ = podgy

**pu|er|ile** /pjʊəraɪl, AM -rᵊl/ If you describe someone or something as **puerile**, you mean that they are silly and childish. ❑ *Concert organisers branded the group's actions as puerile. ...puerile, schoolboy humour.* — ADJ [disapproval]

**puff** /pʌf/ **(puffs, puffing, puffed)** [1] If someone **puffs at** a cigarette, cigar, or pipe, they smoke it. ❑ *He lit a cigar and puffed at it twice.* ♦ **Puff** is also a noun. ❑ *She was taking quick puffs at her cigarette like a beginner.* [2] If you **puff** smoke or moisture from your mouth or if it **puffs** from your mouth, you breathe it out. ❑ *Richard lit another cigarette and puffed smoke towards the ceiling... The weather was dry and cold; wisps of steam puffed from their lips.* ♦ **Puff out** means the same as **puff**. ❑ *He drew heavily on his cigarette and puffed out a cloud of smoke.* [3] If an engine, chimney, or boiler **puffs** smoke or steam, clouds of smoke or steam come out of it. ❑ *As I completed my 26th lap the Porsche puffed blue smoke.* [4] A **puff of** something such as air or smoke is a small amount of it that is blown out from somewhere. ❑ *Wind caught the sudden puff of dust and blew it inland.* [5] If you **are puffing**, you are breathing loudly and quickly with your mouth open because you are out of breath after a lot of physical effort. ❑ *I know nothing about boxing, but I could see he was unfit, because he was puffing.* [6] → See also **puffed**. — VERB: V *at/on* n; N-COUNT = drag; VERB: V n, V prep; PHRASAL VERB: V P n (not pron); VERB: V n; N-COUNT: usu N *of* n; VERB: usu cont, V

♦ **puff out** If you **puff out** your cheeks, you make them larger and rounder by filling them with air. ❑ *He puffed out his fat cheeks and let out a lungful of steamy breath.* → See also **puff 2**. — PHRASAL VERB: V P n (not pron), Also V n P

♦ **puff up** If part of your body **puffs up** as a result of an injury or illness, it becomes swollen. ❑ *Her body bloated and puffed up till pain seemed to burst out through her skin.* → See also **puffed up**. — PHRASAL VERB = swell; V P

**puff|ball** /pʌfbɔːl/ **(puffballs)** also **puff-ball**. A **puffball** is a round fungus which bursts when it is ripe and sends a cloud of seeds into the air. — N-COUNT

**puffed** /pʌft/ [1] If a part of your body is **puffed** or **puffed up**, it is swollen because of an injury or because you are unwell. ❑ *His face was a little puffed.* [2] If you are **puffed** or **puffed out**, you are breathing with difficulty because you have been using a lot of energy. [INFORMAL] ❑ *Do you get puffed out running up and down the stairs?* — ADJ: v-link ADJ = swollen, puffy; ADJ: v-link ADJ = breathless

**puffed up** If you describe someone as **puffed up**, you disapprove of them because they are very proud of themselves and think that they are very important. ❑ *He was too puffed up with his own importance, too blinded by vanity to accept their verdict on him.* → See also **puffed**. — ADJ: oft ADJ *with* n [disapproval]

**puf|fin** /pʌfɪn/ **(puffins)** A **puffin** is a black and white seabird with a large, brightly-coloured beak. — N-COUNT

**puff pas|try** **Puff pastry** is a type of pastry which is very light and consists of a lot of thin layers. — N-UNCOUNT

**puffy** /pʌfi/ **(puffier)** [1] If a part of someone's body, especially their face, is **puffy**, it has a round, swollen appearance. ❑ *Her cheeks were puffy with crying. ...dark-ringed puffy eyes.* ♦ **puffi|ness** *He noticed some slight puffiness beneath her eyes.* — ADJ = swollen; N-UNCOUNT

**pug** /pʌg/ **(pugs)** A **pug** is a small, fat, short-haired dog with a flat face. — N-COUNT

**pu|gi|list** /pjuːdʒɪlɪst/ **(pugilists)** A **pugilist** is a boxer. [OLD-FASHIONED] — N-COUNT

**pug|na|cious** /pʌgneɪʃəs/ Someone who is **pugnacious** is always ready to quarrel or start a fight. [FORMAL] ❑ *The President was in a pugnacious mood when he spoke to journalists about the rebellion.* — ADJ

**pug|nac|ity** /pʌgnæsɪti/ **Pugnacity** is the quality of being pugnacious. [FORMAL] ❑ *He is legendary for his fearlessness and pugnacity.* N-UNCOUNT

**puke** /pjuːk/ **(pukes, puking, puked)** 1 When someone **pukes**, they vomit. [INFORMAL] VERB ❑ *They got drunk and puked out the window.* V ♦ **Puke up** means the same as **puke**. PHRASAL VERB ❑ *He peered at me like I'd just puked up on his jeans...* V P *I figured, why eat when I was going to puke it up again?* V n P 2 **Puke** is the same as **vomit**. [INFORMAL] N-UNCOUNT ❑ *He was fully clothed and covered in puke and piss.*

**puk|ka** /pʌkə/ If you describe something or someone as **pukka**, you mean that they are real or genuine, and of good quality. [BRIT, OLD-FASHIONED] ADJ ❑ *...a pukka English gentleman.*

**pull** /pʊl/ **(pulls, pulling, pulled)** ◆◆◇ 1 When you **pull** something, you hold it firmly and use force in order to move it towards you or away from its previous position. VERB ❑ *They have pulled out patients' teeth unnecessarily...* V n with adv *Erica was solemn, pulling at her blonde curls...* V prep *I helped pull him out of the water...* V n prep *Someone pulled her hair...* V n *He knew he should pull the trigger, but he was suddenly paralysed by fear...* V n *Pull as hard as you can...* V *I let myself out into the street and pulled the door shut.* V n adj ♦ **Pull** is also a noun. N-COUNT: usu sing ❑ *The feather must be removed with a straight, firm pull.* 2 When you **pull** an object from a bag, pocket, or cupboard, you put your hand in and bring the object out. VERB ❑ *Jack pulled the slip of paper from his shirt pocket...* V n prep *Wade walked quickly to the refrigerator and pulled out another beer.* V n with adv 3 When a vehicle, animal, or person **pulls** a cart or piece of machinery, they are attached to it or hold it, so that it moves along behind them when they move forward. VERB ❑ *This is early-20th-century rural Sussex, when horses still pulled the plough.* V n 4 If you **pull yourself** or **pull** a part of your body in a particular direction, you move your body or a part of your body with effort or force. VERB ❑ *Hughes pulled himself slowly to his feet...* V pron-refl prep/adv *He pulled his arms out of the sleeves...* V n prep/adv *She tried to pull her hand free...* V n adj *Lillian brushed his cheek with her fingertips. He pulled away and said, 'Don't!'* V adv 5 When a driver or vehicle **pulls to** a stop or a halt, the vehicle stops. VERB ❑ *He pulled to a stop behind a pickup truck.* V prep 6 In a race or contest, if you **pull ahead of** or **pull away from** an opponent, you gradually increase the amount by which you are ahead of them. VERB ❑ *He pulled away, extending his lead to 15 seconds.* V adv 7 If you **pull** something **apart**, you break or divide it into small pieces, often in order to put them back together again in a different way. VERB ❑ *If I wanted to improve the car significantly I would have to pull it apart and start again.* V n with adv 8 If someone **pulls** a gun or a knife **on** someone else, they take out a gun or knife and threaten the other person with it. [INFORMAL] VERB ❑ *They had a fight. One of them pulled a gun on the other...* V n *on* n *I pulled a knife and threatened her.* V n 9 To **pull** crowds, viewers, or voters means to attract them. [INFORMAL] VERB ❑ *The organisers have to employ performers to pull a crowd.* V n ♦ **Pull in** means the same as **pull**. PHRASAL VERB ❑ *They provided a far better news service and pulled in many more viewers...* V P n (not pron) *She is still beautiful, and still pulling them in at sixty.* V n P 10 A **pull** is a strong physical force which causes things to move in a particular direction. N-COUNT ❑ *...the pull of gravity.* 11 If you **pull** a muscle, you injure it by straining it. VERB ❑ *Dave pulled a back muscle and could barely kick the ball...* V n *He suffered a pulled calf muscle.* V-ed 12 To **pull** a stunt or a trick **on** someone means to do something dramatic or silly in order to get their attention or trick them. [INFORMAL] VERB ❑ *Everyone saw the stunt you pulled on me.* V n *on* n 13 If someone **pulls** someone else, they succeed in attracting them sexually and in spending the rest of the evening or night with them. [BRIT, INFORMAL] VERB 14 to **pull** oneself **up by** one's **bootstraps** → see **bootstraps**. to **pull a face** → see **face**. to **pull** someone's **leg** → see **leg**. to **pull** your **punches** → see **punch**. to **pull rank** → see **rank**. to **pull out all the stops** → see **stop**. to **pull strings** → see **string**. to **pull** your **weight** → see **weight**. to **pull the wool over** someone's **eyes** → see **wool**.

♦ **pull away** 1 When a vehicle or driver **pulls away**, the vehicle starts moving forward. PHRASAL VERB ❑ *I stood in the driveway and watched him back out and pull away.* V P 2 If you **pull away from** someone that you have had close links with, you deliberately become less close to them. PHRASAL VERB ❑ *Other daughters, faced with their mother's emotional hunger, pull away...* V P *He'd pulled away from her as if she had leprosy.* V P *from* n

♦ **pull back** 1 If someone **pulls back from** an action, they decide not to do it or continue with it, because it could have bad consequences. PHRASAL VERB ❑ *They will plead with him to pull back from confrontation...* V P *from* n *The British government threatened to make public its disquiet but then pulled back.* V P 2 If troops **pull back** or if their leader **pulls** them **back**, they go some or all of the way back to their own territory. PHRASAL VERB ❑ *They were asked to pull back from their artillery positions around the city...* V P *He pulled back forces from Mongolia, and he withdrew from Afghanistan.* V P n (not pron) Also V n P

♦ **pull down** To **pull down** a building or statue means to deliberately destroy it. PHRASAL VERB = demolish ❑ *They'd pulled the registry office down which then left an open space...* V n P *A small crowd attempted to pull down a statue.* V P n (not pron)

♦ **pull in** 1 When a vehicle or driver **pulls in** somewhere, the vehicle stops there. PHRASAL VERB ❑ *He pulled in at the side of the road...* V P prep/adv *The van pulled in and waited.* V P 2 → see **pull 9**.

♦ **pull into** When a vehicle or driver **pulls into** a place, the vehicle moves into the place and stops there. PHRASAL VERB ❑ *He pulled into the driveway in front of her garage...* V P n *She pulled the car into a tight parking space on a side street.* V n P n

♦ **pull off** 1 If you **pull off** something very difficult, you succeed in achieving it. PHRASAL VERB ❑ *The National League for Democracy pulled off a landslide victory...* V P n (not pron) *It will be a very, very fine piece of mountaineering if they pull it off.* V n P 2 If a vehicle or driver **pulls off** the road, the vehicle stops by the side of the road. PHRASAL VERB ❑ *I pulled off the road at a small village pub...* V P n *One evening, crossing a small creek, he pulled the car off the road.* V n P n

♦ **pull out** 1 When a vehicle or driver **pulls out**, the vehicle moves out into the road or nearer the centre of the road. PHRASAL VERB ❑ *She pulled out into the street...* V P prep *He was about to pull out to overtake the guy in front of him.* V P 2 If you **pull out of** an agreement, a contest, or an organization, you withdraw from it. PHRASAL VERB ❑ *The World Bank should pull out of the project...* V P *of* n *A racing injury forced Stephen Roche to pull out.* V P 3 If troops **pull out of** a place or if their leader **pulls** them **out**, they leave it. PHRASAL VERB ❑ *The militia in Lebanon has agreed to pull out of Beirut...* V P *of* n *Economic sanctions will be lifted once two-thirds of their forces have pulled out...* V P *His government decided to pull its troops out of Cuba.* V n P *of* n 4 If a country **pulls out of** recession or if someone **pulls** it **out**, it begins to recover from it. PHRASAL VERB ❑ *Sterling has been hit by the economy's failure to pull out of recession...* V P *of* n *What we want to see today are policies to pull us out of this recession.* V n P *of* n 5 → See also **pull-out**.

♦ **pull over** 1 When a vehicle or driver **pulls over**, the vehicle moves closer to the side of the road and stops there. PHRASAL VERB ❑ *He noticed a man behind him in a blue Ford gesticulating to pull over.* V P 2 If the police **pull over** a driver or vehicle, they make the driver stop at the side of the road, usually because the driver has been driving dangerously. PHRASAL VERB ❑ *The officers pulled him over after a high-speed chase...* V n P *Police pulled over his Mercedes near Dieppe.* V P n (not pron) 3 → See also **pullover**.

♦ **pull through** If someone with a serious illness or someone in a very difficult situation **pulls through**, they recover. PHRASAL VERB ❑ *Everyone was very concerned whether he would pull through or not...* V P *It is only our determination to fight that has pulled us* V n P through. ...*ways of helping Russia pull through its upheavals.* V P n

♦ **pull together** [1] If people **pull together**, they help each other or work together in order to deal with a difficult situation. ❑ *The nation was urged to pull together to avoid a slide into complete chaos.* PHRASAL VERB; V P
[2] If you are upset or depressed and someone tells you to **pull yourself together**, they are telling you to control your feelings and behave calmly again. ❑ *Pull yourself together, you stupid woman!.* PHRASAL VERB; V pron-refl P
[3] If you **pull together** different facts or ideas, you link them to form a single theory, argument, or story. ❑ *Let me now pull together the threads of my argument... Data exists but it needs pulling together.* PHRASAL VERB = draw together; V P n; V P; Also V n P

♦ **pull up** [1] When a vehicle or driver **pulls up**, the vehicle slows down and stops. ❑ *The cab pulled up and the driver jumped out.* PHRASAL VERB = draw up; V P
[2] If you **pull up** a chair, you move it closer to something or someone and sit on it. ❑ *He pulled up a chair behind her and put his chin on her shoulder.* PHRASAL VERB = draw up; V P n (not pron); Also V n P

**pul|ley** /pʊli/ **(pulleys)** A **pulley** is a device consisting of a wheel over which a rope or chain is pulled in order to lift heavy objects. N-COUNT

**Pull|man** /pʊlmən/ **(Pullmans)** [1] A **Pullman** is a type of train or railway carriage which is extremely comfortable and luxurious. You can also refer to a **Pullman train** or a **Pullman carriage**. [BRIT] N-COUNT: oft N n
[2] A **Pullman** or a **Pullman car** on a train is a railway car that provides beds for passengers to sleep in. [AM] N-COUNT: oft N n

✔ in BRIT, use **sleeping car**

**pull-out** **(pull-outs)** [1] In a newspaper or magazine, a **pull-out** is a section which you can remove easily and keep. ❑ ...*an eight-page pull-out supplement.* N-COUNT: usu N n
[2] When there is a **pull-out of** armed forces **from** a place, troops which have occupied an area of land withdraw from it. ❑ ...*a pull-out from the occupied territories.* N-SING: oft N *from/of* n

**pull|over** /pʊloʊvəʳ/ **(pullovers)** A **pullover** is a piece of woollen clothing that covers the upper part of your body and your arms. You put it on by pulling it over your head. N-COUNT = jumper, sweater

**pul|mo|nary** /pʌlmənəri, AM -neri/ **Pulmonary** means relating to your lungs. [MEDICAL] ❑ ...*respiratory and pulmonary disease.* ADJ: ADJ n

**pulp** /pʌlp/ **(pulps, pulping, pulped)** [1] If an object is pressed into a **pulp**, it is crushed or beaten until it is soft, smooth, and wet. ❑ *The olives are crushed to a pulp by stone rollers.* N-SING: also no det
[2] In fruit or vegetables, **the pulp** is the soft part inside the skin. ❑ *Make maximum use of the whole fruit, including the pulp which is high in fibre.* N-SING: *the* N, also no det
[3] **Wood pulp** is material made from crushed wood. It is used to make paper. N-UNCOUNT
[4] People refer to stories or novels as **pulp** fiction when they consider them to be of poor quality and intentionally shocking or sensational. ❑ ...*lurid '50s pulp novels.* ADJ: ADJ n
[5] If paper, vegetables, or fruit **are pulped**, they are crushed into a smooth, wet paste. ❑ *Onions can be boiled and pulped to a puree. ...creamed or pulped tomatoes.* VERB: usu passive; be V-ed; V-ed
[6] If money or documents **are pulped**, they are destroyed. This is done to stop the money being used or to stop the documents being seen by the public. ❑ *25 million pounds worth of five pound notes have been pulped because the designers made a mistake.* VERB: usu passive; be V-ed
[7] If someone **is beaten to a pulp** or **beaten to pulp**, they are hit repeatedly until they are very badly injured. PHRASE: V inflects

**pul|pit** /pʊlpɪt/ **(pulpits)** A **pulpit** is a small raised platform with a rail or barrier around it in a church, where a member of the clergy stands to speak. N-COUNT

**pulpy** /pʌlpi/ Something that is **pulpy** is soft, smooth, and wet, often because it has been crushed or beaten. ❑ *The chutney should be a thick, pulpy consistency.* ADJ

**pul|sar** /pʌlsɑːʳ/ **(pulsars)** A **pulsar** is a star that spins very fast and cannot be seen but produces regular radio signals. N-COUNT

**pul|sate** /pʌlseɪt, AM pʌlseɪt/ **(pulsates, pulsating, pulsated)** If something **pulsates**, it beats, moves in and out, or shakes with strong, regular movements. ❑ ...*a star that pulsates. ...a pulsating blood vessel.* VERB; V; V-ing ♦ **pul|sa|tion** /pʌlseɪʃᵊn/ **(pulsations)** *Several astronomers noted that the star's pulsations seemed less pronounced.* N-VAR

**pulse** /pʌls/ **(pulses, pulsing, pulsed)** [1] Your **pulse** is the regular beating of blood through your body, which you can feel when you touch particular parts of your body, especially your wrist. ❑ *Mahoney's pulse was racing, and he felt confused.* N-COUNT: usu sing
[2] In music, a **pulse** is a regular beat, which is often produced by a drum. ❑ ...*the repetitive pulse of the music.* N-COUNT
[3] A **pulse of** electrical current, light, or sound is a temporary increase in its level. ❑ *The switch works by passing a pulse of current between the tip and the surface.* N-COUNT
[4] If you refer to **the pulse of** a group in society, you mean the ideas, opinions, or feelings they have at a particular time. ❑ *The White House insists that the president is in touch with the pulse of the black community.* N-SING: *the* N *of* n
[5] If something **pulses**, it moves, appears, or makes a sound with a strong regular rhythm. ❑ *His temples pulsed a little, threatening a headache... It was a slow, pulsing rhythm that seemed to sway languidly in the air.* VERB = throb; V; V-ing
[6] Some seeds which can be cooked and eaten are called **pulses**, for example peas, beans, and lentils. N-PLURAL

PHRASES [7] If you have your **finger on the pulse of** something, you know all the latest opinions or developments concerning it. ❑ *He claims to have his finger on the pulse of the industry... It's important to keep your finger on the pulse by reading all the right magazines.* PHRASE: Ns inflect, usu PHR after v
[8] When someone **takes** your **pulse** or **feels** your **pulse**, they find out how quickly your heart is beating by feeling the pulse in your wrist. PHRASE: V and N inflect

**pul|ver|ize** /pʌlvəraɪz/ **(pulverizes, pulverizing, pulverized)**

✔ in BRIT, also use **pulverise**

[1] To **pulverize** something means to do great damage to it or to destroy it completely. ❑ ...*the economic policies which pulverised the economy during the 1980s.* VERB; V n
[2] If someone **pulverizes** an opponent in an election or competition, they thoroughly defeat them. [INFORMAL] ❑ *He is set to pulverise his two opponents in the race for the presidency.* VERB = thrash; V n
[3] If you **pulverize** something, you make it into a powder by crushing it. ❑ *Using a pestle and mortar, pulverise the bran to a coarse powder... The fries are made from pellets of pulverised potato.* VERB = grind; V n; V-ed

**puma** /pjuːmə/ **(pumas)** A **puma** is a wild animal that is a member of the cat family. Pumas have brownish-grey fur and live in mountain regions of North and South America. [mainly BRIT] N-COUNT

✔ in AM, use **mountain lion, cougar**

**pum|ice** /pʌmɪs/ **Pumice** is a kind of grey stone from a volcano and is very light in weight. It can be rubbed over surfaces, especially your skin, that you want to clean or make smoother. N-UNCOUNT = pumice stone

**pum|ice stone** **(pumice stones)** [1] A **pumice stone** is a piece of pumice that you rub over your skin in order to clean the skin or make it smoother. N-COUNT
[2] **Pumice stone** is the same as **pumice**. N-UNCOUNT

**pum|mel** /pʌmᵊl/ **(pummels, pummelling, pummelled)**

✔ in AM, use **pummeling, pummeled**

If you **pummel** someone or something, you hit them many times using your fists. ❑ *He trapped Conn in a corner and pummeled him ferociously for thirty seconds.* VERB; V n

**pump** /pʌmp/ **(pumps, pumping, pumped)** ♦◇◇ [1] A **pump** is a machine or device that is used to force a liquid or gas to flow in a particular direction. → See picture on page 1708. ❑ ...*pumps that circulate the fuel around in the engine... You'll need a bicycle pump to keep the tyres topped up with air.* N-COUNT

[2] To **pump** a liquid or gas in a particular direction means to force it to flow in that direction using a pump. ❑ *It's not enough to get rid of raw sewage by pumping it out to sea... The money raised will be used to dig bore holes to pump water into the dried-up lake. ...drill rigs that are busy pumping natural gas... Age diminishes the heart's ability to pump harder and faster under exertion.* (VERB; V n with adv; V n prep; V n; V) [3] A petrol or gas **pump** is a machine with a tube attached to it that you use to fill a car with petrol. ❑ *There are already long queues of vehicles at petrol pumps.* (N-COUNT: oft n N) [4] If someone **has** their stomach **pumped**, doctors remove the contents of their stomach, for example because they have swallowed poison or drugs. ❑ *She was released from hospital yesterday after having her stomach pumped.* (VERB: usu passive; *have* n V-ed) [5] If you **pump** money or other resources **into** something such as a project or an industry, you invest a lot of money or resources in it. [INFORMAL] ❑ *The Government needs to pump more money into community care.* (VERB; V n *into* n) [6] If you **pump** someone **about** something, you keep asking them questions in order to get information. [INFORMAL] ❑ *He ran in every five minutes to pump me about the case... Stop trying to pump information out of me.* (VERB = grill; V n *about/for* n; V n *out of/from* n) [7] **Pumps** are canvas shoes with flat rubber soles which people wear for sports and leisure. [mainly BRIT] (N-COUNT)

☑ in AM, use **trainers**

[8] **Pumps** are women's shoes that do not cover the top part of the foot and are usually made of plain leather. [AM] (N-COUNT)

☑ in BRIT, use **court shoes**

[9] To **prime the pump** means to do something to encourage the success or growth of something, especially the economy. [mainly AM] ❑ *...the use of tax money to prime the pump of the state's economy.* (PHRASE: V inflects)

♦ **pump out** [1] To **pump out** something means to produce or supply it continually and in large amounts. ❑ *Japanese companies have been pumping out plenty of innovative products.* (PHRASAL VERB; V P n; Also V n P) [2] If pop music **pumps out**, it plays very loudly. ❑ *Teenage disco music pumped out at every station.* (PHRASAL VERB; V P)

♦ **pump up** If you **pump up** something such as a tyre, you fill it with air using a pump. ❑ *I tried to pump up my back tyre.* (PHRASAL VERB; V P n (not pron); Also V n P)

**pum|per|nick|el** /pʌmpəʳnɪkəl/ **Pumpernickel** is a dark brown, heavy bread, which is eaten especially in Germany. (N-UNCOUNT)

**pump|kin** /pʌmpkɪn/ **(pumpkins)** A **pumpkin** is a large, round, orange vegetable with a thick skin. ❑ *Quarter the pumpkin and remove the seeds. ...pumpkin pie.* (N-VAR)

**pun** /pʌn/ **(puns)** A **pun** is a clever and amusing use of a word or phrase with two meanings, or of words with the same sound but different meanings. For example, if someone says 'The peasants are revolting', this is a pun because it can be interpreted as meaning either that the peasants are fighting against authority, or that they are disgusting. (N-COUNT)

**punch** /pʌntʃ/ **(punches, punching, punched)** ◆◇◇

[1] If you **punch** someone or something, you hit them hard with your fist. ❑ *After punching him on the chin she wound up hitting him over the head.* ♦ In American English, **punch out** means the same as **punch**. ❑ *'I almost lost my job today.' — 'What happened?' — 'Oh, I punched out this guy.'... In the past, many kids would settle disputes by punching each other out.* ♦ **Punch** is also a noun. ❑ *He was hurting Johansson with body punches in the fourth round.* ♦ **punch|er (punchers)** *...the awesome range of blows which have confirmed him as boxing's hardest puncher.* (VERB; V n; PHRASAL VERB; V P n (not pron); V n P; N-COUNT; N-COUNT: usu supp N) [2] If you **punch the air**, you put one or both of your fists forcefully above your shoulders as a gesture of delight or victory. ❑ *At the end, Graf punched the air in delight, a huge grin on her face.* (VERB; V n) [3] If you **punch** something such as the buttons on a keyboard, you touch them in order to store information on a machine such as a computer or to give the machine a command to do something. ❑ *Mrs. Baylor strode to the elevator and punched the button.* (VERB = push, press; V n) [4] If you **punch** holes **in** something, you make holes in it by pushing or pressing it with something sharp. ❑ *I took a ballpoint pen and punched a hole in the carton.* (VERB; V n *in* n) [5] A **punch** is a tool that you use for making holes in something. ❑ *Make two holes with a hole punch.* (N-COUNT) [6] If you say that something has **punch**, you mean that it has force or effectiveness. ❑ *My nervousness made me deliver the vital points of my address without sufficient punch.* (N-UNCOUNT) [7] **Punch** is a drink made from wine or spirits mixed with things such as sugar, lemons, and spices. (N-MASS) [8] If you say that someone does not **pull** their **punches** when they are criticizing a person or thing, you mean that they say exactly what they think, even though this might upset or offend people. ❑ *She has a reputation for getting at the guts of a subject and never pulling her punches.* (PHRASE: V and N inflect, oft with brd-neg)

♦ **punch in** If you **punch in** a number on a machine or **punch** numbers **into** it, you push the machine's buttons or keys in order to give it a command to do something. ❑ *You can bank by phone in the USA, punching in account numbers on the phone... Punch your credit card number into the keypad.* (PHRASAL VERB; V P n (not pron); V n P)

**Punch and Judy show** /pʌntʃ ən dʒuːdi ʃoʊ/ **(Punch and Judy shows)** A **Punch and Judy show** is a puppet show for children, often performed at fairs or at the seaside. Punch and Judy, the two main characters, are always fighting. (N-COUNT)

**punch|bag** /pʌntʃbæg/ **(punchbags)** also **punch bag.** A **punchbag** is a heavy leather bag, filled with a firm material, that hangs on a rope. Punchbags are used by boxers and other sportsmen for exercise and training. [BRIT] (N-COUNT)

☑ in AM, use **punching bag**

**punch bowl (punch bowls)** A **punch bowl** is a large bowl in which drinks, especially punch, are mixed and served. (N-COUNT)

**punch-drunk** also **punch drunk.** [1] A **punch-drunk** boxer shows signs of brain damage, for example by being unsteady and unable to think clearly, after being hit too often on the head. (ADJ: usu ADJ n) [2] If you say that someone is **punch-drunk**, you mean that they are very tired or confused, for example because they have been working too hard. ❑ *He was punch-drunk with fatigue and depressed by the rain.* (ADJ: usu v-link ADJ)

**punch|ing bag (punching bags)** A **punching bag** is the same as a **punchbag**. [AM] (N-COUNT)

**punch|line** /pʌntʃlaɪn/ **(punchlines)** also **punch line, punch-line.** The **punchline** of a joke or funny story is its last sentence or phrase, which gives it its humour. (N-COUNT)

**punch-up (punch-ups)** A **punch-up** is a fight in which people hit each other. [BRIT, INFORMAL] ❑ *He was involved in a punch-up with Sarah's former lover.* (N-COUNT)

**punchy** /pʌntʃi/ **(punchier, punchiest)** If you describe something as **punchy**, you mean that it expresses its meaning in a forceful or effective way. ❑ *A good way to sound confident is to use short punchy sentences.* (ADJ)

**punc|til|ious** /pʌŋktɪliəs/ Someone who is **punctilious** is very careful to behave correctly. [FORMAL] ❑ *He was punctilious about being ready and waiting in the entrance hall exactly on time... He was a punctilious young man.* (ADJ) ♦ **punc|til|ious|ly** *Given the circumstances, his behaviour to Laura had been punctiliously correct.* (ADV)

**punc|tu|al** /pʌŋktʃuəl/ If you are **punctual**, you do something or arrive somewhere at the right time and are not late. ❑ *He's always very punctual. I'll see if he's here yet.* (ADJ) ♦ **punc|tu|al|ly** *My guest arrived punctually.* (ADV: usu ADV with v) ♦ **punc|tu|al|ity** /pʌŋktʃuælɪti/ *I'll have to have a word with them about punctuality.* (N-UNCOUNT)

**punc|tu|ate** /pʌŋktʃueɪt/ **(punctuates, punctuating, punctuated)** If an activity or situation **is punctuated by** particular things, it is interrupt- (VERB: usu passive) ed by them at intervals. [WRITTEN] ❑ *The silence of the night was punctuated by the distant rumble of traffic.* *be V-ed by/with n*

**punc|tua|tion** /pʌŋktʃueɪʃᵊn/ 1 **Punctuation** is the use of symbols such as full stops or periods, commas, or question marks to divide written words into sentences and clauses. ❑ *He was known for his poor grammar and punctuation.* N-UNCOUNT
2 **Punctuation** is the symbols that you use to divide written words into sentences and clauses. ❑ *Jessica scanned the lines, none of which had any punctuation.* N-UNCOUNT

**punc|tua|tion mark** (**punctuation marks**) A **punctuation mark** is a symbol such as a full stop or period, comma, or question mark that you use to divide written words into sentences and clauses. N-COUNT

**punc|ture** /pʌŋktʃəʳ/ (**punctures, puncturing, punctured**) 1 A **puncture** is a small hole in a car tyre or bicycle tyre that has been made by a sharp object. ❑ *Somebody helped me mend the puncture. ...a tyre that has a slow puncture.* N-COUNT 2 A **puncture** is a small hole in someone's skin that has been made by or with a sharp object. ❑ *An instrument called a trocar makes a puncture in the abdominal wall.* N-COUNT 3 If a sharp object **punctures** something, it makes a hole in it. ❑ *The bullet punctured the skull.* VERB V n 4 If a car tyre or bicycle tyre **punctures** or if something **punctures** it, a hole is made in the tyre. ❑ *The tyre is guaranteed never to puncture or go flat... He punctured a tyre in the last lap.* VERB V V n 5 If someone's feelings or beliefs **are punctured**, their feelings or beliefs are made to seem wrong or foolish, especially when this makes the person feel disappointed or upset. ❑ *His enthusiasm for fishing had been punctured by the sight of what he might catch.* VERB = deflate *be V-ed* Also V n

**pun|dit** /pʌndɪt/ (**pundits**) A **pundit** is a person who knows a lot about a subject and is often asked to give information or opinions about it to the public. ❑ *...a well known political pundit.* N-COUNT: oft supp N = expert

**pun|gent** /pʌndʒᵊnt/ 1 Something that is **pungent** has a strong, sharp smell or taste which is often so strong that it is unpleasant. ❑ *The more herbs you use, the more pungent the sauce will be. ...the pungent smell of burning rubber.* ADJ ≠ delicate ♦ **pun|gen|cy** *...the spices that give Jamaican food its pungency.* N-UNCOUNT: usu with poss 2 If you describe what someone has said or written as **pungent**, you approve of it because it has a direct and powerful effect and often criticizes something very cleverly. [FORMAL] ❑ *He enjoyed the play's shrewd and pungent social analysis.* ADJ approval

**pun|ish** /pʌnɪʃ/ (**punishes, punishing, punished**) 1 To **punish** someone means to make them suffer in some way because they have done something wrong. ❑ *According to present law, the authorities can only punish smugglers with small fines... Don't punish your child for being honest.* VERB V n V n *for* n 2 To **punish** a crime means to punish anyone who commits that crime. ❑ *The government voted to punish corruption in sport with up to four years in jail.* VERB V n

**pun|ish|able** /pʌnɪʃəbᵊl/ If a crime is **punishable** in a particular way, anyone who commits it is punished in that way. ❑ *Treason in this country is still punishable by death.* ADJ: usu v-link ADJ *by/with* n

**pun|ish|ing** /pʌnɪʃɪŋ/ A **punishing** schedule, activity, or experience requires a lot of physical effort and makes you very tired or weak. ❑ *He claimed his punishing work schedule had made him resort to taking the drug.* ADJ: usu ADJ n

**pun|ish|ment** /pʌnɪʃmənt/ (**punishments**) 1 **Punishment** is the act of punishing someone or of being punished. ❑ *...a group which campaigns against the physical punishment of children... I have no doubt that the man is guilty and that he deserves punishment.* N-UNCOUNT 2 A **punishment** is a particular way of punishing someone. ❑ *The government is proposing tougher punishments for officials convicted of corruption.* N-VAR 3 You can use **punishment** to refer to severe physical treatment of any kind. ❑ *Don't expect these types of boot to take the punishment that gardening will give them.* N-UNCOUNT 4 → See also **capital punishment, corporal punishment**.

**pu|ni|tive** /pjuːnɪtɪv/ **Punitive** actions are intended to punish people. [FORMAL] ❑ *Other economists say any punitive measures against foreign companies would hurt US interests.* ADJ: usu ADJ n

**Pun|ja|bi** /pʌndʒɑːbi/ (**Punjabis**) 1 **Punjabi** means belonging or relating to the Punjab region of India or Pakistan, its people, or its language. ADJ: usu ADJ n 2 A **Punjabi** is a person who comes from the Punjab. N-COUNT 3 **Punjabi** is the language spoken by people who live in the Punjab. N-UNCOUNT

**punk** /pʌŋk/ (**punks**) 1 **Punk** or **punk rock** is rock music that is played in a fast, loud, and aggressive way and is often a protest against conventional attitudes and behaviour. Punk rock was particularly popular in the late 1970s. ❑ *I was never really into punk. ...a punk rock band.* N-UNCOUNT: oft N n 2 A **punk** or a **punk rocker** is a young person who likes punk music and dresses in a very noticeable and unconventional way, for example by having brightly coloured hair and wearing metal chains. N-COUNT

**pun|net** /pʌnɪt/ (**punnets**) A **punnet** is a small light box in which soft fruits such as strawberries or raspberries are often sold. You can also use **punnet** to refer to the amount of fruit that a punnet contains. [BRIT] ❑ *...a punnet of strawberries.* N-COUNT

**punt** (**punts**)

> ✔ Pronounced /pʌnt/ for meaning 1 and /pʊnt/ for meaning 2.

1 A **punt** is a long boat with a flat bottom. You move the boat along by standing at one end and pushing a long pole against the bottom of the river. [mainly BRIT] N-COUNT 2 The **punt** was the unit of money used in the Irish Republic before it was replaced by the euro. ❑ *The round-trip fare to Havana is 550 Irish punts ($673).* N-COUNT: num N ♦ **The punt** was also used to refer to the Irish currency system. ❑ *...the cost of defending the punt against speculators.* N-SING: *the* N

**punt|er** /pʌntəʳ/ (**punters**) 1 A **punter** is a person who bets money, especially on horse races. [BRIT, INFORMAL] ❑ *Punters are expected to gamble £70m on the Grand National.* N-COUNT 2 People sometimes refer to their customers or clients as **punters**. [mainly BRIT, INFORMAL] N-COUNT

**puny** /pjuːni/ (**punier, puniest**) Someone or something that is **puny** is very small or weak. ❑ *...a puny, bespectacled youth.* ADJ = feeble

**pup** /pʌp/ (**pups**) 1 A **pup** is a young dog. ❑ *I'll get you an Alsatian pup for Christmas.* N-COUNT = puppy 2 The young of some other animals, for example seals, are called **pups**. ❑ *Two thousand grey seal pups are born there every autumn.* N-COUNT: oft n N

**pupa** /pjuːpə/ (**pupae** /pjuːpiː/) A **pupa** is an insect that is in the stage of development between a larva and a fully grown adult. It has a protective covering and does not move. [TECHNICAL] ❑ *The pupae remain dormant in the soil until they emerge as adult moths in the winter.* N-COUNT

**pu|pil** /pjuːpɪl/ (**pupils**) 1 The **pupils** of a school are the children who go to it. ❑ *Over a third of those now at secondary school in Wales attend schools with over 1,000 pupils.* ◆◇◇ N-COUNT 2 A **pupil** of a painter, musician, or other expert is someone who studies under that expert and learns his or her skills. ❑ *After his education, Goldschmidt became a pupil of the composer Franz Schreker.* N-COUNT: with poss 3 The **pupils** of your eyes are the small, round, black holes in the centre of them. N-COUNT

**pup|pet** /pʌpɪt/ (**puppets**) 1 A **puppet** is a doll that you can move, either by pulling strings which are attached to it or by putting your hand inside its body and moving your fingers. N-COUNT 2 You can refer to a person or country as a **puppet** when you mean that their actions are controlled by a more powerful person or government, even though they may appear to be independent. N-COUNT: oft N n disapproval

❑ *When the invasion occurred he ruled as a puppet of the occupiers.*

**pup|pet|eer** /pʌpɪtɪəʳ/ **(puppeteers)** A **puppeteer** is a person who gives shows using puppets. N-COUNT

**pup|py** /pʌpi/ **(puppies)** A **puppy** is a young dog. ❑ *One Sunday he began trying to teach the two puppies to walk on a leash.* N-COUNT = *pup*

**pup|py fat** also **puppy-fat. Puppy fat** is fat that some children have on their bodies when they are young but that disappears when they grow older and taller. N-UNCOUNT

**pur|chase** /pɜːʳtʃɪs/ **(purchases, purchasing, purchased)** ◆◆◇ 1 When you **purchase** something, you buy it. [FORMAL] ❑ *He purchased a ticket and went up on the top deck.* VERB V n ♦ **pur|chas|er (purchasers)** *The broker will get 5% if he finds a purchaser.* N-COUNT = *buyer* 2 The **purchase of** something is the act of buying it. [FORMAL] ❑ *Some of the receipts had been for the purchase of cars.* → See also **hire purchase**. N-UNCOUNT: oft N *of* n 3 A **purchase** is something that you buy. [FORMAL] ❑ *She opened the tie box and looked at her purchase. It was silk, with maroon stripes.* N-COUNT 4 If you get a **purchase on** something, you manage to get a firm grip on it. [FORMAL] ❑ *I got a purchase on the rope and pulled... I couldn't get any purchase with the screwdriver on the damn screws.* N-UNCOUNT: also *a* N = *grip*

**pur|chas|ing pow|er** 1 The **purchasing power** of a currency is the amount of goods or services that you can buy with it. [BUSINESS] ❑ *The real purchasing power of the rouble has plummeted.* N-UNCOUNT 2 The **purchasing power** of a person or group of people is the amount of goods or services that they can afford to buy. [BUSINESS] ❑ *...the purchasing power of their customers.* N-UNCOUNT

**pur|dah** /pɜːʳdə/ **Purdah** is a custom practised in some Muslim and Hindu societies, in which women either remain in a special part of the house or cover their faces and bodies to avoid being seen by men who are not related to them. If a woman is **in purdah**, she lives according to this custom. N-UNCOUNT: oft *in* N

**pure** /pjʊəʳ/ **(purer, purest)** ◆◇◇ 1 A **pure** substance is not mixed with anything else. ❑ *...a carton of pure orange juice.* ADJ: usu ADJ n 2 Something that is **pure** is clean and does not contain any harmful substances. ❑ *In remote regions, the air is pure and the crops are free of poisonous insecticides. ...demands for purer and cleaner river water.* ADJ ♦ **pu|rity** *They worried about the purity of tap water.* N-UNCOUNT: with poss 3 If you describe something such as a colour, a sound, or a type of light as **pure**, you mean that it is very clear and represents a perfect example of its type. ❑ *...flowers in a whole range of blues with the occasional pure white.* ADJ: usu ADJ n ♦ **pu|rity** *The soaring purity of her voice conjured up the frozen bleakness of the Far North.* N-UNCOUNT 4 If you describe a form of art or a philosophy as **pure**, you mean that it is produced or practised according to a standard or form that is expected of it. [FORMAL] ❑ *Nicholson never swerved from his aim of making pure and simple art.* ADJ: usu ADJ n ♦ **pu|rity** *...verse of great purity, sonority of rhythm, and symphonic form.* N-UNCOUNT 5 **Pure** science or **pure** research is concerned only with theory and not with how this theory can be used in practical ways. ❑ *Physics isn't just about pure science with no immediate applications.* ADJ: ADJ n ≠ *applied* 6 **Pure** means complete and total. ❑ *The old man turned to give her a look of pure surprise.* ADJ [emphasis] = *sheer*

**pure-bred** also **purebred.** A **pure-bred** animal is one whose parents and ancestors all belong to the same breed. ❑ *...pure-bred Arab horses.* ADJ: ADJ n

**pu|ree** /pjʊəreɪ, AM pjʊreɪ/ **(purees, pureeing, pureed)** also **purée.** 1 **Puree** is food which has been crushed or beaten so that it forms a thick, smooth liquid. ❑ *...a can of tomato puree.* N-VAR 2 If you **puree** food, you make it into a puree. ❑ *Puree the apricots in a liquidiser until completely smooth.* VERB V n

**pure|ly** /pjʊəʳli/ 1 You use **purely** to emphasize that the thing you are mentioning is the most important feature or that it is the only thing which should be considered. ❑ *It is a racing machine, designed purely for speed... The government said the moves were purely defensive.* ADV: ADV with cl/group [emphasis] 2 You use **purely and simply** to emphasize that the thing you are mentioning is the only thing involved. ❑ *If Arthur was attracted here by the prospects of therapy, John came down purely and simply to make money.* PHRASE: PHR with cl [emphasis]

**pur|ga|tive** /pɜːʳgətɪv/ **(purgatives)** 1 A **purgative** is a medicine that causes you to get rid of unwanted waste from your body. [FORMAL] N-COUNT = *laxative* 2 A **purgative** substance acts as a purgative. [FORMAL] ❑ *...purgative oils. ...a purgative tea.* ADJ: ADJ n

**pur|ga|tory** /pɜːʳgətri, AM -tɔːri/ 1 **Purgatory** is the place where Roman Catholics believe the spirits of dead people are sent to suffer for their sins before they go to heaven. ❑ *Prayers were said for souls in Purgatory.* N-PROPER 2 You can describe a very unpleasant experience as **purgatory**. ❑ *Every step of the last three miles was purgatory. ...five years of economic purgatory.* N-UNCOUNT = *hell*

**purge** /pɜːʳdʒ/ **(purges, purging, purged)** 1 To **purge** an organization **of** its unacceptable members means to remove them from it. You can also talk about **purging** people **from** an organization. ❑ *The leadership voted to purge the party of 'hostile and anti-party elements'... He recently purged the armed forces, sending hundreds of officers into retirement... They have purged thousands from the upper levels of the civil service.* VERB V n *of* n V n V n *from* n ♦ **Purge** is also a noun. ❑ *The army have called for a more thorough purge of people associated with the late President.* N-COUNT: oft N *of* n 2 If you **purge** something **of** undesirable things, you get rid of them. ❑ *He closed his eyes and lay still, trying to purge his mind of anxiety.* VERB = *rid* V n *of* n Also V n

**pu|ri|fi|er** /pjʊərɪfaɪəʳ/ **(purifiers)** A **purifier** is a device or a substance that is used to purify something such as water, air, or blood. ❑ *...air purifiers.* N-COUNT: oft n N

**pu|ri|fy** /pjʊərɪfaɪ/ **(purifies, purifying, purified)** If you **purify** a substance, you make it pure by removing any harmful, dirty, or inferior substances from it. ❑ *I take wheat and yeast tablets daily to purify the blood... Only purified water is used.* VERB ≠ *contaminate* V n V-ed ♦ **pu|ri|fi|ca|tion** /pjʊərɪfɪkeɪʃᵊn/ *...a water purification plant.* N-UNCOUNT

**pur|ist** /pjʊərɪst/ **(purists)** 1 A **purist** is a person who wants something to be totally correct or unchanged, especially something they know a lot about. ❑ *The new edition of the dictionary carries 7000 additions to the language, which purists say is under threat.* N-COUNT 2 **Purist** attitudes are the kind of attitudes that purists have. ❑ *Britain wanted a 'more purist' approach.* ADJ: usu ADJ n

**pu|ri|tan** /pjʊərɪtᵊn/ **(puritans)** 1 You describe someone as a **puritan** when they live according to strict moral or religious principles, especially when they disapprove of physical pleasures. ❑ *Bykov had forgotten that Malinin was something of a puritan.* N-COUNT [disapproval] 2 **Puritan** attitudes are based on strict moral or religious principles and often involve disapproval of physical pleasures. ❑ *Paul was someone who certainly had a puritan streak in him.* ADJ: usu ADJ n [disapproval]

**Pu|ri|tan (Puritans)** The **Puritans** were a group of English Protestants in the sixteenth and seventeenth centuries who lived in a very strict and religious way. N-COUNT

**pu|ri|tani|cal** /pjʊərɪtænɪkᵊl/ If you describe someone as **puritanical**, you mean that they have very strict moral principles, and often try to make other people behave in a more moral way. ❑ *He has a puritanical attitude towards sex.* ADJ [disapproval]

**pu|ri|tan|ism** /pjʊərɪtənɪzəm/ **Puritanism** is behaviour or beliefs that are based on strict moral or religious principles, especially the principle that people should avoid physical pleasures. ❑ *...the tight-lipped puritanism of the Scottish literary world.* N-UNCOUNT [disapproval]

**Pu|ri|tan|ism** **Puritanism** is the set of beliefs that were held by the Puritans. ❑ *Out of Puritanism came the intense work ethic.* N-UNCOUNT

**pu|rity** /pjʊərɪti/ → see **pure**.

**pur|loin** /pɜːʳlɔɪn/ **(purloins, purloining, purloined)** If someone **purloins** something, they steal it or borrow it without asking permission. [FORMAL] ❑ *Each side purloins the other's private letters.* VERB V n

**pur|ple** /pɜːʳpᵊl/ **(purples)** [1] Something that is **purple** is of a reddish-blue colour. ❑ *She wore purple and green silk. ...sinister dark greens and purples.* [2] **Purple** prose or a **purple patch** is a piece of writing that contains very elaborate language or images. ❑ *...passages of purple prose describing intense experiences.* ◆◆◇ COLOUR; ADJ: usu ADJ n

**Pur|ple Heart** **(Purple Hearts)** The **Purple Heart** is a medal that is given to members of the US Armed Forces who have been wounded during battle. N-COUNT

**pur|plish** /pɜːʳpəlɪʃ/ **Purplish** means slightly purple in colour. ADJ

**pur|port** /pəʳpɔːʳt/ **(purports, purporting, purported)** If you say that someone or something **purports to** do or be a particular thing, you mean that they claim to do or be that thing, although you may not always believe that claim. [FORMAL] ❑ *...a book that purports to tell the whole truth.* VERB V to-inf

**pur|port|ed|ly** /pəʳpɔːʳtɪdli/ If you say that something has **purportedly** been done, you mean that you think that it has been done but you cannot be sure. [FORMAL] ❑ *He was given a letter purportedly signed by the Prime Minister.* ADV: ADV with v, ADV cl/group = supposedly

**pur|pose** /pɜːʳpəs/ **(purposes)** [1] The **purpose** of something is the reason for which it is made or done. ❑ *The purpose of the occasion was to raise money for medical supplies... Various insurance schemes already exist for this purpose. ...the use of nuclear energy for military purposes... He was asked about casualties, but said it would serve no purpose to count bodies.* [2] Your **purpose** is the thing that you want to achieve. ❑ *They might well be prepared to do you harm in order to achieve their purpose... His purpose was to make a profit by improving the company's performance.* [3] **Purpose** is the feeling of having a definite aim and of being determined to achieve it. ❑ *The teachers are enthusiastic and have a sense of purpose.* [4] → See also **cross-purposes**. ◆◆◇ N-COUNT: with supp = aim; N-COUNT: with poss = aim, objective; N-UNCOUNT

PHRASES [5] You use **for all practical purposes** or **to all intents and purposes** to suggest that a situation is not exactly as you describe it, but the effect is the same as if it were. ❑ *For all practical purposes the treaty has already ceased to exist.* [6] If you do something **on purpose**, you do it intentionally. ❑ *Was it an accident or did David do it on purpose?* PHRASE: PHR with cl = in effect; PHRASE: PHR after v = intentionally

**purpose-built** A **purpose-built** building has been specially designed and built for a particular use. [mainly BRIT] ❑ *The company has recently moved into a new purpose-built factory.* ADJ

☑ in AM, usually use **custom-built**

**pur|pose|ful** /pɜːʳpəsfʊl/ If someone is **purposeful**, they show that they have a definite aim and a strong desire to achieve it. ❑ *She had a purposeful air, and it became evident that this was not a casual visit.* ♦ **pur|pose|ful|ly** *He strode purposefully towards the barn.* ADJ ≠ casual; ADV: usu ADV with v ≠ casually

**pur|pose|less** /pɜːʳpəsləs/ If an action is **purposeless**, it does not seem to have a sensible purpose. ❑ *Time may also be wasted in purposeless meetings... Surely my existence cannot be so purposeless?* ADJ = senseless, pointless

**pur|pose|ly** /pɜːʳpəsli/ If you do something **purposely**, you do it intentionally. [FORMAL] ❑ *They are purposely withholding information.* ADV: usu ADV with v, also ADV adj

**purr** /pɜːʳ/ **(purrs, purring, purred)** [1] When a cat **purrs**, it makes a low vibrating sound with its throat because it is contented. ❑ *The plump ginger kitten had settled comfortably in her arms and was purring enthusiastically.* [2] When the engine of a machine such as a car **purrs**, it is working and making a quiet, continuous, vibrating sound. ❑ *Both boats purred out of the cave mouth and into open water.* ♦ **Purr** is also a noun. ❑ *Carmela heard the purr of a motor-cycle coming up the drive.* VERB V; VERB V prep; N-SING

**purse** /pɜːʳs/ **(purses, pursing, pursed)** [1] A **purse** is a very small bag that people, especially women, keep their money in. [BRIT] N-COUNT

☑ in AM, use **change purse**

[2] A **purse** is a small bag that women carry. [AM] ❑ *She looked at me and then reached in her purse for cigarettes.* N-COUNT

☑ in BRIT, use **bag, handbag**

[3] **Purse** is used to refer to the total amount of money that a country, family, or group has. ❑ *The money could simply go into the public purse, helping to lower taxes.* [4] If you **purse** your **lips**, you move them into a small, rounded shape, usually because you disapprove of something or when you are thinking. ❑ *She pursed her lips in disapproval.* N-SING: with supp; VERB V n

**purs|er** /pɜːʳsəʳ/ **(pursers)** On a ship, the **purser** is an officer who deals with the accounts and official papers. On a passenger ship, the purser is also responsible for the welfare of the passengers. N-COUNT

**purse strings** If you say that someone holds or controls **the purse strings**, you mean that they control the way that money is spent in a particular family, group, or country. ❑ *Women control the purse-strings of most families.* N-PLURAL: the N

**pur|su|ance** /pəʳsjuːəns, AM -suː-/ If you do something **in pursuance of** a particular activity, you do it as part of carrying out that activity. [FORMAL] ❑ *He ordered disclosure of a medical report to the Metropolitan Police in pursuance of an investigation of murder.* N-UNCOUNT: usu in N of n

**pur|su|ant** /pəʳsjuːənt, AM -suː-/ If someone does something **pursuant to** a law or regulation, they obey that law or regulation. [FORMAL] ❑ *He should continue to act pursuant to the United Nations Security Council resolutions.* PREP-PHRASE

**pur|sue** /pəʳsjuː, -suː/ **(pursues, pursuing, pursued)** [1] If you **pursue** an activity, interest, or plan, you carry it out or follow it. [FORMAL] ❑ *He said Japan would continue to pursue the policies laid down at the London summit... She had come to England to pursue an acting career.* [2] If you **pursue** a particular aim or result, you make efforts to achieve it, often over a long period of time. [FORMAL] ❑ *Mr. Menendez has aggressively pursued new business.* [3] If you **pursue** a particular topic, you try to find out more about it by asking questions. [FORMAL] ❑ *If your original request is denied, don't be afraid to pursue the matter.* [4] If you **pursue** a person, vehicle, or animal, you follow them, usually in order to catch them. [FORMAL] ❑ *She pursued the man who had stolen a woman's bag.* ◆◇◇ VERB V n V n; VERB V n; VERB = follow up ≠ drop V n; VERB V n

**pur|su|er** /pəʳsjuːəʳ, AM -suː-/ **(pursuers)** Your **pursuers** are the people who are chasing or searching for you. [FORMAL] ❑ *They had shaken off their pursuers.* N-COUNT: oft poss N in pl

**pur|suit** /pəʳsjuːt, AM -suːt/ **(pursuits)** [1] Your **pursuit of** something is your attempts at achieving it. If you do something **in pursuit of** a particular result, you do it in order to achieve that result. ❑ *...a young man whose relentless pursuit of excellence is conducted with single-minded determination.* [2] The **pursuit of** an activity, interest, or plan consists of all the things that you do when you are carrying it out. ❑ *The vigorous pursuit of policies is no guarantee of success.* [3] Someone who is **in pursuit of** a person, vehicle, or animal is chasing them. ❑ *...a police officer who drove a patrol car at more than 120mph in pursuit of a motor cycle.* [4] Your **pursuits** are your activities, usually activities that you enjoy when you are not working. ❑ *They both love outdoor pursuits.* [5] If you are **in hot pursuit of** someone, you are chasing after N-UNCOUNT: N of n, oft in N of n; N-UNCOUNT: N of n; N-UNCOUNT: usu in N of n; N-COUNT: usu pl, with supp; PHRASE

them with great determination. ❑ *I rushed through with Sue in hot pursuit.*

**pur|vey** /pəʳveɪ/ **(purveys, purveying, purveyed)** [1] If you **purvey** something such as information, you tell it to people. [FORMAL] ❑ *...one who would, for a hefty fee, purvey strategic advice to private corporations.* [2] If someone **purveys** goods or services, they provide them. [FORMAL] ❑ *They have two restaurants that purvey dumplings and chicken noodle soup.*
(VERB; V n; VERB = supply, sell; V n)

**pur|vey|or** /pəʳveɪəʳ/ **(purveyors)** A **purveyor of** goods or services is a person or company that provides them. [FORMAL] ❑ *...purveyors of gourmet foods.*
(N-COUNT: usu N *of* n = supplier)

**pur|view** /pɜːʳvjuː/ The **purview of** something such as an organization or activity is the range of things it deals with. [FORMAL] ❑ *That, however, was beyond the purview of the court; it was a diplomatic matter.*
(N-SING: usu N *of* n)

**pus** /pʌs/ **Pus** is a thick yellowish liquid that forms in wounds when they are infected.
(N-UNCOUNT)

**push** /pʊʃ/ **(pushes, pushing, pushed)** ◆◆◇ [1] When you **push** something, you use force to make it move away from you or away from its previous position. ❑ *The woman pushed back her chair and stood up... They pushed him into the car. ...a woman pushing a pushchair... He put both hands flat on the door and pushed as hard as he could... When there was no reply, he pushed the door open.* ♦ **Push** is also a noun. ❑ *He gave me a sharp push... Information is called up at the push of a button.* [2] If you **push through** things that are blocking your way or **push** your **way through** them, you use force in order to move past them. ❑ *I pushed through the crowds and on to the escalator... He pushed his way towards her, laughing.* [3] If an army **pushes into** a country or area that it is attacking or invading, it moves further into it. ❑ *One detachment pushed into the eastern suburbs towards the airfield... The army may push southwards into the Kurdish areas.* ♦ **Push** is also a noun. ❑ *All that was needed was one final push, and the enemy would be vanquished once and for all.* [4] To **push** a value or amount **up** or **down** means to cause it to increase or decrease. ❑ *Any shortage could push up grain prices... Interest had pushed the loan up to $27,000.* [5] If someone or something **pushes** an idea or project in a particular direction, they cause it to develop or progress in a particular way. ❑ *We are continuing to push the business forward... The government seemed intent on pushing local and central government in opposite directions.* [6] If you **push** someone **to** do something or **push** them **into** doing it, you encourage or force them to do it. ❑ *She thanks her parents for keeping her in school and pushing her to study... James did not push her into stealing the money... I knew he was pushing himself to the limit and felt rather anxious... There is no point in pushing them unless they are talented and they enjoy it.* ♦ **Push** is also a noun. ❑ *We need a push to take the first step.* [7] If you **push for** something, you try very hard to achieve it or to persuade someone to do it. ❑ *Britain's health experts are pushing for a ban on all cigarette advertising... Germany is pushing for direct flights to be established.* ♦ **Push** is also a noun. ❑ *In its push for economic growth it has ignored projects that would improve living standards.* [8] If someone **pushes** an idea, a point, or a product, they try in a forceful way to convince people to accept it or buy it. ❑ *Ministers will push the case for opening the plant.* [9] When someone **pushes** drugs, they sell them illegally. [INFORMAL] ❑ *She was sent for trial yesterday accused of pushing drugs.* [10] → See also **pushed, pushing.** [11] If you **get the push** or **are given the push**, you are told that you are not wanted any more, either in your job or by someone you are having a relationship with. [BRIT, INFORMAL] ❑ *Two cabinet ministers also got the push.* [12] to **push the boat out** → see **boat**. to **push** your **luck** → see **luck**. if **push comes to shove** → see **shove**.
(VERB; V n with adv; V n prep; V n; V; V n adj; N-COUNT: usu sing; VERB; V prep/adv; V *way* prep/adv; VERB = advance; V *into* n; V adv *into* n; N-COUNT: usu sing; VERB; V n with adv; V n prep; VERB; V n with adv; V n prep; VERB; V n to-inf; V n *into* -ing; V n prep/adv; V n; N-COUNT: usu sing; VERB; V *for* n; V *for* n to-inf; N-COUNT: usu sing; VERB; V n; VERB = deal; V n; PHRASE: V inflects)

♦ **push ahead** or **push forward** If you **push ahead** or **push forward with** something, you make progress with it. ❑ *The government intends to push ahead with its reform programme.*
(PHRASAL VERB; V P *with* n)

♦ **push around** If someone **pushes** you **around**, they give you orders in a rude and insulting way. [INFORMAL] ❑ *We don't like somebody coming in with lots of money and trying to push people around.*
(PHRASAL VERB; V n P)

♦ **push forward** → see **push ahead.**

♦ **push in** When someone **pushes in**, they unfairly join a queue or line in front of other people who have been waiting longer. ❑ *Nina pushed in next to Liddie.*
(PHRASAL VERB; disapproval; V P)

♦ **push on** When you **push on**, you continue with a journey or task. ❑ *Although the journey was a long and lonely one, Tumalo pushed on.*
(PHRASAL VERB; V P)

♦ **push over** If you **push** someone or something **over**, you push them so that they fall onto the ground. ❑ *People have damaged hedges and pushed over walls... Anna is always attacking other children, pushing them over.* → See also **pushover.**
(PHRASAL VERB; V P n (not pron); V n P)

♦ **push through** If someone **pushes through** a law, they succeed in getting it accepted although some people oppose it. ❑ *The vote will enable the Prime Minister to push through tough policies... He tried to push the amendment through Parliament.*
(PHRASAL VERB; V P n (not pron); V n P n)

**push bike (push bikes)** A **push bike** is a bicycle which you move by turning the pedals with your feet. [BRIT, OLD-FASHIONED]
(N-COUNT)

**push-button** A **push-button** machine or process is controlled by means of buttons or switches. ❑ *...push-button phones.*
(ADJ: ADJ n)

**push|cart** /pʊʃkɑːʳt/ **(pushcarts)** A **pushcart** is a cart from which fruit or other goods are sold in the street. [AM]
(N-COUNT)

✓ in BRIT, use **barrow**

**push|chair** /pʊʃtʃeəʳ/ **(pushchairs)** A **pushchair** is a small chair on wheels, in which a baby or small child can sit and be wheeled around. [BRIT]
(N-COUNT)

✓ in AM, use **stroller**

**pushed** /pʊʃt/ [1] If you are **pushed for** something such as time or money, you do not have enough of it. [BRIT, INFORMAL] ❑ *He's going to be a bit pushed for money.*
(ADJ: v-link ADJ, usu ADJ *for* n)

✓ in AM, use **pressed for**

[2] If you **are hard pushed to** do something, you find it very difficult to do it. [BRIT] ❑ *I'd be hard pushed to teach him anything.*
(PHRASE: V inflects = hard-pressed)

**push|er** /pʊʃəʳ/ **(pushers)** A **pusher** is a person who sells illegal drugs. [INFORMAL] ❑ *He was accused of acting as a carrier for drug pushers.*
(N-COUNT = dealer)

**push|ing** /pʊʃɪŋ/ If you say that someone is **pushing** a particular age, you mean that they are nearly that age. [INFORMAL] ❑ *Pushing 40, he was an ageing rock star.*
(PREP = almost, going on)

**push|over** /pʊʃoʊvəʳ/ **(pushovers)** [1] You say that someone is a **pushover** when you find it easy to persuade them to do what you want. [INFORMAL] ❑ *He is a tough negotiator. We did not expect to find him a pushover and he has not been one.* [2] You say that something is a **pushover** when it is easy to do or easy to get. [INFORMAL] ❑ *You might think Hungarian a pushover to learn. It is not.*
(N-COUNT; N-COUNT: usu sing = doddle)

**push-up (push-ups) Push-ups** are exercises to strengthen your arms and chest muscles. They are done by lying with your face towards the floor and pushing with your hands to raise your body until your arms are straight. [AM]
(N-COUNT)

✓ in BRIT, use **press-ups**

**pushy** /pʊʃi/ **(pushier, pushiest)** If you describe someone as **pushy**, you mean that they try in a forceful way to get things done as they would like or to increase their status or influence. [INFORMAL] ❑ *She was a confident and pushy young woman.*
(ADJ; disapproval)

**pu|sil|lani|mous** /pjuːsɪlænɪməs/ If you say that someone is **pusillanimous**, you mean that they are timid or afraid. [FORMAL] ❑ *The authorities have been too pusillanimous in merely condemning the violence.* ADJ disapproval = cowardly ≠ valiant

**puss** /pʊs/ People sometimes call a cat by saying '**Puss**'. N-VOC

**pussy** /pʊsi/ **(pussies)** 1 **Pussy** is a child's word for a cat. N-COUNT 2 Some people use **pussy** to refer to a woman's genitals. [INFORMAL, ⚠ VERY RUDE] N-COUNT

**pussy|cat** /pʊsikæt/ **(pussycats)** 1 Children or people talking to children often refer to a cat as a **pussycat**. N-COUNT = pussy 2 If you describe someone as a **pussycat**, you think that they are kind and gentle. N-COUNT = sweetie

**pussy|foot** /pʊsifʊt/ **(pussyfoots, pussyfooting, pussyfooted)** If you say that someone **is pussyfooting around**, you are criticizing them for behaving in a too cautious way because they are not sure what to do and are afraid to commit themselves. ❑ *Why don't they stop pussyfooting around and say what they really mean?* VERB disapproval V around/about Also V

**pus|tule** /pʌstʃuːl/ **(pustules)** A **pustule** is a small infected swelling on the skin. [MEDICAL] N-COUNT = boil

**put** /pʊt/ **(puts, putting)** ◆◆◆

> The form **put** is used in the present tense and is the past tense and past participle.

> **Put** is used in a large number of expressions which are explained under other words in this dictionary. For example, the expression **to put someone in the picture** is explained at **picture**.

1 When you **put** something in a particular place or position, you move it into that place or position. ❑ *Leaphorn put the photograph on the desk...* *She hesitated, then put her hand on Grace's arm...* *Mishka put down a heavy shopping bag.* VERB V n prep/adv V n prep/adv V n with adv 2 If you **put** someone somewhere, you cause them to go there and to stay there for a period of time. ❑ *Rather than put him in the hospital, she had been caring for him at home... I'd put the children to bed.* VERB V n prep/adv V n prep/adv 3 To **put** someone or something in a particular state or situation means to cause them to be in that state or situation. ❑ *This is going to put them out of business... He was putting himself at risk... My doctor put me in touch with a psychiatrist.* VERB V n prep/adv V n prep/adv V n prep/adv 4 To **put** something **on** people or things means to cause them to have it, or to cause them to be affected by it. ❑ *The ruling will put extra pressure on health authorities to change working practices and shorten hours... They will also force schools to put more emphasis on teaching basic subjects.* VERB = place V n on n V n on n 5 If you **put** your trust, faith, or confidence **in** someone or something, you trust them or have faith or confidence in them. ❑ *How much faith should we put in anti-ageing products?* VERB = place V n in n 6 If you **put** time, strength, or energy **into** an activity, you use it in doing that activity. ❑ *Eleanor did not put much energy into the discussion.* VERB V n into n/-ing 7 If you **put** money **into** a business or project, you invest money in it. ❑ *Investors should consider putting some money into an annuity.* VERB V n into n 8 When you **put** an idea or remark in a particular way, you express it in that way. You can use expressions like **to put it simply** and **to put it bluntly** before saying something when you want to explain how you are going to express it. ❑ *I had already met Pete a couple of times through – how should I put it – friends in low places... He doesn't, to put it very bluntly, give a damn about the woman or the baby... He admitted the security forces might have made some mistakes, as he put it... You can't put that sort of fear into words.* VERB V it adv/prep V it adv/prep V it V n into n 9 When you **put a question to** someone, you ask them the question. ❑ *Is this fair? Well, I put that question today to Deputy Counsel Craig Gillen... He thinks that some workers may be afraid to put questions publicly.* VERB V n to n V n adv 10 If you **put** a case, opinion, or proposal, you explain it and list the reasons why you support or believe it. ❑ *He always put his point of view with clarity and with courage... He put the case to the Saudi Foreign Minister.* VERB = present V n V n to n 11 If you **put** something **at** a particular value or **in** a particular category, you consider that it has that value or that it belongs in that category. ❑ *I would put her age at about 50 or so... All the more technically advanced countries put a high value on science... It is not easy to put the guilty and innocent into clear-cut categories.* VERB V n at amount V n on n V n into n 12 If you **put** written information somewhere, you write, type, or print it there. ❑ *Mary's family were so pleased that they put an announcement in the local paper to thank them... He crossed out 'Screenplay' and put 'Written by' instead.* VERB V n prep/adv V n

**PHRASES** 13 If you **put it to** someone **that** something is true, you suggest that it is true, especially when you think that they will be unwilling to admit this. ❑ *But I put it to you that they're useless.* PHRASE: V inflects 14 If you say that something is bigger or better than several other things **put together**, you mean that it is bigger or has more good qualities than all of those other things if they are added together. ❑ *London has more pubs and clubs than the rest of the country put together.* PHRASE: n PHR

◆ **put about**

> The forms **put around** and **put round** are also used in British English.

If you **put** something **about**, you tell it to people that you meet and cause it to become well-known. [mainly BRIT] ❑ *Moderates are putting it about that people shouldn't take the things said at the Republican Convention too seriously... The King had been putting about lurid rumours for months.* PHRASAL VERB V it P that V P n (not pron) Also V n P

◆ **put across** or **put over** When you **put** something **across** or **put** it **over**, you succeed in describing or explaining it to someone. ❑ *He has taken out a half-page advertisement in his local paper to put his point across... This is actually a very entertaining book putting over serious health messages.* PHRASAL VERB = get across V n P V P n (not pron)

◆ **put around** → see **put about**.

◆ **put aside** 1 If you **put** something **aside**, you keep it to be dealt with or used at a later time. ❑ *She took up a slice of bread, broke it nervously, then put it aside... Encourage children to put aside some of their pocket-money to buy Christmas presents.* PHRASAL VERB V n P V P n (not pron) 2 If you **put** a feeling or disagreement **aside**, you forget about it or ignore it in order to solve a problem or argument. ❑ *We should put aside our differences and discuss the things we have in common... We admitted that the attraction was there, but decided that we would put the feelings aside.* PHRASAL VERB = forget about V P n (not pron) V n P

◆ **put away** 1 If you **put** something **away**, you put it into the place where it is normally kept when it is not being used, for example in a drawer. ❑ *She finished putting the milk away and turned around... 'Yes, Mum,' replied Cheryl as she slowly put away her doll... Her bed was crisply made, her clothes put away.* PHRASAL VERB V n P V P n (not pron) V-ed P 2 If someone **is put away**, they are sent to prison or to a mental hospital for a long time. [INFORMAL] ❑ *He's an animal! He should be put away... His testimony could put Drago away for life.* PHRASAL VERB be V-ed P V n P

◆ **put back** To **put** something **back** means to delay it or arrange for it to happen later than you previously planned. [mainly BRIT] ❑ *There are always new projects which seem to put the reunion back further... News conferences due to be held by both men have been put back.* PHRASAL VERB = delay V n P be V-ed P Also V P n (not pron)

◆ **put down** 1 If you **put** something **down** somewhere, you write or type it there. ❑ *Never put anything down on paper which might be used in evidence against you at a later date... We've put down on our staff development plan for this year that we would like some technology courses... I had prepared for the meeting by putting down what I wanted from them.* PHRASAL VERB V n P in/on n V P that V P wh Also V P n (not pron) 2 If you **put down** some money, you pay part of the price of something, and will pay the rest later. ❑ *He bought an investment property for $100,000 and put down $20,000... He's got to put cash down.* PHRASAL VERB V P n (not pron) V n P 3 When soldiers, police, or the government **put down** a riot or rebellion, they stop it by using force. ❑ *Soldiers went in to put down a* PHRASAL VERB V P n Also V n P *rebellion.* 4 If someone **puts** you **down**, they treat you in an unpleasant way by criticizing you in front of other people or making you appear foolish. ❑ *I know that I do put people down occasionally... Racist jokes come from wanting to put down other kinds of people we feel threatened by.* → See also **put-down**. 5 When an animal **is put down**, it is killed because it is dangerous or very ill. [mainly BRIT] ❑ *Magistrates ordered his dog Samson to be put down immediately... They think that any legislation that involved putting down dogs was wrong.*

PHRASAL VERB · V n P · V P n (not pron) · PHRASAL VERB · *be* V-ed P · V P n (not pron) · Also V n P

♦ **put down to** If you **put** something **down to** a particular thing, you believe that it is caused by that thing. ❑ *You may be a sceptic and put it down to life's inequalities.*

PHRASAL VERB · V n P P n

♦ **put forward** If you **put forward** a plan, proposal, or name, you suggest that it should be considered for a particular purpose or job. ❑ *He has put forward new peace proposals... I rang the Colonel and asked him to put my name forward for the vacancy in Zurich.*

PHRASAL VERB · = submit · ≠ withdraw · V P n (not pron) · V n P *for* n · Also V n P

♦ **put in** 1 If you **put in** an amount of time or effort doing something, you spend that time or effort doing it. ❑ *They've put in time and effort to keep the strike going... If we don't put money in we will lose our investment.* 2 If you **put in** a request or **put in for** something, you formally request or apply for that thing. ❑ *The ministry ordered 113 of these and later put in a request for 21 more... I decided to put in for a job as deputy secretary.* 3 If you **put in** a remark, you interrupt someone or add to what they have said with the remark. ❑ *'He was a lawyer before that,' Mary Ann put in.* 4 When a ship **puts in** or **puts into** a port, it goes into the port for a short stop. ❑ *It's due to put in at Aden and some other ports before arriving in Basra.*

PHRASAL VERB · V P n (not pron) · V n P · PHRASAL VERB · V P n (not pron) · V P *for* n · PHRASAL VERB · V P with quote · PHRASAL VERB · V P adv/prep

♦ **put off** 1 If you **put** something **off**, you delay doing it. ❑ *Women who put off having a baby often make the best mothers... The Association has put the event off until October.* 2 If you **put** someone **off**, you make them wait for something that they want. ❑ *The old priest tried to put them off, saying that the hour was late.* 3 If something **puts** you **off** something, it makes you dislike it, or decide not to do or have it. ❑ *The high divorce figures don't seem to be putting people off marriage... His personal habits put them off... The country's worsening reputation does not seem to be putting off the tourists... We tried to visit the Abbey but were put off by the queues.* 4 If someone or something **puts** you **off**, they take your attention from what you are trying to do and make it more difficult for you to do it. ❑ *She asked me to be serious – said it put her off if I laughed... It put her off revising for her exams.*

PHRASAL VERB · = postpone · V P -ing/n (not pron) · V n P · PHRASAL VERB · V n P · PHRASAL VERB · V n P n/-ing · V n P · V P n (not pron) · *be* V-ed P · PHRASAL VERB · = distract · V n P · V n P n/-ing

♦ **put on** 1 When you **put on** clothing or make-up, you place it on your body in order to wear it. ❑ *She put on her coat and went out... I haven't even put any lipstick on.* 2 When people **put on** a show, exhibition, or service, they perform it or organize it. ❑ *The band are hoping to put on a UK show before the end of the year... We put it on and everybody said 'Oh it's a brilliant production'.* 3 If someone **puts on** weight, they become heavier. ❑ *I can eat what I want but I never put on weight... Luther's put on three stone.* 4 If you **put on** a piece of equipment or a device, you make it start working, for example by pressing a switch or turning a knob. ❑ *I put the radio on... I put on the light by the bed.* 5 If you **put** a record, tape, or CD **on**, you place it in a record, tape, or CD player and listen to it. ❑ *She poured them drinks, and put a record on loud... Let's go into the study and put on some music.* 6 If you **put** something **on**, you begin to cook or heat it. ❑ *She immediately put the kettle on... Put some rice on now... Put on a pan of water to simmer and gently poach the eggs.* 7 If you **put** a sum of money **on** something, you make a bet about it. For example, if you put £10 on a racehorse, you bet £10 that it will win. ❑ *They each put £20 on Matthew scoring the first goal... I'll put a bet on for you.* 8 To **put** a particular amount **on** the cost or value of something means to add that amount to it. ❑ *The proposal could put 3p on a loaf of bread.* 9 If you **put on** a way of behaving, you behave in a way that is not natural to you or that does not express your real feelings. ❑ *Stop putting on an act and be yourself... It was hard to believe she was ill, she was putting it on.*

PHRASAL VERB · ≠ take off · V P n · V n P · PHRASAL VERB · V P n (not pron) · V n P · PHRASAL VERB · V P n · Also V n P · PHRASAL VERB · V n P · V P n · PHRASAL VERB · ≠ take off · V n P · V P n (not pron) · PHRASAL VERB · V n P · V n P · V P n · PHRASAL VERB · V n P n/-ing · V n P · Also V P n · PHRASAL VERB · ≠ take off · V n P n · PHRASAL VERB · V P n · V it P · Also V n P

♦ **put out** 1 If you **put out** an announcement or story, you make it known to a lot of people. ❑ *The French news agency put out a statement from the Trade Minister.* 2 If you **put out** a fire, candle, or cigarette, you make it stop burning. ❑ *Firemen tried to free the injured and put out the blaze... He lit a half-cigarette and almost immediately put it out again.* 3 If you **put out** an electric light, you make it stop shining by pressing a switch. ❑ *He crossed to the bedside table and put out the light.* 4 If you **put out** things that will be needed, you place them somewhere ready to be used. ❑ *Paula had put out her luggage for the coach... I slowly unpacked the teapot and put it out on the table.* 5 If you **put out** your hand, you move it forward, away from your body. ❑ *He put out his hand to Alfred... She put her hand out and tried to touch her mother's arm.* 6 If you **put** someone **out**, you cause them trouble because they have to do something for you. ❑ *I've always put myself out for others and I'm not doing it any more.* 7 In a sporting competition, to **put out** a player or team means to defeat them so that they are no longer in the competition. ❑ *Another Spaniard, Emilio Sanchez, put out Jens Woehrmann in three sets. ...the debatable goal that put Villa out of the UEFA Cup in Milan.* 8 → See also **put out**.

PHRASAL VERB · V P n · Also V n P · PHRASAL VERB · = extinguish · V P n (not pron) · V n P · PHRASAL VERB · = turn out · ≠ turn on · V P n · Also V n P · PHRASAL VERB · V P n (not pron) · V n P · PHRASAL VERB · = stretch out, extend · V P n · V n P · PHRASAL VERB · V n P · PHRASAL VERB · = knock out · V P n (not pron) · V n P *of* n · Also V n P

♦ **put over** → see **put across**.

♦ **put round** → see **put about**.

♦ **put through** 1 When someone **puts through** someone who is making a telephone call, they make the connection that allows the telephone call to take place. ❑ *The operator will put you through... He asked to be put through to Charley Lunn.* 2 If someone **puts** you **through** an unpleasant experience, they make you experience it. ❑ *She wouldn't want to put them through the ordeal of a huge ceremony.*

PHRASAL VERB · = connect · V n P · *be* V-ed P *to* n · Also V P n · PHRASAL VERB · V n P n

♦ **put together** 1 If you **put** something **together**, you join its different parts to each other so that it can be used. ❑ *He took it apart brick by brick, and put it back together again... The factories no longer relied upon a mechanic to put together looms within the plant.* 2 If you **put together** a group of people or things, you form them into a team or collection. ❑ *It will be able to put together a governing coalition... He is trying to put a team together for next season.* 3 If you **put together** an agreement, plan, or product, you design and create it. ❑ *We wouldn't have time to put together an agreement... We got to work on putting the book together.* → See also **put 14**.

PHRASAL VERB · = assemble · V n P · V P n (not pron) · PHRASAL VERB · V P n (not pron) · V n P · PHRASAL VERB · V P n (not pron) · V n P

♦ **put up** 1 If people **put up** a wall, building, tent, or other structure, they construct it so that it is upright. ❑ *Protesters have been putting up barricades across a number of major intersections.* 2 If you **put up** a poster or notice, you fix it to a wall or board. ❑ *They're putting new street signs up... The teacher training college put up a plaque to the college's founder.* 3 To **put up** resistance to something means to resist it. ❑ *In the end the Kurds surrendered without putting up any resistance... He'd put up a real fight to keep you there.* 4 If you **put up** money for something, you provide the money that is needed to pay for it. ❑ *The state agreed to put up $69,000 to start his company... The merchant banks raise capital for industry. They don't actually put it up themselves.* 5 To **put up** the price of something means to cause it to increase. ❑ *Their friends suggested they should put up their prices... They know he would put their taxes up.* 6 If a person or hotel **puts** you **up** or if you **put up** somewhere, you stay there for one or more nights. ❑ *I wanted to know if she could put me up for a few days... He decid-*

PHRASAL VERB · ≠ take down · V P n (not pron) · PHRASAL VERB · ≠ take down · V n P · V P n (not pron) · PHRASAL VERB · V P n · V P n · PHRASAL VERB · = provide · V P n (not pron) · V n P · PHRASAL VERB · = raise, increase · V P n · V n P · PHRASAL VERB · V n P · V P prep

*ed that he would drive back to town instead of putting up for the night at the hotel.* 7 If a political party **puts up** a candidate in an election or if the candidate **puts up,** the candidate takes part in the election. ❑ *The new party is putting up 15 candidates for 22 seats... He put up as a candidate.* PHRASAL VERB V P n (not pron) V P *as* n

♦ **put up for** If you **put** something **up for** sale or auction, for example, you make it available to be sold or auctioned. ❑ *The old flower and fruit market has been put up for sale... She put up her daughter for adoption in 1967.* PHRASAL VERB V n P P n V P n P n

♦ **put up to** If you **put** someone **up to** something wrong or foolish or something which they would not normally do, you suggest that they do it and you encourage them to do it. ❑ *How do you know he asked me out? You put him up to it.* PHRASAL VERB V n P P n

♦ **put up with** If you **put up with** something, you tolerate or accept it, even though you find it unpleasant or unsatisfactory. ❑ *They had put up with behaviour from their son which they would not have tolerated from anyone else.* PHRASAL VERB V P P n

**pu|ta|tive** /pjuːtətɪv/ If you describe someone or something as **putative**, you mean that they are generally thought to be the thing mentioned. [LEGAL or FORMAL] ❑ *...a putative father.* ADJ: ADJ n

**put-down** **(put-downs)** also **put down.** A **put-down** is something that you say or do to criticize someone or make them appear foolish. [INFORMAL] ❑ *I see the term as a put-down of women.* N-COUNT

**put out** If you feel **put out**, you feel rather annoyed or upset. ❑ *I did not blame him for feeling put out.* ADJ: v-link ADJ

**pu|tre|fac|tion** /pjuːtrɪfækʃᵊn/ **Putrefaction** is the process of decay. [FORMAL] ❑ *...the lingering stench of putrefaction.* N-UNCOUNT

**pu|tre|fy** /pjuːtrɪfaɪ/ **(putrefies, putrefying, putrefied)** When something **putrefies**, it decays and produces a very unpleasant smell. [FORMAL] ❑ *The meat in all of the open flasks putrefied. ...putrefying corpses.* VERB = rot V V-ing

**pu|trid** /pjuːtrɪd/ Something that is **putrid** has decayed and smells very unpleasant. [FORMAL] ❑ *...a foul, putrid stench.* ADJ = rotten

**putsch** /pʊtʃ/ **(putsches)** A **putsch** is a sudden attempt to get rid of a government by force. N-COUNT = coup

**putt** /pʌt/ **(putts, putting, putted)** 1 A **putt** is a stroke in golf that you make when the ball has reached the green in an attempt to get the ball in the hole. ❑ *...a 5-foot putt.* N-COUNT 2 In golf, when you **putt** the ball, you hit a putt. ❑ *Turner, however, putted superbly, twice holing from 40 feet.* VERB V

**putt|er** /pʌtəʳ/ **(putters, puttering, puttered)** 1 A **putter** is a club used for hitting a golf ball a short distance once it is on the green. N-COUNT 2 If you **putter around**, you do unimportant but quite enjoyable things, without hurrying. [AM] ❑ *I started puttering around outside, not knowing what I was doing... She liked to putter in the kitchen.* VERB V *around/about* V

☑ in BRIT, use **potter**

**putt|ing green** /pʌtɪŋ griːn/ **(putting greens)** A **putting green** is a very small golf course on which the grass is kept very short and on which there are no obstacles. N-COUNT

**put|ty** /pʌti/ **Putty** is a stiff paste used to fix sheets of glass into window frames. N-UNCOUNT

**put-upon** also **put upon.** If you are **put-upon**, you are treated badly by someone who takes advantage of your willingness to help them. [INFORMAL] ❑ *Volunteers from all walks of life are feeling put upon.* ADJ

**puz|zle** /pʌzᵊl/ **(puzzles)** 1 If something **puzzles** you, you do not understand it and feel confused. ❑ *My sister puzzles me and causes me anxiety.* VERB V n

♦ **puz|zling** *His letter poses a number of puzzling questions.* ADJ 2 If you **puzzle over** something, you try hard to think of the answer to it or the explanation for it. ❑ *In rehearsing Shakespeare, I puzzle over the complexities of his verse and prose.* VERB V *over/about* n 3 A **puzzle** is a question, game, or toy which you have to think about carefully in order to answer it correctly or put it together properly. ❑ *...a word puzzle.* ➔ See also **crossword.** N-COUNT: oft supp N 4 You can describe a person or thing that is hard to understand as **a puzzle**. ❑ *Data from Voyager II has presented astronomers with a puzzle about why our outermost planet exists.* N-SING: *a* N = *mystery*

**puz|zled** /pʌzᵊld/ Someone who is **puzzled** is confused because they do not understand something. ❑ *Critics remain puzzled by the British election results... Norman looked puzzled.* ADJ: oft ADJ *by/about/at* n

**puz|zle|ment** /pʌzᵊlmənt/ **Puzzlement** is the confusion that you feel when you do not understand something. ❑ *He frowned in puzzlement.* N-UNCOUNT

**PVC** /piː viː siː/ **PVC** is a plastic material that is used for many purposes, for example to make clothing or shoes or to cover chairs. **PVC** is an abbreviation for 'polyvinyl chloride'. N-UNCOUNT: oft N n

**Pvt.** **Pvt.** is used before a person's name as a written abbreviation for the military title **Private**. [AM] ❑ *...Pvt. Carlton McCarthy of the Richmond Howitzers.* N-TITLE

☑ in BRIT, use **Pte**

**pw** **pw** is used especially when stating the weekly cost of something. **pw** is the written abbreviation for 'per week'. ❑ *...single room – £55 pw.*

**pyg|my** /pɪgmi/ **(pygmies)** also **pigmy.** 1 **Pygmy** means belonging to a species of animal which is the smallest of a group of related species. ❑ *Reaching a maximum height of 56cm the pygmy goat is essentially a pet.* ADJ: ADJ n 2 A **pygmy** is a member of a group of very short people who live in Africa or south-east Asia. ❑ *...the pygmy tribes of Papua New Guinea.* N-COUNT

**py|ja|mas** /pɪdʒɑːməz/

☑ The spelling **pajamas** is used in American English. The forms **pyjama** and **pajama** are used as modifiers.

A pair of **pyjamas** consists of loose trousers and a loose jacket that people, especially men, wear in bed. ❑ *My brother was still in his pyjamas. ...a pyjama jacket.* N-PLURAL: also *a pair of* N

**py|lon** /paɪlɒn/ **(pylons)** **Pylons** are very tall metal structures which hold electric cables high above the ground so that electricity can be transmitted over long distances. ❑ *...electricity pylons.* N-COUNT

**pyra|mid** /pɪrəmɪd/ **(pyramids)** 1 **Pyramids** are ancient stone buildings with four triangular sloping sides. The most famous pyramids are those built in ancient Egypt to contain the bodies of their kings and queens. ❑ *We set off to see the Pyramids and Sphinx.* N-COUNT 2 A **pyramid** is a shape, object, or pile of things with a flat base and sloping triangular sides that meet at a point. ❑ *On a plate in front of him was piled a pyramid of flat white biscuits.* N-COUNT: usu N *of* n 3 You can describe something as a **pyramid** when it is organized so that there are fewer people at each level as you go towards the top. ❑ *Traditionally, the Brahmins, or the priestly class, are set at the top of the social pyramid.* N-COUNT

**py|rami|dal** /pɪrəmɪdᵊl, pɪræm-/ Something that is **pyramidal** is shaped like a pyramid. [FORMAL] ❑ *...a black pyramidal tent.* ADJ

**pyra|mid sell|ing** **Pyramid selling** is a method of selling in which one person buys a supply of a particular product direct from the manufacturer and then sells it to a number of other people at an increased price. These people sell it on to others in a similar way, but eventually the final buyers are only able to sell the product for less than they paid for it. [BUSINESS] ❑ *If the scheme appears to be a pyramid selling scam, have nothing to do with it.* N-UNCOUNT

**pyre** /paɪəʳ/ **(pyres)** A **pyre** is a high pile of wood built outside on which people burn a dead body or other things in a ceremony. N-COUNT

**Py|rex** /paɪəreks/ **Pyrex** is a type of strong glass which is used for making bowls and dishes N-UNCOUNT: oft N n that do not break when you cook things in them. [TRADEMARK]

**pyro|ma|ni|ac** /paɪəroʊmeɪniæk/ **(pyromaniacs)** A **pyromaniac** is a person who has an uncontrollable desire to start fires. N-COUNT

**pyro|tech|nics** /paɪroʊteknɪks/ 1 **Pyrotechnics** is the making or displaying of fireworks. N-UNCOUNT ❑ *The festival will feature pyrotechnics, live music, and sculptures.* 2 Impressive and exciting displays of skill are sometimes referred to as **pyrotechnics**. N-PLURAL ❑ *...the soaring pyrotechnics of the singer's voice.*

**Pyr|rhic vic|to|ry** /pɪrɪk vɪktəri/ **(Pyrrhic victories)** also **pyrrhic victory.** If you describe a victory as a **Pyrrhic victory**, you mean that although someone has won or gained something, they have also lost something which was worth even more. N-COUNT

**py|thon** /paɪθən/ **(pythons)** A **python** is a large snake that kills animals by squeezing them with its body. N-COUNT

# Q q

**Q, q** /kjuː/ **(Q's, q's)** **Q** is the seventeenth letter of the English alphabet. N-VAR

**Q & A** /kjuː ən eɪ/ or **Q and A** **Q & A** is a situation in which a person or group of people asks questions and another person or group of people answers them. **Q & A** is short for 'question and answer'. ❑ *...a Q & A session with a prominent politician.* N-UNCOUNT: oft N n

**QC** /kjuː siː/ **(QCs)** In Britain, a **QC** is a senior barrister. **QC** is an abbreviation for 'Queen's Counsel'. ❑ *He hired a top QC to defend him.* N-COUNT

**quack** /kwæk/ **(quacks, quacking, quacked)** 1 If you call someone a **quack** or a **quack doctor**, you mean that they claim to be skilled in medicine but are not. ❑ *I went everywhere for treatment, tried all sorts of quacks.* N-COUNT: oft N n disapproval 2 **Quack remedies** or **quack cures** are medical treatments that you think are unlikely to work because they are not scientific. ADJ: ADJ n disapproval 3 When a duck **quacks**, it makes the noise that ducks typically make. ❑ *There were ducks quacking on the lawn.* VERB V ♦ **Quack** is also a noun. ❑ *Suddenly he heard a quack.* N-COUNT; SOUND

**quack|ery** /kwækəri/ If you refer to a form of medical treatment as **quackery**, you think that it is unlikely to work because it is not scientific. ❑ *To some people, herbal medicine is quackery.* N-UNCOUNT disapproval

**quad** /kwɒd/ **(quads)** 1 **Quads** are the same as **quadruplets**. ❑ *...a 34-year-old mother of quads.* N-COUNT: usu pl 2 A **quad** is the same as a **quadrangle**. [INFORMAL] ❑ *His rooms were on the left-hand side of the quad.* N-COUNT: usu *the* N

**quad bike** **(quad bikes)** A **quad bike** is a kind of motorbike with four large wheels that people ride for fun or in races. N-COUNT

**quad|ran|gle** /kwɒdræŋgᵊl/ **(quadrangles)** A **quadrangle** is an open square area with buildings round it, especially in a college or school. N-COUNT: oft *the* N

**quad|rant** /kwɒdrənt/ **(quadrants)** A **quadrant** is one of four equal parts into which a circle or other shape has been divided. ❑ *A symbol appears in an upper quadrant of the screen.* N-COUNT: usu with supp, adj N, N *of* n

**quad|rille** /kwɒdriːl/ **(quadrilles)** A **quadrille** is a type of old-fashioned dance for four or more couples. N-COUNT

**quad|ri|plegic** /kwɒdrɪpliːdʒɪk/ **(quadriplegics)** A **quadriplegic** is a person who is permanently unable to use their arms and legs. N-COUNT ♦ **Quadriplegic** is also an adjective. ❑ *He is now quadriplegic and confined to a wheelchair.* ADJ

**quad|ru|ped** /kwɒdrʊped/ **(quadrupeds)** A **quadruped** is any animal with four legs. [FORMAL] N-COUNT

**quad|ru|ple** /kwɒdruːpᵊl/ **(quadruples, quadrupling, quadrupled)** 1 If someone **quadruples** an amount or if it **quadruples**, it becomes four times bigger. ❑ *Norway has quadrupled its exports to the EU... The price has quadrupled in the last few years.* VERB V n V 2 If one amount is **quadruple** another amount, it is four times bigger. ❑ *They could sell their merchandise for quadruple the asking price.* PREDET: PREDET det n 3 You use **quadruple** to indicate that something has four parts or happens four times. ❑ *...a quadruple murder.* ADJ: ADJ n

**quad|ru|plet** /kwɒdrʊplət, kwɒdruː-/ **(quadruplets)** **Quadruplets** are four children who are born to the same mother at the same time. N-COUNT: usu pl

**quaff** /kwɒf/ **(quaffs, quaffing, quaffed)** If you **quaff** an alcoholic drink, you drink a lot of it in a short time. [OLD-FASHIONED] ❑ *He's quaffed many a glass of champagne in his time.* VERB V n

**quag|mire** /kwægmaɪəʳ/ **(quagmires)** 1 A **quagmire** is a difficult, complicated, or unpleasant situation which is not easy to avoid or escape from. ❑ *His people had fallen further and further into a quagmire of confusion.* N-COUNT: usu sing with supp 2 A **quagmire** is a soft, wet area of land which your feet sink into if you try to walk across it. ❑ *Rain had turned the grass into a quagmire.* N-COUNT: usu sing

**quail** /kweɪl/ **(quails** or **quail, quails, quailing, quailed)** 1 A **quail** is a type of small bird which is often shot and eaten. N-COUNT 2 If someone or something makes you **quail**, they make you feel very afraid, often so that you hesitate. [LITERARY] ❑ *The very words make many of us quail... He told Naomi she was becoming just like Maya. Naomi quailed at the thought.* VERB V V *at* n

**quaint** /kweɪnt/ **(quainter, quaintest)** Something that is **quaint** is attractive because it is unusual and rather old-fashioned. ❑ *...a small, quaint town with narrow streets and traditional half-timbered houses.* ADJ ♦ **quaint|ly** *This may seem a quaintly old-fashioned idea.* ADV: usu ADV adj ♦ **quaint|ness** *...the quaintness of the rural north.* N-UNCOUNT

**quake** /kweɪk/ **(quakes, quaking, quaked)** 1 A **quake** is the same as an **earthquake**. ❑ *The quake destroyed mud buildings in many remote villages.* N-COUNT 2 If you **quake**, you shake, usually because you are very afraid. ❑ *I just stood there quaking with fear... Her shoulders quaked.* VERB V *with* n V 3 If you **are quaking in your boots** or **quaking in your shoes**, you feel very nervous or afraid, and may be feeling slightly weak as a result. PHRASE: V inflects

**Quak|er** /kweɪkəʳ/ **(Quakers)** A **Quaker** is a person who belongs to a Christian group called the Society of Friends. N-COUNT

**quali|fi|ca|tion** /kwɒlɪfɪkeɪʃᵊn/ **(qualifications)** 1 Your **qualifications** are the examinations that you have passed. ❑ *Lucy wants to study medicine but needs more qualifications.* N-COUNT: usu pl 2 **Qualification** is the act of passing the examinations you need to work in a particular profession. ❑ *Following qualification, he worked as a social worker.* N-UNCOUNT 3 The **qualifications** you need for an activity or task are the qualities and skills that you need to be able to do it. ❑ *Responsibility and reliability are necessary qualifications.* N-COUNT 4 A **qualification** is a detail or explanation that you add to a statement to make it less strong or less general. ❑ *The empirical evidence considered here is subject to many qualifications.* N-VAR ● If something is stated or accepted **without qualification**, it is stated or accepted as it is, without the need for any changes. ❑ *The government conceded to their demands almost without qualification.* PHRASE: PHR with cl/group = *without reservation*

**quali|fied** /kwɒlɪfaɪd/ ◆◇◇ 1 Someone who is **qualified** has passed the examinations that they need to pass in order to work in a particular profession. ❑ *Demand has far outstripped supply of qualified teachers.* ADJ: usu ADJ n 2 If you give someone or something **qualified** support or approval, your support or approval is not total because you have some doubts. ❑ *The government has given qualified support to the idea.* ADJ: ADJ n ≠ *unqualified* 3 If you describe something as a PHRASE:

**qualified success**, you mean that it is only partly successful. ❑ *Even as a humanitarian mission it has been only a qualified success.* v-link PHR

**quali|fi|er** /kwɒlɪfaɪəʳ/ **(qualifiers)** [1] A **qualifier** is an early round or match in some competitions. The players or teams who are successful are able to continue to the next round or to the main competition. ❑ *Last week Wales lost 5-1 to Romania in a World Cup qualifier.* N-COUNT [2] In grammar, a **qualifier** is a word or group of words that comes after a noun and gives more information about the person or thing that the noun refers to. N-COUNT [3] ➔ See also **qualify**.

**quali|fy** /kwɒlɪfaɪ/ **(qualifies, qualifying, qualified)** ◆◇◇ [1] When someone **qualifies**, they pass the examinations that they need to be able to work in a particular profession. ❑ *But when I'd qualified and started teaching it was a different story... I qualified as a doctor from London University over 30 years ago.* VERB V V *as/in* n Also V to-inf [2] If you **qualify** for something or if something **qualifies** you for it, you have the right to do it or have it. ❑ *To qualify for maternity leave you must have worked for the same employer for two years... The basic course does not qualify you to practise as a therapist. ...skills that qualify foreigners for work visas. ...highly trained staff who are well qualified to give unbiased, practical advice.* VERB V *for* n V n to-inf V n *for* n V-ed, Also V, V to-inf [3] To **qualify as** something or to **be qualified as** something means to have all the features that are needed to be that thing. ❑ *13 percent of American households qualify as poor, says Mr. Mishel... These people seem to think that reading a few books on old age qualifies them as experts.* VERB V *as* n V n *as* n Also V [4] If you **qualify** in a competition, you are successful in one part of it and go on to the next stage. ❑ *Nottingham Forest qualified for the final by beating Tranmere on Tuesday... Cameroon have also qualified after beating Sierra Leone. ...a World Cup qualifying match.* VERB V *for* n V V-ing ♦ **quali|fi|er (qualifiers)** *Kenya's Robert Kibe was the fastest qualifier for the 800 metres final.* N-COUNT [5] If you **qualify** a statement, you make it less strong or less general by adding a detail or explanation to it. ❑ *I would qualify that by putting it into context.* VERB V n [6] ➔ See also **qualified**.

**quali|ta|tive** /kwɒlɪtətɪv, AM -teɪt-/ **Qualitative** means relating to the nature or standard of something, rather than to its quantity. [FORMAL] ❑ *There are qualitative differences in the way children and adults think.* ADJ: usu ADJ n ♦ **quali|ta|tive|ly** *The new media are unlikely to prove qualitatively different from the old.* ADV: ADV adj, ADV with v

**qual|ity** /kwɒlɪti/ **(qualities)** ◆◆◇ [1] The **quality** of something is how good or bad it is. ❑ *Everyone can greatly improve the quality of life... Other services vary dramatically in quality. ...high quality paper and plywood.* N-UNCOUNT: usu with supp [2] Something of **quality** is of a high standard. ❑ *...a college of quality... In our work, quality is paramount.* N-UNCOUNT: usu with supp, oft N n [3] Someone's **qualities** are the good characteristics that they have which are part of their nature. ❑ *He wanted to introduce mature people with leadership qualities.* N-COUNT: usu pl, usu supp N [4] You can describe a particular characteristic of a person or thing as a **quality**. ❑ *...a childlike quality. ...the pretentious quality of the poetry.* N-COUNT: oft adj N [5] The **quality papers** or the **quality press** are the more serious newspapers which give detailed accounts of world events, as well as reports on business, culture, and society. [BRIT] ❑ *Even the quality papers agreed that it was a triumph.* ADJ: ADJ n

**qual|ity cir|cle (quality circles)** A **quality circle** is a small group of workers and managers who meet to solve problems and improve the quality of the organization's products or services. [BUSINESS] ❑ *Riddick's first move was to form a quality circle.* N-COUNT

**qual|ity con|trol** In an organization that produces goods or provides services, **quality control** is the activity of checking that the goods or services are of an acceptable standard. [BUSINESS] N-UNCOUNT

**qual|ity time** If people spend **quality time** together, they spend a period of time relaxing or doing things that they both enjoy, and not worrying about work or other responsibilities. N-UNCOUNT approval

**qualm** /kwɑːm/ **(qualms)** If you have no **qualms** about doing something, you are not worried that it may be wrong in some way. ❑ *I have no qualms about recommending this approach.* N-COUNT

**quan|da|ry** /kwɒndəri/ **(quandaries)** If you are **in a quandary**, you have to make a decision but cannot decide what to do. ❑ *The government appears to be in a quandary about what to do with so many people.* N-COUNT: usu sing

**quango** /kwæŋgoʊ/ **(quangos)** In Britain, a **quango** is a committee which is appointed by the government but works independently. A quango has responsibility for a particular area of activity, for example the giving of government grants to arts organizations. N-COUNT

**quan|ti|fi|able** /kwɒntɪfaɪəbᵊl/ Something that is **quantifiable** can be measured or counted in a scientific way. ❑ *A clearly quantifiable measure of quality is not necessary.* ADJ ≠ *unquantifiable*

**quan|ti|fi|er** /kwɒntɪfaɪəʳ/ **(quantifiers)** In grammar, a **quantifier** is a word or phrase such as 'plenty' or 'a lot' which you use to refer to a quantity of something without being precise. It is often followed by 'of', as in 'a lot of money'. N-COUNT

**quan|ti|fy** /kwɒntɪfaɪ/ **(quantifies, quantifying, quantified)** If you try to **quantify** something, you try to calculate how much of it there is. ❑ *It is difficult to quantify an exact figure as firms are reluctant to declare their losses.* VERB: usu with brd-neg V n ♦ **quan|ti|fi|ca|tion** /kwɒntɪfɪkeɪʃᵊn/ *Others are more susceptible to attempts at quantification.* N-UNCOUNT

**quan|ti|ta|tive** /kwɒntɪtətɪv, AM -teɪt-/ **Quantitative** means relating to different sizes or amounts of things. [FORMAL] ❑ *...the advantages of both quantitative and qualitative research.* ADJ: usu ADJ n ♦ **quan|ti|ta|tive|ly** *We cannot predict quantitatively the value or the cost of a new technology.* ADV

**quan|tity** /kwɒntɪti/ **(quantities)** ◆◇◇ [1] A **quantity** is an amount that you can measure or count. ❑ *...a small quantity of water. ...vast quantities of food... Cheap goods are available, but not in sufficient quantities to satisfy demand.* N-VAR [2] Things that are produced or available in **quantity** are produced or available in large amounts. ❑ *After some initial problems, acetone was successfully produced in quantity.* N-UNCOUNT [3] You can use **quantity** to refer to the amount of something that there is, especially when you want to contrast it with its quality. ❑ *...the less discerning drinker who prefers quantity to quality.* N-UNCOUNT = *amount* [4] If you say that someone or something is an **unknown quantity**, you mean that not much is known about what they are like or how they will behave. ❑ *He is an unknown quantity for his rivals.* PHRASE: v-link PHR

**quan|tity sur|vey|or (quantity surveyors)** A **quantity surveyor** is a person who calculates the cost and amount of materials and workers needed for a job such as building a house or a road. [BRIT] N-COUNT

**quan|tum** /kwɒntəm/ [1] In physics, **quantum** theory and **quantum** mechanics are concerned with the behaviour of atomic particles. ❑ *Both quantum mechanics and chaos theory suggest a world constantly in flux.* ADJ: ADJ n [2] A **quantum leap** or **quantum jump** in something is a very great and sudden increase in its size, amount, or quality. ❑ *The vaccine represents a quantum leap in healthcare.* ADJ: ADJ n

**quar|an|tine** /kwɒrəntiːn, AM kwɔːr-/ **(quarantines, quarantining, quarantined)** [1] If a person or animal is **in quarantine**, they are being kept separate from other people or animals for a set period of time, usually because they have or may have a disease. ❑ *She was sent home to Oxford and put in quarantine.* N-UNCOUNT: oft *in/into* n [2] If people or animals **are quarantined**, they are stopped from having contact with other people or animals. If a place **is quarantined**, people and animals are prevented from entering or leaving it. ❑ *Dogs have to be quarantined for six months before they'll let them in.* VERB: usu passive *be* V-ed

**quark** /kwɑːʳk, AM kwɔːrk/ **(quarks)** In physics, a **quark** is one of the basic units of matter. [N-COUNT]

**quar|rel** /kwɒrəl, AM kwɔːr-/ **(quarrels, quarrelling, quarrelled)**

☑ in AM, use **quarreling, quarreled**

1 A **quarrel** is an angry argument between two or more friends or family members. ❑ *I had a terrible quarrel with my other brothers.* [N-COUNT] 2 **Quarrels** between countries or groups of people are disagreements, which may be diplomatic or include fighting. [JOURNALISM] ❑ *...New Zealand's quarrel with France over the Rainbow Warrior incident.* [N-COUNT] 3 When two or more people **quarrel**, they have an angry argument. ❑ *At one point we quarrelled, over something silly... My brother quarrelled with my father.* [V-RECIP; pl-n V; V with n] 4 If you say that you have no **quarrel** with someone or something, you mean that you do not disagree with them. ❑ *We have no quarrel with the people of Spain or of any other country.* [N-SING: with neg]

**quar|rel|some** /kwɒrəlsəm, AM kwɔːr-/ A **quarrelsome** person often gets involved in arguments. ❑ *Benedict had been a wild boy and a quarrelsome young man.* [ADJ: usu ADJ n = argumentative]

**quar|ry** /kwɒri, AM kwɔːri/ **(quarries, quarrying, quarried)** 1 A **quarry** is an area that is dug out from a piece of land or the side of a mountain in order to get stone or minerals. ❑ *...an old limestone quarry.* [N-COUNT] 2 When stone or minerals **are quarried** or when an area **is quarried** for them, they are removed from the area by digging, drilling, or using explosives. ❑ *The large limestone caves are also quarried for cement. ...locally quarried stone.* [VERB; be V-ed; V-ed] ♦ **quar|ry|ing** *Farming, quarrying and other local industries have declined.* [N-UNCOUNT] 3 A person's or animal's **quarry** is the person or animal that they are hunting. [N-SING]

**quart** /kwɔːʳt/ **(quarts)** A **quart** is a unit of volume that is equal to two pints. ❑ *Pick up a quart of milk or a loaf of bread.* [N-COUNT: num N, oft N of n]

**quar|ter** /kwɔːʳtəʳ/ **(quarters, quartering, quartered)** ◆◆◇ 1 A **quarter** is one of four equal parts of something. ❑ *A quarter of the residents are over 55 years old... I've got to go in a quarter of an hour... Prices have fallen by a quarter since January... Cut the peppers into quarters.* [FRACTION] ♦ **Quarter** is also a predeterminer. ❑ *The largest asteroid is Ceres, which is about a quarter the size of the moon.* [PREDET] ♦ **Quarter** is also an adjective. ❑ *...the past quarter century.* [ADJ: ADJ n] 2 A **quarter** is a fixed period of three months. Companies often divide their financial year into four quarters. ❑ *The group said results for the third quarter are due on October 29.* [N-COUNT: usu sing] 3 When you are telling the time, you use **quarter** to talk about the fifteen minutes before or after an hour. For example, 8.15 is **quarter past** eight, and 8.45 is **quarter to** nine. In American English, you can also say that 8.15 is a **quarter after** eight and 8.45 is a **quarter of** nine. ❑ *It was a quarter to six... I got a call at quarter of seven one night.* [N-UNCOUNT: also a N] 4 If you **quarter** something such as a fruit or a vegetable, you cut it into four roughly equal parts. ❑ *Chop the mushrooms and quarter the tomatoes.* [VERB; V n] 5 If the number or size of something **is quartered**, it is reduced to about a quarter of its previous number or size. ❑ *The doses I suggested for adults could be halved or quartered.* [VERB: usu passive; be V-ed] 6 A **quarter** is an American or Canadian coin that is worth 25 cents. ❑ *I dropped a quarter into the slot of the pay phone.* [N-COUNT] 7 A particular **quarter** of a town is a part of the town where a particular group of people traditionally live or work. ❑ *Look for hotels in the French Quarter.* [N-COUNT: supp N] 8 To refer to a person or group you may not want to name, you can talk about the reactions or actions from a particular **quarter**. ❑ *Help came from an unexpected quarter.* [N-COUNT: usu supp N] 9 The rooms provided for soldiers, sailors, or servants to live in are called their **quarters**. ❑ *Mckinnon went down from deck to the officers' quarters.* [N-PLURAL: poss N] 10 If you do something **at close quarters**, you do it very near to a particular person or thing. ❑ *You can watch aircraft take off or land at close quarters.* [PHRASE: PHR after v, v-link PHR]

**quarter|back** /kwɔːʳtəʳbæk/ **(quarterbacks)** In American football, a **quarterback** is the player on the attacking team who begins each play and who decides which play to use. [AM] [N-COUNT]

**quarter-final** **(quarter-finals)**

☑ in AM, use **quarterfinal**

A **quarter-final** is one of the four matches in a competition which decides which four players or teams will compete in the semi-final. ❑ *The very least I'm looking for at Wimbledon is to reach the quarter-finals.* [N-COUNT]

**quarter-finalist** **(quarter-finalists)** A **quarter-finalist** is a person or team that is competing in a quarter-final. [N-COUNT]

**quar|ter|ly** /kwɔːʳtəʳli/ **(quarterlies)** 1 A **quarterly** event happens four times a year, at intervals of three months. ❑ *...the latest Bank of Japan quarterly survey of 5,000 companies.* [ADJ] ♦ **Quarterly** is also an adverb. ❑ *It makes no difference whether dividends are paid quarterly or annually.* [ADV: ADV after v] 2 A **quarterly** is a magazine that is published four times a year, at intervals of three months. [N-COUNT: oft N n]

**quar|ter note** **(quarter notes)** A **quarter note** is a musical note that has a time value equal to two eighth notes. [AM] [N-COUNT]

☑ in BRIT, use **crotchet**

**quar|ter pound|er** **(quarter pounders)** A **quarter pounder** is a hamburger that weighs four ounces before it is cooked. Four ounces is a quarter of a pound. [N-COUNT]

**quar|tet** /kwɔːʳtet/ **(quartets)** 1 A **quartet** is a group of four people who play musical instruments or sing together. ❑ *...a string quartet. ...a quartet of singers.* [N-COUNT-COLL] 2 A **quartet** is a piece of music for four instruments or four singers. [N-COUNT]

**quartz** /kwɔːʳts/ **Quartz** is a mineral in the form of a hard, shiny crystal. It is used in making electronic equipment and very accurate watches and clocks. ❑ *...a quartz crystal.* [N-UNCOUNT: oft N n]

**qua|sar** /kweɪzɑːʳ/ **(quasars)** A **quasar** is an object far away in space that produces bright light and radio waves. [N-COUNT]

**quash** /kwɒʃ/ **(quashes, quashing, quashed)** 1 If a court or someone in authority **quashes** a decision or judgment, they officially reject it. ❑ *The Appeal Court has quashed the convictions of all eleven people.* [VERB; V n] 2 If someone **quashes** rumours, they say or do something to demonstrate that the rumours are not true. ❑ *Graham attempted to quash rumours of growing discontent.* [VERB; V n] 3 To **quash** a rebellion or protest means to stop it, often in a violent way. ❑ *Troops were displaying an obvious reluctance to get involved in quashing demonstrations.* [VERB; V n]

**quasi-** /kweɪzaɪ-/ **Quasi-** is used to form adjectives and nouns that describe something as being in many ways like something else, without actually being that thing. ❑ *The flame is a quasi-religious emblem of immortality.* [COMB in ADJ]

**qua|ver** /kweɪvəʳ/ **(quavers, quavering, quavered)** 1 If someone's voice **quavers**, it sounds unsteady, usually because they are nervous or uncertain. ❑ *Her voice quavered and she fell silent.* [VERB = tremble; V] ♦ **Quaver** is also a noun. ❑ *There was a quaver in Beryl's voice.* [N-COUNT] 2 A **quaver** is a musical note that is half as long as a crotchet. [mainly BRIT] [N-COUNT]

☑ in AM, use **eighth note**

**quay** /kiː/ **(quays)** A **quay** is a long platform beside the sea or a river where boats can be tied up and loaded or unloaded. ❑ *Jack and Stephen were waiting for them on the quay.* [N-COUNT]

**quay|side** /kiːsaɪd/ **(quaysides)** A **quayside** is the same as a **quay**. ❑ *A large group had gathered on the quayside to see them off.* [N-COUNT: oft N n]

**quea|sy** /kwiːzi/ **(queasier, queasiest)** If you feel **queasy** or if you have a **queasy** stomach, you feel rather ill, as if you are going to be sick. [ADJ]

[INFORMAL] ❑ *He was very prone to seasickness and already felt queasy.* ♦ **quea|si|ness** *The food did nothing to stifle her queasiness.* N-UNCOUNT

**queen** /kwiːn/ **(queens)** ◆◆◇ [1] A **queen** is a woman who rules a country as its monarch. ❑ *...Queen Victoria... My grandmother met the Queen last week.* N-TITLE; N-COUNT: oft *the* N [2] A **queen** is a woman who is married to a king. ❑ *The king and queen had fled.* N-TITLE; N-COUNT: oft *the* N [3] If you refer to a woman as **the queen of** a particular activity, you mean that she is well-known for being very good at it. ❑ *...the queen of crime writing.* → See also **beauty queen**. N-COUNT: with supp, N *of* n, n N [4] In chess, the **queen** is the most powerful piece. It can be moved in any direction. N-COUNT [5] A **queen** is a playing card with a picture of a queen on it. ❑ *...the queen of spades.* N-COUNT: oft *the* N *of* n [6] A **queen** or a **queen bee** is a large female bee which can lay eggs. N-COUNT

**queen|ly** /kwiːnli/ You use **queenly** to describe a woman's appearance or behaviour if she looks very dignified or behaves as if she is very important. ❑ *She was a queenly, organizing type.* ADJ: usu ADJ n *= regal*

**Queen Moth|er** **The Queen Mother** is the mother of a ruling king or queen. N-PROPER: *the* N

**queen-size** also **queen-sized.** A **queen-size** bed is larger than a double bed, but smaller than a king-size bed. ADJ: ADJ n

**queer** /kwɪəʳ/ **(queerer, queerest, queers)** [1] Something that is **queer** is strange. [OLD-FASHIONED] ❑ *If you ask me, there's something a bit queer going on.* ADJ [2] People sometimes call homosexual men **queers**. [INFORMAL, OFFENSIVE] N-COUNT ♦ **Queer** is also an adjective. ❑ *...queer men.* ADJ: usu v-link ADJ [3] **Queer** means relating to homosexual people, and is used by some homosexuals. ❑ *...contemporary queer culture.* ADJ: ADJ n *= gay*

**quell** /kwel/ **(quells, quelling, quelled)** [1] To **quell** opposition or violent behaviour means to stop it. ❑ *Troops eventually quelled the unrest.* VERB V n [2] If you **quell** an unpleasant feeling such as fear or anger, you stop yourself or other people from having that feeling. ❑ *The Information Minister is trying to quell fears of a looming oil crisis.* VERB V n

**quench** /kwentʃ/ **(quenches, quenching, quenched)** If someone who is thirsty **quenches** their **thirst**, they lose their thirst by having a drink. ❑ *He stopped to quench his thirst at a stream.* VERB V n

**queru|lous** /kweruləs/ Someone who is **querulous** often complains about things. [FORMAL] ❑ *A querulous male voice said, 'Look, are you going to order, or what?'* ADJ [disapproval]

**que|ry** /kwɪəri/ **(queries, querying, queried)** [1] A **query** is a question, especially one that you ask an organization, publication, or expert. ❑ *If you have any queries about this insurance, please contact Travel Insurance Services Limited.* N-COUNT: oft N *about* n [2] If you **query** something, you check it by asking about it because you are not sure if it is correct. ❑ *It's got a number you can ring to query your bill.* VERB *= question* V n [3] To **query** means to ask a question. ❑ *'Is there something else?' Ryle queried as Helen stopped speaking... One of the journalists queried whether sabotage could have been involved.* VERB V with quote V wh Also V n

**quest** /kwest/ **(quests)** A **quest** is a long and difficult search for something. [LITERARY] ❑ *My quest for a better bank continues.* N-COUNT: oft N *for* n, N to-inf ● If you go **in quest of** something, you try to find or obtain it. ❑ *He went on to say that he was going to New York in quest of peace.* PHRASE: PHR after v, v-link PHR, PHR n

**quest|ing** /kwestɪŋ/ If you **are questing for** something, you are searching for it. [LITERARY] ❑ *He had been questing for religious belief from an early age. ...his questing mind and boundless enthusiasm.* VERB: only cont V *for* n V-ing

**ques|tion** /kwestʃᵊn/ **(questions, questioning, questioned)** ◆◆◆ [1] A **question** is something that you say or write in order to ask a person about something. ❑ *They asked a great many questions about England... The President refused to answer further questions on the subject.* N-COUNT: oft N *about*/*on* n [2] If you **question** someone, you ask them a lot of questions about something. ❑ *This led the therapist to question Jim about his parents and their marriage.* VERB V n ♦ **ques|tion|ing** *The police have detained thirty-two people for questioning.* N-UNCOUNT [3] If you **question** something, you have or express doubts about whether it is true, reasonable, or worthwhile. ❑ *It never occurs to them to question the doctor's decisions.* VERB V n [4] If you say that there is some **question** about something, you mean that there is doubt or uncertainty about it. If something is **in question** or has been **called into question**, doubt or uncertainty has been expressed about it. ❑ *There's no question about their success... The paper says the President's move has called into question the whole basis of democracy in the country... With the loyalty of key military units in question, that could prove an extraordinarily difficult task.* N-SING: with supp, also prep N [5] A **question** is a problem, matter, or point which needs to be considered. ❑ *But the whole question of aid is a tricky political one.* N-COUNT: oft N *of* n/wh [6] The **questions** in an examination are the problems which are set in order to test your knowledge or ability. ❑ *That question did come up in the examination.* N-COUNT [7] → See also **questioning**, **cross-question**, **leading question**, **trick question**.

PHRASES [8] The person, thing, or time **in question** is one which you have just been talking about or which is relevant. ❑ *Add up all the income you've received over the period in question.* PHRASE: n PHR [9] If you say that something is **out of the question**, you are emphasizing that it is completely impossible or unacceptable. ❑ *For the homeless, private medical care is simply out of the question.* PHRASE: v-link PHR [emphasis] [10] If you **pop the question**, you ask someone to marry you. [JOURNALISM, INFORMAL] ❑ *Stuart got serious quickly and popped the question six months later.* PHRASE: V inflects *= propose* [11] If you say **there is no question of** something happening, you are emphasizing that it is not going to happen. ❑ *As far as he was concerned there was no question of betraying his own comrades... There is no question of the tax-payer picking up the bill for the party.* PHRASE: V inflects, PHR -ing, PHR n -ing [emphasis] [12] If you do something **without question**, you do it without arguing or asking why it is necessary. ❑ *...military formations, carrying out without question the battle orders of superior officers.* PHRASE: PHR after v [13] You use **without question** to emphasize the opinion you are expressing. ❑ *He was our greatest storyteller, without question.* PHRASE: PHR with cl [emphasis]

**ques|tion|able** /kwestʃənəbᵊl/ If you say that something is **questionable**, you mean that it is not completely honest, reasonable, or acceptable. [FORMAL] ❑ *He has been dogged by allegations of questionable business practices.* ADJ: oft *it* v-link ADJ wh *= dubious*

**ques|tion|er** /kwestʃənəʳ/ **(questioners)** A **questioner** is a person who is asking a question. ❑ *He agreed with the questioner.* N-COUNT

**ques|tion|ing** /kwestʃənɪŋ/ If someone has a **questioning** expression on their face, they look as if they want to know the answer to a question. [WRITTEN] ❑ *He raised a questioning eyebrow.* → See also **question**. ADJ: ADJ n ♦ **ques|tion|ing|ly** *Brenda looked questioningly at Daniel.* ADV: ADV with v

**ques|tion mark** **(question marks)** [1] A **question mark** is the punctuation mark ? which is used in writing at the end of a question. N-COUNT [2] If there is doubt or uncertainty about something, you can say that there is a **question mark over** it. ❑ *There are bound to be question marks over his future.* N-COUNT: oft N *over* n

**ques|tion|naire** /kwestʃəneəʳ, kes-/ **(questionnaires)** A **questionnaire** is a written list of questions which are answered by a lot of people in order to provide information for a report or a survey. ❑ *Headteachers will be asked to fill in a questionnaire.* N-COUNT

**ques|tion tag** **(question tags)** In grammar, a **question tag** is a very short clause at the end of a statement which changes the statement into a question. For example, in 'She said half price, didn't she?', the words 'didn't she' are a question tag. N-COUNT

**queue** /kjuː/ **(queues, queuing, queued)**

✓ **queueing** can also be used as the continuous form.

[1] A **queue** is a line of people or vehicles that are waiting for something. [mainly BRIT] ❑ *I watched as he got a tray and joined the queue... She waited in the bus queue.* N-COUNT: oft N *for* n, N *of* n

✓ in AM, usually use **line**

[2] If you say there is a **queue of** people who want to do or have something, you mean that a lot of people are waiting for an opportunity to do it or have it. [mainly BRIT] ❑ *Manchester United would be at the front of a queue of potential buyers.* N-COUNT: usu sing, oft N *of* n

✓ in AM, usually use **line**

[3] When people **queue**, they stand in a line waiting for something. [mainly BRIT] ❑ *I had to queue for quite a while. ...a line of women queueing for bread.* VERB V V *for* n

♦ **Queue up** means the same as **queue**. ❑ *A mob of journalists are queuing up at the gate to photograph him... We all had to queue up for our ration books.* PHRASAL VERB V P V P *for* n

✓ in AM, usually use **line up**

[4] A **queue** is a list of computer tasks which will be done in order. [COMPUTING] ❑ *Your print job has been sent to the network print queue.* N-COUNT [5] To **queue** a number of computer tasks means to arrange them to be done in order. [COMPUTING] VERB

♦ **queue up** If you say that people **are queuing up to** do or have something, you mean that a lot of them want the opportunity to do it or have it. [mainly BRIT] ❑ *People are queueing up to work for me!... There are a growing number of countries queueing up for membership.* PHRASAL VERB: usu cont V P to-inf V P *for* n

✓ in AM, usually use **line up**

➔ See also **queue 3**.

**queue-jumping** If you accuse someone of **queue-jumping**, you mean that they are trying to get to the front of a queue or waiting list unfairly. [BRIT] ❑ *...queue-jumping within the National Health Service.* N-UNCOUNT disapproval

**quib|ble** /kwɪbəl/ **(quibbles, quibbling, quibbled)** [1] When people **quibble over** a small matter, they argue about it even though it is not important. ❑ *Council members spent the day quibbling over the final wording of the resolution.* V-RECIP V *over/about/with* n [2] A **quibble** is a small and unimportant complaint about something. ❑ *These are minor quibbles.* N-COUNT

**quiche** /kiːʃ/ **(quiches)** A **quiche** is a pastry case filled with a savoury mixture of eggs, cheese, and often other foods. N-VAR

**quick** /kwɪk/ **(quicker, quickest)** ◆◆◆ [1] Someone or something that is **quick** moves or does things with great speed. ❑ *You'll have to be quick. The flight leaves in about three hours... I think I'm a reasonably quick learner.* ADJ ≠slow ♦ **quick|ly** *Cussane worked quickly and methodically.* ADV: ADV with v ♦ **quick|ness** *...the natural quickness of his mind.* N-UNCOUNT [2] **Quicker** is sometimes used to mean 'at a greater speed', and **quickest** to mean 'at the greatest speed'. **Quick** is sometimes used to mean 'with great speed'. Some people consider this to be non-standard. [INFORMAL] ❑ *Warm the sugar slightly first to make it dissolve quicker.* ADV: ADV after v [3] Something that is **quick** takes or lasts only a short time. ❑ *He took one last quick look about the room... Although this recipe looks long, it is actually very quick to prepare.* ADJ ♦ **quick|ly** *You can become fitter quite quickly and easily.* ADV: ADV with v [4] **Quick** means happening without delay or with very little delay. ❑ *These investors feel the need to make quick profits.* ADJ: usu ADJ n = speedy ♦ **quick|ly** *It quickly became the most popular men's fragrance in the world.* ADV: ADV with v [5] **Quick** is sometimes used to mean 'with very little delay'. [INFORMAL] ❑ *I got away as quick as I could.* ADV: ADV after v [6] If you are **quick to** do something, you do not hesitate to do it. ❑ *Mark says the ideas are Katie's own, and is quick to praise her talent.* ADJ: v-link ADJ, usu ADJ to-inf [7] If someone has a **quick** temper, they are easily made angry. ADJ: ADJ n [8] If something **cuts** you **to the quick**, it makes you feel very upset. [LITERARY] ❑ *I once heard her weeping in her bedroom, which cut me to the quick.* PHRASE: V inflects [9] **quick as a flash** ➔ see **flash**. **quick off the mark** ➔ see **mark**. **quick on the uptake** ➔ see **uptake**.

**quick-** /kwɪk-/ **quick-** is added to words, especially present participles, to form adjectives which indicate that a person or thing does something quickly. ❑ *He was saved by quick-thinking neighbours. ...quick-drying paint.* COMB in ADJ

**quick|en** /kwɪkən/ **(quickens, quickening, quickened)** If something **quickens** or if you **quicken** it, it becomes faster or moves at a greater speed. ❑ *Ainslie's pulse quickened in alarm... He quickened his pace a little.* VERB ≠slow V V n

**quick|fire** /kwɪkfaɪəʳ/ also **quick-fire**. **Quickfire** speech or action is very fast with no pauses in it. ❑ *...that talent for quickfire response.* ADJ: ADJ n

**quick fix (quick fixes)** If you refer to a **quick fix** to a problem, you mean a way of solving a problem that is easy but temporary or inadequate. ❑ *...tax measures enacted as a quick fix.* N-COUNT: oft with neg disapproval

**quickie** /kwɪki/ **(quickies)** A **quickie** is something that only takes a very short time. [INFORMAL] ❑ *...a quickie divorce.* N-COUNT: oft N n

**quick|sand** /kwɪksænd/ **(quicksands)**
[1] **Quicksand** is deep, wet sand that you sink into if you try to walk on it. ❑ *The sandbank was uncertain, like quicksand under his feet.* N-UNCOUNT: also N in pl [2] You can refer to a situation as **quicksand** when you want to suggest that it is dangerous or difficult to escape from, or does not provide a strong basis for what you are doing. ❑ *The research seemed founded on quicksand.* N-UNCOUNT: also N in pl

**quick|silver** /kwɪksɪlvəʳ/ [1] **Quicksilver** is the same as **mercury**. [OLD-FASHIONED] N-UNCOUNT
[2] **Quicksilver** movements or changes are very fast and unpredictable. ❑ *...her quicksilver changes of mood.* ADJ: ADJ n

**quick-tempered** Someone who is **quick-tempered** often gets angry without having a good reason. ADJ

**quick-witted** Someone who is **quick-witted** is intelligent and good at thinking quickly. ADJ

**quid** /kwɪd/ **(quid)** A **quid** is a pound in money. [BRIT, INFORMAL] ❑ *It cost him five hundred quid.* N-COUNT

**quid pro quo (quid pro quos)** A **quid pro quo** is a gift or advantage that is given to someone in return for something that they have done. [FORMAL] ❑ *The statement is emphatic in stating that there must be a quid pro quo.* N-COUNT

**quids** /kwɪdz/ If you **are quids in**, you have more money left than you expected or get more for your money than you expected. [BRIT, INFORMAL] ❑ *Still, we were quids in, we didn't care!* PHRASE: V inflects

**qui|es|cent** /kwiesənt, AM kwaɪ-/ Someone or something that is **quiescent** is quiet and inactive. [LITERARY] ❑ *...a society which was politically quiescent and above all deferential.* ADJ ♦ **qui|es|cence** *...a long period of quiescence.* N-UNCOUNT

**qui|et** /kwaɪət/ **(quieter, quietest, quiets, quieting, quieted)** ◆◆◇ [1] Someone or something that is **quiet** makes only a small amount of noise. ❑ *Tania kept the children reasonably quiet and contented... A quiet murmur passed through the classroom... The airlines have invested enormous sums in new, quieter aircraft.* ADJ ≠noisy ♦ **qui|et|ly** *'This is goodbye, isn't it?' she said quietly.* ADV: ADV with v ♦ **qui|et|ness** *...the smoothness and quietness of the flight.* N-UNCOUNT [2] If a place is **quiet**, there is very little noise there. ❑ *She was received in a small, quiet office... The street was unnaturally quiet.* ADJ ≠noisy ♦ **qui|et|ness** *I miss the quietness of the countryside.* N-UNCOUNT [3] If a place, situation, or time is **quiet**, there is no excitement, activity, or trouble. ❑ *It is very quiet without him... While he wanted Los Angeles and partying, she wanted a quiet life.* ADJ ♦ **qui|et|ly** *His most prized time, though, will be spent quietly on his farm.* ADV: ADV with v ♦ **qui|et|ness** *I do very much appreciate the quietness and privacy here.* N-UNCOUNT
[4] **Quiet** is silence. ❑ *He called for quiet and an-* N-UNCOUNT

*nounced that the next song was in our honor.* 5 If you are **quiet**, you are not saying anything. ❑ *I told them to be quiet and go to sleep.* ♦ **qui|et|ly** *Amy stood quietly in the doorway watching him.* 6 If you refer, for example, to someone's **quiet** confidence or **quiet** despair, you mean that they do not say much about the way they are feeling. ❑ *He has a quiet confidence in his ability.* ♦ **qui|et|ly** *Nigel Deering, the publisher, is quietly confident about the magazine's chances.* 7 You describe activities as **quiet** when they happen in secret or in such a way that people do not notice them. ❑ *The Swedes had sought his freedom through quiet diplomacy.* ♦ **qui|et|ly** *I slipped away quietly... The goal of shifting freight from road to rail has been quietly abandoned.* 8 A **quiet** person behaves in a calm way and is not easily made angry or upset. ❑ *He's a nice quiet man.* 9 If someone or something **quiets** or if you **quiet** them, they become less noisy, less active, or silent. [mainly AM] ❑ *The wind dropped and the sea quieted... Estela started to say something but a gesture from her husband quieted her at once.*

ADJ: v-link ADJ; ADV: ADV with v; ADJ: ADJ n; ADV: ADV adj; ADJ: ADJ n; ADV: usu ADV with v, also ADV adj; ADJ = placid; VERB; V; V n

in BRIT, usually use **quieten**

10 To **quiet** fears or complaints means to persuade people that there is no good reason for them. [mainly AM] ❑ *Music seemed to quiet her anxiety and loneliness.*

VERB; V n

in BRIT, usually use **quieten**

**PHRASES** 11 If someone does not **go quietly**, they do not leave a particular job or a place without complaining or resisting. ❑ *She's not going to go quietly.* 12 If you **keep quiet about** something or **keep** something **quiet**, you do not say anything about it. ❑ *I told her to keep quiet about it.* 13 If something is done **on the quiet**, it is done secretly or in such a way that people do not notice it. ❑ *She'd promised to give him driving lessons, on the quiet, when no one could see.*

PHRASE: V inflects; PHRASE: V inflects; PHRASE: PHR after v

♦ **quiet down** If someone or something **quiets down** or if you **quiet** them **down**, they become less noisy or less active. [mainly AM] ❑ *Once the vote was taken, things quieted down quickly... Try gradually to quiet them down as bedtime approaches.*

PHRASAL VERB; V P; V n P

in BRIT, usually use **quieten down**

**qui|et|en** /kwaɪətᵊn/ **(quietens, quietening, quietened)** 1 If you **quieten** someone or something, or if they **quieten**, you make them become less noisy, less active, or silent. [mainly BRIT] ❑ *She tried to quieten her breathing... A man shouted and the dogs suddenly quietened.*

VERB; V n; V

in AM, usually use **quiet**

2 To **quieten** fears or complaints means to persuade people that there is no good reason for them. [mainly BRIT] ❑ *Russian intelligence will take a long time to quieten the paranoia of the West.*

VERB; V n

in AM, usually use **quiet**

♦ **quieten down** If someone or something **quietens down** or if you **quieten** them **down**, they become less noisy or less active. [mainly BRIT] ❑ *The labour unrest which swept the country last week has quietened down... Somehow I managed to quieten her down... Tom's words before the match might also have quietened down our own supporters.*

PHRASAL VERB = calm down; V P; V n P; V P n (not pron)

in AM, usually use **quiet down**

**qui|etude** /kwaɪətjuːd, AM -tuːd/ **Quietude** is quietness and calm. [FORMAL] N-UNCOUNT = tranquillity

**quiff** /kwɪf/ **(quiffs)** If a man has a **quiff**, his hair has been combed upwards and backwards from his forehead. [mainly BRIT] ❑ *I attempted a classic rock and roll quiff.* N-COUNT

**quill** /kwɪl/ **(quills)** 1 A **quill** is a pen made from a bird's feather. ❑ *She dipped a quill in ink, then began to write.* N-COUNT 2 A bird's **quills** are large, stiff feathers on its wings and tail. N-COUNT 3 The **quills** of a porcupine are the long sharp points on its body. N-COUNT

**quilt** /kwɪlt/ **(quilts)** 1 A **quilt** is a thin cover filled with feathers or some other warm, soft material, which you put over your blankets when you are in bed. ❑ *...an old patchwork quilt.* N-COUNT 2 A **quilt** is the same as a **duvet**. [BRIT] N-COUNT

**quilt|ed** /kwɪltɪd/ Something that is **quilted** consists of two layers of fabric with a layer of thick material between them, often decorated with lines of stitching which form a pattern. ❑ *...a quilted bedspread.* ADJ

**quince** /kwɪns/ **(quinces)** A **quince** is a hard yellow fruit. Quinces are used for making jelly or jam. N-VAR

**qui|nine** /kwɪniːn, AM kwaɪnaɪn/ **Quinine** is a drug that is used to treat fevers such as malaria. N-UNCOUNT

**quin|tes|sence** /kwɪntesᵊns/ 1 **The quintessence of** something is the most perfect or typical example of it. [FORMAL] ❑ *He was the quintessence of all that Eva most deeply loathed.* N-UNCOUNT: with supp, usu the N of n 2 **The quintessence of** something is the aspect of it which seems to represent its central nature. [FORMAL] ❑ *...an old stone cottage, the quintessence of rural England.* N-UNCOUNT: with supp, usu the N of n

**quin|tes|sen|tial** /kwɪntɪsenʃᵊl/ 1 **Quintessential** means representing a perfect or typical example of something. [FORMAL] ❑ *Everybody thinks of him as the quintessential New Yorker.* ♦ **quin|tes|sen|tial|ly** *It is a familiar, and quintessentially British, ritual.* 2 **Quintessential** means representing the central nature of something. [FORMAL] ❑ *...the quintessential charm of his songs.*

ADJ: usu ADJ n; ADV: ADV adj; ADJ: usu ADJ n

**quin|tet** /kwɪntet/ **(quintets)** 1 A **quintet** is a group of five singers or musicians singing or playing together. N-COUNT 2 A **quintet** is a piece of music written for five instruments or five singers. N-COUNT

**quip** /kwɪp/ **(quips, quipping, quipped)** 1 A **quip** is a remark that is intended be amusing or clever. [WRITTEN] ❑ *The commentators make endless quips about the female players' appearance.* N-COUNT 2 To **quip** means to say something that is intended to be amusing or clever. [WRITTEN] ❑ *'He'll have to go on a diet,' Ballard quipped... The chairman quipped that he would rather sell his airline than his computer systems.*

VERB; V with quote; V that

**quirk** /kwɜːʳk/ **(quirks)** 1 A **quirk** is something unusual or interesting that happens by chance. ❑ *By a tantalising quirk of fate, the pair have been drawn to meet in the first round of the championship.* N-COUNT: usu with supp, N of n, adj N 2 A **quirk** is a habit or aspect of a person's character which is odd or unusual. ❑ *Brown was fascinated by people's quirks and foibles.* N-COUNT

**quirky** /kwɜːʳki/ **(quirkier, quirkiest)** Something or someone that is **quirky** is rather odd or unpredictable in their appearance, character, or behaviour. ❑ *We've developed a reputation for being quite quirky and original.* ♦ **quirki|ness** *You will probably notice an element of quirkiness in his behaviour.*

ADJ; N-UNCOUNT

**quis|ling** /kwɪzlɪŋ/ **(quislings)** A **quisling** is someone who helps an enemy army that has taken control of their country. [OLD-FASHIONED] N-COUNT

**quit** /kwɪt/ **(quits, quitting)** ◆◇◇

The form **quit** is used in the present tense and is the past tense and past participle.

1 If you **quit** your job, you choose to leave it. [INFORMAL] ❑ *He quit his job as an office boy in Athens... He figured he would quit before Johnson fired him.* 2 If you **quit** an activity or **quit** doing something, you stop doing it. [mainly AM] ❑ *A nicotine spray can help smokers quit the habit without putting on weight... I was trying to quit smoking at the time.* 3 If you **quit** a place, you leave it completely and do not go back to it. ❑ *...the idea that humans might one day quit the earth to colonise other planets.* 4 If you say that you are going to **call it**

VERB; V n; V; VERB = give up; V n/-ing; V n/-ing; VERB; V n; PHRASE: V inflects

**quits**, you mean that you have decided to stop doing something or being involved in something. ❑ *They raised $630,000 through listener donations, and then called it quits.*

**quite** /kwaɪt/ ◆◆◆ [1] You use **quite** to indicate that something is the case to a fairly great extent. **Quite** is less emphatic than 'very' and 'extremely'. ❑ *I felt quite bitter about it at the time... Well, actually it requires quite a bit of work and research... I was quite a long way away, on the terrace.* (ADV: ADV adj/adv, ADV *a* n, ADV before v; vagueness) [2] You use **quite** to emphasize what you are saying. ❑ *It is quite clear that we were firing in self defence... That's a general British failing. In the USA it's quite different.* (ADV: ADV group, ADV before v; emphasis) [3] You use **quite** after a negative to make what you are saying weaker or less definite. ❑ *Something here is not quite right... After treatment he was able to continue but he was never quite the same.* (ADV: with brd-neg, ADV group, ADV before v) [4] You use **quite** in front of a noun group to emphasize that a person or thing is very impressive or unusual. ❑ *'Oh, he's quite a character,' Sean replied... It's quite a city, Boston.* (PREDET: PREDET *a* n; approval) [5] You can say '**quite**' to express your agreement with someone. [SPOKEN] ❑ *'And if you buy the record it's your choice isn't it.' — 'Quite'.* (ADV: ADV as reply; formulae)

**quit|ter** /kwɪtəʳ/ **(quitters)** If you say that someone is not a **quitter**, you mean that they continue doing something even though it is very difficult. ❑ *He won't resign because he's not a quitter.* (N-COUNT: usu with brd-neg)

**quiv|er** /kwɪvəʳ/ **(quivers, quivering, quivered)** [1] If something **quivers**, it shakes with very small movements. ❑ *Her bottom lip quivered and big tears rolled down her cheeks.* (VERB = tremble; V) [2] If you say that someone or their voice **is quivering with** an emotion such as rage or excitement, you mean that they are strongly affected by this emotion and show it in their appearance or voice. ❑ *Cooper arrived, quivering with rage.* (VERB; V *with* n) ♦ **Quiver** is also a noun. ❑ *I felt a quiver of panic.* (N-COUNT: usu N *of* n)

**quix|ot|ic** /kwɪksɒtɪk/ If you describe someone's ideas or plans as **quixotic**, you mean that they are imaginative or hopeful but unrealistic. [FORMAL] ❑ *He has always lived his life by a hopelessly quixotic code of honour.* (ADJ)

**quiz** /kwɪz/ **(quizzes, quizzing, quizzed)** [1] A **quiz** is a game or competition in which someone tests your knowledge by asking you questions. ❑ *We'll have a quiz at the end of the show.* (N-COUNT) [2] If you **are quizzed** by someone about something, they ask you questions about it. ❑ *He was quizzed about his income, debts and eligibility for state benefits... Sybil quizzed her about life as a working girl.* (VERB; *be* V-ed *about* n; V n *about* n)

**quiz|master** /kwɪzmɑːstəʳ, -mæs-/ **(quizmasters)** A **quizmaster** is the person who asks the questions in a game or quiz on the television or radio. [mainly BRIT] (N-COUNT)

**quiz|zi|cal** /kwɪzɪkəl/ If you give someone a **quizzical** look or smile, you look at them in a way that shows that you are surprised or amused by their behaviour. ❑ *He gave Robin a mildly quizzical glance.* (ADJ: usu ADJ n) ♦ **quiz|zi|cal|ly** *She looked at him quizzically.* (ADV: ADV after v)

**quo** /kwoʊ/ → see **quid pro quo, status quo**.

**quoit** /kɔɪt, AM kwɔɪt/ **(quoits)** [1] **Quoits** is a game which is played by throwing rings over a small post. Quoits is usually played on board ships. (N-UNCOUNT) [2] A **quoit** is a ring used in the game of quoits. (N-COUNT)

**Quon|set hut** /kwɒnsɪt hʌt/ **(Quonset huts)** A **Quonset hut** is a military hut made of metal. The walls and roof form the shape of a semicircle. [AM] (N-COUNT)

✓ in BRIT, use **Nissen hut**

**quor|ate** /kwɔːreɪt/ When a committee is **quorate**, there are enough people present for it to conduct official business and make decisions. [BRIT] ❑ *The session was technically quorate.* (ADJ: v-link ADJ)

**quor|um** /kwɔːrəm/ A **quorum** is the minimum number of people that a committee needs in order to carry out its business officially. When a meeting has a quorum, there are at least that number of people present. ❑ *...enough deputies to make a quorum.* (N-SING)

**quo|ta** /kwoʊtə/ **(quotas)** [1] A **quota** is the limited number or quantity of something which is officially allowed. ❑ *The quota of four tickets per person had been reduced to two.* (N-COUNT: oft N *of* n) [2] A **quota** is a fixed maximum or minimum proportion of people from a particular group who are allowed to do something, such as come and live in a country or work for the government. ❑ *The bill would force employers to adopt a quota system when recruiting workers.* (N-COUNT: oft N *of* n, N n) [3] Someone's **quota of** something is their expected or deserved share of it. ❑ *They have the usual quota of human weaknesses, no doubt.* (N-COUNT: oft N *of* n = share)

**quot|able** /kwoʊtəbəl/ **Quotable** comments are written or spoken comments that people think are interesting and worth quoting. ❑ *...one of his more quotable sayings.* (ADJ)

**quo|ta|tion** /kwoʊteɪʃən/ **(quotations)** [1] A **quotation** is a sentence or phrase taken from a book, poem, or play, which is repeated by someone else. ❑ *He illustrated his argument with quotations from Pasternak.* (N-COUNT = quote) [2] When someone gives you a **quotation**, they tell you how much they will charge to do a particular piece of work. ❑ *Get several written quotations and check exactly what's included in the cost.* (N-COUNT = quote) [3] A company's **quotation** on the stock exchange is its registration on the stock exchange, which enables its shares to be officially listed and traded. [BUSINESS] ❑ *...an American-dominated investment manager with a quotation on the London stock market.* (N-COUNT)

**quo|ta|tion mark (quotation marks)** **Quotation marks** are punctuation marks that are used in writing to show where speech or a quotation begins and ends. They are usually written or printed as "..." or, in Britain, '...'. (N-COUNT: usu pl = inverted commas)

**quote** /kwoʊt/ ◆◆◇ **(quotes, quoting, quoted)** [1] If you **quote** someone as saying something, you repeat what they have written or said. ❑ *He quoted Mr Polay as saying that peace negotiations were already underway... She quoted a great line from a book by Romain Gary... I gave the letter to our local press and they quoted from it.* (VERB; V n *as* -ing; V n; V *from* n) [2] A **quote from** a book, poem, play, or speech is a passage or phrase from it. ❑ *The article starts with a quote from an unnamed member of the Cabinet.* (N-COUNT: oft N *from* n = quotation) [3] If you **quote** something such as a law or a fact, you state it because it supports what you are saying. ❑ *Mr Meacher quoted statistics saying that the standard of living of the poorest people had fallen.* (VERB; V n) [4] If someone **quotes** a price **for** doing something, they say how much money they would charge you for a service they are offering or a for a job that you want them to do. ❑ *A travel agent quoted her £160 for a flight from Bristol to Palma... He quoted a price for the repairs.* (VERB; V n n; V n) [5] A **quote for** a piece of work is the price that someone says they will charge you to do the work. ❑ *Always get a written quote for any repairs needed.* (N-COUNT = quotation) [6] If a company's shares, a substance, or a currency **is quoted** at a particular price, that is its current market price. [BUSINESS] ❑ *In early trading in Hong Kong yesterday, gold was quoted at $368.20 an ounce... Heron is a private company and is not quoted on the Stock Market.* (V-PASSIVE; *be* V-ed *at* amount; *be* V-ed *on* n) [7] **Quotes** are the same as **quotation marks**. [INFORMAL] ❑ *The word 'remembered' is in quotes.* (N-PLURAL) [8] You can say '**quote**' to show that you are about to quote someone's words. [SPOKEN] ❑ *He predicts they will have, quote, 'an awful lot of explaining to do'.* (CONVENTION)

**quoth** /kwoʊθ/ **Quoth** means 'said'. **Quoth** comes before the subject of the verb. [HUMOROUS or OLD-FASHIONED] ❑ *'I blame the selectors,' quoth he.* (VERB; V with quote)

**quo|tid|ian** /kwoʊtɪdiən/ **Quotidian** activities or experiences are basic, everyday activities or experiences. [FORMAL] ❑ *...the minutiae of their quotidian existence.* (ADJ: ADJ n)

**quo|tient** /kwoʊʃənt/ **(quotients)** **Quotient** is used when indicating the presence or degree (N-COUNT: usu sing,

of a characteristic in someone or something. usu n N, N *of* n
❑ *Being rich doesn't actually increase your happiness quotient... The island has an unusually high quotient of clergymen.* **intelligence quotient** → see **IQ**.

**Quran** /kɔːrɑːn/ also **Koran, Qur'an. The Quran** is the holy book on which the religion of Islam is based. N-PROPER: *the* N

**Quran|ic** /kɔːrænɪk/ also **Koranic, Qur'anic. Quranic** is used to describe something which belongs or relates to the Quran. ADJ: ADJ n

**QWER|TY** /kwɜːʳti/ also **Qwerty, qwerty.** A **QWERTY** keyboard on a typewriter or computer is the standard English language keyboard, on which the top line of keys begins with the letters q, w, e, r, t, and y. ADJ: ADJ n

# R r

**R, r** /ɑːʳ/ **(R's, r's)** 1 **R** is the eighteenth letter of the English alphabet. → See also **three Rs**. [N-VAR]
2 In the United States, some cinema films are marked **R** to show that children under 17 years old are only allowed to see them if an adult is with them.

**rab|bi** /ræbaɪ/ **(rabbis)** A **rabbi** is a Jewish religious leader, usually one who is in charge of a synagogue, one who is qualified to teach Judaism, or one who is an expert on Jewish law. [N-COUNT; N-TITLE]

**rab|bini|cal** /ræbɪnɪkᵊl/ or **rabbinic** /ræbɪnɪk/ **Rabbinical** or **rabbinic** refers to the teachings of Jewish religious teachers and leaders. [ADJ] ❑ *...early rabbinic scholars.*

**rab|bit** /ræbɪt/ **(rabbits, rabbiting, rabbited)** A **rabbit** is a small furry animal with long ears. Rabbits are sometimes kept as pets, or live wild in holes in the ground. [N-COUNT]

♦ **rabbit on** If you describe someone as **rabbiting on**, you do not like the way they keep talking for a long time about something that is not very interesting. [BRIT, INFORMAL] [PHRASAL VERB: usu cont] [disapproval] ❑ *What are you rabbiting on about?* [V P *about* n]

**rab|ble** /ræbᵊl/ A **rabble** is a crowd of noisy people who seem likely to cause trouble. [N-SING: usu with supp] ❑ *He seems to attract a rabble of supporters more loyal to the man than to the cause.*

**rabble-rouser** **(rabble-rousers)** A **rabble-rouser** is a clever speaker who can persuade a group of people to behave violently or aggressively, often for the speaker's own political advantage. [N-COUNT] [disapproval]

**rabble-rousing** **Rabble-rousing** is encouragement that a person gives to a group of people to behave violently or aggressively, often for that person's own political advantage. [N-UNCOUNT] [disapproval] ❑ *Critics have accused him of rabble-rousing.*

**rab|id** /ræbɪd, reɪb-/ 1 You can use **rabid** to describe someone who has very strong and unreasonable opinions or beliefs about a subject, especially in politics. [ADJ: usu ADJ n] [disapproval] ❑ *The party has distanced itself from the more rabid nationalist groups in the country.*
♦ **rab|id|ly** *Mead calls the group 'rabidly right-wing'.* [ADV: ADV adj, ADV -ed]
2 A **rabid** dog or other animal has the disease rabies. [ADJ: usu ADJ n]

**ra|bies** /reɪbiːz/ **Rabies** is a serious disease which causes people and animals to go mad and die. Rabies is particularly common in dogs. [N-UNCOUNT]

**rac|coon** /rækuːn/ **(raccoons** or **raccoon)** also **racoon.** A **raccoon** is a small animal that has dark-coloured fur with white stripes on its face and on its long tail. Raccoons live in forests in North and Central America and the West Indies. [N-COUNT]

**race** /reɪs/ **(races, racing, raced)** 1 A **race** is a competition to see who is the fastest, for example in running, swimming, or driving. [◆◆◆ N-COUNT] ❑ *The women's race was won by the American, Patti Sue Plumer.* 2 If you **race**, you take part in a race. [VERB] [V] ❑ *In the 10 years I raced in Europe, 30 drivers were killed... They may even have raced each other – but not regularly.* [V n] [Also V *against* n]
3 **The races** are a series of horse races that are held in a particular place on a particular day. People go to watch and to bet on which horse will win. [N-PLURAL: *the* N] ❑ *The high point of this trip was a day at the races.* 4 A **race** is a situation in which people or organizations compete with each other for power or control. [N-COUNT: usu sing, usu with supp] ❑ *The race for the White House begins in earnest today.* → See also **arms race**, **rat race**.
5 A **race** is one of the major groups which human beings can be divided into according to their physical features, such as the colour of their skin. [N-VAR] ❑ *The College welcomes students of all races, faiths, and nationalities.* → See also **human race**, **race relations**. 6 If you **race** somewhere, you go there as quickly as possible. [VERB] ❑ *He raced across town to the State House building.* [V adv/prep] 7 If something **races** towards a particular state or position, it moves very fast towards that state or position. [VERB] ❑ *Do they realize we are racing towards complete economic collapse?* [V prep/adv]
8 If you **race** a vehicle or animal, you prepare it for races and make it take part in races. [VERB] [V n] ❑ *He still raced sports cars as often as he could.* 9 If your mind **races**, or if thoughts **race** through your mind, you think very fast about something, especially when you are in a difficult or dangerous situation. [VERB] ❑ *I made sure I sounded calm but my mind was racing... Bits and pieces of the past raced through her mind.* [V] [V adv/prep] 10 If your heart **races**, it beats very quickly because you are excited or afraid. [VERB] [V] ❑ *Her heart raced uncontrollably.* 11 → See also **racing**.
12 You describe a situation as a **race against time** when you have to work very fast in order to do something before a particular time, or before another thing happens. [PHRASE] ❑ *An air force spokesman said the rescue operation was a race against time.*

**race|course** /reɪskɔːʳs/ **(racecourses)** also **race course.** A **racecourse** is a track on which horses race. [BRIT] [N-COUNT]

✓ in AM, use **racetrack**

**race|go|er** /reɪsgoʊəʳ/ **(racegoers)** also **race-goer.** **Racegoers** are people who regularly go to watch horse races. [mainly BRIT] [N-COUNT: usu pl]

**race|horse** /reɪshɔːʳs/ **(racehorses)** A **racehorse** is a horse that is trained to run in races. [N-COUNT]

**race meet|ing** **(race meetings)** A **race meeting** is an occasion when a series of horse races are held at the same place, often during a period of several days. [mainly BRIT] [N-COUNT]

**rac|er** /reɪsəʳ/ **(racers)** 1 A **racer** is a person or animal that takes part in races. [N-COUNT] ❑ *Tim Powell is a former champion powerboat racer.* 2 A **racer** is a vehicle such as a car or bicycle that is designed to be used in races and therefore travels fast. [N-COUNT]

**race re|la|tions** **Race relations** are the ways in which people of different races living together in the same community behave towards one another. [N-PLURAL: oft N n]

**race riot** **(race riots)** **Race riots** are violent fights between people of different races living in the same community. [N-COUNT: usu pl]

**race|track** /reɪstræk/ **(racetracks)** also **race track.** 1 A **racetrack** is a track on which horses race. [AM] [N-COUNT]

✓ in BRIT, use **racecourse**

2 A **racetrack** is a track for races, for example car or bicycle races. [N-COUNT]

**ra|cial** /reɪʃᵊl/ **Racial** describes things relating to people's race. [◆◇◇ ADJ: usu ADJ n] ❑ *...the protection of national and racial minorities. ...the elimination of racial discrimination.* ♦ **ra|cial|ly** *We are both children of racially mixed marriages.* [ADV: ADV -ed/adj, ADV with cl]

**ra|cial|ism** /reɪʃəlɪzəm/ **Racialism** means the same as **racism**. [mainly BRIT] N-UNCOUNT

☑ in AM, usually use **racism**

♦ **ra|cial|ist** ❑ *...racialist groups.* ADJ: usu ADJ n

**rac|ing** /reɪsɪŋ/ **Racing** refers to races between animals, especially horses, or between vehicles. ❑ *Mr Honda was himself a keen racing driver in his younger days. ...horse racing.* ◆◇◇ N-UNCOUNT: usu with supp, oft N n

**rac|ism** /reɪsɪzəm/ **Racism** is the belief that people of some races are inferior to others, and the behaviour which is the result of this belief. ❑ *There is a feeling among some black people that the level of racism is declining.* N-UNCOUNT

**rac|ist** /reɪsɪst/ **(racists)** If you describe people, things, or behaviour as **racist**, you mean that they are influenced by the belief that some people are inferior because they belong to a particular race. ❑ *You have to acknowledge that we live in a racist society.* ADJ [disapproval] ♦ A **racist** is someone who is racist. ❑ *He has a hard core of support among white racists.* N-COUNT

**rack** /ræk/ **(racks, racking, racked)**

☑ The spelling **wrack** is also used, mainly for meanings 2 and 3, and mainly in old-fashioned or American English.

1 A **rack** is a frame or shelf, usually with bars or hooks, that is used for holding things or for hanging things on. ❑ *My rucksack was too big for the luggage rack.* ➔ See also **roof rack**, **toast rack**. N-COUNT: oft supp N

2 If someone **is racked by** something such as illness or anxiety, it causes them great suffering or pain. ❑ *His already infirm body was racked by high fever. ...a teenager racked with guilt and anxiety.* ➔ See also **racking**. VERB: usu passive; *be* V-ed *by/with* n; V-ed

**PHRASES** 3 If you **rack** your **brains**, you try very hard to think of something. ❑ *She began to rack her brains to remember what had happened at the nursing home.* PHRASE: V and N inflect

4 If you say that someone is **on the rack**, you mean that they are suffering either physically or mentally. [JOURNALISM] ❑ *Only a year ago, he was on the rack with a heroin addiction that began when he was 13.* PHRASE: usu PHR after v

5 If you say that a place **is going to rack and ruin**, you are emphasizing that it is slowly becoming less attractive or less pleasant because no-one is bothering to look after it. PHRASE: V inflects [emphasis]

6 **Off-the-rack** clothes or goods are made in large numbers, rather than being made specially for a particular person. [AM] ❑ *...the same off-the-rack dress she's been wearing since the night before.* PHRASE: PHR n, PHR after v

☑ in BRIT, use **off-the-peg**

♦ **rack up** If a business **racks up** profits, losses, or sales, it makes a lot of them. If a sportsman, sportswoman, or team **racks up** wins, they win a lot of matches or races. ❑ *Lower rates mean that firms are more likely to rack up profits in the coming months.* PHRASAL VERB: no passive; V P n (not pron)

**rack|et** /rækɪt/ **(rackets)**

☑ The spelling **racquet** is also used for meaning 3.

1 A **racket** is a loud unpleasant noise. ❑ *He makes such a racket I'm afraid he disturbs the neighbours.* N-SING

2 You can refer to an illegal activity used to make money as a **racket**. [INFORMAL] ❑ *A smuggling racket is killing thousands of exotic birds each year.* N-COUNT: oft n N

3 A **racket** is an oval-shaped bat with strings across it. Rackets are used in tennis, squash, and badminton. ❑ *Tennis rackets and balls are provided.* N-COUNT: oft n N

**rack|et|eer** /rækɪtɪəʳ/ **(racketeers)** A **racketeer** is someone who makes money from illegal activities such as threatening people or selling worthless, immoral, or illegal goods or services. N-COUNT

**rack|et|eer|ing** /rækɪtɪərɪŋ/ **Racketeering** is making money from illegal activities such as threatening people or selling worthless, immoral, or illegal goods or services. ❑ *Edwards was indicted on racketeering charges but never convicted.* N-UNCOUNT: oft N n

**rack|ing** /rækɪŋ/ A **racking** pain or emotion is a distressing one which you feel very strongly. ❑ *She was now shaking with long, racking sobs.* ➔ See also **nerve-racking**. ADJ: ADJ n

**rac|on|teur** /rækɒntɜːʳ/ **(raconteurs)** A **raconteur** is someone, usually a man, who can tell stories in an interesting or amusing way. ❑ *He spoke eight languages and was a noted raconteur.* N-COUNT

**ra|coon** /rækuːn/ ➔ see **raccoon**.

**rac|quet** /rækɪt/ ➔ see **racket**.

**racy** /reɪsi/ **(racier, raciest)** **Racy** writing or behaviour is lively, amusing, and slightly shocking. ADJ

**ra|dar** /reɪdɑːʳ/ **(radars)** **Radar** is a way of discovering the position or speed of objects such as aircraft or ships when they cannot be seen, by using radio signals. N-VAR: oft N n

**ra|dial** /reɪdiəl/ **(radials)** **Radial** refers to the pattern that you get when straight lines are drawn from the centre of a circle to a number of points round the edge. ❑ *The white marble floors were inlaid in a radial pattern of brass.* ADJ: usu ADJ n

**ra|di|ance** /reɪdiəns/ 1 **Radiance** is great happiness which shows in someone's face and makes them look very attractive. ❑ *She has the vigour and radiance of someone young enough to be her grand-daughter.* N-UNCOUNT: also *a* N 2 **Radiance** is a glowing light shining from something. ❑ *The dim bulb of the bedside lamp cast a soft radiance over his face.* N-UNCOUNT: also *a* N

**ra|di|ant** /reɪdiənt/ 1 Someone who is **radiant** is so happy that their happiness shows in their face. ❑ *On her wedding day the bride looked truly radiant.* ADJ ♦ **ra|di|ant|ly** *He smiled radiantly and embraced her.* ADV 2 Something that is **radiant** glows brightly. ❑ *The evening sun warms the old red brick wall to a radiant glow.* ADJ ♦ **ra|di|ant|ly** *The sun was still shining radiantly.* ADV

**ra|di|ate** /reɪdieɪt/ **(radiates, radiating, radiated)** 1 If things **radiate** out **from** a place, they form a pattern that is like lines drawn from the centre of a circle to various points on its edge. ❑ *...the various walks which radiate from the Heritage Centre... From here, contaminated air radiates out to the open countryside.* VERB; V *from* n; V prep/adv 2 If you **radiate** an emotion or quality or if it **radiates from** you, people can see it very clearly in your face and in your behaviour. ❑ *She radiates happiness and health... Her voice hadn't changed but I felt the anger that radiated from her.* VERB; V n; V *from* n 3 If something **radiates** heat or light, heat or light comes from it. ❑ *Stoves are meant to radiate heat.* VERB; V n

**ra|dia|tion** /reɪdieɪʃən/ 1 **Radiation** consists of very small particles of a radioactive substance. Large amounts of radiation can cause illness and death. ❑ *They suffer from health problems and fear the long term effects of radiation.* N-UNCOUNT: also N in pl, oft N n 2 **Radiation** is energy, especially heat, that comes from a particular source. ❑ *The satellite will study energy radiation from stars.* N-UNCOUNT: also N in pl, usu with supp

**ra|dia|tion sick|ness** **Radiation sickness** is an illness that people get when they are exposed to too much radiation. N-UNCOUNT

**ra|dia|tor** /reɪdieɪtəʳ/ **(radiators)** 1 A **radiator** is a hollow metal device, usually connected by pipes to a central heating system, that is used to heat a room. N-COUNT 2 The **radiator** in a car is the part of the engine which is filled with water in order to cool the engine. N-COUNT

**radi|cal** /rædɪkəl/ **(radicals)** 1 **Radical** changes and differences are very important and great in degree. ❑ *The country needs a period of calm without more surges of radical change... The Football League has announced its proposals for a radical reform of the way football is run in England.* ◆◆◇ ADJ: usu ADJ n = fundamental ♦ **radi|cal|ly** /rædɪkli/ *...two large groups of people with radically different beliefs and cultures.* ADV = fundamentally 2 **Radical** people believe that there should be great changes in society and try to bring about these changes. ❑ *...threats by left-wing radical groups to disrupt the proceedings.* ADJ: usu ADJ n ≠ conservative ♦ A **radical** is someone who has radical views. N-COUNT

**radi|cal|ism** /rædɪkəlɪzəm/ **Radicalism** is radical beliefs, ideas, or behaviour. ❑ *Jones himself was a curious mixture of radicalism and conservatism.* N-UNCOUNT ≠ conservatism

**radi|cal|ize** /rædɪkəlaɪz/ **(radicalizes, radicalizing, radicalized)**

in BRIT, also use **radicalise**

If something **radicalizes** a process, situation, or person, it makes them more radical. ❑ *He says the opposition will radicalize its demands if these conditions aren't met. ...women radicalized by feminism... The trial was a radicalizing experience for her.* VERB V n V-ed V-ing ♦ **radi|cali|za|tion** /rædɪkəlaɪzeɪʃən/ *...the radicalization of the conservative right.* N-UNCOUNT: oft N of n

**ra|dic|chio** /rædɪkioʊ, AM rɑːdiː-/ **Radicchio** is a vegetable with purple and white leaves that is usually eaten raw in salads. N-UNCOUNT

**ra|dii** /reɪdiaɪ/ **Radii** is the plural of **radius**.

**ra|dio** /reɪdioʊ/ **(radios, radioing, radioed)** ♦♦♦ [1] **Radio** is the broadcasting of programmes for the public to listen to, by sending out signals from a transmitter. ❑ *The announcement was broadcast on radio and television.* N-UNCOUNT: oft N n [2] You can refer to the programmes broadcast by radio stations as **the radio**. ❑ *A lot of people tend to listen to the radio in the mornings.* N-SING: the N [3] A **radio** is the piece of equipment that you use in order to listen to radio programmes. ❑ *He sat down in the armchair and turned on the radio.* N-COUNT [4] **Radio** is a system of sending sound over a distance by transmitting electrical signals. ❑ *They are in twice daily radio contact with the rebel leader.* N-UNCOUNT: oft N n [5] A **radio** is a piece of equipment that is used for sending and receiving messages. ❑ *...the young constable who managed to raise the alarm on his radio.* N-COUNT [6] If you **radio** someone, you send a message to them by radio. ❑ *The officer radioed for advice... A few minutes after take-off, the pilot radioed that a fire had broken out.* VERB V adv/prep V that Also V n, V

**radio|ac|tive** /reɪdioʊæktɪv/ Something that is **radioactive** contains a substance that produces energy in the form of powerful and harmful rays. ❑ *The government has been storing radioactive waste at Fernald for 50 years.* ADJ ♦ **radio|ac|tiv|ity** /reɪdioʊæktɪvɪti/ *...waste which is contaminated with low levels of radioactivity.* N-UNCOUNT

**ra|dio as|trono|my** **Radio astronomy** is a branch of science in which radio telescopes are used to receive and analyse radio waves from space. N-UNCOUNT

**radio|car|bon** /reɪdioʊkɑːʳbən/ also **radio carbon. Radiocarbon** is a type of carbon which is radioactive, and which therefore breaks up slowly at a regular rate. Its presence in an object can be measured in order to find out how old the object is. ❑ *The most frequently used method is radiocarbon dating.* N-UNCOUNT: usu N n

**ra|dio cas|sette** **(radio cassettes)** A **radio cassette** is a radio and a cassette player together in a single machine. [BRIT] ❑ *...a radio cassette player.* N-COUNT: oft N n

**radio-controlled** A **radio-controlled** device works by receiving radio signals which operate it. ❑ *...radio-controlled model planes.* ADJ: usu ADJ n

**ra|di|og|ra|pher** /reɪdiɒgrəfəʳ/ **(radiographers)** A **radiographer** is a person who is trained to take X-rays. N-COUNT

**ra|di|og|ra|phy** /reɪdiɒgrəfi/ **Radiography** is the process of taking X-rays. N-UNCOUNT

**radio|logi|cal** /reɪdiəlɒdʒɪkəl/ [1] **Radiological** means relating to radiology. ❑ *...patients subjected to extensive radiological examinations.* ADJ: ADJ n [2] **Radiological** means relating to radioactive materials. ❑ *...the National Radiological Protection Board's guidelines for storing nuclear waste.* ADJ: ADJ n

**ra|di|olo|gist** /reɪdiɒlədʒɪst/ **(radiologists)** A **radiologist** is a doctor who is trained in radiology. N-COUNT

**ra|di|ol|ogy** /reɪdiɒlədʒi/ **Radiology** is the branch of medical science that uses X-rays and radioactive substances to treat diseases. N-UNCOUNT

**ra|dio tele|phone** **(radio telephones)** A **radio telephone** is a telephone which carries sound by sending radio signals rather than by using wires. Radio telephones are often used in cars. N-COUNT

**ra|dio tele|scope** **(radio telescopes)** A **radio telescope** is an instrument that receives radio waves from space and finds the position of stars and other objects in space. N-COUNT

**radio|thera|pist** /reɪdioʊθerəpɪst/ **(radiotherapists)** A **radiotherapist** is a person who treats diseases such as cancer by using radiation. N-COUNT

**radio|thera|py** /reɪdioʊθerəpi/ **Radiotherapy** is the treatment of diseases such as cancer by using radiation. N-UNCOUNT

**rad|ish** /rædɪʃ/ **(radishes)** **Radishes** are small red or white vegetables that are the roots of a plant. They are eaten raw in salads. N-VAR

**ra|dium** /reɪdiəm/ **Radium** is a radioactive element which is used in the treatment of cancer. N-UNCOUNT

**ra|dius** /reɪdiəs/ **(radii** /reɪdiaɪ/**)** [1] The **radius** around a particular point is the distance from it in any direction. ❑ *Nigel has searched for work in a ten-mile radius around his home.* N-SING: with supp [2] The **radius** of a circle is the distance from its centre to its outside edge. ❑ *He indicated a semicircle with a radius of about thirty miles.* N-COUNT

**ra|don** /reɪdɒn/ **Radon** is a radioactive element in the form of a gas. N-UNCOUNT

**RAF** /ɑːr eɪ ef, ræf/ **The RAF** is the air force of the United Kingdom. **RAF** is an abbreviation for 'Royal Air Force'. ❑ *An RAF helicopter rescued the men after the boat began taking in water.* N-PROPER: the N

**raf|fia** /ræfiə/ **Raffia** is a fibre made from palm leaves. It is used to make mats and baskets. N-UNCOUNT: oft N n

**raff|ish** /ræfɪʃ/ **Raffish** people and places are not very respectable but are attractive and stylish in spite of this. [WRITTEN] ❑ *He was handsome in a raffish kind of way.* ADJ: usu ADJ n

**raf|fle** /ræfəl/ **(raffles, raffling, raffled)** [1] A **raffle** is a competition in which you buy tickets with numbers on them. Afterwards some numbers are chosen, and if your ticket has one of these numbers on it, you win a prize. ❑ *Any more raffle tickets? Twenty-five pence each or five for a pound.* N-COUNT = lottery [2] If someone **raffles** something, they give it as a prize in a raffle. ❑ *During each show we will be raffling a fabulous prize.* VERB V n

**raft** /rɑːft, ræft/ **(rafts)** [1] A **raft** is a floating platform made from large pieces of wood or other materials tied together. ❑ *...a river trip on bamboo rafts through dense rainforest.* N-COUNT [2] A **raft** is a small rubber or plastic boat that you blow air into to make it float. ❑ *The crew spent two days and nights in their raft.* → See also **life raft**. N-COUNT [3] A **raft of** people or things is a lot of them. ❑ *He has surrounded himself with a raft of advisers who are very radical.* N-COUNT: usu sing, N of n = host of

**raft|er** /rɑːftəʳ, ræf-/ **(rafters)** **Rafters** are the sloping pieces of wood that support a roof. ❑ *From the rafters of the thatched roofs hung strings of dried onions and garlic.* N-COUNT: usu pl

**raft|ing** /rɑːftɪŋ, ræf-/ **Rafting** is the sport of travelling down a river on a raft. ❑ *...water sports such as boating, fishing, and rafting.* N-UNCOUNT

**rag** /ræg/ **(rags)** [1] A **rag** is a piece of old cloth which you can use to clean or wipe things. ❑ *He was wiping his hands on an oily rag.* N-VAR [2] **Rags** are old torn clothes. ❑ *There were men, women and small children, some dressed in rags.* N-PLURAL [3] People refer to a newspaper as a **rag** when they have a poor opinion of it. [INFORMAL] ❑ *'This man Tom works for a local rag,' he said.* N-COUNT disapproval [4] → See also **ragged**.

PHRASES [5] You use **rags to riches** to describe the way in which someone quickly becomes very rich after they have been quite poor. ❑ *His was a rags-to-riches story and people admire that.* PHRASE [6] If you describe something as **a red rag to a bull**, you mean that it is certain to make a particular person or group very angry. [mainly BRIT] ❑ *This sort of infor-* PHRASE: v-link PHR, like PHR *mation is like a red rag to a bull for the tobacco companies.*

**raga** /rɑːgə/ **(ragas)** A **raga** is a piece of Indian music based on a traditional scale or pattern of notes which is also called a **raga**. N-COUNT

**raga|muf|fin** /rægəmʌfɪn/ **(ragamuffins)** A **ragamuffin** is someone, especially a child, who is dirty and has torn clothes. [OLD-FASHIONED] ❑ *They looked like little ragamuffins.* N-COUNT

**rag-and-bone man** **(rag-and-bone men)** A **rag-and-bone man** is a person who goes from street to street in a vehicle or with a horse and cart buying things such as old clothes and furniture. [BRIT] N-COUNT

✔ in AM, use **junkman**, **junk dealer**

**rag|bag** /rægbæg/ also **rag-bag.** A **ragbag** of things is a group of things which do not have much in common with each other, but which are being considered together. ❑ *The government was still in effect a ragbag of Social Democrats and Liberals.* N-SING: usu N *of* n

**rag doll** **(rag dolls)** A **rag doll** is a soft doll made of cloth. N-COUNT

**rage** /reɪdʒ/ **(rages, raging, raged)** 1 **Rage** is strong anger that is difficult to control. ❑ *He was red-cheeked with rage... I flew into a rage.* ◆◇◇ N-VAR = fury 2 You say that something powerful or unpleasant **rages** when it continues with great force or violence. ❑ *Train services were halted as the fire raged for more than four hours... The war rages on and the time has come to take sides.* VERB V V *on* 3 If you **rage** about something, you speak or think very angrily about it. ❑ *Monroe was on the phone, raging about her mistreatment by the brothers... Inside, Frannie was raging... 'I can't see it's any of your business,' he raged.* VERB V *about/against/at* n V V with quote 4 You can refer to the strong anger that someone feels in a particular situation as a particular **rage**, especially when this results in violent or aggressive behaviour. ❑ *Cabin crews are reporting up to nine cases of air rage a week.* → See also **road rage**. N-UNCOUNT: n N 5 When something is popular and fashionable, you can say that it is **the rage** or **all the rage**. [INFORMAL] ❑ *The 1950s look is all the rage at the moment.* N-SING: *the* N 6 → See also **raging**.

**rag|ga** /rægə/ **Ragga** is a style of pop music similar to rap music which began in the West Indies. N-UNCOUNT

**rag|ged** /rægɪd/ 1 Someone who is **ragged** looks untidy and is wearing clothes that are old and torn. ❑ *The survivors eventually reached safety, ragged and half-starved.* ♦ **rag|ged|ly** *...dirty, raggedly dressed children.* ADJ ADV: ADV -ed 2 **Ragged** clothes are old and torn. ADJ 3 You can say that something is **ragged** when it is untidy or uneven. ❑ *O'Brien formed the men into a ragged line.* ♦ **rag|ged|ly** *Some people tried to sing, but their voices soon died raggedly away.* ADJ = uneven ADV: ADV after v, ADV -ed

**rag|gedy** /rægɪdi/ People and things that are **raggedy** are dirty and untidy. **Raggedy** clothes are old and torn. [INFORMAL] ❑ *...an old man in a raggedy topcoat.* ADJ

**rag|ing** /reɪdʒɪŋ/ 1 **Raging** water moves very forcefully and violently. ❑ *The field trip involved crossing a raging torrent.* ADJ: ADJ n 2 **Raging** fire is very hot and fierce. ❑ *As he came closer he saw a gigantic wall of raging flame before him.* ADJ: ADJ n 3 **Raging** is used to describe things, especially bad things, that are very intense. ❑ *If raging inflation returns, then interest rates will shoot up... He felt a raging thirst.* ADJ: ADJ n 4 → See also **rage**.

**ra|gout** /rægu:/ **(ragouts)** A **ragout** is a strongly flavoured stew of meat or vegetables or both. N-VAR

**rag rug** **(rag rugs)** A **rag rug** is a small carpet made of old pieces of cloth stitched or woven together. N-COUNT

**rag|tag** /rægtæg/ also **rag-tag.** If you want to say that a group of people or an organization is badly organized and not very respectable, you can describe it as a **ragtag** group or organization. [INFORMAL] ❑ *We started out with a little rag-tag team of 30 people.* ADJ: ADJ n

**rag|time** /rægtaɪm/ **Ragtime** is a kind of jazz piano music that was invented in America in the early 1900s. N-UNCOUNT

**rag trade** **The rag trade** is the business and industry of making and selling clothes, especially women's clothes. ❑ *The rag trade is extremely competitive, and one needs plenty of contacts to survive.* N-SING: *the* N

**raid** /reɪd/ **(raids, raiding, raided)** 1 When soldiers **raid** a place, they make a sudden armed attack against it, with the aim of causing damage rather than occupying any of the enemy's land. ❑ *The guerrillas raided banks and destroyed a police barracks and an electricity substation.* ♦ **Raid** is also a noun. ❑ *The rebels attempted a surprise raid on a military camp.* → See also **air raid**. ◆◇◇ VERB V n N-COUNT: oft N *on/against* n 2 If the police **raid** a building, they enter it suddenly and by force in order to look for dangerous criminals or for evidence of something illegal, such as drugs or weapons. ❑ *Fraud squad officers raided the firm's offices.* ♦ **Raid** is also a noun. ❑ *They were arrested early this morning after a raid on a house by thirty armed police.* VERB V n N-COUNT: oft N *on* n 3 If someone **raids** a building or place, they enter it by force in order to steal something. [BRIT] ❑ *A 19-year-old man has been found guilty of raiding a bank.* ♦ **Raid** is also a noun. ❑ *...an armed raid on a small Post Office.* VERB V n N-COUNT: oft N *on* n 4 If you **raid** the fridge or the larder, you take food from it to eat instead of a meal or in between meals. [INFORMAL] ❑ *She made her way to the kitchen to raid the fridge.* VERB V n

**raid|er** /reɪdəʳ/ **(raiders)** 1 **Raiders** are people who enter a building or place by force in order to steal something. [BRIT] ❑ *The raiders escaped with cash and jewellery.* N-COUNT = robber 2 → See also **corporate raider**.

**rail** /reɪl/ **(rails, railing, railed)** 1 A **rail** is a horizontal bar attached to posts or fixed round the edge of something as a fence or support. ❑ *She gripped the hand rail in the lift.* ◆◇◇ N-COUNT: oft supp N 2 A **rail** is a horizontal bar that you hang things on. ❑ *This pair of curtains will fit a rail up to 7ft 6in wide.* N-COUNT 3 **Rails** are the steel bars which trains run on. ❑ *The train left the rails but somehow forced its way back onto the line.* N-COUNT: usu pl = track 4 If you travel or send something **by rail**, you travel or send it on a train. ❑ *The president traveled by rail to his home town.* N-UNCOUNT: oft N n 5 If you **rail** against something, you criticize it loudly and angrily. [WRITTEN] ❑ *He railed against hypocrisy and greed.* VERB V *against/at* n 6 → See also **railing**.

**PHRASES** 7 If something is **back on the rails**, it is beginning to be successful again after a period when it almost failed. [JOURNALISM] ❑ *They are keen to get the negotiating process back on the rails.* PHRASE 8 If someone **goes off the rails**, they start to behave in a way that other people think is unacceptable or very strange, for example they start taking drugs or breaking the law. ❑ *They've got to do something about these children because clearly they've gone off the rails.* PHRASE: V inflects

**rail|card** /reɪlkɑːʳd/ **(railcards)** A **railcard** is an identity card that allows people to buy train tickets cheaply. [BRIT] N-COUNT

**rail|ing** /reɪlɪŋ/ **(railings)** 1 A fence made from metal bars is called a **railing** or **railings**. ❑ *He walked out on to the balcony where he rested his arms on the railing.* N-COUNT 2 → See also **rail**.

**rail|road** /reɪlroud/ **(railroads, railroading, railroaded)** 1 A **railroad** is a route between two places along which trains travel on steel rails. [AM] ❑ *...railroad tracks that led to nowhere.* N-COUNT

✔ in BRIT, use **railway**

2 A **railroad** is a company or organization that operates railway routes. [AM] ❑ *...The Chicago and Northwestern Railroad.* N-COUNT

✔ in BRIT, use **railway**

3 If you **railroad** someone **into** doing something, you make them do it although they do not VERB

really want to, by hurrying them and putting pressure on them. ❑ *He more or less railroaded the rest of Europe into recognising the new 'independent' states... He railroaded the reforms through.* V n *into* n/-ing; V n *through*

**rail|way** /reɪlweɪ/ **(railways)** 1 A **railway** is a route between two places along which trains travel on steel rails. [mainly BRIT] ❑ *The road ran beside a railway. ...a disused railway line.* ◆◇◇ N-COUNT

☑ in AM, usually use **railroad**

2 A **railway** is a company or organization that operates railway routes. [BRIT] ❑ *...the state-owned French railway. ...the privatisation of the railways.* N-COUNT

☑ in AM, use **railroad**

3 A **railway** is the system and network of tracks that trains travel on. [mainly AM] N-COUNT

**rail|way|man** /reɪlweɪmæn/ **(railwaymen)** **Railwaymen** are men who work for the railway. [BRIT] N-COUNT

☑ in AM, use **rail workers, railroad workers**

**rai|ment** /reɪmənt/ **(raiments)** **Raiment** is clothing. [LITERARY] ❑ *I want nothing but raiment and daily bread.* N-UNCOUNT: also N in pl

**rain** /reɪn/ **(rains, raining, rained)** 1 **Rain** is water that falls from the clouds in small drops. ❑ *I hope you didn't get soaked standing out in the rain.* ◆◆◇ N-UNCOUNT: also *the* N 2 In countries where rain only falls in certain seasons, this rain is referred to as **the rains.** ❑ *...the spring, when the rains came.* N-PLURAL: usu *the* N 3 When rain falls, you can say that **it is raining.** ❑ *It was raining hard, and she hadn't an umbrella.* VERB *it* V 4 If someone **rains** blows, kicks, or bombs **on** a person or place, the person or place is attacked by many blows, kicks, or bombs. You can also say that blows, kicks, or bombs **rain on** a person or place. ❑ *The police, raining blows on rioters and spectators alike, cleared the park... Rockets, mortars and artillery rounds rained on buildings.* VERB V n *on* n; V *on* n ♦ **Rain down** means the same as **rain.** ❑ *Fighter aircraft rained down high explosives... Grenades and mortars rained down on Dubrovnik.* PHRASAL VERB V P n (not pron); V P *on* n 5 If you say that someone does something **rain or shine**, you mean that they do it regularly, without being affected by the weather or other circumstances. ❑ *Frances took her daughter walking every day, rain or shine.* PHRASE

♦ **rain off** If a sports game **is rained off**, it has to stop, or it is not able to start, because of rain. [BRIT] ❑ *Most of the games have been rained off. ...a rained-off cricket match.* PHRASAL VERB *be* V-ed P; V-ed P

☑ in AM, use **rain out**

♦ **rain out** If a sports game **is rained out**, it has to stop, or it is not able to start, because of rain. [AM] ❑ *Saturday's game was rained out.* PHRASAL VERB *be* V-ed P

☑ in BRIT, use **rain off**

**rain|bow** /reɪnboʊ/ **(rainbows)** A **rainbow** is an arch of different colours that you can sometimes see in the sky when it is raining. ❑ *...silk brocade of every colour of the rainbow.* N-COUNT

**rain check** **(rain checks)** 1 If you say you will take a **rain check** on an offer or suggestion, you mean that you do not want to accept it now, but you might accept it at another time. ❑ *Can I take a rain check on that?* N-SING 2 A **rain check** is a free ticket that is given to people when an outdoor game or event is stopped because of rain or bad weather, so that they can go to it when it is held again. [AM] N-COUNT

**rain|coat** /reɪnkoʊt/ **(raincoats)** A **raincoat** is a waterproof coat. N-COUNT

**rain|drop** /reɪndrɒp/ **(raindrops)** A **raindrop** is a single drop of rain. N-COUNT

**rain|fall** /reɪnfɔːl/ **(rainfalls)** **Rainfall** is the amount of rain that falls in a place during a particular period. ❑ *There have been four years of below average rainfall.* N-UNCOUNT: also N in pl

**rain|for|est** /reɪnfɒrɪst, AM -fɔːr-/ **(rainforests)**

☑ in AM, also use **rain forest**

A **rainforest** is a thick forest of tall trees which is found in tropical areas where there is a lot of rain. N-VAR

**rain|storm** /reɪnstɔːʳm/ **(rainstorms)** A **rainstorm** is a fall of very heavy rain. ❑ *His car collided with another car during a heavy rainstorm.* N-COUNT

**rain-swept** also **rainswept.** A **rain-swept** place is a place where it is raining heavily. ❑ *He looked up and down the deserted, rain-swept street.* ADJ: ADJ n

**rain|water** /reɪnwɔːtəʳ/ **Rainwater** is water that has fallen as rain. N-UNCOUNT

**rainy** /reɪni/ **(rainier, rainiest)** 1 During a **rainy** day, season, or period it rains a lot. ❑ *The rainy season in the Andes normally starts in December.* ADJ: usu ADJ n 2 If you say that you are saving something, especially money, **for a rainy day**, you mean that you are saving it until a time in the future when you might need it. ❑ *I'll put the rest in the bank for a rainy day.* PHRASE

**raise** /reɪz/ **(raises, raising, raised)** 1 If you **raise** something, you move it so that it is in a higher position. ❑ *He raised his hand to wave... Milton raised the glass to his lips. ...a small raised platform.* ◆◆◆ VERB V n; V n prep/adv; V-ed 2 If you **raise** a flag, you display it by moving it up a pole or into a high place where it can be seen. ❑ *They had raised the white flag in surrender.* VERB V n 3 If you **raise yourself**, you lift your body so that you are standing up straight, or so that you are no longer lying flat. ❑ *He raised himself into a sitting position.* VERB = lift; V pron-refl 4 If you **raise** the rate or level of something, you increase it. ❑ *The Republic of Ireland is expected to raise interest rates. ...a raised body temperature.* VERB = increase; V n; V-ed 5 To **raise** the standard of something means to improve it. ❑ *...a new drive to raise standards of literacy in Britain's schools.* VERB = improve; V n 6 If you **raise** your **voice**, you speak more loudly, usually because you are angry. ❑ *Don't you raise your voice to me, Henry Rollins!.* VERB V n 7 A **raise** is an increase in your wages or salary. [AM] ❑ *Within two months Kelly got a raise.* N-COUNT

☑ in BRIT, use **rise**

8 If you **raise** money **for** a charity or an institution, you ask people for money which you collect on its behalf. ❑ *...events held to raise money for Help the Aged.* VERB V n *for* n 9 If a person or company **raises** money that they need, they manage to get it, for example by selling their property or by borrowing. ❑ *They raised the money to buy the house and two hundred acres of grounds.* VERB V n 10 If an event **raises** a particular emotion or question, it makes people feel the emotion or consider the question. ❑ *The agreement has raised hopes that the war may end soon... The accident again raises questions about the safety of the plant.* VERB V n; V n 11 If you **raise** a subject, an objection, or a question, you mention it or bring it to someone's attention. ❑ *He had been consulted and had raised no objections.* VERB V n 12 Someone who **raises** a child looks after it until it is grown up. ❑ *My mother was an amazing woman. She raised four of us kids virtually singlehandedly.* VERB = bring up; V n 13 If someone **raises** a particular type of animal or crop, they breed that type of animal or grow that type of crop. ❑ *He raises 2,000 acres of wheat and hay.* VERB V n 14 to **raise the alarm** → see **alarm**. to **raise** your **eyebrows** → see **eyebrow**. to **raise a finger** → see **finger**. to **raise hell** → see **hell**. to **raise a laugh** → see **laugh**. to **raise the roof** → see **roof**.

**rai|sin** /reɪzᵊn/ **(raisins)** **Raisins** are dried grapes. N-COUNT

**rai|son d'etre** /reɪzɒn detrə/ also **raison d'être.** A person's or organization's **raison d'etre** is the most important reason for them existing in the way that they do. ❑ *...a debate about the raison d'etre of the armed forces.* N-SING: usu with poss

**Raj** /rɑːʒ/ **The** British **Raj** was the period of British rule in India which ended in 1947. ❑ *...Indian living conditions under the Raj.* N-SING: *the* N

**rake** /reɪk/ **(rakes, raking, raked)** 1 A **rake** is a garden tool consisting of a row of metal or wooden teeth attached to a long handle. You can use a rake to make the earth smooth and level before you put plants in, or to gather leaves together. N-COUNT
2 If you **rake** a surface, you move a rake across it in order to make it smooth and level. ❑ *Rake the soil, press the seed into it, then cover it lightly.* VERB V n
3 If you **rake** leaves or ashes, you move them somewhere using a rake or a similar tool. ❑ *I watched the men rake leaves into heaps.* VERB V n adv/prep

♦ **rake in** If you say that someone **is raking in** money, you mean that they are making a lot of money very easily, more easily than you think they should. [INFORMAL] ❑ *The privatisation allowed companies to rake in huge profits.* PHRASAL VERB V P n (not pron) Also V n P

♦ **rake over** If you say that someone **is raking over** something that has been said, done, or written in the past, you mean that they are examining and discussing it in detail, in a way that you do not think is very pleasant. ❑ *Nobody wanted to rake over his past history.* PHRASAL VERB V P n (not pron)

♦ **rake up** If someone **is raking up** something unpleasant or embarrassing that happened in the past, they are talking about it when you would prefer them not to mention it. ❑ *Raking up the past won't help anyone.* PHRASAL VERB = drag up V P n (not pron) Also V n P

**raked** /reɪkt/ A **raked** stage or other surface is sloping, for example so that all the audience can see more clearly. ❑ *The action takes place on a steeply raked stage.* ADJ: ADJ n

**rake-off (rake-offs)** If someone who has helped to arrange a business deal takes or gets a **rake-off**, they illegally or unfairly take a share of the profits. [INFORMAL] N-COUNT = cut

**rak|ish** /reɪkɪʃ/ A **rakish** person or appearance is stylish in a confident, bold way. ❑ *...a soft-brimmed hat which he wore at a rakish angle.* ADJ: usu ADJ n
♦ **rak|ish|ly** *...a hat cocked rakishly over one eye.* ADV

**ral|ly** /ræli/ **(rallies, rallying, rallied)** 1 A **rally** is a large public meeting that is held in order to show support for something such as a political party. ❑ *About three thousand people held a rally to mark international human rights day.* ◆◇◇ N-COUNT
2 When people **rally to** something or when something **rallies** them, they unite to support it. ❑ *His supporters have rallied to his defence... He rallied his own supporters for a fight.* VERB V to n V n
3 When someone or something **rallies**, they begin to recover or improve after having been weak. ❑ *He rallied enough to thank his doctors.* ♦ **Rally** is also a noun. ❑ *After a brief rally the shares returned to 126p.* VERB = recover V N-COUNT: usu sing
4 A **rally** is a competition in which vehicles are driven over public roads. ❑ *...an accomplished rally driver.* N-COUNT: usu with supp
5 A **rally** in tennis, badminton, or squash is a continuous series of shots that the players exchange without stopping. ❑ *...a long rally.* N-COUNT

♦ **rally around**

✓ in BRIT, also use **rally round**

When people **rally around** or **rally round**, they work as a group in order to support someone or something at a difficult time. ❑ *So many people have rallied round to help the family... Connie's friends rallied round her.* PHRASAL VERB V P V P n

**ral|ly|ing cry (rallying cries)** A **rallying cry** or **rallying call** is something such as a word or phrase, an event, or a belief which encourages people to unite and to act in support of a particular group or idea. ❑ *...an issue that is fast becoming a rallying cry for many Democrats: national health care.* N-COUNT

**ral|ly|ing point (rallying points)** A **rallying point** is a place, event, or person that people are attracted to as a symbol of a political group or ideal. ❑ *Students used the death of political activists as a rallying point for anti-government protests.* N-COUNT = focus

**ram** /ræm/ **(rams, ramming, rammed)** 1 If a vehicle **rams** something such as another vehicle, it crashes into it with a lot of force, usually deliberately. ❑ *The thieves fled, ramming the policeman's car.* VERB V n
2 If you **ram** something somewhere, you push it there with great force. ❑ *He rammed the key into the lock and kicked the front door open.* VERB V n adv/prep
3 A **ram** is an adult male sheep. N-COUNT
4 → See also **battering ram**.
5 If something **rams home** a message or a point, it makes it clear in a way that is very forceful and that people are likely to listen to. ❑ *The report by Marks & Spencer's chairman will ram this point home.* PHRASE: V inflects
to **ram** something **down** someone's **throat** → see **throat**.

**RAM** /ræm/ **RAM** is the part of a computer in which information is stored while you are using it. **RAM** is an abbreviation for 'Random Access Memory'. [COMPUTING] ❑ *...a PC with 256k RAM minimum.* N-UNCOUNT

**Rama|dan** /ræmədæn/ **Ramadan** is the ninth month of the Muslim year, when Muslims do not eat between the rising and setting of the sun. During Ramadan, Muslims celebrate the fact that it was in this month that God first revealed the words of the Quran to Mohammed. N-UNCOUNT

**ram|ble** /ræmbəl/ **(rambles, rambling, rambled)** 1 A **ramble** is a long walk in the countryside. ❑ *...an hour's ramble through the woods.* N-COUNT
2 If you **ramble**, you go on a long walk in the countryside. ❑ *...freedom to ramble across the moors.* VERB V adv/prep
3 If you say that a person **rambles** in their speech or writing, you mean they do not make much sense because they keep going off the subject in a confused way. ❑ *Sometimes she spoke sensibly; sometimes she rambled.* VERB V

♦ **ramble on** If you say that someone **is rambling on**, you mean that they have been talking for a long time in a boring and rather confused way. ❑ *She only half-listened as Ella rambled on... He stood in my kitchen drinking beer, rambling on about Lillian.* PHRASAL VERB V P V P about n

**ram|bler** /ræmbləʳ/ **(ramblers)** A **rambler** is a person whose hobby is going on long walks in the countryside, often as part of an organized group. [BRIT] N-COUNT

**ram|bling** /ræmblɪŋ/ 1 A **rambling** building is big and old with an irregular shape. ❑ *...that rambling house and its bizarre contents.* ADJ: usu ADJ n
2 If you describe a speech or piece of writing as **rambling**, you are criticizing it for being too long and very confused. ❑ *His actions were accompanied by a rambling monologue.* ADJ: usu ADJ n disapproval

**ram|blings** /ræmblɪŋz/ If you describe a speech or piece of writing as someone's **ramblings**, you are saying that it is meaningless because the person who said or wrote it was very confused or insane. ❑ *The official dismissed the speech as the ramblings of a desperate lunatic.* N-PLURAL: usu with poss disapproval

**ram|bunc|tious** /ræmbʌŋkʃəs/ A **rambunctious** person is energetic in a cheerful, noisy way. [mainly AM] ❑ *...a very rambunctious and energetic class.* ADJ: usu ADJ n = boisterous

✓ in BRIT, usually use **rumbustious**

**ram|ekin** /ræmɪkɪn/ **(ramekins)** A **ramekin** or a **ramekin dish** is a small dish in which food for one person can be baked in the oven. N-COUNT

**rami|fi|ca|tion** /ræmɪfɪkeɪʃən/ **(ramifications)** The **ramifications** of a decision, plan, or event are all its consequences and effects, especially ones which are not obvious at first. ❑ *The book analyses the social and political ramifications of AIDS for the gay community.* N-COUNT: usu pl, oft with poss

**ramp** /ræmp/ **(ramps)** A **ramp** is a sloping surface between two places that are at different levels. ❑ *Lillian was coming down the ramp from the museum.* N-COUNT

**ram|page (rampages, rampaging, rampaged)**

✓ Pronounced /ræmpeɪdʒ/ for meaning 1, and /ræmpeɪdʒ/ for meaning 2.

1 When people or animals **rampage** through a place, they rush about there in a wild or violent way, causing damage or destruction. ❑ *Hundreds of youths rampaged through the town, shop windows* VERB V adv/prep

were smashed and cars overturned... He used a sword to try to defend his shop from a rampaging mob.* [V-ing] 2 If people go **on the rampage**, they rush about in a wild or violent way, causing damage or destruction. ❑ *The prisoners went on the rampage destroying everything in their way.* [PHRASE: v PHR, v-link PHR]

**ram|pant** /ræmpənt/ [ADJ] If you describe something bad, such as a crime or disease, as **rampant**, you mean that it is very common and is increasing in an uncontrolled way. ❑ *Inflation is rampant and industry in decline.*

**ram|part** /ræmpɑːʳt/ **(ramparts)** [N-COUNT: usu pl] The **ramparts** of a castle or city are the earth walls, often with stone walls on them, that were built to protect it. ❑ *...a walk along the ramparts of the Old City.*

**ram-raid** **(ram-raids, ram-raiding, ram-raided)**
1 [N-COUNT] A **ram-raid** is the crime of using a car to drive into and break a shop window in order to steal things from the shop. [BRIT] ❑ *A shop in Station Road was the target of a ram-raid early yesterday.*
2 [VERB] If people **ram-raid**, they use a car to drive into and break a shop window in order to steal things from the shop. [BRIT] ❑ *The kids who are joyriding and ram-raiding are unemployed.* [V, Also V n] ♦ **ram-raider** **(ram-raiders)** [N-COUNT] *Ram-raiders smashed their way into a high-class store.*

**ram|rod** /ræmrɒd/ **(ramrods)** 1 [N-COUNT] A **ramrod** is a long, thin rod which can be used for pushing something into a narrow tube. Ramrods were used, for example, for forcing an explosive substance down the barrel of an old-fashioned gun, or for cleaning the barrel of a gun. 2 [PHRASE] If someone sits or stands **like a ramrod** or **straight as a ramrod**, they have a very straight back and appear rather stiff and formal. ❑ *...a woman with iron grey hair, high cheekbones and a figure like a ramrod.*
3 [ADJ: ADJ n] If someone has a **ramrod** back or way of standing, they have a very straight back and hold themselves in a rather stiff and formal way. ❑ *I don't have the ramrod posture I had when I was in the Navy.* ♦ **Ramrod** is also an adverb. [ADV: ADV adj] ❑ *At 75, she's still ramrod straight.*

**ram|shack|le** /ræmʃækᵊl/ 1 [ADJ: usu ADJ n] A **ramshackle** building is badly made or in bad condition, and looks as if it is likely to fall down. ❑ *They entered the shop, which was a curious ramshackle building.* 2 [ADJ: usu ADJ n] A **ramshackle** system, union, or collection of things has been put together without much thought and is not likely to work very well. ❑ *They joined with a ramshackle alliance of other rebels.*

**ran** /ræn/ **Ran** is the past tense of **run**.

**ranch** /rɑːntʃ, ræntʃ/ **(ranches)** [N-COUNT] A **ranch** is a large farm used for raising animals, especially cattle, horses, or sheep. ❑ *He lives on a cattle ranch in Australia.* → See also **dude ranch**.

**ranch|er** /rɑːntʃəʳ, ræn-/ **(ranchers)** [N-COUNT] A **rancher** is someone who owns or manages a large farm, especially one used for raising cattle, horses, or sheep. ❑ *...a cattle rancher.*

**ranch|ing** /rɑːntʃɪŋ, ræn-/ [N-UNCOUNT] **Ranching** is the activity of running a large farm, especially one used for raising cattle, horses, or sheep.

**ran|cid** /rænsɪd/ [ADJ] If butter, bacon, or other oily foods are **rancid**, they have gone bad and taste old and unpleasant. ❑ *Butter is perishable and can go rancid.*

**ran|cor** /ræŋkər/ → see **rancour**.

**ran|cor|ous** /ræŋkərəs/ [ADJ = acrimonious] A **rancorous** argument or person is full of bitterness and anger. [FORMAL] ❑ *The deal ended after a series of rancorous disputes.*

**ran|cour** /ræŋkəʳ/

✔ in AM, use **rancor**

[N-UNCOUNT] **Rancour** is a feeling of bitterness and anger. [FORMAL] ❑ *'That's too bad,' Teddy said without rancour.*

**rand** /rænd/ **(rands** or **rand)** [N-COUNT: usu num N] The **rand** is the unit of currency used in South Africa. ❑ *...12 million rand.* ♦ **The rand** [N-SING: the N] is also used to refer to the South African currency system. ❑ *The rand slumped by 22% against the dollar.*

**R&B** /ɑːr ən biː/ [N-UNCOUNT: oft N n] **R&B** is a style of popular music developed in the 1940's from blues music, but using electrically amplified instruments. **R&B** is an abbreviation for 'rhythm and blues'.

**R&D** /ɑːr ən diː/ also **R and D.** [N-UNCOUNT: oft *in/on* N] **R&D** refers to the research and development work or department within a large company or organization. **R&D** is an abbreviation for 'Research and Development'. ❑ *Businesses need to train their workers better, and spend more on R&D.*

**ran|dom** /rændəm/ 1 [ADJ: usu ADJ n] A **random** sample or method is one in which all the people or things involved have an equal chance of being chosen. ❑ *The survey used a random sample of two thousand people across England and Wales... The competitors will be subject to random drug testing.* ♦ **ran|dom|ly** [ADV: ADV with v] *...interviews with a randomly selected sample of thirty girls aged between 13 and 18.* 2 [ADJ: usu ADJ n] If you describe events as **random**, you mean that they do not seem to follow a definite plan or pattern. ❑ *...random violence against innocent victims.* ♦ **ran|dom|ly** [ADV: ADV with v] *...drinks and magazines left scattered randomly around.*

PHRASES 3 [PHRASE: PHR after v] If you choose people or things **at random**, you do not use any particular method, so they all have an equal chance of being chosen. ❑ *We received several answers, and we picked one at random.* 4 [PHRASE: PHR after v] If something happens **at random**, it happens without a definite plan or pattern. ❑ *Three black people were killed by shots fired at random from a minibus.*

**ran|dom|ize** /rændəmaɪz/ **(randomizes, randomizing, randomized)**

✔ in BRIT, also use **randomise**

[VERB] If you **randomize** the events or people in scientific experiments or academic research, you use a method that gives them all an equal chance of happening or being chosen. [TECHNICAL] ❑ *The wheel is designed with obstacles in the ball's path to randomise its movement...* [V n] *Properly randomized studies are only now being completed.* [V-ed]

**R&R** /ɑːr ən ɑːr/ also **R and R.** 1 [N-UNCOUNT] **R&R** refers to time that you spend relaxing, when you are not working. **R&R** is an abbreviation for 'rest and recreation'. [mainly AM] ❑ *Winter spas are now the smart set's choice for serious R&R.* 2 [N-UNCOUNT] **R&R** refers to time that members of the armed forces spend relaxing, away from their usual duties. **R&R** is an abbreviation for 'rest and recuperation'. [AM] ❑ *Twenty-five years ago Pattaya was a sleepy fishing village. Then it was discovered by American soldiers on R&R from Vietnam.*

**randy** /rændi/ **(randier, randiest)** [ADJ = horny] Someone who is **randy** is sexually excited and eager to have sex. [BRIT, INFORMAL] ❑ *It was extremely hot and I was feeling rather randy.*

**rang** /ræŋ/ **Rang** is the past tense of **ring**.

**range** /reɪndʒ/ **(ranges, ranging, ranged)** ◆◆◇ 1 [N-COUNT: usu with supp, oft N *of* n] A **range of** things is a number of different things of the same general kind. ❑ *A wide range of colours and patterns are available... The two men discussed a range of issues.* 2 [N-COUNT: usu with supp, oft n N] A **range** is the complete group that is included between two points on a scale of measurement or quality. ❑ *The average age range is between 35 and 55. ...properties available in the price range they are looking for.* 3 [N-COUNT: usu with supp] The **range of** something is the maximum area in which it can reach things or detect things. ❑ *The 120mm mortar has a range of 18,000 yards.* 4 [VERB] If things **range between** two points or **range from** one point to another, they vary within these points on a scale of measurement or quality. ❑ *They range in price from $3 to $15. ...offering merchandise ranging from the everyday to the esoteric. ...temperatures ranging between 5°C and 20°C.* [V *from* amount *to* amount, V *from* n *to* n, V *between* pl-amount] 5 [N-COUNT: usu with supp] A **range** of mountains or hills is a line of them. ❑ *...the massive mountain ranges to the north.* 6 [N-COUNT: usu supp N] A rifle **range** or a shooting **range** is a place where people can practise shooting at targets. ❑ *It reminds me of my days on the rifle range preparing for duty in Vietnam.* [7] A **range** or **kitchen range** is an old-fashioned metal cooker. [BRIT] — N-COUNT: usu with supp

[8] A **range** or **kitchen range** is a large metal device for cooking food using gas or electricity. A range consists of a grill, an oven, and some gas or electric rings. [AM] — N-COUNT

☑ in BRIT, usually use **cooker**

[9] → See also **free-range**.

**PHRASES** [10] If something is **in range** or **within range**, it is near enough to be reached or detected. If it is **out of range**, it is too far away to be reached or detected. ❑ *Cars are driven through the mess, splashing everyone in range. ...a base within range of enemy missiles... The fish stayed 50 yards offshore, well out of range.* — PHRASE: v-link PHR, PHR after v

[11] If you see or hit something **at close range** or **from close range**, you are very close to it when you see it or hit it. If you do something **at a range of** half a mile, for example, you are half a mile away from it when you do it. ❑ *He was shot in the head at close range... The enemy opened fire at a range of only 20 yards.* — PHRASE: PHR after v

**range|finder** /reɪndʒfaɪndə$^{r}$/ **(rangefinders)** A **rangefinder** is an instrument, usually part of a camera or a piece of military equipment, that measures the distance between things that are far away from each other. — N-COUNT

**rang|er** /reɪndʒə$^{r}$/ **(rangers)** A **ranger** is a person whose job is to look after a forest or large park. ❑ *Bill Justice is a park ranger at the Carlsbad Caverns National Park.* — N-COUNT

**rangy** /reɪndʒi/ If you describe a person or animal as **rangy**, you mean that they have long, thin, powerful legs. [WRITTEN] ❑ *...a tall, rangy, redheaded girl.* — ADJ: usu ADJ n = long-legged

**rank** /ræŋk/ **(ranks, ranking, ranked, ranker, rankest)** ◆◇◇ [1] Someone's **rank** is the position or grade that they have in an organization. ❑ *He eventually rose to the rank of captain... The former head of counter-intelligence had been stripped of his rank and privileges.* — N-VAR: with supp

[2] Someone's **rank** is the social class, especially the high social class, that they belong to. [FORMAL] ❑ *He must be treated as a hostage of high rank, not as a common prisoner.* — N-VAR: usu with supp

[3] If an official organization **ranks** someone or something 1st, 5th, or 50th, for example, they calculate that the person or thing has that position on a scale. You can also say that someone or something **ranks** 1st, 5th, or 50th, for example. ❑ *The report ranks the UK 20th out of 22 advanced nations.* (V n ord *in/out of* n) *...the only British woman to be ranked in the top 50 of the women's world rankings...* (*be* V-ed *in* n) *Mr Short does not even rank in the world's top ten.* (V *in/among* n) — VERB

[4] If you say that someone or something **ranks** high or low on a scale or if you **rank** them high or low, you are saying how good or important you think they are. ❑ *His prices rank high among those of other contemporary photographers...* (V adj *among* n) *Investors ranked South Korea high among Asian nations...* (V n adj *among* n) *St Petersburg's night life ranks as more exciting than the capital's...* (V *as* adj) *18 per cent of women ranked sex as very important in their lives...* (V n *as* adj) *The Ritz-Carlton in Aspen has to rank as one of the most extraordinary hotels I have ever been to.* (V *as* n) — VERB

[5] The **ranks** of a group or organization are the people who belong to it. ❑ *There were some misgivings within the ranks of the media too.* — N-PLURAL: with supp

[6] **The ranks** are the ordinary members of an organization, especially of the armed forces. ❑ *Most store managers have worked their way up through the ranks.* — N-PLURAL: *the* N, oft prep N

[7] A **rank of** people or things is a row of them. ❑ *Ranks of police in riot gear stood nervously by.* — N-COUNT: usu N *of* n

[8] A **taxi rank** is a place on a city street where taxis park when they are available for hire. [mainly BRIT] ❑ *The man led the way to the taxi rank.* — N-COUNT

☑ in AM, use **stand**

[9] You can use **rank** to emphasize a bad or undesirable quality that exists in an extreme form. [FORMAL] ❑ *He called it 'rank hypocrisy' that the government was now promoting equal rights.* — ADJ: ADJ n [emphasis] = sheer

[10] You can describe something as **rank** when it has a strong and unpleasant smell. [OLD-FASHIONED, WRITTEN] ❑ *The kitchen was rank with the smell of drying uniforms. ...the rank smell of unwashed clothes.* — ADJ

**PHRASES** [11] If you say that a member of a group or organization **breaks ranks**, you mean that they disobey the instructions of their group or organization. ❑ *Britain appears unlikely to break ranks with other members of the European Union.* — PHRASE: V inflects

[12] If you say that the members of a group **close ranks**, you mean that they are supporting each other only because their group is being criticized. ❑ *Institutions tend to close ranks when a member has been accused of misconduct.* — PHRASE: V inflects

[13] If you experience something, usually something bad, that other people have experienced, you can say that you have **joined** their **ranks**. ❑ *Last month, 370,000 Americans joined the ranks of the unemployed.* — PHRASE: V inflects

[14] If you say that someone in authority **pulls rank**, you mean that they unfairly force other people to do what they want because of their higher rank or position. ❑ *The Captain pulled rank and made his sergeant row the entire way.* — PHRASE: V inflects [disapproval]

**rank and file** **The rank and file** are the ordinary members of an organization or the ordinary workers in a company, as opposed to its leaders or managers. [JOURNALISM] ❑ *There was widespread support for him among the rank and file.* — N-SING: usu *the* N

**-ranked** /-ræŋkt/ **-ranked** is added to words, usually numbers like 'first', 'second', and 'third', to form adjectives which indicate what position someone or something has in a list or scale. ❑ *...Cheryl Thibedeau, Canada's second-ranked sprinter. ...the world's ten highest-ranked players.* — COMB in ADJ: ADJ n

**rank|ing** /ræŋkɪŋ/ **(rankings)** ◆◇◇ [1] In many sports, the list of the best players made by an official organization is called **the rankings**. ❑ *...the 25 leading teams in the world rankings.* — N-PLURAL: *the* N

[2] Someone's **ranking** is their position in an official list of the best players of a sport. ❑ *Agassi was playing well above his world ranking of 12.* — N-COUNT: usu with poss

[3] The **ranking** member of a group, usually a political group, is the most senior person in it. [AM] ❑ *...the ranking Republican on the senate intelligence committee.* — ADJ: ADJ n

**-ranking** /-ræŋkɪŋ/ **-ranking** is used to form adjectives which indicate what rank someone has in an organization. ❑ *...a colonel on trial with three lower-ranking officers.* — COMB in ADJ: ADJ n

**ran|kle** /ræŋk$^{ə}$l/ **(rankles, rankling, rankled)** If an event or situation **rankles**, it makes you feel angry or bitter afterwards, because you think it was unfair or wrong. ❑ *They paid him only £10 for it and it really rankled...* (V) *Britain's refusal to sell Portugal arms in 1937 still rankled with him...* (V *with* n) *The only thing that rankles me is what she says about Ireland.* (V n) — VERB

**ran|sack** /rænsæk/ **(ransacks, ransacking, ransacked)** If people **ransack** a building, they damage things in it or make it very untidy, often because they are looking for something in a quick and careless way. ❑ *Demonstrators ransacked and burned the house where he was staying.* (V n) — VERB

♦ **ran|sack|ing** *...the ransacking of the opposition party's offices.* — N-SING: *the* N *of* n

**ran|som** /rænsəm/ **(ransoms, ransoming, ransomed)** [1] A **ransom** is the money that has to be paid to someone so that they will set free a person they have kidnapped. ❑ *Her kidnapper successfully extorted a £175,000 ransom for her release.* — N-VAR

[2] If you **ransom** someone who has been kidnapped, you pay the money to set them free. ❑ *The same system was used for ransoming or exchanging captives.* (V n) — VERB

**PHRASES** [3] If a kidnapper **is holding** someone **to ransom** or **holding** them **ransom** in British English, or **is holding** a person **for ransom** in American English, they keep that person prisoner until they are given what they want ❑ *He is charged with kidnapping a businessman last year and holding him for ransom.* — PHRASE: V inflects

[4] If you say that someone **is holding** you **to ransom** in British English, or **holding** you **for ransom** in American English, you mean that they are using their power to try to — PHRASE: V inflects [disapproval]

force you to do something which you do not want to do. ❑ *Unison and the other unions have the power to hold the Government to ransom.*

**rant** /ræ̱nt/ **(rants, ranting, ranted)** 1 If you say that someone **rants**, you mean that they talk loudly or angrily, and exaggerate or say foolish things. ❑ *As the boss began to rant, I stood up and went out... Even their three dogs got bored and fell asleep as he ranted on... 'Let's get it over and done with, and to hell with them,' he ranted.* ♦ **Rant** is also a noun. ❑ *Part I is a rant against organised religion.* ♦ **rant\|ing (rantings)** *He had been listening to Goldstone's rantings all night.* 2 If you say that someone **rants and raves**, you mean that they talk loudly and angrily in an uncontrolled way. ❑ *I don't rant and rave or throw tea cups.*
VERB; V; V *on*; V with quote; N-COUNT; N-VAR; PHRASE: Vs inflect; disapproval

**rap** /ræ̱p/ **(raps, rapping, rapped)** 1 **Rap** is a type of music in which the words are not sung but are spoken in a rapid, rhythmic way. ❑ *Her favorite music was by Run DMC, a rap group.* 2 Someone who **raps** performs rap music. ❑ *...the unexpected pleasure of hearing the Kids not only rap but even sing.* 3 A **rap** is a piece of music performed in rap style, or the words that are used in it. ❑ *Every member contributes to the rap, singing either solo or as part of a rap chorus.* 4 If you **rap on** something or **rap** it, you hit it with a series of quick blows. ❑ *Mary Ann turned and rapped on Simon's door. ...rapping the glass with the knuckles of his right hand... A guard raps his stick on a metal hand rail.* ♦ **Rap** is also a noun. ❑ *There was a sharp rap on the door.* 5 A **rap** is a statement in a court of law that someone has committed a particular crime, or the punishment for committing it. [AM, INFORMAL] ❑ *You'll be facing a Federal rap for aiding and abetting an escaped convict.* 6 A **rap** is an act of criticizing or blaming someone. [JOURNALISM] ❑ *FA chiefs could still face a rap and a possible fine.* 7 If you **rap** someone **for** something, you criticize or blame them for it. [JOURNALISM] ❑ *Water industry chiefs were rapped yesterday for failing their customers.* 8 **The rap** about someone or something is their reputation, often a bad reputation which they do not deserve. [AM, INFORMAL] ❑ *The rap on this guy is that he doesn't really care.*
N-UNCOUNT: oft N n; VERB; V; N-COUNT; VERB; V *on* n; V n; V n *on* n; N-COUNT: usu N *on* n; N-COUNT: oft adj N *for* n/-ing; N-COUNT: usu sing; VERB; V n *for/over* n; N-SING: usu with supp

**PHRASES** 9 If someone in authority **raps** your **knuckles** or **raps** you **on the knuckles**, they criticize you or blame you for doing something they think is wrong. [JOURNALISM] ❑ *I joined the workers on strike and was rapped over the knuckles.* 10 If someone in authority gives you **a rap on the knuckles**, they criticize you or blame you for doing something they think is wrong. [JOURNALISM] ❑ *The remark earned him a rap on the knuckles.* 11 If you **take the rap**, you are blamed or punished for something, especially something that is not your fault or for which other people are equally guilty. [INFORMAL] ❑ *When the client was murdered, his wife took the rap, but did she really do it?*
PHRASE: V inflects; PHRASE: PHR after v; PHRASE: V inflects

**ra\|pa\|cious** /rəpe̱ɪʃəs/ If you describe a person or their behaviour as **rapacious**, you disapprove of their greedy or selfish behaviour. [FORMAL] ❑ *...a rapacious exploitation policy.*
ADJ: usu ADJ n; disapproval

**ra\|pac\|ity** /rəpæ̱sɪti/ **Rapacity** is very greedy or selfish behaviour. [FORMAL] ❑ *He argued that the overcrowded cities were the product of a system based on 'selfishness' and 'rapacity'.*
N-UNCOUNT: oft with poss; disapproval

**rape** /re̱ɪp/ **(rapes, raping, raped)** 1 If someone **is raped**, they are forced to have sex, usually by violence or threats of violence. ❑ *A young woman was brutally raped in her own home... They'd held him down and raped him.* 2 **Rape** is the crime of forcing someone to have sex. ❑ *Almost ninety per cent of all rapes and violent assaults went unreported.* 3 **The rape of** an area or of a country is the destruction or spoiling of it. [LITERARY] ❑ *As a result of the rape of the forests, parts of the country are now short of water.* 4 → See also **date rape**, **gang rape**, **oilseed rape**.
◆◇◇ VERB; *be* V-ed; V n; N-VAR; N-SING: *the* N *of* n

**rap\|id** /ræ̱pɪd/ 1 A **rapid** change is one that happens very quickly. ❑ *...the country's rapid economic growth throughout the 1980's. ...the rapid decline in the birth rate.* ♦ **rap\|id\|ly** *...other countries with rapidly growing populations.* ♦ **ra\|pid\|ity** /rəpɪ̱dɪti/ *...the rapidity with which the weather can change here.* 2 A **rapid** movement is one that is very fast. ❑ *He walked at a rapid pace along Charles Street. ...whether the Tunnel will provide more rapid car transport than ferries.* ♦ **rap\|id\|ly** *He was moving rapidly around the room.* ♦ **ra\|pid\|ity** *The water rushed through the holes with great rapidity.*
◆◆◇ ADJ: usu ADJ n; ADV: usu ADV with v, also ADV adj; N-UNCOUNT = speed; ADJ: usu ADJ n; ADV: ADV with v; N-UNCOUNT = speed

**rapid-fire** 1 A **rapid-fire** gun is one that shoots a lot of bullets very quickly, one after the other. ❑ *In the back of the truck was a 12.7 millimeter rapid-fire machine gun.* 2 A **rapid-fire** conversation or speech is one in which people talk or reply very quickly. ❑ *Yul listened to their sophisticated, rapid-fire conversation.* 3 A **rapid-fire** economic activity or development is one that takes place very quickly. [mainly AM, JOURNALISM] ❑ *...the rapid-fire buying and selling of stocks.*
ADJ: ADJ n; ADJ: ADJ n; ADJ: ADJ n

**rap\|ids** /ræ̱pɪdz/ **Rapids** are a section of a river where the water moves very fast, often over rocks. ❑ *His canoe was there, on the river below the rapids.*
N-PLURAL

**rap\|id trans\|it** A **rapid transit** system is a transport system in a city which allows people to travel quickly, using trains that run underground or above the streets. ❑ *...a rapid transit link with the City and London's underground system.*
ADJ: ADJ n

**ra\|pi\|er** /re̱ɪpieʳ/ **(rapiers)** 1 A **rapier** is a very thin sword with a long sharp point. 2 If you say that someone has a **rapier** wit, you mean that they are very intelligent and quick at making clever comments or jokes in a conversation. ❑ *Julie Burchill is famous for her precocity and rapier wit.*
N-COUNT; ADJ: ADJ n

**rap\|ist** /re̱ɪpɪst/ **(rapists)** A **rapist** is a man who has raped someone. ❑ *The convicted murderer and rapist is scheduled to be executed next Friday.*
N-COUNT

**rap\|pel** /ræpe̱l/ **(rappels, rappelling, rappelled)** To **rappel** down a cliff or rock face means to slide down it in a controlled way using a rope, with your feet against the cliff or rock. [AM] ❑ *They learned to rappel down a cliff.*
VERB; V prep

✔ in BRIT, use **abseil**

**rap\|per** /ræ̱pəʳ/ **(rappers)** A **rapper** is a person who performs rap music. ❑ *...rappers like MC Hammer.*
N-COUNT

**rap\|port** /ræpɔ̱ːʳ/ If two people or groups have a **rapport**, they have a good relationship in which they are able to understand each other's ideas or feelings very well. ❑ *He said he wanted 'to establish a rapport with the Indian people'... The success depends on good rapport between interviewer and interviewee.*
N-SING: also no det, oft N *with/between* n

**rap\|por\|teur** /ræ̱pɔːʳtɜ̱ːʳ/ **(rapporteurs)** A **rapporteur** is a person who is officially appointed by an organization to investigate a problem or attend a meeting and to report on it. [FORMAL] ❑ *...the United Nations special rapporteur on torture.*
N-COUNT: usu with supp

**rap\|proche\|ment** /ræprɒ̱ʃmɒn, AM -proʊ̱ʃ-/ A **rapprochement** is an increase in friendliness between two countries, groups, or people, especially after a period of unfriendliness. [FORMAL] ❑ *There have been growing signs of a rapprochement with Vietnam. ...the process of political rapprochement between the two former foes.*
N-SING: also no det, oft N *with/between* n = reconciliation

**rapt** /ræ̱pt/ If someone watches or listens with **rapt** attention, they are extremely interested or fascinated. [LITERARY] ❑ *I noticed that everyone was watching me with rapt attention.* ♦ **rapt\|ly** *...listening raptly to stories about fascinating people.*
ADJ: usu ADJ n; ADV: ADV with v

**rap\|tor** /ræ̱ptəʳ/ **(raptors) Raptors** are birds of prey, such as eagles and hawks. [TECHNICAL]
N-COUNT

**rap\|ture** /ræ̱ptʃəʳ/ **Rapture** is a feeling of extreme happiness or pleasure. [LITERARY] ❑ *The film*
N-UNCOUNT = delight

*was shown to gasps of rapture at the Democratic Convention.*

**rap|tures** /ræptʃəʳz/ If you are **in raptures** or go **into raptures** about something, you are extremely impressed by it and enthusiastic about it. [mainly BRIT, WRITTEN] ❑ *They will be in raptures over the French countryside.* PHRASE: v-link PHR, PHR after v

**rap|tur|ous** /ræptʃərəs/ A **rapturous** feeling or reaction is one of extreme happiness or enthusiasm. [JOURNALISM] ❑ *The students gave him a rapturous welcome.* ADJ: usu ADJ n

**rare** /reəʳ/ **(rarer, rarest)** 1 Something that is **rare** is not common and is therefore interesting or valuable. ❑ *...the black-necked crane, one of the rarest species in the world... She collects rare plants.* ◆◇◇ ADJ ≠ common 2 An event or situation that is **rare** does not occur very often. ❑ *...on those rare occasions when he did eat alone... Heart attacks were extremely rare in babies, he said.* ADJ: oft *it* v-link ADJ to-inf = uncommon ≠ common 3 You use **rare** to emphasize an extremely good or remarkable quality. ❑ *Ferris has a rare ability to record her observations on paper.* ADJ: ADJ n emphasis 4 Meat that is **rare** is cooked very lightly so that the inside is still red. ❑ *Thick tuna steaks are eaten rare, like beef.* ADJ

**rar|efied** /reərɪfaɪd/ 1 If you talk about the **rarefied** atmosphere of a place or institution, you are expressing your disapproval of it, because it has a special social or academic status that makes it very different from ordinary life. ❑ *It is important for the state's future administrators to get out of the rarefied air of the capital.* ADJ: usu ADJ n disapproval 2 **Rarefied** air is air that does not contain much oxygen, for example in mountain areas. ❑ *...living at very high altitudes where the atmosphere is rarefied.* ADJ

**rare|ly** /reəʳli/ If something **rarely** happens, it does not happen very often. ❑ *They battled against other Indian tribes, but rarely fought with the whites... Money was plentiful, and rarely did anyone seem very bothered about levels of expenditure.* ◆◇◇ ADV: ADV before v, ADV with cl/group = seldom ≠ often

**rar|ing** /reərɪŋ/ 1 If you say that you **are raring to go**, you mean that you are very eager to start doing something. ❑ *After a good night's sleep, Paul said he was raring to go.* PHRASE: V inflects 2 If you are **raring to** do something or are **raring for** it, you are very eager to do it or very eager that it should happen. ❑ *He is raring to charge into the fray and lay down the law... Baker suggested the administration wasn't raring for a fight.* ADJ: v-link ADJ, ADJ to-inf, ADJ *for* n

**rar|ity** /reərɪti/ **(rarities)** 1 If someone or something is a **rarity**, they are interesting or valuable because they are so unusual. [JOURNALISM] ❑ *Sontag has always been that rarity, a glamorous intellectual.* N-COUNT: usu sing, oft N *in/among* n 2 The **rarity** of something is the fact that it is very uncommon. ❑ *It was a real prize due to its rarity and good condition.* N-UNCOUNT: oft with poss

**ras|cal** /rɑːskəl, ræs-/ **(rascals)** If you call a man or child a **rascal**, you mean that they behave badly and are rude or dishonest. [OLD-FASHIONED] ❑ *What's that old rascal been telling you?* N-COUNT

**ras|cal|ly** /rɑːskəli, ræs-/ If you describe someone as a **rascally** person, you mean that they behave badly and are wicked or dishonest. [LITERARY] ❑ *They stumble across a ghost town inhabited by a rascally gold prospector.* ADJ: usu ADJ n

**rash** /ræʃ/ **(rashes)** 1 If someone is **rash** or does **rash** things, they act without thinking carefully first, and therefore make mistakes or behave foolishly. ❑ *It would be rash to rely on such evidence... Mr. Major is making no rash promises.* ADJ ♦ **rash|ly** *I made quite a lot of money, but I rashly gave most of it away.* ADV: ADV with cl, ADV after v ♦ **rash|ness** *With characteristic rashness and valor, Peter plunged into the icy water.* N-UNCOUNT 2 A **rash** is an area of red spots that appears on your skin when you are ill or have a bad reaction to something that you have eaten or touched. ❑ *He may break out in a rash when he eats these nuts.* N-COUNT 3 If you talk about a **rash of** events or things, you mean a large number of unpleasant events or undesirable things, which have happened or appeared within a short period of time. ❑ *...one of the few major airlines left untouched by the industry's rash of takeovers.* N-SING: N *of* n = spate

**rash|er** /ræʃəʳ/ **(rashers)** A **rasher** of bacon is a slice of bacon. [BRIT] N-COUNT: oft N *of* n

in AM, use **slice**

**rasp** /rɑːsp, ræsp/ **(rasps, rasping, rasped)** 1 If someone **rasps**, their voice or breathing is harsh and unpleasant to listen to. ❑ *'Where've you put it?' he rasped... He fell back into the water, his breath rasping in his heaving chest.* VERB V with quote V ♦ **Rasp** is also a noun. ❑ *He was still laughing when he heard the rasp of Rennie's voice.* N-SING: with supp 2 If something **rasps** or if you **rasp** it, it makes a harsh, unpleasant sound as it rubs against something hard or rough. ❑ *Sabres rasped from scabbards and the horsemen spurred forward... Foden rasped a hand across his chin.* VERB V prep V n prep ♦ **Rasp** is also a noun. ❑ *...the rasp of something being drawn across the sand.* N-SING: with supp

**rasp|berry** /rɑːzbri, AM ræzberi/ **(raspberries)** **Raspberries** are small, soft, red fruit that grow on bushes. ➔ See picture on page 1711. N-COUNT

**raspy** /rɑːspi, ræs-/ If someone has a **raspy** voice, they make rough sounds as if they have a sore throat or have difficulty in breathing. [LITERARY] ❑ *Both men sang in a deep, raspy tone.* ADJ

**Ras|ta** /ræstə/ **(Rastas)** 1 A **Rasta** is the same as a **Rastafarian**. [INFORMAL] ❑ *The LP was called Rastas Never Die.* N-COUNT 2 **Rasta** means the same as **Rastafarian**. [INFORMAL] ❑ *...Rasta singer Pablo Moses.* ADJ: ADJ n

**Ras|ta|far|ian** /ræstəfeəriən/ **(Rastafarians)** 1 A **Rastafarian** is a member of a Jamaican religious group which considers Haile Selassie, the former Emperor of Ethiopia, to be God. Rastafarians often have long hair which they wear in a hairstyle called dreadlocks. ❑ *He was one of the few thousand committed Rastafarians in South Africa.* N-COUNT 2 **Rastafarian** is used to describe Rastafarians and their beliefs and lifestyle. ❑ *...Rastafarian poet Benjamin Zephaniah.* ADJ: ADJ n

**rat** /ræt/ **(rats, ratting, ratted)** 1 A **rat** is an animal which has a long tail and looks like a large mouse. ❑ *This was demonstrated in a laboratory experiment with rats.* N-COUNT 2 If you call someone a **rat**, you mean that you are angry with them or dislike them, often because they have cheated you or betrayed you. [INFORMAL] ❑ *What did you do with the gun you took from that little rat Turner?* N-COUNT disapproval 3 If someone **rats on** you, they tell someone in authority about things that you have done, especially bad things. [INFORMAL] ❑ *They were accused of encouraging children to rat on their parents.* VERB V *on* n 4 If someone **rats on** an agreement, they do not do what they said they would do. [INFORMAL] ❑ *She claims he ratted on their divorce settlement.* VERB V *on* n 5 If you **smell a rat**, you begin to suspect or realize that something is wrong in a particular situation, for example that someone is trying to deceive you or harm you. ❑ *If I don't send a picture, he will smell a rat.* PHRASE: V inflects

**ra|ta** /rɑːtə/ ➔ see **pro rata**.

**rat-a-tat** You use **rat-a-tat** to represent a series of sharp, repeated sounds, for example the sound of someone knocking at a door. ❑ *...the rat-a-tat at the door.* N-SING; SOUND

**ra|ta|touille** /rætətuːi/ **Ratatouille** is a cooked dish made with vegetables such as tomatoes, onions, aubergines, courgettes, and peppers. N-UNCOUNT: also *a* N

**rat|bag** /rætbæg/ **(ratbags)** If you call someone a **ratbag**, you are insulting them. [BRIT, INFORMAL] ❑ *Lying ratbags, that's what they are.* N-COUNT disapproval

**ratch|et** /rætʃɪt/ **(ratchets, ratcheting, ratcheted)** 1 In a tool or machine, a **ratchet** is a wheel or bar with sloping teeth, which can move only in one direction, because a piece of metal stops the teeth from moving backwards. ❑ *The chair has a ratchet below it to adjust the height.* N-COUNT 2 If a tool or machine **ratchets** or if you **ratchet** it, it makes a clicking noise as it operates, because it has a ratchet in it. ❑ *The rod bent double, the reel shrieked and ratcheted... She took up a sheet and* VERB V V n *ratcheted it into the typewriter.* [3] If you describe a situation as a **ratchet**, you mean that it is bad and can only become worse. [mainly BRIT] ❑ *...another raising of the ratchet of violence in the conflict.* N-SING: with supp

♦ **ratchet down** If something **ratchets down** or **is ratcheted down**, it decreases by a fixed amount or degree, and seems unlikely to increase again. [mainly JOURNALISM] ❑ *We're trying to ratchet down the administrative costs.* PHRASAL VERB ≠ratchet up; V P n (not pron) Also V n P

♦ **ratchet up** If something **ratchets up** or **is ratcheted up**, it increases by a fixed amount or degree, and seems unlikely to decrease again. [JOURNALISM] ❑ *...an attempt to ratchet up the pressure... He fears inflation will ratchet up as the year ends.* PHRASAL VERB ≠ratchet down; V P n (not pron); V P

**rate** /reɪt/ **(rates, rating, rated)** ◆◆◆ [1] The **rate** at which something happens is the speed with which it happens. ❑ *The rate at which hair grows can be agonisingly slow... The world's tropical forests are disappearing at an even faster rate than experts had thought.* N-COUNT: with supp [2] The **rate** at which something happens is the number of times it happens over a period of time. ❑ *New diet books appear at a rate of nearly one a week... His heart rate was 30 beats per minute slower.* N-COUNT: with supp [3] A **rate** is the amount of money that is charged for goods or services. ❑ *Calls cost 36p per minute cheap rate and 48p at all other times. ...specially reduced rates for travellers using Gatwick Airport.* ➔ See also **exchange rate**. N-COUNT: with supp [4] The **rate** of taxation or interest is the amount of tax or interest that needs to be paid. It is expressed as a percentage of the amount that is earned, gained as profit, or borrowed. [BUSINESS] ❑ *The government insisted that it would not be panicked into interest rate cuts.* N-COUNT: with supp [5] If you **rate** someone or something as good or bad, you consider them to be good or bad. You can also say that someone or something **rates** as good or bad. ❑ *Of all the men in the survey, they rate themselves the least fun-loving and the most responsible... Most rated it a hit... We rate him as one of the best... She rated the course highly... Reading books does not rate highly among Britons as a leisure activity. ...the most highly rated player in English football.* VERB: no cont; V n adj; V n n; V n *as* n/adj; V n adv; V adv prep; V-ed [6] If you **rate** someone or something, you think that they are good. [mainly BRIT, INFORMAL] ❑ *It's flattering to know that other clubs have shown interest and seem to rate me.* VERB; V n [7] If someone or something **is rated** at a particular position or rank, they are calculated or considered to be in that position on a list. ❑ *He is generally rated Italy's No. 3 industrialist... He came here rated 100th on the tennis computer.* V-PASSIVE: no cont; *be* V-ed n; *be* V-ed ord [8] If you say that someone or something **rates** a particular reaction, you mean that this is the reaction you consider to be appropriate. ❑ *This is so extraordinary, it rates a medal and a phone call from the President.* VERB: no cont = merit; V n [9] ➔ See also **rating**.

PHRASES [10] You use **at any rate** to indicate that what you have just said might be incorrect or unclear in some way, and that you are now being more precise. ❑ *She modestly suggests that 'sex, or at any rate gender, may account for the difference'.* PHRASE: PHR with cl [11] You use **at any rate** to indicate that the important thing is what you are saying now, and not what was said before. ❑ *Well, at any rate, let me thank you for all you did.* PHRASE: PHR with cl [12] If you say that **at this rate** something bad or extreme will happen, you mean that it will happen if things continue to develop as they have been doing. ❑ *At this rate they'd be lucky to get home before eight-thirty or nine.* PHRASE: PHR with cl

**rate|able value** /reɪtəbəl væljuː/ **(rateable values)** In Britain, the **rateable value** of a building was a value based on its size and facilities, which was used in calculating local taxes called rates. N-COUNT

**rate-cap (rate-caps, rate-capping, rate-capped)** [1] In Britain, when a local council was **rate-capped**, the government prevented it from increasing local taxes called rates, in order to force the council to reduce its spending or make it more efficient. ❑ *Notts County Council is to cut 200 jobs in a bid to escape being rate-capped.* VERB: usu passive; *be* V-ed ♦ **rate-capping** *The project is seriously threatened by rate-capping.* N-UNCOUNT [2] A **rate cap** is a limit placed by the government on the amount of interest that banks or credit card companies can charge their customers. [AM] N-COUNT

**rate of ex|change (rates of exchange)** A **rate of exchange** is the same as an **exchange rate**. ❑ *...four thousand dinars – about four hundred dollars at the official rate of exchange.* N-COUNT = exchange rate

**rate of re|turn (rates of return)** The **rate of return** on an investment is the amount of profit it makes, often shown as a percentage of the original investment. [BUSINESS] ❑ *High rates of return can be earned on these investments.* N-COUNT

**rate|payer** /reɪtpeɪəʳ/ **(ratepayers)** [1] In Britain, a **ratepayer** was a person who owned or rented property and therefore had to pay local taxes called rates. The citizens of a district are sometimes still called the **ratepayers** when their interests and the use of local taxes are being considered. N-COUNT [2] In the United States, a **ratepayer** is a person whose property is served by an electricity, water, or telephone company, and who pays for these services. N-COUNT

**ra|ther** /rɑːðəʳ, ræð-/ ◆◆◆ [1] You use **rather than** when you are contrasting two things or situations. **Rather than** introduces the thing or situation that is not true or that you do not want. ❑ *The problem was psychological rather than physiological... When I'm going out in the evening I use the bike if I can rather than the car.* PREP-PHRASE ♦ **Rather** is also a conjunction. ❑ *She made students think for themselves, rather than telling them what to think.* CONJ [2] You use **rather** when you are correcting something that you have just said, especially when you are describing a particular situation after saying what it is not. ❑ *He explained what the Crux is, or rather, what it was.* ADV: ADV with cl/group [3] If you say that you **would rather** do something or you**'d rather** do it, you mean that you would prefer to do it. If you say that you **would rather not** do something, you mean that you do not want to do it. ❑ *If it's all the same to you, I'd rather work at home... Kids would rather play than study... I would rather Lionel took it on... Sorry. I'd rather not talk about it... Would you like that? Don't hesitate to say no if you'd rather not.* PHRASE; MODAL inf; MODAL inf *than* inf; MODAL that; MODAL *not* inf; MODAL *not* [4] You use **rather** to indicate that something is true to a fairly great extent, especially when you are talking about something unpleasant or undesirable. ❑ *I grew up in rather unusual circumstances... The first speaker began to talk, very fast and rather loudly... I'm afraid it's rather a long story... The reality is rather more complex... The fruit is rather like a sweet chestnut.* ADV: ADV adj/adv, ADV *a* n, ADV compar, ADV *too* adj/adv, ADV prep [5] You use **rather** before verbs that introduce your thoughts and feelings, in order to express your opinion politely, especially when a different opinion has been expressed. ❑ *I rather think he was telling the truth.* ADV: ADV before v; politeness

**rati|fi|ca|tion** /rætɪfɪkeɪʃən/ **(ratifications)** The **ratification** of a treaty or written agreement is the process of ratifying it. ❑ *The EU will now complete ratification of the treaty by June 1.* N-VAR: usu sing, oft N *of* n

**rati|fy** /rætɪfaɪ/ **(ratifies, ratifying, ratified)** When national leaders or organizations **ratify** a treaty or written agreement, they make it official by giving their formal approval to it, usually by signing it or voting for it. ❑ *The parliaments of Australia and Indonesia have yet to ratify the treaty.* VERB; V n

**rat|ing** /reɪtɪŋ/ **(ratings)** ◆◇◇ [1] A **rating** of something is a score or measurement of how good or popular it is. ❑ *...a value-for-money rating of ten out of ten.* ➔ See also **credit rating**. N-COUNT: usu with supp [2] The **ratings** are the statistics published each week which show how popular each television programme is. ❑ *CBS's ratings again showed huge improvement over the previous year.* N-PLURAL

**ra|tio** /reɪʃioʊ, AM -ʃoʊ/ **(ratios)** A **ratio** is a relationship between two things when it is expressed in numbers or amounts. For example, if there are ten boys and thirty girls in a room, the N-COUNT: usu sing, oft N *of* n *to* n ratio of boys to girls is 1:3, or one to three. ❑ *The adult to child ratio is 1 to 6.*

**ra|tion** /ræʃᵊn/ **(rations, rationing, rationed)** 1 *N-COUNT* When there is not enough of something, your **ration** of it is the amount that you are allowed to have. ❑ *The meat ration was down to one pound per person per week.* 2 *VERB* When something **is rationed** by a person or government, you are only allowed to have a limited amount of it, usually because there is not enough of it. ❑ *be V-ed* *Staples such as bread, rice and tea are already being rationed.* *V n* *...the decision to ration food...* *be V-ed to amount* *Motorists will be rationed to thirty litres of petrol a month.* 3 *N-PLURAL* **Rations** are the food which is given to people who do not have enough food or to soldiers. ❑ *Aid officials said that the first emergency food rations of wheat and oil were handed out here last month.* 4 *N-COUNT: usu N of n* Your **ration of** something is the amount of it that you normally have. ❑ *...after consuming his ration of junk food and two cigarettes.* 5 ➔ See also **rationing**.

**ra|tion|al** /ræʃənəl/ 1 *ADJ: usu ADJ n ≠ irrational* **Rational** decisions and thoughts are based on reason rather than on emotion. ❑ *He's asking you to look at both sides of the case and come to a rational decision.* ♦ **ra|tion|al|ly** *ADV: usu ADV with v* *It can be very hard to think rationally when you're feeling so vulnerable and alone.* ♦ **ra|tion|al|ity** /ræʃənælɪti/ *N-UNCOUNT* *We live in an era of rationality.* 2 *ADJ ≠ irrational* A **rational** person is someone who is sensible and is able to make decisions based on intelligent thinking rather than on emotion. ❑ *Did he come across as a sane rational person?*

**ra|tion|ale** /ræʃənɑːl, -næl/ **(rationales)** *N-COUNT: oft N for n/-ing* The **rationale** for a course of action, practice, or belief is the set of reasons on which it is based. [FORMAL] ❑ *However, the rationale for such initiatives is not, of course, solely economic.*

**ra|tion|al|ism** /ræʃənəlɪzəm/ *N-UNCOUNT* **Rationalism** is the belief that your life should be based on reason and logic, rather than emotions or religious beliefs. ❑ *Coleridge was to spend the next thirty years attacking rationalism.*

**ra|tion|al|ist** /ræʃənəlɪst/ **(rationalists)** 1 *ADJ* If you describe someone as **rationalist**, you mean that their beliefs are based on reason and logic rather than emotion or religion. ❑ *White was both visionary and rationalist.* 2 *N-COUNT* If you describe someone as a **rationalist**, you mean that they base their life on rationalist beliefs. 3 ➔ See also **rationalism**.

**ra|tion|al|ize** /ræʃənəlaɪz/ **(rationalizes, rationalizing, rationalized)**

in BRIT, also use **rationalise**

1 *VERB* If you try to **rationalize** attitudes or actions that are difficult to accept, you think of reasons to justify or explain them. ❑ *V n* *He further rationalized his activity by convincing himself that he was actually promoting peace.* 2 *VERB: usu passive = streamline* When a company, system, or industry **is rationalized**, it is made more efficient, usually by getting rid of staff and equipment that are not essential. [mainly BRIT, BUSINESS] ❑ *be V-ed* *The network of 366 local offices is being rationalised to leave the company with 150 to 200 larger branch offices.* ♦ **ra|tion|ali|za|tion** *N-UNCOUNT* *...the rationalization of the textile industry.*

**ra|tion|ing** /ræʃənɪŋ/ *N-UNCOUNT: usu with supp* **Rationing** is the system of limiting the amount of food, water, petrol, or other necessary substances that each person is allowed to have or buy when there is not enough of them. ❑ *The municipal authorities here are preparing for food rationing.*

**rat pack** *N-SING: usu the N [disapproval]* People sometimes refer to the group of journalists and photographers who follow famous people around as **the rat pack**, especially when they think that their behaviour is unacceptable. [BRIT]

**rat race** *N-SING: the N* If you talk about getting out of **the rat race**, you mean leaving a job or way of life in which people compete aggressively with each other to be successful. ❑ *I had to get out of the rat race and take a look at the real world again.*

**rat run** **(rat runs)** *N-COUNT* A **rat run** is a small street which drivers use during busy times in order to avoid heavy traffic on the main roads. [BRIT, INFORMAL]

**rat|tan** /rætæn/ *N-UNCOUNT: usu N n* **Rattan** furniture is made from the woven strips of stems of a plant which grows in South East Asia. ❑ *...a light airy room set with cloth-covered tables and rattan chairs.*

**rat|tle** /rætᵊl/ **(rattles, rattling, rattled)** 1 *VERB* When something **rattles** or when you **rattle** it, it makes short sharp knocking sounds because it is being shaken or it keeps hitting against something hard. ❑ *V* *She slams the kitchen door so hard I hear dishes rattle...* *V n* *He gently rattled the cage and whispered to the canary.* ♦ *N-COUNT* **Rattle** is also a noun. ❑ *There was a rattle of rifle-fire.* ♦ **rat|tling** *N-SING* *At that moment, there was a rattling at the door.* 2 *N-COUNT* A **rattle** is a baby's toy with loose bits inside which make a noise when the baby shakes it. 3 *N-COUNT* A **rattle** is a wooden instrument that people shake to make a loud knocking noise at football matches or tribal ceremonies. 4 *VERB = unnerve* If something or someone **rattles** you, they make you nervous. ❑ *V n* *She refused to be rattled by his £3,000-a-day lawyer.* ♦ **rat|tled** *ADJ: usu v-link ADJ* *He swore in Spanish, another indication that he was rattled.* 5 *VERB* You can say that a bus, train or car **rattles** somewhere when it moves noisily from one place to another. ❑ *V prep/adv* *The bus from Odense rattled into a dusty village called Pozo Almonte.*

♦ **rattle around** *PHRASAL VERB* If you say that someone **rattles around** in a room or other space, you mean that the space is too large for them. ❑ *V P in n* *Also V P n* *We don't want to move, but we're rattling around in our large house.*

♦ **rattle off** *PHRASAL VERB = reel off* If you **rattle off** something, you say it or do it very quickly and without much effort. ❑ *V P n (not pron)* *Also V n P* *Hendry, playing an afternoon match, rattled off a 6-1 win over the Englishman.*

♦ **rattle through** *PHRASAL VERB* If you **rattle through** something, you deal with it quickly in order to finish it. [mainly BRIT] ❑ *V P n* *She rattled through a translation from Virgil's Aeneid.*

**rat|tler** /rætləʳ/ **(rattlers)** *N-COUNT* A **rattler** is the same as a **rattlesnake**. [AM, INFORMAL]

**rattle|snake** /rætᵊlsneɪk/ **(rattlesnakes)** *N-COUNT* A **rattlesnake** is a poisonous American snake which can make a rattling noise with its tail.

**rat|ty** /ræti/ **(rattier, rattiest)** 1 *ADJ = irritable* If someone is **ratty**, they get angry and irritated easily. [BRIT, INFORMAL] ❑ *I had spent too many hours there and was beginning to get a bit ratty and fed up.* 2 *ADJ* **Ratty** clothes and objects are torn or in bad condition, especially because they are old. [AM] ❑ *...my ratty old flannel pyjamas.*

**rau|cous** /rɔːkəs/ *ADJ: usu ADJ n* A **raucous** sound is loud, harsh, and rather unpleasant. ❑ *They heard a bottle being smashed, followed by more raucous laughter.* ♦ **rau|cous|ly** *ADV: usu ADV with v* *They laughed together raucously.*

**raun|chy** /rɔːntʃi/ **(raunchier, raunchiest)** *ADJ* If a film, a person, or the way that someone is dressed is **raunchy**, they are sexually exciting. [INFORMAL] ❑ *...her raunchy new movie.*

**rav|age** /rævɪdʒ/ **(ravages, ravaging, ravaged)** *VERB: usu passive* A town, country, or economy that **has been ravaged** is one that has been damaged so much that it is almost completely destroyed. ❑ *be V-ed* *For two decades the country has been ravaged by civil war and foreign intervention.* *V-ed* *...Nicaragua's ravaged economy.*

**rav|ages** /rævɪdʒiz/ *N-PLURAL: usu the N of n* **The ravages of** time, war, or the weather are the damaging effects that they have. ❑ *...a hi-tech grass pitch that can survive the ravages of a cold, wet climate.*

**rave** /reɪv/ **(raves, raving, raved)** 1 *VERB* If someone **raves**, they talk in an excited and uncontrolled way. ❑ *V* *She cried and raved for weeks, and people did not know what to do...* *V with quote* *'What is wrong with you, acting like that,' she raved, pacing up and down frantically.* 2 *VERB* If you **rave about** something, you speak or write about it with great enthusiasm. ❑ *V about n* *Rachel* *raved about the new foods she ate while she was there... 'Such lovely clothes. I'd no idea Milan was so wonderful,' she raved.* V with quote [3] A **rave** is a big event at which young people dance to electronic music in a large building or in the open air. Raves are often associated with illegal drugs. [BRIT] ❑ *...an all-night rave at Castle Donington.* N-COUNT ♦ **Rave** is also an adjective. ❑ *Old faces and new talents are making it big on the rave scene.* ADJ: ADJ n [4] → See also **raving**. to **rant and rave** → see **rant**.

**ra|ven** /reɪvᵊn/ **(ravens)** A **raven** is a large bird with shiny black feathers and a deep harsh call. N-COUNT

**rav|en|ous** /rævənəs/ If you are **ravenous**, you are extremely hungry. ❑ *Amy realized that she had eaten nothing since leaving Bruton Street, and she was ravenous.* ADJ = starving ♦ **rav|en|ous|ly** *She began to eat ravenously.* ADV

**rav|er** /reɪvəʳ/ **(ravers)** A **raver** is a young person who has a busy social life and goes to a lot of parties, raves, or nightclubs. [BRIT, INFORMAL] N-COUNT

**rave re|view** **(rave reviews)** When journalists write **rave reviews**, they praise something such as a play or book in a very enthusiastic way. ❑ *The play received rave reviews from the critics.* N-COUNT: usu pl

**ra|vine** /rəviːn/ **(ravines)** A **ravine** is a very deep narrow valley with steep sides. ❑ *The bus is said to have overturned and fallen into a ravine.* N-COUNT = gorge

**rav|ing** /reɪvɪŋ/ [1] You use **raving** to describe someone who you think is completely mad. [INFORMAL] ❑ *Malcolm looked at her as if she were a raving lunatic.* ADJ: usu ADJ n ♦ **Raving** is also an adverb. ❑ *I'm afraid Jean-Paul has gone raving mad.* ADV: ADV adj [2] → See also **rave**.

**rav|ings** /reɪvɪŋz/ If you describe what someone says or writes as their **ravings**, you mean that it makes no sense because they are mad or very ill. ❑ *Haig and Robertson saw it as the lunatic ravings of a mad politician.* N-PLURAL: usu the N of n

**ra|vio|li** /rævioʊli/ **(raviolis)** **Ravioli** is a type of pasta that is shaped into small squares, filled with minced meat or cheese and served in a sauce. N-MASS

**rav|ish** /rævɪʃ/ **(ravishes, ravishing, ravished)** If a woman **is ravished** by a man, she is raped by him. [LITERARY] ❑ *She'll never know how close she came to being dragged off and ravished.* VERB: usu passive be V-ed

**rav|ish|ing** /rævɪʃɪŋ/ If you describe someone or something as **ravishing**, you mean that they are very beautiful. [LITERARY] ❑ *She looked ravishing.* ADJ

**raw** /rɔː/ **(rawer, rawest)** [1] **Raw** materials or substances are in their natural state before being processed or used in manufacturing. ❑ *We import raw materials and energy and export mainly industrial products. ...two ships carrying raw sugar from Cuba.* ♦◇◇ ADJ: usu ADJ n [2] **Raw** food is food that is eaten uncooked, that has not yet been cooked, or that has not been cooked enough. ❑ *...a popular dish made of raw fish... This versatile vegetable can be eaten raw or cooked.* ADJ [3] If a part of your body is **raw**, it is red and painful, perhaps because the skin has come off or has been burnt. ❑ *...the drag of the rope against the raw flesh of my shoulders.* ADJ [4] **Raw** emotions are strong basic feelings or responses which are not weakened by other influences. ❑ *Her grief was still raw and he did not know how to help her.* ADJ: usu ADJ n [5] If you describe something as **raw**, you mean that it is simple, powerful, and real. ❑ *...the raw power of instinct.* ADJ: usu ADJ n [6] **Raw** data is facts or information that has not yet been sorted, analysed, or prepared for use. ❑ *Analyses were conducted on the raw data.* ADJ: usu ADJ n [7] If you describe someone in a new job as **raw**, or as a **raw** recruit, you mean that they lack experience in that job. ❑ *...replacing experienced men with raw recruits.* ADJ: usu ADJ n = inexperienced ≠ experienced [8] **Raw** weather feels unpleasantly cold. ❑ *...a raw December morning.* ADJ = bitter [9] **Raw** sewage is sewage that has not been treated to make it cleaner. ❑ *...contamination of bathing water by raw sewage.* ADJ: ADJ n = untreated [10] If you say that you are getting **a raw deal**, you mean that you are being treated unfairly. [INFORMAL] ❑ *I think women have a raw deal.* PHRASE: V PHR ≠ a fair deal [11] to **touch a raw nerve** → see **nerve**.

**raw|hide** /rɔːhaɪd/ **Rawhide** is leather that comes from cattle, and has not been treated or tanned. [AM] ❑ *At his belt he carried a rawhide whip.* N-UNCOUNT: usu N n

**ray** /reɪ/ **(rays)** [1] **Rays** of light are narrow beams of light. ❑ *...the first rays of light spread over the horizon... The sun's rays can penetrate water up to 10 feet.* ♦◇◇ N-COUNT → See also **cosmic rays, gamma rays, X-ray**. [2] A **ray of** hope, comfort, or other positive quality is a small amount of it that you welcome because it makes a bad situation seem less bad. ❑ *They could provide a ray of hope amid the general business and economic gloom.* N-COUNT: N of n = glimmer

**ray|on** /reɪɒn/ **Rayon** is a smooth artificial fabric that is made from cellulose. ❑ *...the old woman's rayon dress.* N-UNCOUNT: oft N n

**raze** /reɪz/ **(razes, razing, razed)** If buildings, villages or towns **are razed** or **razed** to the ground, they are completely destroyed. ❑ *Dozens of villages have been razed... Towns such as Mittelwihr and Bennwihr were virtually razed to the ground.* VERB: usu passive be V-ed be V-ed to n

**ra|zor** /reɪzəʳ/ **(razors)** A **razor** is a tool that people use for shaving. N-COUNT

**ra|zor blade** **(razor blades)** A **razor blade** is a small flat piece of metal with a very sharp edge which is put into a razor and used for shaving. N-COUNT

**razor-sharp** [1] A cutting tool that is **razor-sharp** is extremely sharp. ❑ *...a razor sharp butcher's knife.* ADJ: usu ADJ n [2] If you describe someone or someone's mind as **razor-sharp**, you mean that they have a very accurate and clear understanding of things. ❑ *...his razor-sharp intelligence.* ADJ

**ra|zor wire** **Razor wire** is strong wire with sharp blades sticking out of it. In wars or civil conflict it is sometimes used to prevent people from entering or leaving buildings or areas of land. ❑ *...plans to use razor wire to seal off hostels for migrant workers.* N-UNCOUNT

**razz** /ræz/ **(razzes, razzing, razzed)** To **razz** someone means to tease them, especially in an unkind way. [mainly AM, INFORMAL] ❑ *Molly razzed me about my rotten sense of direction.* VERB V n

**razz|a|ma|tazz** /ræzəmətæz/ **Razzamatazz** is the same as **razzmatazz**. [mainly BRIT] N-UNCOUNT

**razzle-dazzle** /ræzᵊl dæzᵊl/ **Razzle-dazzle** is the same as **razzmatazz**. ❑ *...a razzle-dazzle marketing man.* N-UNCOUNT: oft N n

**razz|ma|tazz** /ræzmətæz/ **Razzmatazz** is a noisy and showy display. ❑ *...the colour and razzmatazz of a US election.* N-UNCOUNT

**RC** /ɑːʳ siː/ also **R.C.** **RC** is an abbreviation for **Roman Catholic**. ❑ *...St Mary's RC Cathedral.* ♦◇◇ ADJ

**Rd** also **Rd.** **Rd** is a written abbreviation for **road**. It is used especially in addresses and on maps or signs. ❑ *St Pancras Library, 100 Euston Rd, London, NW1.*

**-rd** **-rd** is added to numbers that end in 3, except those ending in 13, in order to form ordinal numbers such as 3rd or 33rd. 3rd is pronounced 'third'. ❑ *...September 3rd 1990. ...the 33rd Boston Marathon. ...Canada's 123rd birthday.*

**RDA** /ɑːʳ diː eɪ/ **(RDAs)** The **RDA** of a particular vitamin or mineral is the amount that people need each day to stay healthy. **RDA** is an abbreviation for 'recommended daily amount'. N-COUNT: usu singular

**re** /riː/ You use **re** in business letters, faxes, or other documents to introduce a subject or item which you are going to discuss or refer to in detail. ❑ *Dear Mrs Cox, Re: Household Insurance. We note from our files that we have not yet received your renewal instructions.* = regarding

**re-**

> ✔ Usually pronounced /riː-/ for meaning 1, and before an unstressed syllable for meanings 2 and 3. Otherwise the pronunciation is /ri-/ before a vowel sound and /rɪ-/ before a consonant sound.

1 **Re-** is added to verbs and nouns to form new verbs and nouns that refer to the repeating of an action or process. For example, to 're-read' something means to read it again, and someone's 're-election' is their being elected again. PREFIX 2 **Re-** is added to verbs and nouns to form new verbs and nouns that refer to a process opposite to one that has already taken place. For example, to 'reappear' means to appear after disappearing, and to 'regain' something means to gain it after you have lost it. PREFIX 3 **Re-** is added to verbs and nouns to form new verbs and nouns which describe a change in the position or state of something. For example, to 'relocate' something means to locate it in a different place and to 'rearrange' something means to arrange it in a different way. PREFIX

**R.E.** /ɑːr iː/ **R.E.** is a school subject in which children learn about religion and other social matters. **R.E.** is an abbreviation for 'religious education'. [BRIT] N-UNCOUNT

**-'re** /əʳ/ **-'re** is the usual spoken form of 'are'. It is added to the end of the pronoun or noun which is the subject of the verb. For example, 'they are' can be shortened to 'they're'.

**reach** /riːtʃ/ **(reaches, reaching, reached)** ◆◆◆ 1 When someone or something **reaches** a place, they arrive there. ❑ *He did not stop until he reached the door... He reached Cambridge shortly before three o'clock.* VERB V n V n 2 If someone or something has **reached** a certain stage, level, or amount, they are at that stage, level, or amount. ❑ *The process of political change in South Africa has reached the stage where it is irreversible... We're told the figure could reach 100,000 next year.* VERB V n V n 3 If you **reach** somewhere, you move your arm and hand to take or touch something. ❑ *Judy reached into her handbag and handed me a small printed leaflet... He reached up for an overhanging branch.* VERB V prep/adv V prep/adv 4 If you can **reach** something, you are able to touch it by stretching out your arm or leg. ❑ *Can you reach your toes with your fingertips?* VERB V n 5 If you try to **reach** someone, you try to contact them, usually by telephone. ❑ *Has the doctor told you how to reach him or her in emergencies?* VERB = contact V n 6 If something **reaches** a place, point, or level, it extends as far as that place, point, or level. ❑ *...a nightshirt which reached to his knees... The water level in Lake Taihu has reached record levels.* VERB V to n V n 7 When people **reach** an agreement or a decision, they succeed in achieving it. ❑ *A meeting of agriculture ministers in Luxembourg today has so far failed to reach agreement over farm subsidies... They are meeting in Lusaka in an attempt to reach a compromise.* VERB V n V n 8 Someone's or something's **reach** is the distance or limit to which they can stretch, extend, or travel. ❑ *Isabelle placed a wine cup on the table within his reach.* N-UNCOUNT: oft poss N 9 If a place or thing is within **reach**, it is possible to have it or get to it. If it is out of **reach**, it is not possible to have it or get to it. ❑ *It is located within reach of many important Norman towns, including Bayeux... The price is ten times what it normally is and totally beyond the reach of ordinary people.* N-UNCOUNT

**reaches** /riːtʃiz/ 1 The upper, middle, or lower **reaches** of a river are parts of a river. The upper **reaches** are nearer to the river's source and the lower **reaches** are nearer to the sea into which it flows. ❑ *This year water levels in the middle and lower reaches of the Yangtze are unusually high.* N-PLURAL: usu the adj N of n 2 You can refer to the distant or outer parts of a place or area as the far, farthest, or outer **reaches**. [FORMAL] ❑ *...the outer reaches of the solar system.* N-PLURAL: usu the adj N of n 3 You can refer to the higher or lower levels of an organization as its upper or lower **reaches**. [FORMAL] ❑ *...the upper reaches of the legal profession.* N-PLURAL: usu the adj N of n = echelons

**re|act** /riækt/ **(reacts, reacting, reacted)** ◆◇◇ 1 When you **react to** something that has happened to you, you behave in a particular way because of it. ❑ *They reacted violently to the news... It's natural to react with disbelief if your child is accused of bullying.* VERB = respond V to n V adv/prep Also V 2 If you **react against** someone's way of behaving, you deliberately behave in a different way because you do not like the way they behave. ❑ *My father never saved and perhaps I reacted against that.* VERB = rebel V against n 3 If you **react to** a substance such as a drug, or **to** something you have touched, you are affected unpleasantly or made ill by it. ❑ *Someone allergic to milk is likely to react to cheese.* VERB V to n Also V 4 When one chemical substance **reacts with** another, or when two chemical substances **react**, they combine chemically to form another substance. ❑ *Calcium reacts with water... These two gases react readily to produce carbon dioxide and water.* V-RECIP V with n pl-n V

**re|ac|tion** /riækʃᵊn/ **(reactions)** ◆◆◇ 1 Your **reaction** to something that has happened or something that you have experienced is what you feel, say, or do because of it. ❑ *Reaction to the visit is mixed... He was surprised that his answer should have caused such a strong reaction.* N-VAR: usu with supp 2 A **reaction against** something is a way of behaving or doing something that is deliberately different from what has been done before. ❑ *All new fashion starts out as a reaction against existing convention.* N-COUNT: N against n 3 If there is a **reaction against** something, it becomes unpopular. ❑ *Premature moves in this respect might well provoke a reaction against the reform.* N-SING: also no det, N against n 4 Your **reactions** are your ability to move quickly in response to something, for example when you are in danger. ❑ *The sport requires very fast reactions.* N-PLURAL: oft poss N 5 **Reaction** is the belief that the political or social system of your country should not change. ❑ *Thus, he aided reaction and thwarted progress.* N-UNCOUNT disapproval 6 A chemical **reaction** is a process in which two substances combine together chemically to form another substance. ❑ *Ozone is produced by the reaction between oxygen and ultra-violet light.* N-COUNT 7 If you have a **reaction to** a substance such as a drug, or **to** something you have touched, you are affected unpleasantly or made ill by it. ❑ *Every year, 5000 people have life-threatening reactions to anaesthetics.* N-COUNT: oft adj N to n

**re|ac|tion|ary** /riækʃənri, AM -neri/ **(reactionaries)** A **reactionary** person or group tries to prevent changes in the political or social system of their country. ❑ *It grew ever more clear to everyone that the Minister was too reactionary, too blinkered.* ADJ disapproval ≠ radical ♦ A **reactionary** is someone with reactionary views. ❑ *Critics viewed him as a reactionary.* N-COUNT ≠ radical

**re|ac|ti|vate** /riæktɪveɪt/ **(reactivates, reactivating, reactivated)** If people **reactivate** a system or organization, they make it work again after a period in which it has not been working. ❑ *...a series of economic reforms to reactivate the economy.* VERB V n

**re|ac|tive** /riæktɪv/ 1 Something that is **reactive** is able to react chemically with a lot of different substances. ❑ *Ozone is a highly reactive form of oxygen gas.* ADJ 2 If someone is **reactive**, they behave in response to what happens to them, rather than deciding in advance how they want to behave. ❑ *I want our organization to be less reactive and more pro-active.* ADJ: usu v-link ADJ ≠ proactive

**re|ac|tor** /riæktəʳ/ **(reactors)** A **reactor** is the same as a **nuclear reactor**. N-COUNT

**read** **(reads, reading)** ◆◆◆

> The form **read** is pronounced /riːd/ when it is the present tense, and /red/ when it is the past tense and past participle.

1 When you **read** something such as a book or article, you look at and understand the words that are written there. ❑ *Have you read this book?... I read about it in the paper... He read through the pages slowly and carefully... It was nice to read that the Duke will not be sending his son off to boarding school... She spends her days reading and watching television.* VERB V n V about n V through n V that V ♦ **Read** is also a noun. ❑ *I settled down to have a good read.* N-SING: a N 2 When you **read** a piece of writing to someone, you say the words aloud. ❑ *Jay reads poetry so beautifully... I like it when she reads to us... I sing to the boys or read them a story before tucking them in.* VERB V n V to n V n n 3 People who can **read** have the ability to look at and understand written words. ❑ *He couldn't read or write... He could read words at 18 months.* VERB V V n 4 If you can **read** music, you have the VERB

ability to look at and understand the symbols that are used in written music to represent musical sounds. ❑ *Later on I learned how to read music.* V n

5 When a computer **reads** a file or a document, it takes information from a disk or tape. [COMPUTING] ❑ *How can I read a Microsoft Excel file on a computer that only has Works installed?* VERB; V n

6 You can use **read** when saying what is written on something or in something. For example, if a notice **reads** 'Entrance', the word 'Entrance' is written on it. ❑ *The sign on the bus read 'Private: Not In Service'.* VERB: no cont; V with quote

7 If you refer to how a piece of writing **reads**, you are referring to its style. ❑ *The book reads like a ballad.* VERB; V prep/adv

8 If you say that a book or magazine is a good **read**, you mean that it is very enjoyable to read. ❑ *Ben Okri's latest novel is a good read.* N-COUNT: adj N

9 If something **is read** in a particular way, it is understood or interpreted in that way. ❑ *The play is being widely read as an allegory of imperialist conquest... South Africans were praying last night that he has read the situation correctly.* VERB = interpret; be V-ed as n; V n adv/prep

10 If you **read** someone's mind or thoughts, you know exactly what they are thinking without them telling you. ❑ *As if he could read her thoughts, Benny said, 'You're free to go any time you like.'* VERB; V n

11 If you can **read** someone or you can **read** their gestures, you can understand what they are thinking or feeling by the way they behave or the things they say. ❑ *If you have to work in a team you must learn to read people.* VERB; V n

12 If someone who is trying to talk to you with a radio transmitter says, 'Do you **read** me?', they are asking you if you can hear them. ❑ *We read you loud and clear. Over.* VERB; V n

13 When you **read** a measuring device, you look at it to see what the figure or measurement on it is. ❑ *It is essential that you are able to read a thermometer.* VERB; V n

14 If a measuring device **reads** a particular amount, it shows that amount. ❑ *The thermometer read 105 degrees Fahrenheit.* VERB; V amount

15 If you **read** a subject at university, you study it. [BRIT, FORMAL] ❑ *She read French and German at Cambridge University... He is now reading for a maths degree at Surrey University.* VERB; V n; V for n

✔ in AM, use **major**, **study**

16 If you **take** something **as read**, you accept it as true or right and therefore feel that it does not need to be discussed or proved. ❑ *We took it as read that he must have been a KGB agent.* PHRASE: V inflects

17 → See also **reading**. to **read between the lines** → see **line**.

♦ **read into** If you **read** a meaning **into** something, you think it is there although it may not actually be there. ❑ *The addict often reads disapproval into people's reactions to him even where it does not exist... It would be wrong to try to read too much into such a light-hearted production.* PHRASAL VERB; V n P n; V amount P n

♦ **read out** If you **read out** a piece of writing, you say it aloud. ❑ *He's obliged to take his turn at reading out the announcements... Shall I read them out?* PHRASAL VERB; V P n (not pron); V n P

♦ **read up on** If you **read up on** a subject, you read a lot about it so that you become informed about it. ❑ *I've read up on the dangers of all these drugs.* PHRASAL VERB; V P P n

**read|able** /riːdəbᵊl/ 1 If you say that a book or article is **readable**, you mean that it is enjoyable and easy to read. ❑ *This is an impeccably researched and very readable book.* ADJ

2 A piece of writing that is **readable** is written or printed clearly and can be read easily. ❑ *My secretary worked long hours translating my almost illegible writing into a typewritten and readable script.* ADJ

**read|er** /riːdəʳ/ **(readers)** 1 The **readers** of a newspaper, magazine, or book are the people who read it. ❑ *These texts give the reader an insight into the Chinese mind.* ◆◆◇ N-COUNT

2 A **reader** is a person who reads, especially one who reads for pleasure. ❑ *Thanks to that job I became an avid reader.* N-COUNT: usu with supp

3 A **reader** is a book to help children to learn to read, or to help people to learn a foreign language. It contains passages of text, and often exercises to give practice in reading and writing. N-COUNT

**read|er|ship** /riːdəʳʃɪp/ **(readerships)** The **readership** of a book, newspaper, or magazine is the number or type of people who read it. ❑ *Its readership has grown to over 15,000 subscribers.* N-COUNT: usu sing, usu with supp

**read|ily** /redɪli/ 1 If you do something **readily**, you do it in a way which shows that you are very willing to do it. ❑ *I asked her if she would allow me to interview her, and she readily agreed.* ADV: ADV with v

2 You also use **readily** to say that something can be done or obtained quickly and easily. For example, if you say that something can be readily understood, you mean that people can understand it quickly and easily. ❑ *The components are readily available in hardware shops.* ADV: ADV adj, ADV with v = easily

**readi|ness** /redɪnəs/ 1 If someone is very willing to do something, you can talk about their **readiness to** do it. ❑ *...their readiness to co-operate with the new US envoy.* N-UNCOUNT

2 If you do something **in readiness for** a future event, you do it so that you are prepared for that event. ❑ *Security tightened in the capital in readiness for the president's arrival.* N-UNCOUNT: usu in N

**read|ing** /riːdɪŋ/ **(readings)** 1 **Reading** is the activity of reading books. ❑ *I have always loved reading. ...young people who find reading and writing difficult.* ◆◇◇ N-UNCOUNT

2 A **reading** is an event at which poetry or extracts from books are read to an audience. ❑ *...a poetry reading.* N-COUNT

3 Your **reading of** a word, text, or situation is the way in which you understand or interpret it. ❑ *My reading of her character makes me feel that she was too responsible a person to do those things.* N-COUNT: with supp, usu N of n

4 The **reading** on a measuring device is the figure or measurement that it shows. ❑ *The gauge must be giving a faulty reading.* N-COUNT

5 In the British Parliament or the US Congress, a **reading** is one of the three stages of introducing and discussing a new bill before it can be passed as law. ❑ *The bill is expected to pass its second reading with a comfortable majority.* N-COUNT: usu ord N

6 If you say that a book or an article **makes** interesting **reading** or **makes for** interesting **reading**, you mean that it is interesting to read. ❑ *The list of drinks, a dozen pages long, makes fascinating reading.* PHRASE: V inflects

**read|ing glasses** **Reading glasses** are glasses that are worn by people, for example when they are reading, because they cannot see things close to them very well. N-PLURAL: also a pair of N

**read|ing lamp** **(reading lamps)** A **reading lamp** is a small lamp that you keep on a desk or table. You can move part of it in order to direct the light to where you need it for reading. N-COUNT

**read|ing room** **(reading rooms)** A **reading room** is a quiet room in a library or museum where you can read and study. N-COUNT

**re|adjust** /riːədʒʌst/ **(readjusts, readjusting, readjusted)** 1 When you **readjust to** a new situation, usually one you have been in before, you adapt to it. ❑ *I can understand why astronauts find it difficult to readjust to life on earth... They are bound to take time to readjust after a holiday.* VERB; V to n; V

2 If you **readjust** the level of something, your attitude to something, or the way you do something, you change it to make it more effective or appropriate. ❑ *In the end you have to readjust your expectations.* VERB; V n

3 If you **readjust** something such as a piece of clothing or a mechanical device, you correct or alter its position or setting. ❑ *Readjust your watch. You are now on Moscow time.* VERB; V n

**re|adjust|ment** /riːədʒʌstmənt/ **(readjustments)** 1 **Readjustment** is the process of adapting to a new situation, usually one that you have been in before. ❑ *The next few weeks will be a period of readjustment.* N-VAR: usu with supp

2 A **readjustment** of something is a change that you make to it so that it is more effective or appropriate. ❑ *The organization denies that it is seeking any readjustment of state borders. ...the effects of economic readjustment.* N-VAR: usu with supp

**read|out** /riːdaʊt/ **(readouts)** If an electronic measuring device gives you a **readout**, it displays information about the level of something such as a speed, height, or sound. ❑ *The system provides a digital readout of the vehicle's speed.* N-COUNT

**ready** /redi/ **(readier, readiest, readies, readying, readied)** ◆◆◇ [1] If someone is **ready**, they are properly prepared for something. If something is **ready**, it has been properly prepared and is now able to be used. ❑ *It took her a long time to get ready for church... Are you ready to board, Mr. Daly?... Tomorrow he would tell his pilot to get the aircraft ready.* ADJ: v-link ADJ, oft ADJ *for* n, ADJ to-inf [2] If you are **ready for** something or **ready to** do something, you have enough experience to do it or you are old enough and sensible enough to do it. ❑ *She says she's not ready for marriage... You'll have no trouble getting him into a normal school when you feel he's ready to go.* ADJ: v-link ADJ, usu ADJ *for* n, ADJ to-inf [3] If you are **ready to** do something, you are willing to do it. ❑ *They were ready to die for their beliefs.* ADJ: v-link ADJ to-inf = willing [4] If you are **ready for** something, you need it or want it. ❑ *I don't know about you, but I'm ready for bed.* ADJ: v-link ADJ *for* n [5] To be **ready to** do something means to be about to do it or likely to do it. ❑ *She looked ready to cry.* ADJ: v-link ADJ to-inf [6] You use **ready** to describe things that are able to be used very quickly and easily. ❑ *Why does German industry enjoy such a ready supply of well-trained and well-motivated workers?* ADJ: ADJ n [7] **Ready** money is in the form of notes and coins rather than cheques or credit cards, and so it can be used immediately. ❑ *I'm afraid I don't have enough ready cash.* ADJ: ADJ n [8] When you **ready** something, you prepare it for a particular purpose. [FORMAL] ❑ *John's soldiers were readying themselves for the final assault.* VERB V n *for* n [9] **Ready** combines with past participles to indicate that something has already been done, and that therefore you do not have to do it yourself. ❑ *You can buy ready-printed forms for wills at stationery shops.* COMB in ADJ [10] If you have something **at the ready**, you have it in a position where it can be quickly and easily used. ❑ *Soldiers came charging through the forest, guns at the ready.* PHRASE: usu n PHR

**ready-made** [1] If something that you buy is **ready-made**, you can use it immediately, because the work you would normally have to do has already been done. ❑ *We rely quite a bit on ready-made meals – they are so convenient.* ADJ [2] **Ready-made** means extremely convenient or useful for a particular purpose. ❑ *Those wishing to study urban development have a ready-made example on their doorstep.* ADJ: usu ADJ n

**ready meal** **(ready meals)** **Ready meals** are complete meals that are sold in shops. They are already prepared and you need only heat them before eating them. N-COUNT

**ready-to-wear** **Ready-to-wear** clothes are made in standard sizes so that they fit most people, rather than being made specially for a particular person. ❑ *In 1978 he launched his first major ready-to-wear collection for the Austin Reed stores.* ADJ: ADJ n = off-the-peg

**re|affirm** /riːəfɜːʳm/ **(reaffirms, reaffirming, reaffirmed)** If you **reaffirm** something, you state it again clearly and firmly. [FORMAL] ❑ *He reaffirmed his commitment to the country's economic reform programme... The government has reaffirmed that it will take any steps necessary to maintain law and order.* VERB V n V that

**re|affor|esta|tion** /riːəfɒrɪsteɪʃən, AM -fɔːr-/ **Reafforestation** is the same as **reforestation**. [mainly BRIT] N-UNCOUNT

**re|agent** /rieɪdʒənt/ **(reagents)** A **reagent** is a substance that is used to cause a chemical reaction. Reagents are often used in order to indicate the presence of another substance. [TECHNICAL] N-COUNT

**real** /riːl/ ◆◆◆ [1] Something that is **real** actually exists and is not imagined, invented, or theoretical. ❑ *No, it wasn't a dream. It was real... Legends grew up around a great many figures, both real and fictitious.* ADJ ≠ imaginary [2] If something is **real to** someone, they experience it as though it really exists or happens, even though it does not. ❑ *Whitechild's life becomes increasingly real to the reader.* ADJ: usu v-link ADJ, oft ADJ *to* n [3] A material or object that is **real** is natural or functioning, and not artificial or an imitation. ❑ *...the smell of real leather... Who's to know if they're real guns or not?* ADJ: usu ADJ n = genuine [4] You can use **real** to describe someone or something that has all the characteristics or qualities that such a person or thing typically has. ❑ *...his first real girlfriend... The only real job I'd ever had was as manager of the local cafe.* ADJ: ADJ n = proper [5] You can use **real** to describe something that is the true or original thing of its kind, in contrast to one that someone wants you to believe is true. ❑ *This was the real reason for her call... Her real name had been Miriam Pinckus.* ADJ: ADJ n = true [6] You can use **real** to describe something that is the most important or typical part of a thing. ❑ *When he talks, he only gives glimpses of his real self... The smart executive has people he can trust doing all the real work.* ADJ: ADJ n [7] You can use **real** when you are talking about a situation or feeling to emphasize that it exists and is important or serious. ❑ *Global warming is a real problem... The prospect of civil war is very real... There was never any real danger of the children being affected.* ADJ: usu ADJ n [emphasis] [8] You can use **real** to emphasize a quality that is genuine and sincere. ❑ *Germany has shown real determination to come to terms with the anti-Semitism of its past.* ADJ: ADJ n [emphasis] [9] You can use **real** before nouns to emphasize your description of something or someone. [mainly SPOKEN] ❑ *'It's a fabulous deal, a real bargain.'* ADJ: ADJ n [emphasis] [10] The **real** cost or value of something is its cost or value after other amounts have been added or subtracted and when factors such as the level of inflation have been considered. ❑ *...the real cost of borrowing.* ♦ You can also talk about the cost or value of something **in real terms**. ❑ *In real terms the cost of driving is cheaper than a decade ago.* ADJ: ADJ n = actual, net PHRASE: PHR with cl [11] You can use **real** to emphasize an adjective or adverb. [AM, INFORMAL] ❑ *He is finding prison life 'real tough'.* ADV: ADV adj/adv [emphasis] = really

**PHRASES** [12] If you say that someone does something **for real**, you mean that they actually do it and do not just pretend to do it. ❑ *The sex scenes were just good acting. We didn't do it for real.* PHRASE: usu PHR after v [13] If you think that someone or something is very surprising, you can ask if they are **for real**. [AM, INFORMAL] ❑ *Is this guy for real?* PHRASE: v-link PHR [14] If you say that a thing or event is **the real thing**, you mean that it is the thing or event itself, rather than an imitation or copy. ❑ *The counterfeits sell for about $20 less than the real thing.* PHRASE

**real ale** **(real ales)** **Real ale** is beer which is stored in a barrel and is pumped from it without the use of carbon dioxide. [mainly BRIT] N-MASS

**real es|tate** [1] **Real estate** is property in the form of land and buildings, rather than personal possessions. [mainly AM] ❑ *By investing in real estate, he was one of the richest men in the United States.* N-UNCOUNT = property [2] **Real estate** businesses or **real estate** agents sell houses, buildings, and land. [AM] ❑ *...the real estate agent who sold you your house.* N-UNCOUNT: usu N n

✔ in BRIT, use **estate agency, estate agents**

**re|align** /riːəlaɪn/ **(realigns, realigning, realigned)** If you **realign** your ideas, policies, or plans, you organize them in a different way in order to take account of new circumstances. ❑ *She has, almost single-handedly, realigned British politics.* VERB V n Also V

**re|align|ment** /riːəlaɪnmənt/ **(realignments)** If a company, economy, or system goes through a **realignment**, it is organized or arranged in a new way. ❑ *...a realignment of the existing political structure.* N-VAR: usu N *of* n

**re|al|ise** /riːəlaɪz/ → see **realize**.

**re|al|ism** /riːəlɪzəm/ [1] When people show **realism** in their behaviour, they recognize and accept the true nature of a situation and try to deal with it in a practical way. ❑ *It was time now to show more political realism.* N-UNCOUNT [approval] [2] If things and people are presented with **realism** in paintings, stories, or films, they are presented in a way that is like real life. ❑ *Greene's stories had an edge of realism that made it easy to forget they were fiction.* N-UNCOUNT [approval]

**re|al|ist** /riːəlɪst/ **(realists)** 1 A **realist** is someone who recognizes and accepts the true nature of a situation and tries to deal with it in a practical way. ❑ *I see myself not as a cynic but as a realist.* N-COUNT [approval] 2 A **realist** painter or writer is one who represents things and people in a way that is like real life. ❑ *...perhaps the foremost realist painter of our times.* ADJ: ADJ n

**re|al|is|tic** /riːəlɪstɪk/ 1 If you are **realistic** about a situation, you recognize and accept its true nature and try to deal with it in a practical way. ❑ *Police have to be realistic about violent crime... It's only realistic to acknowledge that something, some time, will go wrong.* ADJ: usu v-link ADJ, oft ADJ *about* n, *it* v-link ADJ to-inf ♦ **re|al|is|ti|cal|ly** *As an adult, you can assess the situation realistically.* ADV: usu ADV with v, also ADV adj 2 Something such as a goal or target that is **realistic** is one which you can sensibly expect to achieve. ❑ *Establish deadlines that are more realistic.* ADJ = *sensible* 3 You say that a painting, story, or film is **realistic** when the people and things in it are like people and things in real life. ❑ *...extraordinarily realistic paintings of Indians.* ADJ ♦ **re|al|is|ti|cal|ly** *The film starts off realistically and then develops into a ridiculous fantasy.* ADV: usu ADV with v

**re|al|is|ti|cal|ly** /riːəlɪstɪkəli/ You use **realistically** when you want to emphasize that what you are saying is true, even though you would prefer it not to be true. ❑ *Realistically, there is never one right answer.* ➔ See also **realistic.** ADV: ADV with cl [emphasis] = *frankly*

**re|al|ity** /riælɪti/ **(realities)** ◆◆◇ 1 You use **reality** to refer to real things or the real nature of things rather than imagined, invented, or theoretical ideas. ❑ *Fiction and reality were increasingly blurred.* ➔ See also **virtual reality.** N-UNCOUNT 2 **The reality of** a situation is the truth about it, especially when it is unpleasant or difficult to deal with. ❑ *...the harsh reality of top international competition.* N-COUNT: usu *the* N *of* n 3 You say that something has become a **reality** when it actually exists or is actually happening. ❑ *...the whole procedure that made this book become a reality.* N-SING 4 You can use **in reality** to introduce a statement about the real nature of something, when it contrasts with something incorrect that has just been described. ❑ *He came across as streetwise, but in reality he was not.* PHRASE: PHR with cl

**re|al|ity TV** **Reality TV** is a type of television programming which aims to show how ordinary people behave in everyday life, or in situations, often created by the programme makers, which are intended to represent everyday life. ❑ *...the Americans' current infatuation with reality TV.* N-UNCOUNT

**re|al|iz|able** /riːəlaɪzəbᵊl/

☑ in BRIT, also use **realisable**

1 If your hopes or aims are **realizable**, there is a possibility that the things that you want to happen will happen. [FORMAL] ❑ *...the reasonless assumption that one's dreams and desires were realizable.* ADJ 2 **Realizable** wealth is money that can be easily obtained by selling something. [FORMAL] ❑ *They must prove they own £250,000 of realisable assets.* ADJ

**re|al|ize** /riːəlaɪz/ **(realizes, realizing, realized)** ◆◆◇

☑ in BRIT, also use **realise**

1 If you **realize** that something is true, you become aware of that fact or understand it. ❑ *As soon as we realised something was wrong, we moved the children away... People don't realize how serious this recession has actually been... Once they realised their mistake the phone was reconnected again... 'That's my brother.' — 'Oh, I hadn't realized.'* VERB V that, V wh, V n, V ♦ **re|ali|za|tion** /riːəlaɪzeɪʃᵊn/ **(realizations)** *There is now a growing realisation that things cannot go on like this for much longer... He nearly cried out at the sudden realization of how much Randall looked like him.* N-VAR: usu N that, N *of* n 2 If your hopes, desires, or fears **are realized**, the things that you hope for, desire, or fear actually happen. ❑ *Straightaway our worst fears were realised.* VERB: usu passive *be* V-ed ♦ **re|ali|za|tion** *...the realization of his worst fears.* N-UNCOUNT: oft *the* N *of* n 3 When someone **realizes** a design or an idea, they make or organize something based on that design or idea. [FORMAL] ❑ *Various textile techniques will be explored to realise design possibilities.* VERB V n 4 If someone or something **realizes** their potential, they do everything they are capable of doing, because they have been given the opportunity to do so. ❑ *The support systems to enable women to realize their potential at work are seriously inadequate.* VERB = *achieve* V n 5 If something **realizes** a particular amount of money when it is sold, that amount of money is paid for it. [FORMAL] ❑ *A selection of correspondence from P G Wodehouse realised £1,232.* VERB V n ♦ **re|ali|za|tion** *I have taken this course solely to assist the realisation of my assets for the benefit of all my creditors.* N-VAR

**real life** If something happens **in real life**, it actually happens and is not just in a story or in someone's imagination. ❑ *In real life men like Richard Gere don't marry street girls.* N-UNCOUNT: usu *in* N ♦ **Real life** is also an adjective. ❑ *...a real-life horror story.* ADJ: ADJ n

**re|allo|cate** /riː æləkeɪt/ **(reallocates, reallocating, reallocated)** When organizations **reallocate** money or resources, they decide to change the way they spend the money or use the resources. ❑ *...a cost-cutting program to reallocate people and resources within the company... Other areas are to lose aid so that money can be reallocated to towns devastated by pit closures.* VERB = *redistribute* V n, V n to n

**re|al|ly** /riːəli/ ◆◆◆ 1 You can use **really** to emphasize a statement. [SPOKEN] ❑ *I'm very sorry. I really am... It really is best to manage without any medication if you possibly can.* ADV: usu ADV with v [emphasis] 2 You can use **really** to emphasize an adjective or adverb. ❑ *It was really good... They were really nice people.* ADV: ADV adj/adv [emphasis] 3 You use **really** when you are discussing the real facts about something, in contrast to the ones someone wants you to believe. ❑ *My father didn't really love her.* ADV: usu ADV with v, also ADV adj 4 People use **really** in questions and negative statements when they want you to answer 'no'. ❑ *Do you really think he would be that stupid?* ADV: ADV before v [emphasis] 5 If you refer to a time when something **really** begins to happen, you are emphasizing that it starts to happen at that time to a much greater extent and much more seriously than before. ❑ *That's when the pressure really started.* ADV: ADV before v [emphasis] 6 People sometimes use **really** to slightly reduce the force of a negative statement. [SPOKEN] ❑ *I'm not really surprised... 'Did they hurt you?' — 'Not really'.* ADV: ADV after neg, usu ADV with v, also ADV with cl [vagueness] 7 You can say **really** to express surprise or disbelief at what someone has said. [SPOKEN] ❑ *'We discovered it was totally the wrong decision.' — 'Really?'.* CONVENTION [feelings]

**realm** /relm/ **(realms)** 1 You can use **realm** to refer to any area of activity, interest, or thought. [FORMAL] ❑ *...the realm of politics.* N-COUNT: usu with supp, oft N *of* n, adj N 2 A **realm** is a country that has a king or queen. [FORMAL] ❑ *Defence of the realm is crucial.* N-COUNT: usu sing 3 If you say that something is not beyond **the realms of possibility**, you mean that it is possible. ❑ *A fall of 50 per cent or more on prices is not beyond the realms of possibility.* PHRASE: *realm* inflects, v-link prep PHR

**real prop|er|ty** **Real property** is property in the form of land and buildings, rather than personal possessions. [AM] N-UNCOUNT = *real estate*

**real time** If something is done **in real time**, there is no noticeable delay between the action and its effect or consequence. ❑ *...umpires, who have to make every decision in real time.* N-UNCOUNT: oft *in* N

**real-time** **Real-time** processing is a type of computer programming or data processing in which the information received is processed by the computer almost immediately. [COMPUTING] ❑ *...real-time language translations.* ADJ: ADJ n

**Real|tor** /riːəltɔːr/ **(Realtors)** also **realtor.** A **Realtor** is a person whose job is to sell houses, buildings, and land, and who is a member of the National Association of Realtors. [AM, TRADEMARK] N-COUNT

☑ in BRIT, use **estate agent**

**real world** If you talk about **the real world**, you are referring to the world and life in general, in contrast to a particular person's own life, experience, and ideas, which may seem untypical N-SING: *the* N and unrealistic. ❑ *When they eventually leave the school they will be totally ill-equipped to deal with the real world.*

**ream** /riːm/ **(reams)** If you say that there are **reams of** paper or **reams of** writing, you mean that there are large amounts of it. [INFORMAL] ❑ *Their specific task is to sort through the reams of information and try to determine what it may mean.* N-COUNT: usu pl, usu N *of* n

**reap** /riːp/ **(reaps, reaping, reaped)** If you **reap** the benefits or the rewards of something, you enjoy the good things that happen as a result of it. ❑ *You'll soon begin to reap the benefits of being fitter.* VERB V n

**reap|er** /riːpəʳ/ **(reapers)** A **reaper** is a machine used to cut and gather crops. → See also **Grim Reaper**. N-COUNT

**re|appear** /riːəpɪəʳ/ **(reappears, reappearing, reappeared)** When people or things **reappear**, they return again after they have been away or out of sight for some time. ❑ *Thirty seconds later she reappeared and beckoned them forward.* VERB V

**re|appear|ance** /riːəpɪərəns/ **(reappearances)** The **reappearance** of someone or something is their return after they have been away or out of sight for some time. ❑ *His sudden reappearance must have been a shock.* N-COUNT: usu with poss

**re|apprais|al** /riːəpreɪzəl/ **(reappraisals)** If there is a **reappraisal** of something such as an idea or plan, people think about the idea carefully and decide whether they want to change it. [FORMAL] ❑ *Britain's worst jail riot will force a fundamental reappraisal of prison policy.* N-VAR = reassessment

**re|appraise** /riːəpreɪz/ **(reappraises, reappraising, reappraised)** If you **reappraise** something such as an idea or a plan, you think carefully about it and decide whether it needs to be changed. [FORMAL] ❑ *It did not persuade them to abandon the war but it did force them to reappraise their strategy.* VERB = rethink V n

**rear** /rɪəʳ/ **(rears, rearing, reared)** ◆◇◇ 1 The **rear** of something such as a building or vehicle is the back part of it. ❑ *He settled back in the rear ofthe taxi. ...a stairway in the rear of the building.* N-SING: *the* N, usu N *of* n = back ≠ front ♦ **Rear** is also an adjective. ❑ *Manufacturers have been obliged to fit rear seat belts in all new cars.* ADJ: ADJ n 2 If you are at the **rear** of a moving line of people, you are the last person in it. [FORMAL] ❑ *Musicians played at the front and rear of the procession.* N-SING: *the* N, usu N *of* n = back ≠ front 3 Your **rear** is the part of your body that you sit on. [INFORMAL] ❑ *I turned away from the phone to see Lewis pat a waitress on her rear.* N-COUNT: usu poss N = behind 4 If you **rear** children, you look after them until they are old enough to look after themselves. ❑ *She reared sixteen children, six her own and ten her husband's.* VERB = bring up, raise V n 5 If you **rear** a young animal, you keep and look after it until it is old enough to be used for work or food, or until it can look after itself. [mainly BRIT] ❑ *She spends a lot of time rearing animals.* VERB V n

✔ in AM, usually use **raise**

6 When a horse **rears**, it moves the front part of its body upwards, so that its front legs are high in the air and it is standing on its back legs. ❑ *The horse reared and threw off its rider.* VERB V 7 If you say that something such as a building or mountain **rears** above you, you mean that is very tall and close to you. ❑ *The exhibition hall reared above me behind a high fence.* VERB = loom V prep/adv

PHRASES 8 If a person or vehicle **is bringing up the rear**, they are the last person or vehicle in a moving line of them. ❑ *...police motorcyclists bringing up the rear of the procession.* PHRASE: V inflects 9 If something unpleasant **rears its head** or **rears its ugly head**, it becomes visible or noticeable. ❑ *The threat of strikes reared its head again this summer.* PHRASE: V and N inflect

**Rear Ad|mi|ral** **(Rear Admirals)** **Rear Admiral** is a rank in the navy. It is the rank below **Vice Admiral**. ❑ *...Rear Admiral Douglas Cap, commander of the USS America.* N-TITLE; N-COUNT

**rear-end** **(rear-ends, rear-ending, rear-ended)** If a driver or vehicle **rear-ends** the vehicle in front, they crash into the back of it. [INFORMAL] ❑ *A few days earlier somebody had rear-ended him.* VERB V n

**rear|guard** /rɪəʳgɑːʳd/ 1 In a battle, **the rearguard** is a group of soldiers who protect the back part of an army, especially when the army is leaving the battle. N-SING: *the* N 2 If someone is **fighting a rearguard action** or **mounting a rearguard action**, they are trying very hard to prevent something from happening, even though it is probably too late for them to succeed. [JOURNALISM] ❑ *Mr Urban looks increasingly like someone fighting a rearguard action to keep their job.* PHRASE: V inflects

**re|arm** /riː ɑːʳm/ **(rearms, rearming, rearmed)** also **re-arm.** If a country **rearms** or **is rearmed**, it starts to build up a new stock of military weapons. ❑ *They neglected to rearm in time and left Britain exposed to disaster. ...NATO's decision to rearm West Germany.* VERB V V n

**re|arma|ment** /riː ɑːʳməmənt/ **Rearmament** is the process of building up a new stock of military weapons. N-UNCOUNT

**re|arrange** /riːəreɪndʒ/ **(rearranges, rearranging, rearranged)** 1 If you **rearrange** things, you change the way in which they are organized or ordered. ❑ *When she returned, she found Malcolm had rearranged all her furniture.* VERB V n 2 If you **rearrange** a meeting or an appointment, you arrange for it to take place at a different time to that originally intended. ❑ *You may cancel or rearrange the appointment.* VERB = reschedule V n

**re|arrange|ment** /riːəreɪndʒmənt/ **(rearrangements)** A **rearrangement** is a change in the way that something is arranged or organized. ❑ *...a rearrangement of the job structure.* N-VAR

**rear-view mir|ror** **(rear-view mirrors)** also **rearview mirror.** Inside a car, the **rear-view mirror** is the mirror that enables you to see the traffic behind you when you are driving. → See picture on page 1707. N-COUNT

**rear|ward** /rɪəʳwəʳd/ If something moves or faces **rearward**, it moves or faces backwards. ❑ *...a rearward facing infant carrier... The centre of pressure moves rearward and the aeroplane becomes unbalanced.* ADV: ADV with v = backward ≠ forward ♦ **Rearward** is also an adjective. ❑ *...the rearward window.* ADJ: ADJ n

**rea|son** /riːzən/ **(reasons, reasoning, reasoned)** ◆◆◆ 1 The **reason for** something is a fact or situation which explains why it happens or what causes it to happen. ❑ *There is a reason for every important thing that happens... Who would have a reason to want to kill her?* N-COUNT: usu with supp, oft N *for* n, N to-inf 2 If you say that you have **reason to** believe something or **to** have a particular emotion, you mean that you have evidence for your belief or there is a definite cause of your feeling. ❑ *They had reason to believe there could be trouble... He had every reason to be upset.* N-UNCOUNT: usu N to-inf 3 The ability that people have to think and to make sensible judgments can be referred to as **reason**. ❑ *...a conflict between emotion and reason.* N-UNCOUNT 4 If you **reason that** something is true, you decide that it is true after thinking carefully about all the facts. ❑ *I reasoned that changing my diet would lower my cholesterol level... 'Listen,' I reasoned, 'it doesn't take a genius to figure out what Adam's up to.'* → See also **reasoned, reasoning**. VERB V that V with quote

PHRASES 5 If one thing happens **by reason of** another, it happens because of it. [FORMAL] ❑ *The boss retains enormous influence by reason of his position.* PHRASE: PHR n 6 If you try to make someone **listen to reason**, you try to persuade them to listen to sensible arguments and be influenced by them. ❑ *The company's top executives had refused to listen to reason.* PHRASE: V inflects 7 If you say that something happened or was done **for no reason**, **for no good reason**, or **for no reason at all**, you mean that there was no obvious reason why it happened or was done. ❑ *The guards, he said, would punch them for no reason... For no reason at all the two men started to laugh.* PHRASE: PHR with cl 8 If a person or thing is someone's **reason for living** or their **reason for being**, they are the most important thing in that person's life. PHRASE: usu poss PHR

❑ *Chloe is my reason for living.* [9] PHRASE: PHR with cl [vagueness] If you say that something happened or is true **for some reason**, you mean that you know it happened or is true, but you do not know why. ❑ *For some inexplicable reason she was attracted to Patrick.* [10] PHRASE: PHR with cl, n PHR If you say that you will do anything **within reason**, you mean that you will do anything that is fair or reasonable and not too extreme. ❑ *I will take any job that comes along, within reason.* [11] **rhyme or reason** → see **rhyme**. to **see reason** → see **see**. **it stands to reason** → see **stand**.

♦ **reason with** PHRASAL VERB If you try to **reason with** someone, you try to persuade them to do or accept something by using sensible arguments. V P n ❑ *I have watched parents trying to reason with their children and have never seen it work.*

**rea|son|able** /riːzənəbᵊl/ ◆◇◇ [1] ADJ ≠*unreasonable* If you think that someone is fair and sensible you can say that they are **reasonable**. ❑ *He's a reasonable sort of chap... Oh, come on, be reasonable.* ♦ **rea|son|ably** ADV /riːzənəbli/ *'I'm sorry, Andrew,' she said reasonably.* ♦ **rea|son|able|ness** N-UNCOUNT *'I can understand how you feel,' Desmond said with great reasonableness.* [2] ADJ If you say that a decision or action is **reasonable**, you mean that it is fair and sensible. ❑ *...a perfectly reasonable decision... At the time, what he'd done had seemed reasonable.* [3] ADJ: oft *it* v-link ADJ to-inf If you say that an expectation or explanation is **reasonable**, you mean that there are good reasons why it may be correct. ❑ *It seems reasonable to expect rapid urban growth.* ♦ **rea|son|ably** ADV: ADV with v *You can reasonably expect your goods to arrive within six to eight weeks.* [4] ADJ If you say that the price of something is **reasonable**, you mean that it is fair and not too high. ❑ *You get an interesting meal for a reasonable price.* ♦ **rea|son|ably** ADV: ADV with v *...reasonably priced accommodation.* [5] ADJ You can use **reasonable** to describe something that is fairly good, but not very good. ❑ *The boy answered him in reasonable French.* ♦ **rea|son|ably** ADV: ADV adj/adv *I can still dance reasonably well.* [6] ADJ A **reasonable** amount of something is a fairly large amount of it. ❑ *They will need a reasonable amount of desk area and good light.* ♦ **rea|son|ably** ADV: ADV adj/adv *From now on events moved reasonably quickly.*

**rea|soned** /riːzᵊnd/ ADJ: usu ADJ n [approval] = *rational* A **reasoned** discussion or argument is based on sensible reasons, rather than on an appeal to people's emotions. ❑ *Abortion is an issue which produces little reasoned argument.*

**rea|son|ing** /riːzənɪŋ/ **(reasonings)** N-VAR **Reasoning** is the process by which you reach a conclusion after thinking about all the facts. ❑ *...the reasoning behind the decision.*

**re|as|sem|ble** /riːəsembᵊl/ **(reassembles, reassembling, reassembled)** [1] VERB If you **reassemble** something, you put it back together after it has been taken apart. V n ❑ *We will now try to reassemble pieces of the wreckage.* [2] VERB If a group of people **reassembles** or if you **reassemble** them, they gather together again in a group. V ❑ *We shall reassemble in the car park in thirty minutes...* V n *Mr Lucas reassembled his team in September.*

**re|as|sert** /riːəsɜːʳt/ **(reasserts, reasserting, reasserted)** [1] VERB If you **reassert** your control or authority, you make it clear that you are still in a position of power, or you strengthen the power that you had. V n ❑ *...the government's continuing effort to reassert its control in the region.* [2] VERB If something such as an idea or habit **reasserts itself**, it becomes noticeable again. V pron-refl ❑ *His sense of humour was beginning to reassert itself.*

**re|as|sess** /riːəses/ **(reassesses, reassessing, reassessed)** VERB If you **reassess** something, you think about it and decide whether you need to change your opinion about it. V n ❑ *I will reassess the situation when I get home.*

**re|as|sess|ment** /riːəsesmənt/ **(reassessments)** N-VAR If you make a **reassessment** of something, you think about it and decide whether you need to change your opinion about it. ❑ *...the moment when we make a reassessment of ourselves.*

**re|assur|ance** /riːəʃʊərəns/ **(reassurances)** [1] N-UNCOUNT If someone needs **reassurance**, they are very worried and need someone to help them stop worrying by saying kind or helpful things. ❑ *She needed reassurance that she belonged somewhere.* [2] N-COUNT **Reassurances** are things that you say to help people stop worrying about something. ❑ *...reassurances that pesticides are not harmful.*

**re|assure** /riːəʃʊəʳ/ **(reassures, reassuring, reassured)** VERB If you **reassure** someone, you say or do things to make them stop worrying about something. V n ❑ *I tried to reassure her, 'Don't worry about it. We won't let it happen again.'...* V n that *She just reassured me that everything was fine.* Also V n *about* n

**re|assured** /riːəʃʊəʳd/ ADJ: usu v-link ADJ If you feel **reassured**, you feel less worried about something, usually because you have received help or advice. ❑ *I feel much more reassured when I've been for a health check.*

**re|assur|ing** /riːəʃʊərɪŋ/ ADJ: oft *it* v-link ADJ to-inf/that If you find someone's words or actions **reassuring**, they make you feel less worried about something. ❑ *It was reassuring to hear John's familiar voice.* ♦ **re|assur|ing|ly** ADV: usu ADV with v, also ADV adj *'It's okay now,' he said reassuringly.*

**re|awak|en** /riːəweɪkən/ **(reawakens, reawakening, reawakened)** VERB = *rekindle* If something **reawakens** an issue, or an interest or feeling that you used to have, it makes you think about it or feel it again. V n ❑ *The King's stand is bound to reawaken the painful debate about abortion.* ♦ **re|awak|en|ing** N-UNCOUNT *...a reawakening of interest in stained glass.*

**re|badge** /riːbædʒ/ **(rebadging, rebadged)** VERB If a product **is rebadged**, it is given a new name, brand, or logo. [BRIT] *be* V-ed ❑ *The car was rebadged as a Vauxhall and sold in Britain.* Also V-ed

**re|bate** /riːbeɪt/ **(rebates)** N-COUNT: usu with supp, oft n N, adj N, N *on* n = *refund* A **rebate** is an amount of money which is paid to you when you have paid more tax, rent, or rates than you needed to. ❑ *...a tax rebate.*

**re|bel** **(rebels, rebelling, rebelled)** ◆◆◇

> The noun is pronounced /rebəl/. The verb is pronounced /rɪbel/.

[1] N-COUNT: usu pl **Rebels** are people who are fighting against their own country's army in order to change the political system there. ❑ *...fighting between rebels and government forces. ...rebel forces in Liberia.* [2] N-COUNT Politicians who oppose some of their own party's policies can be referred to as **rebels**. ❑ *The rebels want another 1% cut in interest rates.* [3] VERB If politicians **rebel** against one of their own party's policies, they show that they oppose it. V *against* n ❑ *More than forty Conservative MPs rebelled against the government and voted against the bill...* V *MPs planning to rebel over the proposed welfare cuts.* [4] N-COUNT You can say that someone is a **rebel** if you think that they behave differently from other people and have rejected the values of society or of their parents. ❑ *She had been a rebel at school.* [5] VERB When someone **rebels**, they start to behave differently from other people and reject the values of society or of their parents. V ❑ *The child who rebels is unlikely to be overlooked...* V *against* n *I was very young and rebelling against everything.*

**re|bel|lion** /rɪbeliən/ **(rebellions)** [1] N-VAR = *insurrection* A **rebellion** is a violent organized action by a large group of people who are trying to change their country's political system. ❑ *The British soon put down the rebellion.* [2] N-VAR = *revolt* A situation in which politicians show their opposition to their own party's policies can be referred to as a **rebellion**. ❑ *There was a Labour rebellion when some left-wing MPs voted against the Chancellor's tax cuts.*

**re|bel|lious** /rɪbeliəs/ [1] ADJ If you think someone behaves in an unacceptable way and does not do what they are told, you can say they are **rebellious**. ❑ *...a rebellious teenager.* ♦ **re|bel|lious|ness** N-UNCOUNT *...the normal rebelliousness of* *youth.* [2] A **rebellious** group of people is a group involved in taking violent action against the rulers of their own country, usually in order to change the system of government there. ❑ *The rebellious officers, having seized the radio station, broadcast the news of the overthrow of the monarchy.* (ADJ: ADJ n)

**re|birth** /riːbɜːʳθ/ You can refer to a change that leads to a new period of growth and improvement in something as its **rebirth**. ❑ *...the rebirth of democracy in Latin America.* (N-UNCOUNT: oft N *of* n)

**re|born** /riːbɔːʳn/ If you say that someone or something **has been reborn**, you mean that they have become active again after a period of being inactive. ❑ *Russia was being reborn as a great power.* (V-PASSIVE; *be* V-ed *as* n)

**re|bound** /rɪbaʊnd/ **(rebounds, rebounding, rebounded)** [1] If something **rebounds** from a solid surface, it bounces or springs back from it. ❑ *His shot in the 21st minute of the game rebounded from a post... The hot liquid splashed down on the concrete and rebounded.* (VERB; V prep; V) [2] If an action or situation **rebounds on** you, it has an unpleasant effect on you, especially when this effect was intended for someone else. ❑ *Mia realised her trick had rebounded on her... The CIA was extremely wary of interfering with the foreign Press; in the past, such interference had rebounded.* (VERB; V *on/upon* n; V) [3] If you say that someone is **on the rebound**, you mean that they have just ended a relationship with a girlfriend or boyfriend. This often makes them do things they would not normally do. ❑ *He took heroin for the first time when he was on the rebound from a broken relationship.* (PHRASE: usu v-link PHR) [4] In basketball, a **rebound** is a shot which someone catches after it has hit the board behind the basket. (N-COUNT)

**re|brand** /riːbrænd/ **(rebrands, rebranding, rebranded)** To **rebrand** a product or organization means to present it to the public in a new way, for example by changing its name or appearance. [BUSINESS] ❑ *There are plans to rebrand many Texas stores.* (VERB; V n)

**re|brand|ing** /riːbrændɪŋ/ **Rebranding** is the process of giving a product or an organization a new image, in order to make it more attractive or successful. [BUSINESS] ❑ *The £85m programme will involve an extensive rebranding of the airline.* (N-UNCOUNT)

**re|buff** /rɪbʌf/ **(rebuffs, rebuffing, rebuffed)** If you **rebuff** someone or **rebuff** a suggestion that they make, you refuse to do what they suggest. ❑ *His proposals have already been rebuffed by the Prime Minister.* ♦ **Rebuff** is also a noun. ❑ *The results of the poll dealt a humiliating rebuff to Mr Jones.* (VERB = *reject*; V n; N-VAR: usu with supp)

**re|build** /riːbɪld/ **(rebuilds, rebuilding, rebuilt)** [1] When people **rebuild** something such as a building or a city, they build it again after it has been damaged or destroyed. ❑ *They say they will stay to rebuild their homes rather than retreat to refugee camps.* (VERB; V n) [2] When people **rebuild** something such as an institution, a system, or an aspect of their lives, they take action to bring it back to its previous condition. ❑ *Everyone would have to work hard together to rebuild the economy... The agency has been rebuilding under new management.* (VERB; V n; V)

**re|buke** /rɪbjuːk/ **(rebukes, rebuking, rebuked)** If you **rebuke** someone, you speak severely to them because they have said or done something that you do not approve of. [FORMAL] ❑ *The president rebuked the House and Senate for not passing those bills within 100 days.* ♦ **Rebuke** is also a noun. ❑ *UN member countries delivered a strong rebuke to both countries for persisting with nuclear testing programs.* (VERB = *reprimand*; V n; N-VAR: usu with supp = *reprimand*)

**re|but** /rɪbʌt/ **(rebuts, rebutting, rebutted)** If you **rebut** a charge or criticism that is made against you, you give reasons why it is untrue or unacceptable. [FORMAL] ❑ *He spent most of his speech rebutting criticisms of his foreign policy.* (VERB = *refute*; V n)

**re|but|tal** /rɪbʌtᵊl/ **(rebuttals)** If you make a **rebuttal of** a charge or accusation that has been made against you, you make a statement which gives reasons why the accusation is untrue. [FORMAL] ❑ *He is conducting a point-by-point rebuttal of charges from former colleagues.* (N-COUNT: oft N *of/to* n)

**re|cal|ci|trant** /rɪkælsɪtrənt/ If you describe someone or something as **recalcitrant**, you mean that they are unwilling to obey orders or are difficult to deal with. [FORMAL] ❑ *The danger is that recalcitrant local authorities will reject their responsibilities.* ♦ **re|cal|ci|trance** /rɪkælsɪtrəns/ *...the government's recalcitrance over introducing even the smallest political reform.* (ADJ: usu ADJ n = *stubborn*; N-UNCOUNT = *stubbornness*)

**re|call** **(recalls, recalling, recalled)** ◆◆◇

> ✓ The verb is pronounced /rɪkɔːl/. The noun is pronounced /riːkɔːl/.

[1] When you **recall** something, you remember it and tell others about it. ❑ *Henderson recalled that he first met Pollard during a business trip to Washington... Her teacher recalled: 'She was always on about modelling.'... Colleagues today recall with humor how meetings would crawl into the early morning hours... I recalled the way they had been dancing together... I have no idea what she said, something about airline travel, I seem to recall.* (VERB; V that; V with quote; V wh; V n; V; Also V -ing) [2] **Recall** is the ability to remember something that has happened in the past or the act of remembering it. ❑ *He had a good memory, and total recall of her spoken words.* (N-UNCOUNT) [3] If you **are recalled** to your home, country, or the place where you work, you are ordered to return there. ❑ *Spain has recalled its Ambassador after a row over refugees seeking asylum at the embassy.* ♦ **Recall** is also a noun. ❑ *The recall of ambassador Alan Green was a public signal of America's concern.* (VERB; V n; N-SING: *the* N *of* n) [4] In sport, if a player is **recalled to** a team, he or she is included in that team again after being left out. ❑ *Dean Richards was recalled to the England squad for the match with Wales.* ♦ **Recall** is also a noun. ❑ *It would be great to get a recall to the England squad for Sweden.* (VERB; V n *to* n; N-SING) [5] If a company **recalls** a product, it asks the shops or the people who have bought that product to return it because there is something wrong with it. ❑ *The company said it was recalling one of its drugs.* (VERB; V n)

**re|cant** /rɪkænt/ **(recants, recanting, recanted)** If you **recant**, you say publicly that you no longer hold a set of beliefs that you had in the past. [FORMAL] ❑ *White House officials ordered Williams to recant. ...a man who had refused after torture to recant his heresy.* (VERB; V; V n)

**re|cap** /riːkæp/ **(recaps, recapping, recapped)** You can say that you are going to **recap** when you want to draw people's attention to the fact that you are going to repeat the main points of an explanation, argument, or description, as a summary of it. ❑ *To recap briefly, an agreement negotiated to cut the budget deficit was rejected 10 days ago... Can you recap the points included in the regional conference proposal?* ♦ **Recap** is also a noun. ❑ *Each report starts with a recap of how we did versus our projections.* (VERB = *sum up, recapitulate*; V; V n; N-SING)

**re|capi|tal|ize** /riːkæpɪtəlaɪz/ **(recapitalizes, recapitalizing, recapitalized)** If a company **recapitalizes**, it changes the way it manages its financial affairs, for example by borrowing money or reissuing shares. [AM, BUSINESS] ❑ *Mr Warnock resigned as the company abandoned a plan to recapitalize... He plans to recapitalize the insurance fund.* ♦ **re|capi|tali|za|tion** /riːkæpɪtəlaɪzeɪʃᵊn/ **(recapitalizations)** *...a recapitalization of the company.* (VERB; V; V n; N-COUNT)

**re|ca|pitu|late** /riːkəpɪtʃʊleɪt/ **(recapitulates, recapitulating, recapitulated)** You can say that you are going to **recapitulate** the main points of an explanation, argument, or description when you want to draw attention to the fact that you are going to repeat the most important points as a summary. ❑ *Let's just recapitulate the essential points... It will shortly be put up for sale under the terms already communicated to you, which, to recapitulate, call for a very minimum of publicity.* ♦ **re|ca|pitu|la|tion** /riːkəpɪtʃʊleɪʃᵊn/ *Chapter* (VERB = *recap, sum up*; V n; V; N-SING)

*9 provides a valuable recapitulation of the material already presented.*

**re|cap|ture** /riːkæptʃəʳ/ **(recaptures, recapturing, recaptured)** 1 When soldiers **recapture** an area of land or a place, they gain control of it again from an opposing army who had taken it from them. VERB ❑ *They said the bodies were found when rebels recaptured the area.* V n ♦ **Recapture** is also a noun. N-SING: usu N *of* n ❑ *...an offensive to be launched for the recapture of the city.* 2 When people **recapture** something that they have lost to a competitor, they get it back again. VERB ❑ *I believe that he would be the best possibility to recapture the centre vote in the forthcoming election.* V n 3 To **recapture** a person or animal which has escaped from somewhere means to catch them again. VERB ❑ *Police have recaptured Alan Lord, who escaped from a police cell in Bolton.* V n ♦ **Recapture** is also a noun. N-SING: usu n *of* n ❑ *...the recapture of a renegade police chief in Panama.* 4 When you **recapture** something such as an experience, emotion, or a quality that you had in the past, you experience it again. VERB When something **recaptures** an experience for you, it makes you remember it. ❑ *He couldn't recapture the form he'd shown in getting to the semi-final.* V n

**re|cast** /riːkɑːst, -kæst/ **(recasts, recasting)**

> ✔ The form **recast** is used in the present tense and is the past tense and past participle.

1 If you **recast** something, you change it by organizing it in a different way. VERB ❑ *The shake-up aims to recast IBM as a federation of flexible and competing subsidiaries.* V n ♦ **re|cast|ing** N-SING: N *of* n *...the recasting of the political map of Europe.* 2 To **recast** an actor's role means to give the role to another actor. VERB ❑ *Stoppard had to recast four of the principal roles.* V n

**rec|ce** /reki/ **(recces, recceing, recced)** If you **recce** an area, you visit that place in order to become familiar with it. VERB People usually recce an area when they are going to return at a later time to do something there. [BRIT, OLD-FASHIONED] ❑ *The first duty of a director is to recce his location.* V n ♦ **Recce** is also a noun. N-COUNT ❑ *Uncle Jim took the air rifle and went on a recce to the far end of the quarry.*

**recd.** In written English, **recd.** can be used as an abbreviation for **received**.

**re|cede** /rɪsiːd/ **(recedes, receding, receded)** 1 If something **recedes** from you, it moves away. VERB ❑ *Luke's footsteps receded into the night... As she receded he waved goodbye.* V prep V 2 When something such as a quality, problem, or illness **recedes**, it becomes weaker, smaller, or less intense. VERB ❑ *Just as I started to think that I was never going to get well, the illness began to recede.* V 3 If a man's hair starts to **recede**, it no longer grows on the front of his head. VERB ❑ *...a youngish man with dark hair just beginning to recede.* V

**re|ceipt** /rɪsiːt/ **(receipts)** 1 A **receipt** is a piece of paper that you get from someone as proof that they have received money or goods from you. N-COUNT In British English a **receipt** is a piece of paper that you get in a shop when you buy something, but in American English the more usual term for this is **sales slip**. ❑ *I wrote her a receipt for the money.* 2 **Receipts** are the amount of money received during a particular period, for example by a shop or theatre. N-PLURAL: usu with supp = takings ❑ *He was tallying the day's receipts.* 3 The **receipt** of something is the act of receiving it. N-UNCOUNT [FORMAL] ❑ *Goods should be supplied within 28 days after the receipt of your order.* 4 If you are **in receipt of** something, you have received it or you receive it regularly. PHRASE [FORMAL] ❑ *We are taking action, having been in receipt of a letter from him.*

**re|ceive** /rɪsiːv/ **(receives, receiving, received)** ◆◆◆ 1 When you **receive** something, you get it after someone gives it to you or sends it to you. VERB = get ❑ *They will receive their awards at a ceremony in Stockholm... I received your letter of November 7.* V n V n 2 You can use **receive** to say that certain kinds of thing happen to someone. VERB For example if they are injured, you can say that they **received** an injury. ❑ *He received more of the blame than anyone when the plan failed to work... She was suffering from whiplash injuries received in a car crash.* V n V n 3 When you **receive** a visitor or a guest, you greet them. VERB ❑ *The following evening the duchess was again receiving guests.* V n 4 If you say that something **is received** in a particular way, you mean that people react to it in that way. VERB: usu passive ❑ *The resolution had been received with great disappointment within the PLO.* *be* V-ed prep/adv 5 When a radio or television **receives** signals that are being transmitted, it picks them up and converts them into sound or pictures. VERB ❑ *The reception was a little faint but clear enough for him to receive the signal.* V n Also V 6 If you **are on the receiving end** or **at the receiving end** of something unpleasant, you are the person that it happens to. PHRASE ❑ *You saw hate in their eyes and you were on the receiving end of that hate.*

**re|ceived** /rɪsiːvd/ The **received** opinion about something or the **received** way of doing something is generally accepted by people as being correct. ADJ: ADJ n [FORMAL] ❑ *He was among the first to question the received wisdom of the time.*

**Re|ceived Pro|nun|cia|tion** **Received Pronunciation** is a way of pronouncing British English that is often used as a standard in the Teaching of English as a Foreign Language. N-UNCOUNT The abbreviation **RP** is also used. The accent represented by the pronunciations in this dictionary is Received Pronunciation.

**re|ceiv|er** /rɪsiːvəʳ/ **(receivers)** 1 A telephone's **receiver** is the part that you hold near to your ear and speak into. N-COUNT 2 A **receiver** is the part of a radio or television that picks up signals and converts them into sound or pictures. N-COUNT ❑ *Autotuning VHF receivers are now common in cars.* 3 **The receiver** is someone who is appointed by a court of law to manage the affairs of a business, usually when it is facing financial failure. N-COUNT: usu *the* N [BUSINESS] ❑ *Between July and September, a total of 1,059 firms called in the receiver.*

**re|ceiv|er|ship** /rɪsiːvəʳʃɪp/ **(receiverships)** If a company goes **into receivership**, it faces financial failure and the administration of its business is handled by the receiver. N-VAR: oft *in/into* N [BUSINESS] ❑ *The company has now gone into receivership with debts of several million.*

**re|cent** /riːsᵊnt/ A **recent** event or period of time happened only a short while ago. ◆◆◆ ADJ: usu ADJ n ❑ *In the most recent attack one man was shot dead and two others were wounded... Sales have fallen by more than 75 percent in recent years.*

**re|cent|ly** /riːsᵊntli/ If you have done something **recently** or if something happened **recently**, it happened only a short time ago. ◆◆◇ ADV: ADV with v, *until* ADV ❑ *The bank recently opened a branch in Germany... He was until very recently the most powerful banker in the city.*

**re|cep|ta|cle** /rɪseptɪkᵊl/ **(receptacles)** A **receptacle** is an object which you use to put or keep things in. N-COUNT = container [FORMAL]

**re|cep|tion** /rɪsepʃᵊn/ **(receptions)** 1 The **reception** in a hotel is the desk or office that books rooms for people and answers their questions. N-SING: *the* N, oft N n, also *at* N [mainly BRIT] ❑ *Have him bring a car round to the reception. ...the hotel's reception desk.*

> ✔ in AM, use **front desk**

2 The **reception** in an office or hospital is the place where people's appointments and questions are dealt with. N-SING: *the* N, oft N n, also *at* N [mainly BRIT] ❑ *Wait at reception for me.* 3 A **reception** is a formal party which is given to welcome someone or to celebrate a special event. N-COUNT ❑ *At the reception they served smoked salmon.* 4 If someone or something has a particular kind of **reception**, that is the way that people react to them. N-COUNT: usu sing, usu supp N ❑ *Mr Mandela was given a tumultuous reception in Washington.* 5 If you get good **reception** from your radio or television, the sound or picture is clear because the signal is strong. N-UNCOUNT If the **reception** is poor, the sound or pic-

ture is unclear because the signal is weak. ❑ *Adjust the aerial's position and direction for the best reception.*

**re|cep|tion cen|tre** **(reception centres)** A **reception centre** is a place where people who have no homes or are being looked after by the government can live until somewhere else is found for them to live. [mainly BRIT] N-COUNT

**re|cep|tion class** **(reception classes)** A **reception class** is a class that children go into when they first start school at the age of four or five. [BRIT] N-COUNT

**re|cep|tion|ist** /rɪse̲pʃənɪst/ **(receptionists)** [1] In a hotel, the **receptionist** is the person whose job is to book rooms for people and answer their questions. [mainly BRIT] N-COUNT

in AM, use **desk clerk**

[2] In an office or hospital, the **receptionist** is the person whose job is to answer the telephone, arrange appointments, and deal with people when they first arrive. N-COUNT

**re|cep|tion room** **(reception rooms)** A **reception room** is a room in a house, for example a living room, where people can sit. This expression is often used in descriptions of houses that are for sale. [BRIT] N-COUNT

**re|cep|tive** /rɪse̲ptɪv/ [1] Someone who is **receptive to** new ideas or suggestions is prepared to consider them or accept them. ❑ *The voters had seemed receptive to his ideas.* ADJ: oft ADJ *to* n ♦ **re|cep|tive|ness** *There was less receptiveness to liberalism in some areas.* N-UNCOUNT [2] If someone who is ill is **receptive to** treatment, they start to get better when they are given treatment. ❑ *...those patients who are not receptive to treatment.* ADJ: v-link ADJ *to* n

**re|cep|tor** /rɪse̲ptəʳ/ **(receptors)** **Receptors** are nerve endings in your body which react to changes and stimuli and make your body respond in a particular way. [TECHNICAL] ❑ *...the information receptors in our brain.* N-COUNT

**re|cess** /rɪse̲s, ri̲ːses/ **(recesses, recessing, recessed)** [1] A **recess** is a break between the periods of work of an official body such as a committee, a court of law, or a government. ❑ *The conference broke for a recess.* N-COUNT: also *in/from* N [2] When formal meetings or court cases **recess**, they stop temporarily. [FORMAL] ❑ *The hearings have now recessed for dinner...* V *for* n *Before the trial recessed today, the lawyer read her opening statement.* V VERB [3] In a room, a **recess** is part of a wall which is built further back than the rest of the wall. Recesses are often used as a place to put furniture such as shelves. ❑ *...a discreet recess next to a fireplace.* N-COUNT [4] **The recesses of** something or somewhere are the parts of it which are hard to see because light does not reach them or they are hidden from view. ❑ *He emerged from the dark recesses of the garage.* N-COUNT: usu pl, usu with supp [5] If you refer to **the recesses of** someone's mind or soul, you are referring to thoughts or feelings they have which are hidden or difficult to describe. ❑ *There was something in the darker recesses of his unconscious that was troubling him.* N-COUNT: usu pl, usu with supp

**re|cessed** /ri̲ːsest/ If something such as a door or window is **recessed**, it is set into the wall that surrounds it. ❑ *...a wide passage, lit from one side by recessed windows.* ADJ

**re|ces|sion** /rɪse̲ʃᵊn/ **(recessions)** A **recession** is a period when the economy of a country is doing badly, for example because industry is producing less and more people are becoming unemployed. ❑ *The oil price increases sent Europe into deep recession.* ◆◆◇ N-VAR

**re|ces|sion|al** /rɪse̲ʃənᵊl/ [1] The **recessional** is a religious song which is sung at the end of a church service. N-SING [2] **Recessional** means related to an economic recession. ❑ *Many home sellers remain stuck in a recessional rut.* ADJ: ADJ n

**re|ces|sion|ary** /rɪse̲ʃᵊnri/ **Recessionary** means relating to an economic recession or having the effect of creating a recession. ❑ *Reduced interest rates would help ease recessionary pressures in the economy.* ADJ: ADJ n

**re|ces|sive** /rɪse̲sɪv/ A **recessive** gene produces a particular characteristic only if a person has two of these genes, one from each parent. Compare **dominant**. [TECHNICAL] ❑ *Sickle-cell anaemia is passed on through a recessive gene.* ADJ: usu ADJ n

**re|charge** /ri̲ːtʃɑ̲ːʳdʒ/ **(recharges, recharging, recharged)** [1] If you **recharge** a battery, you put an electrical charge back into the battery by connecting it to a machine that draws power from another source of electricity such as the mains. ❑ *He is using your mains electricity to recharge his car battery.* VERB V n [2] If you **recharge your batteries**, you take a break from activities which are tiring or difficult in order to relax and feel better when you return to these activities. ❑ *He wanted to recharge his batteries and come back feeling fresh and positive.* PHRASE: V inflects

**re|charge|able** /ri̲ːtʃɑ̲ːʳdʒəbᵊl/ **Rechargeable** batteries can be recharged and used again. Some electrical products are described as **rechargeable** when they contain rechargeable batteries. ❑ *...a rechargeable battery. ...a rechargeable drill.* ADJ: usu ADJ n

**re|cher|ché** /rəʃe̲əʳʃeɪ/ If you describe something as **recherché**, you mean that it is very sophisticated or is associated with people who like things which are unusual and of a very high quality. [FORMAL] ❑ *Only extra-virgin olive oil will do on recherché dinner tables.* ADJ

**re|cidi|vist** /rɪsɪ̲dɪvɪst/ **(recidivists)** A **recidivist** is someone who has committed crimes in the past and has begun to commit crimes again, for example after a period in prison. [FORMAL] ❑ *Six prisoners are still at large along with four dangerous recidivists.* N-COUNT ♦ **re|cidi|vism** /rɪsɪ̲dɪvɪzəm/ *Their basic criticism was that prisons do not reduce the crime rate, they cause recidivism.* N-UNCOUNT

**reci|pe** /re̲sɪpi/ **(recipes)** [1] A **recipe** is a list of ingredients and a set of instructions that tell you how to cook something. ❑ *...a traditional recipe for oatmeal biscuits. ...a recipe book.* N-COUNT [2] If you say that something is **a recipe for** a particular situation, you mean that it is likely to result in that situation. ❑ *Large-scale inflation is a recipe for disaster.* N-SING: *a* N *for* n

**re|cipi|ent** /rɪsɪ̲piənt/ **(recipients)** The **recipient** of something is the person who receives it. [FORMAL] ❑ *...the largest recipient of American foreign aid.* N-COUNT: oft N *of* n

**re|cip|ro|cal** /rɪsɪ̲prəkᵊl/ A **reciprocal** action or agreement involves two people or groups who do the same thing to each other or agree to help each another in a similar way. [FORMAL] ❑ *They expected a reciprocal gesture before more hostages could be freed.* ADJ: usu ADJ n

**re|cip|ro|cate** /rɪsɪ̲prəkeɪt/ **(reciprocates, reciprocating, reciprocated)** If your feelings or actions towards someone **are reciprocated**, the other person feels or behaves in the same way towards you as you have felt or behaved towards them. ❑ *...he reciprocated Mr Prescott's good wishes...* V n *He needs these people to fulfill his ambitions and reciprocates by bringing out the best in each of them.* V *by* -ing VERB ♦ **re|cip|ro|ca|tion** /rɪsɪ̲prəke̲ɪʃᵊn/ *There was no reciprocation of affection.* N-UNCOUNT

**reci|proc|ity** /re̲sɪprɒ̲sɪti/ **Reciprocity** is the exchange of something between people or groups of people when each person or group gives or allows something to the other. [FORMAL] ❑ *They gave assurances they would press for reciprocity with Greece in the issuing of visas.* N-UNCOUNT

**re|cit|al** /rɪsa̲ɪtᵊl/ **(recitals)** [1] A **recital** is a performance of music or poetry, usually given by one person. ❑ *...a solo recital by the harpsichordist Maggie Cole.* N-COUNT: oft with supp [2] If someone speaks for a long time, or says something that is boring or that has been heard many times before, you can describe it as a **recital**. [WRITTEN] ❑ *Before long we all grew bored with his frequent recital of the foods he couldn't eat.* N-COUNT: usu with supp

**reci|ta|tion** /resɪteɪʃən/ **(recitations)** When someone does a **recitation**, they say aloud a piece of poetry or other writing that they have learned. ❑ *The transmission began with a recitation from the Koran.* N-VAR

**re|cite** /rɪsaɪt/ **(recites, reciting, recited)** 1 When someone **recites** a poem or other piece of writing, they say it aloud after they have learned it. ❑ *They recited poetry to one another.* 2 If you **recite** something such as a list, you say it aloud. ❑ *All he could do was recite a list of Government failings.* VERB V n VERB V n

**reck|less** /rekləs/ If you say that someone is **reckless**, you mean that they act in a way which shows that they do not care about danger or the effect their behaviour will have on other people. ❑ *He is charged with causing death by reckless driving.* ♦ **reck|less|ly** *He was leaning recklessly out of the unshuttered window.* ♦ **reck|less|ness** *He felt a surge of recklessness.* ADJ ADV: ADV with v, ADV adj N-UNCOUNT

**reck|on** /rekən/ **(reckons, reckoning, reckoned)** ◆◇◇ 1 If you **reckon** that something is true, you think that it is true. [INFORMAL] ❑ *Toni reckoned that it must be about three o'clock.* 2 If something **is reckoned** to be a particular figure, it is calculated to be roughly that amount. ❑ *The star's surface temperature is reckoned to be minus 75 degrees celcius... There was a proportion of research, which I reckoned at not more than 30 percent, that was basic research.* VERB = think V that VERB: usu passive be V-ed to-inf be V-ed at n

♦ **reckon on** If you **reckon on** something, you feel certain that it will happen and are therefore prepared for it. ❑ *They are typical of couples who plan a family without reckoning on the small fortune it will cost.* PHRASAL VERB V P n/-ing (not pron)

♦ **reckon with** 1 If you say that you had not **reckoned with** something, you mean that you had not expected it and so were not prepared for it. ❑ *Giles had not reckoned with the strength of Sally's feelings for him.* 2 If you say that there is someone or something **to be reckoned with**, you mean that they must be dealt with and it will be difficult. ❑ *This act was a signal to his victim's friends that he was someone to be reckoned with.* PHRASAL VERB: with brd-neg = bargain for, bargain on V P n PHRASE: n PHR

**reck|on|ing** /rekənɪŋ/ **(reckonings)** Someone's **reckoning** is a calculation they make about something, especially a calculation that is not very exact. ❑ *By my reckoning we were seven or eight kilometres from Borj Mechaab.* N-VAR: usu poss N

**re|claim** /rɪkleɪm/ **(reclaims, reclaiming, reclaimed)** 1 If you **reclaim** something that you have lost or that has been taken away from you, you succeed in getting it back. ❑ *In 1986, they got the right to reclaim South African citizenship.* 2 If you **reclaim** an amount of money, for example tax that you have paid, you claim it back. ❑ *There are an estimated eight million people currently thought to be eligible to reclaim income tax.* 3 When people **reclaim** land, they make it suitable for a purpose such as farming or building, for example by draining it or by building a barrier against the sea. ❑ *The Netherlands has been reclaiming farmland from water.* 4 If a piece of land that was used for farming or building **is reclaimed by** a desert, forest, or the sea, it turns back into desert, forest, or sea. ❑ *The diamond towns are gradually being reclaimed by the desert.* VERB V n VERB V n VERB V n VERB: usu passive be V-ed by n

**rec|la|ma|tion** /rekləmeɪʃən/ **Reclamation** is the process of changing land that is unsuitable for farming or building into land that can be used. ❑ *...centuries of sea-wall construction and the reclamation of dry land from the marshes.* N-UNCOUNT

**re|cline** /rɪklaɪn/ **(reclines, reclining, reclined)** 1 If you **recline on** something, you sit or lie on it with the upper part of your body supported at an angle. ❑ *She proceeded to recline on a chaise longue.* 2 When a seat **reclines** or when you **recline** it, you lower the back so that it is more comfortable to sit in. ❑ *Air France first-class seats recline almost like beds... Ramesh had reclined his seat and was lying back smoking.* VERB = lie V prep VERB V V n

**re|cluse** /rɪkluːs, AM rekluːs/ **(recluses)** A **recluse** is a person who lives alone and deliberately avoids other people. ❑ *His widow became a virtual recluse for the remainder of her life.* N-COUNT: usu sing

**re|clu|sive** /rɪkluːsɪv/ A **reclusive** person or animal lives alone and deliberately avoids the company of others. ❑ *She had been living a reclusive life in Los Angeles since her marriage broke up.* ADJ

**rec|og|nise** /rekəgnaɪz/ → see **recognize**.

**rec|og|ni|tion** /rekəgnɪʃən/ ◆◇◇ 1 **Recognition** is the act of recognizing someone or identifying something when you see it. ❑ *He searched for a sign of recognition on her face, but there was none.* 2 **Recognition of** something is an understanding and acceptance of it. ❑ *The CBI welcomed the Chancellor's recognition of the recession and hoped for a reduction in interest rates.* 3 When a government gives diplomatic **recognition** to another country, they officially accept that its status is valid. ❑ *His government did not receive full recognition by Britain until July.* 4 When a person receives **recognition** for the things that they have done, people acknowledge the value or skill of their work. ❑ *At last, her father's work has received popular recognition.* N-UNCOUNT N-UNCOUNT: with supp = acknowledgement N-UNCOUNT: with supp N-UNCOUNT: with supp

PHRASES 5 If you say that someone or something has changed **beyond recognition** or **out of all recognition**, you mean that person or thing has changed so much that you can no longer recognize them. ❑ *The bodies were mutilated beyond recognition... The situation in Eastern Europe has changed out of all recognition.* 6 If something is done **in recognition of** someone's achievements, it is done as a way of showing official appreciation of them. ❑ *Brazil normalised its diplomatic relations with South Africa in recognition of the steps taken to end apartheid.* PHRASE: PHR after v emphasis PREP-PHRASE

**rec|og|niz|able** /rekəgnaɪzəbəl/

✔ in BRIT, also use **recognisable**

If something can be easily recognized or identified, you can say that it is easily **recognizable**. ❑ *The body was found to be well preserved, his features easily recognizable.* ♦ **rec|og|niz|ably** /rekəgnaɪzəbli/ *At seven weeks, an embryo is about three-fourths of an inch long and recognizably human.* ADJ: oft adv ADJ, ADJ as/by/to n ADV: usu ADV n, ADV adj

**rec|og|nize** /rekəgnaɪz/ **(recognizes, recognizing, recognized)** ◆◆◇

✔ in BRIT, also use **recognise**

1 If you **recognize** someone or something, you know who that person is or what that thing is. ❑ *The receptionist recognized him at once... A man I easily recognized as Luke's father sat with a newspaper on his lap.* 2 If someone says that they **recognize** something, they acknowledge that it exists or that it is true. ❑ *I recognize my own shortcomings... Well, of course I recognize that evil exists.* 3 If people or organizations **recognize** something as valid, they officially accept it or approve of it. ❑ *Most doctors appear to recognize homeopathy as a legitimate form of medicine... France is on the point of recognizing the independence of the Baltic States.* 4 When people **recognize** the work that someone has done, they show their appreciation of it, often by giving that person an award of some kind. ❑ *The RAF recognized him as an outstandingly able engineer... Nichols was recognized by the Hall of Fame in 1949.* VERB: no cont V n V n as n VERB: no cont = acknowledge V n V that VERB = accept V n as n V n Also V that VERB V n as n V n

**re|coil** **(recoils, recoiling, recoiled)**

✔ The verb is pronounced /rɪkɔɪl/. The noun is pronounced /riːkɔɪl/.

1 If something makes you **recoil**, you move your body quickly away from it because it frightens, offends, or hurts you. ❑ *For a moment I thought he was going to kiss me. I recoiled in horror... We are attracted by nice smells and recoil from nasty ones.* ♦ **Recoil** is also a noun. ❑ *...his small body jerking in recoil from the volume of his shouting.* 2 If you **recoil from** doing something or **recoil at** the idea VERB V V from n N-UNCOUNT VERB

of something, you refuse to do it or accept it because you dislike it so much. ❑ *People used to recoil from the idea of getting into debt... She recoiled at the number of young girls who had to live by selling their bodies.* (V from n; V at n)

**rec|ol|lect** /rekəlekt/ **(recollects, recollecting, recollected)** If you **recollect** something, you remember it. (VERB = remember) ❑ *Ramona spoke with warmth when she recollected the doctor who used to be at the county hospital... His efforts, the Duke recollected many years later, were distinctly half-hearted.* (V n; V that)

**rec|ol|lec|tion** /rekəlekʃən/ **(recollections)** If you have a **recollection of** something, you remember it. (N-VAR = memory) ❑ *Pat has vivid recollections of the trip... He had no recollection of the crash.*

**re|com|mence** /riːkəmens/ **(recommences, recommencing, recommenced)** If you **recommence** something or if it **recommences**, it begins again after having stopped. [WRITTEN] (VERB) ❑ *He recommenced work on his novel... His course at Sheffield University will not recommence until next year.* (V n; V)

**rec|om|mend** /rekəmend/ **(recommends, recommending, recommended)** ◆◆◇ 1 If someone **recommends** a person or thing to you, they suggest that you would find that person or thing good or useful. (VERB) ❑ *I have just spent a holiday there and would recommend it to anyone... 'You're a good worker, boy,' he told him. 'I'll recommend you for a promotion.'... Ask your doctor to recommend a suitable therapist.* (V n to/for/as n; V n to/for/as n; V n) ♦ **rec|om|mend|ed** *Though ten years old, this book is highly recommended.* (ADJ) 2 If you **recommend** that something is done, you suggest that it should be done. (VERB) ❑ *The judge recommended that he serve 20 years in prison... We strongly recommend reporting the incident to the police... The recommended daily dose is 12 to 24 grams... Many financial planners now recommend against ever fully paying off your home loan.* (V that; V n/-ing; V-ed; V against n/-ing) 3 If something or someone has a particular quality to **recommend** them, that quality makes them attractive or gives them an advantage over similar things or people. (VERB) ❑ *La Noblesse restaurant has much to recommend it... These qualities recommended him to Olivier.* (V n; V n to n)

**rec|om|men|da|tion** /rekəmendeɪʃən/ **(recommendations)** ◆◇◇ 1 The **recommendations** of a person or a committee are their suggestions or advice on what is the best thing to do. (N-VAR: oft with poss) ❑ *The committee's recommendations are unlikely to be made public... The decision was made on the recommendation of the Interior Minister.* 2 A **recommendation** of something is the suggestion that someone should have or use it because it is good. (N-VAR) ❑ *The best way of finding a solicitor is through personal recommendation.*

**rec|om|pense** /rekəmpens/ **(recompenses, recompensing, recompensed)** 1 If you are given something, usually money, **in recompense**, you are given it as a reward or because you have suffered. [FORMAL] (N-UNCOUNT: oft N for n, in N) ❑ *He demands no financial recompense for his troubles... Substantial damages were paid in recompense.* 2 If you **recompense** someone **for** their efforts or their loss, you give them something, usually money, as a payment or reward. [FORMAL] (VERB) ❑ *The fees offered by the NHS do not recompense dental surgeons for their professional time.* (V n for n)

**rec|on|cile** /rekənsaɪl/ **(reconciles, reconciling, reconciled)** 1 If you **reconcile** two beliefs, facts, or demands that seem to be opposed or completely different, you find a way in which they can both be true or both be successful. (VERB) ❑ *It's difficult to reconcile the demands of my job and the desire to be a good father... Negotiators must now work out how to reconcile these demands with American demands for access.* (V pl-n; V n with n) 2 If you **are reconciled with** someone, you become friendly with them again after a quarrel or disagreement. (V-RECIP-PASSIVE) ❑ *He never believed he and Susan would be reconciled... Devlin was reconciled with the Catholic Church in his last few days.* (pl-n be V-ed; be V-ed with n) 3 If you **reconcile** two people, you make them become friends again after a quarrel or disagreement. (VERB) ❑ *...my attempt to reconcile him with Toby.* (V n with n) 4 If you **reconcile yourself to** an unpleasant situation, you accept it, although it does not make you happy to do so. (VERB) ❑ *She had reconciled herself to never seeing him again.* (V pron-refl to n/-ing) ♦ **rec|on|ciled** *She felt a little more reconciled to her lot.* (ADJ: v-link ADJ to n/-ing)

**rec|on|cilia|tion** /rekənsɪlieɪʃən/ **(reconciliations)** 1 **Reconciliation** between two people or countries who have quarrelled is the process of their becoming friends again. A **reconciliation** is an instance of this. (N-VAR: oft N between/with/of n) ❑ *...an appeal for reconciliation between Catholics and Protestants.* 2 The **reconciliation** of two beliefs, facts, or demands that seem to be opposed is the process of finding a way in which they can both be true or both be successful. (N-SING: N between/of/with n) ❑ *...the ideal of democracy based upon a reconciliation of the values of equality and liberty.*

**re|con|dite** /rɪkɒndaɪt, rekən-/ **Recondite** areas of knowledge or learning are difficult to understand, and not many people know about them. [FORMAL] (ADJ: usu ADJ n) ❑ *Her poems are modishly experimental in style and recondite in subject-matter.*

**re|con|di|tion** /riːkəndɪʃən/ **(reconditions, reconditioning, reconditioned)** To **recondition** a machine or piece of equipment means to repair or replace all the parts that are damaged or broken. (VERB) ❑ *He made contact with someone with an idea for reconditioning laser copiers... They sell used and reconditioned motorcycle parts.* (V n; V-ed)

**re|con|firm** /riːkənfɜːʳm/ **(reconfirms, reconfirming, reconfirmed)** **Reconfirm** means the same as **confirm**. (VERB)

**re|con|nais|sance** /rɪkɒnɪsəns/ **Reconnaissance** is the activity of obtaining military information about a place by sending soldiers or planes there, or by the use of satellites. (N-UNCOUNT: oft N n) ❑ *The helicopter was returning from a reconnaissance mission.*

**re|con|nect** /riːkənekt/ **(reconnects, reconnecting, reconnected)** If a company **reconnects** your electricity, water, gas, or telephone after it has been stopped, they provide you with it once again. (VERB) ❑ *They charge a £66.10 fee for reconnecting cut-off customers.* (V n)

**rec|on|noi|tre** /rekənɔɪtəʳ/ **(reconnoitres, reconnoitring, reconnoitred)**

✔ in AM, use **reconnoiter**

To **reconnoitre** an area means to obtain information about its geographical features or about the size and position of an army there. (VERB) ❑ *He was sent to Eritrea to reconnoitre the enemy position... I left a sergeant in command and rode forward to reconnoitre.* (V n; V)

**re|con|quer** /riːkɒŋkəʳ/ **(reconquers, reconquering, reconquered)** If an army **reconquers** a country or territory after having lost it, they win control over it again. (VERB) ❑ *A crusade left Europe in an attempt to reconquer the Holy City.* (V n)

**re|con|sid|er** /riːkənsɪdəʳ/ **(reconsiders, reconsidering, reconsidered)** If you **reconsider** a decision or opinion, you think about it and try to decide whether it should be changed. (VERB) ❑ *We want you to reconsider your decision to resign from the board... If at the end of two years you still feel the same, we will reconsider.* (V n; V) ♦ **re|con|sid|era|tion** /riːkənsɪdəreɪʃən/ *The report urges reconsideration of the decision.* (N-UNCOUNT: oft N of n)

**re|con|sti|tute** /riːkɒnstɪtjuːt, AM -tuːt/ **(reconstitutes, reconstituting, reconstituted)** 1 If an organization or state **is reconstituted**, it is formed again in a different way. (VERB: usu passive) ❑ *Slowly Jewish communities were reconstituted and Jewish life began anew.* (be V-ed) 2 To **reconstitute** dried food means to add water to it so that it can be eaten. (VERB) ❑ *To reconstitute dried tomatoes, simmer in plain water until they are tender... Try eating reconstituted dried prunes, figs or apricots.* (V n; V-ed)

**re|con|struct** /riːkənstrʌkt/ **(reconstructs, reconstructing, reconstructed)** 1 If you **reconstruct** something that has been destroyed or badly damaged, you build it and make it work again. (VERB = rebuild) ❑ *The government must reconstruct the shattered economy... Although this part of Normandy was badly* (V n; V n) *bombed during the war it has been completely reconstructed.* [2] To **reconstruct** a system or policy means to change it so that it works in a different way. ❑ *She actually wanted to reconstruct the state and transform society.* [3] If you **reconstruct** an event that happened in the past, you try to get a complete understanding of it by combining a lot of small pieces of information. ❑ *He began to reconstruct the events of 21 December 1988, when flight 103 disappeared... Elaborate efforts were made to reconstruct what had happened.*

VERB · V n · VERB · V n · V wh

**re|con|struc|tion** /riːkənstrʌkʃᵊn/ **(reconstructions)** [1] **Reconstruction** is the process of making a country normal again after a war, for example by making the economy stronger and by replacing buildings that have been damaged. ❑ *...America's part in the post-war reconstruction of Germany.* [2] The **reconstruction** of a building, structure, or road is the activity of building it again, because it has been damaged. ❑ *Work began on the reconstruction of the road.* [3] The **reconstruction** of a crime or event is when people try to understand or show exactly what happened, often by acting it out. ❑ *Mrs Kerr was too upset to take part in a reconstruction of her ordeal.*

N-UNCOUNT · N-UNCOUNT · N-COUNT: usu with supp

**re|con|struc|tive** /riːkənstrʌktɪv/ **Reconstructive** surgery or treatment involves rebuilding a part of someone's body because it has been badly damaged, or because the person wants to change its shape. ❑ *I needed reconstructive surgery to give me a new nose.*

ADJ: ADJ n

**re|con|vene** /riːkənviːn/ **(reconvenes, reconvening, reconvened)** If a parliament, court, or conference **reconvenes** or if someone **reconvenes** it, it meets again after a break. ❑ *The conference might reconvene after its opening session... It was certainly serious enough for him to reconvene Parliament.*

VERB · V · V n

**rec|ord** **(records, recording, recorded)** ◆◆◆

> ✔ The noun is pronounced /rekɔːʳd, AM -kərd/. The verb is pronounced /rɪkɔːʳd/.

[1] If you keep a **record of** something, you keep a written account or photographs of it so that it can be referred to later. ❑ *Keep a record of all the payments... There's no record of any marriage or children... The result will go on your medical records.* [2] If you **record** a piece of information or an event, you write it down, photograph it, or put it into a computer so that in the future people can refer to it. ❑ *...software packages which record the details of your photographs. ...a place which has rarely suffered a famine in its recorded history.* [3] If you **record** something such as a speech or performance, you put it on tape or film so that it can be heard or seen again later. ❑ *There is nothing to stop viewers recording the films on videotape... The call was answered by a recorded message saying the company had closed early.* [4] If a musician or performer **records** a piece of music or a television or radio show, they perform it so that it can be put onto CD, tape, or film. ❑ *It took the musicians two and a half days to record their soundtrack for the film.* [5] A **record** is a round, flat piece of black plastic on which sound, especially music, is stored, and which can be played on a record player. You can also refer to the music stored on this piece of plastic as a **record**. ❑ *This is one of my favourite records.* [6] If a dial or other measuring device **records** a certain measurement or value, it shows that measurement or value. ❑ *The test records the electrical activity of the brain.* [7] A **record** is the best result that has ever been achieved in a particular sport or activity, for example the fastest time, the furthest distance, or the greatest number of victories. ❑ *Roger Kingdom set the world record of 12.92 seconds. ...the 800 metres, where she is the world record holder.* [8] You use **record** to say that something is higher, lower, better, or worse than has ever been achieved before. ❑ *Profits were at record levels... She won the race in record time.* [9] Someone's **record** is the facts that are known about their achievements or character. ❑ *His record reveals a tough streak.* [10] If someone has a criminal **record**, it is officially known that they have committed crimes in the past. ❑ *...a heroin addict with a criminal record going back 15 years.* [11] ➔ See also **recording, track record**.

N-COUNT · VERB · V n · V-ed · VERB · V n · V-ed · VERB · V n · N-COUNT · VERB · V n · N-COUNT · ADJ: ADJ n · N-COUNT: with supp · N-COUNT

**PHRASES** [12] If you say that what you are going to say next is **for the record**, you mean that you are saying it publicly and officially and you want it to be written down and remembered. ❑ *We're willing to state for the record that it has enormous value.* [13] If you give some information **for the record**, you give it in case people might find it useful at a later time, although it is not a very important part of what you are talking about. ❑ *For the record, most Moscow girls leave school at about 18.* [14] If something that you say is **off the record**, you do not intend it to be considered as official, or published with your name attached to it. ❑ *May I speak off the record?* [15] If you are **on record as** saying something, you have said it publicly and officially and it has been written down. ❑ *The Chancellor is on record as saying that the increase in unemployment is 'a price worth paying' to keep inflation down.* [16] If you keep information **on record**, you write it down or store it in a computer so that it can be used later. ❑ *The practice is to keep on record any analysis of samples.* [17] If something is the best, worst, or biggest **on record**, it is the best, worst, or biggest thing of its kind that has been noticed and written down. ❑ *It's the shortest election campaign on record.* [18] If you **set the record straight** or **put the record straight**, you show that something which has been regarded as true is in fact not true. ❑ *Let me set the record straight on the misconceptions contained in your article.*

PHRASE · PHRASE · PHRASE: usu PHR after v, PHR n · PHRASE · PHRASE · PHRASE · PHRASE

**re|cord|able** /rɪkɔːʳdəbᵊl/ A **recordable** CD or DVD is a CD or DVD that you can record onto. Compare **rewritable**. ❑ *...recordable cds.*

ADJ

**record-breaker** **(record-breakers)** also **record breaker**. A **record-breaker** is someone or something that beats the previous best result in a sport or other activity. ❑ *The movie became a box-office record breaker.*

N-COUNT

**record-breaking** A **record-breaking** success, result, or performance is one that beats the previous best success, result, or performance. ❑ *Australia's rugby union side enjoyed a record-breaking win over France.*

ADJ: ADJ n

**rec|ord|ed de|liv|ery** If you send a letter or parcel **recorded delivery**, you send it using a Post Office service which gives you an official record of the fact that it has been posted and delivered. [BRIT] ❑ *Use recorded delivery for large cheques or money orders.*

N-UNCOUNT

> ✔ in AM, usually use **registered mail**

**re|cord|er** /rɪkɔːʳdəʳ/ **(recorders)** [1] You can refer to a cassette recorder, a tape recorder, or a video recorder as a **recorder**. ❑ *Rodney put the recorder on the desk top and pushed the play button.* ➔ See also **cassette recorder, tape recorder, video recorder**. [2] A **recorder** is a wooden or plastic musical instrument in the shape of a pipe. You play the recorder by blowing into the top of it and covering and uncovering the holes with your fingers. [3] A **recorder** is a machine or instrument that keeps a record of something, for example in an experiment or on a vehicle. ❑ *Data recorders also pin-point mechanical faults rapidly, reducing repair times.* ➔ See also **flight recorder**.

N-COUNT · N-VAR: oft *the* N · N-COUNT

**rec|ord hold|er** **(record holders)** **The record holder** in a particular sport or activity is the person or team that holds the record for doing it fastest or best. ❑ *...the British record holder for the 200m backstroke.*

N-COUNT: usu *the* N

**re|cord|ing** /rɪkɔːʳdɪŋ/ **(recordings)** [1] A **recording of** something is a record, CD, tape, or video of it. ❑ *...a video recording of a police interview.*

◆◇◇ N-COUNT

[2] **Recording** is the process of making records, CDs, tapes, or videos. ❑ *...the recording industry.* N-UNCOUNT: usu N n

**rec|ord play|er** (**record players**) also **record-player**. A **record player** is a machine on which you can play a record in order to listen to the music or other sounds on it. N-COUNT

**re|count** (**recounts, recounting, recounted**)

> ✔ The verb is pronounced /rɪkaʊnt/. The noun is pronounced /riːkaʊnt/.

[1] If you **recount** a story or event, you tell or describe it to people. [FORMAL] ❑ *He then recounted the story of the interview for his first job... He recounted how heavily armed soldiers forced him from the presidential palace.* VERB V n V wh [2] A **recount** is a second count of votes in an election when the result is very close. ❑ *She wanted a recount. She couldn't believe that I had got more votes than her.* N-COUNT

**re|coup** /rɪkuːp/ (**recoups, recouping, recouped**) If you **recoup** a sum of money that you have spent or lost, you get it back. ❑ *Insurance companies are trying to recoup their losses by increasing premiums.* VERB = recover V n

**re|course** /rɪkɔːʳs/ If you achieve something without **recourse to** a particular course of action, you succeed without carrying out that action. To have **recourse to** a particular course of action means to have to do that action in order to achieve something. [FORMAL] ❑ *It enabled its members to settle their differences without recourse to war.* N-UNCOUNT: usu N *to* n

**re|cov|er** /rɪkʌvəʳ/ (**recovers, recovering, recovered**) ◆◇◇ [1] When you **recover from** an illness or an injury, you become well again. ❑ *He is recovering from a knee injury... A policeman was recovering in hospital last night after being stabbed.* VERB V *from* n/-ing V [2] If you **recover from** an unhappy or unpleasant experience, you stop being upset by it. ❑ *...a tragedy from which he never fully recovered... Her plane broke down and it was 18 hours before she got there. It took her three days to recover.* VERB V *from* n V [3] If something **recovers from** a period of weakness or difficulty, it improves or gets stronger again. ❑ *He recovered from a 4-2 deficit to reach the quarter-finals... The stockmarket index fell by 80% before it began to recover.* VERB V *from* n V [4] If you **recover** something that has been lost or stolen, you find it or get it back. ❑ *Police raided five houses in south-east London and recovered stolen goods.* VERB = retrieve V n [5] If you **recover** a mental or physical state, it comes back again. For example, if you **recover** consciousness, you become conscious again. ❑ *She had a severe attack of asthma and it took an hour to recover her breath.* VERB = regain V n [6] If you **recover** money that you have spent, invested, or lent to someone, you get the same amount back. ❑ *Legal action is being taken to try to recover the money.* VERB = recoup V n

**re|cov|er|able** /rɪkʌvərəbᵊl/ If something is **recoverable**, it is possible for you to get it back. ❑ *If you decide not to buy, the money you have spent on the survey is not recoverable.* ADJ

**re|cov|ery** /rɪkʌvəri/ (**recoveries**) ◆◇◇ [1] If a sick person makes a **recovery**, he or she becomes well again. ❑ *He made a remarkable recovery from a shin injury.* N-VAR [2] When there is a **recovery** in a country's economy, it improves. ❑ *Interest-rate cuts have failed to bring about economic recovery.* N-VAR [3] You talk about the **recovery of** something when you get it back after it has been lost or stolen. ❑ *A substantial reward is being offered for the recovery of a painting by Turner.* N-UNCOUNT: usu N *of* n [4] You talk about the **recovery of** someone's physical or mental state when they return to this state. ❑ *...the abrupt loss and recovery of consciousness.* N-UNCOUNT: N *of* n [5] If someone is **in recovery**, they are being given a course of treatment to help them recover from something such as a drug habit or mental illness. ❑ *...Carole, a compulsive pot smoker and alcoholic in recovery.* PHRASE

**re|cre|ate** /riːkrieɪt/ (**recreates, recreating, recreated**) If you **recreate** something, you succeed in making it exist or seem to exist in a different time or place to its original time or place. ❑ *I am trying to recreate family life far from home.* VERB V n

**rec|rea|tion** (**recreations**)

> ✔ Pronounced /rekrieɪʃᵊn/ for meaning 1. Pronounced /riːkrieɪʃᵊn/ and hyphenated re|crea|tion for meaning 2.

[1] **Recreation** consists of things that you do in your spare time to relax. ❑ *Saturday afternoon is for recreation and outings.* N-VAR [2] A **recreation of** something is the process of making it exist or seem to exist again in a different time or place. ❑ *They are seeking to build a faithful recreation of the original Elizabethan theatre.* N-COUNT

**rec|rea|tion|al** /rekrieɪʃənᵊl/ **Recreational** means relating to things people do in their spare time to relax. ❑ *...parks and other recreational facilities. ...recreational use of alcohol.* ADJ: usu ADJ n

**rec|rea|tion|al drug** (**recreational drugs**) **Recreational drugs** are drugs that people take occasionally for enjoyment, especially when they are spending time socially with other people. ❑ *Society largely turns a blind eye to recreational drug use. ...recreational drugs, such as marijuana or cocaine.* N-COUNT: oft N n

**rec|rea|tion|al ve|hi|cle** (**recreational vehicles**) A **recreational vehicle** is a large vehicle that you can live in. The abbreviation **RV** is also used. [mainly AM] N-COUNT

**re|crimi|na|tion** /rɪkrɪmɪneɪʃᵊn/ (**recriminations**) **Recriminations** are accusations that two people or groups make about each other. ❑ *The bitter rows and recriminations have finally ended the relationship.* N-UNCOUNT: also N in pl

**re|cruit** /rɪkruːt/ (**recruits, recruiting, recruited**) ◆◇◇ [1] If you **recruit** people for an organization, you select them and persuade them to join it or work for it. ❑ *The police are trying to recruit more black and Asian officers... In recruiting students to Computer Systems Engineering, the University looks for evidence of all-round ability... He helped to recruit volunteers to go to Pakistan to fight.* VERB V n V n *to/for* n V n to-inf ♦ **re|cruit|er** (**recruiters**) *...a Marine recruiter.* N-COUNT ♦ **re|cruit|ing** *A bomb exploded at an army recruiting office.* N-UNCOUNT: oft N n [2] A **recruit** is a person who has recently joined an organization or an army. N-COUNT

**re|cruit|ment** /rɪkruːtmənt/ The **recruitment** of workers, soldiers, or members is the act or process of selecting them for an organization or army and persuading them to join. ❑ *...the examination system for the recruitment of civil servants.* N-UNCOUNT

**re|cruit|ment con|sult|ant** (**recruitment consultants**) A **recruitment consultant** is a person or service that helps professional people to find work by introducing them to potential employers. [BUSINESS] N-COUNT

**rec|tal** /rektəl/ **Rectal** means relating to the rectum. [MEDICAL] ❑ *...rectal cancer.* ADJ: ADJ n

**rec|tan|gle** /rektæŋgᵊl/ (**rectangles**) A **rectangle** is a four-sided shape whose corners are all ninety degree angles. Each side of a rectangle is the same length as the one opposite to it. N-COUNT

**rec|tan|gu|lar** /rektæŋgjʊləʳ/ Something that is **rectangular** is shaped like a rectangle. ❑ *...a rectangular table.* ADJ

**rec|ti|fi|ca|tion** /rektɪfɪkeɪʃᵊn/ The **rectification** of something that is wrong is the act of changing it to make it correct or satisfactory. ❑ *...the rectification of an injustice.* N-UNCOUNT

**rec|ti|fy** /rektɪfaɪ/ (**rectifies, rectifying, rectified**) If you **rectify** something that is wrong, you change it so that it becomes correct or satisfactory. ❑ *Only an act of Congress could rectify the situation.* VERB V n

**rec|ti|tude** /rektɪtjuːd, AM -tuːd/ **Rectitude** is a quality or attitude that is shown by people who behave honestly and morally according to accepted standards. [FORMAL] ❑ *...people of the utmost moral rectitude.* N-UNCOUNT

**rec|tor** /rektəʳ/ (**rectors**) A **rector** is a priest in the Church of England who is in charge of a particular area. N-COUNT

**rec|tory** /rektəri/ **(rectories)** A **rectory** is a house in which a Church of England rector and his family live. N-COUNT

**rec|tum** /rektəm/ **(rectums)** Someone's **rectum** is the bottom end of the tube down which waste food passes out of their body. [MEDICAL] N-COUNT

**re|cum|bent** /rɪkʌmbənt/ A **recumbent** figure or person is lying down. [FORMAL] ❑ *He looked down at the recumbent figure.* ADJ: usu ADJ n

**re|cu|per|ate** /rɪkuːpəreɪt/ **(recuperates, recuperating, recuperated)** When you **recuperate**, you recover your health or strength after you have been ill or injured. ❑ *I went away to the country to recuperate... He is recuperating from a serious back injury.* VERB = recover V V *from* n ♦ **re|cu|pera|tion** /rɪkuːpəreɪʃən/ *Leonard was very pleased with his powers of recuperation.* N-UNCOUNT = recovery

**re|cu|pera|tive** /rɪkuːpərətɪv/ Something that is **recuperative** helps you to recover your health and strength after an illness or injury. ❑ *Human beings have great recuperative powers.* ADJ: usu ADJ n

**re|cur** /rɪkɜːʳ/ **(recurs, recurring, recurred)** If something **recurs**, it happens more than once. ❑ *...a theme that was to recur frequently in his work. ...a recurring nightmare she has had since childhood.* VERB V V-ing

**re|cur|rence** /rɪkʌrəns, AM -kɜːr-/ **(recurrences)** If there is a **recurrence of** something, it happens again. ❑ *Police are out in force to prevent a recurrence of the violence.* N-VAR: oft N *of* n

**re|cur|rent** /rɪkʌrənt, AM -kɜːr-/ A **recurrent** event or feeling happens or is experienced more than once. ❑ *Race is a recurrent theme in the work.* ADJ: usu ADJ n

**re|cy|clable** /riːsaɪkələbəl/ **Recyclable** waste or materials can be processed and used again. ❑ *...a separate bin for recyclable waste products.* ADJ

**re|cy|cle** /riːsaɪkəl/ **(recycles, recycling, recycled)** If you **recycle** things that have already been used, such as bottles or sheets of paper, you process them so that they can be used again. ❑ *The objective would be to recycle 98 per cent of domestic waste... It is printed on recycled paper.* VERB V n V-ed ♦ **re|cy|cling** *...a recycling scheme.* N-UNCOUNT

**red** /red/ **(reds, redder, reddest)** ♦♦♦ [1] Something that is **red** is the colour of blood or fire. ❑ *...a bunch of red roses.* COLOUR [2] If you say that someone's face is **red**, you mean that it is redder than its normal colour, because they are embarrassed, angry, or out of breath. ❑ *With a bright red face I was forced to admit that I had no real idea.* ADJ [3] You describe someone's hair as **red** when it is between red and brown in colour. ❑ *...a girl with red hair.* ADJ [4] You can refer to red wine as **red**. ❑ *The spicy flavours in these dishes call for reds rather than whites.* N-MASS [5] If you refer to someone as a **red** or a **Red**, you disapprove of the fact that they are a communist, a socialist or have left-wing ideas. [INFORMAL] N-COUNT [disapproval]
PHRASES [6] If a person or company is **in the red** or if their bank account is **in the red**, they have spent more money than they have in their account and therefore they owe money to the bank. ❑ *The theatre is £500,000 in the red.* PHRASE: v-link PHR [7] If you **see red**, you suddenly become very angry. ❑ *I didn't mean to break his nose. I just saw red.* PHRASE: V inflects [8] **like a red rag to a bull** → see **rag**.

**red alert** **(red alerts)** If a hospital, a police force, or a military force is **on red alert**, they have been warned that there may be an emergency, so they can be ready to deal with it. ❑ *All the Plymouth hospitals are on red alert.* N-VAR

**red-blooded** If a man is described as **red-blooded**, he is considered to be strong and healthy and have a strong interest in sex. [INFORMAL] ❑ *Hers is a body which every red-blooded male cannot fail to have noticed.* ADJ: ADJ n

**red|brick** /redbrɪk/ In Britain, a **redbrick** university is one of the universities that were established in large cities outside London in the late 19th and early 20th centuries, as opposed to much older universities such as Oxford and Cambridge. ADJ: ADJ n

**red cab|bage** **(red cabbages)** A **red cabbage** is a cabbage with dark red leaves. N-VAR

**red card** **(red cards)** In football or rugby, if a player is shown the **red card**, the referee holds up a red card to indicate that the player must leave the pitch for breaking the rules. N-COUNT: usu singular

**red car|pet** **(red carpets)** **The red carpet** is special treatment given to an important or honoured guest, for example the laying of a strip of red carpet for them to walk on. ❑ *We'll give her some VIP treatment and roll out the red carpet.* N-COUNT: usu sing

**Red Cres|cent** **The Red Crescent** is an organization in Muslim countries that helps people who are suffering, for example as a result of war, floods, or disease. N-PROPER: *the* N

**Red Cross** **The Red Cross** is an international organization that helps people who are suffering, for example as a result of war, floods, or disease. N-PROPER: *the* N

**red|cur|rant** /redkʌrənt, AM -kɜːr-/ **(redcurrants)** **Redcurrants** are very small, bright red berries that grow in bunches on a bush and can be eaten as a fruit or cooked to make a sauce for meat. The bush on which they grow can also be called a **redcurrant**. [BRIT] N-COUNT

**red|den** /redən/ **(reddens, reddening, reddened)** If someone **reddens** or their face **reddens**, their face turns pink or red, often because they are embarrassed or angry. [WRITTEN] ❑ *He was working himself up to a fury, his face reddening.* VERB V

**red|dish** /redɪʃ/ **Reddish** means slightly red in colour. ❑ *He had reddish brown hair.* ADJ: usu ADJ n

**re|deco|rate** /riːdekəreɪt/ **(redecorates, redecorating, redecorated)** If you **redecorate** a room or a building, you put new paint or wallpaper on it. ❑ *Americans redecorate their houses and offices every few years... Our children have left home, and we now want to redecorate.* VERB V n V ♦ **re|deco|ra|tion** /riːdekəreɪʃən/ *The house is in desperate need of redecoration.* N-UNCOUNT

**re|deem** /rɪdiːm/ **(redeems, redeeming, redeemed)** [1] If you **redeem yourself** or your reputation, you do something that makes people have a good opinion of you again after you have behaved or performed badly. ❑ *He had realized the mistake he had made and wanted to redeem himself... The sole redeeming feature of your behaviour is that you're not denying it.* VERB V n V-ing [2] When something **redeems** an unpleasant thing or situation, it prevents it from being completely bad. ❑ *Work is the way that people seek to redeem their lives from futility... Does this institution have any redeeming features?* VERB V n V-ing [3] If you **redeem** a debt or money that you have promised to someone, you pay money that you owe or that you promised to pay. [FORMAL] ❑ *The amount required to redeem the mortgage was £358,587.* VERB V n [4] If you **redeem** an object that belongs to you, you get it back from someone by repaying them money that you borrowed from them, after using the object as a guarantee. ❑ *Make sure you know exactly what you will be paying back when you plan to redeem the item.* VERB V n [5] In religions such as Christianity, to **redeem** someone means to save them by freeing them from sin and evil. ❑ *...a new female spiritual force to redeem the world.* VERB V n

**re|deem|able** /rɪdiːməbəl/ If something is **redeemable**, it can be exchanged for a particular sum of money or for goods worth a particular sum. ❑ *Their full catalogue costs $5, redeemable against a first order.* ADJ: oft ADJ *against/for* n

**Re|deem|er** /rɪdiːməʳ/ In the Christian religion, **the Redeemer** is Jesus Christ. N-PROPER: *the* N

**re|de|fine** /riːdɪfaɪn/ **(redefines, redefining, redefined)** If you **redefine** something, you cause people to consider it in a new way. ❑ *Feminists have redefined the role of women.* VERB V n

**re|defi|ni|tion** /riːdefɪnɪʃən/ The **redefinition** of something is the act or process of causing people to consider it in a new way. ❑ *...the redefinition of the role of the intellectual.* N-UNCOUNT

**re|demp|tion** /rɪdempʃən/ **(redemptions)** 1 **Redemption** is the act of redeeming something or of being redeemed by something. [FORMAL] ❑ *...redemption of the loan. ...regional differences in the frequency of cash redemptions and quota payment.* N-VAR 2 If you say that someone or something is **beyond redemption**, you mean that they are so bad it is unlikely that anything can be done to improve them. ❑ *No man is beyond redemption.* PHRASE: v-link PHR, PHR after v

**re|demp|tive** /rɪdemptɪv/ In Christianity, a **redemptive** act or quality is something which leads to freedom from the consequences of sin and evil. ❑ *...the redemptive power of Christ.* ADJ: usu ADJ n

**re|deploy** /riːdɪplɔɪ/ **(redeploys, redeploying, redeployed)** 1 If forces or troops **are redeployed** or if they **redeploy**, they go to new positions so that they are ready for action. ❑ *We were forced urgently to redeploy our forces... US troops are redeploying to positions held earlier.* VERB V n V 2 If resources or workers **are redeployed**, they are used for a different purpose or task. ❑ *Some of the workers there will be redeployed to other sites... It would give us an opportunity to redeploy our resources.* VERB be V-ed V n

**re|deploy|ment** /riːdɪplɔɪmənt/ **(redeployments)** The **redeployment** of forces, troops, workers, or resources involves putting them in a different place from where they were before, or using them for a different task or purpose. ❑ *...a redeployment of troops in the border areas.* N-VAR

**re|design** /riːdɪzaɪn/ **(redesigns, redesigning, redesigned)** If a building, vehicle, or system **is redesigned**, it is rebuilt according to a new design in order to improve it. ❑ *The hotel has recently been redesigned and redecorated... The second step is to redesign the school system so that it produces a well-educated population.* VERB be V-ed V n

**re|devel|op** /riːdɪveləp/ **(redevelops, redeveloping, redeveloped)** When an area **is redeveloped**, existing buildings and roads are removed and new ones are built in their place. ❑ *Birmingham is now going to be redeveloped again.* VERB be V-ed

**re|devel|op|ment** /riːdɪveləpmənt/ When **redevelopment** takes place, the buildings in one area of a town are knocked down and new ones are built in their place. N-UNCOUNT

**red-eye (red-eyes)**

> The spelling **redeye** is also used in meaning 2.

1 A **red-eye** or a **red-eye flight** is a plane journey during the night. [INFORMAL] ❑ *She was running to catch a red-eye to New York.* N-COUNT 2 In photography, **redeye** is the unwanted effect that you sometimes get in photographs of people or animals where their eyes appear red because of the reflection of a camera flash or other light. ❑ *The camera incorporates a redeye reduction facility.* N-UNCOUNT: usu N n

**red-faced** A **red-faced** person has a face that looks red, often because they are embarrassed or angry. ❑ *A red-faced Mr Jones was led away by police.* ADJ

**red flag (red flags)** 1 A **red flag** is a flag that is red in colour and is used as a symbol to represent communism and socialism or to indicate danger or as a sign that you should stop. ❑ *Then the rain came and the red flag went up to signal a halt.* N-COUNT 2 If you refer to something as a **red flag**, you mean that it acts as a danger signal. ❑ *The abnormal bleeding is your body's own red flag of danger.* N-COUNT

**red-handed** If someone **is caught red-handed**, they are caught while they are in the act of doing something wrong. ❑ *My boyfriend and I robbed a store and were caught red-handed.* PHRASE: V inflects

**red|head** /redhed/ **(redheads)** A **redhead** is person, especially a woman, whose hair is a colour that is between red and brown. N-COUNT

**red-headed** also **redheaded.** A **red-headed** person is a person whose hair is between red and brown in colour. ADJ: usu ADJ n

**red her|ring (red herrings)** If you say that something is a **red herring**, you mean that it is not important and it takes your attention away from the main subject or problem you are considering. ❑ *As Dr Smith left he said that the inquiry was something of a red herring.* N-COUNT

**red-hot** 1 **Red-hot** metal or rock has been heated to such a high temperature that it has turned red. ❑ *...red-hot iron.* ADJ: usu ADJ n 2 A **red-hot** object is too hot to be touched safely. ❑ *In the main rooms red-hot radiators were left exposed.* ADJ 3 **Red-hot** is used to describe a person or thing that is very popular, especially someone who is very good at what they do or something that is new and exciting. [JOURNALISM] ❑ *Some traders are already stacking the red-hot book on their shelves.* ADJ: usu ADJ n

**Red In|dian (Red Indians)** Native Americans who were living in North America when Europeans arrived there used to be called **Red Indians**. This use could cause offence. [OLD-FASHIONED] N-COUNT

**re|di|rect** /riːdɪrekt, -daɪ-/ **(redirects, redirecting, redirected)** 1 If you **redirect** your energy, resources, or ability, you begin doing something different or trying to achieve something different. ❑ *Controls were used to redistribute or redirect resources.* VERB V n ♦ **re|di|rec|tion** /riːdɪrekʃən, -daɪ-/ *A redirection of resources would then be required.* N-UNCOUNT: also a N, usu N of n 2 If you **redirect** someone or something, you change their course or destination. ❑ *She redirected them to the men's department.* VERB V n

**re|dis|cov|er** /riːdɪskʌvəʳ/ **(rediscovers, rediscovering, rediscovered)** If you **rediscover** something good or valuable that you had forgotten or lost, you become aware of it again or find it again. ❑ *...a one-time rebel who had rediscovered his faith.* VERB V n

**re|dis|cov|ery** /riːdɪskʌvəri/ **(rediscoveries)** The **rediscovery** of something good that you had forgotten or lost is the fact or process of becoming aware of it again or finding it again. ❑ *The best part of his expedition had been the rediscovery of his natural passion for making things.* N-VAR: N of n

**re|dis|trib|ute** /riːdɪstrɪbjuːt/ **(redistributes, redistributing, redistributed)** If something such as money or property **is redistributed**, it is shared among people or organizations in a different way from the way that it was previously shared. ❑ *Wealth was redistributed more equitably among society... Taxes could be used to redistribute income.* VERB be V-ed V n ♦ **re|dis|tri|bu|tion** /riːdɪstrɪbjuːʃən/ *...some redistribution of income so that the better off can help to keep the worse off out of poverty.* N-UNCOUNT: oft N of n

**red-letter day (red-letter days)** A **red-letter day** is a day that you will always remember because something good happens to you then. N-COUNT

**red light (red lights)** 1 A **red light** is a traffic signal which shines red to indicate that drivers must stop. N-COUNT 2 The **red-light** district of a city is the area where prostitutes work. ADJ: ADJ n

**red meat (red meats) Red meat** is meat such as beef or lamb, which is dark brown in colour after it has been cooked. N-MASS ≠ white meat

**red|neck** /rednek/ **(rednecks)** If someone describes a white man, especially a lower class American from the countryside, as a **redneck**, they disapprove of him because they think he is uneducated and has strong, unreasonable opinions. [mainly AM, INFORMAL] ❑ *A large Texan redneck was shouting obscenities at Ali.* N-COUNT disapproval

**red|ness** /rednəs/ **Redness** is the quality of being red. ❑ *Slowly the redness left Sophie's face.* N-UNCOUNT

**redo** /riːduː/ **(redoes, redoing, redid, redone)** If you **redo** a piece of work, you do it again in order to improve it or change it. ❑ *They had redone their sums.* VERB V n

**redo|lent** /redələnt/ If something is **redolent of** something else, it has features that make you think of that other thing. [LITERARY] ❑ *...percussion instruments, redolent of Far Eastern cultures.* ADJ: v-link ADJ, usu ADJ *of* n

**re|dou|ble** /riːdʌbəl/ **(redoubles, redoubling, redoubled)** If you **redouble** your efforts, you try much harder to achieve something. If something **redoubles**, it increases in volume or intensity. ❑ *The president also called on nations to redouble their efforts to negotiate an international trade agreement... The applause redoubled.* VERB; V n; V

**re|doubt** /rɪdaʊt/ **(redoubts)** A **redoubt** is a place or situation in which someone feels safe because they know that nobody can attack them or spoil their peace. [LITERARY] ❑ *...the last redoubt of hippy culture.* N-COUNT = haven

**re|doubt|able** /rɪdaʊtəbəl/ If you describe someone as **redoubtable**, you respect them because they have a very strong character, even though you are slightly afraid of them. ❑ *He is a redoubtable fighter.* ADJ: usu ADJ n = formidable

**re|dound** /rɪdaʊnd/ **(redounds, redounding, redounded)** If an action or situation **redounds** to your benefit or advantage, it gives people a good impression of you or brings you something that can improve your situation. ❑ *The success in the Middle East redounds to his benefit.* VERB; V *to* n

**red pep|per** **(red peppers)** [1] **Red peppers** are peppers which are sweet-tasting and can be used in cooking or eaten raw in salads. N-VAR [2] **Red pepper** is a hot-tasting spicy powder made from the flesh and seeds of small, dried, red peppers. It is used for flavouring food. N-MASS = cayenne pepper

**re|draft** /riːdrɑːft, -dræft/ **(redrafts, redrafting, redrafted)** If you **redraft** something you have written, you write it again in order to improve it or change it. ❑ *The speech had already been redrafted 22 times.* VERB; *be* V-ed

**re|draw** /riːdrɔː/ **(redraws, redrawing, redrew, redrawn)** [1] If people in a position of authority **redraw** the boundaries or borders of a country or region, they change the borders so that the country or region covers a slightly different area than before. ❑ *They have redrawn the country's boundaries along ethnic lines.* VERB; V n [2] If people **redraw** something, for example an arrangement or plan, they change it because circumstances have changed. ❑ *With both countries experiencing economic revolutions, it might be time to redraw the traditional relationship.* VERB; V n

**re|dress** /rɪdres/ **(redresses, redressing, redressed)**

> The noun is also pronounced /riːdres/ in American English.

[1] If you **redress** something such as a wrong or a complaint, you do something to correct it or to improve things for the person who has been badly treated. [FORMAL] ❑ *More and more victims turn to litigation to redress wrongs done to them.* VERB; V n [2] If you **redress** the balance or the imbalance between two things that have become unfair or unequal, you make them fair and equal again. [FORMAL] ❑ *So we're trying to redress the balance and to give teachers a sense that both spoken and written language are equally important.* VERB; V n [3] **Redress** is money that someone pays you because they have caused you harm or loss. [FORMAL] ❑ *They are continuing their legal battle to seek some redress from the government.* N-UNCOUNT = compensation

**red tape** You refer to official rules and procedures as **red tape** when they seem unnecessary and cause delay. ❑ *The little money that was available was tied up in bureaucratic red tape.* N-UNCOUNT [disapproval]

**re|duce** /rɪdjuːs, AM -duːs/ **(reduces, reducing, reduced)** ◆◆◇ [1] If you **reduce** something, you make it smaller in size or amount, or less in degree. ❑ *It reduces the risks of heart disease... The reduced consumer demand is also affecting company profits.* VERB ≠ increase; V n; V-ed [2] If someone **is reduced to** a weaker or inferior state, they become weaker or inferior as a result of something that happens to them. ❑ *They were reduced to extreme poverty.* VERB: usu passive; *be* V-ed *to* n [3] If you say that someone **is reduced to** doing something, you mean that they have to do it, although it is unpleasant or embarrassing. ❑ *He was reduced to begging for a living.* VERB: usu passive; *be* V-ed *to* n/-ing [4] If something is changed to a different or less complicated form, you can say that it **is reduced to** that form. ❑ *All the buildings in the town have been reduced to rubble.* VERB: usu passive; *be* V-ed *to* n [5] If you **reduce** liquid when you are cooking, or if it **reduces**, it is boiled in order to make it less in quantity and thicker. ❑ *Boil the liquid in a small saucepan to reduce it by half... Simmer until mixture reduces.* VERB; V n; V [6] If someone or something **reduces** you **to tears**, they make you feel so unhappy that you cry. ❑ *The attentions of the media reduced her to tears.* PHRASE: V inflects

**re|duc|ible** /rɪdjuːsɪbəl, AM -duːs-/ If you say that an idea, problem, or situation is not **reducible to** something simple, you mean that it is complicated and cannot be described in a simple way. [FORMAL] ❑ *The structure of the universe may not be reducible to a problem in physics.* ADJ: v-link ADJ *to* n, usu with brd-neg

**re|duc|tion** /rɪdʌkʃən/ **(reductions)** ◆◇◇ [1] When there is a **reduction in** something, it is made smaller. ❑ *...a future reduction in UK interest rates.* N-COUNT: usu with supp ≠ increase [2] **Reduction** is the act of making something smaller in size or amount, or less in degree. ❑ *...a new strategic arms reduction agreement.* N-UNCOUNT: usu with supp

**re|duc|tion|ist** /rɪdʌkʃənɪst/ **Reductionist** describes a way of analysing problems and things by dividing them into simpler parts. ❑ *...reductionist science.* ADJ: usu ADJ n

**re|duc|tive** /rɪdʌktɪv/ If you describe something such as a theory or a work of art as **reductive**, you disapprove of it because it reduces complex things to simple elements. [FORMAL] ❑ *...a cynical, reductive interpretation.* ADJ: usu ADJ n [disapproval]

**re|dun|dan|cy** /rɪdʌndənsi/ **(redundancies)** [1] When there are **redundancies**, an organization tells some of its employees to leave because their jobs are no longer necessary or because the organization can no longer afford to pay them. [BRIT, BUSINESS] ❑ *The ministry has said it hopes to avoid compulsory redundancies.* N-COUNT: usu pl

> in AM, use **dismissals, layoffs**

[2] **Redundancy** means being made redundant. [BUSINESS] ❑ *Thousands of bank employees are facing redundancy as their employers cut costs.* N-UNCOUNT

**re|dun|dant** /rɪdʌndənt/ [1] If you are made **redundant**, your employer tells you to leave because your job is no longer necessary or because your employer cannot afford to keep paying you. [BRIT, BUSINESS] ❑ *My husband was made redundant late last year. ...a redundant miner.* ADJ

> in AM, use **be dismissed**

[2] Something that is **redundant** is no longer needed because its job is being done by something else or because its job is no longer necessary or useful. ❑ *Changes in technology may mean that once-valued skills are now redundant.* ADJ: usu v-link ADJ

**red|wood** /redwʊd/ **(redwoods)** A **redwood** is an extremely tall tree which grows in California. N-COUNT ♦ **Redwood** is the wood from this tree. N-UNCOUNT

**reed** /riːd/ **(reeds)** [1] **Reeds** are tall plants that grow in large groups in shallow water or on ground that is always wet and soft. They have strong, hollow stems that can be used for making things such as mats or baskets. N-COUNT: usu pl [2] A **reed** is a small piece of cane or metal inserted into the mouthpiece of a woodwind instrument. The reed vibrates when you blow through it and makes a sound. N-COUNT

**re-educate** **(re-educates, re-educating, re-educated)**

> in AM, also use **reeducate**

If an organization such as a government tries to **re-educate** a group of people, they try to make them adopt new attitudes, beliefs, or types of behaviour. ❑ *We are having to re-educate the public* VERB; V n *very quickly about something they have always taken for granted.* ♦ **re-education** *...a programme of punishment and re-education of political dissidents.* N-UNCOUNT

**reedy** /riːdi/ If you say that someone has a **reedy** voice, you think their voice is unpleasant because it is high and unclear. ❑ *The big man had a high-pitched reedy voice.* ADJ: usu ADJ n

**reef** /riːf/ **(reefs)** A **reef** is a long line of rocks or sand, the top of which is just above or just below the surface of the sea. ❑ *An unspoilt coral reef encloses the bay.* N-COUNT

**reef|er** /riːfəʳ/ **(reefers)** [1] A **reefer** or **reefer coat** is a short thick coat which is often worn by sailors. [BRIT] N-COUNT [2] A **reefer** is a cigarette containing cannabis or marijuana. [INFORMAL, OLD-FASHIONED] N-COUNT

**reek** /riːk/ **(reeks, reeking, reeked)** [1] To **reek of** something, usually something unpleasant, means to smell very strongly of it. VERB = stink ❑ *Your breath reeks of stale cigar smoke...* V *of* n *The entire house reeked for a long time.* V ♦ **Reek** is also a noun. ❑ *He smelt the reek of whisky.* N-SING: usu N *of* n [2] If you say that something **reeks of** unpleasant ideas, feelings, or practices, you disapprove of it because it gives a strong impression that it involves those ideas, feelings, or practices. VERB [disapproval] ❑ *The whole thing reeks of hypocrisy.* V *of* n

**reel** /riːl/ **(reels, reeling, reeled)** [1] A **reel** is a cylindrical object around which you wrap something such as cinema film, magnetic tape, fishing line, or cotton thread. [mainly BRIT] ❑ *...a 30m reel of cable.* ◆◇◇ N-COUNT: oft N *of* n

☑ in AM, usually use **spool**

[2] If someone **reels**, they move about in an unsteady way as if they are going to fall. VERB ❑ *He was reeling a little. He must be very drunk...* V *He lost his balance and reeled back.* V adv/prep [3] If you **are reeling** from a shock, you are feeling extremely surprised or upset because of it. VERB: usu cont ❑ *I'm still reeling from the shock of hearing of it...* V *from* n *It left us reeling with disbelief.* V prep [4] If you say that your brain or your mind **is reeling**, you mean that you are very confused because you have too many things to think about. VERB ❑ *His mind reeled at the question.* V

♦ **reel in** If you **reel in** something such as a fish, you pull it towards you by winding around a reel the wire or line that it is attached to. PHRASAL VERB ❑ *Gleacher reeled in the first fish.* V P n (not pron)

♦ **reel off** If you **reel off** information, you repeat it from memory quickly and easily. PHRASAL VERB ❑ *She reeled off the titles of a dozen or so of the novels.* V P n (not pron) Also V n P

**re-elect** **(re-elects, re-electing, re-elected)**

☑ in AM, also use **reelect**

When someone such as a politician or an official who has been elected **is re-elected**, they win another election and are therefore able to continue in their position as, for example, president, or an official in an organization. VERB ❑ *The president will pursue lower taxes if he is re-elected.* *be* V-ed *...Ramon Mendoza was re-elected president of Real for a third successive four-year term...* *be* V-ed n *He was overwhelmingly re-elected as party leader.* *be* V-ed *as* n ♦ **re-election** /riːɪlekʃᵊn/ *I would like to see him stand for re-election.* N-UNCOUNT

**re-enact** **(re-enacts, re-enacting, re-enacted)** also **reenact.** If you **re-enact** a scene or incident, you repeat the actions that occurred in the scene or incident. VERB ❑ *He re-enacted scenes from his TV series.* V n

**re-enactment** **(re-enactments)** When a **re-enactment** of a scene or incident takes place, people re-enact it. N-COUNT: usu N *of* n

**re-enter** **(re-enters, re-entering, re-entered)**

☑ in AM, also use **reenter**

If you **re-enter** a place, organization, or area of activity that you have left, you return to it. VERB ❑ *Ten minutes later he re-entered the hotel.* V n

**re-entry**

☑ in AM, also use **reentry**

[1] **Re-entry** is the act of returning to a place, organization, or area of activity that you have left. N-UNCOUNT: also *a* N ❑ *The house has been barred and bolted to prevent re-entry.* [2] **Re-entry** is used to refer to the moment when a spacecraft comes back into the earth's atmosphere after being in space. N-UNCOUNT: also *a* N ❑ *The station would burn up on re-entry into the earth's atmosphere.*

**re-examine** **(re-examines, re-examining, re-examined)**

☑ in AM, also use **reexamine**

If a person or group of people **re-examines** their ideas, beliefs, or attitudes, they think about them carefully because they are no longer sure if they are correct. VERB = reassess ❑ *Her husband and children will also have to re-examine their expectations.* V n ♦ **re-examination** **(re-examinations)** *It was time for a re-examination of the situation.* N-VAR: usu N *of* n

**ref** /ref/ **(refs)** [1] **Ref.** is an abbreviation for **reference**. It is written in front of a code at the top of business letters and documents. The code refers to a file where all the letters and documents about the same matter are kept. [BUSINESS] ❑ *Our Ref: JAH/JW.* [2] The **ref** in a sports game, such as football or boxing, is the same as the **referee**. [INFORMAL] ❑ *The ref gave a penalty and Zidane scored.* N-COUNT: usu *the* N

**re|fec|tory** /rɪfektəri/ **(refectories)** A **refectory** is a large room in a school, university or other institution, where meals are served and eaten. N-COUNT = canteen

**re|fer** /rɪfɜːʳ/ **(refers, referring, referred)** [1] If you **refer to** a particular subject or person, you talk about them or mention them. ◆◆◇ VERB ❑ *In his speech, he referred to a recent trip to Canada.* V *to* n [2] If you **refer to** someone or something **as** a particular thing, you use a particular word, expression, or name to mention or describe them. VERB ❑ *Marcia had referred to him as a dear friend.* V *to* n *as* n [3] If a word **refers to** a particular thing, situation, or idea, it describes it in some way. VERB ❑ *The term electronics refers to electrically-induced action.* V *to* n [4] If a person who is ill **is referred to** a hospital or a specialist, they are sent there by a doctor in order to be treated. VERB: usu passive ❑ *Patients are mostly referred to hospital by their general practitioners...* *be* V-ed *to* n *The patient should be referred for tests immediately.* *be* V-ed [5] If you **refer** a task or a problem **to** a person or an organization, you formally tell them about it, so that they can deal with it. VERB ❑ *He could refer the matter to the high court.* V n *to* n [6] If you **refer** someone **to** a person or organization, you send them there for the help they need. VERB ❑ *Now and then I referred a client to him.* V n *to* n [7] If you **refer to** a book or other source of information, you look at it in order to find something out. VERB ❑ *He referred briefly to his notebook.* V *to* n [8] If you **refer** someone **to** a source of information, you tell them the place where they will find the information which they need or which you think will interest them. VERB ❑ *Mr Bryan also referred me to a book by the American journalist Anthony Scaduto.* V n *to* n

**ref|eree** /refəriː/ **(referees, refereeing, refereed)** [1] The **referee** is the official who controls a sports event such as a football game or a boxing match. N-COUNT [2] When someone **referees** a sports event or contest, they act as referee. VERB ❑ *Vautrot has refereed in two World Cups.* V [3] A **referee** is a person who gives you a reference, for example when you are applying for a job. [mainly BRIT] N-COUNT

☑ in AM, use **reference**

**ref|er|ence** /refərəns/ **(references)** [1] **Reference to** someone or something is the act of talking about them or mentioning them. A **reference** is a particular example of this. ◆◇◇ N-VAR ❑ *He made no reference to any agreement.* [2] **Reference** is the act of consulting someone or something in order to get information or advice. N-UNCOUNT ❑ *Please keep this sheet in a safe place for reference.* [3] **Reference** books are ones that you look at when you need specific information or facts about a subject. ADJ: ADJ n ❑ *...a useful reference work for teachers.* [4] A **reference** is a word, phrase, or idea which comes from something such as a book, poem, or play and which you use when making a point about something. N-COUNT

❑ ...*a reference from the Quran.* 5 A **reference** is something such as a number or a name that tells you where you can obtain the information you want. ❑ *Make a note of the reference number shown on the form.* 6 A **reference** is a letter that is written by someone who knows you and which describes your character and abilities. When you apply for a job, an employer might ask for **references**. ❑ *The firm offered to give her a reference.* 7 A **reference** is a person who gives you a reference, for example when you are applying for a job. [mainly AM] N-COUNT N-COUNT N-COUNT

in BRIT, usually use **referee**

PHRASES 8 If you keep information **for future reference**, you keep it because it might be useful in the future. ❑ *Read these notes carefully and keep them for future reference.* 9 You use **with reference to** or **in reference to** in order to indicate what something relates to. ❑ *I am writing with reference to your article on salaries for scientists.* 10 → See also **cross-reference, frame of reference, point of reference, terms of reference.** PHRASE: PHR after v PREP-PHRASE

**ref|er|ence li|brary** **(reference libraries)** A **reference library** is a library that contains books which you can look at in the library itself but which you cannot borrow. N-COUNT

**ref|er|en|dum** /rɛfərɛndəm/ **(referendums** or **referenda** /rɛfərɛndə/**)** If a country holds a **referendum** on a particular policy, they ask the people to vote on the policy and show whether or not they agree with it. ❑ *Estonia said it too planned to hold a referendum on independence.* ◆◇◇ N-COUNT: oft N *on* n

**re|fer|ral** /rɪfɜːrəl/ **(referrals)** **Referral** is the act of officially sending someone to a person or authority that is qualified to deal with them. A **referral** is an instance of this. ❑ *Legal Aid can often provide referral to other types of agencies.* N-VAR: oft N *to* n

**re|fill** **(refills, refilling, refilled)**

The verb is pronounced /riːfɪl/. The noun is pronounced /riːfɪl/.

1 If you **refill** something, you fill it again after it has been emptied. ❑ *I refilled our wine glasses.* ♦ **Refill** is also a noun. [INFORMAL] ❑ *Max held out his cup for a refill.* 2 A **refill** of a particular product, such as soap powder, is a quantity of that product sold in a cheaper container than the one it is usually sold in. You use a refill to fill the more permanent container when it is empty. ❑ *Refill packs are cheaper and lighter.* VERB V n N-COUNT N-COUNT

**re|fi|nance** /riːfaɪnæns/ **(refinances, refinancing, refinanced)** If a person or a company **refinances** a debt or if they **refinance**, they borrow money in order to pay the debt. [BUSINESS] ❑ *A loan was arranged to refinance existing debt... It can be costly to refinance.* VERB V n V

**re|fine** /rɪfaɪn/ **(refines, refining, refined)** 1 When a substance **is refined**, it is made pure by having all other substances removed from it. ❑ *Oil is refined to remove naturally occurring impurities.* ♦ **re|fin|ing** ...*oil refining.* 2 If something such as a process, theory, or machine **is refined**, it is improved by having small changes made to it. ❑ *Surgical techniques are constantly being refined.* VERB: usu passive *be* V-ed N-UNCOUNT VERB: usu passive = improve *be* V-ed

**re|fined** /rɪfaɪnd/ 1 A **refined** substance has been made pure by having other substances removed from it. ❑ ...*refined sugar.* 2 If you say that someone is **refined**, you mean that they are very polite and have good manners and good taste. ❑ ...*refined and well-dressed ladies.* 3 If you describe a machine or a process as **refined**, you mean that it has been carefully developed and is therefore very efficient or elegant. ❑ *This technique is becoming more refined and more acceptable all the time.* ADJ: usu ADJ n ADJ = genteel ADJ

**re|fine|ment** /rɪfaɪnmənt/ **(refinements)** 1 **Refinements** are small changes or additions that you make to something in order to improve it. **Refinement** is the process of making refinements. ❑ *Older cars inevitably lack the latest safety refinements.* 2 **Refinement** is politeness and good manners. ❑ ...*a girl who possessed both dignity and refinement.* N-VAR N-UNCOUNT

**re|fin|er** /rɪfaɪnəʳ/ **(refiners)** **Refiners** are people or organizations that refine substances such as oil or sugar in order to sell them. N-COUNT

**re|fin|ery** /rɪfaɪnəri/ **(refineries)** A **refinery** is a factory where a substance such as oil or sugar is refined. N-COUNT

**re|fit** **(refits, refitting, refitted)**

The verb is pronounced /riːfɪt/. The noun is pronounced /riːfɪt/.

When a ship **is refitted**, it is repaired or is given new parts, equipment, or furniture. ❑ *During the war, Navy ships were refitted here.* ♦ **Refit** is also a noun. ❑ *The ship finished an extensive refit last year.* VERB: usu passive *be* V-ed N-COUNT

**re|flate** /riːfleɪt/ **(reflates, reflating, reflated)** If a government tries to **reflate** its country's economy, it increases the amount of money that is available in order to encourage more economic activity. [BUSINESS] ❑ *The administration may try to reflate the economy next year.* ♦ **re|fla|tion** /riːfleɪʃᵊn/ *Ministers are again talking about reflation and price controls.* VERB V n N-UNCOUNT

**re|flect** /rɪflɛkt/ **(reflects, reflecting, reflected)** 1 If something **reflects** an attitude or situation, it shows that the attitude or situation exists or it shows what it is like. ❑ *The Los Angeles riots reflected the bitterness between the black and Korean communities in the city.* 2 When light, heat or other rays **reflect** off a surface or when a surface **reflects** them, they are sent back from the surface and do not pass through it. ❑ *The sun reflected off the snow-covered mountains... The glass appears to reflect light naturally.* 3 When something **is reflected** in a mirror or in water, you can see its image in the mirror or in the water. ❑ *His image seemed to be reflected many times in the mirror.* 4 When you **reflect on** something, you think deeply about it. ❑ *We should all give ourselves time to reflect... I reflected on the child's future.* 5 You can use **reflect** to indicate that a particular thought occurs to someone. ❑ *Things were very much changed since before the war, he reflected.* 6 If an action or situation **reflects** in a particular way **on** someone or something, it gives people a good or bad impression of them. ❑ *The affair hardly reflected well on the British... Your own personal behavior as a teacher, outside of school hours, reflects on the school itself.* ◆◆◇ VERB = show V n VERB V prep V n VERB: usu passive *be* V-ed VERB V V *on/upon* n VERB V that VERB V adv *on* n V *on* n

**re|flec|tion** /rɪflɛkʃᵊn/ **(reflections)** 1 A **reflection** is an image that you can see in a mirror or in glass or water. ❑ *Meg stared at her reflection in the bedroom mirror.* 2 **Reflection** is the process by which light and heat are sent back from a surface and do not pass through it. ❑ ...*the reflection of a beam of light off a mirror.* 3 If you say that something is a **reflection of** a particular person's attitude or **of** a situation, you mean that it is caused by that attitude or situation and therefore reveals something about it. ❑ *Inhibition in adulthood seems to be very clearly a reflection of a person's experiences as a child.* 4 If something is a **reflection** or a **sad reflection on** a person or thing, it gives a bad impression of them. ❑ *Infection with head lice is no reflection on personal hygiene... The library is unique and its break-up would be a sad reflection on the value we place on our heritage.* 5 **Reflection** is careful thought about a particular subject. Your **reflections** are your thoughts about a particular subject. ❑ *After days of reflection she decided to write back.* ● If someone admits or accepts something **on reflection**, they admit or accept it after having thought carefully about it. ❑ *On reflection, he says, he very much regrets the comments.* N-COUNT N-UNCOUNT N-COUNT: usu N *of* n N-SING: usu N *on* n N-UNCOUNT: also N in pl PHRASE

**re|flec|tive** /rɪflɛktɪv/ 1 If you are **reflective**, you are thinking deeply about something. [WRITTEN] ❑ *I walked on in a reflective mood to the car.* 2 If something is **reflective of** a particular situation or attitude, it is typical of that situation ADJ ADJ: v-link ADJ *of* n or attitude, or is a consequence of it. ❑ *The German government's support of the US is not entirely reflective of German public opinion.* [3] A **reflective** surface or material sends back light or heat. [FORMAL] ❑ *Avoid pans with a shiny, reflective base as the heat will be reflected back.* ADJ

**re|flec|tor** /rɪflektəʳ/ **(reflectors)** [1] A **reflector** is a small piece of specially patterned glass or plastic which is fitted to the back of a bicycle or car or to a post beside the road, and which glows when light shines on it. ➔ See picture on page 1708. [2] A **reflector** is a type of telescope which uses a mirror that is shaped like a ball. N-COUNT N-COUNT

**re|flex** /riːfleks/ **(reflexes)** [1] A **reflex** or a **reflex action** is something that you do automatically and without thinking, as a habit or as a reaction to something. ❑ *Walsh fumbled in his pocket, a reflex from his smoking days.* [2] A **reflex** or a **reflex action** is a normal, uncontrollable reaction of your body to something that you feel, see, or experience. ❑ *...tests for reflexes, like tapping the knee or the heel with a rubber hammer.* [3] Your **reflexes** are your ability to react quickly with your body when something unexpected happens, for example when you are involved in sport or when you are driving a car. ❑ *It takes great skill, cool nerves and the reflexes of an athlete.* N-COUNT N-COUNT N-PLURAL

**re|flex|ive** /rɪfleksɪv/ A **reflexive** reaction or movement occurs immediately in response to something that happens. [FORMAL] ❑ *...that reflexive urge for concealment.* ♦ **re|flex|ive|ly** *He felt his head jerk reflexively.* ADJ: usu ADJ n ADV: usu ADV with v

**re|flex|ive pro|noun** **(reflexive pronouns)** A **reflexive pronoun** is a pronoun such as 'myself' which refers back to the subject of a sentence or clause. For example, in the sentence 'He made himself a cup of tea', the reflexive pronoun 'himself' refers back to 'he'. N-COUNT

**re|flex|ive verb** **(reflexive verbs)** A **reflexive verb** is a transitive verb whose subject and object always refer to the same person or thing, so the object is always a reflexive pronoun. An example is 'to enjoy yourself', as in 'Did you enjoy yourself?'. N-COUNT

**re|flex|ol|ogy** /riːfleksɒlədʒi/ **Reflexology** is the practice of massaging particular areas of the body, especially the feet, in the belief that it can heal particular organs. ♦ **re|flex|olo|gist** **(reflexologists)** ❑ *A reflexologist can often tell what is wrong with his client by the condition of certain parts of the feet.* N-UNCOUNT N-COUNT

**re|for|est** /riːfɒrɪst/ **(reforests, reforesting, reforested)** To **reforest** an area where there used to be a forest means to plant trees over it. ❑ *He decided to do something about reforesting man-made wastes of western Australia.* VERB V n

**re|for|esta|tion** /riːfɒrɪsteɪʃᵊn/ **Reforestation** of an area where there used to be a forest is planting trees over it. ❑ *...the reforestation of the Apennine Mountains.* N-UNCOUNT

**re|form** /rɪfɔːʳm/ **(reforms, reforming, reformed)** ◆◆◇ [1] **Reform** consists of changes and improvements to a law, social system, or institution. A **reform** is an instance of such a change or improvement. ❑ *The party embarked on a programme of economic reform... The Socialists introduced fairly radical reforms.* [2] If someone **reforms** something such as a law, social system, or institution, they change or improve it. ❑ *...his plans to reform the country's economy... A reformed party would have to win the approval of the people.* [3] When someone **reforms** or when something **reforms** them, they stop doing things that society does not approve of, such as breaking the law or drinking too much alcohol. ❑ *When his court case was coming up, James promised to reform... We will try to reform him within the community.* ♦ **re|formed** *...a reformed alcoholic.* [4] ➔ See also **re-form**. N-VAR VERB V n V-ed VERB V V n ADJ: usu ADJ n

**re-form** **(re-forms, re-forming, re-formed)** also **reform.** When an organization, group, or shape **re-forms**, or when someone **re-forms** it, it is created again after a period during which it did not exist or existed in a different form. ❑ *The official trades union council voted to disband itself and re-form as a confederation... The 40-year-old singer reformed his band.* VERB V V n

**ref|or|ma|tion** /refəʳmeɪʃᵊn/ [1] The **reformation** of something is the act or process of changing and improving it. ❑ *He devoted his energies to the reformation of science.* [2] **The Reformation** is the movement to reform the Catholic Church in the sixteenth century, which led to the Protestant church being set up. ❑ *...a famous statue of the Virgin which was destroyed during the Reformation.* N-UNCOUNT N-PROPER: the N

**re|form|er** /rɪfɔːʳməʳ/ **(reformers)** A **reformer** is someone who tries to change and improve something such as a law or a social system. N-COUNT

**re|form|ism** /rɪfɔːʳmɪzəm/ **Reformism** is the belief that a system or law should be reformed. N-UNCOUNT

**re|form|ist** /rɪfɔːʳmɪst/ **(reformists)** **Reformist** groups or policies are trying to reform a system or law. ❑ *...a strong supporter of reformist policies.* ♦ A **reformist** is someone with reformist views. ADJ N-COUNT

**re|fract** /rɪfrækt/ **(refracts, refracting, refracted)** When a ray of light or a sound wave **refracts** or **is refracted**, the path it follows bends at a particular point, for example when it enters water or glass. ❑ *As we age the lenses of the eyes thicken, and thus refract light differently. ...surfaces that cause the light to reflect and refract.* ♦ **re|frac|tion** /rɪfrækʃᵊn/ *...the refraction of the light on the dancing waves.* VERB V n V N-UNCOUNT

**re|frac|tory** /rɪfræktəri/ **Refractory** people are difficult to deal with or control, for example because they are unwilling to obey orders. [FORMAL] ❑ *...refractory priests who refused to side with the king.* ADJ: usu ADJ n = recalcitrant

**re|frain** /rɪfreɪn/ **(refrains, refraining, refrained)** [1] If you **refrain from** doing something, you deliberately do not do it. ❑ *Mrs Hardie refrained from making any comment.* [2] A **refrain** is a short, simple part of a song, which is repeated many times. ❑ *...a refrain from an old song.* [3] A **refrain** is a comment or saying that people often repeat. ❑ *Rosa's constant refrain is that she doesn't have a life.* VERB V from -ing/n N-COUNT N-COUNT

**re|fresh** /rɪfreʃ/ **(refreshes, refreshing, refreshed)** [1] If something **refreshes** you when you have become hot, tired, or thirsty, it makes you feel cooler or more energetic. ❑ *The lotion cools and refreshes the skin.* ♦ **re|freshed** *He awoke feeling completely refreshed.* [2] If you **refresh** something old or dull, you make it as good as it was when it was new. ❑ *Many view these meetings as an occasion to share ideas and refresh friendship.* [3] If someone **refreshes** your memory, they tell you something that you had forgotten. ❑ *He walked on the opposite side of the street to refresh his memory of the building.* [4] If you **refresh** a web page, you click a button in order to get the most recent version of the page. [COMPUTING] ❑ *Press the 'reload' button on your web browser to refresh the site and get the most current version.* VERB V n ADJ: usu v-link ADJ VERB V n VERB V n VERB V n

**re|fresh|er course** **(refresher courses)** A **refresher course** is a training course in which people improve their knowledge or skills and learn about new developments that are related to the job that they do. N-COUNT

**re|fresh|ing** /rɪfreʃɪŋ/ [1] You say that something is **refreshing** when it is pleasantly different from what you are used to. ❑ *It's refreshing to hear somebody speaking common sense.* ♦ **re|fresh|ing|ly** *He was refreshingly honest.* [2] A **refreshing** bath or drink makes you feel energetic or cool again after you have been tired or hot. ❑ *Herbs have been used for centuries to make refreshing drinks.* ADJ ADV ADJ

**re|fresh|ment** /rɪfreʃmənt/ **(refreshments)** [1] **Refreshments** are drinks and small amounts of food that are provided, for example, during a meeting or a journey. N-PLURAL [2] You can refer to food and drink as **refreshment**. [FORMAL] ❑ *May I offer you some refreshment?* N-UNCOUNT

**re|frig|er|ate** /rɪfrɪdʒəreɪt/ **(refrigerates, refrigerating, refrigerated)** If you **refrigerate** food, you make it cold, for example by putting it in a fridge, usually in order to preserve it. ❑ *Refrigerate the dough overnight.* VERB; V n

**re|frig|era|tor** /rɪfrɪdʒəreɪtəʳ/ **(refrigerators)** A **refrigerator** is a large container which is kept cool inside, usually by electricity, so that the food and drink in it stays fresh. N-COUNT = fridge

**re|fu|el** /riːfjuːəl/ **(refuels, refuelling, refuelled)**

✔ in AM, use **refueling, refueled**

When an aircraft or other vehicle **refuels** or when someone **refuels** it, it is filled with more fuel so that it can continue its journey. ❑ *His plane stopped in France to refuel... The airline's crew refuelled the plane.* VERB; V; V n ♦ **re|fu|el|ling** *...in-flight refuelling of Tornados.* N-UNCOUNT

**ref|uge** /refjuːdʒ/ **(refuges)** [1] If you take **refuge** somewhere, you try to protect yourself from physical harm by going there. ❑ *They took refuge in a bomb shelter... His home became a place of refuge for the believers.* N-UNCOUNT [2] A **refuge** is a place where you go for safety and protection, for example from violence or from bad weather. ❑ *...a refuge for battered women.* N-COUNT [3] If you take **refuge in** a particular way of behaving or thinking, you try to protect yourself from unhappiness or unpleasantness by behaving or thinking in that way. ❑ *All too often, they get bored, and seek refuge in drink and drugs.* N-UNCOUNT

**refu|gee** /refjuːdʒiː/ **(refugees)** **Refugees** are people who have been forced to leave their homes or their country, either because there is a war there or because of their political or religious beliefs. ◆◆◇ N-COUNT

**re|fund** **(refunds, refunding, refunded)**

✔ The noun is pronounced /riːfʌnd/. The verb is pronounced /rɪfʌnd/.

[1] A **refund** is a sum of money which is returned to you, for example because you have paid too much or because you have returned goods to a shop. N-COUNT [2] If someone **refunds** your money, they return it to you, for example because you have paid too much or because you have returned goods to a shop. ❑ *We guarantee to refund your money if you're not delighted with your purchase.* VERB; V n

**re|fund|able** /rɪfʌndəbᵊl/ A **refundable** payment will be paid back to you in certain circumstances. ❑ *A refundable deposit is payable on arrival.* ADJ

**re|fur|bish** /riːfɜːʳbɪʃ/ **(refurbishes, refurbishing, refurbished)** To **refurbish** a building or room means to clean it and decorate it and make it more attractive or better equipped. ❑ *We have spent money on refurbishing the offices.* VERB; V n

**re|fur|bish|ment** /riːfɜːʳbɪʃmənt/ **(refurbishments)** The **refurbishment** of something is the act or process of cleaning it, decorating it, and providing it with new equipment or facilities. N-UNCOUNT: also N in pl

**re|fus|al** /rɪfjuːzᵊl/ **(refusals)** [1] Someone's **refusal to** do something is the fact of them showing or saying that they will not do it, allow it, or accept it. ❑ *...her refusal to accept change.* N-VAR [2] If someone has **first refusal** on something that is being sold or offered, they have the right to decide whether or not to buy it or take it before it is offered to anyone else. ❑ *A tenant may have a right of first refusal if a property is offered for sale.* PHRASE: PHR after v

**re|fuse** **(refuses, refusing, refused)** ◆◆◇

✔ The verb is pronounced /rɪfjuːz/. The noun is pronounced /refjuːs/ and is hyphenated ref|use.

[1] If you **refuse to** do something, you deliberately do not do it, or you say firmly that you will not do it. ❑ *He refused to comment after the trial... He expects me to stay on here and I can hardly refuse.* VERB; V to-inf; V [2] If someone **refuses** you something, they do not give it to you or do not allow you to have it. ❑ *The United States has refused him a visa... The town council had refused permission for the march.* VERB; V n n; V n [3] If you **refuse** something that is offered to you, you do not accept it. ❑ *The patient has the right to refuse treatment.* VERB = turn down; V n [4] **Refuse** consists of the rubbish and all the things that are not wanted in a house, shop, or factory, and that are regularly thrown away; used mainly in official language. ❑ *The District Council made a weekly collection of refuse.* N-UNCOUNT = waste, rubbish

**refu|ta|tion** /refjuːteɪʃᵊn/ **(refutations)** A **refutation** of an argument, accusation, or theory is something that proves it is wrong or untrue. [FORMAL] ❑ *He prepared a complete refutation of the Republicans' most serious charges.* N-VAR

**re|fute** /rɪfjuːt/ **(refutes, refuting, refuted)** [1] If you **refute** an argument, accusation, or theory, you prove that it is wrong or untrue. [FORMAL] ❑ *It was the kind of rumour that it is impossible to refute.* VERB = disprove; V n [2] If you **refute** an argument or accusation, you say that it is not true. [FORMAL] ❑ *Isabelle is quick to refute any suggestion of intellectual snobbery.* VERB = deny; V n

**re|gain** /rɪgeɪn/ **(regains, regaining, regained)** If you **regain** something that you have lost, you get it back again. ❑ *Troops have regained control of the city.* VERB; V n

**re|gal** /riːgᵊl/ If you describe something as **regal**, you mean that it is suitable for a king or queen, because it is very impressive or beautiful. ❑ *He sat with such regal dignity.* ADJ ♦ **re|gal|ly** *He inclined his head regally.* ADV

**re|gale** /rɪgeɪl/ **(regales, regaling, regaled)** If someone **regales** you with stories or jokes, they tell you a lot of them, whether you want to hear them or not. ❑ *He was constantly regaled with tales of woe.* VERB; be V-ed n with n

**re|ga|lia** /rɪgeɪliə/ **Regalia** consists of all the traditional clothes and items which someone such as a king or a judge wears and carries on official occasions. ❑ *...officials in full regalia.* N-UNCOUNT

**re|gard** /rɪgɑːʳd/ **(regards, regarding, regarded)** ◆◆◇ [1] If you **regard** someone or something **as** being a particular thing or **as** having a particular quality, you believe that they are that thing or have that quality. ❑ *He was regarded as the most successful Chancellor of modern times... I regard creativity both as a gift and as a skill.* VERB; be V-ed as n; V n as n [2] If you **regard** something or someone **with** a feeling such as dislike or respect, you have that feeling about them. ❑ *He regarded drug dealers with loathing.* VERB; V n with n [3] If you **regard** someone in a certain way, you look at them in that way. [LITERARY] ❑ *She regarded him curiously for a moment... The clerk regarded him with benevolent amusement.* VERB; V n; V n with n [4] If you have **regard for** someone or something, you respect them and care about them. If you hold someone **in** high **regard**, you have a lot of respect for them. ❑ *I have a very high regard for him and what he has achieved... The Party ruled the country without regard for the people's views.* N-UNCOUNT [5] **Regards** are greetings. You use **regards** in expressions such as **best regards** and **with kind regards** as a way of expressing friendly feelings towards someone, especially in a letter. ❑ *Give my regards to your family.* N-PLURAL: oft N to n [formulae]

**PHRASES** [6] You can use **as regards** to indicate the subject that is being talked or written about. ❑ *As regards the war, Haig believed in victory at any price.* PREP-PHRASE [7] You can use **with regard to** or **in regard to** to indicate the subject that is being talked or written about. ❑ *The department is reviewing its policy with regard to immunisation.* PREP-PHRASE = regarding [8] You can use **in this regard** or **in that regard** to refer back to something that you have just said. ❑ *In this regard nothing has changed... I may have made a mistake in that regard.* PHRASE: PHR with cl

**re|gard|ing** /rɪgɑːʳdɪŋ/ You can use **regarding** to indicate the subject that is being talked or written about. ❑ *He refused to divulge any information regarding the man's whereabouts.* PREP = concerning

**re|gard|less** /rɪgɑːʳdləs/ [1] If something happens **regardless of** something else, it is not affected or influenced at all by that other thing. ❑ *It takes in anybody regardless of religion, colour, or creed.* PREP-PHRASE [2] If you say that someone did something **regardless**, you mean that they did it even though there were problems or factors that could have stopped them, or perhaps should have stopped them. ❑ *Despite her recent surgery she has been carrying on regardless.* ADV: ADV after v

**re|gat|ta** /rɪgætə/ **(regattas)** A **regatta** is a sports event consisting of races between yachts or rowing boats. N-COUNT: oft in names

**re|gen|cy** /riːdʒənsi/ **(regencies)**

The spelling **Regency** is usually used for meaning 1.

[1] **Regency** is used to refer to the period in Britain at the beginning of the nineteenth century, and to the style of architecture, literature, and furniture that was popular at the time. ❑ *...a huge, six-bedroomed Regency house.* ADJ: usu ADJ n [2] A **regency** is a period of time when a country is governed by a regent, because the king or queen is unable to rule. N-COUNT

**re|gen|er|ate** /rɪdʒenəreɪt/ **(regenerates, regenerating, regenerated)** [1] To **regenerate** something means to develop and improve it to make it more active, successful, or important, especially after a period when it has been getting worse. VERB ❑ *The government will continue to try to regenerate inner city areas.* V n ♦ **re|gen|era|tion** /rɪdʒenəreɪʃən/ *...the physical and economic regeneration of the area.* N-UNCOUNT [2] If organs or tissues **regenerate** or if something **regenerates** them, they heal and grow again after they have been damaged. VERB ❑ *Nerve cells have limited ability to regenerate if destroyed...* V *Newts can regenerate their limbs.* V n ♦ **re|gen|era|tion** *Vitamin B assists in red-blood-cell regeneration.* N-UNCOUNT

**re|gen|era|tive** /rɪdʒenərətɪv/ **Regenerative** powers or processes cause something to heal or become active again after it has been damaged or inactive. ❑ *...the regenerative power of nature.* ADJ: usu ADJ n

**re|gent** /riːdʒənt/ **(regents)** A **regent** is a person who rules a country when the king or queen is unable to rule, for example because they are too young or too ill. N-COUNT

**reg|gae** /regeɪ/ **Reggae** is a kind of West Indian popular music with a very strong beat. ❑ *Bob Marley provided them with their first taste of Reggae music.* N-UNCOUNT: oft N n

**regi|cide** /redʒɪsaɪd/ **(regicides)** [1] **Regicide** is the act of killing a king. ❑ *He had become czar through regicide.* N-UNCOUNT [2] A **regicide** is a person who kills a king. ❑ *Some of the regicides were sentenced to death.* N-COUNT

**re|gime** /reɪʒiːm/ **(regimes)** [1] If you refer to a government or system of running a country as a **regime**, you are critical of it because you think it is not democratic and uses unacceptable methods. ❑ *...the collapse of the Fascist regime at the end of the war.* ◆◇◇ N-COUNT: oft supp N [disapproval] [2] A **regime** is the way that something such as an institution, company, or economy is run, especially when it involves tough or severe action. ❑ *The authorities moved him to the less rigid regime of an open prison.* N-COUNT [3] A **regime** is a set of rules about food, exercise, or beauty that some people follow in order to stay healthy or attractive. ❑ *He has a new fitness regime to strengthen his back.* N-COUNT: oft supp N

**regi|men** /redʒɪmen/ **(regimens)** A **regimen** is a set of rules about food and exercise that some people follow in order to stay healthy. ❑ *Whatever regimen has been prescribed should be rigorously followed.* N-COUNT = regime

**regi|ment** /redʒɪmənt/ **(regiments)** [1] A **regiment** is a large group of soldiers that is commanded by a colonel. N-COUNT [2] A **regiment of** people is a large number of them. ❑ *...robust food, good enough to satisfy a regiment of hungry customers.* N-COUNT: N *of* n

**regi|men|tal** /redʒɪmentəl/ **Regimental** means belonging to a particular regiment. ❑ *Mills was regimental colonel.* ADJ: ADJ n

**regi|men|ta|tion** /redʒɪmenteɪʃən/ **Regimentation** is very strict control over the way a group of people behave or the way something is done. ❑ *Democracy is incompatible with excessive, bureaucratic regimentation of social life.* N-UNCOUNT

**regi|ment|ed** /redʒɪmentɪd/ Something that is **regimented** is very strictly controlled. ❑ *...the regimented atmosphere of the orphanage.* ADJ

**re|gion** /riːdʒən/ **(regions)** [1] A **region** is a large area of land that is different from other areas of land, for example because it is one of the different parts of a country with its own customs and characteristics, or because it has a particular geographical feature. ❑ *...Barcelona, capital of the autonomous region of Catalonia.* ◆◆◇ N-COUNT [2] **The regions** are the parts of a country that are not the capital city and its surrounding area. [BRIT] ❑ *...London and the regions.* N-PLURAL: *the* N [3] You can refer to a part of your body as a **region**. ❑ *...the pelvic region.* N-COUNT: with supp [4] You say **in the region of** to indicate that an amount that you are stating is approximate. ❑ *The scheme will cost in the region of six million pounds.* PHRASE [vagueness] = around

**re|gion|al** /riːdʒənəl/ **Regional** is used to describe things which relate to a particular area of a country or of the world. ❑ *...the autonomous regional government of Andalucia.* ◆◆◇ ADJ: usu ADJ n ♦ **re|gion|al|ly** *The impact of these trends has varied regionally.* ADV

**re|gion|al|ism** /riːdʒənəlɪzəm/ **Regionalism** is a strong feeling of pride or loyalty that people in a region have for that region, often including a desire to govern themselves. ❑ *A grassroots regionalism appears to be emerging.* N-UNCOUNT

**reg|is|ter** /redʒɪstəʳ/ **(registers, registering, registered)** [1] A **register** is an official list or record of people or things. ❑ *...registers of births, deaths and marriages... He signed the register at the hotel.* ◆◇◇ N-COUNT [2] If you **register** to do something, you put your name on an official list, in order to be able to do that thing or to receive a service. VERB ❑ *Have you come to register at the school?...* V *Thousands lined up to register to vote...* V to-inf *Many students register for these courses to widen skills for use in their current job ...* V *for* n *About 26 million people are not registered with a dentist.* V-ed [3] If you **register** something, such as the name of a person who has just died or information about something you own, you have these facts recorded on an official list. VERB ❑ *In order to register a car in Japan, the owner must have somewhere to park it.* V n *...a registered charity.* V-ed [4] When something **registers on** a scale or measuring instrument, it shows on the scale or instrument. You can also say that something **registers** a certain amount or level **on** a scale or measuring instrument. VERB ❑ *It will only register on sophisticated X-ray equipment...* V *on* n *The earthquake registered 5.3 points on the Richter scale.* V n [5] If you **register** your feelings or opinions about something, you do something that makes them clear to other people. VERB ❑ *Voters wish to register their dissatisfaction with the ruling party.* V n [6] If a feeling **registers on** someone's face, their expression shows clearly that they have that feeling. VERB = show ❑ *Surprise again registered on Rodney's face.* V *on* n [7] If a piece of information does not **register** or if you do not **register** it, you do not really pay attention to it, and so you do not remember it or react to it. VERB ❑ *What I said sometimes didn't register in her brain...* V *The sound was so familiar that she didn't register it.* V n [8] In linguistics, the **register** of a piece of speech or writing is its level and style of language, which is usually appropriate to the situation or circumstances in which it is used. [TECHNICAL] N-VAR [9] → See also **cash register**, **electoral register**.

**reg|is|tered** /redʒɪstəʳd/ A **registered** letter or parcel is sent by a special postal service, for which you pay extra money for insurance in case ADJ: usu ADJ n it gets lost. ❑ *He asked his mother to send it by registered mail.*

**reg|is|tered nurse** **(registered nurses)** N-COUNT A **registered nurse** is someone who is qualified to work as a nurse. [AM, AUSTRALIAN]

**reg|is|ter of|fice** **(register offices)** N-COUNT = *registry office* A **register office** is a place where births, marriages, and deaths are officially recorded, and where people can get married without a religious ceremony. [BRIT]

**reg|is|trar** /re̱dʒɪstrɑːʳ, AM -strɑːr/ **(registrars)** 1 N-COUNT In Britain, a **registrar** is a person whose job is to keep official records, especially of births, marriages, and deaths. 2 N-COUNT A **registrar** is a senior administrative official in a British college or university.

**reg|is|tra|tion** /re̱dʒɪstre͟ɪʃᵊn/ **(registrations)** N-UNCOUNT: usu with supp The **registration** of something such as a person's name or the details of an event is the recording of it in an official list. ❑ *They have campaigned strongly for compulsory registration of dogs.*

**reg|is|tra|tion num|ber** **(registration numbers)** N-COUNT The **registration number** or the **registration** of a car or other road vehicle is the series of letters and numbers that are shown at the front and back of it. [BRIT] ❑ *Another driver managed to get the registration number of the car.*

✔ in AM, use **license number**

**reg|is|try** /re̱dʒɪstri/ **(registries)** N-COUNT A **registry** is a collection of all the official records relating to something, or the place where they are kept. ❑ *It agreed to set up a central registry of arms sales.*

**reg|is|try of|fice** **(registry offices)** N-COUNT A **registry office** is the same as a **register office**. [mainly BRIT]

**re|gress** /rɪgre̱s/ **(regresses, regressing, regressed)** VERB When people or things **regress**, they return to an earlier and less advanced stage of development. [FORMAL] ❑ V to/into n *...if your child regresses to babyish behaviour...* V *Such countries are not 'developing' at all, but regressing.* ♦ **re|gres|sion** /rɪgre̱ʃᵊn/ **(regressions)** N-VAR *This can cause regression in a pupil's learning process.*

**re|gres|sive** /rɪgre̱sɪv/ ADJ **Regressive** behaviour, activities, or processes involve a return to an earlier and less advanced stage of development. [FORMAL] ❑ *This regressive behaviour is more common in boys.*

**re|gret** /rɪgre̱t/ **(regrets, regretting, regretted)** ◆◇◇ 1 VERB If you **regret** something that you have done, you wish that you had not done it. ❑ V n *I simply gave in to him, and I've regretted it ever since...* V that *Ellis seemed to be regretting that he had asked the question...* V -ing *Five years later she regrets having given up her home.* 2 N-VAR **Regret** is a feeling of sadness or disappointment, which is caused by something that has happened or something that you have done or not done. ❑ *Lillee said he had no regrets about retiring.* 3 VERB [politeness] You can say that you **regret** something as a polite way of saying that you are sorry about it. You use expressions such as **I regret to say** or **I regret to inform you** to show that you are sorry about something. ❑ V n *'I very much regret the injuries he sustained,' he said...* V that *I regret that the United States has added its voice to such protests...* V to-inf *Her lack of cooperation is nothing new, I regret to say.* 4 N-UNCOUNT If someone expresses **regret** about something, they say that they are sorry about it. [FORMAL] ❑ *He expressed great regret and said that surgeons would attempt to reverse the operation... She has accepted his resignation with regret.*

**re|gret|ful** /rɪgre̱tfʊl/ ADJ: oft ADJ *about* n, ADJ that If you are **regretful**, you show that you regret something. ❑ *Mr Griffin gave a regretful smile.* ♦ **re|gret|ful|ly** ADV *He shook his head regretfully.*

**re|gret|table** /rɪgre̱təbᵊl/ ADJ [feelings] = *unfortunate* You describe something as **regrettable** when you think that it is bad and that it should not happen or have happened. [FORMAL] ❑ *...an investigation into what the army described as a regrettable incident.* ♦ **re|gret|tably** ADV: ADV with cl, ADV adj *Regrettably we could find no sign of the man and the search was terminated.*

**re|group** /riːgru͟ːp/ **(regroups, regrouping, regrouped)** VERB When people, especially soldiers, **regroup**, or when someone **regroups** them, they form an organized group again, in order to continue fighting. ❑ V *Now the rebel army has regrouped and reorganised...* V n *The rebels may simply be using the truce to regroup their forces.*

**regu|lar** /re̱gjʊləʳ/ **(regulars)** ◆◆◇ 1 ADJ: usu ADJ n **Regular** events have equal amounts of time between them, so that they happen, for example, at the same time each day or each week. ❑ *Take regular exercise... We're going to be meeting there on a regular basis... The cartridge must be replaced at regular intervals.* ♦ **regu|lar|ly** ADV: ADV with v *He also writes regularly for 'International Management' magazine.* ♦ **regu|lar|ity** /re̱gjʊlæ̱rɪti/ N-UNCOUNT *The overdraft arrangements had been generous because of the regularity of the half-yearly payments.* 2 ADJ: usu ADJ n **Regular** events happen often. ❑ *This condition usually clears up with regular shampooing.* ♦ **regu|lar|ly** ADV: ADV with v *Fox, badger, weasel and stoat are regularly seen here.* ♦ **regu|lar|ity** N-UNCOUNT *Closures and job losses are again being announced with monotonous regularity.* 3 ADJ: ADJ n If you are, for example, a **regular** customer at a shop or a **regular** visitor to a place, you go there often. ❑ *She has become a regular visitor to Houghton Hall.* 4 N-COUNT The **regulars** at a place or in a team are the people who often go to the place or are often in the team. ❑ *Regulars at his local pub have set up a fund to help out.* 5 ADJ: det ADJ n = *usual* You use **regular** when referring to the thing, person, time, or place that is usually used by someone. For example, someone's **regular** place is the place where they usually sit. ❑ *The man sat at his regular table near the windows.* 6 ADJ ≠*irregular* A **regular** rhythm consists of a series of sounds or movements with equal periods of time between them. ❑ *...a very regular beat.* ♦ **regu|lar|ly** ADV: ADV with v *Remember to breathe regularly.* ♦ **regu|lar|ity** N-UNCOUNT *Experimenters have succeeded in controlling the rate and regularity of the heartbeat.* 7 ADJ: ADJ n = *ordinary* **Regular** is used to mean 'normal'. [mainly AM] ❑ *The product looks and burns like a regular cigarette.* 8 ADJ: ADJ n In some restaurants, a **regular** drink or quantity of food is of medium size. [mainly AM] ❑ *...a cheeseburger and regular fries.* 9 ADJ ≠*irregular* A **regular** pattern or arrangement consists of a series of things with equal spaces between them. ❑ *...strange small rounded sandy hillocks, that look as if they've been scattered in a regular pattern on the ground.* 10 ADJ ≠*irregular* If something has a **regular** shape, both halves are the same and it has straight edges or a smooth outline. ❑ *...some regular geometrical shape.* ♦ **regu|lar|ity** N-UNCOUNT *...the chessboard regularity of their fields.* 11 ADJ ≠*irregular* In grammar, a **regular** verb, noun, or adjective inflects in the same way as most verbs, nouns, or adjectives in the language.

**regu|lar|ity** /re̱gjʊlæ̱rɪti/ **(regularities)** 1 N-COUNT A **regularity** is the fact that the same thing always happens in the same circumstances. [FORMAL] ❑ *Children seek out regularities and rules in acquiring language.* 2 → See also **regular**.

**regu|lar|ize** /re̱gjʊləraɪz/ **(regularizes, regularizing, regularized)**

✔ in BRIT, also use **regularise**

VERB If someone **regularizes** a situation or system, they make it officially acceptable or put it under a system of rules. [FORMAL] ❑ V n *Cohabiting couples would regularise their unions, they said.*

**regu|late** /re̱gjʊleɪt/ **(regulates, regulating, regulated)** VERB To **regulate** an activity or process means to control it, especially by means of rules. ❑ V n *The powers of the European Commission to regulate competition are increasing.* ♦ **regu|lat|ed** ADJ *...a planned, state-regulated economy.*

**regu|la|tion** /re̱gjʊle͟ɪʃᵊn/ **(regulations)** ◆◇◇ 1 N-COUNT: usu pl = *rule* **Regulations** are rules made by a government or other authority in order to control the way something is done or the way people behave.

❑ *The European Union has proposed new regulations to control the hours worked by its employees.* [2] **Regulation** is the controlling of an activity or process, usually by means of rules. ❑ *Some in the market now want government regulation in order to reduce costs.* N-UNCOUNT: oft N *of* n

**regu|la|tor** /regjʊleɪtəʳ/ **(regulators)** A **regulator** is a person or organization appointed by a government to regulate an area of activity such as banking or industry. ❑ *An independent regulator will be appointed to ensure fair competition.* ◆◇◇ N-COUNT ♦ **regu|la|tory** /regjʊleɪtəri, AM -lətɔːri/ *...the UK's financial regulatory system.* ADJ: ADJ n

**re|gur|gi|tate** /rɪgɜːʳdʒɪteɪt/ **(regurgitates, regurgitating, regurgitated)** [1] If you say that someone is **regurgitating** ideas or facts, you mean that they are repeating them without understanding them properly. ❑ *You can get sick to death of a friend regurgitating her partner's opinions.* VERB disapproval V n [2] If a person or animal **regurgitates** food, they bring it back up from their stomach before it has been digested. [FORMAL] ❑ *Sometimes he regurgitates the food we give him because he cannot swallow.* VERB = bring up V n

**re|hab** /riːhæb/ **Rehab** is the process of helping someone to lead a normal life again after they have been ill, or when they have had a drug or alcohol problem. **Rehab** is short for **rehabilitation**. [INFORMAL] ❑ *...the drug rehab programme.* N-UNCOUNT: oft N n

**re|ha|bili|tate** /riːhəbɪlɪteɪt/ **(rehabilitates, rehabilitating, rehabilitated)** [1] To **rehabilitate** someone who has been ill or in prison means to help them to live a normal life again. To **rehabilitate** someone who has a drug or alcohol problem means to help them stop using drugs or alcohol. ❑ *Considerable efforts have been made to rehabilitate patients who have suffered in this way.* VERB V n ♦ **re|ha|bili|ta|tion** /riːhəbɪlɪteɪʃᵊn/ *...the rehabilitation of young offenders.* N-UNCOUNT [2] If someone **is rehabilitated**, they begin to be considered acceptable again after a period during which they have been rejected or severely criticized. [FORMAL] ❑ *Ten years later, Dreyfus was rehabilitated... His candidacy has divided the party; while most have scorned him, others have sought to rehabilitate him.* VERB be V-ed V n

**re|hash** **(rehashes, rehashing, rehashed)**

> The noun is pronounced /riːhæʃ/. The verb is pronounced /riːhæʃ/.

[1] If you describe something as a **rehash**, you are criticizing it because it repeats old ideas, facts, or themes, though some things have been changed to make it appear new. ❑ *The Observer found the play 'a feeble rehash of familiar Miller themes'.* N-COUNT: usu sing, N *of* n disapproval [2] If you say that someone **rehashes** old ideas, facts, or accusations, you disapprove of the fact that they present them in a slightly different way so that they seem new or original. ❑ *They've taken some of the best bits out of the best things and rehashed them.* VERB disapproval V n

**re|hears|al** /rɪhɜːʳsᵊl/ **(rehearsals)** [1] A **rehearsal** of a play, dance, or piece of music is a practice of it in preparation for a performance. ❑ *The band was scheduled to begin rehearsals for a concert tour.* → See also **dress rehearsal**. N-VAR: oft N *for/of* n [2] You can describe an event or object which is a preparation for a more important event or object as a **rehearsal for** it. ❑ *Daydreams may seem to be rehearsals for real-life situations.* N-COUNT: N *for* n

**re|hearse** /rɪhɜːʳs/ **(rehearses, rehearsing, rehearsed)** [1] When people **rehearse** a play, dance, or piece of music, they practise it in order to prepare for a performance. ❑ *A group of actors are rehearsing a play about Joan of Arc... Tens of thousands of people have been rehearsing for the opening ceremony in the workers' stadium... The cast and crew were only given three and a half weeks to rehearse.* VERB V n V *for* n V [2] If you **rehearse** something that you are going to say or do, you silently practise it by imagining that you are saying or doing it. ❑ *Anticipate any tough questions and rehearse your answers... We encouraged them to rehearse what they were going to say.* VERB V n V wh

**re|house** /riːhaʊz/ **(rehouses, rehousing, rehoused)** If someone **is rehoused**, their council, local government, or other authority provides them with a different house to live in. ❑ *Many of the 100,000 or so families who lost their homes in the earthquake have still not been rehoused... The council has agreed to rehouse the family.* VERB be V-ed V n

**reign** /reɪn/ **(reigns, reigning, reigned)** [1] If you say, for example, that silence **reigns** in a place or confusion **reigns** in a situation, you mean that the place is silent or the situation is confused. [WRITTEN] ❑ *Confusion reigned about how the debate would end... A relative calm reigned over the city.* VERB V V *over* n [2] When a king or queen **reigns**, he or she rules a country. ❑ *...Henry II, who reigned from 1154 to 1189. ...George III, Britain's longest reigning monarch.* VERB V V-ing ♦ **Reign** is also a noun. ❑ *...Queen Victoria's reign.* N-COUNT: with poss [3] If you say that a person **reigns** in a situation or area, you mean that they are very powerful or successful. ❑ *Connors reigned as the world No. 1 for 159 consecutive weeks... Coco Chanel reigned over fashion for half a century.* VERB V V *over* n ♦ **Reign** is also a noun. ❑ *...a new book celebrating Havergal's reign as artistic director of the Citizens' Theatre.* N-COUNT: with poss

**PHRASES** [4] Someone or something that **reigns supreme** is the most important or powerful element in a situation or period of time. ❑ *The bicycle reigned supreme as Britain's most popular mode of transport.* PHRASE: V inflects [5] A **reign of terror** is a period during which there is a lot of violence and killing, especially by people who are in a position of power. ❑ *The commanders accused him of carrying out a reign of terror.* PHRASE

**reign|ing** /reɪnɪŋ/ The **reigning** champion is the most recent winner of a contest or competition at the time you are talking about. ❑ *...the reigning world champion.* ADJ: ADJ n

**re|im|burse** /riːɪmbɜːʳs/ **(reimburses, reimbursing, reimbursed)** If you **reimburse** someone **for** something, you pay them back the money that they have spent or lost because of it. [FORMAL] ❑ *I'll be happy to reimburse you for any expenses you might have incurred... The funds are supposed to reimburse policyholders in the event of insurer failure.* VERB V n *for* n V n

**re|im|burse|ment** /riːɪmbɜːʳsmənt/ **(reimbursements)** If you receive **reimbursement for** money that you have spent, you get your money back, for example because the money should have been paid by someone else. [FORMAL] ❑ *She is demanding reimbursement for medical and other expenses.* N-VAR

**rein** /reɪn/ **(reins, reining, reined)** [1] **Reins** are the thin leather straps attached round a horse's neck which are used to control the horse. N-PLURAL [2] Journalists sometimes use the expression **the reins** or **the reins of power** to refer to the control of a country or organization. ❑ *He was determined to see the party keep a hold on the reins of power.* N-PLURAL: oft *the* N *of* n

**PHRASES** [3] If you **give free rein to** someone, you give them a lot of freedom to do what they want. ❑ *The government continued to believe it should give free rein to the private sector in transport.* PHRASE: V inflects [4] If you **keep a tight rein on** someone, you control them firmly. ❑ *Her parents had kept her on a tight rein with their narrow and inflexible views.* PHRASE: V inflects

♦ **rein back** To **rein back** something such as spending means to control it strictly. ❑ *The government would try to rein back inflation.* PHRASAL VERB V P n (not pron) Also V n P

♦ **rein in** To **rein in** something means to control it. ❑ *His administration's economic policy would focus on reining in inflation... Mary spoiled both her children, then tried too late to rein them in.* PHRASAL VERB V P n (not pron) V n P

**re|incar|nate** /riːɪŋkɑːʳneɪt/ **(reincarnates, reincarnating, reincarnated)** If people believe that they will **be reincarnated** when they die, they believe that their spirit will be born again and will live in the body of another person or animal. VERB: usu passive

❑ *...their belief that human souls were reincarnated in the bodies of turtles.* [be V-ed]

**re|incar|na|tion** /riːɪŋkɑːʳneɪʃᵊn/ **(reincarnations)** 1 [N-UNCOUNT] If you believe in **reincarnation**, you believe that you will be reincarnated after you die. ❑ *Many African tribes believe in reincarnation.* 2 [N-COUNT] A **reincarnation** is a person or animal whose body is believed to contain the spirit of a dead person.

**rein|deer** /reɪndɪəʳ/ **(reindeer)** [N-COUNT] A **reindeer** is a deer with large horns called antlers that lives in northern areas of Europe, Asia, and America.

**re|inforce** /riːɪnfɔːʳs/ **(reinforces, reinforcing, reinforced)** 1 [VERB] If something **reinforces** a feeling, situation, or process, it makes it stronger or more intense. ❑ *A stronger European Parliament would, they fear, only reinforce the power of the larger countries.* [V n] 2 [VERB] If something **reinforces** an idea or point of view, it provides more evidence or support for it. ❑ *The delegation hopes to reinforce the idea that human rights are not purely internal matters.* [V n] 3 [VERB] To **reinforce** an object means to make it stronger or harder. ❑ *Eventually, they had to reinforce the walls with exterior beams.* [V n *with* n] ♦ **re|inforced** [ADJ] *Its windows were of reinforced glass.* 4 [VERB] To **reinforce** an army or a police force means to make it stronger by increasing its size or providing it with more weapons. To **reinforce** a position or place means to make it stronger by sending more soldiers or weapons. ❑ *Both sides have been reinforcing their positions after yesterday's fierce fighting.* [V n]

**re|inforced con|crete** [N-UNCOUNT] **Reinforced concrete** is concrete that is made with pieces of metal inside it to make it stronger.

**re|inforce|ment** /riːɪnfɔːʳsmənt/ **(reinforcements)** 1 [N-PLURAL] **Reinforcements** are soldiers or policemen who are sent to join an army or group of police in order to make it stronger. ❑ *...the despatch of police and troop reinforcements.* 2 [N-VAR: oft N *of* n] The **reinforcement** of something is the process of making it stronger. ❑ *I am sure that this meeting will contribute to the reinforcement of peace and security all over the world.*

**re|instate** /riːɪnsteɪt/ **(reinstates, reinstating, reinstated)** 1 [VERB] If you **reinstate** someone, you give them back a job or position which had been taken away from them. ❑ *The governor is said to have agreed to reinstate five senior workers who were dismissed.* [V n] 2 [VERB] To **reinstate** a law, facility, or practice means to start having it again. ❑ *...the decision to reinstate the grant.* [V n]

**re|instate|ment** /riːɪnsteɪtmənt/ 1 [N-UNCOUNT: usu with poss] **Reinstatement** is the act of giving someone back a job or position which has been taken away from them. ❑ *Parents campaigned in vain for her reinstatement.* 2 [N-UNCOUNT: usu with poss] The **reinstatement** of a law, facility, or practice is the act of causing it to exist again. ❑ *He welcomed the reinstatement of the 10 per cent bank base rate.*

**re|invent** /riːɪnvent/ **(reinvents, reinventing, reinvented)** 1 [VERB] To **reinvent** something means to change it so that it seems different and new. ❑ *They have tried to reinvent their retail stores...* [V n] *He was determined to reinvent himself as a poet and writer.* [V pron-refl] ♦ **re|inven|tion** /riːɪnvenʃən/ [N-UNCOUNT] *...a reinvention of the styles of the 1940s.* 2 [PHRASE: V inflects] If someone is trying **to reinvent the wheel**, they are trying to do something that has already been done successfully. ❑ *Some of these ideas are worth pursuing, but there is no need to reinvent the wheel.*

**re|is|sue** /riː ɪʃuː/ **(reissues, reissuing, reissued)** 1 [N-COUNT] A **reissue** is a book, CD, or film that has not been available for some time but is now published or produced again. ❑ *...this welcome reissue of a 1955 Ingmar Bergman classic.* 2 [VERB: usu passive] If something such as a book, CD, or film **is reissued** after it has not been available for some time, it is published or produced again. ❑ *Her novels have just been reissued with eye-catching new covers.* [be V-ed]

**re|it|er|ate** /riːɪtəreɪt/ **(reiterates, reiterating, reiterated)** [VERB = repeat] If you **reiterate** something, you say it again, usually in order to emphasize it. [FORMAL, JOURNALISM] ❑ *He reiterated his opposition to the creation of a central bank...* [V n] *I want to reiterate that our conventional weapons are superior.* [V that] ♦ **re|it|era|tion** /riːɪtəreɪʃᵊn/ **(reiterations)** [N-VAR: oft N *of* n = repetition] *It was really a reiteration of the same old entrenched positions.*

**re|ject** **(rejects, rejecting, rejected)** ♦♦◇

> ✔ The verb is pronounced /rɪdʒekt/. The noun is pronounced /riːdʒekt/.

1 [VERB] If you **reject** something such as a proposal, a request, or an offer, you do not accept it or you do not agree to it. ❑ *The British government is expected to reject the idea of state subsidy for a new high speed railway.* [V n] ♦ **re|jec|tion** /rɪdʒekʃᵊn/ **(rejections)** [N-VAR: oft N *of* n] *The rejection of such initiatives indicates that voters are unconcerned about the environment.* 2 [VERB] If you **reject** a belief or a political system, you refuse to believe in it or to live by its rules. ❑ *...the children of Eastern European immigrants who had rejected their parents' political and religious beliefs.* [V n] ♦ **re|jec|tion** [N-VAR] *...his rejection of our values.* 3 [VERB] If someone **is rejected** for a job or course of study, it is not offered to them. ❑ *One of my most able students was rejected by another university.* [be V-ed Also V n] ♦ **re|jec|tion** [N-COUNT] *Be prepared for lots of rejections before you land a job.* 4 [VERB] If someone **rejects** another person who expects affection from them, they are cold and unfriendly towards them. ❑ *...people who had been rejected by their lovers.* [V n] ♦ **re|jec|tion** [N-VAR] *These feelings of rejection and hurt remain.* 5 [VERB] If a person's body **rejects** something such as a new heart that has been transplanted into it, it tries to attack and destroy it. ❑ *It was feared his body was rejecting a kidney he received in a transplant four years ago.* [V n] ♦ **re|jec|tion** [N-VAR] *...a special drug which stops rejection of transplanted organs.* 6 [VERB] If a machine **rejects** a coin that you put in it, the coin comes out and the machine does not work. 7 [N-COUNT] A **reject** is a product that has not been accepted for use or sale, because there is something wrong with it.

**re|jig** /riːdʒɪg/ **(rejigs, rejigging, rejigged)** [VERB] If someone **rejigs** an organization or a piece of work, they arrange or organize it in a different way, in order to improve it. [BRIT] ❑ *...adjustments needed to rejig the industry.* [V n]

> ✔ in AM, use **rejigger**

**re|jig|ger** /riːdʒɪgəʳ/ **(rejiggers, rejiggering, rejiggered)** [VERB] If someone **rejiggers** an organization or a piece of work, they arrange or organize it in a different way, in order to improve it. [AM] ❑ *The government is rejiggering some tax assessment methods.* [V n]

> ✔ in BRIT, use **rejig**

**re|joice** /rɪdʒɔɪs/ **(rejoices, rejoicing, rejoiced)** [VERB] If you **rejoice**, you are very pleased about something and you show it in your behaviour. ❑ *Garbo plays the Queen, rejoicing in the love she has found with Antonio...* [V *in/at* n] *Party activists in New Hampshire rejoiced that the presidential campaign had finally started.* [V that Also V] ♦ **re|joic|ing** [N-UNCOUNT] *There was general rejoicing at the news.*

**re|join** /riːdʒɔɪn/ **(rejoins, rejoining, rejoined)** 1 [VERB] If you **rejoin** a group, club, or organization, you become a member of it again after not being a member for a period of time. ❑ *The Prime Minister of Fiji has said Fiji is in no hurry to rejoin the Commonwealth.* [V n] 2 [VERB] If you **rejoin** someone, you go back to them after a short time away from them. ❑ *Mimi and her family went off to Tunisia to rejoin her father.* [V n] 3 [VERB] If you **rejoin** a route, you go back to it after travelling along a different route for a time. ❑ *At Dorset Wharf go left to rejoin the river.* [V n]

**re|join|der** /rɪdʒɔɪndəʳ/ **(rejoinders)** [N-COUNT = retort] A **rejoinder** is a reply, especially a quick, witty, or critical one, to a question or remark. [FORMAL]

**re|ju|venate** /rɪdʒuːvəneɪt/ **(rejuvenates, rejuvenating, rejuvenated)** 1 [VERB] If something **reju-**

**venates** you, it makes you feel or look young again. ❑ *Shelley was advised that the Italian climate would rejuvenate him.* ♦ **re|ju|venat|ing** *The hotel's new Spa offers every kind of rejuvenating treatment and therapy.* [2] If you **rejuvenate** an organization or system, you make it more lively and more efficient, for example by introducing new ideas. ❑ *The government pushed through schemes to rejuvenate the inner cities.* ♦ **re|ju|vena|tion** /rɪdʒuːvəneɪʃən/ *The way Britain organises its politics needs rejuvenation.*

V n
ADJ
VERB
V n
N-UNCOUNT

**re|kin|dle** /riːkɪndəl/ **(rekindles, rekindling, rekindled)** [1] If something **rekindles** an interest, feeling, or thought that you used to have, it makes you think about it or feel it again. ❑ *Ben Brantley's article on Sir Ian McKellen rekindled many memories.* [2] If something **rekindles** an unpleasant situation, it makes the unpleasant situation happen again. ❑ *There are fears that the series could rekindle animosity between the two countries.*

VERB
V n
VERB
V n

**re|lapse** /rɪlæps/ **(relapses, relapsing, relapsed)**

> ✔ The noun can be pronounced /rɪlæps/ or /riːlæps/.

[1] If you say that someone **relapses into** a way of behaving that is undesirable, you mean that they start to behave in that way again. ❑ *'I wish I did,' said Phil Jordan, relapsing into his usual gloom.* ♦ **Relapse** is also a noun. ❑ *...a relapse into the nationalism of the nineteenth century.* [2] If a sick person **relapses**, their health suddenly gets worse after it had been improving. ❑ *In 90 per cent of cases the patient will relapse within six months.* ♦ **Relapse** is also a noun. ❑ *The treatment is usually given to women with a high risk of relapse after surgery.*

VERB
V *into* n
N-COUNT: oft N *into* n
VERB
V
N-VAR

**re|late** /rɪleɪt/ **(relates, relating, related)** [1] If something **relates to** a particular subject, it concerns that subject. ❑ *Other recommendations relate to the details of how such data is stored.* [2] The way that two things **relate**, or the way that one thing **relates to** another, is the sort of connection that exists between them. ❑ *Cornell University offers a course that investigates how language relates to particular cultural codes... Many Christians today feel the need to relate their experience to that of the Hindu, the Buddhist and the Muslim. ...a paper called 'Language and freedom' in which Chomsky tries to relate his linguistic and political views... At the end, we have a sense of names, dates, and events but no sense of how they relate.* [3] If you can **relate to** someone, you can understand how they feel or behave so that you are able to communicate with them or deal with them easily. ❑ *He is unable to relate to other people... When people are cut off from contact with others, they lose all ability to relate.* [4] If you **relate** a story, you tell it. [FORMAL] ❑ *There were officials to whom he could relate the whole story... She related her tale of living rough.*

◆◇◇
VERB
V *to* n
V-RECIP
V *to* n
V n *to* n
V pl-n
V
VERB
V *to* n
V
VERB
V n *to* n
V n

**re|lat|ed** /rɪleɪtɪd/ [1] If two or more things are **related**, there is a connection between them. ❑ *The philosophical problems of chance and of free will are closely related.* [2] People who are **related** belong to the same family. ❑ *...people in countries like Bangladesh who have been able to show they are related to a spouse or parent living in Britain.* [3] If you say that different types of things, such as languages, are **related**, you mean that they developed from the same language. ❑ *Sanskrit is related very closely to Latin, Greek, and the Germanic and Celtic languages. ...closely related species.*

◆◇◇
ADJ = connected
ADJ: v-link ADJ, oft ADJ *to* n
ADJ: oft ADJ *to* n

**-related** /-rɪleɪtɪd/ **-related** combines with nouns to form adjectives with the meaning 'connected with the thing referred to by the noun'. ❑ *...drug-related offences.*

COMB in ADJ: usu ADJ n

**re|la|tion** /rɪleɪʃən/ **(relations)** [1] **Relations** between people, groups, or countries are contacts between them and the way in which they behave towards each other. ❑ *Greece has established full diplomatic relations with Israel.* ➔ See also **industrial relations**, **public relations**, **race relations**. [2] If you talk about the **relation of** one thing **to** another, you are talking about the ways in which they are connected. ❑ *It is a question of the relation of ethics to economics.* [3] Your **relations** are the members of your family. ❑ *...visits to friends and relations.* ➔ See also **poor relation**.

◆◆◇
N-COUNT: usu pl
N-COUNT: usu sing, usu N *of/to/between* n
N-COUNT = relative

**PHRASES** [4] You can talk about something **in relation to** something else when you want to compare the size, condition, or position of the two things. ❑ *The money he'd been ordered to pay was minimal in relation to his salary.* [5] If something is said or done **in relation to** a subject, it is said or done in connection with that subject. ❑ *...a question which has been asked many times in relation to Irish affairs.*

PREP-PHRASE
PREP-PHRASE

**re|la|tion|ship** /rɪleɪʃənʃɪp/ **(relationships)** [1] The **relationship** between two people or groups is the way in which they feel and behave towards each other. ❑ *...the friendly relationship between France and Britain. ...family relationships.* [2] A **relationship** is a close friendship between two people, especially one involving romantic or sexual feelings. ❑ *We had been together for two years, but both of us felt the relationship wasn't really going anywhere.* [3] The **relationship** between two things is the way in which they are connected. ❑ *There is a relationship between diet and cancer.*

◆◆◇
N-COUNT: with supp
N-COUNT
N-COUNT: N *between/to/of* n

**rela|tive** /relətɪv/ **(relatives)** [1] Your **relatives** are the members of your family. ❑ *Get a relative to look after the children.* [2] You use **relative** to say that something is true to a certain degree, especially when compared with other things of the same kind. ❑ *The fighting resumed after a period of relative calm.* [3] You use **relative** when you are comparing the quality or size of two things. ❑ *They chatted about the relative merits of London and Paris as places to live.* [4] **Relative to** something means with reference to it or in comparison with it. ❑ *Japanese interest rates rose relative to America's.* [5] If you say that something is **relative**, you mean that it needs to be considered and judged in relation to other things. ❑ *Fitness is relative; one must always ask 'Fit for what?'.* [6] If one animal, plant, language, or invention is a **relative of** another, they have both developed from the same type of animal, plant, language, or invention. ❑ *The pheasant is a close relative of the Guinea hen.*

◆◇◇
N-COUNT = relation
ADJ: ADJ n = comparative
ADJ: ADJ n
PREP-PHRASE
ADJ: usu v-link ADJ ≠ absolute
N-COUNT: usu N *of* n

**rela|tive clause** **(relative clauses)** In grammar, a **relative clause** is a subordinate clause which specifies or gives information about a person or thing. Relative clauses come after a noun or pronoun and, in English, often begin with a relative pronoun such as 'who', 'which', or 'that'.

N-COUNT

**rela|tive|ly** /relətɪvli/ **Relatively** means to a certain degree, especially when compared with other things of the same kind. ❑ *The sums needed are relatively small.*

◆◇◇
ADV: ADV adj/adv = comparatively

**rela|tive pro|noun** **(relative pronouns)** A **relative pronoun** is a word such as 'who', 'that', or 'which' that is used to introduce a relative clause. 'Whose', 'when', 'where', and 'why' are generally called **relative pronouns**, though they are actually adverbs.

N-COUNT

**rela|tiv|ism** /relətɪvɪzəm/ **Relativism** is the belief that the truth is not always the same but varies according to circumstances. ❑ *Traditionalists may howl, but in today's world, cultural relativism rules.*

N-UNCOUNT ≠ absolutism

**rela|tiv|ist** /relətɪvɪst/ **(relativists)** A **relativist** position or argument is one according to which the truth is not always the same, but varies according to circumstances. ❑ *Bonger advocated a relativist position. In his view, what is considered immoral depends on the social structure.*

ADJ ≠ absolutist

**rela|tiv|ity** /relətɪvɪti/ The theory of **relativity** is Einstein's theory concerning space, time, and motion. [TECHNICAL]

N-UNCOUNT

**re|launch** /riːlɔːntʃ/ **(relaunches, relaunching, relaunched)** To **relaunch** something such as a company, a product, or a scheme means to start it

VERB

again or to produce it in a different way. ❑ *He is hoping to relaunch his film career.* ♦ **Relaunch** is also a noun. ❑ *Football kit relaunches are simply a way of boosting sales.* V n / N-COUNT

**re|lax** /rɪlæks/ **(relaxes, relaxing, relaxed)** ◆◇◇ VERB [1] If you **relax** or if something **relaxes** you, you feel more calm and less worried or tense. ❑ *I ought to relax and stop worrying about it... Do something that you know relaxes you.* V / V n [2] VERB When a part of your body **relaxes**, or when you **relax** it, it becomes less stiff or firm. ❑ *Massage is used to relax muscles, relieve stress and improve the circulation... His face relaxes into a contented smile.* V n / V [3] VERB ≠tighten If you **relax** your grip or hold on something, you hold it less tightly than before. ❑ *He gradually relaxed his grip on the arms of the chair.* V n [4] VERB ≠tighten If you **relax** a rule or your control over something, or if it **relaxes**, it becomes less firm or strong. ❑ *Rules governing student conduct relaxed somewhat in recent years... How much can the President relax his grip over the nation?* V / V n [5] → See also **relaxed**, **relaxing**.

**re|laxa|tion** /riːlækseɪʃᵊn/ [1] N-UNCOUNT: oft N n **Relaxation** is a way of spending time in which you rest and feel comfortable. ❑ *You should be able to find the odd moment for relaxation.* [2] N-UNCOUNT: oft N *of/in* n If there is **relaxation** of a rule or control, it is made less firm or strong. ❑ *...the relaxation of travel restrictions.*

**re|laxed** /rɪlækst/ [1] ADJ If you are **relaxed**, you are calm and not worried or tense. ❑ *As soon as I had made the final decision, I felt a lot more relaxed.* [2] ADJ If a place or situation is **relaxed**, it is calm and peaceful. ❑ *The atmosphere at lunch was relaxed.*

**re|lax|ing** /rɪlæksɪŋ/ ADJ Something that is **relaxing** is pleasant and helps you to relax. ❑ *I find cooking very relaxing.*

**re|lay** **(relays, relaying, relayed)**

> ✔ The noun is pronounced /riːleɪ/. The verb is pronounced /rɪleɪ/.

[1] N-COUNT A **relay** or a **relay race** is a race between two or more teams, for example teams of runners or swimmers. Each member of the team runs or swims one section of the race. ❑ *Britain's prospects of beating the United States in the relay looked poor.* [2] VERB To **relay** television or radio signals means to send them or broadcast them. ❑ *The satellite will be used mainly to relay television programmes... This system continuously monitors levels of radiation and relays the information to a central computer.* V n / V n *to/from* n [3] VERB = pass on If you **relay** something that has been said to you, you repeat it to another person. [FORMAL] ❑ *She relayed the message, then frowned.* V n

**re|lease** /rɪliːs/ **(releases, releasing, released)** ◆◆◆ [1] VERB: usu passive If a person or animal **is released** from somewhere where they have been locked up or looked after, they are set free or allowed to go. ❑ *He was released from custody the next day... He was released on bail.* be V-ed *from* n / be V-ed [2] N-COUNT: with supp When someone is released, you refer to their **release**. ❑ *He called for the immediate release of all political prisoners.* [3] VERB If someone or something **releases** you **from** a duty, task, or feeling, they free you from it. [FORMAL] ❑ *Divorce releases both the husband and wife from all marital obligations to each other... This releases the teacher to work with individuals who are having extreme difficulty.* V n *from* n / V n ♦ N-UNCOUNT: also *a* N, oft N *from* N **Release** is also a noun. ❑ *...release from stored tensions, traumas and grief.* [4] VERB To **release** feelings or abilities means to allow them to be expressed. ❑ *Becoming your own person releases your creativity.* V n ♦ N-UNCOUNT **Release** is also a noun. ❑ *She felt the sudden sweet release of her own tears.* [5] VERB If someone in authority **releases** something such as a document or information, they make it available. ❑ *They're not releasing any more details yet.* V n ♦ N-COUNT: with supp **Release** is also a noun. ❑ *Action had been taken to speed up the release of cheques.* [6] VERB If you **release** someone or something, you stop holding them. [FORMAL] ❑ *He stopped and faced her, releasing her wrist.* V n [7] VERB If you **release** a device, you move it so that it stops holding something. ❑ *Wade released the hand brake and pulled away from the curb.* [8] VERB If something **releases** gas, heat, or a substance, it causes it to leave its container or the substance that it was part of and enter the surrounding atmosphere or area. ❑ *...a weapon which releases toxic nerve gas.* V n ♦ N-COUNT: with supp **Release** is also a noun. ❑ *Under the agreement, releases of cancer-causing chemicals will be cut by about 80 per cent.* [9] VERB When an entertainer or company **releases** a new CD, video, or film, it becomes available so that people can buy it or see it. ❑ *He is releasing an album of love songs.* V n [10] N-COUNT A new **release** is a new CD, video, or film that has just become available for people to buy or see. ❑ *Which of the new releases do you think are really good?* [11] N-UNCOUNT: *on* N If a film or video is **on release** or **on general release**, it is available for people to see in public cinemas or for people to buy. ❑ *The video has sold three million copies in its first three weeks on release.* [12] → See also **day release**, **news release**, **press release**.

**rel|egate** /relɪgeɪt/ **(relegates, relegating, relegated)** [1] VERB If you **relegate** someone or something **to** a less important position, you give them this position. ❑ *Might it not be better to relegate the King to a purely ceremonial function?* V n *to* n [2] VERB: usu passive ≠promote If a sports team that competes in a league **is relegated**, it has to compete in a lower division in the next competition, because it was one of the least successful teams in the higher division. [BRIT] ❑ *If Leigh lose, they'll be relegated.* be V-ed ♦ **rel|ega|tion** /relɪgeɪʃᵊn/ N-UNCOUNT ≠promotion *Relegation to the Third Division would prove catastrophic.*

**re|lent** /rɪlent/ **(relents, relenting, relented)** [1] VERB If you **relent**, you allow someone to do something that you had previously refused to allow them to do. ❑ *Finally his mother relented and gave permission for her youngest son to marry.* V [2] VERB If bad weather **relents**, it improves. ❑ *If the weather relents, the game will be finished today.* V

**re|lent|less** /rɪlentləs/ [1] ADJ Something bad that is **relentless** never stops or never becomes less intense. ❑ *The pressure now was relentless.* ♦ **re|lent|less|ly** ADV *The sun is beating down relentlessly.* [2] ADJ Someone who is **relentless** is determined to do something and refuses to give up, even if what they are doing is unpleasant or cruel. ❑ *Relentless in his pursuit of quality, his technical ability was remarkable.* ♦ **re|lent|less|ly** ADV *She always questioned me relentlessly.*

**rel|evance** /reləvᵊns/ N-UNCOUNT: with supp, oft N *to* n Something's **relevance to** a situation or person is its importance or significance in that situation or to that person. ❑ *Politicians' private lives have no relevance to their public roles.*

**rel|evant** /reləvᵊnt/ [1] ADJ = pertinent ≠irrelevant Something that is **relevant to** a situation or person is important or significant in that situation or to that person. ❑ *Is socialism still relevant to people's lives?* [2] ADJ: *the* ADJ n **The relevant** thing of a particular kind is the one that is appropriate. ❑ *Make sure you enclose all the relevant certificates.*

**re|li|able** /rɪlaɪəbᵊl/ ◆◇◇ [1] ADJ People or things that are **reliable** can be trusted to work well or to behave in the way that you want them to. ❑ *She was efficient and reliable... Japanese cars are so reliable.* ♦ **re|li|ably** /rɪlaɪəbli/ ADV *It's been working reliably for years.* ♦ **re|li|abil|ity** /rɪlaɪəbɪlɪti/ N-UNCOUNT *He's not at all worried about his car's reliability.* [2] ADJ Information that is **reliable** or that is from a **reliable** source is very likely to be correct. ❑ *There is no reliable information about civilian casualties.* ♦ **re|li|ably** ADV *Sonia, we are reliably informed, loves her family very much.* ♦ **re|li|abil|ity** N-UNCOUNT *Both questioned the reliability of recent opinion polls.*

**re|li|ance** /rɪlaɪəns/ N-UNCOUNT: usu poss N *on/upon* n = dependence A person's or thing's **reliance on** something is the fact that they need it and often cannot live or work without it. ❑ *...the country's increasing reliance on foreign aid.*

**re|li|ant** /rɪlaɪənt/ ADJ: v-link ADJ *on/upon* n = dependent A person or thing that is **reliant on** something needs it and often cannot live or work without it. ❑ *These people are not* *wholly reliant on Western charity.* ➔ See also **self-reliant**.

**rel|ic** /relɪk/ **(relics)** 1 If you refer to something or someone as a **relic of** an earlier period, you mean that they belonged to that period but have survived into the present. ❑ *Germany's asylum law is a relic of an era in European history which has passed.* 2 A **relic** is something which was made or used a long time ago and which is kept for its historical significance. ❑ *...a museum of war relics.*
N-COUNT: usu N *of/from* n
N-COUNT: usu with supp

**re|lief** /rɪliːf/ **(reliefs)** 1 If you feel a sense of **relief**, you feel happy because something unpleasant has not happened or is no longer happening. ❑ *I breathed a sigh of relief... The news will come as a great relief to the French authorities.* 2 If something provides **relief from** pain or distress, it stops the pain or distress. ❑ *...a self-help programme which can give lasting relief from the torment of hay fever.* 3 **Relief** is money, food, or clothing that is provided for people who are very poor, or who have been affected by war or a natural disaster. ❑ *Relief agencies are stepping up efforts to provide food, shelter and agricultural equipment.* 4 A **relief** worker is someone who does your work when you go home, or who is employed to do it instead of you when you are sick. ❑ *No relief drivers were available.* 5 ➔ See also **bas-relief**, **tax relief**.
◆◆◇ N-UNCOUNT: also *a* N
N-UNCOUNT: oft N *from* n
N-UNCOUNT: oft N n, n N
N-COUNT: usu N n

**re|lieve** /rɪliːv/ **(relieves, relieving, relieved)** 1 If something **relieves** an unpleasant feeling or situation, it makes it less unpleasant or causes it to disappear completely. ❑ *Drugs can relieve much of the pain.* 2 If someone or something **relieves** you **of** an unpleasant feeling or difficult task, they take it from you. ❑ *A part-time bookkeeper will relieve you of the burden of chasing unpaid invoices and paying bills.* 3 If someone **relieves** you **of** something, they take it away from you. [FORMAL] ❑ *A porter relieved her of the three large cases.* 4 If you **relieve** someone, you take their place and continue to do the job or duty that they have been doing. ❑ *At seven o'clock the night nurse came in to relieve her.* 5 If someone **is relieved of** their duties or **is relieved of** their post, they are told that they are no longer required to continue in their job. [FORMAL] ❑ *The officer involved was relieved of his duties because he had violated strict guidelines.* 6 If an army **relieves** a town or another place which has been surrounded by enemy forces, it frees it. ❑ *The offensive began several days ago as an attempt to relieve the town.* 7 If people or animals **relieve themselves**, they urinate or defecate. [OLD-FASHIONED] ❑ *It is not difficult to train your dog to relieve itself on command.*
VERB / V n
VERB / V n *of* n
VERB / V n *of* n
VERB / V n
VERB: usu passive / *be* V-ed *of* n
VERB / V n
VERB / V pron-refl

**re|lieved** /rɪliːvd/ If you are **relieved**, you feel happy because something unpleasant has not happened or is no longer happening. ❑ *We are all relieved to be back home.*
ADJ: usu v-link ADJ, oft ADJ to-inf/that

**re|li|gion** /rɪlɪdʒᵊn/ **(religions)** 1 **Religion** is belief in a god or gods and the activities that are connected with this belief, such as praying or worshipping in a building such as a church or temple. ❑ *...his understanding of Indian philosophy and religion.* 2 A **religion** is a particular system of belief in a god or gods and the activities that are connected with this system. ❑ *...the Christian religion.*
◆◇◇ N-UNCOUNT
N-COUNT

**re|ligi|os|ity** /rɪlɪdʒiɒsɪti/ If you refer to a person's **religiosity**, you are referring to the fact that they are religious in a way which seems exaggerated and insincere. [FORMAL] ❑ *...their hypocritical religiosity.*
N-UNCOUNT: usu with supp

**re|li|gious** /rɪlɪdʒəs/ 1 You use **religious** to describe things that are connected with religion or with one particular religion. ❑ *...religious groups. ...different religious beliefs.* ♦ **re|li|gious|ly** *India has always been one of the most religiously diverse countries.* 2 Someone who is **religious** has a strong belief in a god or gods. ❑ *They are both very religious and felt it was a gift from God.* 3 ➔ See also **religiously**.
◆◆◇ ADJ: ADJ n
ADV: usu ADV adj/adv, ADV -ed
ADJ

**re|li|gious|ly** /rɪlɪdʒəsli/ 1 If you do something **religiously**, you do it very regularly because you feel you have to. ❑ *Do these exercises religiously every day.* 2 ➔ See also **religious**.
ADV: ADV with v

**re|lin|quish** /rɪlɪŋkwɪʃ/ **(relinquishes, relinquishing, relinquished)** If you **relinquish** something such as power or control, you give it up. [FORMAL] ❑ *He does not intend to relinquish power.*
VERB / V n

**reli|quary** /relɪkwəri, AM -kweri/ **(reliquaries)** A **reliquary** is a container where religious objects connected with a saint are kept.
N-COUNT

**rel|ish** /relɪʃ/ **(relishes, relishing, relished)** 1 If you **relish** something, you get a lot of enjoyment from it. ❑ *I relish the challenge of doing jobs that others turn down.* ♦ **Relish** is also a noun. ❑ *The three men ate with relish.* 2 If you **relish** the idea, thought, or prospect of something, you are looking forward to it very much. ❑ *Jacqueline is not relishing the prospect of another spell in prison.* 3 **Relish** is a sauce or pickle that you eat with other food in order to give the other food more flavour.
VERB / V n
N-UNCOUNT
VERB = look forward to / V n
N-MASS

**re|live** /riːlɪv/ **(relives, reliving, relived)** If you **relive** something that has happened to you in the past, you remember it and imagine that you are experiencing it again. ❑ *There is no point in reliving the past.*
VERB / V n

**re|load** /riːloʊd/ **(reloads, reloading, reloaded)** If someone **reloads** a gun, they load it again by putting in more bullets or explosive. If you **reload** a container, you fill it again. ❑ *She reloaded the gun as quickly as she could... He reloaded and nodded to the gamekeeper.*
VERB / V n / V

**re|lo|cate** /riːloʊkeɪt, AM -loʊkeɪt/ **(relocates, relocating, relocated)** If people or businesses **relocate** or if someone **relocates** them, they move to a different place. ❑ *If the company was to relocate, most employees would move... There will be the problem of where to relocate the returning troops.* ♦ **re|lo|ca|tion** /riːloʊkeɪʃᵊn/ **(relocations)** *The company says the cost of relocation will be negligible.*
VERB / V / V n
N-UNCOUNT: also N in pl

**re|lo|ca|tion ex|penses** **Relocation expenses** are a sum of money that a company pays to someone who moves to a new area in order to work for the company. The money is to help them pay for moving house. [BUSINESS] ❑ *Relocation expenses were paid to encourage senior staff to move to the region.*
N-PLURAL

**re|luc|tant** /rɪlʌktənt/ If you are **reluctant to** do something, you are unwilling to do it and hesitate before doing it, or do it slowly and without enthusiasm. ❑ *Mr Spero was reluctant to ask for help.* ♦ **re|luc|tant|ly** *We have reluctantly agreed to let him go.* ♦ **re|luc|tance** *Ministers have shown extreme reluctance to explain their position to the media.*
◆◇◇ ADJ: usu v-link ADJ to-inf
ADV: ADV with v
N-UNCOUNT: oft N to-inf

**rely** /rɪlaɪ/ **(relies, relying, relied)** 1 If you **rely on** someone or something, you need them and depend on them in order to live or work properly. ❑ *They relied heavily on the advice of their professional advisers.* 2 If you can **rely on** someone to work well or to behave as you want them to, you can trust them to do this. ❑ *I know I can rely on you to sort it out... The Red Cross are relying on us.*
◆◇◇ VERB / V *on/upon* n
VERB / V *on/upon* n to-inf / V *on/upon* n

**REM** /ɑːr iː em/ **REM** sleep is a period of sleep that is very deep, during which your eyes and muscles make many small movements. It is the period during which most of your dreams occur. **REM** is an abbreviation for 'rapid eye movement'.
ADJ: ADJ n

**re|main** /rɪmeɪn/ **(remains, remaining, remained)** 1 If someone or something **remains** in a particular state or condition, they stay in that state or condition and do not change. ❑ *The three men remained silent... The government remained in control... He remained a formidable opponent... It remains possible that bad weather could tear more holes in the tanker's hull.* 2 If you **remain** in a place, you stay there and do not move away. ❑ *He will have to remain in hospital for at least 10 days.* 3 You can say that something **remains** when
◆◆◆ V-LINK / V adj / V prep / V n / it V adj that/to-inf/wh
VERB / V prep / Also V
VERB

it still exists. ❑ *The wider problem remains.* V
[4] If something **remains to be** done, it has not yet been done and still needs to be done. ❑ *Major questions remain to be answered about his work.* V-LINK V to-inf-passive
[5] **The remains of** something are the parts of it that are left after most of it has been taken away or destroyed. ❑ *They were tidying up the remains of their picnic.* N-PLURAL: usu *the* N *of* n
[6] The **remains** of a person or animal are the parts of their body that are left after they have died, sometimes after they have been dead for a long time. ❑ *The unrecognizable remains of a man had been found.* N-PLURAL: usu with supp
[7] Historical **remains** are things that have been found from an earlier period of history, usually buried in the ground, for example parts of buildings and pieces of pottery. ❑ *There are Roman remains all around us.* N-PLURAL: usu supp N
[8] You can use **remain** in expressions such as **the fact remains that** or **the question remains whether** to introduce and emphasize something that you want to talk about. ❑ *The fact remains that inflation is unacceptably high... The question remains whether he was fully aware of the claims.* V-LINK V that V wh
[9] → See also **remaining**. [10] If you say that it **remains to be seen** whether something will happen, you mean that nobody knows whether it will happen. ❑ *It remains to be seen whether her parliamentary colleagues will agree.* PHRASE: usu *it* PHR whether [vagueness]

**re|main|der** /rɪmeɪndəʳ/ **The remainder of** a group are the things or people that still remain after the other things or people have gone or have been dealt with. ❑ *He gulped down the remainder of his coffee.* ♦ **Remainder** is also a pronoun. ❑ *Only 5.9 per cent of the area is now covered in trees. Most of the remainder is farmland.* QUANT: QUANT *of* def-n = rest PRON

**re|main|ing** /rɪmeɪnɪŋ/ ◆◇◇ [1] The **remaining** things or people out of a group are the things or people that still exist, are still present, or have not yet been dealt with. ❑ *The three parties will meet next month to work out remaining differences.* ADJ: ADJ n
[2] → See also **remain**.

**re|make** **(remakes, remaking, remade)**

> ✔ The noun is pronounced /riːmeɪk/. The verb is pronounced /riːmeɪk/.

[1] A **remake** is a film that has the same story, and often the same title, as a film that was made earlier. ❑ *...a 1953 remake of the thirties musical 'Roberta'.* N-COUNT
[2] If a film **is remade**, a new film is made that has the same story, and often the same title, as a film that was made earlier. ❑ *Originally released in 1957, the film was remade as 'The Magnificent Seven'.* VERB: usu passive *be* V-ed
[3] If you have something **remade**, you ask someone to make it again, especially in a way that is better than before. ❑ *He had all the window frames in the room remade.* VERB *have* n V-ed Also V n

**re|mand** /rɪmɑːnd, -mænd/ **(remands, remanding, remanded)** [1] If a person who is accused of a crime **is remanded** in custody or on bail, they are told to return to the court at a later date, when their trial will take place. ❑ *Carter was remanded in custody for seven days.* VERB: usu passive *be* V-ed prep
[2] **Remand** is used to refer to the process of remanding someone in custody or on bail, or to the period of time until their trial begins. ❑ *The remand hearing is often over in three minutes.* N-UNCOUNT: also N in pl, oft N n, *on* N

**re|mand cen|tre** **(remand centres)** In Britain, a **remand centre** is an institution where people who are accused of a crime are sent until their trial begins or until a decision about their punishment has been made. N-COUNT

**re|mark** /rɪmɑːʳk/ **(remarks, remarking, remarked)** ◆◇◇ [1] If you **remark** that something is the case, you say that it is the case. ❑ *I remarked that I would go shopping that afternoon... 'Some people have more money than sense,' Winston had remarked... On several occasions she had remarked on the boy's improvement.* VERB V that V with quote V *on/upon* n/wh
[2] If you make a **remark** about something, you say something about it. ❑ *She has made outspoken remarks about the legalisation of cannabis in Britain.* N-COUNT: with supp = comment

**re|mark|able** /rɪmɑːʳkəbəl/ ◆◇◇ Someone or something that is **remarkable** is unusual or special in a way that makes people notice them and be surprised or impressed. ❑ *He was a remarkable man... It was a remarkable achievement.* ADJ
♦ **re|mark|ably** /rɪmɑːʳkəbli/ *The Scottish labour market has been remarkably successful in absorbing the increase in the number of graduates.* ADV: usu ADV adj/adv, also ADV with cl

**re|mar|riage** /riːmærɪdʒ/ **(remarriages)** **Remarriage** is the act of remarrying. ❑ *The question of divorce and remarriage in church remains highly contentious.* N-VAR

**re|mar|ry** /riːmæri/ **(remarries, remarrying, remarried)** If someone **remarries**, they marry again after they have obtained a divorce from their previous husband or wife, or after their previous husband or wife has died. ❑ *Her mother had never remarried.* VERB V Also V n

**re|mas|ter** /riːmɑːstəʳ, -mæstəʳ/ **(remasters, remastering, remastered)** If a film or musical recording **is remastered**, a new recording is made of the old version, using modern technology to improve the quality. ❑ *A special remastered version of Casablanca is being released.* VERB V-ed Also V n

**re|match** /riːmætʃ/ **(rematches)** [1] A **rematch** is a second game that is played between two people or teams, for example because their first match was a draw or because there was a dispute about some aspect of it. [mainly BRIT] ❑ *Duff said he would be demanding a rematch.* N-COUNT
[2] A **rematch** is a second game or contest between two people or teams who have already faced each other. [mainly AM] ❑ *Stanford will face UCLA in a rematch.* N-COUNT

> ✔ in BRIT, usually use **return match**

**re|medial** /rɪmiːdiəl/ [1] **Remedial** education is intended to improve a person's ability to read, write, or do mathematics, especially when they find these things difficult. ❑ *...children who required special remedial education.* ADJ: usu ADJ n
[2] **Remedial** activities are intended to improve a person's health when they are ill. [FORMAL] ❑ *He is already walking normally and doing remedial exercises.* ADJ: usu ADJ n
[3] **Remedial** action is intended to correct something that has been done wrong or that has not been successful. [FORMAL] ❑ *Some authorities are now having to take remedial action.* ADJ: usu ADJ n

**rem|edy** /remədi/ **(remedies, remedying, remedied)** [1] A **remedy** is a successful way of dealing with a problem. ❑ *The remedy lies in the hands of the government.* N-COUNT
[2] A **remedy** is something that is intended to cure you when you are ill or in pain. ❑ *...natural remedies to help overcome winter infections.* N-COUNT
[3] If you **remedy** something that is wrong or harmful, you correct it or improve it. ❑ *A great deal has been done internally to remedy the situation.* VERB V n

**re|mem|ber** /rɪmembəʳ/ **(remembers, remembering, remembered)** ◆◆◆ [1] If you **remember** people or events from the past, you still have an idea of them in your mind and you are able to think about them. ❑ *You wouldn't remember me. I was in another group... I certainly don't remember talking to you at all... I remembered that we had drunk the last of the coffee the week before... I can remember where and when I bought each one... I used to do that when you were a little girl, remember?* VERB V n/-ing V n/-ing V that V wh V
[2] If you **remember** that something is the case, you become aware of it again after a time when you did not think about it. ❑ *She remembered that she was going to the social club that evening... Then I remembered the cheque, which cheered me up.* VERB V that V n
[3] If you cannot **remember** something, you are not able to bring it back into your mind when you make an effort to do so. ❑ *If you can't remember your number, write it in code in a diary... I can't remember what I said... Don't tell me you can't remember.* VERB: usu with brd-neg V n/-ing V wh V
[4] If you **remember to** do something, you do it when you intend to. ❑ *Please remember to enclose a stamped addressed envelope when writing.* VERB ≠ forget V to-inf
[5] You tell someone to **remember that** something is the case when you want to emphasize its importance. VERB [emphasis]

It may be something that they already know about or a new piece of information. ❑ *It is important to remember that each person reacts differently...* {V that} *It should be remembered that this loss of control can never be regained.* {it modal be V-ed that} 6 If you say that someone will **be remembered** for something that they have done, you mean that people will think of this whenever they think about the person. {VERB: usu passive} ❑ *At his grammar school he is remembered for being bad at games...* {be V-ed for n/-ing} *He will always be remembered as one of the great Chancellors of the Exchequer.* {be V-ed as n} 7 If you ask someone to **remember** you **to** a person who you have not seen for a long time, you are asking them to pass your greetings on to that person. {VERB: no cont, usu imper} ❑ *'Remember me to Lyle, won't you?' I said.* {V n to n} 8 If you make a celebration an occasion **to remember**, you make it very enjoyable for all the people involved. {VERB: only to-inf} ❑ *We'll give everyone a night to remember.* {V}

**re|mem|brance** /rɪme̲mbrəns/ If you do something **in remembrance of** a dead person, you do it as a way of showing that you want to remember them and that you respect them. [FORMAL] {N-UNCOUNT} ❑ *They wore black in remembrance of those who had died.*

**Re|mem|brance Day** In Britain, **Remembrance Day** or **Remembrance Sunday** is the Sunday nearest to the 11th of November, when people honour the memory of those who died in the two world wars. {N-UNCOUNT: oft N n} ❑ *...a Remembrance Day service.*

**re|mind** /rɪma̲ɪnd/ **(reminds, reminding, reminded)** ♦◇◇ 1 If someone **reminds** you **of** a fact or event that you already know about, they say something which makes you think about it. {VERB} ❑ *So she simply welcomed him and reminded him of the last time they had met...* {V n of n} *I had to remind myself that being confident is not the same as being perfect!* {V n that} 2 You use **remind** in expressions such as **Let me remind you that** and **May I remind you that** to introduce a piece of information that you want to emphasize. It may be something that the hearer already knows about or a new piece of information. Sometimes these expressions can sound unfriendly. [SPOKEN] {VERB} {emphasis} ❑ *'Let me remind you,' said Marianne, 'that Manchester is also my home town.'...* {V n that} *Need I remind you who the enemy is?* {V n wh} 3 If someone **reminds** you **to** do a particular thing, they say something which makes you remember to do it. {VERB} ❑ *Can you remind me to buy a bottle of Martini?...* {V n to-inf} *The note was to remind him about something he had to explain to one of his students.* {V n about n} 4 If you say that someone or something **reminds** you **of** another person or thing, you mean that they are similar to the other person or thing and that they make you think about them. {VERB} ❑ *She reminds me of the wife of the pilot who used to work for you.* {V n of n}

**re|mind|er** /rɪma̲ɪndəʳ/ **(reminders)** 1 Something that serves as a **reminder of** another thing makes you think about the other thing. [WRITTEN] {N-COUNT: usu sing, oft N of n/wh, N that} ❑ *The British are about to be given a sharp reminder of what fighting abroad really means.* 2 A **reminder** is a letter or note that is sent to tell you that you have not done something such as pay a bill or return library books. [mainly BRIT] {N-COUNT} ❑ *...the final reminder for the gas bill.*

**remi|nisce** /re̲mɪnɪs/ **(reminisces, reminiscing, reminisced)** If you **reminisce** about something from your past, you write or talk about it, often with pleasure. [FORMAL] {VERB} ❑ *I don't like reminiscing because it makes me feel old.* {V}

**remi|nis|cence** /re̲mɪnɪsəns/ **(reminiscences)** Someone's **reminiscences** are things that they remember from the past, and which they talk or write about. {N-VAR: oft poss N, N of n} **Reminiscence** is the process of remembering these things and talking or writing about them. [FORMAL] ❑ *Here I am boring you with my reminiscences.*

**remi|nis|cent** /re̲mɪnɪsənt/ If you say that one thing is **reminiscent of** another, you mean that it reminds you of it. [FORMAL] {ADJ: v-link ADJ of n} ❑ *The decor was reminiscent of a municipal arts-and-leisure centre.*

**re|miss** /rɪmɪ̲s/ If someone is **remiss**, they are careless about doing things which ought to be done. [FORMAL] {ADJ: v-link ADJ, oft ADJ in n/-ing} ❑ *I would be remiss if I did not do something about it.*

**re|mis|sion** /rɪmɪ̲ʃən/ **(remissions)** 1 If someone who has had a serious disease such as cancer is **in remission** or if the disease is **in remission**, the disease has been controlled so that they are not as ill as they were. {N-VAR} ❑ *Brain scans have confirmed that the disease is in remission.* 2 If someone in prison gets **remission**, their prison sentence is reduced, usually because they have behaved well. [BRIT] {N-UNCOUNT} ❑ *With remission for good behaviour, she could be freed in a year.*

**re|mit** **(remits, remitting, remitted)**

> The noun is pronounced /ri̲ːmɪt/. The verb is pronounced /rɪmɪ̲t/.

1 Someone's **remit** is the area of activity which they are expected to deal with, or which they have authority to deal with. [BRIT] {N-COUNT: usu sing, oft poss N, N of n = brief} ❑ *That issue is not within the remit of the working group.* 2 If you **remit** money to someone, you send it to them. [FORMAL] {VERB} ❑ *Many immigrants regularly remit money to their families.* {V n to n}

**re|mit|tance** /rɪmɪ̲təns/ **(remittances)** A **remittance** is a sum of money that you send to someone. [FORMAL] {N-VAR = payment} ❑ *Please enclose your remittance, making cheques payable to Thames Valley Technology.*

**re|mix** **(remixes, remixing, remixed)**

> The noun is pronounced /ri̲ːmɪks/. The verb is pronounced /ri̲ːmɪ̲ks/.

1 A **remix** is a new version of a piece of music which has been created by putting together the individual instrumental and vocal parts in a different way. {N-COUNT} ❑ *Their new album features remixes of some of their previous hits.* 2 To **remix** a piece of music means to make a new version of it by putting together the individual instrumental and vocal parts in a different way. {VERB} ❑ *The band are remixing some tracks.* {V n}

**rem|nant** /re̲mnənt/ **(remnants)** 1 The **remnants of** something are small parts of it that are left over when the main part has disappeared or been destroyed. {N-COUNT: usu N of n} ❑ *Beneath the present church were remnants of Roman flooring.* 2 A **remnant** is a small piece of cloth that is left over when most of the cloth has been sold. Shops usually sell remnants cheaply. {N-COUNT}

**re|mod|el** /ri̲ːmɒ̲dəl/ **(remodels, remodelling, remodelled)**

> in AM, use **remodeling, remodeled**

To **remodel** something such as a building or a room means to give it a different form or shape. {VERB} ❑ *Workmen were hired to remodel and enlarge the farm buildings.* {V n}

**re|mon|strate** /re̲mənstreɪt, AM rɪmɒ̲nstreɪt/ **(remonstrates, remonstrating, remonstrated)** If you **remonstrate with** someone, you protest to them about something you do not approve of or agree with, and you try to get it changed or stopped. [FORMAL] {VERB} ❑ *He remonstrated with the referee...* {V with n} *I jumped in the car and went to remonstrate.* {V, Also V prep}

**re|morse** /rɪmɔ̲ːʳs/ **Remorse** is a strong feeling of sadness and regret about something wrong that you have done. {N-UNCOUNT} ❑ *He was full of remorse.*

**re|morse|ful** /rɪmɔ̲ːʳsfʊl/ If you are **remorseful**, you feel very guilty and sorry about something wrong that you have done. {ADJ} ❑ *He was genuinely remorseful.* ♦ **re|morse|ful|ly** *'My poor wife!' he said, remorsefully.* {ADV: ADV with v}

**re|morse|less** /rɪmɔ̲ːʳsləs/ 1 If you describe something, especially something unpleasant, as **remorseless**, you mean that it goes on for a long time and cannot be stopped. {ADJ = relentless} ❑ *...the remorseless pressure of recession and financial constraint.* ♦ **re|morse|less|ly** *There have been record bankruptcies and remorselessly rising unemployment.* {ADV: usu ADV with v} 2 Someone who is **remorseless** is prepared to {ADJ}

be cruel to other people and feels no pity for them. ❑ *...the capacity for quick, remorseless violence.*
♦ **re|morse|less|ly** *They remorselessly beat up anyone they suspected of supporting the opposition.* ADV: ADV with v

**re|mote** /rɪmoʊt/ **(remoter, remotest)** ◆◇◇
1 **Remote** areas are far away from cities and places where most people live, and are therefore difficult to get to. ❑ *Landslides have cut off many villages in remote areas.* ADJ: usu ADJ n
2 The **remote** past or **remote** future is a time that is many years distant from the present. ❑ *Slabs of rock had slipped sideways in the remote past, and formed this hole.* ADJ: usu ADJ n = distant
3 If something is **remote from** a particular subject or area of experience, it is not relevant to it because it is very different. ❑ *This government depends on the wishes of a few who are remote from the people.* ADJ: usu v-link ADJ *from* n
4 If you say that there is a **remote** possibility or chance that something will happen, you are emphasizing that there is only a very small chance that it will happen. ❑ *I use a sunscreen whenever there is even a remote possibility that I will be in the sun.* ADJ [emphasis]
5 If you describe someone as **remote**, you mean that they behave as if they do not want to be friendly or closely involved with other people. ❑ *She looked so beautiful, and at the same time so remote.* ADJ

**re|mote ac|cess** **Remote access** is a system which allows you to gain access to a particular computer or network using a separate computer. [COMPUTING] ❑ *The diploma course would offer remote access to course materials via the Internet's world wide web.* N-UNCOUNT

**re|mote con|trol** **(remote controls)**
1 **Remote control** is a system of controlling a machine or a vehicle from a distance by using radio or electronic signals. ❑ *The bomb was detonated by remote control.* N-UNCOUNT
2 The **remote control** for a television or video recorder is the device that you use to control the machine from a distance, by pressing the buttons on it. N-COUNT

**remote-controlled** A **remote-controlled** machine or device is controlled from a distance by the use of radio or electronic signals. ❑ *...a remote-controlled bomb.* ADJ: usu ADJ n

**re|mote|ly** /rɪmoʊtli/ 1 You use **remotely** with a negative statement to emphasize the statement. ❑ *Nobody there was even remotely interested.* ADV: with brd-neg, ADV group, ADV before v [emphasis]
2 If someone or something is **remotely** placed or situated, they are a long way from other people or places. ❑ *...the remotely situated, five bedroom house.* ADV: ADV -ed

**re|mote sens|ing** **Remote sensing** is the gathering of information about something by observing it from space or from the air. N-UNCOUNT: oft N n

**re|mould** **(remoulds, remoulding, remoulded)**

✔ The spelling **remold** is used in American English. The noun is pronounced /riːmoʊld/. The verb is pronounced /riːmoʊld/.

1 A **remould** is an old tyre which has been given a new surface or tread and can be used again. [BRIT] N-COUNT

✔ in AM, use **retread**

2 To **remould** something such as an idea or an economy means to change it so that it has a new structure or is based on new principles. ❑ *...a new phase in the attempt to remould Labour's image.* VERB V n

**re|mount** /riːmaʊnt/ **(remounts, remounting, remounted)** When you **remount** a bicycle or horse, you get back on it after you have got off it or fallen off it. ❑ *He was told to remount his horse and ride back to Lexington... The pony scrabbled up and waited for the rider, who remounted and carried on.* VERB V n V

**re|mov|able** /rɪmuːvəbəl/ A **removable** part of something is a part that can easily be moved from its place or position. ❑ *...a cake tin with a removable base.* ADJ: usu ADJ n

**re|mov|al** /rɪmuːvəl/ **(removals)** 1 The **removal** of something is the act of removing it. ❑ *What they expected to be the removal of a small lump turned out to be major surgery.* N-UNCOUNT: usu with supp
2 **Removal** is the process of transporting furniture or equipment from one building to another. [mainly BRIT] ❑ *Home removals are best done in cool weather.* N-VAR: usu with supp, oft N n

✔ in AM, use **moving**

**re|mov|al man** **(removal men)** **Removal men** are men whose job is to move furniture or equipment from one building to another. [mainly BRIT] N-COUNT

✔ in AM, usually use **movers**

**re|move** /rɪmuːv/ **(removes, removing, removed)** ◆◆◇
1 If you **remove** something from a place, you take it away. [WRITTEN] ❑ *As soon as the cake is done, remove it from the oven... He went to the refrigerator and removed a bottle of wine.* VERB V n *from* n V n
2 If you **remove** clothing, you take it off. [WRITTEN] ❑ *He removed his jacket.* VERB V n
3 If you **remove** a stain from something, you make the stain disappear by treating it with a chemical or by washing it. ❑ *This treatment removes the most stubborn stains.* VERB V n
4 If people **remove** someone **from** power or **from** something such as a committee, they stop them being in power or being a member of the committee. ❑ *The student senate voted to remove Fuller from office.* VERB V n *from* n
5 If you **remove** an obstacle, a restriction, or a problem, you get rid of it. ❑ *The agreement removes the last serious obstacle to the signing of the arms treaty.* VERB V n

**re|moved** /rɪmuːvd/ If you say that an idea or situation is far **removed from** something, you mean that it is very different from it. ❑ *He found it hard to concentrate on conversation so far removed from his present preoccupations.* ADJ: v-link adv ADJ *from* n

**re|mov|er** /rɪmuːvəʳ/ **(removers)** **Remover** is a substance that you use for removing an unwanted stain, mark, or coating from a surface. ❑ *We got some paint remover and scrubbed it off.* N-MASS: usu supp N

**re|mu|ner|ate** /rɪmjuːnəreɪt/ **(remunerates, remunerating, remunerated)** If you **are remunerated** for work that you do, you are paid for it. [FORMAL] ❑ *You will be remunerated and so will your staff.* VERB: usu passive *be* V-ed

**re|mu|nera|tion** /rɪmjuːnəreɪʃən/ **(remunerations)** Someone's **remuneration** is the amount of money that they are paid for the work that they do. [FORMAL] ❑ *...the continuing marked increase in the remuneration of the company's directors.* N-VAR

**re|mu|nera|tive** /rɪmjuːnərətɪv/ **Remunerative** work is work that you are paid for. [FORMAL] ❑ *A doctor advised her to seek remunerative employment.* ADJ: usu ADJ n

**re|nais|sance** /rɪneɪsɒns, AM renɪsɑːns/
1 **The Renaissance** was the period in Europe, especially Italy, in the 14th, 15th, and 16th centuries, when there was a new interest in art, literature, science, and learning. ❑ *...the Renaissance masterpieces in London's galleries.* N-PROPER: *the* N, oft N n
2 If something experiences a **renaissance**, it becomes popular or successful again after a time when people were not interested in it. ❑ *Popular art is experiencing a renaissance.* N-SING = revival

**Re|nais|sance man** **(Renaissance men)** If you describe a man as a **Renaissance man**, you mean that he has a wide range of abilities and interests, especially in the arts and sciences. N-COUNT [approval]

**re|nal** /riːnəl/ **Renal** describes things that concern or are related to the kidneys. [MEDICAL] ❑ *He collapsed from acute renal failure.* ADJ: ADJ n

**re|name** /riːneɪm/ **(renames, renaming, renamed)** If you **rename** something, you change its name to a new name. ❑ *Tel Aviv's Kings Square was renamed Yitzhak Rabin Square.* VERB *be* V-ed n

**rend** /rend/ **(rends, rending, rent)** 1 To **rend** something means to tear it. [LITERARY] ❑ *...pain that rends the heart. ...a twisted urge to rend and tear.* VERB V n V
2 If a loud sound **rends** the air, it is sudden and violent. [LITERARY] ❑ *He bellows, rends the air with anguish.* VERB V n
3 → See also **heart-rending**.

**ren|der** /rendəʳ/ **(renders, rendering, rendered)** [1] You can use **render** with an adjective that describes a particular state to say that someone or something is changed into that state. For example, if someone or something makes a thing harmless, you can say that they **render** it harmless. ❑ *It contained so many errors as to render it worthless.* [2] If you **render** someone help or service, you help them. [FORMAL] ❑ *He had a chance to render some service to his country... Any assistance you can render him will be appreciated.* [3] To **render** something in a particular language or in a particular way means to translate it into that language or in that way. [FORMAL] ❑ *All the signs and announcements were rendered in English and Spanish.*
VERB = make; V n adj; VERB; V n *to* n; V n n; VERB; V n *as/in/into* n

**ren|der|ing** /rendərɪŋ/ **(renderings)** [1] A **rendering of** a play, poem, or piece of music is a performance of it. ❑ *...a rendering of Verdi's Requiem by the BBC Symphony Orchestra.* [2] A **rendering** of an expression or piece of writing or speech is a translation of it. ❑ *This phrase may well have been a rendering of a popular Arabic expression.*
N-COUNT: usu N *of* n = performance; N-COUNT: usu N *of* n

**ren|dez|vous** /rɒndeɪvuː/ **(rendezvousing, rendezvoused)**

> ✔ The form **rendezvous** is pronounced /rɒndeɪvuːz/ when it is the plural of the noun or the third person singular of the verb.

[1] A **rendezvous** is a meeting, often a secret one, that you have arranged with someone for a particular time and place. ❑ *I had almost decided to keep my rendezvous with Tony.* [2] A **rendezvous** is the place where you have arranged to meet someone, often secretly. ❑ *Their rendezvous would be the Penta Hotel at Heathrow Airport.* [3] If you **rendezvous with** someone or if the two of you **rendezvous**, you meet them at a time and place that you have arranged. ❑ *The plan was to rendezvous with him on Sunday afternoon... She wondered where they were going to rendezvous afterwards.*
N-COUNT; N-COUNT; V-RECIP = meet; V *with* n; pl-n V

**ren|di|tion** /rendɪʃᵊn/ **(renditions)** A **rendition of** a play, poem, or piece of music is a performance of it. ❑ *The musicians burst into a rousing rendition of 'Paddy Casey's Reel'.*
N-COUNT: usu N *of* n = performance

**ren|egade** /renɪgeɪd/ **(renegades)** [1] A **renegade** is a person who abandons the religious, political, or philosophical beliefs that he or she used to have, and accepts opposing or different beliefs. [2] **Renegade** is used to describe a member of a group or profession who behaves in a way that is opposed to the normal behaviour or beliefs of that group or profession. ❑ *Three men were shot dead by a renegade policeman.*
N-COUNT; ADJ: ADJ n

**re|nege** /rɪniːg, AM -nɪg/ **(reneges, reneging, reneged)** If someone **reneges on** a promise or an agreement, they do not do what they have promised or agreed to do. ❑ *If someone reneged on a deal, they could never trade here again.*
VERB; V *on* n; Also V

**re|new** /rɪnjuː, AM -nuː/ **(renews, renewing, renewed)** ◆◇◇ [1] If you **renew** an activity, you begin it again. ❑ *He renewed his attack on government policy towards Europe... There was renewed fighting yesterday.* [2] If you **renew** a relationship **with** someone, you start it again after you have not seen them or have not been friendly with them for some time. ❑ *When the two men met again after the war they renewed their friendship... In December 1989 Syria renewed diplomatic relations with Egypt.* [3] When you **renew** something such as a licence or a contract, you extend the period of time for which it is valid. ❑ *Larry's landlord threatened not to renew his lease.* [4] You can say that something **is renewed** when it grows again or is replaced after it has been destroyed or lost. ❑ *Cells are being constantly renewed. ...a renewed interest in public transport systems.*
VERB; V n; V-ed; V-RECIP = resume; pl-n V n; V n *with* n; VERB; V n; VERB: usu passive; *be* V-ed; V-ed

**re|new|able** /rɪnjuːəbᵊl, AM -nuː-/ [1] **Renewable** resources are natural ones such as wind, water, and sunlight, which are always available. ❑ *...renewable energy sources.* [2] If a contract or agreement is **renewable**, it can be extended when it reaches the end of a fixed period of time. ❑ *A formal contract is signed which is renewable annually.*
ADJ: usu ADJ n; ADJ

**re|new|al** /rɪnjuːəl, -nuː-/ **(renewals)** [1] If there is a **renewal of** an activity or a situation, it starts again. ❑ *They will discuss the possible renewal of diplomatic relations.* [2] The **renewal** of a document such as a licence or a contract is an official increase in the period of time for which it remains valid. ❑ *His contract came up for renewal.* [3] **Renewal** of something lost, dead, or destroyed is the process of it growing again or being replaced. ❑ *...urban renewal and regeneration.*
N-SING: usu N *of* n; N-VAR; N-UNCOUNT: oft supp N

**re|nounce** /rɪnaʊns/ **(renounces, renouncing, renounced)** [1] If you **renounce** a belief or a way of behaving, you decide and declare publicly that you no longer have that belief or will no longer behave in that way. ❑ *After a period of imprisonment she renounced terrorism.* [2] If you **renounce** a claim, rank, or title, you officially give it up. ❑ *He renounced his claim to the French throne.*
VERB; V n; VERB = give up; V n

**reno|vate** /renəveɪt/ **(renovates, renovating, renovated)** If someone **renovates** an old building, they repair and improve it and get it back into good condition. ❑ *The couple spent thousands renovating the house.* ♦ **reno|va|tion** /renəveɪʃᵊn/ **(renovations)** *...a property which will need extensive renovation.*
VERB; V n; N-VAR

**re|nown** /rɪnaʊn/ A person **of renown** is well known, usually because they do or have done something good. ❑ *She used to be a singer of some renown.*
N-UNCOUNT: oft n *of* N

**re|nowned** /rɪnaʊnd/ A person or place that is **renowned for** something, usually something good, is well known because of it. ❑ *The area is renowned for its Romanesque churches.*
ADJ: oft ADJ *for/as* n

**rent** /rent/ **(rents, renting, rented)** ◆◇◇ [1] If you **rent** something, you regularly pay its owner a sum of money in order to be able to have it and use it yourself. ❑ *She rents a house with three other girls... He left his hotel in a rented car.* [2] If you **rent** something **to** someone, you let them have it and use it in exchange for a sum of money which they pay you regularly. ❑ *She rented rooms to university students.* ♦ **Rent out** means the same as **rent**. ❑ *He rented out his house while he worked abroad... He repaired the boat, and rented it out for $150.* [3] **Rent** is the amount of money that you pay regularly to use a house, flat, or piece of land. ❑ *She worked to pay the rent while I went to college.* [4] **Rent** is the past tense and past participle of **rend**. [5] → See also **ground rent**, **peppercorn rent**.
VERB; V n; V-ed; VERB; V n *to* n; PHRASAL VERB; V P n (not pron); V n P; N-VAR

♦ **rent out** → see **rent 2**.

**rent|al** /rentᵊl/ **(rentals)** [1] The **rental** of something such as a car or piece of equipment is the activity or process of renting it. ❑ *We can organise car rental from Chicago O'Hare Airport.* [2] The **rental** is the amount of money that you pay when you rent something such as a car, property, or piece of equipment. ❑ *It has been let at an annual rental of £393,000.* [3] You use **rental** to describe things that are connected with the renting out of goods, properties, and services. ❑ *A friend drove her to Oxford, where she picked up a rental car.*
N-UNCOUNT: also N in pl, with supp; N-COUNT; ADJ: ADJ n

**rent boy** **(rent boys)** A **rent boy** is a boy or young man who has sex with men for money. [BRIT, INFORMAL]
N-COUNT

**rent-free** If you have a **rent-free** house or office, you do not have to pay anything to use it. ❑ *He was given a new rent-free apartment.* ♦ **Rent-free** is also an adverb. ❑ *They told James he could no longer live rent-free.*
ADJ: usu ADJ n; ADV: ADV after v

**re|nun|cia|tion** /rɪnʌnsieɪʃᵊn/ **(renunciations)** [1] The **renunciation** of a belief or a way of behaving is the public declaration that you reject it and have decided to stop having that belief or behaving in that way. ❑ *The talks were dependent on a renunciation of terrorism.* [2] The **renunciation of** a claim, title, or privilege is the act of offi-
N-UNCOUNT: also N in pl; N-UNCOUNT

cially giving it up. ❑ *...the renunciation of territory in the Mediterranean.* [3] **Renunciation** is the act of not allowing yourself certain pleasures for moral or religious reasons. N-UNCOUNT = *self-denial* ❑ *Gandhi exemplified the virtues of renunciation, asceticism and restraint.*

**re|open** /riːoʊpən/ **(reopens, reopening, reopened)** [1] If you **reopen** a public building such as a factory, airport, or school, or if it **reopens**, it opens and starts working again after it has been closed for some time. VERB ❑ *Iran reopened its embassy in London...* V n *The Theatre Royal, Norwich, will reopen in November.* V [2] If police or the courts **reopen** a legal case, they investigate it again because it has never been solved or because there was something wrong in the way it was investigated before. VERB ❑ *There was a call today to reopen the investigation into the bombing.* V n [3] If people or countries **reopen** talks or negotiations or if talks or negotiations **reopen**, they begin again after they have stopped for some time. VERB = *resume* ❑ *But now high level delegations will reopen talks that broke up earlier this year.* V n *...the possibility of reopening negotiations with the government...* V n *with* n *Middle East peace talks reopen in Washington on Wednesday.* V [4] If people or countries **reopen** ties or relations, they start being friendly again after a time when they were not friendly. V-RECIP ❑ *He reopened ties with Moscow earlier this year...* V n *with* n *Britain and Argentina reopened diplomatic relations.* pl-n V n [5] If something **reopens** a question or debate, it makes the question or debate relevant again and causes people to start discussing it again. VERB ❑ *His results are likely to reopen the debate on race and education.* V n [6] If a country **reopens** a border or route, or if it **reopens**, it becomes possible to cross or travel along it again after it has been closed. VERB ❑ *Jordan reopened its border with Iraq...* V n *The important Peking Shanghai route has reopened.* V

**re|or|gan|ize** /riɔːʳgənaɪz/ **(reorganizes, reorganizing, reorganized)**

✔ in BRIT, also use **reorganise**

To **reorganize** something or to **reorganize** means to change the way in which something is organized, arranged, or done. VERB ❑ *It is the mother who is expected to reorganize her busy schedule...* V n *Four thousand troops have been reorganized into a fighting force...* V n *into* n *They'll have to reorganise and that might cause them problems.* V ♦ **re|or|gani|za|tion** /riɔːʳgənaɪzeɪʃən/ **(reorganizations)** N-VAR *...the reorganization of the legal system.*

**rep** /rep/ **(reps)** [1] A **rep** is a person whose job is to sell a company's products or services, especially by travelling round and visiting other companies. N-COUNT: oft supp N **Rep** is short for **representative**. ❑ *I'd been working as a sales rep for a photographic company.* → See also **holiday rep**. [2] A **rep** is a person who acts as a representative for a group of people, usually a group of people who work together. N-COUNT: usu supp N ❑ *Contact the health and safety rep at your union.* [3] In the theatre, **rep** is the same as **repertory**. N-UNCOUNT ❑ *A play is tested in rep before ever hitting a West End stage.*

**Rep.** **Rep.** is a written abbreviation for **Representative**. [AM] ❑ *...Rep. Barbara Boxer.*

**re|paid** /rɪpeɪd/ **Repaid** is the past tense and past participle of **repay**.

**re|pair** /rɪpeəʳ/ **(repairs, repairing, repaired)** ◆◇◇ [1] If you **repair** something that has been damaged or is not working properly, you mend it. VERB ❑ *Goldsmith has repaired the roof to ensure the house is wind-proof...* V n *A woman drove her car to the garage to have it repaired.* have n V-ed ♦ **re|pair|er (repairers)** N-COUNT: usu n N *...TV repairers.* [2] If you **repair** a relationship or someone's reputation after it has been damaged, you do something to improve it. VERB ❑ *The government continued to try to repair the damage caused by the minister's interview.* V n [3] A **repair** is something that you do to mend a machine, building, piece of clothing, or other thing that has been damaged or is not working properly. N-VAR ❑ *Many women know how to carry out repairs on their cars... There is no doubt now that her marriage is beyond repair.* [4] If someone **repairs to** a particular place, they go there. VERB [FORMAL] ❑ *We then repaired to the pavilion for lunch.* V *to* n [5] If something such as a building is **in good repair**, it is in good condition. If it is **in bad repair**, it is in bad condition. PHRASE ❑ *The monks of Ettal keep the abbey in good repair.*

**re|pair|man** /rɪpeəʳmæn/ **(repairmen)** A **repairman** is a man who mends broken machines such as televisions and telephones. N-COUNT: usu supp N ❑ *...a cheerful telephone repairman.*

**repa|ra|tion** /repəreɪʃən/ **(reparations)** [1] **Reparations** are sums of money that are paid after a war by the defeated country for the damage and injuries it caused in other countries. N-UNCOUNT: also N in pl ❑ *Israel accepted billions of dollars in war reparations.* [2] **Reparation** is help or payment that someone gives you for damage, loss, or suffering that they have caused you. N-UNCOUNT ❑ *There is a clear demand amongst victims for some sort of reparation from offenders.*

**rep|ar|tee** /repɑːʳtiː, AM -pərteɪ/ **Repartee** is conversation that consists of quick, witty comments and replies. N-UNCOUNT ❑ *She was good at repartee.*

**re|past** /rɪpɑːst, -pæst/ **(repasts)** A **repast** is a meal. N-COUNT [LITERARY]

**re|pat|ri|ate** /riːpætrieɪt, AM -peɪt-/ **(repatriates, repatriating, repatriated)** If a country **repatriates** someone, it sends them back to their home country. VERB ❑ *It was not the policy of the government to repatriate genuine refugees.* V n ♦ **re|pat|ria|tion** /riːpætrieɪʃən, AM -peɪt-/ **(repatriations)** N-VAR *...the forced repatriation of Vietnamese boat people.*

**re|pay** /rɪpeɪ/ **(repays, repaying, repaid)** [1] If you **repay** a loan or a debt, you pay back the money that you owe to the person who you borrowed or took it from. VERB ❑ *He advanced funds of his own to his company, which was unable to repay him.* V n [2] If you **repay** a favour that someone did for you, you do something for them in return. VERB ❑ *It was very kind. I don't know how I can ever repay you.* V n

**re|pay|able** /rɪpeɪəbəl/ A loan that is **repayable** within a certain period of time must be paid back within that time. ADJ: usu v-link ADJ [mainly BRIT] ❑ *The loan is repayable over twenty years.*

✔ in AM, usually use **payable**

**re|pay|ment** /rɪpeɪmənt/ **(repayments)** [1] **Repayments** are amounts of money which you pay at regular intervals to a person or organization in order to repay a debt. N-COUNT ❑ *They were unable to meet their mortgage repayments.* [2] The **repayment of** money is the act or process of paying it back to the person you owe it to. N-UNCOUNT ❑ *He failed to meet last Friday's deadline for repayment of a £114m loan.*

**re|peal** /rɪpiːl/ **(repeals, repealing, repealed)** If the government **repeals** a law, it officially ends it, so that it is no longer valid. VERB ❑ *The government has just repealed the law segregating public facilities.* V n ♦ **Repeal** is also a noun. N-UNCOUNT: N *of* n ❑ *Next year will be the 60th anniversary of the repeal of Prohibition.*

**re|peat** /rɪpiːt/ **(repeats, repeating, repeated)** ◆◆◇ [1] If you **repeat** something, you say or write it again. VERB You can say **I repeat** to show that you feel strongly about what you are repeating. ❑ *He repeated that he had been mis-quoted...* V that *The Libyan leader Colonel Gadaffi repeated his call for the release of hostages...* V n *'You fool,' she kept repeating.* V with quote [2] If you **repeat** something that someone else has said or written, you say or write the same thing, or tell it to another person. VERB ❑ *She had an irritating habit of repeating everything I said to her...* V n *I trust you not to repeat that to anyone else...* V n *to* n *Now, brother, repeat after me, 'All praise to Allah, Lord of All the Worlds'.* V *after* n with quote [3] If you **repeat yourself**, you say something which you have said before, usually by mistake. VERB ❑ *Then he started rambling and repeating himself.* V pron-refl [4] If you **repeat** an action, you do it again. VERB ❑ *The next day I repeated the procedure...* V n *Hold this position for 30 seconds, release and repeat on the other side.* V [5] If an event or series of events **repeats itself**, it hap- VERB pens again. ❑ *The UN will have to work hard to stop history repeating itself.* V pron-refl 6 If there is a **repeat of** an event, usually an undesirable event, it happens again. N-COUNT: usu sing, oft N *of* n = repetition ❑ *There were fears that there might be a repeat of last year's campaign of strikes.* 7 If a company gets **repeat** business or **repeat** customers, people who have bought their goods or services before buy them again. ADJ: ADJ n [BUSINESS] ❑ *Nearly 60% of our bookings come from repeat business and personal recommendation.* 8 A **repeat** is a television or radio programme that has been broadcast before. N-COUNT [BRIT] ❑ *There's nothing except sport and repeats on TV.*

✔ in AM, use **re-run**

9 If there is **a repeat performance** of something, usually something undesirable, it happens again. PHRASE = repeat ❑ *This year can only see a repeat performance of the decline.*

**re|peat|ed** /rɪpiːtɪd/ **Repeated** actions or events are ones which happen many times. ADJ: ADJ n = frequent ❑ *Mr Lawssi apparently did not return the money, despite repeated reminders.*

**re|peat|ed|ly** /rɪpiːtɪdli/ If you do something **repeatedly**, you do it many times. ADV: ADV with v ❑ *Both men have repeatedly denied the allegations.*

**re|peat of|fend|er** **(repeat offenders)** A **repeat offender** is someone who commits the same sort of crime more than once. N-COUNT

**re|peat pre|scrip|tion** **(repeat prescriptions)** A **repeat prescription** is a prescription for a medicine that you have taken before or that you use regularly. N-COUNT [BRIT]

**re|pel** /rɪpel/ **(repels, repelling, repelled)** 1 When an army **repels** an attack, they successfully fight and drive back soldiers from another army who have attacked them. VERB [FORMAL] ❑ *They have fifty thousand troops along the border ready to repel any attack.* V n 2 When a magnetic pole **repels** another magnetic pole, it gives out a force that pushes the other pole away. V-RECIP You can also say that two magnetic poles **repel** each other or that they **repel**. [TECHNICAL] ❑ *Like poles repel, unlike poles attract... As these electrons are negatively charged they will attempt to repel each other.* pl-n V; V n 3 If something **repels** you, you find it horrible and disgusting. VERB: no cont = revolt ❑ *...a violent excitement that frightened and repelled her.* V n ♦ **re|pelled** *She was very striking but in some way I felt repelled.* ADJ

**re|pel|lant** /rɪpelənt/ ➔ see **repellent**.

**re|pel|lent** /rɪpelənt/ **(repellents)**

✔ The spelling **repellant** is also used for meaning 2.

1 If you think that something is horrible and disgusting you can say that it is **repellent**. ADJ [FORMAL] ❑ *...a very large, very repellent toad.* 2 Insect **repellent** is a product containing chemicals that you spray into the air or on your body in order to keep insects away. N-MASS: usu n N ❑ *...mosquito repellent.*

**re|pent** /rɪpent/ **(repents, repenting, repented)** If you **repent**, you show or say that you are sorry for something wrong you have done. VERB ❑ *Those who refuse to repent, he said, will be punished... Did he repent of anything in his life?* V; V *of/for* n

**re|pent|ance** /rɪpentəns/ If you show **repentance** for something wrong that you have done, you make it clear that you are sorry for doing it. N-UNCOUNT = remorse ❑ *They showed no repentance during their trial.*

**re|pent|ant** /rɪpentənt/ Someone who is **repentant** shows or says that they are sorry for something wrong they have done. ADJ ≠ unrepentant ❑ *He was feeling guilty and depressed, repentant and scared.*

**re|per|cus|sion** /riːpəʳkʌʃᵊn/ **(repercussions)** If an action or event has **repercussions**, it causes unpleasant things to happen some time after the original action or event. N-COUNT: usu pl = consequence [FORMAL] ❑ *It was an effort which was to have painful repercussions.*

**rep|er|toire** /repəʳtwɑːʳ/ **(repertoires)** 1 A performer's **repertoire** is all the plays or pieces of music that he or she has learned and can perform. N-COUNT: usu sing, with supp ❑ *Meredith D'Ambrosio has thousands of songs in her repertoire.* 2 The **repertoire** of a person or thing is all the things of a particular kind that the person or thing is capable of doing. N-SING: with supp ❑ *...Mike's impressive repertoire of funny stories.*

**rep|er|tory** /repəʳtri, AM -tɔːri/ 1 A **repertory** company is a group of actors and actresses who perform a small number of plays for just a few weeks at a time. N-UNCOUNT: usu N n They work in a **repertory** theatre. ❑ *...a well-known repertory company in Boston.* 2 A performer's **repertory** is all the plays or pieces of music that he or she has learned and can perform. N-SING: usu poss N = repertoire ❑ *Her repertory was vast and to her it seemed that each song told some part of her life.*

**rep|eti|tion** /repɪtɪʃᵊn/ **(repetitions)** 1 If there is a **repetition of** an event, usually an undesirable event, it happens again. N-VAR: usu N *of* n ❑ *Today the city government has taken measures to prevent a repetition of last year's confrontation.* 2 **Repetition** means using the same words again. N-VAR ❑ *He could also have cut out much of the repetition and thus saved many pages.*

**rep|eti|tious** /repɪtɪʃəs/ Something that is **repetitious** involves actions or elements that are repeated many times and is therefore boring. ADJ [disapproval] = repetitive ❑ *The manifesto is long-winded, repetitious and often ambiguous or poorly drafted.*

**re|peti|tive** /rɪpetɪtɪv/ 1 Something that is **repetitive** involves actions or elements that are repeated many times and is therefore boring. ADJ [disapproval] ❑ *...factory workers who do repetitive jobs.* 2 **Repetitive** movements or sounds are repeated many times. ADJ: usu ADJ n ❑ *...problems that occur as the result of repetitive movements.*

**re|peti|tive strain in|ju|ry** **Repetitive strain injury** is the same as **RSI**. N-UNCOUNT ❑ *...computer users suffering from repetitive strain injury.*

**re|phrase** /riːfreɪz/ **(rephrases, rephrasing, rephrased)** If you **rephrase** a question or statement, you ask it or say it again in a different way. VERB ❑ *Again, the executive rephrased the question.* V n

**re|place** /rɪpleɪs/ **(replaces, replacing, replaced)** ◆◆◇ 1 If one thing or person **replaces** another, the first is used or acts instead of the second. VERB ❑ *The council tax replaces the poll tax next April. ...the city lawyer who replaced Bob as chairman of the company... The smile disappeared to be replaced by a doleful frown.* V n; V n *as* n; *be* V-ed *with/by* n 2 If you **replace** one thing or person **with** another, you put something or someone else in their place to do their job. VERB ❑ *I clean out all the grease and replace it with oil so it works better in very low temperatures... The BBC decided it could not replace her.* V n *with/by* n; V n 3 If you **replace** something that is broken, damaged, or lost, you get a new one to use instead. VERB ❑ *The shower that we put in a few years back has broken and we cannot afford to replace it.* V n 4 If you **replace** something, you put it back where it was before. VERB ❑ *The line went dead. Whitlock replaced the receiver... Replace the caps on the bottles.* V n; V n prep

**re|place|able** /rɪpleɪsəbᵊl/ 1 If something is **replaceable**, you can throw it away when it is finished and put a new one in its place. ADJ = disposable ❑ *...replaceable butane gas cartridges.* 2 If you say that someone is **replaceable**, you mean that they are not so important that someone else could not take their place. ADJ: usu v-link ADJ ≠ irreplaceable ❑ *He would see I was not so easily replaceable.*

**re|place|ment** /rɪpleɪsmənt/ **(replacements)** ◆◇◇ 1 If you refer to the **replacement** of one thing by another, you mean that the second thing takes the place of the first. N-UNCOUNT: with supp ❑ *...the replacement of damaged or lost books.* ➔ See also **hormone replacement therapy**. 2 Someone who takes someone else's place in an organization, government, or team can be referred to as their **replacement**. N-COUNT ❑ *Taylor has nominated Adams as his replacement.*

**re|place|ment value** The **replacement value** of something that you own is the amount of money it would cost you to replace it, for example if it was stolen or damaged. N-SING

**re|play (replays, replaying, replayed)**

> The verb is pronounced /riːpleɪ/. The noun is pronounced /riːpleɪ/.

1 If a match between two sports teams **is replayed**, the two teams play it again, because neither team won the first time, or because the match was stopped because of bad weather. [mainly BRIT] ❑ *Drawn matches were replayed three or four days later.* [VERB: usu passive; be V-ed] ♦ You can refer to a match that is replayed as a **replay**. ❑ *If there has to be a replay we are confident of victory.* [N-COUNT] 2 If you **replay** something that you have recorded on film or tape, you play it again in order to watch it or listen to it. ❑ *He stopped the machine and replayed the message.* [VERB; V n] ♦ **Replay** is also a noun. ❑ *I watched a slow-motion videotape replay of his fall.* [N-COUNT] 3 If you **replay** an event in your mind, you think about it again and again. ❑ *She spends her nights lying in bed, replaying the fire in her mind.* [VERB; V n] 4 → See also **action replay**, **instant replay**.

**re|plen|ish** /rɪplenɪʃ/ **(replenishes, replenishing, replenished)** If you **replenish** something, you make it full or complete again. [FORMAL] ❑ *Three hundred thousand tons of cereals are needed to replenish stocks.* [VERB; V n]

**re|plen|ish|ment** /rɪplenɪʃmənt/ **Replenishment** is the process by which something is made full or complete again. [FORMAL] ❑ *There is a concern about replenishment of the population.* [N-UNCOUNT: usu with supp]

**re|plete** /rɪpliːt/ 1 To be **replete with** something means to be full of it. [FORMAL] ❑ *The Harbor was replete with boats.* [ADJ: v-link ADJ with n] 2 If you are **replete**, you are pleasantly full of food and drink. [FORMAL] ❑ *Replete, guests can then retire to the modern conservatory for coffee.* [ADJ: usu v-link ADJ]

**rep|li|ca** /replɪkə/ **(replicas)** A **replica of** something such as a statue, building, or weapon is an accurate copy of it. ❑ *...a human-sized replica of the Statue of Liberty.* [N-COUNT: usu N of n]

**rep|li|cate** /replɪkeɪt/ **(replicates, replicating, replicated)** If you **replicate** someone's experiment, work, or research, you do it yourself in exactly the same way. [FORMAL] ❑ *He invited her to his laboratory to see if she could replicate the experiment.* [VERB = duplicate; V n]

**re|ply** /rɪplaɪ/ **(replies, replying, replied)** ◆◆◇ 1 When you **reply to** something that someone has said or written to you, you say or write an answer to them. ❑ *'That's a nice dress,' said Michael. 'Thanks,' she replied solemnly... He replied that this was absolutely impossible... Grace was too terrified to reply... To their surprise, hundreds replied to the advertisement.* [VERB = answer; V with quote; V that; V; V to n] 2 A **reply** is something that you say or write when you answer someone or answer a letter or advertisement. ❑ *I called out a challenge, but there was no reply... David has had 12 replies to his ad... He said in reply that the question was unfair.* [N-COUNT: oft N to/from n, also in N = response] 3 If you **reply to** something such as an attack **with** violence or **with** another action, you do something in response. ❑ *Farmers threw eggs and empty bottles at police, who replied with tear gas... The National Salvation Front has already replied to this series of opposition moves with its own demonstrations.* [VERB; V with n; V to n with n]

**re|port** /rɪpɔːʳt/ **(reports, reporting, reported)** ◆◆◆ 1 If you **report** something that has happened, you tell people about it. ❑ *They had been called in to clear drains after local people reported a foul smell... I reported the theft to the police... The officials also reported that two more ships were apparently heading for Malta... 'He seems to be all right now,' reported a relieved Taylor... The foreign secretary is reported as saying that force will have to be used if diplomacy fails... She reported him missing the next day... Between forty and fifty people are reported to have died in the fighting.* [VERB; V n; V n to n; V that; V with quote; be V-ed as -ing/-ed; V n adj; be V-ed to-inf] 2 If you **report on** an event or subject, you tell people about it, because it is your job or duty to do so. ❑ *Many journalists enter the country to report on political affairs... I'll now call at the vicarage and report to you in due course.* [VERB; V on n; V to n] 3 A **report** is a news article or broadcast which gives information about something that has just happened. ❑ *...a report in London's Independent newspaper.* [N-COUNT: usu with supp] 4 A **report** is an official document which a group of people issue after investigating a situation or event. ❑ *After an inspection, the inspectors must publish a report.* [N-COUNT: oft N on n, N by n] 5 If you give someone a **report** on something, you tell them what has been happening. ❑ *She came back to give us a progress report on how the project is going.* [N-COUNT] 6 If you say that there are **reports** that something has happened, you mean that some people say it has happened but you have no direct evidence of it. ❑ *There are unconfirmed reports that two people have been shot in the neighbouring town of Lalitpur.* [N-COUNT: usu pl, N of n, N that] 7 If someone **reports** you **to** a person in authority, they tell that person about something wrong that you have done. ❑ *His ex-wife reported him to police a few days later... The Princess was reported for speeding twice on the same road within a week.* [VERB; V n to n; be V-ed for -ing/n] 8 If you **report to** a person or place, you go to that person or place and say that you are ready to start work or say that you are present. ❑ *Mr Ashwell has to surrender his passport and report to the police every five days... None of the men had reported for duty.* [VERB; V to n; V for n] 9 If you say that one employee **reports to** another, you mean that the first employee is told what to do by the second one and is responsible to them. [FORMAL] ❑ *He reported to a section chief, who reported to a division chief, and so on up the line.* [VERB: no cont; V to n] 10 A school **report** is an official written account of how well or how badly a pupil has done during the term or year that has just finished. [BRIT] ❑ *And now she was getting bad school reports.* [N-COUNT]

> in AM, use **report card**

11 A **report** is a sudden loud noise, for example the sound of a gun being fired or an explosion. [FORMAL] ❑ *Soon afterwards there was a loud report as the fuel tanks exploded.* [N-COUNT] 12 → See also **reporting**.

♦ **report back** 1 If you **report back to** someone, you tell them about something that they asked you to find out about. ❑ *The teams are due to report back to the Prime Minister... I'll report back the moment I have located him... He would, of course, report back on all deliberations... The repairman reported back that the computer had a virus.* [PHRASAL VERB; V P to n; V P; V P on n; V P that, Also V n P, V P n] 2 If you **report back to** a place, you go back there and say that you are ready to start work or say that you are present. ❑ *The authorities have ordered all soldiers who have returned from the front line to report back to barracks... They were sent home and told to report back in the afternoon.* [PHRASAL VERB; V P to n; V P, Also V P for n]

**re|port|age** /rɪpɔːʳtɪdʒ, repɔːʳtɑːʒ/ **Reportage** is the reporting of news and other events of general interest for newspapers, television, and radio. [FORMAL] ❑ *...the magazine's acclaimed mix of reportage and fashion.* [N-UNCOUNT]

**re|port card (report cards)** 1 A **report card** is an official written account of how well or how badly a pupil has done during the term or year that has just finished. [AM] ❑ *The only time I got their attention was when I brought home straight A's on my report card.* [N-COUNT]

> in BRIT, use **report**

2 A **report card** is a report on how well a person, organization, or country has been doing recently. [AM, JOURNALISM] ❑ *The President today issued his final report card on the state of the economy.* [N-COUNT]

**re|port|ed clause (reported clauses)** A **reported clause** is a subordinate clause that indicates what someone said or thought. For example, in 'She said that she was hungry', 'she was hungry' is a reported clause. [BRIT] [N-COUNT]

**re|port|ed|ly** /rɪpɔːʳtɪdli/ If you say that something is **reportedly** true, you mean that someone has said that it is true, but you have no direct evidence of it. [FORMAL] ❑ *More than two hundred people have reportedly been killed in the past week's fighting.* [ADV: ADV with cl/group, ADV before v] [vagueness]

**re|port|ed ques|tion (reported questions)** A **reported question** is a question which is reported using a clause beginning with a word such as [N-COUNT = indirect question] 'why' or 'whether', as in 'I asked her why she'd done it'. [BRIT]

**re|port|ed speech** **Reported speech** is speech which tells you what someone said, but does not use the person's actual words: for example, 'They said you didn't like it', 'I asked him what his plans were', and 'Citizens complained about the smoke'. [BRIT] N-UNCOUNT *= indirect speech*

✔ in AM, use **indirect discourse**

**re|port|er** /rɪpɔːʳtəʳ/ **(reporters)** A **reporter** is someone who writes news articles or who broadcasts news reports. ❑ *...a TV reporter. ...a trainee sports reporter.* ◆◆◇ N-COUNT

**re|port|ing** /rɪpɔːʳtɪŋ/ **Reporting** is the presenting of news in newspapers, on radio, and on television. ❑ *...honest and impartial political reporting.* ◆◆◇ N-UNCOUNT

**re|port|ing clause** **(reporting clauses)** A **reporting clause** is a clause which indicates that you are talking about what someone said or thought. For example, in 'She said that she was hungry', 'She said' is a reporting clause. [BRIT] N-COUNT

**re|port struc|ture** **(report structures)** A **report structure** is a structure containing a reporting clause and a reported clause or a quote. [BRIT] N-COUNT

**re|pose** /rɪpoʊz/ **Repose** is a state in which you are resting and feeling calm. [LITERARY] ❑ *He had a still, almost blank face in repose.* N-UNCOUNT

**re|po|si|tion** /riːpəzɪʃən/ **(repositions, repositioning, repositioned)** [1] To **reposition** an object means to move it to another place or to change its position. ❑ *It is not possible to reposition the carpet without damaging it.* VERB; V n [2] To **reposition** something such as a product or service means to try to interest more or different people in it, for example by changing certain things about it or the way it is marketed. ❑ *The sell-off is aimed at repositioning the company as a publisher principally of business information... Mazda needs to reposition itself if it is to boost its sales and reputation.* VERB; V n; V pron-refl

**re|posi|tory** /rɪpɒzɪtri, AM -tɔːri/ **(repositories)** A **repository** is a place where something is kept safely. [FORMAL] ❑ *A church in Moscow became a repository for police files.* N-COUNT: usu N *for* n *= store*

**re|pos|sess** /riːpəzes/ **(repossesses, repossessing, repossessed)** If your car or house **is repossessed**, the people who supplied it take it back because they are still owed money for it. ❑ *His car was repossessed by the company.* VERB: usu passive; *be* V-ed

**re|pos|ses|sion** /riːpəzeʃən/ **(repossessions)** [1] The **repossession** of someone's house is the act of repossessing it. ❑ *...the problem of home repossessions.* N-VAR [2] You can refer to a house or car that has been repossessed as a **repossession**. ❑ *Many of the cars you will see at auction are repossessions.* N-COUNT

**re|pos|ses|sion or|der** **(repossession orders)** If a bank or building society issues a **repossession order**, they officially tell someone that they are going to repossess their home. [BRIT] N-COUNT

**re|pot** /riːpɒt/ **(repots, repotting, repotted)** If you **repot** a plant, you take it out of its pot and put it in a larger one. ❑ *As your plants flourish, you'll need to repot them in bigger pots.* VERB; V n

**rep|re|hen|sible** /reprɪhensɪbəl/ If you think that a type of behaviour or an idea is very bad and morally wrong, you can say that it is **reprehensible**. [FORMAL] ❑ *Mr Cramer said the violence by anti-government protestors was reprehensible.* ADJ: usu v-link ADJ

**rep|re|sent** /reprɪzent/ **(represents, representing, represented)** [1] If someone such as a lawyer or a politician **represents** a person or group of people, they act on behalf of that person or group. ❑ *...the politicians we elect to represent us.* ◆◆◇ VERB; V n [2] If you **represent** a person or group at an official event, you go there on their behalf. ❑ *The general secretary may represent the president at official ceremonies.* VERB; V n [3] If you **represent** your country or town in a competition or sports event, you take part in it on behalf of the country or town where you live. ❑ *My only aim is to represent Britain at the Olympics.* VERB; V n [4] If a group of people or things **is** well **represented** in a particular activity or in a particular place, a lot of them can be found there. ❑ *Women are already well represented in the area of TV drama... In New Mexico all kinds of cuisines are represented.* V-PASSIVE; *be* adv V-ed; *be* V-ed [5] If you say that something **represents** a change, achievement, or victory, you mean that it is a change, achievement, or victory. [FORMAL or WRITTEN] ❑ *These developments represented a major change in the established order.* V-LINK; V n [6] If a sign or symbol **represents** something, it is accepted as meaning that thing. ❑ *...a black dot in the middle of the circle is supposed to represent the source of the radiation.* VERB: no cont *= symbolize*; V n [7] To **represent** an idea or quality means to be a symbol or an expression of that idea or quality. ❑ *We believe you represent everything British racing needs.* VERB: no cont, no passive *= embody*; V n [8] If you **represent** a person or thing **as** a particular thing, you describe them as being that thing. ❑ *The popular press tends to represent him as an environmental guru.* VERB *= portray*; V n *as* n

**rep|re|sen|ta|tion** /reprɪzenteɪʃən/ **(representations)** [1] If a group or person has **representation** in a parliament or on a committee, someone in the parliament or on the committee supports them and makes decisions on their behalf. ❑ *Puerto Ricans are U.S. citizens but they have no representation in Congress.* → See also **proportional representation**. N-UNCOUNT: oft N prep [2] You can describe a picture, model, or statue of a person or thing as a **representation of** them. [FORMAL] ❑ *...a lifelike representation of Christ.* N-COUNT: usu N *of* n [3] If you make **representations to** a government or other official group, you make formal complaints or requests to them. ❑ *We have made representations to ministers but they just don't seem to be listening.* N-PLURAL: oft N *to/from* n

**rep|re|sen|ta|tion|al** /reprɪzenteɪʃənəl/ In a **representational** painting, the artist attempts to show things as they really are. [FORMAL] ❑ *His painting went through both representational and abstract periods.* ADJ

**rep|re|senta|tive** /reprɪzentətɪv/ **(representatives)** [1] A **representative** is a person who has been chosen to act or make decisions on behalf of another person or a group of people. ❑ *...trade union representatives.* ◆◆◇ N-COUNT [2] A **representative** is a person whose job is to sell a company's products or services, especially by travelling round and visiting other companies. [FORMAL] ❑ *She had a stressful job as a sales representative.* N-COUNT: usu with supp [3] A **representative** group consists of a small number of people who have been chosen to make decisions on behalf of a larger group. ❑ *The new head of state should be chosen by an 87 member representative council.* ADJ: ADJ n [4] Someone who is typical of the group to which they belong can be described as **representative**. ❑ *He was in no way representative of dog-trainers in general.* ADJ: oft ADJ *of* n ♦ **rep|re|senta|tive|ness** *...a process designed to ensure the representativeness of the sample interviewed.* N-UNCOUNT [5] In the United States, a **Representative** is a member of the House of Representatives, the less powerful of the two parts of Congress. N-COUNT [6] → See also **House of Representatives**.

**re|press** /rɪpres/ **(represses, repressing, repressed)** [1] If you **repress** a feeling, you make a deliberate effort not to show or have this feeling. ❑ *It is anger that is repressed that leads to violence and loss of control. ...repressed aggression.* VERB *= suppress*; V n; V-ed [2] If you **repress** a smile, sigh, or moan, you try hard not to smile, sigh, or moan. ❑ *I couldn't repress a sigh of admiration.* VERB; V n [3] If a section of society **is repressed**, their freedom is restricted by the people who have authority over them. ❑ *...a UN resolution banning him from repressing his people.* VERB [disapproval]; V n

**re|pressed** /rɪprest/ A **repressed** person is someone who does not allow themselves to have natural feelings and desires, especially sexual ones. ❑ *Some have charged that the Puritans were sexually repressed and inhibited.* ADJ

**re|pres|sion** /rɪpreʃᵊn/ **(repressions)** 1 **Repression** is the use of force to restrict and control a society or other group of people. ❑ *...a society conditioned by violence and repression.* N-UNCOUNT: also N in pl disapproval = oppression
2 **Repression** of feelings, especially sexual ones, is a person's unwillingness to allow themselves to have natural feelings and desires. ❑ *...the repression of his feelings about men.* N-UNCOUNT

**re|pres|sive** /rɪpresɪv/ A **repressive** government is one that restricts people's freedom and controls them by using force. ❑ *The military regime in power was unpopular and repressive.* ADJ disapproval
♦ **re|pres|sive|ly** *...the country, which had been repressively ruled for ten years.* ADV: ADV with v

**re|prieve** /rɪpriːv/ **(reprieves, reprieving, reprieved)** 1 If someone who has been sentenced in a court **is reprieved**, their punishment is officially delayed or cancelled. ❑ *Fourteen people, waiting to be hanged for the murder of a former prime minister, have been reprieved.* VERB: usu passive, no cont be V-ed ♦ **Reprieve** is also a noun ❑ *A man awaiting death by lethal injection has been saved by a last minute reprieve.* N-VAR 2 A **reprieve** is a delay before a very unpleasant or difficult situation which may or may not take place. ❑ *It looked as though the college would have to shut, but this week it was given a reprieve.* N-COUNT: usu sing

**rep|ri|mand** /reprɪmɑːnd, -mænd/ **(reprimands, reprimanding, reprimanded)** If someone **is reprimanded**, they are spoken to angrily or seriously for doing something wrong, usually by a person in authority. [FORMAL] ❑ *He was reprimanded by a teacher for talking in the corridor... Her attempts to reprimand him were quickly shouted down.* VERB be V-ed for -ing/n V n ♦ **Reprimand** is also a noun. ❑ *He has been fined five thousand pounds and given a severe reprimand.* N-VAR

**re|print** **(reprints, reprinting, reprinted)**

The verb is pronounced /riːprɪnt/. The noun is pronounced /riːprɪnt/.

1 If a book **is reprinted**, further copies of it are printed when all the other ones have been sold. ❑ *It remained an exceptionally rare book until it was reprinted in 1918.* VERB: usu passive be V-ed 2 A **reprint** is a process in which new copies of a book or article are printed because all the other ones have been sold. ❑ *Demand picked up and a reprint was required last November.* N-COUNT 3 A **reprint** is a new copy of a book or article, printed because all the other ones have been sold or because minor changes have been made to the original. ❑ *...a reprint of a 1962 novel.* N-COUNT

**re|pris|al** /rɪpraɪzᵊl/ **(reprisals)** If you do something to a person **in reprisal**, you hurt or punish them because they have done something violent or unpleasant to you. ❑ *Witnesses are unwilling to testify through fear of reprisals.* N-VAR = retaliation

**re|prise** /rɪpriːz/ **(reprises, reprising, reprised)** In music, if there is a **reprise**, an earlier section of music is repeated. N-COUNT

**re|proach** /rɪproʊtʃ/ **(reproaches, reproaching, reproached)** 1 If you **reproach** someone, you say or show that you are disappointed, upset, or angry because they have done something wrong. ❑ *She is quick to reproach anyone who doesn't live up to her own high standards... She had not even reproached him for breaking his promise.* VERB V n V n for -ing/n 2 If you look at or speak to someone with **reproach**, you show or say that you are disappointed, upset, or angry because they have done something wrong. ❑ *He looked at her with reproach... Women in public life must be beyond reproach.* N-VAR 3 If you **reproach yourself**, you think with regret about something you have done wrong. ❑ *You've no reason to reproach yourself, no reason to feel shame... We begin to reproach ourselves for not having been more careful.* VERB = blame V pron-refl V pron-refl for -ing/n

**re|proach|ful** /rɪproʊtʃfʊl/ **Reproachful** expressions or remarks show that you are disappointed, upset, or angry because someone has done something wrong. ❑ *She gave Isabelle a reproachful look.* ADJ ♦ **re|proach|ful|ly** *Luke's mother stopped smiling and looked reproachfully at him.* ADV: ADV after v

**rep|ro|bate** /reprəbeɪt/ **(reprobates)** If you describe someone as a **reprobate**, you mean that they behave in a way that is not respectable or morally correct. [OLD-FASHIONED] ❑ *...a drunken reprobate.* N-COUNT disapproval

**re|pro|duce** /riːprədjuːs, AM -duːs/ **(reproduces, reproducing, reproduced)** 1 If you try to **reproduce** something, you try to copy it. ❑ *I shall not try to reproduce the policemen's English... The effect has proved hard to reproduce.* VERB V n V n 2 If you **reproduce** a picture, speech, or a piece of writing, you make a photograph or printed copy of it. ❑ *We are grateful to you for permission to reproduce this article.* VERB V n 3 If you **reproduce** an action or an achievement, you repeat it. ❑ *If we can reproduce the form we have shown in the last couple of months we will be successful.* VERB = repeat V n 4 When people, animals, or plants **reproduce**, they produce young. ❑ *...a society where women are defined by their ability to reproduce... We are reproducing ourselves at such a rate that our numbers threaten the ecology of the planet.* VERB V V pron-refl ♦ **re|pro|duc|tion** /riːprədʌkʃᵊn/ *Genes are those tiny bits of biological information swapped in sexual reproduction.* N-UNCOUNT

**re|pro|duc|tion** /riːprədʌkʃᵊn/ **(reproductions)** 1 A **reproduction** is a copy of something such as a piece of furniture or a work of art. ❑ *...a reproduction of a popular religious painting.* → See also **reproduce**. N-COUNT: oft N n 2 Sound **reproduction** is the recording of sound onto tapes, CDs, or films so that it can be heard by a large number of people. ❑ *...the increasingly high technology of music reproduction.* N-UNCOUNT

**re|pro|duc|tive** /riːprədʌktɪv/ **Reproductive** processes and organs are concerned with the reproduction of living things. ❑ *...the female reproductive system.* ADJ: usu ADJ n

**re|proof** /rɪpruːf/ **(reproofs)** If you say or do something in **reproof**, you say or do it to show that you disapprove of what someone has done or said. [FORMAL] ❑ *She raised her eyebrows in reproof. ...a reproof that she responded to right away.* N-VAR

**re|prove** /rɪpruːv/ **(reproves, reproving, reproved)** If you **reprove** someone, you speak angrily or seriously to them because they have behaved in a wrong or foolish way. [FORMAL] ❑ *'There's no call for talk like that,' Mrs Evans reproved him... Women were reproved if they did not wear hats in court.* VERB = admonish V with quote V n

**re|prov|ing** /rɪpruːvɪŋ/ If you give someone a **reproving** look or speak in a **reproving** voice, you show or say that you think they have behaved in a wrong or foolish way. [FORMAL] ❑ *'Flatterer,' she said giving him a mock reproving look.* ADJ: usu ADJ n ♦ **reprov|ing|ly** *'I'm trying to sleep,' he lied, speaking reprovingly.* ADV: ADV after v

**rep|tile** /reptaɪl, AM -tɪl/ **(reptiles)** **Reptiles** are a group of cold-blooded animals which have skins covered with small hard plates called scales and lay eggs. Snakes, lizards, and crocodiles are reptiles. N-COUNT

**rep|til|ian** /reptɪliən/ 1 A **reptilian** creature is a reptile. ❑ *...a prehistoric jungle occupied by reptilian creatures.* ADJ: usu ADJ n 2 You can also use the word **reptilian** to describe something that is characteristic of a reptile or that is like a reptile. ❑ *The chick is ugly and almost reptilian in its appearance.* ADJ

**re|pub|lic** /rɪpʌblɪk/ **(republics)** A **republic** is a country where power is held by the people or the representatives that they elect. Republics have presidents who are elected, rather than kings or queens. ❑ *...the Baltic republics. ...the Republic of Ireland.* → See also **banana republic**. ◆◆◇ N-COUNT: oft in names

**re|pub|li|can** /rɪpʌblɪkən/ **(republicans)** ◆◆◇ 1 **Republican** means relating to a republic. In **republican** systems of government, power is held by the people or the representatives that they elect. ❑ *...the nations that had adopted the republican form of government.* ADJ 2 In the United States, if someone is **Republican**, they belong to or support the Republican Party. ❑ *...Republican voters...* ADJ

*Some families have been republican for generations.* ♦ A **Republican** is someone who supports or belongs to the Republican Party. ❑ *What made you decide to become a Republican?* [3] In Northern Ireland, if someone is **Republican**, they believe that Northern Ireland should not be ruled by Britain but should become part of the Republic of Ireland. ❑ *...a Republican paramilitary group.* ♦ A **Republican** is someone who has Republican views. ❑ *...a Northern Ireland republican.*
N-COUNT | ADJ | N-COUNT

**re|pub|li|can|ism** /rɪpʌblɪkənɪzəm/ [1] **Republicanism** is the belief that the best system of government is a republic. [2] **Republicanism** is support for or membership of the Republican Party in the United States.
N-UNCOUNT | N-UNCOUNT

**Re|pub|li|can Par|ty** The **Republican Party** is one of the two main political parties in the United States. It is more right-wing or conservative than the Democratic Party.
N-PROPER

**re|pu|di|ate** /rɪpjuːdieɪt/ **(repudiates, repudiating, repudiated)** If you **repudiate** something or someone, you show that you strongly disagree with them and do not want to be connected with them in any way. [FORMAL or WRITTEN] ❑ *Leaders urged people to turn out in large numbers to repudiate the violence.* ♦ **re|pu|dia|tion** /rɪpjuːdieɪʃᵊn/ **(repudiations)** *...his public repudiation of the conference decision.*
VERB = denounce | V n | N-VAR = denunciation

**re|pug|nant** /rɪpʌgnənt/ If you think that something is horrible and disgusting, you can say that it is **repugnant**. [FORMAL] ❑ *The odour of vitamin in skin is repugnant to insects.* ♦ **re|pug|nance** *She felt a deep sense of shame and repugnance.*
ADJ: oft ADJ *to* n | N-UNCOUNT = disgust

**re|pulse** /rɪpʌls/ **(repulses, repulsing, repulsed)** [1] If you **are repulsed** by something, you think that it is horrible and disgusting and you want to avoid it. ❑ *Evil has charisma. Though people are repulsed by it, they also are drawn to its power.* [2] If an army or other group **repulses** a group of people, they drive it back using force. ❑ *The armed forces were prepared to repulse any attacks.*
VERB: usu passive = repel ≠ attract | *be* V-ed | VERB | V n

**re|pul|sion** /rɪpʌlʃᵊn/ **Repulsion** is an extremely strong feeling of disgust. ❑ *She gave a dramatic shudder of repulsion.*
N-UNCOUNT = revulsion

**re|pul|sive** /rɪpʌlsɪv/ If you describe something or someone as **repulsive**, you mean that they are horrible and disgusting and you want to avoid them. ❑ *...repulsive fat white slugs.* ♦ **re|pul|sive|ly** *...a repulsively large rat.*
ADJ = revolting, disgusting | ADV: ADV adj

**repu|table** /repjʊtəbᵊl/ A **reputable** company or person is reliable and can be trusted. ❑ *You are well advised to buy your car through a reputable dealer.*
ADJ: usu ADJ n

**repu|ta|tion** /repjʊteɪʃᵊn/ **(reputations)** ◆◇◇ [1] To have a **reputation** for something means to be known or remembered for it. ❑ *Alice Munro has a reputation for being a very depressing writer.* [2] Something's or someone's **reputation** is the opinion that people have about how good they are. If they have a good reputation, people think they are good. ❑ *The stories ruined his reputation.* [3] If you know someone **by reputation**, you have never met them but you have heard of their reputation. ❑ *She was by reputation a good organiser.*
N-COUNT: usu with supp | N-COUNT: usu with supp | PHRASE

**re|pute** /rɪpjuːt/ [1] A person or thing **of repute** or **of** high **repute** is respected and known to be good. [FORMAL] ❑ *He was a writer of repute.* [2] A person's or organization's **repute** is their reputation, especially when this is good. [FORMAL] ❑ *Under his stewardship, the UN's repute has risen immeasurably.*
PHRASE: n PHR | N-UNCOUNT: usu with supp = reputation

**re|put|ed** /rɪpjuːtɪd/ If you say that something **is reputed to** be true, you mean that people say it is true, but you do not know if it is definitely true. [FORMAL] ❑ *The monster, which is reputed to live in the deep dark water of a Scottish loch.* ♦ **re|put|ed|ly** /rɪpjuːtɪdli/ *He reputedly earns two million pounds a year.*
V-PASSIVE [vagueness] | *be* V-ed to-inf | ADV: ADV with cl/group, ADV before v

**re|quest** /rɪkwest/ **(requests, requesting, requested)** ◆◆◇ [1] If you **request** something, you ask for it politely or formally. [FORMAL] ❑ *Mr Dennis said he had requested access to a telephone... She had requested that the door to her room be left open.* [2] If you **request** someone **to** do something, you politely or formally ask them to do it. [FORMAL] ❑ *Students are requested to park at the rear of the Department.* [3] If you make a **request**, you politely or formally ask someone to do something. ❑ *France had agreed to his request for political asylum.* [4] A **request** is a song or piece of music which someone has asked a performer or disc jockey to play. ❑ *If you have any requests, I'd be happy to play them for you.*
VERB | V n | V that | VERB | V n to-inf | N-COUNT: oft N *for* n, N that/to-inf | N-COUNT

PHRASES [5] If you do something **at** someone's **request**, you do it because they have asked you to. ❑ *The evacuation is being organised at the request of the United Nations Secretary General.* [6] If something is given or done **on request**, it is given or done whenever you ask for it. ❑ *Leaflets giving details are available on request.*
PHRASE | PHRASE

**requi|em** /rekwiem/ **(requiems)** [1] A **requiem** or a **requiem mass** is a Catholic church service in memory of someone who has recently died. [2] A **requiem** is a piece of music for singers and musicians that can be performed either as part of a requiem mass or as part of a concert. ❑ *...a performance of Verdi's Requiem.*
N-COUNT | N-COUNT: oft in names

**re|quire** /rɪkwaɪəʳ/ **(requires, requiring, required)** ◆◆◇ [1] If you **require** something or if something **is required**, you need it or it is necessary. [FORMAL] ❑ *If you require further information, you should consult the registrar... This isn't the kind of crisis that requires us to drop everything else... Some of the materials required for this technique may be difficult to obtain.* [2] If a law or rule **requires** you **to** do something, you have to do it. [FORMAL] ❑ *The rules also require employers to provide safety training... At least 35 manufacturers have flouted a law requiring prompt reporting of such malfunctions... The law now requires that parents serve on the committees that plan and evaluate school programs... Then he'll know exactly what's required of him.* [3] If you say that something is **required reading** for a particular group of people, you mean that you think it is essential for them to read it because it will give them information which they should have. ❑ *...an important research study that should be required reading for every member of the cabinet.*
VERB | V n | V n to-inf | V-ed | VERB | V n to-inf | V n | V that | *be* V-ed *of* n | PHRASE: v-link PHR, oft PHR *for* n

**re|quire|ment** /rɪkwaɪəʳmənt/ **(requirements)** ◆◇◇ [1] A **requirement** is a quality or qualification that you must have in order to be allowed to do something or to be suitable for something. ❑ *Its products met all legal requirements.* [2] Your **requirements** are the things that you need. [FORMAL] ❑ *Variations of this programme can be arranged to suit your requirements.*
N-COUNT: usu with supp | N-COUNT: usu pl, usu with supp

**requi|site** /rekwɪzɪt/ **(requisites)** [1] You can use **requisite** to indicate that something is necessary for a particular purpose. [FORMAL] ❑ *She filled in the requisite paperwork.* [2] A **requisite** is something which is necessary for a particular purpose. [FORMAL] ❑ *An understanding of accounting techniques is a major requisite for the work of the analysts.*
ADJ: usu *the* ADJ n | N-COUNT: usu with supp

**requi|si|tion** /rekwɪzɪʃᵊn/ **(requisitions, requisitioning, requisitioned)** [1] If people in authority **requisition** a vehicle, building, or food, they formally demand it and take it for official use. [FORMAL] ❑ *Authorities requisitioned hotel rooms to lodge more than 3,000 stranded Christmas vacationers.* [2] A **requisition** is a written document which allows a person or organization to obtain goods. ❑ *...a requisition for a replacement photocopier.*
VERB = commandeer | V n | N-COUNT

**re-route** **(re-routes, re-routing, re-routed)** also **reroute.** If vehicles or planes **are re-routed**, they are directed along a different route because the usual route cannot be used. ❑ *The heavy traffic was re-routed past my front door... They rerouted the planes at La Guardia airport.*
VERB = redirect | *be* V-ed | V n

**re-run** **(re-runs, re-running, re-ran)**

> The spelling **rerun** is also used. The form **re-run** is used in the present tense and is also the past participle of the verb. The noun is pronounced /riːrʌn/. The verb is pronounced /riːrʌn/.

1 If you say that something is **a re-run of** a particular event or experience, you mean that what happens now is very similar to what happened in the past. ❑ *It was the world's second worst air disaster, a horrific re-run of the runway collision in 1977.* N-SING: N *of* n = *repeat*
2 If someone **re-runs** a process or event, they do it or organize it again. ❑ *Edit the input text and re-run the software.* ♦ **Re-run** is also a noun. ❑ *In the re-run he failed to make the final at all, finishing sixth.* VERB V n N-COUNT
3 If an election **is re-run**, it is organized again, for example because the correct procedures were not followed or because no candidate got a large enough majority. ❑ *The ballot was re-run on Mr Todd's insistence after accusations of malpractice.* ♦ **Re-run** is also a noun. ❑ *The opposition has demanded a re-run of parliamentary elections held yesterday.* VERB: usu passive *be* V-ed N-COUNT: oft N *of* n
4 To **re-run** a film, play, or television programme means to show it or put it on again. ❑ *They re-ran the World Cup final on a big screen.* VERB V n
5 A **re-run** is a film, play, or television programme that is shown or put on again. ❑ *Viewers will have to make do with tired re-runs and old movies.* N-COUNT: usu with supp, oft N *of* n = *repeat*

**re|sale** /riːseɪl/ The **resale** price of something that you own is the amount of money that you would get if you sold it. ❑ *...a well-maintained used car with a good resale value.* N-UNCOUNT: N n

**re|sat** /riːsæt/ **Resat** is the past tense and past participle of **resit**.

**re|sched|ule** /riːʃedjuːl, AM -skedʒuːl/ **(reschedules, rescheduling, rescheduled)** 1 If someone **reschedules** an event, they change the time at which it is supposed to happen. ❑ *Since I'll be away, I'd like to reschedule the meeting... They've rescheduled the vigil for February 14th.* ♦ **re|sched|ul|ing** **(reschedulings)** *All this could lead up to a rescheduling of the trip to Asia.* VERB V n V n *for/to* n N-VAR: usu N *of* n
2 To **reschedule** a debt means to arrange for the person, organization, or country that owes money to pay it back over a longer period because they are in financial difficulty. ❑ *...companies that have gone bust or had to reschedule their debts.* ♦ **re|sched|ul|ing** *The President is also expected to request a rescheduling of loan repayments.* VERB V n N-VAR: usu N *of* n

**re|scind** /rɪsɪnd/ **(rescinds, rescinding, rescinded)** If a government or a group of people in power **rescind** a law or agreement, they officially withdraw it and state that it is no longer valid. [FORMAL] ❑ *Trade Union leaders have demanded the government rescind the price rise.* VERB V n

**res|cue** /reskjuː/ **(rescues, rescuing, rescued)** ◆◇◇
1 If you **rescue** someone, you get them out of a dangerous or unpleasant situation. ❑ *Helicopters rescued nearly 20 people from the roof of the burning building.* ♦ **res|cu|er** **(rescuers)** *It took rescuers 90 minutes to reach the trapped men.* VERB V n N-COUNT
2 **Rescue** is help which gets someone out of a dangerous or unpleasant situation. ❑ *A big rescue operation has been launched for a trawler missing in the English Channel.* N-UNCOUNT: oft N n
3 A **rescue** is an attempt to save someone from a dangerous or unpleasant situation. ❑ *A major air-sea rescue is under way.* N-COUNT
4 If you **go to** someone's **rescue** or **come to** their **rescue**, you help them when they are in danger or difficulty. ❑ *The 23-year-old's screams alerted a passerby who went to her rescue.* PHRASE: V inflects

**re|search** /rɪsɜːʳtʃ/ **(researches, researching, researched)** ◆◆◆
1 **Research** is work that involves studying something and trying to discover facts about it. ❑ *65 percent of the 1987 budget went for nuclear weapons research and production.* N-UNCOUNT: also N in pl
2 If you **research** something, you try to discover facts about it. ❑ *She spent two years in South Florida researching and filming her documentary... So far we haven't been able to find anything, but we're still researching.* ♦ **re|search|er** **(researchers)** *He chose to join the company as a market researcher.* VERB V n V N-COUNT

**re|search fel|low** **(research fellows)** A **research fellow** is a member of an academic institution whose job is to do research. N-COUNT

**re|sell** /riːsel/ **(resells, reselling, resold)** If you **resell** something that you have bought, you sell it again. ❑ *Shopkeepers buy them in bulk and resell them for £150 each... It makes sense to buy at dealer prices so you can maximize your profits if you resell.* VERB V n V

**re|sem|blance** /rɪzembləns/ **(resemblances)** If there is a **resemblance** between two people or things, they are similar to each other. ❑ *There was a remarkable resemblance between him and Pete.* N-VAR: oft adj N, N *between/to* n = *similarity*

**re|sem|ble** /rɪzembᵊl/ **(resembles, resembling, resembled)** If one thing or person **resembles** another, they are similar to each other. ❑ *Some of the commercially produced venison resembles beef in flavour.* VERB: no cont V n

**re|sent** /rɪzent/ **(resents, resenting, resented)** If you **resent** someone or something, you feel bitter and angry about them. ❑ *She resents her mother for being so tough on her.* VERB V n/-ing

**re|sent|ful** /rɪzentfʊl/ If you are **resentful**, you feel resentment. ❑ *At first I felt very resentful and angry about losing my job.* ♦ **re|sent|ful|ly** *For a moment she continued to look at him resentfully.* ADJ = *aggrieved* ADV: usu ADV with v

**re|sent|ment** /rɪzentmənt/ **(resentments)** **Resentment** is bitterness and anger that someone feels about something. ❑ *She expressed resentment at being interviewed by a social worker.* N-UNCOUNT: also N in pl

**res|er|va|tion** /rezəʳveɪʃᵊn/ **(reservations)**
1 If you have **reservations about** something, you are not sure that it is entirely good or right. ❑ *I told him my main reservation about his film was the ending.* N-VAR: oft N *about* n
2 If you make a **reservation**, you arrange for something such as a table in a restaurant or a room in a hotel to be kept for you. ❑ *He went to the desk to make a reservation.* N-COUNT = *booking*
3 A **reservation** is an area of land that is kept separate for a particular group of people to live in. ❑ *Seventeen thousand Indians live in Arizona on a reservation.* N-COUNT
4 → See also **central reservation**.

**re|serve** /rɪzɜːʳv/ **(reserves, reserving, reserved)** ◆◆◇
1 If something **is reserved for** a particular person or purpose, it is kept specially for that person or purpose. ❑ *A double room with a balcony overlooking the sea had been reserved for him.* VERB: usu passive = *set aside* *be* V-ed *for* n
2 If you **reserve** something such as a table, ticket, or magazine, you arrange for it to be kept specially for you, rather than sold or given to someone else. ❑ *I'll reserve a table for five.* VERB V n
3 A **reserve** is a supply of something that is available for use when it is needed. ❑ *The Gulf has 65 per cent of the world's oil reserves.* N-COUNT: usu with supp
4 In sports, a **reserve** is someone who is available to play as part of a team if one of the members is ill or cannot play. [mainly BRIT] ❑ *He ended up as a reserve, but still qualified for a team gold medal.* N-COUNT = *substitute*

> in AM, use **substitute**

5 A nature **reserve** is an area of land where the animals, birds, and plants are officially protected. ❑ *Marine biologists are calling for Cardigan Bay to be created a marine nature reserve to protect the dolphins.* N-COUNT: usu supp N
6 If someone shows **reserve**, they keep their feelings hidden. ❑ *His natural reserve made him appear self-conscious.* N-UNCOUNT
7 If you have something **in reserve**, you have it available for use when it is needed. ❑ *...the bottle of whisky that he kept in reserve.* PHRASE: PHR after v
8 to **reserve judgment** → see **judgment**. to **reserve the right** → see **right**.

**re|served** /rɪzɜːʳvd/ 1 Someone who is **reserved** keeps their feelings hidden. ❑ *He was unemotional, quite quiet, and reserved.* ADJ
2 A table in a restaurant or a seat in a theatre that is **reserved** is being kept for someone rather than given or sold to anyone else. ❑ *Seats, or sometimes entire tables, were reserved.* ADJ

**re|serve price** **(reserve prices)** A **reserve price** is the lowest price which is acceptable to the owner of property being auctioned or sold. [BRIT, BUSINESS] N-COUNT

**re|serv|ist** /rɪzɜːʳvɪst/ **(reservists)** Reservists are soldiers who are not serving in the regular army of a country, but who can be called to serve whenever they are needed. N-COUNT

**res|er|voir** /rezəʳvwɑːʳ/ **(reservoirs)** [1] A **reservoir** is a lake that is used for storing water before it is supplied to people. N-COUNT [2] A **reservoir of** something is a large quantity of it that is available for use when needed. ❑ *...the huge oil reservoir beneath the Kuwaiti desert.* N-COUNT: with supp, oft N *of* n, adj N

**re|set** /riːset/ **(resets, resetting)**

✔ The form **reset** is used in the present tense and is the past tense and past participle.

If you **reset** a machine or device, you adjust or set it, so that it is ready to work again or ready to perform a particular function. ❑ *As soon as you arrive at your destination, step out of the aircraft and reset your wrist-watch.* VERB V n

**re|set|tle** /riːsetᵊl/ **(resettles, resettling, resettled)** If people **are resettled** by a government or organization, or if people **resettle**, they move to a different place to live because they are no longer able or allowed to stay in the area where they used to live. ❑ *The refugees were put in camps in Italy before being resettled... In 1990, 200,000 Soviet Jews resettled on Israeli territory.* VERB *be* V-ed V

**re|set|tle|ment** /riːsetᵊlmənt/ **Resettlement** is the process of moving people to a different place to live, because they are no longer allowed to stay in the area where they used to live. ❑ *Only refugees are eligible for resettlement abroad.* N-UNCOUNT: oft N *of* n

**re|shape** /riːʃeɪp/ **(reshapes, reshaping, reshaped)** To **reshape** something means to change its structure or organization. ❑ *If they succeed on Europe, then they will have reshaped the political and economic map of the world.* ♦ **re|shap|ing** *This thesis led to a radical reshaping of Labour policies.* VERB V n N-SING: also no det, usu N *of* n

**re|shuf|fle** **(reshuffles, reshuffling, reshuffled)**

✔ The noun is pronounced /riːʃʌfᵊl/. The verb is pronounced /riːʃʌfᵊl/.

When a political leader **reshuffles** the ministers in a government, he or she changes their jobs so that some of the ministers change their responsibilities. [mainly BRIT] ❑ *The prime minister told reporters this morning that he plans to reshuffle his entire cabinet.* ♦ **Reshuffle** is also a noun. ❑ *He has carried out a partial cabinet reshuffle.* VERB = reorganize V n N-COUNT: usu sing, with supp

**re|side** /rɪzaɪd/ **(resides, residing, resided)** [1] If someone **resides** somewhere, they live there or are staying there. [FORMAL] ❑ *Margaret resides with her invalid mother in a London suburb.* VERB V prep/adv [2] If a quality **resides in** something, the thing has that quality. [FORMAL] ❑ *Happiness does not reside in strength or money.* VERB: no cont V *in* n

**resi|dence** /rezɪdəns/ **(residences)** [1] A **residence** is a house where people live. [FORMAL] ❑ *...hotels and private residences.* N-COUNT [2] Your place of **residence** is the place where you live. [FORMAL] ❑ *...differences among women based on age, place of residence and educational levels.* N-UNCOUNT [3] Someone's **residence** in a particular place is the fact that they live there or that they are officially allowed to live there. ❑ *They had entered the country and had applied for permanent residence.* N-UNCOUNT [4] → See also **hall of residence**.

PHRASES [5] If someone is **in residence** in a particular place, they are living there. ❑ *Windsor is open to visitors when the Royal Family is not in residence.* PHRASE: v-link PHR [6] An artist or writer **in residence** is one who teaches in an institution such as a university or theatre company. ❑ *Wakoski is writer in residence at Michigan State University.* PHRASE: n PHR

**resi|den|cy** /rezɪdənsi/ **(residencies)** [1] Someone's **residency** in a particular place, especially in a country, is the fact that they live there or that they are officially allowed to live there. ❑ *He applied for British residency.* N-UNCOUNT [2] A doctor's **residency** is the period of specialized training in a hospital that he or she receives after leaving university. [AM] ❑ *He completed his pediatric residency at Stanford University Hospital.* N-COUNT

**resi|dent** /rezɪdənt/ **(residents)** ◆◆◇ [1] The **residents** of a house or area are the people who live there. ❑ *The Archbishop called upon the government to build more low cost homes for local residents.* N-COUNT: usu pl, with supp [2] Someone who is **resident in** a country or a town lives there. ❑ *He moved to Belgium in 1990 to live with his son, who had been resident in Brussels since 1967.* ADJ: v-link ADJ, usu ADJ *in* n [3] A **resident** doctor or teacher lives in the place where he or she works. [BRIT] ❑ *The morning after your arrival, you meet with the resident physician for a private consultation.* ADJ: usu ADJ n [4] A **resident** or a **resident** doctor is a doctor who is receiving a period of specialized training in a hospital after leaving university. [AM] N-COUNT

**resi|den|tial** /rezɪdenʃᵊl/ [1] A **residential** area contains houses rather than offices or factories. ❑ *...a smart residential area.* ADJ: usu ADJ n [2] A **residential** institution is one where people live while they are studying there or being cared for there. ❑ *Training involves a two-year residential course. ...a residential home for children with disabilities.* ADJ: usu ADJ n

**resi|dents' as|so|cia|tion** **(residents' associations)** A **residents' association** is an organization of people who live in a particular area. Residents' associations have meetings and take action to make the area more pleasant to live in. N-COUNT

**re|sid|ual** /rɪzɪdʒuəl/ **Residual** is used to describe what remains of something when most of it has gone. ❑ *...residual radiation from nuclear weapons testing.* ADJ: usu ADJ n

**resi|due** /rezɪdjuː, AM -duː/ **(residues)** A **residue** of something is a small amount that remains after most of it has gone. ❑ *Always using the same shampoo means that a residue can build up on the hair.* N-COUNT: usu with supp

**re|sign** /rɪzaɪn/ **(resigns, resigning, resigned)** ◆◇◇ [1] If you **resign** from a job or position, you formally announce that you are leaving it. ❑ *A hospital administrator has resigned over claims he lied to get the job... Mr Robb resigned his position last month.* VERB = quit V V n [2] If you **resign yourself to** an unpleasant situation or fact, you accept it because you realize that you cannot change it. ❑ *Pat and I resigned ourselves to yet another summer without a boat.* VERB = reconcile V pron-refl *to* n/-ing [3] → See also **resigned**.

**res|ig|na|tion** /rezɪgneɪʃᵊn/ **(resignations)** ◆◇◇ [1] Your **resignation** is a formal statement of your intention to leave a job or position. ❑ *Mr Morgan has offered his resignation and it has been accepted. ...his letter of resignation.* N-VAR: usu with poss [2] **Resignation** is the acceptance of an unpleasant situation or fact because you realize that you cannot change it. ❑ *He sighed with profound resignation.* N-UNCOUNT

**re|signed** /rɪzaɪnd/ If you are **resigned to** an unpleasant situation or fact, you accept it without complaining because you realize that you cannot change it. ❑ *He is resigned to the noise and mess.* ADJ: usu v-link ADJ, usu ADJ *to* n/-ing

**re|sili|ent** /rɪzɪliənt/ [1] Something that is **resilient** is strong and not easily damaged by being hit, stretched, or squeezed. ❑ *...an armchair of some resilient plastic material.* ♦ **re|sili|ence** *Do your muscles have the strength and resilience that they should have?* ADJ: usu v-link ADJ N-UNCOUNT: also *a* N [2] People and things that are **resilient** are able to recover easily and quickly from unpleasant or damaging events. ❑ *When the U.S. stock market collapsed in October 1987, the Japanese stock market was the most resilient.* ♦ **re|sili|ence** *...the resilience of human beings to fight after they've been attacked.* ADJ: usu v-link ADJ N-UNCOUNT: also *a* N

**res|in** /rezɪn/ **(resins)** [1] **Resin** is a sticky substance that is produced by some trees. ❑ *The resin from which the oil is extracted comes from a small,* N-MASS *tough tree.* 2 **Resin** is a substance that is produced chemically and used to make plastics. N-MASS

**res|in|ous** /re̲zɪnəs/ Something that is **resinous** is like resin or contains resin. ❑ *Propolis is a hard resinous substance made by bees from the juices of plants.* ADJ

**re|sist** /rɪzɪ̲st/ **(resists, resisting, resisted)** ◆◇◇ 1 If you **resist** something such as a change, you refuse to accept it and try to prevent it. ❑ *She says she will resist a single European currency being imposed... They resisted our attempts to modernize the distribution of books.* VERB = oppose; V n -ing; V n
2 If you **resist** someone or **resist** an attack by them, you fight back against them. ❑ *The man was shot outside his house as he tried to resist arrest... When she had attempted to cut his nails he resisted.* VERB; V n; V
3 If you **resist** doing something, or **resist** the temptation to do it, you stop yourself from doing it although you would like to do it. ❑ *Students should resist the temptation to focus on exams alone.* VERB: oft with neg; V n/-ing
4 If someone or something **resists** damage of some kind, they are not damaged. ❑ *...bodies trained and toughened to resist the cold.* VERB = withstand; V n

**re|sist|ance** /rɪzɪ̲stəns/ **(resistances)** ◆◇◇ 1 **Resistance** to something such as a change or a new idea is a refusal to accept it. ❑ *The US wants big cuts in European agricultural export subsidies, but this is meeting resistance.* N-UNCOUNT: oft N *to* n
2 **Resistance** to an attack consists of fighting back against the people who have attacked you. ❑ *The troops are encountering stiff resistance.* N-UNCOUNT
3 The **resistance** of your body **to** germs or diseases is its power to remain unharmed or unaffected by them. ❑ *This disease is surprisingly difficult to catch as most people have a natural resistance to it.* N-UNCOUNT: oft N *to* n
4 Wind or air **resistance** is a force which slows down a moving object or vehicle. ❑ *The design of the bicycle has managed to reduce the effects of wind resistance and drag.* N-UNCOUNT: usu supp N
5 In electrical engineering or physics, **resistance** is the ability of a substance or an electrical circuit to stop the flow of an electrical current through it. ❑ *...materials that lose all their electrical resistance.* N-VAR
6 In a country which is occupied by the army of another country, or which has a very harsh and strict government, **the resistance** is an organized group of people who are involved in illegal activities against the people in power. ❑ *They managed to escape after being arrested by the resistance.* N-SING: *the* N
7 If you take **the line of least resistance** in a situation, you do what is easiest, even though you think that it may not be the right thing to do. In American English, you usually talk about **the path of least resistance**. ❑ *They would rather take the line of least resistance than become involved in arguments.* PHRASE: PHR after v

**re|sist|ant** /rɪzɪ̲stənt/ 1 Someone who is **resistant to** something is opposed to it and wants to prevent it. ❑ *Some people are very resistant to the idea of exercise.* ADJ: oft ADJ *to* n
2 If something is **resistant to** a particular thing, it is not harmed by it. ❑ *...how to improve plants to make them more resistant to disease.* ADJ: oft ADJ *to* n

**-resistant** /-rɪzɪstənt/ **-resistant** is added to nouns to form adjectives that describe something as not being harmed or affected by the thing mentioned. ❑ *Children's suncare products are normally water-resistant.* COMB in ADJ = -proof

**re|sis|tor** /rɪzɪ̲stəʳ/ **(resistors)** A **resistor** is a device which is designed to increase the ability of an electric circuit to stop the flow of an electric current through it. [TECHNICAL] N-COUNT

**re|sit** **(resits, resitting, resat)**

> ✓ The verb is pronounced /riːsɪ̲t/. The noun is pronounced /riː̲sɪt/.

If someone **resits** a test or examination, they take it again, usually because they failed the first time. [BRIT] ❑ *This year, Jim is resitting the exams he failed... If they fail, they can often resit the next year.* ♦ **Resit** is also a noun. ❑ *He failed his First Year exams and didn't bother about the resits.* VERB = retake; V n; V; N-COUNT = retake

> ✓ in AM, use **retake**

**re|skill** /riːskɪ̲l/ **(reskills, reskilling, reskilled)** If you **reskill**, or if someone **reskills** you, you learn new skills, so that you can do a different job or do your old job in a different way. [BUSINESS] ❑ *We needed to reskill our workforce to cope with massive technological change... You must be willing to reskill.* ♦ **re|skill|ing** *Everyone knows that lifelong learning and reskilling are important.* VERB = retrain; V n; V; N-UNCOUNT

**re|sold** /riːsoʊ̲ld/ **Resold** is the past tense and past participle of **resell**.

**reso|lute** /re̲zəluːt/ If you describe someone as **resolute**, you approve of them because they are very determined not to change their mind or not to give up a course of action. [FORMAL] ❑ *Voters perceive him as a decisive and resolute international leader.* ♦ **reso|lute|ly** *He resolutely refused to speak English unless forced to... The United States remains resolutely opposed to this.* ADJ = determined; ADV: ADV with v, ADV adj

**reso|lu|tion** /re̲zəluː̲ʃᵊn/ **(resolutions)** ◆◆◇ 1 A **resolution** is a formal decision taken at a meeting by means of a vote. ❑ *He replied that the UN had passed two major resolutions calling for a complete withdrawal.* N-COUNT: usu N supp, oft N num
2 If you make a **resolution**, you decide to try very hard to do something. ❑ *They made a resolution to lose all the weight gained during the Christmas period.* → See also **New Year's resolution**. N-COUNT
3 **Resolution** is determination to do something or not do something. ❑ *'I think I'll try a hypnotist,' I said with sudden resolution.* N-UNCOUNT
4 The **resolution** of a problem or difficulty is the final solving of it. [FORMAL] ❑ *...the successful resolution of a dispute involving UN inspectors in Baghdad.* N-SING: oft N *to/of* n
5 The **resolution** of an image is how clear the image is. [TECHNICAL] ❑ *Now this machine gives us such high resolution that we can see very small specks of calcium.* N-UNCOUNT: usu with supp

**re|solve** /rɪzɒ̲lv/ **(resolves, resolving, resolved)** ◆◇◇ 1 To **resolve** a problem, argument, or difficulty means to find a solution to it. [FORMAL] ❑ *We must find a way to resolve these problems before it's too late.* VERB; V n
2 If you **resolve to** do something, you make a firm decision to do it. [FORMAL] ❑ *She resolved to report the matter to the hospital's nursing manager... She resolved that, if Mimi forgot this promise, she would remind her.* VERB; V to-inf; V that
3 **Resolve** is determination to do what you have decided to do. [FORMAL] ❑ *This will strengthen the American public's resolve to go to war.* N-VAR: oft N to-inf = determination

**re|solved** /rɪzɒ̲lvd/ If you are **resolved to** do something, you are determined to do it. [FORMAL] ❑ *Barnes was resolved to moving on when his contract expired.* ADJ: v-link ADJ to-inf

**reso|nance** /re̲zənəns/ **(resonances)** 1 If something has a **resonance for** someone, it has a special meaning or is particularly important to them. ❑ *The ideas of order, security, family, religion and country had the same resonance for them as for Michael.* N-VAR
2 If a sound has **resonance**, it is deep, clear, and strong. ❑ *His voice had lost its resonance; it was tense and strained.* N-UNCOUNT

**reso|nant** /re̲zənənt/ 1 A sound that is **resonant** is deep and strong. ❑ *His voice sounded oddly resonant in the empty room.* ADJ
2 Something that is **resonant** has a special meaning or is particularly important to people. [LITERARY] ❑ *It is a country resonant with cinematic potential, from its architecture to its landscape.* ADJ

**reso|nate** /re̲zəneɪt/ **(resonates, resonating, resonated)** 1 If something **resonates**, it vibrates and produces a deep, strong sound. ❑ *The bass guitar began to thump so loudly that it resonated in my head.* VERB; V
2 You say that something **resonates** when it has a special meaning or when it is particularly important to someone. ❑ *London is confident and alive, resonating with all the qualities of a civilised city.* VERB; V *with* n

**re|sort** /rɪzɔː̲ʳt/ **(resorts, resorting, resorted)** ◆◇◇ 1 If you **resort to** a course of action that you do not really approve of, you adopt it because you cannot see any other way of achieving what you want. ❑ *His punishing work schedule had made him* VERB; V *to* n/-ing

*resort to drugs.* [2] If you achieve something without **resort to** a particular course of action, you succeed without carrying out that action. To have **resort to** a particular course of action means to have to do that action in order to achieve something. ❑ *Congress has a responsibility to ensure that all peaceful options are exhausted before resort to war.* N-UNCOUNT: N *to* n = *recourse*
[3] A **resort** is a place where a lot of people spend their holidays. ❑ *...the ski resorts.* N-COUNT: usu supp N
PHRASES [4] If you do something **as a last resort**, you do it because you can find no other way of getting out of a difficult situation or of solving a problem. ❑ *Nuclear weapons should be used only as a last resort.* PHRASE: PHR with cl [5] You use **in the last resort** when stating the most basic or important fact that will still be true in a situation whatever else happens. ❑ *They would in the last resort support their friends whatever they did.* PHRASE: PHR with cl = *ultimately*

**re|sound** /rɪzaʊnd/ **(resounds, resounding, resounded)** [1] When a noise **resounds**, it is heard very loudly and clearly. [LITERARY] ❑ *A roar of approval resounded through the Ukrainian parliament.* VERB V prep
[2] If a place **resounds with** or **to** particular noises, it is filled with them. [LITERARY] ❑ *The whole place resounded with music... Kabul resounded to the crack of Kalashnikov fire and a flood of artillery.* VERB V *with* n V *to* n

**re|sound|ing** /rɪzaʊndɪŋ/ [1] A **resounding** sound is loud and clear. ❑ *There was a resounding slap as Andrew struck him violently across the face.* ADJ: usu ADJ n [2] You can refer to a very great success as a **resounding** success. ❑ *The good weather helped to make the occasion a resounding success.* ADJ: usu ADJ n [emphasis]

**re|source** /rɪzɔːʳs, AM riːsɔːrs/ **(resources)** ◆◆◇ [1] The **resources** of an organization or person are the materials, money, and other things that they have and can use in order to function properly. ❑ *Some families don't have the resources to feed themselves properly.* N-COUNT: usu pl [2] A country's **resources** are the things that it has and can use to increase its wealth, such as coal, oil, or land. ❑ *...resources like coal, tungsten, oil and copper.* N-COUNT: usu pl

**re|sourced** /rɪzɔːʳst, AM riːsɔːrst/ If an organization is **resourced**, it has all the things, such as money and materials, that it needs to function properly. [BRIT] ❑ *The school is very well resourced – we have a language laboratory and use computers and videos.* ADJ: usu adv ADJ

**re|source|ful** /rɪzɔːʳsfʊl/ Someone who is **resourceful** is good at finding ways of dealing with problems. ❑ *He was amazingly inventive and resourceful, and played a major role in my career.* ADJ
♦ **re|source|ful|ness** *Because of his adventures, he is a person of far greater experience and resourcefulness.* N-UNCOUNT

**re|spect** /rɪspekt/ **(respects, respecting, respected)** ◆◆◇ [1] If you **respect** someone, you have a good opinion of their character or ideas. ❑ *I want him to respect me as a career woman.* VERB V n [2] If you have **respect for** someone, you have a good opinion of them. ❑ *I have tremendous respect for Dean.* ➔ See also **self-respect**. N-UNCOUNT: usu N *for* n [3] If you **respect** someone's wishes, rights, or customs, you avoid doing things that they would dislike or regard as wrong. ❑ *Finally, trying to respect her wishes, I said I'd leave.* VERB V n [4] If you show **respect for** someone's wishes, rights, or customs, you avoid doing anything they would dislike or regard as wrong. ❑ *They will campaign for the return of traditional lands and respect for aboriginal rights and customs.* N-UNCOUNT: usu N *for* n [5] If you **respect** a law or moral principle, you agree not to break it. ❑ *It is about time tour operators respected the law and their own code of conduct.* VERB V n ♦ **Respect** is also a noun. ❑ *...respect for the law and the rejection of the use of violence.* N-UNCOUNT: usu N *for* n
PHRASES [6] You can say **with respect** when you are politely disagreeing with someone or criticizing them. ❑ *With respect, I hardly think that's the point.* PHRASE: PHR with cl [politeness] [7] If you **pay** your **respects to** someone, you go to see them or speak to them. You usually do this to be polite, and not necessarily because you want to do it. [FORMAL] ❑ *Carl had asked him to visit the hospital and to pay his respects to Francis.* PHRASE: V inflects
[8] If you **pay** your **last respects to** someone who has just died, you show your respect or affection for them by coming to see their body or their grave. ❑ *The son had nothing to do with arranging the funeral, but came along to pay his last respects.* PHRASE: V inflects
[9] You use expressions like **in this respect** and **in many respects** to indicate that what you are saying applies to the feature you have just mentioned or to many features of something. ❑ *The children are not unintelligent – in fact, they seem quite normal in this respect.* PHRASE: PHR with cl [10] You use **with respect to** to say what something relates to. In British English, you can also say **in respect of**. [FORMAL] ❑ *Parents often have little choice with respect to the way their child is medically treated.* ➔ See also **respected**. PHRASE: PHR with cl

**re|spect|able** /rɪspektəbᵊl/ [1] Someone or something that is **respectable** is approved of by society and considered to be morally correct. ❑ *He came from a perfectly respectable middle-class family.* ADJ ♦ **re|spect|ably** /rɪspektəbli/ *She's respectably dressed in jeans and sweatshirt.* ADV ♦ **re|spect|abil|ity** /rɪspektəbɪlɪti/ *If she divorced Tony, she would lose the respectability she had as Mrs Tony Tatterton.* N-UNCOUNT [2] You can say that something is **respectable** when you mean that it is good enough or acceptable. ❑ *...investments that offer respectable rates of return.* ADJ = *decent*

**re|spect|ed** /rɪspektɪd/ Someone or something that is **respected** is admired and considered important by many people. ❑ *He is highly respected for his novels and plays.* ADJ: oft adv ADJ

**re|spect|er** /rɪspektəʳ/ **(respecters)** [1] If you say that someone is a **respecter of** something such as a belief or idea, you mean that they behave in a way which shows that they have a high opinion of it. ❑ *Ford was a respecter of proprieties and liked to see things done properly.* N-COUNT: usu N *of* n [2] If you say that someone or something is **no respecter of** a rule or tradition, you mean that the rule or tradition is not important to them. ❑ *Accidents and sudden illnesses are no respecters of age.* PHRASE: v-link PHR

**re|spect|ful** /rɪspektfʊl/ If you are **respectful**, you show respect for someone. ❑ *The children in our family are always respectful to their elders.* ADJ: oft ADJ *of/towards/to* n ♦ **re|spect|ful|ly** *'You are an artist,' she said respectfully.* ADV: usu ADV with v

**re|spec|tive** /rɪspektɪv/ **Respective** means relating or belonging separately to the individual people you have just mentioned. ❑ *Steve and I were at very different stages in our respective careers.* ADJ: ADJ n, usu poss ADJ pl-n

**re|spec|tive|ly** /rɪspektɪvli/ **Respectively** means in the same order as the items that you have just mentioned. ❑ *Their sons, Ben and Jonathan, were three and six respectively.* ADV: ADV with cl/group

**res|pi|ra|tion** /respɪreɪʃᵊn/ Your **respiration** is your breathing. [MEDICAL] ❑ *His respiration grew fainter throughout the day.* ➔ See also **artificial respiration**. N-UNCOUNT

**res|pi|ra|tor** /respɪreɪtəʳ/ **(respirators)** [1] A **respirator** is a device that allows people to breathe when they cannot breathe naturally, for example because they are ill or have been injured. ❑ *She was so ill that she was put on a respirator.* N-COUNT
[2] A **respirator** is a device you wear over your mouth and nose in order to breathe when you are surrounded by smoke or poisonous gas. N-COUNT

**res|pira|tory** /respərətri, AM -tɔːri/ **Respiratory** means relating to breathing. [MEDICAL] ❑ *...people with severe respiratory problems.* ADJ: ADJ n

**res|pite** /respaɪt, -pɪt/ [1] A **respite** is a short period of rest from something unpleasant. [FORMAL] ❑ *It was some weeks now since they had had any respite from shellfire.* N-SING: also no det, oft N *from* n [2] A **respite** is a short delay before a very unpleasant or difficult situation which may or may not take place. [FORMAL] ❑ *Devaluation would only give the economy a brief respite.* N-SING: also no det = *reprieve*

**res|pite care** **Respite care** is short-term care that is provided for very old or very sick peo- N-UNCOUNT ple so that the person who usually cares for them can have a break. ❑ *...respite care for their very ill child for short periods.*

**re|splend|ent** /rɪsplendənt/ [ADJ: oft ADJ *in* n] If you describe someone or something as **resplendent**, you mean that their appearance is very impressive and expensive-looking. [FORMAL] ❑ *Bessie, resplendent in royal blue velvet, was hovering beside the table.*

**re|spond** /rɪspɒnd/ **(responds, responding, responded)** ◆◆◇ [1] [VERB] When you **respond** to something that is done or said, you react to it by doing or saying something yourself. ❑ *They are likely to respond positively to the President's request for aid...* [V *to* n] *The army responded with gunfire and tear gas...* [V *with* n] *'Are you well enough to carry on? — 'Of course,' she responded scornfully...* [V with quote] *The Belgian Minister of Foreign Affairs responded that the protection of refugees was a matter for an international organization.* [V that] [2] [VERB = react] When you **respond to** a need, crisis, or challenge, you take the necessary or appropriate action. ❑ *This modest group size allows our teachers to respond to the needs of each student.* [V *to* n] [3] [VERB] If a patient or their injury or illness **is responding to** treatment, the treatment is working and they are getting better. ❑ *I'm pleased to say that he is now doing well and responding to treatment.* [V *to* n]

**re|spond|ent** /rɪspɒndənt/ **(respondents)** [N-COUNT: usu pl] A **respondent** is a person who replies to something such as a survey or set of questions. ❑ *60 percent of the respondents said they disapproved of the president's performance.*

**re|sponse** /rɪspɒns/ **(responses)** ◆◆◇ [N-COUNT: oft N *to*/*from* n, also *in* N] Your **response** to an event or to something that is said is your reply or reaction to it. ❑ *There has been no response to his remarks from the government.*

**re|sponse time (response times)** [N-COUNT] **Response time** is the time taken for a computer to do something after you have given an instruction. [COMPUTING] ❑ *The only flaw is the slightly slow response times when you press the buttons.*

**re|spon|sibil|ity** /rɪspɒnsɪbɪlɪti/ **(responsibilities)** ◆◆◇ [1] [N-UNCOUNT: oft N *for* n/-ing] If you have **responsibility** for something or someone, or if they are your **responsibility**, it is your job or duty to deal with them and to take decisions relating to them. ❑ *Each manager had responsibility for just under 600 properties.* [2] [N-UNCOUNT: oft N *for* n] If you accept **responsibility for** something that has happened, you agree that you were to blame for it or you caused it. ❑ *No one admitted responsibility for the attacks.* [3] [N-PLURAL: usu with supp] Your **responsibilities** are the duties that you have because of your job or position. ❑ *He handled his responsibilities as a counselor in an intelligent and caring fashion.* [4] [N-UNCOUNT] If someone is given **responsibility**, they are given the right or opportunity to make important decisions or to take action without having to get permission from anyone else. ❑ *She would have loved to have a better-paying job with more responsibility.* [5] [N-SING: usu N to-inf = duty] If you think that you have a **responsibility to** do something, you feel that you ought to do it because it is morally right to do it. ❑ *The court feels it has a responsibility to ensure that customers are not misled.* [6] [N-SING: N *to*/*towards* n] If you think that you have a **responsibility to** someone, you feel that it is your duty to take action that will protect their interests. ❑ *She had decided that as a doctor she had a responsibility to her fellow creatures.*

**re|spon|sible** /rɪspɒnsɪbᵊl/ ◆◆◇ [1] [ADJ: v-link ADJ, usu ADJ *for* n/-ing] If someone or something is **responsible for** a particular event or situation, they are the cause of it or they can be blamed for it. ❑ *He still felt responsible for her death... I want you to do everything you can to find out who's responsible.* [2] [ADJ: v-link ADJ, usu ADJ *for* n/-ing] If you are **responsible for** something, it is your job or duty to deal with it and make decisions relating to it. ❑ *...the minister responsible for the environment.* [3] [ADJ: v-link ADJ *to* n] If you are **responsible to** a person or group, they have authority over you and you have to report to them about what you do. ❑ *I'm responsible to my board of directors.* [4] [ADJ] **Responsible** people behave properly and sensibly, without needing to be supervised. ❑ *He feels that the media should be more responsible in what they report.* ♦ **re|spon|sibly** [ADV: ADV with v] *He urged everyone to act responsibly.* [5] [ADJ: ADJ n] **Responsible** jobs involve making important decisions or carrying out important tasks. ❑ *I work in a government office. It's a responsible position, I suppose, but not very exciting.*

**re|spon|sive** /rɪspɒnsɪv/ [1] [ADJ] A **responsive** person is quick to react to people or events and to show emotions such as pleasure and affection. ❑ *Harriet was an easy, responsive little girl.* ♦ **re|spon|sive|ness** [N-UNCOUNT] *This condition decreases sexual desire and responsiveness.* [2] [ADJ: usu ADJ *to* n] If someone or something is **responsive**, they react quickly and favourably. ❑ *With an election coming soon, your MP should be very responsive to your request.* ♦ **re|spon|sive|ness** [N-UNCOUNT] *Such responsiveness to public pressure is extraordinary.*

| **rest** |
|---|
| ① QUANTIFIER USES |
| ② VERB AND NOUN USES |

**① rest** /rest/ ◆◆◇ [1] [QUANT: QUANT *of* def-n] **The rest** is used to refer to all the parts of something or all the things in a group that remain or that you have not already mentioned. ❑ *It was an experience I will treasure for the rest of my life... He was unable to travel to Barcelona with the rest of the team.* ♦ **Rest** is also a pronoun. [PRON] ❑ *Only 55 per cent of the raw material is canned. The rest is thrown away.* [2] [PHRASE] [vagueness] You can add **and the rest** or **all the rest of it** to the end of a statement or list when you want to refer in a vague way to other things that are associated with the ones you have already mentioned. [SPOKEN] ❑ *...a man with nice clothes, a Range Rover and the rest.*

**② rest** /rest/ **(rests, resting, rested)** ◆◆◇

⇛ Please look at category 18 to see if the expression you are looking for is shown under another headword. [1] [VERB] If you **rest** or if you **rest** your body, you do not do anything active for a time. ❑ *He's tired and exhausted, and has been advised to rest for two weeks...* [V] *Try to rest the injured limb as much as possible.* [V n] [2] [N-VAR] If you get some **rest** or have a **rest**, you do not do anything active for a time. ❑ *'You're worn out, Laura,' he said. 'Go home and get some rest.'.* [3] [VERB = depend] If something such as a theory or someone's success **rests on** a particular thing, it depends on that thing. [FORMAL] ❑ *Such a view rests on a number of incorrect assumptions.* [V *on/upon* n/wh] [4] [VERB] If authority, a responsibility, or a decision **rests with** you, you have that authority or responsibility, or you are the one who will make that decision. [FORMAL] ❑ *The final decision rested with the President.* [V *with* n] [5] [VERB = lean] If you **rest** something somewhere, you put it there so that its weight is supported. ❑ *He rested his arms on the back of the chair.* [V n prep] [6] [VERB] If something **is resting** somewhere, or if you **are resting** it there, it is in a position where its weight is supported. ❑ *His head was resting on her shoulder...* [V prep/adv] *He had been resting his head in his hands, deep in thought.* [V n prep/adv] [7] [VERB = lean] If you **rest** on or against someone or something, you lean on them so that they support the weight of your body. ❑ *He rested on his pickaxe for a while.* [V prep] [8] [N-COUNT: usu n N] A **rest** is an object that is used to support something, especially your head, arms, or feet. ❑ *When you are sitting, keep your elbow on the arm rest.* [9] [VERB] If your eyes **rest on** a particular person or object, you look directly at them, rather than somewhere else. [WRITTEN] ❑ *As she spoke, her eyes rested on her husband's face.* [V *on/upon* n] [10] → See also **rested**.

**PHRASES** [11] [PHRASE: V inflects] When an object that has been moving **comes to rest**, it finally stops. [FORMAL] ❑ *The plane had plowed a path through a patch of forest before coming to rest in a field.* [12] [PHRASE] If you say that someone can **rest easy**, you mean that they don't need to worry about a particular situation. ❑ *How can any woman rest easy now, knowing her breast cancer may be misdiagnosed?* [13] [PHRASE: V inflects] If someone tells you to **give** something **a rest**, they want you to stop doing it because it annoys them or because they think it is harming you. [INFORMAL] ❑ *Give it a rest, will you? We're trying to get some sleep.* [14] If you say that someone who has died **is laid to rest**, you mean that they are buried. ❑ *His dying wish was to be laid to rest at the church near his Somerset home.* PHRASE: V inflects [15] If you **lay** something such as fears or rumours **to rest** or if you **put** them **to rest**, you succeed in proving that they are not true. ❑ *His speech should lay those fears to rest.* PHRASE: V inflects = *allay* [16] If someone refuses to **let** a subject **rest**, they refuse to stop talking about it, especially after they have been talking about it for a long time. ❑ *I am not prepared to let this matter rest.* PHRASE: V inflects = *drop* [17] To **put** someone's **mind at rest** or **set** their **mind at rest** means to tell them something that stops them worrying. ❑ *A brain scan last Friday finally set his mind at rest.* PHRASE: V and N inflect = *reassure* [18] **rest assured** → see **assured**. to **rest on** your **laurels** → see **laurel**. to **rest in peace** → see **peace**.

**rest area** **(rest areas)** A **rest area** is a place beside a motorway or freeway where you can buy petrol and other things, or have a meal. [mainly AM] N-COUNT

☑ in BRIT, use **services**

**re|start** /riːstɑːʳt/ **(restarts, restarting, restarted)** If you **restart** something that has been interrupted or stopped, or if it **restarts**, it starts to happen or function again. ❑ *The commissioners agreed to restart talks as soon as possible... The trial will restart today with a new jury.* VERB V n V ♦ **Restart** is also a noun. ❑ *After a goalless first half, Australia took the lead within a minute of the restart.* N-COUNT

**re|state** /riːsteɪt/ **(restates, restating, restated)** If you **restate** something, you say it again in words or writing, usually in a slightly different way. [FORMAL] ❑ *He continued throughout to restate his opposition to violence.* VERB V n

**re|state|ment** /riːsteɪtmənt/ **(restatements)** A **restatement of** something that has been said or written is another statement that repeats it, usually in a slightly different form. [FORMAL] ❑ *I hope this book is not yet another restatement of the prevailing wisdom.* N-COUNT: usu N *of* n = *reiteration*

**res|tau|rant** /restərɒnt, AM -rənt/ **(restaurants)** A **restaurant** is a place where you can eat a meal and pay for it. In restaurants your food is usually served to you at your table by a waiter or waitress. ❑ *They ate in an Italian restaurant in Forth Street.* ◆◆◇ N-COUNT

**res|tau|rant car** **(restaurant cars)** A **restaurant car** is a carriage on a train where passengers can have a meal. [BRIT] N-COUNT

☑ in AM, use **dining car**

**res|tau|ra|teur** /restərətɜːʳ/ **(restaurateurs)** A **restaurateur** is a person who owns and manages a restaurant. [FORMAL] N-COUNT

**rest|ed** /restɪd/ If you feel **rested**, you feel more energetic because you have just had a rest. ❑ *He looked tanned and well rested after his vacation.* ADJ: v-link ADJ

**rest|ful** /restfʊl/ Something that is **restful** helps you to feel calm and relaxed. ❑ *Adjust the lighting so it is soft and restful.* ADJ

**rest home** **(rest homes)** A **rest home** is the same as an **old people's home**. N-COUNT

**rest|ing place** **(resting places)** [1] A **resting place** is a place where you can stay and rest, usually for a short period of time. ❑ *The area was an important resting place for many types of migrant birds.* N-COUNT [2] You can refer to the place where a dead person is buried as their **resting place** or their final **resting place**. ❑ *The hill is supposed to be the resting place of the legendary King Lud.* N-COUNT: usu with poss

**res|ti|tu|tion** /restɪtjuːʃən, AM -tuː-/ **Restitution** is the act of giving back to a person something that was lost or stolen, or of paying them money for the loss. [FORMAL] ❑ *The victims are demanding full restitution.* N-UNCOUNT

**res|tive** /restɪv/ If you are **restive**, you are impatient, bored, or dissatisfied. [FORMAL] ❑ *The audience grew restive.* ADJ ♦ **res|tive|ness** *There were signs of restiveness among the younger members.* N-UNCOUNT

**rest|less** /restləs/ [1] If you are **restless**, you are bored, impatient, or dissatisfied, and you want to do something else. ❑ *By 1982, she was restless and needed a new impetus for her talent.* ADJ ♦ **rest|less|ness** *From the audience came increasing sounds of restlessness.* N-UNCOUNT [2] If someone is **restless**, they keep moving around because they find it difficult to keep still. ❑ *My father seemed very restless and excited.* ADJ ♦ **rest|less|ness** *Karen complained of hyperactivity and restlessness.* N-UNCOUNT ♦ **rest|less|ly** *He paced up and down restlessly, trying to put his thoughts in order.* ADV: usu ADV with v [3] If you have a **restless** night, you do not sleep properly and when you wake up you feel tired and uncomfortable. ❑ *The shocking revelations of the 700-page report had caused him several restless nights.* ADJ: ADJ n

**re|stock** /riːstɒk/ **(restocks, restocking, restocked)** [1] If you **restock** something such as a shelf, fridge, or shop, you fill it with food or other goods to replace what you have used or sold. ❑ *I have to restock the freezer... Back on Flatbush Avenue, Pong is busy restocking his shelves with cucumbers and coconuts.* VERB V n V n *with* n Also V [2] To **restock** a lake means to put more fish in it because there are very few left. ❑ *The lake was restocked with roach last year.* VERB *be* V-ed *with* n Also V n *with* n, V n

**Res|to|ra|tion** /restəreɪʃən/ [1] **The Restoration** was the event in 1660 when Charles the Second became King of England, Scotland, and Ireland after a period when there had been no King or Queen. ◆◇◇ N-PROPER: *the* N [2] **Restoration** is used to refer to the style of drama and architecture that was popular during and just after the rule of Charles the Second in England. ❑ *...a Restoration comedy.* ADJ: ADJ n

**re|stora|tive** /rɪstɔːrətɪv/ **(restoratives)** [1] Something that is **restorative** makes you feel healthier, stronger, or more cheerful after you have been feeling tired, weak, or miserable. ❑ *She opened the door to her bedroom, thinking how restorative a hot bath would feel tonight.* ADJ [2] If you describe something as a **restorative**, you mean that it makes you feel healthier, stronger, or more cheerful after you have been feeling tired, weak, or miserable. ❑ *Seven days off could be a wonderful restorative.* N-COUNT

**re|store** /rɪstɔːʳ/ **(restores, restoring, restored)** [1] To **restore** a situation or practice means to cause it to exist again. ❑ *The army has recently been brought in to restore order.* ◆◇◇ VERB V n ♦ **res|to|ra|tion** /restəreɪʃən/ *His visit is expected to lead to the restoration of diplomatic relations.* N-UNCOUNT: usu N *of* n [2] To **restore** someone or something **to** a previous condition means to cause them to be in that condition once again. ❑ *We will restore her to health but it may take time... His country desperately needs Western aid to restore its ailing economy.* VERB V n *to* n V n ♦ **res|to|ra|tion** *I owe the restoration of my hearing to this remarkable new technique.* N-UNCOUNT: usu N *of* n [3] When someone **restores** something such as an old building, painting, or piece of furniture, they repair and clean it, so that it looks like it did when it was new. ❑ *...experts who specialise in examining and restoring ancient parchments.* VERB V n ♦ **res|to|ra|tion** **(restorations)** *I specialized in the restoration of old houses.* N-VAR [4] If something that was lost or stolen **is restored to** its owner, it is returned to them. [FORMAL] ❑ *The following day their horses and goods were restored to them.* VERB: usu passive = *return* *be* V-ed *to* n

**re|stor|er** /rɪstɔːrəʳ/ **(restorers)** A **restorer** is someone whose job it is to repair old buildings, paintings, and furniture so that they are look like they did when they were new. ❑ *...an antiques restorer.* N-COUNT: oft n N

**re|strain** /rɪstreɪn/ **(restrains, restraining, restrained)** [1] If you **restrain** someone, you stop them from doing what they intended or wanted to do, usually by using your physical strength. ❑ *Wally gripped my arm, partly to restrain me and partly to reassure me.* VERB V n [2] If you **restrain** an emotion or you **restrain yourself from** doing something, you prevent yourself from showing that VERB emotion or doing what you wanted or intended to do. ❑ *She was unable to restrain her desperate anger... Gladys wanted to ask, 'Aren't you angry with him?' But she restrained herself from doing so.* (V n; V n *from* -ing/n) [3] To **restrain** something that is growing or increasing means to prevent it from getting too large. (VERB = check) ❑ *The radical 500-day plan was very clear on how it intended to try to restrain inflation.* (V n)

**re|strained** /rɪstreɪnd/ [1] Someone who is **restrained** is very calm and unemotional. (ADJ) ❑ *In the circumstances he felt he'd been very restrained.* [2] If you describe someone's clothes or the decorations in a house as **restrained**, you mean that you like them because they are simple and not too brightly-coloured. (ADJ [approval]) ❑ *Her black suit was restrained and expensive.*

**re|strain|ing or|der** **(restraining orders)** A **restraining order** is an order by a court of law that someone should stop doing something until a court decides whether they are legally allowed to continue doing it. (N-COUNT) [mainly AM, LEGAL] ❑ *His estranged wife had taken out a restraining order against him.*

**re|straint** /rɪstreɪnt/ **(restraints)** [1] **Restraints** are rules or conditions that limit or restrict someone or something. (N-VAR: usu with supp, oft N *on* n) ❑ *The Prime Minister is calling for new restraints on trade unions.* [2] **Restraint** is calm, controlled, and unemotional behaviour. (N-UNCOUNT) ❑ *They behaved with more restraint than I'd expected.*

**re|strict** /rɪstrɪkt/ **(restricts, restricting, restricted)** [1] If you **restrict** something, you put a limit on it in order to reduce it or prevent it becoming too great. (VERB = limit) ❑ *There is talk of raising the admission requirements to restrict the number of students on campus... The French, I believe, restrict Japanese imports to a maximum of 3 per cent of their market.* (V n; V n *to* amount) ♦ **re|stric|tion** /rɪstrɪkʃ<sup>ə</sup>n/ *Some restriction on funding was necessary.* (N-UNCOUNT = limit) [2] To **restrict** the movement or actions of someone or something means to prevent them from moving or acting freely. (VERB) ❑ *The government imprisoned dissidents, forbade travel, and restricted the press.* (V n) ♦ **re|stric|tion** *...the justification for this restriction of individual liberty.* (N-UNCOUNT) [3] If you **restrict** someone or their activities **to** one thing, they can only do, have, or deal with that thing. If you **restrict** them **to** one place, they cannot go anywhere else. (VERB = confine) ❑ *For the first two weeks patients are restricted to the grounds.* (*be* V-ed *to* n; Also V n *to* n) [4] If you **restrict** something **to** a particular group, only that group can do it or have it. If you **restrict** something **to** a particular place, it is allowed only in that place. (VERB) ❑ *The hospital may restrict bookings to people living locally.* (V n *to* n)

**re|strict|ed** /rɪstrɪktɪd/ [1] Something that is **restricted** is quite small or limited. (ADJ) ❑ *...the monotony of a heavily restricted diet.* [2] If something is **restricted to** a particular group, only members of that group have it. If it is **restricted to** a particular place, it exists only in that place. (ADJ: v-link ADJ *to* n) ❑ *Discipline problems are by no means restricted to children in families dependent on benefits.* [3] A **restricted** area is one that only people with special permission can enter. (ADJ) ❑ *...a highly restricted area close to the old Khodinka airfield.*

**re|stric|tion** /rɪstrɪkʃ<sup>ə</sup>n/ **(restrictions)** ◆◇◇ [1] A **restriction** is an official rule that limits what you can do or that limits the amount or size of something. (N-COUNT: oft N *on* n) ❑ *...the lifting of restrictions on political parties and the news media.* [2] You can refer to anything that limits what you can do as a **restriction**. (N-COUNT = limitation) ❑ *His parents are trying to make up to him for the restrictions of urban living.* [3] → See also **restrict**.

**re|stric|tive** /rɪstrɪktɪv/ Something that is **restrictive** prevents people from doing what they want to do, or from moving freely. (ADJ) ❑ *Britain is to adopt a more restrictive policy on arms sales.*

**re|stric|tive prac|tice** **(restrictive practices)** **Restrictive practices** are ways in which people involved in an industry, trade, or profession protect their own interests, rather than having a system which is fair to the public, employers, and other workers. (N-COUNT: usu pl) [BRIT, BUSINESS] ❑ *The Act was introduced to end restrictive practices in the docks.*

**rest room** **(rest rooms)** also **restroom**. In a restaurant, theatre, or other public place, a **rest room** is a room with a toilet for customers to use. (N-COUNT) [AM]

☑ in BRIT, usually use **toilet**

**re|struc|ture** /riːstrʌktʃə<sup>r</sup>/ **(restructures, restructuring, restructured)** To **restructure** an organization or system means to change the way it is organized, usually in order to make it work more effectively. (VERB) ❑ *The President called on educators and politicians to help him restructure American education.* (V n) ♦ **re|struc|tur|ing** **(restructurings)** *1,520 workers were laid off as part of a restructuring.* (N-VAR)

**rest stop** **(rest stops)** [1] On a long journey by road, a **rest stop** is a short period when you stop and leave your vehicle, for example to eat or go to the toilet. (N-COUNT) [2] A **rest stop** is a place beside a motorway or freeway where you can buy petrol and other things, or have a meal. (N-COUNT) [mainly AM]

☑ in BRIT, use **services**

**re|sult** /rɪzʌlt/ **(results, resulting, resulted)** ◆◆◆ [1] A **result** is something that happens or exists because of something else that has happened. (N-COUNT: oft *as a* N) ❑ *Compensation is available for people who have developed asthma as a direct result of their work.* [2] If something **results in** a particular situation or event, it causes that situation or event to happen. (VERB) ❑ *Fifty per cent of road accidents result in head injuries.* (V *in* n) [3] If something **results from** a particular event or action, it is caused by that event or action. (VERB) ❑ *Many hair problems result from what you eat... Ignore the early warnings and illness could result.* (V *from* n; V) [4] A **result** is the situation that exists at the end of a contest. (N-COUNT) ❑ *The final election results will be announced on Friday.* [5] A **result** is the number that you get when you do a calculation. (N-COUNT = answer) ❑ *They found their computers producing different results from exactly the same calculation.* [6] Your **results** are the marks or grades that you get for examinations you have taken. (N-COUNT: usu pl) [mainly BRIT] ❑ *Kate's exam results were excellent.*

☑ in AM, usually use **scores**

**re|sult|ant** /rɪzʌltənt/ **Resultant** means caused by the event just mentioned. (ADJ: ADJ n = consequent, ensuing) [FORMAL] ❑ *At least a quarter of a million people have died in the fighting and the resultant famines.*

**re|sume** /rɪzjuːm, AM -zuːm/ **(resumes, resuming, resumed)** ◆◇◇ [1] If you **resume** an activity or if it **resumes**, it begins again. (VERB) [FORMAL] ❑ *After the war he resumed his duties at Emmanuel College... The search is expected to resume early today.* (V n; V) ♦ **re|sump|tion** /rɪzʌmpʃ<sup>ə</sup>n/ *It is premature to speculate about the resumption of negotiations.* (N-UNCOUNT: usu N *of* n) [2] If you **resume** your seat or position, you return to the seat or position you were in before you moved. (VERB) [FORMAL] ❑ *'I changed my mind,' Blanche said, resuming her seat.* (V n) [3] If someone **resumes**, they begin speaking again after they have stopped for a short time. (VERB) [WRITTEN] ❑ *'Hey, Judith,' he resumed, 'tell me all about yourself.'* (V with quote)

**ré|su|mé** /rezjumeɪ, AM -zʊm-/ **(résumés)** also **resumé**. [1] A **résumé** is a short account, either spoken or written, of something that has happened or that someone has said or written. (N-COUNT: oft N of n/wh = summary) ❑ *I will leave with you a resumé of his most recent speech.* [2] Your **résumé** is a brief account of your personal details, your education, and the jobs you have had. You are often asked to send a résumé when you are applying for a job. (N-COUNT) [mainly AM]

☑ in BRIT, usually use **curriculum vitae**

**re|sur|face** /riːsɜː<sup>r</sup>fɪs/ **(resurfaces, resurfacing, resurfaced)** [1] If something such as an idea or problem **resurfaces**, it becomes important or noticeable again. (VERB) ❑ *These ideas resurfaced again in the American civil rights movement.* (V) [2] If someone who has not been seen for a long time **resurfaces**, (VERB = reappear) they suddenly appear again. [INFORMAL] ❑ *It is likely that they would go into hiding for a few weeks, and resurface when the publicity has died down.* V [3] If someone or something that has been under water **resurfaces**, they come back to the surface of the water again. ❑ *George struggled wildly, going under and resurfacing at regular intervals.* VERB V [4] To **resurface** something such as a road means to put a new surface on it. ❑ *Meanwhile the race is on to resurface the road before next Wednesday.* VERB V n

**re|sur|gence** /rɪsɜːʳdʒəns/ If there is a **resurgence of** an attitude or activity, it reappears and grows. [FORMAL] ❑ *Police say drugs traffickers are behind the resurgence of violence.* N-SING: also no det, oft N *of* n

**re|sur|gent** /rɪsɜːʳdʒənt/ You use **resurgent** to say that something is becoming stronger and more popular after a period when it has been weak and unimportant. [FORMAL] ❑ *...the threat from the resurgent nationalist movement.* ADJ: usu ADJ n

**res|ur|rect** /rezərekt/ **(resurrects, resurrecting, resurrected)** If you **resurrect** something, you cause it to exist again after it had disappeared or ended. ❑ *Attempts to resurrect the ceasefire have already failed once.* ♦ **res|ur|rec|tion** /rezərekʃən/ *This is a resurrection of an old story from the mid-70s.* VERB V n N-UNCOUNT

**Res|ur|rec|tion** /rezərekʃən/ In Christian belief, **the Resurrection** is the event in which Jesus Christ came back to life after he had been killed. N-PROPER: the N

**re|sus|ci|tate** /rɪsʌsɪteɪt/ **(resuscitates, resuscitating, resuscitated)** [1] If you **resuscitate** someone who has stopped breathing, you cause them to start breathing again. ❑ *A policeman and then a paramedic tried to resuscitate her.* ♦ **re|sus|ci|ta|tion** /rɪsʌsɪteɪʃən/ *Despite attempts at resuscitation, Mr Lynch died a week later in hospital.* VERB V n N-UNCOUNT [2] If you **resuscitate** something, you cause it to become active or successful again. ❑ *He has submitted a bid to resuscitate the struggling magazine.* ♦ **re|sus|ci|ta|tion** *The economy needs vigorous resuscitation.* VERB = revive V n N-UNCOUNT

**re|tail** /riːteɪl/ **(retails, retailing, retailed)** ◆◇◇ [1] **Retail** is the activity of selling goods direct to the public, usually in small quantities. Compare **wholesale**. [BUSINESS] ❑ *...retail stores... Retail sales grew just 3.8 percent last year.* N-UNCOUNT: usu N n [2] If something is sold **retail**, it is sold in ordinary shops direct to the public. [BUSINESS] ADV: ADV after v [3] If an item in a shop **retails at** or **for** a particular price, it is on sale at that price. [BUSINESS] ❑ *It originally retailed at £23.50.* → See also **retailing**. VERB = sell V *at/for* n

**re|tail|er** /riːteɪləʳ/ **(retailers)** A **retailer** is a person or business that sells goods to the public. [BUSINESS] ❑ *Furniture and carpet retailers are among those reporting the sharpest annual decline in sales.* N-COUNT

**re|tail|ing** /riːteɪlɪŋ/ **Retailing** is the activity of selling goods direct to the public, usually in small quantities. Compare **wholesaling**. [BUSINESS] ❑ *She spent fourteen years in retailing.* N-UNCOUNT: oft N n

**re|tail park** **(retail parks)** A **retail park** is a large specially built area, usually at the edge of a town or city, where there are a lot of large shops and sometimes other facilities such as cinemas and restaurants. N-COUNT

**re|tail price in|dex** **The retail price index** is a list of the prices of typical goods which shows how much the cost of living changes from one month to the next. [BRIT, BUSINESS] ❑ *The retail price index for September is expected to show inflation edging up to about 10.8 per cent.* N-PROPER: the N

> ✓ in AM, use **cost-of-living index**

**re|tain** /rɪteɪn/ **(retains, retaining, retained)** ◆◇◇ [1] To **retain** something means to continue to have that thing. [FORMAL] ❑ *The interior of the shop still retains a nineteenth-century atmosphere.* VERB V n [2] If you **retain** a lawyer, you pay him or her a fee to make sure that he or she will represent you when your case comes before the court. [LEGAL] ❑ *He decided to retain him for the trial.* VERB V n

**re|tain|er** /rɪteɪnəʳ/ **(retainers)** A **retainer** is a fee that you pay to someone in order to make sure that they will be available to do work for you if you need them to. ❑ *Liz was being paid a regular monthly retainer.* N-COUNT

**re|tain|ing wall** **(retaining walls)** A **retaining wall** is a wall that is built to prevent the earth behind it from moving. N-COUNT

**re|take** **(retakes, retaking, retook, retaken)**

> ✓ The verb is pronounced /riːteɪk/. The noun is pronounced /riːteɪk/.

[1] If a military force **retakes** a place or building which it has lost in a war or battle, it captures it again. ❑ *Residents were moved 30 miles away as the rebels retook the town.* VERB = recapture V n [2] If during the making of a film there is a **retake** of a particular scene, that scene is filmed again because it needs to be changed or improved. ❑ *The director, Ron Howard, was dissatisfied with Nicole's response even after several retakes.* N-COUNT [3] If you **retake** a course or an examination, you take it again because you failed it the first time. ❑ *I had one year in the sixth form to retake my GCSEs.* ♦ **Retake** is also a noun. ❑ *Limits will be placed on the number of exam retakes students can sit.* VERB V n N-COUNT = resit

**re|tali|ate** /rɪtælieɪt/ **(retaliates, retaliating, retaliated)** If you **retaliate** when someone harms or annoys you, you do something which harms or annoys them in return. ❑ *I was sorely tempted to retaliate... Christie retaliated by sending his friend a long letter detailing Carl's utter incompetence... The militia responded by saying it would retaliate against any attacks... They may retaliate with sanctions on other products if the bans are disregarded.* ♦ **re|talia|tion** /rɪtælieɪʃən/ *Police said they believed the attack was in retaliation for the death of the drug trafficker.* VERB V V *by* -ing V *against/for* n V *with* n N-UNCOUNT

**re|talia|tory** /rɪtæliətəri, AM -tɔːri/ If you take **retaliatory** action, you try to harm or annoy someone who has harmed or annoyed you. [FORMAL] ❑ *There's been talk of a retaliatory blockade to prevent supplies getting through.* ADJ: usu ADJ n

**re|tard** **(retards, retarding, retarded)**

> ✓ The verb is pronounced /rɪtɑːʳd/. The noun is pronounced /riːtɑːʳd/.

[1] If something **retards** a process, or the development of something, it makes it happen more slowly. [FORMAL] ❑ *Continuing violence will retard negotiations over the country's future.* VERB = slow down V n [2] If you describe someone as a **retard**, you mean that they have not developed normally, either mentally or socially. [INFORMAL, OFFENSIVE] ❑ *What the hell do I want with an emotional retard?* N-COUNT disapproval

**re|tar|da|tion** /riːtɑːʳdeɪʃən/ **Retardation** is the process of making something happen or develop more slowly, or the fact of being less well developed than other people or things of the same kind. [FORMAL] ❑ *...other parents whose children had mental retardation.* N-UNCOUNT: usu supp N

**re|tard|ed** /rɪtɑːʳdɪd/ Someone who is **retarded** is much less advanced mentally than most people of their age. [OLD-FASHIONED] ❑ *...a special school for mentally retarded children.* ADJ

**retch** /retʃ/ **(retches, retching, retched)** If you **retch**, your stomach moves as if you are vomiting. ❑ *The smell made me retch.* VERB = heave V

**retd** **retd** is a written abbreviation for **retired**. It is used after someone's name to indicate that they have retired from the army, navy, or air force. ❑ *...Commander J. R. Simpson, RN (retd).*

**re|tell** /riːtel/ **(retells, retelling, retold)** If you **retell** a story, you write it, tell it, or present it again, often in a different way from its original form. ❑ *Lucilla often asks her sisters to retell the story.* VERB V n

**re|ten|tion** /rɪtenʃən/ The **retention of** something is the keeping of it. [FORMAL] ❑ *They supported the retention of a strong central government.* N-UNCOUNT: oft N *of* n, n N

**re|ten|tive** /rɪtentɪv/ If you have a **retentive** memory, you are able to remember things very well. ❑ *Luke had an amazingly retentive memory.* ADJ: usu ADJ n

**re|think** /riːθɪŋk/ **(rethinks, rethinking, rethought)** 1 If you **rethink** something such as a problem, a plan, or a policy, you think about it again and change it. ❑ *Both major political parties are having to rethink their policies.* ♦ **re|think|ing** *...some fundamental rethinking of the way in which pilots are trained.* 2 If you have a **rethink** of a problem, a plan, or a policy, you think about it again and change it. [JOURNALISM] ❑ *There must be a rethink of government policy towards this vulnerable group.*
VERB; V n; N-UNCOUNT; N-SING: oft N *of/on* n

**re|thought** /riːθɔːt/ **Rethought** is the past tense and past participle of **rethink**.

**reti|cent** /retɪsənt/ Someone who is **reticent** does not tell people about things. ❑ *She is so reticent about her achievements.* ♦ **reti|cence** *Pearl didn't mind his reticence; in fact she liked it.*
ADJ: oft ADJ *about/on* n; N-UNCOUNT

**reti|na** /retɪnə/ **(retinas)** Your **retina** is the area at the back of your eye. It receives the image that you see and then sends the image to your brain.
N-COUNT

**reti|nal** /retɪnᵊl/ **Retinal** means relating to a person's retina. [TECHNICAL] ❑ *...retinal cancer.*
ADJ: ADJ n

**reti|nue** /retɪnjuː, AM -nuː/ **(retinues)** An important person's **retinue** is the group of servants, friends, or assistants who go with them and look after their needs. ❑ *Mind trainers are now part of a tennis star's retinue.*
N-COUNT: usu with supp, oft N *of* n = entourage

**re|tire** /rɪtaɪəʳ/ **(retires, retiring, retired)** ♦◇◇ 1 When older people **retire**, they leave their job and usually stop working completely. ❑ *At the age when most people retire, he is ready to face a new career... In 1974 he retired from the museum.* 2 When a sports player **retires from** their sport, they stop playing in competitions. When they **retire from** a race or a match, they stop competing in it. ❑ *I have decided to retire from Formula One racing at the end of the season.* 3 If you **retire to** another room or place, you go there. [FORMAL] ❑ *Eisenhower left the White House and retired to his farm in Gettysburg.* 4 When a jury in a court of law **retires**, the members of it leave the court in order to decide whether someone is guilty or innocent. ❑ *The jury will retire to consider its verdict today.* 5 When you **retire**, you go to bed. [FORMAL] ❑ *She retires early most nights, exhausted... Some time after midnight, he retired to bed.* 6 → See also **retired**, **retiring**.
VERB; V; V *from* n; VERB; V *from* n; VERB; V *to* n; VERB; V; VERB; V; V *to* n

**re|tired** /rɪtaɪəʳd/ 1 A **retired** person is an older person who has left his or her job and has usually stopped working completely. ❑ *...a seventy-three-year-old retired teacher from Florida.* 2 → See also **retire**.
ADJ: usu ADJ n

**re|tiree** /rɪtaɪəriː/ **(retirees)** A **retiree** is a retired person. [mainly AM] ❑ *...retirees who have completely different expectations of what later life might bring.*
N-COUNT

**re|tire|ment** /rɪtaɪəʳmənt/ **(retirements)** ♦◇◇ 1 **Retirement** is the time when a worker retires. ❑ *...the proportion of the population who are over retirement age.* 2 A person's **retirement** is the period in their life after they have retired. ❑ *...financial support for the elderly during retirement.*
N-VAR: oft N n; N-UNCOUNT

**re|tire|ment home (retirement homes)** A **retirement home** is a place where old people live and are cared for when they are too old to look after themselves.
N-COUNT = rest home, old people's home

**re|tir|ing** /rɪtaɪərɪŋ/ 1 Someone who is **retiring** is shy and avoids meeting other people. ❑ *I'm still that shy, retiring little girl who was afraid to ask for sweets in the shop.* 2 → See also **retire**.
ADJ

**re|told** /riːtoʊld/ **Retold** is the past tense and past participle of **retell**.

**re|took** /riːtʊk/ **Retook** is the past tense of **retake**.

**re|tool** /riːtuːl/ **(retools, retooling, retooled)** If the machines in a factory or the items of equipment used by a firm **are retooled**, they are replaced or changed so that they can do new tasks. ❑ *Each time the product changes, the machines have to be retooled.* ♦ **re|tool|ing** *Retooling, or recasting new toy moulds, is a slow and expensive process.*
VERB; *be* V-ed; Also V n, V; N-UNCOUNT

**re|tort** /rɪtɔːʳt/ **(retorts, retorting, retorted)** To **retort** means to reply angrily to someone. [WRITTEN] ❑ *Was he afraid, he was asked. 'Afraid of what?' he retorted... Others retort that strong central power is a dangerous thing in Russia.* ♦ **Retort** is also a noun. ❑ *His sharp retort clearly made an impact.*
VERB; V with quote; V that; N-COUNT

**re|touch** /riːtʌtʃ/ **(retouches, retouching, retouched)** If someone **retouches** something such as a picture or a photograph, they improve it, for example by painting over parts of it. ❑ *He said the photographs had been retouched... She retouched her make-up.*
VERB; *be* V-ed; V n

**re|trace** /rɪtreɪs/ **(retraces, retracing, retraced)** If you **retrace** your steps or **retrace** your way, you return to the place you started from by going back along the same route. ❑ *He retraced his steps to the spot where he'd left the case.*
VERB; V n

**re|tract** /rɪtrækt/ **(retracts, retracting, retracted)** 1 If you **retract** something that you have said or written, you say that you did not mean it. [FORMAL] ❑ *Mr Smith hurriedly sought to retract the statement, but it had just been broadcast on national radio... He's hoping that if he makes me feel guilty, I'll retract.* ♦ **re|trac|tion** /rɪtrækʃᵊn/ **(retractions)** *Miss Pearce said she expected an unqualified retraction of his comments within twenty four hours.* 2 When a part of a machine or a part of a person's body **retracts** or **is retracted**, it moves inwards or becomes shorter. [FORMAL] ❑ *Torn muscles retract, and lose strength, structure, and tightness.*
VERB; V n; V; N-COUNT: usu sing = withdrawal; VERB; V; Also V n

**re|tract|able** /rɪtræktəbᵊl/ A **retractable** part of a machine or a building can be moved inwards or backwards. ❑ *A 20,000-seat arena with a retractable roof is planned.*
ADJ: usu ADJ n

**re|train** /riːtreɪn/ **(retrains, retraining, retrained)** If you **retrain**, or if someone **retrains** you, you learn new skills, especially in order to get a new job. ❑ *Why not retrain for a job which will make you happier?... Union leaders have called upon the government to help retrain workers.* ♦ **re|train|ing** *...measures such as the retraining of the workforce at their place of work.*
VERB; V; V n; N-UNCOUNT: oft N n

**re|tread** /riːtred/ **(retreads)** 1 If you describe something such as a book, film, or song as a **retread**, you mean that it contains ideas or elements that have been used before, and that it is not very interesting or original. ❑ *His last book, 'Needful Things', was a retread of tired material.* 2 A **retread** is an old tyre which has been given a new surface or tread and can be used again.
N-COUNT: usu sing, oft N *of* n [disapproval]; N-COUNT = remould

**re|treat** /rɪtriːt/ **(retreats, retreating, retreated)** ♦◇◇ 1 If you **retreat**, you move away from something or someone. ❑ *'I've already got a job,' I said quickly, and retreated from the room.* 2 When an army **retreats**, it moves away from enemy forces in order to avoid fighting them. ❑ *The French, suddenly outnumbered, were forced to retreat.* ♦ **Retreat** is also a noun. ❑ *In June 1942, the British 8th Army was in full retreat.* 3 If you **retreat from** something such as a plan or a way of life, you give it up, usually in order to do something safer or less extreme. ❑ *I believe people should live in houses that allow them to retreat from the harsh realities of life.* ♦ **Retreat** is also a noun. ❑ *The President's remarks appear to signal that there will be no retreat from his position.* 4 A **retreat** is a quiet, isolated place that you go to in order to rest or to do things in private. ❑ *He spent yesterday hidden away in his country retreat.* 5 If you **beat a retreat**, you leave a place quickly in order to avoid an embarrassing or dangerous situation. ❑ *Cockburn decided it was time to beat a hasty retreat.*
VERB; V prep; Also V; VERB; V; N-VAR; VERB; V *from/into* n; N-VAR: usu N *from/into* n; N-COUNT: oft supp N; PHRASE: V inflects

**re|trench** /rɪtrentʃ/ **(retrenches, retrenching, retrenched)** If a person or organization **retrenches**, they spend less money. [FORMAL] ❑ *Shortly afterwards, cuts in defence spending forced the aerospace industry to retrench.*
VERB; V

**re|trench|ment** /rɪtrentʃmənt/ **(retrenchments)** **Retrenchment** means spending less money. [FORMAL] ❑ *Defense planners predict an extended period of retrenchment.* N-VAR

**re|tri|al** /riːtraɪəl/ **(retrials)** A **retrial** is a second trial of someone for the same offence. ❑ *Judge Ian Starforth Hill said the jury's task was 'beyond the realms of possibility' and ordered a retrial.* N-COUNT: usu sing

**ret|ri|bu|tion** /retrɪbjuːʃən/ **Retribution** is punishment for a crime, especially punishment which is carried out by someone other than the official authorities. [FORMAL] ❑ *He didn't want any further involvement for fear of retribution.* N-UNCOUNT

**re|triev|al** /rɪtriːvəl/ 1 The **retrieval** of information from a computer is the process of getting it back. ❑ *...electronic storage and retrieval systems.* N-UNCOUNT 2 The **retrieval** of something is the process of getting it back from a particular place, especially from a place where it should not be. ❑ *Its real purpose is the launching and retrieval of small aeroplanes in flight.* N-UNCOUNT = recovery

**re|trieve** /rɪtriːv/ **(retrieves, retrieving, retrieved)** 1 If you **retrieve** something, you get it back from the place where you left it. ❑ *The men were trying to retrieve weapons left when the army abandoned the island.* VERB = recover V n 2 If you manage to **retrieve** a situation, you succeed in bringing it back into a more acceptable state. ❑ *He is the one man who could retrieve that situation.* VERB V n 3 To **retrieve** information from a computer or from your memory means to get it back. ❑ *Computers can instantly retrieve millions of information bits.* VERB V n

**re|triev|er** /rɪtriːvəʳ/ **(retrievers)** A **retriever** is a kind of dog. Retrievers are traditionally used to bring back birds and animals which their owners have shot. N-COUNT

**ret|ro** /retroʊ/ **Retro** clothes, music, and objects are based on the styles of the past. [JOURNALISM] ❑ *...clothes shops where original versions of today's retro looks can be found.* ADJ

**retro-** /retroʊ-/ **Retro-** is used to form adjectives and nouns which indicate that something goes back or goes backwards. ❑ *...exotic effects and retro-style photography.* PREFIX

**retro|ac|tive** /retroʊæktɪv/ If a decision or action is **retroactive**, it is intended to take effect from a date in the past. [FORMAL] ❑ *There are few precedents for this sort of retroactive legislation.* ADJ = retrospective ♦ **retro|ac|tive|ly** *It isn't yet clear whether the new law can actually be applied retroactively.* ADV: ADV with v

**retro|fit** /retroʊfɪt/ **(retrofits, retrofitting, retrofitted)** To **retrofit** a machine or a building means to put new parts or new equipment in it after it has been in use for some time, especially to improve its safety or make it work better. ❑ *Much of this business involves retrofitting existing planes.* VERB V n ♦ **Retrofit** is also a noun. ❑ *A retrofit may involve putting in new door jambs.* N-COUNT; also N n

**retro|grade** /retrəgreɪd/ A **retrograde** action is one that you think makes a situation worse rather than better. [FORMAL] ❑ *The Prime Minister described transferring education to central government funding as 'a retrograde step'.* ADJ: usu ADJ n

**retro|gres|sion** /retrəgreʃən/ **Retrogression** means moving back to an earlier and less efficient stage of development. [FORMAL] ❑ *There has been a retrogression in the field of human rights since 1975.* N-UNCOUNT: also a N = regression

**retro|gres|sive** /retrəgresɪv/ If you describe an action or idea as **retrogressive**, you disapprove of it because it returns to old ideas or beliefs and does not take advantage of recent progress. [FORMAL] ❑ *...the retrogressive policies of the National parties.* ADJ [disapproval] = regressive

**retro|spect** /retrəspekt/ When you consider something **in retrospect**, you think about it afterwards, and often have a different opinion about it from the one that you had at the time. ❑ *In retrospect, I wish that I had thought about alternative courses of action.* PHRASE: PHR with cl

**retro|spec|tive** /retrəspektɪv/ **(retrospectives)** 1 A **retrospective** is an exhibition or showing of work done by an artist over many years, rather than his or her most recent work. ❑ *...a retrospective of the films of Judy Garland.* N-COUNT 2 **Retrospective** feelings or opinions concern things that happened in the past. ❑ *Afterwards, retrospective fear of the responsibility would make her feel almost faint.* ADJ: usu ADJ n ♦ **retro|spec|tive|ly** *Retrospectively, it seems as if they probably were negligent.* ADV: ADV with cl, ADV with v 3 **Retrospective** laws or legal actions take effect from a date before the date when they are officially approved. ❑ *Bankers are quick to condemn retrospective tax legislation.* ADJ: usu ADJ n ♦ **retro|spec|tive|ly** *...a decree which retrospectively changes the electoral law under which last year's national elections were held.* ADV: ADV with v

**re|tune** /riːtjuːn, AM -tuːn/ **(retunes, retuning, retuned)** To **retune** a piece of equipment such as a radio, television, or video means to adjust it so that it receives a different channel, or so that it receives the same channel on a different frequency. ❑ *...this means that listeners in cars should not have to retune as they drive across the country. ...plans to retune VCRs to allow viewers to receive the signal.* VERB V V n

**re|turn** /rɪtɜːʳn/ **(returns, returning, returned)** ◆◆◆ 1 When you **return to** a place, you go back there after you have been away. ❑ *Blair will return to London tonight... So far more than 350,000 people have returned home.* VERB V to/from n V adv 2 Your **return** is your arrival back at a place where you had been before. ❑ *Ryle explained the reason for his sudden return to London.* N-SING: with poss 3 If you **return** something that you have borrowed or taken, you give it back or put it back. ❑ *I enjoyed the book and said so when I returned it.* VERB V n ♦ **Return** is also a noun. ❑ *The main demand of the Indians is for the return of one-and-a-half-million acres of forest to their communities.* N-SING: usu N of n 4 If you **return** something somewhere, you put it back where it was. ❑ *He returned the notebook to his jacket.* VERB V n to n 5 If you **return** someone's action, you do the same thing to them as they have just done to you. If you **return** someone's feeling, you feel the same way towards them as they feel towards you. ❑ *Back at the station the Chief Inspector returned the call.* VERB V n 6 If a feeling or situation **returns**, it comes back or happens again after a period when it was not present. ❑ *Official reports in Algeria suggest that calm is returning to the country.* VERB V ♦ **Return** is also a noun. ❑ *It was like the return of his youth.* N-SING: with supp 7 If you **return to** a state that you were in before, you start being in that state again. ❑ *Life has improved and returned to normal.* VERB V to n ♦ **Return** is also a noun. ❑ *He made an uneventful return to normal health.* N-SING: N to n 8 If you **return to** a subject that you have mentioned before, you begin talking about it again. ❑ *The power of the Church is one theme all these writers return to.* VERB V to n 9 If you **return to** an activity that you were doing before, you start doing it again. ❑ *At that stage he will be 52, young enough to return to politics if he wishes to do so.* VERB V to n ♦ **Return** is also a noun. ❑ *He has not ruled out the shock possibility of a return to football.* N-SING: N to n 10 When a judge or jury **returns** a verdict, they announce whether they think the person on trial is guilty or not. ❑ *They returned a verdict of not guilty.* VERB V n 11 A **return** ticket is a ticket for a journey from one place to another and then back again. [mainly BRIT] ❑ *He bought a return ticket and boarded the next train for home.* ADJ: usu ADJ n ♦ **Return** is also a noun. ❑ *BA and Air France charge more than £400 for a return to Nice.* N-COUNT → See also **day return**.

☑ in AM, usually use **round trip**

12 The **return** trip or journey is the part of a journey that takes you back to where you started from. ❑ *Buy an extra ticket for the return trip.* ADJ: ADJ n ≠ outward 13 The **return on** an investment is the profit that you get from it. [BUSINESS] ❑ *Profits have picked up this year but the return on capital remains tiny.* N-COUNT 14 A tax **return** is an official form that you fill in with details about your income and personal situation, so that the income tax you owe can be calculated. ❑ *He was convicted of filing false income* N-COUNT

*tax returns... Anyone with slight complications in their tax affairs is likely to be asked to fill in a return.* → See also **tax return.** 15 When it is someone's birthday, people sometimes say **'Many happy returns'** to them as a way of greeting them. CONVENTION formulae

PHRASES 16 If you do something **in return for** what someone else has done for you, you do it because they did that thing for you. ❑ *The deal offers an increase in policy value in return for giving up guarantees.* PHRASE 17 If you say that you have reached **the point of no return**, you mean that you now have to continue with what you are doing and it is too late to stop. ❑ *The release of Mr Nelson Mandela marked the point of no return in South Africa's movement away from apartheid.* PHRASE 18 to **return fire** → see **fire.**

**re|turn|able** /rɪtɜːʳnəbᵊl/ 1 **Returnable** containers are intended to be taken back to the place they came from so that they can be used again. ❑ *All beverages must be sold in returnable containers.* ADJ: usu ADJ n ≠ non-returnable 2 If something such as a sum of money or a document is **returnable**, it will eventually be given back to the person who provided it. ❑ *Landlords can charge a returnable deposit.* ADJ: usu ADJ n

**re|turnee** /rɪtɜːʳniː/ **(returnees)** A **returnee** is a person who returns to the country where they were born, usually after they have been away for a long time. ❑ *The number of returnees could go as high as half a million.* N-COUNT: usu pl

**re|turn|er** /rɪtɜːʳnəʳ/ **(returners)** A **returner** is someone who returns to work after a period when they did not work, especially a woman who returns after having children. [BRIT] ❑ *Many returners are far better at working with people than they were when they were younger.* N-COUNT

**re|turn|ing of|fic|er** **(returning officers)** In Britain, the **returning officer** for a particular town or district is an official who is responsible for arranging an election and who formally announces the result. N-COUNT

**re|turn match** **(return matches)** A **return match** is the second of two matches that are played by two sports teams or two players. [BRIT] N-COUNT: usu sing

✔ in AM, use **rematch**

**re|turn vis|it** **(return visits)** If you make a **return visit**, you visit someone who has already visited you, or you go back to a place where you have already been once. ❑ *He made a nostalgic return visit to Germany.* N-COUNT

**re|uni|fi|ca|tion** /riːjuːnɪfɪkeɪʃᵊn/ The **reunification** of a country or city that has been divided into two or more parts for some time is the joining of it together again. ❑ *...the reunification of East and West Beirut in 1991.* N-UNCOUNT: with supp

**re|union** /riːjuːniən/ **(reunions)** 1 A **reunion** is a party attended by members of the same family, school, or other group who have not seen each other for a long time. ❑ *The Association holds an annual reunion.* N-COUNT: usu with supp 2 A **reunion** is a meeting between people who have been separated for some time. ❑ *The children weren't allowed to see her for nearly a week. It was a very emotional reunion.* N-VAR: usu with supp

**re|unite** /riːjuːnaɪt/ **(reunites, reuniting, reunited)** 1 If people **are reunited**, or if they **reunite**, they meet each other again after they have been separated for some time. ❑ *She and her youngest son were finally allowed to be reunited with their family...* VERB be V-ed with n *She spent the post-war years of her marriage trying to reunite father and son...* V n *The band will reunite for this show only.* V 2 If a divided organization or country **is reunited**, or if it **reunites**, it becomes one united organization or country again. ❑ *...a federation under which the divided island would be reunited...* VERB be V-ed *His first job will be to reunite the army.* V n *...celebrations when East and West Germany reunited.* V

**re|us|able** /riːjuːzəbᵊl/ also **re-usable.** Things that are **reusable** can be used more than once. ❑ *...re-usable plastic containers.* ADJ ≠ disposable

**re|use** **(reuses, reusing, reused)**

✔ The verb is pronounced /riːjuːz/. The noun is pronounced /riːjuːs/.

When you **reuse** something, you use it again instead of throwing it away. ❑ *Try where possible to reuse paper.* VERB V n ♦ **Reuse** is also a noun. ❑ *Copper, brass and aluminium are separated for reuse.* N-UNCOUNT

**rev** /rev/ **(revs, revving, revved)** 1 When the engine of a vehicle **revs**, or when you **rev** it, the engine speed is increased as the accelerator is pressed. ❑ *The engine started, revved and the car jerked away down the hill...* VERB V *The old bus was revving its engine, ready to start the journey back towards Madrid.* V n ♦ **Rev up** means the same as **rev.** ❑ *...drivers revving up their engines. ...the sound of a car revving up.* PHRASAL VERB V P n (not pron), V P 2 If you talk about the **revs** of an engine, you are referring to its speed, which is measured in revolutions per minute. ❑ *The engine delivers instant acceleration whatever the revs.* N-PLURAL

**Rev.**

✔ The spelling **Rev** is also used.

**Rev.** is a written abbreviation for **Reverend.** ❑ *...the Rev John Roberts.*

✔ in BRIT, use **Revd**

**re|value** /riːvæljuː/ **(revalues, revaluing, revalued)** 1 When a country **revalues** its currency, it increases the currency's value so that it can buy more foreign currency than before. ❑ *Countries enjoying surpluses will be under no pressure to revalue their currencies.* VERB V n ♦ **re|valua|tion** /riːvæljuːeɪʃᵊn/ **(revaluations)** *There was a general revaluation of other currencies but not the pound.* N-VAR: oft N of n 2 To **revalue** something means to increase the amount that you calculate it is worth so that its value stays roughly the same in comparison with other things, even if there is inflation. ❑ *It is now usual to revalue property assets on a more regular basis.* VERB V n ♦ **re|valua|tion** *Some British banks have used doubtful property revaluations to improve their capital ratios.* N-VAR: oft N of n

**re|vamp** /riːvæmp/ **(revamps, revamping, revamped)** If someone **revamps** something, they make changes to it in order to try and improve it. ❑ *All Italy's political parties have accepted that it is time to revamp the system...* VERB V n *Ricardo Bofill, the Catalan architect, has designed the revamped airport.* V-ed ♦ **Revamp** is also a noun. ❑ *The revamp includes replacing the old navy uniform with a crisp blue and white cotton outfit.* N-SING ♦ **re|vamp|ing** *Expected changes include a revamping of the courts.* N-SING: with supp

**rev coun|ter** A **rev counter** is an instrument in a car or an aeroplane which shows the speed of the engine. [BRIT] → See picture on page 1708. N-SING = tachometer

**Revd** **Revd** is a written abbreviation for **Reverend.** [BRIT] ❑ *...the Revd Alfred Gatty.*

✔ in AM, use **Rev.**

**re|veal** /rɪviːl/ **(reveals, revealing, revealed)** ◆◆◇ 1 To **reveal** something means to make people aware of it. ❑ *She has refused to reveal the whereabouts of her daughter...* VERB V n *A survey of the British diet has revealed that a growing number of people are overweight...* V that *No test will reveal how much of the drug was taken.* V wh 2 If you **reveal** something that has been out of sight, you uncover it so that people can see it. ❑ *A grey carpet was removed to reveal the original pine floor.* VERB = show V n

**re|veal|ing** /rɪviːlɪŋ/ 1 A **revealing** statement, account, or action tells you something that you did not know, especially about the person doing it or making it. ❑ *...a revealing interview.* ADJ ♦ **re|veal|ing|ly** *Even more revealingly, he says: 'There's no such thing as failure.'* ADV 2 **Revealing** clothes allow more of a person's body to be seen than is usual. ❑ *...a tight and revealing dress.* ADJ

**re|veil|le** /rɪvæli, AM revəli/ **Reveille** is the time when soldiers have to get up in the morning. ❑ *It must be nearly six; soon would be reveille and the end of the night's rest.* N-UNCOUNT

**rev|el** /revᵊl/ **(revels, revelling, revelled)**

✔ in AM, use **reveling, reveled**

1 If you **revel in** a situation or experience, you enjoy it very much. ❑ *Revelling in her freedom, she took a hotel room and stayed for several days.* VERB; V *in* n
2 **Revels** are noisy celebrations. [LITERARY] N-COUNT: usu pl

**rev|ela|tion** /revəleɪʃᵊn/ **(revelations)** 1 A **revelation** is a surprising or interesting fact that is made known to people. ❑ *...the seemingly everlasting revelations about his private life.* N-COUNT: oft N *about* n, N that
2 The **revelation of** something is the act of making it known. ❑ *...following the revelation of his affair with a former secretary.* N-VAR: oft N *of* n
3 If you say that something you experienced was **a revelation**, you are saying that it was very surprising or very good. ❑ *Degas's work had been a revelation to her.* N-SING: *a* N, oft N *to* n
4 A divine **revelation** is a sign or explanation from God about his nature or purpose. N-VAR

**rev|ela|tory** /revələtəri, AM -tɔːri/ A **revelatory** account or statement tells you a lot that you did not know. ❑ *...Barbara Stoney's revelatory account of the author's life.* ADJ

**rev|el|ler** /revələʳ/ **(revellers)**

✔ in AM, use **reveler**

**Revellers** are people who are enjoying themselves in a noisy way, often while they are drunk. [LITERARY] ❑ *Many of the revellers are day-trippers.* N-COUNT: usu pl

**rev|el|ry** /revᵊlri/ **(revelries) Revelry** is people enjoying themselves in a noisy way, often while they are drunk. [LITERARY] ❑ *...New Year revelries.* N-UNCOUNT: also N in pl

**re|venge** /rɪvendʒ/ **(revenges, revenging, revenged)** 1 **Revenge** involves hurting or punishing someone who has hurt or harmed you. ❑ *The attackers were said to be taking revenge on the 14-year-old, claiming he was a school bully.* N-UNCOUNT: oft N *on/for/against* n
2 If you **revenge** yourself on someone who has hurt you, you hurt them in return. [WRITTEN] ❑ *The Sunday Mercury accused her of trying to revenge herself on her former lover.* *...relatives wanting to revenge the dead.* VERB = avenge; V pron-refl *on* n; V n

**rev|enue** /revənjuː/ **(revenues) Revenue** is money that a company, organization, or government receives from people. [BUSINESS] ❑ *...a boom year at the cinema, with record advertising revenue and the highest ticket sales since 1980.* → See also **Inland Revenue**. ◆◇◇ N-UNCOUNT: also N in pl, usu with supp

**re|verb** /riːvɜːʳb, rɪvɜːʳb/ **Reverb** is a shaking or echoing effect that is added to a sound, often by an electronic device. ❑ *The unit includes built-in digital effects like reverb.* N-UNCOUNT

**re|ver|ber|ate** /rɪvɜːʳbəreɪt/ **(reverberates, reverberating, reverberated)** 1 When a loud sound **reverberates** through a place, it echoes through it. ❑ *The sound of the tank guns reverberated through the little Bavarian town...* *A woman's shrill laughter reverberated in the courtyard.* VERB; V prep; V
2 You can say that an event or idea **reverberates** when it has a powerful effect which lasts a long time. ❑ *The controversy surrounding the take-over yesterday continued to reverberate around the television industry...* *The news sent shock waves through the community that have continued to reverberate to this day.* VERB; V prep; V

**re|ver|bera|tion** /rɪvɜːʳbəreɪʃᵊn/ **(reverberations)** 1 **Reverberations** are serious effects that follow a sudden, dramatic event. ❑ *The move by the two London colleges is sending reverberations through higher education.* N-COUNT: usu pl
2 A **reverberation** is the shaking and echoing effect that you hear after a loud sound has been made. ❑ *Jason heard the reverberation of the slammed door.* N-VAR = echo

**re|vere** /rɪvɪəʳ/ **(reveres, revering, revered)** If you **revere** someone or something, you respect and admire them greatly. [FORMAL] ❑ *The Chinese revered corn as a gift from heaven.* ♦ **re|vered** *...some of the country's most revered institutions.* VERB; V n; ADJ: usu ADJ n

**rev|er|ence** /revərəns/ **Reverence for** someone or something is a feeling of great respect for them. [FORMAL] ❑ *...showing a deep reverence for their religion.* N-UNCOUNT

**Rev|er|end** /revərənd/ **Reverend** is a title used before the name or rank of an officially appointed religious leader. The abbreviation **Rev** or **Revd** is also used. ❑ *The service was led by the Reverend Jim Simons.* N-TITLE: oft *the* N n

**rev|er|ent** /revərənt/ If you describe someone's behaviour as **reverent**, you mean that they are showing great respect for a person or thing. ❑ *...the reverent hush of a rapt audience.* ♦ **rev|er|ent|ly** *He got up and took the book out almost reverently.* ADJ ≠ irreverent; ADV: usu ADV after v

**rev|er|en|tial** /revərenʃᵊl/ Something that is **reverential** has the qualities of respect and admiration. [FORMAL] ❑ *'That's the old foresters' garden,' she said in reverential tones.* ♦ **rev|er|en|tial|ly** *He reverentially returned the novel to a glass-fronted bookcase.* ADJ; ADV: ADV with v

**rev|erie** /revəri/ **(reveries)** A **reverie** is a state of imagining or thinking about pleasant things, as if you are dreaming. [FORMAL] ❑ *The announcer's voice brought Holden out of his reverie.* N-COUNT = daydream

**re|ver|sal** /rɪvɜːʳsᵊl/ **(reversals)** 1 A **reversal of** a process, policy, or trend is a complete change in it. ❑ *The Financial Times says the move represents a complete reversal of previous US policy.* N-COUNT: oft N *of* n
2 When there is a role **reversal** or a **reversal of** roles, two people or groups exchange their positions or functions. ❑ *When children end up taking care of their parents, it is a strange role reversal indeed.* N-COUNT: n N, N *of* n

**re|verse** /rɪvɜːʳs/ **(reverses, reversing, reversed)** ◆◇◇ 1 When someone or something **reverses** a decision, policy, or trend, they change it to the opposite decision, policy, or trend. ❑ *They have made it clear they will not reverse the decision to increase prices.* VERB; V n
2 If you **reverse** the order of a set of things, you arrange them in the opposite order, so that the first thing comes last. ❑ *The normal word order is reversed in passive sentences.* VERB; *be* V-ed
3 If you **reverse** the positions or functions of two things, you change them so that each thing has the position or function that the other one had. ❑ *He reversed the position of the two stamps.* VERB; V n
4 When a car **reverses** or when you **reverse** it, the car is driven backwards. [mainly BRIT] ❑ *Another car reversed out of the drive...* *He reversed his car straight at the policeman.* VERB; V; V n

✔ in AM, usually use **back up**

5 If your car is **in reverse**, you have changed gear so that you can drive it backwards. ❑ *He lurched the car in reverse along the ruts to the access road.* N-UNCOUNT: usu *in/into* N
6 **Reverse** means opposite to what you expect or to what has just been described. ❑ *The wrong attitude will have exactly the reverse effect.* ADJ: usu ADJ n = opposite
7 If you say that one thing is **the reverse** of another, you are emphasizing that the first thing is the complete opposite of the second thing. ❑ *There is absolutely no evidence at all that spectators want longer cricket matches. Quite the reverse.* N-SING: *the* N
8 A **reverse** is a serious failure or defeat. [FORMAL] ❑ *It's clear that the party of the former Prime Minister has suffered a major reverse.* N-COUNT = setback
9 **The reverse** or **the reverse side** of a flat object which has two sides is the less important or the other side. ❑ *Cheques should be made payable to Country Living and your address written on the reverse.* N-SING: *the* N = back ≠ front

**PHRASES** 10 If something happens **in reverse** or goes **into reverse**, things happen in the opposite way to what usually happens or to what has been happening. ❑ *Amis tells the story in reverse, from the moment the man dies.* PHRASE: v PHR
11 If you **reverse the charges** when you make a telephone call, the person who you are phoning pays the cost of the call and not you. [BRIT] PHRASE: V inflects

✔ in AM, use **call collect**

**re|verse charge call** **(reverse charge calls)** A **reverse charge call** is a telephone call which is paid for by the person who receives the call, rather than the person who makes the call. [BRIT] N-COUNT

✔ in AM, use **collect call**

**re|verse dis|crimi|na|tion** N-UNCOUNT **Reverse discrimination** is the same as **positive discrimination.** ❑ *...a policy of reverse discrimination in favour of children from poor backgrounds.*

**re|verse en|gi|neer|ing** N-UNCOUNT **Reverse engineering** is a process in which a product or system is analysed in order to see how it works, so that a similar version of the product or system can be produced more cheaply. [BUSINESS] ❑ *Xerox set about a process of reverse engineering. It pulled the machines apart and investigated the Japanese factories to find out how they could pull off such feats.*

**re|verse gear** **(reverse gears)** N-VAR The **reverse gear** of a vehicle is the gear which you use in order to make the vehicle go backwards.

**re|verse video** N-UNCOUNT **Reverse video** is the process of reversing the colours of normal characters and background on a computer screen, in order to highlight the display. [COMPUTING]

**re|vers|ible** /rɪvɜːʳsɪbᵊl/ 1 ADJ ≠ irreversible If a process or an action is **reversible**, its effects can be reversed so that the original situation returns. ❑ *Heart disease is reversible in some cases, according to a study published last summer.* 2 ADJ **Reversible** clothes or materials have been made so that either side can be worn or shown as the outside. ❑ *...a reversible waistcoat.*

**re|vers|ing light** **(reversing lights)** N-COUNT: usu pl **Reversing lights** are the white lights on the back of a motor vehicle which shine when the vehicle is in reverse gear. [BRIT]

☑ in AM, use **back-up lights**

**re|ver|sion** /rɪvɜːʳʃᵊn/ **(reversions)** 1 N-SING: also no det, N *to* n = return A **reversion to** a previous state, system, or kind of behaviour is a change back to it. ❑ *This is a reversion to the system under which the Royals were paid for nearly 300 years.* 2 N-VAR: oft *the* N *of* n *to* n **The reversion of** land or property **to** a person, family, or country is the return to them of the ownership or control of the land or property. [LEGAL]

**re|vert** /rɪvɜːʳt/ **(reverts, reverting, reverted)** 1 VERB When people or things **revert to** a previous state, system, or type of behaviour, they go back to it. ❑ V *to* n *Jackson said her boss became increasingly depressed and reverted to smoking heavily.* 2 VERB When someone **reverts to** a previous topic, they start talking or thinking about it again. [WRITTEN] ❑ V *to* n *In the car she reverted to the subject uppermost in her mind.* 3 VERB If property, rights, or money **revert to** someone, they become that person's again after someone else has had them for a period of time. [LEGAL] ❑ V *to* n *When the lease ends, the property reverts to the freeholder.*

**re|view** /rɪvjuː/ ◆◆◇ **(reviews, reviewing, reviewed)** 1 N-COUNT: oft N *of* n, also prep N A **review of** a situation or system is its formal examination by people in authority. This is usually done in order to see whether it can be improved or corrected. ❑ *The president ordered a review of US economic aid to Jordan.* 2 VERB If you **review** a situation or system, you consider it carefully to see what is wrong with it or how it could be improved. ❑ V n *The Prime Minister reviewed the situation with his Cabinet yesterday.* 3 N-COUNT A **review** is a report in the media in which someone gives their opinion of something such as a new book or film. ❑ *We've never had a good review in the music press.* 4 VERB If someone **reviews** something such as a new book or film, they write a report or give a talk on television or radio in which they express their opinion of it. ❑ V n *Richard Coles reviews all of the latest video releases.* 5 VERB When you **review for** an examination, you read things again and make notes in order to be prepared for the examination. [AM] ❑ V *for* *Reviewing for exams gives you a chance to bring together all the individual parts of the course...* V n *Review all the notes you need to cover for each course.* ♦ N-COUNT **Review** is also a noun. ❑ *Begin by planning on three two-hour reviews with four chapters per session.*

☑ in BRIT, use **revise**

**re|view board** **(review boards)** N-COUNT A **review board** is a group of people in authority who examine a situation or system to see if it should be improved, corrected, or changed.

**re|view|er** /rɪvjuːəʳ/ **(reviewers)** N-COUNT A **reviewer** is a person who reviews new books, films, television programmes, CDs, plays, or concerts. ❑ *...the reviewer for the Times Literary Supplement.*

**re|view|ing stand** **(reviewing stands)** N-COUNT A **reviewing stand** is a special raised platform from which military and political leaders watch military parades.

**re|vile** /rɪvaɪl/ **(reviles, reviling, reviled)** VERB = hate If someone or something **is reviled**, people hate them intensely or show their hatred of them. [FORMAL] ❑ *be* V-ed *He was just as feared and reviled as his tyrannical parents...* V n *What right had the crowd to revile the England players for something they could not help...?* ♦ ADJ **re|viled** *He is probably the most reviled man in contemporary theatre.*

**re|vise** /rɪvaɪz/ **(revises, revising, revised)** 1 VERB = change If you **revise** the way you think about something, you adjust your thoughts, usually in order to make them better or more suited to how things are. ❑ V n *He soon came to revise his opinion of the profession.* 2 VERB = change If you **revise** a price, amount, or estimate, you change it to make it more fair, realistic, or accurate. ❑ V n *They realised that some of their prices were higher than their competitors' and revised prices accordingly.* 3 VERB = change When you **revise** an article, a book, a law, or a piece of music, you change it in order to improve it, make it more modern, or make it more suitable for a particular purpose. ❑ V n *for* n *Three editors handled the work of revising the articles for publication...* V n *The staff should work together to revise the school curriculum.* 4 VERB When you **revise for** an examination, you read things again and make notes in order to be prepared for the examination. [BRIT] ❑ V *for* n *I have to revise for maths...* V *I'd better skip the party and stay at home to revise.*

☑ in AM, use **review**

**re|vi|sion** /rɪvɪʒᵊn/ **(revisions)** 1 N-VAR: oft N *of* n To make a **revision of** something that is written or something that has been decided means to make changes to it in order to improve it, make it more modern, or make it more suitable for a particular purpose. ❑ *The phase of writing that is actually most important is revision... A major addition to the earlier revisions of the questionnaire is the job requirement exercise.* 2 N-UNCOUNT: oft poss N When people who are studying do **revision**, they read things again and make notes in order to prepare for an examination. [BRIT] ❑ *Some girls prefer to do their revision at home.*

☑ in AM, use **review**

**re|vi|sion|ism** /rɪvɪʒənɪzəm/ N-UNCOUNT [disapproval] **Revisionism** is a theory of socialism that is more moderate than normal Marxist theory, and is therefore considered unacceptable by most Marxists. [FORMAL] ❑ *The reforms come after decades of hostility to revisionism.*

**re|vi|sion|ist** /rɪvɪʒənɪst/ **(revisionists)** 1 ADJ If you describe a person or their views as **revisionist**, you mean that they reject traditionally held beliefs about a particular historical event or events. [FORMAL] ❑ *...the revisionist interpretation of the French Revolution.* ♦ N-COUNT A **revisionist** is a person who has revisionist views. [FORMAL] ❑ *The reputation of the navigator is under assault from historical revisionists.* 2 ADJ [disapproval] If a socialist describes another socialist's actions or opinions as **revisionist**, they mean that they are unacceptable because they are more moderate than normal Marxist theory allows. [FORMAL] ❑ *This revisionist thesis departs even further from Marxist assertions.* ♦ N-COUNT A **revisionist** is a person who has revisionist views. [FORMAL] ❑ *...ferocious infighting between Stalinist hardliners and revisionists.*

**re|vis|it** /riːvɪzɪt/ **(revisits, revisiting, revisited)** VERB If you **revisit** a place, you return there for a visit after you have been away for a long time, often after the place has changed a lot. ❑ *In the summer, when we returned to Canada, we revisited this lake at dawn.* V n

**re|vi|tal|ize** /riːvaɪtəlaɪz/ **(revitalizes, revitalizing, revitalized)**

✔ in BRIT, also use **revitalise**

To **revitalize** something that has lost its activity or its health means to make it active or healthy again. ❑ *This hair conditioner is excellent for revitalizing dry, lifeless hair.* VERB = revive; V n

**re|viv|al** /rɪvaɪvᵊl/ **(revivals)** 1 When there is a **revival of** something, it becomes active or popular again. ❑ *This return to realism has produced a revival of interest in a number of artists.* N-COUNT: oft N *of* n 2 A **revival** is a new production of a play, an opera, or a ballet. ❑ *...John Clement's revival of Chekhov's 'The Seagull'.* N-COUNT 3 A **revival** meeting is a public religious event that is intended to make people more interested in Christianity. ❑ *He toured South Africa organizing revival meetings.* N-UNCOUNT: usu N n

**re|viv|al|ism** /rɪvaɪvəlɪzəm/ **Revivalism** is a movement whose aim is to make a religion more popular and more influential. ❑ *...a time of intense religious revivalism.* N-UNCOUNT: usu adj N

**re|viv|al|ist** /rɪvaɪvəlɪst/ **(revivalists) Revivalist** people or activities are involved in trying to make a particular religion more popular and more influential. ❑ *...the Hindu revivalist party.* ADJ: ADJ n ♦ **Revivalist** is also a noun. ❑ *Booth was a revivalist intent on his Christian vocation.* N-COUNT

**re|vive** /rɪvaɪv/ **(revives, reviving, revived)** 1 When something such as the economy, a business, a trend, or a feeling **is revived** or when it **revives**, it becomes active, popular, or successful again. ❑ *...an attempt to revive the British economy... There is no doubt that grades have improved and interest in education has revived.* VERB; V n; V 2 When someone **revives** a play, opera, or ballet, they present a new production of it. ❑ *The Gaiety is reviving John B. Kean's comedy 'The Man from Clare'.* VERB; V n 3 If you manage to **revive** someone who has fainted or if they **revive**, they become conscious again. ❑ *She and a neighbour tried in vain to revive him... With a glazed stare she revived for one last instant.* VERB; V n; V

**re|vivi|fy** /riːvɪvɪfaɪ/ **(revivifies, revivifying, revivified)** To **revivify** a situation, event, or activity means to make it more active, lively, or efficient. [FORMAL] ❑ *They've revivified rhythm and blues singing by giving it dance beats.* VERB = revitalize; V n

**re|voke** /rɪvoʊk/ **(revokes, revoking, revoked)** When people in authority **revoke** something such as a licence, a law, or an agreement, they cancel it. [FORMAL] ❑ *The government revoked her husband's license to operate migrant labor crews.* VERB; V n ♦ **revo|ca|tion** /revəkeɪʃᵊn/ *The Montserrat government announced its revocation of 311 banking licences.* N-UNCOUNT

**re|volt** /rɪvoʊlt/ **(revolts, revolting, revolted)** 1 A **revolt** is an illegal and often violent attempt by a group of people to change their country's political system. ❑ *It was undeniably a revolt by ordinary people against their leaders.* N-VAR = rebellion 2 When people **revolt**, they make an illegal and often violent attempt to change their country's political system. ❑ *In 1375 the townspeople revolted.* VERB; V 3 A **revolt** by a person or group against someone or something is a refusal to accept the authority of that person or thing. ❑ *The prime minister is facing a revolt by party activists over his refusal to hold a referendum.* N-VAR = rebellion 4 When people **revolt against** someone or something, they reject the authority of that person or reject that thing. ❑ *The prime minister only reacted when three of his senior cabinet colleagues revolted and resigned in protest on Friday night... Caroline revolted against her ballet training at the age of sixteen.* VERB = rebel; V; V *against* n

**re|volt|ing** /rɪvoʊltɪŋ/ If you say that something or someone is **revolting**, you mean you think they are horrible and disgusting. ❑ *The smell in the cell was revolting.* ADJ = disgusting

**revo|lu|tion** /revəluːʃᵊn/ **(revolutions)** 1 A **revolution** is a successful attempt by a large group of people to change the political system of their country by force. ❑ *The period since the revolution has been one of political turmoil.* ◆◇◇ N-COUNT 2 A **revolution** in a particular area of human activity is an important change in that area. ❑ *The nineteenth century witnessed a revolution in ship design and propulsion.* N-COUNT: with supp

**revo|lu|tion|ary** /revəluːʃənri, AM -neri/ **(revolutionaries)** 1 **Revolutionary** activities, organizations, or people have the aim of causing a political revolution. ❑ *Do you know anything about the revolutionary movement? ...the Cuban revolutionary leader, Jose Marti.* ◆◇◇ ADJ 2 A **revolutionary** is a person who tries to cause a revolution or who takes an active part in one. ❑ *The revolutionaries laid down their arms and its leaders went into voluntary exile.* N-COUNT 3 **Revolutionary** ideas and developments involve great changes in the way that something is done or made. ❑ *Invented in 1951, the rotary engine is a revolutionary concept in internal combustion.* ADJ

**revo|lu|tion|ize** /revəluːʃənaɪz/ **(revolutionizes, revolutionizing, revolutionized)**

✔ in BRIT, also use **revolutionise**

When something **revolutionizes** an activity, it causes great changes in the way that it is done. ❑ *Over the past forty years plastics have revolutionised the way we live.* VERB; V n

**re|volve** /rɪvɒlv/ **(revolves, revolving, revolved)** 1 If you say that one thing **revolves around** another thing, you mean that the second thing is the main feature or focus of the first thing. ❑ *Since childhood, her life has revolved around tennis.* VERB; V *around* n 2 If a discussion or conversation **revolves around** a particular topic, it is mainly about that topic. ❑ *The debate revolves around specific accounting techniques.* VERB; V *around* n 3 If one object **revolves around** another object, the first object turns in a circle around the second object. ❑ *The satellite revolves around the Earth once every hundred minutes.* VERB; V *around* n 4 When something **revolves** or when you **revolve** it, it moves or turns in a circle around a central point or line. ❑ *Overhead, the fan revolved slowly... Monica picked up her Biro and revolved it between her teeth.* VERB; V; V n

**re|volv|er** /rɪvɒlvəʳ/ **(revolvers)** A **revolver** is a kind of hand gun. Its bullets are kept in a revolving cylinder in the gun. N-COUNT

**re|volv|ing door** **(revolving doors)** 1 Some large buildings have **revolving doors** instead of an ordinary door. They consist of four glass doors which turn together in a circle around a vertical post. ❑ *As he went through the revolving doors he felt his courage deserting him.* N-COUNT: usu pl 2 When you talk about a **revolving door**, you mean a situation in which the employees or owners of an organization keep changing. ❑ *They have accepted an offer from another firm with a busy revolving door.* N-COUNT: usu sing [disapproval]

**re|vue** /rɪvjuː/ **(revues)** A **revue** is a theatrical performance consisting of songs, dances, and jokes about recent events. N-COUNT

**re|vul|sion** /rɪvʌlʃᵊn/ Someone's **revulsion** at something is the strong feeling of disgust or disapproval they have towards it. ❑ *...their revulsion at the act of desecration.* N-UNCOUNT: also *a* N = disgust

**revved up** If someone is **revved up**, they are prepared for an important or exciting activity. [INFORMAL] ❑ *My people come to work and I get them all revved up.* ADJ: v-link ADJ = psyched-up

**re|ward** /rɪwɔːʳd/ **(rewards, rewarding, rewarded)** 1 A **reward** is something that you are given, for example because you have behaved well, worked hard, or provided a service to the community. ❑ *He was given the job as a reward for running a successful leadership bid.* ◆◇◇ N-COUNT: oft N *for* n 2 A **reward** is a sum of money offered to anyone who can give information about lost or stolen property or about someone who is wanted by the police. ❑ *The firm* N-COUNT *last night offered a £10,000 reward for information leading to the conviction of the killer.* [3] If you do something and **are rewarded** with a particular benefit, you receive that benefit as a result of doing that thing. ❑ *Make the extra effort to impress the buyer and you will be rewarded with a quicker sale.* [4] The **rewards** of something are the benefits that you receive as a result of doing or having that thing. ❑ *The company is only just starting to reap the rewards of long-term investments.* VERB *be* V-ed Also V n N-COUNT: usu pl

**re|ward|ing** /rɪwɔːʳdɪŋ/ An experience or action that is **rewarding** gives you satisfaction or brings you benefits. ❑ *...a career which she found stimulating and rewarding.* ADJ = *satisfying*

**re|wind** /riːwaɪnd/ **(rewinds, rewinding, rewound)**

✔ The verb is pronounced /riːwaɪnd/. The noun is pronounced /riːwaɪnd/.

[1] When the tape in a video or tape recorder **rewinds** or when you **rewind** it, the tape goes backwards so that you can play it again. Compare **fast forward**. ❑ *Waddington rewound the tape and played the message again... He switched the control to the answer-play mode and waited for the tape to rewind.* [2] If you put a video or cassette tape on **rewind**, you make the tape go backwards. Compare **fast forward**. ❑ *Press the rewind button.* VERB V n V N-UNCOUNT: usu N n

**re|wire** /riːwaɪəʳ/ **(rewires, rewiring, rewired)** If someone **rewires** a building or an electrical appliance, a new system of electrical wiring is put into it. ❑ *Their first job was to rewire the whole house and install central heating... I have had to spend a lot of money having my house replumbed and rewired.* ♦ **re|wir|ing** *The replumbing and rewiring of the flat ran very smoothly.* VERB V n *have* n V-ed N-UNCOUNT

**re|word** /riːwɜːʳd/ **(rewords, rewording, reworded)** When you **reword** something that is spoken or written, you try to express it in a way that is more accurate, more acceptable, or more easily understood. ❑ *All right, I'll reword my question.* VERB = *rephrase* V n

**re|work** /riːwɜːʳk/ **(reworks, reworking, reworked)** If you **rework** something such as an idea or a piece of writing, you reorganize it and make changes to it in order to improve it or bring it up to date. ❑ *See if you can rework your schedule and come up with practical ways to reduce the number of hours you're on call.* ♦ **re|work|ing (reworkings)** *Her latest novel seems at first sight to be a reworking of similar themes.* VERB = *revise* V n N-COUNT: usu N *of* n

**re|wound** /riːwaʊnd/ **Rewound** is the past tense and past participle of **rewind**.

**re|writ|able** /riːraɪtəbᵊl/ also **rewriteable.** A **rewritable** CD or DVD is a CD or DVD that you can record onto more than once. Compare **recordable**. ❑ *...rewritable discs.* ADJ

**re|write** /riːraɪt/ **(rewrites, rewriting, rewrote, rewritten)** [1] If someone **rewrites** a piece of writing such as a book, an article, or a law, they write it in a different way in order to improve it. ❑ *Following this critique, students rewrite their papers and submit them for final evaluation.* [2] If you accuse a government of **rewriting** history, you are criticizing them for selecting and presenting particular historical events in a way that suits their own purposes. ❑ *We have always been an independent people, no matter how they rewrite history.* [3] When journalists say that a sports player **has rewritten** the record books or the history books, they mean that the player has broken a record or several records. ❑ *...the extraordinary West Country team that have rewritten all the record books in those three years.* [4] In the film and television industries, a **rewrite** is the writing of parts of a film again in order to improve it. ❑ *Only after countless rewrites did John consider the script ready.* VERB = *rework* V n VERB disapproval V n VERB V n N-COUNT

**rhap|sod|ic** /ræpsɒdɪk/ Language and feelings that are **rhapsodic** are very powerful and full of delight in something. [FORMAL] ❑ *...a rhapsodic letter about the birth of her first baby.* ADJ

**rhap|so|dize** /ræpsədaɪz/ **(rhapsodizes, rhapsodizing, rhapsodized)**

✔ in BRIT, also use **rhapsodise**

If you **rhapsodize** about someone or something, you express great delight or enthusiasm about them. [FORMAL] ❑ *The critics rhapsodized over her performance in 'Autumn Sonata'.* VERB V *over/about* n

**rhap|so|dy** /ræpsədi/ **(rhapsodies)** A **rhapsody** is a piece of music which has an irregular form and is full of feeling. ❑ *...George Gershwin's Rhapsody In Blue.* N-COUNT: oft in names

**rhe|sus fac|tor** /riːsəs fæktəʳ/ The **rhesus factor** is something that is in the blood of most people. If someone's blood contains this factor, they are rhesus positive. If it does not, they are rhesus negative. N-SING = *Rh factor*

**rheto|ric** /retərɪk/ [1] If you refer to speech or writing as **rhetoric**, you disapprove of it because it is intended to convince and impress people but may not be sincere or honest. ❑ *What is required is immediate action, not rhetoric.* [2] **Rhetoric** is the skill or art of using language effectively. [FORMAL] ❑ *...the noble institutions of political life, such as political rhetoric, public office and public service.* N-UNCOUNT disapproval N-UNCOUNT

**rhe|tori|cal** /rɪtɒrɪkᵊl, AM -tɔːr-/ [1] A **rhetorical** question is one which is asked in order to make a statement rather than to get an answer. ❑ *He grimaced slightly, obviously expecting no answer to his rhetorical question.* ♦ **rhe|tori|cal|ly** /rɪtɒrɪkli, AM -tɔːr-/ *'Do these kids know how lucky they are?' Jackson asked rhetorically.* [2] **Rhetorical** language is intended to be grand and impressive. [FORMAL] ❑ *These arguments may have been used as a rhetorical device to argue for a perpetuation of a United Nations role.* ♦ **rhe|tori|cal|ly** *Suddenly, the narrator speaks in his most rhetorically elevated mode.* ADJ: usu ADJ n ADV: ADV with v ADJ: usu ADJ n ADV

**rhe|tori|cian** /retərɪʃᵊn/ **(rhetoricians)** A **rhetorician** is a person who is good at public speaking or who is trained in the art of rhetoric. ❑ *...an able and fiercely contentious rhetorician.* N-COUNT

**rheu|mat|ic** /ruːmætɪk/ **Rheumatic** is used to describe conditions and pains that are related to rheumatism. **Rheumatic** joints are swollen and painful because they are affected by rheumatism. ❑ *...new treatments for a range of rheumatic diseases.* ADJ: ADJ n

**rheu|mat|ic fe|ver** **Rheumatic fever** is a disease which causes fever, and swelling and pain in your joints. N-UNCOUNT

**rheu|ma|tism** /ruːmətɪzəm/ **Rheumatism** is an illness that makes your joints or muscles stiff and painful. Older people, especially, suffer from rheumatism. N-UNCOUNT

**rheu|ma|toid ar|thri|tis** /ruːmətɔɪd ɑːʳθraɪtɪs/ **Rheumatoid arthritis** is a long-lasting disease that causes your joints, for example your hands or knees, to swell up and become painful. N-UNCOUNT

**rheu|ma|tol|ogy** /ruːmətɒlədʒi/ **Rheumatology** is the area of medicine that is concerned with rheumatism, arthritis, and related diseases. ♦ **rheu|ma|tolo|gist (rheumatologists)** ❑ *He was consultant rheumatologist at the Royal Hampshire Hospital.* N-UNCOUNT N-COUNT

**rheumy** /ruːmi/ If someone has **rheumy** eyes, their eyes are red and watery, usually because they are very ill or old. [LITERARY] ADJ: usu ADJ n

**Rh fac|tor** /ɑːr eɪtʃ fæktəʳ/ The **Rh factor** is the same as the **rhesus factor**. N-UNCOUNT

**rhine|stone** /raɪnstoun/ **(rhinestones)** **Rhinestones** are shiny, glass jewels that are used in cheap jewellery and to decorate clothes. N-COUNT: oft N n

**rhi|ni|tis** /raɪnaɪtɪs/ If you suffer from **rhinitis** or **allergic rhinitis**, your nose is very sore and liquid keeps coming out it. [MEDICAL] N-UNCOUNT

**rhi|no** /raɪnou/ **(rhinos)** A **rhino** is the same as a **rhinoceros**. [INFORMAL] N-COUNT

**rhi|noc|er|os** /raɪnɒsərəs/ **(rhinoceroses)** A **rhinoceros** is a large Asian or African animal N-COUNT with thick grey skin and a horn, or two horns, on its nose.

**rhi|zome** /raɪzoum/ **(rhizomes)** **Rhizomes** are the horizontal stems from which some plants, such as irises, grow. Rhizomes are found on or just under the surface of the earth. N-COUNT

**rho|do|den|dron** /roudədendrən/ **(rhododendrons)** A **rhododendron** is a large bush with large flowers which are usually pink, red, or purple. N-VAR

**rhom|bus** /rɒmbəs/ **(rhombuses)** A **rhombus** is a geometric shape which has four equal sides but is not a square. [TECHNICAL] N-COUNT

**rhu|barb** /ruːbɑːʳb/ **Rhubarb** is a plant with large leaves and long red stems. You can cook the stems with sugar to make jam or puddings. N-UNCOUNT

**rhyme** /raɪm/ **(rhymes, rhyming, rhymed)** 1 If one word **rhymes with** another or if two words **rhyme**, they have a very similar sound. Words that rhyme with each other are often used in poems. ❑ *June always rhymes with moon in old love songs. ...the sort of people who give their children names that rhyme: Donnie, Ronnie, Connie. ...a singer rhyming 'eyes' with 'realise'. ...rhymed couplets.* V-RECIP; V with n; pl-n V; V n with n; V-ed 2 If a poem or song **rhymes**, the lines end with words that have very similar sounds. ❑ *In his efforts to make it rhyme he seems to have chosen the first word that comes into his head. ...rhyming couplets.* VERB; V; V-ing 3 A **rhyme** is a word which rhymes with another word, or a set of lines which rhyme. ❑ *The one rhyme for passion is fashion.* N-COUNT 4 A **rhyme** is a short poem which has rhyming words at the ends of its lines. ❑ *He was teaching Helen a little rhyme.* → See also **nursery rhyme**. N-COUNT = verse 5 **Rhyme** is the use of rhyming words as a technique in poetry. If something is written **in rhyme**, it is written as a poem in which the lines rhyme. ❑ *The plays are in rhyme.* N-UNCOUNT 6 If something happens or is done **without rhyme or reason**, there seems to be no logical reason for it to happen or be done. ❑ *He picked people on a whim, without rhyme or reason.* PHRASE: PHR after v

**rhym|ing slang** **Rhyming slang** is a spoken informal kind of language in which you do not use the normal word for something, but say a word or phrase that rhymes with it instead. In Cockney rhyming slang, for example, people say 'apples and pears' to mean 'stairs'. N-UNCOUNT

**rhythm** /rɪðəm/ **(rhythms)** 1 A **rhythm** is a regular series of sounds or movements. ❑ *He had no sense of rhythm whatsoever.* ◆◇◇ N-VAR 2 A **rhythm** is a regular pattern of changes, for example changes in your body, in the seasons, or in the tides. ❑ *Begin to listen to your own body rhythms.* N-COUNT

**rhythm and blues** **Rhythm and blues** is a style of popular music developed in the 1940's from blues music, but using electrically amplified instruments. The abbreviation **R&B** is also used. N-UNCOUNT

**rhyth|mic** /rɪðmɪk/ or **rhythmical** /rɪðmɪkəl/ A **rhythmic** movement or sound is repeated at regular intervals, forming a regular pattern or beat. ❑ *Good breathing is slow, rhythmic and deep.* ADJ ♦ **rhyth|mi|cal|ly** /rɪðmɪkli/ *She stood, swaying her hips, moving rhythmically.* ADV: ADV after v

**rhythm meth|od** The **rhythm method** is a practice in which a couple try to prevent pregnancy by having sex only at times when the woman is not likely to become pregnant. N-SING: usu *the* N

**rhythm sec|tion** The **rhythm section** of a band is the musicians whose main job is to supply the rhythm. It usually consists of bass and drums, and sometimes keyboard instruments. N-SING

**rib** /rɪb/ **(ribs, ribbing, ribbed)** 1 Your **ribs** are the 12 pairs of curved bones that surround your chest. ❑ *Her heart was thumping against her ribs.* N-COUNT 2 A **rib of** meat such as beef or pork is a piece that has been cut to include one of the animal's ribs. ❑ *...a rib of beef.* N-COUNT: usu N *of* n, n N 3 If you **rib** someone **about** something, you tease them about it in a friendly way. [INFORMAL] ❑ *The guys in my local pub used to rib me about drinking 'girly' drinks.* VERB = tease; V n 4 → See also **ribbed**, **ribbing**.

**rib|ald** /rɪbəld/ A **ribald** remark or sense of humour is rather rude and refers to sex in a humorous way. ❑ *...her ribald comments about a fellow guest's body language.* ADJ: usu ADJ n

**ribbed** /rɪbd/ A **ribbed** surface, material, or garment has a raised pattern of parallel lines on it. ❑ *...ribbed cashmere sweaters.* ADJ: usu ADJ n

**rib|bing** /rɪbɪŋ/ 1 **Ribbing** is friendly teasing. [INFORMAL] ❑ *I got quite a lot of ribbing from my team-mates.* N-UNCOUNT = teasing 2 **Ribbing** is a method of knitting that makes a raised pattern of parallel lines. You use ribbing, for example, round the edge of sweaters so that the material can stretch without losing its shape. N-UNCOUNT = rib

**rib|bon** /rɪbən/ **(ribbons)** 1 A **ribbon** is a long, narrow piece of cloth that you use for tying things together or as a decoration. ❑ *She had tied back her hair with a peach satin ribbon.* N-VAR 2 A typewriter or printer **ribbon** is a long, narrow piece of cloth containing ink and is used in a typewriter or printer. N-COUNT 3 A **ribbon** is a small decorative strip of cloth which is given to someone to wear on their clothes as an award or to show that they are linked with a particular organization. N-COUNT

**rib cage** **(rib cages)** also **ribcage**. Your **rib cage** is the structure of ribs in your chest. It protects your lungs and other organs. N-COUNT

**ri|bo|fla|vin** /raɪboufleɪvɪn/ **Riboflavin** is a vitamin that occurs in green vegetables, milk, fish, eggs, liver, and kidney. N-UNCOUNT

**rice** /raɪs/ **(rices)** **Rice** consists of white or brown grains taken from a cereal plant. You cook rice and usually eat it with meat or vegetables. ❑ *...a meal consisting of chicken, rice and vegetables.* ◆◇◇ N-MASS

**rice pa|per** **Rice paper** is very thin paper made from rice plants. It is used in cooking. N-UNCOUNT

**rice pud|ding** **(rice puddings)** **Rice pudding** is a dessert which is made from rice, milk, and sugar. N-VAR

**rich** /rɪtʃ/ **(richer, richest, riches)** 1 A **rich** person has a lot of money or valuable possessions. ❑ *Their one aim in life is to get rich.* ◆◆◇ ADJ ≠poor ♦ **The rich** are rich people. ❑ *This is a system in which the rich are cared for and the poor are left to suffer.* N-PLURAL: *the* N 2 **Riches** are valuable possessions or large amounts of money. ❑ *An Olympic gold medal can lead to untold riches for an athlete.* N-PLURAL 3 A **rich** country has a strong economy and produces a lot of wealth, so many people who live there have a high standard of living. ❑ *There is hunger in many parts of the world, even in rich countries.* ADJ ≠poor 4 If you talk about the earth's **riches**, you are referring to things that exist naturally in large quantities and that are useful and valuable, for example minerals, wood, and oil. ❑ *...Russia's vast natural riches.* N-PLURAL: usu supp N 5 If something is **rich in** a useful or valuable substance or is a **rich source of** it, it contains a lot of it. ❑ *Liver and kidney are particularly rich in vitamin A.* ADJ: v-link ADJ *in* n, ADJ n 6 **Rich** food contains a lot of fat or oil. ❑ *Additional cream would make it too rich.* ADJ ♦ **rich|ness** *The coffee flavour complemented the richness of the pudding.* N-UNCOUNT 7 **Rich** soil contains large amounts of substances that make it good for growing crops or flowers in. ❑ *Farmers grow rice in the rich soil.* ADJ ≠poor 8 A **rich** deposit of a mineral or other substance is a large amount of it. ❑ *...the country's rich deposits of the metal, lithium.* ADJ ♦ **rich|ness** *...the richness of Tibet's mineral deposits.* N-UNCOUNT 9 If you say that something is a **rich** vein or source of something such as humour, ideas, or information, you mean that it can provide a lot of that thing. ❑ *The director discovered a rich vein of sentimentality.* ADJ: ADJ n 10 **Rich** smells are strong and very pleasant. **Rich** colours and sounds are deep and very pleasant. ❑ *...a rich and luxuriously perfumed bath essence.* ADJ ♦ **rich|ness** *...the richness of colour in Gauguin's paintings.* N-UNCOUNT 11 A **rich** life or history is one that is interesting because it is full of different events and activities. ADJ

❑ *A rich and varied cultural life is essential for this couple.* ♦ **rich|ness** *It all adds to the richness of human life.* N-UNCOUNT 12 A **rich** collection or mixture contains a wide and interesting variety of different things. ADJ ❑ *Visitors can view a rich and colorful array of aquatic plants and animals.* ♦ **rich|ness** *...a huge country, containing a richness of culture and diversity of landscape.* N-UNCOUNT 13 If you say that something a person says or does is **rich**, you are making fun of it because you think it is a surprising and inappropriate thing for them to say or do. [INFORMAL] ADJ: v-link ADJ [feelings] ❑ *Gil says that women can't keep secrets. That's rich, coming from him, the professional sneak.* 14 If you say that someone is **filthy rich** or **stinking rich**, you disapprove of them because they have a lot of money. [INFORMAL] PHRASE: v-link PHR, PHR n [disapproval] = loaded ❑ *He's stinking rich, and with no more talent than he ever had before.*

**-rich** /-rɪtʃ/ **-rich** combines with the names of useful or valuable substances to form adjectives that describe something as containing a lot of a particular substance. COMB in ADJ usu ADJ n ❑ *...Angola's northern oil-rich coastline.*

**rich|ly** /rɪtʃli/ 1 If something is **richly** coloured, flavoured, or perfumed, it has a pleasantly strong colour, flavour, or perfume. ADV: usu ADV -ed/adj ❑ *...an opulent display of richly coloured fabrics.* 2 If something is **richly** decorated, patterned, or furnished, it has a lot of elaborate and beautiful decoration, patterns, or furniture. ADV: usu ADV -ed/adj = lavishly ❑ *Coffee steamed in the richly decorated silver pot.* 3 If you say that someone **richly** deserves an award, success, or victory, you approve of what they have done and feel very strongly that they deserve it. ADV: ADV before v, ADV -ed [feelings] ❑ *He achieved the success he so richly deserved.* 4 If you are **richly** rewarded for doing something, you get something very valuable or pleasant in return for doing it. ADV: ADV before v, ADV -ed ❑ *It is a difficult book to read, but it richly rewards the effort.*

**Richter scale** /rɪktəʳ skeɪl/ **The Richter scale** is a scale which is used for measuring how severe an earthquake is. N-SING: the N ❑ *An earthquake measuring 6.1 on the Richter Scale struck California yesterday.*

**rick** /rɪk/ **(ricks, ricking, ricked)** 1 If you **rick** your neck, you hurt it by pulling or twisting it in an unusual way. [BRIT] VERB ❑ *Kernaghan missed the United game after he ricked his neck...* V n *He recovered from a ricked neck.* V-ed

☑ in AM, use **wrench**

2 A **rick** is a large pile of dried grass or straw that is built in a regular shape and kept in a field until it is needed. N-COUNT

**rick|ets** /rɪkɪts/ **Rickets** is a disease that children can get when their food does not contain enough Vitamin D. It makes their bones soft and causes their liver and spleen to become too large. N-UNCOUNT

**rick|ety** /rɪkɪti/ A **rickety** structure or piece of furniture is not very strong or well made, and seems likely to collapse or break. ADJ: usu ADJ n ❑ *Mona climbed the rickety wooden stairway.*

**rick|shaw** /rɪkʃɔː/ **(rickshaws)** A **rickshaw** is a simple vehicle that is used in Asia for carrying passengers. Some rickshaws are pulled by a man who walks or runs in front. N-COUNT

**rico|chet** /rɪkəʃeɪ, AM -ʃeɪ/ **(ricochets, ricocheting, ricocheted)** When a bullet **ricochets**, it hits a surface and bounces away from it. VERB ❑ *The bullets ricocheted off the bonnet and windscreen.* V prep/adv Also V ♦ **Ricochet** is also a noun. N-COUNT ❑ *He was wounded in the shoulder by a ricochet.*

**rid** /rɪd/ **(rids, ridding)** ♦◇◇

☑ The form **rid** is used in the present tense and is the past tense and past participle of the verb.

1 When you **get rid of** something that you do not want or do not like, you take action so that you no longer have it or suffer from it. PHRASE: V inflects, PHR n ❑ *The owner needs to get rid of the car for financial reasons.* 2 If you **get rid of** someone who is causing problems for you or who you do not like, you do something to prevent them affecting you any more, for example by making them leave. PHRASE: V inflects, PHR n ❑ *He believed that his manager wanted to get rid of him for personal reasons.* 3 If you **rid** a place or person **of** something undesirable or unwanted, you succeed in removing it completely from that place or person. VERB = free ❑ *The proposals are an attempt to rid the country of political corruption.* V n of n 4 If you **rid yourself of** something you do not want, you take action so that you no longer have it or are no longer affected by it. VERB = free ❑ *Why couldn't he ever rid himself of those thoughts, those worries?* V pron-refl of n 5 If you **are rid of** someone or something that you did not want or that caused problems for you, they are no longer with you or causing problems for you. ADJ: v-link ADJ of n ❑ *The family had sought a way to be rid of her and the problems she had caused them.*

**rid|dance** /rɪdᵊns/ You say '**good riddance**' to indicate that you are pleased that someone has left or that something has gone. PHRASE: oft PHR to n [feelings] ❑ *He's gone back to London in a huff and good riddance.*

**rid|den** /rɪdᵊn/ **Ridden** is the past participle of **ride**.

**-ridden** /-rɪdᵊn/ **-ridden** combines with nouns to form adjectives that describe something as having a lot of a particular undesirable thing or quality, or suffering very much because of it. COMB in ADJ ❑ *...the debt-ridden economies of Latin America.*

**rid|dle** /rɪdᵊl/ **(riddles, riddling, riddled)** 1 A **riddle** is a puzzle or joke in which you ask a question that seems to be nonsense but which has a clever or amusing answer. N-COUNT 2 You can describe something as a **riddle** if people have been trying to understand or explain it but have not been able to. N-COUNT = mystery ❑ *Scientists claimed yesterday to have solved the riddle of the birth of the Universe.* 3 If someone **riddles** something **with** bullets or bullet holes, they fire a lot of bullets into it. VERB ❑ *Unknown attackers riddled two homes with gunfire.* V n with n

**rid|dled** /rɪdᵊld/ 1 If something is **riddled with** bullets or bullet holes, it is full of bullet holes. ADJ: usu v-link ADJ with n ❑ *The bodies of four people were found riddled with bullets.* 2 If something is **riddled with** undesirable qualities or features, it is full of them. ADJ: v-link ADJ with n ❑ *They were the principal shareholders in a bank riddled with corruption.*

**-riddled** /-rɪdᵊld/ **-riddled** combines with nouns to form adjectives that describe something as being full of a particular undesirable thing or quality. COMB in ADJ: usu ADJ n ❑ *She pushed the bullet-riddled door open.*

**ride** /raɪd/ **(rides, riding, rode, ridden)** ♦♦◇

1 When you **ride** a horse, you sit on it and control its movements. VERB ❑ *I saw a girl riding a horse...* V n *Can you ride?...* V *He was riding on his horse looking for the castle...* V on n *They still ride around on horses there.* V adv/prep 2 When you **ride** a bicycle or a motorcycle, you sit on it, control it, and travel along on it. VERB ❑ *Riding a bike is great exercise...* V n *Two men riding on motorcycles opened fire on him...* V on n *He rode to work on a bicycle.* V prep/adv 3 When you **ride in** a vehicle such as a car, you travel in it. VERB ❑ *He prefers travelling on the Tube to riding in a limousine...* V in/on n *I remember the village full of American servicemen riding around in jeeps.* V adv/prep 4 A **ride** is a journey on a horse or bicycle, or in a vehicle. N-COUNT ❑ *Would you like to go for a ride?* 5 In a fairground, a **ride** is a large machine that people ride on for fun. N-COUNT 6 If you say that one thing **is riding on** another, you mean that the first thing depends on the second thing. VERB: oft cont = depend ❑ *Billions of pounds are riding on the outcome of the election.* V on n 7 → See also **riding**.

**PHRASES** 8 If you say that someone or something **is riding high**, you mean that they are popular or successful at the present time. PHRASE: V inflects, usu cont ❑ *He was riding high in the public opinion polls.* 9 If you say that someone faces **a rough ride**, you mean that things are going to be difficult for them because people will criticize them a lot or treat them badly. [INFORMAL] PHRASE: usu PHR after v ❑ *The Chancellor could face a rough ride unless the plan works.* 10 If you say that someone **has been taken for a ride**, you mean that they have been deceived or cheated. [INFOR- PHRASE: V inflects

MAL] ❑ *When he had not returned with my money an hour later I realized that I had been taken for a ride.* 11 to **ride roughshod over** → see **roughshod**.

♦ **ride out** If someone **rides out** a storm or a crisis, they manage to survive a difficult period without suffering serious harm. ❑ *The ruling party think they can ride out the political storm... He has to just ride this out and hope that it turns in his favor.*
PHRASAL VERB
V P n (not pron)
V n P

♦ **ride up** If a garment **rides up**, it moves upwards, out of its proper position. ❑ *My underskirt had ridden up into a thick band around my hips.*
PHRASAL VERB
V P

**rid|er** /raɪdəʳ/ **(riders)** 1 A **rider** is someone who rides a horse, a bicycle, or a motorcycle as a hobby or job. You can also refer to someone who is riding a horse, a bicycle, or a motorcycle as a rider. ❑ *She is a very good and experienced rider.* 2 A **rider** is a statement that is added to another statement, especially one which contains a change, an explanation, or further information. ❑ *Mr Casey said he could see no necessity to add any rider on the use of firearms by police... America conventionally attaches a rider to Israeli aid, to the effect that it must not be used in the occupied territories.*
◆◇◇
N-COUNT
N-COUNT: oft N *on/to* n

**ridge** /rɪdʒ/ **(ridges)** 1 A **ridge** is a long, narrow piece of raised land. 2 A **ridge** is a raised line on a flat surface. ❑ *...the bony ridge of the eye socket.*
N-COUNT
N-COUNT: with supp

**ridged** /rɪdʒd/ A **ridged** surface has raised lines on it. ❑ *...boots with thick, ridged soles for walking.*
ADJ: usu ADJ n

**ridi|cule** /rɪdɪkjuːl/ **(ridicules, ridiculing, ridiculed)** 1 If you **ridicule** someone or **ridicule** their ideas or beliefs, you make fun of them in an unkind way. ❑ *I admired her all the more for allowing them to ridicule her and never striking back.* 2 If someone or something is an object of **ridicule** or is held up to **ridicule**, someone makes fun of them in an unkind way. ❑ *As a heavy child, she became the object of ridicule from classmates.*
VERB = mock
V n
N-UNCOUNT

**ri|dicu|lous** /rɪdɪkjʊləs/ If you say that something or someone is **ridiculous**, you mean that they are very foolish. ❑ *It is ridiculous to suggest we are having a romance.*
ADJ: oft *it* v-link ADJ that/to-inf = absurd

**ri|dicu|lous|ly** /rɪdɪkjʊləsli/ You use **ridiculously** to emphasize the fact that you think something is unreasonable or very surprising. ❑ *Dena bought rolls of silk that seemed ridiculously cheap.*
ADV: usu ADV adj/adv
emphasis

**rid|ing** /raɪdɪŋ/ **Riding** is the activity or sport of riding horses. ❑ *The next morning we went riding again.*
N-UNCOUNT

**rife** /raɪf/ If you say that something, usually something bad, is **rife** in a place or that the place is **rife with** it, you mean that it is very common. ❑ *Speculation is rife that he will be sacked... Hollywood soon became rife with rumors.*
ADJ: v-link ADJ, oft ADJ *with* n

**riff** /rɪf/ **(riffs)** 1 In jazz and rock music, a **riff** is a short repeated tune. 2 A **riff** is a short piece of speech or writing that develops a particular theme or idea. ❑ *Rowe does a very clever riff on the nature of prejudice.*
N-COUNT
N-COUNT

**rif|fle** /rɪfᵊl/ **(riffles, riffling, riffled)** If you **riffle** through the pages of a book or **riffle** them, you turn them over quickly, without reading everything that is on them. ❑ *I riffled through the pages until I reached the index.*
VERB = flick
V *through* n
Also V n

**riff-raff** /rɪf ræf/ also **riffraff.** If you refer to a group of people as **riff-raff**, you disapprove of them because you think they are not respectable.
N-UNCOUNT
disapproval

**ri|fle** /raɪfᵊl/ **(rifles, rifling, rifled)** 1 A **rifle** is a gun with a long barrel. ❑ *They shot him at point blank range with an automatic rifle.* 2 If you **rifle through** things or **rifle** them, you make a quick search among them in order to find something or steal something. ❑ *I discovered my husband rifling through the filing cabinet... There were lockers by each seat and I quickly rifled the contents.*
N-COUNT
VERB
V *through* n
V n

**rifle|man** /raɪfᵊlmæn/ **(riflemen)** A **rifleman** is a person, especially a soldier, who is skilled in the use of a rifle.
N-COUNT

**ri|fle range (rifle ranges)** A **rifle range** is a place where you can practise shooting with a rifle.
N-COUNT

**rift** /rɪft/ **(rifts)** 1 A **rift** between people or countries is a serious quarrel or disagreement that stops them having a good relationship. ❑ *The interview reflected a growing rift between the President and the government.* 2 A **rift** is a split that appears in something solid, especially in the ground.
N-COUNT: usu with supp, oft adj N, N prep
N-COUNT

**rig** /rɪg/ **(rigs, rigging, rigged)** 1 If someone **rigs** an election, a job appointment, or a game, they dishonestly arrange it to get the result they want or to give someone an unfair advantage. ❑ *She accused her opponents of rigging the vote.* 2 A **rig** is a large structure that is used for looking for oil or gas and for taking it out of the ground or the sea bed. ❑ *...gas rigs in the North Sea.* 3 A **rig** is a truck or lorry that is made in two or more sections which are joined together by metal bars, so that the vehicle can turn more easily. [AM]
VERB
V n
N-COUNT: oft n N
N-COUNT

✔ in BRIT, usually use **articulated lorry**

4 → See also **rigging**.

♦ **rig up** If you **rig up** a device or structure, you make it or fix it in place using any materials that are available. ❑ *Election officials have rigged up speakers to provide voters with music.*
PHRASAL VERB
V P n (not pron)
Also V n P

**rig|ging** /rɪgɪŋ/ 1 Vote or ballot **rigging** is the act of dishonestly organizing an election to get a particular result. ❑ *She was accused of corruption, of vote rigging on a massive scale.* 2 On a ship, the **rigging** is the ropes which support the ship's masts and sails.
N-UNCOUNT: usu supp N
N-UNCOUNT

**right**

1. CORRECT, APPROPRIATE, OR ACCEPTABLE
2. DIRECTION AND POLITICAL GROUPINGS
3. ENTITLEMENT
4. DISCOURSE USES
5. USED FOR EMPHASIS
6. USED IN TITLES

① **right** /raɪt/ **(rights, righting, righted)** ◆◆◆
⇛ Please look at category 16 to see if the expression you are looking for is shown under another headword. 1 If something is **right**, it is correct and agrees with the facts. ❑ *That's absolutely right... Clocks never told the right time... The barman tells me you saw Ann on Tuesday. Is that right?* ♦ **Right** is also an adverb. ❑ *He guessed right about some things.* ♦ **right|ly** *She attended one meeting only, if I remember rightly.* 2 If you do something in the **right** way or in the **right** place, you do it as or where it should be done or was planned to be done. ❑ *Walking, done in the right way, is a form of aerobic exercise... The chocolate is then melted down to exactly the right temperature.* ♦ **Right** is also an adverb. ❑ *To make sure I did everything right, I bought a fat instruction book.* 3 If you say that someone is seen in **all the right** places or knows **all the right** people, you mean that they go to places which are socially acceptable or know people who are socially acceptable. ❑ *He was always to be seen in the right places.* 4 If someone is **right about** something, they are correct in what they say or think about it. ❑ *Ron has been right about the result of every General Election but one.* ♦ **right|ly** *He rightly assumed that the boy was hiding.* 5 If something such as a choice, action, or decision is the **right** one, it is the best or most suitable one. ❑ *She'd made the right choice in leaving New York... The right decision was made, but probably for the wrong reasons.* ♦ **right|ly** *She hoped she'd decided rightly.* 6 If something is **not right**, there is something unsatisfactory about the situation or thing that you are talking about. ❑ *Ratatouille doesn't taste right with any other oil.* 7 If you think that someone was **right to** do something, you think that there were good moral reasons why they did it. ❑ *You were right to do what you did, under the circumstances.* ♦ **right|ly** *The crowd*
ADJ = correct ≠ wrong
ADV: ADV after v
ADV: ADV after v
ADJ: usu ADJ n = correct ≠ wrong
ADV: ADV after v = correctly
ADJ: usu ADJ n ≠ wrong
ADJ ≠ wrong
ADV
ADJ ≠ wrong
ADV: ADV with v
ADJ: v-link ADJ, with brd-neg ≠ wrong
ADJ: v-link ADJ, usu ADJ to-inf ≠ wrong
ADV:

*screamed for a penalty but the referee rightly ignored them.* 8 **Right** is used to refer to activities or actions that are considered to be morally good and acceptable. ❑ *It's not right, leaving her like this.* ♦ **Right** is also a noun. ❑ *At least he knew right from wrong.* ♦ **right|ness** *Many people have very strong opinions about the rightness or wrongness of abortion.* 9 If you **right** something or if it **rights itself**, it returns to its normal or correct state, after being in an undesirable state. ❑ *They recognise the urgency of righting the economy... Your eyesight rights itself very quickly.* 10 If you **right** a wrong, you do something to make up for a mistake or something bad that you did in the past. ❑ *We've made progress in righting the wrongs of the past.*

ADV before v, ADV with cl
ADJ: v-link ADJ, oft with brd-neg ≠wrong
N-UNCOUNT
N-UNCOUNT: usu N *of* n
VERB
V n
V pron-refl
VERB = rectify
V n

11 If you **right** something that has fallen or rolled over, or if it **rights itself**, it returns to its normal upright position. ❑ *He righted the yacht and continued the race... The helicopter turned at an awful angle before righting itself.* 12 The **right** side of a material is the side that is intended to be seen and that faces outwards when it is made into something.

VERB
V n
V pron-refl
ADJ: ADJ n ≠wrong

**PHRASES** 13 If you say that things **are going right**, you mean that your life or a situation is developing as you intended or expected and you are pleased with it. ❑ *I can't think of anything in my life that's going right.* 14 If someone has behaved in a way which is morally or legally right, you can say that they are **in the right**. You usually use this expression when the person is involved in an argument or dispute. ❑ *She wasn't entirely in the right.* 15 If you **put** something **right**, you correct something that was wrong or that was causing problems. ❑ *We've discovered what's gone wrong and are going to put it right.* 16 **heart in the right place** → see **heart**. **it serves** you **right** → see **serve**. **on the right side of** → see **side**.

PHRASE: V inflects
PHRASE: usu v-link PHR ≠in the wrong
PHRASE: V inflects

② **right** /raɪt/ ◆◆◆

✔ The spelling **Right** is also used for meaning 3.

1 The **right** is one of two opposite directions, sides, or positions. If you are facing north and you turn to the right, you will be facing east. In the word 'to', the 'o' is to the right of the 't'. ❑ *Ahead of you on the right will be a lovely garden.* ♦ **Right** is also an adverb. ❑ *Turn right into the street.* 2 Your **right** arm, leg, or ear, for example, is the one which is on the right side of your body. Your **right** shoe or glove is the one which is intended to be worn on your right foot or hand. 3 You can refer to people who support the political ideals of capitalism and conservatism as **the right**. They are often contrasted with **the left**, who support the political ideals of socialism. ❑ *The Tory Right despise him.* 4 If you say that someone has moved **to the right**, you mean that their political beliefs have become more right-wing. ❑ *They see the shift to the right as a worldwide phenomenon.* 5 If someone is **at** a person's **right hand**, they work closely with that person so they can help and advise them. ❑ *I think he ought to be at the right hand of the president.*

N-SING: usu *the* N ≠left
ADV: ADV after v
ADJ: ADJ n ≠left
N-SING-COLL: *the* N ≠left
N-SING: *the* N ≠left
PHRASE: usu v-link PHR

③ **right** /raɪt/ **(rights)** 1 Your **rights** are what you are morally or legally entitled to do or to have. ❑ *They don't know their rights... You must stand up for your rights.* 2 If you have a **right to** do or to have something, you are morally or legally entitled to do it or to have it. ❑ *...a woman's right to choose.* 3 If someone has **the rights to** a story or book, they are legally allowed to publish it or reproduce it in another form, and nobody else can do so without their permission. ❑ *An agent bought the rights to his life... He'd tried to buy the film rights of all George Bernard Shaw's plays.*

◆◆◆
N-PLURAL: usu poss N
N-SING: usu N to-inf
N-PLURAL: *the* N, usu with supp

**PHRASES** 4 If something is not the case but you think that it should be, you can say that **by rights** it should be the case. ❑ *She did work which by rights should be done by someone else.* 5 If someone is a successful or respected person **in** their **own right**, they are successful or respected because of their own efforts and talents rather than those of the people they are closely connected with. ❑ *Although now a celebrity in her own right, actress Lynn Redgrave knows the difficulties of living in the shadow of her famous older sister.* 6 If you say that you **reserve the right to** do something, you mean that you will do it if you feel that it is necessary. ❑ *He reserved the right to change his mind.* 7 If you say that someone is **within** their **rights to** do something, you mean that they are morally or legally entitled to do it. ❑ *You were quite within your rights to refuse to co-operate with him.*

PHRASE: PHR with cl
PHRASE: usu n adj PHR
PHRASE: V inflects, PHR to-inf
PHRASE: usu v-link PHR = justified

④ **right** /raɪt/ 1 You use **right** in order to attract someone's attention or to indicate that you have dealt with one thing so you can go on to another. [SPOKEN] ❑ *Right, I'll be back in a minute.* 2 You can use **right** to check whether what you have just said is correct. [SPOKEN] ❑ *They have a small plane, right?* 3 You can say '**right**' to show that you are listening to what someone is saying and that you accept it or understand it. [SPOKEN] ❑ *'Your children may well come away speaking with a bit of a broad country accent' — 'Right.' — 'because they're mixing with country children.'* 4 → See also **all right**.

◆◆◆
ADV: ADV cl
CONVENTION
ADV: ADV as reply = yes

⑤ **right** /raɪt/ 1 You can use **right** to emphasize the precise place, position, or time of something. ❑ *The back of a car appeared right in front of him. ...a charming resort right on the Italian frontier.* 2 You can use **right** to emphasize how far something moves or extends or how long it continues. ❑ *...the highway that runs through the Indian zone right to the army positions... She was kept very busy right up to the moment of her departure.* 3 You can use **right** to emphasize that an action or state is complete. ❑ *The candle had burned right down... The handle came right off in my hand.* 4 You can use **right** to emphasize a noun, usually a noun referring to something bad. [BRIT, INFORMAL] ❑ *He gave them a right telling off.* 5 If you say that something happened **right after** a particular time or event or **right before** it, you mean that it happened immediately after or before it. ❑ *All of a sudden, right after the summer, Mother gets married.* 6 If you say **I'll be right there** or **I'll be right back**, you mean that you will get to a place or get back to it in a very short time. ❑ *I'm going to get some water. I'll be right back.*

◆◆◆
ADV: ADV adv/prep [emphasis]
ADV: ADV prep/adv [emphasis]
ADV: ADV adv/prep [emphasis]
ADJ: ADJ n [emphasis] = real
ADV: ADV prep/adv [emphasis] = just
ADV: ADV adv [emphasis]

**PHRASES** 7 If you do something **right away** or **right off**, you do it immediately. [INFORMAL] ❑ *He wants to see you right away... Right off I want to confess that I was wrong.* 8 You can use **right now** to emphasize that you are referring to the present moment. [INFORMAL] ❑ *I'm warning you; stop it right now!*

PHRASE: PHR after v, PHR with cl [emphasis]
PHRASE: PHR with cl [emphasis]

⑥ **Right** /raɪt/ **Right** is used in some British titles. It indicates high rank or status. ❑ *...The Right Reverend John Baker. ...the Right Honourable Lynn Jones MP.*

ADV: ADV adj

**right an|gle (right angles)** also **right-angle.** 1 A **right angle** is an angle of ninety degrees. A square has four right angles. 2 If two things are **at right angles**, they are situated so that they form an angle of 90° where they touch each other. You can also say that one thing is **at right angles to** another. ❑ *...two lasers at right angles.*

N-COUNT
PHRASE: oft PHR *to* n

**right-angled** 1 A **right-angled** triangle has one angle that is a right angle. [BRIT]

ADJ: ADJ n

✔ in AM, use **right triangle**

2 A **right-angled** bend is a sharp bend that turns through approximately ninety degrees.

ADJ: ADJ n

**right-click (right-clicks, right-clicking, right-clicked)** To **right-click** or to **right-click on** something means to press the right-hand button on a computer mouse. [COMPUTING] ❑ *All you have to do is right-click on the desktop and select New Folder.*

VERB ≠left-click
V *on* n

**right|eous** /raɪtʃəs/ If you think that someone behaves or lives in a way that is morally good, you can say that they are **righteous**. People sometimes use **righteous** to express their dis-

ADJ

approval when they think someone is only behaving in this way so that others will admire or support them. [FORMAL] ❑ *Aren't you afraid of being seen as a righteous crusader?* ♦ **right|eous|ness** *Both sides in the dispute have been adopting a tone of moral righteousness.* ♦ **right|eous|ly** *They righteously maintain that they do not practise rationing.* N-UNCOUNT ADV

**right|ful** /raɪtfʊl/ If you say that someone or something has returned to its **rightful** place or position, they have returned to the place or position that you think they should have. ❑ *The Baltics' own democratic traditions would help them to regain their rightful place in Europe.* ♦ **right|ful|ly** *Jealousy is the feeling that someone else has something that rightfully belongs to you.* ADJ: ADJ n; ADV: ADV group

**right-hand** If something is on the **right-hand** side of something, it is positioned on the right of it. ❑ *...a church on the right-hand side of the road.* ADJ: ADJ n ≠ *left-hand*

**right-hand drive** A **right-hand drive** vehicle has its steering wheel on the right side. It is designed to be driven in countries such as Britain, Japan, and Australia where people drive on the left side of the road. ADJ: usu ADJ n ≠ *left-hand drive*

**right-handed** Someone who is **right-handed** uses their right hand rather than their left hand for activities such as writing and sports, and for picking things up. ♦ **Right-handed** is also an adverb. ❑ *I batted left-handed and bowled right-handed.* ADJ ≠ *left-handed*; ADV: ADV after v

**right-hander** **(right-handers)** You can describe someone as a **right-hander** if they use their right hand rather than their left hand for activities such as writing and sports and for picking things up. N-COUNT ≠ *left-hander*

**right-hand man** **(right-hand men)** Someone's **right-hand man** is the person who acts as their chief assistant and helps and supports them a lot in their work. ❑ *He is Rupert Murdoch's right-hand man at News International.* N-COUNT: usu poss N

**right|ist** /raɪtɪst/ **(rightists)** [1] If someone is described as a **rightist**, they are politically conservative and traditional. Rightists support the ideals of capitalism. [2] If someone has **rightist** views or takes part in **rightist** activities, they are politically conservative and traditional and support the ideas of capitalism. N-COUNT ≠ *leftist*; ADJ: usu ADJ n ≠ *leftist*

**right-justify** **(right-justifies, right-justifying, right-justified)** If printed text is **right-justified**, each line finishes at the same distance from the right-hand edge of the page or column. ❑ *Click this option to right-justify the selected text.* VERB ≠ *left-justify*; V n

**right-minded** If you think that someone's opinions or beliefs are sensible and you agree with them, you can describe them as a **right-minded** person. ❑ *He is an able, right-minded, and religious man.* ADJ: usu ADJ n [approval] = *right-thinking*

**righto** /raɪtoʊ/ also **right oh.** Some people say **righto** to show that they agree with a suggestion that someone has made. [BRIT, INFORMAL] ❑ *Righto, Harry. I'll put Russ Clements in charge.* EXCLAM [formulae] = *OK*

**right-of-centre**

✔ in AM, use **right-of-center**

You can describe a person or political party as **right-of-centre** if they have political views which are closer to capitalism and conservatism than to socialism but which are not very extreme. ❑ *...the new right-of-centre government.* ADJ: usu ADJ n ≠ *left-of-centre*

**right of way** **(rights of way)** [1] A **right of way** is a public path across private land. [2] When someone who is driving or walking along a road has **right of way** or **the right of way**, they have the right to continue along a particular road or path, and other people must stop for them. [3] A **right of way** is a strip of land that is used for a road, railway line, or power line. [AM] N-COUNT; N-UNCOUNT; N-COUNT

**right-on** You can describe someone as **right-on** if they have liberal or left-wing ideas, especially if you disagree with them or want to make fun of them. ❑ *The people that come to watch the play are all those right-on left-wing sort of people.* ◆◇◇ ADJ: usu ADJ n = *politically correct*

**rights is|sue** **(rights issues)** A **rights issue** is when a company offers shares at a reduced price to people who already have shares in the company. [BUSINESS] N-COUNT

**right-thinking** If you think that someone's opinions or beliefs are sensible and you agree with them, you can describe them as a **right-thinking** person. ❑ *Every right-thinking American would be proud of them.* ADJ: usu ADJ n [approval] = *right-minded*

**right to life** When people talk about an unborn baby's **right to life**, they mean that a baby has the right to be born, even if it is severely disabled or if its mother does not want it. ❑ *...the Right to Life Campaign.* N-SING: oft N n

**right tri|an|gle** **(right triangles)** A **right triangle** has one angle that is a right angle. [AM] N-COUNT

✔ in BRIT, use **right-angled triangle**

**right|ward** /raɪtwəʳd/ also **rightwards.** If there is a **rightward** trend in the politics of a person or party, their views become more right-wing. ❑ *The result reflects a modest rightward shift in opinion.* ♦ **Rightward** is also an adverb. ❑ *He continued to urge the Conservative Party to tilt rightwards.* ADJ: ADJ n ≠ *leftward*; ADV: ADV after v

**right-wing** ◆◇◇

✔ The spelling **right wing** is also used for meaning 2.

[1] A **right-wing** person or group has conservative or capitalist views. ❑ *...a right-wing government.* [2] **The right wing** of a political party consists of the members who have the most conservative or the most capitalist views. ❑ *...the right wing of the Conservative Party.* ADJ: usu ADJ n ≠ *left-wing*; N-SING: *the* N ≠ *left-wing*

**right-winger** **(right-wingers)** If you think someone has views which are more right-wing than most other members of their party, you can say they are a **right-winger**. N-COUNT ≠ *left-winger*

**rig|id** /rɪdʒɪd/ [1] Laws, rules, or systems that are **rigid** cannot be changed or varied, and are therefore considered to be rather severe. ❑ *Several colleges in our study have rigid rules about student conduct.* ♦ **ri|gid|ity** /rɪdʒɪdɪti/ *...the rigidity of government policy.* ♦ **rig|id|ly** *The caste system was rigidly enforced.* [2] If you disapprove of someone because you think they are not willing to change their way of thinking or behaving, you can describe them as **rigid**. ❑ *She was a fairly rigid person who had strong religious views.* [3] A **rigid** substance or object is stiff and does not bend, stretch, or twist easily. ❑ *...rigid plastic containers.* ♦ **ri|gid|ity** *...the strength and rigidity of glass.* ADJ [disapproval] ≠ *flexible*; N-UNCOUNT; ADV: ADV with v; ADJ [disapproval]; ADJ ≠ *flexible*; N-UNCOUNT

**rig|ma|role** /rɪgməroʊl/ **(rigmaroles)** You can describe a long and complicated process as a **rigmarole**. ❑ *Then the whole rigmarole starts over again.* N-COUNT: usu sing [disapproval]

**ri|gor** /rɪgəʳ/ → see **rigour**.

**ri|gor mor|tis** /rɪgəʳ mɔːʳtɪs/ In a dead body, when **rigor mortis** sets in, the joints and muscles become very stiff. N-UNCOUNT

**rig|or|ous** /rɪgərəs/ [1] A test, system, or procedure that is **rigorous** is very thorough and strict. ❑ *The selection process is based on rigorous tests of competence and experience.* ♦ **rig|or|ous|ly** *...rigorously conducted research.* [2] If someone is **rigorous** in the way that they do something, they are very careful and thorough. ❑ *He is rigorous in his control of expenditure.* ADJ: usu ADJ n; ADV; ADJ: usu v-link ADJ, oft ADJ *in* -ing/n

**rig|our** /rɪgəʳ/ **(rigours)**

✔ in AM, use **rigor**

[1] If you refer to **the rigours of** an activity or job, you mean the difficult, demanding, or unpleasant things that are associated with it. ❑ *He found the rigours of the tour too demanding.* [2] If something is done with **rigour**, it is done in a strict, thorough way. ❑ *The new current affairs series promises to address challenging issues with freshness and rigour.* N-PLURAL: usu *the* N *of* n; N-UNCOUNT

**rile** /raɪl/ **(riles, riling, riled)** If something **riles** you, it makes you angry. ❑ *Cancellations and late departures rarely rile him.* ♦ **riled** *He saw I was riled.*
VERB V n — ADJ

**Riley** /raɪli/ also **Reilly.** If you say that someone is living **the life of Riley**, you mean that they have a very easy and comfortable life with few worries.
PHRASE: usu v PHR

**rim** /rɪm/ **(rims)** 1 The **rim** of a container such as a cup or glass is the edge that goes all the way round the top. ❑ *She looked at him over the rim of her glass.* 2 The **rim** of a circular object is its outside edge. ❑ *...a round mirror with white metal rim.* 3 → See also **rimmed, -rimmed.**
N-COUNT: usu with supp — N-COUNT: usu with supp

**rim|less** /rɪmləs/ **Rimless** glasses are glasses which have no frame around the lenses or which have a frame only along the top of the lenses.
ADJ: usu ADJ n

**rimmed** /rɪmd/ 1 If something **is rimmed with** a substance or colour, it has that substance or colour around its border. ❑ *The plates and glassware were rimmed with gold.* 2 → See also **rim, -rimmed.**
ADJ: usu v-link ADJ *with* n

**-rimmed** /-rɪmd/ 1 **-rimmed** combines with nouns to form adjectives that describe something as having a border or frame made of a particular substance. ❑ *...horn-rimmed spectacles.* 2 → See also **rim, rimmed.**
COMB in ADJ

**rind** /raɪnd/ **(rinds)** 1 The **rind** of a fruit such as a lemon or orange is its thick outer skin. ❑ *...grated lemon rind.* 2 The **rind** of cheese or bacon is the hard outer edge which you do not usually eat. ❑ *Discard the bacon rind and cut each rasher in half.*
N-VAR: usu with supp — N-VAR: usu with supp

**ring**
① TELEPHONING OR MAKING A SOUND
② SHAPES AND GROUPS

① **ring** /rɪŋ/ **(rings, ringing, rang, rung)** ◆◆◇
⇛ Please look at category 11 to see if the expression you are looking for is shown under another headword. 1 When you **ring** someone, you telephone them. [mainly BRIT] ❑ *He rang me at my mother's... I would ring when I got back to the hotel... She has rung home just once... Could someone ring for a taxi?* ♦ **Ring up** means the same as **ring**. ❑ *You can ring us up anytime... John rang up and invited himself over for dinner... A few months ago I rang up about some housing problems... Nobody rings up a doctor in the middle of the night for no reason.*
VERB = phone; V n; V; V adv; V *for* n; PHRASAL VERB; V n P; V P; V P *about* n; V P n (not pron)

☑ in AM, usually use **call**

2 When a telephone **rings**, it makes a sound to let you know that someone is phoning you. ❑ *As soon as he got home, the phone rang.* ♦ **Ring** is also a noun. ❑ *After at least eight rings, an ancient-sounding maid answered the phone.* ♦ **ring|ing** *She was jolted out of her sleep by the ringing of the telephone.* 3 When you **ring** a bell or when a bell **rings**, it makes a sound. ❑ *He heard the school bell ring... The door was opened before she could ring the bell.* ♦ **Ring** is also a noun. ❑ *There was a ring at the bell.* ♦ **ring|ing** *...the ringing of church bells.* 4 If you **ring for** something, you ring a bell to call someone to bring it to you. If you **ring** for someone, you ring a bell so that they will come to you. ❑ *Shall I ring for a fresh pot of tea?* 5 If you say that a place **is ringing with** sound, usually pleasant sound, you mean that the place is completely filled with that sound. [LITERARY] ❑ *The whole place was ringing with music.* 6 You can use **ring** to describe a quality that something such as a statement, discussion, or argument seems to have. For example, if an argument **has a familiar ring**, it seems familiar. ❑ *His proud boast of leading 'the party of low taxation' has a hollow ring.*
VERB; V; N-COUNT; N-UNCOUNT; VERB; V; V n; N-COUNT; N-UNCOUNT; VERB; V *for* n; VERB; V *with* n; N-SING: usu *a* adj N = feel

**PHRASES** 7 If you say that someone **rings the changes**, you mean that they make changes or improvements to the way something is organized or done. ❑ *Ring the changes by adding spices, dried fruit or olives.* 8 If you say that someone's words **ring in** your **ears** or **ring in** your **head**, you mean that you remember them very clearly, usually when you would prefer to forget them. [LITERARY] ❑ *She shivered as the sound of that man's abuse rang in her ears.* 9 If you **give** someone **a ring**, you phone them. [mainly BRIT, INFORMAL] ❑ *We'll give him a ring as soon as we get back.*
PHRASE: V inflects; PHRASE: V and N inflect; PHRASE: V inflects

☑ in AM, usually use **call**

10 If a statement **rings true**, it seems to be true or genuine. If it **rings hollow**, it does not seem to be true or genuine. ❑ *Joanna's denial rang true... The rumpus has made all the optimistic statements about unity and harmony ring a little hollow.* 11 → See also **ringing**. to **ring a bell** → see **bell.**
PHRASE: V inflects

♦ **ring around** → see **ring round.**

♦ **ring back** If you **ring** someone **back**, you phone them either because they phoned you earlier and you were not there or because you did not finish an earlier telephone conversation. [mainly BRIT] ❑ *Tell her I'll ring back in a few minutes... If there's any problem I'll ring you back.*
PHRASAL VERB: no passive; V P; V n P

☑ in AM, usually use **call back**

♦ **ring in** If you **ring in**, you phone a place, such as the place where you work. [mainly BRIT] ❑ *Cecil wasn't there, having rung in to say he was taking the day off.*
PHRASAL VERB; V P

☑ in AM, usually use **call in**

♦ **ring off** When you **ring off**, you put down the receiver at the end of a telephone call. [mainly BRIT] ❑ *She had rung off before he could press her for an answer.*
PHRASAL VERB; V P

☑ in AM, usually use **hang up**

♦ **ring out** If a sound **rings out**, it can be heard loudly and clearly. ❑ *A single shot rang out.*
PHRASAL VERB; V P

♦ **ring round** or **ring around** If you **ring round** or **ring around**, you phone several people, usually when you are trying to organize something or to find some information. [mainly BRIT] ❑ *She'd ring around and get back to me... She immediately started ringing round her friends and relatives.*
PHRASAL VERB; V P; V P n (not pron)

☑ in AM, usually use **call around**

♦ **ring up** 1 → see **ring 1**. 2 If a shop assistant **rings up** a sale on a cash register, he or she presses the keys in order to record the amount that is being spent. ❑ *She was ringing up her sale on an ancient cash register.* 3 If a company **rings up** an amount of money, usually a large amount of money, it makes that amount of money in sales or profits. ❑ *The advertising agency rang up 1.4 billion dollars in yearly sales.*
PHRASAL VERB; V P n; Also V n P; PHRASAL VERB; V P n (not pron)

② **ring** /rɪŋ/ **(rings, ringing, ringed)** ◆◇◇ 1 A **ring** is a small circle of metal or other substance that you wear on your finger as jewellery. ❑ *...a gold wedding ring.* 2 An object or substance that is in the shape of a circle can be described as a **ring**. ❑ *Frank took a large ring of keys from his pocket. ...a ring of blue smoke.* 3 A group of people or things arranged in a circle can be described as a **ring**. ❑ *They then formed a ring around the square.* 4 A gas or electric **ring** is one of the small flat areas on top of a stove which heat up and which you use for cooking. [mainly BRIT]
N-COUNT; N-COUNT: usu with supp; N-COUNT: usu with supp = circle; N-COUNT: usu supp N

☑ in AM, usually use **burner**

5 At a boxing or wrestling match or a circus, the **ring** is the place where the contest or performance takes place. It consists of an enclosed space with seats round it. ❑ *He will never again be allowed inside a British boxing ring.* 6 You can refer to an organized group of people who are involved in an illegal activity as a **ring**. ❑ *Police are investigating the suspected drug ring at the school.* 7 If a building or place **is ringed with** or **by** something, it is surrounded by it. ❑ *The areas are sealed off and ringed by troops.* 8 If you say that someone **runs rings round** you or **runs rings around** you, you mean that they are a lot better or a lot more
N-COUNT: usu with supp; N-COUNT: usu n N; VERB: usu passive; *be* V-ed; PHRASE: V inflects

successful than you at a particular activity. [INFORMAL] ❑ *Mentally, he can still run rings round men half his age!*

**ring bind|er** **(ring binders)** A **ring binder** is a file with hard covers, which you can insert pages into. The pages are held in by metal rings on a bar attached to the inside of the file. N-COUNT

**ring|er** /rɪŋəʳ/ **(ringers)** [1] If you say that one person is **a ringer** or **a dead ringer** for another, you mean that they look exactly like each other. [INFORMAL] PHRASE: usu v-link PHR *for* n [2] A bell **ringer** is someone who rings church bells or hand bells as a hobby. [mainly BRIT] N-COUNT

**ring-fence** **(ring-fences, ring-fencing, ring-fenced)** To **ring-fence** a grant or fund means to put restrictions on it, so that it can only be used for a particular purpose. [BRIT] ❑ *The Treasury has now agreed to ring-fence the money to ensure that it goes directly towards helping elderly people.* VERB V n

**ring fin|ger** **(ring fingers)** Your **ring finger** is the third finger of your left or right hand, without counting your thumb. In some countries, people wear a ring on this finger to show that they are engaged or married. N-COUNT

**ring|ing** /rɪŋɪŋ/ [1] A **ringing** sound is loud and can be heard very clearly. ❑ *He hit the metal steps with a ringing crash.* ADJ: ADJ n = *resounding* [2] A **ringing** statement or declaration is one that is made forcefully and is intended to make a powerful impression. ❑ *...the party's 14th Congress, which gave a ringing endorsement to capitalist-style economic reforms.* ADJ: ADJ n

**ring|leader** /rɪŋliːdəʳ/ **(ringleaders)** The **ringleaders** in a quarrel, disturbance, or illegal activity are the people who started it and who cause most of the trouble. ❑ *The soldiers were well informed about the ringleaders of the protest.* N-COUNT [disapproval]

**ring|let** /rɪŋlət/ **(ringlets)** **Ringlets** are long curls of hair that hang down. N-COUNT: usu pl

**ring|master** /rɪŋmɑːstəʳ, -mæst-/ **(ringmasters)** A circus **ringmaster** is the person who introduces the performers and the animals. N-COUNT

**ring-pull** **(ring-pulls)** A **ring-pull** is a metal strip that you pull off the top of a can of drink in order to open it. [BRIT] N-COUNT

✓ in AM, use **tab**

**ring road** **(ring roads)** A **ring road** is a road that goes round the edge of a town so that traffic does not have to go through the town centre. [mainly BRIT] N-COUNT

✓ in AM, usually use **beltway**

**ring|side** /rɪŋsaɪd/ [1] The **ringside** is the area around the edge of a circus ring, boxing ring, or show jumping ring. ❑ *Most of the top British trainers were at the ringside.* N-SING [2] If you have a **ringside** seat or a **ringside** view, you are close to an event and can see it clearly. ❑ *I had a ringside seat for the whole performance.* ADJ: ADJ n

**ring tone** **(ring tones)** The **ring tone** is the sound made by a telephone, especially a mobile phone, when it rings. ❑ *They offer 70 hours' standby time, 2hr 50min talk time, and 15 ring tones.* N-COUNT

**ring|worm** /rɪŋwɜːʳm/ **Ringworm** is a skin disease caused by a fungus. It produces itchy red patches on a person's or animal's skin, especially on their head and between their legs and toes. [MEDICAL] N-UNCOUNT

**rink** /rɪŋk/ **(rinks)** A **rink** is a large area covered with ice where people go to ice-skate, or a large area of concrete where people go to roller-skate. ❑ *The other skaters were ordered off the rink.* N-COUNT: oft supp N

**rinse** /rɪns/ **(rinses, rinsing, rinsed)** [1] When you **rinse** something, you wash it in clean water in order to remove dirt or soap from it. ❑ *It's important to rinse the rice to remove the starch.* VERB V n ♦ **Rinse** is also a noun. ❑ *A quick rinse isn't sufficient. Use plenty of running water to wash away all traces of shampoo.* N-COUNT [2] If you **rinse** your mouth, you wash it by filling your mouth with water or with a liquid that kills germs, then spitting it out. ❑ *Use a toothbrush on your tongue as well, and rinse your mouth frequently.* VERB V n ♦ **Rinse out** means the same as **rinse**. ❑ *After her meal she invariably rinsed out her mouth... You should rinse your mouth out after eating.* PHRASAL VERB V P n (not pron) V n P ♦ **Rinse** is also a noun. ❑ *...mouth rinses with fluoride.* N-MASS

**riot** /raɪət/ **(riots, rioting, rioted)** [1] When there is a **riot**, a crowd of people behave violently in a public place, for example they fight, throw stones, or damage buildings and vehicles. ❑ *Twelve inmates have been killed during a riot at the prison.* ◆◇◇ N-COUNT [2] If people **riot**, they behave violently in a public place. ❑ *Last year 600 inmates rioted, starting fires and building barricades.* VERB V ♦ **ri|ot|er** **(rioters)** *The militia dispersed the rioters.* N-COUNT ♦ **ri|ot|ing** *At least fifteen people are now known to have died in three days of rioting.* N-UNCOUNT [3] If you say that there is **a riot of** something pleasant such as colour, you mean that there is a large amount of various types of it. ❑ *All the cacti were in flower, so that the desert was a riot of colour.* N-SING: a N *of* n [approval]

PHRASES [4] If someone in authority **reads** you **the riot act**, they tell you that you will be punished unless you start behaving properly. ❑ *I'm glad you read the riot act to Billy. He's still a kid and still needs to be told what to do.* PHRASE: V inflects [5] If people **run riot**, they behave in a wild and uncontrolled manner. ❑ *Rampaging prisoners ran riot through Strangeways jail.* PHRASE: V inflects [6] If something such as your imagination **runs riot**, it is not limited or controlled, and produces ideas that are new or exciting, rather than sensible. ❑ *A conservatory offers the perfect excuse to let your imagination run riot.* PHRASE: V inflects

**riot gear** **Riot gear** is the special clothing and equipment worn by police officers or soldiers when they have to deal with a riot. N-UNCOUNT

**ri|ot|ous** /raɪətəs/ [1] If you say that someone has a **riotous** lifestyle, you mean that they frequently behave in a excessive and uncontrolled way, for example by eating or drinking too much. [FORMAL] ❑ *...aristocrats who wasted their inheritances in riotous living.* ADJ: usu ADJ n = *wild* [2] You can describe someone's behaviour or an event as **riotous** when it is noisy and lively in a rather wild way. ❑ *The dinner was often a riotous affair enlivened by superbly witty speeches.* ADJ: usu ADJ n ♦ **ri|ot|ous|ly** *...a slapstick affair which I found riotously amusing.* ADV: ADV adj/-ed

**riot po|lice** **The riot police** is the section of the police force that is trained to deal with people who cause trouble in public places. ❑ *After about 10 minutes the riot police arrived.* N-SING-COLL

**riot shield** **(riot shields)** **Riot shields** are pieces of equipment made of transparent plastic which are used by the police to protect themselves against angry crowds. N-COUNT: usu pl

**rip** /rɪp/ **(rips, ripping, ripped)** [1] When something **rips** or when you **rip** it, you tear it forcefully with your hands or with a tool such as a knife. ❑ *I felt the banner rip as we were pushed in opposite directions... I tried not to rip the paper as I unwrapped it.* VERB = *tear* V V n [2] A **rip** is a long cut or split in something made of cloth or paper. ❑ *Looking at the rip in her new dress, she flew into a rage.* N-COUNT = *tear* [3] If you **rip** something away, you remove it quickly and forcefully. ❑ *He ripped away a wire that led to the alarm button... He ripped the phone from her hand.* VERB = *tear* V n with adv V n prep [4] If something **rips** into someone or something or **rips** through them, it enters that person or thing so quickly and forcefully that it often goes completely through them. ❑ *A volley of bullets ripped into the facing wall.* VERB = *tear* V prep/adv

PHRASES [5] If you **let rip**, you do something forcefully and without trying to control yourself. [INFORMAL] ❑ *Turn the guitars up full and let rip.* PHRASE: *let* inflects [6] If you **let** something **rip**, you do it as quickly or as forcefully as possible. You can say **'let it rip'** or **'let her rip'** to someone when you want them to make a vehicle go as fast as it possibly can. ❑ *The ecological disaster is partly a product of letting everything rip in order to increase production.* PHRASE: *let* inflects

♦ **rip off** If someone **rips** you **off**, they cheat you by charging you too much money for some- PHRASAL VERB thing or by selling you something that is broken or damaged. [INFORMAL] ❑ *The Consumer Federation claims banks are ripping you off by not passing along savings on interest rates... The airlines have been accused of ripping off customers.* → See also **rip-off**. V n P; V P n (not pron)

♦ **rip up** If you **rip** something **up**, you tear it into small pieces. ❑ *If we wrote I think he would rip up the letter... She took every photograph of me that was in our house and ripped it up.* PHRASAL VERB = tear up; V P n (not pron); V n P

**R.I.P.** /ɑːr aɪ piː/ **R.I.P.** is written on gravestones and expresses the hope that the person buried there may rest in peace. **R.I.P.** is an abbreviation for the Latin expression 'requiescat in pace' or 'requiescant in pace'. CONVENTION

**rip|cord** /rɪpkɔːʳd/ **(ripcords)** also **rip cord.** A **ripcord** is the cord that you pull to open a parachute. N-COUNT

**ripe** /raɪp/ **(riper, ripest)** 1 **Ripe** fruit or grain is fully grown and ready to eat. ❑ *Always choose ripe fruit. ...fields of ripe wheat.* ♦ **ripe|ness** *Test the figs for ripeness.* ADJ; N-UNCOUNT 2 If a situation is **ripe for** a particular development or event, you mean that development or event is likely to happen soon. ❑ *Conditions were ripe for an outbreak of cholera.* ADJ: v-link ADJ *for* n/-ing 3 If someone lives to a **ripe old age**, they live until they are very old. ❑ *He lived to the ripe old age of 95.* PHRASE: prep PHR

**rip|en** /raɪpən/ **(ripens, ripening, ripened)** When crops **ripen** or when the sun **ripens** them, they become ripe. ❑ *I'm waiting for the apples to ripen... You can ripen the tomatoes on a sunny windowsill.* VERB; V; V n

**rip-off** **(rip-offs)** 1 If you say that something that you bought was a **rip-off**, you mean that you were charged too much money or that it was of very poor quality. [INFORMAL] ❑ *If he thinks £5.40 a day for parking at Luton Airport is a rip-off, he should try Heathrow.* N-COUNT 2 If you say that something is a **rip-off of** something else, you mean that it is a copy of that thing and has no original features of its own. [INFORMAL] ❑ *In a rip-off of the hit movie Green Card, Billy marries one of his students so he can stay in the country.* N-COUNT: oft N *of* n

**ri|poste** /rɪpɒst, AM -poʊst/ **(ripostes, riposting, riposted)** 1 A **riposte** is a quick, clever reply to something that someone has said. [WRITTEN] ❑ *Laura glanced at Grace, expecting a cheeky riposte.* N-COUNT 2 If you **riposte**, you make a quick, clever response to something someone has said. [WRITTEN] ❑ *'It's tough at the top,' he said. 'It's tougher at the bottom,' riposted the billionaire.* VERB; V with quote 3 You can refer to an action as a **riposte to** something when it is a response to that thing. [JOURNALISM] ❑ *The operation is being seen as a swift riposte to the killing of a senior army commander.* N-COUNT: oft N *to* n

**rip|ple** /rɪpᵊl/ **(ripples, rippling, rippled)** 1 **Ripples** are little waves on the surface of water caused by the wind or by something moving in or on the water. N-COUNT 2 When the surface of an area of water **ripples** or when something **ripples** it, a number of little waves appear on it. ❑ *You throw a pebble in a pool and it ripples... I could see the dawn breeze rippling the shining water.* VERB; V; V n 3 If something such as a feeling **ripples** over someone's body, it moves across it or through it. [LITERARY] ❑ *A chill shiver rippled over his skin.* VERB; V prep 4 If an event causes **ripples**, its effects gradually spread, causing several other events to happen one after the other. ❑ *The ripples of Europe's currency crisis continue to be felt in most of the member states.* N-COUNT: usu pl, with supp

**rip|ple ef|fect** **(ripple effects)** If an event or action has a **ripple effect**, it causes several other events to happen one after the other. ❑ *Delayed flights have a ripple effect. Just one late flight could be carrying passengers for a dozen connecting services.* N-COUNT = knock-on effect

**rip-roaring** If you describe something as **rip-roaring**, you mean that it is very exciting and full of energy. [INFORMAL] ❑ *...a rip-roaring movie with a great array of special effects.* ADJ: ADJ n

**rip|tide** /rɪptaɪd/ **(riptides)** also **rip-tide.** A **riptide** is an area of sea where two different currents meet or where the water is extremely deep. Riptides make the water very rough and dangerous. N-COUNT

**rise** /raɪz/ **(rises, rising, rose, risen)** ♦♦♦ 1 If something **rises**, it moves upwards. ❑ *He watched the smoke rise from his cigarette... The powdery dust rose in a cloud around him.* VERB; V from/to n; V ♦ **Rise up** means the same as **rise**. ❑ *Spray rose up from the surface of the water... Black dense smoke rose up.* PHRASAL VERB; V P *from/to* n, V P 2 When you **rise**, you stand up. [FORMAL] ❑ *Luther rose slowly from the chair... He looked at Livy and Mark, who had risen to greet him.* VERB; V *from* n; V ♦ **Rise up** means the same as **rise**. ❑ *The only thing I wanted was to rise up from the table and leave this house.* PHRASAL VERB; V P *from* n 3 When you **rise**, you get out of bed. [FORMAL] ❑ *Tony had risen early and gone to the cottage to work.* VERB; V 4 When the sun or moon **rises**, it appears in the sky. ❑ *He wanted to be over the line of the ridge before the sun had risen.* VERB ≠ set; V 5 You can say that something **rises** when it appears as a large tall shape. [LITERARY] ❑ *The building rose before him, tall and stately.* VERB; V prep/adv ♦ **Rise up** means the same as **rise**. ❑ *The White Mountains rose up before me.* PHRASAL VERB; V P prep/adv 6 If the level of something such as the water in a river **rises**, it becomes higher. ❑ *The waters continue to rise as more than 1,000 people are evacuated.* VERB ≠ fall; V 7 If land **rises**, it slopes upwards. ❑ *He looked up the slope of land that rose from the house... The ground begins to rise some 20 yards away.* VERB ≠ fall; V prep/adv; V 8 If an amount **rises**, it increases. ❑ *Pre-tax profits rose from £842,000 to £1.82m... Tourist trips of all kinds in Britain rose by 10.5% between 1977 and 1987... Exports in June rose 1.5% to a record $30.91 billion... The number of business failures has risen... The increase is needed to meet rising costs.* VERB ≠ fall; V *from/to* amount; V *by* amount; V amount; V; V-ing 9 A **rise in** the amount of something is an increase in it. ❑ *...the prospect of another rise in interest rates.* N-COUNT: N *in* n = increase 10 A **rise** is an increase in your wages or your salary. [BRIT] ❑ *He will get a pay rise of nearly £4,000.* N-COUNT = increase

✔ in AM, use **raise**

11 **The rise of** a movement or activity is an increase in its popularity or influence. ❑ *...the rise of racism in America.* N-SING: the N *of* n = increase 12 If the wind **rises**, it becomes stronger. ❑ *The wind was still rising, approaching a force nine gale.* VERB; V 13 If a sound **rises** or if someone's voice **rises**, it becomes louder or higher. ❑ *'Bernard?' Her voice rose hysterically... His voice rose almost to a scream.* VERB; V; V *to* n 14 When the people in a country **rise**, they try to defeat the government or army that is controlling them. ❑ *The National Convention has promised armed support to any people who wish to rise against armed oppression.* VERB; V *against* n ♦ **Rise up** means the same as **rise**. ❑ *He warned that if the government moved against him the people would rise up... A woman called on the population to rise up against the government.* PHRASAL VERB; V P; V P *against* n ♦ **ris|ing** **(risings)** *...popular risings against tyrannical rulers.* N-COUNT 15 If someone **rises to** a higher position or status, they become more important, successful, or powerful. ❑ *She is a strong woman who has risen to the top of a deeply sexist organisation.* VERB; V prep ♦ **Rise up** means the same as **rise**. ❑ *I started with Hoover 26 years ago in sales and rose up through the ranks.* PHRASAL VERB; V P prep 16 The **rise** of someone is the process by which they become more important, successful, or powerful. ❑ *Haig's rise was fuelled by an all-consuming sense of patriotic duty.* N-SING: with poss ≠ fall 17 If something **gives rise to** an event or situation, it causes that event or situation to happen. ❑ *Low levels of choline in the body can give rise to high blood-pressure.* PHRASE: V inflects, PHR n 18 to **rise to the bait** → see **bait**. to **rise to the challenge** → see **challenge**. to **rise to the occasion** → see **occasion**.

♦ **rise above** If you **rise above** a difficulty or problem, you manage not to let it affect you. ❑ *It tells the story of an aspiring young man's attempt to rise above the squalor of the street.* PHRASAL VERB; V P n

♦ **rise up** → see **rise 1, 2, 5, 14, 15.**

**ris|en** /rɪzᵊn/ **Risen** is the past participle of **rise**.

**ris|er** /raɪzəʳ/ **(risers)** 1 An early **riser** is someone who likes to get up early in the morning. A late **riser** is someone who likes to get up late. ❑ *He was an early riser and he would be at the breakfast table at seven.* 2 A **riser** is the flat vertical part of a step or a stair. [TECHNICAL] N-COUNT: supp N / N-COUNT

**ris|ible** /rɪzɪbᵊl/ If you describe something as **risible**, you mean that it is ridiculous and does not deserve to be taken seriously. [FORMAL] ADJ disapproval = ludicrous

**ris|ing damp** If a building has **rising damp**, moisture that has entered the bricks has moved upwards from the floor, causing damage to the walls. [BRIT] N-UNCOUNT

**ris|ing star** **(rising stars)** A **rising star** in a particular sport, art, or area of business is someone who is starting to do very well and who people think will soon be very successful. [JOURNALISM] ❑ *Anna is a rising star in the world of modelling.* N-COUNT

**risk** /rɪsk/ **(risks, risking, risked)** ◆◆◇ 1 If there is a **risk of** something unpleasant, there is a possibility that it will happen. ❑ *There is a small risk of brain damage from the procedure... In all the confusion, there's a serious risk that the main issues will be forgotten.* N-VAR: oft N of n, N that 2 If something that you do is a **risk**, it might have unpleasant or undesirable results. ❑ *You're taking a big risk showing this to Kravis.* N-COUNT 3 If you say that something or someone is a **risk**, you mean they are likely to cause harm. ❑ *It's being overfat that constitutes a health risk... The restaurant has been refurbished – it was found to be a fire risk.* N-COUNT: usu with supp 4 If you are considered a good **risk**, a bank or shop thinks that it is safe to lend you money or let you have goods without paying for them at the time. ❑ *Before providing the cash, they will have to decide whether you are a good or bad risk.* N-COUNT: supp N 5 If you **risk** something unpleasant, you do something which might result in that thing happening or affecting you. ❑ *Those who fail to register risk severe penalties.* VERB V n/-ing 6 If you **risk** doing something, you do it, even though you know that it might have undesirable consequences. ❑ *The captain was not willing to risk taking his ship through the straits in such bad weather.* VERB V -ing/n 7 If you **risk** your life or something else important, you behave in a way that might result in it being lost or harmed. ❑ *She risked her own life to help a disabled woman.* VERB V n

PHRASES 8 To be **at risk** means to be in a situation where something unpleasant might happen. ❑ *Up to 25,000 jobs are still at risk.* PHRASE: v-link PHR, oft PHR of n 9 If you do something **at the risk of** something unpleasant happening, you do it even though you know that the unpleasant thing might happen as a result. ❑ *At the risk of being repetitive, I will say again that statistics are only a guide.* PHRASE: PHR n/-ing 10 If you tell someone that they are doing something **at** their **own risk**, you are warning them that, if they are harmed, it will be their own responsibility. ❑ *Those who wish to come here will do so at their own risk.* PHRASE: PHR after v 11 If you **run** the **risk of** doing or experiencing something undesirable, you do something knowing that the undesirable thing might happen as a result. ❑ *The officers had run the risk of being dismissed.* PHRASE: V and N inflect 12 to **risk** your **neck** → see **neck**.

**risk man|age|ment** **Risk management** is the skill or job of deciding what the risks are in a particular situation and taking action to prevent or reduce them. N-UNCOUNT

**risk-taking** **Risk-taking** means taking actions which might have unpleasant or undesirable results. ❑ *...a more entrepreneurial climate, with positive encouragement of risk-taking and innovation.* N-UNCOUNT

**risky** /rɪski/ **(riskier, riskiest)** If an activity or action is **risky**, it is dangerous or likely to fail. ❑ *Investing in airlines is a very risky business.* ADJ: oft it v-link ADJ to-inf

**ri|sot|to** /rɪzɒtoʊ/ **(risottos)** **Risotto** is an Italian dish consisting of rice cooked with ingredients such as tomatoes, meat, or fish. N-VAR

**ris|qué** /rɪskeɪ, AM rɪskeɪ/ If you describe something as **risqué**, you mean that it is slightly rude because it refers to sex. ❑ *But the risqué headlines don't necessarily reflect a new sexual libertinism in Britain.* ADJ

**ris|sole** /rɪsoʊl, AM rɪsoʊl/ **(rissoles)** **Rissoles** are small balls of chopped meat or vegetables which are fried. [BRIT] N-COUNT: usu pl

**Rita|lin** /rɪtᵊlɪn/ **Ritalin** is a drug that is used especially in the treatment of attention deficit disorder and attention deficit hyperactivity disorder. [TRADEMARK] N-UNCOUNT

**rite** /raɪt/ **(rites)** A **rite** is a traditional ceremony that is carried out by a particular group or within a particular society. ❑ *Most traditional societies have transition rites at puberty.* → See also **last rites**. N-COUNT

**ritu|al** /rɪtʃuəl/ **(rituals)** 1 A **ritual** is a religious service or other ceremony which involves a series of actions performed in a fixed order. ❑ *This is the most ancient, and holiest of the Shinto rituals.* N-VAR 2 **Ritual** activities happen as part of a ritual or tradition. ❑ *...fastings and ritual dancing.* ADJ: ADJ n ♦ **ritu|al|ly** *The statue was ritually bathed and purified.* ADV: ADV with v 3 A **ritual** is a way of behaving or a series of actions which people regularly carry out in a particular situation, because it is their custom to do so. ❑ *The whole Italian culture revolves around the ritual of eating.* N-VAR 4 You can describe something as a **ritual** action when it is done in exactly the same way whenever a particular situation occurs. ❑ *I realized that here the conventions required me to make the ritual noises.* ADJ: ADJ n

**ritu|al|is|tic** /rɪtʃuəlɪstɪk/ 1 **Ritualistic** actions or behaviour follow a similar pattern every time they are used. ❑ *Each evening she bursts into her apartment with a ritualistic shout of 'Honey I'm home!'* ADJ: usu ADJ n 2 **Ritualistic** acts are the fixed patterns of behaviour that form part of a religious service or ceremony. ❑ *...the meditative and ritualistic practices of Buddhism.* ADJ: usu ADJ n

**ritu|al|ized** /rɪtʃuəlaɪzd/

✔ in BRIT, also use **ritualised**

**Ritualized** acts are carried out in a fixed, structured way rather than being natural. ❑ *...highly ritualised courtship displays.* ADJ: usu ADJ n ≠ spontaneous

**ritzy** /rɪtsi/ **(ritzier, ritziest)** If you describe something as **ritzy**, you mean that it is fashionable or expensive. [INFORMAL] ❑ *Palm Springs has ritzy restaurants and glitzy nightlife.* ADJ = fancy

**ri|val** /raɪvᵊl/ **(rivals, rivalling, rivalled)** ◆◆◇

✔ in AM, use **rivaling, rivaled**

1 Your **rival** is a person, business, or organization who you are competing or fighting against in the same area or for the same things. ❑ *The world champion finished more than two seconds ahead of his nearest rival.* N-COUNT 2 If you say that someone or something has **no rivals** or is **without rival**, you mean that it is best of its type. ❑ *...a wonderfully fragrant wine which has no rivals in the Rhone.* N-COUNT: with brd-neg 3 If you say that one thing **rivals** another, you mean that they are both of the same standard or quality. ❑ *Cassette recorders cannot rival the sound quality of CDs.* VERB V n

**ri|val|ry** /raɪvᵊlri/ **(rivalries)** **Rivalry** is competition or fighting between people, businesses, or organizations who are in the same area or want the same things. ❑ *...the rivalry between the Inkatha and the ANC.* N-VAR

**riv|en** /rɪvᵊn/ If a country or organization is **riven by** conflict, it is damaged or destroyed by violent disagreements. ❑ *The four provinces are riven by deep family and tribal conflicts.* ADJ: usu v-link ADJ by/with n

**riv|er** /rɪvəʳ/ **(rivers)** ◆◆◇ A **river** is a large amount of fresh water flowing continuously in a long line across the land. ❑ *...a chemical works on the banks of the river. ...boating on the River Danube.* N-COUNT: oft in names before n

**riv|er bank** **(river banks)** also **riverbank.** A **river bank** is the land along the edge of a river. N-COUNT

**riv|er ba|sin** **(river basins)** A **river basin** is the area of land from which all the water flows into a particular river. N-COUNT

**riv|er bed** **(river beds)** also **riverbed.** A **river bed** is the ground which a river flows over. N-COUNT

**river|boat** /rɪvəʳbout/ **(riverboats)** A **riverboat** is a large boat that carries passengers along a river. N-COUNT: also *by* N

**river|front** /rɪvəʳfrʌnt/ The **riverfront** is an area of land next to a river with buildings such as houses, shops, or restaurants on it. N-SING: *the* N, N n

**river|side** /rɪvəʳsaɪd/ The **riverside** is the area of land by the banks of a river. ❑ *They walked back along the riverside. ...a riverside café.* N-SING: *the* N, N n

**riv|et** /rɪvɪt/ **(rivets, riveting, riveted)** 1 If you **are riveted** by something, it fascinates you and holds your interest completely. ❑ *As a child I remember being riveted by my grandfather's appearance... He was riveted to the John Wayne movie... The scar on her face had immediately riveted their attention.* 2 A **rivet** is a short metal pin with a flat head which is used to fasten flat pieces of metal together. VERB be V-ed be V-ed *to* n V n N-COUNT

**riv|et|ing** /rɪvɪtɪŋ/ If you describe something as **riveting**, you mean that it is extremely interesting and exciting, and that it holds your attention completely. ❑ *I find snooker riveting though I don't play myself.* ADJ

**rivu|let** /rɪvjʊlɪt/ **(rivulets)** A **rivulet** is a small stream. [FORMAL] N-COUNT

**RM** /ɑːr em/ **RM** is written after someone's name to show that they are an officer of the Royal Marines, one of the units which make up the United Kingdom's armed forces. ❑ *...Captain Alastair Rogers, RM.*

**RN** /ɑːr en/ 1 **RN** is a written abbreviation for **Royal Navy**, the navy of the United Kingdom. It is written after someone's name to show that they are an officer of the Royal Navy. [BRIT] ❑ *...RN Museum, Portsmouth. ...Commander Richard Aylard RN.* 2 **RN** is an abbreviation for **registered nurse.** [AM] ❑ *...a pediatric nurse, Kathleen McAdam RN.*

**RNA** /ɑːr en eɪ/ **RNA** is an acid in the chromosomes of the cells of living things which plays an important part in passing information about protein structure between different cells. **RNA** is an abbreviation for 'ribonucleic acid'. [TECHNICAL] N-UNCOUNT

**RNAS** **RNAS** is a written abbreviation for **Royal Naval Air Services**, one of the units which make up the United Kingdom's armed forces.

**roach** /routʃ/ **(roaches)** A **roach** is the same as a **cockroach.** [mainly AM] N-COUNT

**road** /roud/ **(roads)** 1 A **road** is a long piece of hard ground which is built between two places so that people can drive or ride easily from one place to the other. ❑ *There was very little traffic on the roads... We just go straight up the Bristol Road... Buses carry 30 per cent of those travelling by road. ...road accidents.* 2 The **road to** a particular result is the means of achieving it or the process of achieving it. ❑ *We are bound to see some ups and downs along the road to recovery.* ◆◆◆ N-COUNT: oft in names, also *by* N N-COUNT: usu sing, N *to* n

PHRASES 3 If you **hit the road**, you set out on a journey. [INFORMAL] ❑ *I was relieved to get back in the car and hit the road again.* 4 If you are **on the road**, you are going on a long journey or a series of journeys by road. ❑ *He hoped to get a new truck and go back on the road.* 5 If you say that someone is **on the road to** something, you mean that they are likely to achieve it. ❑ *The government took another step on the road to political reform.* 6 **the end of the road** → see **end**. PHRASE: V inflects PHRASE: usu v-link PHR PHRASE: usu PHR after v, PHR *to* n

**road|block** /roudblɒk/ **(roadblocks)** also **road block.** When the police or the army put a **roadblock** across a road, they stop all the traffic going through, for example because they are looking for a criminal. ❑ *The city police set up roadblocks to check passing vehicles.* N-COUNT

**road|hog** /roudhɒg/ **(roadhogs)** also **road hog.** If you describe someone as a **roadhog**, you mean that they drive too fast or in a way which is dangerous to other people. [INFORMAL] N-COUNT disapproval

**road|holding** /roudhouldɪŋ/ A vehicle's **roadholding** is how easy it is to control safely in difficult driving conditions or when going round bends. N-UNCOUNT: usu with supp

**road|house** /roudhaus/ **(roadhouses)** A **roadhouse** is a bar or restaurant on a road outside a city. N-COUNT

**road|ie** /roudi/ **(roadies)** A **roadie** is a person who transports and sets up equipment for a pop band. N-COUNT

**road man|ag|er** **(road managers)** The **road manager** of someone such as a singer or sports player is the person who organizes their travel and other arrangements during a tour. N-COUNT: oft poss N

**road map** **(road maps)** 1 A **road map** is a map which shows the roads in a particular area in detail. 2 A **road map** of something is a detailed account of it, often intended to help people use or understand it. ❑ *The idea was to create a comprehensive road map of the Web.* N-COUNT N-COUNT

**road pric|ing** **Road pricing** is a system of making drivers pay money for driving on certain roads by electronically recording the movement of vehicles on those roads. [BRIT] N-UNCOUNT

**road rage** **Road rage** is anger or violent behaviour caused by someone else's bad driving or the stress of being in heavy traffic. ❑ *...a road rage attack on a male motorist.* N-UNCOUNT: oft N n

**road|show** /roudʃou/ **(roadshows)** also **road show.** 1 A **roadshow** is a travelling show organized by a radio station, magazine, or company. ❑ *The BBC Radio 2 Roadshow will broadcast live from the exhibition.* 2 A **roadshow** is a show presented by travelling actors. [AM] 3 A **roadshow** is a group of people who travel around a country, for example as part of an advertising or political campaign. [mainly AM] ❑ *The Democratic Presidential ticket plans another road show, this time through the industrial Midwest.* N-COUNT: usu supp N N-COUNT N-COUNT

**road|side** /roudsaɪd/ **(roadsides)** The **roadside** is the area at the edge of a road. ❑ *Bob was forced to leave the car at the roadside and run for help.* N-COUNT: usu sing, *the* N, N n

**road|ster** /roudstəʳ/ **(roadsters)** A **roadster** is a car with no roof and only two seats. [OLD-FASHIONED] N-COUNT = *sports car*

**road tax** In Britain, **road tax** is a tax paid every year by the owners of every motor vehicle which is being used on the roads. N-UNCOUNT

**road|way** /roudweɪ/ **(roadways)** The **roadway** is the part of a road that is used by traffic. ❑ *Marks in the roadway seem to indicate that he skidded taking a sharp turn.* N-COUNT: oft *the* N in sing = *road*

**road|works** /roudwɜːʳks/ **Roadworks** are repairs or other work being done on a road. N-PLURAL

**roam** /roum/ **(roams, roaming, roamed)** If you **roam** an area or **roam around** it, you wander or travel around it without having a particular purpose. ❑ *Barefoot children roamed the streets... They're roaming around the country shooting at anything that moves... Farmers were encouraged to keep their livestock in pens rather than letting them roam freely.* VERB V n V prep/adv V

**roam|ing** /roumɪŋ/ **Roaming** refers to the service provided by a mobile phone company which makes it possible for you to use your mobile phone when you travel abroad. ❑ *International Roaming is your digital mobile phone's passport to travel but the cost of calls is high.* N-UNCOUNT

**roan** /roun/ **(roans)** A **roan** is a horse that is brown or black with some white hairs. N-COUNT

**roar** /rɔːʳ/ **(roars, roaring, roared)** 1 If something, usually a vehicle, **roars** somewhere, it goes there very fast, making a loud noise. [WRITTEN] ❑ *The plane roared down the runway for takeoff.* 2 If something **roars**, it makes a very loud VERB V adv/prep VERB noise. [WRITTEN] ❑ *The engine roared, and the vehicle leapt forward. ...the roaring waters of Niagara Falls.* V V-ing ♦ **Roar** is also a noun. ❑ *...the roar of traffic.* N-COUNT: usu sing [3] If someone **roars with** laughter, they laugh in a very noisy way. ❑ *Max threw back his head and roared with laughter.* VERB V with n ♦ **Roar** is also a noun. ❑ *There were roars of laughter as he stood up.* N-COUNT: N of n [4] If someone **roars**, they shout something in a very loud voice. [WRITTEN] ❑ *'I'll kill you for that,' he roared... During the playing of the national anthem the crowd roared and whistled... The audience roared its approval.* VERB V with quote V V n ♦ **Roar** is also a noun. ❑ *There was a roar of approval.* N-COUNT [5] When a lion **roars**, it makes the loud sound that lions typically make. ❑ *The lion roared once, and sprang.* VERB V ♦ **Roar** is also a noun. ❑ *...the roar of lions in the distance.* N-COUNT

**roar|ing** /rɔːrɪŋ/ [1] A **roaring** fire has large flames and is sending out a lot of heat. ADJ: ADJ n [2] If something is a **roaring** success, it is very successful indeed. ❑ *The government's first effort to privatize a company has been a roaring success.* ADJ: ADJ n = resounding [3] → See also **roar**. [4] If someone **does a roaring trade** in a type of goods, they sell a lot of them. ❑ *Salesmen of unofficial souvenirs have also been doing a roaring trade.* PHRASE: V inflects

**roast** /roʊst/ **(roasts, roasting, roasted)** [1] When you **roast** meat or other food, you cook it by dry heat in an oven or over a fire. ❑ *I personally would rather roast a chicken whole.* VERB V n [2] **Roast** meat has been cooked by roasting. ❑ *...roast beef.* ADJ: ADJ n [3] A **roast** is a piece of meat that is cooked by roasting. ❑ *Come into the kitchen. I've got to put the roast in.* N-COUNT

**roast|ing** /roʊstɪŋ/ If someone gives you **a roasting**, they criticize you severely about something in a way that shows that they are very annoyed with you. [BRIT, INFORMAL] ❑ *The team was given a roasting by manager Alex Feguson.* N-SING: usu *a* N

**rob** /rɒb/ **(robs, robbing, robbed)** [1] If someone **is robbed**, they have money or property stolen from them. ❑ *Mrs Yacoub was robbed of her £3,000 designer watch at her West London home... Police said Stefanovski had robbed a man just hours earlier.* VERB be V-ed *of* n V n [2] If someone **is robbed of** something that they deserve, have, or need, it is taken away from them. ❑ *When Miles Davis died, jazz was robbed of its most distinctive voice... I can't forgive Lewis for robbing me of an Olympic gold.* VERB be V-ed *of* n V n *of* n

**rob|ber** /rɒbəʳ/ **(robbers)** A **robber** is someone who steals money or property from a bank, a shop, or a vehicle, often by using force or threats. ❑ *Armed robbers broke into a jeweller's through a hole in the wall.* N-COUNT: oft supp N

**rob|ber bar|on (robber barons)** If you refer to someone as a **robber baron**, you mean that they have made a very large amount of money and have been prepared to act illegally or in an immoral way in order to do so. N-COUNT

**rob|bery** /rɒbəri/ **(robberies) Robbery** is the crime of stealing money or property from a bank, shop, or vehicle, often by using force or threats. ❑ *The gang members committed dozens of armed robberies.* N-VAR: oft supp N

**robe** /roʊb/ **(robes)** [1] A **robe** is a loose piece of clothing which covers all of your body and reaches the ground. You can describe someone as wearing a **robe** or as wearing **robes**. [FORMAL] ❑ *Pope John Paul II knelt in his white robes before the simple altar.* N-COUNT [2] A **robe** is a piece of clothing, usually made of towelling, which people wear in the house, especially when they have just got up or had a bath. ❑ *Ryle put on a robe and went down to the kitchen.* N-COUNT

**-robed** /-roʊbd/ **-robed** combines with the names of colours to indicate that someone is wearing robes of a particular colour. ❑ *...a brown-robed monk.* COMB in ADJ: ADJ n

**rob|in** /rɒbɪn/ **(robins)** [1] A **robin** is a small brown bird found in Europe. The male has an orangey-red neck and breast. N-COUNT [2] A **robin** is a brown bird found in North America. The male has a reddish-brown breast. North American robins are larger than European ones, and are a completely different species of bird. N-COUNT [3] → See also **round-robin**.

**ro|bot** /roʊbɒt, AM -bət/ **(robots)** A **robot** is a machine which is programmed to move and perform certain tasks automatically. ❑ *...very lightweight robots that we could send to the moon for planetary exploration.* N-COUNT

**ro|bot|ic** /roʊbɒtɪk/ **Robotic** equipment can perform certain tasks automatically. ❑ *Astronaut Pierre Thuot tried to latch the 15-foot robotic arm onto the satellite.* ADJ: ADJ n

**ro|bot|ics** /roʊbɒtɪks/ **Robotics** is the science of designing and building robots. [TECHNICAL] N-UNCOUNT

**ro|bust** /roʊbʌst, roʊbʌst/ [1] Someone or something that is **robust** is very strong or healthy. ❑ *More women than men go to the doctor. Perhaps men are more robust or worry less?* ADJ ♦ **ro|bust|ly** *He became robustly healthy.* ADV ♦ **ro|bust|ness** *...the robustness of diesel engines.* N-UNCOUNT [2] **Robust** views or opinions are strongly held and forcefully expressed. ❑ *A British Foreign Office minister has made a robust defence of the agreement.* ADJ: usu ADJ n ♦ **ro|bust|ly** *In the decisions we have to make about Europe, we have to defend our position very robustly indeed.* ADV ♦ **ro|bust|ness** *...a prominent industrialist renowned for the robustness of his right-wing views.* N-UNCOUNT: oft *the* N *of* n

**rock** /rɒk/ **(rocks, rocking, rocked)** [1] **Rock** is the hard substance which the Earth is made of. ❑ *The hills above the valley are bare rock.* ◆◆◇ N-UNCOUNT [2] A **rock** is a large piece of rock that sticks up out of the ground or the sea, or that has broken away from a mountain or a cliff. ❑ *She sat cross-legged on the rock.* N-COUNT [3] A **rock** is a piece of rock that is small enough for you to pick up. ❑ *She bent down, picked up a rock and threw it into the trees.* N-COUNT [4] When something **rocks** or when you **rock** it, it moves slowly and regularly backwards and forwards or from side to side. ❑ *His body rocked from side to side with the train... She sat on the porch and rocked the baby.* VERB V prep/adv V n Also V [5] If an explosion or an earthquake **rocks** a building or an area, it causes the building or area to shake. You can also say that the building or area **rocks**. [JOURNALISM] ❑ *Three people were injured yesterday when an explosion rocked one of Britain's best known film studios... As the buildings rocked under heavy shell-fire, he took refuge in the cellars.* VERB V n V [6] If an event or a piece of news **rocks** a group or society, it shocks them or makes them feel less secure. [JOURNALISM] ❑ *His death rocked the fashion business.* VERB V n [7] **Rock** is loud music with a strong beat that is usually played and sung by a small group of people using instruments such as electric guitars and drums. ❑ *...a rock concert. ...famous rock stars.* N-UNCOUNT: oft N n [8] **Rock** is a sweet that is made in long, hard sticks and is often sold in towns by the sea in Britain. ❑ *...a stick of rock.* N-UNCOUNT

PHRASES [9] If you have an alcoholic drink such as whisky **on the rocks**, you have it with ice cubes in it. ❑ *...a Scotch on the rocks.* PHRASE: usu n PHR = with ice [10] If something such as a marriage or a business is **on the rocks**, it is experiencing very severe difficulties and looks likely to end very soon. ❑ *She confided to her mother six months ago that her marriage was on the rocks.* PHRASE: v-link PHR [11] to **rock the boat** → see **boat**.

**rocka|bil|ly** /rɒkəbɪli/ **Rockabilly** is a kind of fast rock music which developed in the southern United States in the 1950s. N-UNCOUNT

**rock and roll** also **rock'n'roll. Rock and roll** is a kind of popular music developed in the 1950s which has a strong beat and is played on electrical instruments. ❑ *...Elvis Presley – the King of Rock and Roll.* N-UNCOUNT: oft N n

**rock bot|tom** also **rock-bottom.** [1] If something has reached **rock bottom**, it is at such a low level that it cannot go any lower. ❑ *Morale in the armed forces was at rock bottom.* N-UNCOUNT [2] If someone has reached **rock bottom**, they are in such a bad state or are so completely depressed that their N-UNCOUNT situation could not get any worse. ❑ *She was at rock bottom. Her long-term love affair was breaking up and so was she.* 3 A **rock-bottom** price or level is a very low one, mainly in advertisements. ❑ *What they do offer is a good product at a rock-bottom price.* ADJ: usu ADJ n [approval]

**rock climb|er** **(rock climbers)** A **rock climber** is a person whose hobby or sport is climbing cliffs or large rocks. N-COUNT

**rock climb|ing** also **rock-climbing.** **Rock climbing** is the activity of climbing cliffs or large rocks, as a hobby or sport. N-UNCOUNT

**rock|er** /rɒkəʳ/ **(rockers)** 1 A **rocker** is a chair that is built on two curved pieces of wood so that you can rock yourself backwards and forwards while you are sitting in it. [mainly AM] N-COUNT

✓ in BRIT, usually use **rocking chair**

2 A **rocker** is someone who performs rock music. ❑ *...American rockers Guns 'N' Roses.* N-COUNT

**rock|ery** /rɒkəri/ **(rockeries)** A **rockery** is a raised part of a garden which is built of rocks and soil, with small plants growing between the rocks. N-COUNT

**rock|et** /rɒkɪt/ **(rockets, rocketing, rocketed)** ◆◇◇ 1 A **rocket** is a space vehicle that is shaped like a long tube. N-COUNT 2 A **rocket** is a missile containing explosive that is powered by gas. ❑ *There has been a renewed rocket attack on the capital.* N-COUNT: oft N n 3 A **rocket** is a firework that quickly goes high into the air and then explodes. N-COUNT 4 If things such as prices or social problems **rocket**, they increase very quickly and suddenly. [JOURNALISM] ❑ *Fresh food is so scarce that prices have rocketed... The nation has experienced four years of rocketing crime.* VERB = soar V V-ing 5 If something such as a vehicle **rockets** somewhere, it moves there very quickly. ❑ *A train rocketed by, shaking the walls of the row houses.* VERB V prep/adv

**rock|et launch|er** **(rocket launchers)** A **rocket launcher** is a device that can be carried by soldiers and used for firing rockets. N-COUNT

**rock|et sci|ence** If you say that something is **not rocket science**, you mean that you do not have to be clever in order to do it. ❑ *Interviewing politicians may not be rocket science, but it does matter.* N-UNCOUNT

**rock|et sci|en|tist** **(rocket scientists)** If you say that it does not take a **rocket scientist** to do something, you mean that you do not have to be clever to do it. ❑ *It doesn't take a rocket scientist to make a rock record.* N-COUNT: with brd-neg

**rock gar|den** **(rock gardens)** A **rock garden** is a garden which consists of rocks with small plants growing among them. N-COUNT

**rock-hard** also **rock hard.** Something that is **rock-hard** is very hard indeed. ❑ *During the dry season the land is rock hard.* ADJ

**rock|ing chair** **(rocking chairs)** A **rocking chair** is a chair that is built on two curved pieces of wood so that you can rock yourself backwards and forwards when you are sitting in it. N-COUNT

**rock|ing horse** **(rocking horses)** A **rocking-horse** is a toy horse which a child can sit on and which can be made to rock backwards and forwards. N-COUNT

**rock-like** Something that is **rock-like** is very strong or firm, and is unlikely to change. ❑ *...his rock-like integrity.* ADJ: usu ADJ n

**rock'n'roll** /rɒkənroul/ → see **rock and roll.**

**rock pool** **(rock pools)** A **rock pool** is a small pool between rocks on the edge of the sea. N-COUNT

**rock salt** **Rock salt** is salt that is formed in the ground. It is obtained by mining. N-UNCOUNT

**rock-solid** also **rock solid.** 1 Something that is **rock-solid** is extremely hard. ❑ *Freeze it only until firm but not rock solid.* ADJ 2 If you describe someone or something as **rock-solid**, you approve of them because they are extremely reliable or unlikely to change. ❑ *Mayhew is a man of rock-solid integrity.* ADJ [approval]

**rock steady** also **rock-steady.** Something that is **rock steady** is very firm and does not shake or move about. ❑ *He reached for a cigarette and lit it, fingers rock steady.* ADJ

**rocky** /rɒki/ **(rockier, rockiest)** 1 A **rocky** place is covered with rocks or consists of large areas of rock and has nothing growing on it. ❑ *The paths are often very rocky so strong boots are advisable. ...a rocky headland.* ADJ 2 A **rocky** situation or relationship is unstable and full of difficulties. ❑ *They had gone through some rocky times together when Ann was first married.* ADJ

**ro|co|co** /rəkoukou, AM roukəkou/ **Rococo** is a decorative style that was popular in Europe in the eighteenth century. **Rococo** buildings, furniture, and works of art often include complicated curly decoration. N-UNCOUNT: oft N n

**rod** /rɒd/ **(rods)** A **rod** is a long, thin metal or wooden bar. ❑ *...a 15-foot thick roof that was reinforced with steel rods.* → See also **fishing rod, lightning rod.** N-COUNT

**rode** /roud/ **Rode** is the past tense of **ride.**

**ro|dent** /roudənt/ **(rodents)** **Rodents** are small mammals which have sharp front teeth. Rats, mice, and squirrels are rodents. N-COUNT

**ro|deo** /roudiou, roudeɪou/ **(rodeos)** In the United States, a **rodeo** is a public entertainment event in which cowboys show different skills, including riding wild horses and catching cattle with ropes. N-COUNT: usu sing

**roe** /rou/ **(roes)** **Roe** is the eggs or sperm of a fish, which is eaten as food. ❑ *...cod's roe.* N-VAR: oft supp N

**roe deer** **(roe deer)** A **roe deer** is a small deer which lives in woods in Europe and Asia. N-COUNT

**rogue** /roug/ **(rogues)** 1 A **rogue** is a man who behaves in a dishonest or criminal way. ❑ *Mr Ward wasn't a rogue at all.* N-COUNT 2 If a man behaves in a way that you do not approve of but you still like him, you can refer to him as a **rogue.** ❑ *...Falstaff, the loveable rogue.* N-COUNT: oft adj N [feelings] 3 A **rogue** element is someone or something that behaves differently from others of its kind, often causing damage. ❑ *Computer systems throughout the country are being affected by a series of mysterious rogue programs, known as viruses.* ADJ: ADJ n

**rogues' gal|lery** 1 A **rogues' gallery** is a collection of photographs of criminals that is kept by the police and used when they want to identify someone. [JOURNALISM] ❑ *...a Rogues' Gallery of juvenile crime gangs.* N-SING: oft N *of* n 2 You can refer to a group of people or things that you consider undesirable as a **rogues' gallery.** [JOURNALISM] ❑ *He and others in the rogues gallery of international terrorists may be running out of time.* N-SING: oft N *of* n [disapproval]

**ro|guish** /rougɪʃ/ If someone has a **roguish** expression or manner, they look as though they are about to behave badly. ❑ *She was a mature lady with dyed ginger hair and a roguish grin.* ADJ

**roil** /rɔɪl/ **(roils, roiling, roiled)** 1 If water **roils**, it is rough and disturbed. [mainly AM] ❑ *The water roiled to his left as he climbed carefully at the edge of the waterfall.* VERB = churn V 2 Something that **roils** a state or situation makes it disturbed and confused. ❑ *Times of national turmoil generally roil a country's financial markets.* VERB V n

**role** /roul/ **(roles)** 1 If you have a **role** in a situation or in society, you have a particular position and function in it. ❑ *...the drug's role in preventing more serious effects of infection... Both sides have roles to play.* ◆◆◆ N-COUNT: with supp, oft N *in/of/as* n 2 A **role** is one of the characters that an actor or singer can play in a film, play, or opera. ❑ *She has just landed the lead role in The Young Vic's latest production.* N-COUNT: usu with supp

**role mod|el** **(role models)** A **role model** is someone you admire and try to imitate. ❑ *Five out of the ten top role models for British teenagers are black.* N-COUNT

**role play** **(role plays, role playing, role played)** also **role-play.** 1 **Role play** is the act of imitating the character and behaviour of someone N-VAR who is different from yourself, for example as a training exercise. ❑ *Group members have to communicate with each other through role-play.* [2] If people **role play**, they do a role play. ❑ *Rehearse and role-play the interview with a friend beforehand.* ♦ **role play|ing** *We did a lot of role playing.* VERB V n Also V N-UNCOUNT

**role re|ver|sal** **(role reversals)** **Role reversal** is a situation in which two people have chosen or been forced to exchange their duties and responsibilities, so that each is now doing what the other used to do. ❑ *...men who have undertaken the most extreme role reversal and become househusbands.* N-VAR

**roll** /roʊl/ **(rolls, rolling, rolled)** ◆◆◇ [1] When something **rolls** or when you **roll** it, it moves along a surface, turning over many times. ❑ *The ball rolled into the net... I rolled a ball across the carpet.* VERB V prep/adv V n prep [2] If you **roll** somewhere, you move on a surface while lying down, turning your body over and over, so that you are sometimes on your back, sometimes on your side, and sometimes on your front. ❑ *When I was a little kid I rolled down a hill and broke my leg.* VERB V prep/adv [3] When vehicles **roll** along, they move along slowly. ❑ *The lorry quietly rolled forward.* VERB V prep/adv [4] If a machine **rolls**, it is operating. ❑ *He slipped and fell on an airplane gangway as the cameras rolled.* VERB V [5] If drops of liquid **roll** down a surface, they move quickly down it. ❑ *She looked at Ginny and tears rolled down her cheeks.* VERB V *down* n [6] If you **roll** something flexible **into** a cylinder or a ball, you form it into a cylinder or a ball by wrapping it several times around itself or by shaping it between your hands. ❑ *He took off his sweater, rolled it into a pillow and lay down on the grass... He rolled and lit another cigarette.* VERB V n *into* n V n ♦ **Roll up** means the same as **roll**. ❑ *Stein rolled up the paper bag with the money inside.* PHRASAL VERB V P n (not pron) [7] A **roll of** paper, plastic, cloth, or wire is a long piece of it that has been wrapped many times around itself or around a tube. ❑ *The photographers had already shot a dozen rolls of film.* ➔ See also **toilet roll**. N-COUNT: usu N *of* n [8] If you **roll up** something such as a car window or a blind, you cause it to move upwards by turning a handle. If you **roll** it **down**, you cause it to move downwards by turning a handle. ❑ *In mid-afternoon, shopkeepers began to roll down their shutters.* VERB V n with adv [9] If you **roll** your eyes or if your eyes **roll**, they move round and upwards. People sometimes roll their eyes when they are frightened, bored, or annoyed. [WRITTEN] ❑ *People may roll their eyes and talk about overprotective, interfering grandmothers... His eyes rolled and he sobbed.* VERB V n V [10] A **roll** is a small piece of bread that is round or long and is made to be eaten by one person. Rolls can be eaten plain, with butter, or with a filling. ❑ *He spread butter on a roll.* N-COUNT [11] A **roll of** drums is a long, low, fairly loud sound made by drums. ❑ *As the town clock struck two, they heard the roll of drums.* ➔ See also **drum roll**. N-COUNT [12] A **roll** is an official list of people's names. ❑ *...the electoral roll.* N-COUNT: with supp = register [13] ➔ See also **rolling**, **rock and roll**, **sausage roll**.

**PHRASES** [14] If someone is **on a roll**, they are having great success which seems likely to continue. [INFORMAL] ❑ *I made a name for myself and I was on a roll, I couldn't see anything going wrong.* PHRASE: usu v-link PHR [15] If you say **roll on** something, you mean that you would like it to come soon, because you are looking forward to it. [BRIT, INFORMAL] ❑ *Roll on the day someone develops an effective vaccine against malaria.* PHRASE: PHR n [feelings] [16] If something is several things **rolled into one**, it combines the main features or qualities of those things. ❑ *This is our kitchen, sitting and dining room all rolled into one.* PHRASE: pl-n PHR, v-link PHR [17] **to start the ball rolling** ➔ see **ball**. **heads will roll** ➔ see **head**.

♦ **roll back** [1] To **roll back** a change or the power of something means to gradually reduce it or end it. ❑ *Environmentalists regard these moves as the government taking advantage of the national mood to roll back protective measures.* ➔ See also **rollback**. PHRASAL VERB V P n (not pron) Also V n P [2] To **roll back** prices, taxes, or benefits means to reduce them. [mainly AM] ❑ *One provision of the law was to roll back taxes to the 1975 level.* PHRASAL VERB V P n (not pron)

♦ **roll in** or **roll into** [1] If something such as money **is rolling in**, it is appearing or being received in large quantities. [INFORMAL] ❑ *Don't forget, I have always kept the money rolling in.* PHRASAL VERB: usu cont V P [2] If someone **rolls into** a place or **rolls in**, they arrive in a casual way and often late. [mainly BRIT] ❑ *'I've made you late.' — 'No that's all right. I can roll in when I feel like it.'... The brothers usually roll into their studio around midday.* PHRASAL VERB V P V P n

♦ **roll up** [1] If you **roll up** your sleeves or trouser legs, you fold the ends back several times, making them shorter. ❑ *The jacket was too big for him so he rolled up the cuffs... Walking in the surf, she had to roll her pants up to her knees.* ➔ See also **rolled-up**. PHRASAL VERB V P n (not pron) V n P [2] If people **roll up** somewhere, they arrive there, especially in large numbers, to see something interesting. [INFORMAL] ❑ *Roll up, roll up, come and join The Greatest Show on Earth... The first reporters rolled up to the laboratory within minutes.* PHRASAL VERB V P V P prep/adv [3] ➔ See also **roll 6**, **rolled-up**.

**roll|back** /roʊlbæk/ **(rollbacks)** A **rollback** is a reduction in price or some other change that makes something like it was before. [mainly AM] ❑ *Silber says the tax rollback would decimate basic services for the needy.* N-COUNT: usu with supp

**roll call** **(roll calls)** also **roll-call.** [1] If you take a **roll call**, you check which of the members of a group are present by reading their names out. ❑ *We had to stand in the snow every morning for roll call.* N-VAR [2] A **roll call of** a particular type of people or things is a list of them. [JOURNALISM] ❑ *Her list of pupils read like a roll-call of the great and good.* N-SING: N *of* n

**rolled-up** [1] **Rolled-up** objects have been folded or wrapped into a cylindrical shape. ❑ *...a rolled-up newspaper.* ADJ: ADJ n [2] **Rolled-up** sleeves or trouser legs have been made shorter by being folded over at the lower edge. ❑ *...an open-necked shirt, with rolled-up sleeves.* ADJ: ADJ n

**roll|er** /roʊləʳ/ **(rollers)** [1] A **roller** is a cylinder that turns round in a machine or device. N-COUNT [2] **Rollers** are hollow tubes that women roll their hair round in order to make it curly. N-COUNT

**Roll|er|blade** /roʊləʳbleɪd/ **(Rollerblades)** **Rollerblades** are a type of roller skates with a single line of wheels along the bottom. [TRADEMARK] ♦ **roll|er|blader** **(rollerbladers)** ❑ *...a dedicated rollerblader.* ♦ **roll|er|blad|ing** *Rollerblading is great for all ages.* N-COUNT: usu plural N-COUNT N-UNCOUNT

**roller-coaster** **(roller-coasters)** also **rollercoaster.** [1] A **roller-coaster** is a small railway at a fair that goes up and down steep slopes fast and that people ride on for pleasure or excitement. ❑ *It's great to go on the roller coaster five times and not be sick.* N-COUNT [2] If you say that someone or something is on a **roller coaster**, you mean that they go through many sudden or extreme changes in a short time. [JOURNALISM] ❑ *I've been on an emotional roller-coaster since I've been here.* N-COUNT: usu sing

**roller-skate** **(roller-skates, roller-skating, roller-skated)** [1] **Roller-skates** are shoes with four small wheels on the bottom. ❑ *A boy of about ten came up on roller-skates.* N-COUNT: usu pl [2] If you **roller-skate**, you move over a flat surface wearing roller-skates. ❑ *On the day of the accident, my son Gary was roller-skating outside our house.* VERB V ♦ **roller-skating** *The craze for roller skating spread throughout the U.S.* N-UNCOUNT

**rol|lick|ing** /rɒlɪkɪŋ/ [1] A **rollicking** occasion is cheerful and usually noisy. A **rollicking** book or film is entertaining and enjoyable, and not very serious. ❑ *Tony Benn's diaries are a rollicking read.* ♦ **Rollicking** is also an adverb. ❑ *I'm having a rollicking good time.* ADJ: ADJ n ADV: ADV adj [2] If you give someone a **rollicking**, you tell them off in a very angry way. [BRIT, INFORMAL] ❑ *'The boss gave us a rollicking,' said McGoldrick.* N-SING: usu *a* N

**roll|ing** /rəʊlɪŋ/ [1] **Rolling** hills are small hills with gentle slopes that extend a long way into the distance. ❑ *...the rolling countryside of south western France.* ADJ: ADJ n [2] If you say that someone **is rolling in it** or **is rolling in money**, you mean that they are very rich. [INFORMAL] PHRASE: V inflects, emphasis = loaded

**roll|ing mill (rolling mills)** A **rolling mill** is a machine or factory in which metal is rolled into sheets or bars. N-COUNT

**roll|ing pin (rolling pins)** A **rolling pin** is a cylinder that you roll backwards and forwards over uncooked pastry in order to make the pastry flat. N-COUNT

**roll|ing stock** **Rolling stock** is all the engines and carriages that are used on a railway. ❑ *Many stations needed repairs or rebuilding and there was a shortage of rolling stock.* N-UNCOUNT

**roll-neck (roll-necks)** [1] A **roll-neck** sweater or a **roll-necked** sweater is a sweater with a high neck than can be rolled over. [mainly BRIT] ADJ: ADJ n [2] A **roll-neck** is a roll-neck sweater. [mainly BRIT] N-COUNT

**roll of hon|our** A **roll of honour** is a list of the names of people who are admired or respected for something they have done, such as doing very well in a sport or exam. [BRIT] N-SING

✓ in AM, use **honor roll**

**roll-on (roll-ons)** A **roll-on** is a deodorant or cosmetic that you apply to your body using a container with a ball which turns round in the neck of the container. ❑ *I use unperfumed roll-on deodorant.* N-COUNT: oft N n

**roll-on roll-off** A **roll-on roll-off** ship is designed so that cars and lorries can drive on at one end before the ship sails, and then drive off at the other end after the journey. [BRIT] ❑ *...roll-on roll-off ferries.* ADJ: ADJ n

**roll|over** /rəʊləʊvəʳ/ **(rollovers)** [1] In a lottery draw, a **rollover** is a prize that includes the prize money from the previous draw, because nobody won it. N-COUNT: usu singular [2] In finance, a **rollover** is when a loan or other financial arrangement is extended. N-COUNT: usu singular

**roll-top desk (roll-top desks)** also **rolltop desk.** A **roll-top desk** is a desk which has a wooden cover which can be pulled down over the writing surface when the desk is not being used. N-COUNT

**roll-up** /rəʊlʌp/ **(roll-ups)** A **roll-up** is a cigarette that someone makes for themselves, using tobacco and cigarette papers. N-COUNT

**roly-poly** /rəʊli pəʊli/ **Roly-poly** people are pleasantly fat and round. [INFORMAL] ❑ *...a short, roly-poly man with laughing eyes.* ADJ: ADJ n

**ROM** /rɒm/ **ROM** is the permanent part of a computer's memory. The information stored there can be read but not changed. **ROM** is an abbreviation for 'read-only memory'. [COMPUTING] → See also **CD-ROM**. N-UNCOUNT

**Ro|man** /rəʊmən/ **(Romans)** [1] **Roman** means related to or connected with ancient Rome and its empire. ❑ *...the fall of the Roman Empire.* ADJ: usu ADJ n ♦ A **Roman** was a citizen of ancient Rome or its empire. ❑ *When they conquered Britain, the Romans brought this custom with them.* N-COUNT [2] **Roman** means related to or connected with modern Rome. ❑ *...a Roman hotel room.* ADJ: usu ADJ n ♦ A **Roman** is someone who lives in or comes from Rome. ❑ *...soccer-mad Romans.* N-COUNT

**Ro|man al|pha|bet** The **Roman alphabet** is the alphabet that was used by the Romans in ancient times and that is used for writing most western European languages, including English. N-SING: the N

**Ro|man Catho|lic (Roman Catholics)** [1] The **Roman Catholic** Church is the same as the **Catholic** Church. ❑ *...a Roman Catholic priest.* ADJ: usu ADJ n [2] A **Roman Catholic** is the same as a **Catholic**. ❑ *Like her, Maria was a Roman Catholic.* N-COUNT

**Ro|man Ca|tholi|cism** **Roman Catholicism** is the same as **Catholicism**. N-UNCOUNT

**ro|mance** /rəmæns, rəʊmæns/ **(romances)** [1] A **romance** is a relationship between two people who are in love with each other but who are not married to each other. ❑ *After a whirlwind romance the couple announced their engagement in July.* N-COUNT [2] **Romance** refers to the actions and feelings of people who are in love, especially behaviour which is very caring or affectionate. ❑ *He still finds time for romance by cooking candlelit dinners for his girlfriend.* N-UNCOUNT [3] You can refer to the pleasure and excitement of doing something new or exciting as **romance**. ❑ *We want to recreate the romance and excitement that used to be part of rail journeys.* N-UNCOUNT [4] A **romance** is a novel or film about a love affair. ❑ *Her taste in fiction was for chunky historical romances.* N-COUNT [5] **Romance** is used to refer to novels about love affairs. ❑ *Since taking up writing romance in 1967 she has brought out over fifty books.* N-UNCOUNT [6] **Romance** languages are languages such as French, Spanish, and Italian, which come from Latin. [TECHNICAL] ADJ: ADJ n

**Ro|man|esque** /rəʊmənesk/ **Romanesque** architecture is in the style that was common in western Europe around the eleventh century. It is characterized by rounded arches and thick pillars. ADJ: usu ADJ n

**Ro|ma|nian** /ruːmeɪniən/ **(Romanians)** also **Rumanian.** [1] **Romanian** means belonging or relating to Romania, or to its people, language, or culture. ADJ: usu ADJ n [2] A **Romanian** is a Romanian citizen, or a person of Romanian origin. N-COUNT [3] **Romanian** is the language spoken in Romania. N-UNCOUNT

**Ro|man nu|mer|al (Roman numerals)** **Roman numerals** are the letters used by the ancient Romans to represent numbers, for example I, IV, VIII, and XL, which represent 1, 4, 8, and 40. Roman numerals are still sometimes used today. N-COUNT: usu pl

**ro|man|tic** /rəʊmæntɪk/ **(romantics)** ◆◇◇ [1] Someone who is **romantic** or does **romantic** things says and does things that make their wife, husband, girlfriend, or boyfriend feel special and loved. ❑ *When we're together, all he talks about is business. I wish he were more romantic.* ADJ [2] **Romantic** means connected with sexual love. ❑ *He was not interested in a romantic relationship with Ingrid.* ADJ: ADJ n ♦ **ro|man|ti|cal|ly** *We are not romantically involved.* ADV [3] A **romantic** play, film, or story describes or represents a love affair. ❑ *It is a lovely romantic comedy, well worth seeing. ...romantic novels.* ADJ: ADJ n [4] If you say that someone has a **romantic** view or idea of something, you are critical of them because their view of it is unrealistic and they think that thing is better or more exciting than it really is. ❑ *He has a romantic view of rural society.* ADJ: usu ADJ n, disapproval ♦ A **romantic** is a person who has romantic views. ❑ *You're a hopeless romantic.* N-COUNT ≠realist [5] Something that is **romantic** is beautiful in a way that strongly affects your feelings. ❑ *Seacliff House is one of the most romantic ruins in Scotland.* ADJ ♦ **ro|man|ti|cal|ly** *...the romantically named, but very muddy, Cave of the Wild Horses.* ADV [6] **Romantic** means connected with the artistic movement of the eighteenth and nineteenth centuries which was concerned with the expression of the individual's feelings and emotions. ❑ *...the poems and prose of the English romantic poets.* ADJ: ADJ n

**ro|man|ti|cism** /rəʊmæntɪsɪzəm/ [1] **Romanticism** is attitudes, ideals and feelings which are romantic rather than realistic. ❑ *Her determined romanticism was worrying me.* N-UNCOUNT ≠realism [2] **Romanticism** is the artistic movement of the eighteenth and nineteenth centuries which was concerned with the expression of the individual's feelings and emotions. N-UNCOUNT

**ro|man|ti|cize** /rəʊmæntɪsaɪz/ **(romanticizes, romanticizing, romanticized)**

✓ in BRIT, also use **romanticise**

If you **romanticize** someone or something, you think or talk about them in a way which is not at all realistic and which makes them seem better than they really are. ❑ *He romanticized the past as he became disillusioned with his present.* VERB V n

♦ **ro|man|ti|cized** *Mr. Lane's film takes a highly romanticized view of life on the streets.* ADJ

**Roma|ny** /roʊməni/ **(Romanies)** 1 A **Romany** is a member of a race of people who travel from place to place, usually living in caravans, rather than living in one place. N-COUNT 2 **Romany** means related or connected to the Romany people. ADJ: usu ADJ n ❑ *...the Romany community.*

**Romeo** /roʊmioʊ/ **(Romeos)** You can describe a man as a **Romeo** if you want to indicate that he is very much in love with a woman, or that he frequently has sexual relationships with different women. [JOURNALISM, HUMOROUS, INFORMAL] ❑ *...one of Hollywood's most notorious Romeos.* N-COUNT

**romp** /rɒmp/ **(romps, romping, romped)** 1 Journalists use **romp** in expressions like **romp home**, **romp in**, or **romp to victory**, to say that a person or horse has won a race or competition very easily. ❑ *Mr Foster romped home with 141 votes.* VERB V adv/prep 2 When children or animals **romp**, they play noisily and happily. ❑ *Dogs and little children romped happily in the garden.* VERB V

**roof** /ruːf/ **(roofs)** ◆◇◇

> The plural can be pronounced /ruːfs/ or /ruːvz/.

1 The **roof** of a building is the covering on top of it that protects the people and things inside from the weather. ➔ See picture on page 1705. ❑ *...a small stone cottage with a red slate roof.* N-COUNT 2 The **roof** of a car or other vehicle is the top part of it, which protects passengers or goods from the weather. ➔ See picture on page 1707. ❑ *The car rolled onto its roof, trapping him.* N-COUNT 3 **The roof of** your mouth is the highest part of the inside of your mouth. ❑ *She clicked her tongue against the roof of her mouth.* N-COUNT: the N of n

PHRASES 4 If the level of something such as the price of a product or the rate of inflation **goes through the roof**, it suddenly increases very rapidly indeed. [INFORMAL] ❑ *Prices for Korean art have gone through the roof.* PHRASE: V inflects 5 If you **hit the roof** or **go through the roof**, you become very angry indeed, and usually show your anger by shouting at someone. [INFORMAL] ❑ *Sergeant Long will hit the roof when I tell him you've gone off.* PHRASE: V inflects 6 If a group of people inside a building **raise the roof**, they make a very loud noise, for example by singing or shouting. ❑ *He raised the roof at the conference when he sang his own version of the socialist anthem, The Red Flag.* PHRASE: V inflects 7 If a number of things or people are **under one roof** or **under the same roof**, they are in the same building. ❑ *The firms intend to open either together under one roof or alongside each other in shopping malls.* PHRASE: PHR after v, v-link PHR

**roofed** /ruːft, ruːvd/ A **roofed** building or area is covered by a roof. ❑ *...a roofed corridor. ...a peasant hut roofed with branches.* ADJ

**-roofed** /-ruːft, -ruːvd/ **-roofed** combines with adjectives and nouns to form adjectives that describe what kind of roof a building has. ❑ *...a huge flat-roofed concrete and glass building.* COMB in ADJ: usu ADJ n

**roof|er** /ruːfəʳ/ **(roofers)** A **roofer** is a person whose job is to put roofs on buildings and to repair damaged roofs. N-COUNT

**roof gar|den** **(roof gardens)** A **roof garden** is a garden on the flat roof of a building. N-COUNT

**roof|ing** /ruːfɪŋ/ 1 **Roofing** is material used for making or covering roofs. ❑ *A gust of wind pried loose a section of sheet-metal roofing.* N-UNCOUNT: oft N n 2 **Roofing** is the work of putting new roofs on houses. ❑ *...a roofing company.* N-UNCOUNT: oft N n

**roof|less** /ruːfləs/ A **roofless** building has no roof, usually because the building has been damaged or has not been used for a long time. ADJ

**roof rack** **(roof racks)** also **roof-rack.** A **roof rack** is a metal frame that is fixed on top of a car and used for carrying large objects. [BRIT] ➔ See picture on page 1707. N-COUNT

> in AM, use **luggage rack**

**roof|top** /ruːftɒp/ **(rooftops)** also **roof-top.** 1 A **rooftop** is the outside part of the roof of a building. ❑ *Below us you could glimpse the rooftops of a few small villages.* N-COUNT 2 If you shout something **from the rooftops**, you say it or announce it in a very public way. ❑ *When we have something definite to say, we shall be shouting it from the rooftops.* PHRASE: PHR after v

**rook** /rʊk/ **(rooks)** 1 A **rook** is a large black bird. Rooks are members of the crow family. N-COUNT 2 In chess, a **rook** is one of the chess pieces which stand in the corners of the board at the beginning of a game. Rooks can move forwards, backwards, or sideways, but not diagonally. N-COUNT = castle

**rookie** /rʊki/ **(rookies)** 1 A **rookie** is someone who has just started doing a job and does not have much experience, especially someone who has just joined the army or police force. [mainly AM, INFORMAL] ❑ *I don't want to have another rookie to train.* N-COUNT: oft N n 2 A **rookie** is a person who has been competing in a professional sport for less than a year. [AM] N-COUNT: oft N n

**room** /ruːm, rʊm/ **(rooms, rooming, roomed)** ◆◆◆ 1 A **room** is one of the separate sections or parts of the inside of a building. Rooms have their own walls, ceilings, floors, and doors, and are usually used for particular activities. You can refer to all the people who are in a room as **the room**. ❑ *A minute later he excused himself and left the room... The whole room roared with laughter.* N-COUNT 2 If you talk about your **room**, you are referring to the room that you alone use, especially your bedroom at home or your office at work. ❑ *If you're running upstairs, go to my room and bring down my sweater, please.* N-COUNT: poss N 3 A **room** is a bedroom in a hotel. ❑ *Toni booked a room in an hotel not far from Arzfeld.* N-COUNT 4 If you **room with** someone, you share a rented room, apartment, or house with them, for example when you are a student. [AM] ❑ *I had roomed with him in New Haven when we were both at Yale Law School.* VERB V with n Also V together 5 If there is **room** somewhere, there is enough empty space there for people or things to be fitted in, or for people to move freely or do what they want to. ❑ *There is usually room to accommodate up to 80 visitors.* ➔ See also **leg room**, **standing room**. N-UNCOUNT 6 If there is **room for** a particular kind of behaviour or action, people are able to behave in that way or to take that action. ❑ *The intensity of the work left little room for personal grief or anxiety.* N-UNCOUNT: usu N for n 7 If you have **room for manoeuvre**, you have the opportunity to change your plans if it becomes necessary or desirable. ❑ *With an election looming, he has little room for manoeuvre.* PHRASE: PHR after v, poss PHR, with PHR 8 ➔ See also **changing room, chat room, common room, consulting room, dining room, drawing room, dressing room, elbow room, emergency room, ladies' room, leg room, living room, locker room, men's room, morning room, powder room, reading room, reception room, rest room, spare room, standing room.** to **give** something **houseroom** ➔ see **houseroom**.

**-roomed** /-ruːmd/ **-roomed** combines with numbers to form adjectives which tell you how many rooms a house or flat contains. ❑ *They found a little two-roomed flat to rent.* COMB in ADJ: usu ADJ n

**room|ful** /ruːmfʊl/ **(roomfuls)** A **roomful of** things or people is a room that is full of them. You can also refer to the amount or number of things or people that a room can contain as a **roomful**. ❑ *It was like a teacher disciplining a roomful of second-year pupils.* N-COUNT: usu N of n

**room|ing house** **(rooming houses)** A **rooming house** is a building that is divided into small flats or single rooms which people rent to live in. [AM] N-COUNT

**room|mate** /ruːmmeɪt, rʊm-/ **(roommates)** also **room-mate.** 1 Your **roommate** is the person you share a rented room, apartment, or house with, for example when you are at university. [AM] N-COUNT 2 Your **roommate** is the person you N-COUNT share a rented room with, for example when you are at university. [BRIT]

**room ser|vice** Room service is a service in a hotel by which meals or drinks are provided for guests in their rooms. ❑ *The hotel did not normally provide room service.* N-UNCOUNT

**roomy** /ruːmi/ **(roomier, roomiest)** [1] If you describe a place as **roomy**, you mean that you like it because it is large inside and you can move around freely and comfortably. ❑ *The car is roomy and a good choice for anyone who needs to carry equipment.* ADJ approval = *spacious* ≠ *cramped* [2] If you describe a piece of clothing as **roomy**, you mean that you like it because it is large and fits loosely. ❑ *...roomy jackets.* ADJ approval ≠ *tight*

**roost** /ruːst/ **(roosts, roosting, roosted)** [1] A **roost** is a place where birds or bats rest or sleep. N-COUNT [2] When birds or bats **roost** somewhere, they rest or sleep there. ❑ *The peacocks roost in nearby shrubs.* VERB V prep/adv
PHRASES [3] If bad or wrong things that someone has done in the past **have come home to roost**, or if their **chickens have come home to roost**, they are now experiencing the unpleasant effects of these actions. ❑ *Appeasement has come home to roost.* PHRASE: *come* inflects [4] If you say that someone **rules the roost** in a particular place, you mean that they have control and authority over the people there. [INFORMAL] ❑ *Today the country's nationalists rule the roost and hand out the jobs.* PHRASE: V inflects

**roost|er** /ruːstəʳ/ **(roosters)** A **rooster** is an adult male chicken. [AM] N-COUNT
✔ in BRIT, use **cock**

**root** /ruːt/ **(roots, rooting, rooted)** ◆◇◇ [1] The **roots** of a plant are the parts of it that grow under the ground. ❑ *...the twisted roots of an apple tree.* N-COUNT: usu pl [2] If you **root** a plant or cutting or if it **roots**, roots form on the bottom of its stem and it starts to grow. ❑ *Most plants will root in about six to eight weeks... Root the cuttings in a heated propagator.* VERB V, V n [3] **Root** vegetables or **root** crops are grown for their roots which are large and can be eaten. ❑ *...root crops such as carrots and potatoes.* ADJ: ADJ n [4] The **root** of a hair or tooth is the part of it that is underneath the skin. ❑ *...decay around the roots of teeth.* N-COUNT [5] You can refer to the place or culture that a person or their family comes from as their **roots**. ❑ *I am proud of my Brazilian roots.* N-PLURAL: usu poss N [6] You can refer to the cause of a problem or of an unpleasant situation as **the root of** it or **the roots of** it. ❑ *We got to the root of the problem.* N-COUNT: usu *the* N *of* n [7] The **root** of a word is the part that contains its meaning and to which other parts can be added. [TECHNICAL] ❑ *The word 'secretary' comes from the same Latin root as the word 'secret'.* N-COUNT [8] If you **root through** or **in** something, you search for something by moving other things around. ❑ *She rooted through the bag, found what she wanted, and headed toward the door.* VERB = *rummage* V prep [9] ➔ See also **rooted**, **cube root**, **grass roots**, **square root**.
PHRASES [10] If something has been completely changed or destroyed, you can say that it has been changed or destroyed **root and branch**. [WRITTEN] ❑ *The forces of National Socialism were transforming Germany root and branch... Some prison practices are in need of root and branch reform.* PHRASE: PHR after v, PHR n [11] If someone **puts down roots**, they make a place their home, for example by taking part in activities there or by making a lot of friends there. ❑ *When they got to Montana, they put down roots and built a life.* PHRASE: V inflects = *settle down* [12] If an idea, belief, or custom **takes root**, it becomes established among a group of people. ❑ *Time would be needed for democracy to take root.* PHRASE: V inflects

♦ **root around**
✔ in BRIT, also use **root about**

If you **root around** or **root about** in something, you look for something there, moving things around as you search. ❑ *'It's in here somewhere,' he said, rooting about in his desk.* PHRASAL VERB V P prep, Also V P

♦ **root for** If you **are rooting for** someone, you are giving them your support while they are doing something difficult or trying to defeat another person. [INFORMAL] ❑ *Good luck, we'll be rooting for you.* PHRASAL VERB V P n

♦ **root out** [1] If you **root out** a person, you find them and force them from the place they are in, usually in order to punish them. ❑ *The generals have to root out traitors... It shouldn't take too long to root him out.* PHRASAL VERB V P n (not pron), V n P [2] If you **root out** a problem or an unpleasant situation, you find out who or what is the cause of it and put an end to it. ❑ *There would be a major drive to root out corruption.* PHRASAL VERB V P n (not pron)

**root beer** **(root beers)** **Root beer** is a fizzy non-alcoholic drink flavoured with the roots of various plants and herbs. It is popular in the United States. N-UNCOUNT ♦ A glass, can, or bottle of root beer can be referred to as a **root beer**. ❑ *Kevin buys a root beer.* N-COUNT

**root|ed** /ruːtɪd/ [1] If you say that one thing is **rooted in** another, you mean that it is strongly influenced by it or has developed from it. ❑ *The crisis is rooted in deep rivalries between the two groups.* ADJ: v-link ADJ *in* n [2] If someone has deeply **rooted** opinions or feelings, they believe or feel something extremely strongly and are unlikely to change. ❑ *Racism is a deeply rooted prejudice which has existed for thousands of years.* ➔ See also **deep-rooted**. ADJ: usu ADJ n, usu adv ADJ [3] If you are **rooted to the spot**, you are unable to move because you are very frightened or shocked. ❑ *We just stopped there, rooted to the spot.* PHRASE

**root gin|ger** **Root ginger** is the stem of the ginger plant. It is often used in Chinese and Indian cooking. N-UNCOUNT

**root|less** /ruːtləs/ If someone has no permanent home or job and is not settled in any community, you can describe them as **rootless**. ❑ *These rootless young people have nowhere else to go.* ADJ: usu ADJ n

**rope** /roʊp/ **(ropes, roping, roped)** [1] A **rope** is a thick cord or wire that is made by twisting together several thinner cords or wires. Ropes are used for jobs such as pulling cars, tying up boats, or tying things together. ❑ *He tied the rope around his waist. ...a piece of rope.* N-VAR [2] If you **rope** one thing **to** another, you tie the two things together with a rope. ❑ *I roped myself to the chimney.* VERB V n *to* n
PHRASES [3] If you **give** someone **enough rope to hang themselves**, you give them the freedom to do a job in their own way because you hope that their attempts will fail and that they will look foolish. ❑ *The King has merely given the politicians enough rope to hang themselves.* PHRASE: *give* inflects [4] If you **are learning the ropes**, you are learning how a particular task or job is done. [INFORMAL] PHRASE: V inflects [5] If you **know the ropes**, you know how a particular job or task should be done. [INFORMAL] ❑ *The moment she got to know the ropes, there was no stopping her.* PHRASE: V inflects [6] If you describe a payment as **money for old rope**, you are emphasizing that it is earned very easily, for very little effort. [BRIT, INFORMAL] PHRASE: usu v-link PHR emphasis [7] If you **show** someone **the ropes**, you show them how to do a particular job or task. [INFORMAL] PHRASE: V inflects

♦ **rope in** If you say that you **were roped in to** do a particular task, you mean that someone persuaded you to help them do that task. [mainly BRIT, INFORMAL] ❑ *Visitors were roped in for potato picking and harvesting... I got roped in to help with the timekeeping.* PHRASAL VERB: usu passive *be* V-ed P *for* n, *be* V-ed P to-inf, Also *be* V-ed P

♦ **rope off** If you **rope off** an area, you tie ropes between posts all around its edges so that people cannot enter it without permission. ❑ *You should rope off a big field and sell tickets.* PHRASAL VERB V P n (not pron)

**rope lad|der** **(rope ladders)** also **rope-ladder**. A **rope ladder** is a ladder made of two long ropes connected by short pieces of rope, wood, or metal. N-COUNT

**ropey** /roʊpi/ **(ropier, ropiest)** If you say that something is **ropey**, you mean that its quality is poor or unsatisfactory. [BRIT, INFORMAL] ❑ *Your spelling's a bit ropey.* ADJ

**ro|sary** /rouzəri/ **(rosaries)** A **rosary** is a string of beads that members of certain religions, especially Catholics, use for counting prayers. A series of prayers counted in this way is also called a **rosary**. N-COUNT

**rose** /rouz/ **(roses)** [1] **Rose** is the past tense of **rise**. ◆◇◇ [2] A **rose** is a flower, often with a pleasant smell, which grows on a bush with stems that have sharp points called thorns on them. ❑ *...a bunch of yellow roses.* N-COUNT [3] A **rose** is bush that roses grow on. ❑ *Prune rambling roses when the flowers have faded.* N-COUNT [4] Something that is **rose** is reddish-pink in colour. [LITERARY] ❑ *...the rose and violet hues of a twilight sky.* COLOUR [5] If you say that a situation is not **a bed of roses**, you mean that it is not as pleasant as it seems, and that there are some unpleasant aspects to it. ❑ *We all knew that life was unlikely to be a bed of roses back in England.* PHRASE: v-link PHR, usu with brd-neg

**rosé** /rouzeɪ, AM rouzeɪ/ **(rosés) Rosé** is wine which is pink in colour. ❑ *The vast majority of wines produced in this area are reds or rosés.* N-MASS

**rose|bud** /rouzbʌd/ **(rosebuds)** A **rosebud** is a young rose whose petals have not yet opened out fully. N-COUNT

**rose-coloured**

☑ in AM, use **rose-colored**

If you look at a person or situation through **rose-coloured glasses** or **rose-tinted glasses**, you see only their good points and therefore your view of them is unrealistic. In British English, you can also say that someone is looking through **rose-coloured spectacles**. ❑ *Its influence can make you view life through rose-coloured glasses.* PHRASE: usu PHR after v

**rose|hip** /rouzhɪp/ **(rosehips)** A **rosehip** is a bright red or orange fruit that grows on some kinds of rose bushes. N-COUNT

**rose|mary** /rouzməri, AM -meri/ **Rosemary** is a herb used in cooking. It comes from an evergreen plant with small narrow leaves. The plant is also called **rosemary**. N-UNCOUNT

**rose-tinted** → see **rose-coloured**.

**ro|sette** /rouzet/ **(rosettes)** A **rosette** is a large circular decoration made from coloured ribbons which is given as a prize in a competition, or, especially in Britain, is worn to show support for a political party or sports team. N-COUNT

**rose|water** /rouzwɔːtəʳ/ **Rosewater** is a liquid which is made from roses and which has a pleasant smell. It is used as a perfume and in cooking. N-UNCOUNT

**rose win|dow (rose windows)** A **rose window** is a large round stained glass window in a church. N-COUNT

**rose|wood** /rouzwʊd/ **Rosewood** is a hard dark-coloured wood that is used for making furniture. Rosewood comes from a species of tropical tree. ❑ *...a heavy rosewood desk.* N-UNCOUNT

**ros|ter** /rɒstəʳ/ **(rosters)** [1] A **roster** is a list which gives details of the order in which different people have to do a particular job. ❑ *The next day he put himself first on the new roster for domestic chores.* N-COUNT = rota [2] A **roster** is a list, especially of the people who work for a particular organization or are available to do a particular job. It can also be a list of the sports players who are available for a particular team, especially in American English. ❑ *The Amateur Softball Association's roster of umpires has declined to 57,000.* N-COUNT: usu with supp, oft N *of* n = register

**ros|trum** /rɒstrəm/ **(rostrums** or **rostra** /rɒstrə/**)** A **rostrum** is a raised platform on which someone stands when they are speaking to an audience, receiving a prize, or conducting an orchestra. ❑ *As he stood on the winner's rostrum, he sang the words of the national anthem.* N-COUNT

**rosy** /rouzi/ **(rosier, rosiest)** [1] If you say that someone has a **rosy** face, you mean that they have pink cheeks and look very healthy. ❑ *Bethan's round, rosy face seemed hardly to have aged at all.* ADJ [2] If you say that a situation looks **rosy** or that the picture looks **rosy**, you mean that the situation seems likely to be good or successful. ❑ *The job prospects for those graduating in engineering are far less rosy now than they used to be.* ADJ = good

**rot** /rɒt/ **(rots, rotting, rotted)** [1] When food, wood, or another substance **rots**, or when something **rots** it, it becomes softer and is gradually destroyed. ❑ *If we don't unload it soon, the grain will start rotting in the silos... Sugary canned drinks rot your teeth.* VERB V V n [2] If there is **rot** in something, especially something that is made of wood, parts of it have decayed and fallen apart. ❑ *Investigations had revealed extensive rot in the beams under the ground floor.* N-UNCOUNT [3] You can use **the rot** to refer to the way something gradually gets worse. For example, if you are talking about the time when **the rot set in**, you are talking about the time when a situation began to get steadily worse and worse. ❑ *In many schools, the rot is beginning to set in. Standards are falling all the time.* N-SING: the N [4] If you say that someone is being left to **rot** in a particular place, especially in a prison, you mean that they are being left there and their physical and mental condition is being allowed to get worse and worse. ❑ *Most governments simply leave the long-term jobless to rot on the dole.* VERB V prep [5] → See also **dry rot**.

**rota** /routə/ **(rotas)** A **rota** is a list which gives details of the order in which different people have to do a particular job. [mainly BRIT] ❑ *I suggest that you work out a careful rota which will make it clear who tidies the room on which day.* N-COUNT = roster

**ro|ta|ry** /routəri/ [1] **Rotary** means turning or able to turn round a fixed point. ❑ *...turning linear into rotary motion.* ADJ: ADJ n [2] **Rotary** is used in the names of some machines that have parts that turn round a fixed point. ❑ *...a rotary engine.* ADJ: ADJ n

**ro|tate** /routeɪt, AM routeɪt/ **(rotates, rotating, rotated)** [1] When something **rotates** or when you **rotate** it, it turns with a circular movement. ❑ *The Earth rotates round the sun... Take each foot in both your hands and rotate it to loosen and relax the ankle.* VERB V V n [2] If people or things **rotate**, or if someone **rotates** them, they take it in turns to do a particular job or serve a particular purpose. ❑ *The members of the club can rotate and one person can do all the preparation for the evening... They will swap posts in a year's time, according to new party rules which rotate the leadership.* VERB V V n ♦ **ro|tat|ing** *The European Union's rotating presidency passed from Sweden to Belgium.* ADJ: ADJ n

**ro|ta|tion** /routeɪʃᵊn/ **(rotations)** [1] **Rotation** is circular movement. A **rotation** is the movement of something through one complete circle. ❑ *...the daily rotation of the earth upon its axis.* N-VAR [2] The **rotation** of a group of things or people is the fact of them taking turns to do a particular job or serve a particular purpose. If people do something **in rotation**, they take turns to do it. ❑ *Once a month we met for the whole day, and in rotation each one led the group.* N-UNCOUNT: oft *in* N

**rote** /rout/ **Rote** learning or learning **by rote** is learning things by repeating them without thinking about them or trying to understand them. ❑ *He is very sceptical about the value of rote learning.* N-UNCOUNT: N n, *by* N

**ro|tor** /routəʳ/ **(rotors)** The **rotors** or **rotor blades** of a helicopter are the four long, flat, thin pieces of metal on top of it which go round and lift it off the ground. N-COUNT

**rot|ten** /rɒtᵊn/ [1] If food, wood, or another substance is **rotten**, it has decayed and can no longer be used. ❑ *The smell outside this building is overwhelming – like rotten eggs.* ADJ [2] If you describe something as **rotten**, you think it is very unpleasant or of very poor quality. [INFORMAL] ❑ *I personally think it's a rotten idea.* ADJ: usu ADJ n ≠great [3] If you describe someone as **rotten**, you are insulting them or criticizing them because you think that they are very unpleasant or unkind. [INFORMAL] ❑ *You rotten swine! How dare you?* ADJ: usu ADJ n disapproval ≠nice [4] If you feel **rotten**, you feel bad, either because you are ill or because you are sorry ADJ: usu v-link ADJ = awful about something. [INFORMAL] ❑ *I had glandular fever and spent that year feeling rotten.*

**rot|ten ap|ple** **(rotten apples)** You can use **rotten apple** to talk about a person who is dishonest and therefore causes a lot of problems for the group or organization they belong to. ❑ *Police corruption is not just a few rotten apples.* N-COUNT

**rot|ter** /rɒtəʳ/ **(rotters)** If you call someone a **rotter**, you are criticizing them because you think that they have behaved in a very unkind or mean way. [BRIT, INFORMAL, OLD-FASHIONED] N-COUNT disapproval

**Rott|wei|ler** /rɒtvaɪləʳ/ **(Rottweilers)**

☑ in BRIT, also use **rottweiler**

A **Rottweiler** is a large black and brown breed of dog which is often used as a guard dog. N-COUNT

**ro|tund** /roʊtʌnd/ If someone is **rotund**, they are round and fat. [FORMAL] ❑ *A rotund, smiling, red-faced gentleman appeared.* ADJ

**ro|tun|da** /roʊtʌndə/ **(rotundas)** A **rotunda** is a round building or room, especially one with a round bowl-shaped roof. N-COUNT

**rou|ble** /ruːbəl/ **(roubles)** The **rouble** is the unit of money of Russia and some of the other republics that form the Commonwealth of Independent States. N-COUNT: usu num N

**rouge** /ruːʒ/ **(rouges, rouging, rouged)** [1] **Rouge** is a red powder or cream which women and actors can put on their cheeks in order to give them more colour. [OLD-FASHIONED] N-UNCOUNT = blusher [2] If a woman or an actor **rouges** their cheeks or lips, they put red powder or cream on them to give them more colour. ❑ *Florentine women rouged their earlobes... She had curly black hair and rouged cheeks.* VERB V n V-ed

**rough** /rʌf/ **(rougher, roughest, roughs, roughing, roughed)** ◆◇◇ [1] If a surface is **rough**, it is uneven and not smooth. ❑ *His hands were rough and calloused, from years of karate practice.* ADJ ≠smooth ♦ **rough|ness** *She rested her cheek against the roughness of his jacket.* N-UNCOUNT [2] You say that people or their actions are **rough** when they use too much force and not enough care or gentleness. ❑ *Rugby's a rough game at the best of times.* ADJ ≠gentle ♦ **rough|ly** *A hand roughly pushed him aside.* ADV ♦ **rough|ness** *He regretted his roughness.* N-UNCOUNT [3] A **rough** area, city, school, or other place is unpleasant and dangerous because there is a lot of violence or crime there. ❑ *It was quite a rough part of our town.* ADJ [4] If you say that someone has had a **rough** time, you mean that they have had some difficult or unpleasant experiences. ❑ *All women have a rough time in our society.* ADJ: usu ADJ n = tough [5] If you feel **rough**, you feel ill. [BRIT, INFORMAL] ❑ *The virus won't go away and the lad is still feeling a bit rough.* ADJ: v-link ADJ [6] A **rough** calculation or guess is approximately correct, but not exact. ❑ *We were only able to make a rough estimate of how much fuel would be required.* ADJ: usu ADJ n = approximate ♦ **rough|ly** *Gambling and tourism pay roughly half the entire state budget.* ADV: ADV with cl/group [7] If you give someone a **rough** idea, description, or drawing of something, you indicate only the most important features, without much detail. ❑ *I've got a rough idea of what he looks like.* ADJ ♦ **rough|ly** *He knew roughly what was about to be said... Roughly speaking, a scientific humanist is somebody who believes in science and in humanity but not in God.* ADV: ADV with cl/group, ADV after v [8] You can say that something is **rough** when it is not neat and well made. ❑ *...a rough wooden table.* ADJ ♦ **rough|ly** *Roughly chop the tomatoes and add them to the casserole.* ADV: ADV with v [9] If the sea or the weather at sea is **rough**, the weather is windy or stormy and there are very big waves. ❑ *A fishing vessel and a cargo ship collided in rough seas.* ADJ ≠calm [10] When people sleep or live **rough**, they sleep out of doors, usually because they have no home. [BRIT] ❑ *It makes me so sad when I see young people begging or sleeping rough on the streets.* ADV: ADV after v [11] If you have to **rough** it, you have to live without the possessions and comforts that you normally have. ❑ *You won't be roughing it; each room comes equipped with a telephone and a 3-channel radio.* VERB V it [12] **rough justice** → see **justice**.

**rough|age** /rʌfɪdʒ/ **Roughage** consists of the tough parts of vegetables and grains that help you to digest your food and help your bowels to work properly. N-UNCOUNT = fibre

**rough and ready** also **rough-and-ready.** [1] A **rough and ready** solution or method is one that is rather simple and not very exact because it has been thought of or done in a hurry. ❑ *Here is a rough and ready measurement.* ADJ [2] A **rough and ready** person is not very polite or gentle. ❑ *...rough and ready soldiers.* ADJ

**rough and tum|ble** also **rough-and-tumble.** [1] You can use **rough and tumble** to refer to a situation in which the people involved try hard to get what they want, and do not worry about upsetting or harming others, and you think this is acceptable and normal. ❑ *...the rough-and-tumble of political combat.* N-UNCOUNT: oft the N of n [2] **Rough and tumble** is physical playing that involves noisy and slightly violent behaviour. ❑ *He enjoys rough and tumble play.* N-UNCOUNT

**rough|en** /rʌfən/ **(roughens, roughening, roughened)** If something has **been roughened**, its surface has become less smooth. ❑ *...complexions that have been roughened by long periods in the hot sun.* VERB: usu passive be V-ed

**rough-hewn** **Rough-hewn** wood or stone has been cut into a shape but has not yet been smoothed or finished off. ❑ *It is a rough-hewn carving of a cat's head.* ADJ: usu ADJ n

**rough|neck** /rʌfnek/ **(roughnecks)** [1] A **roughneck** is a man who operates an oil well. [mainly AM, INFORMAL] N-COUNT [2] If you describe a man as a **roughneck**, you disapprove of him because you think he is not gentle or polite, and can be violent. [INFORMAL] N-COUNT disapproval

**rough|shod** /rʌfʃɒd/ If you say that someone **is riding roughshod over** a person or their views, you disapprove of them because they are using their power or authority to do what they want, completely ignoring that person's wishes. ❑ *These laws allow the security forces to continue to ride roughshod over the human rights of the people.* PHRASE: V inflects disapproval

**rou|lette** /ruːlet/ **Roulette** is a gambling game in which a ball is dropped onto a wheel with numbered holes in it while the wheel is spinning round. The players bet on which hole the ball will be in when the wheel stops spinning. → See also **Russian roulette**. N-UNCOUNT

**round**

① PREPOSITION AND ADVERB USES
② NOUN USES
③ ADJECTIVE USES
④ VERB USES

**① round** /raʊnd/ ◆◆◇

**Round** is an adverb and preposition that has the same meanings as 'around'. **Round** is often used with verbs of movement, such as 'walk' and 'drive', and also in phrasal verbs such as 'get round' and 'hand round'. **Round** is commoner in British English than American English, and it is slightly more informal.

⇛ Please look at category 20 to see if the expression you are looking for is shown under another headword. [1] To be positioned **round** a place or object means to surround it or be on all sides of it. To move **round** a place means to go along its edge, back to the point where you started. ❑ *They were sitting round the kitchen table... All round us was desert.* PREP ♦ **Round** is also an adverb. ❑ *Visibility was good all round... The goldfish swam round and round in their tiny bowls.* ADV: ADV after v [2] If you move **round** a corner or obstacle, you move to the other side of it. If you look **round** a corner or obstacle, you look to see what is on the other side. ❑ *Suddenly a car came round a corner on the opposite side... One of his* PREP *men tapped and looked round the door.* [3] [PREP] You use **round** to say that something happens in or relates to different parts of a place, or is near a place. ❑ *He happens to own half the land round here... I think he has earned the respect of leaders all round the world.* ♦ [ADV: ADV after v, n ADV] **Round** is also an adverb. ❑ *Shirley found someone to show them round... So you're going to have a look round?* [4] [ADV: ADV after v] If a wheel or object spins **round**, it turns on its axis. ❑ *Holes can be worn remarkably quickly by a wheel going round at 60mph.* [5] [ADV: ADV after v] If you turn **round**, you turn so that you are facing or going in the opposite direction. ❑ *She paused, but did not turn round... The wind veered round to the east.* [6] [ADV: ADV after v] If you move things **round**, you move them so they are in different places. ❑ *I've already moved things round a bit to make it easier for him.* [7] [ADV: ADV after v] If you hand or pass something **round**, it is passed from person to person in a group. ❑ *John handed round the plate of sandwiches.* ♦ [PREP] **Round** is also a preposition. ❑ *They started handing the microphone out round the girls at the front.* [8] [ADV: ADV after v] If you go **round** to someone's house, you visit them. ❑ *I think we should go round and tell Kevin to turn his music down... He came round with a bottle of champagne.* ♦ [PREP] **Round** is also a preposition in non-standard English. ❑ *I went round my wife's house.* [9] [ADV: ADV after v] You use **round** in informal expressions such as **sit round** or **hang round** when you are saying that someone is spending time in a place and is not doing anything very important. [BRIT] ❑ *As we sat round chatting, I began to think I'd made a mistake.* ♦ [PREP] **Round** is also a preposition. ❑ *She would spend the day hanging round street corners.* [10] [PREP] If something is built or based **round** a particular idea, that idea is the basis for it. ❑ *That was for a design built round an existing American engine.* [11] [PREP] If you get **round** a problem or difficulty, you find a way of dealing with it. ❑ *Don't just immediately give up but think about ways round a problem.* [12] [ADV: ADV after v] If you win someone **round**, or if they come **round**, they change their mind about something and start agreeing with you. ❑ *He did his best to talk me round, but I wouldn't speak to him.* [13] [ADV: n ADV, ADV after v] You use **round** in expressions such as **this time round** or **to come round** when you are describing something that has happened before or things that happen regularly. ❑ *In the past, the elections have been marked by hundreds of murders, but this time round the violence has been much more limited.* [14] [PREP] You can use **round** to give the measurement of the outside of something that is shaped like a circle or a cylinder. ❑ *I'm about two inches larger round the waist.* ♦ [ADV] **Round** is also an adverb. ❑ *It's six feet high and five feet round.* [15] [ADV: ADV amount] [vagueness] You use **round** in front of times or amounts to indicate that they are approximate. ❑ *I go to bed round 11:00 at night.*

**PHRASES** [16] [PREP-PHRASE] [vagueness] In spoken English, **round about** means approximately. [mainly BRIT] ❑ *Round about one and a half million people died.* [17] [PHRASE: cl PHR] [emphasis] You say **all round** to emphasize that something affects all parts of a situation or all members of a group. [mainly BRIT] ❑ *It ought to make life much easier all round.* [18] [PHRASE: V inflects] If you say that something **is going round and round** in your head, you mean that you can't stop thinking about it. ❑ *It all keeps going round and round in my head till I don't know where I am.* [19] [PHRASE: PHR after v] If something happens **all year round**, it happens throughout the year. ❑ *Many of these plants are evergreen, so you can enjoy them all year round.* [20] **round the corner** → see **corner**. **the other way round** → see **way**.

**② round** /raʊnd/ **(rounds)** ◆◆◇ [1] [N-COUNT: with supp, oft N *of* n] A **round of** events is a series of related events, especially one which comes after or before a similar series of events. ❑ *This is the latest round of job cuts aimed at making the company more competitive.* [2] [N-COUNT: usu adj N, N num = heat] In sport, a **round** is a series of games in a competition. The winners of these games go on to play in the next round, and so on, until only one player or team is left. ❑ *...in the third round of the Pilkington Cup... After round three, two Americans share the lead.* [3] [N-COUNT: usu adj N, N num] In a boxing or wrestling match, a **round** is one of the periods during which the boxers or wrestlers fight. ❑ *He was declared the victor in the 11th round.* [4] [N-COUNT: usu N *of* n, N *of* num] A **round of** golf is one game, usually including 18 holes. ❑ *...two rounds of golf.* [5] [N-COUNT: usu supp N] If you do your **rounds** or your **round**, you make a series of visits to different places or people, for example as part of your job. [mainly BRIT] ❑ *The consultants still did their morning rounds.*

✔ in AM, usually use **route**

[6] [N-COUNT: usu with supp] If you buy a **round of** drinks, you buy a drink for each member of the group of people that you are with. ❑ *They sat on the clubhouse terrace, downing a round of drinks.* [7] [N-COUNT: usu num N, N *of* n] A **round of** ammunition is the bullet or bullets released when a gun is fired. ❑ *...firing 1650 rounds of ammunition during a period of ten minutes.* [8] [N-COUNT: N *of* n] If there is a **round of applause**, everyone claps their hands to welcome someone or to show that they have enjoyed something. ❑ *Sue got a sympathetic round of applause.* [9] [N-COUNT] In music, a **round** is a simple song sung by several people in which each person sings a different part of the song at the same time.

**PHRASES** [10] [PHRASE: V inflects] If a story, idea, or joke **is going the rounds** or **doing the rounds**, a lot of people have heard it and are telling it to other people. ❑ *This story was going the rounds 20 years ago.* [11] [PHRASE: V inflects, usu PHR *of* n] If you **make the rounds** or **do the rounds**, you visit a series of different places. ❑ *After school, I had picked up Nick and Ted and made the rounds of the dry cleaner and the grocery store.*

**③ round** /raʊnd/ **(rounder, roundest)** [1] [ADJ] Something that is **round** is shaped like a circle or ball. ❑ *She had small feet and hands and a flat, round face. ...the round church known as The New Temple.* [2] [ADJ: ADJ n] A **round** number is a multiple of 10, 100, 1000, and so on. Round numbers are used instead of precise ones to give the general idea of a quantity or proportion. ❑ *A million pounds seemed a suitably round number.*

**④ round** /raʊnd/ **(rounds, rounding, rounded)** [1] [VERB = go round] [V n] If you **round** a place or obstacle, you move in a curve past the edge or corner of it. ❑ *The house disappeared from sight as we rounded a corner.* [2] [VERB] [V n with adv] [be V-ed *to* amount] [V n adv *to* amount] If you **round** an amount **up** or **down**, or if you **round** it **off**, you change it to the nearest whole number or nearest multiple of 10, 100, 1000 and so on. ❑ *We needed to do decimals to round up and round down numbers... The fraction was then multiplied by 100 and rounded to the nearest half or whole number... I'll round it off to about £30.* [3] → See also **rounded**.

♦ **round off** [PHRASAL VERB] [V P n (not pron)] [V n P] [V P *by* -ing] If you **round off** an activity with something, you end the activity by doing something that provides a clear or satisfactory conclusion to it. ❑ *The Italian way is to round off a meal with an ice-cream... This rounded the afternoon off perfectly... He rounds off by proposing a toast to the attendants.*

♦ **round on** [PHRASAL VERB = attack] [V P n] If someone **rounds on** you, they criticize you fiercely and attack you with aggressive words. ❑ *The Conservative Party rounded angrily on him for damaging the Government.*

♦ **round up** [1] [PHRASAL VERB] [V P n (not pron)] [V n P] If the police or army **round up** a number of people, they arrest or capture them. ❑ *The police rounded up a number of suspects... She says the patrolmen rounded them up at the village school and beat them with rifle butts.* [2] [PHRASAL VERB] [V P n (not pron)] If you **round up** animals or things, you gather them together. ❑ *He had sought work as a cowboy, rounding up cattle.* [3] → See also **round 2**, **roundup**.

**round|about** /raʊndəbaʊt/ **(roundabouts)** [1] [N-COUNT] A **roundabout** is a circular structure in the road at a place where several roads meet. You drive round it until you come to the road that you want. [BRIT]

✔ in AM, use **traffic circle**

[2] [N-COUNT] A **roundabout** at a fair is a large, circular mechanical device with seats, often in the shape of

animals or cars, on which children sit and go round and round. [BRIT]

✓ in AM, use **merry-go-round, carousel**

3 A **roundabout** in a park or school play area is a circular platform that children sit or stand on. People push the platform to make it spin round. [BRIT] N-COUNT

✓ in AM, use **merry-go-round**

4 If you go somewhere by a **roundabout** route, you do not go there by the shortest and quickest route. ❑ *He left today on a roundabout route for Jordan and is also due soon in Egypt.* ADJ: usu ADJ n 5 If you do or say something in a **roundabout** way, you do not do or say it in a simple, clear, and direct way. ❑ *We made a bit of a fuss in a roundabout way.* ADJ: usu ADJ n 6 **round about** → see **round**. **swings and roundabouts** → see **swing**.

**round|ed** /raʊndɪd/ 1 Something that is **rounded** is curved in shape, without any points or sharp edges. ❑ *...a low rounded hill.* ADJ 2 You describe something or someone as **rounded** or **well-rounded** when you are expressing approval of them because they have a personality which is fully developed in all aspects. ❑ *...his carefully organised narrative, full of rounded, believable and interesting characters.* ADJ [approval]

**roun|del** /raʊndᵊl/ **(roundels)** A **roundel** is a circular design, for example one painted on a military aircraft. N-COUNT

**round|ers** /raʊndəʳz/ **Rounders** is a game played by two teams of children, in which a player scores points by hitting a ball thrown by a member of the other team and then running round all four sides of a square. N-UNCOUNT

**round|ly** /raʊndli/ If you are **roundly** condemned or criticized, you are condemned or criticized forcefully or by many people. If you are **roundly** defeated, you are defeated completely. ❑ *Political leaders have roundly condemned the shooting.* ADV: usu ADV before v

**round-robin** **(round-robins)** also **round robin.** A **round-robin** is a sports competition in which each player or team plays against every other player or team. ❑ *They beat England 4-1 in their last round-robin match at Nagoya in Japan.* N-COUNT: usu N n ≠ *knock-out*

**round-shouldered** If someone is **round-shouldered**, they bend forward when they sit or stand, and their shoulders are curved rather than straight. ❑ *Cissie was round-shouldered and dumpy.* ADJ [disapproval]

**round ta|ble** **(round tables)** also **round-table, roundtable.** A **round table** discussion is a meeting where experts gather together in order to discuss a particular topic. ❑ *...a round-table conference of the leading heart specialists of America.* N-COUNT: usu N n

**round-the-clock** → see **clock**.

**round trip** **(round trips)** 1 If you make a **round trip**, you travel to a place and then back again. ❑ *The train operates the 2,400-mile round trip once a week.* N-COUNT 2 A **round-trip** ticket is a ticket for a train, bus, or plane that allows you to travel to a particular place and then back again. [AM] ❑ *Mexicana Airlines has announced cheaper round-trip tickets between Los Angeles and cities it serves in Mexico.* ADJ: ADJ n

✓ in BRIT, use **return**

**round|up** /raʊndʌp/ **(roundups)** also **round-up.** 1 In journalism, especially television or radio, a **roundup** of news is a summary of the main events that have happened. ❑ *First, we have this roundup of the day's news.* N-COUNT: usu with supp, oft N *of* n, adj N 2 When there is a **roundup of** people, they are arrested or captured by the police or army and brought to one place. ❑ *There are reports that round ups of westerners are still taking place.* N-COUNT 3 A **roundup** is an occasion when cattle, horses, or other animals are collected together so that they can be counted or sold. [AM] ❑ *What is it that keeps a cowboy looking strong, young and ready for another roundup?* N-COUNT

**round|worm** /raʊndwɜːʳm/ **(roundworms)** A **roundworm** is a very small worm that lives in the intestines of people, pigs, and other animals. N-VAR

**rouse** /raʊz/ **(rouses, rousing, roused)** 1 If someone **rouses** you when you are sleeping or if you **rouse**, you wake up. [LITERARY] ❑ *Hilton roused him at eight-thirty by rapping on the door... When I put my hand on his, he stirs but doesn't quite rouse.* VERB = *wake* V n V 2 If you **rouse yourself**, you stop being inactive and start doing something. ❑ *She seemed to be unable to rouse herself to do anything... He roused himself from his lazy contemplation of the scene beneath him.* VERB V pron-refl to-inf V pron-refl *from* n 3 If something or someone **rouses** you, they make you very emotional or excited. ❑ *He did more to rouse the crowd there than anybody else... Ben says his father was good-natured, a man not quickly roused to anger or harsh opinions.* VERB V n *be* V-ed *to* n ♦ **rous|ing** *...a rousing speech to the convention in support of the president.* ADJ: usu ADJ n 4 If something **rouses** a feeling in you, it causes you to have that feeling. ❑ *It roused a feeling of rebellion in him.* VERB V n

**roust** /raʊst/ **(rousts, rousting, rousted)** If you **roust** someone, you disturb, upset, or hit them, or make them move from their place. [AM] ❑ *Relax, kid, we're not about to roust you. We just want some information... Bruce had gone to bed, but they rousted him out.* VERB V n V n *out* Also V n *from* n

**roust|about** /raʊstəbaʊt/ **(roustabouts)** A **roustabout** is a unskilled worker, especially one who works in a port or at an oil well. [AM] N-COUNT

**rout** /raʊt/ **(routs, routing, routed)** If an army, sports team, or other group **routs** its opponents, it defeats them completely and easily. ❑ *...the Battle of Hastings at which the Norman army routed the English opposition.* VERB V n ♦ **Rout** is also a noun. ❑ *Zidane completed the rout with a low shot from the edge of the penalty area.* N-COUNT

**route** /ruːt/ **(routes, routing, routed)** ◆◆◇

✓ Pronounced /ruːt/ or /raʊt/ in American English.

1 A **route** is a way from one place to another. ❑ *...the most direct route to the town centre... All escape routes were blocked by armed police.* N-COUNT 2 A bus, air, or shipping **route** is the way between two places along which buses, planes, or ships travel regularly. ❑ *...the main shipping routes to Japan.* N-COUNT: oft supp N 3 In the United States, **Route** is used in front of a number in the names of main roads between major cities. ❑ *...the Broadway-Webster exit on Route 580.* N-IN-NAMES: N num 4 Your **route** is the series of visits you make to different people or places, as part of your job. [mainly AM] ❑ *He began cracking open big blue tins of butter cookies and feeding the dogs on his route.* N-COUNT

✓ in BRIT, usually use **round, rounds**

5 You can refer to a way of achieving something as a **route**. ❑ *Researchers are trying to get at the same information through an indirect route.* N-COUNT: usu with supp = *road* 6 If vehicles, goods, or passengers **are routed** in a particular direction, they are made to travel in that direction. ❑ *Double-stack trains are taking a lot of freight that used to be routed via trucks... Approaching cars will be routed into two lanes.* VERB: usu passive *be* V-ed prep/adv

PHRASES 7 **En route to** a place means on the way to that place. **En route** is sometimes spelled **on route** in non-standard English. ❑ *They have arrived in London en route to the United States... One of the bags was lost en route.* PHRASE: oft PHR *to/from/for* n 8 Journalists sometimes use **en route** when they are mentioning an event that happened as part of a longer process or before another event. ❑ *The German set three tournament records and equalled two others en route to grabbing golf's richest prize.* PHRASE: oft PHR *to* n/-ing 9 If you **go the route**, you do something fully or continue with a task until you have completely finished. [AM] ❑ *They have gone the route, in many cases, of just big – big bowls, big statues, big masks, big everything.* PHRASE: *go* inflects

**route map** **(route maps)** 1 A **route map** is a map that shows the main roads in a particular area or the main routes used by buses, trains and other forms of transport in a particular area. N-COUNT 2 If N-COUNT you describe one thing as a **route map** for another thing, you mean that it provides a model showing the best way to achieve or describe it. ❑ *Nowhere could you find a better route map of the troubles of Northern Ireland than in the articles of The Independent's David McKittrick.*

**rout|er** /ruːtəʳ/ **(routers)** On a computer or network of computers, a **router** is a piece of equipment which allows access to other computers or networks, for example the Internet. N-COUNT

**rou|tine** /ruːtiːn/ **(routines)** ◆◇◇ [1] A **routine** is the usual series of things that you do at a particular time. A **routine** is also the practice of regularly doing things in a fixed order. ❑ *The players had to change their daily routine and lifestyle... He checked up on you as a matter of routine.* N-VAR: usu with supp, oft N n, adj N [2] You use **routine** to describe activities that are done as a normal part of a job or process. ❑ *...a series of routine medical tests.* ADJ: usu ADJ n [3] A **routine** situation, action, or event is one which seems completely ordinary, rather than interesting, exciting, or different. ❑ *So many days are routine and uninteresting, especially in winter.* ADJ [disapproval] = ordinary [4] You use **routine** to refer to a way of life that is uninteresting and ordinary, or hardly ever changes. ❑ *...the mundane routine of her life.* N-VAR [disapproval] [5] A **routine** is a computer program, or part of a program, that performs a specific function. [COMPUTING] ❑ *... an installation routine.* N-COUNT [6] A **routine** is a short sequence of jokes, remarks, actions, or movements that forms part of a longer performance. ❑ *...an athletic dance routine.* N-COUNT: usu n N

**rou|tine|ly** /ruːtiːnli/ [1] If something is **routinely** done, it is done as a normal part of a job or process. ❑ *Vitamin K is routinely given in the first week of life to prevent bleeding.* ADV: usu ADV with v, also ADV adj [2] If something happens **routinely**, it happens repeatedly and is not surprising, unnatural, or new. ❑ *Any outside criticism is routinely dismissed as interference.* ADV: ADV with v

**rove** /roʊv/ **(roves, roving, roved)** [1] If someone **roves about** an area or **roves** an area, they wander around it. [LITERARY] ❑ *...roving about the town in the dead of night and seeing something peculiar... She became a photographer, roving the world with her camera in her hand.* VERB = roam; V prep/adv; V n [2] → See also **roving**.

**rov|ing** /roʊvɪŋ/ You use **roving** to describe a person who travels around, rather than staying in a fixed place. ❑ *...a roving reporter.* ADJ: ADJ n

| **row** |
|---|
| ① ARRANGEMENT OR SEQUENCE |
| ② MAKING A BOAT MOVE |
| ③ DISAGREEMENT OR NOISE |

① **row** /roʊ/ **(rows)** ◆◇◇ [1] A **row of** things or people is a number of them arranged in a line. ❑ *...a row of pretty little cottages... Several men are pushing school desks and chairs into neat rows.* N-COUNT: oft N *of* n [2] **Row** is sometimes used in the names of streets. ❑ *...the house at 236 Larch Row.* N-IN-NAMES: n N [3] → See also **death row**, **skid row**. [4] If something happens several times **in a row**, it happens that number of times without a break. If something happens several days **in a row**, it happens on each of those days. ❑ *They have won five championships in a row.* PHRASE: PHR after v

② **row** /roʊ/ **(rows, rowing, rowed)** When you **row**, you sit in a boat and make it move through the water by using oars. If you **row** someone somewhere, you take them there in a boat, using oars. ❑ *He rowed as quickly as he could to the shore... We could all row a boat and swim almost before we could walk... The boatman refused to row him back.* VERB; V prep; V n; V n adv/prep ♦ **Row** is also a noun. ❑ *I took Daniel for a row.* N-COUNT → See also **rowing**.

♦ **row back** If you **row back on** something you have said or written, you express a different or contrary opinion about it. ❑ *The administration has been steadily rowing back from its early opposition to his attendance in London... The government was forced to row back on an austerity plan that would have involved wage cuts.* PHRASAL VERB; V P *from* n; V P *on* n

③ **row** /raʊ/ **(rows, rowing, rowed)** ◆◇◇ [1] A **row** is a serious disagreement between people or organizations. [BRIT, INFORMAL] ❑ *This is likely to provoke a further row about the bank's role in the affair.* N-COUNT: oft adj N, N prep = dispute [2] If two people **row** or if one person **rows with** another, they have a noisy argument. [BRIT, INFORMAL] ❑ *They rowed all the time... He had earlier rowed with his girlfriend.* V-RECIP; pl-n V; V *with* n [3] If you say that someone is making a **row**, you mean that they are making a loud, unpleasant noise. [BRIT, INFORMAL] ❑ *'Whatever is that row?' she demanded. 'Pop festival,' he answered.* N-SING = din, racket

**ro|wan** /roʊən, raʊən/ **(rowans)** A **rowan** or a **rowan tree** is a tree with a silvery trunk that has red berries in autumn. ♦ **Rowan** is the wood of this tree. N-VAR = mountain ash; N-UNCOUNT

**row|boat** /roʊboʊt/ **(rowboats)** A **rowboat** is a small boat that you move through the water by using oars. [AM] N-COUNT

☑ in BRIT, use **rowing boat**

**row|dy** /raʊdi/ **(rowdier, rowdiest)** When people are **rowdy**, they are noisy, rough, and likely to cause trouble. ❑ *He has complained to the police about rowdy neighbours.* ADJ = noisy ♦ **row|di|ness** *...adolescent behaviour like vandalism and rowdiness.* N-UNCOUNT

**row|er** /roʊəʳ/ **(rowers)** A **rower** is a person who rows a boat, especially as a sport. ❑ *...the first rower ever to win golds at four Olympic Games.* N-COUNT

**row house** /roʊ haʊs/ **(row houses)** also **rowhouse.** A **row house** is one of a row of similar houses that are joined together by both of their side walls. [AM] → See picture on page 1706. N-COUNT

☑ in BRIT, use **terraced house**

**row|ing** /roʊɪŋ/ **Rowing** is a sport in which people or teams race against each other in boats with oars. ❑ *...competitions in rowing, swimming and water skiing.* N-UNCOUNT

**row|ing boat** **(rowing boats)** also **rowing-boat.** A **rowing boat** is a small boat that you move through the water by using oars. [BRIT] N-COUNT

☑ in AM, use **rowboat**

**row|ing ma|chine** **(rowing machines)** A **rowing machine** is an exercise machine with moving parts which you move as if you were rowing a rowing boat. N-COUNT

**row|lock** /rɒlək, roʊlɒk/ **(rowlocks)** The **rowlocks** on a rowing boat are the U-shaped pieces of metal that keep the oars in position while you move them backwards and forwards. [BRIT] N-COUNT: usu pl

☑ in AM, use **oarlock**

**roy|al** /rɔɪəl/ **(royals)** ◆◆◇ [1] **Royal** is used to indicate that something is connected with a king, queen, or emperor, or their family. A **royal** person is a king, queen, or emperor, or a member of their family. ❑ *...an invitation to a royal garden party.* ADJ: usu ADJ n [2] **Royal** is used in the names of institutions or organizations that are officially appointed or supported by a member of a royal family. ❑ *...the Royal Academy of Music.* ADJ: ADJ n [3] Members of the royal family are sometimes referred to as **royals**. [INFORMAL] ❑ *The royals have always been patrons of charities pulling in large donations.* N-COUNT: usu pl

**roy|al blue** Something that is **royal blue** is deep blue in colour. COLOUR

**roy|al fami|ly** **(royal families)** The **royal family** of a country is the king, queen, or emperor, and all the members of their family. N-COUNT

**Roy|al High|ness** **(Royal Highnesses)** Expressions such as **Your Royal Highness** and **Their Royal Highnesses** are used to address or refer to members of royal families who are not kings or queens. N-VOC: poss N; PRON: poss PRON [politeness]

**roy|al|ist** /rɔɪəlɪst/ **(royalists)** A **royalist** is someone who supports their country's royal family or who believes that their country should have a king or queen. ❑ *He was hated by the royalists.* N-COUNT: oft N n = monarchist ≠ republican

**roy|al jel|ly** **Royal jelly** is a substance that bees make in order to feed young bees and queen bees. N-UNCOUNT

**roy|al|ly** /rɔɪəli/ If you say that something is done **royally**, you are emphasizing that it is done in an impressive or grand way, or that it is very great in degree. ❑ *They were royally received in every aspect.* ADV: usu ADV with v, also ADV adj [emphasis]

**roy|al|ty** /rɔɪəlti/ **(royalties)** 1 The members of royal families are sometimes referred to as **royalty**. ❑ *Royalty and government leaders from all around the world are gathering in Japan.* N-UNCOUNT
2 **Royalties** are payments made to authors and musicians when their work is sold or performed. They usually receive a fixed percentage of the profits from these sales or performances. ❑ *I lived on about £3,000 a year from the royalties on my book.* N-PLURAL
3 Payments made to someone whose invention, idea, or property is used by a commercial company can be referred to as **royalties**. ❑ *The royalties enabled the inventor to re-establish himself in business.* N-COUNT: usu pl

**RP** /ɑːʳ piː/ **RP** is a way of pronouncing British English that is often considered to be the standard accent. Pronunciations in this dictionary are given in RP. **RP** is an abbreviation for 'Received Pronunciation'.

**rpm** /ɑːʳ piː em/ also **r.p.m.** **rpm** is used to indicate the speed of something by saying how many times per minute it will go round in a circle. **rpm** is an abbreviation for 'revolutions per minute'. ❑ *Both engines were running at 2500 rpm.*

**RSI** /ɑːr es aɪ/ People who suffer from **RSI** have pain in their hands and arms as a result of repeating similar movements over a long period of time, usually as part of their job. **RSI** is an abbreviation for 'repetitive strain injury'. ❑ *The women developed painful RSI because of poor working conditions.* N-UNCOUNT

**RSVP** /ɑːr es viː piː/ also **R.S.V.P.** **RSVP** is an abbreviation for 'répondez s'il vous plaît', which means 'please reply'. It is written on the bottom of a card inviting you to a party or special occasion. [FORMAL]

**Rt Hon.** /raɪt ɒn/ **Rt Hon.** is used in Britain as part of the formal title of some members of the Privy Council and some judges. **Rt Hon.** is an abbreviation for 'Right Honourable'. ❑ *...the Rt Hon. Tony Blair.* ADJ: *the* ADJ n

**rub** /rʌb/ **(rubs, rubbing, rubbed)** 1 If you **rub** a part of your body, you move your hand or fingers backwards and forwards over it while pressing firmly. ❑ *He rubbed his arms and stiff legs... 'I fell in a ditch', he said, rubbing at a scrape on his hand.* VERB; V n; V prep/adv
2 If you **rub against** a surface or **rub** a part of your body **against** a surface, you move it backwards and forwards while pressing it against the surface. ❑ *A cat was rubbing against my leg... He kept rubbing his leg against mine.* VERB; V prep; V n prep
3 If you **rub** an object or a surface, you move a cloth backward and forward over it in order to clean or dry it. ❑ *She took off her glasses and rubbed them hard... He rubbed and rubbed but couldn't seem to get clean.* VERB; V n; V
4 If you **rub** a substance **into** a surface or **rub** something such as dirt **from** a surface, you spread it over the surface or remove it from the surface using your hand or something such as a cloth. ❑ *He rubbed oil into my back.* VERB; V n prep
5 If you **rub** two things **together** or if they **rub together**, they move backwards and forwards, pressing against each other. ❑ *He rubbed his hands together a few times. ...the 650-mile rift that separates the Pacific and North American geological plates as they rub together.* VERB; V n *together*; V *together*
6 If something you are wearing or holding **rubs**, it makes you sore because it keeps moving backwards and forwards against your skin. ❑ *Smear cream on to your baby's skin at the edges of the plaster to prevent it from rubbing.* VERB; V
7 **Rub** is used in expressions such as **there's the rub** and **the rub is** when you are mentioning a difficulty that makes something hard or impossible to achieve. [FORMAL] ❑ *'What do you want to write about?'. And there was the rub, because I didn't yet know.* N-SING: *the* N
8 A massage can be referred to as a **rub**. ❑ *She sometimes asks if I want a back rub.* N-COUNT: usu sing
9 → See also **rubbing**.

**PHRASES** 10 If you **rub shoulders with** famous people, you meet them and talk to them. You can also say that you **rub elbows with** someone, especially in American English. ❑ *He regularly rubbed shoulders with the likes of Elizabeth Taylor and Kylie Minogue.* PHRASE: V inflects, PHR n
11 If you **rub** someone **up the wrong way** in British English, or **rub** someone **the wrong way** in American English, you offend or annoy them without intending to. [INFORMAL] ❑ *What are you going to get out of him if you rub him up the wrong way?* PHRASE: V inflects = annoy
12 to **rub** someone's **nose in it** → see **nose**. to **rub salt into** the **wound** → see **salt**.

♦ **rub in** 1 If you **rub** a substance **in**, you press it into something by continuously moving it over its surface. ❑ *When hair is dry, rub in a little oil to make it smooth and glossy.* PHRASAL VERB; V P n; Also V n P
2 If someone keeps reminding you of something you would rather forget you can say that they **are rubbing it in**. ❑ *Officials couldn't resist rubbing it in... The home side rubbed in their superiority with a further goal.* PHRASAL VERB; V n P; V P n (not pron)

♦ **rub off** If someone's qualities or habits **rub off on** you, you develop some of their qualities or habits after spending time with them. ❑ *He was a tremendously enthusiastic teacher and that rubbed off on all the children... I was hoping some of his genius might rub off.* PHRASAL VERB; V P *on* n; V P

♦ **rub out** If you **rub out** something that you have written on paper or a board, you remove it using a rubber or eraser. ❑ *She began rubbing out the pencilled marks in the margin.* PHRASAL VERB = erase; V P n (not pron)

**rub|ber** /rʌbəʳ/ **(rubbers)** 1 **Rubber** is a strong, waterproof, elastic substance made from the juice of a tropical tree or produced chemically. It is used for making tyres, boots, and other products. ❑ *...the smell of burning rubber.* N-UNCOUNT
2 **Rubber** things are made of rubber. ❑ *...rubber gloves.* ADJ: usu ADJ n
3 A **rubber** is a small piece of rubber or other material that is used to remove mistakes that you have made while writing, drawing, or typing. [BRIT] N-COUNT

✓ in AM, use **eraser**

4 A **rubber** is a condom. [AM, INFORMAL] N-COUNT

**rub|ber band** **(rubber bands)** A **rubber band** is a thin circle of very elastic rubber. You put it around things such as papers in order to keep them together. N-COUNT = elastic band

**rub|ber boot** **(rubber boots)** **Rubber boots** are long boots made of rubber that you wear to keep your feet dry. [AM] N-COUNT: usu pl

✓ in BRIT, use **wellington**

**rub|ber bul|let** **(rubber bullets)** A **rubber bullet** is a bullet made of a metal ball coated with rubber. It is intended to injure people rather than kill them, and is used by police or soldiers to control crowds during a riot. ❑ *Rubber bullets were used to break up the demonstration.* N-COUNT

**rubber|neck** /rʌbəʳnek/ **(rubbernecks, rubbernecking, rubbernecked)** also **rubber-neck**. If someone **is rubbernecking**, they are staring at someone or something, especially in a rude or silly way. [INFORMAL] ❑ *The accident was caused by people slowing down to rubber-neck.* VERB [disapproval]; V
♦ **rubber|necker** **(rubberneckers)** *Pitt planted tall trees outside his home to block rubberneckers.* N-COUNT

**rub|ber plant** **(rubber plants)** A **rubber plant** is a type of plant with shiny leaves. It grows naturally in Asia but is also grown as a house plant in other parts of the world. N-COUNT

**rub|ber stamp** **(rubber stamps, rubber stamping, rubber stamped)** also **rubber-stamp**. 1 A **rubber stamp** is a small device with a name, date, or symbol on it. You press it on to an ink pad and then on to a document in order to show that the document has been officially dealt with. ❑ *In Post Offices, virtually every document that's passed across the counter is stamped with a rubber* N-COUNT *stamp.* 2 When someone in authority **rubber-stamps** a decision, plan, or law, they agree to it without thinking about it much. ❑ *Parliament's job is to rubber-stamp his decisions.* [VERB] [V n]

**rub|bery** /rʌbəri/ 1 Something that is **rubbery** looks or feels soft or elastic like rubber. ❑ *The mask is left on for about 15 minutes while it sets to a rubbery texture.* [ADJ] 2 Food such as meat that is **rubbery** is difficult to chew. [ADJ] [= tough]

**rub|bing** /rʌbɪŋ/ **(rubbings)** 1 A **rubbing** is a picture that you make by putting a piece of paper over a carved surface and then rubbing wax or chalk over it. ❑ *...a brass rubbing.* [N-COUNT: oft n N] 2 → See also **rub**.

**rub|bing al|co|hol** **Rubbing alcohol** is a liquid which is used to clean wounds or surgical instruments. [AM] [N-UNCOUNT]

> ✓ in BRIT, use **surgical spirit**

**rub|bish** /rʌbɪʃ/ **(rubbishes, rubbishing, rubbished)** 1 **Rubbish** consists of unwanted things or waste material such as used paper, empty tins and bottles, and waste food. [mainly BRIT] ❑ *...unwanted household rubbish.* [N-UNCOUNT] [= refuse]

> ✓ in AM, usually use **garbage**, **trash**

2 If you think that something is of very poor quality, you can say that it is **rubbish**. [BRIT, INFORMAL] ❑ *He described her book as absolute rubbish.* [N-UNCOUNT] 3 If you think that an idea or a statement is foolish or wrong, you can say that it is **rubbish**. [mainly BRIT, INFORMAL] ❑ *He's talking rubbish... These reports are total and utter rubbish.* [N-UNCOUNT] [= nonsense] 4 If you think that someone is not very good at something, you can say that they are **rubbish at** it. [BRIT, INFORMAL] ❑ *He was rubbish at his job... I tried playing golf, but I was rubbish.* [ADJ: v-link ADJ, usu ADJ *at* n] [≠ great] 5 If you **rubbish** a person, their ideas or their work, you say they are of little value. [BRIT, INFORMAL] ❑ *Five whole pages of script were devoted to rubbishing her political opponents.* [VERB] [V n]

> ✓ in AM, use **trash**

**rub|bishy** /rʌbɪʃi/ If you describe something as **rubbishy**, you think it is of very poor quality. [BRIT, INFORMAL] ❑ *...some old rubbishy cop movie.* [ADJ: usu ADJ n]

**rub|ble** /rʌbᵊl/ 1 When a building is destroyed, the pieces of brick, stone, or other materials that remain are referred to as **rubble**. ❑ *Thousands of bodies are still buried under the rubble.* [N-UNCOUNT] 2 **Rubble** is used to refer to the small pieces of bricks and stones that are used as a bottom layer on which to build roads, paths, or houses. ❑ *Brick rubble is useful as the base for paths and patios.* [N-UNCOUNT]

**rube** /ruːb/ **(rubes)** If you refer to a man or boy as a **rube**, you consider him stupid and uneducated because he comes from the countryside. [AM, INFORMAL] ❑ *He's no rube. He's a very smart guy.* [N-COUNT] [disapproval] [= hick]

**ru|bel|la** /ruːbelə/ **Rubella** is a disease. The symptoms are a cough, a sore throat, and red spots on your skin. [MEDICAL] [N-UNCOUNT] [= German measles]

**Ru|bi|con** /ruːbɪkɒn/ If you say that someone **has crossed the Rubicon**, you mean that they have reached a point where they cannot change a decision or course of action. [JOURNALISM] ❑ *He's crossed the Rubicon with regard to the use of military force as an option.* [PHRASE: V inflects]

**ru|ble** /ruːbᵊl/ → see **rouble**.

**ru|bric** /ruːbrɪk/ **(rubrics)** 1 A **rubric** is a set of rules or instructions, for example the rules at the beginning of an examination paper. [FORMAL] ❑ *There was a firm rubric in the book about what had to be observed when interrogating anyone under seventeen.* [N-COUNT] 2 A **rubric** is a title or heading under which something operates or is studied. [FORMAL] ❑ *The aid comes under the rubric of technical co-operation between governments.* [N-COUNT] [= title, heading]

**ruby** /ruːbi/ **(rubies)** A **ruby** is a dark red jewel. ❑ *...a ruby and diamond ring.* [N-COUNT]

**ruched** /ruːʃt/ **Ruched** curtains or garments are gathered so that they hang in soft folds. [ADJ]

**ruck** /rʌk/ **(rucks, rucking, rucked)** 1 A **ruck** is a situation where a group of people are fighting or struggling. [BRIT] ❑ *There'll be a huge ruck with the cops as they try to take photographs.* [N-COUNT] [= scrap] 2 In the sport of rugby, a **ruck** is a situation where a group of players struggle for possession of the ball. [N-COUNT]

**ruck|sack** /rʌksæk/ **(rucksacks)** A **rucksack** is a bag with straps that go over your shoulders, so that you can carry things on your back, for example when you are walking or climbing. [BRIT] [N-COUNT]

> ✓ in AM, usually use **knapsack**, **pack**, **backpack**

**ruck|us** /rʌkəs/ If someone or something causes a **ruckus**, they cause a great deal of noise, argument, or confusion. [AM, INFORMAL] ❑ *This caused such a ruckus all over Japan that they had to change their mind.* [N-SING]

**ruc|tion** /rʌkʃᵊn/ **(ructions)** If someone or something causes **ructions**, they cause strong protests, quarrels, or other trouble. [INFORMAL] ❑ *Both activities have caused some ructions.* [N-COUNT: usu pl]

**rud|der** /rʌdəʳ/ **(rudders)** 1 A **rudder** is a device for steering a boat. It consists of a vertical piece of wood or metal at the back of the boat. [N-COUNT] 2 An aeroplane's **rudder** is a vertical piece of metal at the back which is used to make the plane turn to the right or to the left. [N-COUNT]

**rud|der|less** /rʌdəʳləs/ A country or a person that is **rudderless** does not have a clear aim or a strong leader to follow. ❑ *The country was politically rudderless for almost three months.* [ADJ]

**rud|dy** /rʌdi/ **(ruddier, ruddiest)** If you describe someone's face as **ruddy**, you mean that their face is a reddish colour, usually because they are healthy or have been working hard, or because they are angry or embarrassed. ❑ *He had a naturally ruddy complexion.* [ADJ]

**rude** /ruːd/ **(ruder, rudest)** 1 When people are **rude**, they act in an impolite way towards other people or say impolite things about them. ❑ *He's rude to her friends and obsessively jealous.* [ADJ: oft ADJ *to/about* n] [≠ polite] ♦ **rude|ly** *I could not understand why she felt compelled to behave so rudely to a friend.* [ADV: usu ADV with v] ♦ **rude|ness** *She was angry at Steve's rudeness, but I could forgive it.* [N-UNCOUNT: oft with poss] 2 **Rude** is used to describe words and behaviour that are likely to embarrass or offend people, because they relate to sex or to body functions. [mainly BRIT] ❑ *Fred keeps cracking rude jokes with the guests.* [ADJ: usu ADJ n] [= obscene]

> ✓ in AM, usually use **dirty**

3 If someone receives a **rude** shock, something unpleasant happens unexpectedly. ❑ *It will come as a rude shock when their salary or income-tax refund cannot be cashed.* [ADJ: ADJ n] ♦ **rude|ly** *People were awakened rudely by a siren just outside their window.* [ADV: ADV with v] 4 **rude awakening** → see **awakening**.

**ru|di|men|ta|ry** /ruːdɪmentri/ 1 **Rudimentary** things are very basic or simple and are therefore unsatisfactory. [FORMAL] ❑ *...a kind of rudimentary kitchen.* [ADJ] 2 **Rudimentary** knowledge includes only the simplest and most basic facts. [FORMAL] ❑ *He had only a rudimentary knowledge of French.* [ADJ] [= basic]

**ru|di|ments** /ruːdɪmənts/ When you learn **the rudiments of** something, you learn the simplest or most essential things about it. ❑ *She helped to build a house, learning the rudiments of brick-laying as she went along.* [N-PLURAL: usu *the* N *of* n] [= basics]

**rue** /ruː/ **(rues, ruing, rued)** 1 If you **rue** something that you have done, you are sorry that you did it, because it has had unpleasant results. [LITERARY] ❑ *Tavare was probably ruing his decision.* [VERB] [= regret] [V n] 2 If you **rue the day** that you did something, you are sorry that you did it, because it has had unpleasant results. [LITERARY] ❑ *You'll live to rue the day you said that to me, my girl.* [PHRASE: V inflects]

**rue|ful** /ruːfʊl/ If someone is **rueful**, they feel or express regret or sorrow in a quiet and gentle way. [LITERARY] ❑ *He shook his head and gave* [ADJ] *me a rueful smile.* ♦ **rue|ful|ly** *He grinned at her ruefully.* [ADV: usu ADV with v]

**ruff** /rʌf/ **(ruffs)** 1 A **ruff** is a stiff strip of cloth or other material with many small folds in it, which some people wore round their neck in former times. [N-COUNT] ❑ *...an Elizabethan ruff.* 2 A **ruff** is a thick band of feathers or fur round the neck of a bird or animal. [N-COUNT]

**ruf|fian** /rʌfiən/ **(ruffians)** A **ruffian** is a man who behaves violently and is involved in crime. [OLD-FASHIONED] [N-COUNT] ❑ *...gangs of ruffians who lurk about intent on troublemaking.*

**ruf|fle** /rʌfᵊl/ **(ruffles, ruffling, ruffled)** 1 If you **ruffle** someone's hair, you move your hand backwards and forwards through it as a way of showing your affection towards them. [VERB] ❑ *'Don't let that get you down,' he said ruffling Ben's dark curls.* [V n] 2 When the wind **ruffles** something such as the surface of the sea, it causes it to move gently in a wave-like motion. [LITERARY] [VERB] ❑ *The evening breeze ruffled the pond.* [V n] 3 If something **ruffles** someone, it causes them to panic and lose their confidence or to become angry or upset. [VERB] ❑ *I could tell that my refusal to allow him to ruffle me infuriated him.* [V n] 4 If a bird **ruffles** its feathers or if its feathers **ruffle**, they stand out on its body, for example when it is cleaning itself or when it is frightened. [VERB] ❑ *Tame birds, when approached, will stretch out their necks and ruffle their neck feathering...* [V n] *Its body plumage suddenly began to ruffle and swell.* [V] 5 **Ruffles** are folds of cloth at the neck or the ends of the arms of a piece of clothing, or are sometimes sewn on things as a decoration. [N-COUNT: usu pl] ❑ *...a white blouse with ruffles at the neck and cuffs.* 6 To **ruffle** someone's **feathers** means to cause them to become very angry, nervous, or upset. [PHRASE: V inflects] ❑ *His direct, often abrasive approach will doubtless ruffle a few feathers.*

**ruf|fled** /rʌfᵊld/ Something that is **ruffled** is no longer smooth or neat. [ADJ] ❑ *Her short hair was oddly ruffled and then flattened around her head.* → See also **ruffle**.

**rug** /rʌg/ **(rugs)** 1 A **rug** is a piece of thick material that you put on a floor. It is like a carpet but covers a smaller area. [N-COUNT] ❑ *A Persian rug covered the hardwood floors.* 2 A **rug** is a small blanket which you use to cover your shoulders or your knees to keep them warm. [mainly BRIT] [N-COUNT] ❑ *The old lady was seated in her chair at the window, a rug over her knees.* 3 If someone **pulls the rug from under** a person or thing or **pulls the rug from under** someone's **feet**, they stop giving their help or support. [PHRASE: V inflects] ❑ *If the banks opt to pull the rug from under the ill-fated project, it will go into liquidation.* to **sweep** something **under the rug** → see **sweep**.

**rug|by** /rʌgbi/ **Rugby** or **rugby football** is a game played by two teams using an oval ball. Players try to score points by carrying the ball to their opponents' end of the field, or by kicking it over a bar fixed between two posts. [◆◇◇ N-UNCOUNT]

**rug|by tack|le** **(rugby tackles, rugby tackling, rugby tackled)** 1 A **rugby tackle** is a way of making someone fall over by throwing your arms around their legs or hips. [N-COUNT] 2 To **rugby tackle** someone means to make them fall over by throwing your arms around their legs or hips. [VERB] ❑ *He rugby tackled her and stole her bag...* [V n] *He was rugby tackled by a policeman after breaking through police lines.* [be V-ed]

**rug|ged** /rʌgɪd/ 1 A **rugged** area of land is uneven and covered with rocks, with few trees or plants. [LITERARY] [ADJ: usu ADJ n] ❑ *...rugged mountainous terrain.* ♦ **rug|ged|ly** *...a ruggedly beautiful wilderness.* [ADV: ADV adj] ♦ **rug|ged|ness** *The island's ruggedness symbolises our history and the character of the people.* [N-UNCOUNT] 2 If you describe a man as **rugged**, you mean that he has strong, masculine features. [LITERARY] [ADJ: usu ADJ n] [approval] ❑ *A look of pure disbelief crossed Shankly's rugged face.* ♦ **rug|ged|ly** *He was six feet tall and ruggedly handsome.* [ADV: ADV adj, ADV -ed] 3 If you describe someone's character as **rugged**, you mean that they are strong and determined, and have the ability to cope with difficult situations. [ADJ: usu ADJ n] [approval] ❑ *Rugged individualism forged America's frontier society.* 4 A **rugged** piece of equipment is strong and is designed to last a long time, even if it is treated roughly. [ADJ] ❑ *The camera combines rugged reliability with unequalled optical performance and speed.* ♦ **rug|ged|ness** *The body is 90% titanium for ruggedness.* [N-UNCOUNT]

**rug|ger** /rʌgəʳ/ **Rugger** is the same as **rugby**. [BRIT, INFORMAL] [N-UNCOUNT] ❑ *...a rugger match.*

**ruin** /ruːɪn/ **(ruins, ruining, ruined)** 1 To **ruin** something means to severely harm, damage, or spoil it. [◆◇◇ VERB] ❑ *My wife was ruining her health through worry.* [V n] 2 To **ruin** someone means to cause them to no longer have any money. [VERB] ❑ *She accused him of ruining her financially with his taste for the high life.* [V n] 3 **Ruin** is the state of no longer having any money. [N-UNCOUNT] ❑ *The farmers say recent inflation has driven them to the brink of ruin.* 4 **Ruin** is the state of being severely damaged or spoiled, or the process of reaching this state. [N-UNCOUNT] ❑ *The vineyards were falling into ruin.* 5 **The ruins of** something are the parts of it that remain after it has been severely damaged or weakened. [N-PLURAL: the N of n] ❑ *The new Turkish republic he helped to build emerged from the ruins of a great empire.* 6 **The ruins** of a building are the parts of it that remain after the rest has fallen down or been destroyed. [N-COUNT: usu pl] ❑ *One dead child was found in the ruins almost two hours after the explosion.* 7 → See also **ruined**.

PHRASES 8 If something is **in ruins**, it is completely spoiled. [PHRASE: oft v-link PHR] ❑ *Its heavily-subsidized economy is in ruins.* 9 If a building or place is **in ruins**, most of it has been destroyed and only parts of it remain. [PHRASE: usu v-link PHR] ❑ *The abbey was in ruins.*

**ru|ina|tion** /ruːɪneɪʃᵊn/ The **ruination** of someone or something is the act of ruining them or the process of being ruined. [N-UNCOUNT: oft the N of n] ❑ *Money was the ruination of him.*

**ruined** /ruːɪnd/ A **ruined** building or place has been very badly damaged or has gradually fallen down because no-one has taken care of it. [ADJ: ADJ n] ❑ *...a ruined church.*

**ru|in|ous** /ruːɪnəs/ 1 If you describe the cost of something as **ruinous**, you mean that it costs far more money than you can afford or than is reasonable. [ADJ: usu ADJ n] ❑ *Many Britons will still fear the potentially ruinous costs of their legal system.* ♦ **ru|in|ous|ly** *...a ruinously expensive court case.* [ADV: ADV adj] 2 A **ruinous** process or course of action is one that is likely to lead to ruin. [ADJ: usu ADJ n] ❑ *The economy of the state is experiencing the ruinous effects of the conflict.* ♦ **ru|in|ous|ly** *...cities ruinously choked by uncontrolled traffic.* [ADV: usu ADV -ed]

**rule** /ruːl/ **(rules, ruling, ruled)** 1 **Rules** are instructions that tell you what you are allowed to do and what you are not allowed to do. [◆◆◆ N-COUNT: oft N of n, N num] ❑ *...a thirty-two-page pamphlet explaining the rules of basketball... Strictly speaking, this was against the rules.* 2 A **rule** is a statement telling people what they should do in order to achieve success or a benefit of some kind. [N-COUNT: oft N for/of n] ❑ *An important rule is to drink plenty of water during any flight.* 3 The **rules of** something such as a language or a science are statements that describe the way that things usually happen in a particular situation. [N-COUNT: oft N of n] ❑ *...according to the rules of quantum theory.* 4 If something is **the rule**, it is the normal state of affairs. [N-SING: the N] ❑ *However, for many Americans today, weekend work has unfortunately become the rule rather than the exception.* 5 The person or group that **rules** a country controls its affairs. [VERB] ❑ *For four centuries, he says, foreigners have ruled Angola...* [V n] *He ruled for eight months.* [V] *...the long line of feudal lords who had ruled over this land.* [V over n] ♦ **Rule** is also a noun. [N-UNCOUNT: usu supp N] ❑ *...demands for an end to one-party rule.* 6 If something **rules** your life, it influences or restricts your actions in a way that is not good for you. [VERB] ❑ *Scientists have always been aware of how fear can rule our lives and make us ill.* [V n] 7 When someone in authority **rules** that something is true or should happen, they state that they have officially decided that it is true or should happen. [FORMAL] [VERB = pronounce] ❑ *The court ruled* [V that]

*that laws passed by the assembly remained valid... The Israeli court has not yet ruled on the case... A provincial magistrates' court last week ruled it unconstitutional... The committee ruled against all-night opening mainly on safety grounds.* V *on* n / V n adj/n / V *against* n [8] If you **rule** a straight line, you draw it using something that has a straight edge. ❑ *...a ruled grid of horizontal and vertical lines.* VERB / V-ed / Also V n [9] → See also **golden rule**, **ground rule**, **ruling**, **slide rule**.

**PHRASES** [10] If you say that something happens **as a rule**, you mean that it usually happens. ❑ *As a rule, however, such attacks have been aimed at causing damage rather than taking life.* PHRASE: PHR with cl = *generally, usually* [11] If someone in authority **bends the rules** or **stretches the rules**, they do something even though it is against the rules. ❑ *There is a particular urgency in this case, and it would help if you could bend the rules.* PHRASE: V inflects [12] A **rule of thumb** is a rule or principle that you follow which is not based on exact calculations, but rather on experience. ❑ *A good rule of thumb is that a broker must generate sales of ten times his salary if his employer is to make a profit.* PHRASE: *rule* inflects [13] If workers **work to rule**, they protest by working according to the rules of their job without doing any extra work or taking any new decisions. [BRIT] ❑ *Nurses are continuing to work to rule.* PHRASE: V inflects

♦ **rule in** If you say that you **are** not **ruling in** a particular course of action, you mean that you have not definitely decided to take that action. ❑ *We have made no decisions on restructuring yet. We are ruling nothing out and we are ruling nothing in... We must, as I said, take care not to rule in or rule out any one solution.* PHRASAL VERB: usu with brd neg / V n P / V P n (not pron)

♦ **rule out** [1] If you **rule out** a course of action, an idea, or a solution, you decide that it is impossible or unsuitable. ❑ *The Prime Minister is believed to have ruled out cuts in child benefit or pensions.* PHRASAL VERB / V P n (not pron) [2] If something **rules out** a situation, it prevents it from happening or from being possible. ❑ *A serious car accident in 1986 ruled out a permanent future for him in farming.* PHRASAL VERB / V P n (not pron)

♦ **rule out of** If someone **rules** you **out of** a contest or activity, they say that you cannot be involved in it. If something **rules** you **out of** a contest or activity, it prevents you from being involved in it. ❑ *He has ruled himself out of the world championships next year in Stuttgart.* PHRASAL VERB / V n P P n

**rule book** **(rule books)** [1] A **rule book** is a book containing the official rules for a particular game, job, or organization. ❑ *...one of the most serious offences mentioned in the Party rule book.* N-COUNT [2] If you say that someone is doing something by **the rule book**, you mean that they are doing it in the normal, accepted way. ❑ *This was not the time to take risks; he knew he should play it by the rule book.* N-COUNT: *the* N

**rule of law** **The rule of law** refers to a situation in which the people in a society obey its laws and enable it to function properly. [FORMAL] ❑ *I am confident that we can restore peace, stability and respect for the rule of law.* N-SING: usu *the* N

**rul|er** /ruːləʳ/ **(rulers)** [1] The **ruler** of a country is the person who rules the country. ❑ *...the former military ruler of Lesotho.* N-COUNT: oft with poss [2] A **ruler** is a long flat piece of wood, metal, or plastic with straight edges marked in centimetres or inches. Rulers are used to measure things and to draw straight lines. N-COUNT

**rul|ing** /ruːlɪŋ/ **(rulings)** ◆◇◇ [1] The **ruling** group of people in a country or organization is the group that controls its affairs. ❑ *...the Mexican voters' growing dissatisfaction with the ruling party. ...the sport's ruling body, the International Cricket Council.* ADJ: ADJ n [2] A **ruling** is an official decision made by a judge or court. ❑ *Goodwin tried to have the court ruling overturned.* N-COUNT: oft N that [3] Someone's **ruling** passion or emotion is the feeling they have most strongly, which influences their actions. ❑ *Their ruling passion is that of carnal love.* ADJ: ADJ n

**rum** /rʌm/ **(rums)** **Rum** is an alcoholic drink made from sugar. ❑ *...a bottle of rum.* N-MASS

**Ru|ma|nian** /ruːmeɪniən/ → see **Romanian**.

**rum|ba** /rʌmbə/ **(rumbas)** The **rumba** is a popular dance that comes from Cuba, or the music that the dance is performed to. N-COUNT: oft *the* N

**rum|ble** /rʌmbᵊl/ **(rumbles, rumbling, rumbled)** [1] A **rumble** is a low continuous noise. ❑ *The silence of the night was punctuated by the distant rumble of traffic.* N-COUNT: oft N *of* n [2] If a vehicle **rumbles** somewhere, it moves slowly forward while making a low continuous noise. ❑ *A bus rumbled along the road at the top of the path.* VERB / V adv/prep [3] If something **rumbles**, it makes a low, continuous noise. ❑ *The sky, swollen like a black bladder, rumbled and crackled.* VERB / V [4] If your stomach **rumbles**, it makes a vibrating noise, usually because you are hungry. ❑ *Her stomach rumbled. She hadn't eaten any breakfast.* VERB / V [5] If someone **is rumbled**, the truth about them or something they were trying to hide is discovered. [BRIT, INFORMAL] ❑ *When his fraud was rumbled he had just £20.17 in the bank.* VERB: usu passive / *be* V-ed

♦ **rumble on** If you say that something such as an argument **rumbles on**, you mean that it continues for a long time after it should have been settled. [BRIT, JOURNALISM] ❑ *And still the row rumbles on over who is to blame for the steadily surging crime statistics.* PHRASAL VERB / V P

**rum|bling** /rʌmblɪŋ/ **(rumblings)** [1] A **rumbling** is a low continuous noise. ❑ *...the rumbling of an empty stomach.* N-COUNT: usu with supp [2] **Rumblings** are signs that a bad situation is developing or that people are becoming annoyed or unhappy. ❑ *There were rumblings of discontent within the ranks.* N-COUNT: usu pl, oft N prep

**rum|bus|tious** /rʌmbʌstʃuəs/ A **rumbustious** person is energetic in a cheerful, noisy way. [BRIT] ❑ *...the flamboyant and somewhat rumbustious prime minister.* ADJ: usu ADJ n = *boisterous*

☑ in AM, use **rambunctious**

**ru|mi|nate** /ruːmɪneɪt/ **(ruminates, ruminating, ruminated)** [1] If you **ruminate on** something, you think about it very carefully. [FORMAL] ❑ *He ruminated on the terrible wastage that typified American life.* VERB / V *on/about/over* n [2] When animals **ruminate**, they bring food back from their stomach into their mouth and chew it again. [TECHNICAL] VERB

**ru|mi|na|tion** /ruːmɪneɪʃᵊn/ **(ruminations)** Your **ruminations** are your careful thoughts about something. [FORMAL] ❑ *Many of Vasari's ruminations on the subject are not always to be believed.* N-COUNT: oft with poss = *thoughts*

**ru|mi|na|tive** /ruːmɪnətɪv, AM -neɪt-/ If you are **ruminative**, you are thinking very deeply and carefully about something. [FORMAL] ❑ *He was uncharacteristically depressed and ruminative.* ADJ

♦ **ru|mi|na|tive|ly** *He smiles and swirls the ice ruminatively around his almost empty glass.* ADV: ADV with v

**rum|mage** /rʌmɪdʒ/ **(rummages, rummaging, rummaged)** If you **rummage through** something, you search for something you want by moving things around in a careless or hurried way. ❑ *They rummage through piles of second-hand clothes for something that fits.* VERB = *root* / V prep ♦ **Rummage** is also a noun. ❑ *A brief rummage will provide several pairs of gloves.* N-SING: *a* N ♦ **Rummage about** and **rummage around** mean the same as **rummage**. ❑ *I opened the fridge and rummaged about... He rummaged around the post room and found the document.* PHRASAL VERB / V P / V P n (not pron)

**rum|mage sale** **(rummage sales)** A **rummage sale** is a sale of cheap used goods that is usually held to raise money for charity. [AM] N-COUNT

☑ in BRIT, use **jumble sale**

**rum|my** /rʌmi/ **Rummy** is a card game in which players try to collect cards of the same value or cards in a sequence in the same suit. N-UNCOUNT

**ru|mor** /ruːmər/ → see **rumour**.

**ru|mour** /ruːməʳ/ **(rumours)** ◆◇◇

☑ in AM, use **rumor**

A **rumour** is a story or piece of information that may or may not be true, but that people are talking about. ❑ *Simon denied rumours that he was planning to visit Bulgaria later this month.* N-VAR: oft N that, N *of/about* n

**ru|moured** /ruːməʳd/

☑ in AM, use **rumored**

If something **is rumoured to** be the case, people are suggesting that it is the case, but they do not know for certain. ❑ *Her parents are rumoured to be on the verge of splitting up... It was rumoured that he had been interned in an asylum for a while.* V-PASSIVE *be* V-ed to-inf *it be* V-ed that

**ru|mour mill** **(rumour mills)**

☑ in AM, use **rumor mill**

You can refer to the people in a particular place or profession who spread rumours as the **rumour mill**. [mainly JOURNALISM] ❑ *The Washington rumour mill suggests that the president secured his narrow majority only by promising all sorts of concessions.* N-COUNT: oft *the* N

**rumour-monger** /ruːməʳmʌŋgəʳ/ **(rumour-mongers)**

☑ in AM, use **rumormonger**

If you call someone a **rumour-monger**, you disapprove of the fact that they spread rumours. N-COUNT [disapproval]

**rump** /rʌmp/ **(rumps)** [1] The **rump of** a group, organization, or country consists of the members who remain in it after the rest have left. [mainly BRIT] ❑ *The rump of the party does in fact still have considerable assets.* N-SING: with supp [2] An animal's **rump** is its rear end. ❑ *The cows' rumps were marked with a number.* N-COUNT: usu poss N [3] **Rump** or **rump steak** is meat cut from the rear end of a cow. N-UNCOUNT

**rum|ple** /rʌmpəl/ **(rumples, rumpling, rumpled)** VERB = *ruffle* If you **rumple** someone's hair, you move your hand backwards and forwards through it as your way of showing affection to them. ❑ *I leaned forward to rumple his hair, but he jerked out of the way.* V n

**rum|pled** /rʌmpəld/ **Rumpled** means creased or untidy. ❑ *I hurried to the tent and grabbed a few clean, if rumpled, clothes.* ADJ

**rum|pus** /rʌmpəs/ **(rumpuses)** If someone or something causes a **rumpus**, they cause a lot of noise or argument. ❑ *He had actually left the company a year before the rumpus started.* N-COUNT

**run** /rʌn/ **(runs, running, ran)** ◆◆◆

☑ The form **run** is used in the present tense and is also the past participle of the verb.

[1] When you **run**, you move more quickly than when you walk, for example because you are in a hurry to get somewhere, or for exercise. ❑ *I excused myself and ran back to the telephone... He ran the last block to the White House with two cases of gear... Antonia ran to meet them.* ♦ **Run** is also a noun. ❑ *After a six-mile run, Jackie returns home for a substantial breakfast.* VERB V adv/prep V n/amount V N-COUNT: usu sing [2] When someone **runs** in a race, they run in competition with other people. ❑ *...when I was running in the New York Marathon... Phyllis Smith ran a controlled race to qualify in 51.32 sec.* VERB V V n [3] When a horse **runs** in a race or when its owner **runs** it, it competes in a race. ❑ *The owner insisted on Cool Ground running in the Gold Cup... If we have a wet spell, Cecil could also run Armiger in the Derby.* VERB V V n [4] If you say that something long, such as a road, **runs** in a particular direction, you are describing its course or position. You can also say that something **runs** the length or width of something else. ❑ *...the sun-dappled trail which ran through the beech woods.* VERB V prep/adv [5] If you **run** a wire or tube somewhere, you fix it or pull it from, to, or across a particular place. ❑ *Our host ran a long extension cord out from the house and set up a screen and a projector.* VERB V n prep/adv [6] If you **run** your hand or an object **through** something, you move your hand or the object through it. ❑ *He laughed and ran his fingers through his hair.* VERB V n prep [7] If you **run** something through a machine, process, or series of tests, you make it go through the machine, process, or tests. ❑ *They have gathered the best statistics they can find and run them through their own computers.* VERB V n *through* n [8] If someone **runs for** office in an election, they take part as a candidate. ❑ *It was only last February that he announced he would run for president... It is no easy job to run against John Glenn, Ohio's Democratic senator... Women are running in nearly all the contested seats in Los Angeles.* VERB = *stand* V *for* n V *against* n V [9] A **run for** office is an attempt to be elected to office. [mainly AM] ❑ *He was already preparing his run for the presidency.* N-SING: N *for* n

☑ in BRIT, usually use **bid**

[10] If you **run** something such as a business or an activity, you are in charge of it or you organize it. ❑ *His stepfather ran a prosperous paint business... Is this any way to run a country? ...a well-run, profitable organisation.* VERB V n V n V-ed [11] If you talk about how a system, an organization, or someone's life **is running**, you are saying how well it is operating or progressing. ❑ *Officials in charge of the camps say the system is now running extremely smoothly. ...the staff who have kept the bank running.* VERB: usu cont V adv V [12] If you **run** an experiment, computer program, or other process, or start it **running**, you start it and let it continue. ❑ *He ran a lot of tests and it turned out I had an infection called mycoplasma... You can check your program one command at a time while it's running.* VERB V n V [13] When you **run** a cassette or video tape or when it **runs**, it moves through the machine as the machine operates. ❑ *He pushed the play button again and ran the tape... The tape had run to the end but recorded nothing.* VERB = *play* V n V [14] When a machine **is running** or when you **are running** it, it is switched on and is working. ❑ *We told him to wait out front with the engine running. ...with everybody running their appliances all at the same time.* VERB: usu cont V V n [15] A machine or equipment that **runs on** or **off** a particular source of energy functions using that source of energy. ❑ *Black cabs run on diesel.* VERB V *on/off* n [16] If you **run** a car or a piece of equipment, you have it and use it. [mainly BRIT] ❑ *I ran a 1960 Rover 100 from 1977 until 1983.* VERB V n [17] When you say that vehicles such as trains and buses **run** from one place to another, you mean they regularly travel along that route. ❑ *A shuttle bus runs frequently between the Inn and the Country Club. ...a government which can't make the trains run on time.* VERB V prep V [18] If you **run** someone somewhere in a car, you drive them there. [INFORMAL] ❑ *Could you run me up to Baltimore?* VERB = *drive* V n prep/adv [19] If you **run** over or down to a place that is quite near, you drive there. [INFORMAL] ❑ *I'll run over to Short Mountain and check on Mrs Adams.* VERB = *drive* V adv [20] A **run** is a journey somewhere. ❑ *...doing the morning school run.* N-COUNT [21] If a liquid **runs** in a particular direction, it flows in that direction. ❑ *Tears were running down her cheeks... Wash the rice in cold water until the water runs clear.* VERB = *flow* V prep/adv V adj [22] If you **run** water, or if you **run** a tap or a bath, you cause water to flow from a tap. ❑ *She went to the sink and ran water into her empty glass.* VERB V n [23] If a tap or a bath **is running**, water is coming out of a tap. ❑ *You must have left a tap running in the bathroom.* VERB: only cont V [24] If your nose **is running**, liquid is flowing out of it, usually because you have a cold. ❑ *Timothy was crying, mostly from exhaustion, and his nose was running.* VERB: usu cont V [25] If a surface **is running with** a liquid, that liquid is flowing down it. ❑ *After an hour he realised he was completely running with sweat.* VERB: usu cont V *with* n [26] If the dye in some cloth or the ink on some paper **runs**, it comes off or spreads when the cloth or paper gets wet. ❑ *The ink had run on the wet paper.* VERB V [27] If a feeling **runs through** your body or a thought **runs through** your mind, you experience it or think it quickly. ❑ *She felt a surge of excitement run through her.* VERB = *go* V *through* n [28] If a feeling or noise **runs through** a group of people, it spreads among them. ❑ *A buzz of excitement ran through the crowd.* VERB = *go* V *through* n [29] If a theme or feature **runs through** something such as someone's actions or writing, it is present in all of it. ❑ *Another thread running through this series is the role of doctors in the treatment of the mentally ill... There was something of this mood running throughout the Congress's deliberations.* VERB V *through* n V *throughout* n [30] When newspapers or magazines **run** a particular item or story or if it **runs**, it is published or printed. ❑ *The newspaper ran a series of four editorials entitled 'The Choice of Our Lives.' ...an editorial that ran this weekend entitled 'Mr. Cuomo Backs Out.'* VERB V n V

[31] If an amount **is running** at a particular level, it is at that level. ❑ *Today's RPI figure shows inflation running at 10.9 per cent.* VERB = *stand* V *at* n

[32] If a play, event, or legal contract **runs** for a particular period of time, it lasts for that period of time. ❑ *It pleased critics but ran for only three years in the West End... The contract was to run from 1992 to 2020... I predict it will run and run.* VERB V *for* amount V prep V

[33] If someone or something **is running** late, they have taken more time than had been planned. If they **are running** to time or ahead of time, they have taken the time planned or less than the time planned. ❑ *Tell her I'll call her back later, I'm running late again.* VERB: usu cont V adv/prep

[34] If you **are running** a temperature or a fever, you have a high temperature because you are ill. ❑ *The little girl is running a fever and she needs help.* VERB V n

[35] A **run** of a play or television programme is the period of time during which performances are given or programmes are shown. ❑ *The show will transfer to the West End on October 9, after a month's run in Birmingham.* N-COUNT: with supp

[36] A **run of** successes or failures is a series of successes or failures. ❑ *The England skipper is haunted by a run of low scores.* N-SING: usu N *of* n

[37] A **run** of a product is the amount that a company or factory decides to produce at one time. ❑ *Wayne plans to increase the print run to 1,000.* N-COUNT: usu supp N

[38] In cricket or baseball, a **run** is a score of one, which is made by players running between marked places on the field after hitting the ball. ❑ *At 20 he became the youngest player to score 2,000 runs in a season.* N-COUNT

[39] If someone gives you **the run of** a place, they give you permission to go where you like in it and use it as you wish. ❑ *He had the run of the house and the pool.* N-SING: *the* N *of* n

[40] If there is a **run on** something, a lot of people want to buy it or get it at the same time. ❑ *A run on sterling has killed off hopes of a rate cut.* N-SING: N *on* n

[41] A ski **run** or bobsleigh **run** is a course or route that has been designed for skiing or for riding in a bobsleigh. N-COUNT: usu n N

[42] → See also **running**, **dummy run**, **test run**, **trial run**.

**PHRASES** [43] If something happens **against the run of** play or **against the run of** events, it is different from what is generally happening in a game or situation. [BRIT] ❑ *The decisive goal arrived against the run of play.* PHRASE

[44] If you **run** someone **close**, **run** them **a close second**, or **run a close second**, you almost beat them in a race or competition. ❑ *The Under-21 team has defeated Wales and Scotland this season, and ran England very close.* PHRASE: V inflects

[45] If a river or well **runs dry**, it no longer has any water in it. If an oil well **runs dry**, it no longer produces any oil. ❑ *Streams had run dry for the first time in memory.* PHRASE: V inflects = *dry up*

[46] If a source of information or money **runs dry**, no more information or money can be obtained from it. ❑ *Three days into production, the kitty had run dry.* PHRASE: V inflects = *dry up*

[47] If a characteristic **runs in** someone's **family**, it often occurs in members of that family, in different generations. ❑ *The insanity which ran in his family haunted him.* PHRASE: V inflects

[48] If you **make a run for it** or if you **run for it**, you run away in order to escape from someone or something. ❑ *A helicopter hovered overhead as one of the gang made a run for it.* PHRASE: V inflects

[49] If people's feelings **are running high**, they are very angry, concerned, or excited. ❑ *Feelings there have been running high in the wake of last week's killing.* PHRASE: V inflects

[50] If you talk about what will happen **in the long run**, you are saying what you think will happen over a long period of time in the future. If you talk about what will happen **in the short run**, you are saying what you think will happen in the near future. ❑ *Sometimes expensive drugs or other treatments can be economical in the long run... In fact, things could get worse in the short run.* PHRASE: PHR with cl, PHR with v

[51] If you say that someone would **run a mile** if faced with something, you mean that they are very frightened of it and would try to avoid it. ❑ *Yasmin admits she would run a mile if Mark asked her out.* PHRASE: V inflects

[52] If you say that someone could **give** someone else **a run for** their **money**, you mean you think they are almost as good as the other person. ❑ *...a youngster who even now could give Meryl Streep a run for her money.* PHRASE: V inflects

[53] If someone is **on the run**, they are trying to escape or hide from someone such as the police or an enemy. ❑ *Fifteen-year-old Danny is on the run from a local authority home.* PHRASE: v-link PHR, PHR after v

[54] If someone is **on the run**, they are being severely defeated in a contest or competition. ❑ *His opponents believe he is definitely on the run.* PHRASE: usu v-link PHR

[55] If you say that a person or group **is running scared**, you mean that they are frightened of what someone might do to them or what might happen. ❑ *The administration is running scared.* PHRASE: V inflects

[56] If you **are running short of** something or **running low on** something, you do not have much of it left. If a supply of something **is running short** or **running low**, there is not much of it left. ❑ *Government forces are running short of ammunition and fuel... We are running low on drinking water.* PHRASE: V inflects

[57] to **run amok** → see **amok**. to **make** your **blood run cold** → see **blood**. to **run counter to** something → see **counter**. to **run** its **course** → see **course**. to **run deep** → see **deep**. to **run an errand** → see **errand**. to **run the gamut of** something → see **gamut**. to **run the gauntlet** → see **gauntlet**. to **run rings around** someone → see **ring**. to **run riot** → see **riot**. to **run a risk** → see **risk**. to **run to seed** → see **seed**. to **run wild** → see **wild**.

♦ **run across** If you **run across** someone or something, you meet them or find them unexpectedly. ❑ *We ran across some old friends in the village.* PHRASAL VERB = *come across* V P n

♦ **run after** If you **are running after** someone, you are trying to start a relationship with them, usually a sexual relationship. ❑ *By the time she was fifteen Maria was already running after men twice her age.* PHRASAL VERB [disapproval] V P n

♦ **run around** If you **run around**, you go to a lot of places and do a lot of things, often in a rushed or disorganized way. ❑ *No one noticed we had been running around emptying bins and cleaning up... I spend all day running around after the family... I will not have you running around the countryside without my authority.* PHRASAL VERB V P V P *after*/*with* n V P n (not pron)

♦ **run away** [1] If you **run away** from a place, you leave it because you are unhappy there. ❑ *I ran away from home when I was sixteen... After his beating Colin ran away and hasn't been heard of since... Three years ago I ran away to Mexico to live with a circus.* PHRASAL VERB V P *from* n V P V P *to* n

[2] If you **run away** with someone, you secretly go away with them in order to live with them or marry them. ❑ *She ran away with a man called McTavish last year... He and I were always planning to run away together.* PHRASAL VERB = *run off* V P *with* n pl-n V P *together*

[3] If you **run away from** something unpleasant or new, you try to avoid dealing with it or thinking about it. ❑ *They run away from the problem, hoping it will disappear of its own accord... You can't run away for ever.* PHRASAL VERB V P *from* n V P

[4] → See also **runaway**.

♦ **run away with** If you let your imagination or your emotions **run away with** you, you fail to control them and cannot think sensibly. ❑ *You're letting your imagination run away with you.* PHRASAL VERB V P P pron

♦ **run by** If you **run** something **by** someone, you tell them about it or mention it, to see if they think it is a good idea, or can understand it. ❑ *Run that by me again.* PHRASAL VERB V n P n

♦ **run down** [1] If you **run** people or things **down**, you criticize them strongly. ❑ *He last night denounced the British 'genius for running ourselves down'. ...that chap who was running down state schools.* PHRASAL VERB V n P V P n (not pron)

[2] If people **run down** an industry or an organization, they deliberately reduce its size or the amount of work that it does. [mainly BRIT] ❑ *The government is cynically running down Sweden's welfare system.* PHRASAL VERB V P n (not pron)

[3] If someone **runs down** an amount of something, they reduce it or allow it to decrease. [mainly BRIT] ❑ *But the survey also revealed firms were running down stocks instead of making new products.* PHRASAL VERB V P n (not pron)

[4] If a vehicle or its driver **runs** someone **down**, the vehicle hits them and injures them. ❑ *Lozano* PHRASAL VERB = *run down*, *knock over*

*claimed that motorcycle driver Clement Lloyd was trying to run him down.* V n P 5 If a machine or device **runs down**, it gradually loses power or works more slowly. PHRASAL VERB ❑ *The batteries are running down.* V P 6 → See also **run-down**.

♦ **run into** 1 If you **run into** problems or difficulties, you unexpectedly begin to experience them. PHRASAL VERB ❑ *They agreed to sell last year after they ran into financial problems.* V P n (not pron) 2 If you **run into** someone, you meet them unexpectedly. PHRASAL VERB ❑ *He ran into Krettner in the corridor a few minutes later.* V P n 3 If a vehicle **runs into** something, it accidentally hits it. PHRASAL VERB ❑ *The driver failed to negotiate a bend and ran into a tree.* V P n 4 You use **run into** when indicating that the cost or amount of something is very great. PHRASAL VERB ❑ *He said companies should face punitive civil penalties running into millions of pounds.* V P amount

♦ **run off** 1 If you **run off** with someone, you secretly go away with them in order to live with them or marry them. PHRASAL VERB = run away ❑ *The last thing I'm going to do is run off with somebody's husband... We could run off together, but neither of us wants to live the rest of our lives abroad.* V P *with* n pl-n V P *together* 2 If you **run off** copies of a piece of writing, you produce them using a machine. PHRASAL VERB ❑ *If you want to run off a copy sometime today, you're welcome to.* V P n (not pron)

♦ **run out** 1 If you **run out of** something, you have no more of it left. PHRASAL VERB ❑ *They have run out of ideas... We had lots before but now we've run out.* V P *of* n V P to **run out of steam** → see **steam**. 2 If something **runs out**, it becomes used up so that there is no more left. PHRASAL VERB ❑ *Conditions are getting worse and supplies are running out.* V P 3 When a legal document **runs out**, it stops being valid. PHRASAL VERB = expire ❑ *When the lease ran out the family moved to Campigny.* V P

♦ **run over** If a vehicle or its driver **runs** a person or animal **over**, it knocks them down or drives over them. PHRASAL VERB = knock down, run down ❑ *You can always run him over and make it look like an accident... He ran over a six-year-old child as he was driving back from a party.* V n P V P n

♦ **run past** To **run** something **past** someone means the same as to **run** it **by** them. PHRASAL VERB ❑ *Before agreeing, he ran the idea past Johnson.* V n P n

♦ **run through** 1 If you **run through** a list of items, you read or mention all the items quickly. PHRASAL VERB = go through ❑ *I ran through the options with him.* V P n 2 If you **run through** a performance or a series of actions, you practise it. PHRASAL VERB = go through ❑ *Doug stood still while I ran through the handover procedure.* V P n 3 → See also **run-through**.

♦ **run to** 1 If you **run to** someone, you go to them for help or to tell them something. PHRASAL VERB ❑ *If you were at a party and somebody was getting high, you didn't go running to a cop.* V P n 2 If something **runs to** a particular amount or size, it is that amount or size. PHRASAL VERB ❑ *The finished manuscript ran to the best part of fifty double-sided pages.* V P n (not pron) 3 If you cannot **run to** a particular item, you cannot afford to buy it or pay for it. [mainly BRIT] PHRASAL VERB: with brd-neg = afford ❑ *If you can't run to champagne, buy sparkling wine.* V P n

♦ **run up** 1 If someone **runs up** bills or debts, they acquire them by buying a lot of things or borrowing money. PHRASAL VERB ❑ *He ran up a £1,400 bill at the Britannia Adelphi Hotel.* V P n (not pron) 2 → See also **run-up**.

♦ **run up against** If you **run up against** problems, you suddenly begin to experience them. PHRASAL VERB = encounter ❑ *I ran up against the problem of getting taken seriously long before I became a writer.* V P P n

**run|about** /rʌnəbaʊt/ **(runabouts)** 1 A **runabout** is a small car used mainly for short journeys. In American English, **runabout** is used of cars with open tops. N-COUNT ❑ *...a small 1-litre runabout.* 2 A **runabout** is a small, light boat with a motor. [AM] N-COUNT

**run|around** /rʌnəraʊnd/ also **run-around**. If someone **gives** you **the runaround**, they deliberately do not give you all the information or help that you want, and send you to another person or place to get it. [INFORMAL] PHRASE: V inflects

**run|away** /rʌnəweɪ/ **(runaways)** 1 You use **runaway** to describe a situation in which something increases or develops very quickly and cannot be controlled. ADJ: ADJ n ❑ *Our Grand Sale in June was a runaway success. ...a runaway best-seller.* 2 A **runaway** is someone, especially a child, who leaves home without telling anyone or without permission. N-COUNT: oft N n ❑ *...a teenage runaway.* 3 A **runaway** vehicle or animal is moving forward quickly, and its driver or rider has lost control of it. ADJ: ADJ n ❑ *The runaway car careered into a bench, hitting an elderly couple.*

**run-down** also **rundown**.

> The adjective is pronounced /rʌn daʊn/. The noun is pronounced /rʌn daʊn/.

1 If someone is **run-down**, they are tired or slightly ill. [INFORMAL] ADJ: usu v-link ADJ ❑ *...times when you are feeling tired and run-down.* 2 A **run-down** building or area is in very poor condition. ADJ: usu ADJ n ❑ *...one of the most run-down areas in Scotland. ...a run-down block of flats.* 3 A **run-down** place of business is not as active as it used to be or does not have many customers. ADJ: usu ADJ n ❑ *...a run-down slate quarry.* 4 When **the run-down of** an industry or organization takes place, its size or the amount of work that it does is reduced. [mainly BRIT] N-SING: N *of* n ❑ *...the impetus behind the rundown of the coal industry.* 5 If you give someone a **run-down of** a group of things or a **run-down on** something, you give them details about it. [INFORMAL] N-SING: usu N *of/on* n ❑ *Here's a rundown of the options.*

**rune** /ruːn/ **(runes) Runes** are letters from an alphabet that was used by people in Northern Europe in former times. They were carved on wood or stone and were believed to have magical powers. N-COUNT

**rung** /rʌŋ/ **(rungs)** 1 **Rung** is the past participle of **ring**. 2 The **rungs** on a ladder are the wooden or metal bars that form the steps. N-COUNT ❑ *I swung myself onto the ladder and felt for the next rung.* 3 If you reach a particular **rung** in your career, in an organization, or in a process, you reach that level in it. N-COUNT: with supp ❑ *I first worked with him in 1971 when we were both on the lowest rung of our careers.*

**run-in** **(run-ins)** A **run-in** is an argument or quarrel with someone. [INFORMAL] N-COUNT: oft N *with* n = row ❑ *I had a monumental run-in with him a couple of years ago.*

**run|ner** /rʌnəʳ/ **(runners)** 1 A **runner** is a person who runs, especially for sport or pleasure. ◆◇◇ N-COUNT ❑ *...a marathon runner... I am a very keen runner and am out training most days.* 2 The **runners** in a horse race are the horses taking part. N-COUNT ❑ *There are 18 runners in the top race of the day.* 3 A drug **runner** or gun **runner** is someone who illegally takes drugs or guns into a country. N-COUNT: n N 4 Someone who is a **runner** for a particular person or company is employed to take messages, collect money, or do other small tasks for them. N-COUNT ❑ *...a bookie's runner.* 5 **Runners** are thin strips of wood or metal underneath something which help it to move smoothly. N-COUNT: usu pl ❑ *...the runners of his sled.* 6 If someone **does a runner**, they leave a place in a hurry, for example in order to escape arrest or to avoid paying for something. [BRIT, INFORMAL] PHRASE: V inflects = do a bunk ❑ *At this point, the accountant did a runner – with all my bank statements, expenses and receipts.*

**run|ner bean** **(runner beans) Runner beans** are long green beans that are eaten as a vegetable. They grow on a tall climbing plant and are the cases that contain the seeds of the plant. [BRIT] N-COUNT: usu pl = French bean → See picture on page 1712.

> in AM, use **pole beans, scarlet runners**

**runner-up** **(runners-up)** A **runner-up** is someone who has finished in second place in a race or competition. N-COUNT: oft N *to* n ❑ *The ten runners-up will receive a case of wine.*

**run|ning** /rʌnɪŋ/ 1 **Running** is the activity of moving fast on foot, especially as a sport. ◆◆◇ N-UNCOUNT ❑ *We chose to do cross-country running. ...running shoes.* 2 **The running of** something such as a business N-SING:

is the managing or organizing of it. ❑ *...the committee in charge of the day-to-day running of the party.* [3] You use **running** to describe things that continue or keep occurring over a period of time. ❑ *He also began a running feud with Dean Acheson.* [4] A **running** total is a total which changes because numbers keep being added to it as something progresses. ❑ *He kept a running tally of who had called him, who had visited, who had sent flowers.* [5] You can use **running** when indicating that something keeps happening. For example, if something has happened every day for three days, you can say that it has happened for the third day **running** or for three days **running**. ❑ *He said drought had led to severe crop failure for the second year running.* [6] **Running** water is water that is flowing rather than standing still. ❑ *The forest was filled with the sound of running water.* [7] If a house has **running** water, water is supplied to the house through pipes and taps. ❑ *...a house without electricity or running water in a tiny African village.*
the N of n
ADJ: ADJ n = ongoing
ADJ: ADJ n
ADV: n ADV
ADJ: ADJ n
ADJ: ADJ n

**PHRASES** [8] If someone is **in the running for** something, they have a good chance of winning or obtaining it. If they are **out of the running for** something, they have no chance of winning or obtaining it. ❑ *Until this week he appeared to have ruled himself out of the running because of his age.* [9] If someone **is making the running** in a situation, they are more active than the other people involved. [mainly BRIT] ❑ *Republicans are furious that the Democrats currently seem to be making all the running.* [10] If something such as a system or place is **up and running**, it is operating normally. ❑ *We're trying to get the medical facilities up and running again.*
PHRASE
PHRASE: V inflects
PHRASE: v-link PHR, PHR after v

**-running** /-rʌnɪŋ/ **-running** combines with nouns to form nouns which refer to the illegal importing of drugs or guns. ❑ *...a serviceman suspected of drug-running.*
COMB in N-UNCOUNT

**run|ning bat|tle** **(running battles)** When two groups of people fight a **running battle**, they keep attacking each other in various parts of a place. ❑ *They fought running battles in the narrow streets with police.*
N-COUNT

**run|ning com|men|tary** **(running commentaries)** If someone provides a **running commentary** on an event, they give a continuous description of it while it is taking place. ❑ *John gave the police control room a running commentary on the driver's antics as he followed him at 90mph.*
N-COUNT

**run|ning costs** [1] The **running costs** of a business are the amount of money that is regularly spent on things such as salaries, heating, lighting, and rent. [BUSINESS] ❑ *The aim is to cut running costs by £90 million per year.* [2] The **running costs** of a device such as a heater or a fridge are the amount of money that you spend on the gas, electricity, or other type of energy that it uses. ❑ *Always buy a heater with thermostat control to save on running costs.*
N-PLURAL = overheads
N-PLURAL

**run|ning mate** **(running mates)** In an election campaign, a candidate's **running mate** is the person that they have chosen to help them in the election. If the candidate wins, the running mate will become the second most important person after the winner. [mainly AM] ❑ *...Clinton's selection of Al Gore as his running mate.*
N-COUNT: oft poss N

**run|ning or|der** **The running order** of the items in a broadcast, concert, or show is the order in which the items will come. ❑ *We had reversed the running order.*
N-SING: usu the N

**run|ning time** **(running times)** The **running time** of something such as a film, video, or CD is the time it takes to play from start to finish.
N-COUNT

**run|ny** /rʌni/ **(runnier, runniest)** [1] Something that is **runny** is more liquid than usual or than was intended. ❑ *Warm the honey until it becomes runny.* [2] If someone has a **runny** nose or **runny** eyes, liquid is flowing from their nose or eyes. ❑ *Symptoms are streaming eyes, a runny nose, headache and a cough.*
ADJ
ADJ: usu ADJ n

**run-off** **(run-offs)** also **runoff.** A **run-off** is an extra vote or contest which is held in order to decide the winner of an election or competition, because no-one has yet clearly won. ❑ *There will be a run-off between these two candidates on December 9th.*
N-COUNT: usu sing, oft N between pl-n

**run-of-the-mill** also **run of the mill.** A **run-of-the-mill** person or thing is very ordinary, with no special or interesting features. ❑ *I was just a very average run-of-the-mill kind of student.*
ADJ: usu ADJ n disapproval

**runt** /rʌnt/ **(runts)** The **runt** of a group of animals born to the same mother at the same time is the smallest and weakest of them. ❑ *Animals reject the runt of the litter.*
N-COUNT: oft N of n

**run-through** **(run-throughs)** A **run-through** for a show or event is a practice for it. ❑ *Charles and Eddie are getting ready for their final run-through before the evening's recording.*
N-COUNT = rehearsal

**run time** **(run times)** **Run time** is the time during which a computer program is running. [COMPUTING]
N-COUNT

**run-up** **(run-ups)** [1] **The run-up to** an event is the period of time just before it. [mainly BRIT] ❑ *The company believes the products will sell well in the run-up to Christmas.* [2] In sport, a **run-up** is the run made by a player or athlete, for example before throwing a ball or a javelin, or before jumping. ❑ *When I began to compete again, I was struggling with my run-up.*
N-SING: usu the N to n
N-COUNT

**run|way** /rʌnweɪ/ **(runways)** At an airport, the **runway** is the long strip of ground with a hard surface which an aeroplane takes off from or lands on. ❑ *The plane started taxiing down the runway.*
N-COUNT: usu the N

**ru|pee** /ruːpiː/ **(rupees)** A **rupee** is a unit of money that is used in India, Pakistan, and some other countries. ❑ *He earns 20 rupees a day.*
N-COUNT

**rup|ture** /rʌptʃəʳ/ **(ruptures, rupturing, ruptured)** [1] A **rupture** is a severe injury in which an internal part of your body tears or bursts open, especially the part between the bowels and the abdomen. [2] If a person or animal **ruptures** a part of their body or if it **ruptures**, it tears or bursts open. ❑ *His stomach might rupture from all the acid... Whilst playing badminton, I ruptured my Achilles tendon. ...a ruptured appendix.* [3] If you **rupture yourself**, you rupture a part of your body, usually because you have lifted something heavy. ❑ *He ruptured himself playing football.* [4] If an object **ruptures** or if something **ruptures** it, it bursts open. ❑ *Certain truck gasoline tanks can rupture and burn in a collision... Sloshing liquids can rupture the walls of their containers.* [5] If there is a **rupture** between people, relations between them get much worse or end completely. ❑ *The incidents have not yet caused a major rupture in the political ties between countries.* [6] If someone or something **ruptures** relations between people, they damage them, causing them to become worse or to end. ❑ *The incident ruptures a recent and fragile cease-fire.*
N-COUNT
VERB
V
V n
V-ed
VERB
V pron-refl
VERB = burst
V
V n
N-COUNT: usu with supp
VERB
V n

**ru|ral** /rʊərəl/ ◆◇◇ [1] **Rural** places are far away from large towns or cities. ❑ *These plants have a tendency to grow in the more rural areas.* [2] **Rural** means having features which are typical of areas that are far away from large towns or cities. ❑ *...the old rural way of life.*
ADJ: usu ADJ n
ADJ: ADJ n

**ruse** /ruːz, AM ruːs/ **(ruses)** A **ruse** is an action or plan which is intended to deceive someone. [FORMAL] ❑ *It is now clear that this was a ruse to divide them.*
N-COUNT

**rush** /rʌʃ/ **(rushes, rushing, rushed)** ◆◇◇ [1] If you **rush** somewhere, you go there quickly. ❑ *A schoolgirl rushed into a burning flat to save a man's life... I've got to rush. Got a meeting in a few minutes... Shop staff rushed to get help.* [2] If people **rush to** do something, they do it as soon as they can, because they are very eager to do it. ❑ *Russian banks rushed to buy as many dollars as they could.* [3] A **rush** is a situation in which you need to go somewhere or do something very quickly. ❑ *The men*
VERB
V prep/adv
V
V to-inf
VERB
V to-inf
N-SING

*left in a rush... It was all rather a rush.* 4 If there is a **rush for** something, many people suddenly try to get it or do it. ❑ *Record stores are expecting a huge rush for the single.* N-SING: usu N *for* n 5 **The rush** is a period of time when many people go somewhere or do something. ❑ *The shop's opening coincided with the Christmas rush.* N-SING: *the* N, oft supp N 6 If you **rush** something, you do it in a hurry, often too quickly and without much care. ❑ *You can't rush a search... Instead of rushing at life, I wanted something more meaningful.* VERB V n V *at* n ♦ **rushed** *The report had all the hallmarks of a rushed job.* ADJ 7 If you **rush** someone or something to a place, you take them there quickly. ❑ *We got an ambulance and rushed her to hospital... We'll rush it round today if possible.* VERB V n prep V n with adv 8 If you **rush into** something or **are rushed into** it, you do it without thinking about it for long enough. ❑ *He will not rush into any decisions... They had rushed in without adequate appreciation of the task... Ministers won't be rushed into a response... Don't rush him or he'll become confused.* VERB V *into* n V *in* *be* V-ed *into* n V n ♦ **rushed** *At no time did I feel rushed or under pressure.* ADJ: usu v-link ADJ 9 If you **rush** something or someone, you move quickly and forcefully at them, often in order to attack them. ❑ *They rushed the entrance and forced their way in... Tom came rushing at him from another direction.* VERB V n V *at* n 10 If air or liquid **rushes** somewhere, it flows there suddenly and quickly. ❑ *Water rushes out of huge tunnels.* VERB V prep/adv ♦ **Rush** is also a noun. ❑ *A sudden rush of air on my face woke me.* N-COUNT: usu sing, with supp 11 If you experience a **rush of** a feeling, you suddenly experience it very strongly. ❑ *A rush of pure affection swept over him.* N-COUNT: usu sing, with supp 12 If you are **rushed off your feet**, you are extremely busy. [INFORMAL] ❑ *We used to be rushed off our feet at lunchtimes.* PHRASE: usu v-link PHR

♦ **rush out** If a document or product **is rushed out**, it is produced very quickly. ❑ *A statement was rushed out... Studios are rushing out monster movies to take advantage of our new-found enthusiasm for dinosaurs.* PHRASAL VERB *be* V-ed P V P n (not pron) Also V n P

♦ **rush through** If you **rush** something **through**, you deal with it quickly so that it is ready in a shorter time than usual. ❑ *The government rushed through legislation aimed at Mafia leaders... They rushed the burial through so no evidence would show up.* PHRASAL VERB V P n (not pron) V n P

**rush hour** **(rush hours)** also **rush-hour.** The **rush hour** is one of the periods of the day when most people are travelling to or from work. ❑ *During the evening rush hour it was often solid with vehicles... Try to avoid rush-hour traffic.* N-COUNT: also *at/during* N

**rusk** /rʌsk/ **(rusks) Rusks** are hard, dry biscuits that are given to babies and young children. [mainly BRIT] N-VAR

**rus|set** /rʌsɪt/ **(russets) Russet** is used to describe things that are reddish-brown in colour. ❑ *...a russet apple.* COLOUR

**Rus|sian** /rʌʃᵊn/ **(Russians)** 1 **Russian** means belonging or relating to Russia, or to its people, language, or culture. ❑ *...the Russian parliament.* ADJ 2 A **Russian** is a Russian citizen, or a person of Russian origin. ❑ *Three-quarters of Russians live in cities.* N-COUNT

**Rus|sian doll** **(Russian dolls)** A **Russian doll** is a hollow wooden doll that is made in two halves. Inside it are a series of similar wooden dolls, each smaller than the last, placed one inside the other. N-COUNT

**Rus|sian rou|lette** 1 If you say that someone is playing **Russian roulette**, or that what they are doing is like playing **Russian roulette**, you mean that what they are doing is very dangerous because it involves unpredictable risks. ❑ *You are playing Russian roulette every time you have unprotected sex.* N-UNCOUNT 2 If someone plays **Russian roulette**, they fire a gun with only one bullet at their head without knowing whether it will shoot them. N-UNCOUNT

**rust** /rʌst/ **(rusts, rusting, rusted)** 1 **Rust** is a brown substance that forms on iron or steel, for example when it comes into contact with water. ❑ *...a decaying tractor, red with rust.* N-UNCOUNT 2 When a metal object **rusts**, it becomes covered in rust and often loses its strength. ❑ *Copper nails are better than iron nails because the iron rusts.* VERB V 3 **Rust** is sometimes used to describe things that are reddish-brown in colour. ❑ *...turquoise woodwork with accent colours of rust and ochre.* COLOUR

**Rust Belt** also **rust belt.** In the United States and some other countries, **the Rust Belt** is a region which used to have a lot of manufacturing industry, but whose economy is now in difficulty. ❑ *...in the rust belt of the mid-west.* N-SING: *the* N

**rus|tic** /rʌstɪk/ You can use **rustic** to describe things or people that you approve of because they are simple or unsophisticated in a way that is typical of the countryside. ❑ *...the rustic charm of a country lifestyle.* ADJ: usu ADJ n [approval]

**rus|tic|ity** /rʌstɪsɪti/ You can refer to the simple, peaceful character of life in the countryside as **rusticity**. [WRITTEN] ❑ *It pleases me to think of young Tyndale growing up here in deep rusticity.* N-UNCOUNT [approval]

**rus|tle** /rʌsᵊl/ **(rustles, rustling, rustled)** 1 When something thin and dry **rustles** or when you **rustle** it, it makes soft sounds as it moves. ❑ *The leaves rustled in the wind... She rustled her papers impatiently... A snake rustled through the dry grass.* VERB V V n V prep ♦ **Rustle** is also a noun. ❑ *She sat perfectly still, without even a rustle of her frilled petticoats.* N-COUNT: usu sing ♦ **rus|tling** **(rustlings)** *...a rustling sound coming from beneath one of the seats.* N-VAR: oft N *of* n 2 ➔ See also **rustling**.

♦ **rustle up** If you **rustle up** something to eat or drink, you make or prepare it quickly, with very little planning. ❑ *Let's see if somebody can rustle up a cup of coffee.* PHRASAL VERB V P n (not pron)

**rus|tler** /rʌsləʳ/ **(rustlers) Rustlers** are people who steal farm animals, especially cattle, horses, and sheep. [mainly AM] ❑ *...the old Wyoming Trail once used by cattle rustlers and outlaws.* N-COUNT: usu pl, oft n N

**rus|tling** /rʌsəlɪŋ/ 1 **Rustling** is the activity of stealing farm animals, especially cattle. [mainly AM] ❑ *...cattle rustling and horse stealing.* N-UNCOUNT: usu n N 2 ➔ See also **rustle**.

**rusty** /rʌsti/ **(rustier, rustiest)** 1 A **rusty** metal object such as a car or a machine is covered with rust, which is a brown substance that forms on iron or steel when it comes into contact with water. ❑ *...a rusty iron gate.* ADJ: usu ADJ n 2 If a skill that you have or your knowledge of something is **rusty**, it is not as good as it used to be, because you have not used it for a long time. ❑ *You may be a little rusty, but past experience and teaching skills won't have been lost.* ADJ 3 **Rusty** is sometimes used to describe things that are reddish-brown in colour. ADJ

**rut** /rʌt/ **(ruts)** 1 If you say that someone is **in a rut**, you disapprove of the fact that they have become fixed in their way of thinking and doing things, and find it difficult to change. You can also say that someone's life or career is **in a rut**. ❑ *I don't like being in a rut – I like to keep moving on.* N-COUNT: usu sing, usu *in a* N [disapproval] 2 A **rut** is a deep, narrow mark made in the ground by the wheels of a vehicle. ❑ *Our driver slowed up as we approached the ruts in the road.* N-COUNT: oft N *in* n 3 ➔ See also **rutted**, **rutting**.

**ru|ta|ba|ga** /ruːtəbeɪgə/ **(rutabagas)** A **rutabaga** is a round yellow root vegetable with a brown or purple skin. [AM] N-VAR

✓ in BRIT, use **swede**

**ruth|less** /ruːθləs/ 1 If you say that someone is **ruthless**, you mean that you disapprove of them because they are very harsh or cruel, and will do anything that is necessary to achieve what they want. ❑ *The President was ruthless in dealing with any hint of internal political dissent.* ADJ: oft ADJ *in* n [disapproval] ♦ **ruth|less|ly** *The Party has ruthlessly crushed any sign of organised opposition.* ADV: ADV with v ♦ **ruth|less|ness** *...a powerful political figure with a reputation for ruthlessness.* N-UNCOUNT 2 A **ruthless** action or activity is done forcefully and thoroughly, without much concern ADJ: oft ADJ *in* n

for its effects on other people. ❑ *Her lawyers have been ruthless in thrashing out a divorce settlement.*
♦ **ruth|less|ly** *...a ruthlessly efficient woman.* ADV
♦ **ruth|less|ness** *...a woman with a brain and business acumen and a certain healthy ruthlessness.* N-UNCOUNT

**rut|ted** /rʌtɪd/ [1] A **rutted** road or track is very uneven because it has long, deep, narrow marks in it made by the wheels of vehicles. ❑ *...an uncomfortable ride along deeply rutted roads.* ADJ: oft adv ADJ
[2] → See also **rut**.

**rut|ting** /rʌtɪŋ/ [1] **Rutting** male animals such as deer are in a period of sexual excitement and activity. ❑ *...jokes about bitches in heat and rutting stags.* ADJ ♦ **Rutting** is also a noun. ❑ *During the rutting season the big boars have the most terrible mating battles.* N-UNCOUNT: oft N n [2] → See also **rut**.

**RV** /ɑːʳ viː/ **(RVs)** An **RV** is a van which is equipped with such things as beds and cooking equipment, so that people can live in it, usually while they are on holiday. **RV** is an abbreviation for 'recreational vehicle'. [mainly AM] ❑ *...a group of RVs pulled over on the side of the highway.* N-COUNT

✔ in BRIT, usually use **camper, camper van**

**rye** /raɪ/ [1] **Rye** is a cereal grown in cold countries. Its grains can be used to make flour, bread, or other foods. ❑ *One of the first crops that I grew when we came here was rye.* N-UNCOUNT: oft N n [2] **Rye** is bread made from rye. [AM] ❑ *I was eating ham and Swiss cheese on rye.* N-UNCOUNT: usu *on* N

**rye bread** **Rye bread** is brown bread made with rye flour. ❑ *...two slices of rye bread.* N-UNCOUNT

**rye grass** also **ryegrass. Rye grass** is a type of grass that is grown for animals such as cows to eat. N-UNCOUNT

# S s

**S, s** /es/ **(S's, s's)** [1] **S** is the nineteenth letter of the English alphabet. [2] **S** or **s** is an abbreviation for words beginning with s, such as 'south', 'seconds', and 'son'. N-VAR

**-s**

> The form **-es** is also used. The suffix **-s** is pronounced /-s/ after the consonant sounds /p, t, k, f/ or /θ/. After other sounds **-s** is pronounced /-z/. The suffix **-es** is pronounced /-z/ after vowel sounds, and /-ɪz/ after consonant sounds.

[1] **-s** or **-es** is added to a noun to form a plural. ❑ *...her two beloved cats. ...a few problems. ...new houses and flats... Most bosses are traditional.* SUFFIX [2] **-s** or **-es** is added to a verb to form the third person singular, present tense. ❑ *He never thinks about it... She likes her job... No-one wishes to see that.* SUFFIX

**-'s**

> Pronounced /-s/ after the consonant sounds /p, t, k, f/ or /θ/, and /-ɪz/ after the consonant sounds /s, z, ʃ, ʒ, tʃ/ or /dʒ/. After other sounds **-'s** is pronounced /-z/. A final **-s'** is pronounced in the same way as a final **-s.**

[1] **-'s** is added to nouns to form possessives. However, with plural nouns ending in '-s', and sometimes with names ending in '-s', you form the possessive by adding -'. ❑ *...the chairman's son. ...women's rights. ...a boys' boarding-school. ...Sir Charles' car.* [2] **-'s** is the usual spoken form of 'is'. It is added to the end of the pronoun or noun which is the subject of the verb. For example, 'he is' and 'she is' can be shortened to 'he's' and 'she's'. [3] **-'s** is the usual spoken form of 'has', especially where 'has' is an auxiliary verb. It is added to the end of the pronoun or noun which is the subject of the verb. For example, 'It has gone' can be shortened to 'It's gone'. [4] **-'s** is sometimes added to numbers, letters, and abbreviations to form plurals, although many people think you should just add '-s'. ❑ *...new strategies for the 1990's. ...p's and q's.*

**Sab|bath** /sæbəθ/ **The Sabbath** is the day of the week when members of some religious groups do not work. The Jewish Sabbath is on Saturday and the Christian Sabbath is on Sunday. ❑ *...a religious man who kept the Sabbath.* N-PROPER: *the* N, oft N n

**sab|bati|cal** /səbætɪkəl/ **(sabbaticals)** A **sabbatical** is a period of time during which someone such as a university teacher can leave their ordinary work and travel or study. ❑ *He took a year's sabbatical from the Foreign Office... He's been on sabbatical writing a novel.* N-COUNT: also *on* N

**sa|ber** /seɪbəʳ/ → see **sabre**.

**sa|ble** /seɪbəl/ **(sables)** A **sable** is a small furry animal with valued fur. N-COUNT ♦ **Sable** is the fur of a sable. ❑ *...a full-length sable coat.* N-UNCOUNT: oft N n

**sabo|tage** /sæbətɑːʒ/ **(sabotages, sabotaging, sabotaged)** [1] If a machine, railway line, or bridge **is sabotaged**, it is deliberately damaged or destroyed, for example in a war or as a protest. ❑ *The main pipeline supplying water was sabotaged by rebels.* VERB: usu passive, *be* V-ed ♦ **Sabotage** is also a noun. ❑ *The bombing was a spectacular act of sabotage.* N-UNCOUNT [2] If someone **sabotages** a plan or a meeting, they deliberately prevent it from being successful. ❑ *He accused the opposition of trying to sabotage the election.* VERB: V n

**sabo|teur** /sæbətɜːʳ/ **(saboteurs)** A **saboteur** is a person who deliberately damages or destroys things such as machines, railway lines, and bridges in order to weaken an enemy or to make a protest. In Britain, people who try to stop blood sports such as fox hunting are also referred to as **saboteurs**. ❑ *The saboteurs had planned to bomb buses and offices.* N-COUNT

**sa|bre** /seɪbəʳ/ **(sabres)**

> in AM, use **saber**

A **sabre** is a heavy sword with a curved blade that was used in the past by soldiers on horseback. N-COUNT

**sabre-rattling**

> in AM, use **saber-rattling**

If you describe a threat, especially a threat of military action, as **sabre-rattling**, you do not believe that the threat will actually be carried out. ❑ *It is too early to say whether the threats are mere sabre-rattling.* N-UNCOUNT

**sac** /sæk/ **(sacs)** A **sac** is a small part of an animal's body, shaped like a little bag. It contains air, liquid, or some other substance. ❑ *The lungs consist of millions of tiny air sacs.* N-COUNT

**sac|cha|rin** /sækərɪn/ also **saccharine. Saccharin** is a very sweet chemical substance that some people use instead of sugar, especially when they are trying to lose weight. N-UNCOUNT

**sac|cha|rine** /sækərɪn, -riːn/ You describe something as **saccharine** when you find it unpleasantly sweet and sentimental. ❑ *...a saccharine sequel to the Peter Pan story.* ADJ: usu ADJ n [disapproval] = sickly

**sa|chet** /sæʃeɪ, AM sæʃeɪ/ **(sachets)** A **sachet** is a small closed plastic or paper bag, containing a small quantity of something. ❑ *...individual sachets of instant coffee.* N-COUNT: oft N *of* n = packet

**sack** /sæk/ **(sacks, sacking, sacked)** ◆◇◇ [1] A **sack** is a large bag made of rough woven material. Sacks are used to carry or store things such as vegetables or coal. ❑ *...a sack of potatoes.* N-COUNT: oft N *of* n [2] If your employers **sack** you, they tell you that you can no longer work for them because you have done something that they did not like or because your work was not good enough. [BUSINESS] ❑ *Earlier today the Prime Minister sacked 18 government officials for corruption.* VERB = fire, V n ♦ **Sack** is also a noun. ❑ *People who make mistakes can be given the sack the same day.* N-SING: *the* N [3] Some people refer to bed as **the sack.** [INFORMAL] N-SING: *the* N

**sack|cloth** /sækklɒθ/ [1] **Sackcloth** is rough woven material that is used to make sacks. ❑ *He kept the club wrapped in sackcloth.* N-UNCOUNT = hessian [2] If you talk about **sackcloth** or **sackcloth and ashes** you are referring to an exaggerated attempt by someone to show that they are sorry for doing something wrong. N-UNCOUNT

**sack|ful** /sækfʊl/ **(sackfuls)** A **sackful** is the amount of something that a sack contains or could contain. ❑ *...a sackful of presents.* N-COUNT: oft N *of* n = sack

**sack|ing** /sækɪŋ/ **(sackings)** [1] **Sacking** is rough woven material that is used to make sacks. N-UNCOUNT [2] A **sacking** is when an employer tells a worker to leave their job. [BUSINESS] ❑ *...the sacking of twenty-three thousand miners.* N-COUNT

**sac|ra|ment** /sækrəmənt/ **(sacraments)** 1 A **sacrament** is a Christian religious ceremony such as communion, baptism, or marriage. ❑ *...the holy sacrament of baptism.* N-COUNT 2 In the Roman Catholic church, **the Sacrament** is the holy bread eaten at the Eucharist. In the Anglican church, **the Sacrament** is the holy bread and wine taken at Holy Communion. N-SING: *the* N

**sac|ra|men|tal** /sækrəmentəl/ 1 Something that is **sacramental** is connected with a Christian religious ceremony. ❑ *...the sacramental wine.* ADJ 2 **Sacramental** is used to describe something that is considered holy or religious. ❑ *...her view that music is a sacramental art.* ADJ

**sa|cred** /seɪkrɪd/ 1 Something that is **sacred** is believed to be holy and to have a special connection with God. ❑ *The owl is sacred for many Californian Indian people.* ADJ 2 Something connected with religion or used in religious ceremonies is described as **sacred**. ❑ *...sacred songs or music.* ADJ: ADJ n 3 You can describe something as **sacred** when it is regarded as too important to be changed or interfered with. ❑ *My memories are sacred.* ADJ

**sa|cred cow** **(sacred cows)** If you describe a belief, custom, or institution as a **sacred cow**, you disapprove of people treating it with too much respect and being afraid to criticize or question it. ❑ *...the sacred cow of monetarism.* N-COUNT [disapproval]

**sac|ri|fice** /sækrɪfaɪs/ **(sacrifices, sacrificing, sacrificed)** ◆◇◇ 1 If you **sacrifice** something that is valuable or important, you give it up, usually to obtain something else for yourself or for other people. ❑ *She sacrificed family life to her career... Kitty Aldridge has sacrificed all for her first film... He sacrificed himself and so saved his country.* VERB: V n *to/for* n, V n, V pron-refl ♦ **Sacrifice** is also a noun. ❑ *She made many sacrifices to get Anita a good education.* N-VAR ➔ See also **self-sacrifice**. 2 To **sacrifice** an animal or person means to kill them in a special religious ceremony as an offering to a god. ❑ *The priest sacrificed a chicken.* VERB: V n ♦ **Sacrifice** is also a noun. ❑ *...animal sacrifices to the gods.* N-COUNT

**sac|ri|fi|cial** /sækrɪfɪʃəl/ **Sacrificial** means connected with or used in a sacrifice. ❑ *...the sacrificial altar.* ADJ: ADJ n

**sac|ri|fi|cial lamb** **(sacrificial lambs)** If you refer to someone as a **sacrificial lamb**, you mean that they have been blamed unfairly for something they did not do, usually in order to protect another more powerful person or group. ❑ *He was a sacrificial lamb to a system that destroyed him.* N-COUNT = scapegoat

**sac|ri|lege** /sækrɪlɪdʒ/ 1 **Sacrilege** is behaviour that shows great disrespect for a holy place or object. ❑ *Stealing from a place of worship was regarded as sacrilege.* N-UNCOUNT: also *a* N 2 You can use **sacrilege** to refer to disrespect that is shown for someone who is widely admired or for a belief that is widely accepted. ❑ *It is a sacrilege to offend democracy.* N-UNCOUNT: also *a* N

**sac|ri|legious** /sækrɪlɪdʒəs/ If someone's behaviour or actions are **sacrilegious**, they show great disrespect towards something holy or towards something that people think should be respected. ❑ *A number of churches were sacked and sacrilegious acts committed.* ADJ

**sac|ris|ty** /sækrɪsti/ **(sacristies)** A **sacristy** is the room in a church where the priest or minister changes into their official clothes and where holy objects are kept. N-COUNT

**sac|ro|sanct** /sækroʊsæŋkt/ If you describe something as **sacrosanct**, you consider it to be special and are unwilling to see it criticized or changed. ❑ *Freedom of the press is sacrosanct.* ADJ: usu v-link ADJ = sacred

**sad** /sæd/ **(sadder, saddest)** ◆◆◇ 1 If you are **sad**, you feel unhappy, usually because something has happened that you do not like. ❑ *The relationship had been important to me and its loss left me feeling sad and empty... I'm sad that Julie's marriage is on the verge of splitting up... I'd grown fond of our little house and felt sad to leave it... I'm sad about my toys getting burned in the fire.* ADJ: oft ADJ that/to-inf, ADJ *about* n ≠ happy ♦ **sad|ly** *Judy said sadly, 'He has abandoned me.'* ADV: usu ADV with v ♦ **sad|ness** *It is with a mixture of sadness and joy that I say farewell.* N-UNCOUNT ≠ happiness 2 **Sad** stories and **sad** news make you feel sad. ❑ *I received the sad news that he had been killed in a motor-cycle accident.* ADJ: usu ADJ n 3 A **sad** event or situation is unfortunate or undesirable. ❑ *It's a sad truth that children are the biggest victims of passive smoking.* ADJ ♦ **sad|ly** *Sadly, bamboo plants die after flowering... Things are sadly different in Britain.* ADV: usu ADV adj, ADV with cl 4 If you describe someone as **sad**, you do not have any respect for them and think their behaviour or ideas are ridiculous. [INFORMAL] ❑ *...sad old bikers and youngsters who think that Jim Morrison is God.* ADJ: usu ADJ n [disapproval] = pathetic

**SAD** /sæd/ **SAD** is an abbreviation for **seasonal affective disorder**. N-UNCOUNT

**sad|den** /sædən/ **(saddens, saddened)** If something **saddens** you, it makes you feel sad. ❑ *The cruelty in the world saddens me incredibly.* VERB: no cont, V n ♦ **sad|dened** *He was disappointed and saddened that legal argument had stopped the trial.* ADJ: v-link ADJ ♦ **sad|den|ing** *...a saddening experience.* ADJ

**sad|dle** /sædəl/ **(saddles, saddling, saddled)** 1 A **saddle** is a leather seat that you put on the back of an animal so that you can ride the animal. ➔ See also **side-saddle**. N-COUNT 2 If you **saddle** a horse, you put a saddle on it so that you can ride it. ❑ *Why don't we saddle a couple of horses and go for a ride?* VERB: V n ♦ **Saddle up** means the same as **saddle**. ❑ *I want to be gone from here as soon as we can saddle up... She saddled up a horse.* PHRASAL VERB: V P, V P n 3 A **saddle** is a seat on a bicycle or motorcycle. ➔ See picture on page 1708. N-COUNT 4 If you **saddle** someone **with** a problem or **with** a responsibility, you put them in a position where they have to deal with it. ❑ *The war devastated the economy and saddled the country with a huge foreign debt.* VERB: V n *with* n

**saddle|bag** /sædəlbæg/ **(saddlebags)** also **saddle-bag.** A **saddlebag** is a bag fastened to the saddle of a bicycle or motorcycle, or the saddle of a horse. N-COUNT = pannier

**sad|dler** /sædləʳ/ **(saddlers)** A **saddler** is a person who makes, repairs, and sells saddles and other equipment for riding horses. N-COUNT

**sad|dlery** /sædləri/ Saddles and other leather goods made by a saddler can be referred to as **saddlery**. N-UNCOUNT

**saddo** /sædoʊ/ **(saddos)** If you say that someone is a **saddo**, you do not have any respect for them and think their behaviour or ideas are ridiculous. [BRIT, INFORMAL] N-COUNT: oft N n

**sad|ism** /seɪdɪzəm/ **Sadism** is a type of behaviour in which a person obtains pleasure from hurting other people and making them suffer physically or mentally. ❑ *Psychoanalysts tend to regard both sadism and masochism as arising from childhood deprivation.* N-UNCOUNT ♦ **sad|ist** /seɪdɪst/ **(sadists)** *The man was a sadist who tortured animals and people.* N-COUNT

**sa|dis|tic** /sədɪstɪk/ A **sadistic** person obtains pleasure from hurting other people and making them suffer physically or mentally. ❑ *The prisoners rioted against mistreatment by sadistic guards.* ADJ

**sado-masochism** /seɪdoʊ mæsəkɪzəm/ also **sadomasochism. Sado-masochism** is the enjoyment of hurting people and being hurt. ❑ *...the sado-masochism of the Marquis de Sade.* N-UNCOUNT ♦ **sado-masochist** **(sado-masochists)** *...an island resort where sado-masochists can act out their sexual fantasies.* N-COUNT

**sado-masochistic** /seɪdoʊ mæsəkɪstɪk/ also **sadomasochistic.** Something that is **sado-masochistic** is connected with the practice of sado-masochism. ❑ *...a sado-masochistic relationship.* ADJ: usu ADJ n

**s.a.e.** /es eɪ iː/ **(s.a.e.s)** An **s.a.e.** is an envelope on which you have stuck a stamp and written your own name and address. You send it to an organization so that they can reply to you in it. **s.a.e.** is an abbreviation for 'stamped ad- N-COUNT dressed envelope' or 'self addressed envelope'. [BRIT] ❑ *Send an s.a.e. for a free information pack.*

☑ in AM, use **SASE**

**sa|fa|ri** /səfɑːri/ **(safaris)** A **safari** is a trip to observe or hunt wild animals, especially in East Africa. ❑ *He'd like to go on safari to photograph snakes and tigers.* N-COUNT: also *on* N

**sa|fa|ri park** **(safari parks)** A **safari park** is a large enclosed area of land where wild animals, such as lions and elephants, live freely. People can pay to drive through the park and look at the animals. [BRIT] N-COUNT

**sa|fa|ri suit** **(safari suits)** A **safari suit** is a casual suit made from a light-coloured material such as linen or cotton. Safari suits are usually worn in hot weather. N-COUNT

**safe** /seɪf/ **(safer, safest, safes)** ◆◆◇ 1 Something that is **safe** does not cause physical harm or danger. ❑ *Officials arrived to assess whether it is safe to bring emergency food supplies into the city... Most foods that we eat are safe for birds. ...a safe and reliable birth control option.* ADJ: oft *it* v-link ADJ to-inf ≠ *dangerous* 2 If a person or thing is **safe from** something, they cannot be harmed or damaged by it. ❑ *In the future people can go to a football match knowing that they are safe from hooliganism.* ADJ: v-link ADJ, usu ADJ *from* n 3 If you are **safe**, you have not been harmed, or you are not in danger of being harmed. ❑ *Where is Sophy? Is she safe?* ADJ: v-link ADJ ♦ **safe|ly** *All 140 guests were brought out of the building safely by firemen.* ADV: ADV with v 4 A **safe** place is one where it is unlikely that any harm, damage, or unpleasant things will happen to the people or things that are there. ❑ *Many refugees have fled to safer areas.* ADJ ♦ **safe|ly** *The banker keeps the money tucked safely under his bed.* ADV: ADV after v 5 If people or things have a **safe** journey, they reach their destination without harm, damage, or unpleasant things happening to them. ❑ *...the UN plan to deploy 500 troops to ensure the safe delivery of food and other supplies.* ADJ: ADJ n ♦ **safe|ly** *The space shuttle returned safely today from a 10-day mission.* ADV: ADV with v, ADV adv 6 If you are at a **safe** distance from something or someone, you are far enough away from them to avoid any danger, harm, or unpleasant effects. ❑ *I shall conceal myself at a safe distance from the battlefield.* ADJ: ADJ n 7 If something you have or expect to obtain is **safe**, you cannot lose it or be prevented from having it. ❑ *We as consumers need to feel confident that our jobs are safe before we will spend spare cash.* ADJ: usu v-link ADJ = *secure* 8 A **safe** course of action is one in which there is very little risk of loss or failure. ❑ *Electricity shares are still a safe investment.* ADJ: usu ADJ n, also *it* v-link ADJ to-inf ♦ **safe|ly** *We reveal only as much information as we can safely risk at a given time.* ADV: usu ADV before v 9 If you disapprove of something because you think it is not very exciting or original, you can describe it as **safe**. ❑ *...frustrated artists who became lawyers at an early age because it seemed a safe option... Rock'n'roll has become so commercialised and safe since punk.* ADJ disapproval 10 If **it is safe to** say or assume something, you can say it with very little risk of being wrong. ❑ *I think it is safe to say that very few students expend the effort to do quality work in school.* ADJ: oft *it* v-link ADJ to-inf ♦ **safe|ly** *I think you can safely say she will not be appearing in another of my films.* ADV: ADV before v 11 A **safe** is a strong metal cupboard with special locks, in which you keep money, jewellery, or other valuable things. ❑ *The files are now in a safe to which only he has the key.* N-COUNT 12 → See also **safely**.

**PHRASES** 13 If you say that a person or thing is **in safe hands**, or is **safe in** someone's **hands**, you mean that they are being looked after by a reliable person and will not be harmed. ❑ *I had a huge responsibility to ensure these packets remained in safe hands.* PHRASE: usu v-link PHR 14 If you **play safe** or **play it safe**, you do not take any risks. ❑ *If you want to play safe, cut down on the amount of salt you eat.* PHRASE: V inflects 15 If you say you are doing something **to be on the safe side**, you mean that you are doing it in case something undesirable happens, even though this may be unnecessary. ❑ *You might still want to go for an X-ray, however, just to be on the safe side.* PHRASE: PHR with cl 16 If you say **'it's better to be safe than sorry'**, you are advising someone to take action in order to avoid possible unpleasant consequences later, even if this seems unnecessary. ❑ *Don't be afraid to have this checked by a doctor – better safe than sorry!* PHRASE 17 You say that someone is **safe and sound** when they are still alive or unharmed after being in danger. ❑ *All I'm hoping for is that wherever Trevor is he will come home safe and sound.* PHRASE: PHR after v, v-link PHR 18 **a safe pair of hands** → see **pair**. **safe in the knowledge** → see **knowledge**.

**safe area** **(safe areas)** If part of a country that is involved in a war is declared to be a **safe area**, neutral forces will try to keep peace there so that it is safe for people. ❑ *The UN declared it a safe area.* N-COUNT

**safe con|duct** also **safe-conduct.** If you are given **safe conduct**, the authorities officially allow you to travel somewhere, guaranteeing that you will not be arrested or harmed while doing so. ❑ *Her family was given safe conduct to Britain when civil war broke out.* N-UNCOUNT: also *a* N

**safe de|pos|it box** **(safe deposit boxes)** A **safe deposit box** is a small box, usually kept in a special room in a bank, in which you can store valuable objects. N-COUNT

**safe|guard** /seɪfgɑːʳd/ **(safeguards, safeguarding, safeguarded)** 1 To **safeguard** something or someone means to protect them from being harmed, lost, or badly treated. [FORMAL] ❑ *They will press for international action to safeguard the ozone layer... They are taking precautionary measures to safeguard their forces from the effects of chemical weapons.* VERB = *protect* V n V n *from* n 2 A **safeguard** is a law, rule, or measure intended to prevent someone or something from being harmed. ❑ *Many people took second jobs as a safeguard against unemployment.* N-COUNT: oft N *against* n

**safe ha|ven** **(safe havens)** 1 If part of a country is declared a **safe haven**, people who need to escape from a dangerous situation such as a war can go there and be protected. ❑ *Countries overwhelmed by the human tide of refugees want safe havens set up at once.* N-COUNT 2 If a country provides **safe haven** for people from another country who have been in danger, it allows them to stay there under its official protection. [AM] ❑ *Some Democrats support granting the Haitians temporary safe haven in the US.* N-UNCOUNT = *asylum* 3 A **safe haven** is a place, a situation, or an activity which provides people with an opportunity to escape from things that they find unpleasant or worrying. ❑ *...the idea of the family as a safe haven from the brutal outside world.* N-COUNT: usu sing, oft N *from* n

**safe house** **(safe houses)** also **safe-house.** You can refer to a building as a **safe house** when it is used as a place where someone can stay and be protected. Safe houses are often used by spies, criminals, or the police. ❑ *...a farm which operates as a safe house for criminals on the run.* N-COUNT

**safe|keeping** /seɪfkiːpɪŋ/ If something is given to you **for safekeeping**, it is given to you so that you will make sure that it is not harmed or stolen. ❑ *Hampton had been given the bills for safekeeping by a business partner.* N-UNCOUNT: usu *for* N

**safe|ly** /seɪfli/ 1 If something is done **safely**, it is done in a way that makes it unlikely that anyone will be harmed. ❑ *The waste is safely locked away until it is no longer radioactive... 'Drive safely,' he said and waved goodbye.* ADV: usu ADV with v 2 You also use **safely** to say that there is no risk of a situation being changed. ❑ *Once events are safely in the past, this idea seems to become less alarming.* ADV: usu ADV with v 3 → See also **safe**.

**safe pas|sage** If someone is given **safe passage**, they are allowed to go somewhere safely, without being attacked or arrested. ❑ *They were unwilling, or unable, to guarantee safe passage from the city to the aircraft.* N-UNCOUNT: also *a* N, oft N *for/to* n

**safe seat** **(safe seats)** In politics, a **safe seat** is an area in which the candidate from one particular party nearly always wins by a large number of N-COUNT votes. [BRIT] ❑ *The constituency I live in is a safe Labour seat.*

**safe sex** also **safer sex. Safe sex** is sexual activity in which people protect themselves against the risk of AIDS and other diseases, usually by using condoms. N-UNCOUNT

**safe|ty** /seɪfti/ ◆◆◇ 1 **Safety** is the state of being safe from harm or danger. ❑ *The report goes on to make a number of recommendations to improve safety on aircraft.* N-UNCOUNT 2 If you reach **safety**, you reach a place where you are safe from danger. ❑ *He stumbled through smoke and fumes given off from her burning sofa to pull her to safety... Guests ran for safety as the device went off in a ground-floor men's toilet... The refugees were groping their way through the dark, trying to reach safety. ...the safety of one's own home.* N-UNCOUNT: oft prep N 3 If you are concerned about the **safety** of something, you are concerned that it might be harmful or dangerous. ❑ *...consumers are showing growing concern about the safety of the food they buy.* N-SING: with poss 4 If you are concerned for someone's **safety**, you are concerned that they might be in danger. ❑ *The two youths today declined to testify because they said they feared for their safety.* N-SING: with poss 5 **Safety** features or measures are intended to make something less dangerous. ❑ *The built-in safety device compensates for a fall in water pressure.* ADJ: ADJ n 6 If you say that there is **safety in numbers**, you mean that you are safer doing something if there are a lot of people doing it rather than doing it alone. ❑ *Many people still feel there is safety in numbers when belonging to a union.* PHRASE: usu v-link PHR

**safe|ty belt** (safety belts) also **safety-belt.** A **safety belt** is a strap attached to a seat in a car or aeroplane. You fasten it round your body and it stops you being thrown forward if there is an accident. N-COUNT = seat belt

**safe|ty catch** (safety catches) The **safety catch** on a gun is a device that stops you firing the gun accidentally. ❑ *Eddie slipped the safety catch on his automatic back into place.* N-COUNT

**safe|ty glass** **Safety glass** is very strong glass that does not break into sharp pieces if it is hit. N-UNCOUNT

**safe|ty net** (safety nets) 1 A **safety net** is something that you can rely on to help you if you get into a difficult situation. ❑ *Welfare is the only real safety net for low-income workers.* N-COUNT 2 In a circus, a **safety net** is a large net that is placed below performers on a high wire or trapeze in order to catch them and prevent them being injured if they fall off. N-COUNT

**safe|ty of|fic|er** (safety officers) The **safety officer** in a company or an organization is the person who is responsible for the safety of the people who work or visit there. N-COUNT

**safe|ty pin** (safety pins) A **safety pin** is a bent metal pin used for fastening things together. The point of the pin has a cover so that when the pin is closed it cannot hurt anyone. ❑ *...trousers which were held together with safety pins.* N-COUNT

**safe|ty valve** (safety valves) 1 A **safety valve** is a device which allows liquids or gases to escape from a machine when the pressure inside it becomes too great. ❑ *Residents heard an enormous bang as a safety valve on the boiler failed.* N-COUNT 2 A **safety valve** is something that allows you to release strong feelings without hurting yourself or others. ❑ *...crying is a natural safety valve.* N-COUNT

**safe|ty zone** (safety zones) also **safety island.** A **safety zone** is a place in the middle of a road crossing where you can wait before you cross the other half of the road. [AM] N-COUNT

**saf|fron** /sæfrɒn/ 1 **Saffron** is a yellowish-orange powder obtained from a flower and used to give flavour and colouring to some foods. ❑ *...saffron rice.* N-UNCOUNT 2 **Saffron** is a yellowish-orange colour. ❑ *...a Buddhist in saffron robes.* COLOUR

**sag** /sæg/ (sags, sagging, sagged) 1 When something **sags**, it hangs down loosely or sinks downwards in the middle. ❑ *The shirt's cuffs won't sag and lose their shape after washing... He sat down in the sagging armchair.* VERB V V-ing 2 When part of someone's body begins to **sag**, it starts to become less firm and hang down. ❑ *He is heavily built, but beginning to sag.* VERB V 3 To **sag** means to become weaker. ❑ *The pound continued to sag despite four interventions by the Bank of England.* VERB = flag V

**saga** /sɑːgə/ (sagas) 1 A **saga** is a long story, account, or sequence of events. ❑ *...a 600 page saga about 18th century slavery. ...the continuing saga of unexpected failures by leading companies.* N-COUNT 2 A **saga** is a long story composed in medieval times in Norway or Iceland. ❑ *...a Nordic saga of giants and trolls.* N-COUNT

**sa|ga|cious** /səgeɪʃəs/ A **sagacious** person is intelligent and has the ability to make good decisions. [FORMAL] ❑ *...a sagacious leader.* ADJ = wise

**sa|gac|ity** /səgæsɪti/ **Sagacity** is the quality of being sagacious. [FORMAL] ❑ *...a man of great sagacity and immense experience.* N-UNCOUNT = wisdom

**sage** /seɪdʒ/ (sages) 1 A **sage** is a person who is regarded as being very wise. [LITERARY] ❑ *...ancient Chinese sages.* N-COUNT 2 **Sage** means wise and knowledgeable, especially as the result of a lot of experience. [LITERARY] ❑ *He was famous for his sage advice to younger painters.* ♦ **sage|ly** *Susan nodded sagely as if what I had said was profoundly significant.* ADJ = wise ADV: ADV with v = wisely 3 **Sage** is a herb used in cooking. N-UNCOUNT 4 **Sage** is a plant with grey-green leaves and purple, blue, or white flowers. N-VAR

**sag|gy** /sægi/ (saggier, saggiest) If you describe something as **saggy**, you mean that it has become less firm over a period of time and become unattractive. ❑ *Is the mattress lumpy and saggy?* ADJ

**Sag|it|ta|rius** /sædʒɪteəriəs/ 1 **Sagittarius** is one of the twelve signs of the zodiac. Its symbol is a creature that is half horse, half man, shooting an arrow. People who are born approximately between the 22nd of November and the 21st of December come under this sign. N-UNCOUNT 2 A **Sagittarius** is a person whose sign of the zodiac is Sagittarius. N-SING: *a* N

**sago** /seɪgoʊ/ **Sago** is a white substance obtained from the trunk of some palm trees. Sago is used for making sweet puddings. N-UNCOUNT

**sa|hib** /sɑːb, sɑːhɪb/ (sahibs) **Sahib** is a term used by some people in India to address or to refer to a man in a position of authority. Sahib was used especially of white government officials in the period of British rule. N-TITLE; N-COUNT politeness

**said** /sed/ **Said** is the past tense and past participle of **say**.

**sail** /seɪl/ (sails, sailing, sailed) ◆◇◇ 1 **Sails** are large pieces of material attached to the mast of a ship. The wind blows against the sails and pushes the ship along. ❑ *The white sails billow with the breezes they catch.* N-COUNT 2 You say a ship **sails** when it moves over the sea. ❑ *The trawler had sailed from the port of Zeebrugge.* VERB V prep/adv 3 If you **sail** a boat or if a boat **sails**, it moves across water using its sails. ❑ *I shall get myself a little boat and sail her around the world... For nearly two hundred miles she sailed on, her sails hard with ice.* VERB V n prep V adv/prep 4 If a person or thing **sails** somewhere, they move there smoothly and fairly quickly. ❑ *We got into the lift and sailed to the top floor.* VERB V prep/adv 5 → See also **sailing**. 6 When a ship **sets sail**, it leaves a port. ❑ *Christopher Columbus set sail for the New World in the Santa Maria.* PHRASE: V inflects, oft PHR prep 7 **to sail close to the wind** → see **wind**.

♦ **sail through** If someone or something **sails through** a difficult situation or experience, they deal with it easily and successfully. ❑ *While she sailed through her maths exams, he struggled.* PHRASAL VERB V P n

**sail|boat** /seɪlboʊt/ (sailboats) A **sailboat** is the same as a **sailing boat**. [mainly AM] N-COUNT

**sail|cloth** /seɪlklɒθ, AM -klɔːθ/ 1 **Sailcloth** a strong heavy cloth that is used for making things such as sails or tents. ❑ *The mainsails are* N-UNCOUNT *hand-cut and sewn from real sailcloth.* 2 **Sailcloth** is a light canvas material that is used for making clothes. ❑ *...red sailcloth trousers.* N-UNCOUNT

**sail|ing** /seɪlɪŋ/ **(sailings)** 1 **Sailing** is the activity or sport of sailing boats. ❑ *There was swimming and sailing down on the lake.* N-UNCOUNT 2 **Sailings** are trips made by a ship carrying passengers. ❑ *Ferry companies are providing extra sailings from Calais.* N-COUNT: usu pl, oft supp N 3 If you say that a task was not all **plain sailing**, you mean that it was not very easy. ❑ *Pregnancy wasn't all plain sailing and once again there were problems.* PHRASE: usu v-link PHR

**sail|ing boat** **(sailing boats)** also **sailing-boat.** A **sailing boat** is a boat with sails. [BRIT] N-COUNT

✓ in AM, use **sailboat**

**sail|ing ship** **(sailing ships)** A **sailing ship** is a large ship with sails, especially of the kind that were used to carry passengers or cargo. ❑ *American clippers were the ultimate sailing ships.* N-COUNT

**sail|or** /seɪləʳ/ **(sailors)** A **sailor** is someone who works on a ship or sails a boat. N-COUNT

**saint** /seɪnt/ **(saints)** ◆◇◇

✓ The title is usually pronounced /sənt/.

1 A **saint** is someone who has died and been officially recognized and honoured by the Christian church because his or her life was a perfect example of the way Christians should live. ❑ *Every parish was named after a saint. ...Saint John.* N-COUNT; N-TITLE 2 If you refer to a living person as a **saint**, you mean that they are extremely kind, patient, and unselfish. ❑ *My girlfriend is a saint to put up with me.* N-COUNT [approval]

**saint|hood** /seɪnthʊd/ **Sainthood** is the state of being a saint. ❑ *His elevation to sainthood is entirely justified.* N-UNCOUNT: usu supp N

**saint|ly** /seɪntli/ A **saintly** person behaves in a very good or very holy way. ❑ *She has been saintly in her self-restraint.* ADJ [approval]

**sake** /seɪk/ **(sakes)** ◆◇◇ 1 If you do something **for the sake of** something, you do it for that purpose or in order to achieve that result. You can also say that you do it **for** something's **sake**. ❑ *For the sake of historical accuracy, please permit us to state the true facts... For safety's sake, never stand directly behind a horse.* PHRASE: PHR n 2 If you do something **for its own sake**, you do it because you want to, or because you enjoy it, and not for any other reason. You can also talk about, for example, **art for art's sake** or **sport for sport's sake**. ❑ *Economic change for its own sake did not appeal to him.* PHRASE: usu n PHR 3 When you do something **for** someone's **sake**, you do it in order to help them or make them happy. ❑ *I trust you to do a good job for Stan's sake... Linda knew that for both their sakes she must take drastic action.* PHRASE: N inflects, PHR with cl 4 Some people use expressions such as **for God's sake**, **for heaven's sake**, **for goodness sake**, or **for Pete's sake** in order to express annoyance or impatience, or to add force to a question or request. The expressions 'for God's sake' and 'for Christ's sake' could cause offence. [INFORMAL] ❑ *For goodness sake, why didn't you ring me?* PHRASE: N inflects, PHR with cl [feelings]

**saké** /sɑːki, -keɪ/ also **sake.** **Saké** is a Japanese alcoholic drink that is made from rice. N-UNCOUNT

**sa|laam** /səlɑːm/ **(salaams, salaaming, salaamed)** 1 When someone **salaams**, they bow with their right hand on their forehead. This is used as a formal and respectful way of greeting someone in India and Muslim countries. ❑ *He looked from one to the other of them, then salaamed and left.* VERB: V 2 Some Muslims greet people by saying '**Salaam**'. CONVENTION

**sa|la|cious** /səleɪʃəs/ If you describe something such as a book or joke as **salacious**, you think that it deals with sexual matters in an unnecessarily detailed way. ❑ *The newspapers once again filled their columns with salacious details.* ADJ: usu ADJ n = *prurient*

**sal|ad** /sæləd/ **(salads)** 1 A **salad** is a mixture of raw or cold foods such as lettuce, cucumber, and tomatoes. It is often served with other food as part of a meal. ❑ *...a salad of tomato, onion and cucumber. ...potato salad.* ➔ See also **fruit salad**. N-VAR 2 If you refer to your **salad days**, you are referring to a period of your life when you were young and inexperienced. [LITERARY] ❑ *The Grand Hotel did not seem to have changed since her salad days.* PHRASE

**sal|ad bowl** **(salad bowls)** A **salad bowl** is a large bowl from which salad is served at a meal. N-COUNT

**sal|ad cream** **(salad creams)** **Salad cream** is a pale yellow creamy sauce that you eat with salad. N-MASS

**sal|ad dress|ing** **(salad dressings)** **Salad dressing** is a mixture of oil, vinegar, herbs, and other flavourings, which you pour over a salad. ❑ *...low-calorie salad dressings.* N-MASS

**sala|man|der** /sæləmændəʳ/ **(salamanders)** A **salamander** is an animal that looks rather like a lizard, and that can live both on land and in water. N-COUNT

**sa|la|mi** /səlɑːmi/ **(salamis)** **Salami** is a type of strong-flavoured sausage. It is usually thinly sliced and eaten cold. N-VAR

**sala|ried** /sælərid/ **Salaried** people receive a salary from their job. ❑ *...salaried employees... James accepted the generously salaried job at the bank.* ADJ: usu ADJ n

**sala|ry** /sæləri/ **(salaries)** A **salary** is the money that someone is paid each month by their employer, especially when they are in a profession such as teaching, law, or medicine. ❑ *...the lawyer was paid a huge salary... The government has decided to increase salaries for all civil servants.* ◆◇◇ N-VAR

**sale** /seɪl/ **(sales)** ◆◆◆ 1 The **sale** of goods is the act of selling them for money. ❑ *Efforts were made to limit the sale of alcohol. ...a proposed arms sale to Saudi Arabia.* N-SING: usu with supp 2 The **sales** of a product are the quantity of it that is sold. ❑ *The newspaper has sales of 1.72 million. ...retail sales figures.* N-PLURAL 3 The part of a company that deals with **sales** deals with selling the company's products. ❑ *Until 1983 he worked in sales and marketing.* N-PLURAL 4 A **sale** is an occasion when a shop sells things at less than their normal price. ❑ *...a pair of jeans bought half-price in a sale.* N-COUNT 5 A **sale** is an event when goods are sold to the person who offers the highest price. ❑ *The painting was bought by dealers at the Christie's sale.* N-COUNT = *auction* 6 ➔ See also **car boot sale**, **jumble sale**.

**PHRASES** 7 If something is **for sale**, it is being offered to people to buy. ❑ *His former home is for sale at £495,000.* PHRASE 8 Products that are **on sale** can be bought in shops. [mainly BRIT] ❑ *English textbooks and dictionaries are on sale everywhere.* PHRASE 9 If products in a shop are **on sale**, they can be bought for less than their normal price. [AM] ❑ *He bought a sports jacket on sale at Gowings Men's Store.* PHRASE 10 If a property or company is **up for sale**, its owner is trying to sell it. ❑ *The castle has been put up for sale.* PHRASE

**sale|able** /seɪləbᵊl/ also **salable.** Something that is **saleable** is easy to sell to people. ❑ *The Oxfam shops depend on regular supplies of saleable items.* ADJ

**sale|room** /seɪlruːm/ **(salerooms)** A **saleroom** is a place where things are sold by auction. [BRIT] N-COUNT = *auction room*

✓ in AM, use **salesroom**

**sales clerk** **(sales clerks)** also **salesclerk.** A **sales clerk** is a person who works in a shop selling things to customers and helping them to find what they want. [AM] N-COUNT

✓ in BRIT, use **shop assistant**

**sales force** **(sales forces)** also **salesforce.** A company's **sales force** is all the people that work for that company selling its products. N-COUNT

**sales|girl** /seɪlzgɜːʳl/ **(salesgirls)** A **salesgirl** is a young woman who sells things, especially in a shop. Many women prefer to be called a **saleswoman** or a **salesperson** rather than a salesgirl. N-COUNT

**sales|man** /seɪlzmən/ **(salesmen)** A **salesman** is a man whose job is to sell things, especially directly to shops or other businesses on behalf of a company. ❑ *...an insurance salesman.* N-COUNT: usu supp N

**sales|man|ship** /seɪlzmənʃɪp/ **Salesmanship** is the skill of persuading people to buy things. ❑ *I was captured by his brilliant salesmanship.* N-UNCOUNT

**sales|person** /seɪlzpɜːʳsən/ **(salespeople** or **salespersons)** A **salesperson** is a person who sells things, either in a shop or directly to customers on behalf of a company. N-COUNT

**sales pitch (sales pitches)** A salesperson's **sales pitch** is what they say in order to persuade someone to buy something from them. ❑ *His sales pitch was smooth and convincing.* N-COUNT

**sales|room** /seɪlzruːm/ **(salesrooms)** A **salesroom** is a place where things are sold by auction. [AM] N-COUNT = auction room

in BRIT, use **saleroom**

**sales slip (sales slips)** A **sales slip** is a piece of paper that you are given when you buy something in a shop, which shows when you bought it and how much you paid. [AM] N-COUNT

in BRIT, use **receipt**

**sales tax (sales taxes)** The **sales tax** on things that you buy is the amount of money that you pay to the national government, or, in the United States, to the local or state government. N-VAR

**sales|wom|an** /seɪlzwʊmən/ **(saleswomen)** A **saleswoman** is a woman who sells things, either in a shop or directly to customers on behalf of a company. N-COUNT

**sa|li|ent** /seɪliənt/ The **salient** points or facts of a situation are the most important ones. [FORMAL] ❑ *He read the salient facts quickly.* ADJ: usu ADJ n

**sa|line** /seɪlaɪn, AM -liːn/ A **saline** substance or liquid contains salt. ❑ *...a saline solution.* ADJ: usu ADJ n

**sa|li|va** /səlaɪvə/ **Saliva** is the watery liquid that forms in your mouth and helps you to chew and digest food. N-UNCOUNT

**sali|vary gland** /səlaɪvəri glænd, AM sælɪveri -/ **(salivary glands)** Your **salivary glands** are the glands that produce saliva in your mouth. N-COUNT: usu pl

**sali|vate** /sælɪveɪt/ **(salivates, salivating, salivated)** When people or animals **salivate**, they produce a lot of saliva in their mouth, often as a result of seeing or smelling food. ❑ *Any dog will salivate when presented with food.* VERB = drool V

**sal|low** /sæloʊ/ If a person has **sallow** skin, their skin, especially on their face, is a pale yellowish colour and looks unhealthy. ❑ *She had lank hair and sallow skin.* ADJ

**sal|ly** /sæli/ **(sallies, sallying, sallied)** 1 **Sallies** are clever and amusing remarks. [LITERARY] ❑ *He had thus far succeeded in fending off my conversational sallies.* N-COUNT 2 If someone **sallies forth** or **sallies** somewhere, they go out into a rather difficult, dangerous, or unpleasant situation in a brave or confident way. [LITERARY] ❑ *...worrying about her when she sallies forth on her first date... Tamara would sally out on bitterly cold nights.* ♦ **Sally** is also a noun. ❑ *...their first sallies outside the student world.* VERB V forth V prep/adv N-COUNT

**salm|on** /sæmən/ **(salmon)** A **salmon** is a large silver-coloured fish. ♦ **Salmon** is the pink flesh of this fish which is eaten as food. It is often smoked and eaten raw. ❑ *... a splendid lunch of smoked salmon.* N-COUNT N-UNCOUNT

**sal|mo|nel|la** /sælmənelə/ **Salmonella** is a disease caused by bacteria in food. You can also refer to the bacteria itself as **salmonella**. ❑ *He was suffering from salmonella poisoning.* N-UNCOUNT

**salm|on pink** Something that is **salmon pink** or **salmon** is the orangey-pink colour of a salmon's flesh. COLOUR

**sa|lon** /sælɒn, AM səlɑːn/ **(salons)** 1 A **salon** is a place where people have their hair cut or coloured, or have beauty treatments. ❑ *...a new hair salon. ...a beauty salon.* N-COUNT: usu n N 2 A **salon** is a shop where smart, expensive clothes are sold. N-COUNT 3 A **salon** is a sitting room in a large, grand house. N-COUNT

**sa|loon** /səluːn/ **(saloons)** 1 A **saloon** or a **saloon car** is a car with seats for four or more people, a fixed roof, and a boot that is separated from the rear seats. [BRIT] N-COUNT

in AM, use **sedan**

2 A **saloon** is a place where alcoholic drinks are sold and drunk. [AM] N-COUNT = bar

**sal|sa** /sælsə, AM sɑːlsə/ **(salsas)** 1 **Salsa** is a hot, spicy sauce made from onions and tomatoes, usually eaten with Mexican or Spanish food. N-MASS 2 **Salsa** is a type of dance music especially popular in Latin America. ❑ *A band played salsa, and spectators danced wildly.* N-UNCOUNT

**salt** /sɔːlt/ **(salts, salting, salted)** 1 **Salt** is a strong-tasting substance, in the form of white powder or crystals, which is used to improve the flavour of food or to preserve it. Salt occurs naturally in sea water. ❑ *Season lightly with salt and pepper. ...a pinch of salt.* ◆◇◇ N-UNCOUNT 2 When you **salt** food, you add salt to it. ❑ *Salt the stock to your taste and leave it simmering very gently.* ♦ **salt|ed** *Put a pan of salted water on to boil.* VERB V n ADJ: usu ADJ n 3 **Salts** are substances that are formed when an acid reacts with an alkali. ❑ *The rock is rich in mineral salts.* N-COUNT: usu pl 4 ➔ See also **Epsom salts, smelling salts.**

PHRASES 5 If you **take** something **with a pinch of salt**, you do not believe that it is completely accurate or true. ❑ *The more miraculous parts of this account should be taken with a pinch of salt.* PHRASE: V inflects 6 If you say, for example, that any doctor **worth** his or her **salt** would do something, you mean that any doctor who was good at his or her job or who deserved respect would do it. ❑ *Any coach worth his salt would do exactly as I did.* PHRASE: n PHR 7 If someone or something **rubs salt into** the **wound**, they make the unpleasant situation that you are in even worse, often by reminding you of your failures or faults. ❑ *I had no intention of rubbing salt into a friend's wounds, so all I said was that I did not give interviews.* PHRASE: V and *wound* inflect

**salt cel|lar (salt cellars)** A **salt cellar** is a small container for salt with a hole or holes in the top for shaking salt onto food. [BRIT] N-COUNT

in AM, use **salt shaker**

**salt|ine** /sɔːltiːn/ **(saltines)** A **saltine** is a thin square biscuit with salt baked into its surface. [AM] N-COUNT

**salt marsh (salt marshes)** A **salt marsh** is an area of flat, wet ground which is sometimes covered by salt water or contains areas of salt water. N-VAR

**salt shak|er (salt shakers)** A **salt shaker** is the same as a **salt cellar**. [mainly AM] N-COUNT

**salt wa|ter** also **saltwater. Salt water** is water from the sea, which has salt in it. N-UNCOUNT ≠ fresh water

**salty** /sɔːlti/ **(saltier, saltiest)** Something that is **salty** contains salt or tastes of salt. ❑ *...a cool salty sea breeze.* ♦ **salti|ness** *The saltiness of the cheese is balanced by the sweetness of the red peppers.* ADJ N-UNCOUNT

**sa|lu|bri|ous** /səluːbriəs/ 1 A place that is **salubrious** is pleasant and healthy. [FORMAL] ❑ *...your salubrious lochside hotel.* ADJ 2 Something that is described as **salubrious** is respectable or socially desirable. [FORMAL] ❑ *...London's less salubrious quarters.* ADJ

**salu|tary** /sæljʊtəri, AM -teri/ A **salutary** experience is good for you, even though it may seem difficult or unpleasant at first. [FORMAL] ❑ *It was a salutary experience to be in the minority.* ADJ: usu ADJ n

**salu|ta|tion** /sæljʊteɪʃən/ **(salutations) Salutation** or a **salutation** is a greeting to someone. [FORMAL] ❑ *Jackson nodded a salutation... The old man moved away, raising his hand in salutation.* N-COUNT: also in/of N

**sa|lute** /səluːt/ **(salutes, saluting, saluted)** 1 If you **salute** someone, you greet them or show your respect with a formal sign. Soldiers usually salute officers by raising their right hand so that their fingers touch their forehead. ❑ *One of the company stepped out and saluted the General... I stood* VERB V n V

*to attention and saluted.* ♦ **Salute** is also a noun. ❑ *The soldier gave the clenched-fist salute... He raised his hand in salute.* [2] To **salute** a person or their achievements means to publicly show or state your admiration for them. ❑ *I salute him for the leadership role that he is taking.*
N-COUNT: also *in* N
VERB
V n

**sal|vage** /sælvɪdʒ/ **(salvages, salvaging, salvaged)** [1] If something **is salvaged**, someone manages to save it, for example from a ship that has sunk, or from a building that has been damaged. ❑ *The team's first task was to decide what equipment could be salvaged... The investigators studied flight recorders salvaged from the wreckage.*
VERB: usu passive
*be* V-ed
V-ed

[2] **Salvage** is the act of salvaging things from somewhere such as a damaged ship or building. ❑ *The salvage operation went on. ...the cost of salvage.* [3] The **salvage** from somewhere such as a damaged ship or building is the things that are saved from it. ❑ *They climbed up on the rock with their salvage.* [4] If you manage to **salvage** a difficult situation, you manage to get something useful from it so that it is not a complete failure. ❑ *Officials tried to salvage the situation.* [5] If you **salvage** something such as your pride or your reputation, you manage to keep it even though it seems likely you will lose it, or you get it back it after losing it. ❑ *We definitely wanted to salvage some pride for British tennis.*
N-UNCOUNT: oft N n
N-UNCOUNT
VERB
V n
VERB
V n

**sal|va|tion** /sælveɪʃᵊn/ [1] In Christianity, **salvation** is the fact that Christ has saved a person from evil. ❑ *The church's message of salvation has changed the lives of many.* [2] The **salvation** of someone or something is the act of saving them from harm, destruction, or an unpleasant situation. ❑ *...those whose marriages are beyond salvation.* [3] If someone or something is your **salvation**, they are responsible for saving you from harm, destruction, or an unpleasant situation. ❑ *The country's salvation lies in forcing through democratic reforms.*
N-UNCOUNT
N-UNCOUNT
N-SING: with poss

**Sal|va|tion Army** **The Salvation Army** is a Christian organization that aims to spread Christianity and care for the poor. Its members wear military-style uniforms. ❑ *...a Salvation Army hostel.*
N-PROPER: *the* N, N n

**salve** /sælv, AM sæv/ **(salves, salving, salved)** [1] If you do something to **salve** your conscience, you do it in order to feel less guilty. [FORMAL] ❑ *I give myself treats and justify them to salve my conscience.* [2] **Salve** is an oily substance that is put on sore skin or a wound to help it heal. ❑ *...a soothing salve for sore, dry lips.*
VERB = ease
V n
N-MASS = balm

**sal|ver** /sælvəʳ/ **(salvers)** A **salver** is a flat object, usually made of silver, on which things are carried. ❑ *...silver salvers laden with flutes of champagne.*
N-COUNT

**sal|vo** /sælvoʊ/ **(salvoes)** [1] A **salvo** is the firing of several guns or missiles at the same time in a battle or ceremony. ❑ *They were to fire a salvo of blanks, after the national anthem.* [2] A **salvo of** angry words is a lot of them spoken or written at about the same time. ❑ *His testimony, however, was only one in a salvo of new attacks.*
N-COUNT
N-COUNT: with supp

**Sa|mari|tan** /səmærɪtən/ **(Samaritans)** You refer to someone as a **Samaritan** if they help you when you are in difficulty. ❑ *A good Samaritan offered us a room in his house.*
N-COUNT

**sam|ba** /sæmbə/ **(sambas)** A **samba** is a lively Brazilian dance.
N-COUNT

**same** /seɪm/ [1] If two or more things, actions, or qualities are **the same**, or if one is **the same as** another, they are very like each other in some way. ❑ *In essence, all computers are the same... People with the same experience in the job should be paid the same... Driving a boat is not the same as driving a car... I want my son to wear the same clothes as everyone else at the school.* [2] If something is happening **the same as** something else, the two things are happening in a way that is similar or exactly the same. ❑ *I mean, it's a relationship, the same as a marriage is a relationship... He just wanted the war to end, the same as Wally did.* [3] You use **same** to indicate that you are referring to only one place, time, or thing, and not to different ones. ❑ *Bernard works at the same institution as Arlette... It's impossible to get everybody together at the same time... John just told me that your birthday is on the same day as mine.* [4] Something that is still **the same** has not changed in any way. ❑ *Taking ingredients from the same source means the beers stay the same... Only 17% said the economy would improve, but 25% believed it would stay the same.* [5] You use **the same** to refer to something that has previously been mentioned or suggested. ❑ *We made the decision which was right for us. Other parents must do the same... We like him very much and he says the same about us.* ♦ **Same** is also an adjective. ❑ *Dwight Eisenhower possessed much the same ability to appear likeable.* [6] You say **'same here'** in order to suggest that you feel the same way about something as the person who has just spoken to you, or that you have done the same thing. [INFORMAL, SPOKEN] ❑ *'Nice to meet you,' said Michael. 'Same here,' said Mary Ann.* [7] You say **'same to you'** in response to someone who wishes you well with something. [INFORMAL, SPOKEN] ❑ *'Have a nice Easter.' — 'And the same to you Bridie.'*
◆◆◆
ADJ: *the* ADJ, oft ADJ *as* n/-ing
PHRASE
ADJ: *the* ADJ, oft ADJ n *as* n, ADJ n that
ADJ: *the* ADJ
PRON: *the* PRON
ADJ: *the* ADJ
CONVENTION [formulae] = likewise
CONVENTION [formulae]

**PHRASES** [8] You say **'same again'** when you want to order another drink of the same kind as the one you have just had. [INFORMAL, SPOKEN] ❑ *Give Roger another pint, Imogen, and I'll have the same again.* [9] You can say **all the same** or **just the same** to introduce a statement which indicates that a situation or your opinion has not changed, in spite of what has happened or what has just been said. ❑ *...jokes that she did not understand but laughed at just the same.* [10] If you say **'It's all the same to me'**, you mean that you do not care which of several things happens or is chosen. [mainly SPOKEN] ❑ *Whether I've got a moustache or not it's all the same to me.* [11] When two or more people or things are thought to be separate and you say that they are **one and the same**, you mean that they are in fact one single person or thing. ❑ *Luckily, Nancy's father and her attorney were one and the same person... I'm willing to work for the party because its interests and my interests are one and the same.* [12] **at the same time** → see **time**.
PHRASE
PHRASE: PHR with cl
PHRASE
PHRASE: v-link PHR

**same|ness** /seɪmnəs/ The **sameness** of something is its lack of variety. ❑ *He grew bored by the sameness of the speeches.*
N-UNCOUNT: usu with supp

**same-sex** **Same-sex** people are the same sex as each other, or the same sex as a particular person. ❑ *...women's same-sex friends.*
ADJ: usu ADJ n

**samey** /seɪmi/ If you describe a set of things as **samey**, you mean that they are all very similar, and it would be more interesting if they were different from each other. ❑ *He has written a batch of very samey tunes.*
ADJ

**Sami** /sæmi/ **(Sami)** A **Sami** is a member of a people living mainly in northern Scandinavia. ❑ *The Sami have strong views on environmental matters.*
N-COUNT = Lapp

**sa|miz|dat** /sæmɪzdæt, AM sɑːm-/ **Samizdat** referred to a system in the former USSR and Eastern Europe by which books and magazines forbidden by the state were illegally printed by groups who opposed the state. [FORMAL] ❑ *...a publisher specialising in samizdat literature.*
N-UNCOUNT: usu N n

**sa|mo|sa** /səmoʊsə/ **(samosas)** A **samosa** is an Indian food consisting of vegetables, spices, and sometimes meat, wrapped in pastry and fried.
N-COUNT

**samo|var** /sæməvɑːʳ/ **(samovars)** A **samovar** is a large decorated container for heating water, traditionally used in Russia for making tea.
N-COUNT

**sam|ple** /sɑːmpᵊl, sæm-/ **(samples, sampling, sampled)** [1] A **sample** of a substance or product is a small quantity of it that shows you what it is like. ❑ *You'll receive samples of paint, curtains and*
◆◇◇
N-COUNT

*upholstery... We're giving away 2000 free samples... They asked me to do some sample drawings.* 2 A **sample** of a substance is a small amount of it that is examined and analysed scientifically. ❑ *They took samples of my blood. ...urine samples.* N-COUNT = specimen
3 A **sample** of people or things is a number of them chosen out of a larger group and then used in tests or used to provide information about the whole group. ❑ *We based our analysis on a random sample of more than 200 males.* N-COUNT 4 If you **sample** food or drink, you taste a small amount of it in order to find out if you like it. ❑ *We sampled a selection of different bottled waters.* VERB = taste V n 5 If you **sample** a place or situation, you experience it for a short time in order to find out about it. ❑ *...the chance to sample a different way of life.* VERB = try V n

**sam|pler** /sɑːmpləʳ, sæm-/ **(samplers)** 1 A **sampler** is a piece of cloth with words and patterns sewn on it, which is intended to show the skill of the person who made it. N-COUNT 2 A **sampler** is a piece of equipment that is used for copying a piece of music and using it to make a new piece of music. N-COUNT

**samu|rai** /sæmjʊraɪ, AM -mʊr-/ **(samurai)** In former times, a **samurai** was a member of a powerful class of fighters in Japan. N-COUNT

**sana|to|rium** /sænətɔːriəm/ **(sanatoriums** or **sanatoria** /sænətɔːriə/**)**

✔ in AM, also use **sanitarium**

A **sanatorium** is an institution that provides medical treatment and rest, often in a healthy climate, for people who have been ill for a long time. N-COUNT

**sanc|ti|fy** /sæŋktɪfaɪ/ **(sanctifies, sanctifying, sanctified)** If something **is sanctified** by a priest or other holy person, the priest or holy person officially approves of it, or declares it to be holy. ❑ *She is trying to make amends for her marriage not being sanctified.* VERB: usu passive *be* V-ed

**sanc|ti|mo|ni|ous** /sæŋktɪmoʊniəs/ If you say that someone is **sanctimonious**, you disapprove of them because you think that they are trying to appear morally better than other people. ❑ *He writes smug, sanctimonious rubbish.* ADJ [disapproval] = self-righteous

**sanc|tion** /sæŋkʃən/ **(sanctions, sanctioning, sanctioned)** ◆◆◇ 1 If someone in authority **sanctions** an action or practice, they officially approve of it and allow it to be done. ❑ *He may now be ready to sanction the use of force.* ♦ **Sanction** is also a noun. ❑ *The king could not enact laws without the sanction of Parliament.* VERB V n N-UNCOUNT: with supp = approval 2 **Sanctions** are measures taken by countries to restrict trade and official contact with a country that has broken international law. ❑ *The continued abuse of human rights has now led the United States to impose sanctions against the regime.* N-PLURAL: oft N *against/on* n 3 A **sanction** is a severe course of action which is intended to make people obey instructions, customs, or laws. ❑ *As an ultimate sanction, they can sell their shares.* N-COUNT 4 If a country or an authority **sanctions** another country or a person for doing something, it declares that the country or person is guilty of doing it and imposes sanctions on them. ❑ *...their failure to sanction Japan for butchering whales in violation of international conservation treaties.* VERB V n

**sanc|tity** /sæŋktɪti/ If you talk about **the sanctity of** something, you mean that it is very important and must be treated with respect. ❑ *...the sanctity of human life.* N-UNCOUNT: oft *the* N *of* n

**sanc|tu|ary** /sæŋktʃuəri, AM -tʃueri/ **(sanctuaries)** 1 A **sanctuary** is a place where people who are in danger from other people can go to be safe. ❑ *His church became a sanctuary for thousands of people who fled the civil war.* N-COUNT = haven 2 **Sanctuary** is the safety provided in a sanctuary. ❑ *Some of them have sought sanctuary in the church.* N-UNCOUNT 3 A **sanctuary** is a place where birds or animals are protected and allowed to live freely. ❑ *...a bird sanctuary. ...a wildlife sanctuary.* N-COUNT: oft n N

**sanc|tum** /sæŋtəm/ **(sanctums)** 1 If you refer to someone's **inner sanctum**, you mean a room which is private and sometimes secret, where they can be quiet and alone. ❑ *His bedroom's his inner sanctum.* N-COUNT: usu sing 2 A **sanctum** is the holiest place inside a holy building such as a temple or mosque. N-COUNT

**sand** /sænd/ **(sands, sanding, sanded)** ◆◇◇ 1 **Sand** is a substance that looks like powder, and consists of extremely small pieces of stone. Some deserts and many beaches are made up of sand. ❑ *They all walked barefoot across the damp sand to the water's edge. ...grains of sand.* N-UNCOUNT 2 **Sands** are a large area of sand, for example a beach. ❑ *...miles of golden sands.* N-PLURAL 3 If you **sand** a wood or metal surface, you rub sandpaper over it in order to make it smooth or clean. ❑ *Sand the surface softly and carefully.* VERB V n ♦ **Sand down** means the same as **sand**. ❑ *I was going to sand down the chairs and repaint them... Simply sand them down with a fine grade of sandpaper.* PHRASAL VERB V P n (not pron) V n P

**san|dal** /sændəl/ **(sandals) Sandals** are light shoes that you wear in warm weather, which have straps instead of a solid part over the top of your foot. N-COUNT

**sandal|wood** /sændəlwʊd/ 1 **Sandalwood** is the sweet-smelling wood of a tree that is found in South Asia and Australia. It is also the name of the tree itself. N-UNCOUNT 2 **Sandalwood** is the oil extracted from the wood of the tree. It is used to make perfume. N-UNCOUNT

**sand|bag** /sændbæg/ **(sandbags, sandbagging, sandbagged)** 1 A **sandbag** is a cloth bag filled with sand. Sandbags are usually used to build walls for protection against floods or explosions. N-COUNT 2 To **sandbag** something means to protect or strengthen it using sandbags. ❑ *They sandbagged their homes to keep out floods.* VERB V n

**sand|bank** /sændbæŋk/ **(sandbanks)** A **sandbank** is a bank of sand below the surface of the sea or a river. ❑ *The ship hit a sandbank.* N-COUNT

**sand|bar** /sændbɑːʳ/ **(sandbars)** also **sand bar.** A **sandbar** is a sandbank which is found especially at the mouth of a river or harbour. N-COUNT

**sand|box** /sændbɒks/ **(sandboxes)** A **sandbox** is the same as a **sandpit**. [AM] N-COUNT

**sand cas|tle (sand castles)** A **sand castle** is a pile of sand, usually shaped like a castle, which children make when they are playing on the beach. N-COUNT

**sand dune (sand dunes)** A **sand dune** is a hill of sand near the sea or in a sand desert. N-COUNT: usu pl = dune

**sand|er** /sændəʳ/ **(sanders)** A **sander** is a machine for making wood or metal surfaces smoother. N-COUNT

**S & L** /es ən el/ **(S & Ls) S & L** is an abbreviation for **savings and loan**. [BUSINESS] N-COUNT

**S & M** /es ən em/ **S & M** is an abbreviation for **sado-masochism**. N-UNCOUNT

**sand|paper** /sændpeɪpəʳ/ **Sandpaper** is strong paper that has a coating of sand on it. It is used for rubbing wood or metal surfaces to make them smoother. N-UNCOUNT

**sand|pit** /sændpɪt/ **(sandpits)** also **sand-pit.** A **sandpit** is a shallow hole or box in the ground with sand in it where small children can play. [BRIT] N-COUNT

✔ in AM, use **sandbox**

**sand|stone** /sændstoʊn/ **(sandstones) Sandstone** is a type of rock which contains a lot of sand. It is often used for building houses and walls. ❑ *...sandstone cliffs.* N-MASS

**sand|storm** /sændstɔːʳm/ **(sandstorms)** A **sandstorm** is a strong wind in a desert area, which carries sand through the air. N-COUNT

**sand|wich** /sænwɪdʒ, -wɪtʃ/ **(sandwiches, sandwiching, sandwiched)** 1 A **sandwich** usually consists of two slices of bread with a layer of food such as cheese or meat between them. ❑ *...a ham* N-COUNT sandwich. [2] If you **sandwich** two things **together** with something else, you put that other thing between them. If you **sandwich** one thing between two other things, you put it between them. ❑ *Sandwich the two halves of the sponge together with cream.* [3] → See also **sandwiched**. VERB V pl-n together

**sand|wich course** **(sandwich courses)** A **sandwich course** is an educational course in which you have periods of study between periods of being at work. [BRIT] N-COUNT

**sand|wiched** /sænwɪdʒd, -wɪtʃt/ If something is **sandwiched between** two other things, it is in a narrow space between them. ❑ *The original kitchen was sandwiched between the breakfast room and the toilet.* → See also **sandwich**. ADJ: v-link ADJ between pl-n

**sandy** /sændi/ **(sandier, sandiest)** [1] A **sandy** area is covered with sand. ❑ *...long, sandy beaches.* ADJ
[2] **Sandy** hair is light orangey-brown in colour. ADJ

**sane** /seɪn/ **(saner, sanest)** [1] Someone who is **sane** is able to think and behave normally and reasonably, and is not mentally ill. ❑ *He seemed perfectly sane... It wasn't the act of a sane person.* ADJ ≠ insane
[2] If you refer to a **sane** person, action, or system, you mean one that you think is reasonable and sensible. ❑ *No sane person wishes to see conflict or casualties.* ADJ: usu ADJ n ≠ insane

**sang** /sæŋ/ **Sang** is the past tense of **sing**.

**sang-froid** /sɒŋ frwɑː/ also **sangfroid**. A person's **sang-froid** is their ability to remain calm in a dangerous or difficult situation. [FORMAL] ❑ *He behaves throughout with a certain sang-froid.* N-UNCOUNT

**san|gria** /sæŋgriːə/ **Sangria** is a Spanish drink made of red wine, orange or lemon juice, soda, and brandy. N-UNCOUNT

**san|guine** /sæŋgwɪn/ If you are **sanguine about** something, you are cheerful and confident that things will happen in the way you want them to. ❑ *He's remarkably sanguine about the problems involved.* ADJ: usu v-link ADJ, oft ADJ about n

**sani|ta|rium** /sænɪteəriəm/ **(sanitariums)** → see **sanatorium**.

**sani|tary** /sænɪtri, AM -teri/ [1] **Sanitary** means concerned with keeping things clean and healthy, especially by providing a sewage system and a clean water supply. ❑ *Sanitary conditions are appalling.* ADJ: ADJ n
[2] If you say that a place is not **sanitary**, you mean that it is not very clean. ❑ *It's not the most sanitary place one could swim.* ADJ: usu with brd-neg = hygienic

**sani|tary nap|kin** **(sanitary napkins)** A **sanitary napkin** is the same as a **sanitary towel**. [AM] N-COUNT

**sani|tary pro|tec|tion** **Sanitary protection** is sanitary towels or tampons. N-UNCOUNT

**sani|tary tow|el** **(sanitary towels)** A **sanitary towel** is a pad of thick soft material which women wear to absorb the blood during their periods. [BRIT] N-COUNT

✓ in AM, use **sanitary napkin**

**sani|ta|tion** /sænɪteɪʃən/ **Sanitation** is the process of keeping places clean and healthy, especially by providing a sewage system and a clean water supply. ❑ *...the hazards of contaminated water and poor sanitation.* N-UNCOUNT

**sani|tize** /sænɪtaɪz/ **(sanitizes, sanitizing, sanitized)**

✓ in BRIT, also use **sanitise**

To **sanitize** an activity or a situation that is unpleasant or unacceptable means to describe it in a way that makes it seem more pleasant or more acceptable. ❑ *...crime writers who sanitise violence and make it respectable.* VERB V n

**san|ity** /sænɪti/ [1] A person's **sanity** is their ability to think and behave normally and reasonably. ❑ *He and his wife finally had to move from their apartment just to preserve their sanity.* N-UNCOUNT
[2] If there is **sanity** in a situation or activity, there is a purpose and a regular pattern, rather than confusion and worry. ❑ *Rafsanjani has been considering various ways of introducing some sanity into the currency market.* N-UNCOUNT

**sank** /sæŋk/ **Sank** is the past tense of **sink**.

**San|skrit** /sænskrɪt/ **Sanskrit** is an ancient language which used to be spoken in India and is now used only in religious writings and ceremonies. N-UNCOUNT

**Santa Claus** /sæntə klɔːz, AM - klɔːz/ **Santa Claus** or **Santa** is an imaginary old man with a long white beard and a red coat. Traditionally, young children in many countries are told that he brings their Christmas presents. N-PROPER = Father Christmas

**sap** /sæp/ **(saps, sapping, sapped)** [1] If something **saps** your strength or confidence, it gradually weakens or destroys it. ❑ *I was afraid the sickness had sapped my strength.* VERB V n
[2] **Sap** is the watery liquid in plants and trees. ❑ *The leaves, bark and sap are also common ingredients of local herbal remedies.* N-UNCOUNT

**sa|pi|ens** /sæpienz/ → see **homo sapiens**.

**sap|ling** /sæplɪŋ/ **(saplings)** A **sapling** is a young tree. N-COUNT

**sap|per** /sæpəʳ/ **(sappers)** A **sapper** is a soldier whose job is to do building, digging, and similar work. ❑ *They requested sappers to mend bridges or remove mines.* N-COUNT

**sap|phire** /sæfaɪəʳ/ **(sapphires)** [1] A **sapphire** is a precious stone which is blue in colour. ❑ *...a sapphire engagement ring.* N-VAR: oft N n
[2] Something that is **sapphire** is bright blue in colour. [LITERARY] ❑ *...white snow and sapphire skies.* COLOUR

**sap|py** /sæpi/ [1] **Sappy** stems or leaves contain a lot of liquid. ADJ
[2] If you describe someone or something as **sappy**, you think they are foolish. [AM, INFORMAL] ❑ *I wrote this sappy love song.* ADJ disapproval

**Sa|ran wrap** /səræn ræp/ **Saran wrap** is a thin, clear, stretchy plastic which you use to cover food to keep it fresh. [AM, TRADEMARK] N-UNCOUNT

✓ in BRIT, use **clingfilm**

**sar|casm** /sɑːʳkæzəm/ **Sarcasm** is speech or writing which actually means the opposite of what it seems to say. Sarcasm is usually intended to mock or insult someone. ❑ *'What a pity,' Graham said with a hint of sarcasm.* N-UNCOUNT

**sar|cas|tic** /sɑːʳkæstɪk/ Someone who is **sarcastic** says or does the opposite of what they really mean in order to mock or insult someone. ❑ *She poked fun at people's shortcomings with sarcastic remarks.* ♦ **sar|cas|ti|cal|ly** /sɑːʳkæstɪkli/ *'What a surprise!' Caroline murmured sarcastically.* ADJ; ADV: ADV with v

**sar|co|ma** /sɑːʳkoʊmə/ **(sarcomas)** **Sarcoma** is one of the two main forms of cancer. It affects tissues such as muscle and bone. N-VAR

**sar|copha|gus** /sɑːʳkɒfəgəs/ **(sarcophagi** or **sarcophaguses)** A **sarcophagus** is a large decorative container in which a dead body was placed in ancient times. ❑ *...an Egyptian sarcophagus.* N-COUNT

**sar|dine** /sɑːʳdiːn/ **(sardines)** [1] **Sardines** are a kind of small sea fish, often eaten as food. ❑ *They opened a tin of sardines.* N-COUNT
[2] If you say that a crowd of people are **packed like sardines**, you are emphasizing that they are sitting or standing so close together that they cannot move easily. ❑ *The refugees were packed like sardines.* PHRASE: usu v-link PHR emphasis

**sar|don|ic** /sɑːʳdɒnɪk/ If you describe someone as **sardonic**, you mean their attitude to people or things is humorous but rather critical. ❑ *...a big, sardonic man, who intimidated his students.* ADJ: usu ADJ n

**sarge** /sɑːʳdʒ/ A sergeant is sometimes addressed as **sarge** or referred to as **the sarge**. [INFORMAL] ❑ *'Good luck, sarge,' he said.* N-VOC; N-SING: the N

**sari** /sɑːri/ **(saris)** A **sari** is a piece of clothing worn especially by Indian women. It consists of a long piece of thin material that is wrapped around the body. N-COUNT

**sar|in** /sɑːrɪn/ **Sarin** is an extremely poisonous gas that is used in chemical weapons. N-UNCOUNT

**sar|nie** /sɑːʳni/ **(sarnies)** A **sarnie** is a sandwich. [BRIT, INFORMAL] ❑ *...a plate of sarnies.* N-COUNT = butty

**sa|rong** /sərɒŋ, AM -rɔːŋ/ **(sarongs)** A **sarong** is a piece of clothing that is worn especially by Malaysian men and women. It consists of a long piece of cloth wrapped round the waist or body. N-COUNT

**SARS** /sɑːʳz/ **SARS** is a serious disease which affects your ability to breathe. SARS is an abbreviation for 'severe acute respiratory syndrome'. N-UNCOUNT

**sar|to|rial** /sɑːʳtɔːriəl/ **Sartorial** means relating to clothes and to the way they are made or worn. [FORMAL] ❑ *...Sebastian's sartorial elegance.* ADJ: ADJ n

**SAS** /es eɪ es/ **The SAS** is a group of highly trained British soldiers who work on secret or very difficult military operations. **SAS** is an abbreviation for 'Special Air Service'. [BRIT] N-PROPER: *the* N

**SASE** /es eɪ es iː/ **(SASEs)** An **SASE** is an envelope on which you have stuck a stamp and written your own name and address. You send it to a person or organization so that they can reply to you in it. **SASE** is an abbreviation for 'self-addressed stamped envelope'. [AM] N-SING

✔ in BRIT, use **s.a.e.**

**sash** /sæʃ/ **(sashes)** A **sash** is a long piece of cloth which people wear round their waist or over one shoulder, especially with formal or official clothes. ❑ *She wore a white dress with a blue sash.* N-COUNT

**sash|ay** /sæʃeɪ, AM sæʃeɪ/ **(sashays, sashaying, sashayed)** If someone **sashays**, they walk in a graceful but rather noticeable way. ❑ *The models sashayed down the catwalk.* VERB V prep/adv

**sash win|dow (sash windows)** A **sash window** is a window which consists of two frames placed one above the other. The window can be opened by sliding one frame over the other. ➔ See picture on page 1705. N-COUNT

**sas|sy** /sæsi/ [1] If an older person describes a younger person as **sassy**, they mean that they are disrespectful in a lively, confident way. [AM, INFORMAL] ❑ *Are you that sassy with your parents, young lady?* ADJ = cheeky [2] **Sassy** is used to describe things that are smart and stylish. [AM, INFORMAL] ❑ *...colourful and sassy fashion accessories.* ADJ

**sat** /sæt/ **Sat** is the past tense and past participle of **sit**.

**SAT** /es eɪ tiː/ **(SATs)** The **SAT** is an examination which is often taken by students who wish to enter a college or university. **SAT** is an abbreviation for 'Scholastic Aptitude Test'. [AM] N-PROPER

**Sat.** **Sat.** is a written abbreviation for **Saturday**.

**Satan** /seɪtᵊn/ In the Christian religion, **Satan** is the Devil, a powerful evil being who is the chief opponent of God. N-PROPER

**sa|tan|ic** /sətænɪk/ Something that is **satanic** is considered to be caused by or influenced by Satan. ❑ *...satanic cults. ...satanic ritual.* ADJ: usu ADJ n

**Sa|tan|ism** /seɪtənɪzəm/ also **satanism. Satanism** is worship of Satan. ❑ *...black magic and satanism.* N-UNCOUNT ♦ **Sa|tan|ist** /seɪtənɪst/ **(Satanists)** *...a Satanist accused of fire attacks on churches.* N-COUNT

**sa|tay** /sæteɪ, AM sɑːteɪ/ **Satay** is pieces of meat cooked on thin sticks and served with a peanut sauce. ❑ *...chicken satay.* N-UNCOUNT

**satch|el** /sætʃəl/ **(satchels)** A **satchel** is a bag with a long strap that schoolchildren use for carrying books. N-COUNT

**sat|ed** /seɪtɪd/ If you are **sated with** something, you have had more of it than you can enjoy at one time. [FORMAL] ❑ *...children happily sated with ice cream.* ADJ: v-link ADJ

**sat|el|lite** /sætəlaɪt/ **(satellites)** ◆◇◇ [1] A **satellite** is an object which has been sent into space in order to collect information or to be part of a communications system. Satellites move continually round the earth or around another planet. ❑ *The rocket launched two communications satellites... The signals are sent by satellite link.* N-COUNT: also *by* N [2] **Satellite** television is broadcast using a satellite. ❑ *They have four satellite channels.* ADJ: ADJ n [3] A **satellite** is a natural object in space that moves round a planet or star. ❑ *...the satellites of Jupiter.* N-COUNT [4] You can refer to a country, area, or organization as a **satellite** when it is controlled by or depends on a larger and more powerful one. ❑ *Italy became a satellite state of Germany by the end of the 1930s.* N-COUNT: oft N n

**sat|el|lite dish (satellite dishes)** A **satellite dish** is a piece of equipment which people need to have on their house in order to receive satellite television. N-COUNT

**sa|ti|ate** /seɪʃieɪt/ **(satiates, satiating, satiated)** If something such as food or pleasure **satiates** you, you have all that you need or all that you want of it, often so much that you become tired of it. [FORMAL] ❑ *The dinner was enough to satiate the gourmets.* VERB V n

**sat|in** /sætɪn, AM -tᵊn/ **(satins)** [1] **Satin** is a smooth, shiny kind of cloth, usually made from silk. ❑ *...a peach satin ribbon.* N-MASS [2] If something such as a paint, wax, or cosmetic gives something a **satin** finish, it reflects light to some extent but is not very shiny. ADJ: ADJ n

**satin|wood** /sætɪnwʊd/ **Satinwood** is a smooth hard wood which comes from an East Indian tree and is used to make furniture. N-UNCOUNT

**sat|ire** /sætaɪəʳ/ **(satires)** [1] **Satire** is the use of humour or exaggeration in order to show how foolish or wicked some people's behaviour or ideas are. ❑ *The commercial side of the Christmas season is an easy target for satire.* N-UNCOUNT [2] A **satire** is a play, film, or novel in which humour or exaggeration is used to criticize something. ❑ *...a sharp satire on the American political process.* N-COUNT: oft N *on* n

**sa|tir|ic** /sətɪrɪk/ **Satiric** means the same as **satirical**. ❑ *...Ibsen's satiric attack on convention.* ADJ

**sa|tiri|cal** /sətɪrɪkᵊl/ A **satirical** drawing, piece of writing, or comedy show is one in which humour or exaggeration is used to criticize something. ❑ *...a satirical novel about London life in the late 80s.* ADJ

**sati|rist** /sætɪrɪst/ **(satirists)** A **satirist** is someone who writes or uses satire. ❑ *He built a reputation in the 1970s as a social satirist.* N-COUNT

**sati|rize** /sætɪraɪz/ **(satirizes, satirizing, satirized)**

✔ in BRIT, also use **satirise**

If you **satirize** a person or group of people, you use satire to criticize them or make fun of them in a play, film, or novel. ❑ *The newspaper came out weekly. It satirized political leaders.* VERB V n

**sat|is|fac|tion** /sætɪsfækʃᵊn/ [1] **Satisfaction** is the pleasure that you feel when you do something or get something that you wanted or needed to do or get. ❑ *She felt a small glow of satisfaction... Both sides expressed satisfaction with the progress so far.* N-UNCOUNT [2] If you get **satisfaction** from someone, you get money or an apology from them because you have been treated badly. ❑ *If you can't get any satisfaction, complain to the park owner.* N-UNCOUNT [3] If you do something **to** someone's **satisfaction**, they are happy with the way that you have done it. ❑ *It is hard to see how the issue can be resolved to everyone's satisfaction.* PHRASE: PHR after v

**sat|is|fac|tory** /sætɪsfæktəri/ Something that is **satisfactory** is acceptable to you or fulfils a particular need or purpose. ❑ *I never got a satisfactory answer.* ADJ = acceptable

**sat|is|fied** /sætɪsfaɪd/ [1] If you are **satisfied with** something, you are happy because you have got what you wanted or needed. ❑ *We are not satisfied with these results. ...satisfied customers.* ADJ: usu v-link ADJ, oft ADJ *with* n [2] If you are **satisfied that** something is true or has been done properly, you are convinced about this after checking it. ❑ *People must be satisfied that the treatment is safe.* ADJ: v-link ADJ, oft ADJ that

**sat|is|fy** /sætɪsfaɪ/ **(satisfies, satisfying, satisfied)** [1] If someone or something **satisfies** you, they give you enough of what you want or need VERB to make you pleased or contented. ❑ *The pace of change has not been quick enough to satisfy everyone... We just can't find enough good second-hand cars to satisfy demand.* V n / V n [2] To **satisfy** someone **that** something is true or has been done properly means to convince them by giving them more information or by showing them what has been done. ❑ *He has to satisfy the environmental lobby that real progress will be made to cut emissions.* VERB = convince / V n that [3] If you **satisfy** the requirements for something, you are good enough or have the right qualities to fulfil these requirements. ❑ *The procedures should satisfy certain basic requirements.* VERB / V n

**sat|is|fy|ing** /sætɪsfaɪɪŋ/ Something that is **satisfying** makes you feel happy, especially because you feel you have achieved something. ❑ *I found wood carving satisfying.* ADJ

**sat|su|ma** /sætsuːmə/ **(satsumas)** A **satsuma** is a fruit that looks like a small orange. N-COUNT

**satu|rate** /sætʃʊreɪt/ **(saturates, saturating, saturated)** [1] If people or things **saturate** a place or object, they fill it completely so that no more can be added. ❑ *In the last days before the vote, both sides are saturating the airwaves... As the market was saturated with goods and the economy became more balanced, inflation went down.* VERB / V n / be V-ed with n [2] If someone or something **is saturated**, they become extremely wet. ❑ *If the filter has been saturated with motor oil, it should be discarded and replaced.* VERB: usu passive / be V-ed

**satu|rat|ed** /sætʃʊreɪtɪd/ **Saturated** fats are types of fat that are found in some foods, especially meat, eggs, and things such as butter and cheese. They are believed to cause heart disease and some other illnesses if eaten too often. ❑ *...foods rich in cholesterol and saturated fats.* ADJ: usu ADJ n

**satu|ra|tion** /sætʃʊreɪʃᵊn/ [1] **Saturation** is the process or state that occurs when a place or thing is filled completely with people or things, so that no more can be added. ❑ *Reforms have led to the saturation of the market with goods... Road traffic has reached saturation point.* N-UNCOUNT [2] **Saturation** is used to describe a campaign or other activity that is carried out very thoroughly, so that nothing is missed. ❑ *Newspapers, television and radio are all providing saturation coverage.* ADJ: ADJ n

**Sat|ur|day** /sætəʳdeɪ, -di/ **(Saturdays) Saturday** is the day after Friday and before Sunday. ❑ *She had a call from him on Saturday morning at the studio... Every Saturday dad made a beautiful pea and ham soup... The overnight train runs every night of the week except Saturdays.* N-VAR

**sat|ur|nine** /sætəʳnaɪn/ Someone who is **saturnine** is serious and unfriendly. [LITERARY] ❑ *He had a rather forbidding, saturnine manner.* ADJ: usu ADJ n

**sa|tyr** /sætəʳ/ **(satyrs)** In classical mythology a **satyr** is a creature that is half man and half goat. N-COUNT

**sauce** /sɔːs/ **(sauces)** A **sauce** is a thick liquid which is served with other food. ❑ *...pasta cooked in a sauce of garlic, tomatoes, and cheese. ...vanilla ice cream with chocolate sauce.* ◆◇◇ N-MASS

**sauce|pan** /sɔːspən, AM -pæn/ **(saucepans)** A **saucepan** is a deep metal cooking pot, usually with a long handle and a lid. ➔ See picture on page 1710. ❑ *Cook the potatoes and turnips in a large saucepan.* N-COUNT = pan

**sau|cer** /sɔːsəʳ/ **(saucers)** A **saucer** is a small curved plate on which you stand a cup. ➔ See also **flying saucer**. N-COUNT

**saucy** /sɔːsi/ **(saucier, sauciest)** Someone or something that is **saucy** refers to sex in a light-hearted, amusing way. ❑ *...a saucy joke.* ADJ = cheeky

**Sau|di** /saʊdi/ **(Saudis)** [1] **Saudi** or **Saudi Arabian** means belonging or relating to Saudi Arabia or to its people, language, or culture. ❑ *Saudi officials have dismissed such reports as rumours.* ADJ: usu ADJ n [2] The **Saudis** or **Saudi Arabians** are the people who come from Saudi Arabia. N-COUNT

**sau|er|kraut** /saʊəʳkraʊt/ **Sauerkraut** is cabbage which has been cut into very small pieces and pickled. It is eaten mainly in Germany. N-UNCOUNT

**sau|na** /sɔːnə/ **(saunas)** [1] If you have a **sauna**, you sit or lie in a room that is so hot that it makes you sweat. People have saunas in order to relax and to clean their skin thoroughly. N-COUNT [2] A **sauna** is a room or building where you can have a sauna. N-COUNT

**saun|ter** /sɔːntəʳ/ **(saunters, sauntering, sauntered)** If you **saunter** somewhere, you walk there in a slow, casual way. ❑ *We watched our fellow students saunter into the building.* VERB / V prep/adv

**sau|sage** /sɒsɪdʒ, AM sɔːs-/ **(sausages)** A **sausage** consists of minced meat, usually pork, mixed with other ingredients and is contained in a tube made of skin or a similar material. ❑ *...sausages and chips.* N-VAR

**sau|sage meat** **Sausage meat** is minced meat, usually pork, mixed with other ingredients and used to make sausages. N-UNCOUNT

**sau|sage roll** **(sausage rolls)** A **sausage roll** is a small amount of sausage meat which is covered with pastry and cooked. [BRIT] N-COUNT

**sau|té** /soʊteɪ, AM sɔːteɪ/ **(sautés, sautéing, sautéed)** When you **sauté** food, you fry it quickly in hot oil or butter. ❑ *Sauté the chicken until golden brown. ...sautéed mushrooms.* VERB / V n / V-ed

**sav|age** /sævɪdʒ/ **(savages, savaging, savaged)** [1] Someone or something that is **savage** is extremely cruel, violent, and uncontrolled. ❑ *This was a savage attack on a defenceless young girl. ...a savage dog.* ADJ = vicious ♦ **sav|age|ly** *He was savagely beaten.* ADV [2] If you refer to people as **savages**, you dislike them because you think that they do not have an advanced society and are violent. ❑ *...their conviction that the area was a frozen desert peopled with uncouth savages.* N-COUNT: usu pl [disapproval] [3] If someone **is savaged** by a dog or other animal, the animal attacks them violently. ❑ *The animal then turned on him and he was savaged to death.* VERB: usu passive / be V-ed [4] If someone or something that they have done **is savaged** by another person, that person criticizes them severely. ❑ *The show had already been savaged by critics... Speakers called for clearer direction and savaged the Chancellor.* VERB / be V-ed / V n

**sav|age|ry** /sævɪdʒri/ **Savagery** is extremely cruel and violent behaviour. ❑ *...the sheer savagery of war.* N-UNCOUNT

**sa|van|nah** /səvænə/ **(savannahs)** also **savanna**. A **savannah** is a large area of flat, grassy land, usually in Africa. N-VAR

**sa|vant** /sævᵊnt, AM sævɑːnt/ **(savants)** [1] A **savant** is a person of great learning or natural ability. [FORMAL] ❑ *The opinion of savants on the composition of the lunar surface.* N-COUNT [2] You can refer to someone as an **idiot savant** if they seem to be less intelligent than normal people but are unusually good at doing one particular thing. ❑ *...an idiot savant, an autistic with a gift for numbers.* N-COUNT

**save** /seɪv/ **(saves, saving, saved)** [1] If you **save** someone or something, you help them to avoid harm or to escape from a dangerous or unpleasant situation. ❑ *...a final attempt to save 40,000 jobs in Britain's troubled aero industry... A new machine no bigger than a 10p piece could help save babies from cot death... The national health system saved him from becoming a cripple.* ◆◆◇ VERB / V n / V n from n/-ing / V n from n/-ing ♦ **-saving** *His boxing career was ended after two sight-saving operations.* COMB in ADJ [2] If you **save**, you gradually collect money by spending less than you get, usually in order to buy something that you want. ❑ *The majority of people intend to save, but find that by the end of the month there is nothing left... Tim and Barbara are now saving for a house in the suburbs... They could not find any way to save money.* VERB / V / V for n / V n ♦ **Save up** means the same as **save**. ❑ *Julie wanted to put some of her money aside for holidays or save up for something special... People often put money aside in order to save up enough to make one major expenditure.* PHRASAL VERB / V P for n / V P n [3] If you **save** something such as time or money, you prevent the loss or waste of it. ❑ *It saves time in the kitchen to have things you use a lot within reach... I'll try to save him the expense of a flight from Perth... I* VERB ≠ waste / V n / V n n / V on n

*got the fishmonger to skin the fish which helped save on the preparation time.* ♦ **-saving** *...labor-saving devices.* COMB in ADJ [4] If you **save** something, you keep it because it will be needed later. ❑ *Drain the beans thoroughly and save the stock for soup.* VERB V n [5] If someone or something **saves** you **from** an unpleasant action or experience, they change the situation so that you do not have to do it or experience it. ❑ *The scanner will save risk and pain for patients... She was hoping that something might save her from having to make a decision... He arranges to collect the payment from the customer, thus saving the client the paperwork.* VERB V n V n *from* n/-ing V n n [6] If you **save** data in a computer, you give the computer an instruction to store the data on a tape or disk. [COMPUTING] ❑ *Try to get into the habit of saving your work regularly... Import your scanned images from the scanner and save as a JPG file.* VERB V n V *as* n [7] If a goalkeeper **saves**, or **saves** a shot, they succeed in preventing the ball from going into the goal. ❑ *He saved one shot when the ball hit him on the head.* ♦ **Save** is also a noun. ❑ *Spurs could have had several goals but for some brilliant saves from John Hallworth.* VERB V n N-COUNT [8] You can use **save** to introduce the only things, people, or ideas that your main statement does not apply to. [FORMAL] ❑ *There is almost no water at all in Mochudi save that brought up from bore holes.* ● **Save for** means the same as **save**. ❑ *The parking lot was virtually empty save for a few cars clustered to one side.* PREP = apart from PREP-PHRASE = apart from [9] to **save the day** → see **day**. to **save face** → see **face**.
♦ **save up** → see **save 2**.

**sav|er** /seɪvəʳ/ **(savers)** A **saver** is a person who regularly saves money by paying it into a bank account or a building society. ❑ *Low interest rates are bad news for savers.* N-COUNT

**-saver** /-seɪvəʳ/ **(-savers) -saver** combines with words such as 'time' and 'energy' to indicate that something prevents the thing mentioned from being wasted. ❑ *These zip-top bags are great space-savers if storage is limited.* COMB in N-COUNT ≠ -waster

**sav|ing** /seɪvɪŋ/ **(savings)** [1] A **saving** is a reduction in the amount of time or money that is used or needed. ❑ *Fill in the form below and you will be making a saving of £6.60 on a one-year subscription.* ◆◇◇ N-COUNT: usu with supp [2] Your **savings** are the money that you have saved, especially in a bank or a building society. ❑ *Her savings were in the Post Office Savings Bank.* N-PLURAL

**sav|ing grace** **(saving graces)** A **saving grace** is a good quality or feature in a person or thing that prevents them from being completely bad or worthless. ❑ *Ageing's one saving grace is you worry less about what people think.* N-COUNT: with supp

**sav|ings and loan** also **savings and loans.** A **savings and loan** association is a business where people save money to earn interest, and which lends money to savers to buy houses. Compare **building society**. [mainly AM, BUSINESS] N-SING: usu N n

**sav|iour** /seɪvjəʳ/ **(saviours)**

✔ in AM, use **savior**

A **saviour** is a person who saves someone or something from danger, ruin, or defeat. ❑ *...the saviour of his country.* N-COUNT: oft N *of* n

**savoir-faire** /sævwɑːʳ feəʳ/ **Savoir-faire** is the confidence and ability to do the appropriate thing in a social situation. [FORMAL] ❑ *He was full of jocularity and savoir-faire.* N-UNCOUNT

**sa|vour** /seɪvəʳ/ **(savours, savouring, savoured)**

✔ in AM, use **savor**

[1] If you **savour** an experience, you enjoy it as much as you can. ❑ *She savored her newfound freedom.* VERB V n [2] If you **savour** food or drink, you eat or drink it slowly in order to taste its full flavour and to enjoy it properly. ❑ *Savour the flavour of each mouthful, and chew your food well.* VERB V n

**sa|voury** /seɪvəri/ **(savouries)**

✔ in AM, use **savory**

[1] **Savoury** food has a salty or spicy flavour rather than a sweet one. ❑ *Italian cooking is best known for savoury dishes.* ADJ: usu ADJ n [2] **Savouries** are small items of savoury food that are usually eaten as a snack, for example with alcoholic drinks at a party or before a meal. [BRIT] N-COUNT: usu pl

**sav|vy** /sævi/ If you describe someone as having **savvy**, you think that they have a good understanding and practical knowledge of something. [INFORMAL] ❑ *He is known for his political savvy and strong management skills.* N-UNCOUNT: oft supp N

**saw** /sɔː/ **(saws, sawing, sawed, sawn)** [1] **Saw** is the past tense of **see**. [2] A **saw** is a tool for cutting wood, which has a blade with sharp teeth along one edge. Some saws are pushed backwards and forwards by hand, and others are powered by electricity. → See picture on page 1709. → See also **chain saw**. N-COUNT [3] If you **saw** something, you cut it with a saw. ❑ *He escaped by sawing through the bars of his cell... Your father is sawing wood.* VERB V prep/adv V n

**saw|dust** /sɔːdʌst/ **Sawdust** is dust and very small pieces of wood which are produced when you saw wood. ❑ *...a layer of sawdust.* N-UNCOUNT

**sawed-off shot|gun** **(sawed-off shotguns)** A **sawed-off shotgun** is the same as a **sawn-off shotgun**. [AM] N-COUNT

**saw|mill** /sɔːmɪl/ **(sawmills)** A **sawmill** is a factory in which wood from trees is sawn into long flat pieces. N-COUNT

**sawn** /sɔːn/ **Sawn** is the past participle of **saw**.

**sawn-off shot|gun** **(sawn-off shotguns)** A **sawn-off shotgun** is a shotgun on which the barrel has been cut short. Guns like this are often used by criminals because they can be easily hidden. [BRIT] ❑ *The men burst in wearing balaclavas and brandishing sawn-off shotguns.* N-COUNT

✔ in AM, use **sawed-off shotgun**

**sax** /sæks/ **(saxes)** A **sax** is the same as a **saxophone**. [INFORMAL] N-COUNT: oft *the* N

**Sax|on** /sæksᵊn/ **(Saxons)** [1] In former times, **Saxons** were members of a West Germanic tribe. Some members of this tribe settled in Britain and were known as **Anglo-Saxons**. N-COUNT [2] Something that is **Saxon** is related to or characteristic of the ancient Saxons, the Anglo-Saxons, or their descendants. ❑ *...a seventh-century Saxon church.* ADJ

**saxo|phone** /sæksəfoʊn/ **(saxophones)** A **saxophone** is a musical instrument in the shape of a curved metal tube with a narrower part that you blow into and keys that you press. N-VAR: oft *the* N

**sax|opho|nist** /sæksɒfənɪst, AM sæksəfoʊn-/ **(saxophonists)** A **saxophonist** is someone who plays the saxophone. N-COUNT

**say** /seɪ/ **(says** /sez/, **saying, said** /sed/**)** ◆◆◆ [1] When you **say** something, you speak words. ❑ *'I'm sorry,' he said... She said they were very impressed... Forty-one people are said to have been seriously hurt... I packed and said goodbye to Charlie... I hope you didn't say anything about Gretchen... Did he say where he was going?... It doesn't sound exactly orthodox, if I may say so.* VERB V with quote V that *be* V-ed to-inf V n *to* n V n V wh V *so* [2] You use **say** in expressions such as **I would just like to say** to introduce what you are actually saying, or to indicate that you are expressing an opinion or admitting a fact. If you state that you **can't say** something or you **wouldn't say** something, you are indicating in a polite or indirect way that it is not the case. ❑ *I would just like to say that this is the most hypocritical thing I have ever heard in my life... I must say that rather shocked me, too... Dead? Well, I can't say I'm sorry.* VERB V that V that V that [3] You can mention the contents of a piece of writing by mentioning what it **says** or what someone **says** in it. ❑ *The report says there is widespread and routine torture of political prisoners in the country... You can't have one without the other, as the song says... 'Highly inflammable,' it says on the spare canister... Jung believed that God speaks to us in dreams. The Bible says so too.* VERB V that V with quote *it* V with quote V *so* [4] If you **say** something **to yourself**, you think it. ❑ *Perhaps I'm still dreaming, I said to myself.* VERB V *to* pron-refl with quote

5 If you have **a say in** something, you have the right to give your opinion and influence decisions relating to it. ❑ *The students wanted more say in the government of the university.* 6 You indicate the information given by something such as a clock, dial, or map by mentioning what it **says**. ❑ *The clock said four minutes past eleven... The map says there's six of them.* 7 If something **says** something **about** a person, situation, or thing, it gives important information about them. ❑ *I think that says a lot about how well Seles is playing... The appearance of the place and the building says something about the importance of the project.* 8 If something **says** a lot **for** a person or thing, it shows that this person or thing is very good or has a lot of good qualities. ❑ *It says a lot for him that he has raised his game to the level required... It says much for Brookner's skill that the book is sad, but never depressing.* 9 You use **say** in expressions such as **I'll say that for them** and **you can say this for them** after or before you mention a good quality that someone has, usually when you think they do not have many good qualities. ❑ *He's usually smartly-dressed, I'll say that for him... At the very least, he is devastatingly sure of himself, you can say that.* 10 You can use **say** when you want to discuss something that might possibly happen or be true. ❑ *Say you could change anything about the world we live in, what would it be?* 11 You can use **say** or **let's say** when you mention something as an example. ❑ *To see the problem here more clearly, let's look at a different biological system, say, an acorn.*

N-SING: usu *a* N, also *more/some* N; VERB; V n; V that; VERB; V amount *about* n; V pron *about* n; VERB; V amount *for* n; *it* V amount *for* n that; VERB; V pron *for* n; V pron; VERB: only imper = *suppose* V that

**PHRASES** 12 If you say that something **says it all**, you mean that it shows you very clearly the truth about a situation or someone's feelings. ❑ *This is my third visit in a week, which says it all.* 13 You can use **'You don't say'** to express surprise at what someone has told you. People often use this expression to indicate that in fact they are not surprised. ❑ *'I'm a writer.' — 'You don't say. What kind of book are you writing?'* 14 If you say there is a lot **to be said for** something, you mean you think it has a lot of good qualities or aspects. ❑ *There's a lot to be said for being based in the country.* 15 If someone asks **what** you **have to say for yourself**, they are asking what excuse you have for what you have done. ❑ *'Well,' she said eventually, 'what have you to say for yourself?'* 16 If something **goes without saying**, it is obvious. ❑ *It goes without saying that if someone has lung problems they should not smoke.* 17 When one of the people or groups involved in a discussion **has** their **say**, they give their opinion. ❑ *The Football Association have had their say.* 18 You use **'I wouldn't say no'** to indicate that you would like something, especially something that has just been offered to you. [INFORMAL] ❑ *I wouldn't say no to a drink.* 19 You use **to say nothing of** when you mention an additional thing which gives even more strength to the point you are making. ❑ *Unemployment leads to a sense of uselessness, to say nothing of financial problems.* 20 You use **that is to say** or **that's to say** to indicate that you are about to express the same idea more clearly or precisely. [FORMAL] ❑ *...territories that were occupied in 1967, that is to say, in the West Bank and Gaza.* 21 You can use **'You can say that again'** to express strong agreement with what someone has just said. [INFORMAL] ❑ *'Must have been a fiddly job.' — 'You can say that again.'* 22 **to say the least** → see **least**. **needless to say** → see **needless**.

PHRASE: V inflects; CONVENTION [feelings]; PHRASE: amount PHR; PHRASE; PHRASE: oft *it* PHR that; PHRASE: V inflects; CONVENTION [formulae]; PHRASE: PHR n; PHRASE: PHR with cl/group; CONVENTION [emphasis]

**say|ing** /seɪɪŋ/ **(sayings)** 1 A **saying** is a sentence that people often say and that gives advice or information about human life and experience. ❑ *We also realize the truth of that old saying: Charity begins at home.* 2 The **sayings** of a person, especially a religious or political leader, are important things that they said or pieces of advice that they gave. ❑ *The sayings of Confucius offer guidance on this matter.*

N-COUNT; N-COUNT: usu pl

**say-so** If you do something on someone's **say-so**, they tell you to do it or they give you permission to do it. [INFORMAL] ❑ *Directors call the shots and nothing happens on set without their say-so.*

N-SING: oft with poss

**scab** /skæb/ **(scabs)** 1 A **scab** is a hard, dry covering that forms over the surface of a wound. ❑ *The area can be very painful until scabs form after about ten days.* 2 People who continue to work during a strike are called **scabs** by the people who are on strike. ❑ *He hired scabs to replace strikers.* ♦ **Scab** is also an adjective. ❑ *The mill was started up with scab labor.*

N-COUNT; N-COUNT [disapproval]; ADJ: ADJ n

**scab|bard** /skæbəʳd/ **(scabbards)** A **scabbard** is a container for a sword and can hang from a belt.

N-COUNT

**scab|by** /skæbi/ If a person, an animal, or a part of their body is **scabby**, it has scabs on it. ❑ *He had short trousers and scabby knees.*

ADJ

**sca|bies** /skeɪbiːz/ **Scabies** is a very infectious skin disease caused by very small creatures and makes you want to scratch a lot.

N-UNCOUNT

**sca|brous** /skeɪbrəs, skæb-/ If you describe something as **scabrous**, you mean that it deals with sex or describes sex in a shocking way. [LITERARY] ❑ *...the scabrous lower reaches of the film business.*

ADJ [disapproval]

**scaf|fold** /skæfould/ **(scaffolds)** 1 A **scaffold** was a raised platform on which criminals were hanged or had their heads cut off. ❑ *Moore ascended the scaffold and addressed the executioner.* 2 A **scaffold** is a temporary raised platform on which workers stand to paint, repair, or build high parts of a building.

N-COUNT; N-COUNT

**scaf|fold|ing** /skæfəldɪŋ/ **Scaffolding** consists of poles and boards made into a temporary framework that is used by workers when they are painting, repairing, or building high parts of a building, usually outside.

N-UNCOUNT

**scald** /skɔːld/ **(scalds, scalding, scalded)** 1 If you **scald yourself**, you burn yourself with very hot liquid or steam. ❑ *A patient scalded herself in a hot bath. ...a child with a scalded hand.* 2 A **scald** is a burn caused by very hot liquid or steam.

VERB; V n; V-ed; N-COUNT

**scald|ing** /skɔːldɪŋ/ **Scalding** or **scalding hot** liquids are extremely hot. ❑ *I tried to sip the tea but it was scalding. ...scalding hot water.*

ADJ

**scale** /skeɪl/ **(scales, scaling, scaled)** 1 If you refer to the **scale** of something, you are referring to its size or extent, especially when it is very big. ❑ *However, he underestimates the scale of the problem... The break-down of law and order could result in killing on a massive scale.* → See also **full-scale**, **large-scale**, **small-scale**. 2 A **scale** is a set of levels or numbers which are used in a particular system of measuring things or are used when comparing things. ❑ *...an earthquake measuring five-point-five on the Richter scale... The higher up the social scale they are, the more the men have to lose.* → See also **sliding scale**, **timescale**. 3 A pay **scale** or **scale of** fees is a list that shows how much someone should be paid, depending, for example, on their age or what work they do. [BRIT] ❑ *...those on the high end of the pay scale.* 4 The **scale** of a map, plan, or model is the relationship between the size of something in the map, plan, or model and its size in the real world. ❑ *The map, on a scale of 1:10,000, shows over 5,000 individual paths.* → See also **full-scale**, **large-scale**. 5 A **scale** model or **scale** replica of a building or object is a model of it which is smaller than the real thing but has all the same parts and features. ❑ *Franklin made his mother an intricately detailed scale model of the house.* 6 In music, a **scale** is a fixed sequence of musical notes, each one higher than the next, which begins at a particular note. ❑ *...the scale of C major.* 7 The **scales** of a fish or reptile are the small, flat pieces of hard skin that cover its body. 8 **Scales** are a piece of equipment used for weighing things, for example for weighing amounts of food that you need in order

◆◆◇ N-SING: also no det, with supp; N-COUNT: usu with supp; N-COUNT: usu with supp; N-COUNT: usu with supp; ADJ: ADJ n; N-COUNT; N-COUNT: usu pl; N-PLURAL: also *a pair of* N

to make a particular meal. ❑ *...a pair of kitchen scales. ...bathroom scales.* 9 If you **scale** something such as a mountain or a wall, you climb up it or over it. [WRITTEN] ❑ *...Rebecca Stephens, the first British woman to scale Everest.* [VERB = climb] [V n]

**PHRASES** 10 If something is **out of scale with** the things near it, it is too big or too small in relation to them. ❑ *The tower was surmounted by an enormous statue, utterly out of scale with the building.* [PHRASE: usu v-link PHR, oft PHR *with* n]

11 If the different parts of a map, drawing, or model are **to scale**, they are the right size in relation to each other. ❑ *...a miniature garden, with little pagodas and bridges all to scale.* [PHRASE: v-link PHR, PHR after v]

♦ **scale back** To **scale back** means the same as to **scale down**. [mainly AM] ❑ *Despite current price advantage, UK manufacturers are still having to scale back production.* [PHRASAL VERB = reduce] [V P n (not pron)] [Also V n P]

♦ **scale down** If you **scale down** something, you make it smaller in size, amount, or extent than it used to be. ❑ *One Peking factory has had to scale down its workforce from six hundred to only six... The Romanian government yesterday unveiled a new, scaled-down security force.* [PHRASAL VERB = reduce] [V P n (not pron)] [V-ed P]

♦ **scale up** If you **scale up** something, you make it greater in size, amount, or extent than it used to be. ❑ *Since then, Wellcome has been scaling up production to prepare for clinical trials.* [PHRASAL VERB = increase] [V P n (not pron)] [Also V n P]

**scal|lion** /skæljən/ **(scallions)** A **scallion** is a small onion with long green leaves. [AM] [N-COUNT]

☑ in BRIT, use **spring onion**

**scal|lop** /skɒləp, skæl-/ **(scallops)** **Scallops** are large shellfish with two flat fan-shaped shells. Scallops can be eaten. [N-COUNT: usu pl]

**scal|loped** /skɒləpt, skæl-/ **Scalloped** objects are decorated with a series of small curves along the edges. ❑ *The quilt has pretty, scalloped edges and intricate quilting.* [ADJ: usu ADJ n]

**scal|ly|wag** /skæliwæg/ **(scallywags)** If you call a boy or a man a **scallywag**, you mean that he behaves badly but you like him, so you find it difficult to be really angry with him. [INFORMAL, OLD-FASHIONED] ❑ *It's his idea of a joke, I suppose, the scallywag.* [N-COUNT = rascal]

**scalp** /skælp/ **(scalps, scalping, scalped)** 1 Your **scalp** is the skin under the hair on your head. ❑ *He smoothed his hair back over his scalp.* [N-COUNT: usu sing] 2 To **scalp** someone means to remove the skin and hair from the top of their head. ❑ *He pretended to scalp me with his sword.* [VERB] [V n] 3 A **scalp** is the piece of skin and hair that is removed when someone is scalped. [N-COUNT] 4 If someone **scalps** tickets, they sell them outside a sports ground or theatre, usually for more than their original value. [AM] ❑ *He was trying to pick up some cash scalping tickets.* [VERB] [V n]

☑ in BRIT, use **tout**

**scal|pel** /skælpəl/ **(scalpels)** A **scalpel** is a knife with a short, thin, sharp blade. Scalpels are used by surgeons during operations. [N-COUNT]

**scalp|er** /skælpəʳ/ **(scalpers)** A **scalper** is someone who sells tickets outside a sports ground or theatre, usually for more than their original value. [AM] ❑ *Another scalper said he'd charge $1000 for a $125 ticket.* [N-COUNT]

☑ in BRIT, use **tout**

**scaly** /skeɪli/ 1 A **scaly** animal has small pieces of hard skin covering its body. ❑ *The brown rat has prominent ears and a long scaly tail.* [ADJ: usu ADJ n] 2 If someone's skin is **scaly**, it has dry areas and small pieces of it come off. ❑ *If your skin becomes red, sore or very scaly, consult your doctor.* [ADJ]

**scam** /skæm/ **(scams)** A **scam** is an illegal trick, usually with the purpose of getting money from people or avoiding paying tax. [INFORMAL] ❑ *They believed they were participating in an insurance scam, not a murder.* [N-COUNT = swindle]

**scamp** /skæmp/ **(scamps)** If you call a boy a **scamp**, you mean that he is naughty or disrespectful but you like him, so you find it difficult to be angry with him. [INFORMAL] ❑ *Have some respect for me, you scamp!* [N-COUNT = rascal]

**scamp|er** /skæmpəʳ/ **(scampers, scampering, scampered)** When people or small animals **scamper** somewhere, they move there quickly with small, light steps. ❑ *Children scampered off the yellow school bus and into the playground.* [VERB] [V prep/adv]

**scam|pi** /skæmpi/ **Scampi** are large prawns, often served fried in breadcrumbs. [mainly BRIT] [N-UNCOUNT]

**scan** /skæn/ **(scans, scanning, scanned)** 1 When you **scan** written material, you look through it quickly in order to find important or interesting information. ❑ *She scanned the advertisement pages of the newspapers... I haven't read much into it as yet. I've only just scanned through it.* [VERB] [V n] [V *through* n] ♦ **Scan** is also a noun. ❑ *I just had a quick scan through your book again.* [N-SING] 2 When you **scan** a place or group of people, you look at it carefully, usually because you are looking for something or someone. ❑ *The officer scanned the room... She was nervous and kept scanning the crowd for Paul... He raised the binoculars to his eye again, scanning across the scene.* [VERB: no passive] [V n] [V n *for* n] [V prep] 3 If people **scan** something such as luggage, they examine it using a machine that can show or find things inside it that cannot be seen from the outside. ❑ *Their approach is to scan every checked-in bag with a bomb detector.* [VERB] [V n] ♦ **scan|ning** *...routine scanning of luggage.* [N-UNCOUNT] 4 If a computer disk **is scanned**, a program on the computer checks the disk to make sure that it does not contain a virus. [COMPUTING] ❑ *The disk has no viruses – I've scanned it already.* [VERB] [V n] 5 If a picture or document **is scanned** into a computer, a machine passes a beam of light over it to make a copy of it in the computer. [COMPUTING] ❑ *The entire paper contents of all libraries will eventually be scanned into computers... Designs can also be scanned in from paper.* [VERB: usu passive] [*be* V-ed *into/onto* n] [*be* V-ed *in/on*] 6 If a radar or sonar machine **scans** an area, it examines or searches it by sending radar or sonar beams over it. ❑ *The ship's radar scanned the sea ahead.* [VERB] [V n] 7 A **scan** is a medical test in which a machine sends a beam of X-rays over a part of your body in order to check that it is healthy. ❑ *He was rushed to hospital for a brain scan.* [N-COUNT: usu with supp] 8 If a pregnant woman has a **scan**, a machine using sound waves produces an image of her womb on a screen so that a doctor can see if her baby is developing normally. [N-COUNT] 9 If a line of a poem does not **scan**, it is not the right length or does not have emphasis in the right places to match the rest of the poem. ❑ *He had written a few poems. Sid told him they didn't scan.* [VERB: usu with brd-neg] [V]

**scan|dal** /skændəl/ **(scandals)** 1 A **scandal** is a situation or event that is thought to be shocking and immoral and that everyone knows about. ❑ *...a financial scandal.* [◆◇◇] [N-COUNT: usu with supp] 2 **Scandal** is talk about the shocking and immoral aspects of someone's behaviour or something that has happened. ❑ *He loved gossip and scandal.* [N-UNCOUNT] 3 If you say that something is a **scandal**, you are angry about it and think that the people responsible for it should be ashamed. ❑ *It is a scandal that a person can be stopped for no reason by the police.* [N-SING: oft N that] [disapproval] [= disgrace]

**scan|dal|ize** /skændəlaɪz/ **(scandalizes, scandalizing, scandalized)**

☑ in BRIT, also use **scandalise**

If something **scandalizes** people, they are shocked or offended by it. ❑ *She scandalised her family by falling in love with a married man.* [VERB] [V n]

**scan|dal|ous** /skændələs/ 1 **Scandalous** behaviour or activity is considered immoral and shocking. ❑ *He spoke of scandalous corruption and incompetence.* [ADJ: usu ADJ n] ♦ **scan|dal|ous|ly** *He asked only that Ingrid stop behaving so scandalously.* [ADV: ADV with v] 2 **Scandalous** stories or remarks are concerned with the immoral and shocking aspects of someone's behaviour or something that has happened. ❑ *Newspaper columns were full of scandalous tales.* [ADJ: usu ADJ n] 3 You can describe something as **scandalous** if it makes you very angry and you think the [ADJ] [disapproval] [= disgraceful] people responsible for it should be ashamed. ❑ *It is absolutely scandalous that a fantastic building like this is just left to rot away. ...a scandalous waste of money.*

**scan|dal sheet** **(scandal sheets)** N-COUNT You can refer to newspapers and magazines which print mainly stories about sex and crime as **scandal sheets**. [AM]

in BRIT, use **gutter press**

**Scan|di|na|vian** /skændɪneɪviən/ **(Scandinavians)** 1 ADJ **Scandinavian** means belonging or relating to a group of northern European countries that includes Denmark, Norway, and Sweden, or to the people, languages, or culture of those countries. ❑ *The Baltic republics have called on the Scandinavian countries for help.* 2 N-COUNT **Scandinavians** are people from Scandinavian countries.

**scan|ner** /skænəʳ/ **(scanners)** 1 N-COUNT A **scanner** is a machine which is used to examine, identify, or record things, for example by using a beam of light, sound, or X-rays. ❑ *...brain scanners. ...a security scanner that can see through clothes.* 2 N-COUNT A **scanner** is a piece of computer equipment that you use for copying a picture or document onto a computer. [COMPUTING]

**scant** /skænt/ 1 ADJ: usu ADJ n You use **scant** to indicate that there is very little of something or not as much of something as there should be. ❑ *She began to berate the police for paying scant attention to the theft from her car.* 2 ADJ: a ADJ amount [emphasis] = mere If you describe an amount as **scant**, you are emphasizing that it is small. ❑ *This hole was a scant .23 inches in diameter.*

**scanty** /skænti/ **(scantier, scantiest)** 1 ADJ You describe something as **scanty** when there is less of it than you think there should be. ❑ *So far, what scanty evidence we have points to two suspects.* 2 ADJ If someone is wearing **scanty** clothing, he or she is wearing clothes which are sexually revealing. ❑ *...a model in scanty clothing.* ♦ **scanti|ly** ADV: ADV -ed/adj *...a troupe of scantily-clad dancers.*

**scape|goat** /skeɪpgoʊt/ **(scapegoats, scapegoating, scapegoated)** 1 N-COUNT: oft N *for* n If you say that someone is made a **scapegoat for** something bad that has happened, you mean that people blame them and may punish them for it although it may not be their fault. ❑ *I don't deserve to be made the scapegoat for a couple of bad results.* 2 VERB To **scapegoat** someone means to blame them publicly for something bad that has happened, even though it was not their fault. ❑ V n *Ethnic minorities are continually scapegoated for the lack of jobs.*

**scapu|la** /skæpjʊlə/ **(scapulae)** N-COUNT Your **scapula** is your shoulder blade. [MEDICAL]

**scar** /skɑːʳ/ **(scars, scarring, scarred)** 1 N-COUNT A **scar** is a mark on the skin which is left after a wound has healed. ❑ *He had a scar on his forehead. ...facial injuries which have left permanent scars.* 2 VERB: usu passive If your skin **is scarred**, it is badly marked as a result of a wound. ❑ be V-ed *He was scarred for life during a pub fight...* V-ed *His scarred face crumpled with pleasure.* 3 VERB: usu passive If a surface **is scarred**, it is damaged and there are ugly marks on it. ❑ be V-ed *The arena was scarred by deep muddy ruts.* V-ed *...scarred wooden table tops.* 4 N-COUNT If an unpleasant physical or emotional experience leaves a **scar** on someone, it has a permanent effect on their mind. ❑ *The early years of fear and the hostility left a deep scar on the young boy.* 5 VERB If an unpleasant physical or emotional experience **scars** you, it has a permanent effect on your mind. ❑ V n *This is something that's going to scar him forever.*

**scarce** /skeəʳs/ **(scarcer, scarcest)** 1 ADJ: usu v-link ADJ If something is **scarce**, there is not enough of it. ❑ *Food was scarce and expensive. ...the allocation of scarce resources.* 2 PHRASE: V inflects If you **make yourself scarce**, you quickly leave the place you are in, usually in order to avoid a difficult or embarrassing situation. [INFORMAL] ❑ *It probably would be a good idea if you made yourself scarce.*

**scarce|ly** /skeəʳsli/ 1 ADV: ADV before v, ADV group, oft ADV amount [emphasis] You use **scarcely** to emphasize that something is only just true or only just the case. ❑ *He could scarcely breathe... I scarcely knew him... He was scarcely more than a boy.* 2 ADV: ADV before v, ADV group You can use **scarcely** to say that something is not true or is not the case, in a humorous or critical way. ❑ *It can scarcely be coincidence.* 3 ADV: ADV before v If you say **scarcely had** one thing happened when something else happened, you mean that the first event was followed immediately by the second. ❑ *Scarcely had they left before soldiers arrived armed with rifles.*

**scar|city** /skeəʳsɪti/ **(scarcities)** N-VAR = shortage If there is a **scarcity of** something, there is not enough of it for the people who need it or want it. [FORMAL] ❑ *...an ever increasing scarcity of water.*

**scare** /skeəʳ/ **(scares, scaring, scared)** 1 VERB = frighten If something **scares** you, it frightens or worries you. ❑ V n *You're scaring me...* V n adj *The prospect of failure scares me rigid...* it V n to-inf *It scared him to realise how close he had come to losing everything.* ● PHRASE: V inflects [emphasis] If you want to emphasize that something scares you a lot, you can say that it **scares the hell out of** you or **scares the life out of** you. [INFORMAL] 2 N-SING If a sudden unpleasant experience gives you a **scare**, it frightens you. ❑ *Don't you realize what a scare you've given us all?... We got a bit of a scare.* 3 N-COUNT: oft n N A **scare** is a situation in which many people are afraid or worried because they think something dangerous is happening which will affect them all. ❑ *...the doctor at the centre of an Aids scare.* 4 N-COUNT: usu n N = alert A bomb **scare** or a security **scare** is a situation in which there is believed to be a bomb in a place. ❑ *Despite many recent bomb scares, no one has yet been hurt.* 5 → See also **scared**.

♦ **scare away** → see **scare off 1**.

♦ **scare off** PHRASAL VERB 1 If you **scare off** or **scare away** a person or animal, you frighten them so that they go away. ❑ V P n (not pron) *...an alarm to scare off an attacker.* V n P *...the problem of scaring birds away from airport runways.* 2 PHRASAL VERB = put off If you **scare** someone **off**, you accidentally make them unwilling to become involved with you. ❑ V n P *I don't think that revealing your past to your boyfriend scared him off...* V P n (not pron) *The new Democratic Party is not likely to scare off voters.*

♦ **scare up** PHRASAL VERB If you **scare up** something, you provide, produce, or obtain it, often when it is difficult to do so or when you do not have many resources. [mainly AM, INFORMAL] ❑ V P n (not pron) *An all-star game might scare up a little interest.*

**scare|crow** /skeəʳkroʊ/ **(scarecrows)** N-COUNT A **scarecrow** is an object in the shape of a person, which is put in a field where crops are growing in order to frighten birds away.

**scared** /skeəʳd/ 1 ADJ: usu v-link ADJ, oft ADJ *of* n, ADJ to-inf = frightened If you are **scared of** someone or something, you are frightened of them. ❑ *I'm certainly not scared of him... I was too scared to move... Why are you so scared?* 2 ADJ: usu v-link ADJ, oft ADJ that, ADJ *of* -ing = worried If you are **scared that** something unpleasant might happen, you are nervous and worried because you think that it might happen. ❑ *I was scared that I might be sick... He was scared of letting us down.*

**scare|monger|ing** /skeəʳmʌŋgərɪŋ/ N-UNCOUNT If one person or group accuses another person or group of **scaremongering**, they accuse them of deliberately spreading worrying stories to try and frighten people. ❑ *The Government yesterday accused Greenpeace of scaremongering.*

**scare sto|ry** **(scare stories)** N-COUNT A **scare story** is something that is said or written to make people feel frightened and think that a situation is much more unpleasant or dangerous than it really is. ❑ *He described talk of sackings as scare stories.*

**scarf** /skɑːʳf/ **(scarfs** or **scarves)** N-COUNT A **scarf** is a piece of cloth that you wear round your neck or head, usually to keep yourself warm. ❑ *He reached up to loosen the scarf around his neck.*

**scar|let** /skɑːʳlət/ **(scarlets)** COLOUR Something that is **scarlet** is bright red. ❑ *...her scarlet lipstick.*

**scar|let fe|ver** Scarlet fever is an infectious disease which gives you a painful throat, a high temperature, and red spots on your skin. N-UNCOUNT

**scarp|er** /skɑːʳpəʳ/ **(scarpers, scarpering, scarpered)** If someone **scarpers**, they leave a place quickly. [BRIT, INFORMAL] ❑ *He owed Vince money for drugs, so he scarpered.* VERB V

**-scarred** /-skɑːʳd/ [1] **-scarred** is used after nouns such as 'bullet' and 'fire' to form adjectives which indicate that something has been damaged or marked by the thing mentioned. ❑ *...a bullet-scarred bus. ...a lightning-scarred tree.* COMB in ADJ: ADJ n [2] **-scarred** is used after nouns such as 'battle' or 'drug' to form adjectives which indicate that the thing mentioned has had a permanent effect on someone's mind. ❑ *...battle-scarred soldiers.* COMB in ADJ: usu ADJ n [3] → See also **scar**.

**scarves** /skɑːʳvz/ **Scarves** is a plural of **scarf**.

**scary** /skeəri/ **(scarier, scariest)** Something that is **scary** is rather frightening. [INFORMAL] ❑ *I think prison is going to be a scary thing for Harry... There's something very scary about him.* ADJ ♦ **scari|ly** /skeərɪli/ *...the scarily unstable new world order.* ADV: usu ADV adj

**scat** /skæt/ **Scat** is a type of jazz singing in which the singer sings sounds rather than complete words. N-UNCOUNT

**scath|ing** /skeɪðɪŋ/ If you say that someone is being **scathing** about something, you mean that they are being very critical of it. ❑ *His report was scathing about Loyalist and Republican terror groups.* ADJ

**scato|logi|cal** /skætəlɒdʒɪkəl/ If you describe something as **scatological**, you mean that it deliberately refers to or represents faeces in some way. [FORMAL] ❑ *...scatological anecdotes.* ADJ: usu ADJ n

**scat|ter** /skætəʳ/ **(scatters, scattering, scattered)** [1] If you **scatter** things over an area, you throw or drop them so that they spread all over the area. ❑ *She tore the rose apart and scattered the petals over the grave... He began by scattering seed and putting in plants.* VERB V n prep/adv V n [2] If a group of people **scatter** or if you **scatter** them, they suddenly separate and move in different directions. ❑ *After dinner, everyone scattered... The cavalry scattered them and chased them off the field.* VERB V V n [3] → See also **scattered**, **scattering**.

**scatter|brained** /skætəʳbreɪnd/ also **scatter-brained**. If you describe someone as **scatterbrained**, you mean that they often forget things and are unable to organize their thoughts properly. ADJ

**scat|ter cush|ion** **(scatter cushions)** **Scatter cushions** are small cushions for use on sofas and chairs. N-COUNT: usu pl

**scat|tered** /skætəʳd/ [1] **Scattered** things are spread over an area in an untidy or irregular way. ❑ *He picked up the scattered toys... The fridge door was open and food was scattered across the floor.* ADJ: ADJ n, v-link ADJ prep/adv [2] If something is **scattered with** a lot of small things, they are spread all over it. ❑ *Every surface is scattered with photographs.* ADJ: v-link ADJ *with* n

**scatter|gun** /skætəʳgʌn/ **(scatterguns)** also **scatter-gun**. [1] A **scattergun** is a gun that fires a lot of small metal balls at the same time. [AM] N-COUNT = shotgun [2] **Scattergun** means the same as **scattershot**. ❑ *They advocated a scattergun approach of posting dozens of letters.* ADJ: ADJ n

**scat|ter|ing** /skætərɪŋ/ **(scatterings)** A **scattering of** things or people is a small number of them spread over an area. ❑ *...the scattering of houses east of the village.* N-COUNT: usu N *of* n

**scatter|shot** /skætəʳʃɒt/ A **scattershot** approach or method involves doing something to a lot of things or people in disorganized way, rather than focusing on particular things or people. ❑ *The report condemns America's scattershot approach to training workers.* ADJ: usu ADJ n

**scat|ty** /skæti/ If you describe someone as **scatty**, you mean that they often forget things or behave in a silly way. [BRIT, INFORMAL] ❑ *Her mother is scatty and absent-minded.* ADJ = scatter-brained

**scav|enge** /skævɪndʒ/ **(scavenges, scavenging, scavenged)** If people or animals **scavenge for** things, they collect them by searching among waste or unwanted objects. ❑ *Many are orphans, their parents killed as they scavenged for food... Children scavenge through garbage... Cruz had to scavenge information from newspapers and journals.* VERB V *for* n V prep/adv V n Also V ♦ **scav|en|ger** **(scavengers)** *...scavengers such as rats.* N-COUNT

**sce|nario** /sɪnɑːrioʊ, AM -ner-/ **(scenarios)** [1] If you talk about a likely or possible **scenario**, you are talking about the way in which a situation may develop. ❑ *...the nightmare scenario of a divided and irrelevant Royal Family.* N-COUNT [2] The **scenario** of a film is a piece of writing that gives an outline of the story. N-COUNT = outline

**scene** /siːn/ **(scenes)** ◆◆◇ [1] A **scene** in a play, film, or book is part of it in which a series of events happen in the same place. ❑ *I found the scene in which Percy proposed to Olive tremendously poignant. ...the opening scene of 'A Christmas Carol'.* N-COUNT [2] You refer to a place as a **scene** when you are describing its appearance and indicating what impression it makes on you. ❑ *It's a scene of complete devastation... Thick black smoke billowed over the scene.* N-COUNT: usu sing [3] You can describe an event that you see, or that is broadcast or shown in a picture, as a **scene** of a particular kind. ❑ *There were emotional scenes as the refugees enjoyed their first breath of freedom... Television broadcasters were warned to exercise caution over depicting scenes of violence.* N-COUNT: with supp [4] The **scene of** an event is the place where it happened. ❑ *The area has been the scene of fierce fighting for three months... Fire and police crews rushed to the scene, but the couple were already dead.* N-COUNT: usu sing, oft N *of* n [5] You can refer to an area of activity as a particular type of **scene**. ❑ *Sandman is a cult figure on the local music scene.* N-SING: supp N, usu *the* supp N [6] Paintings and drawings of places are sometimes called **scenes**. ❑ *...James Lynch's country scenes.* N-COUNT: usu with supp [7] If you make a **scene**, you embarrass people by publicly showing your anger about something. ❑ *I'm sorry I made such a scene.* N-COUNT: usu sing

PHRASES [8] If something is done **behind the scenes**, it is done secretly rather than publicly. ❑ *But behind the scenes Mr Cain will be working quietly to try to get a deal done.* PHRASE: PHR with cl, PHR n [9] If you refer to what happens **behind the scenes**, you are referring to what happens during the making of a film, play, or radio or television programme. ❑ *It's an exciting opportunity to learn what goes on behind the scenes.* PHRASE: PHR after v, PHR n [10] If you have **a change of scene**, you go somewhere different after being in a particular place for a long time. ❑ *What you need is a change of scene. Why not go on a cruise?* PHRASE: usu v PHR [11] If you **set the scene** for someone, you tell them what they need to know in order to understand what is going to happen or be said next. ❑ *But first to set the scene: I was having a drink with my ex-boyfriend.* PHRASE: V inflects [12] Something that **sets the scene for** a particular event creates the conditions in which the event is likely to happen. ❑ *Gillespie's goal set the scene for an exciting second half.* PHRASE: V inflects [13] When a person or thing appears **on the scene**, they come into being or become involved in something. When they disappear **from the scene**, they are no longer there or are no longer involved. ❑ *He could react rather jealously when and if another child comes on the scene.* PHRASE: usu v PHR

**scen|ery** /siːnəri/ [1] The **scenery** in a country area is the land, water, or plants that you can see around you. ❑ *Sometimes they just drive slowly down the lane enjoying the scenery.* N-UNCOUNT [2] In a theatre, the **scenery** consists of the structures and painted backgrounds that show where the action in the play takes place. N-UNCOUNT [3] If you have **a change of scenery**, you go somewhere different after being in a particular place for a long time. ❑ *A change of scenery might do you the power of good.* PHRASE

**sce|nic** /siːnɪk/ [1] A **scenic** place has attractive scenery. ❑ *This is an extremely scenic part of America.* [2] A **scenic** route goes through attractive scenery and has nice views. ❑ *It was even marked on the map as a scenic route.* ADJ: usu ADJ n; ADJ: usu ADJ n

**scent** /sent/ **(scents, scenting, scented)** [1] The **scent** of something is the pleasant smell that it has. ❑ *Flowers are chosen for their scent as well as their look.* N-COUNT: usu with supp = fragrance [2] If something **scents** a place or thing, it makes it smell pleasant. ❑ *Jasmine flowers scent the air... Scent your drawers and wardrobe with your favourite aromas.* VERB V n V n *with* n [3] **Scent** is a liquid which women put on their necks and wrists to make themselves smell nice. [BRIT] ❑ *She dabbed herself with scent.* N-MASS = perfume

✔ in AM, use **perfume**

[4] The **scent** of a person or animal is the smell that they leave and that other people sometimes follow when looking for them. ❑ *A police dog picked up the murderer's scent.* N-VAR: usu with supp [5] When an animal **scents** something, it becomes aware of it by smelling it. ❑ *...dogs which scent the hidden birds.* VERB: no cont = smell V n

**scent|ed** /sentɪd/ **Scented** things have a pleasant smell, either naturally or because perfume has been added to them. ❑ *The white flowers are pleasantly scented. ...scented body lotion.* ADJ

**scep|ter** /septəʳ/ **(scepters)** → see **sceptre**.

**scep|tic** /skeptɪk/ **(sceptics)**

✔ in AM, use **skeptic**

A **sceptic** is a person who has doubts about things that other people believe. ❑ *But he now has to convince sceptics that he has a serious plan.* N-COUNT

**scep|ti|cal** /skeptɪkəl/

✔ in AM, use **skeptical**

If you are **sceptical about** something, you have doubts about it. ❑ *Other archaeologists are sceptical about his findings.* ♦ **scep|ti|cal|ly** /skeptɪkli/ *I looked at him skeptically, sure he was exaggerating.* ADJ: oft v-link ADJ *about/of* n; ADV: ADV after v

**scep|ti|cism** /skeptɪsɪzəm/

✔ in AM, use **skepticism**

**Scepticism** is great doubt about whether something is true or useful. ❑ *There was considerable scepticism about the Chancellor's forecast of a booming economy.* N-UNCOUNT

**scep|tre** /septəʳ/ **(sceptres)**

✔ in AM, use **scepter**

A **sceptre** is an ornamental rod that a king or queen carries on ceremonial occasions as a symbol of his or her power. N-COUNT

**sched|ule** /ʃedjuːl, AM skedʒuːl/ **(schedules, scheduling, scheduled)** ◆◆◇ [1] A **schedule** is a plan that gives a list of events or tasks and the times at which each one should happen or be done. ❑ *He has been forced to adjust his schedule... We both have such hectic schedules.* N-COUNT = timetable [2] You can use **schedule** to refer to the time or way something is planned to be done. For example, if something is completed **on schedule**, it is completed at the time planned. ❑ *The jet arrived in Johannesburg two minutes ahead of schedule... Everything went according to schedule.* N-UNCOUNT: prep N [3] If something **is scheduled** to happen at a particular time, arrangements are made for it to happen at that time. ❑ *The space shuttle had been scheduled to blast off at 04:38... A presidential election was scheduled for last December... No new talks are scheduled.* VERB: usu passive *be* V-ed to-inf *be* V-ed *for* n V-ed [4] A **schedule** is a written list of things, for example a list of prices, details, or conditions. N-COUNT = list [5] A **schedule** is a list of all the times when trains, boats, buses, or aircraft are supposed to arrive at or leave a particular place. [mainly AM] ❑ *...a bus schedule.* N-COUNT

✔ in BRIT, usually use **timetable**

[6] In a school or college, a **schedule** is a diagram that shows the times in the week at which particular subjects are taught. [AM] N-COUNT

✔ in BRIT, usually use **timetable**

**sche|ma** /skiːmə/ **(schemas** or **schemata** /skiːmətə/**)** A **schema** is an outline of a plan or theory. [FORMAL] ❑ *...a definite position in the schema of the economic process.* N-COUNT = outline

**sche|mat|ic** /skiːmætɪk/ A **schematic** diagram or picture shows something in a simple way. ❑ *This is represented in the schematic diagram below.* ADJ: usu ADJ n

**scheme** /skiːm/ **(schemes, scheming, schemed)** ◆◆◇ [1] A **scheme** is a plan or arrangement involving many people which is made by a government or other organization. [mainly BRIT] ❑ *...schemes to help combat unemployment. ...a private pension scheme.* N-COUNT: oft N to-inf, n N

✔ in AM, use **program**

[2] A **scheme** is someone's plan for achieving something. ❑ *...a quick money-making scheme to get us through the summer.* N-COUNT: oft N to-inf, N *for* -ing [3] If you say that people **are scheming**, you mean that they are making secret plans in order to gain something for themselves. ❑ *Everyone's always scheming and plotting... The bride's family were scheming to prevent a wedding... They claimed that their opponents were scheming against them... You're a scheming little devil, aren't you?* ♦ **schem|ing** *...their favourite pastimes of scheming and gossiping.* VERB: oft cont [disapproval] V V to-inf V *against* n V-ing N-UNCOUNT [4] → See also **colour scheme**, **pension scheme**. [5] When people talk about **the scheme of things** or **the grand scheme of things** , they are referring to the way that everything in the world seems to be organized. ❑ *We realize that we are infinitely small within the scheme of things.* PHRASE

**schem|er** /skiːməʳ/ **(schemers)** If you refer to someone as a **schemer**, you mean that they make secret plans in order to get some benefit for themselves. ❑ *...office schemers who think of nothing but their own advancement.* N-COUNT [disapproval]

**scher|zo** /skeəʳtsoʊ/ **(scherzos)** A **scherzo** is a short, lively piece of classical music which is usually part of a longer piece of music. N-COUNT

**schism** /skɪzəm, sɪz-/ **(schisms)** When there is a **schism**, a group or organization divides into two groups as a result of differences in thinking and beliefs. [FORMAL] ❑ *The church seems to be on the brink of schism.* N-VAR = split

**schiz|oid** /skɪtsɔɪd/ [1] If you describe someone as **schizoid**, you mean that they seem to have very different opinions and purposes at different times. ❑ *...a rather schizoid fellow.* ADJ [2] Someone who is **schizoid** suffers from schizophrenia. ❑ *...a schizoid personality.* ADJ

**schizo|phre|nia** /skɪtsəfriːniə/ **Schizophrenia** is a serious mental illness. People who suffer from it are unable to relate their thoughts and feelings to what is happening around them and often withdraw from society. N-UNCOUNT

**schizo|phren|ic** /skɪtsəfrenɪk/ **(schizophrenics)** [1] A **schizophrenic** is a person who is suffering from schizophrenia. ❑ *He was diagnosed as a paranoid schizophrenic.* ♦ **Schizophrenic** is also an adjective. ❑ *...a schizophrenic patient. ...schizophrenic tendencies.* N-COUNT ADJ [2] Someone's attitude or behaviour can be described as **schizophrenic** when they seem to have very different opinions or purposes at different times. ❑ *...the schizophrenic mood of the American public.* ADJ

**schlep** /ʃlep/ **(schleps, schlepping, schlepped)** also **schlepp.** [1] If you **schlep** something somewhere, you take it there although this is difficult or inconvenient. [AM, INFORMAL] ❑ *You didn't just schlep your guitar around from folk club to folk club.* VERB = lug V n adv/prep [2] If you **schlep** somewhere, you go there. [AM, INFORMAL] ❑ *It's too cold to schlepp around looking at property.* VERB = trudge V adv/prep [3] If you describe someone as a **schlep**, you mean that they are stupid or clumsy. [AM, INFORMAL] N-COUNT [disapproval]

**schlock** /ʃlɒk/ If you refer to films, pop songs, or books as **schlock**, you mean that they have no artistic or social value. [INFORMAL] ❑ *...a showman with a good eye for marketable schlock.* N-UNCOUNT [disapproval]

**schmaltz** /ʃmælts, AM ʃmɑːlts/ If you describe a play, film, or book as **schmaltz**, you do not like it because it is too sentimental. N-UNCOUNT disapproval = slush

**schmaltzy** /ʃmæltsi, AM ʃmɑːltsi/ If you describe songs, films, or books as **schmaltzy**, you do not like them because they are too sentimental. ADJ disapproval = slushy

**schmooze** /ʃmuːz/ **(schmoozes, schmoozing, schmoozed)** If you **schmooze**, you talk casually and socially with someone. [mainly AM, INFORMAL] VERB = chat ❑ *...those coffee houses where you can schmooze for hours.* V

**schnapps** /ʃnæps/ **Schnapps** is a strong alcoholic drink made from potatoes. N-UNCOUNT ♦ A **schnapps** is a glass of schnapps. N-SING

**schol|ar** /skɒləʳ/ **(scholars)** A **scholar** is a person who studies an academic subject and knows a lot about it. [FORMAL] N-COUNT ❑ *The library attracts thousands of scholars and researchers.*

**schol|ar|ly** /skɒləʳli/ 1 A **scholarly** person spends a lot of time studying and knows a lot about academic subjects. ADJ ❑ *He was an intellectual, scholarly man.* 2 A **scholarly** book or article contains a lot of academic information and is intended for academic readers. ADJ ❑ *...the more scholarly academic journals.* 3 **Scholarly** matters and activities involve people who do academic research. ADJ: usu ADJ n ❑ *This has been the subject of intense scholarly debate.*

**schol|ar|ship** /skɒləʳʃɪp/ **(scholarships)** 1 If you get a **scholarship** to a school or university, your studies are paid for by the school or university or by some other organization. N-COUNT ❑ *He got a scholarship to the Pratt Institute of Art.* 2 **Scholarship** is serious academic study and the knowledge that is obtained from it. N-UNCOUNT ❑ *I want to take advantage of your lifetime of scholarship.*

**scho|las|tic** /skəlæstɪk/ Your **scholastic** achievement or ability is your academic achievement or ability while you are at school. [FORMAL] ADJ: ADJ n = academic ❑ *...the values which encouraged her scholastic achievement.*

**school** /skuːl/ **(schools, schooling, schooled)** ♦♦♦ 1 A **school** is a place where children are educated. You usually refer to this place as **school** when you are talking about the time that children spend there and the activities that they do there. N-VAR: usu prep N ❑ *...a boy who was in my class at school... Even the good students say homework is what they most dislike about school... I took the kids for a picnic in the park after school. ...a school built in the Sixties. ...two boys wearing school uniform.* 2 A **school** is the pupils or staff at a school. N-COUNT-COLL ❑ *Deirdre, the whole school's going to hate you.* 3 A privately-run place where a particular skill or subject is taught can be referred to as a **school**. N-COUNT; N-IN-NAMES ❑ *...a riding school and equestrian centre near Chepstow.* 4 A university, college, or university department specializing in a particular type of subject can be referred to as a **school**. N-VAR; N-IN-NAMES ❑ *...a lecturer in the school of veterinary medicine at the University of Pennsylvania... Stella, 21, is at art school training to be a fashion designer.* 5 **School** is used to refer to university or college. [AM] N-UNCOUNT ❑ *Moving rapidly through school, he graduated Phi Beta Kappa from the University of Kentucky at age 18.* 6 A particular **school of** writers, artists, or thinkers is a group of them whose work, opinions, or theories are similar. N-COUNT-COLL: usu with supp ❑ *...the Chicago school of economists.* 7 A **school of** fish or dolphins is a large group of them moving through water together. N-COUNT-COLL: N *of* n 8 If you **school** someone **in** something, you train or educate them to have a certain skill, type of behaviour, or way of thinking. [WRITTEN] VERB ❑ *Many mothers schooled their daughters in the myth of female inferiority...* V n *in* n *He is schooled to spot trouble.* *be* V-ed to-inf 9 To **school** a child means to educate him or her. [AM; also BRIT, FORMAL] VERB ❑ *She's been schooling her kids herself.* V n 10 If you **school** a horse, you train it so that it can be ridden in races or competitions. VERB = train ❑ *She bought him as a £1,000 colt of six months and schooled him.* V n 11 → See also **schooled, schooling, after-school, approved school, boarding school, church school, convent school, driving school, finishing school, grade school, graduate school, grammar school, high school, infant school, junior school, middle school, night school, nursery school, preschool, prep school, primary school, private school, public school, special school, state school, summer school, Sunday school.**

**school age** When a child reaches **school age**, he or she is old enough to go to school. N-UNCOUNT: oft prep N ❑ *Most of them have young children below school age.* ♦ **School age** is also an adjective. ADJ: usu ADJ n ❑ *...families with school-age children.*

**school|bag** /skuːlbæg/ **(schoolbags)** also **school bag.** A **schoolbag** is a bag that children use to carry books and other things to and from school. N-COUNT

**school board** **(school boards)** A **school board** is a committee in charge of education in a particular city or area, or in a particular school, especially in the United States. [AM] N-COUNT-COLL ❑ *Colonel Richard Nelson served on the school board until this year.*

**school book** **(school books)** also **schoolbook. School books** are books giving information about a particular subject, which children use at school. N-COUNT: usu pl

**school|boy** /skuːlbɔɪ/ **(schoolboys)** A **schoolboy** is a boy who goes to school. N-COUNT ❑ *...a group of ten-year-old schoolboys.*

**school bus** **(school buses)** A **school bus** is a special bus which takes children to and from school. N-COUNT

**school|child** /skuːltʃaɪld/ **(schoolchildren)** **Schoolchildren** are children who go to school. N-COUNT: usu pl ❑ *Last year I had an audience of schoolchildren and they laughed at everything.*

**school|days** /skuːldeɪz/ also **school days.** Your **schooldays** are the period of your life when you were at school. N-PLURAL: usu poss N ❑ *He was happily married to a girl he had known since his schooldays.*

**school din|ner** **(school dinners)** **School dinners** are midday meals provided for children at a school. [BRIT] N-VAR ❑ *Overcooked greens are my most vivid recollection of school dinners.*

✔ in AM, use **school lunch**

**schooled** /skuːld/ If you are **schooled in** something, you have learned about it as the result of training or experience. [WRITTEN] ADJ: v-link ADJ *in* n, oft adv ADJ ❑ *They were both well schooled in the ways of the Army.* → See also **school.**

**school friend** **(school friends)** also **schoolfriend.** A **school friend** is a friend of yours who is at the same school as you, or who used to be at the same school when you were children. N-COUNT: oft with poss ❑ *I spent the evening with an old school friend.*

**school|girl** /skuːlgɜːʳl/ **(schoolgirls)** A **schoolgirl** is a girl who goes to school. N-COUNT ❑ *...half a dozen giggling schoolgirls.*

**school|house** /skuːlhaʊs/ **(schoolhouses)** A **schoolhouse** is a small building used as a school. [AM] N-COUNT ❑ *McCreary lives in a converted schoolhouse outside Charlottesville.*

**school|ing** /skuːlɪŋ/ **Schooling** is education that children receive at school. N-UNCOUNT: oft with poss = education ❑ *He had little formal schooling.*

**school kid** **(school kids)** also **schoolkid. School kids** are **schoolchildren**. [INFORMAL] N-COUNT: usu pl ❑ *...young school kids in short pants.*

**school leav|er** **(school leavers)** **School leavers** are young people who have just left school, because they have completed their time there. [BRIT] N-COUNT: usu pl ❑ *...the lack of job opportunities, particularly for school-leavers.*

✔ in AM, use **high school graduate**

**school lunch** **(school lunches)** **School lunches** are midday meals provided for children at a school. N-VAR = school dinner

**school|master** /skuːlmɑːstəʳ, -mæst-/ **(schoolmasters)** A **schoolmaster** is a man who teaches children in a school. [OLD-FASHIONED] N-COUNT

**school|mate** /skuːlmeɪt/ **(schoolmates)** A **schoolmate** is a child who goes to the same school as you, especially one who is your friend. ❑ *He started the magazine with a schoolmate.* N-COUNT: *oft with poss = school-friend*

**school|mistress** /skuːlmɪstrəs/ **(schoolmistresses)** A **schoolmistress** is a woman who teaches children in a school. [OLD-FASHIONED] N-COUNT

**school|room** /skuːlruːm/ **(schoolrooms)** A **schoolroom** is a classroom, especially the only classroom in a small school. N-COUNT

**school|teacher** /skuːltiːtʃəʳ/ **(schoolteachers)** A **schoolteacher** is a teacher in a school. N-COUNT

**school teach|ing** **School teaching** is the work done by teachers in a school. [FORMAL] ❑ *He returned to school teaching.* N-UNCOUNT *= teaching*

**school|work** /skuːlwɜːʳk/ **Schoolwork** is the work that a child does at school or is given at school to do at home. ❑ *My mother would help me with my schoolwork.* N-UNCOUNT

**school|yard** /skuːljɑːʳd/ **(schoolyards)** also **school yard.** The **schoolyard** is the large open area with a hard surface just outside a school building, where the schoolchildren can play and do other activities. ❑ *...the sound of the kids in the schoolyard.* N-COUNT: *usu the N in sing = playground*

**schoon|er** /skuːnəʳ/ **(schooners)** 1 A **schooner** is a medium-sized sailing ship. N-COUNT 2 A **schooner** is a large glass used for drinking sherry. [BRIT] N-COUNT 3 A **schooner** is a tall glass for beer. [AM] N-COUNT

**schtick** /ʃtɪk/ **(schticks)** also **shtick.** An entertainer's **schtick** is a series of funny or entertaining things that they say or do. [mainly AM, INFORMAL] N-VAR

**schwa** /ʃwɑː/ **(schwas)** In the study of language, **schwa** is the name of the neutral vowel sound represented by the symbol ə in this dictionary. N-VAR

**sci|ati|ca** /saɪætɪkə/ **Sciatica** is a severe pain in the nerve in your legs or the lower part of your back. [MEDICAL] N-UNCOUNT

**sci|ence** /saɪəns/ **(sciences)** ◆◆◇ 1 **Science** is the study of the nature and behaviour of natural things and the knowledge that we obtain about them. ❑ *The best discoveries in science are very simple. ...science and technology.* N-UNCOUNT 2 A **science** is a particular branch of science such as physics, chemistry, or biology. ❑ *Physics is the best example of a science which has developed strong, abstract theories.* N-COUNT: *usu with supp* 3 A **science** is the study of some aspect of human behaviour, for example sociology or anthropology. ❑ *...the modern science of psychology.* N-COUNT: *usu with supp* 4 → See also **domestic science**, **exact science**, **Master of Science**, **political science**, **social science**.

**sci|ence fic|tion** **Science fiction** consists of stories in books, magazines, and films about events that take place in the future or in other parts of the universe. N-UNCOUNT

**sci|ence park** **(science parks)** A **science park** is an area, usually linked to a university, where there are a lot of private companies, especially ones concerned with high technology. [BRIT] N-COUNT

**sci|en|tif|ic** /saɪəntɪfɪk/ ◆◇◇ 1 **Scientific** is used to describe things that relate to science or to a particular science. ❑ *Scientific research is widely claimed to be the source of the high standard of living in the US. ...the use of animals in scientific experiments.* ADJ: *usu ADJ n* ♦ **sci|en|tifi|cal|ly** /saɪəntɪfɪkli/ *...scientifically advanced countries.* ADV 2 If you do something in a **scientific** way, you do it carefully and thoroughly, using experiments or tests. ❑ *It's not a scientific way to test their opinions.* ADJ: *usu ADJ n = systematic* ♦ **sci|en|tifi|cal|ly** *Efforts are being made to research it scientifically.* ADV

**sci|en|tist** /saɪəntɪst/ **(scientists)** ◆◆◇ A **scientist** is someone who has studied science and whose job is to teach or do research in science. ❑ *Scientists have collected more data than expected.* → See also **social scientist**. N-COUNT

**sci-fi** /saɪ faɪ/ **Sci-fi** is short for **science fiction**. [INFORMAL] ❑ *...a sci-fi film.* N-UNCOUNT

**scimi|tar** /sɪmɪtəʳ/ **(scimitars)** A **scimitar** is a sword with a curved blade that was used in former times in some Eastern countries. N-COUNT

**scin|til|la** /sɪntɪlə/ If you say that there is **not a scintilla of** evidence, hope, or doubt about something, you are emphasizing that there is none at all. [LITERARY] ❑ *He says there is 'not a scintilla of evidence' to link him to any controversy.* QUANT: *with brd-neg, QUANT of n-uncount* [emphasis] *= shred*

**scin|til|lat|ing** /sɪntɪleɪtɪŋ/ A **scintillating** conversation or performance is very lively and interesting. ❑ *You can hardly expect scintillating conversation from a kid that age.* ADJ: *usu ADJ n = sparkling*

**sci|on** /saɪən/ **(scions)** A **scion of** a rich or famous family is one of its younger or more recent members. [LITERARY] ❑ *Nabokov was the scion of an aristocratic family.* N-COUNT: *usu N of n*

**scis|sors** /sɪzəʳz/ **Scissors** are a small cutting tool with two sharp blades that are screwed together. You use scissors for cutting things such as paper and cloth. → See picture on page 1710. ❑ *He told me to get some scissors... She picked up a pair of scissors from the windowsill.* N-PLURAL: *also a pair of N*

**scle|ro|sis** /sklərəʊsɪs/ **Sclerosis** is a medical condition in which a part inside your body becomes hard. [MEDICAL] → See also **multiple sclerosis.** N-UNCOUNT

**scoff** /skɒf/ **(scoffs, scoffing, scoffed)** 1 If you **scoff at** something, you speak about it in a way that shows you think it is ridiculous or inadequate. ❑ *At first I scoffed at the notion... You may scoff but I honestly feel I'm being cruel only to be kind.* VERB *= mock* V at n V 2 If you **scoff** food, you eat it quickly and greedily. [BRIT, INFORMAL] ❑ *The pancakes were so good that I scoffed the lot.* VERB V n

**scold** /skəʊld/ **(scolds, scolding, scolded)** If you **scold** someone, you speak angrily to them because they have done something wrong. [FORMAL] ❑ *If he finds out, he'll scold me... Later she scolded her daughter for having talked to her father like that... 'You should be at school,' he scolded.* VERB V n V n for n V with quote

**sconce** /skɒns/ **(sconces)** A **sconce** is a decorated object that holds candles or an electric light, and that is attached to the wall of a room. N-COUNT

**scone** /skɒn, skəʊn/ **(scones)** A **scone** is a small cake made from flour and fat, usually eaten with butter. [mainly BRIT] N-COUNT

**scoop** /skuːp/ **(scoops, scooping, scooped)** 1 If you **scoop** a person or thing somewhere, you put your hands or arms under or round them and quickly move them there. ❑ *Michael knelt next to her and scooped her into his arms.* VERB V n prep/adv 2 If you **scoop** something from a container, you remove it with something such as a spoon. ❑ *...the sound of a spoon scooping dog food out of a can.* VERB V n prep/adv 3 A **scoop** is an object like a spoon which is used for picking up a quantity of a food such as ice cream or an ingredient such as flour. ❑ *...a small ice-cream scoop.* N-COUNT 4 You can use **scoop** to refer to an exciting news story which is reported in one newspaper or on one television programme before it appears anywhere else. ❑ *...one of the biggest scoops in the history of newspapers.* N-COUNT 5 If a newspaper **scoops** other newspapers, it succeeds in printing an exciting or important story before they do. ❑ *All the newspapers really want to do is scoop the opposition.* VERB V n 6 If you **scoop** a prize or award, you win it. [JOURNALISM] ❑ *...films which scooped awards around the world.* VERB V n

♦ **scoop up** If you **scoop** something **up**, you put your hands or arms under it and lift it in a quick movement. ❑ *Use both hands to scoop up the leaves... He began to scoop his things up frantically.* PHRASAL VERB V P n (not pron) V n P

**scoot** /skuːt/ **(scoots, scooting, scooted)** If you **scoot** somewhere, you go there very quickly. [INFORMAL] ❑ *Sam said, 'I'm going to hide,' and scooted up the stairs.* VERB *= rush* V prep/adv Also V

**scoot|er** /skuːtə^r/ **(scooters)** 1 A **scooter** is a small light motorcycle which has a low seat. N-COUNT
2 A **scooter** is a type of child's bicycle which has two wheels joined by a wooden board and a handle on a long pole attached to the front wheel. The child stands on the board with one foot, and uses the other foot to move forwards. N-COUNT

**scope** /skoʊp/ 1 If there is **scope for** a particular kind of behaviour or activity, people have the opportunity to behave in this way or do that activity. ❑ *He believed in giving his staff scope for initiative... Banks had increased scope to develop new financial products.* N-UNCOUNT: oft N *for* n, N to-inf 2 The **scope of** an activity, topic, or piece of work is the whole area which it deals with or includes. ❑ *Mr Dobson promised to widen the organisation's scope of activity.* N-SING: usu N *of* n

**scorch** /skɔːʳtʃ/ **(scorches, scorching, scorched)** 1 To **scorch** something means to burn it slightly. ❑ *The bomb scorched the side of the building.* ♦ **scorched** *...scorched black earth.* VERB V n ADJ
2 If something **scorches** or **is scorched**, it becomes marked or changes colour because it is affected by too much heat or by a chemical. ❑ *The leaves are inclined to scorch in hot sunshine... If any of the spray goes onto the lawn it will scorch the grass.* VERB V V n

**scorched earth** A **scorched earth** policy is the deliberate burning, destruction, and removal by an army of everything that would be useful to an enemy coming into the area. ❑ *He employed a scorched-earth policy, destroying villages and burning crops.* N-UNCOUNT: usu N n

**scorch|ing** /skɔːʳtʃɪŋ/ **Scorching** or **scorching hot** weather or temperatures are very hot indeed. [INFORMAL] ❑ *That race was run in scorching weather.* ADJ: usu ADJ n emphasis

**score** /skɔːʳ/ **(scores, scoring, scored)** ◆◆◇

✓ In meaning 9, the plural form is **score**.

1 In a sport or game, if a player **scores** a goal or a point, they gain a goal or point. ❑ *Against which country did Ian Wright score his first international goal?... England scored 282 in their first innings... Gascoigne almost scored in the opening minute.* VERB V n V n V
2 If you **score** a particular number or amount, for example as a mark in a test, you achieve that number or amount. ❑ *Kelly had scored an average of 147 on three separate IQ tests... Congress as an institution scores low in public opinion polls.* VERB V n V adv
3 Someone's **score** in a game or test is a number, for example, a number of points or runs, which shows what they have achieved or what level they have reached. ❑ *The U.S. Open golf tournament was won by Ben Hogan, with a score of 287... There was also a strong link between children's low maths scores and parents' numeracy problems.* N-COUNT
4 The **score** in a game is the result of it or the current situation, as indicated by the number of goals, runs, or points obtained by the two teams or players. ❑ *4-1 was the final score... They beat the Giants by a score of 7 to 3.* N-COUNT 5 If you **score** a success, a victory, or a hit, you are successful in what you are doing. [WRITTEN] ❑ *In recent months, the rebels have scored some significant victories.* VERB V n 6 The **score** of a film, play, or similar production is the music which is written or used for it. ❑ *The dance is accompanied by an original score by Henry Torgue.* N-COUNT
7 The **score** of a piece of music is the written version of it. ❑ *He recognizes enough notation to be able to follow a score.* N-COUNT 8 If you refer to **scores of** things or people, you are emphasizing that there are very many of them. [WRITTEN] ❑ *Campaigners lit scores of bonfires in ceremonies to mark the anniversary.* QUANT: QUANT *of* pl-n emphasis 9 A **score** is twenty or approximately twenty. [WRITTEN] ❑ *A score of countries may be producing or planning to obtain chemical weapons.* NUM: usu *a*/num NUM 10 If you **score** a surface with something sharp, you cut a line or number of lines in it. ❑ *Lightly score the surface of the steaks with a knife.* VERB V n

**PHRASES** 11 If you **keep score** of the number of things that are happening in a certain situation, you count them and record them. ❑ *You can keep score of your baby's movements before birth by recording them on a kick chart.* PHRASE: V inflects, oft PHR *of* n 12 If you **know the score**, you know what the real facts of a situation are and how they affect you, even though you may not like them. [SPOKEN] ❑ *I don't feel sorry for Carl. He knew the score, he knew what he had to do and couldn't do it.* PHRASE: V inflects 13 You can use **on that score** or **on this score** to refer to something that has just been mentioned, especially an area of difficulty or concern. ❑ *I became pregnant easily. At least I've had no problems on that score.* PHRASE 14 If you **score a point over** someone, or **score points off** them, you gain an advantage over them, usually by saying something clever or making a better argument. ❑ *The Prime Minister was trying to score a political point over his rivals... The politicians might be forced to touch on the real issues rather than scoring points off each other.* PHRASE: V and N inflect, PHR n 15 If you **settle a score** or **settle an old score with** someone, you take revenge on them for something they have done in the past. ❑ *The groups had historic scores to settle with each other.* PHRASE: V and N inflect

**score|board** /skɔːʳbɔːʳd/ **(scoreboards)** A **scoreboard** is a large board, for example at a sports ground or stadium, which shows the score in a match or competition. ❑ *The figures flash up on the scoreboard.* N-COUNT

**score|card** /skɔːʳkɑːʳd/ **(scorecards)** also **score card.** 1 A **scorecard** is a printed card that tells you who is taking part in a match, and on which officials, players, or people watching can record each player's score. N-COUNT 2 A **scorecard** is a system or procedure that is used for checking or testing something. [AM] ❑ *This commission would keep environmental scorecards on UN member nations.* N-COUNT: with supp

**score draw** **(score draws)** A **score draw** is the result of a football match in which both teams score at least one goal, and they score the same number of goals. [BRIT] N-COUNT

**score|less** /skɔːʳləs/ In football, baseball, and some other sports, a **scoreless** game is one in which neither team has scored any goals or points. [JOURNALISM] ❑ *Norway had held Holland to a scoreless draw in Rotterdam.* ADJ

**score|line** /skɔːʳlaɪn/ **(scorelines)** The **scoreline** of a football, rugby, or tennis match is the score or the final result of it. [BRIT, JOURNALISM] ❑ *...the excitingly close scoreline of 2-1.* N-COUNT: usu sing, usu *the* N = score

**scor|er** /skɔːrəʳ/ **(scorers)** 1 In football, cricket, and many other sports and games, a **scorer** is a player who scores a goal, runs, or points. ❑ *...David Hirst, the scorer of 11 goals this season.* N-COUNT: usu with supp
2 A **scorer** is an official who writes down the score of a game or competition as it is being played. N-COUNT

**score|sheet** /skɔːʳʃiːt/ also **score sheet.** In football, rugby, and some other sports, if a player **gets on the scoresheet**, he or she scores one or more goals, tries, or points. [BRIT, JOURNALISM] PHRASE: V inflects

**scorn** /skɔːʳn/ **(scorns, scorning, scorned)** 1 If you treat someone or something **with scorn**, you show contempt for them. ❑ *Researchers greeted the proposal with scorn.* N-UNCOUNT: oft *with* N, N *for* n = contempt 2 If you **scorn** someone or something, you feel or show contempt for them. ❑ *Several leading officers have quite openly scorned the peace talks.* VERB V n 3 If you **scorn** something, you refuse to have it or accept it because you think it is not good enough or suitable for you. ❑ *...people who scorned traditional methods.* VERB V n 4 If you **pour scorn on** someone or something or **heap scorn on** them, you say that you think they are stupid and worthless. ❑ *It is fashionable these days to pour scorn on those in public life... He used to heap scorn on Dr Vazquez's socialist ideas.* PHRASE: V inflects = deride

**scorn|ful** /skɔːʳnfəl/ If you are **scornful of** someone or something, you show contempt for them. ❑ *He is deeply scornful of politicians. ...a scornful simile.* ADJ: oft ADJ *of* n = contemptuous

**Scor|pio** /skɔːʳpioʊ/ **(Scorpios)** 1 **Scorpio** is one of the twelve signs of the zodiac. Its symbol is a scorpion. People who are born approximately between the 23rd of October and the 21st of November come under this sign. [2] A **Scorpio** is a person whose sign of the zodiac is Scorpio. N-COUNT

**scor|pi|on** /skɔːʳpiən/ **(scorpions)** A **scorpion** is a small creature which looks like a large insect. Scorpions have a long curved tail, and some of them are poisonous. N-COUNT

**Scot** /skɒt/ **(Scots)** [1] A **Scot** is a person of Scottish origin. N-COUNT [2] **Scots** is a dialect of the English language that is spoken in Scotland. N-UNCOUNT ❑ *There are things you can express in Scots that you can't say in English.* [3] **Scots** means the same as **Scottish**. ADJ: usu ADJ n ❑ *...his guttural Scots accent.*

**scotch** /skɒtʃ/ **(scotches, scotching, scotched)** VERB If you **scotch** a rumour, plan, or idea, you put an end to it before it can develop any further. ❑ *They have scotched rumours that they are planning a special London show.* V n

**Scotch** /skɒtʃ/ **(Scotches)** [1] **Scotch** or **Scotch whisky** is whisky made in Scotland. N-MASS = whisky ❑ *...a bottle of Scotch.* ♦ A **Scotch** is a glass of Scotch. N-COUNT ❑ *He poured himself a Scotch.* [2] **Scotch** means the same as **Scottish**. ADJ: usu ADJ n This use is considered incorrect by many people.

**Scotch egg** **(Scotch eggs)** A **Scotch egg** is a hard boiled egg that is covered with sausage meat and breadcrumbs, then fried. [mainly BRIT] N-COUNT

**Scotch-Irish** If someone, especially an American, is **Scotch-Irish**, they are descended from both Scottish and Irish people, especially from Scottish people who had settled in Northern Ireland. [mainly AM] ADJ ♦ **Scotch-Irish** is also a noun. N-PLURAL: usu *the* N ❑ *...Virginia's Great Valley, where the Scotch-Irish had settled in the eighteenth century.*

**Scotch tape** **Scotch tape** is a clear sticky tape that is sold in rolls and that you use to stick paper or card together or onto a wall. [TRADEMARK] N-UNCOUNT

**scot-free** If you say that someone got away **scot-free**, you are emphasizing that they escaped punishment for something that you believe they should have been punished for. ADV: ADV after v [emphasis] ❑ *Others who were guilty were being allowed to get off scot-free.*

**Scots|man** /skɒtsmən/ **(Scotsmen)** A **Scotsman** is a man of Scottish origin. N-COUNT

**Scots|woman** /skɒtswʊmən/ **(Scotswomen)** A **Scotswoman** is a woman of Scottish origin. N-COUNT

**Scot|tish** /skɒtɪʃ/ Something that is **Scottish** belongs or relates to Scotland, its people, or its language. ADJ

**scoun|drel** /skaʊndrəl/ **(scoundrels)** If you refer to a man as a **scoundrel**, you mean that he behaves very badly towards other people, especially by cheating them or deceiving them. [OLD-FASHIONED] N-COUNT [disapproval] ❑ *He is a lying scoundrel!*

**scour** /skaʊəʳ/ **(scours, scouring, scoured)** [1] If you **scour** something such as a place or a book, you make a thorough search of it to try to find what you are looking for. VERB = search ❑ *Rescue crews had scoured an area of 30 square miles... We scoured the telephone directory for clues.* V n; V n *for* n [2] If you **scour** something such as a sink, floor, or pan, you clean its surface by rubbing it hard with something rough. VERB = scrub ❑ *He decided to scour the sink.* V n

**scourge** /skɜːʳdʒ/ **(scourges, scourging, scourged)** [1] A **scourge** is something that causes a lot of trouble or suffering to a group of people. N-COUNT: oft N *of* n ❑ *...the best chance in 20 years to end the scourge of terrorism.* [2] If something **scourges** a place or group of people, it causes great pain and suffering to people. VERB ❑ *Economic anarchy scourged the post-war world.* V n

**scout** /skaʊt/ **(scouts, scouting, scouted)** [1] A **scout** is someone who is sent to an area of countryside to find out the position of an enemy army. N-COUNT ❑ *They sent two men out in front as scouts.* [2] If you **scout** somewhere **for** something, you go through that area searching for it. VERB = search ❑ *I wouldn't have time to scout the area for junk... A team of four was sent to scout for a nuclear test site... I have people scouting the hills already.* V n *for* n; V *for* n; V n

♦ **scout around**

☑ in BRIT, also use **scout round**

If you **scout around** or **scout round for** something, you go to different places looking for it. PHRASAL VERB = look around ❑ *They scouted around for more fuel... I scouted round in the bushes.* V P *for* n; V P

**Scout** **(Scouts)** [1] **The Scouts** is an organization for children and young people which teaches them to be practical, sensible, and helpful. N-PROPER-COLL: *the* N [2] A **Scout** is a member of the Scouts. N-COUNT ❑ *...a party of seven Scouts and three leaders on a camping trip.*

**scout|master** /skaʊtmɑːstəʳ, -mæs-/ **(scoutmasters)** A **scoutmaster** is a man who is in charge of a troop of Scouts. N-COUNT

**scowl** /skaʊl/ **(scowls, scowling, scowled)** VERB When someone **scowls**, an angry or hostile expression appears on their face. ❑ *He scowled, and slammed the door behind him... She scowled at the two men as they entered the room.* V; V *at* n ♦ **Scowl** is also a noun. N-COUNT ❑ *Chris met the remark with a scowl.*

**scrab|ble** /skræbəl/ **(scrabbles, scrabbling, scrabbled)** [1] If you **scrabble for** something, especially something that you cannot see, you move your hands or your feet about quickly and hurriedly in order to find it. VERB ❑ *He grabbed his jacket and scrabbled in his desk drawer for some loose change... I hung there, scrabbling with my feet to find a foothold.* V *for* n; V to-inf ♦ **Scrabble around** or **scrabble about** means the same as **scrabble**. PHRASAL VERB ❑ *Alberg scrabbled around for pen and paper... Gleb scrabbled about in the hay, pulled out a book and opened it.* V P *for* n; V P [2] If you say that someone **is scrabbling to** do something, you mean that they are having difficulty because they are in too much of a hurry, or because the task is almost impossible. VERB ❑ *The banks are now desperately scrabbling to recover their costs... The opportunity had gone. His mind scrabbled for alternatives.* V to-inf; V *for* n ♦ **Scrabble around** means the same as **scrabble**. PHRASAL VERB ❑ *You get a six-month contract, and then you have to scrabble around for the next job.* V P *for* n; Also V P to-inf

**scrag|gly** /skrægli/ **(scragglier, scraggliest)** **Scraggly** hair or plants are thin and untidy. [mainly AM] ADJ = straggly ❑ *...a scraggly mustache.*

**scrag|gy** /skrægi/ **(scraggier, scraggiest)** If you describe a person or animal as **scraggy**, you mean that they look unattractive because they are so thin. [mainly BRIT] ADJ [disapproval] = scrawny ❑ *...his scraggy neck. ...a flock of scraggy sheep.*

**scram|ble** /skræmbəl/ **(scrambles, scrambling, scrambled)** [1] If you **scramble** over rocks or up a hill, you move quickly over them or up it using your hands to help you. VERB = clamber ❑ *Tourists were scrambling over the rocks looking for the perfect camera angle.* V prep/adv [2] If you **scramble** to a different place or position, you move there in a hurried, awkward way. VERB ❑ *Ann threw back the covers and scrambled out of bed.* V prep/adv [3] If a number of people **scramble for** something, they compete energetically with each other for it. VERB ❑ *More than three million fans are expected to scramble for tickets... Business is booming and foreigners are scrambling to invest.* V *for* n; V to-inf ♦ **Scramble** is also a noun. N-COUNT: usu sing, oft N *for* n, N to-inf ❑ *...a scramble to get a seat on the early morning flight.* [4] If you **scramble** eggs, you break them, mix them together and then heat and stir the mixture in a pan. VERB ❑ *Make the toast and scramble the eggs.* V n ♦ **scram|bled** ADJ: usu ADJ n *...scrambled eggs and bacon.* [5] If a device **scrambles** a radio or telephone message, it interferes with the sound so that the message can only be understood by someone with special equipment. VERB ❑ *The latest machines scramble the messages so that the conversation cannot easily be intercepted.* V n

**scram|bler** /skræmbləʳ/ **(scramblers)** A **scrambler** is an electronic device which alters the sound of a radio or telephone message so that it can only be understood by someone who has special equipment. N-COUNT

**scrap** /skræp/ **(scraps, scrapping, scrapped)**
1 A **scrap of** something is a very small piece or amount of it. ❑ *A crumpled scrap of paper was found in her handbag... They need every scrap of information they can get.* N-COUNT: usu N *of* n
2 **Scraps** are pieces of unwanted food which are thrown away or given to animals. ❑ *...the scraps from the Sunday dinner table.* N-PLURAL
3 If you **scrap** something, you get rid of it or cancel it. [JOURNALISM or INFORMAL] ❑ *President Hussein called on all countries in the Middle East to scrap nuclear or chemical weapons.* VERB; V n
4 **Scrap** metal or paper is no longer wanted for its original purpose, but may have some other use. ❑ *There's always tons of scrap paper in Dad's office.* ADJ: ADJ n
5 **Scrap** is metal from old or damaged machinery or cars. ❑ *Thousands of tanks, artillery pieces and armored vehicles will be cut up for scrap.* N-UNCOUNT

**scrap|book** /skræpbʊk/ **(scrapbooks)** A **scrapbook** is a book with empty pages on which you can stick things such as pictures or newspaper articles in order to keep them. N-COUNT

**scrape** /skreɪp/ **(scrapes, scraping, scraped)**
1 If you **scrape** something from a surface, you remove it, especially by pulling a sharp object over the surface. ❑ *She went round the car scraping the frost off the windows.* VERB; V n with adv
2 If something **scrapes** against something else or if someone or something **scrapes** something else, it rubs against it, making a noise or causing slight damage. ❑ *The only sound is that of knives and forks scraping against china... The car hurtled past us, scraping the wall and screeching to a halt... There was a scraping sound as she dragged the heels of her shoes along the pavement.* VERB; V prep; V n; V-ing
3 If you **scrape** a part of your body, you accidentally rub it against something hard and rough, and damage it slightly. ❑ *She stumbled and fell, scraping her palms and knees.* VERB = graze; V n
4 to **scrape the barrel** → see **barrel**.

♦ **scrape by** If someone **scrapes by**, they earn just enough money to live on with difficulty. ❑ *We're barely scraping by on my salary.* PHRASAL VERB; V P

♦ **scrape through** If you **scrape through** an examination, you just succeed in passing it. If you **scrape through** a competition or a vote, you just succeed in winning it. ❑ *Both my brothers have university degrees. I just scraped through a couple of A-levels... If we can get a draw, we might scrape through.* PHRASAL VERB; V P n; V P

♦ **scrape together** If you **scrape together** an amount of money or a number of things, you succeed in obtaining it with difficulty. ❑ *They only just managed to scrape the money together... It's possible the Congress Party will scrape together a majority.* PHRASAL VERB; V n P; V P n (not pron)

**scrap|er** /skreɪpəʳ/ **(scrapers)** A **scraper** is a tool that has a small handle and a metal or plastic blade and can be used for scraping a particular surface clean. N-COUNT

**scrap|heap** /skræphiːp/ also **scrap heap.**
1 If you say that someone has been thrown on **the scrapheap**, you mean that they have been forced to leave their job by an uncaring employer and are unlikely to get other work. ❑ *Miners have been thrown on the scrapheap with no prospects.* N-SING: usu prep *the* N
2 If things such as machines or weapons are thrown on **the scrapheap**, they are thrown away because they are no longer needed. ❑ *Thousands of Europe's tanks and guns are going to the scrap heap.* N-SING: usu prep *the* N

**scrap|ings** /skreɪpɪŋz/ **Scrapings** are small amounts or pieces that have been scraped off something. ❑ *There might be scrapings under his fingernails.* N-PLURAL

**scrap|py** /skræpi/ If you describe something as **scrappy**, you disapprove of it because it seems to be badly planned or untidy. ❑ *The final chapter is no more than a scrappy addition.* ADJ: usu ADJ n [disapproval]

**scrap|yard** /skræpjɑːʳd/ **(scrapyards)** also **scrap yard.** A **scrapyard** is a place where old machines such as cars or ships are destroyed and where useful parts are saved. [BRIT] N-COUNT

✔ in AM, use **junkyard**

**scratch** /skrætʃ/ **(scratches, scratching, scratched)**
1 If you **scratch yourself**, you rub your fingernails against your skin because it is itching. ❑ *He scratched himself under his arm... The old man lifted his cardigan to scratch his side... I had to wear long sleeves to stop myself scratching.* VERB; V pron-refl; V n; V
2 If a sharp object **scratches** someone or something, it makes small shallow cuts on their skin or surface. ❑ *The branches tore at my jacket and scratched my hands and face... Knives will scratch the worktop.* VERB; V n; V n
3 **Scratches** on someone or something are small shallow cuts. ❑ *The seven-year-old was found crying with scratches on his face and neck.* N-COUNT

PHRASES
4 If you do something **from scratch**, you do it without making use of anything that has been done before. ❑ *Building a home from scratch can be both exciting and challenging.* PHRASE: PHR after v
5 If you say that someone is **scratching** their **head**, you mean that they are thinking hard and trying to solve a problem or puzzle. ❑ *The Institute spends a lot of time scratching its head about how to boost American productivity.* PHRASE: V inflects
6 If you only **scratch the surface of** a subject or problem, you find out or do a small amount, but not enough to understand or solve it. ❑ *Officials say they've only scratched the surface of the drug problem... We had only two weeks to tour Malaysia, which was hardly enough time to scratch the surface.* PHRASE: V inflects, oft PHR *of* n
7 If you say that someone or something is not **up to scratch**, you mean that they are not good enough. ❑ *My mother always made me feel I wasn't coming up to scratch.* PHRASE: PHR after v, v-link PHR, usu with brd-neg

**scratch card** **(scratch cards)** also **scratchcard.** A **scratch card** is a card with hidden words or symbols on it. You scratch the surface off to reveal the words or symbols and find out if you have won a prize. N-COUNT

**scratch file** **(scratch files)** A **scratch file** is a temporary computer file which you use as a work area or as a store while a program is operating. [COMPUTING] N-COUNT

**scratch pad** **(scratch pads)** A **scratch pad** is a temporary storage memory in a computer. [COMPUTING] N-COUNT

**scratchy** /skrætʃi/
1 **Scratchy** sounds are thin and harsh. ❑ *Listening to the scratchy recording, I recognized Walt Whitman almost immediately.* ADJ
2 **Scratchy** clothes or fabrics are rough and uncomfortable to wear next to your skin. ❑ *Wool is so scratchy that it irritates the skin.* ADJ

**scrawl** /skrɔːl/ **(scrawls, scrawling, scrawled)**
1 If you **scrawl** something, you write it in a careless and untidy way. ❑ *He scrawled a hasty note to his wife... Someone had scrawled 'Scum' on his car. ...racist graffiti scrawled on school walls.* VERB; V n prep; V with quote; V-ed
2 You can refer to writing that looks careless and untidy as a **scrawl**. ❑ *The letter was handwritten, in a hasty, barely decipherable scrawl.* N-VAR

**scrawny** /skrɔːni/ **(scrawnier, scrawniest)** If you describe a person or animal as **scrawny**, you mean that they look unattractive because they are so thin. ❑ *...a scrawny woman with dyed black hair.* ADJ [disapproval]

**scream** /skriːm/ **(screams, screaming, screamed)** ◆◇◇
1 When someone **screams**, they make a very loud, high-pitched cry, for example because they are in pain or are very frightened. ❑ *Women were screaming; some of the houses nearest the bridge were on fire... He staggered around the playground, screaming in agony.* ♦ **Scream** is also a noun. ❑ *Hilda let out a scream. ...screams of terror.* VERB; V; V *in* n; N-COUNT
2 If you **scream** something, you shout it in a loud, high-pitched voice. ❑ *'Brigid!' she screamed. 'Get up!'... They started screaming abuse at us.* VERB; V with quote; V n
3 When something makes a loud, high-pitched noise, you can say that it **screams**. [WRITTEN] ❑ *She slammed the car into gear, the tyres screaming as her foot jammed against the accelerator... As he talked, an airforce jet screamed over the town.* ♦ **Scream** is also a noun. ❑ *There was a scream of brakes from the carriageway outside.* VERB = screech; V; V prep/adv; N-COUNT = screech

**scream|ing|ly** /skriːmɪŋli/ If you say that something is, for example, **screamingly** funny or ADV: ADV adj [emphasis]

**screamingly** boring, you mean that it is extremely funny or extremely boring. ❑ *...a screamingly funny joke.*

**scree** /skriː/ **(screes)** **Scree** is a mass of loose stones on the side of a mountain. ❑ *Occasionally scree fell in a shower of dust and noise.* N-VAR

**screech** /skriːtʃ/ **(screeches, screeching, screeched)** [1] If a vehicle **screeches** somewhere or if its tyres **screech**, its tyres make an unpleasant high-pitched noise on the road. ❑ *A black Mercedes screeched to a halt beside the helicopter... The car wheels screeched as they curved and bounced over the rough broken ground.* VERB; V prep/adv; V [2] When you **screech** something, you shout it in a loud, unpleasant, high-pitched voice. ❑ *'Get me some water, Jeremy!' I screeched. ...a player who screeches at you on the field.* VERB = *shriek*; V with quote; V *at* n ♦ **Screech** is also a noun. ❑ *The figure gave a screech.* N-COUNT [3] When a bird, animal, or thing **screeches**, it makes a loud, unpleasant, high-pitched noise. ❑ *A macaw screeched at him from its perch.* VERB; V *at* n ♦ **Screech** is also a noun. ❑ *He heard the screech of brakes.* N-COUNT

**screen** /skriːn/ **(screens, screening, screened)** ◆◆◇
[1] A **screen** is a flat vertical surface on which pictures or words are shown. Television sets and computers have screens, and films are shown on a screen in cinemas. ➔ See also **big screen**, **small screen**, **widescreen**. N-COUNT [2] You can refer to film or television as **the screen**. ❑ *Many viewers have strong opinions about violence on the screen... She was the ideal American teenager, both on and off screen.* N-SING: *the* N, also *on/off* N
[3] When a film or a television programme **is screened**, it is shown in the cinema or broadcast on television. ❑ *The series is likely to be screened in January... TV firms were later banned from screening any pictures of the demo.* VERB; *be* V-ed; V n ♦ **screen|ing (screenings)** *The film-makers will be present at the screenings to introduce their works.* N-COUNT [4] A **screen** is a vertical panel which can be moved around. It is used to keep cold air away from part of a room, or to create a smaller area within a room. ❑ *They put a screen in front of me so I couldn't see what was going on.* N-COUNT [5] If something **is screened by** another thing, it is behind it and hidden by it. ❑ *Most of the road behind the hotel was screened by a block of flats.* VERB: usu passive *be* V-ed *by* n [6] To **screen for** a disease means to examine people to make sure that they do not have it. ❑ *...a quick saliva test that would screen for people at risk of tooth decay.* VERB; V *for* n ♦ **screen|ing** *Britain has an enviable record on breast screening for cancer.* N-VAR: usu N *for* n [7] When an organization **screens** people who apply to join it, it investigates them to make sure that they are not likely to cause problems. ❑ *They will screen all their candidates. ...screening procedures for the regiment.* VERB; V n; V-ing [8] To **screen** people or luggage means to check them using special equipment to make sure they are not carrying a weapon or a bomb. ❑ *The airline had been screening baggage on X-ray machines.* VERB; V n
[9] If you **screen** your telephone calls, calls made to you are connected to an answering machine or are answered by someone else, so that you can choose whether or not to speak to the people phoning you. ❑ *I employ a secretary to screen my calls.* VERB; V n

♦ **screen out** If an organization or country **screens out** certain people, it keeps them out because it thinks they may cause problems. ❑ *The company screened out applicants motivated only by money.* PHRASAL VERB; V P n (not pron)

**screen door (screen doors)** A **screen door** is a door made of fine netting which is on the outside of the main door of a house. It is used to keep insects out when the main door is open. N-COUNT

**screen name (screen names)** Someone's **screen name** is a name that they use when communicating with other people on the Internet. [COMPUTING] ❑ *...someone with the screen name of nirvanakcf.* N-COUNT

**screen|play** /skriːnpleɪ/ **(screenplays)** A **screenplay** is the words to be spoken in a film, and instructions about what will be seen in it. N-COUNT = *script*

**screen|saver** /skriːnseɪvə^r^/ **(screensavers)** also **screen saver**. A **screensaver** is a picture which appears or is put on a computer screen when the computer is not used for a while. [COMPUTING] N-COUNT

**screen test (screen tests)** When a film studio gives an actor a **screen test**, they film a short scene in order to test how good he or she would be in films. N-COUNT

**screen|writer** /skriːnraɪtə^r^/ **(screenwriters)** A **screenwriter** is a person who writes screenplays. N-COUNT

**screen|writing** /skriːnraɪtɪŋ/ **Screenwriting** is the process of writing screenplays. N-UNCOUNT

**screw** /skruː/ **(screws, screwing, screwed)**
[1] A **screw** is a metal object similar to a nail, with a raised spiral line around it. You turn a screw using a screwdriver so that it goes through two things, for example two pieces of wood, and fastens them together. ➔ See picture on page 1709. ❑ *Each bracket is fixed to the wall with just three screws.* N-COUNT [2] If you **screw** something somewhere or if it **screws** somewhere, you fix it in place by means of a screw or screws. ❑ *I had screwed the shelf on the wall myself... Screw down any loose floorboards... I particularly like the type of shelving that screws to the wall.* VERB; V n prep; V n with adv; V prep/adv [3] A **screw** lid or fitting is one that has a raised spiral line on the inside or outside of it, so that it can be fixed in place by twisting. ❑ *...an ordinary jam jar with a screw lid.* ADJ: ADJ n
[4] If you **screw** something somewhere or if it **screws** somewhere, you fix it in place by twisting it round and round. ❑ *Kelly screwed the silencer onto the pistol... Screw down the lid tightly. ...several poles that screw together to give a length of 10 yards.* VERB; V n prep; V n with adv; V prep/adv [5] If you **screw** something such as a piece of paper **into** a ball, you squeeze it or twist it tightly so that it is in the shape of a ball. [BRIT] ❑ *He screwed the paper into a ball and tossed it into the fire.* VERB; V n *into* n

in AM, use **crush**

[6] If you **screw** your face or your eyes **into** a particular expression, you tighten the muscles of your face to form that expression, for example because you are in pain or because the light is too bright. ❑ *He screwed his face into an expression of mock pain.* VERB; V n *into* n [7] If someone **screws** someone else or if two people **screw**, they have sex together. [RUDE] V-RECIP [8] Some people use **screw** in expressions such as **screw you** or **screw that** to show that they are not concerned about someone or something or that they feel contempt for them. [RUDE] VERB: only imper [feelings]
[9] If someone says that they **have been screwed**, they mean that someone else has cheated them, especially by getting money from them dishonestly. [INFORMAL, RUDE] ❑ *They haven't given us accurate information. We've been screwed.* VERB: usu passive; *be* V-ed
[10] If someone **screws** something, especially money, **out of** you, they get it from you by putting pressure on you. [mainly BRIT, INFORMAL] ❑ *For decades rich nations have been screwing money out of poor nations.* VERB; V n *out of* n [11] If you **turn** or **tighten the screw on** someone, you increase the pressure which is already on them, for example by using threats, in order to force them to do a particular thing. ❑ *Parisian taxi drivers are threatening to mount a blockade to turn the screw on the government.* PHRASE: V and N inflect, oft PHR *on* n

♦ **screw up** [1] If you **screw up** your eyes or your face, you tighten your eye or face muscles, for example because you are in pain or because the light is too bright. ❑ *She had screwed up her eyes, as if she found the sunshine too bright... Close your eyes and screw them up tight... His face screwed up in agony.* PHRASAL VERB; V P n (not pron); V n P; V P [2] If you **screw up** a piece of paper, you squeeze it tightly so that it becomes very creased and no longer flat, usually when you are throwing it away. [BRIT] ❑ *He would start writing to his family and would screw the letter up in frustration... He screwed up his first three efforts after only a line or two.* PHRASAL VERB; V n P; V P n (not pron)

in AM, use **crush**

3 To **screw** something **up**, or to **screw up**, means to cause something to fail or be spoiled. [INFORMAL] ❑ *You can't open the window because it screws up the air conditioning... Get out. Haven't you screwed things up enough already!... Somebody had screwed up; they weren't there.* PHRASAL VERB V P n (not pron) V n P V P

**screw|ball** /skruːbɔːl/ **(screwballs)** 1 **Screwball** comedy is silly and eccentric in an amusing and harmless way. [INFORMAL] ❑ *...a remake of a '50s classic screwball comedy.* ADJ: ADJ n 2 If you say that someone is a **screwball**, you mean that they do strange or crazy things. [INFORMAL] N-COUNT disapproval

**screw|driver** /skruːdraɪvəʳ/ **(screwdrivers)** A **screwdriver** is a tool that is used for turning screws. It consists of a metal rod with a flat or cross-shaped end that fits into the top of the screw. ➔ See picture on page 1709. N-COUNT

**screwed up** If you say that someone is **screwed up**, you mean that they are very confused or worried, or that they have psychological problems. [INFORMAL] ❑ *He was really screwed up with his emotional problems.* ADJ

**screw-top** A **screw-top** bottle or jar has a lid that is secured by being twisted on. ADJ: ADJ n

**scrib|ble** /skrɪbᵊl/ **(scribbles, scribbling, scribbled)** 1 If you **scribble** something, you write it quickly and roughly. ❑ *She scribbled a note to tell Mum she'd gone out... As I scribbled in my diary the light went out.* VERB V n V prep/adv 2 To **scribble** means to make meaningless marks or rough drawings using a pencil or pen. ❑ *When Caroline was five she scribbled on a wall.* VERB V prep/adv 3 **Scribble** is something that has been written or drawn quickly and roughly. ❑ *I'm sorry what I wrote was such a scribble.* N-VAR = scrawl

♦ **scribble down** If you **scribble down** something, you write it quickly or roughly. ❑ *I attempted to scribble down the names... He took my name and address, scribbling it down in his notebook.* PHRASAL VERB V P n (not pron) V n P

**scrib|bler** /skrɪbələʳ/ **(scribblers)** People sometimes refer to writers as **scribblers** when they think they are not very good writers. [mainly JOURNALISM] N-COUNT: usu pl disapproval

**scribe** /skraɪb/ **(scribes)** In the days before printing was common, a **scribe** was a person who wrote copies of things such as letters or documents. N-COUNT

**scrimp** /skrɪmp/ **(scrimps, scrimping, scrimped)** If you **scrimp on** things, you live cheaply and spend as little money as possible. ❑ *Scrimping on safety measures can be false economy.* VERB = skimp V on n

**scrip** /skrɪp/ **(scrips)** A **scrip** is a certificate which shows that an investor owns part of a share or stock. [BUSINESS] ❑ *The cash or scrip would be offered as part of a pro rata return of capital to shareholders.* N-COUNT

**script** /skrɪpt/ **(scripts, scripting, scripted)** ◆◇◇ 1 The **script** of a play, film, or television programme is the written version of it. ❑ *Jenny's writing a film script.* N-COUNT 2 The person who **scripts** a film or a radio or television play writes it. ❑ *...James Cameron, who scripted and directed both films.* VERB V n 3 You can refer to a particular system of writing as a particular **script**. ❑ *...a text in the Malay language but written in Arabic script.* N-VAR: usu adj N 4 If you say that something which has happened is not in **the script**, or that someone has not followed **the script**, you mean that something has happened which was not expected or intended to happen. ❑ *Losing was not in the script... The game plan was right. We just didn't follow the script.* N-SING: the N, usu with brd-neg

**script|ed** /skrɪptɪd/ A **scripted** speech has been written in advance, although the speaker may pretend that it is spoken without preparation. ❑ *He had prepared scripted answers.* ADJ: usu ADJ n

**scrip|tur|al** /skrɪptʃərəl/ **Scriptural** is used to describe things that are written in or based on the Christian Bible. ❑ *...scriptural accounts of the process of salvation.* ADJ: ADJ n

**scrip|ture** /skrɪptʃəʳ/ **(scriptures) Scripture** or **the scriptures** refers to writings that are regarded as holy in a particular religion, for example the Bible in Christianity. ❑ *...a quote from scripture. ...the Holy Scriptures.* N-VAR: oft the N

**script|writer** /skrɪptraɪtəʳ/ **(scriptwriters)** A **scriptwriter** is a person who writes scripts for films or for radio or television programmes. N-COUNT

**scroll** /skroʊl/ **(scrolls, scrolling, scrolled)** 1 A **scroll** is a long roll of paper or a similar material with writing on it. ❑ *Ancient scrolls were found in caves by the Dead Sea.* N-COUNT 2 A **scroll** is a painted or carved decoration made to look like a scroll. ❑ *...a handsome suite of chairs incised with Grecian scrolls.* N-COUNT 3 If you **scroll** through text on a computer screen, you move the text up or down to find the information that you need. [COMPUTING] ❑ *I scrolled down to find 'United States of America'.* VERB V prep/adv

**scroll bar (scroll bars)** On a computer screen, a **scroll bar** is a long thin box along one edge of a window, which you click on with the mouse to move the text up, down, or across the window. [COMPUTING] N-COUNT

**Scrooge** /skruːdʒ/ **(Scrooges)** If you call someone a **Scrooge**, you disapprove of them because they are very mean and hate spending money. ❑ *What a bunch of Scrooges.* N-VAR disapproval

**scro|tum** /skroʊtəm/ **(scrotums)** A man's **scrotum** is the bag of skin that contains his testicles. N-COUNT

**scrounge** /skraʊndʒ/ **(scrounges, scrounging, scrounged)** If you say that someone **scrounges** something such as food or money, you disapprove of them because they get it by asking for it, rather than by buying it or earning it. [INFORMAL] ❑ *Williams had to scrounge enough money to get his car out of the car park... The government did not give them money, forcing them to scrounge for food.* VERB disapproval V n V for n

**scrub** /skrʌb/ **(scrubs, scrubbing, scrubbed)** 1 If you **scrub** something, you rub it hard in order to clean it, using a stiff brush and water. ❑ *Surgeons began to scrub their hands and arms with soap and water before operating... The corridors are scrubbed clean.* VERB V n be V-ed adj ♦ **Scrub** is also a noun. ❑ *The walls needed a good scrub.* N-SING: a N 2 If you **scrub** dirt or stains **off** something, you remove them by rubbing hard. ❑ *I started to scrub off the dirt... Matthew stopped and scrubbed the coal dust from his face.* VERB V n with off/away V n prep 3 **Scrub** consists of low trees and bushes, especially in an area that has very little rain. ❑ *...an area of scrub and woodland.* N-UNCOUNT

**scrub|ber** /skrʌbəʳ/ **(scrubbers)** If someone refers to a woman as a **scrubber**, they are suggesting in a very rude way that she has had sex with a lot of men. [BRIT, INFORMAL, OFFENSIVE] N-COUNT disapproval

**scrub|by** /skrʌbi/ **Scrubby** land is rough and dry and covered with scrub. ❑ *...the hot, scrubby hills of western Eritrea.* ADJ: usu ADJ n

**scrub|land** /skrʌblænd/ **(scrublands) Scrubland** is an area of land which is covered with low trees and bushes. ❑ *Thousands of acres of forests and scrubland have been burnt.* N-VAR

**scruff** /skrʌf/ If someone takes you **by the scruff of** the **neck**, they take hold of the back of your neck or collar suddenly and roughly. ❑ *He picked the dog up by the scruff of the neck.* PHRASE: v n PHR

**scruffy** /skrʌfi/ **(scruffier, scruffiest)** Someone or something that is **scruffy** is dirty and untidy. ❑ *...a young man, pale, scruffy and unshaven. ...a scruffy basement flat in London.* ADJ

**scrum** /skrʌm/ **(scrums)** 1 In rugby, a **scrum** is a tight group formed by players from both sides pushing against each other with their heads down in an attempt to get the ball. N-COUNT 2 A **scrum** is a group of people who are close together and pushing against each other. [BRIT] ❑ *She pushed through the scrum of photographers. ...the scrum of shoppers.* N-COUNT: usu sing, oft N of n

**scrum|mage** /skrʌmɪdʒ/ **(scrummages)** In rugby, a **scrummage** is the same as a **scrum**. N-COUNT

**scrump|tious** /skrʌmpʃəs/ If you describe food as **scrumptious**, you mean that it tastes extremely good. [INFORMAL] ❑ *...a scrumptious apple pie.* ADJ = delicious

**scrumpy** /skrʌmpi/ **Scrumpy** is a strong alcoholic drink made from apples. [BRIT, INFORMAL] ❑ *...a pint of scrumpy.* N-UNCOUNT = cider

**scrunch** /skrʌntʃ/ **(scrunches, scrunching, scrunched)** If you **scrunch** something, you squeeze it or bend it so that it is no longer in its natural shape and is often crushed. ❑ *Her father scrunched his nose... Her mother was sitting bolt upright, scrunching her white cotton gloves into a ball.* VERB V n V n *into* n
♦ **Scrunch up** means the same as **scrunch**. ❑ *She scrunched up three pages of notes and threw them in the bin... I scrunched my hat up in my pocket.* PHRASAL VERB V P n (not pron) V n P

**scru|ple** /skruːpᵊl/ **(scruples)** **Scruples** are moral principles or beliefs that make you unwilling to do something that seems wrong. ❑ *...a man with no moral scruples.* N-VAR: usu pl

**scru|pu|lous** /skruːpjʊləs/ 1 Someone who is **scrupulous** takes great care to do what is fair, honest, or morally right. ❑ *I have been scrupulous about telling them the dangers... The Board is scrupulous in its consideration of all applications for licences.* ADJ: usu v-link ADJ [approval] 2 **Scrupulous** means thorough, exact, and careful about details. ❑ *Both readers commend Knutson for his scrupulous attention to detail.* ADJ: usu ADJ n = meticulous

**scru|ti|neer** /skruːtɪnɪəʳ/ **(scrutineers)** A **scrutineer** is a person who checks that an election or a race is carried out according to the rules. [BRIT] N-COUNT

**scru|ti|nize** /skruːtɪnaɪz/ **(scrutinizes, scrutinizing, scrutinized)**

in BRIT, also use **scrutinise**

If you **scrutinize** something, you examine it very carefully, often to find out some information from it or about it. ❑ *Her purpose was to scrutinize his features to see if he was an honest man.* VERB V n

**scru|ti|ny** /skruːtɪni/ If a person or thing is under **scrutiny**, they are being studied or observed very carefully. ❑ *His private life came under media scrutiny.* N-UNCOUNT: oft prep N

**scu|ba div|ing** /skuːbə daɪvɪŋ/ **Scuba diving** is the activity of swimming underwater using special breathing equipment. The equipment consists of cylinders of air which you carry on your back and which are connected to your mouth by rubber tubes. ♦ **scu|ba dive** *I signed up to learn how to scuba dive.* N-UNCOUNT VERB V

**scud** /skʌd/ **(scuds, scudding, scudded)** If clouds **scud** along, they move quickly and smoothly through the sky. [LITERARY] ❑ *...heavy, rain-laden clouds scudding across from the south-west.* VERB V adv/prep

**scuff** /skʌf/ **(scuffs, scuffing, scuffed)** 1 If you **scuff** something or if it **scuffs**, you mark the surface by scraping it against other things or by scraping other things against it. ❑ *Constant wheelchair use will scuff almost any floor surface... Molded plastic scuffs easily.* ♦ **scuffed** *...scuffed brown shoes.* VERB V n V adv ADJ 2 If you **scuff** your feet, you pull them along the ground as you walk. ❑ *Polly, bewildered and embarrassed, dropped her head and scuffed her feet.* VERB = drag V n

**scuf|fle** /skʌfᵊl/ **(scuffles, scuffling, scuffled)** 1 A **scuffle** is a short, disorganized fight or struggle. ❑ *Violent scuffles broke out between rival groups demonstrating for and against independence.* N-COUNT 2 If people **scuffle**, they fight for a short time in a disorganized way. ❑ *Police scuffled with some of the protesters... He and Hannah had been scuffling in the yard outside his house.* V-RECIP V *with* n pl-n V

**scuf|fling** /skʌfəlɪŋ/ A **scuffling** noise is a noise made by a person or animal moving about, usually one that you cannot see. ❑ *There was a scuffling noise in the background.* ADJ: ADJ n

**scuff mark** **(scuff marks)** **Scuff marks** are marks made on a smooth surface when something is rubbed against it. ❑ *Scuff marks from shoes are difficult to remove.* N-COUNT: usu pl

**scull** /skʌl/ **(sculls)** 1 **Sculls** are small oars which are held by one person and used to move a boat through water. N-COUNT: usu pl 2 A **scull** is a small light racing boat which is rowed with two sculls. N-COUNT

**scul|lery** /skʌləri/ **(sculleries)** A **scullery** is a small room next to a kitchen where washing and other household tasks are done. [BRIT, OLD-FASHIONED] N-COUNT

**sculpt** /skʌlpt/ **(sculpts, sculpting, sculpted)** 1 When an artist **sculpts** something, they carve or shape it out of a material such as stone or clay. ❑ *An artist sculpted a full-size replica of her head... When I sculpt, my style is expressionistic.* VERB V n V 2 If something **is sculpted**, it is made into a particular shape. ❑ *More familiar landscapes have been sculpted by surface erosion... Michael smoothed and sculpted Jane's hair into shape.* VERB *be* V-ed V n *into* n

**sculp|tor** /skʌlptəʳ/ **(sculptors)** A **sculptor** is someone who creates sculptures. N-COUNT

**sculp|tur|al** /skʌlptʃərəl/ **Sculptural** means relating to sculpture. ❑ *He enjoyed working with clay as a sculptural form.* ADJ: usu ADJ n

**sculp|ture** /skʌlptʃəʳ/ **(sculptures)** 1 A **sculpture** is a work of art that is produced by carving or shaping stone, wood, clay, or other materials. ❑ *...stone sculptures of figures and animals. ...a collection of 20th-century art and sculpture.* N-VAR 2 **Sculpture** is the art of creating sculptures. ❑ *Both studied sculpture.* N-UNCOUNT

**sculp|tured** /skʌlptʃəʳd/ **Sculptured** objects have been carved or shaped from something. ❑ *...a beautifully sculptured bronze horse.* ADJ

**scum** /skʌm/ 1 If you refer to people as **scum**, you are expressing your feelings of dislike and disgust for them. [INFORMAL] N-PLURAL [disapproval] 2 **Scum** is a layer of a dirty or unpleasant-looking substance on the surface of a liquid. ❑ *...scum marks around the bath.* N-UNCOUNT

**scum|bag** /skʌmbæg/ **(scumbags)** If you refer to someone as a **scumbag**, you are expressing your feelings of dislike and disgust for them. [INFORMAL] N-COUNT [disapproval]

**scup|per** /skʌpəʳ/ **(scuppers, scuppering, scuppered)** To **scupper** a plan or attempt means to spoil it completely. [mainly BRIT, JOURNALISM] ❑ *If Schneider had seen him that would have scuppered all his plans.* VERB V n

**scur|ril|ous** /skʌrɪləs, AM skɜːr-/ **Scurrilous** accusations or stories are untrue and unfair, and are likely to damage the reputation of the person that they relate to. ❑ *Scurrilous and untrue stories were being invented.* ADJ: usu ADJ n

**scur|ry** /skʌri, AM skɜːri/ **(scurries, scurrying, scurried)** 1 When people or small animals **scurry** somewhere, they move there quickly and hurriedly, especially because they are frightened. [WRITTEN] ❑ *The attack began, sending residents scurrying for cover.* VERB V prep/adv 2 If people **scurry to** do something, they do it as soon as they can. [WRITTEN] ❑ *Pictures of starving children have sent many people scurrying to donate money.* VERB = rush V to-inf

**scur|vy** /skɜːʳvi/ **Scurvy** is a disease that is caused by a lack of vitamin C. N-UNCOUNT

**scut|tle** /skʌtᵊl/ **(scuttles, scuttling, scuttled)** 1 When people or small animals **scuttle** somewhere, they run there with short quick steps. ❑ *Two very small children scuttled away in front of them.* VERB V adv/prep 2 To **scuttle** a plan or a proposal means to make it fail or cause it to stop. ❑ *Such threats could scuttle the peace conference.* VERB = scupper V n 3 To **scuttle** a ship means to sink it deliberately by making holes in the bottom. ❑ *He personally had received orders from Commander Lehmann to scuttle the ship.* VERB V n Also V

**scuz|zy** /skʌzi/ **(scuzzier, scuzziest)** Something that is **scuzzy** is dirty or disgusting. [INFORMAL] ❑ *...a scuzzy drug district in New York.* ADJ

**scythe** /saɪð/ **(scythes, scything, scythed)** 1 A **scythe** is a tool with a long curved blade at right N-COUNT angles to a long handle. It is used to cut long grass or grain. [2] If you **scythe** grass or grain, you cut it with a scythe. ❑ *Two men were attempting to scythe the long grass.* VERB · V n

**SE**

✔ in AM, also use **S.E.**

**SE** is a written abbreviation for **south-east**.

**sea** /siː/ **(seas)** ◆◆◇ [1] **The sea** is the salty water that covers about three-quarters of the earth's surface. ❑ *Most of the kids have never seen the sea... All transport operations, whether by sea, rail or road, are closely monitored at all times.* N-SING: the N, also by N = ocean [2] You use **seas** when you are describing the sea at a particular time or in a particular area. [LITERARY] ❑ *He drowned after 30 minutes in the rough seas.* N-PLURAL [3] A **sea** is a large area of salty water that is part of an ocean or is surrounded by land. ❑ *...the North Sea. ...the huge inland sea of Turkana.* N-COUNT; N-IN-NAMES

PHRASES [4] **At sea** means on or under the sea, far away from land. ❑ *The boats remain at sea for an average of ten days at a time.* PHRASE: v-link PHR, PHR after v [5] If you go or look out **to sea**, you go or look across the sea. ❑ *...fishermen who go to sea for two weeks at a time... He pointed out to sea.* PHRASE: PHR after v

**sea air** The **sea air** is the air at the seaside, which is regarded as being good for people's health. ❑ *I took a deep breath of the fresh sea air.* N-UNCOUNT

**sea|bed** /siːbed/ also **sea bed. The seabed** is the ground under the sea. N-SING

**sea|bird** /siːbɜːʳd/ **(seabirds)** also **sea bird. Seabirds** are birds that live near the sea and get their food from it. ❑ *The island is covered with seabirds.* N-COUNT

**sea|board** /siːbɔːʳd/ **(seaboards) The seaboard** is the part of a country that is next to the sea; used especially of the coasts of North America. ❑ *...the Eastern seaboard of the USA.* N-COUNT: usu the N in sing = coast

**sea|borne** /siːbɔːʳn/ also **sea-borne. Seaborne** actions or events take place on the sea in ships. ❑ *...a seaborne invasion.* ADJ: ADJ n

**sea breeze (sea breezes)** A **sea breeze** is a light wind blowing from the sea towards the land. N-COUNT

**sea cap|tain (sea captains)** A **sea captain** is a person in command of a ship, usually a ship that carries goods for trade. N-COUNT

**sea change (sea changes)** A **sea change** in someone's attitudes or behaviour is a complete change. ❑ *A sea change has taken place in young people's attitudes to their parents.* N-COUNT

**sea dog (sea dogs)** also **seadog.** A **sea dog** is a sailor is who has spent many years at sea. [OLD-FASHIONED] N-COUNT

**sea|farer** /siːfeərəʳ/ **(seafarers) Seafarers** are people who work on ships or people who travel regularly on the sea. [WRITTEN] ❑ *The Estonians have always been seafarers.* N-COUNT: usu pl

**sea|faring** /siːfeərɪŋ/ **Seafaring** means working as a sailor or travelling regularly on the sea. ❑ *The Lebanese were a seafaring people.* ADJ: ADJ n

**sea|floor** /siːflɔːʳ/ **The seafloor** is the ground under the sea. N-SING = seabed

**sea|food** /siːfuːd/ **(seafoods) Seafood** is shellfish such as lobsters, mussels, and crabs, and sometimes other sea creatures that you can eat. ❑ *...a seafood restaurant.* N-UNCOUNT: also N in pl

**sea|front** /siːfrʌnt/ **(seafronts) The seafront** is the part of a seaside town that is nearest to the sea. It usually consists of a road with buildings that face the sea. ❑ *They decided to meet on the seafront.* N-COUNT: usu the N in sing

**sea|going** /siːgoʊɪŋ/ also **sea-going. Seagoing** boats and ships are designed for travelling on the sea, rather than on lakes, rivers, or canals. ADJ: ADJ n = ocean-going

**sea-green** also **sea green.** Something that is **sea-green** is a bluish-green colour like the colour of the sea. ❑ *...her sea-green eyes.* COLOUR

**sea|gull** /siːgʌl/ **(seagulls)** A **seagull** is a common kind of bird with white or grey feathers. N-COUNT

**sea|horse** /siːhɔːʳs/ **(seahorses)** also **sea horse.** A **seahorse** is a type of small fish which appears to swim in a vertical position and whose head looks a little like the head of a horse. N-COUNT

**seal**

① CLOSING
② ANIMAL

**① seal** /siːl/ **(seals, sealing, sealed)** ◆◇◇

⇒ Please look at category 11 to see if the expression you are looking for is shown under another headword. [1] When you **seal** an envelope, you close it by folding part of it over and sticking it down, so that it cannot be opened without being torn. ❑ *He sealed the envelope and put on a stamp... Write your letter and seal it in a blank envelope... A courier was despatched with two sealed envelopes.* VERB · V n · V n in n · V-ed [2] If you **seal** a container or an opening, you cover it with something in order to prevent air, liquid, or other material getting in or out. If you **seal** something **in** a container, you put it inside and then close the container tightly. ❑ *She merely filled the containers, sealed them with a cork, and pasted on labels. ...a lid to seal in heat and keep food moist. ...a hermetically sealed, leak-proof packet.* VERB · V n · V n with in · V-ed [3] The **seal** on a container or opening is the part where it has been sealed. ❑ *When assembling the pie, wet the edges where the two crusts join, to form a seal.* N-COUNT [4] A **seal** is a device or a piece of material, for example in a machine, which closes an opening tightly so that air, liquid, or other substances cannot get in or out. ❑ *Check seals on fridges and freezers regularly.* N-COUNT: oft N on n [5] A **seal** is something such as a piece of sticky paper or wax that is fixed to a container or door and must be broken before the container or door can be opened. ❑ *The seal on the box broke when it fell from its hiding-place.* N-COUNT: oft N on n [6] A **seal** is a special mark or design, for example on a document, representing someone or something. It may be used to show that something is genuine or officially approved. ❑ *...a supply of note paper bearing the Presidential seal.* N-COUNT: usu with supp [7] If someone in authority **seals** an area, they stop people entering or passing through it, for example by placing barriers in the way. ❑ *The soldiers were deployed to help paramilitary police seal the border... A wide area round the two-storey building is sealed to all traffic except the emergency services.* VERB · V n · V-ed ♦ **Seal off** means the same as **seal.** ❑ *Police and troops sealed off the area after the attack... Soldiers there are going to seal the airport off.* PHRASAL VERB · V P n (not pron) · V n P [8] To **seal** something means to make it definite or confirm how it is going to be. [WRITTEN] ❑ *McLaren are close to sealing a deal with Renault... His artistic character was sealed by his experiences of the First World War.* VERB · V n · V n

PHRASES [9] If something **sets** or **puts the seal on** something, it makes it definite or confirms how it is going to be. [WRITTEN] ❑ *Such a visit may set the seal on a new relationship between the two governments.* PHRASE: V inflects [10] If a document is **under seal**, it is in a sealed envelope and cannot be looked at, for example because it is private. [FORMAL] ❑ *Because the transcript is still under seal, I am precluded by law from discussing the evidence.* PHRASE: v-link PHR, n PHR [11] to **seal** someone's **fate** → see **fate**.

♦ **seal in** If something **seals in** a smell or liquid, it prevents it from getting out of a food. ❑ *The coffee is freeze-dried to seal in all the flavour.* PHRASAL VERB · V P n · Also V n P

♦ **seal off** [1] If one object or area **is sealed off** from another, there is a physical barrier between them, so that nothing can pass between them. ❑ *Windows are usually sealed off. ...the anti-personnel door that sealed off the chamber.* PHRASAL VERB · be V-ed P · V P n (not pron) [2] → see **seal 7**.

♦ **seal up** If you **seal** something **up**, you close it completely so that nothing can get in or out. ❑ *The paper was used for sealing up holes in walls and roofs.* PHRASAL VERB · V P n (not pron) · Also V n P

**② seal** /siːl/ **(seals)** A **seal** is a large animal with a rounded body and flat legs called flippers. N-COUNT

Seals eat fish and live in and near the sea, usually in cold parts of the world.

**sea lane** **(sea lanes)** Sea lanes are particular routes which ships regularly use in order to cross a sea or ocean. N-COUNT: usu pl

**seal|ant** /siːlənt/ **(sealants)** A **sealant** is a substance that is used to seal holes, cracks, or gaps. N-MASS

**seal|er** /siːləʳ/ **(sealers)** A **sealer** is the same as a **sealant**. N-MASS

**sea lev|el** also **sea-level. Sea level** is the average level of the sea with respect to the land. The height of mountains or other areas is calculated in relation to **sea level**. ❑ *The stadium was 2275 metres above sea level.* N-UNCOUNT

**seal|ing wax** **Sealing wax** is a hard, usually red, substance that melts quickly and is used for putting seals on documents or letters. N-UNCOUNT

**sea lion** **(sea lions)** also **sea-lion.** A **sea lion** is a type of large seal. N-COUNT

**seal|skin** /siːlskɪn/ **Sealskin** is the fur of a seal, used to make coats and other clothing. ❑ *...waterproof sealskin boots.* N-UNCOUNT: oft N n

**seam** /siːm/ **(seams)** [1] A **seam** is a line of stitches which joins two pieces of cloth together. N-COUNT [2] A **seam** of coal is a long, narrow layer of it underneath the ground. ❑ *The average UK coal seam is one metre thick.* N-COUNT: usu with supp

**PHRASES** [3] If something **is coming apart at the seams** or **is falling apart at the seams**, it is no longer working properly and may soon stop working completely. ❑ *Britain's university system is in danger of falling apart at the seams.* PHRASE: V inflects [4] If a place is very full, you can say that it **is bursting at the seams.** ❑ *The hotels of Warsaw, Prague and Budapest were bursting at the seams.* PHRASE: V inflects

**sea|man** /siːmən/ **(seamen)** A **seaman** is a sailor, especially one who is not an officer. ❑ *The men emigrate to work as seamen.* N-COUNT

**sea|man|ship** /siːmənʃɪp/ **Seamanship** is skill in managing a boat and controlling its movement through the sea. ❑ *...the art of seamanship and navigation.* N-UNCOUNT

**seam|less** /siːmləs/ You use **seamless** to describe something that has no breaks or gaps in it or which continues without stopping. ❑ *It was a seamless procession of wonderful electronic music.* ADJ ♦ **seam|less|ly** *He has moved seamlessly from theory to practice.* ADV: ADV with v

**seam|stress** /siːmstrəs, sem-/ **(seamstresses)** A **seamstress** is a woman who sews and makes clothes as her job. [OLD-FASHIONED] N-COUNT

**seamy** /siːmi/ **(seamier, seamiest)** If you describe something as **seamy**, you mean that it involves unpleasant aspects of life such as crime, sex, or violence. ❑ *...Hamburg's seamy St Pauli's district.* ADJ: usu ADJ n = sleazy

**se|ance** /seɪɑːns/ **(seances)** also **séance.** A **seance** is a meeting in which people try to make contact with people who have died. N-COUNT

**sea|plane** /siːpleɪn/ **(seaplanes)** A **seaplane** is a type of aeroplane that can take off from or land on water. N-COUNT

**sea|port** /siːpɔːʳt/ **(seaports)** A **seaport** is a town with a large harbour that is used by ships. ❑ *...the Baltic seaport of Rostock.* N-COUNT

**sea pow|er** **(sea powers)** [1] **Sea power** is the size and strength of a country's navy. ❑ *The transformation of American sea power began in 1940.* N-UNCOUNT [2] A **sea power** is a country that has a large navy. N-COUNT

**sear** /sɪəʳ/ **(sears, searing, seared)** [1] To **sear** something means to burn its surface with a sudden intense heat. ❑ *Grass fires have seared the land near the farming village of Basekhai.* VERB V n [2] If something **sears** a part of your body, it causes a painful burning feeling there. [LITERARY] ❑ *I distinctly felt the heat start to sear my throat.* VERB V n [3] ➔ See also **searing.**

**search** /sɜːʳtʃ/ **(searches, searching, searched)** ◆◆◇ [1] If you **search for** something or someone, you look carefully for them. ❑ *The Turkish security forces have started searching for the missing men... Nonetheless there are signs that both sides may be searching for a compromise.* VERB V for n V for n [2] If you **search** a place, you look carefully for something or someone there. ❑ *Armed troops searched the hospital yesterday... She searched her desk for the necessary information... Relief workers are still searching through collapsed buildings looking for victims.* VERB V n V n for n V prep [3] A **search** is an attempt to find something or someone by looking for them carefully. ❑ *There was no chance of him being found alive and the search was abandoned... Egypt has said there is no time to lose in the search for a Middle East settlement.* N-COUNT: oft N for n [4] If a police officer or someone else in authority **searches** you, they look carefully to see whether you have something hidden on you. ❑ *The man took her suitcase from her and then searched her... His first task was to search them for weapons.* VERB V n V n for n [5] If you **search for** information on a computer, you give the computer an instruction to find that information. [COMPUTING] ❑ *You can use a directory service to search for people on the Internet.* VERB V for n ♦ **Search** is also a noun. ❑ *He was doing a computer search of local news articles.* N-COUNT [6] ➔ See also **searching, strip-search.** [7] If you go **in search of** something or someone, you try to find them. ❑ *Miserable, and unexpectedly lonely, she went in search of Jean-Paul... The law already denies entry to people in search of better economic opportunities.* PHRASE: PHR after v, PHR n [8] You say **'search me'** when someone asks you a question and you want to emphasize that you do not know the answer. [INFORMAL] CONVENTION emphasis

♦ **search out** If you **search** something **out**, you keep looking for it until you find it. ❑ *Traditional Spanish food is delicious and its specialities are worth searching out... Many people want jobs. They try to search them out every day.* PHRASAL VERB = seek out V P n (not pron) V n P

**search en|gine** **(search engines)** A **search engine** is a computer program that searches for documents containing a particular word or words on the Internet. [COMPUTING] N-COUNT

**search|er** /sɜːʳtʃəʳ/ **(searchers)** [1] **Searchers** are people who are looking for someone or something that is missing. ❑ *Searchers have found three mountain climbers missing since Saturday.* N-COUNT: usu pl [2] A **searcher** is someone who is trying to find something such as the truth or the answer to a problem. ❑ *He's not a real searcher after truth.* N-COUNT: oft N after/for n = seeker

**search|ing** /sɜːʳtʃɪŋ/ A **searching** question or look is intended to discover the truth about something. ❑ *They asked her some searching questions on moral philosophy and logic.* ➔ See also **soul-searching.** ADJ: usu ADJ n

**search|light** /sɜːʳtʃlaɪt/ **(searchlights)** A **searchlight** is a large powerful light that can be turned to shine a long way in any direction. N-COUNT

**search par|ty** **(search parties)** A **search party** is an organized group of people who are searching for someone who is missing. N-COUNT

**search war|rant** **(search warrants)** A **search warrant** is a special document that gives the police permission to search a house or other building. ❑ *Officers armed with a search warrant entered the flat.* N-COUNT

**sear|ing** /sɪərɪŋ/ [1] **Searing** is used to indicate that something such as pain or heat is very intense. ❑ *She woke to feel a searing pain in her feet.* ADJ: ADJ n [2] A **searing** speech or piece of writing is very critical. ❑ *...searing criticism.* ADJ: ADJ n

**sea|scape** /siːskeɪp/ **(seascapes)** A **seascape** is a painting or photograph of a scene at sea. N-COUNT

**sea|shell** /siːʃel/ **(seashells)** also **sea shell. Seashells** are the empty shells of small sea creatures. N-COUNT: usu pl = shell

**sea|shore** /siːʃɔːʳ/ **(seashores)** **The seashore** is the part of a coast where the land slopes down into the sea. ❑ *She takes her inspiration from shells and stones she finds on the seashore.* N-COUNT: usu the N in sing

**sea|sick** /siːsɪk/ If someone is **seasick** when they are travelling in a boat, they vomit or feel sick because of the way the boat is moving. ❑ *It was quite rough at times, and she was seasick.* ♦ **sea|sick|ness** *He was very prone to seasickness and already felt queasy.* ADJ: usu v-link ADJ N-UNCOUNT

**sea|side** /siːsaɪd/ You can refer to an area that is close to the sea, especially one where people go for their holidays, as **the seaside**. ❑ *I went to spend a few days at the seaside... The town was Redcar, a seaside resort on the Cleveland coast.* N-SING: *the* N, N n

**sea|son** /siːzᵊn/ **(seasons, seasoning, seasoned)** ◆◆◆ 1 The **seasons** are the main periods into which a year can be divided and which each have their own typical weather conditions. ❑ *Autumn's my favourite season. ...the only region of Brazil where all four seasons are clearly defined. ...the rainy season.* N-COUNT: usu with supp 2 You can use **season** to refer to the period during each year when a particular activity or event takes place. For example, the planting **season** is the period when a particular plant or crop is planted. ❑ *...birds arriving for the breeding season.* N-COUNT: usu sing, usu *the* -ing N 3 You can use **season** to refer to the period when a particular fruit, vegetable, or other food is ready for eating and is widely available. ❑ *The plum season is about to begin... Now British asparagus is in season.* N-COUNT: n N, also *in/out of* N 4 You can use **season** to refer to a fixed period during each year when a particular sport is played. ❑ *...the baseball season... It is his first race this season.* N-COUNT: usu sing, with supp 5 A **season** is a period in which a play or show, or a series of plays or shows, is performed in one place. ❑ *...a season of three new plays.* N-COUNT: with supp 6 A **season of** films is several of them shown as a series because they are connected in some way. ❑ *...a brief season of films in which Artaud appeared.* N-COUNT: usu sing, usu with supp 7 The holiday or vacation **season** is the time when most people have their holiday. ❑ *...the peak holiday season... There are discos and clubs but these are often closed out of season.* N-COUNT: usu sing, usu supp N, also *in/out of* N 8 If you **season** food with salt, pepper, or spices, you add them to it in order to improve its flavour. ❑ *Season the meat with salt and pepper... I believe in seasoning food before putting it on the table.* VERB V n *with* n V n 9 If wood **is seasoned**, it is made suitable for making into furniture or for burning, usually by being allowed to dry out gradually. ❑ *Ensure that new wood has been seasoned.* VERB: usu passive *be* V-ed 10 ➔ See also **seasoned**, **seasoning**. 11 If a female animal is **in season**, she is in a state where she is ready to have sex. PHRASE: usu v-link PHR

**sea|son|al** /siːzənᵊl/ A **seasonal** factor, event, or change occurs during one particular time of the year. ❑ *Seasonal variations need to be taken into account.* ♦ **sea|son|al|ly** *The seasonally adjusted unemployment figures show a rise of twelve-hundred.* ADJ: ADJ n ADV: usu ADV -ed

**sea|son|al af|fec|tive dis|or|der** **Seasonal affective disorder** is a feeling of tiredness and sadness that some people have during the autumn and winter when there is very little sunshine. The abbreviation **SAD** is often used. N-UNCOUNT

**sea|soned** /siːzᵊnd/ You can use **seasoned** to describe a person who has a lot of experience of something. For example, a **seasoned** traveller is a person who has travelled a lot. ❑ *He began acting with the confidence of a seasoned performer.* ADJ: usu ADJ n

**sea|son|ing** /siːzənɪŋ/ **(seasonings)** **Seasoning** is salt, pepper, or other spices that are added to food to improve its flavour. ❑ *Mix the meat with the onion, carrot, and some seasoning.* N-MASS

**sea|son tick|et** **(season tickets)** A **season ticket** is a ticket that you can use repeatedly during a certain period, without having to pay each time. You can buy **season tickets** for things such as buses, trains, regular sporting events, or theatre performances. ❑ *We went to renew our monthly season ticket.* N-COUNT

**seat** /siːt/ **(seats, seating, seated)** ◆◆◇ 1 A **seat** is an object that you can sit on, for example a chair. ❑ *Stephen returned to his seat... Ann could remember sitting in the back seat of their car.* N-COUNT 2 The **seat** of a chair is the part that you sit on. ❑ *The stool had a torn, red plastic seat.* N-COUNT 3 If you **seat yourself** somewhere, you sit down. [WRITTEN] ❑ *He waved towards a chair, and seated himself at the desk. ...a portrait of one of his favourite models seated on an elegant sofa.* VERB V pron-refl V-ed 4 A building or vehicle that **seats** a particular number of people has enough seats for that number. ❑ *The Theatre seats 570.* VERB V amount 5 **The seat of** a piece of clothing is the part that covers your bottom. ❑ *Then he got up and brushed off the seat of his jeans.* N-SING: usu *the* N *of* n 6 When someone is elected to a parliament, congress, or senate, you can say that they, or their party, have won a **seat**. ❑ *Independent candidates won the majority of seats on the local council. ...a Maryland Republican who lost his seat.* N-COUNT 7 If someone has a **seat** on the board of a company or on a committee, they are a member of it. ❑ *He has been unsuccessful in his attempt to win a seat on the board of the company.* N-COUNT 8 The **seat** of an organization, a wealthy family, or an activity is its base. ❑ *Gunfire broke out early this morning around the seat of government in Lagos.* N-COUNT: with supp 9 ➔ See also **deep-seated**, **hot seat**.
PHRASES 10 If you **take a back seat**, you allow other people to have all the power and to make all the decisions. ❑ *You need to take a back seat and think about both past and future.* PHRASE: V inflects 11 If you **take a seat**, you sit down. [FORMAL] ❑ *'Take a seat,' he said in a bored tone... Rachel smiled at him as they took their seats on opposite sides of the table.* PHRASE: V and N inflect 12 **in the driving seat** ➔ see **driving seat**. **by the seat of** your **pants** ➔ see **pants**.

**seat belt** **(seat belts)** also **seatbelt.** A **seat belt** is a strap attached to a seat in a car or an aircraft. You fasten it across your body in order to prevent yourself being thrown out of the seat if there is a sudden movement. ➔ See picture on page 1707. ❑ *The fact I was wearing a seat belt saved my life.* N-COUNT = safety belt

**-seater** /-siːtəʳ/ **(-seaters)** **-seater** combines with numbers to form adjectives and nouns which indicate how many people something such as a car has seats for. ❑ *...a three-seater sofa... The plane is an eight-seater with twin propellers.* ➔ See also **all-seater**. COMB in ADJ and N-COUNT

**seat|ing** /siːtɪŋ/ 1 You can refer to the seats in a place as the **seating**. ❑ *The stadium has been fitted with seating for over eighty thousand spectators.* N-UNCOUNT 2 The **seating** at a public place or a formal occasion is the arrangement of where people will sit. ❑ *She checked the seating arrangements before the guests filed into the dining-room.* N-UNCOUNT: oft N n

**seat of learn|ing** **(seats of learning)** People sometimes refer to a university or a similar institution as a **seat of learning**. [WRITTEN] ❑ *...one department of that great seat of learning.* N-COUNT

**sea tur|tle** **(sea turtles)** A **sea turtle** is a large reptile which has a thick shell covering its body and which lives in the sea most of the time. [AM] N-COUNT

✓ in BRIT, use **turtle**

**sea ur|chin** **(sea urchins)** A **sea urchin** is a small round sea creature that has a hard shell covered with sharp points. N-COUNT

**sea wall** **(sea walls)** A **sea wall** is a wall built along the edge of the sea to stop the sea flowing over the land or destroying it. ❑ *Cherbourg had a splendid harbour enclosed by a long sea wall.* N-COUNT

**sea|ward** /siːwəʳd/

✓ The form **seawards** can also be used for meaning 1.

1 Something that moves or faces **seaward** or **seawards** moves or faces in the direction of the sea or further out to sea. ❑ *A barge was about a hundred yards away, waiting to return seaward... It faced seawards to the north.* ADV: ADV after v ≠ inland 2 The **seaward** side of something faces in the direction of the sea or further out to sea. ❑ *The houses on the seaward side of the road were all in ruins.* ADJ: usu ADJ n

**sea wa|ter** also **seawater.** **Sea water** is salt water from the sea. N-UNCOUNT

**sea|weed** /siːwiːd/ **(seaweeds) Seaweed** is a plant that grows in the sea. There are many kinds of seaweed. ❑ *...seaweed washed up on a beach.* N-MASS

**sea|worthy** /siːwɜːʳði/ A ship or boat which is **seaworthy** is fit to travel at sea. ❑ *The ship was completely seaworthy.* ADJ ♦ **sea|worthiness** *It didn't reach required standards of safety and seaworthiness.* N-UNCOUNT

**se|bum** /siːbəm/ **Sebum** is an oily substance produced by glands in your skin. N-UNCOUNT

**sec** /sek/ **(secs)** If you ask someone to wait a **sec**, you are asking them to wait for a very short time. [INFORMAL] ❑ *Can you just hang on a sec?... Be with you in a sec.* N-COUNT: usu *a* N in sing

**sec.** /sek/ **(secs) Sec.** is a written abbreviation for **second** or **seconds**. ❑ *Grete Waitz finished with a time of 2 hrs, 29 min., 30 sec.*

**seca|teurs** /sekətɜːʳz/ **Secateurs** are a gardening tool that look like a pair of strong, heavy scissors. Secateurs are used for cutting the stems of plants. [BRIT] N-PLURAL: also *a pair of* N

✓ in AM, use **pruning shears**

**se|cede** /sɪsiːd/ **(secedes, seceding, seceded)** If a region or group **secedes from** the country or larger group to which it belongs, it formally becomes a separate country or stops being a member of the larger group. ❑ *Singapore seceded from the Federation of Malaysia and became an independent sovereign state...* (V *from* n) *On 20 August 1960 Senegal seceded.* (V) VERB

**se|ces|sion** /sɪseʃᵊn/ The **secession** of a region or group from the country or larger group to which it belongs is the action of formally becoming separate. ❑ *...the Ukraine's secession from the Soviet Union.* N-UNCOUNT

**se|ces|sion|ist** /sɪseʃənɪst/ **(secessionists) Secessionists** are people who want their region or group to become separate from the country or larger group to which it belongs. ❑ *...Lithuanian secessionists.* N-COUNT: usu pl, N n

**se|clud|ed** /sɪkluːdɪd/ A **secluded** place is quiet and private. ❑ *We were tucked away in a secluded corner of the room... We found a secluded beach a few miles further on.* ADJ: usu ADJ n

**se|clu|sion** /sɪkluːʒᵊn/ If you are living **in seclusion**, you are in a quiet place away from other people. ❑ *She lived in seclusion with her husband on their farm in Panama... They love the seclusion of their garden.* N-UNCOUNT

**second**
① PART OF A MINUTE
② COMING AFTER SOMETHING ELSE
③ SENDING SOMEONE TO DO A JOB

**①sec|ond** /sekənd/ **(seconds)** A **second** is one of the sixty parts that a minute is divided into. People often say '**a second**' or '**seconds**' when they simply mean a very short time. ❑ *For a few seconds nobody said anything... It only takes forty seconds... Her orbital speed must be a few hundred meters per second... Within seconds the other soldiers began firing too.* ◆◆◆ N-COUNT

**②sec|ond** /sekənd/ **(seconds, seconding, seconded)** ◆◆◆

⇛ Please look at category 13 to see if the expression you are looking for is shown under another headword. 1 The **second** item in a series is the one that you count as number two. ❑ *...the second day of his visit to Delhi. ...their second child... My son just got married for the second time... She was the second of nine children. ...King Charles the Second... Britain came second in the Prix St Georges Derby.* ORD 2 **Second** is used before superlative adjectives to indicate that there is only one thing better or larger than the thing you are referring to. ❑ *The party is still the second strongest in Italy. ...the second-largest city in the United States.* ORD: ORD adj-superl 3 You say **second** when you want to make a second point or give a second reason for something. ❑ *The soil is depleted first by having crops grown in it and second by natural weathering and bacterial action.* ADV: ADV cl 4 In Britain, an **upper second** is a good honours degree and a **lower second** is an average honours degree. ❑ *I then went up to Lancaster University and got an upper second.* N-COUNT 5 If you have **seconds**, you have a second helping of food. [INFORMAL] ❑ *There's seconds if you want them.* N-PLURAL 6 **Seconds** are goods that are sold cheaply in shops because they have slight faults. ❑ *It's a new shop selling discounted lines and seconds.* N-COUNT: usu pl 7 The **seconds** of someone who is taking part in a boxing match or chess tournament are the people who assist and encourage them. ❑ *He shouted to his seconds, 'I did it! I did it!'* N-COUNT: usu pl 8 If you **second** a proposal in a meeting or debate, you formally express your agreement with it so that it can then be discussed or voted on. ❑ *...Bryan Sutton, who seconded the motion against fox hunting.* VERB, V n ♦ **sec|ond|er (seconders)** *Candidates need a proposer and seconder whose names are kept secret.* N-COUNT 9 If you **second** what someone has said, you say that you agree with them or say the same thing yourself. ❑ *The Prime Minister seconded the call for discipline in a speech last week.* VERB, V n

PHRASES 10 If you experience something **at second hand**, you are told about it by other people rather than experiencing it yourself. ❑ *Most of them had only heard of the massacre at second hand.* → See also **second-hand**. PHRASE: PHR after v 11 If you say that something is **second to none**, you are emphasizing that it is very good indeed or the best that there is. ❑ *Our scientific research is second to none.* PHRASE: v-link PHR, emphasis 12 If you say that something is **second only to** something else, you mean that only that thing is better or greater than it. ❑ *As a major health risk hepatitis is second only to tobacco.* PHRASE: usu v-link PHR 13 **second nature** → see **nature**. **in the second place** → see **place**.

**③se|cond** /sɪkɒnd/ **(seconds, seconding, seconded)** If you **are seconded** somewhere, you are sent there temporarily by your employer in order to do special duties. [BRIT] ❑ *In 1937 he was seconded to the Royal Canadian Air Force in Ottawa as air armament adviser...* (*be* V-ed prep/adv) *Several hundred soldiers have been seconded to help farmers.* (*be* V-ed to-inf) VERB: usu passive

**sec|ond|ary** /sekəndri, AM -deri/ 1 If you describe something as **secondary**, you mean that it is less important than something else. ❑ *The street erupted in a huge explosion, with secondary explosions in the adjoining buildings... The actual damage to the brain cells is secondary to the damage caused to the blood supply.* ADJ: usu ADJ n, also v-link ADJ *to* n 2 **Secondary** diseases or infections happen as a result of another disease or infection that has already happened. ❑ *He had kidney cancer, with secondary tumours in the brain and lungs.* ADJ: usu ADJ n 3 **Secondary** education is given to pupils between the ages of 11 or 12 and 17 or 18. ❑ *Examinations for the GCSE are taken after about five years of secondary education.* ADJ

**sec|ond|ary mod|ern (secondary moderns) Secondary moderns** were schools which existed until recently in Britain for children aged between about eleven and sixteen, where more attention was paid to practical skills and less to academic study than in a grammar school. N-COUNT

**sec|ond|ary school (secondary schools)** A **secondary school** is a school for pupils between the ages of 11 or 12 and 17 or 18. ❑ *She taught history at a secondary school.* N-VAR

**sec|ond best** also **second-best.** 1 **Second best** is used to describe something that is not as good as the best thing of its kind but is better than all the other things of that kind. ❑ *He put on his second best suit.* ADJ: usu ADJ n 2 You can use **second best** to describe something that you have to accept even though you would have preferred something else. ❑ *He refused to settle for anything that was second best.* ADJ ♦ **Second best** is also a noun. ❑ *Oatmeal is a good second best.* N-SING

**sec|ond cham|ber** The **second chamber** is one of the two groups that a parliament is divided into. In Britain, the second chamber is the House of Lords. In the United States, the second N-SING chamber can be either the Senate or the House of Representatives.

**sec|ond child|hood** If you say that an old person is in their **second childhood**, you mean that their mind is becoming weaker and that their behaviour is similar to that of a young child. N-SING

**second-class** also **second class.** 1 If someone treats you as a **second-class** citizen, they treat you as if you are less valuable and less important than other people. ❑ *Too many airlines treat our children as second-class citizens.* ADJ: ADJ n 2 If you describe something as **second-class**, you mean that it is of poor quality. ❑ *I am not prepared to see children in some parts of this country having to settle for a second-class education.* ADJ: usu ADJ n = second-rate 3 The **second-class** accommodation on a train or ship is the ordinary accommodation, which is cheaper and less comfortable than the first-class accommodation. ❑ *He sat in the corner of a second-class carriage. ...a second-class ticket.* ADJ: ADJ n ♦ **Second class** is also an adverb. ❑ *I recently travelled second class from Pisa to Ventimiglia.* ADV: ADV after v ♦ **Second-class** is second-class accommodation on a train or ship. ❑ *In second class the fare is £85 one-way.* N-UNCOUNT 4 In Britain, **second-class** postage is the slower and cheaper type of postage. In the United States, **second-class** postage is the type of postage that is used for sending newspapers and magazines. ❑ *...a second-class stamp.* ADJ: ADJ n ♦ **Second class** is also an adverb. ❑ *They're going to send it second class.* ADV: ADV after v 5 In Britain, a **second-class** degree is a good university degree, but not as good as a first-class degree. ❑ *A second-class honours degree is the minimum requirement.* ADJ: ADJ n

**sec|ond com|ing** When Christians refer to **the second coming**, they mean the expected return to earth of Jesus Christ. N-SING: the N

**sec|ond cous|in** **(second cousins)** Your **second cousins** are the children of your parents' first cousins. Compare **first cousin**. N-COUNT

**second-degree** 1 In the United States, **second-degree** is used to describe crimes that are considered to be less serious than first-degree crimes. ❑ *The judge reduced the charge to second-degree murder.* ADJ: ADJ n 2 A **second-degree** burn is more severe than a first-degree burn but less severe than a third-degree burn. ❑ *James Bell suffered second-degree burns in an explosion.* ADJ: ADJ n

**second-guess** **(second-guesses, second-guessing, second-guessed)** If you try to **second-guess** something, you try to guess in advance what someone will do or what will happen. ❑ *Editors and contributors are trying to second-guess the future.* VERB V n Also V

**second-hand** 1 **Second-hand** things are not new and have been owned by someone else. ❑ *Buying a second-hand car can be a risky business. ...a stack of second-hand books.* ADJ: usu ADJ n ♦ **Second-hand** is also an adverb. ❑ *Far more boats are bought second-hand than are bought brand new.* ADV: ADV after v 2 A **second-hand** shop sells second-hand goods. ADJ: ADJ n 3 **Second-hand** stories, information, or opinions are those you learn about from other people rather than directly or from your own experience. ❑ *The denunciation was made on the basis of second-hand information.* ADJ: usu ADJ n 4 **at second hand** → see **second**.

**second-in-command** also **second in command.** A **second-in-command** is someone who is next in rank to the leader of a group, and who has authority to give orders when the leader is not there. ❑ *He was posted to Hong Kong as second-in-command of C Squadron.* N-SING

**sec|ond lan|guage** **(second languages)** Someone's **second language** is a language which is not their native language but which they use at work or at school. ❑ *Lucy teaches English as a second language.* N-COUNT

**sec|ond lieu|ten|ant** **(second lieutenants)** 1 A **second lieutenant** is an officer in the army who ranks directly below a lieutenant. [BRIT] N-COUNT 2 A **second lieutenant** is an officer in the army, air force, or marines who ranks directly below a first lieutenant. [AM] N-COUNT

**sec|ond|ly** /sekəndli/ You say **secondly** when you want to make a second point or give a second reason for something. ❑ *You need, firstly, a strong independent board of directors and secondly, an experienced and dedicated staff.* ADV: ADV with cl (not last in cl)

**se|cond|ment** /sɪkɒndmənt/ **(secondments)** Someone who is **on secondment** from their normal employer has been sent somewhere else temporarily in order to do special duties. [BRIT] ❑ *We have two full-time secretaries, one of whom is on secondment from the Royal Navy.* N-VAR: oft *on* N, N *from/to* n

**sec|ond name** **(second names)** Someone's **second name** is their family name, or the name that comes after their first name and before their family name. N-COUNT

**sec|ond opin|ion** **(second opinions)** If you get a **second opinion**, you ask another qualified person for their opinion about something such as your health. ❑ *I would like a second opinion on my doctor's diagnosis.* N-COUNT

**sec|ond per|son** A statement in **the second person** is a statement about the person or people you are talking to. The subject of a statement like this is 'you'. N-SING: the N

**second-rate** If you describe something as **second-rate**, you mean that it is of poor quality. ❑ *...second-rate restaurants. ...another second-rate politician.* ADJ

**sec|ond sight** If you say that someone has **second sight**, you mean that they seem to have the ability to know or see things that are going to happen in the future, or are happening in a different place. N-UNCOUNT

**sec|ond string** also **second-string.** If you describe a person or thing as someone's **second string**, you mean that they are only used if another person or thing is not available. ❑ *...a second string team.* N-SING: oft N n

**sec|ond thought** **(second thoughts)** 1 If you do something without **a second thought**, you do it without thinking about it carefully, usually because you do not have enough time or you do not care very much. ❑ *This murderous lunatic could kill them both without a second thought... Roberto didn't give a second thought to borrowing $2,000 from him.* N-SING: with brd-neg, *a* N 2 If you have **second thoughts about** a decision that you have made, you begin to doubt whether it was the best thing to do. ❑ *I had never had second thoughts about my decision to leave the company.* N-PLURAL: oft N *about* n 3 You can say **on second thoughts** or **on second thought** when you suddenly change your mind about something that you are saying or something that you have decided to do. ❑ *'Wait there!' Kathryn rose. 'No, on second thought, follow me.'* PHRASE: PHR with cl

**sec|ond wind** When you get your **second wind**, you become able to continue doing something difficult or energetic after you have been tired or out of breath. ❑ *Finding a second wind, he rode away from his pursuers.* N-SING

**Sec|ond World War** **The Second World War** is the major war that was fought between 1939 and 1945. N-PROPER: the N

**se|cre|cy** /siːkrəsi/ **Secrecy** is the act of keeping something secret, or the state of being kept secret. ❑ *He shrouds his business dealings in secrecy.* N-UNCOUNT: oft prep N

**se|cret** /siːkrɪt/ **(secrets)** ♦♦◇ 1 If something is **secret**, it is known about by only a small number of people, and is not told or shown to anyone else. ❑ *Soldiers have been training at a secret location... The police have been trying to keep the documents secret.* → See also **top secret.** ADJ: ADJ n, v n ADJ, v-link ADJ ♦ **se|cret|ly** *He wore a hidden microphone to secretly tape-record conversations.* ADV: ADV with v, ADV adj/n 2 A **secret** is a fact that is known by only a small number of people, and is not told to anyone else. ❑ *I think he enjoyed keeping our love* N-COUNT a secret. [3] If you say that a particular way of doing things is **the secret of** achieving something, you mean that it is the best or only way to achieve it. ❑ *The secret of success is honesty and fair dealing.* [4] Something's **secrets** are the things about it which have never been fully explained. ❑ *We have an opportunity now to really unlock the secrets of the universe.* N-SING: the N, oft the N of n; N-COUNT: usu pl, oft with poss

PHRASES [5] If you do something **in secret**, you do it without anyone else knowing. ❑ *Dan found out that I had been meeting my ex-boyfriend in secret.* PHRASE: PHR after v
[6] If you say that someone can **keep a secret**, you mean that they can be trusted not to tell other people a secret that you have told them. ❑ *Tom was utterly indiscreet, and could never keep a secret.* PHRASE: V inflects
[7] If you **make no secret** of something, you tell others about it openly and clearly. ❑ *His wife made no secret of her hatred for the formal occasions.* PHRASE: V inflects, PHR of n

**se|cret agent** **(secret agents)** A **secret agent** is a person who is employed by a government to find out the secrets of other governments. N-COUNT

**sec|re|tar|ial** /sekrəteəriəl/ **Secretarial** work is the work done by a secretary in an office. ❑ *I was doing temporary secretarial work.* ADJ: ADJ n

**sec|re|tari|at** /sekrəteəriæt/ **(secretariats)** A **secretariat** is a department that is responsible for the administration of an international political organization. ❑ *...the UN secretariat.* N-COUNT

**sec|re|tary** /sekrətri, AM -teri/ **(secretaries)** ◆◆◆
[1] A **secretary** is a person who is employed to do office work, such as typing letters, answering phone calls, and arranging meetings. N-COUNT [2] The **secretary** of an organization such as a trade union, a political party, or a club is its official manager. [BRIT] ❑ *My grandfather was secretary of the Scottish Miners' Union.* N-COUNT [3] The **secretary** of a company is the person who has the legal duty of keeping the company's records. N-COUNT [4] **Secretary** is used in the titles of ministers and officials who are in charge of main government departments. ❑ *...the British Foreign Secretary. ...Defense Secretary Caspar Weinberger.* N-COUNT; N-TITLE

**secretary-general** **(secretaries-general)** ◆◇◇ also **Secretary General.** **The secretary-general** of an international political organization is the person in charge of its administration. ❑ *...the United Nations Secretary-General.* N-COUNT: usu the N in sing

**Sec|re|tary of State** **(Secretaries of State)** ◆◇◇
[1] In the United States, **the Secretary of State** is the head of the government department which deals with foreign affairs. N-COUNT: usu the N in sing [2] In Britain, **the Secretary of State** for a particular government department is the head of that department. ❑ *...the Secretary of State for Education.* N-COUNT: usu the N in sing

**se|crete** /sɪkriːt/ **(secretes, secreting, secreted)** [1] If part of a plant, animal, or human **secretes** a liquid, it produces it. ❑ *The sweat glands secrete water.* VERB V n [2] If you **secrete** something somewhere, you hide it there so that nobody will find it. [LITERARY] ❑ *She secreted the gun in the kitchen cabinet.* VERB V n prep/adv

**se|cre|tion** /sɪkriːʃən/ **(secretions)** [1] **Secretion** is the process by which certain liquid substances are produced by parts of plants or from the bodies of people or animals. ❑ *...the secretion of adrenaline. ...insulin secretion.* N-UNCOUNT [2] **Secretions** are liquid substances produced by parts of plants or bodies. ❑ *...gastric secretions.* N-PLURAL

**se|cre|tive** /siːkrətɪv, sɪkriːt-/ If you are **secretive**, you like to have secrets and to keep your knowledge, feelings, or intentions hidden. ❑ *Billionaires are usually fairly secretive about the exact amount that they're worth.* ADJ: oft ADJ about n ♦ **se|cre|tive|ly** *...a banknote handed over secretively in the entrance to a building.* ADV: ADV after v ♦ **se|cre|tive|ness** *He was evasive, to the point of secretiveness.* N-UNCOUNT

**se|cret po|lice** **The secret police** is a police force in some countries that works secretly and deals with political crimes committed against the government. N-UNCOUNT: also the N

**se|cret ser|vice** **(secret services)** [1] A country's **secret service** is a secret government department whose job is to find out enemy secrets and to prevent its own government's secrets from being discovered. N-COUNT [2] **The secret service** is the government department in the United States which protects the president. [AM] N-COUNT

**se|cret weap|on** **(secret weapons)** Someone's **secret weapon** is a thing or person which they believe will help them achieve something and which other people do not know about. ❑ *Discipline was the new coach's secret weapon.* N-COUNT

**sect** /sekt/ **(sects)** A **sect** is a group of people that has separated from a larger group and has a particular set of religious or political beliefs. N-COUNT

**sec|tar|ian** /sekteəriən/ **Sectarian** means resulting from the differences between different religions. ❑ *He was killed in sectarian violence.* ADJ: usu ADJ n

**sec|tari|an|ism** /sekteəriənɪzəm/ **Sectarianism** is strong support for the religious or political group you belong to, and often involves conflict with other groups. ❑ *...political rivalry and sectarianism within our movement.* N-UNCOUNT

**sec|tion** /sekʃən/ **(sections, sectioning, sectioned)** ◆◆◇ [1] A **section** of something is one of the parts into which it is divided or from which it is formed. ❑ *He said it was wrong to single out any section of society for Aids testing... They moulded a complete new bow section for the boat. ...a large orchestra, with a vast percussion section. ...the Georgetown section of Washington, D.C.* → See also **cross-section.** N-COUNT: usu with supp [2] If something **is sectioned**, it is divided into sections. ❑ *It holds vegetables in place while they are being peeled or sectioned.* VERB: usu passive be V-ed [3] A **section** of an official document such as a report, law, or constitution is one of the parts into which it is divided. ❑ *...section 14 of the Trade Descriptions Act 1968.* N-COUNT: usu N num [4] A **section** is a diagram of something such as a building or a part of the body. It shows how the object would appear to you if it were cut from top to bottom and looked at from the side. ❑ *For some buildings a vertical section is more informative than a plan.* N-COUNT [5] **Caesarean section** → see **Caesarean.**
♦ **section off** If an area **is sectioned off**, it is separated by a wall, fence, or other barrier from the surrounding area. ❑ *The kitchen is sectioned off from the rest of the room by a half wall.* PHRASAL VERB: usu passive be V-ed P Also V n P, V P n

**sec|tion|al** /sekʃənəl/ **Sectional** interests are those of a particular group within a community or country. ❑ *He criticized the selfish attitude of certain sectional interests.* ADJ: ADJ n

**sec|tor** /sektəʳ/ **(sectors)** ◆◆◇ [1] A particular **sector** of a country's economy is the part connected with that specified type of industry. ❑ *...the nation's manufacturing sector.* → See also **public sector, private sector.** N-COUNT: supp N [2] A **sector** of a large group is a smaller group which is part of it. ❑ *Workers who went to the Gulf came from the poorest sectors of Pakistani society.* N-COUNT: usu with supp [3] A **sector** is an area of a city or country which is controlled by a military force. ❑ *Officers were going to retake sectors of the city.* N-COUNT: usu with supp [4] A **sector** is a part of a circle which is formed when you draw two straight lines from the centre of the circle to the edge. [TECHNICAL] N-COUNT

**sec|tor|al** /sektərəl/ **Sectoral** means relating to the various economic sectors of a society or to a particular economic sector. [TECHNICAL] ❑ *...sectoral differences within social classes.* ADJ: ADJ n

**secu|lar** /sekjʊləʳ/ You use **secular** to describe things that have no connection with religion. ❑ *He spoke about preserving the country as a secular state.* ADJ: usu ADJ n ≠ religious

**secu|lar|ism** /sekjʊlərɪzəm/ **Secularism** is a system of social organization and education where religion is not allowed to play a part in civil affairs. N-UNCOUNT ♦ **secu|lar|ist** **(secularists)** *...conflict between fundamentalists and secularists.* N-COUNT

**secu|lar|ized** /sekjʊləraɪzd/

✔ in BRIT, also use **secularised**

**Secularized** societies are no longer under the control or influence of religion. ❑ *The Pope had no great sympathy for the secularized West.* ADJ

**se|cure** /sɪkjʊə$^{r}$/ **(secures, securing, secured)** ◆◆◇
[1] VERB If you **secure** something that you want or need, you obtain it, often after a lot of effort. [FORMAL] ❑ *Federal leaders continued their efforts to secure a ceasefire... Graham's achievements helped secure him the job.* (V n; V n n; Also V n *for* n)
[2] VERB If you **secure** a place, you make it safe from harm or attack. [FORMAL] ❑ *Staff withdrew from the main part of the prison but secured the perimeter.* (V n)
[3] ADJ A **secure** place is tightly locked or well protected, so that people cannot enter it or leave it. ❑ *We shall make sure our home is as secure as possible from now on.* ♦ **se|cure|ly** ADV: usu ADV with v *He locked the heavy door securely and kept the key in his pocket.*
[4] VERB If you **secure** an object, you fasten it firmly to another object. ❑ *He helped her close the cases up, and then he secured the canvas straps as tight as they would go.* (V n)
[5] ADJ: usu v-link ADJ If an object is **secure**, it is fixed firmly in position. ❑ *Check joints are secure and the wood is sound.* ♦ **se|cure|ly** ADV: ADV with v *Ensure that the frame is securely fixed to the ground with bolts.*
[6] ADJ If you describe something such as a job as **secure**, it is certain not to change or end. ❑ *...trade union demands for secure wages and employment. ...the failure of financial institutions once thought to be secure.*
[7] ADJ: usu ADJ n A **secure** base or foundation is strong and reliable. ❑ *He was determined to give his family a secure and solid base.*
[8] ADJ: usu v-link ADJ If you feel **secure**, you feel safe and happy and are not worried about life. ❑ *She felt secure and protected when she was with him.*
[9] VERB: usu passive If a loan **is secured**, the person who lends the money may take property such as a house from the person who borrows the money if they fail to repay it. [BUSINESS] ❑ *The loan is secured against your home... His main task is to raise enough finance to repay secured loans.* (*be* V-ed adv/prep; V-ed)

**se|cure unit** **(secure units)** N-COUNT A **secure unit** is a building or part of a building where dangerous prisoners or violent psychiatric patients are kept. ❑ *...the secure unit at Cane Hill hospital.*

**se|cu|rity** /sɪkjʊərɪti/ **(securities)** ◆◆◆
[1] N-UNCOUNT: with supp, oft N n **Security** refers to all the measures that are taken to protect a place, or to ensure that only people with permission enter it or leave it. ❑ *They are now under a great deal of pressure to tighten their airport security... Strict security measures are in force in the capital.*
[2] N-UNCOUNT: usu with supp, oft N *of* n A feeling of **security** is a feeling of being safe and free from worry. ❑ *He loves the security of a happy home life.* ● PHRASE: PHR after v If something gives you **a false sense of security**, it makes you believe that you are safe when you are not. ❑ *Wearing helmets gave cyclists a false sense of security and encouraged them to take risks.*
[3] N-UNCOUNT = *collateral* If something is **security** for a loan, you promise to give that thing to the person who lends you money, if you fail to pay the money back. [BUSINESS] ❑ *The central bank will provide special loans, and the banks will pledge the land as security.*
[4] N-PLURAL **Securities** are stocks, shares, bonds, or other certificates that you buy in order to earn regular interest from them or to sell them later for a profit. [BUSINESS] ❑ *...US government securities and bonds.*
[5] → See also **social security**.

**se|cu|rity blan|ket** **(security blankets)**
[1] N-COUNT If you refer to something as a **security blanket**, you mean that it provides someone with a feeling of safety and comfort when they are in a situation that worries them or makes them feel nervous. ❑ *Alan sings with shy intensity, hiding behind the security blanket of his guitar.*
[2] N-COUNT A baby's **security blanket** is a piece of cloth or clothing which the baby holds and chews in order to feel comforted.

**se|cu|rity cam|era** **(security cameras)** N-COUNT A **security camera** is a video camera that records people's activities in order to detect and prevent crime.

**Se|cu|rity Coun|cil** ◆◇◇ N-PROPER: *the* N **The Security Council** is the committee which governs the United Nations. It has permanent representatives from the United States, Russia, China, France, and the United Kingdom, and temporary representatives from some other countries.

**se|cu|rity guard** **(security guards)** N-COUNT A **security guard** is someone whose job is to protect a building or to collect and deliver large amounts of money.

**se|cu|rity risk** **(security risks)** N-COUNT If you describe someone as a **security risk**, you mean that they may be a threat to the safety of a country or organization.

**se|dan** /sɪdæn/ **(sedans)** N-COUNT A **sedan** is a car with seats for four or more people, a fixed roof, and a boot that is separate from the part of the car that you sit in. [AM]

✓ in BRIT, use **saloon**

**se|dan chair** **(sedan chairs)** N-COUNT A **sedan chair** is an enclosed chair for one person carried on two poles by two men, one in front and one behind. Sedan chairs were used in the 17th and 18th centuries.

**se|date** /sɪdeɪt/ **(sedates, sedating, sedated)**
[1] ADJ: usu ADJ n If you describe someone or something as **sedate**, you mean that they are quiet and rather dignified, though perhaps a bit dull. ❑ *She took them to visit her sedate, elderly cousins.* ♦ **se|date|ly** ADV: ADV with v *...sedately dressed in business suit with waistcoat.*
[2] ADJ: usu ADJ n If you move along at a **sedate** pace, you move slowly, in a controlled way. ❑ *We set off again at a more sedate pace.* ♦ **se|date|ly** ADV: ADV after v *He pulled sedately out of the short driveway.*
[3] VERB If someone **is sedated**, they are given a drug to calm them or to make them sleep. ❑ *The patient is sedated with intravenous use of sedative drugs... Doctors have been told not to sedate children with an anaesthetic that may be linked to five deaths.* (*be* V-ed; V n) ♦ **se|dat|ed** ADJ: v-link ADJ *Grace was asleep, lightly sedated.*

**se|da|tion** /sɪdeɪʃ$^{ə}$n/ N-UNCOUNT: oft *under* N If someone is **under sedation**, they have been given medicine or drugs in order to calm them or make them sleep. ❑ *His mother was under sedation after the boy's body was brought back from Germany.*

**seda|tive** /sedətɪv/ **(sedatives)**
[1] N-COUNT A **sedative** is a medicine or drug that calms you or makes you sleep. ❑ *They use opium as a sedative, rather than as a narcotic.*
[2] ADJ: ADJ n Something that has a **sedative** effect calms you or makes you sleep. ❑ *Amber bath oil has a sedative effect.*

**sed|en|tary** /sedəntəri, AM -teri/ ADJ: usu ADJ n Someone who has a **sedentary** lifestyle or job sits down a lot of the time and does not take much exercise. ❑ *Obesity and a sedentary lifestyle has been linked with an increased risk of heart disease.*

**sedge** /sedʒ/ **(sedges)** N-MASS **Sedge** is a plant that looks like grass and grows in wet ground.

**sedi|ment** /sedɪmənt/ **(sediments)** N-VAR **Sediment** is solid material that settles at the bottom of a liquid, especially earth and pieces of rock that have been carried along and then left somewhere by water, ice, or wind. ❑ *Many organisms that die in the sea are soon buried by sediment.*

**sedi|men|tary** /sedɪmentəri, AM -teri/ ADJ: ADJ n **Sedimentary** rocks are formed from sediment left by water, ice, or wind.

**se|di|tion** /sɪdɪʃ$^{ə}$n/ N-UNCOUNT **Sedition** is speech, writing, or behaviour intended to encourage people to fight against or oppose the government. ❑ *Government officials charged him with sedition.*

**se|di|tious** /sɪdɪʃəs/ ADJ: usu ADJ n A **seditious** act, speech, or piece of writing encourages people to fight against or oppose the government. ❑ *He fell under suspicion for distributing seditious pamphlets.*

**se|duce** /sɪdjuːs, AM -duːs/ **(seduces, seducing, seduced)**
[1] VERB If something **seduces** you, it is so attractive that it makes you do something that you would not otherwise do. ❑ *The view of lake and plunging cliffs seduces visitors... Clever advertising would seduce more people into smoking.* (V n; V n *into* -ing/n)

♦ **se|duc|tion** /sɪdʌkʃᵊn/ **(seductions)** *The country had resisted the seductions of mass tourism.* N-VAR [2] If someone **seduces** another person, they use their charm to persuade that person to have sex with them. ❑ *She has set out to seduce Stephen.* VERB V n

♦ **se|duc|tion** *Her methods of seduction are subtle.* N-VAR

**se|duc|er** /sɪdjuːsəʳ, AM -duːs-/ **(seducers)** A **seducer** is someone, usually a man, who seduces someone else. ❑ *He is proud of his reputation as a seducer of young women.* N-COUNT

**se|duc|tive** /sɪdʌktɪv/ [1] Something that is **seductive** is very attractive or makes you want to do something that you would not otherwise do. ❑ *It's a seductive argument.* ADJ ♦ **se|duc|tive|ly** *...his seductively simple assertion.* ADV [2] A person who is **seductive** is very attractive sexually. ❑ *...a seductive woman.* ADJ ♦ **se|duc|tive|ly** *She was looking seductively over her shoulder.* ADV

**se|duc|tress** /sɪdʌktrəs/ **(seductresses)** A **seductress** is a woman who seduces someone. ❑ *Few males can resist a self-confident seductress.* N-COUNT

**see** /siː/ **(sees, seeing, saw, seen)** ◆◆◆ [1] When you **see** something, you notice it using your eyes. ❑ *You can't see colours at night... I saw a man making his way towards me... She can see, hear, touch, smell, and taste... As he neared the farm, he saw that a police car was parked outside it... Did you see what happened?* VERB: no cont V n V n -ing V V that V wh [2] If you **see** someone, you visit them or meet them. ❑ *Mick wants to see you in his office right away... You need to see a doctor.* VERB V n V n [3] If you **see** an entertainment such as a play, film, concert, or sports game, you watch it. ❑ *He had been to see a Semi-Final of the FA Cup... It was one of the most amazing films I've ever seen.* VERB: no cont = watch V n V n [4] If you **see** that something is true or exists, you realize by observing it that it is true or exists. ❑ *I could see she was lonely. ...a lot of people saw what was happening but did nothing about it... You see young people going to school inadequately dressed for the weather... My taste has changed a bit over the years as you can see... The army must be seen to be taking firm action.* VERB: no cont V that V wh V n -ing V *be* V-ed to-inf [5] If you **see** what someone means or **see** why something happened, you understand what they mean or understand why it happened. ❑ *Oh, I see what you're saying... I really don't see any reason for changing it... Now I see that I was wrong.* VERB: no cont, no passive = understand V wh V n V that [6] If you **see** someone or something **as** a certain thing, you have the opinion that they are that thing. ❑ *She saw him as a visionary, but her father saw him as a man who couldn't make a living... Others saw it as a betrayal... I don't see it as my duty to take sides... As I see it, Llewelyn has three choices open to him... Women are sometimes seen to be less effective as managers.* VERB V n *as* n/-ing V *it as* n V *it as* n to-inf V *it* *be* V-ed to-inf [7] If you **see** a particular quality **in** someone, you believe they have that quality. If you ask what someone **sees in** a particular person or thing, you want to know what they find attractive about that person or thing. ❑ *Frankly, I don't know what Paul sees in her... Young and old saw in him an implacable opponent of apartheid.* VERB: no cont, no passive V n *in* n V *in* n n [8] If you **see** something happening in the future, you imagine it, or predict that it will happen. ❑ *A good idea, but can you see Taylor trying it?... We can see a day where all people live side by side.* VERB: no cont = imagine V n -ing V n [9] If a period of time or a person **sees** a particular change or event, it takes place during that period of time or while that person is alive. ❑ *Yesterday saw the resignation of the acting Interior Minister... He had worked with the General for three years and was sorry to see him go... Mr Frank has seen the economy of his town slashed by the uprising.* VERB: no passive V n V n inf V n -ed [10] You can use **see** in expressions to do with finding out information. For example, if you say **'I'll see what's happening'**, you mean that you intend to find out what is happening. ❑ *Let me just see what the next song is... Shake him gently to see if he responds.* VERB V wh V wh [11] You can use **see** to promise to try and help someone. For example, if you say **'I'll see if I can do it'**, you mean that you will try to do the thing concerned. ❑ *I'll see if I can call her for you... We'll see what we can do, miss.* VERB V if V wh [12] If you **see that** something is done or if you **see to it that** it is done, you make sure that it is done. ❑ *See that you take care of him... Catherine saw to it that the information went directly to Walter.* VERB V that V *to it* that [13] If you **see** someone to a particular place, you accompany them to make sure that they get there safely, or to show politeness. ❑ *He didn't offer to see her to her car... 'Goodnight.' — 'I'll see you out.'* VERB V n prep/adv V n prep/adv [14] If you **see** a lot **of** someone, you often meet each other or visit each other. ❑ *We used to see quite a lot of his wife, Carolyn.* VERB V amount *of* n [15] If you **are seeing** someone, you spend time with them socially, and are having a romantic or sexual relationship. ❑ *My husband was still seeing her and he was having an affair with her.* VERB V n [16] Some writers use **see** in expressions such as **we saw** and **as we have seen** to refer to something that has already been explained or described. ❑ *We saw in Chapter 16 how annual cash budgets are produced... Using the figures given above, it can be seen that machine A pays back the initial investment in two years.* VERB V wh V that [17] **See** is used in books to indicate to readers that they should look at another part of the book, or at another book, because more information is given there. ❑ *See Chapter 7 below for further comments on the textile industry.* VERB: only imper V n

**PHRASES** [18] You can use **seeing that** or **seeing as** to introduce a reason for what you are saying. [mainly BRIT, INFORMAL, SPOKEN] ❑ *Seeing as Mr Moreton is a doctor, I would assume he has a modicum of intelligence.* PHRASE: CONJ SUBORD = since [19] You can say **'I see'** to indicate that you understand what someone is telling you. [SPOKEN] ❑ *'He came home in my car.' — 'I see.'* CONVENTION formulae [20] People say **'I'll see'** or **'We'll see'** to indicate that they do not intend to make a decision immediately, and will decide later. ❑ *We'll see. It's a possibility.* CONVENTION [21] People say **'let me see'** or **'let's see'** when they are trying to remember something, or are trying to find something. ❑ *Let's see, they're six – no, make that five hours ahead of us... Now let me see, who's the man we want?* CONVENTION [22] If you try to make someone **see sense** or **see reason**, you try to make them realize that they are wrong or are being stupid. ❑ *He was hopeful that by sitting together they could both see sense and live as good neighbours.* PHRASE: V inflects [23] You can say **'you see'** when you are explaining something to someone, to encourage them to listen and understand. [SPOKEN] ❑ *Well, you see, you shouldn't really feel that way about it.* CONVENTION [24] **'See you'**, **'be seeing you'**, and **'see you later'** are ways of saying goodbye to someone when you expect to meet them again soon. [INFORMAL, SPOKEN] ❑ *'Talk to you later.' — 'All right. See you love.'* CONVENTION formulae = bye [25] You can say **'You'll see'** to someone if they do not agree with you about what you think will happen in the future, and you believe that you will be proved right. ❑ *The thrill wears off after a few years of marriage. You'll see.* CONVENTION [26] to **have seen better days** → see **day**. to **be seen dead** → see **dead**. **as far as the eye can see** → see **eye**. to **see eye to eye** → see **eye**. **as far as** I **can see** → see **far**. to **see fit** → see **fit**. to **see red** → see **red**. **it remains to be seen** → see **remain**. **wait and see** → see **wait**.

♦ **see about** When you **see about** something, you arrange for it to be done or provided. ❑ *Tony announced it was time to see about lunch... I must see about selling the house.* PHRASAL VERB V P n/-ing V P n/-ing

♦ **see off** [1] If you **see off** an opponent, you defeat them. [BRIT] ❑ *There is no reason why they cannot see off the Republican challenge.* PHRASAL VERB V P n Also V n P [2] When you **see** someone **off**, you go with them to the station, airport, or port that they are leaving from, and say goodbye to them there. ❑ *Ben had planned a steak dinner for himself after seeing Jackie off on her plane.* PHRASAL VERB V n P

♦ **see through** If you **see through** someone or their behaviour, you realize what their intentions are, even though they are trying to hide them. ❑ *I saw through your little ruse from the start.* PHRASAL VERB V P n → See also **see-through**.

♦ **see to** If you **see to** something that needs attention, you deal with it. ❑ *While Franklin saw to the luggage, Sara took Eleanor home.* PHRASAL VERB V P n

**seed** /siːd/ **(seeds, seeding, seeded)** ♦♦◇ [1] A **seed** is the small, hard part of a plant from which a new plant grows. ➔ See pictures on pages 1711 and 1712. ❑ *I sow the seed in pots of soil-based compost. ...sunflower seeds.* N-VAR [2] If you **seed** a piece of land, you plant seeds in it. ❑ *Men mowed the wide lawns and seeded them... The primroses should begin to seed themselves down the steep hillside. ...his newly seeded lawns.* VERB V n V pron-refl V-ed [3] You can refer to the **seeds of** something when you want to talk about the beginning of a feeling or process that gradually develops and becomes stronger or more important. [LITERARY] ❑ *He raised questions meant to plant seeds of doubts in the minds of jurors.* N-PLURAL: N *of* n [4] In sports such as tennis or badminton, a **seed** is a player who has been ranked according to his or her ability. ❑ *...Pete Sampras, Wimbledon's top seed and the world No.1.* N-COUNT: usu supp N, oft ord/num N [5] When a player or a team **is seeded** in a sports competition, they are ranked according to their ability. ❑ *In the UEFA Cup the top 16 sides are seeded for the first round... He is seeded second, behind Brad Beven... The top four seeded nations are through to the semi-finals.* VERB: usu passive *be* V-ed adv/prep V-ed ord V-ed

PHRASES [6] If vegetable plants **go to seed** or **run to seed**, they produce flowers and seeds as well as leaves. ❑ *If unused, winter radishes run to seed in spring.* PHRASE: V inflects [7] If you say that someone or something **has gone to seed** or **has run to seed**, you mean that they have become much less attractive, healthy, or efficient. ❑ *He was a big man in his forties; once he had a lot of muscle but now he was running to seed.* PHRASE: V inflects

**seed|bed** /siːdbed/ **(seedbeds)** also **seed-bed.** [1] A **seedbed** is an area of ground, usually with specially prepared earth, where young plants are grown from seed. N-COUNT [2] You can refer to a place or a situation as a **seedbed** when it seems likely that a particular type of thing or person will develop in that place or situation. ❑ *TV is using radio as a seedbed for ideas.* N-COUNT: oft N *for/of* n

**seed capi|tal** **Seed capital** is an amount of money that a new company needs to pay for the costs of producing a business plan so that they can raise further capital to develop the company. [BUSINESS] ❑ *I am negotiating with financiers to raise seed capital for my latest venture.* N-UNCOUNT

**seed corn** **Seed corn** is money that businesses spend at the beginning of a project in the hope that it will eventually produce profits. [mainly BRIT, BUSINESS] ❑ *The scheme offers seed corn finance with loans at only 4% interest.* N-UNCOUNT

**seed|less** /siːdləs/ A **seedless** fruit has no seeds in it. ❑ *...seedless grapes.* ADJ

**seed|ling** /siːdlɪŋ/ **(seedlings)** A **seedling** is a young plant that has been grown from a seed. N-COUNT

**seed mon|ey** **Seed money** is money that is given to someone to help them start a new business or project. [BUSINESS] N-UNCOUNT

**seedy** /siːdi/ **(seedier, seediest)** If you describe a person or place as **seedy**, you disapprove of them because they look dirty and untidy, or they have a bad reputation. ❑ *Frank ran dodgy errands for a seedy local villain... We were staying in a seedy hotel close to the red light district.* ADJ: usu ADJ n [disapproval] ♦ **seedi|ness** *...the atmosphere of seediness and decay about the city.* N-UNCOUNT

**seeing-eye dog** **(seeing-eye dogs)** also **Seeing Eye dog, seeing eye dog.** A **seeing-eye dog** is a dog that has been trained to lead a blind person. [AM] N-COUNT

✔ in BRIT, use **guide dog**

**seek** /siːk/ **(seeks, seeking, sought)** ♦◇◇ [1] If you **seek** something such as a job or a place to live, you try to find one. [FORMAL] ❑ *They have had to seek work as labourers... Four people who sought refuge in the Italian embassy have left voluntarily... Candidates are urgently sought for the post of Conservative party chairman.* VERB V n V n *be* V-ed *for* n [2] When someone **seeks** something, they try to obtain it. [FORMAL] ❑ *The prosecutors have warned they will seek the death penalty... Haemophiliacs are seeking compensation for being given contaminated blood.* VERB V n V n [3] If you **seek** someone's help or advice, you contact them in order to ask for it. [FORMAL] ❑ *Always seek professional legal advice before entering into any agreement... The couple have sought help from marriage guidance counsellors.* VERB V n V n *from* n [4] If you **seek to** do something, you try to do it. [FORMAL] ❑ *He also denied that he would seek to annex the country.* VERB V to-inf

♦ **seek out** If you **seek out** someone or something or **seek** them **out**, you keep looking for them until you find them. ❑ *Now is the time for local companies to seek out business opportunities in Europe... Ellen spent the day in the hills and sought me out when she returned.* PHRASAL VERB V P n (not pron) V n P

**seek|er** /siːkəʳ/ **(seekers)** A **seeker** is someone who is looking for or trying to get something. ❑ *I am a seeker after truth... The beaches draw sun-seekers from all over Europe.* ➔ See also **asylum seeker, job seeker.** N-COUNT: usu pl, usu n N

**seem** /siːm/ **(seems, seeming, seemed)** ♦♦♦ [1] You use **seem** to say that someone or something gives the impression of having a particular quality, or of happening in the way you describe. ❑ *We heard a series of explosions. They seemed quite close by... Everyone seems busy except us... To everyone who knew them, they seemed an ideal couple... £50 seems a lot to pay... The calming effect seemed to last for about ten minutes... It was a record that seemed beyond reach... The proposal seems designed to break opposition to the government's economic programme... It seems that the attack this morning was very carefully planned to cause few casualties... It seems clear that he has no reasonable alternative... It seemed as if she'd been gone forever... There seems to be a lot of support in Congress for this move... There seems no possibility that such action can be averted... This phenomenon is not as outrageous as it seems.* V-LINK: no cont V adj V adj V n V n V to-inf V prep V -ed *it* V that *it* V adj that *it* V as if *there* V to-inf *there* V n V [2] You use **seem** when you are describing your own feelings or thoughts, or describing something that has happened to you, in order to make your statement less forceful. ❑ *I seem to have lost all my self-confidence... I seem to remember giving you very precise instructions... Excuse me I seem to be a little bit lost.* V-LINK: no cont [vagueness] V to-inf V to-inf V to-inf [3] If you say that you **cannot seem** or **could not seem to** do something, you mean that you have tried to do it and were unable to. ❑ *No matter how hard I try I cannot seem to catch up on all the bills.* PHRASE: PHR to-inf [4] ➔ See also **seeming.**

**seem|ing** /siːmɪŋ/ **Seeming** means appearing to be the case, but not necessarily the case. For example, if you talk about someone's **seeming** ability to do something, you mean that they appear to be able to do it, but you are not certain. [FORMAL] ❑ *Wall Street analysts have been highly critical of the company's seeming inability to control costs.* ADJ: ADJ n [vagueness] = *apparent*

**seem|ing|ly** /siːmɪŋli/ [1] If something is **seemingly** the case, you mean that it appears to be the case, even though it may not really be so. ❑ *A seemingly endless line of trucks waits in vain to load up.* ADV: ADV adj/adv = *apparently* [2] You use **seemingly** when you want to say that something seems to be true. ❑ *He has moved to Spain, seemingly to enjoy a slower style of life.* ADV: ADV with cl/group, ADV before v [vagueness]

**seem|ly** /siːmli/ **Seemly** behaviour or dress is appropriate in the particular circumstances. [OLD-FASHIONED] ❑ *Self-assertion was not thought seemly in a woman.* ADJ

**seen** /siːn/ **Seen** is the past participle of **see.**

**seep** /siːp/ **(seeps, seeping, seeped)** [1] If something such as liquid or gas **seeps** somewhere, it flows slowly and in small amounts into a place where it should not go. ❑ *Radioactive water had seeped into underground reservoirs... The gas is seeping out of the rocks.* VERB V prep/adv V prep/adv ♦ **Seep** is also a noun. ❑ *...an oil seep.* N-COUNT [2] If something such as secret information or an unpleasant emotion **seeps** somewhere, it VERB comes out gradually. ❑ *...the tide of racism which is sweeping Europe seeps into Britain.* V prep/adv

**seep|age** /siːpɪdʒ/ **Seepage** is the slow flow of a liquid through something. ❑ *Chemical seepage has caused untold damage.* N-UNCOUNT

**seer** /siːəʳ/ **(seers)** A **seer** is a person who tells people what will happen in the future. [LITERARY] ❑ *...the writings of the 16th century French seer, Nostradamus.* N-COUNT

**see|saw** /siːsɔː/ **(seesaws, seesawing, seesawed)** also **see-saw.** [1] A **seesaw** is a long board which is balanced on a fixed part in the middle. To play on it, a child sits on each end, and when one end goes up, the other goes down. ❑ *There was a sandpit, a seesaw and a swing in the playground.* N-COUNT [2] In a **seesaw** situation, something continually changes from one state to another and back again. ❑ *...a seesaw price situation.* ♦ **Seesaw** is also a noun. ❑ *Marriage, however, is an emotional seesaw.* ADJ: ADJ n; N-COUNT: usu sing [3] If someone's emotions **see-saw**, or a particular situation **see-saws**, they continually change from one state to another and back again. ❑ *The Tokyo stock market see-sawed up and down.* VERB; V

**seethe** /siːð/ **(seethes, seething, seethed)** [1] When you **are seething**, you are very angry about something but do not express your feelings about it. ❑ *She took it calmly at first but under the surface was seething... She grinned derisively while I seethed with rage... He is seething at all the bad press he is getting. ...a seething anger fueled by decades of political oppression.* VERB; V; V prep; V prep; V-ing [2] If you say that a place **is seething with** people or things, you are emphasizing that it is very full of them and that they are all moving about. ❑ *The forest below him seethed and teemed with life... Madrigueras station was a seething mass of soldiers.* VERB; emphasis; V *with* n; V-ing; Also V

**see-through** **See-through** clothes are made of thin cloth, so that you can see a person's body or underwear through them. ADJ: usu ADJ n = *transparent*

**seg|ment** **(segments, segmenting, segmented)** ◆◇◇

> The noun is pronounced /segmənt/. The verb is pronounced /segment/.

[1] A **segment of** something is one part of it, considered separately from the rest. ❑ *...the poorer segments of society. ...the third segment of his journey.* N-COUNT: N *of* n = *section* [2] A **segment** of fruit such as an orange or grapefruit is one of the sections into which it is easily divided. → See picture on page 1711. N-COUNT [3] A **segment** of a circle is one of the two parts into which it is divided when you draw a straight line through it. N-COUNT: usu N *of* n [4] A **segment** of a market is one part of it, considered separately from the rest. ❑ *Three-to-five day cruises are the fastest-growing segment of the market... Women's tennis is the market leader in a growing market segment – women's sports.* N-COUNT [5] If a company **segments** a market, it divides it into separate parts, usually in order to improve marketing opportunities. [BUSINESS] ❑ *The big six record companies are multinational, and thus can segment the world market into national ones.* VERB; V n *into* n

**seg|men|ta|tion** /segmenteɪʃᵊn/ **Segmentation** is the dividing of something into parts which are loosely connected. [TECHNICAL] N-UNCOUNT

**seg|ment|ed** /segmentɪd/ **Segmented** means divided into parts that are loosely connected to each other. ❑ *...segmented oranges.* ADJ: ADJ n

**seg|re|gate** /segrɪgeɪt/ **(segregates, segregating, segregated)** To **segregate** two groups of people or things means to keep them physically apart from each other. ❑ *Police segregated the two rival camps of protesters... They segregate you from the rest of the community.* VERB; V n; V n prep

**seg|re|gat|ed** /segrɪgeɪtɪd/ **Segregated** buildings or areas are kept for the use of one group of people who are the same race, sex, or religion, and no other group is allowed to use them. ❑ *...racially segregated schools... John grew up in Baltimore when that city was segregated.* ADJ

**seg|re|ga|tion** /segrɪgeɪʃᵊn/ **Segregation** is the official practice of keeping people apart, usually people of different sexes, races, or religions. ❑ *The Supreme Court unanimously ruled that racial segregation in schools was unconstitutional.* N-UNCOUNT: usu with supp

**seg|re|ga|tion|ist** /segrɪgeɪʃənɪst/ **(segregationists)** A **segregationist** is someone who thinks people of different races should be kept apart. ❑ *...a segregationist on the far Right.* N-COUNT: oft N n

**segue** /segweɪ/ **(segues, segueing, segued)** If something such as a piece of music or conversation **segues into** another piece of music or conversation, it changes into it or is followed by it without a break. ❑ *The piece segues into his solo with the strings.* ♦ **Segue** is also a noun. ❑ *...a neat segue into an arrangement of 'Eleanor Rigby'.* VERB; V *into* n; N-COUNT: usu sing

**seis|mic** /saɪzmɪk/ **Seismic** means caused by or relating to an earthquake. ❑ *Earthquakes produce two types of seismic waves.* ADJ: ADJ n

**seis|mo|graph** /saɪzməgrɑːf, -græf/ **(seismographs)** A **seismograph** is an instrument for recording and measuring the strength of earthquakes. N-COUNT

**seis|mol|ogy** /saɪzmɒlədʒi/ **Seismology** is the scientific study of earthquakes. ♦ **seis|mo|logi|cal** ❑ *...the Seismological Society of America.* ♦ **seis|molo|gist** **(seismologists)** *Peter Ward is a seismologist with the US Geological Survey.* N-UNCOUNT; ADJ: usu ADJ n; N-COUNT

**seize** /siːz/ **(seizes, seizing, seized)** ◆◇◇ [1] If you **seize** something, you take hold of it quickly, firmly, and forcefully. ❑ *'Leigh,' he said seizing my arm to hold me back. ...an otter seizing a fish.* VERB; V n; V n [2] When a group of people **seize** a place or **seize** control of it, they take control of it quickly and suddenly, using force. ❑ *Troops have seized the airport and railroad terminals... Army officers plotted a failed attempt yesterday to seize power.* VERB = *take*; V n; V n [3] If a government or other authority **seize** someone's property, they take it from them, often by force. ❑ *Police were reported to have seized all copies of this morning's edition of the newspaper.* VERB; V n [4] When someone **is seized**, they are arrested or captured. ❑ *UN officials say two military observers were seized by the Khmer Rouge yesterday... Men carrying sub-machine guns seized the five soldiers and drove them away.* VERB; *be* V-ed; V n [5] When you **seize** an opportunity, you take advantage of it and do something that you want to do. ❑ *During the riots hundreds of people seized the opportunity to steal property.* VERB; V n

♦ **seize on** If you **seize on** something or **seize upon** it, you show great interest in it, often because it is useful to you. ❑ *Newspapers seized on the results as proof that global warming wasn't really happening.* PHRASAL VERB; V P n

♦ **seize up** [1] If a part of your body **seizes up**, it suddenly stops working, because you have strained it or because you are getting old. ❑ *We are all born flexible but as we grow older, we tend to seize up a little.* PHRASAL VERB; V P [2] If something such as an engine **seizes up**, it stops working, because it has not been properly cared for. ❑ *She put diesel fuel, instead of petrol, into the tank causing the motor to seize up.* PHRASAL VERB; V P

**sei|zure** /siːʒəʳ/ **(seizures)** [1] If someone has a **seizure**, they have a sudden violent attack of an illness, especially one that affects their heart or brain. ❑ *...a mild cardiac seizure... I was prescribed drugs to control seizures.* N-COUNT [2] If there is a **seizure of** power or a **seizure of** an area of land, a group of people suddenly take control of the place, using force. ❑ *...the seizure of territory through force.* N-COUNT: oft N *of* n [3] When an organization such as the police or customs service makes a **seizure of** illegal goods, they find them and take them away. ❑ *Police have made one of the biggest seizures of heroin there's ever been in Britain. ...arms seizures.* N-COUNT: oft N *of* n [4] If a financial institution or a government makes a **seizure of** someone's assets, they take their money or property from them because they have not paid mon- N-COUNT: oft N *of* n ey that they owe. ❑ *A court ordered the seizure of two ships for non-payment of the debt.*

**sel|dom** /seldəm/ If something **seldom** happens, it happens only occasionally. ❑ *They seldom speak... We were seldom at home.* ADV: ADV before v, ADV with cl/group ≠ *often*

**se|lect** /sɪlekt/ **(selects, selecting, selected)** ◆◇◇ [1] If you **select** something, you choose it from a number of things of the same kind. ❑ *Voters are selecting candidates for both US Senate seats... The movie is being shown in selected cities.* VERB V n V-ed, Also V n *for/from* n [2] If you **select** a file or a piece of text on a computer screen, you click on it so that it is marked in a different colour, usually in order for you to give the computer an instruction relating to that file or piece of text. [COMPUTING] ❑ *I selected a file and pressed the Delete key.* VERB V n [3] A **select** group is a small group of some of the best people or things of their kind. ❑ *...a select group of French cheeses.* ADJ: ADJ n [4] If you describe something as **select**, you mean it has many desirable features, but is available only to people who have a lot of money or who belong to a high social class. ❑ *Christian Lacroix is throwing a very lavish and very select party.* ADJ: usu ADJ n = *exclusive*

**se|lect com|mit|tee** **(select committees)** A **select committee** is a committee of members of a parliament which is set up to investigate and report on a particular matter. N-COUNT

**se|lec|tion** /sɪlekʃən/ **(selections)** ◆◇◇ [1] **Selection** is the act of selecting one or more people or things from a group. ❑ *...Darwin's principles of natural selection... Dr. Sullivan's selection to head the Department of Health was greeted with satisfaction.* N-UNCOUNT: with supp [2] A **selection of** people or things is a set of them that have been selected from a larger group. ❑ *...this selection of popular songs.* N-COUNT: oft N *of* n [3] The **selection of** goods in a shop is the particular range of goods that it has available and from which you can choose what you want. ❑ *It offers the widest selection of antiques of every description in a one day market.* N-COUNT: usu sing, usu N *of* n = *range*

**se|lec|tive** /sɪlektɪv/ [1] A **selective** process applies only to a few things or people. ❑ *Selective breeding may result in a greyhound running faster and seeing better than a wolf.* ADJ: ADJ n ♦ **se|lec|tive|ly** *Within the project, trees are selectively cut on a 25-year rotation.* ADV: usu ADV with v ♦ **se|lec|tiv|ity** /sɪlektɪvɪti/ *The soldiers specialized in going out in small groups, to kill with a very high degree of selectivity.* N-UNCOUNT: usu with supp [2] When someone is **selective**, they choose things carefully, for example the things that they buy or do. ❑ *Sales still happen, but buyers are more selective.* ADJ: usu v-link ADJ ♦ **se|lec|tive|ly** *...people on small incomes who wanted to shop selectively.* ADV: ADV with v [3] If you say that someone has a **selective** memory, you disapprove of the fact that they remember certain facts about something and deliberately forget others, often because it is convenient for them to do so. ❑ *We seem to have a selective memory for the best bits of the past.* ADJ: usu ADJ n [disapproval] ♦ **se|lec|tive|ly** *...a tendency to selectively forget all the adverse effects of the drug.* ADV: ADV with v

**se|lec|tive ser|vice** In the United States, **selective service** is a system of selecting and ordering young men to serve in the armed forces for a limited period of time. N-UNCOUNT

**se|lec|tor** /sɪlektə/ **(selectors)** A **selector** is someone whose job is to choose which people will be in a particular sports team or will take part in a particular sports contest. ❑ *...the England cricket selectors.* N-COUNT: usu supp N

**self** /self/ **(selves)** ◆◇◇ [1] Your **self** is your basic personality or nature, especially considered in terms of what you are really like as a person. ❑ *You're looking more like your usual self... She was back to her old self again.* N-COUNT: usu adj N [2] A person's **self** is the essential part of their nature which makes them different from everyone and everything else. ❑ *I want to explore and get in touch with my inner self.* N-COUNT: usu adj N

**self-** /self-/ [1] **Self-** is used to form words which indicate that you do something to yourself or by yourself. ❑ *He is a self-proclaimed racist. ...self-destructive behaviour.* COMB in ADJ and N [2] **Self-** is used to form words which describe something such as a device that does something automatically by itself. ❑ *...a self-loading pistol.* COMB in ADJ and N

**self-absorbed** Someone who is **self-absorbed** thinks so much about things concerning themselves that they do not notice other people or the things around them. ADJ

**self-access** In a school or college, a **self-access** centre is a place where students can choose and use books, tapes, or other materials. [BRIT] ❑ *...a self-access study centre.* ADJ

**self-addressed** A **self-addressed** envelope is an envelope which you have written your address on and which you send to someone in another envelope so that they can send something back to you. ❑ *Please enclose a stamped self-addressed envelope.* ADJ: usu ADJ n

**self-adhesive** Something that is **self-adhesive** is covered on one side with a sticky substance like glue, so that it will stick to surfaces. ❑ *...self-adhesive labels.* ADJ: usu ADJ n

**self-aggrandizement** /self əgrændɪzmənt/

✓ in BRIT, also use **self-aggrandisement**

If you say that someone is guilty of **self-aggrandizement**, you mean that they do certain things in order to make themselves more powerful, wealthy, or important. ❑ *He was interested in service, not self-aggrandisement.* N-UNCOUNT [disapproval]

**self-appointed** A **self-appointed** leader or ruler has taken the position of leader or ruler without anyone else asking them or choosing them to have it. ❑ *...the new self-appointed leaders of the movement.* ADJ: usu ADJ n

**self-assembly** **Self-assembly** is used to refer to furniture and other goods that you buy in parts and that you have to put together yourself. ❑ *...a range of self-assembly bedroom furniture.* ADJ: usu ADJ n

**self-assertion** **Self-assertion** is confidence that you have in speaking firmly about your opinions and demanding the rights that you believe you should have. ❑ *...her silence and lack of self-assertion.* N-UNCOUNT

**self-assertive** Someone who is **self-assertive** acts in a confident way, speaking firmly about their opinions and demanding the rights that they believe they should have. ❑ *If you want good relationships, you must have the confidence to be self-assertive when required.* ADJ

**self-assessment** In Britain, **self-assessment** refers to a system for paying tax in which people have to fill in an official form giving details of how much money they have earned in the previous year. N-SING

**self-assurance** Someone who has **self-assurance** shows confidence in the things that they say and do because they are sure of their abilities. N-UNCOUNT = *self-confidence*

**self-assured** Someone who is **self-assured** shows confidence in what they say and do because they are sure of their own abilities. ❑ *He's a self-assured, confident negotiator.* ADJ = *self-confident*

**self-aware** Someone who is **self-aware** knows and judges their own character well. ❑ *Doing a degree has increased my confidence and I feel much more self-aware.* ADJ: usu v-link ADJ ♦ **self-awareness** *It is assumed that you are interested in achieving greater self-awareness.* N-UNCOUNT

**self-belief** **Self-belief** is confidence in your own abilities or judgment. N-UNCOUNT = *self-confidence*

**self-catering** If you go on a **self-catering** holiday or you stay in **self-catering** accommodation, you stay in a place where you have to make your own meals. [BRIT] ❑ *The self-catering flats are usually reserved for postgraduate students.* N-UNCOUNT: usu N n

**self-centred**

✓ in AM, use **self-centered**

Someone who is **self-centred** is only concerned with their own wants and needs and never thinks about other people. ❑ *He was self-centred, but he wasn't cruel.* ADJ disapproval

**self-confessed** If you describe someone as a **self-confessed** murderer or a **self-confessed** romantic, for example, you mean that they admit openly that they are a murderer or a romantic. ❑ *The self-confessed drug addict was arrested 13 months ago.* ADJ: ADJ n

**self-confidence** If you have **self-confidence**, you behave confidently because you feel sure of your abilities or value. ❑ *With the end of my love affair, I lost all the self-confidence I once had.* N-UNCOUNT

**self-confident** Someone who is **self-confident** behaves confidently because they feel sure of their abilities or value. ❑ *She'd blossomed into a self-confident young woman.* ADJ = self-assured

**self-congratulation** If someone keeps emphasizing how well they have done or how good they are, you can refer to their behaviour as **self-congratulation**. ❑ *This is not a matter for self-congratulation.* N-UNCOUNT disapproval

**self-congratulatory** If you describe someone or their behaviour as **self-congratulatory**, you mean that they keep emphasizing how well they have done or how good they are. ❑ *Officials were self-congratulatory about how well the day had gone.* ADJ disapproval

**self-conscious** 1 Someone who is **self-conscious** is easily embarrassed and nervous because they feel that everyone is looking at them and judging them. ❑ *I felt a bit self-conscious in my swimming costume... Bess was self-conscious about being shorter than her two friends.* ♦ **self-consciously** *She was fiddling self-consciously with her wedding ring.* ♦ **self-consciousness** *...her painful self-consciousness.* 2 If you describe someone or something as **self-conscious**, you mean that they are strongly aware of who or what they are. [FORMAL] ❑ *Putting the work together is a very self-conscious process.* ♦ **self-consciously** *The world which the book inhabits seems too self-consciously literary, too introverted.* ADJ: usu v-link ADJ, oft ADJ *about* n; ADV: ADV with v; N-UNCOUNT; ADJ; ADV: ADV adj

**self-contained** 1 You can describe someone or something as **self-contained** when they are complete and separate and do not need help or resources from outside. ❑ *He seems completely self-contained and he doesn't miss you when you're not there. ...self-contained economic blocs.* 2 **Self-contained** accommodation such as a flat has all its own facilities, so that a person living there does not have to share rooms such as a kitchen or bathroom with other people. ADJ; ADJ: usu ADJ n

**self-contradictory** If you say or write something that is **self-contradictory**, you make two statements which cannot both be true. ❑ *He is notorious for making unexpected, often self-contradictory, comments.* ADJ

**self-control** **Self-control** is the ability to not show your feelings or not do the things that your feelings make you want to do. ❑ *I began to wish I'd shown more self-control.* N-UNCOUNT

**self-controlled** Someone who is **self-controlled** is able to not show their feelings or not do the things that their feelings make them want to do. ❑ *My father, who had always been very self-controlled, became bad-tempered.* ADJ

**self-deception** **Self-deception** involves allowing yourself to believe something about yourself that is not true, because the truth is more unpleasant. ❑ *Human beings have an infinite capacity for self-deception.* N-UNCOUNT = self-delusion

**self-declared** **Self-declared** means the same as **self-proclaimed**. ❑ *...the self-declared interim president... He is a self-declared populist.* ADJ: ADJ n

**self-defeating** A plan or action that is **self-defeating** is likely to cause problems or difficulties instead of producing useful results. ❑ *Dishonesty is ultimately self-defeating.* ADJ

**self-defence**

✔ in AM, use **self-defense**

1 **Self-defence** is the use of force to protect yourself against someone who is attacking you. ❑ *Richards claimed he acted in self-defence after Pagett opened fire on him during a siege. ...courses in karate or some other means of self-defence.* 2 **Self-defence** is the action of protecting yourself against something bad. ❑ *Jokes can be a form of self-defence.* N-UNCOUNT: usu with supp, oft *in/of* N; N-UNCOUNT

**self-delusion** **Self-delusion** is the state of having a false idea about yourself or the situation you are in. ❑ *...the grandiose self-delusion of the addict.* N-UNCOUNT

**self-denial** **Self-denial** is the habit of refusing to do or have things that you would like, either because you cannot afford them, or because you believe it is morally good for you not to do them or have them. ❑ *Should motherhood necessarily mean sacrifice and self-denial?* N-UNCOUNT

**self-denying** Someone who is **self-denying** refuses to do or have things that they would like, either because they cannot afford them, or because they believe it is morally good for them not to do them or have them. ❑ *They believed that good parents should be self-sacrificing and self-denying.* ADJ

**self-deprecating** If you describe someone's behaviour as **self-deprecating**, you mean that they criticize themselves or represent themselves as foolish in a light-hearted way. ❑ *Sharon tells the story of that night with self-deprecating humour.* ADJ: usu ADJ n

**self-destruct** (**self-destructs, self-destructing, self-destructed**) If someone **self-destructs**, they do something that seriously damages their chances of success. ❑ *They're going to be famous, but unless something happens, they're going to self-destruct.* VERB V

**self-destructive** **Self-destructive** behaviour is harmful to the person who behaves in that way. ❑ *He had a reckless, self-destructive streak.* ADJ

**self-determination** **Self-determination** is the right of a country to be independent, instead of being controlled by a foreign country, and to choose its own form of government. N-UNCOUNT = independence

**self-discipline** **Self-discipline** is the ability to control yourself and to make yourself work hard or behave in a particular way without needing anyone else to tell you what to do. ❑ *Exercising at home alone requires a tremendous amount of self-discipline.* N-UNCOUNT

**self-disciplined** Someone who is **self-disciplined** has the ability to control themselves and to make themselves work hard or behave in a particular way without needing anyone else to tell them what to do. ❑ *Most religions teach you to be truthful and self-disciplined.* ADJ

**self-doubt** **Self-doubt** is a lack of confidence in yourself and your abilities. N-UNCOUNT ≠ confidence

**self-drive** 1 A **self-drive** car is one which you hire and drive yourself. [BRIT] ❑ *Any holiday in the USA and Canada is enhanced by renting a self-drive car.* ADJ: ADJ n

✔ in AM, use **rental car**

2 A **self-drive** holiday is one where you drive yourself to the place where you are staying, rather than being taken there by plane or coach. [BRIT] ❑ *...the growth in popularity of self-drive camping holidays.* ADJ: ADJ n

**self-educated** People who are **self-educated** have acquired knowledge or a skill by themselves, rather than being taught it by someone else such as a teacher at school. ❑ *...a self-educated man from a working class background.* ADJ

**self-effacement** Someone's **self-effacement** is their unwillingness to talk about N-UNCOUNT themselves or draw attention to themselves. ❑ *He was modest to the point of self-effacement.*

**self-effacing** Someone who is **self-effacing** does not like talking about themselves or drawing attention to themselves. ❑ *As women we tend to be self-effacing and make light of what we have achieved.* ADJ

**self-employed** If you are **self-employed**, you organize your own work and taxes and are paid by people for a service you provide, rather than being paid a regular salary by a person or a firm. [BUSINESS] ❑ *There are no paid holidays or sick leave if you are self-employed. ...a self-employed builder.* ♦ **The self-employed** are people who are self-employed. ❑ *We want more support for the self-employed.* ADJ; N-PLURAL: the N

**self-esteem** Your **self-esteem** is how you feel about yourself. For example, if you have low **self-esteem**, you do not like yourself, you do not think that you are a valuable person, and therefore you do not behave confidently. ❑ *Poor self-esteem is at the centre of many of the difficulties we experience in our relationships.* N-UNCOUNT

**self-evident** A fact or situation that is **self-evident** is so obvious that there is no need for proof or explanation. ❑ *It is self-evident that we will never have enough resources to meet the demand.* ♦ **self-evidently** *The task was self-evidently impossible.* ADJ: usu v-link ADJ = obvious; ADV: ADV adj, ADV with cl/group

**self-examination** 1 **Self-examination** is thought that you give to your own character and actions, for example in order to judge whether you have been behaving in a way that is acceptable to your own set of values. ❑ *The events in Los Angeles have sparked a new national self-examination.* 2 **Self-examination** is the act of examining your own body to check whether or not you have any signs of a particular disease or illness. ❑ *Breast self-examination is invaluable for detecting cancer in its very early stages.* N-UNCOUNT: also a N; N-UNCOUNT

**self-explanatory** Something that is **self-explanatory** is clear and easy to understand without needing any extra information or explanation. ❑ *I hope the graphs on the following pages are self-explanatory.* ADJ: usu v-link ADJ

**self-expression** **Self-expression** is the expression of your personality, feelings, or opinions, for example through an artistic activity such as drawing or dancing. ❑ *Clothes are a fundamental form of self-expression.* N-UNCOUNT

**self-fulfilling** If you describe a statement or belief about the future as **self-fulfilling**, you mean that what is said or believed comes true because people expect it to come true. ❑ *Fear of failure can become a self-fulfilling prophecy.* ADJ

**self-governing** A **self-governing** region or organization is governed or run by its own people rather than by the people of another region or organization. ❑ *...a self-governing province.* ADJ

**self-government** **Self-government** is government of a country or region by its own people rather than by others. N-UNCOUNT

**self-help** 1 **Self-help** consists of people providing support and help for each other in an informal way, rather than relying on the government, authorities, or other official organizations. ❑ *She helped her Mum set up a self-help group for parents with over-weight children.* 2 **Self-help** consists of doing things yourself to try and solve your own problems without depending on other people. ❑ *...a society that encourages competitiveness and self-help among the very young. ...a self-help book.* N-UNCOUNT: oft N n; N-UNCOUNT

**self-image** **(self-images)** Your **self-image** is the set of ideas you have about your own qualities and abilities. ❑ *Children who have a positive self-image are less likely to present behaviour and discipline problems.* N-COUNT: usu sing

**self-important** If you say that someone is **self-important**, you disapprove of them because they behave as if they are more important than they really are. ❑ *He was self-important, vain and ignorant.* ♦ **self-importance** *Many visitors complained of his bad manners and self-importance.* ADJ disapproval = pompous; N-UNCOUNT

**self-imposed** A **self-imposed** restriction, task, or situation is one that you have deliberately created or accepted for yourself. ❑ *He returned home in the summer of 1974 after eleven years of self-imposed exile.* ADJ: usu ADJ n

**self-indulgence** **(self-indulgences)** **Self-indulgence** is the act of allowing yourself to have or do the things that you enjoy very much. ❑ *Going to the movies in the afternoon is one of my big self-indulgences.* N-VAR

**self-indulgent** If you say that someone is **self-indulgent**, you mean that they allow themselves to have or do the things that they enjoy very much. ❑ *To buy flowers for myself seems wildly self-indulgent.* ADJ

**self-inflicted** A **self-inflicted** wound or injury is one that you do to yourself deliberately. ❑ *He is being treated for a self-inflicted gunshot wound.* ADJ

**self-interest** If you accuse someone of **self-interest**, you disapprove of them because they always want to do what is best for themselves rather than for anyone else. ❑ *Their current protests are motivated purely by self-interest.* N-UNCOUNT disapproval

**self-interested** If you describe someone as **self-interested**, you disapprove of them because they always want to do what is best for themselves rather than for other people. ❑ *Narrowly self-interested behaviour is ultimately self-defeating.* ADJ disapproval

**self|ish** /selfɪʃ/ If you say that someone is **selfish**, you mean that he or she cares only about himself or herself, and not about other people. ❑ *I think I've been very selfish. I've been mainly concerned with myself. ...the selfish interests of a few people.* ♦ **self|ish|ly** *Cabinet Ministers are selfishly pursuing their own vested interests.* ♦ **self|ish|ness** *The arrogance and selfishness of different interest groups never ceases to amaze me.* ADJ disapproval; ADV: usu ADV with v; N-UNCOUNT: usu with supp

**self-knowledge** **Self-knowledge** is knowledge that you have about your own character and nature. ❑ *The more self-knowledge we have, the more control we can exert over our feelings and behaviour.* N-UNCOUNT

**self|less** /selfləs/ If you say that someone is **selfless**, you approve of them because they care about other people more than themselves. ❑ *Perhaps the only all-enduring and selfless love was that of a mother for her child.* ♦ **self|less|ly** *I've never known anyone who cared so selflessly about children.* ♦ **self|less|ness** *I have enormous regard for his selflessness on behalf of his fellow man.* ADJ approval; ADV; N-UNCOUNT

**self-loathing** If someone feels **self-loathing**, they feel great dislike and disgust for themselves. N-UNCOUNT

**self-made** **Self-made** is used to describe people who have become successful and rich through their own efforts, especially if they started life without money, education, or high social status. ❑ *He is a self-made man. ...a self-made millionaire.* ADJ: usu ADJ n

**self-obsessed** If you describe someone as **self-obsessed**, you are criticizing them for spending too much time thinking about themselves or their own problems. ADJ disapproval

**self-parody** **(self-parodies)** **Self-parody** is a way of performing or behaving in which you exaggerate and make fun of the way you normally perform or behave. ❑ *By the end of his life, Presley's vocals often descended close to self-parody.* N-VAR

**self-pity** **Self-pity** is a feeling of unhappiness that you have about yourself and your problems, especially when this is unnecessary or greatly exaggerated. ❑ *Throughout, he showed no trace of self-pity.* N-UNCOUNT disapproval

**self-pitying** Someone who is **self-pitying** is full of self-pity. ❑ *At the risk of sounding self-pitying, I'd say it has been harder on me than it has on Joanne.* ADJ disapproval

**self-portrait** **(self-portraits)** A **self-portrait** is a drawing, painting, or written description that you do of yourself. N-COUNT

**self-possessed** Someone who is **self-possessed** is calm and confident and in control of their emotions. ❑ *She is clearly the most articulate and self-possessed member of her family.* ADJ = self-assured

**self-possession** **Self-possession** is the quality of being self-possessed. ❑ *She found her customary self-possession had deserted her.* N-UNCOUNT = self-assurance

**self-preservation** **Self-preservation** is the action of keeping yourself safe or alive in a dangerous situation, often without thinking about what you are doing. ❑ *The police have the same human urge for self-preservation as the rest of us.* N-UNCOUNT

**self-proclaimed** 1 **Self-proclaimed** is used to show that someone has given themselves a particular title or status rather than being given it by other people. ❑ *...a self-proclaimed expert... He is President of his own self-proclaimed republic.* ADJ: ADJ n = self-confessed
2 **Self-proclaimed** is used to show that someone says themselves that they are a type of person which most people would be embarrassed or ashamed to be. ❑ *One of the prisoners is a self-proclaimed racist who opened fire on a crowd four years ago.* ADJ: ADJ n = self-declared

**self-raising flour** **Self-raising flour** is flour that makes cakes rise when they are cooked because it has chemicals added to it. [BRIT] N-UNCOUNT

☑ in AM, use **self-rising flour**

**self-regulation** **Self-regulation** is the controlling of a process or activity by the people or organizations that are involved in it rather than by an outside organization such as the government. ❑ *Competition between companies is too fierce for self-regulation to work.* N-UNCOUNT

**self-regulatory** also **self-regulating.** **Self-regulatory** systems, organizations, or activities are controlled by the people involved in them, rather than by outside organizations or rules. ❑ *For a self-regulatory system to work, the consent of all those involved is required.* ADJ: usu ADJ n

**self-reliance** **Self-reliance** is the ability to do things and make decisions by yourself, without needing other people to help you. ❑ *People learned self-reliance because they had to.* N-UNCOUNT = independence

**self-reliant** If you are **self-reliant**, you are able to do things and make decisions by yourself, without needing other people to help you. ❑ *She is intelligent and self-reliant, speaking her mind and not suffering fools gladly.* ADJ = independent

**self-respect** **Self-respect** is a feeling of confidence and pride in your own ability and worth. ❑ *They have lost not only their jobs, but their homes, their self-respect and even their reason for living.* N-UNCOUNT

**self-respecting** You can use **self-respecting** with a noun describing a particular type of person to indicate that something is typical of, or necessary for, that type of person. ❑ *He died as any self-respecting gangster should – in a hail of bullets.* ADJ: ADJ n

**self-restraint** If you show **self-restraint**, you do not do something even though you would like to do it, because you think it would be better not to. N-UNCOUNT

**self-righteous** If you describe someone as **self-righteous**, you disapprove of them because they are convinced that they are right in their beliefs, attitudes, and behaviour and that other people are wrong. ❑ *He is critical of the monks, whom he considers narrow-minded and self-righteous.* ♦ **self-righteousness** *...her smug self-righteousness.* ADJ [disapproval] N-UNCOUNT

**self-rising flour** **Self-rising flour** is flour that makes cakes rise when they are cooked because it has chemicals added to it. [AM] N-UNCOUNT

☑ in BRIT, use **self-raising flour**

**self-rule** **Self-rule** is the same as **self-government**. ❑ *The agreement gives the territory limited self-rule.* N-UNCOUNT

**self-sacrifice** **Self-sacrifice** is the giving up of what you want so that other people can have what they need or want. ❑ *I thanked my parents for all their self-sacrifice on my behalf.* N-UNCOUNT

**self-sacrificing** Someone who is **self-sacrificing** gives up what they want so that other people can have what they need or want. ❑ *He was a generous self-sacrificing man.* ADJ

**self-same** also **selfsame.** You use **self-same** when you want to emphasize that the person or thing mentioned is exactly the same as the one mentioned previously. ❑ *You find yourself worshipped by the self-same people who beat you up at school.* ADJ: ADJ n [emphasis]

**self-satisfaction** **Self-satisfaction** is the feeling you have when you are self-satisfied. ❑ *He tried hard not to smile in smug self-satisfaction.* N-UNCOUNT [disapproval] = smugness

**self-satisfied** If you describe someone as **self-satisfied**, you mean that they are too pleased with themselves about their achievements or their situation and they think that nothing better is possible. ❑ *She handed the cigar back to Jason with a self-satisfied smile.* ADJ [disapproval] = smug

**self-seeking** If you describe someone as **self-seeking**, you disapprove of them because they are interested only in doing things which give them an advantage over other people. ❑ *He said that democracy would open the way for self-seeking politicians to abuse the situation.* ADJ [disapproval]

**self-service** A **self-service** shop, restaurant, or garage is one where you get things for yourself rather than being served by another person. ADJ

**self-serving** If you describe someone as **self-serving**, you are critical of them because they are only interested in what they can get for themselves. ❑ *...corrupt, self-serving politicians.* ADJ [disapproval]

**self-standing** 1 An object or structure that is **self-standing** is not supported by other objects or structures. ❑ *...self-standing plastic cases.* ADJ 2 A company or organization that is **self-standing** is independent of other companies or organizations. [BUSINESS] ❑ *Five separate companies, all operating as self-standing units, are now one.* ADJ

**self-study** **Self-study** is study that you do on your own, without a teacher. ❑ *Individuals can enrol on self-study courses in the university's language institute.* N-UNCOUNT: oft N n

**self-styled** If you describe someone as a **self-styled** leader or expert, you disapprove of them because they claim to be a leader or expert but they do not actually have the right to call themselves this. ❑ *Two of those arrested are said to be self-styled area commanders.* ADJ: ADJ n [disapproval]

**self-sufficiency** **Self-sufficiency** is the state of being self-sufficient. N-UNCOUNT

**self-sufficient** 1 If a country or group is **self-sufficient**, it is able to produce or make everything that it needs. ❑ *This enabled the country to become self-sufficient in sugar... Using traditional methods poor farmers can be virtually self-sufficient.* ADJ: usu v-link ADJ
2 Someone who is **self-sufficient** is able to live happily without anyone else. ❑ *Although she had various boyfriends, Madeleine was, and remains, fiercely self-sufficient.* ADJ

**self-supporting** **Self-supporting** is used to describe organizations, schemes, and people who earn enough money to not need financial help from anyone else. ❑ *The income from visitors makes the museum self-supporting.* ADJ

**self-sustaining** A **self-sustaining** process or system is able to continue by itself without anyone or anything else becoming involved. ❑ *Asia's emerging economies will be on a self-sustaining cycle of growth.* ADJ

**self-taught** If you are **self-taught**, you have learned a skill by yourself rather than being taught it by someone else such as a teacher at school. ❑ *...a self-taught musician.* ADJ

**self-will** Someone's **self-will** is their determination to do what they want without caring what other people think. ❑ *She had a little core of self-will.* N-UNCOUNT

**self-willed** Someone who is **self-willed** is determined to do the things that they want to do and will not take advice from other people. ❑ *He was very independent and self-willed.* ADJ

**self-worth** **Self-worth** is the feeling that you have good qualities and have achieved good things. ❑ *Try not to link your sense of self-worth to the opinions of others.* N-UNCOUNT

**sell** /sel/ **(sells, selling, sold)** ◆◆◆ 1 If you **sell** something that you own, you let someone have it in return for money. ❑ *I sold everything I owned except for my car and my books... His heir sold the painting to the London art dealer Agnews... The directors sold the business for £14.8 million... It's not a very good time to sell at the moment.* VERB V n, V n *to* n, V n *for* n, V
2 If a shop **sells** a particular thing, it is available for people to buy there. ❑ *It sells everything from hair ribbons to oriental rugs... Bean sprouts are also sold in cans.* VERB V n, V n
3 If something **sells for** a particular price, that price is paid for it. ❑ *Unmodernised property can sell for up to 40 per cent of its modernised market value.* VERB V *for/at* n
4 If something **sells**, it is bought by the public, usually in fairly large quantities. ❑ *Even if this album doesn't sell and the critics don't like it, we wouldn't ever change... The company believes the products will sell well in the run-up to Christmas.* VERB V, V adv
5 Something that **sells** a product makes people want to buy the product. ❑ *It is only the sensational that sells news magazines. ...car manufacturers' long-held maxim that safety doesn't sell.* VERB V n, V
6 If you **sell** someone an idea or proposal, or **sell** someone **on** an idea, you convince them that it is a good one. ❑ *She tried to sell me the idea of buying my own paper shredder... She is hoping she can sell the idea to clients... An employee sold him on the notion that cable was the medium of the future... You know, I wasn't sold on this trip in the beginning.* VERB V n n, V n *to* n, V n *on* n, V-ed

**PHRASES** 7 If someone **sells** their **body**, they have sex for money. ❑ *85 per cent said they would rather not sell their bodies for a living.* PHRASE: V and N inflect
8 If someone **sells** you **down the river**, they betray you for some personal profit or advantage. ❑ *He has been sold down the river by the people who were supposed to protect him.* PHRASE: V inflects
9 If you **sell** someone **short**, you do not point out their good qualities as much as you should or do as much for them as you should. ❑ *They need to improve their image – they are selling themselves short.* PHRASE: V inflects
10 If you talk about someone **selling** their **soul** in order to get something, you are criticizing them for abandoning their principles. ❑ *...a man who would sell his soul for political viability.* PHRASE: V and N inflect [disapproval]

♦ **sell off** If you **sell** something **off**, you sell it because you need the money. ❑ *The company is selling off some sites and concentrating on cutting debts... We had to sell things off to pay the brewery bill.* → See also **sell-off**. PHRASAL VERB V P n (not pron), V n P

♦ **sell on** If you buy something and then **sell** it **on**, you sell it to someone else soon after buying it, usually in order to make a profit. ❑ *Mr Farrier bought cars at auctions and sold them on... The arms had been sold to a businessman; he sold them on to paramilitary groups.* PHRASAL VERB V n P, V n P *to* n

♦ **sell out** 1 If a shop **sells out** of something, it sells all its stocks of it, so that there is no longer any left for people to buy. ❑ *Hardware stores sold out of water pumps and tarpaulins... The next day the bookshops sold out.* PHRASAL VERB V P *of* n, V P
2 If a performance, sports event, or other entertainment **sells out**, all the tickets for it are sold. ❑ *Football games often sell out well in advance.* PHRASAL VERB V P
3 When things **sell out**, all of them that are available are sold. ❑ *Tickets for the show sold out in 70 minutes.* PHRASAL VERB V P
4 If you accuse someone of **selling out**, you disapprove of the fact that they do something which used to be against their principles, or give in to an opposing group. ❑ *The young in particular see him as a man who will not sell out or be debased by the compromises of politics... Many of his Greenwich Village associates thought Dylan had sold out to commercialism.* PHRASAL VERB [disapproval] V P, V P *to* n
5 **Sell out** means the same as **sell up**. [AM] ❑ *I hear she's going to sell out and move to the city.* PHRASAL VERB V P
6 → See also **sell-out**, **sold out**.

♦ **sell up** If you **sell up**, you sell everything you have, such as your house or your business, because you need the money. [BRIT] ❑ *...all these farmers going out of business and having to sell up... He advised Evans to sell up his flat and move away to the country.* PHRASAL VERB V P, V P n (not pron)

☑ in AM, use **sell out**

**sell-by date** **(sell-by dates)** 1 The **sell-by date** on a food container is the date by which the food should be sold or eaten before it starts to decay. [BRIT] ❑ *...a piece of cheese four weeks past its sell-by date.* N-COUNT

☑ in AM, use **expiration date**

2 If you say that someone or something is **past** their **sell-by date**, you mean they are no longer effective, interesting, or useful. [BRIT] ❑ *As a sportsman, he is long past his sell-by date.* PHRASE: N inflects, v-link PHR [disapproval]

**sell|er** /selə^r/ **(sellers)** 1 A **seller** of a type of thing is a person or company that sells that type of thing. ❑ *...a flower seller. ...Kraft, the largest seller of cheese in the United States.* N-COUNT: n N, N *of* n
2 In a business deal, the **seller** is the person who is selling something to someone else. ❑ *In theory, the buyer could ask the seller to have a test carried out.* N-COUNT: usu *the* N = vendor ≠ buyer
3 If you describe a product as, for example, a big **seller**, you mean that large numbers of it are being sold. ❑ *The gift shop's biggest seller is a photo of Nixon meeting Presley.* → See also **best seller**. N-COUNT: adj N

**sel|ler's mar|ket** When there is a **seller's market** for a particular product, there are fewer of the products for sale than people who want to buy them, so buyers have little choice and prices go up. [BUSINESS] N-SING

**sell|ing point** **(selling points)** A **selling point** is a desirable quality or feature that something has which makes it likely that people will want to buy it. [BUSINESS] N-COUNT

**sell|ing price** **(selling prices)** The **selling price** of something is the price for which it is sold. [BUSINESS] N-COUNT: usu sing

**sell-off** **(sell-offs)** also **selloff.** The **sell-off** of something, for example an industry owned by the state or a company's shares, is the selling of it. [BUSINESS] ❑ *The privatisation of the electricity industry – the biggest sell-off of them all.* N-COUNT: usu with supp

**Sel|lo|tape** /seləteɪp/ **(Sellotapes, Sellotaping, Sellotaped)** 1 **Sellotape** is a clear sticky tape that you use to stick paper or card together or onto a wall. [BRIT, TRADEMARK] N-UNCOUNT

☑ in AM, use **Scotch tape**

2 If you **Sellotape** one thing to another, you stick them together using Sellotape. [BRIT, TRADEMARK] ❑ *I sellotaped the note to his door.* VERB V n adv/prep

☑ in AM, use **tape**

**sell-out** **(sell-outs)** also **sellout.** 1 If a play, sports event, or other entertainment is a **sell-out**, all the tickets for it are sold. ❑ *Their concert there was a sell-out.* N-COUNT: usu sing, oft N n
2 If you describe someone's behaviour as a **sell-out**, you disapprove of the fact that they have done something which used to be against their principles, or given in to an opposing group. ❑ *For some, his decision to become a Socialist candidate at Sunday's election was simply a sell-out.* N-COUNT: usu sing, oft N *to* n [disapproval]

**sell-through** A **sell-through** video is a film on video that you can buy. ADJ: ADJ n

**selves** /selvz/ **Selves** is the plural of **self**.

**se|man|tic** /sɪmæntɪk/ **Semantic** is used to describe things that deal with the meanings of words and sentences. ❑ *He did not want to enter into a semantic debate.* ADJ: usu ADJ n

**se|man|tics** /sɪmæntɪks/ **Semantics** is the branch of linguistics that deals with the meanings of words and sentences. N-UNCOUNT

**sema|phore** /seməfɔː^r/ **Semaphore** is a system of sending messages by using two flags. N-UNCOUNT

You hold a flag in each hand and move your arms to various positions representing different letters of the alphabet.

**sem|blance** /sembləns/ If there is a **semblance of** a particular condition or quality, it appears to exist, even though this may be a false impression. [FORMAL] ❑ *At least a semblance of normality has been restored to parts of the country.* N-UNCOUNT: N *of* n

**se|men** /siːmen/ **Semen** is the liquid containing sperm that is produced by the sex organs of men and male animals. N-UNCOUNT

**se|mes|ter** /sɪmestə^r/ **(semesters)** In colleges and universities in some countries, a **semester** is one of the two main periods into which the year is divided. N-COUNT

**semi** /semi/ **(semis)** 1 A **semi** is a semi-detached house. [BRIT, INFORMAL] N-COUNT 2 In a sporting competition, **the semis** are the semi-finals. [BRIT, INFORMAL] ❑ *He reached the semis after beating Lendl in the quarterfinal.* N-COUNT: usu pl, usu *the* N

**semi-** /semi-/ **Semi-** combines with adjectives and nouns to form other adjectives and nouns that describe someone or something as being partly, but not completely, in a particular state. ❑ *He found Isabel's room in semi-darkness. ...semi-skilled workers.* PREFIX

**semi-annual** A **semi-annual** event happens twice a year. [AM] ❑ *...the semi-annual meeting of the International Monetary Fund.* ADJ: usu ADJ n

✔ in BRIT, usually use **biannual**

**semi|breve** /semibriːv/ **(semibreves)** A **semibreve** is a musical note that has a time value equal to two half notes. [BRIT] N-COUNT

✔ in AM, use **whole note**

**semi-circle** **(semi-circles)** also **semicircle.** A **semi-circle** is one half of a circle, or something having the shape of half a circle. ❑ *They stood in a semi-circle round the teacher's chair and answered questions.* N-COUNT

**semi-circular** also **semicircular.** Something that is **semi-circular** has the shape of half a circle. ❑ *...a semi-circular amphitheatre.* ADJ

**semi-colon** **(semi-colons)**

✔ in AM, usually use **semicolon**

A **semi-colon** is the punctuation mark ; which is used in writing to separate different parts of a sentence or list or to indicate a pause. N-COUNT

**semi|con|duc|tor** /semikəndʌktə^r/ **(semiconductors)** also **semi-conductor.** A **semiconductor** is a substance used in electronics whose ability to conduct electricity increases with greater heat. N-COUNT

**semi-detached** A **semi-detached** house is a house that is joined to another house on one side by a shared wall. [mainly BRIT] ➔ See picture on page 1706. ❑ *...a semi-detached house in Highgate.* ADJ ♦ **Semi-detached** is also a noun. ❑ *It was an ordinary, post-war semi-detached.* N-SING

**semi-final** **(semi-finals)**

✔ in AM, usually use **semifinal**

A **semi-final** is one of the two matches or races in a competition that are held to decide who will compete in the final. ❑ *Steve Lewis won the first semi-final.* N-COUNT ♦ **The semi-finals** is the round of a competition in which these two matches or races are held. ❑ *He was beaten in the semi-finals by Chris Dittmar.* N-PLURAL: usu *the* N

**semi-finalist** **(semi-finalists)**

✔ in AM, usually use **semifinalist**

A **semi-finalist** is a player, athlete, or team that is competing in a semi-final. N-COUNT

**semi|nal** /semɪnəl/ **Seminal** is used to describe things such as books, works, events, and experiences that have a great influence in a particular field. [FORMAL] ❑ *...author of the seminal book 'Animal Liberation'.* ADJ: usu ADJ n

**semi|nar** /semɪnɑː^r/ **(seminars)** 1 A **seminar** is a meeting where a group of people discuss a problem or topic. ❑ *...a series of half-day seminars to help businessmen get the best value from investing in information technology.* N-COUNT 2 A **seminar** is a class at a college or university in which the teacher and a small group of students discuss a topic. ❑ *Students are asked to prepare material in advance of each weekly seminar.* N-COUNT

**semi|nar|ian** /semɪneəriən/ **(seminarians)** A **seminarian** is a student at a seminary. N-COUNT

**semi|nary** /semɪnəri, AM -neri/ **(seminaries)** A **seminary** is a college where priests, ministers, or rabbis are trained. N-COUNT

**se|mi|ot|ics** /semiɒtɪks/ **Semiotics** is the academic study of the relationship of language and other signs to their meanings. N-UNCOUNT

**semi-precious**

✔ in AM, also use **semiprecious**

**Semi-precious** stones are stones such as turquoises and amethysts that are used in jewellery but are less valuable than precious stones such as diamonds and rubies. ADJ: usu ADJ n

**semi-professional**

✔ in AM, also use **semiprofessional**

**Semi-professional** sports players, musicians, and singers receive some money for playing their sport or for performing but they also have an ordinary job as well. ❑ *...a semi-professional country musician.* ADJ

**semi-skilled** also **semiskilled.** A **semi-skilled** worker has some training and skills, but not enough to do specialized work. [BUSINESS] ADJ: usu ADJ n

**semi-skimmed milk** **Semi-skimmed milk** or **semi-skimmed** is milk from which some of the cream has been removed. [BRIT] N-UNCOUNT

✔ in AM, use **one percent milk, two percent milk**

**Se|mit|ic** /sɪmɪtɪk/ 1 **Semitic** languages are a group of languages that include Arabic and Hebrew. ADJ: usu ADJ n 2 **Semitic** people belong to one of the groups of people who speak a Semitic language. ❑ *...the Semitic races.* ADJ: usu ADJ n 3 **Semitic** is sometimes used to mean Jewish. ➔ See also **anti-Semitic**. ADJ: usu ADJ n

**semi|tone** /semitoun/ **(semitones)** In Western music, a **semitone** is the smallest interval between two musical notes. Two semitones are equal to one tone. N-COUNT

**semi-trailer** **(semi-trailers)** also **semitrailer.** A **semi-trailer** is the long rear section of a truck or lorry that can bend when it turns. [AM] N-COUNT

✔ in BRIT, use **trailer**

**semi-tropical** also **semitropical.** 1 **Semi-tropical** places have warm, wet air. ❑ *...a semi-tropical island.* ADJ: usu ADJ n 2 **Semi-tropical** plants and trees grow in places where the air is warm and wet. ❑ *The inn has a garden of semi-tropical vegetation.* ADJ: usu ADJ n

**semo|li|na** /seməliːnə/ **Semolina** consists of small hard grains of wheat that are used for making sweet puddings with milk and for making pasta. N-UNCOUNT

**Sen|ate** /senɪt/ **(Senates)** 1 **The Senate** is the smaller and more important of the two parts of the parliament in some countries, for example the United States and Australia. ❑ *The Senate is expected to pass the bill shortly. ...a Senate committee.* ◆◆◇ N-PROPER-COLL: usu *the* N 2 **Senate** or **the Senate** is the governing council at some universities. ❑ *The new bill would remove student representation from the university Senate.* N-PROPER-COLL

**sena|tor** /senɪtə^r/ **(senators)** A **senator** is a member of a political Senate, for example in the United States or Australia. ◆◇◇ N-COUNT; N-TITLE

**sena|to|rial** /senɪtɔːriəl/ **Senatorial** means belonging to or relating to a Senate. [FORMAL] ❑ *He has senatorial experience in defence and foreign policy.* ADJ: ADJ n

**send** /send/ **(sends, sending, sent)** [1] When you **send** someone something, you arrange for it to be taken and delivered to them, for example by post. *[◆◆◆ VERB]* ❑ *Myra Cunningham sent me a note thanking me for dinner... I sent a copy to the minister for transport... He sent a basket of exotic fruit and a card... Sir Denis took one look and sent it back... More than half a million sheep are sent from Britain to Europe for slaughter every year.* *[V n n; V n to n; V n; V n with adv; be V-ed from n]* [2] If you **send** someone somewhere, you tell them to go there. *[VERB]* ❑ *Inspector Banbury came up to see her, but she sent him away. ...the government's decision to send troops to the region... I suggested that he rest, and sent him for an X-ray... Reinforcements were being sent from the neighbouring region* *[V n with adv; V n to n; V n for n; be V-ed from n]* [3] If you **send** someone **to** an institution such as a school or a prison, you arrange for them to stay there for a period of time. *[VERB]* ❑ *It's his parents' choice to send him to a boarding school, rather than a convenient day school.* *[V n to n]* [4] To **send** a signal means to cause it to go to a place by means of radio waves or electricity. *[VERB]* ❑ *The transmitters will send a signal automatically to a local base station. ...in 1989, after a 12-year journey to Neptune, the space probe Voyager sent back pictures of Triton, its moon.* *[V n to n; V n with adv]* [5] If something **sends** things or people in a particular direction, it causes them to move in that direction. *[VERB]* ❑ *The explosion sent shrapnel flying through the sides of cars on the crowded highway... The slight back and forth motion sent a pounding surge of pain into his skull.* *[V n -ing; V n prep]* [6] To **send** someone or something **into** a particular state means to cause them to go into or be in that state. *[VERB]* ❑ *My attempt to fix it sent Lawrence into fits of laughter. ...before civil war and famine sent the country plunging into anarchy... An obsessive search for our inner selves, far from saving the world, could send us all mad.* *[V n into n; V n -ing; V n adj]* [7] to **send** someone **to Coventry** → see **Coventry**. to **send** someone **packing** → see **pack**.

♦ **send away for** → see **send for 2**.

♦ **send down** [1] If a student **is sent down** from their university or college, they are made to leave because they have behaved very badly. [BRIT] *[PHRASAL VERB: usu passive]* ❑ *She wondered if he had been sent down for gambling.* *[be V-ed P]*

☑ in AM, use **be expelled**

[2] If someone who is on trial **is sent down**, they are found guilty and sent to prison. [BRIT] *[PHRASAL VERB: usu passive]* ❑ *The two rapists were sent down for life in 1983.* *[be V-ed P]*

☑ in AM, use **send up**

♦ **send for** [1] If you **send for** someone, you send them a message asking them to come and see you. *[PHRASAL VERB]* ❑ *I've sent for the doctor.* *[V P n]* [2] If you **send for** something, you write and ask for it to be sent to you. *[PHRASAL VERB]* ❑ *Send for your free catalogue today.* *[V P n]*

♦ **send in** [1] If you **send in** something such as a competition entry or a letter applying for a job, you post it to the organization concerned. *[PHRASAL VERB]* ❑ *Applicants are asked to send in a CV and a covering letter.* *[V P n; Also V n P]* [2] When a government **sends in** troops or police officers, it orders them to deal with a crisis or problem somewhere. *[PHRASAL VERB]* ❑ *He has asked the government to send in troops to end the fighting.* *[V P n; Also V n P]*

♦ **send off** [1] When you **send off** a letter or package, you send it somewhere by post. *[PHRASAL VERB]* ❑ *He sent off copies to various people for them to read and make comments.* *[V P n (not pron); Also V n P]* [2] If a football player **is sent off**, the referee makes them leave the field during a game, as a punishment for seriously breaking the rules. *[PHRASAL VERB: usu passive]* ❑ *The 30-year-old Scottish international was sent off for arguing with a linesman.* *[be V-ed P]* → See also **sending-off**.

♦ **send off for** → see **send for 2**.

♦ **send on** If you **send on** something you have received, especially a document, you send it to another place or person. *[PHRASAL VERB]* ❑ *We coordinate the reports from the overseas divisions, and send them on to headquarters in Athens.* *[V n P; Also V P n (not pron)]*

♦ **send out** [1] If you **send out** things such as letters or bills, you send them to a large number of people at the same time. *[PHRASAL VERB]* ❑ *She had sent out well over four hundred invitations that afternoon.* *[V P n; Also V n P]* [2] To **send out** a signal, sound, light, or heat means to produce it. *[PHRASAL VERB]* ❑ *The crew did not send out any distress signals.* *[V P n; Also V n P]* [3] When a plant **sends out** roots or shoots, they grow. *[PHRASAL VERB = produce]* ❑ *If you cut your rubber plant back, it should send out new side shoots.* *[V P n; Also V n P]*

♦ **send out for** If you **send out for** food, for example pizzas or sandwiches, you phone and ask for it to be delivered to you. *[PHRASAL VERB]* ❑ *Let's send out for a pizza and watch The Late Show.* *[V P P n]*

♦ **send up** [1] If you **send** someone or something **up**, you imitate them in an amusing way that makes them appear foolish. [BRIT, INFORMAL] *[PHRASAL VERB = make fun of]* ❑ *You sense he's sending himself up as well as everything else. ...a spoof that sends up the macho world of fighter pilots.* *[V n P; V P n (not pron)]* → See also **send-up**. [2] If someone who is on trial **is sent up**, they are found guilty and sent to prison. [AM] *[PHRASAL VERB: usu passive]* ❑ *If I'm going to be sent up for killing one guy, then I might as well kill three more.* *[be V-ed P]*

☑ in BRIT, use **send down**

**send|er** /sendəʳ/ **(senders)** **The sender of** a letter, package, or radio message is the person who sent it. *[N-COUNT: the N, oft N of n]* ❑ *The sender of the best letter every week will win a cheque for £20.*

**sending-off** **(sendings-off)** If there is a **sending-off** during a game of football, a player is told to leave the field by the referee, as a punishment for seriously breaking the rules. *[N-COUNT: oft poss N]* ❑ *He is about to begin a three-match ban after his third sending-off of the season.*

**send-off** **(send-offs)** If a group of people give someone who is going away a **send-off**, they come together to say goodbye to them. [INFORMAL] *[N-COUNT: usu adj N]* ❑ *All the people in the buildings came to give me a rousing send-off.*

**send-up** **(send-ups)** A **send-up** is a piece of writing or acting in which someone or something is imitated in an amusing way that makes them appear foolish. [BRIT, INFORMAL] *[N-COUNT: usu sing, oft N of n = parody]* ❑ *...his classic send-up of sixties rock, 'Get Crazy'.*

**Sen|ega|lese** /senɪgəliːz/ **(Senegalese)** [1] **Senegalese** means belonging or relating to Senegal, or to its people or culture. *[ADJ]* ❑ *...the Senegalese navy.* [2] A **Senegalese** is a Senegalese citizen, or a person of Senegalese origin. *[N-COUNT]*

**se|nile** /siːnaɪl/ If old people become **senile**, they become confused, can no longer remember things, and are unable to look after themselves. *[ADJ]*

♦ **se|nil|ity** /sɪnɪlɪti/ ❑ *The old man was showing unmistakable signs of senility.* *[N-UNCOUNT]*

**se|nile de|men|tia** **Senile dementia** is a mental illness that affects some old people and that causes them to become confused and to forget things. *[N-UNCOUNT]* ❑ *She is suffering from senile dementia.*

**sen|ior** /siːnjəʳ/ **(seniors)** [1] The **senior** people in an organization or profession have the highest and most important jobs. *[◆◆◇ ADJ: ADJ n ≠ junior]* ❑ *...senior officials in the Israeli government. ...the company's senior management... Television and radio needed many more women in senior jobs.* [2] If someone is **senior to** you in an organization or profession, they have a higher and more important job than you or they are considered to be superior to you because they have worked there for longer and have more experience. *[ADJ: usu v-link ADJ to n ≠ junior]* ❑ *The position had to be filled by an officer senior to Haig.* ♦ Your **seniors** are the people who are senior to you. *[N-PLURAL: poss N ≠ junior]* ❑ *He was described by his seniors as a model officer.* [3] **Senior** is used when indicating how much older one person is than another. For example, if someone is ten years your **senior**, they are ten years older than you. *[N-SING: poss N ≠ junior]* ❑ *She became involved with a married man many years her senior.* [4] **Seniors** are students in a high school, university, or college who are the oldest and who have reached an advanced level in their studies. [AM] *[N-COUNT]* [5] If you take part in a sport at **senior** level, you take part in competitions with adults and people who have reached a high degree of achievement in that sport. *[ADJ: ADJ n]* ❑ *This will be his* *fifth international championship and his third at senior level.*

**sen|ior citi|zen** **(senior citizens)** A **senior citizen** is an older person who has retired or receives an old age pension. N-COUNT = *pensioner*

**sen|ior|ity** /siːniɒrɪti, AM -ɔːrɪti/ A person's **seniority** in an organization is the importance and power that they have compared with others, or the fact that they have worked there for a long time. ❑ *He has said he will fire editorial employees without regard to seniority.* N-UNCOUNT

**sen|sa|tion** /senseɪʃᵊn/ **(sensations)** 1 A **sensation** is a physical feeling. ❑ *Floating can be a very pleasant sensation... A sensation of burning or tingling may be experienced in the hands.* N-COUNT: with supp = *feeling* 2 **Sensation** is your ability to feel things physically, especially through your sense of touch. ❑ *The pain was so bad that she lost all sensation.* N-UNCOUNT: supp N = *feeling* 3 You can use **sensation** to refer to the general feeling or impression caused by a particular experience. ❑ *It's a funny sensation to know someone's talking about you in a language you don't understand.* N-COUNT: usu adj N = *feeling* 4 If a person, event, or situation is a **sensation**, it causes great excitement or interest. ❑ *...the film that turned her into an overnight sensation.* N-COUNT 5 If a person, event, or situation causes **a sensation**, they cause great interest or excitement. ❑ *She was just 14 when she caused a sensation at the Montreal Olympics.* N-SING: *a* N

**sen|sa|tion|al** /senseɪʃənᵊl/ 1 A **sensational** result, event, or situation is so remarkable that it causes great excitement and interest. ❑ *The world champions suffered a sensational defeat.* ADJ = *dramatic* ♦ **sen|sa|tion|al|ly** *The rape trial was sensationally halted yesterday.* ADV: usu ADV with v 2 You can describe stories or reports as **sensational** if you disapprove of them because they present facts in a way that is intended to cause feelings of shock, anger, or excitement. ❑ *...sensational tabloid newspaper reports.* ADJ: usu ADJ n [disapproval] 3 You can describe something as **sensational** when you think that it is extremely good. ❑ *Her voice is sensational... Experts agreed that this was a truly sensational performance.* ADJ = *amazing* ♦ **sen|sa|tion|al|ly** *...sensationally good food.* ADV

**sen|sa|tion|al|ism** /senseɪʃənəlɪzəm/ **Sensationalism** is the presenting of facts or stories in a way that is intended to produce strong feelings of shock, anger, or excitement. ❑ *The report criticises the newspaper for sensationalism.* N-UNCOUNT [disapproval]

**sen|sa|tion|al|ist** /senseɪʃənəlɪst/ **Sensationalist** news reports and television and radio programmes present the facts in a way that makes them seem worse or more shocking than they really are. ❑ *...sensationalist headlines.* ADJ [disapproval]

**sen|sa|tion|al|ize** /senseɪʃənəlaɪz/ **(sensationalizes, sensationalizing, sensationalized)**

✓ in BRIT, also use **sensationalise**

If someone **sensationalizes** a situation or event, they make it seem worse or more shocking than it really is. ❑ *Local news organizations are being criticized for sensationalizing the story.* VERB [disapproval] V n

**sense** /sens/ **(senses, sensing, sensed)** ♦♦♦ 1 Your **senses** are the physical abilities of sight, smell, hearing, touch, and taste. ❑ *She stared at him again, unable to believe the evidence of her senses. ...a keen sense of smell.* → See also **sixth sense.** N-COUNT 2 If you **sense** something, you become aware of it or you realize it, although it is not very obvious. ❑ *She probably sensed that I wasn't telling her the whole story... He looks about him, sensing danger... Prost had sensed what might happen.* VERB V that V n V wh 3 If you have a **sense that** something is the case, you think that it is the case, although you may not have firm, clear evidence for this belief. ❑ *Suddenly you got this sense that people were drawing themselves away from each other... There is no sense of urgency on either side.* → See also **sense of occasion.** N-SING: N that, N *of* n 4 If you have a **sense of** guilt or relief, for example, you feel guilty or relieved. ❑ *When your child is struggling for life, you feel this overwhelming sense of guilt.* N-SING: N *of* n = *feeling* 5 If you have a **sense of** something such as duty or justice, you are aware of it and believe it is important. ❑ *We must keep a sense of proportion about all this... She needs to regain a sense of her own worth.* N-SING: N *of* n 6 Someone who has a **sense of** timing or style has a natural ability with regard to timing or style. You can also say that someone has a bad **sense of** timing or style. ❑ *He has an impeccable sense of timing... Her dress sense is appalling.* → See also **sense of humour.** N-SING: N *of* n, also n N 7 **Sense** is the ability to make good judgments and to behave sensibly. ❑ *...when he was younger and had a bit more sense... When that doesn't work they sometimes have the sense to seek help.* → See also **common sense.** N-UNCOUNT 8 If you say that there is no **sense** or little **sense in** doing something, you mean that it is not a sensible thing to do because nothing useful would be gained by doing it. ❑ *There's no sense in pretending this doesn't happen.* N-SING: with neg, N *in* -ing, N -ing = *point* 9 A **sense** of a word or expression is one of its possible meanings. ❑ *...a noun which has two senses... Then she remembered that they had no mind in any real sense of that word.* N-COUNT = *meaning*

PHRASES 10 **Sense** is used in several expressions to indicate how true your statement is. For example, if you say that something is true **in a sense**, you mean that it is partly true, or true in one way. If you say that something is true **in a** general **sense**, you mean that it is true in a general way. ❑ *In a sense, both were right... In one sense, the fact that few new commercial buildings can be financed does not matter... He's not the leader in a political sense... Though his background was modest, it was in no sense deprived.* PHRASE: PHR with cl 11 If something **makes sense**, you can understand it. ❑ *He was sitting there saying, 'Yes, the figures make sense.'* PHRASE: V inflects 12 When you **make sense of** something, you succeed in understanding it. ❑ *This is to help her to come to terms with her early upbringing and make sense of past experiences.* PHRASE: V inflects 13 If a course of action **makes sense**, it seems sensible. ❑ *It makes sense to look after yourself... The project should be re-appraised to see whether it made sound economic sense.* PHRASE: V inflects, oft *it* PHR to-inf 14 If you say that someone **has come to** their **senses** or **has been brought to** their **senses**, you mean that they have stopped being foolish and are being sensible again. ❑ *Eventually the world will come to its senses and get rid of them.* PHRASE: V inflects 15 If you say that someone seems to **have taken leave of** their **senses**, you mean that they have done or said something very foolish. [OLD-FASHIONED] ❑ *They looked at me as if I had taken leave of my senses.* PHRASE: V inflects 16 If you say that someone **talks sense**, you mean that what they say is sensible. PHRASE: V inflects 17 If you **have a sense that** something is true or **get a sense that** something is true, you think that it is true. [mainly SPOKEN] ❑ *Do you have the sense that you are loved by the public?* PHRASE: V inflects 18 to **see sense** → see **see.**

**sense|less** /sensləs/ 1 If you describe an action as **senseless**, you think it is wrong because it has no purpose and produces no benefit. ❑ *...people whose lives have been destroyed by acts of senseless violence.* ADJ = *pointless* 2 If someone is **senseless**, they are unconscious. ❑ *They were knocked to the ground, beaten senseless and robbed of their wallets.* ADJ: ADJ after v, v-link ADJ

**sense of di|rec|tion** 1 Your **sense of direction** is your ability to know roughly where you are, or which way to go, even when you are in an unfamiliar place. ❑ *He had a poor sense of direction and soon got lost.* N-SING 2 If you say that someone has a **sense of direction**, you mean that they seem to have clear ideas about what they want to do or achieve. ❑ *The country now had a sense of direction again.* N-SING [approval]

**sense of hu|mour**

✓ in AM, use **sense of humor**

Someone who has a **sense of humour** often finds things amusing, rather than being serious all the time. ❑ *He had enormous charm and a great sense of humour.* N-SING

**sense of oc|ca|sion** If there is a **sense of occasion** when a planned event takes place, people feel that something special and important is happening. ❑ *There is a great sense of occasion and a terrific standard of musicianship.* [N-SING]

**sense or|gan** **(sense organs)** Your **sense organs** are the parts of your body, for example your eyes and your ears, which enable you to be aware of things around you. [FORMAL] [N-COUNT: usu pl]

**sen|sibil|ity** /sɛnsɪbɪlɪti/ **(sensibilities)** 1 **Sensibility** is the ability to experience deep feelings. ❑ *Everything he writes demonstrates the depth of his sensibility.* [N-UNCOUNT: usu supp N] 2 Someone's **sensibility** is their tendency to be influenced or offended by things. ❑ *The challenge offended their sensibilities.* [N-VAR: usu poss N]

**sen|sible** /sɛnsɪbᵊl/ ◆◇◇ 1 **Sensible** actions or decisions are good because they are based on reasons rather than emotions. ❑ *It might be sensible to get a solicitor... The sensible thing is to leave them alone. ...sensible advice.* [ADJ: oft *it* v-link ADJ to-inf] ♦ **sen|sibly** /sɛnsɪbli/ *He sensibly decided to lie low for a while.* [ADV] 2 **Sensible** people behave in a sensible way. ❑ *She was a sensible girl and did not panic... Oh come on, let's be sensible about this.* [ADJ: oft ADJ *about* n/-ing] 3 **Sensible** shoes or clothes are practical and strong rather than fashionable and attractive. ❑ *Wear loose clothing and sensible footwear.* [ADJ: usu ADJ n] ♦ **sen|sibly** *They were not sensibly dressed.* [ADV: ADV after v, ADV -ed]

**sen|si|tive** /sɛnsɪtɪv/ ◆◇◇ 1 If you are **sensitive to** other people's needs, problems, or feelings, you show understanding and awareness of them. ❑ *The classroom teacher must be sensitive to a child's needs... He was always so sensitive and caring.* [ADJ: oft ADJ *to* n] [approval] ♦ **sen|si|tive|ly** *The abuse of women needs to be treated seriously and sensitively.* [ADV: usu ADV with v] ♦ **sen|si|tiv|ity** /sɛnsɪtɪvɪti/ *A good relationship involves concern and sensitivity for each other's feelings.* [N-UNCOUNT: oft N *for* n] 2 If you are **sensitive about** something, you are easily worried and offended when people talk about it. ❑ *Young people are very sensitive about their appearance... Take it easy. Don't be so sensitive.* [ADJ: oft ADJ *about* n] ♦ **sen|si|tiv|ity** **(sensitivities)** *...people who suffer extreme sensitivity about what others think.* [N-VAR: oft N *about* n] 3 A **sensitive** subject or issue needs to be dealt with carefully because it is likely to cause disagreement or make people angry or upset. ❑ *Employment is a very sensitive issue. ...politically sensitive matters.* [ADJ] ♦ **sen|si|tiv|ity** *Due to the obvious sensitivity of the issue he would not divulge any details.* [N-UNCOUNT: oft N *of* n] 4 **Sensitive** documents or reports contain information that needs to be kept secret and dealt with carefully. ❑ *He instructed staff to shred sensitive documents.* [ADJ: usu ADJ n] 5 Something that is **sensitive to** a physical force, substance, or treatment is easily affected by it and often harmed by it. ❑ *...a chemical which is sensitive to light. ...gentle cosmetics for sensitive skin.* [ADJ: oft ADJ *to* n] ♦ **sen|si|tiv|ity** *...the sensitivity of cells to damage by chemotherapy.* [N-UNCOUNT: oft N *of* n] 6 A **sensitive** piece of scientific equipment is capable of measuring or recording very small changes. ❑ *...an extremely sensitive microscope.* [ADJ: usu ADJ n] ♦ **sen|si|tiv|ity** *...the sensitivity of the detector.* [N-UNCOUNT]

**sen|si|tize** /sɛnsɪtaɪz/ **(sensitizes, sensitizing, sensitized)**

> in BRIT, also use **sensitise**

1 If you **sensitize** people **to** a particular problem or situation, you make them aware of it. [FORMAL] ❑ *It seems important to sensitize people to the fact that depression is more than the blues... How many judges in our male-dominated courts are sensitized to women's issues?* [VERB: V n *to* n, V-ed, Also V n] 2 If a substance **is sensitized to** something such as light or touch, it is made sensitive to it. ❑ *Skin is easily irritated, chapped, chafed, and sensitized. ...sensitised nerve endings.* [VERB: usu passive; *be* V-ed, V-ed]

**sen|sor** /sɛnsəʳ/ **(sensors)** A **sensor** is an instrument which reacts to certain physical conditions or impressions such as heat or light, and which is used to provide information. ❑ *The latest Japanese vacuum cleaners contain sensors that detect the amount of dust and type of floor.* [N-COUNT]

**sen|so|ry** /sɛnsəri/ **Sensory** means relating to the physical senses. [FORMAL] ❑ *...sensory information passing through the spinal cord.* [ADJ: ADJ n]

**sen|sual** /sɛnʃuəl/ 1 Someone or something that is **sensual** shows or suggests a great liking for physical pleasures, especially sexual pleasures. ❑ *He was a very sensual person. ...a wide, sensual mouth.* [ADJ] ♦ **sen|su|al|ity** /sɛnʃuælɪti/ *The wave and curl of her blonde hair gave her sensuality and youth.* [N-UNCOUNT] 2 Something that is **sensual** gives pleasure to your physical senses rather than to your mind. ❑ *...sensual dance rhythms.* [ADJ] ♦ **sen|su|al|ity** *These perfumes have warmth and sensuality.* [N-UNCOUNT]

**sen|su|ous** /sɛnʃuəs/ 1 Something that is **sensuous** gives pleasure to the mind or body through the senses. ❑ *The film is ravishing to look at and boasts a sensuous musical score.* [ADJ] ♦ **sen|su|ous|ly** *She lay in the deep bath for a long time, enjoying its sensuously perfumed water.* [ADV: ADV adj, ADV with v] 2 Someone or something that is **sensuous** shows or suggests a great liking for sexual pleasure. ❑ *...his sensuous young mistress, Marie-Therese.* [ADJ = sensual] ♦ **sen|su|ous|ly** *The nose was straight, the mouth sensuously wide and full.* [ADV: ADV adj, ADV with v]

**sent** /sɛnt/ **Sent** is the past tense and past participle of **send**.

**sen|tence** /sɛntəns/ **(sentences, sentencing, sentenced)** ◆◆◇ 1 A **sentence** is a group of words which, when they are written down, begin with a capital letter and end with a full stop, question mark, or exclamation mark. Most sentences contain a subject and a verb. [N-COUNT] 2 In a law court, a **sentence** is the punishment that a person receives after they have been found guilty of a crime. ❑ *They are already serving prison sentences for their part in the assassination... He was given a four-year sentence... The offences carry a maximum sentence of 10 years. ...demands for tougher sentences... The court is expected to pass sentence later today.* → See also **death sentence**, **life sentence**, **suspended sentence**. [N-VAR] 3 When a judge **sentences** someone, he or she states in court what their punishment will be. ❑ *A military court sentenced him to death in his absence... He has admitted the charge and will be sentenced later.* [VERB: V n *to* n, *be* V-ed]

**sen|tence ad|verb** **(sentence adverbs)** Adverbs such as 'fortunately' and 'perhaps' which apply to the whole clause, rather than to part of it, are sometimes called **sentence adverbs**. [N-COUNT]

**sen|ti|ent** /sɛntiənt, -ʃᵊnt/ A **sentient** being is capable of experiencing things through its senses. [FORMAL] [ADJ: usu ADJ n]

**sen|ti|ment** /sɛntɪmənt/ **(sentiments)** 1 A **sentiment** that people have is an attitude which is based on their thoughts and feelings. ❑ *Public sentiment rapidly turned anti-American. ...nationalist sentiments that threaten to split the country.* [N-VAR: supp N = feeling] 2 A **sentiment** is an idea or feeling that someone expresses in words. ❑ *I must agree with the sentiments expressed by John Prescott... The Foreign Secretary echoed this sentiment.* [N-COUNT: usu with supp] 3 **Sentiment** is feelings such as pity or love, especially for things in the past, and may be considered exaggerated and foolish. ❑ *Laura kept that letter out of sentiment.* [N-UNCOUNT]

**sen|ti|ment|al** /sɛntɪmɛntᵊl/ 1 Someone or something that is **sentimental** feels or shows pity or love, sometimes to an extent that is considered exaggerated and foolish. ❑ *I'm trying not to be sentimental about the past.* [ADJ] ♦ **sen|ti|men|tal|ly** *Childhood had less freedom and joy than we sentimentally attribute to it.* [ADV: usu ADV with v] ♦ **sen|ti|men|tal|ity** /sɛntɪmɛntælɪti/ *In this book there is no sentimentality.* [N-UNCOUNT] 2 **Sentimental** means relating to or involving feelings such as pity or love, especially for things in the past. ❑ *Our paintings and photographs are of sentimental value only.* [ADJ: usu ADJ n]

**sen|ti|men|tal|ist** /sentɪmentəlɪst/ **(sentimentalists)** If you describe someone as a **sentimentalist**, you believe that they are sentimental about things. N-COUNT

**sen|ti|men|tal|ize** /sentɪmentəlaɪz/ **(sentimentalizes, sentimentalizing, sentimentalized)**

in BRIT, also use **sentimentalise**

If you **sentimentalize** something, you make it seem sentimental or think about it in a sentimental way. ❑ *He seems either to fear women or to sentimentalize them... He's the kind of filmmaker who doesn't hesitate to over-sentimentalize. ...Rupert Brooke's sentimentalised glorification of war.* VERB V n V V-ed

**sen|ti|nel** /sentɪnəl/ **(sentinels)** A **sentinel** is a sentry. [LITERARY, OLD-FASHIONED] N-COUNT

**sen|try** /sentri/ **(sentries)** A **sentry** is a soldier who guards a camp or a building. ❑ *The sentry would not let her enter.* N-COUNT

**sen|try box (sentry boxes)** also **sentry-box**. A **sentry box** is a narrow shelter with an open front in which a sentry can stand while on duty. N-COUNT

**Sep.** **Sep.** is a written abbreviation for **September**. The more usual abbreviation is **Sept.** ❑ *...Friday Sep. 21, 1990.*

**sepa|rable** /sepərəbəl/ If things are **separable**, they can be separated from each other. ❑ *Character is not separable from physical form but is governed by it.* ADJ: usu v-link ADJ, oft ADJ *from* n

**sepa|rate (separates, separating, separated)** ◆◆◇

The adjective and noun are pronounced /sepərət/. The verb is pronounced /sepəreɪt/.

1 If one thing is **separate from** another, there is a barrier, space, or division between them, so that they are clearly two things. ❑ *Each villa has a separate sitting-room... They are now making plans to form their own separate party... Business bank accounts were kept separate from personal ones.* ADJ: oft ADJ *from* n ♦ **sepa|rate|ness** *...establishing Australia's cultural separateness from Britain.* N-UNCOUNT 2 If you refer to **separate** things, you mean several different things, rather than just one thing. ❑ *Use separate chopping boards for raw meats, cooked meats, vegetables and salads... Men and women have separate exercise rooms... The authorities say six civilians have been killed in two separate attacks.* ADJ: usu ADJ n = different 3 If you **separate** people or things that are together, or if they **separate**, they move apart. ❑ *Police moved in to separate the two groups... The pans were held in both hands and swirled around to separate gold particles from the dirt... The front end of the car separated from the rest of the vehicle... They separated. Stephen returned to the square... They're separated from the adult inmates.* V-RECIP V pl-n V n *from* n V *from* n pl-n V V-ed 4 If you **separate** people or things that have been connected, or if one **separates from** another, the connection between them is ended. ❑ *They want to separate teaching from research... It's very possible that we may see a movement to separate the two parts of the country... He announced a new ministry to deal with Quebec's threat to separate from Canada.* V-RECIP V n *from* n V pl-n V *from* n 5 If a couple who are married or living together **separate**, they decide to live apart. ❑ *Her parents separated when she was very young... Since I separated from my husband I have gone a long way.* V-RECIP pl-n V V *from* n 6 An object, obstacle, distance, or period of time which **separates** two people, groups, or things exists between them. ❑ *...the white-railed fence that separated the yard from the paddock... They had undoubtedly made progress in the six years that separated the two periods... But a group of six women and 23 children got separated from the others.* VERB V n *from* n V pl-n *get* V-ed 7 If you **separate** one idea or fact **from** another, you clearly see or show the difference between them. ❑ *It is difficult to separate legend from truth... It is difficult to separate the two aims.* VERB = distinguish V n *from* n V pl-n ♦ **Separate out** means the same as **separate**. ❑ *How can one ever separate out the act from the attitudes that surround it?* PHRASAL VERB V P n *from* n 8 A quality or factor that **separates** one thing **from** another is the reason why the two things are different from each other. ❑ *The single most important factor that separates ordinary photographs from good photographs is the lighting.* VERB = distinguish V n *from* n 9 If a particular number of points **separate** two teams or competitors, one of them is winning or has won by that number of points. ❑ *In the end only three points separated the two teams.* VERB V pl-n 10 If you **separate** a group of people or things **into** smaller elements, or if a group **separates**, it is divided into smaller elements. ❑ *The police wanted to separate them into smaller groups... Let's separate into smaller groups... So all the colours that make up white light are sent in different directions and they separate.* VERB = split V n *into* n V *into* n V ♦ **Separate out** means the same as **separate**. ❑ *If prepared many hours ahead, the mixture may separate out.* PHRASAL VERB V P 11 **Separates** are clothes such as skirts, trousers, and shirts which cover just the top half or the bottom half of your body. N-PLURAL 12 → See also **separated**. 13 When two or more people who have been together for some time **go** their **separate ways**, they go to different places or end their relationship. ❑ *Sue and her husband decided to go their separate ways.* PHRASE: V inflects

♦ **separate out** If you **separate out** something from the other things it is with, you take it out. ❑ *The ability to separate out reusable elements from other waste is crucial.* → See also **separate 7, 10**. PHRASAL VERB V P n *from* n Also V P n (not pron)

**sepa|rat|ed** /sepəreɪtɪd/ 1 Someone who is **separated** from their wife or husband lives apart from them, but is not divorced. ❑ *Most single parents are either divorced or separated... Tristan had been separated from his wife for two years.* ADJ: v-link ADJ, oft ADJ *from* n 2 If you are **separated** from someone, for example your family, you are not able to be with them. ❑ *The idea of being separated from him, even for a few hours, was torture.* ADJ: oft ADJ *from* n

**sepa|rate|ly** /sepərətli/ If people or things are dealt with **separately** or do something **separately**, they are dealt with or do something at different times or places, rather than together. ❑ *Cook each vegetable separately until just tender.* ADV: ADV with v, oft ADV *from* n ≠together

**sepa|ra|tion** /sepəreɪʃən/ **(separations)** 1 The **separation of** two or more things or groups is the fact that they are separate or become separate, and are not linked. ❑ *...a 'Christian republic' in which there was a clear separation between church and state.* N-VAR: oft N *of/from/between* n 2 During a **separation**, people who usually live together are not together. ❑ *All children will tend to suffer from separation from their parents and siblings.* N-VAR 3 If a couple who are married or living together have a **separation**, they decide to live apart. ❑ *They agreed to a trial separation.* N-VAR

**sepa|ra|tism** /sepərətɪzəm/ **Separatism** is the beliefs and activities of separatists. N-UNCOUNT

**sepa|ra|tist** /sepərətɪst/ **(separatists)** 1 **Separatist** organizations and activities within a country involve members of a group of people who want to establish their own separate government or are trying to do so. ❑ *...the Basque separatist movement.* ADJ: ADJ n 2 **Separatists** are people who want their own separate government or are involved in separatist activities. ❑ *The army has come under attack by separatists.* N-COUNT

**se|pia** /siːpiə/ Something that is **sepia** is deep brown in colour, like the colour of very old photographs. ❑ *The walls are hung with sepia photographs of old school heroes.* COLOUR

**Sept.** **Sept.** is a written abbreviation for **September**. ❑ *I've booked it for Thurs. 8th Sept.*

**Sep|tem|ber** /septembər/ **(Septembers)** **September** is the ninth month of the year in the Western calendar. ❑ *Her son, Jerome, was born in September... They returned to Moscow on 22 September 1930... They spent a couple of nights here last September.* N-VAR

**sep|tic** /septɪk/ If a wound or a part of your body becomes **septic**, it becomes infected. ❑ *...a septic toe.* ADJ

**sep|ti|cae|mia** /septɪsiːmiə/

> in AM, use **septicemia**

**Septicaemia** is blood poisoning. [MEDICAL] N-UNCOUNT

**sep|tic tank** **(septic tanks)** A **septic tank** is an underground tank where faeces, urine, and other waste matter is made harmless using bacteria. N-COUNT

**sep|tua|genar|ian** /septʃuədʒɪneəriən/ **(septuagenarians)** A **septuagenarian** is a person between 70 and 79 years old. [FORMAL] ❑ *...septuagenarian author Mary Wesley.* N-COUNT: oft N n

**se|pul|chral** /sɪpʌlkrəl/ 1 Something that is **sepulchral** is serious or sad and rather frightening. [LITERARY] ❑ *'He's gone,' Rory whispered in sepulchral tones.* ADJ 2 A **sepulchral** place is dark, quiet, and empty. [LITERARY] ❑ *He made his way along the sepulchral corridors.* ADJ

**sep|ul|chre** /sepəlkəʳ/ **(sepulchres)**

> in AM, use **sepulcher**

A **sepulchre** is a building or room in which a dead person is buried. [LITERARY] N-COUNT

**se|quel** /siːkwəl/ **(sequels)** 1 A book or film which is a **sequel to** an earlier one continues the story of the earlier one. ❑ *She is currently writing a sequel to Daphne du Maurier's 'Rebecca'.* N-COUNT: oft N *to* n 2 The **sequel to** something that has happened is an event or situation that happens after it or as a result of it. ❑ *The clash was a sequel to yesterday's strike.* N-COUNT: usu sing

**se|quence** /siːkwəns/ **(sequences)** 1 A **sequence of** events or things is a number of events or things that come one after another in a particular order. ❑ *...the sequence of events which led to the murder. ...a dazzling sequence of novels by John Updike.* N-COUNT: oft N *of* n = series 2 A particular **sequence** is a particular order in which things happen or are arranged. ❑ *...the colour sequence yellow, orange, purple, blue, green and white... The chronological sequence gives the book an element of structure.* N-COUNT 3 A film **sequence** is a part of a film that shows a single set of actions. ❑ *The best sequence in the film occurs when Roth stops at a house he used to live in.* N-COUNT 4 A gene **sequence** or a DNA **sequence** is the order in which the elements making up a particular gene are combined. ❑ *The project is nothing less than mapping every gene sequence in the human body. ...the complete DNA sequence of the human genome.* N-COUNT: supp N

**se|quenc|er** /siːkwənsəʳ/ **(sequencers)** A **sequencer** is an electronic instrument that can be used for recording and storing sounds so that they can be replayed as part of a new piece of music. N-COUNT

**se|quenc|ing** /siːkwənsɪŋ/ Gene **sequencing** or DNA **sequencing** involves identifying the order in which the elements making up a particular gene are combined. ❑ *...the US government's own gene sequencing programme.* N-UNCOUNT: supp N

**se|quen|tial** /sɪkwenʃəl/ Something that is **sequential** follows a fixed order. [FORMAL] ❑ *...the sequential story of the universe.* ADJ: usu ADJ n ♦ **se|quen|tial|ly** *The pages are numbered sequentially.* ADV: ADV after v

**se|ques|ter** /sɪkwestəʳ/ **(sequesters, sequestering, sequestered)** 1 **Sequester** means the same as **sequestrate**. [LEGAL] ❑ *Everything he owned was sequestered.* VERB *be* V-ed Also V n 2 If someone **is sequestered** somewhere, they are isolated from other people. [FORMAL] ❑ *This jury is expected to be sequestered for at least two months.* VERB *be* V-ed

**se|ques|tered** /sɪkwestəʳd/ A **sequestered** place is quiet and far away from busy places. [LITERARY] ADJ = secluded

**se|ques|trate** /siːkwestreɪt/ **(sequestrates, sequestrating, sequestrated)** When property **is sequestrated**, it is taken officially from someone who has debts, usually after a decision in a court of law. If the debts are paid off, the property is returned to its owner. [LEGAL] ❑ *He tried to prevent union money from being sequestrated by the courts.* VERB: usu passive = sequester *be* V-ed ♦ **se|ques|tra|tion** /siːkwestreɪʃən/ *...the sequestration of large areas of land.* N-UNCOUNT

**se|quin** /siːkwɪn/ **(sequins)** **Sequins** are small, shiny discs that are sewn on clothes to decorate them. ❑ *The frocks were covered in sequins, thousands of them.* N-COUNT: usu pl

**se|quinned** /siːkwɪnd/ also **sequined.** A **sequinned** piece of clothing is decorated or covered with sequins. ❑ *...a strapless sequinned evening gown.* ADJ: usu ADJ n

**ser|aph** /serəf/ **(seraphim** /serəfɪm/ or **seraphs)** In the Bible, a **seraph** is a kind of angel. N-COUNT

**Serbo-Croat** /sɜːʳbou krouæt/ **Serbo-Croat** is one of the languages spoken in the former Yugoslavia. N-UNCOUNT

**ser|enade** /serɪneɪd/ **(serenades, serenading, serenaded)** 1 If one person **serenades** another, they sing or play a piece of music for them. Traditionally men did this outside the window of the woman they loved. ❑ *In the interval a blond boy dressed in white serenaded the company on the flute.* VERB V n ♦ **Serenade** is also a noun. ❑ *Placido Domingo sang his serenade of love.* N-COUNT 2 In classical music, a **serenade** is a piece in several parts written for a small orchestra. ❑ *...Vaughan Williams's Serenade to Music.* N-COUNT: oft in names

**ser|en|dipi|tous** /serendɪpɪtəs/ A **serendipitous** event is one that is not planned but has a good result. [LITERARY] ❑ *...a serendipitous discovery.* ADJ

**ser|en|dip|ity** /serendɪpɪti/ **Serendipity** is the luck some people have in finding or creating interesting or valuable things by chance. [LITERARY] ❑ *Some of the best effects in my garden have been the result of serendipity.* N-UNCOUNT

**se|rene** /sɪriːn/ Someone or something that is **serene** is calm and quiet. ❑ *She looked as calm and serene as she always did.* ADJ ♦ **se|rene|ly** *We sailed serenely down the river.* ADV: ADV with v, ADV adj ♦ **se|ren|ity** /sɪrenɪti/ *I had a wonderful feeling of peace and serenity when I saw my husband.* N-UNCOUNT

**serf** /sɜːʳf/ **(serfs)** In former times, **serfs** were a class of people who had to work on a particular person's land and could not leave without that person's permission. N-COUNT

**serf|dom** /sɜːʳfdəm/ 1 The system of **serfdom** was the social and economic system by which the owners of land had serfs. N-UNCOUNT 2 If someone was in a state of **serfdom**, they were a serf. N-UNCOUNT

**serge** /sɜːʳdʒ/ **Serge** is a type of strong woollen cloth used to make clothes such as skirts, coats, and trousers. ❑ *He wore a blue serge suit.* N-UNCOUNT

**ser|geant** /sɑːʳdʒənt/ **(sergeants)** 1 A **sergeant** is a non-commissioned officer of middle rank in the army, marines, or air force. ❑ *A sergeant with a detail of four men came into view. ...Sergeant Black.* N-COUNT; N-TITLE; N-VOC 2 In the British police force, a **sergeant** is an officer with the next to lowest rank. In American police forces, a **sergeant** is an officer with the rank immediately below a captain. ❑ *The unit headed by Sergeant Bell.* N-COUNT; N-TITLE; N-VOC

**ser|geant ma|jor** **(sergeant majors)** also **sergeant-major.** A **sergeant major** is a non-commissioned army or marine officer of the highest rank. N-COUNT; N-TITLE; N-VOC

**se|rial** /sɪəriəl/ **(serials)** 1 A **serial** is a story which is broadcast on television or radio or is published in a magazine or newspaper in a number of parts over a period of time. ❑ *...one of BBC television's most popular serials, Eastenders... Maupin's novels have all appeared originally as serials.* N-COUNT 2 **Serial** killings or attacks are a series of killings or attacks committed by the same person. This person is known as a **serial** killer or attacker. ❑ *The serial killer claimed to have killed 400 people.* ADJ: ADJ n

**se|riali|za|tion** /sɪəriəlaɪzeɪʃən/ **(serializations)**

> in BRIT, also use **serialisation**

1 **Serialization** is the act of serializing a book. N-UNCOUNT 2 A **serialization** is a story, originally written as a book, which is being published or broadcast in a N-COUNT

number of parts. ❑ *...in the serialisation of Jane Austen's Pride and Prejudice.*

**se|rial|ize** /sɪəriəlaɪz/ **(serializes, serializing, serialized)**

✔ in BRIT, also use **serialise**

If a book **is serialized**, it is broadcast on the radio or television or is published in a magazine or newspaper in a number of parts over a period of time. ❑ *A few years ago Tom Brown's Schooldays was serialised on television.* — VERB: usu passive; *be* V-ed

**se|rial num|ber (serial numbers)** [1] The **serial number** of an object is a number on that object which identifies it. ❑ *...the gun's serial number. ...your bike's serial number.* — N-COUNT: oft with poss [2] The **serial number** of a member of the United States military forces is a number which identifies them. — N-COUNT

**se|rial port (serial ports)** A **serial port** on a computer is a place where you can connect the computer to a device such as a modem or a mouse. [COMPUTING] — N-COUNT

**se|ries** /sɪəriːz/ **(series)** ◆◆◇ [1] A **series of** things or events is a number of them that come one after the other. ❑ *...a series of meetings with students and political leaders. ...a series of explosions.* — N-COUNT: usu sing: oft N *of* n = succession [2] A radio or television **series** is a set of programmes of a particular kind which have the same title. ❑ *...the TV series 'The Trials of Life' presented by David Attenborough.* — N-COUNT: usu sing

**se|ri|ous** /sɪəriəs/ ◆◆◆ [1] **Serious** problems or situations are very bad and cause people to be worried or afraid. ❑ *Crime is an increasingly serious problem in Russian society... The government still face very serious difficulties... Doctors said his condition was serious but stable.* — ADJ ♦ **se|ri|ous|ly** *If this ban was to come in it would seriously damage my business... They are not thought to be seriously hurt.* — ADV: ADV adj/adv, ADV with v ♦ **se|ri|ous|ness** *...the seriousness of the crisis.* — N-UNCOUNT: oft N *of* n [2] **Serious** matters are important and deserve careful and thoughtful consideration. ❑ *I regard this as a serious matter... Don't laugh boy. This is serious.* — ADJ [3] When important matters are dealt with in a **serious** way, they are given careful and thoughtful consideration. ❑ *My parents never really faced up to my drug use in any serious way... It was a question which deserved serious consideration.* — ADJ: usu ADJ n ♦ **se|ri|ous|ly** *The management will have to think seriously about their positions.* — ADV: ADV with v [4] **Serious** music or literature requires concentration to understand or appreciate it. ❑ *There is no point reviewing a blockbuster as you might review a serious novel.* — ADJ: ADJ n [5] If someone is **serious about** something, they are sincere about what they are saying, doing, or intending to do. ❑ *You really are serious about this, aren't you?... I hope you're not serious.* — ADJ: oft ADJ *about* n ♦ **se|ri|ous|ly** *Are you seriously jealous of Erica?* — ADV: ADV adj/adv, ADV with v ♦ **se|ri|ous|ness** *In all seriousness, there is nothing else I can do.* — N-UNCOUNT: oft N *of* n [6] **Serious** people are thoughtful and quiet, and do not laugh very often. ❑ *He's quite a serious person.* — ADJ ♦ **se|ri|ous|ly** *They spoke to me very seriously but politely.* — ADV: ADV with v

**se|ri|ous|ly** /sɪəriəsli/ ◆◇◇ [1] You use **seriously** to indicate that you are not joking and that you really mean what you say. ❑ *Seriously, I only smoke in the evenings.* — ADV: ADV with cl [2] You say '**seriously**' when you are surprised by what someone has said, as a way of asking them if they really mean it. [SPOKEN] ❑ *'I tried to chat him up at the general store.' He laughed. 'Seriously?'* — CONVENTION [feelings] [3] ➔ See also **serious**. [4] If you **take** someone or something **seriously**, you believe that they are important and deserve attention. ❑ *It's hard to take them seriously in their pretty grey uniforms.* — PHRASE: V inflects

**ser|mon** /sɜːʳmən/ **(sermons)** A **sermon** is a talk on a religious or moral subject that is given by a member of the clergy as part of a church service. — N-COUNT

**sero|to|nin** /serəʊtəʊnɪn/ **Serotonin** is a chemical produced naturally in your brain that affects the way you feel, for example making you feel happier, calmer, or less hungry. — N-UNCOUNT

**ser|pent** /sɜːʳpənt/ **(serpents)** A **serpent** is a snake. [LITERARY] ❑ *...the serpent in the Garden of Eden.* — N-COUNT

**ser|pen|tine** /sɜːʳpəntaɪn/ Something that is **serpentine** is curving and winding in shape, like a snake when it moves. [LITERARY] ❑ *...serpentine woodland pathways.* — ADJ = winding

**ser|rat|ed** /sereɪtɪd/ A **serrated** object such as a knife or blade has a row of V-shaped points along the edge. ❑ *Bread knives should have a serrated edge.* — ADJ: usu ADJ n

**ser|ried** /serid/ **Serried** things or people are closely crowded together in rows. [LITERARY] ❑ *...serried rows of law books and law reports. ...the serried ranks of fans.* — ADJ: ADJ n

**se|rum** /sɪərəm/ **(serums)** [1] A **serum** is a liquid that is injected into someone's blood to protect them against a poison or disease. — N-VAR [2] **Serum** is the watery, pale yellow part of blood. — N-UNCOUNT

**serv|ant** /sɜːʳvənt/ **(servants)** ◆◇◇ [1] A **servant** is someone who is employed to work at another person's home, for example as a cleaner or a gardener. — N-COUNT [2] You can use **servant** to refer to someone or something that provides a service for people or can be used by them. ❑ *The question is whether technology is going to be our servant or our master.* — N-COUNT ➔ See also **civil servant**.

**serve** /sɜːʳv/ **(serves, serving, served)** ◆◆◇ [1] If you **serve** your country, an organization, or a person, you do useful work for them. ❑ *It is unfair to soldiers who have served their country well for many years... I have always said that I would serve the Party in any way it felt appropriate.* — VERB; V n; V n [2] If you **serve** in a particular place or as a particular official, you perform official duties, especially in the armed forces, as a civil servant, or as a politician. ❑ *During the second world war he served with RAF Coastal Command... For seven years until 1991 he served as a district councillor in Solihull.* — VERB; V prep/adv; V prep/adv [3] If something **serves as** a particular thing or **serves** a particular purpose, it performs a particular function, which is often not its intended function. ❑ *She ushered me into the front room, which served as her office... I really do not think that an inquiry would serve any useful purpose... Their brief visit has served to underline the deep differences between the two countries... The old drawing room serves her as both sitting room and study.* — VERB; V *as/for* n; V n; V to-inf; V n *as/for* n [4] If something **serves** people or an area, it provides them with something that they need. ❑ *This could mean the closure of thousands of small businesses which serve the community... Cuba is well served by motorways.* — VERB; V n; V n [5] Something that **serves** someone's interests benefits them. ❑ *The economy should be organized to serve the interests of all the people.* — VERB; V n [6] When you **serve** food and drink, you give people food and drink. ❑ *Serve it with French bread... Serve the cakes warm... Prepare the garnishes shortly before you are ready to serve the soup. ...the pleasure of having someone serve you champagne and caviar in bed... They are expected to baby-sit, run errands, and help serve at cocktail parties.* — VERB; V n prep; V n adj; V n; V n n; V; Also V n *to* n ♦ **Serve up** means the same as **serve**. ❑ *After all, it is no use serving up TV dinners if the kids won't eat them... He served it up on delicate white plates.* — PHRASAL VERB; V P n (not pron); V n P [7] **Serve** is used to indicate how much food a recipe produces. For example, a recipe that **serves** six provides enough food for six people. ❑ *Garnish with fresh herbs. Serves 4.* — VERB: no cont; V n [8] Someone who **serves** customers in a shop or a bar helps them and provides them with what they want to buy. ❑ *They wouldn't serve me in any pubs 'cos I looked too young... Auntie and Uncle suggested she serve in the shop.* — VERB; V n; V [9] When the police or other officials **serve** someone **with** a legal order or **serve** an order **on** them, they give or send the legal order to them. [LEGAL] ❑ *Immigration officers tried to serve her with a deportation order... Police said they had been unable to serve a summons on 25-year-old Lee Jones.* — VERB; V n *with* n; V n *on* n [10] If you **serve** something such as a prison sentence or an apprenticeship, you spend a period of time doing it. ❑ *...Leo, who is currently serving a life sentence for* — VERB; V n *murder.* 11 When you **serve** in games such as tennis and badminton, you throw up the ball or shuttlecock and hit it to start play. ❑ *He served 17 double faults... If you serve like this nobody can beat you.* ♦ **Serve** is also a noun. ❑ *His second serve clipped the net.* 12 When you describe someone's **serve**, you are indicating how well or how fast they serve a ball or shuttlecock. ❑ *His powerful serve was too much for the defending champion.* 13 → See also **serving**. 14 If you say **it serves** someone **right** when something unpleasant happens to them, you mean that it is their own fault and you have no sympathy for them. ❑ *Serves her right for being so stubborn.*

VERB · V n · V · N-COUNT · N-COUNT · PHRASE: V inflects, oft PHR *for* -ing [feelings]

♦ **serve out** If someone **serves out** their term of office, contract, or prison sentence, they do not leave before the end of the agreed period of time. ❑ *The governor has declared his innocence and says he plans to serve out his term.*

PHRASAL VERB · V P n (not pron) · Also V n P

♦ **serve up** → see **serve 6**.

**serv|er** /sɜːʳvəʳ/ **(servers)** 1 In computing, a **server** is part of a computer network which does a particular task, for example storing or processing information, for all or part of the network. [COMPUTING] 2 In tennis and badminton, the **server** is the player whose turn it is to hit the ball or shuttlecock to start play. ❑ *...a brilliant server and volleyer.* 3 A **server** is something such as a fork or spoon that is used for serving food. ❑ *...salad servers.*

N-COUNT · N-COUNT: oft adj N · N-COUNT: oft n N

**ser|vice** /sɜːʳvɪs/ **(services, servicing, serviced)** ♦♦♦

> For meaning 14, **services** is both the singular and the plural form.

1 A **service** is something that the public needs, such as transport, communications facilities, hospitals, or energy supplies, which is provided in a planned and organized way by the government or an official body. ❑ *Britain still boasts the cheapest postal service... We have started a campaign for better nursery and school services... The authorities have said they will attempt to maintain essential services.* 2 You can sometimes refer to an organization or private company as a particular **service** when it provides something for the public or acts on behalf of the government. ❑ *...the BBC World Service. ...Careers Advisory Services.* 3 If an organization or company provides a particular **service**, they can do a particular job or a type of work for you. ❑ *The kitchen maintains a twenty-four hour service and can be contacted via Reception... The larger firm was capable of providing a better range of services.* 4 **Services** are activities such as tourism, banking, and selling things which are part of a country's economy, but are not concerned with producing or manufacturing goods. ❑ *Mining rose by 9.1%, manufacturing by 9.4% and services by 4.3%.* 5 The level or standard of **service** provided by an organization or company is the amount or quality of the work it can do for you. ❑ *Taking risks is the only way employees can provide effective and efficient customer service.* 6 A bus or train **service** is a route or regular journey that is part of a transport system. ❑ *A bus service operates between Bolton and Salford.* 7 Your **services** are the things that you do or the skills that you use in your job, which other people find useful and are usually willing to pay you for. ❑ *I have obtained the services of a top photographer to take our pictures.* 8 If you refer to someone's **service** or **services to** a particular organization or activity, you mean that they have done a lot of work for it or spent a lot of their time on it. ❑ *You've given a lifetime of service to athletics. ...the two policemen, who have a total of 31 years' service between them.* 9 **The Services** are the army, the navy, and the air force. ❑ *In June 1945, Britain still had forty-five per cent of its workforce in the Services and munitions industries.* 10 **Service** is the work done by people or equipment in the army, navy, or air force, for example during a war. ❑ *The regiment was recruited from the Highlands specifically for service in India.* 11 When you receive **service** in a restaurant, hotel, or shop, an employee asks you what you want or gives you what you have ordered. ❑ *A five-course meal including coffee, service and VAT is £30.* 12 A **service** is a religious ceremony that takes place in a church. ❑ *After the hour-long service, his body was taken to a cemetery in the south of the city.* 13 A **dinner service** or a **tea service** is a complete set of plates, cups, saucers, and other pieces of china. ❑ *...a 60-piece dinner service.* 14 A **services** is a place beside a motorway where you can buy petrol and other things, or have a meal. [BRIT] ❑ *They had to pull up, possibly go to a motorway services or somewhere like that.*

N-COUNT: usu with supp · N-COUNT: oft in names · N-COUNT · N-PLURAL · N-UNCOUNT · N-COUNT: usu n N · N-PLURAL: with poss · N-UNCOUNT: also N in pl, oft N *to* n · N-COUNT: usu pl · N-UNCOUNT · N-UNCOUNT · N-COUNT: also no det · N-COUNT: usu n N · N-COUNT = service station

> in AM, use **rest area**

15 In tennis, badminton, and some other sports, when it is your **service**, it is your turn to serve. ❑ *She conceded just three points on her service during the first set.* 16 **Service** is used to describe the parts of a building or structure that are used by the staff who clean, repair, or look after it, and are not usually used by the public. ❑ *He wheeled the trolley down the corridor and disappeared with it into the service lift.* 17 If you have a vehicle or machine **serviced**, you arrange for someone to examine, adjust, and clean it so that it will keep working efficiently and safely. ❑ *I had had my car serviced at the local garage... Make sure that all gas fires and central heating boilers are serviced annually.* ♦ **Service** is also a noun. ❑ *The car needs a service... The company sends a service engineer to fix the disk drive before it fails.* 18 If a country or organization **services** its debts, it pays the interest on them. ❑ *Almost a quarter of the country's export earnings go to service a foreign debt of $29 billion.* 19 If someone or something **services** an organization, a project, or a group of people, they provide it with the things that it needs in order to function properly or effectively. ❑ *Fossil fuels such as coal, oil and gas will service our needs for some considerable time to come.* 20 → See also **active service, Civil Service, community service, emergency services, in-service, National Health Service, national service, public service, room service.**

N-COUNT: oft with poss · ADJ: ADJ n · VERB · *have* n V-ed · *be* V-ed · Also V n · N-COUNT: usu sing, oft N n · VERB · V n · VERB · V n

PHRASES 21 To be **at the service of** a person or organization means to be available to help or be used by that person or organization. ❑ *The intellectual and moral potential of the world's culture must be put at the service of politics.* 22 You can use '**at your service**' after your name as a formal way of introducing yourself to someone and saying that you are willing to help them in any way you can. ❑ *She bowed dramatically. 'Anastasia Krupnik, at your service,' she said.* 23 If you **do** someone **a service**, you do something that helps or benefits them. ❑ *You are doing me a great service, and I'm very grateful to you.* 24 If a piece of equipment or type of vehicle is **in service**, it is being used or is able to be used. If it is **out of service**, it is not being used, usually because it is not working properly. ❑ *Cuts in funding have meant that equipment has been kept in service long after it should have been replaced.* 25 If someone or something is **of service to** you, they help you or are useful to you. ❑ *That is, after all, the primary reason we live – to be of service to others.*

PHRASE: PHR n, usu PHR after v · CONVENTION [formulae] · PHRASE: V inflects · PHRASE: usu PHR after v, v-link PHR · PHRASE: v-link PHR, oft PHR *to* n

**ser|vice|able** /sɜːʳvɪsəbᵊl/ If you describe something as **serviceable**, you mean that it is good enough to be used and to perform its function. ❑ *His Arabic was not as good as his English, but serviceable enough.* ADJ

**ser|vice area** **(service areas)** A **service area** is a place beside a motorway where you can buy petrol and other things, or have a meal. [BRIT] N-COUNT = service station

> in AM, use **rest area**

**ser|vice charge** **(service charges)** A **service charge** is an amount that is added to your bill in a restaurant to pay for the work of the person N-COUNT who comes and serves you. ❑ *Most restaurants add a 10 per cent service charge.*

**ser|vice in|dus|try** **(service industries)** A **service industry** is an industry such as banking or insurance that provides a service but does not produce anything. N-COUNT

**ser|vice|man** /sɜːʳvɪsmən/ **(servicemen)** A **serviceman** is a man who is in the army, navy, or air force. N-COUNT

**ser|vice pro|vid|er** **(service providers)** A **service provider** is a company that provides a service, especially an Internet service. [COMPUTING] N-COUNT

**ser|vice sta|tion** **(service stations)** 1 A **service station** is a place that sells things such as petrol, oil, and spare parts. Service stations often sell food, drink, and other goods. N-COUNT 2 A **service station** is a place beside a motorway where you can buy petrol and other things, or have a meal. [BRIT] N-COUNT

✔ in AM, use **rest area**

**ser|vice|woman** /sɜːʳvɪswʊmən/ **(service-women)** A **servicewoman** is a woman who is in the army, navy, or air force. N-COUNT

**ser|vi|ette** /sɜːʳviet/ **(serviettes)** A **serviette** is a square of cloth or paper that you use to protect your clothes or to wipe your mouth when you are eating. [BRIT] N-COUNT = *napkin*

✔ in AM, use **napkin**

**ser|vile** /sɜːʳvaɪl, AM -vᵊl/ If you say that someone is **servile**, you disapprove of them because they are too eager to obey someone or do things for them. [FORMAL] ❑ *He was subservient and servile.* ♦ **ser|vil|ity** /sɜːʳvɪlɪti/ *She's a curious mixture of stubbornness and servility.* ADJ [disapproval] = *obsequious*; N-UNCOUNT

**serv|ing** /sɜːʳvɪŋ/ **(servings)** 1 A **serving** is an amount of food that is given to one person at a meal. ❑ *Quantities will vary according to how many servings of soup you want to prepare... Each serving contains 240 calories.* N-COUNT: oft N *of* n 2 A **serving** spoon or dish is used for giving out food at a meal. ❑ *Pile the potatoes into a warm serving dish.* ADJ: ADJ n

**ser|vi|tude** /sɜːʳvɪtjuːd, AM -tuːd/ **Servitude** is the condition of being a slave or of being completely under the control of someone else. ❑ *...a life of servitude.* ➔ See also **penal servitude**. N-UNCOUNT

**sesa|me** /sesəmi/ **Sesame** is a plant grown for its seeds and oil, which are used in cooking. ❑ *...sesame seeds.* N-UNCOUNT: usu N n

**ses|sion** /seʃᵊn/ **(sessions)** ◆◆◇ 1 A **session** is a meeting of a court, parliament, or other official group. ❑ *...an emergency session of parliament... After two late night sessions, the Security Council has failed to reach agreement... The court was in session.* N-COUNT: also *in* N 2 A **session** is a period during which the meetings of a court, parliament, or other official group are regularly held. ❑ *The parliamentary session ends on October 4th.* N-COUNT: also *in* N 3 A **session** of a particular activity is a period of that activity. ❑ *The two leaders emerged for a photo session. ...group therapy sessions.* N-COUNT: usu with supp 4 **Session** musicians are employed to play backing music in recording studios. ❑ *He established himself as a session musician.* ADJ: ADJ n

**set**
① NOUN USES
② VERB AND ADJECTIVE USES

① **set** /set/ **(sets)** ◆◆◆ 1 A **set of** things is a number of things that belong together or that are thought of as a group. ❑ *There must be one set of laws for the whole of the country... I might need a spare set of clothes... The computer repeats a set of calculations... Only she and Mr Cohen had complete sets of keys to the shop... The mattress and base are normally bought as a set. ...a chess set.* N-COUNT: oft N *of* n 2 In tennis, a **set** is one of the groups of six or more games that form part of a match. ❑ *Graf was leading 5-1 in the first set.* N-COUNT: oft supp N 3 In mathematics, a **set** is a group of mathematical quantities that have some characteristic in common. N-COUNT 4 A band's or musician's **set** is the group of songs or tunes that they perform at a concert. ❑ *The band continued with their set after a short break.* N-COUNT 5 You can refer to a group of people as a **set** if they meet together socially or have the same interests and lifestyle. ❑ *He belonged to what the press called 'The Chelsea Set'.* ➔ See also **jet set**. N-SING: supp N 6 The **set** for a play, film, or television show is the furniture and scenery that is on the stage when the play is being performed or in the studio where filming takes place. ❑ *From the first moment he got on the set, he wanted to be a director too. ...his stage sets for the Folies Bergeres.* N-COUNT: also *on/off* N 7 **The set of** someone's face or part of their body is the way that it is fixed in a particular expression or position, especially one that shows determination. ❑ *Matt looked at Hugh and saw the stubbornness in the set of his shoulders.* N-SING: usu *the* N *of* n 8 A **set** is an appliance. For example, a television set is a television. ❑ *Children spend so much time in front of the television set.* N-COUNT: oft supp N

② **set** /set/ **(sets, setting)** ◆◆◆

✔ The form **set** is used in the present tense and is the past tense and past participle of the verb.

⇛ Please look at category 25 to see if the expression you are looking for is shown under another headword. 1 If you **set** something somewhere, you put it there, especially in a careful or deliberate way. ❑ *He took the case out of her hand and set it on the floor... When he set his glass down he spilled a little drink.* VERB = *put, place*; V n prep; V n with adv 2 If something is **set** in a particular place or position, it is in that place or position. ❑ *The castle is set in 25 acres of beautiful grounds.* ADJ: v-link ADJ prep/adv = *situated* 3 If something is **set into** a surface, it is fixed there and does not stick out. ❑ *The man unlocked a gate set in a high wall and let me through.* ADJ: v-link ADJ prep/adv 4 You can use **set** to say that a person or thing causes another person or thing to be in a particular condition or situation. For example, to **set** someone free means to cause them to be free, and to **set** something going means to cause it to start working. ❑ *Set the kitchen timer going... A phrase from the conference floor set my mind wandering... Dozens of people have been injured and many vehicles set on fire... Churchill immediately set into motion a daring plan.* VERB; V n -ing; V n -ing; be V-ed adj/adv; V n with prep 5 When you **set** a clock or control, you adjust it to a particular point or level. ❑ *Set the volume as high as possible... I forgot to set my alarm and I overslept.* VERB; V n adv/prep; V n 6 If you **set** a date, price, goal, or level, you decide what it will be. ❑ *The conference chairman has set a deadline of noon tomorrow... A date will be set for a future meeting.* VERB; V n; V n 7 If you **set** a certain value **on** something, you think it has that value. ❑ *She sets a high value on autonomy.* VERB; V n *on* n/-ing 8 If you **set** something such as a record, an example, or a precedent, you do something that people will want to copy or try to achieve. ❑ *Legal experts said her case would not set a precedent because it was an out-of-court settlement... A new world marathon record of 2 hrs, 8 min, 5 sec, was set by Stephen Jones of Great Britain.* VERB; V n; V n 9 If someone **sets** you a task or aim or if you **set yourself** a task or aim, you need to succeed in doing it. ❑ *I have to plan my academic work very rigidly and set myself clear objectives.* VERB; V n n 10 To **set** an examination or a question paper means to decide what questions will be asked in it. [BRIT] ❑ *He broke with the tradition of setting examinations in Latin.* VERB; V n

✔ in AM, usually use **make up**

11 You use **set** to describe something which is fixed and cannot be changed. ❑ *Investors can apply for a package of shares at a set price.* ADJ: usu ADJ n 12 A **set** book must be studied by students taking a particular course. [BRIT] ❑ *One of the set books is Jane Austen's Emma.* ADJ: ADJ n

✔ in AM, use **required**

13 If a play, film, or story is **set** in a particular place or period of time, the events in it take place in that place or period. ❑ *The play is set in a small Midwestern town.* ADJ: v-link ADJ prep/adv 14 If you are **set to** do some- ADJ:

thing, you are ready to do it or are likely to do it. If something is **set to** happen, it is about to happen or likely to happen. ❑ *Roberto Baggio was set to become one of the greatest players of all time.* (v-link ADJ to-inf)

15 If you are **set on** something, you are strongly determined to do or have it. If you are **set against** something, you are strongly determined not to do or have it. ❑ *She was set on going to an all-girls school.* (ADJ: v-link ADJ *on/against* n/-ing)

16 If you **set** your face or jaw, you put on a fixed expression of determination. ❑ *Instead, she set her jaw grimly and waited in silence.* (VERB; V n)

17 When something such as jelly, melted plastic, or cement **sets**, it becomes firm or hard. ❑ *You can add ingredients to these desserts as they begin to set.* (VERB; V)

18 When the sun **sets**, it goes below the horizon. ❑ *They watched the sun set behind the distant dales. ...the red glow of the setting sun.* (VERB; V; V-ing)

19 To **set** a trap means to prepare it to catch someone or something. ❑ *He seemed to think I was setting some sort of trap for him.* (VERB; V n *for* n)

20 When someone **sets** the table, they prepare it for a meal by putting plates and cutlery on it. (VERB = lay)

21 If someone **sets** a poem or a piece of writing **to** music, they write music for the words to be sung to. ❑ *He has attracted much interest by setting ancient religious texts to music.* (VERB; V n *to* n)

22 → See also **setting**, **set-to**.

**PHRASES** 23 If someone **sets the scene** or **sets the stage for** an event to take place, they make preparations so that it can take place. ❑ *The Democrat convention has set the scene for a ferocious election campaign this autumn.* (PHRASE: V inflects)

24 If you say that someone **is set in** their **ways**, you are being critical of the fact that they have fixed habits and ideas which they will not easily change, even though they may be old-fashioned. (PHRASE: V inflects; disapproval)

25 to **set eyes on** something → see **eye**. to **set fire to** something → see **fire**. to **set foot** somewhere → see **foot**. to **set** your **heart on** something → see **heart**. to **set sail** → see **sail**. to **set great store by** or **on** something → see **store**. to **set to work** → see **work**.

♦ **set against** 1 If one argument or fact **is set against** another, it is considered in relation to it. ❑ *These are relatively small points when set against her expertise on so many other issues.* (PHRASAL VERB; *be* V-ed P n; Also V n P n)

2 To **set** one person **against** another means to cause them to become enemies or rivals. ❑ *The case has set neighbour against neighbour in the village.* (PHRASAL VERB; V n P n)

♦ **set apart** If a characteristic **sets** you **apart from** other people, it makes you different from the others in a noticeable way. ❑ *What sets it apart from hundreds of similar small French towns is the huge factory... Li blends right into the crowd of teenagers. Only his accent sets him apart.* (PHRASAL VERB; V n P *from* n; V n P)

♦ **set aside** 1 If you **set** something **aside for** a special use or purpose, you keep it available for that use or purpose. ❑ *Some doctors advise setting aside a certain hour each day for worry... £130 million would be set aside for repairs to schools.* (PHRASAL VERB; V P n; V P n)

2 If you **set aside** a belief, principle, or feeling, you decide that you will not be influenced by it. ❑ *He urged them to set aside minor differences for the sake of peace.* (PHRASAL VERB; V P n (not pron))

♦ **set back** 1 If something **sets** you **back** or **sets back** a project or scheme, it causes a delay. ❑ *It has set us back in so many respects that I'm not sure how long it will take for us to catch up... There will be a risk of public protest that could set back reforms.* (PHRASAL VERB; V n P; V P n (not pron))

2 If something **sets** you **back** a certain amount of money, it costs you that much money. [INFORMAL] ❑ *In 1981 dinner for two in New York would set you back £5.* (PHRASAL VERB; V n P amount)

3 → See also **setback**.

♦ **set down** 1 If a committee or organization **sets down** rules for doing something, it decides what they should be and officially records them. ❑ *The Convention set down rules for deciding which country should deal with an asylum request.* (PHRASAL VERB = lay down; V P n (not pron))

2 If you **set down** your thoughts or experiences, you write them all down. ❑ *Old Walter is setting down his memories of village life.* (PHRASAL VERB = write down; V P n (not pron))

♦ **set forth** If you **set forth** a number of facts, beliefs, or arguments, you explain them in writing or speech in a clear, organized way. [FORMAL] ❑ *Dr. Mesibov set forth the basis of his approach to teaching students.* (PHRASAL VERB = set out; V P n (not pron))

♦ **set in** If something unpleasant **sets in**, it begins and seems likely to continue or develop. ❑ *Then disappointment sets in as they see the magic is no longer there... Winter is setting in and the population is facing food and fuel shortages.* (PHRASAL VERB; V P; V P)

♦ **set off** 1 When you **set off**, you start a journey. ❑ *Nichols set off for his remote farmhouse in Connecticut... I set off, full of hope and optimism.* (PHRASAL VERB = set out; V P prep/adv; V P)

2 If something **sets off** something such as an alarm or a bomb, it makes it start working so that, for example, the alarm rings or the bomb explodes. ❑ *Any escape, once it's detected, sets off the alarm... It could take months before evidence emerges on how the bomb was made, and who set it off.* (PHRASAL VERB; V P n (not pron); V n P)

3 If something **sets off** an event or a series of events, it causes it to start happening. ❑ *The arrival of the charity van set off a minor riot as villagers scrambled for a share of the aid.* (PHRASAL VERB; V P n (not pron))

♦ **set on** To **set** animals **on** someone means to cause the animals to attack them. ❑ *They brought the young men in and set the dogs on them.* (PHRASAL VERB; V n P n)

♦ **set out** 1 When you **set out**, you start a journey. ❑ *When setting out on a long walk, always wear suitable boots.* (PHRASAL VERB = set off; V P prep/adv)

2 If you **set out to** do something, you start trying to do it. ❑ *He has achieved what he set out to do three years ago.* (PHRASAL VERB; V P to-inf)

3 If you **set** things **out**, you arrange or display them somewhere. ❑ *Set out the cakes attractively, using lacy doilies.* (PHRASAL VERB = arrange; V P n; Also V n P)

4 If you **set out** a number of facts, beliefs, or arguments, you explain them in writing or speech in a clear, organized way. ❑ *He has written a letter to The Times setting out his views.* (PHRASAL VERB; V P n (not pron); Also V n P)

♦ **set up** 1 If you **set** something **up**, you create or arrange it. ❑ *The two sides agreed to set up a commission to investigate claims... Tell us when and why you started your business and how you went about setting it up.* (PHRASAL VERB; V P n (not pron); V n P) ♦ **set|ting up** *The British government announced the setting up of a special fund.* (N-UNCOUNT: usu N *of* n)

2 If you **set up** a temporary structure, you place it or build it somewhere. ❑ *They took to the streets, setting up roadblocks of burning tyres.* (PHRASAL VERB; V P n; Also V n P)

3 If you **set up** a device or piece of machinery, you do the things that are necessary for it to be able to start working. ❑ *I set up the computer so that they could work from home.* (PHRASAL VERB; V P n; Also V n P)

4 If you **set up** somewhere or **set yourself up** somewhere, you establish yourself in a new business or new area. ❑ *The scheme offers incentives to firms setting up in Manhattan... He worked as a dance instructor in London before setting himself up in Bucharest... Grandfather set them up in a liquor business.* (PHRASAL VERB; V P prep/adv; V pron-refl P prep/adv; V n P prep/adv)

5 If you **set up** home or **set up** shop, you buy a house or business of your own and start living or working there. ❑ *They married, and set up home in Ramsgate.* (PHRASAL VERB; V P n)

6 If something **sets up** something such as a process, it creates it or causes it to begin. ❑ *The secondary current sets up a magnetic field inside the tube.* (PHRASAL VERB; V P n; Also V n P)

7 If you **are set up** by someone, they make it seem that you have done something wrong when you have not. [INFORMAL] ❑ *He claimed he had been set up after drugs were discovered at his home... Maybe Angelo tried to set us up.* (PHRASAL VERB; *be* V-ed P; V n P)

8 → See also **set-up**.

♦ **set upon** If you **are set upon** by people, they make a sudden and unexpected physical attack on you. ❑ *We were set upon by about twelve youths and I was kicked unconscious.* (PHRASAL VERB: usu passive; *be* V-ed P)

**set-aside** In the European Union, **set-aside** is a scheme in which some areas of farmland are not used for a period of time, either because too much is being produced already, or so that a crop does not become too cheap. ❑ *A Brockhampton farm is paid £87 per acre for the 1,700 acres it has in set-aside.* (N-UNCOUNT: oft N n)

**set|back** /se̱tbæk/ **(setbacks)** also **set-back.** A **setback** is an event that delays your progress or reverses some of the progress that you have made. (N-COUNT: oft N *for/in/to* n)

❑ *The move represents a setback for the Middle East peace process.*

**set piece** **(set pieces)** also **set-piece.** [1] A **set piece** is an occasion such as a battle or a move in a game of football that is planned and carried out in an ordered way. ❑ *Guerrillas avoid fighting set-piece battles.* N-COUNT: oft N n [2] A **set piece** is a part of a film, novel, or piece of music which has a strong dramatic effect and which is often not an essential part of the main story. ❑ *...the film's martial arts set pieces.* N-COUNT

**sett** /set/ **(setts)** A **sett** is the place where a badger lives. N-COUNT

**set|tee** /setiː/ **(settees)** A **settee** is a long comfortable seat with a back and arms, which two or more people can sit on. N-COUNT = couch, sofa

**set|ter** /setər/ **(setters)** A **setter** is a long-haired dog that can be trained to show hunters where birds and animals are. N-COUNT

**set|ting** /setɪŋ/ **(settings)** [1] A particular **setting** is a particular place or type of surroundings where something is or takes place. ❑ *Rome is the perfect setting for romance.* N-COUNT: usu with supp, oft N *for* n [2] A **setting** is one of the positions to which the controls of a device such as a cooker, stove, or heater can be adjusted. ❑ *You can boil the fish fillets on a high setting.* N-COUNT [3] A table **setting** is the complete set of equipment that one person needs to eat a meal, including knives, forks, spoons, and glasses. N-COUNT

**set|tle** /setəl/ **(settles, settling, settled)** ◆◆◇ [1] If people **settle** an argument or problem, or if something **settles** it, they solve it, for example by making a decision about who is right or about what to do. VERB ❑ *They agreed to try to settle their dispute by negotiation...* V n *Tomorrow's vote is unlikely to settle the question of who will replace their leader.* V n [2] If people **settle** a legal dispute or if they **settle**, they agree to end the dispute without going to a court of law, for example by paying some money or by apologizing. VERB ❑ *In an attempt to settle the case, Molken has agreed to pay restitution...* V n *She got much less than she would have done if she had settled out of court...* V *His company settled with the American authorities by paying a $200 million fine.* V *with* n [3] If you **settle** a bill or debt, you pay the amount that you owe. VERB ❑ *I settled the bill for my coffee and his two glasses of wine...* V n *They settled with Colin at the end of the evening.* V *with* n [4] If something **is settled**, it has all been decided and arranged. VERB: usu passive *be* V-ed ❑ *As far as we're concerned, the matter is settled.* [5] When people **settle** a place or in a place, or when a government **settles** them there, they start living there permanently. VERB ❑ *Refugees settling in Britain suffer from a number of problems...* V prep/adv *Thirty-thousand-million dollars is needed to settle the refugees.* V n Also V [6] If you **settle yourself** somewhere or **settle** somewhere, you sit down or make yourself comfortable. VERB ❑ *Albert settled himself on the sofa...* V pron-refl prep/adv *Jessica settled into her chair with a small sigh of relief.* V prep/adv [7] If something **settles** or if you **settle** it, it sinks slowly down and becomes still. VERB ❑ *A black dust settled on the walls...* V prep/adv *Once its impurities had settled, the oil could be graded...* V *Tap each one firmly on your work surface to settle the mixture.* V n [8] If your eyes **settle on** or **upon** something, you stop looking around and look at that thing for some time. VERB = rest ❑ *The man let his eyes settle upon Cross's face.* V *on/upon* n [9] When birds or insects **settle on** something, they land on it from above. VERB = light ❑ *Moths flew in front of it, eventually settling on the rough painted metal.* V *on* n [10] → See also **settled**. **when the dust settles** → see **dust**. **to settle a score** → see **score**.

♦ **settle down** [1] When someone **settles down**, they start living a quiet life in one place, especially when they get married or buy a house. PHRASAL VERB ❑ *One day I'll want to settle down and have a family...* V P *Before she settled down in Portugal, she had run her own antiques shop in London.* V P prep/adv [2] If a situation or a person that has been going through a lot of problems or changes **settles down**, they become calm. PHRASAL VERB ❑ *It'd be fun, after the situation in Europe settles down, to take a trip over to France.* V P [3] If you **settle down to** do something or to something, you prepare to do it and concentrate on it. PHRASAL VERB ❑ *He got his coffee, came back and settled down to listen...* V P to-inf *They settled down to some serious work.* V P *to* n [4] If you **settle down** for the night, you get ready to lie down and sleep. PHRASAL VERB ❑ *They put up their tents and settled down for the night.* V P

♦ **settle for** If you **settle for** something, you choose or accept it, especially when it is not what you really want but there is nothing else available. PHRASAL VERB ❑ *Virginia was a perfectionist. She was just not prepared to settle for anything mediocre.* V P n

♦ **settle in** If you **settle in**, you become used to living in a new place, doing a new job, or going to a new school. PHRASAL VERB ❑ *I enjoyed King Edward's School enormously once I'd settled in.* V P

♦ **settle on** If you **settle on** a particular thing, you choose it after considering other possible choices. PHRASAL VERB = decide on ❑ *I finally settled on a Mercedes estate.* V P n

♦ **settle up** When you **settle up**, you pay a bill or a debt. PHRASAL VERB ❑ *When we approached the till to settle up, he reduced our bill by 50 per cent.* V P

**set|tled** /setəld/ [1] If you have a **settled** way of life, you stay in one place, in one job, or with one person, rather than moving around or changing. ADJ: usu ADJ n ❑ *He decided to lead a more settled life with his partner.* [2] A **settled** situation or system stays the same all the time. ADJ: usu ADJ n ❑ *There has been a period of settled weather.*

**set|tle|ment** /setəlmənt/ **(settlements)** ◆◆◇ [1] A **settlement** is an official agreement between two sides who were involved in a conflict or argument. N-COUNT: usu with supp ❑ *Our objective must be to secure a peace settlement...* *They are not optimistic about a settlement of the eleven year conflict.* [2] A **settlement** is an agreement to end a disagreement or dispute without going to a court of law, for example by offering someone money. N-COUNT: usu with supp ❑ *She accepted an out-of-court settlement of £4,000.* [3] The **settlement of** a debt is the act of paying back money that you owe. N-UNCOUNT: usu N *of* n ❑ *...ways to delay the settlement of debts.* [4] A **settlement** is a place where people have come to live and have built homes. N-COUNT: usu with supp ❑ *The village is a settlement of just fifty houses.*

**set|tler** /setələr/ **(settlers)** **Settlers** are people who go to live in a new country. N-COUNT ❑ *The village was founded by settlers from the Volga region.*

**set-to** **(set-tos)** A **set-to** is a dispute or fight. [INFORMAL] N-COUNT ❑ *This was the subject of a bit of a set-to between Smith and his record company.*

**set-top box** **(set-top boxes)** A **set-top box** is a piece of equipment that rests on top of your television and receives digital television signals. N-COUNT

**set-up** **(set-ups)** also **setup.** ◆◆◇ [1] A particular **set-up** is a particular system or way of organizing something. [INFORMAL] N-COUNT ❑ *It appears to be an idyllic domestic set-up...* *I gradually got rather disillusioned with the whole setup of the university.* [2] If you describe a situation as a **set-up**, you mean that people have planned it in order to deceive you or to make it look as if you have done something wrong. [INFORMAL] N-COUNT ❑ *He was asked to pick somebody up and bring them to a party, not realizing it was a setup.* [3] The **set-up** of computer hardware or software is the process of installing it and making it ready to use. [COMPUTING] N-SING ❑ *The worst part of the set-up is the poor instruction manual.*

**sev|en** /sevən/ **(sevens)** ◆◆◆ **Seven** is the number 7. NUM ❑ *Sarah and Ella have been friends for seven years.*

**sev|en|teen** /seventiːn/ **(seventeens)** ◆◆◆ **Seventeen** is the number 17. NUM ❑ *Jenny is seventeen years old.*

**sev|en|teenth** /seventiːnθ/ **(seventeenths)** ◆◆◇ [1] The **seventeenth** item in a series is the one that you count as number seventeen. ORD ❑ *She gave birth to Annabel just after her seventeenth birthday.* [2] A **seventeenth** is one of seventeen equal parts of something. FRACTION

**sev|enth** /sevᵊnθ/ **(sevenths)** ◆◆◇ [1] The **seventh** item in a series is the one that you count as number seven. ❑ *I was the seventh child in a family of 11.* ORD [2] A **seventh** is one of seven equal parts of something. ❑ *A million people died, a seventh of the population.* FRACTION

**Sev|enth Day Ad|vent|ist** /sevᵊnθ deɪ ædventɪst/ **(Seventh Day Adventists)** [1] **Seventh Day Adventist** churches are churches that believe that Jesus Christ will return very soon, and that have Saturday as their holy day. ADJ: ADJ n [2] A **Seventh Day Adventist** is a member of the Seventh Day Adventist church. N-COUNT

**sev|enth heav|en** If you say that you are **in seventh heaven**, you mean that you are in a state of complete happiness. [INFORMAL] N-UNCOUNT: *in* N

**sev|en|ti|eth** /sevᵊntiəθ/ **(seventieths)** ◆◆◇ [1] The **seventieth** item in a series is the one that you count as number seventy. ❑ *...the seventieth anniversary of the discovery of Tutankhamun's tomb.* ORD [2] A **seventieth** is one of seventy equal parts of something. FRACTION

**sev|en|ty** /sevᵊnti/ **(seventies)** ◆◆◆ [1] **Seventy** is the number 70. ❑ *Seventy people were killed.* NUM [2] When you talk about the **seventies**, you are referring to numbers between 70 and 79. For example, if you are **in** your **seventies**, you are aged between 70 and 79. If the temperature is **in the seventies**, it is between 70 and 79. ❑ *It's a long way to go for two people in their seventies.* N-PLURAL [3] **The seventies** is the decade between 1970 and 1979. ❑ *In the late Seventies, things had to be new, modern, revolutionary.* N-PLURAL: *the* N

**sev|er** /sevəʳ/ **(severs, severing, severed)** [1] To **sever** something means to cut completely through it or to cut it completely off. [FORMAL] ❑ *Richardson severed his right foot in a motorbike accident. ...oil still gushing from a severed fuel line.* VERB V n V-ed [2] If you **sever** a relationship or connection that you have with someone, you end it suddenly and completely. [FORMAL] ❑ *She severed her ties with England.* VERB V n

**sev|er|al** /sevrəl/ ◆◆◆ **Several** is used to refer to an imprecise number of people or things that is not large but is greater than two. ❑ *I had lived two doors away from this family for several years... Several blue plastic boxes under the window were filled with record albums... Several hundred students gathered on campus.* DET: DET pl-n ♦ **Several** is also a quantifier. ❑ *Several of the delays were caused by the new high-tech baggage system.* QUANT: QUANT *of* pl-n ♦ **Several** is also a pronoun. ❑ *No one drug will suit or work for everyone and sometimes several may have to be tried.* PRON

**sev|er|ance** /sevərəns/ [1] **Severance from** a person or group, or the **severance of** a connection, involves the ending of a relationship or connection. [FORMAL] ❑ *...his bitter sense of severance from his family. ...the complete severance of diplomatic relations.* N-UNCOUNT [2] **Severance** pay is a sum of money that a company gives to its employees when it has to stop employing them. [BUSINESS] ❑ *We were offered 13 weeks' severance pay.* ADJ: ADJ n

**se|vere** /sɪvɪəʳ/ **(severer, severest)** ◆◆◇ [1] You use **severe** to indicate that something bad or undesirable is great or intense. ❑ *...a business with severe cash flow problems... Steve passed out on the floor and woke up blinded and in severe pain... Shortages of professional staff are very severe in some places.* ADJ ♦ **se|vere|ly** *The UN wants to send food aid to 10 countries in Africa severely affected by the drought... An aircraft overshot the runway and was severely damaged.* ADV: usu ADV with v, also ADV adj ♦ **se|ver|ity** /sɪverɪti/ *Several drugs are used to lessen the severity of the symptoms.* N-UNCOUNT: usu with supp [2] **Severe** punishments or criticisms are very strong or harsh. ❑ *This was a dreadful crime and a severe sentence is necessary.* ADJ ♦ **se|vere|ly** *...a campaign to try to change the law to punish dangerous drivers more severely.* ADV: ADV with v ♦ **se|ver|ity** *The Bishop said he was sickened by the severity of the sentence.* N-UNCOUNT: usu with supp

**sew** /soʊ/ **(sews, sewing, sewed, sewn)** [1] When you **sew** something such as clothes, you make them or repair them by joining pieces of cloth together by passing thread through them with a needle. ❑ *She sewed the dresses on the sewing machine... Anyone can sew on a button, including you... Mrs Roberts was a dressmaker, and she taught her daughter to sew.* VERB V n V n with *on* V [2] When something such as a hand or finger **is sewn back** by a doctor, it is joined with the patient's body using a needle and thread. ❑ *The hand was preserved in ice and sewn back on in hospital.* ➔ See also **sewing**. VERB *be* V-ed adv

♦ **sew up** [1] If you **sew up** pieces of cloth or tears in cloth or skin, you join them together using a needle and thread. ❑ *Next day, Miss Stone decided to sew up the rip.* PHRASAL VERB V P n Also V n P [2] If someone **sews up** something such as a business deal, an election, or a game, they make sure that they will get the result they want. [INFORMAL] ❑ *If they didn't move fast, Johnson could sew this deal up within days... The Italians think they've got it all sewn up.* PHRASAL VERB V n P V n P Also V P n (not pron)

**sew|age** /suːɪdʒ/ **Sewage** is waste matter such as faeces or dirty water from homes and factories, which flows away through sewers. ❑ *...the MPs' call for more treatment of raw sewage.* N-UNCOUNT

**sew|er** /suːəʳ/ **(sewers)** A **sewer** is a large underground channel that carries waste matter and rain water away, usually to a place where it is treated and made harmless. ❑ *...the city's sewer system. ...open sewers.* N-COUNT

**sew|er|age** /suːərɪdʒ/ **Sewerage** is the system by which waste matter is carried away in sewers and made harmless. ❑ *...without access to any services such as water or sewerage.* N-UNCOUNT: usu N n

**sew|ing** /soʊɪŋ/ [1] **Sewing** is the activity of making or mending clothes or other things using a needle and thread. ❑ *Her mother had always done all the sewing.* N-UNCOUNT [2] **Sewing** is clothes or other things that are being sewn. ❑ *We all got out our own sewing and sat in front of the log fire.* N-UNCOUNT

**sew|ing ma|chine** **(sewing machines)** A **sewing machine** is a machine that you use for sewing. N-COUNT

**sewn** /soʊn/ **Sewn** is the past participle of **sew**.

**sex** /seks/ **(sexes, sexing, sexed)** ◆◆◇ [1] The two **sexes** are the two groups, male and female, into which people and animals are divided according to the function they have in producing young. ❑ *...an entertainment star who appeals to all ages and both sexes. ...differences between the sexes.* ➔ See also **fair sex**, **opposite sex**, **same-sex**, **single-sex**. N-COUNT: usu with supp [2] The **sex** of a person or animal is their characteristic of being either male or female. ❑ *She continually failed to gain promotion because of her sex... The new technique has been used to identify the sex of foetuses.* N-COUNT: oft with poss = *gender* [3] **Sex** is the physical activity by which people can produce young. ❑ *He was very open in his attitudes about sex... We have a very active sex life.* N-UNCOUNT [4] If two people **have sex**, they perform the act of sex. ❑ *Have you ever thought about having sex with someone other than your husband?* PHRASE: V inflects, pl-n PHR, PHR *with* n

**sex aid** **(sex aids)** A **sex aid** is an object or piece of equipment that is designed to make sex easier or more enjoyable. N-COUNT

**sex ap|peal** Someone's **sex appeal** is their sexual attractiveness. ❑ *She still has the energy and sex appeal of a woman less than half her age.* N-UNCOUNT

**-sexed** /-sekst/ **-sexed** is used after adverbs such as 'over' and 'under' to form adjectives which indicate that someone wants to have sex too often or not often enough. ❑ *My husband has always been a bit over-sexed.* COMB in ADJ

**sex edu|ca|tion** **Sex education** is education in schools on the subject of sexual activity and sexual relationships. N-UNCOUNT

**sex god|dess** **(sex goddesses)** If you refer to a woman, especially a film star, as a **sex goddess**, you mean that many people consider her to be N-COUNT sexually attractive. [JOURNALISM] ❑ *Raquel Welch was at the height of her popularity as a sex goddess.*

**sex|ism** /sɛksɪzəm/ **Sexism** is the belief that the members of one sex, usually women, are less intelligent or less capable than those of the other sex and need not be treated equally. It is also the behaviour which is the result of this belief. ❑ *Groups like ours are committed to eradicating homophobia, racism and sexism.* N-UNCOUNT

**sex|ist** /sɛksɪst/ **(sexists)** If you describe people or their behaviour as **sexist**, you mean that they are influenced by the belief that the members of one sex, usually women, are less intelligent or less capable than those of the other sex and need not be treated equally. ❑ *Old-fashioned sexist attitudes are still common.* ♦ A **sexist** is someone with sexist views or behaviour. ADJ [disapproval] N-COUNT

**sex|less** /sɛksləs/ If you describe a person as **sexless**, you mean that they have no sexual feelings or that they are not sexually active. A **sexless** relationship does not involve sex. ❑ *Malcolm is a brilliant but frustrated surgeon who is married to a neurotic and sexless woman.* ADJ

**sex life (sex lives)** If you refer to someone's **sex life**, you are referring to their sexual relationships and sexual activity. N-COUNT: oft with poss

**sex ob|ject (sex objects)** If someone is described as a **sex object**, he or she is considered only in terms of their physical attractiveness and not their character or abilities. ❑ *He cared for her as a whole person rather than just a sex object.* N-COUNT

**sex|olo|gist** /seksɒlədʒɪst/ **(sexologists)** A **sexologist** is a person who studies sexual relationships and gives advice or makes reports. ❑ *...Alfred Kinsey, the pioneering sexologist.* N-COUNT

**sex|pot** /sɛkspɒt/ **(sexpots)** If you describe someone as a **sexpot**, you mean that they are sexually very attractive. [INFORMAL] N-COUNT

**sex shop (sex shops)** A **sex shop** is a shop that sells products that are associated with sexual pleasure, for example magazines, videos, and special clothing or equipment. N-COUNT

**sex sym|bol (sex symbols)** A **sex symbol** is a famous person, especially an actor or a singer, who is considered by many people to be sexually attractive. ❑ *...Hollywood sex symbols of the Forties.* N-COUNT

**sex|tant** /sɛkstənt/ **(sextants)** A **sextant** is an instrument used for measuring angles, for example between the sun and the horizon, so that the position of a ship or aeroplane can be calculated. N-COUNT

**sex|tet** /sɛkstɛt/ **(sextets)** [1] A **sextet** is a group of six musicians or singers who play or sing together. ❑ *...the Paul Rogers Sextet.* N-COUNT [2] A **sextet** is a piece of music written for six performers. N-COUNT

**sex toy (sex toys)** A **sex toy** is an object that some people use to give themselves or other people sexual pleasure. N-COUNT

**sex|ual** /sɛkʃuəl/ ◆◆◇ [1] **Sexual** feelings or activities are connected with the act of sex or with people's desire for sex. ❑ *This was the first sexual relationship I had had... Men's sexual fantasies often have little to do with their sexual desire.* ♦ **sex|ual|ly** *...sexually transmitted diseases... How many kids in this school are sexually active?* [2] **Sexual** means relating to the differences between male and female people. ❑ *Women's groups denounced sexual discrimination.* ♦ **sex|ual|ly** *If you're sexually harassed, you ought to do something about it.* [3] **Sexual** means relating to the differences between heterosexuals and homosexuals. ❑ *...couples of all sexual persuasions.* [4] **Sexual** means relating to the biological process by which people and animals produce young. ❑ *Girls generally reach sexual maturity two years earlier than boys.* ♦ **sex|ual|ly** *The first organisms that reproduced sexually were plankton.* ADJ: usu ADJ n; ADV: ADV with v, ADV adj; ADJ: usu ADJ n; ADV: ADV with v; ADJ: usu ADJ n; ADJ: usu ADJ n; ADV: ADV with v, ADV adj

**sex|ual abuse** If a child or other person suffers **sexual abuse**, someone forces them to take part in sexual activity with them, often regularly over a period of time. N-UNCOUNT

**sex|ual har|ass|ment** **Sexual harassment** is repeated and unwelcome sexual comments, looks, or physical contact at work, usually a man's actions that offend a woman. N-UNCOUNT

**sex|ual inter|course** **Sexual intercourse** is the physical act of sex between two people. [FORMAL] N-UNCOUNT

**sexu|al|ity** /sɛkʃuælɪti/ [1] A person's **sexuality** is their sexual feelings. ❑ *In Britain, the growing discussion of women's sexuality raised its own disquiet.* N-UNCOUNT: oft poss N [2] You can refer to a person's **sexuality** when you are talking about whether they are sexually attracted to people of the same sex or a different sex. ❑ *He believes he has been discriminated against because of his sexuality.* N-UNCOUNT: oft poss N

**sex|ual|ize** /sɛkʃuəlaɪz/ **(sexualizes, sexualizing, sexualized)**

☑ in BRIT, also use **sexualise**

To **sexualize** something or someone means to make them sexual or consider them in a sexual way. ❑ *Referring to children's friends as girlfriends and boyfriends sexualizes them... Rape is sexualised violence.* VERB; V n; V-ed

**sex|ual ori|en|ta|tion (sexual orientations)** Someone's **sexual orientation** is whether they are sexually attracted to people of the same sex, people of the opposite sex, or both. N-VAR: oft poss N

**sex|ual pref|er|ence (sexual preferences)** Someone's **sexual preference** is the same as their **sexual orientation**. N-VAR: oft poss N

**sexy** /sɛksi/ **(sexier, sexiest)** You can describe people and things as **sexy** if you think they are sexually exciting or sexually attractive. ❑ *It was a wonderful voice which women found incredibly sexy.* ADJ

**SF** /ɛs ɛf/ **SF** is the same as **science fiction**. ❑ *Arthur C Clarke likes to quote his friend and fellow SF writer Ray Bradbury.* N-UNCOUNT: usu N n

**sfx** **Sfx** is an abbreviation for **special effects**. [WRITTEN]

**SGML** /ɛs dʒiː em ɛl/ **SGML** is a computer language for creating files using a system of codes. **SGML** is an abbreviation for 'standard generalized mark-up language'. N-UNCOUNT

**Sgt**

☑ in AM, use **Sgt.**

**Sgt** is the written abbreviation for **Sergeant** when it is used as a title. ❑ *...Sgt Johnston.* N-TITLE

**sh** /ʃ/ also **shh.** You can say **'Sh!'** to tell someone to be quiet. [INFORMAL, SPOKEN] CONVENTION

**shab|by** /ʃæbi/ **(shabbier, shabbiest)** [1] **Shabby** things or places look old and in bad condition. ❑ *His clothes were old and shabby... He walked past her into a tiny, shabby room.* ADJ [2] A person who is **shabby** is wearing old, worn clothes. ❑ *...a shabby, tall man with dark eyes.* ADJ [3] If you describe someone's behaviour as **shabby**, you think they behave in an unfair or unacceptable way. ❑ *It was hard to say why the man deserved such shabby treatment... I knew it was shabby of me, but I couldn't help feeling slightly disappointed.* ADJ [disapproval]

**shack** /ʃæk/ **(shacks, shacking, shacked)** A **shack** is a simple hut built from tin, wood, or other materials. N-COUNT

♦ **shack up** If you say that someone **has shacked up with** someone else or that two people **have shacked up** together, you disapprove of the fact that they have started living together as lovers. [INFORMAL] ❑ *...the deserters who had shacked up with local women... The Government was keen for people to get married rather than shack up... It turned out she was shacked up with a lawyer in New York.* PHRASAL VERB [disapproval] V P *with* n; pl-n V P; *be* V-ed P

**shack|le** /ʃækᵊl/ **(shackles, shackling, shackled)** [1] If you **are shackled by** something, it prevents you from doing what you want to do. [FORMAL] ❑ *The trade unions are shackled by the law. ...people who find themselves shackled to a high-stress job.* VERB: usu passive; *be* V-ed *by/to* n [2] If you throw off the **shackles of** some- N-PLURAL:

thing, you reject it or free yourself from it because it was preventing you from doing what you wanted to do. [LITERARY] ❑ *...a country ready to throw off the shackles of its colonial past.* [3] **Shackles** are two metal rings joined by a chain which are fastened around someone's wrists or ankles in order to prevent them from moving or escaping. ❑ *He unbolted the shackles on Billy's hands.* [4] To **shackle** someone means to put shackles on them. ❑ *...the chains that were shackling his legs.* — with supp; N-PLURAL; VERB; V n

**shade** /ʃeɪd/ **(shades, shading, shaded)** ◆◇◇ [1] A **shade of** a particular colour is one of its different forms. For example, emerald green and olive green are shades of green. ❑ *The walls were painted in two shades of green. ...new eyeshadows in a choice of 80 shades.* [2] **Shade** is an area of darkness under or next to an object such as a tree, where sunlight does not reach. ❑ *Temperatures in the shade can reach forty-eight degrees celsius at this time of year. ...exotic trees provide welcome shade.* [3] If you say that a place or person **is shaded** by objects such as trees, you mean that the place or person cannot be reached, harmed, or bothered by strong sunlight because those objects are in the way. ❑ *...a health resort whose beaches are shaded by palm trees... Umbrellas shade outdoor cafes along winding cobblestone streets.* [4] If you **shade** your eyes, you put your hand or an object partly in front of your face in order to prevent a bright light from shining into your eyes. ❑ *You can't look directly into it; you've got to shade your eyes or close them altogether.* [5] **Shade** is darkness or shadows as they are shown in a picture. ❑ *...Rembrandt's skilful use of light and shade to create the atmosphere of movement.* [6] The **shades of** something abstract are its many, slightly different forms. ❑ *...the capacity to convey subtle shades of meaning.* [7] If something **shades into** something else, there is no clear division between the two things, so that you cannot tell where or when the first thing ends and the second thing begins. ❑ *As the dusk shaded into night, we drove slowly through alleys.* [8] **Shades** are **sunglasses.** [INFORMAL] [9] A **shade** is the same as a **lampshade.** [10] A **shade** is a piece of stiff cloth or heavy paper that you can pull down over a window as a covering. [AM] ❑ *Nancy left the shades down and the lights off.* — N-COUNT: oft N *of* n, *in* N; N-UNCOUNT: oft *in the* N; VERB; *be* V-ed; V n; VERB = shield; V n; N-UNCOUNT ≠ light; N-COUNT: usu pl, N *of* n; VERB; V *into* n; N-PLURAL; N-COUNT; N-COUNT = blind

☑ in BRIT, use **blind**

[11] → See also **shaded, shading.** [12] To **put** someone or something **in the shade** means to be so impressive that the person or thing seems unimportant by comparison. ❑ *...a run that put every other hurdler's performance in the shade.* — PHRASE: V inflects

**shad|ed** /ʃeɪdɪd/ A **shaded** area on something such as a map is one that is coloured darker than the surrounding areas, so that it can be distinguished from them. — ADJ

**-shaded** /-ʃeɪdɪd/ **-shaded** combines with nouns to form adjectives which indicate that sunlight is prevented from reaching a certain place by the thing mentioned. ❑ *...a winding, tree-shaded driveway.* — COMB: COMB in ADJ

**shad|ing** /ʃeɪdɪŋ/ **(shadings)** [1] **Shading** is material such as nets or dark paint that provide shade, especially for plants. ❑ *The conservatory will get very hot in summer unless shading is used.* [2] → See also **shade.** — N-UNCOUNT

**shad|ow** /ʃædoʊ/ **(shadows, shadowing, shadowed)** ◆◇◇ [1] A **shadow** is a dark shape on a surface that is made when something stands between a light and the surface. ❑ *An oak tree cast its shadow over a tiny round pool... Nothing would grow in the shadow of the grey wall... All he could see was his shadow.* [2] **Shadow** is darkness in a place caused by something preventing light from reaching it. ❑ *Most of the lake was in shadow.* [3] If something **shadows** a thing or place, it covers it with a shadow. ❑ *The hood shadowed her face.* [4] If someone **shadows** you, they follow you very closely wherever you go. ❑ *The supporters are being shadowed by a large and highly visible body of police.* [5] A British Member of Parliament who is a member of the **shadow** cabinet or who is a **shadow** cabinet minister belongs to the main opposition party and takes a special interest in matters which are the responsibility of a particular government minister. ❑ *...the shadow chancellor.* ♦ **Shadow** is also a noun. ❑ *Clarke swung at his shadow the accusation that he was 'a tabloid politician'.* — N-COUNT; N-UNCOUNT: oft *in* N = shade; VERB; V n; VERB = follow; V n; ADJ: ADJ n; N-COUNT: poss N

PHRASES [6] If you say that something is true **without a shadow of a doubt** or **without a shadow of doubt**, you are emphasizing that there is no doubt at all that it is true. ❑ *It was without a shadow of a doubt the best we've played.* [7] If you live **in the shadow of** someone or **in** their **shadow**, their achievements and abilities are so great that you are not noticed or valued. ❑ *He has always lived in the shadow of his brother.* [8] If you say that someone is **a shadow of** their **former self**, you mean that they are much less strong or capable than they used to be. ❑ *Johnson returned to the track after his ban but was a shadow of his former self.* — PHRASE: usu with brd-neg [emphasis]; PHRASE: N inflects; PHRASE: Ns inflect

**shad|ow box|ing** [1] **Shadow boxing** is a form of physical exercise or training in which you move your hands and feet as if you are boxing someone. [2] If you describe what two people or groups are doing as **shadow boxing**, you mean that they seem to be taking action against each other but in fact are not serious about the dispute. ❑ *...the tedious shadow boxing that we normally see between bosses and unions in Britain.* — N-UNCOUNT; N-UNCOUNT

**shad|owy** /ʃædoʊi/ [1] A **shadowy** place is dark or full of shadows. ❑ *I watched him from a shadowy corner.* [2] A **shadowy** figure or shape is someone or something that you can hardly see because they are in a dark place. ❑ *...a tall, shadowy figure silhouetted against the pale wall.* [3] You describe activities and people as **shadowy** when very little is known about them. ❑ *...the shadowy world of spies.* — ADJ: usu ADJ n; ADJ: ADJ n; ADJ = mysterious

**shady** /ʃeɪdi/ **(shadier, shadiest)** [1] You can describe a place as **shady** when you like the fact that it is sheltered from bright sunlight, for example by trees or buildings. ❑ *After flowering, place the pot in a shady spot in the garden.* [2] **Shady** trees provide a lot of shade. ❑ *Clara had been reading in a lounge chair under a shady tree.* [3] You can describe activities as **shady** when you think that they might be dishonest or illegal. You can also use **shady** to describe people who are involved in such activities. ❑ *The company was notorious for shady deals.* — ADJ; ADJ: usu ADJ n; ADJ: usu ADJ n [disapproval]

**shaft** /ʃɑːft, ʃæft/ **(shafts)** [1] A **shaft** is a long vertical passage, for example for a lift. ❑ *He was found dead at the bottom of a lift shaft. ...old mine shafts.* [2] In a machine, a **shaft** is a rod that turns round continually in order to transfer movement in the machine. ❑ *...a drive shaft. ...the propeller shaft.* [3] A **shaft** is a long thin piece of wood or metal that forms part of a spear, axe, golf club, or other object. ❑ *...golf clubs with steel shafts.* [4] A **shaft of** light is a beam of light, for example sunlight shining through an opening. ❑ *A brilliant shaft of sunlight burst through the doorway.* — N-COUNT: oft n N; N-COUNT: usu n N; N-COUNT; N-COUNT: usu N *of* n

**shag** /ʃæg/ **(shags, shagging, shagged)** If someone **shags** another person, or if two people **shag**, they have sex together. [BRIT, INFORMAL, RUDE] ♦ **Shag** is also a noun. ❑ *...a spy movie with car chases, a murder, a shag and a happy ending.* — V-RECIP; N-COUNT: usu sing

**shag|gy** /ʃægi/ **(shaggier, shaggiest)** **Shaggy** hair or fur is long and untidy. ❑ *Tim has longish, shaggy hair.* — ADJ

**Shah** /ʃɑː/ **(Shahs)** In former times, **the Shah** of Iran was its ruler. — N-PROPER: *the* N

**shaikh** /ʃeɪk/ **(shaikhs)** → see **sheikh.**

**shake** /ʃeɪk/ **(shakes, shaking, shook, shaken)** ◆◆◇ [1] If you **shake** something, you hold it and move it quickly backwards and forwards or up and down. You can also **shake** a person, for example, — VERB

because you are angry with them or because you want them to wake up. ❑ *The nurse shook the thermometer and put it under my armpit...* V n *Shake the rugs well and hang them for a few hours before replacing on the floor.* V n ♦ **Shake** is also a noun. N-COUNT: usu sing ❑ *She picked up the bag of salad and gave it a shake.* 2 VERB If you **shake yourself** or your body, you make a lot of quick, small, repeated movements without moving from the place where you are. ❑ *As soon as he got inside, the dog shook himself...* V pron-refl *He shook his hands to warm them up.* V n ♦ **Shake** is also a noun. N-COUNT ❑ *Take some slow, deep breaths and give your body a bit of a shake.* 3 VERB If you **shake** your **head**, you turn it from side to side in order to say 'no' or to show disbelief or sadness. ❑ *'Anything else?' Colum asked. Kathryn shook her head wearily.* V n ♦ **Shake** is also a noun. N-COUNT ❑ *Palmer gave a sad shake of his head.* 4 VERB If you **are shaking**, or a part of your body **is shaking**, you are making quick, small movements that you cannot control, for example because you are cold or afraid. ❑ *My hand shook so much that I could hardly hold the microphone...* V *I stood there, crying and shaking with fear.* V *with* n 5 VERB If you **shake** your fist or an object such as a stick **at** someone, you wave it in the air in front of them because you are angry with them. ❑ *The colonel rushed up to Earle, shaking his gun at him.* V n *at* n 6 VERB If a force **shakes** something, or if something **shakes**, it moves from side to side or up and down with quick, small, but sometimes violent movements. ❑ *...an explosion that shook buildings several kilometers away...* V n *The breeze grew in strength, the flags shook, plastic bunting creaked.* V
7 VERB To **shake** something into a certain place or state means to bring it into that place or state by moving it quickly up and down or from side to side. ❑ *Small insects can be collected by shaking them into a jar...* V n prep *Shake off any excess flour before putting livers in the pan.* V n with adv 8 VERB If your voice **is shaking**, you cannot control it properly and it sounds very unsteady, for example because you are nervous or angry. ❑ *His voice shaking with rage, he asked how the committee could keep such a report from the public.* V *with* n Also V 9 VERB If an event or a piece of news **shakes** you, or **shakes** your confidence, it makes you feel upset and unable to think calmly. ❑ *The news of Tandy's escape had shaken them all.* V n ♦ **shak|en** ADJ: usu v-link ADJ *Unhurt, but a bit shaken, she was trying not to cry.* 10 VERB If an event **shakes** a group of people or their beliefs, it causes great uncertainty and makes them question their beliefs. ❑ *It won't shake the football world if we beat Torquay.* V n 11 N-COUNT A **shake** is the same as a **milkshake**. ❑ *He sent his driver to fetch him a strawberry shake.*

PHRASES 12 PHRASE: v-link PHR If you say that someone or something is **no great shakes**, you mean that they are not very skilful or effective. [INFORMAL] ❑ *I'm no great shakes as a detective... The protests have failed partly because the opposition politicians are no great shakes.* 13 PHRASE: V inflects If you **shake** someone's **hand** or **shake** someone **by the hand**, you shake hands with them. ❑ *I said congratulations and walked over to him and shook his hand.* 14 PHRASE: V inflects, PHR *with* n, pl-n PHR If you **shake hands with** someone, you take their right hand in your own for a few moments, often moving it up and down slightly, when you are saying hello or goodbye to them, congratulating them, or agreeing on something. You can also say that two people **shake hands**. ❑ *He nodded greetings to Mary Ann and Michael and shook hands with Burke.* 15 to **shake the foundations of** something → see **foundation**.

♦ **shake down** PHRASAL VERB If someone **shakes** you **down**, they use threats or search you physically in order to obtain something from you. [AM] ❑ *He ordered the dismantling of police checkpoints on highways, which were being used to shake down motorists for bribes.* V P n (not pron) Also V n P

♦ **shake off** 1 PHRASAL VERB If you **shake off** something that you do not want such as an illness or a bad habit, you manage to recover from it or get rid of it. ❑ *Businessmen are trying to shake off habits learned under six decades of a protected economy...* V P n *He was generally feeling bad. He just couldn't shake it off.* V n P 2 PHRASAL VERB If you **shake off** someone who is following you, you manage to get away from them, for example by running faster than them. ❑ *I caught him a lap later, and although I could pass him I could not shake him off...* V n P *He was unaware that they had shaken off their pursuers.* V P n (not pron) 3 PHRASAL VERB If you **shake off** someone who is touching you, you move your arm or body sharply so that they are no longer touching you. ❑ *He grabbed my arm. I shook him off...* V n P *She shook off his restraining hand.* V P n (not pron)

♦ **shake out** PHRASAL VERB If you **shake out** a cloth or a piece of clothing, you hold it by one of its edges and move it up and down one or more times, in order to open it out, make it flat, or remove dust. ❑ *While the water was heating she decided to shake out the carpet...* V P n (not pron) *I took off my poncho, shook it out, and hung it on a peg by the door.* V n P → See also **shake-out**.

♦ **shake up** 1 PHRASAL VERB If someone **shakes up** something such as an organization, an institution, or a profession, they make major changes to it. ❑ *The government wanted to reform the institutions, to shake up the country...* V P n (not pron) *Shareholders are preparing to shake things up in the boardrooms of America.* V n P → See also **shake-up**. 2 PHRASAL VERB If you **are shaken up** or **shook up** by an unpleasant experience, it makes you feel shocked and upset, and unable to think calmly or clearly. ❑ *The jockey was shaken up when he was thrown twice from his horse yesterday...* *be* V-ed P *He was in the car when those people died. That really shook him up.* V n P

**shake|down** /ʃeɪkdaʊn/ **(shakedowns)** 1 N-COUNT If an organization or system is given a **shakedown**, it is thoroughly reorganized in order to make it more efficient. 2 N-COUNT A **shakedown** of a boat, plane, or car is its final test before it starts to be used.

**shak|en** /ʃeɪkən/ **Shaken** is the past participle of **shake**.

**shake-out** **(shake-outs)**

> ✔ in AM, use **shakeout**

N-COUNT: usu sing A **shake-out** is a major set of changes in a system or an organization which results in a large number of companies closing or a large number of people losing their jobs. [JOURNALISM] ❑ *This should be the year of a big shake-out in Italian banking.*

**Shak|er** /ʃeɪkəʳ/ **(Shakers)** 1 N-COUNT A **Shaker** is a member of an American religious group whose members live in communities and have a very simple life. 2 ADJ: ADJ n **Shaker** furniture is usually made of wood and has a very simple design.

**shake-up** **(shake-ups)**

> ✔ in AM, use **shakeup**

N-COUNT: usu with supp, oft N *of/in* n A **shake-up** is a major set of changes in an organization or a system. [JOURNALISM] ❑ *...a radical shake-up of the secondary education system.*

**shaky** /ʃeɪki/ **(shakier, shakiest)** 1 ADJ If you describe a situation as **shaky**, you mean that it is weak or unstable, and seems unlikely to last long or be successful. ❑ *A shaky ceasefire is holding after three days of fighting between rival groups... I'm afraid that this school year is off to a shaky start.* 2 ADJ If your body or your voice is **shaky**, you cannot control it properly and it shakes, for example because you are ill or nervous. ❑ *We have all had a shaky hand and a dry mouth before speaking in public.*

**shale** /ʃeɪl/ **(shales)** N-MASS **Shale** is smooth soft rock that breaks easily into thin layers.

**shall** /ʃəl, STRONG ʃæl/ ◆◆◇

> ✔ **Shall** is a modal verb. It is used with the base form of a verb.

1 MODAL You use **shall** with 'I' and 'we' in questions in order to make offers or suggestions, or to ask for advice. ❑ *Shall I get the keys?... Shall I telephone her and ask her to come here?... Well, shall we go?... Let's have a nice little stroll, shall we?... What shall I do?*
2 MODAL You use **shall**, usually with 'I' and 'we', when

you are referring to something that you intend to do, or when you are referring to something that you are sure will happen to you in the future. ❑ *We shall be landing in Paris in sixteen minutes, exactly on time... I shall know more next month, I hope... I shall miss him terribly.* [3] You use **shall** with 'I' or 'we' during a speech or piece of writing to say what you are going to discuss or explain later. [FORMAL] ❑ *In Chapter 3, I shall describe some of the documentation that I gathered.* MODAL [4] You use **shall** to indicate that something must happen, usually because of a rule or law. You use **shall not** to indicate that something must not happen. ❑ *The president shall hold office for five years.* MODAL [5] You use **shall**, usually with 'you', when you are telling someone that they will be able to do or have something they want. ❑ *'I want to hear all the gossip, all the scandal.' — 'You shall, dearie, you shall!'* MODAL [6] You use **shall** with verbs such as 'look forward to' and 'hope' to say politely that you are looking forward to something or hoping to do something. [FORMAL] ❑ *Well, we shall look forward to seeing him tomorrow.* MODAL, politeness [7] You use **shall** when you are referring to the likely result or consequence of a particular action or situation. ❑ *When big City firms cut down on their entertainments, we shall know that times really are hard.* MODAL

**shal|lot** /ʃəlɒt/ **(shallots)** **Shallots** are small round vegetables that are the roots of a crop and are similar to onions. They have a strong taste and are used for flavouring other food. N-VAR: usu pl

**shal|low** /ʃæloʊ/ **(shallower, shallowest)** [1] A **shallow** container, hole, or area of water measures only a short distance from the top to the bottom. ❑ *Put the milk in a shallow dish... The water is quite shallow for some distance.* ADJ ≠ *deep* [2] If you describe a person, piece of work, or idea as **shallow**, you disapprove of them because they do not show or involve any serious or careful thought. ❑ *I think he is shallow, vain and untrustworthy.* ADJ, disapproval [3] If your breathing is **shallow**, you take only a very small amount of air into your lungs at each breath. ❑ *She began to hear her own taut, shallow breathing.* ADJ ≠ *deep*

**shal|lows** /ʃæloʊz/ **The shallows** are the shallow part of an area of water. ❑ *At dusk more fish come into the shallows.* N-PLURAL: *the* N

**shalt** /ʃəlt, STRONG ʃælt/ **Shalt** is an old-fashioned form of **shall**. ❑ *Thou shalt not kill.* MODAL

**sham** /ʃæm/ **(shams)** Something that is a **sham** is not real or is not really what it seems to be. ❑ *The government's promises were exposed as a hollow sham.* N-COUNT: usu sing, disapproval

**sham|an** /ʃeɪmən/ **(shamans)** [1] A **shaman** is a priest or priestess in shamanism. N-COUNT [2] Among some Native American peoples, a **shaman** is a person who is believed to have powers to heal sick people or to remove evil spirits from them. N-COUNT

**sham|an|ism** /ʃeɪmənɪzəm/ **Shamanism** is a religion which is based on the belief that the world is controlled by good and evil spirits, and that these spirits can be directed by people with special powers. N-UNCOUNT

**sham|bles** /ʃæmbᵊlz/ If a place, event, or situation is **a shambles** or is **in a shambles**, everything is in disorder. ❑ *The ship's interior was an utter shambles... The economy is in a shambles.* N-SING = *mess*

**sham|bo|lic** /ʃæmbɒlɪk/ If you describe a situation, person, or place as **shambolic**, you mean that they are very disorganized. [BRIT] ❑ *...a shambolic public relations disaster.* ADJ

**shame** /ʃeɪm/ **(shames, shaming, shamed)** ◆◇◇ [1] **Shame** is an uncomfortable feeling that you get when you have done something wrong or embarrassing, or when someone close to you has. ❑ *She felt a deep sense of shame... I was, to my shame, a coward.* N-UNCOUNT [2] If someone brings **shame on** you, they make other people lose their respect for you. ❑ *I don't want to bring shame on the family name.* N-UNCOUNT = *disgrace* [3] If something **shames** you, it causes you to feel shame. ❑ *Her son's affair had humiliated and shamed her.* VERB, V n [4] If you **shame** someone **into** doing something, you force them to do it by making them feel ashamed not to. ❑ *He would not let neighbours shame him into silence.* VERB, V n *into/out of* n/-ing [5] If you say that something is **a shame**, you are expressing your regret about it and indicating that you wish it had happened differently. ❑ *It's a crying shame that police have to put up with these mindless attacks.* N-SING: *a* N, oft *it* v-link N that, feelings [6] You can use **shame** in expressions such as **shame on you** and **shame on him** to indicate that someone ought to feel shame for something they have said or done. ❑ *He tried to deny it. Shame on him!* CONVENTION, feelings [7] If someone **puts** you **to shame**, they make you feel ashamed because they do something much better than you do. ❑ *His playing really put me to shame.* PHRASE: V inflects

**shame|faced** /ʃeɪmfeɪst, AM -feɪst/ If you are **shamefaced**, you feel embarrassed because you have done something that you know you should not have done. [FORMAL] ❑ *There was a long silence, and my father looked shamefaced.* ADJ

**shame|ful** /ʃeɪmfʊl/ If you describe a person's action or attitude as **shameful**, you think that it is so bad that the person ought to be ashamed. ❑ *...the most shameful episode in US naval history.* ADJ, disapproval ♦ **shame|ful|ly** *At times they have been shamefully neglected.* ADV: ADV with v, ADV adj

**shame|less** /ʃeɪmləs/ If you describe someone as **shameless**, you mean that they should be ashamed of their behaviour, which is unacceptable to other people. ❑ *...a shameless attempt to stifle democratic debate.* ADJ, disapproval ♦ **shame|less|ly** *...a shamelessly lazy week-long trip.* ADV: ADV with v, ADV adj

**sham|poo** /ʃæmpuː/ **(shampoos, shampooing, shampooed)** [1] **Shampoo** is a soapy liquid that you use for washing your hair. ❑ *...a bottle of shampoo. ...bubble baths, soaps and shampoos.* N-MASS [2] When you **shampoo** your hair, you wash it using shampoo. ❑ *Shampoo your hair and dry it.* VERB, V n

**sham|rock** /ʃæmrɒk/ **(shamrocks)** A **shamrock** is a small plant with three round leaves on each stem. The shamrock is the national symbol of Ireland. N-COUNT

**shan|dy** /ʃændi/ **(shandies)** **Shandy** is a drink which is made by mixing beer and lemonade. [BRIT] ❑ *...half a pint of shandy.* N-UNCOUNT ♦ A glass of shandy can be referred to as a **shandy**. N-COUNT

**shank** /ʃæŋk/ **(shanks)** [1] The **shank** of an object is the long, thin, straight part of the object. ❑ *These hooks are sharp with long shanks.* N-COUNT [2] **Shanks** are the lower parts of the legs; used especially with reference to meat. ❑ *Turn the shanks and baste them once or twice as they cook.* N-COUNT: usu pl

**shan't** /ʃɑːnt, ʃænt/ **Shan't** is the usual spoken form of 'shall not'.

**shan|ty** /ʃænti/ **(shanties)** [1] A **shanty** is a small rough hut which poor people live in, built from tin, cardboard, or other materials that are not very strong. N-COUNT [2] A **shanty** is a song which sailors used to sing while they were doing work on a ship. N-COUNT

**shan|ty town** **(shanty towns)** also **shanty-town.** A **shanty town** is a collection of rough huts which poor people live in, usually in or near a large city. N-COUNT

**shape** /ʃeɪp/ **(shapes, shaping, shaped)** ◆◆◇ [1] The **shape of** an object, a person, or an area is the appearance of their outside edges or surfaces, for example whether they are round, square, curved, or fat. ❑ *Each mirror is made to order and can be designed to almost any shape or size. ...little pens in the shape of baseball bats. ...sofas and chairs of contrasting shapes and colours... The buds are conical or pyramidal in shape... These bras should be handwashed to help them keep their shape.* N-COUNT: oft N *of* n, also *in* N [2] You can refer to something that you can see as a **shape** if you cannot see it clearly, or if its outline is the clearest or most striking aspect of it. ❑ *Lying in bed we often see dark shapes of herons silhouetted against the moon.* N-COUNT [3] A **shape** is a space enclosed by an out- N-COUNT line, for example a circle, a square, or a triangle. ❑ *He suggested that the shapes represented a map of Britain and Ireland.* [4] The **shape of** something that is planned or organized is its structure and character. ❑ *The last two weeks have seen a lot of talk about the future shape of Europe.* [5] Someone or something that **shapes** a situation or an activity has a very great influence on the way it develops. ❑ *Like it or not, our families shape our lives and make us what we are.* [6] If you **shape** an object, you give it a particular shape, using your hands or a tool. ❑ *Cut the dough in half and shape each half into a loaf.* [7] → See also **shaped**.

N-SING: usu N *of* n
VERB
V n
VERB
V n *into* n

**PHRASES** [8] If you say that something is **the shape of things to come**, you mean that it is the start of a new trend or development, and in future things will be like this. ❑ *British Rail says its new Liverpool Street station is the shape of things to come.* [9] If you say, for example, that you will not accept something **in any shape or form**, or **in any way, shape or form**, you are emphasizing that you will not accept it in any circumstances. ❑ *I don't condone violence in any shape or form.* [10] If someone or something is **in shape**, or **in good shape**, they are in a good state of health or in a good condition. If they are **in bad shape**, they are in a bad state of health or in a bad condition. ❑ *He was still in better shape than many young men... The trees were in bad shape from dry rot.* [11] You can use **in the shape of** to state exactly who or what you are referring to, immediately after referring to them in a general way. ❑ *The Prime Minister found a surprise ally today in the shape of Jacques Delors, the Commission President.* [12] If you **lick**, **knock**, or **whip** someone or something **into shape**, you use whatever methods are necessary to change or improve them so that they are in the condition that you want them to be in. ❑ *You'll have four months in which to lick the recruits into shape.* [13] If something is **out of shape**, it is no longer in its proper or original shape, for example because it has been damaged or wrongly handled. ❑ *Once most wires are bent out of shape, they don't return to the original position.* [14] If you are **out of shape**, you are unhealthy and unable to do a lot of physical activity without getting tired. [15] When something **takes shape**, it develops or starts to appear in such a way that it becomes fairly clear what its final form will be. ❑ *In 1912 women's events were added, and the modern Olympic programme began to take shape.*

PHRASE: v-link PHR
PHRASE: PHR after v [emphasis]
PHRASE: PHR after v, v-link PHR
PHRASE: PHR n
PHRASE: V inflects
PHRASE: PHR after v
PHRASE: v-link PHR = *unfit*
PHRASE: V inflects

♦ **shape up** [1] If something **is shaping up**, it is starting to develop or seems likely to happen. ❑ *There are also indications that a major tank battle may be shaping up for tonight... The accident is already shaping up as a significant environmental disaster... It's shaping up to be a terrible winter.* [2] If you ask how someone or something **is shaping up**, you want to know how well they are doing in a particular situation or activity. ❑ *I did have a few worries about how Hugh and I would shape up as parents... Girls are being recruited now. I heard they are shaping up very well.* [3] If you tell someone to **shape up**, you are telling them to start behaving in a sensible and responsible way. ❑ *It is no use simply to tell adolescents to shape up and do something useful.*

PHRASAL VERB
V P
V P *as* n
V P to-inf
PHRASAL VERB
V P *as* n
V P adv
PHRASAL VERB
V P

**shaped** /ʃeɪpt/ Something that is **shaped** like a particular object or in a particular way has the shape of that object or a shape of that type. ❑ *A new perfume from Russia came in a bottle shaped like a tank. ...oddly shaped little packages.*

◆◇◇
ADJ: v-link ADJ *like* n, adv ADJ

**-shaped** /-ʃeɪpt/ **-shaped** combines with nouns to form adjectives that describe the shape of an object. ❑ *...large, heart-shaped leaves. ...an L-shaped settee.*

COMB in ADJ

**shape|less** /ʃeɪpləs/ Something that is **shapeless** does not have a distinct or attractive shape. ❑ *Aunt Mary wore shapeless black dresses.*

ADJ: usu ADJ n

**shape|ly** /ʃeɪpli/ If you describe a woman as **shapely**, you mean that she has an attractive shape. ❑ *...her shapely legs.*

ADJ: usu ADJ n [approval]

**shard** /ʃɑːʳd/ **(shards)** **Shards** are pieces of broken glass, pottery, or metal. ❑ *Eyewitnesses spoke of rocks and shards of glass flying in the air.*

N-COUNT: oft N of n

**share** /ʃeəʳ/ **(shares, sharing, shared)** [1] A company's **shares** are the many equal parts into which its ownership is divided. Shares can be bought by people as an investment. [BUSINESS] ❑ *This is why Sir Colin Marshall, British Airways' chairman, has been so keen to buy shares in US-AIR... For some months the share price remained fairly static.* [2] If you **share** something **with** another person, you both have it, use it, or occupy it. You can also say that two people **share** something. ❑ *...the small income he had shared with his brother from his father's estate... Two Americans will share this year's Nobel Prize for Medicine... Scarce water resources are shared between states who cannot trust each other... Most hostel tenants would prefer single to shared rooms.* [3] If you **share** a task, duty, or responsibility **with** someone, you each carry out or accept part of it. You can also say that two people **share** something. ❑ *You can find out whether they are prepared to share the cost of the flowers with you... The republics have worked out a plan for sharing control of nuclear weapons.* [4] If you **share** an experience **with** someone, you have the same experience, often because you are with them at the time. You can also say that two people **share** something. ❑ *Yes, I want to share my life with you... I felt we both shared the same sense of loss, felt the same pain.* [5] If you **share** someone's opinion, you agree with them. ❑ *We share his view that business can be a positive force for change... Prosperity and economic success remain popular and broadly shared goals.* [6] If one person or thing **shares** a quality or characteristic **with** another, they have the same quality or characteristic. You can also say that two people or things **share** something. ❑ *...newspapers which share similar characteristics with certain British newspapers. ...two groups who share a common language.* [7] If you **share** something that you have **with** someone, you give some of it to them or let them use it. ❑ *The village tribe is friendly and they share their water supply with you... Scientists now have to compete for funding, and do not share information among themselves... Toddlers are notoriously antisocial when it comes to sharing toys.* [8] If you **share** something personal such as a thought or a piece of news **with** someone, you tell them about it. ❑ *It can be beneficial to share your feelings with someone you trust... Film critic Bob Mondello shares his thoughts on the movie 'City of Hope'.* [9] If something is divided or distributed among a number of different people or things, each of them has, or is responsible for, a **share of** it. ❑ *Sara also pays a share of the gas, electricity and phone bills.* [10] If you have or do your **share of** something, you have or do an amount that seems reasonable to you, or to other people. ❑ *Women must receive their fair share of training for good-paying jobs.* [11] → See also **lion's share**, **market share**, **power-sharing**.

◆◆◆
N-COUNT: oft N *in* n
V-RECIP
V n *with* n
pl-n V n
*be* V-ed *between* pl-n
V-ed
V-RECIP
V n *with* n
pl-n V n
V-RECIP
V n *with* n
pl-n V n
VERB: no cont
V n
V-ed
V-RECIP: no cont
V n *with* n
pl-n V n
VERB
V n *with* n
V n *among* pl-n
V n
Also V
VERB
V n *with* n
V n
N-COUNT: usu sing, oft N *of/in* n
N-COUNT: usu sing with poss, N *of* n

♦ **share in** If you **share in** something such as a success or a responsibility, you are one of a number of people who achieve or accept it. ❑ *The company is offering you the chance to share in its success.*

PHRASAL VERB
V P n

♦ **share out** If you **share out** an amount of something, you give each person in a group an equal or fair part of it. ❑ *I drain the pasta, then I share it out between two plates... The company will share out $1.3 billion among 500,000 policyholders.* → See also **share-out**.

PHRASAL VERB
V n P
V P n (not pron)

**share capi|tal** A company's **share capital** is the money that shareholders invest in order to start or expand the business. [BUSINESS] ❑ *The bank has a share capital of almost 100 million dollars.*

N-UNCOUNT

**share|crop|per** /ʃeə^r^krɒpə^r^/ **(sharecroppers)** N-COUNT A **sharecropper** is a farmer who pays the rent for his land with some of the crops they produce.

**share|holder** /ʃeə^r^hoʊldə^r^/ **(shareholders)** ◆◇◇ N-COUNT A **shareholder** is a person who owns shares in a company. [BUSINESS] ❑ *...a shareholders' meeting.*

**share|holding** /ʃeə^r^hoʊldɪŋ/ **(shareholdings)** N-COUNT If you have a **shareholding** in a company, you own some of its shares. [BUSINESS]

**share in|dex** **(share indices** or **share indexes)** N-COUNT A **share index** is a number that indicates the state of a stock market. It is based on the combined share prices of a set of companies. [BUSINESS] ❑ *The FT 30 share index was up 16.4 points to 1,599.6.*

**share is|sue** **(share issues)** N-COUNT When there is a **share issue**, shares in a company are made available for people to buy. [BUSINESS]

**share op|tion** **(share options)** N-COUNT A **share option** is an opportunity for the employees of a company to buy shares at a special price. [BRIT, BUSINESS] ❑ *Only a handful of firms offer share option schemes to all their employees.*

> in AM use **stock option**

**share-out** **(share-outs)** N-COUNT: usu sing If there is a **share-out of** something, several people are given equal or fair parts of it. ❑ *...the share-out of seats in the transitional government.*

**share shop** **(share shops)** N-COUNT A **share shop** is a shop or Internet website where members of the public can buy shares in companies. [BUSINESS]

**share|ware** /ʃeə^r^weə^r^/ N-UNCOUNT: oft N n **Shareware** is computer software that you can try before deciding whether or not to buy the legal right to use it. [COMPUTING] ❑ *...a shareware program.*

**shark** /ʃɑː^r^k/ **(sharks)**

> The form **shark** can also be used as the plural form for meaning 1.

1 N-VAR A **shark** is a very large fish. Some sharks have very sharp teeth and may attack people. 2 N-COUNT disapproval If you refer to a person as a **shark**, you disapprove of them because they trick people out of their money by giving bad advice about buying, selling, or investments. [INFORMAL] ❑ *Beware the sharks when you are making up your mind how to invest.* → See also **loan shark**.

**sharp** /ʃɑː^r^p/ **(sharps, sharper, sharpest)** ◆◆◇ 1 ADJ ≠ blunt A **sharp** point or edge is very thin and can cut through things very easily. A **sharp** knife, tool, or other object has a point or edge of this kind. ❑ *The other end of the twig is sharpened into a sharp point to use as a toothpick... Using a sharp knife, cut away the pith and peel from both fruits.* 2 ADJ You can describe a shape or an object as **sharp** if part of it or one end of it comes to a point or forms an angle. ❑ *His nose was thin and sharp.* 3 ADJ = tight A **sharp** bend or turn is one that changes direction suddenly. ❑ *I was approaching a fairly sharp bend that swept downhill to the left.* ♦ ADV: ADV adv **Sharp** is also an adverb. ❑ *Do not cross the bridge but turn sharp left to go down on to the towpath.* ♦ ADV: ADV after v **sharp|ly** *Room number nine was at the far end of the corridor where it turned sharply to the right.* 4 ADJ approval If you describe someone as **sharp**, you are praising them because they are quick to notice, hear, understand, or react to things. ❑ *He is very sharp, a quick thinker and swift with repartee.* 5 ADJ If someone says something in a **sharp** way, they say it suddenly and rather firmly or angrily, for example because they are warning or criticizing you. ❑ *That ruling had drawn sharp criticism from civil rights groups.* ♦ ADV: ADV with v, ADV adj **sharp|ly** *'You've known,' she said sharply, 'and you didn't tell me?'* 6 ADJ A **sharp** change, movement, or feeling occurs suddenly, and is great in amount, force, or degree. ❑ *There's been a sharp rise in the rate of inflation... He felt a sharp pain in the abductor muscle in his right thigh.* ♦ ADV: ADV with v, ADV adj **sharp|ly** *Unemployment among the over forties has risen sharply in recent years.* 7 ADJ: usu ADJ n A **sharp** difference, image, or sound is very easy to see, hear, or distinguish. ❑ *Many people make a sharp distinction between humans and other animals... We heard a voice sing out in a clear, sharp tone.* ♦ ADV: ADV with v, also ADV adj **sharp|ly** *Opinions on this are sharply divided.* 8 ADJ A **sharp** taste or smell is rather strong or bitter, but is often also clear and fresh. ❑ *...a colourless, almost odourless liquid with a sharp, sweetish taste.* 9 ADV: n ADV = precisely **Sharp** is used after stating a particular time to show that something happens at exactly the time stated. ❑ *She planned to unlock the store at 8.00 sharp this morning.* 10 N-COUNT: usu n N ≠ flat **Sharp** is used after a letter representing a musical note to show that the note should be played or sung half a tone higher. **Sharp** is often represented by the symbol ♯. ❑ *A solitary viola plucks a lonely, soft F sharp.* 11 → See also **razor-sharp**.

**sharp|en** /ʃɑː^r^pən/ **(sharpens, sharpening, sharpened)** 1 VERB If your senses, understanding, or skills **sharpen** or **are sharpened**, you become better at noticing things, thinking, or doing something. ❑ *Her gaze sharpened, as if she had seen something unusual... You can sharpen your skills with rehearsal.* V / V n 2 VERB If you **sharpen** an object, you make its edge very thin or you make its end pointed. ❑ *He started to sharpen his knife. ...sharpened pencils.* V n / V-ed 3 VERB If disagreements or differences between people **sharpen**, or if they **are sharpened**, they become bigger or more important. ❑ *With urbanisation the antagonism between rich and poor sharpened... The case of Harris has sharpened the debate over capital punishment.* V / V n

**sharp|en|er** /ʃɑː^r^pnə^r^/ **(sharpeners)** N-COUNT: usu n N A **sharpener** is a tool or machine used for sharpening pencils or knives. ❑ *...a pencil sharpener.*

**sharp-eyed** ADJ: usu ADJ n A **sharp-eyed** person is good at noticing and observing things. ❑ *A sharp-eyed shop assistant spotted the fake.*

**sharp|ish** /ʃɑː^r^pɪʃ/ ADV: ADV after v If you do something **sharpish**, you do it quickly, without any delay. [BRIT, INFORMAL] ❑ *She was asked to leave, sharpish.*

**sharp prac|tice** N-UNCOUNT disapproval You can use **sharp practice** to refer to an action or a way of behaving, especially in business or professional matters, that you think is clever but dishonest. ❑ *He accused some solicitors of sharp practice.*

**sharp|shooter** /ʃɑː^r^pʃuːtə^r^/ **(sharpshooters)** N-COUNT = marksman A **sharpshooter** is a person who can fire a gun very accurately. [AM]

**sharp tongue** **(sharp tongues)** N-COUNT disapproval If you say that someone has a **sharp tongue**, you are critical of the fact that they say things which are unkind though often clever. ❑ *Despite her sharp tongue, she inspires loyalty from her friends.*

**sharp-tongued** ADJ: usu ADJ n disapproval If you describe someone as **sharp-tongued**, you being critical of them for speaking in a way which is unkind though often clever. ❑ *Julia was a tough, sharp-tongued woman.*

**shat** /ʃæt/ **Shat** is the past tense and past participle of **shit**.

**shat|ter** /ʃætə^r^/ **(shatters, shattering, shattered)** 1 VERB If something **shatters** or **is shattered**, it breaks into a lot of small pieces. ❑ *...safety glass that won't shatter if it's broken... The car shattered into a thousand burning pieces in a 200mph crash... One bullet shattered his skull.* V / V into n / V n ♦ N-UNCOUNT **shat|ter|ing** *...the shattering of glass.* 2 VERB If something **shatters** your dreams, hopes, or beliefs, it completely destroys them. ❑ *A failure would shatter the hopes of many people... Something like that really shatters your confidence.* V n / V n 3 VERB If someone **is shattered** by an event, it shocks and upsets them very much. ❑ *He had been shattered by his son's death. ...the tragedy which had shattered his life.* be V-ed / V n 4 → See also **shattered**, **shattering**.

**shat|tered** /ʃætə^r^d/ 1 ADJ: usu v-link ADJ = devastated If you are **shattered** by something, you are extremely shocked and upset about it. ❑ *It is desperately sad news and I am absolutely shattered to hear it.* 2 ADJ: usu v-link ADJ = exhausted If you say you are **shattered**, you mean you are extremely tired and have no energy left. [BRIT, INFORMAL] ❑ *He was shattered and too tired to concentrate on schoolwork.*

**shat|ter|ing** /ʃætərɪŋ/ 1 Something that is **shattering** shocks and upsets you very much. ❑ *The experience of their daughter's death had been absolutely shattering.* 2 → See also **shatter**, **earth-shattering**. ADJ = devastating

**shave** /ʃeɪv/ **(shaves, shaving, shaved)**
1 When a man **shaves**, he removes the hair from his face using a razor or shaver so that his face is smooth. ❑ *He took a bath and shaved before dinner... He had shaved his face until it was smooth... It's a pity you shaved your moustache off.* ♦ **Shave** is also a noun. ❑ *He never seemed to need a shave.* ♦ **shav|ing** *...a range of shaving products.* VERB; V; V n; V n with *off*; N-COUNT; N-UNCOUNT
2 If someone **shaves** a part of their body, they remove the hair from it so that it is smooth. ❑ *Many women shave their legs... If you have long curly hair, don't shave it off.* VERB; V n; V n with *off*
3 If you **shave** someone, you remove the hair from their face or another part of their body so that it is smooth. ❑ *The doctors shaved his head... She had to call a barber to shave him.* VERB; V n; V n
4 If you **shave off** part of a piece of wood or other material, you cut very thin pieces from it. ❑ *I set the log on the ground and shaved off the bark... She was shaving thin slices off a courgette.* VERB; V n with *off*; V n *off* n
5 If you **shave** a small amount **off** something such as a record, cost, or price, you reduce it by that amount. ❑ *She's already shaved four seconds off the national record for the mile... Supermarket chains have shaved prices.* VERB; V n *off/from* n; V n
6 → See also **shaving**.
7 If you describe a situation as **a close shave**, you mean that there was nearly an accident or a disaster but it was avoided. ❑ *I can't quite believe the close shaves I've had just recently.* PHRASE: N inflects

**shav|en** /ʃeɪvᵊn/ If a part of someone's body is **shaven**, it has been shaved. ❑ *...a small boy with a shaven head.* → See also **clean-shaven**. ADJ

**shav|er** /ʃeɪvəʳ/ **(shavers)** A **shaver** is an electric device, used for shaving hair from the face and body. ❑ *...men's electric shavers.* N-COUNT: oft adj N

**shav|ing** /ʃeɪvɪŋ/ **(shavings)** **Shavings** are small very thin pieces of wood or other material which have been cut from a larger piece. ❑ *The floor was covered with shavings from his wood carvings. ...metal shavings.* → See also **shave**. N-COUNT: usu pl

**shav|ing cream** **(shaving creams)** also **shaving foam.** **Shaving cream** is a soft soapy substance which men put on their face before they shave. ❑ *...a tube of shaving cream.* N-MASS

**shawl** /ʃɔːl/ **(shawls)** A **shawl** is a large piece of woollen cloth which a woman wears over her shoulders or head, or which is wrapped around a baby to keep it warm. N-COUNT

**she** /ʃi, STRONG ʃiː/ ◆◆◆

> **She** is a third person singular pronoun. **She** is used as the subject of a verb.

1 You use **she** to refer to a woman, girl, or female animal who has already been mentioned or whose identity is clear. ❑ *When Ann arrived home that night, she found Brian in the house watching TV... She was seventeen and she had no education or employment.* PRON
2 Some writers may use **she** to refer to a person who is not identified as either male or female. They do this because they wish to avoid using the pronoun 'he' all the time. Some people dislike this use and prefer to use 'he or she' or 'they'. ❑ *The student may show signs of feeling the strain of responsibility and she may give up.* PRON
3 **She** is sometimes used to refer to a country or nation. ❑ *Britain needs new leadership if she is to help shape Europe's future.* PRON
4 Some people use **she** to refer to a car or a machine. People who sail often use **she** to refer to a ship or boat. ❑ *Hundreds of small boats clustered round the yacht as she sailed into Southampton docks.* PRON

**s/he** Some writers use **s/he** instead of either 'he' or 'she' when they are referring to someone who might exist but who has not been identified. By using **s/he**, the writer does not need to say whether the person is male or female. ❑ *Talk to your doctor and see if s/he knows of any local groups.* PRON = he or she

**sheaf** /ʃiːf/ **(sheaves)** 1 A **sheaf of** papers is a number of them held or fastened together. ❑ *He took out a sheaf of papers and leafed through them.* N-COUNT: usu N *of* n
2 A **sheaf of** corn or wheat is a number of corn or wheat plants that have been cut down and tied together. N-COUNT

**shear** /ʃɪəʳ/ **(shears, shearing, sheared, shorn)**
1 To **shear** a sheep means to cut its wool off. ❑ *In the Hebrides they shear their sheep later than anywhere else.* ♦ **shear|ing** *...a display of sheep shearing.* VERB; V n; N-UNCOUNT
2 A pair of **shears** is a garden tool like a very large pair of scissors. Shears are used especially for cutting hedges. ❑ *Trim the shrubs with shears.* N-PLURAL: also *a pair of* N

**sheath** /ʃiːθ/ **(sheaths)** 1 A **sheath** is a covering for the blade of a knife. N-COUNT 2 A **sheath** is a rubber covering for a man's penis and is used during sex as a contraceptive or as a protection against disease. [BRIT] N-COUNT = condom

**sheathe** /ʃiːð/ **(sheathes, sheathing, sheathed)**
1 If something **is sheathed in** a material or other covering, it is closely covered with it. [LITERARY] ❑ *The television was sheathed in a snug coverlet. ...her long legs, sheathed in sheer black tights.* VERB: usu passive; *be* V-ed *in* n; V-ed
2 When someone **sheathes** a knife, they put it in its sheath. [LITERARY] ❑ *He sheathed the knife and strapped it to his shin.* VERB; V n

**sheaves** /ʃiːvz/ **Sheaves** is the plural of **sheaf**.

**she|bang** /ʃɪbæŋ/ **The whole shebang** is the whole situation or business that you are describing. [INFORMAL] PHRASE

**shed** /ʃed/ **(sheds, shedding)** ◆◇◇

> The form **shed** is used in the present tense and in the past tense and past participle of the verb.

1 A **shed** is a small building that is used for storing things such as garden tools. ❑ *...a garden shed.* N-COUNT
2 A **shed** is a large shelter or building, for example at a railway station, port, or factory. ❑ *...disused railway sheds.* N-COUNT: usu n N
3 When a tree **sheds** its leaves, its leaves fall off in the autumn. When an animal **sheds** hair or skin, some of its hair or skin drops off. ❑ *Some of the trees were already beginning to shed their leaves.* VERB; V n
4 To **shed** something means to get rid of it. [FORMAL] ❑ *The firm is to shed 700 jobs.* VERB; V n
5 If a lorry **sheds** its load, the goods that it is carrying accidentally fall onto the road. [mainly BRIT] ❑ *A lorry piled with scrap metal had shed its load.* VERB; V n
6 If you **shed** tears, you cry. ❑ *They will shed a few tears at their daughter's wedding.* VERB; V n
7 To **shed** blood means to kill people in a violent way. If someone **sheds** their blood, they are killed in a violent way, usually when they are fighting in a war. [FORMAL] ❑ *Gunmen in Ulster shed the first blood of the new year.* VERB; V n
8 to **shed light on** something → see **light**.

**she'd** /ʃiːd, ʃɪd/ 1 **She'd** is the usual spoken form of 'she had', especially when 'had' is an auxiliary verb. ❑ *She'd rung up to discuss the divorce.* 2 **She'd** is a spoken form of 'she would'. ❑ *She'd do anything for a bit of money.*

**sheen** /ʃiːn/ If something has a **sheen**, it has a smooth and gentle brightness on its surface. ❑ *The carpet had a silvery sheen to it.* N-SING: oft adj N

**sheep** /ʃiːp/ **(sheep)** 1 A **sheep** is a farm animal which is covered with thick curly hair called wool. Sheep are kept for their wool or for their meat. ❑ *...grassland on which a flock of sheep were grazing.* N-COUNT
2 If you say that a group of people are like **sheep**, you disapprove of them because if one person does something, all the others copy that person. N-PLURAL: usu *like* N [disapproval]
3 → See also **black sheep**.

**sheep|dog** /ʃiːpdɒg/ **(sheepdogs)** A **sheepdog** is a breed of dog. Some sheepdogs are used for controlling sheep. N-COUNT

**sheep|ish** /ʃiːpɪʃ/ If you look **sheepish**, you look slightly embarrassed because you feel foolish or you have done something silly. ❑ *The couple* ADJ *leapt apart when she walked in on them and later came down stairs looking sheepish.*

**sheep|skin** /ʃiːpskɪn/ **(sheepskins)** **Sheepskin** is the skin of a sheep with the wool still attached to it, used especially for making coats and rugs. ❑ *...a sheepskin coat.* N-VAR: oft N n

**sheer** /ʃɪəʳ/ **(sheerer, sheerest)** 1 You can use **sheer** to emphasize that a state or situation is complete and does not involve or is not mixed with anything else. ❑ *His music is sheer delight... Sheer chance quite often plays an important part in sparking off an idea.* ADJ: ADJ n emphasis = pure 2 A **sheer** cliff or drop is extremely steep or completely vertical. ❑ *There was a sheer drop just outside my window.* ADJ: usu ADJ n 3 **Sheer** material is very thin, light, and delicate. ❑ *...sheer black tights.* ADJ

**sheet** /ʃiːt/ **(sheets)** ◆◇◇ 1 A **sheet** is a large rectangular piece of cotton or other cloth that you sleep on or cover yourself with in a bed. ❑ *Once a week, a maid changes the sheets.* N-COUNT 2 A **sheet of** paper is a rectangular piece of paper. ❑ *...a sheet of newspaper... I was able to fit it all on one sheet.* N-COUNT 3 You can use **sheet** to refer to a piece of paper which gives information about something. ❑ *...information sheets on each country in the world.* N-COUNT: usu n N 4 A **sheet of** glass, metal, or wood is a large, flat, thin piece of it. ❑ *...a cracked sheet of glass... Overhead cranes were lifting giant sheets of steel.* N-COUNT: usu N *of* n 5 A **sheet of** something is a thin wide layer of it over the surface of something else. ❑ *...a sheet of ice. ...a blue-grey sheet of dust.* N-COUNT: usu N *of* n 6 → See also **balance sheet, broadsheet, dust sheet, fact sheet, groundsheet, news-sheet, scoresheet, spreadsheet, worksheet. as white as a sheet** → see **white.**

**sheet|ing** /ʃiːtɪŋ/ **Sheeting** is metal, plastic, or other material that is made in the form of sheets. ❑ *They put plastic sheeting on the insides of our windows.* N-UNCOUNT: oft n N

**sheet met|al** **Sheet metal** is metal which has been made into thin sheets. N-UNCOUNT

**sheet mu|sic** **Sheet music** is music that is printed on sheets of paper without a hard cover. ❑ *...a copy of the sheet music to 'Happy Days'.* N-UNCOUNT

**sheikh** /ʃeɪk, AM ʃiːk/ **(sheikhs)** A **sheikh** is a male Arab chief or ruler. ❑ *...Sheikh Khalifa. ...the sheik's role in global oil affairs.* N-TITLE; N-COUNT

**sheikh|dom** /ʃeɪkdəm, AM ʃiːk-/ **(sheikhdoms)** also **sheikdom.** A **sheikhdom** is a country or region that is ruled by a sheikh. N-COUNT

**shelf** /ʃelf/ **(shelves)** 1 A **shelf** is a flat piece of wood, metal, or glass which is attached to a wall or to the sides of a cupboard. Shelves are used for keeping things on. ❑ *He took a book from the shelf. ...the middle shelf of the oven.* N-COUNT 2 A **shelf** is a section of rock on a cliff or mountain or underwater that sticks out like a shelf. ❑ *The house stands on a shelf of rock among pines.* → See also **continental shelf.** N-COUNT 3 If you buy something **off the shelf**, you buy something that is not specially made for you. [BRIT] ❑ *...off-the-shelf software.* PHRASE: PHR after v, PHR n ≠ tailor-made

**shelf life** **(shelf lives)** The **shelf life** of a product, especially food, is the length of time that it can be kept in a shop or at home before it becomes too old to sell or use. ❑ *Mature flour has a longer shelf life.* N-COUNT: usu sing

**shell** /ʃel/ **(shells, shelling, shelled)** ◆◇◇ 1 The **shell** of a nut or egg is the hard covering which surrounds it. ❑ *They cracked the nuts and removed their shells.* N-COUNT ♦ **Shell** is the substance that a shell is made of. ❑ *...beads made from ostrich egg shell.* N-UNCOUNT 2 The **shell** of an animal such as a tortoise, snail, or crab is the hard protective covering that it has around its body or on its back. N-COUNT 3 **Shells** are hard objects found on beaches. They are usually pink, white, or brown and are the coverings which used to surround small sea creatures. ❑ *I collect shells and interesting seaside items. ...sea shells.* N-COUNT 4 If you **shell** nuts, peas, prawns, or other food, you remove their natural outer covering. ❑ *She shelled and ate a few pistachio nuts. ...shelled prawns.* VERB V n V-ed 5 If someone comes out of their **shell**, they become more friendly and interested in other people and less quiet, shy, and reserved. ❑ *Her normally shy son had come out of his shell.* N-COUNT: usu poss N 6 The **shell** of a building, boat, car, or other structure is the outside frame of it. ❑ *...the shells of burned buildings.* N-COUNT: usu with supp 7 A **shell** is a weapon consisting of a metal container filled with explosives that can be fired from a large gun over long distances. N-COUNT 8 To **shell** a place means to fire explosive shells at it. ❑ *The rebels shelled the densely-populated suburbs near the port.* VERB V n ♦ **shell|ing** **(shellings)** *Out on the streets, the shelling continued.* N-VAR

♦ **shell out** If you **shell out for** something, you spend a lot of money on it. [INFORMAL] ❑ *You won't have to shell out a fortune for it. ...insurance which saves you from having to shell out for repairs.* PHRASAL VERB = fork out V P n *for/on* n V P *for/on* n

**she'll** /ʃiːl, ʃɪl/ **She'll** is the usual spoken form of 'she will'. ❑ *Sharon was a wonderful lady and I know she'll be greatly missed.*

**shel|lac** /ʃəlæk/ **Shellac** is a kind of natural varnish which you paint on to wood to give it a shiny surface. N-UNCOUNT

**shell com|pa|ny** **(shell companies)** A **shell company** is a company that another company takes over in order to use its name to gain an advantage. [BUSINESS] N-COUNT

**shell|fire** /ʃelfaɪəʳ/ **Shellfire** is the firing of large military guns. ❑ *The radio said other parts of the capital also came under shellfire.* N-UNCOUNT

**shell|fish** /ʃelfɪʃ/ **(shellfish)** **Shellfish** are small creatures that live in the sea and have a shell. ❑ *Fish and shellfish are the specialities.* N-VAR: usu pl

**shell pro|gram** **(shell programs)** A **shell program** is a basic computer program that provides a framework within which the user can develop the program to suit their own needs. [COMPUTING] N-COUNT

**shell shock** also **shell-shock.** **Shell shock** is the confused or nervous mental condition of people who have been under fire in a war. ❑ *The men were suffering from shell shock.* N-UNCOUNT

**shell-shocked** also **shell shocked.** 1 If you say that someone is **shell-shocked**, you mean that they are very shocked, usually because something bad has happened. [INFORMAL] ❑ *We were shell-shocked when Chelsea took the lead. ...shell-shocked investors.* ADJ = stunned 2 If someone is **shell-shocked**, they have a confused or nervous mental condition as a result of a shocking experience such as being in a war or an accident. ❑ *...a shell-shocked war veteran.* ADJ

**shell suit** **(shell suits)** also **shell-suit.** A **shell suit** is a casual suit which is made of thin nylon. ❑ *...someone in a shell suit from Stirchley.* N-COUNT

**shel|ter** /ʃeltəʳ/ **(shelters, sheltering, sheltered)** ◆◇◇ 1 A **shelter** is a small building or covered place which is made to protect people from bad weather or danger. ❑ *The city's bomb shelters were being prepared for possible air raids. ...a bus shelter.* N-COUNT 2 If a place provides **shelter**, it provides you with a place to stay or live, especially when you need protection from bad weather or danger. ❑ *The number of families seeking shelter rose by 17 percent. ...the hut where they were given food and shelter.* N-UNCOUNT 3 A **shelter** is a building where homeless people can sleep and get food. ❑ *...a shelter for homeless women.* N-COUNT 4 If you **shelter** in a place, you stay there and are protected from bad weather or danger. ❑ *...a man sheltering in a doorway.* VERB V prep/adv 5 If a place or thing **is sheltered** by something, it is protected by that thing from wind and rain. ❑ *...a wooden house, sheltered by a low pointed roof.* VERB: usu passive V-ed 6 If you **shelter** someone, usually someone who is being hunted by police or other people, you provide them with a place to stay or live. ❑ *A neighbor sheltered the boy for seven days.* VERB V n 7 → See also **sheltered.**

**shel|tered** /ʃeltəʳd/ 1 A **sheltered** place is protected from wind and rain. ❑ *...a shallow-sloping beach next to a sheltered bay.* ADJ 2 If you say ADJ:

that someone has led a **sheltered** life, you mean that they have been protected from difficult or unpleasant experiences. ❑ *Perhaps I've just led a really sheltered life.* usu ADJ n 3 **Sheltered** accommodation or work is designed for old or disabled people. It allows them to be independent but also allows them to get help when they need it. ❑ *For the last few years I have been living in sheltered accommodation.* ADJ: ADJ n 4 → See also **shelter**.

**shelve** /ʃelv/ **(shelves, shelving, shelved)** 1 If someone **shelves** a plan or project, they decide not to continue with it, either for a while or permanently. ❑ *Atlanta has shelved plans to include golf in the 1996 Games... Sadly, the project has now been shelved.* VERB V n *be* V-ed 2 If an area of ground next to or under the sea **shelves**, it slopes downwards. ❑ *The shoreline shelves away steeply. ...a gently shelving beach.* VERB V adv/prep V-ing 3 **Shelves** is the plural of **shelf**.

**shelv|ing** /ʃelvɪŋ/ **Shelving** is a set of shelves, or material which is used for making shelves. ❑ *...the shelving on the long, windowless wall.* N-UNCOUNT

**she|nani|gans** /ʃɪnænɪgənz/ You can use **shenanigans** to refer to rather dishonest or immoral behaviour, especially when you think it is amusing or interesting. [INFORMAL] ❑ *...the private shenanigans of public figures.* N-PLURAL

**shep|herd** /ʃepəʳd/ **(shepherds, shepherding, shepherded)** 1 A **shepherd** is a person, especially a man, whose job is to look after sheep. N-COUNT 2 If you **are shepherded** somewhere, someone takes you there to make sure that you arrive at the right place safely. ❑ *She was shepherded by her guards up the rear ramp of the aircraft.* VERB: usu passive *be* V-ed prep/adv

**shep|herd|ess** /ʃepəʳdes/ **(shepherdesses)** A **shepherdess** is a woman whose job is to look after sheep. N-COUNT

**shep|herd's pie** **(shepherd's pies)** **Shepherd's pie** is a dish consisting of minced meat, usually lamb, covered with a layer of mashed potato. [BRIT] N-VAR

**sher|bet** /ʃɜːʳbət/ **(sherbets)** 1 **Sherbet** is a sweet dry powder that tastes fizzy and is eaten as a sweet. [BRIT] ❑ *...sherbet dips.* N-UNCOUNT: oft N n 2 **Sherbet** is like ice cream but made with fruit juice, sugar, and water. [AM] ❑ *...lemon sherbet.* N-VAR

✔ in BRIT, use **sorbet**

**sher|iff** /ʃerɪf/ **(sheriffs)** 1 In the United States, a **sheriff** is a person who is elected to make sure that the law is obeyed in a particular county. ❑ *...the local sheriff.* N-COUNT; N-TITLE 2 In Scotland, a **sheriff** is a legal officer whose chief duty is to act as judge in a Sheriff Court. These courts deal with all but the most serious crimes and with most civil actions. ❑ *...the presiding judge, Sheriff John Mowatt.* N-COUNT; N-TITLE 3 In England and Wales, the **Sheriff of** a city or county is a person who is elected to appointed to carry out mainly ceremonial duties. ❑ *...the Sheriff of Oxford.* N-COUNT: usu N *of* n

**sher|ry** /ʃeri/ **(sherries)** **Sherry** is a type of strong wine that is made in south-western Spain. It is usually drunk before a meal. ❑ *I poured us a glass of sherry. ...some of the world's finest sherries.* N-MASS ♦ A glass of sherry can be referred to as a **sherry**. ❑ *I'll have a sherry please.* N-COUNT

**she's** /ʃiːz, ʃɪz/ 1 **She's** is the usual spoken form of 'she is'. ❑ *She's an exceptionally good cook... She's having a baby in October.* 2 **She's** is a spoken form of 'she has', especially when 'has' is an auxiliary verb. ❑ *She's been married for seven years and has two daughters.*

**shh** /ʃ/ → see **sh**.

**shi|at|su** /ʃiːætsuː/ **Shiatsu** is a form of massage that is used to cure illness and reduce pain. N-UNCOUNT

**shib|bo|leth** /ʃɪbəleθ/ **(shibboleths)** If you describe an idea or belief as a **shibboleth**, you mean that it is thought important by a group of people but may be old-fashioned or wrong. [FORMAL] ❑ *It is time to go beyond the shibboleth that conventional forces cannot deter.* N-COUNT

**shield** /ʃiːld/ **(shields, shielding, shielded)** 1 Something or someone which is a **shield** against a particular danger or risk provides protection from it. ❑ *He used his left hand as a shield against the reflecting sunlight.* N-COUNT: usu sing 2 If something or someone **shields** you **from** a danger or risk, they protect you from it. ❑ *He shielded his head from the sun with an old sack.* VERB = protect V n *from* n 3 If you **shield** your eyes, you put your hand above your eyes to protect them from direct sunlight. ❑ *He squinted and shielded his eyes.* VERB = shade V n 4 A **shield** is a large piece of metal or leather which soldiers used to carry to protect their bodies while they were fighting. N-COUNT 5 A **shield** is a sports prize or badge that is shaped like a shield. N-COUNT

**shift** /ʃɪft/ **(shifts, shifting, shifted)** ◆◇◇ 1 If you **shift** something or if it **shifts**, it moves slightly. ❑ *He stopped, shifting his cane to his left hand... He shifted from foot to foot... The entire pile shifted and slid, thumping onto the floor. ...the squeak of his boots in the snow as he shifted his weight.* VERB V n prep/adv V prep/adv V V n 2 If someone's opinion, a situation, or a policy **shifts** or **is shifted**, it changes slightly. ❑ *Attitudes to mental illness have shifted in recent years... The emphasis should be shifted more towards Parliament.* VERB V *be* V-ed prep/adv ♦ **Shift** is also a noun. ❑ *...a shift in government policy.* N-COUNT: usu N prep 3 If someone **shifts** the responsibility or blame for something onto you, they unfairly make you responsible or make people blame you for it, instead of them. ❑ *It was a vain attempt to shift the responsibility for the murder to somebody else.* VERB [disapproval] V n prep 4 If a shop or company **shifts** goods, they sell goods that are difficult to sell. [BRIT] ❑ *Some suppliers were selling at a loss to shift stock.* VERB 5 If you **shift** gears in a car, you put the car into a different gear. [AM] VERB

✔ in BRIT, use **change**

6 If a group of factory workers, nurses, or other people work **shifts**, they work for a set period before being replaced by another group, so that there is always a group working. Each of these set periods is called a **shift**. You can also use **shift** to refer to a group of workers who work together on a particular shift. ❑ *His father worked shifts in a steel mill.* N-COUNT: oft n N 7 → See also **shifting**.

♦ **shift down** When you **shift down**, you move the gear lever in the vehicle you are driving in order to use a higher gear. [AM] PHRASAL VERB

✔ in BRIT, use **change down**

♦ **shift up** When you **shift up**, you move the gear lever in the vehicle you are driving in order to use a higher gear. [AM] PHRASAL VERB

✔ in BRIT, use **change up**

**shift|ing** /ʃɪftɪŋ/ **Shifting** is used to describe something which is made up of parts that are continuously moving and changing position in relation to other parts. ❑ *The Croatian town of Ilok is a classic case of shifting populations.* → See also **shift**. ADJ: ADJ n

**shift|less** /ʃɪftləs/ If you describe someone as **shiftless**, you mean that they are lazy and have no desire to achieve anything. ❑ *...a shiftless husband.* ADJ [disapproval]

**shifty** /ʃɪfti/ Someone who looks **shifty** gives the impression of being dishonest. [INFORMAL] ❑ *He had a shifty face and previous convictions.* ADJ [disapproval]

**shil|ling** /ʃɪlɪŋ/ **(shillings)** A **shilling** was a unit of money used in Britain until 1971 which was the equivalent of 5p. There were twenty shillings in a pound. N-COUNT

**shilly-shally** /ʃɪli ʃæli/ **(shilly-shallies, shilly-shallying, shilly-shallied)** If you say that someone **is shilly-shallying**, you disapprove of the fact that they are hesitating when they should make a decision. [INFORMAL] ❑ *It's time for Brooke to stop shilly-shallying.* VERB: usu cont [disapproval] = dither V

**shim|mer** /ʃɪməʳ/ **(shimmers, shimmering, shimmered)** If something **shimmers**, it shines VERB with a faint, unsteady light or has an unclear, unsteady appearance. ❑ *The lights shimmered on the water.* V ♦ **Shimmer** is also a noun. ❑ *...a shimmer of starlight.* N-SING

**shim|my** /ʃɪmi/ **(shimmies, shimmying, shimmied)** If you **shimmy**, you dance or move in a way that involves shaking your hips and shoulders from side to side. ❑ *Dancers shimmied in the streets of New Orleans.* VERB; V

**shin** /ʃɪn/ **(shins)** Your **shins** are the front parts of your legs between your knees and your ankles. ❑ *She punched him on the nose and kicked him in the shins.* N-COUNT

**shin|dig** /ʃɪndɪg/ **(shindigs)** A **shindig** is a large, noisy, enjoyable party. [INFORMAL] N-COUNT = *knees-up*

**shine** /ʃaɪn/ **(shines, shining, shined, shone)**
1 When the sun or a light **shines**, it gives out bright light. ❑ *It is a mild morning and the sun is shining... A few scattered lights shone on the horizon.* VERB; V; V
2 If you **shine** a torch or other light somewhere, you point it there, so that you can see something when it is dark. ❑ *One of the men shone a torch in his face... The man walked slowly towards her, shining the flashlight.* VERB; V n prep; V n
3 Something that **shines** is very bright and clear because it is reflecting light. ❑ *Her blue eyes shone and caught the light. ...shining aluminum machines.* VERB = *gleam*; V; V-ing
4 Something that has a **shine** is bright and clear because it is reflecting light. ❑ *This gel gives a beautiful shine to the hair.* N-SING = *sheen*
5 If you **shine** a wooden, leather, or metal object, you make it bright by rubbing or polishing it. ❑ *Let him dust and shine the furniture.* VERB = *polish*; V n
6 Someone who **shines** at a skill or activity does it extremely well. ❑ *Did you shine at school?* VERB = *excel*; V
7 ➔ See also **shining**.
8 If you say that someone has **taken a shine to** another person, you mean that he or she liked them very much at their first meeting. [INFORMAL] ❑ *Seems to me you've taken quite a shine to Miss Richmond.* PHRASE: V inflects
9 **rain or shine** ➔ see **rain**.

**shin|gle** /ʃɪŋgəl/ **(shingles)** 1 **Shingle** is a mass of small rough pieces of stone on the shore of a sea or a river. ❑ *...a beach of sand and shingle.* N-UNCOUNT
2 **Shingles** is a disease in which painful red spots spread in bands over a person's body, especially around their waist. N-UNCOUNT

**shin|ing** /ʃaɪnɪŋ/ A **shining** achievement or quality is a very good one which should be greatly admired. ❑ *She is a shining example to us all.* ➔ See also **shine**. ADJ

**Shin|to** /ʃɪntoʊ/ **Shinto** is the traditional religion of Japan. N-UNCOUNT

**shiny** /ʃaɪni/ **(shinier, shiniest)** **Shiny** things are bright and reflect light. ❑ *Her blonde hair was shiny and clean. ...a shiny new sports car.* ADJ

**ship** /ʃɪp/ **(ships, shipping, shipped)** ◆◆◇ 1 A **ship** is a large boat which carries passengers or cargo. ❑ *Within ninety minutes the ship was ready for departure... We went by ship over to America. ...merchant ships.* N-COUNT: also *by* N
2 If people or things **are shipped** somewhere, they are sent there on a ship or by some other means of transport. ❑ *Food is being shipped to drought-stricken Southern Africa.* VERB: usu passive; *be* V-ed prep/adv
3 ➔ See also **shipping**.
♦ **ship out** If someone **ships out**, they leave a place, especially by ship. ❑ *Sailors hung about while they waited to ship out.* PHRASAL VERB; V P

**ship|board** /ʃɪpbɔːʳd/ **Shipboard** means taking place on a ship. ❑ *...a shipboard romance.* ADJ: ADJ n

**ship|builder** /ʃɪpbɪldəʳ/ **(shipbuilders)** A **shipbuilder** is a company or a person that builds ships. N-COUNT

**ship|building** /ʃɪpbɪldɪŋ/ **Shipbuilding** is the industry of building ships. N-UNCOUNT

**ship|load** /ʃɪploʊd/ **(shiploads)** A **shipload of** people or goods is as many people or goods as a ship can carry. ❑ *...a shipload of refugees.* N-COUNT: usu N *of* n

**ship|mate** /ʃɪpmeɪt/ **(shipmates)** Sailors who work together on the same ship are **shipmates**. ❑ *His shipmates stayed at their stations.* N-COUNT: oft poss N

**ship|ment** /ʃɪpmənt/ **(shipments)** 1 A **shipment** is an amount of a particular kind of cargo that is sent to another country on a ship, train, aeroplane, or other vehicle. ❑ *Food shipments could begin in a matter of weeks. ...a shipment of weapons.* N-COUNT: usu N n, N *of* n
2 The **shipment** of a cargo somewhere is the sending of it there by ship, train, aeroplane, or some other vehicle. ❑ *Bananas are packed before being transported to the docks for shipment overseas.* N-UNCOUNT

**ship|owner** /ʃɪpoʊnəʳ/ **(shipowners)** A **shipowner** is someone who owns a ship or ships or who has shares in a shipping company. N-COUNT

**ship|per** /ʃɪpəʳ/ **(shippers)** **Shippers** are people or companies who ship cargo as a business. N-COUNT: usu pl

**ship|ping** /ʃɪpɪŋ/ 1 **Shipping** is the transport of cargo as a business, especially on ships. ❑ *...the international shipping industry... The Greeks are still powerful players in world shipping.* N-UNCOUNT: usu with supp
2 You can refer to the amount of money that you pay to a company to transport cargo as **shipping**. ❑ *It is $39.95 plus $3 shipping.* N-UNCOUNT
3 You can refer to ships as **shipping** when considering them as a group. ❑ *They sent naval forces to protect merchant shipping.* N-UNCOUNT

**ship|shape** /ʃɪpʃeɪp/ If something is **shipshape**, it looks tidy, neat, and in good condition. ❑ *The house only needs an occasional coat of paint to keep it shipshape.* ADJ: usu v-link ADJ

**ship|wreck** /ʃɪprek/ **(shipwrecks, shipwrecked)** 1 If there is a **shipwreck**, a ship is destroyed in an accident at sea. ❑ *He was drowned in a shipwreck off the coast of Spain.* N-VAR
2 A **shipwreck** is a ship which has been destroyed in an accident at sea. N-COUNT = *wreck*
3 If someone **is shipwrecked**, their ship is destroyed in an accident at sea but they survive and manage to reach land. ❑ *He was shipwrecked after visiting the island.* V-PASSIVE; *be* V-ed

**ship|wright** /ʃɪpraɪt/ **(shipwrights)** A **shipwright** is a person who builds or repairs ships as a job. N-COUNT

**ship|yard** /ʃɪpjɑːʳd/ **(shipyards)** A **shipyard** is a place where ships are built and repaired. N-COUNT

**shire** /ʃaɪəʳ/ **(shires)** 1 **The Shires** or **the shire counties** are the counties of England that have a lot of countryside and farms. ❑ *Smart country people are fleeing back to the shires.* N-COUNT: usu *the* N in pl
2 A **shire** or **shire horse** is a large heavy horse used for pulling loads. [BRIT] N-COUNT

**shirk** /ʃɜːʳk/ **(shirks, shirking, shirked)** If someone does not **shirk** their responsibility or duty, they do what they have a responsibility to do. ❑ *We in the Congress can't shirk our responsibility... The Government will not shirk from considering the need for further action.* VERB: usu with neg; V n; V *from* -ing/n; Also V

**shirt** /ʃɜːʳt/ **(shirts)** ◆◇◇ 1 A **shirt** is a piece of clothing that you wear on the upper part of your body. Shirts have a collar, sleeves, and buttons down the front. N-COUNT
2 ➔ See also **dress shirt**, **stuffed shirt**, **sweatshirt**, **T-shirt**.

**-shirted** /-ʃɜːʳtɪd/ **-shirted** is used to form adjectives which indicate what colour or type of shirt someone is wearing. ❑ *...white-shirted men.* COMB in ADJ

**shirt|sleeve** /ʃɜːʳtsliːv/ **(shirtsleeves)** **Shirtsleeves** are the sleeves of a shirt. If a man is **in shirtsleeves** or **in** his **shirtsleeves**, he is wearing a shirt but not a jacket. ❑ *He rolled up his shirtsleeves.* N-COUNT: usu pl

**shirt-tail** **(shirt-tails)** also **shirttail**. **Shirt-tails** are the long parts of a shirt below the waist. ❑ *He wore sandals and old jeans and his shirt-tails weren't tucked in.* N-COUNT

**shirty** /ʃɜːʳti/ If someone gets **shirty**, they behave in a bad-tempered and rude way because they are annoyed about something. [BRIT, INFORMAL] ❑ *He got quite shirty with me.* ADJ: usu v-link ADJ = *stroppy*

**shit** /ʃɪt/ **(shits, shitting, shat)** 1 Some people use **shit** to refer to solid waste matter from the body of a human being or animal. [INFORMAL, RUDE] N-UNCOUNT
2 To **shit** means to get rid of solid waste matter from the body. [INFORMAL, RUDE] VERB: V
3 To have **a shit** means to get rid of solid waste matter N-SING

from the body. [INFORMAL, RUDE] 4 If someone has **the shits**, liquid waste matter keeps coming out of their body because they are ill or afraid. [INFORMAL, RUDE] 5 People sometimes refer to things that they do not like as **shit**. [INFORMAL, RUDE] ❑ *This is a load of shit.* 6 People sometimes insult someone they do not like by referring to them as a **shit**. [INFORMAL, RUDE] 7 **Shit** is used to express anger, impatience, or disgust. [INFORMAL, RUDE]

N-PLURAL: *the* N
N-UNCOUNT disapproval
N-COUNT disapproval
EXCLAM

**PHRASES** 8 To **beat** or **kick the shit out of** someone means to beat or kick them so violently that they are badly injured. [INFORMAL, RUDE] 9 If someone says that **the shit hit the fan**, they mean that there was suddenly a lot of trouble or angry arguments. [INFORMAL, RUDE] 10 If someone says that they do not **give a shit** about something, they mean that they do not care about it at all. [INFORMAL, RUDE]

PHRASE: V inflects emphasis
PHRASE: V inflects
PHRASE: V inflects, usu with brd-neg feelings

**shite** /ʃaɪt/ If someone describes something as **shite**, they do not like it or think that it is very poor quality. [BRIT, INFORMAL, RUDE]
ADJ disapproval

**shit|less** /ʃɪtləs/ If someone says that they are scared **shitless** or bored **shitless**, they are emphasizing that they are extremely scared or bored. [INFORMAL, RUDE]
ADV: adj ADV emphasis

**shit|ty** /ʃɪti/ **(shittier, shittiest)** If someone describes something as **shitty**, they do not like it or think that it is of poor quality. [INFORMAL, RUDE]
ADJ disapproval

**shiv|er** /ʃɪvəʳ/ **(shivers, shivering, shivered)** When you **shiver**, your body shakes slightly because you are cold or frightened. ❑ *He shivered in the cold... I was sitting on the floor shivering with fear.* ♦ **Shiver** is also a noun. ❑ *The emptiness here sent shivers down my spine.*
VERB = shake; V; V *with* n; N-COUNT

**shiv|ery** /ʃɪvəri/ If you are **shivery**, you cannot stop shivering because you feel cold, frightened, or ill. ❑ *She felt shivery and a little sick.*
ADJ

**shoal** /ʃoʊl/ **(shoals)** A **shoal of** fish is a large group of them swimming together. ❑ *Among them swam shoals of fish. ...tuna shoals.*
N-COUNT: oft N *of* n

**shock** /ʃɒk/ **(shocks, shocking, shocked)** 1 If you have a **shock**, something suddenly happens which is unpleasant, upsetting, or very surprising. ❑ *The extent of the violence came as a shock... He has never recovered from the shock of your brother's death.* 2 **Shock** is a person's emotional and physical condition when something very frightening or upsetting has happened to them. ❑ *She's still in a state of shock.* 3 If someone is **in shock**, they are suffering from a serious physical condition in which their blood is not flowing round their body properly, for example because they have had a bad injury. ❑ *They escaped the blaze but were rushed to hospital suffering from shock.* 4 If something **shocks** you, it makes you feel very upset, because it involves death or suffering and because you had not expected it. ❑ *After forty years in the police force nothing much shocks me.* ♦ **shocked** *This was a nasty attack and the woman is still very shocked.* 5 If someone or something **shocks** you, it upsets or offends you because you think it is rude or morally wrong. ❑ *You can't shock me... They were easily shocked in those days... We were always trying to be creative and to shock.* ♦ **shocked** *Don't look so shocked.* 6 A **shock** announcement or event is one which shocks people because it is unexpected. [JOURNALISM] ❑ *...the shock announcement that she is to resign. ...a shock defeat.* 7 A **shock** is the force of something suddenly hitting or pulling something else. ❑ *Steel barriers can bend and absorb the shock.* 8 A **shock** is the same as an **electric shock**. 9 A **shock of** hair is a very thick mass of hair on a person's head. [WRITTEN] ❑ *...a very old priest with a shock of white hair.* 10 → See also **shocking**, **culture shock**, **electric shock**, **shell shock**.
◆◆◇ N-COUNT; N-UNCOUNT; N-UNCOUNT: oft *in* N; VERB; V n; ADJ; VERB; V n; *be* V-ed; V; ADJ; ADJ: ADJ n; N-VAR; N-COUNT; N-COUNT: N *of* n

**shock ab|sorb|er** **(shock absorbers)** also **shock-absorber.** A **shock absorber** is a device fitted near the wheels of a car or other vehicle to reduce the effects of travelling over uneven ground. ❑ *...a pair of rear shock absorbers.*
N-COUNT

**shock|er** /ʃɒkəʳ/ **(shockers)** A **shocker** is something such as a story, a piece of news, or a film that shocks people or that is intended to shock them. [INFORMAL] ❑ *Marsha Hunt's second novel, 'Free', is a shocker.*
N-COUNT

**shock hor|ror** 1 A **shock horror** story is presented in a way that is intended to cause great shock or anger. [INFORMAL] ❑ *The media is full of shock-horror headlines about under-age crime.* 2 You can say **shock horror!** in reaction to something that other people may find shocking or surprising, to indicate that you do not find it shocking or surprising at all. [HUMOROUS, INFORMAL] ❑ *I felt intellectually superior despite – shock horror – my lack of qualifications.*
ADJ: ADJ n = sensational; EXCLAM feelings

**shock|ing** /ʃɒkɪŋ/ 1 You can say that something is **shocking** if you think that it is very bad. [INFORMAL] ❑ *The media coverage was shocking.* ♦ **shock|ing|ly** *His memory was becoming shockingly bad.* 2 You can say that something is **shocking** if you think that it is morally wrong. ❑ *It is shocking that nothing was said.* ♦ **shock|ing|ly** *Shockingly, this dangerous surgery did not end until the 1930s.* 3 → See also **shock**.
ADJ = appalling; ADV: ADV adj/adv; ADJ: oft *it* v-link ADJ that/to-inf; ADV

**shock|ing pink** Something that is **shocking pink** is very bright pink. ❑ *...a shocking-pink T-shirt.*
COLOUR

**shock jock** **(shock jocks)** A **shock jock** is a radio disc jockey who deliberately uses language or expresses opinions that many people find offensive. [INFORMAL]
N-COUNT

**shock tac|tic** **(shock tactics)** **Shock tactics** are a way of trying to influence people's attitudes to a particular matter by shocking them. ❑ *We must use shock tactics if we are to stop Aids becoming another accepted 20th-century disease.*
N-COUNT: usu pl

**shock thera|py** 1 You can refer to the use of extreme policies or actions to solve a particular problem quickly as **shock therapy**. ❑ *...Prague's policy of economic shock therapy.* 2 **Shock therapy** is a way of treating mentally ill patients by passing an electric current through their brain.
N-UNCOUNT = shock treatment; N-UNCOUNT = shock treatment

**shock treat|ment** **(shock treatments)** **Shock treatment** is the same as **shock therapy**.
N-UNCOUNT: also N in pl

**shock troops** **Shock troops** are soldiers who are specially trained to carry out a quick attack.
N-PLURAL

**shock wave** **(shock waves)** also **shockwave.** 1 A **shock wave** is an area of very high pressure moving through the air, earth, or water. It is caused by an explosion or an earthquake, or by an object travelling faster than sound. ❑ *The shock waves yesterday were felt from Las Vegas to San Diego.* 2 A **shock wave** is the effect of something surprising, such as a piece of unpleasant news, that causes strong reactions when it spreads through a place. ❑ *The crime sent shock waves throughout the country.*
N-COUNT; N-COUNT

**shod** /ʃɒd/ 1 You can use **shod** when you are describing the kind of shoes that a person is wearing. [FORMAL] ❑ *He has demonstrated a strong preference for being shod in running shoes.* 2 **Shod** is the past participle of **shoe**.
ADJ: v-link ADJ *in/with* n, adv ADJ

**shod|dy** /ʃɒdi/ **(shoddier, shoddiest)** **Shoddy** work or a **shoddy** product has been done or made carelessly or badly. ❑ *I'm normally quick to complain about shoddy service.* ♦ **shod|di|ly** *These products are shoddily produced.*
ADJ: usu ADJ n; ADV: usu ADV with v

**shoe** /ʃuː/ **(shoes)** 1 **Shoes** are objects which you wear on your feet. They cover most of your foot and you wear them over socks or stockings. ❑ *...a pair of shoes... You don't mind if I take my shoes off, do you?* → See also **snowshoe**, **training shoe**. 2 A **shoe** is the same as a **horseshoe**. 3 When a blacksmith **shoes** a horse, they fix horseshoes onto its feet. ❑ *Blacksmiths spent most of their time repairing tools and shoeing horses.* 4 → See also **shod**.
◆◇◇ N-COUNT; N-COUNT; VERB; V n

**PHRASES** 5 If you **fill** someone's **shoes** or **step into** their **shoes**, you take their place by doing
PHRASE: V inflects

the job they were doing. ❑ *No one has been able to fill his shoes.* [6] If you talk about being **in** someone's **shoes**, you talk about what you would do or how you would feel if you were in their situation. ❑ *I wouldn't want to be in his shoes.* [PHRASE: usu v-link PHR]

**shoe|horn** /ʃuːhɔːʳn/ **(shoehorns, shoehorning, shoehorned)** [1] A **shoehorn** is a piece of metal or plastic with a slight curve that you put in the back of your shoe so that your heel will go into the shoe easily. [N-COUNT] [2] If you **shoehorn** something **into** a tight place, you manage to get it in there even though it is difficult. ❑ *Their cars are shoehorned into tiny spaces... I was shoehorning myself into my skin-tight ball gown.* [VERB] [*be* V-ed *into* n] [V n *into* n]

**shoe|lace** /ʃuːleɪs/ **(shoelaces)** **Shoelaces** are long, narrow pieces of material like pieces of string that you use to fasten your shoes. ❑ *He began to tie his shoelaces.* [N-COUNT: usu pl]

**shoe|maker** /ʃuːmeɪkəʳ/ **(shoemakers)** A **shoemaker** is a person whose job is making shoes and boots. [N-COUNT]

**shoe|string** /ʃuːstrɪŋ/ **(shoestrings)** [1] **Shoestrings** are long, narrow pieces of material like pieces of string that you use to fasten your shoes. [AM] [N-COUNT: usu pl]

✔ in BRIT, use **shoelaces**

[2] A **shoestring** budget is one where you have very little money to spend. ❑ *The British-produced film was made on a shoestring budget.* [ADJ: ADJ n] [3] If you do something or make something **on a shoestring**, you do it using very little money. ❑ *The theatre will be run on a shoestring.* [PHRASE: PHR after v]

**shone** /ʃɒn, AM ʃoʊn/ **Shone** is the past tense and past participle of **shine**.

**shoo** /ʃuː/ **(shoos, shooing, shooed)** [1] If you **shoo** an animal or a person **away**, you make them go away by waving your hands or arms at them. ❑ *You'd better shoo him away... I shooed him out of the room.* [VERB] [V n with adv] [V n prep] [2] You say '**shoo!**' to an animal when you want it to go away. ❑ *Shoo, bird, shoo.* [EXCLAM]

**shoo-in** **(shoo-ins)** A **shoo-in** is a person or thing that seems sure to succeed. [mainly AM, INFORMAL] ❑ *Ms Brown is still no shoo-in for the November election.* [N-COUNT]

**shook** /ʃʊk/ **Shook** is the past tense of **shake**.

**shoot** /ʃuːt/ **(shoots, shooting, shot)** ◆◆◇ [1] If someone **shoots** a person or an animal, they kill them or injure them by firing a bullet or arrow at them. ❑ *The police had orders to shoot anyone who attacked them... The man was shot dead by the police during a raid on his house... Her father shot himself in the head with a shotgun.* [VERB] [V n] [V n with adj] [V n *in* n] [2] To **shoot** means to fire a bullet from a weapon such as a gun. ❑ *He taunted armed officers by pointing to his head, as if inviting them to shoot... The police came around the corner and they started shooting at us... She had never been able to shoot straight.* [VERB] [V] [V *at* n] [V adv/prep] [3] If someone or something **shoots** in a particular direction, they move in that direction quickly and suddenly. ❑ *They had almost reached the boat when a figure shot past them.* [VERB] [V adv/prep] [4] If you **shoot** something somewhere or if it **shoots** somewhere, it moves there quickly and suddenly. ❑ *Masters shot a hand across the table and gripped his wrist... You'd turn on the water, and it would shoot straight up in the air.* [VERB] [V n prep/adv] [V adv/prep] [5] If you **shoot** a look at someone, you look at them quickly and briefly, often in a way that expresses your feelings. ❑ *Mary Ann shot him a rueful look... The man in the black overcoat shot a penetrating look at the other man.* [VERB] [V n n] [V n *at* n] [6] If someone **shoots to** fame, they become famous or successful very quickly. ❑ *Alina Reyes shot to fame a few years ago with her extraordinary first novel.* [VERB] [V *to* n] [7] When people **shoot** a film or **shoot** photographs, they make a film or take photographs using a camera. ❑ *He'd love to shoot his film in Cuba.* [VERB] [V n] ♦ **Shoot** is also a noun. ❑ *...a barn presently being used for a video shoot.* [N-COUNT] [8] **Shoots** are plants that are beginning to grow, or new parts growing from a plant or tree. [N-COUNT: usu pl] [9] In sports such as football or basketball, when someone **shoots**, they try to score by kicking, throwing, or hitting the ball towards the goal. ❑ *Spencer scuttled away from Young to shoot wide when he should have scored.* [VERB] [V adv/prep] [10] → See also **shooting**, **shot**. [11] If you **shoot the breeze** or **shoot the bull with** someone, you talk to them about things which are not very serious or important. [mainly AM, INFORMAL] ❑ *They expected me to sit up and shoot the breeze with them till one or two in the morning... I also met with Pollack again to kind of shoot the bull.* [PHRASE: V inflects, PHR *with* n, pl-n V] [12] to **shoot from the hip** → see **hip**.

♦ **shoot down** [1] If someone **shoots down** an aeroplane, a helicopter, or a missile, they make it fall to the ground by hitting it with a bullet or missile. ❑ *They claimed to have shot down one incoming missile.* [PHRASAL VERB] [V P n (not pron)] [2] If one person **shoots down** another, they shoot them with a gun. ❑ *He was prepared to suppress rebellion by shooting down protesters... They shot him down in cold blood.* [PHRASAL VERB] [V P n (not pron)] [V n P] [3] If you **shoot** someone **down** or **shoot down** their ideas, you say or show that they are completely wrong. ❑ *She was able to shoot the rumour down in flames with ample documentary evidence.* [PHRASAL VERB] [V n P] [Also V P n (not pron)]

♦ **shoot up** [1] If something **shoots up**, it grows or increases very quickly. ❑ *Sales shot up by 9% last month... The fair market value of the property shot up.* [PHRASAL VERB] [V P *by/to* n] [V P] [2] If a drug addict **shoots up**, they inject a quantity of drugs into their body. [INFORMAL] ❑ *Drug addicts shoot up in the back alleys... We shot up heroin in the playground.* [PHRASAL VERB] [V P] [V P n (not pron)]

**shoot-em-up** **(shoot-em-ups)** A **shoot-em-up** is a computer game that involves shooting and killing characters. [INFORMAL] [N-COUNT]

**shoot|er** /ʃuːtəʳ/ **(shooters)** [1] A **shooter** is a person who shoots a gun. ❑ *An eyewitness identified him as the shooter.* [N-COUNT] [2] A **shooter** is a gun. [INFORMAL] [N-COUNT]

**shoot|ing** /ʃuːtɪŋ/ **(shootings)** [1] A **shooting** is an occasion when someone is killed or injured by being shot with a gun. ❑ *A drug-related gang war led to a series of shootings in the city.* [N-COUNT] [2] **Shooting** is hunting animals with a gun as a leisure activity. [BRIT] ❑ *Grouse shooting begins in August.* [N-UNCOUNT]

✔ in AM, use **hunting**

[3] The **shooting** of a film is the act of filming it. ❑ *Ingrid was busy learning her lines for the next day's shooting.* [N-UNCOUNT: usu with supp]

**shoot|ing gal|lery** **(shooting galleries)** A **shooting gallery** is a place where people use rifles to shoot at targets, especially in order to win prizes. [N-COUNT]

**shoot|ing star** **(shooting stars)** A **shooting star** is a piece of rock or metal that burns very brightly when it enters the earth's atmosphere from space, and is seen from earth as a bright star travelling very fast across the sky. [N-COUNT]

**shoot|ing war** **(shooting wars)** When two countries in conflict engage in a **shooting war**, they fight each other with weapons rather than opposing each other by diplomatic or other means. [JOURNALISM] [N-COUNT]

**shoot-out** **(shoot-outs)** [1] A **shoot-out** is a fight in which people shoot at each other with guns. ❑ *Three IRA men were killed in the shoot-out.* [N-COUNT] [2] In games such as football, a **shoot-out** or a **penalty shoot-out** is a way of deciding the result of a game that has ended in a draw. Players from each team try to score a goal in turn until one player fails to score and their team loses the game. ❑ *The Danes won that UEFA tie in a shoot-out.* [N-COUNT]

**shop** /ʃɒp/ **(shops, shopping, shopped)** ◆◆◇ [1] A **shop** is a building or part of a building where things are sold. [mainly BRIT] ❑ *...health food shops. ...a record shop... It's not available in the shops.* [N-COUNT = store]

✔ in AM, usually use **store**

[2] When you **shop**, you go to shops and buy [VERB]

things. ❑ *He always shopped at the Co-op. ...some advice that's worth bearing in mind when shopping for a new carpet. ...customers who shop once a week.* [V prep/adv; V prep/adv; V]
♦ **shop|per** **(shoppers)** *...crowds of Christmas shoppers.* [N-COUNT] 3 You can refer to a place where a particular service is offered as a particular type of **shop**. ❑ *...the barber shop where Rodney sometimes had his hair cut. ...your local video shop.* [N-COUNT: n N] 4 If you **shop** someone, you report them to the police for doing something illegal. [BRIT, INFORMAL] ❑ *His father was so disgusted to discover his son was dealing drugs he shopped him to police... Fraudsters are often shopped by honest friends and neighbours.* [VERB; V n *to* n; *be* V-ed] 5 → See also **shopping**, **chip shop**, **coffee shop**, **corner shop**, **paper shop**, **pawn shop**, **print shop**, **sex shop**, **tea shop**, **talking shop**, **thrift shop**.

PHRASES 6 If something is happening **all over the shop**, it is happening in many different places or throughout a wide area. [BRIT, INFORMAL] ❑ *This gave them the freedom to make trouble all over the shop without fear of retribution.* [PHRASE: PHR after v] 7 If you **set up shop**, you start a business. ❑ *He set up shop as an independent PR consultant.* [PHRASE: V inflects] 8 If you say that people **are talking shop**, you mean that they are talking about their work, and this is boring for other people who do not do the same work. ❑ *If you hang around with colleagues all the time you just end up talking shop.* [PHRASE: V inflects]

♦ **shop around** If you **shop around**, you go to different shops or companies in order to compare the prices and quality of goods or services before you decide to buy them. ❑ *Prices may vary so it's well worth shopping around before you buy... He shopped around for a firm that would be flexible.* [PHRASAL VERB; V P; V P *for* n]

**shopa|hol|ic** /ʃɒpəhɒlɪk/ **(shopaholics)** A **shopaholic** is someone who greatly enjoys going shopping and buying things, or who cannot stop themselves doing this. [INFORMAL] [N-COUNT]

**shop as|sis|tant** **(shop assistants)** A **shop assistant** is a person who works in a shop selling things to customers. [BRIT] [N-COUNT]

✓ in AM, use **sales clerk**

**shop floor** also **shop-floor**, **shopfloor**. The **shop floor** is used to refer to all the ordinary workers in a factory or the area where they work, especially in contrast to the people who are in charge. [BRIT] ❑ *Cost must be controlled, not just on the shop floor but in the boardroom too.* [N-SING: oft N n]

**shop front** **(shop fronts)** also **shopfront**. A **shop front** is the outside part of a shop which faces the street, including the door and windows. [BRIT] [N-COUNT]

✓ in AM, use **storefront**

**shop|keeper** /ʃɒpkiːpəʳ/ **(shopkeepers)** A **shopkeeper** is a person who owns or manages a small shop. [BRIT] [N-COUNT]

✓ in AM, use **storekeeper**, **merchant**

**shop|lift** /ʃɒplɪft/ **(shoplifts, shoplifting, shoplifted)** If someone **shoplifts**, they steal goods from a shop by hiding them in a bag or in their clothes. ❑ *He openly shoplifted from a supermarket... They had shoplifted thousands of dollars' worth of merchandise.* [VERB; V; V n] ♦ **shop|lifter** **(shoplifters)** *...a shoplifter in court for stealing a bottle of perfume.* [N-COUNT]

**shop|lifting** /ʃɒplɪftɪŋ/ **Shoplifting** is stealing from a shop by hiding things in a bag or in your clothes. ❑ *The grocer accused her of shoplifting and demanded to look in her bag.* [N-UNCOUNT]

**shop|ping** /ʃɒpɪŋ/ ◆◇◇ 1 When you do **the shopping**, you go to shops and buy things. ❑ *I'll do the shopping this afternoon.* → See also **window shopping**. [N-UNCOUNT] 2 Your **shopping** is the things that you have bought from shops, especially food. ❑ *We put the shopping away.* [N-UNCOUNT]

**shop|ping cart** **(shopping carts)** A **shopping cart** is the same as a **shopping trolley**. [AM] [N-COUNT]

**shop|ping cen|tre** **(shopping centres)**

✓ in AM, use **shopping center**

A **shopping centre** is a specially built area containing a lot of different shops. ❑ *The new shopping centre was constructed at a cost of 1.1 million.* [N-COUNT]

**shop|ping chan|nel** **(shopping channels)** A **shopping channel** is a television channel that broadcasts programmes showing products that you can phone the channel and buy. [N-COUNT]

**shop|ping list** **(shopping lists)** A **shopping list** is a list of the things that you want to buy when you go shopping, which you write on a piece of paper. [N-COUNT]

**shop|ping mall** **(shopping malls)** A **shopping mall** is a specially built covered area containing shops and restaurants which people can walk between, and where cars are not allowed. [N-COUNT]

**shop|ping trol|ley** **(shopping trolleys)** A **shopping trolley** is a large metal basket on wheels which is provided by shops such as supermarkets for customers to use while they are in the shop. [BRIT] [N-COUNT]

✓ in AM, use **shopping cart**

**shop stew|ard** **(shop stewards)** A **shop steward** is a trade union member who is elected by the other members in a factory or office to speak for them at official meetings. [BRIT] [N-COUNT]

**shore** /ʃɔːʳ/ **(shores, shoring, shored)** ◆◇◇ The **shores** or the **shore** of a sea, lake, or wide river is the land along the edge of it. Someone who is **on shore** is on the land rather than on a ship. ❑ *They walked down to the shore. ...elephants living on the shores of Lake Kariba... I have spent less time on shore than most men.* [N-COUNT: also prep N]

♦ **shore up** If you **shore up** something that is weak or about to fail, you do something in order to strengthen it or support it. ❑ *The democracies of the West may find it hard to shore up their defences.* [PHRASAL VERB; V P n (not pron)]

**shore|line** /ʃɔːʳlaɪn/ **(shorelines)** A **shoreline** is the edge of a sea, lake, or wide river. [N-COUNT]

**shorn** /ʃɔːʳn/ 1 If grass or hair is **shorn**, it has been cut very short. [LITERARY] ❑ *...his shorn hair.* [ADJ] 2 If a person or thing is **shorn of** something that was an important part of them, it has been removed from them. [LITERARY] ❑ *She looks terrible, shorn of all her beauty.* [ADJ: v-link ADJ *of* n] 3 **Shorn** is the past participle of **shear**.

| **short** |
| --- |
| ① ADJECTIVE AND ADVERB USES |
| ② NOUN USES |

① **short** /ʃɔːʳt/ **(shorter, shortest)** ◆◆◆
⇛ Please look at category 23 to see if the expression you are looking for is shown under another headword. 1 If something is **short** or lasts for a **short** time, it does not last very long. ❑ *The announcement was made a short time ago... How could you do it in such a short period of time?... Kemp gave a short laugh... We had a short meeting.* [ADJ ≠long] 2 If you talk about a **short** hour, day, or year, you mean that it seems to have passed very quickly or will seem to pass very quickly. ❑ *For a few short weeks there was peace.* [ADJ: usu ADJ n ≠long] 3 A **short** speech, letter, or book does not have many words or pages in it. ❑ *They were performing a short extract from Shakespeare's Two Gentlemen of Verona.* [ADJ: usu ADJ n ≠long] 4 Someone who is **short** is not as tall as most people are. ❑ *I'm tall and thin and he's short and fat. ...a short, elderly woman with grey hair.* [ADJ ≠tall] 5 Something that is **short** measures only a small amount from one end to the other. ❑ *The city centre and shops are only a short distance away... His black hair was very short.* [ADJ ≠long] 6 If you are **short of** something or if it is **short**, you do not have enough of it. If you are running **short of** something or if it is running **short**, you do not have much of it left. ❑ *Her father's illness left the family short of money... Supplies of everything are unreliable, food is short.* [ADJ: v-link ADJ, usu ADJ *of* n] 7 If someone or something is or stops **short of** a place, they have not quite reached it. If they are or fall **short of** an amount, they have not quite achieved it. ❑ *He stopped a hundred yards short of the building.* [ADJ: v-link ADJ *of* n] 8 **Short of** a [PREP-PHRASE:]

particular thing means except for that thing or without actually doing that thing. ❑ *Short of climbing railings four metres high, there was no way into the garden from this road.* PREP n/-ing [9] If something is **cut short** or **stops short**, it is stopped before people expect it to or before it has finished. ❑ *His glittering career was cut short by a heart attack.* ADV: ADV after v [10] If a name or abbreviation is **short for** another name, it is the short version of that name. ❑ *Her friend Kes (short for Kesewa) was in tears... 'O.O.B.E.' is short for 'Out Of Body Experience'.* ADJ: v-link ADJ *for* n [11] If you have a **short** temper, you get angry very easily. ❑ *...an awkward, self-conscious woman with a short temper.* → See also **short-tempered**. ADJ [12] If you are **short with** someone, you speak briefly and rather rudely to them, because you are impatient or angry. ❑ *She seemed nervous or tense, and she was definitely short with me.* ADJ: v-link ADJ, usu ADJ *with* n

**PHRASES** [13] If a person or thing is called something **for short**, that is the short version of their name. ❑ *Opposite me was a woman called Jasminder (Jazzy for short).* PHRASE: usu n PHR [14] If you **go short of** something, especially food, you do not have as much of it as you want or need. ❑ *Some people may manage their finances badly and therefore have to go short of essentials.* PHRASE: V inflects, oft PHR *of* n [15] You use **in short** when you have been giving a lot of details and you want to give a conclusion or summary. ❑ *Try tennis, badminton or windsurfing. In short, anything challenging.* PHRASE: PHR with cl [16] You use **nothing short of** or **little short of** to emphasize how great or extreme something is. For example, if you say that something is **nothing short of** a miracle or **nothing short of** disastrous, you are emphasizing that it is a miracle or it is disastrous. ❑ *The results are nothing short of magnificent.* PHRASE: v-link PHR adj/n [emphasis] [17] If you say that someone is, for example, **several cards short of a full deck** or **one sandwich short of a picnic**, you think they are stupid, foolish, or crazy. [INFORMAL] PHRASE: v-link PHR [18] If someone or something **is short on** a particular good quality, they do not have as much of it as you think they should have. ❑ *The proposals were short on detail.* PHRASE: V inflects [disapproval] [19] If someone **stops short of** doing something, they come close to doing it but do not actually do it. ❑ *He stopped short of explicitly criticizing the government.* PHRASE: V inflects, PHR -ing/n [20] If workers are put on **short time**, they are asked to work fewer hours than the normal working week, because their employer can not afford to pay them a full time wage. ❑ *Workers across the country have been put on short time because of the slump in demand... Most manufacturers have had to introduce short-time working.* PHRASE: *on* PHR, PHR n [21] If something **pulls** you **up short** or **brings** you **up short**, it makes you suddenly stop what you are doing. ❑ *The name on the gate pulled me up short.* PHRASE: V inflects [22] If you **make short work of** someone or something, you deal with them or defeat them very quickly. [INFORMAL] ❑ *Agassi made short work of his opponent.* PHRASE: V inflects, PHR n [23] **short of breath** → see **breath**. **at short notice** → see **notice**. **to sell** someone **short** → see **sell**. **to get short shrift** → see **shrift**. **to cut a long story short** → see **story**. **to draw the short straw** → see **straw**. **in short supply** → see **supply**. **in the short term** → see **term**.

② **short** /ʃɔːʳt/ **(shorts)** [1] **Shorts** are trousers with very short legs, that people wear in hot weather or for taking part in sports. ❑ *...two women in bright cotton shorts and tee shirts.* N-PLURAL: also *a pair of* N [2] **Shorts** are men's underpants with short legs. [mainly AM] N-PLURAL: also *a pair of* N [3] A **short** is a small amount of a strong alcoholic drink such as whisky, gin, or vodka, rather than a weaker alcoholic drink that you can drink in larger quantities. [mainly BRIT] N-COUNT [4] A **short** is a short film, especially one that is shown before the main film at the cinema. N-COUNT

**short|age** /ʃɔːʳtɪdʒ/ **(shortages)** If there is a **shortage** of something, there is not enough of it. ❑ *A shortage of funds is preventing the UN from monitoring relief... Vietnam is suffering from food shortage.* ◆◇◇ N-VAR: usu with supp, N *of* n, n N

**short back and sides** also **short-back-and-sides.** If a man has a **short back and sides**, his hair is cut very short at the back and sides with slightly thicker, longer hair on the top of the head. [BRIT] N-SING

**short|bread** /ʃɔːʳtbred/ **(shortbreads)** **Shortbread** is a kind of biscuit made from flour, sugar, and butter. N-VAR

**short|cake** /ʃɔːʳtkeɪk/ [1] **Shortcake** is the same as **shortbread**. [BRIT] N-UNCOUNT [2] **Shortcake** is a cake or dessert which consists of a crisp cake with layers of fruit and cream. [mainly AM] ❑ *...desserts like strawberry shortcake.* N-UNCOUNT

**short-change** **(short-changes, short-changing, short-changed)** [1] If someone **short-changes** you, they do not give you enough change after you have bought something from them. ❑ *The cashier made a mistake and short-changed him.* VERB V n [2] If you **are short-changed**, you are treated unfairly or dishonestly, often because you are given less of something than you deserve. ❑ *Women are in fact still being short-changed in the press.* VERB: usu passive *be* V-ed

**short-circuit** **(short-circuits, short-circuiting, short-circuited)** [1] If an electrical device **short-circuits** or if someone or something **short-circuits** it, a wrong connection or damaged wire causes electricity to travel along the wrong route and damage the device. ❑ *Carbon dust and oil build up in large motors and cause them to short-circuit... Once inside they short-circuited the electronic security.* VERB V, V n ♦ **Short-circuit** is also a noun. ❑ *The fire was started by an electrical short-circuit.* N-COUNT [2] If someone or something **short-circuits** a process or system, they avoid long or difficult parts of it and use a quicker, more direct method to achieve their aim. ❑ *The approach was intended to short-circuit normal complaints procedures.* VERB V n

**short|coming** /ʃɔːʳtkʌmɪŋ/ **(shortcomings)** Someone's or something's **shortcomings** are the faults or weaknesses which they have. ❑ *Marriages usually break down as a result of the shortcomings of both partners.* N-COUNT: usu pl, oft with poss = *failing*

**short|crust** /ʃɔːʳtkrʌst/ **Shortcrust** pastry is a kind of pastry that is used to make pies and tarts. [BRIT] ADJ: ADJ n

**short cut** **(short cuts)** also **short-cut, shortcut.** [1] A **short cut** is a quicker way of getting somewhere than the usual route. ❑ *I tried to take a short cut and got lost.* N-COUNT [2] A **short cut** is a method of achieving something more quickly or more easily than if you use the usual methods. ❑ *Fame can be a shortcut to love and money.* N-COUNT: oft N *to* n [3] On a computer, a **shortcut** is an icon on the desktop that allows you to go immediately to a program, document and so on. [COMPUTING] ❑ *...ways to move or copy icons or create shortcuts in Windows.* N-COUNT [4] On a computer, a **shortcut** is a keystroke or a combination of keystrokes that allows you to give commands without using the mouse. [COMPUTING] ❑ *...a handy keyboard shortcut that takes you to the top of the screen.* N-COUNT

**short|en** /ʃɔːʳtᵊn/ **(shortens, shortening, shortened)** [1] If you **shorten** an event or the length of time that something lasts, or if it **shortens**, it does not last as long as it would otherwise do or as it used to do. ❑ *Smoking can shorten your life... When the days shorten in winter some people suffer depression.* VERB ≠ *lengthen* V n, V [2] If you **shorten** an object or if it **shortens**, it becomes smaller in length. ❑ *Her father paid £1,000 for an operation to shorten her nose... As they shorten, cells become more prone to disease and death.* VERB ≠ *lengthen* V n, V [3] If you **shorten** a name or other word, you change it by removing some of the letters. ❑ *Originally called Lili, she eventually shortened her name to Lee.* VERB V n [4] **to shorten the odds** → see **odds**.

**short|en|ing** /ʃɔːʳtnɪŋ/ **(shortenings)** **Shortening** is cooking fat that you use with flour in order to make pastry or dough. [mainly AM] N-MASS

**short|fall** /ʃɔːʳtfɔːl/ **(shortfalls)** If there is a **shortfall in** something, there is less of it than you need. ❑ *The government has refused to make up a £30,000 shortfall in funding.* N-COUNT: usu with supp = *deficit*

**short|hand** /ʃɔːʳthænd/ 1 **Shorthand** is a quick way of writing and uses signs to represent words or syllables. Shorthand is used by secretaries and journalists to write down what someone is saying. ❑ *Ben took notes in shorthand.* N-UNCOUNT
2 You can use **shorthand** to mean a quick or simple way of referring to something. ❑ *'Third World' is an abstraction, a form of shorthand.* N-UNCOUNT: also *a* N

**short-handed** also **shorthanded.** If a company, organization, or group is **short-handed**, it does not have enough people to work on a particular job or for a particular purpose. ❑ *We're actually a bit short-handed at the moment.* ADJ: usu v-link ADJ = *short-staffed*

**short|hand typ|ist** **(shorthand typists)** A **shorthand typist** is a person who types and writes shorthand, usually in an office. [BRIT] N-COUNT

✔ in AM, use **stenographer**

**short-haul** **Short-haul** is used to describe things that involve transporting passengers or goods over short distances. Compare **long-haul**. ❑ *Short-haul flights operate from Heathrow and Gatwick.* ADJ: ADJ n ≠*long-haul*

**short|ish** /ʃɔːʳtɪʃ/ **Shortish** means fairly short. ❑ *...a shortish man, with graying hair.* ADJ: usu ADJ n

**short|list** /ʃɔːʳtlɪst/ **(shortlists, shortlisting, shortlisted)**

✔ The spelling **short list** is used in American English and sometimes in British English for the noun.

1 If someone is on a **shortlist**, for example for a job or a prize, they are one of a small group of people who have been chosen from a larger group. The successful person is then chosen from the small group. ❑ *If you've been asked for an interview you are probably on a short list of no more than six.* N-COUNT
2 If someone or something **is shortlisted for** a job or a prize, they are put on a shortlist. [mainly BRIT] ❑ *He was shortlisted for the Nobel Prize for literature several times.* VERB: usu passive *be* V-ed *for/as* n

**short-lived** Something that is **short-lived** does not last very long. ❑ *Any hope that the speech would end the war was short-lived.* ADJ ≠*long-lived*

**short|ly** /ʃɔːʳtli/ If something happens **shortly** after or before something else, it happens not long after or before it. If something is going to happen **shortly**, it is going to happen soon. ❑ *Their trial will shortly begin... The work will be completed very shortly... Shortly after moving into her apartment, she found a job.* ◆◇◇ ADV: ADV with v, ADV *after/before* n, ADV adv

**short mes|sage sys|tem** **(short message systems)** also **short message service.** A **short message system** is a way of sending short written messages from one mobile phone to another. The abbreviation **SMS** is also used. N-COUNT

**short-range** **Short-range** weapons or missiles are designed to be fired across short distances. ADJ: ADJ n ≠*long-range*

**short-sighted** also **shortsighted.** 1 If you are **short-sighted**, you cannot see things properly when they are far away, because there is something wrong with your eyes. [mainly BRIT] ❑ *Testing showed her to be very short-sighted.* ADJ ≠*long-sighted*

✔ in AM, usually use **near-sighted**

♦ **short-sightedness** *Radical eye surgery promises to cure short-sightedness.* N-UNCOUNT
2 If someone is **short-sighted** about something, or if their ideas are **short-sighted**, they do not make proper or careful judgments about the future. ❑ *Environmentalists fear that this is a short-sighted approach to the problem of global warming.* ♦ **short-sightedness** *The government now recognises the short-sightedness of this approach.* ADJ; N-UNCOUNT

**short-staffed** A company or place that is **short-staffed** does not have enough people working there. [mainly BRIT] ❑ *The hospital is desperately short-staffed.* ADJ = *short-handed*

✔ in AM, use **short-handed**

**short|stop** /ʃɔːʳtstɒp/ **(shortstops)** In baseball, a **shortstop** is a player who tries to stop balls that go between second and third base. N-COUNT

**short sto|ry** **(short stories)** A **short story** is a written story about imaginary events that is only a few pages long. ❑ *He published a collection of short stories.* N-COUNT

**short-tempered** Someone who is **short-tempered** gets angry very quickly. ❑ *I'm a bit short-tempered sometimes.* ADJ

**short-term** **Short-term** is used to describe things that will last for a short time, or things that will have an effect soon rather than in the distant future. ❑ *Investors weren't concerned about short-term profits over the next few years... This is a cynical manipulation of the situation for short-term political gain... The company has 90 staff, almost all on short-term contracts.* ◆◇◇ ADJ: usu ADJ n ≠*long-term*

**short-termism** If you accuse people of **short-termism**, you mean that they make decisions that produce benefits now or soon, rather than making better decisions that will produce benefits in the future. N-UNCOUNT [disapproval]

**short-time** → see **short**.

**short-wave** also **short wave, shortwave.** **Short-wave** is a range of short radio wavelengths used for broadcasting. ❑ *I use the short-wave radio to get the latest war news.* N-UNCOUNT: oft N n

**shot** /ʃɒt/ **(shots)** 1 **Shot** is the past tense and past participle of **shoot**. ◆◆◇
2 A **shot** is an act of firing a gun. ❑ *He had murdered Perceval at point blank range with a single shot... A man fired a volley of shots at them.* N-COUNT
3 Someone who is a good **shot** can shoot well. Someone who is a bad **shot** cannot shoot well. ❑ *He was not a particularly good shot because of his eyesight.* N-COUNT: adj N
4 In sports such as football, golf, or tennis, a **shot** is an act of kicking, hitting, or throwing the ball, especially in an attempt to score a point. ❑ *He had only one shot at goal.* N-COUNT
5 A **shot** is a photograph or a particular sequence of pictures in a film. ❑ *...a shot of a fox peering from the bushes.* N-COUNT
6 If you have a **shot at** something, you attempt to do it. [INFORMAL] ❑ *The heavyweight champion will be given a shot at Holyfield's world title.* N-COUNT: usu sing, usu N *at* n
7 A **shot of** a drug is an injection of it. ❑ *He administered a shot of Nembutal.* N-COUNT: usu N *of* n
8 A **shot of** a strong alcoholic drink is a small glass of it. [AM] ❑ *...a shot of vodka.* N-COUNT

**PHRASES** 9 If you **give** something your **best shot**, you do it as well as you possibly can. [INFORMAL] ❑ *I don't expect to win. But I am going to give it my best shot.* PHRASE: V inflects
10 The person who **calls the shots** is in a position to tell others what to do. ❑ *The directors call the shots and nothing happens without their say-so.* PHRASE: V inflects
11 If you do something **like a shot**, you do it without any delay or hesitation. [INFORMAL] ❑ *I heard the key turn in the front door and I was out of bed like a shot.* PHRASE: PHR after v
12 If you describe something as **a long shot**, you mean that it is unlikely to succeed, but is worth trying. ❑ *The deal was a long shot, but Bagley had little to lose.* PHRASE: v-link PHR
13 People sometimes use the expression **by a long shot** to emphasize the opinion they are giving. ❑ *The missile-reduction treaty makes sweeping cuts, but the arms race isn't over by a long shot.* PHRASE [emphasis]
14 If something **is shot through with** an element or feature, it contains a lot of that element or feature. ❑ *This is an argument shot through with inconsistency.* PHRASE: V inflects, PHR n
15 **a shot in the dark** → see **dark**.

**shot|gun** /ʃɒtgʌn/ **(shotguns)** A **shotgun** is a gun used for shooting birds and animals which fires a lot of small metal balls at one time. N-COUNT

**shot|gun wed|ding** **(shotgun weddings)** 1 A **shotgun wedding** is a wedding that has to take place quickly, often because the woman is pregnant. N-COUNT
2 A **shotgun wedding** is a merger between two companies which takes place in a N-COUNT

hurry because one or both of the companies is having difficulties. [BUSINESS]

**shot put** In athletics, **the shot put** is a competition in which people throw a heavy metal ball as far as possible. ♦ **shot put|ter (shot putters)** ❑ *...Canadian shot-putter Georgette Reed.* N-SING: usu *the* N; N-COUNT

**should** /ʃəd, STRONG ʃʊd/ ◆◆◆

> **Should** is a modal verb. It is used with the base form of a verb.

1 You use **should** when you are saying what would be the right thing to do or the right state for something to be in. ❑ *I should exercise more... The diet should be maintained unchanged for about a year... He's never going to be able to forget it. And I don't think he should... Sometimes I am not as brave as I should be... Should our children be taught to swim at school?* MODAL 2 You use **should** to give someone an order to do something, or to report an official order. ❑ *All visitors should register with the British Embassy... The European Commission ruled that British Aerospace should pay back tens of millions of pounds.* MODAL 3 If you say that something **should have** happened, you mean that it did not happen, but that you wish it had. If you say that something **should not have** happened, you mean that it did happen, but that you wish it had not. ❑ *I should have gone this morning but I was feeling a bit ill... You should have written to the area manager again... I shouldn't have said what I did.* MODAL 4 You use **should** when you are saying that something is probably the case or will probably happen in the way you are describing. If you say that something **should have** happened by a particular time, you mean that it will probably have happened by that time. ❑ *You should have no problem with reading this language... The doctor said it will take six weeks and I should be fine by then.* MODAL 5 You use **should** in questions when you are asking someone for advice, permission, or information. ❑ *Should I or shouldn't I go to university?... Please could you advise me what I should do?... Should I go back to the motel and wait for you to telephone?* MODAL 6 You say '**I should**', usually with the expression 'if I were you', when you are giving someone advice by telling them what you would do if you were in their position. [FORMAL] ❑ *I should look out if I were you!* MODAL 7 You use **should** in conditional clauses when you are talking about things that might happen. [FORMAL] ❑ *If you should be fired, your health and pension benefits will not be automatically cut off... Should you buy a home from Lovell, the company promises to buy it back at the same price after three years.* MODAL 8 You use **should** in 'that' clauses after certain verbs, nouns, and adjectives when you are talking about a future event or situation. ❑ *He raised his glass and indicated that I should do the same... My father was very keen that I should fulfill my potential.* MODAL 9 You use **should** in expressions such as **I should think** and **I should imagine** to indicate that you think something is true but you are not sure. ❑ *I should think it's going to rain soon.* MODAL vagueness 10 You use **should** in expressions such as **I should like** and **I should be happy** to show politeness when you are saying what you want to do, or when you are requesting, offering, or accepting something. ❑ *I should be happy if you would bring them this evening.* MODAL politeness 11 You use **should** in expressions such as **You should have seen us** and **You should have heard him** to emphasize how funny, shocking, or impressive something that you experienced was. [SPOKEN] ❑ *You should have heard him last night!* MODAL emphasis

**shoul|der** /ʃoʊldəʳ/ **(shoulders, shouldering, shouldered)** ◆◆◇ 1 Your **shoulders** are between your neck and the tops of your arms. ❑ *She led him to an armchair, with her arm round his shoulder... He glanced over his shoulder and saw me watching him.* N-COUNT: oft poss N 2 The **shoulders** of a piece of clothing are the parts that cover your shoulders. ❑ *...extravagant fashions with padded shoulders.* N-COUNT 3 When you talk about someone's problems or responsibilities, you can say that they carry them **on** their **shoulders**. ❑ *No one suspected the anguish he carried on his shoulders.* N-PLURAL: poss N 4 If you **shoulder** the responsibility or the blame for something, you accept it. ❑ *He has had to shoulder the responsibility of his father's mistakes.* VERB = accept V n 5 If you **shoulder** something heavy, you put it across one of your shoulders so that you can carry it more easily. ❑ *The rest of the group shouldered their bags, gritted their teeth and set off.* VERB V n 6 If you **shoulder** someone **aside** or if you **shoulder** your **way** somewhere, you push past people roughly using your shoulder. ❑ *The policemen rushed past him, shouldering him aside... She could do nothing to stop him as he shouldered his way into the house... He shouldered past Harlech and opened the door.* VERB V n with *aside* V *way* prep/adv V *past/through* n 7 A **shoulder** is a joint of meat from the upper part of the front leg of an animal. ❑ *...shoulder of lamb.* N-VAR 8 → See also **cold-shoulder**, **hard shoulder**.

PHRASES 9 If someone offers you **a shoulder to cry on** or is **a shoulder to cry on**, they listen sympathetically as you talk about your troubles. ❑ *Roland sometimes saw me as a shoulder to cry on.* PHRASE: usu PHR after v 10 If you say that someone or something stands **head and shoulders above** other people or things, you mean that they are a lot better than them. ❑ *The two candidates stood head and shoulders above the rest.* PHRASE: PHR *above* n 11 If two or more people stand **shoulder to shoulder**, they are standing next to each other, with their shoulders touching. ❑ *They fell into step, walking shoulder to shoulder with their heads bent against the rain.* PHRASE: PHR after v, v-link PHR 12 If people work or stand **shoulder to shoulder**, they work together in order to achieve something, or support each other. ❑ *They could fight shoulder-to-shoulder against a common enemy.* PHRASE: usu v PHR 13 **a chip on** one's **shoulder** → see **chip**. to **rub shoulders with** → see **rub**.

**shoulder-bag (shoulder-bags)** A **shoulder-bag** is a bag that has a long strap so that it can be carried on a person's shoulder. N-COUNT

**shoul|der blade (shoulder blades)** Your **shoulder blades** are the two large, flat, triangular bones that you have in the upper part of your back, below your shoulders. N-COUNT

**shoulder-high** A **shoulder-high** object is as high as your shoulders. ❑ *...a shoulder-high hedge.* ♦ **Shoulder-high** is also an adverb. ❑ *They picked him up and carried him shoulder high into the garage.* ADJ: usu ADJ n; ADV: ADV after v

**shoulder-length** **Shoulder-length** hair is long enough to reach your shoulders. ADJ: usu ADJ n

**shoul|der pad (shoulder pads)** **Shoulder pads** are small pads that are put inside the shoulders of a jacket, coat, or other article of clothing in order to raise them. N-COUNT

**shoul|der strap (shoulder straps)** 1 The **shoulder straps** on a piece of clothing such as a dress are two narrow straps that go over the shoulders. N-COUNT 2 A **shoulder strap** on a bag is a long strap that you put over your shoulder to carry the bag. N-COUNT

**shouldn't** /ʃʊdᵊnt/ **Shouldn't** is the usual spoken form of 'should not'.

**should've** /ʃʊdəv/ **Should've** is the usual spoken form of 'should have', especially when 'have' is an auxiliary verb.

**shout** /ʃaʊt/ **(shouts, shouting, shouted)** ◆◇◇ 1 If you **shout**, you say something very loudly, usually because you want people a long distance away to hear you or because you are angry. ❑ *He had to shout to make himself heard above the near gale-force wind... 'She's alive!' he shouted triumphantly... Andrew rushed out of the house, shouting for help... You don't have to shout at me... I shouted at mother to get the police... The driver managed to escape from the vehicle and shout a warning.* VERB V V with quote V *for* n V *at* n V *at* n to-inf V n ♦ **Shout** is also a noun. ❑ *The decision was greeted with shouts of protest from opposition MPs... I heard a distant shout.* N-COUNT 2 If you say that someone is **in with a shout of** achieving or winning something, you mean that they have a chance of achieving or PHRASE winning it. [INFORMAL] ❑ *He knew he was be in with a shout of making Craig Brown's squad for Japan.*

♦ **shout down** If people **shout down** someone who is trying to speak, they prevent that person from being heard by shouting at them. PHRASAL VERB ❑ *They shouted him down when he tried to explain why Zaire needed an interim government...* V n P *There were scuffles when UDF hecklers began to shout down the speakers.* V P n (not pron)

♦ **shout out** If you **shout** something **out**, you say it very loudly so that people can hear you clearly. PHRASAL VERB ❑ *They shouted out the names of those detained...* V P n *I shouted out 'I'm OK'...* V P with quote *I wanted to shout it out, let her know what I had overheard.* V n P

**shout|ing match** **(shouting matches)** A **shouting match** is an angry quarrel in which people shout at each other. N-COUNT: oft N *with*/*between* n ❑ *We had a real shouting match with each other.*

**shove** /ʃʌv/ **(shoves, shoving, shoved)** 1 If you **shove** someone or something, you push them with a quick, violent movement. VERB ❑ *He shoved her out of the way...* V n prep/adv *He's the one who shoved me...* V n *She shoved as hard as she could.* V ♦ **Shove** is also a noun. N-COUNT ❑ *She gave Gracie a shove towards the house.* 2 If you **shove** something somewhere, you push it there quickly and carelessly. VERB ❑ *We shoved a copy of the newsletter beneath their door.* V n prep/adv 3 If you talk about what you think will happen **if push comes to shove**, you are talking about what you think will happen if a situation becomes very bad or difficult. PHRASE: V inflects [INFORMAL] ❑ *If push comes to shove, if you should lose your case in the court, what will you do?*

**shov|el** /ʃʌvᵊl/ **(shovels, shovelling, shovelled)**

in AM, use **shoveling, shoveled**

1 A **shovel** is a tool with a long handle that is used for lifting and moving earth, coal, or snow. N-COUNT ❑ *...a coal shovel... She dug the foundation with a pick and shovel.* 2 If you **shovel** earth, coal, or snow, you lift and move it with a shovel. VERB ❑ *He has to get out and shovel snow...* V n *Pendergood had shovelled the sand out of the caravan.* V n prep/adv 3 If you **shovel** something somewhere, you push a lot of it quickly into that place. VERB ❑ *Randall was shoveling food into his mouth.* V n prep/adv

**show** /ʃoʊ/ **(shows, showing, showed, shown)** ♦♦♦ 1 If something **shows that** a state of affairs exists, it gives information that proves it or makes it clear to people. VERB ❑ *Research shows that a high-fibre diet may protect you from bowel cancer...* V that *These figures show an increase of over one million in unemployment...* V n *It was only later that the drug was shown to be addictive...* *be* V-ed to-inf *You'll be given regular blood tests to show whether you have been infected.* V wh 2 If a picture, chart, film, or piece of writing **shows** something, it represents it or gives information about it. VERB ❑ *Figure 4.1 shows the respiratory system...* V n *The cushions, shown left, measure 20 x 12 inches and cost $39.95...* V-ed *Much of the film shows the painter simply going about his task...* V n -ing *Our photograph shows how the plants will turn out.* V wh 3 If you **show** someone something, you give it to them, take them to it, or point to it, so that they can see it or know what you are referring to. VERB ❑ *Cut out this article and show it to your bank manager...* V n *to* n *He showed me the flat he shares with Esther...* V n n *I showed them where the gun was.* V n wh 4 If you **show** someone to a room or seat, you lead them there. VERB ❑ *Let me show you to my study...* V n prep/adv *I'll show you the way.* V n n 5 If you **show** someone how to do something, you do it yourself so that they can watch you and learn how to do it. VERB ❑ *Claire showed us how to make a chocolate roulade...* V n wh *Dr. Reichert has shown us a new way to look at those behavior problems.* V n n 6 If something **shows** or if you **show** it, it is visible or noticeable. VERB ❑ *His beard was just beginning to show signs of grey...* V n *Faint glimmers of daylight were showing through the treetops.* V 7 If you **show** a particular attitude, quality, or feeling, or if it **shows**, you behave in a way that makes this attitude, quality, or feeling clear to other people. VERB ❑ *She showed no interest in her children...* V n *Ferguson was unhappy and it showed...* V *You show me respect...* V n n *Mr Clarke has shown himself to be resolutely opposed to compromise...* V n to-inf *The baby was tugging at his coat to show that he wanted to be picked up.* V that 8 If something **shows** a quality or characteristic or if that quality or characteristic **shows itself**, it can be noticed or observed. VERB ❑ *The story shows a strong narrative gift and a vivid eye for detail...* V n *How else did his hostility to women show itself?* V pron-refl 9 **A show of** a feeling or quality is an attempt by someone to make it clear that they have that feeling or quality. N-COUNT: usu *a* N *of* n ❑ *Miners gathered in the centre of Bucharest in a show of support for the government.* 10 If you say that something is **for show**, you mean that it has no real purpose and is done just to give a good impression. N-UNCOUNT ❑ *The change in government is more for show than for real.* 11 If a company **shows** a profit or a loss, its accounts indicate that it has made a profit or a loss. VERB ❑ *It is the only one of the three companies expected to show a profit for the quarter.* V n 12 If a person you are expecting to meet does not **show**, they do not arrive at the place where you expect to meet them. VERB = turn up [mainly AM] ❑ *There was always a chance he wouldn't show.* V ♦ **Show up** means the same as **show**. PHRASAL VERB ❑ *We waited until five o'clock, but he did not show up.* V P 13 A television or radio **show** is a programme on television or radio. N-COUNT: oft supp N = programme ❑ *I had my own TV show... This is the show in which Loyd Grossman visits the houses of the famous. ...a popular talk show on a Cuban radio station.* 14 A **show** in a theatre is an entertainment or concert, especially one that includes different items such as music, dancing, and comedy. N-COUNT ❑ *How about going shopping and seeing a show in London?* 15 If someone **shows** a film or television programme, it is broadcast or appears on television or in the cinema. VERB ❑ *The BBC World Service Television news showed the same film clip...* V n *American films are showing at Moscow's cinemas.* V ♦ **show|ing** **(showings)** N-COUNT *I gave him a private showing of the film.* 16 A **show** is a public exhibition of things, such as works of art, fashionable clothes, or things that have been entered in a competition. N-COUNT: also *on* N ❑ *The venue for the show is Birmingham's National Exhibition Centre Hall... Two complementary exhibitions are on show at the Africa Centre.* 17 To **show** things such as works of art means to put them in an exhibition where they can be seen by the public. VERB ❑ *50 dealers will show oils, watercolours, drawings and prints from 1900 to 1992.* V n 18 A **show** home, house, or flat is one of a group of new homes. ADJ: ADJ n The building company decorates it and puts furniture in it, and people who want to buy one of the homes come and look round it.

**PHRASES** 19 If a question is decided by a **show of hands**, people vote on it by raising their hands to indicate whether they vote yes or no. PHRASE ❑ *Parliamentary leaders agreed to take all such decisions by a show of hands... Russell then asked for a show of hands concerning each of the targets.* 20 If you **have** something **to show for** your efforts, you have achieved something as a result of what you have done. PHRASE: *have* inflects, PHR n ❑ *I'm nearly 31 and it's about time I had something to show for my time in my job.* 21 You can say **'I'll show you'** to threaten or warn someone that you are going to make them admit that they are wrong. PHRASE ❑ *She shook her fist. 'I'll show you,' she said.* 22 If you say **it just goes to show** or **it just shows that** something is the case, you mean that what you have just said or experienced demonstrates that it is the case. PHRASE: PHR that, PHR n ❑ *This just goes to show that getting good grades in school doesn't mean you're clever.* 23 If you say that someone **steals the show**, you mean that they get a lot of attention or praise because they perform better than anyone else in a show or other event. PHRASE: V inflects ❑ *Brad Pitt steals the show as the young man doomed by his zest for life.* 24 to **show** someone **the door** → see **door**. to **show** your **face** → see **face**.

♦ **show around**

☑ in BRIT, also use **show round**

If you **show** someone **around** or **show** them **round**, you go with them to show them all the interesting, useful, or important features of a place when they first visit it. ❑ *Would you show me around?... Spear showed him around the flat.* PHRASAL VERB V n P V n P n

♦ **show off** [1] If you say that someone **is showing off**, you are criticizing them for trying to impress people by showing in a very obvious way what they can do or what they own. ❑ *All right, there's no need to show off.* PHRASAL VERB [disapproval] V P [2] If you **show off** something that you have, you show it to a lot of people or make it obvious that you have it, because you are proud of it. ❑ *Naomi was showing off her engagement ring... He actually enjoys his new hair-style and has decided to start showing it off.* PHRASAL VERB V P n (not pron) V n P [3] → See also **show-off**.

♦ **show up** [1] If something **shows up** or if something **shows** it **up**, it can be clearly seen or noticed. ❑ *You may have some strange disease that may not show up for 10 or 15 years. ...a telescope so powerful that it can show up galaxies billions of light years away.* PHRASAL VERB V P V P n (not pron) [2] If someone or something **shows** you **up**, they make you feel embarrassed or ashamed of them. ❑ *He wanted to teach her a lesson for showing him up in front of Leonov.* PHRASAL VERB V n P [3] → see **show 12**.

**show|biz** /ʃoʊbɪz/ **Showbiz** is the same as **show business**. [INFORMAL] N-UNCOUNT

**show busi|ness** **Show business** is the entertainment industry of film, theatre, and television. ❑ *He started his career in show business by playing the saxophone and singing.* N-UNCOUNT

**show|case** /ʃoʊkeɪs/ **(showcases, showcasing, showcased)** [1] A **showcase** is a glass container with valuable objects inside it, for example at an exhibition or in a museum. N-COUNT [2] You use **showcase** to refer to a situation or setting in which something is displayed or presented to its best advantage. ❑ *The festival remains a valuable showcase for new talent.* N-COUNT: with supp [3] If something **is showcased**, it is displayed or presented to its best advantage. [JOURNALISM] ❑ *Restored films are being showcased this month at a festival in Paris.* VERB: usu passive *be* V-ed

**show|down** /ʃoʊdaʊn/ **(showdowns)** also **show-down**. A **showdown** is a big argument or conflict which is intended to settle a dispute that has lasted for a long time. ❑ *The Prime Minister is preparing for a showdown with Ministers.* N-COUNT: usu sing

**show|er** /ʃaʊə^r/ **(showers, showering, showered)** [1] A **shower** is a device for washing yourself. It consists of a pipe which ends in a flat cover with a lot of holes in it so that water comes out in a spray. ❑ *She heard him turn on the shower.* N-COUNT [2] A **shower** is a small enclosed area containing a shower. N-COUNT [3] **The showers** or **the shower** in a place such as a sports centre is the area containing showers. ❑ *The showers are a mess... We all stood in the women's shower.* N-COUNT [4] If you have a **shower**, you wash yourself by standing under a spray of water from a shower. ❑ *I think I'll have a shower before dinner... She took two showers a day.* N-COUNT [5] If you **shower**, you wash yourself by standing under a spray of water from a shower. ❑ *There wasn't time to shower or change clothes.* VERB V [6] A **shower** is a short period of rain, especially light rain. ❑ *There'll be bright or sunny spells and scattered showers this afternoon.* N-COUNT [7] You can refer to a lot of things that are falling as a **shower of** them. ❑ *Showers of sparks flew in all directions.* N-COUNT: usu N *of* n [8] If you **are showered with** a lot of small objects or pieces, they are scattered over you. ❑ *They were showered with rice in the traditional manner.* VERB: usu passive *be* V-ed *with* n [9] If you **shower** a person **with** presents or kisses, you give them a lot of presents or kisses in a very generous and extravagant way. ❑ *He showered her with emeralds and furs... Her parents showered her with kisses.* VERB V n *with* n V n *with* n [10] A **shower** is a party or celebration at which the guests bring gifts. [mainly AM] ❑ *...a baby shower.* N-COUNT [11] If you refer to a group of people as a particular kind of **shower**, you disapprove of them. [BRIT, INFORMAL] ...*a shower of wasters.* N-SING: usu sing, oft N of n [disapproval]

**show|er gel** **(shower gels)** **Shower gel** is a type of liquid soap designed for use in the shower. N-VAR

**show|ery** /ʃaʊəri/ If the weather is **showery**, there are showers of rain but it does not rain all the time. ADJ

**show|girl** /ʃoʊgɜː^r l/ **(showgirls)** A **showgirl** is a young woman who sings and dances as part of a group in a musical show. N-COUNT

**show|ground** /ʃoʊgraʊnd/ **(showgrounds)** A **showground** is a large area of land where events such as farming shows or horse riding competitions are held. N-COUNT

**show jump|er** **(show jumpers)** A **show jumper** is a person who takes part in the sport of show jumping. ❑ *I loved horses as a child and was a junior show jumper.* N-COUNT

**show jump|ing** also **showjumping**. **Show jumping** is a sport in which horses are ridden in competitions to demonstrate their skill in jumping over fences and walls. N-UNCOUNT

**show|man** /ʃoʊmæn/ **(showmen)** A **showman** is a person who is very entertaining and dramatic in the way that they perform, or the way that they present things. N-COUNT

**show|man|ship** /ʃoʊmənʃɪp/ **Showmanship** is a person's skill at performing or presenting things in an entertaining and dramatic way. N-UNCOUNT

**shown** /ʃoʊn/ **Shown** is the past participle of **show**.

**show-off** **(show-offs)** also **showoff**. If you say that someone is a **show-off**, you are criticizing them for trying to impress people by showing in a very obvious way what they can do or what they own. [INFORMAL] N-COUNT [disapproval]

**show|piece** /ʃoʊpiːs/ **(showpieces)** also **show-piece**. A **showpiece** is something that is admired because it is the best thing of its type, especially something that is intended to be impressive. ❑ *The factory was to be a showpiece of Western investment in the East.* N-COUNT: with supp

**show|room** /ʃoʊruːm/ **(showrooms)** A **showroom** is a shop in which goods are displayed for sale, especially goods such as cars or electrical or gas appliances. ❑ *...a car showroom.* N-COUNT: usu n N

**show|stopper** /ʃoʊstɒpə^r/ **(showstoppers)** also **show-stopper**. If something is a **showstopper**, it is very impressive. [INFORMAL] ❑ *Her natural creativity and artistic talent make her home a real showstopper.* N-COUNT [approval]

**show-stopping** also **showstopping**. A **show-stopping** performance or product is very impressive. [INFORMAL] ADJ: ADJ n [approval]

**show|time** /ʃoʊtaɪm/ **Showtime** is the time when a particular stage or television show starts. ❑ *It's close to showtime now, so you retire into the dressing room.* N-UNCOUNT

**show tri|al** **(show trials)** People describe a trial as a **show trial** if they believe that the trial is unfair and is held for political reasons rather than in order to find out the truth. ❑ *...the show trials of political dissidents.* N-COUNT [disapproval]

**showy** /ʃoʊi/ **(showier, showiest)** Something that is **showy** is very noticeable because it is large, colourful, or bright. ❑ *Since he was color blind, he favored large, showy flowers.* ADJ

**shrank** /ʃræŋk/ **Shrank** is the past tense of **shrink**.

**shrap|nel** /ʃræpn^əl/ **Shrapnel** consists of small pieces of metal which are scattered from exploding bombs and shells. ❑ *He was hit by shrapnel from a grenade.* N-UNCOUNT

**shred** /ʃred/ **(shreds, shredding, shredded)** [1] If you **shred** something such as food or paper, you cut it or tear it into very small, narrow pieces. ❑ *They may be shredding documents... Finely shred the carrots, cabbage and cored apples.* VERB V n [2] If you cut or N-COUNT: usu pl tear food or paper **into shreds**, you cut or tear it into small, narrow pieces. ❑ *Cut the cabbage into fine long shreds.* [3] If there is not a **shred of** something, there is not even a small amount of it. ❑ *He said there was not a shred of evidence to support such remarks... There is not a shred of truth in the story.* N-COUNT: N *of* n, usu with brd-neg = *scrap*

**shred|der** /ʃre̱də^r/ **(shredders)** A **shredder** is a machine for shredding things such as documents or parts of bushes that have been cut off. ❑ *...a document shredder.* N-COUNT

**shrew** /ʃru̱ː/ **(shrews)** A **shrew** is a small brown animal like a mouse with a long pointed nose. N-COUNT

**shrewd** /ʃru̱ːd/ **(shrewder, shrewdest)** A **shrewd** person is able to understand and judge a situation quickly and to use this understanding to their own advantage. ❑ *She's a shrewd businesswoman.* ADJ

**shriek** /ʃri̱ːk/ **(shrieks, shrieking, shrieked)**
[1] When someone **shrieks**, they make a short, very loud cry, for example because they are suddenly surprised, are in pain, or are laughing. ❑ *She shrieked and leapt from the bed... Miranda shrieked with laughter.* ♦ **Shriek** is also a noun. ❑ *Sue let out a terrific shriek and leapt out of the way.* VERB; V; V *with* n; N-COUNT
[2] If you **shriek** something, you shout it in a loud, high-pitched voice. ❑ *'Stop it!' shrieked Jane... He was shrieking obscenities and weeping.* VERB = *scream*; V with quote; V n

**shrift** /ʃrɪ̱ft/ If someone or something gets **short shrift**, they are paid very little attention. ❑ *The idea has been given short shrift by philosophers.* PHRASE: PHR after v

**shrill** /ʃrɪ̱l/ **(shriller, shrillest)** [1] A **shrill** sound is high-pitched and unpleasant. ❑ *Shrill cries and startled oaths flew up around us as pandemonium broke out... Mary Ann's voice grew shrill.* ♦ **shril|ly** *'What are you doing?' Cathy demanded shrilly.* ♦ **shrill|ness** *...that ugly shrillness in her voice.* ADJ = *piercing*; ADV: usu ADV with v; N-UNCOUNT
[2] If you describe a demand, protest, or statement as **shrill**, you disapprove of it and do not like the strong, forceful way it is said. ❑ *Shrill voices on both sides of the Atlantic are advocating protectionism.* ADJ: usu ADJ n [disapproval]

**shrimp** /ʃrɪ̱mp/ **(shrimps** or **shrimp) Shrimps** are small shellfish with long tails and many legs. ❑ *Add the shrimp and cook for 30 seconds.* N-COUNT

**shrimp cock|tail** **(shrimp cocktails)** A **shrimp cocktail** is a dish that consists of shrimp, salad, and a sauce. It is usually eaten at the beginning of a meal. [mainly AM] N-VAR

✔ in BRIT, use **prawn cocktail**

**shrine** /ʃra̱ɪn/ **(shrines)** [1] A **shrine** is a place of worship which is associated with a particular holy person or object. ❑ *...the holy shrine of Mecca.* N-COUNT
[2] A **shrine** is a place that people visit and treat with respect because it is connected with a dead person or with dead people that they want to remember. ❑ *The monument has been turned into a shrine to the dead and the missing.* N-COUNT

**shrink** /ʃrɪ̱ŋk/ **(shrinks, shrinking, shrank, shrunk)** [1] If cloth or clothing **shrinks**, it becomes smaller in size, usually as a result of being washed. ❑ *All my jumpers have shrunk.* [2] If something **shrinks** or something else **shrinks** it, it becomes smaller. ❑ *The vast forests of West Africa have shrunk... Hungary may have to lower its hopes of shrinking its state sector.* [3] If you **shrink away from** someone or something, you move away from them because you are frightened, shocked, or disgusted by them. ❑ *One child shrinks away from me when I try to talk to him.* [4] If you do not **shrink from** a task or duty, you do it even though it is unpleasant or dangerous. ❑ *We must not shrink from the legitimate use of force if we are to remain credible.* [5] A **shrink** is a psychiatrist. [INFORMAL] ❑ *I've seen a shrink already.* [6] **no shrinking violet** → see **violet**. VERB; V; VERB ≠ *grow*; V; V n; VERB; V prep/adv; VERB: usu with neg; V *from* n; N-COUNT

**shrink|age** /ʃrɪ̱ŋkɪdʒ/ **Shrinkage** is a decrease in the size or amount of something. ❑ *Allow for some shrinkage in both length and width.* N-UNCOUNT

**shrink-wrapped** A **shrink-wrapped** product is sold in a tight covering of thin plastic. ❑ *...a shrink-wrapped cassette.* ADJ: usu ADJ n

**shriv|el** /ʃrɪ̱vᵊl/ **(shrivels, shrivelling, shrivelled)**

✔ in AM, use **shriveling, shriveled**

When something **shrivels** or when something **shrivels** it, it becomes dryer and smaller, often with lines in its surface, as a result of losing the water it contains. ❑ *The plant shrivels and dies. ...dry weather that shrivelled this summer's crops.* ♦ **Shrivel up** means the same as **shrivel**. ❑ *The leaves started to shrivel up.* ♦ **shriv|elled** *It looked old and shrivelled.* VERB; V; V n; PHRASAL VERB; V P; ADJ

**shroud** /ʃra̱ʊd/ **(shrouds, shrouding, shrouded)**
[1] A **shroud** is a cloth which is used for wrapping a dead body. [2] You can refer to something that surrounds an object or situation as a **shroud of** something. ❑ *...a parked car huddled under a shroud of grey snow... Ministers are as keen as ever to wrap their activities in a shroud of secrecy.* [3] If something **has been shrouded in** mystery or secrecy, very little information about it has been made available. ❑ *For years the teaching of acting has been shrouded in mystery. ...the secrecy which has shrouded the whole affair.* [4] If darkness, fog, or smoke **shrouds** an area, it covers it so that it is difficult to see. ❑ *Mist shrouded the outline of Buckingham Palace.* N-COUNT; N-COUNT: N *of* n; VERB; *be* V-ed *in* n; V n; VERB; V n

**Shrove Tues|day** /ʃro̱ʊv tjuːzdeɪ, AM tu̱ːz-/ **Shrove Tuesday** is the Tuesday before Ash Wednesday. People traditionally eat pancakes on Shrove Tuesday. N-UNCOUNT = *Pancake Day*

**shrub** /ʃrʌ̱b/ **(shrubs) Shrubs** are plants that have several woody stems. ❑ *...flowering shrubs.* N-COUNT

**shrub|bery** /ʃrʌ̱bəri/ **(shrubberies)** [1] A **shrubbery** is a part of a garden where a lot of shrubs are growing. [BRIT] [2] You can refer to a lot of shrubs or to shrubs in general as **shrubbery**. N-COUNT; N-UNCOUNT

**shrub|by** /ʃrʌ̱bi/ A **shrubby** plant is like a shrub. ❑ *...a shrubby tree.* ADJ: usu ADJ n

**shrug** /ʃrʌ̱g/ **(shrugs, shrugging, shrugged)** If you **shrug**, you raise your shoulders to show that you are not interested in something or that you do not know or care about something. ❑ *I shrugged, as if to say, 'Why not?'... The man shrugged his shoulders.* ♦ **Shrug** is also a noun. ❑ *'I suppose so,' said Anna with a shrug.* VERB; V; V n; N-COUNT

♦ **shrug off** If you **shrug** something **off**, you ignore it or treat it as if it is not really important or serious. ❑ *He shrugged off the criticism... He just laughed and shrugged it off.* PHRASAL VERB; V P n (not pron); V n P

**shrunk** /ʃrʌ̱ŋk/ **Shrunk** is the past participle of **shrink**.

**shrunk|en** /ʃrʌ̱ŋkən/ Someone or something that is **shrunken** has become smaller than they used to be. ❑ *She now looked small, shrunken and pathetic.* ADJ

**shtick** /ʃtɪ̱k/ → see **schtick**.

**shuck** /ʃʌ̱k/ **(shucks, shucking, shucked)**
[1] The **shuck** of something is its outer covering, for example the leaves round an ear of corn, or the shell of a shellfish. [AM] ❑ *...corn shucks.* [2] If you **shuck** something such as corn or shellfish, you remove it from its outer covering. [AM] ❑ *On a good day, each employee will shuck 3,500 oysters.* [3] If you **shuck** something that you are wearing, you take it off. [AM, INFORMAL] ❑ *He shucked his coat and set to work.* [4] **Shucks** is an exclamation that is used to express embarrassment, disappointment, or annoyance. [AM, INFORMAL] ❑ *Terry actually says 'Oh, shucks!' when complimented on her singing.* N-COUNT; VERB; V n; VERB; V n; EXCLAM [feelings]

**shud|der** /ʃʌ̱də^r/ **(shudders, shuddering, shuddered)** [1] If you **shudder**, you shake with fear, horror, or disgust, or because you are cold. ❑ *Lloyd had urged her to eat caviar. She had shuddered at the thought.* ♦ **Shudder** is also a noun. ❑ *She recoiled with a shudder.* [2] If something such as a machine VERB; V prep/adv; N-COUNT: usu sing; VERB or vehicle **shudders**, it shakes suddenly and violently. ❑ *The train began to pull out of the station – then suddenly shuddered to a halt... The whole ship shuddered and trembled at the sudden strain.* [V prep/adv, V] 3 If something sends **a shudder** or **shudders** through a group of people, it makes them worried or afraid. ❑ *The next crisis sent a shudder of fear through the UN community.* [N-COUNT] 4 If you say that you **shudder to think what** would happen in a particular situation, you mean that you expect it to be so bad that you do not really want to think about it. ❑ *I shudder to think what would have happened if he hadn't acted as quickly as he did.* [PHRASE: V inflects, usu PHR wh] [feelings]

**shuf|fle** /ʃʌfᵊl/ **(shuffles, shuffling, shuffled)** 1 If you **shuffle** somewhere, you walk there without lifting your feet properly off the ground. ❑ *Moira shuffled across the kitchen.* [VERB, V prep/adv] ♦ **Shuffle** is also a noun. ❑ *She noticed her own proud walk had become a shuffle.* [N-SING] 2 If you **shuffle around**, you move your feet about while standing or you move your bottom about while sitting, often because you feel uncomfortable or embarrassed. ❑ *He shuffles around in his chair... He grinned and shuffled his feet.* [VERB, V prep/adv, V n] 3 If you **shuffle** playing cards, you mix them up before you begin a game. ❑ *There are various ways of shuffling and dealing the cards.* [VERB, V n] 4 If you **shuffle** things such as pieces of paper, you move them around so that they are in a different order. ❑ *The silence lengthened as Thorne unnecessarily shuffled some papers.* [VERB, V n]

**shun** /ʃʌn/ **(shuns, shunning, shunned)** If you **shun** someone or something, you deliberately avoid them or keep away from them. ❑ *From that time forward everybody shunned him... He has always shunned publicity.* [VERB, V n, V n]

**shunt** /ʃʌnt/ **(shunts, shunting, shunted)** 1 If a person or thing **is shunted** somewhere, they are moved or sent there, usually because someone finds them inconvenient. ❑ *He has spent most of his life being shunted between his mother, father and various foster families.* [VERB: usu passive] [disapproval] [be V-ed prep/adv] 2 When railway engines **shunt** wagons or carriages, they push or pull them from one railway line to another. ❑ *The GM diesel engine shunted the coaches to Platform 4.* [VERB, V n prep/adv]

**shush** /ʃʊʃ, ʃʌʃ/ **(shushes, shushing, shushed)** 1 You say **shush** when you are telling someone to be quiet. ❑ *Shush! Here he comes. I'll talk to you later.* [CONVENTION] 2 If you **shush** someone, you tell them to be quiet by saying 'shush' or 'sh', or by indicating in some other way that you want them to be quiet. ❑ *Frannie shushed her with a forefinger to the lips.* [VERB, V n, Also V]

**shut** /ʃʌt/ **(shuts, shutting)** ◆◇◇

> The form **shut** is used in the present tense and is the past tense and past participle.

1 If you **shut** something such as a door or if it **shuts**, it moves so that it fills a hole or a space. ❑ *Just make sure you shut the gate after you... The screen door shut gently.* [VERB = close ≠ open, V n, V] ♦ **Shut** is also an adjective. ❑ *They have warned residents to stay inside and keep their doors and windows shut.* [ADJ: v-link ADJ] 2 If you **shut** your eyes, you lower your eyelids so that you cannot see anything. ❑ *Lucy shut her eyes so she wouldn't see it happen.* [VERB = close ≠ open, V n] ♦ **Shut** is also an adjective. ❑ *His eyes were shut and he seemed to have fallen asleep.* [ADJ: v-link ADJ] 3 If your mouth **shuts** or if you **shut** your mouth, you place your lips firmly together. ❑ *Daniel's mouth opened, and then shut again... He opened and shut his mouth, unspeaking.* [VERB = close ≠ open, V, V n] ♦ **Shut** is also an adjective. ❑ *She was silent for a moment, lips tight shut, eyes distant.* [ADJ: v-link ADJ] 4 When a store, bar, or other public building **shuts** or when someone **shuts** it, it is closed and you cannot use it until it is open again. ❑ *There is a tendency to shut museums or shops at a moment's notice... What time do the pubs shut?* [VERB = close ≠ open, V n, V] ♦ **Shut** is also an adjective. ❑ *Make sure you have food to tide you over when the local shop may be shut.* [ADJ: v-link ADJ]

PHRASES 5 If you say that someone **shuts** their **eyes to** something, you mean that they deliberately ignore something which they should deal with. ❑ *We shut our eyes to the plainest facts, refusing to admit the truth.* [PHRASE: V inflects, PHR n] [disapproval] 6 If someone tells you to **keep** your **mouth shut** about something, they are telling you not to let anyone else know about it. [PHRASE: V inflects] 7 If you **keep** your **mouth shut**, you do not express your opinions about something, even though you would like to. ❑ *If she had kept her mouth shut she would still have her job now.* [PHRASE: V inflects]

♦ **shut down** If a factory or business **shuts down** or if someone **shuts** it **down**, work there stops or it no longer trades as a business. ❑ *Smaller contractors had been forced to shut down... It is required by law to shut down banks which it regards as chronically short of capital... Mr Buzetta sold the newspaper's assets to its competitor and shut it down.* [PHRASAL VERB, V P, V P n (not pron), V n P] → See also **shutdown**.

♦ **shut in** 1 If you **shut** someone or something **in** a room, you close the door so that they cannot leave it. ❑ *The door enables us to shut the birds in the shelter in bad weather.* [PHRASAL VERB, V n P n] 2 If you **shut yourself in** a room, you stay in there and make sure nobody else can get in. ❑ *After one particular bad result, he shut himself in the shower room for an hour.* [PHRASAL VERB, V pron-refl P n] 3 → See also **shut-in**.

♦ **shut off** 1 If you **shut off** something such as an engine or an electrical item, you turn it off to stop it working. ❑ *They pulled over and shut off the engine... Will somebody for God's sake shut that alarm off.* [PHRASAL VERB = switch off, V P n (not pron), V n P] 2 If you **shut yourself off**, you avoid seeing other people, usually because you are feeling depressed. ❑ *Billy tends to keep things to himself more and shut himself off.* [PHRASAL VERB, V pron-refl P] 3 If an official organization **shuts off** the supply of something, they no longer send it to the people they supplied in the past. ❑ *The State Water Project has shut off all supplies to farmers.* [PHRASAL VERB, V P n (not pron), Also V n P]

♦ **shut out** 1 If you **shut** something or someone **out**, you prevent them from getting into a place, for example by closing the doors. ❑ *'I shut him out of the bedroom,' says Maureen... I was set to shut out anyone else who came knocking.* [PHRASAL VERB, V n P of n, V P n (not pron)] 2 If you **shut out** a thought or a feeling, you prevent yourself from thinking or feeling it. ❑ *I shut out the memory which was too painful to dwell on... The figures represent such overwhelming human misery that the mind wants to shut it out.* [PHRASAL VERB = block out, V P n (not pron), V n P] 3 If you **shut** someone **out** of something, you prevent them from having anything to do with it. ❑ *She is very reclusive, to the point of shutting me out of her life... She had effectively shut him out by refusing to listen.* [PHRASAL VERB, V n P of n, V n P]

♦ **shut up** If someone **shuts up** or if someone **shuts** them **up**, they stop talking. You can say **'shut up'** as an impolite way to tell a person to stop talking. ❑ *Just shut up, will you?... A sharp put-down was the only way to shut her up.* [PHRASAL VERB, V P, V n P]

**shut|down** /ʃʌtdaʊn/ **(shutdowns)** A **shutdown** is the closing of a factory, shop, or other business, either for a short time or for ever. ❑ *The shutdown is the latest in a series of painful budget measures.* [N-COUNT]

**shut-eye** also **shuteye**. **Shut-eye** is sleep. [INFORMAL] ❑ *Go home and get some shut-eye.* [N-UNCOUNT]

**shut-in** **(shut-ins)** A **shut-in** is someone who is ill for a long time, and has to stay in bed or at home. [AM] ❑ *...Meals on Wheels or similar programs that bring outside life to shut-ins.* [N-COUNT]

**shut|ter** /ʃʌtəʳ/ **(shutters)** 1 The **shutter** in a camera is the part which opens to allow light through the lens when a photograph is taken. ❑ *There are a few things you should check before pressing the shutter release.* [N-COUNT] 2 **Shutters** are wooden or metal covers fitted on the outside of a window. They can be opened to let in the light, or closed to keep out the sun or the cold. ❑ *She opened the shutters and gazed out over village roofs.* [N-COUNT: usu pl]

**shut|tered** /ʃʌtəʳd/ 1 A **shuttered** window, room, or building has its shutters closed. ❑ *I opened a shuttered window.* [ADJ] 2 A **shuttered** window, room, or building has shutters fitted to it. ❑ *...green-shuttered colonial villas.* [ADJ: ADJ n]

**shut|tle** /ʃʌtᵊl/ **(shuttles, shuttling, shuttled)** 1 A **shuttle** is the same as a **space shuttle**. N-COUNT 2 A **shuttle** is a plane, bus, or train which makes frequent journeys between two places. ❑ *...shuttle flights between London and Manchester.* N-COUNT: oft N n 3 If someone or something **shuttles** or **is shuttled** from one place to another place, they frequently go from one place to the other. ❑ *He and colleagues have shuttled back and forth between the three capitals... Machine parts were also being shuttled across the border without authorisation.* VERB V prep/adv be V-ed prep/adv

**shuttle|cock** /ʃʌtᵊlkɒk/ **(shuttlecocks)** A **shuttlecock** is the small object that you hit over the net in a game of badminton. It is rounded at one end and has real or artificial feathers fixed in the other end. N-COUNT

**shut|tle di|plo|ma|cy** **Shuttle diplomacy** is the movement of diplomats between countries whose leaders refuse to talk directly to each other, in order to try to settle the argument between them. ❑ *UN mediators are conducting shuttle diplomacy between the two sides.* N-UNCOUNT

**shy** /ʃaɪ/ **(shyer, shyest, shies, shying, shied)** 1 A **shy** person is nervous and uncomfortable in the company of other people. ❑ *She was a shy and retiring person when she was off-stage... He is painfully shy of women.* ♦ **shy|ly** *The children smiled shyly.* ♦ **shy|ness** *Eventually he overcame his shyness.* ADJ ADV: usu ADV with v N-UNCOUNT 2 If you are **shy of** doing something, you are unwilling to do it because you are afraid of what might happen. ❑ *You should not be shy of having your say in the running of the school.* ADJ: oft ADJ of -ing 3 When a horse **shies**, it moves away suddenly, because something has frightened it. ❑ *Llewelyn's stallion shied as the wind sent sparks flying.* VERB V 4 A number or amount that is just **shy of** another number or amount is just under it. ❑ *...a high-school dropout rate just shy of 53%.* PREP-PHRASE = short of

♦ **shy away from** If you **shy away from** doing something, you avoid doing it, often because you are afraid or not confident enough. ❑ *We frequently shy away from making decisions.* PHRASAL VERB V P P -ing/n

**-shy** /-ʃaɪ/ **-shy** is added to nouns to form adjectives which indicate that someone does not like a particular thing, and tries to avoid it. For example, someone who is camera-shy does not like having their photograph taken. ❑ *...camera-shy red deer.* COMB in ADJ

**shy|ster** /ʃaɪstəʳ/ **(shysters)** If you refer to someone, especially a lawyer or politician, as a **shyster**, you mean that they are dishonest and immoral. [mainly AM, INFORMAL] N-COUNT disapproval

**Sia|mese cat** /saɪəmiːz kæt/ **(Siamese cats)** A **Siamese cat** is a type of cat with short cream and brown fur, blue eyes, dark ears, and a dark tail. N-COUNT

**Sia|mese twin** /saɪəmiːz twɪn/ **(Siamese twins)** **Siamese twins** are twins who are born with their bodies joined. N-COUNT

**sibi|lant** /sɪbɪlənt/ **Sibilant** sounds are soft 's' sounds. [FORMAL] ❑ *A sibilant murmuring briefly pervaded the room.* ADJ: usu ADJ n

**sib|ling** /sɪblɪŋ/ **(siblings)** Your **siblings** are your brothers and sisters. [FORMAL] ❑ *His siblings are mostly in their early twenties.* N-COUNT

**sic** You write **sic** in brackets after a word or expression when you want to indicate to the reader that although the word looks odd or wrong, you intended to write it like that or the original writer wrote it like that. ❑ *The latest school jobs page advertises a 'wide range (sic) of 6th form courses.'*

**Si|cil|ian** /sɪsɪliən/ **(Sicilians)** 1 **Sicilian** means belonging or relating to Sicily, or to its people or culture. ADJ 2 A **Sicilian** is a Sicilian citizen, or a person of Sicilian origin. N-COUNT

**sick** /sɪk/ **(sicker, sickest)** 1 If you are **sick**, you are ill. **Sick** usually means physically ill, but it can sometimes be used to mean mentally ill. ❑ *He's very sick. He needs medication... She found herself with two small children, a sick husband, and no money.* ♦ **The sick** are people who are sick. ❑ *There were no doctors to treat the sick.* ◆◇◇ ADJ N-PLURAL: the N 2 If you are **sick**, the food that you have eaten comes up from your stomach and out of your mouth. If you **feel sick**, you feel as if you are going to be sick. ❑ *She got up and was sick in the handbasin... The very thought of food made him feel sick.* ADJ: v-link ADJ 3 **Sick** is vomit. [BRIT, INFORMAL] N-UNCOUNT 4 If you say that you are **sick of** something or **sick and tired of** it, you are emphasizing that you are very annoyed by it and want it to stop. [INFORMAL] ❑ *I am sick and tired of hearing all these people moaning.* ADJ: v-link ADJ of n/-ing emphasis = fed up 5 If you describe something such as a joke or story as **sick**, you mean that it deals with death or suffering in an unpleasantly humorous way. ❑ *...a sick joke about a cat.* ADJ disapproval

**PHRASES** 6 If you say that something or someone **makes** you **sick**, you mean that they make you feel angry or disgusted. [INFORMAL] ❑ *It makes me sick that people commit offences and never get punished.* PHRASE: V inflects, oft it PHR that 7 If you are **off sick**, you are not at work because you are ill. ❑ *When we are off sick, we only receive half pay.* PHRASE: usu v-link PHR 8 If you say that you are **worried sick**, you are emphasizing that you are extremely worried. [INFORMAL] ❑ *He was worried sick about what our mothers would say.* PHRASE: v-link PHR emphasis

**sick bay** **(sick bays)** also **sick-bay.** A **sick bay** is an area, especially on a ship or navy base, or in Britain in a school or university, where medical treatment is given and where beds are provided for people who are ill. ❑ *...a free 16-bed sick bay for students needing continuous care.* N-COUNT: also prep N

**sick|bed** /sɪkbed/ **(sickbeds)** also **sick-bed.** Your **sickbed** is the bed that you are lying in while you are ill. ❑ *Michael left his sickbed to entertain his house guests.* N-COUNT: usu poss N

**sick build|ing syn|drome** **Sick building syndrome** is a group of conditions, including headaches, sore eyes, and tiredness, which people who work in offices may experience because the air there is not healthy to breathe. N-UNCOUNT

**sick|en** /sɪkən/ **(sickens, sickening, sickened)** If something **sickens** you, it makes you feel disgusted. ❑ *The notion that art should be controlled by intellectuals sickened him.* VERB = disgust V n

**sick|en|ing** /sɪkənɪŋ/ You describe something as **sickening** when it gives you feelings of horror or disgust, or makes you feel sick in your stomach. ❑ *This was a sickening attack on a pregnant and defenceless woman.* ADJ

**sickie** /sɪki/ **(sickies)** If someone takes a **sickie**, they take a day off work saying that they are ill, especially when they are not actually ill. [INFORMAL] ❑ *Broughton took a sickie on Monday.* N-COUNT

**sick|le** /sɪkᵊl/ **(sickles)** A **sickle** is a tool that is used for cutting grass and grain crops. It has a short handle and a long curved blade. N-COUNT

**sick leave** **Sick leave** is the time that a person spends away from work because of illness or injury. [BUSINESS] ❑ *I have been on sick leave for seven months with depression.* N-UNCOUNT: oft on N

**sickle-cell anaemia**

✓ in AM, use **sickle-cell anemia**

**Sickle-cell anaemia** is an inherited illness in which the red blood cells become curved, causing a number of health problems. N-UNCOUNT

**sick|ly** /sɪkli/ **(sicklier, sickliest)** 1 A **sickly** person or animal is weak, unhealthy, and often ill. ❑ *He had been a sickly child.* ADJ 2 A **sickly** smell or taste is unpleasant and makes you feel slightly sick, often because it is extremely sweet. ❑ *...the sickly smell of rum.* ADJ 3 A **sickly** colour or light is unpleasantly pale or weak. ❑ *Wallpapers for children too often come only in sickly pastel shades.* ADJ: usu ADJ n

**sick|ness** /sɪknəs/ **(sicknesses)** 1 **Sickness** is the state of being ill or unhealthy. ❑ *In fifty-two years of working he had one week of sickness... There appears to be another outbreak of sickness among seals in the North Sea.* N-UNCOUNT 2 **Sickness** is the uncomfortable feeling that you are going to vomit. ❑ *Af-* N-UNCOUNT = nausea *ter a while, the sickness gradually passed and she struggled to the mirror.* → See also **morning sickness**, **travel sickness**. [3] A **sickness** is a particular illness. ❑ *...radiation sickness.* N-VAR

**sick|ness ben|efit** **Sickness benefit** is money that you receive regularly from the government when you are unable to work because of illness. [BRIT] N-UNCOUNT

**sick note** **(sick notes)** A **sick note** is an official note signed by a doctor which states that someone is ill and needs to stay off work for a particular period of time. N-COUNT

**sick pay** When you are ill and unable to work, **sick pay** is the money that you get from your employer instead of your normal wages. [BUSINESS] ❑ *They are not eligible for sick pay.* N-UNCOUNT

**sick|room** /sɪkruːm/ **(sickrooms)** also **sick room.** A **sickroom** is a room in which a sick person is lying in bed. ❑ *Close friends were allowed into the sickroom.* N-COUNT

**side** /saɪd/ **(sides, siding, sided)** ◆◆◆ [1] The **side of** something is a position to the left or right of it, rather than in front of it, behind it, or on it. ❑ *On one side of the main entrance there's a red plaque. ...a photograph with me in the centre and Joe and Ken on each side of me. ...the nations on either side of the Pacific... There's nothing but woods on the other side of the highway... There has been a build-up of troops on both sides of the border... PC Dacre knocked on Webb's door and, opening it, stood to one side.* N-COUNT: usu prep N *of* n [2] The **side** of an object, building, or vehicle is any of its flat surfaces which is not considered to be its front, its back, its top, or its bottom. ❑ *We put a notice on the side of the box. ...a van bearing on its side the name of a company... There was a stone staircase against the side of the house... A carton of milk lay on its side.* N-COUNT: usu with poss [3] The **sides** of a hollow or a container are its inside vertical surfaces. ❑ *The rough rock walls were like the sides of a deep canal... Line the base of the dish with greaseproof paper and lightly grease the sides.* N-COUNT [4] The **sides of** an area or surface are its edges. ❑ *Park on the side of the road. ...a small beach on the north side of the peninsula.* N-COUNT: usu prep N *of* n = *edge* [5] The two **sides of** an area, surface, or object are its two halves. ❑ *She turned over on her stomach on the other side of the bed... The major centre for language is in the left side of the brain.* N-COUNT: usu prep N *of* n = *half* [6] The two **sides** of a road are its two halves on which traffic travels in opposite directions. ❑ *It had gone on to the wrong side of the road and hit a car coming in the other direction.* N-COUNT [7] If you talk about the other **side** of a town or of the world, you mean a part of the town or of the world that is very far from where you are. ❑ *He saw the ship that was to transport them to the other side of the world... Are you working on this side of the city?* N-COUNT: with supp [8] Your **sides** are the parts of your body between your front and your back, from under your arms to your hips. ❑ *His arms were limp at his sides... They had laid him on his side.* N-COUNT: usu poss N [9] If someone is **by** your **side** or **at** your **side**, they stay near you and give you comfort or support. ❑ *He was constantly at his wife's side.* N-COUNT: usu sing, *by/at* poss N [10] The two **sides** of something flat, for example a piece of paper, are its two flat surfaces. You can also refer to one side of a piece of paper filled with writing as one **side** of writing. ❑ *The new copiers only copy onto one side of the paper... Fry the chops until brown on both sides.* N-COUNT [11] One **side** of a tape or record is what you can hear or record if you play the tape or record from beginning to end without turning it over. ❑ *We want to hear side A.* N-COUNT [12] **Side** is used to describe things that are not the main or most important ones of their kind. ❑ *She slipped in and out of the theatre by a side door. ...a prawn curry with a lentil side dish.* ADJ: ADJ n ≠ *main* [13] The different **sides** in a war, argument, or negotiation are the groups of people who are opposing each other. ❑ *Both sides appealed for a new ceasefire. ...the elections which his side lost.* N-COUNT: usu with supp [14] The different **sides of** an argument or deal are the different points of view or positions involved in it. ❑ *...those with the ability to see all sides of a question.* N-COUNT: usu N of n [15] If one person or country **sides with** another, they support them in an argument or a war. If people or countries **side against** another person or country, they support each other against them. ❑ *There has been much speculation that America might be siding with the rebels.* VERB V *with/against* n [16] In sport, a **side** is a team. [BRIT] ❑ *Italy were definitely a better side than Germany.* N-COUNT: usu with supp = *team*

☑ in AM, use **team**

[17] A particular **side** of something such as a situation or someone's character is one aspect of it. ❑ *He is in charge of the civilian side of the UN mission... It shows that your child can now see the funny side of things.* N-COUNT: usu supp N [18] The **mother's side** and the **father's side** of your family are your mother's relatives and your father's relatives. ❑ *So was your father's side more well off?* N-COUNT: usu supp N [19] → See also **-sided**, **siding**.

**PHRASES** [20] If two people or things are **side by side**, they are next to each other. ❑ *We sat side by side on two wicker seats.* PHRASE: usu PHR after v [21] If people work or live **side by side**, they work or live closely together in a friendly way. ❑ *...areas where different nationalities have lived side by side for centuries.* PHRASE: usu PHR after v [22] If you say that someone **has let the side down**, you mean that they have embarrassed their family or friends by behaving badly or not doing well at something. [BRIT] ❑ *Brown was constantly letting the side down.* PHRASE: V inflects [23] If something moves **from side to side**, it moves repeatedly to the left and to the right. ❑ *She was shaking her head from side to side.* PHRASE: PHR after v [24] If you are **on** someone's **side**, you are supporting them in an argument or a war. ❑ *He has the Democrats on his side... Some of the younger people seem to be on the side of reform.* PHRASE: PHR after v [25] If something is **on** your **side** or if you have it **on** your **side**, it helps you when you are trying to achieve something. ❑ *The law is not on their side.* PHRASE: PHR after v, v-link PHR [26] If you get **on the wrong side of** someone, you do something to annoy them and make them dislike you. If you stay **on the right side of** someone, you try to please them and avoid annoying them. ❑ *I wouldn't like to get on the wrong side of him.* PHRASE: usu PHR after v [27] If you say that something is **on the** small **side**, you are saying politely that you think it is slightly too small. If you say that someone is **on the** young **side**, you are saying politely that you think they are slightly too young. ❑ *He's quiet and a bit on the shy side.* PHRASE: usu v-link PHR [politeness] [28] If someone does something **on the side**, they do it in addition to their main work. ❑ *...ways of making a little bit of money on the side.* PHRASE: usu PHR after v [29] If you **put** something **to one side** or **put** it **on one side**, you temporarily ignore it in order to concentrate on something else. ❑ *In order to maintain profit margins health and safety regulations are often put to one side.* PHRASE: V inflects [30] If you **take** someone **to one side** or **draw** them **to one side**, you speak to them privately, usually in order to give them advice or a warning. ❑ *He took Sabrina to one side and told her about the safe.* PHRASE: V inflects [31] If you **take sides** or **take** someone's **side** in an argument or war, you support one of the sides against the other. ❑ *We cannot take sides in a civil war.* PHRASE: V inflects [32] to **look on the bright side** → see **bright**. **the other side of the coin** → see **coin**. to **err on the side of** something → see **err**. to **be on the safe side** → see **safe**. someone's **side of the story** → see **story**.

**side|arm** /saɪdɑːʳm/ **(sidearms)** **Sidearms** are weapons, usually small guns, that you can wear on a belt. ❑ *Two guards with sidearms patrolled the wall.* N-COUNT: usu pl

**side|board** /saɪdbɔːʳd/ **(sideboards)** [1] A **sideboard** is a long cupboard which is about the same height as a table. Sideboards are usually kept in dining rooms to put plates and glasses in. N-COUNT [2] **Sideboards** are the same as **sideburns**. [BRIT] N-PLURAL

**side|burns** /saɪdbɜːʳnz/ If a man has **sideburns**, he has a strip of hair growing down the N-PLURAL side of each cheek. ❑ *...a young man with long sideburns.*

**side|car** /saɪdkɑːʳ/ **(sidecars)** A **sidecar** is a kind of box with wheels which you can attach to the side of a motorcycle so that you can carry a passenger in it. N-COUNT

**-sided** /-saɪdɪd/ **-sided** combines with numbers or adjectives to describe how many sides something has, or what kind of sides something has. ❑ *...a three-sided pyramid... We drove up a steep-sided valley.* → See also **one-sided**. COMB in ADJ: usu ADJ n

**side dish (side dishes)** A **side dish** is an amount of a particular food that is served at the same time as the main dish. ❑ *These mushrooms would make a delicious side dish.* N-COUNT

**side-effect (side-effects)** also **side effect.** [1] The **side-effects** of a drug are the effects, usually bad ones, that the drug has on you in addition to its function of curing illness or pain. ❑ *The treatment has a whole host of extremely unpleasant side-effects including weight gain, acne, skin rashes and headaches... Most patients suffer no side-effects.* N-COUNT: usu pl [2] A **side-effect of** a situation is something unplanned and usually unpleasant that happens in addition to the main effects of that situation. ❑ *One side effect of modern life is stress.* N-COUNT: usu N *of* n/-ing

**side-foot (side-foots, side-footing, side-footed)** also **sidefoot.** In football, if a player **side-foots** the ball, they kick it with the side of their foot. [BRIT, JOURNALISM] ❑ *Currie sidefooted his first goal of the season.* ♦ **Side-foot** is also a noun. ❑ *Anthony scored with a simple side-foot.* VERB V n Also V N-COUNT: usu sing

**side is|sue (side issues)** A **side issue** is an issue or subject that is not considered to be as important as the main one. ❑ *I must forget these side issues and remember my mission.* N-COUNT

**side|kick** /saɪdkɪk/ **(sidekicks)** Someone's **sidekick** is a person who accompanies them and helps them, and who you consider to be less intelligent or less important than the other person. [INFORMAL] ❑ *His sons, brother and nephews were his armed sidekicks.* N-COUNT: oft poss N

**side|light** /saɪdlaɪt/ **(sidelights)** [1] The **sidelights** on a vehicle are the small lights at the front that help other drivers to notice the vehicle and to judge its width. [BRIT] N-COUNT

✔ in AM, usually use **parking lights**

[2] The **sidelights** on a vehicle are lights on its sides. [AM] N-COUNT [3] A **sidelight on** a particular situation is a piece of information about that situation which is interesting but which is not particularly important. ❑ *The book is full of amusing sidelights on his family background.* N-COUNT: oft N *on* n

**side|line** /saɪdlaɪn/ **(sidelines, sidelining, sidelined)** [1] A **sideline** is something that you do in addition to your main job in order to earn extra money. ❑ *Mr. Means sold computer disks as a sideline.* N-COUNT [2] The **sidelines** are the lines marking the long sides of the playing area, for example on a football field or tennis court. N-PLURAL [3] If you are **on the sidelines** in a situation, you do not influence events at all, either because you have chosen not to be involved, or because other people have not involved you. ❑ *France no longer wants to be left on the sidelines when critical decisions are taken.* N-PLURAL: the N, usu *on/from* N [4] If someone or something **is sidelined,** they are made to seem unimportant and not included in what people are doing. ❑ *He was under pressure to resign and was about to be sidelined.* VERB: usu passive *be* V-ed

**side|long** /saɪdlɒŋ, AM -lɔːŋ/ If you give someone a **sidelong** look, you look at them out of the corner of your eyes. ❑ *She gave him a quick sidelong glance.* ADJ: ADJ n

**side-on** A **side-on** collision or view is a collision or view from the side of an object. ❑ *...steel beams built into the doors for protection against a side-on crash.* ADJ

**side or|der (side orders)** A **side order** is an amount of a food that you order in a restaurant to be served at the same time as the main dish. ❑ *...a side order of potato salad.* N-COUNT

**side road (side roads)** A **side road** is a road which leads off a busier, more important road. N-COUNT

**side-saddle** When you ride a horse **side-saddle**, you sit on a special saddle with both your legs on one side rather than one leg on each side of the horse. ❑ *Naomi was given a pony and taught to ride side-saddle.* ADV: ADV after v

**side sal|ad (side salads)** A **side salad** is a bowl of salad for one person which is served with a main meal. N-COUNT

**side|show** /saɪdʃoʊ/ **(sideshows)** also **side-show.** [1] A **sideshow** is a less important or less significant event or situation related to a larger, more important one that is happening at the same time. ❑ *In the end, the meeting was a sideshow to a political storm that broke Thursday.* N-COUNT: oft N *to* n [2] At a circus or fair, a **sideshow** is a performance that you watch or a game of skill that you play, that is provided in addition to the main entertainment. N-COUNT

**side-splitting** Something that is **side-splitting** is very funny and makes you laugh a lot. [INFORMAL] ❑ *...a side-splitting joke.* ADJ

**side|step** /saɪdstep/ **(sidesteps, sidestepping, sidestepped)** also **side-step.** [1] If you **sidestep** a problem, you avoid discussing it or dealing with it. ❑ *Rarely, if ever, does he sidestep a question... He was trying to sidestep responsibility.* VERB = avoid V n V n [2] If you **sidestep**, you step sideways in order to avoid something or someone that is coming towards you or going to hit you. ❑ *As I sidestepped, the bottle hit me on the left hip... He made a grab for her but she sidestepped him.* VERB V V n

**side street (side streets)** A **side street** is a quiet, often narrow street which leads off a busier street. N-COUNT

**side|swipe** /saɪdswaɪp/ **(sideswipes)** also **side-swipe.** If you take a **sideswipe at** someone, you make an unexpected critical remark about them while you are talking about something else. ❑ *Despite the increasingly hostile sideswipes at him, the Chancellor is secure in his post.* N-COUNT: usu N *at* n

**side|track** /saɪdtræk/ **(sidetracks, sidetracking, sidetracked)** also **side-track.** If you **are sidetracked** by something, it makes you forget what you intended to do or say, and start instead doing or talking about a different thing. ❑ *He'd managed to avoid being sidetracked by Schneider's problems... The leadership moved to sidetrack the proposal... They have a tendency to try to sidetrack you from your task.* VERB *be* V-ed V n V n *from* n Also *be* V-ed *into* n/-ing

**side|walk** /saɪdwɔːk/ **(sidewalks)** A **sidewalk** is a path with a hard surface by the side of a road. [AM] ❑ *Two men and a woman were walking briskly down the sidewalk toward him.* N-COUNT

✔ in BRIT, use **pavement**

**side|ways** /saɪdweɪz/ [1] **Sideways** means from or towards the side of something or someone. ❑ *Piercey glanced sideways at her... The ladder blew sideways... He was facing sideways.* ♦ **Sideways** is also an adjective. ❑ *Alfred shot him a sideways glance.* ADV: ADV after v ADJ: ADJ n [2] If you are moved **sideways** at work, you move to another job at the same level as your old job. ❑ *He would be moved sideways, rather than demoted.* ♦ **Sideways** is also an adjective. ❑ *...her recent sideways move.* ADV: ADV after v ADJ: ADJ n

**sid|ing** /saɪdɪŋ/ **(sidings)** [1] A **siding** is a short railway track beside the main tracks, where engines and carriages are left when they are not being used. N-COUNT [2] **Siding** is a wooden or metal covering on the outside walls of a building. [AM] N-UNCOUNT

**si|dle** /saɪdᵊl/ **(sidles, sidling, sidled)** If you **sidle** somewhere, you walk there in a quiet or cautious way, as if you do not want anyone to notice you. ❑ *A young man sidled up to me and said, 'May I help you?'* VERB V prep/adv

**SIDS** /sɪdz/ **SIDS** is used to talk about the sudden death of a baby while it is asleep, when it had N-UNCOUNT = cot death not previously been ill. **SIDS** is an abbreviation for 'sudden infant death syndrome'.

**siè|cle** → see **fin de siècle**.

**siege** /siːdʒ/ **(sieges)** [1] A **siege** is a military or police operation in which soldiers or police surround a place in order to force the people there to come out or give up control of the place. ❑ *We must do everything possible to lift the siege... The journalists found a city virtually under siege.* → See also **state of siege**. (N-COUNT: also *under* N)
[2] If police, soldiers, or journalists **lay siege to** a place, they surround it in order to force the people there to come out or give up control of the place. ❑ *The rebels laid siege to the governor's residence.* (PHRASE: V inflects, usu PHR *to* n)

**siege men|tal|ity** If a group of people have a **siege mentality**, they think that other people are constantly trying to harm or defeat them, and so they care only about protecting themselves. ❑ *Police officers had a siege mentality that isolated them from the people they served.* (N-SING: also no det)

**si|es|ta** /siestə/ **(siestas)** A **siesta** is a short sleep or rest which you have in the early afternoon, especially in hot countries. ❑ *They have a siesta during the hottest part of the day.* (N-COUNT)

**sieve** /sɪv/ **(sieves, sieving, sieved)** [1] A **sieve** is a tool used for separating solids from liquids or larger pieces of something from smaller pieces. It consists of a metal or plastic ring with a wire or plastic net underneath, which the liquid or smaller pieces pass through. → See picture on page 1710. ❑ *Press the raspberries through a fine sieve to form a puree.* (N-COUNT)
[2] When you **sieve** a substance, you put it through a sieve. ❑ *Cream the margarine in a small bowl, then sieve the icing sugar into it.* (VERB = *sift*; V n)

**sift** /sɪft/ **(sifts, sifting, sifted)** [1] If you **sift** a powder such as flour or sand, you put it through a sieve in order to remove large pieces or lumps. ❑ *Sift the flour and baking powder into a medium-sized mixing bowl.* (VERB = *sieve*; V n)
[2] If you **sift through** something such as evidence, you examine it thoroughly. ❑ *Police officers have continued to sift through the wreckage following yesterday's bomb attack... Brook has sifted the evidence and summarises it clearly in his report.* (VERB; V *through* n; V n)

**sigh** /saɪ/ **(sighs, sighing, sighed)** ◆◇◇ [1] When you **sigh**, you let out a deep breath, as a way of expressing feelings such as disappointment, tiredness, or pleasure. ❑ *Michael sighed wearily... Dad sighed and stood up.* ♦ **Sigh** is also a noun. ❑ *She kicked off her shoes with a sigh.* (VERB; V prep/adv; V; N-COUNT)
[2] If you **sigh** something, you say it with a sigh. ❑ *'Oh, sorry. I forgot.' — 'Everyone forgets,' the girl sighed.* (VERB; V with quote)
[3] If people breathe or heave a **sigh of relief**, they feel happy that something unpleasant has not happened or is no longer happening. ❑ *There was a big sigh of relief once the economic reform plan was agreed.* (PHRASE: *sigh* inflects, PHR after v)

**sight** /saɪt/ **(sights, sighting, sighted)** ◆◆◇
[1] Someone's **sight** is their ability to see. ❑ *My sight is failing, and I can't see to read any more... I use the sense of sound much more than the sense of sight.* (N-UNCOUNT: oft poss N = *vision*)
[2] **The sight of** something is the act of seeing it or an occasion on which you see it. ❑ *I faint at the sight of blood... The sight of him entering a room could flood her with desire.* (N-SING: *the* N *of* n)
[3] A **sight** is something that you see. ❑ *We encountered the pathetic sight of a family packing up its home.* (N-COUNT: usu with supp, oft adj N)
[4] If you **sight** someone or something, you suddenly see them, often briefly. ❑ *The security forces sighted a group of young men that had crossed the border.* (VERB; V n)
[5] The **sights** of a weapon such as a rifle are the part which helps you aim it more accurately. (N-COUNT: usu pl)
[6] **The sights** are the places that are interesting to see and that are often visited by tourists. ❑ *I am going to show you the sights of our wonderful city.* (N-PLURAL: usu *the* N, oft N *of* n)
[7] You can use **a sight** to mean a lot. For example, if you say that something is **a sight** worse than it was before, you are emphasizing that it is much worse than it was. [INFORMAL] ❑ *She's been no more difficult than most daughters and a sight better than some I could mention.* (ADV: ADV adj/adv; emphasis)
[8] → See also **sighted**, **sighting**.

PHRASES [9] If you **catch sight of** someone, you suddenly see them, often briefly. ❑ *Then he caught sight of her small black velvet hat in the crowd.* (PHRASE: V inflects, PHR n = *see*)
[10] If you say that something seems to have certain characteristics **at first sight**, you mean that it appears to have the features you describe when you first see it but later it is found to be different. ❑ *It promised to be a more difficult undertaking than might appear at first sight.* (PHRASE: PHR with cl)
[11] If something is **in sight** or **within sight**, you can see it. If it is **out of sight**, you cannot see it. ❑ *The Atlantic coast is within sight of the hotel... My companion suggested that we park out of sight of passing traffic to avoid attracting attention.* (PHRASE: usu v-link PHR)
[12] If a result or a decision is **in sight** or **within sight**, it is likely to happen within a short time. ❑ *An agreement on many aspects of trade policy was in sight.* (PHRASE: v-link PHR)
[13] If you **lose sight of** an important aspect of something, you no longer pay attention to it because you are worrying about less important things. ❑ *In some cases, US industry has lost sight of customer needs in designing products.* (PHRASE: V inflects, PHR n = *forget*)
[14] If someone is ordered to do something **on sight**, they have to do it without delay, as soon as a person or thing is seen. ❑ *Troops shot anyone suspicious on sight.* (PHRASE)
[15] If you **set** your **sights on** something, you decide that you want it and try hard to get it. ❑ *They have set their sights on the world record.* (PHRASE: V inflects, PHR n)

**sight|ed** /saɪtɪd/ **Sighted** people have the ability to see. This word is usually used to contrast people who can see with people who are blind. ❑ *Blind children tend to be more passive in this area of motor development than sighted children.* → See also **clear-sighted**, **far-sighted**, **long-sighted**, **near-sighted**, **short-sighted**. (ADJ: ADJ n ≠ *blind*)

**sight|ing** /saɪtɪŋ/ **(sightings)** A **sighting of** something, especially something unusual or unexpected is an occasion on which it is seen. ❑ *...the sighting of a rare sea bird at Lundy island.* (N-COUNT: oft N *of* n)

**sight|less** /saɪtləs/ Someone who is **sightless** is blind. [LITERARY] ❑ *He wiped a tear from his sightless eyes.* (ADJ)

**sight-read (sight-reads, sight-reading)**

> ✔ The form **sight-read** is used in the present tense, where it is pronounced /saɪt riːd/, and is the past tense and past participle, pronounced /saɪt red/.

Someone who can **sight-read** can play or sing music from a printed sheet the first time they see it, without practising it beforehand. ❑ *Symphony musicians cannot necessarily sight-read.* (VERB; V; Also V n)

**sight|see|ing** /saɪtsiːɪŋ/ also **sight-seeing**. If you go **sightseeing** or do some **sightseeing**, you travel around visiting the interesting places that tourists usually visit. ❑ *...a day's sight-seeing in Venice. ...a sightseeing tour.* (N-UNCOUNT)

**sight|seer** /saɪtsiːəʳ/ **(sightseers)** A **sightseer** is someone who is travelling around visiting the interesting places that tourists usually visit. ❑ *...coachloads of sightseers.* (N-COUNT)

**sign** /saɪn/ **(signs, signing, signed)** ◆◆◆ [1] A **sign** is a mark or shape that always has a particular meaning, for example in mathematics or music. ❑ *Equations are generally written with a two-bar equals sign.* (N-COUNT)
[2] A **sign** is a movement of your arms, hands, or head which is intended to have a particular meaning. ❑ *They gave Lavalle the thumbs-up sign... The priest made the sign of the cross over him.* (N-COUNT)
[3] If you **sign**, you communicate with someone using sign language. If a programme or performance **is signed**, someone uses sign language so that deaf people can understand it. ❑ *All programmes will be either 'signed' or subtitled.* (VERB; *be* V-ed; Also V, V n)
[4] A **sign** is a piece of wood, metal, or plastic with words or pictures on it. Signs give you information about something, or give you a warning or an instruction. ❑ *...a sign saying that the highway was closed because of snow.* (N-COUNT)
[5] If there is a **sign of** something, there is something which shows that it exists or is happening. ❑ *They are prepared to* (N-VAR: usu with supp, oft N *of* n)

*hand back a hundred prisoners of war a day as a sign of good will... Your blood would have been checked for any sign of kidney failure.* [6] VERB When you **sign** a document, you write your name on it, usually at the end or in a special space. You do this to indicate that you have written the document, that you agree with what is written, or that you were present as a witness. ❑ *World leaders are expected to sign a treaty pledging to increase environmental protection.* (V n) [7] VERB If an organization **signs** someone or if someone **signs** for an organization, they sign a contract agreeing to work for that organization for a specified period of time. ❑ *The Minnesota Vikings signed Herschel Walker from the Dallas Cowboys...* (V n) *The band then signed to Slash Records.* (V *to/for* n) [8] N-COUNT In astrology, a **sign** or a **sign of the zodiac** is one of the twelve areas into which the heavens are divided. ❑ *The New Moon takes place in your opposite sign of Libra on the 15th.* [9] ➔ See also **signing**, **call sign**. [10] PHRASE: v-link PHR n If you say that there is **no sign of** someone, you mean that they have not yet arrived, although you are expecting them to come. ❑ *The London train was on time, but there was no sign of my Finnish friend.* [11] to **sign** one's **own death warrant** ➔ see **death warrant**.

♦ **sign away** PHRASAL VERB If you **sign** something **away**, you sign official documents that mean that you no longer own it or have a right to it. ❑ *The Duke signed away his inheritance...* (V P n (not pron)) *They signed the rights away when they sold their idea to DC Comics.* (V n P)

♦ **sign for** PHRASAL VERB If you **sign for** something, you officially state that you have received it, by signing a form or book. ❑ *When the postal clerk delivers your order, check the carton before signing for it.* (V P n)

♦ **sign in** PHRASAL VERB If you **sign in**, you officially indicate that you have arrived at a hotel or club by signing a book or form. ❑ *I signed in and crunched across the gravel to my room.* (V P)

♦ **sign off** [1] PHRASAL VERB If someone **signs off**, they write a final message at the end of a letter or they say a final message at the end of a telephone conversation. You can say that people such as entertainers **sign off** when they finish a broadcast. ❑ *O.K. I'll sign off. We'll talk at the beginning of the week.* (V P) [2] PHRASAL VERB When someone who has been unemployed **signs off**, they officially inform the authorities that they have found a job, so that they no longer receive money from the government. [BRIT] ❑ *If you work without signing off the dole you are breaking the law.* (V P n (not pron); Also V P)

♦ **sign on** PHRASAL VERB When an unemployed person **signs on**, they officially inform the authorities that they are unemployed, so that they can receive money from the government in order to live. [BRIT] ❑ *He has signed on at the job centre...* (V P prep) *I had to sign on the dole on Monday.* (V P n (not pron))

♦ **sign over** PHRASAL VERB If you **sign** something **over**, you sign documents that give someone else property, possessions, or rights that were previously yours. ❑ *Two years ago, he signed over his art collection to the New York Metropolitan Museum of Art...* (V P n (not pron)) *Last June, he closed his business voluntarily and signed his assets over to someone else.* (V n P)

♦ **sign up** PHRASAL VERB If you **sign up** for an organization or if an organization **signs** you **up**, you sign a contract officially agreeing to do a job or course of study. ❑ *He signed up as a steward with P&O Lines...* (V P *as/for* n) *He saw the song's potential, and persuaded the company to sign her up.* (V n P)

**sig|nal** /sɪgnəl/ **(signals, signalling, signalled)** ◆◇◇

✔ in AM, use **signaling, signaled**

[1] N-COUNT A **signal** is a gesture, sound, or action which is intended to give a particular message to the person who sees or hears it. ❑ *They fired three distress signals... As soon as it was dark, Mrs Evans gave the signal... You mustn't fire without my signal.* [2] VERB If you **signal to** someone, you make a gesture or sound in order to send them a particular message. ❑ *The United manager was to be seen frantically signalling to McClair...* (V prep/adv) *He stood up, signalling to the officer that he had finished with his client...* (V that) *She signalled a passing taxi and ordered him to take her to the rue Marengo.* (V n; Also V) [3] N-COUNT: with supp = sign If an event or action is a **signal of** something, it suggests that this thing exists or is going to happen. ❑ *Kurdish leaders saw the visit as an important signal of support.* [4] VERB = indicate If someone or something **signals** an event, they suggest that the event is happening or likely to happen. ❑ *She will be signalling massive changes in energy policy...* (V n) *The outcome of that meeting could signal whether there exists a will to begin negotiating.* (V wh) [5] N-COUNT A **signal** is a piece of equipment beside a railway, which indicates to train drivers whether they should stop the train or not. [6] N-COUNT A **signal** is a series of radio waves, light waves, or changes in electrical current which may carry information. ❑ *...high-frequency radio signals.*

**sig|nal box** **(signal boxes)** N-COUNT A **signal box** is a small building near a railway, which contains the switches used to control the signals.

**signal|man** /sɪgnəlmæn/ **(signalmen)** N-COUNT A **signalman** is a person whose job is to control the signals on a particular section of a railway.

**sig|na|tory** /sɪgnətri, AM -tɔːri/ **(signatories)** N-COUNT: oft N *of/to* n The **signatories** of an official document are the people, organizations, or countries that have signed it. [FORMAL] ❑ *Both countries are signatories to the Nuclear Non-Proliferation Treaty.*

**sig|na|ture** /sɪgnətʃəʳ/ **(signatures)** [1] N-COUNT Your **signature** is your name, written in your own characteristic way, often at the end of a document to indicate that you wrote the document or that you agree with what it says. ❑ *I was writing my signature at the bottom of the page.* [2] ADJ: ADJ n A **signature** item is typical of or associated with a particular person. [mainly JOURNALISM] ❑ *Rabbit stew is one of chef Giancarlo Moeri's signature dishes.*

**sig|na|ture tune** **(signature tunes)** N-COUNT A **signature tune** is the tune which is always played at the beginning or end of a particular television or radio programme, or which people associate with a particular performer. [mainly BRIT] ❑ *Doesn't that sound like the signature tune from The Late Late Show?*

✔ in AM, usually use **theme song**

**sign|board** /saɪnbɔːʳd/ **(signboards)** N-COUNT A **signboard** is a piece of wood which has been painted with pictures or words and which gives some information about a particular place, product, or event. ❑ *The signboard outside the factory read 'baby milk plant'.*

**sign|er** /saɪnəʳ/ **(signers)** N-COUNT A **signer** is someone who communicates to deaf people using sign language. ❑ *I'm keen on providing signers for deaf people and readers for the blind.*

**sig|net ring** /sɪgnət rɪŋ/ **(signet rings)** N-COUNT A **signet ring** is a ring which has a flat oval or circular section at the front with a pattern or letters carved into it.

**sig|nifi|cance** /sɪgnɪfɪkəns/ N-UNCOUNT: usu with supp, oft N prep = importance The **significance** of something is the importance that it has, usually because it will have an effect on a situation or shows something about a situation. ❑ *Ideas about the social significance of religion have changed over time.*

**sig|nifi|cant** /sɪgnɪfɪkənt/ ◆◆◇ [1] ADJ: usu ADJ n ≠ insignificant A **significant** amount or effect is large enough to be important or affect a situation to a noticeable degree. ❑ *A small but significant number of 11-year-olds are illiterate. ...foods that offer a significant amount of protein.* ♦ **sig|nifi|cant|ly** ADV: ADV with v, ADV adj/adv/prep *The number of MPs now supporting him had increased significantly.* [2] ADJ A **significant** fact, event, or thing is one that is important or shows something. ❑ *I think it was significant that he never knew his own father.* ♦ **sig|nifi|cant|ly** ADV *Significantly, the company recently opened a huge store in Atlanta.*

**sig|nifi|cant oth|er** **(significant others)** N-COUNT If you refer to your **significant other**, you are referring to your wife, husband, or the person you are having a relationship with.

**sig|ni|fy** /sɪgnɪfaɪ/ **(signifies, signifying, signified)** [1] If an event, a sign, or a symbol **signifies** something, it is a sign of that thing or represents that thing. ❑ *The contrasting approaches to Europe signified a sharp difference between the major parties... The symbol displayed outside a restaurant signifies there's excellent cuisine inside.* [2] If you **signify** something, you make a sign or gesture in order to communicate a particular meaning. ❑ *Two jurors signified their dissent... The UN flag was raised to signify that control had passed into its hands.* VERB V n V that VERB = indicate V n V that

**sign|ing** /saɪnɪŋ/ **(signings)** [1] The **signing of** a document is the act of writing your name to indicate that you agree with what it says or to say that you have been present to witness other people writing their signature. ❑ *Spain's top priority is the signing of an EMU treaty.* [2] A **signing** is someone who has recently signed a contract agreeing to play for a sports team or work for a record company. ❑ *...the salary paid to the club's latest signing.* [3] The **signing of** a player by a sports team or a group by a record company is the act of drawing up a legal document setting out the length and terms of the association between them. ❑ *...Manchester United's signing of the Australian goalkeeper Mark Bosnich.* [4] **Signing** is the use of sign language to communicate with someone who is deaf. ❑ *The two deaf actors converse solely in signing.* N-UNCOUNT: N of n N-COUNT: usu with supp N-UNCOUNT: N of n N-UNCOUNT

**sign lan|guage** **(sign languages)** **Sign language** is movements of your hands and arms used to communicate. There are several official systems of sign language, used for example by deaf people. Movements are also sometimes invented by people when they want to communicate with someone who does not speak the same language. ❑ *Her son used sign language to tell her what happened.* N-VAR

**sign|post** /saɪnpoust/ **(signposts)** A **signpost** is a sign where roads meet that tells you which direction to go in to reach a particular place or different places. ❑ *Turn off at the signpost for Attlebridge.* N-COUNT = sign

**sign|post|ed** /saɪnpoustɪd/ A place or route that is **signposted** has signposts beside the road to show the way. ❑ *The entrance is well signposted and is in Marbury Road.* ADJ

**Sikh** /siːk/ **(Sikhs)** A **Sikh** is a person who follows the Indian religion of Sikhism. ❑ *The rise of racism concerns Sikhs because they are such a visible minority. ...Sikh festivals.* N-COUNT: oft N n

**Sikh|ism** /siːkɪzəm/ **Sikhism** is an Indian religion which separated from Hinduism in the sixteenth century and which teaches that there is only one God. N-UNCOUNT

**si|lage** /saɪlɪdʒ/ **Silage** is food for cattle that is made by cutting a crop such as grass or corn when it is green and then keeping it covered. N-UNCOUNT

**si|lence** /saɪləns/ **(silences, silencing, silenced)** ◆◇◇ [1] If there is **silence**, nobody is speaking. ❑ *They stood in silence... He never lets those long silences develop during dinner... Then he bellowed 'Silence!'* [2] **The silence of** a place is the extreme quietness there. ❑ *She breathed deeply, savouring the silence.* [3] Someone's **silence** about something is their failure or refusal to speak to other people about it. ❑ *The district court ruled that Popper's silence in court today should be entered as a plea of not guilty.* ● If someone **breaks** their **silence** about something, they talk about something that they have not talked about before or for a long time. ❑ *Gary decided to break his silence about his son's suffering in the hope of helping other families.* [4] To **silence** someone or something means to stop them speaking or making a noise. ❑ *A ringing phone silenced her.* [5] If someone **silences** you, they stop you expressing opinions that they do not agree with. ❑ *Like other tyrants, he tried to silence anyone who spoke out against him.* N-VAR: oft in/of N N-UNCOUNT: oft the N of n N-UNCOUNT: oft poss N PHRASE: V inflects VERB V n VERB V n

**si|lenc|er** /saɪlənsəʳ/ **(silencers)** [1] A **silencer** is a device that is fitted onto a gun to make it very quiet when it is fired. ❑ *...a pistol that was equipped with a silencer.* [2] A **silencer** is a device on a car exhaust that makes it quieter. [BRIT] N-COUNT N-COUNT

✔ in AM, use **muffler**

**si|lent** /saɪlənt/ ◆◇◇ [1] Someone who is **silent** is not speaking. ❑ *Trish was silent because she was reluctant to put her thoughts into words... He spoke no English and was completely silent during the visit... They both fell silent.* ♦ **si|lent|ly** *She and Ned sat silently for a moment, absorbing the peace of the lake.* [2] If you describe someone as a **silent** person, you mean that they do not talk to people very much, and sometimes give the impression of being unfriendly. ❑ *He was a serious, silent man.* [3] A place that is **silent** is completely quiet, with no sound at all. Something that is **silent** makes no sound at all. ❑ *The room was silent except for John's crunching.* ♦ **si|lent|ly** *Strange shadows moved silently in the almost permanent darkness.* [4] A **silent** emotion or action is not expressed in speech. ❑ *The attacker still stood there, watching her with silent contempt.* [5] A **silent** film has pictures usually accompanied by music but does not have the actors' voices or any other sounds. ❑ *...one of the famous silent films of Charlie Chaplin.* ADJ: v-link ADJ ADV: ADV with v ADJ: ADJ n = quiet ADJ: usu v-link ADJ ADV: ADV with v ADJ: ADJ n ADJ: ADJ n

**si|lent ma|jor|ity** If you believe that, in society or in a particular group, the opinions of most people are very different from the opinions that are most often heard in public, you can refer to these people as the **silent majority**. ❑ *The silent majority of supportive parents and teachers should make their views known.* N-SING-COLL

**si|lent part|ner** **(silent partners)** A **silent partner** is a person who provides some of the capital for a business but who does not take an active part in managing the business. [AM, BUSINESS] N-COUNT

✔ in BRIT, use **sleeping partner**

**sil|hou|ette** /sɪluet/ **(silhouettes)** [1] A **silhouette** is the solid dark shape that you see when someone or something has a bright light or pale background behind them. ❑ *The dark silhouette of the castle ruins stood out boldly against the fading light.* [2] The **silhouette** of something is the outline that it has, which often helps you to recognize it. ❑ *...the distinctive silhouette of his ears.* N-COUNT N-COUNT

**sil|hou|ett|ed** /sɪluetɪd/ If someone or something is **silhouetted against** a background, you can see their silhouette. ❑ *Silhouetted against the sun stood the figure of a man.* ADJ: usu v-link ADJ against n

**sili|ca** /sɪlɪkə/ **Silica** is silicon dioxide, a compound of silicon which is found in sand, quartz, and flint, and which is used to make glass. N-UNCOUNT

**sili|cate** /sɪlɪkət/ **(silicates)** A **silicate** is a compound of silica which does not dissolve. There are many different kinds of silicate. ❑ *...large amounts of aluminum silicate.* N-MASS

**sili|con** /sɪlɪkən/ **Silicon** is an element that is found in sand and in minerals such as quartz and granite. Silicon is used to make parts of computers and other electronic equipment. ❑ *A chip is a piece of silicon about the size of a postage stamp.* N-UNCOUNT

**sili|con chip** **(silicon chips)** A **silicon chip** is a very small piece of silicon inside a computer. It has electronic circuits on it and can hold large quantities of information or perform mathematical or logical operations. N-COUNT = microchip

**sili|cone** /sɪlɪkoun/ **Silicone** is a tough artificial substance made from silicon, which is used to make polishes, and also used in cosmetic surgery and plastic surgery. ❑ *...silicone breast implants.* N-UNCOUNT: usu N n

**silk** /sɪlk/ **(silks)** **Silk** is a substance which is made into smooth fine cloth and sewing thread. You can also refer to this cloth or thread as **silk**. ❑ *They continued to get their silks from China... Pauline wore a silk dress with a strand of pearls.* N-MASS

**silk|en** /sɪlkən/ [1] **Silken** is used to describe things that are very pleasantly smooth and soft. [LITERARY] ❑ *...her long silken hair.* [2] A **silken** gar- ADJ: usu ADJ n ADJ: ADJ n ment, fabric, or rope is made of silk or a material that looks like silk. [LITERARY] ❑ *...silken cushions.*

**silk-screen** also **silkscreen. Silk-screen** printing is a method of printing patterns onto cloth by forcing paint or dyes through silk or similar material. ❑ *...silk-screen prints.* ADJ: ADJ n

**silk|worm** /sɪlkwɜːʳm/ **(silkworms)** A **silkworm** is the young form of a Chinese moth and it produces silk. N-COUNT

**silky** /sɪlki/ **(silkier, silkiest)** If something has a **silky** texture, it is smooth, soft, and shiny, like silk. ❑ *...dresses in seductively silky fabrics.* ADJ: usu ADJ n

**sill** /sɪl/ **(sills)** A **sill** is a shelf along the bottom edge of a window, either inside or outside a building. ❑ *Whitlock was perched on the sill of the room's only window.* N-COUNT = ledge

**sil|ly** /sɪli/ **(sillier, silliest)** If you say that someone or something is **silly**, you mean that they are foolish, childish, or ridiculous. ❑ *My best friend tells me that I am silly to be upset about this... That's a silly question.* ADJ

**sil|ly sea|son** **The silly season** is the time around August when the newspapers are full of unimportant or silly news stories because there is not much political news to report. [BRIT] N-PROPER: *the* N

**silo** /saɪloʊ/ **(silos)** [1] A **silo** is a tall round metal tower on a farm, in which grass, grain, or some other substance is stored. ❑ *Before silos were invented, cows gave less milk during winter because they had no green grass to eat. ...a grain silo.* N-COUNT [2] A **silo** is a specially built place underground where a nuclear missile is kept. ❑ *...underground nuclear missile silos.* N-COUNT

**silt** /sɪlt/ **Silt** is fine sand, soil, or mud which is carried along by a river. ❑ *The lake was almost solid with silt and vegetation.* N-UNCOUNT

**sil|ver** /sɪlvəʳ/ **(silvers)** [1] **Silver** is a valuable pale grey metal that is used for making jewellery and ornaments. ❑ *...a hand-crafted brooch made from silver. ...silver teaspoons.* ◆◇◇ N-UNCOUNT: oft N n [2] **Silver** consists of coins that are made from silver or that look like silver. ❑ *...the basement where £150,000 in silver was buried.* N-UNCOUNT [3] You can use **silver** to refer to all the things in a house that are made of silver, especially the cutlery and dishes. ❑ *He beat the rugs and polished the silver.* N-UNCOUNT: also *the* N [4] **Silver** is used to describe things that are shiny and pale grey in colour. ❑ *He had thick silver hair which needed cutting.* COLOUR [5] A **silver** is the same as a **silver medal**. ❑ *Britain went on to take bronze and then followed it up by winning silver in the World Cup.* N-VAR [6] **born with a silver spoon in** your **mouth** → see **spoon**.

**sil|ver birch** **(silver birches** or **silver birch)** A **silver birch** is a tree with a greyish-white trunk and branches. N-COUNT

**sil|vered** /sɪlvəʳd/ You can describe something as **silvered** when it has become silver in colour. [LITERARY] ❑ *He had a magnificent head of silvered hair.* ADJ: usu ADJ n

**sil|ver ju|bi|lee** **(silver jubilees)** A **silver jubilee** is the 25th anniversary of an important event such as a person becoming king or queen, or an organization being started. ❑ *She arrived in St Ives to celebrate the Queen's Silver Jubilee.* N-COUNT

**sil|ver lin|ing** [1] If you say that **every cloud has a silver lining**, you mean that every sad or unpleasant situation has a positive side to it. ❑ *As they say, every cloud has a silver lining. We have drawn lessons from the decisions taken.* PHRASE [2] If you talk about a **silver lining**, you are talking about something positive that comes out of a sad or unpleasant situation. ❑ *The fall in inflation is the silver lining of the prolonged recession.* N-SING

**sil|ver med|al** **(silver medals)** If you win a **silver medal**, you come second in a competition, especially a sports contest, and are given a medal made of silver as a prize. ❑ *Gillingham won the silver medal in the 200 metres at Seoul.* N-COUNT

**sil|ver plate** [1] **Silver plate** is metal that has been coated with a thin layer of silver. ❑ *...silver-plate cutlery.* N-UNCOUNT: oft N n [2] **Silver plate** is dishes, bowls, and cups that are made of silver. [BRIT] ❑ *...gold and silver plate, jewellery, and roomfuls of antique furniture.* N-UNCOUNT

✓ in AM, use **silver**, **solid silver**

**silver-plated** Something that is **silver-plated** is covered with a very thin layer of silver. ❑ *...silver-plated cutlery.* ADJ

**sil|ver screen** People sometimes refer to the films that are shown in cinemas as **the silver screen**. ❑ *Marlon Brando, Steve McQueen, and James Dean are now legends of the silver screen.* N-SING: *the* N

**silver|smith** /sɪlvəʳsmɪθ/ **(silversmiths)** A **silversmith** is a person who makes things out of silver. N-COUNT

**silver-tongued** A **silver-tongued** person is very skilful at persuading people to believe what they say or to do what they want them to do. ❑ *...a silver-tongued lawyer.* ADJ: usu ADJ n

**silver|ware** /sɪlvəʳweəʳ/ [1] You can use **silverware** to refer to all the things in a house that are made of silver, especially the cutlery and dishes. ❑ *There was a serving spoon missing when Nina put the silverware back in its box.* N-UNCOUNT = silver [2] Journalists sometimes use **silverware** to refer to silver cups and other prizes won by sports teams or players. ❑ *Everton paraded their recently acquired silverware.* N-UNCOUNT

**sil|ver wed|ding** **(silver weddings)** A married couple's **silver wedding** or **silver wedding anniversary** is the 25th anniversary of their wedding. ❑ *He and Helen celebrated their silver wedding last year.* N-COUNT: usu poss N

**sil|very** /sɪlvəri/ **Silvery** things look like silver or are the colour of silver. ❑ *...a small, intense man with silvery hair.* ADJ: usu ADJ n

**sim** /sɪm/ **(sims)** A **sim** is a computer game that simulates an activity such as playing a sport or flying an aircraft. [COMPUTING] ❑ *The game is a simple sports sim.* N-COUNT

**SIM card** /sɪm kɑːʳd/ **(SIM cards)** A **SIM card** is a microchip in a mobile phone that connects it to a particular phone network. **SIM** is an abbreviation for 'Subscriber Identity Module'. N-COUNT

**sim|ian** /sɪmiən/ [1] If someone has a **simian** face, they look rather like a monkey. [FORMAL] ❑ *Ada had a wrinkled, simian face.* ADJ: usu ADJ n [2] **Simian** is used to describe things relating to monkeys or apes. [TECHNICAL] ❑ *...a simian virus.* ADJ: usu ADJ n

**simi|lar** /sɪmɪləʳ/ If one thing is **similar to** another, or if two things are **similar**, they have features that are the same. ❑ *...a savoury cake with a texture similar to that of carrot cake... The accident was similar to one that happened in 1973. ...a group of similar pictures.* ◆◆◇ ADJ: oft ADJ *to* n ≠ different

**simi|lar|ity** /sɪmɪlærɪti/ **(similarities)** [1] If there is a **similarity between** two or more things, they are similar to each other. ❑ *The astonishing similarity between my brother and my first-born son... She is also 25 and a native of Birmingham, but the similarity ends there.* N-UNCOUNT: oft N *between/in/with* n [2] **Similarities** are features that things have which make them similar to each other. ❑ *There were significant similarities between mother and son.* N-COUNT: usu pl, oft N *between/in/with* n ≠ difference

**simi|lar|ly** /sɪmɪləʳli/ [1] You use **similarly** to say that something is similar to something else. ❑ *Most of the men who now gathered round him again were similarly dressed.* ADV: ADV adj/adv, ADV with v ≠ differently [2] You use **similarly** when mentioning a fact or situation that is similar to the one you have just mentioned. ❑ *A mother recognises the feel of her child's skin when blindfolded. Similarly, she can instantly identify her baby's cry.* ADV: ADV with cl = likewise

**simi|le** /sɪmɪli/ **(similes)** A **simile** is an expression which describes a person or thing as being similar to someone or something else. For example, the sentences 'She runs like a deer' and 'He's as white as a sheet' contain similes. N-COUNT

**sim|mer** /sɪməʳ/ **(simmers, simmering, simmered)** [1] When you **simmer** food or when it **simmers**, you cook it by keeping it at boiling VERB point or just below boiling point. ❑ *Make an infusion by boiling and simmering the rhubarb and camomile together...* V n *Turn the heat down so the sauce simmers gently.* V ♦ **Simmer** is also a noun. N-SING ❑ *Combine the stock, whole onion and peppercorns in a pan and bring to a simmer.* [2] VERB If a conflict or a quarrel **simmers**, it does not actually happen for a period of time, but eventually builds up to the point where it does. ❑ *...bitter divisions that have simmered for more than half a century...* V *The province was attacked a month ago after weeks of simmering tension.* V-ing

**sim|per** /sɪmpəʳ/ **(simpers, simpering, simpered)** VERB When someone **simpers**, they smile in a rather silly way. ❑ *The maid lowered her chin and simpered.* V ♦ **Simper** is also a noun. N-COUNT ❑ *'Thank you doctor,' said the nurse with a simper.*

**sim|ple** /sɪmpəl/ **(simpler, simplest)** ♦♦◇ [1] ADJ ≠ complicated If you describe something as **simple**, you mean that it is not complicated, and is therefore easy to understand. ❑ *...simple pictures and diagrams. ...pages of simple advice on filling in your tax form... Buddhist ethics are simple but its practices are very complex to a western mind.* ♦ **simp|ly** ADV: ADV with v *When applying for a visa state simply and clearly the reasons why you need it.* [2] ADJ If you describe people or things as **simple**, you mean that they have all the basic or necessary things they require, but nothing extra. ❑ *He ate a simple dinner of rice and beans. ...the simple pleasures of childhood... Nothing is simpler than a cool white shirt.* ♦ **simp|ly** ADV: ADV after v *The living room is furnished simply with wicker furniture.* [3] ADJ If a problem is **simple** or if its solution is **simple**, the problem can be solved easily. ❑ *Some puzzles look difficult but once the solution is known are actually quite simple... I cut my purchases dramatically by the simple expedient of destroying my credit cards.* [4] ADJ: oft ADJ to-inf = easy A **simple** task is easy to do. ❑ *The simplest way to install a shower is to fit one over the bath.* ♦ **simp|ly** ADV: ADV with v *Simply dial the number and tell us your area.* [5] ADJ If you say that someone is **simple**, you mean that they are not very intelligent and have difficulty learning things. ❑ *He was simple as a child.* [6] ADJ: ADJ n [emphasis] = plain You use **simple** to emphasize that the thing you are referring to is the only important or relevant reason for something. ❑ *His refusal to talk was simple stubbornness.* [7] ADJ In grammar, **simple** tenses are ones which are formed without an auxiliary verb 'be', for example 'I dressed and went for a walk' and 'This tastes nice'. **Simple** verb groups are used especially to refer to completed actions, regular actions, and situations. Compare **continuous**. [8] ADJ In English grammar, a **simple** sentence consists of one main clause. Compare **compound**, **complex**. [9] → See also **simply**.

**sim|ple in|ter|est** N-UNCOUNT ≠ compound interest **Simple interest** is interest that is calculated on an original sum of money and not also on interest which has previously been added to the sum. Compare **compound interest**. [BUSINESS]

**simple-minded** ADJ [disapproval] If you describe someone as **simple-minded**, you believe that they interpret things in a way that is too simple and do not understand how complicated things are. ❑ *Sylvie was a simple-minded romantic.*

**sim|ple|ton** /sɪmpəltən/ **(simpletons)** N-COUNT [disapproval] If you call someone a **simpleton**, you think they are easily deceived or not very intelligent. ❑ *'But Ian's such a simpleton', she laughed.*

**sim|plic|ity** /sɪmplɪsɪti/ [1] N-UNCOUNT: usu with supp The **simplicity** of something is the fact that it is not complicated and can be understood or done easily. ❑ *The apparent simplicity of his plot is deceptive.* [2] N-UNCOUNT: usu with supp [approval] When you talk about something's **simplicity**, you approve of it because it has no unnecessary parts or complicated details. ❑ *...fussy details that ruin the simplicity of the design.*

**sim|pli|fi|ca|tion** /sɪmplɪfɪkeɪʃən/ **(simplifications)** [1] N-COUNT You can use **simplification** to refer to the thing that is produced when you make something simpler or when you reduce it to its basic elements. ❑ *Like any such diagram, it is a simplification.* [2] N-UNCOUNT **Simplification** is the act or process of making something simpler. ❑ *Everyone favours the simplification of court procedures.*

**sim|pli|fy** /sɪmplɪfaɪ/ **(simplifies, simplifying, simplified)** VERB ≠ complicate If you **simplify** something, you make it easier to understand or you remove the things which make it complex. ❑ *...a plan to simplify the complex social security system.* V n

**sim|plis|tic** /sɪmplɪstɪk/ ADJ A **simplistic** view or interpretation of something makes it seem much simpler than it really is. ❑ *He has a simplistic view of the treatment of eczema.*

**simp|ly** /sɪmpli/ ♦♦◇ [1] ADV: ADV before v, ADV with cl/group [emphasis] = just You use **simply** to emphasize that something consists of only one thing, happens for only one reason, or is done in only one way. ❑ *The table is simply a chipboard circle on a base... Most of the damage that's occurred was simply because of fallen trees.* [2] ADV: ADV before v, ADV adj [emphasis] = just You use **simply** to emphasize what you are saying. ❑ *This sort of increase simply cannot be justified... So many of these questions simply don't have answers.* [3] → See also **simple**.

**simu|late** /sɪmjʊleɪt/ **(simulates, simulating, simulated)** [1] VERB If you **simulate** an action or a feeling, you pretend that you are doing it or feeling it. ❑ *They rolled about on the Gilligan Road, simulating a bloodthirsty fight...* V n *He performed a simulated striptease.* V-ed [2] VERB If you **simulate** an object, a substance, or a noise, you produce something that looks or sounds like it. ❑ *The wood had been painted to simulate stone.* V n [3] VERB If you **simulate** a set of conditions, you create them artificially, for example in order to conduct an experiment. ❑ *The scientist developed one model to simulate a full year of the globe's climate...* V n *Cars are tested to see how much damage they suffer in simulated crashes.* V-ed

**simu|la|tion** /sɪmjʊleɪʃən/ **(simulations)** N-VAR **Simulation** is the process of simulating something or the result of simulating it. ❑ *Training includes realistic simulation of casualty procedures.*

**simu|la|tor** /sɪmjʊleɪtəʳ/ **(simulators)** N-COUNT A **simulator** is a device which artificially creates the effect of being in conditions of some kind. Simulators are used in training people such as pilots or astronauts. ❑ *...pilots practising a difficult landing in a flight simulator.*

**sim|ul|cast** /sɪməlkɑːst, -kæst/ **(simulcasts, simulcasting)**

> ✓ The form **simulcast** is used in the present tense and is the past tense and past participle of the verb.

[1] N-COUNT: oft N *of* n A **simulcast** is a programme which is broadcast at the same time on radio and television, or on more than one channel. ❑ *...tonight's simulcast of Verdi's Aida.* [2] VERB To **simulcast** a programme means to broadcast it at the same time on radio and television, or on more than one channel. ❑ *The show will be simulcast on NBC, Fox and a number of cable networks.* be V-ed Also V n

**sim|ul|ta|neous** /sɪməlteɪniəs, AM saɪm-/ ADJ Things which are **simultaneous** happen or exist at the same time. ❑ *...the simultaneous release of the book and the album... The theatre will provide simultaneous translation in both English and Chinese.* ♦ **sim|ul|ta|neous|ly** ADV: ADV with v, ADV with cl/group *The two guns fired almost simultaneously.*

**sin** /sɪn/ **(sins, sinning, sinned)** [1] N-VAR **Sin** or a **sin** is an action or type of behaviour which is believed to break the laws of God. ❑ *The Vatican's teaching on abortion is clear: it is a sin.* → See also **cardinal sin**, **mortal sin**. [2] VERB If you **sin**, you do something that is believed to break the laws of God. ❑ *The Spanish Inquisition charged him with sinning against God and man...* V *against* n *You have sinned and must repent your ways.* V ♦ **sin|ner** /sɪnəʳ/ **(sinners)** N-COUNT *I am a sinner and I need to repent of my sins.* [3] N-COUNT A **sin** is any action or behaviour that people disapprove of or consider morally wrong. ❑ *The ultimate sin was not infidelity, but public mention which led to scandal.* [4] PHRASE: If you say that a man and a woman

**are living in sin**, you mean that they are living together as a couple although they are not married. [OLD-FASHIONED] ❑ *She was living in sin with her boyfriend.* [5] **a multitude of sins** → see **multitude**. V inflects

**sin-bin** also **sin bin.** In the sports of ice hockey and rugby league, if a player is sent to the **sin-bin**, they are ordered to leave the playing area for a short period of time because they have done something that is against the rules. N-SING

**since** /sɪns/ ◆◆◆ [1] You use **since** when you are mentioning a time or event in the past and indicating that a situation has continued from then until now. PREP ❑ *Jacques Arnold has been a member of parliament since 1987... She had a sort of breakdown some years ago, and since then she has been very shy... I've been here since the end of June.* ♦ **Since** is also an adverb. ADV: ADV with v ❑ *When we first met, we had a row, and we have rowed frequently ever since.* ♦ **Since** is also a conjunction. CONJ ❑ *I've earned my own living since I was seven, doing all kinds of jobs.* [2] You use **since** to mention a time or event in the past when you are describing an event or situation that has happened after that time. PREP ❑ *The percentage increase in reported crime in England and Wales this year is the highest since the war... He turned out to have more battles with the Congress than any president since Andrew Johnson.* ♦ **Since** is also a conjunction. CONJ ❑ *So much has changed in the sport since I was a teenager... Since I have become a mother, the sound of children's voices has lost its charm.* [3] When you are talking about an event or situation in the past, you use **since** to indicate that another event happened at some point later in time. ADV: ADV with v ❑ *About six thousand people were arrested, several hundred of whom have since been released.* [4] If you say that something has **long since** happened, you mean that it happened a long time ago. PHRASE: PHR with v ❑ *Even though her parents have long since died, she still talks about them in the present tense.* [5] You use **since** to introduce reasons or explanations. CONJ = as ❑ *I'm forever on a diet, since I put on weight easily.*

**sin|cere** /sɪnsɪəʳ/ If you say that someone is **sincere**, you approve of them because they really mean the things they say. You can also describe someone's behaviour and beliefs as **sincere**. ADJ approval = genuine ≠ insincere ❑ *He's sincere in his views... There was a sincere expression of friendliness on both their faces.* ♦ **sin|cer|ity** /sɪnserɪti/ *I was impressed with his deep sincerity.* N-UNCOUNT

**sin|cere|ly** /sɪnsɪəʳli/ [1] If you say or feel something **sincerely**, you really mean or feel it, and are not pretending. ADV: usu ADV with v, also ADV adj ❑ *'Congratulations,' he said sincerely... 'I sincerely hope we shall meet again', he said... He sincerely believed he was acting in both women's best interests.* [2] In Britain, people write '**Yours sincerely**' before their signature at the end of a formal letter when they have addressed it to someone by name. In the United States, people usually write '**Sincerely yours**' or '**Sincerely**' instead. CONVENTION ❑ *Yours sincerely, James Brown.*

**si|necure** /sɪnɪkjʊəʳ, saɪn-/ **(sinecures)** A **sinecure** is a job for which you receive payment but which does not involve much work or responsibility. N-COUNT ❑ *She found him an exalted sinecure as a Fellow of the Library of Congress.*

**sine qua non** /sɪni kwɑː noʊn, AM - nɑːn/ **A sine qua non** is something that is essential if you want to achieve a particular thing. [FORMAL] N-SING: *a* N ❑ *Successful agricultural reform is also a sine qua non of Mexico's modernisation.*

**sin|ew** /sɪnjuː/ **(sinews)** A **sinew** is a cord in your body that connects a muscle to a bone. N-COUNT ❑ *...the sinews of the neck.*

**sin|ewy** /sɪnjuːi/ Someone who is **sinewy** has a lean body with strong muscles. ADJ ❑ *A short, sinewy young man.*

**sin|ful** /sɪnfʊl/ If you describe someone or something as **sinful**, you mean that they are wicked or immoral. ADJ ❑ *'I am a sinful man,' he said.* ♦ **sin|ful|ness** *...the sinfulness of apartheid.* N-UNCOUNT

**sing** /sɪŋ/ ◆◆◇ **(sings, singing, sang, sung)** [1] When you **sing**, you make musical sounds with your voice, usually producing words that fit a tune. VERB ❑ *I can't sing... I sing about love most of the time... They were all singing the same song... Go on, then, sing us a song!... 'You're getting to be a habit with me,' sang Eddie.* V / V about n / V n / V n n / V with quote [2] When birds or insects **sing**, they make pleasant high-pitched sounds. VERB ❑ *Birds were already singing in the garden.* V [3] → See also **singing**.

♦ **sing along** If you **sing along with** a piece of music, you sing it while you are listening to someone else perform it. PHRASAL VERB ❑ *We listen to children's shows on the radio, and Janey can sing along with all the tunes... You can sing along to your favourite Elvis hits. ...fifteen hundred people all singing along and dancing.* V P *with* n / V P *to* n / V P → See also **singalong**.

**sing.** **Sing.** is a written abbreviation for **singular**.

**sing|along** /sɪŋəlɒŋ, AM -lɔːŋ/ **(singalongs)** also **sing-along.** A **singalong** is an occasion when a group of people sing songs together for pleasure. N-COUNT ❑ *How about a nice sing-along around the piano?*

**Sin|ga|po|rean** /sɪŋgəpɔːriən/ **(Singaporeans)** [1] **Singaporean** means belonging or relating to Singapore, or to its people or culture. ADJ [2] A **Singaporean** is a citizen of Singapore or a person of Singaporean origin. N-COUNT

**singe** /sɪndʒ/ **(singes, singeing, singed)** If you **singe** something or if it **singes**, it burns very slightly and changes colour but does not catch fire. VERB ❑ *The electric fire had begun to singe the bottoms of his trousers... Toast the dried chillies in a hot pan until they start to singe.* V n / V

**sing|er** /sɪŋəʳ/ ◆◇◇ **(singers)** A **singer** is a person who sings, especially as a job. N-COUNT ❑ *My mother was a singer in a dance band. ...Dame Joan Sutherland, one of the great opera singers of the century.*

**singer-songwriter** **(singer-songwriters)** A **singer-songwriter** is someone who writes and performs their own songs, especially popular songs. N-COUNT ❑ *Twenty years ago singer-songwriter John Prine released his first album.*

**sing|ing** /sɪŋɪŋ/ **Singing** is the activity of making musical sounds with your voice. N-UNCOUNT ❑ *...a people's carnival, with singing and dancing in the streets. ...the singing of a traditional hymn... She's having singing lessons.*

**sin|gle** /sɪŋgəl/ ◆◆◆ **(singles, singling, singled)** [1] You use **single** to emphasize that you are referring to one thing, and no more than one thing. ADJ: ADJ n emphasis ❑ *A single shot rang out... Over six hundred people were wounded in a single day... She hadn't uttered a single word.* [2] You use **single** to indicate that you are considering something on its own and separately from other things like it. ADJ: det ADJ emphasis ❑ *Every single house in town had been damaged... The Middle East is the world's single most important source of oil.* [3] Someone who is **single** is not married. You can also use **single** to describe someone who does not have a girlfriend or boyfriend. ADJ ❑ *Is it difficult being a single mother?... Gay men are now eligible to become foster parents whether they are single or have partners.* [4] A **single** room is a room intended for one person to stay or live in. ADJ: usu ADJ n ❑ *A single room at the Astir Hotel costs £56 a night.* ♦ **Single** is also a noun. N-COUNT ❑ *It's £65 for a single, £98 for a double and £120 for an entire suite.* [5] A **single** bed is wide enough for one person to sleep in. ADJ: ADJ n [6] A **single** ticket is a ticket for a journey from one place to another but not back again. [BRIT] ADJ: usu ADJ n ≠ return ❑ *The price of a single ticket is thirty-nine pounds.* ♦ **Single** is also a noun. N-COUNT ❑ *...a Club Class single to Los Angeles.*

✔ in AM, use **one-way**

[7] A **single** or a **CD single** is a CD which has a few short songs on it. You can also refer to the main song on a CD as a **single**. N-COUNT ❑ *The winners will get a chance to release their own single.* [8] **Singles** N-UNCOUNT

is a game of tennis or badminton in which one player plays another. The plural **singles** can be used to refer to one or more of these matches. ❑ *Becker of Germany won the men's singles.* [9] → See also **single-**. **in single file** → see **file**.

♦ **single out** If you **single** someone **out** from a group, you choose them and give them special attention or treatment. ❑ *The gunman had singled Debilly out and waited for him... His immediate superior has singled him out for a special mention... We wanted to single out the main threat to civilisation.* (PHRASAL VERB; V n P; V n P *for/as* n; V P n (not pron))

**single-** /sɪŋɡᵊl-/ **single-** is used to form words which describe something that has one part or feature, rather than having two or more of them. ❑ *The single-engine plane landed in western Arizona. ...a single-track road.* (COMB in ADJ)

**single-breasted** A **single-breasted** coat, jacket, or suit fastens in the centre of the chest and has only one row of buttons. (ADJ)

**sin|gle cream** **Single cream** is thin cream that does not have a lot of fat in it. [BRIT] (N-UNCOUNT)

☑ in AM, use **light cream**

**single-decker** **(single-deckers)** A **single-decker** or a **single-decker bus** is a bus with only one deck. [BRIT] (N-COUNT)

**single-handed** If you do something **single-handed**, you do it on your own, without help from anyone else. ❑ *I brought up my seven children single-handed.* (ADV: ADV after v)

**single-minded** Someone who is **single-minded** has only one aim or purpose and is determined to achieve it. ❑ *...a single-minded determination to win.* (ADJ)

**sin|gle par|ent** **(single parents)** A **single parent** is someone who is bringing up a child on their own, because the other parent is not living with them. ❑ *I was bringing up my three children as a single parent. ...a single-parent household.* (N-COUNT: oft N n)

**sin|gles bar** **(singles bars)** In North America, a **singles bar** is a bar where single people can go in order to drink and meet other single people. (N-COUNT)

**single-sex** At a **single-sex** school, the pupils are either all boys or all girls. ❑ *Is single-sex education good for girls?* (ADJ: usu ADJ n)

**sin|gle sup|plement** **(single supplements)** also **single person supplement.** A **single supplement** is an additional sum of money that a hotel charges for one person to stay in a room meant for two people. ❑ *You can avoid the single supplement by agreeing to share a twin room.* (N-COUNT)

**sin|glet** /sɪŋɡlət/ **(singlets)** [1] A **singlet** is a sleeveless sports shirt worn by athletes and boxers. [BRIT] ❑ *...a grubby running singlet.* (N-COUNT = vest) [2] A **singlet** is a plain sleeveless piece of underwear which is worn on the upper half of the body. [BRIT] ❑ *He was wearing a blue silk singlet and boxer shorts.* (N-COUNT = vest, undershirt)

**sin|gle|ton** /sɪŋɡᵊltən/ **(singletons)** A **singleton** is someone who is neither married nor in a long-term relationship. ❑ *Bank is a 38-year-old singleton who grew up in Philadelphia.* (N-COUNT)

**sin|gly** /sɪŋɡli/ If people do something **singly**, they each do it on their own, or do it one by one. ❑ *They marched out singly or in pairs.* (ADV: ADV with v)

**sing-song** **(sing-songs)** also **singsong.** [1] A **sing-song** voice repeatedly rises and falls in pitch. ❑ *He started to speak in a nasal sing-song voice.* (ADJ: ADJ n) [2] A **sing-song** is an occasion on which a group of people sing songs together for pleasure. [BRIT] (N-COUNT = singalong)

**sin|gu|lar** /sɪŋɡjʊləʳ/ [1] The **singular** form of a word is the form that is used when referring to one person or thing. ❑ *...the fifteen case endings of the singular form of the Finnish noun... The word 'you' can be singular or plural.* (ADJ ≠ plural) [2] **The singular** of a noun is the form of it that is used to refer to one person or thing. ❑ *The singular of Inuit is Inuk.* (N-SING: the N ≠ plural) [3] **Singular** means very great and remarkable. [FORMAL] ❑ *...a smile of singular sweetness.* (ADJ: ADJ n) ♦ **sin|gu|lar|ly** *It seemed a singularly ill-judged enterprise for Truman to undertake.* (ADV: ADV adj/adv) [4] If you describe someone or something as **singular**, you mean that they are strange or unusual. [OLD-FASHIONED] ❑ *Cardinal Meschia was without doubt a singular character... Where he got that singular notion I just can't think.* (ADJ: usu ADJ n = peculiar) ♦ **sin|gu|lar|ity** /sɪŋɡjʊlærɪti/ *...his abrupt, turbulent style and the singularity of his appearance.* (N-UNCOUNT = peculiarity)

**sin|gu|lar noun** **(singular nouns)** A **singular noun** is a noun such as 'standstill' or 'vicinity' that does not have a plural form and always has a determiner such as 'a' or 'the' in front of it. (N-COUNT)

**sin|is|ter** /sɪnɪstəʳ/ Something that is **sinister** seems evil or harmful. ❑ *There was something sinister about him that she found disturbing.* (ADJ)

**sink** /sɪŋk/ **(sinks, sinking, sank, sunk)** [1] A **sink** is a large fixed container in a kitchen, with taps to supply water. It is mainly used for washing dishes. ❑ *The sink was full of dirty dishes. ...the kitchen sink.* (◆◇◇ N-COUNT) [2] A **sink** is the same as a **washbasin** or **basin**. ❑ *The bathroom is furnished with 2 toilets, 2 showers, and 2 sinks.* (N-COUNT) [3] If a boat **sinks** or if someone or something **sinks** it, it disappears below the surface of a mass of water. ❑ *In a naval battle your aim is to sink the enemy's ship... The boat was beginning to sink fast... The lifeboat crashed against the side of the sinking ship.* (VERB; V n; V; V-ing) ♦ **sink|ing** **(sinkings)** *...the sinking of the Titanic.* (N-COUNT) [4] If something **sinks**, it disappears below the surface of a mass of water. ❑ *A fresh egg will sink and an old egg will float.* (VERB ≠ float; V) [5] If something **sinks**, it moves slowly downwards. ❑ *Far off to the west the sun was sinking.* (VERB; V) [6] If something **sinks to** a lower level or standard, it falls to that level or standard. ❑ *Share prices would have sunk – hurting small and big investors... Pay increases have sunk to around seven per cent... The pound had sunk 10 per cent against the Schilling.* (VERB = fall; V; V to/from/by amount/n; V amount) [7] People use **sink** school or **sink** estate to refer to a school or housing estate that is in a very poor area with few resources. [BRIT, JOURNALISM] ❑ *...unemployed teenagers from sink estates.* (ADJ: ADJ n) [8] If your heart or your spirits **sink**, you become depressed or lose hope. ❑ *My heart sank because I thought he was going to dump me for another girl.* (VERB; V) [9] If something sharp **sinks** or **is sunk into** something solid, it goes deeply into it. ❑ *I sank my teeth into a peppermint cream... The spade sank into a clump of overgrown bushes.* (VERB; V n *into* n; V *into* n) [10] If someone **sinks** a well, mine, or other large hole, they make a deep hole in the ground, usually by digging or drilling. ❑ *...the site where Stephenson sank his first mineshaft.* (VERB; V n) [11] If you **sink** money **into** a business or project, you spend money on it in the hope of making more money. ❑ *He has already sunk $25million into the project.* (VERB = plough; V n *into* n) [12] → See also **sinking, sunk.** [13] If you say that someone will have to **sink or swim**, you mean that they will have to succeed through their own efforts, or fail. ❑ *The government doesn't want to force inefficient firms to sink or swim too quickly.* to **sink without trace** → see **trace**. (PHRASE)

♦ **sink in** When a statement or fact **sinks in**, you finally understand or realize it fully. ❑ *The implication took a while to sink in.* (PHRASAL VERB; V P)

**sink|er** /sɪŋkəʳ/ You can use **hook, line, and sinker** to emphasize that someone is tricked or forced into a situation completely. ❑ *We fell for it hook, line, and sinker.* (PHRASE: PHR after v emphasis)

**sink|ing** /sɪŋkɪŋ/ If you have a **sinking** feeling, you suddenly become depressed or lose hope. ❑ *I began to have a sinking feeling that I was not going to get rid of her.* → See also **sink**. (ADJ: ADJ n)

**Sino-** /saɪnoʊ-/ **Sino-** is added to adjectives indicating nationality to form adjectives which describe relations between China and another country. ❑ *...Sino-Vietnamese friendship.* (COMB in ADJ: ADJ n)

**sinu|ous** /sɪnjuəs/ Something that is **sinuous** moves with smooth twists and turns. [LITERARY] ❑ *...the silent, sinuous approach of a snake through the long grass.* (ADJ: usu ADJ n)

**si|nus** /saɪnəs/ **(sinuses)** Your **sinuses** are the spaces in the bone behind your nose. ❑ *I still suffer from catarrh and sinus problems.*
N-COUNT: usu pl

**si|nusi|tis** /saɪnəsaɪtɪs/ If you have **sinusitis**, the layer of flesh inside your sinuses is swollen and painful, which can cause headaches and a blocked nose.
N-UNCOUNT

**sip** /sɪp/ **(sips, sipping, sipped)** [1] If you **sip** a drink or **sip at** it, you drink by taking just a small amount at a time. ❑ *Jessica sipped her drink thoughtfully... He sipped at the glass and then put it down... He lifted the water-bottle to his lips and sipped.* [2] A **sip** is a small amount of drink that you take into your mouth. ❑ *Harry took a sip of bourbon.*
VERB; V n; V *at/from* n; V; N-COUNT: oft N *of* n

**si|phon** /saɪfᵊn/ **(siphons, siphoning, siphoned)** also **syphon.** [1] If you **siphon** liquid from a container, you make it come out through a tube and down into a lower container by enabling the pressure of the air on it to push it out. ❑ *She puts a piece of plastic tubing in her mouth and starts siphoning gas from a huge metal drum.* ♦ **Siphon off** means the same as **siphon**. ❑ *Surgeons siphoned off fluid from his left lung.* [2] A **siphon** is a tube that you use for siphoning liquid. [3] If you **siphon** money or resources from something, you cause them to be used for a purpose for which they were not intended. ❑ *He had siphoned thousands of pounds a week from the failing business.* ♦ **Siphon off** means the same as **siphon**. ❑ *He had siphoned off a small fortune in aid money from the United Nations.*
VERB; V n prep; PHRASAL VERB; V P n; Also V n P; N-COUNT; VERB; V n prep; PHRASAL VERB; V P n (not pron); Also V n P

**sir** /sɜːʳ/ **(sirs)** [1] People sometimes say **sir** as a very formal and polite way of addressing a man whose name they do not know or a man of superior rank. For example, a shop assistant might address a male customer as **sir**. ❑ *Excuse me sir, but would you mind telling me what sort of car that is?... Good afternoon to you, sir.* [2] **Sir** is the title used in front of the name of a knight or baronet. ❑ *She introduced me to Sir Tobias and Lady Clarke.* [3] You use the expression **Dear sir** at the beginning of a formal letter or a business letter when you are writing to a man. You use **Dear sirs** when you are writing to an organization. ❑ *Dear Sir, Your letter of the 9th October has been referred to us.*
◆◆◇; N-VOC; politeness; N-TITLE; CONVENTION

**sire** /saɪəʳ/ **(sires, siring, sired)** When a male animal, especially a horse, **sires** a young animal, he makes a female pregnant so that she gives birth to it. [TECHNICAL] ❑ *Comet also sired the champion foal out of Spinway Harvest.*
VERB; V n

**si|ren** /saɪərən/ **(sirens)** [1] A **siren** is a warning device which makes a long, loud noise. Most fire engines, ambulances, and police cars have sirens. ❑ *It sounds like an air raid siren.* [2] Some people refer to a woman as a **siren** when they think that she is attractive to men but dangerous in some way. [LITERARY] ❑ *He depicts her as a siren who has drawn him to his ruin.*
N-COUNT: oft supp N; N-COUNT = *femme fatale*

**sir|loin** /sɜːʳlɔɪn/ **(sirloins)** A **sirloin** is a piece of beef which is cut from the bottom and side parts of a cow's back. ❑ *...sirloin steaks.*
N-VAR

**si|sal** /saɪzᵊl/ **Sisal** is the fibre from the leaves of a plant that is grown in the West Indies, South America, and Africa. **Sisal** is used to make rope, cord, and mats.
N-UNCOUNT

**sis|sy** /sɪsi/ **(sissies)** also **cissy.** Some people, especially men, describe a boy as a **sissy** when they disapprove of him because he does not like rough, physical activities or is afraid to do things which might be dangerous. [INFORMAL] ❑ *They were rough kids, and thought we were sissies.*
N-COUNT; disapproval

**sis|ter** /sɪstəʳ/ **(sisters)** [1] Your **sister** is a girl or woman who has the same parents as you. ❑ *His sister Sarah helped him. ...Vanessa Bell, the sister of Virginia Woolf... I didn't know you had a sister.* → See also **half-sister, stepsister.** [2] **Sister** is a title given to a woman who belongs to a religious community. ❑ *Sister Francesca entered the chapel. ...the Hospice of the Sisters of Charity at Lourdes.* [3] A **sister** is a senior female nurse who supervises part of a hospital. [BRIT] ❑ *Ask to speak to the sister on the ward... Sister Middleton followed the coffee trolley.* [4] You can describe a woman as your **sister** if you feel a connection with her, for example because she belongs to the same race, religion, country, or profession. ❑ *Modern woman has been freed from many of the duties that befell her sisters in times past.* [5] You can use **sister** to describe something that is of the same type or is connected in some way to another thing you have mentioned. For example, if a company has a **sister** company, they are connected. ❑ *...the International Monetary Fund and its sister organisation, the World Bank.*
◆◆◆; N-COUNT: oft poss N; N-COUNT; N-TITLE; N-VOC; N-COUNT; N-TITLE; N-VOC; N-COUNT: usu poss N; ADJ: ADJ n

**sis|ter|hood** /sɪstəʳhʊd/ **Sisterhood** is the affection and loyalty that women feel for other women who they have something in common with. ❑ *There was a degree of solidarity and sisterhood among the women.*
N-UNCOUNT

**sister-in-law** **(sisters-in-law)** Someone's **sister-in-law** is the sister of their husband or wife, or the woman who is married to their brother.
N-COUNT: oft poss N

**sis|ter|ly** /sɪstəʳli/ A woman's **sisterly** feelings are the feelings of love and loyalty which you expect a sister to show. ❑ *Bernadette gave him a shy, sisterly kiss.*
ADJ: usu ADJ n

**sit** /sɪt/ **(sits, sitting, sat)** [1] If you **are sitting** somewhere, for example in a chair, your bottom is resting on the chair and the upper part of your body is upright. ❑ *Mother was sitting in her chair in the kitchen... They sat there in shock and disbelief... They had been sitting watching television... He was unable to sit still for longer than a few minutes.* [2] When you **sit** somewhere, you lower your body until you are sitting on something. ❑ *He set the cases against a wall and sat on them... When you stand, they stand; when you sit, they sit.* ♦ **Sit down** means the same as **sit**. ❑ *I sat down, stunned... Hughes beckoned him to sit down on the sofa.* [3] If you **sit** someone somewhere, you tell them to sit there or put them in a sitting position. ❑ *He used to sit me on his lap.* ♦ To **sit** someone **down** somewhere means to **sit** them there. ❑ *She helped him out of the water and sat him down on the rock... They sat me down and had a serious discussion about sex.* [4] If you **sit** an examination, you do it. [BRIT] ❑ *June and July are the traditional months for sitting exams.*
◆◆◆; VERB; V prep/adv; V prep/adv; V; V adj; Also V; VERB; V prep/adv; V; PHRASAL VERB; V P; V P prep/adv; VERB; V n prep/adv; PHRASAL VERB; V n P prep/adv; V n P; VERB = *take*; V n

☑ in AM, use **take**

[5] If you **sit on** a committee or other official group, you are a member of it. ❑ *He was asked to sit on numerous committees.* [6] When a parliament, legislature, court, or other official body **sits**, it officially carries out its work. [FORMAL] ❑ *Parliament sits for only 28 weeks out of 52.* [7] If a building or object **sits** in a particular place, it is in that place. [WRITTEN] ❑ *Our new house sat next to a stream... On the table sat a box decorated with little pearl triangles.* [8] → See also **sitting.** [9] If you **sit tight**, you remain in the same place or situation and do not take any action, usually because you are waiting for something to happen. ❑ *Sit tight. I'll be right back.* to **sit on the fence** → see **fence.**
VERB: no cont; V *on/in* n; VERB; V; VERB = *stand*; V prep/adv; V prep/adv; PHRASE: V inflects

♦ **sit around**

☑ in BRIT, also use **sit about**

If you **sit around** or **sit about**, you spend time doing nothing useful or interesting. [INFORMAL] ❑ *Eve isn't the type to sit around doing nothing.*
PHRASAL VERB; V P

♦ **sit back** If you **sit back** while something is happening, you relax and do not become involved in it. [INFORMAL] ❑ *They didn't have to do anything except sit back and enjoy life.*
PHRASAL VERB; V P

♦ **sit by** If you **sit by** while something wrong or illegal is happening, you allow it to happen and do not do anything about it. ❑ *We can't just sit by and watch you throw your life away.*
PHRASAL VERB = *stand by*; V P

♦ **sit down** [1] → see **sit 2, 3.** [2] If you **sit down** and do something, you spend time and ef-
PHRASAL VERB

fort doing it in order to try to achieve something. ❑ *Have you both sat down and worked out a budget together?* [3] ➔ See also **sit-down**.
V P

♦ **sit in on** If you **sit in on** a lesson, meeting, or discussion, you are present while it is taking place but do not take part in it. ❑ *Will they permit you to sit in on a few classes?*
PHRASAL VERB
V P P n

♦ **sit on** If you say that someone **is sitting on** something, you mean that they are delaying dealing with it. [INFORMAL] ❑ *He had been sitting on the document for at least two months.*
PHRASAL VERB
V P n

♦ **sit out** If you **sit** something **out**, you wait for it to finish, without taking any action. ❑ *The only thing I can do is keep quiet and sit this one out... He can afford to sit out the property slump.*
PHRASAL VERB
V n P
V P n

♦ **sit through** If you **sit through** something such as a film, lecture, or meeting, you stay until it is finished although you are not enjoying it. ❑ *...movies so bad you can hardly bear to sit through them.*
PHRASAL VERB
V P n

♦ **sit up** [1] If you **sit up**, you move into a sitting position when you have been leaning back or lying down. ❑ *Her head spins dizzily as soon as she sits up.*
PHRASAL VERB
V P
[2] If you **sit** someone **up**, you move them into a sitting position when they have been leaning back or lying down. ❑ *She sat him up and made him comfortable.*
PHRASAL VERB
V n P
[3] If you **sit up**, you do not go to bed although it is very late. ❑ *We sat up drinking and talking.* [4] ➔ See also **sit-up**.
PHRASAL VERB
= stay up
V P

**si|tar** /sɪtɑːʳ/ **(sitars)** A **sitar** is an Indian musical instrument with two layers of strings, a long neck, and a round body.
N-VAR: oft *the* N

**sit|com** /sɪtkɒm/ **(sitcoms)** A **sitcom** is an amusing television drama series about a set of characters. **Sitcom** is an abbreviation for 'situation comedy'.
N-COUNT

**sit-down** [1] If you have **a sit-down**, you sit down and rest for a short time. [BRIT, INFORMAL] ❑ *All he wanted was a cup of tea and a sit-down.*
N-SING: *a* N
[2] A **sit-down** meal is served to people sitting at tables. ❑ *A sit-down dinner was followed by a disco.*
ADJ: ADJ n
[3] In a **sit-down** protest, people refuse to leave a place until they get what they want. ❑ *Teachers staged a sit-down protest in front of the president's office.*
ADJ: ADJ n

**site** /saɪt/ **(sites, siting, sited)** [1] A **site** is a piece of ground that is used for a particular purpose or where a particular thing happens. ❑ *He became a hod carrier on a building site. ...a bat sanctuary with special nesting sites.*
◆◆◇
N-COUNT: oft n N
[2] **The site of** an important event is the place where it happened. ❑ *Scientists have described the Aral sea as the site of the worst ecological disaster on earth.*
N-COUNT: usu *the* N *of* n
[3] A **site** is a piece of ground where something such as a statue or building stands or used to stand. ❑ *...the site of Moses' tomb.*
N-COUNT
[4] A **site** is the same as a **website**.
N-COUNT
[5] If something **is sited** in a particular place or position, it is put there or built there. ❑ *He said chemical weapons had never been sited in Germany. ...a damp, old castle, romantically sited on a river estuary.* ♦ **sit|ing** *...controls on the siting of gas storage vessels.*
VERB: usu passive
*be* V-ed prep/adv
V-ed
N-SING: usu *the* N *of* n

**PHRASES** [6] If someone or something is **on site**, they are in a particular area or group of buildings where people work, study, or stay. ❑ *It is cheaper to have extra building work done when the builder is on site.*
PHRASE
[7] If someone or something is **off site**, they are away from a particular area or group of buildings where people work, study, or stay. ❑ *There is ample car parking off site.*
PHRASE

**sit-in** **(sit-ins)** A **sit-in** is a protest in which people go to a public place and stay there for a long time. [BUSINESS] ❑ *The campaigners held a sit-in outside the Supreme Court.*
N-COUNT

**sit|ter** /sɪtəʳ/ **(sitters)** A **sitter** is the same as a **babysitter**.
N-COUNT

**sit|ting** /sɪtɪŋ/ **(sittings)** [1] A **sitting** is one of the periods when a meal is served when there is not enough space for everyone to eat at the same time. ❑ *Dinner was in two sittings.*
N-COUNT
[2] **A sitting** of a parliament, legislature, court, or other official body is one of the occasions when it meets in order to carry out its work. ❑ *...the recent emergency sittings of the UN Security Council.*
N-COUNT: usu N *of* n
= session
[3] A **sitting** president or member of parliament is a present one, not a future or past one. ❑ *...the greatest clash in our history between a sitting president and an ex-president.* [4] ➔ See also **sit**.
ADJ: ADJ n

**sit|ting duck** **(sitting ducks)** If you say that someone is a **sitting duck**, you mean that they are easy to attack, cheat, or take advantage of. [INFORMAL] ❑ *Nancy knew she'd be a sitting duck when she raised the trap door.*
N-COUNT
= sitting target

**sit|ting room** **(sitting rooms)** also **sitting-room.** A **sitting room** is a room in a house where people sit and relax. [BRIT] ➔ See picture on page 1706.
N-COUNT

✔ in AM, usually use **living room**

**sit|ting tar|get** **(sitting targets)** A **sitting target** is the same as a **sitting duck**. ❑ *They know they are a sitting target for the press.*
N-COUNT

**sit|ting ten|ant** **(sitting tenants)** A **sitting tenant** is a person who rents a house or flat as their home and has a legal right to live there. [BRIT] ❑ *1.4 million council homes have been sold, mostly to sitting tenants.*
N-COUNT

**situ|ate** /sɪtʃueɪt/ **(situates, situating, situated)** If you **situate** something such as an idea or fact in a particular context, you relate it to that context, especially in order to understand it better. [FORMAL] ❑ *How do we situate Christianity in the context of modern physics and psychology?*
VERB
V n adv/prep

**situ|at|ed** /sɪtʃueɪtɪd/ If something is **situated** in a particular place or position, it is in that place or position. ❑ *His hotel is situated in one of the loveliest places on the Loire.*
ADJ: v-link ADJ prep, adv ADJ
= located

**situa|tion** /sɪtʃueɪʃᵊn/ **(situations)** [1] You use **situation** to refer generally to what is happening in a particular place at a particular time, or to refer to what is happening to you. ❑ *Army officers said the situation was under control... She's in a hopeless situation.*
◆◆◆
N-COUNT: usu with supp, oft poss N
[2] The **situation** of a building or town is the kind of surroundings that it has. [FORMAL] ❑ *The garden is in a beautiful situation on top of a fold in the rolling Hampshire landscape.*
N-COUNT: usu supp N
= location
[3] **Situations Vacant** is the title of a column or page in a newspaper where jobs are advertised. [mainly BRIT]
PHRASE: oft PHR n

✔ in AM, use **Employment**

**situa|tion com|edy** **(situation comedies)** A **situation comedy** is an amusing television drama series about a set of characters. The abbreviation **sitcom** is also used. ❑ *...a situation comedy that was set in an acupuncture clinic.*
N-VAR

**sit-up** **(sit-ups)**

✔ in AM, also use **situp**

**Sit-ups** are exercises that you do to strengthen your stomach muscles. They involve sitting up from a lying position while keeping your legs straight on the floor.
N-COUNT: usu pl

**six** /sɪks/ **(sixes)** **Six** is the number 6. ❑ *...a glorious career spanning more than six decades.*
◆◆◆
NUM

**six-footer** **(six-footers)** Someone who is six foot tall can be called a **six-footer**. [INFORMAL]
N-COUNT

**six-pack** **(six-packs)** [1] A **six-pack** is a pack containing six bottles or cans sold together. ❑ *He picked up a six-pack of beer.*
N-COUNT: oft N *of* n
[2] If a man has a **six-pack**, his stomach muscles are very well developed. ❑ *He has a six-pack stomach and is extremely well-proportioned.*
N-COUNT: oft N n

**six|pence** /sɪkspəns/ **(sixpences)** A **sixpence** is a small silver coin which was used in Britain before the decimal money system was introduced in 1971. It was the equivalent of 2.5 pence. [BRIT]
N-COUNT

**six-shooter** **(six-shooters)** A **six-shooter** is a small gun that holds six bullets.
N-COUNT

**six|teen** /sɪkstiːn/ **(sixteens)** **Sixteen** is the number 16. ❑ *...exams taken at the age of sixteen... He worked sixteen hours a day.* ◆◆◆ NUM

**six|teenth** /sɪkstiːnθ/ **(sixteenths)** [1] The **sixteenth** item in a series is the one that you count as number sixteen. ❑ *...the sixteenth century AD.* ◆◆◇ ORD [2] A **sixteenth** is one of sixteen equal parts of something. ❑ *...a sixteenth of a second.* FRACTION

**sixth** /sɪksθ/ **(sixths)** [1] The **sixth** item in a series is the one that you count as number six. ❑ *...the sixth round of the World Cup. ...the sixth of December.* ◆◆◇ ORD [2] A **sixth** is one of six equal parts of something. ❑ *The company yesterday shed a sixth of its workforce. ...five-sixths of a mile.* FRACTION

**sixth form** **(sixth forms)** also **sixth-form.** N-COUNT: usu sing The **sixth form** in a British school consists of the classes that pupils go to from 16 to 18 years of age, usually in order to study for A levels. ❑ *She was offered her first modelling job while she was still in the sixth-form.*

**sixth for|mer** **(sixth formers)** also **sixth-former.** A **sixth former** is a pupil who is in the sixth form at a British school. N-COUNT

**sixth sense** If you say that someone has a **sixth sense**, you mean that they seem to have a natural ability to know about things before other people, or to know things that other people do not know. ❑ *The interesting thing about O'Reilly is his sixth sense for finding people who have good ideas.* N-SING

**six|ti|eth** /sɪkstiəθ/ **(sixtieths)** [1] The **sixtieth** item in a series is the one that you count as number sixty. ❑ *He is to retire on his sixtieth birthday.* ◆◆◇ ORD [2] A **sixtieth** is one of sixty equal parts of something. FRACTION

**six|ty** /sɪksti/ **(sixties)** [1] **Sixty** is the number 60. ❑ *...the sunniest April in Britain for more than sixty years.* ◆◆◆ NUM [2] When you talk about the **sixties**, you are referring to numbers between 60 and 69. For example, if you are **in** your **sixties**, you are aged between 60 and 69. If the temperature is **in the sixties**, it is between 60 and 69 degrees. ❑ *...a lively widow in her sixties.* N-PLURAL [3] **The sixties** is the decade between 1960 and 1969. ❑ *In the sixties there were the deaths of the two Kennedy brothers and Martin Luther King.* N-PLURAL: the N

**six-yard box** On a football pitch, **the six-yard box** is the rectangular area marked in front of the goal. N-SING: the N

**siz|able** /saɪzəbᵊl/ → see **sizeable.**

**size** /saɪz/ **(sizes, sizing, sized)** [1] **The size of** something is how big or small it is. Something's size is determined by comparing it to other things, counting it, or measuring it. ❑ *Scientists have found the bones of a hoofed grazing animal about the size of a small horse... In 1970 the average size of a French farm was 19 hectares. ...shelves containing books of various sizes.* ◆◆◇ N-VAR: usu the N of n [2] **The size of** something is the fact that it is very large. ❑ *He knows the size of the task... Jack walked around the hotel and was mesmerized by its sheer size.* N-UNCOUNT: usu the N of n [3] A **size** is one of a series of graded measurements, especially for things such as clothes or shoes. ❑ *My sister is the same height but only a size 12... I tried them on and they were the right size.* N-COUNT

♦ **size up** If you **size up** a person or situation, you carefully look at the person or think about the situation, so that you can decide how to act. [INFORMAL] ❑ *Some US manufacturers have been sizing up the UK as a possible market for their clothes... He spent the evening sizing me up intellectually.* PHRASAL VERB V P n (not pron) V n P

**-size** /-saɪz/ or **-sized** [1] You can use **-size** or **-sized** in combination with nouns to form adjectives which indicate that something is the same size as something else. ❑ *...golfball-sized lumps of coarse black rock.* COMB in ADJ [2] You can use **-size** or **-sized** in combination with adjectives to form adjectives which describe the size of something. ❑ *...full-size gymnasiums. ...a medium-sized college.* COMB in ADJ [3] You can use **-size** or **-sized** in combination with nouns to form adjectives which indicate that something is big enough or small enough to be suitable for a particular job or purpose. ❑ *...a small passport-size photograph. ...a child-sized knife.* COMB in ADJ

**size|able** /saɪzəbᵊl/ also **sizable.** **Sizeable** means fairly large. ❑ *Harry inherited the house and a sizeable chunk of land.* ADJ: usu ADJ n = substantial

**-sized** /-saɪzd/ → see **-size.**

**siz|zle** /sɪzᵊl/ **(sizzles, sizzling, sizzled)** If something such as hot oil or fat **sizzles**, it makes hissing sounds. ❑ *The sausages and burgers sizzled on the barbecue. ...a frying pan of sizzling oil.* VERB V V-ing

**skate** /skeɪt/ **(skates, skating, skated)** [1] **Skates** are ice-skates. N-COUNT [2] **Skates** are roller-skates. N-COUNT [3] If you **skate**, you move about wearing ice-skates or roller-skates. ❑ *I actually skated, and despite some teetering I did not fall on the ice... Dan skated up to him.* VERB V V adv/prep ♦ **skat|ing** *They all went skating together in the winter.* N-UNCOUNT ♦ **skat|er** **(skaters)** *West Lake, an outdoor ice-skating rink, attracts skaters during the day and night.* N-COUNT [4] A **skate** is a kind of flat sea fish. ❑ *Boats had plenty of mackerel and a few skate.* N-COUNT = ray ♦ **Skate** is this fish eaten as food. N-UNCOUNT [5] If you **skate over** or **round** a difficult subject, you avoid discussing it. ❑ *Scientists have tended to skate over the difficulties of explaining dreams... When pressed, he skates around the subject of those women who he met as a 19-year-old.* VERB V over n V round/around n

**skate|board** /skeɪtbɔːʳd/ **(skateboards)** A **skateboard** is a narrow board with wheels at each end, which people stand on and ride for pleasure. N-COUNT

**skate|board|er** /skeɪtbɔːʳdəʳ/ **(skateboarders)** A **skateboarder** is someone who rides on a skateboard. N-COUNT

**skate|board|ing** /skeɪtbɔːʳdɪŋ/ **Skateboarding** is the activity of riding on a skateboard. N-UNCOUNT

**skat|ing rink** **(skating rinks)** A **skating rink** is the same as a **rink.** N-COUNT

**skein** /skeɪn/ **(skeins)** A **skein** is a length of thread, especially wool or silk, wound loosely round on itself. ❑ *...a skein of wool.* N-COUNT

**skel|etal** /skelɪtᵊl/ [1] **Skeletal** means relating to the bones in your body. ❑ *...the skeletal remains of seven adults. ...the skeletal system.* ADJ: ADJ n [2] A **skeletal** person is so thin that you can see their bones through their skin. ❑ *...a hospital filled with skeletal children.* ADJ [3] Something that is **skeletal** has been reduced to its basic structure. ❑ *Passenger services can best be described as skeletal.* ADJ

**skel|eton** /skelɪtᵊn/ **(skeletons)** [1] Your **skeleton** is the framework of bones in your body. ❑ *...a human skeleton.* N-COUNT [2] A **skeleton** staff is the smallest number of staff necessary in order to run an organization or service. ❑ *Only a skeleton staff remains to show anyone interested around the site.* ADJ: ADJ n [3] The **skeleton** of something such as a building or a plan is its basic framework. ❑ *Only skeletons of buildings remained.* N-COUNT: usu N of n [4] If you say that someone has **a skeleton in the closet**, or in British English **a skeleton in the cupboard**, you mean that they are keeping secret a bad or embarrassing fact about themselves. ❑ *Mr Worthing is this election's Mr Nice Guy, without any skeletons in his cupboard.* PHRASE: Ns inflect

**skel|eton key** **(skeleton keys)** A **skeleton key** is a key which has been specially made so that it will open many different locks. N-COUNT

**skep|tic** /skeptɪk/ → see **sceptic.**

**skep|ti|cal** /skeptɪkᵊl/ → see **sceptical.**

**skep|ti|cism** /skeptɪsɪzəm/ → see **scepticism.**

**sketch** /sketʃ/ **(sketches, sketching, sketched)** [1] A **sketch** is a drawing that is done quickly without a lot of details. Artists often use sketches as a preparation for a more detailed painting or drawing. ❑ *...a sketch of a soldier by Orpen.* N-COUNT [2] If you **sketch** something, you make a quick, rough drawing of it. ❑ *Clare and David Astor are sketching a view of far Spanish hills... I always sketch with pen and paper.* VERB V n V [3] A **sketch of** a situation, person, or N-COUNT:

incident is a brief description of it without many details. ❑ *...thumbnail sketches of heads of state and political figures.* [4] If you **sketch** a situation or incident, you give a short description of it, including only the most important facts. ❑ *Cross sketched the story briefly, telling the facts just as they had happened.* ♦ **Sketch out** means the same as **sketch**. ❑ *Luxembourg sketched out an acceptable compromise between Britain, France and Germany.* [5] A **sketch** is a short humorous piece of acting, usually forming part of a comedy show. ❑ *...a five-minute sketch about a folk singer.*
usu N *of* n | VERB *= outline* | V n | PHRASAL VERB | V P n (not pron) | N-COUNT

**sketch|book** /sketʃbʊk/ **(sketchbooks)** also **sketch-book.** A **sketchbook** is a book of plain paper for drawing on.
N-COUNT *= sketchpad*

**sketch|pad** /sketʃpæd/ **(sketchpads)** also **sketch-pad.** A **sketchpad** is the same as a **sketchbook**.
N-COUNT

**sketchy** /sketʃi/ **(sketchier, sketchiest)** **Sketchy** information about something does not include many details and is therefore incomplete or inadequate. ❑ *Details of what actually happened are still sketchy.*
ADJ *= vague*

**skew** /skjuː/ **(skews, skewing, skewed)** If something **is skewed**, it is changed or affected to some extent by a new or unusual factor, and so is not correct or normal. ❑ *The arithmetic of nuclear running costs has been skewed by the fall in the cost of other fuels... Today's election will skew the results in favor of the northern end of the county.*
VERB | *be* V-ed | V n

**skew|er** /skjuːəʳ/ **(skewers, skewering, skewered)** [1] A **skewer** is a long metal pin which is used to hold pieces of food together during cooking. [2] If you **skewer** something, you push a long, thin, pointed object through it. ❑ *He skewered his victim through the neck. ...skewered beef with vegetables.*
N-COUNT | VERB | V n prep | V-ed

**ski** /skiː/ **(skis, skiing, skied)** [1] **Skis** are long, flat, narrow pieces of wood, metal, or plastic that are fastened to boots so that you can move easily on snow or water. ❑ *...a pair of skis.* [2] When people **ski**, they move over snow or water on skis. ❑ *They surf, ski and ride... The whole party then skied off.* ♦ **ski|er** /skiːəʳ/ **(skiers)** *He is an enthusiastic skier.* ♦ **ski|ing** *My hobbies were skiing and scuba diving. ...a skiing holiday.* [3] You use **ski** to refer to things that are concerned with skiing. ❑ *...the Swiss ski resort of Klosters. ...a private ski instructor.* [4] → See also **water-ski**.
◆◇◇ N-COUNT | VERB | V | V adv/prep | N-COUNT | N-UNCOUNT: oft N n | ADJ: ADJ n

**skid** /skɪd/ **(skids, skidding, skidded)** If a vehicle **skids**, it slides sideways or forwards while moving, for example when you are trying to stop it suddenly on a wet road. ❑ *The car pulled up too fast and skidded on the dusty shoulder of the road... The plane skidded off the runway while taking off in a snow storm.* ♦ **Skid** is also a noun. ❑ *I slammed the brakes on and went into a skid.*
VERB | V | V prep | N-COUNT

**skid row** /skɪd roʊ/ also **Skid Row.** You can refer to the poorest part of town, where drunks and homeless people live, as **skid row**. [mainly AM] ❑ *He became a skid row type of drunkard.*
N-UNCOUNT: oft N n

**skiff** /skɪf/ **(skiffs)** A **skiff** is a small light rowing boat or sailing boat, which usually has room for only one person.
N-COUNT

**skif|fle** /skɪfᵊl/ **Skiffle** is a type of music, popular in the 1950s, played by a small group using household objects as well as guitars and drums.
N-UNCOUNT

**ski jump** **(ski jumps)** A **ski jump** is a specially-built steep slope covered in snow whose lower end curves upwards. People ski down it and go into the air at the end.
N-COUNT

**skil|ful** /skɪlfʊl/

✔ in AM, use **skillful**

Someone who is **skilful** at something does it very well. ❑ *He is widely regarded as Hungary's most skilful politician.* ♦ **skil|ful|ly** *He had a clear idea of his company's strengths and skilfully exploited them.*
ADJ | ADV: ADV with v

**ski lift** **(ski lifts)** also **ski-lift.** A **ski lift** is a machine for taking people to the top of a slope so that they can ski down it. It consists of a series of seats hanging down from a moving wire.
N-COUNT

**skill** /skɪl/ **(skills)** [1] A **skill** is a type of work or activity which requires special training and knowledge. ❑ *Most of us will know someone who is always learning new skills, or studying new fields.* [2] **Skill** is the knowledge and ability that enables you to do something well. ❑ *The cut of a diamond depends on the skill of its craftsman.*
◆◆◇ N-COUNT | N-UNCOUNT

**skilled** /skɪld/ [1] Someone who is **skilled** has the knowledge and ability to do something well. ❑ *Not all doctors are skilled in helping their patients make choices.* [2] **Skilled** work can only be done by people who have had some training. ❑ *New industries demanded skilled labour not available locally.*
ADJ: oft ADJ *in/at* n/-ing | ADJ: usu ADJ n *≠ unskilled*

**skil|let** /skɪlɪt/ **(skillets)** A **skillet** is a shallow iron pan which is used for frying.
N-COUNT

**skill|ful** /skɪlfʊl/ → see **skilful**.

**skim** /skɪm/ **(skims, skimming, skimmed)** [1] If you **skim** something **from** the surface of a liquid, you remove it. ❑ *Rough seas today prevented specially equipped ships from skimming oil off the water's surface... Skim off the fat.* [2] If something **skims** a surface, it moves quickly along just above it. ❑ *...seagulls skimming the waves... The little boat was skimming across the sunlit surface of the bay.* [3] If you **skim** a piece of writing, you read through it quickly. ❑ *He skimmed the pages quickly, then read them again more carefully... I only had time to skim through the script before I flew over here.*
VERB | V n *off/from* n | V n with *off* | VERB | V n | V *over/across* n | VERB | V n | V *through* n

♦ **skim off** If someone **skims off** the best part of something, or money which belongs to other people, they take it for themselves. ❑ *He has been accused of skimming the cream off the economy... Rich Italian clubs such as AC Milan cannot simply skim off all of Europe's stars.*
PHRASAL VERB | V n P n | V P n (not pron)

**skimmed milk**

✔ in AM, usually use **skim milk**

**Skimmed milk** is milk from which the cream has been removed.
N-UNCOUNT

**skimp** /skɪmp/ **(skimps, skimping, skimped)** If you **skimp on** something, you use less time, money, or material for it than you really need, so that the result is not good enough. ❑ *Many families must skimp on their food and other necessities just to meet the monthly rent.*
VERB *= scrimp* | V *on* n

**skimpy** /skɪmpi/ **(skimpier, skimpiest)** Something that is **skimpy** is too small in size or quantity. ❑ *...skimpy underwear.*
ADJ

**skin** /skɪn/ **(skins, skinning, skinned)** [1] Your **skin** is the natural covering of your body. ❑ *His skin is clear and smooth... There are three major types of skin cancer... The only difference between us is the colour of our skins.* [2] An animal **skin** is skin which has been removed from a dead animal. Skins are used to make things such as coats and rugs. ❑ *That was real crocodile skin.* [3] The **skin** of a fruit or vegetable is its outer layer or covering. ❑ *The outer skin of the orange is called the 'zest'. ...banana skins.* [4] If a **skin** forms on the surface of a liquid, a thin, fairly solid layer forms on it. ❑ *Stir the custard occasionally to prevent a skin forming.* [5] If you **skin** a dead animal, you remove its skin. ❑ *...with the expertise of a chef skinning a rabbit.* [6] → See also **-skinned**, **banana skin**.
◆◆◇ N-VAR | N-VAR: usu supp N | N-VAR | N-SING | VERB | V n

PHRASES [7] If you do something **by the skin of your teeth**, you just manage to do it. ❑ *He won, but only by the skin of his teeth.* [8] If you say that someone has **a thick skin**, you mean that they are able to listen to criticism about themselves without becoming offended. ❑ *You need a thick skin to be a headmaster.* [9] to **make** your **skin crawl** → see **crawl**.
PHRASE: PHR with cl | PHRASE: N inflects, usu v PHR

**skin care** also **skincare. Skin care** involves keeping your skin clean, healthy-looking, and attractive. ❑ *...a unique range of natural skincare products.*
N-UNCOUNT: oft N n

**skin deep** also **skin-deep.** Something that is only **skin deep** is not a major or important feature of something, although it may appear to be. ❑ *Beauty is only skin deep.* ADJ: usu v-link ADJ

**skin|flint** /skɪnflɪnt/ **(skinflints)** If you describe someone as a **skinflint**, you are saying that they are a mean person who hates spending money. N-COUNT disapproval

**skin|head** /skɪnhed/ **(skinheads)** A **skinhead** is a young person whose hair is shaved or cut very short. Skinheads are usually regarded as violent and aggressive. [BRIT] N-COUNT

**skin|less** /skɪnləs/ **Skinless** meat has had its skin removed. ❑ *...skinless chicken breast fillets.* ADJ: usu ADJ n

**-skinned** /-skɪnd/ **-skinned** is used after adjectives such as 'dark' and 'clear' to form adjectives that indicate what kind of skin someone has. ❑ *Dark-skinned people rarely develop skin cancer... She was smooth-skinned and pretty.* COMB in ADJ

**skin|ny** /skɪni/ **(skinnier, skinniest)** A **skinny** person is extremely thin, often in a way that you find unattractive. [INFORMAL] ❑ *He was quite a skinny little boy.* ADJ

**skinny-dip** **(skinny-dips, skinny-dipping, skinny-dipped)** also **skinny dip.** If you **skinny-dip**, you go swimming with no clothes on. [INFORMAL] ❑ *They used to take off their clothes and go skinny dipping in the creek.* VERB V

**skint** /skɪnt/ If you say that you are **skint**, you mean that you have no money. [BRIT, INFORMAL] ❑ *I'm skint! Lend us a tenner.* ADJ = broke

**skin-tight** also **skintight.** **Skin-tight** clothes fit very tightly so that they show the shape of your body. ❑ *...the youth with the slicked down hair and skin-tight trousers.* ADJ: usu ADJ n

**skip** /skɪp/ **(skips, skipping, skipped)** [1] If you **skip** along, you move almost as if you are dancing, with a series of little jumps from one foot to the other. ❑ *They saw the man with a little girl skipping along behind him... She was skipping to keep up with him.* ♦ **Skip** is also a noun. ❑ *The boxer gave a little skip as he came out of his corner.* [2] When someone **skips**, they jump up and down over a rope which they or two other people are holding at each end and turning round and round. In American English, you say that someone **skips rope**. ❑ *Outside, children were skipping and singing a rhyme... They skip rope and play catch, waiting for the bell.* ♦ **skip|ping** *Skipping is one of the most enjoyable aerobic activities.* [3] If you **skip** something that you usually do or something that most people do, you decide not to do it. ❑ *It is important not to skip meals... Her daughter started skipping school.* [4] If you **skip** or **skip over** a part of something you are reading or a story you are telling, you miss it out or pass over it quickly and move on to something else. ❑ *You might want to skip the exercises in this chapter... She reinvented her own life story, skipping over the war years when she had a German lover.* [5] If you **skip from** one subject or activity **to** another, you move quickly from one to the other although there is no obvious connection between them. ❑ *She kept up a continuous chatter, skipping from one subject to the next.* [6] A **skip** is a large, open, metal container which is used to hold and take away large unwanted items and rubbish. [BRIT] VERB; V adv/prep; V; N-COUNT; VERB; V; V n; N-UNCOUNT; VERB = miss; V n; V n; VERB; V n; V over/to n; VERB = jump; V from n to n; N-COUNT

☑ in AM, use **dumpster**

**skip|per** /skɪpəʳ/ **(skippers, skippering, skippered)** [1] You can use **skipper** to refer to the captain of a ship or boat. ❑ *...the skipper of an English fishing boat... Gunfire, skipper!* [2] You can use **skipper** to refer to the captain of a sports team. ❑ *The England skipper is confident.* [3] To **skipper** a team or a boat means to be the captain of it. ❑ *He skippered the second Rugby XV.* N-COUNT; N-VOC = captain; N-COUNT: usu supp N = captain; VERB = captain; V n

**skip|ping rope** **(skipping ropes)**

☑ in AM, use **skip rope**

A **skipping rope** or **skip rope** is a piece of rope, usually with handles at each end. You exercise or play with it by turning it round and round and jumping over it. N-COUNT

**skir|mish** /skɜːʳmɪʃ/ **(skirmishes, skirmishing, skirmished)** [1] A **skirmish** is a minor battle. ❑ *Border skirmishes between India and Pakistan were common.* [2] If people **skirmish**, they fight. ❑ *They were skirmishing close to the minefield now... Police skirmished with youths on the estate last Friday.* N-COUNT: oft N with/between n; V-RECIP; pl-n V; V with n

**skirt** /skɜːʳt/ **(skirts, skirting, skirted)** [1] A **skirt** is a piece of clothing worn by women and girls. It fastens at the waist and hangs down around the legs. [2] Something that **skirts** an area is situated around the edge of it. ❑ *We raced across a large field that skirted the slope of a hill.* [3] If you **skirt** something, you go around the edge of it. ❑ *We shall be skirting the island on our way... She skirted round the edge of the room to the door.* [4] If you **skirt** a problem or question, you avoid dealing with it. ❑ *He skirted the hardest issues, concentrating on areas of possible agreement... He skirted round his main differences with her.* N-COUNT; VERB; V n; VERB; V n; V round/around n; VERB; V n; V round/around n

**skirt|ing board** **(skirting boards)** **Skirting board** or **skirting** is a narrow length of wood which goes along the bottom of a wall in a room and makes a border between the walls and the floor. [BRIT] N-VAR

☑ in AM, use **baseboard**

**ski slope** **(ski slopes)** A **ski slope** is a sloping surface which you can ski down, either on a snow-covered mountain or on a specially made structure. N-COUNT

**skit** /skɪt/ **(skits)** A **skit** is a short performance in which the actors make fun of people, events, and types of literature by imitating them. ❑ *...clever skits on popular songs.* N-COUNT

**skit|ter** /skɪtəʳ/ **(skitters, skittering, skittered)** If something **skitters**, it moves about very lightly and quickly. ❑ *The rats skittered around them in the drains and under the floorboards.* VERB; V adv/prep

**skit|tish** /skɪtɪʃ/ [1] If you describe a person or animal as **skittish**, you mean that they are easily made frightened or excited. ❑ *The declining dollar gave heart to skittish investors.* [2] Someone who is **skittish** does not concentrate on anything or take life very seriously. ❑ *...his relentlessly skittish sense of humour.* ADJ = nervous; ADJ

**skit|tle** /skɪtᵊl/ **(skittles)** [1] A **skittle** is a wooden object used as a target in the game of skittles. [mainly BRIT] [2] **Skittles** is a game in which players try to knock over as many skittles as they can out of a group of nine by rolling a ball at them. [mainly BRIT] N-COUNT; N-UNCOUNT

**skive** /skaɪv/ **(skives, skiving, skived)** If you **skive**, you avoid working, especially by staying away from the place where you should be working. [BRIT, INFORMAL] ❑ *The company treated me as though I were skiving.* ♦ **Skive off** means the same as **skive**. ❑ *'I absolutely hated school,' Rachel says. 'I skived off all the time.'... Almost everybody's kids skive off school.* VERB; V; PHRASAL VERB; V P; V P n

**skul|dug|gery** /skʌldʌgəri/ **Skulduggery** is behaviour in which someone acts in a dishonest way in order to achieve their aim. [WRITTEN] ❑ *...accusations of political skulduggery.* N-UNCOUNT

**skulk** /skʌlk/ **(skulks, skulking, skulked)** If you **skulk** somewhere, you hide or move around quietly because you do not want to be seen. ❑ *You, meanwhile, will be skulking in the safety of the car.* VERB; V prep/adv

**skull** /skʌl/ **(skulls)** Your **skull** is the bony part of your head which encloses your brain. ❑ *Her husband was later treated for a fractured skull.* N-COUNT

**skull and cross|bones** A **skull and crossbones** is a picture of a human skull above a pair of crossed bones which warns of death or danger. It used to appear on the flags of pirate ships and is now sometimes found on containers holding poisonous substances. ❑ *Skull and cross-* N-SING *bones stickers on the drums aroused the suspicion of the customs officers.*

**skull cap** **(skull caps)** also **skullcap.** A **skull cap** is a small close-fitting cap. N-COUNT

**skunk** /skʌŋk/ **(skunks)** A **skunk** is a small black and white animal which releases an unpleasant smelling liquid if it is frightened or attacked. Skunks live in America. N-COUNT

**sky** /skaɪ/ **(skies)** 1 **The sky** is the space around the earth which you can see when you stand outside and look upwards. ❑ *The sun is already high in the sky. ...warm sunshine and clear blue skies.* 2 **pie in the sky** → see **pie.** ◆◇◇ N-VAR

**sky-blue** Something that is **sky-blue** is a very pale blue in colour. ❑ *Her silk shirtdress was sky-blue, the colour of her eyes.* COLOUR

**sky|div|er** /skaɪdaɪvəʳ/ **(skydivers)** also **sky diver.** A **skydiver** is someone who goes skydiving. N-COUNT

**sky|div|ing** /skaɪdaɪvɪŋ/ **Skydiving** is the sport of jumping out of an aeroplane and falling freely through the air before opening your parachute. N-UNCOUNT

**sky-high** If you say that prices or confidence are **sky-high**, you are emphasizing that they are at a very high level. ❑ *Christie said: 'My confidence is sky high.' ...the effect of falling house prices and sky-high interest rates.* ♦ **Sky high** is also an adverb. ❑ *Their prestige went sky high.* ADJ [emphasis] ADV: ADV after v

**sky|lark** /skaɪlɑːʳk/ **(skylarks)** A **skylark** is a small brown bird that sings while flying high above the ground. N-COUNT

**sky|light** /skaɪlaɪt/ **(skylights)** A **skylight** is a window in a roof. N-COUNT

**sky|line** /skaɪlaɪn/ **(skylines)** **The skyline** is the line or shape that is formed where the sky meets buildings or the land. ❑ *The village church dominates the skyline.* N-COUNT: usu *the* N

**sky|rocket** /skaɪrɒkɪt/ **(skyrockets, skyrocketing, skyrocketed)** If prices or amounts **skyrocket**, they suddenly increase by a very large amount. ❑ *Production has dropped while prices and unemployment have skyrocketed. ...the skyrocketing costs of health care.* VERB V V-ing

**sky|scraper** /skaɪskreɪpəʳ/ **(skyscrapers)** A **skyscraper** is a very tall building in a city. N-COUNT

**sky|ward** /skaɪwəʳd/ also **skywards.** If you look **skyward** or **skywards**, you look up towards the sky. [LITERARY] ❑ *He pointed skywards.* ADV: ADV after v

**slab** /slæb/ **(slabs)** A **slab of** something is a thick, flat piece of it. ❑ *...slabs of stone. ...huge concrete paving slabs.* N-COUNT: with supp

**slack** /slæk/ **(slacker, slackest, slacks, slacking, slacked)** 1 Something that is **slack** is loose and not firmly stretched or tightly in position. ❑ *The boy's jaw went slack.* 2 A **slack** period is one in which there is not much work or activity. ❑ *The workload can be evened out, instead of the shop having busy times and slack periods.* 3 Someone who is **slack** in their work does not do it properly. ❑ *Many publishers have simply become far too slack.* ♦ **slack|ness** *He accused the government of slackness and of complacency.* 4 If someone **is slacking**, they are not working as hard as they should. ❑ *He had never let a foreman see him slacking.* ♦ **Slack off** means the same as **slack.** ❑ *If someone slacks off, Bill comes down hard.* 5 To **take up the slack** or **pick up the slack** means to do or provide something that another person or organization is no longer doing or providing. ❑ *As major airlines give up less-traveled routes, smaller planes are picking up the slack.* ADJ ADJ = quiet ADJ [disapproval] N-UNCOUNT VERB: only cont [disapproval] V PHRASAL VERB V P PHRASE: V inflects

**slack|en** /slækən/ **(slackens, slackening, slackened)** 1 If something **slackens** or if you **slacken** it, it becomes slower, less active, or less intense. ❑ *Inflationary pressures continued to slacken last month... The Conservative government will not slacken the pace of radical reform.* ♦ **slack|en|ing** *There was a slackening of western output during the 1930s.* 2 If your grip or a part of your body **slackens** or if you **slacken** your grip, it becomes looser or more relaxed. ❑ *Her grip slackened on Arnold's arm.* ♦ **slacken off** If something **slackens off**, it becomes slower, less active, or less intense. [mainly BRIT] ❑ *At about five o'clock, business slackened off.* VERB V V n N-SING: oft N *of* n VERB V, Also V n PHRASAL VERB: no passive V P

**slack|er** /slækəʳ/ **(slackers)** If you describe someone as a **slacker**, you mean that they are lazy and do less work than they should. ❑ *He's not a slacker, he's the best worker they've got.* N-COUNT [disapproval]

**slack-jawed** If you say that someone is **slack-jawed**, you mean that their mouth is hanging open, often because they are surprised. ❑ *He just gazed at me slack-jawed.* ADJ

**slacks** /slæks/ **Slacks** are casual trousers. [OLD-FASHIONED] ❑ *She was wearing black slacks and a white sweater.* N-PLURAL: also *a pair of* N = *trousers*

**slag** /slæg/ **(slags, slagging, slagged)** **Slag** is used by some people to refer to a woman who they disapprove of because they think she is sexually immoral. [BRIT, INFORMAL, OFFENSIVE] N-COUNT [disapproval]

♦ **slag off** To **slag** someone **off** means to criticize them in an unpleasant way. [BRIT, INFORMAL] ❑ *All bands slag off their record companies. It's just the way it is... People have been slagging me off.* PHRASAL VERB V P n (not pron) V n P

**slag heap** **(slag heaps)** also **slagheap.** A **slag heap** is a hill made from waste material, such as rock and mud, left over from mining. [mainly BRIT] N-COUNT

**slain** /sleɪn/ **Slain** is the past participle of **slay.**

**slake** /sleɪk/ **(slakes, slaking, slaked)** If you **slake** your thirst, you drink something that stops you being thirsty. VERB

**sla|lom** /slɑːləm/ **(slaloms)** A **slalom** is a race on skis or in canoes in which the competitors have to avoid a series of obstacles in a very twisting and difficult course. N-COUNT

**slam** /slæm/ **(slams, slamming, slammed)** 1 If you **slam** a door or window or if it **slams**, it shuts noisily and with great force. ❑ *She slammed the door and locked it behind her... I was relieved to hear the front door slam... He slammed the gate shut behind him.* 2 If you **slam** something **down**, you put it there quickly and with great force. ❑ *She listened in a mixture of shock and anger before slamming the phone down.* 3 To **slam** someone or something means to criticize them very severely. [JOURNALISM] ❑ *The famed film-maker slammed the claims as 'an outrageous lie'.* 4 If one thing **slams** into or against another, it crashes into it with great force. ❑ *The plane slammed into the building after losing an engine shortly after take-off... He slammed me against the ground.* 5 → See also **Grand Slam.** VERB V n V V n adj VERB V n with adv VERB V n VERB V *into/against* n V n *into/against* n

**slam|mer** /slæməʳ/ **The slammer** is prison. [INFORMAL] N-SING: *the* N

**slan|der** /slɑːndəʳ, slæn-/ **(slanders, slandering, slandered)** 1 **Slander** is an untrue spoken statement about someone which is intended to damage their reputation. Compare **libel.** ❑ *Dr. Bach is now suing the company for slander.* 2 To **slander** someone means to say untrue things about them in order to damage their reputation. ❑ *He has been questioned on suspicion of slandering the Prime Minister.* N-VAR VERB V n

**slan|der|ous** /slɑːndərəs, slæn-/ A spoken statement that is **slanderous** is untrue and intended to damage the reputation of the person that it refers to. ❑ *Herr Kohler wanted an explanation for what he described as 'slanderous' remarks.* ADJ

**slang** /slæŋ/ **Slang** consists of words, expressions, and meanings that are informal and are used by people who know each other very well or who have the same interests. ❑ *Archie liked to think he kept up with current slang.* N-UNCOUNT

**slang|ing match** /slæŋɪŋ mætʃ/ **(slanging matches)** A **slanging match** is an angry quarrel in which people insult each other. [BRIT] ❑ *They conducted a public slanging match.* N-COUNT

**slangy** /slæŋi/ **Slangy** speech or writing has a lot of slang in it. ❑ *The play was full of slangy dialogue.* ADJ: usu ADJ n

**slant** /slɑːnt, slænt/ **(slants, slanting, slanted)** 1 Something that **slants** is sloping, rather than horizontal or vertical. ❑ *The morning sun slanted through the glass roof. ...slanting green eyes.* 2 If something is **on a slant**, it is in a slanting position. ❑ *You're slightly above the garden because the house is on a slant. ...long pockets cut on the slant.* 3 If information or a system **is slanted**, it is made to show favour towards a particular group or opinion. ❑ *The programme was deliberately slanted to make the home team look good.* 4 A particular **slant** on a subject is a particular way of thinking about it, especially one that is unfair. ❑ *The political slant at Focus can be described as centre-right.*

VERB; V adv/prep; V-ing; N-SING; VERB: usu passive; *be* V-ed, Also *be* V-ed prep; N-SING: usu with supp

**slap** /slæp/ **(slaps, slapping, slapped)** 1 If you **slap** someone, you hit them with the palm of your hand. ❑ *He would push or slap her once in a while... I slapped him hard across the face.* ♦ **Slap** is also a noun. ❑ *He reached forward and gave her a slap.* 2 If you **slap** something **onto** a surface, you put it there quickly, roughly, or carelessly. ❑ *The barman slapped the cup on to the waiting saucer.* 3 If journalists say that the authorities **slap** something such as a tax or a ban **on** something, they think it is unreasonable or put on without careful thought. [INFORMAL] ❑ *The government slapped a ban on the export of unprocessed logs.* 4 If you describe something that someone does as **a slap in the face**, you mean that it shocks or upsets you because it shows that they do not support you or respect you. ❑ *'The Sun' calls it a massive slap in the face for the United States government... Britons persist in treating any pay rise of less than 5% as a slap in the face.*

VERB; V n; V n adv/prep; N-COUNT: usu sing; VERB; V n *on/onto* n; VERB; disapproval; = stick; V n *on* n; PHRASE: oft PHR *for* n

**slap bang** also **slap-bang. Slap bang** is used in expressions such as **slap bang in the middle** of somewhere to mean exactly in that place. [BRIT, INFORMAL] ❑ *Of course, slap-bang in the middle of town the rents are high.*

ADV: ADV prep

**slap|dash** /slæpdæʃ/ also **slap-dash.** If you describe someone as **slapdash**, you mean that they do things carelessly without much thinking or planning. ❑ *Malcolm's work methods appear amazingly slapdash.*

ADJ; disapproval

**slap-happy** If you describe someone as **slap-happy**, you believe they are irresponsible and careless. ❑ *...a slap-happy kind of cook.*

ADJ

**slap|stick** /slæpstɪk/ **Slapstick** is a simple type of comedy in which the actors behave in a rough and foolish way. ❑ *...slapstick comedy.*

N-UNCOUNT: oft N n

**slap-up** A **slap-up** meal is a large enjoyable meal. [BRIT, INFORMAL] ❑ *We usually had one slap-up meal a day.*

ADJ: ADJ n

**slash** /slæʃ/ **(slashes, slashing, slashed)** 1 If you **slash** something, you make a long, deep cut in it. ❑ *He came within two minutes of bleeding to death after slashing his wrists.* ♦ **Slash** is also a noun. ❑ *Make deep slashes in the meat and push in the spice paste.* 2 If you **slash at** a person or thing, you quickly hit at them with something such as a knife. ❑ *He slashed at her, aiming carefully.* 3 To **slash** something such as costs or jobs means to reduce them by a large amount. [JOURNALISM] ❑ *Car makers could be forced to slash prices after being accused of overcharging yesterday.* 4 You say **slash** to refer to a sloping line that separates letters, words, or numbers. For example, if you are giving the number 340/2/K you say 'Three four zero, slash two, slash K.' [SPOKEN]

VERB; V n; N-COUNT; VERB; V *at* n; VERB = cut; V n

**slash and burn** also **slash-and-burn. Slash and burn** is a method of farming that involves clearing land by destroying and burning all the trees and plants on it, farming there for a short time, and then moving on to clear a new piece of land. ❑ *Traditional slash and burn farming methods have exhausted the soil.*

N-UNCOUNT: usu N n

**slat** /slæt/ **(slats) Slats** are narrow pieces of wood, metal, or plastic, usually with spaces between them, that are part of things such as Venetian blinds or cupboard doors.

N-COUNT: usu pl

**slate** /sleɪt/ **(slates, slating, slated)** 1 **Slate** is a dark grey rock that can be easily split into thin layers. Slate is often used for covering roofs. ❑ *... a stone-built cottage, with a traditional slate roof.* 2 A **slate** is one of the small flat pieces of slate that are used for covering roofs. 3 A **slate** is a list of candidates for an election, usually from the same party. ❑ *The leadership want to present a single slate of candidates to be approved in an open vote.* 4 If something **is slated to** happen, it is planned to happen at a particular time or on a particular occasion. [mainly AM] ❑ *Bromfield was slated to become U.S. Secretary of Agriculture... Controversial energy measures are slated for Senate debate within days.* 5 If something **is slated**, it is criticized very severely. [BRIT, JOURNALISM] ❑ *Arnold Schwarzenegger's new restaurant has been slated by a top food critic.*

N-UNCOUNT: oft N n; N-COUNT; N-COUNT: usu with supp = list; V-PASSIVE; *be* V-ed to-inf; *be* V-ed *for* n; VERB: usu passive; *be* V-ed

**PHRASES** 6 If you start **with a clean slate**, you do not take account of previous mistakes or failures and make a fresh start. ❑ *The proposal is to pay everything you owe, so that you can start with a clean slate.* 7 If you **wipe the slate clean**, you decide to forget previous mistakes, failures, or debts and to start again. ❑ *Why not wipe the slate clean and start all over again?*

PHRASE; PHRASE: V inflects

**slath|er** /slæðəʳ/ **(slathers, slathering, slathered)** If you **slather** something **with** a substance, or **slather** a substance **onto** something, you put the substance on in a thick layer. ❑ *If your skin is dry, you have to slather on moisturiser. ...pieces of toast slathered with butter and marmalade.*

VERB; V n with adv; *be* V-ed prep; Also V n prep

**slat|ted** /slætɪd/ Something that is **slatted** is made with slats. ❑ *...slatted window blinds.*

ADJ

**slaugh|ter** /slɔːtəʳ/ **(slaughters, slaughtering, slaughtered)** 1 If large numbers of people or animals **are slaughtered**, they are killed in a way that is cruel or unnecessary. ❑ *Thirty four people were slaughtered while queuing up to cast their votes.* ♦ **Slaughter** is also a noun. ❑ *...a war where the slaughter of civilians was commonplace.* 2 To **slaughter** animals such as cows and sheep means to kill them for their meat. ❑ *Lack of chicken feed means that chicken farms are having to slaughter their stock.* ♦ **Slaughter** is also a noun. ❑ *More than 491,000 sheep were exported to the Continent for slaughter last year.*

VERB: usu passive; *be* V-ed; N-UNCOUNT; VERB; V n; N-UNCOUNT

**slaughter|house** /slɔːtəʳhaʊs/ **(slaughterhouses)** A **slaughterhouse** is a place where animals are killed for their meat.

N-COUNT = abattoir

**Slav** /slɑːv/ **(Slavs)** A **Slav** is a member of any of the peoples of Eastern Europe who speak a Slavonic language.

N-COUNT

**slave** /sleɪv/ **(slaves, slaving, slaved)** 1 A **slave** is someone who is the property of another person and has to work for that person. ❑ *The state of Liberia was formed a century and a half ago by freed slaves from the United States.* 2 You can describe someone as a **slave** when they are completely under the control of another person or of a powerful influence. ❑ *Movie stars used to be slaves to the studio system.* 3 If you say that a person **is slaving over** something or **is slaving for** someone, you mean that they are working very hard. ❑ *When you're busy all day the last thing you want to do is spend hours slaving over a hot stove.* ♦ **Slave away** means the same as **slave.** ❑ *He stares at the hundreds of workers slaving away in the intense sun.*

N-COUNT; N-COUNT: with supp; VERB; V *over* n; PHRASAL VERB; V P

♦ **slave away** → see **slave 3**.

**slave la|bour**

in AM, use **slave labor**

1 **Slave labour** refers to slaves or to work done by slaves. ❑ *The children were used as slave labour in gold mines in the jungle.* 2 If people work very hard for long hours for very little money, you can refer to it as **slave labour**. ❑ *He's been forced into slave labour at burger bars to earn a bit of cash.*

N-UNCOUNT; N-UNCOUNT; disapproval

**slav|er** /slævəʳ/ **(slavers, slavering, slavered)** If an animal **slavers**, liquid comes from its mouth, for example because it is about to attack and eat

VERB = slobber

something. ❑ *Mad guard dogs slavered at the end of their chains. ...the wolf's slavering jaws.* V V-ing

**slav|ery** /sleɪvəri/ **Slavery** is the system by which people are owned by other people as slaves. ❑ *My people have survived 400 years of slavery.* N-UNCOUNT

**slave trade** **The slave trade** is the buying and selling of slaves, especially Black Africans, from the 16th to the 19th centuries. ❑ *...profits from the slave trade.* N-SING: the N

**Slav|ic** /slævɪk, slɑːv-/ Something that is **Slavic** belongs or relates to Slavs. ❑ *...Americans of Slavic descent.* ADJ

**slav|ish** /sleɪvɪʃ/ You use **slavish** to describe things that copy or imitate something exactly, without any attempt to be original. ❑ *She herself insists she is no slavish follower of fashion.* ADJ disapproval
♦ **slav|ish|ly** *Most have slavishly copied the design of IBM's big mainframe machines.* ADV: ADV with v, ADV adj

**Sla|von|ic** /sləvɒnɪk/ Something that is **Slavonic** relates to East European languages such as Russian, Czech, and Serbo-Croat, or to the people who speak them. ❑ *The Ukrainians speak a Slavonic language similar to Russian.* ADJ

**slaw** /slɔː/ **Slaw** is a salad of chopped raw carrot, onions, cabbage and other vegetables in mayonnaise. [mainly AM] N-UNCOUNT
✔ in BRIT, usually use **coleslaw**

**slay** /sleɪ/ **(slays, slaying, slew, slayed, slain)** 1 If someone **slays** an animal, they kill it in a violent way. [FORMAL] ❑ *...the hill where St George slew the dragon.* VERB V n 2 If someone **has been slain**, they have been murdered. [mainly AM] ❑ *Two Australian tourists were slain.* V-PASSIVE be V-ed

**slay|ing** /sleɪɪŋ/ **(slayings)** A **slaying** is a murder. [mainly AM] ❑ *...a trail of motiveless slayings.* N-COUNT: usu with supp
✔ in BRIT, usually use **killing**

**sleaze** /sliːz/ You use **sleaze** to describe activities that you consider immoral, dishonest, or not respectable, especially in politics, business, journalism, or entertainment. [INFORMAL] ❑ *She claimed that an atmosphere of sleaze and corruption now surrounded the Government.* N-UNCOUNT disapproval

**slea|zy** /sliːzi/ **(sleazier, sleaziest)** 1 If you describe a place as **sleazy**, you dislike it because it looks dirty and badly cared for, and not respectable. [INFORMAL] ❑ *...sleazy bars.* ADJ disapproval 2 If you describe something or someone as **sleazy**, you disapprove of them because you think they are not respectable and are rather disgusting. [INFORMAL] ❑ *The accusations are making the government's conduct appear increasingly sleazy.* ADJ disapproval

**sled** /sled/ **(sleds, sledding, sledded)** 1 A **sled** is the same as a **sledge**. [AM] N-COUNT 2 If you go **sledding**, you ride on a sled. [AM] ❑ *We got home and went sledding on the small hill in our back yard.* VERB V-ing

**sledge** /sledʒ/ **(sledges, sledging, sledged)** 1 A **sledge** is an object used for travelling over snow. It consists of a framework which slides on two strips of wood or metal. [BRIT] ❑ *She travelled 14,000 miles by sledge across Siberia to Kamchatka.* N-COUNT: also by N = sled 2 If you **sledge** or go **sledging**, you ride on a sledge. [BRIT] ❑ *Our hill is marvellous for sledging and we always have snow in January.* VERB V

**sledge|hammer** /sledʒhæməʳ/ **(sledgehammers)** also **sledge-hammer.** A **sledgehammer** is a large, heavy hammer with a long handle, used for breaking up rocks and concrete. N-COUNT

**sleek** /sliːk/ **(sleeker, sleekest)** 1 **Sleek** hair or fur is smooth and shiny and looks healthy. ❑ *...sleek black hair... The horse's sleek body gleamed.* ADJ 2 If you describe someone as **sleek**, you mean that they look rich and stylish. ❑ *Lord White is as sleek and elegant as any other multi millionaire businessman.* ADJ 3 **Sleek** vehicles, furniture, or other objects look smooth, shiny, and expensive. ❑ *... a sleek white BMW. ...sleek modern furniture.* ADJ

**sleep** /sliːp/ **(sleeps, sleeping, slept)** ♦♦◇ 1 **Sleep** is the natural state of rest in which your eyes are closed, your body is inactive, and your mind does not think. ❑ *They were exhausted from lack of sleep... Try and get some sleep... Be quiet and go to sleep... Often he would have bad dreams and cry out in his sleep.* N-UNCOUNT 2 When you **sleep**, you rest with your eyes closed and your mind and body inactive. ❑ *During the car journey, the baby slept. ...a pool surrounded by sleeping sunbathers.* VERB V V-ing 3 A **sleep** is a period of sleeping. ❑ *I think he may be ready for a sleep soon.* N-COUNT: usu sing 4 If a building or room **sleeps** a particular number of people, it has beds for that number of people. ❑ *The villa sleeps 10 and costs £530 per person for two weeks.* VERB: no cont, no passive V amount 5 → See also **sleeping**.
PHRASES 6 If you cannot **get to sleep**, you are unable to sleep. ❑ *I can't get to sleep with all that singing.* PHRASE: V inflects 7 If you say that you didn't **lose** any **sleep over** something, you mean that you did not worry about it at all. ❑ *I didn't lose too much sleep over that investigation.* PHRASE: V inflects, usu PHR over n 8 If you are trying to make a decision and you say that you will **sleep on it**, you mean that you will delay making a decision on it until the following day, so you have time to think about it. PHRASE: V inflects 9 If a sick or injured animal **is put to sleep**, it is killed by a vet in a way that does not cause it pain. ❑ *I'm going take the dog down to the vet's and have her put to sleep.* PHRASE: V inflects = put down 10 to **sleep rough** → see **rough**.
♦ **sleep around** If you say that someone **sleeps around**, you disapprove of them because they have sex with a lot of different people. [INFORMAL] ❑ *I don't sleep around. ...a drunken husband who slept around with other women.* PHRASAL VERB disapproval V P V P with n
♦ **sleep off** If you **sleep off** the effects of too much travelling, drink, or food, you recover from it by sleeping. ❑ *It's a good idea to spend the first night of your holiday sleeping off the jet lag... They had been up all night and were sleeping it off.* PHRASAL VERB V P n (not pron) V n P
♦ **sleep over** If someone, especially a child, **sleeps over** in a place such as a friend's home, they stay there for one night. ❑ *She said his friends could sleep over in the big room downstairs.* PHRASAL VERB V P
♦ **sleep together** If two people **are sleeping together**, they are having a sexual relationship, but are not usually married to each other. ❑ *I'm pretty sure they slept together before they were married.* PHRASAL VERB V P
♦ **sleep with** If you **sleep with** someone, you have sex with them. ❑ *He was old enough to sleep with a girl and make her pregnant.* PHRASAL VERB V P n

**sleep|er** /sliːpəʳ/ **(sleepers)** 1 You can use **sleeper** to indicate how well someone sleeps. For example, if someone is a light **sleeper**, they are easily woken up. ❑ *I'm a very light sleeper and I can hardly get any sleep at all.* N-COUNT: adj N 2 In British English, a **sleeper** is a carriage on a train containing beds for passengers to sleep in at night, or a section of such a carriage. The usual American words are **sleeping car** for the carriage and **roomette** for the section. N-COUNT 3 A **sleeper** is a train with beds for its passengers to sleep in at night. [BRIT] N-COUNT 4 Railway **sleepers** are large heavy beams that support the rails of a railway track. [BRIT] N-COUNT: oft n N
✔ in AM, use **ties**

**sleep|ing** /sliːpɪŋ/ You use **sleeping** to describe places where people sleep or things concerned with where people sleep. ❑ *On the top floor we have sleeping quarters for women and children.* → See also **sleep**. ADJ: ADJ n

**sleep|ing bag** **(sleeping bags)** A **sleeping bag** is a large deep bag with a warm lining, used for sleeping in, especially when you are camping. N-COUNT

**sleep|ing car** **(sleeping cars)** A **sleeping car** is a railway carriage containing beds for passengers to sleep in at night. N-COUNT

**sleep|ing giant** **(sleeping giants)** If you refer to someone or something as a **sleeping giant**, you mean that they are powerful but they have not yet shown the full extent of their power. [JOURNALISM] ❑ *The trust, which has 2.3 million members, has been characterised as a sleeping giant of the environment movement.* N-COUNT

**sleep|ing part|ner** **(sleeping partners)** [N-COUNT] A **sleeping partner** is a person who provides some of the capital for a business but who does not take an active part in managing the business. [BRIT, BUSINESS]

✔ in AM, use **silent partner**

**sleep|ing pill** **(sleeping pills)** [N-COUNT] A **sleeping pill** is a pill that you can take to help you sleep.

**sleep|ing sick|ness** [N-UNCOUNT] **Sleeping sickness** is a serious tropical disease which causes great tiredness and often leads to death.

**sleep|ing tab|let** **(sleeping tablets)** [N-COUNT] A **sleeping tablet** is the same as a **sleeping pill**.

**sleep|less** /sliːpləs/ 1 [ADJ: usu ADJ n] A **sleepless** night is one during which you do not sleep. ❑ *I have sleepless nights worrying about her.* 2 [ADJ] Someone who is **sleepless** is unable to sleep. ❑ *A sleepless baby can seem to bring little reward.*

**sleep|over** /sliːpoʊvəʳ/ **(sleepovers)** also **sleep-over.** [N-COUNT] A **sleepover** is an occasion when someone, especially a child, sleeps for one night in a place such as a friend's home.

**sleep|walk** /sliːpwɔːk/ **(sleepwalks, sleepwalking, sleepwalked)** [VERB] If someone **is sleepwalking**, they are walking around while they are asleep. [V] ❑ *He once sleepwalked to the middle of the road outside his home at 1 a.m.*

**sleepy** /sliːpi/ **(sleepier, sleepiest)** 1 [ADJ: usu v-link ADJ] If you are **sleepy**, you are very tired and are almost asleep. ❑ *I was beginning to feel amazingly sleepy.* ♦ **sleepi|ly** [ADV: ADV with v] *Joanna sat up, blinking sleepily.* ♦ **sleepi|ness** [N-UNCOUNT] *He tried to fight the sleepiness that overwhelmed him.* 2 [ADJ: usu ADJ n] A **sleepy** place is quiet and does not have much activity or excitement. ❑ *Valence is a sleepy little town just south of Lyon.*

**sleet** /sliːt/ [N-UNCOUNT] **Sleet** is rain that is partly frozen. ❑ *...blinding snow, driving sleet and wind.*

**sleeve** /sliːv/ **(sleeves)** 1 [N-COUNT] The **sleeves** of a coat, shirt, or other item of clothing are the parts that cover your arms. ❑ *His sleeves were rolled up to his elbows... He wore a black band on the left sleeve of his jacket.* 2 [N-COUNT: usu N of n, n N] A record **sleeve** is the stiff envelope in which a record is kept. [mainly BRIT] ❑ *There are to be no pictures of him on the sleeve of the new record.*

✔ in AM, usually use **jacket**

3 [PHRASE: N inflects] If you have something **up** your **sleeve**, you have an idea or plan which you have not told anyone about. You can also say that someone has **an ace, card,** or **trick up** their **sleeve**. ❑ *He wondered what Shearson had up his sleeve.*

**-sleeved** /-sliːvd/ [COMB in ADJ: usu ADJ n] **-sleeved** is added to adjectives such as 'long' and 'short' to form adjectives which indicate that an item of clothing has long or short sleeves. ❑ *...a short-sleeved blue shirt.*

**sleeve|less** /sliːvləs/ [ADJ: usu ADJ n] A **sleeveless** dress, top, or other item of clothing has no sleeves. ❑ *She wore a sleeveless silk dress.*

**sleeve note** **(sleeve notes)** [N-COUNT: usu pl] The **sleeve notes** are short pieces of writing on the covers of records, which tell you something about the music or the musicians. [BRIT]

✔ in AM, use **liner note**

**sleigh** /sleɪ/ **(sleighs)** [N-COUNT] A **sleigh** is a vehicle which can slide over snow. Sleighs are usually pulled by horses.

**sleight of hand** /slaɪt əv hænd/ **(sleights of hand)** [N-VAR] **Sleight of hand** is the deceiving of someone in a skilful way. ❑ *He accused Mr MacGregor of 'sleight of hand'.*

**slen|der** /slendəʳ/ 1 [ADJ] [approval] A **slender** person is attractively thin and graceful. [WRITTEN] ❑ *She was slender, with delicate wrists and ankles. ...a tall, slender figure in a straw hat.* 2 [ADJ: usu ADJ n = slim] You can use **slender** to describe a situation which exists but only to a very small degree. [WRITTEN] ❑ *The United States held a slender lead.*

**slept** /slept/ **Slept** is the past tense and past participle of **sleep**.

**sleuth** /sluːθ/ **(sleuths)** [N-COUNT] A **sleuth** is a detective. [OLD-FASHIONED]

**sleuth|ing** /sluːθɪŋ/ [N-UNCOUNT] **Sleuthing** is the investigation of a crime or mystery by someone who is not a police officer. [LITERARY] ❑ *I did a little sleuthing to see if I could find any footprints.*

**slew** /sluː/ **(slews, slewing, slewed)** 1 **Slew** is the past tense of **slay**. 2 [VERB] If a vehicle **slews** or **is slewed** across a road, it slides across it. [V adv/prep] ❑ *The bus slewed sideways...* [V n prep/adv] *He slewed the car against the side of the building.* 3 [N-COUNT: usu sing, usu N of n] A **slew of** things is a large number of them. [mainly AM] ❑ *There have been a whole slew of shooting incidents.*

**slice** /slaɪs/ **(slices, slicing, sliced)** ◆◇◇ 1 [N-COUNT: usu with supp, oft N of n] A **slice of** bread, meat, fruit, or other food is a thin piece that has been cut from a larger piece. ❑ *Try to eat at least four slices of bread a day. ...water flavored with a slice of lemon.* 2 [VERB] If you **slice** bread, meat, fruit, or other food, you cut it into thin pieces. [V n] ❑ *Helen sliced the cake...* [V n into n] *Slice the steak into long thin slices.* ♦ [PHRASAL VERB] **Slice up** means the same as **slice**. [V P n] ❑ *I sliced up an onion...* [V n P] *He began slicing the pie up.* 3 [N-COUNT: usu N of n] You can use **slice** to refer to a part of a situation or activity. ❑ *Fiction takes up a large slice of the publishing market.* 4 → See also **sliced**, **fish slice**. 5 **slice of the action** → see **action**.
♦ **slice up** → see **slice 2**.

**sliced** /slaɪst/ [ADJ: usu ADJ n] **Sliced** bread has been cut into slices before being wrapped and sold. ❑ *...a sliced white loaf.*

**slick** /slɪk/ **(slicker, slickest)** 1 [ADJ] A **slick** performance, production, or advertisement is skilful and impressive. ❑ *There's a big difference between an amateur video and a slick Hollywood production.* ♦ **slick|ness** [N-UNCOUNT] *These actors and directors brought a new sophistication and slickness to modern theatre.* 2 [ADJ: usu ADJ n] A **slick** action is done quickly and smoothly, and without any obvious effort. ❑ *They were outplayed by the Colombians' slick passing and decisive finishing.* 3 [ADJ] [disapproval] A **slick** person speaks easily in a way that is likely to convince people, but is not sincere. ❑ *Don't be fooled by slick politicians.* 4 [N-COUNT] A **slick** is the same as an **oil slick**. ❑ *Experts are trying to devise ways to clean up the huge slick.*

**slick|er** /slɪkəʳ/ **(slickers)** 1 [N-COUNT] A **slicker** is a long loose waterproof coat. [AM]

✔ in BRIT, use **oilskins**

2 → See also **slick**.

**slide** /slaɪd/ **(slides, sliding, slid)** ◆◇◇ 1 [VERB] When something **slides** somewhere or when you **slide** it there, it moves there smoothly over or against something. [V n with adj] ❑ *She slid the door open...* [V n prep/adv] *I slid the wallet into his pocket...* [V prep/adv] *Tears were sliding down his cheeks.* 2 [VERB] If you **slide** somewhere, you move there smoothly and quietly. [V prep/adv] ❑ *He slid into the driver's seat.* 3 [VERB = slip] To **slide into** a particular mood, attitude, or situation means to gradually start to have that mood, attitude, or situation often without intending to. [V into n] ❑ *She had slid into a depression.* 4 [VERB] If currencies or prices **slide**, they gradually become worse or lower in value. [JOURNALISM] [V] ❑ *The US dollar continued to slide...* [V amount] *Shares slid 11p to 293p after brokers downgraded their profit estimates.* ♦ [N-COUNT] **Slide** is also a noun. ❑ *...the dangerous slide in oil prices.* 5 [N-COUNT] A **slide** is a small piece of photographic film which you project onto a screen so that you can see the picture. ❑ *...a slide show.* 6 [N-COUNT] A **slide** is a piece of glass on which you put something that you want to examine through a microscope. 7 [N-COUNT] A **slide** is a piece of playground equipment that has a steep slope for children to go down for fun. 8 [PHRASE: *let* inflects] If you **let** something **slide**, you allow it to get into a worse state or condition by not attending to it. ❑ *The company had let environmental standards slide.*

**slide rule** **(slide rules)** [N-COUNT] A **slide rule** is an instrument that you use for calculating numbers. It looks like a ruler and has a middle part that slides backwards and forwards.

**slid|ing door** **(sliding doors)** **Sliding doors** are doors which slide together rather than swinging on hinges. N-COUNT

**slid|ing scale** **(sliding scales)** Payments such as wages or taxes that are calculated **on a sliding scale** are higher or lower depending on various different factors. ❑ *Many practitioners have a sliding scale of fees.* N-COUNT: usu sing, oft N *of* n, *on a* N

**slight** /slaɪt/ **(slighter, slightest, slights, slighting, slighted)** ◆◇◇ [1] Something that is **slight** is very small in degree or quantity. ❑ *Doctors say he has made a slight improvement... We have a slight problem... He's not the slightest bit worried.* ADJ: usu ADJ n = *small* [2] A **slight** person has a fairly thin and delicate looking body. ❑ *She is smaller and slighter than Christie. ...a slight, bespectacled figure.* ADJ ♦ **slight|ly** *...a slightly built man.* ADV: ADV -ed [3] If you **are slighted**, someone does or says something that insults you by treating you as if your views or feelings are not important. ❑ *They felt slighted by not being consulted.* VERB: usu passive *feel* V-ed ♦ **Slight** is also a noun. ❑ *It isn't a slight on my husband that I enjoy my evening class.* N-COUNT: usu with supp [4] You use **in the slightest** to emphasize a negative statement. ❑ *That doesn't interest me in the slightest.* PHRASE: with brd-neg [emphasis]

**slight|ly** /slaɪtli/ ◆◆◇ **Slightly** means to some degree but not to a very large degree. ❑ *His family then moved to a slightly larger house... They will be slightly more expensive but they last a lot longer... You can adjust it slightly.* ADV: ADV adj, ADV with v, ADV prep

**slim** /slɪm/ **(slimmer, slimmest, slims, slimming, slimmed)** ◆◇◇ [1] A **slim** person has an attractively thin and well-shaped body. ❑ *The young woman was tall and slim... Jean is pretty, of slim build, with blue eyes.* ADJ [approval] [2] If you **are slimming**, you are trying to make yourself thinner and lighter by eating less food. ❑ *Some people will gain weight, no matter how hard they try to slim.* VERB V Also V n ♦ **Slim down** means the same as **slim**. ❑ *Doctors have told Benny to slim down. ...salon treatments that claim to slim down thighs.* PHRASAL VERB V P, V P n [3] A **slim** book, wallet, or other object is thinner than usual. ❑ *The slim booklets describe a range of services and facilities.* ADJ: usu ADJ n [4] A **slim** chance or possibility is a very small one. ❑ *There's still a slim chance that he may become Prime Minister.* ADJ = *faint* [5] If an organization **slims** its products or workers, it reduces the number of them that it has. [BUSINESS] ❑ *The company recently slimmed its product line.* VERB V n

♦ **slim down** [1] If a company or other organization **slims down** or **is slimmed down**, it employs fewer people, in order to save money or become more efficient. [BUSINESS] ❑ *Many firms have had little choice but to slim down. ...the plan to slim down the coal industry.* PHRASAL VERB V P, V P n (not pron) [2] → see **slim 2**.

**slime** /slaɪm/ **Slime** is a thick, wet substance which covers a surface or comes from the bodies of animals such as snails. ❑ *There was an unappealing film of slime on top of the pond.* N-UNCOUNT

**slim|line** /slɪmlaɪn/ **Slimline** objects are thinner or narrower than normal ones. ❑ *The slimline diary fits easily into a handbag.* ADJ: usu ADJ n

**slimy** /slaɪmi/ **(slimier, slimiest)** [1] **Slimy** substances are thick, wet, and unpleasant. **Slimy** objects are covered in a slimy substance. ❑ *His feet slipped in the slimy mud.* ADJ [2] If you describe someone as **slimy**, you dislike them because they are friendly and pleasant in an insincere way. [BRIT, INFORMAL] ❑ *I've worked hard for what I have and I don't want it taken away by some slimy business partner.* ADJ [disapproval] = *oily*

**sling** /slɪŋ/ **(slings, slinging, slung)** [1] If you **sling** something somewhere, you throw it there carelessly. ❑ *I saw him take off his anorak and sling it into the back seat.* VERB = *fling* V n prep/adv [2] If you **sling** something over your shoulder or over something such as a chair, you hang it there loosely. ❑ *She slung her coat over her desk chair... He had a small green rucksack slung over one shoulder.* VERB V n prep, V n prep [3] If a rope, blanket, or other object **is slung** between two points, someone has hung it loosely between them. ❑ *...two long poles with a blanket slung between them.* VERB: usu passive *be* V-ed prep [4] A **sling** is an object made of ropes, straps, or cloth that is used for carrying things. ❑ *They used slings of rope to lower us from one set of arms to another.* N-COUNT [5] A **sling** is a piece of cloth which supports someone's broken or injured arm and is tied round their neck. ❑ *She was back at work with her arm in a sling.* N-COUNT [6] → See also **mud-slinging**.

**sling|shot** /slɪŋʃɒt/ **(slingshots)** A **slingshot** is a **catapult**. [AM] N-COUNT

**slink** /slɪŋk/ **(slinks, slinking, slunk)** If you **slink** somewhere, you move there quietly because you do not want to be seen. ❑ *He decided that he couldn't just slink away, so he went and sat next to his wife.* VERB = *sneak* V adv/prep

**slinky** /slɪŋki/ **(slinkier, slinkiest)** **Slinky** clothes fit very closely to a woman's body in a way that makes her look sexually attractive. ❑ *She's wearing a slinky black mini-skirt.* ADJ: usu ADJ n

**slip** /slɪp/ **(slips, slipping, slipped)** ◆◆◇ [1] If you **slip**, you accidentally slide and lose your balance. ❑ *He had slipped on an icy pavement... Be careful not to slip.* VERB V, V [2] If something **slips**, it slides out of place or out of your hand. ❑ *His glasses had slipped... The hammer slipped out of her grasp.* VERB V, V prep/adv [3] If you **slip** somewhere, you go there quickly and quietly. ❑ *Amy slipped downstairs and out of the house.* VERB V adv/prep [4] If you **slip** something somewhere, you put it there quickly in a way that does not attract attention. ❑ *I slipped a note under Louise's door... Just slip in a piece of paper.* VERB V n prep, V n with adv [5] If you **slip** something **to** someone, you give it to them secretly. ❑ *Robert had slipped her a note in school... She pulled out a package and slipped it to the man.* VERB V n n, V n *to* n [6] To **slip into** a particular state or situation means to pass gradually into it, in a way that is hardly noticed. ❑ *It amazed him how easily one could slip into a routine.* VERB = *slide* V *into* n [7] If something **slips to** a lower level or standard, it falls to that level or standard. ❑ *Shares slipped to 117p... In June, producer prices slipped 0.1% from May... Overall business activity is slipping.* VERB V *to/from/by* amount/n, V amount, V ♦ **Slip** is also a noun. ❑ *...a slip in consumer confidence.* N-SING: oft N *in* n [8] If you **slip into** or **out of** clothes or shoes, you put them on or take them off quickly and easily. ❑ *She slipped out of the jacket and tossed it on the couch... I slipped off my woollen gloves.* VERB V *into/out of* n, V n with *on/off* [9] A **slip** is a small or unimportant mistake. ❑ *We must be well prepared, there must be no slips.* N-COUNT [10] A **slip of** paper is a small piece of paper. ❑ *...little slips of paper he had torn from a notebook... I put her name on the slip.* N-COUNT: oft N *of* n [11] A **slip** is a thin piece of clothing that a woman wears under her dress or skirt. N-COUNT [12] → See also **Freudian slip**.

**PHRASES** [13] If you **give** someone **the slip**, you escape from them when they are following you or watching you. [INFORMAL] ❑ *He gave reporters the slip by leaving at midnight.* PHRASE: V inflects [14] If you **let slip** information, you accidentally tell it to someone, when you wanted to keep it secret. ❑ *I bet he let slip that I'd gone to America.* PHRASE: *let* inflects [15] If something **slips** your **mind**, you forget about it. ❑ *The reason for my visit had obviously slipped his mind.* PHRASE: V and N inflect [16] to **slip through** your **fingers** → see **finger**. **slip of the tongue** → see **tongue**.

♦ **slip in** If you **slip in** a question or comment, you ask or make it without interrupting the flow of the conversation. ❑ *Slip in a few questions about other things.* PHRASAL VERB V P n (not pron)

♦ **slip through** If something **slips through** a set of checks or rules, it is accepted when in fact it should not be. ❑ *...hardened trouble-makers who have slipped through the security checks... The slightest little bit of inattention can let something slip through.* PHRASAL VERB V P n, V P

♦ **slip up** If you **slip up**, you make a small or unimportant mistake. ❑ *There were occasions when we slipped up.* → See also **slip-up**. PHRASAL VERB V P

**slip-on** **(slip-ons)** **Slip-on** shoes have nothing fastening them. ❑ *...slip-on boat shoes.* ADJ: ADJ n ♦ **Slip-on** is also a noun. ❑ *He removed his brown slip-ons.* N-COUNT

**slip|page** /slɪpɪdʒ/ **(slippages) Slippage** is a failure to maintain a steady position or rate of progress, so that a particular target or standard is not achieved. ❑ *...a substantial slippage in the value of sterling.* N-VAR

**slipped disc** **(slipped discs)** If you have a **slipped disc**, you have a bad back because one of the discs in your spine has moved out of its proper position. N-COUNT

**slip|per** /slɪpəʳ/ **(slippers) Slippers** are loose, soft shoes that you wear at home. N-COUNT

**slip|pery** /slɪpəri/ 1 Something that is **slippery** is smooth, wet, or oily and is therefore difficult to walk on or to hold. ❑ *The tiled floor was wet and slippery... Motorists were warned to beware of slippery conditions.* ADJ 2 You can describe someone as **slippery** if you think that they are dishonest in a clever way and cannot be trusted. ❑ *He is a slippery customer, and should be carefully watched.* ADJ disapproval 3 If someone is on a **slippery slope**, they are involved in a course of action that is difficult to stop and that will eventually lead to failure or trouble. ❑ *The company started down the slippery slope of believing that they knew better than the customer.* PHRASE: N inflects, usu *down/on* PHR, oft PHR *to* n

**slip road** **(slip roads)** A **slip road** is a road which cars use to drive on and off a motorway. [BRIT] N-COUNT

✔ in AM, use **entrance ramp, exit ramp**

**slip|shod** /slɪpʃɒd/ If something is **slipshod**, it has been done in a careless way. ❑ *The hotel had always been run in a slipshod way.* ADJ: usu ADJ n = careless

**slip|stream** /slɪpstriːm/ **(slipstreams)** The **slipstream** of a fast-moving object such as a car, plane, or boat is the flow of air directly behind it. ❑ *He left a host of other riders trailing in his slipstream.* N-COUNT: usu *the* N

**slip-up** **(slip-ups)** A **slip-up** is a small or unimportant mistake. [INFORMAL] ❑ *There's been a slip-up somewhere.* N-COUNT = slip

**slip|way** /slɪpweɪ/ **(slipways)** A **slipway** is a large platform that slopes down into the sea, from which boats are put into the water. N-COUNT

**slit** /slɪt/ **(slits, slitting)**

✔ The form **slit** is used in the present tense and is the past tense and past participle.

1 If you **slit** something, you make a long narrow cut in it. ❑ *They say somebody slit her throat... He began to slit open each envelope... She was wearing a white dress slit to the thigh.* VERB V n V n with *open* V-ed *to/from* n 2 A **slit** is a long narrow cut. ❑ *Make a slit in the stem about half an inch long.* N-COUNT: oft N *in* n 3 A **slit** is a long narrow opening in something. ❑ *She watched them through a slit in the curtains.* N-COUNT: oft N *in* n

**slith|er** /slɪðəʳ/ **(slithers, slithering, slithered)** 1 If you **slither** somewhere, you slide along in an uneven way. ❑ *Robert lost his footing and slithered down the bank.* VERB V prep/adv 2 If an animal such as a snake **slithers**, it moves along in a curving way. ❑ *The snake slithered into the water.* VERB V prep/adv

**slith|ery** /slɪðəri/ Something that is **slithery** is wet or smooth, and so slides easily over things or is easy to slip on. ❑ *...slithery rice noodles.* ADJ = slippery

**sliv|er** /slɪvəʳ/ **(slivers)** A **sliver of** something is a small thin piece or amount of it. ❑ *Not a sliver of glass remains where the windows were.* N-COUNT: usu N *of* n

**Sloane** /sloʊn/ **(Sloanes)** Rich young people from upper middle class backgrounds in London are sometimes called **Sloanes**. [BRIT] N-COUNT

**slob** /slɒb/ **(slobs)** If you call someone a **slob**, you mean that they are very lazy and untidy. [INFORMAL] ❑ *My boyfriend used to call me a fat slob.* N-COUNT disapproval

**slob|ber** /slɒbəʳ/ **(slobbers, slobbering, slobbered)** If a person or an animal **slobbers**, they let liquid fall from their mouth. ❑ *...slobbering on his eternal cigarette end.* VERB = drool V prep Also V

**sloe** /sloʊ/ **(sloes)** A **sloe** is a small, sour fruit that has a dark purple skin. It is often used to flavour gin. N-VAR

**slog** /slɒg/ **(slogs, slogging, slogged)** 1 If you **slog through** something, you work hard and steadily through it. [INFORMAL] ❑ *They secure their degrees by slogging through an intensive 11-month course... She has slogged her way through ballet classes since the age of six.* ♦ **Slog away** means the same as **slog**. ❑ *Edward slogged away, always learning.* VERB V prep V *way through* n PHRASAL VERB V P 2 If you describe a task as a **slog**, you mean that it is tiring and requires a lot of effort. [INFORMAL] ❑ *There is little to show for the two years of hard slog.* N-SING: also no det

**slo|gan** /sloʊgən/ **(slogans)** A **slogan** is a short phrase that is easy to remember. Slogans are used in advertisements and by political parties and other organizations who want people to remember what they are saying or selling. ❑ *They could campaign on the slogan 'We'll take less of your money'.* N-COUNT

**slo|gan|eer|ing** /sloʊgənɪərɪŋ/ **Sloganeering** is the use of slogans by people such as politicians or advertising agencies. ❑ *...the sloganeering of the marketing department.* N-UNCOUNT

**sloop** /sluːp/ **(sloops)** A **sloop** is a small sailing boat with one mast. N-COUNT

**slop** /slɒp/ **(slops, slopping, slopped)** 1 If liquid **slops** from a container or if you **slop** liquid somewhere, it comes out over the edge of the container, usually accidentally. ❑ *A little cognac slopped over the edge of the glass... Refilling his cup, she slopped some tea into the saucer.* VERB V adv/prep V n adv/prep Also V, V n 2 You can use **slop** or **slops** to refer to liquid waste containing the remains of food. ❑ *Breakfast plates were collected and the slops emptied.* N-UNCOUNT: also N in pl

**slope** /sloʊp/ **(slopes, sloping, sloped)** 1 A **slope** is the side of a mountain, hill, or valley. ❑ *Saint-Christo is perched on a mountain slope. ...the lower slopes of the Himalayas.* N-COUNT: usu with supp 2 A **slope** is a surface that is at an angle, so that one end is higher than the other. ❑ *The street must have been on a slope.* N-COUNT: usu sing = incline 3 If a surface **slopes**, it is at an angle, so that one end is higher than the other. ❑ *The bank sloped down sharply to the river... The garden sloped quite steeply.* ♦ **slop|ing** *...a brick building, with a sloping roof. ...the gently sloping beach.* VERB V adv/prep V ADJ 4 If something **slopes**, it leans to the right or to the left rather than being upright. ❑ *The writing sloped backwards.* VERB = slant V adv/prep 5 The **slope** of something is the angle at which it slopes. ❑ *The slope increases as you go up the curve. ...a slope of ten degrees.* N-COUNT: usu sing, oft N *of* n 6 → See also **ski slope**. 7 **slippery slope** → see **slippery**.

**slop|ping out** also **slopping-out**. In prisons where prisoners have to use buckets as toilets, **slopping out** is the practice in which they empty the buckets. [BRIT] N-UNCOUNT

**slop|py** /slɒpi/ **(sloppier, sloppiest)** 1 If you describe someone's work or activities as **sloppy**, you mean they have been done in a careless and lazy way. ❑ *He has little patience for sloppy work from colleagues.* ADJ disapproval 2 If you describe someone or something as **sloppy**, you mean that they are sentimental and romantic. ❑ *It's ideal for people who like a sloppy movie.* ADJ = slushy

**slosh** /slɒʃ/ **(sloshes, sloshing, sloshed)** 1 If a liquid **sloshes around** or if you **slosh** it **around**, it moves around in different directions. ❑ *The water sloshed around the bridge... He took a mouthful of the cheap wine and sloshed it around his mouth... The champagne sloshed and spilt.* VERB V adv/prep V n adv/prep V 2 If you **slosh through** mud or water, you walk through it in an energetic way, so that the mud or water makes sounds as you walk. ❑ *The two girls joined arms and sloshed through the mud together.* VERB V adv/prep

**sloshed** /slɒʃt/ If someone is **sloshed**, they have drunk too much alcohol. [mainly BRIT, INFORMAL] ❑ *Everyone else was getting sloshed.* ADJ: v-link ADJ = drunk

**slot** /slɒt/ **(slots, slotting, slotted)** 1 A **slot** is a narrow opening in a machine or container, for example a hole that you put coins in to make a machine work. ❑ *He dropped a coin into the slot and dialed.* N-COUNT 2 If you **slot** something into something VERB else, or if it **slots** into it, you put it into a space where it fits. ❑ *He was slotting a CD into a CD player... The car seat belt slotted into place easily... She slotted in a fresh filter.* [3] A **slot** in a schedule or scheme is a place in it where an activity can take place. ❑ *Visitors can book a time slot a week or more in advance.* — V n *into/in/onto* n; V n with adv; N-COUNT: oft n N

**sloth** /sloʊθ/ **(sloths)** [1] **Sloth** is laziness, especially with regard to work. [FORMAL] ❑ *He admitted a lack of motivation and a feeling of sloth.* [2] A **sloth** is an animal from Central and South America. Sloths live in trees and move very slowly. — N-UNCOUNT = *idleness*; N-COUNT

**sloth|ful** /sloʊθfʊl/ Someone who is **slothful** is lazy and unwilling to make an effort to work. [FORMAL] ❑ *He was not slothful: he had been busy all night.* — ADJ = *idle*

**slot ma|chine** **(slot machines)** A **slot machine** is a machine from which you can get food or cigarettes or on which you can gamble. You make it work by putting coins into a slot. — N-COUNT

**slot|ted spoon** **(slotted spoons)** A **slotted spoon** is a large plastic or metal spoon with holes in it. It is used to take food out of a liquid. — N-COUNT

**slouch** /slaʊtʃ/ **(slouches, slouching, slouched)** [1] If someone **slouches**, they sit or stand with their shoulders and head bent so they look lazy and unattractive. ❑ *Try not to slouch when you are sitting down... She has recently begun to slouch over her typewriter.* [2] If someone **slouches** somewhere, they walk around slowly with their shoulders and head bent looking lazy or bored. ❑ *Most of the time, they slouch around in the fields.* — VERB; V; V prep/adv; VERB; V adv/prep

**slough** /slʌf/ **(sloughs, sloughing, sloughed)** When a plant **sloughs** its leaves, or an animal such as a snake **sloughs** its skin, the leaves or skin come off naturally. ❑ *All reptiles have to slough their skin to grow.* ♦ **Slough off** means the same as **slough**. ❑ *Our bodies slough off dead cells.* — VERB = *shed*; V n; PHRASAL VERB; V P n; Also V n P

**slov|en|ly** /slʌvᵊnli/ **Slovenly** people are careless, untidy, or inefficient. ❑ *Lisa was irritated by the slovenly attitude of her boyfriend Sean.* — ADJ: usu ADJ n; [disapproval]; = *sloppy*

**slow** /sloʊ/ **(slower, slowest, slows, slowing, slowed)** ◆◆◇ [1] Something that is **slow** moves, happens, or is done without much speed. ❑ *The traffic is heavy and slow... Electric whisks should be used on a slow speed. ...slow, regular breathing.* ♦ **slow|ly** *He spoke slowly and deliberately... Christian backed slowly away.* ♦ **slow|ness** *She lowered the glass with calculated slowness.* [2] In informal English, **slower** is used to mean 'at a slower speed' and **slowest** is used to mean 'at the slowest speed'. In non-standard English, **slow** is used to mean 'with little speed'. ❑ *I began to walk slower and slower... We got there by driving slow all the way.* [3] Something that is **slow** takes a long time. ❑ *The distribution of passports has been a slow process.* ♦ **slow|ly** *My resentment of her slowly began to fade.* ♦ **slow|ness** *...the slowness of political and economic progress.* [4] If someone is **slow** to do something, they do it after a delay. ❑ *The world community has been slow to respond to the crisis.* [5] If something **slows** or if you **slow** it, it starts to move or happen more slowly. ❑ *The rate of bombing has slowed considerably... She slowed the car and began driving up a narrow road.* [6] Someone who is **slow** is not very clever and takes a long time to understand things. ❑ *He got hit on the head and he's been a bit slow since.* [7] If you describe a situation, place, or activity as **slow**, you mean that it is not very exciting. ❑ *The island is too slow for her liking.* [8] If a clock or watch is **slow**, it shows a time that is earlier than the correct time. [9] → See also **slow-**. [10] **slow off the mark** → see **mark**. **slowly but surely** → see **surely**. **slow on the uptake** → see **uptake**. — ADJ ≠ *fast*; ADV: ADV with v; N-UNCOUNT; ADV: ADV after v ≠ *fast*; ADJ ≠ *quick*; ADV: ADV with v; N-UNCOUNT; ADJ: v-link ADJ, usu ADJ to-inf, ADJ *in* -ing; VERB; V; V n; ADJ ≠ *quick*; ADJ = *quiet* ≠ *lively*; ADJ: usu v-link ADJ ≠ *fast*

♦ **slow down** [1] If something **slows down** or is if something **slows** it **down**, it starts to move or happen more slowly. ❑ *The car slowed down as they passed Customs... There is no cure for the disease, although drugs can slow down its rate of development... Damage to the turbine slowed the work down.* [2] If someone **slows down** or if something **slows** them **down**, they become less active. ❑ *You will need to slow down for a while... He was still taking some medication which slowed him down.* [3] → See also **slowdown**. — PHRASAL VERB = *slow up* ≠ *speed up*; V P; V P n (not pron); V n P; PHRASAL VERB; V P; V n P; Also V P n (not pron)

♦ **slow up** **Slow up** means the same as **slow down** 1. ❑ *Sales are slowing up... The introduction of a new code of criminal procedure has also slowed up the system.* — PHRASAL VERB; V P; V P n (not pron); Also V n P

**slow-** /sloʊ-/ **slow-** is used to form words which describe something that happens slowly. ❑ *He was stuck in a line of slow-moving traffic. ...a slow-burning fuse.* — COMB in ADJ

**slow|down** /sloʊdaʊn/ **(slowdowns)** [1] A **slowdown** is a reduction in speed or activity. ❑ *There has been a sharp slowdown in economic growth.* [2] A **slowdown** is a protest in which workers deliberately work slowly and cause problems for their employers. [AM, BUSINESS] ❑ *It's impossible to assess how many officers are participating in the slowdown.* — N-COUNT; N-COUNT

☑ in BRIT, use **go-slow**

**slow lane** **(slow lanes)** [1] On a motorway or freeway, **the slow lane** is the lane for vehicles which are moving more slowly than the other vehicles. [2] If you say that a person, country, or company is in **the slow lane**, you mean that they are not progressing as fast as other people, countries, or companies in a particular area of activity. ❑ *Germany was not trying to push Britain into the slow lane.* — N-COUNT: usu sing, usu *the* N; N-SING: usu *the* N

**slow mo|tion** also **slow-motion.** When film or television pictures are shown **in slow motion**, they are shown much more slowly than normal. ❑ *It seemed almost as if he were falling in slow motion.* — N-UNCOUNT: usu *in* N

**slow-witted** Someone who is **slow-witted** is slow to understand things. — ADJ

**sludge** /slʌdʒ/ **(sludges)** **Sludge** is thick mud, sewage, or industrial waste. ❑ *All dumping of sludge will be banned by 1998.* — N-VAR

**slug** /slʌg/ **(slugs, slugging, slugged)** [1] A **slug** is a small slow-moving creature with a long soft body and no legs, like a snail without a shell. [2] If you take a **slug of** an alcoholic drink, you take a large mouthful of it. [INFORMAL] ❑ *Edgar took a slug of his drink.* [3] If you **slug** someone, you hit them hard. [INFORMAL] ❑ *She slugged her right in the face.* [4] A **slug** is a bullet. [mainly AM, INFORMAL] — N-COUNT; N-COUNT: usu N *of* n = *shot*; VERB = *sock*; V n; N-COUNT

**slug|ger** /slʌgəʳ/ **(sluggers)** In baseball, a **slugger** is a player who hits the ball very hard. [AM] — N-COUNT

**slug|gish** /slʌgɪʃ/ You can describe something as **sluggish** if it moves, works, or reacts much slower than you would like or is normal. ❑ *The economy remains sluggish... Circulation is much more sluggish in the feet than in the hands.* — ADJ

**sluice** /sluːs/ **(sluices, sluicing, sluiced)** [1] A **sluice** is a passage that carries a current of water and has a barrier, called a sluice gate, which can be opened and closed to control the flow of water. [2] If you **sluice** something or **sluice** it down or out, you wash it with a stream of water. ❑ *He sluiced the bath and filled it.* — N-COUNT; VERB; V n

**slum** /slʌm/ **(slums)** A **slum** is an area of a city where living conditions are very bad and where the houses are in bad condition. ❑ *...inner-city slums in the old cities of the north and east.* — N-COUNT: oft N n

**slum|ber** /slʌmbəʳ/ **(slumbers, slumbering, slumbered)** **Slumber** is sleep. [LITERARY] ❑ *He had fallen into exhausted slumber... He roused Charles from his slumbers.* ♦ **Slumber** is also a verb. ❑ *The older three girls are still slumbering peacefully.* — N-VAR; VERB; V

**slum|ber par|ty** **(slumber parties)** A **slumber party** is an occasion when a group of young friends spend the night together at the home of one of the group. [mainly AM] — N-COUNT

**slump** /slʌmp/ **(slumps, slumping, slumped)** [1] If something such as the value of something **slumps**, it falls suddenly and by a large amount. ❑ *Net profits slumped by 41%... Government popularity in Scotland has slumped to its lowest level since the 1970s.* ♦ **Slump** is also a noun. ❑ *...a slump in property prices.* [2] A **slump** is a time when many people in a country are unemployed and poor. ❑ *...the slump of the early 1980s.* [3] If you **slump** somewhere, you fall or sit down there heavily, for example because you are very tired or you feel ill. ❑ *She slumped into a chair... He saw the driver slumped over the wheel.*

VERB; V prep; V prep; Also V; N-COUNT: oft N *in* n; N-COUNT = *recession*; VERB; V prep/adv; V-ed

**slung** /slʌŋ/ **Slung** is the past tense and past participle of **sling**.

**slunk** /slʌŋk/ **Slunk** is the past tense and past participle of **slink**.

**slur** /slɜːʳ/ **(slurs, slurring, slurred)** [1] A **slur** is an insulting remark which could damage someone's reputation. ❑ *This is yet another slur on the integrity of the Metropolitan Police.* [2] If someone **slurs** their speech or if their speech **slurs**, they do not pronounce each word clearly, because they are drunk, ill, or sleepy. ❑ *He repeated himself and slurred his words more than usual... The newscaster's speech began to slur.*

N-COUNT: oft N *on* n = *smear*; VERB; V n; V

**slurp** /slɜːʳp/ **(slurps, slurping, slurped)** [1] If you **slurp** a liquid, you drink it noisily. ❑ *He blew on his soup before slurping it off the spoon... He slurped down a cup of sweet, black coffee.* [2] A **slurp** is a noise that you make with your mouth when you drink noisily, or a mouthful of liquid that you drink noisily. ❑ *He takes a slurp from a cup of black coffee.*

VERB; V n *from/off* n; V adv n; N-COUNT

**slur|ry** /slʌri, AM slɜːri/ **(slurries) Slurry** is a watery mixture of something such as mud, animal waste, or dust. ❑ *...farm slurry and industrial waste.* — N-VAR

**slush** /slʌʃ/ **Slush** is snow that has begun to melt and is therefore very wet and dirty. ❑ *Becker's eyes were as cold and grey as the slush on the pavements outside.* — N-UNCOUNT

**slush fund (slush funds)** A **slush fund** is a sum of money collected to pay for an illegal activity, especially in politics or business. ❑ *He's accused of misusing $17.5 million from a secret government slush fund.* — N-COUNT

**slushy** /slʌʃi/ **(slushier, slushiest)** [1] **Slushy** ground is covered in dirty, wet snow. ❑ *Here and there a drift across the road was wet and slushy.* [2] If you describe a story or idea as **slushy**, you mean you dislike it because it is extremely romantic and sentimental.

ADJ; ADJ [disapproval]

**slut** /slʌt/ **(sluts)** People sometimes refer to a woman as a **slut** when they consider her to be very immoral in her sexual behaviour. [OFFENSIVE] — N-COUNT [disapproval]

**sly** /slaɪ/ [1] A **sly** look, expression, or remark shows that you know something that other people do not know or that was meant to be a secret. ❑ *His lips were spread in a sly smile.* ♦ **sly|ly** *Anna grinned slyly.* [2] If you describe someone as **sly**, you disapprove of them because they keep their feelings or intentions hidden and are clever at deceiving people. ❑ *She is devious and sly and manipulative.*

ADJ: usu ADJ n; ADV; ADJ [disapproval] = *cunning*

**smack** /smæk/ **(smacks, smacking, smacked)** [1] If you **smack** someone, you hit them with your hand. ❑ *She smacked me on the side of the head.* ♦ **Smack** is also a noun. ❑ *Sometimes he just doesn't listen and I end up shouting at him or giving him a smack.* [2] If you **smack** something somewhere, you put it or throw it there so that it makes a loud, sharp noise. ❑ *He smacked his hands down on his knees... Ray Houghton smacked the ball against a post.* [3] If one thing **smacks of** another thing that you consider bad, it reminds you of it or is like it. ❑ *The union was unhappy with the motion, saying it smacked of racism.* [4] Something that is **smack** in a particular place is exactly in that place. [INFORMAL] ❑ *In part that's because industry is smack in the middle of the city.* [5] **Smack** is heroin. [INFORMAL] [6] If you **smack** your **lips**, you open and close your mouth noisily, especially before or after eating, to show that you are eager to eat or enjoyed eating. ❑ *'I really want some dessert,' Keaton says, smacking his lips.*

VERB; V n; N-COUNT; VERB; V n adv/prep; V n adv/prep; VERB; V *of* n; ADV: ADV prep; N-UNCOUNT; PHRASE: V inflects

**small** /smɔːl/ **(smaller, smallest)** [1] A **small** person, thing, or amount of something is not large in physical size. ❑ *She is small for her age... The window was far too small for him to get through... Stick them on using a small amount of glue.* ♦ **small|ness** *Amy had not mentioned the smallness and bareness of Luis's home.* [2] A **small** group or quantity consists of only a few people or things. ❑ *A small group of students meets regularly to learn Japanese... Guns continued to be produced in small numbers.* [3] A **small** child is a very young child. ❑ *I have a wife and two small children... What were you like when you were small?* [4] You use **small** to describe something that is not significant or great in degree. ❑ *It's quite easy to make quite small changes to the way that you work... No detail was too small to escape her attention.* [5] **Small** businesses or companies employ a small number of people and do business with a small number of clients. ❑ *...shops, restaurants and other small businesses.* [6] If someone makes you look or feel **small**, they make you look or feel stupid or ashamed. ❑ *This may just be another of her schemes to make me look small.* [7] **The small of** your **back** is the bottom part of your back that curves in slightly. ❑ *Place your hands on the small of your back and breathe in.* [8] → See also **smalls**. **the small hours** → see **hour**. **small wonder** → see **wonder**.

◆◆◆ ADJ ≠ *large*; N-UNCOUNT; ADJ ≠ *large*; ADJ = *young, little*; ADJ = *minor* ≠ *major*; ADJ; ADJ: v-link ADJ; N-SING: *the* N *of* n

**small ad (small ads) The small ads** in a newspaper are short advertisements in which you can advertise something such as an object for sale or a room to let. ❑ *Prospective buyers should study the small ads in the daily newspaper.* — N-COUNT: usu *the* N in pl

**small arms Small arms** are guns that are light and easy to carry. ❑ *The two sides exchanged small arms fire for about three hours.* — N-PLURAL

**small beer** If you say that something is **small beer**, you mean that it is unimportant in comparison with something else. [BRIT] ❑ *Such roles are small beer compared with the fame she once enjoyed.* — N-UNCOUNT = *peanuts*

**small change Small change** is coins of low value. ❑ *She was counting out 30p, mostly in small change, into my hand.* — N-UNCOUNT

**small fry (small fry) Small fry** is used to refer to someone or something that is considered to be unimportant. ❑ *What they owe to the Inland Revenue is small fry compared to the overall £1.2 million debt.* — N-UNCOUNT: also N in pl

**small|holder** /smɔːlhoʊldəʳ/ **(smallholders)** A **smallholder** is someone who has a smallholding. [BRIT] — N-COUNT

**small|holding** /smɔːlhoʊldɪŋ/ **(smallholdings)** A **smallholding** is a piece of land that is used for farming and is smaller than a normal farm. [BRIT] ❑ *A smallholding in the hills could not support a large family.* — N-COUNT

**small hours** If something happens **in the small hours**, it happens soon after midnight, in the very early morning. ❑ *They were arrested in the small hours of Saturday morning.* — N-PLURAL: usu *in the* N, oft N *of* n

**small|ish** /smɔːlɪʃ/ Something that is **smallish** is fairly small. ❑ *Some smallish firms may close.* — ADJ ≠ *largish*

**small-minded** If you say that someone is **small-minded**, you are critical of them because they have fixed opinions and are unwilling to change them or to think about more general subjects. ❑ *...their small-minded preoccupation with making money.* — ADJ [disapproval]

**small|pox** /smɔːlpɒks/ **Smallpox** is a serious infectious disease that causes spots which leave deep marks on the skin. — N-UNCOUNT

**small print The small print** of a contract or agreement is the part of it that is written in very small print. You refer to it as **the small print** es- — N-UNCOUNT: usu *the* N = *fine print* pecially when you think that it might include unfavourable conditions which someone might not notice or understand. ❑ *Read the small print in your contract to find out exactly what you are insured for.*

**smalls** /smɔːlz/ Your **smalls** are your underwear. [BRIT, INFORMAL] N-PLURAL

**small-scale** A **small-scale** activity or organization is small in size and limited in extent. ❑ *...the small-scale production of farmhouse cheeses in Devon.* ADJ: usu ADJ n ≠ large-scale

**small screen** When people talk about **the small screen**, they are referring to television, in contrast to films that are made for the cinema. ❑ *Now he is also to become a star of the small screen.* N-SING: usu the N ≠ big screen

**small talk** **Small talk** is polite conversation about unimportant things that people make at social occasions. ❑ *Smiling for the cameras, the two men strained to make small talk.* N-UNCOUNT

**small-time** If you refer to workers or businesses as **small-time**, you think they are not very important because their work is limited in extent or not very successful. ❑ *...small time drug dealers.* ADJ ≠ big-time

**small town**

✔ in BRIT, also use **smalltown**

**Small town** is used when referring to small places, usually in the United States, where people are friendly, honest, and polite, or to the people there. **Small town** is also sometimes used to suggest that someone has old-fashioned ideas. [mainly AM] ❑ *...an idealized small-town America of neat, middle-class homes.* ADJ: usu ADJ n

**smarmy** /smɑːʳmi/ **(smarmier, smarmiest)** If you describe someone as **smarmy**, you dislike them because they are unpleasantly polite and flattering, usually because they want you to like them or to do something for them. [BRIT, INFORMAL] ❑ *Rick is slightly smarmy and eager to impress.* ADJ [disapproval]

**smart** /smɑːʳt/ **(smarter, smartest, smarts, smarting, smarted)** ◆◇◇ 1 **Smart** people and things are pleasantly neat and clean in appearance. [mainly BRIT] ❑ *He was smart and well groomed but not good looking... I was dressed in a smart navy blue suit. ...smart new offices.* ADJ ♦ **smart|ly** *He dressed very smartly which was important in those days. ...a smartly-painted door.* ADV: ADV with v ♦ **smart|ness** *The jumper strikes the perfect balance between comfort and smartness.* N-UNCOUNT 2 You can describe someone who is clever as **smart**. ❑ *He thinks he's smarter than Sarah is... Buying expensive furniture is not necessarily the smartest move to make.* → See also **smartly**, **street smart**. ADJ 3 A **smart** place or event is connected with wealthy and fashionable people. ❑ *...smart London dinner parties. ...a smart residential district.* ADJ: usu ADJ n 4 **Smart** bombs and weapons are guided by computers and lasers so that they hit their targets accurately. ADJ: ADJ n 5 If a part of your body or a wound **smarts**, you feel a sharp stinging pain in it. ❑ *My eyes smarted from the smoke.* VERB = sting V 6 If you **are smarting from** something such as criticism or failure, you feel upset about it. [JOURNALISM] ❑ *The Americans were still smarting from their defeat in the Vietnam War.* VERB: usu cont V from n 7 **the smart money** → see **money**.

**smart alec** **(smart alecs)** also **smart aleck**. If you describe someone as a **smart alec**, you dislike the fact that they think they are very clever and always have an answer for everything. [INFORMAL] ❑ *...a fortyish smart-alec TV reporter.* N-COUNT: oft N n [disapproval]

**smart arse** **(smart arses)**

✔ The spellings **smartarse** in British English and **smartass** or **smart-ass** in American English are also used.

If you describe someone as a **smart arse** or **smartass**, you dislike the fact that they think they are very clever and like to show everyone this. [INFORMAL, RUDE] ❑ *...smartass comments.* N-COUNT: oft N n [disapproval]

**smart card** **(smart cards)** A **smart card** is a plastic card which looks like a credit card and can store and process computer data. N-COUNT

**smart drug** **(smart drugs)** **Smart drugs** are drugs which some people think can improve your memory and intelligence. N-COUNT: usu pl

**smart|en** /smɑːʳtᵊn/ **(smartens, smartening, smartened)**

♦ **smarten up** If you **smarten yourself** or a place **up**, you make yourself or the place look neater and tidier. ❑ *...a 10-year programme to smarten up the London Underground... She had wisely smartened herself up. ...a medical student who refused to smarten up.* PHRASAL VERB V P n (not pron) V n P V P

**smart|ly** /smɑːʳtli/ If someone moves or does something **smartly**, they do it quickly and neatly. [WRITTEN] ❑ *The housekeeper moved smartly to the Vicar's desk to answer the call.* → See also **smart**. ADV: ADV with v

**smash** /smæʃ/ **(smashes, smashing, smashed)** ◆◇◇ 1 If you **smash** something or if it **smashes**, it breaks into many pieces, for example when it is hit or dropped. ❑ *Someone smashed a bottle... Two or three glasses fell off and smashed into pieces.* VERB = break V n V into n 2 If you **smash** through a wall, gate, or door, you get through it by hitting and breaking it. ❑ *The demonstrators used trucks to smash through embassy gates... Soldiers smashed their way into his office.* VERB V through n V way prep/adv 3 If something **smashes** or **is smashed** against something solid, it moves very fast and with great force against it. ❑ *The bottle smashed against a wall... He smashed his fist into Anthony's face.* VERB V prep/adv V n prep 4 To **smash** a political group or system means to deliberately destroy it. [INFORMAL] ❑ *Their attempts to clean up politics and smash the power of party machines failed.* VERB V n 5 → See also **smashed**, **smashing**.

♦ **smash down** If you **smash down** a door, building, or other large heavy object, you hit it hard and break it until it falls on the ground. ❑ *The crowd tried to smash down the door of the police station.* PHRASAL VERB = break down V P n (not pron) Also V n P

♦ **smash up** 1 If you **smash** something **up**, you completely destroy it by hitting it and breaking it into many pieces. ❑ *She took revenge on her ex-boyfriend by smashing up his home... You could smash the drawer up with a hammer.* PHRASAL VERB V P n (not pron) V n P 2 If you **smash up** your car, you damage it by crashing it into something. ❑ *All you told me was that he'd smashed up yet another car.* PHRASAL VERB V P n (not pron)

**smash-and-grab** **(smash-and-grabs)** also **smash and grab**. A **smash-and-grab** is a robbery in which a person breaks a shop window, takes the things that are on display there, and runs away with them. ❑ *...a smash and grab raid.* N-COUNT: oft N n

**smashed** /smæʃt/ Someone who is **smashed** is extremely drunk. [INFORMAL] ADJ: usu v-link ADJ

**smash hit** **(smash hits)** A **smash hit** or a **smash** is a very popular show, play, or song. ❑ *The show was a smash hit.* N-COUNT

**smash|ing** /smæʃɪŋ/ If you describe something or someone as **smashing**, you mean that you like them very much. [BRIT, INFORMAL, OLD-FASHIONED] ❑ *She's a smashing girl.* ADJ

**smat|ter|ing** /smætərɪŋ/ **A smattering of** something is a very small amount of it. ❑ *I had acquired a smattering of Greek.* N-SING: usu a N of n

**smear** /smɪəʳ/ **(smears, smearing, smeared)** 1 If you **smear** a surface **with** an oily or sticky substance or **smear** the substance onto the surface, you spread a layer of the substance over the surface. ❑ *My sister smeared herself with suntan oil and slept by the swimming pool... Smear a little olive oil over the inside of the salad bowl.* VERB V n with n V n prep 2 A **smear** is a dirty or oily mark. ❑ *There was a smear of gravy on his chin.* N-COUNT: oft N of n 3 To **smear** someone means to spread unpleasant and untrue rumours or accusations about them in order to damage their reputation. [JOURNALISM] ❑ *...an attempt to smear the director-general of the BBC.* VERB V n 4 A **smear** is an unpleasant and untrue rumour or accusation that is intended to damage someone's reputation. [JOURNALISM] ❑ *He puts all the accusations down to a smear campaign by his political opponents.* N-COUNT: oft N n = slur 5 A **smear** or a **smear test** is a medical test in which a few cells N-COUNT are taken from a woman's cervix and examined to see if any cancer cells are present. [BRIT]

in AM, use **pap smear**, **pap test**

**smeared** /smɪəʳd/ If something is **smeared**, it has dirty or oily marks on it. ❑ *The other child's face was smeared with dirt.* ADJ

**smell** /smel/ **(smells, smelling, smelled, smelt)** ◆◇◇

American English usually uses the form **smelled** as the past tense and past participle. British English uses either **smelled** or **smelt**.

1 The **smell** of something is a quality it has which you become aware of when you breathe in through your nose. ❑ *...the smell of freshly baked bread. ...horrible smells.* N-COUNT: oft N *of* n
2 Your sense of **smell** is the ability that your nose has to detect things. ❑ *...people who lose their sense of smell.* N-UNCOUNT
3 If something **smells** in a particular way, it has a quality which you become aware of through your nose. ❑ *The room smelled of lemons... It smells delicious. ...a crumbly black substance that smells like fresh soil.* V-LINK; V *of* n; V adj; V *like* n
4 If you say that something **smells**, you mean that it smells unpleasant. ❑ *Ma threw that out. She said it smelled... Do my feet smell?* VERB; V; V
5 If you **smell** something, you become aware of it when you breathe in through your nose. ❑ *As soon as we opened the front door we could smell the gas.* VERB; V n
6 If you **smell** something, you put your nose near it and breathe in, so that you can discover its smell. ❑ *I took a fresh rose out of the vase on our table, and smelled it.* VERB = sniff; V n
7 to **smell a rat** → see **rat**.

**-smelling** /-smelɪŋ/ **-smelling** combines with adjectives to form adjectives which indicate how something smells. ❑ *...sweet-smelling dried flowers... The city is covered by a foul-smelling cloud of smoke.* COMB in ADJ

**smell|ing salts** A bottle of **smelling salts** contains a chemical with a strong smell which is used to help someone recover after they have fainted. N-PLURAL

**smelly** /smeli/ **(smellier, smelliest)** Something that is **smelly** has an unpleasant smell. ❑ *He had extremely smelly feet.* ADJ

**smelt** /smelt/ **(smelts, smelting, smelted)**
1 **Smelt** is a past tense and past participle of **smell**. [mainly BRIT]
2 To **smelt** a substance containing metal means to process it by heating it until it melts, so that the metal is extracted and changed chemically. ❑ *Darby was looking for a way to improve iron when he hit upon the idea of smelting it with coke instead of charcoal.* VERB; V n

**smel|ter** /smeltəʳ/ **(smelters)** A **smelter** is a container for smelting metal. N-COUNT

**smid|gen** /smɪdʒɪn/ **(smidgens)** also **smidgeon, smidgin.** A **smidgen** is a small amount of something. [INFORMAL] ❑ *...a smidgen of tobacco. ...a smidgeon of luck.* N-COUNT: oft N *of* n

**smile** /smaɪl/ **(smiles, smiling, smiled)** ◆◆◇
1 When you **smile**, the corners of your mouth curve up and you sometimes show your teeth. People smile when they are pleased or amused, or when they are being friendly. ❑ *When he saw me, he smiled and waved... He rubbed the back of his neck and smiled ruefully at me... His smiling face appears on T-shirts, billboards, and posters.* VERB; V; V *at* n; V-ing
2 A **smile** is the expression that you have on your face when you smile. ❑ *She gave a wry smile... 'There are some sandwiches if you're hungry,' she said with a smile.* N-COUNT
3 If you say that something such as fortune **smiles on** someone, you mean that they are lucky or successful. [LITERARY] ❑ *When fortune smiled on him, he made the most of it.* VERB; V *on/upon* n
4 If you say that someone is **all smiles**, you mean that they look very happy, often when they have previously been worried or upset about something. PHRASE: v-link PHR

**smi|ley** /smaɪli/ **(smileys)** 1 A **smiley** person smiles a lot or is smiling. [INFORMAL] ❑ *Two smiley babies are waiting for their lunch.* ADJ: usu ADJ n
2 A **smiley** is a symbol used in e-mail to show how someone is feeling. :-) is a smiley showing happiness. [COMPUTING] N-COUNT = emoticon

**smil|ing|ly** /smaɪlɪŋli/ If someone does something **smilingly**, they smile as they do it. [WRITTEN] ❑ *He opened the gate and smilingly welcomed the travellers home.* ADV: ADV with v

**smirk** /smɜːʳk/ **(smirks, smirking, smirked)** If you **smirk**, you smile in an unpleasant way, often because you believe that you have gained an advantage over someone else or know something that they do not know. ❑ *Two men looked at me, nudged each other and smirked.* VERB; V

**smite** /smaɪt/ **(smites, smiting, smote, smitten)** To **smite** something means to hit it hard. [LITERARY] ❑ *...the leader charging into battle, sword held high, ready to smite the enemy.* → See also **smitten**. VERB; V n

**smith|er|eens** /smɪðəriːnz/ If something is smashed or blown **to smithereens**, it breaks into very small pieces. ❑ *She dropped the vase and smashed it to smithereens.* N-PLURAL: usu *to* N = pieces, bits

**smithy** /smɪði/ **(smithies)** A **smithy** is a place where a blacksmith works. N-COUNT = forge

**smit|ten** /smɪtᵊn/ 1 If you are **smitten**, you find someone so attractive that you are or seem to be in love with them. ❑ *They were totally smitten with each other.* ADJ: usu v-link ADJ, oft ADJ *with/by* n
2 **Smitten** is the past participle of **smite**.

**smock** /smɒk/ **(smocks)** 1 A **smock** is a loose garment, rather like a long blouse, usually worn by women. ❑ *She was wearing wool slacks and a paisley smock.* N-COUNT
2 A **smock** is a loose garment worn by people such as artists to protect their clothing. N-COUNT

**smocked** /smɒkt/ A **smocked** dress or top is decorated with smocking. ❑ *She was pretty and young, in a loose smocked sundress.* ADJ

**smock|ing** /smɒkɪŋ/ **Smocking** is a decoration on tops and dresses which is made by gathering the material into folds using small stitches. N-UNCOUNT

**smog** /smɒg/ **(smogs)** **Smog** is a mixture of fog and smoke which occurs in some busy industrial cities. ❑ *Cars cause pollution, both smog and acid rain.* N-VAR

**smog|gy** /smɒgi/ **(smoggier, smoggiest)** A **smoggy** city or town is badly affected by smog. ❑ *...the smoggy sprawl of Los Angeles.* ADJ

**smoke** /smoʊk/ **(smokes, smoking, smoked)** ◆◆◇
1 **Smoke** consists of gas and small bits of solid material that are sent into the air when something burns. ❑ *A cloud of black smoke blew over the city... The air was thick with cigarette smoke.* N-UNCOUNT
2 If something **is smoking**, smoke is coming from it. ❑ *The chimney was smoking fiercely. ...a pile of smoking rubble.* VERB; V; V-ing
3 When someone **smokes** a cigarette, cigar, or pipe, they suck the smoke from it into their mouth and blow it out again. If you **smoke**, you regularly smoke cigarettes, cigars, or a pipe. ❑ *He was sitting alone, smoking a big cigar... Do you smoke?* ♦ **Smoke** is also a noun. ❑ *Someone came out for a smoke.* ♦ **smok|er** **(smokers)** *He was not a heavy smoker.* VERB; V n; V; N-SING: *a* N; N-COUNT
4 If fish or meat **is smoked**, it is hung over burning wood so that the smoke preserves it and gives it a special flavour. ❑ *...the grid where the fish were being smoked. ...smoked bacon.* VERB: usu passive; *be* V-ed; V-ed
5 → See also **smoked**, **smoking**.

**PHRASES** 6 If someone says **there's no smoke without fire** or **where there's smoke there's fire**, they mean that there are rumours or signs that something is true so it must be at least partly true. PHRASE
7 If something **goes up in smoke**, it is destroyed by fire. ❑ *More than 900 years of British history went up in smoke in the Great Fire of Windsor.* PHRASE: V inflects
8 If something that is very important to you **goes up in smoke**, it fails or ends without anything being achieved. ❑ *Their dreams went up in smoke after the collapse of their travel agency.* PHRASE: V inflects

♦ **smoke out** If you **smoke out** someone who is hiding, you discover them and make them publicly known. ❑ *The committee have tried dozens* PHRASAL VERB; V n P *of different ways to smoke him out. ...technology to smoke out tax evaders.* V P n (not pron)

**smoke alarm** **(smoke alarms)** also **smoke detector.** A **smoke alarm** or a **smoke detector** is a device fixed to the ceiling of a room which makes a loud noise if there is smoke in the air, to warn people. N-COUNT

**smoke bomb** **(smoke bombs)** A **smoke bomb** is a bomb that produces clouds of smoke when it explodes. N-COUNT

**smoked** /smoʊkt/ **Smoked** glass has been made darker by being treated with smoke. ❑ *...a white van with smoked glass windows.* → See also **smoke**. ADJ

**smoked salm|on** **Smoked salmon** is the flesh of a salmon which is smoked and eaten raw. N-UNCOUNT

**smoke-filled room** **(smoke-filled rooms)** If you talk about a decision being made in a **smoke-filled room**, you mean that it is made by a small group of people in a private meeting, rather than in a more democratic or open way. ❑ *...long discussions in smoke-filled rooms.* N-COUNT [disapproval]

**smoke|less** /smoʊkləs/ **Smokeless** fuel burns without producing smoke. ADJ

**smoke|screen** /smoʊkskriːn/ **(smokescreens)** also **smoke screen.** If something that you do or say is a **smokescreen**, it is intended to hide the truth about your activities or intentions. ❑ *He was accused of putting up a smokescreen to hide poor standards in schools.* N-COUNT

**smoke sig|nal** **(smoke signals)** If someone such as a politician or businessman sends out **smoke signals**, they give an indication of their views and intentions. This indication is often not clear and needs to be worked out. ❑ *The smoke signals from the central bank suggest further cuts are coming.* N-COUNT: usu pl

**smoke|stack** /smoʊkstæk/ **(smokestacks)** A **smokestack** is a very tall chimney that carries smoke away from a factory. N-COUNT = chimney

**smoke|stack in|dus|try** **(smokestack industries)** A **smokestack industry** is a traditional industry such as heavy engineering or manufacturing, rather than a modern industry such as electronics. ❑ *There has been a shift from smokestack industries into high-tech ones.* N-COUNT

**smok|ing** /smoʊkɪŋ/ ◆◇◇ [1] **Smoking** is the act or habit of smoking cigarettes, cigars, or a pipe. ❑ *Smoking is now banned in many places of work. ...a no-smoking area.* N-UNCOUNT [2] A **smoking** area is intended for people who want to smoke. ❑ *...the decision to scrap smoking compartments on Kent trains.* ADJ: ADJ n [3] → See also **smoke**, **passive smoking**.

**smok|ing gun** **(smoking guns)** A **smoking gun** is a piece of evidence that proves that something is true or that someone is responsible for a crime. [mainly AM or JOURNALISM] ❑ *The search for other kinds of evidence tying him to trafficking has not produced a smoking gun.* N-COUNT: usu sing

**smoky** /smoʊki/ **(smokier, smokiest)** also **smokey.** [1] A place that is **smoky** has a lot of smoke in the air. ❑ *His main problem was the extremely smoky atmosphere at work.* ADJ [2] You can use **smoky** to describe something that looks like smoke, for example because it is slightly blue or grey or because it is not clear. ❑ *At the center of the dial is a piece of smoky glass.* ADJ: ADJ n, ADJ colour [3] Something that has a **smoky** flavour tastes as if it has been smoked. ❑ *Cooking with the lid on gives the food that distinctive smoky flavour.* ADJ

**smol|der** /smoʊldəʳ/ → see **smoulder**.

**smooch** /smuːtʃ/ **(smooches, smooching, smooched)** If two people **smooch**, they kiss and hold each other closely. People sometimes smooch while they are dancing. ❑ *I smooched with him on the dance floor... The customers smooch and chat.* V-RECIP V *with* n pl-n V

**smooth** /smuːð/ ◆◇◇ **(smoother, smoothest, smooths, smoothing, smoothed)** [1] A **smooth** surface has no roughness, lumps, or holes. ❑ *...a rich cream that keeps skin soft and smooth. ...a smooth surface such as glass... The flagstones beneath their feet were worn smooth by centuries of use.* ADJ ≠ rough [2] A **smooth** liquid or mixture has been mixed well so that it has no lumps. ❑ *Continue whisking until the mixture looks smooth and creamy.* ADJ ≠ lumpy [3] If you describe a drink such as wine, whisky, or coffee as **smooth**, you mean that it is not bitter and is pleasant to drink. ❑ *This makes the whiskeys much smoother.* ADJ ≠ rough, harsh [4] A **smooth** line or movement has no sudden breaks or changes in direction or speed. ❑ *This exercise is done in one smooth motion.* ADJ ♦ **smooth|ly** *Make sure that you execute all movements smoothly and without jerking.* ADV: ADV with v [5] A **smooth** ride, flight, or sea crossing is very comfortable because there are no unpleasant movements. ❑ *The active suspension system gives the car a very smooth ride.* ADJ ≠ bumpy, rough [6] You use **smooth** to describe something that is going well and is free of problems or trouble. ❑ *Political hopes for a swift and smooth transition to democracy have been dashed.* ADJ ♦ **smooth|ly** *So far, talks at GM have gone smoothly.* ADV: ADV with v [7] If you describe a man as **smooth**, you mean that he is extremely smart, confident, and polite, often in a way that you find rather unpleasant. ❑ *Twelve extremely good-looking, smooth young men have been picked as finalists.* ADJ [8] If you **smooth** something, you move your hands over its surface to make it smooth and flat. ❑ *She stood up and smoothed down her frock... Bardo smoothed his moustache.* VERB V n with adv V n

♦ **smooth out** If you **smooth out** a problem or difficulty, you solve it, especially by talking to the people concerned. ❑ *Baker was smoothing out differences with European allies... It's O.K. I smoothed things out.* PHRASAL VERB V P n (not pron) V n P

♦ **smooth over** If you **smooth over** a problem or difficulty, you make it less serious and easier to deal with, especially by talking to the people concerned. ❑ *...an attempt to smooth over the violent splits that have occurred... The Chancellor is trying to smooth things over.* PHRASAL VERB V P n (not pron) V n P

**smoothie** /smuːði/ **(smoothies)** [1] If you describe a man as a **smoothie**, you mean that he is extremely smart, confident, and polite, often in a way that you find rather unpleasant. [INFORMAL] N-COUNT [2] A **smoothie** is a thick drink made from fruit crushed in a machine, sometimes with yogurt or ice cream added. N-COUNT

**smooth-talking** A **smooth-talking** man talks very confidently in a way that is likely to persuade people, but may not be sincere or honest. ❑ *...the smooth-talking conman who has wrecked their lives.* ADJ = silver-tongued

**smor|gas|bord** /smɔːʳgəsbɔːʳd/ [1] **Smorgasbord** is a meal with a variety of hot and cold savoury dishes, from which people serve themselves. N-SING: also no det [2] A **smorgasbord of** things is a number of different things that are combined together as a whole. [JOURNALISM] ❑ *...a smorgasbord of paintings and sculpture.* N-SING: usu N *of* n

**smote** /smoʊt/ **Smote** is the past tense of **smite**.

**smoth|er** /smʌðəʳ/ **(smothers, smothering, smothered)** [1] If you **smother** a fire, you cover it with something in order to put it out. ❑ *The girl's parents were also burned as they tried to smother the flames.* VERB V n [2] To **smother** someone means to kill them by covering their face with something so that they cannot breathe. ❑ *A father was secretly filmed as he tried to smother his six-week-old son in hospital.* VERB = suffocate V n [3] Things that **smother** something cover it completely. ❑ *Once the shrubs begin to smother the little plants, we have to move them.* VERB V n [4] If you **smother** someone, you show your love for them too much and protect them too much. ❑ *She loved her own children, almost smothering them with love.* VERB V n [5] If you **smother** an emotion or a reaction, you control it so that people do not notice it. ❑ *She summoned up all her pity for him, to smother her self-pity. ...smothered giggles.* VERB = stifle V n V-ed [6] If an activity or process **is smothered**, it is prevented from continu- VERB = stifle ing or developing. ❑ *Intellectual life in France was smothered by the occupation... The debts of both Poland and Hungary are beginning to smother the reform process.* *be* V-ed V n

**smoul|der** /smoʊldəʳ/ **(smoulders, smouldering, smouldered)**

✔ in AM, use **smolder**

1 If something **smoulders**, it burns slowly, producing smoke but not flames. ❑ *A number of buildings around the Parliament were still smouldering today.* VERB V 2 If a feeling such as anger or hatred **smoulders** inside you, you continue to feel it but do not show it. ❑ *Baxter smouldered as he drove home for lunch.* VERB V 3 If you say that someone **smoulders**, you mean that they are sexually attractive, usually in a mysterious or very intense way. ❑ *Melanie Griffith seems to smoulder with sexuality.* VERB V

**SMS** /es em es/ **SMS** is a way of sending short written messages from one mobile phone to another. **SMS** is an abbreviation for 'short message system'. N-UNCOUNT

**smudge** /smʌdʒ/ **(smudges, smudging, smudged)** 1 A **smudge** is a dirty mark. ❑ *There was a dark smudge on his forehead. ...smudges of blood.* N-COUNT 2 If you **smudge** a substance such as ink, paint, or make-up that has been put on a surface, you make it less neat by touching or rubbing it. ❑ *Smudge the outline using a cotton-wool bud... Her lipstick was smudged.* VERB V n V-ed 3 If you **smudge** a surface, you make it dirty by touching it and leaving a substance on it. ❑ *She kissed me, careful not to smudge me with her fresh lipstick.* VERB V n

**smudgy** /smʌdʒi/ **(smudgier, smudgiest)** If something is **smudgy**, its outline is unclear. ❑ *The hand-writing is smudgy. ...smudgy photos.* ADJ = *blurred*

**smug** /smʌg/ If you say that someone is **smug**, you are criticizing the fact they seem very pleased with how good, clever, or lucky they are. ❑ *Thomas and his wife looked at each other in smug satisfaction.* ADJ [disapproval]

**smug|gle** /smʌgəl/ **(smuggles, smuggling, smuggled)** If someone **smuggles** things or people into a place or out of it, they take them there illegally or secretly. ❑ *My message is 'If you try to smuggle drugs you are stupid'... Police have foiled an attempt to smuggle a bomb into Belfast airport... Had it really been impossible to find someone who could smuggle out a letter?* VERB V n V n prep V n with adv ♦ **smug|gling** *An air hostess was arrested and charged with drug smuggling.* N-UNCOUNT

**smug|gler** /smʌgələʳ/ **(smugglers)** **Smugglers** are people who take goods into or out of a country illegally. ❑ *...drug smugglers.* N-COUNT

**smut** /smʌt/ **(smuts)** 1 If you refer to words or pictures that are related to sex as **smut**, you disapprove of them because you think they are rude and unpleasant and have been said or published just to shock or excite people. ❑ *...schoolboy smut.* N-UNCOUNT [disapproval] 2 **Smut** or **smuts** is dirt such as soot which makes a dirty mark on something. N-UNCOUNT: also N in pl

**smut|ty** /smʌti/ **(smuttier, smuttiest)** If you describe something such as a joke, book, or film as **smutty**, you disapprove of it because it shows naked people or refers to sex in a rude or unpleasant way. ❑ *...smutty jokes.* ADJ: usu ADJ n [disapproval]

**snack** /snæk/ **(snacks, snacking, snacked)** 1 A **snack** is a simple meal that is quick to cook and to eat. ❑ *Lunch was a snack in the fields.* N-COUNT 2 A **snack** is something such as a chocolate bar that you eat between meals. ❑ *Do you eat sweets, cakes or sugary snacks?* N-COUNT 3 If you **snack**, you eat snacks between meals. ❑ *Instead of snacking on crisps and chocolate, nibble on celery or carrot.* VERB V *on* n

**snack bar** **(snack bars)** A **snack bar** is a place where you can buy drinks and simple meals such as sandwiches. N-COUNT

**snaf|fle** /snæfəl/ **(snaffles, snaffling, snaffled)** 1 A **snaffle** is an object consisting of two short joined bars of metal that is put in a horse's mouth and attached to the straps that the rider uses to control the horse. N-COUNT 2 If you **snaffle** something, you take it for yourself. [BRIT, INFORMAL] ❑ *Michael Stich then proceeded to snaffle the $2 million first prize.* VERB V n

**snag** /snæg/ **(snags, snagging, snagged)** 1 A **snag** is a small problem or disadvantage. ❑ *A police clampdown on car thieves hit a snag when villains stole one of their cars.* N-COUNT 2 If you **snag** part of your clothing **on** a sharp or rough object or if it **snags**, it gets caught on the object and tears. ❑ *She snagged a heel on a root and tumbled to the ground... Brambles snagged his suit... Local fishermen's nets kept snagging on underwater objects.* VERB V n *on* n V n V *on* n

**snail** /sneɪl/ **(snails)** 1 A **snail** is a small animal with a long, soft body, no legs, and a spiral-shaped shell. Snails move very slowly. N-COUNT 2 If you say that someone does something **at a snail's pace**, you are emphasizing that they are doing it very slowly, usually when you think it would be better if they did it much more quickly. ❑ *The train was moving now at a snail's pace.* PHRASE: PHR after v [emphasis]

**snail mail** Some computer users refer to the postal system as **snail mail**, because it is very slow in comparison with e-mail. N-UNCOUNT

**snake** /sneɪk/ **(snakes, snaking, snaked)** 1 A **snake** is a long, thin reptile without legs. N-COUNT 2 Something that **snakes** in a particular direction goes in that direction in a line with a lot of bends. [LITERARY] ❑ *The road snaked through forested mountains.* VERB = *wind* V prep/adv

**snake|bite** /sneɪkbaɪt/ **(snakebites)** also **snake bite.** A **snakebite** is the bite of a snake, especially a poisonous one. N-VAR

**snake charm|er** **(snake charmers)** also **snake-charmers.** A **snake charmer** is a person who entertains people by controlling the behaviour of a snake, for example by playing music and causing the snake to rise out of a basket and drop back in again. N-COUNT

**snakes and lad|ders** **Snakes and ladders** is a British children's game played with a board and dice. When you go up a ladder, you progress quickly. When you go down a snake, you go backwards. N-UNCOUNT

**snake|skin** /sneɪkskɪn/ **Snakeskin** is the skin of snakes used to make shoes and clothes. N-UNCOUNT: oft N n

**snap** /snæp/ **(snaps, snapping, snapped)** ◆◇◇ 1 If something **snaps** or if you **snap** it, it breaks suddenly, usually with a sharp cracking noise. ❑ *He shifted his weight and a twig snapped... The brake pedal had just snapped off... She gripped the pipe with both hands, trying to snap it in half.* VERB V V adv/prep V n adv/prep Also V n ♦ **Snap** is also a noun. ❑ *Every minute or so I could hear a snap, a crack and a crash as another tree went down.* N-SING 2 If you **snap** something into a particular position, or if it **snaps** into that position, it moves quickly into that position, with a sharp sound. ❑ *He snapped the notebook shut... The bag snapped open.* VERB V n adv/prep V adv ♦ **Snap** is also a noun. ❑ *He shut the book with a snap and stood up.* N-SING 3 If you **snap** your **fingers**, you make a sharp sound by moving your middle finger quickly across your thumb, for example in order to accompany music or to order someone to do something. ❑ *She had millions of listeners snapping their fingers to her first single.* VERB = *click* V n ♦ **Snap** is also a noun. ❑ *I could obtain with the snap of my fingers anything I chose.* N-SING: N *of* n 4 If someone **snaps at** you, they speak to you in a sharp, unfriendly way. ❑ *'Of course I don't know her,' Roger snapped... I'm sorry, Casey, I didn't mean to snap at you like that.* VERB V with quote V *at* n 5 If someone **snaps**, or if something **snaps** inside them, they suddenly stop being calm and become very angry because the situation has become too tense or too difficult for them. ❑ *He finally snapped when she prevented their children from visiting him one weekend.* VERB V 6 If an animal such as a dog **snaps at** you, it opens and shuts its jaws quickly near you, as if it were going to bite you. ❑ *His teeth clicked as he snapped at my ankle... The* VERB V *at* n, V *poodle yapped and snapped.* 7 A **snap** decision or action is one that is taken suddenly, often without careful thought. ❑ *I think this is too important for a snap decision.* 8 A **snap** is a photograph. [INFORMAL] ❑ *...a snap my mother took last year.* 9 If you **snap** someone or something, you take a photograph of them. [INFORMAL] ❑ *He was the first ever non-British photographer to be invited to snap a royal.* 10 → See also **cold snap**. — ADJ: ADJ n; N-COUNT = photo; VERB = photograph, V n

♦ **snap out of** If someone who is depressed **snaps out of it** or **snaps out of** their depression, they suddenly become more cheerful, especially by making an effort. ❑ *Come on, snap out of it!... Often a patient cannot snap out of their negativity that easily.* — PHRASAL VERB; V P P *it*; V P P n

♦ **snap up** If you **snap** something **up**, you buy it quickly because it is cheap or is just what you want. ❑ *Every time we get a new delivery of clothes, people are queuing to snap them up... One eagle-eyed collector snapped up a pair of Schiaparelli earrings for just £6.* — PHRASAL VERB; V n P; V P n (not pron)

**snap|dragon** /snæpdrægən/ **(snapdragons)** A **snapdragon** is a common garden plant with small colourful flowers that can open and shut like a mouth. — N-COUNT

**snap fas|ten|er** **(snap fasteners)** A **snap fastener** is a small metal object used to fasten clothes, made up of two parts which can be pressed together. [AM] — N-COUNT

✓ in BRIT, use **press stud**, **popper**

**snap|per** /snæpəʳ/ **(snappers** or **snapper)** A **snapper** is a fish that has sharp teeth and lives in warm seas. ♦ **Snapper** is this fish eaten as food. — N-COUNT; N-UNCOUNT

**snap|pish** /snæpɪʃ/ If someone is **snappish**, they speak to people in a sharp, unfriendly manner. ❑ *'That is beautiful, Tony,' Momma said, no longer sounding at all snappish.* ♦ **snap|pish|ly** *She said snappishly. 'I'm not pregnant, Brian.'* — ADJ: usu v-link ADJ = snappy; ADV: ADV with v

**snap|py** /snæpi/ **(snappier, snappiest)** 1 If someone has a **snappy** style of speaking, they speak in a quick, clever, brief, and often funny way. ❑ *Each film gets a snappy two-line summary.* 2 If someone is a **snappy** dresser or if they wear **snappy** clothes, they wear smart, stylish clothes. ❑ *She has already made a name for herself as a snappy dresser.* — ADJ: usu ADJ n; ADJ: ADJ n

**snap|shot** /snæpʃɒt/ **(snapshots)** 1 A **snapshot** is a photograph that is taken quickly and casually. 2 If something provides you with a **snapshot of** a place or situation, it gives you a brief idea of what that place or situation is like. ❑ *The interviews present a remarkable snapshot of Britain in these dark days of recession.* — N-COUNT; N-COUNT: usu sing, usu N *of* n

**snare** /sneəʳ/ **(snares, snaring, snared)** 1 A **snare** is a trap for catching birds or small animals. It consists of a loop of wire or rope which pulls tight around the animal. 2 If you describe a situation as a **snare**, you mean that it is a trap from which it is difficult to escape. [FORMAL] ❑ *Given data which are free from bias there are further snares to avoid in statistical work.* 3 If someone **snares** an animal, they catch it using a snare. ❑ *He'd snared a rabbit earlier in the day.* — N-COUNT = trap; N-COUNT = trap; VERB; V n

**snare drum** **(snare drums)** A **snare drum** is a small drum used in orchestras and bands. Snare drums are usually played with wooden sticks, and make a continuous sound. — N-COUNT

**snarl** /snɑːʳl/ **(snarls, snarling, snarled)** 1 When an animal **snarls**, it makes a fierce, rough sound in its throat while showing its teeth. ❑ *He raced ahead up into the bush, barking and snarling... The dogs snarled at the intruders.* ♦ **Snarl** is also a noun. ❑ *With a snarl, the second dog made a dive for his heel.* 2 If you **snarl** something, you say it in a fierce, angry way. ❑ *'Let go of me,' he snarled... I vaguely remember snarling at someone who stepped on my foot... 'Aubrey.' Hyde seemed almost to snarl the name.* ♦ **Snarl** is also a noun. ❑ *His eyes flashed, and his lips were drawn back in a furious snarl.* 3 A **snarl** is a disorganized mass of things. ❑ *She was tangled in a snarl of logs and branches.* — VERB; V; V *at* n; N-COUNT; VERB; V with quote; V *at* n; V n; N-COUNT; N-COUNT: usu with supp

**snarl-up** **(snarl-ups)** A **snarl-up** is a disorganized situation such as a traffic jam, in which things are unable to move or work normally. [BRIT, INFORMAL] — N-COUNT

**snatch** /snætʃ/ **(snatches, snatching, snatched)** 1 If you **snatch** something or **snatch at** something, you take it or pull it away quickly. ❑ *Mick snatched the cards from Archie's hand... He snatched up the telephone... The thin wind snatched at her skirt.* 2 If something **is snatched** from you, it is stolen, usually using force. If a person **is snatched**, they are taken away by force. ❑ *If your bag is snatched, let it go.* 3 If you **snatch** an opportunity, you take it quickly. If you **snatch** something to eat or a rest, you have it quickly in between doing other things. ❑ *I snatched a glance at the mirror... You can even snatch a few hours off.* 4 If you **snatch** victory in a competition, you defeat your opponent by a small amount or just before the end of the contest. ❑ *The American came from behind to snatch victory by a mere eight seconds.* 5 A **snatch of** a conversation or a song is a very small piece of it. ❑ *I heard snatches of the conversation.* — VERB; V n prep; V n with adv; V *at* n; VERB: usu passive; *be* V-ed; VERB; V n; V n; VERB; V n; N-COUNT: usu N *of* n

**snaz|zy** /snæzi/ **(snazzier, snazziest)** Something that is **snazzy** is stylish and attractive, often in a rather bright or noticeable way. [INFORMAL] ❑ *...a snazzy new Porsche.* — ADJ: usu ADJ n

**sneak** /sniːk/ **(sneaks, sneaking, sneaked)**

✓ The form **snuck** is also used in American English for the past tense and past participle.

1 If you **sneak** somewhere, you go there very quietly on foot, trying to avoid being seen or heard. ❑ *Sometimes he would sneak out of his house late at night to be with me.* 2 If you **sneak** something somewhere, you take it there secretly. ❑ *He smuggled papers out each day, photocopied them, and snuck them back... You even snuck me a cigarette.* 3 If you **sneak** a look at someone or something, you secretly have a quick look at them. ❑ *You sneak a look at your watch to see how long you've got to wait.* 4 → See also **sneaking**. — VERB; V adv/prep; VERB; V n prep/adv; V n n; VERB = steal; V n prep

♦ **sneak up on** 1 If someone **sneaks up on** you, they try and approach you without being seen or heard, perhaps to surprise you or do you harm. ❑ *I managed to sneak up on him when you knocked on the door.* 2 If something **sneaks up on** you, it happens or occurs when you are not expecting it. ❑ *Sometimes our expectations sneak up on us unawares.* — PHRASAL VERB = creep up; V P P n; PHRASAL VERB; V P P n

**sneak|er** /sniːkəʳ/ **(sneakers)** **Sneakers** are casual shoes with rubber soles. [mainly AM] — N-COUNT: usu pl

✓ in BRIT, use **trainers**

**sneak|ing** /sniːkɪŋ/ A **sneaking** feeling is a slight or vague feeling, especially one that you are unwilling to accept. ❑ *I have a sneaking suspicion that they are going to succeed.* — ADJ: ADJ n

**sneak pre|view** **(sneak previews)** A **sneak preview of** something is an unofficial opportunity to have a look at it before it is officially published or shown to the public. — N-COUNT: oft N *of* n

**sneaky** /sniːki/ **(sneakier, sneakiest)** If you describe someone as **sneaky**, you disapprove of them because they do things secretly rather than openly. [INFORMAL] ❑ *It is a sneaky and underhand way of doing business.* — ADJ [disapproval] = sly

**sneer** /snɪəʳ/ **(sneers, sneering, sneered)** If you **sneer at** someone or something, you express your contempt for them by the expression on your face or by what you say. ❑ *There is too great a readiness to sneer at anything the Opposition does... 'Hypocrite,' he sneered.* ♦ **Sneer** is also a noun. ❑ *Canete's mouth twisted in a contemptuous sneer.* — VERB; V *at* n; V with quote; N-COUNT

**sneer|ing|ly** /snɪərɪŋli/ To refer **sneeringly** to someone or something means to refer to them in a way that shows your contempt for them. [WRITTEN] ❑ *They were sneeringly dismissive.* — ADV

**sneeze** /sniːz/ **(sneezes, sneezing, sneezed)** 1 When you **sneeze**, you suddenly take in your breath and then blow it down your nose noisily without being able to stop yourself, for example because you have a cold. ❑ *What exactly happens when we sneeze?* ♦ **Sneeze** is also a noun. ❑ *Coughs and sneezes spread infections.* 2 If you say that something is **not to be sneezed at**, you mean that it is worth having. [INFORMAL] ❑ *The money's not to be sneezed at.* VERB V N-COUNT PHRASE

**snick|er** /snɪkəʳ/ **(snickers, snickering, snickered)** If you **snicker**, you laugh quietly in a disrespectful way, for example at something rude or embarrassing. ❑ *We all snickered at Mrs. Swenson.* ♦ **Snicker** is also a noun. ❑ *...a chorus of jeers and snickers.* VERB = *snigger* V at n Also V N-COUNT

**snide** /snaɪd/ A **snide** comment or remark is one which criticizes someone in an unkind and often indirect way. ❑ *He made a snide comment about her weight.* ADJ: usu ADJ n

**sniff** /snɪf/ **(sniffs, sniffing, sniffed)** 1 When you **sniff**, you breathe in air through your nose hard enough to make a sound, for example when you are trying not to cry, or in order to show disapproval. ❑ *She wiped her face and sniffed loudly... Then he sniffed. There was a smell of burning... He sniffed back the tears.* ♦ **Sniff** is also a noun. ❑ *At last the sobs ceased, to be replaced by sniffs.* 2 If you **sniff** something or **sniff at** it, you smell it by sniffing. ❑ *Suddenly, he stopped and sniffed the air... She sniffed at it suspiciously.* 3 You can use **sniff** to indicate that someone says something in a way that shows their disapproval or contempt. ❑ *'Tourists!' she sniffed.* 4 If you say that something is **not to be sniffed at**, you think it is very good or worth having. If someone **sniffs at** something, they do not think it is good enough, or they express their contempt for it. ❑ *The salary was not to be sniffed at either... Foreign Office sources sniffed at reports that British troops might be sent.* 5 If someone **sniffs** a substance such as glue, they deliberately breathe in the substance or the gases from it as a drug. ❑ *He felt light-headed, as if he'd sniffed glue.* ♦ **sniff|er (sniffers)** *...teenage glue sniffers.* 6 If you get a **sniff of** something, you learn or guess that it might be happening or might be near. [INFORMAL] ❑ *You know what they'll be like if they get a sniff of a murder investigation... Have the Press got a sniff yet?... Then, at the first sniff of danger, he was back at his post.* VERB V V, V n with adv N-COUNT VERB V n V at n VERB V with quote VERB: usu passive, usu with brd-neg be V-ed at V at n VERB V n N-COUNT N-SING: usu N of n = *whiff, hint*

♦ **sniff around**

✓ in BRIT, also use **sniff about, sniff round**

1 If a person **is sniffing around**, they are trying to find out information about something, especially information that someone else does not want known. [INFORMAL] ❑ *But really, what harm could it possibly do to pop down there and just sniff around?... A couple of plain-clothes men had been sniffing round his apartment.* 2 If a person or organization **is sniffing around** someone, they are trying to get them, for example as a lover, employee, or client. [INFORMAL] ❑ *When I had to go away to university, I was convinced that other men would be sniffing round her.* PHRASAL VERB = *nose around* V P V P n PHRASAL VERB: no passive V P n

♦ **sniff out** 1 If you **sniff out** something, you discover it after some searching. [INFORMAL] ❑ *...journalists who are trained to sniff out sensation or scandal.* 2 When a dog used by a group such as the police **sniffs out** hidden explosives or drugs, it finds them using its sense of smell. ❑ *A police dog, trained to sniff out explosives, found evidence of a bomb in the apartment.* PHRASAL VERB V P n (not pron) PHRASAL VERB V P n (not pron) Also V n P

♦ **sniff round** → see **sniff around**.

**sniff|er dog (sniffer dogs)** A **sniffer dog** is a dog used by the police or army to find explosives or drugs by their smell. N-COUNT

**snif|fle** /snɪfᵊl/ **(sniffles, sniffling, sniffled)** 1 If you **sniffle**, you keep sniffing, usually because you are crying or have a cold. ❑ *'Please don't yell at me.' She began to sniffle.* 2 A **sniffle** is a slight cold. You can also say that someone has **the sniffles**. [INFORMAL] VERB = *snuffle* V N-COUNT: also *the* N in pl

**snif|fy** /snɪfi/ **(sniffier, sniffiest)** Someone who is **sniffy about** something does not think it is of high quality, perhaps unfairly. [INFORMAL] ❑ *Some people are a bit sniffy about television.* ADJ: oft ADJ *about* n

**snif|ter** /snɪftəʳ/ **(snifters)** 1 A **snifter** is a small amount of an alcoholic drink. [BRIT, INFORMAL] 2 A **snifter** is a bowl-shaped glass used for drinking brandy. [AM] N-COUNT: oft N *of* n N-COUNT

**snig|ger** /snɪgəʳ/ **(sniggers, sniggering, sniggered)** If someone **sniggers**, they laugh quietly in a disrespectful way, for example at something rude or unkind. ❑ *Suddenly, three schoolkids sitting near me started sniggering.* ♦ **Snigger** is also a noun. ❑ *...trying to suppress a snigger.* VERB V N-COUNT

**snip** /snɪp/ **(snips, snipping, snipped)** 1 If you **snip** something, or if you **snip at** or **through** something, you cut it quickly using sharp scissors. ❑ *He has now begun to snip away at the piece of paper... He snipped a length of new bandage and placed it around Peter's chest.* 2 If you say that something is **a snip**, you mean that it is very good value. [BRIT, INFORMAL] ❑ *The beautifully made briefcase is a snip at £74.25.* VERB V adv/prep V n N-SING: *a* N = *bargain*

**snipe** /snaɪp/ **(snipes, sniping, sniped)** 1 If someone **snipes at** you, they criticize you. ❑ *The Spanish media were still sniping at the British press yesterday.* ♦ **snip|ing** *This leaves him vulnerable to sniping from within his own party.* 2 To **snipe at** someone means to shoot at them from a hidden position. ❑ *Gunmen have repeatedly sniped at US Army positions... A member of the security forces was killed in a sniping incident.* VERB V at n N-UNCOUNT VERB V at n V-ing

**snip|er** /snaɪpəʳ/ **(snipers)** A **sniper** is someone who shoots at people from a hidden position. N-COUNT

**snip|pet** /snɪpɪt/ **(snippets)** A **snippet of** something is a small piece of it. ❑ *...snippets of popular classical music.* N-COUNT: oft N *of* n

**snitch** /snɪtʃ/ **(snitches, snitching, snitched)** 1 To **snitch on** a person means to tell someone in authority that the person has done something bad or wrong. [INFORMAL] ❑ *She felt like a fifth-grader who had snitched on a classmate.* 2 A **snitch** is a person who snitches on other people. [INFORMAL] VERB = *grass* V *on* n Also V N-COUNT = *grass*

**sniv|el** /snɪvᵊl/ **(snivels, snivelling, snivelled)**

✓ in AM, use **sniveling, sniveled**

If someone **is snivelling**, they are crying or sniffing in a way that irritates you. ❑ *Billy started to snivel. His mother smacked his hand.* VERB V

**snob** /snɒb/ **(snobs)** 1 If you call someone a **snob**, you disapprove of them because they admire upper-class people and have a low opinion of lower-class people. ❑ *Going to a private school had made her a snob.* 2 If you call someone a **snob**, you disapprove of them because they behave as if they are superior to other people because of their intelligence or taste. ❑ *She was an intellectual snob.* N-COUNT [disapproval] N-COUNT: usu supp N [disapproval]

**snob|bery** /snɒbəri/ **Snobbery** is the attitude of a snob. N-UNCOUNT

**snob|bish** /snɒbɪʃ/ If you describe someone as **snobbish**, you disapprove of them because they are too proud of their social status, intelligence, or taste. ❑ *They had a snobbish dislike for their intellectual and social inferiors.* ADJ [disapproval]

**snob|by** /snɒbi/ **(snobbier, snobbiest)** **Snobby** means the same as **snobbish**. ADJ

**snog** /snɒg/ **(snogs, snogging, snogged)** If one person **snogs** another, they kiss and hold that person for a period of time. You can also say that two people **are snogging**. [BRIT, INFORMAL] ❑ *I'm 15 and I've never snogged a girl... They were snogging under a bridge.* ♦ **Snog** is also a noun. [BRIT, INFORMAL] ❑ *They went for a quick snog behind the bike sheds.* V-RECIP V n n-pl V N-COUNT: usu *a* N

**snook** /snuːk/ If you **cock a snook** at someone in authority or at an organization, you do PHRASE: V inflects something that they cannot punish you for, but which insults them or expresses your contempt. [mainly BRIT, JOURNALISM] ❑ *Tories cocked a snook at their prime minister over this legislation.*

**snook|er** /snuːkəʳ, AM snʊk-/ **(snookers, snookering, snookered)** [1] **Snooker** is a game involving balls on a large table. The players use a long stick to hit a white ball, and score points by knocking coloured balls into the pockets at the sides of the table. ❑ *...a game of snooker... They were playing snooker.* N-UNCOUNT [2] If you **are snookered** by something, it is difficult or impossible for you to take action or do what you want to do. [BRIT, INFORMAL] ❑ *The President has been snookered on this issue.* VERB: usu passive; *be* V-ed

**snoop** /snuːp/ **(snoops, snooping, snooped)** [1] If someone **snoops** around a place, they secretly look around it in order to find out things. ❑ *Ricardo was the one she'd seen snooping around Kim's hotel room.* VERB; V adv/prep ♦ **Snoop** is also a noun. ❑ *The second house that Grossman had a snoop around contained 'strong simple furniture'.* N-COUNT ♦ **snoop|er (snoopers)** *St Barth's strange lack of street names is meant to dissuade journalistic snoopers.* N-COUNT [2] If someone **snoops on** a person, they watch them secretly in order to find out things about their life. ❑ *Governments have been known to snoop on innocent citizens.* VERB; V *on* n

**snooty** /snuːti/ **(snootier, snootiest)** If you say that someone is **snooty**, you disapprove of them because they behave as if they are superior to other people. ❑ *...snooty intellectuals.* ADJ [disapproval]

**snooze** /snuːz/ **(snoozes, snoozing, snoozed)** [1] A **snooze** is a short, light sleep, especially during the day. [INFORMAL] N-COUNT = nap [2] If you **snooze**, you sleep lightly for a short period of time. [INFORMAL] ❑ *Mark snoozed in front of the television.* VERB; V

**snore** /snɔːʳ/ **(snores, snoring, snored)** When someone who is asleep **snores**, they make a loud noise each time they breathe. ❑ *His mouth was open, and he was snoring.* VERB; V ♦ **Snore** is also a noun. ❑ *Uncle Arthur, after a loud snore, woke suddenly.* N-COUNT

**snor|kel** /snɔːʳkəl/ **(snorkels, snorkelling, snorkelled)**

☑ in AM, use **snorkeling, snorkeled**

[1] A **snorkel** is a tube through which a person swimming just under the surface of the sea can breathe. N-COUNT [2] When someone **snorkels**, they swim under water using a snorkel. ❑ *We went snorkelling, and then returned for lunch.* VERB; V

**snort** /snɔːʳt/ **(snorts, snorting, snorted)** [1] When people or animals **snort**, they breathe air noisily out through their noses. People sometimes snort in order to express disapproval or amusement. ❑ *Harrell snorted with laughter... He snorted loudly and shook his head.* VERB; V with n; V ♦ **Snort** is also a noun. ❑ *...snorts of laughter... He turned away with a snort.* N-COUNT: oft N *of* n [2] If someone **snorts** something, they say it in a way that shows contempt. ❑ *'Reports,' he snorted. 'Anyone can write reports.'* VERB; V with quote [3] To **snort** a drug such as cocaine means to breathe it in quickly through your nose. ❑ *He died of cardiac arrest after snorting cocaine.* VERB; V n

**snot** /snɒt/ **Snot** is the substance that is produced inside your nose. [INFORMAL, RUDE] N-UNCOUNT

**snot|ty** /snɒti/ [1] Something that is **snotty** produces or is covered in snot. [INFORMAL, RUDE] ❑ *He suffered from a snotty nose, runny eyes and a slight cough.* ADJ: ADJ n [2] If you describe someone as **snotty**, you disapprove of them because they have a very proud and superior attitude to other people. [INFORMAL] ❑ *...snotty college kids.* ADJ [disapproval]

**snout** /snaʊt/ **(snouts)** The **snout** of an animal such as a pig is its long nose. ❑ *Two alligators rest their snouts on the water's surface.* N-COUNT

**snow** /snoʊ/ **(snows, snowing, snowed)** ◆◇◇ [1] **Snow** consists of a lot of soft white bits of frozen water that fall from the sky in cold weather. ❑ *In Mid-Wales six inches of snow blocked roads... They tramped through the falling snow.* N-UNCOUNT [2] You can refer to a great deal of snow in an area as the **snows**. ❑ *...the first snows of winter.* N-PLURAL [3] When **it snows**, snow falls from the sky. ❑ *It had been snowing all night.* VERB; *it* V [4] If someone **snows** you, they persuade you to do something or convince you of something by flattering or deceiving you. [AM, INFORMAL] ❑ *I'd been a fool letting him snow me with his big ideas.* VERB; V n [5] ➔ See also **snowed in**, **snowed under**.

**snow|ball** /snoʊbɔːl/ **(snowballs, snowballing, snowballed)** [1] A **snowball** is a ball of snow. Children often throw snowballs at each other. N-COUNT [2] If something such as a project or campaign **snowballs**, it rapidly increases and grows. ❑ *From those early days the business has snowballed.* VERB; V

**snow|board** /snoʊbɔːʳd/ **(snowboards)** A **snowboard** is a narrow board that you stand on in order to slide quickly down snowy slopes as a sport or for fun. N-COUNT

**snow|board|ing** /snoʊbɔːʳdɪŋ/ **Snowboarding** is the sport or activity of travelling down snowy slopes using a snowboard. ❑ *New snowboarding facilities should attract more people.* N-UNCOUNT

**snow|bound** /snoʊbaʊnd/ If people or vehicles are **snowbound**, they cannot go anywhere because of heavy snow. ❑ *The village became snowbound.* ADJ = snowed in

**snow-capped** A **snow-capped** mountain is covered with snow at the top. [LITERARY] ❑ *...the snow-capped Himalayan peaks.* ADJ: ADJ n

**snow-covered** **Snow-covered** places and things are covered over with snow. ❑ *...a Swiss chalet set in the snow-covered hills.* ADJ: usu ADJ n

**snow|drift** /snoʊdrɪft/ **(snowdrifts)** A **snowdrift** is a deep pile of snow formed by the wind. N-COUNT

**snow|drop** /snoʊdrɒp/ **(snowdrops)** A **snowdrop** is a small white flower which appears in the early spring. N-COUNT

**snowed in** If you are **snowed in**, you cannot go anywhere because of heavy snow. ❑ *We may all be snowed in here together for days.* ADJ

**snowed un|der** If you say that you are **snowed under**, you are emphasizing that you have a lot of work or other things to deal with. [INFORMAL] ❑ *Ed was snowed under with fan mail when he was doing his television show.* ADJ: v-link ADJ, usu ADJ *with* n [emphasis]

**snow|fall** /snoʊfɔːl/ **(snowfalls)** [1] The **snowfall** in an area or country is the amount of snow that falls there during a particular period. ❑ *The total rain and snowfall amounted to 50mm.* N-UNCOUNT [2] A **snowfall** is a fall of snow. N-COUNT

**snow|field** /snoʊfiːld/ **(snowfields)** A **snowfield** is a large area which is always covered in snow. N-COUNT

**snow|flake** /snoʊfleɪk/ **(snowflakes)** A **snowflake** is one of the soft, white bits of frozen water that fall as snow. N-COUNT

**snow|man** /snoʊmæn/ **(snowmen)** A **snowman** is a large shape which is made out of snow, especially by children, and is supposed to look like a person. N-COUNT

**snow|mobile** /snoʊməbiːl/ **(snowmobiles)** A **snowmobile** is a small vehicle built to move across snow and ice. N-COUNT

**snow pea (snow peas)** **Snow peas** are a type of pea whose pods are eaten as well as the peas inside them. [AM, AUSTRALIAN] N-COUNT: usu pl

☑ in BRIT, use **mangetout**

**snow|plough** /snoʊplaʊ/ **(snowploughs)**

☑ in AM, use **snowplow**

A **snowplough** is a vehicle which is used to push snow off roads or railway lines. N-COUNT

**snow|shoe** /snoʊʃuː/ **(snowshoes)** **Snowshoes** are oval frames which have a strong net stretched across them and which you fasten to your feet so that you can walk on deep snow. N-COUNT: usu pl

**snow|storm** /snoʊstɔːʳm/ **(snowstorms)** A **snowstorm** is a very heavy fall of snow, usually N-COUNT when there is also a strong wind blowing at the same time.

**snow-white** Something that is **snow-white** is of a bright white colour. ❑ *His hair was snow white like an old man's.* ADJ

**snowy** /snoʊi/ **(snowier, snowiest)** A **snowy** place is covered in snow. A **snowy** day is a day when a lot of snow has fallen. ❑ *...the snowy peaks of the Bighorn Mountains.* ADJ: usu ADJ n

**Snr** **Snr** is the written abbreviation for **Senior**. It is used after someone's name to distinguish them from a younger member of their family who has the same name. [mainly BRIT] ❑ *...Robert Trent Jones, Snr.*

☑ in AM, use **Sr.**

**snub** /snʌb/ **(snubs, snubbing, snubbed)** 1 If you **snub** someone, you deliberately insult them by ignoring them or by behaving or speaking rudely towards them. ❑ *He snubbed her in public and made her feel an idiot.* VERB V n 2 If you snub someone, your behaviour or your remarks can be referred to as a **snub**. ❑ *The German move was widely seen as a deliberate snub to Mr Cook.* N-COUNT 3 Someone who has a **snub** nose has a short nose which points slightly upwards. ADJ: ADJ n

**snuck** /snʌk/ **Snuck** is a past tense and past participle of **sneak** in American English.

**snuff** /snʌf/ **(snuffs, snuffing, snuffed)** 1 **Snuff** is powdered tobacco which people take by breathing it in quickly through their nose. N-UNCOUNT 2 If someone **snuffs it**, they die. [BRIT, INFORMAL] ❑ *He thought he was about to snuff it.* VERB V *it*

♦ **snuff out** 1 To **snuff out** something such as a disagreement means to stop it, usually in a forceful or sudden way. ❑ *Every time a new flicker of resistance appeared, the government snuffed it out... The recent rebound in mortgage rates could snuff out the housing recovery.* PHRASAL VERB V n P V P n (not pron) 2 If you **snuff out** a small flame, you stop it burning, usually by using your fingers or by covering it with something for a few seconds. ❑ *Tenzin snuffed out the candle and left the room.* PHRASAL VERB V P n Also V n P

**snuf|fle** /snʌfəl/ **(snuffles, snuffling, snuffled)** If a person or an animal **snuffles**, they breathe in noisily through their nose, for example because they have a cold. ❑ *She snuffled and wiped her nose on the back of her hand.* VERB = sniffle V

**snug** /snʌg/ **(snugger, snuggest)** 1 If you feel **snug** or are in a **snug** place, you are very warm and comfortable, especially because you are protected from cold weather. ❑ *They lay snug and warm amid the blankets. ...a snug log cabin.* ADJ = cosy 2 Something such as a piece of clothing that is **snug** fits very closely or tightly. ❑ *...a snug black T-shirt and skin-tight black jeans.* ADJ 3 A **snug** is a small room in a pub. N-COUNT

**snug|gle** /snʌgəl/ **(snuggles, snuggling, snuggled)** If you **snuggle** somewhere, you settle yourself into a warm, comfortable position, especially by moving closer to another person. ❑ *Jane snuggled up against his shoulder.* VERB V adv/prep

**so** /soʊ/ ♦♦♦

☑ Usually pronounced /soʊ/ for meanings 1, 6, 7, 8, 9, 16 and 17.

1 You use **so** to refer back to something that has just been mentioned. ❑ *'Do you think that made much of a difference to the family?' — 'I think so.'... If you can't play straight, then say so... 'Is he the kind of man who can be as flexible as he needs to be?' — ' Well, I hope so.'.* ADV: ADV after v 2 You use **so** when you are saying that something which has just been said about one person or thing is also true of another one. ❑ *I enjoy Ann's company and so does Martin... They had a wonderful time and so did I.* ADV: ADV cl 3 You use the structures **as...so** and **just as...so** when you want to indicate that two events or situations are similar in some way. ❑ *As computer systems become even more sophisticated, so too do the methods of those who exploit the technology... Just as John has changed, so has his wife.* CONJ 4 If you say that a state of affairs **is so**, you mean that it is the way it has been described. ❑ *Gold has been a poor investment over the past 20 years, and will continue to be so... It is strange to think that he held strong views on many things, but it must have been so.* ADV: v-link ADV 5 You can use **so** with actions and gestures to show a person how to do something, or to indicate the size, height, or length of something. ❑ *Clasp the chain like so.* ADV: ADV after v 6 You use **so** and **so that** to introduce the result of the situation you have just mentioned. ❑ *I am not an emotional type and so cannot bring myself to tell him I love him... People are living longer than ever before, so even people who are 65 or 70 have a surprising amount of time left... There was snow everywhere, so that the shape of things was difficult to identify.* CONJ 7 You use **so**, **so that**, and **so as** to introduce the reason for doing the thing that you have just mentioned. ❑ *Come to my suite so I can tell you all about this wonderful play I saw in Boston... He took her arm and hurried her upstairs so that they wouldn't be overheard... I was beginning to feel alarm, but kept it to myself so as not to worry our two friends.* CONJ 8 You can use **so** in stories and accounts to introduce the next event in a series of events or to suggest a connection between two events. ❑ *The woman asked if he could perhaps mend her fences, and so he stayed... I thought, 'Here's someone who'll understand me.' So I wrote to her... And so Christmas passed.* ADV: ADV cl 9 You can use **so** in conversations to introduce a new topic, or to introduce a question or comment about something that has been said. ❑ *So how was your day?... So you're a runner, huh?... So, as I said to you, natural medicine is also known as holistic medicine... And so, to answer your question, that's why your mother is disappointed... 'I didn't find him funny at all.' — 'So you won't watch the show again then?'.* ADV: ADV cl 10 You can use **so** in conversations to show that you are accepting what someone has just said. ❑ *'It makes me feel, well, important.' — 'And so you are.'... 'You know who Diana was, Grandfather.' — 'So I do!'... 'Why, this is nothing but common vegetable soup!' — 'So it is, madam.'.* ADV: ADV cl 11 You say **'So?'** and **'So what?'** to indicate that you think that something that someone has said is unimportant. [INFORMAL] ❑ *'My name's Bruno.' — 'So?'... 'You take a chance on the weather if you holiday in the UK.' — 'So what?'.* CONVENTION 12 You can use **so** in front of adjectives and adverbs to emphasize the quality that they are describing. ❑ *He was surprised they had married – they had seemed so different... What is so compromising about being an employee of the state?* ADV: ADV adj/adv [emphasis] 13 You can use **so...that** and **so...as** to emphasize the degree of something by mentioning the result or consequence of it. ❑ *The tears were streaming so fast she could not see... The deal seems so attractive it would be ridiculous to say no... He's not so daft as to listen to rumours.* ADV: ADV adj that, ADV adj *as* to-inf [emphasis] 14 → See also **insofar as**.

PHRASES 15 You use **and so on** or **and so forth** at the end of a list to indicate that there are other items that you could also mention. ❑ *...the Government's policies on such important issues as health, education, tax and so on.* PHRASE: cl/group PHR 16 You use **so much** and **so many** when you are saying that there is a definite limit to something but you are not saying what this limit is. ❑ *There is only so much time in the day for answering letters... Even the greatest city can support only so many lawyers.* PHRASE: PHR n 17 You use the structures **not...so much** and **not so much...as** to say that something is one kind of thing rather than another kind. ❑ *I did not really object to Will's behaviour so much as his personality.* PHRASE 18 You use **or so** when you are giving an approximate amount. ❑ *Though rates are heading down, they still offer real returns of 8% or so... Matt got me a room there for a week or so when I first came here.* PHRASE: amount PHR [vagueness] 19 **so much the better** → see **better**. **ever so** → see **ever**. **so far so good** → see **far**. **so long** → see **long**. **so much for** → see **much**. **so much so** → see **much**. **every so often** → see **often**. **so there** → see **there**.

**soak** /səʊk/ **(soaks, soaking, soaked)** [1] If you **soak** something or leave it **to soak**, you put it into a liquid and leave it there. ❑ *Soak the beans for 2 hours... He turned off the water and left the dishes to soak.* VERB V n V
[2] If a liquid **soaks** something or if you **soak** something **with** a liquid, the liquid makes the thing very wet. ❑ *The water had soaked his jacket and shirt... Soak the soil around each bush with at least 4 gallons of water.* VERB V n V n *with* n
[3] If a liquid **soaks through** something, it passes through it. ❑ *There was so much blood it had soaked through my boxer shorts.* VERB V prep/adv
[4] If someone **soaks**, they spend a long time in a hot bath, because they enjoy it. ❑ *What I need is to soak in a hot tub.* VERB V ♦ **Soak** is also a noun. ❑ *I was having a long soak in the bath.* N-COUNT
[5] → See also **soaked**, **soaking**.

♦ **soak up** [1] If a soft or dry material **soaks up** a liquid, the liquid goes into the substance. ❑ *The cells will promptly start to soak up moisture.* PHRASAL VERB V P n Also V n P
[2] If you **soak up** the atmosphere in a place that you are visiting, you observe or get involved in the way of life there, because you enjoy it or are interested in it. [INFORMAL] ❑ *Keaton comes here once or twice a year to soak up the atmosphere.* PHRASAL VERB = *absorb* V P n Also V n P
[3] If something **soaks up** something such as money or other resources, it uses a great deal of money or other resources. ❑ *Defence soaks up forty per cent of the budget.* PHRASAL VERB V P n (not pron)

**soaked** /səʊkt/ If someone or something gets **soaked** or **soaked through**, water or some other liquid makes them extremely wet. ❑ *I have to check my tent – it got soaked last night in the storm... We got soaked to the skin.* ADJ: usu v-link ADJ

**-soaked** /-səʊkt/ **-soaked** combines with nouns such as 'rain' and 'blood' to form adjectives which describe someone or something that is extremely wet or extremely damp because of the thing mentioned. ❑ *He trudged through the rain-soaked woods. ...blood-soaked clothes.* COMB in ADJ: usu ADJ n

**soak|ing** /səʊkɪŋ/ If something is **soaking** or **soaking wet**, it is very wet. ❑ *My face and raincoat were soaking wet.* ADJ

**so-and-so** [1] You use **so-and-so** instead of a word, expression, or name when you are talking generally rather than giving a specific example of a particular thing. [INFORMAL] ❑ *It would be a case of 'just do so-and-so and here's your cash'... If Mrs So-and-so was ill then Mrs So-and-so down the street would go and clean for her.* PRON
[2] People sometimes refer to another person as a **so-and-so** when they are annoyed with them or think that they are foolish. People often use **so-and-so** in order to avoid using a swear word. [INFORMAL] ❑ *All her fault, the wicked little so-and-so.* N-COUNT [disapproval]

**soap** /səʊp/ **(soaps, soaping, soaped)** [1] **Soap** is a substance that you use with water for washing yourself or sometimes for washing clothes. ❑ *...a bar of lavender soap. ...a packet of soap powder. ...a soap bubble.* N-MASS
[2] If you **soap yourself**, you rub soap on your body in order to wash yourself. ❑ *She soaped herself all over .* VERB V pron-refl
[3] A **soap** is the same as a **soap opera**. [INFORMAL] N-COUNT

**soap|box** /səʊpbɒks/ **(soapboxes)** [1] A **soapbox** is a small temporary platform on which a person stands when he or she is making a speech outdoors. ❑ *One of them climbed aboard a soapbox and began informing the locals why gays should be allowed in the military.* N-COUNT
[2] If you say that someone is on their **soapbox**, you mean that they are speaking or writing about something they have strong feelings about. ❑ *We were interested in pushing forward certain issues and getting up on our soapbox about them.* N-COUNT

**soap op|era** **(soap operas)** A **soap opera** is a popular television drama series about the daily lives and problems of a group of people who live in a particular place. N-COUNT

**soapy** /səʊpi/ **(soapier, soapiest)** Something that is **soapy** is full of soap or covered with soap. ❑ *Wash your hands thoroughly with hot soapy water before handling any food.* ADJ: usu ADJ n

**soar** /sɔːʳ/ **(soars, soaring, soared)** [1] If the amount, value, level, or volume of something **soars**, it quickly increases by a great deal. [JOURNALISM] ❑ *Insurance claims are expected to soar. ...figures showed customer complaints had soared to record levels and profits were falling.* VERB V V prep/adv
[2] If something such as a bird **soars** into the air, it goes quickly up into the air. [LITERARY] ❑ *If you're lucky, a splendid golden eagle may soar into view... The two sheets of flame clashed, soaring hundreds of feet high.* VERB V prep/adv V n
[3] If your spirits **soar**, you suddenly start to feel very happy. [LITERARY] ❑ *For the first time in months, my spirits soared.* VERB V

**soar|away** /sɔːrəweɪ/ If you describe something as a **soaraway** success, you mean that its success has suddenly increased. [BRIT, JOURNALISM, INFORMAL] ❑ *...soaraway sales.* ADJ: ADJ n

**sob** /sɒb/ **(sobs, sobbing, sobbed)** [1] When someone **sobs**, they cry in a noisy way, breathing in short breaths. ❑ *She began to sob again, burying her face in the pillow... Her sister broke down, sobbing into her handkerchief.* VERB V V ♦ **sob|bing** *The room was silent except for her sobbing.* N-UNCOUNT
[2] If you **sob** something, you say it while you are crying. ❑ *'Everything's my fault,' she sobbed.* VERB V with quote
[3] A **sob** is one of the noises that you make when you are crying. N-COUNT

**so|ber** /səʊbəʳ/ **(sobers, sobering, sobered)** [1] When you are **sober**, you are not drunk. ❑ *When Dad was sober he was a good father.* ADJ: usu v-link ADJ
[2] A **sober** person is serious and thoughtful. ❑ *We are now far more sober and realistic... The euphoria is giving way to a more sober assessment of the situation.* ADJ ♦ **so|ber|ly** *'There's a new development,' he said soberly.* ADV: usu ADV with v
[3] **Sober** colours and clothes are plain and rather dull. ❑ *He dresses in sober grey suits. ...sober-suited middle-aged men.* ADJ = *sombre* ♦ **so|ber|ly** *She saw Ellis, soberly dressed in a well-cut dark suit.* ADV: ADV with v
[4] → See also **sobering**. [5] **stone-cold sober** → see **stone-cold**.

♦ **sober up** If someone **sobers up**, or if something **sobers** them **up**, they become sober after being drunk. ❑ *He was left to sober up in a police cell. ...the idea that a cup of strong black coffee sobers you up.* PHRASAL VERB V P V n P

**so|ber|ing** /səʊbərɪŋ/ You say that something is a **sobering** thought or has a **sobering** effect when a situation seems serious and makes you become serious and thoughtful. ❑ *Statistics paint a sobering picture – unemployment, tight credit, lower home values, sluggish job growth.* ADJ: usu ADJ n

**so|bri|ety** /səbraɪɪti/ [1] **Sobriety** is the state of being sober rather than drunk. [FORMAL] N-UNCOUNT
[2] **Sobriety** is serious and thoughtful behaviour. [FORMAL] ❑ *...the values society depends upon, such as honesty, sobriety and trust.* N-UNCOUNT

**so|bri|quet** /səʊbrɪkeɪ/ **(sobriquets)** also **soubriquet.** A **sobriquet** is a humorous name that people give someone or something. [WRITTEN] ❑ *From his staff he earned the sobriquet 'Mumbles'.* N-COUNT: usu sing

**sob sto|ry** **(sob stories)** You describe what someone tells you about their own or someone else's difficulties as a **sob story** when you think that they have told you about it in order to get your sympathy. ❑ *Any sob story moved Jarvis to generosity.* N-COUNT

**Soc.** /sɒk/ **Soc.** is the written abbreviation for **Society**.

**so-called** also **so called.** ◆◇◇ [1] You use **so-called** to indicate that you think a word or expression used to describe someone or something is in fact wrong. ❑ *These are the facts that explode their so-called economic miracle.* ADJ: ADJ n
[2] You use **so-called** to indicate that something is generally referred to by the name that you are about to use. ❑ *...a summit of the world's seven leading market economies, the so-called G-7.* ADJ: ADJ n

**soc|cer** /sɒkəʳ/ **Soccer** is a game played by two teams of eleven players using a round ball. Players kick the ball to each other and try to score goals by kicking the ball into a large net. Outside the USA, this game is also referred to as **football**. ◆◇◇ N-UNCOUNT

**so|cia|ble** /soʊʃəbᵊl/ **Sociable** people are friendly and enjoy talking to other people. ❑ *She was, and remained, extremely sociable, enjoying dancing, golf, tennis, skating and bicycling.* ADJ

**so|cial** /soʊʃᵊl/ [1] **Social** means relating to society or to the way society is organized. ❑ *...the worst effects of unemployment, low pay and other social problems. ...long-term social change. ...changing social attitudes. ...the tightly woven social fabric of small towns. ...research into housing and social policy.* ◆◆◆ ADJ: ADJ n ♦ **so|cial|ly** *Let's face it – drinking is a socially acceptable habit. ...one of the most socially deprived areas in Britain.* ADV: ADV adj/-ed [2] **Social** means relating to the status or rank that someone has in society. ❑ *Higher education is unequally distributed across social classes... The guests came from all social backgrounds.* ADJ: ADJ n ♦ **so|cial|ly** *For socially ambitious couples this is a problem. ...socially disadvantaged children.* ADV: usu ADV adj/-ed, also ADV with cl [3] **Social** means relating to leisure activities that involve meeting other people. ❑ *We ought to organize more social events.* ADJ: ADJ n ♦ **so|cial|ly** *We have known each other socially for a long time... The two groups rarely meet socially.* ADV: usu ADV with v, also ADV with cl [4] **Social** animals live in groups and do things together. ❑ *...social insects like bees and ants.* ADJ: ADJ n

**so|cial chap|ter** **The social chapter** is an agreement between countries in the European Union concerning workers' rights and working conditions. N-SING: the N

**so|cial climb|er** **(social climbers)** You describe someone as a **social climber** when they try to get accepted into a higher social class by becoming friendly with people who belong to that class. ❑ *That Rous was a snob and a social climber could scarcely be denied.* N-COUNT disapproval

**so|cial climb|ing** also **social-climbing**. You describe someone's behaviour as **social climbing** when they try to get accepted into a higher social class by becoming friendly with people who belong to that class. ❑ *All that vulgar social-climbing!* ♦ **Social climbing** is also an adjective. ❑ *...Leroy's ambitious social-climbing wife.* N-UNCOUNT disapproval; ADJ: ADJ n

**so|cial club** **(social clubs)** A **social club** is a club where members go in order to meet each other and enjoy leisure activities. N-COUNT

**so|cial de|moc|ra|cy** **(social democracies)** [1] **Social democracy** is a political system according to which social justice and equality can be achieved within the framework of a market economy. ❑ *...western-style social democracy.* N-UNCOUNT [2] A **social democracy** is a country where there is social democracy. N-COUNT

**so|cial demo|crat|ic** A **social democratic** party is a political party whose principles are based on social democracy. ❑ *...relations with the social democratic governments in Europe.* ADJ: ADJ n

**so|cial hous|ing** **Social housing** is housing which is provided for rent or sale at a fairly low cost by organizations such as housing associations and local councils. [BRIT] N-UNCOUNT

**so|ciali|sa|tion** /soʊʃəlaɪzeɪʃᵊn/ → see **socialization**.

**so|cial|ise** /soʊʃəlaɪz/ → see **socialize**.

**so|cial|ism** /soʊʃəlɪzəm/ **Socialism** is a set of left-wing political principles whose general aim is to create a system in which everyone has an equal opportunity to benefit from a country's wealth. Under socialism, the country's main industries are usually owned by the state. N-UNCOUNT

**so|cial|ist** /soʊʃəlɪst/ **(socialists)** [1] **Socialist** means based on socialism or relating to socialism. ❑ *...members of the ruling Socialist party... Ethiopia was declared a socialist state.* ◆◇◇ ADJ: usu ADJ n [2] A **socialist** is a person who believes in socialism or who is a member of a socialist party. ❑ *The French electorate voted out the socialists.* N-COUNT

**so|cial|is|tic** /soʊʃəlɪstɪk/ If you describe a policy or organization as **socialistic**, you mean that it has some of the features of socialism. ❑ *The Conservatives denounced it as socialistic.* ADJ disapproval

**so|cial|ite** /soʊʃəlaɪt/ **(socialites)** A **socialite** is a person who attends many fashionable upper-class social events and who is well known because of this. [JOURNALISM] N-COUNT

**so|ciali|za|tion** /soʊʃəlaɪzeɪʃᵊn/

✓ in BRIT, also use **socialisation**

[1] **Socialization** is the process by which people, especially children, are made to behave in a way which is acceptable in their culture or society. [TECHNICAL] ❑ *Female socialization emphasizes getting along with others.* N-UNCOUNT [2] **Socialization** is the process by which something is made to operate on socialist principles. [TECHNICAL] N-UNCOUNT

**so|cial|ize** /soʊʃəlaɪz/ **(socializes, socializing, socialized)**

✓ in BRIT, also use **socialise**

[1] If you **socialize**, you meet other people socially, for example at parties. ❑ *...an open meeting, where members socialized and welcomed any new members... It distressed her that she and Charles no longer socialized with old friends.* VERB V; V with n ♦ **so|cial|iz|ing** *The hours were terrible, so socialising was difficult.* N-UNCOUNT [2] When people, especially children, **are socialized**, they are made to behave in a way which is acceptable in their culture or society. [TECHNICAL] ❑ *You may have been socialized to do as you are told.* VERB: usu passive; be V-ed

**so|cial life** **(social lives)** Your **social life** involves spending time with your friends, for example at parties or in pubs or bars. N-COUNT: with supp, oft with poss

**so|cial or|der** **(social orders)** The **social order** in a place is the way that society is organized there. ❑ *...the threat to social order posed by right-wing extremists.* N-VAR

**so|cial sci|ence** **(social sciences)** [1] **Social science** is the scientific study of society. N-UNCOUNT [2] The **social sciences** are the various types of social science, for example sociology and politics. N-COUNT: usu pl

**so|cial sci|en|tist** **(social scientists)** A **social scientist** is a person who studies or teaches social science. N-COUNT

**so|cial se|cu|rity** **Social security** is a system under which a government pays money regularly to certain groups of people, for example the sick, the unemployed, or those with no other income. ❑ *...women who did not have jobs and were on social security.* N-UNCOUNT

**so|cial ser|vices** The **social services** in a district are the services provided by the local authority or government to help people who have serious family problems or financial problems. ❑ *I have asked the social services for help, but they have not done anything.* N-PLURAL

**so|cial stud|ies** [1] In Britain, **social studies** is a subject that is taught in schools and colleges, and includes sociology, politics, and economics. N-UNCOUNT [2] In the United States, **social studies** is a subject that is taught in schools, and that includes history, geography, sociology, and politics. N-UNCOUNT

**so|cial work** **Social work** is work which involves giving help and advice to people with serious family problems or financial problems. N-UNCOUNT

**so|cial work|er** **(social workers)** A **social worker** is a person whose job is to do social work. N-COUNT

**so|ci|etal** /səsaɪɪtᵊl/ **Societal** means relating to society or to the way society is organized. [FORMAL] ❑ *...the societal changes that have taken place over the last two decades. ...societal norms.* ADJ: ADJ n = social

**so|ci|ety** /səsaɪɪti/ **(societies)** [1] **Society** is people in general, thought of as a large organized group. ❑ *This reflects attitudes and values prevailing in society... He maintains Islam must adapt to modern* ◆◆◆ N-UNCOUNT

society. [2] A **society** is the people who live in a country or region, their organizations, and their way of life. ❑ *We live in a capitalist society. ...those responsible for destroying our African heritage and the fabric of our society.* [3] A **society** is an organization for people who have the same interest or aim. ❑ *...the North of England Horticultural Society. ...the historical society.* [4] **Society** is the rich, fashionable people in a particular place who meet on social occasions. ❑ *...the high season for society weddings.* [5] → See also **building society**.
N-VAR: with supp / N-COUNT = association / N-UNCOUNT: oft N n

**socio-** /soʊsioʊ-/ **Socio-** is used to form adjectives and nouns which describe or refer to things relating to or involving social factors. ❑ *Fernandez studied the socioeconomic backgrounds of new recruits.*
PREFIX

**socio-economic** also **socioeconomic. Socio-economic** circumstances or developments involve a combination of social and economic factors. ❑ *Suicide is often connected with socio-economic deprivation.*
ADJ: ADJ n

**so|ci|ol|ogy** /soʊsiɒlədʒi/ **Sociology** is the study of society or of the way society is organized. ♦ **so|cio|logi|cal** /soʊsiəlɒdʒɪkəl/ ❑ *Psychological and sociological studies were emphasizing the importance of the family.* ♦ **so|ci|olo|gist (sociologists)** *By the 1950s some sociologists were confident that they had identified the key characteristics of capitalist society.*
N-UNCOUNT / ADJ: usu ADJ n / N-COUNT

**so|cio|path** /soʊsiəpæθ/ **(sociopaths)** A **sociopath** is the same as a **psychopath**.
N-COUNT

**socio-political** also **sociopolitical. Socio-political** systems and problems involve a combination of social and political factors. ❑ *...sociopolitical issues such as ecology and human rights.*
ADJ: ADJ n

**sock** /sɒk/ **(socks) Socks** are pieces of clothing which cover your foot and ankle and are worn inside shoes. ❑ *...a pair of knee-length socks.*
N-COUNT

**sock|et** /sɒkɪt/ **(sockets)** [1] A **socket** is a device on a piece of electrical equipment into which you can put a bulb or plug. [2] A **socket** is a device or point in a wall where you can connect electrical equipment to the power supply. [BRIT]
N-COUNT / N-COUNT

✓ in AM, use **outlet**

[3] You can refer to any hollow part or opening in a structure which another part fits into as a **socket**. ❑ *Her eyes were sunk deep into their sockets.*
N-COUNT

**sod** /sɒd/ **(sods)** [1] If someone calls another person or something such as a job a **sod**, they are expressing anger or annoyance towards that person or thing. [BRIT, INFORMAL, RUDE] [2] If someone uses an expression such as **sod it**, **sod you**, or **sod that**, they are expressing anger or showing that they do not care about something. [BRIT, INFORMAL, RUDE]
N-COUNT [disapproval] / EXCLAM [feelings]

PHRASES [3] **Sod all** means 'nothing at all'. [BRIT, INFORMAL, RUDE] [4] **Sod's Law** or **sod's law** is the idea that if something can go wrong, it will go wrong. [BRIT, INFORMAL]
PHRASE [emphasis] / PHRASE

♦ **sod off** If someone tells someone else to **sod off**, they are telling them in a very rude way to go away or leave them alone. [BRIT, INFORMAL, RUDE]
PHRASAL VERB: only imper

**soda** /soʊdə/ **(sodas)** [1] **Soda** is the same as **soda water**. [2] **Soda** is a sweet fizzy drink. [AM] ❑ *...a glass of diet soda.* ♦ A **soda** is a bottle of soda. ❑ *They had liquor for the adults and sodas for the children.* [3] → See also **bicarbonate of soda**, **caustic soda**.
N-UNCOUNT / N-MASS / N-COUNT

**soda crack|er (soda crackers)** A **soda cracker** is a thin, square, salty biscuit. [AM]
N-COUNT

**soda foun|tain (soda fountains)** A **soda fountain** is a counter in a drugstore or café, where snacks and non-alcoholic drinks are prepared and sold. [AM]
N-COUNT

**soda pop (soda pops) Soda pop** is a sweet fizzy drink. [AM] ♦ A **soda pop** is a bottle or a glass of soda pop.
N-UNCOUNT = soda / N-COUNT

**soda si|phon (soda siphons)** also **soda syphon.** A **soda siphon** is a special bottle for putting soda water in a drink.
N-COUNT

**soda wa|ter** also **soda-water. Soda water** is fizzy water used for mixing with alcoholic drinks and fruit juice.
N-UNCOUNT = soda

**sod|den** /sɒdən/ Something that is **sodden** is extremely wet. ❑ *We stripped off our sodden clothes.*
ADJ

**-sodden** /-sɒdən/ [1] **-sodden** combines with 'drink' and with the names of alcoholic drinks to form adjectives which describe someone who has drunk too much alcohol and is in a bad state as a result. ❑ *He portrays a whisky-sodden Catholic priest.* [2] **-sodden** combines with words such as 'rain' to form adjectives which describe someone or something that has become extremely wet as a result of the thing that is mentioned. ❑ *The porter put our scruffy rain-sodden luggage on a trolley.*
COMB in ADJ: usu ADJ n / COMB in ADJ: usu ADJ n

**sod|ding** /sɒdɪŋ/ **Sodding** is used by some people to emphasize what they are saying, especially when they are angry or annoyed. [BRIT, INFORMAL, RUDE]
ADJ: ADJ n [emphasis]

**so|dium** /soʊdiəm/ [1] **Sodium** is a silvery-white chemical element which combines with other chemicals. Salt is a sodium compound. ❑ *The fish or seafood is heavily salted with pure sodium chloride. ...one level teaspoon of sodium bicarbonate powder.* [2] **Sodium** lighting gives out a strong orange light. ❑ *...the orange glow of the sodium streetlamps.*
N-UNCOUNT / ADJ: ADJ n

**sodo|my** /sɒdəmi/ **Sodomy** is anal sexual intercourse.
N-UNCOUNT

**sofa** /soʊfə/ **(sofas)** A **sofa** is a long, comfortable seat with a back and usually with arms, which two or three people can sit on.
N-COUNT = settee, couch

**sofa bed (sofa beds)** also **sofa-bed.** A **sofa bed** is a type of sofa whose seat folds out so that it can also be used as a bed.
N-COUNT

**soft** /sɒft, AM sɔːft/ **(softer, softest)** ◆◆◇
[1] Something that is **soft** is pleasant to touch, and not rough or hard. ❑ *Regular use of a body lotion will keep the skin soft and supple. ...warm, soft, white towels.* ♦ **soft|ness** *The sea air robbed her hair of its softness.* [2] Something that is **soft** changes shape or bends easily when you press it. ❑ *She lay down on the soft, comfortable bed... Add enough milk to form a soft dough. ...soft cheese.*
ADJ ≠ rough / N-UNCOUNT / ADJ ≠ hard, firm

[3] Something that has a **soft** appearance has smooth curves rather than sharp or distinct edges. ❑ *This is a smart, yet soft and feminine look. ...the soft curves of her body.* ♦ **soft|ly** *She wore a softly tailored suit. ...a fresh, modern hairstyle which has long layers falling softly on the neck.* [4] Something that is **soft** is very gentle and has no force. For example, a **soft** sound or voice is quiet and not harsh. A **soft** light or colour is pleasant to look at because it is not bright. ❑ *There was a soft tapping on my door... When he woke again he could hear soft music.* ♦ **soft|ly** *She crossed the softly lit room... She bent forward and kissed him softly.* [5] If you are **soft on** someone, you do not treat them as strictly or severely as you should do. ❑ *The president says the measure is soft and weak on criminals.* [6] If you say that someone has a **soft heart**, you mean that they are sensitive and sympathetic towards other people. ❑ *Her rather tough and worldly exterior hides a very soft and sensitive heart.* [7] You use **soft** to describe a way of life that is easy and involves very little work. ❑ *The regime at Latchmere could be seen as a soft option.* [8] **Soft** drugs are drugs, such as cannabis, which are illegal but which many people do not consider to be strong or harmful.
ADJ = gentle ≠ hard / ADV: ADV with v / ADJ = gentle / ADV: ADV with v / ADJ: usu v-link ADJ, oft ADJ on n [disapproval] / ADJ [approval] / ADJ = easy ≠ hard / ADJ: ADJ n

[9] A **soft** target is a place or person that can easily be attacked. ❑ *Women who carry cash about in the streets, as they very often have to, are a very soft target.* [10] **Soft** water does not contain much of the mineral calcium and so makes bubbles easily when you use soap. [11] If you have **a soft spot for** someone or something, you feel a great deal of affection for them or like them a lot. ❑ *Terry had a soft spot for me.* **a soft touch** → see **touch**.
ADJ = easy / ADJ ≠ hard / PHRASE: PHR after v, PHR n

**soft|back** /sɒftbæk/ A **softback** is a book with a thin cardboard, paper, or plastic cover. [BRIT] ❑ *This title was a best seller and is now available in softback.* N-SING: also *in* N

in AM, use **softcover**

**soft|ball** /sɒftbɔːl, AM sɔːft-/ **(softballs)** 1 **Softball** is a game similar to baseball, but played with a larger, softer ball. N-UNCOUNT 2 A **softball** is the ball used in the game of softball. N-COUNT

**soft-boiled** A **soft-boiled** egg is one that has been boiled for only a few minutes, so that the yellow part is still liquid. ADJ ≠ hard-boiled

**soft-core** also **softcore. Soft-core** pornography shows or describes sex, but not very violent or unpleasant sex, or not in a very detailed way. Compare **hard-core**. ADJ: ADJ n

**soft|cover** /sɒftkʌvəʳ/ **(softcovers)** also **soft-cover.** A **softcover** is a book with a thin cardboard, paper, or plastic cover. [AM] ❑ *...this set of 6 softcover books.* N-COUNT: also N n, *in* N

in BRIT, use **softback**

**soft drink** **(soft drinks)** A **soft drink** is a cold, non-alcoholic drink such as lemonade or fruit juice, or a fizzy drink. N-COUNT

**sof|ten** /sɒfᵊn, AM sɔːf-/ **(softens, softening, softened)** 1 If you **soften** something or if it **softens**, it becomes less hard, stiff, or firm. ❑ *Soften the butter mixture in a small saucepan... Fry for about 4 minutes, until the onion has softened.* VERB V n V 2 If one thing **softens** the damaging effect of another thing, it makes the effect less severe. ❑ *There were also pledges to soften the impact of the subsidy cuts on the poorer regions. ...He could not think how to soften the blow of what he had to tell her.* VERB V n V n 3 If you **soften** your position, if your position **softens**, or if you **soften**, you become more sympathetic and less hostile or critical towards someone or something. ❑ *The letter shows no sign that the Americans have softened their position... His party's policy has softened a lot in recent years... Livy felt herself soften towards Caroline.* VERB ≠ harden V n V V 4 If your voice or expression **softens** or if you **soften** it, it becomes much more gentle and friendly. ❑ *All at once, Mick's serious expression softened into a grin... She did not smile or soften her voice.* VERB V V n 5 If you **soften** something such as light, a colour, or a sound, you make it less bright or harsh. ❑ *Stark concrete walls have been softened by a show of fresh flowers.* VERB V n 6 Something that **softens** your skin makes it very smooth and pleasant to touch. ❑ *...products designed to moisturize and soften the skin.* VERB V n

♦ **soften up** If you **soften** someone **up**, you put them into a good mood before asking them to do something. [INFORMAL] ❑ *If they'd treated you well it was just to soften you up.* PHRASAL VERB = butter up V n P Also V P n (not pron)

**sof|ten|er** /sɒfənəʳ, AM sɔːf-/ **(softeners)** 1 A water **softener** is a device or substance which removes certain minerals, for example calcium, from water, so that it makes bubbles easily when you use soap to wash things. N-COUNT 2 A fabric **softener** is a chemical substance that you add to water when you wash clothes in order to make the clothes feel softer. N-MASS

**soft fo|cus** If something in a photograph or film is **in soft focus**, it has been made slightly unclear to give it a more romantic effect. ❑ *In the background, in soft focus, we see his smiling wife.* N-UNCOUNT

**soft fruit** **(soft fruits)** **Soft fruits** are small fruits with soft skins, such as strawberries and currants. [BRIT] N-VAR

in AM, use **berries**

**soft fur|nish|ings** **Soft furnishings** are cushions, curtains, and furniture covers. [BRIT] N-PLURAL

in AM, use **soft goods**

**soft goods** **Soft goods** are the same as **soft furnishings**. [AM] N-PLURAL

**soft-hearted** Someone who is **soft-hearted** has a very sympathetic and kind nature. ADJ

**softie** /sɒfti/ **(softies)** also **softy.** If you describe someone as a **softie**, you mean that they are very emotional or that they can easily be made to feel sympathy towards other people. [INFORMAL] ❑ *He's just a big softie.* N-COUNT

**soft land|ing** **(soft landings)** In economics, a **soft landing** is a situation in which the economy stops growing but this does not produce a recession. N-COUNT

**soft loan** **(soft loans)** A **soft loan** is a loan with a very low interest rate. Soft loans are usually made to developing countries or to businesses in developing countries. [BUSINESS] N-COUNT

**softly-softly** also **softly, softly.** A **softly-softly** approach to something is cautious and patient and avoids direct action or force. [BRIT] ❑ *...the government's softly, softly approach to the prison protest.* ADJ: ADJ n

**soft-pedal** **(soft-pedals, soft-pedalling, soft-pedalled)**

in AM, use **soft-pedaling, soft-pedaled**

If you **soft-pedal** something, you deliberately reduce the amount of activity or pressure that you have been using to get something done or seen. ❑ *He refused to soft-pedal an investigation into the scandal.* VERB V n Also V *on* n

**soft porn** **Soft porn** is pornography that shows or describes sex, but not very violent or unpleasant sex, or not in a very detailed way. N-UNCOUNT

**soft sell** also **soft-sell.** A **soft sell** is a method of selling or advertising that involves persuading people in a gentle way rather than putting a lot of pressure on people to buy things. [BUSINESS] ❑ *I think more customers probably prefer a soft sell.* N-SING ≠ hard sell

**soft shoul|der** **(soft shoulders)** On a busy road such as a freeway, **the soft shoulder** is the area at the side of the road where vehicles are allowed to stop in an emergency. [AM] N-COUNT: usu *the* N in sing

in BRIT, use **hard shoulder**

**soft skills** **Soft skills** are interpersonal skills such as the ability to communicate well with other people and to work in a team. N-PLURAL ≠ hard skills

**soft-soap** **(soft-soaps, soft-soaping, soft-soaped)** If you **soft-soap** someone, you flatter them or tell them what you think they want to hear in order to try and persuade them to do something. ❑ *The government is not soft-soaping the voters here.* VERB V n

**soft-spoken** Someone who is **soft-spoken** has a quiet, gentle voice. ❑ *He was a gentle, soft-spoken intelligent man.* ADJ

**soft toy** **(soft toys)** **Soft toys** are toys that are made of cloth filled with a soft material and which look like animals. [BRIT] N-COUNT

in AM, use **stuffed animal, stuffed toy**

**soft|ware** /sɒftweəʳ, AM sɔːf-/ Computer programs are referred to as **software**. Compare **hardware**. [COMPUTING] ❑ *...the people who write the software for big computer projects.* ◆◇◇ N-UNCOUNT

**soft|wood** /sɒftwʊd, AM sɔːft-/ **(softwoods)** **Softwood** is the wood from trees such as pines, that grow quickly and can be cut easily. N-MASS

**softy** /sɒfti, AM sɔːfti/ → see **softie**.

**sog|gy** /sɒgi/ **(soggier, soggiest)** Something that is **soggy** is unpleasantly wet. ❑ *...soggy cheese sandwiches.* ADJ

**soi|gnée** /swɑːnjeɪ, AM -jeɪ/

The spelling **soigné** is also used when referring to a man.

If you describe a person as **soignée**, you mean that they are very elegant. [FORMAL] ❑ *...looking very soignée in black.* ADJ

**soil** /sɔɪl/ **(soils, soiling, soiled)** 1 **Soil** is the substance on the surface of the earth in which plants grow. ❑ *We have the most fertile soil in Europe. ...regions with sandy soils.* ◆◇◇ N-MASS 2 You can use **soil** in expressions like **British soil** to refer to a N-UNCOUNT: with supp = territory

country's territory. ❑ *The issue of foreign troops on Turkish soil is a sensitive one.* [3] [VERB = dirty] If you **soil** something, you make it dirty. [FORMAL] ❑ [V n] *Young people don't want to do things that soil their hands...* [V n] *He raised his eyes slightly as though her words might somehow soil him.* ♦ **soiled** [ADJ] *...a soiled white apron.*

**soi|ree** /swɑːreɪ, AM swɑːreɪ/ **(soirees)** also **soirée.** [N-COUNT] A **soiree** is a social gathering held in the evening. [FORMAL]

**so|journ** /sɒdʒɜːʳn, AM soʊdʒ-/ **(sojourns)** [N-COUNT] A **sojourn** is a short stay in a place that is not your home. [LITERARY]

**sol|ace** /sɒlɪs/ [N-UNCOUNT = comfort] **Solace** is a feeling of comfort that makes you feel less sad. [FORMAL] ❑ *I found solace in writing when my father died three years ago.*

**so|lar** /soʊləʳ/ [1] [ADJ: usu ADJ n] **Solar** is used to describe things relating to the sun. ❑ *A total solar eclipse is due to take place some time tomorrow.* [2] [ADJ: usu ADJ n] **Solar** power is obtained from the sun's light and heat.

**so|lar cell** **(solar cells)** [N-COUNT] A **solar cell** is a device that produces electricity from the sun's rays.

**so|lar|ium** /soʊleəriəm/ **(solariums)** [N-COUNT] A **solarium** is a place equipped with special lamps, where you can go to get an artificial suntan.

**so|lar plex|us** /soʊləʳ pleksəs/ [N-SING: the N, N with poss] Your **solar plexus** is the part of your stomach, below your ribs, where it is painful if you are hit hard.

**so|lar sys|tem** **(solar systems)** [N-COUNT: usu sing, oft the N, poss N] **The solar system** is the sun and all the planets that go round it.

**sold** /soʊld/ **Sold** is the past tense and past participle of **sell**.

**sol|der** /soʊldəʳ, AM sɑːdəʳ/ **(solders, soldering, soldered)** [1] [VERB] If you **solder** two pieces of metal together, you join them by melting a small piece of soft metal and putting it between them so that it holds them together after it has cooled. ❑ [V n] *Fewer workers are needed to solder circuit boards.* [2] [N-UNCOUNT] **Solder** is the soft metal used for soldering.

**sol|der|ing iron** **(soldering irons)** [N-COUNT] A **soldering iron** is a tool used to solder things together.

**sol|dier** /soʊldʒəʳ/ **(soldiers, soldiering, soldiered)** ◆◆◇ [N-COUNT] A **soldier** is a person who works in an army, especially a person who is not an officer.

♦ **soldier on** [PHRASAL VERB] If you **soldier on** at something, you continue to do it although it is difficult or unpleasant. ❑ [V P] *The government has soldiered on as if nothing were wrong.*

**sol|dier|ly** /soʊldʒəʳli/ [ADJ: usu ADJ n] If you act in a **soldierly** way, you behave like a good or brave soldier. [FORMAL] ❑ *There was a great deal of soldierly good fellowship.*

**sol|diery** /soʊldʒəri/ [N-UNCOUNT] **Soldiery** is a group or body of soldiers. [LITERARY] ❑ *...the distant shouts and songs of the drunken soldiery.*

**sold out** [1] [ADJ: v-link ADJ] If a performance, sports event, or other entertainment is **sold out**, all the tickets for it have been sold. ❑ *The premiere on Monday is sold out.* [2] [ADJ: v-link ADJ, oft ADJ of n] If a shop is **sold out of** something, it has sold all of it that it had. ❑ *The stores are sometimes sold out of certain groceries.* → See also **sell out**.

**sole** /soʊl/ **(soles)** [1] [ADJ: ADJ n = only] The **sole** thing or person of a particular type is the only one of that type. ❑ *Their sole aim is to destabilize the Indian government.* [2] [ADJ: ADJ n] If you have **sole** charge or ownership of something, you are the only person in charge of it or who owns it. ❑ *Many women are left as the sole providers in families after their husband has died... Chief Hart had sole control over that fund.* [3] [N-COUNT: usu with supp] The **sole** of your foot or of a shoe or sock is the underneath surface of it. ❑ *...shoes with rubber soles... He had burned the sole of his foot.* [4] [N-COUNT] A **sole** is a kind of flat fish that you can eat. ♦ [N-UNCOUNT] **Sole** is this fish eaten as food.

**-soled** /-soʊld/ [COMB in ADJ: usu ADJ n] **-soled** combines with adjectives and nouns to form adjectives which describe shoes with a particular kind of sole. ❑ *The lad was wearing rubber-soled shoes.*

**sole|ly** /soʊlli/ [ADV: ADV with v, ADV with group/cl] If something involves **solely** one thing, it involves only this thing and no others. ❑ *This program is a production of NPR, which is solely responsible for its content.*

**sol|emn** /sɒləm/ [1] [ADJ = serious] Someone or something that is **solemn** is very serious rather than cheerful or humorous. ❑ *His solemn little face broke into smiles... He looked solemn.* ♦ **so|lem|nity** /səlemnɪti/ [N-UNCOUNT] *The setting for this morning's signing ceremony matched the solemnity of the occasion.* [2] [ADJ] A **solemn** promise or agreement is one that you make in a very formal, sincere way. ❑ *...a solemn pledge that he would never remarry.*

**sole pro|pri|etor** **(sole proprietors)** [N-COUNT] The **sole proprietor** of a business is the owner of the business, when it is owned by only one person. [BUSINESS] ❑ *...a firm of solicitors of which he was the sole proprietor.*

**sole trad|er** **(sole traders)** [N-COUNT] A **sole trader** is a person who owns their own business and does not have a partner or any shareholders. [BUSINESS] ❑ *Finance for a sole trader usually comes from the individual's own savings or from family and friends.*

**so|lic|it** /səlɪsɪt/ **(solicits, soliciting, solicited)** [1] [VERB] If you **solicit** money, help, support, or an opinion **from** someone, you ask them for it. [FORMAL] ❑ [V n] *He's already solicited their support on health care reform...* [V n from n] *No tuition was charged by the school, which solicited contributions from the society's members.* [2] [VERB] When prostitutes **solicit**, they offer to have sex with people in return for money. ❑ [V] *Prostitutes were forbidden to solicit on public roads and in public places.* ♦ **so|lic|it|ing** [N-UNCOUNT] *Girls could get very heavy sentences for soliciting – nine months or more.*

**so|lici|ta|tion** /səlɪsɪteɪʃᵊn/ **(solicitations)** [N-VAR] **Solicitation** is the act of asking someone for money, help, support, or an opinion. [mainly AM] ❑ *Republican leaders are making open solicitation of the Italian-American vote.*

**so|lici|tor** /səlɪsɪtəʳ/ **(solicitors)** ◆◇◇ [1] [N-COUNT] In Britain, a **solicitor** is a lawyer who gives legal advice, prepares legal documents and cases, and represents clients in the lower courts of law. Compare **barrister**. [2] [N-COUNT] In the United States, a **solicitor** is the chief lawyer in a government or city department.

**So|lici|tor Gen|er|al** also **solicitor-general.** [N-SING; N-TITLE] **The Solicitor General** in Britain or the United States, or in an American state, is the second most important legal officer, next in rank below an Attorney General.

**so|lici|tous** /səlɪsɪtəs/ [ADJ: oft ADJ of n] A person who is **solicitous** shows anxious concern for someone or something. [FORMAL] ❑ *He was so solicitous of his guests.* ♦ **so|lici|tous|ly** [ADV: usu ADV with v] *He took her hand in greeting and asked solicitously how everything was.*

**so|lici|tude** /səlɪsɪtjuːd, AM -tuːd/ [N-UNCOUNT] **Solicitude** is anxious concern for someone. [FORMAL] ❑ *He is full of tender solicitude towards my sister.*

**sol|id** /sɒlɪd/ **(solids)** ◆◇◇ [1] [ADJ: usu ADJ n ≠ liquid] A **solid** substance or object stays the same shape whether it is in a container or not. ❑ *...the potential of greatly reducing our solid waste problem... He did not eat solid food for several weeks.* [2] [N-COUNT ≠ liquid] A **solid** is a substance that stays the same shape whether it is in a container or not. ❑ *Solids turn to liquids at certain temperatures. ...the decomposition of solids.* [3] [ADJ] A substance that is **solid** is very hard or firm. ❑ *The snow had melted, but the lake was still frozen solid... The concrete will stay as solid as a rock.* [4] [ADJ: usu ADJ n] A **solid** object or mass does not have a space inside it, or holes or gaps in it. ❑ *...a tunnel carved through 50ft of solid rock. ...a solid mass of colour... The car park was absolutely packed solid with people.* [5] [ADJ: ADJ n] If an object is made of **solid** gold or **solid** wood, for example, it is made of gold or wood all the way through, rather than just on the outside. ❑ *...solid wood doors. ...solid pine furniture.* [6] [ADJ] A structure that is **solid** is strong and is not likely to collapse or fall over. ❑ *Banks are built to look solid to reassure their customers... The car feels very solid.* ♦ **sol|id|ly** [ADV:] *Their house,*

which was solidly built, resisted the main shock. ADV with v
♦ **so|lid|ity** /səlɪdɪti/ *...the solidity of walls and floors.* N-UNCOUNT
7 If you describe someone as **solid**, you mean that they are very reliable and respectable. ADJ [approval] ❑ *Mr Zuma had a solid reputation as a grass roots organiser.* ♦ **sol|id|ly** *Graham is so solidly consistent.* ADV
♦ **so|lid|ity** *He had the proverbial solidity of the English.* N-UNCOUNT
8 **Solid** evidence or information is reliable because it is based on facts. ADJ ❑ *We don't have good solid information on where the people are... He has a solid alibi.*
9 You use **solid** to describe something such as advice or a piece of work which is useful and reliable. ADJ ❑ *The CIU provides churches with solid advice on a wide range of subjects... All I am looking for is a good solid performance.*
♦ **sol|id|ly** *She's played solidly throughout the spring.* ADV: ADV with v
10 You use **solid** to describe something such as the basis for a policy or support for an organization when it is strong, because it has been developed carefully and slowly. ADJ = strong ❑ *...Washington's attempt to build a solid international coalition.*
♦ **sol|id|ly** *The Los Alamos district is solidly Republican... So far, majority public opinion is solidly behind the government.* ADV: ADV adj/prep, ADV with v ♦ **so|lid|ity** *...doubts over the solidity of European backing for the American approach.* N-UNCOUNT
11 If you do something for a **solid** period of time, you do it without any pause or interruption throughout that time. ADJ: ADJ n, -ed ADJ ❑ *We had worked together for two solid years.* ♦ **sol|id|ly** *People who had worked solidly since Christmas enjoyed the chance of a Friday off.* ADV: ADV with v
12 → See also **rock-solid**.

**soli|dar|ity** /sɒlɪdærɪti/ If a group of people show **solidarity**, they show support for each other or for another group, especially in political or international affairs. N-UNCOUNT: oft N *with* n ❑ *Supporters want to march tomorrow to show solidarity with their leaders.*

**sol|id fuel** **(solid fuels)** **Solid fuel** is fuel such as coal or wood, that is solid rather than liquid or gas. [BRIT] N-MASS

**so|lidi|fy** /səlɪdɪfaɪ/ **(solidifies, solidifying, solidified)** 1 When a liquid **solidifies** or **is solidified**, it changes into a solid. VERB ❑ *The thicker lava would have taken two weeks to solidify...* V *The Energy Department plans to solidify the deadly waste in a high-tech billion-dollar factory.* V n *...a frying-pan full of solidified fat.* V-ed
2 If something such as a position or opinion **solidifies**, or if something **solidifies** it, it becomes firmer and more definite and unlikely to change. VERB ❑ *Her attitudes solidified through privilege and habit.* V *...his attempt to solidify his position as chairman.* V n

**solid-state** **Solid-state** electronic equipment is made using transistors or silicon chips, instead of valves or other mechanical parts. [TECHNICAL] ADJ: ADJ n

**so|lilo|quy** /səlɪləkwi/ **(soliloquies)** A **soliloquy** is a speech in a play in which an actor or actress speaks to himself or herself and to the audience, rather than to another actor. N-COUNT

**soli|taire** /sɒlɪteəʳ/ **(solitaires)** 1 **Solitaire** is a game for one person in which you move and remove objects on a board, with the aim of having one object left at the end of the game. N-UNCOUNT
2 **Solitaire** is a card game for only one player. [mainly AM] N-UNCOUNT

✓ in BRIT, use **patience**

3 A **solitaire** is a diamond or other jewel that is set on its own in a ring or other piece of jewellery. N-COUNT

**soli|tary** /sɒlɪtri, AM -teri/ 1 A person or animal that is **solitary** spends a lot of time alone. ADJ: usu ADJ n ❑ *Paul was a shy, pleasant, solitary man... They often have a lonely and solitary life to lead.*
2 A **solitary** activity is one that you do alone. ADJ: ADJ n ❑ *His evenings were spent in solitary drinking.*
3 A **solitary** person or object is alone, with no others near them. ADJ: ADJ n = lone ❑ *...the occasional solitary figure making a study of wildflowers or grasses.*

**soli|tary con|fine|ment** A prisoner who is **in solitary confinement** is being kept alone away from all other prisoners, usually as a punishment. N-UNCOUNT: usu *in* N ❑ *Last night he was being held in solitary confinement in Douglas jail.*

**soli|tude** /sɒlɪtjuːd, AM -tuːd/ **Solitude** is the state of being alone, especially when this is peaceful and pleasant. N-UNCOUNT ❑ *He enjoyed his moments of solitude before the pressures of the day began.*

**solo** /soʊloʊ/ **(solos)** 1 You use **solo** to indicate that someone does something alone rather than with other people. ADJ: usu ADJ n ❑ *He had just completed his final solo album. ...Mick Taylor, who had long since quit the Stones for a solo career.* ♦ **Solo** is also an adverb. ADV: ADV after v ❑ *Charles Lindbergh became the very first person to fly solo across the Atlantic.*
2 A **solo** is a piece of music or a dance performed by one person. N-COUNT ❑ *The original version featured a guitar solo.*

**so|lo|ist** /soʊloʊɪst/ **(soloists)** A **soloist** is a musician or dancer who performs a solo. N-COUNT

**sol|stice** /sɒlstɪs/ **(solstices)** **The summer solstice** is the day of the year with the most hours of daylight, and **the winter solstice** is the day of the year with the fewest hours of daylight. N-COUNT

**sol|uble** /sɒljʊbᵊl/ 1 A substance that is **soluble** will dissolve in a liquid. ADJ ≠ insoluble ❑ *Uranium is soluble in sea water.*
2 If something is **water-soluble** or **fat-soluble**, it will dissolve in water or in fat. COMB in ADJ ❑ *The red dye on the leather is water-soluble. ...fat-soluble vitamins.*

**so|lu|tion** /səluːʃᵊn/ **(solutions)** ◆◆◇ 1 A **solution to** a problem or difficult situation is a way of dealing with it so that the difficulty is removed. N-COUNT: oft N *to* n ❑ *Although he has sought to find a peaceful solution, he is facing pressure to use greater military force. ...the ability to sort out simple, effective solutions to practical problems.*
2 The **solution to** a puzzle is the answer to it. N-COUNT ❑ *...the solution to crossword No. 19721.*
3 A **solution** is a liquid in which a solid substance has been dissolved. N-COUNT: also *in* N ❑ *...a warm solution of liquid detergent.*

**solve** /sɒlv/ **(solves, solving, solved)** ◆◇◇ If you **solve** a problem or a question, you find a solution or an answer to it. VERB ❑ *Their domestic reforms did nothing to solve the problem of unemployment.* V n

**sol|ven|cy** /sɒlvᵊnsi/ A person or organization's **solvency** is their ability to pay their debts. [BUSINESS] N-UNCOUNT: usu with supp

**sol|vent** /sɒlvᵊnt/ **(solvents)** 1 If a person or a company is **solvent**, they have enough money to pay all their debts. [BUSINESS] ADJ: usu v-link ADJ ≠ insolvent ❑ *They're going to have to show that the company is now solvent.*
2 A **solvent** is a liquid that can dissolve other substances. N-MASS ❑ *...a small amount of cleaning solvent. ...industrial solvents.*

**sol|vent abuse** **Solvent abuse** is the dangerous practice of breathing in the gases from substances such as glue in order to feel as if you are drunk. [BRIT, FORMAL] N-UNCOUNT

**som|bre** /sɒmbəʳ/

✓ in AM, use **somber**

1 If someone is **sombre**, they are serious or sad. ADJ ❑ *The pair were in sombre mood... His expression became increasingly sombre.*
2 **Sombre** colours and places are dark and dull. ADJ ❑ *...a worried official in sombre black.*

**som|brero** /sɒmbreəroʊ/ **(sombreros)** A **sombrero** is a hat with a very wide brim which is worn especially in Mexico. N-COUNT

**some** /səm, STRONG sʌm/ ◆◆◆ 1 You use **some** to refer to a quantity of something or to a number of people or things, when you are not stating the quantity or number precisely. DET: DET n-uncount/pl-n ❑ *Robin opened some champagne... He went to fetch some books... Some children refuse to eat at all and others overeat.* ♦ **Some** is also a pronoun. PRON ❑ *This year all the apples are all red. My niece and nephew are going out this morning with step-ladders to pick some.*
2 You use **some** to emphasize that a quantity or number is fairly large. For example, if an activity takes **some** time, it takes quite a lot of time. DET: DET n-uncount/pl-n [emphasis] ❑ *The question of local government finance has been the sub-*

ject of debate for some years... I have discussed this topic in some detail... He remained silent for some time... It took some effort to conceal her relief. [3] You use **some** to emphasize that a quantity or number is fairly small. For example, if something happens to **some** extent, it happens a little. ❑ *'Isn't there some chance that William might lead a normal life?' asked Jill... All mothers share to some extent in the tension of a wedding... Some fishing is still allowed, but limits have been imposed on the size of the catch.* DET: DET n-uncount/sing-n [emphasis]

[4] If you refer to **some of** the people or things in a group, you mean a few of them but not all of them. If you refer to **some of** a particular thing, you mean a part of it but not all of it. ❑ *Some of the people already in work will lose their jobs... Remove the cover and spoon some of the sauce into a bowl... Some of us are sensitive to smells, others find colours easier to remember.* QUANT: QUANT *of* n-uncount/pl-n ≠ *all* ♦ **Some** is also a pronoun. ❑ *When the chicken is cooked I'll freeze some.* PRON [5] If you refer to **some** person or thing, you are referring to that person or thing but in a vague way, without stating precisely which person or thing you mean. ❑ *If you are worried about some aspect of your child's health, call us... She always thinks some guy is going to come along and fix her life.* DET: DET sing-n [vagueness] [6] You can use **some** in front of a number to indicate that it is approximate. ❑ *I have kept birds for some 30 years... He waited some 80 to 100 yards from the big pink villa.* ADV: ADV num [vagueness] = *about* [7] **Some** is used to mean to a small extent or degree. [AM] ❑ *If Susanne is off somewhere, I'll kill time by looking around some.* ADV: ADV after v [8] You can use **some** in front of a noun in order to express your approval or disapproval of the person or thing you are mentioning. [INFORMAL] ❑ *'Some party!' — 'Yep. One hell of a party.'* DET [feelings]

**some|body** /sʌmbədi, AM -bɑːdi/ **Somebody** means the same as **someone**. ◆◆◇ PRON

**some day** also **someday. Some day** means at a date in the future that is unknown or that has not yet been decided. ❑ *Some day I'll be a pilot.* ADV: ADV with v, ADV with cl

**some|how** /sʌmhaʊ/ [1] You use **somehow** to say that you do not know or cannot say how something was done or will be done. ❑ *We'll manage somehow, you and me. I know we will... Somehow Karin managed to cope with the demands of her career... Somehow I knew he would tell me the truth.* ◆◇◇ ADV: ADV with v, ADV adj [2] **somehow or other** → see **other**.

**some|one** /sʌmwʌn/ or **somebody** ◆◆◇ [1] You use **someone** or **somebody** to refer to a person without saying exactly who you mean. ❑ *Her father was shot by someone trying to rob his small retail store... I need someone to help me... If somebody asks me how my diet is going, I say, 'Fine'.* PRON [2] If you say that a person is **someone** or **somebody in** a particular kind of work or **in** a particular place, you mean that they are considered to be important in that kind of work or in that place. ❑ *'Before she came around,' she says, 'I was somebody in this town'.* PRON: usu PRON *in* n

**some|place** /sʌmpleɪs/ **Someplace** means the same as **somewhere**. [AM] ❑ *Maybe if we could go someplace together, just you and I.* ADV: ADV after v

**som|er|sault** /sʌməʳsɔːlt/ **(somersaults, somersaulting, somersaulted)** [1] If someone or something does a **somersault**, they turn over completely in the air. N-COUNT [2] If someone or something **somersaults**, they perform one or more somersaults. ❑ *I hit him back and he somersaulted down the stairs.* VERB V prep

**some|thing** /sʌmθɪŋ/ [1] You use **something** to refer to a thing, situation, event, or idea, without saying exactly what it is. ❑ *He realized right away that there was something wrong... There was something vaguely familiar about him... The garden was something special... 'You said there was something you wanted to ask me,' he said politely... There was something in her attitude that bothered him.* ◆◆◆ PRON: oft PRON adj, PRON adj *about* n [2] You can use **something** to say that the description or amount that you are giving is not exact. ❑ *Clive made a noise, something like a grunt... There was something around a thousand dollars in the office strong box... Their membership seems to have risen to something over 10,000.* PRON: PRON prep [3] If you say that a person or thing is **something** or is really **something**, you mean that you are very impressed by them. [INFORMAL] ❑ *The doors here are really something, all made of good wood like mahogany.* PRON [4] You can use **something** in expressions like **'that's something'** when you think that a situation is not very good but is better that it might have been. ❑ *Well, at least he was in town. That was something.* PRON [5] If you say that a thing is **something of** a disappointment, you mean that it is quite disappointing. If you say that a person is **something of** an artist, you mean that they are quite good at art. ❑ *The city proved to be something of a disappointment... She received something of a surprise when Robert said that he was coming to New York.* PRON: PRON *of* n [6] If you say that there is **something in** an idea or suggestion, you mean that it is quite good and should be considered seriously. ❑ *Christianity has stood the test of time, so there must be something in it... Could there be something in what he said?* PRON: PRON *in* n [7] You use **something** in expressions such as **'or something'** and **'or something like that'** to indicate that you are referring to something similar to what you have just mentioned but you are not being exact. ❑ *This guy, his name was Briarly or Beardly or something... The air fare was about a hundred and ninety-nine pounds or something like that.* PRON [vagueness] [8] **something like** → see **like**.

**-something** /-sʌmθɪŋ/ **(-somethings) -something** is combined with numbers such as twenty and thirty to form adjectives which indicate an approximate amount, especially someone's age. For example, if you say that someone is **thirty-something**, you mean they are between thirty and forty years old. COMB in ADJ

**some|time** /sʌmtaɪm/ You use **sometime** to refer to a time in the future or the past that is unknown or that has not yet been decided. ❑ *The sales figures won't be released until sometime next month... Why don't you come and see me sometime?* ADV: ADV with v, ADV with cl/group

**some|times** /sʌmtaɪmz/ You use **sometimes** to say that something happens on some occasions rather than all the time. ❑ *During the summer, my skin sometimes gets greasy... Sometimes I think he dislikes me... You must have noticed how tired he sometimes looks... Other people's jobs were exactly the same – sometimes good, sometimes bad.* ◆◆◇ ADV: ADV with cl/group, ADV with v

**some|what** /sʌmʰwɒt/ You use **somewhat** to indicate that something is the case to a limited extent or degree. [FORMAL] ❑ *He explained somewhat unconvincingly that the company was paying for everything... Although his relationship with his mother had improved somewhat, he was still depressed.* ◆◇◇ ADV: ADV with cl/group

**some|where** /sʌmʰweəʳ/ [1] You use **somewhere** to refer to a place without saying exactly where you mean. ❑ *I've got a feeling I've seen him before somewhere... I'm not going home yet. I have to go somewhere else first... 'Perhaps we can talk somewhere privately,' said Kesler... Somewhere in Ian's room were some of the letters that she had sent him... I needed somewhere to live in London.* ◆◇◇ ADV: ADV after v, ADV with *be*, oft ADV cl/group, *from* ADV [2] You use **somewhere** when giving an approximate amount, number, or time. ❑ *Caray is somewhere between 73 and 80 years of age... The W.H.O. safety standard for ozone levels is somewhere about a hundred.* ADV: ADV prep [3] If you say that you **are getting somewhere**, you mean that you are making progress towards achieving something. ❑ *At last they were agreeing, at last they were getting somewhere.* PHRASE: V inflects

**som|no|lent** /sɒmnələnt/ If you are **somnolent**, you feel sleepy. [FORMAL] ❑ *The sedative makes people very somnolent.* ADJ: usu ADJ n

**son** /sʌn/ **(sons)** [1] Someone's **son** is their male child. ❑ *He shared a pizza with his son Laurence... Sam is the seven-year-old son of Eric Davies... They have a son.* ◆◆◆ N-COUNT: oft with poss [2] A man, especially a famous man, can be described as a **son** of the place he comes from. [JOURNALISM] ❑ *...New Orleans's most famous son, Louis Armstrong. ...sons of* N-COUNT: with poss

*Africa.* [3] Some people use **son** as a form of address when they are showing kindness or affection to a boy or a man who is younger than them. [INFORMAL] ❑ *Don't be frightened by failure, son.* N-VOC feelings

**so|nar** /soʊnɑːʳ/ **(sonars) Sonar** is equipment on a ship which can calculate the depth of the sea or the position of an underwater object using sound waves. N-VAR

**so|na|ta** /sənɑːtə/ **(sonatas)** A **sonata** is a piece of classical music written either for a single instrument, or for one instrument and a piano. N-COUNT: oft in names

**son et lu|mi|ère** /sɒn eɪ luːmieəʳ/ **Son et lumière** is an entertainment which is held at night in an old building such as a castle. A person describes the history of the place, and at the same time different parts of the building are brightly lit and music is played. N-SING

**song** /sɒŋ, AM sɔːŋ/ **(songs)** ◆◆◇ [1] A **song** is words sung to a tune. ❑ *...a voice singing a Spanish song. ...a love song.* N-COUNT [2] **Song** is the art of singing. ❑ *...dance, music, mime and song. ...the history of American popular song.* N-UNCOUNT [3] A bird's **song** is the pleasant, musical sounds that it makes. ❑ *It's been a long time since I heard a blackbird's song in the evening.* N-COUNT [4] → See also **birdsong**, **song and dance**, **songbird**, **swan song**. [5] If someone **bursts into song** or **breaks into song**, they start singing. ❑ *I feel as if I should break into song.* PHRASE: V inflects

**song and dance** [1] A **song and dance** act is a performance in which a person or group of people sing and dance. N-UNCOUNT: usu N n [2] If you say that someone is making a **song and dance about** something, you mean they are making an unnecessary fuss about it. [BRIT, INFORMAL] ❑ *He used his money to help others – but he never made a song and dance about it.* PHRASE disapproval = fuss

**song|bird** /sɒŋbɜːʳd, AM sɔːŋ-/ **(songbirds)** also **song bird.** A **songbird** is a bird that produces musical sounds which are like singing. There are many different kinds of songbird. N-COUNT

**song sheet (song sheets)** also **songsheet.** A **song sheet** is a piece of paper with the words to one or more songs printed on it. Song sheets are given to groups of people at occasions when they are expected to sing together. to **sing from the same song sheet** → see **sing**. N-COUNT

**song|ster** /sɒŋstəʳ, AM sɔːŋ-/ **(songsters)** Journalists sometimes refer to a popular singer, especially a male singer, as a **songster**. N-COUNT

**song|stress** /sɒŋstrəs, AM sɔːŋ-/ **(songstresses)** Journalists sometimes refer to a female popular singer as a **songstress**. N-COUNT

**song|writer** /sɒŋraɪtəʳ, AM sɔːŋ-/ **(songwriters)** A **songwriter** is someone who writes the words or the music, or both, for popular songs. ❑ *...one of rock'n'roll's greatest songwriters.* → See also **singer-songwriter**. N-COUNT

**son|ic** /sɒnɪk/ **Sonic** is used to describe things related to sound. [TECHNICAL] ❑ *He activated the door with the miniature sonic transmitter.* ADJ: ADJ n

**son-in-law (sons-in-law)** Someone's **son-in-law** is the husband of their daughter. N-COUNT: usu poss N

**son|net** /sɒnɪt/ **(sonnets)** A **sonnet** is a poem that has 14 lines. Each line has 10 syllables, and the poem has a fixed pattern of rhymes. N-COUNT

**son|ny** /sʌni/ Some people address a boy or young man as **sonny**. [INFORMAL] ❑ *Well, sonny, I'll give you a bit of advice.* N-VOC

**son of a bitch (sons of bitches)** also **son-of-a-bitch.** If someone is very angry with another person, or if they want to insult them, they sometimes call them a **son of a bitch**. [INFORMAL, ⚠ VERY RUDE] N-COUNT disapproval

**so|nor|ity** /sənɒrɪti, AM -nɔːr-/ **(sonorities)** The **sonority** of a sound is its deep, rich quality. [FORMAL] ❑ *The lower strings contribute a splendid richness of sonority.* N-UNCOUNT: also N in pl

**so|no|rous** /sɒnərəs, AM sənɔːrəs/ A **sonorous** sound is deep and rich. [LITERARY] ❑ *'Doctor McKee?' the man called in an even, sonorous voice.* ADJ = resonant

**soon** /suːn/ **(sooner, soonest)** ◆◆◆ [1] If something is going to happen **soon**, it will happen after a short time. If something happened **soon** after a particular time or event, it happened a short time after it. ❑ *You'll be hearing from us very soon... This chance has come sooner than I expected... The plane was returning to the airport soon after takeoff when it burst into flames... Soon afterwards he separated from his wife.* ADV: ADV with v, ADV *after* n/cl, ADV *afterwards*

PHRASES [2] If you say that something happens **as soon as** something else happens, you mean that it happens immediately after the other thing. ❑ *As soon as relations improve they will be allowed to go... You'll never guess what happened as soon as I left my room.* PHRASE [3] If you say that you **would just as soon** do something or you**'d just as soon** do it, you mean that you would prefer to do it. ❑ *These people could afford to retire to Florida but they'd just as soon stay put... I'd just as soon not have to make this public... I'd just as soon you put that thing away... She'd just as soon throw your plate in your face as serve you.* PHRASE MODAL inf MODAL *not* inf MODAL that MODAL inf *as* inf

**soon|er** /suːnəʳ/ [1] **Sooner** is the comparative of **soon**.

PHRASES [2] You say **the sooner the better** when you think something should be done as soon as possible. ❑ *Detective Holt said: 'The kidnapper is a man we must catch and the sooner the better'.* PHRASE [3] If you say that something will happen **sooner or later**, you mean that it will happen at some time in the future, even though it might take a long time. ❑ *Sooner or later she would be caught by the police.* PHRASE: PHR with cl = eventually [4] If you say that **no sooner** has one thing happened **than** another thing happens, you mean that the second thing happens immediately after the first thing. ❑ *No sooner had he arrived in Rome than he was kidnapped.* PHRASE = scarcely [5] If you say that you **would sooner** do something or you**'d sooner** do it, you mean that you would prefer to do it. ❑ *Ford vowed that he would sooner burn his factory to the ground than build a single vehicle for war purposes... I'd sooner not talk about it... I'd sooner he didn't know till I've talked to Pete... I would sooner give up sleep than miss my evening class... I'd sooner not, if you don't mind.* PHRASE = would rather MODAL inf MODAL *not* inf MODAL that MODAL inf *than* inf MODAL *not*

**soot** /sʊt/ **Soot** is black powder which rises in the smoke from a fire and collects on the inside of chimneys. ❑ *... a wall blackened by soot.* N-UNCOUNT

**soothe** /suːð/ **(soothes, soothing, soothed)** [1] If you **soothe** someone who is angry or upset, you make them feel calmer. ❑ *He would take her in his arms and soothe her... It did not take long for the central bank to soothe investors' fears.* ♦ **sooth|ing** *Put on some nice soothing music.* VERB V n V n ADJ [2] Something that **soothes** a part of your body where there is pain or discomfort makes the pain or discomfort less severe. ❑ *...a body lotion to soothe dry skin.* ♦ **sooth|ing** *Cold tea is very soothing for burns.* VERB V n ADJ

**sooth|say|er** /suːθseɪəʳ/ **(soothsayers)** In former times, **soothsayers** were people who believed they could see into the future and say what was going to happen. N-COUNT

**sooty** /sʊti/ Something that is **sooty** is covered with soot. ❑ *Their uniforms are torn and sooty.* ADJ

**sop** /sɒp/ **(sops)** You describe something as a **sop to** a person when they are offered something small or unimportant in order to prevent them from getting angry or causing trouble. ❑ *This is an obvious sop to the large Irish-American audience.* N-COUNT: oft N *to* n disapproval

**so|phis|ti|cate** /səfɪstɪkeɪt/ **(sophisticates)** A **sophisticate** is someone who knows about culture, fashion, and other matters that are considered socially important. N-COUNT

**so|phis|ti|cat|ed** /səfɪstɪkeɪtɪd/ ◆◇◇ [1] A **sophisticated** machine, device, or method is more advanced or complex than others. ❑ *Honeybees use one of the most sophisticated communication systems* ADJ *of any insect. ...a large and sophisticated new British telescope.* [2] Someone who is **sophisticated** is comfortable in social situations and knows about culture, fashion, and other matters that are considered socially important. ❑ *Claude was a charming, sophisticated companion.* ADJ = refined [3] A **sophisticated** person is intelligent and knows a lot, so that they are able to understand complicated situations. ❑ *These people are very sophisticated observers of the foreign policy scene.* ADJ

**so|phis|ti|ca|tion** /səfɪstɪkeɪʃən/ [1] The **sophistication** of machines or methods is their quality of being more advanced or complex than others. ❑ *Given the sophistication of modern machines, there is little that cannot be successfully washed at home.* N-UNCOUNT [2] **Sophistication** is the quality of being comfortable in social situations and knowing about culture, fashion, and other matters that are considered socially important. ❑ *James Bond is known for his sophistication, his style and his sense of class.* N-UNCOUNT [3] **Sophistication** is the quality of being intelligent and knowing a lot, so that you are able to understand complicated situations. ❑ *Swift said the growing sophistication among biotech investors presented an opportunity for a more specialist investment fund.* N-UNCOUNT

**soph|ist|ries** /sɒfɪstriz/ **Sophistries** are clever arguments that sound convincing but are in fact false. [FORMAL] ❑ *They refuted the 'sophistries of the economists'.* N-PLURAL

**soph|ist|ry** /sɒfɪstri/ **Sophistry** is the practice of using clever arguments that sound convincing but are in fact false. [FORMAL] ❑ *Political selection is more dependent on sophistry and less on economic literacy.* N-UNCOUNT

**sopho|more** /sɒfəmɔːʳ/ **(sophomores)** A **sophomore** is a student in the second year of college or high school. [AM] N-COUNT

**sopo|rif|ic** /sɒpərɪfɪk/ Something that is **soporific** makes you feel sleepy. [FORMAL] ❑ *...the soporific effect of the alcohol.* ADJ

**sop|ping** /sɒpɪŋ/ Something that is **sopping** or **sopping wet** is extremely wet. [INFORMAL] ❑ *They came back sopping wet.* ADJ

**sop|py** /sɒpi/ **(soppier, soppiest)** If you describe someone or something as **soppy**, you mean that they are foolishly sentimental. [BRIT, INFORMAL] ❑ *He's constantly on the phone to his girlfriend being soppy.* ADJ = slushy

**so|pra|no** /səprɑːnoʊ, -præn-/ **(sopranos)** A **soprano** is a woman, girl, or boy with a high singing voice. ❑ *She was the main soprano at the Bolshoi theatre. ...a pretty girl with a sweet soprano voice.* N-COUNT

**sor|bet** /sɔːʳbeɪ, AM -bɪt/ **(sorbets)** **Sorbet** is a frozen dessert made with fruit juice, sugar, and water. [mainly BRIT] ❑ *...a light lemon sorbet.* N-MASS

☑ in AM, use **sherbet**

**sor|cer|er** /sɔːʳsərəʳ/ **(sorcerers)** In fairy stories, a **sorcerer** is a person who performs magic by using the power of evil spirits. N-COUNT = wizard

**sor|cer|ess** /sɔːʳsərɪs/ **(sorceresses)** In fairy stories, a **sorceress** is a woman who performs magic by using the power of evil spirits. N-COUNT = witch

**sor|cery** /sɔːʳsəri/ **Sorcery** is magic performed by using the power of evil spirits. N-UNCOUNT = witchcraft

**sor|did** /sɔːʳdɪd/ [1] If you describe someone's behaviour as **sordid**, you mean that it is immoral or dishonest. ❑ *I don't want to hear the sordid details of your relationship with Sandra.* ADJ [disapproval] [2] If you describe a place as **sordid**, you mean that it is dirty, unpleasant, or depressing. ❑ *...the attic windows of their sordid little rooms.* ADJ [disapproval] = seedy

**sore** /sɔːʳ/ **(sorer, sorest, sores)** [1] If part of your body is **sore**, it causes you pain and discomfort. ❑ *It's years since I've had a sore throat like I did last night... My chest is still sore from the surgery.* ADJ
♦ **sore|ness** *The soreness lasted for about six weeks.* N-UNCOUNT
[2] If you are **sore** about something, you are angry and upset about it. [mainly AM, INFORMAL] ❑ *The result is that they are now all feeling very sore at you.* ADJ: v-link ADJ, oft ADJ *at/about* n/-ing = annoyed [3] A **sore** is a painful place on the body where the skin is infected. ➔ See also **cold sore**. N-COUNT [4] If something is **a sore point with** someone, it is likely to make them angry or embarrassed if you try to discuss it. ❑ *The continuing presence of American troops on Korean soil remains a very sore point with these students.* PHRASE: oft PHR *with/for/between* n [5] to **stick out like a sore thumb** ➔ see **thumb**.

**sore|ly** /sɔːʳli/ **Sorely** is used to emphasize that a feeling such as disappointment or need is very strong. ❑ *I for one was sorely disappointed. ...the potential to earn sorely needed money for Britain from overseas orders... He will be sorely missed.* ADV: ADV adj/prep, ADV before v [emphasis]

**sor|ghum** /sɔːʳgəm/ **Sorghum** is a type of corn that is grown in warm countries. Its grain can be made into flour or syrup. N-UNCOUNT

**so|ror|ity** /sərɔːrɪti/ **(sororities)** In the United States, a **sorority** is a society of female university or college students. N-COUNT

**sor|rel** /sɒrəl, AM sɔːr-/ **Sorrel** is a plant whose leaves have a bitter taste and are sometimes used in salads and sauces. N-UNCOUNT

**sor|row** /sɒroʊ/ **Sorrow** is a feeling of deep sadness or regret. ❑ *It was a time of great sorrow... Words cannot express my sorrow.* N-UNCOUNT

**sor|row|ful** /sɒroʊfʊl/ **Sorrowful** means very sad. [LITERARY] ❑ *His father's face looked suddenly soft and sorrowful.* ADJ

**sor|rows** /sɒroʊz/ **Sorrows** are events or situations that cause deep sadness. ❑ *...the joys and sorrows of everyday living.* to **drown** one's **sorrows** ➔ see **drown**. N-PLURAL

**sor|ry** /sɒri/ **(sorrier, sorriest)** ◆◆◇ [1] You say **'Sorry'** or **'I'm sorry'** as a way of apologizing to someone for something that you have done which has upset them or caused them difficulties, or when you bump into them accidentally. ❑ *'We're all talking at the same time.' — 'Yeah. Sorry.'... Sorry I took so long... Sorry for barging in like this... I'm really sorry if I said anything wrong... I'm sorry to call so late, but I need a favour... The next morning she came into my room and said she was sorry.* CONVENTION [formulae] [2] If you are **sorry** about a situation, you feel regret, sadness, or disappointment about it. ❑ *She was very sorry about all the trouble she'd caused... I'm sorry about what's happened... I'm sorry he's gone... He was sorry to see them go.* ADJ: v-link ADJ, usu ADJ *about* n, ADJ that/to-inf [3] You use **I'm sorry** or **sorry** as an introduction when you are telling a person something that you do not think they will want to hear, for example when you are disagreeing with them or giving them bad news. ❑ *No, I'm sorry, I can't agree with you... 'I'm sorry,' he told the real estate agent, 'but we really must go now.'... Sorry – no baths after ten o'clock... I'm sorry to have to tell you that Janet West is dead.* CONVENTION [4] You use the expression **I'm sorry to say** to express regret together with disappointment or disapproval. ❑ *I've only done half of it, I'm sorry to say... This, I am sorry to say, is almost entirely wishful thinking.* PHRASE: PHR with cl, PHR that [feelings] [5] You say **'I'm sorry'** to express your regret and sadness when you hear sad or unpleasant news. ❑ *I've heard about Mollie – I'm so sorry... 'I'm afraid he's ill.' — 'I'm sorry to hear that.'* CONVENTION [feelings] [6] If you feel **sorry for** someone who is unhappy or in an unpleasant situation, you feel sympathy and sadness for them. ❑ *I felt sorry for him and his colleagues – it must have been so frustrating for them... I am very sorry for the family.* ADJ: v-link ADJ *for* n [7] You say that someone is feeling **sorry for themselves** when you disapprove of the fact that they keep thinking unhappily about their problems, rather than trying to be cheerful and positive. ❑ *What he must not do is to sit around at home feeling sorry for himself.* ADJ: v-link ADJ *for* pron-refl [disapproval] [8] You say **'Sorry?'** when you have not heard something that someone has said and you want them to repeat it. CONVENTION [formulae] = pardon, excuse me [9] You use **sorry** when you correct yourself and use different words to say what you have just said, especially when what you say the second time does not use the words you would nor- CONVENTION mally choose to use. ❑ *Barcelona will be hoping to bring the trophy back to Spain – sorry, Catalonia – for the first time.* [10] If someone or something is in a **sorry** state, they are in a bad state, mentally or physically. ❑ *The fire left Kuwait's oil industry in a sorry state.* [11] **better safe than sorry** → see **safe**. ADJ: ADJ n

**sort** /sɔːʳt/ **(sorts, sorting, sorted)** [1] If you talk about a particular **sort of** something, you are talking about a class of things that have particular features in common and that belong to a larger group of related things. ❑ *What sort of school did you go to?... There are so many different sorts of mushrooms available these days... He had a nice, serious sort of smile... That's just the sort of abuse that he will be investigating... Eddie was playing a game of some sort.* [2] You describe someone as a particular **sort** when you are describing their character. ❑ *He seemed to be just the right sort for the job... She was a very vigorous sort of person... What sort of men were they?* [3] If you **sort** things, you separate them into different classes, groups, or places, for example so that you can do different things with them. ❑ *The students are sorted into ability groups... He unlatched the box and sorted through the papers... I sorted the laundry.* [4] If you get a problem or the details of something **sorted**, you do what is necessary to solve the problem or organize the details. [INFORMAL] ❑ *I'm trying to get my script sorted.*

◆◆◆ N-COUNT: with supp, usu N *of* n = type, kind
N-SING: with supp = type, kind
VERB
*be* V-ed *into* n
V *through* n
V n
VERB: usu passive = sort out
*get* n V-ed

**PHRASES** [5] **All sorts of** things or people means a large number of different things or people. ❑ *There are all sorts of animals, including bears, pigs, kangaroos, and penguins... Self-help groups of all sorts have been running for more than 20 years.* [6] If you describe something as a thing **of sorts** or as a thing **of a sort**, you are suggesting that the thing is of a rather poor quality or standard. ❑ *He made a living of sorts selling pancakes from a van.* [7] You use **sort of** when you want to say that your description of something is not very accurate. [INFORMAL] ❑ *You could even order windows from a catalogue – a sort of mail order stained glass service.* [8] to **sort the wheat from the chaff** → see **chaff**. **nothing of the sort** → see **nothing**.

PHRASE
PHRASE: n PHR
PHRASE [vagueness]

♦ **sort out** [1] If you **sort out** a group of things, you separate them into different classes, groups, or places, for example so that you can do different things with them. ❑ *Sort out all your bills, receipts, invoices and expenses as quickly as possible and keep detailed accounts... Davina was sorting out scraps of material... How do we sort out fact from fiction?* [2] If you **sort out** a problem or the details of something, you do what is necessary to solve the problem or organize the details. ❑ *India and Nepal have sorted out their trade and security dispute... Have you sorted something out for tomorrow night?* [3] If you **sort** someone **out**, you make them realize that they have behaved wrongly, for example by talking to them or by punishing them. [mainly BRIT] ❑ *It was the older women and young mothers who sorted all the troublemakers out... The crucial skill you need to develop is sorting out the parents.* [4] If you **sort yourself out**, you organize yourself or calm yourself so that you can act effectively and reasonably. ❑ *We're in a state of complete chaos here and I need a little time to sort myself out.*

PHRASAL VERB
V P n (not pron)
V P n (not pron) *from* n
PHRASAL VERB
V P n (not pron)
V n P
PHRASAL VERB
V n P
V P n (not pron)
PHRASAL VERB
V pron-refl P

**sor|tie** /sɔːʳti/ **(sorties)** [1] A **sortie** is a brief trip away from your home base, especially a trip to an unfamiliar place. [FORMAL] ❑ *From here we plan several sorties into the countryside on foot.* [2] If a military force makes a **sortie**, it leaves its own position and goes briefly into enemy territory to make an attack. [FORMAL] ❑ *His men made a sortie to Guazatan and took a prisoner.*

N-COUNT = foray
N-COUNT = raid

**sort|ing of|fice** **(sorting offices)** A **sorting office** is a place where letters and parcels that have been posted are taken and sorted according to where they are being sent. [BRIT] N-COUNT

**SOS** /es oʊ es/ An **SOS** is a signal which indicates to other people that you are in danger and need help quickly. ❑ *The ferry did not even have time to send out an SOS.* N-SING

**so-so** If you say that something is **so-so**, you mean that it is average in quality, rather than being very good or very bad. [INFORMAL] ❑ *Their lunch was only so-so.* ADJ = average

**sot|to voce** /sɒtoʊ voʊtʃeɪ/ If you say something **sotto voce**, you say it in a soft voice. [LITERARY] ADV: usu ADV after v

**sou|bri|quet** /soʊbrɪkeɪ/ **(soubriquets)** → see **sobriquet**.

**souf|flé** /suːfleɪ, AM suːfleɪ/ **(soufflés)** also **souffle**. A **soufflé** is a light food made from a mixture of beaten egg whites and other ingredients that is baked in the oven. It can be either sweet or savoury. ❑ *...a superb cheese soufflé.* N-VAR

**sought** /sɔːt/ **Sought** is the past tense and past participle of **seek**.

**sought-after** Something that is **sought-after** is in great demand, usually because it is rare or of very good quality. ❑ *An Olympic gold medal is the most sought-after prize in world sport.* ADJ

**souk** /suːk/ **(souks)** also **suq**. A **souk** is an outdoor market in a Muslim country, especially in North Africa and the Middle East. N-COUNT

**soul** /soʊl/ **(souls)** [1] Your **soul** is the part of you that consists of your mind, character, thoughts, and feelings. Many people believe that your soul continues existing after your body is dead. ❑ *She went to pray for the soul of her late husband... 'I will put my heart and soul into the job,' he promises.* [2] You can refer to someone as a particular kind of **soul** when you are describing their character or condition. ❑ *He's a jolly soul.* [3] You use **soul** in negative statements like **not a soul** to mean nobody at all. ❑ *I've never harmed a soul in my life... There was not a soul there.* [4] **Soul** or **soul music** is a type of pop music performed mainly by black American musicians. It developed from gospel and blues music and often expresses deep emotions. ❑ *...American soul singer Anita Baker.* [5] to **bare** one's **soul** → see **bare**. **body and soul** → see **body**. **the life and soul of the party** → see **life**.

◆◇◇ N-COUNT: usu with supp
N-COUNT: adj N
N-SING: with brd-neg
N-UNCOUNT

**soul-destroying** Activities or situations that are **soul-destroying** make you depressed, because they are boring or because there is no hope of improvement. ❑ *Believing yourself to be in the wrong job can be soul-destroying.* ADJ ≠ inspiring

**soul food** **Soul food** is used to refer to the kind of food, for example corn bread, ham, and greens, that was popular with black Americans in the southern United States and is considered typical of them. [mainly AM] N-UNCOUNT

**soul|ful** /soʊlfʊl/ Something that is **soulful** expresses deep feelings, especially sadness or love. ❑ *...his great, soulful, brown eyes. ...soulful music.* ♦ **soul|ful|ly** *She gazed at him soulfully.* ADJ ≠ soulless; ADV

**soul|less** /soʊlləs/ If you describe a thing or person as **soulless**, you mean that they lack human qualities and the ability to feel or produce deep feelings. ❑ *...a clean and soulless hotel. ...a grey and soulless existence.* ADJ

**soul mate** **(soul mates)** also **soulmate**. A **soul mate** is someone with whom you share a close friendship and deep personal understanding. ❑ *Steve and I became soul mates, near-constant companions.* N-COUNT

**soul mu|sic** **Soul music** or **soul** is a type of pop music performed mainly by black American musicians. It developed from gospel and blues music and often expresses deep emotions. N-UNCOUNT

**soul-searching** **Soul-searching** is a long and careful examination of your thoughts and feelings, especially when you are trying to make a difficult moral decision or thinking about something that has gone wrong. ❑ *My year was really spent doing a lot of soul-searching and trying to find out what had gone wrong in my life.* N-UNCOUNT

**sound**
① NOUN AND VERB USES
② ADJECTIVE USES

①**sound** /saʊnd/ **(sounds, sounding, sounded)** ◆◆◆
⇒ Please look at category 12 to see if the expression you are looking for is shown under another headword. [1] A **sound** is something that you hear. ❑ *Peter heard the sound of gunfire... Liza was so frightened she couldn't make a sound... There was a splintering sound as the railing gave way. ...the sounds of children playing.* N-COUNT [2] **Sound** is energy that travels in waves through air, water, or other substances, and can be heard. ❑ *The aeroplane will travel at twice the speed of sound.* N-UNCOUNT [3] **The sound** on a television, radio, or CD player is what you hear coming from the machine. Its loudness can be controlled. ❑ *She went and turned the sound down... Compact discs have brought about a vast improvement in recorded sound quality.* N-SING: *the* N [4] A singer's or band's **sound** is the distinctive quality of their music. ❑ *He's got a unique sound and a unique style.* N-COUNT: with supp [5] If something such as a horn or a bell **sounds** or if you **sound** it, it makes a noise. ❑ *The buzzer sounded in Daniel's office... A young man sounds the bell to start the Sunday service.* VERB V V n [6] If you **sound** a warning, you publicly give it. If you **sound** a note of caution or optimism, you say publicly that you are cautious or optimistic. ❑ *The Archbishop of Canterbury has sounded a warning to Europe's leaders on third world debt.* VERB V n [7] When you are describing a noise, you can talk about the way it **sounds**. ❑ *They heard what sounded like a huge explosion... The creaking of the hinges sounded very loud in that silence... It sounded as if he were trying to say something.* V-LINK V *like* n V adj V as if [8] When you talk about the way someone **sounds**, you are describing the impression you have of them when they speak. ❑ *She sounded a bit worried... Murphy sounds like a child... She sounded as if she really cared... I thought she sounded a genuinely caring and helpful person.* V-LINK V adj V *like* n V as if V n [9] When you are describing your impression or opinion of something you have heard about or read about, you can talk about the way it **sounds**. ❑ *It sounds like a wonderful idea to me, does it really work?... It sounds as if they might have made a dreadful mistake... She decided that her doctor's advice sounded pretty good... The book is not as morbid as it sounds... I know this sounds a crazy thing for me to ask you.* V-LINK V *like* n V as if V adj V adj V n [10] You can describe your impression of something you have heard about or read about by talking about **the sound of** it. ❑ *Here's a new idea we liked the sound of... From the sound of things, he might well be the same man.* N-SING: *the* N *of* n [11] → See also **-sounding**, **sounding**. [12] to **sound the alarm** → see **alarm**. to **sound the death knell** → see **death knell**. **safe and sound** → see **safe**.

♦ **sound off** If someone **sounds off**, they express their opinions strongly and rather rudely without being asked. [INFORMAL] ❑ *It is surprising how many people start sounding off about something without really deciding what they think about it.* PHRASAL VERB [disapproval] V P *about/on* n Also V P

♦ **sound out** If you **sound** someone **out**, you question them in order to find out what their opinion is about something. ❑ *He is sounding out Middle Eastern governments on ways to resolve the conflict... Sound him out gradually. Make sure it is what he really wants.* PHRASAL VERB V P n (not pron) V n P

②**sound** /saʊnd/ **(sounder, soundest)** [1] If a structure, part of someone's body, or someone's mind is **sound**, it is in good condition or healthy. ❑ *When we bought the house, it was structurally sound... Although the car is basically sound, I was worried about certain areas.* ADJ: usu v-link ADJ, oft adv ADJ [2] **Sound** advice, reasoning, or evidence is reliable and sensible. ❑ *They are trained nutritionists who can give sound advice on diets... Buy a policy only from an insurance company that is financially sound... His reasoning is perfectly sound, but he misses the point.* ADJ [3] If you describe someone's ideas as **sound**, you mean that you approve of them and think they are correct. ❑ *I am not sure that this is sound democratic practice... I think the idea of secularism is a very sound one.* ADJ [approval] [4] If someone is in a **sound** sleep, they are sleeping very deeply. ❑ *She had woken me out of a sound sleep.* ♦ **Sound** is also an adverb. ❑ *He was lying in bed, sound asleep.* ADJ: ADJ n ADV: ADV adj [5] → See also **soundly**.

**sound|alike** /saʊndəlaɪk/ **(soundalikes)** also **sound-alike**. A **soundalike** is someone, especially a singer, whose voice resembles that of a famous person. ❑ *...an Elvis-soundalike.* N-COUNT: oft n-proper N

**sound bar|ri|er** If an aircraft breaks **the sound barrier**, it reaches a speed that is faster than the speed of sound. N-SING: usu *the* N

**sound|bite** /saʊndbaɪt/ **(soundbites)** also **sound bite, sound-bite.** A **soundbite** is a short sentence or phrase, usually from a politician's speech, which is broadcast during a news programme. N-COUNT

**sound|card** /saʊndkɑːʳd/ **(soundcards)** A **soundcard** is a piece of equipment which can be put inside a computer so that the computer can produce music or other sounds. [COMPUTING] N-COUNT

**sound ef|fect** **(sound effects)** **Sound effects** are the sounds that are created artificially to make a play more realistic, especially a radio play. N-COUNT: usu pl

**sound en|gi|neer** **(sound engineers)** A **sound engineer** is a person who works in a recording studio or for a radio or television company, and whose job it is to alter and balance the levels of different sounds as they are recorded. [mainly BRIT] N-COUNT

✔ in AM, use **sound mixer**

**sound|ing** /saʊndɪŋ/ **(soundings)** [1] **The sounding of** a bell or a horn is the act of causing it to make a sound. ❑ *There were 15 minutes between the first air raid alert and the sounding of the all-clear signal.* N-SING: *the* N *of* n [2] If you take **soundings**, you try to find out people's opinions on a subject. ❑ *She will take soundings of the people's wishes before deciding on a course of action.* N-COUNT: usu pl

**-sounding** /-saʊndɪŋ/ **-sounding** combines with adjectives to indicate a quality that a word, phrase, or name seems to have. ❑ *Many literary academics simply parrot a set of impressive-sounding phrases. ...faraway places with strange-sounding names.* → See also **high-sounding**. COMB in ADJ

**sound|ing board** **(sounding boards)** If you use someone as a **sounding board**, you discuss your ideas with them in order to get another opinion. ❑ *He needed a sounding board rather than thinking alone.* N-COUNT

**sound|less** /saʊndləs/ Something that is **soundless** does not make a sound. [LITERARY] ❑ *My bare feet were soundless over the carpet.* ♦ **sound|less|ly** *Joe's lips moved soundlessly.* ADJ = silent ADV

**sound|ly** /saʊndli/ [1] If someone is **soundly** defeated or beaten, they are severely defeated or beaten. ❑ *Duke was soundly defeated in this month's Louisiana governor's race.* ADV: ADV -ed [2] If a decision, opinion, or statement is **soundly** based, there are sensible or reliable reasons behind it. ❑ *Changes must be soundly based in economic reality.* ADV: ADV -ed [approval] [3] If you sleep **soundly**, you sleep deeply and do not wake during your sleep. ❑ *How can he sleep soundly at night?... She was too soundly asleep to hear Stefano's return.* ADV: ADV after v, ADV adj = deeply

**sound mix|er** **(sound mixers)** A **sound mixer** is a person who works in a recording studio or for a radio or television company, and whose job it is to alter and balance the levels of different sounds as they are recorded. N-COUNT = sound engineer

**sound|proof** /saʊndpruːf/ **(soundproofs, soundproofing, soundproofed)** also **sound-proof.** [1] A **soundproof** room, door, or window is designed to prevent all sound from getting in or out. ❑ *The studio isn't soundproof.* ADJ [2] If you **soundproof** a room, you line it with special materials to stop all sound from getting in or out. ❑ *We've soundproofed our home studio.* VERB V n

**sound stage** **(sound stages)** also **soundstage, soundstage.** A **sound stage** is a stage or set which is suitable for recording sound, especially for a film. N-COUNT

**sound sys|tem** **(sound systems)** A **sound system** is a set of equipment for playing recorded music, or for making a band's music able to be heard by everyone at a concert. N-COUNT

**sound|track** /saʊndtræk/ **(soundtracks)** also **sound track.** The **soundtrack** of a film is its sound, speech, and music. It is used especially to refer to the music. N-COUNT

**sound wave** **(sound waves)** also **soundwave. Sound waves** are the waves of energy that we hear as sound. N-COUNT

**soup** /suːp/ **(soups) Soup** is liquid food made by boiling meat, fish, or vegetables in water. ❑ *...home-made chicken soup.* N-MASS: usu supp N

**soup kitch|en** **(soup kitchens)** also **soup-kitchen.** A **soup kitchen** is a place where homeless people or very poor people are provided with free food. N-COUNT

**soup plate** **(soup plates)** A **soup plate** is a deep plate with a wide edge in which soup is served. N-COUNT

**soup spoon** **(soup spoons)** A **soup spoon** is a spoon used for eating soup. The bowl-like part at the end of it is round. N-COUNT

**soupy** /suːpi/ **Soupy** things are like soup or look like soup. ❑ *...swirling soupy water.* ADJ

**sour** /saʊəʳ/ **(sours, souring, soured)** [1] Something that is **sour** has a sharp, unpleasant taste like the taste of a lemon. ❑ *The stewed apple was sour even with honey.* ➔ See also **sweet and sour**. ADJ
[2] **Sour** milk is milk that has an unpleasant taste because it is no longer fresh. ADJ ≠fresh [3] Someone who is **sour** is bad-tempered and unfriendly. ❑ *She made a sour face in his direction.* ♦ **sour|ly** *'Leave my mother out of it,' he said sourly.* ADJ; ADV: ADV with v [4] If a situation or relationship **turns sour** or **goes sour**, it stops being enjoyable or satisfactory. ❑ *Even the European dream is beginning to turn sour... Their songs are filled with tales of love gone sour.* ADJ [5] If a friendship, situation, or attitude **sours** or if something **sours** it, it becomes less friendly, enjoyable, or hopeful. ❑ *If anything sours the relationship, it is likely to be real differences in their world-views... Her mood soured a little.* VERB; V n; V [6] If you refer to someone's attitude as **sour grapes**, you mean that they say that something is worthless or undesirable because they want it themselves but cannot have it. ❑ *Page's response to the suggestion that this might be sour grapes because his company lost the bid is: 'Life's too short for that.'* PHRASE [disapproval]

**source** /sɔːʳs/ **(sources, sourcing, sourced)** ◆◆◇
[1] The **source of** something is the person, place, or thing which you get it from. ❑ *Renewable sources of energy must be used where practical... Tourism, which is a major source of income for the city, may be seriously affected.* N-COUNT: usu N *of* n [2] In business, if a person or firm **sources** a product or a raw material, they find someone who will supply it. [BUSINESS] ❑ *Together they travel the world, sourcing clothes for the small, privately owned company... About 60 per cent of an average car is sourced from outside of the manufacturer.* VERB; V n; V n [3] A **source** is a person or book that provides information for a news story or for a piece of research. ❑ *Military sources say the boat was heading south at high speed.* N-COUNT: usu with supp [4] The **source of** a difficulty is its cause. ❑ *This gave me a clue as to the source of the problem.* N-COUNT: N *of* n = cause [5] The **source** of a river or stream is the place where it begins. ❑ *...the source of the Tiber.* N-COUNT: usu sing

**sour cream** also **soured cream. Sour cream** is cream that has been artificially made sour by being mixed with bacteria. It is used in cooking. N-UNCOUNT

**south** /saʊθ/ also **South.** [1] **The south** is the direction which is on your right when you are looking towards the direction where the sun rises. ❑ *The town lies ten miles to the south of here... All around him, from east to west, north to south, the stars glittered in the heavens.* ◆◆◆ N-UNCOUNT: also *the* N [2] **The south of** a place, country, or region is the part which is in the south. ❑ *...holidays in the south of France.* N-SING: usu *the* N, oft N *of* n [3] If you go **south**, you travel towards the south. ❑ *We did an extremely fast U-turn and shot south up the Boulevard St. Michel... He went south to climb Taishan, a mountain sacred to the Chinese.* ADV: ADV after v [4] Something that is **south of** a place is positioned to the south of it. ❑ *They now own and operate a farm 50 miles south of Rochester... I was living in a house just south of Market Street.* ADV: ADV *of* n [5] The **south** edge, corner, or part of a place or country is the part which is towards the south. ❑ *...the south coast of Alderney.* ADJ: ADJ n
[6] **'South'** is used in the names of some countries, states, and regions in the south of a larger area. ❑ *Next week the President will visit five South American countries in six days. ...the states of Mississippi and South Carolina.* ADJ [7] A **south** wind is a wind that blows from the south. ADJ [8] **The South** is used to refer to the poorer, less developed countries of the world. ❑ *The debate will pit the industrial North against developing countries in the South.* N-SING: *the* N

**south|bound** /saʊθbaʊnd/ **Southbound** roads or vehicles lead or are travelling towards the south. ❑ *...the southbound train from the Scottish Highlands. ...the southbound carriageway of the M61.* ADJ: usu ADJ n

**south-east** also **southeast.** [1] The **south-east** is the direction which is halfway between south and east. ❑ *The city of Ch'eng Tu lies some seven hundred miles to the South-East.* ◆◆◇ N-UNCOUNT: also *the* N [2] **The south-east of** a place, country, or region is the part which is in the south-east. ❑ *...the regional electricity company serving the South-east of England... The heaviest snowfalls today are expected in the south east.* N-SING: usu *the* N, oft N *of* n [3] If you go **south-east**, you travel towards the south-east. ❑ *We turned south-east, making for Portoferraio.* ADV: ADV after v [4] Something that is **south-east of** a place is positioned to the south-east of it. ❑ *...the potteries of Iznik, some 120km south-east of Istanbul.* ADV: ADV *of* n
[5] The **south-east** part of a place, country, or region is the part which is towards the south-east. ❑ *...South-East Asia. ...an island just off Shetland's south-east coast.* ADJ: ADJ n [6] A **south-east** wind is a wind that blows from the south-east. ADJ: ADJ n

**south-easterly** also **southeasterly.** A **south-easterly** point, area, or direction is to the south-east or towards the south-east. ADJ: usu ADJ n

**south-eastern** also **south eastern. South-eastern** means in or from the south-east of a region or country. ❑ *...this city on the south-eastern edge of the United States.* ADJ: usu ADJ n

**south|er|ly** /sʌðəʳli/ [1] A **southerly** point, area, or direction is to the south or towards the south. ❑ *We set off in a southerly direction. ...the most southerly areas of Zimbabwe and Mozambique.* ADJ: usu ADJ n
[2] A **southerly** wind is a wind that blows from the south. ADJ: usu ADJ n

**south|ern** /sʌðəʳn/ **Southern** means in or from the south of a region, state, or country. ❑ *The Everglades National Park stretches across the southern tip of Florida. ...a place where you can sample southern cuisine.* ◆◆◇ ADJ: ADJ n

**south|ern|er** /sʌðəʳnəʳ/ **(southerners)** A **southerner** is a person who was born in or lives in the south of a country. ❑ *Bob Wilson is a Southerner, from Texas... Southerners smoke less and drink less than those in other parts of the country.* N-COUNT

**south|ern|most** /sʌðəʳnmoust/ The **southernmost** part of an area or the **southernmost** place is the one that is farthest towards the south. ❑ *The ancient province of Satsuma lies in the southernmost part of the Japanese island of Kyushu. ...Aswan, Egypt's southernmost city.* ADJ: usu ADJ n

**South Pole** **The South Pole** is the place on the surface of the earth which is farthest towards the south. N-PROPER: *the* N

**south|ward** /saʊθwəʳd/ also **southwards. Southward** or **southwards** means towards the ADV: usu ADV after v, also n ADV south. ❑ *They drove southward... It was a visit that took him to Mogadishu and southwards to Kismayo.* ♦ **Southward** is also an adjective. (ADJ) ❑ *Instead of her normal southward course towards Alexandria and home, she headed west.*

**south-west** also **southwest.** ◆◆◇ [1] (N-UNCOUNT: also *the* N) **The south-west** is the direction which is halfway between south and west. ❑ *...the village of Popplewell, some six miles to the south-west.* [2] (N-SING: usu *the* N, oft N *of* n) **The south-west of** a place, country, or region is the part which is towards the south-west. ❑ *...the mountains in the south west of the USA.* [3] (ADV: ADV after v) If you go **south-west**, you travel towards the south-west. ❑ *We took a plane south-west across the Anatolian plateau to Cappadocia.* [4] (ADV: ADV *of* n) Something that is **south-west of** a place is positioned to the south-west of it. ❑ *...a gold mine at Orkney, south-west of Johannesburg.* [5] (ADJ: ADJ n) The **south-west** part of a place, country, or region is the part which is towards the south-west. ❑ *...a light aircraft crash near Stranraer in South-West Scotland. ...in the south-west corner of my garden.* [6] (ADJ: ADJ n) A **south-west** wind is a wind that blows from the south-west.

**south-westerly** also **southwesterly.** (ADJ: usu ADJ n) A **south-westerly** point, area, or direction is to the south-west or towards the south-west. ❑ *...the most south-westerly tip of Scotland.*

**south-western** also **south western.** (ADJ: usu ADJ n) **South-western** means in or from the south-west of a region or country. ❑ *...towns and villages in south-western Azerbaijan.*

**sou|venir** /suːvənɪəʳ, AM -nɪr/ **(souvenirs)** (N-COUNT: oft N *of* n) A **souvenir** is something which you buy or keep to remind you of a holiday, place, or event. ❑ *...a souvenir of the summer of 1992.*

**sou'|west|er** /saʊwestəʳ/ **(sou'westers)** (N-COUNT) A **sou'wester** is a waterproof hat that is worn especially by sailors in stormy weather. It has a wide brim at the back to keep your neck dry.

**sov|er|eign** /sɒvrɪn/ **(sovereigns)** [1] (ADJ: usu ADJ n = autonomous) A **sovereign** state or country is independent and not under the authority of any other country. ❑ *The Russian Federation declared itself to be a sovereign republic.* [2] (ADJ) **Sovereign** is used to describe the person or institution that has the highest power in a country. ❑ *Sovereign power will continue to lie with the Supreme People's Assembly.* [3] (N-COUNT = monarch) A **sovereign** is a king, queen, or other royal ruler of a country. ❑ *In March 1889, she became the first British sovereign to set foot on Spanish soil.*

**sov|er|eign|ty** /sɒvrɪnti/ (N-UNCOUNT: also N in pl = autonomy) **Sovereignty** is the power that a country has to govern itself or another country or state. ❑ *Britain's concern to protect national sovereignty is far from new.*

**So|vi|et** /soʊviət, sɒv-/ **(Soviets)** [1] (ADJ: usu ADJ n) **Soviet** is used to describe something that belonged or related to the former Soviet Union. ❑ *...the former Soviet empire.* [2] (N-PLURAL) The **Soviets** were the people of the former Soviet Union. ❑ *In 1957, the Soviets launched Sputnik 1 into outer space.* [3] (N-COUNT) A **soviet** was an elected local, regional, or national council in the former Soviet Union.

**sow**
① VERB USES
② NOUN USE

① **sow** /soʊ/ **(sows, sowing, sowed, sown)** [1] (VERB) If you **sow** seeds or **sow** an area of land **with** seeds, you plant the seeds in the ground. ❑ (V n) *Sow the seed in a warm place in February/March...* (be V-ed *with* n) *Yesterday the field opposite was sown with maize.* [2] (VERB) If someone **sows** an undesirable feeling or situation, they cause it to begin and develop. ❑ (V n) *He cleverly sowed doubts into the minds of his rivals.* [3] (PHRASE: V inflects, PHR n) If one thing **sows the seeds of** another, it starts the process which leads eventually to the other thing. ❑ *Rich industrialised countries have sown the seeds of global warming.*

② **sow** /saʊ/ **(sows)** (N-COUNT) A **sow** is an adult female pig.

**sown** /soʊn/ **Sown** is the past participle of **sow.**

**soy** /sɔɪ/ (N-UNCOUNT: usu N n) **Soy** flour, butter, or other food is made from soybeans. [AM]

✔ in BRIT, use **soya**

**soya** /sɔɪə/ (N-UNCOUNT: usu N n) **Soya** flour, butter, or other food is made from soya beans. [BRIT]

✔ in AM, use **soy**

**soya bean (soya beans)** (N-COUNT) **Soya beans** are beans that can be eaten or used to make flour, oil, or soy sauce. [BRIT]

✔ in AM, use **soybeans**

**soy|bean** /sɔɪbiːn/ **(soybeans)** also **soy bean.** (N-COUNT) **Soybeans** are the same as **soya beans.** [AM]

**soy sauce** /sɔɪ sɔːs/ also **soya sauce.** (N-UNCOUNT) **Soy sauce** is a dark brown liquid made from soya beans and used as a flavouring, especially in Chinese cooking.

**spa** /spɑː/ **(spas)** [1] (N-COUNT) A **spa** is a place where water with minerals in it comes out of the ground. People drink the water or go in it in order to improve their health. ❑ *...Fiuggi, a spa town famous for its water.* [2] (N-COUNT) A health **spa** is a kind of hotel where people go to do exercise and have special treatments in order to improve their health.

**space** /speɪs/ **(spaces, spacing, spaced)** ◆◆◇ [1] (N-VAR) You use **space** to refer to an area that is empty or available. The area can be any size. For example, you can refer to a large area outside as a large open **space** or to a small area between two objects as a small **space.** ❑ *Under the plan, bits of open space – fields, golf-course borders and small parks – will be preserved. ...cutting down yet more trees to make space for houses... I had plenty of space to write and sew... The space underneath could be used as a storage area... List in the spaces below the specific changes you have made.* [2] (N-VAR: usu supp N) A particular kind of **space** is the area that is available for a particular activity or for putting a particular kind of thing in. ❑ *...the high cost of office space... Finding a parking space in the summer months is still a virtual impossibility.* [3] (N-UNCOUNT: oft n *of* N) If a place gives a feeling of **space,** it gives an impression of being large and open. ❑ *Large paintings can enhance the feeling of space in small rooms.* [4] (N-UNCOUNT = room) If you give someone **space** to think about something or to develop as a person, you allow them the time and freedom to do this. ❑ *You need space to think everything over.* [5] (N-UNCOUNT) The amount of **space** for a topic to be discussed in a document is the number of pages available to discuss the topic. ❑ *We can't promise to publish a reply as space is limited.* [6] (N-SING: N *of* n) A **space of** time is a period of time. ❑ *They've come a long way in a short space of time.* [7] (N-UNCOUNT) **Space** is the area beyond the Earth's atmosphere, where the stars and planets are. ❑ *The six astronauts on board will spend ten days in space. ...launching satellites into space. ...outer space.* [8] (N-UNCOUNT) **Space** is the whole area within which everything exists. ❑ *The physical universe is finite in space and time.* [9] (VERB) If you **space** a series of things, you arrange them so that they are not all together but have gaps or intervals of time between them. ❑ (V n adv/prep) *Women once again are having fewer children and spacing them further apart...* (V n) *His voice was angry and he spaced the words for emphasis.* ♦ (PHRASAL VERB) **Space out** means the same as **space.** ❑ (V n P) *He talks quite slowly and spaces his words out...* (V P n (not pron)) *I was spacing out the seedlings into divided trays.* ♦ (N-UNCOUNT) **spac|ing** *Generous spacing gives healthier trees and better crops.* [10] → See also **spacing, airspace, breathing space, outer space, personal space.** [11] (PHRASE: PHR after v) If you are staring **into space,** you are looking straight in front of you, without actually looking at anything in particular, for example because you are thinking or because you are feeling shocked. ❑ *He just sat in the dressing-room staring into space.*

**space age** also **space-age.** [1] (N-SING: *the* N) **The space age** is the present period in the history of the world, when travel in space has become possible. [2] You use **space-age** to describe something that is very modern and makes you think of the technology of the space age. ❑ *...a space-age tower of steel and glass.* ADJ: usu ADJ n = futuristic

**space|craft** /speɪskrɑːft, -kræft/ **(spacecraft)** A **spacecraft** is a rocket or other vehicle that can travel in space. N-COUNT

**spaced-out** also **spaced out.** Someone who is **spaced-out** feels as if nothing around them is real, usually because they have taken drugs or because they are very tired. [INFORMAL] ❑ *He's got this spaced-out look.* ADJ

**space flight** **(space flights)** A **space flight** is a trip into space. ❑ *She made her first and only space flight last September.* N-VAR

**space|man** /speɪsmæn/ **(spacemen)** A **spaceman** is a male astronaut; used mainly by children. N-COUNT = astronaut

**space probe** **(space probes)** A **space probe** is a spacecraft with no people in it which is sent into space in order to study the planets and send information about them back to earth. N-COUNT

**space|ship** /speɪsʃɪp/ **(spaceships)** A **spaceship** is a spacecraft that carries people through space. N-COUNT

**space shut|tle** **(space shuttles)** A **space shuttle** or a **shuttle** is a spacecraft that is designed to travel into space and back to earth several times. N-COUNT

**space sta|tion** **(space stations)** A **space station** is a place built for astronauts to live and work in, which is sent into space and then keeps going around the earth. N-COUNT

**space suit** **(space suits)** also **spacesuit.** A **space suit** is a special protective suit that is worn by astronauts in space. N-COUNT

**space walk** **(space walks)** When an astronaut goes on a **space walk**, he or she leaves the spacecraft and works outside it while floating in space. N-COUNT

**spacey** /speɪsi/ **(spacier, spaciest)** also **spacy.** You can use **spacey** to describe things, especially music, which seem strange, especially because they are very modern or like things in a dream. [INFORMAL] ❑ *...brilliant, spacey guitar sounds.* ADJ

**spac|ing** /speɪsɪŋ/ **Spacing** refers to the way that typing or printing is arranged on a page, especially in relation to the amount of space that is left between words or lines. ❑ *Please type or write clearly in double spacing on one side of A4 paper only.* ➔ See also **space**. N-UNCOUNT

**spa|cious** /speɪʃəs/ A **spacious** room or other place is large in size or area, so that you can move around freely in it. ❑ *The house has a spacious kitchen and dining area.* ADJ: usu ADJ n = roomy

**spacy** /speɪsi/ ➔ see **spacey**.

**spade** /speɪd/ **(spades)** [1] A **spade** is a tool used for digging, with a flat metal blade and a long handle. ❑ *... a garden spade... The girls happily played in the sand with buckets and spades.* N-COUNT [2] **Spades** is one of the four suits in a pack of playing cards. Each card in the suit is marked with one or more black symbols: ♠. ❑ *...the ace of spades.* ♦ A **spade** is a playing card of this suit. N-UNCOUNT-COLL; N-COUNT [3] If you say that someone **calls a spade a spade**, you mean that they speak clearly and directly about things, even embarrassing or unpleasant things. ❑ *I'm not at all secretive, and I'm pretty good at calling a spade a spade.* PHRASE: V inflects [approval]

**spade|work** /speɪdwɜːʳk/ **The spadework** is the uninteresting work that has to be done as preparation before you can start a project or activity. ❑ *It is now that the spadework has to be done to lay firm foundations for later success.* N-SING: usu the N

**spa|ghet|ti** /spəgeti/ **Spaghetti** is a type of pasta. It looks like long pieces of string and is usually served with a sauce. N-UNCOUNT

**spa|ghet|ti west|ern** **(spaghetti westerns)** A **spaghetti western** is a film made in Europe, usually by an Italian director, about life in the American Wild West. N-COUNT

**spake** /speɪk/ **Spake** is the very old-fashioned form of the past tense of **speak**.

**spam** /spæm/ **(spams, spamming, spammed)**

> The form **Spam** can also be used for meaning 1.

[1] **Spam** is a cooked meat product made from pork and ham. [TRADEMARK] N-UNCOUNT [2] In computing, to **spam** people or organizations means to send unwanted e-mails to a large number of them, usually as advertising. [COMPUTING] ❑ *...programs that let you spam the newspapers.* VERB; V n ♦ **Spam** is also a noun. ❑ *...a small group of people fighting the spam plague.* N-VAR ♦ **spam|ming** *The consultant who suggested using spamming to raise the company's profile has been fired.* N-UNCOUNT

**span** /spæn/ **(spans, spanning, spanned)** [1] A **span** is the period of time between two dates or events during which something exists, functions, or happens. ❑ *The batteries had a life span of six hours... Gradually the time span between sessions will increase.* N-COUNT: usu supp N [2] Your concentration **span** or your attention **span** is the length of time you are able to concentrate on something or be interested in it. ❑ *His ability to absorb information was astonishing, but his concentration span was short.* N-COUNT: usu supp N [3] If something **spans** a long period of time, it lasts throughout that period of time or relates to that whole period of time. ❑ *His professional career spanned 16 years... The film, spanning almost a quarter-century, tells the story of Henry Hill.* VERB: no passive; V n; V n [4] If something **spans** a range of things, all those things are included in it. ❑ *Bernstein's compositions spanned all aspects of music, from symphonies to musicals.* VERB: no passive; V n [5] The **span** of something that extends or is spread out sideways is the total width of it from one end to the other. ❑ *It is a very pretty butterfly, with a 2 inch wing span.* N-COUNT: usu with supp [6] A bridge or other structure that **spans** something such as a river or a valley stretches right across it. ❑ *Travellers get from one side to the other by walking across a footbridge that spans a little stream.* VERB; V n [7] ➔ See also **spick and span**.

**span|gle** /spæŋgᵊl/ **(spangles)** **Spangles** are small pieces of shiny metal or plastic which are used to decorate clothing or hair. ❑ *...robes that glittered with spangles.* N-COUNT: usu pl

**span|gled** /spæŋgᵊld/ Something that is **spangled** is covered with small shiny objects. ❑ *...spangled, backless dresses.* ADJ

**span|gly** /spæŋgli/ **Spangly** clothes are decorated with a lot of small shiny objects. ❑ *He certainly liked spangly jackets.* ADJ

**Span|iard** /spænjəʳd/ **(Spaniards)** A **Spaniard** is a Spanish citizen, or a person of Spanish origin. N-COUNT

**span|iel** /spænjəl/ **(spaniels)** A **spaniel** is a type of dog with long ears that hang down. N-COUNT

**Span|ish** /spænɪʃ/ [1] **Spanish** means belonging or relating to Spain, or to its people, language, or culture. ❑ *...a Spanish sherry. ...the Spanish Ambassador.* ADJ: usu ADJ n [2] **Spanish** is the main language spoken in Spain, and in many countries in South and Central America. N-UNCOUNT [3] **The Spanish** are the people who come from Spain. N-PLURAL: usu the N

**spank** /spæŋk/ **(spanks, spanking, spanked)** If someone **spanks** a child, they punish them by hitting them on the bottom several times with their hand. ❑ *When I used to do that when I was a kid, my mom would spank me.* VERB; V n

**spank|ing** /spæŋkɪŋ/ **(spankings)** [1] If someone gives a child a **spanking**, they punish them by hitting them on the bottom several times with their hand. ❑ *Andrea gave her son a sound spanking.* N-COUNT [2] If you describe something as **spanking** new, **spanking** clean, or **spanking** white, you mean that it is very new, very clean, or very white. [INFORMAL] ❑ *...a spanking new Mercedes.* ADV: ADV adj [emphasis]

**span|ner** /spænəʳ/ **(spanners)** 1 A **spanner** is a metal tool whose end fits round a nut so that you can turn it to loosen or tighten it. [mainly BRIT] → See picture on page 1709. N-COUNT

✔ in AM, usually use **wrench**, **monkey wrench**

2 If someone **throws a spanner in the works**, they prevent something happening smoothly in the way that it was planned, by causing a problem or difficulty. [BRIT] ❑ *A bad result is sure to throw a spanner in the works.* PHRASE: V inflects

✔ in AM, use **throw a wrench**, **throw a monkey wrench**

**spar** /spɑːʳ/ **(spars, sparring, sparred)** 1 If you **spar with** someone, you box using fairly gentle blows instead of hitting your opponent hard, either when you are training or when you want to test how quickly your opponent reacts. ❑ *With protective gear on you can spar with a partner... They sparred for a moment, on the brink of a full fight.* V-RECIP; V *with* n; pl-n V 2 If you **spar with** someone, you argue with them but not in an aggressive or serious way. ❑ *Over the years he sparred with his friend Jesse Jackson over political tactics... They had always gotten along, even when they sparred.* V-RECIP; V *with* n; pl-n V

**spare** /speəʳ/ **(spares, sparing, spared)** 1 You use **spare** to describe something that is the same as things that you are already using, but that you do not need yet and are keeping ready in case another one is needed. ❑ *Don't forget to take a few spare batteries... He could have taken a spare key... The wagons carried spare ammunition.* ◆◇◇ ADJ: usu ADJ n ♦ **Spare** is also a noun. ❑ *Give me the trunk key and I'll get the spare.* N-COUNT 2 You use **spare** to describe something that is not being used by anyone, and is therefore available for someone to use. ❑ *The spare bedroom is on the second floor... There was hardly a spare inch of space to be found.* ADJ: usu ADJ n 3 If you have something such as time, money, or space **to spare**, you have some extra time, money, or space that you have not used or which you do not need. ❑ *You got here with ninety seconds to spare... It's not as if he has money to spare.* VERB: only to-inf; V; V 4 If you **spare** time or another resource **for** a particular purpose, you make it available for that purpose. ❑ *She said that she could only spare 35 minutes for our meeting... He suggested that his country could not spare the troops for such an operation.* VERB; V n; V n 5 If a person or a place **is spared**, they are not harmed, even though other people or places have been. [LITERARY] ❑ *We have lost everything, but thank God, our lives have been spared.* VERB: usu passive; *be* V-ed 6 If you **spare** someone an unpleasant experience, you prevent them from suffering it. ❑ *I wanted to spare Frances the embarrassment of discussing this subject... She's just trying to spare Shawna's feelings.* VERB; V n n; V n 7 → See also **sparing**. 8 If you **spare a thought for** an unfortunate person, you make an effort to think sympathetically about them and their bad luck. ❑ *Spare a thought for the nation's shopkeepers – consumer sales slid again in May.* PHRASE: V inflects, PHR n

**spare part** **(spare parts)** **Spare parts** are parts that you can buy separately to replace old or broken parts in a piece of equipment. They are usually parts that are designed to be easily removed or fitted. N-COUNT: usu pl

**spare room** **(spare rooms)** A **spare room** is a bedroom which is kept especially for visitors to sleep in. N-COUNT

**spare time** Your **spare time** is the time during which you do not have to work and you can do whatever you like. ❑ *In her spare time she read books on cooking.* N-UNCOUNT: usu poss N

**spare tyre** **(spare tyres)**

✔ in AM, use **spare tire**

1 A **spare tyre** is a wheel with a tyre on it that you keep in your car in case you get a flat tyre and need to replace one of your wheels. N-COUNT 2 If you describe someone as having a **spare tyre**, you mean that they are fat around the waist. [mainly BRIT, INFORMAL] N-COUNT

**spare wheel** **(spare wheels)** A **spare wheel** is a wheel with a tyre on it that you keep in your car in case you get a flat tyre and need to replace one of your wheels. [mainly BRIT] N-COUNT

✔ in AM, use **spare tire**

**spar|ing** /speərɪŋ/ Someone who is **sparing with** something uses it or gives it only in very small quantities. ❑ *Her sparing use of make-up only seemed to enhance her classically beautiful features.* ADJ ♦ **spar|ing|ly** *Medication is used sparingly.* ADV: ADV after v

**spark** /spɑːʳk/ **(sparks, sparking, sparked)** 1 A **spark** is a tiny bright piece of burning material that flies up from something that is burning. ❑ *The fire gradually got bigger and bigger. Sparks flew off in all directions.* ◆◇◇ N-COUNT 2 A **spark** is a flash of light caused by electricity. It often makes a loud sound. ❑ *He passed an electric spark through a mixture of gases.* N-COUNT 3 If something **sparks**, sparks of fire or light come from it. ❑ *The wires were sparking above me... I stared into the flames of the fire as it sparked to life.* VERB; V; V prep 4 If a burning object or electricity **sparks** a fire, it causes a fire. ❑ *A dropped cigarette may have sparked the fire.* VERB = start; V n 5 A **spark of** a quality or feeling, especially a desirable one, is a small but noticeable amount of it. ❑ *His music lacked that vital spark of imagination.* N-COUNT: N *of* n 6 If one thing **sparks** another, the first thing causes the second thing to start happening. ❑ *What was it that sparked your interest in motoring? ...a row sparked by a comment about his sister.* VERB = cause; V n; V-ed ♦ **Spark off** means the same as **spark**. ❑ *That incident sparked it off... His book, Animal Liberation, sparked off a revolution in the way we think about animals.* PHRASAL VERB; V n P; V P n (not pron) 7 → See also **bright spark**. 8 If **sparks fly** between people, they discuss something in an excited or angry way. ❑ *They are not afraid to tackle the issues or let the sparks fly when necessary.* PHRASE: V inflects

♦ **spark off** → see **spark 6**.

**spar|kle** /spɑːʳkəl/ **(sparkles, sparkling, sparkled)** 1 If something **sparkles**, it is clear and bright and shines with a lot of very small points of light. ❑ *The jewels on her fingers sparkled... His bright eyes sparkled. ...the sparkling blue waters of the ocean.* VERB = glitter; V; V; V-ing ♦ **Sparkle** is also a noun. ❑ *...the sparkle of coloured glass.* N-UNCOUNT 2 **Sparkles** are small points of light caused by light reflecting off a clear bright surface. ❑ *...sparkles of light... There was a sparkle in her eye that could not be hidden.* N-COUNT 3 Someone who **sparkles** is lively, intelligent, and witty. ❑ *She sparkles, and has as much zest as a person half her age.* VERB approval; V ♦ **Sparkle** is also a noun. ❑ *There was little sparkle in their performance.* N-UNCOUNT ♦ **spar|kling** *He is sparkling and versatile in front of the camera.* ADJ 4 → See also **sparkling**.

**spar|kler** /spɑːʳkləʳ/ **(sparklers)** A **sparkler** is a small firework that you can hold as it burns. It looks like a piece of thick wire and burns with a lot of small bright sparks. N-COUNT

**spar|kling** /spɑːʳklɪŋ/ 1 **Sparkling** drinks are slightly fizzy. ❑ *...a glass of sparkling wine. ...a new lightly sparkling drink.* ADJ: usu ADJ n 2 If a company is described as having **sparkling** figures or **sparkling** results, it has performed very well and made a lot of money. [JOURNALISM] ❑ *Top retailer Marks & Spencer has romped in with another set of sparkling results.* ADJ: usu ADJ n 3 → See also **sparkle**.

**spar|kly** /spɑːʳkli/ **Sparkly** things sparkle. [INFORMAL] ❑ *...a sparkly toy necklace... Her eyes were sparkly.* ADJ

**spark plug** **(spark plugs)** A **spark plug** is a device in the engine of a motor vehicle, which produces electric sparks to make the petrol burn. N-COUNT

**sparky** /spɑːʳki/ **(sparkier, sparkiest)** **Sparky** people or events are lively and entertaining. [BRIT, INFORMAL] ❑ *She's a terrific, sparky girl.* ADJ = lively

**spar|ring part|ner** **(sparring partners)** 1 A boxer's **sparring partner** is another boxer who he or she fights regularly in training. N-COUNT 2 Your N-COUNT

**sparring partner** is a person with whom you regularly have friendly arguments.

**spar|row** /spærəʊ/ **(sparrows)** A **sparrow** is a small brown bird that is very common in Britain. N-COUNT

**sparse** /spɑːʳs/ **(sparser, sparsest)** Something that is **sparse** is small in number or amount and spread out over an area. ❑ *Many slopes are rock fields with sparse vegetation... Traffic was sparse on the highway.* ADJ ♦ **sparse|ly** *...the sparsely populated interior region, where there are few roads.* ADV: usu ADV -ed

**spar|tan** /spɑːʳtən/ A **spartan** lifestyle or existence is very simple or strict, with no luxuries. ❑ *Their spartan lifestyle prohibits a fridge or a phone.* ADJ = austere ≠ luxurious

**spasm** /spæzəm/ **(spasms)** 1 A **spasm** is a sudden tightening of your muscles, which you cannot control. ❑ *A muscular spasm in the coronary artery can cause a heart attack... A lack of magnesium causes muscles to go into spasm.* N-VAR: oft into N = convulsion 2 A **spasm** is a sudden strong pain or unpleasant emotion which lasts for a short period of time. [WRITTEN] ❑ *A spasm of pain brought his thoughts back to the present.* N-COUNT: usu N of n

**spas|mod|ic** /spæzmɒdɪk/ Something that is **spasmodic** happens suddenly, for short periods of time, and at irregular intervals. ❑ *He managed to stifle the spasmodic sobs of panic rising in his throat.* ADJ = intermittent

**spas|tic** /spæstɪk/ **(spastics)** Someone who is **spastic** is born with a disability which makes it difficult for them to control their muscles, especially in their arms and legs. This word could cause offence, and most people now refer to someone with this disability as having **cerebral palsy**. ADJ ♦ A **spastic** is someone who is spastic. N-COUNT

**spat** /spæt/ **(spats)** 1 **Spat** is the past tense and past participle of **spit**. 2 A **spat** between people, countries, or organizations is a disagreement between them. ❑ *...a spat between America and Germany over interest rates and currencies.* N-COUNT

**spate** /speɪt/ **(spates)** A **spate of** things, especially unpleasant things, is a large number of them that happen or appear within a short period of time. ❑ *...the recent spate of attacks on horses.* N-COUNT: usu sing, usu N of n = series

**spa|tial** /speɪʃəl/ 1 **Spatial** is used to describe things relating to areas. ❑ *...the spatial distribution of black employment and population in South Africa. ...spatial constraints.* ADJ: ADJ n 2 Your **spatial** ability is your ability to see and understand the relationships between shapes, spaces, and areas. ❑ *His manual dexterity and fine spatial skills were wasted on routine tasks. ...spatial awareness.* ADJ: ADJ n

**spat|ter** /spætəʳ/ **(spatters, spattering, spattered)** If a liquid **spatters** a surface or you **spatter** a liquid over a surface, drops of the liquid fall on an area of the surface. VERB = splatter ❑ *He stared at the rain spattering on the glass...* V prep *Gently turn the fish, being careful not to spatter any hot butter on yourself...* V n prep *Blood spattered the dark concrete.* V n

**-spattered** /-spætəʳd/ **-spattered** is added to nouns to form adjectives which indicate that a liquid has spattered onto something. ❑ *...the blood-spattered body.* COMB in ADJ = -splattered

**spatu|la** /spætʃʊlə/ **(spatulas)** A **spatula** is an object like a knife with a wide, flat blade. Spatulas are used in cooking. ➔ See picture on page 1710. ❑ *Spoon the batter into the prepared pan, smoothing over the top with a spatula.* N-COUNT

**spawn** /spɔːn/ **(spawns, spawning, spawned)** 1 **Spawn** is a soft, jelly-like substance containing the eggs of fish, or of animals such as frogs. ❑ *...her passion for collecting frog spawn.* N-UNCOUNT: usu n N 2 When fish or animals such as frogs **spawn**, they lay their eggs. ❑ *...fish species like salmon and trout which go upstream, spawn and then die.* VERB V 3 If something **spawns** something else, it causes it to happen or to be created. [LITERARY] ❑ *Tyndall's inspired work spawned a whole new branch of science.* VERB V n

**spay** /speɪ/ **(spays, spaying, spayed)** When a female animal **is spayed**, it has its ovaries removed so that it cannot become pregnant. ❑ *All bitches should be spayed unless being used for breeding.* VERB: usu passive = neuter be V-ed

**speak** /spiːk/ **(speaks, speaking, spoke, spoken)** ♦♦♦ 1 When you **speak**, you use your voice in order to say something. ❑ *He tried to speak, but for once, his voice had left him... I rang the hotel and spoke to Louie... She says she must speak with you at once... She cried when she spoke of Oliver. ...as I spoke these idiotic words.* VERB V, V to/with n, V to/with n, V of/about n, V n ♦ **spo|ken** *...a marked decline in the standards of written and spoken English in Britain.* ADJ: ADJ n 2 When someone **speaks to** a group of people, they make a speech. ❑ *When speaking to the seminar Mr Franklin spoke of his experience, gained on a recent visit to Trinidad... He's determined to speak at the Democratic Convention... The President spoke of the need for territorial compromise.* VERB V to n, V, V of n 3 If you **speak for** a group of people, you make their views and demands known, or represent them. ❑ *He said it was the job of the Church to speak for the underprivileged... I speak for all 7,000 members of our organization.* VERB V for n, V for n 4 If you **speak** a foreign language, you know the language and are able to have a conversation in it. ❑ *He doesn't speak English.* VERB V n 5 People sometimes mention something that has been written by saying what the author **speaks of**. ❑ *Throughout the book Liu speaks of the abuse of Party power... St Paul speaks of the body as the 'temple of the Holy Spirit'.* VERB V of n, V of n as n 6 If two people **are not speaking**, they no longer talk to each other because they have quarrelled. ❑ *He is not speaking to his mother because of her friendship with his ex-wife... The co-stars are still not speaking.* V-RECIP: with neg V to n, pl-n V 7 If you say that something **speaks for itself**, you mean that its meaning or quality is so obvious that it does not need explaining or pointing out. ❑ *...the figures speak for themselves – low order books, bleak prospects at home and a worsening outlook for exports.* VERB: no cont V for pron-refl 8 ➔ See also **speaking**. 9 If you say '**Speak for yourself**' when someone has said something, you mean that what they have said is only their opinion or applies only to them. [INFORMAL] ❑ *'We're not blaming you,' Kate said. 'Speak for yourself,' Boris muttered.* CONVENTION

**PHRASES** 10 If a person or thing **is spoken for** or **has been spoken for**, someone has claimed them or asked for them, so no-one else can have them. ❑ *She'd probably drop some comment about her 'fiancé' into the conversation so that he'd think she was already spoken for.* PHRASE: V inflects 11 Nothing **to speak of** means 'hardly anything' or 'only unimportant things'. ❑ *They have no weaponry to speak of... 'Any fresh developments?' — 'Nothing to speak of.'* PHRASE: n PHR, with brd-neg 12 If you **speak well of** someone or **speak highly of** someone, you say good things about them. If you **speak ill of** someone, you criticize them. ❑ *Both spoke highly of the Russian president... It seemed she found it difficult to speak ill of anyone.* PHRASE: V inflects, PHR n 13 You use **so to speak** to draw attention to the fact that you are describing or referring to something in a way that may be amusing or unusual rather than completely accurate. ❑ *I ought not to tell you but I will, since you're in the family, so to speak.* PHRASE: PHR with cl 14 If you are **on speaking terms with** someone, you are quite friendly with them and often talk to them. ❑ *For a long time her mother and her grandmother had hardly been on speaking terms.* PHRASE: usu v-link PHR, oft PHR with n 15 to **speak** your **mind** ➔ see **mind**. to **speak volumes** ➔ see **volume**.

♦ **speak out** If you **speak out** against something or in favour of something, you say publicly that you think it is bad or good. ❑ *As tempers rose, he spoke out strongly against some of the radical ideas for selling off state-owned property... Even then, she continued to speak out at rallies around the country.* PHRASAL VERB V P prep, V P

♦ **speak up** 1 If you **speak up**, you say something, especially to defend a person or protest about something, rather than just saying nothing. ❑ *Uncle Herbert never argued, never spoke up for himself.* PHRASAL VERB V P for n 2 If you ask someone to **speak up**, you are asking them to speak more loudly. ❑ *I'm quite deaf – you'll have to speak up.* PHRASAL VERB: no cont V P

**-speak** /-spiːk/ **-speak** is used to form nouns which refer to the kind of language used by a particular person or by people involved in a particular activity. You use **-speak** when you disapprove of this kind of language because it is difficult for other people to understand. ❑ *Unfortunately, the simplicity of this message is almost lost within his constant management-speak.* COMB in N-UNCOUNT [disapproval]

**speak|easy** /spiːkiːzi/ **(speakeasies)** A **speakeasy** was a place where people could buy alcoholic drinks illegally in the United States between 1920 and 1933, when alcohol was forbidden. N-COUNT

**speak|er** /spiːkəʳ/ **(speakers)** [1] A **speaker** at a meeting, conference, or other gathering is a person who is making a speech or giving a talk. ❑ *Among the speakers at the gathering was Treasury Secretary Nicholas Brady... He was not a good speaker.* ◆◇◇ N-COUNT
[2] A **speaker of** a particular language is a person who speaks it, especially one who speaks it as their first language. ❑ *...in the Ukraine, where a fifth of the population are Russian speakers... The Department has a growing section which teaches English to speakers of other languages.* ➔ See also **native speaker**. N-COUNT: n N, N *of* n
[3] In the parliament or legislature of many countries, the **Speaker** is the person who is in charge of meetings. ❑ *...the Speaker of the Polish Parliament... Mr. Speaker, our message to the president is simple.* N-PROPER; N-VOC: *Mr/Madam* N
[4] A **speaker** is a person who is speaking. ❑ *From a simple gesture or the speaker's tone of voice, the Japanese listener gleans the whole meaning.* N-COUNT: usu *the* N
[5] A **speaker** is a piece of electrical equipment, for example part of a radio or set of equipment for playing CDs or tapes, through which sound comes out. ❑ *For a good stereo effect, the speakers should not be too wide apart.* N-COUNT = *loudspeaker*

**speak|ing** /spiːkɪŋ/ [1] **Speaking** is the activity of giving speeches and talks. ❑ *His work schedule still includes speaking engagements and other public appearances.* N-UNCOUNT: oft supp N
PHRASES [2] You can say '**speaking as** a parent' or '**speaking as** a teacher', for example, to indicate that the opinion you are giving is based on your experience as a parent or as a teacher. ❑ *Well, speaking as a journalist I'm dismayed by the amount of pressure there is for pictures of combat.* PREP-PHRASE
[3] You can say **speaking of** something that has just been mentioned as a way of introducing a new topic which has some connection with that thing. ❑ *There's plenty of time to drop hints for Christmas presents! And speaking of presents, we have 100 exclusive fragrance collections to give away.* PREP-PHRASE = *talking of*
[4] You use **speaking** in expressions such as **generally speaking** and **technically speaking** to indicate which things or which particular aspect of something you are talking about. ❑ *Generally speaking there was no resistance to the idea... Politically speaking, do you think that these moves have been effective?* PHRASE: PHR with cl

**-speaking** /-spiːkɪŋ/ **-speaking** combines with nouns referring to languages to form adjectives which indicate what language someone speaks, or what language is spoken in a particular region. ❑ *Lessons with English-speaking instructors can be booked and paid for in the resort. ...in the mainly French-speaking province of Quebec.* COMB in ADJ: ADJ n

**spear** /spɪəʳ/ **(spears, spearing, speared)** [1] A **spear** is a weapon consisting of a long pole with a sharp metal point attached to the end. N-COUNT
[2] If you **spear** something, you push or throw a pointed object into it. ❑ *Spear a piece of fish with a carving fork and dip it in the batter.* VERB V n
[3] Asparagus or broccoli **spears** are individual stalks of asparagus or broccoli. N-COUNT: with supp

**spear|head** /spɪəʳhed/ **(spearheads, spearheading, spearheaded)** If someone **spearheads** a campaign or an attack, they lead it. [JOURNALISM] ❑ *...Esther Rantzen, who is spearheading a national campaign against bullying.* VERB V n

**spear|mint** /spɪəʳmɪnt/ **Spearmint** is a plant whose leaves have a strong smell and taste. It is often used for flavouring foods, especially sweets. N-UNCOUNT

**spec** /spek/ **(specs)** [1] Someone's **specs** are their glasses. [INFORMAL] ❑ *...a young businessman in his specs and suit.* N-PLURAL: also *a pair of* N
[2] The **spec** for something, especially a machine or vehicle, is its design and the features included in it. [INFORMAL] ❑ *The standard spec includes stainless steel holding tanks.* N-COUNT = *specification*
[3] If you do something **on spec**, you do it hoping to get something that you want, but without being asked or without being certain to get it. [INFORMAL] ❑ *When searching for a job Adrian favours networking and writing letters on spec.* PHRASE: PHR after v

**spe|cial** /speʃᵊl/ **(specials)** [1] Someone or something that is **special** is better or more important than other people or things. ❑ *You're very special to me, darling... There are strong arguments for holidays at Easter and Christmas because these are special occasions... My special guest will be comedian Ben Elton.* ◆◆◆ ADJ
[2] **Special** means different from normal. ❑ *In special cases, a husband can deduct the travel expenses of his wife who accompanies him on a business trip... So you didn't notice anything special about him?* ADJ: ADJ n ≠ *normal*
[3] You use **special** to describe someone who is officially appointed or who has a particular position specially created for them. ❑ *Frank Deford is a special correspondent for Newsweek magazine.* ADJ: ADJ n
[4] **Special** institutions are for people who have serious physical or mental problems. ❑ *Police are still searching for a convicted rapist, who escaped from Broadmoor special hospital yesterday.* ADJ: ADJ n
[5] You use **special** to describe something that relates to one particular person, group, or place. ❑ *Every anxious person will have his or her own special problems or fears. ...it requires a very special brand of courage to fight dictators.* ADJ: ADJ n = *unique*
[6] A **special** is a product, programme, or meal which is not normally available, or which is made for a particular purpose. ❑ *...complaints about the BBC's Hallowe'en special, 'Ghostwatch'... Grocery stores have to offer enough specials to bring people into the store.* N-COUNT

**Spe|cial Branch** The **Special Branch** is the department of the British police that is concerned with political security and deals with things such as terrorism and visits by foreign leaders. N-PROPER: oft *the* N

**spe|cial edu|ca|tion** **Special education** is teaching for pupils who need extra help with their studies. ❑ *The school has a special education unit.* N-UNCOUNT: oft N n

**spe|cial ef|fect** **(special effects)** In film, **special effects** are unusual pictures or sounds that are created by using special techniques. ❑ *...a Hollywood horror film with special effects that are not for the nervous.* N-COUNT: usu pl

**spe|cial|ise** /speʃəlaɪz/ ➔ see **specialize**.

**spe|cial|ism** /speʃəlɪzəm/ **(specialisms)** [1] Someone's **specialism** is a particular subject or skill which they study and know a lot about. ❑ *...a teacher with a specialism in mathematics.* N-COUNT
[2] **Specialism** is the act of specializing in a particular subject. ❑ *The needs of children may not be best met by an over-emphasis on subject specialism.* N-UNCOUNT

**spe|cial|ist** /speʃəlɪst/ **(specialists)** A **specialist** is a person who has a particular skill or knows a lot about a particular subject. ❑ *...a specialist in diseases of the nervous system.* ◆◇◇ N-COUNT: usu N n, n N, N *in/on* n = *expert*

**spe|ci|al|ity** /speʃiælɪti/ **(specialities)** [1] Someone's **speciality** is a particular type of work that they do most or do best, or a subject that they know a lot about. [mainly BRIT] ❑ *My father was a historian of repute. His speciality was the history of Germany.* N-COUNT

✔ in AM, usually use **specialty**

[2] A **speciality** of a particular place is a special food or product that is always very good there. [mainly BRIT] ❑ *Rhineland dishes are a speciality of the restaurant.* N-COUNT: with supp

✔ in AM, usually use **specialty**

**spe|cial|ize** /spe̲ʃəlaɪz/ **(specializes, specializing, specialized)** ◆◇◇

☑ in BRIT, also use **specialise**

If you **specialize in** a thing, you know a lot about it and concentrate a great deal of your time and energy on it, especially in your work or when you are studying or training. You also use **specialize** to talk about a restaurant which concentrates on a particular type of food. ❑ *...a University professor who specializes in the history of the Russian empire. ...a Portuguese restaurant which specializes in seafood.* VERB V *in* n V *in* n ♦ **spe|ciali|za|tion** /spe̲ʃəlaɪze̲ɪʃən/ **(specializations)** *This degree offers a major specialisation in Social Policy alongside a course in Sociology.* N-VAR

**spe|cial|ized** /spe̲ʃəlaɪzd/

☑ in BRIT, also use **specialised**

Someone or something that is **specialized** is trained or developed for a particular purpose or area of knowledge. ❑ *Cocaine addicts get specialized support from knowledgeable staff. ...a specialized knowledge of American History.* ADJ

**spe|cial|ly** /spe̲ʃəli/ [1] If something has been done **specially for** a particular person or purpose, it has been done only for that person or purpose. ❑ *...a soap specially designed for those with sensitive skins... The school is specially for children whose schooling has been disrupted by illness.* ADV: ADV with v, oft ADV *for* n [2] **Specially** is used to mean more than usually or more than other things. [INFORMAL] ❑ *What was specially enjoyable about that job?* ADV: ADV with v, ADV with cl/group

**spe|cial needs** People with **special needs** are people who need special help or care, for example because they are physically or mentally disabled. [BRIT] ❑ *...a school for children with special needs.* N-PLURAL: oft N n

**spe|cial of|fer** **(special offers)** A **special offer** is a product, service, or programme that is offered at reduced prices or rates. ❑ *Ask about special offers on our new 2-week holidays.* N-COUNT

**spe|cial plead|ing** If someone is using **special pleading**, they are trying to persuade you to do something by only telling you the facts that support their case. ❑ *The Secretary of State has given in to special pleading.* N-UNCOUNT

**spe|cial school** **(special schools)** A **special school** is a school for children who have some kind of serious physical or mental problem. [BRIT] N-COUNT

**spe|cial|ty** /spe̲ʃəlti/ **(specialties)** [1] Someone's **specialty** is a particular type of work that they do most or do best, or a subject that they know a lot about. [AM] ❑ *His specialty is international law.* N-COUNT

☑ in BRIT, use **speciality**

[2] A **specialty** of a particular place is a special food or product that is always very good there. [AM] ❑ *...seafood, paella, empanadas and other specialties.* N-COUNT

☑ in BRIT, use **speciality**

**spe|cies** /spi̲ːʃiz/ **(species)** A **species** is a class of plants or animals whose members have the same main characteristics and are able to breed with each other. ❑ *Pandas are an endangered species... There are several thousand species of trees here.* ◆◇◇ N-COUNT

**spe|cif|ic** /spɪsɪ̲fɪk/ [1] You use **specific** to refer to a particular fixed area, problem, or subject. ❑ *Massage may help to increase blood flow to specific areas of the body... There are several specific problems to be dealt with. ...the specific needs of the individual.* ◆◆◇ ADJ: ADJ n = particular [2] If someone is **specific**, they give a description that is precise and exact. You can also use **specific** to describe their description. ❑ *These nerve centres generate rhythmic movements; or to be more specific, rhythmic stomach movements... This report offered the most specific and accurate description of the problems.* ADJ = precise ≠ vague ♦ **speci|fic|ity** /spe̲sɪfɪ̲sɪti/ *...the kind of extreme specificity normally associated only with computer programmes.* N-UNCOUNT [3] Something that is **specific to** a particular thing is connected with that thing only. ❑ *Send your resume with a cover letter that is specific to that particular job.* ADJ: usu v-link ADJ *to* n = peculiar ♦ **Specific** is also used after nouns. ❑ *Most studies of trade have been country-specific. ...a job-specific course.* COMB in ADJ

**spe|cifi|cal|ly** /spɪsɪ̲fɪkli/ [1] You use **specifically** to emphasize that something is given special attention and considered separately from other things of the same kind. ❑ *...the first nursing home designed specifically for people with AIDS... We haven't specifically targeted school children. ...the only book specifically about that event.* ◆◇◇ ADV: ADV with v [emphasis] [2] You use **specifically** to add something more precise or exact to what you have already said. ❑ *...the Christian, and specifically Protestant, religion. ...brain cells, or more specifically, neurons.* ADV: ADV with group [3] You use **specifically** to indicate that something has a restricted nature, as opposed to being more general in nature. ❑ *...a specifically female audience... This is a European, and not a specifically British, problem.* ADV: ADV adj [4] If you state or describe something **specifically**, you state or describe it precisely and clearly. ❑ *I specifically asked for this steak rare.* ADV: ADV with v

**speci|fi|ca|tion** /spe̲sɪfɪke̲ɪʃən/ **(specifications)** A **specification** is a requirement which is clearly stated, for example about the necessary features in the design of something. ❑ *Troll's exclusive, personalized luggage is made to our own exacting specifications in heavy-duty PVC/nylon... Legislation will require UK petrol companies to meet an EU specification for petrol.* N-COUNT

**spe|cif|ics** /spɪsɪ̲fɪks/ The **specifics** of a subject are the details of it that need to be considered. ❑ *Things improved when we got down to the specifics.* N-PLURAL = particulars

**speci|fy** /spe̲sɪfaɪ/ **(specifies, specifying, specified)** [1] If you **specify** something, you give information about what is required or should happen in a certain situation. ❑ *They specified a spacious entrance hall... He has not specified what action he would like them to take.* VERB V n V wh [2] If you **specify** what should happen or be done, you explain it in an exact and detailed way. ❑ *Each recipe specifies the size of egg to be used... One rule specifies that learner drivers must be supervised by adults... Patients eat together at a specified time.* VERB V n V that V-ed

**speci|men** /spe̲sɪmɪn/ **(specimens)** [1] A **specimen** is a single plant or animal which is an example of a particular species or type and is examined by scientists. ❑ *200,000 specimens of fungus are kept at the Komarov Botanical Institute. ...North American fossil specimens.* N-COUNT: usu with supp [2] A **specimen of** something is an example of it which gives an idea of what the whole of it is like. ❑ *Job applicants have to submit a specimen of handwriting. ...a specimen bank note.* N-COUNT: usu with supp [3] A **specimen** is a small quantity of someone's urine, blood, or other body fluid which is examined in a medical laboratory, in order to find out if they are ill or if they have been drinking alcohol or taking drugs. ❑ *He refused to provide a specimen.* N-COUNT = sample

**spe|cious** /spi̲ːʃəs/ Something that is **specious** seems to exist or be true, but is not real or true. [FORMAL] ❑ *It is unlikely that the Duke was convinced by such specious arguments.* ADJ

**speck** /spe̲k/ **(specks)** [1] A **speck** is a very small stain, mark, or shape. ❑ *...a speck of blood.* N-COUNT: oft N *of* n [2] A **speck** is a very small piece of a powdery substance. ❑ *Billy leaned forward and brushed a speck of dust off his shoes.* N-COUNT: oft N *of* n

**speck|led** /spe̲kəld/ A **speckled** surface is covered with small marks, spots, or shapes. ❑ *...a brown speckled egg... The sky was speckled with stars.* ADJ: usu ADJ n

**specs** /spe̲ks/ → see **spec**.

**spec|ta|cle** /spe̲ktəkəl/ **(spectacles)** [1] Glasses are sometimes referred to as **spectacles**. [FORMAL] ❑ *He looked at me over the tops of his spectacles. ...thick spectacle frames.* N-PLURAL: also a pair of N [2] A **spectacle** is a strange or interesting sight. ❑ *It was a spectacle not* N-COUNT = sight *to be missed.* [3] A **spectacle** is a grand and impressive event or performance. ❑ *94,000 people turned up for the spectacle. ...a director passionate about music and spectacle.* [4] **rose-coloured spectacles** → see **rose-coloured**. N-VAR = *extravaganza*

**spec|tacu|lar** /spektækjʊləʳ/ **(spectaculars)** ◆◇◇ [1] Something that is **spectacular** is very impressive or dramatic. ❑ *...spectacular views of the Sugar Loaf Mountain... The results have been spectacular.* ♦ **spec|tacu|lar|ly** *My turnover increased spectacularly.* [2] A **spectacular** is a show or performance which is very grand and impressive. ❑ *...a television spectacular.* ADJ; ADV: ADV with v, ADV adj/adv; N-COUNT: usu n N = *extravaganza*

**spec|ta|tor** /spekteɪtəʳ, AM spekteɪtər/ **(spectators)** A **spectator** is someone who watches something, especially a sporting event. ❑ *Thirty thousand spectators watched the final game.* N-COUNT

**spec|ta|tor sport** **(spectator sports)** A **spectator sport** is a sport that is interesting and entertaining to watch. ❑ *The most popular spectator sport is football.* N-COUNT

**spec|tra** /spektrə/ **Spectra** is a plural form of **spectrum**.

**spec|tral** /spektrəl/ If you describe someone or something as **spectral**, you mean that they look like a ghost. [LITERARY] ❑ *She is compelling, spectral, fascinating, an unforgettably unique performer.* ADJ = *ghostly*

**spec|tre** /spektəʳ/ **(spectres)**

> ✓ in AM, use **specter**

[1] If you refer to the **spectre of** something unpleasant, you are referring to something that you are frightened might occur. ❑ *Failure to arrive at a consensus over the issue raised the spectre of legal action.* [2] A **spectre** is a **ghost**. [LITERARY] N-COUNT: usu *the* N *of* n; N-COUNT

**spec|trum** /spektrəm/ **(spectra** or **spectrums)** [1] **The spectrum** is the range of different colours which is produced when light passes through a glass prism or through a drop of water. A rainbow shows the colours in the spectrum. [2] A **spectrum** is a range of a particular type of thing. ❑ *Politicians across the political spectrum have denounced the act... The term 'special needs' covers a wide spectrum of problems.* [3] A **spectrum** is a range of light waves or radio waves within particular frequencies. ❑ *Vast amounts of energy, from X-rays right through the spectrum down to radio waves, are escaping into space.* N-SING: *the* N; N-COUNT: usu sing, with supp; N-COUNT

**specu|late** /spekjʊleɪt/ **(speculates, speculating, speculated)** ◆◇◇ [1] If you **speculate** about something, you make guesses about its nature or identity, or about what might happen. ❑ *It would be unfair to Debby's family to speculate on the reasons for her suicide... The doctors speculate that he died of a cerebral haemorrhage caused by a blow on the head... The reader can speculate what will happen next.* ♦ **specu|la|tion** /spekjʊleɪʃᵊn/ **(speculations)** *The President has gone out of his way to dismiss speculation over the future of the economy minister.* [2] If someone **speculates** financially, they buy property, stocks, or shares, in the hope of being able to sell them again at a higher price and make a profit. ❑ *The banks made too many risky loans which now can't be repaid, and they speculated in property whose value has now dropped.* VERB; V prep; V that; V wh; N-VAR; VERB; V prep/adv

**specu|la|tive** /spekjʊlətɪv, AM -leɪt-/ [1] A piece of information that is **speculative** is based on guesses rather than knowledge. ❑ *The papers ran speculative stories about the mysterious disappearance of Eddie Donagan.* [2] Someone who has a **speculative** expression seems to be trying to guess something about a person or thing. ❑ *His mother regarded him with a speculative eye.* [3] **Speculative** is used to describe activities which involve buying goods or shares, or buildings and properties, in the hope of being able to sell them again at a higher price and make a profit. ❑ *Thousands of pensioners were persuaded to mortgage their homes to invest in speculative bonds.* ADJ; ADJ; ADJ

**specu|la|tor** /spekjʊleɪtəʳ/ **(speculators)** A **speculator** is a person who speculates financially. N-COUNT

**sped** /sped/ **Sped** is a past tense and past participle of **speed**.

**speech** /spiːtʃ/ **(speeches)** ◆◆◇ [1] **Speech** is the ability to speak or the act of speaking. ❑ *...the development of speech in children. ...a speech therapist specialising in stammering.* [2] Your **speech** is the way in which you speak. ❑ *His speech became increasingly thick and nasal... I'd make fun of her dress and imitate her speech.* [3] **Speech** is spoken language. ❑ *...the way common letter clusters are usually pronounced in speech.* [4] A **speech** is a formal talk which someone gives to an audience. ❑ *She is due to make a speech on the economy next week... He delivered his speech in French. ...a dramatic resignation speech.* [5] A **speech** is a group of lines spoken by a character in a play. ❑ *...the hilarious speech from Alan Bennett's 'Forty Years On'.* [6] → See also **direct speech**, **figure of speech**, **indirect speech**, **maiden speech**, **part of speech**, **reported speech**. N-UNCOUNT; N-SING: usu poss N; N-UNCOUNT; N-COUNT; N-COUNT

**speech day** **(speech days)** In some British schools, **speech day** is a day, usually at the end of the school year, when prizes are presented to pupils and speeches are made by guest speakers and the head teacher. [BRIT] N-VAR

**speechi|fy|ing** /spiːtʃɪfaɪɪŋ/ **Speechifying** is the making of speeches, especially because you want to appear important. ❑ *...five tedious days of speechifying and punditing.* N-UNCOUNT [disapproval]

**speech|less** /spiːtʃləs/ If you are **speechless**, you are temporarily unable to speak, usually because something has shocked you. ❑ *Alex was almost speechless with rage and despair.* ADJ: usu v-link ADJ, oft ADJ *with* n

**speech thera|pist** **(speech therapists)** A **speech therapist** is a person whose job is to help people to overcome speech and language problems. N-COUNT

**speech thera|py** **Speech therapy** is the treatment of people who have speech and language problems. ❑ *A stammering child can benefit from speech therapy.* N-UNCOUNT

**speech|writ|er** /spiːtʃraɪtəʳ/ **(speechwriters)** A **speechwriter** is a person who writes speeches for important people such as politicians. N-COUNT

**speed** /spiːd/ **(speeds, speeding, sped, speeded)** ◆◆◇

> ✓ The form of the past tense and past participle is **sped** in meaning 5 but **speeded** for the phrasal verb.

[1] The **speed** of something is the rate at which it moves or travels. ❑ *He drove off at high speed... With this type of camera, the shutter speed is fixed... An electrical pulse in a wire travels close to the speed of light... Wind speeds reached force five.* [2] The **speed** of something is the rate at which it happens or is done. ❑ *In the late 1850s the speed of technological change quickened... Each learner can proceed at his own speed.* [3] **Speed** is very fast movement or travel. ❑ *Speed is the essential ingredient of all athletics... He put on a burst of speed... The car is quite noisy at speed.* [4] **Speed** is a very fast rate at which something happens or is done. ❑ *I was amazed at his speed of working. ...the sheer speed of the unification process.* [5] If you **speed** somewhere, you move or travel there quickly, usually in a vehicle. ❑ *Trains will speed through the Channel Tunnel at 186mph... The engine noise rises only slightly as I speed along.* [6] Someone who **is speeding** is driving a vehicle faster than the legal speed limit. ❑ *This man was not qualified to drive and was speeding.* ♦ **speed|ing** *He was fined for speeding last year.* [7] **Speed** is an illegal drug such as amphetamine which some people take to increase their energy and excitement. [INFORMAL] [8] → See also **-speed**. [9] to **pick up speed** → see **pick**. [10] If you are **up to speed**, you have all the most recent information that you need about N-VAR: with supp; N-COUNT: with supp = *pace*; N-UNCOUNT; N-UNCOUNT: usu N *of* n/-ing; VERB = *race*; V prep/adv; V prep/adv; VERB: usu cont; V; N-UNCOUNT; N-UNCOUNT; PHRASE: oft PHR *on* n

something. ❑ *A day has been set aside to bring all councillors up to speed on the proposal... Those in charge deluded themselves they were up to speed.*

♦ **speed up** [1] When something **speeds up** or when you **speed** it **up**, it moves or travels faster. ❑ *You notice that your breathing has speeded up a bit... He pushed a lever that speeded up the car.* [2] When a process or activity **speeds up** or when something **speeds** it **up**, it happens at a faster rate. ❑ *Job losses are speeding up... I had already taken steps to speed up a solution to the problem... I kept praying that the DJ would speed the music up.*
PHRASAL VERB; V P; V P n; Also V n P; PHRASAL VERB; V P; V P n (not pron); V n P

**-speed** /-spiːd/ **-speed** is used after numbers to form adjectives that indicate that a bicycle or car has a particular number of gears. ❑ *...a 10-speed bicycle.* COMB in ADJ

**speed|boat** /spiːdbout/ **(speedboats)** A **speedboat** is a boat that can go very fast because it has a powerful engine. N-COUNT

**speed cam|era** **(speed cameras)** A **speed camera** is a camera positioned at the side of a road which automatically photographs vehicles that are going faster than is allowed. The photographs can be used as evidence in a court of law. N-COUNT

**speed dial** **(speed dials)** **Speed dial** is a facility on a telephone that allows you to call a number by pressing a single button rather than by dialling the full number. N-VAR

**speed lim|it** **(speed limits)** The **speed limit** on a road is the maximum speed at which you are legally allowed to drive. N-COUNT: usu *the* N

**speed|om|eter** /spiːdɒmɪtəʳ/ **(speedometers)** A **speedometer** is the instrument in a vehicle which shows how fast the vehicle is moving. ➔ See picture on page 1708. N-COUNT

**speed|way** /spiːdweɪ/ **(speedways)** [1] **Speedway** is the sport of racing motorcycles on special tracks. [2] A **speedway** is a special track for car or motorcycle racing. [AM] N-UNCOUNT; N-COUNT

**speedy** /spiːdi/ **(speedier, speediest)** A **speedy** process, event, or action happens or is done very quickly. ❑ *We wish Bill a speedy recovery.* ADJ: usu ADJ n = *quick* ≠ *slow*

**spell** /spel/ **(spells, spelling, spelled, spelt)** ◆◇◇

> American English uses the form **spelled** as the past tense and past participle. British English uses either **spelled** or **spelt**.

[1] When you **spell** a word, you write or speak each letter in the word in the correct order. ❑ *He gave his name and then helpfully spelt it... How do you spell 'potato'?... 'Tang' is 'Gnat' spelt backwards.* ♦ **Spell out** means the same as **spell**. ❑ *If I don't know a word, I ask them to spell it out for me... I never have to spell out my first name.* [2] Someone who can **spell** knows the correct order of letters in words. ❑ *It's shocking how students can't spell these days... You accused me of inaccuracy yet you can't spell 'Middlesex'.* [3] If something **spells** a particular result, often an unpleasant one, it suggests that this will be the result. ❑ *If the irrigation plan goes ahead, it could spell disaster for the birds.* [4] A **spell of** a particular type of weather or a particular activity is a short period of time during which this type of weather or activity occurs. ❑ *There has been a long spell of dry weather... You join a barrister for two six-month spells of practical experience.* [5] A **spell** is a situation in which events are controlled by a magical power. ❑ *They say she died after a witch cast a spell on her. ...the kiss that will break the spell.* [6] ➔ See also **spelling**.
VERB; V n; V n; V-ed; PHRASAL VERB; V n P; V P n; VERB: no cont; V; V n; VERB: no cont; V n; N-COUNT: usu N *of* n = *period*; N-COUNT

♦ **spell out** [1] If you **spell** something **out**, you explain it in detail or in a very clear way. ❑ *Be assertive and spell out exactly how you feel... How many times do I have to spell it out?* [2] ➔ see **spell 1**.
PHRASAL VERB; V P n (not pron); V n P

**spell|bind|ing** /spelbaɪndɪŋ/ A **spellbinding** image or sound is one that is so fascinating that you can think about nothing else. ❑ *Gray describes in dramatic and spellbinding detail the lives of these five ladies.* ADJ: usu ADJ n = *gripping*

**spell|bound** /spelbaund/ If you are **spellbound by** something or someone, you are so fascinated that you cannot think about anything else. ❑ *His audience had listened like children, spellbound by his words.* ADJ: usu v-link ADJ, oft ADJ *by* n

**spell|check** /speltʃek/ **(spellchecks, spellchecking, spellchecked)** also **spell check.** [1] If you **spellcheck** something you have written on a computer, you use a special program to check whether you have made any spelling mistakes. [COMPUTING] ❑ *This model allows you to spellcheck over 100,000 different words.* [2] If you run a **spellcheck** over something you have written on a computer, you use a special program to check whether you have made any spelling mistakes. [COMPUTING]
VERB; V n; N-COUNT

**spell|check|er** /speltʃekəʳ/ **(spellcheckers)** also **spell checker.** A **spellchecker** is a special program on a computer which you can use to check whether something you have written contains any spelling mistakes. [COMPUTING] N-COUNT

**spell|er** /speləʳ/ **(spellers)** If you describe someone as a good or bad **speller**, you mean that they find it easy or difficult to spell words correctly. ❑ *I am an absolutely appalling speller.* N-COUNT: adj N

**spell|ing** /spelɪŋ/ **(spellings)** [1] A **spelling** is the correct order of the letters in a word. ❑ *In most languages adjectives have slightly different spellings for masculine and feminine.* [2] **Spelling** is the ability to spell words in the correct way. It is also an attempt to spell a word in the correct way. ❑ *His spelling is very bad... Spelling mistakes are often just the result of haste.* [3] ➔ See also **spell**.
N-COUNT; N-UNCOUNT

**spelt** /spelt/ **Spelt** is a past tense and past participle form of **spell**. [mainly BRIT]

**spe|lunk|er** /spɪlʌŋkəʳ/ **(spelunkers)** A **spelunker** is someone who goes into underground caves and tunnels as a leisure activity. [AM] N-COUNT

> in BRIT, use **potholer**

**spe|lunk|ing** /spɪlʌŋkɪŋ/ **Spelunking** is the leisure activity of going into underground caves and tunnels. [AM] N-UNCOUNT

> in BRIT, use **potholing**

**spend** /spend/ **(spends, spending, spent)** ◆◆◆
[1] When you **spend** money, you pay money for things that you want. ❑ *By the end of the holiday I had spent all my money... Businessmen spend enormous amounts advertising their products... Juventus have spent £23m on new players... The survey may cost at least £100 but is money well spent.* ♦ **spend|ing** *Government spending is expected to fall.* [2] If you **spend** time or energy doing something, you use your time or effort doing it. ❑ *Engineers spend much time and energy developing brilliant solutions... This energy could be much better spent taking some positive action.* [3] If you **spend** a period of time in a place, you stay there for a period of time. ❑ *We spent the night in a hotel.* [4] The **spend** on a particular thing is the amount of money that is spent on it, or will be spent. [BUSINESS] ❑ *...the marketing and advertising spend.*
VERB; V n; V n -ing; V amount/n *on* n; V-ed; N-UNCOUNT = *expenditure*; VERB; V n -ing; V n -ing; VERB; V n adv/prep; N-COUNT

**spend|er** /spendəʳ/ **(spenders)** If a person or organization is a big **spender** or a compulsive **spender**, for example, they spend a lot of money or are unable to stop themselves spending money. ❑ *The Swiss are Europe's biggest spenders on food.* N-COUNT: usu adj N

**spend|ing mon|ey** **Spending money** is money that you have or are given to spend on personal things for pleasure, especially when you are on holiday. ❑ *Jo will use her winnings as spending money on her holiday to the Costa Brava.* N-UNCOUNT

**spend|thrift** /spendθrɪft/ **(spendthrifts)** If you call someone a **spendthrift**, you mean that they spend too much money. ♦ **Spendthrift** is also an adjective. ❑ *...his father's spendthrift ways.* N-COUNT [disapproval]; ADJ: usu ADJ n

**spent** /spent/ [1] **Spent** is the past tense and past participle of **spend**. [2] **Spent** substances or ADJ:

containers have been used and cannot be used again. ❑ *Radioactive waste is simply spent fuel.* usu ADJ n

**spent force** If you refer to someone who used to be powerful as **a spent force**, you mean that they no longer have any power or influence. ❑ *As a political leader he was something of a spent force.* N-SING: *a* N

**sperm** /spɜːʳm/ **(sperms** or **sperm)** [1] A **sperm** is a cell which is produced in the sex organs of a male animal and can enter a female animal's egg and fertilize it. ❑ *Any disease which undermines a man's general health will interfere with his sperm production... Doctor believed that his low sperm count was the problem.* N-COUNT [2] **Sperm** is used to refer to the liquid that contains sperm when it is produced. ❑ *...a sperm donor.* N-UNCOUNT

**sper|ma|to|zo|on** /spɜːʳmətəzoʊɒn/ **(spermatozoa** /spɜːʳmətəzoʊə/**)** A **spermatozoon** is a sperm. [TECHNICAL] N-COUNT

**sper|mi|ci|dal** /spɜːʳmɪsaɪdəl/ A **spermicidal** cream or jelly contains spermicide. ADJ: ADJ n

**sper|mi|cide** /spɜːʳmɪsaɪd/ **(spermicides)** **Spermicide** is a substance that kills sperm. ❑ *Although most condoms contain spermicide, there are some manufactured without.* N-MASS

**sperm whale** **(sperm whales)** A **sperm whale** is a large whale with a large head that has a section in it which contains oil. N-COUNT

**spew** /spjuː/ **(spews, spewing, spewed)** [1] When something **spews** out a substance or when a substance **spews** from something, the substance flows out quickly in large quantities. ❑ *The volcano spewed out more scorching volcanic ashes, gases and rocks... Leaking oil spewed from the tanker.* VERB V n with adv V prep [2] If someone **spews** or **spews up**, they vomit. [INFORMAL] VERB

**sphere** /sfɪəʳ/ **(spheres)** [1] A **sphere** is an object that is completely round in shape like a ball. N-COUNT [2] A **sphere of** activity or interest is a particular area of activity or interest. ❑ *...the sphere of international politics. ...nurses, working in all spheres of the health service.* N-COUNT: usu N *of* n = field [3] A **sphere of** people is a group of them who are similar in social status or who have the same interests. ❑ *...the realities of life outside the government and academic spheres of society.* N-COUNT: usu N *of* n

**spheri|cal** /sferɪkəl, AM sfɪr-/ Something that is **spherical** is round like a ball. [FORMAL] ❑ *...purple and gold spherical earrings.* ADJ

**sphinc|ter** /sfɪŋktəʳ/ **(sphincters)** A **sphincter** is a ring of muscle that surrounds an opening to the body and that can tighten to close this opening. [TECHNICAL] ❑ *...the anal sphincter.* N-COUNT

**sphinx** /sfɪŋks/ **(sphinxes)** also **Sphinx. The Sphinx** is a large ancient statue of a creature with a human head and a lion's body that stands near the pyramids in Egypt. In mythology, sphinxes gave people puzzles to solve, and so a person who is mysterious or puzzling is sometimes referred to as a **sphinx**. N-COUNT: usu *the* N in sing

**spice** /spaɪs/ **(spices, spicing, spiced)** [1] A **spice** is a part of a plant, or a powder made from that part, which you put in food to give it flavour. Cinnamon, ginger, and paprika are spices. ❑ *...herbs and spices. ...a row of spice jars.* N-MASS [2] If you **spice** something that you say or do, you add excitement or interest to it. ❑ *They spiced their conversations and discussions with intrigue.* VERB V n *with* n ♦ **Spice up** means the same as **spice**. ❑ *Her publisher wants her to spice up her stories with sex. ...a discovery which spiced the conversation up quite a bit.* PHRASAL VERB V P n (not pron) V n P [3] **Spice** is something which makes life more exciting. ❑ *To add spice to the debate, they disagreed about method and ideology.* N-UNCOUNT

♦ **spice up** → see **spice** 2.

**spiced** /spaɪst/ Food that is **spiced** has had spices or other strong-tasting foods added to it. ❑ *...delicately spiced sauces.* ADJ: usu adv ADJ, oft ADJ *with* n

**spick and span** /spɪk ənd spæn/ also **spick-and-span.** A place that is **spick and span** is very clean and tidy. ❑ *The apartment was spick and span.* ADJ: usu v-link ADJ

**spicy** /spaɪsi/ **(spicier, spiciest)** **Spicy** food is strongly flavoured with spices. ❑ *Thai food is hot and spicy. ...a spicy tomato and coriander sauce.* ADJ

**spi|der** /spaɪdəʳ/ **(spiders)** A **spider** is a small creature with eight legs. Most types of spider make structures called webs in which they catch insects for food. N-COUNT

**spi|dery** /spaɪdəri/ If you describe something such as handwriting as **spidery**, you mean that it consists of thin, dark, pointed lines. ❑ *He saw her spidery writing on the envelope.* ADJ: usu ADJ n

**spiel** /ʃpiːl, AM spiːl/ **(spiels)** Someone's **spiel** is a well-prepared speech that they make, and that they have usually made many times before, often in order to persuade you to buy something. [INFORMAL] N-COUNT = patter

**spif|fing** /spɪfɪŋ/ If someone describes something such as news or an event as **spiffing**, they mean that it is very good. [BRIT, INFORMAL, OLD-FASHIONED] ❑ *I came to give your mother a piece of perfectly spiffing news.* ADJ

**spig|ot** /spɪgət/ **(spigots)** A **spigot** is a faucet or tap. [AM] N-COUNT

**spike** /spaɪk/ **(spikes)** [1] A **spike** is a long piece of metal with a sharp point. ❑ *...a 15-foot wall topped with iron spikes... Yellowing receipts had been impaled on a metal spike.* N-COUNT [2] Any long pointed object can be referred to as a **spike.** ❑ *Her hair stood out in spikes. ...a long spike of white flowers.* N-COUNT: usu with supp [3] If there is a **spike** in the price, volume, or amount of something, the price, volume, or amount of it suddenly increases. ❑ *Although you'd think business would have boomed during the war, there was only a small spike in interest.* N-COUNT: oft N *in* n [4] **Spikes** are a pair of sports shoes with pointed pieces of metal attached to the soles. They help runners' feet to grip the ground when they are running. N-PLURAL: also *a pair of* n [5] → See also **spiked.**

**spiked** /spaɪkt/ [1] Something that is **spiked** has one or more spikes on it. ❑ *...spiked railings.* ADJ: usu ADJ n [2] If someone has **spiked** hair, their hair is short and sticks up all over their head. ADJ: usu ADJ n [3] → See also **spike**.

**spike heels** **Spike heels** are women's shoes with very high narrow heels. [AM] N-PLURAL: also *a pair of* n

✓ in BRIT, use **stilettos**

**spiky** /spaɪki/ Something that is **spiky** has one or more sharp points. ❑ *Her short spiky hair is damp with sweat. ...tall, spiky evergreen trees.* ADJ

**spill** /spɪl/ **(spills, spilling, spilled, spilt)**

✓ American English uses the form **spilled** as the past tense and past participle. British English uses either **spilled** or **spilt**.

[1] If a liquid **spills** or if you **spill** it, it accidentally flows over the edge of a container. ❑ *70,000 tonnes of oil spilled from the tanker... He always spilled the drinks... Don't spill water on your suit.* VERB V adv/prep V n V n adv/prep [2] A **spill** is an amount of liquid that has spilled from a container. ❑ *She wiped a spill of milkshake off the counter... An oil spill could be devastating for wildlife.* N-COUNT: usu with supp [3] If the contents of a bag, box, or other container **spill** or **are spilled**, they come out of the container onto a surface. ❑ *A number of bags had split and were spilling their contents... He carefully balanced the satchel so that its contents would not spill out onto the floor.* VERB V n V adv/prep [4] If people or things **spill** out of a place, they come out of it in large numbers. ❑ *Tears began to spill out of the boy's eyes.* VERB V adv/prep [5] to **spill the beans** → see **bean**. **thrills and spills** → see **thrill**.

♦ **spill out** If you **spill out** information or if it **spills out**, you tell someone about it in a hurried way, because you cannot or do not want to keep it secret. ❑ *The words spilled out in a rush... He was tempted to spill out his problems to Philip.* PHRASAL VERB V P V P n Also V n P

**spill|age** /spɪlɪdʒ/ **(spillages)** If there is a **spillage**, a substance such as oil escapes from its con- N-VAR tainer. **Spillage** is also used to refer to the substance that escapes. ❑ *...an oil spillage off the coast of Texas. ...an accident in the workplace involving blood spillage.*

**spill|over** /spɪloʊvəʳ/ **(spillovers)** A **spillover** is a situation or feeling that starts in one place but then begins to happen or have an effect somewhere else. ❑ *Some jobs are quite likely to have a negative spillover into family life.* N-COUNT: usu with supp

**spilt** /spɪlt/ **Spilt** is a past tense and past participle form of **spill**. [mainly BRIT]

**spin** /spɪn/ **(spins, spinning, spun)** ◆◇◇ [1] If something **spins** or if you **spin** it, it turns quickly around a central point. ❑ *The latest discs, used for small portable computers, spin 3600 times a minute... He spun the wheel sharply and made a U turn in the middle of the road... He spun his car round and went after them.* ♦ **Spin** is also a noun. ❑ *This driving mode allows you to move off in third gear to reduce wheel-spin in icy conditions.* [2] When you **spin** washing, it is turned round and round quickly in a spin drier or a washing machine to get the water out. ❑ *Just spin the washing and it's nearly dry.* ♦ **Spin** is also a noun. ❑ *Set on a cool wash and finish with a short spin.* [3] If your head **is spinning**, you feel unsteady or confused, for example because you are drunk, ill, or excited. ❑ *My head was spinning from the wine.* [4] If someone puts a certain **spin** on an event or situation, they interpret it and try to present it in a particular way. [INFORMAL] ❑ *He interpreted the vote as support for the constitution and that is the spin his supporters are putting on the results today.* → See also **spin doctor**. [5] In politics, **spin** is the way in which political parties try to present everything they do in a positive way to the public and the media. ❑ *The public is sick of spin and tired of promises. It's time for politicians to act.* [6] If you go for **a spin** or take a car for **a spin**, you make a short journey in a car just to enjoy yourself. [7] If someone **spins** a story, they give you an account of something that is untrue or only partly true. ❑ *He was surprised, and annoyed that she had spun a story which was too good to be condemned as a simple lie.* [8] When people **spin**, they make thread by twisting together pieces of a fibre such as wool or cotton using a device or machine. ❑ *Michelle will also spin a customer's wool fleece to specification at a cost of $2.25 an ounce.* ♦ **spin|ning** *They do their own cooking, spinning, and woodworking.* [9] In a game such as tennis or cricket, if you put **spin** on a ball, you deliberately make it spin rapidly when you hit it or throw it.
VERB; V; V n; V n round/around; N-VAR; VERB; V n; N-SING; VERB; V; N-SING: with supp; N-UNCOUNT; N-SING: a N; VERB; V n; Also V n n; VERB; V n; N-UNCOUNT; N-UNCOUNT

♦ **spin off** or **spin out** To **spin off** or **spin off** something such as a company means to create a new company that is separate from the original organization. [BUSINESS] ❑ *He rescued the company and later spun off its textile division into a separate company... Corven plans to help large companies spin out smaller, entrepreneurial firms.* PHRASAL VERB; V P n; V P n

♦ **spin out** [1] If you **spin** something **out**, you make it last longer than it normally would. ❑ *My wife's solicitor was anxious to spin things out for as long as possible... The Government will try to spin out the conference into next autumn.* [2] → See also **spin off**. PHRASAL VERB = prolong; V n P; V P n (not pron)

**spi|na bi|fi|da** /spaɪnə bɪfɪdə/ **Spina bifida** is a condition of the spine that some people are born with. It often makes them unable to use their legs. N-UNCOUNT

**spin|ach** /spɪnɪdʒ, -ɪtʃ/ **Spinach** is a vegetable with large dark green leaves that you chop up and boil in water before eating. N-UNCOUNT

**spi|nal** /spaɪnᵊl/ **Spinal** means relating to your spine. ❑ *...spinal fluid. ...spinal injuries.* ADJ: ADJ n

**spi|nal col|umn** **(spinal columns)** Your **spinal column** is your spine. N-COUNT

**spi|nal cord** **(spinal cords)** Your **spinal cord** is a thick cord of nerves inside your spine which connects your brain to nerves in all parts of your body. N-COUNT

**spin|dle** /spɪndᵊl/ **(spindles)** [1] A **spindle** is a rod in a machine, around which another part of the machine turns. [2] A **spindle** is a pointed rod which you use when you are spinning wool by hand. You twist the wool with the spindle to make it into a thread. N-COUNT; N-COUNT

**spin|dly** /spɪndli/ **(spindlier, spindliest)** Something that is **spindly** is long and thin and looks very weak. ❑ *I did have rather spindly legs.* ADJ

**spin doc|tor** **(spin doctors)** In politics, a **spin doctor** is someone who is skilled in public relations and who advises political parties on how to present their policies and actions. [INFORMAL] N-COUNT

**spine** /spaɪn/ **(spines)** [1] Your **spine** is the row of bones down your back. [2] The **spine** of a book is the narrow stiff part which the pages and covers are attached to. [3] **Spines** are also long, sharp points on an animal's body or on a plant. N-COUNT; N-COUNT; N-COUNT

**spine-chilling** A **spine-chilling** film or story makes you feel very frightened. ADJ: usu ADJ n

**spine|less** /spaɪnləs/ If you say that someone is **spineless**, you mean that they are afraid to take action or oppose people when they should. ❑ *...bureaucrats and spineless politicians.* ADJ [disapproval]

**spine-tingling** A **spine-tingling** film or piece of music is enjoyable because it causes you to feel a strong emotion such as excitement or fear. ❑ *...Martin Scorsese's spine-tingling and stylish thriller.* ADJ

**spin|na|ker** /spɪnəkəʳ/ **(spinnakers)** A **spinnaker** is a large, light, triangular sail that is attached to the front mast of a boat. N-COUNT

**spin|ner** /spɪnəʳ/ **(spinners)** [1] A **spinner** is a cricketer who makes the ball spin when he or she bowls it so that it changes direction when it hits the ground or the bat. [2] A **spinner** is a person who makes thread by spinning. N-COUNT: usu supp N; N-COUNT

**spin|ney** /spɪni/ **(spinneys)** A **spinney** is a small area covered with trees. [BRIT] N-COUNT = copse

✔ in AM, use **copse**

**spin|ning wheel** **(spinning wheels)** also **spinning-wheel**. A **spinning wheel** is a wooden machine that people used in their homes to make thread from wool, in former times. N-COUNT

**spin-off** **(spin-offs)** [1] A **spin-off** is an unexpected but useful or valuable result of an activity that was designed to achieve something else. ❑ *The company put out a report on commercial spin-offs from its research.* [2] A **spin-off** is a book, film, or television series that comes after and is related to a successful book, film, or television series. N-COUNT: usu with supp, oft N from/of n; N-COUNT

**spin|ster** /spɪnstəʳ/ **(spinsters)** A **spinster** is a woman who has never been married; used especially when talking about an old or middle-aged woman. [OLD-FASHIONED] N-COUNT

**spiny** /spaɪni/ A **spiny** plant or animal is covered with long sharp points. ❑ *...a spiny lobster. ...a spiny cactus.* ADJ

**spi|ral** /spaɪərəl/ **(spirals, spiralling, spiralled)**

✔ in AM, use **spiraling**, **spiraled**

[1] A **spiral** is a shape which winds round and round, with each curve above or outside the previous one. ♦ **Spiral** is also an adjective. ❑ *...a spiral staircase.* [2] If something **spirals** or **is spiralled** somewhere, it grows or moves in a spiral curve. ❑ *Vines spiraled upward toward the roof... A joss stick spiralled smoke.* ♦ **Spiral** is also a noun. ❑ *Larks were rising in spirals from the ridge.* [3] If an amount or level **spirals**, it rises quickly and at an increasing rate. ❑ *Production costs began to spiral. ...a spiralling trend of violence... The divorce rate is spiralling upwards.* ♦ **Spiral** is also a noun. ❑ *...an inflationary spiral. ...a spiral of debt.* [4] If an amount or level **spirals** downwards, it falls quickly and at an increasing rate. ❑ *House prices will continue to spiral downwards.*
N-COUNT; ADJ: ADJ n; VERB; V adv/prep; V n, Also V; N-COUNT; VERB; V; V -ing; V adv/prep; N-SING: with supp; VERB; V adv/prep

**spire** /spaɪəʳ/ **(spires)** The **spire** of a building such as a church is the tall pointed structure on the top. N-COUNT

**spir|it** /spɪrɪt/ **(spirits, spiriting, spirited)** ◆◆◇ [1] Your **spirit** is the part of you that is not physical and that consists of your character and feelings. ❑ *The human spirit is virtually indestructible.* ➔ See also **kindred spirit**. N-SING [2] A person's **spirit** is the non-physical part of them that is believed to remain alive after their death. ❑ *His spirit has left him and all that remains is the shell of his body.* N-COUNT: usu poss N = soul [3] A **spirit** is a ghost or supernatural being. ❑ *...protection against evil spirits.* ➔ See also **Holy Spirit**. N-COUNT
[4] **Spirit** is the courage and determination that helps people to survive in difficult times and to keep their way of life and their beliefs. ❑ *She was a very brave girl and everyone who knew her admired her spirit.* N-UNCOUNT [5] **Spirit** is the liveliness and energy that someone shows in what they do. ❑ *They played with spirit.* N-UNCOUNT [6] The **spirit** in which you do something is the attitude you have when you are doing it. ❑ *Their problem can only be solved in a spirit of compromise.* N-SING [7] A particular kind of **spirit** is the feeling of loyalty to a group that is shared by the people who belong to the group. ❑ *There is a great sense of team spirit among the British Olympic squad.* N-UNCOUNT: usu with supp, oft n N
[8] A particular kind of **spirit** is the set of ideas, beliefs, and aims that are held by a group of people. ❑ *...the real spirit of the Labour movement.* N-SING
[9] **The spirit of** something such as a law or an agreement is the way that it was intended to be interpreted or applied. ❑ *The requirement for work permits violates the spirit of the 1950 treaty.* N-SING: the N of n [10] You can refer to a person as a particular kind of **spirit** if they show a certain characteristic or if they show a lot of enthusiasm in what they are doing. ❑ *I like to think of myself as a free spirit.* N-COUNT: usu adj N [11] Your **spirits** are your feelings at a particular time, especially feelings of happiness or unhappiness. ❑ *At supper, everyone was in high spirits.* N-PLURAL [12] If someone or something **is spirited away**, or if they **are spirited out of** somewhere, they are taken from a place quickly and secretly without anyone noticing. [WRITTEN] ❑ *He was spirited away and probably murdered... His parents had spirited him away to the country... It is possible that he has been spirited out of the country.* VERB be V-ed away; V n away; be V-ed prep/adv [13] **Spirits** are strong alcoholic drinks such as whisky and gin. N-PLURAL [14] **Spirit** or **spirits** is an alcoholic liquid that is used as a fuel, for cleaning things, or for other purposes. There are many kinds of spirit. ➔ See also **methylated spirits, surgical spirit**. N-UNCOUNT

**spir|it|ed** /spɪrɪtɪd/ [1] A **spirited** action shows great energy and courage. ❑ *This television program provoked a spirited debate in the United Kingdom.* ADJ: usu ADJ n [2] A **spirited** person is very active, lively, and confident. ❑ *He was by nature a spirited little boy.* ADJ: usu ADJ n

**-spirited** /-spɪrɪtɪd/ **-spirited** combines with adjectives to describe a person's character, attitude, or behaviour. For example, a **mean-spirited** person behaves in a way that is unkind to other people; a **free-spirited** person behaves freely and does as they please. ❑ *That's a mean-spirited thing for a mother to say... Murray was an affable, free-spirited man.* ➔ See also **high-spirited, public-spirited**. COMB in ADJ

**spir|it|less** /spɪrɪtləs/ If someone is **spiritless**, they lack energy, courage, and liveliness. ❑ *They were too spiritless even to resist.* ADJ = apathetic

**spir|it lev|el** **(spirit levels)** also **spirit-level**. A **spirit level** is a device for testing to see if a surface is level. It consists of a plastic, wood, or metal frame containing a glass tube of liquid with an air bubble in it. N-COUNT

**spir|itu|al** /spɪrɪtʃuəl/ **(spirituals)** ◆◇◇ [1] **Spiritual** means relating to people's thoughts and beliefs, rather than to their bodies and physical surroundings. ❑ *She lived entirely by spiritual values, in a world of poetry and imagination.* ADJ ≠ temporal ♦ **spir|itu|al|ly** *Our whole programme is spiritually oriented but not religious.* ADV ♦ **spir|itu|al|ity** /spɪrɪtʃuælɪti/ *...the peaceful spirituality of Japanese culture.* N-UNCOUNT [2] **Spiritual** means relating to people's religious beliefs. ❑ *The spiritual leader of Ireland's 3.7 million Catholics.* ADJ = religious ≠ secular [3] A **spiritual** is a religious song of the type originally sung by black slaves in America. N-COUNT

**spir|itu|al|ism** /spɪrɪtʃuəlɪzəm/ **Spiritualism** is the belief that the spirits of people who are dead can communicate with people who are still alive. N-UNCOUNT ♦ **spir|itu|al|ist** **(spiritualists)** ❑ *He was a poet and an ardent spiritualist.* N-COUNT

**spit** /spɪt/ **(spits, spitting, spat)**

> In American English, the form **spit** is used as the past tense and past participle.

[1] **Spit** is the watery liquid produced in your mouth. You usually use **spit** to refer to an amount of it that has been forced out of someone's mouth. N-UNCOUNT = saliva [2] If someone **spits**, they force an amount of liquid out of their mouth, often to show hatred or contempt. ❑ *The gang thought of hitting him too, but decided just to spit... They spat at me and taunted me... She spit into the little tray of mascara and brushed it on her lashes.* VERB V; V prep; V prep [3] If you **spit** liquid or food somewhere, you force a small amount of it out of your mouth. ❑ *Spit out that gum and pay attention... He felt as if a serpent had spat venom into his eyes.* VERB V n with *out*; V n prep [4] If **it is spitting**, it is raining very lightly. [BRIT] ❑ *It will stop in a minute - it's only spitting.* VERB: usu cont it V

> in AM, use **sprinkle**

[5] A **spit** is a long rod which is pushed through a piece of meat and hung over an open fire to cook the meat. ❑ *She roasted the meat on a spit.* N-COUNT [6] A **spit of** land is a long, flat, narrow piece of land that sticks out into the sea. N-COUNT: N of n
PHRASES [7] If one place is **within spitting distance of** another, they are very close to each other. [INFORMAL] ❑ *...a restaurant within spitting distance of the Tower of London.* PHRASE: usu PHR of n [8] If you say that one person is **the spitting image of** another, you mean that they look very similar. [INFORMAL] ❑ *Nina looks the spitting image of Sissy Spacek.* PHRASE: usu v-link PHR

**spite** /spaɪt/ ◆◇◇ [1] You use **in spite of** to introduce a fact which makes the rest of the statement you are making seem surprising. ❑ *Their love of life comes in spite of, almost in defiance of, considerable hardship.* PREP-PHRASE = despite [2] If you do something **in spite of yourself**, you do it although you did not really intend to or expect to. ❑ *The blunt comment made Richard laugh in spite of himself.* PREP-PHRASE: PREP pron-refl [3] If you do something cruel out of **spite**, you do it because you want to hurt or upset someone. ❑ *I refused her a divorce, out of spite I suppose.* N-UNCOUNT [4] If you do something cruel **to spite** someone, you do it in order to hurt or upset them. ❑ *Pantelaras was giving his art collection away for nothing, to spite Marie and her husband.* VERB: only to-inf V n [5] to **cut off** your **nose to spite** your **face** ➔ see **nose**.

**spite|ful** /spaɪtfʊl/ Someone who is **spiteful** does cruel things to hurt people they dislike. ❑ *He could be spiteful. ...a stream of spiteful telephone calls.* ADJ = malicious ♦ **spite|ful|ly** *We crept into our little sister's bedroom and spitefully defaced her pop posters.* ADV: ADV with v

**spit|tle** /spɪtᵊl/ **Spittle** is the watery liquid which is produced in your mouth. [OLD-FASHIONED] ❑ *Spittle oozed down his jaw.* N-UNCOUNT = spit

**spiv** /spɪv/ **(spivs)** A **spiv** is a man who does not have a regular job and who makes money by business deals which are usually illegal. [BRIT, INFORMAL] N-COUNT = wide boy

**splash** /splæʃ/ **(splashes, splashing, splashed)** [1] If you **splash** about or **splash** around in water, you hit or disturb the water in a noisy way, causing some of it to fly up into the air. ❑ *A lot of people were in the water, swimming or simply splashing about... She could hear the voices of her friends as they splashed in a nearby rock pool... The gliders and their pilots splashed into the lake and had to be fished out.* VERB V about/around; V; V into n [2] If you **splash** a liquid somewhere or if it VERB

**splashes**, it hits someone or something and scatters in a lot of small drops. ❑ *He closed his eyes tight, and splashed the water on his face... A little wave, the first of many, splashed in my face... Beer splashed the carpet... Lorries rumbled past them, splashing them with filthy water from the potholes in the road.* (V n prep; V prep/adv; V n; V n *with* n) [3] A **splash** is the sound made when something hits water or falls into it. ❑ *There was a splash and something fell clumsily into the water.* (N-SING) [4] A **splash** of a liquid is a small quantity of it that falls on something or is added to something. ❑ *Wallcoverings and floors should be able to withstand steam and splashes.* (N-COUNT) [5] A **splash of** colour is an area of a bright colour which contrasts strongly with the colours around it. ❑ *Anne has left the walls white, but added splashes of colour with the tablecloth and the paintings.* (N-COUNT: with supp, oft N *of* n) [6] If a magazine or newspaper **splashes** a story, it prints it in such a way that it is very noticeable. ❑ *The newspapers splashed the story all over their front pages.* (VERB; V n) [7] If you **make a splash**, you become noticed or become popular because of something that you have done. ❑ *Now she's made a splash in the American television show 'Civil Wars'.* (PHRASE: V inflects)

♦ **splash out** If you **splash out on** something, especially on a luxury, you buy it even though it costs a lot of money. [BRIT] ❑ *If he wanted to splash out on a new car it would take him a couple of days to get his hands on the cash.* (PHRASAL VERB: no passive; V P)

**splash|down** /splæʃdaʊn/ **(splashdowns)** A **splashdown** is the landing of a spacecraft in the sea after a flight. (N-COUNT)

**splat** /splæt/ **Splat** is used to describe the sound of something wet hitting a surface with a lot of force. ❑ *The egg landed on my cheek with a splat.* (N-SING; SOUND)

**splat|ter** /splætəʳ/ **(splatters, splattering, splattered)** If a thick wet substance **splatters** on something or is **splattered** on it, it drops or is thrown over it. ❑ *The rain splattered against the french windows... 'Sorry Edward,' I said, splattering the cloth with jam. ...a mud-splattered white shirt.* (VERB = spatter; V adv/prep; V n; V-ed)

**splay** /spleɪ/ **(splays, splaying, splayed)** If things **splay** or **are splayed**, their ends are spread out away from each other. ❑ *He splayed his fingers across his face... His fingers splay out in a star shape... He was on his stomach, his legs splayed apart.* (VERB; V n; V adv/prep; V-ed)

**spleen** /spliːn/ **(spleens)** [1] Your **spleen** is an organ near your stomach that controls the quality of your blood. (N-COUNT) [2] **Spleen** is great and bitter anger. [FORMAL] ❑ *Paul Fussell's latest book vents his spleen against everything he hates about his country.* (N-UNCOUNT: usu poss N)

**splen|did** /splendɪd/ [1] If you say that something is **splendid**, you mean that it is very good. ❑ *Our house has got a splendid view across to the Cotswolds.* (ADJ: usu ADJ n = marvellous) ♦ **splen|did|ly** *I have heard him tell people that we get along splendidly.* (ADV: ADV with v) [2] If you describe a building or work of art as **splendid**, you mean that it is beautiful, impressive, and extremely well made. ❑ *...a splendid Victorian mansion.* (ADJ: usu ADJ n = magnificent) ♦ **splen|did|ly** *The young women are splendidly dressed, some in floor-length ball gowns.* (ADV: ADV adj, ADV with v)

**splen|dour** /splendəʳ/ **(splendours)**

✔ in AM, use **splendor**

[1] The **splendour** of something is its beautiful and impressive appearance. ❑ *The foreign ministers are meeting in the splendour of Oktyabrskaya Hotel in central Moscow.* (N-UNCOUNT) [2] The **splendours of** a place or way of life are its beautiful and impressive features. ❑ *Montagu was extremely impressed by the splendours of the French court.* (N-PLURAL: oft N *of* n)

**sple|net|ic** /splɪnetɪk/ If you describe someone as **splenetic**, you mean that they easily become very angry about things. [FORMAL] ❑ *...retired military men with splenetic opinions.* (ADJ = peevish)

**splice** /splaɪs/ **(splices, splicing, spliced)** If you **splice** two pieces of rope, film, or tape together, you join them neatly at the ends so that they make one continuous piece. ❑ *He taught me to edit and splice film.* (VERB; V n)

**spliff** /splɪf/ **(spliffs)** A **spliff** is a cigarette which contains cannabis or marijuana. [INFORMAL] (N-COUNT = joint)

**splint** /splɪnt/ **(splints)** A **splint** is a long piece of wood or metal that is fastened to a broken arm, leg, or back to keep it still. (N-COUNT)

**splin|ter** /splɪntəʳ/ **(splinters, splintering, splintered)** [1] A **splinter** is a very thin, sharp piece of wood, glass, or other hard substance, which has broken off from a larger piece. ❑ *...splinters of glass. ...a splinter in the finger.* (N-COUNT) [2] If something **splinters** or **is splintered**, it breaks into thin, sharp pieces. ❑ *The ruler cracked and splintered into pieces... The stone rocketed into the glass, splintering it.* (VERB; V prep/adv; V n)

**splin|ter group** **(splinter groups)** A **splinter group** is a group of people who break away from a larger group and form a separate organization, usually because they no longer agree with the views of the larger group. (N-COUNT)

**split** /splɪt/ **(splits, splitting)** ◆◆◇

✔ The form **split** is used in the present tense and is the past tense and past participle of the verb.

[1] If something **splits** or if you **split** it, it is divided into two or more parts. ❑ *In a severe gale the ship split in two... If the chicken is fairly small, you may simply split it in half. ...uniting families split by the war.* (VERB; V *in/into* n; V n *in/into* n; V n) [2] If an organization **splits** or **is split**, one group of members disagrees strongly with the other members, and may form a group of their own. ❑ *Yet it is feared the Republican leadership could split over the agreement... Women priests are accused of splitting the church.* (VERB; V; V n) ♦ **Split** is also an adjective. ❑ *The Kremlin is deeply split in its approach to foreign policy.* (ADJ: usu v-link ADJ) [3] A **split in** an organization is a disagreement between its members. ❑ *They accused both radicals and conservatives of trying to provoke a split in the party.* (N-COUNT) [4] A **split between** two things is a division or difference between them. ❑ *...a split between what is thought and what is felt.* (N-SING: oft N *between* pl-n) [5] If something such as wood or a piece of clothing **splits** or **is split**, a long crack or tear appears in it. ❑ *The seat of his short grey trousers split... Twist the mixture into individual sausages without splitting the skins.* (VERB; V; V n) [6] A **split** is a long crack or tear. ❑ *The plastic-covered seat has a few small splits around the corners.* (N-COUNT) [7] If two or more people **split** something, they share it between them. ❑ *I would rather pay for a meal than watch nine friends pick over and split a bill... All exhibits are for sale, the proceeds being split between Oxfam and the artist.* (VERB; V n; V n *between* pl-n) → See also **splitting**.

♦ **split off** If people **split off from** a group, they stop being part of the group and become separated from it. ❑ *Somehow, Quentin split off from his comrades. ...the Youth Wing which split off the National Liberal party earlier this year.* (PHRASAL VERB; V P; V P n)

♦ **split up** [1] If two people **split up**, or if someone or something **splits** them **up**, they end their relationship or marriage. ❑ *Research suggests that children whose parents split up are more likely to drop out of high school... I was beginning to think that nothing could ever split us up... I split up with my boyfriend last year.* (PHRASAL VERB; V P; V n P; V P *with* n) [2] If a group of people **split up** or **are split up**, they go away in different directions. ❑ *Did the two of you split up in the woods?... This situation has split up the family... Touring the album temporarily split the band up.* (PHRASAL VERB; V P; V P n; V n P) [3] If you **split** something **up**, or if it **splits up**, you divide it so that it is in a number of smaller separate sections. ❑ *Any thought of splitting up the company was unthinkable they said... Even though museums have begged to borrow her collection, she could never split it up... Her company has had to split up and work from two locations.* (PHRASAL VERB; V P n (not pron); V n P; V P)

**split ends** If you have **split ends**, some of your hairs are split at the ends because they are dry or damaged. (N-PLURAL)

**split in|fini|tive** **(split infinitives)** A **split infinitive** is a structure in which an adverb is put between 'to' and the infinitive of a verb, as in 'to (N-COUNT) really experience it'. Some people think it is incorrect to use split infinitives.

**split-level** A **split-level** house or room has part of the ground floor at a different level from another part, usually because the house has been built on ground that slopes.
ADJ: usu ADJ n

**split per|son|al|ity** **(split personalities)** If you say that someone has a **split personality**, you mean that their moods can change so much that they seem to have two separate personalities.
N-COUNT

**split-screen** **(split-screens)** [1] **Split-screen** is used to describe the technique in making films and television programmes in which two different pieces of film are shown at the same time. ❑ *...split-screen movies.* [2] On a computer screen, a **split-screen** is a display of two different things in separate parts of the screen.
ADJ: usu ADJ n
N-COUNT: oft N n

**split se|cond** also **split-second.** A **split second** is an extremely short period of time. ❑ *Her gaze met Michael's for a split second.*
N-SING

**split|ting** /splɪtɪŋ/ A **splitting** headache is a very severe and painful one.
ADJ: ADJ n

**splodge** /splɒdʒ/ **(splodges)** A **splodge** is a large uneven mark or stain, especially one that has been caused by a liquid. [BRIT]
N-COUNT

✓ in AM, use **splotch**

**splotch** /splɒtʃ/ **(splotches)** A **splotch** is a large uneven mark or stain, especially one that has been caused by a liquid.
N-COUNT = *splodge*

**splurge** /splɜːʳdʒ/ **(splurges, splurging, splurged)** If you **splurge on** something, you spend a lot of money, usually on things that you do not need. ❑ *We splurged on Bohemian glass for gifts, and for ourselves.*
VERB = *splash out*
V *on* n

**splut|ter** /splʌtəʳ/ **(splutters, spluttering, spluttered)** [1] If someone **splutters**, they make short sounds and have difficulty speaking clearly, for example because they are embarrassed or angry. ❑ *'But it cannot be,' he spluttered... Molly leapt to her feet, spluttering and howling with rage.* [2] If something **splutters**, it makes a series of short, sharp sounds. ❑ *Suddenly the engine coughed, spluttered and died.*
VERB
V with quote
V
VERB

**spoil** /spɔɪl/ **(spoils, spoiling, spoiled, spoilt)**

✓ American English uses the form **spoiled** as the past tense and past participle. British English uses either **spoiled** or **spoilt**.

[1] If you **spoil** something, you prevent it from being successful or satisfactory. ❑ *It's important not to let mistakes spoil your life... Peaceful summer evenings can be spoilt by mosquitoes.* [2] If you **spoil** children, you give them everything they want or ask for. This is considered to have a bad effect on a child's character. ❑ *Grandparents are often tempted to spoil their grandchildren whenever they come to visit.* ♦ **spoilt, spoiled** *A spoilt child is rarely popular with other children... Oh, that child. He's so spoiled.* [3] If you **spoil yourself** or **spoil** another person, you give yourself or them something nice as a treat or do something special for them. ❑ *Spoil yourself with a new perfume this summer... Perhaps I could employ someone to iron his shirts, but I wanted to spoil him. He was my man.* [4] If food **spoils** or if it **is spoilt**, it is no longer fit to be eaten. ❑ *We all know that fats spoil by becoming rancid... Some organisms are responsible for spoiling food and cause food poisoning.* [5] If someone **spoils** their vote, they write something illegal on their voting paper, usually as a protest about the election, and their vote is not accepted. [BRIT] ❑ *They had broadcast calls for voters to spoil their ballot papers.* [6] The **spoils of** something are things that people get as a result of winning a battle or of doing something successfully. ❑ *True to military tradition, the victors are now treating themselves to the spoils of war.* [7] If you say that someone is **spoilt for choice** or **spoiled for choice**, you mean that they have a great many things of the same type to choose from. ❑ *At lunchtime, MPs are spoilt for choice in 26 restaurants and bars.*
VERB
V n
V n
VERB
V n
ADJ
VERB = *pamper*
V pron-refl
V n
VERB
V
V n
VERB = *deface*
V n
N-PLURAL: usu with supp
PHRASE: v-link PHR

♦ **spoil for** If you **are spoiling for** a fight, you are very eager for it to happen. ❑ *A mob armed with guns was at the border between the two republics, spoiling for a fight.*
PHRASAL VERB: only cont
V P n

**spoil|age** /spɔɪlɪdʒ/ When **spoilage** occurs, something, usually food, decays or is harmed, so that it is no longer fit to be used. [TECHNICAL]
N-UNCOUNT

**spoil|er** /spɔɪləʳ/ **(spoilers)** [1] If you describe someone or something as a **spoiler**, you mean that they try to spoil the performance of other people or things. ❑ *I was a talentless spoiler. If I couldn't be good, why should they?* [2] A **spoiler** is an object which forms part of an aircraft's wings or part of the body of a car. It changes the flow of air around the vehicle, allowing an aircraft to change direction or making a car's forward movement more efficient.
N-COUNT
N-COUNT

**spoil|sport** /spɔɪlspɔːʳt/ **(spoilsports)** If you say that someone is a **spoilsport**, you mean that they are behaving in a way that ruins other people's pleasure or enjoyment. [INFORMAL]
N-COUNT
disapproval
= *killjoy*

**spoilt** /spɔɪlt/ **Spoilt** is a past participle and past tense of **spoil**.

**spoke** /spoʊk/ **(spokes)** [1] **Spoke** is the past tense of **speak**. [2] The **spokes** of a wheel are the bars that connect the outer ring to the centre. ➔ See picture on page 1708.
N-COUNT: usu pl

**spo|ken** /spoʊkən/ **Spoken** is the past participle of **speak**.

**-spoken** /-spoʊkən/ **-spoken** combines with adverbs and adjectives to form adjectives which indicate how someone speaks. ❑ *The woman was smartly dressed and well-spoken. ...a soft-spoken man in his early thirties.*
COMB in ADJ

**spo|ken word** **The spoken word** is used to refer to language expressed in speech, for example in contrast to written texts or music. ❑ *There is a potential educational benefit in allowing pictures to tell the story, rather than the spoken word.*
N-SING: usu *the* N

**spokes|man** /spoʊksmən/ **(spokesmen)** A **spokesman** is a male spokesperson. ❑ *A UN spokesman said that the mission will carry 20 tons of relief supplies.*
◆◆◇
N-COUNT

**spokes|person** /spoʊkspɜːʳsᵊn/ **(spokespersons** or **spokespeople)** A **spokesperson** is a person who speaks as the representative of a group or organization. ❑ *A spokesperson for Amnesty, Norma Johnston, describes some cases.*
N-COUNT

**spokes|woman** /spoʊkswʊmən/ **(spokeswomen)** A **spokeswoman** is a female spokesperson. ❑ *A United Nations spokeswoman in New York said the request would be considered.*
N-COUNT

**sponge** /spʌndʒ/ **(sponges, sponging, sponged)** [1] **Sponge** is a very light soft substance with lots of little holes in it, which can be either artificial or natural. It is used to clean things or as a soft layer. ❑ *...a sponge mattress.* [2] A **sponge** is a sea animal with a soft round body made of natural sponge. [3] A **sponge** is a piece of sponge that you use for washing yourself or for cleaning things. ❑ *He wiped off the table with a sponge.* [4] If you **sponge** something, you clean it by wiping it with a wet sponge. ❑ *Fill a bowl with water and gently sponge your face and body.* ♦ **Sponge down** means the same as **sponge**. ❑ *If your child's temperature rises, sponge her down gently with tepid water.* [5] A **sponge** is a light cake or pudding made from flour, eggs, sugar, and sometimes fat. ❑ *It makes a superb filling for cakes and sponges.* [6] If you say that someone **sponges off** other people or **sponges on** them, you mean that they regularly get money from other people when they should be trying to support themselves. [INFORMAL] ❑ *He should just get an honest job and stop sponging off the rest of us!... He spent his life grumbling about missed opportunities and sponging on his father for money.*
N-COUNT
N-COUNT
N-COUNT
VERB
V n
PHRASAL VERB
V n P
N-VAR
VERB
disapproval
V *off* n
V *on* n

**sponge|bag** /spʌndʒbæg/ **(spongebags)** also **sponge bag.** A **spongebag** is a small bag in which you keep things such as soap and a toothbrush when you are travelling. [BRIT] — N-COUNT = *toilet bag*

**sponge cake (sponge cakes)** A **sponge cake** is a very light cake made from flour, eggs, and sometimes fat. — N-VAR

**spong|er** /spʌndʒəʳ/ **(spongers)** If you describe someone as a **sponger**, you mean that they sponge off other people or organizations. [INFORMAL] — N-COUNT [disapproval] = *scrounger*

**spon|gy** /spʌndʒi/ Something that is **spongy** is soft and can be pressed in, like a sponge. ❑ *The earth was spongy from rain.* — ADJ

**spon|sor** /spɒnsəʳ/ **(sponsors, sponsoring, sponsored)** ◆◇◇ 1 If an organization or an individual **sponsors** something such as an event or someone's training, they pay some or all of the expenses connected with it, often in order to get publicity for themselves. ❑ *The competition was sponsored by Ruinart Champagne.* (VERB = *finance*; V n) 2 In Britain, if you **sponsor** someone who is doing something to raise money for charity, for example trying to walk a certain distance, you agree to give them a sum of money for the charity if they succeed in doing it. ❑ *Please could you sponsor me for my school's campaign for Help the Aged?* (VERB; V n) 3 If you **sponsor** a proposal or suggestion, you officially put it forward and support it. ❑ *Eight senators sponsored legislation to stop the military funding.* (VERB; V n) 4 When a country or an organization such as the United Nations **sponsors** negotiations between countries, it suggests holding the negotiations and organizes them. ❑ *Given the strength of pressure on both sides, the superpowers may well have difficulties sponsoring negotiations.* (VERB; V n) 5 If one country accuses another of **sponsoring** attacks on it, they mean that the other country does not do anything to prevent the attacks, and may even encourage them. ❑ *We have to make the states that sponsor terrorism pay a price.* (VERB = *support*; V n) 6 If a company or organization **sponsors** a television programme, they pay to have a special advertisement shown at the beginning and end of the programme, and at each commercial break. ❑ *Companies will now be able to sponsor programmes on ITV and Channel 4.* (VERB; V n) 7 A **sponsor** is a person or organization that sponsors something or someone. ❑ *I understand Coca-Cola are to be named as the new sponsors of the League Cup later this week.* (N-COUNT)

**spon|sored** /spɒnsəʳd/ In Britain, a **sponsored** event is an event in which people try to do something such as walk or run a certain distance in order to raise money for charity. ❑ *The sponsored walk will raise money for AIDS care.* — ADJ: ADJ n

**spon|sor|ship** /spɒnsəʳʃɪp/ 1 **Sponsorship** is financial support given by a sponsor. ❑ *Campbell is one of an ever-growing number of skiers in need of sponsorship.* (N-UNCOUNT: also N in pl) 2 **Sponsorship** of something is the act of sponsoring it. ❑ *When it is done properly, arts sponsorship can be more effective than advertising.* (N-UNCOUNT: usu with supp)

**spon|ta|neity** /spɒntəneɪɪti/ **Spontaneity** is spontaneous, natural behaviour. ❑ *He had the spontaneity of a child.* — N-UNCOUNT

**spon|ta|neous** /spɒnteɪniəs/ 1 **Spontaneous** acts are not planned or arranged, but are done because someone suddenly wants to do them. ❑ *Diana's house was crowded with happy people whose spontaneous outbursts of song were accompanied by lively music.* (ADJ) ♦ **spon|ta|neous|ly** *As soon as the tremor passed, many people spontaneously arose and cheered.* (ADV: usu ADV with v, also ADV adj) 2 A **spontaneous** event happens because of processes within something rather than being caused by things outside it. ❑ *I had another spontaneous miscarriage at around the 16th to 18th week.* (ADJ) ♦ **spon|ta|neous|ly** *Usually a woman's breasts produce milk spontaneously after the birth.* (ADV: ADV after v)

**spoof** /spuːf/ **(spoofs)** A **spoof** is something such as an article or television programme that seems to be about a serious matter but is actually a joke. ❑ *...a spoof on Hollywood life.* — N-COUNT

**spook** /spuːk/ **(spooks, spooking, spooked)** 1 A **spook** is a ghost. [INFORMAL] (N-COUNT) 2 A **spook** is a spy. [AM, INFORMAL] ❑ *...as a US intelligence spook said yesterday.* (N-COUNT) 3 If people **are spooked**, something has scared them or made them nervous. [mainly AM] ❑ *But was it the wind that spooked her?... Investors were spooked by slowing economies.* (VERB; V n; V n) ♦ **spooked** *He was so spooked that he, too, began to believe that he heard strange clicks and noises on their telephones.* (ADJ: v-link ADJ)

**spooky** /spuːki/ **(spookier, spookiest)** A place that is **spooky** has a frightening atmosphere, and makes you feel that there are ghosts around. [INFORMAL] ❑ *The whole place has a slightly spooky atmosphere.* — ADJ = *creepy*

**spool** /spuːl/ **(spools)** A **spool** is a round object onto which thread, tape, or film can be wound, especially before it is put into a machine. — N-COUNT = *reel*

**spoon** /spuːn/ **(spoons, spooning, spooned)** 1 A **spoon** is an object used for eating, stirring, and serving food. One end of it is shaped like a shallow bowl and it has a long handle. ➔ See picture on page 1710. ❑ *He stirred his coffee with a spoon.* (N-COUNT) 2 You can refer to an amount of food resting on a spoon as a **spoon of** food. ❑ *...tea with two spoons of sugar.* (N-COUNT: usu N *of* n) 3 If you **spoon** food into something, you put it there with a spoon. ❑ *He spooned instant coffee into two of the mugs.* (VERB; V n prep) 4 ➔ See also **greasy spoon, slotted spoon, soup spoon, wooden spoon.** 5 If you think that someone has a lot of advantages because they have a rich or influential family, you can say that they have been **born with a silver spoon in** their **mouth.** ❑ *She was born with a silver spoon in her mouth and everything has been done for her.* (PHRASE: Ns inflect)

**spoon|er|ism** /spuːnərɪzəm/ **(spoonerisms)** A **spoonerism** is a mistake made by a speaker in which the first sounds of two words are changed over, often with a humorous result, for example when someone says 'wrong load' instead of 'long road'. — N-COUNT

**spoon-feed (spoon-feeds, spoon-feeding, spoon-fed)** 1 If you think that someone is being given too much help with something and is not making enough effort themselves, you can say they **are being spoon-fed.** ❑ *Students are unwilling to really work. They want to be spoon-fed.* (VERB: usu passive [disapproval]; *be* V-ed) 2 If you say that someone **is spoon-fed** ideas or information, you mean that they are told about them and are expected to accept them without questioning them. ❑ *They were less willing to be spoon-fed doctrines from Japan.* (VERB: usu passive [disapproval]; *be* V-ed n) 3 If you **spoon-feed** a small child or a sick person, you feed them using a spoon. ❑ *It took two years for me to get better, during which time he spoon-fed me and did absolutely everything around the house.* (VERB; V n)

**spoon|ful** /spuːnfʊl/ **(spoonfuls)** You can refer to an amount of food resting on a spoon as a **spoonful of** food. ❑ *He took a spoonful of the stew and ate it.* — N-COUNT: usu N *of* n

**spoor** /spʊəʳ/ The **spoor** of an animal is the marks or substances that it leaves behind as it moves along, which hunters can follow. — N-SING

**spo|rad|ic** /spərædɪk/ **Sporadic** occurrences of something happen at irregular intervals. ❑ *...a year of sporadic fighting over northern France.* (ADJ ≠ *continuous*) ♦ **spo|radi|cal|ly** *The distant thunder from the coast continued sporadically.* (ADV: ADV with v ≠ *continuously*)

**spore** /spɔːʳ/ **(spores) Spores** are cells produced by bacteria and fungi which can develop into new bacteria or fungi. — N-COUNT

**spor|ran** /spɒrᵊn, AM spɔːrən/ **(sporrans)** A **sporran** is a flat bag made out of leather or fur, which a Scotsman wears on a belt around his waist when he is wearing a skirt called a kilt. — N-COUNT

**sport** /spɔːʳt/ **(sports)** 1 **Sports** are games such as football and basketball and other competitive leisure activities which need physical effort and skill. ❑ *I'd say football is my favourite sport... She excels at sport... Billy turned on a radio to get the sports news.* 2 If you say that someone is a **sport** or a good **sport**, you mean that they cope with a difficult situation or teasing in a cheerful way. [OLD-FASHIONED] ❑ *He was accused of having no sense of humor, of not being a good sport.* ◆◆◇ N-VAR; N-COUNT approval

**sport|ing** /spɔːʳtɪŋ/ 1 **Sporting** means relating to sports or used for sports. ❑ *...major sporting events, such as Wimbledon and the World Cup finals. ...a huge sporting goods store.* 2 If you have **a sporting chance** of doing something, it is quite likely that you will do that thing. ❑ *There was a sporting chance they would meet, but not necessarily at the party.* ADJ: ADJ n; PHRASE

**sports car (sports cars)** A **sports car** is a low, fast car, usually with room for only two people. N-COUNT

**sports|cast** /spɔːʳtskɑːst, -kæst/ **(sportscasts)** A **sportscast** is a radio or television broadcast of a sporting event. [mainly AM] N-COUNT

**sports|caster** /spɔːʳtskɑːstəʳ, -kæst-/ **(sportscasters)** A **sportscaster** is a radio or television broadcaster who describes or comments on sporting events. [mainly AM] N-COUNT

**sports day (sports days)** In British schools, **sports day** is a day or an afternoon when pupils compete in athletics contests such as races and the high jump. Parents are often invited to come and watch the events. N-VAR

**sports jack|et (sports jackets)** A **sports jacket** is a man's jacket, usually made of a woollen material called tweed. It is worn on informal occasions with trousers of a different material. N-COUNT

**sports|man** /spɔːʳtsmən/ **(sportsmen)** A **sportsman** is a man who takes part in sports. N-COUNT

**sports|man|ship** /spɔːʳtsmənʃɪp/ **Sportsmanship** is behaviour and attitudes that show respect for the rules of a game and for the other players. N-UNCOUNT

**sports|wear** /spɔːʳtsweəʳ/ **Sportswear** is the special clothing worn for playing sports or for informal leisure activities. N-UNCOUNT

**sports|woman** /spɔːʳtswʊmən/ **(sportswomen)** A **sportswoman** is a woman who takes part in sports. N-COUNT

**sports writ|er (sports writers)** A **sports writer** is a journalist who writes about sport. N-COUNT

**sport util|ity ve|hi|cle (sport utility vehicles)** also **sports utility vehicle.** A **sport utility vehicle** is a powerful vehicle with four-wheel drive that can be driven over rough ground. The abbreviation **SUV** is often used. N-COUNT

**sporty** /spɔːʳti/ **(sportier, sportiest)** 1 You can describe a car as **sporty** when it performs like a racing car but can be driven on normal roads. ❑ *The steering and braking are exactly what you want from a sporty car.* 2 Someone who is **sporty** likes playing sports. ADJ; ADJ

**spot** /spɒt/ **(spots, spotting, spotted)** 1 **Spots** are small, round, coloured areas on a surface. ❑ *The leaves have yellow areas on the top and underneath are powdery orange spots... The swimsuit comes in navy with white spots or blue with green spots.* 2 **Spots** on a person's skin are small lumps or marks. ❑ *Never squeeze blackheads, spots or pimples.* 3 A **spot of** a liquid is a small amount of it. [mainly BRIT] ❑ *Spots of rain had begun to fall.* 4 If you have a **spot of** something, you have a small amount of it. [mainly BRIT] ❑ *Mr Brooke is undoubtedly in a spot of bother... We've given all the club members tea, coffee and a spot of lunch.* 5 You can refer to a particular place as a **spot**. ❑ *They stayed at several of the island's top tourist spots... They all stood there staring, as if frozen to the spot.* 6 A **spot** in a television or radio show is a part of it that is regularly reserved for a particular performer or type of entertainment. ❑ *Unsuccessful at screen writing, he got a spot on a CNN film show.* 7 If you **spot** something or someone, you notice them. ❑ *Vicenzo failed to spot the error.* → See also **spotted, black spot, blind spot.** ◆◆◇ N-COUNT: usu pl; N-COUNT: usu pl; N-COUNT: N *of* n; QUANT: QUANT *of* n-uncount = bit; N-COUNT: usu supp N; N-COUNT: usu with supp = slot; VERB V n

PHRASES 8 If you are **on the spot**, you are at the actual place where something is happening. ❑ *...areas where troops are on the spot and protecting civilians.* 9 If you do something **on the spot**, you do it immediately. ❑ *James was called to see the producer and got the job on the spot.* 10 If you **put** someone **on the spot**, you cause them to have to answer a difficult question or make a difficult decision. ❑ *He put me on the spot a bit because he invited me right in front of his mum and I didn't particularly want to go... Even clever people are not terribly clever when put on the spot.* 11 **rooted to the spot** → see **rooted**. to **have a soft spot for** someone → see **soft**. PHRASE: v-link PHR; PHRASE: PHR after v, PHR n; PHRASE: V inflects

**spot check (spot checks)** also **spot-check.** If someone carries out a **spot check**, they examine one thing from a group in order to make sure that it is satisfactory. N-COUNT: oft N *on* n

**spot|less** /spɒtləs/ Something that is **spotless** is completely clean. ❑ *Each morning cleaners make sure everything is spotless.* ♦ **spot|less|ly** *The house had huge, spotlessly clean rooms.* ADJ; ADV: ADV adj

**spot|light** /spɒtlaɪt/ **(spotlights, spotlighting, spotlighted)** 1 A **spotlight** is a powerful light, for example in a theatre, which can be directed so that it lights up a small area. 2 If something **spotlights** a particular problem or situation, it makes people notice it and think about it. ❑ *...a new book spotlighting female entrepreneurs.* 3 Someone or something that is **in the spotlight** is getting a great deal of public attention. ❑ *Webb is back in the spotlight.* N-COUNT; VERB = highlight V n; PHRASE: v-link PHR

**spot|lit** /spɒtlɪt/ Something that is **spotlit** is brightly lit up by one or more spotlights. ❑ *She caught a clear view upwards of the spotlit temple.* ADJ

**spot-on** also **spot on. Spot-on** means exactly correct or accurate. [BRIT, INFORMAL] ❑ *Schools were told their exam information had to be spot-on and accurate.* ADJ: usu v-link ADJ

**spot|ted** /spɒtɪd/ 1 Something that is **spotted** has a pattern of spots on it. ❑ *...hand-painted spotted cups and saucers in green and blue... His cheeks were spotted with blackheads.* 2 → See also **spot**. ADJ: oft ADJ *with* n

**spot|ter** /spɒtəʳ/ **(spotters)** A **spotter** of something such as trains or aeroplanes is someone whose hobby is watching and finding out about them. [BRIT] ❑ *I was a devoted train spotter.* N-COUNT: n N

**-spotting** /-spɒtɪŋ/ **-spotting** combines with nouns to form nouns which describe the activity of looking out for things such as birds or trains as a hobby. ❑ *...train-spotting. ...bird-spotting.* COMB in N-UNCOUNT

**spot|ty** /spɒti/ **(spottier, spottiest)** Someone who is **spotty** has spots on their face. ❑ *She was rather fat, and her complexion was muddy and spotty.* ADJ = pimply

**spous|al** /spaʊzəl/ **Spousal** rights and duties are ones which you gain if you are married. [AM, FORMAL] ADJ: ADJ n = marital

**spouse** /spaʊs/ **(spouses)** Someone's **spouse** is the person they are married to. N-COUNT

**spout** /spaʊt/ **(spouts, spouting, spouted)** 1 If something **spouts** liquid or fire, or if liquid or fire **spout** out of something, it comes out very quickly with a lot of force. ❑ *He replaced the boiler when the last one began to spout flames... The main square has a fountain that spouts water 40 feet into the air... In a storm, water spouts out of the blowhole just like a whale.* 2 A **spout of** liquid is a long stream of it which is coming out of something very forcefully. 3 If you say that a person **spouts** something, you disapprove of them because they say something which you do not agree with or which you think they do not honestly feel. ❑ *He used his column to spout ill-informed criticism of the Scots rugby team.* ♦ **Spout forth** and **spout off** mean the same as **spout**. ❑ *...an estate agent spouting forth* VERB V n; V n prep; V adv/prep; N-COUNT = jet; VERB disapproval V n; PHRASAL VERB V P *about* n *about houses.* [4] A **spout** is a long, hollow part of a container through which liquids can be poured out easily. N-COUNT

**sprain** /spreɪn/ **(sprains, spraining, sprained)** [1] If you **sprain** a joint such as your ankle or wrist, you accidentally damage it by twisting it or bending it violently. VERB ❑ *He fell and sprained his ankle.* V n ♦ **sprained** *...a badly sprained ankle... His wrist was sprained.* ADJ: usu ADJ n [2] A **sprain** is the injury caused by spraining a joint. N-COUNT

**sprang** /spræŋ/ **Sprang** is the past tense of **spring**.

**sprat** /spræt/ **(sprats) Sprats** are very small European sea fish which can be eaten. N-COUNT

**sprawl** /sprɔːl/ **(sprawls, sprawling, sprawled)** [1] If you **sprawl** somewhere, you sit or lie down with your legs and arms spread out in a careless way. VERB ❑ *She sprawled on the bed as he had left her, not even moving to cover herself up.* V prep/adv → See also **sprawled**. ♦ **Sprawl out** means the same as **sprawl**. PHRASAL VERB ❑ *He would take two aspirin and sprawl out on his bed.* V P prep [2] If you say that a place **sprawls**, you mean that it covers a large area of land. VERB ❑ *The State Recreation Area sprawls over 900 acres on the southern tip of Key Biscayne.* V prep [3] You can use **sprawl** to refer to an area where a city has grown outwards in an uncontrolled way. N-UNCOUNT: usu with supp ❑ *The whole urban sprawl of Ankara contains over 2.6m people.*

**sprawled** /sprɔːld/ If you are **sprawled** somewhere, you are sitting or lying with your legs and arms spread out in a careless way. ADJ: v-link ADJ, ADJ after v ❑ *People are sprawled on makeshift beds in the cafeteria.*

**spray** /spreɪ/ **(sprays, spraying, sprayed)** ◆◇◇ [1] **Spray** is a lot of small drops of water which are being thrown into the air. N-VAR: oft N *from/of* n ❑ *The moon was casting a rainbow through the spray from the waterfall.* [2] A **spray** is a liquid kept under pressure in a can or other container, which you can force out in very small drops. N-MASS ❑ *...hair spray. ...a can of insect spray.* [3] If you **spray** a liquid somewhere or if it **sprays** somewhere, drops of the liquid cover a place or shower someone. VERB ❑ *A sprayer hooked to a tractor can spray five gallons onto ten acres...* V n prep/adv *Two inmates hurled slates at prison officers spraying them with a hose...* V n *with* n *Drops of blood sprayed across the room.* V prep [4] If a lot of small things **spray** somewhere or if something **sprays** them, they are scattered somewhere with a lot of force. VERB ❑ *A shower of mustard seeds sprayed into the air and fell into the grass...* V prep *The intensity of the blaze shattered windows, spraying glass on the streets below...* V n prep *The bullet slammed into the ceiling, spraying them with bits of plaster.* V n *with* n [5] If someone **sprays** bullets somewhere, they fire a lot of bullets at a group of people or things. VERB ❑ *He ran to the top of the building spraying bullets into shoppers below...* V n prep/adv *The army lorries were sprayed with machine gun fire from guerrillas in the woods.* V n *with* n [6] If something **is sprayed**, it is painted using paint kept under pressure in a container. VERB: usu passive ❑ *The bare metal was sprayed with several coats of primer.* *be* V-ed *with* n [7] When someone **sprays** against insects, they cover plants or crops with a chemical which prevents insects feeding on them. VERB ❑ *He doesn't spray against pests or diseases...* V *against* n *Confine the use of insecticides to the evening and do not spray plants that are in flower...* V n *Because of the immunity of the immature insects, it's important to spray regularly.* V Also V n prep [8] A **spray** is a piece of equipment for spraying water or another liquid, especially over growing plants. N-COUNT [9] A **spray of** flowers or leaves is a number of flowers or leaves on one stem or branch. N-COUNT: N *of* n ❑ *...a small spray of freesias.*

**spray can (spray cans)** also **spray-can.** A **spray can** is a small metal container containing liquid such as paint under pressure so that it can be sprayed. N-COUNT = aerosol

**spray|er** /spreɪəʳ/ **(sprayers)** A **sprayer** is a piece of equipment used for spraying liquid somewhere. N-COUNT = spray

**spray gun (spray guns)** also **spray-gun.** A **spray gun** is a piece of equipment which you use to spray paint under pressure onto a surface. N-COUNT

**spray paint (spray paints, spray painting, spray painted)** also **spray-paint.** [1] **Spray paint** is paint bought in a special can which you spray on a surface by pressing a button on the top of the can. N-MASS ❑ *The walls have been horribly vandalized with spray paint.* [2] If you **spray paint** a surface, you paint it using spray paint. VERB If you **spray paint** something **on** a surface, you paint it on that surface using spray paint. ❑ *The youths are taught how to spray paint cars and mend fences...* V n *He spray-painted his name on the wall.* V n *on* n

**spread** /spred/ **(spreads, spreading, spread)** ◆◆◇ [1] If you **spread** something somewhere, you open it out or arrange it over a place or surface, so that all of it can be seen or used easily. VERB ❑ *She spread a towel on the sand and lay on it.* V n prep ♦ **Spread out** means the same as **spread**. PHRASAL VERB ❑ *He extracted several glossy prints and spread them out on a low coffee table...* V n P *In his room, Tom was spreading out a map of Scandinavia on the bed.* V P n (not pron) [2] If you **spread** your arms, hands, fingers, or legs, you stretch them out until they are far apart. VERB ❑ *Sitting on the floor, spread your legs as far as they will go without overstretching...* V n adv *He stepped back and spread his hands wide. 'You are most welcome to our home.'* V n adj ♦ **Spread out** means the same as **spread**. PHRASAL VERB ❑ *David made a gesture, spreading out his hands as if he were showing that he had no explanation to make...* V P n (not pron) *You need a bed that's large enough to let you spread yourself out.* V n P [3] If you **spread** a substance on a surface or **spread** the surface **with** the substance, you put a thin layer of the substance over the surface. VERB ❑ *Spread the mixture in the cake tin and bake for 30 minutes...* V n prep *Spread the bread with the cheese.* V n *with* n [4] **Spread** is a soft food which is put on bread. N-MASS: usu supp N ❑ *...a wholemeal salad roll with low fat spread.* [5] If something **spreads** or **is spread** by people, it gradually reaches or affects a larger and larger area or more and more people. VERB ❑ *The industrial revolution which started a couple of hundred years ago in Europe is now spreading across the world.* V prep/adv *...the sense of fear spreading in residential neighborhoods...* V *He was fed-up with the lies being spread about him.* V n ♦ **Spread** is also a noun. N-SING: usu *the* N *of* n ❑ *The greatest hope for reform is the gradual spread of information.* [6] If something such as a liquid, gas, or smoke **spreads** or **is spread**, it moves outwards in all directions so that it covers a larger area. VERB ❑ *Fire spread rapidly after a chemical truck exploded...* V *A dark red stain was spreading across his shirt...* V prep *In Northern California, a wildfire has spread a haze of smoke over 200 miles.* V n prep ♦ **Spread** is also a noun. N-SING ❑ *The situation was complicated by the spread of a serious forest fire.* [7] If you **spread** something **over** a period of time, it takes place regularly or continuously over that period, rather than happening at one time. VERB ❑ *There seems to be little difference whether you eat all your calorie allowance in one go, or spread it over the day.* V n *over* n [8] If you **spread** something such as wealth or work, you distribute it evenly or equally. VERB ❑ *...policies that spread the state's wealth more evenly.* V n ♦ **Spread** is also a noun. N-SING: usu N *of* n ❑ *There are easier ways to encourage the even spread of wealth.* [9] A **spread of** ideas, interests, or other things is a wide variety of them. N-SING: usu N *of* n = range ❑ *A topic-based approach can be hard to assess in primary schools with a typical spread of ability.* [10] A **spread** is a large meal, especially one that has been prepared for a special occasion. N-COUNT [11] A **spread** is two pages of a book, magazine, or newspaper that are opposite each other when you open it at a particular place. N-COUNT ❑ *There was a double-page spread of a dinner for 46 people.* [12] **Spread** is used to refer to the difference between the price that a seller wants someone to pay for a particular stock or share and the price that the buyer is willing to pay. N-SING [BUSINESS] ❑ *Market makers earn their livings from the spread between buying and selling prices.* [13] to **spread** your **wings** → see **wing**.

♦ **spread out** [1] If people, animals, or vehicles **spread out**, they move apart from each other. ❑ *Felix watched his men move like soldiers, spreading out into two teams.* [2] If something such as a city or forest **spreads out**, it gets larger and gradually begins to covers a larger area. ❑ *Cities such as Tokyo are spreading out.* [3] → see **spread 1**. [4] → see **spread 2**. PHRASAL VERB V P PHRASAL VERB V P

**spread bet|ting** **Spread betting** is a form of gambling that involves predicting a range of possible scores or results rather than one particular score or result. N-UNCOUNT

**spread|eagled** /spredi:gəld/ also **spread-eagled.** Someone who is **spreadeagled** is lying with their arms and legs spread out. ❑ *They lay spreadeagled on the floor.* ADJ: usu v-link ADJ

**spread out** If people or things are **spread out**, they are a long way apart. ❑ *The Kurds are spread out across five nations.* ADJ: usu v-link ADJ

**spread|sheet** /spredʃi:t/ **(spreadsheets)** A **spreadsheet** is a computer program that is used for displaying and dealing with numbers. Spreadsheets are used mainly for financial planning. [COMPUTING] N-COUNT

**spree** /spri:/ **(sprees)** If you spend a period of time doing something in an excessive way, you can say that you are going **on** a particular kind of **spree**. ❑ *Some Americans went on a spending spree in December to beat the new tax.* N-COUNT: usu n N

**sprig** /sprɪg/ **(sprigs)** A **sprig** is a small stem with leaves on it which has been picked from a bush or plant, especially so that it can be used in cooking or as a decoration. N-COUNT: usu N *of* n

**sprigged** /sprɪgd/ **Sprigged** material or paper has a pattern of small leaves or flowers on it. ❑ *...a sprigged cotton dress.* ADJ: usu ADJ n

**spright|ly** /spraɪtli/ **(sprightlier, sprightliest)** A **sprightly** person, especially an old person, is lively and active. ❑ *...the sprightly 85-year-old President.* ADJ: usu ADJ n = spry

**spring** /sprɪŋ/ **(springs, springing, sprang, sprung)** ◆◆◇ [1] **Spring** is the season between winter and summer when the weather becomes warmer and plants start to grow again. ❑ *We met again in the spring of 1977.* N-VAR [2] A **spring** is a spiral of wire which returns to its original shape after it is pressed or pulled. ❑ *Both springs in the fuel pump were broken.* N-COUNT [3] A **spring** is a place where water comes up through the ground. It is also the water that comes from that place. ❑ *To the north are the hot springs of Banyas de Sant Loan.* N-COUNT: usu pl [4] When a person or animal **springs**, they jump upwards or forwards suddenly or quickly. ❑ *He sprang to his feet, grabbing his keys off the coffee table... Throwing back the sheet, he sprang from the bed... The lion roared once and sprang.* VERB V prep V prep V [5] If something **springs** in a particular direction, it moves suddenly and quickly. ❑ *Sadly when the lid of the boot sprang open, it was empty.* VERB V adj [6] If one thing **springs from** another thing, it is the result of it. ❑ *Ethiopia's art springs from her early Christian as well as her Muslim heritage.* VERB = stem V *from* n [7] If a boat or container **springs a leak**, water or some other liquid starts coming in or out through a crack. ❑ *The yacht has sprung a leak in the hull.* VERB V n [8] If you **spring** some news or a surprise **on** someone, you tell them something that they did not expect to hear, without warning them. ❑ *Mclaren sprang a new idea on him.* VERB V n *on* n [9] to **spring to mind** → see **mind**.

♦ **spring up** If something **springs up**, it suddenly appears or begins to exist. ❑ *New theatres and arts centres sprang up all over the country.* PHRASAL VERB V P

**spring|board** /sprɪŋbɔ:ʳd/ **(springboards)** [1] If something is a **springboard for** something else, it makes it possible for that thing to happen or start. ❑ *The 1981 budget was the springboard for an economic miracle.* N-COUNT: N *for/to* n [2] A **springboard** is a flexible board from which you jump into a swimming pool or onto a piece of gymnastic equipment. N-COUNT

**spring chick|en** **(spring chickens)** If you say that someone is **no spring chicken**, you are saying that they are not young. [HUMOROUS] ❑ *At 85, he is no spring chicken, but Henry Cook is busier than ever.* PHRASE: usu v-link PHR

**spring-clean** **(spring-cleans, spring-cleaning, spring-cleaned)** When you **spring-clean** a house, you thoroughly clean everything in it. ❑ *It's almost as easy these days to give your rooms a new coat of paint as it is to spring-clean them.* VERB V n

**spring on|ion** **(spring onions)** **Spring onions** are small onions with long green leaves. They are often eaten raw in salads. [BRIT] N-VAR: usu pl

☑ in AM, use **scallion**

**spring roll** **(spring rolls)** A **spring roll** is a Chinese food consisting of a small roll of thin pastry filled with vegetables and sometimes meat, and then fried. N-COUNT

**spring tide** **(spring tides)** A **spring tide** is an unusually high tide that happens at the time of a new moon or a full moon. N-COUNT

**spring|time** /sprɪŋtaɪm/ **Springtime** is the period of time during which spring lasts. N-UNCOUNT

**springy** /sprɪŋi/ If something is **springy**, it returns quickly to its original shape after you press it. ❑ *Steam for about 12 mins until the cake is risen and springy to touch in the centre.* ADJ

**sprin|kle** /sprɪŋkəl/ **(sprinkles, sprinkling, sprinkled)** [1] If you **sprinkle** a thing **with** something such as a liquid or powder, you scatter the liquid or powder over it. ❑ *Sprinkle the meat with salt and place in the pan... Cheese can be sprinkled on egg or vegetable dishes.* VERB V n *with* n *be* V-ed *on* n [2] If something **is sprinkled with** particular things, it has a few of them throughout it and they are far apart from each other. ❑ *Unfortunately, the text is sprinkled with errors... Men in green army uniforms are sprinkled throughout the huge auditorium.* VERB *be* V-ed *with* n *be* V-ed prep [3] If **it is sprinkling**, it is raining very lightly. [AM] VERB

☑ in BRIT, use **spit**

**sprin|kler** /sprɪŋkləʳ/ **(sprinklers)** A **sprinkler** is a device used to spray water. Sprinklers are used to water plants or grass, or to put out fires in buildings. N-COUNT

**sprin|kling** /sprɪŋklɪŋ/ A **sprinkling of** something is a small quantity or amount of it, especially if it is spread over a large area. ❑ *...a light sprinkling of snow.* N-SING: usu N *of* n

**sprint** /sprɪnt/ **(sprints, sprinting, sprinted)** [1] **The sprint** is a short, fast running race. ❑ *Rob Harmeling won the sprint in Bordeaux. ...the women's 100-metres sprint.* N-SING: *the* N [2] A **sprint** is a short race in which the competitors run, drive, ride, or swim very fast. ❑ *Lewis will compete in both sprints in Stuttgart.* N-COUNT [3] **A sprint** is a fast run that someone does, either at the end of a race or because they are in a hurry. ❑ *I broke into a sprint.* N-SING: *a* N [4] If you **sprint**, you run or ride as fast as you can over a short distance. ❑ *Sergeant Horne sprinted to the car.* VERB V adv/prep

**sprint|er** /sprɪntəʳ/ **(sprinters)** A **sprinter** is a person who takes part in short, fast races. N-COUNT

**sprite** /spraɪt/ **(sprites)** In fairy stories and legends, a **sprite** is a small, magic creature which lives near water. N-COUNT

**spritz|er** /sprɪtsəʳ/ **(spritzers)** A **spritzer** is a drink consisting of white wine and soda water. N-COUNT

**sprock|et** /sprɒkɪt/ **(sprockets)** A **sprocket** is a wheel with teeth around the outer edge that fit into the holes in a chain or a length of film or tape in order to move it round. N-COUNT

**sprog** /sprɒg/ **(sprogs)** A **sprog** is a baby or child. [BRIT, INFORMAL] N-COUNT

**sprout** /spraʊt/ **(sprouts, sprouting, sprouted)** [1] When plants, vegetables, or seeds **sprout**, they produce new shoots or leaves. ❑ *It only takes a few days for beans to sprout.* VERB V [2] When leaves, shoots, or plants **sprout** somewhere, they grow there. ❑ *Leaf-shoots were beginning to sprout on the hawthorn.* VERB V prep [3] If a garden or other area of land VERB: no passive

**sprouts** plants, they start to grow there. ❑ *...the garden, which had had time to sprout a shocking collection of weeds.* (V n) [4] If something such as hair **sprouts** from a person or animal, or if they **sprout** it, it grows on them. (VERB: no passive) ❑ *She is very old now, with little, round, wire-rimmed glasses and whiskers sprouting from her chin...* (V prep) *As well as sprouting a few grey hairs, Kevin seems to be suffering the occasional memory loss.* (V n) [5] **Sprouts** are vegetables that look like tiny cabbages. They are also called **brussels sprouts**. (N-COUNT: usu pl) [6] **Sprouts** are new shoots on plants. (N-COUNT: usu pl) ❑ *After eleven days of growth the number of sprouts was counted.*

**spruce** /spruːs/ **(spruce; spruces, sprucing, spruced)** [1] A **spruce** is a kind of evergreen tree. (N-VAR) ❑ *Trees such as spruce, pine and oak have been planted. ...a young blue spruce. ...80-year-old spruces.* ♦ **Spruce** is the wood from this tree. (N-UNCOUNT) ❑ *Early settlers built frames of spruce and pine.* [2] Someone who is **spruce** is very neat and smart in appearance. (ADJ) ❑ *Chris was looking spruce in his stiff-collared black shirt and new short hair cut.*

♦ **spruce up** If something **is spruced up**, its appearance is improved. If someone **is spruced up**, they have made themselves look very smart. (PHRASAL VERB) ❑ *Many buildings have been spruced up...* (be V-ed P) *In the evening we spruced ourselves up a bit and went out for dinner.* (V n P)

**sprung** /sprʌŋ/ **Sprung** is the past participle of **spring**.

**spry** /spraɪ/ Someone, especially an old person, who is **spry**, is lively and active. (ADJ: usu v-link ADJ = sprightly) ❑ *The old gentleman was as spry as ever.*

**spud** /spʌd/ **(spuds) Spuds** are potatoes. [INFORMAL] (N-COUNT: usu pl)

**spun** /spʌn/ **Spun** is the past tense and past participle of **spin**.

**spunk** /spʌŋk/ **Spunk** is courage. [INFORMAL] (N-UNCOUNT, approval) ❑ *I admired her independence and her spunk.*

**spunky** /spʌŋki/ **(spunkier, spunkiest)** A **spunky** person shows courage. [INFORMAL] (ADJ, approval = gutsy) ❑ *She's so spunky and spirited.*

**spur** /spɜːʳ/ **(spurs, spurring, spurred)** (◆◇◇) [1] If one thing **spurs** you **to** do another, it encourages you to do it. (VERB = urge) ❑ *It's the money that spurs these fishermen to risk a long ocean journey in their flimsy boats...* (V n to-inf) *His friend's plight had spurred him into taking part.* (V n to/into n/-ing) ♦ **Spur on** means the same as **spur**. (PHRASAL VERB) ❑ *Their attitude, rather than reining him back, only seemed to spur Philip on...* (V n P) *Criticism can be of great use; we may not like it at the time, but it can spur us on to greater things.* (V n P to n) [2] If something **spurs** a change or event, it makes it happen faster or sooner. [JOURNALISM] (VERB) ❑ *The administration may put more emphasis on spurring economic growth.* (V n) [3] Something that acts as a **spur to** something else encourages a person or organization to do that thing or makes it happen more quickly. (N-COUNT: usu sing, oft N to n) ❑ *...a belief in competition as a spur to efficiency.* [4] **Spurs** are small metal wheels with sharp points that are attached to the heels of a rider's boots. The rider uses them to make their horse go faster. (N-COUNT: usu pl) [5] The **spur** of a hill or mountain is a piece of ground which sticks out from its side. (N-COUNT) [6] If you do something **on the spur of the moment**, you do it suddenly, without planning it beforehand. (PHRASE: PHR after v, PHR n) ❑ *They admitted they had taken a vehicle on the spur of the moment.*

**spu|ri|ous** /spjʊəriəs/ [1] Something that is **spurious** seems to be genuine, but is false. (ADJ: usu ADJ n, disapproval) ❑ *He was arrested in 1979 on spurious corruption charges.* [2] A **spurious** argument or way of reasoning is incorrect, and so the conclusion is probably incorrect. (ADJ: usu ADJ n, disapproval) ❑ *...a spurious framework for analysis.*

**spurn** /spɜːʳn/ **(spurns, spurning, spurned)** If you **spurn** someone or something, you reject them. (VERB) ❑ *He spurned the advice of management consultants.* (V n) *...a spurned lover.* (V-ed)

**spur-of-the-moment** → see **spur**.

**spurt** /spɜːʳt/ **(spurts, spurting, spurted)** [1] When liquid or fire **spurts** from somewhere, or when something **spurts** liquid or fire, it comes out quickly in a thin, powerful stream. (VERB) ❑ *They spurted blood all over me. I nearly passed out.* (V n) *...a fountain that spurts water nine stories high...* (V n) *I saw flames spurt from the roof.* (V prep) ♦ **Spurt out** means the same as **spurt**. (Also V; PHRASAL VERB) ❑ *When the washing machine spurts out water at least we can mop it up...* (V P n (not pron)) *Wear eye protection when opening the container, since it's so easy for contents to spurt out.* (V P) [2] A **spurt of** liquid is a stream of it which comes out of something very forcefully. (N-COUNT: oft N of n = jet) ❑ *A spurt of diesel came from one valve and none from the other.* [3] A **spurt of** activity, effort, or emotion is a sudden, brief period of intense activity, effort, or emotion. (N-COUNT: usu with supp = surge) ❑ *At adolescence, muscles go through a growth spurt.* [4] If someone or something **spurts** somewhere, they suddenly increase their speed for a short while in order to get there. (VERB) ❑ *The back wheels spun and the van spurted up the last few feet.* (V prep/adv) [5] If something happens **in spurts**, there are periods of activity followed by periods in which it does not happen. (PHRASE: PHR after v) ❑ *The deals came in spurts: three in 1977, none in 1978, three more in 1979.*

**sput|ter** /spʌtəʳ/ **(sputters, sputtering, sputtered)** If something such as an engine or a flame **sputters**, it works or burns in an uneven way and makes a series of soft popping sounds. (VERB = splutter) ❑ *The truck sputtered and stopped...* (V) *The flame sputters out.* (V prep/adv)

**spu|tum** /spjuːtəm/ **Sputum** is the wet substance which is coughed up from someone's lungs. [MEDICAL] (N-UNCOUNT)

**spy** /spaɪ/ **(spies, spying, spied)** [1] A **spy** is a person whose job is to find out secret information about another country or organization. (N-COUNT) ❑ *He was jailed for five years as an alleged British spy.* [2] A **spy** satellite or **spy** plane obtains secret information about another country by taking photographs from the sky. (ADJ: ADJ n) [3] Someone who **spies for** a country or organization tries to find out secret information about another country or organization. (VERB) ❑ *The agent spied for East Germany for more than twenty years...* (V for n) *East and West are still spying on one another...* (V on n) *I never agreed to spy against the United States.* (V against n) ♦ **spy|ing** *...a ten-year sentence for spying.* (N-UNCOUNT) [4] If you **spy on** someone, you watch them secretly. (VERB) ❑ *That day he spied on her while pretending to work on the shrubs.* (V on n) [5] If you **spy** someone or something, you notice them. [LITERARY] (VERB = spot) ❑ *He was walking down the street when he spied an old friend.* (V n)

**spy|master** /spaɪmɑːstəʳ, -mæs-/ **(spymasters)** A **spymaster** is a spy who is in charge of a group of spies. (N-COUNT)

**sq** also **sq.** **sq** is used as a written abbreviation for **square** when you are giving the measurement of an area. ❑ *The building provides about 25,500 sq ft of air-conditioned offices.*

**squab|ble** /skwɒbəl/ **(squabbles, squabbling, squabbled)** When people **squabble** about something that is not really important. (V-RECIP) ❑ *Mother is devoted to Dad although they squabble all the time...* (pl-n V) *My four-year-old squabbles with his friends.* (V with n) ♦ **squab|bling** *In recent months its government has been paralysed by political squabbling.* (N-UNCOUNT) ♦ **Squabble** is also a noun. (N-COUNT) ❑ *There have been minor squabbles about phone bills.*

**squad** /skwɒd/ **(squads)** (◆◇◇) [1] A **squad** is a section of a police force that is responsible for dealing with a particular type of crime. (N-COUNT: usu sing, usu supp N) ❑ *The building was evacuated and the bomb squad called... The club is under investigation by the fraud squad.* [2] A **squad** is a group of players from which a sports team will be chosen. (N-COUNT) ❑ *Sean O'Leary has been named in the England squad to tour Argentina.* [3] A **squad of** soldiers is a small group of them. (N-COUNT: oft N of n) ❑ *...a squad of commandos.* → See also **death squad**, **firing squad**, **Flying Squad**, **vice squad**.

**squad car** **(squad cars)** A **squad car** is a car used by the police. [AM] (N-COUNT)

✓ in BRIT, usually use **patrol car**, **police car**

**squad|die** /skwɒdi/ **(squaddies)** A **squaddie** is a soldier of the lowest rank in the army. [BRIT, INFORMAL] N-COUNT

**squad|ron** /skwɒdrən/ **(squadrons)** A **squadron** is a section of one of the armed forces, especially the air force. ❑ *The government said it was preparing a squadron of eighteen Mirage fighter planes.* N-COUNT-COLL

**squad|ron lead|er** **(squadron leaders)** A **squadron leader** is an officer in the British air force who has a rank above that of flight lieutenant. N-COUNT; N-TITLE

**squal|id** /skwɒlɪd/ [1] A **squalid** place is dirty, untidy, and in bad condition. ❑ *He followed her up a rickety staircase to a squalid bedsit.* ADJ [2] **Squalid** activities are unpleasant and often dishonest. ❑ *The Tory Party called the bill 'the most squalid measure ever put before the Commons'.* ADJ [disapproval]

**squall** /skwɔːl/ **(squalls, squalling, squalled)** [1] A **squall** is a sudden strong wind which often causes a brief, violent rain storm or snow storm. ❑ *The boat was hit by a squall north of the island.* N-COUNT [2] If a person or animal **squalls**, they make a loud unpleasant noise like the noise made by a crying baby. ❑ *There was an infant squalling in the back of the church. ...squalling guitars.* VERB = wail; V; V-ing

**squal|ly** /skwɔːli/ In **squally** weather, there are sudden strong winds which often cause brief, violent storms. ❑ *The competitors had to contend with squally weather conditions.* ADJ: usu ADJ n

**squal|or** /skwɒləʳ/ You can refer to very dirty, unpleasant conditions as **squalor**. ❑ *He was out of work and living in squalor.* N-UNCOUNT

**squan|der** /skwɒndəʳ/ **(squanders, squandering, squandered)** If you **squander** money, resources, or opportunities, you waste them. ❑ *Hooker didn't squander his money on flashy cars or other vices... He had squandered his chances to win.* VERB; V n *on* n; V n

**square** /skweəʳ/ **(squares, squaring, squared)** ◆◆◇ [1] A **square** is a shape with four sides that are all the same length and four corners that are all right angles. ❑ *Serve the cake warm or at room temperature, cut in squares... Most of the rugs are simple cotton squares.* N-COUNT [2] In a town or city, a **square** is a flat open place, often in the shape of a square. ❑ *The house is located in one of Pimlico's prettiest garden squares. ...St Mark's Square.* N-COUNT; N-IN-NAMES [3] Something that is **square** has a shape the same as a square or similar to a square. ❑ *Round tables seat more people in the same space as a square table... His finger nails were square and cut neatly across.* ADJ: usu ADJ n [4] **Square** is used before units of length when referring to the area of something. For example, if something is three metres long and two metres wide, its area is six square metres. ❑ *Canary Wharf was set to provide 10 million square feet of office space... The Philippines has just 6,000 square kilometres of forest left.* ADJ: ADJ n [5] **Square** is used after units of length when you are giving the length of each side of something that is square in shape. ❑ *...a linen cushion cover, 45 cm square. ...two pieces of wood 4 inches square.* ADJ: amount ADJ [6] To **square** a number means to multiply it by itself. For example, **3 squared** is 3 x 3, or 9. **3 squared** is usually written as $3^2$. ❑ *Take the time in seconds, square it, and multiply by 5.12... A squared plus B squared equals C squared.* VERB; V n; V-ed [7] The **square of** a number is the number produced when you multiply that number by itself. For example, the square of 3 is 9. ❑ *...the square of the speed of light, an exceedingly large number.* N-COUNT: usu with poss [8] If you **square** two different ideas or actions **with** each other or if they **square with** each other, they fit or match each other. ❑ *That explanation squares with the facts, doesn't it... He set out to square his dreams with reality.* VERB; V *with* n; V n *with* n [9] If you **square** something **with** someone, you ask their permission or check with them that what you are doing is acceptable to them. ❑ *She should have squared things with Jay before she went into this business with Walker.* VERB = okay; V n *with* n [10] → See also **squared**, **squarely**.

PHRASES [11] If you say that someone **squares the circle**, you mean that they bring together two things which are normally thought to be so different that they cannot exist together. ❑ *He has squared the circle of keeping the City happy and doing something to improve business cash flow... 'Nirvana' squared the circle by making a record that was both superb pop and rock music at the same time.* PHRASE: V inflects [12] If you are **back to square one**, you have to start dealing with something from the beginning again because the way you were dealing with it has failed. ❑ *If your complaint in not upheld, you may feel you are back to square one.* PHRASE: v-link PHR, PHR after v [13] **fair and square** → see **fair**.

♦ **square off** [1] If you **square** something **off**, you alter it so that it has the shape of a square. ❑ *Peel a thick-skinned orange and square off the ends with a sharp knife.* PHRASAL VERB; V P n (not pron) [2] If one group or person **squares off against** or **with** another, they prepare to fight them. [mainly AM] ❑ *In Florida, farmers are squaring off against cities for rights to groundwater.* PHRASAL VERB; V P *against*

♦ **square up** If you **square up to** a problem, person, or situation, you accept that you have to deal with them and take action to do so. ❑ *The world's most prestigious insurance company was last night squaring up to take on MPs who have accused it of being riddled with corruption.* PHRASAL VERB; V P

**squared** /skweəʳd/ [1] Something that is **squared** has the shape of a square, or has a pattern of squares on it. ❑ *Draw up a scale floor plan on squared paper, marking in the door opening and windows.* ADJ [2] → See also **square**.

**square dance** **(square dances)** [1] A **square dance** is a traditional American dance in which sets of four couples dance together, forming a square at the beginning of the dance. N-COUNT [2] A **square dance** is a social event where people dance square dances. N-COUNT

**square|ly** /skweəʳli/ [1] **Squarely** means directly or in the middle, rather than indirectly or at an angle. ❑ *I kept the gun aimed squarely at his eyes.* ADV: ADV with v [2] If something such as blame or responsibility lies **squarely** with someone, they are definitely the person responsible. ❑ *Responsibility for success or failure lies squarely with the Nigerians.* ADV: ADV with v [3] If you face something **squarely**, you face it directly, without trying to avoid it. ❑ *The management committee have faced the situation squarely.* ADV: ADV with v

**square meal** **(square meals)** A **square meal** is a meal which is big enough to satisfy you. ❑ *They haven't had a square meal for four days.* N-COUNT

**Square Mile** **The Square Mile** is the part of London where many important financial institutions have their main offices. → See also **City**. N-PROPER: *the* N

**square root** **(square roots)** The **square root of** a number is another number which produces the first number when it is multiplied by itself. For example, the square root of 16 is 4. N-COUNT: usu N *of* num

**squash** /skwɒʃ/ **(squashes, squashing, squashed)** [1] If someone or something **is squashed**, they are pressed or crushed with such force that they become injured or lose their shape. ❑ *Robert was lucky to escape with just a broken foot after being squashed against a fence by a car... Whole neighbourhoods have been squashed flat by shelling... She made clay models and squashed them flat again.* VERB; *be* V-ed prep; *be* V-ed adj; V n adj [2] If people or things are **squashed into** a place, they are put or pushed into a place where there is not enough room for them to be. ❑ *The stage is squashed into a small corner of the field.* ADJ: v-link ADJ *into* n = cram [3] If you say that getting a number of people into a small space is **a squash**, you mean that it is only just possible for them all to get into it. [INFORMAL] ❑ *It all looked a bit of a squash as they squeezed inside the small hatchback.* N-SING: *a* N = squeeze [4] If you **squash** something that is causing you trouble, you put a stop to it, often by force. ❑ *The troops would stay in position to squash the first murmur of trouble.* VERB; V n [5] **Squash** is a game in which two N-UNCOUNT players hit a small rubber ball against the walls of a court using rackets. [6] [N-MASS = cordial] **Squash** is a drink made from fruit juice, sugar, and water. Squash is sold in bottles in a concentrated form to which you add water. [BRIT] ❑ *...a glass of orange squash.* [7] [N-VAR] A **squash** is one of a family of vegetables that have thick skin and soft or firm flesh inside.

**squashy** /skwɒʃi/ [ADJ: usu ADJ n] **Squashy** things are soft and able to be squashed easily. ❑ *...deep, squashy sofas.*

**squat** /skwɒt/ **(squats, squatting, squatted)** [1] [VERB = crouch] If you **squat**, you lower yourself towards the ground, balancing on your feet with your legs bent. ❑ [V] *We squatted beside the pool and watched the diver sink slowly down...* [V *on* n] *He came over and squatted on his heels, looking up at the boys.* ♦ [PHRASAL VERB] **Squat down** means the same as **squat**. ❑ [V P] *Albert squatted down and examined it...* [V P prep] *She had squatted down on her heels.* ♦ [N-SING: *a* N] **Squat** is also a noun. ❑ *He bent to a squat and gathered the puppies on his lap.* [2] [ADJ: usu ADJ n] If you describe someone or something as **squat**, you mean they are short and thick, usually in an unattractive way. ❑ *Eddie was a short squat fellow in his forties with thinning hair.* [3] [VERB] People who **squat** occupy an unused building or unused land without having a legal right to do so. ❑ [V] *You can't simply wander around squatting on other people's property...* [V n] *They earn their living by squatting the land and sharecropping.* [4] [N-COUNT] A **squat** is an empty building that people are living in illegally, without paying any rent or any property tax. ❑ *After returning from Paris, David moved to a squat in Brixton.*

**squat|ter** /skwɒtəʳ/ **(squatters)** [N-COUNT] A **squatter** is someone who lives in an unused building without having a legal right to do so and without paying any rent or any property tax.

**squaw** /skwɔː/ **(squaws)** [N-COUNT] In the past, people sometimes referred to a Native American Indian woman as a **squaw**. [OFFENSIVE]

**squawk** /skwɔːk/ **(squawks, squawking, squawked)** [1] [VERB] When a bird **squawks**, it makes a loud harsh noise. ❑ [V] *I threw pebbles at the hens, and that made them jump and squawk.* ♦ [N-COUNT] **Squawk** is also a noun. ❑ *A mallard suddenly took wing, rising steeply into the air with an angry squawk.* [2] [VERB] If a person **squawks**, they complain loudly, often in a high-pitched, harsh tone. [INFORMAL] ❑ [V that] *Mr Arbor squawked that the deal was a double-cross.*

**squeak** /skwiːk/ **(squeaks, squeaking, squeaked)** [1] [VERB] If something or someone **squeaks**, they make a short, high-pitched sound. ❑ [V] *My boots squeaked a little as I walked...* [V adj] *The door squeaked open...* [V *with* n] *She squeaked with delight.* ♦ [N-COUNT] **Squeak** is also a noun. ❑ *He gave an outraged squeak.* [2] [VERB] To **squeak through** or **squeak by** means to only just manage to get accepted, get included in something, or win something. ❑ [V prep/adv] *The President's economic package squeaked through the House of Representatives by 219 votes to 213.* [3] → See also **bubble and squeak**.

**squeaky** /skwiːki/ [ADJ] Something that is **squeaky** makes high-pitched sounds. ❑ *...squeaky floorboards... He had a squeaky voice.*

**squeaky clean** also **squeaky-clean.** [ADJ] If you say that someone is **squeaky clean**, you mean that they live a very moral life and have never done anything wrong. [INFORMAL] ❑ *Maybe this guy isn't so squeaky clean after all.*

**squeal** /skwiːl/ **(squeals, squealing, squealed)** [VERB] If someone or something **squeals**, they make a long, high-pitched sound. ❑ [V *with* n] *Jennifer squealed with delight and hugged me...* [V] *The car's tires squealed again as it sped around the corner.* ♦ [N-COUNT] **Squeal** is also a noun. ❑ *At that moment there was a squeal of brakes and the angry blowing of a car horn.*

**squeam|ish** /skwiːmɪʃ/ [ADJ: usu v-link ADJ] If you are **squeamish**, you are easily upset by unpleasant sights or situations. ❑ *I am not squeamish about blood.*

**squeeze** /skwiːz/ **(squeezes, squeezing, squeezed)** ◆◇◇ [1] [VERB] If you **squeeze** something, you press it firmly, usually with your hands. ❑ [V n] *He squeezed her arm reassuringly...* [V n adj] *Dip the bread briefly in water, then squeeze it dry.* ♦ [N-COUNT: usu sing] **Squeeze** is also a noun. ❑ *I liked her way of reassuring you with a squeeze of the hand.* [2] [VERB] If you **squeeze** a liquid or a soft substance out of an object, you get the liquid or substance out by pressing the object. ❑ [V n prep] *Joe put the plug in the sink and squeezed some detergent over the dishes.* [V-ed] *...freshly squeezed lemon juice.* [3] [VERB] If you **squeeze** your eyes shut or if your eyes **squeeze** shut, you close them tightly, usually because you are frightened or to protect your eyes from something such as strong sunlight. ❑ [V n adj] *Nancy squeezed her eyes shut and prayed...* [V adj] *If you keep your eyes squeezed shut, you'll miss the show.* [4] [VERB] If you **squeeze** a person or thing somewhere or if they **squeeze** there, they manage to get through or into a small space. ❑ [V n prep/adv] *They lowered him gradually into the cockpit. Somehow they squeezed him in the tight space, and strapped him in...* [V prep/adv] *Many break-ins are carried out by youngsters who can squeeze through tiny windows.* [5] [N-SING: *a* N = squash] If you say that getting a number of people into a small space is **a squeeze**, you mean that it is only just possible for them all to get into it. [INFORMAL] ❑ *It was a squeeze in the car with five of them.* [6] [VERB] If you **squeeze** something **out of** someone, you persuade them to give it to you, although they may be unwilling to do this. ❑ [V n *from/out of*] *The investigators complained about the difficulties of squeezing information out of residents.* [7] [VERB] If a government **squeezes** the economy, they put strict controls on people's ability to borrow money or on their own departments' freedom to spend money, in order to control the country's rate of inflation. ❑ [V n] *The government will squeeze the economy into a severe recession to force inflation down.* ♦ [N-SING] **Squeeze** is also a noun. ❑ *The CBI also says the squeeze is slowing down inflation.* [8] [N-COUNT] Someone's **squeeze** is their boyfriend or girlfriend. [INFORMAL, JOURNALISM] ❑ *Jack showed off his latest squeeze at the weekend.*

♦ **squeeze out** [PHRASAL VERB: usu passive] If a person or thing **is squeezed out**, they are no longer included in something that they were previously involved in. ❑ [*be* V-ed P] *Other directors appear happy that Lord Hollick has been squeezed out...* [*be* V-ed P *of* n] *Latin and Greek will be squeezed out of school timetables.*

**squelch** /skweltʃ/ **(squelches, squelching, squelched)** [VERB] To **squelch** means to make a wet, sucking sound, like the sound you make when you are walking on wet, muddy ground. ❑ [V prep/adv] *He squelched across the turf.*

**squib** /skwɪb/ **(squibs)** [PHRASE: N inflects, usu v-link PHR] You can describe something such as an event or a performance as a **damp squib** when it is expected to be interesting, exciting, or impressive, but fails to be any of these things. [BRIT] ❑ *The all-party meeting was a damp squib.*

**squid** /skwɪd/ **(squids** or **squid)** [N-COUNT] A **squid** is a sea creature with a long soft body and many soft arms called tentacles. ♦ [N-UNCOUNT] **Squid** is pieces of this creature eaten as food. ❑ *Add the prawns and squid and cook for 2 minutes.*

**squidgy** /skwɪdʒi/ [ADJ: usu ADJ n = squashy] Something that is **squidgy** is soft and can be squashed easily. [BRIT, INFORMAL] ❑ *...the squidgy end of a melon. ...a squidgy sofa.*

**squig|gle** /skwɪgəl/ **(squiggles)** [N-COUNT] A **squiggle** is a line that bends and curls in an irregular way.

**squig|gly** /skwɪgəli/ [ADJ] **Squiggly** lines are lines that bend and curl in an irregular way. ❑ *He drew three squiggly lines.*

**squint** /skwɪnt/ **(squints, squinting, squinted)** [1] [VERB] If you **squint at** something, you look at it with your eyes partly closed. ❑ [V prep/adv] *The girl squinted at the photograph...* [V] *The bright sunlight made me squint...* [V n] *He squinted his eyes and looked at the floor.* [2] [N-COUNT] If someone has a **squint**, their eyes look in different directions from each other.

**squire** /skwaɪəʳ/ **(squires)** In former times, the **squire** of an English village was the man who owned most of the land in it. N-COUNT; N-TITLE

**squirm** /skwɜːʳm/ **(squirms, squirming, squirmed)** [1] If you **squirm**, you move your body from side to side, usually because you are nervous or uncomfortable. ❑ *He had squirmed and wriggled and screeched when his father had washed his face... He gave a feeble shrug and tried to squirm free... He squirmed out of the straps of his backpack.* VERB = wriggle; V; V adj; V adv/prep [2] If you **squirm**, you are very embarrassed or ashamed. ❑ *Mentioning religion is a sure way to make him squirm.* VERB; V

**squir|rel** /skwɪrəl, AM skwɜːrəl/ **(squirrels)** A **squirrel** is a small animal with a long furry tail. Squirrels live mainly in trees. N-COUNT

**squirt** /skwɜːʳt/ **(squirts, squirting, squirted)** [1] If you **squirt** a liquid somewhere or if it **squirts** somewhere, the liquid comes out of a narrow opening in a thin fast stream. ❑ *He cut open his pie and squirted tomato sauce into it... The water squirted from its throat.* ♦ **Squirt** is also a noun. ❑ *It just needs a little squirt of oil.* VERB; V n prep/adv; V prep/adv; N-COUNT: usu N *of* n [2] If you **squirt** something **with** a liquid, you squirt the liquid at it. ❑ *I squirted him with water.* VERB; V n *with* n

**squishy** /skwɪʃi/ **(squishier, squishiest)** Something that is **squishy** is soft and easy to squash. ❑ *...squishy pink leather chairs.* ADJ

**Sr**

> in AM, use **Sr.**

**Sr** is a written abbreviation for **Senior**, and is written after a man's name. It is used in order to distinguish a man from his son when they both have the same name. ❑ *...Donald Cunningham, Sr.*

**St** also **st.**

> The form **SS** or **SS.** is used as the plural for meaning 2.

[1] **St** is a written abbreviation for **Street**. ❑ *...116 Princess St.* [2] **St** is a written abbreviation for **Saint**. ❑ *...St Thomas. ...the Church of SS Cornelius and Cyprian.*

**st** **st** is used as a written abbreviation for **stone** when you are mentioning someone's weight. [BRIT] ❑ *He weighs 11st 8lb.*

**-st** You add **-st** to numbers written in figures and ending in 1 – but not 11 – in order to form ordinal numbers. ❑ *...Sunday 1st August 1993. ...the 101st Airborne Division.* SUFFIX

**stab** /stæb/ **(stabs, stabbing, stabbed)** [1] If someone **stabs** you, they push a knife or sharp object into your body. ❑ *Somebody stabbed him in the stomach... Stephen was stabbed to death in an unprovoked attack nearly five months ago.* VERB; V n; V *to* n [2] If you **stab** something or **stab at** it, you push at it with your finger or with something pointed that you are holding. ❑ *Bess stabbed a slice of cucumber... Goldstone flipped through the pages and stabbed his thumb at the paragraph he was looking for... He stabbed at the omelette with his fork.* VERB; V n; V n *at* n; V *at* n [3] If you have **a stab at** something, you try to do it. [INFORMAL] ❑ *Several tennis stars have had a stab at acting.* N-SING: *a* N *at* n/-ing [4] You can refer to a sudden, usually unpleasant feeling as **a stab of** that feeling. [LITERARY] ❑ *...a stab of pain just above his eye... She felt a stab of pity for him.* N-SING: *a* N *of* n [5] If you say that someone **has stabbed** you **in the back**, you mean that they have done something very harmful to you when you thought that you could trust them. You can refer to an action of this kind as **a stab in the back**. ❑ *She felt betrayed, as though her daughter had stabbed her in the back.* PHRASE: V inflects [6] **a stab in the dark** → see **dark**.

**stab|bing** /stæbɪŋ/ **(stabbings)** [1] A **stabbing** is an incident in which someone stabs someone else with a knife. N-COUNT [2] A **stabbing** pain is a sudden sharp pain. ❑ *He was struck by a stabbing pain in his midriff.* ADJ: ADJ n

**sta|bil|ity** /stəbɪlɪti/ → see **stable**.

**sta|bi|lize** /steɪbɪlaɪz/ **(stabilizes, stabilizing, stabilized)**

> in BRIT, also use **stabilise**

If something **stabilizes**, or **is stabilized**, it becomes stable. ❑ *Although her illness is serious, her condition is beginning to stabilize... Officials hope the move will stabilize exchange rates.* VERB; V; V n ♦ **sta|bi|li|za|tion** /steɪbɪlaɪzeɪʃən/ *...the stabilisation of property prices.* N-UNCOUNT

**sta|bi|li|zer** /steɪbɪlaɪzəʳ/ **(stabilizers)**

> in BRIT, also use **stabiliser**

A **stabilizer** is a device, mechanism, or chemical that makes something stable. N-COUNT

**sta|ble** /steɪbəl/ **(stabler, stablest, stables)** ◆◆◇ [1] If something is **stable**, it is not likely to change or come to an end suddenly. ❑ *The price of oil should remain stable for the rest of 1992. ...a stable marriage.* ADJ ♦ **sta|bil|ity** /stəbɪlɪti/ *It was a time of political stability and progress.* N-UNCOUNT [2] If someone has a **stable** personality, they are calm and reasonable and their mood does not change suddenly. ❑ *Their characters are fully formed and they are both very stable children.* ADJ ≠ unstable [3] You can describe someone who is seriously ill as **stable** when their condition has stopped getting worse. ❑ *The injured man was in a stable condition.* ADJ [4] Chemical substances are described as **stable** when they tend to remain in the same chemical or atomic state. [TECHNICAL] ❑ *The less stable compounds were converted into a compound called Delta-A THC.* ADJ [5] If an object is **stable**, it is firmly fixed in position and is not likely to move or fall. ❑ *This structure must be stable.* ADJ ≠ unstable [6] A **stable** or **stables** is a building in which horses are kept. N-COUNT [7] A **stable** or **stables** is an organization that breeds and trains horses for racing. ❑ *Miss Curling won on two horses from Mick Trickey's stable.* N-COUNT [8] When horses **are stabled**, they are put into a stable. ❑ *The animals had been fed and stabled.* VERB: usu passive *be* V-ed

**sta|ble boy** **(stable boys)** also **stableboy.** A **stable boy** is a young man who works in a stable looking after the horses. N-COUNT

**sta|ble lad** **(stable lads)** also **stable-lad.** A **stable lad** is the same as a **stable boy**. [BRIT] N-COUNT

> in AM, use **stable boy**

**stable|mate** /steɪbəlmeɪt/ **(stablemates)** **Stablemates** are race horses that come from the same stables and often compete against each other. ❑ *The head groom is responsible for seeing that Milton and his stablemates have safe journeys.* N-COUNT: usu poss N

**stab wound** **(stab wounds)** A **stab wound** is a wound that someone has when they have been stabbed with a knife. N-COUNT

**stac|ca|to** /stəkɑːtoʊ/ A **staccato** noise consists of a series of short, sharp, separate sounds. ❑ *He spoke in Arabic, a short staccato burst.* ADJ: usu ADJ n

**stack** /stæk/ **(stacks, stacking, stacked)** [1] A **stack of** things is a pile of them. ❑ *There were stacks of books on the bedside table and floor.* N-COUNT: usu N *of* n [2] If you **stack** a number of things, you arrange them in neat piles. ❑ *Mme Cathiard was stacking the clean bottles in crates... They are stacked neatly in piles of three.* VERB; V n; V-ed ♦ **Stack up** means the same as **stack**. ❑ *He ordered them to stack up pillows behind his back. ...plates of delicious food stacked up on the counters.* PHRASAL VERB; V P n (not pron); V-ed P [3] If you say that someone has **stacks of** something, you mean that they have a lot of it. [INFORMAL] ❑ *If the job's that good, you'll have stacks of money.* N-PLURAL: N *of* n [4] If someone in authority **stacks** an organization or body, they fill it with their own supporters so that the decisions it makes will be the ones they want it to make. [mainly AM] ❑ *They said they were going to stack the court with anti-abortion judges.* VERB = pack; V n *with* n [5] → See also **stacked**, **chimney stack**. [6] If you say that **the odds are stacked against** someone, or that particular factors **are stacked against** them, you mean that they are unlikely to succeed in what they want to do because the conditions are not favourable. ❑ *The* PHRASE: V inflects, PHR n *odds are stacked against civilians getting a fair trial... Everything seems to be stacked against us.*

♦ **stack up** [1] If you ask how one person or thing **stacks up against** other people or things, you are asking how the one compares with the others. [INFORMAL] ❑ *How does this final presidential debate stack up and compare to the others, do you think?* [2] If facts or figures do not **stack up**, they do not make sense or give the results you expect. ❑ *There have been a number of explanations, but none of them stack up.* [3] → see **stack 2**. PHRASAL VERB: no passive = compare V P PHRASAL VERB V P

**stacked** /stækt/ If a place or surface is **stacked with** objects, it is filled with piles of them. ❑ *Shops in Ho Chi Minh City are stacked with goods.* ADJ: usu v-link ADJ, ADJ *with* n

**sta|dium** /steɪdiəm/ **(stadiums** or **stadia** /steɪdiə/**)** A **stadium** is a large sports ground with rows of seats all round it. ❑ *...a baseball stadium. ...Wembley Stadium.* ♦◇◇ N-COUNT; N-IN-NAMES

**staff** /stɑːf, stæf/ **(staffs, staffing, staffed)** [1] The **staff** of an organization are the people who work for it. ❑ *The staff were very good... He thanked his staff. ...members of staff... Many employers seek diversity in their staffs.* → See also **Chief of Staff**. [2] People who are part of a particular staff are often referred to as **staff**. ❑ *10 staff were allocated to the task... He had the complete support of hospital staff.* [3] If an organization **is staffed by** particular people, they are the people who work for it. ❑ *They are staffed by volunteers... The centre is staffed at all times.* ♦ **staffed** *The house allocated to them was pleasant and spacious, and well-staffed.* → See also **short-staffed**. [4] A **staff** is a strong stick or pole. [5] A **staff** is the five lines that music is written on. [AM] ♦♦♦ N-COUNT-COLL N-PLURAL VERB: usu passive *be* V-ed *by* n *be* V-ed ADJ: adv ADJ N-COUNT

☑ in BRIT, use **stave**

**staff|er** /stɑːfəʳ, stæf-/ **(staffers)** A **staffer** is a member of staff, especially in political organizations or in journalism. [mainly AM] ❑ *The Sky News TV station is largely run by ex-BBC news staffers.* N-COUNT: usu n N

**staff|ing** /stɑːfɪŋ, stæf-/ **Staffing** refers to the number of workers employed to work in a particular organization or building. [BUSINESS] ❑ *Staffing levels in prisons are too low.* N-UNCOUNT

**staff nurse (staff nurses)** A **staff nurse** is a hospital nurse whose rank is just below that of a sister or charge nurse. [BRIT] N-COUNT

**staff of|fic|er (staff officers)** In the army and air force, a **staff officer** is an officer who works for a commander or in the headquarters. N-COUNT

**staff ser|geant (staff sergeants)** also **Staff Sergeant.** A **staff sergeant** is someone who ranks just above sergeant in the British army or the United States army, marines, or air force. ❑ *His father is a staff sergeant in the army. ...Staff Sergeant Robert Daily.* N-COUNT; N-TITLE

**stag** /stæg/ **(stags)** A **stag** is an adult male deer belonging to one of the larger species of deer. Stags usually have large branch-like horns called antlers. N-COUNT

**stage** /steɪdʒ/ **(stages, staging, staged)** [1] A **stage of** an activity, process, or period is one part of it. ❑ *The way children talk about or express their feelings depends on their age and stage of development... Mr Cook has arrived in Greece on the final stage of a tour which also included Egypt and Israel.* [2] In a theatre, the **stage** is an area where actors or other entertainers perform. ❑ *I went on stage and did my show.* [3] You can refer to acting and the production of plays in a theatre as **the stage**. ❑ *He was the first comedian I ever saw on the stage.* [4] If someone **stages** a play or other show, they organize and present a performance of it. ❑ *Maya Angelou first staged the play 'And I Still Rise' in the late 1970s.* [5] If you **stage** an event or ceremony, you organize it and usually take part in it. ❑ *Russian workers have staged a number of strikes in protest at the republic's declaration of independence.* [6] You can refer to a particular area of activity as a particular **stage**, especially when you are talking about politics. ❑ *He was finally forced off the political stage last year by the deterioration of his physical condition.* [7] to **set the stage** → see **set**. ♦♦♦ N-COUNT: usu with supp N-COUNT: also *on* N N-SING: *the* N VERB = put on V n VERB = hold V n N-SING: usu supp N = arena

**stage|coach** /steɪdʒkoʊtʃ/ **(stagecoaches)** also **stage-coach. Stagecoaches** were large carriages pulled by horses which carried passengers and mail. N-COUNT: also *by* N

**stage|craft** /steɪdʒkrɑːft, -kræft/ **Stagecraft** is skill in writing or producing or directing plays in the theatre. N-UNCOUNT

**stage di|rec|tion (stage directions) Stage directions** are the notes in the text of a play which say what the actors should do. N-COUNT

**stage door (stage doors) The stage door** of a theatre is the entrance used by actors and actresses and by employees of the theatre. N-COUNT: usu *the* N in sing

**stage fright** also **stage-fright. Stage fright** is a feeling of fear or nervousness that some people have just before they appear in front of an audience. N-UNCOUNT

**stage|hand** /steɪdʒhænd/ **(stagehands)** also **stage hand.** A **stagehand** is a person whose job is to move the scenery and equipment on the stage in a theatre. N-COUNT

**stage left Stage left** is the left side of the stage for an actor who is standing facing the audience. ❑ *He entered stage left.* ADV: usu ADV after v, also prep ADV

**stage-manage (stage-manages, stage-managing, stage-managed)** If someone **stage-manages** an event, they carefully organize and control it, rather than letting it happen in a natural way. ❑ *Some radicals may oppose him in protest at the attempt of his supporters to stage-manage the congress.* VERB [disapproval] V n

**stage man|ag|er (stage managers)** also **stage-manager.** At a theatre, a **stage manager** is the person who is responsible for the scenery and lights and for the way that actors or other performers move about and use the stage during a performance. N-COUNT

**stage name (stage names)** A **stage name** is a name that an actor or entertainer uses instead of his or her real name when they work. ❑ *Under the stage name of Beverly Brooks, Patricia had small parts in several British films.* N-COUNT

**stage right Stage right** is the right side of the stage for an actor who is standing facing the audience. ADV: usu ADV after v, also prep ADV

**stage-struck** also **stagestruck.** Someone who is **stage-struck** is fascinated by the theatre and wants to become an actor or actress. ADJ

**stage whis|per (stage whispers)** also **stage-whisper.** If someone says something in a **stage whisper**, they say it as if they are speaking privately to one person, although it is actually loud enough to be heard by other people. N-COUNT

**stag|fla|tion** /stægfleɪʃᵊn/ If an economy is suffering from **stagflation**, inflation is high but there is no increase in the demand for goods or in the number of people who have jobs. [BUSINESS] N-UNCOUNT

**stag|ger** /stægəʳ/ **(staggers, staggering, staggered)** [1] If you **stagger**, you walk very unsteadily, for example because you are ill or drunk. ❑ *He lost his balance, staggered back against the rail and toppled over... He was staggering and had to lean on the bar.* [2] If you say that someone or something **staggers on**, you mean that it is only just succeeds in continuing. ❑ *Truman allowed him to stagger on for nearly another two years.* [3] If something **staggers** you, it surprises you very much. ❑ *The whole thing staggers me.* ♦ **stag|gered** *I was simply staggered by the heat of the Argentinian high-summer.* [4] To **stagger** things such as people's holidays or hours of work means to arrange them so that they do not all happen at the same time. ❑ *During the past few years the government has staggered the summer vacation periods for students.* [5] → See also **staggering**. VERB V adv/prep V VERB V adv/prep VERB V n ADJ: v-link ADJ VERB V n

**stag|ger|ing** /stæɡərɪŋ/ Something that is **staggering** is very surprising. ❑ *The results have been quite staggering.* ADJ = astounding

**stag|ing post** **(staging posts)** also **staging-post.** [1] A **staging post** on a long journey is a place where people who are making that journey usually stop, for example to rest or to get new supplies. [BRIT] ❑ *The island is a staging-post for many visiting yachts on their way south.* N-COUNT [2] If you describe an action or achievement as a **staging post**, you mean that it helps you reach a particular goal that you have. [BRIT] ❑ *Privatisation is a necessary staging post to an open market.* N-COUNT

**stag|nant** /stæɡnənt/ [1] If something such as a business or society is **stagnant**, there is little activity or change. ❑ *He is seeking advice on how to revive the stagnant economy... Mass movements are often a factor in the awakening and renovation of stagnant societies.* ADJ [disapproval] [2] **Stagnant** water is not flowing, and therefore often smells unpleasant and is dirty. ADJ

**stag|nate** /stæɡneɪt, AM stæɡneɪt/ **(stagnates, stagnating, stagnated)** If something such as a business or society **stagnates**, it stops changing or progressing. ❑ *Industrial production is stagnating.* VERB [disapproval] V
♦ **stag|na|tion** /stæɡneɪʃᵊn/ *...the stagnation of the steel industry.* N-UNCOUNT

**stag night** **(stag nights)** A **stag night** is a party for a man who is getting married very soon, to which only men are invited. N-COUNT

**stag par|ty** **(stag parties)** A **stag party** is the same as a **stag night**. N-COUNT

**staid** /steɪd/ If you say that someone or something is **staid**, you mean that they are serious, dull, and rather old-fashioned. ❑ *...a staid seaside resort.* ADJ

**stain** /steɪn/ **(stains, staining, stained)** [1] A **stain** is a mark on something that is difficult to remove. ❑ *Remove stains by soaking in a mild solution of bleach. ...a black stain.* N-COUNT: oft supp N [2] If a liquid **stains** something, the thing becomes coloured or marked by the liquid. ❑ *Some foods can stain the teeth, as of course can smoking.* VERB V n ♦ **stained** *His clothing was stained with mud.* ADJ: usu v-link ADJ ♦ **-stained** *...ink-stained fingers.* COMB in ADJ

**stained glass** also **stained-glass.** **Stained glass** consists of pieces of glass of different colours which are fixed together to make decorative windows or other objects. N-UNCOUNT

**stain|less steel** /steɪnləs stiːl/ **Stainless steel** is a metal made from steel and chromium which does not rust. ❑ *...a stainless steel sink.* N-UNCOUNT

**stair** /steəʳ/ **(stairs)** [1] **Stairs** are a set of steps inside a building which go from one floor to another. ❑ *Nancy began to climb the stairs... We walked up a flight of stairs... He stopped at the top of the stairs. ...a stair carpet.* N-PLURAL [2] A **stair** is one of the steps in a flight of stairs. ❑ *Terry was sitting on the bottom stair.* N-COUNT

**stair|case** /steəʳkeɪs/ **(staircases)** A **staircase** is a set of stairs inside a building. ❑ *They walked down the staircase together.* N-COUNT

**stair|way** /steəʳweɪ/ **(stairways)** A **stairway** is a staircase or a flight of steps, inside or outside a building. N-COUNT

**stair|well** /steəʳwel/ **(stairwells)** The **stairwell** is the part of a building that contains the staircase. N-COUNT

**stake** /steɪk/ **(stakes, staking, staked)** ◆◆◇ [1] If something is **at stake**, it is being risked and might be lost or damaged if you are not successful. ❑ *The tension was naturally high for a game with so much at stake... At stake is the success or failure of world trade talks.* PHRASE [2] The **stakes** involved in a contest or a risky action are the things that can be gained or lost. ❑ *By arresting the organisation's two top leaders the government and the army have now raised the stakes.* N-PLURAL: oft supp N [3] If you **stake** something such as your money or your reputation **on** the result of something, you risk your money or reputation on it. ❑ *He has staked his political future on an election victory.* VERB V n *on* n [4] If you have a **stake in** something such as a business, it matters to you, for example because you own part of it or because its success or failure will affect you. ❑ *He was eager to return to a more entrepreneurial role in which he had a big financial stake in his own efforts.* N-COUNT: N *in* n [5] You can use **stakes** to refer to something that is like a contest. For example, you can refer to the choosing of a leader as **the** leadership **stakes**. ❑ *Britain lags behind in the European childcare stakes.* N-PLURAL: *the* supp N [6] A **stake** is a pointed wooden post which is pushed into the ground, for example in order to support a young tree. N-COUNT = post [7] If you **stake a claim**, you say that something is yours or that you have a right to it. ❑ *Jane is determined to stake her claim as an actress.* PHRASE: V inflects
♦ **stake out** If you **stake out** a position that you are stating or a claim that you are making, you are defending the boundaries or limits of the position or claim. ❑ *Those who want to take child abuse seriously today must stake out a humane child protection practice.* PHRASAL VERB V P n (not pron)

**stake|hold|er** /steɪkhoʊldəʳ/ **(stakeholders)** **Stakeholders** are people who have an interest in a company's or organization's affairs. [BUSINESS] N-COUNT

**stake|hold|er pen|sion** **(stakeholder pensions)** In Britain, a **stakeholder pension** is a flexible pension scheme with low charges. Both employees and the state contribute to the scheme, which is optional, and is in addition to the basic state pension. [BUSINESS] N-COUNT

**stake|out** /steɪaʊt/ **(stakeouts)** also **stake-out.** If police officers are on a **stakeout**, they are secretly watching a building for evidence of criminal activity. N-COUNT

**stal|ac|tite** /stæləktaɪt, AM stəlæk-/ **(stalactites)** A **stalactite** is a long piece of rock which hangs down from the roof of a cave. Stalactites are formed by the slow dropping of water containing the mineral lime. N-COUNT

**stal|ag|mite** /stæləɡmaɪt, AM stəlæɡ-/ **(stalagmites)** A **stalagmite** is a long piece of rock which sticks up from the floor of a cave. Stalagmites are formed by the slow dropping of water containing the mineral lime. N-COUNT

**stale** /steɪl/ **(staler, stalest)** [1] **Stale** food is no longer fresh or good to eat. ❑ *Their daily diet consisted of a lump of stale bread, a bowl of rice and stale water.* ADJ ≠ fresh [2] **Stale** air or a **stale** smells is unpleasant because it is no longer fresh. ❑ *A layer of smoke hung low in the stale air. ...the smell of stale sweat.* ADJ [3] If you say that a place, an activity, or an idea is **stale**, you mean that it has become boring because it is always the same. ❑ *Her relationship with Mark has become stale.* ADJ [disapproval]

**stale|mate** /steɪlmeɪt/ **(stalemates)** [1] **Stalemate** is a situation in which neither side in an argument or contest can win or in which no progress is possible. ❑ *President Bush has ended the stalemate over moves to cut the country's budget deficit.* N-VAR = deadlock [2] In chess, **stalemate** is a position in which a player cannot make any move which is allowed by the rules, so that the game ends and no one wins. N-VAR

**stalk** /stɔːk/ **(stalks, stalking, stalked)** [1] The **stalk** of a flower, leaf, or fruit is the thin part that joins it to the plant or tree. → See pictures on pages 1711 and 1712. ❑ *A single pale blue flower grows up from each joint on a long stalk. ...corn stalks.* N-COUNT: usu with supp = stem [2] If you **stalk** a person or a wild animal, you follow them quietly in order to kill them, catch them, or observe them carefully. ❑ *He stalks his victims like a hunter after a deer.* VERB = track V n [3] If someone **stalks** someone else, especially a famous person or a person they used to have a relationship with, they keep following them or contacting them in an annoying and frightening way. ❑ *Even after their divorce he continued to stalk and threaten her.* VERB V n ♦ **stalk|ing** *The Home Secretary is considering a new law against stalking.* N-UNCOUNT [4] If you **stalk** somewhere, you walk there in a stiff, proud, or angry VERB way. ❑ *If his patience is tried at meetings he has been known to stalk out.* V adv/prep

**stalk|er** /stɔːkəʳ/ **(stalkers)** N-COUNT A **stalker** is someone who keeps following or contacting someone else, especially a famous person or a person they used to have a relationship with, in an annoying and frightening way.

**stalk|ing horse** **(stalking horses)** 1 N-COUNT [disapproval] If you describe a person or thing as a **stalking horse**, you mean that it is being used to obtain a temporary advantage so that someone can get what they really want. ❑ *I think the development is a stalking horse for exploitation of the surrounding countryside.* 2 N-COUNT: oft N n In politics, a **stalking horse** is someone who stands against a leader in order to see how strong the opposition is. The stalking horse then withdraws in favour of a stronger challenger. ❑ *The possibility of another stalking horse challenge this autumn cannot be ruled out.*

**stall** /stɔːl/ **(stalls, stalling, stalled)** 1 VERB If a process **stalls**, or if someone or something **stalls** it, the process stops but may continue at a later time. ❑ *The Social Democratic Party has vowed to try to stall the bill until the current session ends.* V n *...but the peace process stalled...* V *Negotiations remained stalled yesterday in New York.* V-ed 2 VERB If you **stall**, you try to avoid doing something until later. ❑ *Some parties have accused the governor of stalling...* V *Thomas had spent all week stalling over his decision.* V *over/on* n 3 VERB If you **stall** someone, you prevent them from doing something until a later time. ❑ *Shop manager Brian Steel stalled the man until the police arrived.* V n 4 VERB If a vehicle **stalls** or if you accidentally **stall** it, the engine stops suddenly. ❑ *The engine stalled...* V *Your foot falls off the pedal and you stall the car.* V n 5 N-COUNT A **stall** is a large table on which you put goods that you want to sell, or information that you want to give people. ❑ *...market stalls selling local fruits.* 6 N-PLURAL: *the* N **The stalls** in a theatre or concert hall are the seats on the ground floor directly in front of the stage. [mainly BRIT]

☑ in AM, use **orchestra**

7 N-COUNT A **stall** is a small enclosed area in a room which is used for a particular purpose, for example a shower. [AM]

☑ in BRIT, usually use **cubicle**

**stall|holder** /stɔːlhouldəʳ/ **(stallholders)** N-COUNT A **stallholder** is a person who sells goods at a stall in a market.

**stal|lion** /stæliən/ **(stallions)** N-COUNT A **stallion** is a male horse, especially one kept for breeding.

**stal|wart** /stɔːlwəʳt/ **(stalwarts)** 1 N-COUNT: usu with supp A **stalwart** is a loyal worker or supporter of an organization, especially a political party. ❑ *His free-trade policies aroused suspicion among Tory stalwarts.* 2 ADJ: usu ADJ n A **stalwart** supporter or worker is loyal, steady, and completely reliable. ❑ *...a stalwart supporter of the colonial government.*

**sta|men** /steɪmen/ **(stamens)** N-COUNT The **stamens** of a flower are the small, delicate stalks which grow at the flower's centre and produce pollen. [TECHNICAL]

**stami|na** /stæmɪnə/ N-UNCOUNT **Stamina** is the physical or mental energy needed to do a tiring activity for a long time. ❑ *You have to have a lot of stamina to be a top-class dancer.*

**stam|mer** /stæməʳ/ **(stammers, stammering, stammered)** 1 VERB If you **stammer**, you speak with difficulty, hesitating and repeating words or sounds. ❑ *Five per cent of children stammer at some point...* V *'Forgive me,' I stammered...* V with quote *People cursed and stammered apologies.* V n ♦ **stam|mer|ing** N-UNCOUNT *Of all speech impediments stammering is probably the most embarrassing.* 2 N-SING Someone who has a **stammer** tends to stammer when they speak. ❑ *A speech-therapist cured his stammer.*

**stamp** /stæmp/ **(stamps, stamping, stamped)** ◆◇◇ 1 N-COUNT A **stamp** or a **postage stamp** is a small piece of paper which you lick and stick on an envelope or package before you post it to pay for the cost of the postage. ❑ *...a book of stamps. ...two first class stamps.* → See also **food stamp**. 2 N-COUNT A **stamp** is a small block of wood or metal which has a pattern or a group of letters on one side. You press it onto an pad of ink and then onto a piece of paper in order to produce a mark on the paper. The mark that you produce is also called a **stamp**. ❑ *...a date stamp and an ink pad... You may live only where the stamp in your passport says you may.* 3 VERB If you **stamp** a mark or word on an object, you press the mark or word onto the object using a stamp or other device. ❑ *Car manufacturers stamp a vehicle identification number at several places on new cars to help track down stolen vehicles...* V n prep *'Eat before JULY 14' was stamped on the label.* V n prep 4 VERB If you **stamp** or **stamp** your **foot**, you lift your foot and put it down very hard on the ground, for example because you are angry or because your feet are cold. ❑ *Often he teased me till my temper went and I stamped and screamed, feeling furiously helpless...* V *His foot stamped down on the accelerator...* V adv/prep *She stamped her feet on the pavement to keep out the cold.* V n prep/adv, Also V n ♦ N-COUNT: usu sing **Stamp** is also a noun. ❑ *...hearing the creak of a door and the stamp of cold feet.* 5 VERB = *stomp* If you **stamp** somewhere, you walk there putting your feet down very hard on the ground because you are angry. ❑ *'I'm going before things get any worse!' he shouted as he stamped out of the bedroom.* V prep/adv 6 VERB If you **stamp on** something, you put your foot down on it very hard. ❑ *He received the original ban last week after stamping on the referee's foot during the supercup final.* V *on* n 7 N-SING: usu *the* N *of* n = *mark* If something bears **the stamp of** a particular quality or person, it clearly has that quality or was done by that person. ❑ *Most of us want to make our home a familiar place and put the stamp of our personality on its walls.* 8 → See also **rubber stamp**.

♦ **stamp on** PHRASAL VERB If someone **stamps on** a dishonest or undesirable activity, they act immediately to stop it happening or spreading. ❑ *The tone of her voice was designed to stamp on this topic of conversation once and for all.* V P n

♦ **stamp out** PHRASAL VERB If you **stamp out** something bad that is happening, you make it stop. ❑ *Dr Muffett stressed that he was opposed to bullying in schools and that action would be taken to stamp it out.* V n P

**stamp col|lect|ing** N-UNCOUNT **Stamp collecting** is the hobby of building up a collection of stamps.

**stamp duty** N-UNCOUNT In Britain, **stamp duty** is a tax that you pay to the government when you buy a house.

**stamped** /stæmpt/ ADJ: usu ADJ n A **stamped** envelope or package has a stamp stuck on it.

**stamped ad|dressed en|velope** **(stamped addressed envelopes)** N-COUNT A **stamped addressed envelope** is an envelope with a stamp on it and your own name and address, which you send to someone so that something can be sent back to you. The abbreviation **s.a.e.** is also used. [BRIT]

☑ in AM, use **SASE**

**stam|pede** /stæmpiːd/ **(stampedes, stampeding, stampeded)** 1 N-COUNT: usu sing If there is a **stampede**, a group of people or animals run in a wild, uncontrolled way. ❑ *There was a stampede for the exit.* 2 VERB If a group of animals or people **stampede** or if something **stampedes** them, they run in a wild, uncontrolled way. ❑ *The crowd stampeded and many were crushed or trampled underfoot...* V *Countryside robbers are learning the ways of the wild west by stampeding cattle to distract farmers before raiding their homes.* V n *...a herd of stampeding cattle.* V-ing 3 N-COUNT: usu sing If a lot of people all do the same thing at the same time, you can describe it as a **stampede**. ❑ *Generous redundancy terms had triggered a stampede of staff wanting to leave.*

**stamp|ing ground** **(stamping grounds)** Someone's **stamping ground** is a place where they like to go often.
N-COUNT: usu with poss = *haunt*

**stance** /stæns/ **(stances)** 1 Your **stance** on a particular matter is your attitude to it. ❑ *The Congress had agreed to reconsider its stance on the armed struggle.*
N-COUNT: usu sing, with supp = *position*
2 Your **stance** is the way that you are standing. [FORMAL] ❑ *Take a comfortably wide stance and flex your knees a little.*
N-COUNT: usu sing, supp N = *position*

**stan|chion** /stæntʃᵊn/ **(stanchions)** A **stanchion** is a pole or bar that stands upright and is used as a support. [FORMAL]
N-COUNT

**stand** /stænd/ **(stands, standing, stood)** ◆◆◆
1 When you **are standing**, your body is upright, your legs are straight, and your weight is supported by your feet. ❑ *She was standing beside my bed staring down at me... They told me to stand still and not to turn round... Overcrowding is so bad that prisoners have to sleep in shifts, while others have to stand.* ♦ **Stand up** means the same as **stand**. ❑ *We waited, standing up, for an hour.*
VERB; V prep; V adj; V; PHRASAL VERB; V P
2 When someone who is sitting **stands**, they change their position so that they are upright and on their feet. ❑ *Becker stood and shook hands with Ben.* ♦ **Stand up** means the same as **stand**. ❑ *When I walked in, they all stood up and started clapping.*
VERB; V; PHRASAL VERB; V P
3 If you **stand aside** or **stand back**, you move a short distance sideways or backwards, so that you are standing in a different place. ❑ *I stood aside to let her pass me... The policemen stood back. Could it be a bomb?*
VERB; V adv/prep; V adv/prep
4 If something such as a building or a piece of furniture **stands** somewhere, it is in that position, and is upright. [WRITTEN] ❑ *The house stands alone on top of a small hill.*
VERB; V prep/adv
5 You can say that a building **is standing** when it remains after other buildings around it have fallen down or been destroyed. ❑ *There are very few buildings left standing.*
VERB; V
6 If you **stand** something somewhere, you put it there in an upright position. ❑ *Stand the plant in the open in a sunny, sheltered place.*
VERB = *place*; V n prep/adv
7 If you leave food or a mixture of something **to stand**, you leave it without disturbing it for some time. ❑ *The salad improves if made in advance and left to stand.*
VERB; V
8 If you take or make a **stand**, you do something or say something in order to make it clear what your attitude to a particular thing is. ❑ *He felt the need to make a stand against racism in South Africa... They must take a stand and cast their votes.*
N-COUNT: usu sing, oft N *against/on* n
9 If you ask someone **where** or **how** they **stand on** a particular issue, you are asking them what their attitude or view is. ❑ *The amendment will force senators to show where they stand on the issue of sexual harassment... So far, the bishop hasn't said where he stands.*
VERB; *where* V *on* n; *where* V
10 If you do not know **where** you **stand with** someone, you do not know exactly what their attitude to you is. ❑ *No-one knows where they stand with him; he is utterly unpredictable.*
VERB; *where* V *with* n
11 You can use **stand** instead of 'be' when you are describing the present state or condition of something or someone. ❑ *The alliance stands ready to do what is necessary... The peace plan as it stands violates basic human rights.*
V-LINK; V adj; V
12 If a decision, law, or offer **stands**, it still exists and has not been changed or cancelled. ❑ *Although exceptions could be made, the rule still stands.*
VERB; V
13 If something that can be measured **stands at** a particular level, it is at that level. ❑ *The inflation rate now stands at 3.6 per cent.*
VERB; V *at* amount
14 You can describe how tall or high someone or something is by saying that they **stand** a particular height. ❑ *She stood five feet five inches tall and weighed 120 pounds... She stood tall and aloof.*
VERB; V amount adj; V adj
15 If something can **stand** a situation or a test, it is good enough or strong enough to experience it without being damaged, harmed, or shown to be inadequate. ❑ *These are the first machines that can stand the wear and tear of continuously crushing glass.*
VERB; V n
16 If you cannot **stand** something, you cannot bear it or tolerate it. ❑ *I can't stand any more. I'm going to run away... How does he stand the pain?*
VERB; V n/-ing; V n/-ing
17 If you cannot **stand** someone or something, you dislike them very strongly. [INFORMAL] ❑ *He can't stand me smoking.*
VERB; V n/-ing
18 If you **stand to gain** something, you are likely to gain it. If you **stand to lose** something, you are likely to lose it. ❑ *The management group would stand to gain millions of dollars if the company were sold.*
VERB; V to-inf
19 If you **stand in** an election, you are a candidate in it. [BRIT] ❑ *He has not yet announced whether he will stand in the election.*
VERB; V *in* n
✔ in AM, use **run**
20 A **stand** is a small shop or stall, outdoors or in a large public building. ❑ *She bought a hot dog from a stand on a street corner.* → See also **newsstand**.
N-COUNT: oft n N = *stall*
21 A **stand** at a sports ground is a large structure where people sit or stand to watch what is happening. [BRIT] ♦ In American English, **stands** is used with same meaning. ❑ *The people in the stands at Candlestick Park are standing and cheering with all their might.*
N-COUNT; N-PLURAL
22 A **stand** is an object or piece of furniture that is designed for supporting or holding a particular kind of thing. ❑ *The teapot came with a stand to catch the drips.*
N-COUNT
23 A **stand** is an area where taxis or buses can wait to pick up passengers. ❑ *Luckily there was a taxi stand nearby.*
N-COUNT: usu n N
24 In a law court, **the stand** is the place where a witness stands to answer questions. ❑ *When the father took the stand today, he contradicted his son's testimony.*
N-SING: *the* N
25 → See also **standing**.

PHRASES 26 If you say **it stands to reason that** something is true or likely to happen, you mean that it is obvious. ❑ *It stands to reason that if you are considerate and friendly to people you will get a lot more back.*
PHRASE: V inflects, usu *it* PHR that
27 If you **stand in the way of** something or **stand in** a person's **way**, you prevent that thing from happening or prevent that person from doing something. ❑ *The British government would not stand in the way of such a proposal.*
PHRASE: V inflects
28 to **stand a chance** → see **chance**. to **stand up and be counted** → see **count**. to **stand firm** → see **firm**. to **stand on** your **own two feet** → see **foot**. to **stand** your **ground** → see **ground**. to **stand** someone **in good stead** → see **stead**. to **stand trial** → see **trial**.

♦ **stand aside** If someone **stands aside**, they resign from an important job or position, often in order to let someone else take their place. [BRIT] ❑ *The President said he was willing to stand aside if that would stop the killing.*
PHRASAL VERB = *stand down*; V P
✔ in AM, use **stand down**

♦ **stand back** If you **stand back** and think about a situation, you think about it as if you were not involved in it. ❑ *Stand back and look objectively at the problem.*
PHRASAL VERB = *step back*; V P

♦ **stand by** 1 If you **are standing by**, you are ready and waiting to provide help or to take action. ❑ *British and American warships are standing by to evacuate their citizens if necessary... We will be holding the auditions from nine o'clock tomorrow night so stand by for details.* → See also **standby**.
PHRASAL VERB; V P to-inf; V P *for* n
2 If you **stand by** and let something bad happen, you do not do anything to stop it. ❑ *The Secretary of Defence has said that he would not stand by and let democracy be undermined.*
PHRASAL VERB; disapproval; V P
3 If you **stand by** someone, you continue to give them support, especially when they are in trouble. ❑ *I wouldn't break the law for a friend, but I would stand by her if she did.*
PHRASAL VERB; approval = *stick by*; V P n
4 If you **stand by** an earlier decision, promise, or statement, you continue to support it or keep it. ❑ *The decision has been made and I have got to stand by it.*
PHRASAL VERB = *stick by*; V P n

♦ **stand down** If someone **stands down**, they resign from an important job or position, often in order to let someone else take their place. ❑ *Four days later, the despised leader finally stood down, just 17 days after taking office... Profits plunged and he stood down as chairman last January.*
PHRASAL VERB = *step down, resign*; V P; V P *as* n

♦ **stand for** 1 If you say that a letter **stands for** a particular word, you mean that it is an abbreviation for that word. ❑ *What does EU stand for?*
PHRASAL VERB; V P n
2 The ideas or attitudes that someone or some-
PHRASAL VERB

thing **stands for** are the ones that they support or represent. ❑ *The party is trying to give the impression that it alone stands for democracy.* [3] If you will **not stand for** something, you will not allow it to happen or continue. ❑ *It's outrageous, and we won't stand for it any more.*
= represent; V P n; PHRASAL VERB: with neg; V P n

♦ **stand in** If you **stand in for** someone, you take their place or do their job, because they are ill or away. ❑ *I had to stand in for her on Tuesday when she didn't show up. ...the acting president, who's standing in while she's out of the country.* ➔ See also **stand-in**.
PHRASAL VERB; V P *for* n; V P

♦ **stand out** [1] If something **stands out**, it is very noticeable. ❑ *Every tree, wall and fence stood out against dazzling white fields.* [2] If something **stands out**, it is much better or much more important than other things of the same kind. ❑ *He played the violin, and he stood out from all the other musicians.* [3] If something **stands out** from a surface, it rises up from it. ❑ *His tendons stood out like rope beneath his skin.*
PHRASAL VERB; V P; PHRASAL VERB; V P *from* n; PHRASAL VERB = stick out; V P

♦ **stand up** [1] ➔ see **stand 1, 2**. [2] If something such as a claim or a piece of evidence **stands up**, it is accepted as true or satisfactory after being carefully examined. ❑ *He made wild accusations that did not stand up... How well does this thesis stand up to close examination?* [3] If a boyfriend or girlfriend **stands** you **up**, they fail to keep an arrangement to meet you. [INFORMAL] ❑ *We were to have had dinner together yesterday evening, but he stood me up.*
PHRASAL VERB; V P; V P *to* n; PHRASAL VERB; V n P

♦ **stand up for** If you **stand up for** someone or something, you defend them and make your feelings or opinions very clear. ❑ *They stood up for what they believed to be right.*
PHRASAL VERB; approval; = stick up for; V P P n

♦ **stand up to** [1] If something **stands up to** bad conditions, it is not damaged or harmed by them. ❑ *Is this building going to stand up to the strongest gales?* [2] If you **stand up to** someone, especially someone more powerful than you are, you defend yourself against their attacks or demands. ❑ *He hit me, so I hit him back – the first time in my life I'd stood up to him.*
PHRASAL VERB; V P P n/-ing; PHRASAL VERB; V P P n

**stand-alone** [1] A **stand-alone** business or organization is independent and does not receive financial support from another organization. [BUSINESS] ❑ *They plan to relaunch it as a stand-alone company.* [2] A **stand-alone** computer is one that can operate on its own and does not have to be part of a network. [COMPUTING] ❑ *...an operating system that can work on networks and stand-alone machines.*
ADJ: ADJ n; ADJ: ADJ n

**stand|ard** /stændəʳd/ **(standards)** [1] A **standard** is a level of quality or achievement, especially a level that is thought to be acceptable. ❑ *The standard of professional cricket has never been lower... There will be new national standards for hospital cleanliness.* [2] A **standard** is something that you use in order to judge the quality of something else. ❑ *...systems that were by later standards absurdly primitive.* [3] **Standards** are moral principles which affect people's attitudes and behaviour. ❑ *My father has always had high moral standards.* ➔ See also **double standard**. [4] You use **standard** to describe things which are usual and normal. ❑ *It was standard practice for untrained clerks to advise in serious cases such as murder.* [5] A **standard** work or text on a particular subject is one that is widely read and often recommended.
◆◆◇ N-COUNT: with supp; N-COUNT: with supp; N-PLURAL: usu with supp; ADJ: usu ADJ n; ADJ: ADJ n

**stand|ard bear|er** **(standard bearers)** also **standard-bearer.** If you describe someone as the **standard bearer** of a group, you mean that they act as the leader or public representative of a group of people who have the same aims or interests. ❑ *Farrakhan was a poor standard-bearer for the causes of African-Americans.*
N-COUNT: usu with supp

**stand|ard|ize** /stændəʳdaɪz/ **(standardizes, standardizing, standardized)**

✔ in BRIT, also use **standardise**

To **standardize** things means to change them so that they all have the same features. ❑ *There is a drive both to standardise components and to reduce the number of models on offer.*
VERB; V n

♦ **stand|ardi|za|tion** /stændəʳdaɪzeɪʃᵊn, AM -dɪz-/ *...the standardisation of working hours in Community countries.*
N-UNCOUNT

**stand|ard lamp** **(standard lamps)** A **standard lamp** is a tall electric light which stands on the floor in a living room. [BRIT]
N-COUNT

✔ in AM, use **floor lamp**

**stand|ard of liv|ing** **(standards of living)** Your **standard of living** is the level of comfort and wealth which you have. ❑ *We'll continue to fight for a decent standard of living for our members.*
N-COUNT

**stand|ard time** **Standard time** is the official local time of a region or country. ❑ *French standard time is GMT plus 1 hr.*
N-UNCOUNT: usu supp N

**stand|by** /stændbaɪ/ **(standbys)** also **stand-by.** [1] A **standby** is something or someone that is always ready to be used if they are needed. ❑ *He sat through the trial as a standby juror.* [2] If someone or something is **on standby**, they are ready to be used if they are needed. ❑ *Security forces have been put on standby in case of violence.* [3] A **standby** ticket for something such as the theatre or a plane journey is a cheap ticket that you buy just before the performance starts or the plane takes off, if there are still some seats left. ❑ *Access International books standby flights from New York to Europe.* ♦ **Standby** is also an adverb. ❑ *Magda was going to fly standby.*
N-COUNT: oft N n; PHRASE: usu v-link PHR, PHR after v; ADJ: ADJ n; ADV: ADV after v

**stand-in** **(stand-ins)** A **stand-in** is a person who takes someone else's place or does someone else's job for a while, for example because the other person is ill or away. ❑ *He was a stand-in for my regular doctor.*
N-COUNT

**stand|ing** /stændɪŋ/ **(standings)** [1] Someone's **standing** is their reputation or status. ❑ *...an artist of international standing... He has improved his country's standing abroad.* [2] A party's or person's **standing** is their popularity. ❑ *But, as the opinion poll shows, the party's standing with the people at large has never been so low.* [3] You use **standing** to describe something which is permanently in existence. ❑ *Israel has a relatively small standing army and its strength is based on its reserves... Elizabeth had a standing invitation to stay with her.* [4] ➔ See also **free-standing, long-standing.** [5] You can use the expression **of many years' standing** to say that something has had a particular function or someone has had a particular role for many years. For example, if a place is your home **of ten years' standing**, it has been your home for ten years. [WRITTEN] ❑ *...a Congressman of 24 years' standing... My girlfriend of long standing left me.*
N-UNCOUNT: with supp, oft adj N, with poss; N-COUNT: usu sing, with poss; ADJ: ADJ n = permanent; PHRASE: n PHR

**stand|ing joke** **(standing jokes)** If something is a **standing joke** among a group of people, they often make jokes about it. ❑ *Her precision became a standing joke with colleagues.*
N-COUNT: usu sing

**stand|ing or|der** **(standing orders)** A **standing order** is an instruction to your bank to pay a fixed amount of money to someone at regular times. [BRIT]
N-COUNT: also *by* N

**stand|ing ova|tion** **(standing ovations)** If a speaker or performer gets a **standing ovation** when they have finished speaking or performing, the audience stands up to clap in order to show its admiration or support.
N-COUNT

**stand|ing room** **Standing room** is space in a room or bus, where people can stand when all the seats have been occupied. ❑ *The place quickly fills up so it's soon standing room only.*
N-UNCOUNT

**stand-off** **(stand-offs)** also **standoff.** A **stand-off** is a situation in which neither of two opposing groups or forces will make a move until the other one does something, so nothing can happen until one of them gives way. ❑ *The State Department was warning that this could lead to anoth-*
N-COUNT

*er diplomatic stand-off.* ➔ See also **Mexican stand-off**.

**stand-offish** also **standoffish.** If you say that someone is **stand-offish**, you mean that they behave in a formal and rather unfriendly way. ❑ *He can be quite stand-offish and rude, even to his friends.* ADJ disapproval = aloof

**stand|out** /stændaʊt/ **(standouts)** also **stand-out.** Journalists use **standout** to refer to a person or thing that is much better than the other people or things involved in something. [AM, AUSTRALIAN] ❑ *In the earlier rounds, Ferguson and Dickinson were the standouts.* N-COUNT: oft N n

**stand|pipe** /stændpaɪp/ **(standpipes)** A **standpipe** is a vertical pipe that is connected to a water supply and stands in a street or other public place. N-COUNT

**stand|point** /stændpɔɪnt/ **(standpoints)** **From** a particular **standpoint** means looking at an event, situation, or idea in a particular way. ❑ *He believes that from a military standpoint, the situation is under control... From my standpoint, you know, this thing is just ridiculous.* N-COUNT: with supp, usu *from* N = point of view, perspective

**stand|still** /stændstɪl/ If movement or activity comes **to** or is brought to **a standstill**, it stops completely. ❑ *Abruptly the group ahead of us came to a standstill... Production is more or less at a standstill.* N-SING: *a* N, usu *to/at* N = halt

**stand-up** also **standup.** [1] A **stand-up** comic or comedian stands alone in front of an audience and tells jokes. ❑ *Women do not normally break into the big time by doing stand-up comedy.* ADJ: ADJ n [2] If people have a **stand-up** argument or fight, they stand up and shout at each other or hit each other violently. ADJ: ADJ n

**stank** /stæŋk/ **Stank** is the past tense of **stink**.

**Stanley knife** /stænli naɪf/ **(Stanley knives)** A **Stanley knife** is a very sharp knife that is used to cut materials such as carpet and paper. It consists of a small blade fixed in the end of a handle. [TRADEMARK] N-COUNT

**stan|za** /stænzə/ **(stanzas)** A **stanza** is one of the parts into which a poem is divided. [TECHNICAL] N-COUNT

**sta|ple** /steɪpᵊl/ **(staples, stapling, stapled)** [1] A **staple** food, product, or activity is one that is basic and important in people's everyday lives. ❑ *The Chinese also eat a type of pasta as part of their staple diet... Staple goods are disappearing from the shops.* ADJ: ADJ n ♦ **Staple** is also a noun. ❑ *Fish is a staple in the diet of many Africans.* N-COUNT [2] A **staple** is something that forms an important part of something else. ❑ *Political reporting has become a staple of American journalism.* N-COUNT: usu N *of* n [3] **Staples** are small pieces of bent wire that are used mainly for holding sheets of paper together firmly. You put the staples into the paper using a device called a stapler. N-COUNT [4] If you **staple** something, you fasten it to something else or fix it in place using staples. ❑ *Staple some sheets of paper together into a book. ...polythene bags stapled to an illustrated card.* VERB V n with adv V-ed

**sta|ple gun** **(staple guns)** A **staple gun** is a small machine used for forcing staples into wood or brick. N-COUNT

**sta|pler** /steɪplər/ **(staplers)** A **stapler** is a device used for putting staples into sheets of paper. N-COUNT

**star** /stɑːr/ **(stars, starring, starred)** [1] A **star** is a large ball of burning gas in space. Stars appear to us as small points of light in the sky on clear nights. ❑ *The night was dark, the stars hidden behind cloud.* ➔ See also **morning star**, **shooting star**. ◆◆◆ N-COUNT [2] You can refer to a shape or an object as a **star** when it has four, five, or more points sticking out of it in a regular pattern. ❑ *Children at school receive coloured stars for work well done.* N-COUNT [3] You can say how many **stars** something such as a hotel or restaurant has as a way of talking about its quality, which is often indicated by a number of star-shaped symbols. The more stars something has, the better it is. ❑ *...five star hotels.* N-COUNT [4] Famous actors, musicians, and sports players are often referred to as **stars**. ❑ *...Gemma, 41, star of the TV series Pennies From Heaven... By now Murphy is Hollywood's top male comedy star... Not all football stars are ill-behaved louts.* N-COUNT: oft supp N [5] If an actor or actress **stars in** a play or film, he or she has one of the most important parts in it. ❑ *The previous year Adolphson had starred in a play in which Ingrid had been an extra.* VERB V *in* n [6] If a play or film **stars** a famous actor or actress, he or she has one of the most important parts in it. ❑ *...a Hollywood film, The Secret of Santa Vittoria, directed by Stanley Kramer and starring Anthony Quinn.* VERB V n [7] Predictions about people's lives which are based on astrology and appear regularly in a newspaper or magazine are sometimes referred to as **the stars**. ❑ *There was nothing in my stars to say I'd have travel problems!* N-PLURAL = horoscope

**star|board** /stɑːrbərd/ In sailing, the **starboard** side of a ship is the right side when you are on it and facing towards the front. [TECHNICAL] ❑ *He detected a ship moving down the starboard side of the submarine.* ADJ ≠ port ♦ **Starboard** is also a noun. ❑ *I could see the fishing boat to starboard.* N-UNCOUNT: usu *to* N

**star|burst** /stɑːrbɜːrst/ **(starbursts)** A **starburst** is a bright light with rays coming from it, or a patch of bright colour with points extending from it. [LITERARY] ❑ *...a starburst of multi-coloured smoke.* N-COUNT

**starch** /stɑːrtʃ/ **(starches)** [1] **Starch** is a substance that is found in foods such as bread, potatoes, pasta, and rice and gives you energy. N-MASS [2] **Starch** is a substance that is used for making cloth stiffer, especially cotton and linen. N-UNCOUNT

**starched** /stɑːrtʃt/ A **starched** garment or piece of cloth has been made stiffer using starch. ❑ *...a starched white shirt. ...starched napkins.* ADJ: usu ADJ n

**starchy** /stɑːrtʃi/ **(starchier, starchiest)** **Starchy** foods contain a lot of starch. ❑ *...starchy and sticky glutinous rices.* ADJ

**star-crossed** If someone is **star-crossed**, they keep having bad luck. [LITERARY] ❑ *...star-crossed lovers parted by war and conflict.* ADJ: usu ADJ n

**star|dom** /stɑːrdəm/ **Stardom** is the state of being very famous, usually as an actor, musician, or sports player. ❑ *In 1929 she shot to stardom on Broadway in a Noel Coward play.* N-UNCOUNT = fame

**stare** /steər/ **(stares, staring, stared)** [1] If you **stare at** someone or something, you look at them for a long time. ❑ *Tamara stared at him in disbelief, shaking her head... Mahoney tried not to stare.* ◆◇◇ VERB V prep/adv V ♦ **Stare** is also a noun. ❑ *Hlasek gave him a long, cold stare.* N-COUNT [2] If a situation or the answer to a problem **is staring** you **in the face**, it is very obvious, although you may not be immediately aware of it. [INFORMAL] ❑ *Then the answer hit me. It had been staring me in the face ever since Lullington.* PHRASE: V inflects

♦ **stare out** If you **stare** someone **out**, you look steadily into their eyes for such a long time that they feel that they have to turn their eyes away from you. ❑ *He glared at Nikitin but the General Secretary stared him out with hard, pebble-like eyes.* PHRASAL VERB V n P

**star|fish** /stɑːrfɪʃ/ **(starfish)** A **starfish** is a flat, star-shaped creature with five arms that lives in the sea. N-COUNT

**star-gazer** **(star-gazers)** also **stargazer.** A **star-gazer** is someone who studies the stars as an astronomer or astrologer. [INFORMAL] N-COUNT

**star-gazing** also **stargazing.** **Star-gazing** is the activity of studying the stars as an astronomer or astrologer. [INFORMAL] N-UNCOUNT

**stark** /stɑːrk/ **(starker, starkest)** [1] **Stark** choices or statements are harsh and unpleasant. ❑ *UK companies face a stark choice if they want to stay competitive... In his celebration speech, he issued a stark warning to Washington and other Western capitals.* ADJ = harsh ♦ **stark|ly** *The point is a starkly simple one.* ADV: ADV with v, ADV adj [2] If two things are in **stark** contrast to one another, they are very different from each other in a way that is very obvious. ❑ *...secret cooperation between London and Washington that was in stark con-* ADJ

trast to official policy. ♦ **stark|ly** *The outlook now is starkly different.* [3] Something that is **stark** is very plain in appearance. ❑ *...the stark white, characterless fireplace in the drawing room.* ♦ **stark|ly** *The desert was luminous, starkly beautiful.*
ADV: ADV with v, ADV adj · ADJ · ADV: ADV adj, ADV with v

**stark na|ked** Someone who is **stark naked** is completely naked. ❑ *All contestants competed stark naked.*
ADJ: ADJ after v, v-link ADJ · emphasis

**star|let** /stɑːʳlɪt/ **(starlets)** A **starlet** is a young actress who is expected to become a film star in the future. [JOURNALISM]
N-COUNT

**star|light** /stɑːʳlaɪt/ **Starlight** is the light that comes from the stars at night.
N-UNCOUNT

**star|ling** /stɑːʳlɪŋ/ **(starlings)** A **starling** is a very common bird with greenish-black feathers covered in pale spots which is found in Europe and North America. Starlings often fly around in large groups.
N-COUNT

**star|lit** /stɑːʳlɪt/ **Starlit** means made lighter or brighter by the stars. ❑ *...a clear starlit sky. ...this cold, starlit night.*
ADJ: ADJ n

**star prize (star prizes)** The **star prize** in a competition is the most valuable prize.
N-COUNT

**star|ry** /stɑːri/ A **starry** night or sky is one in which a lot of stars are visible. ❑ *She stared up at the starry sky.*
ADJ: ADJ n

**starry-eyed** If you say that someone is **starry-eyed**, you mean that they have such a positive or hopeful view of a situation that they do not see what it is really like. ❑ *I'm not starry-eyed about Europe. ...a starry-eyed young couple.*
ADJ

**Stars and Stripes** The Stars and Stripes is the name of the national flag of the United States of America.
N-PROPER: *the* N

**star sign (star signs)** Your **star sign** is the sign of the zodiac under which you were born.
N-COUNT

**star|struck** /stɑːʳstrʌk/ If you describe someone as **starstruck**, you mean that they are very interested in and impressed by famous performers, or that they want to be a performer themselves. ❑ *...a starstruck teenager who auditions for a TV dance show.*
ADJ

**star-studded** A **star-studded** show, event, or cast is one that includes a large number of famous performers. [JOURNALISM] ❑ *...a star-studded production of Hamlet.*
ADJ: ADJ n

**start** /stɑːʳt/ **(starts, starting, started)** [1] If you **start to** do something, you do something that you were not doing before and you continue doing it. ❑ *John then unlocked the front door and I started to follow him up the stairs... It was 1956 when Susanna started the work on the garden... She started cleaning the kitchen.* ♦ **Start** is also a noun. ❑ *After several starts, she read the report properly.* [2] When something **starts**, or if someone **starts** it, it takes place from a particular time. ❑ *The fire is thought to have started in an upstairs room... The Great War started in August of that year... All of the passengers started the day with a swim.* ♦ **Start** is also a noun. ❑ *...1918, four years after the start of the Great War... She demanded to know why she had not been told from the start.* [3] If you **start by** doing something, or if you **start with** something, you do that thing first in a series of actions. ❑ *I started by asking how many day-care centers were located in the United States... He started with a good holiday in Key West, Florida.* [4] You use **start** to say what someone's first job was. For example, if their first job was that of a factory worker, you can say that they **started as** a factory worker. ❑ *Betty started as a shipping clerk at the clothes factory.* ♦ **Start off** means the same as **start**. ❑ *Mr. Dambar had started off as an assistant to Mrs. Spear's husband.* [5] When someone **starts** something such as a new business, they create it or cause it to begin. ❑ *Now is probably as good a time as any to start a business.* ♦ **Start up** means the same as **start**. ❑ *The cost of starting up a day care center for children ranges from $150,000 to $300,000... He said what a good idea it would be to start a community magazine up.* → See also **start-up**. [6] If you **start** an engine, car, or machine, or if it **starts**, it begins to work. ❑ *He started the car, which hummed smoothly... We were just passing one of the parking bays when a car's engine started.* ♦ **Start up** means the same as **start**. ❑ *He waited until they went inside before starting up the car and driving off... Put the key in the ignition and turn it to start the car up... The engine of the seaplane started up.* [7] If you **start**, your body suddenly moves slightly as a result of surprise or fear. ❑ *She put the bottle on the table, banging it down hard. He started at the sound.* ♦ **Start** is also a noun. ❑ *Sylvia woke with a start... He gave a start of surprise and astonishment.* [8] → See also **head start**, **false start**.
♦♦♦ · VERB = begin · V to-inf · V n/-ing · V n/-ing · N-COUNT · VERB = begin · V prep · V prep · V n · N-SING: *the* N = beginning · VERB = begin · V *by* -ing · V *with* n · VERB · V *as* n · PHRASAL VERB · V P *as* n · VERB · V n · PHRASAL VERB = set up · V P n (not pron) · V n P · VERB · V n · V · PHRASAL VERB · V P n (not pron) · V n P · V P · VERB · V · N-COUNT: usu sing

**PHRASES** [9] You use **for a start** or **to start with** to introduce the first of a number of things or reasons that you want to mention or could mention. ❑ *You must get her name and address, and that can be a problem for a start.* [10] If you **get off to a good start**, you are successful in the early stages of doing something. If you **get off to a bad start**, you are not successful in the early stages of doing something. ❑ *The new Prime Minister has got off to a good start, but he still has to demonstrate what manner of leader he is going to be.* [11] **To start with** means at the very first stage of an event or process. ❑ *To start with, the pressure on her was very heavy, but it's eased off a bit now.* [12] **in fits and starts** → see **fit**. to **get off to a flying start** → see **flying**.
PHRASE: PHR with cl/group · PHRASE: V inflects · PHRASE: PHR with cl

♦ **start off** [1] If you **start off by** doing something, you do it as the first part of an activity. ❑ *She started off by accusing him of blackmail but he more or less ignored her... Joe Loss started off playing piano background music for silent films in the 1920s.* [2] To **start** someone **off** means to cause them to begin doing something. ❑ *Her mother started her off acting in children's theatre.* [3] To **start** something **off** means to cause it to begin. ❑ *Best results are obtained by starting the plants off in a warm greenhouse.* [4] → see **start 4**.
PHRASAL VERB · V P *by* -ing · V P -ing · PHRASAL VERB · V n P · PHRASAL VERB · V n P

♦ **start on** If you **start on** something that needs to be done, you start dealing with it. ❑ *No need for you to start on the washing-up yet.*
PHRASAL VERB · V P n

♦ **start out** [1] If someone or something **starts out as** a particular thing, they are that thing at the beginning although they change later. ❑ *Daly was a fast-talking Irish-American who had started out as a salesman... What started out as fun quickly became hard work.* [2] If you **start out by** doing something, you do it at the beginning of an activity. ❑ *We started out by looking at ways in which big projects such as railways could be financed by the private sector.*
PHRASAL VERB · V P *as* n · V P *as* n · PHRASAL VERB · V P *by* -ing

♦ **start over** If you **start over** or **start** something **over**, you begin something again from the beginning. [mainly AM] ❑ *...moving the kids to some other schools, closing them down and starting over with a new staff... It's just not enough money to start life over.*
PHRASAL VERB · V P · V n P

✔ in BRIT, use **start again**

♦ **start up** → see **start 5, 6**.

**start|er** /stɑːʳtəʳ/ **(starters)** [1] A **starter** is a small quantity of food that is served as the first course of a meal. [mainly BRIT]
N-COUNT

✔ in AM, use **appetizer**

[2] The **starter** of a car is the device that starts the engine. [3] The **starters** in a race are the people or animals who take part at the beginning even if they do not finish. ❑ *Of the 10 starters, four were eliminated or retired.*
N-COUNT · N-COUNT: usu pl

**start|er home (starter homes)** A **starter home** is a small, new house or flat which is cheap enough for people who are buying their first home to afford.
N-COUNT

**start|ing block (starting blocks)** **Starting blocks** are blocks which runners put their feet against to help them move quickly forward at the start of a race.
N-COUNT: usu pl

**start|ing point** **(starting points)** also **starting-point.** [1] Something that is a **starting point for** a discussion or process can be used to begin it or act as a basis for it. ❑ *These proposals represent a realistic starting point for negotiation.* N-COUNT: oft N *for* n = *basis*
[2] When you make a journey, your **starting point** is the place from which you start. ❑ *They had already walked a couple of miles or more from their starting point.* N-COUNT: usu with supp

**star|tle** /stɑːʳtᵊl/ **(startles, startling, startled)** If something sudden and unexpected **startles** you, it surprises and frightens you slightly. ❑ *The telephone startled him... The news will startle the City.* VERB; V n; V n
♦ **star|tled** *Martha gave her a startled look.* ADJ

**star|tling** /stɑːʳtəlɪŋ/ Something that is **startling** is so different, unexpected, or remarkable that people react to it with surprise. ❑ *...startling new evidence.* ADJ

**start-up** **(start-ups)** [1] The **start-up** costs of something such as a new business or new product are the costs of starting to run or produce it. [BUSINESS] ❑ *The minimum start-up capital for a Pizza franchise is estimated at $250,000 to $315,000.* ADJ: ADJ n [2] A **start-up** company is a small business that has recently been started by someone. [BUSINESS] ❑ *Thousands and thousands of start-up firms have poured into the computer market.* ADJ: ADJ n ♦ **Start-up** is also a noun. ❑ *For now the only bright spots in the labor market are small businesses and high-tech start-ups.* N-COUNT

**star turn** **(star turns)** **The star turn** of a performance or show is the main item, or the one that is considered to be the most interesting or exciting. [mainly BRIT] N-COUNT: usu *the* N in sing

**star|va|tion** /stɑːʳveɪʃᵊn/ **Starvation** is extreme suffering or death, caused by lack of food. ❑ *Over three hundred people have died of starvation since the beginning of the year.* N-UNCOUNT: usu *of/from* N

**starve** /stɑːʳv/ **(starves, starving, starved)** [1] If people **starve**, they suffer greatly from lack of food which sometimes leads to their death. ❑ *A number of the prisoners we saw are starving... In the 1930s, millions of Ukrainians starved to death or were deported... Getting food to starving people does nothing to stop the war.* VERB; V; V *to* n; V-ing [2] To **starve** someone means not to give them any food. ❑ *He said the only alternative was to starve the people, and he said this could not be allowed to happen... Judy decided I was starving myself.* VERB; V n; V pron-refl [3] If a person or thing **is starved of** something that they need, they are suffering because they are not getting enough of it. ❑ *The electricity industry is not the only one to have been starved of investment.* VERB; *be* V-ed *of* n

**starv|ing** /stɑːʳvɪŋ/ If you say that you are **starving**, you mean that you are very hungry. [INFORMAL] ❑ *Apart from anything else I was starving.* ADJ: v-link ADJ

**stash** /stæʃ/ **(stashes, stashing, stashed)** [1] If you **stash** something valuable in a secret place, you store it there to keep it safe. [INFORMAL] ❑ *We went for the bottle of whiskey that we had stashed behind the bookcase.* VERB; V n prep [2] A **stash of** something valuable is a secret store of it. [INFORMAL] ❑ *A large stash of drugs had been found aboard the yacht.* N-COUNT: with supp, usu N *of* n = *hoard*

**sta|sis** /stæsɪs, AM steɪ-/ **Stasis** is a state in which something remains the same, and does not change or develop. [FORMAL] ❑ *Rock'n'roll had entered a period of stasis.* N-UNCOUNT

**state** /steɪt/ **(states, stating, stated)** ◆◆◆ [1] You can refer to countries as **states**, particularly when you are discussing politics. ❑ *Some weeks ago I recommended to EU member states that we should have discussions with the Americans.* N-COUNT [2] Some large countries such as the USA are divided into smaller areas called **states**. ❑ *Leaders of the Southern states are meeting in Louisville.* N-COUNT [3] The USA is sometimes referred to as **the States**. [INFORMAL] N-PROPER: *the* N [4] You can refer to the government of a country as **the state**. ❑ *The state does not collect enough revenue to cover its expenditure.* N-SING: *the* N [5] **State** industries or organizations are financed and organized by the government rather than private companies. ❑ *...reform of the state social-security system.* ADJ: ADJ n ➔ see **state school**. [6] A **state** occasion is a formal one involving the head of a country. ❑ *The president of Czechoslovakia is in Washington on a state visit.* ADJ: ADJ n [7] When you talk about the **state of** someone or something, you are referring to the condition they are in or what they are like at a particular time. ❑ *For the first few months after Daniel died, I was in a state of clinical depression... Look at the state of my car!* N-COUNT: usu sing, with supp [8] If you **state** something, you say or write it in a formal or definite way. ❑ *Clearly state your address and telephone number... The police report stated that he was arrested for allegedly assaulting his wife... 'Our relationship is totally platonic,' she stated... Buyers who do not apply within the stated period can lose their deposits.* VERB; V n; V that; V with quote; V-ed [9] ➔ See also **head of state**, **nation state**, **police state**, **welfare state**.

PHRASES [10] If you say that someone **is not in a fit state to** do something, you mean that they are too upset or ill to do it. ❑ *When you left our place, you weren't in a fit state to drive.* PHRASE: V inflects, PHR to-inf [11] If you are **in a state** or if you get **into a state**, you are very upset or nervous about something. ❑ *I was in a terrible state because nobody could understand why I had this illness.* PHRASE: v-link PHR [12] If the dead body of an important person **lies in state**, it is publicly displayed for a few days before it is buried. PHRASE: V inflects

**State De|part|ment** ◆◇◇ In the United States, **the State Department** is the government department that is concerned with foreign affairs. ❑ *Officials at the State Department say the issue is urgent. ...a senior State Department official.* N-PROPER: *the* N

**state|hood** /steɪthʊd/ **Statehood** is the condition of being an independent state or nation. N-UNCOUNT

**state|house** /steɪthaʊs/ **(statehouses)** In the United States, a **statehouse** is where the governor of a state has his or her offices, and where the state legislature meets. N-COUNT

**state|less** /steɪtləs/ A person who is **stateless** is not a citizen of any country and therefore has no nationality. ❑ *If I went back I'd be a stateless person.* ADJ

**state|let** /steɪtlət/ **(statelets)** A **statelet** is a small independent state, especially one that until recently was part of a larger country. [JOURNALISM] N-COUNT

**state|ly** /steɪtli/ Something or someone that is **stately** is impressive and graceful or dignified. ❑ *Instead of moving at his usual stately pace, he was almost running.* ADJ

**state|ly home** **(stately homes)** A **stately home** is a very large old house, especially one that people can pay to visit. [mainly BRIT] N-COUNT

**state|ment** /steɪtmənt/ **(statements)** ◆◆◇ [1] A **statement** is something that you say or write which gives information in a formal or definite way. ❑ *'Things are moving ahead.' – I found that statement vague and unclear.* N-COUNT [2] A **statement** is an official or formal announcement that is issued on a particular occasion. ❑ *The statement by the military denied any involvement in last night's attack.* N-COUNT [3] You can refer to the official account of events which a suspect or a witness gives to the police as a **statement**. ❑ *The 350-page report was based on statements from witnesses to the events.* N-COUNT [4] If you describe an action or thing as a **statement**, you mean that it clearly expresses a particular opinion or idea that you have. ❑ *The following recipe is a statement of another kind – food is fun!* N-COUNT [5] A printed document showing how much money has been paid into and taken out of a bank or building society account is called a **statement**. N-COUNT

**state of af|fairs** If you refer to a particular **state of affairs**, you mean the general situation and circumstances connected with someone or something. ❑ *This state of affairs cannot continue for too long, if parliament is to recover.* N-SING: usu with supp

**state of mind** **(states of mind)** Your **state of mind** is your mood or mental state at a particular N-COUNT: usu sing, usu with supp time. ❑ *I want you to get into a whole new state of mind.*

**state of siege** A **state of siege** is a situation in which a government or other authority puts restrictions on the movement of people into or out of a country, town, or building. ❑ *Under the state of siege, the police could arrest suspects without charges or warrants.* N-SING

**state-of-the-art** If you describe something as **state-of-the-art**, you mean that it is the best available because it has been made using the most modern techniques and technology. ❑ *...the production of state-of-the-art military equipment.* ADJ: usu ADJ n

**state|room** /steɪtru:m/ **(staterooms)** 1 On a passenger ship, a **stateroom** is a private room, especially one that is large and comfortable. [OLD-FASHIONED] N-COUNT 2 In a palace or other impressive building, a **stateroom** is a large room for use on formal occasions. [mainly BRIT] N-COUNT

**state school** **(state schools)** A **state school** is a school that is controlled and funded by the government or a local authority, and which children can attend without having to pay. [BRIT] N-COUNT

✔ in AM, use **public school**

**state|side** /steɪtsaɪd/ also **Stateside.** **Stateside** means in, from, or to the United States. [JOURNALISM or INFORMAL] ❑ *The band are currently planning a series of Stateside gigs.* ADJ = American ♦ **Stateside** is also an adverb. ❑ *His debut album was hugely successful Stateside.* ADV: ADV after v

**states|man** /steɪtsmən/ **(statesmen)** A **statesman** is an important and experienced politician, especially one who is widely known and respected. ❑ *Hamilton is a great statesman and political thinker.* ➔ See also **elder statesman**. N-COUNT

**states|man|like** /steɪtsmənlaɪk/ If you describe someone, especially a political leader, as **statesmanlike**, you approve of them because they give the impression of being very able and experienced. ❑ *He was widely respected as a wise and statesmanlike governor.* ADJ [approval]

**states|man|ship** /steɪtsmənʃɪp/ **Statesmanship** is the skill and activities of a statesman. ❑ *He praised the two leaders warmly for their statesmanship.* N-UNCOUNT

**state|wide** /steɪtwaɪd/ **Statewide** means across or throughout the whole of one of the states of the United States. ❑ *These voters often determine the outcome of statewide elections.* ADJ: usu ADJ n ♦ **Statewide** is also an adverb. ❑ *In the weeks since flooding began, 16 people have died statewide.* ADV: ADV after v

**stat|ic** /stætɪk/ 1 Something that is **static** does not move or change. ❑ *The number of young people obtaining qualifications has remained static or decreased.* ADJ 2 **Static** or **static electricity** is electricity which can be caused by things rubbing against each other and which collects on things such as your body or metal objects. N-UNCOUNT 3 If there is **static** on the radio or television, you hear a series of loud noises which spoils the sound. N-UNCOUNT

**sta|tion** /steɪʃən/ **(stations, stationing, stationed)** ◆◆◇ 1 A **station** is a building by a railway line where trains stop so that people can get on or off. ❑ *Ingrid went with him to the railway station to see him off.* N-COUNT: oft n N 2 A bus **station** is a building, usually in a town or city, where buses stop, usually for a while, so that people can get on or off. N-COUNT: n N 3 If you talk about a particular radio or television **station**, you are referring to the programmes broadcast by a particular radio or television company. ❑ *...an independent local radio station... It claims to be the most popular television station in the UK.* N-COUNT: oft n N 4 If soldiers or officials **are stationed** in a place, they are sent there to do a job or to work for a period of time. ❑ *Reports from the capital, Lome, say troops are stationed on the streets.* V-PASSIVE *be* V-ed prep/adv 5 If you **station yourself** somewhere, you go there and wait, usually for a particular purpose. [FORMAL] ❑ *The musicians stationed themselves quickly on either side of the stairs.* VERB = position V pron-refl prep/adv 6 ➔ See also **fire station**, **gas station**, **petrol station**, **police station**, **power station**, **service station**, **space station**, **way station**.

**sta|tion|ary** /steɪʃənri, AM -neri/ Something that is **stationary** is not moving. ❑ *Stationary cars in traffic jams cause a great deal of pollution.* ADJ: usu ADJ n

**sta|tion|er** /steɪʃənəʳ/ **(stationers)** A **stationer** is a person who sells paper, envelopes, pens, and other equipment used for writing. N-COUNT

**sta|tion|ery** /steɪʃənri, AM -neri/ **Stationery** is paper, envelopes, and other materials or equipment used for writing. N-UNCOUNT

**station|master** /steɪʃənmɑːstəʳ, -mæstəʳ/ **(stationmasters)** also **station master.** A **stationmaster** is the official who is in charge of a railway station. N-COUNT

**sta|tion wag|on** **(station wagons)** A **station wagon** is a car with a long body, a door at the rear, and space behind the back seats. [AM] N-COUNT

✔ in BRIT, use **estate car**

**stat|ist** /steɪtɪst/ When a country has **statist** policies, the state has a lot of control over the economy. ❑ *...statist economic controls.* ADJ: usu ADJ n

**sta|tis|tic** /stətɪstɪk/ **(statistics)** ◆◇◇ 1 **Statistics** are facts which are obtained from analysing information expressed in numbers, for example information about the number of times that something happens. ❑ *Official statistics show real wages declining by 24%... There are no reliable statistics for the number of deaths in the battle.* ➔ See also **vital statistics**. N-COUNT: usu pl = figure 2 **Statistics** is a branch of mathematics concerned with the study of information that is expressed in numbers. ❑ *...a professor of Mathematical Statistics.* N-UNCOUNT

**sta|tis|ti|cal** /stətɪstɪkəl/ **Statistical** means relating to the use of statistics. ❑ *The report contains a great deal of statistical information.* ADJ: usu ADJ n ♦ **sta|tis|ti|cal|ly** /stətɪstɪkli/ *The results are not statistically significant.* ADV: ADV with cl/group, ADV with v

**stat|is|ti|cian** /stætɪstɪʃən/ **(statisticians)** A **statistician** is a person who studies statistics or who works using statistics. N-COUNT

**stats** /stæts/ 1 **Stats** are facts which are obtained from analysing information expressed in numbers. **Stats** is an abbreviation for 'statistics'. [INFORMAL] ❑ *...a fall in April's retail sales stats.* N-PLURAL 2 **Stats** is a branch of mathematics concerned with the study of information that is expressed in numbers. [INFORMAL] N-UNCOUNT

**statu|ary** /stætʃuəri, AM -ueri/ If you talk about the **statuary** in a place, you are referring to all the statues and sculpture there. [FORMAL] N-UNCOUNT

**statue** /stætʃu:/ **(statues)** A **statue** is a large sculpture of a person or an animal, made of stone or metal. N-COUNT

**statu|esque** /stætʃuesk/ A **statuesque** woman is big and tall, and stands straight. [WRITTEN] ❑ *She was a statuesque brunette.* ADJ: usu ADJ n

**statu|ette** /stætʃuet/ **(statuettes)** A **statuette** is a very small sculpture of a person or an animal which is often displayed on a shelf or stand. N-COUNT

**stat|ure** /stætʃəʳ/ 1 Someone's **stature** is their height. ❑ *It's more than his physical stature that makes him remarkable... She was a little short in stature.* N-UNCOUNT: usu with poss, *of* supp N, *in* N 2 The **stature** of a person is the importance and reputation that they have. ❑ *Who can deny his stature as the world's greatest cellist?* N-UNCOUNT: usu with poss, *of* supp N, *in* N

**sta|tus** /steɪtəs/ ◆◆◇ 1 Your **status** is your social or professional position. ❑ *People of higher status tend more to use certain drugs. ...women and men of wealth and status. ...his wife's former status as his secretary.* N-UNCOUNT: usu with supp 2 **Status** is the importance and respect that someone has among the public or a particular group. ❑ *Nurses are undervalued, and they never enjoy the same status as doctors.* N-UNCOUNT 3 The **status** of something is the importance that people give it. ❑ *Those things that can be assessed by external tests are being given unduly high status.* N-UNCOUNT = importance 4 A particular **status** is an official description that says what category a person, organization, or place be- N-UNCOUNT: with supp longs to, and gives them particular rights or advantages. ❑ *Bristol regained its status as a city in the local government reorganisation. ...his status as a British citizen.* [5] The **status** of something is its state of affairs at a particular time. [N-UNCOUNT: with supp] ❑ *What is your current financial status?*

**sta|tus quo** /steɪtəs kwoʊ/ **The status quo** is the state of affairs that exists at a particular time, especially in contrast to a different possible state of affairs. [N-SING: usu *the* N] ❑ *They have no wish for any change in the status quo.*

**sta|tus sym|bol** **(status symbols)** A **status symbol** is something that a person has or owns that shows they have money or importance in society. [N-COUNT]

**stat|ute** /stætʃuːt/ **(statutes)** A **statute** is a rule or law which has been made by a government or other organization and formally written down. [N-VAR] ❑ *The new statute covers the care for, bringing up and protection of children.*

**stat|ute book** **(statute books)** **The statute book** is a record of all the laws made by the government. [mainly BRIT] [N-COUNT: *the*/poss N] ❑ *The Bill could reach the statute book by the summer if it attracts the support of Home Office ministers.*

**statu|tory** /stætʃʊtəri, AM -tɔːri/ **Statutory** means relating to rules or laws which have been formally written down. [FORMAL] [ADJ: usu ADJ n] ❑ *We had a statutory duty to report to Parliament.*

**statu|tory rape** In the United States, **statutory rape** is the crime committed by an adult when they have sex with someone who is under the age when they can legally agree to have sex. [N-UNCOUNT]

**staunch** /stɔːntʃ/ **(stauncher, staunchest, staunches, staunching, staunched)** [1] A **staunch** supporter or believer is very loyal to a person, organization, or set of beliefs, and supports them strongly. [ADJ: usu ADJ n = steadfast] ❑ *He's a staunch supporter of controls on government spending.* ♦ **staunch|ly** *He was staunchly opposed to a public confession.* [ADV] [2] To **staunch** the flow of something means to stop it. [FORMAL] [VERB] ❑ *The government claims this is the only way to staunch the annual flow to Germany of hundreds of thousands of refugees.* [V n] [3] To **staunch** a wound, or to **staunch** the blood from a wound, means to stop the wound from bleeding. [FORMAL] [VERB] ❑ *Tom tried to staunch the blood with his handkerchief.* [V n]

**stave** /steɪv/ **(staves, staving, staved)** [1] A **stave** is a strong stick, especially one that is used as a weapon. [N-COUNT = staff] ❑ *Many of the men had armed themselves with staves and pieces of iron.* [2] A **stave** is the five lines that music is written on. [mainly BRIT] [N-COUNT]

☑ in AM, use **staff**

♦ **stave off** If you **stave off** something bad, or if you **stave** it **off**, you succeed in stopping it happening for a while. [PHRASAL VERB] ❑ *In a desperate attempt to stave off defeat, he reluctantly promised wholesale reform of the constitution...* [V P n (not pron)] *But the reality of discovery was a different matter, and he did all he could to stave it off.* [V n P]

**stay** /steɪ/ **(stays, staying, stayed)** ◆◆◆ [1] If you **stay** where you are, you continue to be there and do not leave. [VERB] ❑ *'Stay here,' Trish said. 'I'll bring the car down the drive to take you back.'...* [V adv/prep] *In the old days the woman stayed at home and the man earned the money.* [V adv/prep] [2] If you **stay** in a town, or hotel, or at someone's house, you live there for a short time. [VERB] ❑ *Gordon stayed at The Park Hotel, Milan...* [V prep/adv] *He tried to stay a few months every year in Scotland.* [V n] ♦ **Stay** is also a noun. [N-COUNT: usu supp N] ❑ *An experienced Indian guide is provided during your stay.* [3] If someone or something **stays** in a particular state or situation, they continue to be in it. [V-LINK = remain] ❑ *The Republican candidate said he would 'work like crazy to stay ahead'.* [V adv/prep] *...community care networks that offer classes on how to stay healthy.* [V adj] [4] If you **stay away from** a place, you do not go there. [VERB = keep] ❑ *Government employers and officers also stayed away from work during the strike...* [V away from n] *Every single employee turned up at the meeting, even people who usually stayed away.* [V away] [5] If you **stay out of** something, you do not get involved in it. [VERB] ❑ *In the past, the UN has stayed out of the internal affairs of countries unless invited in.* [V out of n]

**PHRASES** [6] If you **stay put**, you remain somewhere. [PHRASE: V inflects] ❑ *Nigel says for the moment he is very happy to stay put in Lyon.* [7] If you **stay the night** in a place, you sleep there for one night. [PHRASE: V inflects] ❑ *They had invited me to come to supper and stay the night.*

♦ **stay in** If you **stay in** during the evening, you remain at home and do not go out. [PHRASAL VERB ≠ go out; V P] ❑ *Before we had our child the idea of staying in every night would have been horrific.*

♦ **stay on** If you **stay on** somewhere, you remain there after other people have left or after the time when you were going to leave. [PHRASAL VERB] ❑ *He had managed to arrange to stay on in Adelaide...* [V P] *So few teenage Britons stay on at school, compared with the rest of Europe.* [V P]

♦ **stay out** If you **stay out** at night, you remain away from home, especially when you are expected to be there. [PHRASAL VERB ≠ stay in] ❑ *That was the first time Elliot stayed out all night.* [V P]

♦ **stay up** If you **stay up**, you remain out of bed at a time when most people have gone to bed or at a time when you are normally in bed yourself. [PHRASAL VERB] ❑ *I used to stay up late with my mom and watch movies.* [V P adv/prep]

**stay-at-home** **(stay-at-homes)** If you describe someone as a **stay-at-home**, you mean that they stay at home rather than going out to work or travelling. [N-COUNT: usu N n] ❑ *I was a stay-at-home mum until 1980 when my husband lost his job.*

**stay|ing pow|er** also **staying-power.** If you have **staying power**, you have the strength or determination to keep going until you reach the end of what you are doing. [N-UNCOUNT = stamina] ❑ *Someone who lacks staying power and persistence is unlikely to make a good researcher.*

**stay of ex|ecu|tion** **(stays of execution)** If you are given a **stay of execution**, you are legally allowed to delay obeying an order of a court of law. [LEGAL] [N-COUNT]

**STD** /es tiː diː/ **(STDs)** **STD** is an abbreviation for 'sexually transmitted disease'. [MEDICAL] [N-COUNT: usu N n] ❑ *...an STD clinic.*

**stead** /sted/ [1] If you do something **in** someone's **stead**, you replace them and do it instead of them. [FORMAL] [PHRASE: PHR after v] ❑ *We hope you will consent to act in his stead.* [2] If you say that something will **stand** someone **in good stead**, you mean that it will be very useful to them in the future. [PHRASE: V inflects] ❑ *My years of teaching stood me in good stead.*

**stead|fast** /stedfɑːst, -fæst/ If someone is **steadfast in** something that they are doing, they are convinced that what they are doing is right and they refuse to change it or to give up. [ADJ: oft ADJ *in* n] ❑ *He remained steadfast in his belief that he had done the right thing.*

**steady** /stedi/ **(steadier, steadiest, steadies, steadying, steadied)** ◆◇◇ [1] A **steady** situation continues or develops gradually without any interruptions and is not likely to change quickly. [ADJ] ❑ *Despite the steady progress of building work, the campaign against it is still going strong... The improvement in standards has been steady and persistent, but has attracted little comment from educationalists... A student doesn't have a steady income.* ♦ **steadi|ly** /stedɪli/ *Relax as much as possible and keep breathing steadily.* [ADV: ADV with v] [2] If an object is **steady**, it is firm and does not shake or move about. [ADJ ≠ unsteady] ❑ *Get as close to the subject as you can and hold the camera steady.* [3] If you look at someone or speak to them in a **steady** way, you look or speak in a calm, controlled way. [ADJ] ❑ *'Well, go on,' said Camilla, her voice fairly steady.* ♦ **steadi|ly** *He moved back a little and stared steadily at Elaine.* [ADV: ADV after v] [4] If you describe a person as **steady**, you mean that they are sensible and reliable. [ADJ: usu v-link ADJ] ❑ *He was firm and steady unlike other men she knew.* [5] If you **steady** something or if it **steadies**, it stops shaking or moving about. [VERB] ❑ *Two men* [V n] *were on the bridge-deck, steadying a ladder... Lovelock eased back the throttles and the ship steadied.* V [6] If you **steady yourself**, you control your voice or expression, so that people will think that you are calm and not nervous. VERB = compose ❑ *Somehow she steadied herself and murmured, 'Have you got a cigarette?'... She breathed in to steady her voice.* V pron-refl V n [7] You say **'steady on'** to someone to tell them to calm down or to be careful about what they are saying. EXCLAM ❑ *'What if there's another murder?' — 'Steady on!'.*

**steak** /steɪk/ **(steaks)** [1] A **steak** is a large flat piece of beef without much fat on it. You cook it by grilling or frying it. → See also **rump steak**, **T-bone steak**. N-VAR [2] **Steak** is beef that is used for making stews. It is often cut into cubes to be sold. N-UNCOUNT ❑ *...steak and kidney pie.* → See also **stewing steak**. [3] A fish **steak** is a large piece of fish that contains few bones. N-COUNT: usu n N ❑ *...fresh salmon steaks.*

**steak house** **(steak houses)** also **steakhouse.** A **steak house** is a restaurant that serves mainly steaks. N-COUNT

**steal** /stiːl/ **(steals, stealing, stole, stolen)** ◆◇◇ [1] If you **steal** something **from** someone, you take it away from them without their permission and without intending to return it. VERB ❑ *He was accused of stealing a small boy's bicycle... Bridge stole the money from clients' accounts... People who are drug addicts come in and steal... She has since been jailed for six months for stealing from the tills.* V n, V n from n, V, V-ing ♦ **sto|len** *We have now found the stolen car.* ADJ [2] If you **steal** someone else's ideas, you pretend that they are your own. VERB ❑ *A writer is suing director Steven Spielberg for allegedly stealing his film idea.* V n [3] If someone **steals** somewhere, they move there quietly, in a secret way. VERB [LITERARY] ❑ *They can steal away at night and join us... Leroy stole up the hall to the parlor.* V adv/prep, V adv/prep **to steal a glance** → see **glance**. **to steal a march on** someone → see **march**. **to steal the show** → see **show**. **to steal** someone's **thunder** → see **thunder**.

**stealth** /stelθ/ If you use **stealth** when you do something, you do it quietly and carefully so that no one will notice what you are doing. N-UNCOUNT: oft by N ❑ *He claimed Tony Blair is trying to get us into the euro by stealth.*

**stealthy** /stelθi/ **(stealthier, stealthiest)** ADJ **Stealthy** actions or movements are performed quietly and carefully, so that no one will notice what you are doing. ❑ *I would creep in and with stealthy footsteps explore the second-floor.* ♦ **stealthi|ly** /stelθɪli/ *Slowly and stealthily, someone was creeping up the stairs.* ADV: ADV with v

**steam** /stiːm/ **(steams, steaming, steamed)** ◆◇◇ [1] **Steam** is the hot mist that forms when water boils. **Steam** vehicles and machines are operated using steam as a means of power. N-UNCOUNT ❑ *In an electric power plant the heat converts water into high-pressure steam. ...the invention of the steam engine.* [2] If something **steams**, it gives off steam. VERB ❑ *...restaurants where coffee pots steamed on their burners. ...a basket of steaming bread rolls.* V, V-ing [3] If you **steam** food or if it **steams**, you cook it in steam rather than in water. VERB ❑ *Steam the carrots until they are just beginning to be tender... Leave the vegetables to steam over the rice for the 20 minutes cooking time. ...steamed clams and broiled chicken.* V n, V, V-ed

**PHRASES** [4] If something such as a plan or a project goes **full steam ahead**, it progresses quickly. PHRASE: v PHR ❑ *The Government was determined to go full steam ahead with its privatisation programme.* [5] If you **let off steam**, you get rid of your energy, anger, or strong emotions with physical activity or by behaving in a noisy or violent way. PHRASE: V inflects [INFORMAL] ❑ *Regular exercise helps to combat unwanted stress and is a good way of relaxing or letting off steam.* [6] If you **run out of steam**, you stop doing something because you have no more energy or enthusiasm left. PHRASE: V inflects [INFORMAL] ❑ *I decided to paint the bathroom ceiling but ran out of steam halfway through.*

♦ **steam ahead** If an economy or company **steams ahead**, it becomes stronger and more successful. PHRASAL VERB ❑ *The latest figures show industrial production steaming ahead at an 8.8 per cent annual rate.* V P

♦ **steam up** [1] If someone **gets steamed up about** something, they are very annoyed about it. PHRASAL VERB ❑ *The general manager may have got steamed up about nothing.* get V-ed P about n [2] When a window, mirror, or pair of glasses **steams up**, it becomes covered with steam or mist. PHRASAL VERB ❑ *...the irritation of living with lenses that steam up when you come in from the cold.* V P

**steam|boat** /stiːmbout/ **(steamboats)** A **steamboat** is a boat or ship that has an engine powered by steam. N-COUNT = steamer

**steam|er** /stiːməʳ/ **(steamers)** [1] A **steamer** is a ship that has an engine powered by steam. N-COUNT [2] A **steamer** is a special container used for steaming food such as vegetables and fish. N-COUNT

**steam iron** **(steam irons)** A **steam iron** is an electric iron that produces steam from water that you put into it. The steam makes it easier to get the creases out of your clothes. N-COUNT

**steam|roller** /stiːmroʊləʳ/ **(steamrollers, steamrollering, steamrollered)** [1] A **steamroller** is a large, heavy vehicle with wide, solid metal wheels, which is used to make the surface of a road flat. In the past steamrollers were powered by steam. N-COUNT [2] If you **steamroller** someone who disagrees with you or opposes you, you defeat them or you force them to do what you want by using your power or by putting a lot of pressure on them. VERB ❑ *They could simply steamroller all opposition.* V n

**steam|ship** /stiːmʃɪp/ **(steamships)** A **steamship** is a ship that has an engine powered by steam. N-COUNT = steamer

**steamy** /stiːmi/ [1] **Steamy** means involving exciting sex. ADJ: usu ADJ n [INFORMAL] ❑ *He'd had a steamy affair with an office colleague.* [2] A **steamy** place has hot, wet air. ADJ: usu ADJ n ❑ *...a steamy cafe.*

**steed** /stiːd/ **(steeds)** A **steed** is a large strong horse used for riding. N-COUNT [LITERARY]

**steel** /stiːl/ **(steels, steeling, steeled)** ◆◇◇ [1] **Steel** is a very strong metal which is made mainly from iron. Steel is used for making many things, for example bridges, buildings, vehicles, and cutlery. N-MASS: oft N n ❑ *...steel pipes. ...the iron and steel industry... The front wall is made of corrugated steel.* → See also **stainless steel**. [2] **Steel** is used to refer to the industry that produces steel and items made of steel. N-UNCOUNT: oft N n ❑ *...a three-month study of European steel.* [3] If you **steel yourself**, you prepare to deal with something unpleasant. VERB ❑ *Those involved are steeling themselves for the coming battle... I was steeling myself to call round when Simon arrived.* V pron-refl for/against n, V pron-refl to-inf

**steel band** **(steel bands)** A **steel band** is a band of people who play music on special metal drums. Steel bands started in the West Indies. N-COUNT

**steel|maker** /stiːlmeɪkeʳ/ **(steelmakers)** A **steelmaker** is a company that makes steel. N-COUNT

**steel wool** **Steel wool** is a mass of fine steel threads twisted together into a small ball and used for cleaning hard surfaces or removing paint. N-UNCOUNT

**steel|worker** /stiːlwɜːʳkəʳ/ **(steelworkers)** also **steel worker.** A **steelworker** is a person who works in a factory where steel is made. N-COUNT

**steel|works** /stiːlwɜːʳks/ **(steelworks)** A **steelworks** is a factory where steel is made. N-COUNT

**steely** /stiːli/ [1] **Steely** is used to emphasize that a person is hard, strong, and determined. ADJ: usu ADJ n emphasis ❑ *Their indecision has been replaced by confidence and steely determination.* [2] You use **steely** to describe something that has the grey colour of steel. ADJ: usu ADJ n ❑ *...steely grey hair.*

**steep** /stiːp/ **(steeper, steepest)** [1] A **steep** slope rises at a very sharp angle and is difficult to go up. ADJ ❑ *San Francisco is built on 40 hills and some are very steep. ...a narrow, steep-sided valley.* ♦ **steep|ly** *The road climbs steeply, with good views* ADV: ADV with v *of Orvieto through the trees. ...steeply terraced valleys. ...houses with steeply sloping roofs.* [2] A **steep** increase or decrease in something is a very big increase or decrease. ❑ *Consumers are rebelling at steep price increases.* {ADJ = sharp} ♦ **steep|ly** *Unemployment is now rising steeply.* {ADV: ADV with v} [3] If you say that the price of something is **steep**, you mean that it is expensive. [INFORMAL] ❑ *The premium can be a little steep, but will be well worth it if your dog is injured.* {ADJ: usu v-link ADJ}

**steeped** /stiːpt/ If a place or person is **steeped in** a quality or characteristic, they are surrounded by it or deeply influenced by it. ❑ *The castle is steeped in history and legend.* {ADJ: v-link ADJ *in* n}

**steep|en** /stiːpən/ **(steepens, steepening, steepened)** If a slope or an angle **steepens**, it becomes steeper. [LITERARY] ❑ *The road steepened and then levelled out suddenly.* {VERB} {V}

**stee|ple** /stiːpᵊl/ **(steeples)** A **steeple** is a tall pointed structure on top of the tower of a church. {N-COUNT = spire}

**steeple|chase** /stiːpᵊltʃeɪs/ **(steeplechases)** [1] A **steeplechase** is a long horse race in which the horses have to jump over obstacles such as hedges and water jumps. {N-COUNT} [2] A **steeplechase** is a 3000 metres race around a track, during which people jump over obstacles and water jumps. {N-COUNT}

**steer** /stɪəʳ/ **(steers, steering, steered)** [1] When you **steer** a car, boat, or plane, you control it so that it goes in the direction that you want. ❑ *What is it like to steer a ship this size?... When I was a kid, about six or seven, she would often let me steer the car along our driveway.* {VERB} {V n} {V n prep} [2] If you **steer** people towards a particular course of action or attitude, you try to lead them gently in that direction. ❑ *The new government is seen as one that will steer the country in the right direction.* {VERB} {V n prep} [3] If you **steer** someone in a particular direction, you guide them there. ❑ *Nick steered them into the nearest seats.* {VERB = guide} {V n prep} [4] If you **steer** a particular **course**, you take a particular line of action. ❑ *Prime Minister Hun Sen has sought to steer a course between the two groups.* {VERB} {V n prep} [5] → See also **steering**. [6] If you **steer clear of** someone or something, you deliberately avoid them. ❑ *I think a lot of people, women in particular, steer clear of these sensitive issues.* {PHRASE: V inflects}

**steer|ing** /stɪərɪŋ/ [1] The **steering** in a car or other vehicle is the mechanical parts of it which make it possible to steer. {N-UNCOUNT} [2] A **steering** committee or a **steering** group is a group of people that organizes the early stages of a project, and makes sure it progresses in a satisfactory way. ❑ *There will be an economic steering committee with representatives of each of the republics.* {ADJ: ADJ n}

**steer|ing col|umn** **(steering columns)** In a car or other vehicle, the **steering column** is the rod on which the steering wheel is fixed. {N-COUNT}

**steer|ing wheel** **(steering wheels)** In a car or other vehicle, the **steering wheel** is the wheel which the driver holds when he or she is driving. → See picture on page 1708. {N-COUNT}

**stel|lar** /stelәʳ/ [1] **Stellar** is used to describe anything connected with stars. ❑ *A stellar wind streams outward from the star.* {ADJ: ADJ n} [2] A **stellar** person or thing is considered to be very good. ❑ *The French companies are registering stellar profits.* {ADJ: usu ADJ n = outstanding}

**stem** /stem/ **(stems, stemming, stemmed)** {◆◇◇} [1] If a condition or problem **stems from** something, it was caused originally by that thing. ❑ *Much of the instability stems from the economic effects of the war.* {VERB} {V *from* n} [2] If you **stem** something, you stop it spreading, increasing, or continuing. [FORMAL] ❑ *Austria has sent three army battalions to its border with Hungary to stem the flow of illegal immigrants.* {VERB} {V n} [3] The **stem** of a plant is the thin, upright part on which the flowers and leaves grow. ❑ *He stooped down, cut the stem for her with his knife and handed her the flower.* {N-COUNT = stalk} [4] The **stem** of a wine glass is the long thin part which connects the bowl to the base. {N-COUNT} [5] The **stem** of a pipe is the long thin part through which smoke is sucked. {N-COUNT} [6] In grammar, the **stem** of a word is the main part of it, which does not change when the ending changes. {N-COUNT}

**stem cell** **(stem cells)** A **stem cell** is a type of cell that can produce other cells which are able to develop into any kind of cell in the body. {N-COUNT}

**-stemmed** /-stemd/ **-stemmed** is added to adjectives to form adjectives which indicate what the stem of something is like. ❑ *...an enormous bouquet of long-stemmed roses.* {COMB in ADJ: usu ADJ n}

**stench** /stentʃ/ **(stenches)** A **stench** is a strong and very unpleasant smell. ❑ *The stench of burning rubber was overpowering.* {N-COUNT: oft N *of* n}

**sten|cil** /stensᵊl/ **(stencils, stencilling, stencilled)**

> ✔ in AM, use **stenciling**, **stenciled**

[1] A **stencil** is a piece of paper, plastic, or metal which has a design cut out of it. You place the stencil on a surface and paint it so that paint goes through the holes and leaves a design on the surface. {N-COUNT} [2] If you **stencil** a design or if you **stencil** a surface **with** a design, you put a design on a surface using a stencil. ❑ *He then stencilled the ceiling with a moon and stars motif.* {VERB} {V n *with* n}

**ste|nog|ra|pher** /stәnɒgrәfәʳ/ **(stenographers)** A **stenographer** is a person who types and writes shorthand, usually in an office. [AM] {N-COUNT}

> ✔ in BRIT, use **shorthand typist**

**sten|to|rian** /stentɔːriәn/ A **stentorian** voice is very loud and strong. [FORMAL] ❑ *He bellowed in a stentorian voice.* {ADJ: usu ADJ n}

**step** /step/ **(steps, stepping, stepped)** {◆◆◆} [1] If you take a **step**, you lift your foot and put it down in a different place, for example when you are walking. ❑ *I took a step towards him... She walked on a few steps... He heard steps in the corridor.* {N-COUNT} [2] If you **step on** something or **step** in a particular direction, you put your foot on the thing or move your foot in that direction. ❑ *This was the moment when Neil Armstrong became the first man to step on the Moon... She accidentally stepped on his foot on a crowded commuter train.* {VERB} {V prep/adv} {V prep/adv} [3] **Steps** are a series of surfaces at increasing or decreasing heights, on which you put your feet in order to walk up or down to a different level. ❑ *This little room was along a passage and down some steps... A flight of stone steps leads to the terrace.* {N-COUNT} [4] A **step** is a raised flat surface in front of a door. ❑ *A little girl was sitting on the step of the end house.* → See also **doorstep**. {N-COUNT} [5] A **step** is one of a series of actions that you take in order to achieve something. ❑ *He greeted the agreement as the first step towards peace... She is not content with her present lot and wishes to take steps to improve it.* {N-COUNT: oft N prep/adv} [6] A **step** in a process is one of a series of stages. ❑ *The next step is to put the theory into practice.* {N-COUNT = stage} [7] The **steps** of a dance are the sequences of foot movements which make it up. {N-COUNT = movement} [8] Someone's **step** is the way they walk. ❑ *He quickened his step.* {N-SING: poss N}

**PHRASES** [9] If you stay **one step ahead of** someone or something, you manage to achieve more than they do or avoid competition or danger from them. ❑ *Successful travel is partly a matter of keeping one step ahead of the crowd.* {PHRASE: PHR after v, v-link PHR} [10] If people who are walking or dancing are **in step**, they are moving their feet forward at exactly the same time as each other. If they are **out of step**, their feet are moving forward at different times. ❑ *They were almost the same height and they moved perfectly in step.* {PHRASE: PHR after v} [11] If people are **in step with** each other, their ideas or opinions are the same. If they are **out of step with** each other, their ideas or opinions are different. ❑ *Moscow is anxious to stay in step with Washington.* {PHRASE: usu PHR *with* n} [12] If you tell someone to **step on it**, you are telling them to go faster or hurry up. [INFORMAL] ❑ *We've only got thirty-five minutes so step on it.* {PHRASE = get a move on} [13] If you do something **step by step**, you do it by progressing gradually from one stage to the next. ❑ *I am not rushing things and I'm taking it step by step... Follow our sim-* {PHRASE: PHR with v, PHR n} ple step-by-step instructions. 14 If someone tells you to **watch** your **step**, they are warning you to be careful about how you behave or what you say so that you do not get into trouble. PHRASE

♦ **step aside** → see **step down**.

♦ **step back** If you **step back** and think about a situation, you think about it as if you were not involved in it. ❑ *I stepped back and analysed the situation... It was necessary to step back from the project and look at it as a whole.* PHRASAL VERB = stand back; V P; V P from n

♦ **step down** or **step aside** If someone **steps down** or **steps aside**, they resign from an important job or position, often in order to let someone else take their place. ❑ *Judge Ito said that if his wife was called as a witness, he would step down as trial judge... Many would prefer to see him step aside in favour of a younger man.* PHRASAL VERB = stand down; V P as n; V P

♦ **step in** If you **step in**, you get involved in a difficult situation because you think you can or should help with it. ❑ *There are circumstances in which the State must step in to protect children.* PHRASAL VERB = intervene; V P

♦ **step out** If someone **steps out of** a role or situation, they leave it. ❑ *I don't regret stepping out of the security of marriage.* PHRASAL VERB; V P of n; Also V P

♦ **step up** If you **step up** something, you increase it or increase its intensity. ❑ *He urged donors to step up their efforts to send aid to Somalia.* PHRASAL VERB = increase; V P n (not pron)

**step|brother** /stepbrʌðə^r/ **(stepbrothers)** also **step-brother**. Someone's **stepbrother** is the son of their stepfather or stepmother. N-COUNT: oft poss N

**step-by-step** → see **step**.

**step change** **(step changes)** A **step change** is a sudden or major change in the way that something happens or the way that someone behaves. ❑ *We now need a step change in our secondary schools to match that achieved in our primaries.* N-COUNT: usu sing, usu N in n

**step|child** /steptʃaɪld/ **(stepchildren)** also **step-child**. Someone's **stepchild** is a child that was born to their husband or wife during a previous relationship. N-COUNT: oft poss N

**step|daughter** /stepdɔːtə^r/ **(stepdaughters)** also **step-daughter**. Someone's **stepdaughter** is a daughter that was born to their husband or wife during a previous relationship. N-COUNT: oft poss N

**step|father** /stepfɑːðə^r/ **(stepfathers)** also **step-father**. Someone's **stepfather** is the man who has married their mother after the death or divorce of their father. N-COUNT: oft poss N

**step|ladder** /steplædə^r/ **(stepladders)** A **stepladder** is a portable ladder that is made of two sloping parts that are hinged together at the top so that it will stand up on its own. N-COUNT = steps

**step|mother** /stepmʌðə^r/ **(stepmothers)** also **step-mother**. Someone's **stepmother** is the woman who has married their father after the death or divorce of their mother. N-COUNT: oft poss N

**step|parent** /steppeərənt/ **(stepparents)** also **step-parent**. Someone's **stepparent** is their stepmother or stepfather. N-COUNT: oft poss N

**steppe** /step/ **(steppes)** **Steppes** are large areas of flat grassy land where there are no trees, especially the area that stretches from Eastern Europe across the south of the former Soviet Union to Siberia. N-UNCOUNT: also N in pl

**step|ping stone** **(stepping stones)** also **stepping-stone**. 1 You can describe a job or event as a **stepping stone** when it helps you to make progress, especially in your career. ❑ *Many students now see university as a stepping stone to a good job.* N-COUNT: oft N to n 2 **Stepping stones** are a line of large stones which you can walk on in order to cross a shallow stream or river. N-COUNT: usu pl

**step|sister** /stepsɪstə^r/ **(stepsisters)** also **step-sister**. Someone's **stepsister** is the daughter of their stepfather or stepmother. N-COUNT: oft poss N

**step|son** /stepsʌn/ **(stepsons)** also **step-son**. Someone's **stepson** is a son born to their husband or wife during a previous relationship. N-COUNT: oft poss N

**ste|reo** /steriou/ **(stereos)** 1 **Stereo** is used to describe a sound system in which the sound is played through two speakers. Compare **mono**. ❑ *...loudspeakers that give all-around stereo sound.* ADJ 2 A **stereo** is a cassette or CD player with two speakers. N-COUNT

**ste|reo|type** /steriətaɪp/ **(stereotypes, stereotyping, stereotyped)** 1 A **stereotype** is a fixed general image or set of characteristics that a lot of people believe represent a particular type of person or thing. ❑ *Many men feel their body shape doesn't live up to the stereotype of the ideal man.* N-COUNT 2 If someone **is stereotyped** as something, people form a fixed general idea or image of them, so that it is assumed that they will behave in a particular way. ❑ *He was stereotyped by some as a rebel... I get very worked up about the way women are stereotyped in a lot of mainstream films.* VERB: usu passive; be V-ed as n; be V-ed

**ste|reo|typi|cal** /sterioutɪpɪk^əl/ A **stereotypical** idea of a type of person or thing is a fixed general idea that a lot of people have about it, that may be false in many cases. ❑ *Dara challenges our stereotypical ideas about gender and femininity.* ADJ

**ster|ile** /steraɪl, AM -rəl/ 1 Something that is **sterile** is completely clean and free from germs. ❑ *He always made sure that any cuts were protected by sterile dressings.* ♦ **ste|ril|ity** /stərɪlɪti/ *...the antiseptic sterility of the hospital.* ADJ: usu ADJ n; N-UNCOUNT 2 A person or animal that is **sterile** is unable to have or produce babies. ❑ *George was sterile. ...a sterile male.* ♦ **ste|ril|ity** *This disease causes sterility in both males and females.* ADJ; N-UNCOUNT 3 A **sterile** situation is lacking in energy and new ideas. ❑ *Too much time has been wasted in sterile debate.* ♦ **ste|ril|ity** *...the sterility of Dorothea's life in industry.* ADJ: usu ADJ n [disapproval]; N-UNCOUNT

**steri|lize** /sterɪlaɪz/ **(sterilizes, sterilizing, sterilized)**

> in BRIT, also use **sterilise**

1 If you **sterilize** a thing or a place, you make it completely clean and free from germs. ❑ *Sulphur is also used to sterilize equipment.* ♦ **steri|li|za|tion** /sterɪlaɪzeɪʃ^ən, AM -lɪz-/ *...the pasteurization and sterilization of milk.* VERB; V n; N-UNCOUNT 2 If a person or an animal **is sterilized**, they have a medical operation that makes it impossible for them to have or produce babies. ❑ *My wife was sterilized after the birth of her fourth child.* ♦ **steri|li|za|tion** **(sterilizations)** *In some cases, a sterilization is performed through the vaginal wall.* VERB: usu passive; be V-ed; N-VAR

**ster|ling** /stɜːʳlɪŋ/ ◆◆◇ 1 **Sterling** is the money system of Great Britain. ❑ *The stamps had to be paid for in sterling.* N-UNCOUNT 2 **Sterling** means very good in quality; used to describe someone's work or character. [FORMAL] ❑ *Those are sterling qualities to be admired in anyone.* ADJ: usu ADJ n [approval] = excellent, outstanding

**stern** /stɜːʳn/ **(sterner, sternest, sterns)** 1 **Stern** words or actions are very severe. ❑ *Mr Straw issued a stern warning to those who persist in violence.* ♦ **stern|ly** *'We will take the necessary steps,' she said sternly.* ADJ; ADV: ADV with v, ADV adj 2 Someone who is **stern** is very serious and strict. ❑ *Her father was stern and hard to please.* ADJ 3 The **stern** of a boat is the back part of it. **From stem to stern** → see **stem**. N-COUNT ≠ prow

**ster|num** /stɜːʳnəm/ **(sternums)** Your **sternum** is the long flat bone which goes from your throat to the bottom of your ribs and to which your ribs are attached. [MEDICAL] N-COUNT = breastbone

**ster|oid** /sterɔɪd, AM stɪr-/ **(steroids)** A **steroid** is a type of chemical substance found in your body. Steroids can be artificially introduced into the bodies of athletes to improve their strength. N-COUNT

**stetho|scope** /steθəskoup/ **(stethoscopes)** A **stethoscope** is an instrument that a doctor uses to listen to your heart and breathing. It consists of a small disc that is placed on your body, connected to a hollow tube with two pieces that the doctor puts in his or her ears. N-COUNT

**Stet|son** /stets^ən/ **(Stetsons)** A **Stetson** is a type of hat with a wide brim that is traditionally worn by cowboys. [TRADEMARK] N-COUNT

**stew** /stjuː, AM stuː/ **(stews, stewing, stewed)**
1 A **stew** is a meal which you make by cooking meat and vegetables in liquid at a low temperature. N-VAR ❑ *She served him a bowl of beef stew... They made a stew.* 2 When you **stew** meat, vegetables, or fruit, you cook them slowly in liquid in a closed dish. VERB ❑ *Stew the apple and blackberries to make a thick pulp.* V n

**stew|ard** /stjuːəʳd, AM stuː-/ **(stewards)** 1 A **steward** is a man who works on a ship, plane, or train, looking after passengers and serving meals to them. N-COUNT 2 A **steward** is a man or woman who helps to organize a race, march, or other public event. N-COUNT → See also **shop steward**.

**stew|ard|ess** /stjuːəʳdes, stuː-/ **(stewardesses)** A **stewardess** is a woman who works on a ship, plane, or train, looking after passengers and serving meals to them. N-COUNT = *air hostess*

**stew|ard|ship** /stjuːəʳdʃɪp, AM stuː-/ **Stewardship** is the responsibility of looking after property. [FORMAL] N-UNCOUNT: usu N *of* n

**stew|ing steak** **Stewing steak** is beef which is suitable for cooking slowly in a stew. [BRIT] N-UNCOUNT

✔ in AM, use **stew meat**

**stew meat** **Stew meat** is the same as **stewing steak**. [AM] N-UNCOUNT

**stick**
① NOUN USES
② VERB USES

① **stick** /stɪk/ **(sticks)** ◆◇◇ 1 A **stick** is a thin branch which has fallen off a tree. N-COUNT ❑ *...people carrying bundles of dried sticks to sell for firewood.* 2 A **stick** is a long thin piece of wood which is used for supporting someone's weight or for hitting people or animals. N-COUNT ❑ *He looks old and walks with a stick... Crowds armed with sticks and stones took to the streets.* → See also **carrot and stick**. 3 A **stick** is a long thin piece of wood which is used for a particular purpose. N-COUNT: usu n N ❑ *...kebab sticks. ...lolly sticks. ...drum sticks.* 4 Some long thin objects that are used in sports are called **sticks**. N-COUNT: usu n N ❑ *...lacrosse sticks. ...hockey sticks. ...ski-sticks.* 5 A **stick of** something is a long thin piece of it. N-COUNT: usu N *of* n, n N ❑ *...a stick of celery. ...cinnamon sticks.* 6 If you give someone some **stick**, you criticize them or tease them roughly. N-UNCOUNT [BRIT, INFORMAL] ❑ *It's not motorists who give you the most stick, it's the general public... I get some stick from the lads because of my faith but I don't mind.* 7 If you say that someone lives in **the sticks**, you mean that they live a long way from any large cities. N-PLURAL: *the* N disapproval [INFORMAL] ❑ *He lived out in the sticks somewhere.* 8 If someone **gets the wrong end of the stick** or **gets hold of the wrong end of the stick**, they do not understand something correctly and get the wrong idea about it. PHRASE: V inflects [INFORMAL]

② **stick** /stɪk/ **(sticks, sticking, stuck)** ◆◆◇
⇛ Please look at category 9 to see if the expression you are looking for is shown under another headword. 1 If you **stick** something somewhere, you put it there in a rather casual way. VERB [INFORMAL] ❑ *He folded the papers and stuck them in his desk drawer... Jack opened his door and stuck his head out.* V n prep/adv, V n prep/adv 2 If you **stick** a pointed object **in** something, or if it **sticks in** something, it goes into it or through it by making a cut or hole. VERB ❑ *Some punk stuck a knife in her last night... The soldiers went at once to the mound and began to stick their bayonets through it... The knife stuck in the ground at his feet.* V n *in/into/through* n, V n *in/into/through* n, V *in* n 3 If something **is sticking out** from a surface or object, it extends up or away from it. If something **is sticking into** a surface or object, it is partly in it. VERB ❑ *They lay where they had fallen from the crane, sticking out of the water... His hair sticks up in half a dozen directions. ...when we see her with lots of tubes and needles sticking into her little body.* V adv/prep, V adv/prep, V adv/prep 4 If you **stick** one thing to another, you attach it using glue, sticky tape, or another sticky substance. VERB ❑ *We just stuck it to the window... He has nowhere to stick up his posters... Stick down any loose bits of flooring.* V n prep, V n with adv, V n with adv 5 If one thing **sticks to** another, it becomes attached to it and is difficult to remove. VERB ❑ *Peel away the waxed paper if it has stuck to the bottom of the cake... If left to stand, cooked pasta sticks together.* V *to* n, V *together* 6 If something **sticks in** your mind, you remember it for a long time. VERB ❑ *The incident stuck in my mind because it was the first example I had seen of racism in that country.* V *in* n 7 If something which can usually be moved **sticks**, it becomes fixed in one position. VERB ❑ *The needle on the dial went right round to fifty feet, and there it stuck.* V 8 → See also **stuck**. 9 to **stick in** your **throat** → see **throat**.

♦ **stick around** If you **stick around**, you stay where you are, often because you are waiting for something. PHRASAL VERB [INFORMAL] ❑ *Stick around a while and see what develops.* V P

♦ **stick at** If you **stick at** a task or activity, you continue doing it, even if it is difficult. PHRASAL VERB ❑ *You will find it hard at first, but stick at it.* V P n

♦ **stick by** 1 If you **stick by** someone, you continue to give them help or support. PHRASAL VERB ❑ *...friends who stuck by me during the difficult times as Council Leader.* V P n 2 If you **stick by** a promise, agreement, decision, or principle, you do what you said you would do, or do not change your mind. PHRASAL VERB = *stick to* ❑ *But I made my decision then and stuck by it.* V P n

♦ **stick out** 1 If you **stick out** part of your body, you extend it away from your body. PHRASAL VERB ❑ *She made a face and stuck out her tongue at him... He stuck his hand out and he said, 'Good evening.'* V P n (not pron), V n P to **stick** your **neck out** → see **neck**. 2 If something **sticks out**, it is very noticeable because it is unusual. PHRASAL VERB = *stand out* ❑ *What had Cutter done to make him stick out from the crowd?* V P *from* n to **stick out a mile** → see **mile**. to **stick out like a sore thumb** → see **thumb**. 3 If someone in an unpleasant or difficult situation **sticks it out**, they do not leave or give up. PHRASE: V inflects ❑ *I really didn't like New York, but I wanted to stick it out a little bit longer.*

♦ **stick to** 1 If you **stick to** something or someone when you are travelling, you stay close to them. PHRASAL VERB ❑ *There are interesting hikes inland, but most ramblers stick to the clifftops.* V P n 2 If you **stick to** something, you continue doing, using, saying, or talking about it, rather than changing to something else. PHRASAL VERB ❑ *Perhaps he should have stuck to writing.* V P n 3 If you **stick to** a promise, agreement, decision, or principle, you do what you said you would do, or do not change your mind. PHRASAL VERB = *stick by* ❑ *Immigrant support groups are waiting to see if he sticks to his word... But one problem is that few people can stick to a diet for long.* V P n, V P n to **stick to** your **guns** → see **gun**. 4 If you **stick to** rules, you do what they say you must do. PHRASAL VERB ❑ *Obviously we are disappointed but the committee could do nothing less than stick to the rules... Police must stick to the highest standards if they are to win back public confidence.* V P n, V P n

♦ **stick together** If people **stick together**, they stay with each other and support each other. PHRASAL VERB ❑ *If we all stick together, we ought to be okay.* V P

♦ **stick up for** If you **stick up for** a person or a principle, you support or defend them forcefully. PHRASAL VERB = *stand up for* ❑ *I can stick up for myself.* V P P n

♦ **stick with** 1 If you **stick with** something, you do not change to something else. PHRASAL VERB ❑ *They prefer, in the end, to stick with what they know.* V P n 2 If you **stick with** someone, you stay close to them. PHRASAL VERB ❑ *Tugging the woman's arm, she pulled her to her side saying: 'You just stick with me, dear.'* V P n

**stick|er** /stɪkəʳ/ **(stickers)** A **sticker** is a small piece of paper or plastic, with writing or a picture on one side, which you can stick onto a surface. N-COUNT → See also **bumper sticker**.

**stick|ing plas|ter** **(sticking plasters)** **Sticking plaster** is material that you can stick over a cut or wound in order to protect it. A **sticking plaster** is a piece of this material. N-VAR [BRIT]

✔ in AM, use **Band-Aid**

**stick|ing point** **(sticking points)** also **sticking-point.** A **sticking point** in a discussion or series of negotiations is a point on which the people involved cannot agree and which may delay or stop the talks. A **sticking point** is also one aspect of a problem which you have trouble dealing with. ❑ *The main sticking point was the question of taxes.* N-COUNT: usu sing

**stick in|sect** **(stick insects)** also **stick-insect.** A **stick insect** is an insect with a long body and thin legs. It looks like a small stick. N-COUNT

**stick-in-the-mud** **(stick-in-the-muds)** If you describe someone as a **stick-in-the-mud**, you disapprove of them because they do not like doing anything that is new or fun. [INFORMAL] N-COUNT [disapproval] = fuddy-duddy

**stickle|back** /stɪkəlbæk/ **(sticklebacks)** A **stickleback** is a small fish which has sharp points along its back. N-COUNT

**stick|ler** /stɪkləʳ/ **(sticklers)** If you are a **stickler for** something, you always demand or require it. ❑ *Lucy was a stickler for perfection, and everything had to be exactly right.* N-COUNT: usu N *for* n

**stick-on** **Stick-on** labels, shapes, and objects have a sticky material on one side so that they will stick to things. ADJ: ADJ n = adhesive

**stick shift** **(stick shifts)** A **stick shift** is the lever that you use to change gear in a car or other vehicle. [AM] N-COUNT = gearshift

☑ in BRIT, usually use **gear lever**

**sticky** /stɪki/ **(stickier, stickiest)** 1 A **sticky** substance is soft, or thick and liquid, and can stick to other things. **Sticky** things are covered with a sticky substance. ❑ *...sticky toffee... If the dough is sticky, add more flour... Peel away the sticky paper.* ADJ 2 A **sticky** situation involves problems or is embarrassing. [mainly BRIT, INFORMAL] ❑ *Inevitably the transition will yield some sticky moments.* ADJ: usu ADJ n 3 **Sticky** weather is unpleasantly hot and damp. ❑ *...four desperately hot, sticky days in the middle of August.* ADJ = muggy

**sticky tape** **Sticky tape** is clear sticky tape that is sold in rolls and that you use, for example to stick paper or card together, or to stick things onto a wall. [BRIT] N-UNCOUNT

☑ in AM, use **Scotch tape**

**stiff** /stɪf/ **(stiffer, stiffest)** 1 Something that is **stiff** is firm or does not bend easily. ❑ *His waterproof trousers were brand new and stiff... Clean the mussels with a stiff brush under cold running water.* ADJ = rigid ♦ **stiff|ly** *Moira sat stiffly upright in her straight-backed chair.* ADV: ADV adj, ADV with v 2 Something such as a door or drawer that is **stiff** does not move as easily as it should. ❑ *Train doors have handles on the inside. They are stiff so that they cannot be opened accidentally.* ADJ 3 If you are **stiff**, your muscles or joints hurt when you move, because of illness or because of too much exercise. ❑ *The Mud Bath is particularly recommended for relieving tension and stiff muscles... I'm stiff all over right now – I hope I can recover for tomorrow's race.* ADJ ♦ **stiff|ly** *He climbed stiffly from the Volkswagen.* ADV 4 **Stiff** behaviour is rather formal and not very friendly or relaxed. ❑ *They always seemed a little awkward with each other, a bit stiff and formal.* ADJ ♦ **stiff|ly** *'Why don't you borrow your sister's car?' said Cassandra stiffly. ...a stiffly worded letter of complaint.* ADV: ADV with v, ADV adj 5 **Stiff** can be used to mean difficult or severe. ❑ *The film faces stiff competition for the Best Film nomination... Under Greece's stiff anti-drugs laws they could face twenty years in jail.* ADJ: usu ADJ n 6 A **stiff** drink is a large amount of a strong alcoholic drink. ❑ *...a stiff whisky.* ADJ: ADJ n = large 7 If you are bored **stiff**, worried **stiff**, or scared **stiff**, you are extremely bored, worried, or scared. [INFORMAL] ❑ *Anna tried to look interested. Actually, she was bored stiff.* ADV: adj ADV [emphasis] ♦ **Stiff** is also an adjective. ❑ *Even if he bores you stiff, it is good manners not to let him know it.* ADJ: v n ADJ

**stiff|en** /stɪfən/ **(stiffens, stiffening, stiffened)** 1 If you **stiffen**, you stop moving and stand or sit with muscles that are suddenly tense, for example because you feel afraid or angry. ❑ *Ada stiffened at the sound of his voice.* VERB V 2 If your muscles or joints **stiffen**, or if something **stiffens** them, they become difficult to bend or move. ❑ *The blood supply to the skin is reduced when muscles stiffen.* VERB V Also V n ♦ **Stiffen up** means the same as **stiffen**. ❑ *These clothes restrict your freedom of movement and stiffen up the whole body.* PHRASAL VERB V P n (not pron) 3 If something such as cloth **is stiffened**, it is made firm so that it does not bend easily. ❑ *This special paper was actually thin, soft Sugiwara paper that had been stiffened with a kind of paste.* VERB: usu passive *be* V-ed

♦ **stiffen up** → see **stiffen 2**.

**stiff-necked** also **stiffnecked.** If you say that someone is **stiff-necked**, you mean that they are proud and unwilling to do what other people want. ADJ [disapproval]

**sti|fle** /staɪfəl/ **(stifles, stifling, stifled)** 1 If someone **stifles** something you consider to be a good thing, they prevent it from continuing. ❑ *Critics have accused the US of trying to stifle debate.* VERB [disapproval] = repress V n 2 If you **stifle** a yawn or laugh, you prevent yourself from yawning or laughing. ❑ *She makes no attempt to stifle a yawn.* VERB = suppress V n 3 If you **stifle** your natural feelings or behaviour, you prevent yourself from having those feelings or behaving in that way. ❑ *It is best to stifle curiosity and leave birds' nests alone.* VERB = suppress V n

**sti|fling** /staɪfəlɪŋ/ 1 **Stifling** heat is so intense that it makes you feel uncomfortable. You can also use **stifling** to describe a place that is extremely hot. ❑ *The stifling heat of the little room was beginning to make me nauseous.* ADJ 2 If a situation is **stifling**, it makes you feel uncomfortable because you cannot do what you want. ❑ *Life at home with her parents and two sisters was stifling. ...a stifling bureaucracy.* ADJ 3 → See also **stifle**.

**stig|ma** /stɪgmə/ **(stigmas)** 1 If something has a **stigma** attached to it, people think it is something to be ashamed of. ❑ *There is a strong argument for remaining an unmarried mother. There's no stigma attached any more.* N-VAR 2 The **stigma** of a flower is the top of the centre part which takes in pollen. [TECHNICAL] N-COUNT

**stig|ma|ta** /stɪgmɑːtə/ **Stigmata** are marks that appear on a person's body in the same places where Christ was wounded when he was nailed to the cross. Some Christians believe that these marks are a sign of holiness. N-PLURAL

**stig|ma|tize** /stɪgmətaɪz/ **(stigmatizes, stigmatizing, stigmatized)**

☑ in BRIT, also use **stigmatise**

If someone or something **is stigmatized**, they are unfairly regarded by many people as being bad or having something to be ashamed of. ❑ *Children in single-parent families must not be stigmatised... The AIDS epidemic further stigmatised gays.* VERB *be* V-ed V n

**stile** /staɪl/ **(stiles)** A **stile** is an entrance to a field or path consisting of a step on either side of a fence or wall to help people climb over it. N-COUNT

**sti|let|to** /stɪletoʊ/ **(stilettos)** **Stilettos** are women's shoes that have high, very narrow heels. [mainly BRIT] N-COUNT: usu pl

☑ in AM, usually use **spike heels**

**still**

① ADVERB USES
② NOT MOVING OR MAKING A NOISE
③ EQUIPMENT

**① still** /stɪl/ ◆◆◆ 1 If a situation that used to exist **still** exists, it has continued and exists now. ❑ *I still dream of home... Brian's toe is still badly swollen and he cannot put on his shoe... If you don't like the job, why are you still there?* ADV: ADV before v, ADV group 2 If something that has not yet happened could **still** happen, it is possible that it will happen. If something that has not yet happened is **still to** happen, it will hap- ADV: ADV before v pen at a later time. ❑ *Big money could still be made if the crisis keeps oil prices high... The details have still to be worked out.* [3] If you say that there **is still** an amount of something left, you are emphasizing that there is that amount left. ❑ *There are still some outstanding problems... There's still time to catch up with them.* ADV: *be* ADV n [4] You use **still** to emphasize that something remains the case or is true in spite of what you have just said. ❑ *I'm average for my height. But I still feel I'm fatter than I should be... Despite the ruling, Boreham was still found guilty.* ADV: ADV before v = nonetheless [5] You use **still** to indicate that a problem or difficulty is not really worth worrying about. ❑ *'Any idea who is going to be here this weekend?' — 'No. Still, who cares?'* ADV: ADV with cl [6] You use **still** in expressions such as **still further**, **still another**, and **still more** to show that you find the number or quantity of things you are referring to surprising or excessive. ❑ *We look forward to strengthening still further our already close co-operation with the police service.* ADV: ADV n/adv [emphasis] = even [7] You use **still** with comparatives to indicate that something has even more of a quality than something else. ❑ *Formula One motor car racing is supposed to be dangerous. 'Indycar' racing is supposed to be more dangerous still.* ADV: ADV with compar [emphasis]

**② still** /stɪl/ **(stiller, stillest, stills)** ◆◆◆ [1] If you stay **still**, you stay in the same position and do not move. ❑ *David had been dancing about like a child, but suddenly he stood still and looked at Brad... He played the tape through once, then sat very still for several minutes... Gladys was still, then she shook her head slowly.* ADJ: ADJ after v, v-link ADJ [2] If air or water is **still**, it is not moving. ❑ *The night air was very still... He watched the still water over the side of the boat.* ADJ [3] Drinks that are **still** do not contain any bubbles of carbon dioxide. ❑ *...a glass of still orange.* ADJ ≠ sparkling [4] If a place is **still**, it is quiet and shows no sign of activity. ❑ *In the room it was very still.* ADJ = quiet ♦ **still|ness** *Four deafening explosions shattered the stillness of the night air.* N-UNCOUNT [5] A **still** is a photograph taken from a cinema film which is used for publicity purposes. N-COUNT: oft N n

**③ still** /stɪl/ **(stills)** A **still** is a piece of equipment used to make strong alcoholic drinks by a process called distilling. N-COUNT

**still|birth** /stɪlbɜːʳθ/ **(stillbirths)** A **stillbirth** is the birth of a dead baby. N-VAR

**still|born** /stɪlbɔːʳn/ [1] A **stillborn** baby is dead when it is born. ❑ *It was a miracle that she survived the birth of her stillborn baby.* ADJ [2] An idea, action, or attempt which is **stillborn** is completely ineffective or unsuccessful. ❑ *The ceasefire itself could prove stillborn if rebel units in the bush keep on fighting.* ADJ

**still life (still lifes)** A **still life** is a painting or drawing of an arrangement of objects such as flowers or fruit. It also refers to this type of painting or drawing. N-VAR

**stilt** /stɪlt/ **(stilts)** [1] **Stilts** are long upright pieces of wood or metal on which some buildings are built, especially where the ground is wet or very soft. ❑ *They inhabit reed huts built on stilts above the water.* N-COUNT: usu pl, oft *on* N [2] **Stilts** are two long pieces of wood with pieces for the feet fixed high up on the sides so that people can stand on them and walk high above the ground. N-COUNT

**stilt|ed** /stɪltɪd/ If someone speaks in a **stilted** way, they speak in a formal or unnatural way, for example because they are not relaxed. ❑ *We made polite, stilted conversation.* ADJ = laboured ≠ easy

**stimu|lant** /stɪmjʊlənt/ **(stimulants)** A **stimulant** is a drug that makes your body work faster, often increasing your heart rate and making you less likely to sleep. N-COUNT

**stimu|late** /stɪmjʊleɪt/ **(stimulates, stimulating, stimulated)** ◆◇◇ [1] To **stimulate** something means to encourage it to begin or develop further. ❑ *America's priority is rightly to stimulate its economy... The Russian health service has stimulated public interest in home cures.* VERB V n ♦ **stimu|la|tion** /stɪmjʊleɪʃᵊn/ *...an economy in need of stimulation.* N-UNCOUNT [2] If you **are stimulated by** something, it makes you feel full of ideas and enthusiasm. ❑ *Bill was stimulated by the challenge... I was stimulated to examine my deepest thoughts.* VERB: usu passive *be* V-ed *be* V-ed to-inf ♦ **stimu|lat|ing** *It is a complex yet stimulating book... The atmosphere was always stimulating.* ADJ ♦ **stimu|la|tion** *Many enjoy the mental stimulation of a challenging job.* N-UNCOUNT: usu with supp [3] If something **stimulates** a part of a person's body, it causes it to move or start working. ❑ *Exercise stimulates the digestive and excretory systems... The body is stimulated to build up resistance.* VERB V n *be* V-ed to-inf ♦ **stimu|lat|ing** *...the stimulating effect of adrenaline.* ADJ ♦ **stimu|la|tion** *...physical stimulation. ...the chemical stimulation of drugs.* N-UNCOUNT: usu with supp

**stimu|la|tive** /stɪmjʊlətɪv/ If a government policy has a **stimulative** effect on the economy, it encourages the economy to grow. ❑ *It is possible that a tax cut might have some stimulative effect.* ADJ: usu ADJ n

**stimu|lus** /stɪmjʊləs/ **(stimuli** /stɪmjʊlaɪ/**)** A **stimulus** is something that encourages activity in people or things. ❑ *Interest rates could fall soon and be a stimulus to the US economy.* N-VAR

**sting** /stɪŋ/ **(stings, stinging, stung)** [1] If a plant, animal, or insect **stings** you, a sharp part of it, usually covered with poison, is pushed into your skin so that you feel a sharp pain. ❑ *The nettles stung their legs... This type of bee rarely stings.* VERB V n V [2] The **sting** of an insect or animal is the part that stings you. ❑ *Remove the bee sting with tweezers.* N-COUNT [3] If you feel a **sting**, you feel a sharp pain in your skin or other part of your body. ❑ *This won't hurt – you will just feel a little sting.* N-COUNT: usu sing [4] If a part of your body **stings**, or if a substance **stings** it, you feel a sharp pain there. ❑ *His cheeks were stinging from the icy wind... Sprays can sting sensitive skin.* VERB V V n [5] If someone's remarks **sting** you, they make you feel hurt and annoyed. ❑ *He's a sensitive lad and some of the criticism has stung him.* VERB: no cont = hurt V n

**sting|ray** /stɪŋreɪ/ **(stingrays)** A **stingray** is a type of large flat fish with a long tail which it can use as a weapon. N-COUNT

**stin|gy** /stɪndʒi/ **(stingier, stingiest)** If you describe someone as **stingy**, you are criticizing them for being unwilling to spend money. [INFORMAL] ❑ *Winston was not a stingy man.* ADJ [disapproval] = mean ≠ generous

**stink** /stɪŋk/ **(stinks, stinking, stank, stunk)** [1] To **stink** means to smell extremely unpleasant. ❑ *Get away from me – your breath stinks... The place stinks of fried onions... The pond stank like a sewer.* VERB V V *of* n V *like* n ♦ **Stink** is also a noun. ❑ *He was aware of the stink of stale beer on his breath.* N-SING ♦ **stink|ing** *They were locked up in a stinking cell.* ADJ [2] If you say that something **stinks**, you mean that you disapprove of it because it involves ideas, feelings, or practices that you do not like. [INFORMAL] ❑ *I think their methods stink... The whole thing stinks of political corruption.* VERB [disapproval] V V *of* n [3] If someone makes **a stink** about something they are angry about, they show their anger in order to make people take notice. [INFORMAL] ❑ *The tabloid press kicked up a stink about his seven-day visit.* N-SING: *a* N = fuss

**stink|er** /stɪŋkəʳ/ **(stinkers)** If you describe someone or something as a **stinker**, you mean that you think they are very unpleasant or bad. [INFORMAL] ❑ *I think he's an absolute stinker to do that to her.* N-COUNT [disapproval]

**stink|ing** /stɪŋkɪŋ/ [1] You use **stinking** to describe something that is unpleasant or bad. [INFORMAL] ❑ *I had a stinking cold.* ADJ: ADJ n [2] ➔ See also **stink**.

**stinky** /stɪŋki/ **(stinkier, stinkiest)** If something is **stinky**, it smells extremely unpleasant. ❑ *...sweaty, stinky socks.* ADJ: usu ADJ n

**stint** /stɪnt/ **(stints)** A **stint** is a period of time which you spend doing a particular job or activity or working in a particular place. ❑ *He is returning to this country after a five-year stint in Hong Kong.* N-COUNT: with supp, oft adj N, N prep

**sti|pend** /staɪpend/ **(stipends)** [1] A **stipend** is a sum of money that is paid regularly, especially to a magistrate or a member of the clergy, as a N-COUNT

salary or for their living expenses. [mainly BRIT]
[2] A **stipend** is a sum of money that is paid to a student for their living expenses. [mainly AM] N-COUNT

**sti|pen|di|ary** /staɪpe̲ndiəri, AM -dieri/ ADJ: ADJ n A **stipendiary** magistrate or member of the clergy receives a stipend.

**stip|pled** /stɪ̲pəld/ ADJ A surface that is **stippled** is covered with tiny spots. ❑ *The room remains simple with bare, stippled green walls.*

**stipu|late** /stɪ̲pjʊleɪt/ **(stipulates, stipulating, stipulated)** VERB = specify If you **stipulate** a condition or **stipulate that** something must be done, you say clearly that it must be done. ❑ *She could have stipulated that she would pay when she collected the computer...* V that/wh *International rules stipulate the number of foreign entrants.* V n ♦ **stipu|la|tion** /stɪpjʊle̲ɪʃən/ N-COUNT = condition **(stipulations)** *Clifford's only stipulation is that his clients obey his advice.*

**stir** /stɜ̲ːr/ **(stirs, stirring, stirred)** ◆◇◇ [1] VERB If you **stir** a liquid or other substance, you move it around or mix it in a container using something such as a spoon. ❑ *Stir the soup for a few seconds...* V n *There was Mrs Bellingham, stirring sugar into her tea...* V n *into* n *You don't add the peanut butter until after you've stirred in the honey.* V n with *in* [2] VERB = move If you **stir**, you move slightly, for example because you are uncomfortable or beginning to wake up. [WRITTEN] ❑ *Eileen shook him, and he started to stir...* V *The two women lay on their backs, not stirring.* V [3] VERB: usu with brd-neg, V *from* n If you do not **stir from** a place, you do not move from it. [WRITTEN] ❑ *She had not stirred from the house that evening.* [4] VERB = move If something **stirs** or if the wind **stirs** it, it moves gently in the wind. [WRITTEN] ❑ *Palm trees stir in the soft Pacific breeze...* V *Not a breath of fresh air stirred the long white curtains.* V n [5] VERB If a particular memory, feeling, or mood **stirs** or **is stirred in** you, you begin to think about it or feel it. [WRITTEN] ❑ *Then a memory stirs in you and you start feeling anxious...* V *in* n *Amy remembered the anger he had stirred in her...* V n *in* n *Deep inside the awareness was stirring that something was about to happen.* V [6] N-SING = commotion If an event causes a **stir**, it causes great excitement, shock, or anger among people. ❑ *His film has caused a stir in America.*
[7] ➔ See also **stirring**.

♦ **stir up** [1] PHRASAL VERB If something **stirs up** dust or **stirs up** mud in water, it causes it to rise up and move around. ❑ *They saw first a cloud of dust and then the car that was stirring it up.* V n P [2] PHRASAL VERB disapproval If you **stir up** a particular mood or situation, usually a bad one, you cause it. ❑ *As usual, Harriet is trying to stir up trouble...* V P n (not pron) *I thought at first that Jay had been stirring things up.* V n P

**sti̲r-fry** **(stir-fries, stir-frying, stir-fried)** [1] VERB If you **stir-fry** vegetables, meat, or fish, you cook small pieces of them quickly by stirring them in a small quantity of very hot oil. This method is often used in Chinese cookery. ❑ *Stir-fry the vegetables until crisp.* V n ...*stir-fried vegetables.* V-ed [2] N-COUNT A **stir-fry** is a Chinese dish consisting of small pieces of vegetables, meat, or fish which have been stir-fried. ❑ *Serve the stir-fry with 'instant' noodles.* [3] ADJ: ADJ n **Stir-fry** vegetables, meat, or fish or **stir-fry** dishes are cooked by the stir-fry method.

**stir|rer** /stɜ̲ːrər/ **(stirrers)** N-COUNT disapproval If you refer to someone as a **stirrer**, you disapprove of them because they often try to cause trouble. [BRIT, INFORMAL]

**stir|ring** /stɜ̲ːrɪŋ/ **(stirrings)** [1] ADJ: usu ADJ n = rousing A **stirring** event, performance, or account of something makes people very excited or enthusiastic. ❑ *The Prime Minister made a stirring speech...* *Stowe gives a stirring performance as a strong spirited female.* [2] N-COUNT: usu N *of* n A **stirring of** a feeling or thought is the beginning of one. ❑ *I feel a stirring of curiosity.*

**stir|rup** /stɪ̲rəp, AM stɜ̲ːr-/ **(stirrups)** N-COUNT **Stirrups** are the two metal loops which are attached to a horse's saddle by long pieces of leather. You place your feet in the stirrups when riding a horse.

**stitch** /stɪ̲tʃ/ **(stitches, stitching, stitched)** [1] VERB = sew If you **stitch** cloth, you use a needle and thread to join two pieces together or to make a decoration. ❑ *Fold the fabric and stitch the two layers together...* V n adv/prep *We stitched incessantly.* V ...*those patient ladies who stitched the magnificent medieval tapestries.* V n [2] N-COUNT **Stitches** are the short pieces of thread that have been sewn in a piece of cloth. ❑ ...*a row of straight stitches.* [3] N-COUNT In knitting and crochet, a **stitch** is a loop made by one turn of wool around a knitting needle or crochet hook. ❑ *Her mother counted the stitches on her knitting needles.* [4] N-UNCOUNT: usu n N If you sew or knit something in a particular **stitch**, you sew or knit in a way that produces a particular pattern. ❑ *The design can be worked in cross stitch.* [5] VERB When doctors **stitch** a wound, they use a special needle and thread to sew the skin together. ❑ *Jill washed and stitched the wound.* V n ♦ **Stitch up** PHRASAL VERB means the same as **stitch**. ❑ *Dr Armonson stitched up her wrist wounds...* V P n (not pron) *They've taken him off to hospital to stitch him up.* V n P [6] N-COUNT A **stitch** is a piece of thread that has been used to sew the skin of a wound together. ❑ *He had six stitches in a head wound.* [7] N-SING A **stitch** is a sharp pain in your side, usually caused by running or laughing a lot. [8] PHRASE: PHR after v, v-link PHR If you are **in stitches**, you cannot stop laughing. [INFORMAL] ❑ *Here's a book that will have you in stitches.*

♦ **stitch up** [1] PHRASAL VERB = frame, set up To **stitch** someone **up** means to trick them so that they are put in a difficult or unpleasant situation, especially one where they are blamed for something they have not done. [BRIT, INFORMAL] ❑ *He claimed that a police officer had threatened to stitch him up and send him to prison.* V n P Also V P n (not pron) [2] PHRASAL VERB = secure To **stitch up** an agreement, especially a complicated agreement between several people, means to arrange it. [mainly BRIT, INFORMAL] ❑ *Shiraz has stitched up major deals all over the world to boost sales.* V P n [3] ➔ see **stitch 5**.

**stitch|ing** /stɪ̲tʃɪŋ/ N-UNCOUNT **Stitching** is a row of stitches that have been sewn in a piece of cloth. ❑ *The stitching had begun to fray at the edges.*

**sti̲tch-up** **(stitch-ups)** also **stitch up.** N-COUNT: usu sing If you describe a situation as a **stitch-up**, you mean that it has been arranged in a way that makes it unfair. [BRIT, INFORMAL] ❑ *My view is that this is a stitch up.*

**stoat** /sto̲ʊt/ **(stoats)** N-COUNT A **stoat** is a small, thin, wild animal that has brown fur. Some stoats that live in northern Europe have fur that turns white in winter.

**stock** /stɒ̲k/ **(stocks, stocking, stocked)** ◆◆◇ [1] N-COUNT: usu pl **Stocks** are shares in the ownership of a company, or investments on which a fixed amount of interest will be paid. [BUSINESS] ❑ ...*the buying and selling of stocks and shares.* [2] N-UNCOUNT: usu poss N A company's **stock** is the amount of money which the company has through selling shares. [BUSINESS] ❑ *Two years later, when Compaq went public, their stock was valued at $38 million.* [3] VERB: no cont If a shop **stocks** particular goods, it keeps a supply of them to sell. ❑ *The shop stocks everything from cigarettes to recycled loo paper.* V n [4] N-UNCOUNT A shop's **stock** is the total amount of goods which it has available to sell. ❑ *We took the decision to withdraw a quantity of stock from sale.* [5] VERB If you **stock** something such as a cupboard, shelf, or room, you fill it with food or other things. ❑ *I worked stocking shelves in a grocery store...* V n *Some families stocked their cellars with food and water...* V n *with* n *The kitchen cupboard was stocked with tins of soup.* V-ed ♦ **Stock up** PHRASAL VERB means the same as **stock**. ❑ *I had to stock the boat up with food...* V n P *with* n *Start planning for Christmas now by stocking up the freezer with some festive dishes.* V P n (not pron) *with* n [6] N-COUNT: with supp, usu N *of* n If you have a **stock of** things, you have a supply of them stored in a place ready to be used. ❑ *Stocks of ammunition were running low.* [7] N-SING: with supp The **stock** of something is the total amount of it that is available in a particular area. [mainly BRIT] ❑ ...*the stock of accommodation available to be rented.* [8] N-UNCOUNT: usu supp N If you are from a particular **stock**, you are descended from a particular group of people. [FORMAL] ❑ *We are both from working class stock.* [9] N-PLURAL = livestock **Stock** are cattle, sheep, pigs, or other animals which are kept by a farmer, usually ones which have been specially bred. ❑ *I am carefully selecting the breeding stock.* [10] ADJ: ADJ n A **stock** answer, expression, or way of doing something is one that is very commonly used, especially because people cannot be bothered to think of something new. ❑ *My boss had a stock response – 'If it ain't broke, don't fix it!'.* = standard

11 **Stock** is a liquid, usually made by boiling meat, bones, or vegetables in water, that is used to give flavour to soups and sauces. N-MASS

12 → See also **stocking, laughing stock, rolling stock**.

**PHRASES** 13 If goods are **in stock**, a shop has them available to sell. If they are **out of stock**, it does not. ❑ *Check that your size is in stock... Lemon and lime juice were both temporarily out of stock.* PHRASE: usu v-link PHR

14 If you **take stock**, you pause to think about all the aspects of a situation or event before deciding what to do next. ❑ *It was time to take stock of the situation.* PHRASE: V inflects, usu PHR *of* n

15 **lock, stock, and barrel** → see **barrel**.

♦ **stock up** 1 → see **stock 5**. 2 If you **stock up on** something, you buy a lot of it, in case you cannot get it later. ❑ *The authorities have urged people to stock up on fuel.* PHRASAL VERB V P *on/with* n

**stock|ade** /stɒkeɪd/ **(stockades)** A **stockade** is a wall of large wooden posts built around an area to keep out enemies or wild animals. ❑ *...the inner stockade.* N-COUNT

**stock|broker** /stɒkbroʊkəʳ/ **(stockbrokers)** A **stockbroker** is a person whose job is to buy and sell stocks and shares for people who want to invest money. [BUSINESS] N-COUNT

**stock|broker belt** **(stockbroker belts)** **The stockbroker belt** is an area outside a city, especially London, where rich people who travel to work in the city live. [BRIT] ❑ *He grew up in the comfort of the Surrey stockbroker belt.* N-COUNT: usu *the* N

**stock|broking** /stɒkbroʊkɪŋ/ **Stockbroking** is the professional activity of buying and selling stocks and shares for clients. [BUSINESS] ❑ *His stockbroking firm was hit by the 1987 crash.* N-UNCOUNT: usu N n

**stock car** **(stock cars)** A **stock car** is an old car which has had changes made to it so that it is suitable for races in which the cars often crash into each other. ❑ *He acted as grand marshal of a stock car race.* N-COUNT

**stock con|trol** **Stock control** is the activity of making sure that a company always has exactly the right amount of goods available to sell. [BUSINESS] N-UNCOUNT

**stock cube** **(stock cubes)** A **stock cube** is a solid cube made from dried meat or vegetable juices and other flavourings. Stock cubes are used to add flavour to dishes such as stews and soups. N-COUNT

**stock ex|change** **(stock exchanges)** A **stock exchange** is a place where people buy and sell stocks and shares. **The stock exchange** is also the trading activity that goes on there and the trading organization itself. [BUSINESS] ❑ *The shortage of good stock has kept some investors away from the stock exchange. ...the New York Stock Exchange.* ◆◇◇ N-COUNT: usu *the* N in sing = stock market

**stock|holder** /stɒkhoʊldəʳ/ **(stockholders)** A **stockholder** is a person who owns shares in a company. [AM, BUSINESS] N-COUNT

☑ in BRIT, use **shareholder**

**stock|ing** /stɒkɪŋ/ **(stockings)** 1 **Stockings** are items of women's clothing which fit closely over their feet and legs. Stockings are usually made of nylon or silk and are held in place by suspenders. ❑ *...a pair of nylon stockings.* N-COUNT 2 A **stocking** is the same as a **Christmas stocking**. N-COUNT 3 → See also **stock, body stocking**.

**stock|inged** /stɒkɪŋd/ If someone is in their **stockinged** feet, they are wearing socks, tights, or stockings, but no shoes. [LITERARY] ❑ *He tip-toed to the door in his stockinged feet.* ADJ: ADJ n

**stock|ing fill|er** **(stocking fillers)** also **stocking-filler.** A **stocking filler** is a small present that is suitable for putting in a Christmas stocking. [mainly BRIT] N-COUNT

☑ in AM, usually use **stocking stuffer**

**stock|ing stuff|er** **(stocking stuffers)** A **stocking stuffer** is the same as a **stocking filler**. [mainly AM] N-COUNT

**stock-in-trade** also **stock in trade.** If you say that something is someone's **stock-in-trade**, you mean that it is a usual part of their behaviour or work. ❑ *Patriotism is every politician's stock-in-trade.* N-SING: with poss = staple

**stock|ist** /stɒkɪst/ **(stockists)** A **stockist** of a particular product is someone who sells this product in their shop. [BRIT] ❑ *The name of your nearest stockist is available from the company.* N-COUNT = retailer

**stock mar|ket** **(stock markets)** **The stock market** consists of the general activity of buying stocks and shares, and the people and institutions that organize it. [BUSINESS] ❑ *The company's shares promptly fell by 300 lire on the stock market.* ◆◇◇ N-COUNT: *the* N

**stock op|tion** **(stock options)** A **stock option** is an opportunity for the employees of a company to buy shares at a special price. [AM, BUSINESS] ❑ *He made a huge profit from the sale of shares purchased under the company's stock option program.* N-COUNT

☑ in BRIT use **share option**

**stock|pile** /stɒkpaɪl/ **(stockpiles, stockpiling, stockpiled)** 1 If people **stockpile** things such as food or weapons, they store large quantities of them for future use. ❑ *People are stockpiling food for the coming winter.* VERB = hoard V n 2 A **stockpile of** things is a large quantity of them that have been stored for future use. ❑ *The two leaders also approved treaties to cut stockpiles of chemical weapons.* N-COUNT: oft N *of* n = stock

**stock|room** /stɒkruːm/ **(stockrooms)** also **stock-room.** A **stockroom** is a room, especially in a shop or a factory, where a stock of goods is kept. N-COUNT

**stock-still** If someone stands or sits **stock-still**, they do not move at all. ❑ *The lieutenant stopped and stood stock-still.* ADJ: ADJ after v

**stock|taking** /stɒkteɪkɪŋ/ **Stocktaking** is the activity of counting and checking all the goods that a shop or business has. [BUSINESS] N-UNCOUNT

**stocky** /stɒki/ **(stockier, stockiest)** A **stocky** person has a body that is broad, solid, and often short. ADJ: usu ADJ n

**stodgy** /stɒdʒi/ **(stodgier, stodgiest)** **Stodgy** food is very solid and heavy. It makes you feel very full, and is difficult to digest. ❑ *He was disgusted with the stodgy pizzas on sale in London.* ADJ: usu ADJ n

**sto|gie** /stoʊgi/ **(stogies)** A **stogie** is a long thin cigar. [AM] N-COUNT

**sto|ic** /stoʊɪk/ **(stoics)** 1 **Stoic** means the same as **stoical**. [FORMAL] ❑ *The kids of Kobe try to be as stoic as their parents in this tragic situation.* ADJ [approval] 2 If you say that someone is a **stoic**, you approve of them because they do not complain or show they are upset in bad situations. [FORMAL] N-COUNT [approval]

**stoi|cal** /stoʊɪkᵊl/ If you say that someone behaves in a **stoical** way, you approve of them because they do not complain or show they are upset in bad situations. [FORMAL] ❑ *She never ceased to admire the stoical courage of those in Northern Ireland.* ADJ [approval] ♦ **stoi|cal|ly** *She put up with it all stoically for years.* ADV: usu ADV with v

**stoi|cism** /stoʊɪsɪzəm/ **Stoicism** is stoical behaviour. [FORMAL] ❑ *They bore their plight with stoicism and fortitude.* N-UNCOUNT [approval]

**stoke** /stoʊk/ **(stokes, stoking, stoked)** 1 If you **stoke** a fire, you add coal or wood to it to keep it burning. ❑ *She was stoking the stove with sticks of maple.* VERB V n ♦ **Stoke up** means the same as **stoke**. ❑ *He stoked up the fire in the hearth.* PHRASAL VERB V P n 2 If you **stoke** something such as a feeling, you cause it to be felt more strongly. ❑ *These demands are helping to stoke fears of civil war.* VERB V n ♦ **Stoke up** means the same as **stoke**. ❑ *He has sent his proposals in the hope of stoking up interest for the idea.* PHRASAL VERB V P n (not pron)

**stok|er** /stoʊkəʳ/ **(stokers)** In former times a **stoker** was a person whose job was to stoke fires, especially on a ship or a steam train. N-COUNT

**stole** /stoʊl/ **(stoles) Stole** is the past tense of **steal**.

**sto|len** /stoʊlᵊn/ **Stolen** is the past participle of **steal**.

**stol|id** /stɒlɪd/ If you describe someone as **stolid**, you mean that they do not show much emotion or are not very exciting or interesting. ❑ *He glanced furtively at the stolid faces of the two detectives.* ADJ: usu ADJ n

**stom|ach** /stʌmək/ **(stomachs, stomaching, stomached)** ◆◇◇ 1 Your **stomach** is the organ inside your body where food is digested before it moves into the intestines. ❑ *He had an upset stomach... My stomach is completely full.* N-COUNT 2 You can refer to the front part of your body below your waist as your **stomach**. ❑ *The children lay down on their stomachs. ...stomach muscles.* N-COUNT: oft poss N 3 If the front part of your body below your waist feels uncomfortable because you are feeling worried or frightened, you can refer to it as your **stomach**. ❑ *His stomach was in knots.* N-COUNT: oft poss N 4 If you say that someone has a strong **stomach**, you mean that they are not disgusted by things that disgust most other people. ❑ *Surgery often demands actual physical strength, as well as the possession of a strong stomach.* N-COUNT 5 If you cannot **stomach** something, you cannot accept it because you dislike it or disapprove of it. ❑ *I could never stomach the cruelty involved in the wounding of animals.* VERB: with brd-neg V n/-ing

**PHRASES** 6 If you do something **on an empty stomach**, you do it without having eaten. ❑ *Avoid drinking on an empty stomach.* PHRASE: PHR after v 7 If you say that something **turns** your **stomach** or makes your **stomach turn**, you mean that it is so unpleasant or offensive that it makes you feel sick. ❑ *The true facts will turn your stomach... I saw the shots of what happened on television and my stomach just turned over.* PHRASE: V inflects 8 **butterflies in** your **stomach** → see **butterfly**.

**stom|ach ache (stomach aches)** also **stomachache.** If you have a **stomach-ache**, you have a pain in your stomach. N-VAR

**stomach-churning** If you describe something as **stomach-churning**, you mean that it is so unpleasant that it makes you feel physically sick. ❑ *The stench from rotting food is stomach-churning.* ADJ

**stomp** /stɒmp/ **(stomps, stomping, stomped)** If you **stomp** somewhere, you walk there with very heavy steps, often because you are angry. ❑ *He stomped out of the room.* VERB V prep/adv

**stone** /stoʊn/ **(stones, stoning, stoned)** ◆◆◇

✓ The plural is usually **stone** in meaning 10.

1 **Stone** is a hard solid substance found in the ground and often used for building houses. ❑ *He could not tell whether the floor was wood or stone... People often don't appreciate that marble is a natural stone. ...stone walls.* N-MASS 2 A **stone** is a small piece of rock that is found on the ground. ❑ *He removed a stone from his shoe... The crowd began throwing stones.* N-COUNT 3 A **stone** is a large piece of stone put somewhere in memory of a person or event, or as a religious symbol. ❑ *The monument consists of a circle of gigantic stones.* N-COUNT 4 **Stone** is used in expressions such as **set in stone** and **tablets of stone** to suggest that an idea or rule is firm and fixed, and cannot be changed. ❑ *Scientific opinions are not carved on tablets of stone; they change over the years.* N-UNCOUNT: oft with brd-neg 5 You can refer to a jewel as a **stone**. ❑ *...a diamond ring with three stones.* N-COUNT 6 A **stone** is a small hard ball of minerals and other substances which sometimes forms in a person's kidneys or gall bladder. ❑ *He had kidney stones.* N-COUNT: usu n N 7 The **stone** in a plum, cherry, or other fruit is the large hard seed in the middle of it. [mainly BRIT] → See picture on page 1711. N-COUNT

✓ in AM, usually use **pit**

8 If you **stone** a fruit, you remove its stone. [mainly BRIT] ❑ *Then stone the fruit and process the plums to a puree.* VERB V n

✓ in AM, usually use **pit**

9 If people **stone** someone or something, they throw stones at them. ❑ *A post office was set on fire and vehicles were stoned by looters.* VERB V n 10 A **stone** is a measurement of weight, especially the weight of a person, equal to 14 pounds or 6.35 kilograms. [BRIT] ❑ *I weighed around 16 stone.* N-COUNT: usu num N 11 → See also **stoned, foundation stone, paving stone, precious stone, stepping stone.**

**PHRASES** 12 If you say that one place is **a stone's throw from** another, you mean that the places are close to each other. ❑ *...a two-bedroom apartment just a stone's throw from the beach... Just a stone's throw away is the City Art Gallery.* PHRASE: PHR prep/adv 13 If you say that you will **leave no stone unturned**, you are emphasizing that you will try every way you can think of in order to achieve what you want. ❑ *He said he would leave no stone unturned in the search for peace.* PHRASE: V inflects [emphasis] 14 **kill two birds with one stone** → see **bird**.

**Stone Age** The **Stone Age** is a very early period of human history, when people used tools and weapons made of stone, not metal. N-PROPER: *the* N

**stone-cold** 1 If something that should be warm is **stone-cold**, it is very cold. ❑ *Hillsden took a sip of tea, but it was stone cold.* ADJ 2 If someone is **stone-cold sober**, they are not drunk at all. [INFORMAL] PHRASE: v-link PHR

**stoned** /stoʊnd/ If someone is **stoned**, their mind is greatly affected by a drug such as cannabis. [INFORMAL] ADJ: usu v-link ADJ

**stone-dead** If you **kill** something such as an idea or emotion **stone-dead**, you completely destroy it. ❑ *The prospect of having to pay a graduate tax until retirement would kill the students' enthusiasm stone dead.* PHRASE: V inflects [emphasis]

**stone deaf** also **stone-deaf.** Someone who is **stone deaf** cannot hear at all. ADJ: usu v-link ADJ

**stone-ground** also **stoneground. Stone-ground** flour or bread is made from grain that has been crushed between two large, heavy pieces of stone. ADJ: usu ADJ n

**stone|mason** /stoʊnmeɪsᵊn/ **(stonemasons)** A **stonemason** is a person who is skilled at cutting and preparing stone so that it can be used for walls and buildings. N-COUNT

**stone|wall** /stoʊnwɔːl, AM -wɔːl/ **(stonewalls, stonewalling, stonewalled)** If you say that someone **stonewalls**, you disapprove of them because they delay giving a clear answer or making a clear decision, often because there is something that they want to hide or avoid doing. ❑ *The administration is just stonewalling in an attempt to hide their political embarrassment.* VERB [disapproval] V ♦ **stone|wall|ing** *After 18 days of stonewalling, he at last came out and faced the issue.* N-UNCOUNT

**stone|ware** /stoʊnweəʳ/ **Stoneware** is hard clay pottery which is baked at a high temperature. ❑ *...hand-painted blue-and-white stoneware.* N-UNCOUNT: oft N n

**stone-washed** also **stonewashed. Stone-washed** jeans are jeans which have been specially washed with small pieces of stone so that when you buy them they are fairly pale and soft. ADJ

**stone|work** /stoʊnwɜːʳk/ **Stonework** consists of objects or parts of a building that are made of stone. ❑ *...the crumbling stonework of the derelict church.* N-UNCOUNT = *masonry*

**stony** /stoʊni/ **(stonier, stoniest)** 1 **Stony** ground is rough and contains a lot of stones. ❑ *The steep, stony ground is well drained. ...a stony track.* ADJ 2 A **stony** expression or attitude does not show any sympathy or friendliness. ❑ *He drove us home in stony silence.* ADJ

**stood** /stʊd/ **Stood** is the past tense and past participle of **stand**.

**stooge** /stuːdʒ/ **(stooges)** If you refer to someone as a **stooge**, you are criticizing them because they are used by someone else to do unpleasant or dishonest tasks. ❑ *He has vehemently rejected claims that he is a government stooge.* N-COUNT: usu with supp [disapproval]

**stool** /stuːl/ **(stools)** [1] A **stool** is a seat with legs but no support for your arms or back. ❑ *O'Brien sat on a bar stool and leaned his elbows on the counter.* N-COUNT [2] If someone **has fallen between two stools**, they are unable to decide which of two courses of action to take and as a result they have not done either of them successfully. PHRASE: V inflects
[3] **Stools** are the pieces of solid waste matter that are passed out of a person's body through their bowels. [mainly MEDICAL] N-COUNT: usu pl = faeces

**stoop** /stuːp/ **(stoops, stooping, stooped)** [1] If you **stoop**, you stand or walk with your shoulders bent forwards. ❑ *She was taller than he was and stooped slightly.* VERB V ♦ **Stoop** is also a noun. ❑ *He was a tall, thin fellow with a slight stoop.* N-SING ♦ **stoop|ing** *...a slender slightly stooping American.* ADJ: usu ADJ n [2] If you **stoop**, you bend your body forwards and downwards. ❑ *He stooped to pick up the carrier bag of groceries... Two men in shirt sleeves stooped over the car... Stooping down, he picked up a big stone and hurled it.* VERB V V over n V down/over [3] If you say that a person **stoops to** doing something, you are criticizing them because they do something wrong or immoral that they would not normally do. ❑ *He had not, until recently, stooped to personal abuse... How could anyone stoop so low?* VERB [disapproval] V to n/-ing V adj [4] A **stoop** is a small platform at the door of a building, with steps leading up to it. [AM] ❑ *They stood together on the stoop and rang the bell.* N-COUNT

**stop** /stɒp/ **(stops, stopping, stopped)** ◆◆◆ [1] If you have been doing something and then you **stop** doing it, you no longer do it. ❑ *He can't stop thinking about it... I've been told to lose weight and stop smoking... I stopped working last year to have a baby... Does either of the parties want to stop the fighting?... She stopped in mid-sentence.* VERB V -ing V -ing V -ing V n V [2] If you **stop** something happening, you prevent it from happening or prevent it from continuing. ❑ *He proposed a new diplomatic initiative to try to stop the war... If the fire isn't stopped, it could spread to 25,000 acres... I think she really would have liked to stop us seeing each other... Motherhood won't stop me from pursuing my acting career.* VERB V n V n V n -ing V n from -ing [3] If an activity or process **stops**, it is no longer happening. ❑ *The rain had stopped and a star or two was visible over the mountains... The system overheated and filming had to stop.* VERB V V [4] If something such as machine **stops** or **is stopped**, it is no longer moving or working. ❑ *The clock had stopped at 2.12 a.m... Arnold stopped the engine and got out of the car.* VERB V V n [5] When a moving person or vehicle **stops** or **is stopped**, they no longer move and they remain in the same place. ❑ *The car failed to stop at an army checkpoint... He stopped and let her catch up with him... The event literally stopped the traffic.* VERB = halt V V V n [6] If something that is moving comes **to a stop** or is brought **to a stop**, it slows down and no longer moves. ❑ *People often wrongly open doors before the train has come to a stop... He slowed the car almost to a stop.* N-SING: to a N = halt [7] If someone does not **stop to** think or **to** explain, they continue with what they are doing without taking any time to think about or explain it. ❑ *She doesn't stop to think about what she's saying... There is something rather strange about all this if one stops to consider it... People who lead busy lives have no time to stop and reflect.* VERB = pause V to-inf V to-inf V [8] If you say that a quality or state **stops** somewhere, you mean that it exists or is true up to that point, but no further. ❑ *The cafe owner has put up the required 'no smoking' signs, but thinks his responsibility stops there.* VERB = end V adv [9] A **stop** is a place where buses or trains regularly stop so that people can get on and off. ❑ *They waited at a bus stop.* N-COUNT: oft supp N [10] If you **stop** somewhere on a journey, you stay there for a short while. ❑ *He insisted we stop at a small restaurant just outside of Atlanta.* VERB V prep/adv [11] A **stop** is a time or place at which you stop during a journey. ❑ *The last stop in Mr Cook's lengthy tour was Paris.* N-COUNT: usu with supp [12] In music, organ **stops** are the knobs at the side of the organ, which you pull or push in order to control the type of sound that comes out of the pipes. N-COUNT: usu pl
**PHRASES** [13] If you say that someone will **stop at nothing to** get something, you are emphasizing that they are willing to do things that are extreme, wrong, or dangerous in order to get it. ❑ *Their motive is money, and they will stop at nothing to get it.* PHRASE: V inflects [emphasis] [14] If you **pull out all the stops**, you do everything you can to make something happen or succeed. ❑ *New Zealand police vowed yesterday to pull out all the stops to find the killer.* PHRASE: V inflects [15] If you **put a stop to** something that you do not like or approve of, you prevent it from happening or continuing. ❑ *His daughter should have stood up and put a stop to all these rumours.* PHRASE: V inflects [16] If you say that someone does not **know when to stop**, you mean that they do not control their own behaviour very well and so they often annoy or upset other people. ❑ *Like many politicians before him, Mr Bentley did not know when to stop.* PHRASE: *know* inflects [17] to **stop dead** → see **dead**. to **stop short of** → see **short**. to **stop** someone **in** their **tracks** → see **track**.
♦ **stop by** If you **stop by** somewhere, you make a short visit to a person or place. [INFORMAL] ❑ *Perhaps I'll stop by the hospital... I'll stop by to see Leigh before going home.* PHRASAL VERB V P n V P
♦ **stop off** If you **stop off** somewhere, you stop for a short time in the middle of a journey. ❑ *The president stopped off in Poland on his way to Munich for the economic summit.* PHRASAL VERB V P

**stop|cock** /stɒpkɒk/ **(stopcocks)** A **stopcock** is a tap on a pipe, which you turn in order to allow something to pass through the pipe or to stop it from passing through. N-COUNT

**stop|gap** /stɒpgæp/ **(stopgaps)** A **stopgap** is something that serves a purpose for a short time, but is replaced as soon as possible. ❑ *Gone are the days when work was just a stopgap between leaving school and getting married.* N-COUNT: oft N n

**stop-go**

✓ in AM, also use **stop-and-go**

**Stop-go** is used to describe processes in which there are periods of inactivity between periods of activity. ❑ *...stop-go economic cycles.* ADJ: usu ADJ n

**stop|light** /stɒplaɪt/ **(stoplights)** also **stop light.** [1] A **stoplight** is a set of coloured lights which controls the flow of traffic on a road. [AM] N-COUNT

✓ in BRIT, use **traffic light**

[2] The **stoplights** on a car or other vehicle are the two red lights at the back. [AM] N-COUNT

✓ in BRIT, use **tail-lights**

**stop|over** /stɒpoʊvəʳ/ **(stopovers)** A **stopover** is a short stay in a place in between parts of a journey. ❑ *The Sunday flights will make a stopover in Paris.* N-COUNT

**stop|page** /stɒpɪdʒ/ **(stoppages)** [1] When there is a **stoppage**, people stop working because of a disagreement with their employers. [BUSINESS] ❑ *Mineworkers in the Ukraine have voted for a one-day stoppage next month.* N-COUNT: oft supp N = strike [2] In football and some other sports, when there is a **stoppage**, the game stops for a short time, for example because a player is injured. The referee may add some extra time at the end of the game because of this. [mainly BRIT] N-COUNT

✓ in AM, use **time out**

**stop|per** /stɒpəʳ/ **(stoppers)** A **stopper** is a piece of glass, plastic, or cork that fits into the top of a bottle or jar to close it. ❑ *...a bottle of colourless liquid sealed with a cork stopper.* → See also **show-stopper**. N-COUNT

**stop press** **Stop press** is sometimes printed next to an article in a newspaper to indicate that this is very recent news and was added after the rest of the newspaper had been printed. [BRIT] ❑ *STOP PRESS – Crisis in Chechnya.*

**stop|watch** /stɒpwɒtʃ/ **(stopwatches)** also **stop-watch.** A **stopwatch** is a watch with buttons which you press at the beginning and end of an event, so that you can measure exactly how long it takes. N-COUNT

**stor|age** /stɔːrɪdʒ/ 1 If you refer to the **storage** of something, you mean that it is kept in a special place until it is needed. ❑ *...the storage of toxic waste... Some of the space will at first be used for storage... The collection has been in storage for decades.* N-UNCOUNT 2 **Storage** is the process of storing data in a computer. ❑ *His task is to ensure the fair use and storage of personal information held on computer.* N-UNCOUNT 3 → See also **cold storage**.

**store** /stɔːʳ/ **(stores, storing, stored)** ◆◆◇ 1 A **store** is a building or part of a building where things are sold. In British English, **store** is used mainly to refer to a large shop selling a variety of goods, but in American English a **store** can be any size of shop. ❑ *...grocery stores. ...a local record store.* N-COUNT 2 When you **store** things, you put them in a container or other place and leave them there until they are needed. ❑ *Store the cookies in an airtight tin... Some types of garden furniture must be stored inside in the winter.* VERB = keep; V n prep/adv; V n prep/adv ♦ **Store away** means the same as **store**. ❑ *He simply stored the tapes away... He's stored away nearly one ton of potatoes.* PHRASAL VERB; V n P; V P n 3 When you **store** information, you keep it in your memory, in a file, or in a computer. ❑ *Where in the brain do we store information about colours? ...chips for storing data in electronic equipment.* VERB; V n; V n 4 A **store of** things is a supply of them that you keep somewhere until you need them. ❑ *I handed over my secret store of chocolate biscuits.* N-COUNT: usu N *of* n 5 A **store** is a place where things are kept while they are not being used. ❑ *...a decision taken in 1982 to build a store for spent fuel from submarines. ...a grain store.* N-COUNT: usu with supp 6 If you have a **store of** knowledge, jokes, or stories, you have a large amount of them ready to be used. ❑ *He possessed a vast store of knowledge.* N-COUNT: usu N *of* n 7 → See also **chain store**, **cold store**, **department store**.

PHRASES 8 If something is **in store for** you, it is going to happen at some time in the future. ❑ *There were also surprises in store for me... Who knows what lies in store for the President?* PHRASE: PHR after v, v-link PHR, usu PHR *for* n 9 If you **set great store by** something, you think that it is extremely important or necessary. [FORMAL] ❑ *...a retail group which sets great store by traditional values.* PHRASE: V inflects, PHR n

♦ **store away** → see **store 2**.

♦ **store up** If you **store** something **up**, you keep it until you think that the time is right to use it. ❑ *Investors were storing up a lot of cash in anticipation of disaster.* PHRASAL VERB; V P n (not pron)

**store|card** /stɔːʳkɑːʳd/ **(storecards)** also **store card.** A **storecard** is a plastic card that you use to buy goods on credit from a particular store or group of stores. [mainly BRIT] N-COUNT

✓ in AM, usually use **charge card**

**store de|tec|tive (store detectives)** A **store detective** is someone who is employed by a shop to walk around the shop looking for people who are secretly stealing goods. N-COUNT

**store|front** /stɔːʳfrʌnt/ **(storefronts)** 1 A **storefront** is the outside part of a shop which faces the street, including the door and windows. [mainly AM] N-COUNT

✓ in BRIT, usually use **shop front**

2 A **storefront** is a small shop or office that opens onto the street and is part of a row of shops or offices. [AM] ❑ *...a tiny storefront office on the main street.* N-COUNT: oft N n

**store|house** /stɔːʳhaʊs/ **(storehouses)** A **storehouse** is a building in which things, usually food, are stored. N-COUNT

**store|keeper** /stɔːʳkiːpəʳ/ **(storekeepers)** A **storekeeper** is a shopkeeper. [mainly AM] N-COUNT

**store|room** /stɔːruːm/ **(storerooms)** A **storeroom** is a room in which you keep things until they are needed. ❑ *...a storeroom filled with massive old furniture covered with dust.* N-COUNT

**sto|rey** /stɔːri/ **(storeys)**

✓ in AM, use **story**

A **storey** of a building is one of its different levels, which is situated above or below other levels. ❑ *...the upper storeys of the Empire State Building.* N-COUNT: usu supp N = floor

**-storey** /-stɔːri/

✓ in AM, use **-story**

**-storey** is used after numbers to form adjectives that indicate that a building has a particular number of floors or levels. ❑ *...a modern three-storey building.* → See also **multi-storey**. COMB in ADJ

**-storeyed** /-stɔːrid/

✓ in AM, use **-storied**

**-storeyed** means the same as **-storey**. ❑ *The streets were lined with two-storeyed houses.* COMB in ADJ

**stork** /stɔːʳk/ **(storks)** A **stork** is a large bird with a long beak and long legs, which lives near water. N-COUNT

**storm** /stɔːʳm/ **(storms, storming, stormed)** ◆◇◇ 1 A **storm** is very bad weather, with heavy rain, strong winds, and often thunder and lightning. ❑ *...the violent storms which whipped America's East Coast.* N-COUNT 2 If something causes a **storm**, it causes an angry or excited reaction from a large number of people. ❑ *The photos caused a storm when they were first published. ...the storm of publicity that Richard's book had generated.* N-COUNT: oft N *of* n 3 A **storm of** applause or other noise is a sudden loud amount of it made by an audience or other group of people in reaction to something. ❑ *His speech was greeted with a storm of applause.* N-COUNT: usu sing, usu N *of* n 4 If you **storm into** or **out of** a place, you enter or leave it quickly and noisily, because you are angry. ❑ *He stormed into an office, demanding to know where the head of department was.* VERB; V adv/prep 5 If a place that is being defended **is stormed**, a group of people attack it, usually in order to get inside it. ❑ *Government buildings have been stormed and looted... The refugees decided to storm the embassy.* VERB; *be* V-ed; V n ♦ **storm|ing** *...the storming of the Bastille.* N-UNCOUNT: N *of* n 6 → See also **firestorm**.

PHRASES 7 If someone or something **takes** a place **by storm**, they are extremely successful. ❑ *Kenya's long distance runners have taken the athletics world by storm.* PHRASE: V inflects 8 If someone **weathers the storm**, they succeed in reaching the end of a very difficult period without much harm or damage. ❑ *He insists he will not resign and will weather the storm.* PHRASE: V and N inflect 9 **a storm in a teacup** → see **teacup**.

**storm cloud (storm clouds)** also **stormcloud.** 1 **Storm clouds** are the dark clouds which are seen before a storm. N-COUNT: usu pl 2 You can use **storm clouds** to refer to a sign that something very unpleasant is going to happen. [FORMAL] ❑ *Over the past three weeks, the storm clouds have gathered again over the government.* N-COUNT: usu pl

**storm troop|er (storm troopers)** also **stormtrooper. Storm troopers** were members of a private Nazi army who were well-known for being violent. N-COUNT

**stormy** /stɔːʳmi/ **(stormier, stormiest)** 1 If there is **stormy** weather, there are strong winds and heavy rain. ❑ *It had been a night of stormy weather, with torrential rain and high winds.* ADJ: usu ADJ n ≠ calm 2 **Stormy** seas have very large strong waves because there are strong winds. ❑ *They make the treacherous journey across stormy seas.* ADJ: usu ADJ n ≠ calm 3 If you describe a situation as **stormy**, you mean it involves a lot of angry argument or criticism. ❑ *The letter was read at a stormy meeting.* ADJ

**sto|ry** /stɔːri/ **(stories)** ◆◆◆ 1 A **story** is a description of imaginary people and events, which is written or told in order to entertain. ❑ *I shall tell* N-COUNT *you a story about four little rabbits. ...a popular love story with a happy ending.* [2] N-COUNT A **story** is a description of an event or something that happened to someone, especially a spoken description of it. ❑ *The parents all shared interesting stories about their children... Isak's story is typical of a child who has a specific learning disability.* [3] N-COUNT: usu N *of* n The **story of** something is a description of all the important things that have happened to it since it began. ❑ *...the story of the women's movement in Ireland.* [4] N-COUNT = *tale, yarn* If someone invents a **story**, they give a false explanation or account of something. ❑ *He invented some story about a cousin.* [5] N-COUNT A news **story** is a piece of news in a newspaper or in a news broadcast. ❑ *Those are some of the top stories in the news... They'll do anything for a story. ...front-page news stories.* [6] → see **storey, -storey**. [7] → See also **cock-and-bull story, short story, sob story, success story, tall story**.

**PHRASES** [8] PHRASE: V inflects In British English, you use **to cut a long story short** to indicate that you are going to state the final result of an event and not give any more details. In American English, you say **to make a long story short**. ❑ *To cut a long story short, I ended up as managing director.* [9] PHRASE: usu v-link PHR You use **a different story** to refer to a situation, usually a bad one, which exists in one set of circumstances when you have mentioned that it does not exist in another set of circumstances. ❑ *Where Marcella lives, the rents are fairly cheap, but a little further north it's a different story.* [10] PHRASE: v-link PHR If you say **it's the same old story** or **it's the old story**, you mean that something unpleasant or undesirable seems to happen again and again. ❑ *It's the same old story. They want one person to do three people's jobs.* [11] PHRASE: usu v-link PHR If you say that something is **only part of the story** or is **not the whole story**, you mean that the explanation or information given is not enough for a situation to be fully understood. ❑ *This may be true but it is only part of the story... Jane goes to great lengths to explain that this is not the whole story.* [12] PHRASE: *side* inflects If someone tells you their **side of the story**, they tell you why they behaved in a particular way and why they think they were right, when other people think that person behaved wrongly. ❑ *He had already made up his mind before even hearing her side of the story.*

**story|board** /stɔːribɔːʳd/ **(storyboards)** N-COUNT A **storyboard** is a set of pictures which show what will happen in something such as a film or advertisement that is being planned.

**story|book** /stɔːribʊk/ **(storybooks)** N-COUNT A **storybook** is a book of stories for children.

**story|line** /stɔːrilaɪn/ **(storylines)** N-COUNT = *plot* The **storyline** of a book, film, or play is its story and the way in which it develops. ❑ *The surprise twists in the storyline are the film's greatest strength.*

**story|teller** /stɔːritelәʳ/ **(storytellers)** also **story-teller**. N-COUNT A **storyteller** is someone who tells or writes stories. ❑ *He was the one who first set down the stories of the Celtic storytellers.*

**story|telling** /stɔːritelɪŋ/ also **story-telling**. N-UNCOUNT **Storytelling** is the activity of telling or writing stories. ❑ *The programme is 90 minutes of dynamic Indian folk dance, live music and storytelling.*

**stout** /staʊt/ **(stouter, stoutest)** [1] ADJ A **stout** person is rather fat. ❑ *He was a tall, stout man with gray hair.* [2] ADJ = *sturdy* **Stout** shoes, branches, or other objects are thick and strong. ❑ *I hope you've both got stout shoes. ...a stout oak door.* [3] ADJ approval = *robust* If you use **stout** to describe someone's actions, attitudes, or beliefs, you approve of them because they are strong and determined. ❑ *He produced a stout defence of the car business.* ♦ **stout|ly** ADV: ADV with v, ADV adj *She stoutly defended her husband during the trial. ...stoutly anti-imperialist nations.*

**stove** /stoʊv/ **(stoves)** N-COUNT A **stove** is a piece of equipment which provides heat, either for cooking or for heating a room. ❑ *She put the kettle on the gas stove.*

**stow** /stoʊ/ **(stows, stowing, stowed)** VERB If you **stow** something somewhere, you carefully put it there until it is needed. ❑ *I helped her stow her bags in the boot of the car.* V n prep/adv Also V n

♦ **stow away** PHRASAL VERB V P ❑ *He stowed away on a ferry and landed in North Shields.*

**stow|age** /stoʊɪdʒ/ N-UNCOUNT **Stowage** is the space that is available for stowing things on a ship or aeroplane. ❑ *Stowage is provided in lined lockers beneath the berths.*

**stow|away** /stoʊәweɪ/ **(stowaways)** N-COUNT A **stowaway** is a person who hides in a ship, aeroplane, or other vehicle in order to make a journey secretly or without paying. ❑ *The crew discovered the stowaway about two days into their voyage.*

**strad|dle** /strædәl/ **(straddles, straddling, straddled)** [1] VERB If you **straddle** something, you put or have one leg on either side of it. ❑ *He sat down, straddling the chair.* V n [2] VERB If something **straddles** a river, road, border, or other place, it stretches across it or exists on both sides of it. ❑ *A small wooden bridge straddled the dike. ...this town that straddles the US-Mexico border.* V n V n [3] VERB Someone or something that **straddles** different periods, groups, or fields of activity exists in, belongs to, or takes elements from them all. ❑ *He straddles two cultures, having been brought up in Britain and later converted to Islam.* V n

**strafe** /streɪf/ **(strafes, strafing, strafed)** VERB To **strafe** an enemy means to attack them with a lot of bombs or bullets from a low-flying aircraft. ❑ *It seemed that the plane was going to swoop down and strafe the town, so we dived for cover.* V n

**strag|gle** /strægәl/ **(straggles, straggling, straggled)** [1] VERB If people **straggle** somewhere, they move there slowly, in small groups with large, irregular gaps between them. ❑ *They came straggling up the cliff road.* V prep/adv [2] VERB If a small quantity of things **straggle** over an area, they cover it in an uneven or untidy way. ❑ *Her grey hair straggled in wisps about her face... They were beyond the last straggling suburbs now.* V prep V-ing

**strag|gler** /strægәlәʳ/ **(stragglers)** N-COUNT: usu pl The **stragglers** are the people in a group who are moving more slowly or making less progress than the others. ❑ *There were two stragglers twenty yards back.*

**strag|gly** /strægәli/ ADJ **Straggly** hair or a **straggly** plant is thin and grows or spreads out untidily in different directions. ❑ *Her long fair hair was knotted and straggly.*

**straight** /streɪt/ **(straighter, straightest, straights)** ◆◆◇ [1] ADJ A **straight** line or edge continues in the same direction and does not bend or curve. ❑ *Keep the boat in a straight line... Using the straight edge as a guide, trim the cloth to size... There wasn't a single straight wall in the building.* ♦ ADV: ADV after v **Straight** is also an adverb. ❑ *Stand straight and stretch the left hand to the right foot.* [2] ADJ: usu ADJ n **Straight** hair has no curls or waves in it. ❑ *Grace had long straight dark hair which she wore in a bun.* [3] ADV: ADV prep/adv You use **straight** to indicate that the way from one place to another is very direct, with no changes of direction. ❑ *The ball fell straight to the feet of Klinsmann... He finished his conversation and stood up, looking straight at me... Straight ahead were the low cabins of the motel.* [4] ADV: ADV prep/adv If you go **straight** to a place, you go there immediately. ❑ *As always, we went straight to the experts for advice.* [5] ADJ: ADJ n If you give someone a **straight** answer, you answer them clearly and honestly. ❑ *What a shifty arguer he is, refusing ever to give a straight answer.* ♦ ADV: ADV after v **Straight** is also an adverb. ❑ *I lost my temper and told him straight that I hadn't been looking for any job.* [6] ADJ: ADJ n **Straight** means following one after the other, with no gaps or intervals. ❑ *They'd won 12 straight games before they lost.* ♦ ADV: n ADV **Straight** is also an adverb. ❑ *He called from Weddington, having been there for 31 hours straight.* [7] ADJ: ADJ n A **straight** choice or a **straight** fight involves only two people or things. ❑ *It's a straight choice between low-paid jobs and no jobs.* [8] ADJ If you describe someone as **straight**, you mean that they are normal and conventional, for example in their opinions and in the way they live. ❑ *Dorothy was described as a very straight woman, a very strict Christian who was married to her job.* 9 If you describe someone as **straight**, you mean that they are heterosexual rather than homosexual. [INFORMAL] ❑ *His sexual orientation was a lot more gay than straight.* ♦ **Straight** is also a noun. ❑ *...a standard of sexual conduct that applies equally to gays and straights.* 10 A **straight** drink, especially an alcoholic drink, has not had another liquid such as water added to it. ❑ *...a large straight whiskey without ice.* 11 On a racetrack, a **straight** is a section of the track that is straight, rather than curved. ❑ *I went to overtake him on the back straight on the last lap.* → See also **home straight**.

ADJ: usu v-link ADJ ≠ gay | N-COUNT | ADJ: ADJ n, v n ADJ = neat | N-COUNT

**PHRASES** 12 If you **get** something **straight**, you make sure that you understand it properly or that someone else does. [SPOKEN] ❑ *Let's get things straight. I didn't lunch with her.* 13 If a criminal **is going straight**, they are no longer involved in crime. 14 If something keeps people **on the straight and narrow**, it helps to keep them living an honest or healthy life. ❑ *All her efforts to keep him on the straight and narrow have been rewarded.* 15 **a straight face** → see **face**. to **set the record straight** → see **record**.

PHRASE: V inflects | PHRASE: V inflects | PHRASE: PHR after v

**straight ar|row (straight arrows)** A **straight arrow** is someone who is very traditional, honest, and moral. [mainly AM] ❑ *...a well-scrubbed, straight-arrow group of young people.*

N-COUNT: oft N n

**straight away** also **straightaway**. If you do something **straight away**, you do it immediately and without delay. ❑ *I should go and see a doctor straight away.*

ADV: ADV with v = immediately

**straight|en** /streɪt$^{ə}$n/ **(straightens, straightening, straightened)** 1 If you **straighten** something, you make it tidy or put it in its proper position. ❑ *She sipped her coffee and straightened a picture on the wall. ...tidying, straightening cushions and organising magazines.* 2 If you are standing in a relaxed or slightly bent position and then you **straighten**, you make your back or body straight and upright. ❑ *The three men straightened and stood waiting.* ♦ **Straighten up** means the same as **straighten**. ❑ *He straightened up and slipped his hands in his pockets.* 3 If you **straighten** something, or it **straightens**, it becomes straight. ❑ *Straighten both legs until they are fully extended... The road straightened and we were on a plateau.* ♦ **Straighten out** means the same as **straighten**. ❑ *No one would dream of straightening out the knobbly spire at Empingham Church... The road twisted its way up the mountain then straightened out for the last two hundred yards.*

VERB | V n | V n | VERB | V | PHRASAL VERB | V P | VERB | V n | V | PHRASAL VERB | V P n (not pron) | V P

♦ **straighten out** 1 If you **straighten out** a confused situation, you succeed in getting it organized and tidied up. ❑ *He would make an appointment with him to straighten out a couple of things... My sister had come in with her common sense and straightened them out.* 2 → see **straighten 3**.

PHRASAL VERB = sort out | V P n (not pron) | V n P

♦ **straighten up** → see **straighten 2**.

**straight-faced** A **straight-faced** person appears not to be amused in a funny situation. ❑ *...a straight-faced, humourless character... 'Whatever gives you that idea?' she replied straight-faced.*

ADJ: usu ADJ n, ADJ after v

**straight|forward** /streɪtfɔːʳwəʳd/ 1 If you describe something as **straightforward**, you approve of it because it is easy to do or understand. ❑ *Disposable nappies are fairly straightforward to put on... The question seemed straightforward enough.* 2 If you describe a person or their behaviour as **straightforward**, you approve of them because they are honest and direct, and do not try to hide their feelings. ❑ *She is very blunt, very straightforward and very honest.*

ADJ: oft ADJ to-inf [approval] | ADJ [approval]

**straight-laced** → see **strait-laced**.

**strain** /streɪn/ **(strains, straining, strained)** ◆◇◇ 1 If **strain** is put **on** an organization or system, it has to do more than it is able to do. ❑ *The prison service is already under considerable strain... The vast expansion in secondary education is putting an enormous strain on the system.* 2 To **strain** something means to make it do more than it is able to do. ❑ *The volume of scheduled flights is straining the air traffic control system.* 3 **Strain** is a state of worry and tension caused by a difficult situation. ❑ *She was tired and under great strain. ...the stresses and strains of a busy and demanding career.* 4 If you say that a situation is **a strain**, you mean that it makes you worried and tense. ❑ *I sometimes find it a strain to be responsible for the mortgage.* 5 **Strain** is a force that pushes, pulls, or stretches something in a way that may damage it. ❑ *Place your hands under your buttocks to take some of the strain off your back.* 6 **Strain** is an injury to a muscle in your body, caused by using the muscle too much or twisting it. ❑ *Avoid muscle strain by warming up with slow jogging.* 7 If you **strain** a muscle, you injure it by using it too much or twisting it. ❑ *He strained his back during a practice session.* 8 If you **strain to** do something, you make a great effort to do it when it is difficult to do. ❑ *I had to strain to hear... They strained their eyes, but saw nothing.* 9 When you **strain** food, you separate the liquid part of it from the solid parts. ❑ *Strain the stock and put it back into the pan.* 10 You can use **strain** to refer to a particular quality in someone's character, remarks, or work. ❑ *There was a strain of bitterness in his voice. ...this cynical strain in the book.* 11 A **strain of** a germ, plant, or other organism is a particular type of it. ❑ *Every year new strains of influenza develop.* 12 → See also **eye strain**, **repetitive strain injury**.

N-VAR: oft *under* N, N *on* n = pressure | VERB = stretch | V n | N-UNCOUNT: also N in pl = stress | N-SING: *a* N | N-UNCOUNT | N-VAR: usu n N | VERB | V n | VERB | V to-inf | V n | VERB | V n | N-SING: with supp | N-COUNT: usu N *of* n

**strained** /streɪnd/ 1 If someone's appearance, voice, or behaviour is **strained**, they seem worried and nervous. ❑ *Gil sensed something wrong from her father's strained voice.* 2 If relations between people are **strained**, those people do not like or trust each other. ❑ *...a period of strained relations between the prime minister and his deputy.*

ADJ ≠ relaxed | ADJ

**strain|er** /streɪnəʳ/ **(strainers)** A **strainer** is an object with holes which you pour a liquid through in order to separate the liquid from the solids in it. ❑ *Pour the broth through a strainer. ...a tea strainer.*

N-COUNT

**strait** /streɪt/ **(straits)** 1 You can refer to a narrow strip of sea which joins two large areas of sea as a **strait** or **the straits**. ❑ *An estimated 1600 vessels pass through the strait annually. ...the Straits of Gibraltar.* 2 If someone is **in** dire or desperate **straits**, they are in a very difficult situation, usually because they do not have much money. ❑ *The company's closure has left many small businessmen in desperate financial straits.*

N-COUNT; N-IN-NAMES | N-PLURAL: adj N

**strait|ened** /streɪt$^{ə}$nd/ If someone is living in **straitened** circumstances, they do not have as much money as they used to, and are finding it very hard to buy or pay for everything that they need. [FORMAL] ❑ *His father died when he was ten, leaving the family in straitened circumstances.*

ADJ: usu ADJ n

**strait|jacket** /streɪtdʒækɪt/ **(straitjackets)** 1 A **straitjacket** is a special jacket used to tie the arms of a violent person tightly around their body. 2 If you describe an idea or a situation as a **straitjacket**, you mean that it is very limited and restricting. ❑ *The national curriculum must be a guide, not a straitjacket.*

N-COUNT | N-COUNT

**strait-laced** also **straight-laced, straitlaced.** If you describe someone as **strait-laced**, you disapprove of them because they have very strict views about what kind of behaviour is moral or acceptable. ❑ *He was criticised for being boring, strait-laced and narrow-minded.*

ADJ [disapproval]

**strand** /strænd/ **(strands, stranding, stranded)** 1 A **strand of** something such as hair, wire, or thread is a single thin piece of it. ❑ *She tried to blow a gray strand of hair from her eyes. ...high fences, topped by strands of barbed-wire.* 2 A **strand** of a plan or theory is a part of it. ❑ *There had been two strands to his tactics... He's trying to bring together various strands of radical philosophic thought.* 3 If

N-COUNT: usu N *of* n | N-COUNT = element | VERB

you **are stranded**, you are prevented from leaving a place, for example because of bad weather. ❑ *The climbers had been stranded by a storm.* *be* V-ed

**strange** /streɪndʒ/ **(stranger, strangest)** ◆◆◇ [1] Something that is **strange** is unusual or unexpected, and makes you feel slightly nervous or afraid. ❑ *Then a strange thing happened... There was something strange about the flickering blue light... It's strange how things turn out.* ♦ **strange|ly** *She noticed he was acting strangely... The hut suddenly seemed strangely silent.* ♦ **strange|ness** *...the breathy strangeness of the music.* [2] A **strange** place is one that you have never been to before. A **strange** person is someone that you have never met before. ❑ *I ended up alone in a strange city... She was faced with a new job, in unfamiliar surroundings with strange people.* [3] → See also **stranger**. ADJ: oft *it* v-link ADJ that/to-inf/*how* = odd; ADV: ADV with v, ADV adj; N-UNCOUNT; ADJ: ADJ n = unfamiliar ≠ familiar

**strange|ly** /streɪndʒli/ You use **strangely** to emphasize that what you are saying is surprising. ❑ *Strangely, the race didn't start until 8.15pm... No, strangely enough, this is not the case.* → See also **strange**. ADV: ADV with cl [emphasis] = surprisingly

**stran|ger** /streɪndʒəʳ/ **(strangers)** [1] A **stranger** is someone you have never met before. ❑ *Telling a complete stranger about your life is difficult... Sometimes I feel like I'm living with a stranger.* [2] If two people are **strangers**, they do not know each other. ❑ *The women knew nothing of the dead girl. They were strangers.* [3] If you are a **stranger** in a place, you do not know the place well. ❑ *'You don't know much about our town, do you?' — 'No, I'm a stranger here.'* [4] If you are a **stranger to** something, you have had no experience of it or do not understand it. ❑ *He is no stranger to controversy... We were both strangers to diplomatic life.* [5] → See also **strange**. N-COUNT; N-PLURAL; N-COUNT ≠ local; N-COUNT: oft with brd-neg, N *to* n

**stran|gle** /stræŋɡəl/ **(strangles, strangling, strangled)** [1] To **strangle** someone means to kill them by squeezing their throat tightly so that they cannot breathe. ❑ *He tried to strangle a border policeman and steal his gun.* [2] To **strangle** something means to prevent it from succeeding or developing. ❑ *The country's economic plight is strangling its scientific institutions.* VERB = throttle; V n; VERB; V n

**stran|gled** /stræŋɡəld/ A **strangled** voice or cry sounds unclear because the throat muscles of the person speaking or crying are tight. [LITERARY] ❑ *In a strangled voice he said, 'This place is going to be unthinkable without you.'* ADJ: ADJ n

**strangle|hold** /stræŋɡəlhoʊld/ To have a **stranglehold on** something means to have control over it and prevent it from being free or from developing. ❑ *These companies are determined to keep a stranglehold on the banana industry.* N-SING

**stran|gu|la|tion** /stræŋɡjʊleɪʃən/ **Strangulation** is the act of killing someone by squeezing their throat tightly so that they cannot breathe. ❑ *He is charged with the strangulation of two students.* N-UNCOUNT

**strap** /stræp/ **(straps, strapping, strapped)** [1] A **strap** is a narrow piece of leather, cloth, or other material. Straps are used to carry things, fasten things together, or to hold a piece of clothing in place. ❑ *Nancy gripped the strap of her beach bag... She pulled the strap of her nightgown onto her shoulder... I undid my watch strap.* [2] If you **strap** something somewhere, you fasten it there with a strap. ❑ *Strapping the skis on the roof, we boarded the hovercraft in Dover... Through the basement window I saw him strap on his pink cycling helmet.* N-COUNT; VERB; V n prep; V n with *on/in/down*

**strap|less** /stræpləs/ A **strapless** dress or bra does not have the usual narrow bands of material over the shoulders. ❑ *...a black, strapless evening dress.* ADJ: usu ADJ n

**strapped** /stræpt/ If someone is **strapped for** money, they do not have enough money to buy or pay for the things they want or need. ❑ *My husband and I are really strapped for cash.* → See also **cash-strapped**. ADJ: oft ADJ *for* n, adv ADJ

**strap|ping** /stræpɪŋ/ If you describe someone as **strapping**, you mean that they are tall and strong, and look healthy. ❑ *He was a bricklayer – a big, strapping fellow.* ADJ: usu ADJ n [approval]

**stra|ta** /strɑːtə, AM streɪtə/ **Strata** is the plural of **stratum**.

**strata|gem** /strætədʒəm/ **(stratagems)** A **stratagem** is a plan that is intended to achieve a particular effect, often by deceiving people. [FORMAL] ❑ *Trade discounts may be used as a competitive stratagem to secure customer loyalty.* N-COUNT = ploy

**stra|tegic** /strətiːdʒɪk/ [1] **Strategic** means relating to the most important, general aspects of something such as a military operation or political policy, especially when these are decided in advance. ❑ *...the new strategic thinking which NATO leaders produced at the recent London summit... The island is of strategic importance to France.* ♦ **stra|tegi|cal|ly** /strətiːdʒɪkli/ *...strategically important roads, bridges and buildings.* [2] **Strategic** weapons are very powerful missiles that can be fired only after a decision to use them has been made by a political leader. ❑ *...strategic nuclear weapons.* [3] If you put something in a **strategic** position, you place it cleverly in a position where it will be most useful or have the most effect. ❑ *...the marble benches Eve had placed at strategic points throughout the gardens, where the views were spectacular.* ♦ **stra|tegi|cal|ly** *We had kept its presence hidden with a strategically placed chair.* ◆◇◇ ADJ: usu ADJ n; ADV; ADJ: usu ADJ n ≠ tactical; ADJ: usu ADJ n; ADV: usu ADV -ed

**strat|egist** /strætədʒɪst/ **(strategists)** A **strategist** is someone who is skilled in planning the best way to gain an advantage or to achieve success, especially in war. ❑ *Military strategists had devised a plan that guaranteed a series of stunning victories.* N-COUNT

**strat|egy** /strætədʒi/ **(strategies)** [1] A **strategy** is a general plan or set of plans intended to achieve something, especially over a long period. ❑ *Next week, health ministers gather in Amsterdam to agree a strategy for controlling malaria... What should our marketing strategy have achieved?* [2] **Strategy** is the art of planning the best way to gain an advantage or achieve success, especially in war. ❑ *I've just been explaining the basic principles of strategy to my generals.* ◆◆◇ N-VAR = policy; N-UNCOUNT

**strati|fi|ca|tion** /strætɪfɪkeɪʃən/ **Stratification** is the division of something, especially society, into different classes or layers. [FORMAL] ❑ *She was concerned about the stratification of American society.* N-UNCOUNT

**strati|fied** /strætɪfaɪd/ A **stratified** society is one that is divided into different classes or social layers. [FORMAL] ❑ *...a highly stratified, unequal and class-divided society.* ADJ

**strato|sphere** /strætəsfɪəʳ/ [1] **The stratosphere** is the layer of the earth's atmosphere which lies between 10 and 50 kilometres above the earth. [2] If you say that someone or something climbs or is sent into **the stratosphere**, you mean that they reach a very high level. [JOURNALISM] ❑ *This was enough to launch their careers into the stratosphere.* N-SING: the N; N-SING: the N

**strato|spher|ic** /strætəsferɪk, AM -fɪrɪk/ **Stratospheric** means found in or related to the stratosphere. ❑ *...stratospheric ozone.* ADJ: ADJ n

**stra|tum** /strɑːtəm, AM streɪtəm/ **(strata)** [1] A **stratum** of society is a group of people in it who are similar in their education, income, or social status. [FORMAL] ❑ *It was an enormous task that affected every stratum of society.* [2] **Strata** are different layers of rock. [TECHNICAL] ❑ *Contained within the rock strata is evidence that the region was intensely dry 15,000 years ago.* N-COUNT: usu with supp; N-COUNT: usu pl

**straw** /strɔː/ **(straws)** [1] **Straw** consists of the dried, yellowish stalks from crops such as wheat or barley. ❑ *The barn was full of bales of straw. ...a wide-brimmed straw hat.* [2] A **straw** is a thin tube of paper or plastic, which you use to suck a drink N-UNCOUNT; N-COUNT into your mouth. ❑ *...a bottle of lemonade with a straw in it.*

PHRASES [3] If you **are clutching at straws** or **grasping at straws**, you are trying unusual or extreme ideas or methods because other ideas or methods have failed. ❑ *...a badly thought-out scheme from a Government clutching at straws.* PHRASE: V inflects [4] If an event is **the last straw** or **the straw that broke the camel's back**, it is the latest in a series of unpleasant or undesirable events, and makes you feel that you cannot tolerate a situation any longer. ❑ *For him the Church's decision to allow the ordination of women had been the last straw.* PHRASE: usu v-link PHR [5] If you draw **the short straw**, you are chosen from a number of people to perform a job or duty that you will not enjoy. ❑ *...if a few of your guests have drawn the short straw and agreed to drive others home after your summer barbecue.* PHRASE: usu v PHR

**straw|berry** /strɔ͟ːbri, AM -beri/ **(strawberries)** A **strawberry** is a small red fruit which is soft and juicy and has tiny yellow seeds on its skin. ➔ See picture on page 1711. ❑ *...strawberries and cream. ...homemade strawberry jam.* N-COUNT

**stra͟w|berry blo͟nde (strawberry blondes)** also **strawberry blond.** [1] **Strawberry blonde** hair is reddish blonde. ADJ [2] A **strawberry blonde** is a person, especially a woman, who has strawberry blonde hair. N-COUNT

**stra͟w po͟ll (straw polls)** A **straw poll** is the unofficial questioning of a group of people to find out their opinion about something. ❑ *A straw poll conducted at the end of the meeting found most people agreed with Mr Forth.* N-COUNT

**stray** /stre͟ɪ/ **(strays, straying, strayed)** [1] If someone **strays** somewhere, they wander away from where they are supposed to be. ❑ *Tourists often get lost and stray into dangerous areas... A railway line crosses the park so children must not be allowed to stray.* VERB; V prep/adv; V [2] A **stray** dog or cat has wandered away from its owner's home. ❑ *...a refuge for stray cats.* ADJ: ADJ n ♦ **Stray** is also a noun. ❑ *The dog was a stray which had been adopted.* N-COUNT [3] If your mind or your eyes **stray**, you do not concentrate on or look at one particular subject, but start thinking about or looking at other things. ❑ *Even with the simplest cases I find my mind straying.* VERB = wander; V [4] You use **stray** to describe something that exists separated from other similar things. ❑ *An 8-year-old boy was killed by a stray bullet... She shrugged a stray lock of hair out of her eyes.* ADJ: ADJ n

**streak** /stri͟ːk/ **(streaks, streaking, streaked)** [1] A **streak** is a long stripe or mark on a surface which contrasts with the surface because it is a different colour. ❑ *There are these dark streaks on the surface of the moon... The flames begin as a few streaks of red against the pale brown of the walls.* N-COUNT [2] If something **streaks** a surface, it makes long stripes or marks on the surface. ❑ *Rain had begun to streak the window-panes... His face was pale and streaked with dirt.* VERB; V n; be V-ed with n [3] If someone has a **streak** of a particular type of behaviour, they sometimes behave in that way. ❑ *He's still got a mean streak.* N-COUNT: usu sing, with supp [4] If something or someone **streaks** somewhere, they move there very quickly. ❑ *A meteorite streaked across the sky.* VERB = dart; V prep/adv [5] A winning **streak** or a lucky **streak** is a continuous series of successes, for example in gambling or sport. A losing **streak** or an unlucky **streak** is a series of failures or losses. ❑ *The casinos had better watch out since I'm obviously on a lucky streak!* N-COUNT: adj N

**streak|er** /stri͟ːkəʳ/ **(streakers)** A **streaker** is someone who runs quickly through a public place wearing no clothes, as a joke. N-COUNT

**streaky** /stri͟ːki/ **(streakier, streakiest)** Something that is **streaky** is marked with long stripes that are a different colour to the rest of it. ❑ *She has streaky fair hair and blue eyes. ...the empty house with its streaky windows.* ADJ

**stre͟aky ba|con** **Streaky bacon** is bacon which has stripes of fat between stripes of meat. [BRIT] N-UNCOUNT

**stream** /stri͟ːm/ **(streams, streaming, streamed)** ◆◇◇ [1] A **stream** is a small narrow river. ❑ *There was a small stream at the end of the garden. ...a mountain stream.* N-COUNT [2] A **stream** of smoke, air, or liquid is a narrow moving mass of it. ❑ *He breathed out a stream of cigarette smoke... Add the oil in a slow, steady stream.* N-COUNT: with supp, usu N *of* n [3] A **stream** of vehicles or people is a long moving line of them. ❑ *There was a stream of traffic behind him.* N-COUNT: with supp, usu N *of* n [4] A **stream of** things is a large number of them occurring one after another. ❑ *We had a constant stream of visitors.* N-COUNT: with supp, usu N *of* n [5] If a liquid **streams** somewhere, it flows or comes out in large amounts. ❑ *Tears streamed down their faces... She came in, rain streaming from her clothes and hair.* VERB; V prep/adv; V prep/adv [6] If your eyes **are streaming**, liquid is coming from them, for example because you have a cold. You can also say that your nose **is streaming**. ❑ *Her eyes were streaming now from the wind... A cold usually starts with a streaming nose and dry throat.* VERB: usu cont; V; V-ing [7] If people or vehicles **stream** somewhere, they move there quickly and in large numbers. ❑ *Refugees have been streaming into Travnik for months.* VERB; V prep/adv [8] When light **streams** into or out of a place, it shines strongly into or out of it. ❑ *Sunlight was streaming into the courtyard.* VERB; V prep/adv [9] If something such as a new factory or a new system comes **on stream** or is brought **on stream**, it begins to operate or becomes available. ❑ *As new mines come on stream, Chile's share of world copper output will increase sharply.* PHRASE: usu V PHRASE [10] ➔ See also **jet stream**.

**stream|er** /stri͟ːməʳ/ **(streamers)** **Streamers** are long rolls of coloured paper used for decorating rooms at parties. N-COUNT

**stream|ing** /stri͟ːmɪŋ/ **Streaming** is a method of transmitting data from the Internet directly to a user's computer screen without the need to download it. [COMPUTING] ❑ *...web sites that feature streaming media.* ➔ See also **stream**. N-UNCOUNT: usu N n

**stream|line** /stri͟ːmlaɪn/ **(streamlines, streamlining, streamlined)** To **streamline** an organization or process means to make it more efficient by removing unnecessary parts of it. ❑ *They're making efforts to streamline their normally cumbersome bureaucracy.* VERB; V n

**stream|lined** /stri͟ːmlaɪnd/ A **streamlined** vehicle, animal, or object has a shape that allows it to move quickly or efficiently through air or water. ❑ *...these beautifully streamlined and efficient cars.* ADJ: usu ADJ n

**stre͟am of co͟n|scious|ness (streams of consciousness)** also **stream-of-consciousness.** If you describe what someone writes or says as a **stream of consciousness**, you mean that it expresses their thoughts as they occur, rather than in a structured way. [FORMAL] ❑ *The novel is an intensely lyrical stream-of-consciousness about an Indian woman who leaves her family home to be married.* N-VAR: oft N n

**street** /stri͟ːt/ **(streets)** ◆◆◆ [1] A **street** is a road in a city, town, or village, usually with houses along it. ❑ *He lived at 66 Bingfield Street... Boppard is a small, quaint town with narrow streets.* N-COUNT; N-IN-NAMES [2] You can use **street** or **streets** when talking about activities that happen out of doors in a town rather than inside a building. ❑ *Changing money on the street is illegal-always use a bank... Their aim is to raise a million pounds to get the homeless off the streets. ...a New York street gang.* N-COUNT: *the* N, usu *on/off* N [3] ➔ See also **back street**, **civvy street**, **Downing Street**, **Fleet Street**, **high street**, **Wall Street**.

PHRASES [4] If someone is **streets ahead of** you, they are much better at something than you are. ❑ *He was streets ahead of the other contestants.* PHRASE: usu v-link PHR, oft PHR *of* n [5] If you talk about **the man in the street** or **the man or woman in the street**, you mean ordinary people in general. ❑ *The average man or woman in the street doesn't know very much about immune disorders.* PHRASE [6] If a job or activity is **up** your **street**, it is the kind of job or activity that you are very PHRASE: usu v-link PHR interested in. [BRIT] ❑ *She loved it, this was just up her street.*

☑ in AM, use **up** your **alley**

**street|car** /striːtkɑːʳ/ **(streetcars)** A **streetcar** is an electric vehicle for carrying people which travels on rails in the streets of a town. [AM] N-COUNT

☑ in BRIT, use **tram**

**street child** **(street children)** **Street children** are homeless children who live outdoors in a city and live by begging or stealing. N-COUNT: usu pl

**street cred** also **street-cred.** If someone says that you have **street cred**, they mean that ordinary young people would approve of you and consider you to be part of their culture, usually because you share their sense of fashion or their views. [BRIT, INFORMAL] ❑ *Having children was the quickest way to lose your street cred.* N-UNCOUNT [approval] = cred

**street cred|ibil|ity** **Street credibility** is the same as **street cred.** [mainly BRIT] N-UNCOUNT

**street crime** **Street crime** refers to crime such as vandalism, car theft and mugging that are usually committed outdoors. N-UNCOUNT

**street|lamp** /striːtlæmp/ **(streetlamps)** also **street-lamp.** A **streetlamp** is the same as a **streetlight.** ❑ *He paused under a streetlamp and looked across at the cafe.* N-COUNT = streetlight

**street|light** /striːtlaɪt/ **(streetlights)** also **street light.** A **streetlight** is a tall post with a light at the top, which stands by the side of a road to light it up, usually in a town. ❑ *As the day darkened the streetlights came on.* N-COUNT = streetlamp

**street map** **(street maps)** A **street map** is a map of a town or city, showing the positions and names of all the streets. N-COUNT

**street peo|ple** **Street people** are homeless people who live outdoors in a town or city. N-PLURAL

**street smart** also **street-smart.** Someone who is **street smart** knows how to deal with difficult or dangerous situations, especially in big cities. [mainly AM, INFORMAL] ❑ *He is street smart and is not afraid of this neighborhood.* ADJ = streetwise

**street smarts** You can use **street smarts** to refer to the skills and intelligence people need to be successful in difficult situations, especially in a city. [AM, INFORMAL] ❑ *The boys learned their street smarts early.* N-PLURAL

**street value** The **street value** of a drug is the price that is paid for it when it is sold illegally to drug users. [JOURNALISM] ❑ *...cocaine with a street value of two million pounds.* N-SING: usu N *of* amount

**street|walker** /striːtwɔːkəʳ/ **(streetwalkers)** A **streetwalker** is a prostitute who stands or walks in the streets in order to get customers. [OLD-FASHIONED] N-COUNT

**street|wise** /striːtwaɪz/ Someone who is **streetwise** knows how to deal with difficult or dangerous situations in big cities. [INFORMAL] ❑ *Salt and Peppa are two streetwise and sassy girls from Queens.* ADJ

**strength** /streŋθ/ **(strengths)** ◆◆◇ [1] Your **strength** is the physical energy that you have, which gives you the ability to perform various actions, such as lifting or moving things. ❑ *She has always been encouraged to swim to build up the strength of her muscles... He threw it forward with all his strength... He leant against the wall, fighting for strength to continue.* N-UNCOUNT [2] Someone's **strength** in a difficult situation is their confidence or courage. ❑ *Something gave me the strength to overcome the difficulty... His strength is an inspiration to me in my life... You need strength of mind to stand up for yourself.* N-UNCOUNT: also *a* N ≠weakness [3] The **strength** of an object or material is its ability to be treated roughly, or to carry heavy weights, without being damaged or destroyed. ❑ *He checked the strength of the cables. ...the properties of a material, such as strength or electrical conductivity.* N-UNCOUNT: also N in pl [4] The **strength** of a person, organization, or country is the power or influence that they have. ❑ *America values its economic leadership, and the political and military strength that goes with it... The Alliance in its first show of strength drew a hundred thousand-strong crowd to a rally... They have their own independence movement which is gathering strength.* N-UNCOUNT: also N in pl [5] If you refer to the **strength of** a feeling, opinion, or belief, you are talking about how deeply it is felt or believed by people, or how much they are influenced by it. ❑ *He was surprised at the strength of his own feeling... What makes a mayor successful in Los Angeles is the strength of his public support.* N-UNCOUNT = intensity, depth [6] Someone's **strengths** are the qualities and abilities that they have which are an advantage to them, or which make them successful. ❑ *Take into account your own strengths and weaknesses... Tact was never Mr Moore's strength... Organisation is the strength of any good army.* N-VAR ≠weakness [7] If you refer to the **strength** of a currency, economy, or industry, you mean that its value or success is steady or increasing. ❑ *...the long-term competitive strength of the American economy... The drop was caused partly by the pound's strength against the dollar.* N-UNCOUNT ≠weakness [8] The **strength** of a group of people is the total number of people in it. ❑ *...elite forces, comprising about one-tenth of the strength of the army.* N-UNCOUNT: also N in pl [9] The **strength** of a wind, current, or other force is its power or speed. ❑ *A tropical storm is gaining strength in the eastern Atlantic.* N-UNCOUNT: also N in pl [10] The **strength** of a drink, chemical, or drug is the amount of the particular substance in it that gives it its particular effect. ❑ *Each capsule contains between 30 and 100 pellets of morphine sulphate according to the strength of dose required.* N-UNCOUNT: also N in pl [11] You can talk about the **strength** of a flavour, smell, colour, sound, or light to describe how intense or easily noticed it is. ❑ *The wine has lots of strength of flavour.* N-UNCOUNT: also N in pl

PHRASES [12] If a person or organization **goes from strength to strength**, they become more and more successful or confident. ❑ *A decade later, the company has gone from strength to strength.* PHRASE: V inflects [13] If a team or army is at **full strength**, all the members that it needs or usually has are present. ❑ *He needed more time to bring US forces there up to full strength. ...a full-strength team.* PHRASE: PHR after v, v-link PHR, PHR n [14] If a group turns out **in strength**, they arrive in large numbers. ❑ *Mr Gore called on voters and party workers to turn out in strength... Security forces have been out in strength.* PHRASE: PHR after v [15] If one thing is done **on the strength of** another, it is done because of the influence of that other thing. ❑ *He was elected to power on the strength of his charisma.* PHRASE: PHR after v [16] If an army or team is **under strength** or **below strength**, it does not have all the members that it needs or usually has. ❑ *His regiments were considerably under strength... They had been beaten three days earlier by a below-strength Brazilian side.* PHRASE: PHR after v, v-link PHR, PHR n

**strength|en** /streŋθən/ **(strengthens, strengthening, strengthened)** ◆◇◇ [1] If something **strengthens** a person or group or if they **strengthen** their position, they become more powerful and secure, or more likely to succeed. ❑ *...the new constitution, which strengthens the government and enables it to balance and check the powers of parliament and president... He hoped to strengthen the position of the sciences in the leading universities.* VERB V n V n [2] If something **strengthens** a case or argument, it supports it by providing more reasons or evidence for it. ❑ *He does not seem to be familiar with research which might have strengthened his own arguments.* VERB = reinforce V n [3] If a currency, economy, or industry **strengthens**, or if something **strengthens** it, it increases in value or becomes more successful. ❑ *The dollar strengthened against most other currencies... If the Government wants to save the Pound it should start by strengthening the British economy.* VERB ≠weaken V V n [4] If a government **strengthens** laws or measures or if they **strengthen**, they are made more severe. ❑ *I am also looking urgently at how we can strengthen the law... Community leaders want to strengthen controls at external frontiers... Because of the war, security procedures have strengthened.* VERB V n V n V [5] If VERB something **strengthens** you or **strengthens** your resolve or character, it makes you more confident and determined. ≠ weaken ❑ *Any experience can teach and strengthen you, but particularly the more difficult ones... This merely strengthens our resolve to win the league.* V n, V n [6] VERB If something **strengthens** a relationship or link, or if a relationship or link **strengthens**, it makes it closer and more likely to last for a long time. ❑ *His visit is intended to strengthen ties between the two countries... In a strange way, his affair caused our relationship to strengthen.* V n, V [7] VERB = deepen If something **strengthens** an impression, feeling, or belief, or if it **strengthens**, it becomes greater or affects more people. ❑ *His speech strengthens the impression he is the main power in the organization... Every day of sunshine strengthens the feelings of optimism... Amy's own Republican sympathies strengthened as the days passed.* V n, V n, V [8] VERB If something **strengthens** your body or a part of your body, it makes it healthier, often in such a way that you can move or carry heavier things. ❑ *Cycling is good exercise. It strengthens all the muscles of the body.* V n [9] VERB = reinforce If something **strengthens** an object or structure, it makes it able to be treated roughly or able to support heavy weights, without being damaged or destroyed. ❑ *The builders will have to strengthen the existing joists with additional timber.* V n

**strenu|ous** /strenjuəs/ ADJ A **strenuous** activity or action involves a lot of energy or effort. ❑ *Avoid strenuous exercise in the evening... Strenuous efforts had been made to improve conditions in the jail.*

**stress** /stres/ **(stresses, stressing, stressed)** ◆◆◇ [1] VERB = emphasize If you **stress** a point in a discussion, you put extra emphasis on it because you think it is important. ❑ *The spokesman stressed that the measures did not amount to an overall ban... They also stress the need for improved employment opportunities, better transport and health care... 'We're not saying we're outside and above all this,' he stresses.* V that, V n, V with quote ♦ N-VAR: N *on* n = emphasis **Stress** is also a noun. ❑ *Japanese car makers are laying ever more stress on European sales.* [2] N-VAR: oft *under* N If you feel under **stress**, you feel worried and tense because of difficulties in your life. ❑ *Katy could think clearly when not under stress. ...a wide range of stress-related problems.* [3] N-VAR **Stresses** are strong physical pressures applied to an object. ❑ *Earthquakes happen when stresses in rock are suddenly released as the rocks fracture.* [4] VERB If you **stress** a word or part of a word when you say it, you put emphasis on it so that it sounds slightly louder. ❑ *'Sit down,' she replied, stressing each word.* V n ♦ N-VAR **Stress** is also a noun. ❑ *...the misplaced stress on the first syllable of this last word.*

**stressed** /strest/ [1] ADJ: usu v-link ADJ ≠ relaxed If you are **stressed**, you feel tense and anxious because of difficulties in your life. ❑ *Work out what situations or people make you feel stressed and avoid them.* [2] ADJ ≠ unstressed If a word or part of a word is **stressed**, it is pronounced with emphasis.

**stressed out** ADJ If someone is **stressed out**, they are very tense and anxious because of difficulties in their lives. [INFORMAL]

**stress|ful** /stresfʊl/ ADJ If a situation or experience is **stressful**, it causes the person involved to feel stress. ❑ *I think I've got one of the most stressful jobs there is.*

**stretch** /stretʃ/ **(stretches, stretching, stretched)** ◆◇◇ [1] VERB: no cont = extend Something that **stretches** over an area or distance covers or exists in the whole of that area or distance. ❑ *The procession stretched for several miles. ...an artificial reef stretching the length of the coast.* V prep/adv, V n [2] N-COUNT: usu N *of* n A **stretch of** road, water, or land is a length or area of it. ❑ *It's a very dangerous stretch of road.* [3] VERB When you **stretch**, you put your arms or legs out straight and tighten your muscles. ❑ *He yawned and stretched... Try stretching your legs and pulling your toes upwards... She arched her back and stretched herself.* V, V n, V n ♦ N-COUNT **Stretch** is also a noun. ❑ *At the end of a workout spend time cooling down with some slow stretches.* ♦ N-UNCOUNT **stretch|ing** *Make sure no awkward stretching is required.* [4] N-COUNT: oft N *of* n A **stretch of** time is a period of time. ❑ *...after an 18-month stretch in the army... He would study for eight to ten hours at a stretch.* [5] VERB If something **stretches from** one time **to** another, it begins at the first time and ends at the second, which is longer than expected. ❑ *...a working day that stretches from seven in the morning to eight at night.* V *from* n *to* n [6] VERB = range If a group of things **stretch from** one type of thing **to** another, the group includes a wide range of things. ❑ *...a trading empire, with interests that stretched from chemicals to sugar.* V *from* n *to* n [7] VERB When something soft or elastic **stretches** or **is stretched**, it becomes longer or bigger as well as thinner, usually because it is pulled. ❑ *The cables are designed not to stretch... Ease the pastry into the corners of the tin, making sure you don't stretch it.* V, V n [8] ADJ: ADJ n **Stretch** fabric is soft and elastic and stretches easily. ❑ *...stretch fabrics such as Lycra. ...stretch cotton swimsuits.* [9] VERB If you **stretch** an amount of something or if it **stretches**, you make it last longer than it usually would by being careful and not wasting any of it. ❑ *They're used to stretching their budgets... During his senior year his earnings stretched far enough to buy an old car.* V n, V [10] VERB: no cont If your resources can **stretch to** something, you can just afford to do it. ❑ *She suggested to me that I might like to start regular savings and I said Well, I don't know whether I can stretch to that.* V *to* n [11] VERB If something **stretches** your money or resources, it uses them up so you have hardly enough for your needs. ❑ *The drought there is stretching American resources... Public expenditure was being stretched to the limit by having to support 3 million unemployed people.* V n, *be* V-ed prep/adv [12] VERB [approval] = push If you say that a job or task **stretches** you, you mean that you like it because it makes you work hard and use all your energy and skills so that you do not become bored or achieve less than you should. ❑ *I'm trying to move on and stretch myself with something different... They criticised the quality of teaching, claiming pupils were not stretched enough.* V pron-refl, V n

**PHRASES** [13] PHRASE: PHR after v If you are **at full stretch**, you are using the maximum amount of effort or energy. ❑ *Everyone would be working at full stretch.* [14] PHRASE [emphasis] If you say that something is not true or possible **by any stretch of the imagination**, you are emphasizing that it is completely untrue or absolutely impossible. ❑ *Her husband was not a womaniser by any stretch of the imagination.* [15] PHRASE: V inflects If you **stretch** your **legs**, you go for a short walk, usually after you have been sitting down for a long time. ❑ *I stopped at the square and got out to stretch my legs.*

♦ **stretch out** [1] PHRASAL VERB If you **stretch out** or **stretch yourself out**, you lie with your legs and body in a straight line. ❑ *The jacuzzi was too small to stretch out in... Moira stretched herself out on the lower bench.* V P adv/prep, V pron-refl P prep/adv [2] PHRASAL VERB If you **stretch out** a part of your body, you hold it out straight. ❑ *He was about to stretch out his hand to grab me.* V P n, Also V n P

**stretch|er** /stretʃəʳ/ **(stretchers, stretchered)** [1] N-COUNT A **stretcher** is a long piece of canvas with a pole along each side, which is used to carry an injured or sick person. ❑ *The two ambulance attendants quickly put Plover on a stretcher and got him into the ambulance.* [2] V-PASSIVE If someone **is stretchered** somewhere, they are carried there on a stretcher. ❑ *I was close by as Lester was stretchered into the ambulance.* *be* V-ed prep/adv

**stretch limo** **(stretch limos)** N-COUNT A **stretch limo** is a very long and luxurious car in which a rich, famous, or important person is driven somewhere.

**stretch marks** N-PLURAL **Stretch marks** are lines or marks on someone's skin caused by the skin stretching after the person's weight has changed rapidly. Women who have had children often have stretch marks.

**stretchy** /stretʃi/ **(stretchier, stretchiest)** ADJ **Stretchy** material is slightly elastic and stretches easily.

**strew** /struː/ **(strews, strewing, strewed, strewn)** VERB To **strew** things somewhere, or to **strew** a place **with** things, means to scatter them there.

❑ *The racoons knock over the rubbish bins in search of food, and strew the contents all over the ground... An elderly woman was strewing the floor with French chalk so that the dancing shoes would not slip... By the end, bodies were strewn all round the headquarters building.* V n prep/adv V n *with* n V-ed

**strewn** /struːn/ 1 If a place is **strewn with** things, they are lying scattered there. ❑ *The front room was strewn with books and clothes... The riverbed was strewn with big boulders.* ♦ **Strewn** is also a combining form. ❑ *...a litter-strewn street. ...a rock-strewn hillside.* 2 **Strewn** is the past participle of **strew**. ADJ: v-link ADJ *with* n COMB in ADJ

**strick|en** /strɪkən/ 1 **Stricken** is the past participle of some meanings of **strike**. 2 If a person or place is **stricken by** something such as an unpleasant feeling, an illness, or a natural disaster, they are severely affected by it. ❑ *...a family stricken by genetically inherited cancer... Foreign aid workers will not be allowed into the stricken areas.* ♦ **Stricken** is also a combining form. ❑ *He was panic-stricken at the thought he might never play again. ...drought-stricken areas.* ADJ: oft ADJ *by/with* n COMB in ADJ

**strict** /strɪkt/ **(stricter, strictest)** 1 A **strict** rule or order is very clear and precise or severe and must always be obeyed completely. ❑ *The officials had issued strict instructions that we were not to get out of the jeep... French privacy laws are very strict... All your replies will be treated in the strictest confidence.* ♦ **strict|ly** *The acceptance of new members is strictly controlled.* 2 If a parent or other person in authority is **strict**, they regard many actions as unacceptable and do not allow them. ❑ *My parents were very strict. ...a few schools selected for their high standards and their strict discipline.* ♦ **strict|ly** *My own mother was brought up very strictly and correctly.* 3 If you talk about the **strict** meaning of something, you mean the precise meaning of it. ❑ *It's not quite peace in the strictest sense of the word, rather the absence of war.* ♦ **strict|ly** *Actually, that is not strictly true... Strictly speaking, it is not one house at all, but three houses joined together.* → See also **strict**. 4 You use **strict** to describe someone who never does things that are against their beliefs. ❑ *Four million Britons are now strict vegetarians.* ◆◇◇ ADJ ADV: ADV with v ADJ ADV ADJ: ADJ n ADV: ADV adj ADJ: ADJ n

**strict|ly** /strɪktli/ You use **strictly** to emphasize that something is of one particular type, or intended for one particular thing or person, rather than any other. ❑ *This session was strictly for the boys.* ADV: ADV group [emphasis] = purely

**stric|ture** /strɪktʃəʳ/ **(strictures)** 1 You can use **strictures** to refer to severe criticism or disapproval of something. [FORMAL] ❑ *...Mencken's strictures on the 1920s, with its self-righteous prohibition on alcohol and unconventional ideas.* 2 You can refer to things that limit what you can do as **strictures** of a particular kind. [mainly FORMAL] ❑ *Your goals are hindered by financial strictures.* N-COUNT: usu pl, oft N *on/against* n N-COUNT: usu pl, usu with supp = restriction

**stride** /straɪd/ **(strides, striding, strode)** 1 If you **stride** somewhere, you walk there with quick, long steps. ❑ *They were joined by a newcomer who came striding across a field... He turned abruptly and strode off down the corridor.* 2 A **stride** is a long step which you take when you are walking or running. ❑ *With every stride, runners hit the ground with up to five times their body-weight... He walked with long strides.* 3 Someone's **stride** is their way of walking with long steps. ❑ *He lengthened his stride to keep up with her.* 4 If you **make strides** in something that you are doing, you make rapid progress in it. ❑ *The country has made enormous strides politically but not economically.* VERB V prep/adv V prep/adv N-COUNT N-SING: usu poss N N-COUNT: usu pl, usu adj N

PHRASES 5 If you **get into** your **stride** or **hit** your **stride**, you start to do something easily and confidently, after being slow and uncertain. ❑ *The campaign is just getting into its stride.* 6 In British English, if you **take** a problem or difficulty **in** your **stride**, you deal with it calmly and easily. The American expression is **take** something **in stride**. ❑ *Beth was struck by how Naomi took the mistake in her stride.* PHRASE: V inflects PHRASE: V inflects

**stri|den|cy** /straɪdənsi/ **Stridency** is the quality of being strident. ❑ *Many voters were alarmed by the President's new stridency.* N-UNCOUNT

**stri|dent** /straɪdənt/ 1 If you use **strident** to describe someone or the way they express themselves, you mean that they make their feelings or opinions known in a very strong way that perhaps makes people uncomfortable. ❑ *...the unnecessarily strident tone of the President's remarks.* 2 If a voice or sound is **strident**, it is loud, harsh, and unpleasant to listen to. ❑ *She tried to laugh, and the sound was harsh and strident.* ADJ [disapproval] ADJ

**strife** /straɪf/ **Strife** is strong disagreement or fighting. [FORMAL] ❑ *Money is a major cause of strife in many marriages.* N-UNCOUNT = conflict

**strike** /straɪk/ **(strikes, striking, struck, stricken)** ◆◆◇

> The form **struck** is the past tense and past participle. The form **stricken** can also be used as the past participle for meanings 6 and 17.

1 When there is a **strike**, workers stop doing their work for a period of time, usually in order to try to get better pay or conditions for themselves. [BUSINESS] ❑ *French air traffic controllers have begun a three-day strike in a dispute over pay... Staff at the hospital went on strike in protest at the incidents. ...a call for strike action.* 2 When workers **strike**, they go on strike. [BUSINESS] ❑ *...their recognition of the workers' right to strike... They shouldn't be striking for more money... The government agreed not to sack any of the striking workers.* ♦ **strik|er (strikers)** *The strikers want higher wages, which state governments say they can't afford.* 3 If you **strike** someone or something, you deliberately hit them. [FORMAL] ❑ *She took two quick steps forward and struck him across the mouth... It is impossible to say who struck the fatal blow.* 4 If something that is falling or moving **strikes** something, it hits it. [FORMAL] ❑ *His head struck the bottom when he dived into the 6ft end of the pool... One 16-inch shell struck the control tower.* 5 If you **strike** one thing against another, or if one thing **strikes** against another, the first thing hits the second thing. [FORMAL] ❑ *Wilde fell and struck his head on the stone floor... My right toe struck against a submerged rock.* 6 If something such as an illness or disaster **strikes**, it suddenly happens. ❑ *Bank of England officials continued to insist that the pound would soon return to stability but disaster struck... A powerful earthquake struck the Italian island of Sicily early this morning.* 7 To **strike** means to attack someone or something quickly and violently. ❑ *The attacker struck as she was walking near a housing estate at Monacurra.* 8 A military **strike** is a military attack, especially an air attack. ❑ *...a punitive air strike. ...a nuclear strike.* 9 If something **strikes at** the heart or root of something, it attacks or conflicts with the basic elements or principles of that thing. [LITERARY] ❑ *...a rejection of her core beliefs and values, which strikes at the very heart of her being.* 10 If an idea or thought **strikes** you, it suddenly comes into your mind. ❑ *A thought struck her. Was she jealous of her mother, then?... At this point, it suddenly struck me that I was wasting my time.* 11 If something **strikes** you **as** being a particular thing, it gives you the impression of being that thing. ❑ *He struck me as a very serious but friendly person... You've always struck me as being an angry man.* 12 If you **are struck** by something, you think it is very impressive, noticeable, or interesting. ❑ *She was struck by his simple, spellbinding eloquence... What struck me about the firm is how genuinely friendly and informal it is.* 13 If you **strike** a deal or a bargain with someone, you come to an agreement with them. ❑ *They struck a deal with their paper supplier, getting two years of newsprint on credit... The two struck a deal in which Rendell took half of what a manager would... He insists he has struck no bargains for their release.* 14 If you **strike** a balance, you do something that is halfway between two extremes. ❑ *At times like that you*

N-COUNT: also *on* N; VERB; V; V *for* n; V-ing; N-COUNT; VERB; V n prep/adv; V n; VERB = hit; V n; V n; VERB = bang; V n *on/against* n; V *against* n; VERB; V; V n; VERB; V; N-COUNT: with supp, oft N *against* n; VERB; V *at* n; VERB: no cont; V n; *it* V n *that/how*; VERB; V n *as* n/adj; V n *as* -ing; VERB; *be* V-ed *by/with* n; V n; V-RECIP; V n *with* n; pl-n V n; V n (non-recip); VERB; V n *have to strike a balance between sleep and homework.*

15 If you **strike** a pose or attitude, you put yourself in a particular position, for example when someone is taking your photograph. ❑ *She struck a pose, one hand on her hip and the other waving an imaginary cigarette.* VERB = adopt; V n

16 If something **strikes** fear **into** people, it makes them very frightened or anxious. [LITERARY] ❑ *If there is a single subject guaranteed to strike fear in the hearts of parents, it is drugs.* VERB; V n *into* n

17 If you **are struck** dumb or blind, you suddenly become unable to speak or to see. [WRITTEN] ❑ *I was struck dumb by this and had to think it over for a moment.* VERB: usu passive; *be* V-ed adj

18 When a clock **strikes**, its bells make a sound to indicate what the time is. ❑ *The clock struck nine... Finally, the clock strikes.* VERB; V n, V

19 If you **strike** words **from** a document or an official record, you remove them. [FORMAL] ❑ *Strike that from the minutes.* ♦ **Strike out** means the same as **strike**. ❑ *The censor struck out the next two lines.* VERB; V n *from* n; Also V n; PHRASAL VERB; V P n; Also V n P

20 When you **strike** a match, you make it produce a flame by moving it quickly against something rough. ❑ *Robina struck a match and held it to the crumpled newspaper in the grate.* VERB; V n

21 If someone **strikes** oil or gold, they discover it in the ground as a result of mining or drilling. ❑ *Hamilton Oil announced that it had struck oil in the Liverpool Bay area of the Irish Sea.* VERB; V n

22 When a coin or medal **is struck**, it is made. ❑ *Another medal was specially struck for him.* VERB: usu passive; *be* V-ed

23 → See also **stricken, striking, hunger strike.**

**PHRASES** 24 If you **strike gold**, you find, do, or produce something that brings you a lot of money or success. [JOURNALISM] ❑ *The company has struck gold with its new holiday development, Center Parcs.* PHRASE: V inflects

25 If you **strike it rich**, you make a lot of money, especially in a short time. [INFORMAL] ❑ *He hoped to strike it rich by investing in ginseng.* PHRASE: V inflects

26 to **strike a chord** → see **chord**. to **strike home** → see **home**. to **strike it lucky** → see **lucky**. to **strike a happy medium** → see **medium**.

♦ **strike back** If you **strike back**, you harm or criticize someone who has harmed or criticized you. ❑ *Our instinctive reaction when someone causes us pain is to strike back... Sometimes, Kappy got angry and struck back at him in whatever way she could.* PHRASAL VERB; V P; V P *at* n

♦ **strike down** If someone **is struck down**, especially by an illness, they are killed or severely harmed by it. [WRITTEN] ❑ *Frank had been struck down by a massive heart attack.* PHRASAL VERB: usu passive; *be* V-ed P

♦ **strike off** If someone such as a doctor or lawyer **is struck off**, their name is removed from the official register and they are not allowed to do medical or legal work any more. [BRIT] ❑ *...a company lawyer who had been struck off for dishonest practices... He could be struck off the medical register.* PHRASAL VERB: usu passive; *be* V-ed P; *be* V-ed P n

♦ **strike out** 1 If you **strike out**, you begin to do something different, often because you want to become more independent. ❑ *She wanted me to strike out on my own, buy a business. ...a desire to make changes and to strike out in new directions.* PHRASAL VERB; V P; V P

2 If you **strike out at** someone, you hit, attack, or speak angrily to them. ❑ *He seemed always ready to strike out at anyone and for any cause... Frampton struck out blindly, hitting not Waddington, but an elderly man.* PHRASAL VERB; V P *at* n; V P

3 If someone **strikes out**, they fail. [AM, INFORMAL] ❑ *The lawyer admitted that he was the firm's second lawyer. The first one had struck out completely.* PHRASAL VERB; V P

4 → See also **strike 19**.

♦ **strike up** 1 When you **strike up** a conversation or friendship with someone, you begin one. [WRITTEN] ❑ *I trailed her into Penney's and struck up a conversation.* PHRASAL VERB; V P n (not pron)

2 When musicians **strike up** a piece of music, or when music **strikes up**, the music begins. ❑ *And then the orchestra struck up the National Anthem... The band struck up, and riders paraded round the ring.* PHRASAL VERB; V P n (not pron); V P

**strike-breaker** **(strike-breakers)** also **strikebreaker**. A **strike-breaker** is a person who continues to work during a strike, or someone who takes over the work of a person who is on strike. N-COUNT

**strik|er** /straɪkəʳ/ **(strikers)** 1 In football and some other team sports, a **striker** is a player who mainly attacks and scores goals, rather than defends. ❑ *...and the England striker scored his sixth goal of the season.* N-COUNT

2 → See also **strike**.

**strik|ing** /straɪkɪŋ/ ◆◇◇ 1 Something that is **striking** is very noticeable or unusual. ❑ *The most striking feature of those statistics is the high proportion of suicides... He bears a striking resemblance to Lenin.* ♦ **strik|ing|ly** *In one respect, however, the men really were strikingly similar. ...a strikingly handsome man.* ADJ; ADV: usu ADV adj

2 Someone who is **striking** is very attractive, in a noticeable way. ❑ *She was a striking woman with long blonde hair.* ADJ

3 → See also **strike**.

**Strim|mer** /strɪməʳ/ **(Strimmers)** A **Strimmer** is an electric tool used for cutting long grass or grass at the edge of a lawn. It cuts the grass with a piece of plastic cord which goes round very fast. [TRADEMARK] N-COUNT

**string** /strɪŋ/ **(strings, stringing, strung)** ◆◇◇

1 **String** is thin rope made of twisted threads, used for tying things together or tying up parcels. ❑ *He held out a small bag tied with string. ...a shiny metallic coin on a string.* N-VAR

2 A **string of** things is a number of them on a piece of string, thread, or wire. ❑ *She wore a string of pearls around her neck. ...a string of fairy lights.* N-COUNT: usu N *of* n

3 A **string of** places or objects is a number of them that form a line. ❑ *The landscape is broken only by a string of villages... A string of five rowing boats set out from the opposite bank.* N-COUNT: usu sing, usu N *of* n

4 A **string of** similar events is a series of them that happen one after the other. ❑ *The incident was the latest in a string of attacks.* N-COUNT: usu sing, usu N *of* n

5 The **strings** on a musical instrument such as a violin or guitar are the thin pieces of wire or nylon stretched across it that make sounds when the instrument is played. ❑ *He went off to change a guitar string. ...a twenty-one-string harp.* N-COUNT

6 **The strings** are the section of an orchestra which consists of stringed instruments played with a bow. ❑ *The strings provided a melodic background to the passages played by the soloist... There was a 20-member string section.* N-PLURAL: oft N n

7 In computing, a **string** is a particular series of letters, numbers, symbols, or spaces, for example a word or phrase that you want to search for in a document. N-COUNT

8 If you **string** something somewhere, you hang it up between two or more objects. ❑ *He had strung a banner across the wall.* ♦ **String up** means the same as **string**. ❑ *People were stringing up decorations on the fronts of their homes.* VERB; V n prep/adv; PHRASAL VERB; V P n (not pron); Also V n P

9 → See also **highly strung, purse strings, second string, strung out.**

**PHRASES** 10 If something is offered to you with **no strings attached** or with **no strings**, it is offered without any special conditions. ❑ *Aid should be given to developing countries with no strings attached. ...no-strings grants that last for five years.* PHRASE

11 If you **pull strings**, you use your influence with other people in order to get something done, often unfairly. PHRASE: V inflects

♦ **string along** If you **string** someone **along**, you deceive them by letting them believe you have the same desires, beliefs, or hopes as them. [INFORMAL] ❑ *She took advantage of him, stringing him along even after they were divorced.* PHRASAL VERB; V n P

♦ **string together** If you **string** things **together**, you form something from them by adding them to each other, one at a time. ❑ *As speech develops, the child starts to string more words together... The speaker strung together a series of jokes.* PHRASAL VERB; V n P; V P n

♦ **string up** To **string** someone **up** means to kill them by hanging them. [INFORMAL] ❑ *Guards rushed into his cell and strung him up.* PHRASAL VERB; V n P; Also V P n (not pron)

**string bean** **(string beans)** 1 **String beans** are long, very narrow green vegetables consisting of the cases that contain the seeds of a climbing plant. [AM] N-COUNT: usu pl

in BRIT, use **French beans**

2 **String beans** are vegetables similar to French beans, but thicker. [BRIT] N-COUNT: usu pl

**stri̲nged i̲n|stru|ment (stringed instruments)** A **stringed instrument** is a musical instrument that has strings, such as a violin or a guitar. N-COUNT

**strin|gen|cy** /strɪndʒənsi/ Financial **stringency** is a situation in which a government or person does not have much money or is trying not to spend much. [FORMAL] ❑ *In times of financial stringency it is clear that public expenditure has to be closely scrutinized.* N-UNCOUNT: supp N

**strin|gent** /strɪndʒənt/ **Stringent** laws, rules, or conditions are very severe or are strictly controlled. [FORMAL] ❑ *He announced that there would be more stringent controls on the possession of weapons... Its drug-testing procedures are the most stringent in the world.* ♦ **strin|gent|ly** *He is determined to see the Act enforced more stringently.* ADJ; ADV: ADV with v

**string|er** /strɪŋər/ **(stringers)** A **stringer** is a journalist who is employed part-time by a newspaper or news service in order to report on a particular area. [JOURNALISM] ❑ *He picked up extra money as a local stringer for the New York Herald.* N-COUNT

**stri̲ng quar|te̲t (string quartets)** 1 A **string quartet** is a group of four musicians who play stringed instruments together. The instruments are two violins, a viola, and a cello. ❑ *...a recital by the Borodin String Quartet.* N-COUNT 2 A **string quartet** is a piece of music played on two violins, a viola, and a cello. ❑ *...Dvorak's String Quartet Opus 34.* N-COUNT

**stringy** /strɪŋi/ **(stringier, stringiest)** **Stringy** food contains long, thin pieces that are difficult or unpleasant to eat. ❑ *The meat was stringy.* ADJ

**strip** /strɪp/ **(strips, stripping, stripped)** ◆◇◇ 1 A **strip of** something such as paper, cloth, or food is a long, narrow piece of it. ❑ *...a new kind of manufactured wood made by pressing strips of wood together and baking them... Serve dish with strips of fresh raw vegetables.* N-COUNT: usu N *of* n 2 A **strip of** land or water is a long narrow area of it. ❑ *The coastal cities of Liguria sit on narrow strips of land lying under steep mountains. ...a short boat ride across a narrow strip of water.* N-COUNT: usu N *of* n = stretch 3 A **strip** is a long street in a city or town, where there are a lot of stores, restaurants, and hotels. [AM] ❑ *...Goff's Charcoal Hamburgers on Lover's Lane, a busy commercial strip in North Dallas.* N-COUNT 4 If you **strip**, you take off your clothes. ❑ *They stripped completely, and lay in the damp grass... Women residents stripped naked in protest.* VERB V, V adj ♦ **Strip off** means the same as **strip**. ❑ *The children were brazenly stripping off and leaping into the sea.* PHRASAL VERB V P 5 If someone **is stripped**, their clothes are taken off by another person, for example in order to search for hidden or illegal things. ❑ *One prisoner claimed he'd been dragged to a cell, stripped and beaten.* ➔ See also **strip-search**. VERB: usu passive, *be* V-ed 6 To **strip** something means to remove everything that covers it. ❑ *After Mike left for work I stripped the beds and vacuumed the carpets... The floorboards in both this room and the dining room have been stripped, sanded and sealed.* VERB V n, V n 7 If you **strip** an engine or a piece of equipment, you take it to pieces so that it can be cleaned or repaired. ❑ *Volvo's three-man team stripped the car and restored it.* VERB V n ♦ **Strip down** means the same as **strip**. ❑ *In five years I had to strip the water pump down four times... I stripped down the two SU carburettors, cleaned and polished the pieces and rebuilt the units.* PHRASAL VERB V n P, V P n (not pron) 8 To **strip** someone **of** their property, rights, or titles means to take those things away from them. ❑ *A senior official was stripped of all his privileges for publicly criticising his employer.* VERB *be* V-ed *of* n, Also V n *of* n 9 In a newspaper or magazine, a **strip** is a series of drawings which tell a story. The words spoken by the characters are often written on the drawings. [AM] ❑ *...the Doonesbury strip.* N-COUNT 10 ➔ See also **landing strip**.

♦ **strip away** 1 To **strip away** something, especially something that hides the true nature of a thing, means to remove it completely. ❑ *Altman strips away the pretence and mythology to expose the film industry as a business like any other.* PHRASAL VERB V P n (not pron) 2 To **strip away** a layer of something means to remove it completely. ❑ *Sensitive Cream will not strip away the skin's protective layer... She'd managed to strip the bloodied rags away from Nellie's body.* PHRASAL VERB V P n (not pron), V n P *from* n

♦ **strip down** ➔ see **strip 7**.

♦ **strip off** If you **strip off** your clothes, you take them off. ❑ *He stripped off his wet clothes and stepped into the shower.* ➔ See also **strip 4**. PHRASAL VERB V P n (not pron)

**stri̲p car|to̲on (strip cartoons)** A **strip cartoon** is the same as a **comic strip**. [BRIT] N-COUNT

**stri̲p club (strip clubs)** A **strip club** is a club which people go to in order to see striptease. N-COUNT

**stripe** /straɪp/ **(stripes)** 1 A **stripe** is a long line which is a different colour from the areas next to it. ❑ *She wore a bright green jogging suit with a white stripe down the sides... The walls in the front bedroom are painted with broad, pale blue and white stripes.* N-COUNT 2 In the armed forces or the police, **stripes** are V-shaped bands of material sewn onto a uniform to indicate the rank of corporal or sergeant. In the United States, **stripes** can also show the length of time that a person has served in an organization. ❑ *...a soldier with a corporal's stripes on his arms.* N-COUNT: usu pl

**striped** /straɪpt/ Something that is **striped** has stripes on it. ❑ *...a bottle green and maroon striped tie. ...striped wallpaper.* ADJ: usu ADJ n

**strip|ey** /straɪpi/ ➔ see **stripy**.

**stri̲p joint (strip joints)** A **strip joint** is the same as a **strip club**. [INFORMAL] N-COUNT

**stri̲p light (strip lights)** also **strip-light.** A **strip light** is an electric light in the form of a long tube. [BRIT] N-COUNT

**stri̲p light|ing** also **strip-lighting. Strip lighting** is a method of lighting which uses long tubes rather than light bulbs. [BRIT] ❑ *Other causes of migraine are VDU screens and strip-lighting.* N-UNCOUNT

**strip|ling** /strɪplɪŋ/ **(striplings)** People sometimes refer to a young man as a **stripling** when they want to indicate in a slightly humorous way that although he is no longer a boy, he is not yet really a man. [OLD-FASHIONED] ❑ *...a stripling of 20.* N-COUNT

**stri̲p mine (strip mines)** A **strip mine** is a mine in which the coal, metal, or mineral is near the surface, and so underground passages are not needed. [AM] N-COUNT

☑ in BRIT, use **opencast mine**

**stri̲p min|ing** also **strip-mining. Strip mining** is a method of mining that is used when a mineral is near the surface and underground passages are not needed. [AM] N-UNCOUNT

☑ in BRIT, use **opencast mining**

**strip|per** /strɪpər/ **(strippers)** A **stripper** is a person who earns money by taking their clothes off in public, especially as part of a show. ❑ *She worked as a stripper and did some acting. ...a male stripper.* N-COUNT

**stri̲p-search (strip-searches, strip-searching, strip-searched)** also **strip search.** If a person is **strip-searched**, someone such as a police officer makes them take off all their clothes and searches them, usually to see if they are carrying drugs or weapons. Compare **body search**. ❑ *All 23 of them were strip-searched for drugs.* VERB: usu passive, *be* V-ed *for* n, Also *be* V-ed

**strip|tease** /strɪptiːz, AM -tiːz/ **(stripteases)** also **strip-tease. Striptease** is a form of entertainment in which someone slowly takes off their clothes in a sexually exciting way, usually while music is played. N-VAR

**stripy** /straɪpi/ also **stripey.** Something that is **stripy** has stripes on it. [INFORMAL] ❑ *He was wearing a stripy shirt and baggy blue trousers.* ADJ: usu ADJ n = stripey

**strive** /straɪv/ **(strives, striving)**

☑ The past tense is either **strove** or **strived**, and the past participle is either **striven** or **strived**.

If you **strive to** do something or **strive for** something, you make a great effort to do it or get it. ❑ *He strives hard to keep himself very fit... Mr* VERB V to-inf

*Annan said the region must now strive for economic development as well as peace.* V for n

**strobe** /stroʊb/ **(strobes)** A **strobe** or a **strobe light** is a very bright light which flashes on and off very quickly. N-COUNT: oft N n

**strode** /stroʊd/ **Strode** is the past tense and past participle of **stride**.

**stroke** /stroʊk/ **(strokes, stroking, stroked)** ◆◇◇
[1] If you **stroke** someone or something, you move your hand slowly and gently over them. ❑ *Carla, curled up on the sofa, was smoking a cigarette and stroking her cat... She walked forward and embraced him and stroked his tousled white hair.* VERB; V n; V n
[2] If someone has a **stroke**, a blood vessel in their brain bursts or becomes blocked, which may kill them or make them unable to move one side of their body. ❑ *He had a minor stroke in 1987, which left him partly paralysed.* N-COUNT: usu sing
[3] The **strokes** of a pen or brush are the movements or marks that you make with it when you are writing or painting. ❑ *Fill in gaps by using short, upward strokes of the pencil.* N-COUNT: usu pl
[4] When you are swimming or rowing, your **strokes** are the repeated movements that you make with your arms or the oars. ❑ *I turned and swam a few strokes further out to sea.* N-COUNT: usu pl
[5] A swimming **stroke** is a particular style or method of swimming. ❑ *She spent hours practising the breast stroke.* N-COUNT: usu sing, supp N
[6] The **strokes** of a clock are the sounds that indicate each hour. ❑ *On the stroke of 12, fireworks suddenly exploded into the night.* N-COUNT
[7] In sports such as tennis, baseball, cricket, and golf, a **stroke** is the action of hitting the ball. ❑ *Compton was sending the ball here, there, and everywhere with each stroke.* N-COUNT
[8] **A stroke of** luck or good fortune is something lucky that happens. ❑ *It didn't rain, which turned out to be a stroke of luck.* N-SING: *a* N *of* n
[9] **A stroke of** genius or inspiration is a very good idea that someone suddenly has. ❑ *At the time, his appointment seemed a stroke of genius.* N-SING: *a* N *of* n
PHRASES [10] If something happens **at a stroke** or **in one stroke**, it happens suddenly and completely because of one single action. ❑ *The disease wiped out 40 million rabbits at a stroke... How can Britain reduce its prison population in one stroke?* PHRASE: PHR after v
[11] If someone does not **do a stroke of** work, they are very lazy and do no work at all. [INFORMAL] ❑ *I never did a stroke of work at college.* PHRASE: with brd-neg, V inflects [emphasis]

**stroll** /stroʊl/ **(strolls, strolling, strolled)** If you **stroll** somewhere, you walk there in a slow, relaxed way. ❑ *He collected some orange juice from the refrigerator and, glass in hand, strolled to the kitchen window.* ♦ **Stroll** is also a noun. ❑ *After dinner, I took a stroll round the city.* VERB; V prep/adv; N-COUNT

**stroll|er** /stroʊləʳ/ **(strollers)** A **stroller** is a small chair on wheels, in which a baby or small child can sit and be wheeled around. [AM] N-COUNT

✓ in BRIT, use **pushchair**

**strong** /strɒŋ, AM strɔːŋ/ **(stronger** /strɒŋgəʳ, AM strɔːŋgər/, **strongest** /strɒŋgɪst, AM strɔːŋgɪst/**)** ◆◆◆
[1] Someone who is **strong** is healthy with good muscles and can move or carry heavy things, or do hard physical work. ❑ *I'm not strong enough to carry him... I feared I wouldn't be able to control such a strong horse.* ADJ ≠weak
[2] Someone who is **strong** is confident and determined, and is not easily influenced or worried by other people. ❑ *He is sharp and manipulative with a strong personality... It's up to managers to be strong and do what they believe is right.* ADJ ≠weak
[3] **Strong** objects or materials are not easily broken and can support a lot of weight or resist a lot of strain. ❑ *The vacuum flask has a strong casing, which won't crack or chip... Glue the mirror in with a strong adhesive.* ♦ **strong|ly** *The fence was very strongly built, with very large posts.* ADJ ≠weak; ADV: ADV -ed
[4] A **strong** wind, current, or other force has a lot of power or speed, and can cause heavy things to move. ❑ *Strong winds and torrential rain combined to make conditions terrible for golfers in the Scottish Open... A fairly strong current seemed to be moving the whole boat.* ♦ **strong|ly** *The metal is strongly attracted to the surface.* ADJ = powerful; ADV: ADV with v
[5] A **strong** impression or influence has a great effect on someone. ❑ *We're glad if our music makes a strong impression, even if it's a negative one... Teenage idols have a strong influence on our children.* ♦ **strong|ly** *He is strongly influenced by Spanish painters such as Goya and El Greco.* ADJ; ADV: ADV with v
[6] If you have **strong** opinions on something or express them using **strong** words, you have extreme or very definite opinions which you are willing to express or defend. ❑ *She is known to hold strong views on Cuba... There has been strong criticism of the military regime... It condemned in extremely strong language what it called Britain's iniquitous campaign.* ♦ **strong|ly** *Obviously you feel very strongly about this... We are strongly opposed to the presence of America in this region.* ADJ: usu ADJ n; ADV: usu ADV with v
[7] If someone in authority takes **strong** action, they act firmly and severely. ❑ *The government has said it will take strong action against any further strikes.* ADJ: usu ADJ n
[8] If there is a **strong** case or argument for something, it is supported by a lot of evidence. ❑ *The testimony presented offered a strong case for acquitting her on grounds of self-defense... The evidence that such investment promotes growth is strong.* ♦ **strong|ly** *He argues strongly for retention of NATO as a guarantee of peace... These are conditions said by doctors to be strongly indicative of heart failure.* ADJ; ADV: ADV with v, ADV adj/adv
[9] If there is a **strong** possibility or chance that something is true or will happen, it is very likely to be true or to happen. ❑ *There is a strong possibility that the cat contracted the condition by eating contaminated pet food.* ADJ
[10] Your **strong** points are your best qualities or talents, or the things you are good at. ❑ *Discretion is not Jeremy's strong point... Cynics argue that the EU is stronger on rhetoric than on concrete action.* ADJ: ADJ n, v-link ADJ *on* n
[11] A **strong** competitor, candidate, or team is good or likely to succeed. ❑ *She was a strong contender for Britain's Olympic team.* ADJ: usu ADJ n
[12] If a relationship or link is **strong**, it is close and likely to last for a long time. ❑ *He felt he had a relationship strong enough to talk frankly to Sarah... Delhi first began to develop strong ties with Moscow in the 1950s.* ADJ
[13] A **strong** currency, economy, or industry has a high value or is very successful. ❑ *The US dollar continued its strong performance in Tokyo today... The local economy is strong and the population is growing.* ADJ = robust ≠weak
[14] If something is a **strong** element or part of something else, it is an important or large part of it. ❑ *We are especially encouraged by the strong representation, this year, of women in information technology disciplines.* ADJ
[15] You can use **strong** when you are saying how many people there are in a group. For example, if a group is twenty strong, there are twenty people in it. ❑ *Ukraine indicated that it would establish its own army, 400,000 strong. ...a 1,000-strong crowd.* ADJ: num ADJ
[16] A **strong** drink, chemical, or drug contains a lot of the particular substance which makes it effective. ❑ *Strong coffee or tea late at night may cause sleeplessness.* ADJ
[17] A **strong** colour, flavour, smell, sound, or light is intense and easily noticed. ❑ *As she went past there was a gust of strong perfume... The wine goes with strong and mild cheese alike.* ♦ **strong|ly** *He leaned over her, smelling strongly of sweat.* ADJ; ADV: ADV with v
[18] If someone has a **strong** accent, they speak in a distinctive way that shows very clearly what country or region they come from. ❑ *'Good, Mr Ryle,' he said in English with a strong French accent.* ADJ = pronounced ≠slight
[19] You can say that someone has **strong** features or a **strong** face if their face has large, distinctive features. ❑ *He had a strong Greek nose and olive-black eyes.* ADJ
[20] If someone or something is still **going strong**, they are still alive, in good condition, or popular after a long time. [INFORMAL] ❑ *The old machinery was still going strong.* PHRASE: v-link PHR

**strong-arm** If you refer to someone's behaviour as **strong-arm** tactics or methods, you disapprove of it because it consists of using threats or force in order to achieve something. ❑ *The money has been recovered without resorting to verbal abuse or strong-arm tactics.* ADJ: ADJ n [disapproval]

**strong|hold** /strɒŋhoʊld, AM strɔːŋ-/ **(strongholds)** N-COUNT: oft N *of* n = *bastion* If you say that a place or region is a **stronghold of** a particular attitude or belief, you mean that most people there share this attitude or belief. ❑ *The seat was a stronghold of the Labour party.*

**strong|man** /strɒŋmæn, AM strɔːŋ-/ **(strongmen)** N-COUNT If you refer to a male political leader as a **strongman**, you mean that he has great power and control over his country, although his methods may sometimes be violent or morally wrong. [JOURNALISM] ❑ *He was a military strongman who ruled the country after a coup.*

**strong-minded** ADJ [approval] If you describe someone, especially a woman, as **strong-minded**, you approve of them because they have their own firm attitudes and opinions, and are not easily influenced by other people. ❑ *She is a strong-minded, independent woman.*

**strong-willed** ADJ = *headstrong* ≠ *weak-willed* Someone who is **strong-willed** has a lot of determination and always tries to do what they want, even though other people may advise them not to. ❑ *He is a very determined and strong-willed person.*

**strop|py** /strɒpi/ **(stroppier, stroppiest)** ADJ Someone who is **stroppy** is bad-tempered and gets angry or upset with people. [BRIT, INFORMAL] ❑ *The gas people haven't called to repair the cooker so I shall have to get stroppy with them.*

**strove** /stroʊv/ **Strove** is a past tense of **strive**.

**struck** /strʌk/ **Struck** is the past tense and past participle of **strike**.

**struc|tur|al** /strʌktʃərəl/ ADJ: usu ADJ n **Structural** means relating to or affecting the structure of something. ❑ *The explosion caused little structural damage to the office towers themselves.* ♦ **struc|tur|al|ly** ADV: ADV adj/-ed, ADV with cl *When we bought the house, it was structurally sound, but I decided to redecorate throughout.*

**struc|tur|al en|gi|neer** **(structural engineers)** N-COUNT A **structural engineer** is an engineer who works on large structures such as roads, bridges, and large buildings.

**struc|tur|al|ism** /strʌktʃərəlɪzəm/ N-UNCOUNT **Structuralism** is a method of interpreting and analysing such things as language, literature, and society, which focuses on contrasting ideas or elements of structure and attempts to show how they relate to the whole structure. [TECHNICAL]

**struc|tur|al|ist** /strʌktʃərəlɪst/ **(structuralists)** 1 N-COUNT A **structuralist** is someone whose work is based on structuralism. 2 ADJ: ADJ n **Structuralist** is used to refer to people and things that are connected with structuralism. ❑ *There are two main structuralist techniques incorporated into critical social research.*

**struc|ture** /strʌktʃəʳ/ **(structures, structuring, structured)** ◆◆◇ 1 N-VAR: usu with supp, oft N *of* n The **structure of** something is the way in which it is made, built, or organized. ❑ *The typical family structure of Freud's patients involved two parents and two children... The chemical structure of this particular molecule is very unusual.* 2 N-COUNT: usu with supp A **structure** is something that consists of parts connected together in an ordered way. ❑ *The feet are highly specialised structures made up of 26 small delicate bones.* 3 N-COUNT = *building* A **structure** is something that has been built. ❑ *About half of those funds has gone to repair public roads, structures and bridges.* 4 VERB If you **structure** something, you arrange it in a careful, organized pattern or system. V n ❑ *By structuring the course this way, we're forced to produce something the companies think is valuable.* 5 → See also **report structure**.

**strug|gle** /strʌgəl/ **(struggles, struggling, struggled)** ◆◆◇ 1 VERB If you **struggle to** do something, you try hard to do it, even though other people or things may be making it difficult for you to succeed. V prep ❑ *They had to struggle against all kinds of adversity...* V to-inf *Those who have lost their jobs struggle to pay their supermarket bills.* 2 N-VAR: oft N prep, N to-inf A **struggle** is a long and difficult attempt to achieve something such as freedom or political rights. ❑ *Life became a struggle for survival. ...a young lad's struggle to support his poverty-stricken family... He is currently locked in a power struggle with his Prime Minister.* 3 VERB If you **struggle** when you are being held, you twist, kick, and move violently in order to get free. V ❑ *I struggled, but he was a tall man, well-built.* 4 V-RECIP If two people **struggle with** each other, they fight. pl-n V ❑ *She screamed at him to 'stop it' as they struggled on the ground...* V *with* n *There were signs that she struggled with her attacker.* ♦ N-COUNT **Struggle** is also a noun. ❑ *He died in a struggle with prison officers less than two months after coming to Britain.* 5 VERB If you **struggle to** move yourself or **to** move a heavy object, you try to do it, but it is difficult. V to-inf ❑ *I could see the young boy struggling to free himself...* V prep *I struggled with my bags, desperately looking for a porter.* 6 VERB: only cont If a person or organization **is struggling**, they are likely to fail in what they are doing, even though they might be trying very hard. V to-inf ❑ *The company is struggling to find buyers for its new product...* V prep *One in five young adults was struggling with everyday mathematics...* V *By the 1960s, many shipyards were struggling.* 7 N-SING: *a* N An action or activity that is **a struggle** is very difficult to do. ❑ *Losing weight was a terrible struggle.*

♦ **struggle on** PHRASAL VERB If you **struggle on**, you continue doing something rather than stopping, even though it is difficult. V P ❑ *Why should I struggle on to please my parents?...* V P *with* n *The rest of the world struggles on with its perpetual problems, poverty and debt.*

**strum** /strʌm/ **(strums, strumming, strummed)** VERB If you **strum** a stringed instrument such as a guitar, you play it by moving your fingers backwards and forwards across the strings. V n ❑ *In the corner, one youth sat alone, softly strumming a guitar...* V prep/adv *Vaska strummed away on his guitar.* ♦ N-SING: oft N *of* n **Strum** is also a noun. ❑ *A little while later, I heard the strum of my father's guitar as he began to sing.*

**strung** /strʌŋ/ **Strung** is the past tense and past participle of **string**.

**strung out** 1 ADJ: usu v-link ADJ, usu ADJ prep If things are **strung out** somewhere, they are spread out in a line. ❑ *Buildings were strung out on the north side of the river.* 2 ADJ: v-link ADJ, usu ADJ *on* n If someone is **strung out on** drugs, they are heavily affected by drugs. [INFORMAL] ❑ *He was permanently strung out on heroin.*

**strut** /strʌt/ **(struts, strutting, strutted)** 1 VERB [disapproval] Someone who **struts** walks in a proud way, with their head held high and their chest out, as if they are very important. V prep/adv ❑ *He struts around town like he owns the place.* 2 N-COUNT A **strut** is a piece of wood or metal which holds the weight of other pieces in a building or other structure. ❑ *...the struts of a suspension bridge.*

**strych|nine** /strɪkniːn, AM -naɪn/ N-UNCOUNT **Strychnine** is a very poisonous drug which is sometimes used in very small amounts as a medicine.

**stub** /stʌb/ **(stubs, stubbing, stubbed)** 1 N-COUNT: with supp The **stub** of a cigarette or a pencil is the last short piece of it which remains when the rest has been used. ❑ *He pulled the stub of a pencil from behind his ear. ...an ashtray of cigarette stubs.* 2 N-COUNT: usu n N A ticket **stub** is the part that you keep when you go in to watch a performance. ❑ *Fans who still have their original ticket stubs should contact Sheffield Arena by July 3.* 3 N-COUNT: usu n N A cheque **stub** is the small part that you keep as a record of what you have paid. 4 VERB If you **stub** your **toe**, you hurt it by accidentally kicking something. V n ❑ *I stubbed my toes against a table leg.*

♦ **stub out** PHRASAL VERB = *put out* When someone **stubs out** a cigarette, they put it out by pressing it against something hard. V P n (not pron) ❑ *Signs across the entrances warn all visitors to stub out their cigarettes.*

**stub|ble** /stʌbəl/ 1 N-UNCOUNT **Stubble** is the short stalks which are left standing in fields after corn or wheat has been cut. ❑ *The stubble was burning in the fields.* 2 N-UNCOUNT The very short hairs on a man's face when he has not shaved recently are referred to as **stubble**. ❑ *His face was covered with the stubble of several nights.*

**stub|bly** /stʌbəli/ If a man has not shaved recently, he has a **stubbly** chin. ❑ *He had long unkempt hair and a stubbly chin.* ADJ: usu ADJ n

**stub|born** /stʌbəʳn/ [1] Someone who is **stubborn** or who behaves in a **stubborn** way is determined to do what they want and is very unwilling to change their mind. ❑ *He is a stubborn character used to getting his own way.* ADJ = obstinate ♦ **stub|born|ly** *He stubbornly refused to tell her how he had come to be in such a state.* ADV ♦ **stub|born|ness** *I couldn't tell if his refusal to talk was simple stubbornness.* N-UNCOUNT [2] A **stubborn** stain or problem is difficult to remove or to deal with. ❑ *This treatment removes the most stubborn stains.* ADJ: usu ADJ n = persistent ♦ **stub|born|ly** *Some interest rates have remained stubbornly high.* ADV

**stub|by** /stʌbi/ An object that is **stubby** is shorter and thicker than usual. ❑ *He pointed a stubby finger at a wooden chair opposite him.* ADJ = stumpy

**stuc|co** /stʌkoʊ/ **Stucco** is a type of plaster used for covering walls and decorating ceilings. N-UNCOUNT: oft N n

**stuck** /stʌk/ [1] **Stuck** is the past tense and past participle of **stick**. [2] If something is **stuck** in a particular position, it is fixed tightly in this position and is unable to move. ❑ *He said his car had got stuck in the snow... She had got something stuck between her teeth.* ADJ: v-link ADJ, oft ADJ prep/adv [3] If you are **stuck** in a place, you want to get away from it, but are unable to. ❑ *I was stuck at home with flu.* ADJ: v-link ADJ prep/adv [4] If you are **stuck** in a boring or unpleasant situation, you are unable to change it or get away from it. ❑ *I don't want to get stuck in another job like that.* ADJ: v-link ADJ prep/adv = trapped [5] If something is **stuck** at a particular level or stage, it is not progressing or changing. ❑ *The negotiations have got stuck on a number of key issues... US unemployment figures for March showed the jobless rate stuck at 7 per cent.* ADJ: v-link ADJ prep/adv [6] If you are **stuck with** something that you do not want, you cannot get rid of it. ❑ *Many people are now stuck with expensive fixed-rate mortgages.* ADJ: v-link ADJ *with* n [7] If you get **stuck** when you are trying to do something, you are unable to continue doing it because it is too difficult. ❑ *They will be there to help if you get stuck.* ADJ: v-link ADJ, oft ADJ *on* n [8] If you **get stuck in**, you do something with enthusiasm and determination. [BRIT, INFORMAL] ❑ *We're bottom of the league and we have to get stuck in.* PHRASE: V inflects

**stuck-up** If you say that someone is **stuck-up**, you mean that are very proud and unfriendly because they think they are very important. [INFORMAL] ❑ *She was a famous actress, but she wasn't a bit stuck-up.* ADJ [disapproval]

**stud** /stʌd/ **(studs)** [1] A **studs** are small pieces of metal which are attached to a surface for decoration. ❑ *You see studs on lots of London front doors.* N-COUNT [2] A **stud** is an earring consisting of a small shape attached to a bar which goes through a hole in your ear. ❑ *...plain gold studs.* N-COUNT [3] **Studs** are small round objects attached to the bottom of boots, especially sports boots, so that the person wearing them does not slip. [BRIT] N-COUNT

✔ in AM, use **cleats**

[4] Horses or other animals that are kept for **stud** are kept to be used for breeding. ❑ *He was voted horse of the year and then was retired to stud.* N-UNCOUNT [5] ➔ See also **press stud**.

**stud book** **(stud books)** also **studbook.** A **stud book** is a written record of the breeding of a particular horse, especially a racehorse. N-COUNT

**stud|ded** /stʌdɪd/ [1] Something that is **studded** is decorated with studs or things that look like studs. ❑ *...studded leather jackets.* ADJ: oft ADJ *with* n [2] ➔ See also **star-studded**.

**stu|dent** /stjuːdᵊnt, stuː-/ **(students)** [1] A **student** is a person who is studying at a university or college. ❑ *Warren's eldest son is an art student, at St Martin's. ...a 23-year-old medical student.* ➔ See also **mature student**. ◆◆◆ N-COUNT [2] A **student** is a child who is studying at a secondary school. N-COUNT = pupil [3] Someone who is a **student of** a particular subject is interested in the subject and spends time learning about it. ❑ *...a passionate student of nineteenth century history.* N-COUNT: N *of* n

**stu|dents' un|ion** **(students' unions)** or **student union** [1] **The students' union** is the students' organization in a university or college which organizes leisure activities, provides welfare services, and represents students' political interests. [BRIT] N-COUNT: oft *the* N, oft in names [2] **The students' union** is the building where the students' union organization has its offices and which usually has a shop, a coffee bar, and a meeting place. N-SING: *the* N

**stud farm** **(stud farms)** A **stud farm** is a place where horses are bred. N-COUNT

**stud|ied** /stʌdid/ A **studied** action is deliberate or planned. ❑ *'We both have an interesting 10 days coming up,' said Alex Ferguson with studied understatement.* ➔ See also **study**. ADJ: ADJ n ≠ unstudied

**stu|dio** /stjuːdioʊ, stuː-/ **(studios)** [1] A **studio** is a room where a painter, photographer, or designer works. ❑ *She was in her studio again, painting onto a large canvas.* ◆◆◇ N-COUNT [2] A **studio** is a room where radio or television programmes are recorded, CDs are produced, or films are made. ❑ *She's much happier performing live than in a recording studio.* N-COUNT [3] You can also refer to film-making or recording companies as **studios**. ❑ *She wrote to Paramount Studios and asked if they would audition her.* N-COUNT: usu pl [4] A **studio** is a small flat with one room for living and sleeping in, a kitchen, and a bathroom. You can also talk about a **studio flat** in British English or a **studio apartment** in American English. ❑ *I live on my own in a studio flat.* N-COUNT

**stu|dio audi|ence** **(studio audiences)** A **studio audience** is a group of people who are in a television or radio studio watching while a programme is being made, so that their clapping, laughter, or questions are recorded on the programme. N-COUNT-COLL

**stu|di|ous** /stjuːdiəs, stuː-/ Someone who is **studious** spends a lot of time reading and studying books. ❑ *I was a very quiet, studious little girl.* ADJ

**stu|di|ous|ly** /stjuːdiəsli, stuː-/ If you do something **studiously**, you do it carefully and deliberately. ❑ *When I looked at Clive, he studiously avoided my eyes.* ADV: usu ADV with v, also ADV adj

**study** /stʌdi/ **(studies, studying, studied)** [1] If you **study**, you spend time learning about a particular subject or subjects. ❑ *...a relaxed and happy atmosphere that will allow you to study to your full potential... He went to Hull University, where he studied History and Economics... The rehearsals make it difficult for her to study for law school exams.* ◆◆◆ VERB V, V n, V *for* n [2] **Study** is the activity of studying. ❑ *...the use of maps and visual evidence in the study of local history... She gave up her studies to have Alexander.* N-UNCOUNT: also N in pl [3] A **study** of a subject is a piece of research on it. ❑ *Recent studies suggest that as many as 5 in 1000 new mothers are likely to have this problem.* N-COUNT: usu with supp [4] You can refer to educational subjects or courses that contain several elements as **studies** of a particular kind. ❑ *...a new centre for Islamic studies... She is currently doing a business studies course at Leeds.* N-PLURAL: supp N [5] If you **study** something, you look at it or watch it very carefully, in order to find something out. ❑ *Debbie studied her friend's face for a moment.* VERB V n [6] If you **study** something, you consider it or observe it carefully in order to be able to understand it fully. ❑ *I know that you've been studying chimpanzees for thirty years now... I invite every citizen to carefully study the document.* VERB V n, V n [7] A **study** by an artist is a drawing which is done in preparation for a larger picture. N-COUNT [8] A **study** is a room in a house which is used for reading, writing, and studying. N-COUNT [9] ➔ See also **studied**, **case study**.

**stuff** /stʌf/ **(stuffs, stuffing, stuffed)** [1] You can use **stuff** to refer to things such as a substance, a collection of things, events, or ideas, or the contents of something in a general way without mentioning the thing itself by name. [INFORMAL] ❑ *I'd like some coffee, and I don't object to the* ◆◆◇ N-UNCOUNT: usu with supp *powdered stuff if it's all you've got... 'What do you want to know?' — 'About life and stuff.'... He pointed to a duffle bag.'That's my stuff.'* [2] If you **stuff** something somewhere, you push it there quickly and roughly. ❑ *I stuffed my hands in my pockets... He stuffed the newspapers into a litter bin and headed down the street.* [3] If you **stuff** a container or space **with** something, you fill it with something or with a quantity of things until it is full. ❑ *He grabbed my purse, opened it and stuffed it full, then gave it back to me... He still stood behind his cash register stuffing his mouth with popcorn.* [4] If you **stuff yourself**, you eat a lot of food. [INFORMAL] ❑ *I could stuff myself with ten chocolate bars and half an hour later eat a big meal.* ♦ **stuffed** *But you're just so stuffed you won't be able to drink anything.* [5] If you **stuff** a bird such as a chicken or a vegetable such as a pepper, you put a mixture of food inside it before cooking it. ❑ *Will you stuff the turkey and shove it in the oven for me? ...stuffed tomatoes.* [6] If a dead animal **is stuffed**, it is filled with a substance so that it can be preserved and displayed. [7] **Stuff** is used in front of nouns to emphasize that you do not care about something, or do not want it. [INFORMAL] ❑ *Ultimately my attitude was: stuff them... Stuff your money. We don't want a handout.* [8] If you say that someone **knows** their **stuff**, you mean that they are good at doing something because they know a lot about it. [INFORMAL] ❑ *These chaps know their stuff after seven years of war.*

VERB = *shove* | V n prep/adv | V n prep/adv | VERB = *cram* | V n adj | V n *with* n | VERB | V pron-refl prep | ADJ: v-link ADJ | VERB | V n | V-ed | VERB: usu passive | VERB: only imper | emphasis | V n | V n | PHRASE: V inflects | approval

**stuffed ani|mal** **(stuffed animals)** **Stuffed animals** are toys that are made of cloth filled with a soft material and which look like animals. [AM]
N-COUNT = *stuffed toy*

✔ in BRIT, use **soft toy**

**stuffed shirt** **(stuffed shirts)** If you describe someone, especially someone with an important position, as a **stuffed shirt**, you mean that they are extremely formal and old-fashioned. [INFORMAL] ❑ *In a pinstriped suit he instantly looked like a stuffed shirt.*
N-COUNT | disapproval

**stuffed toy** **(stuffed toys)** A **stuffed toy** is the same as a **stuffed animal**. [AM]
N-COUNT

✔ in BRIT, use **soft toy**

**stuff|ing** /stʌfɪŋ/ **(stuffings)** [1] **Stuffing** is a mixture of food that is put inside a bird such as a chicken, or a vegetable such as a pepper, before it is cooked. ❑ *Chestnuts can be used at Christmas time, as a stuffing for turkey, guinea fowl or chicken.* [2] **Stuffing** is material that is used to fill things such as cushions or toys in order to make them firm or solid.
N-MASS | N-UNCOUNT

**stuffy** /stʌfi/ **(stuffier, stuffiest)** [1] **Stuffy** people or institutions are formal and old-fashioned. ❑ *Why were grown-ups always so stuffy and slow to recognize good ideas? ...a firm of lawyers in Lincoln's Inn, immensely stuffy and respectable.* [2] If it is **stuffy** in a place, it is unpleasantly warm and there is not enough fresh air. ❑ *It was hot and stuffy in the classroom.*
ADJ | disapproval | ADJ

**stul|ti|fy** /stʌltɪfaɪ/ **(stultifies, stultifying, stultified)** If something **stultifies** you, it makes you feel empty or dull in your mind, because it is so boring. [FORMAL] ❑ *This attitude stultifies scientific progress.* ♦ **stul|ti|fy|ing** *A rigid routine can be stultifying and boring.*
VERB | V n | ADJ

**stum|ble** /stʌmbᵊl/ **(stumbles, stumbling, stumbled)** [1] If you **stumble**, you put your foot down awkwardly while you are walking or running and nearly fall over. ❑ *He stumbled and almost fell... I stumbled into the telephone box and dialed 999.* ♦ **Stumble** is also a noun. ❑ *I make it into the darkness with only one stumble.* [2] If you **stumble** while you are reading aloud or speaking, you make a mistake, and have to pause before saying the words properly. ❑ *...his voice wavered and he stumbled over the words at one point.*
VERB | V | V prep/adv | N-COUNT: usu sing | VERB | V *over* n Also V

♦ **stumble across** or **stumble on** If you **stumble across** something or **stumble on** it, you find it or discover it unexpectedly. ❑ *I stumbled across an extremely simple but very exact method for understanding where my money went... History relates that they stumbled on a magnificent waterfall.*
PHRASAL VERB = *come across* | V P n | V P n

**stum|bling block** **(stumbling blocks)** A **stumbling block** is a problem which stops you from achieving something. ❑ *Perhaps the major stumbling block to reunification is the military presence in South Korea.*
N-COUNT: oft N *to/in* n

**stump** /stʌmp/ **(stumps, stumping, stumped)** [1] A **stump** is a small part of something that remains when the rest of it has been removed or broken off. ❑ *If you have a tree stump, check it for fungus... The tramp produced a stump of candle from his deep pockets.* [2] In cricket, the **stumps** are the three wooden sticks that are placed upright in the ground to form the wicket. [3] If you **are stumped** by a question or problem, you cannot think of any solution or answer to it. ❑ *John is stumped by an unexpected question... Well, maybe I stumped you on that one.* [4] If politicians **stump** the country or **stump for** a candidate, they travel around making campaign speeches before an election. [mainly AM] ❑ *When candidates went stumping around the country, people traveled for miles on foot, by horse, by carriage to hear them speak... He was in Georgia stumping for Senator Wyche Fowler, a Democrat.* [5] If politicians are **on the stump**, they are campaigning for an election. [mainly AM] ❑ *The presidential candidates are on the stump today.*
N-COUNT: usu with supp | N-COUNT | VERB | *be* V-ed | V n | VERB | V n | V *for* n Also V | PHRASE: usu v-link PHR

♦ **stump up** If you **stump up** a sum of money, you pay it, often unwillingly. [BRIT, INFORMAL] ❑ *Customers do not have to stump up any cash for at least four weeks.*
PHRASAL VERB = *cough up* | V P n (not pron) Also V P

**stumpy** /stʌmpi/ **Stumpy** things are short and thick. ❑ *Does this dress make my legs look too stumpy?*
ADJ

**stun** /stʌn/ **(stuns, stunning, stunned)** [1] If you **are stunned** by something, you are extremely shocked or surprised by it and are therefore unable to speak or do anything. ❑ *Many cinema-goers were stunned by the film's violent and tragic end.* ♦ **stunned** *When they told me she had gone missing I was totally stunned.* [2] If something such as a blow on the head **stuns** you, it makes you unconscious or confused and unsteady. ❑ *Sam stood his ground and got a blow that stunned him.* [3] → See also **stunning**.
VERB: usu passive | *be* V-ed | ADJ | VERB | V n

**stung** /stʌŋ/ **Stung** is the past tense and past participle of **sting**.

**stunk** /stʌŋk/ **Stunk** is the past participle of **stink**.

**stun|ner** /stʌnəʳ/ **(stunners)** A **stunner** is an extremely attractive woman. [INFORMAL] ❑ *One of the girls was an absolute stunner.*
N-COUNT

**stun|ning** /stʌnɪŋ/ [1] A **stunning** person or thing is extremely beautiful or impressive. ❑ *She was 55 and still a stunning woman.* [2] A **stunning** event is extremely unusual or unexpected. ❑ *The minister resigned last night after a stunning defeat in Sunday's vote.*
ADJ: usu ADJ n | ADJ: usu ADJ n

**stunt** /stʌnt/ **(stunts, stunting, stunted)** [1] A **stunt** is something interesting that is done in order to attract attention and get publicity for the person or company responsible for it. ❑ *In a bold promotional stunt for the movie, he smashed his car into a passing truck.* [2] A **stunt** is a dangerous and exciting piece of action in a film. ❑ *Sean Connery insisted on living dangerously for his new film by performing his own stunts.* [3] If something **stunts** the growth or development of a person or thing, it prevents it from growing or developing as much as it should. ❑ *The heart condition had stunted his growth a bit... High interest rates have stunted economic growth.* ♦ **stunt|ed** *Damage may result in stunted growth and sometimes death of the plant.*
N-COUNT | N-COUNT | VERB | V n | V n | ADJ

**stunt man** **(stunt men)** also **stuntman.** A **stunt man** is a man whose job is to do dangerous things, either for publicity, or in a film instead of
N-COUNT

an actor so that the actor does not risk being injured.

**stunt wom|an** **(stunt women)** also **stuntwoman.** A **stunt woman** is a woman whose job is to do dangerous things, either for publicity, or in a film instead of an actor so that the actor does not risk being injured. N-COUNT

**stu|pefy** /stjuːpɪfaɪ, stuː-/ **(stupefies, stupefying, stupefied)** If something **stupefies** you, it shocks or surprises you so much that you cannot think properly for a while. [FORMAL] ❑ *...a violent slap on the side of the head, which stunned and stupefied him.* VERB; V n

**stu|pen|dous** /stjuːpendəs, AM stuː-/ Something that is **stupendous** is surprisingly impressive or large. ❑ *He was a man of stupendous stamina and energy... This stupendous novel keeps you gripped to the end.* ADJ: usu ADJ n

**stu|pid** /stjuːpɪd, AM stuː-/ **(stupider, stupidest)** ◆◇◇ [1] If you say that someone or something is **stupid**, you mean that they show a lack of good judgment or intelligence and they are not at all sensible. ❑ *I'll never do anything so stupid again... I made a stupid mistake... Your father wouldn't have asked such a stupid question.* ADJ = foolish ♦ **stu|pid|ly** *We had stupidly been looking at the wrong column of figures.* ADV: usu ADV with v, also ADV adj ♦ **stu|pid|ity** /stjuːpɪdɪti, AM stuː-/ **(stupidities)** *I just stared at him, astonished by his stupidity.* N-VAR: usu with poss [2] You say that something is **stupid** to indicate that you do not like it or care about it, or that it annoys you. ❑ *I wouldn't call it art. It's just stupid and tasteless... Friendship is much more important to me than a stupid old ring!* ADJ [disapproval] = silly

**stu|por** /stjuːpəʳ, AM stuː-/ **(stupors)** Someone who is **in a stupor** is almost unconscious and is unable to act or think normally, especially as a result of drink or drugs. ❑ *He fell back onto the sofa in a drunken stupor.* N-COUNT: usu sing, oft *in/into a* N

**stur|dy** /stɜːʳdi/ **(sturdier, sturdiest)** Someone or something that is **sturdy** looks strong and is unlikely to be easily injured or damaged. ❑ *The camera was mounted on a sturdy tripod.* ADJ = robust ♦ **stur|di|ly** *It was a good table too, sturdily constructed of elm.* ADV: usu ADV with v

**stur|geon** /stɜːʳdʒᵊn/ **(sturgeon)** A **sturgeon** is a large fish which lives in northern parts of the world. Sturgeon are usually caught for their eggs, which are known as caviar. N-VAR

**stut|ter** /stʌtəʳ/ **(stutters, stuttering, stuttered)** [1] If someone has a **stutter**, they find it difficult to say the first sound of a word, and so they often hesitate or repeat it two or three times. ❑ *He spoke with a pronounced stutter.* N-COUNT: usu sing = stammer [2] If someone **stutters**, they have difficulty speaking because they find it hard to say the first sound of a word. ❑ *I was trembling so hard, I thought I would stutter when I spoke.* VERB = stammer; V ♦ **stut|ter|ing** *He had to stop talking because if he'd kept on, the stuttering would have started.* N-UNCOUNT [3] If something **stutters** along, it progresses slowly and unevenly. ❑ *The old truck stuttered along the winding road... The political debate stutters on.* VERB; V prep/adv; V prep/adv

**sty** /staɪ/ **(sties)** A **sty** is the same as a **pigsty**. N-COUNT

**stye** /staɪ/ **(styes)** also **sty.** If you have a **stye**, your eyelid is red and swollen because part of it is infected. N-COUNT

**style** /staɪl/ **(styles, styling, styled)** ◆◆◇ [1] The **style** of something is the general way in which it is done or presented, which often shows the attitudes of the people involved. ❑ *Our children's different needs and learning styles created many problems... Belmont Park is a broad sweeping track which will suit the European style of running.* N-COUNT: with supp, also *in* adj N [2] If people or places have **style**, they are smart and elegant. ❑ *Bournemouth, you have to admit, has style... Both love doing things in style... She had not lost her grace and style.* N-UNCOUNT: oft *in* N [3] The **style** of a product is its design. ❑ *His 50 years of experience have given him strong convictions about style... Several styles of hat were available.* N-VAR [4] In the arts, a particular **style** is characteristic of a particular period or group of people. ❑ *...six scenes in the style of a classical Greek tragedy. ...a mixture of musical styles.* N-COUNT: usu with supp [5] If something such as a piece of clothing, a vehicle, or someone's hair **is styled** in a particular way, it is designed or shaped in that way. ❑ *His thick blond hair had just been styled before his trip.* VERB: usu passive; *be* V-ed [6] → See also **old-style**, **self-styled**, **styling**. [7] to **cramp** someone's **style** → see **cramp**.

**-style** /-staɪl/ [1] **-style** combines with nouns and adjectives to form adjectives which describe the style or characteristics of something. ❑ *...the development of a Western-style political system. ...a hearty country-style dinner.* COMB in ADJ: usu ADJ n [2] **-style** combines with adjectives and nouns to form adverbs which describe how something is done. ❑ *Guests have been asked to dress 1920s-style.* COMB in ADV: ADV after v

**styl|ing** /staɪlɪŋ/ [1] The **styling** of an object is the design and appearance of it. ❑ *The car neatly blends classic styling into a smooth modern package.* N-UNCOUNT: oft supp N [2] The **styling** of someone's hair is the way in which it is cut and arranged. ❑ *...shampoos and styling products.* N-UNCOUNT: oft N n [3] → See also **style**.

**styl|ised** /staɪlaɪzd/ → see **stylized**.

**styl|ish** /staɪlɪʃ/ Someone or something that is **stylish** is smart, elegant, and fashionable. ❑ *...a very attractive and very stylish woman of 27. ...a varied choice of stylish designs.* ADJ ♦ **styl|ish|ly** *...stylishly dressed middle-aged women.* ADV

**styl|ist** /staɪlɪst/ **(stylists)** [1] A **stylist** is a person whose job is to cut and arrange people's hair. ❑ *Choose a stylist recommended by someone whose hair you like.* N-COUNT = hairdresser [2] A **stylist** is someone whose job is to create the style of something such as an advertisement or the image of people such as pop singers. ❑ *She is now a writer and fashion stylist.* N-COUNT

**sty|lis|tic** /staɪlɪstɪk/ **Stylistic** describes things relating to the methods and techniques used in creating a piece of writing, music, or art. ❑ *There are some stylistic elements in the statue that just don't make sense.* ADJ: usu ADJ n

**styl|ized** /staɪlaɪzd/

✔ in BRIT, also use **stylised**

Something that is **stylized** is shown or done in a way that is not natural in order to create an artistic effect. ❑ *Some of it has to do with recent stage musicals, which have been very, very stylised.* ADJ

**sty|lus** /staɪləs/ **(styluses)** [1] The **stylus** on a record player is the small needle that picks up the sound signals on the records. N-COUNT = needle [2] A **stylus** is a device like a pen with which you can input written text or drawing directly into a computer. [COMPUTING] ❑ *It has a stylus-operated on-screen keyboard that takes great skill to master.* N-COUNT

**sty|mie** /staɪmi/ **(stymies, stymieing, stymied)** If you **are stymied by** something, you find it very difficult to take action or to continue what you are doing. [INFORMAL] ❑ *Companies have been stymied by the length of time it takes to reach an agreement.* VERB: usu passive; *be* V-ed

**styro|foam** /staɪərəfoum/ **Styrofoam** is a very light, plastic substance, used especially to make containers. [AM] N-UNCOUNT

✔ in BRIT, use **polystyrene**

**suave** /swɑːv/ **(suaver, suavest)** Someone who is **suave** is charming, polite, and elegant, but may be insincere. ❑ *He is a suave, cool and cultured man.* ADJ ♦ **suave|ly** *...the skills needed to deal suavely with a company's senior managers.* ADV

**sub** /sʌb/ **(subs)** [1] In team games such as football, a **sub** is a player who is brought into a match to replace another player. [INFORMAL] ❑ *We had a few injuries and had to use youth team kids as subs.* N-COUNT = substitute [2] A **sub** is the same as a **submarine**. [INFORMAL] N-COUNT [3] A fixed amount of money that you pay regularly in order to be a member of a club or society is called your **subs**. [BRIT, OLD-FASHIONED] ❑ *Subs will be raised as from next year.* N-PLURAL = subscription fees

**sub-** /sʌb-/ [1] **Sub-** is used at the beginning of words that have 'under' as part of their mean- PREFIX ing. ❑ *The waters were rising about the rock and would soon submerge it. ...a nuclear-powered submarine.* [2] **Sub-** is added to the beginning of nouns in order to form other nouns that refer to things that are part of a larger thing. ❑ *...a subcommittee on family values and individual rights. ...the subdivision of farms into smallholdings.* PREFIX [3] **Sub-** is added to the beginning of adjectives in order to form other adjectives that describe someone or something as inferior, for example inferior to normal people or to normal things. ❑ *The cold has made already substandard living conditions even worse.* PREFIX

**sub|al|tern** /sʌbəltəʳn/ **(subalterns)** A **subaltern** is any commissioned officer in the army below the rank of captain. [BRIT] N-COUNT

**sub|atom|ic** /sʌbətɒmɪk/ A **subatomic** particle is a particle which is part of an atom, for example an electron, a proton, or a neutron. [TECHNICAL] ADJ: ADJ n

**sub|com|mit|tee** /sʌbkəmɪti/ **(subcommittees)** also **sub-committee.** A **subcommittee** is a small committee made up of members of a larger committee. N-COUNT-COLL

**sub|con|scious** /sʌbkɒnʃəs/ [1] Your **subconscious** is the part of your mind that can influence you or affect your behaviour even though you are not aware of it. ❑ *...the hidden power of the subconscious... The memory of it all was locked deep in my subconscious.* N-SING: *the* N, N with poss [2] A **subconscious** feeling or action exists in or is influenced by your subconscious. ❑ *He caught her arm in a subconscious attempt to detain her. ...a subconscious cry for affection.* ADJ: usu ADJ n ≠ *conscious*

♦ **sub|con|scious|ly** *Subconsciously I had known that I would not be in personal danger.* ADV: usu ADV with v, also ADV adj

**sub|con|ti|nent** /sʌbkɒntɪnənt/ **(subcontinents)** also **sub-continent.** A **subcontinent** is part of a larger continent, made up of a number of countries that form a large mass of land. **The subcontinent** is often used to refer to the area that contains India, Pakistan, and Bangladesh. N-COUNT: usu sing

**sub|con|tract** /sʌbkəntrækt/ **(subcontracts, subcontracting, subcontracted)**

✔ The verb is pronounced /sʌbkəntrækt/. The noun is pronounced /sʌbkɒntrækt/.

[1] If one firm **subcontracts** part of its work **to** another firm, it pays the other firm to do part of the work that it has been employed to do. [BUSINESS] ❑ *The company is subcontracting production of most of the parts... They are cutting costs by subcontracting work out to other local firms.* VERB = *contract out* V n, V n *to* n [2] A **subcontract** is a contract between a firm which is being employed to do a job and another firm which agrees to do part of that job. N-COUNT

**sub|con|trac|tor** /sʌbkəntræktəʳ, AM -kɑːntræk-/ **(subcontractors)** also **sub-contractor.** A **subcontractor** is a person or firm that has a contract to do part of a job which another firm is responsible for. [BUSINESS] ❑ *The company was considered as a possible subcontractor to build the aeroplane.* N-COUNT

**sub|cul|ture** /sʌbkʌltʃəʳ/ **(subcultures)** also **sub-culture.** A **subculture** is the ideas, art, and way of life of a group of people within a society, which are different from the ideas, art, and way of life of the rest of the society. ❑ *...the latest American subculture.* N-COUNT: usu with supp

**sub|cu|ta|neous** /sʌbkjuteɪniəs/ **Subcutaneous** is used to indicate that something is situated, used, or put under your skin. ❑ *...subcutaneous fat.* ADJ: ADJ n

**sub|di|vide** /sʌbdɪvaɪd/ **(subdivides, subdividing, subdivided)** also **sub-divide.** If something **is subdivided**, it is divided into several smaller areas, parts, or groups. ❑ *The verbs were subdivided into transitive and intransitive categories.* VERB: usu passive, *be* V-ed *into* n

**sub|di|vi|sion** /sʌbdɪvɪʒən/ **(subdivisions)** also **sub-division.** [1] A **subdivision** is an area, part, or section of something which is itself a part of something larger. ❑ *Months are a conventional subdivision of the year.* N-COUNT [2] A **subdivision** is an area of land for building houses on. [AM] ❑ *Rammick lives high on a ridge in a 400-home subdivision.* N-COUNT

**sub|due** /səbdjuː, AM -duː/ **(subdues, subduing, subdued)** [1] If soldiers or the police **subdue** a group of people, they defeat them or bring them under control by using force. ❑ *Senior government officials admit they have not been able to subdue the rebels.* VERB, V n [2] To **subdue** feelings means to make them less strong. ❑ *He forced himself to subdue and overcome his fears.* VERB, V n

**sub|dued** /səbdjuːd, AM -duːd/ [1] Someone who is **subdued** is very quiet, often because they are sad or worried about something. ❑ *The audience are strangely subdued, clapping politely after each song.* ADJ [2] **Subdued** sounds are not very loud. ❑ *The conversation around them was resumed, but in subdued tones.* ADJ [3] **Subdued** lights or colours are not very bright. ❑ *The lighting was subdued.* ADJ

**sub-editor** **(sub-editors)** also **subeditor.** A **sub-editor** is a person whose job it is to check and correct articles in newspapers or magazines before they are printed. [BRIT] N-COUNT

✔ in AM, use **copy editor**

**sub|group** /sʌbgruːp/ **(subgroups)** also **sub-group.** A **subgroup** is a group that is part of a larger group. ❑ *The Action Group worked by dividing its tasks among a large number of subgroups.* N-COUNT

**sub|head|ing** /sʌbhedɪŋ/ **(subheadings)** also **sub-heading.** **Subheadings** are titles that divide part of a piece of writing into shorter sections. N-COUNT

**sub|hu|man** /sʌbhjuːmən/ also **sub-human.** If you describe someone or their situation as **subhuman**, you mean that they behave or live in a much worse way than human beings normally do. ❑ *The Greeks treated women as sub-human.* ADJ

**sub|ject** **(subjects, subjecting, subjected)** ◆◆◇

✔ The noun and adjective are pronounced /sʌbdʒɪkt/. The verb is pronounced /səbdʒekt/.

[1] The **subject** of something such as a conversation, letter, or book is the thing that is being discussed or written about. ❑ *It was I who first raised the subject of plastic surgery. ...the president's own views on the subject.* N-COUNT [2] Someone or something that is the **subject of** criticism, study, or an investigation is being criticized, studied, or investigated. ❑ *Over the past few years, some of the positions Mr. Meredith has adopted have made him the subject of criticism... He's now the subject of an official inquiry.* N-COUNT: N *of* n [3] A **subject** is an area of knowledge or study, especially one that you study at school, college, or university. ❑ *...a tutor in maths and science subjects.* N-COUNT [4] In an experiment or piece of research, the **subject** is the person or animal that is being tested or studied. [FORMAL] ❑ *'White noise' was played into the subject's ears through headphones.* N-COUNT [5] An artist's **subjects** are the people, animals, or objects that he or she paints, models, or photographs. ❑ *Her favourite subjects are shells spotted on beach walks.* N-COUNT: with supp [6] In grammar, the **subject** of a clause is the noun group that refers to the person or thing that is doing the action expressed by the verb. For example, in 'My cat keeps catching birds', 'my cat' is the subject. N-COUNT [7] To be **subject to** something means to be affected by it or to be likely to be affected by it. ❑ *Prices may be subject to alteration... In addition, interest on Treasury issues isn't subject to state and local income taxes.* ADJ: v-link ADJ *to* n [8] If someone is **subject to** a particular set of rules or laws, they have to obey those rules or laws. ❑ *The tribunal is unique because Mr Jones is not subject to the normal police discipline code.* ADJ: v-link ADJ *to* n [9] If you **subject** someone **to** something unpleasant, you make them experience it. ❑ *...the man who had subjected her to four years of beatings and abuse.* VERB, V n *to* n [10] The people who live in or belong to a particular country, usually one ruled by a monarch, are the **subjects** N-COUNT: with supp

of that monarch or country. ❑ *Roughly half of them are British subjects.*

**PHRASES** [11] When someone involved in a conversation **changes the subject**, they start talking about something else, often because the previous subject was embarrassing. ❑ *He tried to change the subject, but she wasn't to be put off.* PHRASE: V inflects [12] If an event will take place **subject to** a condition, it will take place only if that thing happens. ❑ *They denied a report that Egypt had agreed to a summit, subject to certain conditions.* PREP-PHRASE

**sub|jec|tion** /səbdʒekʃən/ **Subjection to** someone involves being completely controlled by them. ❑ *...their complete subjection to their captors. ...the worst forms of economic subjection and drudgery.*

**sub|jec|tive** /səbdʒektɪv/ ADJ ≠ *objective* Something that is **subjective** is based on personal opinions and feelings rather than on facts. ❑ *We know that taste in art is a subjective matter... The way they interpreted their past was highly subjective.* ♦ **sub|jec|tive|ly** ADV ≠ *objectively* *Our preliminary results suggest that people do subjectively find the speech clearer.* ♦ **sub|jec|tiv|ity** N-UNCOUNT ≠ *objectivity* /sʌbdʒəktɪvɪti/ *They accused her of flippancy and subjectivity in her reporting of events in their country.*

**sub|ject mat|ter** also **subject-matter.** N-UNCOUNT = *subject* The **subject matter** of something such as a book, lecture, film, or painting is the thing that is being written about, discussed, or shown. ❑ *Then, attitudes changed and artists were given greater freedom in their choice of subject matter... Her subject matter is herself.*

**sub ju|di|ce** /sʌb dʒuːdɪsi/ also **sub-judice.** ADJ: usu v-link ADJ When something is **sub judice**, it is the subject of a trial in a court of law. In Britain, this means that people are not allowed to discuss it in the media. [LEGAL] ❑ *He declined further comment on the grounds that the case was sub judice.*

**sub|ju|gate** /sʌbdʒʊgeɪt/ **(subjugates, subjugating, subjugated)** [1] VERB If someone **subjugates** a group of people, they take complete control of them, especially by defeating them in a war. [FORMAL] ❑ *Their costly and futile attempt to subjugate the Afghans lasted just 10 years.* V n ♦ **sub|ju|ga|tion** N-UNCOUNT: usu N *of* n /sʌbdʒʊgeɪʃən/ *...the brutal subjugation of native tribes.* [2] VERB: usu passive If your wishes or desires **are subjugated to** something, they are treated as less important than that thing. [FORMAL] ❑ *After having been subjugated to ambition, your maternal instincts are at last starting to assert themselves.* *be* V-ed *to* n Also *be* V-ed

**sub|junc|tive** /səbdʒʌŋktɪv/ N-SING: *the* N In English, a clause expressing a wish or suggestion can be put in **the subjunctive**, or in the **subjunctive** mood, by using the base form of a verb or 'were'. Examples are 'He asked that they be removed' and 'I wish I were somewhere else'. These structures are formal. [TECHNICAL]

**sub|let** /sʌblet/ **(sublets, subletting)**

> ✓ The form **sublet** is used in the present tense and is the past tense and past participle of the verb.

VERB If you **sublet** a building or part of a building, you allow someone to use it and you take rent from them, although you are not the owner and pay rent for it yourself. ❑ *The company rented the building, occupied part and sublet the rest.* V n

**sub|li|mate** /sʌblɪmeɪt/ **(sublimates, sublimating, sublimated)** VERB If you **sublimate** a strong desire or feeling, you express it in a way that is socially acceptable. [TECHNICAL or FORMAL] ❑ *He could try to sublimate the problem by writing, in detail, about it.* V n

**sub|lime** /səblaɪm/ [1] ADJ: usu ADJ n [approval] If you describe something as **sublime**, you mean that it has a wonderful quality that affects you deeply. [LITERARY] ❑ *Sublime music floats on a scented summer breeze to the spot where you lie.* ♦ N-SING: *the* N You can refer to sublime things as **the sublime.** ❑ *She elevated every rare small success to the sublime.* ♦ **sub|lime|ly** ADV: usu ADV adj *...the most sublimely beautiful of all living things.* ● PHRASE: PHR after v If you describe something as going **from the sublime to the ridiculous**, you mean that it involves a change from something very good or serious to something silly or unimportant. ❑ *At times the show veered from the sublime to the ridiculous.* [2] ADJ: usu ADJ n [emphasis] You can use **sublime** to emphasize a quality that someone or something has, usually a quality that is undesirable or negative. [FORMAL or LITERARY] ❑ *The administration's sublime incompetence is probably temporary... He displayed a sublime indifference to the distinction between right and wrong.* ♦ **sub|lime|ly** ADV: usu ADV adj *Mrs Trollope was sublimely uninterested in what she herself wore.*

**sub|limi|nal** /sʌblɪmɪnəl/ ADJ: usu ADJ n **Subliminal** influences or messages affect your mind without you being aware of it. ❑ *Colour has a profound, though often subliminal influence on our senses and moods. ...subliminal advertising.*

**sub-machine gun** **(sub-machine guns)** also **sub-machine-gun, submachine gun.** N-COUNT A **sub-machine gun** is a light portable type of machine gun.

**sub|ma|rine** /sʌbməriːn, AM -riːn/ **(submarines)** [1] N-COUNT A **submarine** is a type of ship that can travel both above and below the surface of the sea. The abbreviation **sub** is also used. ❑ *...a nuclear submarine.* [2] ADJ: ADJ n **Submarine** means existing below the surface of the sea. [FORMAL] ❑ *...submarine caves. ...submarine plants.* [3] N-COUNT: usu N n A **submarine** sandwich is a long soft bread roll filled with a combination of things such as meat, cheese, eggs, and salad. The abbreviation **sub** is also used. [AM]

**sub|ma|rin|er** /sʌbmærɪnəʳ, AM also sʌbməriːnəʳ/ **(submariners)** N-COUNT A **submariner** is a sailor or other person who goes in a submarine.

**sub|merge** /səbmɜːʳdʒ/ **(submerges, submerging, submerged)** [1] VERB If something **submerges** or if you **submerge** it, it goes below the surface of some water or another liquid. ❑ *Hippos are unable to submerge in the few remaining water holes...* V *The river burst its banks, submerging an entire village.* V n [2] VERB If you **submerge yourself in** an activity, you give all your attention to it and do not think about anything else. ❑ *He submerges himself in the world of his imagination.* V pron-refl *in* n

**sub|merged** /səbmɜːʳdʒd/ ADJ If something is **submerged**, it is below the surface of some water. ❑ *My right toe struck against a submerged rock.*

**sub|mers|ible** /səbmɜːʳsɪbəl/ ADJ If something is **submersible**, it can go or operate under water. ❑ *...a submersible pump.*

**sub|mis|sion** /səbmɪʃən/ **(submissions)** [1] N-UNCOUNT: oft *into* N **Submission** is a state in which people can no longer do what they want to do because they have been brought under the control of someone else. ❑ *The army intends to take the city or simply starve it into submission.* [2] N-UNCOUNT: usu *the* N *of* n **The submission of** a proposal, report, or other document is the act of formally sending it to someone, so that they can consider it or decide about it. [FORMAL] ❑ *Diploma and certificate courses do not normally require the submission of a dissertation.* [3] N-COUNT A **submission** is a proposal, report, or other document that is formally sent or presented to someone, so that they can consider or decide about it. ❑ *A written submission has to be prepared.*

**sub|mis|sive** /səbmɪsɪv/ ADJ If you are **submissive**, you obey someone without arguing. ❑ *Most doctors want their patients to be submissive.* ♦ **sub|mis|sive|ly** ADV *The troops submissively laid down their weapons.*

**sub|mit** /səbmɪt/ **(submits, submitting, submitted)** [1] VERB If you **submit to** something, you unwillingly allow something to be done to you, or you do what someone wants, for example because you are not powerful enough to resist. ❑ *In desperation, Mrs. Jones submitted to an operation on her right knee to relieve the pain...* V *to* n *If I submitted to their demands, they would not press the allegations.* V *to* n [2] VERB = *present* If you **submit** a proposal, report, or request **to** someone, you formally send it to them so that they can consider it or decide about it. ❑ *They submitted their reports to the Chancellor yesterday... Head teachers yesterday submitted a claim for a 9 per cent pay rise.* V n *to* n / V n

**sub|nor|mal** /sʌbnɔːʳməl/ also **sub-normal.** If someone is **subnormal**, they have less ability or intelligence than a normal person of their age. [OLD-FASHIONED] ❑ *...educationally subnormal children.* ADJ ♦ **The subnormal** are people who are subnormal. ❑ *She attended a school for the educationally subnormal.* N-PLURAL: *the* N

**sub|or|di|nate** **(subordinates, subordinating, subordinated)**

> ✔ The noun and adjective are pronounced /səbɔːʳdɪnət/. The verb is pronounced /səbɔːʳdɪneɪt/.

1 If someone is your **subordinate**, they have a less important position than you in the organization that you both work for. ❑ *Haig tended not to seek guidance from subordinates.* N-COUNT: oft poss N ≠ superior 2 Someone who is **subordinate to** you has a less important position than you and has to obey you. ❑ *Sixty of his subordinate officers followed his example... Women were regarded as subordinate to free men.* ADJ: oft ADJ *to* n ≠ superior 3 Something that is **subordinate to** something else is less important than the other thing. ❑ *It was an art in which words were subordinate to images.* ADJ: oft ADJ *to* n 4 If you **subordinate** something **to** another thing, you regard it or treat it as less important than the other thing. ❑ *He was both willing and able to subordinate all else to this aim.* VERB V n *to* n ♦ **sub|or|di|na|tion** /səbɔːʳdɪneɪʃən/ *...the social subordination of women.* N-UNCOUNT: oft N *of/to* n

**sub|or|di|nate clause** **(subordinate clauses)** A **subordinate clause** is a clause in a sentence which adds to or completes the information given in the main clause. It cannot usually stand alone as a sentence. Compare **main clause**. [TECHNICAL] N-COUNT

**sub|or|di|nat|ing con|junc|tion** **(subordinating conjunctions)** A **subordinating conjunction** is a word such as 'although', 'because', or 'when' which begins a subordinate clause. Compare **co-ordinating conjunction**. [TECHNICAL] N-COUNT

**sub-plot** **(sub-plots)** also **subplot.** The **sub-plot** in a play, film, or novel is a story that is separate from and less important than the main story. ❑ *...a fascinating sub-plot to the main drama.* N-COUNT

**sub|poe|na** /səpiːnə/ **(subpoenas, subpoenaing, subpoenaed)** 1 A **subpoena** is a legal document telling someone that they must attend a court of law and give evidence as a witness. ❑ *He has been served with a subpoena to answer the charges in court.* N-COUNT 2 If someone **subpoenas** a person, they give them a legal document telling them to attend a court of law and give evidence. If someone **subpoenas** a piece of evidence, the evidence must be produced in a court of law. ❑ *Select committees have the power to subpoena witnesses... The investigation will rely on existing powers to subpoena documents.* VERB V n / V n

**sub|scribe** /səbskraɪb/ **(subscribes, subscribing, subscribed)** 1 If you **subscribe to** an opinion or belief, you are one of a number of people who have this opinion or belief. ❑ *I've personally never subscribed to the view that either sex is superior to the other.* VERB V *to* n 2 If you **subscribe to** a magazine or a newspaper, you pay to receive copies of it regularly. ❑ *My main reason for subscribing to New Scientist is to keep abreast of advances in science.* VERB V *to* n 3 If you **subscribe to** an online newsgroup or service, you send a message saying that you wish to receive it or belong to it. [COMPUTING] ❑ *Usenet is a collection of discussion groups, known as newsgroups, to which anybody can subscribe.* VERB V *to* n Also V 4 If you **subscribe for** shares in a company, you apply to buy shares in that company. [BUSINESS] ❑ *Employees subscribed for far more shares than were available.* VERB V *for* n Also V n

**sub|scrib|er** /səbskraɪbəʳ/ **(subscribers)** 1 A magazine's or a newspaper's **subscribers** are the people who pay to receive copies of it regularly. ❑ *I have been a subscriber to Railway Magazine for many years.* N-COUNT: usu pl, oft N *to* n 2 **Subscribers to** a service are the people who pay to receive the service. ❑ *China has almost 15 million subscribers to satellite and cable television.* N-COUNT: usu pl, oft N *to* n

**sub|scrip|tion** /səbskrɪpʃən/ **(subscriptions)** 1 A **subscription** is an amount of money that you pay regularly in order to belong to an organization, to help a charity or campaign, or to receive copies of a magazine or newspaper. ❑ *You can become a member by paying the yearly subscription.* N-COUNT 2 **Subscription** television is television that you can watch only if you pay a subscription. A **subscription** channel is a channel that you can watch only if you pay a subscription. ADJ: ADJ n

**sub|sec|tion** /sʌbsekʃən/ **(subsections)** also **sub-section.** A **subsection** of a text or a document such as a law is one of the smaller parts into which its main parts are divided. N-COUNT: also N num

**sub|se|quent** /sʌbsɪkwənt/ 1 You use **subsequent** to describe something that happened or existed after the time or event that has just been referred to. [FORMAL] ❑ *...the increase of population in subsequent years... Those concerns were overshadowed by subsequent events.* ◆◇◇ ADJ: ADJ n ≠ previous ♦ **sub|se|quent|ly** *She subsequently became the Faculty's President.* ADV 2 If something happened **subsequent to** something else, it happened after that thing. [FORMAL] ❑ *They won only one more game subsequent to their Cup semi-final win last year.* PHRASE: PHR n/-ing ≠ prior to

**sub|ser|vi|ent** /səbsɜːʳviənt/ 1 If you are **subservient**, you do whatever someone wants you to do. ❑ *She is expected to be subservient to her uncle.* ADJ: oft ADJ *to* n ♦ **sub|ser|vi|ence** /səbsɜːʳviəns/ *...an austere regime stressing obedience and subservience to authority.* N-UNCOUNT 2 If you treat one thing as **subservient to** another, you treat it as less important than the other thing. ❑ *The woman's needs are seen as subservient to the group interest.* ADJ: v-link ADJ *to* n

**sub|set** /sʌbset/ **(subsets)** A **subset of** a group of things is a smaller number of things that belong together within that group. ❑ *...subsets of the population such as men, women, ethnic groups, etc.* N-COUNT: oft N *of* n

**sub|side** /səbsaɪd/ **(subsides, subsiding, subsided)** 1 If a feeling or noise **subsides**, it becomes less strong or loud. ❑ *The pain had subsided during the night.* VERB V 2 If fighting **subsides**, it becomes less intense or general. ❑ *Violence has subsided following two days of riots.* VERB V 3 If the ground or a building **is subsiding**, it is very slowly sinking to a lower level. ❑ *Does that mean the whole house is subsiding?* VERB V 4 If a level of water, especially flood water, **subsides**, it goes down. ❑ *Local officials say the flood waters have subsided.* VERB V

**sub|sid|ence** /səbsaɪdəns, sʌbsɪdəns/ When there is **subsidence** in a place, the ground there sinks to a lower level. N-UNCOUNT

**sub|sid|iari|ty** /səbsɪdiærɪti/ **Subsidiarity** is the principle of allowing the individual members of a large organization to make decisions on issues that affect them, rather than leaving those decisions to be made by the whole group. [TECHNICAL] ❑ *The chancellor knows that the principle of subsidiarity must be guaranteed and shown to work.* N-UNCOUNT

**sub|sidi|ary** /səbsɪdiəri, AM -dieri/ **(subsidiaries)** 1 A **subsidiary** or a **subsidiary** company is a company which is part of a larger and more important company. [BUSINESS] ❑ *...British Asia Airways, a subsidiary of British Airways.* N-COUNT: oft N *of* n, N n 2 If something is **subsidiary**, it is less important than something else with which it is connected. ❑ *The economics ministry has increasingly played a subsidiary role to the finance ministry.* ADJ = secondary

**sub|si|dize** /sʌbsɪdaɪz/ **(subsidizes, subsidizing, subsidized)**

> ✔ in BRIT, also use **subsidise**

VERB
If a government or other authority **subsidizes** something, they pay part of the cost of it. ❑ *At the moment they are existing on pensions that are subsidised by the government.* (V n) ♦ **sub|si|dized** *...heavily subsidized prices for housing, bread, and meat.* (ADJ) ♦ **sub|si|diz|ing** *...the subsidising of London's transport.* (N-UNCOUNT) ♦ **sub|si|di|za|tion** /sʌbsɪdaɪzeɪʃᵊn/ *...the federal government's subsidisation of poorer parts of the country.* (N-UNCOUNT: usu N *of* n)

**sub|si|dy** /sʌbsɪdi/ **(subsidies)** ◆◇◇ N-COUNT
A **subsidy** is money that is paid by a government or other authority in order to help an industry or business, or to pay for a public service. ❑ *European farmers are planning a massive demonstration against farm subsidy cuts.*

**sub|sist** /səbsɪst/ **(subsists, subsisting, subsisted)** VERB
If people **subsist**, they are just able to obtain the food or money that they need in order to stay alive. [FORMAL] ❑ *The prisoners subsisted on one mug of the worst quality porridge three times a day.* (V *on* n)

**sub|sist|ence** /səbsɪstəns/ 1 N-UNCOUNT: oft N n
**Subsistence** is the condition of just having enough food or money to stay alive. ❑ *...below the subsistence level... The standard of living today is on the edge of subsistence.* 2 ADJ: ADJ n
In **subsistence** farming or **subsistence** agriculture, farmers produce food to eat themselves rather than to sell. ❑ *Many black Namibians are subsistence farmers who live in the arid borderlands.*

**sub|soil** /sʌbsɔɪl/ N-UNCOUNT: also *a* N
The **subsoil** is a layer of earth that is just below the surface soil but above hard rock. ❑ *...the chalk subsoil on the site.*

**sub|son|ic** /sʌbsɒnɪk/ ADJ: ADJ n
**Subsonic** speeds or aeroplanes are very fast but slower than the speed of sound. ❑ *This is 20,000 feet higher than most subsonic airliners.*

**sub-species** **(sub-species)** also **subspecies.** N-COUNT: oft N *of* n
A **sub-species of** a plant or animal is one of the types that a particular species is divided into. ❑ *Several other sub-species of gull are found in the region.*

**sub|stance** /sʌbstəns/ **(substances)** ◆◇◇
1 N-COUNT: usu with supp
A **substance** is a solid, powder, liquid, or gas with particular properties. ❑ *There's absolutely no regulation of cigarettes to make sure that they don't include poisonous substances... The substance that's causing the problem comes from the barley.*
2 N-UNCOUNT: oft with brd-neg
**Substance** is the quality of being important or significant. [FORMAL] ❑ *It's questionable whether anything of substance has been achieved... Syria will attend only if the negotiations deal with issues of substance.*
3 N-SING: *the* N *of* n
**The substance of** what someone says or writes is the main thing that they are trying to say. ❑ *The substance of his discussions doesn't really matter.*
4 N-UNCOUNT = truth
If you say that something has no **substance**, you mean that it is not true. [FORMAL] ❑ *There is no substance in any of these allegations.*

**sub-standard** also **substandard.** ADJ
A **sub-standard** service or product is unacceptable because it is below a required standard. ❑ *Residents in general are poor and undereducated, and live in substandard housing.*

**sub|stan|tial** /səbstænʃᵊl/ ◆◇◇ ADJ: usu ADJ n = significant
**Substantial** means large in amount or degree. [FORMAL] ❑ *The party has just lost office and with it a substantial number of seats.*

**sub|stan|tial|ly** /səbstænʃəli/
1 ADV: ADV with v, ADV adj/prep = significantly
If something changes **substantially** or is **substantially** different, it changes a lot or is very different. [FORMAL] ❑ *The percentage of girls in engineering has increased substantially... The price was substantially higher than had been expected.*
2 ADV: ADV adj
If you say that something is **substantially** correct or unchanged, you mean that it is mostly correct or mostly unchanged. [FORMAL] ❑ *He checked the details given and found them substantially correct.*

**sub|stan|ti|ate** /səbstænʃieɪt/ **(substantiates, substantiating, substantiated)** VERB = validate
To **substantiate** a statement or a story means to supply evidence which proves that it is true. [FORMAL] ❑ *There is little scientific evidence to substantiate the claims.* (V n) ♦ **sub|stan|tia|tion** /səbstænʃieɪʃᵊn/ *There may be alternative methods of substantiation other than written records.* (N-UNCOUNT)

**sub|stan|tive** /səbstæntɪv/ ADJ: usu ADJ n
**Substantive** negotiations or issues deal with the most important and central aspects of a subject. [FORMAL] ❑ *They plan to meet again in Rome very soon to begin substantive negotiations.*

**sub|sta|tion** /sʌbsteɪʃᵊn/ **(substations)** also **sub-station.** N-COUNT
A **substation** is a place where high-voltage electricity from power plants is converted to lower-voltage electricity for homes or factories.

**sub|sti|tute** /sʌbstɪtjuːt, AM -tuːt/ **(substitutes, substituting, substituted)** ◆◇◇
1 VERB
If you **substitute** one thing **for** another, or if one thing **substitutes for** another, it takes the place or performs the function of the other thing. ❑ *They were substituting violence for dialogue...* (V n *for* n) *You could always substitute a low-fat soft cheese...* (V n) *Would phone conversations substitute for cosy chats over lunch or in the pub after work?...* (V *for* n) *He was substituting for the injured William Wales.* (V *for* n) ♦ **sub|sti|tu|tion** /sʌbstɪtjuːʃᵊn, AM -tuː-/ **(substitutions)** *In my experience a straight substitution of carob for chocolate doesn't work.* (N-VAR: usu with supp, oft N *of* n)
2 N-COUNT: oft N *for* n
A **substitute** is something that you have or use instead of something else. ❑ *...tests on humans to find a blood substitute made from animal blood.*
3 N-COUNT: with neg, usu sing, N *for* n
If you say that one thing is no **substitute for** another, you mean that it does not have certain desirable features that the other thing has, and is therefore unsatisfactory. If you say that there is no **substitute for** something, you mean that it is the only thing which is really satisfactory. ❑ *The printed word is no substitute for personal discussion with a great thinker... There is no substitute for practical experience.*
4 N-COUNT
In team games such as football, a **substitute** is a player who is brought into a match to replace another player. ❑ *Coming on as a substitute, he scored four crucial goals for Cameroon.*

**sub|sti|tute teach|er** **(substitute teachers)** N-COUNT
A **substitute teacher** is a teacher whose job is to take the place of other teachers at different schools when they are unable to be there. [AM]

☑ in BRIT, use **supply teacher**

**sub|stra|tum** /sʌbstrɑːtəm, AM -streɪt-/ **(substrata)** N-COUNT: with supp, usu N *of* n
A **substratum of** something is a layer that lies under the surface of another layer, or a feature that is less obvious than other features. [FORMAL] ❑ *...its deep substratum of chalk.*

**sub|sume** /səbsjuːm, AM -suːm/ **(subsumes, subsuming, subsumed)** VERB
If something **is subsumed** within a larger group or class, it is included within it, rather than being considered as something separate. [FORMAL] ❑ *After that the two alliances might be subsumed into a new European security system...* (*be* V-ed prep) *With unification, East Germany was subsumed by capitalist West Germany.* (*be* V-ed; Also V n, V n prep)

**sub|ter|fuge** /sʌbtəʳfjuːdʒ/ **(subterfuges)** N-VAR
**Subterfuge** is a trick or a dishonest way of getting what you want. ❑ *Most people can see right through that type of subterfuge.*

**sub|ter|ra|nean** /sʌbtəreɪniən/ ADJ: usu ADJ n = underground
A **subterranean** river or tunnel is under the ground. [FORMAL] ❑ *London has 9 miles of such subterranean passages.*

**sub|text** /sʌbtekst/ **(subtexts)** N-VAR: usu with supp
The **subtext** is the implied message or subject of something that is said or written. ❑ *Europe's divisions are the subtext of a new movie thriller called Zentropa.*

**sub|ti|tle** /sʌbtaɪtᵊl/ **(subtitles)**
1 N-COUNT
The **subtitle** of a piece of writing is a second title which is often longer and explains more than the main title. ❑ *'Kathleen' was, as its 1892 subtitle asserted, 'An Irish Drama'.*
2 N-PLURAL
**Subtitles** are a printed translation of the words of a foreign film that are shown at the bottom of the picture. ❑ *The dialogue is in Spanish, with English subtitles.*

**sub|ti|tled** /sʌbtaɪtəld/ [1] If you say how a book or play **is subtitled**, you say what its subtitle is. ❑ *'Lorna Doone' is subtitled 'a Romance of Exmoor'.* [2] If a foreign film is **subtitled**, a printed translation of the words is shown at the bottom of the picture. ❑ *Much of the film is subtitled. ...subtitled films.*
V-PASSIVE; *be* V-ed with quote; ADJ

**sub|tle** /sʌtəl/ **(subtler, subtlest)** [1] Something that is **subtle** is not immediately obvious or noticeable. ❑ *...the slow and subtle changes that take place in all living things... Intolerance can take subtler forms too.* ♦ **sub|tly** *The truth is subtly different.* [2] A **subtle** person cleverly uses indirect methods to achieve something. ❑ *I even began to exploit him in subtle ways.* ♦ **sub|tly** *What I've tried very subtly to do is to reclaim language.* [3] **Subtle** smells, tastes, sounds, or colours are pleasantly complex and delicate. ❑ *...subtle shades of brown. ...delightfully subtle scents.* ♦ **sub|tly** *...a white sofa teamed with subtly coloured rugs.*
ADJ; ADV; ADJ; ADV: ADV with v; ADJ; ADV

**sub|tle|ty** /sʌtəlti/ **(subtleties)** [1] **Subtleties** are very small details or differences which are not obvious. ❑ *His fascination with the subtleties of human behaviour makes him a good storyteller... When a book goes into translation, all those linguistic subtleties get lost.* [2] **Subtlety** is the quality of being not immediately obvious or noticeable, and therefore difficult to describe. ❑ *Many of the resulting wines lack the subtlety of the original model.* [3] **Subtlety** is the ability to notice and recognize things which are not obvious, especially small differences between things. ❑ *She analyses herself with great subtlety.* [4] **Subtlety** is the ability to use indirect methods to achieve something, rather than doing something that is obvious. ❑ *They had obviously been hoping to approach the topic with more subtlety.*
N-COUNT: usu pl, usu with supp, oft N *of* n; N-UNCOUNT; N-UNCOUNT; N-UNCOUNT

**sub|to|tal** /sʌbtoʊtəl/ **(subtotals)** also **subtotal.** A **subtotal** is a figure that is the result of adding some numbers together but is not the final total.
N-COUNT

**sub|tract** /səbtrækt/ **(subtracts, subtracting, subtracted)** If you **subtract** one number **from** another, you do a calculation in which you take it away from the other number. For example, if you subtract 3 from 5, you get 2. ❑ *Mandy subtracted the date of birth from the date of death... We have subtracted $25 per adult to arrive at a basic room rate.*
VERB ≠ add; V n *from* n; V n

♦ **sub|trac|tion** /səbtrækʃən/ **(subtractions)** *She's ready to learn simple addition and subtraction... I looked at what he'd given me and did a quick subtraction.*
N-VAR ≠ addition

**sub-tropical** also **subtropical. Sub-tropical** places have a climate that is warm and wet, and are often near tropical regions. ❑ *...the sub-tropical region of the Chapare.*
ADJ = semi-tropical

**sub|urb** /sʌbɜːʳb/ **(suburbs)** [1] A **suburb of** a city or large town is a smaller area which is part of the city or large town but is outside its centre. ❑ *Anna was born in 1923 in Ardwick, a suburb of Manchester.* [2] If you live **in the suburbs**, you live in an area of houses outside the centre of a large town or city. ❑ *His family lived in the suburbs. ...Bombay's suburbs.*
N-COUNT: usu with supp, oft N *of* n; N-PLURAL: oft *in the* N

**sub|ur|ban** /səbɜːʳbən/ **Suburban** means relating to a suburb. ❑ *...a suburban shopping centre in Sydney.*
ADJ: ADJ n

**sub|ur|bia** /səbɜːʳbiə/ Journalists often use **suburbia** to refer to the suburbs of cities and large towns considered as a whole. ❑ *...images of bright summer mornings in leafy suburbia.*
N-UNCOUNT

**sub|ver|sion** /səbvɜːʳʃən, AM -ʒən/ **Subversion** is the attempt to weaken or destroy a political system or a government. ❑ *He was arrested in parliament on charges of subversion for organizing the demonstration.*
N-UNCOUNT

**sub|ver|sive** /səbvɜːʳsɪv/ **(subversives)** [1] Something that is **subversive** is intended to weaken or destroy a political system or government. ❑ *This courageous and subversive movie has attracted widespread critical support.* [2] **Subversives** are people who attempt to weaken or destroy a political system or government. ❑ *Agents regularly rounded up suspected subversives.*
ADJ; N-COUNT

**sub|vert** /səbvɜːʳt/ **(subverts, subverting, subverted)** To **subvert** something means to destroy its power and influence. [FORMAL] ❑ *...an alleged plot to subvert the state.*
VERB = undermine; V n

**sub|way** /sʌbweɪ/ **(subways)** [1] A **subway** is an underground railway. [mainly AM] ❑ *...the Bay Area Rapid Transit subway system... I don't ride the subway late at night.*
N-COUNT: oft N n, also *by* N

☑ in BRIT, use **underground, tube**

[2] A **subway** is a passage underneath a busy road or a railway track for people to walk through. [BRIT]
N-COUNT

☑ in AM, use **underpass**

**sub-zero** also **subzero. Sub-zero** temperatures are below 0° centigrade or, in the United States, below 0° Fahrenheit. ❑ *...passengers stranded in sub-zero temperatures.*
ADJ

**suc|ceed** /səksiːd/ **(succeeds, succeeding, succeeded)** ◆◆◇ [1] If you **succeed in** doing something, you manage to do it. ❑ *We have already succeeded in working out ground rules with the Department of Defense... Some people will succeed in their efforts to stop smoking.* [2] If something **succeeds**, it works in a satisfactory way or has the result that is intended. ❑ *...a move which would make any future talks even more unlikely to succeed.* [3] Someone who **succeeds** gains a high position in what they do, for example in business or politics. ❑ *...the skills and qualities needed to succeed in small and medium-sized businesses.* [4] If you **succeed** another person, you are the next person to have their job or position. ❑ *David Rowland is almost certain to succeed him as chairman on January 1... The present ruler, Prince Rainier III, succeeded to the throne on 9 May 1949.* [5] If one thing **is succeeded by** another thing, the other thing happens or comes after it. ❑ *A quick divorce can be succeeded by a much longer – and more agonising – period of haggling over the fate of the family.*
VERB ≠ fail; V *in* -ing/n; V *in* -ing/n; VERB ≠ fail; V; VERB ≠ fail; V; VERB; V n; V *to* n; VERB: usu passive; *be* V-ed

**suc|cess** /səkses/ **(successes)** ◆◆◇ [1] **Success** is the achievement of something that you have been trying to do. ❑ *It's important for the long-term success of any diet that you vary your meals. ...the success of European business in building a stronger partnership between management and workers.* [2] **Success** is the achievement of a high position in a particular field, for example in business or politics. ❑ *Nearly all of the young people interviewed believed that work was the key to success.* [3] The **success** of something is the fact that it works in a satisfactory way or has the result that is intended. ❑ *Most of the cast was amazed by the play's success.* [4] Someone or something that is a **success** achieves a high position, makes a lot of money, or is admired a great deal. ❑ *We hope it will be a commercial success.*
N-UNCOUNT ≠ failure; N-UNCOUNT ≠ failure; N-UNCOUNT: usu with poss ≠ failure; N-COUNT ≠ failure

**suc|cess|ful** /səksesfʊl/ ◆◆◇ [1] Something that is **successful** achieves what it was intended to achieve. Someone who is **successful** achieves what they intended to achieve. ❑ *How successful will this new treatment be?... I am looking forward to a long and successful partnership with him... She has been comparatively successful in maintaining her privacy.* ♦ **suc|cess|ful|ly** *The doctors have successfully concluded preliminary tests.* [2] Something that is **successful** is popular or makes a lot of money. ❑ *...the hugely successful movie that brought Robert Redford an Oscar for his directing... One of the keys to successful business is careful planning.* [3] Someone who is **successful** achieves a high position in what they do, for example in business or politics. ❑ *Women do not necessarily have to imitate men to be successful in business... She is a successful lawyer.*
ADJ: oft ADJ *in* -ing ≠ unsuccessful; ADV: ADV with v; ADJ; ADJ: oft ADJ *in* n ≠ unsuccessful

**suc|ces|sion** /səkseʃən/ **(successions)** [1] A **succession of** things of the same kind is a number of them that exist or happen one after the other. ❑ *Adams took a succession of jobs which have*
N-SING: oft N *of* n, also *in* N

*stood him in good stead... Scoring three goals in quick succession, he made it 10-8.* [2] **Succession** is the fact or right of being the next person to have an important job or position. ❑ *She is now seventh in line of succession to the throne.* N-UNCOUNT: also N in pl

**suc|ces|sive** /səksesɪv/ **Successive** means happening or existing one after another without a break. ❑ *Jackson was the winner for a second successive year.* ADJ

**suc|ces|sor** /səksesəʳ/ **(successors)** Someone's **successor** is the person who takes their job after they have left. ❑ *He set out several principles that he hopes will guide his successors.* N-COUNT: oft poss N, N *to* n

**suc|cess sto|ry (success stories)** Someone or something that is a **success story** is very successful, often unexpectedly or in spite of unfavourable conditions. ❑ *Sock Shop was one of the high-street success stories of the 80s.* N-COUNT

**suc|cinct** /səksɪŋkt/ Something that is **succinct** expresses facts or ideas clearly and in few words. ❑ *The book gives an admirably succinct account of the technology and its history.* ADJ [approval] = *concise*
♦ **suc|cinct|ly** *He succinctly summed up his manifesto as 'Work hard, train hard and play hard'.* ADV: ADV with v

**suc|cor** /sʌkəʳ/ → see **succour**.

**suc|cour** /sʌkəʳ/ **(succours, succouring, succoured)**

✔ in AM, use **succor**

[1] **Succour** is help given to people who are suffering or in difficulties. [FORMAL] ❑ *...a commitment to give succour to populations involved in the conflict.* N-UNCOUNT = *assistance*
[2] If you **succour** someone who is suffering or in difficulties, you help them. [FORMAL] ❑ *Helicopters fly in appalling weather to succour shipwrecked mariners.* VERB = *assist, aid* V n

**suc|cu|lent** /sʌkjʊlənt/ **(succulents)** [1] **Succulent** food, especially meat or vegetables, is juicy and good to eat. ❑ *Cook pieces of succulent chicken with ample garlic and a little sherry.* ADJ [approval]
[2] **Succulents** or **succulent** plants are types of plants which have thick, fleshy leaves. N-COUNT

**suc|cumb** /səkʌm/ **(succumbs, succumbing, succumbed)** If you **succumb to** temptation or pressure, you do something that you want to do, or that other people want you to do, although you feel it might be wrong. [FORMAL] ❑ *Don't succumb to the temptation to have just one cigarette... The Minister said his country would never succumb to pressure.* VERB = *give in* V *to* n V *to* n

**such** /sʌtʃ/ ♦♦♦

✔ When **such** is used as a predeterminer, it is followed by 'a' and a count noun in the singular. When it is used as a determiner, it is followed by a count noun in the plural or by an uncount noun.

[1] You use **such** to refer back to the thing or person that you have just mentioned, or a thing or person like the one that you have just mentioned. You use **such as** and **such...as** to introduce a reference to the person or thing that has just been mentioned. ❑ *There have been previous attempts at coups. We regard such methods as entirely unacceptable... There'd be no telling how John would react to such news as this.* DET: DET n, DET n *as* pron ♦ **Such** is also a predeterminer. ❑ *If your request is for information about a child, please contact the Registrar to find out how to make such a request... How can we make sense of such a story as this?* PREDET: PREDET *a* n ♦ **Such** is also used before **be**. ❑ *We are scared because we are being watched – such is the atmosphere in Pristina and other cities in Kosovo.* *such be* ♦ **As such** is also used. ❑ *There should be a law ensuring products tested on animals have to be labelled as such.* -ed *as such* ♦ **Such as** is also used. ❑ *Issues such as these were not really his concern.* *such as* pron [2] You use **such...as** to link something or someone with a clause in which you give a description of the kind of thing or person that you mean. ❑ *Each member of the alliance agrees to take such action as it deems necessary, including the use of armed force... Britain is not enjoying such prosperity as it was in the mid-1980s.* DET: DET n *as* cl ♦ **Such as** is also used. ❑ *Children do not use inflections such as are used in mature adult speech.* n *such as* cl [3] You use **such...as** to introduce one or more examples of the kind of thing or person that you have just mentioned. ❑ *...such careers as teaching, nursing, hairdressing and catering. ...delays caused by such things as bad weather or industrial disputes.* DET: DET n *as* n ♦ **Such as** is also used. ❑ *...serious offences, such as assault on a police officer.* *such as* n [4] You use **such** before noun groups to emphasize the extent of something or to emphasize that something is remarkable. ❑ *I think most of us don't want to read what's in the newspaper anyway in such detail... The economy was not in such bad shape, he says.* DET [emphasis] ♦ **Such** is also a predeterminer. ❑ *You know the health service is in such a state and it's getting desperate now... It was such a pleasant surprise.* PREDET: PREDET *a* n [5] You use **such...that** in order to emphasize the degree of something by mentioning the result or consequence of it. ❑ *The weather has brought such a demand for beer that one brewery will operate over the weekend... This is something where you can earn such a lot of money that there is not any risk that you will lose it... He was in such a hurry that he almost pushed me over on the stairs.* PREDET: PREDET *a* n that [emphasis] ♦ **Such** is also a determiner. ❑ *She looked at him in such distress that he had to look away.* DET: DET n that ♦ **Such** is also used after **be**. ❑ *Though Vivaldi had earned a great deal in his lifetime, his extravagance was such that he died in poverty.* *be such* that [6] You use **such...that** or **such...as** in order to say what the result or consequence of something that you have just mentioned is. ❑ *The operation has uncovered such backstreet dealing in stolen property that police might now press for changes in the law.* DET: DET n that ♦ **Such** is also a predeterminer. ❑ *He could put an idea in such a way that Alan would believe it was his own.* PREDET: PREDET *a* n that/*as to* ♦ **Such** is also used after **be**. ❑ *OFSTED's brief is such that it can conduct any inquiry or provide any advice which the Secretary of State requires.* *be such* that

**PHRASES** [7] You use **such and such** to refer to a thing or person when you do not want to be exact or precise. [SPOKEN] ❑ *I said, 'Well what time'll I get to Leeds?' and he said such and such a time but I missed my connection.* PHRASE: PHR *a* n, PHR after v [vagueness] [8] You use **such as it is** or **such as they are** to suggest that the thing you have just mentioned is not very good, important, or useful. ❑ *The British Women's Movement, such as it is these days, came up with a programme of speeches at the House of Commons.* PHRASE: n PHR [9] You use **as such** with a negative to indicate that a word or expression is not a very accurate description of the actual situation. ❑ *I am not a learner as such – I used to ride a bike years ago.* PHRASE: usu n PHR [10] You use **as such** after a noun to indicate that you are considering that thing on its own, separately from other things or factors. ❑ *Mr Simon said he was not against taxes as such, 'but I do object when taxation is justified on spurious or dishonest grounds,' he says.* PHRASE: n PHR [11] **no such thing** → see **thing**.

**such|like** /sʌtʃlaɪk/ You use **suchlike** to refer to other things that are like the ones you have already mentioned. ❑ *...objets d'art, gold, silver, and ivory assortments, ceramics, and suchlike.* PRON = *the like* ♦ **Suchlike** is also a determiner. ❑ *The prices of polymers and suchlike materials will decrease.*

**suck** /sʌk/ **(sucks, sucking, sucked)** [1] If you **suck** something, you hold it in your mouth and pull at it with the muscles in your cheeks and tongue, for example in order to get liquid out of it. ❑ *They waited in silence and sucked their sweets... He sucked on his cigarette... Doran was clutching the bottle with both hands and sucking intently.* VERB V n V *on/at* n V [2] If something **sucks** a liquid, gas, or object in a particular direction, it draws it there with a powerful force. ❑ *The pollution-control team is at the scene and is due to start sucking up oil any time now. ...the airline pilot who was almost sucked from the cockpit of his plane when a window shattered.* VERB V n with adv *be* V-ed prep [3] If you **are sucked into** a bad situation, you are unable to prevent yourself from becoming involved in it. V-PASSIVE

❑ *...the extent to which they have been sucked into the cycle of violence.* [4] If someone says that something **sucks**, they are indicating that they think it is very bad. [INFORMAL, RUDE] ❑ *The system sucks.* [5] to **suck** someone **dry** → see **dry**. be V-ed *into* n; VERB: no cont [feelings]; V

♦ **suck up** You say that someone **is sucking up to** a person in authority when you do not like the fact that they are trying to please the person because of the person's position. [INFORMAL] ❑ *She kept sucking up to the teachers, especially Mrs Clements.* PHRASAL VERB [disapproval]; V P *to* n; Also V P

**suck|er** /sʌkəʳ/ **(suckers)** [1] If you call someone a **sucker**, you mean that it is very easy to cheat them. [INFORMAL] ❑ *But that is what the suckers want so you give it them.* [2] If you describe someone as a **sucker for** something, you mean that they find it very difficult to resist it. [INFORMAL] ❑ *I'm such a sucker for romance.* [3] The **suckers** on some animals and insects are the parts on the outside of their body which they use in order to stick to a surface. [4] A **sucker** is a small device used for attaching things to surfaces. It consists of a cup-shaped piece of rubber that sticks to a surface when it is pressed flat. ❑ *...sucker pads.* N-COUNT; N-VOC [disapproval]; N-COUNT: N *for* n; N-COUNT; N-COUNT

**suck|le** /sʌkəl/ **(suckles, suckling, suckled)** [1] When a mother **suckles** her baby, she feeds it by letting it suck milk from her breast. [OLD-FASHIONED] ❑ *A young woman suckling a baby is one of life's most natural and delightful scenes.* [2] When a baby **suckles**, it sucks milk from its mother's breast. [FORMAL] ❑ *As the baby suckles, a further supply of milk is generated.* VERB = breastfeed; V n; VERB = breastfeed; V

**su|crose** /suːkroʊs/ **Sucrose** is a common type of sugar. [TECHNICAL] N-UNCOUNT

**suc|tion** /sʌkʃən/ **(suctions, suctioning, suctioned)** [1] **Suction** is the process by which liquids, gases, or other substances are drawn out of somewhere. ❑ *Dustbags act as a filter and suction will be reduced if they are too full.* [2] If a doctor or nurse **suctions** a liquid, they remove it by using a machine which sucks it away. ❑ *Michael was showing the nurse how to suction his saliva.* [3] **Suction** is the process by which two surfaces stick together when the air between them is removed. ❑ *...their pneumatic robot which uses air to move and sticks to surfaces by suction.* N-UNCOUNT; VERB; V n; N-UNCOUNT: oft N n

**Su|da|nese** /suːdəniːz/ **(Sudanese)** [1] **Sudanese** means belonging or relating to Sudan, or to its people or culture. [2] The **Sudanese** are the people of Sudan. ADJ; N-PLURAL

**sud|den** /sʌdən/ [1] **Sudden** means happening quickly and unexpectedly. ❑ *He had been deeply affected by the sudden death of his father-in-law... She started to thank him, but a sudden movement behind him caught her attention... It was all very sudden.* ♦ **sud|den|ness** *The enemy seemed stunned by the suddenness of the attack.* [2] If something happens **all of a sudden**, it happens quickly and unexpectedly. ❑ *All of a sudden she didn't look sleepy any more.* ♦◇◇ ADJ: usu ADJ n; N-UNCOUNT: oft *the* N *of* n; PHRASE: usu PHR with cl, PHR with v

**sud|den death** **Sudden death** is a way of quickly deciding the winner of something such as a football or basketball game or a golf tournament when there are equal scores at the time when it would normally end. In a **sudden-death** situation, the first team to score a goal or the first golfer to win a hole is the winner. N-UNCOUNT: oft N n

**sud|den|ly** /sʌdənli/ If something happens **suddenly**, it happens quickly and unexpectedly. ❑ *Suddenly, she looked ten years older... Her expression suddenly altered... He sat down suddenly.* ♦♦◇ ADV: usu ADV with cl, ADV with v, also ADV adj

**suds** /sʌdz/ **Suds** are the bubbles that are produced when a substance such as soap is mixed with water. ❑ *He had soap suds in his ears.* N-PLURAL

**sue** /suː/ **(sues, suing, sued)** If you **sue** someone, you start a legal case against them, usually in order to claim money from them because they have harmed you in some way. ❑ *Mr Warren sued him for libel over the remarks... One former patient has already indicated his intention to sue.* VERB; V n *for* n; V

**suede** /sweɪd/ **Suede** is leather with a soft, slightly rough surface. ❑ *Albert wore a brown suede jacket and jeans.* N-UNCOUNT: oft N n

**suet** /suːɪt/ **Suet** is hard animal fat that is used in cooking. N-UNCOUNT: oft N n

**suf|fer** /sʌfəʳ/ **(suffers, suffering, suffered)** ♦♦◇ [1] If you **suffer** pain, you feel it in your body or in your mind. ❑ *Within a few days she had become seriously ill, suffering great pain and discomfort... Can you assure me that my father is not suffering?* [2] If you **suffer from** an illness or from some other bad condition, you are badly affected by it. ❑ *He was eventually diagnosed as suffering from terminal cancer... I realized he was suffering from shock.* [3] If you **suffer** something bad, you are in a situation in which something painful, harmful, or very unpleasant happens to you. ❑ *The peace process has suffered a serious blow now... Romania suffered another setback in its efforts to obtain financial support for its reforms.* [4] If you **suffer**, you are badly affected by an event or situation. ❑ *There are few who have not suffered... It is obvious that Syria will suffer most from this change of heart.* [5] If something **suffers**, it does not succeed because it has not been given enough attention or is in a bad situation. ❑ *I'm not surprised that your studies are suffering... Without a major boost in tourism, the economy will suffer even further.* [6] → See also **suffering**. VERB; V n; V; VERB; V *from* n; V *from* n; VERB; V n; V n; VERB; V; V *from* n; VERB; V; V

**suf|fer|ance** /sʌfrəns/ If you are allowed to do something **on sufferance**, you can do it, although you know that the person who gave you permission would prefer that you did not do it. ❑ *His party held office on sufferance.* N-UNCOUNT: usu *on* N

**suf|fer|er** /sʌfərəʳ/ **(sufferers)** A **sufferer from** an illness or some other bad condition is a person who is affected by the illness or condition. ❑ *Frequently sufferers of this kind of allergy are also sufferers of asthma. ...hay-fever sufferers.* N-COUNT: oft N *from/of* n, n N

**suf|fer|ing** /sʌfərɪŋ/ **(sufferings)** **Suffering** is serious pain which someone feels in their body or their mind. ❑ *It has caused terrible suffering to animals... His many novels have portrayed the sufferings of his race.* → See also **long-suffering**. N-UNCOUNT: also N in pl = torment

**suf|fice** /səfaɪs/ **(suffices, sufficing, sufficed)** [1] If you say that something will **suffice**, you mean it will be enough to achieve a purpose or to fulfil a need. [FORMAL] ❑ *A cover letter should never exceed one page; often a far shorter letter will suffice.* [2] **Suffice it to say** or **suffice to say** is used at the beginning of a statement to indicate that what you are saying is obvious, or that you will only give a short explanation. ❑ *Suffice it to say that afterwards we never met again.* VERB: no cont = do; V; PHRASE: PHR that, PHR with cl

**suf|fi|cien|cy** /səfɪʃənsi/ **Sufficiency of** something is enough of that thing to achieve a purpose or to fulfil a need. [FORMAL] ❑ *There's a sufficiency of drama in these lives to sustain your interest.* → See also **self-sufficiency**. N-UNCOUNT: also *a* N, oft N *of* n ≠ insufficiency

**suf|fi|cient** /səfɪʃənt/ If something is **sufficient for** a particular purpose, there is enough of it for the purpose. ❑ *One metre of fabric is sufficient to cover the exterior of an 18-in-diameter hatbox... There was not sufficient evidence to secure a conviction.* ♦ **suf|fi|cient|ly** *She recovered sufficiently to accompany Chou on his tour of Africa in 1964.* ♦◇◇ ADJ: oft ADJ to-inf, ADJ n to-inf, ADJ *for* n ≠ insufficient; ADV

**suf|fix** /sʌfɪks/ **(suffixes)** [1] A **suffix** is a letter or group of letters, for example '-ly' or '-ness', which is added to the end of a word in order to form a different word, often of a different word class. For example, the suffix '-ly' is added to 'quick' to form 'quickly'. Compare **affix** and **prefix**. [2] A **suffix** is one or more numbers or letters added to the end of a code number to indicate, for example, what area something belongs to. ❑ *These ships were all numbered with the suffix LBK.* N-COUNT; N-COUNT

**suf|fo|cate** /sʌfəkeɪt/ **(suffocates, suffocating, suffocated)** [1] If someone **suffocates** or **is suffocated**, they die because there is no air for them to breathe. ❑ *He either suffocated, or froze* VERB; V to death... They were suffocated as they slept. [be V-ed] ♦ **suf|fo|ca|tion** /sʌfəkeɪʃᵊn/ [N-UNCOUNT] *Many of the victims died of suffocation.* 2 [VERB] If you say that you **are suffocating** or that something **is suffocating** you, you mean that you feel very uncomfortable because there is not enough fresh air and it is difficult to breathe. ❑ *That's better. I was suffocating in that cell of a room...* [V] *The airlessness of the room suffocated her.* [V n] 3 [VERB] You say that a person or thing **is suffocating**, or that something **is suffocating** them, when the situation that they are in does not allow them to act freely or to develop. ❑ *After a few weeks with her parents, she felt she was suffocating...* [V] *The governor's proposals would actually cost millions of jobs and suffocate the economy.* [V n]

**suf|frage** /sʌfrɪdʒ/ [N-UNCOUNT] **Suffrage** is the right of people to vote for a government or national leader. [FORMAL] ❑ *...the women's suffrage movement.*

**suf|fra|gette** /sʌfrədʒet/ (**suffragettes**) [N-COUNT] In the early twentieth century in Britain, a **suffragette** was a woman who was involved in the campaign for women to have the right to vote. ❑ *She was a suffragette and a birth control pioneer.*

**suf|fra|gist** /sʌfrədʒɪst/ (**suffragists**) [N-COUNT] A **suffragist** is a person who is in favour of women having the right to vote, especially in societies where women are not allowed to vote. [mainly AM]

**suf|fuse** /səfjuːz/ (**suffuses, suffusing, suffused**) 1 [VERB] If something, especially a colour or feeling, **suffuses** a person or thing, it gradually spreads over or through them. [LITERARY] ❑ *A dull red flush suffused Selby's face.* [V n] 2 [VERB] If something such as a book, film, or piece of music **is suffused with** a quality, it is full of that quality. [FORMAL] ❑ *This book is suffused with Shaw's characteristic wry Irish humour.* [be V-ed with n]

**Sufi** /suːfi/ (**Sufis**) [N-COUNT: oft N n] A **Sufi** is a member of a very spiritual group of Muslims. ❑ *...the teachings of the Sufi mystics.*

**sug|ar** /ʃʊgəʳ/ (**sugars, sugaring, sugared**) ◆◇◇ 1 [N-UNCOUNT] **Sugar** is a sweet substance that is used to make food and drinks sweet. It is usually in the form of small white or brown crystals. ❑ *...bags of sugar... Ice cream is high in fat and sugar.* ➔ See also **caster sugar**, **confectioners' sugar**, **demerara sugar**, **granulated sugar**, **icing sugar**. 2 [N-COUNT] If someone has one **sugar** in their tea or coffee, they have one small spoon of sugar or one sugar lump in it. ❑ *How many sugars do you take? ...a mug of tea with two sugars.* 3 [VERB] If you **sugar** food or drink, you add sugar to it. ❑ *He sat down and sugared and stirred his coffee.* [V n] 4 [N-COUNT: usu pl] **Sugars** are substances that occur naturally in food. When you eat them, the body converts them into energy. ❑ *Plants produce sugars and starch to provide themselves with energy.* 5 to **sugar the pill** ➔ see **pill**.

**sug|ar beet** (**sugar beets**) [N-VAR] **Sugar beet** is a crop with a large round root. It is grown for the sugar which can be obtained from this root.

**sug|ar bowl** (**sugar bowls**) [N-COUNT] A **sugar bowl** is a small bowl in which sugar is kept.

**sug|ar cane** also **sugarcane.** [N-UNCOUNT] **Sugar cane** is a tall tropical plant. It is grown for the sugar that can be obtained from its thick stems.

**sugar-coated** 1 [ADJ: usu ADJ n] **Sugar-coated** food is covered with a sweet substance made of sugar. ❑ *Some sugar-coated cereals are 50% sugar.* 2 [ADJ: usu ADJ n] [disapproval] If you describe something such as a story as **sugar-coated**, you disapprove of it because it appears to be pleasant or attractive but in fact describes something very unpleasant. ❑ *...a sugar-coated view of a boy's introduction to sex.*

**sug|ar dad|dy** (**sugar daddies**) also **sugar-daddy.** [N-COUNT: usu poss N] A woman's **sugar daddy** is a rich older man who gives her money and presents in return for her company, affection, and usually sexual intercourse. [INFORMAL] ❑ *Actor John Goodman played Melanie Griffith's sugar daddy in the film.*

**sug|ared al|mond** (**sugared almonds**) [N-COUNT: usu pl] **Sugared almonds** are nuts which have been covered with a hard sweet coating.

**sug|ar lump** (**sugar lumps**) also **sugar-lump.** [N-COUNT] **Sugar lumps** are small cubes of sugar. You put them in cups of tea and coffee.

**sug|ary** /ʃʊgəri/ [ADJ: usu ADJ n] **Sugary** food or drink contains a lot of sugar. ❑ *Sugary canned drinks rot your teeth. ...sugary tea.*

**sug|gest** /sədʒest, AM səgdʒ-/ (**suggests, suggesting, suggested**) ◆◆◆ 1 [VERB] If you **suggest** something, you put forward a plan or idea for someone to think about. ❑ *He suggested a link between class size and test results of seven-year-olds...* [V n] *I suggest you ask him some specific questions about his past...* [V that] *I suggested to Mike that we go out for a meal with his colleagues...* [V to n that] *No one has suggested how this might occur...* [V wh] *'Could he be suffering from amnesia?' I suggested...* [V with quote] *So instead I suggested taking her out to dinner for a change.* [V -ing] 2 [VERB] If you **suggest** the name of a person or place, you recommend them to someone. ❑ *Could you suggest someone to advise me how to do this?...* [V n] *They can suggest where to buy one.* [V wh to-inf] 3 [VERB] If you **suggest that** something is the case, you say something which you believe is the case. ❑ *I'm not suggesting that is what is happening...* [V that] *It is wrong to suggest that there are easy alternatives...* [V that] *Their success is conditional, I suggest, on this restriction.* [V that] 4 [VERB] If one thing **suggests** another, it implies it or makes you think that it might be the case. ❑ *Earlier reports suggested that a meeting would take place on Sunday...* [V that] *Its hairy body suggests a mammal.* [V n] 5 [VERB] If one thing **suggests** another, it brings it to your mind through an association of ideas. ❑ *This onomatopoeic word suggests to me the sound a mousetrap makes when it snaps shut.* [V n]

**sug|gest|ible** /sədʒestɪbᵊl, AM səgdʒ-/ [ADJ] Someone who is **suggestible** can be easily influenced by other people. ❑ *...highly suggestible and compliant individuals.*

**sug|ges|tion** /sədʒestʃᵊn, AM səgdʒ-/ (**suggestions**) ◆◇◇ 1 [N-COUNT: oft N of/for n/-ing] If you make a **suggestion**, you put forward an idea or plan for someone to think about. ❑ *The dietitian was helpful, making suggestions as to how I could improve my diet... Perhaps he'd followed her suggestion of a stroll to the river.* 2 [N-COUNT: oft N that] A **suggestion** is something that a person says which implies that something is the case. ❑ *We reject any suggestion that the law needs amending... There are suggestions that he might be supported by the Socialists.* 3 [N-SING: usu with brd-neg, N that, N of n] If there is no **suggestion that** something is the case, there is no reason to think that it is the case. ❑ *There is no suggestion whatsoever that the two sides are any closer to agreeing.* 4 [N-COUNT: usu sing, N of n = hint] If there is a **suggestion of** something, there is a slight amount or sign of it. ❑ *...that fashionably faint suggestion of a tan. ...a firm, well-sprung mattress with not one suggestion of a sag.* 5 [N-UNCOUNT] **Suggestion** means giving people a particular idea by associating it with other ideas. ❑ *The power of suggestion is very strong.*

**sug|ges|tive** /sədʒestɪv, AM səgdʒ-/ 1 [ADJ: v-link ADJ of n] Something that is **suggestive of** something else is quite like it or may be a sign of it. ❑ *The fingers were gnarled, lumpy, with long, curving nails suggestive of animal claws.* 2 [ADJ] **Suggestive** remarks or looks cause people to think about sex, often in a way that makes them feel uncomfortable. ❑ *...another former employee who claims Thomas made suggestive remarks to her.*

**sui|cid|al** /suːɪsaɪdᵊl/ 1 [ADJ] People who are **suicidal** want to kill themselves. ❑ *I was suicidal and just couldn't stop crying.* 2 [ADJ: oft it v-link ADJ to-inf] If you describe an action or behaviour as **suicidal**, you mean that it is very dangerous. ❑ *They realized it would be suicidal to resist in the face of overwhelming military superiority.*

**sui|cide** /suːɪsaɪd/ (**suicides**) ◆◇◇ 1 [N-VAR] People who commit **suicide** deliberately kill themselves because they do not want to continue living. ❑ *She tried to commit suicide on several occasions. ...a grow-*

*ing number of suicides in the community.* [2] You say that people commit **suicide** when they deliberately do something which ruins their career or position in society. ❑ *They say it would be political suicide for the party to abstain.* [3] The people involved in a **suicide** attack, mission, or bombing do not expect to survive. ❑ *According to the army, the teenager said he was on a 'suicide mission' for the movement. ...a suicide bomber.*
N-UNCOUNT: supp N
ADJ: ADJ n

**sui|cide note** **(suicide notes)** A **suicide note** is a note written by someone who intends to kill themselves saying that this is what they are going to do and sometimes explaining why.
N-COUNT

**sui|cide pact** **(suicide pacts)** A **suicide pact** is an arrangement that two or more people make to kill themselves at the same time and usually in the same place. ❑ *Police refused to say if the couple died in a suicide pact.*
N-COUNT

**sui gen|eris** /suːi dʒenərɪs/ If you describe a person or thing as **sui generis**, you mean that there is no-one else or nothing else of the same kind and so you cannot make judgments about them based on other things. [FORMAL] ❑ *Japanese politics are sui generis.*
ADJ
= unique

**suit** /suːt/ **(suits, suiting, suited)** [1] A man's **suit** consists of a jacket, trousers, and sometimes a waistcoat, all made from the same fabric. ❑ *...a dark pin-striped business suit. ...a smart suit and tie.* [2] A woman's **suit** consists of a jacket and skirt, or sometimes trousers, made from the same fabric. ❑ *I was wearing my tweed suit.* [3] A particular type of **suit** is a piece of clothing that you wear for a particular activity. ❑ *...a completely revolutionary atmospheric diving suit.* [4] If something **suits** you, it is convenient for you or is the best thing for you in the circumstances. ❑ *They will only release information if it suits them... They should be able to find you the best package to suit your needs.* [5] If something **suits** you, you like it. ❑ *I don't think a sedentary life would altogether suit me.* [6] If a piece of clothing or a particular style or colour **suits** you, it makes you look attractive. ❑ *Green suits you.* [7] If you **suit yourself**, you do something just because you want to do it, without bothering to consider other people. ❑ *These large institutions make – and change – the rules to suit themselves... He made a dismissive gesture. 'Suit yourself.'* [8] In a court of law, a **suit** is a case in which someone tries to get a legal decision against a person or company, often so that the person or company will have to pay them money for having done something wrong to them. ❑ *Up to 2,000 former employees have filed personal injury suits against the company.* ♦ In American English, you can say that someone **files** or **brings suit against** another person. ❑ *One insurance company has already filed suit against the city of Chicago.* [9] A **suit** is one of the four types of card in a set of playing cards. These are hearts, diamonds, clubs, and spades. [10] → See also **bathing suit**, **birthday suit**, **boiler suit**, **trouser suit**. [11] If people **follow suit**, they do the same thing that someone else has just done. ❑ *Efforts to persuade the remainder to follow suit have continued.*
◆◆◇
N-COUNT
N-COUNT
N-COUNT: n N
VERB: no cont
V n
V n
VERB: no cont
V n
VERB: no cont
V n
VERB
= please
V pron-refl
V pron-refl
N-COUNT
= lawsuit
N-UNCOUNT
N-COUNT
PHRASE: V inflects

**suit|able** /suːtəbᵊl/ Someone or something that is **suitable for** a particular purpose or occasion is right or acceptable for it. ❑ *Employers usually decide within five minutes whether someone is suitable for the job... The authority must make suitable accommodation available to the family.* ♦ **suit|abil|ity** /suːtəbɪlɪti/ *...information on the suitability of a product for use in the home.*
◆◇◇
ADJ: oft ADJ *for* n/-ing
N-UNCOUNT: with supp

**suit|ably** /suːtəbli/ [1] You use **suitably** to indicate that someone or something has the right qualities or things for a particular activity, purpose, or situation. ❑ *There are problems in recruiting suitably qualified scientific officers for NHS laboratories... Unfortunately I'm not suitably dressed for gardening.* [2] If you say that someone or something is, for example, **suitably** impressed or **suitably** dramatic, you mean that they have as much of that quality as you would expect in that situation. ❑ *She flicked her eyes up to make certain I was suitably impressed... Her exit seemed suitably dramatic.*
ADV: ADV adj/-ed
ADV: ADV adj

**suit|case** /suːtkeɪs/ **(suitcases)** A **suitcase** is a box or bag with a handle and a hard frame in which you carry your clothes when you are travelling. ❑ *It did not take Andrew long to pack a suitcase.*
N-COUNT

**suite** /swiːt/ **(suites)** [1] A **suite** is a set of rooms in a hotel or other building. ❑ *They had a fabulous time during their week in a suite at the Paris Hilton. ...a new suite of offices.* → See also **en suite**. [2] A **suite** is a set of matching armchairs and a sofa. ❑ *...a three-piece suite.* [3] A bathroom **suite** is a matching bath, washbasin, and toilet.
N-COUNT
N-COUNT
N-COUNT

**suit|ed** /suːtɪd/ If something is well **suited to** a particular purpose, it is right or appropriate for that purpose. If someone is well **suited to** a particular job, they are right or appropriate for that job. ❑ *The area is well suited to road cycling as well as off-road riding... Satellites are uniquely suited to provide this information.*
ADJ: v-link ADJ, usu adv ADJ *to* n/-ing, ADJ to-inf

**suit|ing** /suːtɪŋ/ **(suitings)** **Suiting** is cloth from which trousers, jackets, skirts, and men's suits are made.
N-MASS

**suit|or** /suːtəʳ/ **(suitors)** [1] A woman's **suitor** is a man who wants to marry her. [OLD-FASHIONED] ❑ *My mother had a suitor who adored her.* [2] A **suitor** is a company or organization that wants to buy another company. [BUSINESS] ❑ *The company was making little progress in trying to find a suitor.*
N-COUNT
N-COUNT

**sul|fate** /sʌlfeɪt/ → see **sulphate**.

**sul|fide** /sʌlfaɪd/ → see **sulphide**.

**sul|fur** /sʌlfəʳ/ → see **sulphur**.

**sul|fu|ric acid** /sʌlfjʊərɪk æsɪd/ → see **sulphuric acid**.

**sul|fur|ous** /sʌlfərəs/ → see **sulphurous**.

**sulk** /sʌlk/ **(sulks, sulking, sulked)** If you **sulk**, you are silent and bad-tempered for a while because you are annoyed about something. ❑ *He turned his back and sulked.* ♦ **Sulk** is also a noun. ❑ *He went off in a sulk... Now she must be tired of my sulks.*
VERB
V
N-COUNT: oft *in/into* a N

**sulky** /sʌlki/ Someone who is **sulky** is sulking or is unwilling to enjoy themselves. ❑ *I was quite sulky, so I didn't take part in much. ...a sulky adolescent.*
ADJ

**sul|len** /sʌlᵊn/ Someone who is **sullen** is bad-tempered and does not speak much. ❑ *The offenders lapsed into a sullen silence.*
ADJ

**sul|ly** /sʌli/ **(sullies, sullying, sullied)** [1] If something **is sullied by** something else, it is damaged so that it is no longer pure or of such high value. [FORMAL] ❑ *The City's reputation has been sullied by scandals like those at Lloyd's... She claimed they were sullying her good name.* [2] If someone **sullies** something, they make it dirty. [FORMAL] ❑ *I felt loath to sully the gleaming brass knocker by handling it.*
VERB
be V-ed
V n
VERB
V n

**sul|phate** /sʌlfeɪt/ **(sulphates)**

✓ in AM, use **sulfate**

A **sulphate** is a salt of sulphuric acid. ❑ *...copper sulphate. ...sulphate of potash.*
N-MASS: oft n N, N *of* n

**sul|phide** /sʌlfaɪd/ **(sulphides)**

✓ in AM, use **sulfide**

A **sulphide** is a compound of sulphur with some other chemical elements. ❑ *...hydrogen sulphide.*
N-MASS: oft n N

**sul|phur** /sʌlfəʳ/

✓ in AM, use **sulfur**

**Sulphur** is a yellow chemical which has a strong smell. ❑ *The air reeks of sulphur.*
N-UNCOUNT

**sul|phu|ric acid** /sʌlfjʊərɪk æsɪd/

✓ in AM, use **sulfuric acid**

**Sulphuric acid** is a colourless, oily, and very powerful acid.
N-UNCOUNT

**sul|phur|ous** /sʌlfərəs/

✓ in AM, use **sulfurous**

**Sulphurous** air or places contain sulphur or smell of sulphur. ❑ *...sulphurous volcanic gases.* ADJ: usu ADJ n

**sul|tan** /sʌltən/ **(sultans)** A **sultan** is a ruler in some Muslim countries. ❑ *...during the reign of Sultan Abdul Hamid.* N-TITLE; N-COUNT

**sul|tana** /sʌltɑːnə, -tæn-/ **(sultanas) Sultanas** are dried white grapes. [BRIT] N-COUNT: usu pl

**sul|try** /sʌltri/ 1 **Sultry** weather is hot and damp. [WRITTEN] ❑ *The climax came one sultry August evening.* 2 Someone who is **sultry** is attractive in a way that suggests hidden passion. [WRITTEN] ❑ *...a dark-haired sultry woman.* ADJ: usu ADJ n; ADJ

**sum** /sʌm/ **(sums, summing, summed)** 1 A **sum of** money is an amount of money. ❑ *Large sums of money were lost... Even the relatively modest sum of £50,000 now seems beyond his reach.* 2 A **sum** is a simple calculation in arithmetic. ❑ *I can't do my sums.* 3 In mathematics, **the sum of** two numbers is the number that is obtained when they are added together. ❑ *The sum of all the angles of a triangle is 180 degrees.* 4 **The sum of** something is all of it. ❑ *'Public opinion' is only the sum of the views of thousands of people like yourself.* 5 → See also **lump sum.** 6 If you say that something is **more than the sum of** its **parts** or **greater than the sum of** its **parts**, you mean that it is better than you would expect from the individual parts, because the way they combine adds a different quality. ❑ *As individual members' solo careers have proved, each band was greater than the sum of its parts.* ◆◇◇ N-COUNT: oft N *of* n; N-COUNT; N-SING: *the* N *of* n; N-SING: *the* N *of* n; PHRASE: v-link PHR

♦ **sum up** 1 If you **sum** something **up**, you describe it as briefly as possible. ❑ *One voter in Brasilia summed up the mood – 'Politicians have lost credibility,' he complained... Obree summed his weekend up in one word: 'Disastrous.'* 2 If something **sums** a person or situation **up**, it represents their most typical characteristics. ❑ *'I love my wife, my horse and my dog,' he said, and that summed him up... Sadly, the feud sums up the relationship between Lord Bath and the man who succeeds him.* 3 If you **sum up** after a speech or at the end of a piece of writing, you briefly state the main points again. When a judge **sums up** after a trial, he reminds the jury of the evidence and the main arguments of the case they have heard. ❑ *When the judge summed up, it was clear he wanted a guilty verdict.* 4 → See also **summing-up.** PHRASAL VERB V P n (not pron) V n P; PHRASAL VERB = epitomize V n P; V P n (not pron); PHRASAL VERB V P

**sum|ma|rize** /sʌməraɪz/ **(summarizes, summarizing, summarized)**

✓ in BRIT, also use **summarise**

If you **summarize** something, you give a summary of it. ❑ *Table 3.1 summarizes the information given above... Basically, the article can be summarized in three sentences... To summarise, this is a clever approach to a common problem.* VERB V n; *be* V-ed prep/adv; V

**sum|mary** /sʌməri/ **(summaries)** 1 A **summary of** something is a short account of it, which gives the main points but not the details. ❑ *What follows is a brief summary of the process... Here's a summary of the day's news.* ● You use **in summary** to indicate that what you are about to say is a summary of what has just been said. ❑ *In summary, it is my opinion that this complete treatment process was very successful.* 2 **Summary** actions are done without delay, often when something else should have been done first or done instead. [FORMAL] ❑ *It says torture and summary execution are common.* N-COUNT: oft N *of* n = résumé; PHRASE: PHR with cl; ADJ: ADJ n

**sum|mat** /sʌmət/ **Summat** is a British dialect form of the word 'something'. ❑ *Are we going to write a story or summat?*

**sum|ma|tion** /sʌmeɪʃᵊn/ **(summations)** A **summation** is a summary of what someone has said or done. [FORMAL] ❑ *Her introduction is a model of fairness, a lively summation of Irish history.* N-COUNT: usu sing, oft N *of* n = summary

**sum|mer** /sʌməʳ/ **(summers) Summer** is the season between spring and autumn. In the summer the weather is usually warm or hot. ❑ *I escaped the heatwave in London earlier this summer and flew to Cork... It was a perfect summer's day. ...in the summer of 1987. ...the summer holidays... He used to spend childhood summers with his grandparents.* → See also **high summer, Indian summer.** ◆◆◇ N-VAR

**sum|mer camp (summer camps)** In the United States, a **summer camp** is a place in the country where parents can pay to send their children during the school summer holidays. The children staying there can take part in many outdoor and social activities. N-COUNT

**sum|mer house (summer houses)** also **summerhouse.** 1 A **summer house** is a small building in a garden. It contains seats, and people can sit there in the summer. 2 Someone's **summer house** is a house in the country or by the sea where they spend the summer. ❑ *He visited relatives at their summer house on the river.* N-COUNT; N-COUNT

**sum|mer school (summer schools)** 1 A **summer school** is an educational course on a particular subject that is run during the summer. The students usually stay at the place where the summer school is being held. [mainly BRIT] ❑ *...a summer school for young professional singers.* 2 **Summer school** is a summer term at a school, college, or university, for example for students who need extra teaching or who want to take extra courses. [mainly AM] N-VAR; N-VAR

**sum|mer time** also **summertime.** 1 **Summer time** is the period of time during which the summer lasts. ❑ *It's a very beautiful place in the summertime.* 2 → See also **British Summer Time.** N-UNCOUNT: also *the* N

**sum|mery** /sʌməri/ Something that is **summery** is suitable for summer or characteristic of summer. ❑ *...light summery fruit salads.* ADJ

**summing-up (summings-up)** also **summing up.** In a trial, the judge's **summing-up** is the speech the judge makes at the end of the trial to remind the jury of the evidence and the main arguments of the case they have heard. ❑ *There was pandemonium in court as the judge gave his summing-up.* N-COUNT

**sum|mit** /sʌmɪt/ **(summits)** 1 A **summit** is a meeting at which the leaders of two or more countries discuss important matters. ❑ *...next week's Washington summit. ...the NATO summit meeting in Rome.* 2 The **summit** of a mountain is the top of it. ❑ *...the first man to reach the summit of Mount Everest.* ◆◆◇ N-COUNT; N-COUNT

**sum|mon** /sʌmən/ **(summons, summoning, summoned)** 1 If you **summon** someone, you order them to come to you. [FORMAL] ❑ *Howe summoned a doctor and hurried over... Suddenly we were summoned to the interview room... He has been summoned to appear in court on charges of incitement to law-breaking.* 2 If you **summon** a quality, you make a great effort to have it. For example, if you **summon** the courage or strength to do something, you make a great effort to be brave or strong, so that you will be able to do it. ❑ *It took her a full month to summon the courage to tell her mother.* ♦ **Summon up** means the same as **summon.** ❑ *Painfully shy, he finally summoned up courage to ask her to a game.* VERB V n; *be* V-ed prep/adv; *be* V-ed to-inf; VERB V n; PHRASAL VERB V P n (not pron)

♦ **summon up** If something **summons up** a memory or thought, it causes it to come to your mind. [LITERARY] ❑ *The oddest events will summon up memories.* PHRASAL VERB V P n (not pron)

**sum|mons** /sʌmənz/ **(summonses, summonsing, summonsed)** 1 A **summons** is an order to come and see someone. ❑ *I received a summons to the Palace from Sir Robert Fellowes, the Queen's private secretary.* 2 A **summons** is an official order to appear in court. ❑ *She had received a summons to appear in court.* 3 If someone **is summonsed**, they are officially ordered to appear in court. ❑ *The men were summonsed and last week 30 appeared before Hove magistrates.* N-COUNT; N-COUNT; VERB: usu passive *be* V-ed

**sumo** /suːmoʊ/ **Sumo** is the Japanese style of wrestling. ❑ *...a sumo wrestler.* N-UNCOUNT: oft N n

**sump** /sʌmp/ **(sumps)** 1 The **sump** is the place under an engine which holds the engine oil. [mainly BRIT] N-COUNT: oft N n

in AM, use **oil pan**

2 A **sump** is a deep cave which is often filled with water. N-COUNT

**sump|tu|ous** /sʌmptʃuəs/ Something that is **sumptuous** is grand and obviously very expensive. ❑ *She produces elegant wedding gowns in a variety of sumptuous fabrics.* ADJ

**sum to|tal** The **sum total of** a number of things is all the things added or considered together. You often use this expression to indicate that you are disappointed because the total amount is rather small. ❑ *That small room contained the sum total of the family's possessions.* N-SING: usu the N of n = sum

**sun** /sʌn/ **(suns)** 1 **The sun** is the ball of fire in the sky that the Earth goes round, and that gives us heat and light. ❑ *The sun was now high in the southern sky... The sun came out, briefly. ...the sun's rays... The sun was shining.* ◆◆◇ N-SING: usu the N 2 You refer to the light and heat that reach us from the sun as **the sun**. ❑ *Dena took them into the courtyard to sit in the sun.* N-UNCOUNT: usu the N 3 A **sun** is any star which has planets going around it. N-COUNT 4 **Everything under the sun** means a very great number of things. **Anything under the sun** means anything at all. ❑ *We sat there for hours talking about everything under the sun.* PHRASE: PHR after v 5 **a place in the sun** → see **place**.

**Sun.** **Sun.** is a written abbreviation for **Sunday**. ❑ *The Palace is open Mon-Sun.*

**sun-baked** **Sun-baked** land or earth has been made hard and dry by the sun shining on it. ❑ *...a dry, sun-baked lawn.* ADJ: ADJ n

**sun|bathe** /sʌnbeɪθ/ **(sunbathes, sunbathing, sunbathed)** When people **sunbathe**, they sit or lie in a place where the sun shines on them, so that their skin becomes browner. ❑ *Franklin swam and sunbathed at the pool every morning.* VERB V ♦ **sun|bather** **(sunbathers)** *A week ago Bournemouth beach was thronged with sunbathers soaking up the 80 degrees heat.* N-COUNT ♦ **sun|bath|ing** *Nearby there is a stretch of white sand beach perfect for sunbathing.* N-UNCOUNT

**sun|beam** /sʌnbiːm/ **(sunbeams)** A **sunbeam** is a ray of sunlight. ❑ *A sunbeam slants through the west window.* N-COUNT

**sun|bed** /sʌnbed/ **(sunbeds)** A **sunbed** is a piece of equipment with ultraviolet lights. You lie on it to make your skin browner. N-COUNT

**sun|belt** /sʌnbelt/ The warmer, sunnier parts of a country or continent, especially the southern United States, are sometimes referred to as **the sunbelt**. ❑ *During the last recession, migration to the sunbelt accelerated.* N-SING: usu the N

**sun|block** /sʌnblɒk/ **(sunblocks)** **Sunblock** is a cream which you put on your skin to protect it completely from the sun. N-MASS

**sun|burn** /sʌnbɜːʳn/ **(sunburns)** If someone has **sunburn**, their skin is bright pink and sore because they have spent too much time in hot sunshine. ❑ *The risk and severity of sunburn depend on the body's natural skin colour... I was concerned that I was not protected and would get a sunburn.* N-VAR

**sun|burnt** /sʌnbɜːʳnt/ also **sunburned.** 1 Someone who is **sunburnt** has sore bright pink skin because they have spent too much time in hot sunshine. ❑ *A badly sunburned face or back is extremely painful.* ADJ = burnt 2 Someone who is **sunburnt** has very brown skin because they have spent a lot of time in the sunshine. ❑ *Mr Cooper looked fit and sunburnt.* ADJ = tanned

**sun|burst** /sʌnbɜːʳst/ **(sunbursts)** A **sunburst** is a pattern or design that resembles the sun with rays coming from it. ❑ *...a bronze sunburst pendant.* N-COUNT

**sun|dae** /sʌndeɪ, -di/ **(sundaes)** A **sundae** is a tall glass of ice cream with whipped cream and nuts or fruit on top. ❑ *...a chocolate sundae.* N-COUNT: usu n N

**Sun|day** /sʌndeɪ, -di/ **(Sundays)** **Sunday** is the day after Saturday and before Monday. ❑ *I thought we might go for a drive on Sunday... Naomi used to go to church in Granville every Sunday.* N-VAR

**Sun|day best** If you are in your **Sunday best**, you are wearing your best clothes, which you only wear for special occasions. N-SING: poss N

**Sun|day school** **(Sunday schools)** **Sunday school** is a class organized by a church that some children go to on Sundays in order to learn about Christianity. ❑ *...a Sunday School teacher.* N-VAR

**sun|der** /sʌndəʳ/ **(sunders, sundering, sundered)** If people or things **are sundered**, they are separated or split by something. [LITERARY] ❑ *The city is being sundered by racial tension... Police moved in to separate the two groups, already sundered by distrust.* VERB: usu passive be V-ed V-ed

**sun|dial** /sʌndaɪəl/ **(sundials)** A **sundial** is a device used for telling the time when the sun is shining. The shadow of an upright rod falls onto a flat surface that is marked with the hours, and points to the correct hour. N-COUNT

**sun|down** /sʌndaʊn/ **Sundown** is the time when the sun sets. [AM] ❑ *The fighting broke out about two hours after sundown.* N-UNCOUNT

in BRIT, usually use **sunset**

**sun-drenched** also **sundrenched.** **Sun-drenched** places have a lot of hot sunshine. ❑ *He sat on the terrace of his sun-drenched villa in the South of France.* ADJ: ADJ n

**sun|dries** /sʌndriz/ When someone is making a list of things, items that are not important enough to be listed separately are sometimes referred to together as **sundries**. [FORMAL] ❑ *The inn gift shop stocks quality Indian crafts and sundries.* N-PLURAL

**sun|dry** /sʌndri/ 1 If someone refers to **sundry** people or things, they are referring to several people or things that are all different from each other. [FORMAL] ❑ *Scientists, business people, and sundry others gathered on Monday for the official opening.* ADJ: ADJ n 2 **All and sundry** means everyone. ❑ *He was well known to all and sundry.* PHRASE: usu prep PHR

**sun|flower** /sʌnflaʊəʳ/ **(sunflowers)** A **sunflower** is a very tall plant with large yellow flowers. Oil from sunflower seeds is used in cooking and to make margarine. N-COUNT

**sung** /sʌŋ/ **Sung** is the past participle of **sing**.

**sun|glasses** /sʌnglɑːsɪz, -glæs-/ **Sunglasses** are glasses with dark lenses which you wear to protect your eyes from bright sunlight. ❑ *She slipped on a pair of sunglasses.* N-PLURAL: also a pair of N

**sun hat** **(sun hats)** also **sunhat.** A **sun hat** is a wide-brimmed hat that protects your head from the sun. N-COUNT

**sunk** /sʌŋk/ 1 **Sunk** is the past participle of **sink**. 2 If you say that someone is **sunk**, you mean that they have no hope of avoiding trouble or failure. [INFORMAL] ❑ *Without him we'd be well and truly sunk.* ADJ: v-link ADJ

**sunk|en** /sʌŋkən/ 1 **Sunken** ships have sunk to the bottom of a sea, ocean, or lake. ❑ *The sunken sailing-boat was a glimmer of white on the bottom... Try diving for sunken treasure.* ADJ: ADJ n 2 **Sunken** gardens, roads, or other features are below the level of their surrounding area. ❑ *The room was dominated by a sunken bath.* ADJ: ADJ n 3 **Sunken** eyes, cheeks, or other parts of the body curve inwards and make you look thin and unwell. ❑ *Her eyes were sunken and black-ringed.* ADJ

**sun lamp** **(sun lamps)** also **sunlamp.** A **sun lamp** is a lamp that produces ultraviolet light. People use sun lamps to make their skin browner. N-COUNT

**sun|less** /sʌnləs/ 1 On **sunless** days, the sun does not shine. ❑ *The day dawned sunless and with a low cloud base.* ADJ ≠ sunny 2 **Sunless** places are not lit by the sun. ❑ *Carmen stayed behind in the dark, sunless room.* ADJ: ADJ n

**sun|light** /sʌnlaɪt/ **Sunlight** is the light that comes from the sun during the day. ❑ *I saw her sitting at a window table, bathed in sunlight.* N-UNCOUNT

**sun|lit** /sʌnlɪt/ **Sunlit** places are brightly lit by the sun. ❑ *Her house has two big sunlit rooms with floor-to-ceiling windows.* ADJ: ADJ n

**sun|ny** /sʌni/ **(sunnier, sunniest)** [1] When it is **sunny**, the sun is shining brightly. ❑ *The weather was surprisingly warm and sunny... There is a chance of sunny spells in the West.* ADJ = *bright* [2] **Sunny** places are brightly lit by the sun. ❑ *Most roses like a sunny position in a fairly fertile soil.* ADJ [3] Someone who has a **sunny** disposition is usually cheerful and happy. ❑ *He was a nice lad – bright and with a sunny disposition... The staff wear big sunny smiles.* ADJ = *cheery*

**sun|rise** /sʌnraɪz/ **(sunrises)** [1] **Sunrise** is the time in the morning when the sun first appears in the sky. ❑ *The rain began before sunrise.* N-UNCOUNT ≠ *sunset* [2] A **sunrise** is the colours and light that you see in the eastern part of the sky when the sun first appears. ❑ *There was a spectacular sunrise yesterday.* N-COUNT ≠ *sunset*

**sun|roof** /sʌnruːf/ **(sunroofs)** A **sunroof** is a panel in the roof of a car that opens to let sunshine and air enter the car. N-COUNT

**sun|screen** /sʌnskriːn/ **(sunscreens)** A **sunscreen** is a cream that protects your skin from the sun's rays, especially in hot weather. N-MASS

**sun|set** /sʌnset/ **(sunsets)** [1] **Sunset** is the time in the evening when the sun disappears out of sight from the sky. ❑ *The dance ends at sunset.* N-UNCOUNT ≠ *sunrise* [2] A **sunset** is the colours and light that you see in the western part of the sky when the sun disappears in the evening. ❑ *There was a red sunset over Paris.* N-COUNT ≠ *sunrise*

**sun|shine** /sʌnʃaɪn/ **Sunshine** is the light and heat that comes from the sun. ❑ *She was sitting outside a cafe in bright sunshine... I awoke next morning to brilliant sunshine streaming into my room.* N-UNCOUNT

**sun|spot** /sʌnspɒt/ **(sunspots)** **Sunspots** are dark cool patches that appear on the surface of the sun and last for about a week. N-COUNT

**sun|stroke** /sʌnstroʊk/ **Sunstroke** is an illness caused by spending too much time in hot sunshine. N-UNCOUNT

**sun|tan** /sʌntæn/ **(suntans)** also **sun-tan.** [1] If you have a **suntan**, the sun has turned your skin an attractive brown colour. N-COUNT = *tan* [2] **Suntan** lotion, oil, or cream protects your skin from the sun. ❑ *She playfully rubs suntan lotion on his neck.* ADJ: ADJ n

**sun|tanned** /sʌntænd/ Someone who is **suntanned** has an attractive brown colour from being in the sun. ❑ *He is always suntanned and incredibly fit.* ADJ = *tanned*

**sun-up** also **sunup. Sun-up** is the time of day when the sun rises. [AM] ❑ *We worked from sun-up to sunset.* N-UNCOUNT

✔ in BRIT, use **sunrise**

**sup** /sʌp/ **(sups, supping, supped)** [1] If you **sup** something, you drink it, especially by taking small amounts. [LITERARY or OLD-FASHIONED] ❑ *We supped mulled wine.* VERB V n [2] If you **sup**, you eat dinner in the evening. [LITERARY or OLD-FASHIONED] ❑ *He had been invited to sup with a colleague and his wife.* VERB = *dine* V

**su|per** /suːpəʳ/ [1] Some people use **super** to mean very nice or very good. [mainly BRIT, INFORMAL, OLD-FASHIONED] ❑ *We had a super time... That's a super idea... 'I think I could find you something.' — 'That would be super.'* ◆◇◇ ADJ = *great* [2] **Super** is used before adjectives to indicate that something has a lot of a quality. ❑ *I'm going to Greece in the summer so I've got to be super slim.* ADV: ADV adj [3] **Super** is used before nouns to indicate that something is larger, better, or more advanced than similar things. ❑ *...building Russia into a super state. ...a chance to test-drive a stunning Lotus super-car.* ADJ: ADJ n

**super-** /suːpəʳ-/ **Super-** is used to form adjectives which indicate that something is at a higher level than something else. ❑ *...a fragment of crystal with supernormal powers.* PREFIX

**super|an|nu|at|ed** /suːpərænjueɪtɪd/ If you describe something as **superannuated**, you mean that it is old and no longer used for its original purpose. [FORMAL] ❑ *...the superannuated idealism of the Sixties.* ADJ: usu ADJ n

**super|an|nua|tion** /suːpərænjueɪʃᵊn/ **Superannuation** is money which people pay regularly into a special fund so that when they retire from their job they will receive money regularly as a pension. [mainly BRIT, BUSINESS] ❑ *The union pressed for a superannuation scheme.* N-UNCOUNT = *pension*

**su|perb** /suːpɜːʳb/ [1] If something is **superb**, its quality is very good indeed. ❑ *There is a superb 18-hole golf course 6 miles away... The waters are crystal clear and offer a superb opportunity for swimming.* ◆◇◇ ADJ = *excellent, outstanding* ♦ **su|perb|ly** *The orchestra played superbly.* ADV: ADV with v, ADV adv/adj [2] If you say that someone has **superb** confidence, control, or skill, you mean that they have very great confidence, control, or skill. ❑ *With superb skill he managed to make a perfect landing.* ADJ ♦ **su|perb|ly** *...his superbly disciplined opponent.* ADV: ADV with v, ADV adj/adv

**su|per|bug** /suːpəʳbʌg/ **(superbugs)** Journalists refer to a type of bacteria as a **superbug** when it is very difficult to deal with because it cannot be killed by antibiotics. N-COUNT

**super|charged** /suːpəʳtʃɑːʳdʒd/ If a car engine is **supercharged**, it has more air than normal forced into it so that the petrol burns more quickly and the car has more power. ADJ

**super|cili|ous** /suːpəʳsɪliəs/ If you say that someone is **supercilious**, you disapprove of them because they behave in a way that shows they think they are better than other people. ❑ *His manner is supercilious and arrogant.* ADJ [disapproval] = *disdainful*

**super|com|put|er** /suːpəʳkəmpjuːtəʳ/ **(supercomputers)** A **supercomputer** is a powerful computer that can process large amounts of data very quickly. N-COUNT

**super|con|duc|tiv|ity** /suːpəʳkɒndʌktɪvɪti/ **Superconductivity** is the ability of certain metals to allow electricity to pass through them without any resistance at very low temperatures. [TECHNICAL] N-UNCOUNT

**super|con|duc|tor** /suːpəʳkəndʌktəʳ/ **(superconductors)** A **superconductor** is a metal that allows electricity to pass through it without resistance at very low temperatures. [TECHNICAL] N-COUNT

**super-ego** **(super-egos)** also **superego.** Your **super-ego** is the part of your mind which makes you aware of what is right and wrong, and which causes you to feel guilty when you have done something wrong. [TECHNICAL] N-COUNT

**super|fi|cial** /suːpəʳfɪʃᵊl/ [1] If you describe someone as **superficial**, you disapprove of them because they do not think deeply, and have little understanding of anything serious or important. ADJ [disapproval] [2] If you describe something such as an action, feeling, or relationship as **superficial**, you mean that it includes only the simplest and most obvious aspects of that thing, and not those aspects which require more effort to deal with or understand. ❑ *Their arguments do not withstand the most superficial scrutiny... His roommate had been pleasant on a superficial level.* ADJ [3] **Superficial** is used to describe the appearance of something or the impression that it gives, especially if its real nature is very different. ❑ *Despite these superficial resemblances, this is a darker work than her earlier novels.* ADJ [4] **Superficial** injuries are not very serious, and affect only the surface of the body. You can also describe damage to an object as **superficial**. ❑ *The 69-year-old clergyman escaped with superficial wounds.* ADJ = *slight*

**super|flu|ity** /suːpəʳfluːɪti/ **(superfluities)** If there is a **superfluity of** something, there is more of it than is needed. [FORMAL] ❑ *The city has a superfluity of five-star hotels.* N-COUNT: usu N *of* n

**super|flu|ous** /suːpɜːʳfluəs/ Something that is **superfluous** is unnecessary or is no longer needed. ❑ *My presence at the afternoon's proceedings was superfluous.* ADJ

**super|grass** /suːpəʳgrɑːs, -græs/ **(supergrasses)** A **supergrass** is a person who gives the police information about a large group of criminals. [BRIT, INFORMAL] N-COUNT

**super|group** /suːpəʳgruːp/ **(supergroups)** A **supergroup** is a pop group that has become very popular and famous. ❑ *Supergroup U2 will appear at Wembley Stadium on April 20.* N-COUNT

**super|heat|ed** /suːpəʳhiːtəd/ If a liquid is **superheated**, it has been heated to a temperature that is higher than its boiling point without being allowed to boil. [TECHNICAL] ADJ

**super|he|ro** /suːpəʳhɪəroʊ/ **(superheroes)** A **superhero** is a character in a cartoon or film who has special powers and fights against evil. ❑ *...superheroes like Batman and Superman.* N-COUNT

**super|high|way** /suːpəʳhaɪweɪ/ **(superhighways)** 1 A **superhighway** is a large, fast motorway or freeway with several lanes. [AM] ❑ *He took off for the city on the eight-lane superhighway.* N-COUNT 2 The information **superhighway** is the network of computer links that enables computer users all over the world to communicate with each other. [COMPUTING] N-COUNT

**super|hu|man** /suːpəʳhjuːmən/ If you describe a quality that someone has as **superhuman**, you mean that it seems to be much greater than that of ordinary people. ❑ *Officers were terrified of his superhuman strength.* ADJ: usu ADJ n

**super|im|pose** /suːpərɪmpoʊz/ **(superimposes, superimposing, superimposed)** 1 If one image **is superimposed on** another, it is put on top of it so that you can see the second image through it. ❑ *His picture was superimposed on a muscular body... You can superimpose the lettering directly onto one of your pictures.* VERB: usu passive; be V-ed on/over n; V n onto n 2 If features or characteristics from one situation **are superimposed onto** or **on** another, they are transferred onto or used in the second situation, though they may not fit. ❑ *Patterns of public administration and government are superimposed on traditional societies.* VERB: usu passive; be V-ed on n

**super|in|tend** /suːpərɪntend/ **(superintends, superintending, superintended)** If you **superintend** something, you have responsibility for ensuring that it is carried out properly. [FORMAL] ❑ *During the interval, Linton superintended a prize draw.* VERB; V n

**super|in|ten|dent** /suːpərɪntendənt/ **(superintendents)** 1 In Britain, a **superintendent** is a senior police officer of the rank above an inspector. In the United States, a **superintendent** is the head of a police department. ❑ *He was stopped at the airport by an assistant superintendent of police. ...Detective Superintendent Kirby.* N-COUNT; N-TITLE 2 A **superintendent** is a person who is responsible for a particular thing or the work done in a particular department. ❑ *He became superintendent of the bank's East African branches.* N-COUNT: N of n 3 A **superintendent** is a person whose job is to look after a large building such as a school or a block of flats and deal with small repairs to it. [AM] N-COUNT

☑ in BRIT, use **caretaker**

**su|peri|or** /suːpɪəriəʳ/ **(superiors)** 1 If one thing or person is **superior to** another, the first is better than the second. ❑ *We have a relationship infinitely superior to those of many of our friends... Long-term stock market investments have produced superior returns compared with cash deposits.* ◆◇◇ ADJ: oft ADJ to n ≠ inferior ♦ **su|peri|or|ity** *The technical superiority of laser discs over tape is well established.* N-UNCOUNT: oft N over/to n 2 If you describe something as **superior**, you mean that it is good, and better than other things of the same kind. ❑ *A few years ago it was virtually impossible to find superior quality coffee in local shops... Lulu was said to be of very superior intelligence.* ADJ 3 A **superior** person or thing is more important than another person or thing in the same organization or system. ❑ *...negotiations between the mutineers and their superior officers.* ADJ: oft ADJ to n 4 Your **superior** in an organization that you work for is a person who has a higher rank than you. ❑ *Other army units are completely surrounded and cut-off from communication with their superiors.* N-COUNT: poss N ≠ subordinate 5 If you describe someone as **superior**, you disapprove of them because they behave as if they are better, more important, or more intelligent than other people. ❑ *Finch gave a superior smile.* ADJ [disapproval] ♦ **su|peri|or|ity** *...a false sense of his superiority over mere journalists.* N-UNCOUNT: oft N over n 6 If one group of people has **superior** numbers to another group, the first has more people than the second, and therefore has an advantage over it. [FORMAL] ❑ *The demonstrators fled when they saw the authorities' superior numbers.* ADJ

**su|peri|or|ity** /suːpɪəriɒrɪti, AM -ɔːrɪti/ If one side in a war or conflict has **superiority**, it has an advantage over its enemy, for example because it has more soldiers or better equipment. [FORMAL] ❑ *The US will need a three-to-one superiority in forces to be sure of a successful attack... We have air superiority.* → See also **superior**. N-UNCOUNT: oft N over/in n

**super|la|tive** /suːpɜːʳlətɪv/ **(superlatives)** 1 If you describe something as **superlative**, you mean that it is extremely good. ❑ *Some superlative wines are made in this region... The Regent hotel has a superlative view of Hong Kong island.* ADJ 2 If someone uses **superlatives** to describe something, they use adjectives and expressions which indicate that it is extremely good. ❑ *...a spectacle which has critics world-wide reaching for superlatives.* N-COUNT: usu pl 3 In grammar, the **superlative** form of an adjective or adverb is the form that indicates that something has more of a quality than anything else in a group. For example, 'biggest' is the superlative form of 'big'. Compare **comparative**. ADJ: ADJ n ♦ **Superlative** is also a noun. ❑ *...his tendency towards superlatives and exaggeration.* N-COUNT

**super|man** /suːpəʳmæn/ **(supermen)** A **superman** is a man who has very great physical or mental abilities. ❑ *Collor nurtured the idea that he was a superman, who single-handedly could resolve Brazil's crisis.* N-COUNT

**super|mar|ket** /suːpəʳmɑːʳkɪt/ **(supermarkets)** A **supermarket** is a large shop which sells all kinds of food and some household goods. ❑ *Most of us do our food shopping in the supermarket.* ◆◇◇ N-COUNT

**super|mini** /suːpəʳmɪni/ **(superminis)** also **super-mini**. A **supermini** is a small car which has been designed to be comfortable and easy to drive. N-COUNT

**super|model** /suːpəʳmɒdəl/ **(supermodels)** A **supermodel** is a very famous fashion model. N-COUNT

**super|natu|ral** /suːpəʳnætʃrəl/ **Supernatural** creatures, forces, and events are believed by some people to exist or happen, although they are impossible according to scientific laws. ❑ *The Nakani were evil spirits who looked like humans and possessed supernatural powers. ...supernatural beings.* ADJ ♦ **The supernatural** is things that are supernatural. ❑ *He writes short stories with a touch of the supernatural.* N-SING: the N

**super|no|va** /suːpəʳnoʊvə/ **(supernovas** or **supernovae** /suːpəʳnoʊviː/**)** A **supernova** is an exploding star. ❑ *At least one supernova occurs per decade in our galaxy.* N-COUNT

**super|pow|er** /suːpəʳpaʊəʳ/ **(superpowers)** A **superpower** is a very powerful and influential country, usually one that is rich and has nuclear weapons. ❑ *The United States could claim to be both a military and an economic superpower.* N-COUNT

**super|sede** /suːpəʳsiːd/ **(supersedes, superseding, superseded)** If something **is superseded by** something newer, it is replaced because it has become old-fashioned or unacceptable. ❑ *Hand tools are relics of the past that have now been superseded by the machine.* VERB: usu passive; be V-ed; Also V n

**super|son|ic** /suːpəʳsɒnɪk/ **Supersonic** aircraft travel faster than the speed of sound. ❑ *There was a huge bang; it sounded like a supersonic jet.* ADJ: ADJ n

**super|star** /su:pəʳstɑ:ʳ/ **(superstars)** A **superstar** is a very famous entertainer or sports player. [INFORMAL] ❑ *...a Hollywood superstar.* [N-COUNT]

**su|per|state** /su:pəʳsteɪt/ **(superstates)** A **superstate** is a group of several countries that are very closely linked politically. ❑ *...a European superstate.* [N-COUNT]

**super|sti|tion** /su:pəʳstɪʃᵊn/ **(superstitions)** [N-VAR] **Superstition** is belief in things that are not real or possible, for example magic. ❑ *Fortune-telling is a very much debased art surrounded by superstition.*

**super|sti|tious** /su:pəʳstɪʃəs/ [1] People [ADJ: usu v-link ADJ] who are **superstitious** believe in things that are not real or possible, for example magic. ❑ *Jean was extremely superstitious and believed the colour green brought bad luck.* [2] **Superstitious** fears or beliefs [ADJ: ADJ n] are irrational and not based on fact. ❑ *A wave of superstitious fear spread among the townspeople.*

**super|store** /su:pəʳstɔ:ʳ/ **(superstores)** [N-COUNT] **Superstores** are very large supermarkets or shops selling household goods and equipment. Superstores are usually built outside city centres away from other shops. ❑ *...a Do-It-Yourself superstore.*

**super|struc|ture** /su:pəʳstrʌktʃəʳ/ **(superstructures)** The **superstructure** of a ship is the [N-COUNT: usu sing] part of it that is above its main deck. ❑ *We might try to clear up some of the cabins in the superstructure.*

**super|tank|er** /su:pəʳtæŋkəʳ/ **(supertankers)** [N-COUNT] A **supertanker** is an extremely large ship that is used for transporting oil.

**super|vise** /su:pəʳvaɪz/ **(supervises, supervising, supervised)** [1] If you **supervise** an activity or [VERB] a person, you make sure that the activity is done correctly or that the person is doing a task or behaving correctly. ❑ *University teachers have refused* [V n] *to supervise students' examinations.* [2] If you [VERB] **supervise** a place where work is done, you ensure that the work there is done properly. ❑ *He makes* [V n] *the wines and supervises the vineyards.*

**super|vi|sion** /su:pəʳvɪʒᵊn/ **Supervision** is [N-UNCOUNT: oft N *of* n, *under* N] the supervising of people, activities, or places. ❑ *A toddler requires close supervision and firm control at all times... The plan calls for a cease-fire and UN supervision of the country.*

**super|vi|sor** /su:pəʳvaɪzəʳ/ **(supervisors)** A [N-COUNT] **supervisor** is a person who supervises activities or people, especially workers or students. ❑ *...a full-time job as a supervisor at a factory... Each student has a supervisor to advise on the writing of the dissertation.*

**super|vi|sory** /su:pəʳvaɪzəri/ **Supervisory** [ADJ: ADJ n] means involved in supervising people, activities, or places. ❑ *Most supervisory boards meet only twice a year. ...staff with a minor supervisory role.*

**super|woman** /su:pəʳwʊmən/ **(superwomen)** **Superwoman** is used to refer to a type [N-VAR] of ideal woman who is able to do many things in her life successfully at the same time, such as have a job, bring up children, care for her home, and be attractive. ❑ *Superwoman exists only in the minds of journalists and Hollywood producers.*

**su|pine** /su:paɪn/ If you are **supine**, you are [ADJ] lying flat on your back. [FORMAL] ❑ *...bedridden persons confined to the supine position.* ♦ **Supine** is also [ADV: ADV after v] an adverb. ❑ *I lay supine on the poolside grass.*

**sup|per** /sʌpəʳ/ **(suppers)** [1] Some people re- [N-VAR] fer to the main meal eaten in the early part of the evening as **supper**. ❑ *Some guests like to dress for supper.* [2] **Supper** is a simple meal eaten just be- [N-VAR] fore you go to bed at night. ❑ *She gives the children their supper, then puts them to bed.*

**sup|per club** **(supper clubs)** In the United [N-COUNT] States, a **supper club** is a small expensive nightclub.

**sup|per|time** /sʌpəʳtaɪm/ **Suppertime** is [N-UNCOUNT] the period of the day when people have their supper. It can be in the early part of the evening or just before they go to bed at night. ❑ *They'll be back by suppertime.*

**sup|plant** /səplɑ:nt, -plænt/ **(supplants, supplanting, supplanted)** If a person or thing **is supplanted**, another person or thing takes their [VERB = usurp] place. [FORMAL] ❑ *He may be supplanted by a younger* [be V-ed] *man... By the 1930s the wristwatch had almost com-* [V n] *pletely supplanted the pocket watch.*

**sup|ple** /sʌpᵊl/ **(suppler, supplest)** [1] A **sup-** [ADJ] **ple** object or material bends or changes shape easily without cracking or breaking. ❑ *The leather is supple and sturdy enough to last for years.* [2] A [ADJ] **supple** person can move and bend their body very easily. ❑ *Try these simple exercises to keep your feet supple.*

**sup|plement** /sʌplɪmənt/ **(supplements, supplementing, supplemented)** [1] If you **sup-** [VERB] **plement** something, you add something to it in order to improve it. ❑ *...people doing extra jobs out-* [V n] *side their regular jobs to supplement their incomes... I* [V n *with* n] *suggest supplementing your diet with vitamins E and A.* ♦ **Supplement** is also a noun. ❑ *Business sponsor-* [N-COUNT: oft N *to* n] *ship must be a supplement to, not a substitute for, public funding.* [2] A **supplement** is a pill that you [N-COUNT] take or a special kind of food that you eat in order to improve your health. ❑ *...a multiple vitamin and mineral supplement.* [3] A **supplement** is a sepa- [N-COUNT] rate part of a magazine or newspaper, often dealing with a particular topic. ❑ *...a special supplement to a monthly financial magazine.* ➔ See also **colour supplement**. [4] A **supplement to** a book is an [N-COUNT: oft N *to* n] additional section, written some time after the main text and published either at the end of the book or separately. ❑ *...the supplement to the Encyclopedia Britannica.* [5] A **supplement** is an extra [N-COUNT] amount of money that you pay in order to obtain special facilities or services, for example when you are travelling or staying at a hotel. ❑ *If you are travelling alone, the single room supplement is £11 a night.* [6] A **supplement** is an extra amount of [N-COUNT: usu N n, N *to* n] money that is paid to someone, in addition to their normal pension or income. ❑ *Some people may be entitled to a housing benefit supplement. ...people who need a supplement to their basic pension.*

**sup|plemen|tal** /sʌplɪmentᵊl/ **Sup-** [ADJ: ADJ n] **plemental** means the same as **supplementary**. [mainly AM, FORMAL] ❑ *You'll probably be able to buy supplemental insurance at an extra cost.*

**sup|plemen|ta|ry** /sʌplɪmentri, AM -teri/ [ADJ: usu ADJ n = extra] **Supplementary** things are added to something in order to improve it. ❑ *...the question of whether or not we need to take supplementary vitamins... Provide them with additional background or with supplementary information.*

**sup|plemen|ta|tion** /sʌplɪmənteɪʃᵊn/ [N-UNCOUNT] **Supplementation** is the use of pills or special types of food in order to improve your health. [MEDICAL] ❑ *The product provided inadequate vitamin and mineral supplementation.*

**sup|pli|cant** /sʌplɪkənt/ **(supplicants)** A **sup-** [N-COUNT] **plicant** is a person who prays to God or respectfully asks an important person to help them or to give them something that they want very much. [FORMAL] ❑ *He flung himself down in the flat submissive posture of a mere supplicant.*

**sup|pli|ca|tion** /sʌplɪkeɪʃᵊn/ **(supplications)** [N-VAR] A **supplication** is a prayer to God or a respectful request to someone in authority for help. [FORMAL] ❑ *He raised his arms in a gesture of supplication.*

**sup|plied** /səplaɪd/ If you say that a person [ADJ: v-link ADJ *with* n] or place is well **supplied with** particular things, you mean that they have a large number of them. ❑ *France is abundantly supplied with excellent family-run hotels.* ➔ See also **supply**.

**sup|pli|er** /səplaɪəʳ/ **(suppliers)** A **supplier** is [N-COUNT: oft N n, N *of* n] a person, company, or organization that sells or supplies something such as goods or equipment to customers. [BUSINESS] ❑ *...Hillsdown Holdings, one of the UK's biggest food suppliers.*

**sup|ply** /səplaɪ/ **(supplies, supplying, supplied)** ◆◆◇ [1] If you **supply** someone with something that [VERB] they want or need, you give them a quantity of it.

❑ ...*an agreement not to produce or supply chemical weapons. ...a pipeline which will supply the major Greek cities with Russian natural gas. ...the blood vessels supplying oxygen to the brain.* V n / V n *with* n / V n *to* n
2 You can use **supplies** to refer to food, equipment, and other essential things that people need, especially when these are provided in large quantities. ❑ *What happens when food and gasoline supplies run low?... The country's only supplies are those it can import by lorry from Vietnam.* N-PLURAL: oft n N
3 A **supply of** something is an amount of it which someone has or which is available for them to use. ❑ *The brain requires a constant supply of oxygen... Most urban water supplies in the United States now contain fluoride in varying amounts.* N-VAR: N *of* n, n N
4 **Supply** is the quantity of goods and services that can be made available for people to buy. [BUSINESS] ❑ *Prices change according to supply and demand.* N-UNCOUNT ≠ *demand*
5 If something is **in short supply**, there is very little of it available and it is difficult to find or obtain. ❑ *Food is in short supply all over the country.* PHRASE: usu v-link PHR

**sup|ply line** **(supply lines)** A **supply line** is a route along which goods and equipment are transported to an army during a war. ❑ *The bombing campaign appears aimed at cutting the supply lines between Germany and its army in occupied France.* N-COUNT

**sup|ply teach|er** **(supply teachers)** A **supply teacher** is a teacher whose job is to take the place of other teachers at different schools when they are unable to be there. [BRIT] N-COUNT

in AM, use **substitute teacher**

**sup|port** /səpɔːʳt/ **(supports, supporting, supported)** ◆◆◆
1 If you **support** someone or their ideas or aims, you agree with them, and perhaps help them because you want them to succeed. ❑ *The vice president insisted that he supported the hard-working people of New York... The National Union of Mineworkers pressed the party to support a total ban on imported coal.* VERB = *back* ≠ *oppose* / V n / V n
♦ **Support** is also a noun. ❑ *The prime minister gave his full support to the government's reforms.* N-UNCOUNT: usu with supp
2 If you give **support** to someone during a difficult or unhappy time, you are kind to them and help them. ❑ *It was hard to come to terms with her death after all the support she gave to me and the family.* N-UNCOUNT
3 Financial **support** is money provided to enable an organization to continue. This money is usually provided by the government. ❑ ...*the government's proposal to cut agricultural support by only about 15%.* N-UNCOUNT: oft supp N = *funding*
4 If you **support** someone, you provide them with money or the things that they need. ❑ *I have children to support, money to be earned, and a home to be maintained... She sold everything she'd ever bought in order to support herself through art school.* VERB / V n / V pron-refl
5 If a fact **supports** a statement or a theory, it helps to show that it is true or correct. ❑ *The Freudian theory about daughters falling in love with their father has little evidence to support it.* VERB = *substantiate* / V n
♦ **Support** is also a noun. ❑ *The two largest powers in any system must always be major rivals. History offers some support for this view.* N-UNCOUNT = *evidence*
6 If something **supports** an object, it is underneath the object and holding it up. ❑ ...*the thick wooden posts that supported the ceiling.* VERB = *hold up* / V n
7 A **support** is a bar or other object that supports something. N-COUNT
8 If you **support yourself**, you prevent yourself from falling by holding onto something or by leaning on something. ❑ *He supported himself by means of a nearby post.* VERB / V pron-refl
♦ **Support** is also a noun. ❑ *Alice, very pale, was leaning against him as if for support.* N-UNCOUNT
9 If you **support** a sports team, you always want them to win and perhaps go regularly to their games. ❑ *Tim, 17, supports Manchester United.* VERB / V n
10 → See also **supporting**.

**sup|port|er** /səpɔːʳtəʳ/ **(supporters)** ◆◆◇ **Supporters** are people who support someone or something, for example a political leader or a sports team. ❑ *The fourth night of violence in the German city of Rostock was triggered by football supporters... Bradley was a major supporter of the 1986 tax reform plan.* N-COUNT: usu pl, with supp

**sup|port group** **(support groups)** A **support group** is an organization run by and for people who have a particular problem or medical condition. ❑ *She attended a cancer support group at her local hospital.* N-COUNT: oft with supp

**sup|port|ing** /səpɔːʳtɪŋ/ 1 In a film or play, a **supporting** actor or actress is one who has an important part, but not the most important part. ❑ ...*the winner of the best supporting actress award.* ADJ: ADJ n
2 → See also **support**.

**sup|port|ive** /səpɔːʳtɪv/ If you are **supportive**, you are kind and helpful to someone at a difficult or unhappy time in their life. ❑ *They were always supportive of each other.* ADJ: oft ADJ *of* n

**sup|pose** /səpoʊz/ **(supposes, supposing, supposed)** ◆◆◇
1 You can use **suppose** or **supposing** before mentioning a possible situation or action. You usually then go on to consider the effects that this situation or action might have. ❑ *Suppose someone gave you an egg and asked you to describe exactly what was inside... Supposing he's right and I do die tomorrow? Maybe I should take out an extra insurance policy.* VERB / V that / V that
2 If you **suppose that** something is true, you believe that it is probably true, because of other things that you know. ❑ *The policy is perfectly clear and I see no reason to suppose that it isn't working... It had been supposed that by then Peter would be married.* VERB / V that / *it be* V-ed that / Also V n

PHRASES
3 You can say '**I suppose**' when you want to express slight uncertainty. [SPOKEN] ❑ *I get a bit uptight these days. Hormones, I suppose... I suppose I'd better do some homework... Is that the right way up? — Yeah. I suppose so... There's nothing to keep us here, is there? — I suppose not.* PHRASE: oft PHR that, PHR *so/not* [vagueness]
4 You can say '**I suppose**' or '**I don't suppose**' before describing someone's probable thoughts or attitude, when you are impatient or slightly angry with them. [SPOKEN] ❑ *I suppose you think you're funny.* PHRASE: PHR that [feelings]
5 You can say '**I don't suppose**' as a way of introducing a polite request. [SPOKEN] ❑ *I don't suppose you could tell me where James Street is could you?* PHRASE: PHR that [politeness]
6 You can use '**do you suppose**' to introduce a question when you want someone to give their opinion about something, although you know that they are unlikely to have any more knowledge or information about it than you. [SPOKEN] ❑ *Do you suppose he was telling the truth?* PHRASE: PHR that
7 You can use '**do you suppose**' as a polite way of suggesting or requesting that someone does something. ❑ *Do you suppose we could get together for a little chat sometime soon?* PHRASE: PHR that [politeness]

**sup|posed** ◆◆◇

Pronounced /səpoʊzd/ or /səpoʊst/ for meanings 1 to 4, and /səpoʊzɪd/ for meaning 5.

1 If you say that something **is supposed to** happen, you mean that it is planned or expected. Sometimes this use suggests that the thing does not really happen in this way. ❑ *He produced a hand-written list of nine men he was supposed to kill... Public spending is supposed to fall, not rise, in the next few years.* PHRASE
2 If something **was supposed to** happen, it was planned or intended to happen, but did not in fact happen. ❑ *He was supposed to go back to Bergen on the last bus, but of course the accident prevented him.* PHRASE
3 If you say that something **is supposed to** be true, you mean that people say it is true but you do not know for certain that it is true. ❑ *'The Whipping Block' has never been published, but it's supposed to be a really good poem... 'The President cannot be disturbed,' his son is supposed to have told an early morning caller.* PHRASE
4 You can use '**be supposed to**' to express annoyance at someone's ideas, or because something is not happening in the proper way. ❑ *You're supposed to be my friend!... What am I supposed to have done wrong now?* PHRASE [feelings]
5 You can use **supposed** to suggest that something that people talk about or believe in may not in fact exist, happen, or be as it is described. ❑ *Not all indigenous regimes were willing to* ADJ: ADJ n = *alleged*

*accept the supposed benefits of British trade.* ♦ **sup|pos|ed|ly** /səpoʊzɪdli/ *He was more of a victim than any of the women he supposedly offended.* ADV: ADV with v, ADV with cl/group

**sup|po|si|tion** /sʌpəzɪʃən/ **(suppositions)** 1 A **supposition** is an idea or statement which someone believes or assumes to be true, although they may have no evidence for it. [FORMAL] ❑ *There's a popular supposition that we're publicly funded but the bulk of our money comes from competitive contracts.* N-COUNT: oft N that = *assumption* 2 You can describe someone's ideas or statements as **supposition** if you disapprove of the fact that they have no evidence to support them. ❑ *The report has been rejected by the authorities, who said much of it was based on supposition or inaccuracy.* N-UNCOUNT disapproval

**sup|posi|tory** /səpɒzɪtri, AM -tɔːri/ **(suppositories)** A **suppository** is a solid block of medicine that is put into the rectum, where it gradually dissolves. N-COUNT

**sup|press** /səpres/ **(suppresses, suppressing, suppressed)** 1 If someone in authority **suppresses** an activity, they prevent it from continuing, by using force or making it illegal. ❑ *...drug traffickers, who continue to flourish despite international attempts to suppress them. ...nationwide demonstrations for democracy, suppressed after 7 weeks by the army.* ♦ **sup|pres|sion** /səpreʃən/ *...people who were imprisoned after the violent suppression of the pro-democracy movement protests.* VERB V n V-ed N-UNCOUNT: usu N *of* n 2 If a natural function or reaction of your body **is suppressed**, it is stopped, for example by drugs or illness. ❑ *The reproduction and growth of the cancerous cells can be suppressed by bombarding them with radiation.* ♦ **sup|pres|sion** *Eye problems can indicate an unhealthy lifestyle with subsequent suppression of the immune system.* VERB *be* V-ed N-UNCOUNT: usu N *of* n 3 If you **suppress** your feelings or reactions, you do not express them, even though you might want to. ❑ *Liz thought of Barry and suppressed a smile... The Professor said that deep sleep allowed suppressed anxieties to surface.* ♦ **sup|pres|sion** *A mother's suppression of her own feelings can cause problems.* VERB V n V-ed N-UNCOUNT: usu N *of* n 4 If someone **suppresses** a piece of information, they prevent other people from learning it. ❑ *At no time did they try to persuade me to suppress the information.* ♦ **sup|pres|sion** *The inspectors found no evidence which supported any allegation of suppression of official documents.* VERB V n N-UNCOUNT: N *of* n 5 If someone or something **suppresses** a process or activity, they stop it continuing or developing. ❑ *'The Government is suppressing inflation by devastating the economy,' he said.* VERB V n

**sup|pres|sant** /səpresənt/ **(suppressants)** A **suppressant** is a drug which is used to stop one of the natural functions of the body. [MEDICAL] ❑ *...the brief period in her life when she took Dexedrine as an appetite suppressant.* N-COUNT: n N

**sup|pres|sor** /səpresəʳ/ **Suppressor** cells or genes are ones that prevent a cancer from developing or spreading. [MEDICAL] ADJ: ADJ n

**supra|na|tion|al** /suːprənæʃənəl/ also **supra-national.** A **supranational** organization or authority involves or relates to more than one country. ❑ *...NATO and other Western supranational institutions.* ADJ: ADJ n

**su|prema|cist** /suːpreməsɪst/ **(supremacists)** A **supremacist** is someone who believes that one group of people, usually white people, should be more powerful and have more influence than another group. ❑ *...a white supremacist group.* N-COUNT: oft N n

**su|prema|cy** /suːpreməsi/ 1 If one group of people has **supremacy** over another group, they have more political or military power than the other group. ❑ *The conservative old guard had re-established its political supremacy.* N-UNCOUNT: usu with poss, oft N *over* n 2 If someone or something has **supremacy** over another person or thing, they are better. ❑ *In the United States Open final, Graf retained overall supremacy.* N-UNCOUNT: usu with poss, oft N *over* n = *superiority*

**su|preme** /suːpriːm/ ◆◆◇ 1 **Supreme** is used in the title of a person or an official group to indicate that they are at the highest level in a particular organization or system. ❑ *MacArthur was Supreme Commander for the allied powers in the Pacific. ...the Supreme Court.* ADJ: ADJ n 2 You use **supreme** to emphasize that a quality or thing is very great. ❑ *Her approval was of supreme importance.* ♦ **su|preme|ly** *She gets on with her job and does it supremely well.* ADJ emphasis ADV: ADV adj/adv

**su|pre|mo** /suːpriːmoʊ/ **(supremos)** A **supremo** is someone who is considered to have the most authority or skill in a particular organization, situation, or area of activity. [BRIT, JOURNALISM] ❑ *Her new role as fashion supremo is something she can really get her teeth into.* N-COUNT: usu supp N

**Supt**

✔ in AM, use **Supt.**

**Supt** is a written abbreviation for **superintendent** when it is part of the title of someone in the police force. ❑ *Det Supt Bassett was in charge of the murder enquiry.*

**sur|charge** /sɜːʳtʃɑːʳdʒ/ **(surcharges)** A **surcharge** is an extra payment of money in addition to the usual payment for something. It is added for a specific reason, for example by a company because costs have risen or by a government as a tax. ❑ *The prices of overseas holidays are subject to surcharges.* N-COUNT: oft N *on/for* n

**sure** /ʃʊəʳ/ **(surer, surest)** ◆◆◆ 1 If you are **sure** that something is true, you are certain that it is true. If you are not **sure** about something, you do not know for certain what the true situation is. ❑ *He'd never been in a class before and he was not even sure that he should have been teaching... The president has never been sure which direction he wanted to go in on this issue... It is impossible to be sure about the value of land.* ADJ: v-link ADJ, ADJ that, ADJ wh, ADJ *about/of* n = *certain* ≠ *doubtful* 2 If someone is **sure of** getting something, they will definitely get it or they think they will definitely get it. ❑ *A lot of people think that it's better to pay for their education so that they can be sure of getting quality.* ADJ: v-link ADJ *of* -ing/n 3 If you say that something **is sure to** happen, you are emphasizing your belief that it will happen. ❑ *With over 80 beaches to choose from, you are sure to find a place to lay your towel.* PHRASE emphasis 4 **Sure** is used to emphasize that something such as a sign or ability is reliable or accurate. ❑ *Sharpe's leg and shoulder began to ache, a sure sign of rain... She has a sure grasp of social issues such as literacy, poverty and child care.* ADJ: ADJ n emphasis 5 If you tell someone to **be sure to** do something, you mean that they must not forget to do it. ❑ *Be sure to read about how mozzarella is made, on page 65... Be sure you get your daily quota of calcium.* ADJ: v-link ADJ, ADJ to-inf, ADJ that emphasis 6 **Sure** is an informal way of saying 'yes' or 'all right'. ❑ *'He rang you?' — 'Sure. Last night.'... 'I'd like to be alone, O.K?' — 'Sure. O.K.'.* CONVENTION formulae 7 You can use **sure** in order to emphasize what you are saying. [INFORMAL] ❑ *'Has the whole world just gone crazy?' — 'Sure looks that way, doesn't it.'* ADV: ADV before v emphasis = *certainly*

**PHRASES** 8 You say **sure enough**, especially when telling a story, to confirm that something was really true or was actually happening. ❑ *We found the English treacle pudding too good to resist. Sure enough, it was delicious.* PHRASE: PHR with cl (not last in cl) 9 If you say that something is **for sure** or that you know it **for sure**, you mean that it is definitely true. ❑ *One thing's for sure, Astbury's vocal style hasn't changed much over the years.* PHRASE: PHR with cl (not first in cl) 10 If you **make sure that** something is done, you take action so that it is done. ❑ *Make sure that you follow the instructions carefully.* PHRASE: V inflects, usu PHR that 11 If you **make sure that** something is the way that you want or expect it to be, you check that it is that way. ❑ *He looked in the bathroom to make sure that he was alone.* PHRASE: V inflects, usu PHR that 12 If you say that something is a **sure thing**, you mean that you are certain that it will happen or be successful. [INFORMAL] ❑ *This proposal is by no means a sure thing.* PHRASE 13 If you are **sure of yourself**, you are very confident about your own abilities or opinions. ❑ *I'd never seen him like this, so sure of himself, so in command.* PHRASE: v-link PHR

**sure-fire** also **surefire.** A **sure-fire** thing is something that is certain to succeed or win. [INFORMAL] ❑ *...a surefire best seller.* ADJ: ADJ n

**sure-footed** also **surefooted.** 1 A person or animal that is **sure-footed** can move easily over steep or uneven ground without falling. ❑ *My horse is small but wiry and sure-footed.* ADJ 2 If someone is **sure-footed**, they are confident in what they are doing. ❑ *The Labour Party was growing increasingly sure-footed.* ADJ = confident

**sure|ly** /ʃʊəʳli/ ◆◇◇ 1 You use **surely** to emphasize that you think something should be true, and you would be surprised if it was not true. ❑ *You're an intelligent woman, surely you realize by now that I'm helping you... If I can accept this situation, surely you can.* ADV: ADV with cl/group [emphasis] 2 If something will **surely** happen or is **surely** the case, it will definitely happen or is definitely the case. [FORMAL] ❑ *He knew that under the surgeon's knife he would surely die... He is an artist, just as surely as Rembrandt or any other first-rate portrait painter is one.* ADV: ADV with cl, ADV before v = certainly 3 If you say that something is happening **slowly but surely**, you mean that it is happening gradually but it is definitely happening. ❑ *Slowly but surely she started to fall in love with him.* PHRASE: PHR with cl

**sure|ty** /ʃʊərɪti/ **(sureties)** A **surety** is money or something valuable which you give to someone to show that you will do what you have promised. ❑ *The insurance company will take warehouse stocks or treasury bonds as surety.* N-VAR

**surf** /sɜːʳf/ **(surfs, surfing, surfed)** 1 **Surf** is the mass of white bubbles that is formed by waves as they fall upon the shore. ❑ *...surf rolling onto white sand beaches.* N-UNCOUNT 2 If you **surf**, you ride on big waves in the sea on a special board. ❑ *I'm going to buy a surfboard and learn to surf... I'm going to be surfing bigger waves when I get to Australia!* VERB V V n ♦ **surf|er (surfers)** *...this small fishing village, which continues to attract painters and surfers.* N-COUNT 3 If you **surf** the Internet, you spend time finding and looking at things on the Internet. [COMPUTING] ❑ *No one knows how many people currently surf the Net.* VERB V n ♦ **surf|er (surfers)** *Net surfers can use their credit cards to pay for anything from toys to train tickets.* N-COUNT

**sur|face** /sɜːʳfɪs/ ◆◆◇ **(surfaces, surfacing, surfaced)** 1 The **surface** of something is the flat top part of it or the outside of it. ❑ *Ozone forms a protective layer between 12 and 30 miles above the Earth's surface. ...tiny little waves on the surface of the water... Its total surface area was seven thousand square feet.* N-COUNT: usu with supp 2 A work **surface** is a flat area, for example the top of a table, desk, or kitchen cupboard, on which you can work. ❑ *It can simply be left on the work surface.* N-COUNT: usu with supp 3 When you refer to **the surface** of a situation, you are talking about what can be seen easily rather than what is hidden or not immediately obvious. ❑ *Back in Britain, things appear, on the surface, simpler... Social unrest, never far below the surface in Brazil, has erupted over the last few days.* N-SING: usu the N 4 **Surface** is used to describe the parts of the armed forces which travel by ship or by land rather than underwater or in the air. ❑ *In contrast with its surface fleet, Britain's submarine force was relatively small.* ADJ: ADJ n 5 If someone or something under water **surfaces**, they come up to the surface of the water. ❑ *He surfaced, gasping for air.* VERB V 6 When something such as a piece of news, a feeling, or a problem **surfaces**, it becomes known or becomes obvious. ❑ *The paper says the evidence, when it surfaces, is certain to cause uproar.* VERB = emerge V 7 When someone **surfaces**, they appear after not being seen for some time, for example because they have been asleep. [INFORMAL] ❑ *What time do you surface?* VERB V

**sur|face mail** **Surface mail** is the system of sending letters and parcels by road, rail, or sea, not by air. N-UNCOUNT

**surface-to-air** **Surface-to-air** missiles are fired from the ground or a boat and aimed at aircraft or at other missiles. ADJ: ADJ n

**surface-to-surface** **Surface-to-surface** missiles are fired from the ground or a boat and aimed at targets on the ground or at other boats. ❑ *The surface-to-surface missiles were fired from the west of the capital.* ADJ: ADJ n

**surf|board** /sɜːʳfbɔːʳd/ **(surfboards)** A **surfboard** is a long narrow board that is used for surfing. N-COUNT

**sur|feit** /sɜːʳfɪt/ A **surfeit of** something is an amount which is too large. [FORMAL] ❑ *Rationing had put an end to a surfeit of biscuits long ago.* N-SING: usu N of n = surplus

**surf|ing** /sɜːʳfɪŋ/ 1 **Surfing** is the sport of riding on the top of a wave while standing or lying on a special board. N-UNCOUNT 2 **Surfing** is the activity of looking at different sites on the Internet, especially when you are not looking for anything in particular. [COMPUTING] ❑ *The simple fact is that, for most people, surfing is too expensive.* N-UNCOUNT

**surge** /sɜːʳdʒ/ **(surges, surging, surged)** 1 A **surge** is a sudden large increase in something that has previously been steady, or has only increased or developed slowly. ❑ *Specialists see various reasons for the recent surge in inflation... The anniversary is bound to bring a new surge of interest in Dylan's work.* N-COUNT: usu sing, usu N in/of n 2 If something **surges**, it increases suddenly and greatly, after being steady or developing only slowly. ❑ *The Freedom Party's electoral support surged from just under 10 per cent to nearly 17 per cent... Surging imports will add to the demand for hard currency.* VERB V from/to/by amount V-ing 3 If a crowd of people **surge** forward, they suddenly move forward together. ❑ *The photographers and cameramen surged forward. ...the crowd surging out from the church.* VERB V adv/prep 4 A **surge** is a sudden powerful movement of a physical force such as wind or water. ❑ *The whole car shuddered with an almost frightening surge of power.* N-COUNT: usu sing with supp, oft N of n 5 If a physical force such as water or electricity **surges** through something, it moves through it suddenly and powerfully. ❑ *Thousands of volts surged through his car after he careered into a lamp post, ripping out live wires.* VERB V adv/prep

**sur|geon** /sɜːʳdʒəⁿn/ **(surgeons)** A **surgeon** is a doctor who is specially trained to perform surgery. ❑ *...a heart surgeon.* → See also **plastic surgeon**. N-COUNT

**sur|gery** /sɜːʳdʒəri/ ◆◇◇ **(surgeries)** 1 **Surgery** is medical treatment in which someone's body is cut open so that a doctor can repair, remove, or replace a diseased or damaged part. ❑ *His father has just recovered from heart surgery... Mr Clark underwent five hours of emergency surgery.* → See also **cosmetic surgery, keyhole surgery, plastic surgery**. N-UNCOUNT 2 A **surgery** is the room or house where a doctor or dentist works. [BRIT] ❑ *Bill was in the doctor's surgery demanding to know what was wrong with him.* N-COUNT

☑ in AM, use **doctor's office, dentist's office**

3 A doctor's **surgery** is the period of time each day when a doctor sees patients at his or her surgery. [BRIT] ❑ *His surgery always ends at eleven.* N-COUNT: oft with poss

☑ in AM, use **office hours**

4 In Britain, when someone such as an MP or a local councillor holds a **surgery**, they go to an office where members of the public can come and talk to them about problems or issues that concern them. N-COUNT: usu sing 5 A **surgery** is the room in a hospital where surgeons operate on their patients. [AM] N-COUNT

☑ in BRIT, use **theatre, operating theatre**

**sur|gi|cal** /sɜːʳdʒɪkəˡl/ 1 **Surgical** equipment and clothing is used in surgery. ❑ *...an array of surgical instruments. ...a pair of surgical gloves.* ADJ: ADJ n 2 **Surgical** treatment involves surgery. ❑ *A biopsy is usually a minor surgical procedure. ...surgical removal of a tumor.* ADJ: ADJ n ♦ **sur|gi|cal|ly** *In very severe cases, bunions may be surgically removed.* ADV: ADV with v 3 **Surgical** military actions are designed to destroy a particular target without harming other people or damaging other buildings near it. ❑ *The new figures cast doubt on the government's claim to have achieved a surgical strike against military targets.* ADJ: ADJ n

**sur|gi|cal spir|it** **Surgical spirit** is a liquid which is used to clean wounds or surgical instruments. It consists mainly of alcohol. [BRIT] N-UNCOUNT

✓ in AM, use **rubbing alcohol**

**sur|ly** /sɜːʳli/ **(surlier, surliest)** Someone who is **surly** behaves in a rude bad-tempered way. [WRITTEN] ❑ *He became surly and rude towards me.* ADJ

**sur|mise** /səʳmaɪz/ **(surmises, surmising, surmised)** [1] If you **surmise** that something is true, you guess it from the available evidence, although you do not know for certain. [FORMAL] ❑ *There's so little to go on, we can only surmise what happened... He surmised that he had discovered one of the illegal streets.* VERB V wh V that Also V, V n [2] If you say that a particular conclusion is **surmise**, you mean that it is a guess based on the available evidence and you do not know for certain that it is true. [FORMAL] ❑ *It is mere surmise that Bosch had Brant's poem in mind when doing this painting... His surmise proved correct.* N-VAR = *conjecture*

**sur|mount** /səʳmaʊnt/ **(surmounts, surmounting, surmounted)** If you **surmount** a problem or difficulty, you deal successfully with it. ❑ *I realized I had to surmount the language barrier.* VERB = *overcome* V n

**sur|name** /sɜːʳneɪm/ **(surnames)** Your **surname** is the name that you share with other members of your family. In English speaking countries and many other countries it is your last name. ❑ *She'd never known his surname.* N-COUNT

**sur|pass** /səʳpɑːs, -pæs/ **(surpasses, surpassing, surpassed)** [1] If one person or thing **surpasses** another, the first is better than, or has more of a particular quality than, the second. ❑ *He was determined to surpass the achievements of his older brothers... Warwick Arts Centre is the second largest Arts Centre in Britain, surpassed in size only by London's Barbican.* VERB V n V-ed [2] If something **surpasses** expectations, it is much better than it was expected to be. ❑ *Conrad Black gave an excellent party that surpassed expectations.* VERB V n

**sur|plice** /sɜːʳplɪs/ **(surplices)** A **surplice** is a loose white knee-length garment which is worn over a longer garment by priests and members of the choir in some churches. ❑ *...the priest and choir in their lace surplices.* N-COUNT

**sur|plus** /sɜːʳpləs/ **(surpluses)** [1] If there is a **surplus of** something, there is more than is needed. ❑ *Germany suffers from a surplus of teachers.* ◆◇◇ N-VAR [2] **Surplus** is used to describe something that is extra or that is more than is needed. ❑ *Few people have large sums of surplus cash... The houses are being sold because they are surplus to requirements.* ADJ: usu ADJ n, also v-link ADJ *to* n [3] If a country has a trade **surplus**, it exports more than it imports. ❑ *Japan's annual trade surplus is in the region of 100 billion dollars.* N-COUNT: usu n N [4] If a government has a budget **surplus**, it has spent less than it received in taxes. ❑ *Norway's budget surplus has fallen from 5.9% in 1986 to an expected 0.1% this year.* N-COUNT: usu n N

**sur|prise** /səʳpraɪz/ **(surprises, surprising, surprised)** [1] A **surprise** is an unexpected event, fact, or piece of news. ❑ *I have a surprise for you: We are moving to Switzerland!... It may come as a surprise to some that a normal, healthy child is born with many skills... It is perhaps no surprise to see another 60s singing star attempting a comeback.* ◆◆◇ N-COUNT: oft N *to* n ♦ **Surprise** is also an adjective. ❑ *Baxter arrived here this afternoon, on a surprise visit.* ADJ: ADJ n [2] **Surprise** is the feeling that you have when something unexpected happens. ❑ *The Foreign Office in London has expressed surprise at these allegations... 'You mean he's going to vote against her?' Scobie asked in surprise... I started working hard for the first time in my life. To my surprise, I found I liked it.* N-UNCOUNT [3] If something **surprises** you, it gives you a feeling of surprise. ❑ *We'll solve the case ourselves and surprise everyone... It surprised me that a driver of Alain's experience should make those mistakes... It wouldn't surprise me if there was such chaos after this election that another had to be held... They were served lamb and rosemary and she surprised herself by eating greedily.* VERB V n *it* V n that/if *it* V n that/if V pron-refl [4] If you **surprise** someone, you give them, tell them, or do something pleasant that they are not expecting. ❑ *Surprise a new neighbour with one of your favourite home-made dishes.* VERB V n *with* n [5] If you describe someone or something as a **surprise**, you mean that they are very good or pleasant although you were not expecting this. ❑ *...Senga MacFie, one of the surprises of the World Championships three months ago.* N-COUNT [6] If you **surprise** someone, you attack, capture, or find them when they are not expecting it. ❑ *Marlborough led his armies across the Rhine and surprised the French and Bavarian armies near the village of Blenheim.* VERB V n [7] → See also **surprised**, **surprising**. [8] If something **takes** you **by surprise**, it happens when you are not expecting it or when you are not prepared for it. ❑ *His question took his two companions by surprise.* PHRASE: V inflects

**sur|prised** /səʳpraɪzd/ [1] If you are **surprised** at something, you have a feeling of surprise, because it is unexpected or unusual. ❑ *This lady was genuinely surprised at what happened to her pet... Chang seemed surprised to find the big living-room empty.* ◆◇◇ ADJ: usu v-link ADJ, oft ADJ *at/by* n, ADJ to-inf, ADJ that/how [2] → See also **surprise**.

**sur|pris|ing** /səʳpraɪzɪŋ/ [1] Something that is **surprising** is unexpected or unusual and makes you feel surprised. ❑ *It is not surprising that children learn to read at different rates... A surprising number of customers order the same sandwich every day.* ◆◇◇ ADJ: oft *it* v-link ADJ that/to-inf ♦ **sur|pris|ing|ly** *...the Flemish Bloc, which did surprisingly well in the general election last year.* ADV: ADV with cl, ADV adj/adv [2] → See also **surprise**.

**sur|re|al** /sərɪːəl/ If you describe something as **surreal**, you mean that the elements in it are combined in a strange way that you would not normally expect, like in a dream. ❑ *'Performance' is undoubtedly one of the most surreal movies ever made.* ADJ

**sur|re|al|ism** /sərɪːəlɪzəm/ **Surrealism** is a style in art and literature in which ideas, images, and objects are combined in a strange way, like in a dream. N-UNCOUNT

**sur|re|al|ist** /sərɪːəlɪst/ **(surrealists)** [1] **Surrealist** means related to or in the style of surrealism. ❑ *Dali's shoe hat was undoubtedly the most surrealist idea he ever worked on with Schiaparelli.* ADJ [2] A **surrealist** is an artist or writer whose work is based on the ideas of surrealism. N-COUNT

**sur|re|al|is|tic** /sərɪːəlɪstɪk/ [1] **Surrealistic** means the same as **surreal**. ❑ *...the surrealistic way the movie plays with time.* ADJ [2] **Surrealistic** means related to or in the style of surrealism. ❑ *...Man Ray's surrealistic study of a woman's face with glass teardrops.* ADJ: ADJ n

**sur|ren|der** /sərendəʳ/ **(surrenders, surrendering, surrendered)** [1] If you **surrender**, you stop fighting or resisting someone and agree that you have been beaten. ❑ *General Martin Bonnet called on the rebels to surrender... She surrendered to the police in London last December.* ◆◇◇ VERB V V *to* n ♦ **Surrender** is also a noun. ❑ *...the government's apparent surrender to demands made by the religious militants.* N-VAR: oft N *to* n [2] If you **surrender** something you would rather keep, you give it up or let someone else have it, for example after a struggle. ❑ *Nadja had to fill out forms surrendering all rights to her property.* VERB V n ♦ **Surrender** is also a noun. ❑ *...the sixteen-day deadline for the surrender of weapons and ammunition.* N-UNCOUNT: usu N *of* n [3] If you **surrender** something such as a ticket or your passport, you give it to someone in authority when they ask you to. [FORMAL] ❑ *They have been ordered to surrender their passports.* VERB V n

**sur|ren|der value** **(surrender values)** The **surrender value** of a life insurance policy is the amount of money you receive if you decide that you no longer wish to continue with the policy. [BUSINESS] N-COUNT

**sur|rep|ti|tious** /sʌrəptɪʃəs, AM sɜːr-/ A **surreptitious** action is done secretly. ❑ *He made a surreptitious entrance to the club through the little door in the brick wall.* ADJ = *furtive* ♦ **sur|rep|ti|tious|ly** *Surreptitiously Mark looked at his watch.* ADV: ADV with v

**sur|ro|ga|cy** /sʌrəgəsi, AM sɜːr-/ **Surrogacy** is an arrangement by which a woman gives birth to a baby on behalf of a woman who is physically unable to have babies herself, and then gives the baby to her. ❑ *In this country it is illegal to pay for surrogacy.* N-UNCOUNT

**sur|ro|gate** /sʌrəgeɪt, AM sɜːr-/ **(surrogates)** You use **surrogate** to describe a person or thing that is given a particular role because the person or thing that should have the role is not available. ❑ *Martin had become Howard Cosell's surrogate son.* ADJ: ADJ n ♦ **Surrogate** is also a noun. ❑ *Arms control should not be made into a surrogate for peace.* N-COUNT

**sur|ro|gate moth|er** **(surrogate mothers)** A **surrogate mother** is a woman who has agreed to give birth to a baby on behalf of another woman. N-COUNT

**sur|round** /səraʊnd/ **(surrounds, surrounding, surrounded)** ◆◆◇ 1 If a person or thing **is surrounded** by something, that thing is situated all around them. VERB ❑ *The small churchyard was surrounded by a rusted wrought-iron fence...* be V-ed *The shell surrounding the egg has many important functions.* V n *...the snipers and artillerymen in the surrounding hills.* V-ing 2 If you **are surrounded** by soldiers or police, they spread out so that they are in positions all the way around you. VERB = encircle ❑ *When the car stopped in the town square it was surrounded by soldiers and militiamen...* be V-ed *He tried to run away but gave up when he found himself surrounded.* V-ed 3 The circumstances, feelings, or ideas which **surround** something are those that are closely associated with it. VERB ❑ *The decision had been agreed in principle before today's meeting, but some controversy surrounded it.* V n 4 If you **surround yourself with** certain people or things, you make sure that you have a lot of them near you all the time. VERB ❑ *He had made it his business to surround himself with a hand-picked group of bright young officers...* V n with/by n *They love being surrounded by familiar possessions.* V n with/by n

**sur|round|ings** /səraʊndɪŋz/ When you are describing the place where you are at the moment, or the place where you live, you can refer to it as your **surroundings**. ❑ *Schumacher adapted effortlessly to his new surroundings.* N-PLURAL: oft poss N, in N with supp

**sur|tax** /sɜːʳtæks/ **Surtax** is an additional tax on incomes higher than the level at which ordinary tax is paid. [BUSINESS] ❑ *...a 10% surtax for Americans earning more than $250,000 a year.* N-UNCOUNT

**sur|ti|tle** /sɜːʳtaɪtᵊl/ **(surtitles)** At an opera or play that is being performed in a foreign language, **surtitles** are a translation or summary of the words, which appear on a screen above the stage. N-COUNT: usu pl

**sur|veil|lance** /səʳveɪləns/ **Surveillance** is the careful watching of someone, especially by an organization such as the police or the army. ❑ *He was arrested after being kept under constant surveillance... Police keep track of the kidnapper using electronic surveillance equipment.* N-UNCOUNT

**sur|vey** **(surveys, surveying, surveyed)** ◆◆◇

> ✔ The noun is pronounced /sɜːʳveɪ/. The verb is pronounced /səʳveɪ/, and can also be pronounced /sɜːʳveɪ/ in meanings 2 and 5.

1 If you carry out a **survey**, you try to find out detailed information about a lot of different people or things, usually by asking people a series of questions. ❑ *According to the survey, overall world trade has also slackened.* N-COUNT 2 If you **survey** a number of people, companies, or organizations, you try to find out information about their opinions or behaviour, usually by asking them a series of questions. VERB ❑ *Business Development Advisers surveyed 211 companies for the report...* V n *Only 18 percent of those surveyed opposed the idea.* V-ed 3 If you **survey** something, you look at or consider the whole of it carefully. VERB ❑ *He pushed himself to his feet and surveyed the room.* V n 4 If someone carries out a **survey** of an area of land, they examine it and measure it, usually in order to make a map of it. N-COUNT ❑ *...the organizer of the geological survey of India.* 5 If someone **surveys** an area of land, they examine it and measure it, usually in order to make a map of it. VERB ❑ *Scarborough Council commissioned geological experts earlier this year to survey the cliffs.* V n 6 A **survey** is a careful examination of the condition and structure of a house, usually carried out in order to give information to a person who wants to buy it. [mainly BRIT] N-COUNT ❑ *...a structural survey undertaken by a qualified surveyor.*

> ✔ in AM, use **inspection**

7 If someone **surveys** a house, they examine it carefully and report on its structure, usually in order to give advice to a person who is thinking of buying it. [mainly BRIT] VERB ❑ *...the people who surveyed the house for the mortgage.* V n

> ✔ in AM, use **inspect**

**sur|vey|or** /səʳveɪəʳ/ **(surveyors)** 1 A **surveyor** is a person whose job is to survey land. N-COUNT ❑ *...the surveyor's maps of the Queen Alexandra Range.* 2 A **surveyor** is a person whose job is to survey buildings. [BRIT] N-COUNT ❑ *Our surveyor warned us that the house needed totally rebuilding.*

> ✔ in AM, use **structural engineer**, **inspector**

3 → See also **quantity surveyor**.

**sur|viv|al** /səʳvaɪvᵊl/ ◆◇◇ 1 If you refer to the **survival** of something or someone, you mean that they manage to continue or exist in spite of difficult circumstances. N-UNCOUNT ❑ *...companies which have been struggling for survival in the advancing recession... Ask for the free booklet 'Debt: a Survival Guide'.* 2 If you refer to the **survival** of a person or living thing, you mean that they live through a dangerous situation in which it was possible that they might die. N-UNCOUNT ❑ *If cancers are spotted early there's a high chance of survival... An animal's sense of smell is still crucial to its survival.* 3 You can use **the survival of the fittest** to refer to a situation in which only the strongest people or things continue to live or be successful, while the others die or fail. PHRASE

**sur|vive** /səʳvaɪv/ **(survives, surviving, survived)** ◆◆◇ 1 If a person or living thing **survives** in a dangerous situation such as an accident or an illness, they do not die. VERB ❑ *...the sequence of events that left the eight pupils battling to survive in icy seas for over four hours...* V *Those organisms that are most suited to the environment will be those that will survive...* V *Drugs that dissolve blood clots can help people survive heart attacks.* V n 2 If you **survive** in difficult circumstances, you manage to live or continue in spite of them and do not let them affect you very much. VERB ❑ *...people who are struggling to survive without jobs.* V *...a man who had survived his share of boardroom coups.* V n 3 If something **survives**, it continues to exist even after being in a dangerous situation or existing for a long time. VERB ❑ *When the market economy is introduced, many factories will not survive...* V *The chances of a planet surviving a supernova always looked terribly slim.* V n 4 If you **survive** someone, you continue to live after they have died. VERB ❑ *Most women will survive their spouses.* V n

**sur|vi|vor** /səʳvaɪvəʳ/ **(survivors)** 1 A **survivor of** a disaster, accident, or illness is someone who continues to live afterwards in spite of coming close to death. N-COUNT: oft N of n ❑ *Officials said there were no survivors of the plane crash.* 2 A **survivor of** a very unpleasant experience is a person who has had such an experience, and who is still affected by it. N-COUNT: oft N of n ❑ *This book is written with survivors of child sexual abuse in mind.* 3 A person's **survivors** are the members of their family who continue to live after they have died. [AM] N-COUNT: usu pl, usu poss N, N of ❑ *The compensation bill offers the miners or their survivors as much as $100,000 apiece.* 4 If you describe someone as a **survivor**, you approve of the fact that they are able to carry on with their life even though they experience many difficulties. N-COUNT approval ❑ *Above all Susie is a great survivor, with a bright, indomitable spirit.*

**sus|cep|tibil|ity** /səseptɪbɪlɪti/ **(susceptibilities)** [1] If you have a **susceptibility to** something unpleasant, you are likely to be affected by it. ❑ *...his increased susceptibility to infections.* [2] A person's **susceptibilities** are feelings which can be easily hurt. [FORMAL] ❑ *I am well aware that in saying this I shall outrage a few susceptibilities.*
N-VAR = vulnerability
N-PLURAL = sensibilities

**sus|cep|tible** /səseptɪbᵊl/ [1] If you are **susceptible to** something or someone, you are very likely to be influenced by them. ❑ *Young people are the most susceptible to advertisements... James was extremely susceptible to flattery.* [2] If you are **susceptible to** a disease or injury, you are very likely to be affected by it. ❑ *Walking with weights makes the shoulders very susceptible to injury.*
ADJ: v-link ADJ *to* n
ADJ: usu v-link ADJ *to* n = vulnerable

**su|shi** /suːʃi/ **Sushi** is a Japanese dish of rice with sweet vinegar, often served with raw fish.
N-UNCOUNT

**sus|pect** **(suspects, suspecting, suspected)** ◆◆◇

The verb is pronounced /səspekt/. The noun and adjective are pronounced /sʌspekt/.

[1] You use **suspect** when you are stating something that you believe is probably true, in order to make it sound less strong or direct. ❑ *I suspect they were right... The above complaints are, I suspect, just the tip of the iceberg... Do women really share such stupid jokes? We suspect not.* [2] If you **suspect** that something dishonest or unpleasant has been done, you believe that it has probably been done. If you **suspect** someone **of** doing an action of this kind, you believe that they probably did it. ❑ *He suspected that the woman staying in the flat above was using heroin... It was perfectly all right, he said, because the police had not suspected him of anything... You don't really think Webb suspects you?... Frears was rushed to hospital with a suspected heart attack.* [3] A **suspect** is a person who the police or authorities think may be guilty of a crime. ❑ *Police have arrested a suspect in a series of killings and sexual assaults in the city.* [4] **Suspect** things or people are ones that you think may be dangerous or may be less good or genuine than they appear. ❑ *Delegates evacuated the building when a suspect package was found.*
VERB [vagueness] V that; V that; V *not/so*
VERB V that; V n *of* n; V n; V-ed
N-COUNT
ADJ

**sus|pend** /səspend/ **(suspends, suspending, suspended)** ◆◇◇ [1] If you **suspend** something, you delay it or stop it from happening for a while or until a decision is made about it. ❑ *A UN official said aid programs will be suspended until there's adequate protection for relief convoys.* [2] If someone **is suspended**, they are prevented from holding a particular job or position for a fixed length of time or until a decision is made about them. ❑ *Julie was suspended from her job shortly after the incident... The Lawn Tennis Association suspended Mr Castle from the British team.* [3] If something **is suspended** from a high place, it is hanging from that place. ❑ *...a mobile of birds or nursery rhyme characters which could be suspended over the cot.*
VERB V n
VERB *be* V-ed; V n
VERB: usu passive *be* V-ed

**sus|pend|ed ani|ma|tion** [1] **Suspended animation** is a state in which an animal is unconscious, with its body functioning very slowly, for example so that the animal can survive the winter. [2] If you describe someone as being in a state of **suspended animation**, you mean that they have become inactive and are doing nothing. ❑ *She lay in a state of suspended animation, waiting for dawnlight, when she would rise.*
N-UNCOUNT
N-UNCOUNT

**sus|pend|ed sen|tence** **(suspended sentences)** If a criminal is given a **suspended sentence**, they are given a prison sentence which they have to serve if they commit another crime within a specified period of time. ❑ *John was given a four-month suspended sentence.*
N-COUNT

**sus|pend|er** /səspendəʳ/ **(suspenders)** [1] **Suspenders** are the fastenings which hold up a woman's stockings. [BRIT]
N-COUNT: usu pl

in AM, use **garters**

[2] **Suspenders** are a pair of straps that go over someone's shoulders and are fastened to their trousers at the front and back to prevent the trousers from falling down. [AM]
N-PLURAL: also *a pair of* N

in BRIT, use **braces**

**sus|pend|er belt** **(suspender belts)** A **suspender belt** is a piece of underwear for women that is used for holding up stockings. [BRIT]
N-COUNT

in AM, use **garter belt**

**sus|pense** /səspens/ [1] **Suspense** is a state of excitement or anxiety about something that is going to happen very soon, for example about some news that you are waiting to hear. ❑ *The suspense over the two remaining hostages ended last night when the police discovered the bullet ridden bodies.* [2] If you **keep** or **leave** someone **in suspense**, you deliberately delay telling them something that they are very eager to know about. ❑ *Keppler kept all his men in suspense until that morning before announcing which two would be going.*
N-UNCOUNT
PHRASE: V inflects, PHR after v

**sus|pense|ful** /səspensfʊl/ A **suspenseful** story makes you feel excited or anxious about what is going to happen in the story next. ❑ *...a suspenseful and sinister tale.*
ADJ: usu ADJ n

**sus|pen|sion** /səspenʃᵊn/ **(suspensions)** [1] The **suspension** of something is the act of delaying or stopping it for a while or until a decision is made about it. ❑ *A strike by British Airways ground staff has led to the suspension of flights between London and Manchester.* [2] Someone's **suspension** is their removal from a job or position for a period of time or until a decision is made about them. ❑ *The minister warned that any civil servant not at his desk faced immediate suspension.* [3] A vehicle's **suspension** consists of the springs and other devices attached to the wheels, which give a smooth ride over uneven ground.
N-UNCOUNT
N-VAR
N-VAR

**sus|pen|sion bridge** **(suspension bridges)** A **suspension bridge** is a type of bridge that is supported from above by cables.
N-COUNT

**sus|pi|cion** /səspɪʃᵊn/ **(suspicions)** [1] **Suspicion** or a **suspicion** is a belief or feeling that someone has committed a crime or done something wrong. ❑ *There was a suspicion that this runner attempted to avoid the procedures for dope testing... The police said their suspicions were aroused because Mr Owens had other marks on his body... Scotland Yard had assured him he was not under suspicion.* [2] If there is **suspicion of** someone or something, people do not trust them or consider them to be reliable. ❑ *...the traditional British suspicion of psychotherapy... He may have had some suspicions of Michael Foster, the editor of the journal.* [3] A **suspicion** is a feeling that something is probably true or is likely to happen. ❑ *I have a sneaking suspicion that they are going to succeed.* [4] A **suspicion of** something is a very small amount of it. [WRITTEN] ❑ *...large blooms of white with a suspicion of pale pink.*
◆◇◇ N-VAR: oft N that, N *of* n, *under* N, *on* N *of* n
N-VAR: oft N *of* n
N-COUNT: oft N that
N-SING: usu N *of* n = hint

**sus|pi|cious** /səspɪʃəs/ [1] If you are **suspicious of** someone or something, you do not trust them, and are careful when dealing with them. ❑ *He was rightly suspicious of meeting me until I reassured him I was not writing about him... He has his father's suspicious nature.* ♦ **sus|pi|cious|ly** *'What is it you want me to do?' Adams asked suspiciously.* [2] If you are **suspicious of** someone or something, you believe that they are probably involved in a crime or some dishonest activity. ❑ *Two officers on patrol became suspicious of two men in a car... A woman kept prisoner in a basement was rescued after suspicious neighbours tipped off police.* [3] If you describe someone or something as **suspicious**, you mean that there is some aspect of them which makes you think that they are involved in a crime or a dishonest activity. ❑ *He reported that two suspicious-looking characters had approached Callendar.* ♦ **sus|pi|cious|ly** *They'll question them as to whether anyone was seen acting suspiciously in the area over the last few days... Police were told to arrest voters found with suspiciously large sums of money in their pockets.* [4] → See also **suspiciously**.
ADJ: oft ADJ *of* n/-ing
ADJ: ADV after v
ADJ: oft ADJ *of* n
ADJ
ADV: ADV with v, ADV adj/adv

**sus|pi|cious|ly** /səspɪʃəsli/ [1] If you say that one thing looks or sounds **suspiciously** like another thing, you mean that it probably is that thing, or something very similar to it, although it may be intended to seem different. ❑ *The tan-coloured dog looks suspiciously like an American pit bull terrier.* ADV: ADV prep [2] You can use **suspiciously** when you are describing something that you think is slightly strange or not as it should be. ❑ *He lives alone in a suspiciously tidy flat in Notting Hill Gate.* ADV: ADV adj/adv [3] → See also **suspicious**.

**suss** /sʌs/ **(susses, sussing, sussed)** If you **suss** a person or situation, you realize or work out what their real character or nature is. [BRIT, INFORMAL] VERB ❑ *I think I've sussed the reason for it...* V n *The women began to suss that there was no reason why they should be impressed by him...* V that *We're getting the problem sussed.* *get* n V-ed Also V wh ♦ **Suss out** means the same as **suss**. PHRASAL VERB ❑ *They're sussing out the area to see how strong the police presence is...* V P n (not pron) *He susses his colleagues out and he knows who he can trust...* V n P *I'd had the training to suss out what he was up to.* V P wh Also V that

**sussed** /sʌst/ If someone is **sussed**, they are clever and know a lot about something such as clothes, pop music, or politics. [BRIT, INFORMAL] ADJ = *smart*

**sus|tain** /səsteɪn/ **(sustains, sustaining, sustained)** ◆◇◇ [1] If you **sustain** something, you continue it or maintain it for a period of time. VERB ❑ *But he has sustained his fierce social conscience from young adulthood through old age.* V n *...a period of sustained economic growth throughout 1995.* V-ed [2] If you **sustain** something such as a defeat, loss, or injury, it happens to you. [FORMAL] VERB ❑ *Every aircraft in there has sustained some damage...* V n *A seventeen-year-old tourist died late last night of injuries sustained in yesterday's bomb blast.* V-ed [3] If something **sustains** you, it supports you by giving you help, strength, or encouragement. [FORMAL] VERB ❑ *The cash dividends they get from the cash crop would sustain them during the lean season.* V n

**sus|tain|able** /səsteɪnəbᵊl/ [1] You use **sustainable** to describe the use of natural resources when this use is kept at a steady level that is not likely to damage the environment. ADJ ❑ *Try to buy wood that you know has come from a sustainable source.* [2] A **sustainable** plan, method, or system is designed to continue at the same rate or level of activity without any problems. ADJ ❑ *The creation of an efficient and sustainable transport system is critical to the long-term future of London.*

**sus|te|nance** /sʌstɪnəns/ **Sustenance** is food or drink which a person, animal, or plant needs to remain alive and healthy. [FORMAL] N-UNCOUNT ❑ *The state provided a basic quantity of food for daily sustenance, but little else.*

**su|ture** /suːtʃəʳ/ **(sutures)** A **suture** is a stitch made to join together the open parts of a wound, especially one made after a patient has been operated on. [MEDICAL] N-COUNT

**SUV** /es juː viː/ **(SUVs)** An **SUV** is a powerful vehicle with four-wheel drive that can be driven over rough ground. **SUV** is an abbreviation for 'sport utility vehicle'. N-COUNT

**svelte** /svelt, sfelt/ Someone who is **svelte** is slim and looks attractive and elegant. ADJ [approval]

**SW**

✔ in AM, also use **S.W.**

**SW** is a written abbreviation for **south-west**. ❑ *...King's Road, London SW 3.*

**swab** /swɒb/ **(swabs, swabbing, swabbed)** [1] A **swab** is a small piece of cotton wool used by a doctor or nurse for cleaning a wound or putting a substance on it. N-COUNT [2] If you **swab** something, you clean it using a wet cloth or a tool called a mop. VERB ❑ *I noticed a lone man in the cafeteria swabbing the floor as I passed.* V n

**swad|dle** /swɒdᵊl/ **(swaddles, swaddling, swaddled)** If you **swaddle** a baby, you wrap cloth around it in order to keep it warm or to prevent it from moving. [OLD-FASHIONED] VERB ❑ *Swaddle your new-born baby so that she feels secure.* V n *...a baby swaddled in silk brocade.* V-ed

**swag** /swæg/ **(swags)** [1] **Swag** is stolen goods, or money obtained illegally. [INFORMAL, OLD-FASHIONED] N-UNCOUNT [2] A **swag** is a piece of material that is put above a window and hangs down in a decorative way. N-COUNT

**swag|ger** /swægəʳ/ **(swaggers, swaggering, swaggered)** If you **swagger**, you walk in a very proud, confident way, holding your body upright and swinging your hips. VERB ❑ *A broad shouldered man wearing a dinner jacket swaggered confidently up to the bar...* V prep/adv *John Steed was an arrogant, swaggering young man.* V-ing ♦ **Swagger** is also a noun. N-SING ❑ *He walked with something of a swagger.*

**swain** /sweɪn/ **(swains)** A **swain** is a young man who is in love. [OLD-FASHIONED] N-COUNT

**swal|low** /swɒloʊ/ **(swallows, swallowing, swallowed)** [1] If you **swallow** something, you cause it to go from your mouth down into your stomach. VERB ❑ *You are asked to swallow a capsule containing vitamin B...* V n *Polly took a bite of the apple, chewed and swallowed.* V ♦ **Swallow** is also a noun. N-COUNT ❑ *Jan lifted her glass and took a quick swallow.* [2] If you **swallow**, you make a movement in your throat as if you are swallowing something, often because you are nervous or frightened. VERB ❑ *Nancy swallowed hard and shook her head.* V [3] If someone **swallows** a story or a statement, they believe it completely. VERB ❑ *It was vital that he swallowed the story about Juanita being in that motel room that night.* V n [4] A **swallow** is a kind of small bird with pointed wings and a forked tail. N-COUNT [5] **a bitter pill to swallow** → see **pill**.

♦ **swallow up** [1] If one thing **is swallowed up** by another, it becomes part of the first thing and no longer has a separate identity of its own. PHRASAL VERB ❑ *During the 1980s monster publishing houses started to swallow up smaller companies.* V P n Also V n P [2] If something **swallows up** money or resources, it uses them entirely while giving very little in return. PHRASAL VERB ❑ *A seven-day TV ad campaign could swallow up the best part of £50,000...* V P n (not pron) *Farmers could see a quarter of their income swallowed up by the interest rate rise.* V-ed P Also V n P [3] If a person or thing **is swallowed up** by something, they disappear into it so that you cannot see them any more. PHRASAL VERB ❑ *He headed back towards the flea market and was swallowed up in the crowd...* *be* V-ed P *Weeds had swallowed up the garden.* V P n (not pron) Also V n P

**swam** /swæm/ **Swam** is the past tense of **swim**.

**swamp** /swɒmp/ **(swamps, swamping, swamped)** [1] A **swamp** is an area of very wet land with wild plants growing in it. N-VAR [2] If something **swamps** a place or object, it fills it with water. VERB ❑ *A rogue wave swamped the boat.* V n [3] If you **are swamped** by things or people, you have more of them than you can deal with. VERB: usu passive ❑ *He is swamped with work.* *be* V-ed

**swamp|land** /swɒmplænd/ **(swamplands)** **Swampland** is an area of land that is always very wet. N-VAR

**swampy** /swɒmpi/ **(swampier, swampiest)** A **swampy** area of land is always very wet. ADJ

**swan** /swɒn/ **(swans, swanning, swanned)** [1] A **swan** is a large bird with a very long neck. Swans live on rivers and lakes and are usually white. N-COUNT [2] If you describe someone as **swanning around** or **swanning off**, you mean that they go and have fun, rather than working or taking care of their responsibilities. [BRIT, INFORMAL] VERB ❑ *She spends her time swanning around the world.* V prep/adv

**swank** /swæŋk/ **(swanks, swanking, swanked)** If someone **is swanking**, they are speaking about things they own or things they have achieved, in order to impress other people. [mainly BRIT, INFORMAL] VERB [disapproval] = *boast, brag* ❑ *I have always been against swanking about all the things I have been lucky enough to win.* V *about* n Also V

**swanky** /swæŋki/ **(swankier, swankiest)** If you describe something as **swanky**, you mean that it ADJ: usu ADJ n = *ritzy* is fashionable and expensive. [INFORMAL] ❑ *...one of the swanky hotels that line the shore at Acapulco.*

**swan song** also **swan-song.** Someone's **swan song** is the last time that they do something for which they are famous, for example the last time that an actor gives a performance in the theatre. ❑ *I competed in the Commonwealth Games in Christchurch, which was my swan song.* N-SING

**swap** /swɒp/ **(swaps, swapping, swapped)** also **swop.** [1] If you **swap** something with someone, you give it to them and receive a different thing in exchange. ❑ *Next week they will swap places and will repeat the switch weekly... I'd gladly swap places with mummy any day... I know a sculptor who swaps her pieces for drawings by a well-known artist... Some hostages were swapped for convicted prisoners.* V-RECIP = exchange; V pl-n; V pl-n *with* n; V n *for/with* n; V n *for/with* n ♦ **Swap** is also a noun. ❑ *If she ever fancies a job swap, I could be interested.* N-COUNT: oft n N [2] If you **swap** one thing **for** another, you remove the first thing and replace it with the second, or you stop doing the first thing and start doing the second. ❑ *Despite the heat, he'd swapped his overalls for a suit and tie... Both sides swapped their goalies in the 30th minute.* VERB; V n *for* n; V n

**swarm** /swɔːʳm/ **(swarms, swarming, swarmed)** [1] A **swarm of** bees or other insects is a large group of them flying together. N-COUNT-COLL: oft N *of* n [2] When bees or other insects **swarm**, they move or fly in a large group. ❑ *A dark cloud of bees comes swarming out of the hive.* VERB; V prep/adv [3] When people **swarm** somewhere, they move there quickly in a large group. ❑ *People swarmed to the shops, buying up everything in sight.* VERB; V prep/adv [4] A **swarm of** people is a large group of them moving about quickly. ❑ *Today at the crossing there were swarms of tourists taking photographs.* N-COUNT-COLL: oft N *of* n = horde [5] If a place **is swarming with** people, it is full of people moving about in a busy way. ❑ *Within minutes the area was swarming with officers who began searching a nearby wood.* VERB: usu cont; V *with* n

**swarthy** /swɔːʳði/ A **swarthy** person has a dark face. ❑ *He had a broad swarthy face.* ADJ

**swash|buck|ling** /swɒʃbʌklɪŋ/ If you describe someone or something as **swashbuckling**, you mean that they are connected with adventure and excitement. ❑ *...a swashbuckling adventure story.* ADJ

**swas|ti|ka** /swɒstɪkə/ **(swastikas)** A **swastika** is a symbol in the shape of a cross with each arm bent over at right angles. It is used in India as a good luck sign, but it was also used by the Nazis in Germany as their official symbol. N-COUNT

**swat** /swɒt/ **(swats, swatting, swatted)** If you **swat** something such as an insect, you hit it with a quick, swinging movement, using your hand or a flat object. ❑ *Hundreds of flies buzz around us, and the workman keeps swatting them.* VERB; V n

**swathe** /sweɪð, AM swɑːð/ **(swathes, swathing, swathed)**

✔ The noun is also spelled **swath.**

[1] A **swathe of** land is a long strip of land. ❑ *Year by year great swathes of this small nation's countryside disappear.* N-COUNT: usu N *of* n [2] A **swathe of** cloth is a long strip of cloth, especially one that is wrapped around someone or something. ❑ *...swathes of white silk.* N-COUNT: usu N *of* n [3] To **swathe** someone or something **in** cloth means to wrap them in it completely. ❑ *She swathed her enormous body in thin black fabrics... His head was swathed in bandages made from a torn sheet.* VERB; V n *in* n; V-ed

**SWAT team** /swɒt tiːm/ **(SWAT teams)** A **SWAT team** is a group of policemen who have been specially trained to deal with very dangerous or violent situations. **SWAT** is an abbreviation for 'Special Weapons and Tactics'. [mainly AM] N-COUNT

**sway** /sweɪ/ **(sways, swaying, swayed)** [1] When people or things **sway**, they lean or swing slowly from one side to the other. ❑ *The people swayed back and forth with arms linked... The whole boat swayed and tipped. ...a coastal highway lined with tall, swaying palm trees.* VERB; V adv/prep; V; V-ing [2] If you **are swayed by** someone or something, you are influenced by them. ❑ *Don't ever be swayed by fashion. ...last minute efforts by the main political parties to sway the voters in tomorrow's local elections.* VERB; *be* V-ed; V n

PHRASES [3] If someone or something **holds sway**, they have great power or influence over a particular place or activity. ❑ *South of the Usk, a completely different approach seems to hold sway.* PHRASE: V inflects, oft PHR *over* n [4] If you are **under the sway of** someone or something, they have great influence over you. ❑ *How mothers keep daughters under their sway is the subject of the next five sections.* PHRASE: PHR after v, v-link PHR

**swear** /sweəʳ/ **(swears, swearing, swore, sworn)** [1] If someone **swears**, they use language that is considered to be rude or offensive, usually because they are angry. ❑ *It's wrong to swear and shout... They swore at them and ran off.* VERB; V; V *at* n [2] If you **swear to** do something, you promise in a serious way that you will do it. ❑ *Alan swore that he would do everything in his power to help us... We have sworn to fight cruelty wherever we find it... The police are the only civil servants who have to swear allegiance to the Crown... I have sworn an oath to defend her.* VERB; V that; V to-inf; V n; V n [3] If you say that you **swear** that something is true or that you can **swear** to it, you are saying very firmly that it is true. ❑ *I swear I've told you all I know... I swear on all I hold dear that I had nothing to do with this... Behind them was a confusion of noise, perhaps even a shot, but he couldn't swear to it.* VERB emphasis; V that; V *on/by* n that; V *to* n [4] If someone **is sworn to** secrecy or **is sworn to** silence, they promise another person that they will not reveal a secret. ❑ *She was bursting to announce the news but was sworn to secrecy.* VERB: usu passive; *be* V-ed *to* n [5] → See also **sworn.**

♦ **swear by** If you **swear by** something, you believe that it can be relied on to have a particular effect. [INFORMAL] ❑ *Many people swear by vitamin C's ability to ward off colds.* PHRASAL VERB; V P n

♦ **swear in** When someone **is sworn in**, they formally promise to fulfil the duties of a new job or appointment. ❑ *Soon after the New Year, the new Congress will come to Washington to be sworn in.* PHRASAL VERB: usu passive; *be* V-ed P

**swearing-in** The **swearing-in** at the beginning of a trial or official appointment is the act of making formal promises to fulfil the duties it involves. N-SING

**swear word** **(swear words)** also **swear-word.** A **swear word** is a word which is considered to be rude or offensive. Swear words are usually used when people are angry. N-COUNT

**sweat** /swet/ **(sweats, sweating, sweated)** [1] **Sweat** is the salty colourless liquid which comes through your skin when you are hot, ill, or afraid. ❑ *Both horse and rider were dripping with sweat within five minutes.* N-UNCOUNT [2] When you **sweat**, sweat comes through your skin. ❑ *Already they were sweating as the sun beat down upon them.* VERB; V ♦ **sweat|ing** *...symptoms such as sweating, irritability, anxiety and depression.* N-UNCOUNT [3] If someone is **in a sweat**, they are sweating a lot. ❑ *Every morning I would break out in a sweat... I really don't feel a bit sick, no night sweats, no fevers.* N-COUNT [4] If someone is **in a cold sweat** or **in a sweat**, they feel frightened or embarrassed. ❑ *The very thought brought me out in a cold sweat.* PHRASE: PHR after v, v-link ADJ [5] to **sweat blood** → see **blood.**

**sweat|er** /swetəʳ/ **(sweaters)** A **sweater** is a warm knitted piece of clothing which covers the upper part of your body and your arms. N-COUNT = jumper, pullover

**sweat|pants** /swetpænts/ also **sweat pants.** **Sweatpants** are the part of a sweatsuit that covers your legs. N-PLURAL

**sweat|shirt** /swetʃɜːʳt/ **(sweatshirts)** also **sweat shirt.** A **sweatshirt** is a loose warm piece of casual clothing, usually made of thick stretchy cotton, which covers the upper part of your body and your arms. N-COUNT

**sweat|shop** /swetʃɒp/ **(sweatshops)** also **sweat shop.** If you describe a small factory as a **sweatshop**, you mean that many people work there in poor conditions for low pay. N-COUNT disapproval

**sweat|suit** /swetsuːt/ **(sweatsuits)** also **sweat suit.** A **sweatsuit** is a loose, warm, stretchy suit consisting of long trousers and a top which people wear to relax and do exercise. N-COUNT = *tracksuit*

**sweaty** /sweti/ **(sweatier, sweatiest)** 1 If parts of your body or your clothes are **sweaty**, they are soaked or covered with sweat. ❑ *...sweaty hands... She was hot and sweaty.* ADJ 2 A **sweaty** place or activity makes you sweat because it is hot or tiring. ❑ *...a sweaty nightclub.* ADJ

**swede** /swiːd/ **(swedes)** A **swede** is a round yellow root vegetable with a brown or purple skin. [BRIT] N-VAR

☑ in AM, use **rutabaga**

**Swede** /swiːd/ **(Swedes)** A **Swede** is a Swedish citizen, or a person of Swedish origin. N-COUNT

**Swe|dish** /swiːdɪʃ/ 1 **Swedish** means belonging or relating to Sweden, or to its people, language, or culture. ADJ 2 **Swedish** is the language spoken in Sweden. N-UNCOUNT

**sweep** /swiːp/ **(sweeps, sweeping, swept)** ◆◇◇
1 If you **sweep** an area of floor or ground, you push dirt or rubbish off it using a brush with a long handle. ❑ *The owner of the store was sweeping his floor when I walked in... She was in the kitchen sweeping crumbs into a dust pan... Norma picked up the broom and began sweeping.* VERB V n V n prep/adv V, Also V n with adv 2 If you **sweep** things off something, you push them off with a quick smooth movement of your arm. ❑ *With a gesture of frustration, she swept the cards from the table... 'Thanks friend,' he said, while sweeping the money into his pocket.* VERB V n prep/adv V n prep/adv 3 If someone with long hair **sweeps** their hair into a particular style, they put it into that style. ❑ *...stylish ways of sweeping your hair off your face... Her long, fine hair was swept back in a ponytail.* VERB V n prep/adv V-ed 4 If your arm or hand **sweeps** in a particular direction, or if you **sweep** it there, it moves quickly and smoothly in that direction. ❑ *His arm swept around the room... Daniels swept his arm over his friend's shoulder. ...the long sweeping arm movements of a violinist.* VERB V prep/adv V n prep/adv V-ing ♦ **Sweep** is also a noun. ❑ *With one sweep of her hand she threw back the sheets.* N-COUNT 5 If wind, a stormy sea, or another strong force **sweeps** someone or something along, it moves them quickly along. ❑ *...landslides that buried homes and swept cars into the sea... Suddenly, she was swept along by the crowd.* VERB V n prep/adv V n prep/adv 6 If you **are swept** somewhere, you are taken there very quickly. ❑ *The visitors were swept past various monuments... A limousine swept her along the busy freeway to the airport.* VERB be V-ed prep/adv V n prep/adv 7 If something **sweeps** from one place to another, it moves there extremely quickly. [WRITTEN] ❑ *An icy wind swept through the streets... The car swept past the gate house.* VERB V prep/adv V prep/adv 8 If events, ideas, or beliefs **sweep** through a place, they spread quickly through it. ❑ *A flu epidemic is sweeping through Moscow. ...the wave of patriotism sweeping the country.* VERB V through/across n V n 9 If someone **sweeps** into a place, they walk into it in a proud, confident way, often when they are angry. [WRITTEN] ❑ *She swept into the conference room... Scarlet with rage, she swept past her employer and stormed up the stairs... The Chief turned and swept out.* VERB V prep/adv V prep/adv V prep/adv 10 If a person or group **sweeps** an election or **sweeps to** victory, they win the election easily. ❑ *...a man who's promised to make radical changes to benefit the poor has swept the election... In both republics, centre-right parties swept to power.* VERB V n V to n 11 If someone makes a **sweep of** a place, they search it, usually because they are looking for people who are hiding or for an illegal activity. ❑ *Two of the soldiers swiftly began making a sweep of the premises.* N-COUNT: usu sing 12 → See also **sweeping**, **chimney sweep**.

**PHRASES** 13 If someone **sweeps** something bad or wrong **under the carpet**, or if they **sweep** it **under the rug**, they try to prevent people from hearing about it. ❑ *For a long time this problem has been swept under the carpet.* PHRASE: V inflects 14 If you **make a clean sweep of** something such as a series of games or tournaments, you win them all. ❑ *...the first club to make a clean sweep of all three trophies.* PHRASE: PHR n, usu v PHR 15 to **sweep the board** → see **board**.

♦ **sweep up** If you **sweep up** rubbish or dirt, you push it together with a brush and then remove it. ❑ *Get a broom and sweep up that glass will you?... He started working for a gallery sweeping up and making the tea.* PHRASAL VERB V P n (not pron) V P Also V n P

**sweep|er** /swiːpəʳ/ **(sweepers)** In football, a **sweeper** is a player whose position is behind the main defenders but in front of the goalkeeper. N-COUNT

**sweep|ing** /swiːpɪŋ/ 1 A **sweeping** curve is a long wide curve. ❑ *...the long sweeping curve of Rio's Guanabara Bay.* ADJ: ADJ n 2 If someone makes a **sweeping** statement or generalization, they make a statement which applies to all things of a particular kind, although they have not considered all the relevant facts carefully. ❑ *It is far too early to make sweeping statements about gene therapy.* ADJ: usu ADJ n [disapproval] 3 **Sweeping** changes are large and very important or significant. ❑ *The new government has started to make sweeping changes in the economy.* ADJ: usu ADJ n = *far-reaching* 4 → See also **sweep**.

**sweep|stake** /swiːpsteɪk/ **(sweepstakes)** A **sweepstake** is a method of gambling in which each person pays a small amount of money and is given the name of a competitor before a race or contest. The person who has the name of the winner receives all the money. N-COUNT

**sweet** /swiːt/ **(sweeter, sweetest, sweets)** ◆◇◇
1 **Sweet** food and drink contains a lot of sugar. ❑ *...a mug of sweet tea... If the sauce seems too sweet, add a dash of red wine vinegar.* ADJ ♦ **sweet|ness** *Florida oranges have a natural sweetness.* N-UNCOUNT 2 **Sweets** are small sweet things such as toffees, chocolates, and mints. [BRIT] N-COUNT

☑ in AM, use **candy**

3 A **sweet** is something sweet, such as fruit or a pudding, that you eat at the end of a meal, especially in a restaurant. [BRIT] ❑ *The sweet was a mousse flavoured with whisky.* N-VAR = *dessert*

☑ in AM, use **dessert**

4 A **sweet** smell is a pleasant one, for example the smell of a flower. ❑ *She'd baked some bread which made the air smell sweet.* ADJ 5 If you describe something such as air or water as **sweet**, you mean that it smells or tastes pleasantly fresh and clean. ❑ *I gulped a breath of sweet air.* ADJ 6 A **sweet** sound is pleasant, smooth, and gentle. ❑ *Her voice was as soft and sweet as a young girl's. ...the sweet sounds of Mozart.* ADJ ♦ **sweet|ly** *He sang much more sweetly than he has before.* ADV: usu ADV with v 7 If you describe something as **sweet**, you mean that it gives you great pleasure and satisfaction. [WRITTEN] ❑ *There are few things quite as sweet as revenge.* ADJ ≠ *bitter* 8 If you describe someone as **sweet**, you mean that they are pleasant, kind, and gentle towards other people. ❑ *How sweet of you to think of me!* ADJ ♦ **sweet|ly** *I just smiled sweetly and said no.* ADV: usu ADV with v 9 If you describe a small person or thing as **sweet**, you mean that they are attractive in a simple or unsophisticated way. [INFORMAL] ❑ *...a sweet little baby girl... The house was really sweet.* ADJ = *cute* 10 → See also **sweetly**, **sweetness**. 11 **a sweet tooth** → see **tooth**.

**sweet and sour** also **sweet-and-sour.** **Sweet and sour** is used to describe Chinese food that contains both a sweet flavour and something sharp or sour such as lemon or vinegar. ADJ: ADJ n

**sweet|bread** /swiːtbred/ **(sweetbreads)** **Sweetbreads** are meat obtained from the pancreas of a calf or a lamb. N-COUNT

**sweet|corn** /swiːtkɔʳn/ also **sweet corn.** **Sweetcorn** is a long rounded vegetable covered in small yellow seeds. It is part of the maize plant. The seeds themselves can also be referred to as **sweetcorn**. N-UNCOUNT

**sweet|en** /swiːtᵊn/ **(sweetens, sweetening, sweetened)** 1 If you **sweeten** food or drink, you add sugar, honey, or another sweet substance to it. ❑ *He liberally sweetened his coffee... The Australians* VERB V n *fry their bananas and sweeten them with honey.* V n *with* n

2 If you **sweeten** something such as an offer or a business deal, you try to make someone want it more by improving it or by increasing the amount you are willing to pay. ❑ *Kalon Group has sweetened its takeover offer for Manders.* VERB · V n

**sweet|en|er** /swiːtənəʳ/ **(sweeteners)** 1 **Sweetener** is an artificial substance that can be used in drinks instead of sugar. N-MASS 2 A **sweetener** is something that you give or offer someone in order to persuade them to accept an offer or business deal. N-COUNT

**sweet|heart** /swiːthɑːʳt/ **(sweethearts)** 1 You call someone **sweetheart** if you are very fond of them. ❑ *Happy birthday, sweetheart.* N-VOC = *darling* 2 Your **sweetheart** is your boyfriend or your girlfriend. [JOURNALISM or OLD-FASHIONED] ❑ *I married Shurla, my childhood sweetheart, in Liverpool.* N-COUNT: usu supp N

**sweetie** /swiːti/ **(sweeties)** 1 You can call someone **sweetie** if you are fond of them, especially if they are younger than you. [INFORMAL] N-VOC 2 If you say that someone is a **sweetie**, you mean that they are kind and nice. [INFORMAL] N-COUNT 3 Sweets are sometimes referred to as **sweeties** by children or by adults speaking to children. [BRIT] N-COUNT

**sweet|ish** /swiːtɪʃ/ A **sweetish** smell or taste is fairly sweet. ADJ

**sweet|ly** /swiːtli/ 1 If an engine or machine is running **sweetly**, it is working smoothly and efficiently. ❑ *He heard the car engine running sweetly beyond the open door.* ADV: ADV with v 2 If you kick or hit a ball **sweetly**, you kick or hit it in the very middle of it so that it goes firmly and accurately to the place you are aiming for. ❑ *He could strike the ball as sweetly as when he was 28 years younger.* ADV: ADV with v 3 → See also **sweet**.

**sweet|meat** /swiːtmiːt/ **(sweetmeats)** **Sweetmeats** are sweet items of food, especially ones that are considered special. [OLD-FASHIONED] N-COUNT: usu pl

**sweet|ness** /swiːtnəs/ 1 If you say that a relationship or situation is not **all sweetness and light**, you mean that it is not as pleasant as it appears to be. ❑ *It has not all been sweetness and light between him and the Prime Minister.* PHRASE: with brd-neg, usu v-link PHR 2 → See also **sweet**.

**sweet noth|ings** If someone whispers **sweet nothings** to you, they quietly say nice, loving, and flattering things to you. N-PLURAL

**sweet pea** **(sweet peas)** also **sweetpea.** A **sweet pea** is a climbing plant which has delicate, sweet-smelling flowers. N-COUNT

**sweet pep|per** **(sweet peppers)** A **sweet pepper** is a hollow green, red, or yellow vegetable. N-COUNT = *capsicum*

**sweet po|ta|to** **(sweet potatoes)** **Sweet potatoes** are vegetables that look like large ordinary potatoes but taste sweet. They have pinkish-brown skins and yellow flesh. N-VAR

**sweet shop** **(sweet shops)** also **sweetshop.** A **sweet shop** is a small shop that sells sweets and cigarettes, and sometimes newspapers and magazines. [BRIT] N-COUNT: oft *the* N

✔ in AM, use **candy store**

**sweet talk** **(sweet talks, sweet talking, sweet talked)** also **sweet-talk.** If you **sweet talk** someone, you talk to them very nicely so that they will do what you want. ❑ *She could always sweet-talk Pamela into letting her stay up late... He even tried to sweet-talk the policewoman who arrested him.* VERB · V n *into* -ing/n · V n

**swell** /swel/ **(swells, swelling, swelled, swollen)**

✔ The forms **swelled** and **swollen** are both used as the past participle.

1 If the amount or size of something **swells** or if something **swells** it, it becomes larger than it was before. ❑ *The human population swelled, at least temporarily, as migrants moved south... His bank balance has swelled by £222,000 in the last three weeks... Offers from other countries should swell the force to 35,000.* VERB = *increase* · V · V *to/by* n · V n *to* n 2 If something such as a part of your body **swells**, it becomes larger and rounder than normal. ❑ *Do your ankles swell at night?... The limbs swell to an enormous size.* ♦ **Swell up** means the same as **swell**. ❑ *When you develop a throat infection or catch a cold the glands in the neck swell up.* VERB · V · V *to* n · PHRASAL VERB · V P 3 If you **swell with** a feeling, you are suddenly full of that feeling. [LITERARY] ❑ *She could see her two sons swell with pride.* VERB · V *with* n 4 You can describe something as **swell** if you think it is really nice. [AM, INFORMAL] ❑ *I've had a swell time.* ADJ 5 → See also **swelling, swollen, groundswell.**

♦ **swell up** → see **swell 2.**

**swell|ing** /swelɪŋ/ **(swellings)** A **swelling** is a raised, curved shape on the surface of your body which appears as a result of an injury or an illness. ❑ *His eye was partly closed, and there was a swelling over his lid.* N-VAR

**swel|ter** /sweltəʳ/ **(swelters, sweltering, sweltered)** If you **swelter**, you are very uncomfortable because the weather is extremely hot. ❑ *They sweltered in temperatures rising to a hundred degrees.* VERB · V

**swel|ter|ing** /sweltərɪŋ/ If you describe the weather as **sweltering**, you mean that it is extremely hot and makes you feel uncomfortable. ADJ

**swept** /swept/ **Swept** is the past tense and past participle of **sweep**.

**swerve** /swɜːʳv/ **(swerves, swerving, swerved)** If a vehicle or other moving thing **swerves** or if you **swerve** it, it suddenly changes direction, often in order to avoid hitting something. ❑ *Drivers coming in the opposite direction swerved to avoid the bodies... Her car swerved off the road into a 6ft high brick wall... Suddenly Ned swerved the truck, narrowly missing a blond teenager on a skateboard.* ♦ **Swerve** is also a noun. ❑ *He swung the car to the left and that swerve saved Malone's life.* VERB · V · V prep/adv · V n · N-COUNT

**swift** /swɪft/ **(swifter, swiftest, swifts)** 1 A **swift** event or process happens very quickly or without delay. ❑ *Our task is to challenge the UN to make a swift decision... The police were swift to act.* ♦ **swift|ly** *The French have acted swiftly and decisively to protect their industries.* ADJ = *quick* · ADV 2 Something that is **swift** moves very quickly. ❑ *With a swift movement, Matthew Jerrold sat upright.* ♦ **swift|ly** *Lenny moved swiftly and silently across the front lawn.* ADJ = *quick* · ADV: ADV with v 3 A **swift** is a small bird with long curved wings. N-COUNT

**swig** /swɪg/ **(swigs, swigging, swigged)** If you **swig** a drink, you drink it from a bottle or cup quickly and in large amounts. ❑ *I swigged down two white wines... He was still hanging around, swigging the Coke out of the can.* ♦ **Swig** is also a noun. ❑ *Brian took a swig of his beer.* VERB · V n with *down/back* · V n · N-COUNT

**swill** /swɪl/ **(swills, swilling, swilled)** 1 If you **swill** an alcoholic drink, you drink a lot of it. ❑ *A crowd of men were standing around swilling beer.* VERB · V n 2 If a liquid **swills around**, or if you **swill** it **around**, it moves around the area that it is contained in. ❑ *Gallons of sea water had rushed into the cabin and were now swilling about in the bilges... She swilled the whisky slowly around in her glass.* VERB · V *around/about* · V n *around/about* 3 **Swill** is a liquid mixture containing waste food that is given to pigs to eat. N-UNCOUNT

**swim** /swɪm/ **(swims, swimming, swam, swum)** ◆◇◇ 1 When you **swim**, you move through water by making movements with your arms and legs. ❑ *She learned to swim when she was really tiny... I went round to Jonathan's to see if he wanted to go swimming... He was rescued only when an exhausted friend swam ashore... I swim a mile a day.* ♦ **Swim** is also a noun. ❑ *When can we go for a swim, Mam?* VERB · V · V · V adv/prep · V amount/n · N-SING 2 If you **swim** a race, you take part in a swimming race. ❑ *She swam the 400 metres medley ten seconds slower than she did in 1980.* VERB · V n 3 If you **swim** a stretch of water, you keep swimming until you have crossed it. ❑ *In 1875, Captain Matthew Webb became the first man to swim the English Channel.* VERB · V n 4 When a fish **swims**, it moves through water by moving its body. ❑ *The barriers are lethal to fish try-* VERB · V adv/prep · Also V *ing to swim upstream.* [5] If objects **swim**, they seem to be moving backwards and forwards, usually because you are ill. ❑ *Alexis suddenly could take no more: he felt too hot, he couldn't breathe, the room swam.* [6] If your head **is swimming**, you feel unsteady and slightly ill. ❑ *The musty aroma of incense made her head swim.* [7] **sink or swim** → see **sink**. VERB V VERB = spin V

**swim|mer** /swɪməʳ/ **(swimmers)** A **swimmer** is a person who swims, especially for sport or pleasure, or a person who is swimming. ❑ *You don't have to worry about me. I'm a good swimmer.* N-COUNT

**swim|ming** /swɪmɪŋ/ **Swimming** is the activity of swimming, especially as a sport or for pleasure. ❑ *...swimming lessons.* N-UNCOUNT

**swim|ming bath** **(swimming baths)** [1] A **swimming baths** or **swimming bath** is a building that contains an indoor public swimming pool. The plural **swimming baths** can be used to refer to one or more than one of these places. [BRIT] ❑ *It had been two years since I had been to the swimming baths.* N-COUNT

✓ in AM, use **pool, swimming pool**

[2] A **swimming bath** is a public swimming pool, especially an indoor one. [BRIT] N-COUNT

✓ in AM, use **pool, swimming pool**

**swim|ming cap** **(swimming caps)** A **swimming cap** is a rubber cap which you wear to keep your hair dry when you are swimming. [BRIT] N-COUNT

✓ in AM, use **bathing cap**

**swim|ming cos|tume** **(swimming costumes)** A **swimming costume** is the same as a **swimsuit**. [BRIT] N-COUNT = swimsuit

**swim|ming|ly** /swɪmɪŋli/ If you say that something **is going swimmingly**, you mean that everything is happening in a satisfactory way, without any problems. [INFORMAL] ❑ *The work has been going swimmingly.* PHRASE: V inflects

**swim|ming pool** **(swimming pools)** A **swimming pool** is a large hole in the ground that has been made and filled with water so that people can swim in it. N-COUNT

**swim|ming trunks** **Swimming trunks** are the shorts that a man wears when he goes swimming. [BRIT] N-PLURAL: also *a pair of* N

✓ in AM, use **trunks**

**swim|suit** /swɪmsuːt/ **(swimsuits)** A **swimsuit** is a piece of clothing that is worn for swimming, especially by women and girls. N-COUNT

**swim|wear** /swɪmweəʳ/ **Swimwear** is the things people wear for swimming. N-UNCOUNT

**swin|dle** /swɪndᵊl/ **(swindles, swindling, swindled)** If someone **swindles** a person or an organization, they deceive them in order to get something valuable from them, especially money. ❑ *A City businessman swindled investors out of millions of pounds.* ♦ **Swindle** is also a noun. ❑ *He fled to Switzerland rather than face trial for a tax swindle.* VERB V n *out of* n N-COUNT

**swine** /swaɪn/ **(swines)**

✓ The form **swines** is used as the plural for meaning 1; **swine** is used as both the singular and plural for meaning 2.

[1] If you call someone a **swine**, you dislike them or think that they are a bad person, usually because they have behaved unpleasantly towards you. [INFORMAL] [2] A **swine** is a pig. [TECHNICAL or OLD-FASHIONED] ❑ *...imports of live swine from Canada.* N-COUNT disapproval N-COUNT

**swing** /swɪŋ/ **(swings, swinging, swung)** [1] If something **swings** or if you **swing** it, it moves repeatedly backwards and forwards or from side to side from a fixed point. ❑ *The sail of the little boat swung crazily from one side to the other... She was swinging a bottle of wine by its neck... Ian lit a cigarette and sat on the end of the table, one leg swinging.* ♦ **Swing** is also a noun. ❑ *...a woman in a tight red dress, walking with a slight swing to her hips.* ◆◇◇ VERB V adv/prep V n V-ing N-COUNT: usu with supp

[2] If something **swings** in a particular direction or if you **swing** it in that direction, it moves in that direction with a smooth, curving movement. ❑ *The torchlight swung across the little beach and out over the water, searching... The canoe found the current and swung around... Roy swung his legs carefully off the couch and sat up.* ♦ **Swing** is also a noun. ❑ *When he's not on the tennis court, you'll find him practising his golf swing.* [3] If a vehicle **swings** in a particular direction, or if the driver **swings** it in a particular direction, they turn suddenly in that direction. ❑ *Joanna swung back on to the main approach and headed for the airport... The tyres dug into the grit as he swung the car off the road.* [4] If someone **swings around**, they turn around quickly, usually because they are surprised. ❑ *She swung around to him, spilling her tea without noticing it.* [5] If you **swing at** a person or thing, you try to hit them with your arm or with something that you are holding. ❑ *Blanche swung at her but she moved her head back and Blanche missed... I picked up his baseball bat and swung at the man's head.* ♦ **Swing** is also a noun. ❑ *I often want to take a swing at someone to relieve my feelings.* [6] A **swing** is a seat hanging by two ropes or chains from a metal frame or from the branch of a tree. You can sit on the seat and move forwards and backwards through the air. [7] **Swing** is a style of jazz dance music that was popular in the 1930's. It was played by big bands. [8] A **swing** in people's opinions, attitudes, or feelings is a change in them, especially a sudden or big change. ❑ *There was a massive twenty per cent swing away from the Conservatives to the Liberal Democrats... Dieters suffer from violent mood swings.* [9] If people's opinions, attitudes, or feelings **swing**, they change, especially in a sudden or extreme way. ❑ *In two years' time there is a presidential election, and the voters could swing again... The mood amongst Tory MPs seems to be swinging away from their leader.* VERB V prep/adv V prep/adv V n prep/adv N-COUNT VERB V adv/prep V n prep/adv VERB V adv VERB V *at* n V *at* n N-COUNT = swipe N-COUNT N-UNCOUNT N-COUNT: usu with supp VERB V V adv/prep

**PHRASES** [10] If something is **in full swing**, it is operating fully and is no longer in its early stages. ❑ *When we returned, the party was in full swing and the dance floor was crowded.* [11] If you **get into the swing of** something, you become very involved in it and enjoy what you are doing. ❑ *Everyone understood how hard it was to get back into the swing of things after such a long absence.* [12] If you say that a situation is **swings and roundabouts**, you mean that there are as many gains as there are losses. [BRIT] [13] **no room to swing a cat** → see **cat**. PHRASE: v-link PHR PHRASE: V inflects, PHR n PHRASE

**swing bridge** **(swing bridges)** A **swing bridge** is a low bridge that can be opened either in the middle or on one side in order to let ships pass through. N-COUNT

**swing door** **(swing doors)** **Swing doors** are doors that can open both towards you and away from you. [mainly BRIT] N-COUNT: usu pl

✓ in AM, usually use **swinging door**

**swinge|ing** /swɪndʒɪŋ/ A **swingeing** action, such as an attack or cut, is very great or severe. [BRIT, mainly JOURNALISM] ❑ *...the book mounted a swingeing attack on the materialist, growth-oriented economics of the day.* ADJ: ADJ n

**swing|er** /swɪŋəʳ/ **(swingers)** [1] A **swinger** is a person who is lively and fashionable. [INFORMAL, OLD-FASHIONED] [2] **Swingers** are people who are married or in a long-term relationship and who like to have sex with other couples. N-COUNT N-COUNT

**swing|ing** /swɪŋɪŋ/ If you describe something or someone as **swinging**, you mean that they are lively and fashionable. [INFORMAL, OLD-FASHIONED] ❑ *The stuffy '50s gave way to the swinging '60s.* ADJ: usu ADJ n

**swing|ing door** **(swinging doors)** **Swinging doors** are doors that can open both towards you and away from you. [AM] N-COUNT: usu pl

✓ in BRIT, use **swing door**

**swing vote** **(swing votes)** In a situation when people are about to vote, the **swing vote** is used to talk about the vote of a person or group which is difficult to predict and which will be important in deciding the result. [mainly AM, JOURNALISM] ❑ *...a Democrat who holds the swing vote on the committee.* N-COUNT

**swing vot|er** **(swing voters)** A **swing voter** is a person who is not a firm supporter of any political party, and whose vote in an election is difficult to predict. [AM] N-COUNT

☑ in BRIT, use **floating voter**

**swipe** /swaɪp/ **(swipes, swiping, swiped)** 1 If you **swipe at** a person or thing, you try to hit them with a stick or other object, making a swinging movement with your arm. ❑ *She swiped at Rusty as though he was a fly... He swiped me across the shoulder with the poker.* ♦ **Swipe** is also a noun. ❑ *He took a swipe at Andrew that deposited him on the floor.* 2 If you **swipe** something, you steal it quickly. [INFORMAL] ❑ *Five soldiers were each fined £140 for swiping a wheelchair from a disabled tourist.* 3 If you take a **swipe at** a person or an organization, you criticize them, usually in an indirect way. ❑ *In a swipe at the president, he called for an end to 'begging for aid around the world'.* 4 If you **swipe** a credit card or swipe card through a machine, you pass it through a narrow space in the machine so that the machine can read information on the card's magnetic strip. ❑ *Swipe your card through the phone, then dial.*
VERB; V *at* n; V n; N-COUNT; VERB = pinch V n; N-COUNT; VERB; V n *through* n; Also V n

**swipe card** **(swipe cards)** also **swipecard.** A **swipe card** is a plastic card with a magnetic strip on it which contains information that can be read or transferred by passing the card through a special machine. ❑ *They use a swipe card to go in and out of their offices.* N-COUNT

**swirl** /swɜːʳl/ **(swirls, swirling, swirled)** If you **swirl** something liquid or flowing, or if it **swirls**, it moves round and round quickly. ❑ *She smiled, swirling the wine in her glass... The black water swirled around his legs, reaching almost to his knees... She swirled the ice-cold liquid around her mouth. ...Carmen with her swirling gypsy skirts.* ♦ **Swirl** is also a noun. ❑ *...small swirls of chocolate cream... He breathes out a swirl of cigarette smoke.*
VERB; V n; V prep/adv; V n prep; V-ing; N-COUNT

**swish** /swɪʃ/ **(swishes, swishing, swished, swisher, swishest)** 1 If something **swishes** or if you **swish** it, it moves quickly through the air, making a soft sound. ❑ *A car swished by heading for the coast... He swished his cape around his shoulders... He heard a swishing sound.* ♦ **Swish** is also a noun. ❑ *She turned with a swish of her skirt.* 2 If you describe something as **swish**, you mean that it is smart and fashionable. [BRIT, INFORMAL, OLD-FASHIONED] ❑ *...a swish cocktail bar.*
VERB; V adv/prep; V n prep/adv; V-ing; N-COUNT; ADJ

**Swiss** /swɪs/ **(Swiss)** 1 **Swiss** means belonging or relating to Switzerland, or to its people or culture. 2 **The Swiss** are the people of Switzerland.
ADJ; N-COUNT: usu pl, *the* N

**Swiss cheese** **(Swiss cheeses)** Swiss cheese is hard cheese with holes in it. N-VAR

**swiss roll** **(swiss rolls)** also **swiss-roll.** A **swiss roll** is a cylindrical cake made from a thin flat sponge which is covered with jam or cream on one side, then rolled up. [BRIT] N-VAR

☑ in AM, use **jelly roll**

**switch** /swɪtʃ/ **(switches, switching, switched)** ◆◇◇ 1 A **switch** is a small control for an electrical device which you use to turn the device on or off. ❑ *Leona put some detergent into the dishwasher, shut the door and pressed the switch. ...a light switch.* 2 If you **switch to** something different, for example to a different system, task, or subject of conversation, you change to it from what you were doing or saying before. ❑ *Estonia is switching to a market economy... The law would encourage companies to switch from coal to cleaner fuels... The encouragement of a friend spurred Chris into switching jobs.* ♦ **Switch** is also a noun. ❑ *New technology made a switch to oil possible... The spokesman implicitly condemned the United States policy switch.* ♦ **Switch over** means the same as **switch.** ❑ *...a professional man who started out in law but switched over to medicine.* 3 If you **switch** your attention from one thing **to** another or if your attention **switches**, you stop paying attention to the first thing and start paying attention to the second. ❑ *My mother's interest had switched to my health... As the era wore on, she switched her attention to films.* 4 If you **switch** two things, you replace one with the other. ❑ *In half an hour, they'd switched the tags on every cable... The ballot boxes have been switched.*
N-COUNT; VERB = change; V *to* n; V *from* n *to* n; V pl-n; N-COUNT: usu with supp; PHRASAL VERB V P *to* n; VERB; V *to* n; V n *to* n; VERB = swap; V pl-n; V pl-n

♦ **switch off** 1 If you **switch off** a light or other electrical device, you stop it working by operating a switch. ❑ *She switched off the coffee-machine... Glass parked the car and switched the engine off.* 2 If you **switch off**, you stop paying attention or stop thinking or worrying about something. [INFORMAL] ❑ *You may find you've got so many things to think about that it's difficult to switch off.*
PHRASAL VERB = turn off; V P n (not pron); V n P; PHRASAL VERB; V P

♦ **switch on** If you **switch on** a light or other electrical device, you make it start working by operating a switch. ❑ *She emptied both their mugs and switched on the electric kettle... He pointed the light at his feet and tried to switch it on.*
PHRASAL VERB = turn on; V P n (not pron); V n P

♦ **switch over** 1 If you **switch over** when you are watching television, you change to another channel. ❑ *I just happened to switch over although I haven't been watching the Olympics... Let's switch over to Channel 4.* 2 → see **switch 2.**
PHRASAL VERB; V P; V P *to* n

**switch|back** /swɪtʃbæk/ **(switchbacks)** 1 A **switchback** is a road which rises and falls sharply many times, or a sharp rise and fall in a road. [BRIT] ❑ *...a dizzy bus ride over a switchback road.* 2 A **switchback** is a road which goes up a steep hill in a series of sharp bends, or a sharp bend in a road. [AM]
N-COUNT: oft N n; N-COUNT

**switch|blade** /swɪtʃbleɪd/ **(switchblades)** A **switchblade** is a knife with a blade that is hidden in the handle and that springs out when a button is pressed. [AM] N-COUNT

☑ in BRIT, use **flick-knife**

**switch|board** /swɪtʃbɔːʳd/ **(switchboards)** A **switchboard** is a place in a large office or business where all the telephone calls are connected. ❑ *He asked to be connected to the central switchboard at London University.* N-COUNT

**switched-on** If you describe someone as **switched-on**, you mean that they are aware of the latest developments in a particular area or activity. [INFORMAL] ❑ *I am very impressed with Brian Hanlon, who seems a switched-on sort of guy.* ADJ

**swiv|el** /swɪvᵊl/ **(swivels, swivelling, swivelled)**

☑ in AM, use **swiveling, swiveled**

1 If something **swivels** or if you **swivel** it, it turns around a central point so that it is facing in a different direction. ❑ *She swivelled her chair round and stared out across the back lawn... His chairs can swivel, but they can't move up or down.* 2 If you **swivel** in a particular direction, you turn suddenly in that direction. ❑ *He swivelled round to face Sarah.*
VERB; V n adv/prep; V; Also V n; VERB; V adv/prep

**swiv|el chair** **(swivel chairs)** A **swivel chair** is a chair whose seat can be turned around a central point to face in a different direction without moving the legs. N-COUNT: usu sing

**swol|len** /swoʊlᵊn/ 1 If a part of your body is **swollen**, it is larger and rounder than normal, usually as a result of injury or illness. ❑ *My eyes were so swollen I could hardly see.* 2 A **swollen** river has more water in it and flows faster than normal, usually because of heavy rain. 3 **Swollen** is the past participle of **swell.**
ADJ; ADJ

**swoon** /swuːn/ **(swoons, swooning, swooned)** If you **swoon**, you are strongly affected by your feelings for someone you love or admire very much. ❑ *Virtually every woman in the '20s swooned*
VERB; V *over* n

*over Valentino... The ladies shriek and swoon at his every word.* V Also V adv

**swoop** /swuːp/ **(swoops, swooping, swooped)** [1] If police or soldiers **swoop on** a place, they go there suddenly and quickly, usually in order to arrest someone or to attack the place. [JOURNALISM] ❑ *The terror ended when armed police swooped on the car... The drugs squad swooped and discovered 240 kilograms of cannabis.* ♦ **Swoop** is also a noun. ❑ *Police held 10 suspected illegal immigrants after a swoop on a German lorry.* [2] When a bird or aeroplane **swoops**, it suddenly moves downwards through the air in a smooth curving movement. ❑ *More than 20 helicopters began swooping in low over the ocean... The hawk swooped and soared away carrying something.* [3] If something is done **in one fell swoop** or **at one fell swoop**, it is done on a single occasion or by a single action. ❑ *In one fell swoop the bank wiped away the tentative benefits of this policy.* VERB; V *on* n; V; N-COUNT; VERB; V adv/prep; V; PHRASE: PHR with cl

**swop** /swɒp/ → see **swap**.

**sword** /sɔːʳd/ **(swords)** [1] A **sword** is a weapon with a handle and a long sharp blade. N-COUNT

**PHRASES** [2] If you **cross swords with** someone, you disagree with them and argue with them about something. ❑ *...a candidate who's crossed swords with Labor by supporting the free-trade pact.* PHRASE: V inflects, PHR *with* n, pl-n PHR [3] If you say that something is a **double-edged sword** or a **two-edged sword**, you mean that it has negative effects as well as positive effects. PHRASE: N inflects [4] **Sword of Damocles** → see **Damocles**.

**sword|fish** /sɔːʳdfɪʃ/ **(swordfish)** A **swordfish** is a large sea fish with a very long upper jaw. ♦ **Swordfish** is this fish eaten as food. ❑ *...grilled swordfish with a yogurt dressing.* N-VAR; N-UNCOUNT

**swords|man** /sɔːʳdzmən/ **(swordsmen)** A **swordsman** is a man who is skilled at fighting with a sword. N-COUNT

**swore** /swɔːʳ/ **Swore** is the past tense of **swear**.

**sworn** /swɔːʳn/ [1] **Sworn** is the past participle of **swear**. [2] If you make a **sworn** statement or declaration, you swear that everything that you have said in it is true. ❑ *The allegations against them were made in sworn evidence to the inquiry.* ADJ: ADJ n [3] If two people or two groups of people are **sworn** enemies, they dislike each other very much. ❑ *It somehow seems hardly surprising that Ms Player is now his sworn enemy.* ADJ: ADJ n

**swot** /swɒt/ **(swots, swotting, swotted)** [1] If you **swot**, you study very hard, especially when you are preparing for an examination. [BRIT, INFORMAL] ❑ *They swotted for their A levels.* [2] If you call someone a **swot**, you disapprove of the fact that they study extremely hard and are not interested in other things. [BRIT, INFORMAL] VERB; V *for* n; N-COUNT disapproval

**swum** /swʌm/ **Swum** is the past participle of **swim**.

**swung** /swʌŋ/ **Swung** is the past tense and past participle of **swing**.

**syba|rit|ic** /sɪbərɪtɪk/ Someone who has a **sybaritic** way of life spends a lot of time relaxing in a luxurious way. [FORMAL] ADJ: usu ADJ n

**syca|more** /sɪkəmɔːʳ/ **(sycamores)** A **sycamore** or a **sycamore tree** is a tree that has yellow flowers and large leaves with five points. ♦ **Sycamore** is the wood of this tree. ❑ *The furniture is made of sycamore, beech and leather.* N-VAR; N-UNCOUNT

**syco|phan|cy** /sɪkəfænsi, AM -fənsi/ **Sycophancy** is the quality or action of being sycophantic. [FORMAL] N-UNCOUNT disapproval

**syco|phant** /sɪkəfænt, AM -fənt/ **(sycophants)** A **sycophant** is a person who behaves in a sycophantic way. [FORMAL] ❑ *...a dictator surrounded by sycophants, frightened to tell him what he may not like.* N-COUNT disapproval

**syco|phan|tic** /sɪkəfæntɪk/ If you describe someone as **sycophantic**, you disapprove of them because they flatter people who are more important and powerful than they are in order to gain an advantage for themselves. ❑ *...his clique of sycophantic friends.* ADJ disapproval

**syl|la|ble** /sɪləbᵊl/ **(syllables)** A **syllable** is a part of a word that contains a single vowel sound and that is pronounced as a unit. So, for example, 'book' has one syllable, and 'reading' has two syllables. ❑ *We children called her Oma, accenting both syllables.* N-COUNT

**syl|la|bus** /sɪləbəs/ **(syllabuses)** [1] You can refer to the subjects that are studied in a particular course as the **syllabus**. [mainly BRIT] ❑ *...the GCSE history syllabus.* N-COUNT [2] A **syllabus** is an outline or summary of the subjects to be covered in a course. [mainly AM] N-COUNT

**syl|van** /sɪlvən/ **Sylvan** is used to describe things that have an association with woods and trees. [LITERARY] ADJ: usu ADJ n

**sym|bio|sis** /sɪmbioʊsɪs, -baɪ-/ [1] **Symbiosis** is a close relationship between two organisms of different kinds which benefits both organisms. [TECHNICAL] ❑ *...the link between bacteria, symbiosis, and the evolution of plants and animals.* N-UNCOUNT [2] **Symbiosis** is any relationship between different things, people, or groups that benefits all the things or people concerned. ❑ *...the cosy symbiosis of the traditional political parties.* N-UNCOUNT

**sym|bi|ot|ic** /sɪmbiɒtɪk, -baɪ-/ A **symbiotic** relationship is one in which organisms, people, or things exist together in a way that benefits them all. ❑ *...fungi that have a symbiotic relationship with the trees of these northwestern forests.* ADJ: usu ADJ n

**sym|bol** /sɪmbᵊl/ **(symbols)** ◆◇◇ [1] Something that is a **symbol of** a society or an aspect of life seems to represent it because it is very typical of it. ❑ *To them, the monarchy is the special symbol of nationhood... She was put under house arrest two years ago but remained a powerful symbol in last year's election.* N-COUNT: with supp [2] A **symbol of** something such as an idea is a shape or design that is used to represent it. ❑ *I frequently use sunflowers as symbols of strength.* N-COUNT: with supp [3] A **symbol for** an item in a calculation or scientific formula is a number, letter, or shape that represents that item. ❑ *What's the chemical symbol for mercury?* N-COUNT [4] → See also **sex symbol**, **status symbol**.

**sym|bol|ic** /sɪmbɒlɪk/ [1] If you describe an event, action, or procedure as **symbolic**, you mean that it represents an important change, although it has little practical effect. ❑ *A lot of Latin-American officials are stressing the symbolic importance of the trip... The move today was largely symbolic.* ♦ **sym|boli|cal|ly** /sɪmbɒlɪkli/ *It was a simple enough gesture, but symbolically important.* ADJ; ADV: ADV adj, ADV with cl [2] Something that is **symbolic of** a person or thing is regarded or used as a symbol of them. ❑ *Yellow clothes are worn as symbolic of spring.* ♦ **sym|boli|cal|ly** *Each circle symbolically represents the whole of humanity.* ADJ: usu v-link ADJ *of* n; ADV: ADV with v [3] **Symbolic** is used to describe things involving or relating to symbols. ❑ *...symbolic representations of landscape.* ADJ: ADJ n

**sym|bol|ise** /sɪmbəlaɪz/ → see **symbolize**.

**sym|bol|ism** /sɪmbəlɪzəm/ [1] **Symbolism** is the use of symbols in order to represent something. ❑ *The scene is so rich in symbolism that any explanation risks spoiling the effect.* N-UNCOUNT [2] You can refer to the **symbolism** of an event or action when it seems to show something important about a situation. ❑ *The symbolism of every gesture will be of vital importance during the short state visit.* N-UNCOUNT: usu N *of* n

**sym|bol|ize** /sɪmbəlaɪz/ **(symbolizes, symbolizing, symbolized)**

✔ in BRIT, also use **symbolise**

If one thing **symbolizes** another, it is used or regarded as a symbol of it. ❑ *The fall of the Berlin Wall symbolised the end of the Cold War between East and West. ...the post-war world order symbolised by the United Nations.* VERB; V n; V-ed

**sym|met|ri|cal** /sɪmetrɪkᵊl/ If something is **symmetrical**, it has two halves which are exactly the same, except that one half is the mirror image ADJ of the other. ❑ *...the neat rows of perfectly symmetrical windows.* ♦ **sym|met|ri|cal|ly** /sɪmetrɪkl/ ADV: ADV with v *The south garden at Sissinghurst was composed symmetrically.*

**sym|me|try** /sɪmɪtri/ **(symmetries)** [1] N-VAR Something that has **symmetry** is symmetrical in shape, design, or structure. ❑ *...the incredible beauty and symmetry of a snowflake... I loved the house because it had perfect symmetry.* [2] N-UNCOUNT **Symmetry** in a relationship or agreement is the fact of both sides giving and receiving an equal amount. ❑ *The superpowers pledged to maintain symmetry in their arms shipments.*

**sym|pa|thet|ic** /sɪmpəθetɪk/ [1] ADJ: oft v-link ADJ *to* n If you are **sympathetic** to someone who is in a bad situation, you are kind to them and show that you understand their feelings. ❑ *She was very sympathetic to the problems of adult students... It may be that he sees you only as a sympathetic friend.* ♦ **sym|pa|theti|cal|ly** /sɪmpəθetɪkli/ ADV: ADV with v *She nodded sympathetically.* [2] ADJ: oft v-link ADJ *to* n If you are **sympathetic to** a proposal or action, you approve of it and are willing to support it. ❑ *She met people in London who were sympathetic to the Indian freedom struggle.* ♦ **sym|pa|theti|cal|ly** ADV: ADV with v *After a year we will sympathetically consider an application for reinstatement.* [3] ADJ You describe someone as **sympathetic** when you like them and approve of the way that they behave. ❑ *She sounds a most sympathetic character.*

**sym|pa|thize** /sɪmpəθaɪz/ **(sympathizes, sympathizing, sympathized)**

in BRIT, also use **sympathise**

[1] VERB If you **sympathize** with someone who is in a bad situation, you show that you are sorry for them. ❑ *I must tell you how much I sympathize with you for your loss, Professor... He would sympathize but he wouldn't understand.* (V *with* n; V) [2] VERB If you **sympathize with** someone's feelings, you understand them and are not critical of them. ❑ *Some Europeans sympathize with the Americans over the issue... He liked Max, and sympathized with his ambitions.* (V *with* n; V *with* n) [3] VERB If you **sympathize with** a proposal or action, you approve of it and are willing to support it. ❑ *Most of the people living there sympathized with the guerrillas.* (V *with* n)

**sym|pa|thiz|er** /sɪmpəθaɪzəʳ/ **(sympathizers)**

in BRIT, also use **sympathiser**

N-COUNT: usu pl, oft supp N The **sympathizers** of an organization or cause are the people who approve of it and support it. ❑ *These villagers are guerrilla sympathizers.*

**sym|pa|thy** /sɪmpəθi/ **(sympathies)** ◆◇◇ [1] N-UNCOUNT: also N in pl If you have **sympathy** for someone who is in a bad situation, you are sorry for them, and show this in the way you behave towards them. ❑ *I have had very little help from doctors and no sympathy whatsoever... I wanted to express my sympathies on your resignation.* [2] N-UNCOUNT: also N in pl, oft N *with/for* n If you have **sympathy** with someone's ideas or opinions, you agree with them. ❑ *I have some sympathy with this point of view... Lithuania still commands considerable international sympathy for its cause... She has frequently expressed Republican sympathies.* [3] N-UNCOUNT: oft N *with* n If you take some action **in sympathy with** someone else, you do it in order to show that you support them. ❑ *Milne resigned in sympathy because of the way Donald had been treated.*

**sym|phon|ic** /sɪmfɒnɪk/ ADJ: usu ADJ n **Symphonic** means relating to or like a symphony.

**sym|pho|ny** /sɪmfəni/ **(symphonies)** N-COUNT; N-IN-NAMES A **symphony** is a piece of music written to be played by an orchestra. Symphonies are usually made up of four separate sections called movements.

**sym|pho|ny or|ches|tra** **(symphony orchestras)** N-COUNT; N-IN-NAMES A **symphony orchestra** is a large orchestra that plays classical music.

**sym|po|sium** /sɪmpoʊziəm/ **(symposia** /sɪmpoʊziə/ or **symposiums)** N-COUNT: oft N *on* n A **symposium** is a conference in which experts or academics discuss a particular subject. ❑ *He had been taking part in an international symposium on population.*

**symp|tom** /sɪmptəm/ **(symptoms)** ◆◇◇ [1] N-COUNT A **symptom** of an illness is something wrong with your body or mind that is a sign of the illness. ❑ *One of the most common symptoms of schizophrenia is hearing imaginary voices. ...patients with flu symptoms.* [2] N-COUNT: oft N *of* n A **symptom of** a bad situation is something that happens which is considered to be a sign of this situation. ❑ *Your problem with keeping boyfriends is just a symptom of a larger problem: making and keeping friends.*

**symp|to|mat|ic** /sɪmptəmætɪk/ ADJ: v-link ADJ, usu ADJ *of* n If something is **symptomatic of** something else, especially something bad, it is a sign of it. [FORMAL] ❑ *The city's problems are symptomatic of the crisis that is spreading throughout the country.*

**syna|gogue** /sɪnəgɒg/ **(synagogues)** N-COUNT; N-IN-NAMES A **synagogue** is a building where Jewish people meet to worship or to study their religion.

**syn|apse** /saɪnæps, AM sɪnæps/ **(synapses)** N-COUNT A **synapse** is one of the points in the nervous system at which a signal passes from one nerve cell to another. [TECHNICAL]

**sync** /sɪŋk/ also **synch.** PHRASE: usu v-link PHR, oft PHR *with* n If two things are **out of sync**, they do not match or do not happen together as they should. If two things are **in sync**, they match or happen together as they should. [INFORMAL] ❑ *Normally, when demand and supply are out of sync, you either increase the supply, or you adjust the price mechanism.*

**synch** /sɪŋk/ → see **sync**.

**syn|chro|nize** /sɪŋkrənaɪz/ **(synchronizes, synchronizing, synchronized)**

in BRIT, also use **synchronise**

V-RECIP If you **synchronize** two activities, processes, or movements, or if you **synchronize** one activity, process, or movement **with** another, you cause them to happen at the same time and speed as each other. ❑ *It was virtually impossible to synchronise our lives so as to take holidays and weekends together... Synchronise the score with the film action. ...a series of unexpected, synchronized attacks.* (V pl-n; V n *with* n; V-ed)

**syn|chro|nized swim|ming**

in BRIT, also use **synchronised swimming**

N-UNCOUNT **Synchronized swimming** is a sport in which two or more people perform complicated and carefully planned movements in water in time to music.

**syn|co|pat|ed** /sɪŋkəpeɪtɪd/ ADJ In **syncopated** music, the weak beats in the bar are stressed instead of the strong beats. ❑ *Some spirituals are based on syncopated rhythms.*

**syn|co|pa|tion** /sɪŋkəpeɪʃᵊn/ **(syncopations)** N-VAR **Syncopation** is the quality that music has when the weak beats in a bar are stressed instead of the strong ones.

**syn|di|cate** **(syndicates, syndicating, syndicated)**

The noun is pronounced /sɪndɪkət/. The verb is pronounced /sɪndɪkeɪt/.

[1] N-COUNT A **syndicate** is an association of people or organizations that is formed for business purposes or in order to carry out a project. ❑ *...a syndicate of 152 banks. ...a major crime syndicate.* [2] VERB: usu passive When newspaper articles or television programmes **are syndicated**, they are sold to several different newspapers or television stations, who then publish the articles or broadcast the programmes. ❑ *Today his programme is syndicated to 500 stations.* (*be* V-ed prep/adv) ♦ **syn|di|ca|tion** /sɪndɪkeɪʃᵊn/ N-UNCOUNT *The show was ready for syndication in early 1987.* [3] N-COUNT A press **syndicate** is a group of newspapers or magazines that are all owned by the same person or company.

**syn|drome** /sɪndroʊm/ **(syndromes)** [1] N-COUNT; N-IN-NAMES A **syndrome** is a medical condition that is characterized by a particular group of signs and symptoms. ❑ *Irritable bowel syndrome seems to affect more women than men.* → See also **Down's syndrome**, **premenstrual syndrome**. [2] You can refer to an undesirable condition that is characterized by a particular type of activity or behaviour as a **syndrome**. ❑ *It's a bit like the exam syndrome where you write down everything you know regardless of what has been asked.* N-COUNT: usu sing, usu supp N

**syn|er|gy** /sɪnəʳdʒi/ **(synergies)** If there is **synergy** between two or more organizations or groups, they are more successful when they work together than when they work separately. [BUSINESS] ❑ *Of course, there's quite obviously a lot of synergy between the two companies... The synergies gained from the merger, Pirelli claimed, would create savings of about £130m over four years.* N-VAR

**syn|od** /sɪnɒd/ **(synods)** A **synod** is a special council of members of a Church, which meets regularly to discuss religious issues. N-COUNT

**syno|nym** /sɪnənɪm/ **(synonyms)** A **synonym** is a word or expression which means the same as another word or expression. ❑ *The term 'industrial democracy' is often used as a synonym for worker participation.* N-COUNT: oft N *for* n

**syn|ony|mous** /sɪnɒnɪməs/ If you say that one thing is **synonymous with** another, you mean that the two things are very closely associated with each other so that one suggests the other or one cannot exist without the other. ❑ *Paris has always been synonymous with elegance, luxury and style.* ADJ: usu v-link ADJ, oft ADJ *with* n

**syn|op|sis** /sɪnɒpsɪs/ **(synopses** /sɪnɒpsiːz/**)** A **synopsis** is a summary of a longer piece of writing or work. ❑ *For each title there is a brief synopsis of the book.* N-COUNT = summary

**syn|tac|tic** /sɪntæktɪk/ **Syntactic** means relating to syntax. [TECHNICAL] ❑ *...three common syntactic devices in English.* ADJ: ADJ n

**syn|tax** /sɪntæks/ **Syntax** is the ways that words can be put together, or are put together, in order to make sentences. [TECHNICAL] ❑ *His grammar and syntax, both in oral and written expression, were much better than the average.* N-UNCOUNT

**synth** /sɪnθ/ **(synths)** A **synth** is the same as a **synthesizer**. [INFORMAL] N-COUNT

**syn|the|sis** /sɪnθɪsɪs/ **(syntheses** /sɪnθɪsiːz/**)**
[1] A **synthesis of** different ideas or styles is a mixture or combination of these ideas or styles. [FORMAL] ❑ *His novels are a rich synthesis of Balkan history and mythology.* [2] The **synthesis** of a substance is the production of it by means of chemical or biological reactions. [TECHNICAL] ❑ *...the genes that regulate the synthesis of these compounds.* N-COUNT: usu sing, N *of* n; N-VAR: usu with supp

**syn|the|size** /sɪnθɪsaɪz/ **(synthesizes, synthesizing, synthesized)**

✔ in BRIT, also use **synthesise**

[1] To **synthesize** a substance means to produce it by means of chemical or biological reactions. [TECHNICAL] ❑ *After extensive research, Albert Hoffman first succeeded in synthesizing the acid in 1938.* [2] If you **synthesize** different ideas, facts, or experiences, you combine them to form a single idea or impression. [FORMAL] ❑ *The movement synthesised elements of modern art that hadn't been brought together before, such as Cubism and Surrealism.* VERB; V n; VERB = fuse; V n

**syn|the|sized** /sɪnθɪsaɪzd/

✔ in BRIT, also use **synthesised**

**Synthesized** sounds are produced electronically using a synthesizer. ❑ *...synthesised dance music.* ADJ: ADJ n

**syn|the|siz|er** /sɪnθɪsaɪzəʳ/ **(synthesizers)**

✔ in BRIT, also use **synthesiser**

A **synthesizer** is an electronic machine that produces speech, music, or other sounds, usually by combining individual syllables or sounds that have been previously recorded. ❑ *Now he can only communicate through a voice synthesiser.* N-COUNT

**syn|thet|ic** /sɪnθetɪk/ **Synthetic** products are made from chemicals or artificial substances rather than from natural ones. ❑ *Boots made from synthetic materials can usually be washed in a machine. ...synthetic rubber.* ♦ **syn|theti|cal|ly** *...the therapeutic use of natural and synthetically produced hormones.* ADJ: usu ADJ n = man-made, artificial; ADV: ADV with v

**syn|thet|ics** /sɪnθetɪks/ You can refer to synthetic clothing, fabric, or materials as **synthetics**. ❑ *Natural fabrics like silk and wool are better insulators than synthetics.* N-PLURAL

**syphi|lis** /sɪfɪlɪs/ **Syphilis** is a serious disease which is passed on through sexual intercourse. N-UNCOUNT

**sy|phon** /saɪfəⁿ/ → see **siphon**.

**Syr|ian** /sɪriən/ **(Syrians)** [1] **Syrian** means belonging or relating to Syria, or to its people or culture. [2] A **Syrian** is a Syrian citizen, or a person of Syrian origin. ADJ; N-COUNT

**sy|ringe** /sɪrɪndʒ/ **(syringes)** A **syringe** is a small tube with a thin hollow needle at the end. Syringes are used for putting liquids into things and for taking liquids out, for example for injecting drugs or for taking blood from someone's body. N-COUNT

**syr|up** /sɪrəp/ **(syrups)** [1] **Syrup** is a sweet liquid made by cooking sugar with water, and sometimes with fruit juice as well. ❑ *...canned fruit with sugary syrup.* [2] **Syrup** is a very sweet thick liquid made from sugar. ❑ *...a heavy syrup pudding.* → See also **golden syrup**, **maple syrup**. [3] **Syrup** is a medicine in the form of a thick, sweet liquid. ❑ *...cough syrup.* N-MASS; N-UNCOUNT: oft supp N; N-MASS: usu supp N

**syr|upy** /sɪrəpi/ [1] Liquid that is **syrupy** is sweet or thick like syrup. [2] If you describe something as **syrupy**, you dislike it because it is too sentimental. ❑ *...this syrupy film version of Conroy's novel.* ADJ; ADJ disapproval

**sys|tem** /sɪstəm/ **(systems)** [1] A **system** is a way of working, organizing, or doing something which follows a fixed plan or set of rules. You can use **system** to refer to an organization or institution that is organized in this way. ❑ *...a flexible and relatively efficient filing system. ...a multi-party system of government.* [2] A **system** is a set of devices powered by electricity, for example a computer or an alarm. ❑ *Viruses tend to be good at surviving when a computer system crashes.* [3] A **system** is a set of equipment or parts such as water pipes or electrical wiring, which is used to supply water, heat, or electricity. ❑ *...a central heating system.* [4] A **system** is a network of things that are linked together so that people or things can travel from one place to another or communicate. ❑ *...Australia's road and rail system. ...a news channel on a local cable system.* [5] Your **system** is your body's organs and other parts that together perform particular functions. ❑ *These gases would seriously damage the patient's respiratory system.* [6] A **system** is a particular set of rules, especially in mathematics or science, which is used to count or measure things. ❑ *...the decimal system of metric weights and measures.* [7] People sometimes refer to the government or administration of a country as **the system**. ❑ *These feelings are likely to make people attempt to overthrow the system.* [8] → See also **central nervous system**, **digestive system**, **ecosystem**, **immune system**, **metric system**, **nervous system**, **public address system**, **solar system**, **sound system**. [9] If you **get** something **out of** your **system**, you take some action so that you no longer want to do it or no longer have strong feelings about it. ❑ *I want to get boxing out of my system and settle down to enjoy family life.* ◆◆◆ N-COUNT: usu with supp; N-COUNT: usu supp N; N-COUNT: usu supp N; N-COUNT: usu supp N = network; N-COUNT: usu supp N; N-COUNT: usu supp N; N-SING: the N; PHRASE: V inflects

**sys|tem|at|ic** /sɪstəmætɪk/ Something that is done in a **systematic** way is done according to a fixed plan, in a thorough and efficient way. ❑ *They had not found any evidence of a systematic attempt to rig the ballot.* ♦ **sys|tem|ati|cal|ly** /sɪstəmætɪkli/ *The army has systematically violated* ADJ: usu ADJ n; ADV: ADV with v *human rights... She began applying systematically to colleges.*

**sys|tema|tize** /sɪstəmətaɪz/ **(systematizes, systematizing, systematized)**

✔ in BRIT, also use **systematise**

If you **systematize** things, you make them organized. [FORMAL] ❑ *You need to systematize your approach to problem solving.* ♦ **sys|tema|ti|za|tion** /sɪstəmətaɪzeɪʃən, AM -tɪz-/ *...a systematization of management practice.* VERB V n Also V N-UNCOUNT: usu N *of* n

**sys|tem|ic** /sɪstiːmɪk/ [1] **Systemic** means affecting the whole of something. [FORMAL] ❑ *The economy is locked in a systemic crisis.* ADJ: usu ADJ n [2] **Systemic** chemicals or drugs are absorbed into the whole of an organism such as a plant or person, rather than being applied to one area. [TECHNICAL] ADJ

**sys|tems ana|lyst** **(systems analysts)** A **systems analyst** is someone whose job is to decide what computer equipment and software a company needs, and to provide it. N-COUNT

# T t

**T, t** /tiː/ **(T's, t's)** T is the twentieth letter of the English alphabet. N-VAR

**ta** /tɑː/ **Ta** means 'thank you'. [BRIT, INFORMAL] CONVENTION

**tab** /tæb/ **(tabs)** 1 A **tab** is a small piece of cloth or paper that is attached to something, usually with information about that thing written on it. ❑ *A stupid medical clerk had slipped the wrong tab on his X-ray.* N-COUNT = *label* 2 A **tab** is the total cost of goods or services that you have to pay, or the bill or check for those goods or services. [mainly AM] ❑ *At least one estimate puts the total tab at $7 million.* N-COUNT = *bill* 3 A **tab** is a metal strip that you pull off the top of a can of drink in order to open it. N-COUNT 4 A **tab** is a drug, especially one that is sold illegally, which is in tablet form. [INFORMAL] ❑ *One tab of Ecstasy costs at least £15.* N-COUNT

PHRASES 5 If someone **keeps tabs on** you, they make sure that they always know where you are and what you are doing, often in order to control you. [INFORMAL] PHRASE: V inflects: PHR n 6 If you **pick up the tab**, you pay a bill on behalf of a group of people or provide the money that is needed for something. [INFORMAL] ❑ *Pollard picked up the tab for dinner that night.* PHRASE: V inflects

**Ta|bas|co** /tæbæskoʊ/ **Tabasco** is a hot spicy sauce made from peppers. [TRADEMARK] N-UNCOUNT

**tab|by** /tæbi/ **(tabbies)** A **tabby** or a **tabby cat** is a cat whose fur has dark stripes on a lighter background. N-COUNT

**tab|er|nac|le** /tæbəʳnækəl/ **(tabernacles)** 1 A **tabernacle** is a church used by certain Christian Protestant groups and by Mormons. N-COUNT: oft in names 2 **The Tabernacle** was a small tent which contained the most holy writings of the ancient Jews and which they took with them when they were travelling. N-PROPER: *the* N

**ta|ble** /teɪbəl/ **(tables, tabling, tabled)** ◆◆◇ 1 A **table** is a piece of furniture with a flat top that you put things on or sit at. ❑ *She was sitting at the kitchen table eating a currant bun... I placed his drink on the small table at his elbow.* N-COUNT 2 If someone **tables** a proposal, they say formally that they want it to be discussed at a meeting. [mainly BRIT] ❑ *They've tabled a motion criticising the Government for doing nothing about the problem.* VERB = *propose* V n 3 If someone **tables** a proposal or plan which has been put forward, they decide to discuss it or deal with it at a later date, rather than straight away. [AM] ❑ *We will table that for later.* VERB V n 4 A **table** is a written set of facts and figures arranged in columns and rows. ❑ *Consult the table on page 104... Other research supports the figures in Table 3.3.* N-COUNT: also N num 5 → See also **coffee table, dressing table, negotiating table, round table, tea table**.

PHRASES 6 If you put something **on the table**, you present it at a meeting for it to be discussed. ❑ *This is one of the best packages we've put on the table in years.* PHRASE: PHR after v, v-link PHR 7 If you **turn the tables on** someone, you change the situation completely, so that instead of them causing problems for you, you are causing problems for them. ❑ *The only question is whether the President can use his extraordinary political skills to turn the tables on his opponents.* PHRASE: V inflects, oft PHR *on* n 8 to **put** your **cards on the table** → see **card**.

**tab|leau** /tæbloʊ/ **(tableaux)** 1 A **tableau** is a scene, for example from the Bible, history, or mythology, that consists of a group of people in costumes who do not speak or move. The people are sometimes on a float in a procession. ❑ *...tableaux depicting the foundation of Barcelona.* N-COUNT 2 A **tableau** is a piece of art such as a sculpture or painting that shows a scene, especially one from the Bible, history, or mythology. ❑ *...Gaudi's luxuriant stone tableau of the Nativity on the cathedral's east face.* N-COUNT

**table|cloth** /teɪbəlklɒθ, AM -klɔːθ/ **(tablecloths)** A **tablecloth** is a cloth used to cover a table. N-COUNT

**ta|ble danc|ing** **Table dancing** is a type of entertainment in a bar or club in which a woman who is wearing very few clothes dances in a sexy way close to a customer or group of customers. N-UNCOUNT

**ta|ble lamp** **(table lamps)** A **table lamp** is a small electric lamp which stands on a table or other piece of furniture. N-COUNT

**ta|ble man|ners** You can use **table manners** to refer to the way you behave when you are eating a meal at a table. ❑ *He attacked the food as quickly as decent table manners allowed.* N-PLURAL: usu supp N

**table|spoon** /teɪbəlspuːn/ **(tablespoons)** 1 A **tablespoon** is a fairly large spoon used for serving food and in cooking. N-COUNT 2 You can refer to an amount of food resting on a tablespoon as a **tablespoon** of food. ❑ *...a tablespoon of sugar.* N-COUNT: usu N *of* n

**table|spoon|ful** /teɪbəlspuːnfʊl/ **(tablespoonfuls** or **tablespoonsful)** You can refer to an amount of food resting on a tablespoon as a **tablespoonful** of food. ❑ *Grate a tablespoonful of fresh ginger into a pan.* N-COUNT: usu N *of* n

**tab|let** /tæblət/ **(tablets)** 1 A **tablet** is a small solid round mass of medicine which you swallow. ❑ *It is never a good idea to take sleeping tablets regularly.* N-COUNT: oft n N = *pill* 2 Clay **tablets** or stone **tablets** are the flat pieces of clay or stone which people used to write on before paper was invented. **tablets of stone** → see **stone**. N-COUNT: oft n N

**ta|ble ten|nis** also **table-tennis. Table tennis** is a game played inside by two or four people. The players stand at each end of a table which has a low net across the middle and hit a small light ball over the net, using small bats. N-UNCOUNT

**ta|ble top** **(table tops)** also **tabletop.** A **table top** is the flat surface on a table. N-COUNT

**table|ware** /teɪbəlweəʳ/ **Tableware** consists of the objects used on the table at meals, for example plates, glasses, or cutlery. [FORMAL] N-UNCOUNT

**ta|ble wine** **(table wines)** **Table wine** is fairly cheap wine that is drunk with meals. N-MASS

**tab|loid** /tæblɔɪd/ **(tabloids)** A **tabloid** is a newspaper that has small pages, short articles, and lots of photographs. Tabloids are often considered to be less serious than other newspapers. Compare **broadsheet**. N-COUNT

**ta|boo** /tæbuː/ **(taboos)** If there is a **taboo** on a subject or activity, it is a social custom to avoid doing that activity or talking about that subject, because people find them embarrassing or offensive. ❑ *The topic of addiction remains something of a taboo.* N-COUNT ♦ **Taboo** is also an adjective. ❑ *Cancer is a taboo subject and people are frightened or embarrassed to talk openly about it.* ADJ

**tabu|late** /tæbjʊleɪt/ **(tabulates, tabulating, tabulated)** To **tabulate** information means to ar- VERB range it in columns on a page so that it can be analysed. ❑ *Results for the test program haven't been tabulated.* V n

**tacho|graph** /tækəgrɑːf, -græf/ **(tachographs)** A **tachograph** is a device that is put in vehicles such as lorries and coaches in order to record information such as how fast the vehicle goes, how far it travels, and the number of breaks the driver takes. [BRIT] N-COUNT

**tac|it** /tæsɪt/ If you refer to someone's **tacit** agreement or approval, you mean they are agreeing to something or approving it without actually saying so, often because they are unwilling to admit to doing so. ❑ *The question was a tacit admission that a mistake had indeed been made.* ADJ: usu ADJ n
♦ **tac|it|ly** *He tacitly admitted that the government had breached regulations.* ADV: ADV with v

**taci|turn** /tæsɪtɜːʳn/ A **taciturn** person does not say very much and can seem unfriendly. ❑ *A taciturn man, he replied to my questions in monosyllables.* ADJ

**tack** /tæk/ **(tacks, tacking, tacked)** 1 A **tack** is a short nail with a broad, flat head, especially one that is used for fastening carpets to the floor. → See also **thumbtack**. to **get down to brass tacks** → see **brass**. N-COUNT
2 If you **tack** something to a surface, you pin it there with tacks or drawing pins. ❑ *He had tacked this note to her door... She had recently taken a canvas from the theater and tacked it up on the wall.* VERB; V n *to* n; V n with adv
3 If you change **tack** or try a different **tack**, you try a different method for dealing with a situation. ❑ *In desperation I changed tack... This report takes a different tack from the 20 that have come before.* N-SING: also no det = approach
4 If a sailing boat **is tacking** or if the people in it **tack** it, it is sailing towards a particular point in a series of sideways movements rather than in a straight line. ❑ *We were tacking fairly close inshore... The helmsman could tack the boat singlehanded.* VERB; V; V n, Also V n prep/adv
5 If you **tack** pieces of material together, you sew them together with big, loose stitches in order to hold them firmly or check that they fit, before sewing them properly. ❑ *Tack them together with a 1.5 cm seam... Tack the cord around the cushion.* VERB; V pl-n with *together*; V n prep/adv
♦ **tack on** If you say that something **is tacked on** to something else, you think that it is added in a hurry and in an unsatisfactory way. ❑ *The child-care bill is to be tacked on to the budget plan now being worked out in the Senate.* PHRASAL VERB; *be* V-ed P *to* n; Also V n P

**tack|le** /tækəl/ **(tackles, tackling, tackled)** ♦◇◇
1 If you **tackle** a difficult problem or task, you deal with it in a very determined or efficient way. ❑ *The first reason to tackle these problems is to save children's lives.* VERB; V n
2 If you **tackle** someone in a game such as hockey or football, you try to take the ball away from them. If you **tackle** someone in rugby or American football, you knock them to the ground. ❑ *Foley tackled the quarterback.* ♦ **Tackle** is also a noun. ❑ *...a tackle by full-back Brian Burrows.* VERB; V n; N-COUNT
3 If you **tackle** someone about a particular matter, you speak to them honestly about it, usually in order to get it changed or done. ❑ *I tackled him about how anyone could live amidst so much poverty.* VERB = confront; V n *about* wh/n
4 If you **tackle** someone, you attack them and fight them. ❑ *He claims Pasolini overtook and tackled him, pushing him into the dirt.* VERB; V n
5 **Tackle** is the equipment that you need for a sport or activity, especially fishing. ❑ *...fishing tackle.* N-UNCOUNT

**tacky** /tæki/ **(tackier, tackiest)** 1 If you describe something as **tacky**, you dislike it because it is cheap and badly made or vulgar. [INFORMAL] ❑ *...a woman in a fake leopard-skin coat and tacky red sunglasses.* ADJ: usu ADJ n; disapproval
2 If something such as paint or glue is **tacky**, it is slightly sticky and not yet dry. ❑ *Test to see if the finish is tacky, and if it is, leave it to harden.* ADJ = sticky

**taco** /tækoʊ/ **(tacos)** A **taco** is a crispy Mexican pancake made from corn and eggs, which is folded and filled with meat, vegetables, and a spicy sauce. N-COUNT

**tact** /tækt/ **Tact** is the ability to avoid upsetting or offending people by being careful not to say or do things that would hurt their feelings. ❑ *On this occasion the press have not been intrusive and they have shown great tact.* N-UNCOUNT = diplomacy

**tact|ful** /tæktfʊl/ If you describe a person or what they say as **tactful** you approve of them because they are careful not to offend or upset another person. ❑ *He had been extremely tactful in dealing with the financial question.* ADJ: oft *it* v-link ADJ to-inf; approval; = diplomatic
♦ **tact|ful|ly** *Alex tactfully refrained from further comment.* ADV: usu ADV with v

**tac|tic** /tæktɪk/ **(tactics)** **Tactics** are the methods that you choose to use in order to achieve what you want in a particular situation. ❑ *What sort of tactics will the President use to rally the people behind him?* ♦◇◇ N-COUNT: usu pl

**tac|ti|cal** /tæktɪkəl/ 1 You use **tactical** to describe an action or plan which is intended to help someone achieve what they want in a particular situation. ❑ *It's not yet clear whether the Prime Minister's resignation offer is a serious one, or whether it's simply a tactical move.* ADJ: usu ADJ n
♦ **tac|ti|cal|ly** /tæktɪkli/ *The electorate is astute enough to vote tactically against the Government.* ADV: ADV adj, ADV after v, ADV with cl
2 **Tactical** weapons or forces are those which a military leader can decide for themselves to use in a battle, rather than waiting for a decision by a political leader. ❑ *They have removed all tactical nuclear missiles that could strike Europe.* ADJ: ADJ n

**tac|ti|cal vot|ing** **Tactical voting** is the act of voting for a particular person or political party in order to prevent someone else from winning, rather than because you support that person or party. [BRIT] N-UNCOUNT

**tac|ti|cian** /tæktɪʃən/ **(tacticians)** If you say that someone is a good **tactician**, you mean that they are skilful at choosing the best methods in order to achieve what they want. ❑ *He is an extremely astute political tactician.* N-COUNT: usu supp N

**tac|tile** /tæktaɪl, AM -təl/ 1 If you describe someone as **tactile**, you mean that they tend to touch other people a lot when talking to them. ❑ *The children are very tactile with warm, loving natures.* ADJ
2 Something such as fabric which is **tactile** is pleasant or interesting to touch. ❑ *Tweed is timeless, tactile and tough.* ADJ
3 **Tactile** experiences or sensations are received or felt by touch. [FORMAL] ❑ *Babies who sleep with their parents receive much more tactile stimulation than babies who sleep in a cot.* ADJ: usu ADJ n

**tact|less** /tæktləs/ If you describe someone as **tactless**, you think what they say or do is likely to offend other people. ❑ *He had alienated many people with his tactless remarks.* ADJ ≠ tactful

**tad** /tæd/ You can use **a tad** in expressions such as **a tad big** or **a tad small** when you mean that it is slightly too big or slightly too small. [INFORMAL] ❑ *It was a tad confusing.* PHRASE: PHR adj/adv

**tad|pole** /tædpoʊl/ **(tadpoles)** **Tadpoles** are small water creatures which grow into frogs or toads. N-COUNT

**taf|fe|ta** /tæfɪtə/ **Taffeta** is shiny stiff material made of silk or nylon that is used mainly for making women's clothes. N-UNCOUNT

**taf|fy** /tæfi/ **Taffy** is a sticky sweet that you chew. It is made by boiling sugar and butter together with water. [AM] N-UNCOUNT

✔ in BRIT, use **toffee**

**tag** /tæg/ **(tags, tagging, tagged)** 1 A **tag** is a small piece of card or cloth which is attached to an object or person and has information about that object or person on it. ❑ *Staff wore name tags. ...baggage tags.* → See also **dog tag, price tag**. N-COUNT
2 An electronic **tag** is a device that is firmly attached to someone or something and sets off an alarm if that person or thing moves away or is removed. ❑ *A hospital is to fit new-born babies with electronic tags to foil kidnappers.* → See also **electronic tagging**. N-COUNT
3 If you **tag** something, you attach something to it or mark it so that it can be VERB

identified later. ❑ *Professor Orr has developed interesting ways of tagging chemical molecules using existing laboratory lasers.* V n 4 You can refer to a phrase that is used to describe someone or something as a **tag**. [JOURNALISM] ❑ *In Britain, jazz is losing its elitist tag and gaining a much broader audience.* N-COUNT: usu with supp = label 5 If you **tag** someone in a particular way, you keep describing them using a particular phrase or thinking of them as a particular thing. [JOURNALISM] ❑ *...the pundits were still tagging him with that age-old label, 'best of a bad bunch'... She has always lived in John's house and is still tagged 'Dad's girlfriend' by his children.* VERB = label; V n *with* n; *be* V-ed n; Also V n *as* n, V n 6 ➔ See also **question tag**.

♦ **tag along** If someone goes somewhere and you **tag along**, you go with them, especially when they have not asked you to. ❑ *I let him tag along because he had not been too well recently... She seems quite happy to tag along with them.* PHRASAL VERB; V P; V P *with* n

♦ **tag on** If you **tag** something **on**, you add it. [INFORMAL] ❑ *It is also worth tagging on an extra day or two to see the capital.* PHRASAL VERB = tack on; V P n (not pron)

**tag line** (**tag lines**) also **tag-line.** The **tag line** of something such as a television commercial or a joke is the phrase that comes at the end and is meant to be amusing or easy to remember. N-COUNT

**Tai Chi** /taɪ tʃiː/ also **tai chi. Tai Chi** is a type of Chinese physical exercise in which you make slow, controlled movements. N-UNCOUNT

**tail** /teɪl/ (**tails, tailing, tailed**) ◆◇◇ 1 The **tail** of an animal, bird, or fish is the part extending beyond the end of its body. ❑ *...a black dog with a long tail.* N-COUNT ♦ **-tailed** *...white-tailed deer.* COMB in ADJ 2 You can use **tail** to refer to the end or back of something, especially something long and thin. ❑ *...the horizontal stabilizer bar on the plane's tail.* N-COUNT: usu with supp 3 If a man is wearing **tails**, he is wearing a formal jacket which has two long pieces hanging down at the back. N-PLURAL 4 To **tail** someone means to follow close behind them and watch where they go and what they do. [INFORMAL] ❑ *Officers had tailed the gang from London during a major undercover inquiry... He trusted her so little that he had her tailed.* VERB = shadow; V n; *have* n V-ed 5 If you toss a coin and it comes down **tails**, you can see the side of it that does not have a picture of a head on it. ADV: ADV after v 6 If you say that you have your **tail between** your **legs**, you are emphasizing that you feel defeated and ashamed. ❑ *His team retreated last night with tails tucked firmly between their legs.* PHRASE: PHR after v, *with* PHR [emphasis] 7 cannot **make head or tail of** something ➔ see **head**.

♦ **tail away** or **tail off** When a person's voice **tails away** or **tails off**, it gradually becomes quieter and then silent. ❑ *His voice tailed away in the bitter cold air.* PHRASAL VERB; V P

♦ **tail off** When something **tails off**, it gradually becomes less in amount or value, often before coming to an end completely. ❑ *Last year, economic growth tailed off to below four percent.* ➔ See also **tail away**. PHRASAL VERB; V P

**tail|back** /teɪlbæk/ (**tailbacks**) A **tailback** is a long line of traffic stretching back along a road, which moves very slowly or not at all, for example because of road works or an accident. [BRIT] ❑ *The flooding led to six-mile tailbacks between west London and Heathrow Airport.* N-COUNT

✔ in AM, use **backup**

**tail|coat** /teɪlkoʊt/ (**tailcoats**) also **tail coat.** A **tailcoat** is a man's coat which is short at the front with long pieces at the back. Tailcoats were popular in the 19th century and are now worn only for very formal occasions, such as weddings. N-COUNT = tails

**tail end** also **tail-end.** The **tail end** of an event, situation, or period of time is the last part of it. ❑ *Barry had obviously come in on the tail-end of the conversation.* N-SING: usu N *of* n

**tail|gate** /teɪlgeɪt/ (**tailgates, tailgating, tailgated**) 1 A **tailgate** is a door at the back of a truck or car, that is hinged at the bottom so that it opens downwards. N-COUNT 2 If you **tailgate** someone, you drive very closely behind them. ❑ *Perhaps the fact that the car was tailgating him made him accelerate... Police pulled him over doing 120km/h, making rapid changes and tailgating.* VERB; V n; V

**tail-light** (**tail-lights**) also **taillight.** The **tail-lights** on a car or other vehicle are the two red lights at the back. ➔ See picture on page 1707. N-COUNT = rear light

**tai|lor** /teɪləʳ/ (**tailors, tailoring, tailored**) 1 A **tailor** is a person whose job is to make men's clothes. N-COUNT 2 If you **tailor** something such as a plan or system **to** someone's needs, you make it suitable for a particular person or purpose by changing the details of it. ❑ *We can tailor the program to the patient's needs.* VERB; V n *to* n

**tai|lored** /teɪləʳd/ **Tailored** clothes are designed to fit close to the body, rather than being loose. ❑ *...a white tailored shirt.* ADJ: usu ADJ n = fitted

**tailor-made** 1 If something is **tailor-made**, it has been specially designed for a particular person or purpose. ❑ *Each client's portfolio is tailor-made.* ADJ 2 If you say that someone or something is **tailor-made for** a particular task, purpose, or need, you are emphasizing that they are perfectly suitable for it. ❑ *He was tailor-made, it was said, for the task ahead.* ADJ: oft ADJ *for* n [emphasis] 3 **Tailor-made** clothes have been specially made to fit a particular person. ❑ *He was wearing a tweed suit that looked tailor-made.* ADJ

**tailor-make** (**tailor-makes, tailor-making, tailor-made**) If someone **tailor-makes** something for you, they make or design it to suit your requirements. ❑ *The company can tailor-make your entire holiday.* ➔ See also **tailor-made**. VERB; V n

**tail|pipe** /teɪlpaɪp/ (**tailpipes**) A **tailpipe** is the end pipe of a car's exhaust system. [AM] ➔ See picture on page 1707. N-COUNT

**tail|wind** /teɪlwɪnd/ (**tailwinds**) also **tail wind.** A **tailwind** is a wind that is blowing from behind an aeroplane, boat, or other vehicle, making it move faster. N-COUNT ≠ headwind

**taint** /teɪnt/ (**taints, tainting, tainted**) 1 If a person or thing **is tainted by** something bad or undesirable, their status or reputation is harmed because they are associated with it. ❑ *Opposition leaders said that the elections had been tainted by corruption. ...a series of political scandals that has tainted the political stars of a generation.* VERB; *be* V-ed; V n ♦ **taint|ed** *He came out only slightly tainted by telling millions of viewers he and his wife had had marital problems.* ADJ 2 A **taint** is an undesirable quality which spoils the status or reputation of someone or something. ❑ *Her government never really shook off the taint of corruption.* N-COUNT: usu sing, usu with supp 3 If an unpleasant substance **taints** food or medicine, the food or medicine is spoiled or damaged by it. ❑ *Rancid oil will taint the flavour. ...blood tainted with the AIDS and hepatitis viruses.* VERB; V n; V-ed

**take**

① USED WITH NOUNS DESCRIBING ACTIONS

② OTHER USES

① **take** /teɪk/ (**takes, taking, took, taken**) ◆◆◆

**Take** is used in combination with a wide range of nouns, where the meaning of the combination is mostly given by the noun. Many of these combinations are common idiomatic expressions whose meanings can be found at the appropriate nouns. For example, the expression **take care** is explained at **care**.

1 You can use **take** followed by a noun to talk about an action or event, when it would also be possible to use the verb that is related to that noun. For example, you can say **'she took a shower'** instead of 'she showered'. ❑ *Betty took a photograph of us... I've never taken a holiday since starting this job... There's not enough people willing to take the risk.* VERB; V n; V n; V n 2 In ordinary spoken or written English, people use **take** with a range of nouns instead of using a more specific verb. For example VERB

people often say **'he took control'** or **'she took a positive attitude'** instead of 'he assumed control' or 'she adopted a positive attitude'. ❑ *The Patriotic Front took power after a three-month civil war...* V n *I felt it was important for women to join and take a leading role.* V n

**② take** /teɪk/ **(takes, taking, took, taken)** ◆◆◆

⇛ Please look at category 46 to see if the expression you are looking for is shown under another headword. **1** If you **take** something, you reach out for it and hold it. VERB ❑ *Here, let me take your coat...* V n *Colette took her by the shoulders and shook her...* V n *by* n *She took her in her arms and tried to comfort her.* V n prep **2** If you **take** something with you when you go somewhere, you carry it or have it with you. VERB ❑ *Mark often took his books to Bess's house to study...* V n prep/adv *You should take your passport with you when changing money...* V n *with* n *Don't forget to take your camera.* V n **3** If a person, vehicle, or path **takes** someone somewhere, they transport or lead them there. VERB ❑ *The school bus takes them to school and brings them back.* V n prep/adv **4** If something such as a job or interest **takes** you to a place, it is the reason for you going there. VERB ❑ *He was a poor student from Madras whose genius took him to Cambridge.* V n prep/adv **5** If you **take** something such as your problems or your business to someone, you go to that person when you have problems you want to discuss or things you want to buy. VERB ❑ *You need to take your problems to a trained counsellor.* V n prep/adv **6** If one thing **takes** another **to** a particular level, condition, or state, it causes it to reach that level or condition. VERB ❑ *Her latest research takes her point further.* V n prep/adv **7** If you **take** something from a place, you remove it from there. VERB ❑ *He took a handkerchief from his pocket and lightly wiped his mouth...* V n with prep/adv *Opening a drawer, she took out a letter.* **8** If you **take** something from someone who owns it, you steal it or go away with it without their permission. VERB ❑ *He has taken my money, and I have no chance of getting it back.* V n **9** If an army or political party **takes** something or someone, they win them from their enemy or opponent. VERB ❑ *Marines went in, taking 15 prisoners.* V n **10** If you **take** one number or amount from another, you subtract it or deduct it. VERB ❑ *Take off the price of the house, that's another hundred thousand.* V n with adv/prep **11** If you cannot **take** something difficult, painful, or annoying, you cannot tolerate it without becoming upset, ill, or angry. VERB: no passive, usu with brd-neg = stand, bear ❑ *Don't ever ask me to look after those kids again. I just can't take it!.* V n **12** If you **take** something such as damage or loss, you suffer it, especially in war or in a battle. VERB ❑ *They have taken heavy casualties.* V n **13** If something **takes** a certain amount of time, that amount of time is needed in order to do it. VERB: no passive ❑ *Since the roads are very bad, the journey took us a long time...* V n n *I had heard an appeal could take years...* V n *The sauce takes 25 minutes to prepare and cook...* V n to-inf *The game took her less than an hour to finish...* V n n to-inf *You must beware of those traps – you could take all day getting out of them...* V n -ing *It takes 15 minutes to convert the plane into a car by removing the wings and the tail...* it V n to-inf *It had taken Masters about twenty hours to reach the house...* it V n n to-inf *It took thirty-five seconds for the hour to strike.* it V n *for* n to-inf **14** If something **takes** a particular quality or thing, that quality or thing is needed in order to do it. VERB: no passive = need ❑ *At one time, walking across the room took all her strength...* V n *It takes courage to say what you think...* it V n to-inf *It takes a pretty bad level of performance before the teachers will criticize the students.* it V n *before* cl **15** If you **take** something that is given or offered to you, you agree to accept it. VERB = accept ❑ *His sons took his advice.* V n **16** If you **take** a feeling such as pleasure, pride, or delight in a particular thing or activity, the thing or activity gives you that feeling. VERB = derive ❑ *They take great pride in their heritage...* V n *in* n/-ing *The government will take comfort from the latest opinion poll.* V n *from* n/-ing **17** If a shop, restaurant, theatre, or other business **takes** a certain amount of money, they get that amount from people buying goods or services. VERB [mainly BRIT, BUSINESS] ❑ *The firm took £100,000 in bookings.* V amount

✔ in AM, usually use **take in**

**18** You can use **take** to refer to the amount of money that a business such as a store or theatre gets from selling its goods or tickets during a particular period. N-SING: usu *the* N [mainly AM, BUSINESS] ❑ *It added another $11.8 million to the take, for a grand total of $43 million.*

✔ in BRIT, usually use **takings**

**19** If you **take** a prize or medal, you win it. VERB ❑ *'Poison' took first prize at the 1991 Sundance Film Festival.* V n **20** If you **take** the blame, responsibility, or credit for something, you agree to accept it. VERB = accept ❑ *His brother Raoul did it, but Leonel took the blame and kept his mouth shut.* V n **21** If you **take** patients or clients, you accept them as your patients or clients. VERB ❑ *Some universities would be forced to take more students than they wanted.* V n **22** If you **take** a telephone call, you speak to someone who is telephoning you. VERB ❑ *Douglas telephoned Catherine at her office. She refused to take his calls.* V n **23** If you **take** something in a particular way, you react in the way mentioned to a situation or to someone's beliefs or behaviour. VERB ❑ *Unfortunately, no one took my messages seriously.* V n adv/prep **24** You use **take** when you are discussing or explaining a particular question, in order to introduce an example or to say how the question is being considered. VERB: usu imper = consider ❑ *There's confusion and resentment, and it's almost never expressed out in the open. Take this office, for example.* V n **25** If you **take** someone's meaning or point, you understand and accept what they are saying. VERB ❑ *They've turned sensible, if you take my meaning.* V n **26** If you **take** someone **for** something, you believe wrongly that they are that thing. VERB ❑ *She had taken him for a journalist...* V n *for* n *I naturally took him to be the owner of the estate.* V n to-inf **27** If you **take** something from among a number of things, you choose to have or buy it. VERB ❑ *'I'll take the grilled tuna,' Mary Ann told the waiter.* V n **28** If you **take** a road or route, you choose to travel along it. VERB ❑ *From Wrexham centre take the Chester Road to the outskirts of town...* V n prep/adv *The road forked in two directions. He had obviously taken the wrong fork.* V n **29** If you **take** a car, train, bus, or plane, you use it to go from one place to another. VERB ❑ *It's the other end of the High Street. We'll take the car, shall we?...* V n *She took the train to New York every weekend.* V n prep/adv **30** If you **take** a subject or course at school or university, you choose to study it. VERB ❑ *Students are allowed to take European history and American history.* V n **31** If you **take** a test or examination, you do it in order to obtain a qualification. VERB ❑ *She took her driving test in Greenford.* V n **32** If you **take** someone **for** a subject, you give them lessons in that subject. VERB = teach [mainly BRIT] ❑ *The teacher who took us for economics was Miss Humphrey.* V n *for* n **33** If someone **takes** drugs, pills, or other medicines, they take them into their body, for example by swallowing them. VERB ❑ *She's been taking sleeping pills.* V n **34** If you **take** a note or a letter, you write down something you want to remember or the words that someone says. VERB ❑ *She sat expressionless, carefully taking notes.* V n **35** If you **take** a particular measurement, you use special equipment to find out what something measures. VERB ❑ *If he feels hotter than normal, take his temperature.* V n **36** If a place or container **takes** a particular amount or number, there is enough space for that amount or number. VERB: no passive ❑ *The place could just about take 2,000 people.* V amount **37** If you **take** a particular size in shoes or clothes, that size fits you. VERB ❑ *47 per cent of women in the UK take a size 16 or above.* V n **38** A **take** is a short piece of action which is filmed in one continuous process for a cinema or television film. N-COUNT ❑ *She couldn't get it right – she never knew the lines and we had to do several takes.* **39** Someone's **take on** a particular situation or fact is their attitude to it or their interpretation of it. N-SING: N *on* n, usu supp N = perspective ❑ *What's your take on the new government? Do you think it can work?*

PHRASES **40** You can say **'I take it'** to check with someone that what you believe to be the case or PHRASE: PHR with cl, oft PHR that what you understand them to mean is in fact the case, or is in fact what they mean. ❑ *I take it you're a friend of the Kellings, Mr Burr.* (= *I presume*)

41 You can say '**take it from me**' to tell someone that you are absolutely sure that what you are saying is correct, and that they should believe you. ❑ *Take it from me – this is the greatest achievement by any Formula One driver ever.* (PHRASE: PHR with cl = *believe me*)

42 If you say to someone '**take it or leave it**', you are telling them that they can accept something or not accept it, but that you are not prepared to discuss any other alternatives. ❑ *A 72-hour week, 12 hours a day, six days a week, take it or leave it.* (CONVENTION)

43 If someone **takes** an insult or attack **lying down**, they accept it without protesting. ❑ *The government is not taking such criticism lying down.* (PHRASE: *take* inflects)

44 If something **takes a lot out of** you or **takes it out of** you, it requires a lot of energy or effort and makes you feel very tired and weak afterwards. ❑ *He looked tired, as if the argument had taken a lot out of him.* (PHRASE: V inflects, PHR n)

45 If someone tells you to **take five** or to **take ten**, they are telling you to have a five or ten minute break from what you are doing. [mainly AM, INFORMAL] (PHRASE: V inflects)

46 to **be taken aback** → see **aback**. to **take up arms** → see **arm**. to **take the biscuit** → see **biscuit**. to **take the bull by the horns** → see **bull**. to **take** your **hat off to** someone → see **hat**. to **take the mickey** → see **mickey**. to **take the piss out of** someone → see **piss**. to **take** something **as read** → see **read**. to **be taken for a ride** → see **ride**. to **take** someone **by surprise** → see **surprise**. **take my word for it** → see **word**.

♦ **take after** If you **take after** a member of your family, you resemble them in your appearance, your behaviour, or your character. ❑ *Ted's always been difficult, Mr Kemp – he takes after his dad.* (PHRASAL VERB: no passive; V P n)

♦ **take apart** 1 If you **take** something **apart**, you separate it into the different parts that it is made of. ❑ *When the clock stopped, he took it apart, found what was wrong, and put the whole thing together again.* (PHRASAL VERB = *dismantle*; V n P)

2 If you **take apart** something such as an argument or an idea, you show what its weaknesses are, usually by analyzing it carefully. ❑ *They will take that problem apart and analyze it in great detail... He proceeds to take apart every preconception anyone might have ever had about him.* (PHRASAL VERB; V n P; V P n (not pron))

♦ **take away** 1 If you **take** something **away from** someone, you remove it from them, so that they no longer possess it or have it with them. ❑ *They're going to take my citizenship away... 'Give me the knife,' he said softly, 'or I'll take it away from you.'... In prison they'd taken away his watch and everything he possessed.* (PHRASAL VERB; V n P; V n P *from* n; V P n (not pron))

2 If you **take** one number or amount **away from** another, you subtract one number from the other. ❑ *Add up the bills for each month. Take this away from the income.* (PHRASAL VERB = *subtract* ≠ *add*; V n P *from* n; Also V P n, V n P)

3 To **take** someone **away** means to bring them from their home to an institution such as a prison or hospital. ❑ *Two men claiming to be police officers called at the pastor's house and took him away... Soldiers took away four people one of whom was later released.* (PHRASAL VERB = *take off*; V n P; V P n (not pron))

4 → See also **takeaway**.

♦ **take away from** If something **takes away from** an achievement, success, or quality, or **takes** something **away from** it, it makes it seem lower in value or worth than it should be. ❑ *'It's starting to rain again.' — 'Not enough to take away from the charm of the scene.'... The victory looks rather hollow. That takes nothing away from the courage and skill of the fighting forces.* (PHRASAL VERB = *detract*; V P P n; V n P P n)

♦ **take back** 1 If you **take** something **back**, you return it to the place where you bought it or where you borrowed it from, because it is unsuitable or broken, or because you have finished with it. ❑ *If I buy something and he doesn't like it I'll take it back... I once took back a pair of shoes that fell apart after a week.* (PHRASAL VERB; V n P; V P n (not pron))

2 If you **take** something **back**, you admit that something that you said or thought is wrong. ❑ *I take it back, I think perhaps I am an extrovert... Take back what you said about Jeremy!* (PHRASAL VERB; V n P; V P n)

3 If you **take** someone **back**, you allow them to come home again, after they have gone away because of a quarrel or other problem. ❑ *Why did she take him back?... The government has agreed to take back those people who are considered economic rather than political refugees.* (PHRASAL VERB; V n P; V P n (not pron))

4 If you say that something **takes** you **back**, you mean that it reminds you of a period of your past life and makes you think about it again. ❑ *I enjoyed experimenting with colours – it took me back to being five years old... This takes me back.* (PHRASAL VERB; V n P *to* n/-ing; V n P)

♦ **take down** 1 If you **take** something **down**, you reach up and get it from a high place such as a shelf. ❑ *Alberg took the portrait down from the wall... Gil rose and went to his bookcase and took down a volume.* (PHRASAL VERB; V n P; V P n (not pron))

2 If you **take down** a structure, you remove each piece of it. ❑ *The Canadian army took down the barricades erected by the Indians... They put up the bird table, but it got in everyone else's way so Les tried to take it down.* (PHRASAL VERB ≠ *put up*; V P n (not pron); V n P)

3 If you **take down** a piece of information or a statement, you write it down. ❑ *We've been trying to get back to you, Tom, but we think we took your number down incorrectly... I took down his comments in shorthand.* (PHRASAL VERB = *write down*; V n P; V P n (not pron))

♦ **take in** 1 If you **take** someone **in**, you allow them to stay in your house or your country, especially when they do not have anywhere to stay or are in trouble. ❑ *He persuaded Jo to take him in... The monastery has taken in 26 refugees.* (PHRASAL VERB; V n P; V P n)

2 If the police **take** someone **in**, they remove them from their home in order to question them. ❑ *The police have taken him in for questioning in connection with the murder of a girl.* (PHRASAL VERB; V n P; Also V P n (not pron))

3 If you **are taken in by** someone or something, you are deceived by them, so that you get a false impression of them. ❑ *I married in my late teens and was taken in by his charm – which soon vanished... I know I was a naive fool to trust him but he is a real charmer who totally took me in.* (PHRASAL VERB; *be* V-ed P; V n P)

4 If you **take** something **in**, you pay attention to it and understand it when you hear it or read it. ❑ *Lesley explains possible treatments but you can tell she's not taking it in... Gazing up into his eyes, she seemed to take in all he said.* (PHRASAL VERB; V n P; V P n (not pron))

5 If you **take** something **in**, you see all of it at the same time or with just one look. ❑ *The eyes behind the lenses were dark and quick-moving, taking in everything at a glance.* (PHRASAL VERB; V P n (not pron); Also V n P)

6 If you **take in** something such as a film or a museum, you go to see it. [INFORMAL] ❑ *I was wondering if you might want to take in a movie with me this evening.* (PHRASAL VERB: no passive; V P n (not pron); Also V n P)

7 If people, animals, or plants **take in** air, drink, or food, they allow it to enter their body, usually by breathing or swallowing. ❑ *They will certainly need to take in plenty of liquid.* (PHRASAL VERB; V P n; Also V n P)

8 If you **take in** a dress, jacket, or other item of clothing, you make it smaller and tighter. ❑ *She had taken in the grey dress so that it hugged her thin body.* (PHRASAL VERB ≠ *let out*; V P n; Also V n P)

9 If a store, restaurant, theatre, or other business **takes in** a certain amount of money, they get that amount from people buying goods or services. [mainly AM, BUSINESS] ❑ *They plan to take in $1.6 billion.* (PHRASAL VERB; V P amount)

✔ in BRIT, usually use **take**

♦ **take off** 1 When an aeroplane **takes off**, it leaves the ground and starts flying. ❑ *We eventually took off at 11 o'clock and arrived in Venice at 1.30.* (PHRASAL VERB ≠ *land*; V P)

2 If something such as a product, an activity, or someone's career **takes off**, it suddenly becomes very successful. ❑ *In 1944, he met Edith Piaf, and his career took off.* (PHRASAL VERB; V P)

3 If you **take off** or **take yourself off**, you go away, often suddenly and unexpectedly. ❑ *He took off at once and headed back to the motel... He took himself off to Mexico.* (PHRASAL VERB; V P; V pron-refl P)

4 If you **take** a garment **off**, you remove it. ❑ *He wouldn't take his hat off... She took off her spectacles.* (PHRASAL VERB ≠ *put on*; V n P; V P n)

5 If you **take** time **off**, you obtain permission not to go to work for a short period of time. ❑ *Mitchel's schedule had not permitted him to take time off... She took two days off work.* (PHRASAL VERB; V n P; V n P n)

6 If you **take** someone **off**, you make them go with you to a particular place, especially when they do not want (PHRASAL VERB = *take away*)

to go there. ❑ *The police stopped her and took her off to a police station.* V n P prep/adv [7] If you **take** someone **off**, you imitate them and the things that they do and say, in such a way that you make other people laugh. [mainly BRIT] PHRASAL VERB = mimic ❑ *Mike can take off his father to perfection.* V P n (not pron) Also V n P [8] → See also **takeoff**.

♦ **take on** [1] If you **take on** a job or responsibility, especially a difficult one, you accept it. PHRASAL VERB ❑ *No other organisation was able or willing to take on the job.* V P n (not pron) [2] If something **takes on** a new appearance or quality, it develops that appearance or quality. PHRASAL VERB: no passive = assume ❑ *Believing he had only a year to live, his writing took on a feverish intensity.* V P n (not pron) [3] If a vehicle such as a bus or ship **takes on** passengers, goods, or fuel, it stops in order to allow them to get on or to be loaded on. PHRASAL VERB ❑ *This is a brief stop to take on passengers and water.* V P n (not pron) [4] If you **take** someone **on**, you employ them to do a job. PHRASAL VERB ❑ *He's spoken to a publishing firm. They're going to take him on... The party has been taking on staff, including temporary organisers.* V n P; V P n (not pron) [5] If you **take** someone **on**, you fight them or compete against them, especially when they are bigger or more powerful than you are. PHRASAL VERB: no passive ❑ *Democrats were reluctant to take on a president whose popularity ratings were historically high... I knew I couldn't take him on.* V P n (not pron); V n P [6] If you **take** something **on** or **upon yourself**, you decide to do it without asking anyone for permission or approval. PHRASAL VERB: no passive ❑ *Knox had taken it on himself to choose the wine... He took upon himself the responsibility for protecting her... The President absolved his officers and took the blame upon himself.* V *it* P pron-refl to-inf; V P pron-refl n; V n P pron-refl

♦ **take out** [1] If you **take** something **out**, you remove it permanently from its place. PHRASAL VERB ❑ *I got an abscess so he took the tooth out... When you edit the tape you can take out the giggles.* V n P; V P n (not pron) [2] If you **take out** something such as a loan, a licence, or an insurance policy, you obtain it by fulfilling the conditions and paying the money that is necessary. PHRASAL VERB ❑ *They find a house, agree a price, and take out a mortgage through their building society.* V P n (not pron) [3] If you **take** someone **out**, they go to something such as a restaurant or theatre with you after you have invited them, and usually you pay for them. PHRASAL VERB ❑ *Jessica's grandparents took her out for the day... Reichel took me out to lunch. ...a father taking out his daughter for a celebratory dinner.* V n P; V n P *to* n; V P n (not pron)

♦ **take out on** If you **take** something **out on** someone, you behave in an unpleasant way towards them because you feel angry or upset, even though this is not their fault. PHRASAL VERB ❑ *Jane's always annoying her and she takes it out on me sometimes.* V n P P n

♦ **take over** [1] If you **take over** a company, you get control of it, for example by buying its shares. [BUSINESS] PHRASAL VERB ❑ *A British newspaper says British Airways plan to take over Trans World Airways.* V P n Also V n P [2] If someone **takes over** a country or building, they get control of it by force, for example with the help of the army. PHRASAL VERB ❑ *The Belgians took over Rwanda under a League of Nations mandate.* V P n (not pron) [3] If you **take over** a job or role or if you **take over**, you become responsible for the job after someone else has stopped doing it. PHRASAL VERB ❑ *His widow has taken over the running of his empire, including six London theatres... In 1966, Pastor Albertz took over from him as governing mayor... She took over as chief executive of the Book Trust.* V P n (not pron); V P *from* n; V P [4] If one thing **takes over** from something else, it becomes more important, successful, or powerful than the other thing, and eventually replaces it. PHRASAL VERB ❑ *Cars gradually took over from horses... When the final vote came, rationality took over.* V P *from* n; V P [5] → See also **takeover**.

♦ **take to** [1] If you **take to** someone or something, you like them, especially after knowing them or thinking about them for only a short time. PHRASAL VERB ❑ *Did the children take to him?* V P n [2] If you **take to** doing something, you begin to do it as a regular habit. PHRASAL VERB ❑ *They had taken to wandering through the streets arm-in-arm.* V P -ing

♦ **take up** [1] If you **take up** an activity or a subject, you become interested in it and spend time doing it, either as a hobby or as a career. PHRASAL VERB ❑ *He did not particularly want to take up a competitive sport... Angela used to be a model and has decided to take it up again.* V P n; V n P [2] If you **take up** a question, problem, or cause, you act on it or discuss how you are going to act on it. PHRASAL VERB ❑ *Most scientists who can present evidence of an environmental threat can reasonably assume that a pressure group will take up the issue... Dr Mahathir intends to take up the proposal with the prime minister... If the bank is unhelpful take it up with the Ombudsman.* V P n (not pron); V P n *with* n; V n P *with* n Also V n P [3] If you **take up** a job, you begin to work at it. PHRASAL VERB ❑ *He will take up his post as the head of the civil courts at the end of next month.* V P n (not pron) Also V n P [4] If you **take up** an offer or a challenge, you accept it. PHRASAL VERB ❑ *Increasingly, more wine-makers are taking up the challenge of growing Pinot Noir.* V P n (not pron) [5] If something **takes up** a particular amount of time, space, or effort, it uses that amount. PHRASAL VERB ❑ *I know how busy you must be and naturally I wouldn't want to take up too much of your time... A good deal of my time is taken up with reading critical essays and reviews... The aim was not to take up valuable time with the usual boring pictures.* V P n (not pron); *be* V-ed P *with* -ing/n; V P n *with* n/-ing [6] If you **take up** a particular position, you get into a particular place in relation to something else. PHRASAL VERB: no passive ❑ *He had taken up a position in the centre of the room.* V P n (not pron) [7] If you **take up** something such as a task or a story, you begin doing it after it has been interrupted or after someone else has begun it. PHRASAL VERB ❑ *Gerry's wife Jo takes up the story... 'No, no, no,' says Damon, taking up where Dave left off.* V P n (not pron); V P *wh* Also V n P [8] → See also **take-up**.

♦ **take up on** If you **take** someone **up on** their offer or invitation, you accept it. PHRASAL VERB ❑ *Since she'd offered to babysit, I took her up on it.* V n P P n

♦ **take upon** → see **take on 6**.

♦ **take up with** If you **are taken up with** something, it keeps you busy or fully occupied. PHRASAL VERB ❑ *His mind was wholly taken up with the question.* *be* V-ed P P n

**take|away** /teɪkəweɪ/ **(takeaways)** [1] A **takeaway** is a shop or restaurant which sells hot cooked food that you eat somewhere else. [BRIT] N-COUNT

✓ in AM, use **takeout**

[2] A **takeaway** is hot cooked food that you buy from a shop or restaurant and eat somewhere else. [BRIT] N-COUNT ❑ *...a Chinese takeaway.*

✓ in AM, use **takeout**

**take-home pay** Your **take-home pay** is the amount of your wages or salary that is left after income tax and other payments have been subtracted. [BUSINESS] N-UNCOUNT ❑ *He was earning £215 a week before tax: take-home pay, £170.*

**tak|en** /teɪkən/ [1] **Taken** is the past participle of **take**. [2] If you are **taken with** something or someone, you are very interested in them or attracted to them. [INFORMAL] ADJ: v-link ADJ, usu ADJ *with* n ❑ *She seems very taken with the idea.*

**take|off** /teɪkɒf, AM -ɔːf/ **(takeoffs)** also **take-off.** [1] **Takeoff** is the beginning of a flight, when an aircraft leaves the ground. N-VAR [2] A **takeoff of** someone is a humorous imitation of the way in which they behave. N-COUNT: usu sing, usu N *of* n ❑ *The programme was worth watching for an inspired takeoff of the Collins sisters.*

**take|out** /teɪkaʊt/ **(takeouts)** [1] A **takeout** is a store or restaurant which sells hot cooked food that you eat somewhere else. [AM] N-COUNT

✓ in BRIT, use **takeaway**

[2] A **takeout** or **takeout** food is hot cooked food which you buy from a store or restaurant and eat somewhere else. [AM] N-COUNT: oft N n

✓ in BRIT, use **takeaway**

**take|over** /teɪkoʊvəʳ/ **(takeovers)** ◆◇◇ [1] A **takeover** is the act of gaining control of a company by buying more of its shares than anyone else. [BUSINESS] N-COUNT ❑ *...the government's takeover of the Bank of New England Corporation.* [2] A **takeover** is the act of taking control of a country, political party, N-COUNT: usu with supp = coup or movement by force. ❑ *There's been a military takeover of some kind.*

**tak|er** /teɪkəʳ/ **(takers)** If there are no **takers for** something such as an investment or a challenge, nobody is willing to accept it. ❑ *Over 100 buyers or investors were approached, but there were no takers.*

N-COUNT: usu with brd-neg, usu pl, oft N *for* n

**-taker** /-teɪkəʳ/ **(-takers) -taker** combines with nouns to form other nouns which refer to people who take things, for example decisions or notes. ❑ *Of these, 40% told census-takers they were Muslims... They've got some terrific penalty-takers.*

COMB in N-COUNT

**take-up** **Take-up** is the rate at which people apply for or buy something which is offered, for example financial help from the government or shares in a company. [mainly BRIT] ❑ *...a major campaign to increase the take-up of welfare benefits.*

N-UNCOUNT: usu with supp, oft N *of* n

**tak|ings** /teɪkɪŋz/ You can use **takings** to refer to the amount of money that a business such as a shop or a cinema gets from selling its goods or tickets during a particular period. [BUSINESS] ❑ *The pub said that their takings were fifteen to twenty thousand pounds a week.*

N-PLURAL

**talc** /tælk/ **Talc** is the same as **talcum powder**. [INFORMAL]

N-UNCOUNT

**tal|cum pow|der** /tælkəm paʊdəʳ/ **Talcum powder** is fine powder with a pleasant smell which people put on their bodies after they have had a bath or a shower.

N-UNCOUNT

**tale** /teɪl/ **(tales)** 1 A **tale** is a story, often involving magic or exciting events. ❑ *...a collection of stories, poems and folk tales.* 2 You can refer to an interesting, exciting, or dramatic account of a real event as a **tale**. ❑ *The media have been filled with tales of horror and loss resulting from Monday's earthquake.* 3 ➔ See also **fairy tale, old wives' tale, tall tale**.

◆◇◇ N-COUNT; N-IN-NAMES; N-COUNT: usu with supp, oft N *of* n = story

PHRASES 4 If you survive a dangerous or frightening experience and so are able to tell people about it afterwards, you can say that you **lived to tell the tale**. ❑ *You lived to tell the tale this time but who knows how far you can push your luck.* 5 If someone **tells tales about** you, they tell other people things about you which are untrue or which you wanted to be kept secret. ❑ *I hesitated, not wanting to tell tales about my colleague.* ➔ See also **tell-tale**.

PHRASE: V inflects; PHRASE: V inflects

**tal|ent** /tælənt/ **(talents) Talent** is the natural ability to do something well. ❑ *The player was given hardly any opportunities to show off his talents... He's got lots of talent.* ➔ See also **talent show**.

◆◇◇ N-VAR: oft N *for* n

**tal|ent|ed** /tæləntɪd/ Someone who is **talented** has a natural ability to do something well. ❑ *Howard is a talented pianist.*

ADJ = gifted

**tal|ent scout** **(talent scouts)** A **talent scout** is someone whose job is to find people who have talent, for example as actors, footballers, or musicians, so that they can be offered work.

N-COUNT

**tal|ent show** **(talent shows)** A **talent show**, **talent competition**, or **talent contest** is a show where ordinary people perform an act on stage, usually in order to try to win a prize for the best performance.

N-COUNT

**tal|is|man** /tælɪzmən/ **(talismans)** A **talisman** is an object which you believe has magic powers to protect you or bring you luck.

N-COUNT = charm

**talk** /tɔːk/ **(talks, talking, talked)** 1 When you **talk**, you use spoken language to express your thoughts, ideas, or feelings. ❑ *He was too distressed to talk... The boys all began to talk at once.* ♦ **Talk** is also a noun. ❑ *That's not the kind of talk one usually hears from accountants.* 2 If you **talk to** someone, you have a conversation with them. You can also say that two people **talk**. ❑ *We talked and laughed a great deal... I talked to him yesterday... When she came back, they were talking about American food... Can't you see I'm talking? Don't interrupt.* ♦ **Talk** is also a noun. ❑ *We had a long talk about her father, Tony, who was a friend of mine.* 3 If you **talk to** someone, you tell them about the things that are worrying you. You can also say that two people **talk**. ❑ *Your first step should be to talk to a teacher or school counselor... We need to talk alone... Do ring if you want to talk about it... I just have to sort some things out. We really needed to talk.* ♦ **Talk** is also a noun. ❑ *I think it's time we had a talk.* 4 If you **talk on** or **about** something, you make an informal speech telling people what you know or think about it. ❑ *She will talk on the issues she cares passionately about including education and nursery care... He intends to talk to young people about the dangers of AIDS.* ♦ **Talk** is also a noun. ❑ *A guide gives a brief talk on the history of the site.* 5 **Talks** are formal discussions intended to produce an agreement, usually between different countries or between employers and employees. ❑ *Talks between striking railway workers and the Polish government have broken down.* 6 If one group of people **talks to** another, or if two groups **talk**, they have formal discussions in order to do a deal or produce an agreement. ❑ *We're talking to some people about opening an office in London... The company talked with many potential investors... It triggered broad speculation that GM and Jaguar might be talking.* 7 When different countries or different sides in a dispute **talk**, or **talk to** each other, they discuss their differences in order to try and settle the dispute. ❑ *The Foreign Minister said he was ready to talk to any country that had no hostile intentions... They are collecting information in preparation for the day when the two sides sit down and talk... John Reid has to find a way to make both sides talk to each other... The speed with which the two sides came to the negotiating table shows that they are ready to talk.* 8 If people **are talking about** another person or **are talking**, they are discussing that person. ❑ *Everyone is talking about him... People will talk, but you have to get on with your life.* ♦ **Talk** is also a noun. ❑ *There has been a lot of talk about me getting married.* 9 If someone **talks** when they are being held by police or soldiers, they reveal important or secret information, usually unwillingly. ❑ *They'll talk, they'll implicate me.* 10 If you **talk** a particular language or **talk** with a particular accent, you use that language or have that accent when you speak. ❑ *You don't sound like a foreigner talking English... They were amazed that I was talking in an Irish accent.* 11 If you **talk** something such as politics or sport, you discuss it. ❑ *The guests were mostly middle-aged men talking business.* 12 You can use **talk** to say what you think of the ideas that someone is expressing. For example, if you say that someone **is talking sense**, you mean that you think the opinions they are expressing are sensible. ❑ *You must admit George, you're talking absolute rubbish.* 13 You can say that you **are talking** a particular thing to draw attention to your topic or to point out a characteristic of what you are discussing. [SPOKEN] ❑ *We're talking megabucks this time.* 14 If you say that something such as an idea or threat is just **talk**, or **all talk**, you mean that it does not mean or matter much, because people are exaggerating about it or do not really intend to do anything about it. ❑ *Has much of this actually been tried here? Or is it just talk?*

◆◆◆ VERB; V; N-UNCOUNT; V-RECIP; pl-n V; V *to/with* n; pl-n V *about* n; V (non-recip); N-COUNT; V-RECIP; V *to* n; pl-n V; V *about* n (non-recip); V (non-recip); N-COUNT; VERB = speak; V *on/about* n; V *to* n; N-COUNT: oft N *on/about* n; N-PLURAL: oft N *with/between* n, N *on/about* n; V-RECIP; V *to* n *about* n/-ing; V *with/to* n; pl-n V; V-RECIP; V *to* n; pl-n V; V *to/with* pron-recip; V (non-recip); VERB; V *about/of* n; V; N-UNCOUNT: N *about/of* n/-ing, N that; VERB; V; VERB: no passive; V n; V prep/adv; VERB: no passive; V n; VERB; V n; VERB: no passive; V n; N-UNCOUNT

PHRASES 15 You can say **talk about** before mentioning a particular expression or situation, when you mean that something is a very striking or clear example of that expression or situation. [INFORMAL] ❑ *Took us quite a while to get here, didn't it? Talk about Fate moving in a mysterious way!* 16 You can use the expression **talking of** to introduce a new topic that you want to discuss, and to link it to something that has already been mentioned. ❑ *Belvoir Farms produce a delicious elderflower tea. Talking of elderflower, you might wish to try Elderflower Champagne.* 17 to **talk shop** ➔ see **shop**.

PHRASE: PHR n/-ing emphasis; PHRASE: PHR n/-ing

♦ **talk around** ➔ see **talk round**.

♦ **talk back** If you **talk back** to someone in authority such as a parent or teacher, you answer them in a rude way. ❑ *How dare you talk back to me!... I talked back and asked questions.*
PHRASAL VERB; V P *to* n; V P

♦ **talk down** [1] To **talk down** someone who is flying an aircraft in an emergency means to give them instructions so that they can land safely. ❑ *The pilot began to talk him down by giving instructions over the radio.* [2] If someone **talks down** a particular thing, they make it less interesting, valuable, or likely than it originally seemed. ❑ *They even blame the government for talking down the nation's fourth biggest industry... Businessmen are tired of politicians talking the economy down.*
PHRASAL VERB; V n P; PHRASAL VERB ≠ *talk up*; V P n (not pron); V n P

♦ **talk down to** If you say that someone **talks down to** you, you disapprove of the way they talk to you, treating you as if you are not very intelligent or not very important. ❑ *She was a gifted teacher who never talked down to her students.*
PHRASAL VERB; [disapproval]; = *patronize*; V P P n

♦ **talk into** If you **talk** a person **into** doing something they do not want to do, especially something wrong or stupid, you persuade them to do it. ❑ *He talked me into marrying him. He also talked me into having a baby.*
PHRASAL VERB ≠ *talk out of*; V n P -ing/n

♦ **talk out** If you **talk out** something such as a problem, you discuss it thoroughly in order to settle it. ❑ *Talking things out with someone else can be helpful... Talk out your problems. Do not keep them bottled up.*
PHRASAL VERB = *talk through*; V n P; V P n (not pron)

♦ **talk out of** If you **talk** someone **out of** doing something they want or intend to do, you persuade them not to do it. ❑ *My mother tried to talk me out of getting a divorce.*
PHRASAL VERB ≠ *talk into*; V n P P -ing/n

♦ **talk over** If you **talk** something **over**, you discuss it thoroughly and honestly. ❑ *He always talked things over with his friends... We should go somewhere quiet, and talk it over... Talk over problems, don't bottle them up inside.*
PHRASAL VERB; V n P *with* n; V n P; V P n (not pron)

♦ **talk round**

✔ in AM, usually use **talk around**

If you **talk** someone **round**, you persuade them to change their mind so that they agree with you, or agree to do what you want them to do ❑ *He went to the house to try to talk her round... It advises salesmen to talk round reluctant customers over a cup of tea.*
PHRASAL VERB; V n P; V P n (not pron)

♦ **talk through** [1] If you **talk** something **through** with someone, you discuss it with them thoroughly. ❑ *He and I have talked through this whole tricky problem... Now her children are grown-up and she has talked through with them what happened... It had all seemed so simple when they'd talked it through, so logical... He had talked it through with Judith.* [2] If someone **talks** you **through** something that you do not know, they explain it to you carefully. ❑ *Now she must talk her sister through the process a step at a time.*
PHRASAL VERB; pl-n V P n (not pron); V P *with* n n; pl-n V n P; V n P *with* n; PHRASAL VERB; V n P n

♦ **talk up** [1] If someone **talks up** a particular thing, they make it sound more interesting, valuable, or likely than it originally seemed. ❑ *Politicians accuse the media of talking up the possibility of a riot.* [2] To **talk** someone or something **up** in negotiations means to persuade someone to pay more money than they originally offered or wanted to. [mainly BRIT] ❑ *Clarke kept talking the price up, while Wilkinson kept knocking it down.*
PHRASAL VERB; V P n; Also V n P; PHRASAL VERB; V n P; Also V P n (not pron)

**talka|tive** /tɔːkətɪv/ Someone who is **talkative** talks a lot. ❑ *He suddenly became very talkative, his face slightly flushed, his eyes much brighter.*
ADJ

**talk|er** /tɔːkəʳ/ **(talkers)** You can use **talker** to refer to someone when you are considering how much they talk, or how good they are at talking to people. ❑ *...a fluent talker.*
N-COUNT: usu supp N

**talkie** /tɔːki/ **(talkies)** A **talkie** is a cinema film made with sound, as opposed to a silent film. [OLD-FASHIONED]
N-COUNT

**talk|ing head** **(talking heads)** **Talking heads** are people who appear in television discussion programmes and interviews to give their opinions about a topic. [JOURNALISM]
N-COUNT = *pundit*

**talk|ing point** **(talking points)** A **talking point** is an interesting subject for discussion or argument. ❑ *It's bound to be the main talking point during discussions between the Prime Minister and the President.*
N-COUNT

**talk|ing shop** **(talking shops)** If you say that a conference or a committee is just a **talking shop**, you disapprove of it because nothing is achieved as a result of what is discussed. [mainly BRIT]
N-COUNT; [disapproval]

**talking-to** If you give someone **a talking-to**, you speak to them severely, usually about something unacceptable that they have done, in order to show them they were wrong. [INFORMAL]
N-SING: *a* N

**talk show** **(talk shows)** also **talk-show.** A **talk show** is a television or radio show in which famous people talk to each other in an informal way and are asked questions about different topics.
N-COUNT = *chat show*

**tall** /tɔːl/ **(taller, tallest)** [1] Someone or something that is **tall** has a greater height than is normal or average. ❑ *Being tall can make you feel incredibly self-confident... The windows overlooked a lawn of tall waving grass.* [2] You use **tall** to ask or talk about the height of someone or something. ❑ *How tall are you?... I'm only 5ft tall, and I look younger than my age.*
♦◇◇ ADJ; ADJ: *how* ADJ, amount ADJ, *as* ADJ *as*, ADJ-compar *than*

PHRASES [3] If something is **a tall order**, it is very difficult. ❑ *Financing your studies may seem like a tall order, but there is plenty of help available.* [4] If you say that someone **walks tall**, you mean that they behave in a way that shows that they have pride in themselves and in what they are doing.
PHRASE: N inflects, v-link PHR; PHRASE: V inflects

**tal|low** /tæloʊ/ **Tallow** is hard animal fat that is used for making candles and soap.
N-UNCOUNT

**tall ship** **(tall ships)** A **tall ship** is a sailing ship which has very tall masts and square sails.
N-COUNT

**tall sto|ry** **(tall stories)** A **tall story** is the same as a **tall tale**.
N-COUNT

**tall tale** **(tall tales)** A **tall tale** is a long and complicated story that is difficult to believe because most of the events it describes seem unlikely or impossible. ❑ *...the imaginative tall tales of sailors.*
N-COUNT

**tal|ly** /tæli/ **(tallies, tallying, tallied)** [1] A **tally** is a record of amounts or numbers which you keep changing and adding to as the activity which affects it progresses. ❑ *They do not keep a tally of visitors to the palace, but it is very popular.* [2] If one number or statement **tallies with** another, they agree with each other or are exactly the same. You can also say that two numbers or statements **tally**. ❑ *Its own estimate of three hundred tallies with that of another survey... The figures didn't seem to tally.* [3] If you **tally** numbers, items, or totals, you count them. ❑ *...as we tally the number of workers who have been laid off this year.* ♦ **Tally up** means the same as **tally**. ❑ *Bookkeepers haven't yet tallied up the total cost.*
N-COUNT: usu sing, oft N *of* n; V-RECIP = *correspond*; V *with* n; pl-n V; VERB; V n; PHRASAL VERB; V P n (not pron); Also V n P

**Tal|mud** /tælmʊd/ **The Talmud** is the collection of ancient Jewish laws which governs the religious and non-religious life of Orthodox Jews.
N-PROPER: *the* N

**tal|on** /tælən/ **(talons)** The **talons** of a bird of prey are its hooked claws.
N-COUNT: usu pl

**tama|rind** /tæmərɪnd/ **(tamarinds)** A **tamarind** is a fruit which grows on a tropical evergreen tree which has pleasant-smelling flowers. You can also refer to the tree on which this fruit grows as a **tamarind**.
N-VAR

**tama|risk** /tæmərɪsk/ **(tamarisks)** A **tamarisk** is a bush or small tree which grows mainly around the Mediterranean and in Asia, and has pink or white flowers.
N-COUNT

**tam|bou|rine** /tæmbəriːn/ **(tambourines)** A **tambourine** is a musical instrument which you shake or hit with your hand. It consists of a drum skin on a circular frame with pairs of small round pieces of metal all around the edge.
N-COUNT: oft *the* N

**tame** /teɪm/ **(tamer, tamest, tames, taming, tamed)** [1] A **tame** animal or bird is one that is not afraid of humans. ❑ *The deer never became tame; they would run away if you approached them.* ADJ
[2] If you say that something or someone is **tame**, you are criticizing them for being weak and uninteresting, rather than forceful or shocking. ❑ *Some of today's political demonstrations look rather tame.* ADJ [disapproval]
♦ **tame|ly** *There was no excuse though when Thomas shot tamely wide from eight yards.* ADV: ADV with v
[3] If someone **tames** a wild animal or bird, they train it not to be afraid of humans and to do what they say. ❑ *The Amazons were believed to have been the first to tame horses.* VERB; V n

**ta|moxi|fen** /təmɒksɪfen/ **Tamoxifen** is a drug that is used for treating women who have breast cancer. N-UNCOUNT

**tamp** /tæmp/ **(tamps, tamping, tamped)** If you **tamp** something, you press it down by tapping it several times so that it becomes flatter and more solid. ❑ *Then I tamp down the soil with the back of a rake... Philpott tamped a wad of tobacco into his pipe.* VERB; V n with adv; V n prep/adv; Also V n

**tam|per** /tæmpəʳ/ **(tampers, tampering, tampered)** If someone **tampers with** something, they interfere with it or try to change it when they have no right to do so. ❑ *I don't want to be accused of tampering with the evidence.* VERB; V with n

**tam|pon** /tæmpɒn/ **(tampons)** A **tampon** is a tube made of cotton wool that a woman puts inside her vagina in order to absorb blood during menstruation. N-COUNT

**tan** /tæn/ **(tans, tanning, tanned)** [1] If you have a **tan**, your skin has become darker than usual because you have been in the sun. ❑ *She is tall and blonde, with a permanent tan.* N-SING: usu *a* N = suntan
[2] If a part of your body **tans** or if you **tan** it, your skin becomes darker than usual because you spend a lot of time in the sun. ❑ *I have very pale skin that never tans... Leigh rolled over on her stomach to tan her back.* VERB; V; V n
♦ **tanned** *Their skin was tanned and glowing from their weeks at the sea.* ADJ
[3] Something that is **tan** is a light brown colour. ❑ *...a tan leather jacket.* COLOUR
[4] To **tan** animal skins means to make them into leather by treating them with tannin or other chemicals. ❑ *...the process of tanning animal hides.* VERB; V n

**tan|dem** /tændəm/ **(tandems)** [1] A **tandem** is a bicycle designed for two riders, on which one rider sits behind the other. N-COUNT
**PHRASES** [2] If one thing happens or is done **in tandem with** another thing, the two things happen at the same time. ❑ *Malcolm's contract will run in tandem with his existing one.* PHRASE: usu PHR after v, oft PHR *with* n
[3] If one person does something **in tandem with** another person, the two people do it by working together. ❑ *He is working in tandem with officials of the Serious Fraud Office.* PHRASE: usu PHR after v, oft PHR *with* n

**tan|doori** /tændʊəri/ **Tandoori** dishes are Indian meat dishes which are cooked in a clay oven. ADJ: usu ADJ n

**tang** /tæŋ/ A **tang** is a strong, sharp smell or taste. ❑ *She could smell the salty tang of the sea.* N-SING

**tan|gent** /tændʒᵊnt/ **(tangents)** [1] A **tangent** is a line that touches the edge of a curve or circle at one point, but does not cross it. N-COUNT
[2] If someone **goes off at a tangent**, they start saying or doing something that is not directly connected with what they were saying or doing before. ❑ *The conversation went off at a tangent.* PHRASE: V and N inflect

**tan|gen|tial** /tændʒenʃᵊl/ [1] If you describe something as **tangential**, you mean that it has only a slight or indirect connection with the thing you are concerned with, and is therefore not worth considering seriously. [FORMAL] ❑ *Too much time was spent discussing tangential issues.* ADJ
[2] If something is **tangential to** something else, it is at a tangent to it. ❑ *...point T, where the demand curve is tangential to the straight line L.* ADJ: oft ADJ *to* n

**tan|ge|rine** /tændʒəriːn/ **(tangerines)** A **tangerine** is a small sweet orange. N-COUNT

**tan|gible** /tændʒɪbᵊl/ If something is **tangible**, it is clear enough or definite enough to be easily seen, felt, or noticed. ❑ *There should be some tangible evidence that the economy is starting to recover.* ADJ
♦ **tan|gibly** *This tangibly demonstrated that the world situation could be improved.* ADV: usu ADV with v, also ADV adj

**tan|gle** /tæŋgᵊl/ **(tangles, tangling, tangled)** [1] A **tangle of** something is a mass of it twisted together in an untidy way. ❑ *A tangle of wires is all that remains of the computer and phone systems.* N-COUNT: usu N *of* n
[2] If something **is tangled** or **tangles**, it becomes twisted together in an untidy way. ❑ *Animals get tangled in fishing nets and drown... She tried to kick the pajamas loose, but they were tangled in the satin sheet... Her hair tends to tangle... He suggested that tangling fishing gear should be made a criminal offence.* VERB; *get/be* V-ed *in* n; V-ed; V; V n; Also *get/be* V-ed
[3] You can refer to a confusing or complicated situation as a **tangle**. ❑ *I was thinking what a tangle we had got ourselves into.* N-SING: oft N *of* n
[4] If ideas or situations **are tangled**, they become confused and complicated. ❑ *The themes get tangled in Mr. Mahfouz's epic storytelling... You are currently in a muddle where financial and emotional concerns are tangled together.* VERB: usu passive; *get/be* V-ed; V-ed
♦ **tan|gled** *His personal life has become more tangled than ever.* ADJ

♦ **tangle up** [1] If a person or thing is **tangled up in** something such as wire or ropes, they are caught or trapped in it. ❑ *Sheep kept getting tangled up in it and eventually the wire was removed... The teeth are like razors. Once you get tangled up it will never let you go.* PHRASAL VERB: usu passive; *get/be* V-ed P *in* n; *get/be* V-ed P
[2] If you are **tangled up in** a complicated or unpleasant situation, you are involved in it and cannot get free of it. ❑ *Politicians normally avoid getting tangled up in anything to do with their electorate's savings.* PHRASAL VERB: usu passive; *get/be* V-ed P *in/with* n
♦ **tan|gled up** *For many days now Buddy and Joe had appeared to be more and more tangled up in secrets.* ADJ: v-link ADJ

**tan|go** /tæŋgoʊ/ **(tangos, tangoing, tangoed)** [1] The **tango** is a South American dance in which two people hold each other closely, walk quickly in one direction, then walk quickly back again. N-SING: usu *the* N
[2] A **tango** is a piece of music intended for tango dancing. ❑ *A tango was playing on the jukebox... The sounds of tango filled the air.* N-VAR
[3] If you **tango**, you dance the tango. ❑ *They can rock and roll, they can tango, but they can't bop.* VERB; V
[4] **it takes two to tango** → see **two**.

**tangy** /tæŋi/ **(tangier, tangiest)** A **tangy** flavour or smell is one that is sharp, especially a flavour like that of lemon juice or a smell like that of sea air. ADJ

**tank** /tæŋk/ **(tanks)** [1] A **tank** is a large container for holding liquid or gas. ❑ *...an empty fuel tank... Two water tanks provide a total capacity of 400 litres.* ◆◇◇ N-COUNT: oft n N
[2] A **tank** is a large military vehicle that is equipped with weapons and moves along on metal tracks that are fitted over the wheels. N-COUNT
[3] → See also **septic tank**, **think-tank**.

**tank|ard** /tæŋkəʳd/ **(tankards)** A **tankard** is a large metal cup with a handle, which you can drink beer from. N-COUNT
♦ A **tankard** of beer is an amount of it contained in a tankard. ❑ *...a tankard of ale.* N-COUNT: usu N *of* n

**tanked** /tæŋkt/
✔ in BRIT, also use **tanked up**
If someone is **tanked** or **tanked up**, they are drunk. [INFORMAL] ADJ: usu v-link ADJ

**tank|er** /tæŋkəʳ/ **(tankers)** [1] A **tanker** is a very large ship used for transporting large quantities of gas or liquid, especially oil. ❑ *A Greek oil tanker has run aground.* N-COUNT: oft supp N, also *by* N
[2] A **tanker** is a large truck, railway vehicle, or aircraft used for transporting large quantities of a substance. N-COUNT: usu supp N, also *by* N

**tank top** **(tank tops)** [1] A **tank top** is a knitted piece of clothing that covers the upper part of your body and has no sleeves. [BRIT] N-COUNT
[2] A **tank top** is a soft cotton shirt with no sleeves, collar, or buttons. [AM] N-COUNT

**tan|ner** /tænəʳ/ **(tanners)** A **tanner** is someone whose job is making leather from animal skins. N-COUNT

**tan|nin** /tænɪn/ **Tannin** is a yellow or brown chemical that is found in plants such as tea. It is used in the process of making leather and in dyeing. N-UNCOUNT

**Tan|noy** /tænɔɪ/ A **Tannoy** is a system of loudspeakers used to make public announcements, for example at a fair or at a sports stadium. [BRIT, TRADEMARK] N-SING: oft *over* N

☑ in AM, use **public address system**

**tan|ta|lize** /tæntəlaɪz/ **(tantalizes, tantalizing, tantalized)**

☑ in BRIT, also use **tantalise**

If someone or something **tantalizes** you, they make you feel hopeful and excited about getting what you want, usually before disappointing you by not letting you have what they appeared to offer. ❑ *...the dreams of democracy that have so tantalized them.* ♦ **tan|ta|liz|ing** *A tantalising aroma of roast beef fills the air.* ♦ **tan|ta|liz|ing|ly** *She went away disappointed after getting tantalisingly close to breaking the record.* VERB; V n; ADJ; ADV: ADV adj, ADV with v, ADV with cl

**tan|ta|mount** /tæntəmaʊnt/ If you say that one thing is **tantamount to** a second, more serious thing, you are emphasizing how bad, unacceptable, or unfortunate the first thing is by comparing it to the second. [FORMAL] ❑ *What Bracey is saying is tantamount to heresy.* ADJ: v-link ADJ *to* n/-ing [emphasis]

**tan|tric** /tæntrɪk/ also **Tantric. Tantric** is used to describe things relating to or connected with a particular movement in Buddhism and Hinduism. ❑ *...tantric yoga.* ADJ: ADJ n

**tan|trum** /tæntrəm/ **(tantrums)** If a child has a **tantrum**, they lose their temper in a noisy and uncontrolled way. If you say that an adult is throwing a **tantrum**, you are criticizing them for losing their temper and acting in a childish way. ❑ *He immediately threw a tantrum, screaming and stomping up and down like a child.* N-COUNT [disapproval]

**Taoi|seach** /tiːʃək/ The prime minister of the Republic of Ireland is called the **Taoiseach**. N-SING: usu *the* N

**Tao|ism** /taʊɪzəm/ **Taoism** is a Chinese religious philosophy which believes that people should lead a simple honest life and not interfere with the course of natural events. N-UNCOUNT

**tap** /tæp/ **(taps, tapping, tapped)** 1 A **tap** is a device that controls the flow of a liquid or gas from a pipe or container, for example on a sink. [mainly BRIT] ❑ *She turned on the taps. ...a cold-water tap.* ◆◇◇ N-COUNT

☑ in AM, use **faucet**

2 If you **tap** something, you hit it with a quick light blow or a series of quick light blows. ❑ *He tapped the table to still the shouts of protest... Grace tapped on the bedroom door and went in.* ♦ **Tap** is also a noun. ❑ *A tap on the door interrupted him and Sally Pierce came in.* VERB; V n; V adv/prep; N-COUNT: usu N *on/at* n 3 If you **tap** your fingers or feet, you make a regular pattern of sound by hitting a surface lightly and repeatedly with them, especially while you are listening to music. ❑ *The song's so catchy it makes you bounce round the living room or tap your feet.* VERB; V n 4 If you **tap** a resource or situation, you make use of it by getting from it something that you need or want. ❑ *He owes his election to having tapped deep public disillusion with professional politicians... The company is tapping shareholders for £15.8 million... The Campbell Soup Company says it will try to tap into Japan's rice market.* VERB; V n; V n *for* n; V *into* n 5 If someone **taps** your telephone, they attach a special device to the line so that they can secretly listen to your conversations. ❑ *The government passed laws allowing the police to tap telephones.* → See also **phone-tapping**, **wiretap**. ♦ **Tap** is also a noun. ❑ *He assured MPs that ministers and MPs were not subjected to phone taps.* VERB = bug; V n; N-COUNT: oft n N

**PHRASES** 6 If drinks are **on tap**, they come from a tap rather than from a bottle. ❑ *Filtered water is always on tap, making it very convenient to use.* PHRASE: usu v-link PHR 7 If something is **on tap**, you can have as much of it as you want whenever you want. [INFORMAL] ❑ *The advantage of group holidays is company on tap but time alone if you want it.* PHRASE: usu v-link PHR

**tap|as** /tæpæs/ In Spain, **tapas** are small plates of food that are served with drinks or before a main meal. N-PLURAL

**tap danc|er (tap dancers)** A **tap dancer** is a dancer who does tap dancing. N-COUNT

**tap danc|ing** also **tap-dancing. Tap dancing** is a style of dancing in which the dancers wear special shoes with pieces of metal on the heels and toes. The shoes make loud sharp sounds as the dancers move their feet. N-UNCOUNT

**tape** /teɪp/ **(tapes, taping, taped)** 1 **Tape** is a narrow plastic strip covered with a magnetic substance. It is used to record sounds, pictures, and computer information. ❑ *Many students declined to be interviewed on tape.* ◆◆◇ N-UNCOUNT: oft *on* N 2 A **tape** is a cassette or spool with magnetic tape wound round it. ❑ *She still listens to the tapes I made her.* N-COUNT 3 If you **tape** music, sounds, or television pictures, you record them using a tape recorder or a video recorder. ❑ *She has just taped an interview... He shouldn't be taping without the singer's permission. ...taped evidence from prisoners.* VERB; V n; V; V-ed 4 A **tape** is a strip of cloth used to tie things together or to identify who a piece of clothing belongs to. ❑ *The books were all tied up with tape.* N-VAR 5 A **tape** is a ribbon that is stretched across the finishing line of a race. ❑ *...the finishing tape.* N-COUNT: supp N 6 **Tape** is a sticky strip of plastic used for sticking things together. N-UNCOUNT 7 If you **tape** one thing to another, you attach it using sticky tape. ❑ *I taped the base of the feather onto the velvet... The envelope has been tampered with and then taped shut again.* VERB; V n *onto/to* n; *be* V-ed adj 8 → See also **magnetic tape**, **masking tape**, **red tape**, **sticky tape**, **videotape**.

**tape deck (tape decks)** also **tape-deck.** A **tape deck** is the machine on which you can play or record cassette tapes. N-COUNT

**tape meas|ure (tape measures)** A **tape measure** is a strip of metal, plastic, or cloth which has numbers marked on it and is used for measuring. N-COUNT

**ta|per** /teɪpəʳ/ **(tapers, tapering, tapered)** 1 If something **tapers**, or if you **taper** it, it becomes gradually thinner at one end. ❑ *Unlike other trees, it doesn't taper very much. It stays fat all the way up... Taper the shape of your eyebrows towards the outer corners.* ♦ **ta|pered** *...the elegantly tapered legs of the dressing-table.* VERB; V; V n; ADJ 2 If something **tapers** or **is tapered**, it gradually becomes reduced in amount, number, or size until it is greatly reduced. ❑ *There are signs that inflation is tapering... If you take these drugs continuously, withdrawal must be tapered.* ♦ **Taper off** means the same as **taper**. ❑ *Immigration is expected to taper off... I suggested that we start to taper off the counseling sessions.* VERB; V; *be* V-ed; PHRASAL VERB; V P; V P n; Also V n P 3 A **taper** is a long, thin candle or a thin wooden strip that is used for lighting fires. N-COUNT

♦ **taper off** → see **taper 2**.

**tape-record (tape-records, tape-recording, tape-recorded)** also **tape record.** If you **tape-record** speech, music, or another kind of sound, you record it on tape, using a tape recorder or a tape deck. ❑ *The conversation was tape-recorded and played in court. ...a tape-recorded interview.* VERB = tape; *be* V-ed; V-ed

**tape re|cord|er (tape recorders)** also **tape-recorder.** A **tape recorder** is a machine used for recording and playing music, speech, or other sounds. N-COUNT

**tape re|cord|ing (tape recordings)** A **tape recording** is a recording of sounds that has been made on tape. N-COUNT: oft N *of* n

**tape stream|er (tape streamers)** A **tape streamer** is a piece of computer equipment that you use for copying data from a hard disk onto magnetic tape for security or storage. [COMPUTING] N-COUNT

**tap|es|try** /tæpɪstri/ **(tapestries)** 1 A **tapestry** is a large piece of heavy cloth with a picture sewn on it using coloured threads. 2 You can re- N-VAR; N-COUNT:

fer to something as a **tapestry** when it is made up of many varied types of people or things. [LITERARY] ❑ *Hedgerows and meadows are thick with a tapestry of wild flowers.* with supp

**tape|worm** /teɪpwɜːʳm/ **(tapeworms)** A **tapeworm** is a long, flat parasite which lives in the stomach and intestines of animals or people. N-COUNT

**tapio|ca** /tæpioʊkə/ **Tapioca** is a food consisting of white grains, rather like rice, which come from the cassava plant. N-UNCOUNT

**tap wa|ter** **Tap water** is the water that comes out of a tap in a building such as a house or a hotel. N-UNCOUNT

**tar** /tɑːʳ/ **(tars, tarring, tarred)** 1 **Tar** is a thick black sticky substance that is used especially for making roads. N-UNCOUNT 2 **Tar** is one of the poisonous substances contained in tobacco. N-UNCOUNT 3 If some people in a group behave badly and if people then wrongly think that all of the group is equally bad, you can say that the whole group **is tarred with the same brush**. PHRASE: V inflects ❑ *I am a football supporter and I have to often explain that I'm not one of the hooligan sort because we'll all get tarred with the same brush when there's trouble.* 4 → See also **tarred**.

**ta|ra|ma|sa|la|ta** /tærəməsəlɑːtə/ **Taramasalata** is a pink creamy food made from the eggs of a fish such as cod or mullet. It is usually eaten at the beginning of a meal. N-UNCOUNT

**ta|ran|tu|la** /təræntʃʊlə/ **(tarantulas)** A **tarantula** is a large hairy spider which has a poisonous bite. N-COUNT

**tar|dy** /tɑːʳdi/ **(tardier, tardiest)** 1 If you describe something or someone as **tardy**, you think that they are later than they should be or later than expected. ADJ [LITERARY] ❑ *He wept for the loss of his mother and his tardy recognition of her affection.* ♦ **tar|di|ness** *His legendary tardiness left audiences waiting for hours.* N-UNCOUNT 2 If you describe someone or something as **tardy**, you are criticizing them because they are slow to act. ADJ: oft ADJ *in* -ing/n disapproval ❑ *...companies who are tardy in paying bills.* ♦ **tar|di|ness** *...England's tardiness in giving talented young players greater international experience.* N-UNCOUNT: oft N *in* -ing/n

**tar|get** /tɑːʳgɪt/ **(targets, targeting** or **targetting, targeted** or **targetted)** ◆◆◇ 1 A **target** is something at which someone is aiming a weapon or other object. N-COUNT ❑ *The missiles missed their target.* 2 A **target** is a result that you are trying to achieve. N-COUNT ❑ *He's won back his place too late to achieve his target of 20 goals this season.* 3 To **target** a particular person or thing means to decide to attack or criticize them. VERB ❑ *He targets the economy as the root cause of the deteriorating law and order situation.* V n ♦ **Target** is also a noun. ❑ *In the past they have been the target of racist abuse.* N-COUNT: oft N *of/for* n 4 If you **target** a particular group of people, you try to appeal to those people or affect them. VERB ❑ *The campaign will target American insurance companies.* V n ♦ **Target** is also a noun. ❑ *Yuppies are a prime target group for marketing strategies.* N-COUNT 5 If someone or something is **on target**, they are making good progress and are likely to achieve the result that is wanted. PHRASE: v-link PHR ❑ *We were still right on target for our deadline.*

**tar|get mar|ket** **(target markets)** A **target market** is a market in which a company is trying to sell its products or services. N-COUNT [BUSINESS] ❑ *We decided that we needed to change our target market from the over-45s to the 35-45s.*

**tar|iff** /tærɪf/ **(tariffs)** 1 A **tariff** is a tax that a government collects on goods coming into a country. N-COUNT: oft N *on* n [BUSINESS] ❑ *America wants to eliminate tariffs on items such as electronics.* 2 A **tariff** is the rate at which you are charged for public services such as gas and electricity, or for accommodation and services in a hotel. N-COUNT: usu supp N [BRIT, FORMAL] ❑ *The daily tariff includes accommodation and unlimited use of the pool and gymnasium.*

**tar|mac** /tɑːʳmæk/ 1 **Tarmac** is a material used for making road surfaces, consisting of crushed stones mixed with tar. N-UNCOUNT [BRIT, TRADEMARK] ❑ *...a strip of tarmac. ...tarmac paths.*

☑ in AM, usually use **blacktop**

2 **The tarmac** is an area with a surface made of tarmac, especially the area from which planes take off at an airport. N-SING: *the* N ❑ *Standing on the tarmac were two American planes.*

**tarn** /tɑːʳn/ **(tarns)** A **tarn** is a small lake in an area of mountains. N-COUNT: oft in names

**tar|nish** /tɑːʳnɪʃ/ **(tarnishes, tarnishing, tarnished)** 1 If you say that something **tarnishes** someone's reputation or image, you mean that it causes people to have a worse opinion of them than they would otherwise have had. VERB ❑ *The affair could tarnish the reputation of the prime minister.* V n ♦ **tar|nished** *He says he wants to improve the tarnished image of his country.* ADJ 2 If a metal **tarnishes** or if something **tarnishes** it, it becomes stained and loses its brightness. VERB ❑ *It never rusts or tarnishes...* V *Wear cotton gloves when cleaning silver, because the acid in your skin can tarnish the metal.* V n ♦ **tar|nished** *...its brown surfaces of tarnished brass.* ADJ 3 **Tarnish** is a substance which forms on the surface of some metals and which stains them or causes them to lose their brightness. N-UNCOUNT

**Ta|rot** /tæroʊ/ **The Tarot** is a pack of cards with pictures on them that is used to predict what will happen to people in the future. N-UNCOUNT: also *the* N, oft N n **Tarot** is also used to refer to the system of predicting people's futures using these cards. ❑ *...tarot cards.*

**tarp** /tɑːʳp/ **(tarps)** A **tarp** is a sheet of heavy waterproof material that is used as a protective cover. N-COUNT [mainly AM]

☑ in BRIT, usually use **tarpaulin**

**tar|pau|lin** /tɑːʳpɔːlɪn/ **(tarpaulins)** 1 **Tarpaulin** is a fabric made of canvas or similar material coated with tar, wax, paint, or some other waterproof substance. N-UNCOUNT: oft N n ❑ *...a piece of tarpaulin. ...tarpaulin covers.* 2 A **tarpaulin** is a sheet of heavy waterproof material that is used as a protective cover. N-COUNT

**tar|ra|gon** /tærəgɒn/ **Tarragon** is a European herb with narrow leaves which are used to add flavour to food. N-UNCOUNT

**tarred** /tɑːʳd/ A **tarred** road or roof has a surface of tar. ADJ

**tar|ry** **(tarries, tarrying, tarried)**

☑ The verb is pronounced /tæri/. The adjective is pronounced /tɑːri/.

1 If you **tarry** somewhere, you stay there longer than you meant to and delay leaving. VERB = linger [OLD-FASHIONED] ❑ *Two old boys tarried on the street corner discussing cattle.* V 2 If you describe something as **tarry**, you mean that it has a lot of tar in it or is like tar. ADJ ❑ *I smelled tarry melted asphalt. ...cups of tarry coffee.*

**tart** /tɑːʳt/ **(tarts, tarting, tarted)** 1 A **tart** is a shallow pastry case with a filling of food, especially sweet food. N-VAR ❑ *...jam tarts. ...a slice of home-made tart.* 2 If something such as fruit is **tart**, it has a sharp taste. ADJ = sharp ❑ *The blackberries were a bit too tart on their own, so we stewed them gently with some apples.* 3 A **tart** remark or way of speaking is sharp and unpleasant, often in a way that is rather cruel. ADJ = acid ❑ *The words were more tart than she had intended.* ♦ **tart|ly** *'There are other patients on the ward, Lovell,' the staff nurse reminded her tartly.* ADV: usu ADV with v 4 If someone refers to a woman or girl as a **tart**, they are criticizing her because they think she is sexually immoral or dresses in a way that makes her look sexually immoral. N-COUNT disapproval [INFORMAL, OFFENSIVE]

♦ **tart up** If someone **tarts up** a room or building, they try to improve its appearance, often with the result that it looks vulgar. PHRASAL VERB disapproval [BRIT, INFORMAL] ❑ *'Have you ever wondered why British Rail would rather tart up their stations than improve services?' he asked.* V P n (not pron) *...tarted-up pubs.* V-ed P Also V n P

**tar|tan** /tɑːʳtᵊn/ **(tartans) Tartan** is a design for cloth traditionally associated with Scotland, and which has a number of distinctive types. The design is made up of lines of different widths and colours crossing each other at right angles. **Tartan** is also used to refer to cloth which has this pattern. N-VAR: oft N n

**tar|tar** /tɑːʳtəʳ/ **(tartars)** 1 **Tartar** is a hard yellowish substance that forms on your teeth and causes them to decay if it is not removed. N-UNCOUNT 2 If you describe someone, especially a woman in a position of authority, as a **tartar**, you mean that they are fierce, bad-tempered, and strict. [INFORMAL] ❑ *She can be quite a tartar.* N-COUNT 3 → See also **cream of tartar**.

**tar|tare sauce** also **tartar sauce. Tartare sauce** is a thick cold sauce, usually eaten with fish, consisting of chopped onions and capers mixed with mayonnaise. N-UNCOUNT

**tarty** /tɑːʳti/ **(tartiest)** If you describe a woman or her clothes as **tarty**, you are critical of her because she tries to make herself look sexually attractive in a vulgar way. [INFORMAL] ❑ *That coat made her look so tarty.* ADJ disapproval

**task** /tɑːsk, tæsk/ **(tasks, tasking, tasked)** ◆◆◇ 1 A **task** is an activity or piece of work which you have to do, usually as part of a larger project. ❑ *She used the day to catch up with administrative tasks.* N-COUNT: usu N *of* -ing, supp N 2 If you **are tasked with** doing a particular activity or piece of work, someone in authority asks you to do it. ❑ *The minister was tasked with checking that British aid money was being spent wisely.* VERB be V-ed *with* n/-ing 3 If you **take** someone **to task**, you criticize them or tell them off because of something bad or wrong that they have done. ❑ *The country's intellectuals are also being taken to task for their failure to speak out against the regime.* PHRASE: V inflects, oft PHR *for* n/-ing = *rebuke*

**task force** **(task forces)** also **taskforce.** ◆◇◇ 1 A **task force** is a small section of an army, navy, or air force that is sent to a particular place to deal with a military crisis. ❑ *The United States is sending a naval task force to the area to evacuate American citizens.* N-COUNT 2 A **task force** is a group of people working together on a particular task. ❑ *We have set up a task force to look at the question of women returning to work.* N-COUNT

**task|master** /tɑːskmɑːstəʳ, tæskmæstəʳ/ **(taskmasters)** If you refer to someone as a hard **taskmaster**, you mean that they expect the people they supervise to work very hard. N-COUNT: usu adj N

**tas|sel** /tæsᵊl/ **(tassels) Tassels** are bunches of short pieces of wool or other material tied together at one end and attached as decorations to something such as a piece of clothing or a lampshade. N-COUNT

**tas|selled** /tæsᵊld/

✓ in AM, use **tasseled**

**Tasselled** means decorated with tassels. ❑ *...tasselled cushions.* ADJ

**taste** /teɪst/ **(tastes, tasting, tasted)** ◆◆◇ 1 **Taste** is one of the five senses that people have. When you have food or drink in your mouth, your sense of taste makes it possible for you to recognize what it is. ❑ *...a keen sense of taste.* N-UNCOUNT 2 The **taste** of something is the individual quality which it has when you put it in your mouth and which distinguishes it from other things. For example, something may have a sweet, bitter, sour, or salty taste. ❑ *I like the taste of wine and enjoy trying different kinds.* N-COUNT: usu with supp 3 If you have a **taste** of some food or drink, you try a small amount of it in order to see what the flavour is like. ❑ *We have a taste of the white wine he's brought.* N-SING 4 If food or drink **tastes of** something, it has that particular flavour, which you notice when you eat or drink it. ❑ *It tastes like chocolate... The pizza tastes delicious without any cheese at all.* VERB: no cont V *of/like* n V adj 5 If you **taste** some food or drink, you eat or drink a small amount of it in order to try its flavour, for example to see if you like it or not. ❑ *He finished his aperitif and tasted the wine the waiter had produced.* VERB V n 6 If you can **taste** something that you are eating or drinking, you are aware of its flavour. ❑ *You can taste the chilli in the dish but it is a little sweet.* VERB: no passive V n 7 If you have a **taste of** a particular way of life or activity, you have a brief experience of it. ❑ *This voyage was his first taste of freedom.* N-SING: N *of* n 8 If you **taste** something such as a way of life or a pleasure, you experience it for a short period of time. ❑ *Anyone who has tasted this life wants it to carry on for as long as possible.* VERB: no passive V n 9 If you have a **taste for** something, you have a liking or preference for it. ❑ *That gave me a taste for reading.* N-SING: N *for* n/-ing 10 A person's **taste** is their choice **in** the things that they like or buy, for example their clothes, possessions, or music. If you say that someone has good **taste**, you mean that you approve of their choices. If you say that they have poor **taste**, you disapprove of their choices. ❑ *His taste in clothes is extremely good... Oxford's social circle was far too liberal for her taste.* N-UNCOUNT: also N in pl

**PHRASES** 11 If you say that something that is said or done is **in bad taste** or **in poor taste**, you mean that it is offensive, often because it concerns death or sex and is inappropriate for the situation. If you say that something is **in good taste**, you mean that it is not offensive and that it is appropriate for the situation. ❑ *He rejects the idea that his film is in bad taste.* PHRASE: v-link PHR, PHR after v 12 When a recipe tells you to add a particular spice or other flavouring **to taste**, it means that you can add as much of that ingredient as you like. ❑ *Add tomato paste, salt and pepper to taste.* PHRASE: PHR after v

**taste bud** **(taste buds)** also **tastebud.** Your **taste buds** are the little points on the surface of your tongue which enable you to recognize the flavour of a food or drink. N-COUNT: usu pl, oft poss N

**taste|ful** /teɪstfʊl/ If you say that something is **tasteful**, you consider it to be attractive, elegant, and in good taste. ❑ *The decor is tasteful and restrained.* ♦ **taste|ful|ly** *...a large and tastefully decorated home.* ADJ ≠*tasteless* ADV: usu ADV with v, also ADV adj

**taste|less** /teɪstləs/ 1 If you describe something such as furniture, clothing, or the way that a house is decorated as **tasteless**, you consider it to be vulgar and unattractive. ❑ *...a flat crammed with spectacularly tasteless objets d'art.* ADJ 2 If you describe something such as a remark or joke as **tasteless**, you mean that it is offensive. ❑ *I think that is the most vulgar and tasteless remark I ever heard in my life.* ADJ 3 If you describe food or drink as **tasteless**, you mean that it has very little or no flavour. ❑ *The fish was mushy and tasteless.* ADJ = *flavourless* ≠*tasty*

**tast|er** /teɪstəʳ/ **(tasters)** 1 A **taster** is someone whose job is to taste different wines, teas, or other foods or drinks, in order to test their quality. ❑ *...a wine taster.* N-COUNT 2 If you refer to something as **a taster of** something greater, or of something that will come later, you mean that it gives you an idea what that thing is like, and often makes you interested in it or want more of it. [mainly BRIT] ❑ *The book is essentially a taster for those unfamiliar with the subject.* N-COUNT: usu sing, oft N *of* n

✓ in AM, usually use **taste**

**tast|ing** /teɪstɪŋ/ **(tastings) Tasting** is used in expressions such as **wine tasting** to refer to a social event at which people try different kinds of the specified drink or food in small amounts. N-COUNT: usu supp N

**tasty** /teɪsti/ **(tastier, tastiest)** If you say that food, especially savoury food, is **tasty**, you mean that it has a fairly strong and pleasant flavour which makes it good to eat. ❑ *Try this tasty dish for supper with a crispy salad.* ADJ

**tat** /tæt/ You can use **tat** to refer to ornaments, used goods, cheap clothes, or other items which you think are cheap and of bad quality. [BRIT, INFORMAL] ❑ *...souvenir shops selling an astounding variety of tat.* N-UNCOUNT

**ta-ta** /tæ tɑː/ also **ta ta. Ta-ta** is used to say goodbye. [BRIT, INFORMAL or DIALECT] ❑ *Okay John. See you again. Ta-ta... Ta-ta for now.* CONVENTION formulae = *bye*

**tat|tered** /tætəʳd/ [1] If something such as clothing or a book is **tattered**, it is damaged or torn, especially because it has been used a lot over a long period of time. ❑ *He fled wearing only a sarong and a tattered shirt.* [2] If you describe something as **tattered**, you mean that it has been badly damaged or has failed completely. ❑ *But, two-and-a-half years later, things haven't quite gone to plan and Stanley's dreams of fame and fortune lie tattered and torn.* ADJ ADJ

**tat|ters** /tætəʳz/ [1] Clothes that are **in tatters** are badly torn in several places, so that pieces can easily come off. ❑ *His jersey was left in tatters.* [2] If you say that something such as a plan or a person's state of mind is **in tatters**, you are emphasizing that it is weak, has suffered a lot of damage, and is likely to fail completely. ❑ *The economy is in tatters.* N-PLURAL: usu *in* N; N-PLURAL: usu *in* N emphasis

**tat|tle** /tætəl/ → see **tittle-tattle**.

**tat|too** /tætuː/ **(tattoos, tattooing, tattooed)** [1] A **tattoo** is a design that is drawn on someone's skin using needles to make little holes and filling them with coloured dye. [2] If someone **tattoos** you, they give you a tattoo. ❑ *In the old days, they would paint and tattoo their bodies for ceremonies... He had the words 'Angie loves Ian' tattooed on his left shin.* [3] A military **tattoo** is a public display of exercises and music given by members of the armed forces. [BRIT] N-COUNT; VERB V n V-ed; N-COUNT

**tat|ty** /tæti/ If you describe something as **tatty**, you think it is untidy, rather dirty, and looks as if it has not been cared for. [mainly BRIT] ❑ *...a very tatty old bathrobe.* ADJ = scruffy

**taught** /tɔːt/ **Taught** is the past tense and past participle of **teach**.

**taunt** /tɔːnt/ **(taunts, taunting, taunted)** If someone **taunts** you, they say unkind or insulting things to you, especially about your weaknesses or failures. ❑ *A gang taunted a disabled man... Other youths taunted him about his clothes.* ♦ **Taunt** is also a noun. ❑ *For years they suffered racist taunts.* VERB V n V n *about* n; N-COUNT

**taupe** /toʊp/ Something that is **taupe** is a pale brownish-grey colour. COLOUR

**Tau|rus** /tɔːrəs/ [1] **Taurus** is one of the twelve signs of the zodiac. Its symbol is a bull. People who are born approximately between the 20th of April and the 20th of May come under this sign. [2] **A Taurus** is a person whose sign of the zodiac is Taurus. N-UNCOUNT; N-SING: *a* N

**taut** /tɔːt/ **(tauter, tautest)** [1] Something that is **taut** is stretched very tight. ❑ *The clothes line is pulled taut and secured.* [2] If someone has a **taut** expression, they look very worried and tense. ❑ *Ben sat up quickly, his face taut and terrified.* ADJ; ADJ

**taut|en** /tɔːtən/ **(tautens, tautening, tautened)** If a part of your body **tautens** or if you **tauten** it, it becomes stiff or firm. ❑ *Her whole body tautened violently... There are exercises that tauten facial muscles.* VERB V V n

**tau|to|logi|cal** /tɔːtəlɒdʒɪkəl/ A **tautological** statement involves tautology. ADJ

**tau|tol|ogy** /tɔːtɒlədʒi/ **(tautologies)** **Tautology** is the use of different words to say the same thing twice in the same statement. 'The money should be adequate enough' is an example of tautology. N-VAR

**tav|ern** /tævəʳn/ **(taverns)** A **tavern** is a bar or pub. [OLD-FASHIONED] N-COUNT; N-IN-NAMES

**taw|dry** /tɔːdri/ **(tawdrier, tawdriest)** [1] If you describe something such as clothes or decorations as **tawdry**, you mean that they are cheap and show a lack of taste. ❑ *...tawdry jewellery.* [2] If you describe something such as a story or an event as **tawdry**, you mean that it is unpleasant or immoral. ❑ *...the yawning gulf between her fantasies and the tawdry reality.* ADJ = tacky; ADJ: usu ADJ n

**taw|ny** /tɔːni/ **Tawny** hair, fur, or skin is a pale brown colour. ❑ *She had tawny hair.* COLOUR

**tax** /tæks/ **(taxes, taxing, taxed)** [1] **Tax** is an amount of money that you have to pay to the government so that it can pay for public services. ❑ *They are calling for large spending cuts and tax increases. ...a pledge not to raise taxes on people below a certain income.* [2] When a person or company **is taxed**, they have to pay a part of their income or profits to the government. When goods **are taxed**, a percentage of their price has to be paid to the government. ❑ *Husband and wife are now taxed separately on their incomes... The Bonn government taxes profits of corporations at a rate that is among the highest in Europe.* [3] If something **taxes** your strength, your patience, or your resources, it uses nearly all of them, so that you have great difficulty in carrying out what you are trying to do. ❑ *Overcrowding has taxed the city's ability to deal with waste.* [4] → See also **taxing**, **council tax**, **income tax**, **poll tax**, **value added tax**. ◆◆◆ N-VAR; VERB *be* V-ed V n Also V; VERB V n

**tax|able** /tæksəbəl/ **Taxable** income is income on which you have to pay tax. ADJ: usu ADJ n

**taxa|tion** /tækseɪʃən/ [1] **Taxation** is the system by which a government takes money from people and spends it on things such as education, health, and defence. [2] **Taxation** is the amount of money that people have to pay in taxes. ❑ *The result will be higher taxation.* N-UNCOUNT; N-UNCOUNT

**tax avoid|ance** **Tax avoidance** is the use of legal methods to pay the smallest possible amount of tax. N-UNCOUNT

**tax break** **(tax breaks)** If the government gives a **tax break** to a particular group of people or type of organization, it reduces the amount of tax they have to pay or changes the tax system in a way that benefits them. [mainly AM] ❑ *Today they'll consider tax breaks for businesses that create jobs in inner cities.* N-COUNT

**tax cred|it** **(tax credits)** A **tax credit** is an amount of money on which you do not have to pay tax. N-COUNT

**tax-deductible** /tæks dɪdʌktɪbəl/ If an expense is **tax-deductible**, it can be paid out of the part of your income on which you do not pay tax, so that the amount of tax you pay is reduced. ❑ *Keep track of tax-deductible expenses, such as the supplies and equipment you buy.* ADJ

**tax disc** **(tax discs)** In Britain, a **tax disc** is a small round piece of paper displayed on cars and motorcycles which proves that the owner has paid road tax. N-COUNT

**tax eva|sion** **Tax evasion** is the crime of not paying the full amount of tax that you should pay. N-UNCOUNT

**tax-free** **Tax-free** is used to describe income on which you do not have to pay tax. ❑ *...a tax-free investment plan.* ADJ: ADJ n, amount ADJ, v-link ADJ

**tax ha|ven** **(tax havens)** A **tax haven** is a country or place which has a low rate of tax so that people choose to live there or register companies there in order to avoid paying higher tax in their own countries. N-COUNT

**taxi** /tæksi/ **(taxis, taxiing, taxied)** [1] A **taxi** is a car driven by a person whose job is to take people where they want to go in return for money. ❑ *The taxi drew up in front of the Riviera Club... He set off by taxi.* [2] When an aircraft **taxis** along the ground, or when a pilot **taxis** a plane somewhere, it moves slowly along the ground. ❑ *She gave permission to the plane to taxi into position and hold for take-off... The pilot taxied the plane to the end of the runway.* N-COUNT: also *by* N = cab; VERB V prep/adv V n prep/adv Also V, V n

**taxi|cab** /tæksikæb/ **(taxicabs)** also **taxi-cab.** A **taxicab** is the same as a **taxi**. [mainly AM] N-COUNT = cab

**taxi|der|mist** /tæksidɜːʳmɪst/ **(taxidermists)** A **taxidermist** is a person whose job is to prepare the skins of dead animals and birds and fill them with a special material to make them look as if they are alive. N-COUNT

**taxi|der|my** /tæksidɜːʳmi/ **Taxidermy** is the craft of preparing the skins of dead animals and N-UNCOUNT birds and filling them with a special material to make them look as if they are alive.

**tax|ing** /tæksɪŋ/ A **taxing** task or problem is one that requires a lot of mental or physical effort. ❑ *It's unlikely that you'll be asked to do anything too taxing.* ADJ = demanding

**taxi rank** **(taxi ranks)** A **taxi rank** is a place where taxis wait for passengers, for example at an airport or outside a station. [BRIT] N-COUNT

☑ in AM, use **taxi stand**

**taxi stand** **(taxi stands)** A **taxi stand** is the same as a **taxi rank**. [mainly AM] N-COUNT

**tax|ono|my** /tæksɒnəmi/ **(taxonomies)** **Taxonomy** is the process of naming and classifying things such as animals and plants into groups within a larger system, according to their similarities and differences. [TECHNICAL] N-VAR

**tax|payer** /tækspeɪəʳ/ **(taxpayers)** **Taxpayers** are people who pay a percentage of their income to the government as tax. N-COUNT

**tax re|lief** **Tax relief** is a reduction in the amount of tax that a person or company has to pay, for example because of expenses associated with their business or property. ❑ *...mortgage interest tax relief.* N-UNCOUNT

**tax re|turn** **(tax returns)** A **tax return** is an official form that you fill in with details about your income and personal situation, so that the tax you owe can be calculated. N-COUNT

**tax shel|ter** **(tax shelters)** A **tax shelter** is a way of arranging the finances of a business or a person so that they have to pay less tax. N-COUNT

**tax year** **(tax years)** A **tax year** is a particular period of twelve months which is used by the government as a basis for calculating taxes and for organizing its finances and accounts. In Britain, the tax year begins on April 6th and ends on April 5th. In the United States, the tax year begins on January 1st and ends on December 31st. N-COUNT

**TB** /tiː biː/ **TB** is an extremely serious infectious disease that affects someone's lungs and other parts of their body. **TB** is an abbreviation for 'tuberculosis'. N-UNCOUNT

**tba** also **TBA.** **tba** is sometimes written in announcements to indicate that something such as the place where something will happen or the people who will take part is not yet known and will be announced at a later date. **tba** is an abbreviation for 'to be announced'. ❑ *July 24: Australia v New Zealand (venue TBA).*

**tbc** also **TBC.** **tbc** is sometimes written in announcements about future events to indicate that details of the event are not yet certain and will be confirmed later. **tbc** is an abbreviation for 'to be confirmed'.

**T-bone steak** **(T-bone steaks)** A **T-bone steak** is a thick piece of beef that contains a T-shaped bone. N-VAR

**tbs.** In recipes, **tbs.** is a written abbreviation for **tablespoonful**.

**tbsp.** **(tbsps)** In recipes, **tbsp.** is a written abbreviation for **tablespoonful**. N-COUNT

**T-cell** **(T-cells)** A **T-cell** is a type of white blood cell. N-COUNT

**tea** /tiː/ **(teas)** [1] **Tea** is a drink made by adding hot water to tea leaves or tea bags. Many people add milk to the drink and some add sugar. ❑ *...a cup of tea... Would you like some tea?... Four or five men were drinking tea from flasks.* ♦ A cup of tea can be referred to as a **tea**. ❑ *Would anybody like a tea or coffee?* [2] The chopped dried leaves of the plant that tea is made from is referred to as **tea**. ❑ *...a packet of tea.* [3] **Tea** is a meal some people eat in the late afternoon. It consists of food such as sandwiches and cakes, with tea to drink. [BRIT] ❑ *I'm doing the sandwiches for tea.* → See also **afternoon tea, high tea.** [4] Some people refer to the main meal that they eat in the early part of the evening as **tea**. [BRIT] ❑ *At five o'clock he comes back for his tea.* [5] If you say that someone or something is **not** your **cup of tea**, you mean that they are not the kind of person or thing that you like. ❑ *Politics was not his cup of tea.* ◆◆◇ N-MASS; N-COUNT; N-MASS; N-VAR; N-VAR; PHRASE: v-link PHR, usu with brd-neg

**tea bag** **(tea bags)** also **teabag.** **Tea bags** are small paper bags with tea leaves in them. You put them into hot water to make tea. N-COUNT

**tea break** **(tea breaks)** If you have a **tea break**, you stop working and have a cup of tea or coffee. [mainly BRIT] N-COUNT

☑ in AM, use **coffee break**

**tea cad|dy** **(tea caddies)** A **tea caddy** is a small tin in which you keep tea. [mainly BRIT] N-COUNT

**tea|cake** /tiːkeɪk/ **(teacakes)** **Teacakes** are round flat bread cakes. They usually contain raisins and are often toasted and eaten with butter. [BRIT] N-COUNT

**teach** /tiːtʃ/ **(teaches, teaching, taught)** [1] If you **teach** someone something, you give them instructions so that they know about it or how to do it. ❑ *The trainers have a programme to teach them vocational skills... George had taught him how to ride a horse... She taught Julie to read... The computer has simplified the difficult task of teaching reading to the deaf.* [2] To **teach** someone something means to make them think, feel, or act in a new or different way. ❑ *Their daughter's death had taught him humility... He taught his followers that they could all be members of the kingdom of God... Teach them to voice their feelings.* [3] If you **teach** or **teach** a subject, you help students to learn about it by explaining it or showing them how to do it, usually as a job at a school, college, or university. ❑ *Ingrid is currently teaching Mathematics at Shimla Public School... She taught English to Japanese business people... She has taught for 34 years... She taught children French. ...this twelve month taught course.* [4] → See also **teaching**. to **teach** someone **a lesson** → see **lesson**. ◆◆◇ VERB: V n n; V n wh; V n to-inf; V n *to* n; VERB: V n n; V n that; V n to-inf; VERB: V n; V n *to* n; V; V n n; V-ed

**teach|er** /tiːtʃəʳ/ **(teachers)** A **teacher** is a person who teaches, usually as a job at a school or similar institution. ❑ *...her chemistry teacher.* → See also **supply teacher**. ◆◆◇ N-COUNT

**tea chest** **(tea chests)** A **tea chest** is a large wooden box in which tea is packed when it is exported. People also use tea chests for putting things in when they move from one house to another. [BRIT] N-COUNT

**teach-in** **(teach-ins)** A **teach-in** is a meeting, usually between students and teachers, with discussions on important and interesting topics. Teach-ins are not usually part of a formal academic course. N-COUNT

**teach|ing** /tiːtʃɪŋ/ **(teachings)** [1] **Teaching** is the work that a teacher does in helping students to learn. ❑ *The Government funds university teaching. ...the teaching of English in schools.* [2] The **teachings** of a particular person, group of people, or religion are all the ideas and principles that they teach. ❑ *...their teachings on sexuality and marriage.* ◆◇◇ N-UNCOUNT; N-COUNT: usu pl, with poss

**teach|ing hos|pi|tal** **(teaching hospitals)** A **teaching hospital** is a hospital that is linked with a medical school, where medical students and newly qualified doctors receive practical training. N-COUNT

**teach|ing prac|tice** **Teaching practice** is a period that a student teacher spends teaching at a school as part of his or her training. [mainly BRIT] N-UNCOUNT

☑ in AM, usually use **practice teaching**

**tea cloth** **(tea cloths)** also **tea-cloth.** A **tea cloth** is the same as a **tea towel**. [BRIT] N-COUNT

**tea cosy** **(tea cosies)** also **tea-cosy.** A **tea cosy** is a soft knitted or fabric cover which you put over a teapot in order to keep the tea hot. [BRIT] N-COUNT

☑ in AM, use **tea cozy**

**tea|cup** /tiːkʌp/ **(teacups)** also **tea-cup.** 1 A **teacup** is a cup that you use for drinking tea. N-COUNT 2 If you describe a situation as **a storm in a teacup**, you think that a lot of fuss is being made about something that is not important. [BRIT] PHRASE: PHR after v, v-link PHR ❑ *Both are trying to present the disagreement as a storm in a teacup.*

✔ in AM, use **a tempest in a teapot**

**tea dance** **(tea dances)** A **tea dance** is a social event that takes place in the afternoon, where people meet to dance and have tea. Tea dances are especially popular with older people. N-COUNT

**teak** /tiːk/ **Teak** is the wood of a tall tree with very hard, light-coloured wood which grows in South-East Asia. N-UNCOUNT ❑ *The door is beautifully made in solid teak.*

**tea|kettle** /tiːketəl/ **(teakettles)** also **tea kettle.** A **teakettle** is a kettle that is used for boiling water to make tea. [mainly AM] N-COUNT

**teal** /tiːl/ **(teals** or **teal)** A **teal** is a small duck found in Europe and Asia. N-COUNT

**tea leaf** **(tea leaves)** also **tea-leaf. Tea leaves** are the small pieces of dried leaves that you use to make tea. N-COUNT: usu pl

**team** /tiːm/ **(teams, teaming, teamed)** ◆◆◆ 1 A **team** is a group of people who play a particular sport or game together against other similar groups of people. N-COUNT-COLL ❑ *The team failed to qualify for the African Nations Cup finals... He had lost his place in the England team.* 2 You can refer to any group of people who work together as a **team**. N-COUNT-COLL ❑ *Each specialist consultant has a team of doctors under him.*

♦ **team up** If you **team up with** someone, you join them in order to work together for a particular purpose. You can also say that two people or groups **team up**. PHRASAL VERB ❑ *Elton teamed up with Eric Clapton to wow thousands at a Wembley rock concert...* V P *with* n *Recently a friend suggested that we team up for a working holiday in Europe in the summer.* pl-n V

**team-mate** **(team-mates)** also **teammate.** In a game or sport, your **team-mates** are the other members of your team. N-COUNT: oft poss N

**team play|er** **(team players)** If you refer to someone as a **team player**, you mean that they work well with other people in order to achieve things. N-COUNT [approval]

**team spir|it** **Team spirit** is the feeling of pride and loyalty that exists among the members of a team and that makes them want their team to do well or to be the best. N-UNCOUNT

**team|ster** /tiːmstəʳ/ **(teamsters)** A **teamster** is a person who drives a truck. [AM] N-COUNT = *trucker*

✔ in BRIT, use **lorry driver**

**team|work** /tiːmwɜːʳk/ **Teamwork** is the ability a group of people have to work well together. N-UNCOUNT ❑ *Today's complex buildings require close teamwork between the architect and the builders.*

**tea par|ty** **(tea parties)** also **tea-party.** A **tea party** is a social gathering in the afternoon at which tea, cakes, and sandwiches are served. [OLD-FASHIONED] N-COUNT

**tea|pot** /tiːpɒt/ **(teapots)** also **tea pot.** 1 A **teapot** is a container with a lid, a handle, and a spout, used for making and serving tea. N-COUNT 2 If you describe a situation as **a tempest in a teapot**, you think that a lot of fuss is being made about something that is not important. [AM] PHRASE: PHR after v, v-link PHR ❑ *On Capitol Hill, senators today appear to view the matter as something of a tempest in a teapot.*

✔ in BRIT, use **a storm in a teacup**

**tear**
① CRYING
② DAMAGING OR MOVING

① **tear** /tɪəʳ/ **(tears)** ◆◇◇ 1 **Tears** are the drops of salty liquid that come out of your eyes when you are crying. N-COUNT: usu pl ❑ *Her eyes filled with tears... I didn't shed a single tear.* 2 You can use **tears** in expressions such as **in tears**, **burst into tears**, and **close to tears** to indicate that someone is crying or is almost crying. N-PLURAL ❑ *He was in floods of tears on the phone... She burst into tears and ran from the kitchen.* 3 → See also **crocodile tears**.

② **tear** /teəʳ/ **(tears, tearing, tore, torn)** ◆◆◇
⇛ Please look at category 8 to see if the expression you are looking for is shown under another headword. 1 If you **tear** paper, cloth, or another material, or if it **tears**, you pull it into two pieces or you pull it so that a hole appears in it. VERB ❑ *She very nearly tore my overcoat...* V n *Mary Ann tore the edge off her napkin...* V n prep *He took a small notebook from his jacket pocket and tore out a page...* V n with adv *Too fine a material may tear...* V *Nancy quickly tore open the envelope...* V n with adj *He noticed that fabric was tearing away from the plane's wing...* V prep/adv *He went ashore leaving me to start repairing the torn sail.* V-ed ♦ **Tear up** means the same as **tear**. PHRASAL VERB ❑ *She tore the letter up...* V n P *Don't you dare tear up her ticket.* V P n *...a torn up photograph.* V-ed P 2 A **tear** in paper, cloth, or another material is a hole that has been made in it. N-COUNT ❑ *I peered through a tear in the van's curtains.* 3 If you **tear** one of your muscles or ligaments, or if it **tears**, you injure it by accidentally moving it in the wrong way. VERB ❑ *He tore a muscle in his right thigh...* V n *If the muscle is stretched again it could even tear.* V *...torn ligaments.* V-ed 4 To **tear** something from somewhere means to remove it roughly and violently. VERB ❑ *She tore the windscreen wipers from his car...* V n prep *He tore down the girl's photograph, and crumpled it into a ball.* V n with adv 5 If a person or animal **tears at** something, they pull it violently and try to break it into pieces. VERB = *rip* ❑ *Female fans fought their way past bodyguards and tore at his clothes.* V *at* n 6 If you **tear** somewhere, you move there very quickly, often in an uncontrolled or dangerous way. VERB = *rush* ❑ *The door flew open and Miranda tore into the room.* V prep/adv 7 If you say that a place **is torn by** particular events, you mean that unpleasant events which cause suffering and division among people are happening there. V-PASSIVE ❑ *...a country that has been torn by civil war and foreign invasion since its independence.* be V-ed *by* n ♦ **-torn** *...the riot-torn areas of Los Angeles.* COMB in ADJ 8 → See also **torn, wear and tear**.

♦ **tear apart** 1 If something **tears** people **apart**, it causes them to quarrel or to leave each other. PHRASAL VERB ❑ *War and revolution have torn families apart.* V n P 2 If something **tears** you **apart**, it makes you feel very upset, worried, and unhappy. PHRASAL VERB ❑ *Don't think it hasn't torn me apart to be away from you.* V n P

♦ **tear away** If you **tear** someone **away from** a place or activity, you force them to leave the place or stop doing the activity, even though they want to remain there or carry on. PHRASAL VERB: oft with brd-neg ❑ *Fame hasn't torn her away from her beloved Liverpool...* V n P *from* n *Japan's education ministry ordered the change to encourage students to tear themselves away from textbooks...* V pron-refl P *from* n *I stared at the man, couldn't tear my eyes away.* V n P

♦ **tear down** If you **tear** something **down**, you destroy it or remove it completely. PHRASAL VERB = *pull down* ❑ *Angry Russians may have torn down the statue of Felix Dzerzhinsky...* V P n (not pron) *I imagine they'll be tearing the building down sooner or later.* V n P

♦ **tear into** If you **tear into** someone, you criticize them very angrily and strongly. [INFORMAL] PHRASAL VERB ❑ *I had a real row with him. I tore into him.* V P n

♦ **tear off** If you **tear off** your clothes, you take them off in a rough and violent way. PHRASAL VERB ❑ *Totally exhausted, he tore his clothes off and fell into bed...* V n P *Fuentes tore off his hat and flung it to the ground.* V P n

♦ **tear up** 1 If something such as a road, railway, or area of land **is torn up**, it is completely removed or destroyed. PHRASAL VERB ❑ *Dozens of miles of railway track have been torn up...* be V-ed P *The company came under furious attack from environmentalists for tearing up the forests.* V P n (not pron) 2 → see **tear 1**.

**tear|away** /teərəweɪ/ **(tearaways)** If you refer to a young person as a **tearaway**, you mean that they behave in a wild and uncontrolled way. [BRIT] N-COUNT ❑ *He blamed lack of parental control for the young tearaways' behaviour.*

**tear|drop** /tɪəʳdrɒp/ **(teardrops)** A **teardrop** is a large tear that comes from your eye when you are crying quietly. N-COUNT = tear

**tear|ful** /tɪəʳfʊl/ If someone is **tearful**, their face or voice shows signs that they have been crying or that they want to cry. ❑ *She became very tearful when pressed to talk about it.* ♦ **tear|ful|ly** *Gwendolen smiled tearfully.* ADJ; ADV: usu ADV with v

**tear gas** /tɪəʳ gæs/ **Tear gas** is a gas that causes your eyes to sting and fill with tears so that you cannot see. It is sometimes used by the police or army to control crowds. ❑ *Police used tear gas to disperse the demonstrators.* N-UNCOUNT

**tear-jerker** /tɪəʳ dʒɜːʳkəʳ/ **(tear-jerkers)** also **tearjerker.** If you refer to a play, film, or book as a **tear-jerker**, you are indicating that it is very sad or sentimental. [INFORMAL] N-COUNT

**tea room** **(tea rooms)** also **tearoom.** A **tea room** is the same as a **tea shop**. N-COUNT; N-IN-NAMES

**tease** /tiːz/ **(teases, teasing, teased)** [1] To **tease** someone means to laugh at them or make jokes about them in order to embarrass, annoy, or upset them. ❑ *He told her how the boys in East Poldown had set on him, teasing him... He teased me mercilessly about going Hollywood... 'You must be expecting a young man,' she teased.* ♦ **Tease** is also a noun. ❑ *Calling her by her real name had always been one of his teases.* ♦ **teas|ing** *She tolerated the teasing, until the fourth grade.* [2] If you refer to someone as a **tease**, you mean that they like laughing at people or making jokes about them. ❑ *My brother's such a tease.* [3] If you say that someone **is teasing**, you mean that they are pretending to offer you something that you want, especially sex, but then not giving it to you. ❑ *I thought she was teasing, playing the innocent, but looking back, I'm not so sure... When did you last flirt with him or tease him?* [4] If you refer to someone as a **tease**, you mean that they pretend to offer someone what they want, especially sex, but then do not give it to them. ❑ *Later she heard he had told one of her friends she was a tease.* [5] ➔ See also **teasing**, **striptease**. VERB; V n; V n about n/-ing; V with quote; N-COUNT; N-UNCOUNT: also the N; N-COUNT: usu sing; VERB; V; V n; N-COUNT: usu sing disapproval

♦ **tease out** If you **tease out** information or a solution, you succeed in obtaining it even though this is difficult. ❑ *They try to tease out the answers without appearing to ask... There had to be an answer – he was sure he could tease it out if only he had time.* PHRASAL VERB; V P n (not pron); V n P; Also V n P of n

**teas|er** /tiːzəʳ/ **(teasers)** [1] A **teaser** is a difficult question, especially one in a competition. [INFORMAL] [2] A **teaser** is someone who makes fun of people in a slightly cruel way. N-COUNT = poser; N-COUNT

**tea ser|vice** **(tea services)** A **tea service** is the same as a **tea set**. N-COUNT

**tea set** **(tea sets)** A **tea set** is a set of cups, saucers, and plates, with a milk jug, sugar bowl, and teapot. N-COUNT

**tea shop** **(tea shops)** also **teashop.** A **tea shop** is a small restaurant where tea, coffee, cakes, sandwiches, and light meals are served. [BRIT] N-COUNT; N-IN-NAMES = tea room

**teas|ing** /tiːzɪŋ/ A **teasing** expression or manner shows that the person is not completely serious about what they are saying or doing. ❑ *'But we're having such fun, aren't we?' he protested with a teasing smile.* ADJ

**tea|spoon** /tiːspuːn/ **(teaspoons)** [1] A **teaspoon** is a small spoon that you use to put sugar into tea or coffee. [2] You can refer to an amount of food resting on a teaspoon as a **teaspoon** of food. ❑ *He wants three teaspoons of sugar in his coffee.* N-COUNT; N-COUNT: usu N of n

**tea|spoon|ful** /tiːspuːnfʊl/ **(teaspoonfuls** or **teaspoonsful)** You can refer to an amount of food resting on a teaspoon as a **teaspoonful** of food. ❑ *...a heaped teaspoonful of salt.* N-COUNT: usu N of n

**teat** /tiːt/ **(teats)** [1] A **teat** is a pointed part on the body of a female animal which her babies suck in order to get milk. [2] A **teat** is a piece of rubber or plastic that is shaped like a teat, especially one that is fitted to a bottle so that a baby can drink from it. [mainly BRIT] N-COUNT; N-COUNT

**tea ta|ble** also **tea-table.** You refer to a table as **the tea table** when it is being used for a meal eaten in the late afternoon or early evening. [mainly BRIT] ❑ *...cakes and sandwiches on the tea-table.* N-SING: the N

**tea|time** /tiːtaɪm/ **(teatimes)** **Teatime** is the period of the day when people have their tea. It can be eaten in the late afternoon or in the early part of the evening. [BRIT] N-VAR

**tea tow|el** **(tea towels)** A **tea towel** is a cloth used to dry dishes after they have been washed. [BRIT] N-COUNT = tea cloth

> in AM, use **dish towel**

**tech** /tek/ **(techs)** A **tech** is the same as a **technical college**. [BRIT, INFORMAL] N-COUNT: also at N

**techie** /teki/ **(techies)** Some people refer to someone who works in a technological industry, especially computing, as a **techie**. [INFORMAL] N-COUNT

**tech|ni|cal** /teknɪkəl/ [1] **Technical** means involving the sorts of machines, processes, and materials that are used in industry, transport, and communications. ❑ *...jobs that require technical knowledge.* ♦ **tech|ni|cal|ly** /teknɪkli/ *...the largest and most technically advanced furnace company in the world.* [2] You use **technical** to describe the practical skills and methods used to do an activity such as an art, a craft, or a sport. ❑ *Their technical ability is exceptional.* ♦ **tech|ni|cal|ly** *While Sade's voice isn't technically brilliant it has a quality which is unmistakable.* [3] **Technical** language involves using special words to describe the details of a specialized activity. ❑ *The technical term for sunburn is erythema.* [4] ➔ See also **technically**. ◆◇◇ ADJ: usu ADJ n; ADV: ADV adj; ADJ: usu ADJ n; ADV: ADV adj; ADJ

**tech|ni|cal col|lege** **(technical colleges)** In Britain, a **technical college** is a college where you can study arts and technical subjects, often as part of the qualifications and training required for a particular job. N-VAR: oft in names

**tech|ni|cal|ity** /teknɪkælɪti/ **(technicalities)** [1] The **technicalities** of a process or activity are the detailed methods used to do it or to carry it out. ❑ *...the technicalities of classroom teaching.* [2] A **technicality** is a point, especially a legal one, that is based on a strict interpretation of the law or of a set of rules. ❑ *The earlier verdict was overturned on a legal technicality.* N-PLURAL: usu N of n; N-COUNT

**tech|ni|cal|ly** /teknɪkli/ If something is **technically** the case, it is the case according to a strict interpretation of facts, laws, or rules, but may not be important or relevant in a particular situation. ❑ *Nude bathing is technically illegal but there are plenty of unspoilt beaches where no one would ever know.* ➔ See also **technical**. ADV: ADV adj, ADV with cl

**tech|ni|cal sup|port** **Technical support** is a repair and advice service that some companies such as computer companies provide for their customers, usually by telephone, fax, or e-mail. N-UNCOUNT

**tech|ni|cian** /teknɪʃən/ **(technicians)** [1] A **technician** is someone whose job involves skilled practical work with scientific equipment, for example in a laboratory. ❑ *...a laboratory technician.* [2] A **technician** is someone who is very good at the detailed technical aspects of an activity. ❑ *...a versatile, veteran player, a superb technician.* N-COUNT; N-COUNT

**Tech|ni|col|or** /teknɪkʌləʳ/

> The spelling **technicolour** is also used in British English for meaning 2.

[1] **Technicolor** is a system of colour photography used in making cinema films. [TRADEMARK] ❑ *...films in Technicolor.* [2] You can use **technicolor** to describe real or imagined scenes when you want to emphasize that they are very colourful, especially in an exaggerated way. [INFORMAL] ❑ *I was seeing it all in glorious technicolour: mountains, valleys, lakes, summer sunshine. ...Technicolor dreams.* N-UNCOUNT; N-UNCOUNT

**tech|nique** /tekniːk/ **(techniques)** 1 A **technique** is a particular method of doing an activity, usually a method that involves practical skills. ❑ *...tests performed using a new technique.* ◆◆◇ N-COUNT: with supp
2 **Technique** is skill and ability in an artistic, sporting, or other practical activity that you develop through training and practice. ❑ *He went off to the Amsterdam Academy to improve his technique.* N-UNCOUNT

**tech|no** /teknoʊ/ **Techno** is a form of modern electronic music with a very fast beat. N-UNCOUNT

**techno-** /teknoʊ-/ **Techno-** is used at the beginning of words that refer to technology. ❑ *He tried to implement a technocratic economic policy. ...a group of futurist technofreaks.* PREFIX

**tech|noc|ra|cy** /teknɒkrəsi/ **(technocracies)** 1 A **technocracy** is a group of scientists, engineers, and other experts who have political power as well as technical knowledge. ❑ *...the power of the Brussels technocracy.* N-COUNT-COLL 2 A **technocracy** is a country or society that is controlled by scientists, engineers, and other experts. ❑ *...a centralised technocracy.* N-COUNT

**tech|no|crat** /teknəkræt/ **(technocrats)** A **technocrat** is a scientist, engineer, or other expert who is one of a group of similar people who have political power as well as technical knowledge. N-COUNT

**tech|no|crat|ic** /teknəkrætɪk/ **Technocratic** means consisting of or influenced by technocrats. ❑ *...the current technocratic administration.* ADJ: usu ADJ n

**tech|no|logi|cal** /teknəlɒdʒɪkᵊl/ **Technological** means relating to or associated with technology. ❑ *...an era of very rapid technological change.* ADJ: ADJ n
♦ **tech|no|logi|cal|ly** /teknəlɒdʒɪkli/ *...technologically advanced aircraft.* ADV: usu ADV adj

**tech|nol|ogy** /teknɒlədʒi/ **(technologies)** **Technology** refers to methods, systems, and devices which are the result of scientific knowledge being used for practical purposes. ❑ *Technology is changing fast... They should be allowed to wait for cheaper technologies to be developed.* ◆◆◇ N-VAR
♦ **tech|nolo|gist** /teknɒlədʒɪst/ **(technologists)** *...the scientists and technologists that we will need for the future.* N-COUNT

**tech|no|phobe** /teknoʊfoʊb/ **(technophobes)** If you refer to someone as a **technophobe**, you mean that they do not like new technology, such as computers or mobile telephones, and are afraid to use it. N-COUNT

**tec|ton|ic** /tektɒnɪk/ **Tectonic** means relating to the structure of the earth's surface or crust. [TECHNICAL] ❑ *...the tectonic plates of the Pacific region.* ADJ: ADJ n

**tec|ton|ics** /tektɒnɪks/ → see **plate tectonics**.

**Ted** /ted/ **(Teds)** A **Ted** is the same as a **Teddy boy**. [BRIT, INFORMAL] N-COUNT

**ted|dy** /tedi/ **(teddies)** A **teddy** is the same as a **teddy bear**. Children often call their teddies 'Teddy' when they are talking to them or about them. N-COUNT

**ted|dy bear** **(teddy bears)** also **teddy-bear**. A **teddy bear** is a children's toy, made from soft or furry material, which looks like a friendly bear. N-COUNT

**Teddy boy** **(Teddy boys)** A **Teddy boy** is a man who dresses in a style that became popular in the 1950's. Teddy boys were associated with early rock and roll music, and often regarded as bad or violent. [BRIT] N-COUNT

**te|di|ous** /tiːdiəs/ If you describe something such as a job, task, or situation as **tedious**, you mean it is boring and rather frustrating. ❑ *Such lists are long and tedious to read.* ADJ = boring ♦ **te|di|ous|ly** *...the most tediously boring aspects of international relations.* ADV: usu ADV adj

**te|dium** /tiːdiəm/ If you talk about **the tedium of** a job, task, or situation, you think it is boring and rather frustrating. ❑ *She began to wonder whether she wouldn't go mad with the tedium of the job.* N-UNCOUNT: oft N *of* n = boredom

**tee** /tiː/ **(tees, teeing, teed)** 1 In golf, a **tee** is a small piece of wood or plastic which is used to support the ball before it is hit at the start of each hole. N-COUNT 2 On a golf course, a **tee** is one of the small flat areas of ground from which people hit the ball at the start of each hole. N-COUNT 3 **to a tee** → see **T**.
♦ **tee off** 1 If someone or something **tees** you **off**, they make you angry or annoyed. [mainly AM, INFORMAL] ❑ *Something the boy said to him teed him off... That remark really teed off the old boy.* PHRASAL VERB = tick off V pron P V P n Also V n P 2 In golf, when you **tee off**, you hit the ball from a tee at the start of a hole. ❑ *In a few hours time the world's top golfers tee off in the US Masters.* PHRASAL VERB V P

**teem** /tiːm/ **(teems, teeming, teemed)** If you say that a place **is teeming with** people or animals, you mean that it is crowded and the people and animals are moving around a lot. ❑ *For most of the year, the area is teeming with tourists.* VERB: usu cont = swarm V *with* n

**teen** /tiːn/ **(teens)** 1 If you are in your **teens**, you are between thirteen and nineteen years old. ❑ *Most people who smoke began smoking in their teens.* N-PLURAL: with supp, usu poss N 2 **Teen** is used to describe things such as films, magazines, bands, or activities that are aimed at or are done by people who are in their teens. ❑ *...a teen movie starring George Carlin.* ADJ: ADJ n = teenage

**teen|age** /tiːneɪdʒ/ 1 **Teenage** children are aged between thirteen and nineteen years old. ❑ *Almost one in four teenage girls now smoke.* ADJ: ADJ n 2 **Teenage** is used to describe things such as films, magazines, bands, or activities that are aimed at or are done by teenage children. ❑ *...'Smash Hits', a teenage magazine.* ADJ: ADJ n

**teen|aged** /tiːneɪdʒd/ **Teenaged** people are aged between thirteen and nineteen. ❑ *She is the mother of two teenaged daughters.* ADJ: ADJ n

**teen|ager** /tiːneɪdʒəʳ/ **(teenagers)** A **teenager** is someone who is between thirteen and nineteen years old. ❑ *As a teenager he attended Tulse Hill Senior High School.* ◆◇◇ N-COUNT

**tee|ny** /tiːni/ **(teenier, teeniest)** If you describe something as **teeny**, you are emphasizing that it is very small. [INFORMAL] ❑ *...little teeny bugs.* ADJ: ADJ n [emphasis] = tiny

**teeny|bopper** /tiːnibɒpəʳ/ **(teenyboppers)** also **teeny-bopper**. A **teenybopper** is a teenager, usually a girl, who is very interested in pop music. [INFORMAL, OLD-FASHIONED] N-COUNT

**tee|pee** /tiːpiː/ → see **tepee**.

**tee-shirt** → see **T-shirt**.

**tee|ter** /tiːtəʳ/ **(teeters, teetering, teetered)** 1 **Teeter** is used in expressions such as **teeter on the brink** and **teeter on the edge** to emphasize that something seems to be in a very unstable situation or position. ❑ *Three of the hotels are in receivership, and others are teetering on the brink of bankruptcy... His voice teetered on the edge of hysteria.* VERB [emphasis] V *on* n V *on* n 2 If someone or something **teeters**, they shake in an unsteady way, and seem to be about to lose their balance and fall over. ❑ *Hyde shifted his weight and felt himself teeter forward, beginning to overbalance.* VERB V adv/prep

**teeth** /tiːθ/ **Teeth** is the plural of **tooth**.

**teeth|ing** /tiːðɪŋ/ When babies **are teething**, their teeth are starting to appear through their gums, often causing them pain. ❑ *Emma broke off a bit of rusk and gave it to Jacinta, who was teething.* VERB: only cont V ♦ **Teething** is also a noun. ❑ *Teething can be painful and make your baby irritable.* N-UNCOUNT

**teeth|ing prob|lems** If a project or new product has **teething problems**, it has problems in its early stages or when it first becomes available. [BRIT] ❑ *There are bound to be teething problems with something so new.* N-PLURAL

**teeth|ing trou|bles** **Teething troubles** are the same as **teething problems**. [BRIT] ❑ *As the director of the project explains, there are still a few teething troubles to overcome.* N-PLURAL

**tee|to|tal** /tiːtoʊtᵊl, AM tiːtoʊtᵊl/ Someone who is **teetotal** does not drink alcohol. ADJ: usu v-link ADJ

**tee|to|tal|ler** /tiːtoʊtələʳ/ **(teetotallers)** A **teetotaller** is someone who does not drink alcohol. N-COUNT

**TEFL** /tefᵊl/ **TEFL** is the teaching of English to people whose first language is not English, especially people from a country where English is not spoken. **TEFL** is an abbreviation for 'teaching English as a foreign language'. N-UNCOUNT

**Tef|lon** /teflɒn/ **Teflon** is a type of plastic which is often used to coat pans. Teflon provides a very smooth surface which food does not stick to, so the pan can be cleaned easily. [TRADEMARK] N-UNCOUNT

**tel.** **Tel.** is a written abbreviation for **telephone number**.

**tele|cast** /telɪkɑːst, -kæst/ **(telecasts)** A **telecast** is a programme that is broadcast on the television, especially a programme that is broadcast live. [AM] N-COUNT

**tele|com|mu|ni|ca|tions** /telɪkəmjuːnɪkeɪʃᵊnz/

☑ The form **telecommunication** is used as a modifier.

**Telecommunications** is the technology of sending signals and messages over long distances using electronic equipment, for example by radio and telephone. ❑ *...a Japanese telecommunication company.* N-UNCOUNT: usu N n

**tele|com|mut|er** /telɪkəmjuːtəʳ/ **(telecommuters)** **Telecommuters** are the same as **teleworkers**. [BUSINESS] N-COUNT

**tele|com|mut|ing** /telɪkəmjuːtɪŋ/ **Telecommuting** is the same as **teleworking**. [BUSINESS] N-UNCOUNT

**tele|con|fer|ence** /telɪkɒnfrəns/ **(teleconferences)** A **teleconference** is a meeting involving people in various places around the world who use telephones or video links to communicate with each other. [BUSINESS] N-COUNT
♦ **tele|con|fer|enc|ing** ❑ *...teleconferencing facilities.* N-UNCOUNT

**tele|gen|ic** /telɪdʒenɪk/ Someone who is **telegenic** behaves confidently and looks attractive when they are on the television. ❑ *The bright and telegenic Miss Foster is being paid around £90,000 a year for her exclusive deal.* ADJ

**tele|gram** /telɪgræm/ **(telegrams)** A **telegram** is a message that is sent by telegraph and then printed and delivered to someone's home or office. ❑ *The President received a briefing by telegram.* N-COUNT: also *by* N

**tele|graph** /telɪgrɑːf, -græf/ **(telegraphs, telegraphing, telegraphed)** [1] **Telegraph** is a system of sending messages over long distances, either by means of electricity or by radio signals. Telegraph was used more often before the invention of telephones. N-UNCOUNT: also *the* N [2] To **telegraph** someone means to send them a message by telegraph. ❑ *Churchill telegraphed an urgent message to Wavell.* VERB V n *to* n [3] If someone **telegraphs** something that they are planning or intending to do, they make it obvious, either deliberately or accidentally, that they are going to do it. ❑ *The commission telegraphed its decision earlier this month by telling an official to prepare the order.* VERB V n

**tele|graph pole** **(telegraph poles)** A **telegraph pole** is a tall wooden pole with telephone wires attached to it, connecting several different buildings to the telephone system. [BRIT] N-COUNT

☑ in AM, use **telephone pole**

**tele|mar|ket|ing** /telɪmɑːʳkɪtɪŋ/ **Telemarketing** is a method of selling in which someone employed by a company telephones people to try and persuade them to buy the company's products or services. [BUSINESS] N-UNCOUNT

**te|lem|etry** /təlemɪtri/ **Telemetry** is the science of using automatic equipment to make scientific measurements and transmit them by radio to a receiving station. [TECHNICAL] N-UNCOUNT

**tele|path|ic** /telɪpæθɪk/ If you believe that someone is **telepathic**, you believe that they have mental powers which cannot be explained by science, such as being able to communicate with other people's minds, and know what other people are thinking. ❑ *I could not know that. I'm not telepathic.* ADJ ♦ **tele|pathi|cal|ly** /telɪpæθɪkli/ *I used to communicate with her telepathically.* ADV: ADV with v

**te|lepa|thy** /tɪlepəθi/ If you refer to **telepathy**, you mean the direct communication of thoughts and feelings between people's minds, without the need to use speech, writing, or any other normal signals. ❑ *Many of us find it very difficult to state our needs. We expect people to know by telepathy what we are feeling.* N-UNCOUNT

**tele|phone** /telɪfoʊn/ **(telephones, telephoning, telephoned)** ◆◆◇ [1] The **telephone** is the electrical system of communication that you use to talk directly to someone else in a different place. You use the telephone by dialling a number on a piece of equipment and speaking into it. ❑ *They usually exchanged messages by telephone... I dread to think what our telephone bill is going to be... She was wanted on the telephone.* N-UNCOUNT = phone [2] A **telephone** is the piece of equipment that you use when you talk to someone by telephone. ❑ *He got up and answered the telephone.* N-COUNT = phone [3] If you **telephone** someone, you dial their telephone number and speak to them by telephone. ❑ *I felt so badly I had to telephone Owen to say I was sorry... They usually telephone first to see if she is at home.* VERB = call, ring, phone V n V [4] If you are **on the telephone**, you are speaking to someone by telephone. ❑ *Linda remained on the telephone to the police for three hours.* PHRASE: v-link PHR, PHR after v

**tele|phone book** **(telephone books)** The **telephone book** is a book that contains an alphabetical list of the names, addresses, and telephone numbers of the people in a particular area. N-COUNT = telephone directory, phone book

**tele|phone booth** **(telephone booths)** A **telephone booth** is a place in a public building or in the street where there is a telephone that can be used by the public. [FORMAL] N-COUNT

**tele|phone box** **(telephone boxes)** A **telephone box** is a small shelter in the street in which there is a public telephone. [BRIT] N-COUNT = phone box, call box

☑ in AM, use **phone booth**

**tele|phone di|rec|tory** **(telephone directories)** A **telephone directory** is the same as a **telephone book**. N-COUNT

**tele|phone ex|change** **(telephone exchanges)** A **telephone exchange** is a building where connections are made between telephone lines. [mainly BRIT] N-COUNT

**tele|phone num|ber** **(telephone numbers)** Your **telephone number** is the number that other people dial when they want to talk to you on the telephone. N-COUNT = phone number

**tele|phone pole** **(telephone poles)** A **telephone pole** is a tall wooden pole with telephone wires attached to it, connecting several different buildings to the telephone system. [AM] N-COUNT

☑ in BRIT, use **telegraph pole**

**te|lepho|nist** /tɪlefənɪst/ **(telephonists)** A **telephonist** is someone who works at a telephone exchange or whose job is to answer the telephone for a business or other organization. [BRIT] N-COUNT = operator

**te|lepho|ny** /tɪlefəni/ **Telephony** is a system of sending voice signals using electronic equipment. ❑ *These optical fibres may be used for new sorts of telephony.* N-UNCOUNT

**tele|photo lens** /telɪfoʊtoʊ lenz/ **(telephoto lenses)** A **telephoto lens** is a powerful camera lens which allows you to take close-up pictures of something that is far away. N-COUNT

**Tele|prompt|er** /telɪprɒmptəʳ/ **(Teleprompters)** A **Teleprompter** is a device used by people speaking on television or at a public event, which displays words for them to read. [mainly AM, TRADEMARK] N-COUNT

☑ in BRIT, usually use **Autocue**

**tele|sales** /teliseilz/ **Telesales** is the selling of a company's products or services by telephone, either by phoning possible customers or by answering calls from customers. [BUSINESS] N-UNCOUNT: oft N n

**tele|scope** /teliskoup/ **(telescopes)** A **telescope** is a long instrument shaped like a tube. It has lenses inside it that make distant things seem larger and nearer when you look through it. N-COUNT

**tele|scop|ic** /teliskɒpik/ 1 **Telescopic** lenses and instruments are used to make things seem larger and nearer, and are usually longer than others of the same type. ❑ *...a sporting rifle fitted with a telescopic sight.* ADJ: usu ADJ n 2 A **telescopic** object is made of cylindrical sections that fit or slide into each other, so that it can be made longer or shorter, for example to save space when it is not being used. ❑ *...this new lightweight telescopic ladder.* ADJ: usu ADJ n

**tele|van|gelist** /telivændʒəlist/ **(televangelists)** A **televangelist** is someone who makes regular television broadcasts to promote a particular form of Christianity and raise money for particular Christian groups or projects. N-COUNT

**tele|vise** /telivaiz/ **(televises, televising, televised)** If an event or programme **is televised**, it is broadcast so that it can be seen on television. ❑ *The Grand Prix will be televised by the BBC.* VERB: usu passive *be* V-ed

**tele|vi|sion** /telivɪʒᵊn, -vɪʒ-/ **(televisions)** ◆◆◇ 1 A **television** or **television set** is a piece of electrical equipment consisting of a box with a glass screen on it on which you can watch programmes with pictures and sounds. ❑ *She turned the television on and flicked around between news programmes.* N-COUNT = *TV, telly* 2 **Television** is the system of sending pictures and sounds by electrical signals over a distance so that people can receive them on a television in their home. ❑ *Toy manufacturers began promoting some of their products on television.* N-UNCOUNT = *TV* 3 **Television** refers to all the programmes that you can watch. ❑ *I don't have much time to watch very much television.* N-UNCOUNT = *TV* 4 **Television** is the business or industry concerned with making programmes and broadcasting them on television. ❑ *British commercial television has been steadily losing its lead as the most advanced sector of the industry in Europe.* N-UNCOUNT

**tele|vis|ual** /teləvɪʒuəl/ **Televisual** means broadcast on or related to television. [mainly BRIT] ❑ *...a televisual masterpiece.* ADJ: ADJ n = *television*

**tele|work|er** /teliwɜːʳkəʳ/ **(teleworkers)** **Teleworkers** are people who work from home using equipment such as telephones, fax machines, and modems to contact the people they work with and their customers. [BUSINESS] N-COUNT = *telecommuter*

**tele|work|ing** /teliwɜːʳkɪŋ/ **Teleworking** is working from home using equipment such as telephones, fax machines, and modems to contact people. [BUSINESS] N-UNCOUNT = *telecommuting*

**tel|ex** /teleks/ **(telexes, telexing, telexed)** 1 **Telex** is an international system of sending written messages. Messages are converted into signals which are transmitted, either by electricity or by radio signals, and then printed out by a machine in another place. N-UNCOUNT 2 A **telex** is a machine that transmits and receives telex messages. N-COUNT 3 A **telex** is a message that you send or that has been received and printed by telex. N-COUNT 4 If you **telex** a message to someone, you send it to them by telex. ❑ *The embassy says it has telexed their demands to the foreign ministry... They telexed British Airways.* VERB V n *to* n V n

**tell** /tel/ **(tells, telling, told)** ◆◆◆ 1 If you **tell** someone something, you give them information. ❑ *In the evening I returned to tell Phyllis our relationship was over... I called Andie to tell her how spectacular the stuff looked... Claire had made me promise to tell her the truth... I only told the truth to the press when the single was released as it seemed the perfect time to do it... Tell us about your moment on the summit... Her voice breaking with emotion, she told him: 'It doesn't seem fair'.* VERB V n that V n wh V n n V n *to* n V n *about* n V with quote 2 If you **tell** something such as a joke, a story, or your personal experiences, you communicate it to other people using speech. ❑ *His friends say he was always quick to tell a joke... He told his story to The Sunday Times and produced photographs... Will you tell me a story?* VERB V n V n *to* n V n n 3 If you **tell** someone **to** do something, you order or advise them to do it. ❑ *A passer-by told the driver to move his car so that it was not causing an obstruction.* VERB V n to-inf 4 If you **tell yourself** something, you put it into words in your own mind because you need to encourage or persuade yourself about something. ❑ *'Come on', she told herself... I told myself I would be satisfied with whatever I could get from it all.* VERB V pron-refl with quote V pron-refl that 5 If you can **tell** what is happening or what is true, you are able to judge correctly what is happening or what is true. ❑ *It was already impossible to tell where the bullet had entered... You can tell he's joking.* VERB: no cont, oft with brd-neg V wh V that 6 If you can **tell** one thing **from** another, you are able to recognize the difference between it and other similar things. ❑ *I can't really tell the difference between their policies and ours... How do you tell one from another?... I had to look twice to tell which was Martinez; they all looked alike.* VERB: no cont, oft with brd-neg V n *between* pl-n V n *from* n V wh 7 If you **tell**, you reveal or give away a secret. [INFORMAL] ❑ *Many of the children know who they are but are not telling.* VERB V 8 If facts or events **tell** you something, they reveal certain information to you through ways other than speech. ❑ *The facts tell us that this is not true... I don't think the unemployment rate ever tells us much about the future... The evidence of our eyes tells us a different story... While most of us feel fairly complacent about the nutrients we're getting from our diets, the facts tell a very different story.* VERB V n that V n amount V n n V n 9 If an unpleasant or tiring experience begins to **tell**, it begins to have a serious effect. ❑ *The pressure began to tell as rain closed in after 20 laps.* VERB V 10 → See also **telling**, **kiss and tell**. 11 You use **as far as** I **can tell** or **so far as** I **could tell** to indicate that what you are saying is based on the information you have, but that there may be things you do not know. ❑ *As far as I can tell, Jason is basically a nice guy.* PHRASE [vagueness] 12 You can say **'I tell you'**, **'I can tell you'**, or **'I can't tell you'** to add emphasis to what you are saying. [INFORMAL] ❑ *I tell you this, I will not rest until that day has come... This little letter gave us a few chuckles, I can tell you.* CONVENTION [emphasis] 13 If you say **'You never can tell'**, you mean that the future is always uncertain and it is never possible to know exactly what will happen. ❑ *You never can tell what life is going to bring you.* CONVENTION 14 If someone disagrees with you or refuses to do what you suggest and you are eventually proved to be right, you can say **'I told you so'**. [INFORMAL] ❑ *Her parents did not approve of her decision and, if she failed, her mother would say, 'I told you so.'* CONVENTION 15 You use **I'll tell you what** or **I tell you what** to introduce a suggestion or a new topic of conversation. [SPOKEN] ❑ *I tell you what, I'll bring the water in a separate glass.* CONVENTION 16 to **tell the time** → see **time**. **time will tell** → see **time**.

♦ **tell apart** If you can **tell** people or things **apart**, you are able to recognize the differences between them and can therefore identify each of them. ❑ *Perhaps it is the almost universal use of flavourings that makes it so hard to tell the products apart.* PHRASAL VERB V n P

♦ **tell off** If you **tell** someone **off**, you speak to them angrily or seriously because they have done something wrong. ❑ *He never listened to us when we told him off... I'm always being told off for being so awkward... Dutch police told off two of the gang, aged 10 and 11.* PHRASAL VERB V n P V n P *for* n/-ing V P n (not pron)

♦ **tell on** If you **tell on** someone, you give information about them to a person in authority, especially if they have done something wrong. [INFORMAL] ❑ *Never mind, I won't tell on you... I'll tell my mummy on you.* PHRASAL VERB V P n V n P n

**tell|er** /teləʳ/ **(tellers)** A **teller** is someone who works in a bank and who customers pay money to or get money from. [mainly AM or SCOTTISH] N-COUNT = *cashier*

**tell|ing** /telɪŋ/ **(tellings)** 1 The **telling** of a story or of something that has happened is the reporting of it to other people. ❑ *Herbert sat quietly* N-VAR through the telling of this saga. [2] If something is **telling**, it shows the true nature of a person or situation. ❑ *How a man shaves may be a telling clue to his age.* ♦ **tell|ing|ly** *Most tellingly, perhaps, chimpanzees do not draw as much information from the world around them as we do.* [3] A **telling** argument or criticism is a very effective one. ❑ *The most telling condemnation of the system was that it failed to fulfil its function.* [4] You use **there's no telling** to introduce a statement when you want to say that it is impossible to know what will happen in a situation. ❑ *There's no telling how long the talks could drag on.* ADJ = *revealing*; ADV: ADV with cl, ADV with v; ADJ: usu ADJ n; PHRASE: usu PHR wh

**telling-off** **(tellings-off)** also **telling off.** If you give someone a **telling-off**, you tell them that you are very angry with them about something they have done. [INFORMAL] ❑ *I got a severe telling off for not phoning him.* N-COUNT: usu sing

**tell-tale** also **telltale.** Something that is described as **telltale** gives away information, often about something bad that would otherwise not be noticed. ❑ *Only occasionally did the telltale redness around his eyes betray the fatigue he was suffering.* ADJ: ADJ n

**tel|ly** /teli/ **(tellies)** A **telly** is a television. [BRIT, INFORMAL] ❑ *After a hard day's work most people want to relax in front of the telly.* N-VAR = *box, TV*

☑ in AM, use **TV**

**te|maze|pam** /tɪmæzɪpæm/ **Temazepam** is a drug that is used to make people feel calmer or less anxious. N-UNCOUNT

**te|mer|ity** /tɪmerɪti/ If you say that a person has the **temerity to** do something, you are annoyed about something they have done which you think showed a lack of respect. ❑ *...'difficult' patients who have the temerity to challenge their doctors' decisions.* N-UNCOUNT: usu N to-inf; disapproval; = *presumption*

**temp** /temp/ **(temps, temping, temped)** [1] A **temp** is a person who is employed by an agency that sends them to work in different offices for short periods of time, for example to replace someone who is ill or on holiday. [2] If someone **is temping**, they are working as a temp. ❑ *Mrs Reynolds has been temping since losing her job.* N-COUNT; VERB: only cont V

**tem|per** /tempəʳ/ **(tempers, tempering, tempered)** [1] If you refer to someone's **temper** or say that they have a **temper**, you mean that they become angry very easily. ❑ *He had a temper and could be nasty... I hope he can control his temper.* [2] Your **temper** is the way you are feeling at a particular time. If you are **in** a good **temper**, you feel cheerful. If you are **in** a bad **temper**, you feel angry and impatient. ❑ *I was in a bad temper last night.* [3] To **temper** something means to make it less extreme. [FORMAL] ❑ *For others, especially the young and foolish, the state will temper justice with mercy... He had to learn to temper his enthusiasm.* N-VAR; N-VAR: with supp, oft adj N, oft *in* N; VERB: V n *with* n, V n

PHRASES [4] If someone is **in a temper** or gets **into a temper**, the way that they are behaving shows that they are feeling angry and impatient. ❑ *She was still in a temper when Colin arrived... When I try to explain how I feel he just flies into a temper.* [5] If you **lose** your **temper**, you become so angry that you shout at someone or show in some other way that you are no longer in control of yourself. ❑ *I've never seen him get cross or lose his temper.* PHRASE: v-link PHR, PHR after v; PHRASE: V inflects

**tem|pera|ment** /temprəmənt/ **(temperaments)** [1] Your **temperament** is your basic nature, especially as it is shown in the way that you react to situations or to other people. ❑ *His impulsive temperament regularly got him into difficulties... She was furtive and vicious by temperament.* [2] **Temperament** is the tendency to behave in an uncontrolled, bad-tempered, or unreasonable way. ❑ *Some of the models were given to fits of temperament.* N-VAR; N-UNCOUNT

**tem|pera|men|tal** /temprəmentᵊl/ [1] If you say that someone is **temperamental**, you are criticizing them for not being calm or quiet by nature, but having moods that change often and suddenly. ❑ *He is very temperamental and critical.* [2] If you describe something such as a machine or car as **temperamental**, you mean that it often does not work properly. ❑ *I first started cruising in yachts with temperamental petrol engines.* ADJ disapproval; ADJ

**tem|pera|men|tal|ly** /temprəmentəli/ **Temperamentally** means because of someone's basic nature or related to someone's basic nature. ❑ *He is a quitter who is temperamentally unsuited to remaining a champion.* ADV: ADV with cl/group, ADV after v

**tem|per|ance** /tempərəns/ [1] If you believe in **temperance**, you disapprove of drinking alcohol. ❑ *...a reformed alcoholic extolling the joys of temperance.* [2] A person who shows **temperance** has a strong mind and does not eat too much, drink too much, or do too much of anything. [FORMAL] ❑ *The age of hedonism is being ushered out by a new era of temperance.* N-UNCOUNT; N-UNCOUNT = *moderation*

**tem|per|ate** /tempərɪt/ [1] **Temperate** is used to describe a climate or a place which is never extremely hot or extremely cold. ❑ *The Nile Valley keeps a temperate climate throughout the year.* [2] If a person's behaviour is **temperate**, it is calm and reasonable, so that they do not get angry or lose their temper easily. [FORMAL] ❑ *His final report to the President was far more temperate and balanced than the earlier memorandum.* ADJ: usu ADJ n; ADJ = *moderate*

**tem|pera|ture** /temprətʃəʳ/ **(temperatures)** ◆◇◇ [1] The **temperature** of something is a measure of how hot or cold it is. ❑ *The temperature soared to above 100 degrees in the shade... Coping with severe drops in temperature can be very difficult.* [2] Your **temperature** is the temperature of your body. A normal temperature is about 37° centigrade. ❑ *His temperature continued to rise alarmingly.* [3] You can use **temperature** to talk about the feelings and emotions that people have in particular situations. ❑ *There's also been a noticeable rise in the political temperature.* N-VAR; N-UNCOUNT: oft poss N; N-COUNT: usu sing

PHRASES [4] If something is at **room temperature**, its temperature is neither hot nor cold. ❑ *Stir the parsley into the potatoes and serve at room temperature.* [5] If you **are running a temperature** or if you **have a temperature**, your temperature is higher than it usually is. ❑ *He began to run an extremely high temperature.* [6] If you **take** someone's **temperature** you use an instrument called a thermometer to measure the temperature of their body in order to see if they are ill. ❑ *He will probably take your child's temperature too.* PHRASE: usu PHR after v, v-link PHR; PHRASE: V inflects; PHRASE: V inflects

**tem|pest** /tempɪst/ **(tempests)** [1] A **tempest** is a very violent storm. [LITERARY] [2] You can refer to a situation in which people are very angry or excited as a **tempest**. [LITERARY] ❑ *I hadn't foreseen the tempest my request would cause.* **a tempest in a teapot** → see **teapot**. N-COUNT; N-COUNT: usu with supp = *storm*

**tem|pes|tu|ous** /tempestʃuəs/ If you describe a relationship or a situation as **tempestuous**, you mean that very strong and intense emotions, especially anger, are involved. ❑ *For years, the couple's tempestuous relationship made the headlines.* ADJ: usu ADJ n = *stormy*

**tem|pi** /tempi/ **Tempi** is a plural of **tempo**.

**tem|plate** /templeɪt, AM -plɪt/ **(templates)** [1] A **template** is a thin piece of metal or plastic which is cut into a particular shape. It is used to help you cut wood, paper, metal, or other materials accurately, or to reproduce the same shape many times. ❑ *Trace around your template and transfer the design onto a sheet of card.* [2] If one thing is a **template for** something else, the second thing is based on the first thing. ❑ *The deal is likely to provide a template for other agreements.* N-COUNT; N-COUNT: usu sing

**tem|ple** /tempᵊl/ **(temples)** ◆◇◇ [1] A **temple** is a building used for the worship of a god or gods, especially in the Buddhist and Hindu religions, and in ancient Greek and Roman times. ❑ *...a small Hindu temple. ...the Temple of Diana at Ephesus.* [2] Your **temples** are the flat parts on each side of the front part of your head, near your forehead. N-COUNT; N-IN-NAMES; N-COUNT: usu pl

❑ *Threads of silver ran through his beard and the hair at his temples.*

**tem|po** /tempoʊ/ **(tempos** or **tempi)** [1] The **tempo** of an event is the speed at which it happens. ❑ *...owing to the slow tempo of change in an overwhelmingly rural country.* N-SING = pace [2] The **tempo** of a piece of music is the speed at which it is played. ❑ *In a new recording, the Boston Philharmonic tried the original tempo.* N-VAR

**tem|po|ral** /tempərəl/ [1] **Temporal** powers or matters relate to ordinary institutions and activities rather than to religious or spiritual ones. [FORMAL] ❑ *...the spiritual and temporal leader of the Tibetan people.* ADJ: ADJ n = secular ≠ spiritual [2] **Temporal** means relating to time. [FORMAL] ❑ *One is also able to see how specific acts are related to a temporal and spatial context.* ADJ: ADJ n

**tem|po|rary** /tempərəri, AM -reri/ Something that is **temporary** lasts for only a limited time. ❑ *His job here is only temporary. ...a temporary loss of memory.* ◆◇◇ ADJ ≠ permanent ♦ **tem|po|rari|ly** /tempəreərɪli/ *The peace agreement has at least temporarily halted the civil war.* ADV: ADV with v, ADV adj ≠ permanently

**tem|po|rize** /tempəraɪz/ **(temporizes, temporizing, temporized)**

> ✔ in BRIT, also use **temporise**

If you say that someone **is temporizing**, you mean that they keep doing unimportant things in order to delay something important such as making a decision or stating their real opinion. [FORMAL] ❑ *They are still temporizing in the face of what can only be described as a disaster... 'Not exactly, sir,' temporized Sloan.* VERB V V with quote

**tempt** /tempt/ **(tempts, tempting, tempted)** [1] Something that **tempts** you attracts you and makes you want it, even though it may be wrong or harmful. ❑ *Reducing the income will further impoverish these families and could tempt an offender into further crime... It is the fresh fruit that tempts me at this time of year... Can I tempt you with a little puff pastry?... The fact that she had become wealthy did not tempt her to alter her frugal way of life.* VERB V n *into* n/-ing V n V n *with* n V n to-inf [2] If you **tempt** someone, you offer them something they want in order to encourage them to do what you want them to do. ❑ *...a million dollar marketing campaign to tempt American tourists back to Britain... Don't let credit tempt you to buy something you can't afford... She will be offering a package worth about 40 million dollars, to tempt the rebels into agreeing to disarm.* VERB V n prep/adv V n to-inf V n *into* -ing/n [3] → See also **tempted**. [4] If someone says that something they say or do **is tempting fate** or **is tempting providence**, they mean they are worried that it may cause the good luck they have had so far to end. ❑ *As soon as you start to talk about never having played on a losing side, it is tempting fate.* PHRASE: V inflects

**temp|ta|tion** /tempteɪʃən/ **(temptations)** If you feel you want to do something or have something, even though you know you really should avoid it, you can refer to this feeling as **temptation**. You can also refer to the thing you want to do or have as a **temptation**. ❑ *Will they be able to resist the temptation to buy?* N-VAR

**tempt|ed** /temptɪd/ If you say that you are **tempted to** do something, you mean that you would like to do it. ❑ *I'm very tempted to sell my house.* ADJ: v-link ADJ, usu ADJ to-inf

**tempt|ing** /temptɪŋ/ If something is **tempting**, it makes you want to do it or have it. ❑ *In the end, I turned down Raoul's tempting offer of the Palm Beach trip.* ADJ ♦ **tempt|ing|ly** *The good news is that prices are still temptingly low.* ADV

**tempt|ress** /temptrəs/ **(temptresses)** If you describe a woman as a **temptress**, you mean that she uses her female charm to encourage men to have sexual relations with her. N-COUNT

**ten** /ten/ **(tens) Ten** is the number 10. ❑ *Over the past ten years things have changed.* → See also **Number Ten**. **ten a penny** → see **penny**. ◆◆◆ NUM

**ten|able** /tenəbᵊl/ If you say that an argument, point of view, or situation is **tenable**, you believe that it is reasonable and could be successfully defended against criticism. ❑ *This argument is simply not tenable.* ADJ ≠ untenable

**te|na|cious** /tɪneɪʃəs/ [1] If you are **tenacious**, you are very determined and do not give up easily. ❑ *He is regarded at the BBC as a tenacious and persistent interviewer.* ADJ ♦ **te|na|cious|ly** *In spite of his illness, he clung tenaciously to his job.* ADV: usu ADV after v [2] If you describe something such as an idea or belief as **tenacious**, you mean that it has a strong influence on people and is difficult to change or remove. ❑ *...a remarkably tenacious belief that was to dominate future theories of military strategy.* ADJ = deep-seated

**te|nac|ity** /tɪnæsɪti/ If you have **tenacity**, you are very determined and do not give up easily. ❑ *Talent, hard work and sheer tenacity are all crucial to career success.* N-UNCOUNT

**ten|an|cy** /tenənsi/ **(tenancies) Tenancy** is the use that you have of land or property belonging to someone else, for which you pay rent. ❑ *His father took over the tenancy of the farm 40 years ago.* N-VAR

**ten|ant** /tenənt/ **(tenants)** A **tenant** is someone who pays rent for the place they live in, or for land or buildings that they use. → See also **sitting tenant**. N-COUNT

**tench** /tentʃ/ **(tench) Tench** are dark green European fish that live in lakes and rivers. N-VAR

**tend** /tend/ **(tends, tending, tended)** [1] If something **tends to** happen, it usually happens or it often happens. ❑ *A problem for manufacturers is that lighter cars tend to be noisy.* ◆◆◇ VERB V to-inf [2] If you **tend towards** a particular characteristic, you often display that characteristic. ❑ *Artistic and intellectual people tend towards left-wing views.* VERB V *towards* n Also V *to* n [3] You can say that you **tend to** think something when you want to give your opinion, but do not want it to seem too forceful or definite. ❑ *I tend to think that members of parliament by and large do a good job.* VERB [vagueness] V to-inf [4] If you **tend** someone or something, you do what is necessary to keep them in a good condition or to improve their condition. [FORMAL] ❑ *For years he tended her in her painful illness.* VERB = look after V n [5] If you **tend to** someone or something, you pay attention to them and deal with their problems and needs. ❑ *In our culture, girls are brought up to tend to the needs of others.* VERB = attend V *to* n

**ten|den|cy** /tendənsi/ **(tendencies)** [1] A **tendency** is a worrying or unpleasant habit or action that keeps occurring. ❑ *...the government's tendency towards secrecy in recent years.* ◆◇◇ N-COUNT: with supp [2] A **tendency** is a part of your character that makes you behave in an unpleasant or worrying way. ❑ *He is spoiled, arrogant and has a tendency towards snobbery.* N-COUNT: with supp

**ten|den|tious** /tendenʃəs/ Something that is **tendentious** expresses a particular opinion or point of view very strongly, especially one that many people disagree with. [FORMAL] ❑ *His analysis was rooted in a somewhat tendentious reading of French history.* ADJ = controversial

> **tender**
> ① ADJECTIVE USES
> ② NOUN AND VERB USES

**①ten|der** /tendəʳ/ **(tenderer, tenderest)** [1] Someone or something that is **tender** expresses gentle and caring feelings. ❑ *Her voice was tender, full of pity.* ADJ ♦ **ten|der|ly** *Mr. White tenderly embraced his wife.* ADV: ADV with v ♦ **ten|der|ness** *She smiled, politely rather than with tenderness or gratitude.* N-UNCOUNT [2] If you say that someone does something at a **tender** age, you mean that they do it when they are still young and have not had much experience. ❑ *He had become attracted to the game at the tender age of seven.* ADJ: ADJ n [3] Meat or other food that is **tender** is easy to cut or chew. ❑ *Cook for a minimum of 2 hours, or until the meat is tender.* ADJ ≠ tough [4] If part of your body is **tender**, it is sensitive and painful when it is touched. ❑ *My tummy felt very tender.* ADJ = sore

♦ **ten|der|ness** *There is still some tenderness in her tummy.* N-UNCOUNT

② **ten|der** /tendəʳ/ **(tenders, tendering, tendered)** [1] A **tender** is a formal offer to supply goods or to do a particular job, and a statement of the price that you or your company will charge. If a contract is **put out to tender**, formal offers are invited. If a company **wins a tender**, their offer is accepted. [BUSINESS] ❑ *Builders will then be sent the specifications and asked to submit a tender for the work.* N-VAR [2] If a company **tenders for** something, it makes a formal offer to supply goods or do a job for a particular price. [BUSINESS] ❑ *The staff are forbidden to tender for private-sector work.* VERB V *for* n [3] If you **tender** something such as a suggestion, your resignation, or money, you formally offer or present it. ❑ *She quickly tendered her resignation.* VERB V n [4] → See also **legal tender**.

**tender-hearted** If you are **tender-hearted**, you have a gentle and caring nature. ADJ

**ten|der|ize** /tendəraɪz/ **(tenderizes, tenderizing, tenderized)**

✔ in BRIT, also use **tenderise**

If you **tenderize** meat, you make it softer by preparing it in a particular way. ❑ *Wine vinegar tenderises meat.* VERB V n

**ten|don** /tendən/ **(tendons)** A **tendon** is a strong cord in a person's or animal's body which joins a muscle to a bone. → See also **Achilles tendon**. N-COUNT

**ten|dril** /tendrɪl/ **(tendrils)** [1] A **tendril** is something light and thin, for example a piece of hair which hangs loose and is away from the main part. ❑ *Tendrils of hair strayed to the edge of her pillow.* N-COUNT [2] **Tendrils** are thin stems which grow on some plants so that they can attach themselves to supports such as walls or other plants. N-COUNT: usu pl

**ten|ement** /tenəmənt/ **(tenements)** [1] A **tenement** is a large, old building which is divided into a number of individual flats. ❑ *...elegant 19th century tenement buildings.* N-COUNT [2] A **tenement** is one of the flats in a tenement. N-COUNT

**ten|et** /tenɪt/ **(tenets)** The **tenets** of a theory or belief are the main principles on which it is based. [FORMAL] ❑ *Non-violence and patience are the central tenets of their faith.* N-COUNT: with supp, oft N *of* n = *principle*

**ten|ner** /tenəʳ/ **(tenners)** A **tenner** is ten pounds or a ten-pound note. [BRIT, INFORMAL] N-COUNT

**ten|nis** /tenɪs/ **Tennis** is a game played by two or four players on a rectangular court. The players use an oval bat with strings across it to hit a ball over a net across the middle of the court. ♦◇◇ N-UNCOUNT

**ten|or** /tenəʳ/ **(tenors)** [1] A **tenor** is a male singer whose voice is fairly high. N-COUNT: oft N n [2] A **tenor** saxophone or other musical instrument has a range of notes that are of a fairly low pitch. ❑ *...one of the best tenor sax players ever.* ADJ [3] The **tenor** of something is the general meaning or mood that it expresses. [FORMAL] ❑ *The whole tenor of discussions has changed.* N-SING: with poss

**ten-pin bowl|ing** also **tenpin bowling**. **Ten-pin bowling** is a game in which you try to knock down ten objects shaped like bottles by rolling a heavy ball towards them. It is usually played in a place called a bowling alley. [mainly BRIT] N-UNCOUNT

✔ in AM, usually use **bowling**

**tense** /tens/ **(tenser, tensest, tenses, tensing, tensed)** [1] A **tense** situation or period of time is one that makes people anxious, because they do not know what is going to happen next. ❑ *This gesture of goodwill did little to improve the tense atmosphere at the talks... After three very tense weeks he phoned again.* ADJ [2] If you are **tense**, you are anxious and nervous and cannot relax. ❑ *Dart, who had at first been very tense, at last relaxed.* ADJ ♦ **tense|ly** *She waited tensely for the next bulletin.* ADV: usu ADV with v ♦ **tense|ness** *McKay walked slowly toward this screen, feeling a growing tenseness.* N-UNCOUNT [3] If your body is **tense**, your muscles are tight and not relaxed. ❑ *A bath can relax tense muscles.* ADJ ♦ **tense|ness** *If you feel a tenseness around the eyes, relax your muscles.* N-UNCOUNT [4] If your muscles **tense**, if you **tense**, or if you **tense** your muscles, your muscles become tight and stiff, often because you are anxious or frightened. ❑ *Newman's stomach muscles tensed... Jane tensed her muscles to stop them from shaking.* VERB V V n ♦ **Tense up** means the same as **tense**. ❑ *When we are under stress our bodies tend to tense up... Tense up the muscles in both of your legs.* PHRASAL VERB V P V P n Also V n P [5] The **tense** of a verb group is its form, which usually shows whether you are referring to past, present, or future time. N-COUNT

♦ **tense up** → see **tense 4**.

**ten|sile** /tensaɪl, AM -sɪl/ You use **tensile** when you are talking about the amount of stress that materials such as wire, rope, and concrete can take without breaking; a technical term in engineering. ❑ *Certain materials can be manufactured with a high tensile strength.* ADJ: ADJ n

**ten|sion** /tenʃən/ **(tensions)** [1] **Tension** is the feeling that is produced in a situation when people are anxious and do not trust each other, and when there is a possibility of sudden violence or conflict. ❑ *The tension between the two countries is likely to remain.* ♦◇◇ N-UNCOUNT: also N in pl [2] **Tension** is a feeling of worry and anxiety which makes it difficult for you to relax. ❑ *Smiling and laughing has actually been shown to relieve tension and stress.* N-UNCOUNT: also N in pl [3] If there is a **tension** between forces, arguments, or influences, there are differences between them that cause difficulties. ❑ *The film explored the tension between public duty and personal affections.* N-VAR: usu N *between* pl-n [4] The **tension** in something such as a rope or wire is the extent to which it is stretched tight. N-UNCOUNT

**tent** /tent/ **(tents)** A **tent** is a shelter made of canvas or nylon which is held up by poles and ropes, and is used mainly by people who are camping. N-COUNT

**ten|ta|cle** /tentəkəl/ **(tentacles)** [1] The **tentacles** of an animal such as an octopus are the long thin parts that are used for feeling and holding things, for getting food, and for moving. N-COUNT: usu pl [2] If you talk about the **tentacles** of a political, commercial, or social organization, you are referring to the power and influence that it has in the outside community. ❑ *Free speech is being gradually eroded year after year by new tentacles of government control.* N-COUNT: usu pl, with supp [disapproval]

**ten|ta|tive** /tentətɪv/ [1] **Tentative** agreements, plans, or arrangements are not definite or certain, but have been made as a first step. ❑ *Political leaders have reached a tentative agreement to hold a preparatory conference next month.* ADJ = *provisional* ≠ *firm* ♦ **ten|ta|tive|ly** *The next round of talks is tentatively scheduled to begin October 21st in Washington.* ADV: ADV with v [2] If someone is **tentative**, they are cautious and not very confident because they are uncertain or afraid. ❑ *My first attempts at complaining were rather tentative.* ADJ ≠ *confident* ♦ **ten|ta|tive|ly** *Perhaps, he suggested tentatively, they should send for Dr Band.* ADV: ADV with v

**tent|ed** /tentɪd/ [1] A **tented** field or a **tented** camp is an area where a number of people are living in tents. ADJ: usu ADJ n [2] A **tented** room has long pieces of material hanging down from the centre of the ceiling to the walls, so that the room has the appearance of the inside of a large tent. ❑ *...a tented dining area.* ADJ: usu ADJ n

**tenter|hooks** /tentəʳhʊks/ If you are **on tenterhooks**, you are very nervous and excited because you are wondering what is going to happen in a particular situation. ❑ *He was still on tenterhooks waiting for his directors' decision about the job.* PHRASE: v-link PHR

**tenth** /tenθ/ **(tenths)** [1] The **tenth** item in a series is the one that you count as number ten. ♦♦◇ ORD [2] A **tenth** is one of ten equal parts of something. ❑ *We received only two tenths of an inch of rain during the entire month of June.* FRACTION

**tenu|ous** /tenjuəs/ If you describe something such as a connection, a reason, or someone's position as **tenuous**, you mean that it is very uncertain or weak. ❑ *The cultural and historical links between the many provinces were seen to be very tenuous.* ♦ **tenu|ous|ly** *The sub-plots are only tenuously interconnected.* ADJ ≠strong; ADV: ADV with v

**ten|ure** /tenjəʳ/ [1] **Tenure** is the legal right to live in a particular building or to use a particular piece of land during a fixed period of time. ❑ *Lack of security of tenure was a reason for many families becoming homeless.* N-UNCOUNT [2] **Tenure** is the period of time during which someone holds an important job. ❑ *...the three-year tenure of President Bush.* N-UNCOUNT: with supp [3] If you have **tenure** in your job, you have the right to keep it until you retire. N-UNCOUNT

**te|pee** /tiːpiː/ **(tepees)** also **teepee.** A **tepee** is a round tent. Tepees were first made by Native American peoples from animal skins or the outer covering of trees. N-COUNT = wigwam

**tep|id** /tepɪd/ [1] Water or another liquid that is **tepid** is slightly warm. ❑ *She bent her mouth to the tap and drank the tepid water.* ADJ = lukewarm [2] If you describe something such as a feeling or reaction as **tepid**, you mean that it lacks enthusiasm. ❑ *His nomination, while strongly backed by the President, has received tepid support in the Senate.* ADJ = lukewarm

**te|qui|la** /tɪkiːlə/ **(tequilas) Tequila** is a strong alcoholic drink made in Mexico from a type of cactus plant. N-MASS

**ter|cen|te|nary** /tɜːʳsentiːnəri, AM -ten-/ A **tercentenary** is a day or a year which is exactly three hundred years after an important event such as the birth of a famous person. ❑ *...the tercentenary of Purcell's death.* N-SING: oft *the* N *of* n

**term** /tɜːʳm/ **(terms, terming, termed)** ♦♦♦ [1] If you talk about something **in terms of** something or **in** particular **terms**, you are specifying which aspect of it you are discussing or from what point of view you are considering it. ❑ *Our goods compete in terms of product quality, reliability and above all variety... Paris has played a dominant role in France, not just in political terms but also in economic power.* PHRASE: PHR after v, PHR with cl [2] If you say something **in** particular **terms**, you say it using a particular type or level of language or using language which clearly shows your attitude. ❑ *The video explains in simple terms how the new tax works.* PHRASE: usu PHR after v, PHR with cl [3] A **term** is a word or expression with a specific meaning, especially one which is used in relation to a particular subject. ❑ *Myocardial infarction is the medical term for a heart attack.* N-COUNT: usu with supp [4] If you say that something **is termed** a particular thing, you mean that that is what people call it or that is their opinion of it. ❑ *He had been termed a temporary employee... He termed the war a humanitarian nightmare.* VERB *be* V-ed n, V n n [5] A **term** is one of the periods of time that a school, college, or university divides the year into. ❑ *...the summer term. ...the last day of term.* N-VAR [6] A **term** is a period of time between two elections during which a particular party or government is in power. ❑ *Felipe Gonzalez won a fourth term of office in Spain's election.* N-COUNT: with supp [7] A **term** is a period of time that someone spends doing a particular job or in a particular place. ❑ *...a 12 month term of service... Offenders will be liable to a seven-year prison term.* N-COUNT: with supp [8] A **term** is the period for which a legal contract or insurance policy is valid. ❑ *Premiums are guaranteed throughout the term of the policy.* N-COUNT: with supp [9] The **term** of a woman's pregnancy is the nine month period that it lasts. **Term** is also used to refer to the end of the nine month period. ❑ *Women over 40 seem to be just as capable of carrying a baby to term as younger women.* N-UNCOUNT [10] The **terms** of an agreement, treaty, or other arrangement are the conditions that must be accepted by the people involved in it. ❑ *...the terms of the Helsinki agreement.* N-PLURAL: usu with supp

PHRASES [11] If you **come to terms with** something difficult or unpleasant, you learn to accept and deal with it. ❑ *She had come to terms with the fact that her husband would always be crippled.* PHRASE: V inflects, PHR n [12] If two people or groups compete **on equal terms** or **on the same terms**, neither of them has an advantage over the other. ❑ *I had at last found a sport where I could compete on equal terms with able-bodied people.* PHRASE: PHR after v [13] If two people are **on good terms** or **on friendly terms**, they are friendly with each other. ❑ *Madeleine is on good terms with Sarah.* PHRASE: v-link PHR, PHR after v [14] You use the expressions **in the long term, in the short term**, and **in the medium term** to talk about what will happen over a long period of time, over a short period of time, and over a medium period of time. ❑ *The agreement should have very positive results in the long term.* → See also **long-term, medium-term, short-term.** PHRASE: PHR with cl [15] If you do something **on** your **terms**, you do it under conditions that you decide because you are in a position of power. ❑ *They will sign the union treaty only on their terms.* PHRASE: PHR after v [16] If you say that you **are thinking in terms of** doing a particular thing, you mean that you are considering it. ❑ *United should be thinking in terms of winning the European Cup.* PHRASE: V inflects, PHR -ing/n [17] **in no uncertain terms** → see **uncertain. in real terms** → see **real. on speaking terms** → see **speak.**

**ter|mi|nal** /tɜːʳmɪnəl/ **(terminals)** [1] A **terminal** illness or disease causes death, often slowly, and cannot be cured. ❑ *...terminal cancer. ...his illness was terminal.* ♦ **ter|mi|nal|ly** *The patient is terminally ill.* ADJ: usu ADJ n; ADV: ADV adj [2] A **terminal** is a place where vehicles, passengers, or goods begin or end a journey. ❑ *Plans are underway for a fifth terminal at Heathrow airport.* N-COUNT: usu supp N [3] A computer **terminal** is a piece of equipment consisting of a keyboard and a screen that is used for putting information into a computer or getting information from it. [COMPUTING] ❑ *Carl sits at a computer terminal 40 hours a week.* N-COUNT [4] On a piece of electrical equipment, a **terminal** is one of the points where electricity enters or leaves it. ❑ *...the positive terminal of the battery.* N-COUNT

**ter|mi|nate** /tɜːʳmɪneɪt/ **(terminates, terminating, terminated)** [1] When you **terminate** something or when it **terminates**, it ends completely. [FORMAL] ❑ *Her next remark abruptly terminated the conversation... His contract terminates at the end of the season.* ♦ **ter|mi|na|tion** /tɜːʳmɪneɪʃən/ *...a dispute which led to the abrupt termination of trade.* VERB V n, V; N-UNCOUNT [2] To **terminate** a pregnancy means to end it. [MEDICAL] ❑ *After a lot of agonizing she decided to terminate the pregnancy.* ♦ **ter|mi|na|tion (terminations)** *You should also have a medical check-up after the termination of a pregnancy.* VERB V n; N-VAR [3] When a train or bus **terminates** somewhere, it ends its journey there. [FORMAL] ❑ *This train will terminate at Taunton.* VERB V prep/adv

**ter|mi|ni** /tɜːʳmɪnaɪ/ **Termini** is a plural of **terminus.**

**ter|mi|nol|ogy** /tɜːʳmɪnɒlədʒi/ **(terminologies)** The **terminology** of a subject is the set of special words and expressions used in connection with it. ❑ *...gastritis, which in medical terminology means an inflammation of the stomach.* N-VAR: usu with supp

**ter|mi|nus** /tɜːʳmɪnəs/ **(termini)** On a bus or train route, the **terminus** is the last stop, where the bus or train turns round or starts a journey in the opposite direction. N-COUNT

**ter|mite** /tɜːʳmaɪt/ **(termites) Termites** are small white insects which live in hot countries in homes made of earth. Termites do a lot of damage by eating wood. N-COUNT

**term pa|per (term papers)** A **term paper** is an essay or report which a student writes on a subject that he or she has studied during a term at a school, college, or university. [AM] N-COUNT

**terms of ref|er|ence Terms of reference** are the instructions given to someone when they are asked to consider or investigate a particular subject, telling them what they must deal with and what they can ignore. [FORMAL] ❑ *The government has announced the terms of reference for its proposed committee of inquiry.* N-PLURAL

**tern** /tɜːʳn/ **(terns)** A **tern** is a small black and white seabird with long wings and a forked tail. N-COUNT

**ter|race** /terɪs/ **(terraces)** [1] A **terrace** is a row of similar houses joined together by their side walls. [BRIT] ❑ *...a terrace of stylish Victorian houses. ...3 Queensborough Terrace.* N-COUNT; N-IN-NAMES [2] A **terrace** is a flat area of stone or grass next to a building where people can sit. N-COUNT [3] **Terraces** are a series of flat areas built like steps on the side of a hill so that crops can be grown there. ❑ *...massive terraces of maize and millet carved into the mountainside like giant steps.* N-COUNT: usu pl [4] **The terraces** at a football ground are wide steps that people can stand on when they are watching a game. [BRIT] N-PLURAL: the N

**ter|raced** /terɪst/ A **terraced** slope or side of a hill has flat areas like steps cut into it, where crops or other plants can be grown. ADJ: usu ADJ n

**ter|raced house** **(terraced houses)** A **terraced house** or a **terrace house** is one of a row of similar houses joined together by their side walls. [BRIT] → See picture on page 1706. N-COUNT

✓ in AM, use **row house**

**ter|rac|ing** /terəsɪŋ/ **Terracing** is a sloping piece of land that has had flat areas like steps built on it, for example so that people can grow crops there. N-UNCOUNT

**terra|cotta** /terəkɒtə/ also **terra-cotta.** [1] **Terracotta** is a brownish-red clay that has been baked and is used for making things such as flower pots, small statues, and tiles. ❑ *...plants in terracotta pots.* N-UNCOUNT: oft N n [2] **Terracotta** is used to describe things that are brownish-red in colour. ❑ *...the soft tones of blue, cream and terracotta.* COLOUR

**ter|ra fir|ma** /terə fɜːʳmə/ If you describe the ground as **terra firma**, you mean that it feels safe in contrast to being in the air or at sea. ❑ *...his relief on finding himself once more on terra firma.* N-UNCOUNT

**ter|rain** /təreɪn/ **(terrains)** **Terrain** is used to refer to an area of land or a type of land when you are considering its physical features. ❑ *The terrain changed quickly from arable land to desert.* N-VAR: usu with supp

**ter|ra|pin** /terəpɪn/ **(terrapins)** A **terrapin** is a reptile which has a thick shell covering its body and which lives partly in water and partly on land. N-COUNT

**ter|res|trial** /tɪrestriəl/ [1] **Terrestrial** means relating to the planet Earth rather than to some other part of the universe. ❑ *...terrestrial life forms.* ADJ: ADJ n [2] **Terrestrial** television channels are transmitted using equipment situated at ground level, and not by satellite. [BRIT] ADJ: usu ADJ n

**ter|ri|ble** /terɪbᵊl/ ◆◆◇ [1] A **terrible** experience or situation is very serious or very unpleasant. ❑ *Tens of thousands more suffered terrible injuries in the world's worst industrial disaster... I often have the most terrible nightmares.* ADJ = dreadful ♦ **ter|ri|bly** *My son has suffered terribly. He has lost his best friend.* ADV: ADV after v [2] If something is **terrible**, it is very bad or of very poor quality. ❑ *She admits her French is terrible.* ADJ = dreadful [3] You use **terrible** to emphasize the great extent or degree of something. ❑ *I was a terrible fool, you know. I remember that now.* ADJ: ADJ n [emphasis] ♦ **ter|ri|bly** *I'm terribly sorry to bother you at this hour.* ADV: usu ADV adj

**ter|ri|er** /teriəʳ/ **(terriers)** A **terrier** is a small breed of dog. There are many different types of terrier. → See also **bull terrier**, **pit bull terrier**. N-COUNT

**ter|rif|ic** /tərɪfɪk/ [1] If you describe something or someone as **terrific**, you are very pleased with them or very impressed by them. [INFORMAL] ❑ *What a terrific idea!... Everybody there was having a terrific time.* ADJ = great [2] **Terrific** means very great in amount, degree, or intensity. ❑ *All of a sudden there was a terrific bang and a flash of smoke.* ADJ: ADJ n [emphasis] = tremendous ♦ **ter|rifi|cal|ly** /tərɪfɪkli/ *...the only child of terrifically repressed parents.* ADV: usu ADV adj/-ed

**ter|ri|fy** /terɪfaɪ/ **(terrifies, terrifying, terrified)** If something **terrifies** you, it makes you feel extremely frightened. ❑ *Flying terrifies him.* VERB V n

♦ **ter|ri|fied** *He was absolutely terrified of heights... She was terrified that Ronnie would kidnap Sam.* ADJ: oft ADJ of n, ADJ that, ADJ to-inf

**ter|ri|fy|ing** /terɪfaɪɪŋ/ If something is **terrifying**, it makes you very frightened. ❑ *I still find it terrifying to find myself surrounded by horses.* ADJ: oft ADJ to-inf = frightening

**ter|ri|to|rial** /terɪtɔːriəl/ [1] **Territorial** means concerned with the ownership of a particular area of land or water. ❑ *It is the only republic which has no territorial disputes with the others.* ADJ: usu ADJ n [2] If you describe an animal or its behaviour as **territorial**, you mean that it has an area which it regards as its own, and which it defends when other animals try to enter it. ❑ *Two cats or more in one house will also exhibit territorial behaviour.* ADJ

**Ter|ri|to|rial Army** **The Territorial Army** is a British armed force whose members are not professional soldiers but train as soldiers in their spare time. N-PROPER: the N

**ter|ri|to|rial wa|ters** A country's **territorial waters** are the parts of the sea close to its coast which are recognized by international agreement to be under its control, especially with regard to fishing rights. N-PLURAL: usu poss/adj N

**ter|ri|tory** /terətri, AM -tɔːri/ **(territories)** ◆◆◇ [1] **Territory** is land which is controlled by a particular country or ruler. ❑ *The government denies that any of its territory is under rebel control. ...Russian territory.* N-VAR [2] A **territory** is a country or region that is controlled by another country. ❑ *He toured some of the disputed territories now under UN control.* N-COUNT [3] You can use **territory** to refer to an area of knowledge or experience. ❑ *Following the futuristic The Handmaid's Tale, Margaret Atwood's seventh novel, Cat's Eye, returns to more familiar territory.* **virgin territory** → see **virgin**. N-UNCOUNT: with supp = terrain [4] An animal's **territory** is an area which it regards as its own and which it defends when other animals try to enter it. N-VAR: usu with supp [5] **Territory** is land with a particular character. ❑ *...mountainous territory. ...a vast and uninhabited territory.* N-UNCOUNT: with supp, usu adj N [6] If you say that something **comes with the territory**, you mean that you accept it as a natural result of the situation you are in. ❑ *You can't expect not to have a debate; that's what comes with the territory in a democracy.* PHRASE: V inflects

**ter|ror** /terəʳ/ **(terrors)** [1] **Terror** is very great fear. ❑ *I shook with terror whenever I was about to fly in an aeroplane.* N-UNCOUNT [2] **Terror** is violence or the threat of violence, especially when it is used for political reasons. ❑ *The bomb attack on the capital could signal the start of a pre-election terror campaign.* N-UNCOUNT: oft N n [3] A **terror** is something that makes you very frightened. ❑ *As a boy, he had a real terror of facing people. ...the terrors of violence.* N-COUNT [4] If someone describes a child as a **terror**, they think that he or she is naughty and difficult to control. [INFORMAL] ❑ *He was a terror. He had been a difficult child for as long as his parents could remember.* N-COUNT [disapproval] [5] **reign of terror** → see **reign**.

**ter|ror|ise** /terəraɪz/ → see **terrorize**.

**ter|ror|ism** /terərɪzəm/ **Terrorism** is the use of violence, especially murder and bombing, in order to achieve political aims or to force a government to do something. N-UNCOUNT [disapproval]

**ter|ror|ist** /terərɪst/ **(terrorists)** A **terrorist** is a person who uses violence, especially murder and bombing, in order to achieve political aims. ❑ *One American was killed and three were wounded in terrorist attacks.* ◆◇◇ N-COUNT: oft N n [disapproval]

**ter|ror|ize** /terəraɪz/ **(terrorizes, terrorizing, terrorized)**

✓ in BRIT, also use **terrorise**

If someone **terrorizes** you, they keep you in a state of fear by making it seem likely that they will attack you. ❑ *Bands of gunmen have hijacked food shipments and terrorized relief workers.* VERB V n

**ter|ry** /teri/ **Terry** or **terry cloth** is a type of fabric which has a lot of very small loops covering both sides. It is used especially for making things like towels and babies' nappies. ❑ *...a terry nappy.* N-UNCOUNT: usu N n

**terse** /tɜːʳs/ **(terser, tersest)** A **terse** statement or comment is brief and unfriendly. ❑ *He issued a terse statement, saying he is discussing his future with colleagues before announcing his decision on Monday.* ADJ = curt
♦ **terse|ly** *'It's too late,' he said tersely.* ADV: ADV with v

**ter|tiary** /tɜːʳʃəri, AM -ʃieri/ [1] **Tertiary** means third in order, third in importance, or at a third stage of development. [FORMAL] ❑ *He must have come to know those philosophers through secondary or tertiary sources.* ADJ [2] **Tertiary education** is education at university or college level. [BRIT] ❑ *...institutions of tertiary education.* ADJ: ADJ n

☑ in AM, use **higher education**

**ter|tiary sec|tor** **(tertiary sectors)** The **tertiary sector** consists of industries which provide a service, such as transport and finance. [BUSINESS] ❑ *...economies that are slowly increasing the proportion of their labour force in the tertiary sector.* N-COUNT

**TESL** /tesᵊl/ **TESL** is the teaching of English to people who live in an English-speaking country, but whose first language is not English. **TESL** is an abbreviation for 'teaching English as a second language'. N-UNCOUNT

**TESOL** /tiːsɒl/ **TESOL** is the teaching of English to people whose first language is not English. **TESOL** is an abbreviation for 'teaching English to speakers of other languages'. N-UNCOUNT

**test** /test/ **(tests, testing, tested)** ◆◆◆ [1] When you **test** something, you try it, for example by touching it or using it for a short time, in order to find out what it is, what condition it is in, or how well it works. ❑ *The drug must first be tested in clinical trials to see if it works on other cancers.* VERB V n [2] A **test** is a deliberate action or experiment to find out how well something works. ❑ *...the banning of nuclear tests.* N-COUNT [3] If you **test** someone, you ask them questions or tell them to perform certain actions in order to find out how much they know about a subject or how well they are able to do something. ❑ *There was a time when each teacher spent an hour, one day a week, testing pupils in every subject... She decided to test herself with a training run in London.* VERB V n V pron-refl [4] A **test** is a series of questions that you must answer or actions that you must perform in order to show how much you know about a subject or how well you are able to do something. ❑ *Out of a total of 2,602 pupils only 922 passed the test... She had sold her bike, taken a driving test and bought a car.* N-COUNT [5] If you **test** someone, you deliberately make things difficult for them in order to see how they react. ❑ *She may be testing her mother to see how much she can take before she throws her out.* VERB V n [6] If an event or situation is a **test of** a person or thing, it reveals their qualities or effectiveness. ❑ *It is a commonplace fact that holidays are a major test of any relationship.* N-COUNT: usu sing, oft N *of* n [7] If you **are tested for** a particular disease or medical condition, you are examined or go through various procedures in order to find out whether you have that disease or condition. ❑ *My doctor wants me to be tested for diabetes... Girls in an affected family can also be tested to see if they carry the defective gene.* VERB: usu passive *be* V-ed *for* n *be* V-ed [8] A medical **test** is an examination of a part of your body in order to check that you are healthy or to find out what is wrong with you. ❑ *If necessary X-rays and blood tests will also be used to aid diagnosis.* N-COUNT [9] A **test** is a sports match between two international teams, usually in cricket, rugby union, or rugby league. [BRIT] N-COUNT [10] → See also **testing**, **acid test**, **breath test**, **means test**, **litmus test**, **test match**.

**PHRASES** [11] If you **put** something **to the test**, you find out how useful or effective it is by using it. ❑ *The Liverpool team are now putting their theory to the test.* PHRASE: V inflects [12] If new circumstances or events **put** something **to the test**, they put a strain on it and indicate how strong or stable it really is. ❑ *Sooner or later, life will put the relationship to the test.* PHRASE: V inflects [13] If you say that something **will stand the test of time**, you mean that it is strong or effective enough to last for a very long time. ❑ *It says a lot for her culinary skills that so many of her recipes have stood the test of time.* PHRASE: V inflects [14] to **test the waters** → see **water**.

**tes|ta|ment** /testəmənt/ **(testaments)** [1] If one thing is a **testament to** another, it shows that the other thing exists or is true. [FORMAL] ❑ *Braka's house, just off Sloane Square, is a testament to his Gothic tastes.* N-VAR: usu N *to* n = testimony [2] Someone's **last will and testament** is the most recent will that they have made, especially the last will that they make before they die. [LEGAL] PHRASE: Ns inflect, usu with poss [3] → See also **New Testament**, **Old Testament**.

**test bed** **(test beds)** A **test bed** is a piece of equipment used for testing new machines. N-COUNT

**test case** **(test cases)** A **test case** is a legal case which becomes an example for deciding other similar cases. N-COUNT

**test|er** /testəʳ/ **(testers)** [1] A **tester** is a person who has been asked to test a particular thing. N-COUNT [2] A **tester** is a machine or device that you use to test whether another machine or device is working properly. ❑ *I have a battery tester in my garage.* N-COUNT: usu n N

**tes|ti|cle** /testɪkᵊl/ **(testicles)** A man's **testicles** are the two sex glands between his legs that produce sperm. N-COUNT

**tes|ticu|lar** /testɪkjʊləʳ/ **Testicular** means relating to or involving the testicles. ❑ *...testicular cancer.* ADJ: ADJ n

**tes|ti|fy** /testɪfaɪ/ **(testifies, testifying, testified)** [1] When someone **testifies** in a court of law, they give a statement of what they saw someone do or what they know of a situation, after having promised to tell the truth. ❑ *Several eyewitnesses testified that they saw the officers hit Miller in the face... Eva testified to having seen Herndon with his gun on the stairs... He hopes to have his 12-year prison term reduced by testifying against his former colleagues.* VERB V that V *to* -ing/n V *against/for/about* n Also V [2] If one thing **testifies to** another, it supports the belief that the second thing is true. [FORMAL] ❑ *Recent excavations testify to the presence of cultivated inhabitants on the hill during the Arthurian period.* VERB V *to* n

**tes|ti|mo|nial** /testɪmoʊniəl/ **(testimonials)** [1] A **testimonial** is a written statement about a person's character and abilities, often written by their employer. ❑ *She could hardly expect her employer to provide her with testimonials to her character and ability.* N-COUNT = reference [2] A **testimonial** is a sports match which is specially arranged so that part of the profit from the tickets sold can be given to a particular player or to a particular player's family. N-COUNT

**tes|ti|mo|ny** /testɪməni, AM -moʊni/ **(testimonies)** [1] In a court of law, someone's **testimony** is a formal statement that they make about what they saw someone do or what they know of a situation, after having promised to tell the truth. ❑ *His testimony was an important element of the Prosecution case.* N-VAR: oft poss N [2] If you say that one thing is **testimony to** another, you mean that it shows clearly that the second thing has a particular quality. ❑ *This book is testimony to a very individual kind of courage.* N-UNCOUNT: also *a* N, usu N *to* n

**test|ing** /testɪŋ/ ◆◇◇ [1] A **testing** problem or situation is very difficult to deal with and shows a lot about the character of the person who is dealing with it. ❑ *The most testing time is undoubtedly in the early months of your return to work.* ADJ [2] **Testing** is the activity of testing something or someone in order to find out information. ❑ *The National Collegiate Athletic Association introduced drug testing in the mid-1980s.* N-UNCOUNT

**tes|tis** /testɪs/ **(testes** /testiːz/**)** A man's **testes** are his **testicles**. [MEDICAL] N-COUNT: usu pl

**test match** **(test matches)** In cricket and rugby, a **test match** is a one of a series of matches played between teams representing two countries. [BRIT] N-COUNT = test

**tes|tos|ter|one** /testɒstəroʊn/ **Testosterone** is a hormone found in men and male ani- N-UNCOUNT mals, which can also be produced artificially. It is thought to be responsible for the male sexual instinct and other male characteristics.

**test pi|lot** **(test pilots)** A **test pilot** is a pilot who flies aircraft of a new design in order to test their performance. N-COUNT

**test run** **(test runs)** If you give a machine or system a **test run**, you try it out to see if it will work properly when it is actually in use. N-COUNT = *trial run*

**test tube** **(test tubes)** also **test-tube.** A **test tube** is a small tube-shaped container made from glass. Test tubes are used in laboratories. N-COUNT

**test-tube baby** **(test-tube babies)** also **test tube baby.** A **test-tube baby** is a baby that develops from an egg which has been removed from the mother's body, fertilized, and then replaced in her womb in order that it can continue developing. N-COUNT

**tes|ty** /testi/ If you describe someone as **testy**, you mean that they easily become impatient or angry. [mainly LITERARY] ❑ *Ben's getting a little testy in his old age.* ♦ **tes|ti|ly** *He reacted testily to reports that he'd opposed military involvement.* ADJ: usu v-link ADJ; ADV: ADV with v

**teta|nus** /tetənəs/ **Tetanus** is a serious painful disease caused by bacteria getting into wounds. It makes your muscles, especially your jaw muscles, go stiff. N-UNCOUNT

**tetchy** /tetʃi/ **(tetchier, tetchiest)** If you say that someone is **tetchy**, you mean they are bad-tempered and likely to get angry suddenly without an obvious reason. [mainly BRIT, INFORMAL] ❑ *You always get tetchy when you're hungry... He was in a particularly tetchy mood yesterday.* ADJ

**teth|er** /teðəʳ/ **(tethers, tethering, tethered)** 1 If you say that you are **at the end of** your **tether**, you mean that you are so worried, tired, and unhappy because of your problems that you feel you cannot cope. ❑ *She was jealous, humiliated, and emotionally at the end of her tether.* PHRASE: *tether* inflects, usu *at* PHR, v PHR 2 A **tether** is a rope or chain which is used to tie an animal to a post or fence so that it can only move around within a small area. N-COUNT 3 If you **tether** an animal or object **to** something, you attach it there with a rope or chain so that it cannot move very far. ❑ *The officer dismounted, tethering his horse to a tree.* VERB: V n *to* n

**Teu|ton|ic** /tju:tɒnɪk, AM tu:-/ **Teutonic** means typical of or relating to German people. [FORMAL] ❑ *The coach was a masterpiece of Teutonic engineering.* ADJ: usu ADJ n

**Tex-Mex** /teksmeks/ You use **Tex-Mex** to describe things such as food or music that combine typical elements from Mexico and the south-western United States. [AM, INFORMAL] ❑ *...Tex-Mex restaurants.* ADJ: usu ADJ n

**text** /tekst/ **(texts, texting, texted)** ◆◇◇ 1 The **text** of a book is the main part of it, rather than the introduction, pictures, or notes. ❑ *The text is precise and informative.* N-SING: *the* N 2 **Text** is any written material. ❑ *A CD-ROM can store more than 250,000 pages of typed text.* N-UNCOUNT 3 The **text** of a speech, broadcast, or recording is the written version of it. ❑ *A spokesman said a text of Dr Runcie's speech had been circulated to all of the bishops.* N-COUNT: usu sing, usu N *of* n 4 A **text** is a book or other piece of writing, especially one connected with science or learning. ❑ *Her text is believed to be the oldest surviving manuscript by a female physician.* N-COUNT 5 A **text** is a written or spoken passage, especially one that is used in a school or university for discussion or in an examination. ❑ *His early plays are set texts in universities.* N-COUNT 6 A **text** is the same as a **text message**. ❑ *I borrowed my wife's mobile phone last week and a text arrived from another man.* N-COUNT 7 If you **text** someone, you send them a text message on a mobile phone. ❑ *Mary texted me when she got home.* VERB: V n

**text|book** /tekstbʊk/ **(textbooks)** also **text book.** 1 A **textbook** is a book containing facts about a particular subject that is used by people studying that subject. ❑ *...a chemistry textbook.* N-COUNT 2 If you say that something is a **textbook** case or example, you are emphasizing that it provides a clear example of a type of situation or event. ❑ *The house is a textbook example of medieval domestic architecture.* ADJ: ADJ n [emphasis]

**tex|tile** /tekstaɪl/ **(textiles)** 1 **Textiles** are types of cloth or fabric, especially ones that have been woven. ❑ *...the Scottish textile industry.* N-COUNT: usu pl, usu with supp 2 **Textiles** are the industries concerned with the manufacture of cloth. ❑ *Another 75,000 jobs will be lost in textiles and clothing.* N-PLURAL: no det

**text|ing** /tekstɪŋ/ **Texting** is the same as **text messaging**. N-UNCOUNT

**text mes|sage** **(text messages)** A **text message** is a written message that you send using a mobile phone. N-COUNT

**text mes|sag|ing** **Text messaging** is sending written messages using a mobile phone. N-UNCOUNT

**text|phone** /tekstfoʊn/ **(textphones)** A **textphone** is a telephone with a screen and a keyboard, designed for people with hearing problems. N-COUNT

**tex|tu|al** /tekstʃuəl/ **Textual** means relating to written texts, especially literary texts. ❑ *...close textual analysis of Shakespeare.* ADJ: ADJ n

**tex|ture** /tekstʃəʳ/ **(textures)** 1 The **texture** of something is the way that it feels when you touch it, for example how smooth or rough it is. ❑ *Aloe Vera is used in moisturisers to give them a wonderfully silky texture.* N-VAR 2 The **texture** of something, especially food or soil, is its structure, for example whether it is light with lots of holes, or very heavy and solid. ❑ *This cheese has an open, crumbly texture with a strong flavour.* N-VAR

**tex|tured** /tekstʃəʳd/ A **textured** surface is not smooth, but has a particular texture, for example, it feels rough. ❑ *The shoe's sole had a slightly textured surface.* ADJ: usu ADJ n

**-th** /-θ/ You add **-th** to numbers written in figures and ending in 4, 5, 6, 7, 8, 9, 10, 11, 12, or 13 in order to form ordinal numbers. These numbers are pronounced as if they were written as words. For example, 7th is pronounced the same as 'seventh', and 5th is pronounced the same as 'fifth'. ❑ *...Thursday, 10th May, 1990. ...between Broadway and 6th Avenue. ...the 25th amendment to the American constitution.* SUFFIX

**Thai** /taɪ/ **(Thais)** 1 **Thai** means belonging or relating to Thailand, or to its people, language, or culture. ADJ 2 A **Thai** is a citizen of Thailand, or a person of Thai origin. N-COUNT 3 **Thai** is the language spoken in Thailand. N-UNCOUNT

**tha|lido|mide** /θəlɪdəmaɪd/ 1 **Thalidomide** is a drug which used to be given to pregnant women, before it was discovered that it resulted in babies being born with wrongly shaped arms and legs. N-UNCOUNT 2 **Thalidomide** is used to describe someone whose arms and legs are wrongly shaped because their mother took thalidomide when she was pregnant. ❑ *...the special needs of thalidomide children.* ADJ: ADJ n

**than** /ðən, STRONG ðæn/ ◆◆◆ 1 You use **than** after a comparative adjective or adverb in order to link two parts of a comparison. ❑ *The radio only weighs a few ounces and is smaller than a cigarette packet... Indian skins age far more slowly than American or Italian ones.* PREP: compar PREP group ♦ **Than** is also a conjunction. ❑ *He wished he could have helped her more than he did... Sometimes patients are more depressed six months later than when they first hear the bad news.* CONJ: compar CONJ cl 2 You use **than** when you are stating a number, quantity, or value approximately by saying that it is above or below another number, quantity, or value. ❑ *They talked on the phone for more than an hour. ...the three-match Test series in England, starting in less than two months time.* PREP: *more/less* PREP n 3 You use **than** in order to link two parts of a contrast, for example in order to state a preference. ❑ *The arrangement was more a formality than a genuine partnership of two nations.* CONJ 4 **less than** → see **less**. **more than**

→ see **more**. **more often than not** → see **often**. **other than** → see **other**. **rather than** → see **rather**.

**thank** /θæŋk/ **(thanks, thanking, thanked)** ◆◆◆

1 You use **thank you** or, in more informal English, **thanks** to express your gratitude when someone does something for you or gives you what you want. ❑ *Thank you very much for your call... Thanks for the information... Thanks a lot, Suzie. You've been great.* CONVENTION formulae

2 You use **thank you** or, in more informal English, **thanks** to politely accept or refuse something that has just been offered to you. ❑ *'You'd like a cup as well, would you, Mr Secombe?' — 'Thank you, Jane, I'd love one.'... 'Would you like a cigarette?' — 'No thank you.'.* CONVENTION formulae

3 You use **thank you** or, in more informal English, **thanks** to politely acknowledge what someone has said to you, especially when they have answered your question or said something nice to you. ❑ *The policeman smiled at her. 'Pretty dog.' — 'Oh well, thank you.'... 'It's great to see you.' — 'Thanks. Same to you.'* CONVENTION formulae

4 You use **thank you** or **thank you very much** in order to say firmly that you do not want someone's help or to tell them that you do not like the way that they are behaving towards you. ❑ *I can stir my own tea, thank you... We know where we can get it, thank you very much.* CONVENTION emphasis

5 When you **thank** someone **for** something, you express your gratitude to them for it. ❑ *I thanked them for their long and loyal service... When the decision was read out Mrs Gardner thanked the judges.* VERB V n *for* n V n

6 When you express your **thanks** to someone, you express your gratitude to them for something. ❑ *They accepted their certificates with words of thanks.* N-PLURAL

7 → See also **thankyou**.

**PHRASES** 8 You say **'Thank God'**, **'Thank Goodness'**, or **'Thank heavens'** when you are very relieved about something. ❑ *I was wrong, thank God... Thank heavens we have you here.* PHRASE: oft PHR with cl, PHR that feelings

9 If you say that you **have** someone **to thank for** something, you mean that you are grateful to them because they caused it to happen. ❑ *I have her to thank for my life.* PHRASE: V inflects, oft PHR *for* n

10 If you say that something happens **thanks to** a particular person or thing, you mean that they are responsible for it happening or caused it to happen. ❑ *It is thanks to this committee that many new sponsors have come forward.* PHRASE: PHR n, usu PHR with cl, v-link PHR, PHR after v

11 If you say that something happens **no thanks to** a particular person or thing, you mean that they did not help it to happen, or that it happened in spite of them. ❑ *It is no thanks to the Government that net assets did rise.* PHRASE: PHR n, usu PHR with cl, v-link PHR

**thank|ful** /θæŋkfʊl/ When you are **thankful**, you are very happy and relieved that something has happened. ❑ *Most of the time I'm just thankful that I've got a job.* ADJ: usu v-link ADJ, oft ADJ that, ADJ *for* n = *grateful*

**thank|ful|ly** /θæŋkfʊli/ You use **thankfully** in order to express approval or happiness about a statement that you are making. ❑ *Thankfully, she was not injured.* ADV: ADV with cl/group

**thank|less** /θæŋkləs/ If you describe a job or task as **thankless**, you mean that it is hard work and brings very few rewards. ❑ *Soccer referees have a thankless task.* ADJ: usu ADJ n

**thanks|giving** /θæŋksgɪvɪŋ/ **Thanksgiving** is the giving of thanks to God, especially in a religious ceremony. ❑ *The Prince's unexpected recovery was celebrated with a thanksgiving service in St Paul's.* N-UNCOUNT

**Thanks|giving (Thanksgivings)** In the United States, **Thanksgiving** or **Thanksgiving Day** is a public holiday on the fourth Thursday in November. It was originally a day when people celebrated the end of the harvest and thanked God for it. N-VAR

**thank|you** /θæŋkjuː/ **(thankyous)** also **thank-you.** If you refer to something as a **thankyou** for what someone has done for you, you mean that it is intended as a way of thanking them. ❑ *The surprise gift is a thankyou for our help. ...a thank-you note.* → See also **thank**. N-COUNT: oft N n

**that**

① DEMONSTRATIVE USES
② CONJUNCTION AND RELATIVE PRONOUN USES

**① that** /ðæt/ ◆◆◆

⇛ Please look at category 20 to see if the expression you are looking for is shown under another headword.

1 You use **that** to refer back to an idea or situation expressed in a previous sentence or sentences. ❑ *They said you particularly wanted to talk to me. Why was that?... Some members feared Germany might raise its interest rates on Thursday. That could have set the scene for a confrontation with the US.* PRON ♦ **That** is also a determiner. ❑ *The most important purpose of our Health Care is to support you when making a claim for medical treatment. For that reason the claims procedure is as simple and helpful as possible.* DET

2 You use **that** to refer to someone or something already mentioned. ❑ *The Commissioners get between £50,000 and £60,000 a year in various allowances. But that amount can soar to £90,000 a year.* DET

3 When you have been talking about a particular period of time, you use **that** to indicate that you are still referring to the same period. You use expressions such as **that morning** or **that afternoon** to indicate that you are referring to an earlier period of the same day. ❑ *The story was published in a Sunday newspaper later that week.* DET

4 You use **that** in expressions such as **that of** and **that which** to introduce more information about something already mentioned, instead of repeating the noun which refers to it. [FORMAL] ❑ *A recession like that of 1973-74 could put one in ten American companies into bankruptcy.* PRON: PRON *of* n, PRON pron-rel

5 You use **that** in front of words or expressions which express agreement, responses, or reactions to what has just been said. ❑ *'She said she'd met you in England.' — 'That's true.'... 'I've never been to Paris.' — 'That's a pity. You should go one day.'* PRON

6 You use **that** to introduce a person or thing that you are going to give details or information about. [FORMAL] ❑ *In my case I chose that course which I considered right.* DET

7 You use **that** when you are referring to someone or something which is a distance away from you in position or time, especially when you indicate or point to them. When there are two or more things near you, **that** refers to the more distant one. ❑ *Look at that guy. He's got red socks... Where did you get that hat?* DET ♦ **That** is also a pronoun. ❑ *That looks heavy. May I carry it for you?* PRON

8 You use **that** when you are identifying someone or asking about their identity. ❑ *That's my wife you were talking to... I answered the phone and this voice went, 'Hello? Is that Alison?'* PRON

9 You can use **that** when you expect the person you are talking to to know what or who you are referring to, without needing to identify the particular person or thing fully. [SPOKEN] ❑ *Did you get that cheque I sent?* DET ♦ **That** is also a pronoun. ❑ *That was a terrible case of blackmail in the paper today.* PRON

10 If something is **not that** bad, funny, or expensive for example, it is not as bad, funny, or expensive as it might be or as has been suggested. ❑ *Not even Gary, he said, was that stupid.* ADV: with brd-neg, ADV adj/adv

11 You can use **that** to emphasize the degree of a feeling or quality. [INFORMAL] ❑ *I would have walked out, I was that angry.* ADV: ADV adj/adv emphasis = *so*

12 → See also **those**.

**PHRASES** 13 You use **and all that** or **and that** to refer generally to everything else which is associated with what you have just mentioned. [INFORMAL] ❑ *I'm not a cook myself but I am interested in nutrition and that.* PHRASE: cl/group PHR vagueness

14 You use **at that** after a statement which modifies or emphasizes what you have just said. ❑ *Success never seems to come but through hard work, often physically demanding work at that.* PHRASE: n/adj PHR emphasis

15 You use **that is** or **that is to say** to indicate that you are about to express the same idea more clearly or precisely. ❑ *I am a disappointing, though generally dutiful, student. That is, I do as I'm told.* PHRASE: PHR with cl/group

16 You use **that's it** to indicate that PHRASE:

nothing more needs to be done or that the end has been reached. ❑ *When he left the office, that was it, the workday was over.* V inflects

17 You use **that's it** to express agreement with or approval of what has just been said or done. ❑ *'You got married, right?' — 'Yeah, that's it.'* CONVENTION formulae = *exactly*

18 You use **just like that** to emphasize that something happens or is done immediately or in a very simple way, often without much thought or discussion. [INFORMAL] ❑ *Just like that, I was in love.* PHRASE: PHR with cl emphasis

19 You use **that's that** to say there is nothing more you can do or say about a particular matter. [SPOKEN] ❑ *'Well, if that's the way you want it,' he replied, tears in his eyes, 'I guess that's that.'* PHRASE: V inflects

20 **like that** → see **like**. **this and that** → see **this**. **this, that and the other** → see **this**.

② **that** /ðət, STRONG ðæt/ ◆◆◆ 1 You can use **that** after many verbs, adjectives, nouns, and expressions to introduce a clause in which you report what someone has said, or what they think or feel. ❑ *He called her up one day and said that he and his wife were coming to New York... We were worried that she was going to die.* CONJ

2 You use **that** after 'it' and a link verb and an adjective to comment on a situation or fact. ❑ *I've made up my mind, but it's obvious that you need more time to think.* CONJ: *it* v-link adj CONJ cl

3 You use **that** to introduce a clause which gives more information to help identify the person or thing you are talking about. ❑ *...pills that will make the problem disappear. ...a car that won't start.* PRON

4 You use **that** after expressions with 'so' and 'such' in order to introduce the result or effect of something. ❑ *She became so nervous that she shook violently.* CONJ: *so/such* group CONJ cl

**thatch** /θætʃ/ **(thatches)** 1 A **thatch** or a **thatch roof** is a roof made from straw or reeds. ❑ *They would live in a small house with a green door and a new thatch.* N-COUNT

2 **Thatch** is straw or reeds used to make a roof. N-UNCOUNT

3 You can refer to someone's hair as their **thatch of** hair, especially when it is very thick and untidy. ❑ *Teddy ran thick fingers through his unruly thatch of hair.* N-SING: oft N *of* n

**thatched** /θætʃt/ A **thatched** house or a house with a **thatched** roof has a roof made of straw or reeds. → See picture on page 1706. ADJ: usu ADJ n

**thatch|er** /θætʃəʳ/ **(thatchers)** A **thatcher** is a person whose job is making roofs from straw or reeds. N-COUNT

**thatch|ing** /θætʃɪŋ/ 1 **Thatching** is straw or reeds used to make a roof. N-UNCOUNT 2 **Thatching** is the skill or activity of making roofs from straw or reeds. N-UNCOUNT

**that'd** /ðætəd/ **That'd** is a spoken form of 'that would', or of 'that had' when 'had' is an auxiliary verb.

**that'll** /ðætəl/ **That'll** is a spoken form of 'that will'.

**that's** /ðæts/ **That's** is a spoken form of 'that is'.

**thaw** /θɔː/ **(thaws, thawing, thawed)** 1 When ice, snow, or something else that is frozen **thaws**, it melts. ❑ *It's so cold the snow doesn't get a chance to thaw.* VERB V

2 A **thaw** is a period of warmer weather when snow and ice melt, usually at the end of winter. ❑ *We slogged through the mud of an early spring thaw.* N-COUNT

3 When you **thaw** frozen food or when it **thaws**, you leave it in a place where it can reach room temperature so that it is ready for use. ❑ *Always thaw pastry thoroughly... The food in the freezer had thawed during a power cut.* ♦ **Thaw out** means the same as **thaw**. ❑ *Thaw it out completely before reheating in a saucepan... I remember to thaw out the chicken before I leave home.* VERB V n V PHRASAL VERB V n P V P n Also V P

4 If something **thaws** relations between people or if relations **thaw**, they become friendly again after a period of being unfriendly. ❑ *At least this second meeting had helped to thaw the atmosphere... It took up to Christmas for political relations to thaw.* ♦ **Thaw** is also a noun. ❑ *His visit is one of the most striking results of the thaw in relations between East and West.* VERB V n V N-SING

♦ **thaw out** 1 → see **thaw 3**.

**the** ◆◆◆

> **The** is the definite article. It is used at the beginning of noun groups. **The** is usually pronounced /ðə/ before a consonant and /ði/ before a vowel, but pronounced /ðiː/ when you are emphasizing it.

1 You use **the** at the beginning of noun groups to refer to someone or something that you have already mentioned or identified. ❑ *A waiter came and hovered. John caught my look and we both got up and, ignoring the waiter, made our way to the buffet... Six of the 38 people were Russian citizens.* DET

2 You use **the** at the beginning of a noun group when the first noun is followed by an 'of' phrase or a clause which identifies the person or thing. ❑ *There has been a slight increase in the consumption of meat... Of the 9,660 cases processed last year, only 10 per cent were totally rejected.* DET

3 You use **the** in front of some nouns that refer to something in our general experience of the world. ❑ *It's always hard to speculate about the future... Amy sat outside in the sun.* DET

4 You use **the** in front of nouns that refer to people, things, services, or institutions that are associated with everyday life. ❑ *The doctor's on his way... Who was that on the phone?* DET

5 You use **the** instead of a possessive determiner, especially when you are talking about a part of someone's body or a member of their family. ❑ *'How's the family?' — 'Just fine, thank you.'... I patted him on the head.* DET

6 You use **the** in front of a singular noun when you want to make a general statement about things or people of that type. ❑ *An area in which the computer has made considerable strides in recent years is in playing chess... After dogs, the horse has had the closest relationship with man.* DET: DET sing-n

7 You use **the** with the name of a musical instrument when you are talking about someone's ability to play the instrument. ❑ *She was trying to teach him to play the guitar.* DET

8 You use **the** with nationality adjectives and nouns to talk about the people who live in a country. ❑ *The Japanese, Americans, and even the French and Germans, judge economic policies by results.* DET: DET pl-n

9 You use **the** with words such as 'rich', 'poor', 'old', or 'unemployed' to refer to all people of a particular type. ❑ *...care for the elderly and the disabled.* DET: DET pl-n

10 If you want to refer to a whole family or to a married couple, you can make their surname into a plural and use **the** in front of it. ❑ *The Taylors decided that they would employ an architect to do the work.* DET: DET pl-n-proper

11 You use **the** in front of an adjective when you are referring to a particular thing that is described by that adjective. ❑ *He knows he's wishing for the impossible... I thought you might like to read the enclosed.* DET: DET adj/-ed

12 You use **the** to indicate that you have enough of the thing mentioned for a particular purpose. ❑ *She may not have the money to maintain or restore her property... We must have the patience to continue to work until we will find a peaceful solution.* DET: DET n to-inf, DET n *for* n = *sufficient*

13 You use **the** with some titles, place names, and other names. ❑ *The company was alleged to have leaked the news to the Daily Mail. ...the Albert Hall.* DET

14 You use **the** in front of numbers such as first, second, and third. ❑ *The meeting should take place on the fifth of May... Marco Polo is said to have sailed on the Pacific on his way to Java in the thirteenth century.* DET: DET ord

15 You use **the** in front of numbers when they refer to decades. ❑ *It's sometimes hard to imagine how bad things were in the thirties.* DET: DET pl-num

16 You use **the** in front of superlative adjectives and adverbs. ❑ *Brisk daily walks are still the best exercise for young and old alike.* DET: DET superl

17 You use **the** in front of each of two comparative adjectives or adverbs when you are describing how one amount or quality changes in relation to another. ❑ *The longer you have been in shape in the past, the quicker you will regain fitness in future.* DET: DET compar DET compar

18 When you express rates, prices, and measurements, you can use **the** to say how many units apply to each of the items being measured. ❑ *New Japanese cars averaged 13 km to the litre in 1981... Some analysts predicted that the exchange rate would* DET: DET sing-n

*soon be $2 to the pound.* [19] You use **the** to indicate that something or someone is the most famous, important, or best thing of its kind. In spoken English, you put more stress on it, and in written English, you often underline it or write it in capitals or italics. ❑ *Camden Market is the place to be on a Saturday or Sunday.* DET

**thea|tre** /θiːətəʳ/ **(theatres)** ◆◆◇

✔ in AM, use **theater**

[1] A **theatre** is a building with a stage in it, on which plays, shows, and other performances take place. ❑ *I worked at the Grand Theatre.* N-COUNT; N-IN-NAMES [2] You can refer to work in the theatre such as acting or writing plays as **the theatre.** ❑ *You can work in films and the theatre.* N-SING: *the* N [3] **Theatre** is entertainment that involves the performance of plays. N-UNCOUNT [4] A **theater** or a **movie theater** is a place where people go to watch films for entertainment. [AM] N-COUNT

✔ in BRIT, use **cinema**

[5] In a hospital, a **theatre** is a special room where surgeons carry out medical operations. ❑ *She is back from theatre and her condition is comfortable.* N-COUNT: also prep N = *operating theatre* [6] A **theatre of** war or other conflict is the area or region in which the war or conflict is happening. ❑ *The Middle East has often been a theatre of war.* N-COUNT: usu sing, usu N *of* n

**theatre-goer (theatre-goers)**

✔ in AM, use **theatergoer**

**Theatre-goers** are people who are at the theatre to see a play, or who regularly go to the theatre to see plays. N-COUNT

**the|at|ri|cal** /θiætrɪkᵊl/ [1] **Theatrical** means relating to the theatre. ❑ *These are the prizes given for the most outstanding British theatrical performances of the year.* ADJ: ADJ n ♦ **the|at|ri|cal|ly** /θiætrɪkli/ *Shaffer's great gift lies in his ability to animate ideas theatrically.* ADV [2] **Theatrical** behaviour is exaggerated and unnatural, and intended to create an effect. ❑ *In a theatrical gesture Glass clamped his hand over his eyes.* ADJ ♦ **the|at|ri|cal|ly** *He looked theatrically at his watch.* ADV [3] **Theatrical** can be used to describe something that is grand and dramatic, as if it is part of a performance in a theatre. ❑ *There was a theatrical air about the whole scene which had a great appeal for me.* ADJ ♦ **the|at|ri|cal|ly** *...a white hotel theatrically set along a ridge.* ADV

**thee** /ðiː/ **Thee** is an old-fashioned, poetic, or religious word for 'you' when you are talking to only one person. It is used as the object of a verb or preposition. ❑ *I miss thee, beloved father.* PRON: v PRON, prep PRON

**theft** /θeft/ **(thefts) Theft** is the crime of stealing. ❑ *Art theft is now part of organised crime.* N-VAR: oft n N, N *of* n

**their** /ðeəʳ/ ◆◆◆

✔ **Their** is the third person plural possessive determiner.

[1] You use **their** to indicate that something belongs or relates to the group of people, animals, or things that you are talking about. ❑ *Janis and Kurt have announced their engagement... Horses were poking their heads over their stall doors.* DET [2] You use **their** instead of 'his or her' to indicate that something belongs or relates to a person without saying whether that person is a man or a woman. Some people think this use is incorrect. ❑ *Every member will receive their own 'Welcome to Labour' brochure.* DET

**theirs** /ðeəʳz/

✔ **Theirs** is the third person plural possessive pronoun.

[1] You use **theirs** to indicate that something belongs or relates to the group of people, animals, or things that you are talking about. ❑ *There was a big group of a dozen people at the table next to theirs... It would cost about £3000 to install a new heating system in a flat such as theirs.* PRON [2] You use **theirs** instead of 'his or hers' to indicate that something belongs or relates to a person without saying whether that person is a man or a woman. Some people think this use is incorrect. ❑ *He would leave the trailer unlocked. If there was something inside someone wanted, it would be theirs for the taking.* PRON

**them** /ðəm, STRONG ðem/ ◆◆◆

✔ **Them** is a third person plural pronoun. **Them** is used as the object of a verb or preposition.

[1] You use **them** to refer to a group of people, animals, or things. ❑ *Kids these days have no one to tell them what's right and wrong... His dark socks, I could see, had a stripe on them.* PRON: v PRON, prep PRON [2] You use **them** instead of 'him or her' to refer to a person without saying whether that person is a man or a woman. Some people think this use is incorrect. ❑ *It takes great courage to face your child and tell them the truth.* PRON: v PRON, prep PRON [3] In non-standard spoken English, **them** is sometimes used instead of 'those'. ❑ *'Our Billy doesn't eat them ones,' Helen said.* DET

**the|mat|ic** /θiːmætɪk/ **Thematic** means concerned with the subject or theme of something, or with themes and topics in general. [FORMAL] ❑ *...assembling this material into thematic groups.* ADJ: usu ADJ n ♦ **the|mati|cal|ly** /θiːmætɪkli/ *...a thematically-linked threesome of songs.* ADV

**theme** /θiːm/ **(themes)** [1] A **theme** in a piece of writing, a talk, or a discussion is an important idea or subject that runs through it. ❑ *The theme of the conference is renaissance Europe.* ◆◇◇ N-COUNT: usu with supp [2] A **theme** in an artist's work or in a work of literature is an idea in it that the artist or writer develops or repeats. ❑ *The novel's central theme is the perennial conflict between men and women.* N-COUNT: usu with supp [3] A **theme** is a short simple tune on which a piece of music is based. ❑ *...variations on themes from Mozart's The Magic Flute.* N-COUNT [4] **Theme** music or a **theme** song is a piece of music that is played at the beginning and end of a film or of a television or radio programme. ❑ *...the theme from Dr Zhivago.* N-COUNT: usu N n

**themed** /θiːmd/ A **themed** place or event has been created so that it shows a particular historical time or way of life, or tells a well-known story. [mainly BRIT] ❑ *...themed restaurants, bars, and nightclubs.* ADJ: usu ADJ n

**theme park (theme parks)** A **theme park** is a large outdoor area where people pay to go to enjoy themselves. All the different activities in a theme park are usually based on a particular idea or theme. N-COUNT

**theme pub (theme pubs)** A **theme pub** is a pub that has been decorated and furnished in a style that is often based on a particular country or type of activity. [mainly BRIT] ❑ *...Irish theme pubs.* N-COUNT

**them|self** /ðəmself/ **Themself** is sometimes used instead of 'themselves' when it clearly refers to a singular subject. Some people consider this use to be incorrect. ❑ *No one perceived themself to be in a position to hire such a man.* PRON: v PRON, prep PRON

**them|selves** /ðəmselvz/ ◆◆◆

✔ **Themselves** is the third person plural reflexive pronoun.

[1] You use **themselves** to refer to people, animals, or things when the object of a verb or preposition refers to the same people or things as the subject of the verb. ❑ *They all seemed to be enjoying themselves... The men talked amongst themselves.* PRON: v PRON, prep PRON [2] You use **themselves** to emphasize the people or things that you are referring to. **Themselves** is also sometimes used instead of 'them' as the object of a verb or preposition. ❑ *Many mentally ill people are themselves unhappy about the idea of community care.* PRON [emphasis] [3] You use **themselves** instead of 'himself or herself' to refer back to the person who is the subject of sentence without saying whether it is a man or a woman. Some people think this use is incorrect. ❑ *What can a patient with emphysema do to help themselves?* PRON: v PRON, prep PRON [4] You use **themselves** instead of 'himself or herself' to em- PRON [emphasis]

phasize the person you are referring to without saying whether it is a man or a woman. **Themselves** is also sometimes used as the object of a verb or preposition. Some people think this use is incorrect. ❑ *Each student makes only one item themselves.*

**then** /ðen/ ◆◆◆ [1] **Then** means at a particular time in the past or in the future. ❑ *He wanted to have a source of income after his retirement; until then, he wouldn't require additional money... The clinic opened for business last October and since then has treated more than 200 people.* ADV: ADV with cl, oft prep ADV [2] **Then** is used when you refer to something which was true at a particular time in the past but is not true now. ❑ *...the Race Relations Act of 1976 (enacted by the then Labour Government).* ADJ: ADJ n ♦ **Then** is also an adverb. ❑ *Richard Strauss, then 76 years old, suffered through the war years in silence.* ADV: ADV group [3] You use **then** to say that one thing happens after another, or is after another on a list. ❑ *Add the oil and then the scallops to the pan, leaving a little space for the garlic.* ADV: ADV cl/group, ADV before v [4] You use **then** in conversation to indicate that what you are about to say follows logically in some way from what has just been said or implied. ❑ *'I wasn't a very good scholar at school.' — 'What did you like doing best then?'.* ADV: cl/group ADV [5] You use **then** at the end of a topic or at the end of a conversation. ❑ *'I'll talk to you on Friday anyway.' — 'Yep. Okay then.'* ADV: cl/group ADV [6] You use **then** with words like 'now', 'well', and 'okay', to introduce a new topic or a new point of view. ❑ *Now then, you say you walk on the fields out the back?* ADV: adv ADV [7] You use **then** to introduce the second part of a sentence which begins with 'if'. The first part of the sentence describes a possible situation, and **then** introduces the result of the situation. ❑ *If the answer is 'yes', then we must decide on an appropriate course of action.* ADV: ADV cl [8] You use **then** at the beginning of a sentence or after 'and' or 'but' to introduce a comment or an extra piece of information to what you have already said. ❑ *He sounded sincere, but then, he always did.* ADV: ADV cl [9] **now and then** → see **now**. **there and then** → see **there**.

**thence** /ðens/ [1] **Thence** means from a particular place, especially when you are giving directions about how to get somewhere. [FORMAL] ❑ *I ran straight up to Columbia County, then turned East, came down the Harlem Valley and thence home.* ADV: usu ADV adv/prep, also ADV before v [2] **Thence** is used to say that something changes from one state or condition to another. [FORMAL] ❑ *...the conversion of sunlight into heat and thence into electricity.* ADV: usu ADV prep, also ADV before v

**thence|forth** /ðensfɔːʳθ/ **Thenceforth** means starting from a particular time in the past that you have mentioned. [FORMAL] ❑ *My life was totally different thenceforth.* ADV: ADV with cl = *thereafter*

**the|oc|ra|cy** /θiɒkrəsi/ **(theocracies)** A **theocracy** is a society which is ruled by priests who represent a god. [TECHNICAL] N-VAR

**theo|crat|ic** /θiːəkrætɪk/ A **theocratic** society is ruled by priests who represent a god. [TECHNICAL] ADJ: usu ADJ n ≠ *secular*

**theo|lo|gian** /θiːəloʊdʒᵊn/ **(theologians)** A **theologian** is someone who studies the nature of God, religion, and religious beliefs. N-COUNT

**the|ol|ogy** /θiɒlədʒi/ **Theology** is the study of the nature of God and of religion and religious beliefs. ❑ *...questions of theology.* N-UNCOUNT ♦ **theo|logi|cal** /θiːəlɒdʒɪkᵊl/ *...theological books.* ADJ: usu ADJ n

**theo|rem** /θiːərəm/ **(theorems)** A **theorem** is a statement in mathematics or logic that can be proved to be true by reasoning. N-COUNT

**theo|reti|cal** /θiːəretɪkᵊl/ [1] A **theoretical** study or explanation is based on or uses the ideas and abstract principles that relate to a particular subject, rather than the practical aspects or uses of it. ❑ *...theoretical physics.* ADJ: usu ADJ n [2] If you describe a situation as a **theoretical** one, you mean that although it is supposed to be true or to exist in the way stated, it may not in fact be true or exist in that way. ❑ *This is certainly a theoretical risk but in practice there is seldom a problem.* ADJ: usu ADJ n

**theo|reti|cal|ly** /θiːəretɪkəli/ You use **theoretically** to say that although something is supposed to be true or to happen in the way stated, it may not in fact be true or happen in that way. ❑ *Theoretically, the price is supposed to be marked on the shelf.* ADV: ADV with cl/group

**theo|reti|cian** /θɪərətɪʃᵊn/ **(theoreticians)** A **theoretician** is the same as a **theorist**. N-COUNT

**theo|rist** /θiːərɪst/ **(theorists)** A **theorist** is someone who develops an abstract idea or set of ideas about a particular subject in order to explain it. N-COUNT

**theo|rize** /θiːəraɪz/ **(theorizes, theorizing, theorized)**

> ✔ in BRIT, also use **theorise**

If you **theorize** that something is true or **theorize** about it, you develop an abstract idea or set of ideas about something in order to explain it. ❑ *Police are theorizing that the killers may be posing as hitchhikers... By studying the way people behave, we can theorize about what is going on in their mind.* VERB V that V *about* n Also V ♦ **theo|riz|ing** *This was no time for theorizing.* N-UNCOUNT

**theo|ry** /θɪəri/ **(theories)** ◆◆◇ [1] A **theory** is a formal idea or set of ideas that is intended to explain something. ❑ *Einstein formulated the Theory of Relativity in 1905.* N-VAR: usu with supp [2] If you have a **theory** about something, you have your own opinion about it which you cannot prove but which you think is true. ❑ *There was a theory that he wanted to marry her.* N-COUNT [3] The **theory** of a practical subject or skill is the set of rules and principles that form the basis of it. ❑ *He taught us music theory.* N-UNCOUNT: usu with supp, supp N, N *of* n [4] You use **in theory** to say that although something is supposed to be true or to happen in the way stated, it may not in fact be true or happen in that way. ❑ *A school dental service exists in theory, but in practice, there are few dentists to work in them.* PHRASE: PHR with cl = *theoretically*

**thera|peu|tic** /θerəpjuːtɪk/ [1] If something is **therapeutic**, it helps you to relax or to feel better about things, especially about a situation that made you unhappy. ❑ *Astanga Yoga is a therapeutic physical exercise that focuses on breathing and relaxation.* ADJ [2] **Therapeutic** treatment is designed to treat an illness or to improve a person's health, rather than to prevent an illness. [MEDICAL] ❑ *...therapeutic drugs.* ADJ: usu ADJ n

**thera|pist** /θerəpɪst/ **(therapists)** A **therapist** is a person who is skilled in a particular type of therapy. N-COUNT: usu supp N

**thera|py** /θerəpi/ **(therapies)** ◆◇◇ [1] **Therapy** is the treatment of someone with mental or physical illness without the use of drugs or operations. ❑ *He is having therapy to conquer his phobia.* N-UNCOUNT [2] A **therapy** is a particular treatment of someone with a particular illness. [MEDICAL] ❑ *...hormonal therapies. ...conventional drug therapy.* N-VAR: with supp

**there** ◆◆◆

> ✔ Pronounced /ðəʳ/, STRONG ðeəʳ/ for meanings 1 and 2, and /ðeəʳ/ for meanings 3 to 20.

[1] **There** is used as the subject of the verb 'be' to say that something exists or does not exist, or to draw attention to it. ❑ *There are roadworks between Camblesforth and Carlton... Are there some countries that have been able to tackle these problems successfully?... There were differences of opinion, he added, on very basic issues.* PRON: PRON *be* n [2] You use **there** in front of certain verbs when you are saying that something exists, develops, or can be seen. Whether the verb is singular or plural depends on the noun which follows the verb. ❑ *There remains considerable doubt over when the intended high-speed rail link will be complete... There appeared no imminent danger.* PRON: PRON v n [3] **There** is used after 'hello' or 'hi' when you are greeting someone. ❑ *Oh, hi there. You must be Sidney.* CONVENTION [4] If something is **there**, it exists or is available. ❑ *The group of old buildings on the corner* ADV: *be* ADV, oft ADV *for*

*by the main road is still there today... The book is there for people to read and make up their own mind.* n, ADV to-inf

5 You use **there** to refer to a place which has already been mentioned. ❑ *The next day we drove the 33 miles to Siena (the Villa Arceno is a great place to stay while you are there) for the Palio... 'Come on over, if you want.' — 'How do I get there?'... It's one hell of a train trip, about five days there and back.* ADV: be ADV, ADV with v, n ADV, oft prep ADV

6 You use **there** to indicate a place that you are pointing to or looking at, in order to draw someone's attention to it. ❑ *There it is, on the corner over there... There she is on the left up there... The toilets are over there, dear.* ADV: ADV with be, ADV after v, oft prep ADV

7 You use **there** in expressions such as **'there he was'** or **'there we were'** to sum up part of a story or to slow a story down for dramatic effect. [SPOKEN] ❑ *So there we were with Amy and she was driving us crazy.* ADV: ADV cl

8 You use **there** when speaking on the telephone to ask if someone is available to speak to you. ❑ *Hello, is Gordon there please?* ADV: ADV with be

9 You use **there** to refer to a point that someone has made in a conversation. ❑ *I think you're right there John.* ADV: ADV after v

10 You use **there** to refer to a stage that has been reached in an activity or process. ❑ *We are making further investigations and will take the matter from there.* ADV: ADV with cl, oft prep ADV

11 You use **there** to indicate that something has reached a point or level which is completely successful. ❑ *We had hoped to fill the back page with extra news; we're not quite there yet... Life has not yet returned to normal but we are getting there.* ADV: be ADV, ADV after v

12 You can use **there** in expressions such as **there you go** or **there we are** when accepting that an unsatisfactory situation cannot be changed. [SPOKEN] ❑ *I'm the oldest and, according to all the books, should be the achiever, but there you go.* ADV: ADV cl

13 You can use **there** in expressions such as **there you go** and **there we are** when emphasizing that something proves that you were right. [SPOKEN] ❑ *You see? There you go. That's why I didn't mention it earlier. I knew you'd take it the wrong way.* ADV: ADV cl [emphasis]

**PHRASES** 14 You use **there again** to introduce an extra piece of information which either contradicts what has been said or gives an alternative to it. ❑ *At 18 stone, I can't run around the way I used to. There again, some people say I never did.* PHRASE: PHR cl

15 Phrases such as **there** you **go again** are used to show annoyance at someone who is repeating something that has annoyed you in the past. [SPOKEN] ❑ *'There you go again, upsetting the child!' said Shirley.* PHRASE: V inflects

16 You can add **'so there'** to what you are saying to show that you will not change your mind about a decision you have made, even though the person you are talking to disagrees with you. [INFORMAL] ❑ *I think that's sweet, so there.* PHRASE: cl PHR

17 If something happens **there and then** or **then and there**, it happens immediately. ❑ *Many felt that he should have resigned there and then.* PHRASE: PHR after v, PHR with cl

18 You say **'there there'** to someone who is very upset, especially a small child, in order to comfort them. [SPOKEN] ❑ *'There, there,' said Mum. 'You've been having a really bad dream.'* CONVENTION

19 You say **'there you are'** or **'there you go'** when you are offering something to someone. [SPOKEN] ❑ *Nora picked up the boy, and gave him a biscuit. 'There you are, Lennie, you take the nice biscuit.'* CONVENTION [formulae]

20 If someone **is there for** you, they help and support you, especially when you have problems. [INFORMAL] ❑ *Despite what happened in the past I want her to know I am there for her.* PHRASE: V inflects

**there|abouts** /ðeərəbaʊts/ You add **or thereabouts** after a number or date to indicate that it is approximate. ❑ *He told us that her age was forty-eight or thereabouts.* PHRASE: n/num PHR

**there|after** /ðeərɑːftəʳ, -æftəʳ/ **Thereafter** means after the event or date mentioned. [FORMAL] ❑ *It was the only time she had ever discouraged him from dangerous activities and she regretted it thereafter.* ADV: ADV with cl = *subsequently*

**there|by** /ðeəʳbaɪ/ You use **thereby** to introduce an important result or consequence of the event or action you have just mentioned. [FORMAL] ❑ *Our bodies can sweat, thereby losing heat by evaporation.* ADV: ADV with cl = *thus*

**there|fore** /ðeəʳfɔːʳ/ You use **therefore** to introduce a logical result or conclusion. ❑ *Muscle cells need lots of fuel and therefore burn lots of calories.* ◆◆◇ ADV: ADV with cl/group = *thus*

**there|in** /ðeərɪn/ 1 **Therein** means contained in the place that has been mentioned. [FORMAL] ❑ *By burning tree branches, pine needles, and pine cones, many not only warm their houses but improve the smell therein.* ADV: n ADV

2 **Therein** means relating to something that has just been mentioned. [FORMAL] ❑ *Afternoon groups relate to the specific addictions and problems therein.* ADV: n ADV

3 When you say **therein lies** a situation or problem, you mean that an existing situation has caused that situation or problem. [FORMAL or OLD-FASHIONED] ❑ *Santa Maria di Castellabate is barely mentioned in guidebooks; therein lies its charm.* PHRASE: V inflects, PHR n

**there|of** /ðeərɒv/ **Thereof** is used after a noun to relate that noun to a situation or thing that you have just mentioned. [FORMAL] ❑ *...his belief in God – or the lack thereof.* ADV: n ADV

**there|on** /ðeərɒn/ 1 **Thereon** means on the object or surface just mentioned. [FORMAL] ❑ *There was a card on each door with a guest's name inscribed thereon.* ADV: ADV after v

2 **Thereon** can be used to refer back to a thing that has previously been mentioned to show that the word just used relates to that thing. [FORMAL] ❑ *You will, in addition, pay to the Bank any losses, costs, expenses or legal fees (including VAT thereon).* ADV: n ADV, ADV after v

**there|upon** /ðeərəpɒn/ **Thereupon** means happening immediately after something else has happened and usually as a result of it. [FORMAL] ❑ *Some months ago angry demonstrators mounted a noisy demonstration beneath his window. His neighbours thereupon insisted upon more security.* ADV: ADV with cl

**therm** /θɜːʳm/ **(therms)** A **therm** is a measurement of heat. N-COUNT: num N

**ther|mal** /θɜːʳməl/ **(thermals)** 1 **Thermal** means relating to or caused by heat or by changes in temperature. ❑ *...thermal power stations.* ADJ: ADJ n

2 **Thermal** streams or baths contain water which is naturally hot or warm. ❑ *Volcanic activity has created thermal springs and boiling mud pools.* ADJ: ADJ n

3 **Thermal** clothes are specially designed to keep you warm in cold weather. ❑ *My feet were like blocks of ice despite the thermal socks.* ADJ: ADJ n ♦ **Thermals** are thermal clothes. ❑ *Have you got your thermals on?* N-PLURAL

4 A **thermal** is a movement of rising warm air. ❑ *Birds use thermals to lift them through the air.* N-COUNT

**ther|mo** /θɜːʳmoʊ/ **Thermo** means using or relating to heat. ❑ *The main thermo power station in the area has been damaged.* ADJ: ADJ n ♦ **Thermo** is also a combining form. ❑ *...the dangers of thermo-nuclear war.* COMB in ADJ ♦ **Thermo** also combines to form nouns. ❑ *The body is made of mineral-reinforced thermoplastic.* COMB in NOUNS

**ther|mo|dy|nam|ics** /θɜːʳmoʊdaɪnæmɪks/

> ✓ The form **thermodynamic** is used as a modifier.

**Thermodynamics** is the branch of physics that is concerned with the relationship between heat and other forms of energy. N-UNCOUNT

**ther|mom|eter** /θəʳmɒmɪtəʳ/ **(thermometers)** A **thermometer** is an instrument for measuring temperature. It usually consists of a narrow glass tube containing a thin column of a liquid which rises and falls as the temperature rises and falls. N-COUNT

**ther|mo|nu|clear** /θɜːʳmoʊnjuːkliəʳ, AM -nuːk-/ also **thermo-nuclear.** A **thermonuclear** weapon or device is one which uses the high temperatures that result from a nuclear reaction in order to cause it to explode. ADJ: ADJ n

**ther|mo|plas|tic** /θɜːʳmoʊplæstɪk/ **(thermoplastics)** **Thermoplastic** materials are types of plastic which becomes soft when they are heated and hard when they cool down. N-COUNT: usu N n

**Ther|mos** /θɜːʳmɒs/ **(Thermoses)** A **Thermos**, **Thermos flask**, or in American English **Thermos bottle**, is a container which is used to keep hot drinks hot or cold drinks cold. It has two thin shiny glass walls with no air between them. [TRADEMARK] N-COUNT = *vacuum flask, flask*

**ther|mo|stat** /θɜːʳməstæt/ **(thermostats)** A **thermostat** is a device that switches a system or motor on or off according to the temperature. Thermostats are used, for example, in central heating systems and fridges. N-COUNT

**the|sau|rus** /θɪsɔːrəs/ **(thesauruses)** A **thesaurus** is a reference book in which words with similar meanings are grouped together. N-COUNT

**these** ◆◆◆

> The determiner is pronounced /ðiːz/. The pronoun is pronounced /ðiːz/.

1 You use **these** at the beginning of noun groups to refer to someone or something that you have already mentioned or identified. ❑ *Switch to an interest-paying current account and stay in credit. Most banks and larger building societies now offer these accounts... A steering committee has been formed. These people can make decisions in ten minutes which would usually take us months.* DET: DET pl-n ♦ **These** is also a pronoun. ❑ *AIDS kills mostly the young population of a nation. These are the people who contribute most to a country's economic development.* PRON 2 You use **these** to introduce people or things that you are going to talk about. ❑ *Your camcorder should have these basic features: autofocus, playback facility, zoom lens.* DET: DET pl-n ♦ **These** is also a pronoun. ❑ *Look after yourself properly while you are pregnant. These are some of the things you can do for yourself.* PRON 3 In spoken English, people use **these** to introduce people or things into a story. ❑ *I was on my own and these fellows came along towards me.* DET: DET pl-n 4 You use **these** when you are identifying someone or asking about their identity. ❑ *These are my children.* PRON 5 You use **these** to refer to people or things that are near you, especially when you touch them or point to them. ❑ *These scissors are awfully heavy.* DET: DET pl-n ♦ **These** is also a pronoun. ❑ *These are the people who are doing our loft conversion for us.* PRON 6 You use **these** when you refer to something which you expect the person you are talking to to know about, or when you are checking that you are both thinking of the same person or thing. ❑ *You know these last few months when we've been expecting it to warm up a little bit?* DET: DET pl-n 7 You use **these** in the expression **these days** to mean 'at the present time'. ❑ *Living in Bootham these days can be depressing.* DET: DET pl-n

**the|sis** /θiːsɪs/ **(theses** /θiːsiːz/**)** 1 A **thesis** is an idea or theory that is expressed as a statement and is discussed in a logical way. ❑ *This thesis does not stand up to close inspection.* N-COUNT = *argument* 2 A **thesis** is a long piece of writing based on your own ideas and research that you do as part of a university degree, especially a higher degree such as a PhD. N-COUNT

**thes|pian** /θespiən/ **(thespians)** 1 A **thespian** is an actor or actress. [HUMOROUS or OLD-FASHIONED] N-COUNT 2 **Thespian** means relating to drama and the theatre. [OLD-FASHIONED] ADJ: ADJ n

**they** /ðeɪ/ ◆◆◆

> **They** is a third person plural pronoun. **They** is used as the subject of a verb.

1 You use **they** to refer to a group of people, animals, or things. ❑ *The two men were far more alike than they would ever admit... People matter because of what they are, not what they have.* PRON 2 You use **they** instead of 'he or she' to refer to a person without saying whether that person is a man or a woman. Some people think this use is incorrect. ❑ *The teacher is not responsible for the student's success or failure. They are only there to help the student learn.* PRON 3 You use **they** in expressions such as 'they say' or 'they call it' to refer to people in general when you are making general statements about what people say, think, or do. ❑ *They say there's plenty of opportunities out there, you just have to look carefully and you'll find them.* PRON [vagueness]

**they'd** /ðeɪd/ 1 **They'd** is a spoken form of 'they had', especially when 'had' is an auxiliary verb. ❑ *They'd both lived in this road all their lives.* 2 **They'd** is a spoken form of 'they would'. ❑ *He agreed that they'd visit her after they stopped at Jan's for coffee.*

**they'll** /ðeɪəl/ **They'll** is the usual spoken form of 'they will'. ❑ *They'll probably be here Monday and Tuesday.*

**they're** /ðeəʳ, ðeɪəʳ/ **They're** is the usual spoken form of 'they are'. ❑ *People eat when they're depressed.*

**they've** /ðeɪv/ **They've** is the usual spoken form of 'they have', especially when 'have' is an auxiliary verb. ❑ *The worst thing is when you call friends and they've gone out.*

**thick** /θɪk/ **(thicker, thickest)** ◆◇◇ 1 Something that is **thick** has a large distance between its two opposite sides. ❑ *For breakfast I had a thick slice of bread and syrup... This material is very thick and this needle doesn't go through it.* ADJ ≠ *thin* ♦ **thick|ly** *Slice the meat thickly.* ADV: ADV with v 2 You can use **thick** to talk or ask about how wide or deep something is. ❑ *The folder was two inches thick... How thick are these walls?* ADJ: n ADJ, *how* ADJ, amount ADJ, *as* ADJ *as* ♦ **Thick** is also a combining form. ❑ *His life was saved by a quarter-inch-thick bullet-proof steel screen.* COMB in ADJ: ADJ n ♦ **thick|ness (thicknesses)** *The size of the fish will determine the thickness of the steaks. ...a layer of gases about 200 miles in thickness.* N-VAR: oft N *of* n, N *of* amount, amount *in* N 3 If something that consists of several things is **thick**, it has a large number of them very close together. ❑ *She inherited our father's thick, wavy hair... They walked through thick forest.* ADJ = *dense* ♦ **thick|ly** *I rounded a bend where the trees and brush grew thickly.* ADV: ADV -ed, ADV after v 4 If something is **thick with** another thing, the first thing is full of or covered with the second. ❑ *The air is thick with acrid smoke from the fires.* ADJ: v-link ADJ *with* n 5 **Thick** clothes are made from heavy cloth, so that they will keep you warm in cold weather. ❑ *In the winter she wears thick socks, Wellington boots and gloves.* ADJ ≠ *thin* 6 **Thick** smoke, fog, or cloud is difficult to see through. ❑ *The smoke was bluish-black and thick.* ADJ 7 **Thick** liquids are fairly stiff and solid and do not flow easily. ❑ *They had to battle through thick mud to reach construction workers.* ADJ 8 If someone's voice is **thick**, they are not speaking clearly, for example because they are ill, upset, or drunk. ❑ *When he spoke his voice was thick with bitterness.* ADJ: usu v-link ADJ ♦ **thick|ly** *'It's all my fault,' he mumbled thickly.* ADV: ADV after v 9 A **thick** accent is very obvious and easy to identify. ❑ *He answered our questions in English but with a thick accent.* ADJ: usu ADJ n = *strong* 10 If you describe someone as **thick**, you think they are stupid. [BRIT, INFORMAL] ❑ *How could she have been so thick?* ADJ: usu v-link ADJ [disapproval] = *stupid*

PHRASES 11 If things happen **thick and fast**, they happen very quickly and in large numbers. ❑ *The rumours have been coming thick and fast.* PHRASE: PHR after v 12 If you are **in the thick of** an activity or situation, you are very involved in it. ❑ *I enjoy being in the thick of things.* PHRASE: PHR n, usu v-link PHR, PHR after v 13 If you do something **through thick and thin**, you do it although the conditions or circumstances are very bad. ❑ *She'd stuck by Bob through thick and thin.* PHRASE: PHR after v 14 **a thick skin** → see **skin**.

**thick|en** /θɪkən/ **(thickens, thickening, thickened)** 1 When you **thicken** a liquid or when it **thickens**, it becomes stiffer and more solid. ❑ *Thicken the broth with the cornflour... Keep stirring until the sauce thickens.* VERB V n V 2 If something **thickens**, it becomes more closely grouped together or more solid than it was before. ❑ *The crowds around him began to thicken.* VERB V 3 People sometimes say **'the plot thickens'** when a situation or series of events is getting more and more complicated and mysterious. ❑ *'Find anything?' he asked. 'Yeah. The plot thickens,' I said.* PHRASE: V inflects

**thick|en|er** /θɪkənəʳ/ **(thickeners)** A **thickener** is a substance that is added to a liquid in order N-MASS to make it stiffer and more solid. ❑ *...cornstarch, used as a thickener... How much thickener is used?*

**thick|et** /θɪkɪt/ **(thickets)** A **thicket** is a small group of trees or bushes which are growing closely together. N-COUNT

**thick|set** /θɪkset/ also **thick-set.** A man who is **thickset** is broad and heavy, with a solid-looking body. ❑ *He was of middle height, thick-set. ...his stout, thickset figure.* ADJ = stocky

**thick-skinned** If you say that someone is **thick-skinned**, you mean that they are not easily upset by criticism or unpleasantness. ❑ *He was thick-skinned enough to cope with her taunts.* ADJ: usu v-link ADJ ≠ thin-skinned

**thief** /θiːf/ **(thieves** /θiːvz/**)** A **thief** is a person who steals something from another person. ❑ *The thieves snatched the camera. ...car thieves.* N-COUNT

**thiev|ing** /θiːvɪŋ/ 1 **Thieving** is the act of stealing things from people. [OLD-FASHIONED] ❑ *...an ex-con who says he's given up thieving.* N-UNCOUNT 2 **Thieving** means involved in stealing things or intending to steal something. ❑ *He vowed to wreak vengeance on his unfaithful, thieving wife.* ADJ: ADJ n

**thigh** /θaɪ/ **(thighs)** Your **thighs** are the top parts of your legs, between your knees and your hips. N-COUNT

**thim|ble** /θɪmbᵊl/ **(thimbles)** A **thimble** is a small metal or plastic object which you use to protect your finger when you are sewing. N-COUNT

**thin** /θɪn/ **(thinner, thinnest, thins, thinning, thinned)** ◆◇◇ 1 Something that is **thin** is much narrower than it is long. ❑ *A thin cable carries the signal to a computer... James's face was thin, finely boned, and sensitive.* ADJ 2 A person or animal that is **thin** has no extra fat on their body . ❑ *He was a tall, thin man with grey hair.* ADJ ≠ fat ♦ **thin|ness** *There was something familiar about him, his fawn raincoat, his thinness, the way he moved.* N-UNCOUNT 3 Something such as paper or cloth that is **thin** is flat and has only a very small distance between its two opposite surfaces. ❑ *...a small, blue-bound book printed in fine type on thin paper.* ADJ ≠ thick ♦ **thin|ly** *Peel and thinly slice the onion.* ADV: ADV with v 4 Liquids that are **thin** are weak and watery. ❑ *The soup was thin and clear, yet mysteriously rich.* ADJ ≠ thick 5 A crowd or audience that is **thin** does not have many people in it. ❑ *The crowd, which had been thin for the first half of the race, had now grown considerably.* ADJ ♦ **thin|ly** *The island is thinly populated.* ADV: ADV -ed 6 **Thin** clothes are made from light cloth and are not warm to wear. ❑ *Her gown was thin, and she shivered, partly from cold.* ADJ ≠ thick ♦ **thin|ly** *Mrs Brown wrapped the thinly clad man in her fur coat.* ADV: ADV adj/-ed 7 If you describe an argument or explanation as **thin**, you mean that it is weak and difficult to believe. ❑ *However, the evidence is thin and, to some extent, ambiguous.* ADJ = weak ≠ strong ♦ **thin|ly** *Much of the speech was a thinly disguised attack on the management of the company.* ADV: usu ADV -ed, also ADV before v 8 If someone's hair is described as **thin**, they do not have a lot of hair. ❑ *She had pale thin yellow hair she pulled back into a bun.* ADJ ≠ thick 9 When you **thin** something or when it **thins**, it becomes less crowded because people or things have been removed from it. ❑ *It would have been better to have thinned the trees over several winters rather than all at one time... By midnight the crowd had thinned.* VERB V n V ♦ **Thin out** means the same as **thin**. ❑ *NATO will continue to thin out its forces... When the crowd began to thin out, I realized that most of the food was still there.* PHRASAL VERB V P n (not pron) V P 10 To **thin** a sauce or liquid means to make it weaker and more watery by adding another liquid to it. ❑ *It may be necessary to thin the sauce slightly.* VERB V n ♦ **Thin down** means the same as **thin**. ❑ *Thin down your mayonnaise with soured cream.* PHRASAL VERB V P n (not pron) 11 If a man's hair **is thinning**, it has begun to fall out. ❑ *His hair is thinning and his skin has lost all hint of youth.* VERB V **thin on top** → see **top**. 12 If someone's patience, for example, **is wearing thin**, they are beginning to become impatient or angry with someone. ❑ *Parliament has not yet begun to combat the deepening economic crisis, and public patience is wearing thin.* PHRASE 13 **on thin ice** → see **ice**. **thin air** → see **air**.

♦ **thin down** → see **thin 10**.

♦ **thin out** → see **thin 9**.

**thine** /ðaɪn/ **Thine** is an old-fashioned, poetic, or religious word for 'yours' when you are talking to only one person. ❑ *I am Thine, O Lord, I have heard Thy voice.* PRON

**thing** /θɪŋ/ **(things)** ◆◆◆ 1 You can use **thing** to refer to any object, feature, or event when you cannot, need not, or do not want to refer to it more precisely. ❑ *'What's that thing in the middle of the fountain?' — 'Some kind of statue, I guess.'... She was in the middle of clearing the breakfast things... If you could change one thing about yourself, what would it be?... A strange thing happened.* N-COUNT: usu with supp 2 **Thing** is used in lists and descriptions to give examples or to increase the range of what you are referring to. ❑ *These are genetic disorders that only affect males normally. They are things like muscular dystrophy and haemophilia... The Earth is made mainly of iron and silicon and things like that.* N-COUNT: usu pl, usu with supp 3 **Thing** is often used after an adjective, where it would also be possible just to use the adjective. For example, you can say **it's a different thing** instead of **it's different**. ❑ *To be a parent is a terribly difficult thing.* N-COUNT: adj N 4 **Thing** is often used instead of the pronouns 'anything,' or 'everything' in order to emphasize what you are saying. ❑ *It isn't going to solve a single thing... Don't you worry about a thing.* N-SING: oft with brd-neg [emphasis] 5 **Thing** is used in expressions such as **such a thing** or **things like that**, especially in negative statements, in order to emphasize the bad or difficult situation you are referring back to. ❑ *I don't believe he would tell Leo such a thing.* N-COUNT: usu with brd-neg, with supp [emphasis] 6 You can use **thing** to refer in a vague way to a situation, activity, or idea, especially when you want to suggest that it is not very important. [INFORMAL] ❑ *I'm a bit unsettled tonight. This war thing's upsetting me.* N-COUNT: supp N, usu n N [vagueness] 7 You often use **thing** to indicate to the person you are addressing that you are about to mention something important, or something that you particularly want them to know. ❑ *One thing I am sure of was that she was scared... The funny thing is that the rest of us have known that for years.* N-COUNT: with supp, oft adj N 8 **Thing** is often used to refer back to something that has just been mentioned, either to emphasize it or to give more information about it. ❑ *I never wanted to be normal. It was not a thing I ever thought desirable.* N-COUNT 9 A **thing** is a physical object that is considered as having no life of its own. ❑ *It's not a thing, Beauchamp. It's a human being!* N-COUNT 10 **Thing** is used to refer to something, especially a physical object, when you want to express contempt or anger towards it. [SPOKEN] ❑ *Turn that thing off!* N-COUNT [disapproval] 11 You can call a person or an animal a particular **thing** when you want to mention a particular quality that they have and express your feelings towards them, usually affectionate feelings. [INFORMAL] ❑ *You really are quite a clever little thing.* N-COUNT: adj N 12 Your **things** are your clothes or possessions. ❑ *Sara told him to take all his things and not to return.* N-PLURAL: poss N 13 **Things** can refer to the situation or life in general and the way it is changing or affecting you. ❑ *Everyone agrees things are getting better.* N-PLURAL 14 If you say that something is **the thing**, you mean that it is fashionable or popular. ❑ *I feel under pressure to go out and get drunk because it's the thing to do.* N-SING: the N, oft N to-inf

**PHRASES** 15 If, for example, you **do the** right **thing** or **do the** decent **thing** in a situation, you do something which is considered correct or socially acceptable in that situation. ❑ *People want to do the right thing and buy 'green'... Carrington did the honourable thing and resigned.* PHRASE: V inflects 16 If you say that something is **the done thing**, you mean it is the most socially acceptable way to behave. [BRIT] ❑ *It was not the done thing. In those days the man was supposed to be the provider.* PHRASE: oft with brd-neg, v-link PHR 17 If you do something **first thing**, you do it at the beginning of the day, before you do anything else. If you do it **last thing**, you do it at the end of the day, before you go to bed or go to sleep. ❑ *I'll go see her, first* PHRASE: PHR after v, PHR with cl, oft PHR prep thing... *I always do it last thing on a Saturday.* 18 If you **have a thing about** someone or something, you have very strong feelings about them. [INFORMAL] ❑ *I had always had a thing about red hair... He's got this thing about ties.* (PHRASE: V inflects, PHR n/-ing)

19 You say **it is a** good **thing to** do something to introduce a piece of advice or a comment on a situation or activity. ❑ *Can you tell me whether it is a good thing to prune an apple tree?* (PHRASE: PHR inf)

20 If you **make a thing of** something or **make a thing about** it, you talk about it or do it in an exaggerated way, so that it seems much more important than it really is. [INFORMAL] ❑ *Gossips made a big thing about him going on shopping trips with her.* (PHRASE: V inflects, PHR n/-ing)

21 You can say that the first of two ideas, actions, or situations **is one thing** when you want to contrast it with a second idea, action, or situation and emphasize that the second one is much more difficult, important, or extreme. ❑ *It was one thing to talk about leaving; it was another to physically walk out the door.* (PHRASE: V inflects, oft *it* PHR to-inf; emphasis)

22 You can say **for one thing** when you are explaining a statement or answering a question, to suggest that you are not giving the whole explanation or answer, and that there are other points that you could add to it. ❑ *She was a monster. For one thing, she really enjoyed cruelty.* (PHRASE: PHR with cl)

23 You can use the expression **'one thing and another'** to suggest that there are several reasons for something or several items on a list, but you are not going to explain or mention them all. [SPOKEN] ❑ *What with one thing and another, it was fairly late in the day when we returned to Shrewsbury.* (PHRASE: oft *with* PHR)

24 If you say **it is just one of those things** you mean that you cannot explain something because it seems to happen by chance. ❑ *'I wonder why.' Mr. Dambar shrugged. 'It must be just one of those things, I guess.'* (PHRASE: V inflects)

25 You say **one thing led to another** when you are explaining how something happened, but you do not really want to give the details or you think people will be able to imagine the details. ❑ *He came by on Saturday to see if she was lonely. One thing led to another and he stayed the night.* (PHRASE: V inflects)

26 If you **do** your **own thing**, you live, act, or behave in the way you want to, without paying attention to convention or depending on other people. [INFORMAL] ❑ *We accept the right of all men and women to do their own thing, however bizarre.* (PHRASE: V inflects)

27 If something is **a thing of the past**, it no longer exists or happens, or is being replaced by something new. ❑ *Painful typhoid injections are a thing of the past, thanks to the introduction of an oral vaccine.* (PHRASE: v-link PHR, PHR after v)

28 If you say that someone **is seeing** or **hearing things**, you mean that they believe they are seeing or hearing something that is not really there. ❑ *Dr Payne led Lana back into the examination room and told her she was seeing things.* (PHRASE: V inflects, usu cont)

29 You can say there is **no such thing as** something to emphasize that it does not exist or is not possible. ❑ *There really is no such thing as a totally risk-free industry.* (PHRASE: usu v-link PHR, oft PHR *as* n; emphasis)

30 You say **the thing is** to introduce an explanation, comment, or opinion, that relates to something that has just been said. **The thing is** is often used to identify a problem relating to what has just been said. [SPOKEN] ❑ *'What does your market research consist of?' — 'Well, the thing is, it depends on our target age group.'.* (PHRASE: PHR cl)

31 If you say that something is **just the thing** or is **the very thing**, you are emphasizing that it is exactly what is wanted or needed. ❑ *Kiwi fruit are just the thing for a healthy snack.* (PHRASE: usu v-link PHR, oft PHR *for* n, PHR to-inf; emphasis)

32 If you say that a person knows **a thing or two** about something or could teach someone **a thing or two** about it, you mean that they know a lot about it or are good at it. ❑ *Patricia Hewitt knows a thing or two about how to be well-organised... The peace movement has learnt a thing or two from Vietnam.* (PHRASE: PHR after v, oft PHR *about* n)

33 **other things being equal** → see **equal**. **first things first** → see **first**. **the real thing** → see **real**. **the shape of things to come** → see **shape**.

**thingum|my** /θɪŋəmi/ **(thingummies)** You refer to something or someone as **thingummy**, **thingummyjig** or **thingummybob** when you do not know or cannot be bothered to use the proper word or name for them. [INFORMAL, SPOKEN] ❑ *I once bought a thingummy out of one of those catalogues... I must say, I mean, it sounded like er thingummyjig all over again without the politics.* (N-COUNT)

**thingy** /θɪŋi/ **(thingies)** You refer to something or someone as **thingy** when you do not know or cannot be bothered to use the proper word or name for them. [INFORMAL, SPOKEN] ❑ *...the new phone thingy. ...what's his name, Sir Jack Thingy.* (N-COUNT)

**think** /θɪŋk/ **(thinks, thinking, thought)** ◆◆◆ 1 If you **think** that something is the case, you have the opinion that it is the case. ❑ *I certainly think there should be a ban on tobacco advertising... A generation ago, it was thought that babies born this small could not survive... Tell me, what do you think of my theory?... Peter is useless, far worse than I thought... He manages a good deal better than I thought possible... 'It ought to be stopped.' — 'Yes, I think so.'* (VERB: no cont; V that; *it be* V-ed that; V *of/about* n; V; V adj; V *so/not*)

2 If you say that you **think** that something is true or will happen, you mean that you have the impression that it is true or will happen, although you are not certain of the facts. ❑ *Nora thought he was seventeen years old... The storm is thought to be responsible for as many as four deaths... 'Did Mr Stevens ever mention her to you?' — 'No, I don't think so.'* (VERB: no cont; V that; *be* V-ed to-inf; V *so/not*)

3 If you **think** in a particular way, you have those general opinions or attitudes. ❑ *You were probably brought up to think like that... If you think as I do, vote as I do... I don't blame you for thinking that way.* (VERB: no cont, no passive; V *like* n; V *as/like* cl; V n)

4 When you **think** about ideas or problems, you make a mental effort to consider them. ❑ *She closed her eyes for a moment, trying to think... I have often thought about this problem... Let's think what we can do... We had to think what to do next.* (VERB; V; V *about* n/wh; V wh; V wh-to-inf) ♦ **Think** is also a noun. [mainly BRIT] ❑ *I'll have a think about that.* (N-SING: *a* N)

5 If you **think** in a particular way, you consider things, solve problems, or make decisions in this way, for example because of your job or your background. ❑ *To make the computer work at full capacity, the programmer has to think like the machine... The referee has to think the way the players do.* (VERB: no passive; V prep; V n)

6 If you **think of** something, it comes into your mind or you remember it. ❑ *Nobody could think of anything to say... I was trying to think what else we had to do.* (VERB: no cont; V *of* n; V wh)

7 If you **think of** an idea, you make a mental effort and use your imagination and intelligence to create it or develop it. ❑ *He thought of another way of getting out of the marriage.* (VERB; V *of* n)

8 If you **are thinking** something at a particular moment, you have words or ideas in your mind without saying them out loud. ❑ *She must be ill, Tatiana thought... I remember thinking how lovely he looked... I'm trying to think positive thoughts.* (VERB: no passive; V with quote; V wh/that; V n)

9 If you **think of** someone or something as having a particular quality or purpose, you regard them as having this quality or purpose. ❑ *We all thought of him as a father... Nobody had thought him capable of that kind of thing.* (VERB: no cont; V *of* n *as* n/-ing; V n adj)

10 If you **think** a lot **of** someone or something, you admire them very much or think they are very good. ❑ *To tell the truth, I don't think much of psychiatrists... People at the club think very highly of him.* (VERB: no cont; V amount *of* n; V adv *of* n)

11 If you **think of** someone, you show consideration for them and pay attention to their needs. ❑ *I'm only thinking of you... You don't have to think about me and Hugh.* (VERB; V *of* n; V *about* n)

12 If you **are thinking of** taking a particular course of action, you are considering it as a possible course of action. ❑ *Martin was thinking of taking legal action against Zuckerman.* (VERB; V *of* -ing/n)

13 You can say that you **are thinking of** a particular aspect or subject, in order to introduce an example or explain more exactly what you are talking about. ❑ *I'm primarily thinking of the first year.* (VERB: usu cont; V *of* n)

14 You use **think** in questions where you are expressing your anger or shock at someone's behaviour. ❑ *What were you thinking of? You shouldn't steal.* (VERB: only interrog; disapproval; V *of* n/-ing)

15 You use **think** when you are commenting on something which you did or experienced in the past and which now seems sur- (VERB: no cont, no passive)

prising, foolish, or shocking to you. ❑ *To think I left you alone in a place with a madman at large!...*
V that
*When I think of how you've behaved and the trouble you've got into!*
V *of* n
16 You can use **think** in expressions such as **you would think** or **I would have thought** when you are criticizing someone because they ought to or could be expected to do something, but have not done it. ❑ *You'd think you'd remember to wash your ears... 'Surely to God she should have been given some proper help.' — 'Well I would have thought so.'*
VERB: no cont
disapproval
V that
V *so*
Also V
17 You can use **think** in expressions such as **anyone would think** and **you would think** to express your surprise or disapproval at the way someone is behaving. ❑ *Anyone would think you were in love with the girl.*
VERB: no cont
V that
18 → See also **thinking**, **thought**.

**PHRASES** 19 You use expressions such as **come to think of it**, **when you think about it**, or **thinking about it**, when you mention something that you have suddenly remembered or realized. ❑ *He was her distant relative, as was everyone else on the island, come to think of it.*
PHRASE: PHR with cl
20 You use '**I think**' as a way of being polite when you are explaining or suggesting to someone what you want to do, or when you are accepting or refusing an offer. ❑ *I think I'll go home and have a shower... We need a job, and I thought we could go around and ask if people need odd jobs done.*
PHRASE: PHR that, PHR with cl, PHR *so/not*
politeness
21 You use '**I think**' in conversations or speeches to make your statements and opinions sound less forceful, rude, or direct. ❑ *I think he means 'at' rather than 'to'... Thanks, but I think I can handle it.*
PHRASE: PHR that, PHR with cl, PHR *so/not*
vagueness
22 You say **just think** when you feel excited, fascinated, or shocked by something, and you want the person to whom you are talking to feel the same. ❑ *Just think; tomorrow we shall walk out of this place and leave it all behind us forever.*
PHRASE: PHR with cl, PHR wh
= *imagine*
23 If you **think again about** an action or decision, you consider it very carefully, often with the result that you change your mind and decide to do things differently. ❑ *It has forced politicians to think again about the wisdom of trying to evacuate refugees.*
PHRASE: oft PHR *about* n/-ing
24 If you **think nothing of** doing something that other people might consider difficult, strange, or wrong, you consider it to be easy or normal, and you do it often or would be quite willing to do it. ❑ *I thought nothing of betting £1,000 on a horse.*
PHRASE: V inflects, PHR -ing
25 If something happens and you **think nothing of it**, you do not pay much attention to it or think of it as strange or important, although later you realize that it is. ❑ *When she went off to see her parents for the weekend I thought nothing of it.*
PHRASE: V inflects
26 you **can't hear** yourself **think** → see **hear**. to **shudder to think** → see **shudder**. to **think better of it** → see **better**. to **think big** → see **big**. to **think twice** → see **twice**. to **think the world of** someone → see **world**.

♦ **think back** If you **think back**, you make an effort to remember things that happened to you in the past. ❑ *I thought back to the time in 1975 when my son was desperately ill... Thinking back, I don't know how I had the courage.*
PHRASAL VERB = *look back*
V P prep
V P

♦ **think out** If you **think** something **out**, you consider all the aspects and details of it before doing anything or making a decision. ❑ *I need time alone to think things out... The book is detailed and well thought out... He chewed at the end of his pencil, thinking out the next problem.*
PHRASAL VERB
V n P
V-ed P
V P n (not pron)

♦ **think over** If you **think** something **over**, you consider it carefully before making a decision. ❑ *She said she needs time to think it over... I suggest you think over your position very carefully.*
PHRASAL VERB
V n P
V P n (not pron)

♦ **think through** If you **think** a situation **through**, you consider it thoroughly, together with all its possible effects or consequences. ❑ *I didn't think through the consequences of promotion... It was the first time she'd had a chance to think it through.*
PHRASAL VERB
V P n (not pron)
V n P

♦ **think up** If you **think** something **up**, for example an idea or plan, you invent it using mental effort. ❑ *Julian has been thinking up new ways of raising money... 'Where do you get that idea about the piano?' — 'Well, I just thought it up.'*
PHRASAL VERB
V P n (not pron)
V n P

**think|er** /θɪŋkəʳ/ **(thinkers)** A **thinker** is a person who spends a lot of time thinking deeply about important things, especially someone who is famous for thinking of new or interesting ideas.
N-COUNT

**think|ing** /θɪŋkɪŋ/ ◆◆◇ 1 The general ideas or opinions of a person or group can be referred to as their **thinking**. ❑ *There was undeniably a strong theoretical dimension to his thinking.*
N-UNCOUNT: with poss
2 **Thinking** is the activity of using your brain by considering a problem or possibility or creating an idea. ❑ *This is a time of decisive action and quick thinking.*
N-UNCOUNT
3 If you describe someone as a **thinking** man or woman, you mean that they are intelligent and take an interest in important events and issues, and you approve of this. ❑ *Thinking people on both sides will applaud this book... A newspaper called him 'the thinking man's Tory'.*
ADJ: ADJ n
approval
4 → See also **wishful thinking**. **to** my **way of thinking** → see **way**.

**think piece** **(think pieces)** also **think-piece**. A **think piece** is an article in a newspaper or magazine that discusses a particular subject in a serious and thoughtful way.
N-COUNT

**think-tank** **(think-tanks)** A **think-tank** is a group of experts who are gathered together by an organization, especially by a government, in order to consider various problems and try and work out ways to solve them. ❑ *...Moscow's leading foreign policy think-tank.*
N-COUNT-COLL

**thin-skinned** If you say that someone is **thin-skinned**, you mean that they are easily upset by criticism or unpleasantness. ❑ *Some fear he is too thin-skinned to survive the rough-and-tumble of a presidential campaign.*
ADJ: usu v-link ADJ
disapproval
= *sensitive*
≠ *thick-skinned*

**third** /θɜːʳd/ **(thirds)** ◆◆◇ 1 The **third** item in a series is the one that you count as number three. ❑ *I sleep on the third floor... It was the third time one of his cars had gone up in flames.*
ORD
2 A **third** is one of three equal parts of something. ❑ *A third of the cost went into technology and services.*
FRACTION
3 You say **third** when you want to make a third point or give a third reason for something. ❑ *First, interest rates may take longer to fall than is hoped. Second, in real terms, lending may fall. Third, bad loans could wipe out much of any improvement.*
ADV: ADV with cl (not last in cl)
= *thirdly*
4 A **third** is the lowest honours degree that can be obtained from a British university.
N-COUNT: usu sing

**third-class** A **third-class** degree is the lowest honours degree that can be obtained from a British university.
ADJ: ADJ n

**third-degree** 1 **Third-degree** burns are very severe, destroying tissue under the skin. ❑ *He suffered third-degree burns over 98 per cent of his body.*
ADJ: ADJ n
2 If you say that someone has been given **the third degree**, you mean that they have been questioned or criticized extremely severely, sometimes with physical violence. [INFORMAL] ❑ *The next thing you know, she's phoned to complain and you're suddenly being given the third degree.*
N-SING: usu *the* N

**third|ly** /θɜːʳdli/ You use **thirdly** when you want to make a third point or give a third reason for something. ❑ *First of all, there are not many of them, and secondly, they have little money and, thirdly, they have few big businesses.*
ADV: ADV with cl (not last in cl)
= *third*

**third par|ty** **(third parties)** 1 A **third party** is someone who is not one of the main people involved in a business agreement or legal case, but who is involved in it in a minor role. ❑ *You can instruct your bank to allow a third party to remove money from your account.*
N-COUNT
2 **Third-party** insurance is a type of insurance that pays money to people who are hurt or whose property is damaged as a result of something you have done. It does not pay you any money for damage you suffer as a result of your own actions. [BRIT] ❑ *Premiums for third-party cover are set to rise by up to 25 per cent.*
ADJ

**third per|son** In grammar, a statement in **the third person** is a statement about another
N-SING: *the* N

person or thing, and not directly about yourself or about the person you are talking to. The subject of a statement like this is 'he', 'she', 'it', or a name or noun.

**third-rate** If you describe something as **third-rate**, you mean that it is of a very poor quality or standard. ❑ *...a third-rate movie.* [ADJ: usu ADJ n]

**Third Way** The **Third Way** is used to refer to a set of political beliefs and principles that is neither extremely right-wing nor extremely left-wing. [N-SING]

**Third World** The countries of Africa, Asia, and South America are sometimes referred to all together as **the Third World**, especially those parts that are poor, do not have much power, and are not considered to be highly developed. Compare **First World**. ❑ *...development in the Third World. ...Third World debt.* [◆◇◇ N-PROPER: *the* N, N n]

**thirst** /θɜːʳst/ **(thirsts, thirsting, thirsted)** [1] **Thirst** is the feeling that you need to drink something. ❑ *Instead of tea or coffee, drink water to quench your thirst... I had such a thirst.* [N-VAR] [2] **Thirst** is the condition of not having enough to drink. ❑ *They died of thirst on the voyage.* [N-UNCOUNT] [3] A **thirst for** something is a very strong desire for that thing. ❑ *Children show a real thirst for learning.* [N-SING: usu N *for* n = hunger] [4] If you say that someone **thirsts for** something, you mean that they have a strong desire for it. [LITERARY] ❑ *We all thirst for the same things.* [VERB = hunger; V *for/after* n]

**thirsty** /θɜːʳsti/ **(thirstier, thirstiest)** [1] If you are **thirsty**, you feel a need to drink something. ❑ *Drink whenever you feel thirsty during exercise.* [ADJ: usu v-link ADJ] ♦ **thirsti|ly** /θɜːʳstɪli/ *The child nodded, drinking her milk thirstily.* [ADV: ADV after v] [2] If you are **thirsty for** something, you have a strong desire for it. [LITERARY] ❑ *People should understand how thirsty for revenge they are.* [ADJ: v-link ADJ *for* n = hungry]

**thir|teen** /θɜːʳtiːn/ **(thirteens)** **Thirteen** is the number 13. [◆◆◆ NUM]

**thir|teenth** /θɜːʳtiːnθ/ The **thirteenth** item in a series is the one that you count as number thirteen. [◆◆◇ ORD]

**thir|ti|eth** /θɜːʳtiəθ/ The **thirtieth** item in a series is the one that you count as number thirty. [◆◆◇ ORD]

**thir|ty** /θɜːʳti/ **(thirties)** [1] **Thirty** is the number 30. [◆◆◆ NUM] [2] When you talk about the **thirties**, you are referring to numbers between 30 and 39. For example, if you are **in** your **thirties**, you are aged between 30 and 39. If the temperature is **in the thirties**, the temperature is between 30 and 39 degrees. [N-PLURAL] [3] **The thirties** is the decade between 1930 and 1939. ❑ *She became quite a notable director in the thirties and forties.* [N-PLURAL: *the* N]

**this** [◆◆◆]

> The determiner is pronounced /ðɪs/. In other cases, **this** is pronounced /ðɪs/.

[1] You use **this** to refer back to a particular person or thing that has been mentioned or implied. ❑ *When food comes out of any oven, it should stand a while. During this delay the centre carries on cooking... On 1 October the US suspended a proposed $574 million aid package for 1991. Of this amount, $250 million is for military purchases.* [DET: DET sing-n/ n-uncount] ♦ **This** is also a pronoun. ❑ *I don't know how bad the injury is, because I have never had one like this before.* [PRON] [2] You use **this** to introduce someone or something that you are going to talk about. ❑ *This is what I will do. I will telephone Anna and explain.* [PRON] ♦ **This** is also a determiner. ❑ *This report is from David Cook of our Science Unit: 'Why did the dinosaurs become extinct?'* [DET: DET sing-n/ n-uncount] [3] You use **this** to refer back to an idea or situation expressed in a previous sentence or sentences. ❑ *You feel that it's uneconomic to insist that people work together in groups. Why is this?* [PRON] ♦ **This** is also a determiner. ❑ *There have been continual demands for action by the political authorities to put an end to this situation.* [DET: DET sing-n/ n-uncount] [4] In spoken English, people use **this** to introduce a person or thing into a story. ❑ *I came here by chance and was just watching what was going on, when this girl attacked me.* [DET: DET sing-n] [5] You use **this** to refer to a person or thing that is near you, especially when you touch them or point to them. When there are two or more people or things near you, **this** refers to the nearest one. ❑ *'If you'd prefer something else I'll gladly have it changed for you.' — 'No, this is great.'... 'Is this what you were looking for?' Bradley produced the handkerchief.* [PRON] ♦ **This** is also a determiner. ❑ *This church was built in the eleventh century.* [DET: DET sing-n] [6] You use **this** when you refer to a general situation, activity, or event which is happening or has just happened and which you feel involved in. ❑ *I thought, this is why I've travelled thousands of miles... Tim, this is awful. I know what you must think, but it's not so.* [PRON: PRON with *be*] [7] You use **this** when you refer to the place you are in now or to the present time. ❑ *We've stopped transporting weapons to this country by train... I think coffee is probably the best thing at this point.* [DET: DET sing-n/ n-uncount] ♦ **This** is also a pronoun. ❑ *This is the worst place I've come across.* [PRON] [8] You use **this** to refer to the next occurrence in the future of a particular day, month, season, or festival. ❑ *We're getting married this June.* [DET: DET sing-n] [9] You use **this** when you are indicating the size or shape of something with your hands. ❑ *They'd said the wound was only about this big you see and he showed me with his fingers.* [ADV: ADV adj] [10] You use **this** when you are going to specify how much you know or how much you can tell someone. ❑ *I am not going to reveal what my seven-year plan is, but I will tell you this much, if it works out, the next seven years will be very interesting.* [ADV: ADV adv] [11] If you say **this is it**, you are agreeing with what someone else has just said. ❑ *'You know, people conveniently forget the things they say.' — 'Well this is it.'* [CONVENTION formulae] [12] You use **this** in order to say who you are or what organization you are representing, when you are speaking on the telephone, radio, or television. ❑ *Hello, this is John Thompson.* [PRON] [13] You use **this** to refer to the medium of communication that you are using at the time of speaking or writing. ❑ *What I'm going to do in this lecture is focus on something very specific.* [DET: DET sing-n] [14] → See also **these**. [15] If you say that you are doing or talking about **this and that**, or **this, that, and the other** you mean that you are doing or talking about a variety of things that you do not want to specify. ❑ *'And what are you doing now?' — 'Oh this and that.'* [PHRASE]

**this|tle** /θɪsᵊl/ **(thistles)** A **thistle** is a wild plant which has leaves with sharp points and purple flowers. [N-COUNT]

**thith|er** /ðɪðəʳ/ **Thither** means to the place that has already been mentioned. [OLD-FASHIONED] ❑ *They have dragged themselves thither for shelter.* [ADV: ADV after v = there]

**hither and thither** → see **hither**.

**tho'** also **tho. Tho'** and **tho** are very informal written forms of **though**.

**thong** /θɒŋ, AM θɔːŋ/ **(thongs)** [1] A **thong** is a long thin strip of leather, plastic, or rubber. [N-COUNT] [2] A **thong** is a narrow band of cloth that is worn between a person's legs to cover up his or her sexual organs, and that is held up by a piece of string around the waist. [N-COUNT] [3] **Thongs** are open shoes which are held on your foot by a V-shaped strap that goes between your big toe and the toe next to it. [mainly AM] [N-COUNT: usu pl]

> in BRIT, usually use **flip-flops**

**tho|rac|ic** /θɔːræsɪk/ **Thoracic** means relating to or affecting your thorax. [MEDICAL] ❑ *...diseases of the thoracic area.* [ADJ: ADJ n]

**thor|ax** /θɔːræks/ **(thoraxes** or **thoraces** /θɔːrəsiːz/) [1] Your **thorax** is the part of your body between your neck and your waist. [MEDICAL] [N-COUNT: usu sing] [2] An insect's **thorax** is the central part of its body to which the legs and wings are attached. [TECHNICAL] [N-COUNT: usu sing]

**thorn** /θɔːʳn/ **(thorns)** [1] **Thorns** are the sharp points on some plants and trees, for example on a rose bush. [N-COUNT] [2] A **thorn** or a **thorn bush** or a **thorn tree** is a bush or tree which has a lot of thorns on it. ❑ *...the shade of a thorn bush.* [N-VAR] [3] If you describe someone or something as a **thorn in** [PHRASE: v-link PHR] your **side** or **a thorn in** your **flesh**, you mean that they are a continuous problem to you or annoy you. ❑ *The Party was a thorn in the flesh of his coalition.*

**thorny** /θɔ͟ːni/ **(thornier, thorniest)** [1] A **thorny** plant or tree is covered with thorns. ❑ *...thorny hawthorn trees.* ADJ: usu ADJ n [2] If you describe a problem as **thorny**, you mean that it is very complicated and difficult to solve, and that people are often unwilling to discuss it. ❑ *...the thorny issue of immigration policy.* ADJ: usu ADJ n

**thor|ough** /θʌ͟rə, AM θɜ͟ːroʊ/ ◆◇◇ [1] A **thorough** action or activity is one that is done very carefully and in a detailed way so that nothing is forgotten. ❑ *We are making a thorough investigation... How thorough is the assessment?* ADJ: usu ADJ n ♦ **thor|ough|ly** *Food that is being offered hot must be reheated thoroughly.* ADV: ADV with v ♦ **thor|ough|ness** *The thoroughness of the evaluation process we went through was impressive.* N-UNCOUNT [2] Someone who is **thorough** is always very careful in their work, so that nothing is forgotten. ❑ *Martin would be a good judge, I thought. He was calm and thorough.* ADJ: usu v-link ADJ ♦ **thor|ough|ness** *His thoroughness and attention to detail is legendary.* N-UNCOUNT [3] **Thorough** is used to emphasize the great degree or extent of something. ❑ *We regard the band as a thorough shambles.* ADJ: det ADJ [emphasis] = complete ♦ **thor|ough|ly** *I thoroughly enjoy your programme.* ADV: ADV before v, ADV adj

**thorough|bred** /θʌ͟rəbred, AM θɜ͟ːroʊ-/ **(thoroughbreds)** [1] A **thoroughbred** is a horse that has parents that are of the same high quality breed. N-COUNT [2] A **thoroughbred** is a particular breed of racing horse. ❑ *...a thoroughbred stallion.* N-COUNT: oft N n

**thorough|fare** /θʌ͟rəfeəʳ, AM θɜ͟ːroʊ-/ **(thoroughfares)** A **thoroughfare** is a main road in a town or city which usually has shops along it and a lot of traffic. [FORMAL] ❑ *...a busy thoroughfare.* N-COUNT: usu supp N

**thorough|going** /θʌ͟rəgoʊɪŋ, AM θɜ͟ːroʊ-/ also **thorough-going.** [1] You use **thoroughgoing** to emphasize that someone or something is fully or completely the type of person or thing specified. ❑ *...a thoroughgoing conservative. ...readers who are unhappy with such thoroughgoing materialism.* ADJ: usu ADJ n [emphasis] [2] If you describe a piece of work as **thoroughgoing**, you approve of it because it has been carefully and thoroughly put together. ❑ *...a thoroughgoing review of prison conditions.* ADJ: usu ADJ n [approval] = thorough

**those** ◆◆◆

> ✔ The determiner is pronounced /ðoʊz/. The pronoun is pronounced /ðo͟ʊz/.

[1] You use **those** to refer to people or things which have already been mentioned. ❑ *Theoretically he had control over more than $400 million in US accounts. But, in fact, it was the US Treasury and State Department who controlled those accounts... They have the aircraft capable of doing significant damage, because most of those aircraft are capable of launching anti-ship missiles.* DET: DET pl-n ♦ **Those** is also a pronoun. ❑ *I understand that there are a number of projects going on. Could you tell us a little bit about those?* PRON [2] You use **those** when you are referring to people or things that are a distance away from you in position or time, especially when you indicate or point to them. ❑ *What are those buildings?... Oh, those books! I meant to put them away before this afternoon.* DET: DET pl-n ♦ **Those** is also a pronoun. ❑ *Those are nice shoes. Where'd you get them?* PRON [3] You use **those** to refer to someone or something when you are going to give details or information about them. [FORMAL] ❑ *Those people who took up weapons to defend themselves are political prisoners.* DET: DET pl-n [4] You use **those** to introduce more information about something already mentioned, instead of repeating the noun which refers to it. [FORMAL] ❑ *The interests he is most likely to enjoy will be those which enable him to show off himself or his talents.* PRON: PRON pron-rel, PRON *of* n [5] You use **those** to mean 'people'. ❑ *A little selfish behaviour is unlikely to cause real damage to those around us.* PRON: PRON prep/adj/-ed, PRON pron-rel [6] You use **those** when you refer to things that you expect the person you are talking to to know about or when you are checking that you are both thinking of the same people or things. ❑ *He did buy me those daffodils a week or so ago.* DET: DET pl-n

**thou** /ðaʊ/ **Thou** is an old-fashioned, poetic, or religious word for 'you' when you are talking to only one person. It is used as the subject of a verb. → See also **holier-than-thou**. PRON

**though** ◆◆◆

> ✔ Pronounced /ðoʊ/ for meanings 1 and 2, and /ðo͟ʊ/ for meanings 3 to 5.

[1] You use **though** to introduce a statement in a subordinate clause which contrasts with the statement in the main clause. You often use **though** to introduce a fact which you regard as less important than the fact in the main clause. ❑ *Gaelic has been a dying language for many years, though children are nowadays taught it in school... After news of this new court case Ford broke down again, though he blamed the breakdown on his work.* CONJ = although [2] You use **though** to introduce a subordinate clause which gives some information that is relevant to the main clause and weakens the force of what it is saying. ❑ *I look back on it as the bloodiest (though not literally) winter of the war.* CONJ = although [3] You use **though** to indicate that the information in a clause contrasts with or modifies information given in a previous sentence or sentences. ❑ *I like him. Though he makes me angry sometimes.* ADV: ADV with cl [4] You can say **though I say so myself** or **even though I say it myself** when you are praising yourself or something you have done, but do not want to sound too proud. [mainly SPOKEN] ❑ *I'm a good cook, though I say it myself.* PHRASE: PHR with cl [5] **as though** → see **as**. **even though** → see **even**.

**thought** /θɔ͟ːt/ **(thoughts)** ◆◆◆ [1] **Thought** is the past tense and past participle of **think**. [2] A **thought** is an idea that you have in your mind. ❑ *The thought of Nick made her throat tighten... He pushed the thought from his mind... I've just had a thought.* N-COUNT: oft N *of* n/-ing, N that [3] A person's **thoughts** are their mind, or all the ideas in their mind when they are concentrating on one particular thing. ❑ *I jumped to my feet so my thoughts wouldn't start to wander... If he wasn't there physically, he was always in her thoughts.* N-PLURAL: usu poss N [4] A person's **thoughts** are their opinions on a particular subject. ❑ *Many of you have written to us to express your thoughts on the conflict... Mr Goodman, do you have any thoughts on that?* N-PLURAL: oft poss N, N *on/about* n [5] **Thought** is the activity of thinking, especially deeply, carefully, or logically. ❑ *Alice had been so deep in thought that she had walked past her car without even seeing it... He had given some thought to what she had told him.* N-UNCOUNT [6] A **thought** is an intention, hope, or reason for doing something. ❑ *Sarah's first thought was to run back and get Max... They had no thought of surrender.* N-COUNT: oft N *of* n [7] A **thought** is an act of kindness or an offer of help; used especially when you are thanking someone, or expressing admiration of someone. ❑ *'Would you like to move into the ward?' — 'A kind thought, but no, thank you.'* N-SING: with supp, oft adj N [8] **Thought** is the group of ideas and beliefs which belongs, for example, to a particular religion, philosophy, science, or political party. ❑ *Aristotle's scientific theories dominated Western thought for fifteen hundred years.* N-UNCOUNT [9] → See also **second thought**.

**thought|ful** /θɔ͟ːtfʊl/ [1] If you are **thoughtful**, you are quiet and serious because you are thinking about something. ❑ *Nancy, who had been thoughtful for some time, suddenly spoke.* ADJ = pensive ♦ **thought|ful|ly** *Daniel nodded thoughtfully.* ADV: ADV with v [2] If you describe someone as **thoughtful**, you approve of them because they remember what other people want, need, or feel, and try not to upset them. ❑ *...a thoughtful and caring man... Thank you. That's very thoughtful of you.* ADJ: oft ADJ *of* n [approval] = considerate ≠ thoughtless ♦ **thought|ful|ly** *...the bottle of wine he had thoughtfully purchased for the celebrations.* ADV: ADV with v

♦ **thought|ful|ness** *I can't tell you how much I appreciate your thoughtfulness.* N-UNCOUNT
[3] If you describe something such as a book, film, or speech as **thoughtful**, you mean that it is serious and well thought out. ❑ *...a thoughtful and scholarly book.* ADJ
♦ **thought|ful|ly** *...these thoughtfully designed machines.* ADV: ADV with v

**thought|less** /θɔːtləs/ If you describe someone as **thoughtless**, you are critical of them because they forget or ignore other people's wants, needs, or feelings. ❑ *It was thoughtless of her to mention it.* ADJ [disapproval] ≠ *thoughtful*
♦ **thought|less|ly** *They thoughtlessly planned a picnic without him.* ADV: ADV with v

**thought-provoking** If something such as a book or a film is **thought-provoking**, it contains interesting ideas that make people think seriously. ❑ *This is an entertaining yet thought-provoking film.* ADJ

**thou|sand** /θaʊzənd/ **(thousands)** ♦♦♦

> ✓ The plural form is **thousand** after a number, or after a word or expression referring to a number, such as 'several' or 'a few'.

[1] **A thousand** or **one thousand** is the number 1,000. ❑ *...five thousand acres... Visitors can expect to pay about a thousand pounds a day.* NUM: usu *a*/num NUM
[2] If you refer to **thousands of** things or people, you are emphasizing that there are very many of them. ❑ *Thousands of refugees are packed into over-crowded towns and villages.* QUANT: QUANT *of* pl-n [emphasis]
♦ You can also use **thousands** as a pronoun. ❑ *Hundreds have been killed in the fighting and thousands made homeless.* PRON
[3] **a thousand and one** ➔ see **one**.

**thou|sandth** /θaʊzənθ/ **(thousandths)** [1] The **thousandth** item in a series is the one that you count as number one thousand. ❑ *The magazine has just published its six thousandth edition.* ORD
♦ If you say that something has happened for the **thousandth** time, you are emphasizing that it has happened again and that it has already happened a great many times. ❑ *The phone rings for the thousandth time.* ORD [emphasis]
[2] A **thousandth** is one of a thousand equal parts of something. ❑ *...a dust particle weighing only a thousandth of a gram.* FRACTION

**thrall** /θrɔːl/ If you say that someone is **in thrall to** a person or thing, you mean that they are completely in their power or are greatly influenced by them. [FORMAL] ❑ *He is not in thrall to the media... Tomorrow's children will be even more in the thrall of the silicon chip.* N-UNCOUNT: oft *in* N *to* n

**thrash** /θræʃ/ **(thrashes, thrashing, thrashed)** [1] If one player or team **thrashes** another in a game or contest, they defeat them easily or by a large score. [INFORMAL] ❑ *Second-placed Rangers thrashed St Johnstone 5-nil.* VERB = *hammer* V n amount Also V n
[2] If you **thrash** someone, you hit them several times as a punishment. ❑ *'Liar!' Sarah screamed, as she thrashed the child. 'You stole it.'* VERB V n
[3] If someone **thrashes about**, or **thrashes** their arms or legs **about**, they move in a wild or violent way, often hitting against something. You can also say that someone's arms or legs **thrash about**. ❑ *Many of the crew died a terrible death as they thrashed about in shark-infested waters... Jimmy collapsed on the floor, thrashing his legs about like an injured racehorse.* VERB V adv/prep V n adv/prep
[4] If a person or thing **thrashes** something, or **thrashes at** something, they hit it continually in a violent or noisy way. ❑ *...a magnificent paddle-steamer on the mighty Mississippi, her huge wheel thrashing the muddy water... Three shaggy-haired men thrash tunelessly at their guitars.* VERB V n V *at* n
[5] ➔ See also **thrashing**.

♦ **thrash out** [1] If people **thrash out** something such as a plan or an agreement, they decide on it after a great deal of discussion. ❑ *The foreign ministers have thrashed out a suitable compromise formula.* PHRASAL VERB = *hammer out* V P n (not pron)
[2] If people **thrash out** a problem or a dispute, they discuss it thoroughly until they reach an agreement. ❑ *...a sincere effort by two people to thrash out differences about which they have strong feelings.* PHRASAL VERB = *hammer out* V P n (not pron) Also V n P

**thrash|ing** /θræʃɪŋ/ **(thrashings)** [1] If one player or team gives another one a **thrashing**, they defeat them easily or by a large score. [INFORMAL] ❑ *Can the New Zealand bowlers fight back after their thrashing at Christchurch?* N-COUNT: usu with supp
[2] If someone gives someone else a **thrashing**, they hit them several times as a punishment. ❑ *If Sarah caught her, she would get a thrashing.* N-COUNT = *hiding, beating*
[3] ➔ See also **thrash**.

**thread** /θred/ **(threads, threading, threaded)** [1] **Thread** or a **thread** is a long very thin piece of a material such as cotton, nylon, or silk, especially one that is used in sewing. ❑ *...a tiny Nepalese hat embroidered with golden threads.* N-VAR
[2] The **thread** of an argument, a story, or a situation is an aspect of it that connects all the different parts together. ❑ *The thread running through many of these proposals was the theme of individual power and opportunity.* N-COUNT: usu with supp
[3] A **thread of** something such as liquid, light, or colour is a long thin line or piece of it. ❑ *A thin, glistening thread of moisture ran along the rough concrete sill.* N-COUNT: usu N *of* n
[4] The **thread** on a screw, or on something such as a lid or a pipe, is the raised spiral line of metal or plastic around it which allows it to be fixed in place by twisting. ➔ See picture on page 1709. ❑ *The screw threads will be able to get a good grip.* N-COUNT
[5] If you **thread** your **way** through a group of people or things, or **thread through** it, you move through it carefully or slowly, changing direction frequently as you move. ❑ *Slowly she threaded her way back through the moving mass of bodies... We threaded through a network of back streets.* VERB V *way* prep/adv V prep
[6] If you **thread** a long thin object **through** something, you pass it through one or more holes or narrow spaces. ❑ *...threading the laces through the eyelets of his shoes... Instruments developed at the hospital allow doctors to thread microscopic telescopes into the digestive tract.* VERB V n *through* n V n *into* n
[7] If you **thread** small objects such as beads onto a string or thread, you join them together by pushing the string through them. ❑ *Wipe the mushrooms clean and thread them on a string.* VERB V n prep
[8] When you **thread** a needle, you put a piece of thread through the hole in the top of the needle in order to sew with it. ❑ *I sit down, thread a needle, snip off an old button.* VERB V n

PHRASES [9] If you say that something **is hanging by a thread**, you mean that it is in a very uncertain state and is unlikely to survive or succeed. ❑ *The fragile peace was hanging by a thread as thousands of hardliners took to the streets.* PHRASE: V inflects
[10] If you **pick up the threads of** an activity, you start it again after an interruption. If you **pick up the threads of** your **life**, you become more active again after a period of failure or bad luck. ❑ *Many women have been able to pick up the threads of their former career.* PHRASE: V inflects

**thread|bare** /θredbeər/ [1] **Threadbare** clothes, carpets, and other pieces of cloth look old, dull, and very thin, because they have been worn or used too much. ❑ *She sat cross-legged on a square of threadbare carpet.* ADJ = *worn*
[2] If you describe an activity, an idea, or an argument as **threadbare**, you mean that it is very weak, or inadequate, or old and no longer interesting. ❑ *...the government's threadbare domestic policies.* ADJ

**threat** /θret/ **(threats)** ♦♦◇ [1] A **threat to** a person or thing is a danger that something unpleasant might happen to them. A **threat** is also the cause of this danger. ❑ *Some couples see single women as a threat to their relationships... The Hurricane Center warns people not to take the threat of tropical storms lightly.* N-VAR: with supp, oft N *to*/*from* n, N *of* n
[2] A **threat** is a statement by someone that they will do something unpleasant, especially if you do not do what they want. ❑ *He may be forced to carry out his threat to resign... The priest remains in hiding after threats by former officials of the ousted dictatorship.* N-COUNT: usu with supp, oft N to-inf
[3] If a person or thing is **under threat**, there is a danger that something unpleasant might be done to them, or that they might cease to exist. ❑ *His position as* PHRASE: oft PHR *of*/*from* n

*leader will be under threat at a party congress due next month... She lives daily under threat of violence.*

**threat|en** /θretᵊn/ **(threatens, threatening, threatened)** ◆◆◇ [1] VERB If a person **threatens to** do something unpleasant to you, or if they **threaten** you, they say or imply that they will do something unpleasant to you, especially if you do not do what they want. ❑ V to-inf *He said army officers had threatened to destroy the town...* V n *with* n *He tied her up and threatened her with a six-inch knife...* V n *If you threaten me or use any force, I shall inform the police.* Also V that [2] VERB If something or someone **threatens** a person or thing, they are likely to harm that person or thing. ❑ V n *The newcomers directly threaten the livelihood of the established workers...* be V-ed *with* n *30 percent of reptiles, birds, and fish are currently threatened with extinction.* [3] VERB If something unpleasant **threatens to** happen, it seems likely to happen. ❑ V to-inf *The fighting is threatening to turn into full-scale war.* [4] → See also **threatened, threatening.**

**threat|ened** /θretᵊnd/ ADJ: v-link ADJ, oft ADJ *by* n If you feel **threatened**, you feel as if someone is trying to harm you. ❑ *Anger is the natural reaction we experience when we feel threatened or frustrated.* → See also **threaten.**

**threat|en|ing** /θretənɪŋ/ ◆◇◇ ADJ: usu ADJ n You can describe someone's behaviour as **threatening** when you think that they are trying to harm you. ❑ *The police could have charged them with threatening behaviour.* ♦ **threat|en|ing|ly** ADV: usu ADV with v *'This ain't no affair of yours, boy!' McClosky said threateningly.* → See also **threaten, life-threatening.**

**three** /θriː/ **(threes) Three** is the number 3. ◆◆◆ NUM ❑ *We waited three months before going back to see the specialist.*

**three-cornered** ADJ: usu ADJ n If you describe something such as a disagreement, competition, or game as **three-cornered**, you mean that it involves three people, groups, or teams. [mainly BRIT] ❑ *...the three-cornered struggle between employers and male and female workers.*

**three-dimensional** [1] ADJ A **three-dimensional** object is solid rather than flat, because it can be measured in three different directions, usually the height, length, and width. The abbreviation **3-D** can also be used. ❑ *...a three-dimensional model.* [2] ADJ A **three-dimensional** picture, image, or film looks as though it is deep or solid rather than flat. The abbreviation **3-D** can also be used. ❑ *...new software, which generates both two-dimensional drawings and three-dimensional images.* [3] ADJ [approval] If you describe fictional characters as **three-dimensional** you mean that they seem real and natural. ❑ *She emerges as a full, three-dimensional character in a way that few horror genre heroines ever do.* [4] ADJ: ADJ n **Three-dimensional** art or design is produced by carving or shaping stone, wood, clay, or other materials. The abbreviation **3-D** can also be used. ❑ *...a degree in three-dimensional art.*

**three-fourths** QUANT: QUANT *of* n In American English, people sometimes use **three-fourths** to mean **three-quarters**. ❑ *Three-fourths of the apartments in the ghetto had no heat.* ♦ PRON **Three-fourths** is also a pronoun. ❑ *He has just under 1,600 delegates, about three-fourths what he needs to win the Democratic presidential nomination.*

**three-line whip (three-line whips)** N-COUNT A **three-line whip** is a situation where the MPs in a political party are ordered to attend parliament and vote in a particular way on a particular issue. [BRIT]

**three-piece** [1] ADJ: ADJ n A **three-piece** suit is a set of three pieces of matching clothing, usually a man's jacket, waistcoat, and trousers. [2] ADJ: ADJ n A **three-piece** suite is a sofa and two matching armchairs. [mainly BRIT]

**three-point turn (three-point turns)** N-COUNT When the driver of a vehicle does a **three-point turn**, he or she turns the vehicle by driving forwards in a curve, then backwards in a curve, and then forwards in a curve.

**three-quarter** also **three quarter.** ADJ: ADJ n You can use **three-quarter** to describe something which is three fourths of the usual size or three fourths of a standard measurement. ❑ *Choose short or three-quarter sleeves for summer. ...a session which lasted one and three-quarter hours.*

**three-quarters** QUANT: QUANT *of* n **Three-quarters** is an amount that is three out of four equal parts of something. ❑ *Three-quarters of the country's workers took part in the strike... It took him about three-quarters of an hour.* ♦ PRON **Three-quarters** is also a pronoun. ❑ *Road deaths have increased by three-quarters.* ♦ ADV: ADV adj/-ed **Three-quarters** is also an adverb. ❑ *We were left with an open bottle of champagne three-quarters full.*

**three Rs** N-PLURAL: *the* N When talking about children's education, **the three Rs** are the basic skills of reading, writing, and arithmetic.

**three|some** /θriːsəm/ **(threesomes)** N-COUNT A **threesome** is a group of three people.

**three-wheeler (three-wheelers)** N-COUNT A **three-wheeler** is a bicycle or car with three wheels.

**thresh** /θreʃ/ **(threshes, threshing, threshed)** VERB: usu passive When a cereal such as corn, wheat, or rice **is threshed**, it is beaten in order to separate the grains from the rest of the plant. ❑ be V-ed *The corn was still sown, cut and threshed as it was a hundred years ago.* Also V

**thresh|old** /θreʃhoʊld/ **(thresholds)** [1] N-COUNT: usu sing The **threshold** of a building or room is the floor in the doorway, or the doorway itself. ❑ *He stopped at the threshold of the bedroom.* [2] N-COUNT: usu with supp, oft N *of* n, n N A **threshold** is an amount, level, or limit on a scale. When the **threshold** is reached, something else happens or changes. ❑ *She has a low threshold of boredom and needs the constant stimulation of physical activity... Fewer than forty per cent voted – the threshold for results to be valid.* [3] PHRASE: PHR n/-ing If you are **on the threshold of** something exciting or new, you are about to experience it. ❑ *We are on the threshold of a new era in astronomy.*

**threw** /θruː/ **Threw** is the past tense of **throw.**

**thrice** /θraɪs/ [1] ADV: ADV with v, ADV adv, ADV n Something that happens **thrice** happens three times. [OLD-FASHIONED] ❑ *They should think not twice, but thrice, before ignoring such advice... She plays tennis thrice weekly.* [2] ADV: ADV n You can use **thrice** to indicate that something is three times the size, value, or intensity of something else. [OLD-FASHIONED] ❑ *...moving at thrice the speed of sound.*

**thrift** /θrɪft/ **(thrifts)** [1] N-UNCOUNT [approval] ≠extravagance **Thrift** is the quality and practice of being careful with money and not wasting things. ❑ *They were rightly praised for their thrift and enterprise.* [2] N-COUNT A **thrift** or a **thrift institution** is a kind of savings bank. [AM, BUSINESS]

**thrift shop (thrift shops)** N-COUNT A **thrift shop** or **thrift store** is a shop that sells used goods cheaply and gives its profits to a charity. [AM]

✔ in BRIT, use **charity shop**

**thrifty** /θrɪfti/ **(thriftier, thriftiest)** ADJ [approval] If you say that someone is **thrifty**, you are praising them for saving money, not buying unnecessary things, and not wasting things. ❑ *My mother taught me to be thrifty. ...thrifty shoppers.*

**thrill** /θrɪl/ **(thrills, thrilling, thrilled)** [1] N-COUNT: usu sing, oft N *of* n/-ing If something gives you a **thrill**, it gives you a sudden feeling of great excitement, pleasure, or fear. ❑ *I can remember the thrill of not knowing what I would get on Christmas morning... It's a great thrill for a cricket-lover like me to play at the home of cricket.* [2] VERB If something **thrills** you, or if you **thrill at** it, it gives you a feeling of great pleasure and excitement. ❑ V n *The electric atmosphere both terrified and thrilled him...* V *at/to* n *The children will thrill at all their favourite characters.* [3] → See also **thrilled, thrilling.** [4] PHRASE If you refer to **thrills and spills**, you are referring to an experience which is exciting and full of surprises. ❑ *Its prime audience lies in the 17 to 24 age group, and they want instant thrills and spills.*

**thrilled** /θrɪld/ 1 If someone is **thrilled**, they are extremely pleased about something. ❑ *I was so thrilled to get a good report from him... Sue and John were especially thrilled with this award.* [*ADJ: v-link ADJ, oft ADJ to-inf, ADJ prep, ADJ that; = delighted*] ● If you say that someone is **thrilled to bits**, you are emphasizing the fact that they are extremely pleased about something. You can also say **thrilled to pieces**, especially in American English. ❑ *I'm thrilled to bits to have won the cash.* [*PHRASE: v-link PHR, oft PHR to-inf, PHR at/with n/-ing; emphasis*] 2 → See also **thrill**.

**thrill|er** /θrɪləʳ/ **(thrillers)** A **thriller** is a book, film, or play that tells an exciting fictional story about something such as criminal activities or spying. ❑ *...a tense psychological thriller.* [*N-COUNT*]

**thrill|ing** /θrɪlɪŋ/ 1 Something that is **thrilling** is very exciting and enjoyable. ❑ *Our wildlife trips offer a thrilling encounter with wildlife in its natural state.* [*ADJ; = exciting*] ♦ **thrill|ing|ly** *Watson has a wonderful voice, with thrillingly clear top notes.* [*ADV: ADV adj, ADV with v*] 2 → See also **thrill**.

**thrive** /θraɪv/ **(thrives, thriving, thrived)** 1 If someone or something **thrives**, they do well and are successful, healthy, or strong. ❑ *Today his company continues to thrive. ...the river's thriving population of kingfishers.* [*VERB; V; V-ing*] 2 If you say that someone **thrives on** a particular situation, you mean that they enjoy it or that they can deal with it very well, especially when other people find it unpleasant or difficult. ❑ *Many people thrive on a stressful lifestyle.* [*VERB; V on n/-ing*]

**thro'** also **thro. Thro'** is sometimes used as a written abbreviation for **through**.

**throat** /θrəʊt/ **(throats)** 1 Your **throat** is the back of your mouth and the top part of the tubes that go down into your stomach and your lungs. ❑ *She had a sore throat... As she stared at him she felt her throat go dry.* [*◆◇◇ N-COUNT: oft poss N*] 2 Your **throat** is the front part of your neck. ❑ *His striped tie was loosened at his throat.* [*N-COUNT: oft poss N*]

**PHRASES** 3 If you **clear** your **throat**, you cough once in order to make it easier to speak or to attract people's attention. ❑ *Cross cleared his throat and spoke in low, polite tones.* [*PHRASE: V inflects*] 4 If you **ram** something **down** someone's **throat** or **force** it **down** their **throat**, you keep mentioning a situation or idea in order to make them accept it or believe it. ❑ *I've always been close to my dad but he's never rammed his career down my throat.* [*PHRASE: V inflects*] 5 If two people or groups are **at each other's throats**, they are quarrelling or fighting violently with each other. ❑ *The idea that Billy and I are at each other's throats couldn't be further from the truth.* [*PHRASE: v-link PHR, PHR after v*] 6 If something **sticks in** your **throat**, you find it unacceptable. ❑ *What sticks in my throat is that I wasn't able to win the trophy.* [*PHRASE: V inflects*] 7 a **lump in** your **throat** → see **lump**.

**throaty** /θrəʊti/ A **throaty** voice or laugh is low and rather rough. [*ADJ; = hoarse*]

**throb** /θrɒb/ **(throbs, throbbing, throbbed)** 1 If part of your body **throbs**, you feel a series of strong and usually painful beats there. ❑ *His head throbbed.* [*VERB; V*] ♦ **Throb** is also a noun. ❑ *The bruise on his stomach ached with a steady throb.* [*N-SING*] 2 If something **throbs**, it vibrates and makes a steady noise. [LITERARY] ❑ *The engines throbbed.* [*VERB; V*] ♦ **Throb** is also a noun. ❑ *Jake's head jerked up at the throb of the engine.* [*N-SING*]

**throes** /θrəʊz/ 1 If someone is experiencing something very unpleasant or emotionally painful, you can say that they are in the **throes** of it, especially when it is in its final stages. [FORMAL] ❑ *...when the country was going through the final throes of civil war.* [*N-PLURAL: usu prep N, N of n*] 2 If you are **in the throes of** doing or experiencing something, especially something difficult, you are busy doing it or are deeply involved in it. [FORMAL] ❑ *The country is in the throes of a general election.* [*PREP-PHRASE*] 3 → See also **death throes**.

**throm|bo|sis** /θrɒmbəʊsɪs/ **(thromboses** /θrɒmbəʊsiːz/**)** **Thrombosis** is the formation of a blood clot in a person's heart or in one of their blood vessels, which can cause death. [MEDICAL] [*N-VAR*] → See also **coronary thrombosis, deep vein thrombosis**.

**throne** /θrəʊn/ **(thrones)** 1 A **throne** is a decorative chair used by a king, queen, or emperor on important official occasions. [*N-COUNT*] 2 You can talk about **the throne** as a way of referring to the position of being king, queen, or emperor. ❑ *...the Queen's 50th anniversary on the throne.* [*N-SING: the N*]

**throng** /θrɒŋ, AM θrɔːŋ/ **(throngs, thronging, thronged)** 1 A **throng** is a large crowd of people. [LITERARY] ❑ *An official pushed through the throng.* [*N-COUNT; = crowd*] 2 When people **throng** somewhere, they go there in great numbers. [LITERARY] ❑ *The crowds thronged into the mall.* [*VERB; = flock; V to/into/around n*] 3 If people **throng** a place, they are present there in great numbers. ❑ *They throng the beaches between late June and early August.* [*VERB; = crowd; V n*] ♦ **thronged** *The streets are thronged with people.* [*ADJ: v-link ADJ with n*]

**throt|tle** /θrɒtᵊl/ **(throttles, throttling, throttled)** 1 To **throttle** someone means to kill or injure them by squeezing their throat or tightening something around it and preventing them from breathing. ❑ *The attacker then tried to throttle her with wire.* [*VERB; = strangle; V n*] 2 If you say that something or someone **is throttling** a process, institution, or group, you mean that they are restricting it severely or destroying it. ❑ *He said the over-valuation of sterling was throttling industry.* [*VERB; V n*] 3 The **throttle** of a motor vehicle or aircraft is the device, lever, or pedal that controls the quantity of fuel entering the engine and is used to control the vehicle's speed. ❑ *He gently opened the throttle, and the ship began to ease forward.* [*N-COUNT*] 4 **Throttle** is the power that is obtained by using a throttle. ❑ *...motor bikes revving at full throttle.* [*N-UNCOUNT*] 5 If you say that something is done **at full throttle**, you mean that it is done with great speed and enthusiasm. ❑ *He lived his life at full throttle.* [*PHRASE: PHR after v, v-link PHR*]

**through** ◆◆◆

✓ The preposition is pronounced /θruː/. In other cases, **through** is pronounced /θruː/

In addition to the uses shown below, **through** is used in phrasal verbs such as 'see through', 'think through', and 'win through'.

1 To move **through** something such as a hole, opening, or pipe means to move directly from one side or end of it to the other. ❑ *The theatre was evacuated when rain poured through the roof at the Liverpool Playhouse... Go straight through that door under the EXIT sign... Visitors enter through a side entrance.* [*PREP*] ♦ **Through** is also an adverb. ❑ *He went straight through to the kitchen and took a can of beer from the fridge... She opened the door and stood back to allow the man to pass through.* [*ADV: ADV after v*] 2 To cut **through** something means to cut it in two pieces or to make a hole in it. ❑ *Use a proper fish knife and fork if possible as they are designed to cut through the flesh but not the bones... Rabbits still manage to find a way in. I am sure that some have even taken to gnawing through the metal.* [*PREP*] ♦ **Through** is also an adverb. ❑ *Score lightly at first and then repeat, scoring deeper each time until the board is cut through.* [*ADV: ADV after v*] 3 To go **through** a town, area, or country means to travel across it or in it. ❑ *Go up to Ramsgate, cross into France, go through Andorra and into Spain. ...travelling through pathless woods.* [*PREP*] ♦ **Through** is also an adverb. ❑ *Few know that the tribe was just passing through.* [*ADV: ADV after v*] 4 If you move **through** a group of things or a mass of something, it is on either side of you or all around you. ❑ *We made our way through the crowd to the river... Sybil's fingers ran* [*PREP*]

*through the water.* ♦ **Through** is also an adverb. ❑ *He pushed his way through to the edge of the crowd where he waited.* ADV: ADV after v

[5] To get **through** a barrier or obstacle means to get from one side of it to the other. ❑ *Allow twenty-five minutes to get through Passport Control and Customs... He was one of the last of the crowd to pass through the barrier.* PREP ♦ **Through** is also an adverb. ❑ *...a maze of concrete and steel barriers, designed to prevent vehicles driving straight through.* ADV: ADV after v

[6] If a driver goes **through** a red light, they keep driving even though they should stop. ❑ *He was killed at a road junction by a van driver who went through a red light.* PREP

[7] If something goes into an object and comes out of the other side, you can say that it passes **through** the object. ❑ *The ends of the net pass through a wooden bar at each end.* PREP ♦ **Through** is also an adverb. ❑ *I bored a hole so that the fixing bolt would pass through.* ADV: ADV after v

[8] To go **through** a system means to move around it or to pass from one end of it to the other. ❑ *...electric currents travelling through copper wires... What a lot of cards you've got through the post!* PREP ♦ **Through** is also an adverb. ❑ *It is also expected to consider a resolution which would allow food to go through immediately with fewer restrictions.* ADV: ADV after v

[9] If you see, hear, or feel something **through** a particular thing, that thing is between you and the thing you can see, hear, or feel. ❑ *Alice gazed pensively through the wet glass.* PREP

[10] If something such as a feeling, attitude, or quality, happens **through** an area, organization, or a person's body, it happens everywhere in it or affects all of it. ❑ *An atmosphere of anticipation vibrated through the crowd... What was going through his mind when he spoke those amazing words?* PREP

[11] If something happens or exists **through** a period of time, it happens or exists from the beginning until the end. ❑ *She kept quiet all through breakfast.* PREP ♦ **Through** is also an adverb. ❑ *We've got a tough programme, hard work right through to the summer.* ADV: ADV after v

[12] If something happens from a particular period of time **through** another, it starts at the first period and continues until the end of the second period. [AM] ❑ *...open Monday through Sunday from 7:00 am to 10:00 pm.* PREP

☑ in BRIT, use **to**

[13] If you go **through** a particular experience or event, you experience it, and if you behave in a particular way **through** it, you behave in that way while it is happening. ❑ *Men go through a change of life emotionally just like women.* PREP

[14] If you are **through with** something or if it is **through**, you have finished doing it and will never do it again. If you are **through with** someone, you do not want to have anything to do with them again. ❑ *I'm through with the explaining.* ADJ: v-link ADJ, oft ADJ *with* n

[15] You use **through** in expressions such as **half-way through** and **all the way through** to indicate to what extent an action or task is completed. ❑ *A thirty-nine-year-old competitor collapsed half-way through the marathon and died shortly afterwards.* PREP: n PREP n ♦ **Through** is also an adverb. ❑ *Stir the pork about until it turns white all the way through.* ADV: n ADV

[16] If something happens because of something else, you can say that it happens **through** it. ❑ *They are understood to have retired through age or ill health.* PREP

[17] You use **through** when stating the means by which a particular thing is achieved. ❑ *Those who seek to grab power through violence deserve punishment.* PREP

[18] If you do something **through** someone else, they take the necessary action for you. ❑ *Do I need to go through my doctor or can I make an appointment direct?* PREP = *via*

[19] If something such as a proposal or idea goes **through**, it is accepted by people in authority and is made legal or official. ❑ *It is possible that the present Governor General will be made interim President, if the proposals go through.* ADV: ADV after v ♦ **Through** is also a preposition. ❑ *They want to get the plan through Congress as quickly as possible.* PREP

[20] If someone gets **through** an examination or a round of a competition, they succeed or win. ❑ *She was bright, learned languages quickly, and sailed through her exams.* PREP ♦ **Through** is also an adverb. ❑ *Nigeria also go through from that group.* ADV: ADV after v

[21] When you get **through** while making a telephone call, the call is connected and you can speak to the person you are phoning. ❑ *He may find the line cut on the telephone so that he can't get through.* ADV: ADV after v

[22] If you look or go **through** a lot of things, you look at them or deal with them one after the other. ❑ *Let's go through the numbers together and see if a workable deal is possible.* PREP

[23] If you read **through** something, you read it from beginning to end. ❑ *She read through pages and pages of the music I had brought her.* PREP ♦ **Through** is also an adverb. ❑ *He read the article straight through, looking for any scrap of information that might have passed him by.* ADV: ADV after v

[24] A **through** train goes directly to a particular place, so that the people who want to go there do not have to change trains. ❑ *...Britain's longest through train journey, 685 miles.* ADJ: ADJ n

[25] If you say that someone or something is wet **through**, you are emphasizing how wet they are. ❑ *I returned to the inn cold and wet, soaked through by the drizzling rain.* ADV: adj ADV [emphasis]

[26] **Through and through** means completely and to the greatest extent possible. ❑ *I've gotten my feet thoroughly soaked and feel frozen through and through.* PHRASE: usu n/adj PHR, PHR after v

**through|out** /θruːaʊt/ ♦♦◇ [1] If you say that something happens **throughout** a particular period of time, you mean that it happens during the whole of that period. ❑ *The national tragedy of rival groups killing each other continued throughout 1990... Movie music can be made memorable because its themes are repeated throughout the film.* PREP ♦ **Throughout** is also an adverb. ❑ *The first song, 'Blue Moon', didn't go too badly except that everyone talked throughout.* ADV: ADV with cl

[2] If you say that something happens or exists **throughout** a place, you mean that it happens or exists in all parts of that place. ❑ *'Sight Savers', founded in 1950, now runs projects throughout Africa, the Caribbean and South East Asia.* PREP ♦ **Throughout** is also an adverb. ❑ *The route is well sign-posted throughout.* ADV: ADV with cl

**through|put** /θruːpʊt/ The **throughput** of an organization or system is the amount of things it can do or deal with in a particular period of time. ❑ *...technologies which will allow us to get much higher throughput.* N-UNCOUNT

**through|way** /θruːweɪ/ → see **thruway**.

**throw** /θroʊ/ **(throws, throwing, threw, thrown)** ♦♦◇ [1] When you **throw** an object that you are holding, you move your hand or arm quickly and let go of the object, so that it moves through the air. ❑ *He spent hours throwing a tennis ball against a wall... The crowd began throwing stones... Sophia jumps up and throws down her knitting... He threw Brian a rope.* VERB V n prep/adv, V n, V n with adv, V n n ♦ **Throw** is also a noun. ❑ *One of the judges thought it was a foul throw... A throw of the dice allows a player to move himself forward.* N-COUNT: oft N *of* n ♦ **throw|ing** *He didn't really know very much about javelin throwing.* N-UNCOUNT: usu with supp

[2] If you **throw** your body or part of your body into a particular position or place, you move it there suddenly and with a lot of force. ❑ *She threw her arms around his shoulders... She threatened to throw herself in front of a train... He set his skinny legs apart and threw back his shoulders.* VERB V n prep, V pron-refl prep/adv, V n with adv

[3] If you **throw** something into a particular place or position, you put it there in a quick and careless way. ❑ *He struggled out of his bulky jacket and threw it on to the back seat.* VERB V n prep/adv

[4] To **throw** someone into a particular place or position means to force them roughly into that place or position. ❑ *He threw me to the ground and started to kick... The device exploded, throwing Mr Taylor from his car.* VERB V n prep/adv, V n prep/adv

[5] If you say that someone **is thrown into** prison, you mean that they are put there by the authorities, especially if this seems unfair or cruel. ❑ *Those two should have been thrown in jail... Police should have the power to fine people who hamper rescue efforts. In fact I'd throw them into prison for a night.* VERB *be* V-ed *in/into* n, V n *in/into* n

[6] If a horse **throws** its rider, it makes him or her fall off, by suddenly jumping or moving VERB

violently. ❑ *The horse reared, throwing its rider and knocking down a youth standing beside it.* V n

7 VERB If a person or thing **is thrown into** an unpleasant situation or state, something causes them to be in that situation or state. ❑ *Abidjan was thrown into turmoil because of a protest by taxi drivers...* *be* V-ed prep *Economic recession had thrown millions out of work.* V n prep

8 VERB = *cast* If something **throws** light or a shadow **on** a surface, it causes that surface to have light or a shadow on it. ❑ *The sunlight is white and blinding, throwing hard-edged shadows on the ground.* V n *on/onto* n

9 VERB = *cast* If something **throws** doubt **on** a person or thing, it causes people to doubt or suspect them. ❑ *This new information does throw doubt on their choice.* V n *on/upon* n

10 VERB: no cont If you **throw** a look or smile at someone or something, you look or smile at them quickly and suddenly. ❑ *Emily turned and threw her a suggestive grin.* V n n, Also V n *at* n

11 VERB If you **throw** yourself, your energy, or your money **into** a particular job or activity, you become involved in it very actively or enthusiastically. ❑ *She threw herself into a modelling career...* V pron-refl *into* n *They threw all their military resources into the battle.* V n *into* n

12 VERB If you **throw** a fit or a tantrum, you suddenly start to behave in an uncontrolled way. ❑ *I used to get very upset and scream and swear, throwing tantrums all over the place.* V n

13 VERB If something such as a remark or an experience **throws** you, it surprises you or confuses you because it is unexpected. ❑ *The professor rather threw me by asking if I went in for martial arts.* V n

14 VERB If you **throw** a punch, you punch someone. ❑ *Everything was fine until someone threw a punch.* V n

15 VERB When someone **throws** a party, they organize one, usually in their own home. [INFORMAL] ❑ *Why not throw a party for your friends?* V n

16 VERB In sports, if a player **throws** a game or contest, they lose it as a result of a deliberate action or intention. ❑ *...offering him a bribe to throw the game.* V n

17 N-COUNT A **throw** is a light rug, blanket, or cover for a sofa or bed.

PHRASES 18 PHRASE: amount PHR If things cost a particular amount of money **a throw**, they cost that amount each. [INFORMAL] ❑ *Most applications software for personal computers cost over $500 a throw.*

19 PHRASE: V inflects If someone **throws** themselves **at** you, they make it very obvious that they want to begin a relationship with you, by behaving as though they are sexually attracted to you. ❑ *I'll say you started it, that you threw yourself at me.*

20 to **throw** someone **in at the deep end** → see **end**. to **throw down the gauntlet** → see **gauntlet**. to **throw light on** something → see **light**. to **throw in** your **lot with** someone → see **lot**. to **throw money at** something → see **money**. to **throw good money after bad** → see **money**. to **throw a spanner in the works** → see **spanner**. **a stone's throw** → see **stone**. to **throw in the towel** → see **towel**. to **throw** your **weight about** → see **weight**. to **throw a wrench** → see **wrench**.

♦ **throw away** or **throw out** 1 PHRASAL VERB When you **throw away** or **throw out** something that you do not want, you get rid of it, for example by putting it in a rubbish container. ❑ *I never throw anything away...* V n P *I'm not advising you to throw away your makeup or forget about your appearance.* V P n (not pron)

2 PHRASAL VERB If you **throw away** an opportunity, advantage, or benefit, you waste it, rather than using it sensibly. ❑ *Failing to tackle the deficit would be throwing away an opportunity we haven't had for a generation...* V P n (not pron) *We should have won. We threw it away.* V n P → See also **throwaway**.

♦ **throw back** 1 PHRASAL VERB If you **throw** something **back at** a person, you remind them of something bad they did in the past, in order to upset them. ❑ *I should never have told you that. I knew you'd throw it back at me.* V n P *at* n, Also V P *at* n n

2 PHRASAL VERB: usu passive If someone **is thrown back on** their own powers or resources, they have to use them, because there is nothing else they can use. ❑ *We are constantly thrown back on our own resources.* *be* V-ed P *on* n

♦ **throw down** PHRASAL VERB If you **throw down** a challenge to someone, you do something new or unexpected in a bold or forceful manner that will probably cause them to reply or react equally strongly. ❑ *The regional parliament threw down a new challenge to the central authorities by passing a law allowing private ownership of businesses...* V P n (not pron) *Government ministers have been responding to the challenge thrown down by their former colleague.* V-ed P

♦ **throw in** 1 PHRASAL VERB = *toss in* If you **throw in** a remark when having a conversation, you add it in a casual or unexpected way. ❑ *Occasionally Farling threw in a question.* V P n, Also V n P

2 PHRASAL VERB = *include* If a person who is selling something **throws in** something extra, they give you the extra thing and only ask you to pay for the first thing. ❑ *Pay £4.80 for larger prints and they throw in a free photo album...* V P n (not pron) *They were offering me a weekend break in Paris – with free beer thrown in.* V-ed P, Also V n P

♦ **throw off** 1 PHRASAL VERB = *cast off* If you **throw off** something that is restricting you or making you unhappy, you get rid of it. ❑ *...a country ready to throw off the shackles of its colonial past...* V P n (not pron) *One day depression descended upon him, and wherever he went after that he could never throw it off.* V n P

2 PHRASAL VERB = *give off* If something **throws off** a substance, it produces it and releases it into the air. ❑ *The belt may make a squealing noise and throw off sooty black particles of rubber.* V P n (not pron)

3 PHRASAL VERB If you **throw off** people who are chasing you or trying to find you, you do something unexpected that makes them unable to catch you or find you. ❑ *He threw off pursuers by pedaling across the state line...* V P n *He tried to throw police off the track of his lover.* V n P n, Also V n P

♦ **throw out** 1 PHRASAL VERB → see **throw away 1**.

2 If a judge **throws out** a case, he or she rejects it and the accused person does not have to stand trial. ❑ *The defense wants the district Judge to throw out the case.* V P n, Also V n P

3 PHRASAL VERB If you **throw** someone **out**, you force them to leave a place or group. ❑ *He was thrown out of the Olympic team after testing positive for drugs...* *be/get* V-ed P *of* n *I wanted to kill him, but instead I just threw him out of the house...* V n P *of* n *The party threw out the Trotskyist Militant Tendency.* V P n (not pron), Also V n P

♦ **throw together** 1 PHRASAL VERB If you **throw** something **together**, for example a meal or a costume, you make it quickly and not very carefully. [INFORMAL] ❑ *Too often, picnic preparation consists of throwing together some sandwiches and grabbing an apple.* V P n (not pron), Also V n P

2 PHRASAL VERB If people **are thrown together** by a situation or event, it causes them to get to know each other, even though they may not want to. ❑ *The cast and crew were thrown together for 12 hours a day, six days a week.* pl-n *be* V-ed P *...men and women thrown together in inhospitable surroundings...* V-ed P *My husband is constantly thrown together with young people through his work.* *be* V-ed P *with* n, Also V pl-n P, V P pl-n

♦ **throw up** 1 PHRASAL VERB When someone **throws up**, they vomit. [INFORMAL] ❑ *She said she had thrown up after reading reports of the trial.* V P

2 PHRASAL VERB If something **throws up** dust, stones, or water, when it moves or hits the ground, it causes them to rise up into the air. ❑ *If it had hit the Earth, it would have made a crater 100 miles across and thrown up an immense cloud of dust.* V P n (not pron), Also V n P

3 PHRASAL VERB To **throw up** a particular person or thing means to produce them or cause them to become noticeable. [mainly BRIT] ❑ *The political struggle threw up a strong leader.* V P n (not pron)

**throw|away** /θrouəweɪ/ 1 ADJ: ADJ n A **throwaway** product is intended to be used only for a short time, and then to be thrown away. ❑ *Now they are producing throwaway razors.*

2 ADJ: ADJ n If you say that someone makes a **throwaway** remark or gesture, you mean that they make it in a casual way, although it may be important, or have some serious or humorous effect. ❑ *...a throwaway remark she later regretted.*

**throw|back** /θroubæk/ **(throwbacks)** N-COUNT: usu sing, oft N *to* n If you say that something is a **throwback** to a former time, you mean that it is like something that existed a long time ago. ❑ *The hall is a throwback to another era with its old prints and stained-glass.*

**throw-in** **(throw-ins)** When there is a **throw-in** in a football or rugby match, the ball is thrown back onto the field after it has been kicked off it. N-COUNT

**thrown** /θroun/ **Thrown** is the past participle of **throw**.

**thru'** also **thru.** **Thru'** is sometimes used a written abbreviation for **through**. [mainly AM]

**thrum** /θrʌm/ **(thrums, thrumming, thrummed)** When something such as a machine or engine **thrums**, it makes a low beating sound. ❑ *The air-conditioner thrummed.* ♦ **Thrum** is also a noun. ❑ *...the thrum of refrigeration motors... My head was going thrum thrum thrum.* VERB; V; N-COUNT; SOUND

**thrush** /θrʌʃ/ **(thrushes)** [1] A **thrush** is a fairly small bird with a brown back and a spotted breast. [2] **Thrush** is a medical condition caused by a fungus. It most often occurs in a baby's mouth or in a woman's vagina. N-COUNT; N-UNCOUNT

**thrust** /θrʌst/ **(thrusts, thrusting, thrust)** [1] If you **thrust** something or someone somewhere, you push or move them there quickly with a lot of force. ❑ *They thrust him into the back of a jeep.* ♦ **Thrust** is also a noun. ❑ *Two of the knife thrusts were fatal.* [2] If you **thrust** your **way** somewhere, you move there, pushing between people or things which are in your way. ❑ *She thrust her way into the crowd.* [3] If something **thrusts** up or out of something else, it sticks up or sticks out in a noticeable way. [LITERARY] ❑ *An aerial thrust up from the grass verge... A ray of sunlight thrust out through the clouds.* [4] **Thrust** is the power or force that is required to make a vehicle move in a particular direction. ❑ *It provides the thrust that makes the craft move forward.* [5] The **thrust** of an activity or of an idea is the main or essential things it expresses. ❑ *The main thrust of the research will be the study of the early Universe and galaxy formation.* [6] **cut and thrust** → see **cut**. VERB = shove; V n prep/adv; N-COUNT; VERB = push; V *way* prep/adv; VERB; V adv/prep; V adv/prep; N-UNCOUNT; N-SING: adj N, usu N *of* n

♦ **thrust upon** If something **is thrust upon** you, you are forced to have it, deal with it, or experience it. ❑ *Why has such sadness been thrust upon us?... Some are born great, some achieve greatness, and some have greatness thrust upon them.* PHRASAL VERB: usu passive; *be* V-ed P n; *have* n V-ed P n

**thru|way** /θruːweɪ/ **(thruways)** also **throughway.** A **thruway** is a wide road that is specially designed so that a lot of traffic can move along it very quickly. It is usually divided along the middle, so that traffic travelling in one direction is separated from the traffic travelling in the opposite direction. [AM] N-COUNT = express-way

**Thu.** → see **Thurs.**

**thud** /θʌd/ **(thuds, thudding, thudded)** [1] A **thud** is a dull sound, such as that which a heavy object makes when it hits something soft. ❑ *She tripped and fell with a sickening thud.* [2] If something **thuds** somewhere, it makes a dull sound, usually when it falls onto or hits something else. ❑ *She ran up the stairs, her bare feet thudding on the wood... There was a heavy thudding noise against the bedroom door.* ♦ **thud|ding** *...the thudding of the bombs beyond the hotel.* [3] When your heart **thuds**, it beats strongly and rather quickly, for example because you are very frightened or very happy. ❑ *My heart had started to thud, and my mouth was dry.* N-COUNT: usu sing, oft N *of* n; SOUND = thump; VERB; V prep/adv; V-ing; N-UNCOUNT: oft N *of* n; VERB = pound; V

**thug** /θʌg/ **(thugs)** You can refer to a violent person or criminal as a **thug**. ❑ *...the cowardly thugs who mug old people.* N-COUNT [disapproval]

**thug|gery** /θʌgəri/ **Thuggery** is rough, violent behaviour. N-UNCOUNT

**thug|gish** /θʌgɪʃ/ If you describe a person or their behaviour as **thuggish**, you mean they behave in a violent, rough, or threatening way. ❑ *The owner of the stall, a large, thuggish man, grabbed Dai by the collar.* ADJ [disapproval]

**thumb** /θʌm/ **(thumbs, thumbing, thumbed)** [1] Your **thumb** is the short thick part on the side of your hand next to your four fingers. ❑ *She bit the tip of her left thumb, not looking at me.* [2] If you **thumb** a lift or **thumb** a ride, you stand by the side of the road holding out your thumb until a driver stops and gives you a lift. ❑ *It may interest you to know that a boy answering Rory's description thumbed a ride to Howth... Thumbing a lift had once a carefree, easy-going image.* [3] → See also **well-thumbed**. N-COUNT; VERB = hitch; V n *to* n; V n

PHRASES [4] If you say that someone or something **sticks out like a sore thumb** or **stands out like a sore thumb**, you are emphasizing that they are very noticeable, usually because they are unusual or inappropriate. ❑ *Does the new housing stick out like a sore thumb or blend into its surroundings?* [5] If you say that someone is **twiddling** their **thumbs**, you mean that they do not have anything to do and are waiting for something to happen. ❑ *The prospect of waiting around just twiddling his thumbs was appalling.* [6] If you are **under** someone's **thumb**, you are under their control, or very heavily influenced by them. ❑ *I cannot tell you what pain I feel when I see how much my mother is under my father's thumb.* [7] **green thumb** → see **green**. to **thumb** your **nose at** someone → see **nose**. **rule of thumb** → see **rule**. PHRASE: V and N inflect [emphasis]; PHRASE: V inflects; PHRASE: v-link PHR, PHR after v

♦ **thumb through** If you **thumb through** something such as a book or magazine, you turn the pages quickly rather than reading each page carefully. ❑ *He had the drawer open and was thumbing through the files.* PHRASAL VERB; V P n

**thumb|nail** /θʌmneɪl/ **(thumbnails)** also **thumb-nail.** [1] Your **thumbnail** is the nail on your thumb. [2] A **thumbnail** sketch or account is a very short description of an event, idea, or plan which gives only the main details. N-COUNT; ADJ: ADJ n

**thumb|print** /θʌmprɪnt/ **(thumbprints)** also **thumb print.** [1] A **thumbprint** is a mark made by a person's thumb which shows the pattern of lines on its surface. [2] If you say that something such as a project has someone's **thumbprint** on it, you mean that it has features that make it obvious that they have been involved with it. ❑ *It's got your thumbprint all over it.* N-COUNT; N-COUNT

**thumb|screw** /θʌmskruː/ **(thumbscrews)** also **thumb screw.** [1] A **thumbscrew** is an object that was used in the past to torture people by crushing their thumbs. [2] If someone puts the **thumbscrews** on you, they start to put you under extreme pressure in order to force you to do something. N-COUNT; N-COUNT

**thumbs down** also **thumbs-down.** If you say that someone gives a plan, idea, or suggestion **the thumbs-down**, you are indicating that they do not approve of it and refuse to accept it. [INFORMAL] N-SING ≠ thumbs-up

**thumbs-up** also **thumbs up.** [1] A **thumbs-up** or a **thumbs-up sign** is a sign that you make by raising your thumb to show that you agree with someone, that you are happy with an idea or situation, or that everything is all right. ❑ *She checked the hall, then gave the others a thumbs-up sign.* [2] If you give a plan, idea, or suggestion **the thumbs-up**, you indicate that you approve of it and are willing to accept it. [INFORMAL] ❑ *The financial markets have given the thumbs up to the new policy.* N-SING; N-SING: the N ≠ thumbs-down

**thumb|tack** /θʌmtæk/ **(thumbtacks)** A **thumbtack** is a short pin with a broad flat top which is used for fastening papers or pictures to a board, wall, or other surface. [AM] N-COUNT

✔ in BRIT, use **drawing pin**

**thump** /θʌmp/ **(thumps, thumping, thumped)** [1] If you **thump** something, you hit it hard, usually with your fist. ❑ *He thumped my shoulder affectionately, nearly knocking me over... I heard you thumping on the door.* ♦ **Thump** is also a noun. ❑ *He felt a thump on his shoulder.* [2] If you **thump** someone, you attack them and hit them with your fist. [mainly BRIT, INFORMAL] ❑ *Don't say it serves me right or I'll thump you.* [3] If you **thump** something somewhere or if it **thumps** there, it makes VERB = bang; V n; V *on* n; N-COUNT; VERB; V n; VERB a loud, dull sound by hitting something else. ❑ *She thumped her hand on the witness box... Waiters went scurrying down the aisles, thumping down tureens of soup. ...paving stones and bricks which have been thumping down on police shields and helmets.* V n prep V n with adv V prep/adv ♦ **Thump** is also a noun. ❑ *There was a loud thump as the horse crashed into the van.* N-COUNT = thud [4] When your heart **thumps**, it beats strongly and quickly, usually because you are afraid or excited. ❑ *My heart was thumping wildly but I didn't let my face show any emotion.* VERB = pound, thud V [5] → See also **thumping**.

**thump|ing** /θʌmpɪŋ/ [1] **Thumping** is used to emphasize that something is very great or severe. [BRIT, INFORMAL] ❑ *The Right has a thumping majority.* ADJ: ADJ n emphasis = whopping [2] → See also **thump**.

**thun|der** /θʌndəʳ/ **(thunders, thundering, thundered)** [1] **Thunder** is the loud noise that you hear from the sky after a flash of lightning, especially during a storm. ❑ *...a distant clap of thunder.* N-UNCOUNT [2] When **it thunders**, a loud noise comes from the sky after a flash of lightning. ❑ *The day was heavy and still. It would probably thunder later.* VERB it V [3] The **thunder of** something that is moving or making a sound is the loud deep noise it makes. ❑ *The thunder of the sea on the rocks seemed to blank out other thoughts.* N-UNCOUNT: N of n = roar [4] If something or someone **thunders** somewhere, they move there quickly and with a lot of noise. ❑ *A lorry thundered by.* VERB V prep/adv [5] If something **thunders**, it makes a very loud noise, usually continuously. ❑ *She heard the sound of the guns thundering in the fog. ...thundering applause.* VERB = resound V V-ing [6] If you **thunder** something, you say it loudly and forcefully, especially because you are angry. [WRITTEN] ❑ *'It's your money. Ask for it!' she thundered... The Prosecutor looked toward Napoleon, waiting for him to thunder an objection.* VERB = bellow V with quote V n [7] If you **steal** someone's **thunder**, you get the attention or praise that they thought they would get, usually by saying or doing what they had intended to say or do. ❑ *He had no intention of letting the Foreign Secretary steal any of his thunder.* PHRASE: V inflects

**thunder|bolt** /θʌndəʳboʊlt/ **(thunderbolts)** A **thunderbolt** is a flash of lightning, accompanied by thunder, which strikes something such as a building or a tree. N-COUNT

**thunder|clap** /θʌndəʳklæp/ **(thunderclaps)** A **thunderclap** is a short loud noise that you hear in the sky just after you see a flash of lightning. N-COUNT

**thunder|cloud** /θʌndəʳklaʊd/ **(thunderclouds)** A **thundercloud** is a large dark cloud that is likely to produce thunder and lightning. N-COUNT

**thun|der|ous** /θʌndərəs/ If you describe a noise as **thunderous**, you mean that it is very loud and deep. ❑ *The audience responded with thunderous applause.* ADJ: usu ADJ n = deafening

**thunder|storm** /θʌndəʳstɔːʳm/ **(thunderstorms)** A **thunderstorm** is a storm in which there is thunder and lightning and a lot of heavy rain. N-COUNT

**thunder|struck** /θʌndəʳstrʌk/ If you say that someone is **thunderstruck**, you mean that they are extremely surprised or shocked. [FORMAL] ADJ: usu v-link ADJ = stunned

**thun|dery** /θʌndəri/ When the weather is **thundery**, there is a lot of thunder, or there are heavy clouds which make you think that there will be thunder soon. ❑ *Heavy thundery rain fell throughout Thursday.* ADJ

**Thurs.** also **Thur., Thu. Thurs.** is a written abbreviation for **Thursday**.

**Thurs|day** /θɜːʳzdeɪ, -di/ **(Thursdays) Thursday** is the day after Wednesday and before Friday. ❑ *On Thursday Barrett invited me for a drink... I'm always terribly busy on Thursdays.* N-VAR

**thus** /ðʌs/ ◆◆◇ [1] You use **thus** to show that what you are about to mention is the result or consequence of something else that you have just mentioned. [FORMAL] ❑ *Even in a highly skilled workforce some people will be more capable and thus better paid than others.* ADV: ADV with cl/group = therefore, hence [2] If you say that something is **thus** or happens **thus** you mean that it is, or happens, as you have just described or as you are just about to describe. [FORMAL] ❑ *Joanna was pouring the drink. While she was thus engaged, Charles sat on one of the bar-stools.* ADV: ADV with v, ADV cl

**thwack** /θwæk/ **(thwacks)** A **thwack** is a sound made when two solid objects hit each other hard. ❑ *I listened to the thwack of the metal balls... Then the woodcutter let his axe fly – Thwack! Everyone heard it.* N-COUNT; SOUND

**thwart** /θwɔːʳt/ **(thwarts, thwarting, thwarted)** If you **thwart** someone or **thwart** their plans, you prevent them from doing or getting what they want. ❑ *The accounting firm deliberately destroyed documents to thwart government investigators.* VERB V n

**thy** /ðaɪ/ **Thy** is an old-fashioned, poetic, or religious word for 'your' when you are talking to one person. ❑ *Honor thy father and thy mother.* DET

**thyme** /taɪm/ **Thyme** is a type of herb used in cooking. N-UNCOUNT

**thy|roid** /θaɪrɔɪd/ **(thyroids)** Your **thyroid** or your **thyroid gland** is a gland in your neck that produces chemicals which control the way your body grows and functions. N-COUNT

**thy|self** /ðaɪself/ **Thyself** is an old-fashioned, poetic, or religious word for 'yourself' when you are talking to only one person. ❑ *Love thy neighbour as thyself.* PRON

**ti|ara** /tiɑːrə/ **(tiaras)** A **tiara** is a metal band shaped like half a circle and decorated with jewels which a woman of very high social rank wears on her head at formal social occasions; also used of similar ornaments that girls or women wear on their heads. N-COUNT

**Ti|bet|an** /tɪbetᵊn/ **(Tibetans)** [1] **Tibetan** means belonging or relating to Tibet, or to its people, language, or culture. ADJ [2] A **Tibetan** is a Tibetan citizen or a person of Tibetan origin. N-COUNT [3] **Tibetan** is a language spoken by people who live in Tibet. N-COUNT

**tibia** /tɪbiə/ **(tibias)** Your **tibia** is the inner bone of the two bones in the lower part of your leg. [MEDICAL] N-COUNT

**tic** /tɪk/ **(tics)** If someone has a **tic**, a part of their face or body keeps making a small uncontrollable movement, for example because they are tired or have a nervous illness. ❑ *...people with nervous tics.* N-COUNT

**tick** /tɪk/ **(ticks, ticking, ticked)** [1] A **tick** is a written mark like a V: ✓. It is used to show that something is correct or has been selected or dealt with. [mainly BRIT] ❑ *Place a tick in the appropriate box.* N-COUNT

> in AM, usually use **check**

[2] If you **tick** something that is written on a piece of paper, you put a tick next to it. [mainly BRIT] ❑ *Please tick this box if you do not wish to receive such mailings.* VERB V n

> in AM, usually use **check**

[3] When a clock or watch **ticks**, it makes a regular series of short sounds as it works. ❑ *A wind-up clock ticked busily from the kitchen counter.* VERB V ♦ **Tick away** means the same as **tick**. ❑ *A grandfather clock ticked away in a corner.* PHRASAL VERB V P ♦ **tick|ing** *...the endless ticking of clocks.* N-UNCOUNT: oft N of n [4] The **tick** of a clock or watch is the series of short sounds it makes when it is working, or one of those sounds. ❑ *He sat listening to the tick of the grandfather clock.* N-COUNT [5] You can use **tick** to refer to a very short period of time. [BRIT, INFORMAL] ❑ *I'll be back in a tick.* N-COUNT = sec [6] If you talk about what makes someone **tick**, you are talking about the beliefs, wishes, and feelings that make them behave in the way that they do. [INFORMAL] ❑ *He wanted to find out what made them tick.* VERB V [7] A **tick** is a small creature which lives on the bodies of people or animals and uses their blood as food. ❑ *...chemicals that destroy ticks and mites.* N-COUNT

♦ **tick away** or **tick by** or **tick on** If you say that the clock or time is **ticking away**, PHRASAL VERB

**ticking by**, or **ticking on**, you mean that time is passing, especially when there is something that needs to be done or when you are waiting for something to happen. ❑ *The clock ticks away, leaving little time for talks.* V P

♦ **tick by** → see **tick away**.

♦ **tick off** [1] If you **tick off** items on a list, you write a tick or other mark next to them, in order to show that they have been dealt with. [mainly BRIT] ❑ *He ticked off my name on a piece of paper... Tick it off in the box.* PHRASAL VERB V P n (not pron) V n P

✔ in AM, usually use **check off**

[2] If you **tick** someone **off**, you speak angrily to them because they have done something wrong. [BRIT, INFORMAL] ❑ *His mum ticked him off at home... Abdel felt free to tick him off for smoking too much... Traffic police ticked off a pensioner for jumping a red light.* → See also **ticking off**. PHRASAL VERB = tell off V n P V n P *for* -ing/n V P n *for* -ing/n Also V P n

[3] If you say that something **ticks** you **off**, you mean that it annoys you. [AM, INFORMAL] ❑ *I just think it's rude and it's ticking me off... She's still ticked off at him for brushing her off and going out with you instead.* PHRASAL VERB V n P V-ed P

♦ **tick on** → see **tick away**.

♦ **tick over** [1] If an engine **is ticking over**, it is running at a low speed or rate, for example when it is switched on but you are not actually using it. [BRIT] ❑ *Very slowly he moved forward, the engine ticking over.* PHRASAL VERB = idle V P

[2] If a person, system, or business **is ticking over**, they are working steadily, but not producing very much or making much progress. [BRIT] ❑ *The market is at least ticking over.* PHRASAL VERB V P

**tick|er** /tɪkəʳ/ **(tickers)** Your **ticker** is your heart. [INFORMAL, OLD-FASHIONED] N-COUNT

**tick|er tape** **Ticker tape** consists of long narrow strips of paper on which information such as stock exchange prices is printed by a machine. In American cities, people sometimes throw ticker tape from high windows as a way of celebrating and honouring someone in public. ❑ *A half million people watched the troops march in New York's ticker tape parade.* N-UNCOUNT: oft N n

**tick|et** /tɪkɪt/ **(tickets)** [1] A **ticket** is a small, official piece of paper or card which shows that you have paid to enter a place such as a theatre or a sports ground, or shows that you have paid for a journey. ❑ *I queued for two hours to get a ticket to see the football game... I love opera and last year I got tickets for Covent Garden... Entrance is free, but by ticket only.* ◆◆◇ N-COUNT: also *by* N

[2] A **ticket** is an official piece of paper which orders you to pay a fine or to appear in court because you have committed a driving or parking offence. ❑ *I want to know at what point I break the speed limit and get a ticket.* N-COUNT

[3] A **ticket** for a game of chance such as a raffle or a lottery is a piece of paper with a number on it. If the number on your ticket matches the number chosen, you win a prize. ❑ *She bought a lottery ticket and won more than $33 million.* N-COUNT: usu n N

[4] The particular **ticket** on which a person fights an election is the party they represent or the policies they support. [BRIT] ❑ *He first ran for president on a far-left ticket.* N-SING: usu with supp = platform

[5] A **ticket** is the list of candidates who are representing a particular political party or group in an election. [AM] ❑ *He plans to remain on the Republican ticket for the November election.* N-COUNT: usu ADJ n

[6] If you say that something is **just the ticket**, you mean that it is exactly what is needed. [INFORMAL] ❑ *Young kids need all the energy and protein they can get and whole milk is just the ticket.* PHRASE: usu v-link PHR

[7] → See also **ticketing**, **big-ticket**, **dream ticket**, **meal ticket**, **parking ticket**, **season ticket**.

**tick|et|ing** /tɪkɪtɪŋ/ **Ticketing** is the act or activity of selling tickets. ❑ *...automatic ticketing machines.* N-UNCOUNT: oft N n

**tick|ing off** **(tickings off)** If you give someone a **ticking off**, you speak angrily to them because they have done something wrong. [BRIT, INFORMAL] ❑ *They got a ticking off from the police.* N-COUNT: usu sing = telling-off

**tick|le** /tɪkəl/ **(tickles, tickling, tickled)** [1] When you **tickle** someone, you move your fingers lightly over a sensitive part of their body, often in order to make them laugh. ❑ *I was tickling him, and he was laughing and giggling.* VERB V n

[2] If something **tickles** you or **tickles**, it causes an irritating feeling by lightly touching a part of your body. ❑ *...a yellow hat with a great feather that tickled her ear... A beard doesn't scratch, it just tickles.* VERB V n V

[3] If a fact or a situation **tickles** you, it amuses you or gives you pleasure. ❑ *It tickles me to see him riled... The story was really funny – it tickled me.* VERB it V n to-inf V n

♦ **tick|led** *They all sounded just as tickled.* ADJ: usu v-link ADJ

**tick|lish** /tɪkəlɪʃ/ [1] A **ticklish** problem, situation, or task is difficult and needs to be dealt with carefully. ❑ *So car makers are faced with the ticklish problem of how to project products at new buyers.* ADJ: usu ADJ n = delicate

[2] Someone who is **ticklish** is sensitive to being tickled, and laughs as soon as you tickle them. ❑ *This massage method is not recommended for anyone who is very ticklish.* ADJ

**tid|al** /taɪdəl/ **Tidal** means relating to or produced by tides. ❑ *The tidal stream or current gradually decreases in the shallows.* ADJ: usu ADJ n

**tid|al wave** **(tidal waves)** [1] A **tidal wave** is a very large wave, often caused by an earthquake, that flows onto the land and destroys things. ❑ *...a massive tidal wave swept the ship up and away.* N-COUNT

[2] If you describe a very large number of emotions, things, or people as a **tidal wave**, you mean that they all occur at the same time. ❑ *The trade union movement was swept along by the same tidal wave of patriotism which affected the country as a whole.* N-COUNT: usu sing, usu N *of* n = deluge

**tid|bit** /tɪdbɪt/ → see **titbit**.

**tid|dler** /tɪdləʳ/ **(tiddlers)** [1] A **tiddler** is a very small fish of any kind. [BRIT, INFORMAL] N-COUNT

[2] If you refer to a person or thing as a **tiddler**, you mean that they are very unimportant or small, especially when compared to other people or things of the same type. [BRIT, INFORMAL] ❑ *On a world scale the earthquake was a tiddler.* N-COUNT: usu with supp

**tid|dly** /tɪdəli/ [1] If someone is **tiddly**, they are slightly drunk. [BRIT, INFORMAL] ADJ = tipsy

[2] If you describe a thing as **tiddly**, you mean that it is very small. [BRIT, INFORMAL] ❑ *...a tiddly picture.* ADJ = tiny

**tiddly|wink** /tɪdəliwɪŋk/ **(tiddlywinks)** [1] **Tiddlywinks** is a game in which the players try to make small round pieces of plastic jump into a container, by pressing their edges with a larger piece of plastic. N-UNCOUNT

[2] **Tiddlywinks** are the small round piece of plastic used in the game of tiddlywinks. N-COUNT

**tide** /taɪd/ **(tides, tiding, tided)** [1] **The tide** is the regular change in the level of the sea on the shore. ❑ *The tide was at its highest... The tide was going out, and the sand was smooth and glittering.* ◆◇◇ N-COUNT

[2] A **tide** is a current in the sea that is caused by the regular and continuous movement of large areas of water towards and away from the shore. ❑ *Roman vessels used to sail with the tide from Boulogne to Richborough.* N-COUNT

[3] The **tide of** opinion, for example, is what the majority of people think at a particular time. ❑ *The tide of opinion seems overwhelmingly in his favour.* N-SING: N *of* n

[4] People sometimes refer to events or forces that are difficult or impossible to control as **the tide of** history, for example. ❑ *They talked of reversing the tide of history.* N-SING: the N *of* n

[5] You can talk about a **tide of** something, especially something which is unpleasant, when there is a large and increasing amount of it. ❑ *...an ever increasing tide of crime.* N-SING: N *of* n

[6] → See also **high tide**, **low tide**.

♦ **tide over** If you do something for someone to **tide** them **over**, you help them through a period when they are having difficulties, especially by lending them money. ❑ *He wanted money to tide him over... The banks were prepared to put up 50 million euros to tide over the company.* PHRASAL VERB V n P V P n (not pron)

**tid|ings** /taɪdɪŋz/ You can use **tidings** to refer to news that someone tells you. [FORMAL, OLD- N-PLURAL: usu adj N, oft N *of* n

FASHIONED] ❑ *He hated always to be the bearer of bad tidings.*

**tidy** /taɪdi/ **(tidier, tidiest, tidies, tidying, tidied)**

1 Something that is **tidy** is neat and is arranged in an organized way. ❑ *Having a tidy desk can seem impossible if you have a busy, demanding job.* ADJ ≠ untidy
♦ **tidi|ly** /taɪdɪli/ *...books and magazines stacked tidily on shelves.* ADV ♦ **tidi|ness** *Employees are expected to maintain a high standard of tidiness in their dress and appearance.* N-UNCOUNT
2 Someone who is **tidy** likes everything to be neat and arranged in an organized way. ❑ *She's obsessively tidy, always hoovering and polishing.* ADJ ≠ untidy ♦ **tidi|ness** *I'm very impressed by your tidiness and order.* N-UNCOUNT
3 When you **tidy** a place such as a room or cupboard, you make it neat by putting things in their proper places. ❑ *She made her bed, and tidied her room.* VERB V n
4 A **tidy** amount of money is a large amount. [INFORMAL] ❑ *The opportunities are there to make a tidy profit.* ADJ: ADJ n = sizeable

♦ **tidy away** When you **tidy** something **away**, you put it in something else so that it is not in the way. [mainly BRIT] ❑ *The large log basket can be used to tidy toys away... When they'd gone, McMinn tidied away the glasses and tea-cups.* PHRASAL VERB V n P, V P n (not pron)

♦ **tidy up** When you **tidy up** or **tidy** a place **up**, you put things back in their proper places so that everything is neat. ❑ *I really must start tidying the place up... He tried to tidy up, not wanting the maid to see the disarray... Anne made the beds and tidied up the nursery.* PHRASAL VERB V n P, V P, V P n (not pron)

**tie** /taɪ/ **(ties, tying, tied)** ◆◆◇

1 If you **tie** two things **together** or **tie** them, you fasten them together with a knot. ❑ *He tied the ends of the plastic bag together... Mr Saunders tied her hands and feet.* VERB V n adv/prep, V n
2 If you **tie** something or someone in a particular place or position, you put them there and fasten them using rope or string. ❑ *He had tied the dog to one of the trees near the canal... He tied her hands behind her back.* VERB V n to n, V n prep/adv
3 If you **tie** a piece of string or cloth around something or **tie** something **with** a piece of string or cloth, you put the piece of string or cloth around it and fasten the ends together. ❑ *She tied her scarf over her head... Roll the meat and tie it with string... Dad handed me a big box wrapped in gold foil and tied with a red ribbon.* VERB V n prep/adv, V n with n, V-ed
4 If you **tie** a knot or bow **in** something or **tie** something **in** a knot or bow, you fasten the ends together. ❑ *He took a short length of rope and swiftly tied a slip knot... She tied a knot in her scarf... She wore a checked shirt tied in a knot above the navel.* VERB V n, V n in n, V-ed
5 When you **tie** something or when something **ties**, you close or fasten it using a bow or knot. ❑ *He pulled on his heavy suede shoes and tied the laces. ...a long white thing around his neck that tied in front in a floppy bow.* VERB V n, V
6 A **tie** is a long narrow piece of cloth that is worn round the neck under a shirt collar and tied in a knot at the front. Ties are worn mainly by men. ❑ *Jason had taken off his jacket and loosened his tie.* N-COUNT
7 If one thing **is tied to** another or two things **are tied**, the two things have a close connection or link. ❑ *Their cancers are not so clearly tied to radiation exposure... My social life and business life are closely tied.* VERB: usu passive = link, connect; be V-ed to n; pl-n be V-ed
8 If you **are tied to** a particular place or situation, you are forced to accept it and cannot change it. ❑ *They had children and were consequently tied to the school holidays.* VERB: usu passive; be V-ed to n/-ing
9 **Ties** are the connections you have with people or a place. ❑ *Quebec has always had particularly close ties to France.* N-COUNT: usu pl, oft N prep = connection
10 Railroad **ties** are large heavy beams that support the rails of a railway track. [AM] N-COUNT

in BRIT, use **sleepers**

11 If two people **tie** in a competition or game or if they **tie with** each other, they have the same number of points or the same degree of success. ❑ *Both teams had tied on points and goal difference... Ronan Rafferty had tied with Frank Nobilo.* V-RECIP = draw; pl-n V; V with n ♦ **Tie** is also a noun. ❑ *The first game ended in a tie.* N-COUNT
12 In sport, a **tie** is a match that is part of a competition. The losers leave the competition and the winners go on to the next round. [mainly BRIT] ❑ *They'll meet the winners of the first round tie.* N-COUNT
13 → See also **tied**, **black tie**, **bow tie**, **old school tie**. **your hands are tied** → see **hand**. **to tie the knot** → see **knot**. **to tie yourself in knots** → see **knot**.

♦ **tie down** A person or thing that **ties** you **down** restricts your freedom in some way. ❑ *We'd agreed from the beginning not to tie each other down... The reason he didn't have a family was that he didn't want to be tied down.* PHRASAL VERB V n P, V n P

♦ **tie in with** or **tie up with** If something such as an idea or fact **ties in with** or **ties up with** something else, it is consistent with it or connected with it. ❑ *Our wedding had to tie in with David leaving the army... I've got a feeling that the death may be tied up with his visit in some way.* PHRASAL VERB V P P n, V P P n, Also V n P P n

♦ **tie up** 1 When you **tie** something **up**, you fasten string or rope round it so that it is firm or secure. ❑ *He tied up the bag and took it outside.* PHRASAL VERB V P n, Also V n P
2 If someone **ties** another person **up**, they fasten ropes or chains around them so that they cannot move or escape. ❑ *Masked robbers broke in, tied him up, and made off with $8,000... At about 5 a.m. they struck again in Fetcham, tying up a couple and ransacking their house.* PHRASAL VERB V n P, V P n (not pron)
3 If you **tie** an animal **up**, you fasten it to a fixed object with a piece of rope so that it cannot run away. ❑ *Would you go and tie your horse up please... They dismounted, tied up their horses and gave them the grain they had brought.* PHRASAL VERB = tether; V n P, V P n (not pron)
4 If you **tie up** an issue or problem, you deal with it in a way that gives definite conclusions or answers. ❑ *Kingfisher confirmed that it hopes to tie up a deal within the next two weeks... We could have tied the whole case up without getting you and Smith shot at.* PHRASAL VERB V P n (not pron), V n P
5 → See also **tied up**, **tie-up**.

♦ **tie up with** → see **tie in with**.

**tie-break** **(tie-breaks)** A **tie-break** is an extra game which is played in a tennis match when the score in a set is 6-6. The player who wins the tie-break wins the set. [mainly BRIT] N-COUNT

in AM, usually use **tie-breaker**

**tie-breaker** **(tie-breakers)** A **tie-breaker** is an extra question or round that decides the winner of a competition or game when two or more people have the same score at the end. N-COUNT

**tied** /taɪd/ 1 A **tied** cottage or house belongs to a farmer or other employer and is rented to someone who works for him or her. [BRIT] ❑ *He lives with his wife in a tied cottage in Hamsey.* ADJ: usu ADJ n
2 → See also **tie**.

**tied up** If someone or something is **tied up**, they are busy or being used, with the result that they are not available for anything else. [INFORMAL] ❑ *He's tied up with his new book. He's working hard, you know.* ADJ: v-link ADJ, oft ADJ with/in n

**tie-dye** **(tie-dyes, tie-dyeing, tie-dyed)** 1 If a piece of cloth or a garment **is tie-dyed**, it is tied in knots and then put into dye, so that some parts become more deeply coloured than others. ❑ *He wore a T-shirt that had been tie-dyed in bright colours... I bought a great tie-dyed silk scarf.* VERB: usu passive; be V-ed; V-ed
2 A **tie-dye** is a garment or piece of cloth that has been tie-dyed. ❑ *They wore tie-dyes and ponchos. ...a hideous tie-dye shirt.* N-VAR: usu N n

**tie-pin** **(tie-pins)** also **tiepin**. A **tie-pin** is a thin narrow object with a pin on it and is used to pin a person's tie to their shirt. N-COUNT

**tier** /tɪəʳ/ **(tiers)** 1 A **tier** is a row or layer of something that has other layers above or below it. ❑ *...the auditorium with the tiers of seats around and above it.* N-COUNT: oft N of n ♦ **Tier** is also a combining form. ❑ *...a three-tier wedding cake.* COMB in ADJ
2 A **tier** is a level in an organization or system. ❑ *Islanders have campaigned for the abolition of one of the three tiers of municipal power on the island.* N-COUNT: oft N of n ♦ **Tier** is also a combining form. ❑ *...the possibility of a two-tier system of universities.* COMB in ADJ

**tie-up** **(tie-ups)** 1 A **tie-up** or a **traffic tie-up** is a long line of vehicles that cannot move for- N-COUNT ward because there is too much traffic, or because the road is blocked by something. [AM] ❑ *In some cities this morning, there were traffic tie-ups up to 40 miles long.*

✔ in BRIT, use **traffic jam**

2 A **tie-up** between two organizations is a business connection that has been arranged between them. ❑ *The deal is expected to result in similar tie-ups between big media companies and telecommunications operators.* — N-COUNT: oft N *between* pl-n, N *with* n

**tiff** /tɪf/ **(tiffs)** A **tiff** is a small unimportant quarrel, especially between two close friends or between people in a romantic relationship. — N-COUNT

**ti|ger** /taɪgəʳ/ **(tigers)** A **tiger** is a large fierce animal belonging to the cat family. Tigers are orange with black stripes. → See also **paper tiger**. — N-COUNT

**tight** /taɪt/ **(tighter, tightest)** ◆◇◇ 1 **Tight** clothes or shoes are rather small and fit closely to your body. ❑ *His jeans were too tight.* [ADJ ≠ loose] ♦ **tight|ly** *He buttoned his collar tightly round his thick neck.* [ADV: ADV with v] 2 If you hold someone or something **tight**, you hold them firmly and securely. ❑ *She just fell into my arms, clutching me tight for a moment... Hold on tight!* [ADV: ADV after v] ♦ **Tight** is also an adjective. ❑ *As he and Henrietta passed through the gate he kept a tight hold of her arm.* [ADJ: usu ADJ n] ♦ **tight|ly** *She climbed back into bed and wrapped her arms tightly round her body.* [ADV: ADV after v] 3 **Tight** controls or rules are very strict. ❑ *The measures include tight control of media coverage... Security is tight this week at the polling sites.* [ADJ] ♦ **tight|ly** *The internal media was tightly controlled by the government during the war.* [ADV: ADV after v, ADV -ed] 4 Something that is shut **tight** is shut very firmly. ❑ *I keep the flour and sugar in individual jars, sealed tight with their glass lids... She kept her eyes tight closed.* [ADV: ADV -ed, ADV after v] ♦ **tight|ly** *Pemberton frowned and closed his eyes tightly.* [ADV: ADV after v, ADV -ed] 5 Skin, cloth, or string that is **tight** is stretched or pulled so that it is smooth or straight. ❑ *My skin feels tight and lacking in moisture.* [ADJ] ♦ **tight|ly** *Her sallow skin was drawn tightly across the bones of her face.* [ADV: ADV with v] 6 **Tight** is used to describe a group of things or an amount of something that is closely packed together. ❑ *She curled up in a tight ball, with her knees tucked up at her chin... The men came in a tight group.* [ADJ: usu ADJ n] ♦ **Tight** is also an adverb. ❑ *The people sleep on sun loungers packed tight, end to end.* [ADV] ♦ **tight|ly** *Many animals travel in tightly packed lorries and are deprived of food, water and rest.* [ADV: ADV after v, ADV -ed] 7 If a part of your body is **tight**, it feels rather uncomfortable and painful, for example because you are ill, anxious, or angry. ❑ *It is better to stretch the tight muscles first.* [ADJ = taut] ♦ **tight|ness** *Heart disease often shows itself first as pain or tightness in the chest.* [N-UNCOUNT] 8 A **tight** group of people is one whose members are closely linked by beliefs, feelings, or interests. ❑ *We're a tight group, so we do keep in touch.* [ADJ = close] 9 A **tight** bend or corner is one that changes direction very quickly so that you cannot see very far round it. ❑ *They collided on a tight bend and both cars were extensively damaged.* [ADJ: usu ADJ n = sharp] 10 A **tight** schedule or budget allows very little time or money for unexpected events or expenses. ❑ *It's difficult to cram everything into a tight schedule... Financially things are a bit tight.* [ADJ] 11 A **tight** contest is one where none of the competitors has a clear advantage or looks likely to win, so that it is difficult to say who the winner will be. ❑ *It was a very tight match.* [ADJ] 12 If you say that someone is **tight**, you disapprove of them because they are unwilling to spend their money. [INFORMAL] ❑ *What about getting new ones – Are you so tight you won't even spend three roubles?* [ADJ disapproval = tight-fisted, mean, stingy] 13 → See also **airtight**, **skin-tight**. 14 If you are in **a tight corner** or in **a tight spot**, you are in a difficult situation. [INFORMAL] ❑ *That puts the president in a tight spot if the vote is not a resounding 'yes'.* [PHRASE: usu prep PHR] 15 You can say '**sleep tight**' to someone when they are going to bed as an affectionate way of saying that you hope they will sleep well. ❑ *Good night, Davey. Sleep tight.* [CONVENTION] 16 to **keep a tight rein on** → see **rein**. to **sit tight** → see **sit**.

**tight|en** /taɪtᵊn/ **(tightens, tightening, tightened)** 1 If you **tighten** your grip on something, or if your grip **tightens**, you hold the thing more firmly or securely. ❑ *Luke answered by tightening his grip on her shoulder... Her arms tightened about his neck in gratitude... Stefano's grip tightened and his tone became colder.* [VERB ≠ loosen; V n; V prep; V] 2 If you **tighten** a rope or chain, or if it **tightens**, it is stretched or pulled hard until it is straight. ❑ *The anchorman flung his whole weight back, tightening the rope... The cables tightened and he was lifted gradually from the deck.* [VERB ≠ slacken; V n; V] 3 If a government or organization **tightens** its grip on a group of people or an activity, or if its grip **tightens**, it begins to have more control over it. ❑ *He knows he has considerable support for his plans to tighten his grip on the machinery of central government... As the regime's grip on the mainland tightened over the next few years, hundreds of thousands more people fled south.* [VERB; V n; V] 4 When you **tighten** a screw, nut, or other device, you turn it or move it so that it is more firmly in place or holds something more firmly. ❑ *I used my thumbnail to tighten the screw on my lamp.* [VERB; V n] ♦ **Tighten up** means the same as **tighten**. ❑ *It's important to tighten up the wheels properly, otherwise they vibrate loose and fall off.* [PHRASAL VERB; V P n (not pron); Also V n P] 5 If a part of your body **tightens**, the muscles in it become tense and stiff, for example because you are angry or afraid. ❑ *Sofia's throat had tightened and she couldn't speak.* [VERB ≠ relax; V] ♦ **tight|en|ing** *...a headache caused by tension which results in tightening of the muscles in the neck.* [N-UNCOUNT: usu N *of* n] 6 If someone in authority **tightens** a rule, a policy, or a system, they make it stricter or more efficient. ❑ *The United States plans to tighten the economic sanctions currently in place... Take-off and landing procedures have been tightened after two jets narrowly escaped disaster.* [VERB ≠ relax; V n; V n] ♦ **Tighten up** means the same as **tighten**. ❑ *Until this week, every attempt to tighten up the law had failed... He accused ministers of breaking election pledges to tighten up on immigration.* [PHRASAL VERB; V P n (not pron); V P *on* n; Also V n P] ♦ **tight|en|ing** *...the tightening of state control over press and broadcasting.* [N-UNCOUNT: oft N *of* n] 7 to **tighten** your **belt** → see **belt**. to **tighten the screw** → see **screw**.

♦ **tighten up** If a group, team, or organization **tightens up**, they make an effort to control what they are doing more closely, in order to become more efficient and successful. ❑ *I want us to be a bit more sensible this time and tighten up.* → See also **tighten 4, 6**. [PHRASAL VERB ≠ loosen up; V P]

**tight-fisted** If you describe someone as **tight-fisted**, you disapprove of them because they are unwilling to spend money. ❑ *He had the reputation of being one of the most tight-fisted and demanding of employers.* [ADJ disapproval = mean, stingy ≠ generous]

**tight-lipped** 1 If you describe someone as **tight-lipped**, you mean that they are unwilling to give any information about something. ❑ *Military officials are still tight-lipped about when or whether their forces will launch a ground offensive.* [ADJ: oft ADJ *about* n/wh ≠ forthcoming] 2 Someone who is **tight-lipped** has their lips pressed tightly together, especially because they are angry or disapproving. ❑ *He was sitting at the other end of the table, tight-lipped and angry.* [ADJ]

**tight|rope** /taɪtroʊp/ **(tightropes)** 1 A **tightrope** is a tightly stretched piece of rope on which someone balances and performs tricks in a circus. [N-COUNT] 2 You can use **tightrope** in expressions such as **walk a tightrope** and **live on a tightrope** to indicate that someone is in a difficult situation and has to be very careful about what they say or do. ❑ *School administrators walk a tightrope between the demands of the community and the realities of how children really behave.* [N-COUNT: usu sing]

**tights** /taɪts/ 1 **Tights** are a piece of clothing, usually worn by women and girls. They are usually made of nylon and cover the hips, legs and feet. [BRIT] ❑ *...a new pair of tights.* [N-PLURAL: also *a pair of* N]

✔ in AM, use **pantyhose**

2 **Tights** are a piece of tight clothing, usually [N-PLURAL:]

worn by dancers, acrobats, or people in exercise classes, and covering the hips and each leg. also *a pair of* N

**ti|gress** /taɪgrɪs/ **(tigresses)** A **tigress** is a female **tiger**. N-COUNT

**til|de** /tɪldə/ **(tildes)** A **tilde** is a symbol that is written over the letter 'n' in Spanish ñ and the letters 'o' õ and 'a' ã in Portuguese to indicate the way in which they should be pronounced. N-COUNT

**tile** /taɪl/ **(tiles, tiling, tiled)** [1] **Tiles** are flat, square pieces of baked clay, carpet, cork, or other substance, which are fixed as a covering onto a floor or wall. ❑ *Amy's shoes squeaked on the tiles as she walked down the corridor... The cabins had lino-leum tile floors.* N-VAR [2] **Tiles** are flat pieces of baked clay which are used for covering roofs. ➔ See picture on page 1705. ❑ *...a fine building, with a neat little porch and ornamental tiles on the roof.* N-VAR [3] When someone **tiles** a surface such as a roof or floor, they cover it with tiles. ❑ *He wants to tile the bathroom.* VERB V n [4] ➔ See also **tiling**.

**til|ing** /taɪlɪŋ/ [1] You can refer to a surface that is covered by tiles as **tiling**. ❑ *The kitchen has smart black tiling, worksurfaces and cupboards.* N-UNCOUNT [2] ➔ See also **tile**.

**till** /tɪl/ **(tills)** [1] In spoken English and informal written English, **till** is often used instead of **until**. ❑ *They had to wait till Monday to ring the bank manager... I've survived till now, and will go on doing so without help from you.* ◆◇◇ PREP ♦ **Till** is also a conjunction. ❑ *They slept till the alarm bleeper woke them at four.* CONJ [2] In a shop or other place of business, a **till** is a counter or cash register where money is kept, and where customers pay for what they have bought. [BRIT] ❑ *...long queues at tills that make customers angry.* N-COUNT

✔ in AM, use **cash register**

[3] A **till** is the drawer of a cash register, in which the money is kept. [AM] ❑ *He checked the register. There was money in the till.* N-COUNT: usu *the* N

**till|er** /tɪləʳ/ **(tillers)** The **tiller** of a boat is a handle that is fixed to the rudder. It is used to turn the rudder, which then steers the boat. N-COUNT

**tilt** /tɪlt/ **(tilts, tilting, tilted)** [1] If you **tilt** an object or if it **tilts**, it moves into a sloping position with one end or side higher than the other. ❑ *She tilted the mirror and began to comb her hair... Leonard tilted his chair back on two legs and stretched his long body... The boat instantly tilted, filled and sank.* VERB V n V n adv/prep V [2] If you **tilt** part of your body, usually your head, you move it slightly upwards or to one side. ❑ *Mari tilted her head back so that she could look at him... His wife tilted his head to the side and inspected the wound... She tilted her face to kiss me quickly on the chin.* VERB V n with adv V n prep V n ♦ **Tilt** is also a noun. ❑ *He opened the rear door for me with an apologetic tilt of his head.* N-COUNT: usu sing [3] The **tilt** of something is the fact that it tilts or slopes, or the angle at which it tilts or slopes. ❑ *...calculations based on our understanding of the tilt of the earth's axis... The 3-metre-square slabs are on a tilt.* N-COUNT: usu sing, oft N *of* n [4] If a person or thing **tilts towards** a particular opinion or if something **tilts** them **towards** it, they change slightly so that they become more in agreement with that opinion or position. ❑ *When the political climate tilted towards fundamentalism he was threatened... The paper has done much to tilt American public opinion in favour of intervention.* VERB V prep/adv V n prep/adv [5] If there is a **tilt towards** a particular opinion or position, that opinion or position is favoured or begins to be favoured. ❑ *The chairman also criticised the plan for its tilt towards higher taxes rather than lower spending.* N-SING: N *towards* n [6] A **tilt at** something is an attempt to win or obtain it. [JOURNALISM] ❑ *His first tilt at Parliament came in the same year but he failed to win the seat.* N-COUNT: N *at* n [7] To move **full tilt** or **at full tilt** means to move with as much speed, energy, or force as possible. ❑ *As John approached at full tilt he saw a queue of traffic blocking the road.* PHRASE: PHR after v

**tilt|ing train** **(tilting trains)** A **tilting train** is a type of train that can travel faster than ordinary trains because it tilts when the track curves. N-COUNT

**tim|ber** /tɪmbəʳ/ **Timber** is wood that is used for building houses and making furniture. You can also refer to trees that are grown for this purpose as **timber**. ❑ *These Severn Valley woods have been exploited for timber since Saxon times.* N-UNCOUNT

**tim|bered** /tɪmbəʳd/ A **timbered** building has a wooden frame or wooden beams showing on the outside. ➔ See also **half-timbered**. ADJ: usu ADJ n

**tim|ber yard** **(timber yards)** A **timber yard** is a place where timber is stored and sold. [BRIT] N-COUNT

✔ in AM, use **lumberyard**

**tim|bre** /tæmbəʳ/ **(timbres)** The **timbre** of someone's voice or of a musical instrument is the particular quality of sound that it has. [FORMAL] ❑ *His voice had a deep timbre... The timbre of the violin is far richer than that of the mouth organ.* N-COUNT: usu sing, oft N *of* n

**time** /taɪm/ **(times, timing, timed)** [1] **Time** is what we measure in minutes, hours, days, and years. ❑ *...a two-week period of time... Time passed, and still Ma did not appear... The social significance of religion has changed over time.* ◆◆◆ N-UNCOUNT [2] You use **time** to ask or talk about a specific point in the day, which can be stated in hours and minutes and is shown on clocks. ❑ *'What time is it?' — 'Eight o'clock.'... He asked me the time... What time did he leave?... The time is now 19 minutes past the hour.* N-SING: *wh/the* N [3] The **time** when something happens is the point in the day when it happens or is supposed to happen. ❑ *Departure times are 08:15 from St Quay, and 18:15 from St Helier.* ➔ See also **opening time**. N-COUNT [4] You use **time** to refer to the system of expressing time and counting hours that is used in a particular part of the world. ❑ *The incident happened just after ten o'clock local time.* N-UNCOUNT: supp N [5] You use **time** to refer to the period that you spend doing something or when something has been happening. ❑ *Adam spent a lot of time in his grandfather's office... He wouldn't have the time or money to take care of me... Listen to me, I haven't got much time... The route was blocked for some time... For a long time I didn't tell anyone... A short time later they sat down to eat.* N-UNCOUNT: also *a* N [6] If you say that something has been happening for **a time**, you mean that it has been happening for a fairly long period of time. ❑ *He stayed for quite a time... After a time they came to a pond.* N-SING: *a* N [7] You use **time** to refer to a period of time or a point in time, when you are describing what is happening then. For example, if something happened **at** a particular **time**, that is when it happened. If it happens **at all times**, it always happens. ❑ *We were in the same college, which was male-only at that time... By this time he was thirty... It was a time of terrible uncertainty... Homes are more affordable than at any time in the past five years... It seemed like a good time to tell her.* N-COUNT: with supp, oft prep N [8] You use **time** or **times** to talk about a particular period in history or in your life. ❑ *We'll be alone together, quite like old times... We are in one of the most severe recessions in modern times.* N-COUNT: with supp, usu adj N, N *of* n [9] You can use **the times** to refer to the present time and to modern fashions, tastes, and developments. For example, if you say that someone **keeps up with the times**, you mean they are fashionable or aware of modern developments. If you say they are **behind the times**, you mean they are unfashionable or not aware of them. ❑ *This approach is now seriously out of step with the times... Johnny has changed his image to fit the times.* N-PLURAL: *the* N [10] When you describe the **time** that you had on a particular occasion or during a particular part of your life, you are describing the sort of experience that you had then. ❑ *Sarah and I had a great time while the kids were away... She's had a really tough time the last year and a half.* N-COUNT: adj N [11] Your **time** is the amount of time that you have to live, or to do a particular thing. ❑ *Now Martin has begun to suffer the effects of AIDS, and he says his time is running out.* N-SING: poss N [12] If you say it is **time for** something, **time to** do something, or **time** you did something, you mean that this thing ought to happen or be done now. ❑ *Opinion polls indicated a feeling among the public that it was* N-UNCOUNT: oft N *for* n, N to-inf, N that *time for a change... It was time for him to go to work... This was no time to make a speech.* **13** N-COUNT: with supp When you talk about a **time** when something happens, you are referring to a specific occasion when it happens. ❑ *Every time she travels on the bus it's delayed by at least three hours... The last time I saw her was about sixteen years ago.* **14** N-COUNT: usu num/ord N You use **time** after numbers to say how often something happens. ❑ *It was her job to make tea three times a day.* **15** N-PLURAL: num N compar, num N *as* adj/adv, num N n You use **times** after numbers when comparing one thing to another and saying, for example, how much bigger, smaller, better, or worse it is. ❑ *Its profits are rising four times faster than the average company. ...an area five times the size of Britain.* **16** CONJ You use **times** in arithmetic to link numbers or amounts that are multiplied together to reach a total. ❑ *Four times six is 24.* **17** N-COUNT: with supp, oft poss N, N *of* n Someone's **time** in a race is the amount of time it takes them to finish the race. ❑ *He was over a second faster than his previous best time.* **18** N-UNCOUNT: usu supp N, oft *in* N The **time** of a piece of music is the number of beats that the piece has in each bar. ❑ *A reel is in four-four time, and a jig is in six-eight time.* **19** VERB If you **time** something for a particular time, you plan or decide to do it or cause it to happen at this time. ❑ V n to-inf *He timed the election to coincide with new measures to boost the economy...* V n *for* n *We had timed our visit for March 7...* V n adv *He had timed his intervention well...* V-ed *Operation Amazon is timed to coincide with the start of the dry season.* Also V n **20** VERB If you **time** an action or activity, you measure how long someone takes to do it or how long it lasts. ❑ V n *He timed each performance with a stopwatch.* **21** ➔ See also **timing.**

**PHRASES** **22** PHRASE: *it* v-link PHR that, PHR as reply [emphasis] If you say it is **about time** that something was done, you are saying in an emphatic way that it should happen or be done now, and really should have happened or been done sooner. ❑ *It's about time a few movie makers with original ideas were given a chance.* **23** PHRASE: PHR after v If you do something **ahead of time**, you do it before a particular event or before you need to, in order to be well prepared. ❑ *Find out ahead of time what regulations apply to your situation.* **24** PHRASE: v-link PHR, oft PHR *in* -ing If someone is **ahead of** their **time** or **before** their **time**, they have new ideas a long time before other people start to think in the same way. ❑ *My mother was ahead of her time. She surrounded me with culture and art.* **25** PHRASE: PHR after v = *continually* If something happens or is done **all the time**, it happens or is done continually. ❑ *We can't be together all the time.* **26** PHRASE: amount PHR You say **at a time** after an amount to say how many things or how much of something is involved in one action, place, or group. ❑ *Beat in the eggs, one at a time.* **27** PHRASE: PHR with cl If something could happen **at any time**, it is possible that it will happen very soon, though nobody can predict exactly when. ❑ *Conditions are still very tense and the fighting could escalate at any time.* **28** PHRASE: PHR with cl [emphasis] You say **at the best of times** when you are making a negative or critical comment to emphasize that it is true even when the circumstances are as favourable as possible. ❑ *A trade war would be bad at the best of times, but in the current economic climate, it would be a disaster.* **29** PHRASE: PHR with cl If you say that something was the case **at one time**, you mean that it was the case during a particular period in the past. ❑ *At one time 400 men, women and children lived in the village.* **30** PHRASE: PHR with cl If two or more things exist, happen, or are true **at the same time**, they exist, happen, or are true together although they seem to contradict each other. ❑ *I was afraid of her, but at the same time I really liked her.* **31** PHRASE: PHR with cl **At the same time** is used to introduce a statement that slightly changes or contradicts the previous statement. ❑ *I don't think I set out to come up with a different sound for each album. At the same time, I do have a sense of what is right for the moment.* **32** PHRASE: PHR with cl/group You use **at times** to say that something happens or is true on some occasions or at some moments. ❑ *The debate was highly emotional at times.* **33** PHRASE: usu v-link PHR If you say that something was **before** your **time**, you mean that it happened or existed before you were born or before you were able to know about it or remember it. ❑ *'You've never seen the Marilyn Monroe film?' — 'No, I think it was a bit before my time.'* **34** PHRASE: PHR after v If someone has reached a particular stage in life **before** their **time**, they have reached it at a younger age than is normal. ❑ *The small print has forced me, years before my time, to buy spectacles.* **35** PHRASE: PHR with cl [emphasis] If you say **not before time** after a statement has been made about something that has been done, you are saying in an emphatic way that you think it should have been done sooner. [BRIT] ❑ *The virus is getting more and more attention, and not before time.* **36** PHRASE: V inflects If you **call time on** something, you end it. [mainly BRIT, JOURNALISM] ❑ *Scott Hastings has called time on his international career by cutting short his contract.* **37** PHRASE: V inflects Someone who **is doing time** is in prison. [INFORMAL] ❑ *He is serving 11 years for robbery, and did time for a similar offence before that.* **38** PHRASE: usu PHR with v, PHR with group If you say that something will be the case **for all time**, you mean that it will always be the case. ❑ *The desperate condition of the world is that madness has always been here, and that it will remain so for all time.* **39** PHRASE: PHR with cl If something is the case or will happen **for the time being**, it is the case or will happen now, but only until something else becomes possible or happens. ❑ *For the time being, however, immunotherapy is still in its experimental stages.* **40** PHRASE: PHR with v, PHR with cl If you do something **from time to time**, you do it occasionally but not regularly. ❑ *Her daughters visited him from time to time when he was ill.* **41** PHRASE: PHR with cl If you say that something is the case **half the time** you mean that it often is the case. [INFORMAL] ❑ *Half the time, I don't have the slightest idea what he's talking about.* **42** PHRASE: V inflects, PHR n If you say that you **have no time for** a person or thing, you mean you do not like them or approve of them, and if you say that you **have a lot of time for** a person or thing, you mean you like them or approve of them very much. ❑ *When I think of what he's done to my mother and me, I've just got no time for him.* **43** PHRASE: V inflects, PHR that, PHR to-inf [emphasis] If you say that **it is high time** that something happened or was done, you are saying in an emphatic way that it should happen or be done now, and really should have happened or been done sooner. ❑ *It is high time the Government displayed a more humanitarian approach towards victims of the recession.* **44** PHRASE: PHR after v, oft PHR *for* n, PHR to-inf If you are **in time for** a particular event, you are not too late for it. ❑ *I arrived just in time for my flight to London.* **45** PHRASE: PHR with cl If you say that something will happen **in time** or **given time**, you mean that it will happen eventually, when a lot of time has passed. ❑ *He would sort out his own problems, in time... Tina believed that, given time, her business would become profitable.* **46** PHRASE: PHR after v, oft PHR *with* n If you are playing, singing, or dancing **in time** with a piece of music, you are following the rhythm and speed of the music correctly. If you are **out of time** with it, you are not following the rhythm and speed of the music correctly. ❑ *Her body swayed in time with the music... We were standing onstage playing completely out of time.* **47** PHRASE: PHR with cl If you say that something will happen, for example, **in** a week **'s time** or **in** two years **' time**, you mean that it will happen a week from now or two years from now. ❑ *Presidential elections are due to be held in ten days' time.* **48** PHRASE: PHR after v, oft PHR *for* n If you arrive somewhere **in good time**, you arrive early so that there is time to spare before a particular event. ❑ *If we're out, we always make sure we're home in good time for the programme.* **49** PHRASE: PHR after v, PHR as reply If you tell someone that something will happen **in good time** or **all in good time**, you are telling them to be patient because it will happen eventually. ❑ *There will be many advanced exercises that you won't be able to do at first. You will get to them in good time.* **50** PHRASE: PHR with cl If something happens **in no time** or **in next to no time**, it happens almost immediately or very quickly. ❑ *He expects to be out of prison in next to no time.* **51** PHRASE: PHR with cl If you do something **in** your **own time**, you do it at the speed that you choose, rather than allowing anyone to hurry you. ❑ *Now,* *in your own time, tell me what happened.*

[52] PHRASE: PHR with cl — If you do something such as work **in** your **own time** in British English, or **on** your **own time** in American English, you do it in your free time rather than, for example, at work or school. ❑ *If I choose to work on other projects in my own time, then I say that is my business.*

[53] PHRASE: V inflects — If you **keep time** when playing or singing music, you follow or play the beat, without going too fast or too slowly. ❑ *As he sang he kept time on a small drum.*

[54] PHRASE: V inflects — When you talk about how well a watch or clock **keeps time**, you are talking about how accurately it measures time. ❑ *Some pulsars keep time better than the earth's most accurate clocks.*

[55] PHRASE: V inflects, oft PHR *for* n, PHR to-inf — If you **make time for** a particular activity or person, you arrange to have some free time so that you can do the activity or spend time with the person. ❑ *Before leaving the city, be sure to make time for a shopping trip.*

[56] PHRASE: V inflects — If you say that you **made good time** on a journey, you mean it did not take you very long compared to the length of time you expected it to take. ❑ *They had left early in the morning, on quiet roads, and made good time.*

[57] PHRASE: V inflects — If someone **is making up for lost time**, they are doing something actively and with enthusiasm because they have not had the opportunity to do it before or when they were younger. ❑ *Five years older than the majority of officers of his same rank, he was determined to make up for lost time.*

[58] PHRASE: V inflects — If you **are marking time**, you are doing something that is not particularly useful or interesting while you wait for something more important or interesting to happen. ❑ *He's really just marking time until he's old enough to leave.*

[59] PHRASE: PHR with cl — If you say that something happens or is the case **nine times out of ten** or **ninety-nine times out of a hundred**, you mean that it happens on nearly every occasion or is almost always the case. ❑ *When they want something, nine times out of ten they get it.*

[60] PHRASE: n PHR, usu PHR after adj-superl — If you say that someone or something is, for example, the best writer **of all time**, or the most successful film **of all time**, you mean that they are the best or most successful there has ever been. ❑ *'Monopoly' is one of the best-selling games of all time.*

[61] PHRASE: v-link PHR, PHR after v — If you are **on time**, you are not late. ❑ *Don't worry, she'll be on time.*

[62] PHRASE: v-link PHR, oft *it* v-link PHR *before* cl — If you say that it is **only a matter of time** or **only a question of time** before something happens, you mean that it cannot be avoided and will definitely happen at some future date. ❑ *It now seems only a matter of time before they resign.*

[63] PHRASE: usu *of/in/for* PHR — When you refer to **our time** or **our times** you are referring to the present period in the history of the world. ❑ *It would be wrong to say that the Church doesn't enter the great moral debates of our time.*

[64] PHRASE: V inflects — If you do something to **pass the time** you do it because you have some time available and not because you really want to do it. ❑ *Without particular interest and just to pass the time, I read a story.*

[65] PHRASE: V inflects — If you **play for time**, you try to make something happen more slowly, because you do not want it to happen or because you need time to think about what to do if it happens. ❑ *The president's decision is being seen as an attempt to play for time.*

[66] PHRASE: V inflects, oft *it* PHR to-inf — If you say that something will **take time**, you mean that it will take a long time. ❑ *Change will come, but it will take time.*

[67] PHRASE: V inflects, oft PHR -ing — If you **take** your **time** doing something, you do it quite slowly and do not hurry. ❑ *'Take your time,' Cross told him. 'I'm in no hurry.'*

[68] PHRASE: V inflects — If a child can **tell the time**, they are able to find out what the time is by looking at a clock or watch. ❑ *My four-year-old daughter cannot quite tell the time.*

[69] PHRASE: PHR with cl, PHR after v = *repeatedly* — If something happens **time after time**, it happens in a similar way on many occasions. ❑ *Burns had escaped from jail time after time.*

[70] PHRASE: V inflects — If you say that **time flies**, you mean that it seems to pass very quickly. ❑ *Time flies when you're having fun.*

[71] PHRASE: Ns inflect, PHR after v, v-link PHR — If you have **the time of** your **life**, you enjoy yourself very much indeed. ❑ *We're taking our little grandchild away with us. We'll make sure he has the time of his life.*

[72] PHRASE: v-link PHR, PHR after v — If you say there is **no time to lose** or **no time to be lost**, you mean you must hurry as fast as you can to do something. ❑ *He rushed home, realising there was no time to lose.*

[73] PHRASE: oft PHR whether/if — If you say that **time will tell** whether something is true or correct, you mean that it will not be known until some time in the future whether it is true or correct. ❑ *Only time will tell whether Broughton's optimism is justified.*

[74] PHRASE: V inflects, usu PHR *in* -ing — If you **waste no time in** doing something, you take the opportunity to do it immediately or quickly. ❑ *Tom wasted no time in telling me why he had come.*

[75] **time and again** → see **again**. **in the fullness of time** → see **fullness**.

**time and mo|tion** N-UNCOUNT: usu N n — A **time and motion** study is a study of the way that people do a particular job, or the way they work in a particular place in order to discover the most efficient methods of working.

**time bomb** **(time bombs)** also **time-bomb.**
[1] N-COUNT — A **time bomb** is a bomb with a mechanism that causes it to explode at a particular time.
[2] N-COUNT: oft adj N — If you describe something as a **time bomb**, you mean that it is likely to have a serious effect on a person or situation at a later date, especially if you think it will cause a lot of damage. ❑ *This proposal is a political time bomb that could cost the government the next election.*

**time-consuming** also **time consuming.** ADJ: oft *it* v-link ADJ to-inf — If something is **time-consuming**, it takes a lot of time. ❑ *It's just very time consuming to get such a large quantity of data.*

**time frame** **(time frames)** N-COUNT = *timescale* — The **time frame** of an event is the length of time during which it happens or develops. [FORMAL] ❑ *The time frame within which all this occurred was from September 1985 to March 1986.*

**time-honoured** ADJ: ADJ n = *age-old* — A **time-honoured** tradition or way of doing something is one that has been used and respected for a very long time. ❑ *The beer is brewed in the time-honoured way at the Castle Eden Brewery.*

**time|keeper** /taɪmkiːpəʳ/ **(timekeepers)** also **time-keeper.**
[1] N-COUNT — A **timekeeper** is a person or an instrument that records or checks the time.
[2] N-COUNT: supp N — If you say that someone is a good **timekeeper**, you mean that they usually arrive on time for things. If you say that they are a poor **timekeeper**, you mean that they are often late. [BRIT]

**time|keeping** /taɪmkiːpɪŋ/
[1] N-UNCOUNT: poss N, adj N — If you talk about someone's **timekeeping**, you are talking about how good they are at arriving in time for things. [BRIT] ❑ *I am trying to improve my timekeeping.*
[2] N-UNCOUNT — **Timekeeping** is the process or activity of timing an event or series of events. ❑ *Who did the timekeeping?*

**time lag** **(time lags)** also **time-lag.** N-COUNT: usu sing, oft N *between* pl-n — A **time lag** is a fairly long interval of time between one event and another related event that happens after it. ❑ *...the time-lag between theoretical research and practical applications.*

**time|less** /taɪmləs/ ADJ — If you describe something as **timeless**, you mean that it is so good or beautiful that it cannot be affected by changes in society or fashion. ❑ *There is a timeless quality to his best work.* ♦ **time|less|ness** N-UNCOUNT — *Maybe it was the trees that gave this place its atmosphere of mystery and timelessness.*

**time lim|it** **(time limits)** N-COUNT — A **time limit** is a date before which a particular task must be completed. ❑ *We have extended the time limit for claims until July 30.*

**time|line** /taɪmlaɪn/ **(timelines)** also **time line.**
[1] N-COUNT — A **timeline** is a visual representation of a sequence of events, especially historical events.
[2] N-COUNT — A **timeline** is the length of time that a project is expected to take. ❑ *Use your deadlines to establish the timeline for your research plan.*

**time|ly** /taɪmli/ ADJ [approval] — A **timely** event happens at a moment when it is useful, effective, or relevant.

❑ *The recent outbreaks of cholera are a timely reminder that this disease is still a serious health hazard.*

**time out** **(time outs)** also **time-out.** [1] In basketball, American football, ice hockey, and some other sports, when a team calls a **time out**, they call a stop to the game for a few minutes in order to rest and discuss how they are going to play. N-VAR [2] If you take **time out from** a job or activity, you have a break from it and do something different instead. ❑ *He took time out from campaigning to accompany his mother to dinner.* N-UNCOUNT: oft N *from* n, N to-inf

**time|piece** /taɪmpiːs/ **(timepieces)** also **time piece.** A **timepiece** is a clock, watch, or other device that measures and shows time. [OLD-FASHIONED] N-COUNT

**tim|er** /taɪməʳ/ **(timers)** A **timer** is a device that measures time, especially one that is part of a machine and causes it to start or stop working at specific times. ❑ *...electronic timers that automatically switch on the lights when it gets dark.* ➔ See also **egg timer**. N-COUNT

**time|scale** /taɪmskeɪl/ **(timescales)** also **time scale.** The **timescale** of an event is the length of time during which it happens or develops. ❑ *He gave no timescale for these steps.* N-COUNT: oft *on* N with supp

**time-server** **(time-servers)** also **timeserver.** If you refer to someone as a **time-server**, you disapprove of them because they are making very little effort at work and are just waiting until they retire or leave for a new job. N-COUNT [disapproval]

**time-share** **(time-shares)** also **time share.** If you have a **time-share**, you have the right to use a particular property as holiday accommodation for a specific amount of time each year. N-VAR

**time sig|nal** **(time signals)** The **time signal** is the series of high-pitched sounds that are broadcast at certain times on the radio, for example at exactly one o'clock or exactly six o'clock. [BRIT] N-COUNT: usu *the* N in sing

**time sig|na|ture** **(time signatures)** The **time signature** of a piece of music consists of two numbers written at the beginning that show how many beats there are in each bar. N-COUNT

**time slot** **(time slots)** A television or radio programme's **time slot** is the time when it is broadcast. ❑ *90 per cent of listeners had stayed with the programme when it changed its time slot.* N-COUNT

**time switch** **(time switches)** A **time switch** is a device that causes a machine to start or stop working at specific times. N-COUNT

**time|table** /taɪmteɪbᵊl/ **(timetables, timetabling, timetabled)** [1] A **timetable** is a plan of the times when particular events are to take place. ❑ *Don't you realize we're working to a timetable? We have to have results... The two countries are to try to agree a timetable for formal talks.* N-COUNT = schedule [2] In a school or college, a **timetable** is a list that shows the times in the week at which particular subjects are taught. You can also refer to the range of subjects that a student learns or the classes that a teacher teaches as their **timetable**. [BRIT] ❑ *Options are offered subject to staff availability and the constraints of the timetable.* N-COUNT

✔ in AM, usually use **class schedule**

[3] A **timetable** is a list of the times when trains, boats, buses, or aeroplanes are supposed to arrive at or leave from a particular place. [mainly BRIT] ❑ *For a local bus timetable, contact Dyfed County Council.* N-COUNT

✔ in AM, usually use **schedule**

[4] If something **is timetabled**, it is scheduled to happen or do something at a particular time. [mainly BRIT] ❑ *On both days, three very different trains will be timetabled... Opie is timetabled to work a four-day week.* VERB: usu passive = schedule *be* V-ed *be* V-ed to-inf

**time tri|al** **(time trials)** In cycling and some other sports, a **time trial** is a contest in which competitors race along a course individually, in as fast a time as possible, instead of racing directly against each other. N-COUNT

**time wast|er** **(time wasters)** also **time-waster.** If you say that someone or something is a **time waster**, you mean that they cause you to spend a lot of time doing something that is unnecessary or does not produce any benefit. ❑ *Surfing the Internet is fun, but it's also a time waster.* N-COUNT [disapproval]

**time-worn** also **timeworn.** Something that is **time-worn** is old or has been used a lot over a long period of time. ❑ *Even in the dim light the equipment looked old and time-worn.* ADJ

**time zone** **(time zones)** also **time-zone.** A **time zone** is one of the areas into which the world is divided where the time is calculated as being a particular number of hours behind or ahead of GMT. N-COUNT

**tim|id** /tɪmɪd/ [1] **Timid** people are shy, nervous, and have no courage or confidence in themselves. ❑ *A timid child, Isabella had learned obedience at an early age.* ♦ **ti|mid|ity** /tɪmɪdɪti/ *She doesn't ridicule my timidity.* ♦ **tim|id|ly** *The little boy stepped forward timidly and shook Leo's hand.* ADJ ≠ confident N-UNCOUNT ADV: usu ADV with v [2] If you describe someone's attitudes or actions as **timid**, you are criticizing them for being too cautious or slow to act, because they are nervous about the possible consequences of their actions. ❑ *The President's critics say he has been too timid in responding to changing international developments.* ♦ **ti|mid|ity** *He was soon disillusioned by the government's timidity on social reform.* ♦ **tim|id|ly** *A number of these states are moving timidly towards multi-party democracy.* ADJ [disapproval] = hesitant ≠ assertive N-UNCOUNT ADV: ADV with v

**tim|ing** /taɪmɪŋ/ [1] **Timing** is the skill or action of judging the right moment in a situation or activity at which to do something. ❑ *His photo is a wonderful happy moment caught with perfect timing.* N-UNCOUNT: usu supp N [2] **Timing** is used to refer to the time at which something happens or is planned to happen, or to the length of time that something takes. ❑ *The timing of the minister's visit, however, could somewhat detract from the goodwill it's supposed to generate.* N-UNCOUNT: usu N *of* n [3] ➔ See also **time**.

**tim|or|ous** /tɪmərəs/ [1] If you describe someone as **timorous**, you mean that they are frightened and nervous of other people and situations. [LITERARY] ❑ *He is a reclusive, timorous creature.* ADJ = timid [2] If you describe someone's actions or decisions as **timorous**, you are criticizing them for being too cautious or weak, because the person is not very confident and is worried about the possible consequences of their actions. ❑ *Some delegates believe the final declaration is likely to be too timorous.* ADJ [disapproval] = feeble

**tim|pa|ni** /tɪmpəni/ **Timpani** are large drums that are played in an orchestra. N-PLURAL = kettle-drum

**tin** /tɪn/ **(tins)** [1] **Tin** is a soft silvery-white metal. ❑ *...a factory that turns scrap metal into tin cans. ...a tin-roofed hut.* N-UNCOUNT [2] A **tin** is a metal container which is filled with food and sealed in order to preserve the food for long periods of time. [mainly BRIT] ❑ *She popped out to buy a tin of soup.* ♦ A **tin of** food is the amount of food contained in a tin. [mainly BRIT] ❑ *He had survived by eating a small tin of fruit every day.* N-COUNT: oft N *of* n N-COUNT: oft N *of* n

✔ in AM, use **can**

[3] A **tin** is a metal container with a lid in which things such as biscuits, cakes, or tobacco can be kept. ❑ *Store the cookies in an airtight tin.* ♦ A **tin of** something is the amount contained in a tin. ❑ *They emptied out the remains of the tin of paint and smeared it on the inside of the van.* N-COUNT: oft supp N, N *of* n N-COUNT: oft N *of* n [4] A baking **tin** is a metal container used for baking things such as cakes and bread in an oven. [BRIT] ❑ *Pour the mixture into the cake tin and bake for 45 minutes.* N-COUNT: usu supp N

✔ in AM, use **pan, baking pan**

**tinc|ture** /tɪŋktʃəʳ/ **(tinctures)** A **tincture** is a medicine consisting of alcohol and a small amount of a drug. ❑ *...a few drops of tincture of iodine.* N-VAR: oft N *of* n

**tin|der** /tɪndəʳ/ **Tinder** consists of small pieces of something dry, especially wood or grass, N-UNCOUNT = kindling that burns easily and can be used for lighting a fire.

**tinder|box** /tɪndəʳbɒks/ **(tinderboxes)** also **tinder box.** If you say that a situation is a **tinderbox**, you mean that it is very tense and something dangerous or unpleasant is likely to happen very soon. N-COUNT: usu sing

**tine** /taɪn/ **(tines)** The **tines** of something such as a fork are the long pointed parts. [FORMAL] N-COUNT

**tin|foil** /tɪnfɔɪl/ also **tin foil. Tinfoil** consists of shiny metal in the form of a thin sheet which is used for wrapping food. N-UNCOUNT = *foil*

**tinge** /tɪndʒ/ **(tinges)** A **tinge** of a colour, feeling, or quality is a small amount of it. ❑ *His skin had an unhealthy greyish tinge... Could there have been a slight tinge of envy in Eva's voice?* N-COUNT: usu with supp

**tinged** /tɪndʒd/ **1** If something is **tinged with** a particular colour, it has a small amount of that colour in it. ❑ *His dark hair was just tinged with grey.* ADJ: usu v-link ADJ, oft ADJ *with* n, ADJ colour **2** If something is **tinged with** a particular feeling or quality, it has or shows a small amount of that feeling or quality. ❑ *Her homecoming was tinged with sadness.* ADJ: usu v-link ADJ, oft ADJ *with* n

**tin|gle** /tɪŋgᵊl/ **(tingles, tingling, tingled)** **1** When a part of your body **tingles**, you have a slight stinging feeling there. ❑ *The backs of his thighs tingled.* VERB V ♦ **tin|gling** *Its effects on the nervous system include weakness, paralysis, and tingling in the hands and feet.* N-UNCOUNT **2** If you **tingle with** a feeling such as excitement, you feel it very strongly. ❑ *She tingled with excitement... When I look over and see Terry I tingle all over.* VERB V *with* n V ♦ **Tingle** is also a noun. ❑ *I felt a sudden tingle of excitement.* N-COUNT: usu sing

**tin|gly** /tɪŋgli/ **1** If something makes your body feel **tingly**, it gives you a slight stinging feeling. ❑ *These lotions tend to give the skin a tingly sensation.* ADJ **2** If something pleasant or exciting makes you feel **tingly**, it gives you a pleasant warm feeling. ❑ *He had a way of sounding so sincere. It made me warm and tingly.* ADJ

**tink|er** /tɪŋkəʳ/ **(tinkers, tinkering, tinkered)** If you **tinker with** something, you make some small changes to it, in an attempt to improve it or repair it. ❑ *Instead of the Government admitting its error, it just tinkered with the problem... It is not enough to tinker at the edges; our objective must be to reconstruct the entire system.* VERB V *with* n V ♦ **tink|er|ing** *No amount of tinkering is going to improve matters.* N-UNCOUNT

**tin|kle** /tɪŋkᵊl/ **(tinkles, tinkling, tinkled)** **1** If something **tinkles**, it makes a clear, high-pitched, ringing noise, especially as small parts of it strike a surface. ❑ *A fresh cascade of splintered glass tinkled to the floor... We strolled past tinkling fountains and perfumed gardens.* VERB V prep/adv V-ing, Also V ♦ **Tinkle** is also a noun. ❑ *...a tinkle of broken glass.* N-COUNT: usu sing **2** If a bell **tinkles** or if you **tinkle** it, it makes a quiet ringing noise as you shake it. ❑ *An old-fashioned bell tinkled as he pushed open the door... Miss Peel tinkled her desk bell and they all sat down again.* VERB V V n ♦ **Tinkle** is also a noun. ❑ *...the tinkle of goat bells.* N-COUNT: usu sing

**tinned** /tɪnd/ **Tinned** food is food that has been preserved by being sealed in a tin. [mainly BRIT] ❑ *...tinned tomatoes. ...tinned salmon.* ADJ: usu ADJ n

✔ in AM, usually use **canned**

**tin|ny** /tɪni/ **1** If you describe a sound as **tinny**, you mean that it has an irritating, high-pitched quality. ❑ *He could hear the tinny sound of a radio playing a pop song.* ADJ **2** If you use **tinny** to describe something such as a cheap car, you mean that it is made of thin metal and is of poor quality. ❑ *It is one of the cheapest cars on the market, with tinny bodywork.* ADJ

**tin open|er** **(tin openers)** also **tin-opener.** A **tin opener** is a tool that is used for opening tins of food. [BRIT] → See picture on page 1710. N-COUNT

✔ in AM, use **can opener**

**tin|pot** /tɪnpɒt/ also **tin-pot.** You can use **tinpot** to describe a leader, country, or government that you consider to be unimportant and inferior to most others. [mainly BRIT] ❑ *...a tinpot dictator.* ADJ: ADJ n [disapproval]

**tin|sel** /tɪnsᵊl/ **Tinsel** consists of small strips of shiny paper attached to long pieces of thread. People use tinsel as a decoration at Christmas. N-UNCOUNT

**Tin|sel|town** /tɪnsᵊltaʊn/ People sometimes refer to Hollywood as **Tinseltown**, especially when they want to show that they disapprove of it or when they are making fun of it. N-PROPER

**tint** /tɪnt/ **(tints, tinting, tinted)** **1** A **tint** is a small amount of colour. ❑ *Its large leaves often show a delicate purple tint.* N-COUNT **2** If you put a **tint** on your hair, you dye it a slightly different colour. ❑ *You've had a tint on your hair.* N-COUNT **3** If something **is tinted**, it has a small amount of a particular colour or dye in it. ❑ *Eyebrows can be tinted with the same dye... Most of the dirt was on the outside of the tinted glass.* VERB: usu passive *be* V-ed V-ed ♦ **-tinted** *He wore green-tinted glasses.* COMB in ADJ

**tin whis|tle** **(tin whistles)** A **tin whistle** is a simple musical instrument in the shape of a metal pipe with holes. Tin whistles make a high sound and are often used in folk music, for example Irish music. N-COUNT

**tiny** /taɪni/ **(tinier, tiniest)** Something or someone that is **tiny** is extremely small. ❑ *The living room is tiny... Though she was tiny, she had a very loud voice.* ◆◇◇ ADJ

**-tion** /-ʃᵊn/ **(-tions)** → see **-ation.**

**tip** /tɪp/ **(tips, tipping, tipped)** **1** The **tip** of something long and narrow is the end of it. ❑ *The sleeves covered his hands to the tips of his fingers... She poked and shifted things with the tip of her walking stick.* ◆◇◇ N-COUNT: oft N *of* n **2** If you **tip** an object or part of your body or if it **tips**, it moves into a sloping position with one end or side higher than the other. ❑ *He leaned away from her, and she had to tip her head back to see him... A young boy is standing on a stool, reaching for a cookie jar, and the stool is about to tip.* VERB V n adv/prep V **3** If you **tip** something somewhere, you pour it there. ❑ *Tip the vegetables into a bowl... Tip away the salt and wipe the pan.* VERB V n prep V n with adv **4** To **tip** rubbish means to get rid of it by leaving it somewhere. [BRIT] ❑ *...the costs of tipping rubbish in landfills... How do you stop people tipping?... We live in a street off Soho Road and there's rubbish tipped everywhere.* VERB V n V V-ed

✔ in AM, use **dump**

**5** A **tip** is a place where rubbish is left. [BRIT] N-COUNT

✔ in AM, use **garbage dump**

**6** If you describe a place as **a tip**, you mean it is very untidy. [BRIT, INFORMAL] ❑ *The flat is an absolute tip.* N-COUNT **7** If you **tip** someone such as a waiter in a restaurant, you give them some money in order to thank them for their services. ❑ *Do you really think it's customary to tip the waiters?... She tipped the barmen 10 dollars and bought drinks all round.* VERB V n V n amount ♦ **tip|ping** *A 10 percent service charge is added in lieu of tipping.* N-UNCOUNT **8** If you give a **tip** to someone such as a waiter in a restaurant, you give them some money to thank them for their services. ❑ *I gave the barber a tip.* N-COUNT **9** A **tip** is a useful piece of advice. ❑ *It shows how to prepare a CV, and gives tips on applying for jobs.* N-COUNT: oft N *on/for* -ing/n **10** If a person **is tipped to** do something or **is tipped for** success at something, experts or journalists believe that they will do that thing or achieve that success. [BRIT] ❑ *He is tipped to be the country's next foreign minister... He was widely tipped for success.* VERB: usu passive *be* V-ed to-inf *be* V-ed *for* n **11** Someone's **tip** for a race or competition is their advice on its likely result, especially to someone who wants to bet money on the result. ❑ *United are still my tip for the Title.* N-COUNT: oft N *for* n

PHRASES **12** If you say that a problem is **the tip of the iceberg**, you mean that it is one small part of a much larger problem. ❑ *Unless we're all a lot more careful, the people who have died so far will be just the tip of the iceberg.* PHRASE: v-link PHR **13** If something **tips the scales** or **tips the balance**, it gives someone a slight advantage. ❑ *Today's slightly shorter race could well help to tip the scales in his favour.* PHRASE: V inflects, oft PHR prep **14** If a PHRASE:

comment or question is **on the tip of** your **tongue**, you really want to say it or ask it, but you decide not to say it. ❑ *It was on the tip of Mahoney's tongue to say the boss was out.* v-link PHR

♦ **tip off** If someone **tips** you **off**, they give you information about something that has happened or is going to happen. ❑ *Greg tipped police off on his car phone about a suspect drunk driver... He was arrested two days later after a friend tipped off the FBI.* PHRASAL VERB V n P V P n (not pron)

♦ **tip over** If you **tip** something **over** or if it **tips over**, it falls over or turns over. ❑ *He tipped the table over in front of him... She tipped over the chair and collapsed into the corner with a splintering crash... We grabbed it just as it was about to tip over.* PHRASAL VERB V n P V P n (not pron) V P

♦ **tip up** If you **tip** something **up** or if it **tips up**, it moves into a sloping position with one end or side higher than the other. ❑ *We had to tip up the bed and the model was in grave danger of falling off it!... Tip the bottle up so it's in the same position as it would be when feeding the baby... The aircraft leveled out, and tipped up again for its climb to 20,000 feet.* PHRASAL VERB V P n (not pron) V n P V P

**tip-off** **(tip-offs)** A **tip-off** is a piece of information or a warning that you give to someone, often privately or secretly. ❑ *The man was arrested at his home after a tip-off to police from a member of the public.* N-COUNT

**-tipped** /-tɪpt/ **-tipped** combines with nouns to form adjectives that describe something as having a tip made of a particular substance or covered with a particular material. ❑ *In his hand, he carried a gold-tipped crook. ...poison-tipped arrows.* COMB in ADJ

**tip|ple** /tɪpəl/ **(tipples)** A person's **tipple** is the alcoholic drink that they usually drink. [mainly BRIT, INFORMAL] ❑ *My favourite tipple is a glass of port.* N-COUNT: usu supp N

**tip|ster** /tɪpstər/ **(tipsters)** A **tipster** is someone who tells you, usually in exchange for money, which horses they think will win particular races, so that you can bet money on the horses. N-COUNT

**tip|sy** /tɪpsi/ If someone is **tipsy**, they are slightly drunk. ❑ *I'm feeling a bit tipsy.* ADJ = tiddly

**tip|toe** /tɪptoʊ/ **(tiptoes, tiptoeing, tiptoed)**
1 If you **tiptoe** somewhere, you walk there very quietly without putting your heels on the floor when you walk. ❑ *She slipped out of bed and tiptoed to the window.* VERB V prep/adv 2 If you do something **on tiptoe** or **on tiptoes**, you do it standing or walking on the front part of your foot, without putting your heels on the ground. ❑ *She leaned her bike against the stone wall and stood on tiptoe to peer over it.* PHRASE: PHR after v, v-link PHR

**tip-top** also **tiptop.** You can use **tip-top** to indicate that something is extremely good. [INFORMAL, OLD-FASHIONED] ❑ *Her hair was thick, glossy and in tip-top condition.* ADJ: usu ADJ n

**ti|rade** /taɪreɪd/ **(tirades)** A **tirade** is a long angry speech in which someone criticizes a person or thing. ❑ *She launched into a tirade against the policies that ruined her business.* N-COUNT

**tire** /taɪər/ **(tires, tiring, tired)** 1 If something **tires** you or if you **tire**, you feel that you have used a lot of energy and you want to rest or sleep. ❑ *If driving tires you, take the train... He tired easily, though he was unable to sleep well at night.* VERB V n V 2 If you **tire of** something, you no longer wish to do it, because you have become bored of it or unhappy with it. ❑ *He felt he would never tire of international cricket.* VERB: no passive = weary V of n/-ing 3 A **tire** is the same as a **tyre**. [AM] N-COUNT
→ See pictures on pages 1707 and 1708.

♦ **tire out** If something **tires** you **out**, it makes you exhausted. ❑ *The oppressive afternoon heat had quite tired him out... His objective was to tire out the climbers.* PHRASAL VERB = wear out V n P V P n ♦ **tired out** *He was obviously tired out.* ADJ

**tired** /taɪərd/ 1 If you are **tired**, you feel that you want to rest or sleep. ❑ *Michael is tired and he has to rest after his long trip.* ◆◇◇ ADJ ♦ **tired|ness** *He had to cancel some engagements because of tiredness.* N-UNCOUNT 2 You can describe a part of your body as **tired** if it looks or feels as if you need to rest it or to sleep. ❑ *My arms are tired, and my back is tense.* ADJ 3 If you are **tired of** something, you do not want it to continue because you are bored of it or unhappy with it. ❑ *I am tired of all the speculation... I was tired of being a bookkeeper.* ADJ: v-link ADJ of n/-ing = sick 4 If you describe something as **tired**, you are critical of it because you have heard it or seen it many times. ❑ *I didn't want to hear another one of his tired excuses.* ADJ: usu ADJ n [disapproval]

**tire|less** /taɪərləs/ If you describe someone or their efforts as **tireless**, you approve of the fact that they put a lot of hard work into something, and refuse to give up or take a rest. ❑ *...Mother Teresa's tireless efforts to help the poor.* ADJ [approval] ♦ **tire|less|ly** *He worked tirelessly for the cause of health and safety.* ADV: ADV with v

**tire|some** /taɪərsəm/ If you describe someone or something as **tiresome**, you mean that you find them irritating or boring. ❑ *...the tiresome old lady next door.* ADJ

**tir|ing** /taɪərɪŋ/ If you describe something as **tiring**, you mean that it makes you tired so that you want to rest or sleep. ❑ *It had been a long and tiring day... Travelling is tiring.* ADJ

**tis|sue** /tɪʃuː, tɪsjuː/ **(tissues)** 1 In animals and plants, **tissue** consists of cells that are similar to each other in appearance and that have the same function. ❑ *As we age we lose muscle tissue.* ◆◇◇ N-UNCOUNT: also N in pl 2 **Tissue** or **tissue paper** is thin paper that is used for wrapping things that are easily damaged, such as objects made of glass or china. N-UNCOUNT 3 A **tissue** is a piece of thin soft paper that you use to blow your nose. ❑ *...a box of tissues.* N-COUNT

**tit** /tɪt/ **(tits)** 1 A **tit** is a small European bird that eats insects and seeds. There are several kinds of tit. → See also **blue tit**. N-COUNT 2 A woman's **tits** are her breasts. [INFORMAL, RUDE] N-COUNT: usu pl 3 If you call someone a **tit**, you are insulting them and saying that they are stupid. [BRIT, INFORMAL, RUDE] N-COUNT [disapproval]

**ti|tan** /taɪtən/ **(titans)** If you describe someone as a **titan** of a particular field, you mean that they are very important and powerful or successful in that field. ❑ *...the country's two richest business titans.* N-COUNT: usu N n, N of n

**ti|tan|ic** /taɪtænɪk/ If you describe something as **titanic**, you mean that it is very big or important, and usually that it involves very powerful forces. ❑ *The world had witnessed a titanic struggle between two visions of the future.* ADJ: usu ADJ n = monumental

**ti|ta|nium** /taɪteɪniəm/ **Titanium** is a light strong white metal. N-UNCOUNT

**tit|bit** /tɪtbɪt/ **(titbits)**

in AM, use **tidbit**

1 You can refer to a small piece of information about someone's private affairs as a **titbit**, especially when it is interesting and shocking. ❑ *...titbits of gossip gleaned from the corridors of power.* N-COUNT 2 A **titbit** is a small piece of food. N-COUNT

**tit-for-tat** A **tit-for-tat** action is one where someone takes revenge on another person for what they have done by doing something similar to them. ❑ *The two countries have each expelled another diplomat following a round of tit-for-tat expulsions.* ADJ: usu ADJ n

**tithe** /taɪð/ **(tithes)** A **tithe** is a fixed amount of money or goods that is given regularly in order to support a church, a priest, or a charity. N-COUNT

**tit|il|late** /tɪtɪleɪt/ **(titillates, titillating, titillated)** If something **titillates** someone, it pleases and excites them, especially in a sexual way. ❑ *The pictures were not meant to titillate audiences.* VERB V n ♦ **tit|il|lat|ing** *...deliberately titillating lyrics.* ADJ

**ti|tle** /taɪtəl/ **(titles, titling, titled)** 1 The **title** of a book, play, film, or piece of music is its name. ❑ *'Patience and Sarah' was first published in 1969 under the title 'A Place for Us'.* ◆◆◇ N-COUNT 2 When a writer, composer, or artist **titles** a work, they give it a title. ❑ *Pirandello titled his play 'Six Characters in Search of an Author'... The single is titled 'White Love'... Their story is the subject of a new book titled 'The Golden* VERB V n n be V-ed n V-ed

*Thirteen'.* ♦ **-titled** *...his aptly titled autobiography, Life is Meeting.* [3] Publishers and booksellers often refer to books or magazines as **titles**. ❑ *It has become the biggest publisher of new poetry in Britain, with 50 new titles a year.* [4] A person's **title** is a word such as 'Sir', 'Lord', or 'Lady' that is used in front of their name, or a phrase that is used instead of their name, and indicates that they have a high rank in society. ❑ *Her husband was also honoured with his title 'Sir Denis'.* [5] Someone's **title** is a word such as 'Mr', 'Mrs', or 'Doctor', that is used before their own name in order to show their status or profession. ❑ *She has been awarded the title Professor.* [6] Someone's **title** is a name that describes their job or status in an organization. ❑ *'Could you tell me your official job title?' — 'It's Data Processing Manager.'* [7] If a person or team wins a particular **title**, they win a sports competition that is held regularly. Usually a person keeps a title until someone else defeats them. ❑ *He became Jamaica's first Olympic gold medallist when he won the 400m title in 1948.*

COMB in ADJ; N-COUNT: usu pl; N-COUNT: oft poss N; N-COUNT: oft poss N; N-COUNT: oft poss N; N-COUNT: usu with supp, oft poss N

**ti|tled** /taɪtəld/ Someone who is **titled** has a title such as 'Lord', 'Lady', 'Sir', or 'Princess' before their name, showing that they have a high rank in society. ❑ *Her mother was a titled lady.* ◆◇◇ ADJ

**title-holder** (**title-holders**) also **title holder.** The **title-holder** is the person who most recently won a sports competition that is held regularly. ❑ *Kasparov became the youngest world title-holder at 22.* N-COUNT

**ti|tle role** (**title roles**) **The title role** in a play or film is the role referred to in the name of the play or film. ❑ *My novel 'The Rector's Wife' is being adapted for TV, with Lindsay Duncan in the title role.* N-COUNT: *the* N

**ti|tle track** (**title tracks**) The **title track** on a CD, record, or tape is a song or piece of music that has the same title as the CD, record, or tape. ❑ *They come from Tuam, a place they refer to on the title track of their album, 'All the Way From Tuam'.* N-COUNT: usu sing

**tit|ter** /tɪtəʳ/ (**titters, tittering, tittered**) If someone **titters**, they give a short nervous laugh, especially when they are embarrassed about something. ❑ *Mention sex therapy and most people will titter in embarrassment.* ♦ **Titter** is also a noun. ❑ *Mollie gave an uneasy little titter.* ♦ **tit|ter|ing** *There was nervous tittering from among the studio audience.* VERB = *snigger*; V; N-COUNT; N-UNCOUNT

**tittle-tattle** /tɪtəl tætəl/ If you refer to something that a group of people talk about as **tittle-tattle**, you mean that you disapprove of it because it is not important, and there is no real evidence that it is true. ❑ *...tittle-tattle about the private lives of minor celebrities.* N-UNCOUNT [disapproval] = *gossip*

**titu|lar** /tɪtʃʊləʳ/ A **titular** job or position has a name that makes it seem important, although the person who has it is not really important or powerful. ❑ *He is titular head, and merely signs laws occasionally.* ADJ: ADJ n = *nominal*

**tiz|zy** /tɪzi/ If you get **in a tizzy** or **into a tizzy**, you get excited, worried, or nervous about something, especially something that is not important. [INFORMAL] ❑ *He was in a right tizzy, muttering and swearing... Male journalists have been sent into a tizzy by the idea of female fighter pilots.* PHRASE: v-link PHR, PHR after v

**T-junction** (**T-junctions**) If you arrive at a **T-junction**, the road that you are on joins at right angles to another road, so that you have to turn either left or right to continue. [BRIT] N-COUNT

**TM** /tiː em/ [1] **TM** is a kind of meditation, in which people mentally relax by silently repeating special words over and over again. **TM** is an abbreviation for 'transcendental meditation'. [2] **TM** is a written abbreviation for **trademark**. N-UNCOUNT

**TNT** /tiː en tiː/ **TNT** is a powerful explosive substance. **TNT** is an abbreviation for 'trinitrotoluene'. N-UNCOUNT

**to**

① PREPOSITION AND ADVERB USES
② USED BEFORE THE BASE FORM OF A VERB

## ① to ◆◆◆

✔ Usually pronounced /tə/ before a consonant and /tu/ before a vowel, but pronounced /tuː/ when you are emphasizing it.

In addition to the uses shown below, **to** is used in phrasal verbs such as 'see to' and 'come to'. It is also used with some verbs that have two objects in order to introduce the second object.

[1] You use **to** when indicating the place that someone or something visits, moves towards, or points at. ❑ *Two friends and I drove to Florida during college spring break. ...a five-day road and rail journey to Peking... She went to the window and looked out... He pointed to a chair, signalling for her to sit.* PREP

[2] If you go **to** an event, you go where it is taking place. ❑ *We went to a party at the leisure centre... He came to dinner.* PREP

[3] If something is attached **to** something larger or fixed **to** it, the two things are joined together. ❑ *There was a piece of cloth tied to the dog's collar... Scrape off all the meat juices stuck to the bottom of the pan.* PREP

[4] You use **to** when indicating the position of something. For example, if something is **to** your left, it is nearer your left side than your right side. ❑ *Hemingway's studio is to the right... Atlanta was only an hour's drive to the north.* PREP

[5] When you give something **to** someone, they receive it. ❑ *He picked up the knife and gave it to me... Firms should be allowed to offer jobs to the long-term unemployed at a lower wage.* PREP: v n PREP n

[6] You use **to** to indicate who or what an action or a feeling is directed towards. ❑ *Marcus has been most unkind to me today... I have had to pay for repairs to the house.* PREP: adj/n PREP n

[7] You use **to** with certain nouns and adjectives to show that a following noun is related to them. ❑ *He is a witty man, and an inspiration to all of us... Marriage is not the answer to everything.* PREP: adj/n PREP n

[8] If you say something **to** someone, you want that person to listen and understand what you are saying. ❑ *I'm going to have to explain to them that I can't pay them.* PREP

[9] You use **to** when indicating someone's reaction to something or their feelings about a situation or event. For example, if you say that something happens **to** someone's surprise you mean that they are surprised when it happens. ❑ *He survived, to the amazement of surgeons.* PREP

[10] You use **to** when indicating the person whose opinion you are stating. ❑ *It was clear to me that he respected his boss... Everyone seemed to her to be amazingly kind.* PREP

[11] You use **to** when indicating what something or someone is becoming, or the state or situation that they are progressing towards. ❑ *The shouts changed to screams of terror. ...an old ranch house that has been converted to a nature centre.* PREP

[12] **To** can be used as a way of introducing the person or organization you are employed by, when you perform some service for them. ❑ *Rickman worked as a dresser to Nigel Hawthorne... He was an official interpreter to the government of Nepal.* PREP: n PREP n

[13] You use **to** to indicate that something happens until the time or amount mentioned is reached. ❑ *From 1977 to 1985 the United States gross national product grew 21 percent... The annual rate of inflation in Britain has risen to its highest level for eight years.* PREP

[14] You use **to** when indicating the last thing in a range of things, usually when you are giving two extreme examples of something. ❑ *I read everything from fiction to history.* PREP: *from* n PREP n

[15] If someone goes from place **to** place or from job **to** job, they go to several places, or work in several jobs, and spend only a short time in each one. ❑ *Larry and Andy had drifted from place to place, worked at this and that.* PREP: *from* n PREP n

[16] If someone moves **to and fro**, they move repeatedly from PHRASE: PHR after v

one place to another and back again, or from side to side. ❑ *She stood up and began to pace to and fro.* 17 You use **to** when you are stating a time which is less than thirty minutes before an hour. For example, if it is 'five **to** eight', it is five minutes before eight o'clock. ❑ *At twenty to six I was waiting by the entrance to the station... At exactly five minutes to nine, Ann left her car and entered the building.* PREP: num/n PREP num 18 You use **to** when giving ratios and rates. ❑ *...engines that can run at 60 miles to the gallon.* PREP: amount PREP amount 19 You use **to** when indicating that two things happen at the same time. For example, if something is done **to** music, it is done at the same time as music is being played. ❑ *Romeo left the stage, to enthusiastic applause... Amy woke up to the sound of her doorbell ringing.* PREP 20 If you say **'There's nothing to it'**, **'There's not much to it'**, or **'That's all there is to it'**, you are emphasizing how simple you think something is. ❑ *Once they have tried growing orchids, they will see there is really nothing to it.* CONVENTION [emphasis] 21 If you push or shut a door **to**, you close it but may not shut it completely. ❑ *He slipped out, pulling the door to.* ADV: ADV after v 22 → See also **according to**.

**②to** ◆◆◆

> ✔ Pronounced /tə/ before a consonant and /tu/ before a vowel.

1 You use **to** before the base form of a verb to form the to-infinitive. You use the to-infinitive after certain verbs, nouns, and adjectives, and after words such as 'how', 'which', and 'where'. ❑ *The management wanted to know what I was doing there... She told ministers of her decision to resign.* *to inf* 2 You use **to** before the base form of a verb to indicate the purpose or intention of an action. ❑ *...using the experience of big companies to help small businesses... He was doing this to make me more relaxed.* **in order to** → see **order**. *to inf* *= in order to* 3 You use **to** before the base form of a verb when you are commenting on a statement that you are making, for example when saying that you are being honest or brief, or that you are summing up or giving an example. ❑ *I'm disappointed, to be honest... Well, to sum up, what is the message that you are trying to get across?* *to inf* 4 You use **to** before the base form of a verb when indicating what situation follows a particular action. ❑ *From the garden you walk down to discover a large lake... He awoke to find Charlie standing near the bed.* *to inf* 5 You use **to** with 'too' and 'enough' in expressions like **too much to** and **old enough to**; see **too** and **enough**.

**toad** /təʊd/ **(toads)** A **toad** is a creature which is similar to a frog but which has a drier skin and spends less time in water. N-COUNT

**toad|stool** /təʊdstuːl/ **(toadstools)** A **toadstool** is a fungus that you cannot eat because it is poisonous. N-COUNT

**toady** /təʊdi/ **(toadies, toadying, toadied)** 1 If you refer to someone as a **toady**, you disapprove of them because they flatter or are pleasant towards an important or powerful person in the hope of getting some advantage from them. N-COUNT [disapproval] 2 If you say that someone **is toadying to** an important or powerful person, you disapprove of them because they are flattering or being pleasant towards that person in the hope of getting some advantage from them. ❑ *They came backstage afterward, cooing and toadying to him.* VERB [disapproval] V *to* n Also V

**toast** /təʊst/ **(toasts, toasting, toasted)** 1 **Toast** is bread which has been cut into slices and made brown and crisp by cooking at a high temperature. ❑ *...a piece of toast.* N-UNCOUNT 2 When you **toast** something such as bread, you cook it at a high temperature so that it becomes brown and crisp. ❑ *Toast the bread lightly on both sides. ...a toasted sandwich.* VERB V n V-ed 3 When you drink a **toast to** someone or something, you drink some wine or another alcoholic drink as a symbolic gesture, in order to show your appreciation of them or to wish them success. ❑ *Eleanor and I drank a toast to Miss Jacobs.* N-COUNT 4 When you **toast** someone or something, you drink a toast to them. ❑ *Party officials and generals toasted his health.* VERB V n 5 If someone is **the toast of** a place, they are very popular and greatly admired there, because they have done something very successfully or well. ❑ *She was the toast of Paris.* N-SING: *the* N *of* n

**toast|er** /təʊstəʳ/ **(toasters)** A **toaster** is a piece of electrical equipment used to toast bread. N-COUNT

**toastie** /təʊsti/ **(toasties)** A **toastie** is a toasted sandwich. [BRIT] N-COUNT

**toast|master** /təʊstmɑːstəʳ, -mæs-/ **(toastmasters)** At a special ceremony or formal dinner, the **toastmaster** is the person who proposes toasts and introduces the speakers. N-COUNT

**toast rack** **(toast racks)** A **toast rack** is an object that is designed to hold pieces of toast in an upright position and separate from each other, ready for people to eat. N-COUNT

**toasty** /təʊsti/ **(toastier, toastiest)** If something is **toasty**, it is comfortably warm. [INFORMAL] ❑ *The heating system knows to make the temperature toasty on a cold morning.* ADJ

**to|bac|co** /təbækoʊ/ **(tobaccos)** 1 **Tobacco** is dried leaves which people smoke in pipes, cigars, and cigarettes. You can also refer to pipes, cigars, and cigarettes as a whole as **tobacco**. ❑ *Try to do without tobacco and alcohol.* N-MASS 2 **Tobacco** is the plant from which tobacco is obtained. N-UNCOUNT

**to|bac|co|nist** /təbækənɪst/ **(tobacconists)** A **tobacconist** or a **tobacconist's** is a shop that sells things such as tobacco, cigarettes, and cigars. N-COUNT: oft *the* N

**to|bog|gan** /təbɒgən/ **(toboggans)** A **toboggan** is a light wooden board with a curved front, used for travelling down hills on snow or ice. N-COUNT *= sled, sledge*

**toc|ca|ta** /təkɑːtə/ **(toccatas)** A **toccata** is a fast piece of music for the piano, organ, or other keyboard instrument. N-COUNT: oft in names

**to|day** /tədeɪ/ ◆◆◆ 1 You use **today** to refer to the day on which you are speaking or writing. ❑ *How are you feeling today?... I wanted him to come with us today, but he couldn't.* ADV: ADV with cl ♦ **Today** is also a noun. ❑ *The Prime Minister remains the main story in today's newspapers.* N-UNCOUNT 2 You can refer to the present period of history as **today**. ❑ *He thinks pop music today is as exciting as it's ever been.* ADV: ADV with cl, n ADV ♦ **Today** is also a noun. ❑ *In today's America, health care is one of the very biggest businesses.* N-UNCOUNT

**tod|dle** /tɒdᵊl/ **(toddles, toddling, toddled)** When a child **toddles**, it walks unsteadily with short quick steps. ❑ *...once your baby starts toddling... She fell while toddling around.* VERB V V adv/prep

**tod|dler** /tɒdləʳ/ **(toddlers)** A **toddler** is a young child who has only just learned to walk or who still walks unsteadily with small, quick steps. N-COUNT

**tod|dy** /tɒdi/ **(toddies)** A **toddy** is a drink that is made by adding hot water and sugar to a strong alcoholic drink such as whisky, rum, or brandy. ❑ *...a hot toddy.* N-VAR: usu supp N

**to-do** /tə duː/ When there is a **to-do**, people are very excited, confused, or angry about something. [INFORMAL] N-SING

**toe** /təʊ/ **(toes, toeing, toed)** 1 Your **toes** are the five movable parts at the end of each foot. N-COUNT: usu pl

PHRASES 2 If you **dip** your **toes into** something or **dip** your **toes into the waters of** something, you start doing that thing slowly and carefully, because you are not sure whether it will be successful or whether you will like it. ❑ *This may encourage gold traders to dip their toes back into the markets.* PHRASE: V inflects, usu PHR n 3 If you say that someone or something **keeps** you **on** your **toes**, you mean that they cause you to remain alert and ready for anything that might happen. ❑ *His fiery campaign rhetoric has kept opposition parties on their toes for months.* PHRASE: V inflects 4 If you **toe the line**, you behave in the way that people in authority expect you to. ❑ *...attempts to persuade the rebel members to toe the line.* PHRASE: V inflects 5 If you **tread on** someone's **toes**, you offend them by criticizing the way that they do some- PHRASE: V inflects thing or by interfering in their affairs. [INFORMAL] ❑ *I must be careful not to tread on their toes. My job is to challenge, but not threaten them.*

**toe|cap** /toʊkæp/ **(toecaps)** also **toe-cap.** A **toecap** is a piece of leather or metal which is fitted over the end of a shoe or boot in order to protect or strengthen it. N-COUNT

**toe-curling** If you describe something as **toe-curling**, you mean that it makes you feel very embarrassed. ❑ *...toe-curling home videos.* ADJ

**TOEFL** /toʊfəl/ **TOEFL** is an English language examination which is often taken by foreign students who want to study at universities in English-speaking countries. **TOEFL** is an abbreviation of 'Test of English as a Foreign Language'. N-PROPER

**toe|hold** /toʊhoʊld/ **(toeholds)** also **toe-hold.** If you have a **toehold in** a situation, you have managed to gain an uncertain position or a small amount of power in it, which you hope will give you the opportunity to get a better or more powerful position. ❑ *Mitsubishi Motors were anxious to get a toehold in the European market.* N-COUNT: usu sing, usu N *in/on* n

**toe|nail** /toʊneɪl/ **(toenails)** also **toe nail.** Your **toenails** are the thin hard areas at the end of each of your toes. N-COUNT: usu pl

**toff** /tɒf/ **(toffs)** If you refer to someone as a **toff**, you are saying in an unkind way that they come from the upper classes or are very rich. [BRIT, INFORMAL] N-COUNT [disapproval] = *nob*

**tof|fee** /tɒfi, AM tɔːfi/ **(toffees)** [1] **Toffee** is a sticky sweet that you chew. It is made by boiling sugar and butter together with water. [BRIT] N-UNCOUNT

✔ in AM, use **taffy**

[2] A **toffee** is an individual piece of toffee. N-COUNT

**toffee-nosed** If you say that someone is **toffee-nosed**, you disapprove of them because they have a high opinion of themselves and a low opinion of other people. [BRIT, INFORMAL] ADJ [disapproval] = *stuck-up*

**tog** /tɒg/ **(togs)** [1] A **tog** is an official measurement that shows how warm a blanket or quilt is. [BRIT] ❑ *The range of tog values has been extended to 15 togs.* ♦ **Tog** is also a combining form. ❑ *...a snug 13.5-tog winter duvet.* [2] **Togs** are clothes, especially ones for a particular purpose. [INFORMAL] ❑ *The photograph showed him wearing football togs.* N-COUNT: usu N n, num N; COMB in ADJ; N-PLURAL

**toga** /toʊgə/ **(togas)** A **toga** is a piece of clothing which was worn by the ancient Romans. N-COUNT

**to|geth|er** /təgeðəʳ/ ♦♦♦

> In addition to the uses shown below, **together** is used in phrasal verbs such as 'piece together', 'pull together', and 'sleep together'.

[1] If people do something **together**, they do it with each other. ❑ *We went on long bicycle rides together... They all live together in a three-bedroom house... Together they swam to the ship.* ADV: usu ADV after v, also ADV cl ≠ *alone*

[2] If things are joined **together**, they are joined with each other so that they touch or form one whole. ❑ *Mix the ingredients together thoroughly... She clasped her hands together on her lap.* ADV: ADV after v

[3] If things or people are situated **together**, they are in the same place and very near to each other. ❑ *The trees grew close together... Ginette and I gathered our things together.* ADV: ADV after v

[4] If a group of people are held or kept **together**, they are united with each other in some way. ❑ *He has done enough to pull the party together.* ♦ **Together** is also an adjective. ❑ *We are together in the way we're looking at this situation.* ADV: ADV after v; ADJ: v-link ADJ = *united*

[5] If two people are **together**, they are married or having a sexual relationship with each other. ❑ *We were together for five years.* ADJ: v-link ADJ, n ADJ, v n ADJ

[6] If two things happen or are done **together**, they happen or are done at the same time. ❑ *Three horses crossed the finish line together... 'Yes,' they said together.* ADV: ADV after v ≠ *separately*

[7] You use **together** when you are adding two or more amounts or things to each other in order to consider a total amount or effect. ❑ *Together they account for less than five per cent of the population.* ADV: ADV before v, n ADV, ADV cl

[8] If you say that two things **go together**, or that one thing **goes together with** another, you mean that they go well with each other or cannot be separated from each other. ❑ *I can see that some colours go together and some don't.* PHRASE: pl-n PHR, PHR *with* n/-ing

[9] If you describe someone as **together**, you admire them because they are very confident, organized, and know what they want. [INFORMAL] ❑ *She was very headstrong, and very together.* ADJ [approval]

[10] You use **together with** to mention someone or something else that is also involved in an action or situation. ❑ *Every month we'll deliver the very best articles, together with the latest fashion and beauty news.* PREP-PHRASE

[11] to **get** your **act together** → see **act**. to **put** your **heads together** → see **head**. **put together** → see **put**.

**to|geth|er|ness** /təgeðəʳnəs/ **Togetherness** is a happy feeling of affection and closeness to other people, especially your friends and family. ❑ *Nothing can ever take the place of real love and family togetherness.* N-UNCOUNT

**tog|gle** /tɒgəl/ **(toggles)** A **toggle** is a small piece of wood or plastic which is sewn to something such as a coat or bag, and which is pushed through a loop or hole to fasten it. N-COUNT

**toil** /tɔɪl/ **(toils, toiling, toiled)** [1] When people **toil**, they work very hard doing unpleasant or tiring tasks. [LITERARY] ❑ *People who toiled in dim, dank factories were too exhausted to enjoy their family life... Workers toiled long hours.* ♦ **Toil away** means the same as **toil**. ❑ *She has toiled away at the violin for years... Nora toils away serving burgers at the local cafe.* VERB; V; V n; PHRASAL VERB; V P *at/on* n; V P

[2] **Toil** is unpleasant work that is very tiring physically. [LITERARY] N-UNCOUNT

**toi|let** /tɔɪlət/ **(toilets)** [1] A **toilet** is a large bowl with a seat, or a platform with a hole, which is connected to a water system and which you use when you want to get rid of urine or faeces from your body. N-COUNT

[2] A **toilet** is a room in a house or public building that contains a toilet. [BRIT] → See picture on page 1706. ❑ *Annette ran and locked herself in the toilet... Fred never uses public toilets.* N-COUNT

✔ in AM, use **bathroom, rest room**

[3] You can say that someone **goes to the toilet** to mean that they get rid of waste substances from their body, especially when you want to avoid using words that you think may offend people. [mainly BRIT] PHRASE: V inflects

✔ in AM, usually use **go to the bathroom**

**toi|let bag** **(toilet bags)** A **toilet bag** is a small bag in which you keep things such as soap, a flannel, and a toothbrush when you are travelling. N-COUNT = *sponge bag*

**toi|let pa|per** **Toilet paper** is thin soft paper that people use to clean themselves after they have got rid of urine or faeces from their body. N-UNCOUNT

**toi|let|ries** /tɔɪlətriz/ **Toiletries** are things that you use when washing or taking care of your body, for example soap and toothpaste. N-PLURAL

**toi|let roll** **(toilet rolls)** A **toilet roll** is a long narrow strip of toilet paper that is wound around a small cardboard tube. N-VAR

**toi|let trained** If a child is **toilet trained**, he or she has learned to use the toilet. ADJ = *potty trained*

**toi|let train|ing** **Toilet training** is the process of teaching a child to use the toilet. N-UNCOUNT = *potty training*

**toi|let wa|ter** **(toilet waters)** **Toilet water** is fairly weak and inexpensive perfume. N-MASS

**to-ing and fro-ing** If you say that there is a lot of **to-ing and fro-ing**, you mean that the same actions or movements or the same arguments are being repeated many times. [mainly BRIT] ❑ *After some to-ing and fro-ing, Elsie and the children moved back to London.* N-UNCOUNT

**to|ken** /toʊkən/ **(tokens)** [1] You use **token** to describe things or actions which are small or unimportant but are meant to show particular intentions or feelings which may not be sincere. ❑ *The announcement was welcomed as a step in the right direction, but was widely seen as a token gesture.* ADJ: ADJ n

2 A **token** is a piece of paper or card that can be exchanged for goods, either in a particular shop or as part of a special offer. [BRIT] ❑ *Here is the fifth token towards our offer. You need six of these tokens.* — N-COUNT: oft n N

☑ in AM, use **coupon**

3 A **token** is a round flat piece of metal or plastic that is sometimes used instead of money. ❑ *Some of the older telephones still only accept tokens.* — N-COUNT
4 If you give something to a person or do something for them as a **token of** your feelings, you give it or do it as a way of expressing those feelings. ❑ *As a token of goodwill, I'm going to write another letter.* — N-COUNT: usu with supp, oft N *of* n
5 You use **by the same token** to introduce a statement that you think is true for the same reasons that were given for a previous statement. ❑ *If you give up exercise, your muscles shrink and fat increases. By the same token, if you expend more energy you will lose fat.* — PHRASE: PHR with cl

**to|ken|ism** /toʊkənɪzəm/ If you refer to an action as **tokenism**, you disapprove of it because you think it is just done for effect, in order to show a particular intention or to impress a particular type of person. ❑ *Is his promotion evidence of the minorities' advance, or mere tokenism?* — N-UNCOUNT [disapproval]

**told** /toʊld/ 1 **Told** is the past tense and past participle of **tell**. 2 You can use **all told** to introduce or follow a summary, general statement, or total. ❑ *All told there were 104 people on the payroll.* — PHRASE: PHR with cl, amount PHR

**tol|er|able** /tɒlərəbᵊl/ 1 If you describe something as **tolerable**, you mean that you can bear it, even though it is unpleasant or painful. ❑ *He described their living conditions as tolerable.* — ADJ ≠ *intolerable*
♦ **tol|er|ably** /tɒlərəbli/ *Their captors treated them tolerably well. ...tolerably hot water.* — ADV: usu ADV adj/adv
2 If you describe something as **tolerable**, you mean that it is fairly good and reasonably satisfactory, but not of the highest quality or standard. [FORMAL] ❑ *He fell asleep just past midnight with tolerable ease.* — ADJ = *reasonable*
♦ **tol|er|ably** *He can see tolerably well and he can read.* — ADV

**tol|er|ance** /tɒlərəns/ **(tolerances)** 1 **Tolerance** is the quality of allowing other people to say and do as they like, even if you do not agree or approve of it. ❑ *...his tolerance and understanding of diverse human nature.* — N-UNCOUNT: oft N *of* n [approval] ≠ *intolerance*
2 **Tolerance** is the ability to bear something painful or unpleasant. ❑ *There is lowered pain tolerance, lowered resistance to infection. ...a low tolerance of errors.* — N-UNCOUNT: usu with supp, n N, N *of* n
3 If someone or something has a **tolerance to** a substance, they are exposed to it so often that it does not have very much effect on them. ❑ *As with any drug taken in excess, your body can build up a tolerance to it.* — N-VAR: with supp, usu N *to* n

**tol|er|ant** /tɒlərənt/ 1 If you describe someone as **tolerant**, you approve of the fact that they allow other people to say and do as they like, even if they do not agree with or like it. ❑ *They need to be tolerant of different points of view.* — ADJ: oft v-link ADJ *of* n [approval] ≠ *intolerant*
♦ **tol|er|ant|ly** *She had listened tolerantly to his jumbled account.* — ADV: ADV with v
2 If a plant, animal, or machine is **tolerant of** particular conditions or types of treatment, it is able to bear them without being damaged or hurt. ❑ *...plants which are more tolerant of dry conditions.* — ADJ: v-link ADJ *of* n

**tol|er|ate** /tɒləreɪt/ **(tolerates, tolerating, tolerated)** 1 If you **tolerate** a situation or person, you accept them although you do not particularly like them. ❑ *She can no longer tolerate the position that she's in.* — VERB = *put up with*; V n
2 If you can **tolerate** something unpleasant or painful, you are able to bear it. ❑ *The ability to tolerate pain varies from person to person.* — VERB = *bear*; V n

**toll** /toʊl/ **(tolls, tolling, tolled)** 1 When a bell **tolls** or when someone **tolls** it, it rings slowly and repeatedly, often as a sign that someone has died. ❑ *Church bells tolled and black flags fluttered... The pilgrims tolled the bell.* — VERB; V; V n
2 A **toll** is a small sum of money that you have to pay in order to use a particular bridge or road. — N-COUNT
3 A **toll** road or **toll** bridge is a road or bridge where you have to pay in order to use it. — N-COUNT: N n
4 A **toll** is a total number of deaths, accidents, or disasters that occur in a particular period of time. [JOURNALISM] ❑ *There are fears that the casualty toll may be higher.* ➔ See also **death toll**. — N-COUNT: usu sing, supp N
5 If you say that something **takes** its **toll** or **takes a heavy toll**, you mean that it has a bad effect or causes a lot of suffering. ❑ *Winter takes its toll on your health.* — PHRASE: V inflects, oft PHR *on* n

**toll-free** A **toll-free** telephone number is one which you can dial without having to pay for the call. [AM] ♦ **Toll-free** is also an adverb. ❑ *Call our customer-service staff toll-free.* — ADJ: usu ADJ n; ADV: ADV after v

☑ in BRIT, use **freefone**

**tom** /tɒm/ **(toms)** A **tom** is a male cat. — N-COUNT

**toma|hawk** /tɒməhɔːk/ **(tomahawks)** A **tomahawk** is a small light axe that is used by Native American peoples. — N-COUNT

**to|ma|to** /təmɑːtoʊ, AM -meɪ-/ **(tomatoes)** **Tomatoes** are small, soft, red fruit that you can eat raw in salads or cooked as a vegetable. ➔ See picture on page 1712. — N-VAR

**tomb** /tuːm/ **(tombs)** A **tomb** is a large grave that is above ground and that usually has a sculpture or other decoration on it. — N-COUNT

**tom|boy** /tɒmbɔɪ/ **(tomboys)** If you say that a girl is a **tomboy**, you mean that she likes playing rough or noisy games, or doing things that were traditionally considered to be things that boys enjoy. — N-COUNT

**tomb|stone** /tuːmstoʊn/ **(tombstones)** A **tombstone** is a large stone with words carved into it, which is placed on a grave. — N-COUNT = *gravestone, headstone*

**tom cat** **(tomcats)** also **tomcat.** A **tom cat** is a male cat. — N-COUNT = *tom*

**tome** /toʊm/ **(tomes)** A **tome** is a very large, heavy book. [FORMAL] — N-COUNT

**tom|fool|ery** /tɒmfuːləri/ **Tomfoolery** is playful behaviour, usually of a rather silly, noisy, or rough kind. ❑ *Were you serious, or was that a bit of tomfoolery?* — N-UNCOUNT

**to|mor|row** /təmɒroʊ, AM -mɔːr-/ **(tomorrows)** ◆◆◇ 1 You use **tomorrow** to refer to the day after today. ❑ *Bye, see you tomorrow... The first official results will be announced tomorrow.* — ADV: ADV with cl
♦ **Tomorrow** is also a noun. ❑ *Davies plays for the Barbarians in tomorrow's match against England.* — N-UNCOUNT
2 You can refer to the future, especially the near future, as **tomorrow**. ❑ *What is education going to look like tomorrow?* — ADV: ADV with cl
♦ **Tomorrow** is also a noun. ❑ *...tomorrow's computer industry.* — N-UNCOUNT: also N in pl

**tom-tom** **(tom-toms)** A **tom-tom** is a tall narrow drum that is usually played with the hands. — N-COUNT

**ton** /tʌn/ **(tons)** ◆◇◇ 1 A **ton** is a unit of weight that is equal to 2240 pounds in Britain and to 2000 pounds in the United States. ❑ *Hundreds of tons of oil spilled into the sea... Getting rid of rubbish can cost $100 a ton.* — N-COUNT: num N, oft N *of* n
2 A **ton** is the same as a **tonne**. — N-COUNT

**PHRASES** 3 If someone **comes down on** you **like a ton of bricks**, they are extremely angry with you and tell you off because of something wrong that you have done. [INFORMAL] ❑ *If you do something awful they all come down on you like a ton of bricks.* — PHRASE: V inflects
4 If you say that something **weighs a ton**, you mean that it is extremely heavy. [INFORMAL] — PHRASE: V inflects

**to|nal** /toʊnᵊl/ **Tonal** means relating to the qualities or pitch of a sound or to the tonality of a piece of music. ❑ *There is little tonal variety in his voice. ...tonal music.* — ADJ: usu ADJ n

**to|nal|ity** /toʊnælɪti/ **(tonalities)** **Tonality** is the presence of a musical key in a piece of music. [TECHNICAL] — N-VAR

**tone** /toʊn/ **(tones, toning, toned)** ◆◇◇ 1 The **tone** of a sound is its particular quality. ❑ *Cross could hear him speaking in low tones to Sarah. ...the clear tone of the bell.* — N-COUNT: with supp, usu pl
2 Someone's **tone** is a quality in their voice which shows what they are feel- — N-COUNT: usu with supp

ing or thinking. ❑ *I still didn't like his tone of voice... Her tone implied that her patience was limited.* [3] The **tone** of a speech or piece of writing is its style and the opinions or ideas expressed in it. ❑ *The spokesman said the tone of the letter was very friendly... His comments to reporters were conciliatory in tone.* [4] The **tone** of a place or an event is its general atmosphere. ❑ *The service desk at the entrance, with its friendly, helpful and efficient staff, sets the tone for the rest of the store.* [5] The **tone** of someone's body, especially their muscles, is its degree of firmness and strength. ❑ *...stretch exercises that aim to improve muscle tone.* [6] Something that **tones** your body makes it firm and strong. ❑ *This movement lengthens your spine and tones the spinal nerves... Try these toning exercises before you start the day. ...finely toned muscular bodies.* ♦ **Tone up** means the same as **tone**. ❑ *Exercise tones up your body... Although it's not strenuous exercise, you feel toned-up, supple and relaxed.* [7] A **tone** is one of the lighter, darker, or brighter shades of the same colour. ❑ *Each brick also varies slightly in tone, texture and size.* [8] A **tone** is one of the sounds that you hear when you are using a telephone, for example the sound that tells you that a number is engaged or busy, or no longer exists. [9] → See also **dialling tone**, **ring tone**. [10] If you say that something **lowers the tone of** a place or event, you mean that it is not appropriate and makes the place or event seem less respectable. ❑ *Councillors say plastic-framed windows lower the tone of the neighbourhood.*

N-SING: also *in* N · N-SING: *the* N, usu with supp · N-UNCOUNT · VERB V n · V-ing · V-ed · PHRASAL VERB V P n · V-ed P · N-VAR · N-SING: usu with supp · PHRASE: V inflects

♦ **tone down** [1] If you **tone down** something that you have written or said, you make it less forceful, severe, or offensive. ❑ *The fiery right-wing leader toned down his militant statements after the meeting... We have had to ask the agency and their client to tone their ads down.* [2] If you **tone down** a colour or a flavour, you make it less bright or strong. ❑ *When Ken Hom wrote his first book for the BBC he was asked to tone down the spices and garlic in his recipes.*

PHRASAL VERB V P n (not pron) · V n P · PHRASAL VERB V P n (not pron) Also V n P

♦ **tone up** → see **tone 6**.

**-toned** /-toʊnd/ **-toned** combines with adjectives to indicate that something has a particular kind of tone. ❑ *...soft, pastel-toned drawings.* COMB in ADJ

**tone-deaf** If you say that someone is **tone-deaf**, you mean that they cannot sing in tune or recognize different tunes. ADJ

**tone|less** /toʊnləs/ A **toneless** voice is dull and does not express any feeling. [WRITTEN] ADJ

♦ **tone|less|ly** ❑ *'That's most kind of him,' Eleanor said tonelessly.* ADV: ADV after v

**ton|er** /toʊnəʳ/ **(toners)** A **toner** is a substance which you can put on your skin, for example to clean it or make it less oily. N-MASS

**tongs** /tɒŋz, AM tɔːŋz/ **Tongs** are a tool that you use to grip and pick up objects that you do not want to touch. They consist of two long narrow pieces of metal joined together at one end. **hammer and tongs** → see **hammer**. N-PLURAL: also *a pair of* N

**tongue** /tʌŋ/ **(tongues)** [1] Your **tongue** is the soft movable part inside your mouth which you use for tasting, eating, and speaking. ❑ *I walked over to the mirror and stuck my tongue out... She ran her tongue around her lips.* [2] You can use **tongue** to refer to the kind of things that a person says. ❑ *She had a nasty tongue, but I liked her.* [3] A **tongue** is a language. [LITERARY] ❑ *The French feel passionately about their native tongue.* → See also **mother tongue**. [4] **Tongue** is the cooked tongue of an ox or sheep. It is usually eaten cold. [5] The **tongue** of a shoe or boot is the piece of leather which is underneath the laces. [6] A **tongue of** something such as fire or land is a long thin piece of it. [LITERARY] ❑ *A yellow tongue of flame shot upwards.*

N-COUNT: usu poss N · N-COUNT: usu supp N · N-COUNT = language · N-VAR · N-COUNT · N-COUNT: N *of* n

PHRASES [7] A **tongue-in-cheek** remark or attitude is not serious, although it may seem to be. ❑ *...a lighthearted, tongue-in-cheek approach.* [8] If you **hold** your **tongue**, you do not say anything even though you might want to or be expected to, because it is the wrong time to say it. ❑ *Douglas held his tongue, preferring not to speak out on a politically sensitive issue.* [9] If you describe something you said as **a slip of the tongue**, you mean that you said it by mistake. ❑ *At one stage he referred to Anna as John's fiancée, but later said that was a slip of the tongue.* [10] to **bite** your **tongue** → see **bite**.

PHRASE: PHR n, v-link PHR, PHR after v · PHRASE: V inflects · PHRASE: *slip* inflects

**tongue-in-cheek** → see **tongue**.

**tongue-lashing** **(tongue-lashings)** also **tongue lashing**. If someone gives you a **tongue-lashing**, they shout at you or criticize you in a very forceful way. [INFORMAL] ❑ *After a cruel tongue lashing, he threw the girl out of the group.* N-COUNT

**tongue-tied** If someone is **tongue-tied**, they are unable to say anything because they feel shy or nervous. ❑ *In their presence I became self-conscious and tongue-tied.* ADJ: usu v-link ADJ

**tongue-twister** **(tongue-twisters)** also **tongue twister**. A **tongue-twister** is a sentence or expression which is very difficult to say properly, especially when you try to say it quickly. An example of a tongue-twister is 'Red leather, yellow leather'. N-COUNT

**ton|ic** /tɒnɪk/ **(tonics)** [1] **Tonic** or **tonic water** is a colourless fizzy drink that has a slightly bitter flavour and is often mixed with alcoholic drinks, especially gin. ❑ *Keeler sipped at his gin and tonic. ...low-calorie tonics.* [2] A **tonic** is a medicine that makes you feel stronger, healthier, and less tired. ❑ *Britons are spending twice as much on health tonics as they were five years ago.* [3] A **tonic** is anything that makes you feel stronger, more cheerful, or more enthusiastic. ❑ *Seeing Marcus at that moment was a great tonic.*

N-MASS · N-MASS · N-COUNT: oft adj N, N *for* n = boost

**to|night** /tənaɪt/ **Tonight** is used to refer to the evening of today or the night that follows today. ❑ *I'm at home tonight... Tonight, I think he proved to everybody what a great player he was... There they will stay until 11 o'clock tonight.* ♦ **Tonight** is also a noun. ❑ *...tonight's flight to London.*

◆◆◇ ADV: ADV with cl, n ADV · N-UNCOUNT

**ton|nage** /tʌnɪdʒ/ **(tonnages)** [1] The **tonnage** of a ship is its size or the amount of space that it has inside it for cargo. [TECHNICAL] [2] **Tonnage** is the total number of tons that something weighs, or the total amount that there is of it.

N-VAR · N-VAR

**tonne** /tʌn/ **(tonnes)** A **tonne** is a metric unit of weight that is equal to 1000 kilograms. ❑ *...65.5 million tonnes of coal.* N-COUNT: num N, oft N *of* n

**ton|sil|li|tis** /tɒnsɪlaɪtɪs/ **Tonsillitis** is a painful swelling of your tonsils caused by an infection. N-UNCOUNT

**ton|sils** /tɒnsɪlz/

✓ The form **tonsil** is used as a modifier.

Your **tonsils** are the two small soft lumps in your throat at the back of your mouth. N-PLURAL

**tony** /toʊni/ **(tonier, toniest)** If you describe something as **tony**, you mean it is stylish and sophisticated. [AM] ❑ *...a tony dance club in Manhattan.* ADJ = classy

**too**

① ADDING SOMETHING OR RESPONDING
② INDICATING EXCESS

①**too** /tuː/ [1] You use **too** after mentioning another person, thing, or aspect that a previous statement applies to or includes. ❑ *'Nice to talk to you.' — 'Nice to talk to you too.'... 'I've got a great feeling about it.' — 'Me too.'... He doesn't want to meet me. I, too, have been afraid to talk to him... We talked to her agent. He's your agent, too, right?* [2] You use **too** after adding a piece of information or a comment to a statement, in order to emphasize that it is surprising or important. ❑ *We did learn to read, and quickly too... People usually think of it as a 'boys' book', which of course it is, and a very*

◆◆◆ ADV: cl/group ADV · ADV: cl/group ADV emphasis

*good one too.* 3 You use **too** at the end of a sentence to emphasize an opinion that you have added after a statement made by you or by another person. ❑ *'That money's mine.' — 'Of course it is, and quite right too.'... 'Oh excuse me.' — 'I should think so too.'* ADV: cl ADV [emphasis]

**② too** /tuː/ ◆◆◆
⇛ Please look at category 4 to see if the expression you are looking for is shown under another headword. 1 You use **too** in order to indicate that there is a greater amount or degree of something than is desirable, necessary, or acceptable. ❑ *Leather jeans that are too big will make you look larger... Eggs shouldn't be kept in the fridge, it's too cold... She was drinking too much, eating too much, having too many late nights.* ADV: ADV adj/adv, oft ADV adj/adv to-inf 2 You use **too** with a negative to make what you are saying sound less forceful or more polite or cautious. ❑ *I wasn't too happy with what I'd written so far... He won't be too pleased to see you.* ADV: with brd-neg, ADV adj [vagueness] = *very* 3 You use **all too** or **only too** to emphasize that something happens to a greater extent or degree than is pleasant or desirable. ❑ *She remembered it all too well... The letter spoke only too clearly of his anxiety for her.* PHRASE: PHR adv/adj [emphasis] 4 **too bad** → see **bad**. **none too** → see **none**.

**took** /tʊk/ **Took** is the past tense of **take**.

**tool** /tuːl/ **(tools)** 1 A **tool** is any instrument or simple piece of equipment that you hold in your hands and use to do a particular kind of work. For example, spades, hammers, and knives are all tools. ❑ *I find the best tool for the purpose is a pair of shears.* → See also **machine tool**. ◆◇◇ N-COUNT 2 You can refer to anything that you use for a particular purpose as a particular type of **tool**. ❑ *The video has become an invaluable teaching tool.* N-COUNT: usu with supp, oft N *for* -ing/n 3 If you describe someone as a **tool** of a particular person, group, or system, you mean that they are controlled and used by that person, group, or system, especially to do unpleasant or dishonest things. ❑ *He became the tool of the security services.* N-COUNT: usu N *of* n [disapproval] = *puppet*
PHRASES 4 If you say that workers **down tools**, you mean that they stop working suddenly in order to strike or to make a protest of some kind. [BRIT] PHRASE: V inflects 5 **The tools of** your **trade** or **the tools of the trade** are the skills, instruments, and other equipment that you need in order to do your job properly. ❑ *They're here to learn the tools of their trade from their American colleagues.* PHRASE: PHR after v, oft v-link PHR

**tool|bar** /tuːlbɑːʳ/ **(toolbars)** A **toolbar** is a narrow grey strip across a computer screen containing pictures, called icons, which represent different computer functions. When you want to use a particular function, you move the cursor onto its icon using a mouse. [COMPUTING] N-COUNT

**tool box** **(tool boxes)** A **tool box** is a metal or plastic box which contains general tools that you need at home, for example to do repairs in your house or car. N-COUNT

**tool kit** **(tool kits)** A **tool kit** is a special set of tools that are kept together and that are often used for a particular purpose. N-COUNT

**toot** /tuːt/ **(toots, tooting, tooted)** If someone **toots** their car horn or if a car horn **toots**, it produces a short sound or series of sounds. ❑ *People set off fireworks and tooted their car horns... Car horns toot as cyclists dart precariously through the traffic.* VERB = *hoot* V n V ♦ **Toot** is also a noun. ❑ *The driver gave me a wave and a toot.* N-SING

**tooth** /tuːθ/ **(teeth)** 1 Your **teeth** are the hard white objects in your mouth, which you use for biting and chewing. ❑ *If a tooth feels very loose, your dentist may recommend that it's taken out.* ◆◇◇ N-COUNT: oft poss N 2 The **teeth** of something such as a comb, saw, cog, or zip are the parts that stick out in a row on its edge. → See picture on page 1709. N-PLURAL 3 If you say that something such as an official group or a law has **teeth**, you mean that it has power and is able to be effective. ❑ *The opposition argues that the new council will be unconstitutional and without teeth... The law must have teeth, and it must be enforced.* N-PLURAL 4 → See also **wisdom tooth**.
PHRASES 5 If you say that someone **cut** their **teeth** doing a particular thing, at a particular time, or in a particular place, you mean that that is how, when, or where they began their career and learned some of their skills. ❑ *...director John Glen, who cut his teeth on Bond movies.* PHRASE: V inflects, PHR prep, PHR -ing 6 If you say that something **sets** your **teeth on edge**, you mean that you find it extremely unpleasant or irritating. ❑ *Their voices set your teeth on edge.* PHRASE: V inflects 7 If you **fight tooth and nail** to do something, you do everything you can in order to achieve it. If you **fight** something **tooth and nail**, you do everything you can in order to prevent it. ❑ *He fought tooth and nail to keep his job.* PHRASE: V inflects, oft PHR to-inf 8 If you describe a task or activity as something you can **get** your **teeth into**, you mean that you like it because it is interesting, complex, and makes you think hard. [INFORMAL] ❑ *This role gave her something to get her teeth into.* PHRASE: V inflects, oft PHR n [approval] 9 If you do something **in the teeth of** a difficulty or danger, you do it in spite of the difficulty or danger. ❑ *I was battling my way along the promenade in the teeth of a force ten gale... In the teeth of the longest recession since the 1930s, the company continues to perform well.* PHRASE: PHR n 10 If you say that someone **is lying through** their **teeth**, you are emphasizing that they are telling lies. [INFORMAL] PHRASE: V inflects [emphasis] 11 If you describe someone as **long in the tooth**, you are saying unkindly or humorously that they are old or getting old. [INFORMAL] ❑ *Aren't I a bit long in the tooth to start being an undergraduate?* PHRASE: v-link PHR [disapproval] 12 If you have **a sweet tooth**, you like sweet food very much. PHRASE: usu PHR after v 13 to **get the bit between** your **teeth** → see **bit**. to **give** one's **eye teeth for** something → see **eye**. to **gnash** one's **teeth** → see **gnash**. to **grit** your **teeth** → see **grit**. a **kick in the teeth** → see **kick**. **by the skin of** your **teeth** → see **skin**.

**tooth|ache** /tuːθeɪk/ **Toothache** is pain in one of your teeth. N-UNCOUNT

**tooth|brush** /tuːθbrʌʃ/ **(toothbrushes)** A **toothbrush** is a small brush that you use for cleaning your teeth. N-COUNT

**tooth de|cay** If you have **tooth decay**, one or more of your teeth has become decayed. N-UNCOUNT

**tooth fairy** **(tooth fairies)** The **tooth fairy** is an imaginary creature. Children are told that if they put a tooth that comes out under their pillow, the tooth fairy will take it away while they are sleeping and leave a coin in its place. N-COUNT: usu *the* N in sing

**tooth|less** /tuːθləs/ 1 You use **toothless** to describe a person or their smile when they have no teeth. ADJ: usu ADJ n 2 If you describe something such as an official group or a law as **toothless**, you mean it has no real power and is not effective. ❑ *In his view, the Commission remains a toothless and ineffectual body.* ADJ

**tooth|paste** /tuːθpeɪst/ **(toothpastes)** **Toothpaste** is a thick substance which you put on your toothbrush and use to clean your teeth. N-MASS

**tooth|pick** /tuːθpɪk/ **(toothpicks)** A **toothpick** is a small stick which you use to remove food from between your teeth. N-COUNT

**tooth|some** /tuːθsəm/ If you describe food as **toothsome**, you mean that it tastes very good. ❑ *...the toothsome honey-sweetened gingerbread.* ADJ

**toothy** /tuːθi/ A **toothy** smile is one in which a person shows a lot of teeth. ADJ: ADJ n

**too|tle** /tuːtᵊl/ **(tootles, tootling, tootled)** 1 If you **tootle** somewhere, you travel or go there without rushing or without any particular aim. [mainly BRIT, INFORMAL] ❑ *I'm sure Ted is tootling down the motorway at this very moment.* VERB V prep/adv 2 If you **tootle** a tune on an instrument, you play it quietly, without concentrating or taking it seriously. [INFORMAL] ❑ *McCann tootled a tune on the piano.* VERB V n, Also V

**top** /tɒp/ **(tops, topping, topped)** 1 The **top** of something is its highest point or part. ❑ *I waited at the top of the stairs. ...the picture at the top of the page... Bake the biscuits for 20-25 minutes, until* ◆◆◆ N-COUNT: usu *the* N in sing, oft N *of* n ≠ *bottom* *the tops are lightly browned.* ♦ **Top** is also an adjective. ❑ *...the top corner of his newspaper.* ADJ: ADJ n ≠ bottom 2 The **top** thing or layer in a series of things or layers is the highest one. ❑ *I can't reach the top shelf... Our new flat was on the top floor.* ADJ: ADJ n 3 The **top** of something such as a bottle, jar, or tube is a cap, lid, or other device that fits or screws onto one end of it. ❑ *...the plastic tops from aerosol containers. ...a bottle top.* N-COUNT 4 The **top** of a street, garden, bed, or table is the end of it that is farthest away from where you usually enter it or from where you are. [mainly BRIT] ❑ *...a little shop at the top of the street... He moved to the empty chair at the top of the table.* N-SING: the N, oft N *of* n = end, head ♦ **Top** is also an adjective. ❑ *...the hill near the top end of the garden. ...the top corridor of the main building.* ADJ: ADJ n 5 A **top** is a piece of clothing that you wear on the upper half of your body, for example a blouse or shirt. [INFORMAL] ❑ *Look at my new top.* N-COUNT 6 You can use **top** to indicate that something or someone is at the highest level of a scale or measurement. ❑ *The vehicles have a top speed of 80 kilometres per hour. ...a top-ranking Saudi officer.* ADJ: ADJ n ≠ bottom 7 The **top** of an organization or career structure is the highest level in it. ❑ *We started from the bottom and we had to work our way up to the top. ...his dramatic rise to the top of the military hierarchy.* N-SING: the N, oft N *of* n ≠ bottom ♦ **Top** is also an adjective. ❑ *I need to have the top people in this company pull together.* ADJ: ADJ n 8 You can use **top** to describe the most important or famous people or things in a particular area of work or activity. ❑ *The President met this afternoon with his top military advisers.* ADJ: ADJ n 9 If someone is **at the top of** a table or league or is **the top of** the table or league, their performance is better than that of all the other people involved. ❑ *The United States will be at the top of the medal table... Labour was top of the poll with forty-six percent.* N-SING: the N ≠ bottom ♦ **Top** is also an adjective. ❑ *I usually came top in English.* ADJ 10 You can use **top** to indicate that something is the first thing you are going to do, because you consider it to be the most important. ❑ *Cleaning up the water supply is their top priority... On arrival, a six-course meal was top of the agenda.* ADJ: oft ADJ *of* n 11 You can use **top** to indicate that someone does a particular thing more times than anyone else or that something is chosen more times than anything else. ❑ *He was Italy's top scorer during the World Cup matches.* ADJ: ADJ n 12 To **top** a list means to be mentioned or chosen more times than anyone or anything else. [JOURNALISM] ❑ *It was the first time a Japanese manufacturer had topped the list for imported vehicles.* VERB V n 13 If something **tops** a particular amount, it is larger than that amount. [JOURNALISM] ❑ *Imports topped £10 billion last month.* VERB V n 14 If something **is topped with** something, it has that thing as its highest part. ❑ *The holiest of their chapels are topped with gilded roofs... To serve, top the fish with the cooked leeks.* VERB *be* V-ed *with/by* n V n *with* n ♦ **-topped** *...the glass-topped table.* Also V n COMB in ADJ 15 If you **top** a story, remark, or action, you follow it with a better or more impressive one. ❑ *How are you going to top that?* VERB V n 16 You can use **tops** after mentioning a quantity, to say that it is the maximum possible. [INFORMAL] ❑ *The publisher expected the book to sell 1,500 copies, tops.* ADV: num ADV = max 17 → See also **topping**.

**PHRASES** 18 If someone **blows** their **top**, they become very angry about something. [INFORMAL] ❑ *He blew his top after airport officials refused to let him on a plane.* PHRASE: V inflects 19 If a person, organization, or country **comes out on top**, they are more successful than the others that they have been competing with. ❑ *The only way to come out on top is to adopt a different approach.* PHRASE: V inflects 20 If someone pays **top dollar** for something, they pay the highest possible price for it. [INFORMAL] ❑ *People will always pay top dollar for something exclusive.* PHRASE: v PHR, PHR n 21 If you say that you clean, tidy, or examine something **from top to bottom**, you are emphasizing that you do it completely and thoroughly. ❑ *She would clean the house from top to bottom.* PHRASE: PHR after v emphasis 22 You can use **from top to toe** to emphasize that the whole of someone's body is covered or dressed in a particular thing or type of clothing. ❑ *They were sensibly dressed from top to toe in rain gear.* PHRASE: PHR after v emphasis 23 When something **gets on top of** you, it makes you feel unhappy or depressed because it is very difficult or worrying, or because it involves more work than you can manage. ❑ *Things have been getting on top of me lately.* PHRASE: V inflects, PHR n 24 If you say something **off the top of** your **head**, you say it without thinking about it much before you speak, especially because you do not have enough time. ❑ *It was the best I could think of off the top of my head.* PHRASE: PHR after v, PHR with cl 25 If one thing is **on top** of another, it is placed over it or on its highest part. ❑ *...the vacuum flask that was resting on top of the stove.* PHRASE: v-link PHR, PHR after v, oft PHR *of* n 26 You can use **on top** or **on top of** to indicate that a particular problem exists in addition to a number of other problems. ❑ *An extra 700 jobs are being cut on top of the 2,000 that were lost last year.* PHRASE 27 You say that someone is **on top** when they have reached the most important position in an organization or business. ❑ *How does he stay on top, 17 years after becoming foreign minister?* PHRASE: usu v-link PHR 28 If you **are on top of** or **get on top of** something that you are doing, you are dealing with it successfully. ❑ *...the government's inability to get on top of the situation.* PHRASE: V inflects, PHR n 29 If you say that you feel **on top of the world**, you are emphasizing that you feel extremely happy and healthy. ❑ *Two months before she gave birth to Jason she left work feeling on top of the world.* PHRASE: usu v-link PHR emphasis 30 If one thing is **over the top** of another, it is placed over it so that it is completely covering it. ❑ *I have overcome this problem by placing a sheet of polythene over the top of the container.* PHRASE: PHR after v, v-link PHR, oft PHR *of* n 31 You describe something as **over the top** when you think that it is exaggerated, and therefore unacceptable. [mainly BRIT, INFORMAL] ❑ *The special effects are a bit over the top but I enjoyed it.* PHRASE: usu v-link PHR = OTT 32 If you say something **at the top of** your **voice**, you say it very loudly. ❑ *'Stephen!' shouted Marcia at the top of her voice.* PHRASE: PHR after v 33 **at the top of the heap** → see **heap**.

♦ **top off** If you **top off** an event or period with a particular thing, you end it in an especially satisfactory, dramatic, or annoying way by doing that thing. ❑ *He topped off his career with an Olympic gold medal... To top it all off one of the catering staff managed to slice their finger cutting cheese.* PHRASAL VERB = round off V P n (not pron) V n P

♦ **top up** If you **top** something **up**, you make it full again when part of it has been used. [mainly BRIT] ❑ *We topped up the water tanks... He topped her glass up after complaining she was a slow drinker.* PHRASAL VERB V P n (not pron) V n P → See also **top-up**.

**to|paz** /toupæz/ **(topazes)** A **topaz** is a precious stone which is usually yellowish-brown in colour. N-VAR

**top brass** In the army or in other organizations, **the top brass** are the people in the highest positions. [BRIT, INFORMAL] ❑ *...a reshuffle of the army's top brass.* N-SING-COLL: also no det, oft with supp

**top-class** also **top class. Top-class** means among the finest of its kind. ❑ *We think he'll turn into a top-class player.* ADJ

**top|coat** /tɒpkout/ **(topcoats)** also **top coat.** 1 A **topcoat** is a coat that you wear over your other clothes. N-COUNT 2 A **topcoat** is the final layer of paint or varnish that is put on something. **Topcoat** is the type of paint or varnish that you use for the final layer. Compare **undercoat**. N-VAR

**top dog (top dogs)** If a person or organization is **top dog**, they are the most successful or powerful one in a particular group. [INFORMAL] ❑ *Reynolds has never concealed his ambition to be the top dog.* N-COUNT

**top-dollar** → see **top**.

**top-drawer** If you describe someone or something as **top-drawer**, you are saying, often in a humorous way, that they have a high social standing or are of very good quality. ADJ: usu ADJ n

**top-end** **Top-end** products are expensive and of extremely high quality. [BUSINESS] ❑ *...top-end camcorders.* ADJ

**top hat** **(top hats)** A **top hat** is a man's tall hat with a narrow brim. Top hats are now worn only on special occasions, for example at some weddings. N-COUNT

**top-heavy** [1] Something that is **top-heavy** is larger or heavier at the top than at the bottom, and might therefore fall over. ❑ *...top-heavy flowers such as sunflowers.* ADJ [2] If you describe a business or other organization as **top-heavy**, you mean that it has too many senior managers in relation to the number of junior managers or workers. ❑ *...top-heavy bureaucratic structures.* ADJ [disapproval]

**to|pi|ary** /toʊpiəri, AM -eri/ **Topiary** is the art of cutting trees and bushes into different shapes, for example into the shapes of birds or animals. N-UNCOUNT

**top|ic** /tɒpɪk/ **(topics)** A **topic** is a particular subject that you discuss or write about. ❑ *The main topic for discussion is political union.* N-COUNT

**topi|cal** /tɒpɪkəl/ **Topical** is used to describe something that concerns or relates to events that are happening at the present time. ❑ *The magazine's aim is to discuss topical issues within a Christian framework.* ADJ ♦ **topi|cal|ity** /tɒpɪkælɪti/ *The book has all the lively topicality of first-rate journalism.* N-UNCOUNT

**top|knot** /tɒpnɒt/ **(topknots)** also **top-knot.** If someone, especially a woman, has her hair in a **topknot**, her hair is arranged in a small neat pile on top of her head. N-COUNT

**top|less** /tɒpləs/ [1] If a woman goes **topless**, she does not wear anything to cover her breasts. ❑ *I wouldn't sunbathe topless if I thought I might offend anyone.* ADJ: ADJ after v, ADJ n, v-link ADJ [2] A **topless** show or bar is one in which the female entertainers or staff do not wear anything to cover their breasts. ADJ: ADJ n

**top-level** A **top-level** discussion or activity is one that involves the people with the greatest amount of power and authority in an organization or country. ❑ *...a top-level meeting of American generals at the Pentagon.* ADJ: ADJ n

**top|most** /tɒpmoʊst/ The **topmost** thing in a number of things is the one that is highest or nearest the top. ❑ *...the topmost branches of a gigantic oak tree.* ADJ: ADJ n = *uppermost, highest*

**top-notch** also **top notch.** If you describe someone or something as **top-notch**, you mean that they are of a very high standard or quality. [INFORMAL, OLD-FASHIONED] ADJ = *first-rate*

**topo|graphi|cal** /tɒpəgræfɪkəl/ A **topographical** survey or map relates to or shows the physical features of an area of land, for example its hills, valleys, and rivers. ADJ: usu ADJ n

**to|pog|ra|phy** /təpɒgrəfi/ **(topographies)** [1] **Topography** is the study and description of the physical features of an area, for example its hills, valleys, or rivers, or the representation of these features on maps. N-UNCOUNT [2] The **topography** of a particular area is its physical shape, including its hills, valleys, and rivers. ❑ *The topography of the river's basin has changed significantly since the floods.* N-COUNT: usu sing, with poss

**top|ping** /tɒpɪŋ/ **(toppings)** A **topping** is food, such as cream or cheese, that is poured or put on top of other food in order to decorate it or add to its flavour. ➔ See also **top**. N-MASS

**top|ple** /tɒpəl/ **(topples, toppling, toppled)** [1] If someone or something **topples** somewhere or if you **topple** them, they become unsteady or unstable and fall over. ❑ *He just released his hold and toppled slowly backwards... Winds and rain toppled trees and electricity lines.* VERB, V adv/prep, V n ♦ **Topple over** means the same as **topple**. ❑ *The tree is so badly damaged they are worried it might topple over.* PHRASAL VERB, V P [2] To **topple** a government or leader, especially one that is not elected by the people, means to cause them to lose power. [JOURNALISM] ❑ *...the revolution which toppled the regime.* VERB = *overthrow*, V n

**top-ranked** A **top-ranked** sports player or team is the most successful player or team in a particular sport. [JOURNALISM] ADJ: ADJ n

**top-ranking** A **top-ranking** person is someone who has a very high rank or status in a particular organization or field of activity. ❑ *...400 of Germany's top-ranking military officials.* ADJ: ADJ n

**top-rated** A **top-rated** show or service is the most successful or highly regarded of its kind. [JOURNALISM] ❑ *...the top-rated American television series.* ADJ: ADJ n

**top round** **Top round** is a joint of beef that is cut from the upper part of the cow's leg. It is usually cooked by roasting or stewing. [AM] N-UNCOUNT

✔ in BRIT, use **topside**

**top se|cret** **Top secret** information or activity is intended to be kept completely secret, for example in order to prevent a country's enemies from finding out about it. ❑ *The top secret documents had to do with the most advanced military equipment.* ADJ: usu ADJ n

**top|side** /tɒpsaɪd/ **(topsides)** [1] **Topside** is a joint of beef that is cut from the upper part of the cow's leg. It is usually cooked by roasting or stewing. [BRIT] N-UNCOUNT

✔ in AM, use **top round**

[2] On a ship, if you go **topside**, you go up onto the top deck. [TECHNICAL] ❑ *He left the control station and went topside.* ADV: ADV after v [3] The **topside** or **topsides** of a ship or boat are the top deck or the parts which you can see above the water. [TECHNICAL] N-COUNT: usu pl

**top|soil** /tɒpsɔɪl/ **Topsoil** is the layer of soil nearest the surface of the ground. N-UNCOUNT

**topsy-turvy** /tɒpsi tɜːʳvi/ Something that is **topsy-turvy** is in a confused or disorganized state. [INFORMAL] ❑ *The world has turned topsy-turvy in my lifetime.* ADJ

**top-up** **(top-ups)** [1] A **top-up** is another serving of a drink in the same glass that you have just used. [BRIT] N-COUNT [2] A **top-up** loan or payment is added to an amount of money in order to bring it up to a required level. [BRIT] ❑ *Student grants will be frozen at existing levels and top-up loans made available.* ADJ: ADJ n

**torch** /tɔːʳtʃ/ **(torches, torching, torched)** [1] A **torch** is a small electric light which is powered by batteries and which you can carry in your hand. [BRIT] N-COUNT

✔ in AM, use **flashlight**

[2] A **torch** is a long stick with burning material at one end, used to provide light or to set things on fire. ❑ *They lit a torch and set fire to the chapel's thatch.* N-COUNT [3] A **torch** is a device that produces a hot flame and is used for tasks such as cutting or joining pieces of metal. ❑ *The gang worked for up to ten hours with acetylene torches to open the vault.* ➔ See also **blowtorch**. N-COUNT: supp N [4] If someone **torches** a building or vehicle, they set fire to it deliberately. ❑ *The rioters torched the local library.* VERB, V n

**PHRASES** [5] If you say that someone **is carrying a torch for** someone else, you mean that they secretly admire them or love them. ❑ *He has always carried a torch for Barbara.* PHRASE: V inflects, PHR n [6] If you say that someone is **carrying the torch** of a particular belief or movement, you mean that they are working hard to ensure that it is not forgotten and continues to grow stronger. ❑ *This group aims to carry the torch for the millions who demonstrated and the thousands who died.* PHRASE: V inflects, usu PHR *for/of* n

**torch|light** /tɔːʳtʃlaɪt/ If you do something **by torchlight**, you do it using the light that is produced by a torch or torches. ❑ *Surgeons are performing operations in tents by torchlight.* N-UNCOUNT: oft *by* N, N n

**torch song** **(torch songs)** A **torch song** is a sentimental popular song about love, usually sung by a woman. N-COUNT

**tore** /tɔːʳ/ **Tore** is the past tense of **tear**.

**tor|ment** **(torments, tormenting, tormented)**

> ✔ The noun is pronounced /tɔːʳment/. The verb is pronounced /tɔːʳment/.

1 **Torment** is extreme suffering, usually mental suffering. ❑ *The torment of having her baby kidnapped is written all over her face.* N-UNCOUNT = anguish 2 A **torment** is something that causes extreme suffering, usually mental suffering. ❑ *Sooner or later most writers end up making books about the torments of being a writer.* N-COUNT 3 If something **torments** you, it causes you extreme mental suffering. ❑ *At times the memories returned to torment her.* VERB = torture V n 4 If you **torment** a person or animal, you annoy them in a playful, rather cruel way for your own amusement. ❑ *My older brother used to torment me by singing it to me.* VERB V n

**tor|men|tor** /tɔːʳmentəʳ/ **(tormentors)** Someone's **tormentor** is a person who deliberately causes them physical or mental pain. ❑ *...cases where women subjected to years of brutality lose control and kill their tormentors.* N-COUNT: usu poss N

**torn** /tɔːʳn/ 1 **Torn** is the past participle of **tear**. 2 If you are **torn between** two or more things, you cannot decide which to choose, and so you feel anxious or troubled. ❑ *Robb is torn between becoming a doctor and a career in athletics.* ADJ: usu v-link ADJ, oft ADJ *between* pl-n

**tor|na|do** /tɔːʳneɪdoʊ/ **(tornadoes** or **tornados)** A **tornado** is a violent wind storm consisting of a tall column of air which spins round very fast and causes a lot of damage. N-COUNT

**tor|pe|do** /tɔːʳpiːdoʊ/ **(torpedoes, torpedoing, torpedoed)** 1 A **torpedo** is bomb that is shaped like a tube and that travels under water. N-COUNT 2 If a ship **is torpedoed**, it is hit, and usually sunk, by a torpedo or torpedoes. ❑ *More than a thousand people died when the Lusitania was torpedoed.* VERB: usu passive *be* V-ed 3 If someone **torpedoes** negotiations or plans, they deliberately prevent them from being completed or from being successful. [INFORMAL] ❑ *These attacks are seen as an effort to torpedo the talks.* VERB = sabotage, wreck V n

**tor|pid** /tɔːʳpɪd/ If you are **torpid**, you are mentally or physically inactive, especially because you are feeling lazy or sleepy. [FORMAL] ADJ = lethargic

**tor|por** /tɔːʳpəʳ/ **Torpor** is the state of being completely inactive mentally or physically, for example because of illness or laziness. [FORMAL] ❑ *He had slumped into a state of torpor from which nothing could rouse him... The sick person gradually falls into a torpor.* N-UNCOUNT: also *a* N

**torque** /tɔːʳk/ **Torque** is a force that causes something to spin around a central point such as an axle. [TECHNICAL] N-UNCOUNT

**tor|rent** /tɒrənt, AM tɔːr-/ **(torrents)** 1 A **torrent** is a lot of water falling or flowing rapidly or violently. ❑ *Torrents of water gushed into the reservoir.* N-COUNT: oft N *of* n 2 A **torrent of** abuse or questions is a lot of abuse or questions directed continuously at someone. ❑ *He directed a torrent of abuse at me.* N-COUNT: usu N *of* n

**tor|ren|tial** /tərenʃəl, AM tɔːr-/ **Torrential** rain pours down very rapidly and in great quantities. ADJ: usu ADJ n

**tor|rid** /tɒrɪd, AM tɔːrɪd/ 1 **Torrid** weather is extremely hot and dry. [LITERARY] ❑ *...the torrid heat of a Spanish summer.* ADJ: usu ADJ n 2 A **torrid** relationship or incident involves very strong emotions connected with love and sex. ❑ *She began a torrid love affair with a theatrical designer.* ADJ: usu ADJ n = passionate 3 If someone or something has a **torrid** time, they experience a lot of difficulties. [BRIT, JOURNALISM] ❑ *Seles, the victim of a death threat earlier this week, has had a torrid time during the Championships.* ADJ: usu ADJ n

**tor|sion** /tɔːʳʃən/ **Torsion** is a twisting effect on something such as a piece of metal or an organ of the body. [TECHNICAL] N-UNCOUNT

**tor|so** /tɔːʳsoʊ/ **(torsos)** Your **torso** is the main part of your body, and does not include your head, arms, and legs. [FORMAL] N-COUNT: oft poss N

**tort** /tɔːʳt/ **(torts)** A **tort** is something that you do or fail to do which harms someone else and for which you can be sued for damages. [LEGAL] N-VAR

**tor|til|la** /tɔːʳtiːjə/ **(tortillas)** A **tortilla** is a piece of thin flat bread that first came from Mexico, and is made from corn and eggs. N-VAR

**tor|til|la chip** **(tortilla chips)** **Tortilla chips** are thick crisps made from corn which are often served with dips such as salsa. N-COUNT: usu pl

**tor|toise** /tɔːʳtəs/ **(tortoises)** A **tortoise** is a slow-moving animal with a shell into which it can pull its head and legs for protection. N-COUNT

**tortoise|shell** /tɔːʳtəsʃel/ **(tortoiseshells)** 1 **Tortoiseshell** is the hard shell of a kind of sea turtle. It is brown and yellow in colour and is often polished and used to make jewellery and ornaments. N-UNCOUNT 2 **Tortoiseshell** means made of tortoiseshell or made of a material which resembles tortoiseshell. ❑ *He wears huge spectacles with thick tortoiseshell frames.* ADJ: usu ADJ n

**tor|tu|ous** /tɔːʳtʃuəs/ 1 A **tortuous** road is full of bends and twists. ❑ *The only road access is a tortuous mountain route.* ADJ: usu ADJ n 2 A **tortuous** process or piece of writing is very long and complicated. ❑ *...these long and tortuous negotiations aimed at ending the conflict.* ADJ: usu ADJ n

**tor|ture** /tɔːʳtʃəʳ/ **(tortures, torturing, tortured)** ◆◇◇ 1 If someone **is tortured**, another person deliberately causes them great pain over a period of time, in order to punish them or to make them reveal information. ❑ *French police are convinced that she was tortured and killed... They never again tortured a prisoner in his presence.* VERB *be* V-ed V n ♦ **Torture** is also a noun. ❑ *...alleged cases of torture and murder by the security forces.* N-VAR 2 To **torture** someone means to cause them to suffer mental pain or anxiety. ❑ *He would not torture her further by trying to argue with her... She tortured herself with fantasies of Bob and his new girlfriend.* VERB = torment V n V pron-refl 3 If you say that something is **torture** or a **torture**, you mean that it causes you great mental or physical suffering. [INFORMAL] ❑ *Waiting for the result was torture.* N-UNCOUNT: also *a* N

**tor|tur|er** /tɔːʳtʃərəʳ/ **(torturers)** A **torturer** is someone who tortures people. N-COUNT

**tor|tur|ous** /tɔːʳtʃərəs/ Something that is **torturous** is extremely painful and causes great suffering. ❑ *This is a torturous, agonizing way to kill someone.* ADJ

**Tory** /tɔːri/ **(Tories)** ◆◆◇ In Britain, a **Tory** politician or voter is a member of or votes for the Conservative Party. ❑ *...the former Tory Party chairman, Chris Patten.* ADJ ♦ **Tory** is also a noun. ❑ *...the first female leader of the Tories.* N-COUNT

**toss** /tɒs, AM tɔːs/ **(tosses, tossing, tossed)** 1 If you **toss** something somewhere, you throw it there lightly, often in a rather careless way. ❑ *He screwed the paper into a ball and tossed it into the fire... He tossed Malone a can of beer, and took one himself.* VERB V n prep/adv V n n 2 If you **toss** your head or **toss** your hair, you move your head backwards, quickly and suddenly, often as a way of expressing an emotion such as anger or contempt. ❑ *'I'm sure I don't know.' Cook tossed her head... Gasping, she tossed her hair out of her face.* VERB V n V n prep/adv ♦ **Toss** is also a noun. ❑ *With a toss of his head and a few hard gulps, Bob finished the last of his beer.* N-COUNT 3 In sports and informal situations, if you decide something by **tossing** a coin, you spin a coin into the air and guess which side of the coin will face upwards when it lands. ❑ *We tossed a coin to decide who would go out and buy the buns.* VERB V n ♦ **Toss** is also a noun. ❑ *It would be better to decide it on the toss of a coin.* N-COUNT: usu sing 4 **The toss** is a way of deciding something, such as who is going to go first in a game, that consists of spinning a coin into the air and guessing which side of the coin will face upwards when it lands. ❑ *Bangladesh won the toss and decided to bat first.* N-SING: *the* N 5 If something such as the wind or sea **tosses** an object, it causes it to move from side to side or up and down. [LITERARY] ❑ *The seas grew turbulent, tossing the small boat like a cork... As the plane was tossed up and down, the pilot tried to stabilise it.* VERB V n *be* V-ed adv/prep 6 If you **toss** food while preparing it, you put pieces of it into a VERB liquid and lightly shake them so that they become covered with the liquid. ❑ *Do not toss the salad until you're ready to serve...* [V n] *Add the grated orange rind and toss the apple slices in the mixture...* [V n *in* n] *Serve straight from the dish with a tossed green salad.* [V-ed] 7 → See also **toss-up**.

PHRASES 8 If you say that someone **argues the toss**, you are criticizing them for continuing to argue for longer than is necessary about something that is not very important. [BRIT] ❑ *They were still arguing the toss about the first goal.* [PHRASE: V inflects, oft PHR prep] [disapproval] 9 If you say that you do not **give a toss** about someone or something, you are emphasizing that you do not care about them at all. [BRIT, INFORMAL] ❑ *Well, who gives a toss about sophistication anyway?* [PHRASE: with brd-neg, V inflects, oft PHR *about* n, PHR wh] [emphasis] 10 If you **toss and turn**, you keep moving around in bed and cannot sleep properly, for example because you are ill or worried. [PHRASE: Vs inflect]

**toss-up** **(toss-ups)** If you say that it is a **toss-up** whether one thing will happen or another thing will happen, you mean that either result seems equally likely. ❑ *It's a toss-up whether oil prices will go up or down over the days ahead.* [N-COUNT: usu *a* N in sing, oft N wh, N *between* pl-n]

**tot** /tɒt/ **(tots, totting, totted)** 1 A **tot** is a very young child. [INFORMAL] [N-COUNT] 2 A **tot of** a strong alcoholic drink such as whisky or brandy is a small amount of it in a glass. [mainly BRIT] [N-COUNT: usu N *of* n]

♦ **tot up** To **tot up** a total or a list of numbers means to add up several numbers in order to reach a total. [mainly BRIT] ❑ *I finally sat down to tot up the full extent of my debt.* [PHRASAL VERB = add up] [V P n (not pron)]

**to|tal** /toʊtəl/ **(totals, totalling, totalled)** ◆◆◆ 1 A **total** is the number that you get when you add several numbers together or when you count how many things there are in a group. ❑ *The companies have a total of 1,776 employees.* [N-COUNT] 2 The **total** number or cost of something is the number or cost that you get when you add together or count all the parts in it. ❑ *The total cost of the project would be more than $240 million.* [ADJ: ADJ n] 3 If there are a number of things **in total**, there are that number when you count or add them all together. ❑ *I was with my husband for eight years in total.* [PHRASE: PHR after v, PHR with cl, amount PHR] 4 If several numbers or things **total** a certain figure, that figure is the total of all the numbers or all the things. ❑ *The unit's exports will total $85 million this year.* [VERB] [V amount] 5 When you **total** a set of numbers or objects, you add them all together. ❑ *They haven't totalled the exact figures.* [VERB] [V n] 6 You can use **total** to emphasize that something is as great in extent, degree, or amount as it possibly can be. ❑ *Why should we trust a total stranger?* [ADJ: usu ADJ n] [emphasis] [= complete] ♦ **to|tal|ly** *Young people want something totally different from the old ways.* [ADV: ADV adj/adv, ADV with v = completely]

**to|tali|tar|ian** /toʊtælɪteəriən/ A **totalitarian** political system is one in which there is only one political party which controls everything and does not allow any opposition parties. [ADJ] [disapproval]

**to|tali|tari|an|ism** /toʊtælɪteəriənɪzəm/ **Totalitarianism** is the ideas, principles, and practices of totalitarian political systems. [N-UNCOUNT]

**to|tal|ity** /toʊtælɪti/ The **totality of** something is the whole of it. [FORMAL] ❑ *...a process of social, economic and political change which involves the totality of human experience.* [N-UNCOUNT: oft N *of* n, *in its/their* N]

**to|tal qual|ity man|age|ment** **Total quality management** is a set of management principles aimed at improving performance throughout a company, especially by involving employees in decision-making. The abbreviation **TQM** is also used. [BUSINESS] ❑ *He is a firm believer in total quality management.* [N-UNCOUNT]

**tote** /toʊt/ **(totes, toting, toted)** 1 **The Tote** is a system of betting money on horses in races. [BRIT] [N-SING: *the* N]

in AM, use **parimutuel**

2 To **tote** something, especially a gun, means to carry it with you in such a way that people can see it. [JOURNALISM] ❑ *The demonstrators fled when soldiers toting machine guns advanced on the crowd.* [VERB] [V n]

♦ **-toting** *They are too frightened to speak out against the gun-toting thugs.* [COMB in ADJ]

**to|tem** /toʊtəm/ **(totems)** 1 In some societies, a family's **totem** is the particular animal, plant, or natural object which they regard as a special symbol and which they believe has spiritual significance. [N-COUNT] 2 Something that is a **totem of** another thing is a symbol of it. [WRITTEN] ❑ *This opera is one of the cultural totems of Western civilisation.* [N-COUNT: oft N *of* n]

**to|tem pole** **(totem poles)** A **totem pole** is a long wooden pole with symbols and pictures carved and painted on it. Totem poles are made by some Native American peoples and placed outside their homes. [N-COUNT]

**tot|ter** /tɒtəʳ/ **(totters, tottering, tottered)** 1 If someone **totters** somewhere, they walk there in an unsteady way, for example because they are ill or drunk. ❑ *He tottered to the fridge, got a beer and slumped at the table.* [VERB] [V prep/adv] 2 If something such as a market or government **is tottering**, it is weak and likely to collapse or fail completely. ❑ *The property market is tottering.* [VERB] [V] *...further criticism of the tottering government.* [V-ing]

**tou|can** /tuːkən, AM -kæn/ **(toucans)** A **toucan** is a South American bird with a large brightly-coloured beak. [N-COUNT]

**touch** /tʌtʃ/ **(touches, touching, touched)** ◆◆◇ 1 If you **touch** something, you put your hand onto it in order to feel it or to make contact with it. ❑ *Her tiny hands gently touched my face...* [VERB] [V n] *The virus is not passed on through touching or shaking hands.* [V-ing] ♦ **Touch** is also a noun. ❑ *Sometimes even a light touch on the face is enough to trigger off this pain.* [N-COUNT: usu sing] 2 If two things **are touching**, or if one thing **touches** another, or if you **touch** two things, their surfaces come into contact with each other. ❑ *Their knees were touching ...* [V-RECIP] [pl-n V] *A cyclist crashed when he touched wheels with another rider...* [V pl-n *with* n] *If my arm touches the wall, it has to be washed again...* [V n] *In some countries people stand close enough to touch elbows...* [V pl-n] *He touched the cow's side with his stick.* [V n *with* n] 3 Your sense of **touch** is your ability to tell what something is like when you feel it with your hands. ❑ *The evidence suggests that our sense of touch is programmed to diminish with age.* [N-UNCOUNT] 4 To **touch** something means to strike it, usually quite gently. ❑ *As the aeroplane went down the runway the wing touched a pile of rubble.* [VERB] [V n] 5 If something **has** not **been touched**, nobody has dealt with it or taken care of it. ❑ *When John began to restore the house in the 1960s, nothing had been touched for 40 years.* [VERB: usu passive, with brd-neg *be* V-ed] 6 If you say that you did not **touch** someone or something, you are emphasizing that you did not attack, harm or destroy them, especially when you have been accused of doing so. ❑ *Pearce remained adamant, saying 'I didn't touch him'...* [VERB: with brd-neg] [emphasis] [V n] *I was in the garden. I never touched the sandwiches.* [V n] 7 You say that you never **touch** something or that you have not **touched** something for a long time to emphasize that you never use it, or you have not used it for a long time. ❑ *He doesn't drink much and doesn't touch drugs.* [VERB: no passive, with brd-neg] [emphasis] [V n] 8 If you **touch on** a particular subject or problem, you mention it or write briefly about it. ❑ *The film touches on these issues, but only superficially.* [VERB] [V *on/upon* n] 9 If something **touches** you, it affects you in some way for a short time. ❑ *...a guilt that in some sense touches everyone.* [VERB] [V n] 10 If something that someone says or does **touches** you, it affects you emotionally, often because you see that they are suffering a lot or that they are being very kind. ❑ *It has touched me deeply to see how these people live...* [VERB = move] [*it* V n to-inf] *Her enthusiasm touched me.* [V n] ♦ **touched** *I was touched to find that he regards me as engaging.* [ADJ: v-link ADJ] 11 If something **is touched with** a particular quality, it has a certain amount of that quality. [WRITTEN] ❑ *His crinkly hair was touched with grey...* [VERB: usu passive] [*be* V-ed *with* n] *The boy was touched with genius.* [*be* V-ed *with* n] 12 If you say about someone that nobody can **touch** him or her **for** a particular thing, you mean that he or she is much better at [VERB: no cont, no passive, with brd-neg]

it than anyone else. ❑ *No one can touch these girls for professionalism.* 13 To **touch** a particular level, amount, or score, especially a high one, means to reach it. [mainly BRIT] ❑ *By the third lap Kinkead had touched 289 m.p.h.* 14 A **touch** is a detail which is added to something to improve it. ❑ *They called the event 'a tribute to heroes', which was a nice touch.*
V n *for* n; Also V n; VERB: no passive; V n; N-COUNT: supp N

15 If someone has a particular kind of **touch**, they have a particular way of doing something. ❑ *The dishes he produces all have a personal touch.*
N-SING: with supp

16 **A touch of** something is a very small amount of it. ❑ *She thought she just had a touch of flu.*
QUANT: QUANT *of* n-uncount

PHRASES 17 You can use **a touch** to mean slightly or to a small extent, especially in order to make something you say seem less extreme. For example, if you say that something is **a touch** expensive, you might really think that it is very expensive. [mainly BRIT] ❑ *We were all a touch uneasy, I think... I found it a touch distasteful.* 18 ➔ See also **touching**. 19 You use **at the touch of** in expressions such as **at the touch of a button** and **at the touch of a key** to indicate that something is possible by simply touching a switch or one of the keys of a keyboard. ❑ *Staff will be able to trace calls at the touch of a button.* 20 If you say that someone has **the common touch**, you mean that they have the natural ability to have a good relationship with ordinary people and be popular with them. 21 If you get **in touch with** someone, you contact them by writing to them or telephoning them. If you are, keep, or stay **in touch with** them, you write, phone, or visit each other regularly. ❑ *The organisation would be in touch with him tomorrow.* 22 If you are **in touch with** a subject or situation, or if someone keeps you **in touch with** it, you know the latest news or information about it. If you are **out of touch with** it, you do not know the latest news or information about it. ❑ *...keeping the unemployed in touch with the labour market... Mr Cavazos' problem was that he was out of touch.* 23 If you **lose touch with** someone, you gradually stop writing, telephoning, or visiting them. ❑ *In my job one tends to lose touch with friends.* 24 If you **lose touch with** something, you no longer have the latest news or information about it. ❑ *Their leaders have lost touch with what is happening in the country.* 25 If you say that something is **touch and go**, you mean that you are uncertain whether it will happen or succeed. ❑ *It was touch and go whether we'd go bankrupt.* 26 If you say that someone is **a soft touch** or **an easy touch**, you mean that they can easily be persuaded to lend you money or to do things for you. [INFORMAL] ❑ *Pamela was an easy touch when she needed some cash.* 27 **would not touch** someone or something **with a barge pole** ➔ see **barge pole**. **the finishing touch** ➔ see **finish**. **touch wood** ➔ see **wood**.
PHRASE: PHR adj/adv/prep; vagueness; = a bit; PHRASE: PHR n, usu PHR after v; PHRASE: usu PHR after v; approval; PHRASE: PHR after v, v-link PHR, usu PHR *with* n; PHRASE: PHR after v, v-link PHR, usu PHR *with* n; PHRASE: V inflects, PHR *with* n, pl-n PHR; PHRASE: V inflects, usu PHR *with* n; PHRASE: v-link PHR, oft PHR *wh*; PHRASE: v-link PHR

♦ **touch down** When an aircraft **touches down**, it lands. ❑ *Spacecraft Columbia touched down yesterday.*
PHRASAL VERB = land; V P

♦ **touch off** If something **touches off** a situation or series of events, it causes it to start happening. ❑ *Is the massacre likely to touch off a new round of violence?*
PHRASAL VERB = spark off; V P n (not pron); Also V n P

**touch|down** /tʌtʃdaʊn/ **(touchdowns)** 1 **Touchdown** is the landing of an aircraft or spacecraft. ❑ *The astronauts are preparing for touchdown tomorrow morning.* 2 In rugby and American football, a **touchdown** is when a team scores points by taking the ball over the opposition's goal line.
N-VAR = landing; N-COUNT

**tou|ché** /tuːʃeɪ/ You say '**touché**' when you want to admit that the other person in an argument has won a point, usually with a short and witty remark.
CONVENTION

**touch|ing** /tʌtʃɪŋ/ If something is **touching**, it causes feelings of sadness or sympathy. ❑ *Her story is the touching tale of a wife who stood by the husband she loved.* ➔ See also **touch**.
ADJ = moving

**touch|line** /tʌtʃlaɪn/ In sports such as rugby and football, **the touchline** is one of the two lines which mark the side of the playing area. [mainly BRIT]
N-SING: usu *the* N

**touch pa|per** also **touchpaper.** If someone **lights the touch paper** or **lights the blue touch paper**, they do something which causes anger or excitement. [BRIT, JOURNALISM] ❑ *This kind of remark is guaranteed to light the blue touch paper with some Labour politicians.*
PHRASE: V inflects

**touch-screen** **(touch-screens)** A **touch-screen** is a computer screen that allows the user to give commands to the computer by touching parts of the screen rather than by using the keyboard or mouse. [COMPUTING]
N-COUNT: oft N n

**touch|stone** /tʌtʃstoʊn/ **(touchstones)** If you use one thing as a **touchstone** of another, you use it as a test or standard by which you judge the second thing. ❑ *Job security has become the touchstone of a good job for many employees.*
N-COUNT: usu N *of/for* n

**touch-tone** A **touch-tone** telephone has numbered buttons that make different sounds when you press them. Some automatic telephone services can only be used with this kind of telephone.
ADJ: ADJ n

**touchy** /tʌtʃi/ **(touchier, touchiest)** 1 If you describe someone as **touchy**, you mean that they are easily upset, offended, or irritated. ❑ *She is very touchy about her past.* 2 If you say that something is a **touchy** subject, you mean that it is a subject that needs to be dealt with carefully and in a sensitive way, because it might upset or offend people. ❑ *...the touchy question of political reform.*
ADJ: oft ADJ *about* n; disapproval; = sensitive; ADJ: usu ADJ n; = delicate

**touchy-feely** /tʌtʃi fiːli/ If you describe something as **touchy-feely**, you mean that it involves people expressing emotions such as love and affection openly in a way which you find embarrassing and silly. ❑ *...a touchy-feely song about making your life worth living.*
ADJ; disapproval

**tough** /tʌf/ **(tougher, toughest, toughs)** 1 A **tough** person is strong and determined, and can tolerate difficulty or suffering. ❑ *He built up a reputation as a tough businessman... She is tough and ambitious.* ♦ **tough|ness** *Mrs Potter has won a reputation for toughness and determination on her way to the top.* 2 If you describe someone as **tough**, you mean that they are rough and violent. ❑ *He had shot three people dead earning himself a reputation as a tough guy.* ♦ A **tough** is a tough person. ❑ *Three burly toughs elbowed their way to the front.* 3 A **tough** place or area is considered to have a lot of crime and violence. ❑ *She doesn't seem cut out for this tough neighbourhood.* 4 A **tough** way of life or period of time is difficult or full of suffering. ❑ *He was having a tough time at work.* 5 A **tough** task or problem is difficult to do or solve. ❑ *It was a very tough decision but we feel we made the right one.* 6 **Tough** policies or actions are strict and firm. ❑ *He is known for taking a tough line on security.* 7 A **tough** substance is strong, and difficult to break, cut, or tear. ❑ *In industry, diamond can form a tough, non-corrosive coating for tools.* 8 **Tough** meat is difficult to cut and chew. ❑ *The steak was tough and the peas were like bullets.* 9 If someone who is trying to achieve something **hangs tough**, they remain determined and do not give up, even when there are difficulties or problems. [AM, INFORMAL] ❑ *The White House is hanging tough for a good agreement to be reached.*
◆◆◇ ADJ; N-UNCOUNT; ADJ; N-COUNT; ADJ: usu ADJ n = rough; ADJ: usu ADJ n = rough; ADJ: oft *it* v-link ADJ to-inf, ADJ to-inf = hard; ADJ = strong; ADJ; ADJ; PHRASE: V inflects

**tough cookie** **(tough cookies)** If you describe someone as a **tough cookie**, you mean that they are unemotional and are not easily hurt by what people say or do.
N-COUNT

**tough|en** /tʌfᵊn/ **(toughens, toughening, toughened)** 1 If you **toughen** something or if it **toughens**, you make it stronger so that it will not break easily. ❑ *Do not add salt to beans when cooking as this tends to toughen the skins.* 2 If a person, institution, or law **toughens** its policies,
VERB; V n; Also V; VERB

regulations, or punishments, it makes them firmer or stricter. ❑ *Talks are under way to toughen trade restrictions.* (V n) ♦ **Toughen up** means the same as **toughen**. ❑ *The new law toughens up penalties for those that misuse guns.* (PHRASAL VERB; V P n; Also V n P) 3 If an experience **toughens** you, it makes you stronger and more independent in character. ❑ *They believe that participating in fights toughens boys and shows them how to be men.* (VERB; V n) ♦ **Toughen up** means the same as **toughen**. ❑ *He thinks boxing is good for kids, that it toughens them up... My father tried to teach me to toughen up.* (PHRASAL VERB; V n P; V P)

**tough love** **Tough love** is the practice of being very strict with a relative or friend who has an addiction or other problem in order to help them overcome the problem. ❑ *...the activities of black communities in identifying their own law-breaking youths and then administering tough love.* (N-UNCOUNT)

**tou|pee** /tuːpeɪ, AM tuːpeɪ/ **(toupees)** A **toupee** is a piece of artificial hair worn by a man to cover a patch on his head where he has lost his hair. (N-COUNT)

**tour** /tʊəʳ/ **(tours, touring, toured)** ◆◆◇ 1 A **tour** is an organized trip that people such as musicians, politicians, or theatre companies go on to several different places, stopping to meet people or perform. ❑ *The band are currently on a two-month tour of Europe. ...a presidential campaign tour in Illinois.* (N-COUNT: usu with supp) ● When people are travelling on a tour, you can say that they are **on tour**. ❑ *The band will be going on tour.* (PHRASE: PHR after v, v-link PHR) 2 When people such as musicians, politicians, or theatre companies **tour**, they go on a tour, for example in order to perform or to meet people. ❑ *A few years ago they toured the country in a roadshow... He toured for nearly two years and played 500 sell-out shows.* (VERB; V n; V) 3 A **tour** is a journey during which you visit several places that interest you. ❑ *It was week five of my tour of the major cities of Europe.* (N-COUNT: oft N *of* n) 4 A **tour** is a short trip that you make round a place, for example round a historical building, so that you can look at it. ❑ *...a guided tour of a ruined Scottish castle.* (N-COUNT: oft N *of* n) 5 If you **tour** a place, you go on a journey or trip round it. ❑ *You can also tour the site on modern coaches equipped with videos.* (VERB; V n)

**tour de force** /tʊəʳ də fɔːʳs/ **(tours de force)** also **tour-de-force.** If you call something such as a performance, speech, or production a **tour de force**, you are emphasizing that it is extremely good or extremely well done or made. ❑ *Stevenson's deeply felt performance is a tour-de-force.* (N-COUNT: usu sing; emphasis)

**Tourette's syn|drome** /tʊəʳets sɪndroʊm/ or **Tourette syndrome, Tourette's. Tourette's syndrome** is a brain disorder that causes the sufferer to make sudden uncontrolled movements and sometimes swear and spit. ❑ *...a Tourette's sufferer* (N-UNCOUNT)

**tour|ism** /tʊərɪzəm/ **Tourism** is the business of providing services for people on holiday, for example hotels, restaurants, and trips. (N-UNCOUNT)

**tour|ist** /tʊərɪst/ **(tourists)** ◆◇◇ A **tourist** is a person who is visiting a place for pleasure and interest, especially when they are on holiday. ❑ *...foreign tourists... Blackpool is the top tourist attraction in England.* (N-COUNT: oft N n)

**tour|isty** /tʊərɪsti/ If you describe a place as **touristy**, you do not like it because it is full of tourists or full of things for tourists to buy and do. [INFORMAL] ❑ *Visit some of the less touristy islands.* (ADJ; disapproval)

**tour|na|ment** /tʊəʳnəmənt/ **(tournaments)** ◆◇◇ A **tournament** is a sports competition in which players who win a match continue to play further matches in the competition until just one person or team is left. (N-COUNT: oft supp N)

**tour|ni|quet** /tʊəʳnɪkeɪ/ **(tourniquets)** A **tourniquet** is a strip of cloth that is tied tightly round an injured arm or leg in order to stop it bleeding. (N-COUNT)

**tour op|era|tor** **(tour operators)** A **tour operator** is a company that provides holidays in which your travel and accommodation are booked for you. (N-COUNT)

**tour rep** **(tour reps)** A **tour rep** is the same as a **holiday rep**. [BRIT] (N-COUNT)

**tou|sled** /taʊzəld/ If you have **tousled** hair, it is untidy and looks as if it has not been brushed or combed. (ADJ; = dishevelled)

**tout** /taʊt/ **(touts, touting, touted)** 1 If someone **touts** something, they try to sell it or convince people that it is good. ❑ *It has the trappings of an election campaign in the United States, with slick television ads touting the candidates.* (VERB; disapproval; V n) 2 If someone **touts for** business or custom, they try to obtain it. [mainly BRIT] ❑ *He visited Thailand and Singapore to tout for investment.* (VERB; V *for* n) 3 If someone **touts** tickets, they sell them outside a sports ground or theatre, usually for more than their original value. [BRIT] ❑ *...a man who made his money touting tickets.* (VERB; V n)

✔ in AM, use **scalp**

4 A **tout** is someone who sells things such as tickets unofficially, usually at prices which are higher than the official ones. [BRIT] (N-COUNT)

✔ in AM, use **scalper**

**tow** /toʊ/ **(tows, towing, towed)** 1 If one vehicle **tows** another, it pulls it along behind it. ❑ *He had been using the vehicle to tow his work trailer... They threatened to tow away my car... The British navy boarded the vessel and towed it to New York.* (VERB; V n; V n with adv; V n prep) 2 If you have someone **in tow**, they are following you closely because you are looking after them or you are leading them somewhere. [INFORMAL] ❑ *There she was on my doorstep with child in tow.* (PHRASE: *with* n PHR, PHR after v)

**to|wards** /təwɔːʳdz, AM tɔːʳdz/ or **toward** ◆◆◆

In addition to the uses shown below, **towards** is used in phrasal verbs such as 'count towards' and 'lean towards'.

1 If you move, look, or point **towards** something or someone, you move, look, or point in their direction. ❑ *Caroline leant across the table towards him... Anne left Artie and walked down the corridor towards the foyer... When he looked towards me, I smiled and waved.* (PREP) 2 If things develop **towards** a particular situation, that situation becomes nearer in time or more likely to happen. ❑ *The talks made little evident progress towards agreement.* (PREP: PREP n/-ing) 3 If you have a particular attitude **towards** something or someone, you have that attitude when you think about them or deal with them. ❑ *It's the business of the individual to determine his own attitude towards religion... Not everyone in the world will be kind and caring towards you.* (PREP) 4 If something happens **towards** a particular time, it happens just before that time. ❑ *The Channel tunnel was due to open towards the end of 1993.* (PREP) 5 If something is **towards** part of a place or thing, it is near that part. ❑ *The home of the Morgan family was up Gloucester Road, towards the top of the hill.* (PREP) 6 If you give money **towards** something, you give it to help pay for that thing. ❑ *He gave them £50,000 towards a house.* (PREP)

**tow|el** /taʊəl/ **(towels, towelling, towelled)**

✔ in AM, use **toweling, toweled**

1 A **towel** is a piece of thick soft cloth that you use to dry yourself. ❑ *...a bath towel.* (N-COUNT) 2 If you **towel** something or **towel** it dry, you dry it with a towel. ❑ *James came out of his bedroom, toweling his wet hair... I towelled myself dry... He stepped out of the shower and began towelling himself down.* (VERB; V n; V n adj; V n *down/off*) 3 If you **throw in the towel**, you stop trying to do something because you realize that you cannot succeed. [INFORMAL] ❑ *It seemed as if the police had thrown in the towel and were abandoning the investigation.* (PHRASE: V inflects) 4 → See also **sanitary towel**, **tea towel**.

**tow|el|ling** /taʊəlɪŋ/
in AM, use **toweling**

**Towelling** is a kind of fairly thick soft cloth that is used especially for making towels. ❑ *...a towelling bathrobe.* N-UNCOUNT: oft N n

**tow|er** /taʊə^r/ **(towers, towering, towered)** ◆◇◇
1 A **tower** is a tall, narrow building, that either stands alone or forms part of another building such as a church or castle. ❑ *...an eleventh century castle with 120-foot high towers. ...the Leaning Tower of Pisa.* N-COUNT; N-IN-NAMES 2 Someone or something that **towers over** surrounding people or things is a lot taller than they are. ❑ *He stood up and towered over her.* VERB V *over/above* n 3 A **tower** is a tall structure that is used for sending radio or television signals. ❑ *Troops are still in control of the television and radio tower.* N-COUNT 4 A **tower** is the same as a **tower block**. ❑ *...his design for a new office tower in Frankfurt.* N-COUNT 5 A **tower** is a tall box that contains the main parts of a computer, such as the hard disk and the drives. [COMPUTING] N-COUNT 6 → See also **clock tower**, **control tower**, **ivory tower**. 7 If you refer to someone as **a tower of strength**, you appreciate them because they give you a lot of help, support, and encouragement when you have problems or are in a difficult situation. ❑ *Pat was a tower of strength to our whole family.* PHRASE: *tower* inflects, v-link PHR, oft PHR *to* n [approval]

**tow|er block** **(tower blocks)** A **tower block** is a tall building divided into flats or offices. [BRIT] ❑ *...a 23-storey tower block.* N-COUNT
in AM, use **high-rise building, high-rise**

**tow|er|ing** /taʊərɪŋ/ 1 If you describe something such as a mountain or cliff as **towering**, you mean that it is very tall and therefore impressive. [LITERARY] ❑ *...towering cliffs of black granite which rise straight out of the sea.* ADJ: ADJ n 2 If you describe someone or something as **towering**, you are emphasizing that they are impressive because of their importance, skill, or intensity. [LITERARY] ❑ *He remains a towering figure in British politics.* ADJ: ADJ n [emphasis]

**town** /taʊn/ **(towns)** ◆◆◆ 1 A **town** is a place with many streets and buildings, where people live and work. Towns are larger than villages and smaller than cities. Many places that are called towns in Britain would be called cities in the United States. ❑ *...Saturday night in the small town of Braintree, Essex... Parking can be tricky in the town centre.* N-COUNT ♦ You can use **the town** to refer to the people of a town. ❑ *The town takes immense pride in recent achievements.* N-COUNT: usu sing 2 You use **town** in order to refer to the town where you live. ❑ *He admits he doesn't even know when his brother is in town... She left town.* N-UNCOUNT 3 You use **town** in order to refer to the central area of a town where most of the shops and offices are. ❑ *I walked around town... I caught a bus into town.* N-UNCOUNT 4 → See also **ghost town**, **hometown**, **new town**.
PHRASES 5 If you say that someone **goes to town** on something, you mean that they deal with it with a lot of enthusiasm or intensity. ❑ *We really went to town on it, turning it into a full, three-day show.* PHRASE: V inflects, oft PHR *on* n 6 If you go out **on the town** or go for a night **on the town**, you enjoy yourself by going to a town centre in the evening and spending a long time there visiting several places of entertainment. ❑ *My idea of luxury used to be going out on the town and coming back in the early hours of the morning.* PHRASE: prep PHR, n PHR = *on the tiles*

**town coun|cil** **(town councils)** A **town council** is a group of people who have been elected to govern a British town. N-COUNT-COLL: oft in names

**town cri|er** **(town criers)** In former times, a **town crier** was a man whose job was to walk through the streets of a town shouting out news and official announcements. N-COUNT

**town hall** **(town halls)** also **Town Hall**. 1 In Britain, a **town hall** in a town is a large building owned and used by the town council, often as its main office. You can also use **town hall** to refer to the town council that uses this building. N-COUNT 2 In the United States, especially in New England, a **town hall** is a building or hall used for local government business. N-COUNT

**town house** **(town houses)** 1 A **town house** is a tall narrow house in a town, usually in a row of similar houses. N-COUNT 2 The **town house** of a wealthy person is the house that they own in a town or city, rather than another house that they own in the country. N-COUNT: with poss

**townie** /taʊni/ **(townies)** If someone who lives in the countryside refers to someone from a town or city as a **townie**, they disapprove of that person because they think they have no knowledge of the countryside or country life. N-COUNT [disapproval]

**town plan|ning** **Town planning** is the planning and design of all the new buildings, roads, and parks in a place in order to make them attractive and convenient for the people who live there. N-UNCOUNT: oft N n

**towns|folk** /taʊnzfoʊk/ The **townsfolk** of a town or city are the people who live there. [OLD-FASHIONED] N-PLURAL = *towns-people*

**town|ship** /taʊnʃɪp/ **(townships)** 1 In South Africa, a **township** was a town where only black people lived. ❑ *...the South African township of Soweto.* N-COUNT 2 In the United States and Canada, a **township** is an area of land, especially a part of a county which is organized as a unit of local government. N-COUNT

**towns|people** /taʊnzpiːpəl/ The **townspeople** of a town or city are the people who live there. ❑ *Food shortages forced many townspeople into the country to grow their own food.* N-PLURAL

**tow|path** /toʊpɑːθ, -pæθ/ **(towpaths)** A **towpath** is a path along the side of a canal or river, which horses used to walk on when they pulled boats. N-COUNT

**tow|rope** /toʊroʊp/ **(towropes)** also **tow rope**. A **towrope** is a strong rope that is used for pulling vehicles. N-COUNT

**tow truck** **(tow trucks)** A **tow truck** is a motor vehicle which is used to pull broken or damaged vehicles. N-COUNT

**tox|ic** /tɒksɪk/ A **toxic** substance is poisonous. ❑ *...the cost of cleaning up toxic waste... These products are not toxic to humans.* ADJ = *poisonous* ♦ **tox|ic|ity** /tɒksɪsɪti/ **(toxicities)** *...data on the toxicity of chemicals.* N-VAR

**toxi|col|ogy** /tɒksɪkɒlədʒi/ **Toxicology** is the study of poisons. [TECHNICAL] N-UNCOUNT ♦ **toxi|co|logi|cal** /tɒksɪkəlɒdʒɪkəl/ ❑ *There were no adverse toxicological effects.* ADJ: ADJ n ♦ **toxi|colo|gist** **(toxicologists)** *Toxicologists attempt to identify and understand toxic hazards.* N-COUNT

**tox|in** /tɒksɪn/ **(toxins)** A **toxin** is any poisonous substance produced by bacteria, animals, or plants. ❑ *Tests showed increased levels of toxin in shellfish.* N-VAR

**toy** /tɔɪ/ **(toys, toying, toyed)** ◆◇◇ 1 A **toy** is an object that children play with, for example a doll or a model car. ❑ *He was really too old for children's toys. ...a toy telephone.* → See also **soft toy**. N-COUNT 2 You can refer to objects that adults use for fun rather than for a serious purpose as **toys**. ❑ *Computers have become household toys.* N-COUNT: oft supp N
♦ **toy with** 1 If you **toy with** an idea, you consider it casually without making any decisions about it. ❑ *He toyed with the idea of going to China.* PHRASAL VERB V P n 2 If you **toy with** food or drink, you do not eat or drink it with any enthusiasm, but only take a bite or a little drink from time to time. ❑ *She had no appetite, and merely toyed with the bread and cheese.* PHRASAL VERB V P n

**toy|boy** /tɔɪbɔɪ/ **(toyboys)** People sometimes refer to a woman's lover as her **toyboy** when he is much younger than she is. [BRIT, HUMOROUS, INFORMAL] N-COUNT

**toy|town** /tɔɪtaʊn/ You use **toytown** to show that you think something is silly, childish, or worthless. [BRIT] ❑ *He denounced what he called* ADJ: ADJ n [disapproval] *toytown revolutionaries advocating non-payment of taxes... Inflation has turned the rouble into a toytown currency.*

**TQM** /tiː kjuː em/ **TQM** is a set of management principles aimed at improving performance throughout a company, especially by involving employees in decision-making. **TQM** is an abbreviation for 'total quality management'. [BUSINESS] ❑ *One of the main themes of TQM is employee involvement... Under TQM principles the search for quality is continuous.* N-UNCOUNT

**trace** /treɪs/ **(traces, tracing, traced)** 1 If you **trace** the origin or development of something, you find out or describe how it started or developed. ❑ *The exhibition traces the history of graphic design in America from the 19th century to the present... The psychiatrist successfully traced some of her problems to severe childhood traumas.* ♦ **Trace back** means the same as **trace**. ❑ *Britain's Parliament can trace its history back to the English Parliament of the 13th century... She has never traced back her lineage, but believes her grandparents were from Aberdeenshire.* ◆◇◇ VERB V n V n to n PHRASAL VERB V n P to n V P n (not pron) 2 If you **trace** someone or something, you find them after looking for them. ❑ *Police are anxious to trace two men seen leaving the house just before 8am.* VERB V n 3 If you **trace** something such as a pattern or a shape, for example with your finger or toe, you mark its outline on a surface. ❑ *I traced the course of the river on the map.* VERB V n 4 If you **trace** a picture, you copy it by covering it with a piece of transparent paper and drawing over the lines underneath. ❑ *She learned to draw by tracing pictures out of old storybooks.* VERB V n 5 A **trace of** something is a very small amount of it. ❑ *Wash them in cold water to remove all traces of sand.* N-COUNT: usu N of n 6 A **trace** is a sign which shows you that someone or something has been in a place. ❑ *There's been no trace of my aunt and uncle... Finally, and mysteriously, Hoffa disappeared without trace.* N-COUNT: usu N of n, also without N 7 If you say that someone or something **sinks without trace** or **sinks without a trace**, you mean that they stop existing or stop being successful very suddenly and completely. ❑ *The Social Democratic Party has sunk without trace at these elections.* PHRASE: V inflects

♦ **trace back** → see **trace 1**.

**trace|able** /treɪsəbəl/ If one thing is **traceable to** another, there is evidence to suggest that the first thing was caused by or is connected to the second thing. ❑ *The probable cause of his death is traceable to an incident in 1724.* ADJ: usu v-link ADJ, usu ADJ to n

**trace el|ement** **(trace elements)** 1 A **trace element** is a chemical element such as iron or zinc that occurs in very small amounts in living things and is necessary for normal growth and development. N-COUNT 2 A **trace element** is a very small amount of a chemical element that is found in a metal or other substance. N-COUNT

**tra|chea** /trəkiːə, AM treɪkiə/ **(tracheas** or **tracheae** /trəkiːi, AM treɪkiiː/ **)** Your **trachea** is your **windpipe**. [MEDICAL] N-COUNT

**trac|ing pa|per** **Tracing paper** is transparent paper which you put over a picture so that you can draw over its lines in order to produce a copy of it. N-UNCOUNT

**track** /træk/ **(tracks, tracking, tracked)** 1 A **track** is a narrow road or path. ❑ *We set off once more, over a rough mountain track.* ◆◆◇ N-COUNT = path 2 A **track** is a piece of ground, often oval-shaped, that is used for races involving athletes, cars, bicycles, horses, or dogs called greyhounds. ❑ *The two men turned to watch the horses going round the track. ...the athletics track.* N-COUNT 3 Railway **tracks** are the rails that a train travels along. ❑ *A woman fell on to the tracks.* N-COUNT: usu pl 4 A **track** is one of the songs or pieces of music on a CD, record, or tape. N-COUNT 5 **Tracks** are marks left in the ground by the feet of animals or people. ❑ *The only evidence of pandas was their tracks in the snow.* N-PLURAL: oft supp N 6 If you **track** animals or people, you try to follow them by looking for the signs that they have left behind, for example the marks left by their feet. ❑ *He thought he had better track this wolf and kill it.* VERB V n 7 To **track** someone or something means to follow their movements by means of a special device, such as a satellite or radar. ❑ *Our radar began tracking the jets.* VERB V n 8 If you **track** someone or something, you investigate them, because you are interested in finding out more about them. ❑ *If it's possible, track the rumour back to its origin.* VERB V n 9 In a school, a **track** is a group of children of the same age and ability who are taught together. [AM] N-COUNT

☑ in BRIT, use **stream**

10 To **track** students means to divide them into groups according to their ability. [AM] ❑ *Students are already being tracked.* VERB be V-ed Also V n

☑ in BRIT, use **stream**

♦ **track|ing** *Tracking assigns some students to college prep and others to vocational programs.* N-UNCOUNT

11 → See also **backtrack**, **fast track**, **racetrack**, **sidetrack**, **soundtrack**, **title track**.

**PHRASES** 12 If someone **covers** their **tracks**, they hide or destroy evidence of their identity or their actions, because they want to keep them secret. ❑ *He covered his tracks, burnt letters and diaries.* PHRASE: V inflects 13 If you say that someone **has the inside track**, you mean that they have an advantage, for example special knowledge about something. [mainly AM or JOURNALISM] ❑ *Denver has the inside track among 10 sites being considered.* PHRASE: V inflects 14 If you **keep track of** a situation or a person, you make sure that you have the newest and most accurate information about them all the time. ❑ *With eleven thousand employees, it's very difficult to keep track of them all.* PHRASE: V inflects, PHR n 15 If you **lose track of** someone or something, you no longer know where they are or what is happening. ❑ *You become so deeply absorbed in an activity that you lose track of time.* PHRASE: V inflects, PHR n 16 If you **make tracks**, you leave the place where you are, especially when you are in a hurry. [INFORMAL] ❑ *We'd better make tracks soon, hadn't we?* PHRASE: V inflects 17 If someone or something is **on track**, they are acting or progressing in a way that is likely to result in success. ❑ *It may take some time to get the British economy back on track.* PHRASE: PHR after v, v-link PHR 18 If you are **on the track of** someone or something, you are trying to find them, or find information about them. ❑ *He was on the track of an escaped criminal.* PHRASE: PHR n, usu v-link PHR = on the trail of 19 If you are **on the right track**, you are acting or progressing in a way that is likely to result in success. If you are **on the wrong track**, you are acting or progressing in a way that is likely to result in failure. ❑ *Guests are returning in increasing numbers – a sure sign that we are on the right track... The country was headed on the wrong track, economically.* PHRASE: v-link PHR, PHR after v 20 If someone or something **stops** you **in** your **tracks**, or if you **stop dead in** your **tracks**, you suddenly stop moving because you are very surprised, impressed, or frightened. ❑ *The thought almost stopped me dead in my tracks.* PHRASE: V inflects 21 If someone or something **stops** a process or activity **in its tracks**, or if it **stops dead in its tracks**, they prevent the process or activity from continuing. ❑ *U.S. manufacturers may find the export boom stopping dead in its tracks.* PHRASE: V inflects 22 **off the beaten track** → see **beaten**.

♦ **track down** If you **track down** someone or something, you find them, or find information about them, after a difficult or long search. ❑ *She had spent years trying to track down her parents... I don't know where that old story came from, I've never been able to track it down.* PHRASAL VERB V P n (not pron) V n P

**track and field** **Track and field** refers to athletics as opposed to other sports. N-UNCOUNT

**track|ball** /trækbɔːl/ **(trackballs)** also **track ball, tracker ball.** A **trackball** is a ball on some computers that you turn in order to move the cursor. [COMPUTING] N-COUNT

**track|er** /trækəʳ/ **(trackers)** A **tracker** is a person or animal that finds other people or animals by following the marks left by their feet and other signs that show where they have been. N-COUNT

**track|er fund** /trækəʳfʌnd/ **(tracker funds)** A **tracker fund** is an investment in which shares in different companies are bought and sold so that the value of the shares held always matches the average value of shares in all or part of a stock market. [mainly BRIT, BUSINESS] N-COUNT

**track event** **(track events)** A **track event** is an event in athletics which involves running or walking around a racetrack, in contrast to events that involve only jumping or throwing. N-COUNT

**track|pad** /trækpæd/ **(trackpads)** A **trackpad** is a flat pad on some computers that you slide your finger over in order to move the cursor. [COMPUTING] ❑ *...with enhancements like a trackpad instead of a trackball.* N-COUNT

**track rec|ord** **(track records)** If you talk about the **track record** of a person, company, or product, you are referring to their past performance, achievements, or failures in it. ❑ *The job needs someone with a good track record in investment.* N-COUNT: usu with supp, oft N *in* n, N *of* -ing

**track|suit** /træksuːt/ **(tracksuits)** also **track suit.** A **tracksuit** is a loose, warm suit consisting of trousers and a top which people wear to relax and to do exercise. [BRIT] N-COUNT

✔ in AM, use **sweatsuit**

**tract** /trækt/ **(tracts)** [1] A **tract of** land is a very large area of land. ❑ *A vast tract of land is ready for development.* N-COUNT: usu N *of* n [2] A **tract** is a short article expressing a strong opinion on a religious, moral, or political subject in order to try to influence people's attitudes. ❑ *She produced a feminist tract, 'Comments on Birth-Control', in 1930.* N-COUNT = pamphlet [3] A **tract** is a system of organs and tubes in an animal's or person's body that has a particular function, especially the function of processing a substance in the body. [MEDICAL] ❑ *Foods are broken down in the digestive tract. ...urinary tract infections.* N-COUNT: usu supp N

**trac|table** /træktəbᵊl/ If you say that a person, problem, or device is **tractable**, you mean that they can be easily controlled or dealt with. [FORMAL] ❑ *...the country's least tractable social problems.* ADJ ≠ intractable

**trac|tion** /trækʃᵊn/ [1] **Traction** is a form of medical treatment, in which weights and pulleys are used to gently pull or stretch an injured part of the body for a period of time. You say that a person who is having this treatment is **in traction.** ❑ *Isabelle's legs were in traction for about two and a half weeks.* N-UNCOUNT: oft *in* N [2] **Traction** is a particular form of power that makes a vehicle move. N-UNCOUNT: usu supp N [3] **Traction** is the grip that something has on the ground, especially the wheels of a vehicle. N-UNCOUNT

**trac|tor** /træktəʳ/ **(tractors)** A **tractor** is a farm vehicle that is used to pull farm machinery and to provide the energy needed for the machinery to work. N-COUNT

**trad** /træd/ **Trad** or **trad jazz** is a kind of jazz based on the jazz that was played in the 1920s. [BRIT] N-UNCOUNT

**trade** /treɪd/ **(trades, trading, traded)** ◆◆◆ [1] **Trade** is the activity of buying, selling, or exchanging goods or services between people, firms, or countries. ❑ *The ministry had direct control over every aspect of foreign trade. ...negotiations on a new international trade agreement... Texas has a long history of trade with Mexico.* N-UNCOUNT: usu with supp [2] When people, firms, or countries **trade**, they buy, sell, or exchange goods or services between themselves. ❑ *They may refuse to trade, even when offered attractive prices... They had years of experience of trading with the West... He has been trading in antique furniture for 25 years.* ♦ **trad|ing** *Trading on the stock exchange may be suspended.* VERB; V; V *with* n; V *in* n; N-UNCOUNT: usu with supp [3] A **trade** is a particular area of business or industry. ❑ *They've completely ruined the tourist trade for the next few years. ...the arms trade.* N-COUNT: usu supp N [4] Someone's **trade** is the kind of work that they do, especially when they have been trained to do it over a period of time. ❑ *He learnt his trade as a diver in the North Sea... Allyn was a jeweller by trade.* N-COUNT: oft poss N, also *by* N [5] If someone **trades** one thing **for** another or if two people **trade** things, they agree to exchange one thing for the other thing. [mainly AM] ❑ *They traded land for goods and money... Kids used to trade baseball cards... They suspected that Neville had traded secret information with Mr Foster.* V-RECIP; V n *for* n (non-recip); pl-n V n; V n *with* n ♦ **Trade** is also a noun. ❑ *I am willing to make a trade with you.* N-COUNT

✔ in BRIT, use **exchange**

[6] If you **trade** places **with** someone or if the two of you **trade** places, you move into the other person's position or situation, and they move into yours. [mainly AM] ❑ *Mike asked George to trade places with him so he could ride with Tod... The receiver and the quarterback are going to trade positions.* V-RECIP = exchange; V n *with* n; pl-n V n [7] In professional sports, for example football or baseball, if a player **is traded** from one team to another, they leave one team and begin playing for another. [AM] ❑ *He was traded from the Giants to the Yankees... The A's have not won a game since they traded him.* VERB; *be* V-ed; V n

✔ in BRIT, use **transfer**

[8] If two people or groups **trade** something such as blows, insults, or jokes, they hit each other, insult each other, or tell each other jokes. [mainly AM] ❑ *Children would settle disputes by trading punches or insults in the schoolyard... They traded artillery fire with government forces inside the city.* V-RECIP = exchange; pl-n V n; V n *with* n

♦ **trade down** If someone **trades down**, they sell something such as their car or house and buy a less expensive one. ❑ *They are selling their five-bedroom house and trading down to a two-bedroom cottage.* PHRASAL VERB; V P *to* n

♦ **trade in** If you **trade in** an old car or appliance, you give it to the person you are buying a new one from so that you pay less. ❑ *He had a Rolls-Royce, and he traded it in for two matching silver Range Rovers... Richard refused to trade in his old Canon cameras.* → See also **trade-in.** PHRASAL VERB; V n P; V P n (not pron)

♦ **trade off** If you **trade off** one thing **against** another, you exchange all or part of one thing for another, as part of a negotiation or compromise. ❑ *They cynically tried to trade off a reduction in the slaughter of dolphins against a resumption of commercial whaling... There is a possibility of being able to trade off information for a reduced sentence.* → See also **trade-off.** PHRASAL VERB; V P n *against* n; V P n *for* n

♦ **trade up** If someone **trades up**, they sell something such as their car or their house and buy a more expensive one. ❑ *Mini-car owners are trading up to 'real' cars... Homeowners will feel more comfortable and they may feel ready to trade up.* PHRASAL VERB; V P *to* n; V P

**trade as|so|cia|tion** **(trade associations)** A **trade association** is a body representing organizations within the same trade. It aims to protect their collective interests, especially in negotiations with governments and trade unions. ❑ *...one of the two main trade associations for antiques dealers.* N-COUNT

**Trade De|scrip|tions Act** also **Trades Descriptions Act.** In Britain, **the Trade Descriptions Act** or **the Trades Descriptions Act** is a law designed to prevent companies from presenting their goods or services in a dishonest or misleading way. ❑ *Last year it was convicted and fined under the Trades Descriptions Act for placing For Sale boards on empty homes in the area.* N-SING: *the* N

**trade fair** **(trade fairs)** A **trade fair** is an exhibition where manufacturers show their products to other people in industry and try to get business. N-COUNT

**trade gap** **(trade gaps)** If a country imports goods worth more than the value of the goods that it exports, this is referred to as a **trade gap.** [BUSINESS] N-COUNT: usu sing

**trade-in** **(trade-ins)** A **trade-in** is an arrangement in which someone buys something such as a new car or washing machine at a reduced price by giving their old one, as well as money, in payment. ❑ *...the trade-in value of the car.* N-COUNT: oft N n

**trade|mark** /treɪdmɑːʳk/ **(trademarks)** also **trade mark.** 1 A **trademark** is a name or symbol that a company uses on its products and that cannot legally be used by another company. N-COUNT
2 If you say that something is the **trademark** of a particular person or place, you mean that it is characteristic of them or typically associated with them. ❑ *...the spiky punk hairdo that became his trademark.* N-COUNT: with poss

**trade name** **(trade names)** A **trade name** is the name which manufacturers give to a product or to a range of products. ❑ *It's marketed under the trade name 'Tattle'.* N-COUNT = brand name

**trade-off** **(trade-offs)** also **tradeoff.** A **trade-off** is a situation where you make a compromise between two things, or where you exchange all or part of one thing for another. [JOURNALISM] ❑ *...the trade-off between inflation and unemployment.* N-COUNT

**trad|er** /treɪdəʳ/ **(traders)** A **trader** is a person whose job is to trade in goods or stocks. ❑ *Market traders display an exotic selection of the island's produce.* ◆◇◇ N-COUNT: oft n N

**trade route** **(trade routes)** A **trade route** is a route, often covering long distances, that is used by traders. N-COUNT

**trade se|cret** **(trade secrets)** 1 A **trade secret** is information that is known, used, and kept secret by a particular firm, for example about a method of production or a chemical process. ❑ *The nature of the polymer is currently a trade secret.* N-COUNT
2 A **trade secret** is a piece of knowledge that you have, especially about how to do something, that you are not willing to tell other people. ❑ *I'd rather not talk about it too much because I don't like giving trade secrets away.* N-COUNT

**trades|man** /treɪdzmən/ **(tradesmen)** A **tradesman** is a person, usually a man, who sells goods or services, especially one who owns and runs a shop. N-COUNT

**trades un|ion** **(trades unions)** → see **trade union.**

**Trades Un|ion Con|gress** The **Trades Union Congress** in Britain is the same as the **TUC**. N-PROPER: the N

**trade sur|plus** **(trade surpluses)** If a country has a **trade surplus**, it exports more than it imports. [BUSINESS] ❑ *The country's trade surplus widened to 16.5 billion dollars.* N-COUNT

**trade un|ion** **(trade unions)** also **trades union.** A **trade union** is an organization that has been formed by workers in order to represent their rights and interests to their employers, for example in order to improve working conditions or wages. [mainly BRIT] N-COUNT: oft N n

☑ in AM, usually use **labor union**

**trade un|ion|ism** **Trade unionism** is the system, practices, and beliefs of trade unions. N-UNCOUNT

**trade un|ion|ist** **(trade unionists)** also **trades unionist.** A **trade unionist** is an active member of a trade union. [BRIT] N-COUNT

**trad|ing es|tate** **(trading estates)** A **trading estate** is the same as an **industrial estate**. [BRIT] N-COUNT: oft in names

**tra|di|tion** /trədɪʃən/ **(traditions)** 1 A **tradition** is a custom or belief that has existed for a long time. ❑ *...the rich traditions of Afro-Cuban music, and dance... Mary has carried on the family tradition of giving away plants.* ◆◇◇ N-VAR 2 If you say that something or someone is **in the tradition of** a person or thing from the past, you mean that they have many features that remind you of that person or thing. ❑ *They're marvellous pictures in the tradition of Gainsborough.* PREP-PHRASE

**tra|di|tion|al** /trədɪʃənəl/ 1 **Traditional** customs, beliefs, or methods are ones that have existed for a long time without changing. ❑ *...traditional teaching methods. ...traditional Indian music.* ◆◆◇ ADJ: usu ADJ n
♦ **tra|di|tion|al|ly** *Married women have traditionally been treated as dependent on their husbands.* ADV: ADV with cl/group
2 A **traditional** organization or person prefers older methods and ideas to modern ones. ❑ *We're still a traditional school in a lot of ways.* ADJ: usu ADJ n ≠ progressive
♦ **tra|di|tion|al|ly** *He is loathed by some of the more traditionally minded officers.* ADV: ADV -ed, ADV adj

**tra|di|tion|al|ism** /trədɪʃənəlɪzəm/ **Traditionalism** is behaviour and ideas that support established customs and beliefs, rather than modern ones. N-UNCOUNT ≠ modernity

**tra|di|tion|al|ist** /trədɪʃənəlɪst/ **(traditionalists)** 1 A **traditionalist** is a person who supports the established customs and beliefs of his or her society or group, and does not want to change them. N-COUNT ≠ progressive 2 A **traditionalist** idea, argument, or organization supports the established customs and beliefs of a society or group, rather than modern ones. ADJ ≠ progressive

**tra|duce** /trədjuːs, AM -duːs/ **(traduces, traducing, traduced)** If someone has **been traduced**, unpleasant and untrue things have deliberately been said about them. [FORMAL] ❑ *We have been traduced in the press as xenophobic bigots.* VERB: usu passive be V-ed

**traf|fic** /træfɪk/ **(traffics, trafficking, trafficked)** 1 **Traffic** refers to all the vehicles that are moving along the roads in a particular area. ❑ *There was heavy traffic on the roads. ...the problems of city life, such as traffic congestion.* → See also **traffic jam.** ◆◇◇ N-UNCOUNT: also the N 2 **Traffic** refers to the movement of ships, trains, or aircraft between one place and another. **Traffic** also refers to the people and goods that are being transported. ❑ *Air traffic had returned to normal... The railways will carry a far higher proportion of freight traffic.* → See also **air traffic control.** N-UNCOUNT: with supp, usu n N
3 **Traffic in** something such as drugs or stolen goods is an illegal trade in them. ❑ *Traffic in illicit drugs was now worth some 500 thousand million dollars a year.* N-UNCOUNT: with supp, usu N in n 4 Someone who **traffics in** something such as drugs or stolen goods buys and sells them even though it is illegal to do so. ❑ *The president said illegal drugs are hurting the entire world and anyone who traffics in them should be brought to justice.* VERB V in n ♦ **traf|fick|ing** *He was sentenced to ten years in prison on charges of drug trafficking.* N-UNCOUNT: usu n N

**traf|fic calm|ing** also **traffic-calming. Traffic calming** consists of measures designed to make roads safer, for example making them narrower or placing obstacles in them, so that drivers are forced to slow down. ❑ *...traffic calming schemes.* N-UNCOUNT: usu N n

**traf|fic cir|cle** **(traffic circles)** A **traffic circle** is a circular structure in the road at a place where several roads meet. You drive round it until you come to the road that you want. [AM] N-COUNT

☑ in BRIT, use **roundabout**

**traf|fic cone** **(traffic cones)** A **traffic cone** is a plastic object with a pointed top that is placed on a road to prevent people from driving or parking there. N-COUNT

**traf|fic jam** **(traffic jams)** A **traffic jam** is a long line of vehicles that cannot move forward because there is too much traffic, or because the road is blocked by something. N-COUNT

**traf|fick|er** /træfɪkəʳ/ **(traffickers)** A **trafficker** in particular goods, especially drugs, is a person who illegally buys or sells these goods. ❑ *They have been arrested as suspected drug traffickers.* N-COUNT: usu n N

**traf|fic light** **(traffic lights)** **Traffic lights** are sets of red, amber, and green lights at the places where roads meet. They control the traffic by signalling when vehicles have to stop and when they can go. Traffic lights can also be referred to as a **traffic light.** N-COUNT: usu pl

**traf|fic war|den** **(traffic wardens)** A **traffic warden** is a person whose job is to make sure that cars are not parked illegally. [mainly BRIT] N-COUNT

**trag|edy** /trædʒɪdi/ **(tragedies)** 1 A **tragedy** is an extremely sad event or situation. ❑ *They have suffered an enormous personal tragedy... Maskell's life had not been without tragedy.* ◆◇◇ N-VAR
2 **Tragedy** is a type of literature, especially dra- N-VAR

ma, that is serious and sad, and often ends with the death of the main character. ❑ *The story has elements of tragedy and farce.*

**trag|ic** /trædʒɪk/ [ADJ] 1 A **tragic** event or situation is extremely sad, usually because it involves death or suffering. ❑ *It was just a tragic accident... The circumstances are tragic but we have to act within the law.* ♦ **tragi|cal|ly** /trædʒɪkli/ [ADV: ADV with cl, ADV with v, ADV adj/adv] *Tragically, she never saw the completed building because she died before it was finished.* 2 [ADJ: ADJ n] **Tragic** is used to refer to tragedy as a type of literature. ❑ *...Michael Henchard, the tragic hero of 'The Mayor of Casterbridge'.*

**tragi-comedy** /trædʒi kɒmədi/ **(tragi-comedies)** also **tragicomedy.** [N-COUNT] A **tragi-comedy** is a play or other written work that is both sad and amusing.

**tragi-comic** /trædʒi kɒmɪk/ also **tragi-comic.** [ADJ] Something that is **tragi-comic** is both sad and amusing at the same time.

**trail** /treɪl/ **(trails, trailing, trailed)** ◆◇◇ 1 [N-COUNT = track] A **trail** is a rough path across open country or through forests. ❑ *He was following a broad trail through the trees.* 2 [N-COUNT] A **trail** is a route along a series of paths or roads, often one that has been planned and marked out for a particular purpose. ❑ *...a large area of woodland with hiking and walking trails.* 3 [N-COUNT: usu sing, oft N *of* n] A **trail** is a series of marks or other signs of movement or other activities left by someone or something. ❑ *Everywhere in the house was a sticky trail of orange juice.* 4 [VERB = follow] If you **trail** someone or something, you follow them secretly, often by finding the marks or signs that they have left. ❑ [V n] *Two detectives were trailing him...* [V n prep/adv] *I trailed her to a shop in Kensington.* 5 [N-COUNT: n N] You can refer to all the places that a politician visits in the period before an election as their campaign **trail**. ❑ *During a recent speech on the campaign trail, he was interrupted by hecklers.* 6 [VERB] If you **trail** something or it **trails**, it hangs down loosely behind you as you move along. ❑ [V n] *She came down the stairs slowly, trailing the coat behind her...* [V prep] *He let his fingers trail in the water.* 7 [VERB] If someone **trails** somewhere, they move there slowly, without any energy or enthusiasm, often following someone else. ❑ [V adv/prep] *He trailed through the wet Manhattan streets.* 8 [VERB: usu cont] If a person or team in a sports match or other contest **is trailing**, they have a lower score than their opponents. ❑ [V amount] *He scored again, leaving Dartford trailing 3-0 at the break...* [V *behind* n] *The polls showed the Tories trailing behind the Government by 17 per cent.* 9 [PHRASE: usu v-link PHR] If you are **on the trail of** a person or thing, you are trying hard to find them or find out about them. ❑ *The police were hot on his trail.* 10 → See also **nature trail**, **paper trail**. to **blaze a trail** → see **blaze**.

♦ **trail off** or **trail away** [PHRASAL VERB = tail away] If a speaker's voice or a speaker **trails off** or **trails away**, their voice becomes quieter and they hesitate until they stop speaking completely. ❑ [V P] *'But he had no reason. He of all men...' Kate's voice trailed off.*

**trail|blazer** /treɪlbleɪzəʳ/ **(trailblazers)** [N-COUNT] A **trailblazer** is a person who is the leader in a particular field, especially who does a particular thing before anyone else does. ❑ *He has been the trailblazer and given British sprinters the belief that we are able to take on and beat the world's best.*

**trail-blazing** also **trailblazing.** [ADJ: ADJ n] A **trail-blazing** idea, event, or organization is new, exciting, and original. ❑ *...a trail-blazing agreement that could lead to a global ban on nuclear weapons.*

**trail|er** /treɪləʳ/ **(trailers)** 1 [N-COUNT] A **trailer** is a container on wheels which is pulled by a car or other vehicle and which is used for transporting large or heavy items. 2 [N-COUNT] A **trailer** is the long rear section of a lorry or truck, in which the goods are carried. 3 [N-COUNT] A **trailer** is a long vehicle without an engine which people use as a home or as an office and which can be pulled behind a car. [mainly AM]

✔ in BRIT, use **caravan**

4 [N-COUNT: oft N *for* n] A **trailer** for a film or television programme is a set of short extracts which are shown to advertise it.

**trail|er park** **(trailer parks)** also **trailer court.** [N-COUNT] A **trailer park** is an area where people can pay to park their trailers and live in them. [AM]

✔ in BRIT, use **caravan site**

**trail|er trash** [N-UNCOUNT-COLL] [disapproval] Some people use **trailer trash** to refer to poor people who live in trailer parks and who they think are vulgar or worthless. This use could cause offence. [AM, INFORMAL]

**trail|er truck** **(trailer trucks)** [N-COUNT] A **trailer truck** is a truck or lorry that is made in two or more sections which are joined together by metal bars, so that the vehicle can turn more easily. [AM]

✔ in BRIT, usually use **articulated lorry**

**train**
① NOUN USES
② VERB USES

① **train** /treɪn/ **(trains)** ◆◆◇ 1 [N-COUNT: also *by* N] A **train** is a number of carriages, cars, or trucks which are all connected together and which are pulled by an engine along a railway. Trains carry people and goods from one place to another. ❑ *The train pulled into a station... We can catch the early morning train... He arrived in Shenyang by train yesterday.* 2 [N-COUNT: with supp, usu N *of* n] A **train of** vehicles, people, or animals is a long line of them travelling slowly in the same direction. ❑ *...a long train of oil tankers.* 3 [N-COUNT: usu sing, N *of* n] A **train of** thought or a **train of** events is a connected sequence, in which each thought or event seems to occur naturally or logically as a result of the previous one. ❑ *He lost his train of thought for a moment, then recovered it... Giles set in motion a train of events which would culminate in tragedy.* 4 [N-COUNT] The **train** of a woman's formal dress or wedding dress is the long part at the back of it which flows along the floor behind her. 5 [PHRASE: v-link PHR, PHR after v] If a process or event is **in train** or has been set **in train**, it is happening or starting to happen. [mainly BRIT] ❑ *He praised the economic reforms set in train by the government.*

✔ in AM, usually use **in motion**

② **train** /treɪn/ **(trains, training, trained)** ◆◆◇ 1 [VERB] If someone **trains** you **to** do something, they teach you the skills that you need in order to do it. If you **train to** do something, you learn the skills that you need in order to do it. ❑ [V n to-inf] *The US was ready to train its troops to participate...* [V to-inf] *Stavros was training to be a priest...* [V *as/in* n] *Psychiatrists initially train as doctors...* [V n *as/in* n] *We don't train them only in bricklaying, but also in other building techniques...* [V] *Companies favour the lawyer who has trained with a City firm...* [V-ed] *I'm a trained nurse.* ♦ **-trained** [COMB in ADJ] *Mr. Koutab is an American-trained lawyer.* ♦ **train|er (trainers)** [N-COUNT] *...a book for both teachers and teacher trainers.* 2 [VERB] To **train** a natural quality or talent that someone has, for example their voice or musical ability, means to help them to develop it. ❑ [V n] *I see my degree as something which will train my mind and improve my chances of getting a job.* 3 [VERB] If you **train for** a physical activity such as a race or if someone **trains** you **for** it, you prepare for it by doing particular physical exercises. ❑ [V *for* n] *Strachan is training for the new season...* [V n *for* n, Also V, V n] *He has spent a year training crews for next month's round the world race.* ♦ **train|er** [N-COUNT] *She went to the gym with her trainer.* 4 [VERB] If an animal or bird **is trained to** do particular things, it is taught to do them, for example in order to be able to work for someone or to be a good pet. ❑ [*be* V-ed to-inf] *Sniffer dogs could be trained to track them down.* [V n, Also V n to-inf] *...a man who trained hundreds of dogs.* ♦ **train|er** [N-COUNT] *The horse made a winning start for his new trainer.* 5 [VERB] If you **train** something such as a gun, a camera, or a light **on** a person or thing, you aim it at them and keep it towards them. ❑ [V n *on* n] *She trained her binoculars on the horizon.* 6 [VERB] If you **train** a tree, bush, or plant in a particular direction, you tie it and cut it so that it grows in that direction. ❑ [V n prep] *Instead of training the shoots up the* *fence, lay them flat in both directions alongside it... You could even put a trellis on your walls and train plants to grow up it.* V n to-inf 7 → See also **training**.

♦ **train up** PHRASAL VERB If someone **trains** you **up**, they teach you new skills or give you the necessary preparation so that you will reach the standard required for a particular job or activity. [BRIT, INFORMAL] ❑ *The first companies to go in took a policy of employing East Germans and training them up...* V n P *He usually preferred to train up a crew of enthusiastic young sailors from scratch.* V P n (not pron)

**trainee** /treɪniː/ **(trainees)** N-COUNT: oft N n A **trainee** is someone who is employed at a low level in a particular job in order to learn the skills needed for that job. ❑ *He is a 24-year-old trainee reporter.*

**train|er** /treɪnəʳ/ **(trainers)** N-COUNT: usu pl **Trainers** are shoes that people wear, especially for running and other sports. [BRIT] → See also **train**.

> ✔ in AM, use **sneakers**

**train|ing** /treɪnɪŋ/ ♦◇◇ 1 N-UNCOUNT **Training** is the process of learning the skills that you need for a particular job or activity. ❑ *He called for much higher spending on education and training. ...a one-day training course.* 2 N-UNCOUNT **Training** is physical exercise that you do regularly in order to keep fit or to prepare for an activity such as a race. ❑ *The emphasis is on developing fitness through exercises and training. ...her busy training schedule.* ● PHRASE: v-link PHR, PHR after v If you are **in training**, you are preparing yourself for a physical activity such as a race, by taking a lot of exercise and eating special food. ❑ *He will soon be back in training for next year's National.* 3 → See also **circuit training**, **potty training**.

**train|ing camp** **(training camps)** N-COUNT A **training camp** for soldiers or sports players is an organized period of training at a particular place.

**train|ing shoe** **(training shoes)** N-COUNT: usu pl **Training shoes** are the same as **trainers**.

**train|spotter** /treɪnspɒtəʳ/ **(trainspotters)** also **train spotter, train-spotter.** N-COUNT A **trainspotter** is someone who is very interested in trains and spends time going to stations and recording the numbers of the trains that they see. [BRIT]

**train|spot|ting** /treɪnspɒtɪŋ/ also **train spotting, train-spotting.** N-UNCOUNT **Trainspotting** is the hobby of going to railway stations and recording the numbers of the trains that you see. [BRIT]

**traipse** /treɪps/ **(traipses, traipsing, traipsed)** 1 VERB If you **traipse** somewhere, you go there unwillingly, often because you are tired or unhappy. ❑ *If traipsing around shops does not appeal to you, perhaps using a catalogue will.* V prep/adv 2 VERB [disapproval] If you talk about people **traipsing** somewhere, you mean that they are going there or moving about there in a way that annoys someone or gets in their way. ❑ *You will have to get used to a lot of people traipsing in and out of your home.* V prep/adv

**trait** /treɪt, treɪ/ **(traits)** N-COUNT: with supp A **trait** is a particular characteristic, quality, or tendency that someone or something has. ❑ *The study found that some alcoholics had clear personality traits showing up early in childhood.*

**trai|tor** /treɪtəʳ/ **(traitors)** 1 N-COUNT: oft N *to* n [disapproval] If you call someone a **traitor**, you mean that they have betrayed beliefs that they used to hold, or that their friends hold, by their words or actions. ❑ *Some say he's a traitor to the working class.* 2 N-COUNT If someone is a **traitor**, they betray their country or a group of which they are a member by helping its enemies, especially during time of war. ❑ *...rumours that there were traitors among us who were sending messages to the enemy.*

**trai|tor|ous** /treɪtərəs/ ADJ A **traitorous** action will betray or bring danger to a country or to the group of people that someone belongs to. ❑ *...the monstrous betrayal of men by their most traitorous companions. ...the movement could be labeled as divisive, even traitorous.*

**tra|jec|tory** /trədʒektəri/ **(trajectories)** 1 N-COUNT: with supp The **trajectory** of a moving object is the path that it follows as it moves. ❑ *...the trajectory of an artillery shell.* 2 N-COUNT: with supp The **trajectory** of something such as a person's career is the course that it follows over time. ❑ *...a relentlessly upward career trajectory.*

**tram** /træm/ **(trams)** N-COUNT: also *by* N A **tram** is a public transport vehicle, usually powered by electricity from wires above it, which travels along rails laid in the surface of a street. [mainly BRIT]

> ✔ in AM, usually use **streetcar**

**tram|line** /træmlaɪn/ **(tramlines)** N-COUNT A **tramline** is one of the rails laid in the surface of a road that trams travel along. [BRIT]

> ✔ in AM, use **streetcar line**

**tramp** /træmp/ **(tramps, tramping, tramped)** 1 N-COUNT A **tramp** is a person who has no home or job, and very little money. Tramps go from place to place, and get food or money by asking people or by doing casual work. 2 VERB = trudge If you **tramp** somewhere, you walk there slowly and with regular, heavy steps, for a long time. ❑ *They put on their coats and tramped through the falling snow...* V prep/adv *She spent all day yesterday tramping the streets, gathering evidence.* V n 3 N-UNCOUNT: usu N *of* n The **tramp** of people is the sound of their heavy, regular walking. ❑ *He heard the slow, heavy tramp of feet on the stairs.* 4 N-COUNT [disapproval] If someone refers to a woman as a **tramp**, they are insulting her, because they think that she is immoral in her sexual behaviour. [mainly AM, OFFENSIVE]

**tram|ple** /træmpᵊl/ **(tramples, trampling, trampled)** 1 VERB To **trample on** someone's rights or values or to **trample** them means to deliberately ignore them. ❑ *They say loggers are destroying rain forests and trampling on the rights of natives...* V *on* n *Diplomats denounced the leaders for trampling their citizens' civil rights.* V n 2 VERB: usu passive If someone **is trampled**, they are injured or killed by being stepped on by animals or by other people. ❑ *Many people were trampled in the panic that followed.* be V-ed 3 VERB If someone **tramples** something or **tramples on** it, they step heavily and carelessly on it and damage it. ❑ *They don't want people trampling the grass, pitching tents or building fires...* V n *Please don't trample on the azaleas.* V *on* n

**tram|po|line** /træmpəliːn/ **(trampolines)** N-COUNT A **trampoline** is a piece of equipment on which you jump up and down as a sport. It consists of a large piece of strong cloth held by springs in a frame.

**tram|way** /træmweɪ/ **(tramways)** N-COUNT A **tramway** is a set of rails laid in the surface of a road for trams to travel along. [mainly BRIT]

**trance** /trɑːns, træns/ **(trances)** N-COUNT: oft prep N A **trance** is a state of mind in which someone seems to be asleep and to have no conscious control over their thoughts or actions, but in which they can see and hear things and respond to commands given by other people. ❑ *Like a man in a trance, Blake found his way back to his rooms.*

**tranche** /trɑːnʃ/ **(tranches)** 1 N-COUNT: usu N *of* n In economics, a **tranche** of shares in a company, or a **tranche** of a company, is a number of shares in that company. [mainly BRIT, BUSINESS] ❑ *On February 12th he put up for sale a second tranche of 32 state-owned companies.* 2 N-COUNT: usu N *of* n A **tranche** of something is a piece, section, or part of it. A **tranche** of things is a group of them. [FORMAL] ❑ *They risk losing the next tranche of funding.*

**tran|quil** /træŋkwɪl/ ADJ = serene Something that is **tranquil** is calm and peaceful. ❑ *The tranquil atmosphere of The Connaught allows guests to feel totally at home.* ♦ **tran|quil|lity** /træŋkwɪlɪti/ N-UNCOUNT *The hotel is a haven of peace and tranquillity.*

**tran|quil|lize** /træŋkwɪlaɪz/ **(tranquillizes, tranquillizing, tranquillized)**

> ✔ The spellings **tranquilize** in American English, and **tranquillise** in British English, are also used.

VERB To **tranquillize** a person or an animal means to

make them become calm, sleepy, or unconscious by means of a drug. ❑ *This powerful drug is used to tranquilize patients undergoing surgery.* = sedate V n

**tran|quil|liz|er** /trǽŋkwɪlaɪzəʳ/ **(tranquillizers)**

> ✔ The spellings **tranquilizer** in American English, and **tranquilliser** in British English, are also used.

N-COUNT A **tranquillizer** is a drug that makes people feel calmer or less anxious. Tranquillizers are sometimes used to make people or animals become sleepy or unconscious.

**trans.** **trans.** is a written abbreviation for 'translated by'.

**trans-** /trǽnz-/ PREFIX [1] **trans-** is used to form adjectives which indicate that something involves or enables travel from one side of an area to the other. For example, a trans-continental journey is a journey across a continent. ❑ *...trans-Pacific flights between Asia and America. ...the Trans-Siberian railway.* PREFIX [2] **trans-** is used to form words which indicate that someone or something moves from one group, thing, state, or place to another. ❑ *...trans-racial adoption.*

**trans|act** /trænzǽkt/ **(transacts, transacting, transacted)** VERB If you **transact** business, you enter into a deal with someone, for example by buying or selling something. [FORMAL] ❑ *This would free them to transact business across state lines.* V n

**trans|ac|tion** /trænzǽkʃən/ **(transactions)** ◆◇◇ N-COUNT A **transaction** is a piece of business, for example an act of buying or selling something. [FORMAL]

**trans|at|lan|tic** /trænzətlǽntɪk/ ADJ: ADJ n [1] **Transatlantic** flights or signals go across the Atlantic Ocean, usually between the United States and Britain. ❑ *Many transatlantic flights land there.* ADJ: ADJ n [2] **Transatlantic** is used to refer to something that happens, exists, or begins in the United States. [BRIT] ❑ *...transatlantic fashions.*

**trans|cend** /trænsénd/ **(transcends, transcending, transcended)** VERB Something that **transcends** normal limits or boundaries goes beyond them, because it is more significant than them. ❑ *...issues like European union that transcend party loyalty.* V n

**tran|scend|ence** /trænséndəns/ N-UNCOUNT **Transcendence** is the quality of being able to go beyond normal limits or boundaries. ❑ *...the transcendence of class differences.*

**trans|cend|ent** /trænséndənt/ ADJ Something that is **transcendent** goes beyond normal limits or boundaries, because it is more significant than them. ❑ *...the idea of a transcendent God who stood apart from mankind.*

**tran|scen|den|tal** /trǽnsendéntəl/ ADJ: usu ADJ n **Transcendental** refers to things that lie beyond the practical experience of ordinary people, and cannot be discovered or understood by ordinary reasoning. ❑ *...the transcendental nature of God.*

**tran|scen|den|tal medi|ta|tion** N-UNCOUNT **Transcendental meditation** is a kind of meditation in which people mentally relax by silently repeating special words over and over again. The abbreviation **TM** is also used.

**trans|con|ti|nen|tal** /trǽnskɒntɪnéntəl/ ADJ: usu ADJ n A **transcontinental** journey or route goes from one side of a continent to the other. In American English, **transcontinental** usually means from one side of the United States to the other. ❑ *...in mid-nineteenth-century America, before the transcontinental railroad was built.*

**tran|scribe** /trænskráɪb/ **(transcribes, transcribing, transcribed)** VERB [1] If you **transcribe** a speech or text, you write it out in a different form from the one in which it exists, for example by writing it out in full from notes or from a tape recording. ❑ *She is transcribing, from his dictation, the diaries of Simon Forman.* V n VERB [2] If you **transcribe** a piece of music for an instrument which is not the one for which it was originally written, you rewrite it so that it can be played on that instrument. ❑ *He gave up trying to write for the guitar and decided to transcribe the work for piano.* V n for n Also V n

**tran|script** /trǽnskrɪpt/ **(transcripts)** N-COUNT: oft N of n A **transcript of** a conversation or speech is a written text of it, based on a recording or notes.

**tran|scrip|tion** /trænskrɪ́pʃən/ **(transcriptions)** N-UNCOUNT [1] **Transcription** of speech or text is the process of transcribing it. N-COUNT [2] A **transcription** of a conversation or speech is a written text of it, based on a recording or notes.

**trans|der|mal** /trænzdɜ́ːʳməl/ ADJ **Transdermal** medicine is absorbed through the skin, for example by means of a skin patch. ❑ *...a transdermal cream.*

**tran|sept** /trǽnsept/ **(transepts)** N-COUNT In a cathedral or church, the **transept** is the part which projects to the north or south of the main part of the building.

**trans|fer** **(transfers, transferring, transferred)** ◆◆◇

> ✔ The verb is pronounced /trænsfɜ́ːʳ/. The noun is pronounced /trǽnsfɜːʳ/.

VERB [1] If you **transfer** something or someone **from** one place **to** another, or they **transfer from** one place **to** another, they go from the first place to the second. ❑ *Remove the wafers with a spoon and transfer them to a plate... The person can transfer from wheelchair to seat with relative ease.* ♦ **Transfer** is also a noun. ❑ *Arrange for the transfer of medical records to your new doctor.* V n from/to n; V from/to n; N-VAR: oft N of n

VERB [2] If something **is transferred**, or **transfers**, **from** one person or group of people **to** another, the second person or group gets it instead of the first. ❑ *I realized she'd transferred all her love from me to you... On 1 December the presidency of the Security Council automatically transfers from the US to Yemen.* ♦ **Transfer** is also a noun. ❑ *...the transfer of power from the old to the new regimes.* V n from/to n; V from/to n; N-VAR: usu N of n

N-VAR: supp N, N of n [3] Technology **transfer** is the process or act by which a country or organization which has developed new technology enables another country or organization to use the technology. ❑ *The Philippines needs capital and technology transfer.*

VERB [4] In professional sports, if a player **transfers** or **is transferred** from one club to another, they leave one club and begin playing for another. [BRIT] ❑ *...Nick Barmby who transferred from Spurs to Middlesbrough... He was transferred from Crystal Palace to Arsenal for £2.5 million.* ♦ **Transfer** is also a noun. ❑ *...Gascoigne's transfer to the Italian club, Lazio.* V from/to n; be V-ed from/to n; N-COUNT

> ✔ in AM, use **trade**

VERB [5] If you **are transferred**, or if you **transfer, to** a different job or place, you move to a different job or start working in a different place. ❑ *I was transferred to the book department... I suspect that she is going to be transferred... Anton was able to transfer from Lavine's to an American company.* ♦ **Transfer** is also a noun. ❑ *They will be offered transfers to other locations.* be V-ed from/to n; be V-ed; V from/to n; Also V n; N-VAR: oft N to n

VERB [6] When information **is transferred onto** a different medium, it is copied from one medium to another. ❑ *Such information is easily transferred onto microfilm. ...systems to create film-quality computer effects and then transfer them to film.* ♦ **Transfer** is also a noun. ❑ *It can be connected to a PC for the transfer of information. ...data transfer.* be V-ed onto/to n; V n onto/to n; N-UNCOUNT: usu with supp, N of n, n N

VERB [7] When property or land **is transferred**, it stops being owned by one person or institution and becomes owned by another. [LEGAL] ❑ *He has already transferred ownership of most of the works to a British foundation... Certain kinds of property are transferred automatically at death.* ♦ **Transfer** is also a noun. ❑ *...an outright transfer of property.* V n from/to n; be V-ed; Also V n; N-VAR: oft N of n

VERB [8] If you **transfer** or **are transferred** when you are on a journey, you change from one vehicle to another. ❑ *He likes to transfer from the bus to the Blue Line at 103rd Street in Watts... 1,654 passengers were transferred at sea to a Norwegian cruise ship.* V from/to n; be V-ed from/to n

N-COUNT [9] **Transfers** are pieces of paper with a design on one side. The design can be transferred by heat or pressure onto material, paper, or china for decoration. ❑ *...gold letter transfers.*

**trans|fer|able** /trænsfɜːrəbəl/ ADJ If something is **transferable**, it can be passed or moved from one person or organization to another and used by them. ❑ *Your Railcard is not transferable to anyone else.*

**trans|fer|ence** /trænsfərəns/ N-UNCOUNT: oft N *of* n = transfer The **transference** of something such as power, information, or affection from one person or place to another is the action of transferring it. ❑ *It is a struggle for a transference of power.*

**trans|fer list** **(transfer lists)** N-COUNT In football, a **transfer list** is a list of players at a club who may be sold to other clubs. [BRIT]

**trans|fig|ure** /trænsfɪgər, AM -fɪgjər/ **(transfigures, transfiguring, transfigured)** VERB To **be transfigured** means to be changed into something great or beautiful. [LITERARY] ❑ *They are transfigured by the healing powers of art...* (be V-ed) *He smiled back, which for an instant transfigured his unrevealing features.* (V n)

**trans|fix** /trænsfɪks/ **(transfixes, transfixing, transfixed)** VERB = mesmerize If you **are transfixed** by something, it captures all of your interest or attention, so that you are unable to think of anything else or unable to act. ❑ *We were all transfixed by the images of the war.* (be V-ed) ♦ **trans|fixed** ADJ: v-link ADJ, ADJ after v *Her eyes were transfixed with terror... For hours he stood transfixed.*

**trans|form** /trænsfɔːrm/ ◆◇◇ **(transforms, transforming, transformed)** 1 VERB To **transform** something **into** something else means to change or convert it into that thing. ❑ *Your metabolic rate is the speed at which your body transforms food into energy...* (V n *into* n) *Delegates also discussed transforming them from a guerrilla force into a regular army.* (V n *from* n *into* n; Also V n) ♦ **trans|for|ma|tion** /trænsfərmeɪʃən/ **(transformations)** N-VAR: usu with supp *Norah made plans for the transformation of an attic room into a study... Chemical transformations occur.* 2 VERB To **transform** something or someone means to change them completely and suddenly so that they are much better or more attractive. ❑ *The Minister said the Urban Development Corporation was now transforming the area...* (V n) *He said she had transformed him from a hard-drinking womaniser into a devoted husband and father.* (V n *from* n *into* n; Also V n *into* n) ♦ **trans|for|ma|tion** N-VAR: usu with supp *In the last five years he's undergone a personal transformation.*

**trans|form|er** /trænsfɔːrmər/ **(transformers)** N-COUNT A **transformer** is a piece of electrical equipment which changes a voltage to a higher or lower voltage.

**trans|fu|sion** /trænsfjuːʒən/ **(transfusions)** N-VAR A **transfusion** is the same as a **blood transfusion**.

**trans|gen|der** /trænzdʒendər/ **(transgenders)** ADJ **Transgender** people, such as transsexuals, do not have a straightforward gender identity. ❑ *...a three-year-project designed to overcome prejudice towards gay, lesbian, bisexual and transgender people.* ♦ **Transgender** is also a noun. N-COUNT ❑ *Karen said she is a transgender – a man who wants to be a woman and is attracted to women.*

**trans|gen|ic** /trænzdʒenɪk/ ADJ: ADJ n **Transgenic** plants or animals contain genetic material that has been added to them from another species. [TECHNICAL] ❑ *...transgenic sheep that secrete a human protein into their milk.*

**trans|gress** /trænzgres/ **(transgresses, transgressing, transgressed)** VERB If someone **transgresses**, they break a moral law or a rule of behaviour. ❑ *If a politician transgresses, that is not the fault of the media.* (V) *...a monk who had transgressed against the law of celibacy...* (V *against* n) *It seemed to me that he had transgressed the boundaries of good taste.* (V n) ♦ **trans|gres|sion** /trænzgreʃən/ **(transgressions)** N-VAR *Tales of the candidate's alleged past transgressions have begun springing up.*

**trans|gres|sive** /trænzgresɪv/ ADJ **Transgressive** is used to describe actions that break a moral law or a rule of behaviour. [FORMAL] ❑ *To write and publish this poem was a daring, transgressive act.*

**trans|gres|sor** /trænzgresər/ **(transgressors)** N-COUNT A **transgressor** is someone who has broken a particular rule or law or has done something that is generally considered unacceptable. [FORMAL]

**tran|si|ence** /trænziəns, AM -nʃəns/ N-UNCOUNT If you talk about the **transience** of a situation, you mean that it lasts only a short time or is constantly changing. [FORMAL] ❑ *...the superficiality and transience of the club scene.*

**tran|si|ent** /trænziənt, AM -nʃənt/ ADJ **Transient** is used to describe a situation that lasts only a short time or is constantly changing. [FORMAL] ❑ *...the transient nature of high fashion.*

**tran|sis|tor** /trænzɪstər/ **(transistors)** 1 N-COUNT A **transistor** is a small electronic part in something such as a television or radio, which controls the flow of electricity. 2 N-COUNT A **transistor** or a **transistor radio** is a small portable radio. [OLD-FASHIONED]

**trans|it** /trænzɪt/ 1 N-UNCOUNT **Transit** is the carrying of goods or people by vehicle from one place to another. ❑ *During their talks, the two presidents discussed the transit of goods between the two countries.* ● PHRASE: v-link PHR, PHR after v If people or things are **in transit**, they are travelling or being taken from one place to another. ❑ *They were in transit to Bombay.* 2 ADJ: ADJ n A **transit** area is an area where people wait or where goods are kept between different stages of a journey. ❑ *...refugees arriving at the two transit camps.* 3 N-UNCOUNT: oft N n = transport A **transit system** is a system for moving people or goods from one place to another, for example using buses or trains. [AM]

> in BRIT, use **transport system**

**tran|si|tion** /trænzɪʃən/ ◆◇◇ **(transitions, transitioning, transitioned)** 1 N-VAR **Transition** is the process in which something changes from one state to another. ❑ *The transition to a multi-party democracy is proving to be difficult. ...a period of transition.* 2 VERB If someone **transitions from** one state or activity to another, they move gradually from one to the other. ❑ *Most of the discussion was on what needed to be done now as we transitioned from the security issues to the challenging economic issues...* (V *from* n) *There was a significant decline in the size of the business as the company transitioned to an intellectual property company.* (V *to* n; Also V n)

**tran|si|tion|al** /trænzɪʃənəl/ 1 ADJ: ADJ n A **transitional** period is one in which things are changing from one state to another. ❑ *...a transitional period following more than a decade of civil war.* 2 ADJ: ADJ n **Transitional** is used to describe something that happens or exists during a transitional period. ❑ *The main rebel groups have agreed to join in a meeting to set up a transitional government.*

**tran|si|tive** /trænzɪtɪv/ ADJ ≠ intransitive A **transitive** verb has a direct object.

**tran|si|tiv|ity** /trænzɪtɪvɪti/ N-UNCOUNT The **transitivity** of a verb is whether or not it is used with a direct object.

**tran|si|tory** /trænzɪtəri, AM -tɔːri/ ADJ = transient If you say that something is **transitory**, you mean that it lasts only for a short time. ❑ *Most teenage romances are transitory.*

**Trans|it van** **(Transit vans)** N-COUNT A **Transit van** is a type of van that is used for carrying goods. [BRIT, TRADEMARK]

**trans|late** /trænzleɪt/ **(translates, translating, translated)** 1 VERB If something that someone has said or written **is translated from** one language **into** another, it is said or written again in the second language. ❑ *Only a small number of Kadare's books have been translated into English...* (be V-ed *into/from* n) *Martin Luther translated the Bible into German...* (V n *into/from* n) *The Celtic word 'geis' is usually translated as 'taboo'...* (be V-ed *as* n) *The girls waited for Mr Esch to translate.* (V) *...Mr Mani by Yehoshua, translated from Hebrew by Hillel Halkin.* (V-ed; Also V n, V n *as* n) ♦ **trans|la|tion** N-UNCOUNT *The papers have been sent to Saudi Arabia for translation.* 2 VERB If a name, a word, or an expression **translates as** something in a different language, that is what it means in that language.

❑ *His family's Cantonese nickname for him translates as Never Sits Still.* [V as n] **3** If one thing **translates** or **is translated into** another, the second happens or is done as a result of the first. [VERB] ❑ *Reforming Warsaw's stagnant economy requires harsh measures that would translate into job losses...* [V into n] *Your decision must be translated into specific, concrete actions.* [be V-ed into n] **4** If you say that a remark, a gesture, or an action **translates as** something, or that you **translate** it **as** something, you decide that this is what its significance is. [VERB] ❑ *'I love him' often translates as 'He's better than nothing'...* [V as n] *I translated this as a mad desire to lock up every single person with HIV.* [V n as n] **5** → See also **translation**.

**trans|la|tion** /trænzleɪʃᵊn/ **(translations)** A **translation** is a piece of writing or speech that has been translated from a different language. [N-COUNT: also in N] ❑ *...MacNiece's excellent English translation of 'Faust'... I've only read Solzhenitsyn in translation.*

**trans|la|tor** /trænzleɪtəʳ/ **(translators)** A **translator** is a person whose job is translating writing or speech from one language to another. [N-COUNT]

**trans|lu|cent** /trænzluːsᵊnt/ **1** If a material is **translucent**, some light can pass through it. [ADJ] ❑ *The building is roofed entirely with translucent corrugated plastic.* **2** You use **translucent** to describe something that has a glowing appearance, as if light is passing through it. [ADJ] ❑ *She had fair hair, blue eyes and translucent skin.*

**trans|mis|sion** /trænzmɪʃᵊn/ **(transmissions)** **1** The **transmission** of something is the passing or sending of it to a different person or place. [N-UNCOUNT: usu with supp, n N, N of n] ❑ *Heterosexual contact is responsible for the bulk of HIV transmission. ...the transmission of knowledge and skills.* **2** The **transmission** of television or radio programmes is the broadcasting of them. [N-UNCOUNT] **3** A **transmission** is a broadcast. [N-COUNT] **4** The **transmission** on a car or other vehicle is the system of gears and shafts by which the power from the engine reaches and turns the wheels. [N-VAR] ❑ *The car was fitted with automatic transmission. ...a four-speed manual transmission.*

**trans|mit** /trænzmɪt/ **(transmits, transmitting, transmitted)** **1** When radio and television programmes, computer data, or other electronic messages **are transmitted**, they are sent from one place to another, using wires, radio waves, or satellites. [VERB] ❑ *The game was transmitted live in Spain and Italy...* [be V-ed] *This is currently the most efficient way to transmit certain types of data like electronic mail...* [V n] *The device is not designed to transmit to satellites.* [V to n] **2** If one person or animal **transmits** a disease to another, they have the disease and cause the other person or animal to have it. [FORMAL] [VERB] ❑ *...mosquitoes that transmit disease to humans...* [V n to n] *There was no danger of transmitting the infection through operations.* [V n] **3** If you **transmit** an idea or feeling to someone else, you make them understand and share the idea or feeling. [LITERARY] [VERB = convey] ❑ *He transmitted his keen enjoyment of singing to the audience.* [V n to n] **4** If an object or substance **transmits** something such as sound or electrical signals, the sound or signals are able to pass through it. [VERB] ❑ *These thin crystals transmit much of the power.* [V n]

**trans|mit|ter** /trænzmɪtəʳ/ **(transmitters)** A **transmitter** is a piece of equipment that is used for broadcasting television or radio programmes. [N-COUNT]

**trans|mute** /trænzmjuːt/ **(transmutes, transmuting, transmuted)** If something **transmutes** or **is transmuted into** a different form, it is changed into that form. [FORMAL] [VERB] ❑ *She ceased to think, as anger transmuted into passion...* [V into n] *Scientists transmuted matter into pure energy and exploded the first atomic bomb.* [V n into n, Also V n] ♦ **trans|mu|ta|tion** **(transmutations)** *...the transmutation of food into energy.* [N-VAR: oft N of n]

**trans|par|en|cy** /trænspærənsi, AM -per-/ **(transparencies)** **1** A **transparency** is a small piece of photographic film with a frame around it which can be projected onto a screen so that you can see the picture. [N-COUNT = slide] **2** **Transparency** is the quality that an object or substance has when you can see through it. [N-UNCOUNT] ❑ *Cataracts is a condition that affects the transparency of the lenses.* **3** The **transparency** of a process, situation, or statement is its quality of being easily understood or recognized, for example because there are no secrets connected with it, or because it is expressed in a clear way. [N-UNCOUNT] ❑ *The Chancellor emphasised his determination to promote openness and transparency in the Government's economic decision-making.*

**trans|par|ent** /trænspærənt, AM -per-/ **1** If an object or substance is **transparent**, you can see through it. [ADJ] ❑ *...a sheet of transparent coloured plastic.* **2** If a situation, system, or activity is **transparent**, it is easily understood or recognized. [ADJ] ❑ *The company has to make its accounts and operations as transparent as possible.* ♦ **trans|par|ent|ly** *The system was clearly not functioning smoothly or transparently.* [ADV: ADV adj, ADV with v] **3** You use **transparent** to describe a statement or action that is obviously dishonest or wrong, and that you think will not deceive people. [ADJ] ❑ *He thought he could fool people with transparent deceptions.* ♦ **trans|par|ent|ly** *To force this agreement on the nation is transparently wrong.* [ADV: ADV adj]

**tran|spire** /trænspaɪəʳ/ **(transpires, transpiring, transpired)** **1** When **it transpires that** something is the case, people discover that it is the case. [FORMAL] [VERB = turn out] ❑ *It transpired that Paolo had left his driving licence at home...* [it V that] *As it transpired, the Labour government did not dare go against the pressures exerted by the City.* [it V] **2** When something **transpires**, it happens. Some speakers of English consider this use to be incorrect. [VERB] ❑ *Nothing is known as yet about what transpired at the meeting.* [V]

**trans|plant** **(transplants, transplanting, transplanted)**

> The noun is pronounced /trænsplɑːnt, -plænt/. The verb is pronounced /trænsplɑːnt, -plænt/.

**1** A **transplant** is a medical operation in which a part of a person's body is replaced because it is diseased. [N-VAR] ❑ *He was recovering from a heart transplant operation. ...the controversy over the sale of human organs for transplant.* **2** If doctors **transplant** an organ such as a heart or a kidney, they use it to replace a patient's diseased organ. [VERB] ❑ *The operation to transplant a kidney is now fairly routine.* [V n] *...transplanted organs such as hearts and kidneys.* [V-ed] ♦ **trans|plan|ta|tion** /trænzplænteɪʃᵊn/ *...a shortage of kidneys for transplantation.* [N-UNCOUNT: usu with supp] **3** To **transplant** someone or something means to move them to a different place. [VERB] ❑ *Marriage had transplanted Rebecca from London to Manchester...* [V n from/to/into n] *Farmers will be able to seed it directly, rather than having to transplant seedlings.* [V n]

**trans|port** **(transports, transporting, transported)** ◆◆◇

> The noun is pronounced /trænspɔːʳt/. The verb is pronounced /trænspɔːʳt/.

**1** **Transport** refers to any vehicle that you can travel in or carry goods in. [mainly BRIT] [N-UNCOUNT] ❑ *Have you got your own transport?*

> in AM, usually use **transportation**

**2** **Transport** is a system for taking people or goods from one place to another, for example using buses or trains. [mainly BRIT] [N-UNCOUNT] ❑ *The extra money could be spent on improving public transport.*

> in AM, usually use **transportation**

**3** **Transport** is the activity of taking goods or people from one place to another in a vehicle. [mainly BRIT] [N-UNCOUNT] ❑ *Local production virtually eliminates transport costs.*

> in AM, usually use **transportation**

**4** To **transport** people or goods somewhere is to take them from one place to another in a vehicle. [VERB] ❑ *There's no petrol, so it's very difficult to transport goods...* [V n] *They use tankers to transport the oil to Los Angeles.* [V n prep/adv] **5** If you say that you **are transported** to [VERB] another place or time, you mean that something causes you to feel that you are living in the other place or at the other time. [mainly LITERARY] ❑ *Dr Drummond felt that he had been transported into a world that rivalled the Arabian Nights... This delightful musical comedy transports the audience to the innocent days of 1950s America.* — *be* V-ed prep/adv; V n prep/adv

**trans|por|ta|tion** /trænspɔːʳteɪʃᵊn/
1 **Transportation** refers to any type of vehicle that you can travel in or carry goods in. [mainly AM] ❑ *The company will provide transportation.* — N-UNCOUNT

✔ in BRIT, usually use **transport**

2 **Transportation** is a system for taking people or goods from one place to another, for example using buses or trains. [mainly AM] ❑ *Campuses are usually accessible by public transportation.* — N-UNCOUNT

✔ in BRIT, usually use **transport**

3 **Transportation** is the activity of taking goods or people from one place to another in a vehicle. [mainly AM] ❑ *Oxfam may also help with the transportation of refugees.* — N-UNCOUNT

✔ in BRIT, usually use **transport**

**trans|port|er** /trænspɔːʳtəʳ/ **(transporters)** A **transporter** is a large vehicle or an aeroplane that is used for carrying very large or heavy objects, for example cars. [mainly BRIT] — N-COUNT

**trans|pose** /trænspoʊz/ **(transposes, transposing, transposed)** 1 If you **transpose** something **from** one place or situation **to** another, you move it there. ❑ *Genetic engineers transpose or exchange bits of hereditary material from one organism to the next.* — VERB = transfer; V n *from* n *to* n ♦ **trans|po|si|tion** /trænspəzɪʃᵊn/ **(transpositions)** *...a transposition of 'Macbeth' to third century BC China.* — N-VAR: oft N *of* n 2 If you **transpose** two things, you reverse them or put them in each other's place. ❑ *Many people inadvertently transpose digits of the ZIP code.* — VERB = reverse; V n ♦ **trans|po|si|tion** *His pen name represented the transposition of his initials and his middle name.* — N-VAR: oft N *of* n

**trans|put|er** /trænspjuːtəʳ/ **(transputers)** A **transputer** is a type of fast powerful microchip. [COMPUTING] — N-COUNT

**trans|sex|ual** /trænsekʃuəl/ **(transsexuals)** A **transsexual** is a person who has decided that they want to live as a person of the opposite sex, and so has changed their name and appearance in order to do this. Transsexuals sometimes have an operation to change their sex. — N-COUNT

**trans|verse** /trænzvɜːʳs/ **Transverse** is used to describe something that is at right angles to something else. — ADJ: usu ADJ n

**trans|ves|tism** /trænzvestɪzəm/ **Transvestism** is the practice of wearing clothes normally worn by a person of the opposite sex, usually for pleasure. — N-UNCOUNT = cross-dressing

**trans|ves|tite** /trænzvestaɪt/ **(transvestites)** A **transvestite** is a person, usually a man, who enjoys wearing clothes normally worn by people of the opposite sex. — N-COUNT = cross-dresser

**trap** /træp/ **(traps, trapping, trapped)** 1 A **trap** is a device which is placed somewhere or a hole which is dug somewhere in order to catch animals or birds. — ◆◇◇ N-COUNT 2 If a person **traps** animals or birds, he or she catches them using traps. ❑ *The locals were encouraged to trap and kill the birds.* — VERB; V n 3 A **trap** is a trick that is intended to catch or deceive someone. ❑ *He was trying to decide whether the question was some sort of a trap.* — N-COUNT 4 If you **trap** someone **into** doing or saying something, you trick them so that they do or say it, although they did not want to. ❑ *Were you just trying to trap her into making some admission?... She had trapped him so neatly that he wanted to slap her.* — VERB; V n *into* -ing/n; V n 5 To **trap** someone, especially a criminal, means to capture them. [JOURNALISM] ❑ *The police knew that to trap the killer they had to play him at his own game.* — VERB; V n 6 A **trap** is an unpleasant situation that you cannot easily escape from. ❑ *The Government has found it's caught in a trap of its own making.* — N-COUNT: usu sing 7 If you **are trapped** somewhere, something falls onto you or blocks your way and prevents you from moving or escaping. ❑ *The train was trapped underground by a fire... The light aircraft then cartwheeled, trapping both men... Until he saw the trapped wagons and animals, he did not realize the full extent of the catastrophe.* — VERB; *be* V-ed; V n; V-ed 8 When something **traps** gas, water, or energy, it prevents it from escaping. ❑ *Wool traps your body heat, keeping the chill at bay... The volume of gas trapped on these surfaces can be considerable.* — VERB; V n; V-ed 9 → See also **trapped**, **booby-trap**, **death trap**, **poverty trap**.

PHRASES 10 If someone **falls into** the **trap of** doing something, they think or behave in a way which is not wise or sensible. ❑ *Many people fall into the trap of believing that home decorating must always be done on a large scale.* — PHRASE: V inflects, oft PHR *of* -ing 11 If someone tells you to **shut** your **trap** or **keep** your **trap shut**, they are telling you rudely that you should be quiet and not say anything. [INFORMAL, RUDE] — PHRASE: V inflects = shut up

**trap|door** **(trapdoors** /træpdɔːʳ/) also **trap door**. A **trapdoor** is a small horizontal door in a floor, a ceiling, or on a stage. — N-COUNT

**tra|peze** /trəpiːz/ **(trapezes)** A **trapeze** is a bar of wood or metal hanging from two ropes on which people in a circus swing and perform skilful movements. — N-COUNT

**trapped** /træpt/ If you feel **trapped**, you are in an unpleasant situation in which you lack freedom, and you feel you cannot escape from it. ❑ *...people who think of themselves as trapped in mundane jobs.* → See also **trap**. — ADJ: usu v-link ADJ

**trap|per** /træpəʳ/ **(trappers)** A **trapper** is a person who traps animals, especially for their fur. — N-COUNT

**trap|pings** /træpɪŋz/ The **trappings** of power, wealth, or a particular job are the extra things, such as decorations and luxury items, that go with it. — N-PLURAL: usu N *of* n [disapproval]

**trash** /træʃ/ **(trashes, trashing, trashed)**
1 **Trash** consists of unwanted things or waste material such as used paper, empty containers and bottles, and waste food. [AM] — N-UNCOUNT: also *the* N

✔ in BRIT, use **rubbish**

2 If you say that something such as a book, painting, or film is **trash**, you mean that it is of very poor quality. [INFORMAL] ❑ *Pop music doesn't have to be trash, it can be art.* — N-UNCOUNT = rubbish 3 If someone **trashes** a place or vehicle, they deliberately destroy it or make it very dirty. [INFORMAL] ❑ *Would they trash the place when the party was over?* — VERB = wreck; V n 4 If you **trash** people or their ideas, you criticize them very strongly and say that they are worthless. [mainly AM, INFORMAL] ❑ *People asked why the candidates spent so much time trashing each other.* — VERB = rubbish; V n 5 → See also **white trash**.

**trash can** **(trash cans)** A **trash can** is a large round container which people put their rubbish in and which is usually kept outside their house. [AM] — N-COUNT = garbage can

✔ in BRIT, use **dustbin**

**trashy** /træʃi/ **(trashier, trashiest)** If you describe something as **trashy**, you think it is of very poor quality. [INFORMAL] ❑ *I was reading some trashy romance novel.* — ADJ [disapproval] = rubbishy

**trat|to|ria** /trætəriːə/ **(trattorias)** A **trattoria** is an Italian restaurant. — N-COUNT

**trau|ma** /trɔːmə, AM traʊmə/ **(traumas)** **Trauma** is a very severe shock or very upsetting experience, which may cause psychological damage. ❑ *I'd been through the trauma of losing a house... The officers are claiming compensation for trauma after the disaster.* — N-VAR

**trau|mat|ic** /trɔːmætɪk, AM traʊ-/ A **traumatic** experience is very shocking and upsetting, and may cause psychological damage. ❑ *I suffered a nervous breakdown. It was a traumatic experience.* — ADJ

**trau|ma|tize** /trɔːmətaɪz, AM traʊ-/ **(traumatizes, traumatizing, traumatized)**

✔ in BRIT, also use **traumatise**

If someone **is traumatized** by an event or situation, it shocks or upsets them very much, and may cause them psychological damage. ❑ *My wife was traumatized by the experience... Did his parents traumatize him?... Traumatising a child with an abnormal fear of strangers probably won't do much good. ...young children traumatised by their parents' deaths.* VERB; *be* V-ed; V n; V n *with* n; V-ed
♦ **trau|ma|tized** *He left her in the middle of the road, shaking and deeply traumatized.* ADJ

**trav|ail** /trævеɪl, AM trəveɪl/ **(travails)** You can refer to unpleasant hard work or difficult problems as **travail**. [LITERARY] ❑ *He did whatever he could to ease their travail.* N-VAR

**trav|el** /trævᵊl/ **(travels, travelling, travelled)** ◆◆◇

✔ in AM, use **traveling, traveled**

[1] If you **travel**, you go from one place to another, often to a place that is far away. ❑ *You had better travel to Helsinki tomorrow... I've been traveling all day... Students often travel hundreds of miles to get here... I had been travelling at 150 kilometres an hour... He was a charming travelling companion.* VERB; V prep/adv; V; V amount/n; V *at* amount; V-ing
♦ **trav|el|ling** *I love travelling.* N-UNCOUNT [2] **Travel** is the activity of travelling. ❑ *He detested air travel. ...a writer of travel books.* N-UNCOUNT [3] If you **travel** the world, the country, or the area, you go to many different places in the world or in a particular country or area. ❑ *Dr Ryan travelled the world gathering material for his book.* VERB; V n [4] When light or sound from one place reaches another, you say that it **travels** to the other place. ❑ *When sound travels through water, strange things can happen... Light travels at around 300,000,000 metres per second.* VERB; V prep/adv; V *at* amount [5] When news becomes known by people in different places, you can say that it **travels** to them. ❑ *News of his work traveled all the way to Asia.* VERB; V adv/prep [6] Someone's **travels** are the journeys that they make to places a long way from their home. ❑ *He also collects things for the house on his travels abroad.* N-PLURAL: with poss, usu poss N [7] → See also **travelling**, **much-travelled**, **well-travelled**. [8] If you **travel light**, you travel without taking much luggage. PHRASE: V inflects

**trav|el agen|cy** **(travel agencies)** A **travel agency** is a business which makes arrangements for people's holidays and journeys. N-COUNT

**trav|el agent** **(travel agents)** [1] A **travel agent** or **travel agent's** is a shop or office where you can go to arrange a holiday or journey. ❑ *He worked in a travel agent's.* N-COUNT [2] A **travel agent** is a person or business that arranges people's holidays and journeys. N-COUNT

**trav|el|ler** /trævələʳ/ **(travellers)** ◆◇◇

✔ in AM, use **traveler**

[1] A **traveller** is a person who is making a journey or a person who travels a lot. ❑ *Many air travellers suffer puffy ankles and feet during long flights.* N-COUNT: oft supp N [2] A **traveller** is a person who travels from place to place, often living in a van or other vehicle, rather than living in one place. [BRIT] → See also **New Age traveller**. N-COUNT

**trav|el|ler's cheque** **(traveller's cheques)**

✔ in AM, use **traveler's check**

**Traveller's cheques** are cheques that you buy at a bank and take with you when you travel, for example so that you can exchange them for the currency of the country that you are in. N-COUNT: usu pl

**trav|el|ling** /trævəlɪŋ/

✔ in AM, use **traveling**

A **travelling** actor or musician, for example, is one who travels around an area or country performing in different places. ❑ *...travelling entertainers.* ADJ: ADJ n = *itinerant*

**trav|el|ling sales|man** **(travelling salesmen)**

✔ in AM, use **traveling salesman**

A **travelling salesman** is a salesman who travels to different places and meets people in order to sell goods or take orders. N-COUNT

**trav|elogue** /trævəlɒg, -lɔːg/ **(travelogues)** A **travelogue** is a talk or film about travel or about a particular person's travels. N-COUNT

**trav|el rep** **(travel reps)** A **travel rep** is the same as a **holiday rep**. [BRIT] N-COUNT

**trav|el sick|ness** If someone has **travel sickness**, they feel sick as a result of travelling in a vehicle. N-UNCOUNT

**trav|erse** /trævɜːʳs, trəvɜːʳs/ **(traverses, traversing, traversed)** If someone or something **traverses** an area of land or water, they go across it. [LITERARY] ❑ *I traversed the narrow pedestrian bridge.* VERB = *cross*; V n

**trav|es|ty** /trævəsti/ **(travesties)** If you describe something as a **travesty of** another thing, you mean that it is a very bad representation of that other thing. ❑ *Her research suggests that Smith's reputation today is a travesty of what he really stood for.* N-COUNT: oft N *of* n

**trawl** /trɔːl/ **(trawls, trawling, trawled)** [1] If you **trawl through** a large number of similar things, you search through them looking for something that you want or something that is suitable for a particular purpose. [BRIT] ❑ *A team of officers is trawling through the records of thousands of petty thieves... Her private secretary has carefully trawled the West End for a suitable show.* VERB; V *through* n; V n [2] When fishermen **trawl for** fish, they pull a wide net behind their ship in order to catch fish. ❑ *They had seen him trawling and therefore knew that there were fish... We came upon a fishing boat trawling for Dover sole.* VERB; V; V *for* n; Also V n

**trawl|er** /trɔːləʳ/ **(trawlers)** A **trawler** is a fishing boat that is used for trawling. N-COUNT

**tray** /treɪ/ **(trays)** A **tray** is a flat piece of wood, plastic, or metal, which usually has raised edges and which is used for carrying things, especially food and drinks. N-COUNT

**treach|er|ous** /tretʃərəs/ [1] If you describe someone as **treacherous**, you mean that they are likely to betray you and cannot be trusted. ❑ *He publicly left the party and denounced its treacherous leaders.* ADJ [disapproval] [2] If you say that something is **treacherous**, you mean that it is very dangerous and unpredictable. ❑ *The current of the river is fast flowing and treacherous.* ADJ

**treach|ery** /tretʃəri/ **(treacheries)** **Treachery** is behaviour or an action in which someone betrays their country or betrays a person who trusts them. N-UNCOUNT: also N in pl

**trea|cle** /triːkᵊl/ **Treacle** is a thick, sweet, sticky liquid that is obtained when sugar is processed. It is used in making cakes and puddings. [BRIT] N-UNCOUNT

✔ in AM, use **molasses**

**tread** /tred/ **(treads, treading, trod, trodden)**
[1] If you **tread on** something, you put your foot on it when you are walking or standing. ❑ *Oh, sorry, I didn't mean to tread on your foot.* VERB; V *on* n [2] If you **tread** in a particular way, you walk that way. [LITERARY] ❑ *She trod casually, enjoying the touch of the damp grass on her feet.* VERB; V adv [3] A person's **tread** is the sound that they make with their feet as they walk. [WRITTEN] ❑ *We could now very plainly hear their heavy tread.* N-SING: supp N, N *of* n [4] If you **tread** carefully, you behave in a careful or cautious way. ❑ *If you are hoping to form a new relationship tread carefully and slowly to begin with.* VERB; V adv [5] The **tread** of a step or stair is its flat upper surface. ❑ *He walked up the stairs. The treads were covered with a kind of rubber and very quiet.* N-COUNT [6] The **tread** of a tyre or shoe is the pattern of thin lines cut into its surface that stops it slipping. ❑ *The fat, broad tyres had a good depth of tread.* N-VAR
PHRASES [7] If someone is **treading a** fine **line** or **path**, they are acting carefully because they have to avoid making a serious mistake, especially in a situation where they have to deal with two opposing demands. ❑ *They have to tread the delicate path between informing children and boring them.* PHRASE: V inflects, oft PHR *between* pl-n [8] If you **tread** a particular **path**, you take a particular course of action or do something in a particular PHRASE: V inflects

way. ❑ *He continues to tread an unconventional path.* [9] If someone who is in deep water **treads water**, they float in an upright position by moving their legs slightly. PHRASE: V inflects [10] If you say that someone **is treading water**, you mean that they are in an unsatisfactory situation where they are not progressing, but are just continuing doing the same things. PHRASE: V inflects ❑ *I could either tread water until I was promoted, which looked to be a few years away, or I could change what I was doing.* [11] to **tread on** someone's **toes** → see **toe**.

**trea|dle** /tredᵊl/ **(treadles)** N-COUNT The **treadle** on a spinning wheel or sewing machine is a lever that you operate with your foot in order to turn a wheel in the machine.

**tread|mill** /tredmɪl/ **(treadmills)** [1] N-COUNT: usu sing You can refer to a task or a job as a **treadmill** when you have to keep doing it although it is unpleasant and exhausting. ❑ *Mr Stocks can expect a gruelling week on the publicity treadmill.* [2] N-COUNT A **treadmill** is a piece of equipment, for example an exercise machine, consisting of a wheel with steps around its edge or a continuous moving belt. The weight of a person or animal walking on it causes the wheel or belt to turn.

**trea|son** /triːzᵊn/ N-UNCOUNT **Treason** is the crime of betraying your country, for example by helping its enemies or by trying to remove its government using violence.

**trea|son|able** /triːzənəbᵊl/ ADJ **Treasonable** activities are criminal activities which someone carries out with the intention of helping their country's enemies or removing its government using violence. ❑ *They were brought to trial for treasonable conspiracy.*

**treas|ure** /treʒəʳ/ **(treasures, treasuring, treasured)** [1] N-UNCOUNT **Treasure** is a collection of valuable old objects such as gold coins and jewels that has been hidden or lost. [LITERARY] ❑ *It was here, the buried treasure, she knew it was.* [2] N-COUNT: usu pl **Treasures** are valuable objects, especially works of art and items of historical value. ❑ *The house was large and full of art treasures.* [3] VERB = cherish If you **treasure** something that you have, you keep it or care for it carefully because it gives you great pleasure and you think it is very special. ❑ V n *She treasures her memories of those joyous days.* ♦ N-COUNT **Treasure** is also a noun. ❑ *His greatest treasure is his collection of rock records.* ♦ ADJ: ADJ n **treas|ured** *These books are still among my most treasured possessions.* [4] N-COUNT = gem If you say that someone is a **treasure**, you mean that they are very helpful and useful to you. [INFORMAL] ❑ *Charlie? Oh, he's a treasure, loves children.*

**treas|ure chest** **(treasure chests)** [1] N-COUNT A **treasure chest** is a box containing treasure. [2] N-COUNT: usu N *of* n If you describe something as a **treasure chest of** a particular thing, you mean that it is very good source of that thing. ❑ *This book is a treasure chest of information.*

**treas|ur|er** /treʒərəʳ/ **(treasurers)** N-COUNT: oft N *of* n The **treasurer** of a society or organization is the person who is in charge of its finances and keeps its accounts.

**treas|ure trove** **(treasure troves)** [1] N-COUNT: usu sing, N *of* n If you describe something or someone as a **treasure trove of** a particular thing, you mean that they are a very good or rich source of that thing. ❑ *The dictionary is a vast treasure trove of information.* [2] N-COUNT: usu sing, oft N *for* n You can refer to a collection of valuable objects as a **treasure trove**.

**treas|ury** /treʒəri/ **(treasuries)** ◆◇◇ N-COUNT-COLL: usu *the* N in sing In Britain, the United States, and some other countries, **the Treasury** is the government department that deals with the country's finances.

**treat** /triːt/ **(treats, treating, treated)** ◆◆◇ [1] VERB If you **treat** someone or something in a particular way, you behave towards them or deal with them in that way. ❑ V n *with* n *Artie treated most women with indifference...* V n *as/like* n *Police say they're treating it as a case of attempted murder...* V n adv *She adored Paddy but he didn't treat her well.* [2] VERB When a doctor or nurse **treats** a patient or an illness, he or she tries to make the patient well again. ❑ V n *with* n *Doctors treated her with aspirin...* V n *for* n *The boy was treated for a minor head wound...* V n *An experienced nurse treats all minor injuries.* [3] VERB If something **is treated with** a particular substance, the substance is put onto or into it in order to clean it, to protect it, or to give it special properties. ❑ *be* V-ed *with* n *About 70% of the cocoa acreage is treated with insecticide...* V n *It was many years before the city began to treat its sewage.* [4] VERB If you **treat** someone **to** something special which they will enjoy, you buy it or arrange it for them. ❑ V n *to* n *She was always treating him to ice cream...* V pron-refl *to* n *Tomorrow I'll treat myself to a day's gardening...* V pron-refl *If you want to treat yourself, the Malta Hilton offers high international standards.* Also V n [5] N-COUNT If you give someone a **treat**, you buy or arrange something special for them which they will enjoy. ❑ *Lettie had never yet failed to return from town without some special treat for him.* [6] N-SING: poss N If you say that something is your **treat**, you mean that you are paying for it as a treat for someone else. [SPOKEN] [7] PHRASE: PHR after v If you say, for example, that something looks or works **a treat**, you mean that it looks very good or works very well. [BRIT, INFORMAL] ❑ *The first part of the plan works a treat.* [8] to **treat** someone **like dirt** → see **dirt**.

**treat|able** /triːtəbᵊl/ ADJ A **treatable** disease is one which can be cured or controlled, usually by the use of drugs. ❑ *This is a treatable condition... Depression is treatable.*

**trea|tise** /triːtɪz, AM -tɪs/ **(treatises)** N-COUNT: usu with supp, oft N *on* n A **treatise** is a long, formal piece of writing about a particular subject. ❑ *...Locke's Treatise on Civil Government.*

**treat|ment** /triːtmənt/ **(treatments)** ◆◆◇ [1] N-VAR: oft supp N, N *of/for* n **Treatment** is medical attention given to a sick or injured person or animal. ❑ *Many patients are not getting the medical treatment they need. ...an effective treatment for eczema.* [2] N-UNCOUNT: usu supp N, N *of* n Your **treatment** of someone is the way you behave towards them or deal with them. ❑ *We don't want any special treatment.* [3] N-VAR: usu N *of* n, supp N **Treatment** of something involves putting a particular substance onto or into it, in order to clean it, to protect it, or to give it special properties. ❑ *There should be greater treatment of sewage before it is discharged... As with all oily hair treatments, shampoo needs to be applied first.* [4] PHRASE: PHR after v If you say that someone is given **the full treatment**, you mean either that they are treated extremely well or that they are treated extremely severely. [INFORMAL] ❑ *If you've got friends or family coming to stay, make it really special by giving them the full treatment.*

**trea|ty** /triːti/ **(treaties)** ◆◆◇ N-COUNT A **treaty** is a written agreement between countries in which they agree to do a particular thing or to help each other. ❑ *...negotiations over a 1992 treaty on global warming.*

**tre|ble** /trebᵊl/ **(trebles, trebling, trebled)** [1] VERB = triple If something **trebles** or if you **treble** it, it becomes three times greater in number or amount than it was. ❑ V *They will have to pay much more when rents treble in January...* V n *The city has trebled the number of its prisoners to 21,000.* ♦ N-SING: oft N *of* n **tre|bling** *A new threat to Bulgaria's stability is the week-old miners' strike for a trebling of minimum pay.* [2] PREDET: PREDET det n = triple If one thing is **treble** the size or amount of another thing, it is three times greater in size or amount. ❑ *More than 7 million shares changed hands, treble the normal daily average.* [3] N-COUNT A **treble** is a boy with a very high singing voice. [4] N-COUNT In sport, a **treble** is three successes one after the other, for example winning three horse races on the same day, or winning three competitions in the same season. [mainly BRIT, JOURNALISM] ❑ *The win completed a treble for them – they already claimed a league and cup double this year.*

**tree** /triː/ **(trees)** ◆◆◇ [1] N-COUNT: oft n N A **tree** is a tall plant that has a hard trunk, branches, and leaves. ❑ *I planted those apple trees. ...a variety of shrubs and trees.* → See also **Christmas tree**, **family tree**.

**PHRASES** [2] PHRASE: If you say that someone **is barking**

**up the wrong tree**, you mean that they are following the wrong course of action because their beliefs or ideas about something are incorrect. [INFORMAL] ❑ *Scientists in Switzerland realised that most other researchers had been barking up the wrong tree.* — V inflects, usu cont
[3] If someone **can't see the wood for the trees** in British English, or **can't see the forest for the trees** in American English, they are very involved in the details of something and so they do not notice what is important about the thing as a whole. — PHRASE: V inflects
[4] **the top of the tree** → see **top**.

**tree|less** /triːləs/ A **treeless** area or place has no trees in it. — ADJ

**tree-lined** A **tree-lined** road or street has trees on either side. ❑ *...the broad, tree-lined avenues.* — ADJ: usu ADJ n

**tree|top** /triːtɒp/ **(treetops)** also **tree tops.** The **treetops** are the top branches of the trees in a wood or forest. — N-COUNT: usu pl

**tree trunk** **(tree trunks)** A **tree trunk** is the wide central part of a tree, from which the branches grow. — N-COUNT

**trek** /trek/ **(treks, trekking, trekked)** [1] If you **trek** somewhere, you go on a journey across difficult country, usually on foot. ❑ *...trekking through the jungles... This year we're going trekking in Nepal.* ♦ **Trek** is also a noun. ❑ *He is on a trek through the South Gobi desert.* [2] If you **trek** somewhere, you go there rather slowly and unwillingly, usually because you are tired. ❑ *They trekked from shop to shop in search of white knee-length socks.* — VERB; V prep/adv; V-ing; N-COUNT; VERB; V prep/adv

**trel|lis** /trelɪs/ **(trellises)** A **trellis** is a frame which supports climbing plants. — N-VAR

**trem|ble** /trembᵊl/ **(trembles, trembling, trembled)** [1] If you **tremble**, you shake slightly because you are frightened or cold. ❑ *His mouth became dry, his eyes widened, and he began to tremble all over... Gil was white and trembling with anger... With trembling fingers, he removed the camera from his pocket.* ♦ **Tremble** is also a noun. ❑ *I will never forget the look on the patient's face, the tremble in his hand.* [2] If something **trembles**, it shakes slightly. [LITERARY] ❑ *He felt the earth tremble under him.* [3] If your voice **trembles**, it sounds unsteady and uncertain, usually because you are upset or nervous. [LITERARY] ❑ *His voice trembled, on the verge of tears.* ♦ **Tremble** is also a noun. ❑ *'Please understand this,' she began, a tremble in her voice.* — VERB = shake; V; V with n; V-ing; N-SING: usu N in/of n; VERB = quiver; V; VERB = shake; V; N-SING: usu N in/of n

**tre|men|dous** /trɪmendəs/ [1] You use **tremendous** to emphasize how strong a feeling or quality is, or how large an amount is. [INFORMAL] ❑ *I felt a tremendous pressure on my chest.* ♦ **tre|men|dous|ly** *The business is tremendously profitable... I enjoyed the show tremendously.* [2] You can describe someone or something as **tremendous** when you think they are very good or very impressive. [INFORMAL] ❑ *I thought it was absolutely tremendous.* ♦ **tre|men|dous|ly** *I thought they played tremendously well, didn't you?* — ◆◇◇ ADJ: usu ADJ n [emphasis] = terrific; ADV: ADV adj/adv/-ed, ADV after v; ADJ = terrific; ADV: ADV adj/adv/-ed, ADV after v

**tremo|lo** /treməloʊ/ If someone's singing or speaking voice has a **tremolo** in it, it moves up and down instead of staying on the same note. — N-UNCOUNT: also a N

**trem|or** /tremər/ **(tremors)** [1] A **tremor** is a small earthquake. [2] If an event causes a **tremor** in a group or organization, it threatens to make the group or organization less strong or stable. ❑ *News of 160 redundancies had sent tremors through the community.* [3] A **tremor** is a shaking of your body or voice that you cannot control. ❑ *He felt a tremor in his arms.* — N-COUNT; N-COUNT: usu with supp; N-COUNT

**tremu|lous** /tremjʊləs/ If someone's voice, smile, or actions are **tremulous**, they are unsteady because the person is uncertain, afraid, or upset. [LITERARY] ❑ *She fidgeted in her chair as she took a deep, tremulous breath.* ♦ **tremu|lous|ly** *'He was so good to me,' she said tremulously.* — ADJ; ADV: ADV with v

**trench** /trentʃ/ **(trenches)** [1] A **trench** is a long narrow channel that is cut into the ground, for example in order to lay pipes or get rid of water. [2] A **trench** is a long narrow channel in the ground used by soldiers in order to protect themselves from the enemy. People often refer to the battle grounds of the First World War in Northern France and Belgium as **the trenches**. ❑ *We fought with them in the trenches. ...trench warfare.* — N-COUNT; N-COUNT: usu the N in pl, N n

**trench|ant** /trentʃənt/ You can use **trenchant** to describe something such as a criticism or comment that is very clear, effective, and forceful. [FORMAL] ❑ *He was shattered and bewildered by this trenchant criticism... His comment was trenchant and perceptive.* — ADJ

**trench coat** **(trench coats)** also **trenchcoat.** A **trench coat** is a type of raincoat with pockets and a belt. Trench coats are often similar in design to military coats. — N-COUNT

**trend** /trend/ **(trends)** [1] A **trend** is a change or development towards something new or different. ❑ *This is a growing trend. ...a trend towards part-time employment.* [2] To set a **trend** means to do something that becomes accepted or fashionable, and that a lot of other people copy. ❑ *The record has already proved a success and may well start a trend.* — ◆◇◇ N-COUNT; N-COUNT: usu sing

**trend-setter** **(trend-setters)** also **trendsetter.** A **trend-setter** is a person or institution that starts a new fashion or trend. — N-COUNT

**trendy** /trendi/ **(trendier, trendiest)** [1] If you say that something or someone is **trendy**, you mean that they are very fashionable and modern. [INFORMAL] ❑ *...a trendy London night club.* [2] If you describe someone who follows new ideas as **trendy**, you disapprove of them because they are more interested in being fashionable than in thinking seriously about these ideas. [INFORMAL] ❑ *Trendy teachers are denying children the opportunity to study classic texts.* — ADJ; ADJ: usu ADJ n [disapproval]

**trepi|da|tion** /trepɪdeɪʃᵊn/ **Trepidation** is fear or anxiety about something that you are going to do or experience. [FORMAL] ❑ *It was with some trepidation that I viewed the prospect of cycling across Uganda.* — N-UNCOUNT: oft with N = anxiety

**tres|pass** /trespəs/ **(trespasses, trespassing, trespassed)** [1] If someone **trespasses**, they go onto someone else's land without their permission. ❑ *They were trespassing on private property... You're trespassing!* ♦ **Trespass** is the act of trespassing. ❑ *You could be prosecuted for trespass.* ♦ **tres|pass|er** **(trespassers)** *Trespassers will be prosecuted.* [2] If you say that someone **is trespassing** on something, you mean that they are involving themselves in something that is not their concern. ❑ *They were acting to prevent the state from trespassing on family matters such as sex education.* — VERB; V prep; V; N-VAR; N-COUNT; VERB; V prep Also V

**tress** /tres/ **(tresses)** A woman's **tresses** are her long flowing hair. [LITERARY] — N-COUNT: usu pl

**tres|tle** /tresᵊl/ **(trestles)** A **trestle** is a wooden or metal structure that is used, for example, as one of the supports for a table. It has two pairs of sloping legs which are joined by a flat piece across the top. — N-COUNT

**tres|tle ta|ble** **(trestle tables)** A **trestle table** is a table made of a long board that is supported on trestles. — N-COUNT

**tri-** /traɪ-/ **Tri-** is used at the beginning of nouns and adjectives that have 'three' as part of their meaning. ❑ *...a tri-partite meeting... It was triangular in shape.* — PREFIX

**tri|ad** /traɪæd/ **(triads)**

> ✔ The spelling **Triad** is also used for meaning 1.

[1] The **Triads** were Chinese secret societies in old China that were often associated with organized crime. [2] A **triad** is a group of three similar things. [FORMAL] ❑ *For the faculty, there exists the triad of responsibilities: teaching, research, and service.* — N-COUNT: usu pl, oft N n; N-COUNT: oft N of n

**tri|age** /triːɑːʒ/ **Triage** is the process of quickly examining sick or injured people, for example after an accident or a battle, so that those — N-UNCOUNT: oft N n who are in the most serious condition can be treated first. [MEDICAL] ❑ *...the triage process.*

**tri|al** /traɪəl/ **(trials)** 1 A **trial** is a formal meeting in a law court, at which a judge and jury listen to evidence and decide whether a person is guilty of a crime. ❑ *New evidence showed the police lied at the trial... He's awaiting trial in a military court on charges of plotting against the state... They believed that his case would never come to trial.* 2 A **trial** is an experiment in which you test something by using it or doing it for a period of time to see how well it works. If something is **on trial**, it is being tested in this way. ❑ *They have been treated with this drug in clinical trials... The robots have been on trial for the past year.* 3 If someone gives you a **trial** for a job, or if you are **on trial**, you do the job for a short period of time to see if you are suitable for it. ❑ *He had just given a trial to a young woman who said she had previous experience.* 4 If you refer to the **trials of** a situation, you mean the unpleasant things that you experience in it. ❑ *...the trials of adolescence.* 5 In some sports or outdoor activities, **trials** are a series of contests that test a competitor's skill and ability. ❑ *He has been riding in horse trials for less than a year. ...Dovedale Sheepdog Trials.*
◆◆◇ N-VAR; N-VAR; N-COUNT: usu sing, also *on* N; N-COUNT: usu pl, N *of* n; N-COUNT: usu pl, supp N

PHRASES 6 If you do something **by trial and error**, you try several different methods of doing it until you find the method that works properly. ❑ *Many drugs were found by trial and error.* 7 If someone is **on trial**, they are being tried in a court of law. ❑ *He is currently on trial accused of serious drugs charges.* 8 If you say that someone or something is **on trial**, you mean that they are in a situation where people are observing them to see whether they succeed or fail. ❑ *The President will be drawn into a damaging battle in which his credentials will be on trial.* 9 If someone **stands trial**, they are tried in court for a crime they are accused of.
PHRASE: oft *by/through* PHR; PHRASE: v-link PHR, PHR after v; PHRASE: v-link PHR, PHR after v; PHRASE: V inflects, oft PHR *for* n

**tri|al bal|loon (trial balloons)** A **trial balloon** is a proposal that you mention or an action that you try in order to find out other people's reactions to it, especially if you think they are likely to oppose it. [mainly AM] ❑ *They floated the trial balloon of actually cutting Social Security.* N-COUNT

**tri|al run (trial runs)** A **trial run** is a first attempt at doing something to make sure you can do it properly. N-COUNT

**tri|an|gle** /traɪæŋgəl/ **(triangles)** 1 A **triangle** is an object, arrangement, or flat shape with three straight sides and three angles. ❑ *Its outline roughly forms an equilateral triangle. ...triangles of fried bread.* 2 The **triangle** is a musical instrument that consists of a piece of metal shaped like a triangle. You play it by hitting it with a short metal bar. 3 If you describe a group of three people as a **triangle**, you mean that they are all connected with each other in a particular situation, but often have different interests. ❑ *She plays a French woman in a love triangle with Jonathan Pryce and Christopher Walken.* ➔ See also **eternal triangle**.
N-COUNT; N-COUNT: usu sing, *the* N; N-COUNT: usu sing, with supp

**tri|an|gu|lar** /traɪæŋgjʊlər/ 1 Something that is **triangular** is in the shape of a triangle. ❑ *...cottages around a triangular green.* 2 You can describe a relationship or situation as **triangular** if it involves three people or things. ❑ *One particular triangular relationship became the model of Simone's first novel.* ADJ; ADJ

**tri|ath|lete** /traɪæθliːt/ **(triathletes)** A **triathlete** is someone who takes part in a **triathlon**. N-COUNT

**tri|ath|lon** /traɪæθlɒn/ **(triathlons)** A **triathlon** is an athletics competition in which each competitor takes part in three events; swimming, cycling, and running. N-COUNT: usu sing

**trib|al** /traɪbəl/ **Tribal** is used to describe things relating to or belonging to tribes and the way that they are organized. ❑ *They would go back to their tribal lands.* ADJ: usu ADJ n

**trib|al|ism** /traɪbəlɪzəm/ 1 **Tribalism** is the state of existing as a tribe. ❑ *Apartheid used tribalism as the basis of its 'divide-and-rule' homeland policies.* 2 You can use **tribalism** to refer to the loyalties that people feel towards particular social groups and to the way these loyalties affect their behaviour and their attitudes towards others. ❑ *His argument was that multi-party systems encourage tribalism.* N-UNCOUNT; N-UNCOUNT disapproval

**tribe** /traɪb/ **(tribes)** 1 **Tribe** is sometimes used to refer to a group of people of the same race, language, and customs, especially in a developing country. Some people disapprove of this use. ❑ *...three-hundred members of the Xhosa tribe.* 2 You can use **tribe** to refer to a group of people who are all doing the same thing or who all behave in the same way. [mainly HUMOROUS, INFORMAL] ❑ *...tribes of talented young people.* N-COUNT-COLL; N-COUNT-COLL: usu N *of* n, adj N

**tribes|man** /traɪbzmən/ **(tribesmen)** A **tribesman** is a man who belongs to a tribe. N-COUNT

**tribu|la|tion** /trɪbjʊleɪʃən/ **(tribulations)** You can refer to the suffering or difficulty that you experience in a particular situation as **tribulations**. [FORMAL] ❑ *...the trials and tribulations of everyday life.* N-VAR

**tri|bu|nal** /traɪbjuːnəl/ **(tribunals)** A **tribunal** is a special court or committee that is appointed to deal with particular problems. ❑ *His case comes before an industrial tribunal in March.* N-COUNT-COLL

**tribu|tary** /trɪbjʊtəri, AM -teri/ **(tributaries)** A **tributary** is a stream or river that flows into a larger one. ❑ *...the Napo river, a tributary of the Amazon.* N-COUNT: oft N n

**trib|ute** /trɪbjuːt/ **(tributes)** 1 A **tribute** is something that you say, do, or make to show your admiration and respect for someone. ❑ *The song is a tribute to Roy Orbison... He paid tribute to the organising committee.* 2 If one thing is **a tribute to** another, the first thing is the result of the second and shows how good it is. ❑ *His success has been a tribute to hard work, to professionalism.* N-VAR: usu N *to* n; N-SING: *a* N, usu N *to* n, N *to* n that

**trice** /traɪs/ If someone does something **in a trice**, they do it very quickly. ❑ *He will sew it up in a trice... She was back in a trice.* PHRASE: PHR with v, PHR with cl

**tri|ceps** /traɪseps/ **(triceps)** Your **triceps** is the muscle in the back part of your upper arm. N-COUNT

**trick** /trɪk/ **(tricks, tricking, tricked)** 1 A **trick** is an action that is intended to deceive someone. ❑ *We are playing a trick on a man who keeps bothering me.* 2 If someone **tricks** you, they deceive you, often in order to make you do something. ❑ *Stephen is going to be pretty upset when he finds out how you tricked him... His family tricked him into going to Pakistan, and once he was there, they took away his passport... His real purpose is to trick his way into your home to see what he can steal.* 3 A **trick** is a clever or skilful action that someone does in order to entertain people. ❑ *He shows me card tricks.* 4 A **trick** is a clever way of doing something. ❑ *Tiffany revamped her sitting room with simple decorative tricks.* 5 ➔ See also **confidence trick, conjuring trick, hat-trick**.
◆◇◇ N-COUNT; VERB; V n; V n *into* -ing/n; V *way* prep/adv; N-COUNT; N-COUNT

PHRASES 6 If something **does the trick**, it achieves what you wanted. [INFORMAL] ❑ *Sometimes a few choice words will do the trick.* 7 If someone tries **every trick in the book**, they try every possible thing that they can think of in order to achieve something. [INFORMAL] ❑ *Companies are using every trick in the book to stay one step in front of their competitors.* 8 If you say that something is a **trick of the light**, you mean that what you are seeing is an effect caused by the way that the light falls on things, and does not really exist in the way that it appears. ❑ *Her head appears to be on fire but that is only a trick of the light.* 9 If you say that someone does not **miss a trick**, you mean that they always know what is happening and take advantage of every situation. [INFORMAL] 10 The **tricks of the trade** are the quick and clever ways of doing something that are known by people who regularly do a particular activity. 11 If you
PHRASE: V inflects; PHRASE: v PHR; PHRASE: v-link PHR; PHRASE: V inflects, with brd-neg; PHRASE: *trick* inflects; PHRASE:

v-link PHR, disapproval — say that someone is **up to** their **tricks** or **up to** their **old tricks**, you disapprove of them because they are behaving in the dishonest or deceitful way in which they typically behave. [INFORMAL] ❑ *I have no respect for my father who, having remarried, is still up to his old tricks.*

**trick|ery** /trɪkəri/ N-UNCOUNT **Trickery** is the use of dishonest methods in order to achieve something.

**trick|le** /trɪkᵊl/ **(trickles, trickling, trickled)** [1] VERB When a liquid **trickles**, or when you **trickle** it, it flows slowly in very small amounts. ❑ V prep/adv *A tear trickled down the old man's cheek...* V n *Trickle water gently over the back of your baby's head.* ♦ N-COUNT: usu sing **Trickle** is also a noun. ❑ *There was not so much as a trickle of water.* [2] VERB When people or things **trickle** in a particular direction, they move there slowly in small groups or amounts, rather than all together. ❑ V adv/prep *Some donations are already trickling in.* ♦ N-COUNT: usu sing **Trickle** is also a noun. ❑ *The flood of cars has now slowed to a trickle.*

**trickle-down** ADJ: ADJ n The **trickle-down** theory is the theory that benefits given to people at the top of a system will eventually be passed on to people lower down the system. For example, if the rich receive tax cuts, they will pass these benefits on to the poor by creating jobs. ❑ *The government is not simply relying on trickle-down economics to tackle poverty.*

**trick or treat** N-UNCOUNT **Trick or treat** is an activity in which children knock on the doors of houses at Halloween and shout 'trick or treat'. If the person who answers the door does not give the children a treat, such as sweets or candy, they play a trick on him or her.

**trick ques|tion** N-COUNT **(trick questions)** If someone asks you a **trick question**, they ask you a question which is very difficult to answer, for example because there is a hidden difficulty or because the answer that seems obvious is not the correct one.

**trick|ster** /trɪkstəʳ/ N-COUNT **(tricksters)** A **trickster** is a person who deceives or cheats people, often in order to get money from them. [INFORMAL]

**tricky** /trɪki/ **(trickier, trickiest)** [1] ADJ If you describe a task or problem as **tricky**, you mean that it is difficult to do or deal with. ❑ *Parking can be tricky in the town centre.* [2] ADJ: usu ADJ n If you describe a person as **tricky**, you mean that they are likely to deceive you or cheat you.

**tri|col|our** /trɪkələʳ/ **(tricolours)** also **tricolor**. N-COUNT A **tricolour** is a flag which is made up of blocks of three different colours.

**tri|cy|cle** /traɪsɪkᵊl/ N-COUNT **(tricycles)** A **tricycle** is a cycle with three wheels, two at the back and one at the front. Tricycles are usually ridden by children.

**tried** /traɪd/ ADJ: ADJ *and* adj **Tried** is used in the expressions **tried and tested**, **tried and trusted**, and **tried and true**, which describe a product or method that has already been used and has been found to be successful. ❑ *...over 1000 tried-and-tested recipes.* → See also **try**, **well-tried**.

**tri|er** /traɪəʳ/ N-COUNT, approval **(triers)** If you say that someone is a **trier**, you approve of them because they try very hard at things that they do, although they are not often successful. [BRIT] ❑ *He may not always achieve greatness but at least he's a trier.*

**tri|fle** /traɪfᵊl/ **(trifles, trifling, trifled)** [1] PHRASE: PHR adj/adv/prep, vagueness You can use **a trifle** to mean slightly or to a small extent, especially in order make something you say seem less extreme. ❑ *As a photographer, he'd found both locations just a trifle disappointing.* [2] N-COUNT A **trifle** is something that is considered to have little importance, value, or significance. ❑ *He had no money to spare on trifles.* [3] N-VAR **Trifle** is a cold dessert made of layers of sponge cake, jelly, fruit, and custard, and usually covered with cream.

♦ **trifle with** PHRASAL VERB: usu with brd-neg If you say that someone is **not** a person **to be trifled with**, you are indicating to other people that they must treat that person with respect. ❑ be V-ed P *He was not someone to be trifled with...* V P n *No man in Tabriz trifled with the executioner.*

**tri|fling** /traɪfəlɪŋ/ ADJ: oft *a* ADJ amount = *trivial* A **trifling** matter is small and unimportant. ❑ *Outside California these difficulties may seem fairly trifling. ...a comparatively trifling 360 yards.*

**trig|ger** /trɪgəʳ/ ◆◇◇ **(triggers, triggering, triggered)** [1] N-COUNT The **trigger** of a gun is a small lever which you pull to fire it. ❑ *A man pointed a gun at them and pulled the trigger.* [2] N-COUNT: oft N n The **trigger** of a bomb is the device which causes it to explode. ❑ *...trigger devices for nuclear weapons.* [3] VERB = *activate* To **trigger** a bomb or system means to cause it to work. ❑ V n *The thieves must have deliberately triggered the alarm and hidden inside the house.* [4] VERB If something **triggers** an event or situation, it causes it to begin to happen or exist. ❑ V n *...the incident which triggered the outbreak of the First World War.* ♦ PHRASAL VERB **Trigger off** means the same as **trigger**. ❑ V P n (not pron) Also V n P *It is still not clear what events triggered off the demonstrations.* [5] N-COUNT: oft N *for* n If something acts as a **trigger for** another thing such as an illness, event, or situation, the first thing causes the second thing to begin to happen or exist. ❑ *Stress may act as a trigger for these illnesses.*

**trigger-happy** also **trigger happy**. ADJ, disapproval If you describe someone as **trigger-happy**, you disapprove of them because they are too ready and willing to use violence and weapons, especially guns. [INFORMAL] ❑ *Some of them are a bit trigger-happy – they'll shoot at anything that moves.*

**trigo|nom|etry** /trɪgənɒmɪtri/ N-UNCOUNT **Trigonometry** is the branch of mathematics that is concerned with calculating the angles of triangles or the lengths of their sides.

**trike** /traɪk/ N-COUNT **(trikes)** A **trike** is a child's **tricycle**. [INFORMAL]

**tril|by** /trɪlbi/ N-COUNT **(trilbies)** A **trilby** or a **trilby hat** is a man's hat which is made of felt and has a groove along the top from front to back. [BRIT]

**trill** /trɪl/ **(trills, trilling, trilled)** [1] VERB If a bird **trills**, it sings with short, high-pitched, repeated notes. ❑ V *At one point a bird trilled in the Conservatory.* [2] VERB If you say that a woman **trills**, you mean that she talks or laughs in a high-pitched voice which sounds rather musical but which also sounds rather irritating. ❑ V with quote *'How adorable!' she trills.* [3] N-COUNT A **trill** is the playing of two musical notes repeatedly and quickly one after the other. [TECHNICAL]

**tril|lion** /trɪljən/ **(trillions)**

> ✓ The plural form is **trillion** after a number, or after a word or expression referring to a number, such as 'several' or 'a few'.

NUM: usu *a*/num NUM A **trillion** is a million million. ❑ *Between July 1st and October 1st, the central bank printed over 2 trillion roubles.*

**tril|ogy** /trɪlədʒi/ N-COUNT: oft N *of* n, supp N **(trilogies)** A **trilogy** is a series of three books, plays, or films that have the same subject or the same characters.

**trim** /trɪm/ **(trimmer, trimmest, trims, trimming, trimmed)** [1] ADJ Something that is **trim** is neat, tidy, and attractive. ❑ *The neighbours' gardens were trim and neat.* [2] ADJ, approval If you describe someone's figure as **trim**, you mean that it is attractive because there is no extra fat on their body. ❑ *The driver was a trim young woman of perhaps thirty.* [3] VERB If you **trim** something, for example someone's hair, you cut off small amounts of it in order to make it look neater and tidier. ❑ V n *My friend trims my hair every eight weeks.* ♦ N-SING **Trim** is also a noun. ❑ *His hair needed a trim.* [4] VERB If a government or other organization **trims** something such as a plan, policy, or amount, they reduce it slightly in extent or size. ❑ V n *American companies looked at ways they could trim these costs.* [5] VERB: usu passive If something such as a piece of clothing **is trimmed with** a type of material or design, it is decorated with it, usually along its edges. ❑ be V-ed *with* n *...jackets, which are then trimmed with crocheted flowers.* ♦ COMB in ADJ **-trimmed** *He wears a fur-trimmed* *coat.* 6 The **trim** on something such as a piece of clothing is a decoration, for example along its edges, that is in a different colour or material. ❑ *...a white satin scarf with black trim.* N-VAR = trimming 7 When people are **in trim** or **in good trim**, they are in good physical condition. ❑ *He is already getting in trim for the big day.* PHRASE: v-link PHR, PHR after v

**tri|ma|ran** /traɪmərӕn/ **(trimarans)** A **trimaran** is a fast sailing boat similar to a catamaran, but with three hulls instead of two. N-COUNT

**trim|ming** /trɪmɪŋ/ **(trimmings)** 1 The **trimming** on something such as a piece of clothing is the decoration, for example along its edges, that is in a different colour or material. ❑ *...the lace trimming on her satin nightgown.* N-VAR: usu supp N = trim 2 **Trimmings** are pieces of something, usually food, which are left over after you have cut what you need. ❑ *Use any pastry trimmings to decorate the apples.* N-PLURAL 3 If you say that something comes with **all the trimmings**, you mean that it has many extra things added to it to make it more special. ❑ *They were married with all the trimmings, soon after graduation.* PHRASE: with/and PHR

**Trini|ty** /trɪnɪti/ In the Christian religion, **the Trinity** or **the Holy Trinity** is the union of the Father, the Son, and the Holy Spirit in one God. N-PROPER: the N

**trin|ket** /trɪŋkɪt/ **(trinkets)** A **trinket** is a pretty piece of jewellery or small ornament that is inexpensive. N-COUNT

**trio** /triːoʊ/ **(trios)** A **trio** is a group of three people together, especially musicians or singers, or a group of three things that have something in common. N-COUNT-COLL

**trip** /trɪp/ **(trips, tripping, tripped)** ◆◆◇ 1 A **trip** is a journey that you make to a particular place. ❑ *On the Thursday we went out on a day trip... Mark was sent to the Far East on a business trip.* ➔ See also **round trip**. N-COUNT 2 If you **trip** when you are walking, you knock your foot against something and fall or nearly fall. ❑ *She tripped and fell last night and broke her hip... He tried to follow Jack's footsteps in the snow and tripped on a rock.* VERB V V on/over n ♦ **Trip up** means the same as **trip**. ❑ *I tripped up and hurt my foot... Make sure trailing flexes are kept out of the way so you don't trip up over them.* PHRASAL VERB V P V P on/over n 3 If you **trip** someone who is walking or running, you put your foot or something else in front of them, so that they knock their own foot against it and fall or nearly fall. ❑ *One guy stuck his foot out and tried to trip me.* VERB V n ♦ **Trip up** means the same as **trip**. ❑ *He made a sudden dive for Uncle Jim's legs to try to trip him up.* PHRASAL VERB V n P 4 If you say that someone is, for example, on a power **trip**, a guilt **trip**, or a nostalgia **trip**, you mean that their behaviour is motivated by power, guilt, or nostalgia. [INFORMAL] ❑ *There's such pressure to be happy in Hawaii, if you're unhappy you're on a guilt trip... The biggest star perk, and the biggest power trip, must be the private plane.* N-COUNT: usu on n N [disapproval] 5 A **trip** is an experience that someone has when their mind is affected by a drug such as LSD. [INFORMAL] N-COUNT 6 If someone **is tripping**, they are having an experience in which their mind is affected by a drug such as LSD. [INFORMAL] ❑ *One night I was tripping on acid.* VERB: usu cont V on n Also V 7 If someone **trips** somewhere, they walk there with light, quick steps. [LITERARY] ❑ *A girl in a red smock tripped down the hill.* VERB V prep/adv

♦ **trip up** If someone or something **trips** a person **up**, or if they **trip up**, they fail or make a mistake. ❑ *Your own lies will trip you up... He will do all he can to trip up the new right-wing government... The two occasions she tripped up tell you nothing about how often she got away with it.* ➔ See also **trip 2, 3**. PHRASAL VERB V n P V P n (not pron) V P

**tri|par|tite** /traɪpɑːʳtaɪt/ You can use **tripartite** to describe something that has three parts or that involves three groups of people. [FORMAL] ❑ *...tripartite meetings between Government ministers, trades union leaders and industrialists.* ADJ: usu ADJ n

**tripe** /traɪp/ 1 **Tripe** is the stomach of a pig, cow, or ox which is eaten as food. N-UNCOUNT 2 You refer to something that someone has said or written as **tripe** when you think that it is silly and worthless. [INFORMAL] ❑ *I've never heard such a load of tripe in all my life.* N-UNCOUNT = rubbish

**tri|ple** /trɪpᵊl/ **(triples, tripling, tripled)** 1 **Triple** means consisting of three things or parts. ❑ *...a triple somersault... In 1882 Germany, Austria, and Italy formed the Triple Alliance.* ADJ: ADJ n 2 If something **triples** or if you **triple** it, it becomes three times as large in size or number. ❑ *I got a fantastic new job and my salary tripled... The Exhibition has tripled in size from last year... The merger puts the firm in a position to triple its earnings.* VERB = treble V V in n V n 3 If something is **triple the** amount or size of another thing, it is three times as large. ❑ *The mine reportedly had an accident rate triple the national average.* PREDET: PREDET the n = treble

**tri|ple jump** **The triple jump** is an athletic event in which competitors have to jump as far as they can, and are allowed to touch the ground once with each foot in the course of the jump. N-SING: usu the N

**tri|plet** /trɪplət/ **(triplets)** **Triplets** are three children born at the same time to the same mother. N-COUNT: usu pl

**tri|pod** /traɪpɒd/ **(tripods)** A **tripod** is a stand with three legs that is used to support something such as a camera or a telescope. N-COUNT

**trip|per** /trɪpəʳ/ **(trippers)** A **tripper** is a person who is on a trip or on holiday. [mainly BRIT, INFORMAL] ❑ *...when the shops shut and the trippers go home.* ➔ See also **day-tripper**. N-COUNT

**trip|tych** /trɪptɪk/ **(triptychs)** A **triptych** is a painting or a carving on three panels that are usually joined together by hinges. N-COUNT

**trip|wire** /trɪpwaɪəʳ/ **(tripwires)** also **trip wire.** A **tripwire** is a wire stretched just above the ground, which sets off something such as a trap or an explosion if someone touches it. N-COUNT

**trite** /traɪt/ If you say that something such as an idea, remark, or story is **trite**, you mean that it is dull and boring because it has been said or told too many times. ❑ *The movie is teeming with obvious and trite ideas.* ADJ = clichéd

**tri|umph** /traɪʌmf/ **(triumphs, triumphing, triumphed)** ◆◇◇ 1 A **triumph** is a great success or achievement, often one that has been gained with a lot of skill or effort. ❑ *The championships proved to be a personal triumph for the coach, Dave Donovan... Cataract operations are a triumph of modern surgery, with a success rate of more than 90 percent.* N-VAR 2 **Triumph** is a feeling of great satisfaction and pride resulting from a success or victory. ❑ *Her sense of triumph was short-lived.* N-UNCOUNT 3 If someone or something **triumphs**, they gain complete success, control, or victory, often after a long or difficult struggle. ❑ *All her life, Kelly had stuck with difficult tasks and challenges, and triumphed... The whole world looked to her as a symbol of good triumphing over evil.* VERB V V over n

**tri|um|phal** /traɪʌmfᵊl/ **Triumphal** is used to describe things that are done or made to celebrate a victory or great success. ❑ *He made a triumphal entry into the city.* ADJ: usu ADJ n

**tri|um|phal|ism** /traɪʌmfəlɪzəm/ People sometimes refer to behaviour which celebrates a great victory or success as **triumphalism**, especially when this behaviour is intended to upset the people they have defeated. [mainly BRIT, JOURNALISM] ❑ *There was a touch of triumphalism about the occasion.* N-UNCOUNT

**tri|umph|al|ist** /traɪʌmfəlɪst/ **Triumphalist** behaviour is behaviour in which politicians or organizations celebrate a victory or a great success, especially when this is intended to upset the people they have defeated. [mainly BRIT, JOURNALISM] ❑ *...a triumphalist celebration of their supremacy.* ADJ: ADJ n

**tri|um|phant** /traɪʌmfənt/ Someone who is **triumphant** has gained a victory or succeeded in something and feels very happy about it. ❑ *The captain's voice was triumphant... This trip was not like his first triumphant return home in 1990.* ADJ

♦ **tri|um|phant|ly** *They marched triumphantly into the capital.* [ADV: ADV with v, ADV with cl]

**tri|um|vi|rate** /traɪʌmvɪrət/ A **triumvirate** is a group of three people who work together, especially when they are in charge of something. [FORMAL] ❑ *...the triumvirate of women who worked together on the TV dramatisation of the novel.* [N-SING-COLL: oft N *of* n]

**trivia** /trɪviə/ 1 **Trivia** is unimportant facts or details that are considered to be amusing rather than serious or useful. ❑ *The two men chatted about such trivia as their favourite kinds of fast food.* [N-UNCOUNT] 2 A **trivia** game or competition is one where the competitors are asked questions about interesting but unimportant facts in many subjects. ❑ *...a pub trivia game.* [ADJ: ADJ n]

**triv|ial** /trɪviəl/ If you describe something as **trivial**, you think that it is unimportant and not serious. ❑ *The director tried to wave aside these issues as trivial details that could be settled later.* [ADJ]

**trivi|al|ity** /trɪviælɪti/ **(trivialities)** If you refer to something as a **triviality**, you think that it is unimportant and not serious. ❑ *He accused me of making a great fuss about trivialities... Interviews with politicians were juxtaposed with news items of quite astonishing triviality.* [N-VAR]

**trivi|al|ize** /trɪviəlaɪz/ **(trivializes, trivializing, trivialized)**

✔ in BRIT, also use **trivialise**

If you say that someone **trivializes** something important, you disapprove of them because they make it seem less important, serious, and complex than it is. ❑ *It never ceases to amaze me how the business world continues to trivialize the world's environmental problems.* [VERB] [disapproval] [V n]

**trod** /trɒd/ **Trod** is the past tense of **tread**.

**trod|den** /trɒdᵊn/ **Trodden** is the past participle of **tread**.

**trog|lo|dyte** /trɒglədaɪt/ **(troglodytes)** 1 A **troglodyte** is someone who lives in a cave. [FORMAL] [N-COUNT] 2 If you refer to someone as a **troglodyte**, you mean that they are unsophisticated and do not know very much about anything. ❑ *He dismissed advocates of a completely free market as economic troglodytes with no concern for the social consequences.* [N-COUNT] [disapproval]

**troi|ka** /trɔɪkə/ **(troikas)** Journalists sometimes refer to a group of three powerful politicians or states as a **troika**. ❑ *...leader of the troika of past, present and future presidents.* [N-COUNT: usu sing, oft N *of* n]

**Tro|jan horse** /troʊdʒən hɔːʳs/ **(Trojan horses)** 1 If you describe a person or thing as a **Trojan horse**, you mean that they are being used to hide someone's true purpose or intentions. ❑ *Was Colombo the emissary of Pope Paul, his Trojan horse within the Commission?* [N-COUNT: usu sing, oft N *for/of* n] [disapproval] 2 A **Trojan horse** is a computer virus which is inserted into a program or system and is designed to take effect after a particular period of time or a certain number of operations. [COMPUTING] [N-COUNT]

**troll** /trɒl, troʊl/ **(trolls, trolling, trolled)** 1 In Scandinavian mythology, **trolls** are creatures who look like ugly people. They live in caves or on mountains and steal children. [N-COUNT] 2 If you **troll** somewhere, you go there in a casual and unhurried way. [mainly BRIT, INFORMAL] ❑ *I trolled along to see Michael Frayn's play, 'Noises Off'.* [VERB] [V prep/adv] 3 If you **troll through** papers or files, you look through them in a fairly casual way. [mainly BRIT, INFORMAL] ❑ *Trolling through the files revealed a photograph of me drinking coffee in the office.* [VERB] [V *through* n]

**trol|ley** /trɒli/ **(trolleys)** 1 A **trolley** is an object with wheels that you use to transport heavy things such as shopping or luggage. [BRIT] ❑ *A porter relieved her of the three large cases she had been pushing on a trolley. ...supermarket trolleys.* [N-COUNT]

✔ in AM, use **cart**

2 A **trolley** is a small table on wheels which is used for serving drinks or food. [BRIT] [N-COUNT]

✔ in AM, use **cart**

3 A **trolley** is a bed on wheels for moving patients in hospital. [BRIT] [N-COUNT]

✔ in AM, use **gurney**

4 A **trolley** or **trolley car** is an electric vehicle for carrying people which travels on rails in the streets of a town. [AM] ❑ *He took a northbound trolley on State Street.* [N-COUNT] [= streetcar]

✔ in BRIT, use **tram**

5 If you say that someone is **off** their **trolley**, you mean that their ideas or behaviour are very strange. [BRIT, INFORMAL] [PHRASE: usu v-link PHR] [= mad]

**trol|ley bus** **(trolley buses)** A **trolley bus** is a bus that is driven by electric power taken from cables above the street. [N-COUNT: also *by* N]

**trom|bone** /trɒmboʊn/ **(trombones)** A **trombone** is a large musical instrument of the brass family. It consists of two long oval tubes, one of which can be pushed backwards and forwards to play different notes. [N-VAR: oft *the* N]

**trom|bon|ist** /trɒmboʊnɪst/ **(trombonists)** A **trombonist** is someone who plays the trombone. [N-COUNT]

**trompe l'oeil** /trɒmp lɔɪ/ **(trompe l'oeils)** 1 **Trompe l'oeil** is a technique used in art in which objects are painted their normal size in a very realistic way, to make people think that the objects are solid and real. ❑ *...a trompe l'oeil painting.* [N-UNCOUNT: oft N n] 2 A **trompe l'oeil** is a trompe l'oeil painting. [N-COUNT]

**troop** /truːp/ **(troops, trooping, trooped)** ◆◆◇ 1 **Troops** are soldiers, especially when they are in a large organized group doing a particular task. ❑ *The next phase of the operation will involve the deployment of more than 35,000 troops from a dozen countries.* [N-PLURAL] 2 A **troop** is a group of soldiers within a cavalry or armoured regiment. ❑ *...a troop of enemy cavalry trotting towards the Dutch right flank.* [N-COUNT-COLL] 3 A **troop of** people or animals is a group of them. ❑ *Amy was aware of the little troop of travellers watching the two of them.* [N-COUNT: N *of* n] 4 If people **troop** somewhere, they walk there in a group, often in a sad or tired way. [INFORMAL] ❑ *They all trooped back to the house for a rest.* [VERB] [V adv/prep]

**troop|er** /truːpəʳ/ **(troopers)** 1 A **trooper** is a soldier of low rank in the cavalry or in an armoured regiment in the army. ❑ *...a trooper from the 7th Cavalry.* [N-COUNT; N-TITLE] 2 In the United States, a **trooper** is a police officer in a state police force. ❑ *Once long ago he had considered becoming a state trooper.* [N-COUNT] 3 → See also **storm trooper**.

**troop|ship** /truːpʃɪp/ **(troopships)** also **troop ship**. A **troopship** is a ship on which large numbers of soldiers are taken from one place to another. [N-COUNT]

**tro|phy** /troʊfi/ **(trophies)** 1 A **trophy** is a prize, for example a silver cup, that is given to the winner of a competition or race. [N-COUNT] 2 **Trophy** is used in the names of some competitions and races in which the winner receives a trophy. ❑ *He finished third in the Tote Gold Trophy.* [N-IN-NAMES] 3 A **trophy** is something that you keep in order to show that you have done something very difficult. ❑ *His office was lined with animal heads, trophies of his hunting hobby.* [N-COUNT]

**tropi|cal** /trɒpɪkᵊl/ 1 **Tropical** means belonging to or typical of the tropics. ❑ *...tropical diseases. ...a plan to preserve the world's tropical forests.* [ADJ: ADJ n] 2 **Tropical** weather is hot and damp weather that people believe to be typical of the tropics. [ADJ]

**trop|ics** /trɒpɪks/ **The tropics** are the parts of the world that lie between two lines of latitude, the tropic of Cancer, $23\frac{1}{2}°$ north of the equator, and the tropic of Capricorn, $23\frac{1}{2}°$ south of the equator. [N-PLURAL: *the* N]

**trot** /trɒt/ **(trots, trotting, trotted)** 1 If you **trot** somewhere, you move fairly fast at a speed between walking and running, taking small quick steps. ❑ *I trotted down the steps and out to the shed... A small shabby man was trotting beside Bardi trying to get his attention.* [VERB] [V prep/adv] [V] ♦ **Trot** is also a noun. ❑ *He walked* [N-SING]

*briskly, but without breaking into a trot.* 2 When an animal such as a horse **trots**, it moves fairly fast, taking quick small steps. You can also say that the rider of the animal **is trotting**. ❑ *Alan took the reins and the small horse started trotting... Pete got on his horse and started trotting across the field.* ♦ **Trot** is also a noun. ❑ *As they started up again, the horse broke into a brisk trot.* 3 If something happens several times **on the trot**, it happens that number of times without a break. [BRIT, INFORMAL] ❑ *She lost five games on the trot.*
VERB; V; V prep/adv; N-SING; PHRASE: PHR after v = *in a row*

♦ **trot out** If you say that a person **trots out** old ideas or information, you are criticizing him or her for repeating them in a way that is not new or interesting. [INFORMAL] ❑ *Was it really necessary to trot out the same old stereotypes about Ireland?*
PHRASAL VERB [disapproval]; V P n (not pron) Also V n P

**Trot|sky|ist** /trɒtskiɪst/ **(Trotskyists)** A **Trotskyist** is someone who supports the revolutionary left-wing ideas of Leon Trotsky.
N-COUNT

**trot|ter** /trɒtəʳ/ **(trotters) Trotters** are pig's feet which you can cook and eat. [BRIT]
N-COUNT: usu pl

**trou|ba|dour** /truːbədɔːʳ/ **(troubadours)** 1 **Troubadours** were poets and singers who used to travel around and perform to noble families in Italy and France in the twelfth and thirteenth centuries. 2 People sometimes refer to popular singers as **troubadours**, especially when the words of their songs are an important part of their music.
N-COUNT; N-COUNT

**trou|ble** /trʌbᵊl/ **(troubles, troubling, troubled)** ♦♦◇ 1 You can refer to problems or difficulties as **trouble**. ❑ *I had trouble parking... You've caused us a lot of trouble... The plane developed engine trouble soon after taking off... The crew are in serious trouble in 50-knot winds and huge seas... The Sullivans continued to have financial troubles.* 2 If you say that one aspect of a situation is **the trouble**, you mean that it is the aspect which is causing problems or making the situation unsatisfactory. ❑ *The trouble is that these restrictions have remained while other things have changed... Your trouble is that you can't take rejection.* 3 Your **troubles** are the things that you are worried about. ❑ *She kept her troubles to herself.* 4 If you have kidney **trouble** or back **trouble**, for example, there is something wrong with your kidneys or your back. ❑ *Her husband had never before had any heart trouble... He began to have trouble with his right knee.* 5 If there is **trouble** somewhere, especially in a public place, there is fighting or rioting there. ❑ *Riot police are being deployed throughout the city to prevent any trouble. ...the first victim of the troubles in Northern Ireland.* 6 If you tell someone that it is **no trouble** to do something for them, you are saying politely that you can or will do it, because it is easy or convenient for you. ❑ *It's no trouble at all; on the contrary, it will be a great pleasure to help you.* 7 If you say that a person or animal is **no trouble**, you mean that they are very easy to look after. ❑ *My little grandson is no trouble at all, but his 6-year-old elder sister is rude and selfish.* 8 If something **troubles** you, it makes you feel rather worried. ❑ *Is anything troubling you?... He was troubled by the lifestyle of his son.* ♦ **trou|bling** *But most troubling of all was the simple fact that nobody knew what was going on.* 9 If a part of your body **troubles** you, it causes you physical pain or discomfort. ❑ *The ulcer had been troubling her for several years.* 10 If you say that someone does **not trouble to** do something, you are critical of them because they do not behave in the way that they should do, and you think that this would require very little effort. ❑ *He yawns, not troubling to cover his mouth... He hadn't troubled himself to check his mirrors.* 11 You use **trouble** in expressions such as **I'm sorry to trouble you** when you are apologizing to someone for disturbing them in order to ask them something. ❑ *I'm sorry to trouble you, but I wondered if by any chance you know where he is.*
N-UNCOUNT: oft *in* N, also N in pl; N-SING: usu *the* N = *problem*; N-PLURAL: usu poss N; N-UNCOUNT: n N, N *with* n; N-UNCOUNT: also N in pl; N-UNCOUNT: with brd-neg, oft N to-inf [politeness] = *bother*; N-UNCOUNT: with brd-neg; VERB; V n; V n; ADJ; VERB; V n; VERB: with brd-neg [disapproval]; V to-inf; V pron-refl to-inf; VERB [formulae] = *bother*

PHRASES 12 If someone is **in trouble**, they are in a situation in which a person in authority is angry with them or is likely to punish them because they have done something wrong. ❑ *He was in trouble with his teachers.* 13 If you **take the trouble to** do something, you do something which requires a small amount of additional effort. ❑ *He did not take the trouble to see the film before he attacked it.* 14 If you say that someone or something is **more trouble than** they are **worth**, you mean that they cause you a lot of problems or take a lot of time and effort and you do not achieve or gain very much in return. ❑ *Some grumbled that Johnson was more trouble than he was worth.*
PHRASE: usu v-link PHR, PHR after v; PHRASE: V inflects, usu PHR to-inf, oft with brd-neg; PHRASE: V inflects, v-link PHR

**trou|bled** /trʌbᵊld/ 1 Someone who is **troubled** is worried because they have problems. ❑ *Rose sounded deeply troubled.* 2 A **troubled** place, situation, organization, or time has many problems or conflicts. ❑ *There is much we can do to help this troubled country.* 3 to **pour oil on troubled waters** → see **oil**.
ADJ; ADJ: usu ADJ n

**trouble-free** Something that is **trouble-free** does not cause any problems or difficulties. ❑ *The carnival got off to a virtually trouble-free start with the police reporting only one arrest.*
ADJ

**trouble|maker** /trʌbᵊlmeɪkəʳ/ **(troublemakers)** If you refer to someone as a **troublemaker**, you mean that they cause unpleasantness, quarrels, or fights, especially by encouraging people to oppose authority.
N-COUNT [disapproval]

**trouble|shooter** /trʌbᵊlʃuːtəʳ/ **(troubleshooters)** also **trouble-shooter.** A **troubleshooter** is a person whose job is to solve major problems or difficulties that occur in a company or government.
N-COUNT

**trouble|shooting** /trʌbᵊlʃuːtɪŋ/ **Troubleshooting** is the activity or process of solving major problems or difficulties that occur in a company or government.
N-UNCOUNT

**trou|ble|some** /trʌbᵊlsəm/ 1 You use **troublesome** to describe something or someone that causes annoying problems or difficulties. ❑ *He needed surgery to cure a troublesome back injury.* 2 A **troublesome** situation or issue is full of complicated problems or difficulties. ❑ *The economy has become a troublesome issue for the party.*
ADJ; ADJ

**trou|ble spot (trouble spots)** also **trouble-spot.** A **trouble spot** is a country or an area of a country where there is repeated fighting between two or more groups of people.
N-COUNT

**trough** /trɒf, AM trɔːf/ **(troughs)** 1 A **trough** is a long narrow container from which farm animals drink or eat. 2 A **trough** is a low area between two big waves on the sea. ❑ *The boat rolled heavily in the troughs between the waves.* 3 A **trough** is a low point in a process that has regular high and low points, for example a period in business when people do not produce as much as usual. ❑ *Looking back afterwards you will see that this was not a terminal trough in your career.* 4 A **trough of** low pressure is a long narrow area of low air pressure between two areas of higher pressure. [TECHNICAL]
N-COUNT; N-COUNT; N-COUNT; N-COUNT

**trounce** /traʊns/ **(trounces, trouncing, trounced)** If you **trounce** someone in a competition or contest, you defeat them easily or by a large score. [INFORMAL] ❑ *In Rugby League, Australia trounced France by sixty points to four.*
VERB = *thrash*; V n

**troupe** /truːp/ **(troupes)** A **troupe** is a group of actors, singers, or dancers who work together and often travel around together, performing in different places. ❑ *...troupes of travelling actors.*
N-COUNT-COLL: oft N *of* n = *company*

**troup|er** /truːpəʳ/ **(troupers)** You can refer to an actor or other performer as a **trouper**, especially when you want to suggest that they have a lot of experience and can deal with difficult situations in a professional way. ❑ *Like the old trouper he is, he timed his entry to perfection.*
N-COUNT

**trou|ser** /traʊzəʳ/ **(trousers, trousering, troused)** If you say that someone **trousers** a sum of money, you mean that they receive it, usually when they do not deserve it or should not take it. [BRIT, INFORMAL] ❑ *Many people think that ex-ministers are trousering £25,000 in fees simply for going to a few board meetings a year.*
VERB; V n

**trou|sers** /traʊzəʳz/

✓ The form **trouser** is used as a modifier.

1 **Trousers** are a piece of clothing that you wear over your body from the waist downwards, and that cover each leg separately. [mainly BRIT] ❑ *He was smartly dressed in a shirt, dark trousers and boots... Alexander rolled up his trouser legs.*
N-PLURAL: also *a pair of* N

✓ in AM, usually use **pants**

2 to **wear the trousers** → see **wear**.

**trou|ser suit (trouser suits)** A **trouser suit** is women's clothing consisting of a pair of trousers and a jacket which are made from the same material. [BRIT]
N-COUNT

✓ in AM, use **pantsuit, pants suit**

**trous|seau** /truːsoʊ/ **(trousseaux)** A **trousseau** is a collection of clothes and other possessions that a bride brings with her when she gets married. [OLD-FASHIONED]
N-COUNT

**trout** /traʊt/ **(trout** or **trouts)** A **trout** is a fairly large fish that lives in rivers and streams. ♦ **Trout** is this fish eaten as food.
N-VAR; N-UNCOUNT

**trove** /troʊv/ → see **treasure trove**.

**trow|el** /traʊəl/ **(trowels)** 1 A **trowel** is a small garden tool which you use for digging small holes or removing weeds. 2 A **trowel** is a small tool with a flat blade that you use for spreading things such as cement and plaster onto walls and other surfaces.
N-COUNT; N-COUNT

**tru|an|cy** /truːənsi/ **Truancy** is when children stay away from school without permission.
N-UNCOUNT

**tru|ant** /truːənt/ **(truants, truanting, truanted)** 1 A **truant** is a pupil who stays away from school without permission. 2 If a pupil **truants**, he or she stays away from school without permission. ❑ *In his fourth year he was truanting regularly.* ♦ **tru|ant|ing** *Truanting is a small but growing problem in primary schools.* 3 If a pupil **plays truant**, he or she stays away from school without permission. ❑ *She was getting into trouble over playing truant from school.*
N-COUNT; VERB; V; N-UNCOUNT = truancy; PHRASE: V inflects, oft PHR *from* n

**truce** /truːs/ **(truces)** A **truce** is an agreement between two people or groups of people to stop fighting or quarrelling for a short time. ❑ *The fighting of recent days has given way to an uneasy truce between the two sides... Let's call a truce.*
N-COUNT

**truck** /trʌk/ **(trucks, trucking, trucked)** 1 A **truck** is a large vehicle that is used to transport goods by road. [mainly AM]
◆◇◇ N-COUNT

✓ in BRIT, usually use **lorry**

2 A **truck** is an open vehicle used for carrying goods on a railway. [BRIT] ❑ *They were loaded on the railway trucks to go to Liverpool.*
N-COUNT: usu supp N

✓ in AM, use **freight car**

3 When something or someone **is trucked** somewhere, they are driven there in a lorry. [mainly AM] ❑ *The liquor was sold legally and trucked out of the state.* 4 If you say that you will **have no truck with** someone or something, you are refusing to be involved with them in any way. ❑ *He would have no truck with deceit.*
VERB: usu passive; *be* V-ed prep/adv; PHRASE: V inflects, PHR n

**truck|er** /trʌkəʳ/ **(truckers)** A **trucker** is someone who drives a truck as their job. [mainly AM]
N-COUNT

✓ in BRIT, use **lorry driver**

**truck|ing** /trʌkɪŋ/ **Trucking** is the activity of transporting goods from one place to another using trucks. [mainly AM] ❑ *...the deregulation of the trucking industry.*
N-UNCOUNT: usu N n

✓ in BRIT, use **haulage**

**truck|load** /trʌkloʊd/ **(truckloads)** also **truck load**. A **truckload** of goods or people is the amount of them that a truck can carry. ❑ *Truckloads of food, blankets, and other necessities reached the city.*
N-COUNT: usu N *of* n

**truck stop (truck stops)** A **truck stop** is a place where drivers, especially truck or lorry drivers, can stop, for example to rest or to get something to eat. [mainly AM]
N-COUNT

**trucu|lent** /trʌkjʊlənt/ If you say that someone is **truculent**, you mean that they are bad-tempered and aggressive. ♦ **trucu|lence** /trʌkjʊləns/ ❑ *'Your secretary said you'd be wanting a cleaner,' she announced with her usual truculence.*
ADJ = belligerent; N-UNCOUNT = belligerence

**trudge** /trʌdʒ/ **(trudges, trudging, trudged)** If you **trudge** somewhere, you walk there slowly and with heavy steps, especially because you are tired or unhappy. ❑ *We had to trudge up the track back to the station.* ♦ **Trudge** is also a noun. ❑ *We were reluctant to start the long trudge home.*
VERB; V prep/adv; N-SING

**true** /truː/ **(truer, truest)** 1 If something is **true**, it is based on facts rather than being invented or imagined, and is accurate and reliable. ❑ *Everything I had heard about him was true... The film tells the true story of a group who survived in the Andes in sub-zero temperatures.* 2 You use **true** to emphasize that a person or thing is sincere or genuine, often in contrast to something that is pretended or hidden. ❑ *I allowed myself to acknowledge my true feelings... The true cost often differs from that which had first been projected.* 3 If you use **true** to describe something or someone, you approve of them because they have all the characteristics or qualities that such a person or thing typically has. ❑ *Maybe one day you'll find true love... The ability to work collaboratively is a true test of leadership... I think he's a true genius.* 4 If you say that a fact is **true of** a particular person or situation, you mean that it is valid or relevant for them. ❑ *I accept that the romance may have gone out of the marriage, but surely this is true of many couples... Expenditure on health in most of these countries has gone down, and the same is true for education.* 5 If you are **true to** someone, you remain committed and loyal to them. If you are **true to** an idea or promise, you remain committed to it and continue to act according to it. ❑ *David was true to his wife... India has remained true to democracy... She's been true to her word from day one.*
◆◆◇ ADJ: oft *it* v-link ADJ that; ADJ: ADJ n emphasis = real; ADJ: ADJ n approval = real; ADJ: v-link ADJ *of/for* n; ADJ: v-link ADJ *to* n = faithful

PHRASES 6 If a dream, wish, or prediction **comes true**, it actually happens. ❑ *Owning a place of their own is a dream come true for the couple.* 7 If a general statement **holds true** in particular circumstances, or if your previous statement **holds true** in different circumstances, it is true or valid in those circumstances. [FORMAL] ❑ *This law is known to hold true for galaxies at a distance of at least several billion light years.* 8 If you say that something seems **too good to be true**, you are suspicious of it because it seems better than you had expected, and you think there may something wrong with it that you have not noticed. ❑ *On the whole the celebrations were remarkably good-humoured and peaceful. Indeed, it seemed almost too good to be true.* 9 If you say that something such as a story or a film is **true to life**, you approve of it because it seems real. ❑ *The opening scenes of this movie are just not true to life.* 10 **true colours** → see **colour**. **true to form** → see **form**. **to ring true** → see **ring**. **tried and true** → see **tried**.
PHRASE: V inflects; PHRASE: V inflects, oft PHR *for* n; PHRASE: v-link PHR; PHRASE: v-link PHR approval

**true-blue** also **true blue**. 1 If you describe someone as **true-blue**, you mean that they are right-wing in their ideas and opinions. [BRIT] ❑ *Her husband is a true blue Tory.* 2 A **true-blue** supporter of something is someone who is very loyal and reliable. [AM]
ADJ; ADJ

**truf|fle** /trʌfᵊl/ **(truffles)** 1 A **truffle** is a soft round sweet made with chocolate and usually flavoured with rum. 2 A **truffle** is a round type of
N-COUNT; N-COUNT

fungus which is expensive and considered very good to eat.

**trug** /trʌg/ **(trugs)** A **trug** is a wide, shallow, oval basket used for carrying garden tools, flowers, or plants. [BRIT] N-COUNT

**tru|ism** /truːɪzəm/ **(truisms)** A **truism** is a statement that is generally accepted as obviously true and is repeated so often that it has become boring. N-COUNT

**tru|ly** /truːli/ ◆◇◇ [1] You use **truly** to emphasize that something has all the features or qualities of a particular thing, or is the case to the fullest possible extent. ❑ *...a truly democratic system... Not all doctors truly understand the reproductive cycle.* ADV: ADV group, ADV before v emphasis [2] You can use **truly** in order to emphasize your description of something. ❑ *...a truly splendid man... They were truly appalling.* ADV: ADV adj emphasis [3] You use **truly** to emphasize that feelings are genuine and sincere. ❑ *Believe me, Susan, I am truly sorry.* ADV: ADV adj, ADV before v emphasis [4] **well and truly** → see **well**. [5] You write **Yours truly** at the end of a formal letter to someone you do not know very well. You write your signature after the words 'Yours truly'. ❑ *Yours truly, Phil Turner.* CONVENTION [6] You can say **yours truly** as a way of referring to yourself. [HUMOROUS, INFORMAL] ❑ *Yours truly was awoken by a shout: 'Ahoy there!'* PHRASE

**trump** /trʌmp/ **(trumps, trumping, trumped)** [1] In a game of cards, **trumps** is the suit which is chosen to have the highest value in one particular game. ❑ *Hearts are trumps.* N-UNCOUNT-COLL [2] In a game of cards, a **trump** is a playing card which belongs to the suit which has been chosen as trumps. ❑ *He played a trump.* N-COUNT [3] If you **trump** what someone has said or done, you beat it by saying or doing something else that seems better. ❑ *The Socialists tried to trump this with their slogan.* VERB V n

PHRASES [4] Your **trump card** is something powerful that you can use or do, which gives you an advantage over someone. ❑ *In the end, the Ten took their appeal to the Supreme Court; this, they had believed, would be their trump card.* PHRASE: poss PHR [5] If you say that someone **came up trumps**, you mean that they did something successfully, often when they were not expected to. [BRIT] ❑ *Dwayne has come up trumps with a goal worthy of winning any match.* PHRASE: V inflects

**trumped-up** **Trumped-up** charges are untrue, and made up in order to punish someone unfairly. ADJ: usu ADJ n = *false*

**trum|pet** /trʌmpɪt/ **(trumpets, trumpeting, trumpeted)** [1] A **trumpet** is a musical instrument of the brass family which plays quite high notes. N-VAR: oft *the* N [2] If someone **trumpets** something that they are proud of or that they think is important, they speak about it publicly in a very forceful way. ❑ *The government has been trumpeting tourism as a growth industry... Nobody should be trumpeting about chemical weapons... It was trumpeted that the nation's health was improving.* VERB V n *as* n V *about* n *it be* V-ed that

**trum|pet|er** /trʌmpɪtəʳ/ **(trumpeters)** A **trumpeter** is someone who plays a trumpet. N-COUNT

**trun|cat|ed** /trʌŋkeɪtɪd, AM trʌŋkeɪtɪd/ A **truncated** version of something is one that has been shortened. ❑ *The review body has produced a truncated version of its annual report.* ADJ: usu ADJ n

**trun|cheon** /trʌntʃən/ **(truncheons)** A **truncheon** is a short, thick stick that is carried as a weapon by a policeman. [BRIT] N-COUNT

☑ in AM, use **billy**

**trun|dle** /trʌndəl/ **(trundles, trundling, trundled)** [1] If a vehicle **trundles** somewhere, it moves there slowly, often with difficulty or an irregular movement. ❑ *The train eventually trundled in at 7.54.* VERB V prep/adv [2] If you **trundle** something somewhere, especially a small, heavy object with wheels, you move or roll it along slowly. ❑ *The old man lifted the barrow and trundled it away.* VERB V n adv/prep [3] If you say that someone **is trundling** somewhere, you mean that they are walking slowly, often in a tired way or with heavy steps. ❑ *Girls trundle in carrying heavy book bags.* VERB V adv/prep

**trunk** /trʌŋk/ **(trunks)** [1] The **trunk** of a tree is the large main stem from which the branches grow. ❑ *...the gnarled trunk of a birch tree.* N-COUNT: usu N *of* n, n N [2] A **trunk** is a large, strong case or box used for storing things or for taking on a journey. N-COUNT [3] An elephant's **trunk** is its very long nose that it uses to lift food and water to its mouth. N-COUNT: usu with poss [4] The **trunk** of a car is a covered space at the back or front in which you put luggage or other things. [AM] → See picture on page 1707. N-COUNT

☑ in BRIT, use **boot**

[5] **Trunks** are shorts that a man wears when he goes swimming. N-PLURAL [6] Your **trunk** is the central part of your body, from your neck to your waist. [FORMAL] N-COUNT: usu sing

**trunk road** **(trunk roads)** A **trunk road** is a major road that has been specially built for travelling long distances. A trunk road is not as wide or as fast as a motorway. [BRIT] N-COUNT

**truss** /trʌs/ **(trusses, trussing, trussed)** [1] To **truss** someone means to tie them up very tightly so that they cannot move. [WRITTEN] ❑ *She trussed him quickly with stolen bandage, and gagged his mouth.* VERB = *bind* V n ♦ **Truss up** means the same as **truss**. ❑ *She was trussed up with yellow nylon rope.* PHRASAL VERB: usu passive *be* V-ed P [2] A **truss** is a special belt with a pad that a man wears when he has a hernia in order to prevent it from getting worse. N-COUNT

♦ **truss up** → see **truss 1**.

**trust** /trʌst/ **(trusts, trusting, trusted)** ◆◆◇ [1] If you **trust** someone, you believe that they are honest and sincere and will not deliberately do anything to harm you. ❑ *'I trust you completely,' he said... He did argue in a general way that the president can't be trusted.* VERB V n V n ♦ **trust|ed** *After speaking to a group of her most trusted advisers, she turned her anger into action.* ADJ: ADJ n [2] Your **trust in** someone is your belief that they are honest and sincere and will not deliberately do anything to harm you. ❑ *He destroyed me and my trust in men... You've betrayed their trust... There's a feeling of warmth and trust here.* N-UNCOUNT: oft poss N *in* n [3] If you **trust** someone **to** do something, you believe that they will do it. ❑ *That's why I must trust you to keep this secret.* VERB V n to-inf [4] If you **trust** someone **with** something important or valuable, you allow them to look after it or deal with it. ❑ *This could make your superiors hesitate to trust you with major responsibilities... I'd trust him with my life.* VERB V n *with* n V n *with* n ♦ **Trust** is also a noun. ❑ *She was organizing and running a large household, a position of trust which was generously paid.* N-UNCOUNT: also *a* N [5] If you do not **trust** something, you feel that it is not safe or reliable. ❑ *She nodded, not trusting her own voice... For one thing, he didn't trust his legs to hold him up... I still can't trust myself to remain composed in their presence.* VERB V n V n to-inf V pron-refl to-inf [6] If you **trust** someone's judgment or advice, you believe that it is good or right. ❑ *I blame myself and will never be able to trust my instinct again.* VERB V n [7] If you say you **trust that** something is true, you mean you hope and expect that it is true. [FORMAL] ❑ *I trust you will take the earliest opportunity to make a full apology.* VERB V that [8] If you **trust in** someone or something, you believe strongly in them, and do not doubt their powers or their good intentions. [FORMAL] ❑ *He was a pastor who trusted in the Lord who lived to preach.* VERB V *in* n [9] A **trust** is a financial arrangement in which a group of people or an organization keeps and invests money for someone. ❑ *The money will be put in trust until she is 18.* N-COUNT: also *in* N [10] A **trust** is a group of people or an organization that has control of an amount of money or property and invests it on behalf of other people or as a charity. ❑ *He had set up two charitable trusts.* N-COUNT: supp N, oft in names [11] In Britain, a **trust** or a **trust hospital** is a public hospital that receives its funding directly from the national government. It has its own board of governors and is not controlled by the local health authority. N-COUNT: supp N, N n [12] → See also **trusting**, **unit trust**.

PHRASES [13] If something valuable is kept **in trust**, it is held and protected by a group of peo- PHRASE: PHR after v, v-link PHR, ple or an organization on behalf of other people. ❑ *The British Library holds its collection in trust for the nation.* [14] If you **take** something **on trust** after having heard or read it, you believe it completely without checking it. ❑ *He was adamant that the allegations were untrue, so I took him on trust.* [15] **tried and trusted** → see **tried**.

oft PHR *for* n — PHRASE: V inflects

♦ **trust to** If you **trust to** luck or instinct, you hope that it will enable you to achieve what you are trying to do, because you have nothing else to help you. ❑ *I set off for the valley, trusting to luck... Gardiner is simply trusting to instinct and experience.*

PHRASAL VERB: no passive = *rely on* — V P n — V P n

**trus|tee** /trʌstiː/ **(trustees)** A **trustee** is someone with legal control of money or property that is kept or invested for another person, company, or organization. — N-COUNT

**trust fund** **(trust funds)** A **trust fund** is an amount of money or property that someone owns, usually after inheriting it, but which is kept and invested for them. — N-COUNT

**trust|ing** /trʌstɪŋ/ A **trusting** person believes that people are honest and sincere and do not intend to harm him or her. ❑ *She has an open, trusting nature.* — ADJ

**trust|worthy** /trʌstwɜːʳði/ A **trustworthy** person is reliable, responsible, and can be trusted completely. ❑ *He is a trustworthy and level-headed leader.* ♦ **trust|worthi|ness** *He wrote a reference for him, describing his reliability and trustworthiness as 'above questioning'.* — ADJ — N-UNCOUNT

**trusty** /trʌsti/ **Trusty** things, animals, or people are reliable and have always worked well in the past. ❑ *She still drives her trusty black Corvette.* — ADJ: ADJ n = *faithful*

**truth** /truːθ/ **(truths)** [1] **The truth** about something is all the facts about it, rather than things that are imagined or invented. ❑ *I must tell you the truth about this business... The truth of the matter is that we had no other choice... In the town very few know the whole truth.* [2] If you say that there is some **truth in** a statement or story, you mean that it is true, or at least partly true. ❑ *There is no truth in this story... Is there any truth to the rumors?* [3] A **truth** is something that is believed to be true. ❑ *It is an almost universal truth that the more we are promoted in a job, the less we actually exercise the skills we initially used to perform it.* [4] → See also **home truth**, **moment of truth**.

◆◆◇ N-UNCOUNT — N-UNCOUNT: oft N *of/in* n — N-COUNT

**PHRASES** [5] You say **in truth** in order to indicate that you are giving your honest opinion about something. ❑ *In truth, we were both unhappy.* — PHRASE: PHR with cl

[6] You say **to tell you the truth** or **truth to tell** in order to indicate that you are telling someone something in an open and honest way, without trying to hide anything. ❑ *To tell you the truth, I was afraid to see him.* — PHRASE: PHR with cl

**truth|ful** /truːθfʊl/ If a person or their comments are **truthful**, they are honest and do not tell any lies. ❑ *We've all learnt to be fairly truthful about our personal lives... She could not give him a truthful answer.* ♦ **truth|ful|ly** *I answered all their questions truthfully.* ♦ **truth|ful|ness** *I can say, with absolute truthfulness, that I did not injure her.* — ADJ — ADV: ADV with v — N-UNCOUNT

**try** /traɪ/ **(tries, trying, tried)** [1] If you **try** to do something, you want to do it, and you take action which you hope will help you to do it. ❑ *He secretly tried to block her advancement in the Party... Does it annoy you if others do things less well than you would, or don't seem to try hard enough?... I tried calling him when I got here but he wasn't at home... No matter how bad you feel, keep trying.* ♦ **Try** is also a noun. ❑ *It wasn't that she'd really expected to get any money out of him; it had just seemed worth a try.*

◆◆◆ VERB — V to-inf — V adv — V -ing — V — N-COUNT

[2] To **try and** do something means to try to do it. [INFORMAL] ❑ *I must try and see him.* [3] If you **try for** something, you make an effort to get it or achieve it. ❑ *My partner and I have been trying for a baby for two years... He said he was going to try for first place next year.* [4] If you **try** something new or different, you use it, do it, or experience it in order to discover its qualities or effects. ❑ *It's best not to try a new recipe for the first time on such an important occasion... I have tried painting the young shoots with weed poisoner, but this does not kill them off.* ♦ **Try** is also a noun. ❑ *If you're still sceptical about exercising, we can only ask you to trust us and give it a try.* [5] If you **try** a particular place or person, you go to that place or person because you think that they may be able to provide you with what you want. ❑ *Have you tried the local music shops?* [6] If you **try** a door or window, you try to open it. ❑ *Bob tried the door. To his surprise it opened.* [7] When a person **is tried**, he or she has to appear in a law court and is found innocent or guilty after the judge and jury have heard the evidence. When a legal case **is tried**, it is considered in a court of law. ❑ *He suggested that those responsible should be tried for crimes against humanity... Whether he is innocent or guilty is a decision that will be made when the case is tried in court... The military court which tried him excluded two of his lawyers.*

VERB — V *and* inf — VERB — V *for* n — V *for* n — VERB — V n — V -ing — N-COUNT: usu sing — VERB — V n — VERB — V n — VERB — *be* V-ed *for* n — *be* V-ed — V n

[8] In the game of rugby, a **try** is the action of scoring by putting the ball down behind the goal line of the opposing team. ❑ *The French, who led 21-3 at half time, scored eight tries.* [9] → See also **tried**, **trying**. [10] If you say that something fails but not **for want of trying** or not **for lack of trying**, you mean that everything possible was done to make it succeed. ❑ *Not all is perfect, but it isn't for want of trying.* [11] to **try** your **best** → see **best**. to **try** your **hand** → see **hand**. to **try** your **luck** → see **luck**. to **try** someone's **patience** → see **patience**.

N-COUNT — PHRASE: with neg, *it* v-link PHR, PHR with cl

♦ **try on** [1] If you **try on** a piece of clothing, you put it on to see if it fits you or if it looks nice. ❑ *Try on clothing and shoes to make sure they fit.* [2] If you say that a person **is trying it on**, you mean that they are trying to obtain something or to impress someone, often in a slightly dishonest way and without much hope of success. [BRIT, INFORMAL] ❑ *They're just trying it on – I don't believe they'll go this far.*

PHRASAL VERB — V P n — Also V n P — PHRASAL VERB: usu cont — V *it* P — Also V *it* P *with* n

♦ **try out** If you **try** something **out**, you test it in order to find out how useful or effective it is or what it is like. ❑ *She knew I wanted to try the boat out at the weekend... London Transport hopes to try out the system in September.* — PHRASAL VERB — V n P — V P n (not pron)

**try|ing** /traɪɪŋ/ If you describe something or someone as **trying**, you mean that they are difficult to deal with and make you feel impatient or annoyed. ❑ *Support from those closest to you is vital in these trying times.* → See also **try**. — ADJ

**try|out** /traɪaʊt/ **(tryouts)** also **try-out.** If you give something a **tryout**, you try it or test it to see how useful it is. ❑ *The recycling scheme gets its first try-out in rural Dorset.* — N-COUNT = *trial*

**tryst** /trɪst/ **(trysts)** A **tryst** is a meeting between lovers in a quiet secret place. [LITERARY] — N-COUNT = *assignation*

**tsar** /zɑːʳ/ **(tsars)** also **czar.** [1] In former times, the **tsar** was the king of Russia. [2] A particular kind of **tsar** is a person who has been appointed by the government to deal with a particular problem that is affecting the country. ❑ *...the former New York police chief who was appointed as 'drug tsar' by Bill Clinton.* — N-COUNT; N-TITLE — N-COUNT: supp N

**tsa|ri|na** /zɑːriːnə/ **(tsarinas)** also **czarina.** In former times, a **tsarina** was the queen of Russia or the wife of the tsar. — N-COUNT; N-TITLE

**tsar|ist** /zɑːrɪst/ also **czarist. Tsarist** means belonging to or supporting the system of government by a tsar, especially in Russia before 1917. — ADJ: usu ADJ n

**tset|se fly** /tsetsi flaɪ/ **(tsetse flies)** also **tsetse.** A **tsetse fly** or a **tsetse** is an African fly that feeds on blood and can cause serious diseases in the people and animals that it bites. — N-VAR

**T-shirt** **(T-shirts)** also **tee-shirt.** A **T-shirt** is a cotton shirt with no collar or buttons. T-shirts usually have short sleeves. — N-COUNT

**tsp.** **(tsps)** In a recipe, **tsp.** is a written abbreviation for **teaspoonful**.

**tsu|na|mi** /tsʊnɑːmi/ **(tsunamis)** A **tsunami** is a very large wave, often caused by an earthquake, that flows onto the land and destroys things. N-COUNT = tidal wave

**tub** /tʌb/ **(tubs)** [1] A **tub** is a deep container of any size. ❑ *He peeled the paper top off a little white tub and poured the cream into his coffee.* N-COUNT ♦ A **tub of** something is the amount of it contained in a tub. ❑ *She would eat four tubs of ice cream in one sitting.* N-COUNT: N *of* n [2] A **tub** is the same as a **bathtub**. [AM] ❑ *She lay back in the tub.* N-COUNT = bath [3] → See also **hot tub**.

**tuba** /tjuːbə, AM tuː-/ **(tubas)** A **tuba** is a large musical instrument of the brass family which produces very low notes. It consists of a long metal tube folded round several times with a wide opening at the end. N-VAR: oft *the* N

**tub|by** /tʌbi/ **(tubbier, tubbiest)** If you describe someone as **tubby**, you mean that they are rather fat. [INFORMAL] ADJ = chubby

**tube** /tjuːb, AM tuːb/ **(tubes)** [1] A **tube** is a long hollow object that is usually round, like a pipe. ❑ *He is fed by a tube that enters his nose. ...a cardboard tube.* ◆◇◇ N-COUNT [2] A **tube of** something such as paste is a long, thin container which you squeeze in order to force the paste out. ❑ *...a tube of toothpaste. ...a small tube of moisturizer.* N-COUNT: oft N *of* n [3] Some long, thin, hollow parts in your body are referred to as **tubes**. ❑ *The lungs are in fact constructed of thousands of tiny tubes.* N-COUNT [4] **The tube** is the underground railway system in London. [BRIT] ❑ *I took the tube then the train and came straight here.* N-SING: *the* N, also *by* N [5] You can refer to the television as **the tube**. [AM, INFORMAL] ❑ *The only baseball he saw was on the tube.* N-COUNT: *the* N = TV

✔ in BRIT, use **the box**

[6] If a business, economy, or institution **goes down the tubes** or **goes down the tube**, it fails or collapses completely. [mainly AM, INFORMAL] ❑ *The country was going down the tubes economically.* PHRASE: V inflects [7] → See also **bronchial tube**, **cathode-ray tube**, **fallopian tube**, **inner tube**, **test tube**.

**tu|ber** /tjuːbəʳ, AM tuː-/ **(tubers)** A **tuber** is the swollen underground stem of particular types of plants. N-COUNT

**tu|ber|cu|lar** /tjuːbɜːʳkjʊləʳ, AM tuː-/ **Tubercular** means suffering from, relating to, or causing tuberculosis. ❑ *...tubercular patients... He died of tubercular meningitis. ...tubercular bacteria.* ADJ

**tu|ber|cu|lo|sis** /tjuːbɜːʳkjʊloʊsɪs, AM tuː-/ **Tuberculosis** is a serious infectious disease that affects someone's lungs and other parts of their body. The abbreviation **TB** is also used. N-UNCOUNT

**tube top** **(tube tops)** A **tube top** is a piece of women's clothing that is made of stretchy material and covers her chest but leaves her shoulders bare. [AM] N-COUNT

✔ in BRIT, use **boob tube**

**tub|ing** /tjuːbɪŋ, AM tuː-/ **Tubing** is plastic, rubber, or another material in the shape of a tube. ❑ *...metres of plastic tubing.* N-UNCOUNT

**tubu|lar** /tjuːbjʊləʳ, AM tuː-/ Something that is **tubular** is long, round, and hollow in shape, like a tube. ❑ *...a modern table with chrome tubular legs.* ADJ

**TUC** /tiː juː siː/ In Britain, **the TUC** is an organization which represents trade unions, and to which most trade unions belong. **TUC** is an abbreviation for 'Trades Union Congress'. N-PROPER: *the* N

**tuck** /tʌk/ **(tucks, tucking, tucked)** [1] If you **tuck** something somewhere, you put it there so that it is safe, comfortable, or neat. ❑ *He tried to tuck his flapping shirt inside his trousers... She found a rose tucked under the windscreen wiper of her car one morning.* VERB V n prep V-ed [2] You can use **tuck** to refer to a form of plastic surgery which involves reducing the size of a part of someone's body. ❑ *She'd undergone 13 operations, including a tummy tuck.* N-COUNT: usu supp N

♦ **tuck away** [1] If you **tuck away** something such as money, you store it in a safe place. ❑ *The extra income has meant Phillippa can tuck away the rent... I tucked the box away in the linen drawer.* PHRASAL VERB V P n (not pron) V n P [2] If someone or something **is tucked away**, they are well hidden in a quiet place where very few people go. ❑ *We were tucked away in a secluded corner of the room.* PHRASAL VERB: usu passive *be* V-ed P

♦ **tuck in** [1] If you **tuck in** a piece of material, you keep it in position by placing one edge or end of it behind or under something else. For example, if you **tuck in** your shirt, you place the bottom part of it inside your trousers or skirt. ❑ *'Probably,' I said, tucking in my shirt... Tuck the sheets in firmly.* PHRASAL VERB V P n V n P [2] If you **tuck** a child **in** bed or **tuck** them **in**, you make them comfortable by straightening the sheets and blankets and pushing the loose ends under the mattress. ❑ *I read Lili a story and tucked her in her own bed... My mother would tuck me in, turn out the lights and tiptoe out.* PHRASAL VERB V n P n V n P

♦ **tuck into** or **tuck in** If someone **tucks into** a meal or **tucks in**, they start eating enthusiastically or hungrily. [BRIT, INFORMAL] ❑ *She tucked into a breakfast of bacon and eggs... Tuck in, it's the last hot food you'll get for a while.* PHRASAL VERB V P n V P

♦ **tuck up** If you **tuck** a child **up** in bed, you tuck them in. [BRIT] ❑ *She tucked them up in bed... He mostly stayed at home tucking up the children... She had gone to work believing Helen was safely tucked up in bed.* PHRASAL VERB V n P V P n (not pron) V-ed P

**tuck|er** /tʌkəʳ/ **Tucker** is food. [mainly AUSTRALIAN, INFORMAL] ❑ *...a man who knows what constitutes decent tucker and how to go about serving it up.* N-UNCOUNT

**tuck|ered out** /tʌkəʳd aʊt/ or **tuckered.** If you are **tuckered** or **tuckered out**, you are extremely tired. [mainly AM, INFORMAL] ADJ

**Tues.** also **Tue. Tues.** is a written abbreviation for **Tuesday**.

**Tues|day** /tjuːzdeɪ, -di, AM tuːz-/ **(Tuesdays)** **Tuesday** is the day after Monday and before Wednesday. ❑ *He phoned on Tuesday, just before you came... On Tuesdays and Saturdays the market comes to town.* N-VAR

**tuft** /tʌft/ **(tufts)** A **tuft of** something such as hair or grass is a small amount of it which is growing together in one place or is held together at the bottom. ❑ *He had a small tuft of hair on his chin.* N-COUNT: oft N *of* n

**tuft|ed** /tʌftɪd/ Something that is **tufted** has a tuft or tufts on it. ADJ

**tug** /tʌg/ **(tugs, tugging, tugged)** [1] If you **tug** something or **tug at** it, you give it a quick and usually strong pull. ❑ *A little boy came running up and tugged at his sleeve excitedly... She kicked him, tugging his thick hair.* VERB V *at* n V n ♦ **Tug** is also a noun. ❑ *I felt a tug at my sleeve.* Also V N-COUNT [2] A **tug** or a **tug boat** is a small powerful boat which pulls large ships, usually when they come into a port. N-COUNT

**tug-of-love** Journalists sometimes use **tug-of-love** to refer to a situation in which the parents of a child are divorced and one of the parents tries to get the child from the other, for example by taking him or her illegally. [BRIT] ❑ *A mother yesterday won a tug-of-love battle for custody of her twin daughters.* N-SING: usu N n

**tug-of-war** **(tugs-of-war)** also **tug of war.** [1] A **tug-of-war** is a sports event in which two teams test their strength by pulling against each other on opposite ends of a rope. N-VAR [2] You can use **tug-of-war** to refer to a situation in which two people or groups both want the same thing and are fairly equally matched in their struggle to get it. ❑ *Chelsea and Aston Villa were involved in a tug of war for Liverpool's Ray Houghton last night.* N-VAR

**tui|tion** /tjuɪʃᵊn, AM tu-/ [1] If you are given **tuition** in a particular subject, you are taught about that subject. ❑ *The courses will give the beginner personal tuition in all types of outdoor photography.* N-UNCOUNT: oft supp N, N *in* n [2] You can use **tuition** to refer to the amount of money that you have to pay for being taught particular subjects, especially in a univer- N-UNCOUNT sity, college, or private school. ❑ *Angela's $7,000 tuition at University this year will be paid for with scholarships.*

**tu|lip** /tjuːlɪp, AM tuː-/ **(tulips)** **Tulips** are brightly coloured flowers that grow in the spring, and have oval or pointed petals packed closely together. N-COUNT

**tulle** /tjuːl, AM tuːl/ **Tulle** is a soft nylon or silk cloth similar to net, that is used for making evening dresses. N-UNCOUNT

**tum** /tʌm/ **(tums)** Your **tum** is your stomach. [BRIT, INFORMAL] N-COUNT = *tummy*

**tum|ble** /tʌmbᵊl/ **(tumbles, tumbling, tumbled)** 1 If someone or something **tumbles** somewhere, they fall there with a rolling or bouncing movement. ❑ *A small boy tumbled off a third floor fire escape... He fell to the ground, and the gun tumbled out of his hand.* ♦ **Tumble** is also a noun. ❑ *He injured his ribs in a tumble from his horse.* 2 If prices or levels of something **are tumbling**, they are decreasing rapidly. [JOURNALISM] ❑ *House prices have tumbled by almost 30 per cent in real terms since mid-1989... Share prices continued to tumble today on the Tokyo stock market. ...tumbling inflation.* ♦ **Tumble** is also a noun. ❑ *Oil prices took a tumble yesterday.* 3 If water **tumbles**, it flows quickly over an uneven surface. ❑ *Waterfalls crash and tumble over rocks. ...the aromatic pines and tumbling streams of the Zonba Plateau.* 4 If you say that someone **tumbles into** a situation or place, you mean that they get into it without being fully in control of themselves or knowing what they are doing. [mainly BRIT] ❑ *Many mothers and children tumble into poverty after divorce.* 5 ➔ See also **rough and tumble**.
VERB; V prep/adv; V prep/adv; N-COUNT: usu sing; VERB; V by/from/to amount; V; V-ing; N-COUNT: usu sing; VERB; V prep; V-ing; VERB; V into n

♦ **tumble down** If a building **tumbles down**, it collapses or parts of it fall off, usually because it is old and no-one has taken care of it. ❑ *The outer walls looked likely to tumble down in a stiff wind.* PHRASAL VERB; V P

**tumble|down** /tʌmbᵊldaʊn/ A **tumble-down** building is in such a bad condition that it is partly falling down or has holes in it. ADJ: usu ADJ n = *ram-shackle*

**tum|ble dry|er** **(tumble dryers)** also **tumble drier.** A **tumble dryer** is an electric machine which dries washing by turning it over and over and blowing warm air onto it. [mainly BRIT] N-COUNT

☑ in AM, use **dryer**

**tum|bler** /tʌmbləʳ/ **(tumblers)** A **tumbler** is a drinking glass with straight sides. N-COUNT

**tumble|weed** /tʌmbᵊlwiːd/ **Tumbleweed** is a plant that grows in desert areas in North America. It breaks off from its roots at the end of its life and then blows around on the ground. [AM] N-UNCOUNT

**tum|my** /tʌmi/ **(tummies)** 1 Your **tummy** is the part of the front of your body below your waist. **Tummy** is often used by children or by adults talking to children. ❑ *Your baby's tummy should feel warm, but not hot.* 2 You can use **tummy** to refer to the parts inside your body where food is digested. **Tummy** is often used by children or by adults talking to children. ❑ *It's easy to get a tummy upset from river water.*
N-COUNT = *stomach*; N-COUNT = *stomach*

**tu|mour** /tjuːməʳ, AM tuː-/ **(tumours)**

☑ in AM, use **tumor**

A **tumour** is a mass of diseased or abnormal cells that has grown in a person's or animal's body. N-COUNT

**tu|mult** /tjuːmʌlt, AM tuː-/ 1 A **tumult** is a state of great confusion or excitement. ❑ *A tumult of feelings inside her fought for supremacy. ...the recent tumult in global financial markets.* 2 A **tumult** is a lot of noise made by a crowd of people. ❑ *Round one ends, to a tumult of whistles, screams and shouts.*
N-SING: also no det, oft N *of* n; N-SING: also no det, oft N *of* n

**tu|mul|tu|ous** /tjuːmʌltʃuəs, AM tuː-/ 1 A **tumultuous** event or period of time involves many exciting and confusing events or feelings. ❑ *...the tumultuous changes in Eastern Europe... It's been a tumultuous day at the international trade negotiations in Brussels.* 2 A **tumultuous** reaction to something is very noisy, because the people involved are very happy or excited. ❑ *Delegates greeted the news with tumultuous applause.*
ADJ: usu ADJ n; ADJ: usu ADJ n

**tuna** /tjuːnə, AM tuːnə/ **(tuna** or **tunas)** **Tuna** or **tuna fish** are large fish that live in warm seas and are caught for food. ♦ **Tuna** or **tuna fish** is this fish eaten as food. ❑ *She began opening a tin of tuna.*
N-VAR; N-UNCOUNT

**tun|dra** /tʌndrə/ **(tundras)** **Tundra** is one of the large flat areas of land in the north of Europe, Asia, and America. The ground below the top layer of soil is always frozen and no trees grow there. N-VAR

**tune** /tjuːn, AM tuːn/ **(tunes, tuning, tuned)** ◆◇◇ 1 A **tune** is a series of musical notes that is pleasant and easy to remember. ❑ *She was humming a merry little tune.* 2 You can refer to a song or a short piece of music as a **tune**. ❑ *She'll also be playing your favourite pop tunes.* 3 When someone **tunes** a musical instrument, they adjust it so that it produces the right notes. ❑ *'We do tune our guitars before we go on,' he insisted.* ♦ **Tune up** means the same as **tune**. ❑ *Others were quietly tuning up their instruments.* 4 When an engine or machine **is tuned**, it is adjusted so that it works well. ❑ *Drivers are urged to make sure that car engines are properly tuned.* ♦ **Tune up** means the same as **tune**. ❑ *The shop charges up to $500 to tune up a Porsche.* 5 If your radio or television **is tuned to** a particular broadcasting station, you are listening to or watching the programmes being broadcast by that station. ❑ *A small colour television was tuned to an afternoon soap opera.* 6 ➔ See also **fine-tune**, **signature tune**, **tuning fork**.
N-COUNT = *melody*; N-COUNT; VERB; V n; PHRASAL VERB; V P n; VERB: usu passive; *be* V-ed; PHRASAL VERB; V P n; VERB: usu passive; *be* V-ed *to* n

**PHRASES** 7 If you say that a person or organization **is calling the tune**, you mean that they are in a position of power or control in a particular situation. ❑ *Who would then be calling the tune in Parliament?* 8 If you say that someone **has changed** their **tune**, you are criticizing them because they have changed their opinion or way of doing things. ❑ *You've changed your tune since this morning, haven't you?* 9 If you say that someone is **dancing to** someone else's **tune**, you mean that they are allowing themselves to be controlled by the other person. ❑ *The danger of commercialism is that the churches end up dancing to the tune of their big business sponsors.* 10 A person or musical instrument that is **in tune** produces exactly the right notes. A person or musical instrument that is **out of tune** does not produce exactly the right notes. ❑ *It was just an ordinary voice, but he sang in tune... Many of the notes are out of tune.* 11 If you are **in tune with** a group of people, you are in agreement or sympathy with them. If you are **out of tune with** them, you are not in agreement or sympathy with them. ❑ *Today, his change of direction seems more in tune with the times... The peace campaigners were probably out of tune with most Britons.* 12 **To the tune of** a particular amount of money means to the extent of that amount. ❑ *They've been sponsoring the World Cup to the tune of a million and a half pounds.* 13 **he who pays the piper calls the tune** ➔ see **piper**.
PHRASE: V inflects; PHRASE: V inflects, disapproval; PHRASE: V inflects, disapproval; PHRASE: PHR after v, v-link PHR; PHRASE: v-link PHR, PHR n; PREP-PHRASE: PREP amount

♦ **tune in** 1 If you **tune in** to a particular television or radio station or programme, you watch or listen to it. ❑ *More than six million youngsters tune in to Blockbusters every day... The idea that people plan their radio listening is nonsense; most tune in impulsively.* 2 If you **tune in to** something such as your own or other people's feelings, you become aware of them. ❑ *You can start now to tune in to your own physical, social and spiritual needs.* ➔ See also **tuned in**.
PHRASAL VERB; V P *to* n; V P; PHRASAL VERB; V P *to* n

♦ **tune up** When a group of musicians **tune up**, they adjust their instruments so that they produce the right notes. ❑ *I could hear the sound of a band tuning up.* ➔ See also **tune 4**. PHRASAL VERB; V P

**tuned in** If someone is **tuned in to** something, they are aware of it and concentrating on it. ❑ *He's just not tuned in to the child's feelings.* ADJ: usu v-link ADJ *to* n

**tune|ful** /tjuːnfʊl, AM tuːn-/ A piece of music that is **tuneful** has a pleasant tune. ADJ

**tune|less** /tjuːnləs, AM tuːn-/ **Tuneless** music and voices do not sound pleasant. ❑ *Someone walked by, singing a tuneless song.* ADJ: usu ADJ n ♦ **tune|less|ly** *My dad whistled tunelessly through his teeth.* ADV: ADV after v

**tun|er** /tjuːnəʳ, AM tuːn-/ **(tuners)** The **tuner** in a radio or television set is the part which you adjust to receive different radio or television signals, so that you can watch or listen to the programme that you want. N-COUNT: oft supp N

**tung|sten** /tʌŋstən/ **Tungsten** is a greyish-white metal. N-UNCOUNT

**tu|nic** /tjuːnɪk, AM tuː-/ **(tunics)** A **tunic** is a sleeveless garment that is worn on the top part of your body. N-COUNT

**tun|ing fork** **(tuning forks)** A **tuning fork** is a small steel instrument which is used to tune instruments by striking it against something to produce a note of fixed musical pitch. N-COUNT

**Tu|ni|sian** /tjuːnɪziən, AM tuːn-/ **(Tunisians)**
1 **Tunisian** means belonging to or relating to Tunisia, or to its people or culture. ADJ 2 A **Tunisian** is a Tunisian citizen, or a person of Tunisian origin. N-COUNT

**tun|nel** /tʌnᵊl/ **(tunnels, tunnelling, tunnelled)** ◆◇◇
✓ in AM, use **tunneling, tunneled**
1 A **tunnel** is a long passage which has been made under the ground, usually through a hill or under the sea. ❑ *...two new railway tunnels through the Alps.* N-COUNT: oft supp N 2 To **tunnel** somewhere means to make a tunnel there. ❑ *The rebels tunnelled out of a maximum security jail.* VERB V prep/adv 3 → See also **wind tunnel**.

**tun|nel vi|sion** 1 If you suffer from **tunnel vision**, you are unable to see things that are not straight in front of you. N-UNCOUNT 2 If you say that someone has **tunnel vision**, you disapprove of them because they are concentrating completely on achieving a particular aim, and do not notice or consider all the different aspects of what they are doing. N-UNCOUNT [disapproval]

**tup|pence** /tʌpəns/ In Britain, **tuppence** was two old pence. [INFORMAL] N-UNCOUNT

**Tup|per|ware** /tʌpəʳweəʳ/ **Tupperware** is a range of plastic containers with tight-fitting lids that are used for storing food. [TRADEMARK] ❑ *...a Tupperware box.* N-UNCOUNT: oft N n

**tur|ban** /tɜːʳbən/ **(turbans)** A **turban** is a long piece of cloth that is wound round the head. It is worn by Sikh men and by some Hindu and Muslim men. N-COUNT

**tur|bine** /tɜːʳbaɪn, AM -bɪn/ **(turbines)** A **turbine** is a machine or engine which uses a stream of air, gas, water, or steam to turn a wheel and produce power. N-COUNT

**turbo** /tɜːʳboʊ/ **(turbos)** A **turbo** is a fan in the engine of a car or plane that improves its performance by using exhaust gases to blow fuel vapour into the engine. N-COUNT

**turbo-charged** also **turbocharged.** A **turbo-charged** engine or vehicle is fitted with a turbo. ADJ: usu ADJ n

**tur|bo|prop** /tɜːʳboʊprɒp/ **(turboprops)** also **turbo-prop.** 1 A **turboprop** is a turbine engine that makes an aircraft propeller go round. N-COUNT 2 A **turboprop** is an aircraft with one or more turboprops. N-COUNT

**tur|bot** /tɜːʳbət/ **(turbot)** **Turbot** are a type of edible flat fish that live in European seas. N-VAR ♦ **Turbot** is this fish eaten as food. N-UNCOUNT

**tur|bu|lence** /tɜːʳbjʊləns/ 1 **Turbulence** is a state of confusion and disorganized change. ❑ *The 1960s and early 1970s were a time of change and turbulence.* N-UNCOUNT 2 **Turbulence** is violent and uneven movement within a particular area of air, liquid, or gas. ❑ *His plane encountered severe turbulence and winds of nearly two-hundred miles an hour.* N-UNCOUNT

**tur|bu|lent** /tɜːʳbjʊlənt/ 1 A **turbulent** time, place, or relationship is one in which there is a lot of change, confusion, and disorder. ❑ *They had been together for five or six turbulent years of rows and reconciliations.* ADJ: usu ADJ n 2 **Turbulent** water or air contains strong currents which change direction suddenly. ❑ *I had to have a boat that could handle turbulent seas.* ADJ: usu ADJ n

**turd** /tɜːʳd/ **(turds)** A **turd** is a lump of faeces. [INFORMAL, RUDE] N-COUNT

**tu|reen** /tjʊəriːn, AM tʊr-/ **(tureens)** A **tureen** is a large bowl with a lid from which you can serve soup or vegetables. N-COUNT

**turf** /tɜːʳf/ **(turfs, turfing, turfed)** 1 **Turf** is short, thick, even grass. ❑ *They shuffled slowly down the turf towards the cliff's edge.* N-UNCOUNT: also *the* N 2 Someone's **turf** is the area which is most familiar to them or where they feel most confident. ❑ *Their turf was Paris: its streets, theaters, homes, and parks.* N-UNCOUNT: usu poss N = *territory*

♦ **turf out** If someone **is turfed out** of a place or position, they are forced to leave. [BRIT, INFORMAL] ❑ *We hear stories of people being turfed out and ending up on the streets... The party was turfed out of office after 15 years. ...the right wing landslide which has turfed out the Socialist government.* PHRASAL VERB be V-ed P be V-ed P *of* n V P n Also V n P

**turf war** **(turf wars)** or **turf battle** 1 A **turf war** is a struggle between criminals or gangs over who controls a particular area. [mainly JOURNALISM] ❑ *The estate is at the centre of a bitter turf war between rival drug gangs.* N-COUNT: oft N *between* n, N *over* n 2 A **turf war** is a struggle between people over who controls a particular activity. [mainly JOURNALISM] ❑ *Both sides say this is more than just a turf war between big and small banks.* N-COUNT: oft N *between* n, N *over* n

**tur|gid** /tɜːʳdʒɪd/ If you describe something such as a piece of writing or a film as **turgid**, you think it is boring and difficult to understand. ❑ *He used to make extremely dull, turgid and frankly boring speeches.* ADJ

**Turk** /tɜːʳk/ **(Turks)** A **Turk** is a Turkish citizen, or a person of Turkish origin. N-COUNT

**tur|key** /tɜːʳki/ **(turkeys)** A **turkey** is a large bird that is kept on a farm for its meat. N-COUNT ♦ **Turkey** is the flesh of this bird eaten as food. ❑ *It's a proper Christmas dinner, with turkey and bread sauce.* N-UNCOUNT → See also **cold turkey**.

**Turk|ish** /tɜːʳkɪʃ/ 1 **Turkish** means belonging or relating to Turkey, or to its people, language, or culture. ADJ 2 **Turkish** is the main language spoken in Turkey. N-UNCOUNT

**Turk|ish bath** **(Turkish baths)** 1 A **Turkish bath** is a type of bath in which you sit in a very hot steamy room, then wash, have a massage, and finally swim or shower in very cold water. N-COUNT 2 A **Turkish bath** is a place where you can have a Turkish bath. N-COUNT

**Turk|ish de|light** **(Turkish delights)** **Turkish delight** is a jelly-like sweet that is covered with powdered sugar or chocolate. N-VAR

**tur|mer|ic** /tɜːʳmərɪk/ **Turmeric** is a yellow spice that is used to flavour food such as curry. N-UNCOUNT

**tur|moil** /tɜːʳmɔɪl/ **(turmoils)** **Turmoil** is a state of confusion, disorder, uncertainty, or great anxiety. ❑ *...the political turmoil of 1989... Her marriage was in turmoil.* N-VAR: usu with supp, oft *in* N

**turn** /tɜːʳn/ **(turns, turning, turned)** ◆◆◆

> **Turn** is used in a large number of other expressions which are explained under other words in the dictionary. For example, the expression 'turn over a new leaf' is explained at **leaf**.

1 When you **turn** or when you **turn** part of your body, you move your body or part of your body so that it is facing in a different or opposite direction. ❑ *He turned abruptly and walked away... He sighed, turning away and surveying the sea... He turned his head left and right.* VERB V V prep/adv V n adv/prep ♦ **Turn around** or **turn round** means the same as **turn**. ❑ *I felt a tapping on my shoulder and I turned around... Turn your upper body round so that your shoulders are fac-* PHRASAL VERB V P V n P

*ing to the side.* 2 When you **turn** something, you move it so that it is facing in a different or opposite direction, or is in a very different position. ❑ *They turned their telescopes towards other nearby galaxies... She had turned the bedside chair to face the door... The lid, turned upside down, served as a coffee table.* VERB V n prep/adv V n to-inf V-ed

3 When something such as a wheel **turns**, or when you **turn** it, it continually moves around in a particular direction. ❑ *As the wheel turned, the potter shaped the clay... The engine turned a propeller.* VERB V V n

4 When you **turn** something such as a key, knob, or switch, or when it **turns**, you hold it and twist your hand, in order to open something or make it start working. ❑ *Turn a special key, press the brake pedal, and your car's brakes lock... Turn the heat to very low and cook for 20 minutes... I tried the doorknob and it turned.* VERB V n V n prep/adv V

5 When you **turn** in a particular direction or **turn** a corner, you change the direction in which you are moving or travelling. ❑ *Now turn right to follow West Ferry Road... The man with the umbrella turned the corner again.* ♦ **Turn** is also a noun. ❑ *You can't do a right-hand turn here.* VERB V prep/adv V n N-COUNT

6 The point where a road, path, or river **turns**, is the point where it has a bend or curve in it. ❑ *...the corner where Tenterfield Road turned into the main road.* ♦ **Turn** is also a noun. ❑ *...a sharp turn in the road.* VERB V prep/adv Also V N-COUNT

7 When the tide **turns**, it starts coming in or going out. ❑ *There was not much time before the tide turned.* VERB V

8 When you **turn** a page of a book or magazine, you move it so that is flat against the previous page, and you can read the next page. ❑ *He turned the pages of a file in front of him.* VERB V n

9 If you **turn** a weapon or an aggressive feeling **on** someone, you point it at them or direct it at them. ❑ *He tried to turn the gun on me... The crowd than turned their anger on Prime Minister James Mitchell.* VERB V n *on* n V n *on* n

10 If you **turn to** a particular page in a book or magazine, you open it at that page. ❑ *To order, turn to page 236.* VERB V *to* n

11 If you **turn** your attention or thoughts **to** a particular subject or if you **turn to** it, you start thinking about it or discussing it. ❑ *We turned our attention to the practical matters relating to forming a company... We turn now to the British news.* VERB V n *to* n V *to* n

12 If you **turn to** someone, you ask for their help or advice. ❑ *For assistance, they turned to one of the city's most innovative museums.* VERB V *to* n

13 If you **turn to** a particular activity, job, or way of doing something, you start doing or using it. ❑ *These communities are now turning to recycling in large numbers.* VERB V *to/from* n/-ing

14 To **turn** or **be turned into** something means to become that thing. ❑ *A prince turns into a frog in this cartoon fairytale... The hated dictator had turned his country into one of the poorest police states in Europe.* VERB V *into/to* n V n *into/to* n

15 You can use **turn** before an adjective to indicate that something or someone changes by acquiring the quality described by the adjective. ❑ *If the bailiff thinks that things could turn nasty he will enlist the help of the police.* V-LINK = *become* V adj

16 If something **turns** a particular colour or if something **turns** it a particular colour, it becomes that colour. ❑ *The sea would turn pale pink and the sky blood red... Her contact lenses turned her eyes green.* V-LINK V colour V n colour

17 You can use **turn** to indicate that there is a change to a particular kind of weather. For example, if it **turns** cold, the weather starts being cold. ❑ *If it turns cold, cover plants.* V-LINK V adj

18 If a situation or trend takes a particular kind of **turn**, it changes so that it starts developing in a different or opposite way. ❑ *The scandal took a new turn over the weekend.* N-COUNT: with supp, oft N *in* n

19 If a business **turns** a profit, it earns more money than it spends. [AM, BUSINESS] ❑ *The firm will be able to service debt and still turn a modest profit.* VERB: no passive V n

✔ in BRIT, use **make**, **return**

20 When someone **turns** a particular age, they pass that age. When it **turns** a particular time, it passes that time. ❑ *It was his ambition to accumulate a million dollars before he turned thirty.* VERB V n

21 **Turn** is used in expressions such as **the turn of the century** and **the turn of the year** to refer to a period of time when one century or year is ending and the next one is beginning. ❑ *They fled to South America around the turn of the century.* N-SING: *the* N *of* n

22 When someone **turns** a wooden or metal object that they are making, they shape it using a special tool. ❑ *...the joys of making a living from turning wood.* VERB V n

23 If it is your **turn to** do something, you now have the duty, chance, or right to do it, when other people have done it before you or will do it after you. ❑ *Tonight it's my turn to cook... Let each child have a turn at fishing.* N-COUNT: usu with poss, oft N to-inf, N *at* -ing, N -ing

24 If you say that someone is having a **turn**, you mean they feel suddenly very unwell for a short period of time. [BRIT, INFORMAL] N-COUNT

25 → See also **turning**.

PHRASES 26 You can use **by turns** to indicate that someone has two particular emotions or qualities, one after the other. ❑ *His tone was by turns angry and aggrieved.* PHRASE: PHR with group, PHR with v

27 If there is a particular **turn of events**, a particular series of things happen. ❑ *They were horrified at this unexpected turn of events.* PHRASE

28 If you say that something happens **at every turn**, you are emphasizing that it happens frequently or all the time, usually so that it prevents you from achieving what you want. ❑ *Its operations were hampered at every turn by inadequate numbers of trained staff.* PHRASE: PHR after v, PHR with cl [emphasis]

29 If you do someone **a good turn**, you do something that helps or benefits them. ❑ *He did you a good turn by resigning.* PHRASE: usu PHR after v

30 If someone **turns** a place **inside out** or **upside down**, they search it very thoroughly and usually make it very untidy. ❑ *They hadn't found a scrap of evidence though they had turned his flat inside out.* PHRASE: V inflects

31 If something such as a system or way of life **is turned inside out** or **upside down**, it is changed completely, making people confused or upset. ❑ *He felt too shocked to move. His world had been turned upside down.* PHRASE: V inflects

32 You use **in turn** to refer to actions or events that are in a sequence one after the other, for example because one causes the other. ❑ *One of the members of the surgical team leaked the story to a fellow physician who, in turn, confided in a reporter.* PHRASE: PHR with cl/group

33 If each person in a group does something **in turn**, they do it one after the other in a fixed or agreed order. ❑ *There were cheers for each of the women as they spoke in turn.* PHRASE: PHR after v

34 If you **speak out of turn** or **talk out of turn**, you say something that you do not have the right or authority to say. ❑ *I hope I haven't spoken out of turn.* PHRASE: V inflects

35 If two or more people **take turns to** do something, or in British English **take it in turns to** do something, they do it one after the other several times, rather than doing it together. ❑ *We took turns to drive the car.* PHRASE: V inflects, oft PHR to-inf

36 If a situation **takes a turn for the worse**, it suddenly becomes worse. If a situation **takes a turn for the better**, it suddenly becomes better. ❑ *Her condition took a sharp turn for the worse.* PHRASE: V inflects

♦ **turn against** If you **turn against** someone or something, or if you **are turned against** them, you stop supporting them, trusting them, or liking them. ❑ *A kid I used to be friends with turned against me after being told that I'd been insulting him... Working with the police has turned me against the use of violent scenes as entertainment.* PHRASAL VERB V P n V n P n

♦ **turn around** or **turn round** 1 → see **turn 1**.

2 If you **turn** something **around**, or if it **turns around**, it is moved so that it faces the opposite direction. ❑ *Bud turned the truck around, and started back for Dalton Pond... He had reached over to turn round a bottle of champagne so that the label didn't show... There was enough room for a wheelchair to get in but not to turn round.* PHRASAL VERB V n P V P n (not pron) V P

3 If something such as a business or economy **turns around**, or if someone **turns** it **around**, it becomes successful, after being unsuccessful for a period of time. [BUSINESS] ❑ *Turning the company around won't be easy... In his long career at BP, Horton turned around two entire divisions... If the economy turned round the Prime Minister's authority would quickly increase.* PHRASAL VERB V n P V P n (not pron) V P

4 If you say that someone **turns around** and says something, you are indicating that they say it unexpectedly or angrily, es- PHRASAL VERB

pecially in order to criticize another person or to defend themselves. [INFORMAL] ❑ *I feel that if I say how tired I get, David will turn around and say, 'I told you so'.* V P *and* v [5] If you **turn around** a question, sentence, or idea, you change the way in which it is expressed, in order to consider it differently. PHRASAL VERB ❑ *Now turn the question around and start looking not for what you did wrong in the past, but for what you can do to make things better in the future...* V n P *It's an example of how you can turn around the sentence and create a whole new meaning.* V P n (not pron) [6] ➔ See also **turnaround**.

♦ **turn away** [1] If you **turn** someone **away**, you do not allow them to enter your country, home, or other place. PHRASAL VERB ❑ *Turning refugees away would be an inhumane action...* V n P *Hard times are forcing community colleges to turn away students.* V P n (not pron) [2] To **turn away from** something such as a method or an idea means to stop using it or to become different from it. PHRASAL VERB ❑ *Japanese corporations have been turning away from production and have diverted into finance and real estate.* V P *from* n

♦ **turn back** [1] If you **turn back** or if someone **turns** you **back** when you are going somewhere, you change direction and go towards where you started from. PHRASAL VERB ❑ *She turned back towards the crossroads...* V P prep/adv *They were very nearly forced to turn back...* V P *Police attempted to turn back protesters marching towards the offices of President Ershad.* V P n Also V n P [2] If you **cannot turn back**, you cannot change your plans and decide not to do something, because the action you have already taken makes it impossible. PHRASAL VERB: with brd-neg ❑ *The administration has now endorsed the bill and can't turn back.* V P

♦ **turn down** [1] If you **turn down** a person or their request or offer, you refuse their request or offer. PHRASAL VERB = reject ❑ *Before this I'd have smiled and turned her down...* V n P *Would you turn down $7,000,000 to appear nude in a magazine?* V P n (not pron) [2] When you **turn down** a radio, heater, or other piece of equipment, you reduce the amount of sound or heat being produced, by adjusting the controls. PHRASAL VERB ≠ turn up ❑ *He kept turning the central heating down...* V n P *She could not bear the relentless music and turned down the volume.* V P n (not pron)

♦ **turn in** [1] When you **turn in**, you go to bed. [INFORMAL] PHRASAL VERB ❑ *Would you like some tea before you turn in?* V P [2] If you **turn** someone **in**, you take them to the police or tell the police where they are because they are suspected of committing a crime. If you **turn** yourself **in**, you go to the police because you have been involved in a crime. PHRASAL VERB ❑ *He has been given until noon today to turn himself in to authorities...* V n P *to* n *There would be strong incentives to turn someone in...* V n P *I might today hesitate to turn in a burglar.* V P n Also V P n *to* n [3] When you **turn in** a completed piece of work, especially written work, you give it to the person who asked you to do it. PHRASAL VERB = hand in ❑ *Now we wait for them to turn in their essays...* V P n *I want everybody to turn a report in.* V n P [4] If you **turn** something **in**, you return it to the place or person you borrowed it from. [mainly AM] PHRASAL VERB = return ❑ *I went back to the station-house to turn in my badge and gun.* V P n

♦ **turn off** [1] If you **turn off** the road or path you are going along, you start going along a different road or path which leads away from it. PHRASAL VERB ❑ *The truck turned off the main road along the gravelly track which led to the farm...* V P n (not pron) *He turned off only to find he was trapped in a town square with no easy exit.* V P [2] When you **turn off** a piece of equipment or a supply of something, you stop heat, sound, or water being produced by adjusting the controls. PHRASAL VERB = switch off ≠ turn on ❑ *The light's a bit too harsh. You can turn it off...* V n P *I have to get up and turn off the radio.* V P n [3] If something **turns** you **off** a particular subject or activity, it makes you have no interest in it. PHRASAL VERB ❑ *What turns teenagers off science and technology?...* V n P n *Teaching off a blackboard is boring, and undoubtedly turns people off.* V n P Also V P n ➔ See also **turn-off**. [4] If something or someone **turns** you **off**, you do not find them sexually attractive or they stop you feeling sexually excited. PHRASAL VERB ≠ turn on [INFORMAL] ❑ *Aggressive men turn me off completely.* V n P Also V P n (not pron) ➔ See also **turn-off**.

♦ **turn on** [1] When you **turn on** a piece of equipment or a supply of something, you cause heat, sound, or water to be produced by adjusting the controls. PHRASAL VERB = switch on ≠ turn off ❑ *I want to turn on the television...* V P n (not pron) *She asked them why they hadn't turned the lights on.* V n P [2] If someone or something **turns** you **on**, they attract you and make you feel sexually excited. PHRASAL VERB ≠ turn off [INFORMAL] ❑ *The body that turns men on doesn't have to be perfect.* V n P ➔ See also **turn-on**. [3] If you say that someone **turns on** a particular way of behaving, you mean that they suddenly start behaving in that way, and you are often also suggesting that this is insincere. PHRASAL VERB [INFORMAL] ❑ *He could also turn on the style when the occasion demanded.* V P n (not pron) Also V n P [4] If someone **turns on** you, they attack you or speak angrily to you. PHRASAL VERB ❑ *Demonstrators turned on police, overturning vehicles and setting fire to them.* V P n [5] If something **turns on** a particular thing, its success or truth depends on that thing. PHRASAL VERB = hinge on ❑ *The plot turns on whether Ilsa will choose her lover or her husband.* V P n

♦ **turn out** [1] If something **turns out** a particular way, it happens in that way or has the result or degree of success indicated. PHRASAL VERB = work out ❑ *If I had known my life was going to turn out like this, I would have let them kill me...* V P prep *Sometimes things don't turn out the way we think they're going to...* V P n *I was positive things were going to turn out fine.* V P adj [2] When you are commenting on pleasant weather, you can say that is has **turned out** nice or fine, especially if this is unexpected. PHRASAL VERB [BRIT, SPOKEN] ❑ *It's turned out nice again.* *it* V P adj [3] If something **turns out to** be a particular thing, it is discovered to be that thing. PHRASAL VERB ❑ *Cosgrave's forecast turned out to be quite wrong...* V P to-inf *It turned out that I knew the person who got shot.* *it* V-ed P that [4] When you **turn out** something such as a light or gas, you move the switch or knob that controls it so that it stops giving out light or heat. PHRASAL VERB = turn off ❑ *I'll just play until the janitor comes round to turn the lights out.* V n P Also V P n (not pron) [5] If a business or other organization **turns out** something, it produces it. PHRASAL VERB ❑ *They have been turning out great blades for 400 years.* V P n Also V n P [6] If you **turn** someone **out of** a place, especially the place where they have been living, you force them to leave that place. PHRASAL VERB = throw out ❑ *Surely nobody would suggest turning him out of the house...* V n P *of/from* n *It was previously a small monastery but the authorities turned all the monks out.* V n P Also V P n [7] If you **turn out** the contents of a container, you empty it by removing them or letting them fall out. PHRASAL VERB ❑ *Turn out the dough on to a floured surface...* V P n *Turn the plants out of their pots.* V n P *of/from* n [8] If people **turn out for** a particular event or activity, they go and take part in it or watch it. PHRASAL VERB ❑ *Thousands of people turned out for the funeral...* V P *for* n *It was no wonder the fans turned out. The matches yielded 259 goals.* V P [9] ➔ See also **turnout**, **turned out**.

♦ **turn over** [1] If you **turn** something **over**, or if it **turns over**, it is moved so that the top part is now facing downwards. PHRASAL VERB ❑ *Liz picked up the blue envelope and turned it over curiously...* V n P *I don't suppose you thought to turn over the tape, did you?...* V P n (not pron) *The buggy turned over and Nancy was thrown out.* V P [2] If you **turn over**, for example when you are lying in bed, you move your body so that you are lying in a different position. PHRASAL VERB ❑ *Ann turned over in her bed once more.* V P [3] If you **turn** something **over in** your mind, you think carefully about it. PHRASAL VERB ❑ *Even when she didn't say anything you could see her turning things over in her mind.* V n P *in* n [4] If you **turn** something **over to** someone, you give it to them when they ask for it, because they have a right to it. PHRASAL VERB = hand over ❑ *I would turn the evidence over to the police...* V n P (not pron) *to* n *The lawyer turned over the release papers.* V P n [5] If you **turn over** a job or responsibility that you have, you give it to someone else, so that you no longer have it. PHRASAL VERB ❑ *The King may turn over some of his official posts to his son.* V P n *to* n [6] If you **turn over** when you are watching television, you change to another channel. PHRASAL VERB ❑ *Whenever he's on TV, I turn over.* V P [7] ➔ See also **turnover**.

♦ **turn over to** If you **turn** something **over to** a different function or use, you change its function or use. ❑ *When he first leased the land in the late 1970s, he planned to turn it over to cereal production.* PHRASAL VERB V n P P n Also V P n (not pron) P n

♦ **turn round** → see **turn around**.

♦ **turn up** [1] If you say that someone or something **turns up**, you mean that they arrive, often unexpectedly or after you have been waiting a long time. ❑ *Richard had turned up on Christmas Eve with Tony.* PHRASAL VERB = show up V P [2] If you **turn** something **up** or if it **turns up**, you find, discover, or notice it. ❑ *Investigations have never turned up any evidence. ...a very rare 15th-Century spoon, which turned up in an old house in Devon.* PHRASAL VERB V P n (not pron) V P [3] When you **turn up** a radio, heater, or other piece of equipment, you increase the amount of sound, heat, or power being produced, by adjusting the controls. ❑ *Bill would turn up the TV in the other room... I turned the volume up... Turn the heat up high.* PHRASAL VERB ≠ turn down V P n (not pron) V n P V n P adj

**turn|about** /tɜːʳnəbaʊt/ A **turnabout** is a complete change in opinion, attitude, or method. ❑ *As her confidence grows you may well see a considerable turnabout in her attitude.* N-SING: oft N *in* n = turnaround

**turn|around** /tɜːʳnəraʊnd/ **(turnarounds)** [1] A **turnaround** is a complete change in opinion, attitude, or method. ❑ *I have personally never done such a complete turnaround in my opinion of a person.* N-COUNT: oft N *in* n [2] A **turnaround** is a sudden improvement, especially in the success of a business or a country's economy. ❑ *The deal marks a turnaround in the fortunes of South Wales Electricity.* N-COUNT: usu sing, oft N *in* n [3] The **turnaround** or **turnaround time** of a task, for example the unloading of an aircraft or ship, is the amount of time that it takes. ❑ *It is possible to produce a result within 34 hours but the standard turnaround is 12 days... The agency should reduce turnaround time by 11 per cent.* N-VAR

**turn|coat** /tɜːʳnkoʊt/ **(turncoats)** If you describe someone as a **turncoat**, you think they are disloyal or deceitful, because they have left their party or organization and joined an opposing one. N-COUNT [disapproval]

**turned out** If you are well **turned out** or smartly **turned out**, you are dressed smartly. ❑ *...a well-turned-out young chap in a black suit.* ♦◇◇ ADJ: adv ADJ

**turn|ing** /tɜːʳnɪŋ/ **(turnings)** If you take a particular **turning**, you go along a road which leads away from the side of another road. ❑ *Take the next turning on the right.* → See also **turn**. N-COUNT = turn

**turn|ing point** **(turning points)** A **turning point** is a time at which an important change takes place which affects the future of a person or thing. ❑ *The vote yesterday appears to mark something of a turning point in the war.* N-COUNT: usu sing, oft N *in/for* n

**tur|nip** /tɜːʳnɪp/ **(turnips)** A **turnip** is a round vegetable with a greenish-white skin that is the root of a crop. → See picture on page 1712. N-VAR

**turn-off** **(turn-offs)** [1] A **turn-off** is a road leading away from a major road or a motorway. N-COUNT [2] Something that is a **turn-off** causes you to lose interest or sexual excitement. [INFORMAL] N-COUNT: usu sing

**turn-on** **(turn-ons)** Something or someone that is a **turn-on** is sexually exciting. [INFORMAL] N-COUNT: usu sing

**turn|out** /tɜːʳnaʊt/ **(turnouts)** also **turn-out.** [1] The **turnout** at an event is the number of people who go to it or take part in it. ❑ *On the big night there was a massive turnout.* N-COUNT: usu sing, oft supp N [2] The **turnout** in an election is the number of people who vote in it, as a proportion of the number of people who have the right to vote in it. ❑ *Election officials said the turnout of voters was low... A high turnout was reported at the polling booths.* N-COUNT: usu sing

**turn|over** /tɜːʳnoʊvəʳ/ **(turnovers)** [1] The **turnover** of a company is the value of the goods or services sold during a particular period of time. [BUSINESS] ❑ *The company had a turnover of £3.8 million.* N-VAR: usu with supp, supp N, N *of* n [2] The **turnover** of people in an organization or place is the rate at which people leave and are replaced. [BUSINESS] ❑ *Short-term contracts increase staff turnover.* N-VAR: usu with supp, supp N, N *of* n

**turn|pike** /tɜːʳnpaɪk/ **(turnpikes)** A **turnpike** is a road, especially an expressway, which people have to pay to drive on. [mainly AM] N-COUNT

**turn|round** /tɜːʳnraʊnd/ A **turnround** is the same as a **turnaround**. N-SING

**turn sig|nal** **(turn signals)** A car's **turn signals** are the flashing lights that tell you it is going to turn left or right. [AM] → See picture on page 1707. N-COUNT

✔ in BRIT, use **indicators**

**turn|stile** /tɜːʳnstaɪl/ **(turnstiles)** A **turnstile** is a mechanical barrier at the entrance to a place such as a museum or a football ground. Turnstiles have metal arms that you push round as you go through them and enter the building or area. N-COUNT

**turn|table** /tɜːʳnteɪbᵊl/ **(turntables)** A **turntable** is the flat, round part of a record player on which a record is put when it is played. N-COUNT

**turn-up** **(turn-ups)** The **turn-ups** on a pair of trousers are the parts which are folded over at the ends of the legs. [BRIT] N-COUNT: usu pl

✔ in AM, use **cuffs**

**tur|pen|tine** /tɜːʳpəntaɪn/ **Turpentine** is a colourless liquid used, for example, for cleaning paint off brushes. N-UNCOUNT

**tur|pi|tude** /tɜːʳpɪtjuːd, AM -tuːd/ **Turpitude** is very immoral behaviour. [FORMAL] N-UNCOUNT: usu supp N

**tur|quoise** /tɜːʳkwɔɪz/ **(turquoises)** **Turquoise** or **turquoise blue** is used to describe things that are of a light greenish-blue colour. ❑ *...a clear turquoise sea.* COLOUR

**tur|ret** /tʌrɪt, AM tɜːr-/ **(turrets)** [1] A **turret** is a small narrow tower on top of a building or a larger tower. N-COUNT [2] The **turret** on a tank or warship is the part where the guns are fixed, which can be turned in any direction. N-COUNT: oft n N

**tur|tle** /tɜːʳtᵊl/ **(turtles)** [1] A **turtle** is a large reptile which has a thick shell covering its body and which lives in the sea most of the time. [BRIT] N-COUNT

✔ in AM, use **sea turtle**

[2] A **turtle** is any reptile that has a thick shell around its body, for example a tortoise or terrapin. [AM] N-COUNT

**tur|tle dove** **(turtle doves)** also **turtle-dove.** A **turtle dove** is a type of light-brown dove which makes a soft pleasant sound and which is said to behave in a very affectionate way towards its sexual partner and its young. N-COUNT

**turtle|neck** /tɜːʳtᵊlnek/ **(turtlenecks)** [1] A **turtleneck** or **turtleneck sweater** is a sweater with a short round collar that fits closely around your neck. [BRIT] N-COUNT

✔ in AM, use **mock turtleneck**

[2] A **turtleneck** or **turtleneck sweater** is a sweater with a high neck which folds over. [AM] N-COUNT

✔ in BRIT, use **polo neck**

**tusk** /tʌsk/ **(tusks)** The **tusks** of an elephant, wild boar, or walrus are its two very long, curved, pointed teeth. N-COUNT

**tus|sle** /tʌsᵊl/ **(tussles, tussling, tussled)** [1] If one person **tussles with** another, or if they **tussle**, they get hold of each other and struggle or fight. ❑ *They ended up ripping down perimeter fencing and tussling with the security staff... He grabbed my microphone and we tussled over that... James and Elliott tussled.* ♦ **Tussle** is also a noun. ❑ *The referee booked him for a tussle with the goalie.* V-RECIP V *with* n pl-n V *over* n pl-n V N-COUNT [2] If one person **tussles with** another for something, or if they **tussle** for it, they try to beat each other in order to get it. [JOURNALISM] ❑ *Pezzo tussled for fourth place with Orvosova... Officials tussled over who had responsibility for the newly fashionable unemployment agenda.* ♦ **Tussle** is also a noun. ❑ *...a legal tussle over who gets custody of the children.* V-RECIP V *for* n *with* n pl-n V *for/over* n N-COUNT: usu with supp [3] If someone **tussles with** a difficult problem or is- VERB = wrestle sue, they try hard to solve it. [JOURNALISM] ❑ *He is tussling with the problem of what to do about inflation.* V *with* n

**tus|sock** /tʌsək/ **(tussocks)** A **tussock** is a small piece of grass which is much longer and thicker than the grass around it. N-COUNT: oft N *of* n

**tut** /tʌt/ **(tuts, tutting, tutted)** [1] **Tut** is used in writing to represent the sound that you make with your tongue touching the top of your mouth when you want to indicate disapproval, annoyance, or sympathy. [2] If you **tut**, you make a sound with your tongue touching the top of your mouth when you want to indicate disapproval, annoyance, or sympathy. ❑ *He tutted and shook his head.* VERB V

**tu|telage** /tjuːtɪlɪdʒ, AM tuːt-/ If one person, group, or country does something **under the tutelage of** another, they do it while they are being taught or guided by them. [FORMAL] N-UNCOUNT: usu *under* N

**tu|tor** /tjuːtəʳ, AM tuːt-/ **(tutors, tutoring, tutored)** [1] A **tutor** is a teacher at a British university or college. In some American universities or colleges, a **tutor** is a teacher of the lowest rank. ❑ *He is course tutor in archaeology at the University of Southampton.* [2] A **tutor** is someone who gives private lessons to one pupil or a very small group of pupils. [3] If someone **tutors** a person or a subject, they teach that person or subject. ❑ *The old man was tutoring her in the stringed instruments. ...at the college where I tutored a two-day Introduction to Chairmaking course... I tutored in economics.* N-COUNT N-COUNT VERB V n *in* n V n V *in* n

**tu|to|rial** /tjuːtɔːriəl, AM tuːt-/ **(tutorials)** [1] In a university or college, a **tutorial** is a regular meeting between a tutor and one or several students, for discussion of a subject that is being studied. ❑ *...teaching in small tutorial groups.* [2] **Tutorial** means relating to a tutor or tutors, especially one at a university or college. ❑ *...the tutorial staff.* N-COUNT: oft N n ADJ: ADJ n

**tut-tut** **(tut-tuts, tut-tutting, tut-tutted)** also **tut tut.** [1] **Tut-tut** is used in writing to represent the sound that you make with your tongue touching the top of your mouth when you want to indicate disapproval, annoyance, or sympathy. [2] If you **tut-tut about** something, you express your disapproval of it, especially by making a sound with your tongue touching the top of your mouth. ❑ *We all spent a lot of time tut-tutting about Angie and her lifestyle... The doctor tut-tutted, dismissing my words as excuses.* CONVENTION [feelings] = *tut* VERB V *about* n V

**tutu** /tuːtuː/ **(tutus)** A **tutu** is a costume worn by female ballet dancers. It has a very short stiff skirt made of many layers of material that sticks out from the waist. N-COUNT

**tux** /tʌks/ **(tuxes)** A **tux** is the same as a **tuxedo.** [INFORMAL] N-COUNT

**tux|edo** /tʌksiːdoʊ/ **(tuxedos)** A **tuxedo** is a black or white jacket worn by men for formal social events. [mainly AM] N-COUNT

☑ in BRIT, usually use **dinner jacket**

**TV** /tiː viː/ **(TVs)** **TV** means the same as **television.** ❑ *The TV was on... I prefer going to the cinema to watching TV. ...a TV commercial.* ◆◆◇ N-VAR

**TV din|ner** **(TV dinners)** A **TV dinner** is a complete meal that is sold in a single container. It can be heated up quickly and eaten from the container it is cooked in. N-COUNT

**twad|dle** /twɒdəl/ If you refer to something that someone says as **twaddle**, you mean that it is silly or untrue. [INFORMAL] N-UNCOUNT [disapproval] = *drivel*

**twang** /twæŋ/ **(twangs, twanging, twanged)** [1] If you **twang** something such as a tight string or elastic band, or if it **twangs**, it makes a fairly loud, ringing sound because it has been pulled and then released. ❑ *...people who sat at the back of class and twanged an elastic band... The song is a fiery mix of twanging guitar with relentless drumming... The fiddle began to twang.* ♦ **Twang** is also a noun. ❑ *Something gave a loud discordant twang.* [2] A **twang** is a quality in someone's way of speaking in which sound seems to be coming through the nose. ❑ *...her broad Australian twang.* VERB V n V-ing V N-COUNT; SOUND N-COUNT: usu sing

**twat** /twɒt/ **(twats)** If someone calls another person a **twat**, they are insulting them and showing that they do not like or respect them. [INFORMAL, OFFENSIVE] N-COUNT [disapproval]

**tweak** /twiːk/ **(tweaks, tweaking, tweaked)** [1] If you **tweak** something, especially part of someone's body, you hold it between your finger and thumb and twist it or pull it. ❑ *He tweaked Guy's ear roughly.* [2] If you **tweak** something such as a system or a design, you improve it by making a slight change. [INFORMAL] ❑ *He expects the system to get even better as the engineers tweak its performance.* ♦ **Tweak** is also a noun. ❑ *The camera has undergone only two minor tweaks since its introduction.* VERB V n VERB V n N-COUNT

**twee** /twiː/ If you say that something is **twee**, it is pretty or sentimental in a way that you think is excessive or silly. [BRIT] ADJ: usu v-link ADJ [disapproval]

**tweed** /twiːd/ **(tweeds)** [1] **Tweed** is a thick woollen cloth, often woven from different coloured threads. [2] Someone who is wearing **tweeds** is wearing a tweed suit. ❑ *...an academic, dressed in tweeds and smoking a pipe.* N-MASS N-PLURAL

**tweedy** /twiːdi/ [1] If you describe someone as **tweedy**, you mean that they have an upper-class but plain appearance, and look as if they live in the country, for example because they are wearing tweed. ❑ *An older woman, pink-cheeked and tweedy, appeared in the doorway.* [2] **Tweedy** clothes are made from tweed. ADJ ADJ

**tweet** /twiːt/ **(tweets)** A **tweet** is a short, high-pitched sound made by a small bird. N-COUNT; SOUND

**twee|zers** /twiːzəʳz/ **Tweezers** are a small tool that you use for tasks such as picking up small objects or pulling out hairs. Tweezers consist of two strips of metal or plastic joined together at one end. N-PLURAL: oft *a pair of* N

**twelfth** /twelfθ/ **(twelfths)** [1] The **twelfth** item in a series is the one that you count as number twelve. ❑ *...the twelfth anniversary of the April revolution. ...a twelfth-century church.* [2] A **twelfth** is one of twelve equal parts of something. ❑ *She is entitled to a twelfth of the cash.* ◆◆◇ ORD FRACTION

**twelve** /twelv/ **(twelves)** **Twelve** is the number 12. ◆◆◆ NUM

**twen|ti|eth** /twentiəθ/ **(twentieths)** [1] The **twentieth** item in a series is the one that you count as number twenty. ❑ *...the twentieth century.* [2] A **twentieth** is one of twenty equal parts of something. ❑ *A few twentieths of a gram can be critical.* ◆◆◇ ORD FRACTION

**twen|ty** /twenti/ **(twenties)** [1] **Twenty** is the number 20. [2] When you talk about the **twenties**, you are referring to numbers between 20 and 29. For example, if you are **in** your **twenties**, you are aged between 20 and 29. If the temperature is **in the twenties**, the temperature is between 20 and 29 degrees. ❑ *They're both in their twenties and both married with children of their own.* [3] **The twenties** is the decade between 1920 and 1929. ❑ *It was written in the Twenties, but it still really stands out.* ◆◆◆ NUM N-PLURAL N-PLURAL: *the* N

**24-7** /twentifɔːʳsevᵊn/ also **twenty-four seven.** If something happens **24-7**, it happens all the time without ever stopping. **24-7** means twenty-four hours a day, seven days a week. [mainly AM, INFORMAL] ❑ *I feel like sleeping 24-7.* ♦ **24-7** is also an adjective. ❑ *...a 24-7 radio station.* ADV: ADV after v ADJ: ADJ n

**twerp** /twɜːʳp/ **(twerps)** If you call someone a **twerp**, you are insulting them and saying that they are silly or stupid. [INFORMAL] N-COUNT [disapproval] = *twit*

**twice** /twaɪs/ [1] If something happens **twice**, there are two actions or events of the same kind. ❑ *He visited me twice that fall and called me on the telephone often... Thoroughly brush teeth and gums twice daily.* [2] You use **twice** in expressions such as **twice a day** and **twice a week** to indicate that two events or actions of the same kind ◆◆◆ ADV: ADV with v, ADV adv, ADV n ADV: ADV *a* n happen in each day or week. ❑ *I phoned twice a day, leaving messages with his wife.* [3] If one thing is, for example, **twice as** big or old **as** another, the first thing is two times as big or old as the second. People sometimes say that one thing is **twice as** good or hard **as** another when they want to emphasize that the first thing is much better or harder than the second. ❑ *The figure of seventy-million pounds was twice as big as expected.* ADV: ADV *as* adj/adv

♦ **Twice** is also a predeterminer. ❑ *Unemployment in Northern Ireland is twice the national average.* PREDET: PREDET *the* n

[4] If you **think twice** about doing something, you consider it again and decide not to do it, or decide to do it differently. ❑ *She'd better shut her mouth and from now on think twice before saying stupid things.* PHRASE: V inflects [5] **once or twice** → see **once**. **twice over** → see **over**.

**twid|dle** /twɪdəl/ **(twiddles, twiddling, twiddled)** [1] If you **twiddle** something, you twist it or turn it quickly with your fingers. ❑ *He twiddled a knob on the dashboard... She had sat there twiddling nervously with the clasp of her handbag.* VERB V n V *with* n [2] to **twiddle** your **thumbs** → see **thumb**.

**twig** /twɪg/ **(twigs, twigging, twigged)** [1] A **twig** is a very small thin branch that grows out from a main branch of a tree or bush. N-COUNT [2] If you **twig**, you suddenly realize or understand something. [INFORMAL] ❑ *Then I twigged that they were illegal immigrants... By the time she'd twigged what it was all about it was too late.* VERB V that V wh Also V

**twi|light** /twaɪlaɪt/ [1] **Twilight** is the time just before night when the daylight has almost gone but when it is not completely dark. N-UNCOUNT = dusk [2] **Twilight** is the small amount of light that there is outside just after the sun has gone down. ❑ *...the deepening autumn twilight.* N-UNCOUNT [3] **The twilight of** a particular period of time is the final stages of it, when the most important events have already happened. ❑ *Now both men are in the twilight of their careers.* N-SING: *the* N *of* n, N n [4] A **twilight** state or a **twilight** zone is a situation of confusion or uncertainty, which seems to exist between two different states or categories. ❑ *They fell into that twilight zone between military personnel and civilian employees.* ADJ: ADJ n

**twill** /twɪl/ **Twill** is cloth, usually cotton, that is woven in a way which produces parallel sloping lines across it. N-UNCOUNT

**twin** /twɪn/ **(twins, twinning, twinned)** [1] If two people are **twins**, they have the same mother and were born on the same day. ❑ *Sarah was looking after the twins... She had a twin brother and a younger brother.* ◆◇◇ N-COUNT: oft N n [2] **Twin** is used to describe a pair of things that look the same and are close together. ❑ *...the twin spires of the cathedral. ...the world's largest twin-engined aircraft.* ADJ: ADJ n [3] **Twin** is used to describe two things or ideas that are similar or connected in some way. ❑ *...the twin concepts of liberty and equality.* ADJ: ADJ n [4] When a place or organization in one country **is twinned with** a place or organization in another country, a special relationship is formally established between them. [BRIT] ❑ *Five Polish banks are to be twinned with counterparts in Western Europe... The borough is twinned with Kasel in Germany.* VERB: usu passive *be* V-ed *with* n V-ed [5] **Twin** towns or cities are twinned with each other. [BRIT] ❑ *This led Zagreb's twin town, Mainz, to donate £70,000-worth of high-quality equipment.* ADJ: ADJ n

in AM, use **sister cities**

[6] → See also **identical twin**, **Siamese twin**.

**twin bed** **(twin beds)** **Twin beds** are two single beds in one bedroom. N-COUNT: usu pl

**twin-bedded** also **twin bedded**. A **twin-bedded** room, for example in a hotel, has two single beds. [mainly BRIT] ADJ: ADJ n

**twine** /twaɪn/ **(twines, twining, twined)** [1] **Twine** is strong string used especially in gardening and farming. N-UNCOUNT [2] If you **twine** one thing around another, or if one thing **twines** around another, the first thing is twisted or wound around the second. ❑ *He had twined his chubby arms around Vincent's neck... These strands of molecules twine around each other to form cable-like structures.* VERB V n prep V prep

**twinge** /twɪndʒ/ **(twinges)** [1] A **twinge** is a sudden sharp feeling or emotion, usually an unpleasant one. ❑ *For a moment, Arnold felt a twinge of sympathy for Mr Wilson.* N-COUNT: with supp, usu N *of* n = pang [2] A **twinge** is a sudden sharp pain. ❑ *He felt a slight twinge in his damaged hamstring.* N-COUNT

**twin|kle** /twɪŋkəl/ **(twinkles, twinkling, twinkled)** [1] If a star or a light **twinkles**, it shines with an unsteady light which rapidly and constantly changes from bright to faint. ❑ *At night, lights twinkle in distant villages across the valleys. ...a band of twinkling diamonds.* VERB V V-ing [2] If you say that someone's eyes **twinkle**, you mean that their face expresses good humour or amusement. ❑ *She saw her mother's eyes twinkle with amusement.* VERB V

♦ **Twinkle** is also a noun. ❑ *A kindly twinkle came into her eyes.* N-SING

**twin|set** /twɪnset/ **(twinsets)** also **twin set**, **twin-set**. A **twinset** is a set of women's clothing, consisting of a cardigan and sweater of the same colour. [BRIT] N-COUNT

**twirl** /twɜːrl/ **(twirls, twirling, twirled)** [1] If you **twirl** something or if it **twirls**, it turns around and around with a smooth, fairly fast movement. ❑ *Bonnie twirled her empty glass in her fingers... All around me leaves twirl to the ground.* VERB V n V prep/adv [2] If you **twirl**, you turn around and around quickly, for example when you are dancing. ❑ *Several hundred people twirl around the ballroom dance floor.* VERB = whirl V prep/adv [3] If you **twirl** something such as your hair, you twist it around your finger. ❑ *Sarah lifted her hand and started twirling a strand of hair.* VERB V n

**twist** /twɪst/ **(twists, twisting, twisted)** [1] If you **twist** something, you turn it to make a spiral shape, for example by turning the two ends of it in opposite directions. ❑ *Her hands began to twist the handles of the bag she carried... Twist the string carefully around the second stem with the other hand.* ◆◇◇ VERB V n V n adv/prep [2] If you **twist** something, especially a part of your body, or if it **twists**, it moves into an unusual, uncomfortable, or bent position, for example because of being hit or pushed, or because you are upset. ❑ *He twisted her arms behind her back and clipped a pair of handcuffs on her wrists... Sophia's face twisted in pain... The body was twisted, its legs at an awkward angle.* VERB V n prep V V-ed [3] If you **twist** part of your body such as your head or your shoulders, you turn that part while keeping the rest of your body still. ❑ *She twisted her head sideways and looked towards the door... Susan twisted round in her seat until she could see Graham and Sabrina behind her.* VERB V n adv V adv/prep [4] If you **twist** a part of your body such as your ankle or wrist, you injure it by turning it too sharply, or in an unusual direction. ❑ *He fell and twisted his ankle... Rupert Moon is out of today's session with a twisted knee.* VERB V n V-ed [5] If you **twist** something, you turn it so that it moves around in a circular direction. ❑ *She was staring down at her hands, twisting the ring on her finger... Reaching up to a cupboard he takes out a jar and twists the lid off.* VERB V n V n with adv

♦ **Twist** is also a noun. ❑ *The bag is resealed with a simple twist of the valve.* N-COUNT: oft N *of* n

[6] If a road or river **twists**, it has a lot of sudden changes of direction in it. ❑ *The roads twist round hairpin bends... The lane twists and turns between pleasant but unspectacular cottages.* VERB V prep V

♦ **Twist** is also a noun. ❑ *It allows the train to maintain a constant speed through the twists and turns of existing track.* N-COUNT: usu pl

[7] If you say that someone **has twisted** something that you have said, you disapprove of them because they have repeated it in a way that changes its meaning, in order to harm you or benefit themselves. ❑ *It's a shame the way that the media can twist your words and misrepresent you.* VERB [disapproval] = distort V n [8] A **twist** in something is an unexpected and significant development. ❑ *The battle of the sexes also took a new twist.* N-COUNT [9] A **twist** is the shape that something has when it has been twisted. ❑ *...bunches of violets in twists of paper.* N-COUNT: usu N *of* n [10] If some- PHRASE:

thing happens by **a twist of fate**, it happens by chance, and it is strange, interesting, or unfortunate in some way. ❑ *By a curious twist of fate, cricket was also my favourite sport.* [11] → See also **twisted**. to **twist** someone**'s arm** → see **arm**. to **get** your **knickers in a twist** → see **knickers**. to **twist the knife** → see **knife**. — *twist* inflects, usu *by/in* PHR

**twist|ed** /twɪstɪd/ If you describe a person as **twisted**, you dislike them because you think they are strange in an unpleasant way. ❑ *...a twisted man who shot at the president.* — ADJ [disapproval]

**twist|er** /twɪstəʳ/ **(twisters)** A **twister** is the same as a **tornado**. [AM] — N-COUNT

**twisty** /twɪsti/ A **twisty** road, track, or river has a lot of sharp bends and corners. — ADJ

**twit** /twɪt/ **(twits)** If you call someone as a **twit**, you are insulting them and saying that they are silly or stupid. [BRIT, INFORMAL] — N-COUNT [disapproval] = twerp

**twitch** /twɪtʃ/ **(twitches, twitching, twitched)** If something, especially a part of your body, **twitches** or if you **twitch** it, it makes a little jumping movement. ❑ *When I stood up to her, her right cheek would begin to twitch... Stern twitched his shoulders.* ♦ **Twitch** is also a noun. ❑ *He developed a nervous twitch and began to blink constantly.* — VERB; V; V n; N-COUNT

**twitch|er** /twɪtʃəʳ/ **(twitchers)** A **twitcher** is an enthusiastic bird-watcher. [BRIT, INFORMAL] — N-COUNT

**twitchy** /twɪtʃi/ If you are **twitchy**, you are behaving in a rather nervous way that shows you feel anxious and cannot relax. [INFORMAL] ❑ *Afraid of bad publicity, the department had suddenly become very twitchy about journalists.* — ADJ = jumpy

**twit|ter** /twɪtəʳ/ **(twitters, twittering, twittered)** [1] When birds **twitter**, they make a lot of short high-pitched sounds. ❑ *There were birds twittering in the eucalyptus trees. ...a tree filled with twittering birds.* ♦ **Twitter** is also a noun. ❑ *Naomi would waken to the twitter of birds.* [2] If you say that someone **is twittering about** something, you mean that they are speaking about silly or unimportant things, usually rather fast or in a high-pitched voice. ❑ *...debutantes twittering excitedly about Christian Dior dresses... She laughs, blushes and twitters: 'Oh, doesn't Giles have just the most charming sense of humour?'* — VERB; V; V-ing; N-UNCOUNT: usu N *of* n; VERB; V *about* n; V with quote; Also V

**two** /tuː/ **(twos)** [1] **Two** is the number 2. — ◆◆◆ NUM
PHRASES [2] If you say **it takes two** or **it takes two to tango**, you mean that a situation or argument involves two people and they are both therefore responsible for it. ❑ *Divorce is never the fault of one partner; it takes two... It takes two to tango and so far our relationship has been one-sided.* — PHRASE
[3] If you **put two and two together**, you work out the truth about something for yourself, by using the information that is available to you. ❑ *Putting two and two together, I assume that this was the car he used.* [4] to **kill two birds with one stone** → see **bird**. **two a penny** → see **penny**. — PHRASE: V inflects

**two-bit** You use **two-bit** to describe someone or something that you have no respect for or that you think is inferior. [AM, INFORMAL] ❑ *...some two-bit little dictator... That may be two-bit psychology, but it's the only explanation I have.* — ADJ: ADJ n [disapproval]

**two-dimensional** also **two dimensional.** [1] A **two-dimensional** object or figure is flat rather than solid so that only its length and width can be measured. ❑ *...new software, which generates both two-dimensional drawings and three-dimensional images.* [2] If you describe fictional characters as **two-dimensional**, you are critical of them because they are very simple and not realistic enough to be taken seriously. ❑ *I found the characters very two-dimensional, not to say dull.* — ADJ: usu ADJ n; ADJ [disapproval]

**two-faced** If you describe someone as **two-faced**, you are critical of them because they say they do or believe one thing when their behaviour or words show that they do not do it or do not believe it. ❑ *He had been devious and two-faced.* — ADJ: usu v-link ADJ [disapproval]

**two|fold** /tuːfoʊld/ also **two-fold.** You can use **twofold** to introduce a topic that has two equally important parts. [FORMAL] ❑ *The case against is twofold: too risky and too expensive.* — ADJ

**two-handed** A **two-handed** blow or catch is done using both hands. — ADJ: usu ADJ n, also ADJ after v

**two-horse** If you describe a contest as a **two-horse** race, you mean that only two of the people or things taking part have any chance of winning. ❑ *The election may not be the traditional two-horse race between the preferred Democrat and Republican party candidates.* — ADJ: ADJ n

**two-percent milk** **Two-percent milk** is milk from which some of the cream has been removed. [AM] — N-UNCOUNT

✓ in BRIT, use **semi-skimmed milk**

**two-piece** **(two-pieces)** also **two piece.** [1] You can use **two-piece** to describe something, especially a set of clothing, that is in two parts. ❑ *...a two-piece bathing suit.* [2] A **two-piece** is a woman's suit which consists of a jacket and a skirt or pair of trousers. — ADJ: ADJ n; N-COUNT

**two|some** /tuːsəm/ **(twosomes)** A **twosome** is a group of two people. — N-COUNT

**two-thirds** also **two thirds.** **Two-thirds of** something is an amount that is two out of three equal parts of it. ❑ *Two-thirds of householders in this country live in a mortgaged home.* ♦ **Two-thirds** is also a pronoun. ❑ *The United States and Russia hope to conclude a treaty to cut their nuclear arsenals by two-thirds.* ♦ **Two-thirds** is also an adverb. ❑ *Do not fill the container more than two-thirds full... A second book has already been commissioned and is two-thirds finished.* ♦ **Two-thirds** is also an adjective. ❑ *...the two thirds majority in parliament needed to make constitutional changes.* — QUANT: QUANT *of* n; PRON; ADV: ADV adj/-ed; ADJ: ADJ n

**two-way** [1] **Two-way** means moving or working in two opposite directions or allowing something to move or work in two opposite directions. ❑ *The bridge is now open to two-way traffic.* [2] A **two-way** radio can send and receive signals. [3] If there is **two-way** help or learning, two people or groups are both helping each other or both learning from each other. ❑ *Trust is a two way thing.* — ADJ: usu ADJ n; ADJ: ADJ n; ADJ: ADJ n

**ty|coon** /taɪkuːn/ **(tycoons)** A **tycoon** is a person who is successful in business and so has become rich and powerful. — N-COUNT = magnate

**tyke** /taɪk/ **(tykes)** You can refer to a child, especially a naughty or playful one, as a **tyke** when you want to show affection for them. [INFORMAL] — N-COUNT [approval]

**type**
① SORT OR KIND
② WRITING AND PRINTING

**① type** /taɪp/ **(types)** [1] A **type of** something is a group of those things that have particular features in common. ❑ *There are various types of the disease... In 1990, 25% of households were of this type.* [2] If you refer to a particular thing or person as a **type of** something more general, you are considering that thing or person as an example of that more general group. ❑ *Have you done this type of work before?... Rates of interest for this type of borrowing can be high... I am a very determined type of person.* [3] If you refer to a person as a particular **type**, you mean that they have that particular appearance, character, or way of behaving. ❑ *It's the first time I, a fair-skinned, freckly type, have sailed in the sun without burning.* [4] If you say that someone is **not** your **type**, you mean that they are not the sort of person who you usually find attractive. [INFORMAL] ❑ *At first I thought he was rather ordinary looking, a little chubby, not my type.* [5] → See also **blood type**. — ◆◆◇ N-COUNT: usu with supp, oft N *of* n = sort, kind; N-COUNT: with supp, usu N *of* n = sort, kind; N-COUNT: usu supp N = sort; PHRASE: v-link PHR

**② type** /taɪp/ **(types, typing, typed)** [1] If you **type** something, you use a typewriter or word processor to write it. ❑ *I can type your essays for you... I had never really learnt to type properly... The letter consists of six closely typed pages.* [2] **Type** is — ◆◆◇ VERB; V n; V; V-ed; N-UNCOUNT printed text as it appears in a book or newspaper, or the small pieces of metal that are used to create this. ❑ *The correction had already been set in type.* [3] → See also **typing**.

♦ **type in** or **type into** If you **type** information **into** a computer or **type** it **in**, you press keys on the keyboard so that the computer stores or processes the information. ❑ *Officials type each passport number into a computer... You have to type in commands, such as 'help' and 'print'... You type things in, and it responds.* PHRASAL VERB = key in; V n P n; V P n (not pron); V n P

♦ **type out** If you **type** something **out**, you write it in full using a typewriter or word processor. ❑ *The two of us stood by while two typists typed out the whole document again... I read it down the phone to a man called Dave, who typed it out.* PHRASAL VERB = type; V P n (not pron); V n P

♦ **type up** If you **type up** a text that has been written by hand, you produce a typed copy of it. ❑ *They didn't get around to typing up the letter... When the first draft was completed, Nichols typed it up.* PHRASAL VERB; V P n (not pron); V n P

**type|cast** /taɪpkɑːst, -kæst/ **(typecasts, typecasting)**

☑ The form **typecast** is used in the present tense and is the past tense and past participle.

If an actor **is typecast**, they play the same type of character in every play or film that they are in. ❑ *I didn't want to be typecast and I think I've maintained a large variety in the roles I've played... African-Americans were often typecast as servants, entertainers or criminals.* VERB: usu passive; *be* V-ed; *be* V-ed *as* n

**type|face** /taɪpfeɪs/ **(typefaces)** In printing, a **typeface** is a set of alphabetical characters, numbers, and other characters that all have the same design. There are many different typefaces. N-COUNT

**type|script** /taɪpskrɪpt/ **(typescripts)** A **typescript** is a typed copy of an article or literary work. N-VAR

**type|writ|er** /taɪpraɪtəʳ/ **(typewriters)** A **typewriter** is a machine with keys which are pressed in order to print letters, numbers, or other characters onto paper. N-COUNT

**type|writ|ten** /taɪprɪtən/ A **typewritten** document has been typed on a typewriter or word processor. ADJ

**ty|phoid** /taɪfɔɪd/ **Typhoid** or **typhoid fever** is a serious infectious disease that produces fever and diarrhoea and can cause death. It is spread by dirty water or food. N-UNCOUNT

**ty|phoon** /taɪfuːn/ **(typhoons)** A **typhoon** is a very violent tropical storm. N-COUNT

**ty|phus** /taɪfəs/ **Typhus** is a serious infectious disease that produces spots on the skin, a high fever, and a severe headache. N-UNCOUNT

**typi|cal** /tɪpɪkəl/ ◆◇◇ [1] You use **typical** to describe someone or something that shows the most usual characteristics of a particular type of person or thing, and is therefore a good example of that type. ❑ *Cheney is everyone's image of a typical cop: a big white guy, six foot, 220 pounds.* ADJ [2] If a particular action or feature is **typical of** someone or something, it shows their usual qualities or characteristics. ❑ *This reluctance to move towards a democratic state is typical of totalitarian regimes... With typical energy he found new journalistic outlets.* ADJ: usu v-link ADJ, oft ADJ *of* n = characteristic [3] If you say that something is **typical of** a person, situation, or thing, you are criticizing them or complaining about them and saying that they are just as bad or disappointing as you expected them to be. ❑ *She threw her hands into the air. 'That is just typical of you, isn't it?'* ADJ: usu v-link ADJ, oft ADJ *of* n [feelings]

**typi|cal|ly** /tɪpɪkəli/ [1] You use **typically** to say that something usually happens in the way that you are describing. ❑ *It typically takes a day or two, depending on size.* ADV: ADV with cl/group = normally [2] You use **typically** to say that something shows all the most usual characteristics of a particular type of person or thing. ❑ *Philip paced the floor, a typically nervous expectant father.* ADV: ADV adj = characteristically [3] You use **typically** to indicate that someone has behaved in the way that they normally do. ❑ *Typically, the Norwegians were on the mountain two hours before anyone else.* ADV: ADV with cl, ADV adj = characteristically

**typi|fy** /tɪpɪfaɪ/ **(typifies, typifying, typified)** If something or someone **typifies** a situation or type of thing or person, they have all the usual characteristics of it and are a typical example of it. ❑ *These two buildings typify the rich extremes of Irish architecture.* VERB = epitomize; V n

**typ|ing** /taɪpɪŋ/ [1] **Typing** is the work or activity of typing something by means of a typewriter or word processor. ❑ *She didn't do any typing till the evening.* N-UNCOUNT [2] **Typing** is the skill of using a typewriter or keyboard quickly and accurately. ❑ *My typing is quite dreadful.* N-UNCOUNT: usu with supp, oft poss N

**typ|ist** /taɪpɪst/ **(typists)** A **typist** is someone who works in an office typing letters and other documents. N-COUNT

**ty|po|graphi|cal** /taɪpəgræfɪkəl/ **Typographical** relates to the way in which printed material is presented. ❑ *Owing to a typographical error, the town of Longridge was spelt as Longbridge.* ADJ: ADJ n

**ty|pog|ra|phy** /taɪpɒgrəfi/ **Typography** is the way in which written material is arranged and prepared for printing. N-UNCOUNT

**ty|pol|ogy** /taɪpɒlədʒi/ **(typologies)** A **typology** is a system for dividing things into different types, especially in science and the social sciences. [FORMAL] N-COUNT

**ty|ran|ni|cal** /tɪrænɪkəl/ [1] If you describe someone as **tyrannical**, you mean that they are severe or unfair towards the people that they have authority over. ❑ *He killed his tyrannical father with a blow to the head.* ADJ [2] If you describe a government or organization as **tyrannical**, you mean that it acts without considering the wishes of its people and treats them cruelly or unfairly. ❑ *...one of the world's most oppressive and tyrannical regimes.* ADJ

**tyr|an|nize** /tɪrənaɪz/ **(tyrannizes, tyrannizing, tyrannized)**

☑ in BRIT, also use **tyrannise**

If you say that one person **tyrannizes** another, you mean that the first person uses their power over the second person in order to treat them very cruelly and unfairly. ❑ *...fathers who tyrannize their families... Armed groups use their power to tyrannise over civilians.* VERB; V n; V *over* n; Also V

**tyr|an|ny** /tɪrəni/ **(tyrannies)** [1] A **tyranny** is a cruel, harsh, and unfair government in which a person or small group of people have power over everyone else. ❑ *Self-expression and individuality are the greatest weapons against tyranny.* N-VAR [2] If you describe someone's behaviour and treatment of others that they have authority over as **tyranny**, you mean that they are severe with them or unfair to them. ❑ *I'm the sole victim of Mother's tyranny.* N-UNCOUNT [3] You can describe something that you have to use or have as a **tyranny** if you think it is undesirable or unpleasant. ❑ *The telephone is one of the great tyrannies of modern life.* N-COUNT: oft N *of* n

**ty|rant** /taɪərənt/ **(tyrants)** You can use **tyrant** to refer to someone who treats the people they have authority over in a cruel and unfair way. ❑ *...households where the father was a tyrant.* N-COUNT

**tyre** /taɪəʳ/ **(tyres)**

☑ in AM, use **tire**

A **tyre** is a thick piece of rubber which is fitted onto the wheels of vehicles such as cars, buses, and bicycles. → See pictures on pages 1707 and 1708. → See also **spare tyre**. N-COUNT

**tyro** /taɪroʊ/ **(tyros)** A **tyro** is a person who is just beginning to learn something or who has very little experience of something. [JOURNALISM] ❑ *...a tyro journalist.* N-COUNT: oft N n

# U u

**U, u** /juː/ **(U's, u's)** **U** is the twenty-first letter of the English alphabet. *N-VAR*

**uber-** /uːbəʳ-/ **Uber** combines with nouns and adjectives to form nouns and adjectives that refer to a great or extreme example of something. [JOURNALISM] ❑ *Uber-babe Jenny McCarthy has hinted at the trials young actresses must undergo in Hollywood's seedier realms... McNally now owns a clutch of uberchic downtown celebrity hang-outs.* *COMB in N-COUNT, COMB in ADJ*

**ubiqui|tous** /juːbɪkwɪtəs/ If you describe something or someone as **ubiquitous**, you mean that they seem to be everywhere. [FORMAL] ❑ *Sugar is ubiquitous in the diet... She is one of the wealthiest, most ubiquitous media personalities around.* *ADJ*

**ubiquity** /juːbɪkwɪti/ If you talk about **the ubiquity of** something, you mean that it seems to be everywhere. [FORMAL] *N-UNCOUNT: oft N of n*

**ud|der** /ʌdəʳ/ **(udders)** A cow's **udder** is the organ that hangs below its body and produces milk. *N-COUNT*

**UFO** /juː ef oʊ, juːfoʊ/ **(UFOs)** A **UFO** is an object seen in the sky or landing on earth which cannot be identified and which is often believed to be from another planet. **UFO** is an abbreviation for 'unidentified flying object'. ❑ *There has been a surge of UFO sightings in America.* *N-COUNT*

**Ugan|dan** /juːgændən/ **(Ugandans)** 1 **Ugandan** means belonging or relating to Uganda or to its people or culture. *ADJ* 2 A **Ugandan** is a Ugandan citizen, or a person of Ugandan origin. *N-COUNT*

**ugh** **Ugh** is used in writing to represent the sound that people make if they think something is unpleasant, horrible, or disgusting. ❑ *Ugh – it was horrible.* *EXCLAM*

**ugly** /ʌgli/ **(uglier, ugliest)** 1 If you say that someone or something is **ugly**, you mean that they are very unattractive and unpleasant to look at. ❑ *...an ugly little hat... She makes me feel dowdy and ugly.* *ADJ ≠ beautiful* ♦ **ug|li|ness** *...the raw ugliness of his native city.* *N-UNCOUNT ≠ beauty* 2 If you refer to an event or situation as **ugly**, you mean that it is very unpleasant, usually because it involves violent or aggressive behaviour. ❑ *There have been some ugly scenes... The confrontation turned ugly.* *ADJ* ♦ **ug|li|ness** *...the subtlety and ugliness of sexual harassment.* *N-UNCOUNT: usu with supp* 3 **to rear its ugly head** → see **head**.

**ugly duck|ling** **(ugly ducklings)** If you say that someone, especially a child, is an **ugly duckling**, you mean that they are unattractive or awkward now, but will probably develop into an attractive and successful person. *N-COUNT: usu sing*

**UHF** /juː eɪtʃ ef/ **UHF** is a range of radio waves which allows a radio or television receiver to produce a good quality of sound. **UHF** is an abbreviation for 'ultra-high frequency'. ❑ *...Boston UHF channels.* *N-UNCOUNT: oft N n*

**uh huh** also **uh-huh.** **Uh huh** is used in writing to represent a sound that people make when they are agreeing with you, when they want to show that they understand what you are saying, or when they are answering 'yes' to a question. [INFORMAL] ❑ *'Did she?' — 'Uh huh.'* ◆◇◇ *CONVENTION*

**UHT** /juː eɪtʃ tiː/ **UHT** is used to describe milk which has been treated at a very high temperature so that it can be kept for a long time if the container is not opened. **UHT** is an abbreviation for 'ultra-heat-treated'. [BRIT] *ADJ: usu ADJ n = long-life*

**UK** /juː keɪ/ **The UK** is Great Britain and Northern Ireland. **UK** is an abbreviation for 'United Kingdom'. *N-PROPER: the N*

**uku|lele** /juːkəleɪli/ **(ukuleles)** also **ukelele.** A **ukulele** is a small guitar with four strings. *N-COUNT*

**ul|cer** /ʌlsəʳ/ **(ulcers)** An **ulcer** is a sore area on the outside or inside of your body which is very painful and may bleed or produce an unpleasant poisonous substance. ❑ *...stomach ulcers.* *N-COUNT*

**ul|cer|at|ed** /ʌlsəreɪtɪd/ If a part of someone's body is **ulcerated**, ulcers have developed on it. ❑ *...ulcerated mouths... Every inch of his arms and legs was ulcerated.* *ADJ*

**ul|te|ri|or** /ʌltɪəriəʳ/ If you say that someone has an **ulterior** motive for doing something, you believe that they have a hidden reason for doing it. ❑ *Sheila had an ulterior motive for trying to help Stan.* *ADJ: ADJ n*

**ul|ti|mate** /ʌltɪmət/ 1 You use **ultimate** to describe the final result or aim of a long series of events. ❑ *He said it is still not possible to predict the ultimate outcome... The ultimate aim is to expand the network further.* ◆◇◇ *ADJ: ADJ n = eventual* 2 You use **ultimate** to describe the original source or cause of something. ❑ *Plants are the ultimate source of all foodstuffs... The ultimate cause of what's happened seems to have been the advertising campaign.* *ADJ: ADJ n = fundamental* 3 You use **ultimate** to describe the most important or powerful thing of a particular kind. ❑ *...the ultimate power of the central government... Of course, the ultimate authority remained the presidency.* *ADJ: ADJ n* 4 You use **ultimate** to describe the most extreme and unpleasant example of a particular thing. ❑ *Bringing back the death penalty would be the ultimate abuse of human rights.* *ADJ: ADJ n* 5 You use **ultimate** to describe the best possible example of a particular thing. ❑ *Caviar and oysters on ice are generally considered the ultimate luxury foods.* *ADJ: ADJ n = definitive* 6 **The ultimate in** something is the best or most advanced example of it. ❑ *This hotel is the ultimate in luxury.* *PHRASE: PHR n/-ing, usu v-link PHR, PHR after v*

**ul|ti|mate|ly** /ʌltɪmətli/ 1 **Ultimately** means finally, after a long and often complicated series of events. ❑ *...a tough but ultimately worthwhile struggle.* ◆◇◇ *ADV: ADV adj, ADV with v = eventually* 2 You use **ultimately** to indicate that what you are saying is the most important point in a discussion. ❑ *Ultimately, Bismarck's revisionism scarcely affected or damaged British interests at all.* *ADV: ADV with cl*

**ul|ti|ma|tum** /ʌltɪmeɪtəm/ **(ultimatums)** An **ultimatum** is a warning to someone that unless they act in a particular way, action will be taken against them. ❑ *They issued an ultimatum to the police to rid an area of racist attackers, or they will take the law into their own hands.* *N-COUNT*

**ultra-** /ʌltrə-/ **Ultra-** is added to adjectives to form other adjectives that emphasize that something or someone has a quality to an extreme degree. ❑ *...a wide range of ultra-modern equipment. ...an ultra-ambitious executive.* *PREFIX* [emphasis]

**ultra|ma|rine** /ʌltrəməriːn/ **Ultramarine** is used to describe things that are very bright blue in colour. ❑ *...an ultramarine sky.* *COLOUR*

**ultra|son|ic** /ʌltrəsɒnɪk/ **Ultrasonic** sounds have very high frequencies, which human beings cannot hear. *ADJ: usu ADJ n*

**ultra|sound** /ʌltrəsaʊnd/ **Ultrasound** is sound waves which travel at such a high frequency that they cannot be heard by humans. Ultrasound is used in medicine to get pictures of the inside of people's bodies. ❑ *I had an ultrasound scan to see how the pregnancy was progressing.*
N-UNCOUNT: usu N n

**ultra|vio|let** /ʌltrəvaɪələt/ **Ultraviolet** light or radiation is what causes your skin to become darker in colour after you have been in sunlight. In large amounts ultraviolet light is harmful. ❑ *The sun's ultraviolet rays are responsible for both tanning and burning.*
ADJ: usu ADJ n

**ulu|late** /juːljʊleɪt, AM ʌl-/ **(ululates, ululating, ululated)** If someone **ululates**, they make quickly repeated loud sounds, often to express sorrow or happiness. [LITERARY] ❑ *They ululated like Red Indians... He let out this long ululating moan.*
VERB; V; V-ing

**um** **Um** is used in writing to represent a sound that people make when they are hesitating, usually while deciding what they want to say next. ❑ *She felt her face going red – 'I'm sorry Rob, it's just that I'm, um, overwhelmed.'*

**um|ber** /ʌmbəʳ/ **Umber** is used to describe things that are yellowish or reddish brown in colour. ❑ *...umber paint.*
COLOUR

**um|bili|cal cord** /ʌmbɪlɪkəl kɔːʳd/ **(umbilical cords)** The **umbilical cord** is the tube that connects an unborn baby to its mother, through which it receives oxygen and food.
N-COUNT: usu sing

**um|brage** /ʌmbrɪdʒ/ If you say that a person **takes umbrage**, you mean that they are upset or offended by something that someone says or does to them, often without much reason. [FORMAL] ❑ *He takes umbrage against anyone who criticises him.*
PHRASE: V inflects = take offence

**um|brel|la** /ʌmbrelə/ **(umbrellas)** 1 An **umbrella** is an object which you use to protect yourself from the rain or hot sun. It consists of a long stick with a folding frame covered in cloth. ❑ *Harry held an umbrella over Dawn.* 2 **Umbrella** is used to refer to a single group or description that includes a lot of different organizations or ideas. ❑ *Does coincidence come under the umbrella of the paranormal?... Within the umbrella term 'dementia' there are many different kinds of disease.* 3 **Umbrella** is used to refer to a system or agreement which protects a country or group of people. ❑ *The major powers have chosen to act under the moral umbrella of the United Nations.*
N-COUNT; N-SING: usu N *of* n, supp N, N n; N-SING: N *of* n, supp N

**um|laut** /ʊmlaʊt/ **(umlauts)** An **umlaut** is a symbol that is written over vowels in German and some other languages to indicate the way in which they should be pronounced. For example, the word 'für' has an umlaut over the 'u'.
N-COUNT

**um|pire** /ʌmpaɪəʳ/ **(umpires, umpiring, umpired)** 1 An **umpire** is a person whose job is to make sure that a sports match or contest is played fairly and that the rules are not broken. ❑ *The umpire's decision is final.* 2 To **umpire** means to be the umpire in a sports match or contest. ❑ *He umpired baseball games... He umpired for school football matches until he was in his late 50s.*
N-COUNT; VERB; V n; V

**ump|teen** /ʌmptiːn/ **Umpteen** can be used to refer to an extremely large number of things or people. [INFORMAL] ❑ *He was interrupted by applause umpteen times... He has produced umpteen books, plays and television series.*
DET: DET pl-n; emphasis; = countless

**ump|teenth** /ʌmptiːnθ/ You use **umpteenth** to indicate that an occasion, thing, or person happens or comes after many others. [INFORMAL] ❑ *He checked his watch for the umpteenth time... She was now on her umpteenth gin.*
ORD; emphasis

**un-** /ʌn-/ 1 **Un-** is added to the beginning of adjectives, adverbs, and nouns, in order to form words that have the opposite meaning. ❑ *My father was an unemployed labourer... He had sensed his mother's unhappiness.* 2 **Un-** is added to the beginning of a verb that describes a process, in order to form another verb that describes the reverse of that process. ❑ *He undressed and draped his clothes neatly over the back of the chair... She was anxious for me to unwrap the other gifts.* 3 **Un-** is added to the beginning of the past participle of a verb, in order to form an adjective that means that the process described by the verb has not happened. ❑ *The theory remains untested... Dealers across the country continue to complain about huge stocks of unsold cars.*
PREFIX; PREFIX; PREFIX

**UN** /juː en/ The **UN** is the same as the **United Nations**. ❑ *...a UN peacekeeping mission.*
◆◆◇ N-PROPER

**un|abashed** /ʌnəbæʃt/ If you describe someone as **unabashed**, you mean that they are not ashamed, embarrassed, or shy about something, especially when you think most people would be. ❑ *He seems unabashed by his recent defeat... He's an unabashed, old-fashioned romantic.*
ADJ

**un|abat|ed** /ʌnəbeɪtɪd/ If something continues **unabated**, it continues without any reduction in intensity or amount. ❑ *The fighting has continued unabated for over 24 hours. ...his unabated enthusiasm for cinema.*
ADJ: usu ADJ after v, also ADJ n, v-link ADJ

**un|able** /ʌneɪbəl/ If you are **unable to** do something, it is impossible for you to do it, for example because you do not have the necessary skill or knowledge, or because you do not have enough time or money. ❑ *The military may feel unable to hand over power to a civilian President next year.*
◆◇◇ ADJ: v-link ADJ to-inf ≠ able

**un|abridged** /ʌnəbrɪdʒd/ An **unabridged** piece of writing, for example a book or article, is complete and not shortened in any way.
ADJ = full-length ≠ abridged

**un|ac|cep|table** /ʌnəkseptəbəl/ If you describe something as **unacceptable**, you strongly disapprove of it or object to it and feel that it should not be allowed to continue. ❑ *It is totally unacceptable for children to swear... Joanna left her husband because of his unacceptable behaviour.* ♦ **un|ac|cept|ably** /ʌnəkseptəbli/ *The reform program has brought unacceptably high unemployment and falling wages.*
ADJ ≠ acceptable; ADV: usu ADV adj, also ADV after v

**un|ac|com|pa|nied** /ʌnəkʌmpənid/ 1 If someone is **unaccompanied**, they are alone. ❑ *It is estimated that every year 50 unaccompanied children arrive in Britain... Kelly's too young to go unaccompanied.* 2 **Unaccompanied** luggage or goods are being sent or transported separately from their owner. ❑ *Unaccompanied bags are either searched or removed.* 3 An **unaccompanied** voice or instrument sings or plays alone, with no other instruments playing at the same time. ❑ *...an unaccompanied flute... The piece is most often sung unaccompanied.*
ADJ: ADJ n, ADJ after v, v-link ADJ; ADJ: ADJ n; ADJ: ADJ n, ADJ after v

**un|ac|count|able** /ʌnəkaʊntəbəl/ 1 Something that is **unaccountable** does not seem to have any sensible explanation. ❑ *For some unaccountable reason, it struck me as extremely funny.* ♦ **un|ac|count|ably** /ʌnəkaʊntəbli/ *And then, unaccountably, she giggled.* 2 If you describe a person or organization as **unaccountable**, you are critical of them because they are not responsible to anyone for their actions, or do not feel they have to explain their actions to anyone. ❑ *Economic policy in Europe should not be run by an unaccountable committee of governors of central banks.*
ADJ: usu ADJ n = inexplicable; ADV; ADJ; disapproval

**un|ac|count|ed for** /ʌnəkaʊntɪd fɔːʳ/ If people or things are **unaccounted for**, you do not know where they are or what has happened to them. ❑ *5,000 American servicemen who fought in Korea are still unaccounted for... About £50 million from the robbery five years ago is unaccounted for.*
ADJ: v-link ADJ

**un|ac|cus|tomed** /ʌnəkʌstəmd/ 1 If you are **unaccustomed to** something, you do not know it very well or have not experienced it very often. [WRITTEN] ❑ *They were unaccustomed to such military setbacks... It is a part of Britain as yet largely unaccustomed to tourists.* 2 If you describe someone's behaviour or experiences as **unaccustomed**, you mean that they do not usually behave like this or have experiences of this kind. [WRITTEN] ❑ *He began to comfort me with such unaccustomed gentleness.*
ADJ: v-link ADJ *to* n/-ing = unused ≠ accustomed; ADJ: ADJ n

**un|ac|knowl|edged** /ʌnæknɒlɪdʒd/ [1] If you describe something or someone as **unacknowledged**, you mean that people ignore their existence or presence, or are not aware of it. ❑ *Unresolved or unacknowledged fears can trigger sleepwalking.* — ADJ: usu ADJ n
[2] If you describe something or someone as **unacknowledged**, you mean that their existence or importance is not recognized officially or publicly. ❑ *This tradition goes totally unacknowledged in official guidebooks.* — ADJ

**un|ac|quaint|ed** /ʌnəkweɪntɪd/ If you are **unacquainted with** something, you do not know about it or do not have not any experience of it. ❑ *I was then totally unacquainted with his poems.* — ADJ: v-link ADJ *with* n; = unfamiliar

**un|adorned** /ʌnədɔːʳnd/ Something that is **unadorned** is plain, rather than having decoration on it. ❑ *The room is typically simple and unadorned, with white walls and a tiled floor.* — ADJ

**un|adul|ter|at|ed** /ʌnədʌltəreɪtɪd/ [1] Something that is **unadulterated** is completely pure and has had nothing added to it. ❑ *Organic food is unadulterated food produced without artificial chemicals or pesticides.* — ADJ; ≠ adulterated
[2] You can also use **unadulterated** to emphasize a particular quality, often a bad quality. ❑ *It was pure, unadulterated hell.* — ADJ: ADJ n; [emphasis]

**un|af|fect|ed** /ʌnəfektɪd/ [1] If someone or something is **unaffected by** an event or occurrence, they are not changed by it in any way. ❑ *She seemed totally unaffected by what she'd drunk... The strike shut down 50 airports, but most international flights were unaffected.* — ADJ: v-link ADJ, oft ADJ *by* n
[2] If you describe someone as **unaffected**, you mean that they are natural and genuine in their behaviour, and do not act as though they are more important than other people. ❑ *...this unaffected, charming couple.* — ADJ; [approval]; = genuine

**un|afraid** /ʌnəfreɪd/ If you are **unafraid to** do something, you are confident and not at all nervous about doing it. ❑ *He is a man with a reputation for being tough and unafraid of unpopular decisions... She was a forceful intellectual unafraid to speak her mind.* — ADJ: v-link ADJ, ADJ after v, oft ADJ *of* n, ADJ to-inf; ≠ afraid

**un|aid|ed** /ʌneɪdɪd/ If you do something **unaided**, you do it without help from anyone or anything else. ❑ *There have been at least thirteen previous attempts to reach the North Pole unaided.* — ADJ: usu ADJ after v, also ADJ n

**un|al|loyed** /ʌnəlɔɪd/ If you describe a feeling such as happiness or relief as **unalloyed**, you are emphasizing that it is a strong feeling and no other feeling is involved. [LITERARY] ❑ *...an occasion of unalloyed joy.* — ADJ: usu ADJ n; [emphasis]

**un|al|ter|able** /ʌnɔːltərəbᵊl/ Something that is **unalterable** cannot be changed. ❑ *...an unalterable fact of life.* — ADJ: usu ADJ n; = unchangeable

**un|al|tered** /ʌnɔːltəʳd/ Something that remains **unaltered** has not changed or been changed. ❑ *The rest of the apartment had fortunately remained unaltered since that time... These were my opinions, and they continue unaltered.* — ADJ: v-link ADJ, ADJ after v, ADJ n; = unchanged

**un|am|bigu|ous** /ʌnæmbɪgjuəs/ If you describe a message or comment as **unambiguous**, you mean that it is clear and cannot be understood wrongly. ❑ *...an election result that sent the party an unambiguous message.* — ADJ; ≠ ambiguous
♦ **un|am|bigu|ous|ly** *He has failed to dissociate himself clearly and unambiguously from the attack.* — ADV: usu ADV with v, also ADV adj

**un|am|bi|tious** /ʌnæmbɪʃəs/ [1] An **unambitious** person is not particularly interested in improving their position in life or in being successful, rich, or powerful. — ADJ; ≠ ambitious
[2] An **unambitious** idea or plan is not very complicated, risky, or new, and is easy to carry out successfully. — ADJ; ≠ ambitious

**una|nim|ity** /juːnənɪmɪti/ When there is **unanimity** among a group of people, they all agree about something or all vote for the same thing. ❑ *All decisions would require unanimity.* — N-UNCOUNT

**unani|mous** /juːnænɪməs/ [1] When a group of people are **unanimous**, they all agree about something or all vote for the same thing. ❑ *Editors were unanimous in their condemnation of the proposals... They were unanimous that Chortlesby Manor must be preserved.* — ADJ: usu v-link ADJ, oft ADJ *in* n, ADJ that
♦ **unani|mous|ly** *Today its executive committee voted unanimously to reject the proposals... The board of ministers unanimously approved the project last week.* — ADV: ADV with v
[2] A **unanimous** vote, decision, or agreement is one in which all the people involved agree. ❑ *...the unanimous vote for Hungarian membership... Their decision was unanimous.* — ADJ

**un|an|nounced** /ʌnənaʊnst/ If someone arrives or does something **unannounced**, they do it unexpectedly and without anyone having being told about it beforehand. ❑ *He had just arrived unannounced from South America... My first night in Saigon I paid an unannounced visit to my father's cousins.* — ADJ: usu ADJ after v, ADJ n, also v-link ADJ

**un|an|swer|able** /ʌnɑːnsərəbᵊl, -æns-/ [1] If you describe a question as **unanswerable**, you mean that it has no possible answer or that a particular person cannot possibly answer it. ❑ *They would ask their mother unanswerable questions.* — ADJ
[2] If you describe a case or argument as **unanswerable**, you think that it is obviously true or correct and that nobody could disagree with it. ❑ *The argument for recruiting McGregor was unanswerable.* — ADJ

**un|an|swered** /ʌnɑːnsəʳd, -æns-/ Something such as a question or letter that is **unanswered** has not been answered. ❑ *Some of the most important questions remain unanswered... He had always had difficulty leaving questions unanswered.* — ADJ: v-link ADJ, ADJ n, ADJ after v

**un|ap|peal|ing** /ʌnəpiːlɪŋ/ If you describe someone or something as **unappealing**, you find them unpleasant and unattractive. ❑ *He's wearing a deeply unappealing baseball hat... The town is scruffy and unappealing.* — ADJ; ≠ appealing

**un|ap|pe|tiz|ing** /ʌnæpɪtaɪzɪŋ/
✔ in BRIT, also use **unappetising**
If you describe food as **unappetizing**, you think it will be unpleasant to eat because of its appearance. ❑ *...cold and unappetizing chicken.* — ADJ; ≠ appetizing

**un|ap|proach|able** /ʌnəproʊtʃəbᵊl/ If you describe someone as **unapproachable**, you mean that they seem to be difficult to talk to and not very friendly. — ADJ; ≠ approachable

**un|ar|gu|able** /ʌnɑːʳgjuəbᵊl/ If you describe a statement or opinion as **unarguable**, you think that it is obviously true or correct and that nobody could disagree with it. ❑ *He is making the unarguable point that our desires and preferences have a social component.* — ADJ; ≠ arguable
♦ **un|ar|gu|ably** /ʌnɑːʳgjuəbli/ *He is unarguably an outstanding man.* — ADV: ADV with cl/group

**un|armed** /ʌnɑːʳmd/ If a person or vehicle is **unarmed**, they are not carrying any weapons. ❑ *The soldiers concerned were unarmed at the time... Thirteen unarmed civilians died in that attack.* — ADJ
♦ **Unarmed** is also an adverb. ❑ *He says he walks inside the prison without guards, unarmed.* — ADV: ADV after v

**un|ashamed** /ʌnəʃeɪmd/ If you describe someone's behaviour or attitude as **unashamed**, you mean that they are open and honest about things that other people might find embarrassing or shocking. ❑ *I grinned at him in unashamed delight. ...a man rightly unashamed of his own talent.* — ADJ
♦ **un|asham|ed|ly** /ʌnəʃeɪmɪdli/ *Drugs are sold unashamedly in broad daylight.* — ADV: ADV with v, ADV adj/n

**un|asked** /ʌnɑːskt, -æskt/ [1] An **unasked** question is one that has not been asked, although people are wondering what the answer is. ❑ *She was undernourished, an observation that prompted yet another unasked question... Significant questions will go unasked.* — ADJ
[2] If someone says or does something **unasked**, they say or do it without being asked to do it. ❑ *His advice, offered to her unasked, was to stay home and make the best of things.* — ADJ: ADJ after v; = unprompted

**un|as|sail|able** /ʌnəseɪləbᵊl/ If you describe something or someone as **unassailable**, you mean that nothing can alter, destroy, or challenge — ADJ them. ❑ *That was enough to give Mansell an unassailable lead... His legal position is unassailable.*

**un|as|sist|ed** /ʌnəsɪstɪd/ If you do something **unassisted**, you do it on your own and no-one helps you. ❑ *At other times, he'd force her to walk totally unassisted. ...a mother who has had an unassisted delivery.* — ADJ: ADJ after v, ADJ n; = *unaided*

**un|as|sum|ing** /ʌnəsjuːmɪŋ, AM -suːm-/ If you describe a person or their behaviour as **unassuming**, you approve of them because they are quiet and do not try to appear important. ❑ *He's a man of few words, very polite and unassuming.* — ADJ; approval

**un|at|tached** /ʌnətætʃt/ Someone who is **unattached** is not married or does not have a girlfriend or boyfriend. ❑ *I knew only two or three unattached men.* — ADJ; = *single*

**un|at|tain|able** /ʌnəteɪnəbᵊl/ If you say that something is **unattainable**, you mean that it cannot be achieved or is not available. ❑ *There are those who argue that true independent advice is unattainable. ...an unattainable dream.* — ADJ

**un|at|tend|ed** /ʌnətendɪd/ When people or things are left **unattended**, they are not being watched or looked after. ❑ *Never leave young children unattended near any pool or water tank... An unattended bag was spotted near the platform at Gatwick.* — ADJ: ADJ after v, ADJ n, v-link ADJ

**un|at|trac|tive** /ʌnətræktɪv/ 1 **Unattractive** people and things are unpleasant in appearance. ❑ *I'm 27, have a nice flat, a good job and I'm not unattractive. ...an unattractive and uninteresting city.* — ADJ; ≠ *attractive* 2 If you describe something as **unattractive**, you mean that people do not like it and do not want to be involved with it. ❑ *The market is still unattractive to many insurers... It is not an unattractive option to make programmes for other companies.* — ADJ; ≠ *attractive*

**un|author|ized** /ʌnɔːθəraɪzd/

✔ in BRIT, also use **unauthorised**

If something is **unauthorized**, it has been produced or is happening without official permission. ❑ *...the unauthorized use of a military vehicle... It has also been made quite clear that the trip was unauthorised.* — ADJ; = *unofficial*

**un|avail|able** /ʌnəveɪləbᵊl/ When things or people are **unavailable**, you cannot obtain them, meet them, or talk to them. ❑ *Mr Hicks is out of the country and so unavailable for comment... Basic food products are frequently unavailable in the state shops.* — ADJ: usu v-link ADJ; ≠ *available*

**un|avail|ing** /ʌnəveɪlɪŋ/ An **unavailing** attempt to do something does not succeed. ❑ *Efforts to reach the people named in the report proved unavailing... He died after a brave but unavailing fight against a terminal illness.* — ADJ; = *unsuccessful*

**un|avoid|able** /ʌnəvɔɪdəbᵊl/ If something is **unavoidable**, it cannot be avoided or prevented. ❑ *Managers said the job losses were unavoidable... The recession has resulted in an unavoidable increase in spending on unemployment benefit.* — ADJ
♦ **un|avoid|ably** /ʌnəvɔɪdəbli/ *Prince Khalid was unavoidably detained in Saudi Arabia.* — ADV

**un|aware** /ʌnəweəʳ/ If you are **unaware of** something, you do not know about it. ❑ *Many people are unaware of just how much food and drink they consume... She was unaware that she was being filmed.* — ADJ: v-link ADJ, usu ADJ *of* n, ADJ that; ≠ *aware*

**un|awares** /ʌnəweəʳz/ If something **catches** you **unawares** or **takes** you **unawares**, it happens when you are not expecting it. ❑ *Investors and currency dealers were caught completely unawares by the Bundesbank's action... The suspect was taken unawares, without the chance to dispose of the evidence.* — PHRASE: V inflects

**un|bal|ance** /ʌnbæləns/ **(unbalances, unbalancing, unbalanced)** 1 If something **unbalances** a relationship, system, or group, it disturbs or upsets it so that it is no longer successful or functioning properly. ❑ *The interplay between the new politics and the modern media will unbalance the political process and inhibit its workings.* — VERB; = *destabilize*; V n 2 To **unbalance** something means to make it unsteady and likely to tip over. ❑ *Her whole body began to buckle, unbalancing the ladder... Don't lean in – you're unbalancing the horse.* — VERB; V n; V n

**un|bal|anced** /ʌnbælənst/ 1 If you describe someone as **unbalanced**, you mean that they appear disturbed and upset or they seem to be slightly mad. ❑ *I knew how unbalanced Paula had been since my uncle Peter died.* — ADJ; = *disturbed* 2 If you describe something such as a report or argument as **unbalanced**, you think that it is unfair or inaccurate because it emphasizes some things and ignores others. ❑ *UN officials argued that the report was unbalanced. ...unbalanced and unfair reporting.* — ADJ; = *biased*; ≠ *balanced*

**un|bear|able** /ʌnbeərəbᵊl/ If you describe something as **unbearable**, you mean that it is so unpleasant, painful, or upsetting that you feel unable to accept it or deal with it. ❑ *War has made life almost unbearable for the civilians remaining in the capital... I was in terrible, unbearable pain.* — ADJ; = *intolerable*
♦ **un|bear|ably** /ʌnbeərəbli/ *By the evening it had become unbearably hot.* — ADV: usu ADV adj/-ed

**un|beat|able** /ʌnbiːtəbᵊl/ 1 If you describe something as **unbeatable**, you mean that it is the best thing of its kind. ❑ *These resorts, like Magaluf and Arenal, remain unbeatable in terms of price. ...unbeatable Italian cars.* — ADJ; emphasis 2 In a game or competition, if you describe a person or team as **unbeatable**, you mean that they win so often, or perform so well that they are unlikely to be beaten by anyone. ❑ *The opposition was unbeatable... With two more days of competition to go China is in an unbeatable position.* — ADJ; = *invincible*

**un|beat|en** /ʌnbiːtᵊn/ In sport, if a person or their performance is **unbeaten**, nobody else has performed well enough to beat them. ❑ *He's unbeaten in 20 fights... Sampdoria lost their unbeaten record with a 2-1 home defeat against Genoa.* — ADJ

**un|be|com|ing** /ʌnbɪkʌmɪŋ/ 1 If you describe things such as clothes as **unbecoming**, you mean that they look unattractive. [OLD-FASHIONED] — ADJ; ≠ *becoming* 2 If you describe a person's behaviour or remarks as **unbecoming**, you mean that they are shocking and unsuitable for that person. [FORMAL] ❑ *His conduct was totally unbecoming to an officer in the British armed services... Those involved had performed acts unbecoming of university students.* — ADJ: oft ADJ *to/of* n

**un|be|known** /ʌnbɪnoʊn/

✔ The form **unbeknownst** /ʌnbɪnoʊnst/ is also used.

If something happens **unbeknown to** you or **unbeknownst to** you, you do not know about it. ❑ *I am appalled that children can mount up debts unbeknown to their parents... Unbeknownst to her father, she began taking dancing lessons.* — PREP-PHRASE

**un|be|liev|able** /ʌnbɪliːvəbᵊl/ 1 If you say that something is **unbelievable**, you are emphasizing that it is very good, impressive, intense, or extreme. ❑ *His guitar solos are just unbelievable... It was an unbelievable moment when Chris won the gold medal.* — ADJ; emphasis; = *incredible*
♦ **un|be|liev|ably** /ʌnbɪliːvəbli/ *Our car was still going unbelievably well... He beamed: 'Unbelievably, we have now made it to the final twice.'* — ADV: ADV with cl/group; = *incredibly*
2 You can use **unbelievable** to emphasize that you think something is very bad or shocking. ❑ *I find it unbelievable that people can accept this sort of behaviour.* — ADJ: oft *it* v-link ADJ that; emphasis; = *incredible*
♦ **un|be|liev|ably** *What you did was unbelievably stupid... Unbelievably, our Government are now planning to close this magnificent institution.* — ADV: ADV with cl/group; = *incredibly*
3 If an idea or statement is **unbelievable**, it seems so unlikely to be true that you cannot believe it. ❑ *I still find this story both fascinating and unbelievable... I know it sounds unbelievable but I never wanted to cheat.* — ADJ; = *incredible*
♦ **un|be|liev|ably** *Lainey was, unbelievably, pregnant again.* — ADV: ADV with cl/group

**un|be|liev|er** /ʌnbɪliːvəʳ/ **(unbelievers)** People who do not believe in a particular religion are sometimes referred to as **unbelievers**. — N-COUNT; ≠ *believer*

**un|be|liev|ing** /ʌnbɪliːvɪŋ/ [ADJ] If you describe someone as **unbelieving**, you mean that they do not believe something that they have been told. ❑ *He looked at me with unbelieving eyes.*

**un|bend** /ʌnbend/ **(unbends, unbending, unbent)** [VERB] [V] If someone **unbends**, their attitude becomes less strict than it was. ❑ *In her dying days the old Queen unbent a little.*

**un|bend|ing** /ʌnbendɪŋ/ [ADJ = inflexible] If you describe a person or their behaviour as **unbending**, you mean that they have very strict beliefs and attitudes, which they are unwilling to change. ❑ *He was rigid and unbending. ...her unbending opposition to the old regime.*

**un|bi|ased** /ʌnbaɪəst/ also **unbiassed.** [ADJ = impartial ≠ biased] If you describe someone or something as **unbiased**, you mean they are fair and not likely to support one particular person or group involved in something. ❑ *There is no clear and unbiased information available for consumers... The researchers were expected to be unbiased. ...an unbiased jury.*

**un|bid|den** /ʌnbɪdən/ [ADJ: ADJ after v, v-link ADJ, ADJ n] If something happens **unbidden**, it happens without you expecting or wanting it to happen. [LITERARY] ❑ *The name came unbidden to Cook's mind – Ashley Stoker.*

**un|bind** /ʌnbaɪnd/ **(unbinds, unbinding, unbound)** [VERB] If you **unbind** something or someone, you take off a piece of cloth, string, or rope that has been tied round them. ❑ [V n] *She unbound her hair and let it flow loose in the wind...* [V-ed] *Many cultures still have fairly strict rules about women displaying unbound hair.*

**un|blem|ished** /ʌnblemɪʃt/ [ADJ: usu ADJ n = untarnished] 1 If you describe something such as someone's record, reputation, or character as **unblemished**, you mean it has not been harmed or spoiled. ❑ *...Lee's unblemished reputation as a man of honor and principle.* [ADJ: usu ADJ n] 2 If you describe something as **unblemished**, you mean that it has no marks or holes on its surface. ❑ *Be sure to select firm, unblemished fruit.*

**un|blink|ing** /ʌnblɪŋkɪŋ/ [ADJ] If you describe someone's eyes or expression as **unblinking**, you mean that they are looking steadily at something without blinking. [LITERARY] ❑ *He stared into Leo's unblinking eyes.* ♦ [ADV: usu ADV after v] **un|blink|ing|ly** *She looked at him unblinkingly.*

**un|born** /ʌnbɔːrn/ [ADJ] An **unborn** child has not yet been born and is still inside its mother's womb. ❑ *...her unborn baby... They will affect generations of Britons still unborn.* ♦ [N-PLURAL: the N] **The unborn** are children who are not born yet.

**un|bound** /ʌnbaʊnd/ **Unbound** is the past tense and past participle of **unbind**.

**un|bound|ed** /ʌnbaʊndɪd/ [ADJ = boundless] If you describe something as **unbounded**, you mean that it has, or seems to have, no limits. ❑ *...an unbounded capacity to imitate and adopt the new... His advice was always sensible and his energy unbounded.*

**un|break|able** /ʌnbreɪkəbəl/ [ADJ] 1 **Unbreakable** objects cannot be broken, usually because they are made of a very strong material. ❑ *Tableware for outdoor use should ideally be unbreakable.* [ADJ] 2 An **unbreakable** rule or limit must be obeyed. ❑ *One unbreakable rule in our school is that no child can be tested without written parental permission.*

**un|bridge|able** /ʌnbrɪdʒəbəl/ [ADJ] An **unbridgeable** gap or divide between two sides in an argument is so great that the two sides seem unlikely ever to agree. [JOURNALISM] ❑ *...the apparently unbridgeable gulf between the SIS and the Security Service... The gap between the President and his opponents is unbridgeable.*

**un|bri|dled** /ʌnbraɪdəld/ [ADJ: usu ADJ n] If you describe behaviour or feelings as **unbridled**, you mean that they are not controlled or limited in any way. ❑ *...a tale of lust and unbridled passion.*

**un|bro|ken** /ʌnbroʊkən/ [ADJ = uninterrupted] If something is **unbroken**, it is continuous or complete and has not been interrupted or broken. ❑ *...an unbroken run of 38 match wins... We've had ten days of almost unbroken sunshine.*

**un|buck|le** /ʌnbʌkəl/ **(unbuckles, unbuckling, unbuckled)** [VERB] If you **unbuckle** something such as a belt or a shoe, you undo the buckle fastening it. ❑ [V n] *He unbuckled his seat belt.*

**un|bur|den** /ʌnbɜːrdən/ **(unburdens, unburdening, unburdened)** [VERB] If you **unburden yourself** or your problems to someone, you tell them about something which you have been secretly worrying about. ❑ [V pron-refl] *The Centre became a place where many came to unburden themselves, to talk about their hopes and fears...* [V n to n] *Somehow he had to unburden his soul to somebody, and it couldn't be to Laura...* [V pron-refl of n] *Some students unburden themselves of emotional problems that faculty members feel ill equipped to handle.* [Also V pron-refl, V n]

**un|but|ton** /ʌnbʌtən/ **(unbuttons, unbuttoning, unbuttoned)** [VERB] If you **unbutton** an item of clothing, you undo the buttons fastening it. ❑ [V n] *She had begun to unbutton her blouse.* [V-ed] *...his unbuttoned blue coat.*

**un|called for** /ʌnkɔːld fɔːr/ [ADJ = unwarranted] If you describe a remark or criticism as **uncalled for**, you mean that it should not have been made, because it was unkind or unfair. ❑ *I'm sorry. That was uncalled for. ...Leo's uncalled-for remarks about her cousin.*

**un|can|ny** /ʌnkæni/ [ADJ] If you describe something as **uncanny**, you mean that it is strange and difficult to explain. ❑ *The hero, Danny, bears an uncanny resemblance to Kirk Douglas... I had this uncanny feeling that Alice was warning me.* ♦ [ADV: usu ADV adj/adv] **un|can|ni|ly** /ʌnkænɪli/ *They have uncannily similar voices.*

**un|cared for** /ʌnkeərd fɔːr/ [ADJ: usu v-link ADJ] If you describe people or animals as **uncared for**, you mean that they have not been looked after properly and as a result are hungry, dirty, or ill. ❑ *...people who feel unwanted, unloved, and uncared for.*

**un|caring** /ʌnkeərɪŋ/ [ADJ disapproval ≠ caring] If you describe someone as **uncaring**, you are critical of them for not caring about other people, especially people who are in a bad situation. ❑ *It portrays him as cold and uncaring. ...this uncaring attitude towards the less well off.*

**un|ceas|ing** /ʌnsiːsɪŋ/ [ADJ: usu ADJ n emphasis] If you describe something as **unceasing**, you are emphasizing that it continues without stopping. ❑ *...his unceasing labours.* ♦ [ADV: ADV with v] **un|ceas|ing|ly** *Paul talked unceasingly from dawn to dusk.*

**un|cer|emo|ni|ous|ly** /ʌnserɪmoʊniəsli/ [ADV: ADV with v] If someone or something is removed, left, or put somewhere **unceremoniously**, this is done in a sudden or rude way that shows they are not thought to be important. ❑ *She was unceremoniously dumped to be replaced by a leader who could win the election... He had to be bundled unceremoniously out of the way.*

**un|cer|tain** /ʌnsɜːrtən/ [ADJ: usu v-link ADJ, oft ADJ about/of n, ADJ wh/that = unsure ≠ certain] 1 If you are **uncertain about** something, you do not know what you should do, what is going to happen, or what the truth is about something. ❑ *He was uncertain about his brother's intentions... They were uncertain of the total value of the transaction... He stopped, uncertain how to put the question tactfully... With some hesitation and an uncertain smile, she held out her hand.* ♦ [ADV: usu ADV after v] **un|cer|tain|ly** *He entered the hallway and stood uncertainly.* [ADJ: usu v-link ADJ, oft it v-link ADJ wh] 2 If something is **uncertain**, it is not known or definite. ❑ *How far the republics can give practical help, however, is uncertain... It's uncertain whether they will accept the plan... Students all over the country are facing an uncertain future.* [PHRASE: PHR after v emphasis] 3 If you say that someone tells a person something **in no uncertain terms**, you are emphasizing that they say it strongly and clearly so that there is no doubt about what they mean. ❑ *She told him in no uncertain terms to go away.*

**un|cer|tain|ty** /ʌnsɜːrtənti/ **(uncertainties)** [N-VAR] **Uncertainty** is a state of doubt about the future or about what is the right thing to do. ❑ *...a period* *of political uncertainty. ...the uncertainties of life on the West Coast.*

**un|chal|lenged** /ʌntʃælɪndʒd/ [1] When something goes **unchallenged** or is **unchallenged**, people accept it without asking questions about whether it is right or wrong. ❑ *These views have not gone unchallenged. ...the unchallenged principle of parliamentary sovereignty.* [2] If you say that someone's position of authority is **unchallenged**, you mean that it is strong and no one tries to replace them. ❑ *He is the unchallenged leader of the strongest republic. ...the man who has led his party unchallenged for over thirty years.* [3] If you do something **unchallenged**, nobody stops you and asks you questions, for example about who you are or why you are doing it. ❑ *I managed to walk around unchallenged for 10 minutes before an alert nurse spotted me.*

ADJ: ADJ after v, ADJ n, v-link ADJ
ADJ: ADJ n, ADJ after v, v-link ADJ
ADJ: ADJ after v

**un|change|able** /ʌntʃeɪndʒəbəl/ Something that is **unchangeable** cannot be changed at all. ❑ *The doctrine is unchangeable. ...a thoroughly organised and almost unchangeable system of laws and customs.*

ADJ = *unalterable*

**un|changed** /ʌntʃeɪndʒd/ If something is **unchanged**, it has stayed the same for a particular period of time. ❑ *For many years prices have remained virtually unchanged.*

ADJ: usu v-link ADJ

**un|chang|ing** /ʌntʃeɪndʒɪŋ/ Something that is **unchanging** always stays the same. ❑ *...eternal and unchanging truths.*

ADJ

**un|char|ac|ter|is|tic** /ʌnkærɪktərɪstɪk/ If you describe something as **uncharacteristic of** someone, you mean that it is not typical of them. ❑ *It was uncharacteristic of her father to disappear like this. ...an uncharacteristic lack of modesty.* ♦ **un|char|ac|ter|is|ti|cal|ly** /ʌnkærɪktərɪstɪkli/ *Owen has been uncharacteristically silent... Uncharacteristically for Keegan, he decided to have a snooze.*

ADJ: oft ADJ *of* n ≠ *typical, characteristic*
ADV: usu ADV adj, also ADV with v, ADV with cl

**un|chari|table** /ʌntʃærɪtəbəl/ If you describe someone's remarks, thoughts, or behaviour as **uncharitable**, you think they are being unkind or unfair to someone. ❑ *This was an uncharitable assessment of the reasons for the failure.*

ADJ

**un|chart|ed** /ʌntʃɑːrtɪd/ If you describe a situation, experience, or activity as **uncharted** territory or waters, you mean that it is new or unfamiliar. ❑ *Carter's fourth album definitely moves into uncharted territory. ...a largely uncharted area of medical science.*

ADJ: usu ADJ n = *unexplored*

**un|checked** /ʌntʃekt/ If something harmful or undesirable is left **unchecked**, nobody controls it or prevents it from growing or developing. ❑ *If left unchecked, weeds will flourish. ...a world in which brutality and lawlessness are allowed to go unchecked.*

ADJ: ADJ after v, ADJ n, v-link ADJ

**un|civi|lized** /ʌnsɪvɪlaɪzd/

✓ in BRIT, also use **uncivilised**

If you describe someone's behaviour as **uncivilized**, you find it unacceptable, for example because it is very cruel or very rude. ❑ *The campaign has abounded in mutual accusations of uncivilised behaviour... I think any sport involving animals where the animals do not have a choice is barbaric and uncivilized.*

ADJ [disapproval]

**un|claimed** /ʌnkleɪmd/ If something is **unclaimed**, nobody has claimed it or said that it belongs to them. ❑ *Her luggage remained unclaimed at Frankfurt Departures. ...unclaimed prizes.*

ADJ

**un|clas|si|fied** /ʌnklæsɪfaɪd/ [1] If information or a document is **unclassified**, it is not secret and is available to the general public. [2] If something is **unclassified**, it has not been given a grade or put into a category, for example because it is of a low or basic standard. ❑ *...an unclassified honours degree.*

ADJ ≠ *classified*
ADJ ≠ *classified*

**un|cle** /ʌŋkəl/ **(uncles)** Someone's **uncle** is the brother of their mother or father, or the husband of their aunt. ❑ *My uncle was the mayor of Memphis... A telegram from Uncle Fred arrived.*

◆◆◇ N-FAMILY; N-TITLE

**un|clean** /ʌnkliːn/ [1] Something that is **unclean** is dirty and likely to cause disease. ❑ *...the Western attitude to insects as being dirty and unclean... By bathing in unclean water, they expose themselves to contamination.* [2] If you describe someone or something as **unclean**, you consider them to be spiritually or morally bad. ❑ *They felt as though they had done something discreditable and unclean. ...unclean thoughts.*

ADJ = *dirty* ≠ *clean*
ADJ

**un|clear** /ʌnklɪər/ [1] If something is **unclear**, it is not known or not certain. ❑ *It is unclear how much popular support they have among the island's population... Just what the soldier was doing in Bireij is unclear.* [2] If you are **unclear** about something, you do not understand it properly or are not sure about it. ❑ *He is still unclear about his own future.*

ADJ: usu v-link ADJ, oft *it* v-link ADJ wh = *uncertain*
ADJ: v-link ADJ, oft ADJ *about* n/wh, ADJ *as to* wh/n, ADJ wh

**Uncle Sam** /ʌŋkəl sæm/ Some people refer to the United States of America or its government as **Uncle Sam**. [mainly AM; also BRIT, JOURNALISM] ❑ *They are ready to defend themselves against Uncle Sam's imperialist policies.*

N-PROPER

**Uncle Tom (Uncle Toms)** In the past, some black people used **Uncle Tom** to refer to a black man when they disapproved of him because he was too respectful or friendly towards white people. This use could cause offence. ❑ *To the radical blacks of the Sixties, he was an Uncle Tom.*

N-COUNT [disapproval]

**un|clothed** /ʌnkloʊðd/ If someone is **unclothed**, they are not wearing any clothes. [FORMAL] ❑ *He learned how to draw the unclothed human frame... It's considered improper to be unclothed in public.*

ADJ: ADJ n, v-link ADJ, ADJ after v = *naked*

**un|clut|tered** /ʌnklʌtərd/ If you describe something as **uncluttered**, you mean that it is simple and does not contain or consist of a lot of unnecessary things. ❑ *If you keep a room uncluttered it makes it seem lighter and bigger... The portraits are simple, uncluttered compositions.*

ADJ ≠ *cluttered*

**un|coil** /ʌnkɔɪl/ **(uncoils, uncoiling, uncoiled)** If something **uncoils** or if you **uncoil** it, it becomes straight after it has been wound or curled up. If someone who is curled up **uncoils**, they move so that their body becomes straight. ❑ *He uncoiled the hose and gave them a thorough drenching... Dan played with the tangerine peel, letting it uncoil and then coil again... Mack seemed to uncoil slowly up into a standing position.*

VERB
V n
V
V

**un|combed** /ʌnkoʊmd/ If someone's hair is **uncombed**, it is untidy because it has not been brushed or combed.

ADJ

**un|com|fort|able** /ʌnkʌmftəbəl/ [1] If you are **uncomfortable**, you are slightly worried or embarrassed, and not relaxed and confident. ❑ *The request for money made them feel uncomfortable... If you are uncomfortable with your counsellor or therapist, you must discuss it... I feel uncomfortable lying.* ♦ **un|com|fort|ably** /ʌnkʌmftəbli/ *Sandy leaned across the table, his face uncomfortably close to Brad's... He smiled uncomfortably.* [2] Something that is **uncomfortable** makes you feel slight pain or physical discomfort when you experience it or use it. ❑ *Wigs are hot and uncomfortable to wear constantly. ...an old and uncomfortable chair.* ♦ **un|com|fort|ably** *The water was uncomfortably cold.* [3] If you are **uncomfortable**, you are not physically content and relaxed, and feel slight pain or discomfort. ❑ *I sometimes feel uncomfortable after eating in the evening... People living or working with smokers can find it uncomfortable to wear contact lenses because the smoke causes irritation.* ♦ **un|com|fort|ably** *He felt uncomfortably hot... He awoke to find himself lying uncomfortably on a pile of firewood.* [4] You can describe a situation or fact as **uncomfortable** when it is difficult to deal with and causes problems and worries. ❑ *It is uncomfortable to think of our own death, but we need*

ADJ: usu v-link ADJ, oft ADJ *with/about* n, ADJ -ing = *awkward*
ADV: usu ADV adj/-ed, also ADV after v
ADJ: oft ADJ to-inf
ADV: ADV adj
ADJ: usu v-link ADJ
ADV: ADV adj, ADV after v
ADJ: oft *it* v-link ADJ to-inf, ADJ to-inf

*to... The decree put the president in an uncomfortable position.*

**un|com|mit|ted** /ʌnkəmɪtɪd/ [1] If you are **uncommitted**, you have not yet decided to support a particular idea, belief, group, or person, or you are unwilling to show your support. ❑ *The allegiance of uncommitted voters will be crucial... I was still uncommitted to the venture when we reached Kanpur.* ♦ **The uncommitted** are people who are uncommitted. ❑ *It was the uncommitted that Labour needed to reach.* [2] If resources are **uncommitted**, it has not yet been decided what to use them for. ❑ *...£32.3m of uncommitted loans.*
ADJ ≠committed; N-PLURAL: the N; ADJ

**un|com|mon** /ʌnkɒmən/ [1] If you describe something as **uncommon**, you mean that it does not happen often or is not often seen. ❑ *Cancer of the breast in young women is uncommon... A 15-year lifespan is not uncommon for a dog.* [2] If you describe a quality, usually a good quality, as **uncommon**, you mean that it is unusually great in degree or amount. [LITERARY] ❑ *Both are blessed with uncommon ability to fix things... She read Cecelia's last letter with uncommon interest.* ♦ **un|com|mon|ly** *Mary was uncommonly good at tennis.*
ADJ: usu v-link ADJ = unusual ≠common; ADJ: ADJ n = unusual; ADV: usu ADV adj/adv

**un|com|mu|ni|ca|tive** /ʌnkəmjuːnɪkətɪv/ If you describe someone as **uncommunicative**, you are critical of them because they do not talk to other people very much and are unwilling to express opinions or give information. ❑ *My daughter is very difficult, uncommunicative and moody.*
ADJ [disapproval]

**un|com|plain|ing** /ʌnkəmpleɪnɪŋ/ If you describe someone as **uncomplaining**, you approve of them because they do difficult or unpleasant things and do not complain about them. ❑ *He was a cheerful and uncomplaining travel companion.*
ADJ [approval]

**un|com|pli|cat|ed** /ʌnkɒmplɪkeɪtɪd/ If you describe someone or something as **uncomplicated**, you approve of them because they are easy to deal with or understand. ❑ *She is a beautiful, uncomplicated girl. ...good, fresh British cooking with its uncomplicated, direct flavours.*
ADJ [approval] ≠complex

**un|com|pre|hend|ing** /ʌnkɒmprɪhendɪŋ/ If you describe someone as **uncomprehending**, you mean that they do not understand what is happening or what someone has said. ❑ *He gave the bottle a long, uncomprehending look.*
ADJ

**un|com|pro|mis|ing** /ʌnkɒmprəmaɪzɪŋ/ [1] If you describe someone as **uncompromising**, you mean that they are determined not to change their opinions or aims in any way. ❑ *Mrs Thatcher was a tough and uncompromising politician.* ♦ **un|com|pro|mis|ing|ly** *The company had once been uncompromisingly socialist... He states uncompromisingly that he is opposed to any practices which oppress animals.* [2] If you describe something as **uncompromising**, you mean that it does not attempt to make something that is shocking or unpleasant any more acceptable to people. ❑ *...a film of uncompromising brutality.* ♦ **un|com|pro|mis|ing|ly** *...the uncompromisingly modern decor.*
ADJ; ADV: usu ADV adj, also ADV after v; ADJ; ADV: ADV adj

**un|con|cealed** /ʌnkənsiːld/ An **unconcealed** emotion is one that someone has made no attempt to hide. ❑ *His message was received with unconcealed anger.*
ADJ: usu ADJ n = open

**un|con|cern** /ʌnkənsɜːʳn/ A person's **unconcern** is their lack of interest in or anxiety about something, often something that most people would be concerned about. ❑ *She'd mentioned it casually once, surprising him by her unconcern.*
N-UNCOUNT ≠concern

**un|con|cerned** /ʌnkənsɜːʳnd/ If a person is **unconcerned about** something, usually something that most people would care about, they are not interested in it or worried about it. ❑ *Paul was unconcerned about what he had done... He seems totally unconcerned by real dangers.*
ADJ: usu v-link ADJ, oft ADJ about/by n ≠concerned

**un|con|di|tion|al** /ʌnkəndɪʃənəl/ If you describe something as **unconditional**, you mean that the person doing or giving it does not require anything to be done by other people in exchange. ❑ *Children need unconditional love... The leader of the revolt made an unconditional surrender early this morning.* ♦ **un|con|di|tion|al|ly** *The hostages were released unconditionally.*
ADJ: usu ADJ n ≠conditional; ADV: ADV with v

**un|con|firmed** /ʌnkənfɜːʳmd/ If a report or a rumour is **unconfirmed**, there is no definite proof as to whether it is true or not. ❑ *There are unconfirmed reports of several small villages buried by mudslides.*
ADJ

**un|con|gen|ial** /ʌnkəndʒiːniəl/ If you describe a person or place as **uncongenial**, you mean that they are unfriendly and unpleasant. ❑ *He continued to find the Simpsons uncongenial bores... Hollywood was an uncongenial place to work.*
ADJ ≠congenial

**un|con|nect|ed** /ʌnkənektɪd/ If one thing is **unconnected with** another or the two things are **unconnected**, the things are not related to each other in any way. ❑ *She was known to have had personal problems unconnected with her marriage... I can't believe that those two murders are unconnected.*
ADJ: oft ADJ with/to n = unrelated

**un|con|scion|able** /ʌnkɒnʃənəbəl/ If you describe something as **unconscionable**, you mean that the person responsible for it ought to be ashamed of it, especially because its effects are so great or severe. [LITERARY] ❑ *It's unconscionable for the government to do anything for a man who admits to smuggling 135 tons of cocaine into the United States.*
ADJ

**un|con|scious** /ʌnkɒnʃəs/ [1] Someone who is **unconscious** is in a state similar to sleep, usually as the result of a serious injury or a lack of oxygen. ❑ *By the time ambulancemen arrived he was unconscious.* ♦ **un|con|scious|ness** *He knew that he might soon lapse into unconsciousness.* [2] If you are **unconscious of** something, you are unaware of it. ❑ *He himself seemed totally unconscious of his failure.* ♦ **un|con|scious|ly** *'I was very unsure of myself after the divorce,' she says, unconsciously sweeping back the curls from her forehead.* [3] If feelings or attitudes are **unconscious**, you are not aware that you have them, but they show in the way that you behave. ❑ *Unconscious envy manifests itself very often as this kind of arrogance.* ♦ **un|con|scious|ly** *I think racism is unconsciously inherent in practically everyone.* [4] Your **unconscious** is the part of your mind that contains feelings and ideas that you do not know about or cannot control. ❑ *In examining the content of the unconscious, Freud called into question some deeply-held beliefs.*
ADJ: v-link ADJ, ADJ n, ADJ after v ≠conscious; N-UNCOUNT; ADJ: v-link ADJ of n = oblivious ≠conscious; ADV: usu ADV with v, also ADV adj; ADJ; ADV: ADV adj ADV with v; N-SING: the/poss N

**un|con|sti|tu|tion|al** /ʌnkɒnstɪtjuːʃənəl, AM -tuː-/ If something is **unconstitutional**, it breaks the rules of a political system. ❑ *The Moldavian parliament has declared the elections unconstitutional... Banning cigarette advertising would be unconstitutional, since selling cigarettes is legal.*
ADJ ≠constitutional

**un|con|trol|lable** /ʌnkəntroʊləbəl/ [1] If you describe a feeling or physical action as **uncontrollable**, you mean that you cannot control it or prevent yourself from feeling or doing it. ❑ *It had been a time of almost uncontrollable excitement... He burst into uncontrollable laughter at something I'd said.* ♦ **un|con|trol|lably** /ʌnkəntroʊləbli/ *I started shaking uncontrollably and began to cry.* [2] If you describe a person as **uncontrollable**, you mean that their behaviour is bad and that nobody can make them behave more sensibly. ❑ *Mark was withdrawn and uncontrollable... Uncontrollable children grow into young criminals.* [3] If you describe a situation or series of events as **uncontrollable**, you believe that nothing can be done to control them or to prevent things from getting worse. ❑ *If political and ethnic problems are not resolved the situation could become uncontrollable.*
ADJ: usu ADJ n; ADV: usu ADV after v; ADJ; ADJ

**un|con|trolled** /ʌnkəntroʊld/ [1] If you describe someone's behaviour as **uncontrolled**, you mean they appear unable to stop it or to make it less extreme. ❑ *His uncontrolled behavior disturbed the entire class... Julia blows her nose, but*
ADJ: ADJ n, ADJ after v, v-link ADJ

*her sobbing goes on uncontrolled.* [2] If a situation or activity is **uncontrolled**, no-one is controlling it or preventing it from continuing or growing. ❑ *...the central bank's uncontrolled printing of money.* ADJ = unchecked

**un|con|ven|tion|al** /ʌnkənvenʃənəl/ [1] If you describe a person or their attitude or behaviour as **unconventional**, you mean that they do not behave in the same way as most other people in their society. ❑ *Linus Pauling is an unconventional genius... He had rather unconventional work habits, preferring to work through the night.* [2] An **unconventional** way of doing something is not the usual way of doing it, and may be rather surprising. ❑ *The vaccine had been produced by an unconventional technique... Despite his unconventional methods, he has inspired pupils more than anyone else.* ADJ ≠conventional; ADJ ≠conventional

**un|con|vinced** /ʌnkənvɪnst/ If you are **unconvinced** that something is true or right, you are not at all certain that it is true or right. ❑ *Most consumers seem unconvinced that the recession is over.* ADJ: usu v-link ADJ, oft ADJ that

**un|con|vinc|ing** /ʌnkənvɪnsɪŋ/ [1] If you describe something such as an argument or explanation as **unconvincing**, you find it difficult to believe because it does not seem real. ❑ *Mr Patel phoned the University for an explanation, and he was given the usual unconvincing excuses... To many readers it sounded unconvincing.* ♦ **un|con|vinc|ing|ly** *'It's not that I don't believe you, Meg,' Jack said, unconvincingly.* [2] If you describe a story or a character in a story as **unconvincing**, you think they do not seem likely or real. ❑ *...an unconvincing love story.* ADJ ≠convincing; ADV: ADV with v; ADJ ≠convincing

**un|cooked** /ʌnkʊkt/ **Uncooked** food has not yet been cooked. ADJ = raw

**un|co|opera|tive** /ʌnkoʊɒpərətɪv/ If you describe someone as **uncooperative**, you mean that they make no effort at all to help other people or to make other people's lives easier. ❑ *She became uncooperative: unwilling to do her homework or help with any household chores. ...a bunch of stupid, cranky, uncooperative old fools.* ADJ: usu v-link ADJ = unhelpful ≠cooperative

**un|co|ordi|nat|ed** /ʌnkoʊɔːʳdɪneɪtɪd/ also **unco-ordinated.** [1] If you describe someone as **uncoordinated** you mean that their movements are not smooth or controlled. ❑ *They were unsteady on their feet and rather uncoordinated. ...an uncoordinated toddler.* [2] If you describe actions or plans as **uncoordinated**, you mean they are not well-organized. ❑ *Government action has been half-hearted and uncoordinated. ...late, uncoordinated and piecemeal enemy responses.* ADJ; ADJ

**un|cork** /ʌnkɔːʳk/ **(uncorks, uncorking, uncorked)** When you **uncork** a bottle, you open it by pulling the cork out of it. ❑ *Steve uncorked bottles of champagne to toast the achievement.* VERB = open; V n

**un|cor|robo|rat|ed** /ʌnkərɒbəreɪtɪd/ An **uncorroborated** statement or claim is not supported by any evidence or information. ❑ *Uncorroborated confessions should no longer be accepted by courts.* ADJ: usu ADJ n

**un|count|able noun** /ʌnkaʊntəbəl naʊn/ **(uncountable nouns)** An **uncountable noun** is the same as an **uncount noun.** N-COUNT

**un|count noun** /ʌnkaʊnt naʊn/ **(uncount nouns)** An **uncount noun** is a noun such as 'gold', 'information', or 'furniture' which has only one form and can be used without a determiner. N-COUNT

**un|couth** /ʌnkuːθ/ If you describe a person as **uncouth**, you mean that their behaviour is rude, noisy, and unpleasant. ADJ [disapproval] = coarse

**un|cov|er** /ʌnkʌvəʳ/ **(uncovers, uncovering, uncovered)** [1] If you **uncover** something, especially something that has been kept secret, you discover or find out about it. ❑ *Auditors said they had uncovered evidence of fraud.* [2] When people who are digging somewhere **uncover** something, they find a thing or a place that has been under the ground for a long time. ❑ *Archaeologists have uncovered an 11,700-year-old hunting camp in Alaska.* [3] To **uncover** something means to remove something that is covering it. ❑ *When the seedlings sprout, uncover the tray.* VERB = discover; V n; VERB = unearth; V n; VERB; V n

**un|cov|ered** /ʌnkʌvəʳd/ Something that is left **uncovered** does not have anything covering it. ❑ *Minor cuts and grazes can usually be left uncovered to heal by themselves... The uncovered bucket in the corner stank.* ADJ: ADJ after v, ADJ n, v-link ADJ

**un|criti|cal** /ʌnkrɪtɪkəl/ If you describe a person or their behaviour as **uncritical**, you mean that they do not judge whether someone or something is good or bad, right or wrong, before supporting or believing them. ❑ *...the conventional notion of women as uncritical purchasers of heavily advertised products.* ♦ **un|criti|cal|ly** /ʌnkrɪtɪkli/ *Politicians want a lap-dog press which will uncritically report their propaganda.* ADJ; ADV: usu ADV with v, also ADV adj

**unc|tu|ous** /ʌŋktʃuəs/ [1] If you describe someone as **unctuous**, you are critical of them because they seem to be full of praise, kindness, or interest, but are obviously insincere. [FORMAL] ❑ *...the kind of unctuous tone that I've heard often at diplomatic parties.* [2] If you describe food or drink as **unctuous**, you mean that it is creamy or oily. [FORMAL] ADJ [disapproval]; ADJ

**un|cul|ti|vat|ed** /ʌnkʌltɪveɪtɪd/ If land is **uncultivated**, there are no crops growing on it. ❑ *...the flat, largely uncultivated plains. ...an area left uncultivated to attract insects and small animals.* ADJ: ADJ n, ADJ after v, v-link ADJ

**un|cul|tured** /ʌnkʌltʃəʳd/ If you describe someone as **uncultured**, you are critical of them because they do not seem to know much about art, literature, and other cultural topics. ADJ [disapproval]

**un|cut** /ʌnkʌt/ [1] Something that is **uncut** has not been cut. ❑ *...a patch of uncut grass... Trees were to be left uncut, roads unpaved.* [2] An **uncut** book, play, or film has not had parts removed. ❑ *We saw the uncut version of 'Caligula' when we were in Europe.* [3] **Uncut** diamonds and other precious stones have not been cut into a regular shape. ADJ; ADJ: usu ADJ n; ADJ: usu ADJ n

**un|dam|aged** /ʌndæmɪdʒd/ Something that is **undamaged** has not been damaged or spoilt in any way. ❑ *The Korean ship was apparently undamaged... Choose a golden-orange-coloured pineapple with undamaged leaves.* ADJ ≠damaged

**un|dat|ed** /ʌndeɪtɪd/ Something that is **undated** does not have a date written on it. ❑ *In each packet there are batches of letters, most of which are undated.* ADJ ≠dated

**un|daunt|ed** /ʌndɔːntɪd/ If you are **undaunted**, you are not at all afraid or worried about dealing with something, especially something that would frighten or worry most people. ❑ *Undaunted by the scale of the job, Lesley set about planning how each room should look.* ADJ: usu v-link ADJ, oft ADJ *by* n

**un|de|cid|ed** /ʌndɪsaɪdɪd/ If someone is **undecided**, they cannot decide about something or have not yet decided about it. ❑ *After university she was still undecided as to what career she wanted to pursue... He says he's counting on undecided voters to help him win next week's election.* ADJ

**un|de|feat|ed** /ʌndɪfiːtɪd/ If a sports player or team is **undefeated**, nobody has beaten them over a particular period of time. ❑ *She was undefeated for 13 years.* ADJ = unbeaten

**un|de|mand|ing** /ʌndɪmɑːndɪŋ/ [1] If you describe something such as a job as **undemanding**, you mean that it does not require you to work very hard or to think a great deal about it. ❑ *Over a tenth of the population have secure, undemanding jobs... The book is an enjoyable and undemanding read.* [2] If you describe someone as **undemanding**, you mean they are easy to be with and do not ask other people to do a great deal for them. ❑ *...an undemanding companion.* ADJ: usu ADJ n ≠challenging; ADJ ≠demanding

**un|demo|crat|ic** /ʌndeməkrætɪk/ A system, process, or decision that is **undemocratic** is one that is controlled or made by one person or a small number of people, rather than by all the people involved. ❑ *...the undemocratic rule of the* ADJ ≠democratic *former political establishment... Opponents denounced the decree as undemocratic and unconstitutional.*

**un|de|mon|stra|tive** /ʌndɪmɒnstrətɪv/ Someone who is **undemonstrative** does not often show affection. ❑ *Lady Ainslie is an undemonstrative woman who rarely touches even her own son.* ADJ = *reserved*

**un|de|ni|able** /ʌndɪnaɪəbəl/ If you say that something is **undeniable**, you mean that it is definitely true. ❑ *Her charm is undeniable. ...the undeniable fact that she was driving with almost twice the legal limit of alcohol in her blood.* ADJ

♦ **un|de|ni|ably** /ʌndɪnaɪəbli/ *Bringing up a baby is undeniably hard work.* ADV

**un|der** /ʌndər/ ◆◆◆

> In addition to the uses shown below, **under** is also used in phrasal verbs such as 'go under' and 'knuckle under'.

1 If a person or thing is **under** something, they are at a lower level than that thing, and may be covered or hidden by it. ❑ *...swimming in the pool or lying under an umbrella... Under a wide shelf that holds coffee jars stands a pile of magazines... She buried her head under the covers, pretending to be asleep... A path runs under the trees.* PREP

2 In a place such as a sea, river, or swimming pool, if someone or something is **under** the water, they are fully in the water and covered by it. ❑ *They said he'd been held under the water and drowned... Goldfish were swimming lazily in a group just under the surface.* PREP

♦ **Under** is also an adverb. ❑ *When the water was up to his neck, a hand came from behind and pushed his head under.* ADV: ADV after v

3 If you go **under** something, you move from one side to the other of something that is at a higher level than you. ❑ *He went under a brick arch... A river boat passed under the bridge.* PREP

4 Something that is **under** a layer of something, especially clothing, is covered by that layer. ❑ *I was wearing two sweaters under the green army jacket... It was hard to see the colours under the layer of dust.* PREP

5 You can use **under** before a noun to indicate that a person or thing is being affected by something or is going through a particular process. ❑ *...fishermen whose livelihoods are under threat... I'm rarely under pressure and my co-workers are always nice to me... Firemen said they had the blaze under control... He was rushed to court yesterday under armed guard.* PREP

6 If something happens **under** particular circumstances or conditions, it happens when those circumstances or conditions exist. ❑ *His best friend was killed by police under extremely questionable circumstances... Under normal conditions, only about 20 to 40 per cent of vitamin E is absorbed.* PREP

7 If something happens **under** a law, agreement, or system, it happens because that law, agreement, or system says that it should happen. ❑ *Under law, your employer has the right to hire a temporary worker to replace you... Under the Constitution, you cannot be tried twice for the same crime.* PREP

8 If something happens **under** a particular person or government, it happens when that person or government is in power. ❑ *There would be no new taxes under his leadership. ...the realities of life under a brutal dictatorship.* PREP

9 If you study or work **under** a particular person, that person teaches you or tells you what to do. ❑ *Kiefer was just one of the artists who had studied under Beuys in the early Sixties... I am the new manager and you will be working under me.* PREP

10 If you do something **under** a particular name, you use that name instead of your real name. ❑ *Were any of your books published under the name Amanda Fairchild?... The patient was registered under a false name.* PREP

11 You use **under** to say which section of a list, book, or system something is in. ❑ *This study is described under 'General Diseases of the Eye'... 'Where would it be?' — 'Filed under C, second drawer down.'* PREP

12 If something or someone is **under** a particular age or amount, they are less than that age or amount. ❑ *...jobs for those under 65... Expenditure this year should be just under 15 billion pounds.* PREP: PREP amount ≠ *over*

♦ **Under** is also an adverb. ❑ *...free childminding service for 5's and under.* ADV: amount *and* ADV

13 **under wraps** → see **wrap**.

**under-** /ʌndər-/ 1 **Under-** is used to form words that express the idea that there is not enough of something. For example if people are underfed, they are not getting enough food. ❑ *Make sure that you are not underinsured... Victorian cut glass is perhaps the most underpriced area of the antique glass market.* PREFIX

2 **Under-** is added to the beginning of nouns that refer to a job or rank in order to form nouns that refer to a less important job or rank. ❑ *...the new undersecretary of education. ...clients who wouldn't deal with an undermanager.* PREFIX

**under|achieve** /ʌndərətʃiːv/ **(underachieves, underachieving, underachieved)** If someone **underachieves** in something such as school work or a job, they do not perform as well as they could. ❑ *Some people might think I've underachieved in my job.* VERB ≠ *excel* V

♦ **under|achiev|er (underachievers)** *He just wanted people to stop calling him disadvantaged, an underachiever.* N-COUNT

**un|der age** also **underage.** 1 A person who is **under age** is legally too young to do something, for example to drink alcohol, have sex, or vote. ❑ *Underage youths can obtain alcohol from their older friends. ...girls who have babies when they are under age.* ADJ

2 **Under age** activities such as drinking or smoking are carried out by people who are legally too young to do them. ❑ *...his efforts to stop under age drinking and drug abuse.* ADJ: ADJ n

**under|arm** /ʌndərɑːrm/ **(underarms)** 1 **Underarm** means in or for the areas under your arms, where they are joined to your body. ❑ *...underarm deodorants.* ADJ: ADJ n

♦ **Underarm** is also a noun. ❑ *Wash the feet, underarms and body surface using a soap.* N-COUNT: usu pl = *armpit*

2 You use **underarm** to describe actions, such as throwing a ball, in which you do not raise your arm above your shoulder. [BRIT] ❑ *...an underarm throw.* ADJ: ADJ n ≠ *overarm*

♦ **Underarm** is also an adverb. ❑ *Practise throwing a ball underarm.* ADV: ADV after v ≠ *overarm*

✔ in AM, use **underhand, underhanded**

**under|belly** /ʌndərbeli/ **(underbellies)** 1 The **underbelly** of something is the part of it that can be most easily attacked or criticized. ❑ *The ANC are attacking rugby because it is the soft underbelly of South African sport.* N-COUNT: usu with supp, usu N *of* n

2 The **underbelly** of an animal or a vehicle is the underneath part of it. ❑ *The missiles emerge from the underbelly of the transport plane.* N-COUNT: usu with supp, usu N *of* n

**under|brush** /ʌndərbrʌʃ/ **Underbrush** consists of bushes and plants growing close together under trees in a forest. [AM] ❑ *...the cool underbrush of the rain forest.* N-UNCOUNT

✔ in BRIT, use **undergrowth**

**under|carriage** /ʌndərkærɪdʒ/ **(undercarriages)** The **undercarriage** of an aeroplane is the part, including the wheels, which supports the aeroplane when it is on the ground and when it is landing or taking off. [mainly BRIT] N-COUNT

✔ in AM, use **landing gear**

**under|class** /ʌndərklɑːs, -klæs/ **(underclasses)** A country's **underclass** consists of those members of its population who are poor, and who have little chance of improving their situation. ❑ *The basic problems of the inner-city underclass are inadequate housing and lack of jobs.* N-COUNT: usu sing

**under|clothes** /ʌndərkloʊðz/ Your **underclothes** are the items of clothing that you wear next to your skin and under your other clothes. ❑ *...from multi-patterned sweaters to attractive underclothes.* N-PLURAL = *underwear*

**under|cloth|ing** /ʌndərkloʊðɪŋ/ **Underclothing** is the same as **underclothes**. ❑ *...a common brand of men's underclothing.* N-UNCOUNT

**under|coat** /ʌndərkoʊt/ **(undercoats)** An **undercoat** is a covering of paint or varnish put onto a surface as a base for a final covering of paint or varnish. Compare **topcoat**. N-VAR

**under|cov|er** /ʌndəʳkʌvəʳ/ **Undercover** work involves secretly obtaining information for the government or the police. ❑ *...an undercover operation designed to catch drug smugglers. ...undercover reporters.* ♦ **Undercover** is also an adverb. ❑ *Swanson persuaded Hubley to work undercover to capture the killer.*
ADJ: usu ADJ n
ADV: ADV after v

**under|cur|rent** /ʌndəʳkʌrənt, -kɜːr-/ **(undercurrents)** 1 If there is an **undercurrent of** a feeling, you are hardly aware of the feeling, but it influences the way you think or behave. ❑ *...a deep undercurrent of racism in British society.* 2 An **undercurrent** is a strong current of water that is moving below the surface current and in a different direction to it. ❑ *Colin tried to swim after him but the strong undercurrent swept them apart.*
N-COUNT: usu with supp, usu N *of* n
N-COUNT

**under|cut** /ʌndəʳkʌt/ **(undercuts, undercutting)**

> ✓ The form **undercut** is used in the present tense and is also the past tense and past participle.

1 If you **undercut** someone or **undercut** their prices, you sell a product more cheaply than they do. [BUSINESS] ❑ *The firm will be able to undercut its competitors whilst still making a profit. ...promises to undercut air fares on some routes by 40 per cent.* 2 If your attempts to achieve something **are undercut** by something, that thing prevents your attempts from being effective. ❑ *Popular support would be undercut by political developments.*
VERB
V n
V n
VERB: usu passive = undermine *be* V-ed

**under|de|vel|oped** /ʌndəʳdɪveləpt/ An **underdeveloped** country or region does not have modern industries and usually has a low standard of living. Some people dislike this term and prefer to use **developing**. ❑ *Underdeveloped countries should be assisted by allowing them access to modern technology. ...public-health problems in the underdeveloped world.*
ADJ: usu ADJ n = developing ≠ developed

**under|dog** /ʌndəʳdɒg, AM -dɔːg/ **(underdogs)** **The underdog** in a competition or situation is the person who seems least likely to succeed or win. ❑ *Most of the crowd were cheering for the underdog to win just this one time.*
N-COUNT: usu *the* N

**under|done** /ʌndəʳdʌn/ **Underdone** food has been cooked for less time than necessary, and so is not pleasant to eat. ❑ *The second batch of bread came out underdone. ...underdone meat.*
ADJ ≠ overdone

**under|em|ployed** /ʌndərɪmplɔɪd/ If someone is **underemployed**, they have not got enough work to do, or their work does not make full use of their skills or abilities.
ADJ

**under|es|ti|mate** /ʌndərestɪmeɪt/ **(underestimates, underestimating, underestimated)** 1 If you **underestimate** something, you do not realize how large or great it is or will be. ❑ *None of us should ever underestimate the degree of difficulty women face in career advancement... Never underestimate what you can learn from a group of like-minded people.* ♦ **under|es|ti|ma|tion** /ʌndərestɪmeɪʃᵊn/ *...a serious underestimation of harm to the environment.* 2 If you **underestimate** someone, you do not realize what they are capable of doing. ❑ *The first lesson I learnt as a soldier was never to underestimate the enemy.*
VERB
V n
V wh
N-UNCOUNT: also *a* N
VERB
V n

**under|ex|posed** /ʌndərɪkspoʊzd/ If a photograph is **underexposed**, it is darker than it should be because the film was not exposed to enough light.
ADJ ≠ overexposed

**under|fed** /ʌndəʳfed/ People who are **underfed** do not get enough food to eat. ❑ *Kate still looks pale and underfed. ...ill-trained and underfed young soldiers.*
ADJ

**under|fi|nanced** /ʌndəʳfaɪnænst/ also **under-financed. Underfinanced** means the same as **underfunded.** ❑ *From the beginning, the project was underfinanced.*
ADJ: usu v-link ADJ

**under|foot** /ʌndəʳfʊt/ 1 You describe something as being **underfoot** when you are standing or walking on it. ❑ *...a room, high and square with carpet underfoot and tapestries on the walls... It was still wet underfoot.* 2 If you trample or crush something **underfoot**, you spoil or destroy it by stepping on it. ❑ *Morgan dropped his cigarette and crushed it underfoot.*
ADV: ADV after v, n ADV
ADV: ADV after v

**under|fund|ed** /ʌndəʳfʌndɪd/ also **under-funded.** An organization or institution that is **underfunded** does not have enough money to spend, and so it cannot function properly. ❑ *For years we have argued that the health service is underfunded. ...underfunded pensions.*
ADJ: usu v-link ADJ

**under|gar|ment** /ʌndəʳgɑːʳmənt/ **(undergarments) Undergarments** are items of clothing that you wear next to your skin and under your other clothes. [OLD-FASHIONED]
N-COUNT: usu pl = underwear, underclothes

**under|go** /ʌndəʳgoʊ/ **(undergoes, undergoing, underwent, undergone)** If you **undergo** something necessary or unpleasant, it happens to you. ❑ *New recruits have been undergoing training in recent weeks... He underwent an agonising 48-hour wait for the results of tests.*
VERB
V n
V n

**under|grad** /ʌndəʳgræd/ **(undergrads)** An **undergrad** is a student at a university or college who is studying for his or her first degree. [INFORMAL]
N-COUNT

**under|gradu|ate** /ʌndəʳgrædʒuət/ **(undergraduates)** An **undergraduate** is a student at a university or college who is studying for his or her first degree. ❑ *Economics undergraduates are probably the brightest in the university. ...undergraduate degree programmes.*
N-COUNT: oft N n

**under|ground** ◆◇◇

> ✓ The adverb is pronounced /ʌndəʳgraʊnd/. The noun and adjective are pronounced /ʌndəʳgraʊnd/.

1 Something that is **underground** is below the surface of the ground. ❑ *Solid low-level waste will be disposed of deep underground... The plane hit so hard that one engine was buried 16 feet underground.* ♦ **Underground** is also an adjective. ❑ *...a rundown shopping area with an underground car park. ...underground water pipes.* 2 **The underground** in a city is the railway system in which electric trains travel below the ground in tunnels. [BRIT] ❑ *...a woman alone in the underground waiting for a train... He crossed London by underground.*
ADV: ADV after v
ADJ: ADJ n
N-SING: *the* N, also *by* N

> ✓ in AM, use **subway**

3 In a country which is controlled by an enemy or has a harsh government, **the underground** is an organized group of people who are involved in illegal activities against the people in power. ❑ *These US dollars were smuggled into the country during the war, to aid the underground.* 4 **Underground** groups and activities are secret because their purpose is to oppose the government and they are illegal. ❑ *They are accused of organising and financing an underground youth movement.* 5 If you go **underground**, you hide from the authorities or the police because your political ideas or activities are illegal. ❑ *After the violent clashes of 1981 they either went underground or left the country.*
N-SING: *the* N
ADJ: ADJ n
ADV: ADV after v

**under|growth** /ʌndəʳgroʊθ/ **Undergrowth** consists of bushes and plants growing together under the trees in a forest. [BRIT] ❑ *...plunging through the undergrowth.*
N-UNCOUNT

> ✓ in AM, use **underbrush**

**under|hand** /ʌndəʳhænd/ or **underhanded** 1 If an action is **underhand** or if it is done in an **underhand** way, it is done secretly and dishonestly. ❑ *...underhand financial deals. ...a list of the underhanded ways in which their influence operates in the United States... Mr Livingstone accused the government of being underhand.* 2 You use **underhand** or **underhanded** to describe actions, such as throwing a ball, in which you do not raise your arm above your shoulder. [AM] ❑ *...an underhanded pitch.* ♦ **Underhand** is also an adverb. ❑ *In softball, pitches are tossed underhand.*
ADJ: usu ADJ n [disapproval]
ADJ: ADJ n ≠ overarm
ADV: ADV after v ≠ overarm

> ✓ in BRIT, use **underarm**

**under|lay (underlays)**

✔ The noun is pronounced /ˈʌndəʳleɪ/. The verb is pronounced /ˌʌndəʳˈleɪ/.

1 **Underlay** is a layer of thick material that you place between a carpet and the floor to protect the carpet and make it feel warmer and softer. [BRIT] 2 **Underlay** is the past tense of **underlie**. N-MASS

**under|lie** /ˌʌndəʳˈlaɪ/ **(underlies, underlying, underlay, underlain)** If something **underlies** a feeling or situation, it is the cause or basis of it. ❑ *Try to figure out what feeling underlies your anger.* ➔ See also **underlying**. VERB V n

**under|line** /ˌʌndəʳˈlaɪn/ **(underlines, underlining, underlined)** 1 If one thing, for example an action or an event, **underlines** another, it draws attention to it and emphasizes its importance. ❑ *The report underlined his concern that standards were at risk... But the incident underlines how easily things can go wrong.* 2 If you **underline** something such as a word or a sentence, you draw a line underneath it in order to make people notice it or to give it extra importance. ❑ *Take two coloured pens and underline the positive and negative words.* VERB = underscore V n V wh Also V that VERB V n

**under|ling** /ˈʌndəʳlɪŋ/ **(underlings)** You refer to someone as an **underling** when they are inferior in rank or status to someone else and take orders from them. You use this word to show that you do not respect someone. ❑ *...underlings who do the dirty work.* N-COUNT disapproval = minion

**under|ly|ing** /ˌʌndəʳˈlaɪɪŋ/ 1 The **underlying** features of an object, event, or situation are not obvious, and it may be difficult to discover or reveal them. ❑ *To stop a problem you have to understand its underlying causes... I think that the underlying problem is education, unemployment and bad housing.* 2 You describe something as **underlying** when it is below the surface of something else. ❑ *...hills with the hard underlying rock poking through the turf.* 3 ➔ See also **underlie**. ADJ: ADJ n ADJ: ADJ n

**under|manned** /ˌʌndəʳˈmænd/ If an organization is **undermanned**, it does not have enough employees to function properly. ❑ *In some stores we were undermanned and customer service was suffering.* ADJ: usu v-link ADJ = understaffed

**under|mine** /ˌʌndəʳˈmaɪn/ **(undermines, undermining, undermined)** ◆◇◇ 1 If you **undermine** something such as a feeling or a system, you make it less strong or less secure than it was before, often by a gradual process or by repeated efforts. ❑ *Offering advice on each and every problem will undermine her feeling of being adult... Western intelligence agencies are accused of trying to undermine the government.* 2 If you **undermine** someone or **undermine** their position or authority, you make their authority or position less secure, often by indirect methods. ❑ *She undermined him and destroyed his confidence in his own talent... The conversations were designed to undermine her authority so she felt that she could no longer work for the company.* 3 If you **undermine** someone's efforts or **undermine** their chances of achieving something, you behave in a way that makes them less likely to succeed. ❑ *The continued fighting threatens to undermine efforts to negotiate an agreement.* VERB V n V n VERB V n V n VERB V n

**under|neath** /ˌʌndəʳˈniːθ/ 1 If one thing is **underneath** another, it is directly under it, and may be covered or hidden by it. ❑ *The device exploded underneath a van. ...using dogs to locate people trapped underneath collapsed buildings. ...a table for two underneath the olive trees... Her apartment was underneath a bar, called 'The Lift'.* ♦ **Underneath** is also an adverb. ❑ *He has on a denim shirt with a T-shirt underneath. ...if we could maybe pull back a bit of this carpet to see what's underneath.* 2 The part of something which is **underneath** is the part which normally touches the ground or faces towards the ground. ❑ *Check the actual construction of the chair by looking underneath... His bare feet were smooth on top and rough-skinned underneath.* ♦ **Underneath** is also an adjective. ❑ *Some objects had got entangled with the underneath mechanism of the engine.* ♦ **Underneath** is also a noun. ❑ *Now I know what the underneath of a car looks like.* 3 You use **underneath** when talking about feelings and emotions that people do not show in their behaviour. ❑ *He was as violent as Nick underneath.* ♦ **Underneath** is also a preposition. ❑ *Underneath his outgoing behaviour Luke was shy.* PREP = beneath ADV: n ADV, ADV after v, *be* ADV, *from* ADV ADV: ADV after v, n/adj ADV ADJ: ADJ n N-SING: *the* N ADV: ADV with cl PREP

**under|nour|ished** /ˌʌndəʳˈnʌrɪʃt, AM -ˈnɜːr-/ If someone is **undernourished**, they are weak and unhealthy because they have not been eating enough food or the right kind of food. ❑ *...undernourished children.* ADJ: usu v-link ADJ = underfed, malnourished

**under|nour|ish|ment** /ˌʌndəʳˈnʌrɪʃmənt, AM -ˈnɜːr-/ If someone is suffering from **undernourishment**, they have poor health because they are not eating enough food or are eating the wrong kind of food. N-UNCOUNT = malnutrition

**under|paid** /ˌʌndəʳˈpeɪd/ People who are **underpaid** are not paid enough money for the job that they do. ❑ *Women are frequently underpaid for the work that they do. ...underpaid factory workers.* ADJ: usu v-link ADJ ≠ overpaid

**under|pants** /ˈʌndəʳpænts/ **Underpants** are a piece of underwear which have two holes to put your legs through and elastic around the top to hold them up round your waist or hips. In British English, **underpants** refers to only men's underwear but in American English it refers to both men's and women's. N-PLURAL: also *a pair of* N

**under|pass** /ˈʌndəʳpɑːs, -pæs/ **(underpasses)** An **underpass** is a road or path that goes underneath a railway or another road. ❑ *The Hanger Lane underpass was closed through flooding.* N-COUNT

**under|pin** /ˌʌndəʳˈpɪn/ **(underpins, underpinning, underpinned)** If one thing **underpins** another, it helps the other thing to continue or succeed by supporting and strengthening it. ❑ *...mystical themes that underpin all religions.* ♦ **under|pin|ning (underpinnings)** *...the economic underpinning of ancient Mexican society. ...the violent woman-hating underpinnings of films like 'Cape Fear'.* VERB V n N-VAR

**under|play** /ˌʌndəʳˈpleɪ/ **(underplays, underplaying, underplayed)** If you **underplay** something, you make it seem less important than it really is. [mainly BRIT] ❑ *We often underplay the skills we have... The problem of alcoholism was, and still is, often underplayed.* VERB = play down, downplay V n V n

✔ in AM, usually use **play down**

**under|popu|lat|ed** /ˌʌndəʳˈpɒpjuleɪtɪd/ You describe a country or region as **underpopulated** when it could support a much larger population than it has. ❑ *Many of the islands are mainly wild and underpopulated.* ADJ ≠ overpopulated

**under|privi|leged** /ˌʌndəʳˈprɪvɪlɪdʒd/ **Underprivileged** people have less money and fewer possessions and opportunities than other people in their society. ❑ *...helping underprivileged children to learn to read. ...the hideous effects of government cuts on underprivileged families.* ♦ **The underprivileged** are people who are underprivileged. ❑ *...government plans to make more jobs available to the underprivileged.* ADJ: usu ADJ n = deprived, disadvantaged N-PLURAL: *the* N

**under|rate** /ˌʌndəʳˈreɪt/ **(underrates, underrating, underrated)** If you **underrate** someone or something, you do not recognize how clever, important, or significant they are. ❑ *We women have a lot of good business skills, although we tend to underrate ourselves... He underrated the seriousness of William's head injury.* ♦ **under|rat|ed** *He is a very underrated poet.* VERB ≠ overrate V n V n ADJ: usu ADJ n

**under|score** /ˌʌndəʳˈskɔːʳ/ **(underscores, underscoring, underscored)** 1 If something such as an action or an event **underscores** another, it draws attention to the other thing and emphasizes its importance. [mainly AM] ❑ *The Labor Department figures underscore the shaky state of the economic recovery.* VERB = underline V n Also V that, V *the fact* that

✔ in BRIT, usually use **underline**

[2] If you **underscore** something such as a word or a sentence, you draw a line underneath it in order to make people notice it or give it extra importance. [mainly AM] ❑ *He heavily underscored his note to Shelley.*
VERB = *underline*; V n

✔ in BRIT, usually use **underline**

**under|sea** /ʌndəʳsiː/ **Undersea** things or activities exist or happen below the surface of the sea. ❑ *...an undersea pipeline running to Europe. ...undersea exploration.*
ADJ: ADJ n

**under-secretary** **(under-secretaries)** also **undersecretary.** An **under-secretary** is a senior official with an important post in a government department. ❑ *...Under-Secretary of State Reginald Bartholomew.*
N-COUNT

**under|shirt** /ʌndəʳʃɜːʳt/ **(undershirts)** An **undershirt** is a piece of clothing that you wear on the top half of your body next to your skin in order to keep warm. [AM] ❑ *He put on a pair of short pants and an undershirt.*
N-COUNT

✔ in BRIT, use **vest**

**under|side** /ʌndəʳsaɪd/ **(undersides)** The **underside** of something is the part of it which normally faces towards the ground. ❑ *...the underside of the car.*
N-COUNT: usu with supp, N *of* n = *underneath*

**under|signed** /ʌndəʳsaɪnd/ On a legal document, the **undersigned** people are the ones who have signed their names at the bottom of the document. [LEGAL] ❑ *The undersigned buyers agree to pay a 5,000 pound deposit.* ♦ **The undersigned** are the people who have signed a legal document. ❑ *...we the undersigned, all prominent doctors in our fields.*
ADJ: ADJ n; N-PLURAL: *the* N

**under|sized** /ʌndəʳsaɪzd/ **Undersized** people or things are smaller than usual, or smaller than they should be. ❑ *...undersized and underweight babies... They squashed into an undersized reception room... He was undersized, as were all the children I was to meet.*
ADJ: usu ADJ n ≠ *oversized*

**under|spend** /ʌndəʳspend/ **(underspends, underspending, underspent)** If an organization or country **underspends**, it spends less money than it plans to or less money than it can afford. ❑ *...a country that underspends on health and overspends on statisticians.* ♦ **Underspend** is also a noun. ❑ *There has been an underspend in the department's budget.*
VERB; V; Also V n; N-COUNT

**under|staffed** /ʌndəʳstɑːft, -stæft/ If an organization is **understaffed**, it does not have enough employees to do its work properly. ❑ *Many institutions offering child care are understaffed and underequipped. ...an understaffed police force.*
ADJ: usu v-link ADJ = *undermanned*

**under|stand** /ʌndəʳstænd/ **(understands, understanding, understood)** ◆◆◆ [1] If you **understand** someone or **understand** what they are saying, you know what they mean. ❑ *Rusty nodded as though she understood the old woman... I don't understand what you are talking about... He was speaking poor English, trying to make himself understood.* [2] If you **understand** a language, you know what someone is saying when they are speaking that language. ❑ *I couldn't read or understand a word of Yiddish, so I asked him to translate.* [3] To **understand** someone means to know how they feel and why they behave in the way that they do. ❑ *It would be nice to have someone who really understood me, a friend... Trish had not exactly understood his feelings... She understands why I get tired and grumpy.* [4] You say that you **understand** something when you know why or how it happens. ❑ *They are too young to understand what is going on... In the effort to understand AIDS, attention is moving from the virus to the immune system.* [5] If you **understand** that something is the case, you think it is true because you have heard or read that it is. You can say that something **is understood** to be the case to mean that people generally think it is true. ❑ *We understand that she's in the studio recording her second album... As I understand it, you came round the corner by the cricket field and there was the man in the road... The management is understood to be very unwilling to agree to this request... It is understood that the veteran reporter had a heart attack.* [6] If someone **is given to understand** that something is the case, it is communicated to them that it is the case, usually without them being told directly. ❑ *I am given to understand that he was swearing throughout the game at our fans.* [7] You can use **understand** in expressions like **do you understand?** or **is that understood?** after you have told someone what you want, to make sure that they have understood you and will obey you. ❑ *You do not hit my grandchildren, do you understand?... I don't need it, understand?... I don't want to hear another word about it. Is that understood, Emma?*
VERB: no cont; V n; V wh; *make* pron-refl V-ed; VERB: no cont; V n; VERB: no cont; V n; V n; V wh; VERB: no cont; V wh; V n; VERB: no cont; V that; V *it*; *be* V-ed to-inf; *it be* V-ed that/to-inf; PHRASE: *give* inflects, usu PHR that; CONVENTION

**under|stand|able** /ʌndəʳstændəbᵊl/ [1] If you describe someone's behaviour or feelings as **understandable**, you think that they have reacted to a situation in a natural way or in the way you would expect. ❑ *His unhappiness was understandable.* ♦ **under|stand|ably** /ʌndəʳstændəbli/ *The duke is understandably proud of Lady Helen and her achievements... Most organizations are, quite understandably, suspicious of new ideas.* [2] If you say that something such as a statement or theory is **understandable**, you mean that people can easily understand it. ❑ *Roger Neuberg writes in a simple and understandable way.*
ADJ; ADV: ADV adj, ADV with cl; ADJ = *comprehensible*

**under|stand|ing** /ʌndəʳstændɪŋ/ **(understandings)** ◆◇◇ [1] If you have an **understanding of** something, you know how it works or know what it means. ❑ *They have to have a basic understanding of computers in order to use the advanced technology.* [2] If you are **understanding** towards someone, you are kind and forgiving. ❑ *Her boss, who was very understanding, gave her time off... Fortunately for John, he had an understanding wife.* [3] If you show **understanding**, you show that you realize how someone feels or why they did something, and are not hostile towards them. ❑ *We would like to thank them for their patience and understanding.* [4] If there is **understanding between** people, they are friendly towards each other and trust each other. ❑ *There was complete understanding between Wilson and myself.* [5] An **understanding** is an informal agreement about something. ❑ *We had not set a date for marriage but there was an understanding between us.* [6] If you say that it is your **understanding that** something is the case, you mean that you believe it to be the case because you have heard or read that it is. ❑ *It is my understanding that this torture has been going on for many years.* [7] If you agree to do something **on the understanding that** something else will be done, you do it because you have been told that the other thing will definitely be done. ❑ *Kevin had treatment on the understanding that he would attempt to overcome his drinking problem.*
N-VAR: N *of* n = *grasp*; ADJ = *sympathetic*; N-UNCOUNT; N-UNCOUNT: usu N *between* pl-n; N-COUNT: N prep; N-SING: poss N, oft N that; PHRASE

**under|state** /ʌndəʳsteɪt/ **(understates, understating, understated)** If you **understate** something, you describe it in a way that suggests that it is less important or serious than it really is. ❑ *The government chooses deliberately to understate the increase in prices.*
VERB ≠ *overstate, exaggerate*; V n

**under|stat|ed** /ʌndəʳsteɪtɪd/ If you describe a style, colour, or effect as **understated**, you mean that it is not obvious. ❑ *I have always liked understated clothes – simple shapes which take a lot of hard work to get right. ...his typically understated humour.*
ADJ: ADJ n = *subtle*

**under|state|ment** /ʌndəʳsteɪtmənt/ **(understatements)** [1] If you say that a statement is an **understatement**, you mean that it does not fully express the extent to which something is true. ❑ *To say I'm disappointed is an understatement... He was getting very hard to live with, and that's the understatement of the year.* [2] **Understatement** is the practice of suggesting that things have much less of a particular quality
N-COUNT; N-UNCOUNT

than they really have. ❑ *He informed us with massive understatement that he was feeling disappointed. ...typical British understatement.*

**under|stood** /ʌndəʳstʊd/ **Understood** is the past tense and past participle of **understand**.

**under|study** /ʌndəʳstʌdi/ **(understudies)** An actor's or actress's **understudy** is the person who has learned their part in a play and can act the part if the actor or actress is ill. ❑ *He was an understudy to Charlie Chaplin on a tour of the USA.* N-COUNT

**under|take** /ʌndəʳteɪk/ **(undertakes, undertaking, undertook, undertaken)** 1 When you **undertake** a task or job, you start doing it and accept responsibility for it. ❑ *She undertook the arduous task of monitoring the elections.* VERB; V n 2 If you **undertake to** do something, you promise that you will do it. ❑ *He undertook to edit the text himself.* VERB; V to-inf

**under|tak|er** /ʌndəʳteɪkəʳ/ **(undertakers)** An **undertaker** is a person whose job is to deal with the bodies of people who have died and to arrange funerals. N-COUNT

**under|tak|ing** /ʌndəʳteɪkɪŋ/ **(undertakings)** 1 An **undertaking** is a task or job, especially a large or difficult one. ❑ *Organizing the show has been a massive undertaking.* N-COUNT 2 If you give an **undertaking** to do something, you formally promise to do it. ❑ *The MOD gave an undertaking to Saville that it had provided him with all relevant material.* N-COUNT: oft N to-inf

**under|tone** /ʌndəʳtoʊn/ **(undertones)** 1 If you say something **in** an **undertone**, you say it very quietly. ❑ *'What d'you think?' she asked in an undertone... Well-dressed clients were talking in polite undertones as they ate.* N-COUNT: in N 2 If something has **undertones** of a particular kind, it suggests ideas or attitudes of this kind without expressing them directly. ❑ *...a witty, racy story with surprisingly serious undertones.* N-COUNT: with supp

**under|took** /ʌndəʳtʊk/ **Undertook** is the past tense of **undertake**.

**under|tow** /ʌndəʳtoʊ/ **(undertows)** 1 If there is an **undertow** of a feeling, that feeling exists in such a weak form that you are hardly aware of it, but it influences the way you think or behave. ❑ *...an undertow of sadness.* N-COUNT: usu with supp = undercurrent 2 An **undertow** is a strong current of water that is moving below the surface current and in a different direction to it. N-COUNT = undercurrent

**under|used** /ʌndəʳjuːzd/ also **underused.** Something useful that is **underused** is not used as much for people's benefit as it could be. ❑ *At present many schools' sports grounds are grossly underused. ...areas where muscles are underused and underdeveloped. ...underused land.* ADJ = underutilized

**under|uti|lized** /ʌndəʳjuːtɪlaɪzd/

✔ in BRIT, also use **underutilised**

**Underutilized** is a more formal word for **underused**. ❑ *They had to sell off 10 percent of all underutilized farmland.* ADJ: usu ADJ n = underused

**under|value** /ʌndəʳvæljuː/ **(undervalues, undervaluing, undervalued)** If you **undervalue** something or someone, you fail to recognize how valuable or important they are. ❑ *We must never undervalue freedom.* ♦ **under|val|ued** *Even the best teacher can feel undervalued.* VERB; V n; ADJ = underrated

**under|wa|ter** /ʌndəʳwɔːtəʳ/ 1 Something that exists or happens **underwater** exists or happens below the surface of the sea, a river, or a lake. ❑ *...giant submarines able to travel at high speeds underwater... Some stretches of beach are completely underwater at high tide.* ♦ **Underwater** is also an adjective. ❑ *...underwater exploration. ...a retired underwater photographer.* ADV: ADV after v, n ADV; ADJ: ADJ n 2 **Underwater** devices are specially made so that they can work in water. ❑ *...underwater camera equipment. ...a pool of clear water lit by underwater lights.* ADJ: ADJ n

**un|der way** also **underway.** If an activity is **under way**, it has already started. If an activity gets **under way**, it starts. ❑ *An investigation is underway to find out how the disaster happened... The conference gets under way later today with a debate on the family.* ADJ: v-link ADJ

**under|wear** /ʌndəʳweəʳ/ **Underwear** is clothing such as vests and pants which you wear next to your skin under your other clothes. ❑ *...a couple who went for a late-night swim in their underwear. ...a change of underwear.* N-UNCOUNT

**under|weight** /ʌndəweɪt/ If someone is **underweight**, they are too thin, and therefore not healthy. ❑ *Nearly a third of the children were severely underweight.* ADJ: usu v-link ADJ ≠ overweight

**under|went** /ʌndəʳwent/ **Underwent** is the past tense of **undergo**.

**under|whelmed** /ʌndəʳʰwelmd/ If you are **underwhelmed by** something, you are not impressed or excited by it. [INFORMAL] ❑ *He was underwhelmed by the prospect of meeting the Queen.* ADJ: usu v-link ADJ, oft ADJ *by* n ≠ overwhelmed

**under|whelm|ing** /ʌndəʳʰwelmɪŋ/ If you use **underwhelming** to describe the response or reaction to something, you mean that people were not very impressed or excited by it. [INFORMAL] ❑ *...the distinctly underwhelming response to their second album.* ADJ

**under|world** /ʌndəʳwɜːʳld/ 1 The **underworld** in a city is the organized crime there and the people who are involved in it. ❑ *Some claim that she still has connections to the criminal underworld. ...a wealthy businessman with underworld connections.* N-SING: oft N n, n N 2 In many ancient religions and legends, **the underworld** is a place under the earth's surface where people go after they die. ❑ *...Persephone, goddess of the underworld.* N-SING: *the* N

**under|write** /ʌndəʳraɪt/ **(underwrites, underwriting, underwrote, underwritten)** If an institution or company **underwrites** an activity or **underwrites** the cost of it, they agree to provide any money that is needed to cover losses or buy special equipment, often for an agreed fee. [BUSINESS] ❑ *The government will have to create a special agency to underwrite small business loans.* VERB; V n

**under|writ|er** /ʌndəʳraɪtəʳ/ **(underwriters)** 1 An **underwriter** is someone whose job involves agreeing to provide money for a particular activity or to pay for any losses that are made. [BUSINESS] ❑ *If the market will not buy the shares, the underwriter buys them.* N-COUNT 2 An **underwriter** is someone whose job is to judge the risks involved in certain activities and decide how much to charge for insurance. [BUSINESS] N-COUNT

**un|de|served** /ʌndɪzɜːʳvd/ If you describe something such as a reaction, treatment, or result as **undeserved**, you mean that the person who experiences it has not earned it and should not really have it. ❑ *Douglas has an undeserved reputation for being dull and dry... Jim's treatment was harsh and undeserved.* ADJ = unmerited

**un|de|sir|able** /ʌndɪzaɪərəbᵊl/ **(undesirables)** 1 If you describe something or someone as **undesirable**, you think they will have harmful effects. ❑ *Inflation is considered to be undesirable because of its adverse effects on income distribution... A large group of undesirable strangers crashed her party.* ADJ 2 **Undesirables** are people who a particular government considers to be dangerous or a threat to society, and therefore wants to get rid of. ❑ *The Home Office is usually quick to deport undesirables.* N-COUNT

**un|de|tect|ed** /ʌndɪtektɪd/ If you are **undetected** or if you do something **undetected**, people do not find out where you are or what you are doing. ❑ *...the spy ring had a fifth member as yet still undetected... They managed to get away from the coast undetected. ...an undetected cancer.* ADJ: ADJ after v, ADJ n, v-link ADJ

**un|de|vel|oped** /ʌndɪveləpt/ 1 An **undeveloped** country or region does not have modern industries and usually has a low standard of living. ❑ *The big losers will be the undeveloped countries, especially sub-Saharan Africa.* ADJ: usu ADJ n 2 **Undeveloped** ADJ land has not been built on or used for activities such as mining and farming. ❑ *Vast tracts of the country are wild and undeveloped. ...the world's largest undeveloped gold deposit outside of South Africa.*

**un|did** /ʌndɪd/ **Undid** is the past tense of **undo**.

**un|dies** /ʌndiz/ You can refer to a woman or girl's underwear as their **undies**. [INFORMAL] N-PLURAL: oft poss N

**un|dig|ni|fied** /ʌndɪgnɪfaɪd/ If you describe someone's actions as **undignified**, you mean they are foolish or embarrassing. ❑ *It is sad to see a county confine its activities to undignified public bickering... All this public outpouring is so undignified.* ADJ ≠ dignified

**un|di|lut|ed** /ʌndaɪluːtɪd/ 1 If you describe someone's feelings or characteristics as **undiluted**, you are emphasizing that they are very strong and not mixed with any other feeling or quality. ❑ *I will look back at this one with undiluted pleasure... Her Irish accent, after thirty-odd years in London, is undiluted.* ADJ: usu ADJ n 2 A liquid that is **undiluted** has not been made weak by mixing it with water. ADJ

**un|dis|ci|plined** /ʌndɪsɪplɪnd/ If you describe someone as **undisciplined**, you mean that they behave badly or in a disorganized way. ❑ *...a noisy and undisciplined group of students... Teachers often view youth workers as undisciplined and ineffectual.* ADJ

**un|dis|closed** /ʌndɪsklouzd/ **Undisclosed** information is not revealed to the public. ❑ *The company has been sold for an undisclosed amount.* ADJ: usu ADJ n

**un|dis|cov|ered** /ʌndɪskʌvəʳd/ Something that is **undiscovered** has not been discovered or noticed. ❑ *The name Vulcan was given to the undiscovered planet... This site remained undiscovered, though long sought, until recent times.* ADJ

**un|dis|guised** /ʌndɪsgaɪzd/ If you describe someone's feelings as **undisguised**, you mean that they show them openly and do not make any attempt to hide them. ❑ *Hean looked down at Bauer in undisguised disgust... By mid-season the hostility between the two was undisguised.* ADJ: usu ADJ n

**un|dis|mayed** /ʌndɪsmeɪd/ If you say that someone is **undismayed** by something unpleasant or unexpected, you mean that they do not feel any fear, worry, or sadness about it. [FORMAL] ❑ *He was undismayed by the prospect of failure.* ADJ: v-link ADJ = undaunted

**un|dis|put|ed** /ʌndɪspjuːtɪd/ 1 If you describe a fact or opinion as **undisputed**, you are trying to persuade someone that it is generally accepted as true or correct. ❑ *...the undisputed fact that he had broken the law. ...his undisputed genius.* ADJ 2 If you describe someone as the **undisputed** leader or champion, you mean that everyone accepts their position as leader or champion. ❑ *At 78 years of age, he's still undisputed leader of his country. ...after 10 years of undisputed power.* ADJ

**un|dis|tin|guished** /ʌndɪstɪŋgwɪʃt/ If you describe someone or something as **undistinguished**, you mean they are not attractive, interesting, or successful. ❑ *...his short and undistinguished career as an art student.* ADJ = mediocre

**un|dis|turbed** /ʌndɪstɜːʳbd/ 1 Something that remains **undisturbed** is not touched, moved, or used by anyone. ❑ *The desk looked undisturbed... Peonies react badly to being moved and are best left undisturbed.* ADJ: v-link ADJ, ADJ after v, ADJ n 2 A place that is **undisturbed** is peaceful and has not been affected by changes that have happened in other places. ❑ *In the Balearics pockets of rural life and inland villages are undisturbed... The war had not left Bargate undisturbed.* ADJ: v-link ADJ, ADJ after v, ADJ n 3 If you are **undisturbed** in something that you are doing, you are able to continue doing it and are not affected by something that is happening. ❑ *I can spend the whole day undisturbed at the warehouse... There was a small restaurant on Sullivan Street where we could talk undisturbed... They want undisturbed rest.* ADJ: ADJ after v, ADJ n, v-link ADJ = uninterrupted 4 If someone is **undisturbed by** something, it does not affect, bother, or upset them. ❑ *Victoria was strangely undisturbed by this symptom, even though her husband and family were frightened.* ADJ: usu v-link ADJ *by* n = unconcerned

**un|di|vid|ed** /ʌndɪvaɪdɪd/ 1 If you give someone or something your **undivided** attention, you concentrate on them fully and do not think about anything else. ❑ *Eldest children are the only ones to have experienced the undivided attention of their parents. ...any task that requires undivided concentration.* ADJ: usu ADJ n 2 **Undivided** feelings are ones that are very strong and not mixed with other feelings. ❑ *The paintings she produced in those months won undivided admiration... He has my undivided loyalty.* ADJ: usu ADJ n = wholehearted 3 An **undivided** country or organization is one that is not separated into smaller parts or groups. ❑ *Mandela said, 'We want a united, undivided South Africa'. ...the goal of an undivided Church.* ADJ

**undo** /ʌnduː/ **(undoes, undoing, undid, undone)** 1 If you **undo** something that is closed, tied, or held together, or if you **undo** the thing holding it, you loosen or remove the thing holding it. ❑ *I managed secretly to undo a corner of the parcel... Some clamps that had held the device together came undone.* VERB V n V-ed 2 To **undo** something that has been done means to reverse its effect. ❑ *She knew it would be difficult to undo the damage that had been done... If Michael won, he would undo everything I have fought for.* VERB V n V n 3 → See also **undoing**, **undone**.

**un|do|ing** /ʌnduːɪŋ/ If something is someone's **undoing**, it is the cause of their failure. ❑ *His lack of experience may prove to be his undoing.* N-SING: with poss = downfall

**un|done** /ʌndʌn/ 1 Work that is **undone** has not yet been done. ❑ *He left nothing undone that needed attention.* ADJ: ADJ after v 2 → See also **undo**.

**un|doubt|ed** /ʌndaʊtɪd/ You can use **undoubted** to emphasize that something exists or is true. ❑ *The event was an undoubted success. ...a man of your undoubted ability.* ADJ: usu ADJ n [emphasis] ♦ **un|doubt|ed|ly** *Undoubtedly, political and economic factors have played their part... Hanley is undoubtedly a great player.* ADV: ADV with cl/group, ADV before v

**un|dreamed of** /ʌndriːmd ɒv, AM - ʌv/

✓ in BRIT, also use **undreamt of**

If you describe something as **undreamed of**, you are emphasizing that it is much better, worse, or more unusual than you thought was possible. ❑ *This new design will offer undreamed-of levels of comfort, safety and speed... They have freedoms that were undreamed-of even ten years ago.* ADJ [emphasis]

**un|dress** /ʌndres/ **(undresses, undressing, undressed)** When you **undress** or **undress** someone, you take off your clothes or someone else's clothes. ❑ *She went out, leaving Rachel to undress and have her shower... She undressed the child before putting her in the tin bath.* VERB V V n

**un|dressed** /ʌndrest/ If you are **undressed**, you are wearing no clothes or your night clothes. If you get **undressed**, you take off your clothes. ❑ *Fifteen minutes later he was undressed and in bed... He got undressed in the bathroom.* ADJ

**un|due** /ʌndjuː, AM -duː/ If you describe something bad as **undue**, you mean that it is greater or more extreme than you think is reasonable or appropriate. ❑ *This would help the families to survive the drought without undue suffering... It is unrealistic to put undue pressure on ourselves by saying we are the best.* ADJ: ADJ n = excessive

**un|du|late** /ʌndʒuleɪt/ **(undulates, undulating, undulated)** Something that **undulates** has gentle curves or slopes, or moves gently and slowly up and down or from side to side in an attractive manner. [LITERARY] ❑ *As we travel south, the countryside begins to undulate as the rolling hills sweep down to the riverbanks... His body slowly undulated in time to the music.* VERB V V Also V n ♦ **un|du|lat|ing** *...gently undulating hills.* ADJ

**un|du|ly** /ʌndjuːli, AM -duːli/ If you say that something does not happen or is not done **unduly**, you mean that it does not happen or is not done to an excessive or unnecessary extent. ❑ *'But* ADV: ADV with v, ADV adj, oft with brd-neg *you're not unduly worried about doing this report?' — 'No.'... He appealed to firms not to increase their prices unduly.*

**un|dy|ing** /ʌndaɪɪŋ/ If you refer to someone's **undying** feelings, you mean that the feelings are very strong and are unlikely to change. [LITERARY] ❑ *Dianne declared her undying love for Sam... He had won her undying gratitude.*
ADJ: usu ADJ n

**un|earned in|come** /ʌnɜːʳnd ɪŋkʌm/ **Unearned income** is money that people gain from interest or profit from property or investment, rather than money that they earn from a job. ❑ *Reduction in the tax on unearned income could be a boost for small businesses.*
N-UNCOUNT

**un|earth** /ʌnɜːʳθ/ **(unearths, unearthing, unearthed)** 1 If someone **unearths** facts or evidence about something bad, they discover them with difficulty, usually because they were being kept secret or were being lied about. ❑ *Researchers have unearthed documents indicating her responsibility for the forced adoption of children.*
VERB = uncover; V n
2 If someone **unearths** something that is buried, they find it by digging in the ground. ❑ *Fossil hunters have unearthed the bones of an elephant believed to be 500,000 years old.*
VERB; V n
3 If you say that someone **has unearthed** something, you mean that they have found it after it had been hidden or lost for some time. ❑ *From somewhere, he had unearthed a black silk suit.*
VERB = dig out; V n

**un|earth|ly** /ʌnɜːʳθli/ 1 You use **unearthly** to describe something that seems very strange and unnatural. ❑ *For a few seconds we watched the unearthly lights on the water... The sound was so serene that it seemed unearthly.*
ADJ: usu ADJ n
2 If you refer to a time as an **unearthly** hour, you are emphasizing that it is very early in the morning. ❑ *They arranged to meet in Riverside Park at the unearthly hour of seven in the morning.*
ADJ: ADJ n [emphasis] = ungodly
3 An **unearthly** noise is unpleasant because it sounds frightening and unnatural. ❑ *She heard the sirens scream their unearthly wail.*
ADJ: usu ADJ n

**un|ease** /ʌniːz/ 1 If you have a feeling of **unease**, you feel rather anxious or afraid, because you think that something is wrong. ❑ *Sensing my unease about the afternoon ahead, he told me,'These men are pretty easy to talk to.'... We left with a deep sense of unease, because we knew something was being hidden from us.*
N-UNCOUNT: oft with poss = anxiety
2 If you say that there is **unease** in a situation, you mean that people are dissatisfied or angry, but have not yet started to take any action. ❑ *He faces growing unease among the Democrats about the likelihood of war. ...the depth of public unease about the economy.*
N-UNCOUNT

**un|easy** /ʌniːzi/ 1 If you are **uneasy**, you feel anxious, afraid, or embarrassed, because you think that something is wrong or that there is danger. ❑ *He looked uneasy and refused to answer questions... I had an uneasy feeling that he was going to spoil it.* ♦ **un|easi|ly** /ʌniːzɪli/ *Meg shifted uneasily on her chair... He laughed uneasily.* ♦ **un|easi|ness** *With a small degree of uneasiness, he pushed it open and stuck his head inside.*
ADJ = uncomfortable; ADV: usu ADV after v, also ADV adj; N-UNCOUNT
2 If you are **uneasy about** doing something, you are not sure that it is correct or wise. ❑ *Richard was uneasy about how best to approach his elderly mother.* ♦ **un|easi|ness** *I felt a great uneasiness about meeting her again.*
ADJ: usu v-link ADJ about n; N-UNCOUNT
3 If you describe a situation or relationship as **uneasy**, you mean that the situation is not settled and may not last. [JOURNALISM] ❑ *An uneasy calm has settled over Los Angeles... The uneasy alliance between these two men offered a glimmer of hope.* ♦ **un|easi|ly** *...a country whose component parts fit uneasily together.*
ADJ: usu ADJ n; ADV: usu ADV after v, also ADV adj

**un|eco|nom|ic** /ʌniːkənɒmɪk, -ek-/ 1 If you describe something such as an industry or business as **uneconomic**, you mean that it does not produce enough profit. [BUSINESS] ❑ *...the closure of uneconomic factories... The company said the service was uneconomic.*
ADJ = unprofitable ≠ profitable
2 If you say that an action or plan is **uneconomic**, you think it will cost a lot of money and not be successful or not be worth the expense. ❑ *It would be uneconomic to try and repair it.*
ADJ: v-link ADJ ≠ cost-effective

**un|eco|nomi|cal** /ʌniːkənɒmɪkᵊl, -ek-/ If you say that an action, a method, or a product is **uneconomical**, you mean that it does not make a profit. [BUSINESS] ❑ *It would be uneconomical to send a brand new tape... The methods employed are old-fashioned and uneconomical... Even the successful flying boats proved, in the end, uneconomical.*
ADJ = unprofitable

**un|edu|cat|ed** /ʌnedʒukeɪtɪd/ Someone who is **uneducated** has not received much education. ❑ *Though an uneducated man, Chavez was not a stupid one.* ♦ **The uneducated** are people who are uneducated. ❑ *The poor and uneducated did worst under these reforms.*
ADJ ≠ educated; N-PLURAL: the N

**un|emo|tion|al** /ʌnɪmoʊʃənᵊl/ If you describe someone as **unemotional**, you mean that they do not show any feelings. ❑ *British men are often seen as being reserved and unemotional... She began to read in a brisk, unemotional voice.* ♦ **un|emo|tion|al|ly** *McKinnon looked at him unemotionally.*
ADJ ≠ emotional; ADV: ADV after v

**un|em|ploya|ble** /ʌnɪmplɔɪəbᵊl/ Someone who is **unemployable** does not have a job and is unlikely to get a job, because they do not have the skills or abilities that an employer might want. ❑ *He freely admits he is unemployable and will probably never find a job.*
ADJ

**un|em|ployed** /ʌnɪmplɔɪd/ Someone who is **unemployed** does not have a job. ❑ *This workshop helps young unemployed people in Grimsby... Have you been unemployed for over six months?* ♦ **The unemployed** are people who are unemployed. ❑ *We want to create jobs for the unemployed.*
ADJ; N-PLURAL: the N

**un|em|ploy|ment** /ʌnɪmplɔɪmənt/ **Unemployment** is the fact that people who want jobs cannot get them. ❑ *...an area that had the highest unemployment rate in western Europe... Unemployment is so damaging both to individuals and to communities.*
◆◇◇ N-UNCOUNT

**un|em|ploy|ment ben|efit** **(unemployment benefits)** **Unemployment benefit** is money that some people receive from the state when they do not have a job and are unable to find one. ❑ *In 1986 more than three million were receiving unemployment benefit.*
N-UNCOUNT: also N in pl

**un|em|ploy|ment line** **(unemployment lines)** When people talk about **the unemployment line**, they are talking about the state of being unemployed, especially when saying how many people are unemployed. [AM] ❑ *Many white-collar workers, like stock brokers and investment bankers, find themselves in the unemployment lines.*
N-COUNT

✔ in BRIT, use **dole queue**

**un|end|ing** /ʌnendɪŋ/ If you describe something as **unending**, you mean that it continues without stopping for a very long time. ❑ *...the country's seemingly unending cycle of political violence.*
ADJ: usu ADJ n = endless

**un|en|dur|able** /ʌnɪndjʊərəbᵊl, AM -dʊr-/ If you describe a bad situation as **unendurable**, you mean that it is so extremely unpleasant that you have to end it. [FORMAL] ❑ *Isaac had found the work unendurable and walked out of the job... It has placed an almost unendurable strain on their marriage.*
ADJ = intolerable ≠ bearable

**un|en|vi|able** /ʌnenviəbᵊl/ If you describe a situation or task as **unenviable**, you mean that nobody would enjoy dealing with it because it is very difficult, dangerous, or unpleasant. ❑ *She had the unenviable task of making the first few phone calls... It put me in the unenviable position of having to lie.*
ADJ: usu ADJ n ≠ enviable

**un|equal** /ʌniːkwəl/ 1 An **unequal** system or situation is unfair because it gives more power or privileges to one person or group of people than to others. ❑ *This country still had a deeply oppressive, unequal and divisive political system. ...the unequal power relationships between men and women. ...unequal pay.* ♦ **un|equal|ly** *...unequally distributed assets... The victims were treated unequally.*
ADJ: usu ADJ n; ADV: ADV with v
2 If someone is **unequal to** a task they have to
ADJ:

do, they do not have the abilities needed to do it well. [FORMAL] ❑ *He felt unequal to the job and wished there were someone he could go to for advice.*
v-link ADJ *to* n

[3] **Unequal** means being different in size, strength, or amount. ❑ *The Egyptians probably measured their day in twenty-four hours of unequal length.*
ADJ

**un|equalled** /ʌniːkwəld/

✔ in AM, use **unequaled**

If you describe something as **unequalled**, you mean that it is greater, better, or more extreme than anything else of the same kind. ❑ *This record figure was unequalled for 13 years. ...an unequalled level of service. ...a feat unequaled in the history of polar exploration.*
ADJ = *unparalleled*

**un|equivo|cal** /ʌnɪkwɪvəkəl/ If you describe someone's attitude as **unequivocal**, you mean that it is completely clear and very firm. [FORMAL] ❑ *...Richardson's unequivocal commitment to fair play... Yesterday, the message to him was unequivocal: 'Get out.'*
ADJ
♦ **un|equivo|cal|ly** /ʌnɪkwɪvəkli/ *Temperature records have unequivocally confirmed the existence of global warming.*
ADV: ADV with v, ADV adj

**un|err|ing** /ʌnɜːrɪŋ/ If you describe someone's judgment or ability as **unerring**, you mean that they are always correct and never mistaken. ❑ *She has an unerring instinct for people's weak spots.*
ADJ: usu ADJ n = *infallible*
♦ **un|err|ing|ly** *It was wonderful to watch her fingers moving deftly and unerringly.*
ADV: ADV with v, ADV adj

**un|escort|ed** /ʌnɪskɔːtɪd/ If someone or something is **unescorted**, they are not protected or supervised. ❑ *Unescorted children are not allowed beyond this point... They advise against foreign delegates wandering unescorted in various parts of town.*
ADJ: ADJ n, ADJ after v, v-link ADJ = *unaccompanied*

**un|ethi|cal** /ʌneθɪkəl/ If you describe someone's behaviour as **unethical**, you think it is wrong and unacceptable according to a society's rules or people's beliefs. ❑ *It's simply unethical to promote and advertise such a dangerous product.*
ADJ ≠ *ethical*

**un|even** /ʌniːvən/ [1] An **uneven** surface or edge is not smooth, flat, or straight. ❑ *He staggered on the uneven surface of the car park. ...uneven teeth.*
ADJ ≠ *even*
♦ **un|even|ly** *...wearing dresses that pinched at the armholes, that hung as unevenly as flags.*
ADV: ADV with v
[2] Something that is **uneven** is not regular or consistent. ❑ *He could hear that her breathing was uneven.*
ADJ ≠ *even*
♦ **un|even|ly** *The steaks were unevenly cooked.*
ADV: ADV with v
[3] If you describe something as **uneven**, you think it is not very good because it is not consistent in quality. ❑ *This was, for him, an oddly uneven performance.*
ADJ = *patchy*
[4] An **uneven** system or situation is unfairly arranged or organized. ❑ *Some of the victims are complaining loudly about the uneven distribution of emergency aid... It was an uneven contest.*
ADJ: usu ADJ n = *unequal*
♦ **un|even|ly** *Within a free enterprise capitalist society, resources are very unevenly distributed.*
ADV: ADV with v

**un|event|ful** /ʌnɪventfʊl/ If you describe a period of time as **uneventful**, you mean that nothing interesting, exciting, or important happened during it. ❑ *The return journey was uneventful, the car running perfectly... It was rare for her to have an opportunity to discuss her dull, uneventful life.*
ADJ
♦ **un|event|ful|ly** *The five years at that school passed fairly uneventfully.*
ADV: ADV after v

**un|ex|cep|tion|able** /ʌnɪksepʃənəbəl/ If you describe someone or something as **unexceptionable**, you mean that they are unlikely to be criticized or objected to, but are not new or exciting, and may have some hidden bad qualities. [FORMAL] ❑ *The candidate was quite unexceptionable, a well-known travel writer and TV personality... The school's unexceptionable purpose is to involve parents more closely in the education of their children.*
ADJ

**un|ex|cep|tion|al** /ʌnɪksepʃənəl/ If you describe something as **unexceptional**, you mean that it is ordinary, not very interesting, and often disappointing. ❑ *Since then, Michael has lived an unexceptional life... The rest of the summer was unexceptional.*
ADJ = *unremarkable* ≠ *exceptional*

**un|ex|cit|ing** /ʌnɪksaɪtɪŋ/ If you describe someone or something as **unexciting**, you think they are rather boring, and not likely to shock or surprise you in any way. ❑ *He is regarded as very capable but unexciting... It was a methodical, unexciting chore.*
ADJ = *dull* ≠ *exciting*

**un|ex|pec|ted** /ʌnɪkspektɪd/ If an event or someone's behaviour is **unexpected**, it surprises you because you did not think that it was likely to happen. ❑ *His death was totally unexpected... He made a brief, unexpected appearance at the office.*
◆◇◇ ADJ
♦ **un|ex|pect|ed|ly** *Moss had clamped an unexpectedly strong grip on his arm.*
ADV: ADV adj, ADV with v

**un|ex|plained** /ʌnɪkspleɪnd/ If you describe something as **unexplained**, you mean that the reason for it or cause of it is unclear or is not known. ❑ *The demonstrations were provoked by the unexplained death of an opposition leader... Soon after leaving Margate, for some unexplained reason, the train was brought to a standstill.*
ADJ: usu ADJ n

**un|fail|ing** /ʌnfeɪlɪŋ/ If you describe someone's good qualities or behaviour as **unfailing**, you mean that they never change. ❑ *He had the unfailing care and support of Erica, his wife... He continued to appear in the office with unfailing regularity thereafter.*
ADJ: usu ADJ n
♦ **un|fail|ing|ly** *He was unfailingly polite to customers... Foreigners unfailingly fall in love with the place.*
ADV: usu ADV adj, also ADV with v

**un|fair** /ʌnfeər/ [1] An **unfair** action or situation is not right or fair. ❑ *She was awarded £5,000 in compensation for unfair dismissal... America decided that imported steel had an unfair advantage over steel made at home... It was unfair that he should suffer so much... The union said it was unfair to ask workers to adopt a policy of wage restraint.*
◆◇◇ ADJ: oft *it* v-link ADJ that/to-inf
♦ **un|fair|ly** *An industrial tribunal has no jurisdiction to decide whether an employee was fairly or unfairly dismissed... He unfairly blamed Frances for the failure.*
ADV: ADV adj, ADV with v
[2] An **unfair** system or situation does not give equal treatment or equal opportunities to everyone involved. ❑ *The American plane makers continue to accuse Airbus of unfair competition... Some have been sentenced to long prison terms after unfair trials.*
ADJ: usu ADJ n
♦ **un|fair|ness** *What about the unfairness of life? Why do bad things happen to good people?*
N-UNCOUNT

**un|fair dis|mis|sal** If an employee claims **unfair dismissal**, they begin a legal action against their employer in which they claim that they were dismissed from their job unfairly. [BUSINESS] ❑ *His former chauffeur is claiming unfair dismissal on the grounds of racial discrimination.*
N-UNCOUNT

**un|faith|ful** /ʌnfeɪθfʊl/ If someone is **unfaithful to** their lover or to the person they are married to, they have a sexual relationship with someone else. ❑ *James had been unfaithful to Christine for the entire four years they'd been together. ...her unfaithful husband.*
ADJ: oft ADJ *to* n

**un|fa|mil|iar** /ʌnfəmɪlɪər/ [1] If something is **unfamiliar to** you, you know nothing or very little about it, because you have not seen or experienced it before. ❑ *She grew many wonderful plants that were unfamiliar to me... I was alone in an unfamiliar city.*
ADJ: oft ADJ *to* n ≠ *familiar*
♦ **un|fa|mili|ar|ity** /ʌnfəmɪliærɪti/ *...problems which arise from the newness of the approach and its unfamiliarity to prisoners.*
N-UNCOUNT: oft with poss ≠ *familiarity*
[2] If you are **unfamiliar with** something, it is unfamiliar to you. ❑ *She speaks no Japanese and is unfamiliar with Japanese culture.*
ADJ: v-link ADJ *with* n
♦ **un|fa|mili|ar|ity** *...her unfamiliarity with the politics of the region.*
N-UNCOUNT: N *with* n

**un|fash|ion|able** /ʌnfæʃənəbəl/ If something is **unfashionable**, it is not approved of or done by most people. ❑ *Wearing fur has become deeply unfashionable... The couple hold the unfashionable view that marriage is a sacred union.*
ADJ ≠ *fashionable*
♦ **un|fash|ion|ably** *He wears his blonde hair unfashionably long.*
ADV: usu ADV adj

**un|fas|ten** /ʌnfɑːsən, -fæsən/ **(unfastens, unfastening, unfastened)** If you **unfasten** something that is closed, tied, or held together, or if you un-
VERB = *undo* ≠ *fasten*

**fasten** the thing holding it, you loosen or remove the thing holding it. ❑ *When Ted was six we decided that he needed to know how to fasten and unfasten his seat belt... Reaching down, he unfastened the latch on the gate... He once emerged from the toilets with his flies unfastened.* V n / V n / V-ed

**un|fath|om|able** /ʌnfæðəməbᵊl/ [1] If you describe something as **unfathomable**, you mean that it cannot be understood or explained, usually because it is very strange or complicated. ❑ *For some unfathomable reason, there are no stairs where there should be... How odd life was, how unfathomable, how profoundly unjust.* ADJ = inexplicable [2] If you use **unfathomable** to describe a person or the expression on their face, you mean that you cannot tell what they are thinking or what they intend to do. [LITERARY] ❑ *...a strange, unfathomable and unpredictable individual. ...the dark eyes that right now seemed opaque and unfathomable.* ADJ = inscrutable

**un|fa|vour|able** /ʌnfeɪvərəbᵊl/

✔ in AM, use **unfavorable**

[1] **Unfavourable** conditions or circumstances cause problems for you and reduce your chances of success. ❑ *Unfavourable economic conditions were blocking a recovery of the American insurance market... Unfavourable weather has had damaging effects on this year's harvest... The whole international economic situation is very unfavourable for the countries in the south.* ADJ: usu ADJ n ≠favourable [2] If you have an **unfavourable** reaction to something, you do not like it. ❑ *A more unfavourable response was given today by the Prime Minister... First reactions have been distinctly unfavourable.* ADJ ≠favourable ♦ **un|fa|vour|ably** /ʌnfeɪvərəbli/ *When the body reacts unfavourably to food, the pulse rate will go up.* ADV: ADV after v [3] If you make an **unfavourable** comparison between two things, you say that one thing seems worse than the other. ❑ *He makes unfavourable comparisons between British and French cooking.* ADJ: ADJ n ≠favourable ♦ **un|fa|vour|ably** *Childcare facilities in Britain compare unfavourably with other European countries.* ADV: ADV with v

**un|fea|sible** /ʌnfiːzɪbᵊl/ If you say that something is **unfeasible**, you mean that you do not think it can be done, made, or achieved. ❑ *The weather made it unfeasible to be outdoors... The board said the idea was unfeasible.* ADJ = impractical ≠feasible

**un|feel|ing** /ʌnfiːlɪŋ/ If you describe someone as **unfeeling**, you are criticizing them for their lack of kindness or sympathy for other people. [WRITTEN] ❑ *He was branded an unfeeling bully... There's no way anyone could accuse this woman of being cold and unfeeling.* ADJ [disapproval] = insensitive

**un|fet|tered** /ʌnfetəʳd/ If you describe something as **unfettered**, you mean that it is not controlled or limited by anyone or anything. [FORMAL] ❑ *...unfettered free trade... Unfettered by the bounds of reality, my imagination flourished. ...city slums, where drug traffickers reign virtually unfettered.* ADJ: ADJ n, v-link ADJ, ADJ after v

**un|fin|ished** /ʌnfɪnɪʃt/ If you describe something such as a work of art or a piece of work as **unfinished**, you mean that it is not complete, for example because it was abandoned or there was no time to complete it. ❑ *...Jane Austen's unfinished novel... The cathedral was eventually completed in 1490, though the Gothic facade remains unfinished.* ADJ: ADJ n, v-link ADJ, ADJ after v = incomplete

**un|fit** /ʌnfɪt/ [1] If you are **unfit**, your body is not in good condition because you have not been taking regular exercise. ❑ *Many children are so unfit they are unable to do even basic exercises.* ADJ: usu v-link ADJ ≠fit [2] If someone is **unfit** for something, he or she is unable to do it because of injury or illness. ❑ *He had a third examination and was declared unfit for duty... Mr Abel's doctor has said he is unfit to travel.* ADJ: usu v-link ADJ, ADJ for n, ADJ to-inf [3] If you say that someone or something is **unfit** for a particular purpose or job, you are criticizing them because they are not good enough for that purpose or job. ❑ *Existing houses are becoming totally unfit for human habitation... They were utterly unfit to govern America... She is an unfit mother.* ADJ: oft ADJ for n, ADJ to-inf [disapproval] ≠fit

**un|flag|ging** /ʌnflægɪŋ/ If you describe something such as support, effort, or enthusiasm as **unflagging**, you mean that it does not stop or get less as time passes. ❑ *He was sustained by the unflagging support of his family... The book is not one word too long and its narrative pace is unflagging.* ADJ [approval]

**un|flap|pable** /ʌnflæpəbᵊl/ Someone who is **unflappable** is always calm and never panics or gets upset or angry. ADJ

**un|flat|ter|ing** /ʌnflætərɪŋ/ If you describe something as **unflattering**, you mean that it makes a person or thing seem less attractive than they really are. ❑ *He depicted the town's respectable families in an unflattering light... The knee-length dresses were unflattering and ugly.* ADJ ≠flattering

**un|flinch|ing** /ʌnflɪntʃɪŋ/ You can use **unflinching** in expressions such as **unflinching honesty** and **unflinching support** to indicate that a good quality which someone has is strong and steady, and never weakens. ❑ *...the armed forces, all of whom had pledged their unflinching support and loyalty to the government.* ADJ ♦ **un|flinch|ing|ly** *They were unflinchingly loyal to their friends.* ADV

**un|fo|cused** /ʌnfoʊkəst/ also **unfocussed.** [1] If someone's eyes are **unfocused**, they are open, but not looking at anything. ❑ *Her eyes were unfocused, as if she were staring inside at her memories of the day. ...his unfocused gaze.* ADJ [2] If you describe someone's feelings or plans as **unfocused**, you are criticizing them because they do not seem to be clearly formed or have any clear purpose. ❑ *But for now, she is in the grip of a blind, unfocused anger... It is not perhaps surprising that the administration now appears so indecisive and unfocused.* ADJ [disapproval]

**un|fold** /ʌnfoʊld/ **(unfolds, unfolding, unfolded)** [1] If a situation **unfolds**, it develops and becomes known or understood. ❑ *The outcome depends on conditions as well as how events unfold.* VERB V [2] If a story **unfolds** or if someone **unfolds** it, it is told to someone else. ❑ *Don's story unfolded as the cruise got under way... Mr Wills unfolds his story with evident enjoyment.* VERB V / V n [3] If someone **unfolds** something which has been folded or if it **unfolds**, it is opened out and becomes flat. ❑ *He quickly unfolded the blankets and spread them on the mattress... When the bird lifts off into flight, its wings unfold to an impressive six-foot span.* VERB ≠fold V n / V

**un|fore|see|able** /ʌnfɔːʳsiːəbᵊl/ An **unforeseeable** problem or unpleasant event is one which you did not expect and could not have predicted. ❑ *This is such an unforeseeable situation that anything could happen.* ADJ

**un|fore|seen** /ʌnfəʳsiːn/ If something that has happened was **unforeseen**, it was not expected to happen or known about beforehand. ❑ *Radiation may damage cells in a way that was previously unforeseen... Unfortunately, due to unforeseen circumstances, this year's show has been cancelled.* ADJ

**un|for|get|table** /ʌnfəʳgetəbᵊl/ If you describe something as **unforgettable**, you mean that it is, for example, extremely beautiful, enjoyable, or unusual, so that you remember it for a long time. You can also refer to extremely unpleasant things as **unforgettable**. ❑ *A visit to the Museum is an unforgettable experience. ...the leisure activities that will make your holiday unforgettable.* ADJ ♦ **un|for|get|tably** /ʌnfəʳgetəbli/ *...an unforgettably unique performer.* ADV: usu ADV cl/group

**un|for|giv|able** /ʌnfəʳgɪvəbᵊl/ If you say that something is **unforgivable**, you mean that it is very bad, cruel, or socially unacceptable. ❑ *These people are animals and what they did was unforgivable.* ADJ = inexcusable

**un|for|giv|ing** /ʌnfəʳgɪvɪŋ/ [1] If you describe someone as **unforgiving**, you mean that they are unwilling to forgive other people. [FORMAL] ❑ *He was an unforgiving man who never forgot a slight... He finds human foibles endearing, but is unforgiving of pretension.* ADJ ≠forgiving [2] If you describe a situation or activity as **unforgiving**, you mean that it ADJ causes a lot of people to experience great difficulty or failure, even people who deserve to succeed. ❑ *Business is a competitive activity. It is very fierce and very unforgiving.*

**un|formed** /ʌnfɔːʳmd/ ADJ = undeveloped If you describe someone or something as **unformed**, you mean that they are in an early stage of development and not fully formed or matured. [FORMAL] ❑ *The market for which they are competing is still unformed. ...the unformed minds of children.*

**un|for|tu|nate** /ʌnfɔːʳtʃʊnət/ **(unfortunates)** 1 ADJ = unlucky If you describe someone as **unfortunate**, you mean that something unpleasant or unlucky has happened to them. You can also describe the unpleasant things that happen to them as **unfortunate**. ❑ *Some unfortunate person passing below could all too easily be seriously injured... Apparently he had been unfortunate enough to fall victim to a gang of thugs... Through some unfortunate accident, the information reached me a day late... It was unfortunate for Davey that his teacher did not take kindly to him.* 2 ADJ If you describe something that has happened as **unfortunate**, you think that it is inappropriate, embarrassing, awkward, or undesirable. ❑ *It really is desperately unfortunate that this should have happened just now. ...the unfortunate incident of the upside-down Canadian flag.* 3 ADJ You can describe someone as **unfortunate** when they are poor or have a difficult life. ❑ *Every year we have charity days to raise money for unfortunate people.* ♦ N-COUNT An **unfortunate** is someone who is unfortunate. ❑ *Dorothy was another of life's unfortunates.*

**un|for|tu|nate|ly** /ʌnfɔːʳtʃʊnətli/ ◆◇◇ ADV: ADV with cl, oft ADV *for* n [feelings] = regrettably You can use **unfortunately** to introduce or refer to a statement when you consider that it is sad or disappointing, or when you want to express regret. ❑ *Unfortunately, my time is limited... Unfortunately for the Prince, his title brought obligations as well as privileges.*

**un|found|ed** /ʌnfaʊndɪd/ ADJ = groundless If you describe a rumour, belief, or feeling as **unfounded**, you mean that it is wrong and is not based on facts or evidence. ❑ *There were unfounded rumours of alcohol abuse... The allegations were totally unfounded.*

**un|friend|ly** /ʌnfrendli/ ADJ ≠friendly If you describe a person, organization, or their behaviour as **unfriendly**, you mean that they behave towards you in an unkind or rather hostile way. ❑ *It is not fair for him to be permanently unfriendly to someone who has hurt him... People always complain that the big banks and big companies are unfriendly and unhelpful... Judy spoke in a loud, rather unfriendly voice.*

**-unfriendly** /-ʌnfrendli/ COMB in ADJ ≠-friendly **-unfriendly** combines with nouns, and sometimes adverbs, to form adjectives which describe something which is bad for a particular thing. ❑ *It's couched in such very user-unfriendly terminology. ...this harsh, and environmentally-unfriendly, action.*

**un|ful|filled** /ʌnfʊlfɪld/ 1 ADJ: usu ADJ n ≠fulfilled If you use **unfulfilled** to describe something such as a promise, ambition, or need, you mean that what was promised, hoped for, or needed has not happened. ❑ *...angry at unfulfilled promises of jobs and decent housing... The election had raised hopes that remain unfulfilled.* 2 ADJ: usu v-link ADJ ≠fulfilled If you describe someone as **unfulfilled**, you mean that they feel dissatisfied with life or with what they have done. ❑ *You must let go of the idea that to be single is to be unhappy and unfulfilled.*

**un|fun|ny** /ʌnfʌni/ ADJ ≠funny If you describe something or someone as **unfunny**, you mean that they do not make you laugh, although this was their intention or purpose. ❑ *We became increasingly fed up with his increasingly unfunny and unintelligent comments.*

**un|furl** /ʌnfɜːʳl/ **(unfurls, unfurling, unfurled)** 1 VERB If you **unfurl** something rolled or folded such as an umbrella, sail, or flag, you open it, so that it is spread out. You can also say that it **unfurls**. ❑ *Once outside the inner breakwater, we began to unfurl all the sails.* (V n) *...two weeks later when the leaves unfurl.* (V) 2 VERB = unfold If you say that events, stories, or scenes **unfurl** before you, you mean that you are aware of them or can see them as they happen or develop. ❑ *...as the dramatic changes in Europe continue to unfurl.* (V)

**un|fur|nished** /ʌnfɜːʳnɪʃt/ ADJ: usu ADJ n, also ADJ after v, v-link ADJ If you rent an **unfurnished** house, flat, or apartment, no furniture is provided by the owner.

**un|gain|ly** /ʌngeɪnli/ ADJ = clumsy If you describe a person, animal, or vehicle as **ungainly**, you mean that they look awkward or clumsy, often because they are big. ❑ *The dog, an ungainly mongrel pup, was loping about the road... Paul swam in his ungainly way to the side of the pool.*

**un|gen|er|ous** /ʌndʒenərəs/ 1 ADJ ≠generous If you describe someone's remarks, thoughts, or actions as **ungenerous**, you mean that they are unfair or unkind. [FORMAL] ❑ *This was a typically ungenerous response.* 2 ADJ ≠generous You can use **ungenerous** when you are describing a person or organization that is unwilling to give much money to other people. [FORMAL] ❑ *The company had a good pension scheme for the salaried employees and an ungenerous scheme for the hourly paid.*

**un|glued** /ʌngluːd/ 1 PHRASE: V inflects If something **comes unglued**, it becomes separated from the thing that it was attached to. ❑ *I wear my old shoes every day. One sole has come unglued.* 2 PHRASE: V inflects = fail To **come unglued** means to fail. [mainly AM, INFORMAL] ❑ *Their marriage finally came unglued.*

✓ in BRIT, usually use **come unstuck**

3 PHRASE: V inflects If someone **comes unglued**, they become very upset and emotional, and perhaps confused or mentally ill. [mainly AM, INFORMAL] ❑ *If she hears what you're saying, she's going to come unglued.*

**un|god|ly** /ʌngɒdli/ 1 ADJ = unholy If you describe someone or something as **ungodly**, you mean that they are morally bad or are opposed to religion. 2 ADJ: ADJ n [emphasis] = unearthly If you refer to a time as an **ungodly** hour, you are emphasizing that it is very early in the morning. ❑ *...at the ungodly hour of 4.00am.* 3 ADJ: ADJ n If you refer to the amount or volume of something as **ungodly**, you mean that it is excessive or unreasonable. ❑ *...a power struggle of ungodly proportions.*

**un|gov|ern|able** /ʌngʌvəʳnəbᵊl/ 1 ADJ: usu v-link ADJ If you describe a country or region as **ungovernable**, you mean that it seems impossible to control or govern it effectively, for example because of violence or conflict among the population. ❑ *The country has become virtually ungovernable.* 2 ADJ: usu ADJ n = uncontrollable If you describe feelings as **ungovernable**, you mean that they are so strong that they cannot be controlled. ❑ *He was filled with an ungovernable rage.*

**un|gra|cious** /ʌngreɪʃəs/ ADJ = discourteous If you describe a person or their behaviour as **ungracious**, you mean that they are not polite or friendly in their speech or behaviour. [FORMAL] ❑ *...his ungracious behaviour during the Queen's recent visit... I was often rude and ungracious in refusing help.*

**un|grate|ful** /ʌngreɪtfʊl/ ADJ [disapproval] ≠grateful If you describe someone as **ungrateful**, you are criticizing them for not showing thanks or for being unkind to someone who has helped them or done them a favour. ❑ *I thought it was rather ungrateful... You ungrateful brat.*

**un|guard|ed** /ʌngɑːʳdɪd/ 1 ADJ: ADJ after v, v-link ADJ, ADJ n If something is **unguarded**, nobody is protecting it or looking after it. ❑ *I should not leave my briefcase and camera bag unguarded.* 2 ADJ: usu ADJ n If you do or say something in an **unguarded** moment, you do or say it carelessly and without thinking, especially when it is something that you did not want anyone to see or know. ❑ *The photographers managed to capture Jane in an unguarded moment.*

**un|ham|pered** /ʌnhæmpəʳd/ ADJ: usu ADJ after v, ADJ *by* n If you are **unhampered by** a problem or obstacle, you are free from it, and so you are able to do what you want to. [WRITTEN] ❑ *...her belief that things go best if* *businessmen are allowed to make money unhampered by any kind of regulations.*

**un|hap|pi|ly** /ʌnhæpɪli/ You use **unhappily** to introduce or refer to a statement when you consider it is sad and wish that it was different. ❑ *On May 23rd, unhappily, the little boy died... Unhappily for Berkowitz, he never got a penny.* ADV: ADV with cl = unfortunately

**un|hap|py** /ʌnhæpi/ **(unhappier, unhappiest)** ◆◇◇ 1 If you are **unhappy**, you are sad and depressed. ❑ *Her marriage is in trouble and she is desperately unhappy... He was a shy, sometimes unhappy man.* ADJ = miserable ≠ happy ♦ **un|hap|pi|ly** *'I don't have your imagination,' King said unhappily. ...an unhappily married woman.* ADV: usu ADV with v ♦ **un|hap|pi|ness** *There was a lot of unhappiness in my adolescence.* N-UNCOUNT 2 If you are **unhappy about** something, you are not pleased about it or not satisfied with it. ❑ *He has been unhappy with his son's political leanings... I suspect he isn't altogether unhappy about my absence... A lot of Republicans are unhappy that the government isn't doing more.* ADJ: v-link ADJ, oft ADJ *about/at* n/-ing, ADJ that ♦ **un|hap|pi|ness** *He has, by submitting his resignation, signalled his unhappiness with the government's decision.* N-UNCOUNT: oft N *with/about* n, N that 3 An **unhappy** situation or choice is not satisfactory or desirable. ❑ *...this unhappy chapter in the history of relations between our two countries. ...unhappy experiences of writing for television.* ADJ: ADJ n

**un|harmed** /ʌnhɑːʳmd/ If someone or something is **unharmed** after an accident or violent incident, they are not hurt or damaged in any way. ❑ *The car was a write-off, but everyone escaped unharmed.* ADJ: ADJ after v, v-link ADJ = unhurt

**un|healthy** /ʌnhelθi/ **(unhealthier, unhealthiest)** 1 Something that is **unhealthy** is likely to cause illness or poor health. ❑ *Avoid unhealthy foods such as hamburger and chips... He worked in the notoriously unhealthy environment of a coal mine.* ADJ ≠ healthy 2 If you are **unhealthy**, you are not very fit or well. ❑ *I'm quite unhealthy really. ...a poorly dressed, unhealthy looking fellow with a poor complexion.* ADJ ≠ healthy 3 An **unhealthy** economy or company is financially weak and unsuccessful. [BUSINESS] ❑ *The redundancy of skilled and experienced workers is a terrible waste and a clear sign of an unhealthy economy.* ADJ = weak ≠ strong 4 If you describe someone's behaviour or interests as **unhealthy**, you do not consider them to be normal and think they may involve mental problems. ❑ *Frank has developed what I would term an unhealthy relationship with these people... MacGregor believes it is unhealthy to lead a life with no interests beyond politics.* ADJ ≠ healthy

**un|heard** /ʌnhɜːʳd/ 1 If you say that a person or their words go **unheard**, you are expressing criticism because someone refuses to pay attention to what is said or take it into consideration. [WRITTEN] ❑ *His impassioned pleas went unheard.* ADJ: usu v-link ADJ, ADJ after v, also ADJ n [disapproval] 2 If you describe spoken comments or pieces of music as **unheard**, you mean that most people are not familiar with them because they have not been expressed or performed in public. ❑ *...a country where social criticism was largely unheard until this year.* ADJ 3 If someone's words or cries go **unheard**, nobody can hear them, or a particular person cannot hear them. [WRITTEN] ❑ *Martin's weak cries for help went unheard until 6.40pm yesterday.* ADJ: usu v-link ADJ

**un|heard of** 1 You can say that an event or situation is **unheard of** when it never happens. ❑ *Meals are taken communally with other guests in the dining-room. Private bathrooms and toilets are unheard of... It's almost unheard of in France for a top politician not to come from the social elite.* ADJ: v-link ADJ 2 You can say that an event or situation is **unheard of** when it happens for the first time and is very surprising or shocking. ❑ *Mom announced that she was going to visit her family for a couple of weeks, which was absolutely unheard of.* ADJ

**un|heed|ed** /ʌnhiːdɪd/ If you say that something such as a warning or danger goes **unheeded**, you mean that it has not been taken seriously or dealt with. [WRITTEN] ❑ *The advice of experts went unheeded. ...a damning picture of lax banking standards and unheeded warnings.* ADJ: usu v-link ADJ, also ADJ n, ADJ after v

**un|help|ful** /ʌnhelpfʊl/ If you say that someone or something is **unhelpful**, you mean that they do not help you or improve a situation, and may even make things worse. ❑ *The criticism is both unfair and unhelpful. ...unhelpful hotel staff.* ADJ ≠ helpful

**un|her|ald|ed** /ʌnherəldɪd/ 1 If you describe an artist or sports player as **unheralded**, you mean that people have not recognized their talent or ability. [JOURNALISM] ❑ *They are inviting talented, but unheralded film-makers to submit examples of their work.* ADJ: usu ADJ n = unsung ≠ acclaimed 2 If you describe something that happens as **unheralded**, you mean that you did not expect it, because nobody mentioned it beforehand. [WRITTEN] ❑ *...Sandi's unheralded arrival on her doorstep... The complete reversal of this policy was unheralded.* ADJ

**un|hesi|tat|ing|ly** /ʌnhezɪteɪtɪŋli/ If you say that someone does something **unhesitatingly**, you mean that they do it immediately and confidently, without any doubt or anxiety. ❑ *I would unhesitatingly choose the latter option... So is there any taboo she wouldn't touch? Unhesitatingly she replies, 'Politics.'* ADV: usu ADV with v, also ADV with cl

**un|hinge** /ʌnhɪndʒ/ **(unhinges, unhinging, unhinged)** If you say that an experience **has unhinged** someone, you mean that it has affected them so deeply that they have become mentally ill. ❑ *The stress of war temporarily unhinged him.* VERB V n ♦ **un|hinged** *...feelings that make you feel completely unhinged and crazy.* ADJ

**un|hinged** /ʌnhɪndʒd/ If you describe someone's behaviour or performance as **unhinged**, you are critical of it because it seems wild and uncontrollable. [JOURNALISM] ❑ *The phrase 'yeah yeah yeah' can rarely have been delivered with so much unhinged passion.* ADJ [disapproval]

**un|hip** /ʌnhɪp/ If you describe someone or something as **unhip**, you mean that they are not at all fashionable or modern. [INFORMAL] ❑ *...two rather stiff, unhip, middle-aged men.* ADJ ≠ hip

**un|ho|ly** /ʌnhoʊli/ 1 You use **unholy** to emphasize how unreasonable or unpleasant you think something is. ❑ *She protested that it wasn't traditional jazz at all, but an unholy row... The economy is still an unholy mess.* ADJ: ADJ n [emphasis] = horrendous 2 If you refer to two or more people or groups working together as an **unholy** alliance, you mean that this arrangement is unusual because the people usually oppose each other. ❑ *If the government does fall it will be because of this unholy alliance between the far right and the left... Westerners charged that the party was run by an unholy coalition between North and South.* ADJ: ADJ n [disapproval] 3 If you describe something as **unholy**, you mean that it is wicked or bad. ❑ *'This ought to be fun,' he told Alex, eyes gleaming with an almost unholy relish.* ADJ: usu ADJ n

**un|hook** /ʌnhʊk/ **(unhooks, unhooking, unhooked)** 1 If you **unhook** a piece of clothing that is fastened with hooks, you undo the hooks. ❑ *She unhooked her dress.* VERB V n 2 If you **unhook** something that is held in place by hooks, you open it or remove it by undoing the hooks. ❑ *Chris unhooked the shutters and went out on the balcony.* VERB V n

**un|hur|ried** /ʌnhʌrɪd/ If you describe something as **unhurried**, you approve of it because it is relaxed and slow, and is not rushed or anxious. ❑ *...an unhurried pace of life.* ADJ [approval] = leisurely

**un|hurt** /ʌnhɜːʳt/ If someone who has been attacked, or involved in an accident, is **unhurt**, they are not injured. ❑ *The lorry driver escaped unhurt, but a pedestrian was injured... The two girls suddenly emerged from among the trees. Both seemed to be calm and unhurt.* ADJ: ADJ after v, v-link ADJ ≠ hurt

**un|hy|gien|ic** /ʌnhaɪdʒiːnɪk, AM -dʒienɪk/ If you describe something as **unhygienic**, you mean that it is dirty and likely to cause infection or disease. ❑ *Parts of the shop were very dirty, unhygienic, and an ideal breeding ground for bacteria. ...unhygienic conditions.* ADJ = insanitary ≠ hygienic

**uni|corn** /juːnɪkɔːʳn/ **(unicorns)** In stories and legends, a **unicorn** is an imaginary animal that looks like a white horse and has a horn growing from its forehead. N-COUNT

**un|iden|ti|fi|able** /ʌnaɪdentɪfaɪəbᵊl/ If something or someone is **unidentifiable**, you are not able to say exactly what it is or who they are. ❑ *...unidentifiable howling noises... All the bodies were totally unidentifiable.* ADJ = unrecognizable

**un|iden|ti|fied** /ʌnaɪdentɪfaɪd/ ◆◇◇ [1] If you describe someone or something as **unidentified**, you mean that nobody knows who or what they are. ❑ *He was shot this morning by unidentified intruders at his house. ...unidentified cancer-causing substances in the environment.* ADJ: usu ADJ n = unknown [2] If you use **unidentified** to describe people, groups, and organizations, you do not want to give their names. [JOURNALISM] ❑ *...his claims, which were based on the comments of anonymous and unidentified sources.* ADJ: usu ADJ n = unnamed

**uni|fi|ca|tion** /juːnɪfɪkeɪʃᵊn/ **Unification** is the process by which two or more countries join together and become one country. ❑ *...the process of general European unification.* N-UNCOUNT

**uni|form** /juːnɪfɔːʳm/ **(uniforms)** ◆◇◇ [1] A **uniform** is a special set of clothes which some people, for example soldiers or the police, wear to work in and which some children wear at school. ❑ *The town police wear dark blue uniforms and flat caps... Philippe was in uniform, wearing a pistol holster on his belt... She will probably take great pride in wearing school uniform.* N-VAR [2] You can refer to the particular style of clothing which a group of people wear to show they belong to a group or a movement as their **uniform**. ❑ *Mark's is the uniform of the young male traveller – green Army trousers, T-shirt and shirt.* N-COUNT: with supp [3] If something is **uniform**, it does not vary, but is even and regular throughout. ❑ *Chips should be cut into uniform size and thickness... The price rises will not be uniform across the country.* ADJ ♦ **uni|form|ity** /juːnɪfɔːʳmɪti/ *...the caramel that was used to maintain uniformity of color in the brandy.* N-UNCOUNT ♦ **uni|form|ly** *Beyond the windows, a November midday was uniformly grey... Microwaves heat water uniformly.* ADV: ADV adj, ADV with v [4] If you describe a number of things as **uniform**, you mean that they are all the same. ❑ *Along each wall stretched uniform green metal filing cabinets.* ADJ: usu ADJ n = identical ♦ **uni|form|ity** *...the dull uniformity of the houses.* N-UNCOUNT ♦ **uni|form|ly** *The natives uniformly agreed on this important point.* ADV: ADV adj, ADV with v

**uni|formed** /juːnɪfɔːʳmd/ If you use **uniformed** to describe someone who does a particular job, you mean that they are wearing a uniform. ❑ *...uniformed policemen.* ADJ: usu ADJ n

**uni|form|ity** /juːnɪfɔːʳmɪti/ If there is **uniformity** in something such as a system, organization, or group of countries, the same rules, ideas, or methods are applied in all parts of it. ❑ *Spanish liberals sought to create linguistic as well as administrative uniformity.* → See also **uniform**. N-UNCOUNT

**uni|fy** /juːnɪfaɪ/ **(unifies, unifying, unified)** If someone **unifies** different things or parts, or if the things or parts **unify**, they are brought together to form one thing. ❑ *A flexible retirement age is being considered by Ministers to unify men's and women's pension rights... He said he would seek to unify the Conservative Party and win the next general election... The plan has been for the rival armies to demobilise, to unify, and then to hold elections to decide who rules. ...the benefits of unifying with the West.* V-RECIP; V pl-n; V n; pl-n V; V *with* n ♦ **uni|fied** *...a unified German state. ...a unified system of taxation.* ADJ: usu ADJ n

**uni|lat|er|al** /juːnɪlætərᵊl/ A **unilateral** decision or action is taken by only one of the groups, organizations, or countries that are involved in a particular situation, without the agreement of the others. ❑ *...unilateral nuclear disarmament.* ADJ: usu ADJ n ♦ **uni|lat|er|al|ly** *The British Government was careful not to act unilaterally.* ADV: ADV with v

**uni|lat|er|al|ism** /juːnɪlætərəlɪzəm/ [1] **Unilateralism** is the belief that one country should get rid of all its own nuclear weapons, without waiting for other countries to do the same. N-UNCOUNT [2] **Unilateralism** is used to refer to a policy in which one country or group involved in a situation takes a decision or action on its own, without the agreement of the other countries or groups involved. ❑ *...the recent history of American aggressive unilateralism on trade.* N-UNCOUNT

**un|im|agi|nable** /ʌnɪmædʒɪnəbᵊl/ If you describe something as **unimaginable**, you are emphasizing that it is difficult to imagine or understand properly, because it is not part of people's normal experience. ❑ *The scale of the fighting is almost unimaginable... The children here have lived through unimaginable horrors.* ADJ [emphasis] = unbelievable ♦ **un|im|agi|nably** /ʌnɪmædʒɪnəbli/ *Conditions in prisons out there are unimaginably bad.* ADV: ADV adj

**un|im|agi|na|tive** /ʌnɪmædʒɪnətɪv/ [1] If you describe someone as **unimaginative**, you are criticizing them because they do not think of new methods or things to do. ❑ *Her second husband was a steady, unimaginative, corporate lawyer. ...unimaginative teachers.* ADJ [disapproval] ≠ imaginative [2] If you describe something as **unimaginative**, you mean that it is boring or unattractive because very little imagination or effort has been used on it. ❑ *...unimaginative food.* ADJ: usu ADJ n [disapproval] ≠ imaginative

**un|im|paired** /ʌnɪmpeəʳd/ If something is **unimpaired** after something bad or unpleasant has happened to it, it is not damaged or made worse. [FORMAL] ❑ *His health and vigour were unimpaired by a stroke... Queen Milena possessed great beauty, which she retained unimpaired in advancing years.* ADJ: v-link ADJ, ADJ after v, ADJ n = unharmed

**un|im|peach|able** /ʌnɪmpiːtʃəbᵊl/ If you describe someone as **unimpeachable**, you mean that they are completely honest and reliable. [FORMAL] ❑ *He said all five were men of unimpeachable character. ...an unimpeachable source.* ADJ

**un|im|ped|ed** /ʌnɪmpiːdɪd/ If something moves or happens **unimpeded**, it continues without being stopped or interrupted by anything. [FORMAL] ❑ *We drove, unimpeded by anyone, to Arras... He promised to allow justice to run its course unimpeded... U.N. aid convoys have unimpeded access to the city.* ADJ: ADJ after v, ADJ n, v-link ADJ

**un|im|por|tant** /ʌnɪmpɔːʳtᵊnt/ If you describe something or someone as **unimportant**, you mean that they do not have much influence, effect, or value, and are therefore not worth serious consideration. ❑ *It was an unimportant job, and paid very little... When they had married, six years before, the difference in their ages had seemed unimportant.* ADJ ≠ important

**un|im|pressed** /ʌnɪmprest/ If you are **unimpressed by** something or someone, you do not think they are very good, clever, or useful. ❑ *He was also very unimpressed by his teachers... Graham Fletcher was unimpressed with the idea of filling in a lengthy questionnaire.* ADJ: v-link ADJ, oft ADJ *by/with* n ≠ impressed

**un|im|pres|sive** /ʌnɪmpresɪv/ If you describe someone or something as **unimpressive**, you mean they appear very ordinary, without any special or exciting qualities. ❑ *...even though Manchester United have looked unimpressive over recent weeks... Rainey was an unimpressive, rather dull lecturer.* ADJ ≠ impressive

**un|in|formed** /ʌnɪnfɔːʳmd/ If you describe someone as **uninformed**, you mean that they have very little knowledge or information about a particular situation or subject. ❑ *He could not complain that he was uninformed about the true nature of the regime... Cases of child abuse often go unreported or ignored by uninformed citizens.* ADJ

**un|in|hab|it|able** /ʌnɪnhæbɪtəbᵊl/ If a place is **uninhabitable**, it is impossible for people to live there, for example because it is dangerous or unhealthy. ❑ *As parts of the world become uninhabitable, millions of people will try to migrate to more hospitable areas. ...a young couple turning an uninhabitable wreck into their first home.* ADJ ≠ habitable

**un|in|hab|it|ed** /ʌnɪnhæbɪtɪd/ An **uninhabited** place is one where nobody lives. ❑ *...an uninhabited island in the North Pacific... The area is largely uninhabited.* ADJ = deserted

**un|in|hib|it|ed** /ʌnɪnhɪbɪtɪd/ If you describe a person or their behaviour as **uninhibited**, you mean that they express their opinions and feelings openly, and behave as they want to, without worrying what other people think. ❑ *...a commanding and uninhibited entertainer... The dancing is uninhibited and as frenzied as an aerobics class.* ADJ ≠ inhibited

**un|ini|ti|at|ed** /ʌnɪnɪʃieɪtɪd/ You can refer to people who have no knowledge or experience of a particular subject or activity as **the uninitiated**. ❑ *For the uninitiated, Western Swing is a fusion of jazz, rhythm & blues, rock & roll and country music.* N-PLURAL: the N
♦ **Uninitiated** is also an adjective. ❑ *For those uninitiated in scientific ocean drilling, the previous record was a little over 4 km.* ADJ

**un|in|jured** /ʌnɪndʒəʳd/ If someone is **uninjured** after an accident or attack, they are not hurt, even though you would expect them to be. ❑ *The man's wife, a passenger in the van, was uninjured in the accident.* ADJ: ADJ after v, v-link ADJ = unhurt

**un|in|spired** /ʌnɪnspaɪəʳd/ If you describe something or someone as **uninspired**, you are criticizing them because they do not seem to have any original or exciting qualities. ❑ *The script was singularly uninspired... Food in the dining car was adequate, if uninspired.* ADJ [disapproval] ≠ inspired

**un|in|spir|ing** /ʌnɪnspaɪərɪŋ/ If you describe something or someone as **uninspiring**, you are criticizing them because they have no special or exciting qualities, and make you feel bored. ❑ *The series of speeches on the economy was uninspiring and a rehash of old subjects... The house had a tiny kitchen with an uninspiring view.* ADJ [disapproval] ≠ inspiring

**un|in|stall** /ʌnɪnstɔːl/ **(uninstalls, uninstalling, uninstalled)** If you **uninstall** a computer program, you remove it permanently from your computer. [COMPUTING] ❑ *If you don't like the program, just uninstall it and forget it.* VERB V n

**un|in|tel|li|gent** /ʌnɪntelɪdʒənt/ If you describe a person as **unintelligent**, you mean that they are stupid, or do not show any sensible ideas or thoughts. ❑ *He believes him to be a weak and unintelligent man... He certainly was not unintelligent.* ADJ ≠ intelligent

**un|in|tel|li|gible** /ʌnɪntelɪdʒɪbəl/ **Unintelligible** language is impossible to understand, for example because it is not written or pronounced clearly, or because its meaning is confused or complicated. ❑ *He muttered something unintelligible. ...the unintelligible phrases and images of his earlier poems.* ADJ = incomprehensible

**un|in|tend|ed** /ʌnɪntendɪd/ **Unintended** results were not planned to happen, although they happened. ❑ *...the unintended consequences of human action. ...unintended pregnancies.* ADJ ≠ intended

**un|in|ten|tion|al** /ʌnɪntenʃənəl/ Something that is **unintentional** is not done deliberately, but happens by accident. ❑ *Perhaps he had slightly misled them, but it was quite unintentional... There are moments of unintentional humour.* ADJ = inadvertent
♦ **un|in|ten|tion|al|ly** *...an overblown and unintentionally funny adaptation of 'Dracula'. ...a scientist who unintentionally absorbed a small quantity of the mind-altering drug through the skin on his fingers.* ADV: ADV adj, ADV with v

**un|in|ter|est|ed** /ʌnɪntrəstɪd/ If you are **uninterested in** something or someone, you do not want to know any more about them, because you think they have no special or exciting qualities. ❑ *I was so uninterested in the result that I didn't even bother to look at it. ...unhelpful and uninterested shop staff.* ADJ: usu v-link ADJ, oft ADJ in n/-ing

**un|in|ter|est|ing** /ʌnɪntrəstɪŋ/ If you describe something or someone as **uninteresting**, you mean they have no special or exciting qualities. ❑ *Their media has earned the reputation for being rather dull and uninteresting.* ADJ = boring, dull

**un|in|ter|rupt|ed** /ʌnɪntərʌptɪd/ [1] If something is **uninterrupted**, it is continuous and has no breaks or interruptions in it. ❑ *This enables the healing process to continue uninterrupted. ...five years of rapid and uninterrupted growth.* ADJ: ADJ after v, v-link ADJ, ADJ n [2] An **uninterrupted** view of something is a clear view of it, without any obstacles in the way. ❑ *Diners can enjoy an uninterrupted view of the garden.* ADJ: usu ADJ n

**un|in|vit|ed** /ʌnɪnvaɪtɪd/ If someone does something or goes somewhere **uninvited**, they do it or go there without being asked, often when their action or presence is not wanted. ❑ *He came uninvited to one of Stein's parties. ...a hundred invited guests and many more who were uninvited. ...an uninvited question from a reporter.* ADJ: ADJ after v, v-link ADJ, ADJ n ≠ invited

**un|ion** /juːnjən/ **(unions)** ◆◆◆ [1] A **union** is a workers' organization which represents its members and which aims to improve things such as their working conditions and pay. ❑ *I feel that women in all types of employment can benefit from joining a union. ...union officials.* N-COUNT = trade union [2] When the **union** of two or more things occurs, they are joined together and become one thing. ❑ *In 1918 the Romanian majority in this former tsarist province voted for union with Romania.* N-UNCOUNT: oft N with/of n [3] When two or more things, for example countries or organizations, have been joined together to form one thing, you can refer to them as a **union**. ❑ *Tanzania is a union of the states of Tanganyika and Zanzibar. ...the question of which countries should join the currency union.* N-SING: usu with supp, oft N of pl-n [4] **Union** is used in the name of some clubs, societies, and organizations. ❑ *The naming of stars is at the discretion of the International Astronomical Union.* N-IN-NAMES

**un|ion|ism** /juːnjənɪzəm/ **Unionism** is any set of political principles based on the idea that two or more political or national units should be joined or remain together, for example that Northern Ireland should remain part of the United Kingdom. ♦ **un|ion|ist** **(unionists)** ❑ *...traditional unionists fearful of home rule.* N-UNCOUNT N-COUNT

**un|ioni|za|tion** /juːnjənaɪzeɪʃən/

☑ in BRIT, also use **unionisation**

The **unionization** of workers or industries is the process of workers becoming members of trade unions. ❑ *Increasing unionization led to demands for higher wages and shorter hours.* N-UNCOUNT

**un|ion|ized** /juːnjənaɪzd/

☑ in BRIT, also use **unionised**

**Unionized** workers belong to trade unions. If a company or place is **unionized**, most of the workers there belong to trade unions. ❑ *The company is unionized.* ADJ

**Un|ion Jack** **(Union Jacks)** **The Union Jack** is the national flag of the United Kingdom. It consists of a blue background with red and white crosses on it. N-COUNT: usu sing, oft the N

**un|ion suit** **(union suits)** A **union suit** is a piece of underwear, worn by men or boys, that covers the body and legs. [AM] N-COUNT

**unique** /juːniːk/ ◆◇◇ [1] Something that is **unique** is the only one of its kind. ❑ *Each person's signature is unique... The area has its own unique language, Catalan.* ADJ ♦ **unique|ly** *Because of the extreme cold, the Antarctic is a uniquely fragile environment... Uniquely among the great world religions, Buddhism is rooted only in the universal experience of suffering known to all human beings.* ADV: ADV group, ADV with v ♦ **unique|ness** *Each time I returned I was struck by the uniqueness of Australia and its people.* N-UNCOUNT [2] You can use **unique** to describe things that you admire because they are very unusual and special. ❑ *Brett's vocals are just unique... Kauffman was a woman of unique talent and determination.* ADJ [approval] ♦ **unique|ly** *...people who consider themselves uniquely qualified to be president of the United States.* ADV: ADV group, ADV with v [3] If something is **unique to** one thing, person, group, or place, it concerns or belongs only to that thing, person, group, or place. ❑ *No one knows for sure why adolescence is unique to* ADJ: v-link ADJ to n *humans... This interesting and charming creature is unique to Borneo.* ♦ **unique|ly** *The problem isn't uniquely American.* ADV: ADV adj

**uni|sex** /juːnɪseks/ **Unisex** is used to describe things, usually clothes or places, which are designed for use by both men and women rather than by only one sex. ❑ *...the unisex hair salon.* ADJ

**uni|son** /juːnɪsən, -zən/ [1] If two or more people do something **in unison**, they do it together at the same time. ❑ *The students gave him a rapturous welcome, chanting in unison: 'We want the king!'... Michael and the landlady nodded in unison.* PHRASE: PHR after v [2] If people or organizations act **in unison**, they act the same way because they agree with each other or because they want to achieve the same aims. ❑ *The international community is ready to work in unison against him.* PHRASE: PHR after v

**unit** /juːnɪt/ **(units)** [1] If you consider something as a **unit**, you consider it as a single, complete thing. ❑ *Agriculture was based in the past on the family as a unit.* ◆◆◇ N-COUNT [2] A **unit** is a group of people who work together at a specific job, often in a particular place. ❑ *...the health services research unit.* N-COUNT [3] A **unit** is a group within an armed force or police force, whose members fight or work together or carry out a particular task. ❑ *One secret military unit tried to contaminate the drinking water of the refugees... Two small Marine units have been trapped inside the city for the last 36 hours.* N-COUNT: oft supp N [4] A **unit** is a small machine which has a particular function, often part of a larger machine. ❑ *The unit plugs into any TV set.* N-COUNT [5] A **unit** of measurement is a fixed standard quantity, length, or weight that is used for measuring things. The litre, the centimetre, and the ounce are all units. N-COUNT [6] A **unit** is one of the parts that a textbook is divided into. N-COUNT = module

**uni|tary** /juːnɪtri, AM -teri/ A **unitary** country or organization is one in which two or more areas or groups have joined together, have the same aims, and are controlled by a single government. ❑ *...a call for the creation of a single unitary state.* ADJ: ADJ n

**unit cost** **(unit costs)** **Unit cost** is the amount of money that it costs a company to produce one article. [BUSINESS] ❑ *They aim to reduce unit costs through extra sales.* N-COUNT

**unite** /juːnaɪt/ **(unites, uniting, united)** If a group of people or things **unite** or if something **unites** them, they join together and act as a group. ❑ *The two parties have been trying to unite since the New Year... The vast majority of nations have agreed to unite their efforts to bring peace.* VERB V V n

**unit|ed** /juːnaɪtɪd/ [1] When people are **united** about something, they agree about it and act together. ❑ *Every party is united on the need for parliamentary democracy... A united effort is always more effective than an isolated complaint.* ◆◇◇ ADJ [2] **United** is used to describe a country which has been formed from two or more states or countries. ❑ *...the first elections held in a united Germany for 58 years.* ADJ [3] **United** is used in the names of countries which are made up from several states or smaller countries. ❑ *...the United States of America.* ADJ: ADJ n, in names

**Unit|ed King|dom** **The United Kingdom** is the official name for the country consisting of Great Britain and Northern Ireland. N-PROPER: the N

**Unit|ed Na|tions** **The United Nations** is an organization which most countries belong to. Its role is to encourage international peace, cooperation, and friendship. ◆◆◇ N-PROPER: the N

**unit sales** **Unit sales** refers to the number of individual items that a company sells. [BUSINESS] ❑ *Unit sales of T-shirts increased 6%.* N-PLURAL

**unit trust** **(unit trusts)** A **unit trust** is an organization which invests money in many different types of business and which offers units for sale to the public as an investment. You can also refer to an investment of this type as a **unit trust**. [BRIT, BUSINESS] N-COUNT

✔ in AM, use **mutual fund**

**unity** /juːnɪti/ [1] **Unity** is the state of different areas or groups being joined together to form a single country or organization. ❑ *Senior politicians met today to discuss the future of European economic unity. ...German unity.* ◆◇◇ N-UNCOUNT: oft adj N = union [2] When there is **unity**, people are in agreement and act together for a particular purpose. ❑ *...a renewed unity of purpose... Speakers at the rally mouthed sentiments of unity... The choice was meant to create an impression of party unity.* N-UNCOUNT

**Univ** also **Univ.** **Univ** is a written abbreviation for **University** which is used especially in the names of universities. ❑ *...the Wharton School, Univ. of Pennsylvania.*

**uni|ver|sal** /juːnɪvɜːʳsəl/ **(universals)** [1] Something that is **universal** relates to everyone in the world or everyone in a particular group or society. ❑ *The insurance industry has produced its own proposals for universal health care... The desire to look attractive is universal.* ♦ **uni|ver|sal|ity** /juːnɪvɜːʳsælɪti/ *I have been amazed at the universality of all of our experiences, whatever our origins, sex or age.* ADJ: usu ADJ n; N-UNCOUNT: oft N of n [2] Something that is **universal** affects or relates to every part of the world or the universe. ❑ *...universal diseases.* ADJ [3] A **universal** is a principle that applies in all cases or a characteristic that is present in all members of a particular class. ❑ *There are no economic universals.* N-COUNT

**uni|ver|sal bank** **(universal banks)** A **universal bank** is a bank that offers both banking and stockbroking services to its clients. [BUSINESS] ❑ *...universal banks offering a wide range of services.* N-COUNT

**uni|ver|sal|ly** /juːnɪvɜːʳsəli/ [1] If something is **universally** believed or accepted, it is believed or accepted by everyone with no disagreement. ❑ *...a universally accepted point of view... The scale of the problem is now universally recognised.* ADV: usu ADV -ed/adj [2] If something is **universally** true, it is true everywhere in the world or in all situations. ❑ *The disadvantage is that it is not universally available.* ADV: usu ADV adj, also ADV with v, be ADV n

**uni|verse** /juːnɪvɜːʳs/ **(universes)** [1] **The universe** is the whole of space and all the stars, planets, and other forms of matter and energy in it. ❑ *Early astronomers thought that our planet was the centre of the universe.* ◆◇◇ N-COUNT: usu the N in sing [2] If you talk about someone's **universe**, you are referring to the whole of their experience or an important part of it. ❑ *Good writers suck in what they see of the world, re-creating their own universe on the page.* N-COUNT: usu sing, oft with poss = world

**uni|ver|sity** /juːnɪvɜːʳsɪti/ **(universities)** A **university** is an institution where students study for degrees and where academic research is done. ❑ *Patrick is now at London University... They want their daughter to go to university, but they are also keen that she get a summer job... The university refused to let Dick Gregory speak on campus.* ◆◆◆ N-VAR; N-IN-NAMES

**un|just** /ʌndʒʌst/ If you describe an action, system, or law as **unjust**, you think that it treats a person or group badly in a way that they do not deserve. ❑ *The attack on Charles was deeply unjust... He spent 25 years campaigning against racist and unjust immigration laws.* ♦ **un|just|ly** *She was unjustly accused of stealing money and then given the sack.* ADJ = unfair; ADV: usu ADV with v

**un|jus|ti|fi|able** /ʌndʒʌstɪfaɪəbəl, ʌndʒʌstɪfaɪəbəl/ If you describe an action, especially one that harms someone, as **unjustifiable**, you mean there is no good reason for it. ❑ *Using these missiles to down civilian aircraft is simply immoral and totally unjustifiable.* ♦ **un|jus|ti|fi|ably** *The press invade people's privacy unfairly and unjustifiably every day.* ADJ ≠ justifiable; ADV ≠ justifiably

**un|jus|ti|fied** /ʌndʒʌstɪfaɪd/ If you describe a belief or action as **unjustified**, you think that there is no good reason for having it or doing it. ❑ *Your report last week was unfair. It was based upon wholly unfounded and totally unjustified allegations... The commission concluded that the police action was unjustified.* ADJ

**un|kempt** /ʌnkempt/ If you describe something or someone as **unkempt**, you mean that ADJ they are untidy, and not looked after carefully or kept neat. ❑ *His hair was unkempt and filthy. ...the unkempt grass. ...an unkempt old man.*

**un|kind** /ʌnkaɪnd/ **(unkinder, unkindest)** 1 If someone is **unkind**, they behave in an unpleasant, unfriendly, or slightly cruel way. You can also describe someone's words or actions as **unkind**. ❑ *All last summer he'd been unkind to her... No one has an unkind word to say about him... Without wishing to be unkind, she's not the most interesting company.* ADJ: oft ADJ *to* n, *it* v-link ADJ to-inf ≠*kind* ♦ **un|kind|ly** *Several viewers commented unkindly on her costumes... 'He's a bit of an eccentric old fatty,' Thomas thought, unkindly.* ADV: ADV with v, ADV with cl ≠*kindly* ♦ **un|kind|ness** *He realized the unkindness of the remark and immediately regretted having hurt her with it.* N-UNCOUNT ≠*kindness* 2 If you describe something bad that happens to someone as **unkind**, you mean that they do not deserve it. [WRITTEN] ❑ *The weather was unkind to those pipers who played in the morning. ...a shared conviction that some unkind fate or chance is keeping them apart.* ADJ: oft ADJ *to* n ≠*kind*

**un|know|able** /ʌnnoʊəbᵊl/ If you describe something as **unknowable**, you mean that it is impossible for human beings to know anything about it. [WRITTEN] ❑ *Any investment in shares is a bet on an unknowable future flow of profits... The specific impact of the greenhouse effect is unknowable.* ADJ

**un|know|ing** /ʌnnoʊɪŋ/ If you describe a person as **unknowing**, you mean that they are not aware of what is happening or of what they are doing. ❑ *Some governments have been victims and perhaps unknowing accomplices in the bank's activities.* ADJ: usu ADJ n = *unwitting*

**un|know|ing|ly** /ʌnnoʊɪŋli/ If someone does something **unknowingly**, they do it without being aware of it. ❑ *...if people unknowingly move into more contaminated areas of the river. ...the extent to which the workforce colludes knowingly or unknowingly with such criminal activity.* ADV: ADV with v, ADV with cl ≠*knowingly*

**un|known** /ʌnnoʊn/ **(unknowns)** ◆◇◇ 1 If something is **unknown** to you, you have no knowledge of it. ❑ *An unknown number of demonstrators were arrested... How did you expect us to proceed on such a perilous expedition, through unknown terrain... The motive for the killing is unknown.* ADJ ♦ An **unknown** is something that is unknown. ❑ *The length of the war is one of the biggest unknowns.* N-COUNT 2 An **unknown** person is someone whose name you do not know or whose character you do not know anything about. ❑ *Unknown thieves had forced their way into the apartment... I could not understand how someone with so many awards could be unknown to me.* ADJ 3 An **unknown** person is not famous or publicly recognized. ❑ *He was an unknown writer. ...a popular environment where both established and unknown artists can meet, talk and drink.* ADJ ♦ An **unknown** is a person who is unknown. ❑ *Within a short space of time a group of complete unknowns had established a wholly original form of humour.* N-COUNT 4 If you say that a particular problem or situation is **unknown**, you mean that it never occurs. ❑ *A hundred years ago coronary heart disease was virtually unknown in Europe and America.* ADJ: usu v-link ADJ = *unheard of* 5 **The unknown** refers generally to things or places that people do not know about or understand. ❑ *Ignorance of people brings fear, fear of the unknown.* N-SING: *the* N

**un|law|ful** /ʌnlɔːfʊl/ If something is **unlawful**, the law does not allow you to do it. [FORMAL] ❑ *...employees who believe their dismissal was unlawful... A pushed-in window indicated unlawful entry.* ADJ = *illegal* ≠*lawful* ♦ **un|law|ful|ly** *...the councils' assertion that the government acted unlawfully in imposing the restrictions.* ADV: ADV with v

**un|law|ful kill|ing** **(unlawful killings)** **Unlawful killing** is used to refer to crimes which involve one person killing another. [LEGAL] N-VAR

**un|lead|ed** /ʌnledɪd/ **Unleaded** fuel contains a smaller amount of lead than most fuels so that it produces fewer harmful substances when it is burned. ❑ *The new Metro is designed to run on unleaded fuel.* ADJ ♦ **Unleaded** is also a noun. ❑ *All its V8 engines will run happily on unleaded.* N-UNCOUNT

**un|learn** /ʌnlɜːʳn/ **(unlearns, unlearning, unlearned)**

✔ in BRIT, also use **unlearnt**

If you **unlearn** something that you have learned, you try to forget it or ignore it, often because it is wrong or it is having a bad influence on you. ❑ *They learn new roles and unlearn old ones... Before you know it, you will have unlearned the debt habit.* VERB ≠*learn* V n V n

**un|leash** /ʌnliːʃ/ **(unleashes, unleashing, unleashed)** If you say that someone or something **unleashes** a powerful force, feeling, activity, or group, you mean that they suddenly start it or send it somewhere. ❑ *Then he unleashed his own, unstoppable, attack... The officers were still reluctant to unleash their troops in pursuit of a defeated enemy.* VERB V n V n

**un|leav|ened** /ʌnlevᵊnd/ **Unleavened** bread or dough is made without any yeast. ADJ: usu ADJ n

**un|less** /ʌnles/ ◆◆◇ You use **unless** to introduce the only circumstances in which an event you are mentioning will not take place or in which a statement you are making is not true. ❑ *Unless you are trying to lose weight to please yourself, it's going to be tough to keep your motivation level high... We cannot understand disease unless we understand the person who has the disease.* CONJ

**un|like** /ʌnlaɪk/ ◆◇◇ 1 If one thing is **unlike** another thing, the two things have different qualities or characteristics from each other. ❑ *This was a foreign country, so unlike San Jose... She was unlike him in every way except for her coal black eyes.* PREP ≠*like* 2 You can use **unlike** to contrast two people, things, or situations, and show how they are different. ❑ *Unlike aerobics, walking entails no expensive fees for classes or clubs.* PREP ≠*like* 3 If you describe something that a particular person has done as being **unlike** them, you mean that you are surprised by it because it is not typical of their character or normal behaviour. ❑ *It was so unlike him to say something like that, with such intensity, that I was astonished... 'We'll all be arrested!' Thomas yelled, which was most unlike him.* PREP ≠*like*

**un|like|ly** /ʌnlaɪkli/ **(unlikeliest)** ◆◆◇ If you say that something is **unlikely** to happen or **unlikely** to be true, you believe that it will not happen or that it is not true, although you are not completely sure. ❑ *A military coup seems unlikely... As with many technological revolutions, you are unlikely to be aware of it... It's now unlikely that future parliaments will bring back the death penalty... In the unlikely event of anybody phoning, could you just scribble a message down?* ADJ: usu v-link ADJ, oft ADJ to-inf, *it* v-link ADJ that ≠*likely*

**un|lim|it|ed** /ʌnlɪmɪtɪd/ If there is an **unlimited** quantity of something, you can have as much or as many of that thing as you want. ❑ *An unlimited number of copies can still be made from the original... You'll also have unlimited access to the swimming pool.* ADJ ≠*limited*

**un|list|ed** /ʌnlɪstɪd/ 1 If a person or their telephone number is **unlisted**, the number is not listed in the telephone book, and the telephone company will refuse to give it to people who ask for it. [mainly AM] ADJ

✔ in BRIT, usually use **ex-directory**

2 An **unlisted** company or **unlisted** stock is not listed officially on a stock exchange. [BUSINESS] ❑ *Its shares are traded on the Unlisted Securities Market.* ADJ

**un|lis|ten|able** /ʌnlɪsᵊnəbᵊl/ If you describe music as **unlistenable**, you mean that is very poor in quality. ❑ *The early stuff is mostly unlistenable.* ADJ disapproval

**un|lit** /ʌnlɪt/ 1 An **unlit** fire or cigarette has not been made to start burning. ADJ 2 An **unlit** street or building is dark because there are no lights switched on in it. ADJ

**un|load** /ʌnloʊd/ **(unloads, unloading, unloaded)** 1 If you **unload** goods from a vehicle, or VERB you **unload** a vehicle, you remove the goods from the vehicle, usually after they have been transported from one place to another. ❑ *Unload everything from the boat and clean it thoroughly...* V n *from* n *They were reported to be unloading trucks filled with looted furniture.* V n [2] If someone **unloads** investments, they get rid of them or sell them. [BUSINESS] VERB ❑ *Since March, he has unloaded 1.3 million shares.* V n

**un|lock** /ʌnlɒk/ **(unlocks, unlocking, unlocked)** [1] If you **unlock** something such as a door, a room, or a container that has a lock, you open it using a key. VERB ≠ lock ❑ *He unlocked the car and threw the coat on to the back seat.* V n [2] If you **unlock** the potential or the secrets of something or someone, you release them. VERB ❑ *Education and training is the key that will unlock our nation's potential.* V n

**un|lov|able** /ʌnlʌvəbəl/ If someone is **unlovable**, they are not likely to be loved by anyone, because they do not have any attractive qualities. ADJ ≠ lovable

**un|loved** /ʌnlʌvd/ If someone feels **unloved**, they feel that nobody loves them. ADJ ≠ loved ❑ *I think she feels desperately wounded and unloved at the moment. ...a lonely, unloved child.*

**un|love|ly** /ʌnlʌvli/ If you describe something as **unlovely**, you mean that it is unattractive or unpleasant in some way. [WRITTEN] ADJ = ugly ❑ *She found a small, inexpensive motel on the outskirts of the town; it was barren and unlovely.*

**un|lov|ing** /ʌnlʌvɪŋ/ If you describe a person as **unloving**, you believe that they do not love, or show love to, the people they ought to love. ADJ ≠ loving ❑ *The overworked, overextended parent may be seen as unloving, but may simply be exhausted.*

**un|lucki|ly** /ʌnlʌkɪli/ You use **unluckily** as a comment on something bad or unpleasant that happens to someone, in order to suggest sympathy for them or that it was not their fault. ADV: ADV with cl, ADV with v, oft ADV *for* n = unfortunately ≠ luckily ❑ *Unluckily for him, the fraud officers were watching this flight too.*

**un|lucky** /ʌnlʌki/ **(unluckier, unluckiest)** [1] If someone is **unlucky**, they have bad luck. ADJ: oft ADJ to-inf = unfortunate ≠ lucky ❑ *Owen was unlucky not to score on two occasions... Others were unlucky victims of falling debris.* [2] You can use **unlucky** to describe unpleasant things which happen to someone, especially when you feel that the person does not deserve them. ADJ ≠ lucky ❑ *...Argentina's unlucky defeat by Ireland.* [3] **Unlucky** is used to describe something that is thought to cause bad luck. ADJ ≠ lucky ❑ *Some people think it is unlucky to look at a new moon through glass.*

**un|made** /ʌnmeɪd/ An **unmade** bed has not had the sheets and covers neatly arranged after it was last slept in. ADJ

**un|man|age|able** /ʌnmænɪdʒəbəl/ [1] If you describe something as **unmanageable**, you mean that it is difficult to use, deal with, or control. ADJ ❑ *People were visiting the house every day, sometimes in unmanageable numbers. ...her freckles and unmanageable hair.* [2] If you describe someone, especially a young person, as **unmanageable**, you mean that they behave in an unacceptable way and are difficult to control. ADJ = uncontrollable ❑ *The signs are that indulged children tend to become unmanageable when they reach their teens.*

**un|man|ly** /ʌnmænli/ If you describe a boy's or man's behaviour as **unmanly**, you are critical of the fact that they are behaving in a way that you think is inappropriate for a man. ADJ: usu v-link ADJ [disapproval] = effeminate ❑ *Your partner can feel the loss as acutely as you, but may feel that it is unmanly to cry.*

**un|manned** /ʌnmænd/ [1] **Unmanned** vehicles such as spacecraft do not have any people in them and operate automatically or are controlled from a distance. ADJ: usu ADJ n ❑ *...a special unmanned spacecraft. ...unmanned rockets.* [2] If a place is **unmanned**, there is nobody working there. ADJ ❑ *Unmanned post offices meant millions of letters went unsorted.*

**un|marked** /ʌnmɑːʳkt/ [1] Something that is **unmarked** has no marks on it. ADJ: usu v-link ADJ ❑ *Her shoes are still white and unmarked.* [2] Something that is **unmarked** has no marking on it which identifies what it is or whose it is. ADJ: usu ADJ n ❑ *He had seen them come out and get into the unmarked police car... He lies in an unmarked grave at Elmton.* [3] In a sport such as football, hockey, or basketball, if a player is **unmarked**, there are no players from the opposing team who are watching them in order to challenge them when they have control of the ball. [BRIT] ADJ: usu v-link ADJ, also ADJ after v ❑ *Sheringham was unmarked as he met Anderton's free kick and headed in after nine minutes.*

**un|mar|ried** /ʌnmærid/ Someone who is **unmarried** is not married. ADJ ❑ *They refused to rent an apartment to an unmarried couple.*

**un|mask** /ʌnmɑːsk, -mæsk/ **(unmasks, unmasking, unmasked)** If you **unmask** someone or something bad, you show or make known their true nature or character, when they had previously been thought to be good. VERB = expose ❑ *Elliott unmasked and confronted the master spy and traitor Kim Philby.* V n

**un|matched** /ʌnmætʃt/ If you describe something as **unmatched**, you are emphasizing that it is better or greater than all other things of the same kind. ADJ [emphasis] = unrivalled ❑ *...a landscape of unmatched beauty... Brian's old-fashioned cuisine was unmatched for flavour.*

**un|men|tion|able** /ʌnmenʃənəbəl/ If you describe something as **unmentionable**, you mean that it is too embarrassing or unpleasant to talk about. ADJ ❑ *Has he got some unmentionable disease?*

**un|mer|ci|ful|ly** /ʌnmɜːʳsɪfʊli/ If you do something **unmercifully**, you do it a lot, showing no pity. ADV: usu ADV with v, also ADV adj = mercilessly ❑ *Uncle Sebastian used to tease Mother and Daddy unmercifully that all they could produce was girls.*

**un|met** /ʌnmet/ **Unmet** needs or demands are not satisfied. ADJ: ADJ n, v-link ADJ, ADJ after v ❑ *...the unmet demand for quality family planning services... This need routinely goes unmet.*

**un|me|tered** /ʌnmiːtəʳd/ An **unmetered** service for something such as water supply or telephone access is one that allows you to use as much as you want for a basic cost, rather than paying for the amount you use. ADJ ❑ *Clients are not charged by the minute but given unmetered access to the Internet for a fixed fee.*

**un|miss|able** /ʌnmɪsəbəl/ If you say that something such as an event or a film is **unmissable**, you are emphasizing that it is so good that everyone should try to go to it or see it. [BRIT, INFORMAL] ADJ [emphasis] ❑ *His new show is unmissable.*

**un|mis|tak|able** /ʌnmɪsteɪkəbəl/ also **unmistakeable.** If you describe something as **unmistakable**, you mean that it is so obvious that it cannot be mistaken for anything else. ADJ ❑ *He didn't give his name, but the voice was unmistakable. ...the unmistakable smell of marijuana drifted down.* ♦ **un|mis|tak|ably** /ʌnmɪsteɪkəbli/ *It's still unmistakably a Minnelli movie... She's unmistakably Scandinavian.* ADV: usu ADV group, also ADV with v

**un|miti|gat|ed** /ʌnmɪtɪgeɪtɪd/ You use **unmitigated** to emphasize that a bad situation or quality is totally bad. ADJ: ADJ n [emphasis] = absolute, utter ❑ *Last year's cotton crop was an unmitigated disaster... She leads a life of unmitigated misery.*

**un|mo|lest|ed** /ʌnməlestɪd/ If someone does something **unmolested**, they do it without being stopped or interfered with. ADJ: usu ADJ after v, also v-link ADJ, ADJ n ❑ *Like many fugitives, he lived in Argentina unmolested for many years... We now have a community where kids and adults can go to the park unmolested.*

**un|moved** /ʌnmuːvd/ If you are **unmoved by** something, you are not emotionally affected by it. ADJ: v-link ADJ ❑ *Mr Bird remained unmoved by the corruption allegations... His face was unmoved, but on his lips there was a trace of displeasure.*

**un|mu|si|cal** /ʌnmjuːzɪkᵊl/ 1 An **unmusical** sound is unpleasant to listen to. ❑ *Lainey had a terrible voice, unmusical and sharp.* — ADJ
2 An **unmusical** person cannot play or appreciate music. ❑ *They're completely unmusical.* — ADJ

**un|named** /ʌnneɪmd/ 1 **Unnamed** people or things are talked about but their names are not mentioned. ❑ *An unnamed man collapsed and died while he was walking near Dundonald... The cash comes from an unnamed source.* — ADJ: usu ADJ n
2 **Unnamed** things have not been given a name. ❑ *...unnamed comets and asteroids.* — ADJ: usu ADJ n

**un|natu|ral** /ʌnnætʃərᵊl/ 1 If you describe something as **unnatural**, you mean that it is strange and often frightening, because it is different from what you normally expect. ❑ *The aircraft rose with unnatural speed on take-off... The altered landscape looks unnatural and weird.* — ADJ
♦ **un|natu|ral|ly** *The house was unnaturally silent. ...unnaturally cold conditions.* — ADV: ADV adj
2 Behaviour that is **unnatural** seems artificial and not normal or genuine. ❑ *She gave him a bright, determined smile which seemed unnatural.* — ADJ: usu v-link ADJ = false
♦ **un|natu|ral|ly** *Try to avoid shouting or speaking unnaturally.* — ADV: ADV with v

**un|natu|ral|ly** /ʌnnætʃərəli/ You can use **not unnaturally** to indicate that the situation you are describing is exactly as you would expect in the circumstances. ❑ *It was a question that Roy not unnaturally found impossible to answer.* → See also **unnatural**. — PHRASE: PHR with cl

**un|nec|es|sary** /ʌnnesəsri, AM -seri/ If you describe something as **unnecessary**, you mean that it is not needed or does not have to be done, and is undesirable. ❑ *The slaughter of whales is unnecessary and inhuman... He accused Diana of making an unnecessary fuss.* — ADJ = needless ≠necessary
♦ **un|nec|es|sari|ly** /ʌnnesəserɪli/ *I didn't want to upset my husband or my daughter unnecessarily... A bad keyboard can make life unnecessarily difficult.* — ADV: ADV with v, ADV adj = needlessly

**un|nerve** /ʌnnɜːʳv/ (**unnerves, unnerving, unnerved**) If you say that something **unnerves** you, you mean that it worries or troubles you. ❑ *The news about Dermot had unnerved me.* — VERB V n

**un|nerv|ing** /ʌnnɜːʳvɪŋ/ If you describe something as **unnerving**, you mean that it makes you feel worried or uncomfortable. ❑ *It is very unnerving to find out that someone you see every day is carrying a potentially deadly virus.* — ADJ = disconcerting

**un|no|ticed** /ʌnnoʊtɪst/ If something happens or passes **unnoticed**, it is not seen or noticed by anyone. ❑ *I tried to slip up the stairs unnoticed... Her forty-fourth birthday had just passed, unnoticed by all but herself.* — ADJ: usu ADJ after v, also v-link ADJ, ADJ n

**un|ob|served** /ʌnəbzɜːʳvd/ If you do something **unobserved**, you do it without being seen by other people. ❑ *Looking round to make sure he was unobserved, he slipped through the door... John had been sitting, unobserved, in the darkness.* — ADJ: v-link ADJ, ADJ after v, ADJ n = unseen

**un|ob|tain|able** /ʌnəbteɪnəbᵊl/ If something or someone is **unobtainable**, you cannot get them. ❑ *Fish was unobtainable in certain sections of Tokyo.* — ADJ ≠available

**un|ob|tru|sive** /ʌnəbtruːsɪv/ If you describe something or someone as **unobtrusive**, you mean that they are not easily noticed or do not draw attention to themselves. [FORMAL] ❑ *The coffee-table is glass, to be as unobtrusive as possible.* — ADJ ≠conspicuous
♦ **un|ob|tru|sive|ly** *They slipped away unobtrusively.* — ADV: usu ADV with v

**un|oc|cu|pied** /ʌnɒkjʊpaɪd/ If a building is **unoccupied**, there is nobody in it. ❑ *The house was unoccupied at the time of the explosion... The fire broke out in two unoccupied cabins.* — ADJ: v-link ADJ, ADJ n, ADJ after v

**un|of|fi|cial** /ʌnəfɪʃᵊl/ An **unofficial** action or statement is not organized or approved by a person or group in authority. ❑ *Staff voted to continue an unofficial strike in support of seven colleagues who were dismissed last week... Official reports put the death toll at under one hundred, but unofficial estimates speak of at least two hundred dead.* — ADJ: usu ADJ n ≠official
♦ **un|of|fi|cial|ly** *Some workers are legally employed, but the majority work unofficially with neither health nor wage security.* — ADV: usu ADV with v, also ADV with cl

**un|opened** /ʌnoʊpənd/ If something is **unopened**, it has not been opened yet. ❑ *...unopened bottles of olive oil... The letter lay unopened in the travel firm's pigeonhole... Catherine put all the envelopes aside unopened.* — ADJ: ADJ n, v-link ADJ, ADJ after v

**un|op|posed** /ʌnəpoʊzd/ In something such as an election or a war, if someone is **unopposed**, there are no opponents competing or fighting against them. ❑ *The council re-elected him unopposed as party leader.* — ADJ: usu ADJ after v, also v-link ADJ, ADJ n

**un|ortho|dox** /ʌnɔːʳθədɒks/ 1 If you describe someone's behaviour, beliefs, or customs as **unorthodox**, you mean that they are different from what is generally accepted. ❑ *She spent an unorthodox girlhood travelling with her father throughout Europe... His methods were unorthodox, and his lifestyle eccentric.* — ADJ = unconventional ≠orthodox
2 If you describe ways of doing things as **unorthodox**, you are criticizing them because they are unusual or illegal. ❑ *The charity says the journalists appear to have obtained confidential documents in an unorthodox manner.* — ADJ [disapproval] ≠orthodox

**un|pack** /ʌnpæk/ (**unpacks, unpacking, unpacked**) 1 When you **unpack** a suitcase, box, or similar container, or you **unpack** the things inside it, you take the things out of the container. ❑ *He unpacked his bag.* — VERB ≠pack V n, Also V
2 If you **unpack** an idea or problem, you analyse it and consider it in detail. ❑ *A lot of ground has been covered in unpacking the issues central to achieving this market-led strategic change.* — VERB = analyse V n

**un|paid** /ʌnpeɪd/ 1 If you do **unpaid** work or are an **unpaid** worker, you do a job without receiving any money for it. ❑ *Even unpaid work for charity is better than nothing... The unpaid volunteers do the work because they love it.* — ADJ: ADJ n ≠paid
2 **Unpaid** taxes or bills, for example, are bills or taxes which have not been paid yet. ❑ *The taxman caught up with him and demanded £17,000 in unpaid taxes... The bills remained unpaid because of a dispute over the quality of the company's work.* — ADJ = outstanding

**un|pal|at|able** /ʌnpælɪtəbᵊl/ 1 If you describe an idea as **unpalatable**, you mean that you find it unpleasant and difficult to accept. ❑ *It is an unpalatable fact that rape makes a good news story... It was only then that I began to learn the unpalatable truth about John.* — ADJ = distasteful
2 If you describe food as **unpalatable**, you mean that it is so unpleasant that you can hardly eat it. ❑ *...a lump of dry, unpalatable cheese.* — ADJ

**un|par|al|leled** /ʌnpærəleld/ If you describe something as **unparalleled**, you are emphasizing that it is, for example, bigger, better, or worse than anything else of its kind, or anything that has happened before. ❑ *Germany's unparalleled prosperity is based on wise investments... The country is facing a crisis unparalleled since the Second World War.* — ADJ: oft ADJ *since/in* n [emphasis] = unequalled

**un|par|don|able** /ʌnpɑːʳdənəbᵊl/ If you say that someone's behaviour is **unpardonable**, you mean that it is very wrong or offensive, and completely unacceptable. ❑ *...an unpardonable lack of discipline... I must ask a question you may find unpardonable.* — ADJ = unforgivable, inexcusable

**un|pick** /ʌnpɪk/ (**unpicks, unpicking, unpicked**) 1 If you **unpick** a piece of sewing, you remove the stitches from it. ❑ *You can always unpick the hems on the dungarees if you don't like them.* — VERB = undo V n
2 If someone **unpicks** a plan or policy, they disagree with it and examine it thoroughly in order to find any mistakes that they can use to defeat it. [BRIT] ❑ *A statesman who ought to know better wants to unpick last year's reform of Europe's common agricultural policy.* — VERB V n

**un|play|able** /ʌnpleɪəbᵊl/ In some sports, if you describe a player as **unplayable**, you mean that they are playing extremely well and are diffi- — ADJ cult to beat. If you describe a ball as **unplayable**, you mean that it is difficult to hit. [BRIT]

**un|pleas|ant** /ʌnplezᵊnt/ 1 If something is **unpleasant**, it gives you bad feelings, for example by making you feel upset or uncomfortable. ❑ *The symptoms can be uncomfortable, unpleasant and serious... The vacuum has an unpleasant smell... It was a very unpleasant and frightening attack.* ♦ **un|pleas|ant|ly** *The water moved darkly around the body, unpleasantly thick and brown... The smell was unpleasantly strong... My heart was hammering unpleasantly.* 2 An **unpleasant** person is very unfriendly and rude. ❑ *She thought him an unpleasant man... Don't start giving me problems otherwise I'll have to be very unpleasant indeed. ...a thoroughly unpleasant person.* ♦ **un|pleas|ant|ly** *Melissa laughed unpleasantly... The Heidlers are an unpleasantly hypocritical pair.* ♦ **un|pleas|ant|ness** *There had to be a reason for the unpleasantness some people habitually displayed.*

ADJ ≠pleasant / ADV: ADV adj, ADV with v ≠pleasantly / ADJ ≠pleasant / ADV ≠pleasantly / N-UNCOUNT

**un|plug** /ʌnplʌg/ **(unplugs, unplugging, unplugged)** If you **unplug** an electrical device or telephone, you pull a wire out of a socket so that it stops working. ❑ *I had to unplug the phone.*

VERB ≠plug in / V n

**un|plugged** /ʌnplʌgd/ If a pop group or musician performs **unplugged**, they perform without any electric instruments. [JOURNALISM] ❑ *Do you remember when everyone got a bit tired of electronic clutter and went unplugged and acoustic?*

ADJ: ADJ after v, ADJ n

**un|pol|lut|ed** /ʌnpəluːtɪd/ Something that is **unpolluted** is free from pollution.

ADJ ≠polluted

**un|popu|lar** /ʌnpɒpjʊləʳ/ If something or someone is **unpopular**, most people do not like them. ❑ *It was a painful and unpopular decision... In high school, I was very unpopular, and I did encounter a little prejudice... The Chancellor is deeply unpopular with voters.* ♦ **un|popu|lar|ity** /ʌnpɒpjʊlærɪti/ *...his unpopularity among his colleagues.*

ADJ: oft ADJ *with* n ≠popular / N-UNCOUNT: usu with poss ≠popularity

**un|prec|edent|ed** /ʌnpresɪdentɪd/ 1 If something is **unprecedented**, it has never happened before. ❑ *Such a move is rare, but not unprecedented... In 1987 the Socialists took the unprecedented step of appointing a civilian to command the force.* 2 If you describe something as **unprecedented**, you are emphasizing that it is very great in quality, amount, or scale. ❑ *Each home boasts an unprecedented level of quality throughout... The scheme has been hailed as an unprecedented success.*

ADJ / ADJ: usu ADJ n [emphasis]

**un|pre|dict|able** /ʌnprɪdɪktəbᵊl/ If you describe someone or something as **unpredictable**, you mean that you cannot tell what they are going to do or how they are going to behave. ❑ *He is utterly unpredictable. ...Britain's notoriously unpredictable weather.* ♦ **un|pre|dict|ably** *Monthly costs can rise or fall unpredictably. ...her husband's unpredictably violent behavior to others.* ♦ **un|pre|dict|abil|ity** /ʌnprɪdɪktəbɪlɪti/ *...the unpredictability of the weather.*

ADJ ≠predictable / ADV: usu ADV with v, ADV adj / N-UNCOUNT: oft with poss

**un|pre|pared** /ʌnprɪpeəʳd/ 1 If you are **unprepared for** something, you are not ready for it, and you are therefore surprised or at a disadvantage when it happens. ❑ *I was totally unprepared for the announcement on the next day... Faculty members complain that their students are unprepared to do college-level work... We were caught completely unprepared.* 2 If you are **unprepared to** do something, you are not willing to do it. ❑ *He was unprepared to co-operate, or indeed to communicate.*

ADJ: usu v-link ADJ, oft ADJ *for* n ≠prepared / ADJ: v-link ADJ to-inf ≠prepared

**un|pre|pos|sess|ing** /ʌnpriːpəzesɪŋ/ If you describe someone or something as **unprepossessing**, you mean that they look rather plain or ordinary, although they may have good or special qualities that are hidden. [FORMAL] ❑ *We found the tastiest and most imaginative paella and tapas in the most unprepossessing bars and cafés.*

ADJ

**un|pre|ten|tious** /ʌnprɪtenʃəs/ If you describe a place, person, or thing as **unpretentious**, you approve of them because they are simple in appearance or character, rather than sophisticated or luxurious. ❑ *The Tides Inn is both comfortable and unpretentious. ...good, unpretentious pop music.*

ADJ [approval]

**un|prin|ci|pled** /ʌnprɪnsɪpᵊld/ If you describe a person or their actions as **unprincipled**, you are criticizing them for their lack of moral principles and because they do things which are immoral or dishonest. ❑ *It is a market where people can be very unprincipled and unpleasant. ...the unprincipled behaviour of the prosecutor's office during the crisis.*

ADJ [disapproval] = unscrupulous ≠principled

**un|print|able** /ʌnprɪntəbᵊl/ If you describe something that someone has said or done as **unprintable**, you mean that it is so rude or shocking that you do not want to say exactly what it was. ❑ *Her reply was unprintable. ...some quite unprintable stories.*

ADJ

**un|pro|duc|tive** /ʌnprədʌktɪv/ Something that is **unproductive** does not produce any good results. ❑ *Research workers are well aware that much of their time and effort is unproductive. ...increasingly unproductive land.*

ADJ ≠productive

**un|pro|fes|sion|al** /ʌnprəfeʃənᵊl/ If you use **unprofessional** to describe someone's behaviour at work, you are criticizing them for not behaving according to the standards that are expected of a person in their profession. ❑ *What she did was very unprofessional. She left abruptly about 90 minutes into the show... He was also fined $150 for unprofessional conduct.*

ADJ [disapproval] ≠professional

**un|prof|it|able** /ʌnprɒfɪtəbᵊl/ 1 An industry, company, or product that is **unprofitable** does not make any profit or does not make enough profit. [BUSINESS] ❑ *...unprofitable state-owned industries... The newspaper is believed to have been unprofitable for at least the past decade.* 2 **Unprofitable** activities or efforts do not produce any useful or helpful results. ❑ *...an endless, unprofitable argument... The day proved frustratingly unprofitable.*

ADJ ≠profitable / ADJ = fruitless

**un|prom|is|ing** /ʌnprɒmɪsɪŋ/ If you describe something as **unpromising**, you think that it is unlikely to be successful or produce anything good in the future. ❑ *In fact, his business career had distinctly unpromising beginnings... Their land looked so unpromising that the colonists eventually gave most of it back.*

ADJ ≠promising

**un|pro|nounce|able** /ʌnprənaʊnsəbᵊl/ An **unpronounceable** word or name is too difficult to say.

ADJ

**un|pro|tect|ed** /ʌnprətektɪd/ 1 An **unprotected** person or place is not looked after or defended, and so they may be harmed or attacked. ❑ *What better target than an unprotected girl, going along that river walkway in the dark... The landing beaches would be unprotected.* 2 If something is **unprotected**, it is not covered or treated with anything, and so it may easily be damaged. ❑ *Exposure of unprotected skin to the sun carries the risk of developing skin cancer... This leaves fertile soil unprotected and prone to erosion.* 3 If two people have **unprotected** sex, they do not use a condom when they have sex.

ADJ: ADJ n, v-link ADJ, ADJ after v / ADJ: ADJ n, v-link ADJ, ADJ after v / ADJ: ADJ n

**un|prov|en** /ʌnpruːvᵊn, -proʊv-/ or **unproved** If something is **unproven**, it has not definitely been proved to be true. ❑ *There are a lot of unproven allegations flying around.*

ADJ

**un|pro|voked** /ʌnprəvoʊkt/ If someone makes an **unprovoked** attack, they attack someone who has not tried to harm them in any way.

ADJ

**un|pub|lished** /ʌnpʌblɪʃt/ An **unpublished** book, letter, or report has never been published. An unpublished writer has never had his or her work published.

ADJ

**un|pun|ished** /ʌnpʌnɪʃt/ If a criminal or crime goes **unpunished**, the criminal is not punished. ❑ *Persistent criminals who have gone unpunished by the courts have been dealt with by local people... I have been amazed at times that cruelty can go unpunished.*

ADJ: v-link ADJ, ADJ n, ADJ after v

**un|quali|fied** /ʌnkwɒlɪfaɪd/ [ADJ ≠ qualified] 1 If you are **unqualified**, you do not have any qualifications, or you do not have the right qualifications for a particular job. ❑ *She was unqualified for the job... Unqualified members of staff at the hospital were not sufficiently supervised.* 2 [ADJ: usu ADJ n, emphasis] **Unqualified** means total or unlimited. ❑ *The event was an unqualified success... Egypt has given almost unqualified backing to Washington.*

**un|ques|tion|able** /ʌnkwestʃənəbᵊl/ [ADJ, emphasis, = undoubted ≠ questionable] If you describe something as **unquestionable**, you are emphasizing that it is so obviously true or real that nobody can doubt it. ❑ *He inspires affection and respect as a man of unquestionable integrity... There is an unquestionable link between job losses and deteriorating services.* ♦ **un|ques|tion|ably** [ADV: ADV with cl/group] /ʌnkwestʃənəbli/ *They have seen the change as unquestionably beneficial to the country... He is unquestionably a star.*

**un|ques|tioned** /ʌnkwestʃənd/ [ADJ, emphasis, = unequivocal] 1 You use **unquestioned** to emphasize that something is so obvious, real, or great that nobody can doubt it or disagree with it. ❑ *His commitment has been unquestioned... The play was an immediate and unquestioned success in London.* 2 [ADJ = undisputed] If something or someone is **unquestioned**, they are accepted by everyone, without anyone doubting or disagreeing. ❑ *Stalin was the unquestioned ruler of the Soviet Union from the late 1920s until his death in 1953.* 3 [ADJ: ADJ n, emphasis, = unquestioning] If you describe someone's belief or attitude as **unquestioned**, you are emphasizing that they accept something without any doubt or disagreement. ❑ *Royalty is regarded with unquestioned reverence.*

**un|ques|tion|ing** /ʌnkwestʃənɪŋ/ [ADJ: usu ADJ n, emphasis] If you describe a person or their beliefs as **unquestioning**, you are emphasizing that they accept something without any doubt or disagreement. ❑ *Isabella had been taught unquestioning obedience... For the last 20 years, I have been an unquestioning supporter of comprehensive schools.* ♦ **un|ques|tion|ing|ly** [ADV: ADV with v] *She supported him unquestioningly.*

**un|quote** /ʌnkwoʊt/ [PHRASE] You can say **quote** before and **unquote** after a word or phrase, or **quote, unquote** before or after it, to show that you are quoting someone or that you do not believe that a word or phrase used by others is accurate. [SPOKEN] ❑ *He drowned in a boating quote 'accident' unquote.*

**un|rav|el** /ʌnrævᵊl/ **(unravels, unravelling, unravelled)**

☑ in AM, use **unraveling, unraveled**

1 [VERB V] If something such as a plan or system **unravels**, it breaks up or begins to fail. ❑ *His government began to unravel because of a banking scandal.* 2 [VERB V n, V] If you **unravel** something that is knotted, woven, or knitted, or if it **unravels**, it becomes one straight piece again or separates into its different threads. ❑ *He was good with his hands and could unravel a knot or untangle yarn that others wouldn't even attempt... The stairway carpet is so frayed it threatens to unravel.* 3 [VERB V n, V] If you **unravel** a mystery or puzzle, or if it **unravels**, it gradually becomes clearer and you can work out the answer to it. ❑ *A young mother has flown to Iceland to unravel the mystery of her husband's disappearance... Gradually, with an intelligent use of flashbacks, Yves' story unravels.*

**un|read** /ʌnred/ [ADJ: ADJ after v, ADJ n, v-link ADJ] If a book or other piece of writing is **unread**, you or other people have not read it, for example because it is boring or because you have no time. ❑ *All his unpublished writing should be destroyed unread... He caught up on months of unread periodicals.*

**un|read|able** /ʌnriːdəbᵊl/ 1 [ADJ, disapproval, = unintelligible] If you use **unreadable** to describe a book or other piece of writing, you are criticizing it because it is very boring, complicated, or difficult to understand. ❑ *For some this is the greatest novel in the world. For others it is unreadable.* 2 [ADJ: usu v-link ADJ = illegible] If a piece of writing is **unreadable**, it is impossible to read because the letters are unclear, especially because it has been damaged in some way. ❑ *...if contracts are unreadable because of the microscopic print.* 3 [ADJ = impenetrable] If someone's face or expression is **unreadable**, it is impossible to tell what they are thinking or feeling. [LITERARY] ❑ *He looked back at the woman for approval, but her face was unreadable.*

**un|real** /ʌnriːl/ 1 [ADJ: v-link ADJ = bizarre] If you say that a situation is **unreal**, you mean that it is so strange that you find it difficult to believe it is happening. ❑ *It was unreal. Like some crazy childhood nightmare... It felt so unreal to be talking about our son like this.* ♦ **un|re|al|ity** [N-UNCOUNT] /ʌnriælɪti/ *To his surprise he didn't feel too weak. Light-headed certainly, and with a sense of unreality, but able to walk.* 2 [ADJ, disapproval, = unrealistic] If you use **unreal** to describe something, you are critical of it because you think that it is not like, or not related to, things you expect to find in the real world. ❑ *...unreal financial targets... Almost all fictional detectives are unreal.*

**un|re|al|is|tic** /ʌnriəlɪstɪk/ [ADJ: oft *it* v-link ADJ to-inf ≠ realistic] If you say that someone is being **unrealistic**, you mean that they do not recognize the truth about a situation, especially about the difficulties involved in something they want to achieve. ❑ *There are many who feel that the players are being completely unrealistic in their demands... It would be unrealistic to expect such a process ever to be completed. ...their unrealistic expectations of parenthood.* ♦ **un|re|al|is|ti|cal|ly** [ADV: ADV with v, ADV adj ≠ realistically] /ʌnriəlɪstɪkli/ *Tom spoke unrealistically of getting a full-time job that paid an enormous sum. ...unrealistically high standards of expectation.*

**un|rea|son|able** /ʌnriːzənəbᵊl/ 1 [ADJ ≠ reasonable] If you say that someone is being **unreasonable**, you mean that they are behaving in a way that is not fair or sensible. ❑ *The strikers were being unreasonable in their demands, having rejected the deal two weeks ago... It was her unreasonable behaviour with a Texan playboy which broke up her marriage... It's unreasonable to expect your child to behave in a caring way if you behave selfishly.* ♦ **un|rea|son|ably** [ADV] /ʌnriːzənəbli/ *We unreasonably expect near perfect behaviour from our children.* 2 [ADJ ≠ reasonable] An **unreasonable** decision, action, price, or amount seems unfair and difficult to justify. ❑ *...unreasonable increases in the price of petrol... One in four consumers now say water prices are very unreasonable.* ♦ **un|rea|son|ably** [ADV: usu ADV adj] *The banks' charges are unreasonably high.*

**un|rea|son|ing** /ʌnriːzənɪŋ/ [ADJ: ADJ n = irrational] **Unreasoning** feelings or actions are not logical, sensible, or controlled. [LITERARY] ❑ *At this moment of success I found only an unreasoning sense of futility... Niki's voice provoked a new bout of unreasoning anger.*

**un|rec|og|niz|able** /ʌnrekəgnaɪzəbl, -naɪz-/

☑ in BRIT, also use **unrecognisable**

[ADJ: oft ADJ *to* n ≠ recognizable] If someone or something is **unrecognizable**, they have become impossible to recognize or identify, for example because they have been greatly changed or damaged. ❑ *The corpses of the prisoners were nearly unrecognizable from the number of bullet wounds they'd received... The new town would have been unrecognisable to the original inhabitants.*

**un|rec|og|nized** /ʌnrekəgnaɪzd/

☑ in BRIT, also use **unrecognised**

1 [ADJ: ADJ after v, v-link ADJ] If someone does something **unrecognized**, nobody knows or recognizes them while they do it. ❑ *He is believed to have worked unrecognised as a doorman at East End clubs.* 2 [ADJ: ADJ after v, v-link ADJ, ADJ n] If something is **unrecognized**, people are not aware of it. ❑ *There is the possibility that hypothermia can go unrecognized... There must be many vases, bowls or bottles sitting unrecognised in people's homes.* 3 [ADJ: ADJ after v, v-link ADJ, ADJ n] If you or your achievements or qualities are **unrecognized**, you have not been properly appreciated or acknowledged by other people for what you have done. ❑ *Hard work and talent so often go unrecognised and unrewarded... There really is a wealth of unrecognised*

*talent out there.* [4] An **unrecognized** meeting, agreement, or political party is not formally acknowledged as legal or valid by the authorities. ❑ *Local authorities are likely to refuse to hire facilities to unrecognised martial arts organisations.* ADJ: usu ADJ n

**un|re|con|struct|ed** /ʌnriːkənstrʌktɪd/ If you describe systems, beliefs, policies, or people as **unreconstructed**, you are critical of them because they have not changed at all, in spite of new ideas and circumstances. ❑ *...the unreconstructed racism of the official opposition... She accused him of being an unreconstructed male chauvinist.* ADJ: usu ADJ n disapproval

**un|re|cord|ed** /ʌnrɪkɔːʳdɪd/ You use **unrecorded** to describe something that has not been written down or recorded officially, especially when it should have been. ❑ *The statistics don't reveal of course unrecorded crime... Much of Poland's private industry goes unrecorded.* ADJ: ADJ n, v-link ADJ, ADJ after v

**un|re|fined** /ʌnrɪfaɪnd/ An **unrefined** food or other substance is in its natural state and has not been processed. ❑ *Unrefined carbohydrates include brown rice and other grains. ...the price of unrefined oil as it comes out of the ground.* ADJ: usu ADJ n ≠ refined

**un|re|hearsed** /ʌnrɪhɜːʳst/ **Unrehearsed** activities or performances have not been prepared, planned, or practised beforehand. ❑ *In fact, the recordings were mostly unrehearsed improvisations.* ADJ

**un|re|lat|ed** /ʌnrɪleɪtɪd/ [1] If one thing is **unrelated to** another, there is no connection between them. You can also say that two things are **unrelated**. ❑ *My line of work is entirely unrelated to politics... Two of them died from apparently unrelated causes.* ADJ: oft ADJ *to* n = unconnected ≠ related [2] If one person is **unrelated to** another, they are not members of the same family. You can also say that two people are **unrelated**. [WRITTEN] ❑ *Jimmy is adopted and thus unrelated to Beth by blood.* ADJ: oft ADJ *to* n ≠ related

**un|re|lent|ing** /ʌnrɪlentɪŋ/ [1] If you describe someone's behaviour as **unrelenting**, you mean that they are continuing to do something in a very determined way, often without caring whether they hurt or embarrass other people. ❑ *She established her authority with unrelenting thoroughness... In the face of severe opposition and unrelenting criticism, the task seemed overwhelming.* ADJ = relentless [2] If you describe something unpleasant as **unrelenting**, you mean that it continues without stopping. ❑ *...an unrelenting downpour of rain.* ADJ

**un|re|li|able** /ʌnrɪlaɪəbᵊl/ If you describe a person, machine, or method as **unreliable**, you mean that you cannot trust them. ❑ *Diplomats can be a notoriously unreliable and misleading source of information... He had an unreliable car.* ADJ ≠ reliable
♦ **un|re|li|abil|ity** /ʌnrɪlaɪəbɪlɪti/ *...his lateness and unreliability.* N-UNCOUNT

**un|re|lieved** /ʌnrɪliːvd/ If you describe something unpleasant as **unrelieved**, you mean that it is very severe and is not replaced by anything better, even for a short time. ❑ *...unrelieved misery... The sun baked down on the concrete, unrelieved by any breeze.* ADJ: oft ADJ *by* n

**un|re|mark|able** /ʌnrɪmɑːʳkəbᵊl/ If you describe someone or something as **unremarkable**, you mean that they are very ordinary, without many exciting, original, or attractive qualities. ❑ *...a tall, lean man, with an unremarkable face. ...a rather unremarkable town in North Wales.* ADJ ≠ remarkable

**un|re|marked** /ʌnrɪmɑːʳkt/ If something happens or goes **unremarked**, people say nothing about it, because they consider it normal or do not notice it. [FORMAL] ❑ *His departure, in fact, went almost unremarked... It did not pass unremarked that three-quarters of the petitions were instituted by women.* ADJ: v-link ADJ, ADJ after v, ADJ n = unnoticed

**un|re|mit|ting** /ʌnrɪmɪtɪŋ/ Something that is **unremitting** continues without stopping or becoming less intense. [FORMAL] ❑ *I was sent to boarding school, where I spent six years of unremitting misery... He watched her with unremitting attention.* ADJ: usu ADJ n
♦ **un|re|mit|ting|ly** *The weather was unremittingly awful.* ADV: usu ADV adj

**un|re|pent|ant** /ʌnrɪpentənt/ If you are **unrepentant**, you are not ashamed of your beliefs or actions. ❑ *Pamela was unrepentant about her strong language and abrasive remarks. ...unrepentant defenders of the death penalty.* ADJ

**un|rep|re|senta|tive** /ʌnreprɪzentətɪv/ If you describe a group of people as **unrepresentative**, you mean that their views are not typical of the community or society to which they belong. ❑ *The President denounced the demonstrators as unrepresentative of the Romanian people.* ADJ: oft ADJ *of* n ≠ representative

**un|rep|re|sent|ed** /ʌnreprɪzentɪd/ If you are **unrepresented** in something such as a parliament, legislature, law court, or meeting, there is nobody there speaking or acting for you, for example to give your opinions or instructions. ❑ *...groups who feel they've been officially unrecognized or unrepresented in international councils.* ADJ ≠ represented

**un|re|quit|ed** /ʌnrɪkwaɪtɪd/ If you have **unrequited** love for someone, they do not love you. [LITERARY] ❑ *...his unrequited love for a married woman.* ADJ

**un|re|served** /ʌnrɪzɜːʳvd/ An **unreserved** opinion or statement is one that expresses a feeling or opinion completely and without any doubts. ❑ *Charles displays unreserved admiration for his grandfather... Jones' lawyers are seeking an unreserved apology from the newspaper.* ADJ: usu ADJ n
♦ **un|re|serv|ed|ly** /ʌnrɪzɜːʳvɪdli/ *We apologise unreservedly for any imputation of incorrect behaviour by Mr Taylor.* ADV: ADV with v = wholeheartedly

**un|re|solved** /ʌnrɪzɒlvd/ If a problem or difficulty is **unresolved**, no satisfactory solution has been found to it. [FORMAL] ❑ *The murder remains unresolved. ...unresolved issues.* ADJ: v-link ADJ, ADJ n, ADJ after v

**un|re|spon|sive** /ʌnrɪspɒnsɪv/ [1] An **unresponsive** person does not react or pay enough attention to something, for example to an urgent situation or to people's needs. [FORMAL] ❑ *He was totally unresponsive to the pressing social and economic needs of the majority of the population. ...a cold, unresponsive man.* ADJ: oft ADJ *to* n ≠ responsive [2] If a person or their body is **unresponsive**, they do not react physically in a normal way, or do not make any movements. [FORMAL] ❑ *I found her in a coma, totally unresponsive.* ADJ

**un|rest** /ʌnrest/ If there is **unrest** in a particular place or society, people are expressing anger and dissatisfaction about something, often by demonstrating or rioting. [JOURNALISM] ❑ *The real danger is civil unrest in the east of the country... There is growing unrest among students in several major cities.* N-UNCOUNT

**un|re|strained** /ʌnrɪstreɪnd/ If you describe someone's behaviour as **unrestrained**, you mean that it is extreme or intense, for example because they are expressing their feelings strongly or loudly. ❑ *There was unrestrained joy on the faces of the people.* ADJ ≠ restrained

**un|re|strict|ed** /ʌnrɪstrɪktɪd/ [1] If an activity is **unrestricted**, you are free to do it in the way that you want, without being limited by any rules. ❑ *Freedom to pursue extra-curricular activities is totally unrestricted... The Commissioner has absolutely unrestricted access to all the files.* ADJ [2] If you have an **unrestricted** view of something, you can see it fully and clearly, because there is nothing in the way. ❑ *Nearly all seats have an unrestricted view.* ADJ

**un|re|ward|ed** /ʌnrɪwɔːʳdɪd/ You can say that someone goes **unrewarded**, or that their activities go **unrewarded**, when they do not achieve what they are trying to achieve. ❑ *The jockey rushed back from America to ride at Nottingham on Monday but went unrewarded. ...a long and unrewarded struggle.* ADJ

**un|re|ward|ing** /ʌnrɪwɔːʳdɪŋ/ If you describe an activity as **unrewarding**, you mean that it does not give you any feelings of achieve- ADJ ≠ rewarding ment or pleasure. ❑ *...dirty and unrewarding work... Listening to it in its entirety is also fairly unrewarding.*

**un|ripe** /ʌnraɪp/ **Unripe** fruit or vegetables are not yet ready to eat. ADJ ≠ *ripe*

**un|ri|valled** /ʌnraɪvəld/
in AM, use **unrivaled**

If you describe something as **unrivalled**, you are emphasizing that it is better than anything else of the same kind. ❑ *He had an unrivalled knowledge of south Arabian society, religion, law and customs... It's a team unrivalled in stature, expertise and credibility.* ADJ [emphasis] = *unequalled*

**un|roll** /ʌnroʊl/ **(unrolls, unrolling, unrolled)** If you **unroll** something such as a sheet of paper or cloth, or if it **unrolls**, it opens up and becomes flat when it was previously rolled in a cylindrical shape. ❑ *I unrolled my sleeping bag as usual... Guests bring movies on tape, and show them on the screen that unrolls from the ceiling.* VERB V n V

**un|ruf|fled** /ʌnrʌfəld/ If you describe someone as **unruffled**, you mean that they are calm and do not seem to be affected by surprising or frightening events. ADJ = *unperturbed*

**un|ru|ly** /ʌnruːli/ 1 If you describe people, especially children, as **unruly**, you mean that they behave badly and are difficult to control. ❑ *It's not good enough just to blame the unruly children. ...unruly behaviour.* ADJ 2 **Unruly** hair is difficult to keep tidy. ❑ *The man had a huge head of remarkably black, unruly hair.* ADJ: usu ADJ n

**un|safe** /ʌnseɪf/ 1 If a building, machine, activity, or area is **unsafe**, it is dangerous. ❑ *Critics claim the trucks are unsafe... She was also warned it was unsafe to run early in the morning in the neighbourhood.* ADJ = *dangerous* ≠ *safe* 2 If you are **unsafe**, you are in danger of being harmed. ❑ *In the larger neighbourhood, I felt very unsafe.* ADJ: v-link ADJ ≠ *safe* 3 If a criminal conviction is **unsafe**, it is not based on enough evidence or is based on false evidence. [BRIT, LEGAL] ❑ *An appeal court decided their convictions were unsafe.* ADJ

**un|said** /ʌnsed/ If something is **left unsaid** or **goes unsaid** in a particular situation, it is not said, although you might have expected it to be said. ❑ *Some things, Donald, are better left unsaid... Bill Bradley says too much is going unsaid between blacks and whites.* ADJ: usu ADJ after v, also v-link ADJ, ADJ n

**un|sale|able** /ʌnseɪləbəl/
in AM, use **unsalable**

If something is **unsaleable**, it cannot be sold because nobody wants to buy it. ❑ *Most developers reserve the right to turn down a property they think is virtually unsaleable.* ADJ

**un|sani|tary** /ʌnsænɪtri, AM -teri/ Something that is **unsanitary** is dirty and unhealthy, so that you may catch a disease from it. ❑ *...diseases caused by unsanitary conditions... Discharge of raw sewage into the sea is unsanitary and unsafe.* ADJ = *insanitary, unhygienic*

**un|sat|is|fac|tory** /ʌnsætɪsfæktəri/ If you describe something as **unsatisfactory**, you mean that it is not as good as it should be, and cannot be considered acceptable. ❑ *The inspectors said just under a third of lessons were unsatisfactory... He asked a few more questions, to which he received unsatisfactory answers.* ADJ = *inadequate* ≠ *satisfactory*

**un|sat|is|fied** /ʌnsætɪsfaɪd/ 1 If you are **unsatisfied with** something, you are disappointed because you have not got what you hoped to get. ❑ *The game ended a few hours too early, leaving players and spectators unsatisfied... The centre helps people who are unsatisfied with the solicitors they are given.* ADJ: usu v-link ADJ, oft ADJ *with* n = *dissatisfied* 2 If a need or demand is **unsatisfied**, it is not dealt with. ❑ *The poll suggests that the strongest unsatisfied appetite for home computers isn't among the richest consumers.* ADJ: usu ADJ n = *unmet*

**un|sat|is|fy|ing** /ʌnsætɪsfaɪɪŋ/ If you find something **unsatisfying**, you do not get any satisfaction from it. ❑ *Rose says so far the marriage has been unsatisfying... The boredom is caused as much by people's unsatisfying home lives as by lack of work.* ADJ ≠ *satisfying*

**un|sa|voury** /ʌnseɪvəri/
in AM, use **unsavory**

If you describe a person, place, or thing as **unsavoury**, you mean that you find them unpleasant or morally unacceptable. ❑ *The sport has long been associated with unsavoury characters.* ADJ: usu ADJ n [disapproval]

**un|scathed** /ʌnskeɪðd/ If you are **unscathed** after a dangerous experience, you have not been injured or harmed by it. ❑ *Tony emerged unscathed apart from a severely bruised finger... East Los Angeles was left relatively unscathed by the riots.* ADJ: ADJ after v, v-link ADJ = *unharmed*

**un|sched|uled** /ʌnʃedjuːld, AM -sked-/ An **unscheduled** event was not planned to happen, but happens unexpectedly or because someone changes their plans at a late stage. ❑ *...an unscheduled meeting with Robin Cook... The ship made an unscheduled stop at Hawaii.* ADJ: usu ADJ n

**un|schooled** /ʌnskuːld/ An **unschooled** person has had no formal education. [LITERARY] ❑ *...unskilled work done by unschooled people... He was almost completely unschooled.* ADJ = *uneducated* ≠ *educated*

**un|sci|en|tif|ic** /ʌnsaɪəntɪfɪk/ Research or treatment that is **unscientific** is not likely to be good because it is not based on facts or is not done in the proper way. ❑ *No member of the team was medically qualified and its methods were considered totally unscientific. ...this small, unscientific sample of voters.* ADJ

**un|scram|ble** /ʌnskræmbəl/ **(unscrambles, unscrambling, unscrambled)** To **unscramble** things that are in a state of confusion or disorder means to arrange them so that they can be understood or seen clearly. ❑ *All you have to do to win is unscramble the words here to find four names of birds. ...electronic circuits which can be programmed to allow the user to unscramble transmitted signals.* VERB V n V n

**un|screw** /ʌnskruː/ **(unscrews, unscrewing, unscrewed)** 1 If you **unscrew** something such as a lid, or if it **unscrews**, you keep turning it until you can remove it. ❑ *She unscrewed the cap of her water bottle and gave him a drink... The base of the lamp unscrews for wiring and mounting.* VERB V n V 2 If you **unscrew** something such as a sign or mirror which is fastened to something by screws, you remove it by taking out the screws. ❑ *He unscrewed the back of the telephone and started connecting it to the cable.* VERB V n

**un|script|ed** /ʌnskrɪptɪd/ An **unscripted** talk or speech is made without detailed preparation, rather than being read out. ❑ *...unscripted radio programmes.* ADJ: usu ADJ n

**un|scru|pu|lous** /ʌnskruːpjʊləs/ If you describe a person as **unscrupulous**, you are critical of the fact that they are prepared to act in a dishonest or immoral way in order to get what they want. ❑ *These kids are being exploited by very unscrupulous people. ...the unscrupulous use of hostages.* ADJ [disapproval]

**un|sea|son|ably** /ʌnsiːzənəbli/ **Unseasonably** warm, cold, or mild weather is warmer, colder, or milder than it usually is at the time of year. ❑ *...a spell of unseasonably warm weather... It was unseasonably mild for late January.* ADV: ADV adj

**un|seat** /ʌnsiːt/ **(unseats, unseating, unseated)** When people try to **unseat** a person who is in an important job or position, they try to remove him or her from that job or position. ❑ *It is still not clear who was behind Sunday's attempt to unseat the President.* VERB V n

**un|secured** /ʌnsɪkjʊəd/ **Unsecured** is used to describe loans or debts that are not guaranteed by a particular asset such as a person's home. ❑ *We can arrange unsecured loans for any amount from £500 to £7,500.* ADJ: usu ADJ n

**un|seed|ed** /ʌnsiːdɪd/ In tennis and badminton competitions, an **unseeded** player is someone who has not been ranked among the top 16 players by the competition's organizers. ❑ *He was understandably dejected after losing in the first round to an unseeded American.* ADJ ≠ *seeded*

**un|see|ing** /ʌnsiːɪŋ/ If you describe a person or their eyes as **unseeing**, you mean that they are not looking at anything, or not noticing something, although their eyes are open. [LITERARY] ❑ *In the hallway Greenfield was staring at the wood panelling with unseeing eyes... He stared unseeing out of the window.* ADJ: ADJ n, ADJ after v, v-link ADJ

**un|seem|ly** /ʌnsiːmli/ If you say that someone's behaviour is **unseemly**, you disapprove of it because it is not polite or not suitable for a particular situation or occasion. [LITERARY] ❑ *It would be unseemly for judges to receive pay increases when others are having to tighten their belts. ...unseemly drinking, brawling and gambling.* ADJ [disapproval]

**un|seen** /ʌnsiːn/ 1 If you describe something as **unseen**, you mean that it has not been seen for a long time. ❑ *...a spectacular ballroom, unseen by the public for over 30 years... We print a selection of previously unseen photos from the Spanish rider's early years.* ADJ 2 You can use **unseen** to describe things which people cannot see. ❑ *For me, a performance is in front of a microphone, over the radio, to an unseen audience... There was barely time for the two boys to escape unseen.* ADJ: ADJ n, ADJ after v

**un|self|ish** /ʌnselfɪʃ/ If you describe someone as **unselfish**, you approve of the fact that they regard other people's wishes and interests as more important than their own. ❑ *She started to get a reputation as an unselfish girl with a heart of gold... As a player he was unselfish, a true team man.* ADJ [approval] = selfless ≠ selfish ♦ **un|self|ish|ly** *She has loyally and unselfishly spent every single day at her husband's side.* ADV: ADV with v ♦ **un|self|ish|ness** *...acts of unselfishness and care.* N-UNCOUNT

**un|sen|ti|men|tal** /ʌnsentɪmentᵊl/ If you describe someone as **unsentimental**, you mean that they do not allow emotions like pity or affection to interfere with their work or decisions. ❑ *She was a practical, unsentimental woman... They are unsentimental about their impact on employees.* ADJ

**un|set|tle** /ʌnsetᵊl/ **(unsettles, unsettling, unsettled)** If something **unsettles** you, it makes you feel rather worried or uncertain. ❑ *The presence of the two policemen unsettled her.* VERB = disturb V n

**un|set|tled** /ʌnsetᵊld/ 1 In an **unsettled** situation, there is a lot of uncertainty about what will happen. ❑ *Britain's unsettled political scene also worries some investors.* ADJ = unstable 2 If you are **unsettled**, you cannot concentrate on anything because you are worried. ❑ *A lot of people wake up every day with a sense of being unsettled and disturbed.* ADJ: v-link ADJ 3 An **unsettled** argument or dispute has not yet been resolved. ❑ *They were in the process of resolving all the unsettled issues.* ADJ = unresolved 4 **Unsettled** places are places where no people have yet lived. ❑ *Until very recently Texas was an unsettled frontier.* ADJ: usu ADJ n 5 **Unsettled** weather is unpredictable and changes a lot. ❑ *Despite the unsettled weather, we had a marvellous weekend.* ADJ ≠ settled

**un|set|tling** /ʌnsetəlɪŋ/ If you describe something as **unsettling**, you mean that it makes you feel rather worried or uncertain. ❑ *The prospect of change of this kind has an unsettling effect on any organisation.* ADJ = disturbing ♦ **un|set|tling|ly** *It was unsettlingly quiet.* ADV: ADV adj

**un|shad|ed** /ʌnʃeɪdɪd/ An **unshaded** light or light bulb has no shade fitted to it. ADJ: ADJ n = naked

**un|shake|able** /ʌnʃeɪkəbᵊl/ also **unshakable.** If you describe someone's beliefs as **unshakeable**, you are emphasizing that they are so strong that they cannot be destroyed or altered. ❑ *She had an unshakeable faith in human goodness and natural honesty.* ADJ: usu ADJ n [emphasis]

**un|shak|en** /ʌnʃeɪkən/ 1 If your beliefs are **unshaken**, you still have those beliefs, although they have been attacked or challenged. ❑ *His faith that men such as the Reverend John Leale tried to do their best is unshaken.* ADJ: usu v-link ADJ = firm 2 If you are **unshaken by** something, you are not emotionally affected by it. ❑ *Mona remains unshaken by her ordeal and is matter-of-fact about her courage.* ADJ: usu v-link ADJ

**un|shav|en** /ʌnʃeɪvᵊn/ If a man is **unshaven**, he has not shaved recently and there are short hairs on his face or chin. ADJ

**un|sight|ly** /ʌnsaɪtli/ If you describe something as **unsightly**, you mean that it is unattractive to look at. ❑ *My mother has had unsightly varicose veins for years.* ADJ = ugly

**un|signed** /ʌnsaɪnd/ 1 An **unsigned** document does not have anyone's signature on it. ADJ 2 An **unsigned** band has not signed a contract with a company to produce CDs. ADJ: usu ADJ n

**un|skilled** /ʌnskɪld/ 1 People who are **unskilled** do not have any special training for a job. ❑ *He went to Paris in search of work as an unskilled labourer.* ADJ ≠ skilled 2 **Unskilled** work does not require any special training. ❑ *In the US, minorities and immigrants have generally gone into low-paid, unskilled jobs.* ADJ: usu ADJ n ≠ skilled

**un|smil|ing** /ʌnsmaɪlɪŋ/ An **unsmiling** person is not smiling, and looks serious or unfriendly. [LITERARY] ❑ *He was unsmiling and silent. ...the unsmiling woman in the ticket booth.* ADJ

**un|so|ciable** /ʌnsoʊʃəbᵊl/ Someone who is **unsociable** does not like talking to other people and tries to avoid meeting them. ❑ *My marriage has broken up. It has made me reclusive and unsociable... I am by no means an unsociable person.* ADJ ≠ sociable

**un|so|cial** /ʌnsoʊʃᵊl/ If someone works **unsocial** hours, they work late at night, early in the morning, at weekends, or on public holidays. In Britain, people are often paid extra for working unsocial hours. [BRIT] ADJ

**un|sold** /ʌnsoʊld/ **Unsold** goods have been available for people to buy but nobody has bought them. ❑ *...piles of unsold books... Thirteen per cent of Christie's coin and banknote auction went unsold.* ADJ

**un|so|lic|it|ed** /ʌnsəlɪsɪtɪd/ Something that is **unsolicited** has been given without being asked for and may not have been wanted. ❑ *'If I were you,' she adds by way of some unsolicited advice, 'I'd watch out for that girl of yours.'* ADJ: usu ADJ n

**un|solved** /ʌnsɒlvd/ An **unsolved** mystery or problem has never been solved. ❑ *...America's unsolved problems of poverty and racism... David's murder remains unsolved.* ADJ

**un|so|phis|ti|cat|ed** /ʌnsəfɪstɪkeɪtɪd/ 1 **Unsophisticated** people do not have a wide range of experience or knowledge and have simple tastes. ❑ *It was music of a rather crude kind which unsophisticated audiences enjoyed listening to... She was quite unsophisticated in the ways of the world.* ADJ ≠ sophisticated 2 An **unsophisticated** method or device is very simple and often not very effective. ❑ *...an unsophisticated alarm system.* ADJ = crude ≠ sophisticated

**un|sound** /ʌnsaʊnd/ 1 If a conclusion or method is **unsound**, it is based on ideas that are wrong. ❑ *The thinking is good-hearted, but muddled and fundamentally unsound... The national tests were educationally unsound.* ADJ: usu v-link ADJ ≠ sound 2 If something or someone is **unsound**, they are unreliable. ❑ *No sensible person would put his money in a bank he knew to be unsound.* ADJ = unreliable 3 If you say that something is **unsound** in some way, you mean that it is damaging in that way or to the thing mentioned. ❑ *The project is environmentally unsound... A diet extremely low in calories can also be a diet that is nutritionally unsound.* ADJ: usu v-link ADJ, usu adv ADJ ≠ sound 4 If a building or other structure is **unsound**, it is in poor condition and is likely to collapse. ❑ *The church was structurally unsound.* ADJ: usu v-link ADJ

**un|speak|able** /ʌnspiːkəbᵊl/ If you describe something as **unspeakable**, you are emphasizing that it is extremely unpleasant. ❑ *...the unspeakable horrors of chemical weapons. ...unspeakable crimes.* ADJ [emphasis] = appalling ♦ **un|speak|ably** /ʌnspiːkəbli/ *The novel was unspeakably boring.* ADV: usu ADV adj

**un|speci|fied** /ʌnspesɪfaɪd/ You say that something is **unspecified** when you are not told ADJ: usu ADJ n exactly what it is. ❑ *The government said an unspecified number of bandits were killed... He was arrested on unspecified charges.*

**un|spec|tacu|lar** /ʌnspektækjʊlər/ If you describe something as **unspectacular**, you mean that it is rather dull and not remarkable in any way. ❑ *His progress at school had been unspectacular compared to his brother. ...pleasant, if largely unspectacular, countryside.* ADJ

**un|spoiled** /ʌnspɔɪld/

in BRIT, also use **unspoilt** /ʌnspɔɪlt/

If you describe a place as **unspoiled**, you think it is beautiful because it has not been changed or built on for a long time. ❑ *The port is quiet and unspoiled. ...the unspoiled island of Cozumel.* ADJ

**un|spo|ken** /ʌnspoʊkən/ 1 If your thoughts, wishes, or feelings are **unspoken**, you do not speak about them. ❑ *His face was expressionless, but Alex felt the unspoken criticism... The other unspoken fear here is of an outbreak of hooliganism.* ADJ
2 When there is an **unspoken** agreement or understanding between people, their behaviour shows that they agree about something or understand it, even though they have never spoken about it. ❑ *There had been an unspoken agreement between them that he would not call for her at Seymour House.* ADJ: ADJ n = *tacit*

**un|sport|ing** /ʌnspɔːrtɪŋ/ If you describe someone playing a game as **unsporting**, you are critical of them because they have done something that is unfair to their opponent. ❑ *Players are warned, fined and can even be disqualified for unsporting actions in the heat of contest.* ADJ [disapproval]

**un|sta|ble** /ʌnsteɪbəl/ 1 You can describe something as **unstable** if it is likely to change suddenly, especially if this creates difficulty or danger. ❑ *After the fall of Pitt in 1801 there was a decade of unstable government... The situation is unstable and potentially dangerous.* ADJ ≠ *stable* 2 **Unstable** objects are likely to move or fall. ❑ *Both clay and sandstone are unstable rock formations.* ADJ ≠ *stable* 3 If people are **unstable**, their emotions and behaviour keep changing because their minds are disturbed or upset. ❑ *He was emotionally unstable.* ADJ ≠ *stable*

**un|stat|ed** /ʌnsteɪtɪd/ You say that something is **unstated** when it has not been expressed in words. ❑ *The implication was plain, if left unstated... An additional, unstated reason for his resignation may have been a lawsuit filed against him.* ADJ

**un|steady** /ʌnstedi/ 1 If you are **unsteady**, you have difficulty doing something, for example walking, because you cannot completely control your legs or your body. ❑ *The boy was very unsteady and had staggered around when he got up... He poured coffee into the mugs, and with an unsteady hand, held one of them out to David.* ADJ ♦ **un|steadi|ly** /ʌnstedɪli/ *She pulled herself unsteadily from the bed to the dresser.* ADV: ADV with v 2 If you describe something as **unsteady**, you mean that it is not regular or stable, but unreliable or unpredictable. ❑ *His voice was unsteady and only just audible.* ADJ 3 **Unsteady** objects are not held, fixed, or balanced securely. ❑ *...a slightly unsteady item of furniture.* ADJ: usu ADJ n

**un|stick** /ʌnstɪk/ (**unsticks, unsticking, unstuck**) If you **unstick** something or if it **unsticks**, it becomes separated from the thing that it was stuck to. ❑ *Mike shook his head, to unstick his hair from his sweating forehead... The stewards' badges are made so they do not unstick from a car and therefore cannot be passed around.* → See also **unstuck**. VERB V n V

**un|stint|ing** /ʌnstɪntɪŋ/ **Unstinting** help, care, or praise is great in amount or degree and is given generously. ❑ *The task of producing the text was made easier by the unstinting help and generosity extended to me.* ADJ: usu ADJ n

**un|stop|pable** /ʌnstɒpəbəl/ Something that is **unstoppable** cannot be prevented from continuing or developing. ❑ *The progress of science is unstoppable. ...the country's seemingly unstoppable economy.* ADJ

**un|stressed** /ʌnstrest/ If a word or syllable is **unstressed**, it is pronounced without emphasis. [TECHNICAL] ❑ *...the unstressed syllable of words like 'above', 'surround' or 'arrive'.* ADJ ≠ *stressed*

**un|struc|tured** /ʌnstrʌktʃərd/ Something such as a meeting, interview, or activity that is **unstructured** is not organized in a complete or detailed way. ❑ *Our aim was that these meetings be unstructured and informal.* ADJ ≠ *structured*

**un|stuck** /ʌnstʌk/ 1 If something **comes unstuck**, it becomes separated from the thing that it was attached to. ❑ *The brown vinyl covering all the horizontal surfaces is coming unstuck in several places.* PHRASE: V inflects 2 To **come unstuck** means to fail. [mainly BRIT, INFORMAL] ❑ *Where economics comes unstuck is when it doesn't take account of the anticipated actions of human beings.* PHRASE: V inflects = *fail*

in AM, usually use **come unglued**

→ See also **unstick**.

**un|sub|scribe** /ʌnsəbskraɪb/ (**unsubscribes, unsubscribing, unsubscribed**) If you **unsubscribe** from an online service, you send a message saying that you no longer wish to receive that service. [COMPUTING] ❑ *Go to the website today and you can unsubscribe online.* VERB V

**un|sub|stan|ti|at|ed** /ʌnsəbstænʃieɪtɪd/ A claim, accusation, or story that is **unsubstantiated** has not been proved to be valid or true. ❑ *I do object to their claim, which I find totally unsubstantiated. ...unsubstantiated rumours about his private life.* ADJ = *unconfirmed*

**un|suc|cess|ful** /ʌnsəksesfʊl/ 1 Something that is **unsuccessful** does not achieve what it was intended to achieve. ❑ *His efforts were unsuccessful. ...a second unsuccessful operation on his knee... There were reports last month of unsuccessful negotiations between guerrillas and commanders.* ADJ ≠ *successful* ♦ **un|suc|cess|ful|ly** *He has been trying unsuccessfully to sell the business in one piece since early last year.* ADV: ADV with v ≠ *successfully* 2 Someone who is **unsuccessful** does not achieve what they intended to achieve, especially in their career. ❑ *The difference between successful and unsuccessful people is that successful people put into practice the things they learn... He and his friend Boris were unsuccessful in getting a job.* ADJ ≠ *successful*

**un|suit|able** /ʌnsuːtəbəl/ Someone or something that is **unsuitable for** a particular purpose or situation does not have the right qualities for it. ❑ *Amy's shoes were unsuitable for walking any distance.* ADJ: oft ADJ *for* n/-ing ≠ *suitable*

**un|suit|ed** /ʌnsuːtɪd/ 1 If someone or something is **unsuited to** a particular job, situation, or place, they do not have the right qualities or characteristics for it. ❑ *He's totally unsuited to the job... The snow cruiser proved hopelessly unsuited to Antarctic conditions.* ADJ: oft ADJ *to* n/-ing ≠ *suited* 2 If two people, especially a man and a woman, are **unsuited to** each other, they have different personalities or interests, and so are unlikely to have a successful relationship. ❑ *By the end of that first year, I knew how totally unsuited we were to each other.* ADJ: oft ADJ *to* n = *incompatible* ≠ *suited*

**un|sul|lied** /ʌnsʌlid/ If something is **unsullied**, it has not been spoiled or made less pure by the addition of something unpleasant or unacceptable. [LITERARY] ❑ *She had the combined talents of toughness, intellect, experience and unsullied reputation... He smiled, unsullied by doubt.* ADJ ≠ *sullied, tainted*

**un|sung** /ʌnsʌŋ/ **Unsung** is used to describe people, things, or places that are not appreciated or praised, although you think they deserve to be. [WRITTEN] ❑ *They are among the unsung heroes of our time.* ADJ

**un|sup|port|ed** /ʌnsəpɔːrtɪd/ 1 If a statement or theory is **unsupported**, there is no evidence which proves that it is true or correct. ❑ *It was a theory unsupported by evidence... The letters contained unsupported allegations.* ADJ 2 An **unsupported** person does not have anyone to provide them with money and the things they need. ADJ: usu ADJ n

❑ *Unsupported mothers are one of the fastest-growing groups of welfare claimants.* 3 An **unsupported** building or person is not being physically supported or held up by anything. ❑ *...the vast unsupported wall of the Ajuda Palace in Lisbon. ...the child's first unsupported step.*
ADJ: usu ADJ n

**un|sure** /ʌnʃʊəʳ/ 1 If you are **unsure of yourself**, you lack confidence. ❑ *He made her feel hot, and awkward, and unsure of herself... The evening show was terrible, with hesitant unsure performances from all.* 2 If you are **unsure about** something, you feel uncertain about it. ❑ *Fifty-two per cent were unsure about the idea... Scientists are becoming increasingly unsure of the validity of this technique.*
ADJ: usu v-link ADJ, oft ADJ *of* n ≠ confident, sure
ADJ: v-link ADJ, oft ADJ *about*/*of* n ≠ certain

**un|sur|passed** /ʌnsəʳpɑːst, -pæst/ If you describe something as **unsurpassed**, you are emphasizing that it is better or greater than anything else of its kind. ❑ *The quality of Smallbone furniture is unsurpassed. ...the Hamburg weekly, surely unsurpassed in the world for its intellectual range and quality.*
ADJ [emphasis] = unrivalled

**un|sur|pris|ing** /ʌnsəʳpraɪzɪŋ/ If something is **unsurprising**, you are not surprised by it because you would expect it to happen or be like it is. ❑ *It is unsurprising that he remains so hated... His choice was unsurprising.* ♦ **un|sur|pris|ing|ly** *Unsurprisingly, not everyone agrees that things are better... The proposals were swiftly and unsurprisingly rejected by Western ministers.*
ADJ: usu v-link ADJ, oft ADJ that ≠ surprising
ADV: ADV with cl, ADV with v ≠ surprisingly

**un|sus|pect|ed** /ʌnsəspektɪd/ If you describe something as **unsuspected**, you mean that people do not realize it or are not aware of it. ❑ *A surprising number of ailments are caused by unsuspected environmental factors.*
ADJ: usu ADJ n

**un|sus|pect|ing** /ʌnsəspektɪŋ/ You can use **unsuspecting** to describe someone who is not at all aware of something that is happening or going to happen. ❑ *The co-defendants are charged with selling worthless junk bonds to thousands of unsuspecting depositors. ...his unsuspecting victim.*
ADJ: usu ADJ n

**un|sweet|ened** /ʌnswiːtᵊnd/ **Unsweetened** food or drink does not have any sugar or other sweet substance added to it.
ADJ: usu ADJ n ≠ sweetened

**un|swerv|ing** /ʌnswɜːʳvɪŋ/ If you describe someone's attitude, feeling, or way of behaving as **unswerving**, you mean that it is strong and firm and does not weaken or change. ❑ *In his diary of 1944 he proclaims unswerving loyalty to the monarchy.*
ADJ: usu ADJ n = unwavering

**un|sym|pa|thet|ic** /ʌnsɪmpəθetɪk/ 1 If someone is **unsympathetic**, they are not kind or helpful to a person in difficulties. ❑ *Her husband was unsympathetic and she felt she had no one to turn to. ...an unsympathetic doctor.* 2 An **unsympathetic** person is unpleasant and difficult to like. ❑ *...a very unsympathetic main character... He's unsympathetic, but charismatic and complex.* 3 If you are **unsympathetic to** a particular idea or aim, you are not willing to support it. ❑ *I'm highly unsympathetic to what you are trying to achieve.*
ADJ ≠ sympathetic
ADJ
ADJ: v-link ADJ *to* n

**un|tamed** /ʌnteɪmd/ An **untamed** area or place is in its original or natural state and has not been changed or affected by people. [LITERARY] ❑ *...the wild, untamed undergrowth... The interior of Corsica is high and untamed.*
ADJ

**un|tan|gle** /ʌntæŋgᵊl/ (**untangles, untangling, untangled**) 1 If you **untangle** something that is knotted or has become twisted around something, you undo the knots in it or free it. ❑ *He was found desperately trying to untangle several reels of film. ...a light, non-sticky mousse which untangles hair and adds brilliant shine.* 2 If you **untangle** a confused or complicated situation, you make the different things involved clear, or put the situation right. ❑ *Lawyers and accountants began trying to untangle the complex affairs of the bank.*
VERB; V n; V n
VERB = disentangle; V n

**un|tapped** /ʌntæpt/ An **untapped** supply or source of something has not yet been used. ❑ *Mongolia, although poor, has considerable untapped resources of oil and minerals.*
ADJ: usu ADJ n

**un|ten|able** /ʌntenəbᵊl/ An argument, theory, or position that is **untenable** cannot be defended successfully against criticism or attack. ❑ *This argument is untenable from an intellectual, moral and practical standpoint.*
ADJ: usu v-link ADJ

**un|test|ed** /ʌntestɪd/ 1 If something or someone is **untested**, they have not yet been tried out or have not yet experienced a particular situation, so you do not know what they will be like. ❑ *The Egyptian Army remained an untested force.* 2 If you describe something such as a drug or chemical as **untested**, you mean that it has not been subject to scientific tests to find out if it is safe to use. ❑ *...the dangers of giving untested drugs to people.*
ADJ = untried
ADJ: usu ADJ n

**un|think|able** /ʌnθɪŋkəbᵊl/ 1 If you say that something is **unthinkable**, you are emphasizing that it cannot possibly be accepted or imagined as a possibility. ❑ *Her strong Catholic beliefs made abortion unthinkable.* ♦ **The unthinkable** is something that is unthinkable. ❑ *Edward VIII had done the unthinkable and abdicated the throne.* 2 You can use **unthinkable** to describe a situation, event, or action which is extremely unpleasant to imagine or remember. ❑ *This place is going to be unthinkable without you.*
ADJ: usu v-link ADJ [emphasis]
N-SING: the N
ADJ

**un|think|ing** /ʌnθɪŋkɪŋ/ If you say that someone is **unthinking**, you are critical of them because you consider that they do not think carefully about the effects of their behaviour. ❑ *He doesn't say those silly things that unthinking people say.* ♦ **un|think|ing|ly** *Many motor accidents are the result of unthinkingly mixing speed and alcohol.*
ADJ [disapproval] = thoughtless
ADV: usu ADV with v, also ADV adj

**un|ti|dy** /ʌntaɪdi/ 1 If you describe something as **untidy**, you mean that it is not neat or well arranged. ❑ *The place quickly became untidy. ...a thin man with untidy hair... Clothes were thrown in the luggage in an untidy heap.* ♦ **un|ti|di|ly** /ʌntaɪdɪli/ *Her long hair tumbles untidily around her shoulders. ...the desk piled untidily with books and half-finished homework.* ♦ **un|ti|di|ness** *The dust and untidiness in her room no longer bothered her.* 2 If you describe a person as **untidy**, you mean that they do not care about whether things are neat and well arranged, for example in their house. ❑ *I'm untidy in most ways.*
ADJ ≠ tidy
ADV: usu ADV with v, also ADV adj
N-UNCOUNT ≠ tidiness
ADJ ≠ tidy

**un|tie** /ʌntaɪ/ (**unties, untying, untied**) 1 If you **untie** something that is tied to another thing or if you **untie** two things that are tied together, you remove the string or rope that holds them or that has been tied round them. ❑ *Nicholas untied the boat from her mooring... Just untie my hands.* 2 If you **untie** something such as string or rope, you undo it so that there is no knot or so that it is no longer tying something. ❑ *She hurriedly untied the ropes binding her ankles... Then she untied her silk scarf.* 3 When you **untie** your shoelaces or your shoes, you loosen or undo the laces of your shoes. ❑ *She untied the laces on one of her sneakers... Your boot lace is untied.*
VERB; V n; V n
VERB; V n; V n
VERB = undo; V n; V-ed

**un|til** /ʌntɪl/ 1 If something happens **until** a particular time, it happens during the period before that time and stops at that time. ❑ *Until 1971, he was a high-ranking official in the Central Committee. ...consumers who have waited until after the Christmas holiday to do that holiday shopping.* ♦ **Until** is also a conjunction. ❑ *I waited until it got dark... Stir with a metal spoon until the sugar has dissolved.* 2 You use **until** with a negative to emphasize the moment in time after which the rest of your statement becomes true, or the condition which would make it true. ❑ *The traffic laws don't take effect until the end of the year... It was not until 1911 that the first of the vitamins was identified.* ♦ **Until** is also a conjunction. ❑ *The EU will not lift its sanctions until that country makes political changes.* 3 **up until** → see **up**.
◆◆◆ PREP: PREP n/prep = till
CONJ = till
PREP: PREP after neg = till
CONJ: CONJ after neg = till

**un|time|ly** /ʌntaɪmli/ 1 If you describe an event as **untimely**, you mean that it happened earlier than it should, or sooner than you expected. ❑ *His mother's untimely death had a catastrophic*
ADJ: usu ADJ n = premature

*effect on him.* [2] You can describe something as **untimely** if it happens at an unsuitable time. ❑ *...an untimely visit from the milkman... I am sure your readers would have seen the article as at best untimely.*
ADJ = ill-timed

**un|tir|ing** /ʌntaɪərɪŋ/ If you describe a person or their efforts as **untiring**, you approve of them because they continue what they are doing without slowing down or stopping. ❑ *...an untiring fighter for justice, democracy and tolerance.*
ADJ: usu ADJ n approval = tireless

**un|tit|led** /ʌntaɪtəld/ [1] If something such as a book, film, or song is **untitled**, it does not have a title. ❑ *The full-length feature, as yet untitled, will include interviews plus footage of their live gigs.*
ADJ
[2] Someone who is **untitled** does not have a title such as 'Sir' or 'Lord'.
ADJ

**unto** /ʌntu/ [1] **Unto** was used to indicate that something was done or given to someone. [LITERARY or OLD-FASHIONED] ❑ *And he said unto him, 'Who is my neighbor?'... I will do unto others what they did to me.*
PREP = to
[2] **Unto** was used to indicate that something continued until a particular time. [LITERARY or OLD-FASHIONED] ❑ *Be ye faithful unto the end.*
PREP = until

**un|told** /ʌntoʊld/ [1] You can use **untold** to emphasize how bad or unpleasant something is. ❑ *The demise of the industry has caused untold misery to thousands of hard-working tradesmen... This might do untold damage to her health.*
ADJ: ADJ n emphasis
[2] You can use **untold** to emphasize that an amount or quantity is very large, especially when you are not sure how large it is. ❑ *...the nation's untold millions of anglers.*
ADJ: ADJ n emphasis

**un|touch|able** /ʌntʌtʃəbəl/ **(untouchables)** [1] If you say that someone is **untouchable**, you mean that they cannot be affected or punished in any way. ❑ *I want to make it clear, however, that no one is untouchable in this investigation.* ♦ An **untouchable** is someone who is untouchable. ❑ *...an anti-corruption squad nicknamed the 'Untouchables'.*
ADJ; N-COUNT
[2] If you describe someone, especially a sports player or entertainer, as **untouchable**, you are emphasizing that they are better than anyone else in what they do. ❑ *A lot of the players began to feel they were untouchable.*
ADJ emphasis
[3] Some people refer to Hindus of the lowest social rank as **untouchables**. ❑ *He was born an untouchable in a very poor village in south India.*
N-COUNT

**un|touched** /ʌntʌtʃt/ [1] Something that is **untouched by** something else is not affected by it. ❑ *Asian airlines remain untouched by the deregulation that has swept America.*
ADJ: v-link ADJ, ADJ after v
[2] If something is **untouched**, it is not damaged in any way, although it has been in a situation where it could easily have been damaged. ❑ *Michael pointed out to me that amongst the rubble, there was one building that remained untouched... The desk had been rifled for money, some banknotes taken but cheque-book and credit cards left untouched.*
ADJ: v-link ADJ, ADJ after v
[3] An **untouched** area or place is thought to be beautiful because it is still in its original state and has not been changed or damaged in any way. ❑ *Ducie is one of the world's last untouched islands, nearly 5,000km from Australia.*
ADJ: ADJ n, v-link ADJ, ADJ after v
[4] If food or drink is **untouched**, none of it has been eaten or drunk. ❑ *The coffee was untouched, the toast had cooled.*
ADJ: v-link ADJ, ADJ after v, ADJ n

**un|to|ward** /ʌntəwɔːʳd, AM -tɔːʳd/ If you say that something **untoward** happens, you mean that something happens that is unexpected and causes difficulties. [FORMAL] ❑ *The surveyor's report didn't highlight anything untoward... Tampering with a single enzyme can lead to untoward effects elsewhere.*
ADJ: pron-indef ADJ, ADJ n

**un|trace|able** /ʌntreɪsəbəl/ If someone or something is **untraceable**, it is impossible to find them. ❑ *...a world where electronic crime is untraceable.*
ADJ

**un|trained** /ʌntreɪnd/ [1] Someone who is **untrained** has not been taught the skills that they need for a particular job, activity, or situation. ❑ *It is a nonsense to say we have untrained staff dealing with emergencies... Our Intelligence Service was untrained, cumbersome, and almost wholly ineffectual.*
ADJ
[2] If you describe a voice or a mind, for example, as **untrained**, you mean that it has not been developed through formal education or training. ❑ *It was often said that he had the best untrained mind in politics.*
ADJ: usu ADJ n

**un|tram|melled** /ʌntræməld/

✓ in AM, use **untrammeled**

Someone who is **untrammelled** is able to act freely in the way they want to, rather than being restricted by something. [LITERARY] ❑ *...the only place where the royal family could really relax and lead an untrammelled domestic life... She thought of herself as a free woman, untrammelled by family relationships.*
ADJ: oft ADJ by n

**un|treat|ed** /ʌntriːtɪd/ [1] If an injury or illness is left **untreated**, it is not given medical treatment. ❑ *If left untreated the condition may become chronic. ...the consequences of untreated tuberculosis.*
ADJ: ADJ after v, ADJ n, v-link ADJ
[2] **Untreated** materials, water, or chemicals are harmful and have not been made safe. ❑ *...the dumping of nuclear waste and untreated sewage.*
ADJ: usu ADJ n
[3] **Untreated** materials are in their natural or original state, often before being prepared for use in a particular process. ❑ *All the bedding is made of simple, untreated cotton... In its untreated state the carbon fibre material is rather like cloth.*
ADJ: usu ADJ n = raw

**un|tried** /ʌntraɪd/ If someone or something is **untried**, they have not yet experienced certain situations or have not yet been tried out, so you do not know what they will be like. ❑ *He was young and untried, with no reputation of his own. ...a long legal battle through untried areas of law.*
ADJ = untested

**un|trou|bled** /ʌntrʌbəld/ If you are **untroubled by** something, you are not affected or worried by it. ❑ *She is untroubled by the fact that she didn't win. ...an untroubled night's sleep.*
ADJ ≠ troubled

**un|true** /ʌntruː/ If a statement or idea is **untrue**, it is false and not based on facts. ❑ *The allegations were completely untrue... It was untrue to say that all political prisoners have been released... Such remarks are both offensive and untrue.*
ADJ: usu v-link ADJ ≠ true

**un|trust|wor|thy** /ʌntrʌstwɜːʳði/ If you say that someone is **untrustworthy**, you think they are unreliable and cannot be trusted. ❑ *I think he is shallow, vain and untrustworthy... His opponents still say he's a fundamentally untrustworthy figure.*
ADJ

**un|truth** /ʌntruːθ/ **(untruths** /ʌntruːðz/**)** An **untruth** is a lie. [FORMAL] ❑ *The Advertising Standards Authority accused estate agents of using blatant untruths... I have never uttered one word of untruth.*
N-VAR = falsehood

**un|truth|ful** /ʌntruːθfʊl/ If someone is **untruthful** or if they say **untruthful** things, they are dishonest and say things that they know are not true. ❑ *He must not be untruthful, or a coward... Some people may be tempted to give untruthful answers.*
ADJ ≠ truthful

**un|tu|tored** /ʌntjuːtəʳd, AM -tuːt-/ If someone is **untutored**, they have not been formally trained to do something, although they may be quite skilled at it. [FORMAL] ❑ *This untutored mathematician had an obsession with numbers... They had left school at fifteen and were quite untutored in writing.*
ADJ

**un|typi|cal** /ʌntɪpɪkəl/ If someone or something is **untypical of** a particular type of person or thing, they are not a good example of the way that type of person or thing normally is. People sometimes say something is **not untypical** when they mean that it is quite normal. ❑ *Anita Loos was in many respects untypical of the screenwriting trade... I believe our results are not untypical.* ♦ **un|typi|cal|ly** /ʌntɪpɪkli/ *Untypically for a man in that situation he became interested in Buddhism.*
ADJ: usu v-link ADJ; ADV: ADV adj/-ed, ADV with cl = unusually

**un|us|able** /ʌnjuːzəbəl/ Something that is **unusable** is not in a good enough state or condition to be used. ❑ *Bombing had made roads and railways unusable.*
ADJ

**un|used**

> Pronounced /ʌnjuːzd/ for meaning 1, and /ʌnjuːst/ for meaning 2.

1 Something that is **unused** has not been used or is not being used at the moment. ❑ *...unused containers of food and drink.* ADJ: ADJ n, ADJ after v, v-link ADJ
2 If you are **unused to** something, you have not often done it or experienced it before, so it feels unusual and unfamiliar to you. ❑ *Mother was entirely unused to such hard work.* ADJ: v-link ADJ *to* n

**un|usual** /ʌnjuːʒuəl/ ◆◇◇ 1 If something is **unusual**, it does not happen very often or you do not see it or hear it very often. ❑ *They have replanted many areas with rare and unusual plants... To be appreciated as a parent is quite unusual.* ADJ
2 If you describe someone as **unusual**, you think that they are interesting and different from other people. ❑ *...an unusual man with business talents.* ADJ

**un|usu|al|ly** /ʌnjuːʒuəli/ 1 You use **unusually** to emphasize that someone or something has more of a particular quality than is usual. ❑ *He was an unusually complex man. ...this year's unusually harsh winter.* ADV: ADV adj [emphasis]
2 You can use **unusually** to suggest that something is not what normally happens. ❑ *Unusually among British prime ministers, he was not a man of natural authority.* ADV: ADV with cl, oft ADV *for* n

**un|ut|ter|able** /ʌnʌtərəbᵊl/ You can use **unutterable** to emphasize that something, especially a bad quality, is great in degree or intensity. [WRITTEN] ❑ *...unutterable rubbish.* ADJ: ADJ n [emphasis]
♦ **un|ut|ter|ably** /ʌnʌtərəbli/ *I suddenly felt unutterably depressed.* ADV: usu ADV adj

**un|vary|ing** /ʌnveəriŋ/ If you describe something as **unvarying**, you mean that it stays the same and never changes. ❑ *...her unvarying refusal to make public appearances.* ADJ: usu ADJ n

**un|veil** /ʌnveɪl/ (**unveils, unveiling, unveiled**)
1 If someone formally **unveils** something such as a new statue or painting, they draw back the curtain which is covering it. ❑ *...a ceremony to unveil a monument to the victims.* VERB, V n ♦ **un|veil|ing** *...the unveiling of a monument to one of the Croatian heroes of the past.* N-UNCOUNT: oft N *of* n
2 If you **unveil** a plan, new product, or some other thing that has been kept secret, you introduce it to the public. ❑ *Companies from across Europe are here to unveil their latest models.* VERB, V n ♦ **un|veil|ing** *...the unveiling of a detailed peace plan.* N-UNCOUNT: oft N *of* n

**un|waged** /ʌnweɪdʒd/ You can refer to people who do not have a paid job as **the unwaged**. [BRIT, BUSINESS] ❑ *There are special rates for the under 18s, full-time students, over 60s and the unwaged.* N-PLURAL: usu *the* N ♦ **Unwaged** is also an adjective. ❑ *...the effect on male wage-earners, unwaged females, and children.* ADJ

**un|want|ed** /ʌnwɒntɪd/ If you say that something or someone is **unwanted**, you mean that you do not want them, or that nobody wants them. ❑ *...the misery of unwanted pregnancies... She felt unwanted... Every year thousands of unwanted animals are abandoned.* ADJ

**un|war|rant|ed** /ʌnwɒrəntɪd, AM -wɔːr-/ If you describe something as **unwarranted**, you are critical of it because there is no need or reason for it. [FORMAL] ❑ *Any attempt to discuss the issue of human rights was rejected as an unwarranted interference in the country's internal affairs... He accused the police of using unwarranted brutality.* ADJ [disapproval]

**un|wary** /ʌnweəri/ If you describe someone as **unwary**, you mean that they are not cautious or experienced and are therefore likely to be harmed or deceived. [FORMAL] ❑ *With its quicksands the river usually drowns a few unwary visitors every season.* ADJ: usu ADJ n ♦ **The unwary** are people who are unwary. ❑ *Specialist subjects are full of pitfalls for the unwary.* N-SING: *the* N

**un|washed** /ʌnwɒʃt/ 1 **Unwashed** people or objects are dirty and need to be washed. ❑ *Leftover food and unwashed dishes cover the dirty counters.* ADJ
2 **The unwashed** or **the great unwashed** is a way of referring to poor or ordinary people. [HUMOROUS] ❑ *A scowling man briskly led the Queen's husband away from the great unwashed.* PHRASE

**un|wa|ver|ing** /ʌnweɪvərɪŋ/ If you describe a feeling or attitude as **unwavering**, you mean that it is strong and firm and does not weaken. ❑ *She has been encouraged by the unwavering support of her family... His attitude was unwavering.* ADJ = unswerving

**un|wel|come** /ʌnwelkəm/ 1 An **unwelcome** experience is one that you do not like and did not want. ❑ *The media has brought more unwelcome attention to the Royal Family... A colleague made unwelcome sexual advances towards her.* ADJ = unwanted
2 If you say that a visitor is **unwelcome**, you mean that you did not want them to come. ❑ *...an unwelcome guest... She was, quite deliberately, making him feel unwelcome.* ADJ ≠ welcome

**un|wel|com|ing** /ʌnwelkəmɪŋ/ 1 If someone is **unwelcoming**, or if they behave in an **unwelcoming** way, they are unfriendly or hostile when you visit or approach them. ❑ *His manner was cold and unwelcoming... Both women were unwelcoming, making little attempt to put Kathryn at her ease.* ADJ [disapproval]
2 If you describe a place as **unwelcoming**, you mean that it looks unattractive or difficult to live or work in. ❑ *My room was cold and unwelcoming.* ADJ

**un|well** /ʌnwel/ If you are **unwell**, you are ill. ❑ *He had been riding in Hyde Park, but felt unwell as he was being driven back to his office late this afternoon.* ADJ: v-link ADJ

**un|whole|some** /ʌnhoʊlsəm/ 1 **Unwholesome** food or drink is not healthy or good for you. ❑ *The fish were unwholesome and old.* ADJ
2 If you describe someone's feelings or behaviour as **unwholesome**, you are critical of them because they are unpleasant or unnatural. ❑ *My desire to be rich was an insane, unwholesome, oppressive desire.* ADJ [disapproval]

**un|wieldy** /ʌnwiːldi/ 1 If you describe an object as **unwieldy**, you mean that it is difficult to move or carry because it is so big or heavy. ❑ *They came panting up to his door with their unwieldy baggage.* ADJ = awkward
2 If you describe a system as **unwieldy**, you mean that it does not work very well as a result of it being too large or badly organized. ❑ *His firm must contend with the unwieldy Russian bureaucracy. ...an unwieldy legal system.* ADJ = cumbersome

**un|will|ing** /ʌnwɪlɪŋ/ 1 If you are **unwilling to** do something, you do not want to do it and will not agree to do it. ❑ *Initially the government was unwilling to accept the defeat... For months I had been either unwilling or unable to go through with it.* ADJ: usu v-link, usu ADJ to-inf ≠ willing ♦ **un|will|ing|ness** *...their unwillingness to accept responsibility for mistakes.* N-UNCOUNT: oft N to-inf
2 You can use **unwilling** to describe someone who does not really want to do the thing they are doing. ❑ *A youthful teacher, he finds himself an unwilling participant in school politics.* ADJ: usu ADJ n = reluctant ♦ **un|will|ing|ly** *My beard had started to grow, and I had unwillingly complied with the order to shave it off... Unwillingly, she moved aside.* ADV: ADV with v, ADV with cl = reluctantly

**un|wind** /ʌnwaɪnd/ (**unwinds, unwinding, unwound**) 1 When you **unwind**, you relax after you have done something that makes you tense or tired. ❑ *It helps them to unwind after a busy day at work.* VERB, V
2 If you **unwind** a length of something that is wrapped round something else or round itself, you loosen it and make it straight. You can also say that it **unwinds**. ❑ *One of them unwound a length of rope from around his waist... The thread unwound a little more.* VERB, V n, V

**un|wise** /ʌnwaɪz/ If you describe something as **unwise**, you think that it is foolish and likely to lead to a bad result. ❑ *It would be unwise to expect too much. ...a series of unwise investments in plastics and shipping.* ADJ: oft *it* v-link ADJ to-inf ≠ sensible ♦ **un|wise|ly** *She accepted that she had acted unwisely and mistakenly.* ADV: usu ADV with v, also ADV with cl

**un|wit|ting** /ʌnwɪtɪŋ/ If you describe a person or their actions as **unwitting**, you mean that the person does something or is involved in something without realizing it. ❑ *We're unwitting victims of the system... It had been an unwitting blun-* ADJ: usu ADJ n *der on Blair's part.* ♦ **un|wit|ting|ly** *He was unwittingly caught up in the confrontation.* ADV: usu ADV with v

**un|work|able** /ʌnwɜːʳkəbəl/ If you describe something such as a plan, law, or system as **unworkable**, you believe that it cannot be successful. ❑ *There is the strong possibility that such cooperation will prove unworkable... Washington is unhappy with the peace plan which it views as unworkable.* ADJ: usu v-link ADJ

**un|world|ly** /ʌnwɜːʳldli/ [1] If you describe someone as **unworldly**, you mean that they have not experienced many things in their life and do not know what sort of things usually happen to other people during their lives. ❑ *She was so young, so unworldly... He is a little unworldly about such matters.* ADJ = naive [2] If you describe someone as **unworldly**, you mean that they are not interested in having a lot of money or possessions. ❑ *Kitty's family was unworldly, unimpressed by power, or money.* ADJ ≠ worldly

**un|wor|thy** /ʌnwɜːʳði/ [1] If a person or thing is **unworthy of** something good, they do not deserve it. ❑ *He felt unworthy of being married to such an attractive woman.* ADJ: oft ADJ *of* n/-ing, ADJ to-inf ≠ worthy [2] If you say that an action is **unworthy of** someone, you mean that it is not a nice thing to do and someone with their reputation or position should not do it. [LITERARY] ❑ *His accusations are unworthy of a prime minister.* ADJ: oft ADJ *of* n

**un|wound** /ʌnwaʊnd/ **Unwound** is the past tense and past participle of **unwind**.

**un|wrap** /ʌnræp/ **(unwraps, unwrapping, unwrapped)** When you **unwrap** something, you take off the paper, plastic, or other covering that is around it. ❑ *I untied the bow and unwrapped the small box.* VERB ≠ wrap; V n

**un|writ|ten** /ʌnrɪtən/ [1] Something such as a book that is **unwritten** has not been printed or written down. ❑ *Universal have agreed to pay £2.5 million for Grisham's next, as yet unwritten, novel.* ADJ: usu ADJ n [2] An **unwritten** rule, law, or agreement is one that is understood and accepted by everyone, although it may not have been formally or officially established. ❑ *They obey the one unwritten rule that binds them all – no talking.* ADJ: usu ADJ n

**un|yield|ing** /ʌnjiːldɪŋ/ [1] You describe someone as **unyielding** when they have very strong, fixed ideas about something and are unlikely to change their mind. [WRITTEN] ❑ *The authorities proved unyielding on one crucial opposition demand... His unyielding attitude on this subject was that since he had done it, so could everyone.* ADJ [2] If a barrier or surface is **unyielding**, it is very solid or hard. [LITERARY] ❑ *...the troopers, who had to build roads through those unyielding mountains... He sat on the edge of an unyielding armchair, a cup of tea in his hand.* ADJ

**un|zip** /ʌnzɪp/ **(unzips, unzipping, unzipped)** [1] When you **unzip** something which is fastened by a zip or when it **unzips**, you open it by pulling open the zip. ❑ *James unzipped his bag... This padded changing bag unzips to form a convenient and comfortable mat for nappy changing.* VERB; V n; V [2] To **unzip** a computer file means to open a file that has been compressed. [COMPUTING] ❑ *Unzip the icons into a sub-directory.* VERB; V n

**up**

① PREPOSITION, ADVERB, AND ADJECTIVE USES
② USED IN COMBINATION AS A PREPOSITION
③ VERB USES

## ① up ♦♦♦

The preposition is pronounced /ʌp/. The adverb and adjective are pronounced /ʌp/.

**Up** is often used with verbs of movement such as 'jump' and 'pull', and also in phrasal verbs such as 'give up' and 'wash up'.

⇛ Please look at category 22 to see if the expression you are looking for is shown under another headword. [1] If a person or thing goes **up** something such as a slope, ladder, or chimney, they move away from the ground or to a higher position. ❑ *They were climbing up a narrow mountain road... I ran up the stairs and saw Alison lying at the top... The heat disappears straight up the chimney.* PREP ≠ down ♦ **Up** is also an adverb. ❑ *Finally, after an hour, I went up to Jeremy's room... Intense balls of flame rose up into the sky... He put his hand up.* ADV: ADV after v, oft ADV prep/adv ≠ down [2] If a person or thing is **up** something such as a ladder or a mountain, they are near the top of it. ❑ *He was up a ladder sawing off the tops of his apple trees... The Newton Hotel is halfway up a steep hill.* PREP ≠ down ♦ **Up** is also an adverb. ❑ *...a research station perched 4000 metres up on the lip of the crater.* ADV: ADV after v [3] You use **up** to indicate that you are looking or facing in a direction that is away from the ground or towards a higher level. ❑ *Paul answered, without looking up... Keep your head up, and look around you from time to time.* ADV: ADV after v [4] If someone stands **up**, they move so that they are standing. ❑ *He stood up and went to the window... He got up and went out into the foyer.* ADV: ADV after v [5] If you go or look **up** something such as a road or river, you go or look along it. If you are **up** a road or river, you are somewhere along it. ❑ *A line of tanks came up the road from the city... We leaned on the wooden rail of the bridge and looked up the river... He had a relation who lived up the road.* PREP: v PREP n ≠ down [6] If you are travelling to a particular place, you can say that you are going **up** to that place, especially if you are going towards the north or to a higher level of land. If you are already in such a place, you can say that you are **up** there. [mainly SPOKEN] ❑ *I'll be up to see you tomorrow... He was living up North... I live here now, but I've spent all my time up in Swaziland.* ADV: ADV after v, *be* ADV, oft ADV prep/adv [7] If you go **up** to something or someone, you move to the place where they are and stop there. ❑ *The girl ran the rest of the way across the street and up to the car... On the way out a boy of about ten came up on roller skates... He brought me up to the bar and introduced me to Dave.* ADV: ADV after v, usu ADV *to* n [8] If an amount of something goes **up**, it increases. If an amount of something is **up**, it has increased and is at a higher level than it was. ❑ *They recently put my rent up... Tourism is up, jobs are up, individual income is up... Germany's rate has also risen sharply, up from 3 percent to 4.5 percent... Over the decade, women in this category went up by 120%.* ADV: ADV after v, *be* ADV, oft ADV *to/by* amount ≠ down [9] If you are **up**, you are not in bed. ❑ *Are you sure you should be up?... Soldiers are up at seven for three hours of exercises.* ADJ: v-link ADJ [10] If a period of time is **up**, it has come to an end. ❑ *The moment the half-hour was up, Brooks rose... When the six weeks were up, everybody was sad that she had to leave.* ADJ: v-link ADJ = over [11] You say that a road is **up** when it is being repaired and cannot be used. [BRIT] ❑ *Half the road was up in Leadenhall Street, so their taxi was obliged to make a detour.* ADJ: v-link ADJ [12] If a baseball player is **up**, it is their turn to bat. ADJ: v-link ADJ [13] If a computer or computer system is **up**, it is working. Compare **down**. ADJ: v-link ADJ [14] People sometimes say '**Up yours!**' as an insult when you have said something to annoy them or make them angry. [INFORMAL, RUDE] ❑ *'Up yours,' said the reporter and stormed out into the street.* EXCLAM

**PHRASES** [15] If someone who has been in bed for some time, for example because they have been ill, is **up and about**, they are now out of bed and living their normal life. ❑ *How are you Lennox? Good to see you up and about.* PHRASE: v-link PHR [16] If you say that **something is up**, you mean that something is wrong or that something worrying is happening. [INFORMAL] ❑ *What is it then? Something's up, isn't it?... Mr. Gordon stopped talking, and his friends knew something was up.* PHRASE: V inflects [17] If you say to someone '**What's up?**' or if you tell them **what's up**, you are asking them or telling them what is wrong or what is worrying them. [INFORMAL] ❑ *'What's up?', I said to him. — 'Nothing much,' he answered... Let's sit down and then you can say what's up.* PHRASE [18] If you PHRASE:

move **up and down** somewhere, you move there repeatedly in one direction and then in the opposite direction. ❑ *He continued to jump up and down like a boy at a football match... I strolled up and down thoughtfully before calling a taxi... There's a lot of rushing up and down the gangways.* PHR after v **19** If you have **ups and downs**, you experience a mixture of good things and bad things. ❑ *Every relationship has a lot of ups and downs... The organisation has had its ups and downs. ...the ups and downs of parenthood.* PHRASE **20** If something is **on the up** or **on the up and up**, it is becoming more successful. [BRIT, INFORMAL] ❑ *They're saying that the economy is on the up... It was a great year for music, people had money, opportunities, hope – things were on the up and up.* PHRASE: usu v-link PHR **21** If someone is **on the up and up**, they are honest and sincere. [AM, INFORMAL] ❑ *I'm a pretty good judge of men. If you're honest and on the up and up, I'll be able to tell it.* PHRASE: usu v-link PHR **22** **up in arms** → see **arm**.

② **up** /ʌp/ ◆◆◆
⇛ Please look at category 9 to see if the expression you are looking for is shown under another headword. **1** If you feel **up to** doing something, you are well enough to do it. ❑ *Those patients who were up to it could move to the adjacent pool... His fellow-directors were not up to running the business without him.* PREP-PHRASE: PREP n/-ing **2** To be **up to** something means to be secretly doing something that you should not be doing. [INFORMAL] ❑ *Why did you need a room unless you were up to something?... They must have known what their father was up to.* PREP-PHRASE **3** If you say that it is **up to** someone to do something, you mean that it is their responsibility to do it. ❑ *It was up to him to make it right, no matter how long it took... I'm sure I'd have spotted him if it had been up to me.* PREP-PHRASE: oft v-link PREP n to-inf **4** **Up until** or **up to** are used to indicate the latest time at which something can happen, or the end of the period of time that you are referring to. ❑ *Please feel free to call me any time up until half past nine at night... Up to 1989, the growth of per capita income averaged 1 per cent per year.* PREP-PHRASE **5** You use **up to** to say how large something can be or what level it has reached. ❑ *Up to twenty thousand students paid between five and six thousand dollars... It could be up to two years before the process is complete.* PREP-PHRASE: PREP amount **6** If you say that something is **not up to much**, you mean that it is of poor quality. [BRIT, INFORMAL] ❑ *My own souffles aren't up to much.* PHRASE: v-link PHR **7** If someone or something is **up for** election, review, or discussion, they are about to be considered. ❑ *A third of the Senate and the entire House are up for re-election.* PREP-PHRASE **8** If you are **up against** something, you have a very difficult situation or problem to deal with. ❑ *The chairwoman is up against the greatest challenge to her position... They were up against a good team but did very well.* PREP-PHRASE **9** **up to** your **ears** → see **ear**. **up to par** → see **par**. **up to scratch** → see **scratch**.

③ **up** /ʌp/ **(ups, upping, upped)** **1** If you **up** something such as the amount of money you are offering for something, you increase it. ❑ *He upped his offer for the company.* VERB = *increase* V n **2** If you **up and** leave a place, you go away from it, often suddenly or unexpectedly. ❑ *One day he just upped and left.* VERB V *and* v

**up-and-coming** **Up-and-coming** people are likely to be successful in the future. ❑ *...his readiness to share the limelight with young, up-and-coming stars... Mr Hurford is an up-and-coming player.* ADJ: ADJ n

**up|beat** /ʌpbiːt/ **(upbeats)** **1** If people or their opinions are **upbeat**, they are cheerful and hopeful about a situation. [INFORMAL] ❑ *The Defense Secretary gave an upbeat assessment of the war so far... Neil's colleagues say he was actually in a joking, upbeat mood.* ADJ: usu ADJ n = *positive* **2** In music, the **upbeat** is the beat before the first beat of the bar. N-COUNT ≠ *downbeat*

**up|braid** /ʌpbreɪd/ **(upbraids, upbraiding, upbraided)** If you **upbraid** someone, you tell them that they have done something wrong and criticize them for doing it. [FORMAL] ❑ *His mother summoned him, upbraided him, wept and prayed... His wife set about upbraiding him for neglecting the children.* VERB = *reproach* ≠ *praise* V n V n *for* n/-ing

**up|bring|ing** /ʌpbrɪŋɪŋ/ Your **upbringing** is the way that your parents treat you and the things that they teach you when you are growing up. ❑ *Martin's upbringing shaped his whole life... Sam's mother said her son had a good upbringing and schooling.* N-UNCOUNT: usu with supp

**up|chuck** /ʌptʃʌk/ **(upchucks, upchucking, upchucked)** If you **upchuck**, food and drink comes back up from your stomach and out through your mouth. [AM, INFORMAL] VERB = *vomit*
✔ in BRIT, use **throw up**

**up|com|ing** /ʌpkʌmɪŋ/ **Upcoming** events will happen in the near future. ❑ *...the upcoming Asian Games in Beijing... We'll face a tough fight in the upcoming election.* ADJ: ADJ n

**up|country** /ʌpkʌntri/ also **up-country**. **Upcountry** places are towards the middle or north of a large country, usually in the countryside. ❑ *...a collection of upcountry hamlets.* ADJ: ADJ n ♦ **Upcountry** is also an adverb. ❑ *I run a cattle station some miles up-country... We went up-country to Ballarat.* ADV: *be* ADV, ADV after v

**up|date** **(updates, updating, updated)**
✔ The verb is pronounced /ʌpdeɪt/. The noun is pronounced /ʌpdeɪt/.

**1** If you **update** something, you make it more modern, usually by adding new parts to it or giving new information. ❑ *He was back in the office, updating the work schedule on the computer... Airlines would prefer to update rather than retrain crews. ...an updated edition of the book.* VERB V n V V-ed **2** An **update** is a news item containing the latest information about a particular situation. ❑ *She had heard the news-flash on a TV channel's news update. ...a weather update. ...football results update.* N-COUNT: usu with supp **3** If you **update** someone **on** a situation, you tell them the latest developments in that situation. ❑ *We'll update you on the day's top news stories.* VERB V n *on* n

**up|end** /ʌpend/ **(upends, upending, upended)** If you **upend** something, you turn it upside down. ❑ *He upended the beer, and swallowed. ...upended flower pots.* VERB V n V-ed

**up front** also **up-front, upfront.** **1** If you are **up front about** something, you act openly or publicly so that people know what you are doing or what you believe. [INFORMAL] ❑ *You can't help being biased so you may as well be up front about it... They tended to have a much more up-front attitude.* ADJ: usu v-link ADJ = *open* **2** If a payment is made **up front**, it is made in advance and openly, so that the person being paid can see that the money is there. ❑ *For the first time the government's actually put some money up front... Some companies charge a fee up front, but we don't think that's right.* ADV: ADV after v ♦ **Up front** is also an adjective. ❑ *The eleven percent loan has no up-front costs. ...up-front charges.* ADJ: ADJ n

**up|grade** **(upgrades, upgrading, upgraded)**
✔ The verb is pronounced /ʌpgreɪd/. The noun is pronounced /ʌpgreɪd/.

**1** If equipment or services **are upgraded**, they are improved or made more efficient. ❑ *Helicopters have been upgraded and modernized. ...upgraded catering facilities.* VERB: usu passive *be* V-ed V-ed ♦ **Upgrade** is also a noun. ❑ *...equipment which needs expensive upgrades. ...upgrades in the level of security.* N-COUNT: usu pl **2** If someone **is upgraded**, their job or status is changed so that they become more important or receive more money. ❑ *He was upgraded to security guard.* VERB: usu passive = *promote* ≠ *downgrade* *be* V-ed *to* n **3** If you **upgrade** or **are upgraded**, you change something such as your air ticket or your hotel room to one that is more expensive. ❑ *You can upgrade from self-catering accommodation to a hotel.* VERB V Also V n

**up|heav|al** /ʌphiːvᵊl/ **(upheavals)** An **upheaval** is a big change which causes a lot of trouble, confusion, and worry. ❑ *Wherever there is political upheaval, invariably there are refugees... Having a baby will mean the greatest upheaval in your life.* N-COUNT: usu adj N

**up|held** /ʌphe̲ld/ **Upheld** is the past tense and past participle of **uphold**.

**up|hill** /ʌ̲phɪl/ [1] If something or someone is **uphill** or is moving **uphill**, they are near the top of a hill or are going up a slope. ❑ *He had been running uphill a long way.* ♦ **Uphill** is also an adjective. ❑ *...a long, uphill journey... The walk from the village to Greystones was uphill all the way.* [2] If you refer to something as an **uphill** struggle or an **uphill** battle, you mean that it requires a great deal of effort and determination, but it should be possible to achieve it. ❑ *It had been an uphill struggle to achieve what she had wanted... It's an uphill battle but I think we're going to win.*
ADV: ADV after v, be ADV, ADV *from* n ≠ downhill
ADJ: usu ADJ n ≠ downhill
ADJ: ADJ n

**up|hold** /ʌpho̲ʊld/ **(upholds, upholding, upheld)** [1] If you **uphold** something such as a law, a principle, or a decision, you support and maintain it. ❑ *Our policy has been to uphold the law. ...upholding the artist's right to creative freedom.* [2] If a court of law **upholds** a legal decision that has already been made, it decides that it was the correct decision. ❑ *The crown court, however, upheld the magistrate's decision.*
VERB V n V n
VERB V n

**up|hold|er** /ʌpho̲ʊldəʳ/ **(upholders)** An **upholder** of a particular tradition or system is someone who believes strongly in it and will support it when it is threatened. [FORMAL] ❑ *...upholders of the traditional family unit.*
N-COUNT

**up|hol|stered** /ʌpho̲ʊlstəʳd/ **Upholstered** chairs and seats have a soft covering that makes them comfortable to sit on. ❑ *All of their furniture was upholstered in flowery materials.*
ADJ: oft ADJ *in* n

**up|hol|ster|er** /ʌpho̲ʊlstərəʳ/ **(upholsterers)** An **upholsterer** is someone whose job is to make and fit the soft covering on chairs and seats.
N-COUNT

**up|hol|stery** /ʌpho̲ʊlstəri/ **Upholstery** is the soft covering on chairs and seats that makes them more comfortable to sit on. ❑ *...white leather upholstery... Simon rested his head against the upholstery.*
N-UNCOUNT

**up|keep** /ʌ̲pki:p/ [1] The **upkeep** of a building or place is the work of keeping it in good condition. ❑ *The money will be used for the estate's upkeep... The maintenance department is responsible for the general upkeep of the park.* [2] The **upkeep** of a group of people or services is the process of providing them with the things that they need. ❑ *He offered to pay £100 a month towards his son's upkeep.*
N-UNCOUNT: usu with poss = maintenance
N-UNCOUNT: usu with poss = maintenance

**up|land** /ʌ̲plənd/ **(uplands)** [1] **Upland** places are situated on high land. ❑ *...San Marino, the tiny upland republic... It's important that these upland farms continue to survive.* [2] **Uplands** are areas of high land. ❑ *...a deep valley ringed about by green uplands.*
ADJ: ADJ n
N-PLURAL ≠ lowland

**up|lift** **(uplifts, uplifting, uplifted)**

✓ The verb is pronounced /ʌplɪ̲ft/. The noun is pronounced /ʌ̲plɪft/.

[1] If something **uplifts** people, it helps them to have a better life, for example by making them feel happy or by improving their social conditions. [LITERARY] ❑ *We need a little something to help sometimes, to uplift us and make us feel better... Art was created to uplift the mind and the spirit.* ♦ **Uplift** is also a noun. ❑ *This victory was a massive uplift for us.* [2] In economics, an **uplift** in something such as the price of shares is an increase in their value. [BUSINESS] ❑ *...an uplift in the stock market... Its shares were down across the first quarter, but are now showing a 20 per cent uplift.*
VERB V n V n
N-VAR
N-COUNT: usu sing, oft N *in* n

**up|lift|ed** /ʌplɪ̲ftɪd/ [1] If people's faces or arms are **uplifted**, they are pointing them upwards or are holding them up. [LITERARY] ❑ *The men support the ballerinas, who pose with their uplifted arms. ...her white, uplifted chin.* [2] If something makes you feel **uplifted**, it makes you feel very cheerful and happy. ❑ *...people whose presence left you feeling uplifted, happy and full of energy. ...a smile so radiant that he felt uplifted by it.*
ADJ: usu ADJ n
ADJ: v-link ADJ, oft ADJ *by* n

**up|lift|ing** /ʌplɪ̲ftɪŋ/ You describe something as **uplifting** when it makes you feel very cheerful and happy. ❑ *...a charming and uplifting love story... I like a film to be uplifting.*
ADJ

**up|load** /ʌplo̲ʊd/ **(uploads, uploading, uploaded)** If you **upload** data, you transfer it to your computer or from your computer to another computer. [COMPUTING]
VERB

**up|market** /ʌpmɑ̲:ʳkɪt/ also **up-market.** **Upmarket** products or services are expensive, of good quality, and intended to appeal to people in a high social class. [mainly BRIT] ❑ *Anne chose an upmarket agency aimed at professional people. ...restaurants which years ago weren't quite so upmarket as they are today.* ♦ **Upmarket** is also an adverb. ❑ *Japanese firms have moved steadily upmarket.*
ADJ: usu ADJ n ≠ downmarket
ADV: ADV after v ≠ downmarket

✓ in AM, usually use **upscale**

**upon** /əpɒ̲n/ ◆◆◇

In addition to the uses shown below, **upon** is used in phrasal verbs such as 'come upon' and 'look upon', and after some other verbs such as 'decide' and 'depend'.

[1] If one thing is **upon** another, it is on it. [FORMAL] ❑ *He set the tray upon the table... He bent forward and laid a kiss softly upon her forehead.* [2] You use **upon** when mentioning an event that is followed immediately by another event. [FORMAL] ❑ *The door on the left, upon entering the church, leads to the Crypt of St Issac... Upon conclusion of these studies, the patient was told that she had a severe problem.* [3] You use **upon** between two occurrences of the same noun in order to say that there are large numbers of the thing mentioned. ❑ *Row upon row of women surged forwards.* [4] If an event is **upon** you, it is just about to happen. ❑ *The long-threatened storm was upon us.*
PREP = on
PREP: PREP -ing/n = on
PREP: n PREP n
PREP: PREP pron

**up|per** /ʌ̲pəʳ/ ◆◇◇ [1] You use **upper** to describe something that is above something else. ❑ *There is a smart restaurant on the upper floor... Students travel the cheap lower deck and tourists the upper.* [2] You use **upper** to describe the higher part of something. ❑ *...the upper part of the foot. ...the upper rungs of the ladder.* [3] If you have **the upper hand** in a situation, you have more power than the other people involved and can make decisions about what happens. ❑ *The government was beginning to gain the upper hand... It was easy to see who had the upper hand.* [4] The **upper** of a shoe is the top part of it, which is attached to the sole and the heel. ❑ *Leather uppers allow the feet to breathe.*
ADJ: ADJ n, the ADJ ≠ lower
ADJ: ADJ n ≠ lower
PHRASE: PHR after v
N-COUNT: usu pl

**up|per case** **Upper case** letters are capital letters. ❑ *Most schools teach children lower case letters first, and upper case letters later.* ♦ **Upper case** is also a noun. ❑ *I'm wondering if 'per capita' ought to have upper case, or should it be lower case?*
ADJ: usu ADJ n ≠ lower case
N-UNCOUNT ≠ lower case

**up|per class** **(upper classes)** also **upper-class.** The **upper class** or the **upper classes** are the group of people in a society who own the most property and have the highest social status, and who may not need to work for money. ❑ *...goods specifically designed to appeal to the tastes of the upper class.* ♦ **Upper class** is also an adjective. ❑ *All of them came from wealthy, upper class families.*
N-COUNT-COLL: usu *the* N
ADJ: usu ADJ n

**upper|class|man** /ʌ̲pəʳklɑ:smən/ **(upperclassmen)** An **upperclassman** is a junior or senior student in an American high school, college, or university. [AM]
N-COUNT

**up|per crust** also **upper-crust.** The **upper crust** are the upper classes. [INFORMAL] ❑ *...the kind of lifestyle of the privileged upper crust.* ♦ **Upper crust** is also an adjective. ❑ *Sergeant Parrott normally spoke with an upper-crust accent.*
N-SING-COLL
ADJ: ADJ n

**upper|cut** /ʌ̲pəʳkʌt/ **(uppercuts)** An **uppercut** is a type of punch used in boxing. It is a hard upward blow to the chin.
N-COUNT

**Up|per House** **(Upper Houses)** [1] In Britain, **the Upper House** is **the House of Lords**.
N-PROPER

❑ *The decision was announced after objections were raised in the Upper House of Parliament.* [2] In the United States, **the Upper House** is **the Senate**. N-PROPER
[3] In other countries where the parliament is divided into two groups of members, **the Upper House** is the more senior of these groups, although it may not be more powerful. ❑ *The Upper House of the German parliament is to meet today in Berlin.* N-COUNT: also N-PROPER

**up|per lip** **(upper lips)** [1] Your **upper lip** is the part of your face between your mouth and your nose. ❑ *The beginnings of a moustache showed on his upper lip.* N-COUNT: usu sing [2] Your **upper lip** is the higher of your two lips. ❑ *His upper lip was flat, but the lower one sagged.* N-COUNT ≠ lower lip

**upper|most** /ʌpəʳmoʊst/ [1] **The uppermost** part of something is the part that is higher than the rest of it. **The uppermost** thing is the highest one of a group of things. ❑ *John was on the uppermost floor of the three-storey gatehouse... The rain spattered on the uppermost leaves.* ADJ: usu ADJ n = topmost ♦ **Uppermost** is also an adverb. ❑ *Lift the fish and carefully place it on a large board, flat side uppermost.* ADV: n ADV = up [2] If something is **uppermost in** a particular situation, it is the most important thing in that situation. ❑ *The economy appears to be uppermost in people's minds.* ADJ: usu v-link ADJ

**up|pi|ty** /ʌpɪti/ If you say that someone is **uppity**, you mean that they are behaving as if they were very important and you do not think that they are important. [INFORMAL] ❑ *If you just tried to show normal dignity, you were viewed as uppity.* ADJ disapproval

**up|raised** /ʌpreɪzd/ If your hand or an object is **upraised**, you are holding it up in the air. ❑ *A soldier stood on the centre line of the road, his arm upraised. ...the landlady's upraised glass.* ADJ

**up|right** /ʌpraɪt/ **(uprights)** [1] If you are sitting or standing **upright**, you are sitting or standing with your back straight, rather than bending or lying down. ❑ *Helen sat upright in her chair... Jerrold pulled himself upright on the bed... He moved into an upright position.* ADJ: usu ADJ after v, v-link ADJ, also ADJ n [2] An **upright** vacuum cleaner or freezer is tall rather than wide. ❑ *...the latest state-of-the-art upright vacuum cleaners.* ADJ: ADJ n [3] An **upright** chair has a straight back and no arms. ❑ *He was sitting on an upright chair beside his bed, reading.* ADJ [4] You can refer to vertical posts or the vertical parts of an object as **uprights**. ❑ *...the uprights of a four-poster bed.* N-COUNT [5] You can describe people as **upright** when they are careful to follow acceptable rules of behaviour and behave in a moral way. ❑ *...a very upright, trustworthy man.* ADJ: usu ADJ n

**up|right pia|no** **(upright pianos)** An **upright piano** is a piano in which the strings are arranged vertically, rather than horizontally as they are in a grand piano. N-COUNT

**up|ris|ing** /ʌpraɪzɪŋ/ **(uprisings)** When there is an **uprising**, a group of people start fighting against the people who are in power in their country, because they want to bring about a political change. ❑ *...a popular uprising against the authoritarian government... Isolated attacks in the north-east of the country have now turned into a full-scale uprising.* N-COUNT: usu sing = rebellion, revolt

**up-river** also **upriver.** Something that is moving **up-river** is moving towards the source of a river, from a point down the river. Something that is **up-river** is towards the source of a river. ❑ *Heavy goods could be brought up-river in barges... He has a house down there but it's miles up river... The vineyards of Anjou extend from west of Angers to up-river of Saumur. ...La Reole, up-river from St-Macaire.* ADV: ADV after v, be ADV, oft ADV of/from n ≠ down-river ♦ **Up-river** is also an adjective. ❑ *...an upriver trip in Central Africa.* ADJ: ADJ n

**up|roar** /ʌprɔːʳ/ [1] If there is **uproar**, there is a lot of shouting and noise because people are very angry or upset about something. ❑ *The announcement caused uproar in the crowd... The courtroom was in an uproar.* N-UNCOUNT: also a N, oft in N [2] You can also use **uproar** to refer to a lot of public criticism and debate about something that has made people angry. ❑ *The town is in uproar over the dispute... The surprise announcement could cause an uproar in the United States.* N-UNCOUNT: also a N

**up|roari|ous** /ʌprɔːriəs/ When events or people are **uproarious**, they make people laugh in a very noisy way. [LITERARY] ❑ *He had spent several uproarious evenings at the Embassy Club... The noise of talk and laughter was uproarious.* ADJ ♦ **up|roari|ous|ly** *Bob laughed uproariously. ...an uproariously funny story.* ADV: ADV after v, ADV adj

**up|root** /ʌpruːt/ **(uproots, uprooting, uprooted)** [1] If you **uproot yourself** or if you **are uprooted**, you leave, or are made to leave, a place where you have lived for a long time. ❑ *...the trauma of uprooting themselves from their homes... He had no wish to uproot Dena from her present home. ...refugees who were uprooted during Ethiopia's civil war.* VERB V pron-refl V n be V-ed [2] If someone **uproots** a tree or plant, or if the wind **uproots** it, it is pulled out of the ground. ❑ *...fallen trees which have been uprooted by the storm. ...uprooted trees.* VERB V n V-ed

**up|scale** /ʌpskeɪl/ **Upscale** is used to describe products or services that are expensive, of good quality, and intended to appeal to people in a high social class. [AM] ❑ *...upscale department-store chains such as Bloomingdale's and Saks Fifth Avenue.* ADJ: usu ADJ n ♦ **Upscale** is also an adverb. ❑ *T-shirts, the epitome of American casualness, have moved upscale.* ADV: ADV after v

✓ in BRIT, use **upmarket**

**up|set** **(upsets, upsetting, upset)** ◆◇◇

✓ The verb and adjective are pronounced /ʌpset/. The noun is pronounced /ʌpset/.

[1] If you are **upset**, you are unhappy or disappointed because something unpleasant has happened to you. ❑ *After she died I felt very, very upset... Marta looked upset... She sounded upset when I said you couldn't give her an appointment... They are terribly upset by the break-up of their parents' marriage.* ADJ: usu v-link ADJ, oft ADJ by/about n ♦ **Upset** is also a noun. ❑ *...stress and other emotional upsets.* N-COUNT [2] If something **upsets** you, it makes you feel worried or unhappy. ❑ *She warned me not to say anything to upset him... Don't upset yourself, Ida.* VERB V n V pron-refl ♦ **up|set|ting** *Childhood illness can be upsetting for children and parents alike... I will never see him again and that is a terribly upsetting thought.* ADJ: usu v-link ADJ = distressing
[3] If events **upset** something such as a procedure or a state of affairs, they cause it to go wrong. ❑ *...a deal that would upset the balance of power in the world's gold markets.* VERB V n ♦ **Upset** is also a noun. ❑ *Markets are very sensitive to any upsets in the Japanese economic machine.* N-COUNT [4] If you **upset** an object, you accidentally knock or push it over so that it scatters over a large area. ❑ *Don't upset the piles of sheets under the box.* VERB V n [5] A stomach **upset** is a slight illness in your stomach caused by an infection or by something that you have eaten. ❑ *Paul was unwell last night with a stomach upset.* N-COUNT: supp N ♦ **Upset** is also an adjective. ❑ *Larry is suffering from an upset stomach.* ADJ: ADJ n [6] to **upset the applecart** → see **applecart**.

**up|shot** /ʌpʃɒt/ **The upshot** of a series of events or discussions is the final result of them, usually a surprising result. ❑ *The upshot is that we have lots of good but not very happy employees.* N-SING: the N = outcome

**up|side down** /ʌpsaɪd daʊn/ also **upside-down.** [1] If something has been moved **upside down**, it has been turned round so that the part that is usually lowest is above the part that is usually highest. ❑ *The painting was hung upside down... Salter held the bag by the corners and shook it upside down.* ADV: ADV after v, n ADV ♦ **Upside down** is also an adjective. ❑ *His eyes were open and everything he saw was upside down... Tony had an upside-down map of Britain on his wall.* ADJ [2] to **turn** something **upside down** → see **turn**.

**up|stage** /ʌpsteɪdʒ/ **(upstages, upstaging, upstaged)** [1] When an actor is **upstage** or moves **upstage**, he or she is or moves towards the back ADV: ADV after v, be ADV, part of the stage. [TECHNICAL] ❑ *Upstage and right of centre, Robert Morris stands with his back to the audience... Position a camera upstage... They slowly moved from upstage left into the centre.* (prep ADV ≠downstage) ♦ **Upstage** is also an adjective. ❑ *...the large upstage box that Noble used for his 1990 production of King Lear.* (ADJ: ADJ n ≠downstage) [2] If someone **upstages** you, they draw attention away from you by being more attractive or interesting. (VERB) ❑ *He had a younger brother who always publicly upstaged him.* (V n)

**up|stairs** /ʌpsteəʳz/ [1] If you go **upstairs** in a building, you go up a staircase towards a higher floor. (ADV: ADV after v ≠downstairs) ❑ *He went upstairs and changed into fresh clothes.* [2] If something or someone is **upstairs** in a building, they are on a floor that is higher than the ground floor. (ADV: be ADV, n ADV ≠downstairs) ❑ *The restaurant is upstairs and consists of a large, open room... The boys are curled asleep in the small bedroom upstairs.* [3] An **upstairs** room or object is situated on a floor of a building that is higher than the ground floor. (ADJ: ADJ n) ❑ *Marsani moved into the upstairs apartment. ...an upstairs balcony.* [4] **The upstairs** of a building is the floor or floors that are higher than the ground floor. (N-SING: the N ≠downstairs) ❑ *Frances invited them to occupy the upstairs of her home.*

**up|stand|ing** /ʌpstændɪŋ/ **Upstanding** people behave in a morally acceptable way. [FORMAL] (ADJ: usu ADJ n = upright) ❑ *You look like a nice upstanding young man.*

**up|start** /ʌpstɑːʳt/ **(upstarts)** You can refer to someone as an **upstart** when they behave as if they are important, but you think that they are too new in a place or job to be treated as important. (N-COUNT [disapproval]) ❑ *Many prefer a familiar authority figure to a young upstart.*

**up|state** /ʌpsteɪt/ **Upstate** means belonging or relating to the parts of a state that are furthest to the north or furthest from the main city. [mainly AM] (ADJ: ADJ n) ❑ *...an idyllic village in upstate New York.* ♦ **Upstate** is also an adverb. ❑ *These buses will carry families upstate to visit relatives in prison.* (ADV: ADV after v, n ADV)

**up|stream** /ʌpstriːm/ Something that is moving **upstream** is moving towards the source of a river, from a point further down the river. Something that is **upstream** is towards the source of a river. (ADV: ADV after v, be ADV, n ADV, oft ADV of/from n ≠downstream) ❑ *The water rose high enough for them to continue upstream. ...the river police, whose headquarters are just upstream of the Isle St Louis.* ♦ **Upstream** is also an adjective. ❑ *Steps lead down to the subway from the upstream side.* (ADJ: ADJ n ≠downstream)

**up|surge** /ʌpsɜːʳdʒ/ If there is an **upsurge in** something, there is a sudden, large increase in it. [FORMAL] (N-SING: oft N in/of n) ❑ *...the upsurge in oil prices... Saudi bankers say there's been an upsurge of business confidence since the end of the war.*

**up|swing** /ʌpswɪŋ/ **(upswings)** An **upswing** is a sudden improvement in something such as an economy, or an increase in an amount or level. (N-COUNT: usu sing, oft N in n, on the N ≠downswing) ❑ *...an upswing in the economy... Violent crime is on the upswing.*

**up|take** /ʌpteɪk/ [1] A person's **uptake of** something is the amount of it that they use. [TECHNICAL] (N-SING: usu with supp) ❑ *The drug increases the number of red cells in the blood, enhancing oxygen uptake by 10 per cent. ...research in relation to the uptake of nitrate into vegetables.* [2] You say that someone is **quick on the uptake** when they understand things quickly. You say that someone is **slow on the uptake** when they have difficulty understanding simple or obvious things. (PHRASE: v-link PHR) ❑ *She is not an intellectual, but is quick on the uptake... Carol was absent-minded and a little slow on the uptake.*

**up-tempo** also **uptempo.** An **up-tempo** piece of music has a fast beat. (ADJ: usu ADJ n) ❑ *...an up-tempo arrangement of 'Some Enchanted Evening'.*

**up|tight** /ʌptaɪt/ Someone who is **uptight** is tense, nervous, or annoyed about something and so is difficult to be with. [INFORMAL] (ADJ: usu v-link ADJ ≠relaxed) ❑ *Penny never got uptight about exams.*

**up-to-date** also **up to date.** [1] If something is **up-to-date**, it is the newest thing of its kind. (ADJ ≠out of date) ❑ *...Germany's most up to date electric power station. ...enhancing the system and bringing it up to date... This production is bang up-to-date.* [2] If you are **up-to-date** about something, you have the latest information about it. (ADJ: usu v-link ADJ) ❑ *We'll keep you up to date with any news.*

**up-to-the-minute** also **up to the minute. Up-to-the-minute** information is the latest information that you can get about something. (ADJ: usu ADJ n) ❑ *...24 hours a day up-to-the-minute instant news... Computers give them up-to-the-minute information on sales and stocks.*

**up|town** /ʌptaʊn/ If you go **uptown**, or go to a place **uptown**, you go away from the centre of a town or city towards the edge. **Uptown** sometimes refers to a part of the city other than the main business district. [mainly AM] (ADV: ADV after v ≠downtown) ❑ *He rode uptown and made his way to Bob's apartment... Susan continued to live uptown... There's a skating rink uptown.* ♦ **Uptown** is also an adjective. (ADJ: ADJ n ≠downtown) ❑ *...uptown clubs. ...a small uptown radio station. ...uptown New York.*

**up|trend** /ʌptrend/ An **uptrend** is a general improvement in something such as a market or the economy. (N-SING ≠downtrend) ❑ *Racal Electronics shares have been in a strong uptrend... Many analysts think the dollar is on an uptrend.*

**up|turn** /ʌptɜːʳn/ **(upturns)** If there is an **upturn** in the economy or in a company or industry, it improves or becomes more successful. (N-COUNT: oft N in n ≠downturn) ❑ *They do not expect an upturn in the economy until the end of the year... There has been a modest upturn in most parts of the industry.*

**up|turned** /ʌptɜːʳnd/ [1] Something that is **upturned** points upwards. (ADJ: usu ADJ n) ❑ *...his eyes closed and his palms upturned.* [2] Something that is **upturned** is upside down. (ADJ: usu ADJ n) ❑ *...upturned buckets... He clung to the upturned boat, screaming for help.*

**up|ward** /ʌpwəʳd/ [1] An **upward** movement or look is directed towards a higher place or a higher level. (ADJ: ADJ n ≠downward) ❑ *She started once again on the steep upward climb... She gave him a quick, upward look, then lowered her eyes.* [2] If you refer to an **upward** trend or an **upward** spiral, you mean that something is increasing in quantity or price. (ADJ: ADJ n ≠downward) ❑ *...the Army's concern that the upward trend in the numbers avoiding military service may continue.*

**up|ward|ly mo|bile** If you describe someone as **upwardly mobile**, you mean that they are moving, have moved, or are trying to move to a higher social position. (ADJ) ❑ *The Party has been unable to attract upwardly mobile voters.* ♦ **The upwardly mobile** are people who are upwardly mobile. (N-PLURAL: the N) ❑ *...the large detached houses of the upwardly mobile with their double garages and array of cars.*

**up|wards** /ʌpwəʳdz/ also **upward.** [1] If someone moves or looks **upwards**, they move or look up towards a higher place. (ADV: ADV after v, n ADV ≠downwards) ❑ *'There,' said Jack, pointing upwards... They climbed upward along the steep cliffs surrounding the village... Hunter nodded again and gazed upwards in fear... Lie face upwards with a cushion under your head.* [2] If an amount or rate moves **upwards**, it increases. (ADV: ADV after v ≠downwards) ❑ *...with prices soon heading upwards in high street stores... Unemployment will continue upward for much of this year... The share price is likely to leap upwards.* [3] A quantity that is **upwards of** a particular number is more than that number. (PREP-PHRASE: PREP amount) ❑ *...projects worth upwards of 200 million pounds... It costs upward of $40,000 a year to keep some prisoners in prison.*

**up|wind** /ʌpwɪnd/ If something moves **upwind**, it moves in the opposite direction to the wind. If something is **upwind**, the wind is blowing away from it. (ADV: ADV after v, be ADV, oft ADV of n ≠downwind) ❑ *...riding a bike upwind... The rich went to live in the west of London, upwind of the smell of people and industry.* ♦ **Upwind** is also an adjective. (ADJ: ADJ n) ❑ *...big trees at the forest's upwind edge.*

**ura|nium** /jʊreɪniəm/ **Uranium** is a naturally occurring radioactive metal that is used to produce nuclear energy and weapons. N-UNCOUNT

**ur|ban** /ɜːʳbən/ **Urban** means belonging to, or relating to, a town or city. ❑ *Most of the population is an urban population... Most urban areas are close to a park. ...urban planning.* ◆◇◇ ADJ: usu ADJ n ≠ *rural*

**ur|bane** /ɜːʳbeɪn/ Someone who is **urbane** is polite and appears comfortable in social situations. ❑ *She describes him as urbane and charming... In conversation, he was suave and urbane.* ADJ = *cultured* ≠ *gauche* ♦ **ur|ban|ity** /ɜːʳbænɪti/ *Fearey had all the charm and urbanity of the trained diplomat.* N-UNCOUNT

**ur|bani|za|tion** /ɜːʳbənaɪzeɪʃᵊn/

✔ in BRIT, also use **urbanisation**

**Urbanization** is the process of creating towns in country areas. N-UNCOUNT

**ur|ban|ized** /ɜːʳbənaɪzd/

✔ in BRIT, also use **urbanised**

1 An **urbanized** country or area has many buildings and a lot of industry and business. ❑ *Zambia is black Africa's most urbanised country... All the nice areas in Florida are becoming more and more urbanized.* ADJ: usu ADJ n 2 An **urbanized** population consists of people who live and work in a town. ADJ

**ur|ban myth** **(urban myths)** or **urban leg|end** An **urban myth** is a strange or surprising story which many people believe, but which is not actually true. N-COUNT

**ur|chin** /ɜːʳtʃɪn/ **(urchins)** An **urchin** is a young child who is dirty and poorly dressed. [OLD-FASHIONED] ❑ *We were in the bazaar with all the little urchins watching us.* ➔ See also **sea urchin**. N-COUNT

**Urdu** /ʊəʳduː, ɜːʳ-/ **Urdu** is an official language of Pakistan. Urdu is also spoken in India. N-UNCOUNT

**urge** /ɜːʳdʒ/ **(urges, urging, urged)** 1 If you **urge** someone **to** do something, you try hard to persuade them to do it. ❑ *They urged parliament to approve plans for their reform programme.* ◆◆◇ VERB V n to-inf 2 If you **urge** someone somewhere, you make them go there by touching them or talking to them. ❑ *He slipped his arm around her waist and urged her away from the window... 'Come on, Grace,' he was urging her, 'don't wait, hurry up.'* VERB V n prep/adv V n 3 If you **urge** a course of action, you strongly advise that it should be taken. ❑ *He urged restraint on the security forces... We urge vigorous action to be taken immediately.* VERB V n *on* n V n 4 If you have an **urge to** do or have something, you have a strong wish to do or have it. ❑ *He had an urge to open a shop of his own.* N-COUNT: oft N to-inf

♦ **urge on** If you **urge** someone **on**, you encourage them to do something. ❑ *She had a strong and supportive sister who urged her on... Visitors remember a lean, cheerful figure on horseback urging on his men.* PHRASAL VERB = *encourage* V n P V P n (not pron)

**ur|gent** /ɜːʳdʒᵊnt/ 1 If something is **urgent**, it needs to be dealt with as soon as possible. ❑ *There is an urgent need for food and water... He had urgent business in New York.* ◆◇◇ ADJ = *pressing* ♦ **ur|gen|cy** *The urgency of finding a cure attracted some of the best minds in medical science... It is a matter of utmost urgency.* N-UNCOUNT ♦ **ur|gent|ly** *Red Cross officials said they urgently needed bread and water... The money was most urgently required.* ADV: ADV with v 2 If you speak in an **urgent** way, you show that you are anxious for people to notice something or to do something. ❑ *His voice was low and urgent... His mother leaned forward and spoke to him in urgent undertones.* ADJ ♦ **ur|gen|cy** *She was surprised at the urgency in his voice.* N-UNCOUNT ♦ **ur|gent|ly** *They hastened to greet him and asked urgently, 'Did you find it?'* ADV: ADV with v

**uri|nal** /jʊraɪnᵊl, AM jʊrɪnᵊl/ **(urinals)** A **urinal** is a bowl fixed to the wall of a men's public toilet for men to urinate in. N-COUNT

**uri|nary** /jʊərɪnəri, AM -neri/ **Urinary** means belonging to or related to the parts of a person's body through which urine flows. [MEDICAL] ❑ *...urinary tract infections.* ADJ: ADJ n

**uri|nate** /jʊərɪneɪt/ **(urinates, urinating, urinated)** When someone **urinates**, they get rid of urine from their body. VERB

**urine** /jʊərɪn/ **Urine** is the liquid that you get rid of from your body when you go to the toilet. N-UNCOUNT

**URL** /juː ɑːr el/ **(URLs)** A **URL** is an address that shows where a particular page can be found on the World Wide Web. **URL** is an abbreviation for 'Uniform Resource Locator'. [COMPUTING] ❑ *The URL for the Lonely Planet travel centre is http://www.lonelyplanet.com.* N-COUNT

**urn** /ɜːʳn/ **(urns)** 1 An **urn** is a container in which a dead person's ashes are kept. N-COUNT 2 An **urn** is a metal container used for making a large quantity of tea or coffee and keeping it hot. N-COUNT: usu supp N

**us** /əs, STRONG ʌs/ ◆◆◆

✔ **Us** is the first person plural pronoun. **Us** is used as the object of a verb or a preposition.

1 A speaker or writer uses **us** to refer both to himself or herself and to one or more other people. You can use **us** before a noun to make it clear which group of people you are referring to. ❑ *Neither of us forgot about it... Heather went to the kitchen to get drinks for us... They don't like us much... He showed us aspects of the game that we had never seen before... Another time of great excitement for us boys was when war broke out.* PRON: v PRON, prep PRON 2 **Us** is sometimes used to refer to people in general. ❑ *All of us will struggle fairly hard to survive if we are in danger... Each of us will have our own criteria for success.* PRON: v PRON, prep PRON 3 A speaker or writer may use **us** instead of 'me' in order to include the audience or reader in what they are saying. [mainly FORMAL] ❑ *This brings us to the second question I asked.* PRON: v PRON, prep PRON 4 In non-standard English, **us** is sometimes used instead of 'me'. [BRIT, SPOKEN] ❑ *'Hang on a bit,' said Eileen. 'I'm not finished yet. Give us a chance.'* PRON: v PRON, prep PRON

**US** /juː es/ also **U.S.** **The US** is an abbreviation for **the United States**. ❑ *The first time I saw TV was when I arrived in the US in 1956... They are to inherit 100,000 US dollars.* N-PROPER: *the* N, N n

**USA** /juː es eɪ/ also **U.S.A.** **The USA** is an abbreviation for **the United States of America**. N-PROPER: *the* N

**us|able** /juːzəbᵊl/ If something is **usable**, it is in a good enough state or condition to be used. ❑ *Charity shops and jumble sales welcome usable clothes... Half of the island's population has no usable English.* ADJ

**USAF** /juː es eɪ ef/ also **U.S.A.F.** **The USAF** is an abbreviation for **the United States Air Force**. N-PROPER: usu *the* N

**us|age** /juːsɪdʒ/ **(usages)** 1 **Usage** is the way in which words are actually used in particular contexts, especially with regard to their meanings. ❑ *The word 'undertaker' had long been in common usage... He was a stickler for the correct usage of English.* N-UNCOUNT: usu with supp 2 A **usage** is a meaning that a word has or a way in which it can be used. ❑ *It's very definitely a usage which has come over to Britain from America.* N-COUNT 3 **Usage** is the degree to which something is used or the way in which it is used. ❑ *Parts of the motor wore out because of constant usage... If your water usage is very small it may be worthwhile opting for a meter.* N-UNCOUNT: usu with supp

**USB** /juː es biː/ **(USBs)** A **USB** on a computer is a place where you can attach another piece of equipment, for example a printer. **USB** is an abbreviation for 'Universal Serial Bus'. [COMPUTING] ❑ *The device plugs into one of the laptop's USB ports.* N-COUNT

**use**

① VERB USES
② NOUN USES

① **use** /juːz/ **(uses, using, used)** 1 If you **use** something, you do something with it in order to do a job or to achieve a particular result or effect. ❑ *Trim off the excess pastry using a sharp knife... He had simply used a little imagination... Officials used loud hailers to call for calm... The show uses Zondo's* ◆◆◆ VERB V n V n V n to-inf V n prep

*trial and execution as its framework.* 2 If you **use** a supply of something, you finish it so that none of it is left. ❑ *You used all the ice cubes and didn't put the ice trays back... They've never had anything spare – they've always used it all.* ♦ **Use up** means the same as **use**. ❑ *It isn't them who use up the world's resources... We were breathing really fast, and using the air up quickly.*
VERB; V n; V n; PHRASAL VERB; V P n (not pron); V n P

3 If someone **uses** drugs, they take drugs regularly, especially illegal ones. ❑ *He denied he had used drugs.*
VERB; = take, do; V n

4 You can say that someone **uses** the toilet or bathroom as a polite way of saying that they go to the toilet. ❑ *Wash your hands after using the toilet... He asked whether he could use my bathroom.*
VERB; politeness; V n; V n

5 If you **use** a particular word or expression, you say or write it, because it has the meaning that you want to express. ❑ *The judge liked using the word 'wicked' of people he had sent to jail.*
VERB; V n

6 If you **use** a particular name, you call yourself by that name, especially when it is not the name that you usually call yourself. ❑ *Now I use a false name if I'm meeting people for the first time.*
VERB; V n

7 If you say that someone **uses** people, you disapprove of them because they make others do things for them in order to benefit or gain some advantage from it, and not because they care about the other people. ❑ *Be careful she's not just using you... Why do I have the feeling I'm being used again?*
VERB; disapproval; = exploit; V n; V n

8 → See also **used**.

② **use** /juːs/ **(uses)** 1 Your **use** of something is the action or fact of your using it. ❑ *The treatment does not involve the use of any artificial drugs. ...research related to microcomputers and their use in classrooms... We are denied use of the land by the ruling classes... He would support a use of force if the UN deemed it necessary.*
◆◆◇ N-UNCOUNT: also *a* N, usu N *of* n

2 If you have **a use for** something, you need it or can find something to do with it. ❑ *You will no longer have a use for the magazines... They both loved the fabric, but couldn't find a use for it.*
N-SING: *a* N *for* n

3 If something has a particular **use**, it is intended for a particular purpose. ❑ *Infrared detectors have many uses... It's an interesting scientific phenomenon, but of no practical use whatever... French furniture was designed for every use... The report outlined possible uses for the new weapon. ...Elderflower Water for use as an eye and skin lotion... We need to recognize that certain uses of the land upon which we live are simply wrong.*
N-VAR: with supp, oft adj N, N *of/for* n, N *as/in* n

4 If you have the **use of** something, you have the permission or ability to use it. ❑ *She will have the use of the car one night a week. ...young people who at some point in the past have lost the use of their limbs... You will have full use of all the new leisure club facilities.*
N-UNCOUNT: also *the* N, usu N *of* n

5 A **use** of a word is a particular meaning that it has or a particular way in which it can be used. ❑ *There are new uses of words coming in and old uses dying out.*
N-COUNT: with supp, oft N *of* n

6 Your **use of** a particular name is the fact of your calling yourself by it. ❑ *Police have been hampered by Mr Urquhart's use of bogus names.*
N-UNCOUNT: N *of* n

**PHRASES** 7 If something is **for the use of** a particular person or group of people, it is for that person or group to use. ❑ *The leisure facilities are there for the use of guests... He raises crops mainly for the use of his family.*
PHRASE: PHR n

8 If you say that being something or knowing someone **has** its **uses**, you mean that it makes it possible for you to do what you otherwise would not be able to do. [INFORMAL] ❑ *Being a hospital Sister had its uses.*
PHRASE: V inflects

9 If something such as a technique, building, or machine is **in use**, it is used regularly by people. If it has gone **out of use**, it is no longer used regularly by people. ❑ *...the methods of making Champagne which are still in use today... The site has been out of use for many years.*
PHRASE: usu v-link PHR

10 If you **make use of** something, you do something with it in order to do a job or achieve a particular result or effect. [WRITTEN] ❑ *Not all nursery schools make use of the opportunities open to them. ...making use of the same bottle time after time.*
PHRASE: V inflects, PHR n

11 You use expressions such as **it's no use**, **there's no use**, and **what's the use** to indicate that a particular action will not achieve anything. ❑ *It's no use arguing with a drunk... There's no use you asking me any more questions... What's the use of complaining?*
PHRASE: V inflects, usu PHR -ing

12 If you say **it's no use**, you mean that you have failed to do something and realize that it is useless to continue trying because it is impossible. ❑ *It's no use. Let's hang up and try for a better line.*
PHRASE: V inflects

13 If something or someone is **of use**, they are useful. If they are **no use**, they are not at all useful. ❑ *The contents of this booklet should be of use to all students... I'm sorry, I've been no use to you.*
PHRASE: usu v-link PHR, oft PHR *to* n

| **used** |
|---|
| ① MODAL USES AND PHRASES |
| ② ADJECTIVE USES |

① **used** /juːst/ 1 If something **used to** be done or **used to** be the case, it was done regularly in the past or was the case in the past. ❑ *People used to come and visit him every day... He used to be one of the professors at the School of Education... I feel more compassion and less anger than I used to.*
◆◆◇ PHRASE

2 If something **used not to** be done or **used not to** be the case, it was not done in the past or was not the case in the past. The forms **did not use to** and **did not used to** are also found, especially in spoken English. ❑ *Borrowing used not to be recommended... At some point kids start doing things they didn't use to do. They get more independent... He didn't used to like anyone walking on the lawns in the back garden.*
PHRASE: with neg

3 If you **are used to** something, you are familiar with it because you have done it or experienced it many times before. ❑ *I'm used to having my sleep interrupted... It doesn't frighten them. They're used to it.*
PHRASE: V inflects, PHR n/-ing

4 If you **get used to** something or someone, you become familiar with it or get to know them, so that you no longer feel that the thing or person is unusual or surprising. ❑ *This is how we do things here. You'll soon get used to it... He took some getting used to.*
PHRASE: V inflects

② **used** /juːzd/ 1 A **used** object is dirty or spoiled because it has been used, and usually needs to be thrown away or washed. ❑ *...a used cotton ball stained with makeup... He took a used envelope bearing an Irish postmark.*
ADJ: usu ADJ n ≠ unused

2 A **used** car has already had one or more owners. ❑ *Would you buy a used car from this man?... His only big purchase has been a used Ford.*
ADJ: usu ADJ n = second-hand

**use|ful** /juːsfʊl/ 1 If something is **useful**, you can use it to do something or to help you in some way. ❑ *The slow cooker is very useful for people who go out all day... Hypnotherapy can be useful in helping you give up smoking... The police gained a great deal of useful information about the organization.* ♦ **use|ful|ly** *...the problems to which computers could be usefully applied... We need to find ways of dealing creatively and usefully with our feelings.* ♦ **use|ful|ness** *His interest lay in the usefulness of his work, rather than in any personal credit.*
◆◆◇ ADJ ≠ useless; ADV: ADV with v; N-UNCOUNT

2 If an object or skill **comes in useful**, it can help you achieve something in a particular situation. ❑ *The accommodation is some distance from the clubhouse, so a hire car comes in useful.*
PHRASE: V inflects

**use|less** /juːsləs/ 1 If something is **useless**, you cannot use it. ❑ *He realised that their money was useless in this country... Computers would be useless without software writers.* ♦ **use|less|ly** *His right arm hung rather uselessly.* ♦ **use|less|ness** *The car had rusted almost to the point of uselessness.*
ADJ: usu v-link ADJ ≠ useful; ADV; N-UNCOUNT

2 If something is **useless**, it does not achieve anything helpful or good. ❑ *She knew it was useless to protest. ...a useless punishment which fails to stop drug trafficking.* ♦ **use|less|ly** *Uselessly, he checked the same pockets he'd checked before.* ♦ **use|less|ness** *...the uselessness of their research.*
ADJ: oft *it* v-link ADJ to-inf = pointless; ADV; N-UNCOUNT

3 If you say that someone or something is **useless**, you mean that they are no good at all. [INFORMAL] ❑ *Their education system is useless... He was useless at any game with a ball.*
ADJ: oft ADJ *at* n = hopeless

4 If someone feels **useless**, they feel bad because they are unable to help someone or achieve anything. ❑ *She sits at home all day, watching TV and feeling useless.*
ADJ

♦ **use|less|ness** *...the sense of uselessness and the boredom of empty days.*
N-UNCOUNT

**Use|net** /juːznet/ **Usenet** is a computer network that links newsgroups on the Internet. [COMPUTING]
N-UNCOUNT

**user** /juːzəʳ/ **(users)** A **user** is a person or thing that uses something such as a place, facility, product, or machine. ❑ *Beach users have complained about people walking their dogs on the sand. ...a regular user of Holland's health-care system. ...a user of electric current, such as an electric motor, a lamp, or a toaster.*
◆◇◇ N-COUNT: with supp

**user-friendly** If you describe something such as a machine or system as **user-friendly**, you mean that it is well designed and easy to use. ❑ *This an entirely computer operated system which is very user friendly. ...user-friendly libraries.*
ADJ

**user group** **(user groups)** A **user group** is a group of people with the same interests, who use a particular product or service. ❑ *PLATFORM is an alliance of more than 80 rail-user groups. ...the IBM PC User Group.*
N-COUNT

**ush|er** /ʌʃəʳ/ **(ushers, ushering, ushered)** [1] If you **usher** someone somewhere, you show them where they should go, often by going with them. [FORMAL] ❑ *I ushered him into the office... They were quickly ushered away.*
VERB; V n prep/adv; V n prep/adv

[2] An **usher** is a person who shows people where to sit, for example at a wedding or at a concert. ❑ *He did part-time work as an usher in a theatre.*
N-COUNT

[3] An **usher** is a person who organizes people who are attending a law court in Britain.
N-COUNT

♦ **usher in** If one thing **ushers in** another thing, it indicates that the other thing is about to begin. [FORMAL] ❑ *...a unique opportunity to usher in a new era of stability in Europe.*
PHRASAL VERB; V P n (not pron)

**USMC** /juː es em siː/ also **U.S.M.C.** **USMC** is an abbreviation for **United States Marine Corps**.
N-PROPER: usu *the* N

**USN** /juː es en/ also **U.S.N.** **USN** is an abbreviation for **United States Navy**.
N-PROPER: usu *the* N

**USP** /juː es piː/ **(USPs)** The **USP** of a product or service is a particular feature of it which can be used in advertising to show how it is different from, and better than, other similar products or services. **USP** is an abbreviation for 'Unique Selling Point'. [BUSINESS] ❑ *With Volvo, safety was always the USP.*
N-COUNT

**usu.** **usu.** is a written abbreviation for **usually**.

**usu|al** /juːʒuəl/ [1] **Usual** is used to describe what happens or what is done most often in a particular situation. ❑ *It is a neighborhood beset by all the usual inner-city problems... She's smiling her usual friendly smile... After lunch there was a little more clearing up to do than usual... It is usual to tip waiters, porters, guides and drivers.*
◆◆◇ ADJ: det ADJ, v-link ADJ, oft it v-link ADJ to-inf = *normal*

♦ **Usual** is also a noun. ❑ *The stout barman in a bow tie presented himself to take their order. 'Good morning, sir. The usual?'*
N-SING: *the* N

PHRASES [2] You use **as usual** to indicate that you are describing something that normally happens or that is normally the case. ❑ *As usual there will be the local and regional elections on June the twelfth... The front pages are, as usual, a mixture of domestic and foreign news.*
PHRASE: PHR with cl

[3] If something happens **as usual**, it happens in the way that it normally does, especially when other things have changed. ❑ *When somebody died everything went on as usual, as if it had never happened.*
PHRASE: PHR after v

[4] **business as usual** → see **business**.

**usu|al|ly** /juːʒuəli/ [1] If something **usually** happens, it is the thing that most often happens in a particular situation. ❑ *The best information about hotels usually comes from friends and acquaintances who have been there... They ate, as they usually did, in the kitchen... Usually, the work is boring... Offering only one loan, usually an installment loan, is part of the plan.*
◆◆◇ ADV: ADV before v, ADV with cl/group = *generally, normally*

[2] You use **more than usually** to show that something shows even more of a particular quality than it normally does. ❑ *She felt more than usually hungry after her excursion... He was more than usually depressed by problems at work.*
PHRASE: v-link PHR adj = *unusually*

**usurp** /juːzɜːʳp/ **(usurps, usurping, usurped)** If you say that someone **usurps** a job, role, title, or position, they take it from someone when they have no right to do this. [FORMAL] ❑ *Did she usurp his place in his mother's heart?*
VERB; V n

**usurp|er** /juːzɜːʳpəʳ/ **(usurpers)** A **usurper** is someone who takes another person's title or position when they have no right to. [FORMAL]
N-COUNT

**usu|ry** /juːʒəri/ **Usury** is the practice of lending money at a high rate of interest.
N-UNCOUNT disapproval

**ute** /juːt/ **(utes)** A **ute** is a vehicle that is designed to travel over rough ground. **Ute** is an abbreviation for 'utility vehicle'. [AUSTRALIAN, INFORMAL]
N-COUNT

**uten|sil** /juːtensᵊl/ **(utensils)** **Utensils** are tools or objects that you use in order to help you to cook or to do other tasks in your home. ❑ *...utensils such as bowls, steamers and frying pans.*
N-COUNT: usu pl

**u|ter|ine** /juːtəraɪn, AM -rɪn/ **Uterine** means relating to the uterus of a woman or female mammal. [MEDICAL]
ADJ

**uter|us** /juːtərəs/ **(uteruses)** The **uterus** of a woman or female mammal is her womb. [MEDICAL] ❑ *...an ultrasound scan of the uterus.*
N-COUNT

**uti|lise** /juːtɪlaɪz/ → see **utilize**.

**utili|tar|ian** /juːtɪlɪteəriən/ **(utilitarians)** [1] **Utilitarian** means based on the idea that the morally correct course of action is the one that produces benefit for the greatest number of people. [TECHNICAL] ❑ *It was James Mill who was the best publicist for utilitarian ideas on government.*
ADJ

♦ A **utilitarian** is someone with utilitarian views. ❑ *One of the greatest utilitarians was Claude Helvetius.*
N-COUNT

[2] **Utilitarian** objects and buildings are designed to be useful rather than attractive. ❑ *Bruce's office is a corner one, utilitarian and unglamorous.*
ADJ = *functional*

**utili|tari|an|ism** /juːtɪlɪteəriənɪzəm/ **Utilitarianism** is the idea that the morally correct course of action is the one that produces benefit for the greatest number of people. [TECHNICAL]
N-UNCOUNT

**util|ity** /juːtɪlɪti/ **(utilities)** [1] The **utility** of something is its usefulness. [FORMAL] ❑ *Belief in the utility of higher education is shared by students nationwide... He inwardly questioned the utility of his work.*
N-UNCOUNT: with supp = *usefulness*

[2] A **utility** is an important service such as water, electricity, or gas that is provided for everyone, and that everyone pays for. ❑ *...public utilities such as gas, electricity and phones.*
N-COUNT

**util|ity room** **(utility rooms)** A **utility room** is a room in a house which is usually connected to the kitchen and which contains things such as a washing machine, sink, and cleaning equipment.
N-COUNT

**util|ity ve|hi|cle** **(utility vehicles)** A **utility vehicle** is a vehicle that is designed to travel over rough ground. [AUSTRALIAN]
N-COUNT

**uti|lize** /juːtɪlaɪz/ **(utilizes, utilizing, utilized)**

✓ in BRIT, also use **utilise**

If you **utilize** something, you use it. [FORMAL] ❑ *Sound engineers utilize a range of techniques to enhance the quality of the recordings... Minerals can be absorbed and utilized by the body in a variety of different forms.*
VERB = *use*; V n; V n

♦ **uti|li|za|tion** /juːtɪlaɪzeɪʃᵊn/ *...the utilisation of human resources.*
N-UNCOUNT: usu N *of* n, n N

**ut|most** /ʌtmoʊst/ [1] You can use **utmost** to emphasize the importance or seriousness of something or to emphasize the way that it is done. ❑ *It is a matter of the utmost urgency to find out what has happened to these people... Security matters are treated with the utmost seriousness... You should proceed with the utmost caution.*
ADJ: ADJ n emphasis

[2] If you say that you are doing your **utmost to** do something, you are emphasizing that you are trying as hard as you can to do it. [FORMAL] ❑ *He would have done his utmost to help her, of that she was certain.*
N-SING: poss N emphasis

[3] If you say that something is done **to the utmost**, you are emphasizing that it is done to the greatest extent, amount, or degree possible.
PHRASE: usu PHR after v emphasis

❑ *My limited diplomatic skills were tested to the utmost... The best plan is to continue to attack him to the utmost of our power.*

**uto|pia** /juːtoʊpiə/ **(utopias)** If you refer to an imaginary situation as a **utopia**, you mean that it is one in which society is perfect and everyone is happy, but which you feel is not possible. ❑ *We weren't out to design a contemporary utopia. ...the social utopias of revolutionary peasants.* N-VAR

**uto|pian** /juːtoʊpiən/ 1 If you describe a plan or idea as **utopian**, you are criticizing it because it is unrealistic and shows a belief that things can be improved much more than is possible. ❑ *He was pursuing a utopian dream of world prosperity... A complete absence of national border controls is as utopian today as the vision of world government.* ADJ disapproval = idealistic 2 **Utopian** is used to describe political or religious philosophies which claim that it is possible to build a new and perfect society in which everyone is happy. [FORMAL] ❑ *His was a utopian vision of nature in its purest form.* ADJ: usu ADJ n

**ut|ter** /ʌtəʳ/ **(utters, uttering, uttered)** 1 If someone **utters** sounds or words, they say them. [LITERARY] ❑ *He uttered a snorting laugh... They departed without uttering a word.* VERB V n V n 2 You use **utter** to emphasize that something is great in extent, degree, or amount. ❑ *This, of course, is utter nonsense. ...this utter lack of responsibility... A look of utter confusion swept across his handsome face.* ADJ: ADJ n emphasis = absolute, total

**ut|ter|ance** /ʌtərəns/ **(utterances)** 1 Someone's **utterances** are the things that they say. [FORMAL] ❑ *...the Queen's public utterances. ...a host of admirers who hung on her every utterance.* N-COUNT: oft poss N 2 **Utterance** is the expression in words of ideas, thoughts, and feelings. [FORMAL] ❑ *She could choose her own partner in matrimony, as long as she gave no utterance to her passions and emotions.* N-UNCOUNT

**ut|ter|ly** /ʌtəʳli/ You use **utterly** to emphasize that something is very great in extent, degree, or amount. ❑ *Everything about the country seemed utterly different from what I'd experienced before... The new laws coming in are utterly ridiculous.* ADV: ADV adj/prep, ADV with v emphasis = totally

**U-turn** **(U-turns)** 1 If you make a **U-turn** when you are driving or cycling, you turn in a half circle in one movement, so that you are then going in the opposite direction. N-COUNT 2 If you describe a change in a politician's policy, plans, or actions as a **U-turn**, you mean that it is a complete change and that they made the change because they were weak or were wrong. ❑ *...a humiliating U-turn by the Prime Minister.* N-COUNT disapproval

# V v

**V, v** /viː/ **(V's, v's)** 1 **V** is the twenty-second letter of the English alphabet. 2 **V** or **v** is an abbreviation for words beginning with v, such as 'verse', 'versus', 'very', and 'volt'. ❑ *...Newcastle United v Leicester City.* N-VAR

**vac** /væk/ **(vacs)** 1 A **vac** is a period of the year when universities and colleges are officially closed. **Vac** is an abbreviation for 'vacation'. [BRIT, INFORMAL] ❑ *..the summer vac.* N-COUNT: usu sing 2 A **vac** is an electric machine which sucks up dust and dirt from carpets. **Vac** is an abbreviation for 'vacuum cleaner'. [INFORMAL] N-COUNT

**va|can|cy** /veɪkənsi/ **(vacancies)** 1 A **vacancy** is a job or position which has not been filled. ❑ *Most vacancies are at senior level, requiring appropriate qualifications.* N-COUNT 2 If there are **vacancies** at a building such as a hotel, some of the rooms are available to rent. N-COUNT

**va|cant** /veɪkənt/ 1 If something is **vacant**, it is not being used by anyone. ❑ *Half way down the coach was a vacant seat.* ADJ: usu ADJ n = empty 2 If a job or position is **vacant**, no one is doing it or in it at present, and people can apply for it. ❑ *The post of chairman has been vacant for some time.* ADJ 3 A **vacant** look or expression is one that suggests that someone does not understand something or that they are not thinking about anything in particular. ❑ *She had a kind of vacant look on her face.* ADJ = blank ♦ **va|cant|ly** *He looked vacantly out of the window.* ADV: ADV after v

**va|cate** /veɪkeɪt, AM veɪkeɪt/ **(vacates, vacating, vacated)** If you **vacate** a place or a job, you leave it or give it up, making it available for other people. [FORMAL] ❑ *He vacated the flat and went to stay with an uncle... He recently vacated his post as NHS Personnel Director.* VERB = leave; V n; V n

**va|ca|tion** /vəkeɪʃᵊn, AM veɪ-/ **(vacations, vacationing, vacationed)** 1 A **vacation** is a period of the year when universities and colleges, and in the United States also schools, are officially closed. ❑ *During his summer vacation he visited Russia.* N-COUNT = holiday 2 A **vacation** is a period of time during which you relax and enjoy yourself away from home. [AM] ❑ *They planned a late summer vacation in Europe... We went on vacation to Puerto Rico.* N-COUNT: also on/from N

> ✔ in BRIT, use **holiday**

3 If you have a particular number of days' or weeks' **vacation**, you do not have to go to work for that number of days or weeks. [AM] N-UNCOUNT

> ✔ in BRIT, use **holiday**

4 If you **are vacationing** in a place away from home, you are on vacation there. [AM] ❑ *Myles vacationed in Jamaica... He was vacationing and couldn't be reached for comment.* VERB; V prep/adv; V

> ✔ in BRIT, use **holiday**

**va|ca|tion|er** /veɪkeɪʃənəʳ/ **(vacationers)** **Vacationers** are people who are on vacation in a particular place. [mainly AM] N-COUNT: usu pl

> ✔ in BRIT, usually use **holidaymakers**

**vac|ci|nate** /væksɪneɪt/ **(vaccinates, vaccinating, vaccinated)** If a person or animal **is vaccinated**, they are given a vaccine, usually by injection, to prevent them from getting a disease. ❑ *Dogs must be vaccinated against distemper... Have you had your child vaccinated against whooping cough?... Measles, mumps and whooping cough are spreading again because children are not being vaccinated.* VERB: usu passive; be V-ed against n; have n V-ed against n; be/get V-ed

♦ **vac|ci|na|tion** /væksɪneɪʃᵊn/ **(vaccinations)** *Parents were too frightened to bring their children for vaccination... Anyone who wants to avoid the flu should consider getting a vaccination.* N-VAR

**vac|cine** /væksiːn, AM væksiːn/ **(vaccines)** A **vaccine** is a substance containing a harmless form of the germs that cause a particular disease. It is given to people, usually by injection, to prevent them getting that disease. ❑ *Anti-malarial vaccines are now undergoing trials... Seven million doses of vaccine are annually given to British children.* N-MASS

**vac|il|late** /væsɪleɪt/ **(vacillates, vacillating, vacillated)** If you **vacillate between** two alternatives or choices, you keep changing your mind. [FORMAL] ❑ *She vacillates between men twice her age and men younger than she... We cannot vacillate on the question of the party's leadership.* VERB; V between pl-n; V

**va|cu|ity** /vækjuːɪti/ If you refer to the **vacuity** of something or someone, you are critical of them because they lack intelligent thought or ideas. [FORMAL] ❑ *His vacuity was a handicap in these debates. ...a campaign notable for its intellectual vacuity and personal nastiness.* N-UNCOUNT: usu with poss [disapproval]

**vacu|ous** /vækjuəs/ If you describe a person or their comments as **vacuous**, you are critical of them because they lack intelligent thought or ideas. ❑ *Male models are not always so vacuous as they are made out to be.* ADJ [disapproval]

**vacuum** /vækjuːm, -juːəm/ **(vacuums, vacuuming, vacuumed)** 1 If someone or something creates a **vacuum**, they leave a place or position which then needs to be filled by another person or thing. ❑ *His presence should fill the power vacuum which has been developing over the past few days.* N-COUNT: usu sing, oft supp N 2 If something is done **in a vacuum**, it is not affected by any outside influences or information. ❑ *Moral values cannot be taught in a vacuum.* PHRASE: PHR after v 3 If you **vacuum** something, you clean it using a vacuum cleaner. ❑ *I vacuumed the carpets today... It's important to vacuum regularly.* VERB; V n; V 4 A **vacuum** is a space that contains no air or other gas. N-COUNT: usu sing

**vacuum bot|tle** **(vacuum bottles)** A **vacuum bottle** is the same as a **vacuum flask**. [AM] N-COUNT

**vacuum clean|er** **(vacuum cleaners)** also **vacuum-cleaner.** A **vacuum cleaner** or a **vacuum** is an electric machine which sucks up dust and dirt from carpets. N-COUNT

**vacuum flask** **(vacuum flasks)** A **vacuum flask** is a container which is used to keep hot drinks hot or cold drinks cold. It has two thin silvery glass walls with a vacuum between them. [BRIT] N-COUNT

> ✔ in AM, usually use **Thermos, vacuum bottle**

**vacuum-packed** Food that is **vacuum-packed** is packed in a bag from which most of the air has been removed, in order to keep the food fresh. ADJ

**vaga|bond** /vægəbɒnd/ **(vagabonds)** A **vagabond** is someone who wanders from place to place and has no home or job. [OLD-FASHIONED] N-COUNT = tramp, vagrant

**va|gary** /veɪgəri/ **(vagaries)** **Vagaries** are unexpected and unpredictable changes in a situation or in someone's behaviour which you have no N-COUNT: usu pl, usu N of n control over. [FORMAL] ❑ *...the perplexing vagaries of politics.*

**va|gi|na** /vədʒaɪnə/ **(vaginas)** N-COUNT A woman's **vagina** is the passage connecting her outer sex organs to her womb.

**vagi|nal** /vədʒaɪnᵊl/ ADJ: ADJ n **Vaginal** means relating to or involving the vagina. ❑ *The creams have been used to reduce vaginal infections.*

**va|gran|cy** /veɪgrənsi/ N-UNCOUNT **Vagrancy** is a way of life in which someone moves a lot from place to place because they have no permanent home or job, and have to ask for or steal things in order to live. ❑ *Vagrancy and begging has become common-place in London.*

**va|grant** /veɪgrənt/ **(vagrants)** N-COUNT = tramp A **vagrant** is someone who moves a lot from place to place because they have no permanent home or job, and have to ask for or steal things in order to live. ❑ *He lived on the street as a vagrant.*

**vague** /veɪg/ **(vaguer, vaguest)** 1 ADJ ≠ precise If something written or spoken is **vague**, it does not explain or express things clearly. ❑ *The description was pretty vague. ...vague information.* ♦ **vague|ly** ADV *'I'm not sure,' Liz said vaguely... They issued a vaguely worded statement.* ♦ **vague|ness** N-UNCOUNT: oft N of n *...the vagueness of the language in the text.* 2 ADJ = faint If you have a **vague** memory or idea of something, the memory or idea is not clear. ❑ *They have only a vague idea of the amount of water available... Waite's memory of that first meeting was vague.* ♦ **vague|ly** ADV: ADV with v *Judith could vaguely remember her mother lying on the sofa.* 3 ADJ If you are **vague** about something, you deliberately do not tell people much about it. ❑ *He was vague, however, about just what U.S. forces might actually do... Democratic leaders under election pressure tend to respond with vague promises of action.* 4 ADJ If you describe someone as **vague**, you mean that they do not seem to be thinking clearly. ❑ *She had married a charming but rather vague Englishman... His eyes were always so vague when he looked at her.* 5 ADJ: usu ADJ n If something such as a feeling is **vague**, you experience it only slightly. ❑ *He was conscious of that vague feeling of irritation again.* 6 ADJ: usu ADJ n A **vague** shape or outline is not clear and is therefore not easy to see. ❑ *The bus was a vague shape in the distance.*

**vague|ly** /veɪgli/ 1 ADV: ADV adj **Vaguely** means to some degree but not to a very large degree. ❑ *The voice on the line was vaguely familiar, but Crook couldn't place it at first.* 2 → See also **vague**.

**vain** /veɪn/ **(vainer, vainest)** 1 ADJ: ADJ n = fruitless A **vain** attempt or action is one that fails to achieve what was intended. ❑ *The drafting committee worked through the night in a vain attempt to finish on schedule.* ♦ **vain|ly** ADV: ADV with v *He hunted vainly through his pockets for a piece of paper.* 2 ADJ: ADJ n If you describe a hope that something will happen as a **vain** hope, you mean that there is no chance of it happening. ❑ *He married his fourth wife, Susan, in the vain hope that she would improve his health.* ♦ **vain|ly** ADV: ADV with v *He then set out for Virginia for what he vainly hoped would be a peaceful retirement.* 3 ADJ [disapproval] If you describe someone as **vain**, you are critical of their extreme pride in their own beauty, intelligence, or other good qualities. ❑ *I think he is shallow, vain and untrustworthy.*

PHRASES 4 PHRASE: PHR after v, v-link PHR If you do something **in vain**, you do not succeed in achieving what you intend. ❑ *He stopped at the door, waiting in vain for her to acknowledge his presence.* 5 PHRASE: PHR after v, v-link PHR If you say that something such as someone's death, suffering, or effort was **in vain**, you mean that it was useless because it did not achieve anything. ❑ *He wants the world to know his son did not die in vain.*

**vain|glo|ri|ous** /veɪnglɔːriəs/ ADJ: ADJ n [disapproval] If you describe someone as **vainglorious**, you are critical of them because they are very proud of what they have done and boast a lot about it. [LITERARY]

**val|ance** /væləns/ **(valances)** 1 N-COUNT A **valance** is a piece of cloth that hangs down over the sides of a bed in order to make it look nice. 2 N-COUNT A **valance** is a long narrow piece of wood or fabric which is fitted at the top of a window for decoration and to hide the curtain rail. [AM]

✔ in BRIT, use **pelmet**

**vale** /veɪl/ **(vales)** N-COUNT; N-IN-NAMES: oft in names A **vale** is a valley. [LITERARY] ❑ *...a small vale, sheltering under mist-shrouded hills.*

**vale|dic|to|ri|an** /vælɪdɪktɔːriən/ **(valedictorians)** N-COUNT A **valedictorian** is the student who has the highest marks in their class when they graduate from high school, college, or university, and who gives a speech at their graduation ceremony. [AM]

**val|edic|tory** /vælɪdɪktəri/ **(valedictories)** 1 ADJ: usu ADJ n = farewell A **valedictory** speech, letter, or performance is one that is intended as a way of saying goodbye when someone leaves another person, a place, or a job. [FORMAL] ❑ *...Mr Walker, making his valedictory address after two years as chairman.* 2 N-COUNT: oft N n A **valedictory** is a speech that is given by the student with the highest marks in their class at their graduation ceremony. [AM]

**val|en|tine** /væləntaɪn/ **(valentines)** N-COUNT A **valentine** or a **valentine card** is a greetings card that you send to someone who you are in love with or are attracted to, usually without signing your name, on St Valentine's Day, the 14th of February.

**val|et** /væleɪ, -lɪt/ **(valets, valeting, valeted)** 1 N-COUNT A **valet** is a male servant who looks after his employer by doing things such as caring for his clothes and cooking for him. 2 VERB: V n If someone **valets** a vehicle, they are paid to clean it thoroughly inside and out.

**val|iant** /væliənt/ ADJ: usu ADJ n A **valiant** action is very brave and determined, though it may lead to failure or defeat. ❑ *Despite valiant efforts by the finance minister, inflation rose to 36%.* ♦ **val|iant|ly** ADV: ADV with v = bravely *He suffered further heart attacks and strokes, all of which he fought valiantly.*

**val|id** /vælɪd/ 1 ADJ: oft it v-link ADJ to-inf A **valid** argument, comment, or idea is based on sensible reasoning. ❑ *They put forward many valid reasons for not exporting.* ♦ **va|lid|ity** /vəlɪdɪti/ N-UNCOUNT: usu with poss *The editorial in the Financial Times says this argument has lost much of its validity.* 2 ADJ Something that is **valid** is important or serious enough to make it worth saying or doing. ❑ *Most designers share the unspoken belief that fashion is a valid form of visual art.* ♦ **va|lid|ity** N-UNCOUNT: usu N of n/-ing *...the validity of making children wear cycle helmets.* 3 ADJ If a ticket or other document is **valid**, it can be used and will be accepted by people in authority. ❑ *All tickets are valid for two months.* 4 → See also **validity**.

**vali|date** /vælɪdeɪt/ **(validates, validating, validated)** 1 VERB = substantiate V n To **validate** something such as a claim or statement means to prove or confirm that it is true or correct. [FORMAL] ❑ *This discovery seems to validate the claims of popular astrology.* ♦ **vali|da|tion** /vælɪdeɪʃᵊn/ **(validations)** N-VAR *This validation process ensures that the data conforms to acceptable formats.* 2 VERB V n To **validate** a person, state, or system means to prove or confirm that they are valuable or worthwhile. ❑ *The Academy Awards appear to validate his career.* ♦ **vali|da|tion** N-VAR: usu N of n *I think the film is a validation of our lifestyle.*

**va|lid|ity** /vəlɪdɪti/ N-UNCOUNT: usu the N of n **The validity of** something such as a result or a piece of information is whether it can be trusted or believed. ❑ *Shocked by the results of the elections, they now want to challenge the validity of the vote... Some people, of course, denied the validity of any such claim.* → See also **valid**.

**Va|lium** /væliəm/ **(Valium)** N-VAR **Valium** is a drug given to people to calm their nerves when they are very depressed or upset. [TRADEMARK]

**val|ley** /væli/ **(valleys)** ◆◇◇ N-COUNT; N-IN-NAMES: oft in names A **valley** is a low stretch of land between hills, especially one that has a river flowing through it. ❑ *...a wooded valley set against the backdrop of Monte Rosa. ...the Loire valley.*

**val|our** /vælə^r/

in AM, use **valor**

**Valour** is great bravery, especially in battle. [LITERARY] N-UNCOUNT = gallantry

**valu|able** /væljuəb^əl/ ◆◇◇ 1 If you describe something or someone as **valuable**, you mean that they are very useful and helpful. ❑ *Many of our teachers also have valuable academic links with Heidelberg University... The experience was very valuable.* ADJ 2 **Valuable** objects are objects which are worth a lot of money. ❑ *Just because a camera is old does not mean it is valuable. ...valuable books.* ADJ

**valu|ables** /væljuəb^əlz/ **Valuables** are things that you own that are worth a lot of money, especially small objects such as jewellery. ❑ *Leave your valuables in the hotel safe.* N-PLURAL

**valua|tion** /væljueɪʃ^ən/ **(valuations)** A **valuation** is a judgment that someone makes about how much money something is worth. ❑ *...an independent valuation of the company... Valuation lies at the heart of all takeovers.* N-VAR

**value** /vælju:/ ◆◆◆ **(values, valuing, valued)** 1 The **value** of something such as a quality, attitude, or method is its importance or usefulness. If you place a particular **value** on something, that is the importance or usefulness you think it has. ❑ *Further studies will be needed to see if these therapies have any value... Ronnie put a high value on his appearance.* N-UNCOUNT: also *a* N, usu with supp ● If something is **of value**, it is useful or important. If it is **of no value**, it has no usefulness or importance. ❑ *This weekend course will be of value to everyone interested in the Pilgrim Route.* PHRASE: v-link PHR 2 If you **value** something or someone, you think that they are important and you appreciate them. ❑ *I've done business with Mr Weston before. I value the work he gives me.* VERB V n ♦ **val|ued** As you are a valued customer, I am writing to you to explain the situation. ADJ 3 The **value** of something is how much money it is worth. ❑ *The value of his investment has risen by more than $50,000... The country's currency went down in value by 3.5 per cent.* N-VAR ● If something is **of value**, it is worth a lot of money. If it is **of no value**, it is worth very little money. ❑ *...a brooch which is really of no value... It might contain something of value.* PHRASE: v-link PHR 4 When experts **value** something, they decide how much money it is worth. ❑ *Your lender will then send their own surveyor to value the property... I asked him if he would have my jewellery valued for insurance purposes... Spanish police have seized cocaine valued at around $53 million.* VERB V n *have* n V-ed V-ed 5 You use **value** in certain expressions to say whether something is worth the money that it costs. For example, if something is or gives **good value**, it is worth the money that it costs. ❑ *The restaurant is informal, stylish and extremely good value... This wine highlights the quality and value for money of South African wines.* N-UNCOUNT 6 The **values** of a person or group are the moral principles and beliefs that they think are important. ❑ *The countries of South Asia also share many common values.* N-PLURAL: with supp, oft with poss, supp N 7 **Value** is used after another noun when mentioning an important or noticeable feature about something. ❑ *The script has lost all of its shock value over the intervening 24 years.* N-UNCOUNT: n N 8 ➔ See also **face value**.

**value-added tax** also **value added tax**. **Value-added tax** is a tax that is added to the price of goods or services. The abbreviation **VAT** is also used. [BRIT] N-UNCOUNT

**value judg|ment** **(value judgments)**

in BRIT, also use **value judgement**

If you make a **value judgment** about something, you form an opinion about it based on your principles and beliefs and not on facts which can be checked or proved. ❑ *Social scientists have grown extremely unwilling to make value judgments about cultures.* N-COUNT

**value|less** /vælju:ləs/ If you describe something as **valueless**, you mean that it is not at all useful. ❑ *Such attitudes are valueless unless they reflect inner cognition and certainty. ...commercially valueless trees.* ADJ = worthless

**valu|er** /vælju:ə^r/ **(valuers)** A **valuer** is someone whose job is to estimate the cost or value of something, for example a house, or objects that are going to be sold in an auction. [BRIT] N-COUNT

in AM, use **appraiser**

**value sys|tem** **(value systems)** The **value system** of a group of people is the set of beliefs and attitudes that they all share. N-COUNT

**valve** /vælv/ **(valves)** 1 A **valve** is a device attached to a pipe or a tube which controls the flow of air or liquid through the pipe or tube. ➔ See picture on page 1708. N-COUNT 2 A **valve** is a small piece of tissue in your heart or in a vein which controls the flow of blood and keeps it flowing in one direction only. ❑ *He also has problems with a heart valve.* N-COUNT 3 ➔ See also **safety valve**.

**vamp** /væmp/ **(vamps)** If you describe a woman as a **vamp**, you mean that she uses her sexual attractiveness to get what she wants from men. N-COUNT disapproval

**vam|pire** /væmpaɪə^r/ **(vampires)** A **vampire** is a creature in legends and horror stories. Vampires are said to come out of graves at night and suck the blood of living people. N-COUNT

**vam|pire bat** **(vampire bats)** A **vampire bat** is a bat from South America which feeds by sucking the blood of other animals. N-COUNT

**van** /væn/ ◆◇◇ **(vans)** 1 A **van** is a small or medium-sized road vehicle with one row of seats at the front and a space for carrying goods behind. N-COUNT 2 A **van** is a railway carriage, often without windows, which is used to carry luggage, goods, or mail. [BRIT] ❑ *In the guard's van lay my tin trunk.* N-COUNT: usu supp N

in AM, use **baggage car, boxcar**

**van|dal** /vænd^əl/ **(vandals)** A **vandal** is someone who deliberately damages things, especially public property. N-COUNT

**van|dal|ise** /vændəlaɪz/ ➔ see **vandalize**.

**van|dal|ism** /vændəlɪzəm/ **Vandalism** is the deliberate damaging of things, especially public property. ❑ *...acts of vandalism.* N-UNCOUNT

**van|dal|ize** /vændəlaɪz/ **(vandalizes, vandalizing, vandalized)**

in BRIT, also use **vandalise**

If something such as a building or part of a building **is vandalized** by someone, it is damaged on purpose. ❑ *The walls had been horribly vandalized with spray paint... About 1,000 rioters vandalized buildings and looted stores.* VERB *be* V-ed V n

**vane** /veɪn/ **(vanes)** A **vane** is a flat blade which pushes or is pushed by wind or water, and forms part of a machine such as a fan, a windmill, or a ship's propeller. ➔ See also **weather vane**. N-COUNT

**van|guard** /vængɑ:^rd/ 1 If someone is **in the vanguard of** something such as a revolution or an area of research, they are involved in the most advanced part of it. You can also refer to the people themselves as **the vanguard**. ❑ *Such thinking puts Kodak in the vanguard of a movement reshaping the computer industry. ...the role of the Party as the political vanguard.* N-SING: usu *the* N, oft *in the* N *of* n 2 **The vanguard** of an army is the part of it that goes into battle first. ❑ *...a force of mobile reserve units that could strike quickly and effectively at the vanguard of an invading army.* N-SING: *the* N

**va|nil|la** /vənɪlə/ 1 **Vanilla** is a flavouring used in ice cream and other sweet food. ❑ *I added a dollop of vanilla ice-cream to the pie.* N-UNCOUNT: usu N n 2 If you describe a person or thing as **vanilla**, you mean that they are ordinary, with no special or extra features. ❑ *...just plain vanilla couples like me and Tony.* ADJ

**van|ish** /vænɪʃ/ **(vanishes, vanishing, vanished)** 1 If someone or something **vanishes**, they disappear suddenly or in a way that cannot be explained. ❑ *He just vanished and was never seen* VERB = disappear V *again... Anne vanished from outside her home last Wednesday... The gunmen paused only to cut the wires to the house, then vanished into the countryside.* V from n; V into n. 2 If something such as a species of animal or a tradition **vanishes**, it stops existing. ❑ *Near the end of Devonian times, thirty percent of all animal life vanished... In the past two years, one-party rule has vanished from Eastern Europe.* VERB = disappear; V; V from n

**van|ish|ing point** (vanishing points) 1 The **vanishing point** is the point in the distance where parallel lines seem to meet. ❑ *The highway stretched out ahead of me until it narrowed to a vanishing point some miles away.* N-COUNT: usu sing. 2 If you say that something has reached **vanishing point**, you mean it has become very small or unimportant. ❑ *By 1973, this gap had narrowed almost to vanishing point.* N-UNCOUNT

**van|ity** /vænɪti/ If you refer to someone's **vanity**, you are critical of them because they take great pride in their appearance or abilities. ❑ *Men who use steroids are motivated by sheer vanity.* N-UNCOUNT: also N in pl [disapproval]

**van|quish** /væŋkwɪʃ/ **(vanquishes, vanquishing, vanquished)** To **vanquish** someone means to defeat them completely in a battle or a competition. [LITERARY] ❑ *A happy ending is only possible because the hero has first vanquished the dragons.* VERB = overcome; V n

**van|tage point** /vɑːntɪdʒ pɔɪnt, vænt-/ **(vantage points)** 1 A **vantage point** is a place from which you can see a lot of things. ❑ *From a concealed vantage point, he saw a car arrive.* N-COUNT = viewpoint. 2 If you view a situation **from** a particular **vantage point**, you have a clear understanding of it because of the particular period of time you are in. ❑ *From today's vantage point, the 1987 crash seems just a blip in the upward progress of the market.* N-COUNT: oft with poss = viewpoint

**vap|id** /væpɪd/ If you describe someone or something as **vapid**, you are critical of them because they are dull and uninteresting. ❑ *...the Minister's young and rather vapid wife... She made a vapid comment about the weather.* ADJ [disapproval] = vacuous

**va|por** /veɪpəʳ/ → see **vapour**.

**va|por|ize** /veɪpəraɪz/ **(vaporizes, vaporizing, vaporized)**

☑ in BRIT, also use **vaporise**

If a liquid or solid **vaporizes** or if you **vaporize** it, it changes into vapour or gas. ❑ *The benzene vaporized and formed a huge cloud of gas... The blast may have vaporised the meteorite.* VERB; V; V n

**va|pour** /veɪpəʳ/ **(vapours)**

☑ in AM, use **vapor**

**Vapour** consists of tiny drops of water or other liquids in the air, which appear as mist. ❑ *...water vapour.* N-VAR

**va|pour trail** (vapour trails)

☑ in AM, use **vapor trail**

A **vapour trail** is a white line of water vapour left in the sky by an aeroplane, a rocket, or a missile. N-COUNT

**vari|able** /veəriəbᵊl/ **(variables)** 1 Something that is **variable** changes quite often, and there usually seems to be no fixed pattern to these changes. ❑ *The potassium content of foodstuffs is very variable. ...a variable rate of interest.* ADJ ♦ **vari|abil|ity** /veəriəbɪlɪti/ *There's a great deal of variability between individuals.* N-UNCOUNT 2 A **variable** is a factor that can change in quality, quantity, or size, which you have to take into account in a situation. ❑ *Decisions could be made on the basis of price, delivery dates, after-sales service or any other variable.* N-COUNT 3 A **variable** is a quantity that can have any one of a set of values. [TECHNICAL] ❑ *It is conventional to place the independent variable on the right-hand side of an equation.* N-COUNT

**vari|ance** /veəriəns/ **(variances)** 1 If one thing is **at variance with** another, the two things seem to contradict each other. [FORMAL] ❑ *Many of his statements were at variance with the facts.* PHRASE: v-link PHR, oft PHR with n 2 The **variance** between things is the difference between them. [FORMAL] ❑ *...the variances in the stock price.* N-VAR: usu with supp = variation

**vari|ant** /veəriənt/ **(variants)** A **variant** of a particular thing is something that has a different form to that thing, although it is related to it. ❑ *The quagga was a strikingly beautiful variant of the zebra.* N-COUNT: usu with supp, oft N of n

**vari|ation** /veərieɪʃᵊn/ **(variations)** 1 A **variation on** something is the same thing presented in a slightly different form. ❑ *This delicious variation on an omelette is quick and easy to prepare.* N-COUNT: usu N on n 2 A **variation** is a change or slight difference in a level, amount, or quantity. ❑ *The survey found a wide variation in the prices charged for canteen food... Every day without variation my grandfather ate a plate of cold ham.* N-VAR

**vari|cose vein** /værɪkoʊs veɪn/ **(varicose veins)** **Varicose veins** are swollen and painful veins in a person's legs, which sometimes require a medical operation. N-COUNT: usu pl

**var|ied** /veərid/ Something that is **varied** consists of things of different types, sizes, or qualities. ❑ *It is essential that your diet is varied and balanced.* → See also **vary**. ADJ = diverse

**varie|gat|ed** /veəriəgeɪtɪd/ 1 A **variegated** leaf or plant has different colours on it. [TECHNICAL] ❑ *The leaves are a variegated red.* ADJ: usu ADJ n 2 Something that is **variegated** consists of many different parts or types. [FORMAL] ❑ *...our variegated dialects.* ADJ = varied

**va|ri|ety** /vəraɪɪti/ **(varieties)** ◆◆◇ 1 If something has **variety**, it consists of things which are different from each other. ❑ *Susan's idea of freedom was to have variety in her life style.* N-UNCOUNT = diversity 2 A **variety of** things is a number of different kinds or examples of the same thing. ❑ *The island offers such a wide variety of scenery and wildlife... People change their mind for a variety of reasons.* N-SING: usu N of n 3 A **variety of** something is a type of it. ❑ *She has 12 varieties of old-fashioned roses.* N-COUNT: oft N of n = kind

**vari|ous** /veəriəs/ ◆◆◇ 1 If you say that there are **various** things, you mean there are several different things of the type mentioned. ❑ *The school has received various grants from the education department.* ADJ: usu ADJ n 2 If a number of things are described as **various**, they are very different from one another. ❑ *The methods are many and various. ...the country's rich and various heritage.* ADJ = varied

**vari|ous|ly** /veəriəsli/ You can use **variously** to introduce a number of different ways in which something can be described. ❑ *...the crowds, which were variously estimated at two to several thousand.* ADV: usu ADV with v, also ADV adj

**var|nish** /vɑːʳnɪʃ/ **(varnishes, varnishing, varnished)** 1 **Varnish** is an oily liquid which is painted onto wood or other material to give it a hard, clear, shiny surface. ❑ *The varnish comes in six natural wood shades.* N-MASS 2 The **varnish** on an object is the hard, clear, shiny surface that it has when it has been painted with varnish. ❑ *He brought out the fiddle, its varnish cracked and blistered.* N-SING 3 If you **varnish** something, you paint it with varnish. ❑ *Varnish the table with two or three coats of water-based varnish. ...the varnished floorboards.* VERB; V n; V-ed 4 → See also **nail varnish**.

**var|sity** /vɑːʳsɪti/ **(varsities)** 1 People sometimes use **varsity** to describe things that relate to universities, especially sports activities or teams at a university or competitions between universities. [BRIT, mainly JOURNALISM] ❑ *The school has not given them the same opportunities to participate in varsity sports that men receive.* ADJ: ADJ n 2 The **varsity** is the main or first team for a particular sport at a high school, college, or university. [AM] ❑ *She has been in the playoffs every year since she made the varsity.* N-COUNT: oft N n

**vary** /veəri/ **(varies, varying, varied)** ◆◇◇ 1 If things **vary**, they are different from each other in size, amount, or degree. ❑ *As they're handmade, each one varies slightly... The text varies from the earlier versions... Different writers will prepare to varying degrees.* VERB = differ; V; V from n; V-ing 2 If something **varies** or if you **vary** it, VERB

it becomes different or changed. ❑ *The cost of the alcohol duty varies according to the amount of wine in the bottle... You are welcome to vary the diet.* [= change] [V] [V n]
3 → See also **varied**.

**vas|cu|lar** /væskjʊləʳ/ **Vascular** is used to describe the channels and veins through which fluids pass in the bodies of animals and plants. [TECHNICAL] ❑ *...the oldest known vascular plants. ...vascular diseases of the legs.* [ADJ: ADJ n]

**vase** /vɑːz, AM veɪs/ **(vases)** A **vase** is a jar, usually made of glass or pottery, used for holding cut flowers or as an ornament. ❑ *...a vase of red roses.* [N-COUNT]

**vas|ec|to|my** /vəsektəmi/ **(vasectomies)** A **vasectomy** is a surgical operation in which the tube that carries sperm to a man's penis is cut, usually as a means of contraception. [N-VAR]

**Vas|eline** /væsəliːn/ **Vaseline** is a soft clear jelly made from petroleum, which is used to protect the skin and for other purposes. [TRADEMARK] [N-UNCOUNT] [= petroleum jelly]

**vas|sal** /væsəl/ **(vassals)** 1 In feudal society, a **vassal** was a man who gave military service to a lord, in return for which he was protected by the lord and received land to live on. [N-COUNT] 2 If you say that one country is a **vassal** of another, you mean that it is controlled by it. [WRITTEN] ❑ *Opponents of the treaty argue that monetary union will turn France into a vassal of Germany.* [N-COUNT: usu sing] [disapproval]

**vast** /vɑːst, væst/ **(vaster, vastest)** Something that is **vast** is extremely large. ❑ *...Afrikaner farmers who own vast stretches of land... The vast majority of the eggs would be cracked.* ♦ **vast|ness** *...the vastness of the desert.* [◆◇◇] [ADJ: usu ADJ n] [= huge] [N-UNCOUNT]

**vast|ly** /vɑːstli, væst-/ **Vastly** means to an extremely great degree or extent. ❑ *The jury has heard two vastly different accounts of what happened.* [ADV: usu ADV compar]

**vat** /væt/ **(vats)** A **vat** is a large barrel or tank in which liquids can be stored. [N-COUNT]

**VAT** /viː eɪ tiː, væt/ **VAT** is a tax that is added to the price of goods or services. **VAT** is an abbreviation for 'value added tax'. [BRIT] [◆◇◇] [N-UNCOUNT]

**Vati|can** /vætɪkən/ **The Vatican** is the city state in Rome ruled by the Pope which is the centre of the Roman Catholic Church. You can also use **the Vatican** to refer to the Pope or his officials. ❑ *The president had an audience with the Pope in the Vatican.* [N-PROPER: the N, N n]

**vat|man** /vætmæn/ also **VAT man.** You can refer to the government department which advises and checks the accounts of people who have to pay VAT as **the vatman**. [BRIT, INFORMAL] ❑ *If you have had a problem with the vatman, let us know.* [N-SING: the N]

**vau|de|ville** /vɔːdəvɪl/ **Vaudeville** is a type of entertainment consisting of short acts such as comedy, singing, and dancing. Vaudeville was especially popular in the early part of the twentieth century. [mainly AM] [N-UNCOUNT]

✔ in BRIT, usually use **music hall**

**vault** /vɔːlt/ **(vaults, vaulting, vaulted)** 1 A **vault** is a secure room where money and other valuable things can be kept safely. ❑ *Most of the money was in storage in bank vaults.* [N-COUNT] 2 A **vault** is a room underneath a church or in a cemetery where people are buried, usually the members of a single family. ❑ *He ordered that Matilda's body should be buried in the family vault.* [N-COUNT] [= tomb] 3 A **vault** is an arched roof or ceiling. ❑ *...the vault of a great cathedral.* [N-COUNT] 4 If you **vault** something or **vault over** it, you jump quickly onto or over it, especially by putting a hand on top of it to help you balance while you jump. ❑ *He could easily vault the wall... Ned vaulted over a fallen tree.* [VERB] [V n] [V prep]

**vaunt|ed** /vɔːntɪd/ If you describe something as **vaunted** or **much vaunted**, you mean that people praise it more than it deserves. [FORMAL] ❑ *Simpson's much vaunted discoveries are in fact commonplace in modern sociology.* [ADJ: usu ADJ n]

**vb Vb** is a written abbreviation for **verb**.

**VC** /viː siː/ **(VCs)** 1 The **VC** is a medal awarded to soldiers, sailors, and airmen in Britain and the Commonwealth for acts of great bravery in battle. **VC** is an abbreviation for 'Victoria Cross'. [N-COUNT] ♦ A **VC** is a soldier who has been awarded a Victoria Cross. ❑ *Aren't you the boy whose father was a VC in the war?* [N-COUNT] 2 **VC** is a written abbreviation for **vice-chancellor**.

**VCR** /viː siː ɑːʳ/ **(VCRs)** A **VCR** is a machine that can be used to record television programmes or films onto videotapes, so that people can play them back and watch them later on a television set. **VCR** is an abbreviation for 'video cassette recorder'. [N-COUNT] [= video]

**VD** /viː diː/ **VD** is used to refer to diseases such as syphilis and gonorrhoea which are passed on by sexual intercourse. **VD** is an abbreviation for 'venereal disease'. [N-UNCOUNT]

**VDT** /viː diː tiː/ **(VDTs)** A **VDT** is the same as a **VDU**. **VDT** is an abbreviation for 'visual display terminal'. [mainly AM] [N-COUNT] [= monitor]

**VDU** /viː diː juː/ **(VDUs)** A **VDU** is a machine with a screen which is used to display information from a computer. **VDU** is an abbreviation for 'visual display unit'. [BRIT] [N-COUNT] [= monitor]

✔ in AM, use **VDT**

**-'ve** /-əv/ **'ve** is the usual spoken form of 'have', especially when 'have' is an auxiliary verb. It is added to the end of the pronoun which is the subject of the verb. For example, 'you have' can be shortened to 'you've'.

**veal** /viːl/ **Veal** is meat from a calf. [N-UNCOUNT]

**vec|tor** /vektəʳ/ **(vectors)** 1 A **vector** is a variable quantity, such as force, that has size and direction. [TECHNICAL] [N-COUNT] 2 A **vector** is an insect or other organism that causes a disease by carrying a germ or parasite from one person or animal to another. [MEDICAL] [N-COUNT]

**veep** /viːp/ **(veeps)** A **veep** is a vice-president, especially the vice-president of the United States. [AM, INFORMAL] [N-COUNT]

**veer** /vɪəʳ/ **(veers, veering, veered)** 1 If something **veers** in a certain direction, it suddenly moves in that direction. ❑ *The plane veered off the runway and careered through the perimeter fence.* [VERB] [= swerve] [V prep/adv] 2 If someone or something **veers** in a certain direction, they change their position or direction in a particular situation. ❑ *He is unlikely to veer from his boss's strongly held views.* [VERB] [V prep/adv]

**veg** /vedʒ/ **(veg) Veg** are plants such as cabbages, potatoes, and onions which you can cook and eat. **Veg** is an abbreviation for 'vegetables'. [mainly BRIT, INFORMAL] ❑ *...fruit and veg.* [N-VAR]

✔ in AM, usually use **veggies**

**ve|gan** /viːgən/ **(vegans)** Someone who is **vegan** never eats meat or any animal products such as milk, butter, or cheese. ❑ *The menu changes weekly and usually includes a vegan option.* [ADJ] ♦ A **vegan** is someone who is vegan. [N-COUNT]

**veg|eburg|er** /vedʒibɜːʳgəʳ/ **(vegeburgers)** also **veggieburger. Vegeburgers** are flat round cakes of food made from vegetables mixed with flour and flavourings. You grill or fry them. [N-COUNT]

**veg|eta|ble** /vedʒtəbəl/ **(vegetables)** 1 **Vegetables** are plants such as cabbages, potatoes, and onions which you can cook and eat. ❑ *A good general diet should include plenty of fresh vegetables. ...vegetable soup.* [◆◇◇] [N-COUNT] 2 **Vegetable** matter comes from plants. [FORMAL] ❑ *...compounds, of animal, vegetable or mineral origin.* [ADJ: usu ADJ n]

**veg|etar|ian** /vedʒɪteəriən/ **(vegetarians)** 1 Someone who is **vegetarian** never eats meat or fish. ❑ *Yasmin sticks to a strict vegetarian diet.* [ADJ] ♦ A **vegetarian** is someone who is vegetarian. ❑ *...a special menu for vegetarians.* [N-COUNT] 2 **Vegetarian** food does not contain any meat or fish. ❑ *...vegetarian lasagnes.* [ADJ]

**veg|etari|an|ism** /vedʒɪteəriənɪzəm/ If someone practises **vegetarianism**, they never eat meat or fish. N-UNCOUNT

**veg|etate** /vedʒɪteɪt/ **(vegetates, vegetating, vegetated)** If someone **vegetates**, they spend their time doing boring or worthless things. ❑ *He spends all his free time at home vegetating in front of the TV.* VERB V

**veg|etat|ed** /vedʒɪteɪtɪd/ If an area is **vegetated**, it is covered with plants and trees. [FORMAL] ❑ *That part of Castle Walk is not thickly vegetated.* ADJ: usu adv ADJ

**veg|eta|tion** /vedʒɪteɪʃən/ Plants, trees, and flowers can be referred to as **vegetation**. [FORMAL] ❑ *The inn has a garden of semi-tropical vegetation.* N-UNCOUNT: usu with supp

**veg|eta|tive** /vedʒɪtətɪv, AM -teɪt-/ If someone is in a **vegetative** state, they are unable to move, think, or speak, and their condition is not likely to improve. [MEDICAL] ❑ *She was in what was described as a vegetative state.* ADJ: usu ADJ n

**veg|gie** /vedʒi/ **(veggies)** 1 **Veggie** means the same as **vegetarian**. [mainly BRIT, INFORMAL] ❑ *You can cook a cheap veggie chilli in 15 minutes.* ADJ
♦ A **veggie** is someone who is vegetarian. N-COUNT
2 **Veggies** are plants such as cabbages, potatoes, and onions which you can cook and eat. [mainly AM, INFORMAL] ❑ *...well-balanced meals of fresh fruit and veggies, chicken, fish, pasta, and no red meat.* N-COUNT: usu pl

✔ in BRIT, usually use **veg**

**veg|gie|burg|er** /vedʒibɜːʳgəʳ/ → see **vegeburger**.

**ve|he|ment** /viːəmənt/ If a person or their actions or comments are **vehement**, the person has very strong feelings or opinions and expresses them forcefully. ❑ *She suddenly became very vehement and agitated, jumping around and shouting... One vehement critic is Michael Howard.* ADJ
♦ **ve|he|mence** *He spoke more loudly and with more vehemence than he had intended.* N-UNCOUNT
♦ **ve|he|ment|ly** *Krabbe has always vehemently denied using drugs.* ADV: ADV with v, ADV prep/adj

**ve|hi|cle** /viːɪkəl/ **(vehicles)** 1 A **vehicle** is a machine such as a car, bus, or truck which has an engine and is used to carry people from place to place. ❑ *...a vehicle which was somewhere between a tractor and a truck.* ◆◆◇ N-COUNT
2 You can use **vehicle** to refer to something that you use in order to achieve a particular purpose. ❑ *Her art became a vehicle for her political beliefs.* N-COUNT: usu with supp, oft N *for* n = medium

**ve|hicu|lar** /vɪhɪkjʊləʳ/ **Vehicular** is used to describe something which relates to vehicles and traffic. [FORMAL] ❑ *...vehicular traffic... There is no vehicular access.* ADJ: usu ADJ n

**veil** /veɪl/ **(veils)** 1 A **veil** is a piece of thin soft cloth that women sometimes wear over their heads and which can also cover their face. ❑ *She's got long fair hair but she's got a veil over it.* N-COUNT
2 You can refer to something that hides or partly hides a situation or activity as a **veil**. ❑ *The country is ridding itself of its disgraced prime minister in a veil of secrecy... The chilling facts behind this veil of silence were slow to emerge.* N-COUNT: usu sing, N *of* n
3 You can refer to something that you can partly see through, for example a mist, as a **veil**. [LITERARY] ❑ *The eruption has left a thin veil of dust in the upper atmosphere.* N-COUNT: oft N *of* n = haze
4 If you **draw a veil over** something, you stop talking about it because it is too unpleasant to talk about. ❑ *The clamour to draw a veil over the minister's extra-marital activities reeks of hypocrisy.* PHRASE: V inflects, PHR n

**veiled** /veɪld/ 1 A **veiled** comment is expressed in a disguised form rather than directly and openly. ❑ *He made only a veiled reference to international concerns over human rights issues... This last clause is a thinly-veiled threat to those who might choose to ignore the decree.* ADJ: ADJ n
2 A woman or girl who is **veiled** is wearing a veil. ❑ *A veiled woman gave me a kindly smile.* ADJ

**vein** /veɪn/ **(veins)** 1 Your **veins** are the thin tubes in your body through which your blood flows towards your heart. Compare **artery**. ❑ *Many veins are found just under the skin.* → See also **varicose vein**. N-COUNT: usu pl
2 Something that is written or spoken **in** a particular **vein** is written or spoken in that style or mood. ❑ *It is one of his finest works in a lighter vein.* N-COUNT: usu sing, with supp, usu adj N
3 A **vein of** a particular quality is evidence of that quality which someone often shows in their behaviour or work. ❑ *This Spanish drama has a vein of black humour running through it.* N-COUNT: usu sing, with supp
4 A **vein of** a particular metal or mineral is a layer of it lying in rock. ❑ *...a rich and deep vein of limestone.* N-COUNT: N *of* n = seam
5 The **veins** on a leaf are the thin lines on it. ❑ *...the serrated edges and veins of the feathery leaves.* N-COUNT

**veined** /veɪnd/ 1 **Veined** skin has a lot of veins showing through it. ❑ *Helen's hands were thin and veined.* ADJ
2 Something that is **veined** has a pattern or colouring like that of veins showing through skin. ❑ *...a bronze ashtray shaped like a veined leaf.* ADJ

**Vel|cro** /velkroʊ/ **Velcro** is a material consisting of two strips of nylon fabric which you press together to close things such as pockets and bags. [TRADEMARK] N-UNCOUNT: oft N n

**veldt** /velt, felt/ also **veld. The veldt** is a high area of flat grassy land with very few trees in southern Africa. N-SING: usu *the* N

**vel|lum** /veləm/ **Vellum** is strong paper of good quality for writing on. N-UNCOUNT

**ve|loc|ity** /vɪlɒsɪti/ **(velocities) Velocity** is the speed at which something moves in a particular direction. [TECHNICAL] ❑ *...the velocities at which the stars orbit. ...high velocity rifles.* N-VAR

**ve|lour** /vəlʊəʳ/ **Velour** is a silk or cotton fabric similar to velvet. ❑ *...a gold Mercedes with red velour seats.* N-UNCOUNT: usu N n

**vel|vet** /velvɪt/ **(velvets) Velvet** is soft material made from cotton, silk, or nylon, which has a thick layer of short cut threads on one side. ❑ *...a charcoal-gray overcoat with a velvet collar.* N-MASS: usu N n

**vel|vet|een** /velvɪtiːn/ **Velveteen** is a soft fabric which looks and feels like velvet and is sometimes used as a cheaper alternative to velvet. ❑ *...a black velveteen coat. ...loose blouses of bright-coloured velveteen.* N-UNCOUNT: usu N n

**vel|vety** /velvɪti/ If you describe something as **velvety**, you mean that it is pleasantly soft to touch and has the appearance or quality of velvet. ❑ *The grass grew thick and velvety.* ADJ

**ve|nal** /viːnəl/ If you describe someone as **venal**, you disapprove of them because they are prepared to do almost anything in return for money, even things which are dishonest or immoral. ❑ *Ian Trimmer is corrupt and thoroughly venal. ...venal politicians.* ADJ [disapproval]

**ven|det|ta** /vendetə/ **(vendettas)** If one person has a **vendetta against** another, the first person wants revenge for something the second person did to them in the past. ❑ *The vice president said the cartoonist has a personal vendetta against him.* N-VAR: oft N *against* n

**vend|ing ma|chine** /vendɪŋ məʃiːn/ **(vending machines)** A **vending machine** is a machine from which you can get things such as cigarettes, chocolate, or coffee by putting in money and pressing a button. N-COUNT

**ven|dor** /vendəʳ/ **(vendors)** 1 A **vendor** is someone who sells things such as newspapers, cigarettes, or food from a small stall or cart. ❑ *...ice-cream vendors.* N-COUNT: usu supp N = seller
2 The **vendor** of a house or piece of land is the person who owns it and is selling it. [LEGAL] ❑ *Remember, the estate agent is working for the vendor.* N-COUNT = seller

**ve|neer** /vɪnɪəʳ/ **(veneers)** 1 If you refer to the pleasant way that someone or something appears as a **veneer**, you are critical of them because you believe that their true, hidden nature is not good. ❑ *His super-clean image gave a veneer of respectability to the new professional set-up.* N-SING: usu with supp, oft N *of* n, adj N [disapproval]
2 **Veneer** is a thin layer of wood or plastic N-VAR

which is used to improve the appearance of something. ❑ *The wood was cut into large sheets of veneer.*

**ven|er|able** /venərəbəl/ [1] A **venerable** person deserves respect because they are old and wise. ❑ *...a venerable old man with white hair.* ADJ: usu ADJ n

[2] Something that is **venerable** is impressive because it is old or important historically. ❑ *May Day has become a venerable institution.* ADJ: usu ADJ n

**ven|er|ate** /venəreɪt/ **(venerates, venerating, venerated)** If you **venerate** someone or something, you value them or feel great respect for them. [FORMAL] ❑ *My father venerated General Eisenhower.* ♦ **ven|er|at|ed** *Jerusalem is Christianity's most venerated place.* ♦ **ven|era|tion** *Churchill was held in near veneration during his lifetime.* VERB = revere V n ADJ N-UNCOUNT

**ve|nereal dis|ease** /vɪnɪəriəl dɪziːz/ **(venereal diseases) Venereal disease** is used to refer to diseases such as syphilis and gonorrhoea which are passed on by sexual intercourse. The abbreviation **VD** is also used. N-VAR

**Ve|netian blind** /vəniːʃən blaɪnd/ **(Venetian blinds)** A **Venetian blind** is a window blind made of thin horizontal strips which can be adjusted to let in more or less light. N-COUNT

**venge|ance** /vendʒəns/ [1] **Vengeance** is the act of killing, injuring, or harming someone because they have harmed you. ❑ *He swore vengeance on everyone involved in the murder.* [2] If you say that something happens **with a vengeance**, you are emphasizing that it happens to a much greater extent than was expected. ❑ *It began to rain again with a vengeance.* N-UNCOUNT = revenge PHRASE: PHR after v [emphasis]

**venge|ful** /vendʒfʊl/ If you describe someone as **vengeful**, you are critical of them because they feel a great desire for revenge. ❑ *He was stabbed to death by his vengeful wife.* ADJ [disapproval]

**veni|son** /venɪzən/ **Venison** is the meat of a deer. N-UNCOUNT

**ven|om** /venəm/ **(venoms)** [1] You can use **venom** to refer to someone's feelings of great bitterness and anger towards someone. ❑ *He reserved particular venom for critics of his foreign policy.* N-UNCOUNT

[2] The **venom** of a creature such as a snake or spider is the poison that it puts into your body when it bites or stings you. ❑ *...snake handlers who grow immune to snake venom.* N-MASS = poison

**ven|om|ous** /venəməs/ [1] If you describe a person or their behaviour as **venomous**, you mean that they show great bitterness and anger towards someone. ❑ *He heaped abuse on Waite and made venomous personal attacks.* [2] A **venomous** snake, spider, or other creature uses poison to attack other creatures. ❑ *The adder is Britain's only venomous snake.* ADJ: usu ADJ n; ADJ = poisonous

**ve|nous** /viːnəs/ **Venous** is used to describe something which is related to veins. [MEDICAL] ❑ *...venous blood.* ADJ: ADJ n

**vent** /vent/ **(vents, venting, vented)** [1] A **vent** is a hole in something through which air can come in and smoke, gas, or smells can go out. → See picture on page 1708. ❑ *There was a small air vent in the ceiling.* [2] If you **vent** your feelings, you express them forcefully. ❑ *She telephoned her best friend to vent her frustration... The rioters were prevented from venting their anger on the police.* [3] If you **give vent to** your feelings, you express them forcefully. [FORMAL] ❑ *She gave vent to her anger and jealousy.* N-COUNT = duct; VERB V n V n *on* n; PHRASE: V inflects

**ven|ti|late** /ventɪleɪt/ **(ventilates, ventilating, ventilated)** If you **ventilate** a room or building, you allow fresh air to get into it. ❑ *Ventilate the room properly when paint stripping. ...badly ventilated rooms.* ♦ **ven|ti|la|tion** /ventɪleɪʃən/ *The only ventilation comes from tiny sliding windows.* VERB V n V-ed N-UNCOUNT

**ven|ti|la|tor** /ventɪleɪtər/ **(ventilators)** [1] A **ventilator** is a machine that helps people breathe when they cannot breathe naturally, for example because they are very ill or have been seriously injured. [2] A **ventilator** is a device that lets fresh air into a room or building and lets old or dirty air out. N-COUNT; N-COUNT

**ven|tri|cle** /ventrɪkəl/ **(ventricles)** A **ventricle** is a part of the heart that pumps blood to the arteries. [MEDICAL] N-COUNT

**ven|trilo|quist** /ventrɪləkwɪst/ **(ventriloquists)** A **ventriloquist** is someone who can speak without moving their lips and who entertains people by making their words appear to be spoken by a puppet. N-COUNT

**ven|ture** /ventʃər/ **(ventures, venturing, ventured)** [1] A **venture** is a project or activity which is new, exciting, and difficult because it involves the risk of failure. ❑ *...his latest writing venture. ...a Russian-American joint venture.* [2] If you **venture** somewhere, you go somewhere that might be dangerous. [LITERARY] ❑ *People are afraid to venture out for fear of sniper attacks.* [3] If you **venture** a question or statement, you say it in an uncertain way because you are afraid it might be stupid or wrong. [WRITTEN] ❑ *'So you're Leo's girlfriend?' he ventured... He ventured that plants draw part of their nourishment from the air... Stephen ventured a few more sentences in halting Welsh.* [4] If you **venture to** do something that requires courage or is risky, you do it. ❑ *'Don't ask,' he said, whenever Ginny ventured to raise the subject.* [5] If you **venture into** an activity, you do something that involves the risk of failure because it is new and different. ❑ *He enjoyed little success when he ventured into business.* ◆◇◇ N-COUNT: usu supp N; VERB V adv/prep; VERB V with quote V that V n; VERB = dare V to-inf; VERB V *into* n

**ven|ture capi|tal Venture capital** is capital that is invested in projects that have a high risk of failure, but that will bring large profits if they are successful. [BUSINESS] N-UNCOUNT

**ven|ture capi|tal|ist (venture capitalists)** A **venture capitalist** is someone who makes money by investing in high risk projects. [BUSINESS] N-COUNT

**ven|ture|some** /ventʃərsəm/ If you describe someone as **venturesome**, you mean that they are willing to take risks and try out new things. [FORMAL] ❑ *...the venturesome graduate who is determined to succeed.* ADJ = adventurous

**venue** /venjuː/ **(venues)** The **venue** for an event or activity is the place where it will happen. ❑ *Birmingham's International Convention Centre is the venue for a three-day arts festival.* ◆◇◇ N-COUNT

**ve|rac|ity** /vəræsɪti/ **Veracity** is the quality of being true or the habit of telling the truth. [FORMAL] ❑ *We have total confidence in the veracity of our research.* N-UNCOUNT

**ve|ran|da** /vərændə/ **(verandas)** also **verandah.** A **veranda** is a roofed platform along the outside of a house. N-COUNT

**verb** /vɜːrb/ **(verbs)** A **verb** is a word such as 'sing', 'feel', or 'die' which is used with a subject to say what someone or something does or what happens to them, or to give information about them. → See also **phrasal verb**. N-COUNT

**ver|bal** /vɜːrbəl/ [1] You use **verbal** to indicate that something is expressed in speech rather than in writing or action. ❑ *They were jostled and subjected to a torrent of verbal abuse... We have a verbal agreement with her.* ♦ **ver|bal|ly** *Teachers were threatened with kitchen knives, physically assaulted and verbally abused.* [2] You use **verbal** to indicate that something is connected with words and the use of words. ❑ *The test has scores for verbal skills, mathematical skills, and abstract reasoning skills.* ADJ: usu ADJ n; ADV; ADJ: ADJ n

[3] In grammar, **verbal** means relating to a verb. ❑ *...a verbal noun.* ADJ: usu ADJ n

**ver|bal|ize** /vɜːrbəlaɪz/ **(verbalizes, verbalizing, verbalized)**

✔ in BRIT, also use **verbalise**

If you **verbalize** your feelings, thoughts, or ideas, you express them in words. [FORMAL] ❑ *...his inability to verbalize his feelings.* VERB V n Also V

**ver|ba|tim** /vərbeɪtɪm/ If you repeat something **verbatim**, you use exactly the same words as were used originally. ❑ *The President's speeches* ADV: ADV after v *are regularly reproduced verbatim in the state-run newspapers.* ♦ **Verbatim** is also an adjective. ❑ *I was treated to a verbatim report of every conversation she's taken part in over the past week.* [ADJ: ADJ n]

**verb group** **(verb groups)** A **verb group** or **verbal group** consists of a verb, or of a main verb following a modal or one or more auxiliaries. Examples are 'walked', 'can see', and 'had been waiting'. [N-COUNT]

**ver|bi|age** /vɜːʳbiɪdʒ/ If you refer to someone's speech or writing as **verbiage**, you are critical of them because they use too many words, which makes their speech or writing difficult to understand. [FORMAL] ❑ *Stripped of their pretentious verbiage, his statements come dangerously close to inviting racial hatred.* [N-UNCOUNT] [disapproval] [= waffle]

**ver|bose** /vɜːʳboʊs/ If you describe a person or a piece of writing as **verbose**, you are critical of them because they use more words than are necessary, and so make you feel bored or annoyed. [FORMAL] ❑ *...verbose politicians... His writing is difficult and often verbose.* [ADJ] [disapproval] [= long-winded]

**ver|dant** /vɜːʳdᵊnt/ If you describe a place as **verdant**, you mean that it is covered with green grass, trees, and plants. [LITERARY] ❑ *...a small verdant garden with a view out over Paris.* [ADJ] [= lush]

**ver|dict** /vɜːʳdɪkt/ **(verdicts)** 1 In a court of law, the **verdict** is the decision that is given by the jury or judge at the end of a trial. ❑ *The jury returned a unanimous guilty verdict... Three judges will deliver their verdict in October.* [◆◇◇ N-COUNT] 2 Someone's **verdict** on something is their opinion of it, after thinking about it or investigating it. ❑ *The doctor's verdict was that he was entirely healthy.* [N-COUNT: oft with poss, oft N *on* n]

**ver|di|gris** /vɜːʳdɪgrɪs, -griːs/ **Verdigris** is a greenish-blue substance that forms on the metals copper, brass, and bronze after they have been left in wet or damp conditions. [N-UNCOUNT]

**verge** /vɜːʳdʒ/ **(verges, verging, verged)** 1 If you are **on the verge of** something, you are going to do it very soon or it is likely to happen or begin very soon. ❑ *The country was on the verge of becoming prosperous and successful... Carole was on the verge of tears.* [PREP-PHRASE: v-link PREP -ing/n] [= brink] 2 The **verge** of a road is a narrow piece of ground by the side of a road, which is usually covered with grass or flowers. [mainly BRIT] [N-COUNT]

☑ in AM, usually use **shoulder**

♦ **verge on** If someone or something **verges on** a particular state or quality, they are almost the same as that state or quality. ❑ *...a fury that verged on madness.* [PHRASAL VERB] [V P n (not pron)]

**veri|fi|able** /verɪfaɪəbᵊl/ Something that is **verifiable** can be proved to be true or genuine. ❑ *This is not a romantic notion but verifiable fact.* [ADJ]

**veri|fy** /verɪfaɪ/ **(verifies, verifying, verified)** 1 If you **verify** something, you check that it is true by careful examination or investigation. ❑ *I verified the source from which I had that information... A clerk simply verifies that the payment and invoice amount match.* [VERB] [V n] [V that] ♦ **veri|fi|ca|tion** /verɪfɪkeɪʃᵊn/ *All charges against her are dropped pending the verification of her story.* [N-UNCOUNT: oft N *of* n] 2 If you **verify** something, you state or confirm that it is true. ❑ *The government has not verified any of those reports... I can verify that it takes about thirty seconds.* [VERB: no cont] [= confirm] [V n] [V that]

**veri|ly** /verɪli/ **Verily** is an old-fashioned or religious word meaning 'truly'. It is used to emphasize a statement or opinion. ❑ *Verily I say unto you, that one of you shall betray me.* [ADV: usu ADV with cl, also ADV adj/adv] [emphasis]

**veri|si|mili|tude** /verɪsɪmɪlɪtjuːd, AM -tuːd/ **Verisimilitude** is the quality of seeming to be true or real. [FORMAL] ❑ *At the required level of visual verisimilitude, computer animation is costly.* [N-UNCOUNT] [= authenticity]

**veri|table** /verɪtəbᵊl/ You can use **veritable** to emphasize the size, amount, or nature of something. ❑ *...a veritable feast of pre-match entertainment.* [ADJ: usu *a* ADJ n] [emphasis]

**ver|ity** /verɪti/ **(verities)** The **verities** of something are all the things that are believed to be true about it. [FORMAL] ❑ *...some verities of human nature.* [N-COUNT: usu pl, usu with supp]

**ver|mil|ion** /vəʳmɪliən/ **Vermilion** is used to describe things that are bright red in colour. [LITERARY] ❑ *...her vermilion lip gloss... The furniture on it is glossy vermilion.* [COLOUR]

**ver|min** /vɜːʳmɪn/ **Vermin** are small animals such as rats and mice which cause problems to humans by carrying disease and damaging crops or food. [N-PLURAL]

**ver|mouth** /vɜːʳməθ/ **(vermouths)** **Vermouth** is a strong alcoholic drink made from red or white wine flavoured with herbs. [N-MASS]

**ver|nacu|lar** /vəʳnækjʊləʳ/ **(vernaculars)** **The vernacular** is the language or dialect that is most widely spoken by ordinary people in a region or country. ❑ *...books or plays written in the vernacular.* [N-COUNT: usu *the* N in sing]

**ver|ru|ca** /vəruːkə/ **(verrucas)** A **verruca** is a small infectious lump which grows on the bottom of your foot. [BRIT] [N-COUNT]

**ver|sa|tile** /vɜːʳsətaɪl, AM -tᵊl/ 1 If you say that a person is **versatile**, you approve of them because they have many different skills. ❑ *He had been one of the game's most versatile athletes.* [ADJ] [approval] ♦ **ver|sa|til|ity** /vɜːʳsətɪlɪti/ *Aileen stands out for her incredible versatility as an actress.* [N-UNCOUNT] 2 A tool, machine, or material that is **versatile** can be used for many different purposes. ❑ *Never before has computing been so versatile.* [ADJ] ♦ **ver|sa|til|ity** *Velvet is not known for its versatility.* [N-UNCOUNT]

**verse** /vɜːʳs/ **(verses)** 1 **Verse** is writing arranged in lines which have rhythm and which often rhyme at the end. ❑ *I have been moved to write a few lines of verse.* ➔ See also **blank verse**. [N-UNCOUNT] [= poetry] 2 A **verse** is one of the parts into which a poem, a song, or a chapter of the Bible or the Koran is divided. ❑ *This verse describes three signs of spring.* [N-COUNT]

**versed** /vɜːʳst/ If you are **versed in** or **well versed in** something, you know a lot about it. ❑ *Page is well versed in many styles of jazz.* [ADJ: v-link ADJ *in* n, adv ADJ]

**ver|sion** /vɜːʳʃᵊn, -ʒᵊn/ **(versions)** 1 A **version of** something is a particular form of it in which some details are different from earlier or later forms. ❑ *...an updated version of his book... Ludo is a version of an ancient Indian racing game.* [◆◆◇ N-COUNT: oft N *of* n] 2 Someone's **version of** an event is their own description of it, especially when it is different to other people's. ❑ *Yesterday afternoon the White House put out a new version of events.* [N-COUNT: with supp, oft poss N, N *of* n]

**ver|sus** /vɜːʳsəs/ 1 You use **versus** to indicate that two figures, ideas, or choices are opposed. ❑ *Only 18.8% of the class of 1982 had some kind of diploma four years after high school, versus 45% of the class of 1972. ...bottle-feeding versus breastfeeding.* [PREP] 2 **Versus** is used to indicate that two teams or people are competing against each other in a sporting event. ❑ *Italy versus Japan is turning out to be a surprisingly well matched competition.* [PREP] [= against]

**ver|te|bra** /vɜːʳtɪbrə/ **(vertebrae** /vɜːʳtɪbreɪ/**)** **Vertebrae** are the small circular bones that form the spine of a human being or animal. [N-COUNT: usu pl]

**ver|te|brate** /vɜːʳtɪbrɪt/ **(vertebrates)** A **vertebrate** is a creature which has a spine. Mammals, birds, reptiles, and fish are vertebrates. [N-COUNT: oft N n] [≠ invertebrate]

**ver|ti|cal** /vɜːʳtɪkᵊl/ 1 Something that is **vertical** stands or points straight up. ❑ *The gadget can be attached to any vertical or near vertical surface.* [ADJ] [≠ horizontal] ♦ **ver|ti|cal|ly** *Cut each bulb in half vertically.* [ADV: ADV after v] 2 **The vertical** is the direction that points straight up, at an angle of 90 degrees to a flat surface. ❑ *Pluto seems to have suffered a major collision that tipped it 122 degrees from the vertical.* [N-SING: *the* N]

**ver|tigi|nous** /vɜːʳtɪdʒɪnəs/ A **vertiginous** cliff or mountain is very high and steep. [LITERARY] [ADJ: usu ADJ n]

**ver|ti|go** /vɜːʳtɪgoʊ/ If you get **vertigo** when you look down from a high place, you feel unsteady and sick. [N-UNCOUNT]

**verve** /vɜːʳv/ **Verve** is lively and forceful enthusiasm. [WRITTEN] ❑ *He looked for the dramatic, like the sunset in this painting, and painted it with great verve.* N-UNCOUNT

**very** /veri/ ◆◆◆ [1] **Very** is used to give emphasis to an adjective or adverb. ❑ *The problem and the answer are very simple... It is very, very strong evidence indeed... I'm very sorry... They are getting the hang of it very quickly... Thank you very much... The men were very much like my father.* ADV: ADV adj/adv [emphasis] [2] **Not very** is used with an adjective or adverb to say that something is not at all true, or that it is true only to a small degree. ❑ *She's not very impressed with them... It's obviously not used very much... 'How well do you know her?' — 'Not very.'* PHRASE: usu PHR adj/adv [3] You use **very** to give emphasis to a superlative adjective or adverb. For example, if you say that something is **the very best**, you are emphasizing that it is the best. ❑ *They will be helped by the very latest in navigation aids... At the very least, the Government must offer some protection to mothers who fear domestic violence.* ADV: ADV superl [emphasis] [4] You use **very** with certain nouns in order to specify an extreme position or extreme point in time. ❑ *At the very back of the yard, several feet from Lenny, was a wooden shack... I turned to the very end of the book, to read the final words... He was wrong from the very beginning... We still do not have enough women at the very top.* ADJ: ADJ n [emphasis] [5] You use **very** with nouns to emphasize that something is exactly the right one or exactly the same one. ❑ *Everybody says he is the very man for the case... She died in this very house.* ADJ: ADJ n [emphasis] [6] You use **very** with nouns to emphasize the importance or seriousness of what you are saying. ❑ *At one stage his very life was in danger... The very basis of Indian politics has been transformed... History is taking place before your very eyes.* ADJ: ADJ n [emphasis]
PHRASES [7] The expression **very much so** is an emphatic way of answering 'yes' to something or saying that it is true or correct. ❑ *'Are you enjoying your holiday?' — 'Very much so.'* PHRASE: PHR as reply, cl PHR [emphasis] [8] **Very well** is used to say that you agree to do something or you accept someone's answer, even though you might not be completely satisfied with it. ❑ *'We need proof, sir.' Another pause. Then, 'Very well.'... Very well, please yourself.* CONVENTION [formulae] = all right [9] If you say that you **cannot very well** do something, you mean that it would not be right or possible to do it. ❑ *He couldn't very well go to her office and force her to write a check... I said yes. I can't very well say no.* PHRASE: V inflects, PHR inf

**ves|pers** /vespəʳz/ In some Christian churches, **vespers** is a service in the evening. N-UNCOUNT

**ves|sel** /vesᵊl/ ◆◇◇ (**vessels**) [1] A **vessel** is a ship or large boat. [FORMAL] ❑ *...a New Zealand navy vessel.* N-COUNT [2] A **vessel** is a bowl or other container in which liquid is kept. [FORMAL] N-COUNT [3] ➔ See also **blood vessel**.

**vest** /vest/ (**vests, vesting, vested**) [1] A **vest** is a piece of underwear which you can wear on the top half of your body in order to keep warm. [BRIT] N-COUNT

✔ in AM, use **undershirt**

[2] A **vest** is a sleeveless piece of clothing with buttons which people usually wear over a shirt. [AM] N-COUNT

✔ in BRIT, use **waistcoat**

[3] If something **is vested in** you, or if you **are vested with** it, it is given to you as a right or responsibility. [FORMAL] ❑ *All authority was vested in the woman, who discharged every kind of public duty... The mass media have been vested with significant power as social and political agents in modern developed societies... There's an extraordinary amount of power vested in us.* VERB: usu passive; be V-ed in n; be V-ed with n; V-ed

**vest|ed in|ter|est** (**vested interests**) If you have a **vested interest in** something, you have a very strong reason for acting in a particular way, for example to protect your money, power, or reputation. ❑ *The administration has no vested interest in proving whether public schools were good or bad.* N-VAR: usu N in n/-ing

**ves|ti|bule** /vestɪbjuːl/ (**vestibules**) A **vestibule** is an enclosed area between the outside door of a building and the inside door. [FORMAL] N-COUNT = entrance hall

**ves|tige** /vestɪdʒ/ (**vestiges**) A **vestige of** something is a very small part that still remains of something that was once much larger or more important. [FORMAL] ❑ *We represent the last vestige of what made this nation great – hard work.* N-COUNT: usu N of n

**ves|tig|ial** /vestɪdʒiəl/ **Vestigial** is used to describe the small amounts of something that still remain of a larger or more important thing. [FORMAL] ❑ *Vestigial remains of these plays are now seen in the Christmas pantomime.* ADJ: usu ADJ n

**vest|ments** /vestmənts/ **Vestments** are the special clothes worn by priests during church ceremonies. N-PLURAL

**ves|try** /vestri/ (**vestries**) A **vestry** is a room in a church which the clergy use as an office or to change into their ceremonial clothes for church services. N-COUNT

**vet** /vet/ (**vets, vetting, vetted**) [1] A **vet** is someone who is qualified to treat sick or injured animals. [mainly BRIT] N-COUNT

✔ in AM, usually use **veterinarian**

[2] A **vet** is someone who has served in the armed forces of their country, especially during a war. [AM, INFORMAL] ❑ *All three are Vietnam vets.* N-COUNT: oft supp N = veteran [3] If something **is vetted**, it is checked carefully to make sure that it is acceptable to people in authority. [mainly BRIT] ❑ *He can find no trace of a rule requiring research to be vetted before publication... He had not been allowed to read any book until his mother had vetted it.* VERB: be V-ed; V n [4] If someone **is vetted**, they are investigated fully before being given a particular job, role, or position, especially one which involves military or political secrets. [BRIT] ❑ *She was secretly vetted before she ever undertook any work for me.* VERB: usu passive = screen; be V-ed ♦ **vet|ting** *The government is to make major changes to the procedure for carrying out security vetting.* N-UNCOUNT

**vetch** /vetʃ/ (**vetches**) **Vetch** is a wild plant. Some types of vetch are sometimes grown as a crop. N-MASS

**vet|er|an** /vetərən/ ◆◇◇ (**veterans**) [1] A **veteran** is someone who has served in the armed forces of their country, especially during a war. ❑ *They approved a $1.1 billion package of pay increases for the veterans of the Persian Gulf War.* N-COUNT: oft N of n [2] You use **veteran** to refer to someone who has been involved in a particular activity for a long time. ❑ *...Tony Benn, the veteran Labour MP and former Cabinet minister.* N-COUNT: usu N n

**Vet|er|ans Day** In the United States, **Veterans Day** is November 11, when people honour those who have served or are serving in the armed forces. N-UNCOUNT

**vet|eri|nar|ian** /vetərɪneəriən/ (**veterinarians**) A **veterinarian** is a person who is qualified to treat sick or injured animals. [mainly AM] N-COUNT

✔ in BRIT, usually use **vet**

**vet|eri|nary** /vetərənəri, AM -neri/ **Veterinary** is used to describe the work of a person whose job is to treat sick or injured animals, or to describe the medical treatment of animals. ❑ *It was decided that our veterinary screening of horses at events should be continued.* ADJ: ADJ n

**vet|eri|nary sur|geon** (**veterinary surgeons**) A **veterinary surgeon** is someone who is qualified to treat sick or injured animals. [BRIT, FORMAL] N-COUNT = vet

✔ in AM, usually use **veterinarian**

**veto** /viːtoʊ/ (**vetoes, vetoing, vetoed**) [1] If someone in authority **vetoes** something, they forbid it, or stop it being put into action. ❑ *The President vetoed the economic package passed by Congress.* VERB = block; V n ♦ **Veto** is also a noun. ❑ *The veto was a calculated political risk.* N-COUNT [2] **Veto** is the right that someone in authority has to forbid something. ❑ *...the President's power of veto.* N-UNCOUNT

**vex** /veks/ **(vexes, vexing, vexed)** If someone or something **vexes** you, they make you feel annoyed, puzzled, and frustrated. ❑ *It vexed me to think of others gossiping behind my back.* ♦ **vexed** *Exporters, farmers and industrialists alike are vexed and blame the government.* ♦ **vex|ing** *There remains, however, another and more vexing problem.* ➔ See also **vexed**. VERB = *annoy* V n ADJ: usu v-link ADJ ADJ

**vexa|tion** /vekseɪʃᵊn/ **(vexations) Vexation** is a feeling of being annoyed, puzzled, and frustrated. [FORMAL] ❑ *He kicked the broken machine in vexation.* N-UNCOUNT: also N in pl = *annoyance*

**vexed** /vekst/ A **vexed** problem or question is very difficult and causes people a lot of trouble. ❑ *Ministers have begun work on the vexed issue of economic union... Later Mr Moi raised the vexed question of refugees.* ➔ See also **vex**. ADJ: usu ADJ n = *thorny*

**VHF** /viː eɪtʃ ef/ **VHF** is used to refer to a range of frequencies that is often used for transmitting radio broadcasts in stereo. **VHF** is an abbreviation for 'very high frequency'. N-UNCOUNT: oft N n

**via** /vaɪə, viːə/ 1 If you go somewhere **via** a particular place, you go through that place on the way to your destination. ❑ *Mr Baker will return home via Britain and France.* 2 If you do something **via** a particular means or person, you do it by making use of that means or person. ❑ *Translators can now work from home, via electronic mail systems.* ◆◇◇ PREP PREP

**vi|able** /vaɪəbᵊl/ 1 Something that is **viable** is capable of doing what it is intended to do. ❑ *Cash alone will not make Eastern Europe's banks viable. ...commercially viable products.* ♦ **vi|abil|ity** /vaɪəbɪlɪti/ *...the shaky financial viability of the nuclear industry.* 2 Foetuses, seeds, or eggs are described as **viable** if they are capable of developing into living beings without outside help. [TECHNICAL] ❑ *Five viable pregnancies were established.* ADJ N-UNCOUNT ADJ

**via|duct** /vaɪədʌkt/ **(viaducts)** A **viaduct** is a long, high bridge that carries a road or a railway across a valley. N-COUNT

**Vi|ag|ra** /vaɪægrə/ **Viagra** is a drug that is given to men with certain sexual problems in order to help them to have sexual intercourse. [TRADEMARK] N-UNCOUNT

**vial** /vaɪəl/ **(vials)** A **vial** is a very small bottle which is used to hold something such as perfume or medicine. [FORMAL] N-COUNT = *phial*

**vibe** /vaɪb/ **(vibes) Vibes** are the good or bad atmosphere that you sense with a person or in a place. [INFORMAL] ❑ *Sorry, Chris, but I have bad vibes about this guy.* N-COUNT: usu pl

**vi|brant** /vaɪbrənt/ 1 Someone or something that is **vibrant** is full of life, energy, and enthusiasm. ❑ *Tom felt himself being drawn towards her vibrant personality... Orlando itself is vibrant, full of affordable accommodation and great places to eat.* ♦ **vi|bran|cy** /vaɪbrənsi/ *She was a woman with extraordinary vibrancy and extraordinary knowledge.* 2 **Vibrant** colours are very bright and clear. ❑ *Horizon Blue, Corn Yellow and Pistachio Green are just three of the vibrant colours in this range.* ♦ **vi|brant|ly** *...a selection of vibrantly coloured French cast-iron saucepans.* ADJ N-UNCOUNT = *vitality* ADJ: usu ADJ n = *brilliant* ADV: ADV adj

**vi|bra|phone** /vaɪbrəfoʊn/ **(vibraphones)** A **vibraphone** is an electronic musical instrument which consists of a set of metal bars in a frame. When you hit the bars they produce ringing notes that last for some time. N-COUNT

**vi|brate** /vaɪbreɪt, AM vaɪbreɪt/ **(vibrates, vibrating, vibrated)** If something **vibrates** or if you **vibrate** it, it shakes with repeated small, quick movements. ❑ *The ground shook and the cliffs seemed to vibrate... The noise vibrated the table.* ♦ **vi|bra|tion** /vaɪbreɪʃᵊn/ **(vibrations)** *The vibrations of the vehicles rattled the shop windows.* VERB V V n N-VAR

**vi|bra|to** /vɪbrɑːtoʊ/ **(vibratos) Vibrato** is a rapidly repeated slight change in the pitch of a musical note. Singers and musicians use vibrato to make the music sound more emotional. ❑ *I encourage oboe and clarinet players to use plenty of vibrato.* N-VAR

**vi|bra|tor** /vaɪbreɪtəʳ, AM vaɪbreɪtər/ **(vibrators)** A **vibrator** is an electric device which vibrates. It is used in massage to reduce pain, or to give sexual pleasure. N-COUNT

**vic|ar** /vɪkəʳ/ **(vicars)** 1 A **vicar** is an Anglican priest who is in charge of a church and the area it is in, which is called a parish. [mainly BRIT] 2 A **vicar** is a priest who is in charge of a chapel that is associated with a parish church in the Episcopal Church in the United States. [AM] N-COUNT; N-VOC N-COUNT; N-VOC

**vic|ar|age** /vɪkərɪdʒ/ **(vicarages)** A **vicarage** is a house in which a vicar lives. [BRIT] N-COUNT

**vi|cari|ous** /vɪkeəriəs, AM vaɪkæriəs/ A **vicarious** pleasure or feeling is experienced by watching, listening to, or reading about other people doing something, rather than by doing it yourself. ❑ *She invents fantasy lives for her own vicarious pleasure.* ♦ **vi|cari|ous|ly** *...a father who lived vicariously through his sons' success.* ADJ: ADJ n ADV: usu ADV with v

**vice** /vaɪs/ **(vices)** 1 A **vice** is a habit which is regarded as a weakness in someone's character, but not usually as a serious fault. ❑ *Intellectual pretension was never one of his vices.* 2 **Vice** refers to criminal activities, especially those connected with pornography or prostitution. ❑ *He said those responsible for offences connected with vice, gaming and drugs should be deported on conviction.* 3 A **vice** is a tool with a pair of parts that hold an object tightly while you do work on it. [BRIT] ◆◇◇ N-COUNT N-UNCOUNT N-COUNT

☑ in AM, use **vise**

**vice-** /vaɪs-/ **Vice-** is used before a rank or title to indicate that someone is next in importance to the person who holds the rank or title mentioned. ❑ *...America's vice-president... Tim Munton becomes the new vice-captain.* PREFIX

**vice-chancellor (vice-chancellors)** 1 In a British university, the **vice-chancellor** is the person in charge of academic and administrative matters. 2 In an American university, the **vice-chancellor** is the person next in rank below the chancellor, who acts as the chancellor's deputy or substitute. N-COUNT N-COUNT

**vice|roy** /vaɪsrɔɪ/ **(viceroys)** In former times, a **viceroy** was the person who ruled a colony on behalf of his king, queen, or government. N-COUNT

**vice squad (vice squads) The vice squad** is the section of a police force that deals with crime relating to pornography, prostitution, and gambling. ❑ *...ten vice-squad officers.* N-COUNT: usu *the* N in sing, N n

**vice ver|sa** /vaɪsə vɜːʳsə/ **Vice versa** is used to indicate that the reverse of what you have said is true. For example 'women may bring their husbands with them, and vice versa' means that men may also bring their wives with them. ❑ *Teachers qualified to teach in England are not accepted in Scotland and vice versa.* PHRASE: usu *and/or/not* PHR

**vi|cin|ity** /vɪsɪnɪti/ If something is **in the vicinity of** a particular place, it is near it. [FORMAL] ❑ *There were a hundred or so hotels in the vicinity of the railway station.* N-SING: *the* N, oft *in* N, N *of* n

**vi|cious** /vɪʃəs/ 1 A **vicious** person or a **vicious** blow is violent and cruel. ❑ *He was a cruel and vicious man... He suffered a vicious attack by a gang of white youths... The blow was so sudden and vicious that he dropped to his knees.* ♦ **vi|cious|ly** *She had been viciously attacked with a hammer.* ♦ **vi|cious|ness** *...the intensity and viciousness of these attacks.* 2 A **vicious** remark is cruel and intended to upset someone. ❑ *It is a deliberate, nasty and vicious attack on a young man's character.* ♦ **vi|cious|ly** *'He deserved to die,' said Penelope viciously.* ADJ = *brutal* ADV: usu ADV with v, also ADV adj N-UNCOUNT ADJ = *savage* ADV: ADV with v

**vi|cious cir|cle (vicious circles)** or **vicious cycle** A **vicious circle** is a problem or difficult situation that has the effect of creating new problems which then cause the original problem or situation to occur again. ❑ *The more pesticides are* N-COUNT: usu sing, oft N *of* n ≠ *virtuous circle* *used, the more resistant the insects become so the more pesticides have to be used. It's a vicious circle.*

**vi|cis|si|tudes** /vɪsɪsɪtjuːdz, AM -tuːdz/ N-PLURAL: oft N *of* n You use **vicissitudes** to refer to changes, especially unpleasant ones, that happen to someone or something at different times in their life or development. [FORMAL] ❑ *Whatever the vicissitudes of her past life, Jill now seems to have come through.*

**vic|tim** /vɪktɪm/ **(victims)** ◆◆◇ 1 N-COUNT A **victim** is someone who has been hurt or killed. ❑ *Not all the victims survived... Statistically our chances of being the victims of violent crime are remote.* 2 N-COUNT A **victim** is someone who has suffered as a result of someone else's actions or beliefs, or as a result of unpleasant circumstances. ❑ *He was a victim of racial prejudice... Infectious diseases are spreading among many of the flood victims.* 3 PHRASE: V inflects, PHR n If you **fall victim to** something or someone, you suffer as a result of them, or you are killed by them. ❑ *In the early 1960s, Blyton fell victim to Alzheimer's disease.*

**vic|tim|ize** /vɪktɪmaɪz/ **(victimizes, victimizing, victimized)** ◆◇◇

in BRIT, also use **victimise**

VERB: *be* V-ed, Also V n If someone **is victimized**, they are deliberately treated unfairly. ❑ *He felt the students had been victimized because they'd voiced opposition to the government.* ♦ **vic|timi|za|tion** /vɪktɪmaɪzeɪʃən/ N-UNCOUNT *...society's cruel victimization of women.*

**vic|tim|less** /vɪktɪmləs/ ADJ: usu ADJ n A **victimless** crime is a crime which is considered to be less serious than other crimes because nobody suffers directly as a result of it. [JOURNALISM] ❑ *...the so-called victimless crime of prostitution.*

**vic|tim sup|port** N-UNCOUNT **Victim support** is the giving of help and advice to people who are victims of crime. ❑ *When the attack took place, there were no victim support schemes.*

**vic|tor** /vɪktəʳ/ **(victors)** N-COUNT The **victor** in a battle or contest is the person who wins. [LITERARY]

**Vic|to|rian** /vɪktɔːriən/ **(Victorians)** 1 ADJ: usu ADJ n **Victorian** means belonging to, connected with, or typical of Britain in the middle and last parts of the 19th century, when Victoria was Queen. ❑ *We have a lovely old Victorian house. ...The Early Victorian Period.* 2 ADJ You can use **Victorian** to describe people who have old-fashioned attitudes, especially about good behaviour and morals. ❑ *Victorian values are much misunderstood... My grandfather was very Victorian.* 3 N-COUNT: usu pl The **Victorians** were the British people who lived in the time of Queen Victoria.

**Vic|to|ri|ana** /vɪktɔːriɑːnə/ N-UNCOUNT Interesting or valuable objects made in the time of Queen Victoria are sometimes referred to as **Victoriana**.

**vic|to|ri|ous** /vɪktɔːriəs/ ADJ = winning You use **victorious** to describe someone who has won a victory in a struggle, war, or competition. ❑ *In 1978 he played for the victorious Argentinian side in the World Cup.*

**vic|to|ry** /vɪktəri/ **(victories)** ◆◆◇ 1 N-VAR ≠ defeat A **victory** is a success in a struggle, war, or competition. ❑ *Union leaders are heading for victory in their battle over workplace rights. ...the former Welsh rugby union skipper who led Great Britain to victory over France.* 2 PHRASE: N inflects, PHR after v, v-link PHR If you say that someone has won a **moral victory**, you mean that although they have officially lost a contest or dispute, they have succeeded in showing they are right about something. ❑ *She said her party had won a moral victory.*

**video** /vɪdioʊ/ **(videos, videoing, videoed)** ◆◆◇ 1 N-COUNT A **video** is a film or television programme recorded on tape for people to watch on a television set. ❑ *...the makers of films and videos.* 2 N-UNCOUNT: oft *on* N **Video** is the system of recording films and events on tape so that people can watch them on a television set. ❑ *She has watched the race on video. ...manufacturers of audio and video equipment.* 3 N-COUNT = video recorder, VCR A **video** is a machine that you can use to record television programmes and play videotapes on a television set. [mainly BRIT] ❑ *He'd set the video for 8.00.*

in AM, usually use **VCR**

4 VERB = videotape, tape; V n If you **video** a television programme or event, you record it on tape using a video recorder or video camera, so that you can watch it later. [mainly BRIT] ❑ *She had been videoing the highlights of the tournament.*

in AM, usually use **tape, videotape**

5 N-COUNT **Video** is a system by which you see television images or films on your computer, rather than on a television set.

**video cam|era** **(video cameras)** N-COUNT A **video camera** is a camera that you use to record something that is happening, so that you can watch it later.

**video cas|sette** **(video cassettes)** N-COUNT = videotape A **video cassette** is a cassette containing videotape, on which you can record or watch moving pictures and sounds.

**video-con|ference** **(video-conferences)** N-COUNT A **video-conference** is a meeting that takes place using video conferencing. [BUSINESS]

**video con|fer|enc|ing** /vɪdioʊ kɒnfrənsɪŋ/ also **videoconferencing, videoconferencing.** N-UNCOUNT **Video conferencing** is a system that enables people in various places around the world to have a meeting by seeing and hearing each other on a screen. [BUSINESS]

**video dia|ry** **(video diaries)** N-COUNT A **video diary** is a film that someone makes of the things that happen to them over a period of time, recorded using a video camera.

**video game** **(video games)** N-COUNT A **video game** is a computer game that you play on your television or on a similar device.

**video nas|ty** **(video nasties)** N-COUNT A **video nasty** is an extremely violent or frightening film which people can only buy on video. [BRIT]

**video|phone** /vɪdioʊfoʊn/ **(videophones)** also **video phone.** N-COUNT A **videophone** is a telephone which has a camera and screen so that people who are using the phone can see and hear each other.

**video re|cord|er** **(video recorders)** N-COUNT = video A **video recorder** or a **video cassette recorder** is the same as a **VCR**.

**video|tape** /vɪdioʊteɪp/ **(videotapes, videotaping, videotaped)** also **video tape.** 1 N-UNCOUNT **Videotape** is magnetic tape that is used to record moving pictures and sounds to be shown on television. 2 N-COUNT A **videotape** is the same as a **video cassette.** 3 VERB = video; V n If you **videotape** a television programme or event, you record it on tape using a video recorder or video camera, so that you can watch it later. [mainly AM] ❑ *She videotaped the entire trip.*

**video wall** **(video walls)** N-COUNT A **video wall** is a set of video screens that are connected together, so that each screen shows a part of the whole picture or so that the same picture is repeated on each screen.

**vie** /vaɪ/ **(vies, vying, vied)** V-RECIP = compete; V *with* n to-inf; pl-n V to-inf; V *with* n *for* n; pl-n V *for* n If one person or thing **is vying with** another for something, the people or things are competing for it. [FORMAL] ❑ *California is vying with other states to capture a piece of the growing communications market... Four rescue plans are vying to save the zoo... In hospitals, business plans vie with patients for doctors' attention... The two are vying for the support of New York voters.*

**view** /vjuː/ **(views, viewing, viewed)** ◆◆◆ 1 N-COUNT: usu with supp, oft N *on* n, N that Your **views** on something are the beliefs or opinions that you have about it, for example whether you think it is good, bad, right, or wrong. ❑ *Washington and Moscow are believed to have similar views on Kashmir... My own view is absolutely clear. What I did was right... You should also make your views known to your local MP.* 2 N-SING: with supp, oft N *of* n Your **view of** a particular subject is the way that you understand and think about it. ❑ *The drama takes an idealistic, even a naive view of the subject... The whole point was to get away from a Christian-centred view of religion.* 3 VERB = regard If you **view** something in a particular way, you think of it in that way. ❑ *First-generation Americans view the United States as a land of golden opportunity... Abigail's mother Linda views her daughter's talent with a mixture of pride and worry... We would view favourably any sensible suggestion for maintaining the business.* (V n *as* n/-ing; V n *with/in* n; V n with adv) [4] The **view** from a window or high place is everything which can be seen from that place, especially when it is considered to be beautiful. ❑ *The view from our window was one of beautiful green countryside.* (N-COUNT) [5] If you have a **view of** something, you can see it. ❑ *He stood up to get a better view of the blackboard.* (N-SING: with supp, oft N *of* n, poss N) [6] You use **view** in expressions to do with being able to see something. For example, if something is **in view**, you can see it. If something is **in full view of everyone**, everyone can see it. ❑ *She was lying there in full view of anyone who walked by... A group of riders came into view on the dirt road.* (N-UNCOUNT: *in/into* N) [7] If you **view** something, you look at it for a particular purpose. [FORMAL] ❑ *They came back to view the house again.* (VERB; V n) [8] If you **view** a television programme, video, or film, you watch it. [FORMAL] ❑ *We have viewed the video recording of the incident... 'Elizabeth R', a TV portrait of the Queen, had record viewing figures.* (VERB; V n; V-ing) [9] **View** refers to the way in which a piece of text or graphics is displayed on a computer screen. [COMPUTING] ❑ *To see the current document in full-page view, click the Page Zoom Full button.* (N-UNCOUNT)

**PHRASES** [10] If you **take a dim view** or **a poor view of** someone or something, you disapprove of them or have a low opinion of them. ❑ *They took a dim view of local trade unionists.* (PHRASE: v PHR, usu PHR *of* n) [11] You use **in my view** when you want to indicate that you are stating a personal opinion, which other people might not agree with. ❑ *In my view things won't change.* (PHRASE: PHR with cl) [12] You use **in view of** when you are taking into consideration facts that have just been mentioned or are just about to be mentioned. ❑ *In view of the fact that Hobson was not a trained economist his achievements were remarkable.* (PREP-PHRASE: PREP n) [13] If you have something **in view**, you are aware of it and your actions are aimed towards it. ❑ *They have very clear career aims in view... Ackroyd worked out this whole plot with one objective in view.* (PHRASE: usu PHR after v; = in mind) [14] If you **take the long view**, you consider what is likely to happen in the future over a long period, rather than thinking only about things that are going to happen soon. ❑ *Some investors are taking the long view.* (PHRASE: V inflects, oft PHR *of* n) [15] If something such as a work of art is **on view**, it is shown in public for people to look at. ❑ *A significant exhibition of contemporary sculpture will be on view at the Portland Gallery.* (PHRASE: usu v-link PHR) [16] If you do something **with a view to** doing something else, you do it because you hope it will result in that other thing being done. ❑ *He has called a meeting of all parties tomorrow, with a view to forming a national reconciliation government.* (PHRASE: PHR -ing/n)

**view|er** /vjuːə$^{r}$/ **(viewers)** [1] **Viewers** are people who watch television, or who are watching a particular programme on television. ❑ *These programmes are each watched by around 19 million viewers every week.* (◆◇◇ N-COUNT: usu pl) [2] A **viewer** is someone who is looking carefully at a picture or other interesting object. ❑ *...the relationship between the art object and the viewer.* (N-COUNT)

**view|finder** /vjuːfaɪndə$^{r}$/ **(viewfinders)** A **viewfinder** is a small square of glass in a camera that you look through in order to see what you are going to photograph. (N-COUNT)

**view|point** /vjuːpɔɪnt/ **(viewpoints)** [1] Someone's **viewpoint** is the way that they think about things in general, or the way they think about a particular thing. ❑ *The novel is shown from the girl's viewpoint.* (N-COUNT: usu with supp; = point of view) [2] A **viewpoint** is a place from which you can get a good view of something. ❑ *You have to know where to stand for a good viewpoint.* (N-COUNT: with supp; = vantage point)

**vig|il** /vɪdʒɪl/ **(vigils)** A **vigil** is a period of time when people remain quietly in a place, especially at night, for example because they are praying or are making a political protest. ❑ *Protesters are holding a twenty-four hour vigil outside the socialist party headquarters.* (N-COUNT) ● If someone **keeps a vigil** or **keeps vigil** somewhere, they remain there quietly for a period of time, especially at night, for example because they are praying or are making a political protest. ❑ *She kept a vigil at Patrick's bedside.* (PHRASE: V inflects, usu PHR prep/adv)

**vigi|lant** /vɪdʒɪlənt/ Someone who is **vigilant** gives careful attention to a particular problem or situation and concentrates on noticing any danger or trouble that there might be. ❑ *He warned the public to be vigilant and report anything suspicious.* (ADJ; = alert) ♦ **vigi|lance** *Drugs are a problem that requires constant vigilance.* (N-UNCOUNT)

**vigi|lan|te** /vɪdʒɪlænti/ **(vigilantes)** **Vigilantes** are people who organize themselves into an unofficial group to protect their community and to catch and punish criminals. ❑ *...vigilante patrols.* (N-COUNT)

**vi|gnette** /vɪnjet/ **(vignettes)** A **vignette** is a short description, picture, or piece of acting which expresses very clearly and neatly the typical characteristics of the thing that it represents. [FORMAL] ❑ *The book is an excellent vignette of some of the major debates in science.* (N-COUNT: oft N *of* n)

**vig|or|ous** /vɪgərəs/ [1] **Vigorous** physical activities involve using a lot of energy, usually to do short and repeated actions. ❑ *Very vigorous exercise can increase the risk of heart attacks... African dance is vigorous, but full of subtlety.* (ADJ) ♦ **vig|or|ous|ly** *He shook his head vigorously.* (ADV: ADV after v) [2] A **vigorous** person does things with great energy and enthusiasm. A **vigorous** campaign or activity is done with great energy and enthusiasm. ❑ *Sir Robert was a strong and vigorous politician. ...a vigorous campaign against GM food.* (ADJ: usu ADJ n) ♦ **vig|or|ous|ly** *The police vigorously denied that excessive force had been used.* (ADV: ADV with v)

**vig|our** /vɪgə$^{r}$/

✔ in AM, use **vigor**

**Vigour** is physical or mental energy and enthusiasm. ❑ *His body lacks the bounce and vigour of a normal two-year-old.* (N-UNCOUNT)

**Vi|king** /vaɪkɪŋ/ **(Vikings)** The **Vikings** were men who sailed from Scandinavia and attacked villages in most parts of north-western Europe from the 8th to the 11th centuries. (N-COUNT)

**vile** /vaɪl/ **(viler, vilest)** If you say that someone or something is **vile**, you mean that they are very unpleasant. ❑ *She was in too vile a mood to work.* (ADJ; = foul)

**vili|fy** /vɪlɪfaɪ/ **(vilifies, vilifying, vilified)** If you **are vilified** by someone, they say or write very unpleasant things about you, so that people will have a low opinion of you. [FORMAL] ❑ *The agency has been vilified by some doctors for being unnecessarily slow to approve life-saving drugs... He was vilified, hounded, and forced into exile by the FBI.* (VERB; *be* V-ed *for* -ing/n; *be* V-ed; Also V n, V n *as* n) ♦ **vili|fi|ca|tion** /vɪlɪfɪkeɪʃən/ *Clare did not deserve the vilification she had been subjected to.* (N-UNCOUNT)

**vil|la** /vɪlə/ **(villas)** A **villa** is a fairly large house, especially one that is used for holidays in Mediterranean countries. (N-COUNT)

**vil|lage** /vɪlɪdʒ/ **(villages)** A **village** consists of a group of houses, together with other buildings such as a church and a school, in a country area. ❑ *He lives quietly in the country in a village near Lahti. ...the village school.* (◆◆◇ N-COUNT)

**vil|lag|er** /vɪlɪdʒə$^{r}$/ **(villagers)** You refer to the people who live in a village, especially the people who have lived there for most or all of their lives, as the **villagers**. ❑ *Soon the villagers couldn't afford to buy food for themselves.* (N-COUNT: usu pl)

**vil|lain** /vɪlən/ **(villains)** [1] A **villain** is someone who deliberately harms other people or breaks the law in order to get what he or she wants. (N-COUNT) [2] The **villain** in a novel, film, or play is the main bad character. (N-COUNT; ≠ hero)

**vil|lain|ous** /vɪlənəs/ A **villainous** person is very bad and willing to harm other people or break the law in order to get what he or she wants. ❑ *...her villainous father.* (ADJ: usu ADJ n)

**vil|lainy** /vɪləni/ **Villainy** is very bad or criminal behaviour. [FORMAL] ❑ *They justify every villainy in the name of high ideals.* N-UNCOUNT

**vinai|grette** /vɪnɪgret/ **(vinaigrettes)** **Vinaigrette** is a dressing made by mixing oil, vinegar, salt, pepper, and herbs, which is used on salad. N-MASS = French dressing

**vin|di|cate** /vɪndɪkeɪt/ **(vindicates, vindicating, vindicated)** If a person or their decisions, actions, or ideas **are vindicated**, they are proved to be correct, after people have said that they were wrong. [FORMAL] ❑ *The director said he had been vindicated by the experts' report.* ♦ **vin|di|ca|tion** /vɪndɪkeɪʃᵊn/ *He called the success a vindication of his party's free-market economic policy.* VERB be V-ed N-UNCOUNT: also a N, usu N of n

**vin|dic|tive** /vɪndɪktɪv/ If you say that someone is **vindictive**, you are critical of them because they deliberately try to upset or cause trouble for someone who they think has done them harm. ❑ *...a vindictive woman desperate for revenge against the man who loved and left her.* ♦ **vin|dic|tive|ness** *...a dishonest person who is operating completely out of vindictiveness.* ADJ [disapproval] N-UNCOUNT

**vine** /vaɪn/ **(vines)** A **vine** is a plant that grows up or over things, especially one which produces grapes. N-VAR = grapevine

**vin|egar** /vɪnɪgəʳ/ **(vinegars)** **Vinegar** is a sharp-tasting liquid, usually made from sour wine or malt, which is used to make things such as salad dressing. N-MASS

**vin|egary** /vɪnɪgəri/ If something has a **vinegary** taste or smell, it tastes or smells of vinegar. ❑ *The salads taste too vinegary.* ADJ

**vine|yard** /vɪnjəʳd/ **(vineyards)** A **vineyard** is an area of land where grape vines are grown in order to produce wine. You can also use **vineyard** to refer to the set of buildings in which the wine is produced. N-COUNT

**vin|tage** /vɪntɪdʒ/ **(vintages)** 1 The **vintage** of a good quality wine is the year and place that it was made before being stored to improve it. You can also use **vintage** to refer to the wine that was made in a certain year. ❑ *This wine is from one of the two best vintages of the decade in this region.* N-COUNT
2 **Vintage** wine is good quality wine that has been stored for several years in order to improve its quality. ❑ *If you can buy only one case at auction, it should be vintage port.* ADJ: ADJ n 3 **Vintage** cars or aeroplanes are old but are admired because they are considered to be the best of their kind. ❑ *The museum will have a permanent exhibition of 60 vintage cars.* ADJ: ADJ n 4 You can use **vintage** to describe something which is the best and most typical of its kind. ❑ *This is vintage comedy at its best.* ADJ: usu ADJ n

**vint|ner** /vɪntnəʳ/ **(vintners)** 1 A **vintner** is someone whose job is to buy and sell wine. [FORMAL] N-COUNT 2 A **vintner** is someone who grows grapes and makes wine. [FORMAL] N-COUNT

**vi|nyl** /vaɪnɪl/ **(vinyls)** 1 **Vinyl** is a strong plastic used for making things such as floor coverings and furniture. ❑ *...a modern vinyl floor covering. ...a reclining chair upholstered in shiny blue vinyl.* N-MASS: oft N n
2 You can use **vinyl** to refer to records, especially in contrast to cassettes or compact discs. ❑ *This compilation was first issued on vinyl in 1984.* N-UNCOUNT: oft on N

**viol** /vaɪəl/ **(viols)** **Viols** are a family of musical instruments that are made of wood and have six strings. You play the viol with a bow while sitting down. N-VAR: oft the N

**vio|la** /vioʊlə/ **(violas)** A **viola** is a musical instrument with four strings that is played with a bow. It is like a violin, but is slightly larger and can play lower notes. N-VAR: oft the N

**vio|late** /vaɪəleɪt/ **(violates, violating, violated)** 1 If someone **violates** an agreement, law, or promise, they break it. [FORMAL] ❑ *They went to prison because they violated the law.* ♦ **vio|la|tion** /vaɪəleɪʃᵊn/ **(violations)** *To deprive the boy of his education is a violation of state law... He was in violation of his contract.* ♦ **vio|la|tor (violators)** *...a government which is a known violator of human rights.* ◆◇◇ VERB = break V n N-VAR: usu N of n N-COUNT
2 If you **violate** someone's privacy or peace, you disturb it. [FORMAL] ❑ *These men were violating her family's privacy.* VERB V n 3 If someone **violates** a special place, for example a grave, they damage it or treat it with disrespect. ❑ *Detectives are still searching for those who violated the graveyard.* ♦ **vio|la|tion** *The violation of the graves is not the first such incident.* VERB = desecrate V n N-UNCOUNT: usu N of n

**vio|lence** /vaɪələns/ 1 **Violence** is behaviour which is intended to hurt, injure, or kill people. ❑ *Twenty people were killed in the violence... They threaten them with violence.* ◆◆◇ N-UNCOUNT 2 If you do or say something with **violence**, you use a lot of force and energy in doing or saying it, often because you are angry. [LITERARY] ❑ *The violence in her tone gave Alistair a shock.* N-UNCOUNT

**vio|lent** /vaɪələnt/ 1 If someone is **violent**, or if they do something which is **violent**, they use physical force or weapons to hurt, injure, or kill other people. ❑ *A quarter of current inmates have committed violent crimes. ...violent anti-government demonstrations... Sometimes the men get violent.* ♦ **vio|lent|ly** *Some opposition activists have been violently attacked.* ◆◇◇ ADJ ADV: ADV with v 2 A **violent** event happens suddenly and with great force. ❑ *A violent explosion seemed to jolt the whole ground.* ♦ **vio|lent|ly** *A nearby volcano erupted violently, sending out a hail of molten rock and boiling mud.* ADJ: usu ADJ n ADV: ADV with v
3 If you describe something as **violent**, you mean that it is said, done, or felt very strongly. ❑ *Violent opposition to the plan continues... He had violent stomach pains. ...an outburst of violent emotion.* ♦ **vio|lent|ly** *He was violently scolded.* ADJ: usu ADJ n = intense ADV 4 A **violent** death is painful and unexpected, usually because the person who dies has been murdered. ❑ *...an innocent man who had met a violent death.* ♦ **vio|lent|ly** *...a girl who had died violently nine years earlier.* ADJ ADV: ADV with v 5 A **violent** film or television programme contains a lot of scenes which show violence. ❑ *It was the most violent film that I have ever seen.* ADJ

**vio|let** /vaɪəlɪt/ **(violets)** 1 A **violet** is a small plant that has purple or white flowers in the spring. N-COUNT 2 Something that is **violet** is a bluish-purple colour. ❑ *The light was beginning to drain from a violet sky.* COLOUR 3 If you say that someone is no **shrinking violet**, you mean that they are not at all shy. ❑ *When it comes to expressing himself he is no shrinking violet.* PHRASE: usu with brd-neg, N inflects, v-link PHR

**vio|lin** /vaɪəlɪn/ **(violins)** A **violin** is a musical instrument. Violins are made of wood and have four strings. You play the violin by holding it under your chin and moving a bow across the strings. ❑ *Lizzie used to play the violin.* N-VAR: oft the N

**vio|lin|ist** /vaɪəlɪnɪst/ **(violinists)** A **violinist** is someone who plays the violin. N-COUNT

**VIP** /viː aɪ piː/ **(VIPs)** A **VIP** is someone who is given better treatment than ordinary people because they are famous, influential, or important. **VIP** is an abbreviation for 'very important person'. N-COUNT

**vi|per** /vaɪpəʳ/ **(vipers)** A **viper** is a small poisonous snake found mainly in Europe. N-COUNT = adder

**vi|ral** /vaɪərəl/ A **viral** disease or infection is caused by a virus. ❑ *...a 65-year-old patient suffering from severe viral pneumonia.* ADJ: usu ADJ n

**vir|gin** /vɜːʳdʒɪn/ **(virgins)** 1 A **virgin** is someone who has never had sex. ❑ *I was a virgin until I was thirty years old.* N-COUNT 2 You use **virgin** to describe something such as land that has never been used or spoiled. ❑ *Within 40 years there will be no virgin forest left.* ADJ: usu ADJ n 3 If you say that a situation is **virgin territory**, you mean that you have no experience of it and it is completely new for you. PHRASE: v-link PHR, PHR after v
4 You can use **virgin** to describe someone who has never done or used a particular thing before. ❑ *Until he appeared in 'In the Line of Fire' Malkovich had been an action-movie virgin.* N-COUNT: oft n N

**vir|gin|al** /vɜːʳdʒɪnᵊl/ 1 If you describe someone as **virginal**, you mean that they look young and innocent, as if they have had no ex- ADJ = pure perience of sex. ❑ *Somehow she'd always been a child in his mind, pure and virginal.* 2 Something that is **virginal** looks new and clean, as if it has not been used or spoiled. ❑ *...abandoning worn-out land to cultivate virginal pasture.* ADJ

**vir|gin|ity** /vəˈdʒɪnɪti/ **Virginity** is the state of never having had sex. ❑ *She lost her virginity when she was 20.* ● When you **lose** your **virginity**, you have sex for the first time. N-UNCOUNT; PHRASE: V inflects

**Vir|go** /vɜːˈɡoʊ/ **(Virgos)** 1 **Virgo** is one of the twelve signs of the zodiac. Its symbol is a young woman. People who are born approximately between the 23rd of August and the 22nd of September come under this sign. N-UNCOUNT 2 A **Virgo** is a person whose sign of the zodiac is Virgo. N-COUNT

**vir|ile** /vɪraɪl, AM -rəl/ 1 If you describe a man as **virile**, you mean that he has the qualities that a man is traditionally expected to have, such as strength and sexual power. ❑ *He wanted his sons to become strong, virile, and athletic like himself.* ADJ ♦ **vi|ril|ity** /vɪrɪlɪti/ *Children are also considered proof of a man's virility.* N-UNCOUNT 2 Something that is described as **virile** is considered to be very strong and forceful. [LITERARY] ❑ *...Prokofiev's most virile, aggressive music.* ADJ

**vir|tual** /vɜːˈtʃuəl/ 1 You can use **virtual** to indicate that something is so nearly true that for most purposes it can be regarded as true. ❑ *Argentina came to a virtual standstill while the game was being played. ...conditions of virtual slavery.* ADJ: ADJ n 2 **Virtual** objects and activities are generated by a computer to simulate real objects and activities. [COMPUTING] ❑ *This is a virtual shopping centre offering visitors entry to a clutch of well-known e-tailers without going to their different websites.* ADJ: ADJ n ♦ **vir|tu|al|ity** *People speculate about virtuality systems, but we're already working on it.* N-UNCOUNT

**vir|tu|al|ly** /vɜːˈtʃuəli/ You can use **virtually** to indicate that something is so nearly true that for most purposes it can be regarded as true. ❑ *Virtually all cooking was done over coal-fired ranges... It would have been virtually impossible to research all the information.* ◆◇◇ ADV: ADV with group = almost

**vir|tual memo|ry** **Virtual memory** is a computing technique in which you increase the size of a computer's memory by arranging or storing the data in it in a different way. [COMPUTING] N-UNCOUNT

**vir|tual re|al|ity** **Virtual reality** is an environment which is produced by a computer and seems very like reality to the person experiencing it. [COMPUTING] N-UNCOUNT

**vir|tual stor|age** **Virtual storage** is the same as **virtual memory**. [COMPUTING] N-UNCOUNT

**vir|tue** /vɜːˈtʃuː/ **(virtues)** 1 **Virtue** is thinking and doing what is right and avoiding what is wrong. ❑ *She could have established her own innocence and virtue easily enough.* N-UNCOUNT = goodness ≠ vice 2 A **virtue** is a good quality or way of behaving. ❑ *His virtue is patience... Humility is considered a virtue.* N-COUNT 3 The **virtue** of something is an advantage or benefit that it has, especially in comparison with something else. ❑ *There was no virtue in returning to Calvi the way I had come.* N-COUNT

**PHRASES** 4 You use **by virtue of** to explain why something happens or is true. [FORMAL] ❑ *The article stuck in my mind by virtue of one detail.* PREP-PHRASE 5 If you **make a virtue of** something, you pretend that you did it because you chose to, although in fact you did it because you had to. ❑ *The movie makes a virtue out of its economy.* PHRASE: V inflects, PHR n

**vir|tu|os|ity** /vɜːˈtʃuɒsɪti/ The **virtuosity** of someone such as an artist or sports player is their great skill. ❑ *At that time, his virtuosity on the trumpet had no parallel in jazz.* N-UNCOUNT: oft with poss

**vir|tuo|so** /vɜːˈtʃuoʊzoʊ/ **(virtuosos** or **virtuosi** /vɜːˈtʃuoʊzi/**)** 1 A **virtuoso** is someone who is extremely good at something, especially at playing a musical instrument. ❑ *He was gaining a reputation as a remarkable virtuoso.* N-COUNT 2 A **virtuoso** performance or display shows great skill. ❑ *England's football fans were hoping for a virtuoso performance against Cameroon.* ADJ: ADJ n

**vir|tu|ous** /vɜːˈtʃuəs/ 1 A **virtuous** person behaves in a moral and correct way. ❑ *Louis was shown as an intelligent, courageous and virtuous family man.* ADJ = good 2 If you describe someone as **virtuous**, you mean that they have done what they ought to do and feel very pleased with themselves, perhaps too pleased. ❑ *I cleaned the flat, which left me feeling virtuous.* ADJ ♦ **vir|tu|ous|ly** *'I've already done that,' said Ronnie virtuously.* ADV: usu ADV with v, also ADV adj

**vir|tu|ous cir|cle** If you describe a situation as a **virtuous circle**, you mean that once one good thing starts happening, other good things happen, which cause the first thing to continue happening. ❑ *Exercise creates its own virtuous circle. Once you start a programme and do it regularly, you'll feel so good you'll want to continue. ...a virtuous circle of investment and growth.* N-SING ≠ vicious circle

**viru|lence** /vɪrjʊləns/ 1 **Virulence** is great bitterness and hostility. [FORMAL] ❑ *The virulence of the café owner's anger had appalled her.* N-UNCOUNT: oft N *of* n 2 The **virulence** of a disease or poison is its ability to harm or kill people or animals. ❑ *Medical authorities were baffled, both as to its causes and its virulence.* N-UNCOUNT

**viru|lent** /vɪrjʊlənt/ 1 **Virulent** feelings or actions are extremely bitter and hostile. [FORMAL] ❑ *Now he faces virulent attacks from the Italian media.* ADJ: usu ADJ n = vicious ♦ **viru|lent|ly** *The talk was virulently hostile to the leadership.* ADV: usu ADV adj 2 A **virulent** disease or poison is extremely powerful and dangerous. ❑ *A very virulent form of the disease appeared in Belgium.* ADJ

**vi|rus** /vaɪərəs/ **(viruses)** 1 A **virus** is a kind of germ that can cause disease. ❑ *There are many different strains of flu virus.* ◆◇◇ N-COUNT 2 In computer technology, a **virus** is a program that introduces itself into a system, altering or destroying the information stored in the system. [COMPUTING] N-COUNT

**visa** /viːzə/ **(visas)** A **visa** is an official document, or a stamp put in your passport, which allows you to enter or leave a particular country. ❑ *His visitor's visa expired. ...an exit visa. ...a tightening of U.S. visa requirements.* N-COUNT: oft supp N

**vis|age** /vɪzɪdʒ/ **(visages)** Someone's **visage** is their face. [LITERARY] ❑ *...his milky-white innocent visage.* N-COUNT: oft with poss = face

**vis-à-vis** /viːz ɑː viː/ You use **vis-à-vis** when you are considering a relationship or comparison between two things or quantities. [FORMAL] ❑ *Each currency is given a value vis-à-vis the other currencies.* PREP

**vis|cera** /vɪsərə/ **Viscera** are the large organs inside the body, such as the heart, liver, and stomach. [MEDICAL] N-PLURAL

**vis|cer|al** /vɪsərəl/ **Visceral** feelings are feelings that you feel very deeply and find it difficult to control or ignore, and that are not the result of thought. [LITERARY] ❑ *...the sheer visceral joy of being alive.* ADJ: usu ADJ n = instinctive

**vis|cose** /vɪskoʊs/ **Viscose** is a smooth artificial fabric. [mainly BRIT] ❑ *...a black viscose floral dress.* N-UNCOUNT: oft N n

✓ in AM, usually use **rayon**

**vis|cos|ity** /vɪskɒsɪti/ **Viscosity** is the quality that some liquids have of being thick and sticky. ❑ *...the viscosity of the paint.* N-UNCOUNT: oft N *of* n

**vis|count** /vaɪkaʊnt/ **(viscounts)** A **viscount** is a British nobleman who is below an earl and above a baron in rank. ❑ *...a biography of Viscount Mourne.* N-COUNT; N-TITLE

**vis|count|ess** /vaɪkaʊntɪs/ **(viscountesses)** A **viscountess** is the wife of a viscount or a woman who holds the same position as a viscount. N-COUNT; N-TITLE

**vis|cous** /vɪskəs/ A **viscous** liquid is thick and sticky. ❑ *...dark, viscous blood.* ADJ

**vise** /vaɪs/ → see **vice 3**.

**vis|ibil|ity** /vɪzɪbɪlɪti/ 1 **Visibility** means how far or how clearly you can see in particular weather conditions. ❑ *Visibility was poor.* N-UNCOUNT 2 If you N-UNCOUNT refer to the **visibility** of something such as a situation or problem, you mean how much it is seen or noticed by other people. ❑ *The plight of the Kurds gained global visibility.*

**vis|ible** /vɪzɪb$^{ə}$l/ ◆◇◇ 1 ADJ: usu v-link ADJ, oft ADJ *to/from* n If something is **visible**, it can be seen. ❑ *The warning lights were clearly visible... They found a bacterium visible to the human eye.* 2 ADJ You use **visible** to describe something or someone that people notice or recognize. ❑ *The most visible sign of the intensity of the crisis is unemployment... He was making a visible effort to control himself.* ♦ **vis|ibly** /vɪzɪbli/ ADV: ADV with v, ADV adj *They emerged visibly distressed and weeping.* 3 ADJ: ADJ n ≠ *invisible* In economics, **visible** earnings are the money that a country makes as a result of producing goods, rather than from services such as banking and tourism. [BUSINESS] ❑ *In the UK visible imports have traditionally been greater than visible exports.*

**vi|sion** /vɪʒ$^{ə}$n/ **(visions)** ◆◇◇ 1 N-COUNT: usu N *of* n Your **vision of** a future situation or society is what you imagine or hope it would be like, if things were very different from the way they are now. ❑ *I have a vision of a society that is free of exploitation and injustice... That's my vision of how the world could be.* 2 N-COUNT: usu N *of* n = *image* If you have a **vision of** someone in a particular situation, you imagine them in that situation, for example because you are worried that it might happen, or hope that it will happen. ❑ *He had a vision of Cheryl, slumped on a plastic chair in the waiting-room... Maybe you had visions of being surrounded by happy, smiling children.* 3 N-COUNT A **vision** is the experience of seeing something that other people cannot see, for example in a religious experience or as a result of madness or taking drugs. ❑ *It was on 24th June 1981 that young villagers first reported seeing the Virgin Mary in a vision.* 4 N-UNCOUNT = *sight* Your **vision** is your ability to see clearly with your eyes. ❑ *It causes blindness or serious loss of vision.* 5 N-UNCOUNT = *view* Your **vision** is everything that you can see from a particular place or position. ❑ *Jane blocked Cross's vision and he could see nothing.* 6 → See also **tunnel vision**.

**vi|sion|ary** /vɪʒənri, AM -neri/ **(visionaries)** 1 N-COUNT If you refer to someone as a **visionary**, you mean that they have strong, original ideas about how things might be different in the future, especially about how things might be improved. ❑ *An entrepreneur is more than just a risk taker. He is a visionary.* 2 ADJ You use **visionary** to describe the strong, original ideas of a visionary. ❑ *...the visionary architecture of Etienne Boulleé.*

**vis|it** /vɪzɪt/ **(visits, visiting, visited)** ◆◆◆ 1 VERB If you **visit** someone, you go to see them and spend time with them. ❑ *He wanted to visit his brother in* V n *Worcester... Bill would visit on weekends.* V ♦ **Visit** is also a noun. N-COUNT ❑ *Helen had recently paid him a visit.* 2 VERB If you **visit** a place, you go there for a short time. ❑ *He'll be visiting four cities including Cagliari in* V n *Sardinia... Caroline visited all the big stores.* V n *...a visiting truck driver.* V-ing ♦ **Visit** is also a noun. N-COUNT: usu N *to* n ❑ *I paid a visit to my local print shop.* 3 VERB If you **visit** a website, you look at it. [COMPUTING] ❑ *For details visit our website* V n *at www.cobuild.collins.co.uk.* 4 VERB = *see* If you **visit** a professional person such as a doctor or lawyer, you go and see them in order to get professional advice. If they **visit** you, they come to see you in order to give you professional advice. [mainly BRIT] ❑ *If necessary the patient can then visit his doctor for* V n *further advice.* ♦ **Visit** is also a noun. N-COUNT: usu with supp ❑ *You may have regular home visits from a neonatal nurse.*

♦ **visit with** PHRASAL VERB If you **visit with** someone, you go to see them and spend time with them. [AM] ❑ *I visited with him in San Francisco.* V P n

**vis|ita|tion** /vɪzɪteɪʃ$^{ə}$n/ **(visitations)** 1 N-COUNT A **visitation** is an event in which God or another non-human being seems to appear to someone or contact them. ❑ *The young people have claimed almost daily visitations from the Virgin Mary.* 2 N-COUNT People sometimes refer humorously to a visit from someone, especially from someone in authority, as a **visitation**. ❑ *They had another visitation from Essex police.* 3 N-UNCOUNT: usu with supp **Visitation** is the act of officially visiting someone. [FORMAL] ❑ *House-to-house visitation has been carried on, under the regulations of the General Board of Health... I had visitation rights.*

**vis|it|ing fire|man** **(visiting firemen)** N-COUNT A **visiting fireman** is an important visitor, who gets special treatment. [AM]

**visi|tor** /vɪzɪtə$^{r}$/ **(visitors)** ◆◇◇ N-COUNT: oft N *from/to* n A **visitor** is someone who is visiting a person or place. ❑ *The other day we had some visitors from Switzerland... As a student I lived in Oxford but was a frequent visitor to Belfast.*

**vi|sor** /vaɪzə$^{r}$/ **(visors)** 1 N-COUNT A **visor** is a movable part of a helmet which can be pulled down to protect a person's eyes or face. ❑ *He pulled on a battered old crash helmet with a scratched visor.* 2 N-COUNT: usu n N A **visor** is a piece of plastic or other material fixed above the windscreen inside a car, which can be turned down to protect the driver's eyes from bright sunshine.

**vis|ta** /vɪstə/ **(vistas)** 1 N-COUNT: with supp = *panorama* A **vista** is a view from a particular place, especially a beautiful view from a high place. [WRITTEN] ❑ *From my bedroom window I looked out on a crowded vista of hills and rooftops.* 2 N-COUNT = *vision* A **vista** is a vision of a situation or of a range of possibilities. [FORMAL] ❑ *These uprisings come from desperation and a vista of a future without hope.*

**vis|ual** /vɪʒuəl/ **(visuals)** 1 ADJ: usu ADJ n **Visual** means relating to sight, or to things that you can see. ❑ *...the graphic visual depiction of violence. ...music, film, dance, and the visual arts.* ♦ **visu|al|ly** ADV: usu ADV adj *...visually handicapped boys and girls.* 2 N-COUNT A **visual** is something such as a picture, diagram, or piece of film that is used to show or explain something. ❑ *Remember you want your visuals to reinforce your message, not detract from what you are saying.*

**vis|ual aid** **(visual aids)** N-COUNT: usu pl **Visual aids** are things that you can look at, such as a film, model, map, or slides, to help you understand something or to remember information.

**visu|al|ize** /vɪʒuəlaɪz/ **(visualizes, visualizing, visualized)**

✔ in BRIT, also use **visualise**

VERB = *imagine* If you **visualize** something, you imagine what it is like by forming a mental picture of it. ❑ *Susan* V n *visualized her wedding day and saw herself walking down the aisle on her father's arm... He could not visualize her as old...* V n prep *She visualized him stomping to his* V n -ing *car, the picture of self-righteousness... It was hard* V wh *to visualize how it could have been done.* ♦ **visu|ali|za|tion** /vɪʒuəlaɪzeɪʃ$^{ə}$n/ **(visualizations)** N-VAR *...a perfect visualization of reality.*

**vi|tal** /vaɪt$^{ə}$l/ ◆◇◇ 1 ADJ = *crucial* If you say that something is **vital**, you mean that it is necessary or very important. ❑ *The port is vital to supply relief to millions of drought victims... Nick Wileman is a school caretaker so it is vital that he gets on well with young people... After her release she was able to give vital information about her kidnapper.* ♦ **vi|tal|ly** ADV: usu ADV adj *Lesley's career in the church is vitally important to her.* 2 ADJ = *lively* If you describe someone or something as **vital**, you mean that they are very energetic and full of life. ❑ *They are both very vital people and a good match.*

**vi|tal|ity** /vaɪtælɪti/ N-UNCOUNT = *vigour* If you say that someone or something has **vitality**, you mean that they have great energy and liveliness. ❑ *Without continued learning, graduates will lose their intellectual vitality.*

**vi|tal signs** N-PLURAL The **vital signs** of a seriously ill person are the things such as their blood pressure and temperature which show that they are alive.

**vi|tal sta|tis|tics** 1 N-PLURAL: usu with poss The **vital statistics** of a population are statistics such as the number of births, deaths, or marriages which take place in it. 2 N-PLURAL: usu with poss Someone's **vital statistics**, especially a woman's, are the measurements of their body at certain points, for example at their chest, waist, and hips.

**vita|min** /vɪtəmɪn, AM vaɪt-/ **(vitamins)** **Vitamins** are substances that you need in order to remain healthy, which are found in food or can be eaten in the form of pills. ❑ *Butter, margarine, and oily fish are all good sources of vitamin D.* ◆◇◇ N-COUNT: oft N n

**vi|ti|ate** /vɪʃieɪt/ **(vitiates, vitiating, vitiated)** If something **is vitiated**, its effectiveness is spoiled or weakened. [FORMAL] ❑ *Strategic policy during the War was vitiated because of a sharp division between 'easterners' and 'westerners'... But this does not vitiate his scholarship.* VERB be V-ed V n

**vit|re|ous** /vɪtriəs/ **Vitreous** means made of glass or resembling glass. [TECHNICAL] ADJ: usu ADJ n

**vit|ri|ol** /vɪtrioul/ If you refer to what someone says or writes as **vitriol**, you disapprove of it because it is full of bitterness and hate, and so causes a lot of distress and pain. ❑ *The vitriol he hurled at members of the press knew no bounds.* N-UNCOUNT [disapproval] = acrimony, venom

**vit|ri|ol|ic** /vɪtriɒlɪk/ If you describe someone's language or behaviour as **vitriolic**, you disapprove of it because it is full of bitterness and hate, and so causes a lot of distress and pain. ❑ *There was a vicious and vitriolic attack on him in one of the Sunday newspapers two weeks ago.* ADJ: usu ADJ n [disapproval] = venomous

**vitro** /viːtrou/ → see **in vitro**.

**vi|tu|pera|tion** /vɪtjuːpəreɪʃən, AM vaɪtuːp-/ **(vituperations)** **Vituperation** is language that is full of hate, anger, or insults. [FORMAL] N-UNCOUNT: also N in pl

**vi|tu|pera|tive** /vɪtjuːpərətɪv, AM vaɪtuːp-/ **Vituperative** remarks are full of hate, anger, or insults. [FORMAL] ❑ *He is often the victim of vituperative remarks concerning his wealth. ...one of journalism's most vituperative critics.* ADJ: ADJ n = vitriolic

**viva** /vaɪvə/ **(vivas)** A **viva** is a university examination in which a student answers questions in speech rather than writing. [BRIT] N-COUNT

**vi|va|cious** /vɪveɪʃəs/ If you describe someone as **vivacious**, you mean that they are lively, exciting, and attractive. [WRITTEN] ❑ *She's beautiful, vivacious, and charming.* ADJ [approval]

**vi|vac|ity** /vɪvæsɪti/ If you say that someone has **vivacity**, you mean that they are lively, exciting, and attractive. [WRITTEN] N-UNCOUNT [approval]

**viv|id** /vɪvɪd/ 1 If you describe memories and descriptions as **vivid**, you mean that they are very clear and detailed. ❑ *People who lived through World War II have vivid memories of confusion and incompetence... On Wednesday night I had a very vivid dream which really upset me.* ♦ **viv|id|ly** *I can vividly remember the feeling of panic that overwhelmed me.* ADJ; ADV: usu ADV with v, also ADV adj
2 Something that is **vivid** is very bright in colour. ❑ *...a vivid blue sky.* ♦ **viv|id|ly** *...vividly coloured birds.* ADJ; ADV: ADV -ed/adj

**vivi|sec|tion** /vɪvɪsekʃən/ **Vivisection** is the practice of using live animals for scientific experiments. ❑ *...a fierce opponent of vivisection.* N-UNCOUNT

**vix|en** /vɪksən/ **(vixens)** A **vixen** is a female fox. N-COUNT

**viz.** **viz.** is used in written English to introduce a list of specific items or examples. ❑ *The school offers two modules in Teaching English as a Foreign Language, viz. Principles and Methods of Language Teaching and Applied Linguistics.* = namely

**V-neck** **(V-necks)** A **V-neck** or a **V-neck** sweater is a sweater with a neck that is in the shape of the letter V. N-COUNT: oft N n

**vo|cabu|lary** /voukæbjʊləri, AM -leri/ **(vocabularies)** 1 Your **vocabulary** is the total number of words you know in a particular language. ❑ *His speech is immature, his vocabulary limited.* N-VAR: oft with poss
2 The **vocabulary** of a language is all the words in it. ❑ *...a new word in the German vocabulary.* N-SING
3 The **vocabulary** of a subject is the group of words that are typically used when discussing it. ❑ *...the vocabulary of natural science.* N-VAR: with supp

**vo|cal** /voukəl/ 1 You say that people are **vocal** when they speak forcefully about something that they feel strongly about. ❑ *He has been very vocal in his displeasure over the results... A public inquiry earlier this year produced vocal opposition from residents.* ♦ **vo|cal|ly** *Both these proposals were resisted by the developed countries, most vocally by the United States.* ADJ; ADV: usu ADV with v
2 **Vocal** means involving the use of the human voice, especially in singing. ❑ *...a wider range of vocal styles.* ♦ **vo|cal|ly** *Vocally, it is often a very accomplished performance.* ADJ: ADJ n; ADV: ADV with cl/group, ADV with v

**vo|cal cords** also **vocal chords.** Your **vocal cords** are the part of your throat that vibrates when you speak. N-PLURAL

**vo|cal|ist** /voukəlɪst/ **(vocalists)** A **vocalist** is a singer who sings with a pop group. N-COUNT = singer

**vo|cal|ize** /voukəlaɪz/ **(vocalizes, vocalizing, vocalized)**

✔ in BRIT, also use **vocalise**

1 If you **vocalize** a feeling or an idea, you express it in words. ❑ *Archbishop Hunthausen also vocalized his beliefs that women and homosexuals should be more active in the church.* VERB = express V n
2 When you **vocalize** a sound, you use your voice to make it, especially by singing it. ❑ *In India and Bali students learn to vocalize music before ever picking up instruments.* VERB V n Also V

**vo|cals** /voukəlz/ In a pop song, the **vocals** are the singing, in contrast to the playing of instruments. ❑ *Johnson now sings backing vocals for Mica Paris.* N-PLURAL

**vo|ca|tion** /voukeɪʃən/ **(vocations)** 1 If you have a **vocation**, you have a strong feeling that you are especially suited to do a particular job or to fulfil a particular role in life, especially one which involves helping other people. ❑ *It could well be that he has a real vocation... Diana was a young mission school teacher convinced of her vocation to provide support for her schoolgirl pupils.* N-VAR
2 If you refer to your job or profession as your **vocation**, you feel that you are particularly suited to it. ❑ *Her vocation is her work as an actress.* N-VAR: oft poss N

**vo|ca|tion|al** /voukeɪʃənəl/ **Vocational** training and skills are the training and skills needed for a particular job or profession. ❑ *...a course designed to provide vocational training in engineering.* ♦ **vo|ca|tion|al|ly** *...a variety of vocationally oriented courses.* ADJ: usu ADJ n; ADV: ADV -ed/adj

**voca|tive** /vɒkətɪv/ **(vocatives)** A **vocative** is a word such as 'darling' or 'madam' which is used to address someone or attract their attention. [TECHNICAL] N-COUNT

**vo|cif|er|ous** /vəsɪfərəs, AM vous-/ If you describe someone as **vociferous**, you mean that they speak with great energy and determination, because they want their views to be heard. ❑ *He was a vociferous opponent of Conservatism.* ♦ **vo|cif|er|ous|ly** *He vociferously opposed the state of emergency imposed by the government.* ADJ = strident; ADV: usu ADV with v, also ADV adj

**vod|ka** /vɒdkə/ **(vodkas)** **Vodka** is a strong, clear, alcoholic drink. N-MASS

**vogue** /voug/ 1 If there is a **vogue for** something, it is very popular and fashionable. ❑ *Despite the vogue for so-called health teas, there is no evidence that they are any healthier.* N-SING: oft N for n = trend, fad
2 If something is **in vogue**, is very popular and fashionable. If it comes **into vogue**, it becomes very popular and fashionable. ❑ *Pale colours are much more in vogue than autumnal bronzes and coppers. ...the hippie-ethnic look which came into vogue in the late 60s.* PHRASE: v-link PHR, PHR after v

**voice** /vɔɪs/ **(voices, voicing, voiced)** 1 When someone speaks or sings, you hear their **voice**. ❑ *Miriam's voice was strangely calm... 'The police are here,' she said in a low voice... There was a sound of loud voices from the kitchen.* ◆◆◇ N-COUNT: oft poss N, adj N
2 Someone's **voice** is their opinion on a particular topic and what they say about it. ❑ *What does one do when a government simply refuses to listen to the voice of the opposition?* N-COUNT
3 If you have a **voice in** something, you have the right to express an opinion on it. ❑ *Egypt is once again accepted as an important voice in Arab politics.* N-SING: N in n
4 If you **voice** something such as an opinion or an emotion, you say what you think or feel. ❑ *Some scientists have voiced concern that the disease could be passed on to humans... The predomi-* VERB = express V n V-ed

*nant opinion voiced by Detroit's Arab population seems to be one of frustration.* 5 In grammar, if a verb is in **the active voice**, the person who performs the action is the subject of the verb. If a verb is in **the passive voice**, the thing or person affected by the action is the subject of the verb.
N-SING: *the* adj N

**PHRASES** 6 If you **give voice to** an opinion, a need, or a desire, you express it aloud. ❑ *...a community radio run by the Catholic Church which gave voice to the protests of the slum-dwellers.*
PHRASE: V inflects, PHR n = *express*

7 If someone tells you to **keep** your **voice down**, they are asking you to speak more quietly. ❑ *Keep your voice down, for goodness sake.*
PHRASE: V inflects

8 If you **lose** your **voice**, you cannot speak for a while because of an illness. ❑ *I had to be careful not to get a sore throat and lose my voice.*
PHRASE: V inflects

9 If you **raise** your **voice**, you speak more loudly. If you **lower** your **voice**, you speak more quietly. ❑ *He raised his voice for the benefit of the other two women... She'd lowered her voice until it was barely audible.*
PHRASE: V inflects

10 If you say something **at the top of** your **voice**, you say it as loudly as possible. ❑ *'Damn!' he yelled at the top of his voice.*
PHRASE: Ns inflect [emphasis]

11 If a number of people say something **with one voice**, they all express the same opinion about something. ❑ *This would enable the community to speak with one voice in world affairs.*
PHRASE

**voice box** **(voice boxes)** Your **voice box** is the top part of the tube that leads from your throat to your lungs, which contains your vocal cords.
N-COUNT = *larynx*

**voiced** /vɔɪst/ A **voiced** speech sound is one that is produced with vibration of the vocal cords. [TECHNICAL]
ADJ

**voice|less** /vɔɪsləs/ A **voiceless** speech sound is one that is produced without vibration of the vocal cords. [TECHNICAL]
ADJ

**voice mail** **Voice mail** is a system of sending messages over the telephone. Calls are answered by a machine which connects you to the person you want to leave a message for, and they can listen to their messages later.
N-UNCOUNT

**voice-over** **(voice-overs)** also **voiceover.** The **voice-over** of a film, television programme, or advertisement consists of words which are spoken by someone who is not seen. ❑ *89% of advertisements had a male voice-over.*
N-COUNT

**void** /vɔɪd/ **(voids, voiding, voided)** 1 If you describe a situation or a feeling as a **void**, you mean that it seems empty because there is nothing interesting or worthwhile about it. ❑ *His death has left a void in the cricketing world which can never be filled.*
N-COUNT: usu sing

2 You can describe a large or frightening space as a **void**. ❑ *He stared into the dark void where the battle had been fought.*
N-COUNT

3 Something that is **void** or **null and void** is officially considered to have no value or authority. ❑ *The original elections were declared void by the former military ruler... The agreement will be considered null and void.*
ADJ: v-link ADJ = *invalid*

4 If you are **void of** something, you do not have any of it. [FORMAL] ❑ *He rose, his face void of emotion as he walked towards the door.*
ADJ: v-link ADJ *of* n

5 To **void** something means to officially say that it is not valid. [FORMAL] ❑ *The Supreme Court threw out the confession and voided his conviction for murder.*
VERB: V n

**voile** /vɔɪl/ **Voile** is thin material which is used for making women's clothing, for example dresses, blouses, and scarves.
N-UNCOUNT: oft N n

**vol.** **(vols) Vol.** is used as a written abbreviation for **volume** when you are referring to one or more books in a series of books.
◆◇◇

**vola|tile** /vɒlətaɪl, AM -təl/ 1 A situation that is **volatile** is likely to change suddenly and unexpectedly. ❑ *The international oil markets have been highly volatile since the early 1970s.*
ADJ = *unstable*

♦ **vola|til|ity** /vɒlətɪlɪti/ *He is keen to see a general reduction in arms sales given the volatility of the region.*
N-UNCOUNT = *instability*

2 If someone is **volatile**, their mood often changes quickly. ❑ *He has a volatile temper.*
ADJ

3 A **volatile** liquid or substance is one that will quickly change into a gas. [TECHNICAL] ❑ *It's thought that the blast occurred when volatile chemicals exploded.*
ADJ

**vol|can|ic** /vɒlkænɪk/ **Volcanic** means coming from or created by volcanoes. ❑ *Over 200 people have been killed by volcanic eruptions.*
ADJ: usu ADJ n

**vol|ca|no** /vɒlkeɪnoʊ/ **(volcanoes)** A **volcano** is a mountain from which hot melted rock, gas, steam, and ash from inside the earth sometimes burst. ❑ *The volcano erupted last year killing about 600 people.*
N-COUNT

**vole** /voʊl/ **(voles)** A **vole** is a small animal that looks like a mouse but has very small ears and a short tail. Voles usually live in fields or near rivers. → See also **water vole.**
N-COUNT

**vo|li|tion** /vəlɪʃən, AM voʊl-/ 1 Your **volition** is the power you have to decide something for yourself. [FORMAL] ❑ *We like to think that everything we do and everything we think is a product of our volition.*
N-UNCOUNT = *free will*

2 If you do something **of** your **own volition**, you do it because you have decided for yourself that you will do it and not because someone else has told you to do it. [FORMAL] ❑ *Makin said Mr Coombes had gone to the police of his own volition.*
PHRASE: PHR after v = *voluntarily*

**vol|ley** /vɒli/ **(volleys, volleying, volleyed)** 1 In sport, if someone **volleys** the ball, they hit it before it touches the ground. ❑ *He volleyed the ball spectacularly into the far corner of the net... McNeil volleyed more effectively in the second set.*
VERB: V n prep/adv, V

♦ **Volley** is also a noun. ❑ *She hit most of the winning volleys.*
N-COUNT

2 A **volley of** gunfire is a lot of bullets that travel through the air at the same time. ❑ *It's still not known how many died in the volleys of gunfire.*
N-COUNT: oft N *of* n

**volley|ball** /vɒlibɔːl/ **Volleyball** is a game in which two teams hit a large ball with their hands backwards and forwards over a high net. If you allow the ball to touch the ground, the other team wins a point.
N-UNCOUNT

**volt** /voʊlt/ **(volts)** A **volt** is a unit used to measure the force of an electric current.
N-COUNT

**volt|age** /voʊltɪdʒ/ **(voltages)** The **voltage** of an electrical current is its force measured in volts. ❑ *The systems are getting smaller and using lower voltages. ...high-voltage power lines.*
N-VAR

**volte-face** /vɒlt fɑːs/ **(volte-faces)** If you say that someone's behaviour is a **volte-face**, you mean that they have changed their opinion or decision completely, so that it is the opposite of what it was before. [FORMAL] ❑ *The day's events were a remarkable volte-face.*
N-COUNT: usu sing = *about-face*

**vol|uble** /vɒljʊbəl/ If you say that someone is **voluble**, you mean that they talk a lot with great energy and enthusiasm. [FORMAL] ❑ *She was voluble with excitement... Bert is a voluble, gregarious man.*
ADJ

♦ **vol|ubly** /vɒljʊbli/ *In the next booth along he could see an elderly lady, talking volubly.*
ADV: ADV with v

**vol|ume** /vɒljuːm/ **(volumes)** 1 The **volume of** something is the amount of it that there is. ❑ *Senior officials will be discussing how the volume of sales might be reduced. ...the sheer volume of traffic and accidents.*
◆◆◇ N-COUNT: usu sing, usu N *of* n

2 The **volume** of an object is the amount of space that it contains or occupies. ❑ *When egg whites are beaten they can rise to seven or eight times their original volume.*
N-COUNT: usu sing

3 A **volume** is a book. [FORMAL] ❑ *...a 125-page volume.*
N-COUNT

4 A **volume** is one book in a series of books. ❑ *...the first volume of his autobiography.*
N-COUNT: usu supp N

5 A **volume** is a collection of several issues of a magazine, for example all the issues for one year. ❑ *...bound volumes of the magazine.*
N-COUNT: usu with supp

6 **The volume** of a radio, television, or sound system is the loudness of the sound it produces. ❑ *He turned down the volume... He came to complain about the volume of the music.*
N-UNCOUNT

7 If something such as an action **speaks volumes about** a person or thing, it gives you a lot of information about them. ❑ *What you wear speaks volumes about you.*
PHRASE: V inflects, oft PHR *about* n

**vo|lu|mi|nous** /vəluːmɪnəs/ Something that is **voluminous** is very large or contains a lot of
ADJ: usu ADJ n

things. [FORMAL] ❑ *The FBI kept a voluminous file on Pablo Picasso.*

**vol|un|tary** /vɒləntri, AM -teri/ ◆◇◇ [1] **Voluntary** actions or activities are done because someone chooses to do them and not because they have been forced to do them. ❑ *Attention is drawn to a special voluntary course in Commercial French... The scheme, due to begin next month, will be voluntary.* ADJ ≠ compulsory ♦ **vol|un|tar|ily** /vɒləntrəli, AM -terɪli/ *I would only leave here voluntarily if there was a big chance to work abroad.* ADV: ADV with v [2] **Voluntary** work is done by people who are not paid for it, but who do it because they want to do it. ❑ *He'd been working at the local hostel for the handicapped on a voluntary basis.* ADJ: usu ADJ n [3] A **voluntary** worker is someone who does work without being paid for it, because they want to do it. ❑ *Apna Arts has achieved more with voluntary workers in three years than most organisations with paid workers have achieved in ten... We depend solely upon our voluntary helpers.* ADJ: usu ADJ n [4] A **voluntary** organization is controlled and organized by the people who have chosen to work for it, often without being paid, rather than receiving help or money from the government. ❑ *Some local authorities and voluntary organizations also run workshops for disabled people.* ADJ: ADJ n

**vol|un|teer** /vɒləntɪəʳ/ ◆◇◇ **(volunteers, volunteering, volunteered)** [1] A **volunteer** is someone who does work without being paid for it, because they want to do it. ❑ *She now helps in a local school as a volunteer three days a week... Mike was a member of the local volunteer fire brigade.* N-COUNT [2] A **volunteer** is someone who offers to do a particular task or job without being forced to do it. ❑ *Right. What I want now is two volunteers to come down to the front.* N-COUNT [3] If you **volunteer to** do something, you offer to do it without being forced to do it. ❑ *Aunt Mary volunteered to clean up the kitchen... He volunteered for the army in 1939... She volunteered as a nurse in a soldiers' rest-home... He's volunteered his services as a chauffeur.* VERB V to-inf V *for* n V *as* n V n Also V [4] If you **volunteer** information, you tell someone something without being asked. [FORMAL] ❑ *The room was quiet; no one volunteered any further information... 'They were both great supporters of Franco,' Ryle volunteered... The next week, Phillida volunteered that they were getting on better.* VERB V n V with quote V that [5] A **volunteer** is someone who chooses to join the armed forces, especially during a war, as opposed to someone who is forced to join by law. ❑ *They fought as volunteers with the Afghan guerrillas.* N-COUNT

**vo|lup|tu|ous** /vəlʌptʃuəs/ If you describe a woman as **voluptuous**, you mean that she has large breasts and hips and is considered attractive in a sexual way. ❑ *...a voluptuous, well-rounded lady with glossy black hair.* ADJ

**vom|it** /vɒmɪt/ **(vomits, vomiting, vomited)** [1] If you **vomit**, food and drink comes back up from your stomach and out through your mouth. ❑ *Any product made from cow's milk made him vomit... She began to vomit blood a few days before she died... He vomited up all he had just eaten.* VERB V V n V n with *up* ♦ **vom|it|ing** *Nausea, diarrhoea, and vomiting may accompany migraine.* N-UNCOUNT [2] **Vomit** is partly digested food and drink that has come back up from someone's stomach and out through their mouth. N-UNCOUNT = sick

**voo|doo** /vuːduː/ **Voodoo** is a form of religion involving magic which is practised by some people in the West Indies, especially Haiti. N-UNCOUNT

**vo|ra|cious** /vəreɪʃəs, AM vɔːr-/ If you describe a person, or their appetite for something, as **voracious**, you mean that they want a lot of something. [LITERARY] ❑ *Joseph Smith was a voracious book collector. ...the band's voracious appetite for fun.* ADJ: usu ADJ n = insatiable ♦ **vo|ra|cious|ly** *He read voraciously.* ADV

**vor|tex** /vɔːʳteks/ **(vortexes** or **vortices** /vɔːʳtɪsiːz/**)** [1] A **vortex** is a mass of wind or water that spins round so fast that it pulls objects down into its empty centre. ❑ *The polar vortex is a system of wintertime winds.* N-COUNT [2] If you refer to a situation as a **vortex**, you feel that you are being forced into it without being able to prevent it. ❑ *When marriages break down children are swept into the vortex of their parents' embittered emotions.* N-COUNT: usu sing, with supp

**vote** /voʊt/ ◆◆◆ **(votes, voting, voted)** [1] A **vote** is a choice made by a particular person or group in a meeting or an election. ❑ *He walked to the local polling centre to cast his vote... The government got a massive majority – well over 400 votes... Mr Reynolds was re-elected by 102 votes to 60.* N-COUNT [2] **A vote** is an occasion when a group of people make a decision by each person indicating his or her choice. The choice that most people support is accepted by the group. ❑ *Why do you think we should have a vote on that?... They took a vote and decided not to do it.* N-COUNT: usu *a* N in sing [3] **The vote** is the total number of votes or voters in an election, or the number of votes received or cast by a particular group. ❑ *Opposition parties won about fifty-five per cent of the vote.* N-SING: usu *the* N [4] If you have **the vote** in an election, or have **a vote** in a meeting, you have the legal right to indicate your choice. ❑ *Before that, women did not have a vote at all.* N-SING [5] When you **vote**, you indicate your choice officially at a meeting or in an election, for example by raising your hand or writing on a piece of paper. ❑ *Two-thirds of the national electorate had the chance to vote in these elections... It seems many people would vote for the government, at a general election, if there was a new leader... The residents of Leningrad voted to restore the city's original name of St Petersburg... The parliament has voted by an overwhelming majority to suspend its declaration of independence... The Bridgeport Common Council voted 9:8 for a five percent tax increase.* VERB V V prep V to-inf V *by* n to-inf/prep V num prep/to-inf ♦ **vot|ing** *Voting began about two hours ago.* N-UNCOUNT [6] If you **vote** a particular political party or leader, or **vote yes** or **no**, you make that choice with the vote that you have. ❑ *52.5% of those questioned said they'd vote Labour... A single candidate is put forward and the people vote yes or no.* VERB V n V *yes/no* [7] If people **vote** someone a particular title, they choose that person to have that title. ❑ *His class voted him the man 'who had done the most for Yale.'.* VERB = elect V n n [8] → See also **block vote**.

**PHRASES** [9] If you **vote with** your **feet**, you show that you do not support something by leaving the place where it is happening or leaving the organization that is supporting it. ❑ *Thousands of citizens are already voting with their feet, and leaving the country.* PHRASE: V inflects [10] If you say **'I vote that'** a particular thing should happen, you are suggesting that this is what should happen. [INFORMAL] ❑ *I vote that we all go to Holland immediately.* PHRASE: PHR that [11] **One man one vote** or **one person one vote** is a system of voting in which every person in a group or country has the right to cast their vote, and in which each individual's vote is counted and has equal value. ❑ *Mr Gould called for a move towards 'one man one vote'.* PHRASE

♦ **vote in** If people **vote in** a particular person or political party, they give enough votes to that person or party in an official election for them to hold a position of power. ❑ *If he fails, then he will have little excuse in the eyes of those who voted him in... The members of the national assembly will vote in a prime minister by a simple majority.* PHRASAL VERB = elect V n P V P n (not pron)

♦ **vote out** If people **vote out** a particular person or political party, they give that person or party so few votes in an official election that they no longer hold a position of power. ❑ *And if the President doesn't make things better, other voters say, we'll vote him out, too... They cannot join forces to vote her out of office... And of course we all know we can vote out our councillors.* PHRASAL VERB V n P V n P *of* n V P n (not pron)

**vote of con|fi|dence** **(votes of confidence)** [1] A **vote of confidence** is a vote in which members of a group are asked to indicate that they still support the person or group in power, usually the government. ❑ *The Indian Prime Minister, V P Singh, lost a vote of confidence in the Indian parliament.* N-COUNT: usu sing [2] A **vote of confidence** is something that you say or do which shows that you approve of or support a person or a group. ❑ *The* N-COUNT: usu sing *ten-year deal is a vote of confidence in coal-fired power stations.*

**vote of no con|fi|dence** **(votes of no confidence)** A **vote of no confidence** is a vote in which members of a group are asked to indicate that they do not support the person or group in power, usually the government. ❑ *The opposition has called for a vote of no confidence in the government.* N-COUNT: usu sing

**vote of thanks** **(votes of thanks)** A **vote of thanks** is an official speech in which the speaker formally thanks a person for doing something. ❑ *I would like to propose a vote of thanks to our host.* N-COUNT: usu sing

**vot|er** /voʊtəʳ/ **(voters)** **Voters** are people who have the legal right to vote in elections, or people who are voting in a particular election. ❑ *Austrian voters went to the polls this weekend to elect a successor to the President.* ◆◆◇ N-COUNT: usu pl

**vouch** /vaʊtʃ/ **(vouches, vouching, vouched)**
♦ **vouch for** [1] If you say that you can or will **vouch for** someone, you mean that you can guarantee their good behaviour. ❑ *Kim's mother agreed to vouch for Maria and get her a job.* PHRASAL VERB V P n [2] If you say that you can **vouch for** something, you mean that you have evidence from your own personal experience that it is true or correct. ❑ *He cannot vouch for the accuracy of the story.* PHRASAL VERB V P n

**vouch|er** /vaʊtʃəʳ/ **(vouchers)** A **voucher** is a ticket or piece of paper that can be used instead of money to pay for something. ❑ *...gift vouchers.* N-COUNT: usu N *for* n, n N

**vouch|safe** /vaʊtʃseɪf/ **(vouchsafes, vouchsafing, vouchsafed)** If you **are vouchsafed** something or it **is vouchsafed to** you, you are given or granted it. [FORMAL] ❑ *As we approached the summit we were vouchsafed a rare vision... Eric gritted his teeth and vouchsafed them a few more drops of brandy... 'He drives like a madman,' was all the information he vouchsafed.* VERB *be* V-ed n, V n n, V n, Also V n *to* n

**vow** /vaʊ/ **(vows, vowing, vowed)** [1] If you **vow to** do something, you make a serious promise or decision that you will do it. ❑ *While many models vow to go back to college, few do... I solemnly vowed that someday I would return to live in Europe... 'I'll kill him,' she vowed... They have vowed a quick and decisive response.* VERB V to-inf, V that, V with quote, V n [2] A **vow** is a serious promise or decision to do a particular thing. ❑ *I made a silent vow to be more careful in the future.* N-COUNT: oft N to-inf, N that [3] **Vows** are a particular set of serious promises, such as the promises two people make when they are getting married. ❑ *He had broken his vow of poverty.* N-COUNT: usu pl, with supp

**vow|el** /vaʊəl/ **(vowels)** A **vowel** is a sound such as the ones represented in writing by the letters 'a', 'e' 'i', 'o' and 'u', which you pronounce with your mouth open, allowing the air to flow through it. Compare **consonant**. ❑ *The vowel in words like 'my' and 'thigh' is not very difficult.* N-COUNT

**vox pop** /vɒks pɒp/ **(vox pops)** In a radio or television programme, a **vox pop** is an item consisting of a series of short interviews with ordinary members of the public. [mainly BRIT, JOURNALISM] N-VAR

**voy|age** /vɔɪɪdʒ/ **(voyages, voyaging, voyaged)** [1] A **voyage** is a long journey on a ship or in a spacecraft. ❑ *...the first space shuttle voyage to be devoted entirely to astronomy.* N-COUNT: usu sing, usu with supp [2] To **voyage** to a place means to travel there, especially by sea. [FORMAL] ❑ *The Greenpeace flagship is voyaging through the Arctic cold of the Barents Sea.* VERB = *journey, travel* V prep/adv ♦ **voy|ag|er** **(voyagers)** *...fifteenth-century voyagers to the lands now called America and the Caribbean.* N-COUNT ♦ **voy|ag|ing** *Our boat would not have been appropriate for ocean voyaging.* N-UNCOUNT: supp N

**vo|yeur** /vwaɪɜːʳ, AM vɔɪ-/ **(voyeurs)** [1] A **voyeur** is someone who gets sexual pleasure from secretly watching other people having sex or taking their clothes off. N-COUNT [2] If you describe someone as a **voyeur**, you disapprove of them because you think they enjoy watching other people's suffering or problems. ❑ *The media has made unfeeling voyeurs of all of us.* N-COUNT [disapproval]

**vo|yeur|ism** /vwaɪərɪzəm, AM vɔɪɜːr-/ [1] **Voyeurism** is the practice of getting sexual pleasure by secretly watching other people having sex or taking their clothes off. N-UNCOUNT [2] If you describe someone's behaviour as **voyeurism**, you disapprove of them because you think they enjoy watching other people's suffering or problems. ❑ *The BBC yesterday defended a series featuring dramatic crime reconstructions against suggestions of voyeurism.* N-UNCOUNT [disapproval]

**vo|yeur|is|tic** /vwaɪərɪstɪk, AM vɔɪ-/ [1] **Voyeuristic** behaviour involves getting sexual pleasure from secretly watching other people having sex or taking their clothes off. ADJ [2] If you describe someone's behaviour as **voyeuristic**, you disapprove of them because you think they enjoy watching other people's suffering or problems. ❑ *We as a society are growing more commercial and voyeuristic all the time.* ADJ [disapproval]

**vs.** **vs.** is a written abbreviation for **versus**. ❑ *...England vs. Brazil in the U.S. Cup.*

**V-sign** **(V-signs)** [1] In Britain, a **V-sign** is a rude gesture which is made by sticking up your first two fingers in a V shape, with the palm of your hand facing you. N-COUNT [2] A **V-sign** is a gesture which is made by sticking up your first two fingers in a V shape, with the palm of your hand facing away from you, as a sign of victory. N-COUNT

**VSO** /viː es oʊ/ **VSO** is a British organization that sends skilled people to developing countries to work on projects that help the local community. **VSO** is an abbreviation for 'Voluntary Service Overseas'. N-PROPER

**vul|gar** /vʌlgəʳ/ [1] If you describe something as **vulgar**, you think it is in bad taste or of poor artistic quality. ❑ *The film is tasteless, vulgar and even badly shot.* ADJ [disapproval] ♦ **vul|gar|ity** /vʌlgærɪti/ *I hate the vulgarity of this room.* N-UNCOUNT [2] If you describe pictures, gestures, or remarks as **vulgar**, you dislike them because they refer to sex or parts of the body in a rude way that you find unpleasant. ❑ *The women laughed coarsely at some vulgar jokes... The lyrics were vulgar.* ADJ [disapproval] ♦ **vul|gar|ity** *There's a good deal of vulgarity.* N-UNCOUNT [3] If you describe a person or their behaviour as **vulgar**, you mean that they lack taste or behave rudely. ❑ *He was a vulgar old man, but he never swore in front of a woman.* ADJ [disapproval] = *crude* ♦ **vul|gar|ity** *It's his vulgarity that I can't take.* N-UNCOUNT

**vul|ner|able** /vʌlnərəbᵊl/ [1] Someone who is **vulnerable** is weak and without protection, with the result that they are easily hurt physically or emotionally. ❑ *Old people are particularly vulnerable members of our society.* ◆◇◇ ADJ ♦ **vul|ner|abil|ity** /vʌlnərəbɪlɪti/ **(vulnerabilities)** *David accepts his own vulnerability.* N-VAR [2] If a person, animal, or plant is **vulnerable to** a disease, they are more likely to get it than other people, animals, or plants. ❑ *People with high blood pressure are especially vulnerable to diabetes.* ADJ: usu v-link ADJ *to* n = *prone, susceptible* ♦ **vul|ner|abil|ity** *Taking long-term courses of certain medicines may increase vulnerability to infection.* N-UNCOUNT [3] Something that is **vulnerable** can be easily harmed or affected by something bad. ❑ *Their tanks would be vulnerable to attack from the air... Goodyear could be vulnerable in a prolonged economic slump.* ADJ: oft ADJ *to* n ♦ **vul|ner|abil|ity** *...anxieties about the country's vulnerability to invasion.* N-UNCOUNT

**vul|ture** /vʌltʃəʳ/ **(vultures)** [1] A **vulture** is a large bird which lives in hot countries and eats the flesh of dead animals. N-COUNT [2] If you describe a person as a **vulture**, you disapprove of them because you think they are trying to gain from another person's troubles. [JOURNALISM] ❑ *With no buyer in sight for the company as a whole, the vultures started to circle.* N-COUNT [disapproval]

**vul|va** /vʌlvə/ **(vulvas)** The **vulva** is the outer part of a woman's sexual organs. [TECHNICAL] N-COUNT

**vy|ing** /vaɪɪŋ/ **Vying** is the present participle of **vie**.

# Ww

**W, w** /dʌbᵊlju:/ **(W's, w's)** [1] **W** is the twenty-third letter of the English alphabet. [2] **W** or **w** is an abbreviation for words beginning with w, such as 'west' or 'watt'. N-VAR

**wacko** /wækoʊ/ If you say that someone is **wacko**, you are saying in an unkind way that they are strange and eccentric. [INFORMAL] ❑ *Lampley was obviously completely wacko.* ADJ disapproval = mad

**wacky** /wæki/ **(wackier, wackiest)** also **whacky.** If you describe something or someone as **wacky**, you mean that they are eccentric, unusual, and often funny. [INFORMAL] ❑ *...a wacky new television comedy series.* ADJ

**wad** /wɒd/ **(wads)** A **wad of** something such as paper or cloth is a tight bundle or ball of it. ❑ *...a wad of banknotes. ...a wad of cotton soaked in cleaning fluid.* N-COUNT: oft N *of* n

**wad|ding** /wɒdɪŋ/ **Wadding** is soft material which is put around things to protect them, for example in packing. N-UNCOUNT

**wad|dle** /wɒdᵊl/ **(waddles, waddling, waddled)** To **waddle** somewhere means to walk there with short, quick steps, swinging slightly from side to side. A person or animal that waddles usually has short legs and a fat body. ❑ *McGinnis pushed himself laboriously out of the chair and waddled to the window.* VERB; V prep/adv

**wade** /weɪd/ **(wades, wading, waded)** [1] If you **wade** through something that makes it difficult to walk, usually water or mud, you walk through it. ❑ *Rescuers had to wade across a river to reach them.* [2] To **wade through** a lot of documents or pieces of information means to spend a lot of time and effort reading them or dealing with them. ❑ *It has taken a long time to wade through the 'incredible volume' of evidence.* VERB; V prep/adv; VERB; V *through* n

♦ **wade in** or **wade into** If someone **wades in** or **wades into** something, they get involved in a very determined and forceful way, often without thinking enough about the consequences of their actions. ❑ *They don't just listen sympathetically, they wade in with remarks like, 'If I were you...'... Police waded into a crowd of protesters.* PHRASAL VERB; V P; V P n

**wad|er** /weɪdəʳ/ **(waders)** [1] A **wader** is a bird with long legs and a long neck, which lives near water and feeds on fish. There are several different kinds of waders. [2] **Waders** are long rubber boots which cover all of the legs and are worn by fishermen when they are standing in water. N-COUNT; N-COUNT: usu pl

**wadge** /wɒdʒ/ → see **wodge**.

**wadi** /wɒdi/ **(wadis)** A **wadi** is a river in North Africa or Arabia which is dry except in the rainy season. [TECHNICAL] N-COUNT

**wad|ing pool** **(wading pools)** A **wading pool** is a shallow artificial pool for children to play in. [AM] N-COUNT

✔ in BRIT, use **paddling pool**

**wa|fer** /weɪfəʳ/ **(wafers)** [1] A **wafer** is a thin crisp biscuit which is usually eaten with ice cream. [2] A **wafer** is a circular, thin piece of special bread which the priest gives people to eat in the Christian service of Holy Communion. N-COUNT; N-COUNT

**wafer-thin** **Wafer-thin** means extremely thin and flat. ❑ *Cut the fennel into wafer-thin slices.* ADJ: ADJ n, v-link ADJ

**waf|fle** /wɒfᵊl/ **(waffles, waffling, waffled)** [1] If you say that someone **waffles**, you are critical of them because they talk or write a lot without actually making any clear or important points. [BRIT, INFORMAL] ❑ *My wife often tells me I waffle... There was some bloke on the phone waffling about an airline ticket.* ♦ **Waffle on** means the same as **waffle**. ❑ *Whenever I open my mouth I don't half waffle on.* ♦ **Waffle** is also a noun. ❑ *He writes smug, sanctimonious waffle.* [2] If someone **waffles** on an issue or question, they cannot decide what to do or what their opinion is about it. [AM] ❑ *He's waffled on abortion and gay rights... He kept waffling and finding excuses not to close the deal.* [3] A **waffle** is a kind of square cake made of batter with squares marked on it. Waffles are usually eaten with syrup poured over them. VERB disapproval; V; V *about* n; PHRASAL VERB; V P; N-UNCOUNT; VERB = waver; V *on/about/over* n; V; N-COUNT

**waft** /wɒft, wæft/ **(wafts, wafting, wafted)** If sounds or smells **waft** through the air, or if something such as a light wind **wafts** them, they move gently through the air. ❑ *The scent of climbing roses wafts through the window... A slight breeze rose, wafting the heavy scent of flowers past her.* ♦ **Waft** is also a noun. ❑ *A waft of perfume drifted into Ingrid's nostrils.* VERB; V prep/adv; V n prep/adv; N-COUNT: N *of* n

**wag** /wæg/ **(wags, wagging, wagged)** [1] When a dog **wags** its tail, it repeatedly waves its tail from side to side. ❑ *The dog was biting, growling and wagging its tail.* [2] If you **wag** your finger, you shake it repeatedly and quickly from side to side, usually because you are annoyed with someone. ❑ *He wagged a disapproving finger.* [3] If you **wag** your head, you move it from side to side, often because you are unhappy about a situation. ❑ *He wags his head unhappily.* VERB; V n; VERB; V n; VERB = shake; V n

**wage** /weɪdʒ/ **(wages, waging, waged)** ◆◇◇ [1] Someone's **wages** are the amount of money that is regularly paid to them for the work that they do. ❑ *His wages have gone up... This may end efforts to set a minimum wage well above the poverty line.* [2] If a person, group, or country **wages** a campaign or a war, they start it and continue it over a period of time. ❑ *...the three factions that had been waging a civil war.* N-COUNT; VERB; V n

**waged** /weɪdʒd/ [1] **Waged** is the past tense and past participle of **wage**. [2] **Waged** workers receive money regularly for doing a job. **Waged** work is work that you are paid to do. ❑ *...the influx of women into the waged workforce... They want secure, waged employment.* ADJ: usu ADJ n

**wage pack|et** **(wage packets)** People's wages can be referred to as their **wage packet**. [mainly BRIT] ❑ *They work long hours in order to take home a fat wage packet.* N-COUNT

✔ in AM, usually use **paycheck**

**wa|ger** /weɪdʒəʳ/ **(wagers, wagering, wagered)** [1] If you **wager on** the result of a horse race, football match, or other event, you give someone a sum of money which they give you back with extra money if the result is what you predicted, or which they keep if it is not. [JOURNALISM] ❑ *Just because people wagered on the Yankees did not mean that they liked them... Golfers had wagered a good deal of money on Nick Faldo winning the championship.* ♦ **Wager** is also a noun. ❑ *There have been various wagers on certain candidates since the Bishop* VERB = bet, gamble; V *on* n; V n *on* n; N-COUNT *announced his retirement.* [2] If you say that you will **wager that** something is the case, you mean you are confident that it is the case. ❑ *She was willing to wager that he didn't own the apartment he lived in.* VERB = bet V that

**wag|gle** /wægᵊl/ **(waggles, waggling, waggled)** If you **waggle** something, or if something **waggles**, it moves up and down or from side to side with short quick movements. ❑ *He was waggling his toes in his socks. ...puppet animals with eyes that move and ears that waggle.* VERB = wiggle V n V

**wag|on** /wægən/ **(wagons)**

✓ in BRIT, also use **waggon**

[1] A **wagon** is a strong vehicle with four wheels, usually pulled by horses or oxen and used for carrying heavy loads. [2] A **wagon** is a large container on wheels which is pulled by a train. [mainly BRIT] N-COUNT = cart N-COUNT

✓ in AM, use **freight car**

[3] Someone who is **on the wagon** has stopped drinking alcohol. [INFORMAL] ❑ *I'm on the wagon for a while. Cleaning out my system.* [4] ➔ See also **station wagon**. PHRASE: v-link PHR, PHR after v

**wag|tail** /wægteɪl/ **(wagtails)** A **wagtail** is a type of small bird which moves its tail quickly up and down as it walks. N-COUNT

**wah-wah** /wɑːwɑː/ In music, **wah-wah** is used to describe the sound produced by covering and uncovering the open end of a brass instrument. This sound can also be produced electronically, especially when playing the electric guitar. ❑ *He played some wah-wah guitar.* N-UNCOUNT: usu N n

**waif** /weɪf/ **(waifs)** If you refer to a child or young woman as a **waif**, you mean that they are very thin and look as if they have nowhere to live. ❑ *...a dirty-faced waif of some five or six years.* N-COUNT

**wail** /weɪl/ **(wails, wailing, wailed)** [1] If someone **wails**, they make long, loud, high-pitched cries which express sorrow or pain. ❑ *The women began to wail in mourning. ...a mother wailing for her lost child.* ♦ **Wail** is also a noun. ❑ *Wails of grief were heard as visitors filed past the site of the disaster.* [2] If you **wail** something, you say it in a loud, high-pitched voice that shows that you are unhappy or in pain. ❑ *'Now look what you've done!' Shirley wailed... Primrose, stupefied by tiredness, began to wail that she was hungry.* [3] If something such as a siren or an alarm **wails**, it makes a long, loud, high-pitched sound. ❑ *Police cars, their sirens wailing, accompanied the lorries.* ♦ **Wail** is also a noun. ❑ *The wail of the bagpipe could be heard in the distance.* ♦ **wail|ing** *Our artillery opened up and we heard a fearful wailing and screeching.* VERB V V for n N-COUNT: oft N of n VERB V with quote V that VERB V N-UNCOUNT: oft N of n N-UNCOUNT

**waist** /weɪst/ **(waists)** [1] Your **waist** is the middle part of your body where it narrows slightly above your hips. ❑ *Ricky kept his arm round her waist... He was stripped to the waist.* ♦ **-waisted** *Sarah looked slender-waisted, fragile and very beautiful.* [2] The **waist** of a garment such as a dress, coat, or pair of trousers is the part of it which covers the middle part of your body. ♦ **-waisted** ❑ *...high-waisted dresses.* N-COUNT: oft poss N COMB in ADJ N-COUNT COMB in ADJ

**waist|band** /weɪstbænd/ **(waistbands)** A **waistband** is a narrow piece of material which is sewn on to a pair of trousers, a skirt, or other item of clothing at the waist in order to strengthen it. N-COUNT

**waist|coat** /weɪstkout, weskət/ **(waistcoats)** A **waistcoat** is a sleeveless piece of clothing with buttons which people usually wear over a shirt. [BRIT] N-COUNT

✓ in AM, use **vest**

**waist|line** /weɪstlaɪn/ **(waistlines)** [1] Your **waistline** is your waist measurement. ❑ *A passion for cooking does not necessarily have to be bad for your waistline.* [2] The **waistline** of a piece of clothing is the place where the upper and lower parts are sewn together, which is near to your waist when you wear it. N-COUNT: oft poss N = waist N-COUNT = waist

**wait** /weɪt/ **(waits, waiting, waited)** [1] When you **wait for** something or someone, you spend some time doing very little, because you cannot act until that thing happens or that person arrives. ❑ *I walk to a street corner and wait for the school bus... Stop waiting for things to happen. Make them happen... I waited to see how she responded... Angus got out of the car to wait... We will have to wait a week or so before we know whether the operation is a success... He told waiting journalists that he did not expect a referendum to be held for several months.* ♦ **wait|ing** *The waiting became almost unbearable.* [2] A **wait** is a period of time in which you do very little, before something happens or before you can do something. ❑ *...the four-hour wait for the organizers to declare the result.* [3] If something **is waiting for** you, it is ready for you to use, have, or do. ❑ *There'll be a car waiting for you... When we came home we had a meal waiting for us... Ships with unfurled sails wait to take them aboard.* [4] If you say that something can **wait**, you mean that it is not important or urgent and so you will deal with it or do it later. ❑ *I want to talk to you, but it can wait... Any changes will have to wait until sponsors can be found.* [5] You can use **wait** when you are trying to make someone feel excited, or to encourage or threaten them. ❑ *If you think this all sounds very exciting, just wait until you read the book... As soon as you get some food inside you, you'll feel more cheerful. Just you wait.* [6] **Wait** is used in expressions such as **wait a minute**, **wait a second**, and **wait a moment** to interrupt someone when they are speaking, for example because you object to what they are saying or because you want them to repeat something. [SPOKEN] ❑ *'Wait a minute!' he broke in. 'This is not giving her a fair hearing!'* [7] If an employee **waits on** you, for example in a restaurant or hotel, they take orders from you and bring you what you want. ❑ *There were plenty of servants to wait on her... Each student is expected to wait at table for one week each semester.* ◆◆◆ VERB: no passive V for n V for n to-inf V to-inf V V n V-ing Also V n for n N-UNCOUNT N-COUNT: usu sing VERB: usu cont V for n have n V-ing for n V to-inf VERB: no cont V V VERB: only imper V until cl/n V VERB: only imper = hold on, hang on V n VERB V on n V at n

**PHRASES** [8] If you say that you **can't wait** to do something or **can hardly wait** to do it, you are emphasizing that you are very excited about it and eager to do it. [SPOKEN] ❑ *We can't wait to get started... It's gonna be great. I can hardly wait.* [9] If you tell someone to **wait and see**, you tell them that they must be patient or that they must not worry about what is going to happen in the future because they have no control over it. ❑ *We'll have to wait and see what happens. ...a wait-and-see attitude.* PHRASE: oft PHR to-inf [emphasis] PHRASE: oft PHR n, PHR wh

♦ **wait around**

✓ in BRIT, also use **wait about**

If you **wait around** or **wait about**, you stay in the same place, usually doing very little, because you cannot act before something happens or before someone arrives. ❑ *The attacker may have been waiting around for an opportunity to strike... I waited around to speak to the doctor. ...the ghastly tedium of waiting about at the airport.* PHRASAL VERB V P for n V P to-inf V P

♦ **wait in** If you **wait in**, you deliberately stay at home and do not go out, for example because someone is coming to see you. [mainly BRIT] ❑ *If I'd waited in for you I could have waited all day.* PHRASAL VERB = stay in V P for n

♦ **wait on** If you **are waiting on** something, you are waiting for it to happen, for example before you do or decide anything. [AM] ❑ *Since then I've been waiting on events.* PHRASAL VERB V P n

♦ **wait up** [1] If you **wait up**, you deliberately do not go to bed, especially because you are expecting someone to return home late at night. ❑ *I hope he doesn't expect you to wait up for him... Don't wait up.* [2] If you ask someone to **wait up**, you are asking them to go more slowly or to stop and wait for you. [AM, INFORMAL] ❑ *I was running down the hill shouting, 'Michael, Michael, man, wait up'.* PHRASAL VERB = stay up V P for n V P PHRASAL VERB: usu imper = wait V P

**wait|er** /weɪtəʳ/ **(waiters)** A **waiter** is a man who works in a restaurant, serving people with food and drink. ➔ See also **dumb waiter**. N-COUNT

**wait|ing game** **(waiting games)** If you play a **waiting game**, you deal with a situation by deliberately doing nothing, because you believe you will gain an advantage by acting later, or because you are waiting to see how other people are going to act. ❑ *He's playing a waiting-game. He'll hope to hang on as long as possible until the pressure is off.* N-COUNT: usu sing

**wait|ing list** **(waiting lists)** A **waiting list** is a list of people who have asked for something which cannot be given to them immediately, for example medical treatment, housing, or training, and who must therefore wait until it is available. ❑ *There were 20,000 people on the waiting list for a home.* N-COUNT: oft *on* N

**wait|ing room** **(waiting rooms)** also **waiting-room.** A **waiting room** is a room in a place such as a railway station or a clinic, where people can sit down while they wait. N-COUNT

**wait|ress** /weɪtrəs/ **(waitresses, waitressing, waitressed)** 1 A **waitress** is a woman who works in a restaurant, serving people with food and drink. N-COUNT 2 A woman who **waitresses** works in a restaurant serving food and drink. ❑ *She had been working in a pub, cooking and waitressing.* VERB V
♦ **wait|ress|ing** *She does a bit of waitressing as a part-time job.* N-UNCOUNT

**waive** /weɪv/ **(waives, waiving, waived)** 1 If you **waive** your right to something, for example legal representation, you choose not to have it or do it. ❑ *He pleaded guilty to the murders of three boys and waived his right to appeal.* VERB V n 2 If someone **waives** a rule, they say that people do not have to obey it in a particular situation. ❑ *The art gallery waives admission charges on Sundays.* VERB V n

**waiv|er** /weɪvəʳ/ **(waivers)** A **waiver** is when a person, government, or organization agrees to give up a right or says that people do not have to obey a particular rule or law. ❑ *...a waiver of constitutional rights.* N-COUNT: usu with supp

**wake** /weɪk/ **(wakes, waking, woke, woken)** ◆◇◇

> The form **waked** is used in American English for the past tense.

1 When you **wake** or when someone or something **wakes** you, you become conscious again after being asleep. ❑ *It was cold and dark when I woke at 6.30... Bob woke slowly to sunshine pouring in his window... She woke to find her dark room lit by flashing lights... She went upstairs to wake Milton.* VERB V, V *to* n, V to-inf, V n
♦ **Wake up** means the same as **wake**. ❑ *One morning I woke up and felt something was wrong... At dawn I woke him up and said we were leaving.* PHRASAL VERB V P, V n P
2 The **wake** of a boat or other object moving in water is the track of waves that it makes behind it as it moves through the water. ❑ *Dolphins sometimes play in the wake of the boats.* N-COUNT: usu sing, with poss
3 A **wake** is a gathering or social event that is held before or after someone's funeral. ❑ *A funeral wake was in progress.* N-COUNT: usu sing

**PHRASES** 4 If one thing follows **in the wake of** another, it happens after the other thing is over, often as a result of it. ❑ *The governor has enjoyed a huge surge in the polls in the wake of last week's convention.* PREP-PHRASE = following
5 Your **waking hours** are the times when you are awake rather than asleep. ❑ *It was work which consumed most of his waking hours.* PHRASE: usu with poss
6 If you leave something or someone **in** your **wake**, you leave them behind you as you go. ❑ *Adam stumbles on, leaving a trail of devastation in his wake.* PHRASE: PHR after v
7 If you are following **in** someone's **wake**, you are following them or their example. ❑ *In his wake came a waiter wheeling a trolley. ...the endless stream of female artists who released albums in her wake.* PHRASE: PHR after v

♦ **wake up** If something such as an activity **wakes** you **up**, it makes you more alert and ready to do things after you have been lazy or inactive. ❑ *A cool shower wakes up the body and boosts circulation.* → See also **wake 1**. PHRASAL VERB V P n (not pron) Also V n P

♦ **wake up to** If you **wake up to** something, you become aware of it. ❑ *People should wake up to the fact that people with disabilities have got a vote as well.* PHRASAL VERB V P P n

**wake|ful** /weɪkfʊl/ Someone who is **wakeful** finds it difficult to get to sleep and wakes up very often when they should be sleeping. ADJ
♦ **wake|ful|ness** ❑ *It is never a good idea to take sleeping tablets regularly for this kind of wakefulness.* N-UNCOUNT

**wak|en** /weɪkən/ **(wakens, wakening, wakened)** When you **waken**, or when someone or something **wakens** you, you wake from sleep. [LITERARY] ❑ *The noise of a door slamming wakened her... Women are much more likely than men to waken because of noise.* VERB = wake V n V
♦ **Waken up** means the same as **waken**. ❑ *'Drink this coffee – it will waken you up.'... If you do waken up during the night, start the exercises again.* PHRASAL VERB V n P V P

**wake-up call** **(wake-up calls)** 1 A **wake-up call** is a telephone call that you can book through an operator or at a hotel to make sure that you wake up at a particular time. N-COUNT: usu sing 2 If you say that something is a **wake-up call** to a person or group of people, you mean that it will make them notice something and start to take action. ❑ *The Ambassador said he hoped the statement would serve as a wake-up call to the government.* N-COUNT: usu sing, oft N *to* n

**walk** /wɔːk/ **(walks, walking, walked)** ◆◆◆
1 When you **walk**, you move forward by putting one foot in front of the other in a regular way. ❑ *Rosanna and Forbes walked in silence for some while... She turned and walked away... They would stop the car and walk a few steps... When I was your age I walked five miles to school.* VERB V, V prep/adv, V n, V n *to* n
2 A **walk** is a journey that you make by walking, usually for pleasure. ❑ *I went for a walk... He often took long walks in the hills.* N-COUNT
3 A **walk** of a particular distance is the distance which a person has to walk to get somewhere. ❑ *It was only a three-mile walk to Kabul from there... The church is a short walk from Piazza Dante.* N-SING: supp N, N *of* n
4 A **walk** is a route suitable for walking along for pleasure. ❑ *There is a 2 mile coastal walk from Craster to Newton.* N-COUNT
5 **A walk** is the action of walking rather than running. ❑ *She slowed to a steady walk.* N-SING: *a* N
6 Someone's **walk** is the way that they walk. ❑ *George, despite his great height and gangling walk, was a keen dancer.* N-SING: poss N
7 If you **walk** someone somewhere, you walk there with them in order to show politeness or to make sure that they get there safely. ❑ *She walked me to my car.* VERB = escort V n prep/adv
8 If you **walk** your dog, you take it for a walk in order to keep it healthy. ❑ *I walk my dog each evening around my local streets.* VERB V n
9 to be **walking on air** → see **air**. to **walk tall** → see **tall**.

♦ **walk away** If you **walk away** from a problem or a difficult situation, you do nothing about it or do not face any bad consequences from it. ❑ *The most appropriate strategy may simply be to walk away from the problem... No one knows you're a part of this. You can just walk away.* PHRASAL VERB V P *from* n, V P

♦ **walk away with** If you **walk away with** something such as a prize, you win it or get it very easily. [JOURNALISM] ❑ *Enter our competition and you could walk away with £10,000.* PHRASAL VERB = walk off with V P P n

♦ **walk in on** If you **walk in on** someone, you enter the room that they are in while they are doing something private, and this creates an embarrassing situation. ❑ *His wife walked in on him making love.* PHRASAL VERB V P P n

♦ **walk into** 1 If you **walk into** an unpleasant situation, you become involved in it without expecting to, especially because you have been careless. ❑ *He's walking into a situation that he absolutely can't control.* PHRASAL VERB V P n 2 If you **walk into** a job, you manage to get it very easily. [INFORMAL] ❑ *When I left school, I could walk into any job.* PHRASAL VERB V P n

♦ **walk off with** If you **walk off with** something such as a prize, you win it or get it very easily. [JOURNALISM] ❑ *The delighted pensioner walked off with a £2,000 prize.* PHRASAL VERB = walk away with V P P n

♦ **walk out** 1 If you **walk out of** a meeting, a performance, or an unpleasant situation, you leave it suddenly, usually in order to show that PHRASAL VERB you are angry or bored. ❑ *Several dozen councillors walked out of the meeting in protest... Mr. Mason walked out during the performance.* VP *of* n VP [2] If someone **walks out on** their family or their partner, they leave them suddenly and go to live somewhere else. ❑ *Her husband walked out on her.* PHRASAL VERB VP *on* n [3] If workers **walk out**, they stop doing their work for a period of time, usually in order to try to get better pay or conditions for themselves. ❑ *Nationwide industrial action began earlier this week, when staff at most banks walked out.* PHRASAL VERB VP

♦ **walk over** If someone **walks over** you, they treat you very badly. [INFORMAL] ❑ *Do you think you can walk over me? Well, you won't, ever!* PHRASAL VERB VP n

**walk|about** /wɔːkəbaʊt/ **(walkabouts)** A **walkabout** is a walk by a king, queen, or other important person through a public place in order to meet people in an informal way. [mainly BRIT] ❑ *He was ambushed by angry protesters during a walkabout in Bolton.* ● If a king, queen, or other important person **goes walkabout** or **goes on a walkabout**, he or she walks through crowds in a public place in order to meet people in an informal way. [BRIT] ❑ *The Prime Minister insisted on going walkabout in Belfast.* N-COUNT PHRASE: V inflects

**walk|er** /wɔːkəʳ/ **(walkers)** [1] A **walker** is a person who walks, especially in the countryside for pleasure or in order to keep healthy. N-COUNT [2] A **walker** is a special kind of frame which is designed to help babies or disabled or ill people to walk. ❑ *She eventually used a cane, then a walker, and finally was confined to the house.* N-COUNT: oft supp N

**walkie-talkie** /wɔːki tɔːki/ **(walkie-talkies)** A **walkie-talkie** is a small portable radio which you can talk into and hear messages through so that you can communicate with someone far away. N-COUNT

**walk|ing** /wɔːkɪŋ/ [1] **Walking** is the activity of taking walks for exercise or pleasure, especially in the country. ❑ *Recently I've started to do a lot of walking and cycling. ...a walking holiday.* N-UNCOUNT [2] You can use **walking** in expressions like **a walking disaster** or **a walking dictionary** in order to emphasize, for example, that someone causes a lot of disasters, or knows a lot of difficult words. [HUMOROUS] ❑ *He was a walking encyclopaedia.* ADJ: ADJ n [emphasis]

**walk|ing stick** **(walking sticks)** A **walking stick** is a long wooden stick which a person can lean on while walking. N-COUNT

**Walk|man** /wɔːkmən/ **(Walkmans)** A **Walkman** is a small cassette player with light headphones which people carry around so that they can listen to music, for example while they are travelling. [TRADEMARK] N-COUNT = *personal stereo*

**walk of life** **(walks of life)** The **walk of life** that you come from is the position that you have in society and the kind of job you have. ❑ *One of the greatest pleasures of this job is meeting people from all walks of life.* N-COUNT: usu pl = *background*

**walk-on** A **walk-on** part in a play or film is a very small part which usually does not involve any speaking. ❑ *He and his family have walk-on parts in the latest film.* ADJ: ADJ n

**walk|out** /wɔːkaʊt/ **(walkouts)** [1] A **walkout** is a strike. N-COUNT [2] If there is a **walkout** during a meeting, some or all of the people attending it leave in order to show their disapproval of something that has happened at the meeting. ❑ *The commission's proceedings have been wrecked by tantrums and walkouts.* N-COUNT

**walk|over** /wɔːkoʊvəʳ/ **(walkovers)** If you say that a competition or contest is a **walkover**, you mean that it is won very easily. N-COUNT: usu sing

**walk-up** **(walk-ups)** A **walk-up** is a tall apartment block which has no lift. You can also refer to an apartment in such a block as a **walk-up**. [AM] ❑ *She lives in a tiny fifth floor walk-up in New York's East Village.* N-COUNT

**walk|way** /wɔːkweɪ/ **(walkways)** A **walkway** is a passage or path for people to walk along. Walkways are often raised above the ground. N-COUNT

**wall** /wɔːl/ **(walls)** ♦♦♦ [1] A **wall** is one of the vertical sides of a building or room. → See picture on page 1705. ❑ *Kathryn leaned against the wall of the church... The bedroom walls would be painted light blue... She checked the wall clock.* ♦ **-walled** *...a glass-walled elevator.* N-COUNT COMB in ADJ [2] A **wall** is a long narrow vertical structure made of stone or brick that surrounds or divides an area of land. ❑ *He sat on the wall in the sun.* N-COUNT [3] The **wall** of something that is hollow is its side. ❑ *He ran his fingers along the inside walls of the box.* N-COUNT: with supp [4] A **wall of** something is a large amount of it forming a high vertical barrier. ❑ *She gazed at the wall of books... I was just hit by a wall of water.* N-COUNT: with supp, usu N *of* n [5] You can describe something as a **wall of** a particular kind when it acts as a barrier and prevents people from understanding something. ❑ *The police say they met the usual wall of silence.* N-COUNT: with supp, usu N *of* n [6] → See also **cavity wall**, **dry-stone wall**, **fly-on-the-wall**, **hole-in-the-wall**, **off-the-wall**, **retaining wall**, **sea wall**, **stonewall**, **wall-to-wall**.

PHRASES [7] If you say that you **are banging your head against a wall**, you are emphasizing that you are frustrated because someone is stopping you from making progress in something. [INFORMAL] ❑ *I appealed for help but felt I was always banging my head against a wall... I wondered if I was banging my head against a brick wall.* PHRASE: V inflects, usu cont [emphasis] [8] If you have your **back to the wall**, you are in a very difficult situation and can see no way out of it. [INFORMAL] ❑ *Their threat to hire replacement workers has the union with its back to the wall.* PHRASE: *back* inflects [9] If you say that something or someone **is driving** you **up the wall**, you are emphasizing that they annoy and irritate you. [INFORMAL] ❑ *The heat is driving me up the wall... I sang in the bath and drove my parents up the wall.* PHRASE: V inflects [emphasis] [10] If a person or company **goes to the wall**, they lose all their money and their business fails. [INFORMAL] ❑ *Even quite big companies are going to the wall these days.* PHRASE: V inflects [11] **fly on the wall** → see **fly**. **the writing is on the wall** → see **writing**.

♦ **wall in** If someone or something **is walled in**, they are surrounded or enclosed by a wall or barrier. ❑ *He is walled in by a mountain of papers in his cluttered Broadway office.* PHRASAL VERB: usu passive *be* V-ed P

**wal|la|by** /wɒləbi/ **(wallabies)** A **wallaby** is an animal similar to a small kangaroo. Wallabies live in Australia and New Guinea. N-COUNT

**wall|covering** /wɔːlkʌvərɪŋ/ **(wallcoverings)** also **wall covering**. A **wallcovering** is a material such as wallpaper that is used to decorate the walls on the inside of a building. N-VAR

**walled** /wɔːld/ If an area of land or a city is **walled**, it is surrounded or enclosed by a wall. ❑ *...a walled rose garden.* ADJ

**wal|let** /wɒlɪt/ **(wallets)** A **wallet** is a small flat folded case, usually made of leather or plastic, in which you can keep banknotes and credit cards. N-COUNT: oft poss N

**wall|flower** /wɔːlflaʊəʳ/ **(wallflowers)** [1] A **wallflower** is a plant that is grown in gardens and has sweet-smelling yellow, red, orange, or purple flowers. N-COUNT [2] If you say that someone is a **wallflower**, you mean that they are shy and do not get involved in dancing or talking to people at social events. N-COUNT

**wal|lop** /wɒləp/ **(wallops, walloping, walloped)** If you **wallop** someone or something, you hit them very hard, often causing a dull sound. [INFORMAL] ❑ *Once, she walloped me over the head with a frying pan.* ♦ **Wallop** is also a noun. ❑ *With one brutal wallop, Clarke flattened him.* VERB = *whack* V n prep N-COUNT: usu sing; SOUND

**wal|low** /wɒloʊ/ **(wallows, wallowing, wallowed)** [1] If you say that someone **is wallowing in** an unpleasant situation, you are criticizing them for being deliberately unhappy. ❑ *His tired* VERB [disapproval] V *in* n *mind continued to wallow in self-pity.* [2] If a person or animal **wallows in** water or mud, they lie or roll about in it slowly for pleasure. ❑ *Never have I had such a good excuse for wallowing in deep warm baths.* VERB V *in* n

**wall|paper** /wɔːlpeɪpəʳ/ **(wallpapers, wallpapering, wallpapered)** [1] **Wallpaper** is thick coloured or patterned paper that is used for covering and decorating the walls of rooms. ❑ *...the wallpaper in the bedroom.* N-MASS [2] If someone **wallpapers** a room, they cover the walls with wallpaper. ❑ *We were going to wallpaper that room anyway.* VERB V n [3] **Wallpaper** is the background on a computer screen. [COMPUTING] ❑ *... pre-installed wallpaper images.* N-UNCOUNT

**Wall Street** ◆◇◇ **Wall Street** is a street in New York where the Stock Exchange and important banks are. **Wall Street** is often used to refer to the financial business carried out there and to the people who work there. [BUSINESS] ❑ *On Wall Street, stocks closed at their second highest level today... Wall Street seems to be ignoring other indications that consumers are spending less.* N-PROPER

**wall-to-wall** [1] A **wall-to-wall** carpet covers the floor of a room completely. ADJ: usu ADJ n [2] You can use **wall-to-wall** to describe something that fills or seems to fill all the available space. ❑ *...television's wall-to-wall soccer coverage.* ADJ: usu ADJ n

**wal|ly** /wɒli/ **(wallies)** If you refer to someone as a **wally**, you think that they are stupid or foolish. [BRIT, INFORMAL] N-COUNT disapproval

**wal|nut** /wɔːlnʌt/ **(walnuts)** [1] **Walnuts** are edible nuts which have a wrinkled shape and a hard round shell that is light brown in colour. ❑ *...chopped walnuts.* N-VAR [2] A **walnut tree** or a **walnut** is a tree on which walnuts grow. N-VAR ♦ **Walnut** is the wood of this tree. ❑ *...a handsome walnut desk.* N-UNCOUNT

**wal|rus** /wɔːlrəs/ **(walruses)** A **walrus** is a large, fat animal which lives in the sea. It has two long teeth called tusks that point downwards. N-COUNT

**waltz** /wɔːlts/ **(waltzes, waltzing, waltzed)** [1] A **waltz** is a piece of music with a rhythm of three beats in each bar, which people can dance to. ❑ *...Tchaikovsky's 'Waltz of the Flowers'.* N-COUNT; N-IN-NAMES: oft in names [2] A **waltz** is a dance in which two people hold each other and move around the floor doing special steps in time to waltz music. ❑ *Arthur Murray taught the foxtrot, the tango and the waltz.* N-COUNT [3] If you **waltz** with someone, you dance a waltz with them. ❑ *'Waltz with me,' he said, taking her hand... Couples are waltzing round the wooden floor.* V-RECIP V *with* n pl-n V adv/prep [4] If you say that someone **waltzes** somewhere, you mean that they do something in a relaxed and confident way. [INFORMAL] ❑ *She's probably got herself a new man and gone waltzing off with him.* VERB V adv/prep

**wan** /wɒn/ If you describe someone as **wan**, you mean that they look pale and tired. [LITERARY] ❑ *He looked wan and tired.* ADJ = washed-out

**wand** /wɒnd/ **(wands)** A **wand** is the same as a **magic wand**. ❑ *You can't simply wave a wand and get rid of nuclear weapons.* N-COUNT

**wan|der** /wɒndəʳ/ **(wanders, wandering, wandered)** [1] If you **wander** in a place, you walk around there in a casual way, often without intending to go in any particular direction. ❑ *They wandered off in the direction of the nearest store... Those who do not have relatives to return to are left to wander the streets and sleep rough.* VERB V prep/adv V n ♦ **Wander** is also a noun. ❑ *A wander around any market will reveal stalls piled high with vegetables.* N-SING: *a* N = stroll [2] If a person or animal **wanders** from a place where they are supposed to stay, they move away from the place without going in a particular direction. ❑ *Because Mother is afraid we'll get lost, we aren't allowed to wander far... To keep their bees from wandering, beekeepers feed them sugar solutions.* VERB = stray V adv/prep V [3] If your mind **wanders** or your thoughts **wander**, you stop concentrating on something and start thinking about other things. ❑ *His mind would wander, and he would lose track of what he was doing.* VERB = stray V [4] If your eyes **wander**, you stop looking at one thing and start looking around at other things. ❑ *His eyes wandered restlessly around the room.* VERB V prep/adv

**wan|der|er** /wɒndərəʳ/ **(wanderers)** A **wanderer** is a person who travels around rather than settling in one place. N-COUNT = drifter

**wan|der|ing** /wɒndərɪŋ/ **Wandering** is used to describe people who travel around rather than staying in one place for a long time. [LITERARY] ❑ *...a band of wandering musicians.* ADJ: ADJ n = itinerant

**wan|der|ings** /wɒndərɪŋz/ Someone's **wanderings** are journeys that they make from place to place without staying in one place for a long time. ❑ *On his wanderings he's picked up Spanish, Italian, French and a smattering of Russian.* N-PLURAL: usu with poss

**wan|der|lust** /wɒndəʳlʌst/ Someone who has **wanderlust** has a strong desire to travel. ❑ *His wanderlust would not allow him to stay long in one spot.* N-UNCOUNT

**wane** /weɪn/ **(wanes, waning, waned)** [1] If something **wanes**, it becomes gradually weaker or less, often so that it eventually disappears. ❑ *While his interest in these sports began to wane, a passion for rugby developed. ...her mother's waning strength.* VERB = fade V V-ing **wax and wane** → see **wax**. [2] If something is **on the wane**, it is becoming weaker or less. ❑ *In 1982, with his career prospects on the wane, he sold a script for £5,000.* PHRASE: v-link PHR = diminishing [3] When the moon **is waning**, it is showing a smaller area of brightness each day as it changes from a full moon to a new moon. ❑ *The moon was waning, and each day it rose later.* VERB: usu cont V

**wan|gle** /wæŋgəl/ **(wangles, wangling, wangled)** If you **wangle** something that you want, you manage to get it by being clever or persuading someone. [INFORMAL] ❑ *We managed to wangle a few days' leave... He had wangled his way into the country without a visa... I asked the Captain to wangle us three tickets to Athens... Amanda had wangled a job for Robyn with the council.* VERB V n V *way* prep/adv V n n V n *for* n

**wank** /wæŋk/ **(wanks, wanking, wanked)** To **wank** means to masturbate. [BRIT, ⚠ VERY RUDE] VERB ♦ **Wank** is also a noun. N-SING

**wank|er** /wæŋkəʳ/ **(wankers)** If someone calls a man a **wanker**, they do not like him and they think he is very stupid or unpleasant. [BRIT, ⚠ VERY RUDE] N-COUNT disapproval

**wan|na** /wɒnə/ **Wanna** is used in written English to represent the words 'want to' when they are pronounced informally. ❑ *I wanna be married to you. Do you wanna be married to me?*

**wanna|be** /wɒnəbiː/ **(wannabes)** also **wannabee.** If you call someone a **wannabe**, you are saying in an unkind way that they are trying very hard to be like another person or group of people. [INFORMAL] ❑ *...a feeble James Dean wannabe.* N-COUNT: usu n N, N n disapproval

**want** ◆◆◆ /wɒnt/ **(wants, wanting, wanted)** [1] If you **want** something, you feel a desire or a need for it. ❑ *I want a drink... Ian knows exactly what he wants in life... People wanted to know who this talented designer was... They began to want their father to be the same as other daddies... They didn't want people staring at them as they sat on the lawn, so they put up high walls... He wanted his power recognised... I want my car this colour... And remember, we want him alive.* VERB: no cont, no passive V n V to-inf V n to-inf V n -ing V n -ed V n n V n adj/prep [2] You can say that you **want to** say something to indicate that you are about to say it. ❑ *Look, I wanted to apologize for today. I think I was a little hard on you.* VERB: no cont, no passive V to-inf [3] You use **want** in questions as a way of making an offer or inviting someone to do something. ❑ *Do you want another cup of coffee?... Do you want to leave your bike here?* VERB: no cont, no passive V n V to-inf [4] If you say to someone that you **want** something, or ask them if they **want to** do it, you are firmly telling them what you want or what you want them to do. ❑ *I want an explanation from you, Jeremy... If you have a problem with that, I want you to tell me right now... Do you want to tell me what all this is about?... I want my money back!* VERB: no cont, no passive V n V n to-inf V to-inf V n adv/prep [5] If you say that something **wants** doing, you VERB: no cont,

think that it needs to be done. [mainly BRIT, INFORMAL] ❑ *Her hair wants cutting.* (no passive; V -ing) 6 If you tell someone that they **want to** do a particular thing, you are advising them to do it. [INFORMAL] ❑ *You want to be very careful not to have a man like Crevecoeur for an enemy.* (VERB: no cont, no passive; V to-inf) 7 If someone **is wanted** by the police, the police are searching for them because they are thought to have committed a crime. ❑ *He was wanted for the murder of a magistrate.* (VERB: usu passive; be V-ed *for* n)
♦ **want|ed** *He is one of the most wanted criminals in Europe.* (ADJ: ADJ n) 8 If you **want** someone, you have a great desire to have sex with them. ❑ *Come on, darling. I want you.* (VERB; V n) 9 If a child **is wanted**, its mother or another person loves it and is willing to look after it. ❑ *Children should be wanted and planned... I want this baby very much, because it certainly will be the last.* (VERB; be V-ed; V n) 10 A **want of** something is a lack of it. [FORMAL] ❑ *...a want of manners and charm.* (N-SING: also no det, N *of* n = *lack*) 11 Your **wants** are the things that you want. ❑ *Supermarkets often claim that they are responding to the wants of consumers by providing packaged foods.* (N-PLURAL: usu with poss) 12 If you do something **for want of** something else, you do it because the other thing is not available or not possible. ❑ *Many of them had gone into teaching for want of anything better to do.* (PHRASE: PHR n, PHR with v)

♦ **want out** If you **want out**, you no longer want to be involved in a plan, project, or situation that you are part of. [INFORMAL] ❑ *We've had enough, John. We want out.* (PHRASAL VERB; V P)

**want ad** **(want ads)** The **want ads** in a newspaper or magazine are small advertisements, usually offering things for sale or offering jobs. [mainly AM] (N-COUNT: usu pl = *classified ads*)

**want|ing** /wɒntɪŋ/ If you find something or someone **wanting**, they are not of as high a standard as you think they should be. ❑ *He analysed his game and found it wanting.* (ADJ: v-link ADJ, oft ADJ *in* n)

**wan|ton** /wɒntən/ 1 A **wanton** action deliberately causes harm, damage, or waste without having any reason to. ❑ *...this unnecessary and wanton destruction of our environment.* (ADJ: usu ADJ n) 2 If someone describes a woman as **wanton**, they disapprove of her because she clearly enjoys sex or has sex with a lot of men. ❑ *...the idea that only wanton women have sexual passions.* (ADJ; disapproval)

**WAP** /wæp/ **WAP** is a system which allows devices such as mobile phones to connect to the Internet. **WAP** is an abbreviation for 'Wireless Application Protocol'. (N-UNCOUNT)

**war** /wɔːʳ/ **(wars)** 1 A **war** is a period of fighting or conflict between countries or states. ❑ *He spent part of the war in the National Guard... They've been at war for the last fifteen years.* (◆◆◆ N-VAR ≠ *peace*) 2 **War** is intense economic competition between countries or organizations. ❑ *The most important thing is to reach an agreement and to avoid a trade war.* (N-VAR: usu with supp) 3 If you make **war on** someone or something that you are opposed to, you do things to stop them succeeding. ❑ *She has been involved in the war against organised crime. ...if the United States is to be successful in its war on drugs.* (N-VAR: oft N *against*/*on* n) 4 → See also **warring, civil war, Cold War, council of war.**

PHRASES 5 If a country **goes to war**, it starts fighting a war. ❑ *Do you think this crisis can be settled without going to war?* (PHRASE: V inflects) 6 If two people, countries, or organizations have a **war of words**, they criticize each other because they strongly disagree about something. [JOURNALISM] ❑ *Animal rights activists have been engaged in an increasingly bitter war of words with many of the nation's zoos.* (PHRASE: oft PHR *between*/*with* n) 7 **to lose the battle but win the war** → see **battle**.

**war|ble** /wɔːʳbᵊl/ **(warbles, warbling, warbled)** 1 When a bird **warbles**, it sings pleasantly. ❑ *The bird continued to warble... A flock of birds was already warbling a cheerful morning chorus.* (VERB; V; V n) 2 If someone **warbles**, they sing in a high-pitched, rather unsteady voice. ❑ *She warbled as she worked. ...singers warbling 'Over the Rainbow'.* (VERB; V; V n)

**war|bler** /wɔːʳbləʳ/ **(warblers)** **Warblers** are a family of small birds that have a pleasant song. (N-COUNT: usu supp N)

**war chest** **(war chests)** A **war chest** is a fund to finance a project such as a political campaign. ❑ *Governor Caperton has the largest campaign war chest.* (N-COUNT)

**ward** /wɔːʳd/ **(wards, warding, warded)** 1 A **ward** is a room in a hospital which has beds for many people, often people who need similar treatment. ❑ *A toddler was admitted to the emergency ward with a wound in his chest.* (N-COUNT) 2 A **ward** is a district which forms part of a political constituency or local council. ❑ *...the marginal wards of Reading Kentwood and Tilehurst West.* (N-COUNT) 3 A **ward** or a **ward of court** is a child who is the responsibility of a person called a guardian, or of a court of law, because their parents are dead or because they are believed to be in need of protection. ❑ *Alex was made a ward of court.* (N-COUNT)

♦ **ward off** To **ward off** a danger or illness means to prevent it from affecting you or harming you. ❑ *She may have put up a fight to try to ward off her assailant... Mass burials are now under way in an effort to ward off an outbreak of cholera.* (PHRASAL VERB; V P n (not pron) Also V n P)

**war|den** /wɔːʳdᵊn/ **(wardens)** 1 A **warden** is a person who is responsible for a particular place or thing, and for making sure that the laws or regulations that relate to it are obeyed. ❑ *He was a warden at the local parish church... Game wardens were appointed to enforce hunting laws in New Hampshire.* → See also **traffic warden.** (N-COUNT: usu with supp) 2 The **warden** of a prison is the person in charge of it. [AM] ❑ *A new warden took over the prison.* (N-COUNT)

✔ in BRIT, use **governor**

**war|der** /wɔːʳdəʳ/ **(warders)** A **warder** is someone who works in a prison supervising the prisoners. [BRIT] (N-COUNT)

✔ in AM, use **guard**

**ward|robe** /wɔːʳdroʊb/ **(wardrobes)** 1 A **wardrobe** is a tall cupboard or cabinet in which you can hang your clothes. (N-COUNT) 2 Someone's **wardrobe** is the total collection of clothes that they have. ❑ *Her wardrobe consists primarily of huge cashmere sweaters and tiny Italian sandals.* (N-COUNT: oft poss N) 3 The **wardrobe** in a theatre company is the actors' and actresses' costumes. ❑ *In the wardrobe department were rows of costumes.* (N-UNCOUNT: also *the* N)

**-ware** /-weəʳ/ **-ware** combines with nouns to refer to objects that are made of a particular material or that are used for a particular purpose in the home. ❑ *...boxes of cheap glassware.* (COMB in N-UNCOUNT)

**ware|house** /weəʳhaʊs/ **(warehouses)** A **warehouse** is a large building where raw materials or manufactured goods are stored until they are exported to other countries or distributed to shops to be sold. (N-COUNT)

**ware|house club** **(warehouse clubs)** A **warehouse club** is a large shop which sells goods at reduced prices to people who pay each year to become members of the organization that runs the shop. (N-COUNT)

**ware|hous|ing** /weəʳhaʊzɪŋ/ **Warehousing** is the act or process of storing large quantities of goods so that they can be sold or used at a later date. ❑ *All donations go towards the cost of warehousing.* (N-UNCOUNT)

**wares** /weəʳz/ Someone's **wares** are the things that they sell, usually in the street or in a market. [OLD-FASHIONED] ❑ *Vendors displayed their wares in baskets or on the ground.* (N-PLURAL)

**war|fare** /wɔːʳfeəʳ/ 1 **Warfare** is the activity of fighting a war. ❑ *...the threat of chemical warfare.* (N-UNCOUNT: oft supp N) 2 **Warfare** is sometimes used to refer to any violent struggle or conflict. ❑ *Much of the violence is related to drugs and gang warfare... At times party rivalries have broken out into open warfare.* (N-UNCOUNT: oft supp N)

**war game** **(war games)** 1 **War games** are military exercises that are carried out for the purpose of training, and that are designed to imitate a real war as closely as possible. (N-COUNT: usu pl) 2 A **war game** is a game in which model soldiers are used to re- (N-COUNT) create battles that happened in the past. War games can also be played on computers.

**war|head** /wɔːʳhed/ **(warheads)** A **warhead** is the front part of a bomb or missile where the explosives are carried. ❑ *...nuclear warheads.* N-COUNT

**war|horse** /wɔːʳhɔːʳs/ **(warhorses)** also **warhorse, war horse.** You can refer to someone such as an old soldier or politician who is still active and aggressive as a **warhorse**. N-COUNT

**war|like** /wɔːʳlaɪk/ **Warlike** people seem aggressive and eager to start a war. ❑ *The Scythians were a fiercely warlike people.* ADJ: usu ADJ n

**war|lord** /wɔːʳlɔːʳd/ **(warlords)** If you describe a leader of a country or organization as a **warlord**, you are critical of them because they have achieved power by behaving in an aggressive and violent way. ❑ *He had been a dictator and a warlord who had oppressed and degraded the people of the South. ...a drug warlord.* N-COUNT disapproval

**warm** /wɔːʳm/ **(warmer, warmest, warms, warming, warmed)** ◆◆◇ [1] Something that is **warm** has some heat but not enough to be hot. ❑ *Because it was warm, David wore only a white cotton shirt... Dissolve the salt in the warm water.* ADJ: oft *it* v-link ADJ ≠cool [2] **Warm** clothes and blankets are made of a material such as wool which protects you from the cold. ❑ *They have been forced to sleep in the open without food or warm clothing.* ADJ ≠cool ♦ **warm|ly** *Remember to wrap up warmly on cold days. ...warmly dressed.* ADV: ADV after v, ADV -ed [3] **Warm** colours have red or yellow in them rather than blue or green, and make you feel comfortable and relaxed. ❑ *The basement hallway is painted a warm yellow.* ADJ: usu ADJ n [4] A **warm** person is friendly and shows a lot of affection or enthusiasm in their behaviour. ❑ *She was a warm and loving mother... I would like to express my warmest thanks to the doctors.* ADJ ♦ **warm|ly** *New members are warmly welcomed... He greeted me warmly.* ADV: ADV with v [5] If you **warm** a part of your body or if something hot **warms** it, it stops feeling cold and starts to feel hotter. ❑ *The sun had come out to warm his back... She went to warm her hands by the log fire.* VERB V n V n [6] If you **warm to** a person or an idea, you become fonder of the person or more interested in the idea. ❑ *Those who got to know him better warmed to his openness and honesty.* VERB V *to* n

♦ **warm down** If you **warm down** after doing a physical activity, you do special exercises to help relax your muscles and joints. ❑ *He always warms down after training.* ➔ See also **warm-down**. PHRASAL VERB V P

♦ **warm up** [1] If you **warm** something **up** or if it **warms up**, it gets hotter. ❑ *He blew on his hands to warm them up... All that she would have to do was warm up the pudding... The weather had warmed up.* PHRASAL VERB V n P V P n (not pron) V P [2] If you **warm up** for an event such as a race, you prepare yourself for it by doing exercises or by practising just before it starts. ❑ *In an hour the drivers will be warming up for the main event.* ➔ See also **warm-up**. PHRASAL VERB V P [3] When a machine or engine **warms up** or someone **warms** it **up**, it becomes ready for use a little while after being switched on or started. ❑ *He waited for his car to warm up... We spent a frustrating five minutes while the pilot warmed up the engines.* PHRASAL VERB V P, V P n (not pron) Also V n P [4] If a comedian or speaker **warms up** an audience or the audience **warms up**, the audience is prepared for the main show or speaker by being told jokes, so that they are in a good mood. ❑ *They would always come out and warm up the audience... The crowd began to warm up.* PHRASAL VERB V P n (not pron) V P

**warm-blooded** A **warm-blooded** animal, for example a bird or a mammal, has a fairly high body temperature which does not change much and is not affected by the surrounding temperature. ADJ ≠cold-blooded

**warm-down** **(warm-downs)** A **warm-down** is a series of special exercises that you do after doing a physical activity to help relax your muscles and joints. N-COUNT: usu sing

**warm-hearted** A **warm-hearted** person is friendly and affectionate. ADJ

**war|monger** /wɔːʳmʌŋgəʳ/ **(warmongers)** If you describe a politician or leader as a **warmonger**, you disapprove of them because you think they are encouraging people to start or join a war. N-COUNT disapproval

**warmth** /wɔːʳmθ/ [1] The **warmth** of something is the heat that it has or produces. ❑ *She went further into the room, drawn by the warmth of the fire.* N-UNCOUNT [2] The **warmth** of something such as a garment or blanket is the protection that it gives you against the cold. ❑ *The blanket will provide additional warmth and comfort in bed.* N-UNCOUNT [3] Someone who has **warmth** is friendly and enthusiastic in their behaviour towards other people. ❑ *He greeted us both with warmth and affection.* N-UNCOUNT

**warm-up** **(warm-ups)** A **warm-up** is something that prepares you for an activity or event, usually because it is a short practice or example of what the activity or event will involve. ❑ *The exercises can be fun and a good warm-up for the latter part of the programme... The criticism was merely a warm-up for what is being prepared for the finance minister.* N-COUNT: usu sing, oft N *for* n, N n

**warn** /wɔːʳn/ **(warns, warning, warned)** ◆◆◇ [1] If you **warn** someone about something such as a possible danger or problem, you tell them about it so that they are aware of it. ❑ *When I had my first baby friends warned me that children were expensive... They warned him of the dangers of sailing alone... Analysts warned that Europe's most powerful economy may be facing trouble... He also warned of a possible anti-Western backlash.* VERB V n that V n *of/about* n V that V *of* n [2] If you **warn** someone not **to** do something, you advise them not to do it so that they can avoid possible danger or punishment. ❑ *Mrs. Blount warned me not to interfere... 'Don't do anything yet,' he warned. 'Too risky.'... 'Keep quiet, or they'll all come out,' they warned him... I wish I'd listened to the people who warned me against having the operation.* VERB V n to-inf V with quote V n with quote V n *against* n/-ing

♦ **warn off** If you **warn** someone **off**, you tell them to go away or to stop doing something because of possible danger or punishment. ❑ *The police warned the intruder off... He spends his spare time visiting schools to warn pupils off drugs.* PHRASAL VERB V n P V n P n/-ing Also V P n (not pron)

**warn|ing** /wɔːʳnɪŋ/ **(warnings)** ◆◇◇ [1] A **warning** is something which is said or written to tell people of a possible danger, problem, or other unpleasant thing that might happen. ❑ *The minister gave a warning that if war broke out, it would be catastrophic... The government has unveiled new health warnings for cigarette packets.* N-COUNT: oft N that, N to-inf [2] A **warning** is an advance notice of something that will happen, often something unpleasant or dangerous. ❑ *The soldiers opened fire without warning... With no warning, he was fired from his job.* N-VAR: oft *without* N [3] **Warning** actions or signs give a warning. ❑ *She ignored the warning signals... Some fog warning signs had been put up with flashing yellow lights.* ADJ: ADJ n

**war of nerves** A **war of nerves** is a conflict in which the opposing sides try to make each other feel less confident. ❑ *...the continuing war of nerves between the army and the leadership.* N-SING

**warp** /wɔːʳp/ **(warps, warping, warped)** [1] If something **warps** or **is warped**, it becomes damaged by bending or curving, often because of the effect of heat or water. ❑ *Left out in the heat of the sun, tapes easily warp or get stuck in their cases... It should have prevented rain water warping the door trim.* VERB V V n [2] If something **warps** someone's character, it damages them or it influences them in a bad way. ❑ *I never had any toys, my father thought that they would warp my personal values... Their lives have been warped by war.* VERB V n V n [3] A **warp** in time or space is an imaginary break or sudden change in the normal experience of time or space. ❑ *When a divorced woman re-enters the world of dating and romance, she's likely to feel as though she has entered a time warp.* N-COUNT: n N [4] In weaving, **the warp** is the threads which are held in a frame or machine called a N-SING: the N loom while another thread is passed across through them. Compare **weft**.

**war paint** also **warpaint. War paint** is the paint which some groups of people used to decorate their faces and bodies before they fought a battle. [N-UNCOUNT]

**war|path** /wɔːʳpɑːθ, -pæθ/ If you say that someone is or has gone **on the warpath**, you mean that they are angry and getting ready for a fight or conflict. [INFORMAL] ❑ *I had warned the children that daddy was on the warpath.* [PHRASE: PHR after v, oft v-link PHR]

**war|plane** /wɔːʳpleɪn/ **(warplanes)** also **war plane.** A **warplane** is an aircraft that is designed to be used for fighting, for example to attack other aircraft or to drop bombs. [N-COUNT]

**war|rant** /wɒrənt, AM wɔːr-/ **(warrants, warranting, warranted)** 1 If something **warrants** a particular action, it makes the action seem necessary or appropriate for the circumstances. ❑ *The allegations are serious enough to warrant an investigation.* [VERB = merit] [V n] ♦ **war|rant|ed** *Do you think this fear is warranted?* [ADJ] 2 A **warrant** is a legal document that allows someone to do something, especially one that is signed by a judge or magistrate and gives the police permission to arrest someone or search their house. ❑ *Police confirmed that they had issued a warrant for his arrest. ...a search warrant.* [N-COUNT: oft N *for* n, also *by* N] 3 → See also **death warrant**.

**war|rant of|fic|er** **(warrant officers)** A **warrant officer** is a person in the army, the air force, or the marines who is above the rank of sergeant and below the rank of lieutenant. In the United States Navy, a **warrant officer** is above the rank of petty officer and below the rank of ensign. [N-COUNT]

**war|ran|ty** /wɒrənti, AM wɔːr-/ **(warranties)** A **warranty** is a written promise by a company that, if you find a fault in something they have sold you within a certain time, they will repair it or replace it free of charge. ❑ *...a twelve month warranty... The equipment is still under warranty.* [N-COUNT: also *under* N = guarantee]

**war|ren** /wɒrən, AM wɔːr-/ **(warrens)** 1 A **warren** is a group of holes in the ground which are connected by tunnels and which rabbits live in. [N-COUNT: oft n N] 2 If you describe a building or an area of a city as a **warren**, you mean that there are many narrow passages or streets. ❑ *...a warren of narrow streets.* [N-COUNT: usu with supp, oft N *of* n = maze]

**war|ring** /wɔːrɪŋ/ **Warring** is used to describe groups of people who are involved in a conflict or quarrel with each other. ❑ *The warring factions have not yet turned in all their heavy weapons. ...warring husbands and wives.* [ADJ: ADJ n]

**war|ri|or** /wɒriəʳ, AM wɔːr-/ **(warriors)** A **warrior** is a fighter or soldier, especially one in former times who was very brave and experienced in fighting. [N-COUNT]

**war|ship** /wɔːʳʃɪp/ **(warships)** A **warship** is a ship with guns that is used for fighting in wars. [N-COUNT]

**wart** /wɔːʳt/ **(warts)** A **wart** is a small lump which grows on your skin. [N-COUNT]

**wart|hog** /wɔːʳthɒg, AM -hɔːg/ **(warthogs)** A **warthog** is a wild pig with two large teeth that curve upwards at the sides of its mouth. Warthogs live in Africa. [N-COUNT]

**war|time** /wɔːʳtaɪm/ also **war-time. Wartime** is a period of time when a war is being fought. ❑ *...his wartime experiences in France.* [N-UNCOUNT: oft *in* N, N n]

**war wid|ow** **(war widows)** A **war widow** is a woman whose husband was killed while he was in the armed forces during a war. [N-COUNT]

**wary** /weəri/ **(warier, wariest)** If you are **wary of** something or someone, you are cautious because you do not know much about them and you believe they may be dangerous or cause problems. ❑ *People did not teach their children to be wary of strangers... They were very wary about giving him a contract.* [ADJ: usu v-link ADJ, oft ADJ *of*/*about* n/-ing] ♦ **wari|ly** /weərɪli/ *She studied me warily, as if I might turn violent.* [ADV: usu ADV with v]

**was** /wəz, STRONG wɒz, AM wʌz/ **Was** is the first and third person singular of the past tense of **be**.

**wash** /wɒʃ/ **(washes, washing, washed)** 1 If you **wash** something, you clean it using water and usually a substance such as soap or detergent. ❑ *He got a job washing dishes in a pizza parlour... It took a long time to wash the mud out of his hair... Rub down the door and wash off the dust before applying the varnish.* [♦◇◇ VERB] [V n] [V n prep] [V n with adv] ♦ **Wash** is also a noun. ❑ *That coat could do with a wash... The treatment leaves hair glossy and lasts 10 to 16 washes.* [N-COUNT] 2 If you **wash** or if you **wash** part of your body, especially your hands and face, you clean part of your body using soap and water. ❑ *They looked as if they hadn't washed in days... She washed her face with cold water... You are going to have your dinner, get washed, and go to bed.* [VERB] [V] [V n] [*get* V-ed] ♦ **Wash** is also a noun. ❑ *She had a wash and changed her clothes.* [N-COUNT: usu *a* N in sing] 3 If a sea or river **washes** somewhere, it flows there gently. You can also say that something carried by a sea or river **washes** or **is washed** somewhere. ❑ *The sea washed against the shore... The force of the water washed him back into the cave.* [VERB] [V prep/adv] [V n with adv] [Also V n prep] 4 **The wash** of a boat is the wave that it causes on either side as it moves through the water. ❑ *...the wash from large ships.* [N-SING: *the* N] 5 If a feeling **washes over** you, you suddenly feel it very strongly and cannot control it. [WRITTEN] ❑ *A wave of self-consciousness can wash over her when someone new enters the room.* [VERB] [V *over/through* n] 6 If you say that an excuse or idea will not **wash**, you mean that people will not accept or believe it. [INFORMAL] ❑ *He said her policies didn't work and the excuses didn't wash... If they believe that solution would wash with the Haitian people, they are making a dramatic error.* [VERB: usu with brd-neg] [V] [V *with* n] 7 → See also **washing**. 8 If you say that something such as an item of clothing **is in the wash**, you mean that it is being washed, is waiting to be washed, or has just been washed and should therefore not be worn or used. [INFORMAL] ❑ *Your jeans are in the wash.* [PHRASE: V inflects] 9 to **wash** your **dirty linen in public** → see **dirty**. to **wash** your **hands of** something → see **hand**.

♦ **wash away** If rain or floods **wash away** something, they destroy it and carry it away. ❑ *Flood waters washed away one of the main bridges in Pusan.* [PHRASAL VERB] [V P n (not pron)] [Also V n P]

♦ **wash down** 1 If you **wash** something, especially food, **down** with a drink, you drink the drink after eating the food, especially to make the food easier to swallow or digest. ❑ *He took two aspirin immediately and washed them down with three cups of water.* [PHRASAL VERB] [V n P] [Also V P n (not pron)] 2 If you **wash down** an object, you wash it all, from top to bottom. ❑ *The prisoner started to wash down the walls of his cell.* [PHRASAL VERB] [V P n (not pron)] [Also V n P]

♦ **wash out** 1 If you **wash out** a container, you wash the inside of it. ❑ *It was my job to wash out the fish tank.* [PHRASAL VERB = clean out] [V P n (not pron)] 2 If dye or dirt **washes out**, it can be removed by washing. ❑ *With permanent tints, the result won't wash out.* [PHRASAL VERB] [V P] 3 If rain **washes out** a sports game or other event, it spoils it or prevents it from continuing. ❑ *Rain washed out five of the last seven games.* [PHRASAL VERB] [V P n (not pron)] 4 → See also **washed-out**, **washout**.

♦ **wash over** If something someone does or says **washes over** you, you do not notice it or it does not affect you in any way. ❑ *The television headlines seemed to wash over her without meaning anything.* [PHRASAL VERB] [V P n]

♦ **wash up** 1 If you **wash up**, you wash the plates, cups, cutlery, and pans which have been used for cooking and eating a meal. [BRIT] ❑ *I ran some hot water and washed up... I bet you make breakfast and wash up their plates, too.* [PHRASAL VERB] [V P] [V P n (not pron)] [Also V n P]

☑ in AM, use **wash the dishes**

2 If you **wash up**, you clean part of your body with soap and water, especially your hands and face. [AM] ❑ *He headed to the bathroom to wash up.* [PHRASAL VERB] [V P]

☑ in BRIT, use **wash**

3 If something **is washed up on** a piece of [PHRASAL VERB:]

land, it is carried by a river or sea and left there. ❑ *Thousands of herring and crab are washed up on the beaches during every storm... The fossils appear to be an early form of seaweed washed up on a beach.* [4] → See also **washed up**, **washing-up**. — usu passive; be V-ed P; prep/adv V-ed P

**wash|able** /wɒʃəbᵊl/ **Washable** clothes or materials can be washed in water without being damaged. ❑ *Choose washable curtains.* — ADJ

**wash|basin** /wɒʃbeɪsᵊn/ **(washbasins)** also **wash basin.** A **washbasin** is a large bowl, usually with taps for hot and cold water, for washing your hands and face. [mainly BRIT] — N-COUNT = basin, sink

> ✓ in AM, usually use **sink**

**wash|cloth** /wɒʃklɒθ, AM -klɔːθ/ **(washcloths)** A **washcloth** is a small cloth that you use for washing yourself. [AM] — N-COUNT

> ✓ in BRIT, use **flannel, facecloth**

**washed-out** also **washed out.** [1] **Washed-out** colours are very pale. ❑ *He stared at me out of those washed-out blue eyes.* — ADJ: usu ADJ n [2] If someone looks **washed-out**, they look very tired and lacking in energy. ❑ *She looked washed out and listless.* — ADJ: usu v-link ADJ

**washed up** also **washed-up.** If you say that someone is **washed up**, you mean that their career or success has ended. [INFORMAL] ❑ *He's all washed up, but he still yells at everyone.* — ADJ

**wash|er** /wɒʃəʳ/ **(washers)** [1] A **washer** is a thin flat ring of metal or rubber which is placed over a bolt before the nut is screwed on. — N-COUNT [2] A **washer** is the same as a **washing machine**. [INFORMAL] — N-COUNT

**wash|ing** /wɒʃɪŋ/ **Washing** is a collection of clothes, sheets, and other things which are waiting to be washed, are being washed, or have just been washed. ❑ *...plastic bags full of dirty washing.* — N-UNCOUNT

**wash|ing line** **(washing lines)** A **washing line** is a strong cord which you can hang wet clothes on while they dry. — N-COUNT

**wash|ing ma|chine** **(washing machines)** A **washing machine** is a machine that you use to wash clothes in. — N-COUNT

**wash|ing pow|der** **(washing powders)** **Washing powder** is a powder that you use with water to wash clothes. [BRIT] — N-MASS

> ✓ in AM, usually use **soap powder, laundry detergent**

**washing-up** [1] To **do** the **washing-up** means to wash the plates, cups, cutlery, and pans which have been used for cooking and eating a meal. [BRIT] ❑ *Martha volunteered to do the washing-up.* — N-UNCOUNT

> ✓ in AM, use **wash the dishes**

[2] **Washing-up** is the plates, cups, cutlery, and pans which you have to wash after a meal. [BRIT] ❑ *...a brimming bowl of washing-up.* — N-UNCOUNT

> ✓ in AM, use **dirty dishes, the dishes**

**washing-up liq|uid** **(washing-up liquids)** **Washing-up liquid** is a thick soapy liquid which you add to hot water to clean dirty dishes. [BRIT] — N-MASS

> ✓ in AM, use **dishwashing liquid, dish soap**

**wash|out** /wɒʃaʊt/ **(washouts)** If an event or plan is a **washout**, it fails completely. [INFORMAL] ❑ *The mission was a washout.* — N-COUNT

**wash-rag** **(wash-rags)** also **washrag.** A **wash-rag** is the same as a **washcloth**. [AM] — N-COUNT

**wash|room** /wɒʃruːm/ **(washrooms)** A **washroom** is a room with toilets and washing facilities, situated in a large building such as a factory or an office block. — N-COUNT

**wash|stand** /wɒʃstænd/ **(washstands)** A **washstand** is a piece of furniture designed to hold a bowl for washing your hands and face in, which was used in former times before washbasins had taps on them. — N-COUNT

**wasn't** /wɒzᵊnt, AM wʌz-/ **Wasn't** is the usual spoken form of 'was not'.

**wasp** /wɒsp/ **(wasps)** A **wasp** is an insect with wings and yellow and black stripes across its body. Wasps have a painful sting like a bee but do not produce honey. — N-COUNT

**WASP** /wɒsp/ **(WASPs)** **WASP** is used to refer to the people in American society whose ancestors came from northern Europe, especially England, and who are considered to have a lot of power and influence. **WASP** is an abbreviation for 'White Anglo-Saxon Protestant'. [AM] — N-COUNT: also N n; disapproval

**wasp|ish** /wɒspɪʃ/ A **waspish** remark or sense of humour is sharp and critical. — ADJ

**wast|age** /weɪstɪdʒ/ [1] **Wastage** of something is the act of wasting it or the amount of it that is wasted. ❑ *...a series of measures to prevent the wastage of water... There was a lot of wastage and many wrong decisions were hastily taken.* — N-UNCOUNT [2] **Wastage** is the process by which part of someone's body gets weaker or smaller because they are very ill or have not eaten enough. ❑ *This can lead to bodily weakness and muscle wastage.* — N-UNCOUNT [3] **Wastage** refers to the number of people who leave a company, college, or other organization, especially before they have completed their education or training. [BRIT] ❑ *British universities have very little wastage and their graduates are good.* → See also **natural wastage**. — N-UNCOUNT

**waste** /weɪst/ **(wastes, wasting, wasted)** [1] If you **waste** something such as time, money, or energy, you use too much of it doing something that is not important or necessary, or is unlikely to succeed. ❑ *There could be many reasons and he was not going to waste time speculating on them... I resolved not to waste money on a hotel... The system wastes a large amount of water.* ♦ **Waste** is also a noun. ❑ *It is a waste of time going to the doctor with most mild complaints... I think that is a total waste of money.* — ◆◆◇ VERB; V n -ing; V n *on* n; V n; N-SING: a N *of* n [2] **Waste** is the use of money or other resources on things that do not need it. ❑ *The packets are measured to reduce waste... I hate waste.* — N-UNCOUNT [3] **Waste** is material which has been used and is no longer wanted, for example because the valuable or useful part of it has been taken out. ❑ *Congress passed a law that regulates the disposal of waste... Up to 10 million tonnes of toxic wastes are produced every year in the UK. ...the process of eliminating body waste.* — N-UNCOUNT: also N in pl [4] If you **waste** an opportunity for something, you do not take advantage of it when it is available. ❑ *Let's not waste an opportunity to see the children... It was a wasted opportunity.* — VERB; V n; V-ed [5] **Waste** land is land, especially in or near a city, which is not used or looked after by anyone, and so is covered by wild plants and rubbish. ❑ *Yarrow can be found growing wild in fields and on waste ground.* — ADJ: usu ADJ n [6] **Wastes** are a large area of land, for example a desert, in which there are very few people, plants, or animals. ❑ *...the barren wastes of the Sahara.* — N-PLURAL: adj N, N *of* n [7] → See also **wasted**. [8] If something **goes to waste**, it remains unused or has to be thrown away. ❑ *Mexican cookery is economical, she says. Nothing goes to waste.* — PHRASE: V inflects [9] to **waste no time** → see **time**.

♦ **waste away** If someone **wastes away**, they become extremely thin or weak because they are ill or worried and they are not eating properly. ❑ *Persons dying from cancer visibly waste away.* — PHRASAL VERB; V P

**waste|basket** /weɪstbɑːskɪt, -bæsk-/ **(wastebaskets)** A **wastebasket** is the same as a **wastepaper basket**. [AM] — N-COUNT

**wast|ed** /weɪstɪd/ [1] A **wasted** action is one that is unnecessary. ❑ *I'm sorry you had a wasted journey.* — ADJ [2] Someone who is **wasted** is very tired and weak, often because of an illness. ❑ *They look too wasted to care about much.* — ADJ

**waste dis|pos|al** **(waste disposals)** A **waste disposal** or a **waste disposal unit** is a small machine in a kitchen sink that chops up vegetable waste. [BRIT] — N-COUNT

> ✓ in AM, use **garbage disposal**

**waste|ful** /weɪstfʊl/ Action that is **wasteful** uses too much of something valuable such as time, money, or energy. ❑ *This kind of training is ineffective, and wasteful of scarce resources... Try to avoid wasteful duplication of effort.* ADJ

**waste|land** /weɪstlænd/ **(wastelands)** [1] A **wasteland** is an area of land on which not much can grow or which has been spoiled in some way. ❑ *The pollution has already turned vast areas into a wasteland.* N-VAR: oft adj N, N *of* n [2] If you refer to a place, situation, or period in time as a **wasteland**, you are criticizing it because you think there is nothing interesting or exciting in it. ❑ *...the cultural wasteland of Franco's repressive rule.* N-COUNT: oft adj N, N *of* n [disapproval] = *desert*

**waste|paper bas|ket** **(wastepaper baskets)** A **wastepaper basket** is a container for rubbish, especially paper, which is usually placed on the floor in the corner of a room or next to a desk. N-COUNT

**wast|ing** /weɪstɪŋ/ A **wasting** disease is one which makes you gradually become thinner and weaker. ADJ: ADJ n

**wast|rel** /weɪstrəl/ **(wastrels)** If you describe someone as a **wastrel** you mean that they are lazy and spend their time and money on foolish things. [LITERARY] N-COUNT

**watch**
① LOOKING AND PAYING ATTENTION
② INSTRUMENT THAT TELLS THE TIME

**①watch** /wɒtʃ/ **(watches, watching, watched)** ◆◆◆
⇛ Please look at category 15 to see if the expression you are looking for is shown under another headword. [1] If you **watch** someone or something, you look at them, usually for a period of time, and pay attention to what is happening. ❑ *The man was standing in his doorway watching him... He watched the barman prepare the beer he had ordered... Chris watched him sipping his brandy... I watched as Amy ate a few nuts.* VERB V n, V n inf, V n -ing, V [2] If you **watch** something on television or an event such as a sports match, you spend time looking at it, especially when you see it from the beginning to the end. ❑ *I'd stayed up late to watch the film... They spent a great deal of time watching television.* VERB V n [3] If you **watch** a situation or event, you pay attention to it or you are aware of it, but you do not influence it. ❑ *Human rights groups have been closely watching the case... Annoyed commuters could only watch as the departure time ticked by.* VERB V n, V [4] If you **watch** people, especially children or animals, you are responsible for them, and make sure that they are not in danger. ❑ *Parents can't be expected to watch their children 24 hours a day.* VERB V n [5] If you **watch** someone, you follow them secretly or spy on them. ❑ *Ella was scared that someone was watching her.* VERB V n [6] If you tell someone to **watch** a particular person or thing, you are warning them to be careful that the person or thing does not get out of control or do something unpleasant. ❑ *You really ought to watch these quiet types... If you're watching the calories, don't have mayonnaise.* VERB V n, V n [7] A **watch** is a period of carefully looking and listening, often while other people are asleep and often as a military duty, so that you can warn them of danger or an attack. ❑ *I had the first watch that May evening.* N-COUNT

**PHRASES** [8] If someone **keeps watch**, they look and listen all the time, while other people are asleep or doing something else, so that they can warn them of danger or an attack. ❑ *Jose, as usual, had climbed a tree to keep watch.* PHRASE: V inflects [9] If you **keep watch on** events or a situation, you pay attention to what is happening, so that you can take action at the right moment. ❑ *US officials have been keeping close watch on the situation.* PHRASE: V inflects, usu PHR *on* n [10] You say '**watch it**' in order to warn someone to be careful, especially when you want to threaten them about what will happen if they are not careful. ❑ *'Now watch it, Patsy,' the Sergeant told her.* PHRASE [11] If someone is **on watch**, they have the job of carefully looking and listening, often while other people are asleep and often as a military duty, so that they can warn them of danger or an attack. ❑ *Apart from two men on watch in the engine-room, everyone was asleep.* PHRASE: v-link PHR, PHR after v [12] If you are **on the watch for** something, you are expecting it to happen and you therefore pay attention to events so that you will notice it when it does happen. ❑ *Environmentalists will be on the watch for damage to wildlife.* PHRASE: v-link PHR, oft PHR *for* n = *on the lookout* [13] If someone is being kept **under watch**, they are being guarded or observed all the time. PHRASE: PHR after v, v-link PHR [14] You say to someone '**you watch**' or '**just watch**' when you are predicting that something will happen, and you are very confident that it will happen as you say. ❑ *You watch. Things will get worse before they get better.* PHRASE [15] to **watch** your **step** → see **step**.

♦ **watch for** or **watch out for** If you **watch for** something or **watch out for** it, you pay attention so that you notice it, either because you do not want to miss it or because you want to avoid it. ❑ *We'll be watching for any developments... He called out to them to watch out for the unexploded mine.* PHRASAL VERB = *look out for* V P n, V P P n

♦ **watch out** If you tell someone to **watch out**, you are warning them to be careful, because something unpleasant might happen to them or they might get into difficulties. ❑ *You have to watch out because there are land mines all over the place.* PHRASAL VERB = *look out* V P

♦ **watch out for** → see **watch for**.

♦ **watch over** If you **watch over** someone or something, you pay attention to them to make sure that nothing bad happens to them. ❑ *The guards were originally hired to watch over the houses as they were being built.* PHRASAL VERB = *watch* V P n

**②watch** /wɒtʃ/ **(watches)** A **watch** is a small clock which you wear on a strap on your wrist, or on a chain. ◆◇◇ N-COUNT

**watch|dog** /wɒtʃdɒg, AM -dɔːg/ **(watchdogs)** A **watchdog** is a person or committee whose job is to make sure that companies do not act illegally or irresponsibly. ❑ *...an anti-crime watchdog group funded by New York businesses.* N-COUNT: oft supp N, N n

**-watcher** /-wɒtʃəʳ/ **(-watchers)** **-watcher** combines with nouns to form other nouns that refer to people who are interested in a group of animals or people, and who study them closely. ❑ *The bird-watchers crept about in the bushes... Royal-watcher Mary Hayes said: 'It looks like it is going to be an unhappy time for the Queen.'* COMB in N-COUNT

**watch|ful** /wɒtʃfʊl/ Someone who is **watchful** notices everything that is happening. ❑ *The best thing is to be watchful and see the family doctor for any change in your normal health.* ADJ

**-watching** /-wɒtʃɪŋ/ **-watching** combines with nouns to form other nouns which refer to the activity of looking at a group of animals or people and studying them because they interest you. ❑ *Whale-watching has become a growth leisure industry... He is said to have invented the sport of celebrity-watching.* COMB in N-UNCOUNT

**watch|man** /wɒtʃmən/ **(watchmen)** A **watchman** is a person whose job is to guard a building or area. → See also **nightwatchman**. N-COUNT

**watch|tower** /wɒtʃtaʊəʳ/ **(watchtowers)** A **watchtower** is a high building which gives a person a good view of the area around the place that they are guarding. N-COUNT

**watch|word** /wɒtʃwɜːʳd/ **(watchwords)** Someone's **watchword** is a word or phrase that sums up their attitude or approach to a particular subject or to things in general. ❑ *Caution has been one of Mr Allan's watchwords.* N-COUNT: oft with poss

**wa|ter** /wɔːtəʳ/ **(waters, watering, watered)** ◆◆◆ [1] **Water** is a clear thin liquid that has no colour or taste when it is pure. It falls from clouds as rain and enters rivers and seas. All animals and people N-UNCOUNT need water in order to live. ❑ *Get me a glass of water. ...the sound of water hammering on the metal roof. ...a trio of children playing along the water's edge.* [2] You use **waters** to refer to a large area of sea, especially the area of sea which is near to a country and which is regarded as belonging to it. ❑ *The ship will remain outside Chinese territorial waters. ...the open waters of the Arctic Ocean.* N-PLURAL: with supp [3] You sometimes use **waters** to refer to a situation which is very complex or difficult. ❑ *...the man brought in to guide him through troubled waters... The British Government may be in stormy economic waters.* N-PLURAL: adj N [4] If you **water** plants, you pour water over them in order to help them to grow. ❑ *He went out to water the plants.* VERB V n [5] If your eyes **water**, tears build up in them because they are hurting or because you are upset. ❑ *His eyes watered from cigarette smoke.* VERB V [6] If you say that your mouth **is watering**, you mean that you can smell or see some nice food and you might mean that your mouth is producing a liquid. ❑ *...cookies to make your mouth water.* → See also **mouth-watering**. VERB V

PHRASES [7] When a pregnant woman's **waters break**, the fluid in her womb that surrounds the baby passes out of her body, showing that the baby is ready to be born. A doctor or midwife can **break** a woman's **waters** so that the birth can begin. ❑ *My waters broke at six in the morning and within four hours Jamie was born.* PHRASE: V inflects [8] If you say that an event or incident is **water under the bridge**, you mean that it has happened and cannot now be changed, so there is no point in worrying about it any more. ❑ *He was relieved his time in jail was over and regarded it as water under the bridge.* PHRASE: v-link PHR [9] If you are **in deep water**, you are in a difficult or awkward situation. ❑ *I could tell that we were getting off the subject and into deep water.* PHRASE [10] If an argument or theory does not **hold water**, it does not seem to be reasonable or be in accordance with the facts. ❑ *This argument simply cannot hold water in Europe.* PHRASE: V inflects, usu with brd-neg [11] If you are **in hot water**, you are in trouble. [INFORMAL] ❑ *The company has already been in hot water over high prices this year.* PHRASE: v-link PHR, PHR after v [12] If you **pour cold water on** an idea or suggestion, you show that you have a low opinion of it. ❑ *City economists pour cold water on the idea that the economic recovery has begun.* PHRASE: V inflects, PHR n [13] If you **test the water** or **test the waters**, you try to find out what reaction an action or idea will get before you do it or tell it to people. ❑ *You should be cautious when getting involved and test the water before committing yourself.* PHRASE: V and N inflect [14] **like water off a duck's back** → see **duck**. to **take to** something **like a duck to water** → see **duck**. to **keep** your **head above water** → see **head**.

♦ **water down** [1] If you **water down** a substance, for example food or drink, you add water to it to make it weaker. ❑ *You can water down a glass of wine and make it last twice as long... I bought a water-based paint, then decided to water it down even more.* PHRASAL VERB = *dilute* V P n (not pron) V n P [2] If something such as a proposal, speech, or statement **is watered down**, it is made much weaker and less forceful, or less likely to make people angry. ❑ *Proposed legislation affecting bird-keepers has been watered down.* → See also **watered-down**. VERB = *tone down* *be* V-ed P

**water|bed** /wɔːtəʳbed/ **(waterbeds)** also **water bed.** A **waterbed** is a bed which consists of a plastic case filled with water. N-COUNT

**wa|ter bird (water birds)** A **water bird** is a bird that swims or walks in water, especially lakes and rivers. There are many kinds of water bird. N-COUNT

**water-borne** also **waterborne.** [1] A **water-borne** disease or infection is one that people can catch from infected water. ADJ: ADJ n [2] Something that is **water-borne** travels or is transported on water. ❑ *...a waterborne safari down the Nile... Environmental pressures are strengthening the case for waterborne freight.* ADJ: ADJ n

**wa|ter bot|tle (water bottles)** A **water bottle** is a small container for carrying water to drink on a long journey. → See also **hot-water bottle**. N-COUNT

**wa|ter buf|fa|lo (water buffaloes** or **water buffalo)** A **water buffalo** is an animal like a large cow with long horns that curve upwards. In some countries water buffalo are kept for their milk and are used to draw ploughs. N-COUNT = *buffalo*

**wa|ter butt (water butts)** A **water butt** is a large barrel for collecting rain as it flows off a roof. [BRIT] N-COUNT

in AM, use **rain barrel**

**wa|ter can|non (water cannons** or **water cannon)** A **water cannon** is a machine which shoots out a large, powerful stream of water. It is used by police to break up crowds of people who are protesting or fighting. N-COUNT

**wa|ter chest|nut (water chestnuts)** A **water chestnut** is the thick bottom part of the stem of a plant which grows in China. It is used in Chinese cookery. N-COUNT

**water|colour** /wɔːtəʳkʌləʳ/ **(watercolours)**

in AM, use **watercolor**

[1] **Watercolours** are coloured paints, used for painting pictures, which you apply with a wet brush or dissolve in water first. ❑ *...a collection of rich paintings in watercolour, acrylic and oil.* N-VAR [2] A **watercolour** is a picture which has been painted with watercolours. ❑ *...a lovely watercolour by J. M. W. Turner.* N-COUNT

**wa|ter cool|er (water coolers)** [1] A **water cooler** is a machine that dispenses drinking water, especially in an office. [mainly AM] N-COUNT [2] **Water cooler** is used in expressions that refer to the informal conversations that people have in their office or workplace. ❑ *Three out of four Americans watched Roots, and then the next day could talk about race relations at the water cooler.* N-SING

**water|course** /wɔːtəʳkɔːʳs/ **(watercourses)** also **water course.** A **watercourse** is a stream or river, or the channel that it flows along. [FORMAL] N-COUNT

**water|cress** /wɔːtəʳkres/ **Watercress** is a small plant with white flowers which grows in streams and pools. Its leaves taste hot and are eaten raw in salads. N-UNCOUNT

**watered-down** also **watered down.** If you describe something such as a proposal, speech, or statement as **watered-down**, you mean that it is weaker or less forceful than its original form. ❑ *The British government introduced a watered-down version of the proposals.* → See also **water down**. ADJ

**water|fall** /wɔːtəʳfɔːl/ **(waterfalls)** A **waterfall** is a place where water flows over the edge of a steep, high cliff in hills or mountains, and falls into a pool below. ❑ *...Angel Falls, the world's highest waterfall.* N-COUNT

**wa|ter fea|ture (water features)** A **water feature** is something such as an artificial pond or waterfall, usually in a garden. N-COUNT

**water|fowl** /wɔːtəʳfaʊl/ **(waterfowl) Waterfowl** are birds that swim in water, especially ducks, geese, and swans. N-COUNT

**water|front** /wɔːtəʳfrʌnt/ **(waterfronts)** A **waterfront** is a street or piece of land which is next to an area of water, for example a harbour or the sea. ❑ *They went for a stroll along the waterfront.* N-COUNT: usu sing

**wa|ter hole (water holes)** also **waterhole.** In a desert or other dry area, a **water hole** is a pool of water where animals can drink. N-COUNT

**wa|ter|ing can (watering cans)** A **watering can** is a container with a long spout which is used to water plants. N-COUNT

**wa|ter|ing hole (watering holes)** You can refer to a pub or bar where people go to drink and meet their friends as a **watering hole**. ❑ *I was in* N-COUNT *my favorite watering hole, waiting for the game to start.*

**wa|ter jump** **(water jumps)** A **water jump** is a fence with a pool of water on the far side of it, which people or horses jump over as part of a race or competition. N-COUNT

**wa|ter lily** **(water lilies)** also **waterlily.** A **water lily** is a plant with large flat leaves and colourful flowers which floats on the surface of lakes and rivers. N-COUNT

**water|line** /wɔːtəʳlaɪn/ **(waterlines)** also **water line.** The **waterline** is a line, either real or imaginary, on the side of a ship representing the level the water reaches when the ship is at sea. ❑ *Ray painted below the waterline with a special anti-rust paint.* N-COUNT: usu sing

**water|logged** /wɔːtəʳlɒgd, AM -lɔːgd/ also **water-logged.** Something such as soil or land that is **waterlogged** is so wet that it cannot absorb any more water, so that a layer of water remains on its surface. ❑ *The match is off because of a waterlogged pitch.* ADJ

**wa|ter main** **(water mains)** A **water main** is a very large underground pipe used for supplying water to houses and factories. N-COUNT

**water|mark** /wɔːtəʳmɑːʳk/ **(watermarks)** A **watermark** is a design which is put into paper when it is made, and which you can only see if you hold the paper up to the light. Banknotes often have a watermark, to make them harder to copy illegally. → See also **high-water mark.** N-COUNT

**wa|ter mead|ow** **(water meadows)** **Water meadows** are wet fields of grass near a river, which are often flooded. [mainly BRIT] N-COUNT: usu pl

**water|melon** /wɔːtəʳmelən/ **(watermelons)** A **watermelon** is a large round fruit with green skin, pink flesh, and black seeds. N-VAR

**water|mill** /wɔːtəʳmɪl/ **(watermills)** also **water mill.** A **watermill** is a mill powered by a water wheel. N-COUNT

**wa|ter pis|tol** **(water pistols)** A **water pistol** is a small toy gun which shoots out water. N-COUNT

**wa|ter polo** **Water polo** is a game played in a swimming pool in which two teams of swimmers try to score goals with a ball. N-UNCOUNT

**water|proof** /wɔːtəʳpruːf/ **(waterproofs, waterproofing, waterproofed)** 1 Something which is **waterproof** does not let water pass through it. ❑ *Take waterproof clothing – Orkney weather is unpredictable.* ADJ 2 **Waterproofs** are items of clothing which do not let water in. [mainly BRIT] ❑ *For staying dry you'll want nice lightweight waterproofs to wear over your leathers.* N-COUNT: usu pl 3 If something **is waterproofed**, it is treated so that water cannot pass through it or damage it. ❑ *The whole boat has been totally waterproofed.* VERB: usu passive *be* V-ed

**wa|ter rate** **(water rates)** In Britain, the charges made for the use of water from the public water supply are known as the **water rates.** N-COUNT: usu pl

**water-resistant** Something that is **water-resistant** does not allow water to pass through it easily, or is not easily damaged by water. ❑ *Microfibre fabrics are both water resistant and windproof.* ADJ

**water|shed** /wɔːtəʳʃed/ **(watersheds)** 1 If something such as an event is a **watershed in** the history or development of something, it is very important because it represents the beginning of a new stage in it. ❑ *The election of Mary Robinson in 1990 was a watershed in Irish politics.* N-COUNT: usu sing, oft N *in* n = *turning point* 2 **The watershed** is a time before which television broadcasters have agreed not to show programmes unsuitable for children, for example programmes that contain scenes of sex or violence. [BRIT] ❑ *The advert should only be shown after the 9pm watershed.* N-COUNT: usu *the* N in sing

**water|side** /wɔːtəʳsaɪd/ The **waterside** is the area beside a stretch of water such as a river or lake. ❑ *Her garden stretches down to the waterside.* N-SING: oft N n = *waterfront*

**water-ski** **(water-skis, water-skiing, water-skied)** also **waterski.** If you **water-ski**, you stand on skis in the water while being pulled along by a boat. ❑ *The staff will be happy to help arrange for you to swim, sail, or water-ski.* ♦ **water-skiing** *He offered to teach them water-skiing.* VERB V N-UNCOUNT

**water-soluble** also **water soluble.** Something that is **water-soluble** dissolves in water. ❑ *Vitamin C is water soluble. ...oat bran and other water-soluble fibres.* ADJ

**wa|ter sup|ply** **(water supplies)** The **water supply** in an area is the water which is collected and passed through pipes to buildings for people to use. ❑ *The town is without electricity and the water supply has been cut off.* N-COUNT

**wa|ter ta|ble** **(water tables)** **The water table** is the level below the surface of the ground where water can be found. ❑ *Environmentalists say that diverting water from the river will lower the water table and dry out wells.* N-COUNT: usu *the* N

**water|tight** /wɔːtəʳtaɪt/ also **water-tight.** 1 Something that is **watertight** does not allow water to pass through it, for example because it is tightly sealed. ❑ *The flask is completely watertight, even when laid on its side.* ADJ 2 A **watertight** case, argument, or agreement is one that has been so carefully put together that nobody will be able to find a fault in it. ❑ *The police had a watertight case. They even got his fingerprints from that glass cabinet.* ADJ

**wa|ter tow|er** **(water towers)** A **water tower** is a large tank of water which is placed on a high metal structure so that water can be supplied at a steady pressure to surrounding buildings. N-COUNT

**wa|ter vole** **(water voles)** A **water vole** is a small furry animal that can swim. Water voles live in holes in the banks of rivers. [mainly BRIT] N-COUNT

**water|way** /wɔːtəʳweɪ/ **(waterways)** A **waterway** is a canal, river, or narrow channel of sea which ships or boats can sail along. N-COUNT

**wa|ter wheel** **(water wheels)** also **waterwheel.** A **water wheel** is a large wheel which is turned by water flowing through it. Water wheels are used to provide power to drive machinery. N-COUNT

**water|works** /wɔːtəʳwɜːʳks/ **(waterworks)** A **waterworks** is a building where a supply of water is stored and cleaned before being distributed to the public. N-COUNT

**wa|tery** /wɔːtəri/ 1 Something that is **watery** is weak or pale. ❑ *A watery light began to show through the branches... Martha managed to produce a dim, watery smile.* ADJ: usu ADJ n 2 If you describe food or drink as **watery**, you dislike it because it contains too much water, or has no flavour. ❑ *...watery beer.* ADJ: usu ADJ n [disapproval] 3 Something that is **watery** contains, resembles, or consists of water. ❑ *Emma's eyes went red and watery.* ADJ

**watt** /wɒt/ **(watts)** A **watt** is a unit of measurement of electrical power. ❑ *Use a 3 amp fuse for equipment up to 720 watts. ...a 100-watt lightbulb.* N-COUNT: usu num N

**watt|age** /wɒtɪdʒ/ The **wattage** of a piece of electrical equipment is the amount of electrical power which it produces or uses, expressed in watts. N-UNCOUNT

**wat|tle** /wɒtᵊl/ **Wattle** is a framework made by weaving thin sticks through thick sticks which is used for making fences and walls. [BRIT] ❑ *...the native huts of mud and wattle. ...wattle fencing.* N-UNCOUNT

**wave** /weɪv/ **(waves, waving, waved)** 1 If you **wave** or **wave** your hand, you move your hand from side to side in the air, usually in order to say hello or goodbye to someone. ❑ *He waved at the waiter, who rushed to the table... He grinned, waved, and said, 'Hi!'... Elaine turned and waved her hand lazily and left.* ♦ **Wave** is also a noun. ❑ *Steve stopped him with a wave of the hand... Paddy spotted Mary Ann and gave her a cheery wave.* ◆◆◇ VERB V *to/at* n V V n Also V n prep N-COUNT: usu with supp 2 If you **wave** someone away or **wave** them on, you make a movement with your hand to indicate that they should move in a particular direction. VERB

❑ *Leshka waved him away with a show of irritation.* V n adv/prep

[3] VERB If you **wave** something, you hold it up and move it rapidly from side to side. ❑ V n *Hospital staff were outside to welcome him, waving flags and applauding... She was apt to raise her voice and wave her hands about.* V n adv/prep ♦ COMB in ADJ **-waving** *Hundreds of banner-waving demonstrators took to the streets. ...a flag-waving crowd.* ♦ COMB in N-UNCOUNT **-waving** *There will be marching bands and plenty of flag-waving at the parade.*

[4] VERB = sway If something **waves**, it moves gently from side to side or up and down. ❑ V *...grass and flowers waving in the wind.*

[5] N-COUNT A **wave** is a raised mass of water on the surface of water, especially the sea, which is caused by the wind or by tides making the surface of the water rise and fall. ❑ *...the sound of the waves breaking on the shore.*

[6] N-COUNT If someone's hair has **waves**, it curves slightly instead of being straight.

[7] N-COUNT: with supp A **wave** is a sudden increase in heat or energy that spreads out from an earthquake or explosion. ❑ *The shock waves of the earthquake were felt in Teheran.*

[8] N-COUNT: usu pl, oft supp N **Waves** are the form in which things such as sound, light, and radio signals travel. ❑ *Sound waves, light waves, and radio waves have a certain frequency, or number of waves per second.*

[9] N-COUNT: usu N *of* n If you refer to a **wave of** a particular feeling, you mean that it increases quickly and becomes very intense, and then often decreases again. ❑ *She felt a wave of panic, but forced herself to leave the room calmly.*

[10] N-COUNT: usu N *of* n A **wave** is a sudden increase in a particular activity or type of behaviour, especially an undesirable or unpleasant one. ❑ *...the current wave of violence. ...an even newer crime wave.*

[11] → See also **long wave**, **medium wave**, **Mexican wave**, **new wave**, **short-wave**, **tidal wave**.

**wave|band** /weɪvbænd/ **(wavebands)** N-COUNT A **waveband** is a group of radio waves of similar length which are used for particular types of radio communication.

**wave|length** /weɪvleŋθ/ **(wavelengths)** [1] N-COUNT: usu with supp A **wavelength** is the distance between a part of a wave of energy such as light or sound and the next similar part. ❑ *Sunlight consists of different wavelengths of radiation.* [2] N-COUNT: with supp A **wavelength** is the size of radio wave which a particular radio station uses to broadcast its programmes. ❑ *She found the wavelength of their broadcasts, and left the radio tuned to their station.* [3] PHRASE: v-link PHR If two people are **on the same wavelength**, they find it easy to understand each other and they tend to agree, because they share similar interests or opinions. ❑ *It's great to work with people who are on the same wavelength.*

**wave|let** /weɪvlət/ **(wavelets)** N-COUNT: usu pl **Wavelets** are small waves on the surface of a sea or lake. [LITERARY]

**wa|ver** /weɪvəʳ/ **(wavers, wavering, wavered)** [1] VERB If you **waver**, you cannot decide about something or you consider changing your mind about something. ❑ V *Some military commanders wavered over whether to support the coup...* V *Coleman has never wavered in his claim that he is innocent.* [2] VERB If something **wavers**, it shakes with very slight movements or changes. ❑ V *The shadows of the dancers wavered continually.*

**wavy** /weɪvi/ **(wavier, waviest)** [1] ADJ **Wavy** hair is not straight or curly, but curves slightly. ❑ *She had short, wavy brown hair.* [2] ADJ: usu ADJ n A **wavy** line has a series of regular curves along it. ❑ *The boxes were decorated with a wavy gold line.*

**wax** /wæks/ **(waxes, waxing, waxed)** [1] N-MASS **Wax** is a solid, slightly shiny substance made of fat or oil which is used to make candles and polish. It melts when it is heated. ❑ *There were coloured candles which had spread pools of wax on the furniture... She loved the scent in the house of wax polish.* [2] VERB If you **wax** a surface, you put a thin layer of wax onto it, especially in order to polish it. ❑ V n *We'd have long talks while she helped me wax the floor.* [3] VERB If you have your legs **waxed**, you have the hair removed from your legs by having wax put on them and then pulled off quickly. ❑ *have* n V-ed *She has just had her legs waxed at the local beauty parlour...* V n *She could go shopping, and wax her legs.* [4] N-UNCOUNT **Wax** is the sticky yellow substance found in your ears. [5] VERB If you say that someone, for example, **waxes** lyrical or **waxes** indignant about a subject, you mean that they talk about it in an enthusiastic or indignant way. ❑ V adj *He waxed lyrical about the skills and commitment of his employees...* V adj *My mother waxed eloquent on the theme of wifely duty.* [6] PHRASE: Vs inflect If something **waxes and wanes**, it first increases and then decreases over a period of time. ❑ *Portugal and Spain had possessed vast empires that waxed and waned.*

**waxed pa|per** N-UNCOUNT **Waxed paper** is the same as **wax paper**.

**wax|en** /wæksᵊn/ ADJ A **waxen** face is very pale and looks very unhealthy. [LITERARY]

**wax pa|per** N-UNCOUNT = waxed paper **Wax paper** is paper that has been covered with a thin layer of wax. It is used mainly in cooking or to wrap food. [AM]

✔ in BRIT, use **greaseproof paper**

**wax|work** /wækswɜːʳk/ **(waxworks)** [1] N-COUNT A **waxwork** is a model of a person, especially a famous person, made out of wax. [2] N-COUNT A **waxworks** is a place where waxworks are displayed for the public to look at. **Waxworks** is both the singular and the plural form.

**waxy** /wæksi/ ADJ: usu ADJ n Something that is **waxy** looks or feels like wax. ❑ *Choose small waxy potatoes for the salad. ...the waxy coating on the insect's body.*

**way** /weɪ/ **(ways)** ◆◆◆ [1] N-COUNT: oft N *of* -ing, N to-inf If you refer to a **way of** doing something, you are referring to how you can do it, for example the action you can take or the method you can use to achieve it. ❑ *Another way of making new friends is to go to an evening class... I worked myself into a frenzy plotting ways to make him jealous... I can't think of a worse way to spend my time... There just might be a way... 'All right, Mrs Bates,' she said. 'We'll do it your way'.* [2] N-COUNT: usu sing, usu adj N If you talk about the **way** someone does something, you are talking about the qualities their action has. ❑ *She smiled in a friendly way... He had a strange way of talking.* [3] N-COUNT: with supp, oft *in* N If a general statement or description is true **in** a particular **way**, this is the form of it that is true in a particular case. ❑ *Computerized reservation systems help airline profits in several ways... She was afraid in a way that was quite new to her.* [4] N-COUNT: *in* N with supp = respect You use **way** in expressions such as **in some ways**, **in many ways**, and **in every way** to indicate the degree or extent to which a statement is true. ❑ *In some ways, the official opening is a formality... She described her lover as 'perfect in every way'.* [5] N-PLURAL: with supp The **ways** of a particular person or group of people are their customs or their usual behaviour. ❑ *He denounces people who urge him to alter his ways... He said he was against returning to old authoritarian ways.* [6] N-SING: with poss If you refer to someone's **way**, you are referring to their usual or preferred type of behaviour. ❑ *She is now divorced and, in her usual resourceful way, has started her own business... Direct confrontation was not his way.* [7] N-COUNT: with supp You use **way** to refer to one particular opinion or interpretation of something, when others are possible. ❑ *I suppose that's one way of looking at it... With most of Dylan's lyrics, however, there are other ways of interpreting the words... Sometimes, the bank manager just doesn't see it your way.* [8] N-COUNT: with supp You use **way** when mentioning one of a number of possible, alternative results or decisions. ❑ *There is no indication which way the vote could go... The judge could have decided either way.* [9] N-SING: with supp The **way** you feel about something is your attitude to it or your opinion about it. ❑ *I'm terribly sorry – I had no idea you felt that way.* [10] N-SING: *the* N that If you mention **the way** that something happens, you are mentioning the fact that it happens. ❑ *I hate the way he manipulates people... You may remember the way each scene ended with someone looking pensive or significant.* [11] N-SING: poss N You use **way** in expressions such as **push** your **way**, **work** your **way**, or **eat** your **way**, followed by a prepositional phrase or adverb, in order to indicate movement, progress, or force as well as the action described by the verb. ❑ *She thrust her way into the crowd... He thought we were trying to buy our way into his company.*

12 N-COUNT: usu *the* N in sing, oft N *to* n — **The way** somewhere consists of the different places that you go through or the route that you take in order to get there. ❑ *Does anybody know the way to the bathroom?... I'm afraid I can't remember the way... We're not even a third of the way there.*

13 N-SING: with supp — If you go or look a particular **way**, you go or look in that direction. ❑ *As he strode into the kitchen, he passed Pop coming the other way... They paused at the top of the stairs, doubtful as to which way to go next... Could you look this way?*

14 N-SING: poss N — You can refer to the direction you are travelling in as your **way**. [SPOKEN] ❑ *She would say she was going my way and offer me a lift.*

15 N-SING: poss N — If you lose your **way**, you take a wrong or unfamiliar route, so that you do not know how to get to the place that you want to go to. If you find your **way**, you manage to get to the place that you want to go to. ❑ *The men lost their way in a sandstorm and crossed the border by mistake.*

16 N-COUNT: poss N — You talk about people going their different **ways** in order to say that their lives develop differently and they have less contact with each other. ❑ *It wasn't until we each went our separate ways that I began to learn how to do things for myself... You go your way and I'll go mine.*

17 N-SING: poss N — If something comes your **way**, you get it or receive it. ❑ *Take advantage of the opportunities coming your way in a couple of months... If I run into anything that might interest you, I'll send it your way.*

18 N-SING: *the*/poss N, *in/out of* N — If someone or something is in **the way**, they prevent you from moving forward or seeing clearly. ❑ *'You're standing in the way,' she said. 'Would you mind moving aside'... Get out of my way!*

19 N-SING: with supp — You use **way** in expressions such as **the right way up** and **the other way around** to refer to one of two or more possible positions or arrangements that something can have. ❑ *The flag was held the wrong way up by some spectators... It's important to fit it the right way round.*

20 ADV: ADV adv/prep [emphasis] — You can use **way** to emphasize, for example, that something is a great distance away or is very much below or above a particular level or amount. ❑ *Way down in the valley to the west is the town of Freiburg... These exam results are way above average.*

21 N-PLURAL: num N — If you split something a number of **ways**, you divide it into a number of different parts or quantities, usually fairly equal in size. ❑ *The region was split three ways, between Greece, Serbia and Bulgaria... Splitting the price six ways had still cost them each a bundle.* ♦ COMB in ADJ: ADJ n — **Way** is also a combining form. ❑ *...a simple three-way division.*

22 N-SING: *a* N, usu supp N — **Way** is used in expressions such as **a long way**, **a little way**, and **quite a way**, to say how far away something is or how far you have travelled. ❑ *Some of them live in places quite a long way from here... A little way further down the lane we passed the driveway to a house.*

23 N-SING: *a* N, usu supp N — **Way** is used in expressions such as **a long way, a little way,** and **quite a way**, to say how far away in time something is. ❑ *Success is still a long way off... August is still an awfully long way away.*

24 N-SING: predet/quant *the* N — You use **way** in expressions such as **all the way, most of the way** and **half the way** to refer to the extent to which an action has been completed. ❑ *He had unscrewed the caps most of the way... When was the last time you listened to an album all the way through?*

**PHRASES**

25 PHRASE: oft PHR adv/prep — You use **all the way** to emphasize how long a distance is. ❑ *He had to walk all the way home.*

26 PHRASE: PHR after v [emphasis] — You can use **all the way** to emphasize that your remark applies to every part of a situation, activity, or period of time. ❑ *Having started a revolution we must go all the way.*

27 PHRASE: V inflects — If someone says that you **can't have it both ways**, they are telling you that you have to choose between two things and cannot do or have them both. ❑ *Countries cannot have it both ways: the cost of a cleaner environment may sometimes be fewer jobs in dirty industries.*

28 PHRASE: PHR with cl = *incidentally* — You say **by the way** when you add something to what you are saying, especially something that you have just thought of. [SPOKEN] ❑ *The name Latifah, by the way, means 'delicate'... By the way, how did your seminar go?*

29 PREP-PHRASE: PREP n — You use **by way of** when you are explaining the purpose of something that you have said or are about to say. For example, if you say something **by way of an introduction**, you say it as an introduction. ❑ *'I get very superstitious about things like that,' she said by way of explanation.*

30 PHRASE: V inflects = *reform* — If someone **changes** their **ways** or **mends** their **ways**, they permanently improve their behaviour or their way of doing something. ❑ *What can be done to encourage convicted offenders to change their ways?*

31 PHRASE: V inflects, usu PHR *for* n — If you **clear the way**, **open the way**, or **prepare the way** for something, you create an opportunity for it to happen. ❑ *The talks are meant to clear the way for formal negotiations on a new constitution... The decision could open the way for other children to sue their parents.*

32 PHRASE: PHR after v, v-link PHR [disapproval] — If you say that someone takes **the easy way out**, you disapprove of them because they do what is easiest for them in a difficult situation, rather than dealing with it properly. ❑ *It is the easy way out to blame others for our failure.*

33 PHRASE: PHR with cl — You use **either way** in order to introduce a statement which is true in each of the two possible or alternative cases that you have just mentioned. ❑ *The sea may rise or the land may fall; either way the sand dunes will be gone in a short time.*

34 PHRASE: usu v-link PHR [approval] — If you say that a particular type of action or development is **the way forward**, you approve of it because it is likely to lead to success. ❑ *...people who genuinely believe that anarchy is the way forward.*

35 PHRASE: V inflects — If someone **gets** their **way** or **has** their **way**, nobody stops them doing what they want to do. You can also say that someone **gets** their **own** way or **has** their **own way**. ❑ *She is very good at using her charm to get her way.*

36 PHRASE: V inflects, PHR n — If one thing **gives way to** another, the first thing is replaced by the second. ❑ *First he had been numb. Then the numbness gave way to anger.*

37 PHRASE: V inflects — If an object that is supporting something **gives way**, it breaks or collapses, so that it can no longer support that thing. ❑ *The hook in the ceiling had given way and the lamp had fallen blazing on to the table.*

38 PHRASE: V inflects, usu PHR *to* n = *give in, yield* — If you **give way to** someone or something that you have been resisting, you stop resisting and allow yourself to be persuaded or controlled by them. [WRITTEN] ❑ *It seems the President has given way to pressure from the hardliners.*

39 PHRASE: V inflects, oft PHR *to* n — If a moving person, a vehicle, or its driver **gives way**, they slow down or stop in order to allow other people or vehicles to pass in front of them. [BRIT] ❑ *Give way to traffic coming from the left.*

✔ in AM, use **yield**

40 PHRASE: V inflects, PHR -ing — If you say that someone or something **has a way of** doing a particular thing, you mean that they often do it. ❑ *Bosses have a way of always finding out about such things.*

41 PHRASE: V inflects, PHR n [approval] — If you say that a person **has a way** with something or someone, you mean that that person seems to have a natural skill or instinct for dealing with them. [mainly SPOKEN] ❑ *Constance doesn't have a way with words like you do.*

42 PHRASE [emphasis] — You use **in no way** or **not in any way** to emphasize that a statement is not at all true. ❑ *A spokesman insisted the two events were 'in no way related'.*

43 PHRASE: PHR with cl [vagueness] — If you say that something is true **in a way**, you mean that although it is not completely true, it is true to a limited extent or in certain respects. You use **in a way** to reduce the force of a statement. ❑ *In a way, I suppose I'm frightened of failing... It made things very unpleasant in a way.*

44 PHRASE: V inflects — If you say that someone **gets in the way** or **is in the way**, you are annoyed because their presence or their actions stop you doing something properly. ❑ *'We wouldn't get in the way,' Suzanne promised. 'We'd just stand quietly in a corner.'*

45 PHRASE: V inflects, oft PHR *of* n — To **get in the way of** something means to make it difficult for it to happen, continue, or be appreciated properly. ❑ *She had a job which never got in the way of her leisure interests.*

46 If you **know** your **way around** a particular subject, system, or job, or if you **know** your **way about** it, you know all the procedures and facts about it. ❑ *He knows his way around the intricate maze of European law.*
PHRASE: V inflects, PHR n

47 If you **lead the way** along a particular route, you go along it in front of someone in order to show them where to go. ❑ *She grabbed his suitcase and led the way.*
PHRASE: V inflects

48 If a person or group **leads the way in** a particular activity, they are the first person or group to do it or they make the most new developments in it. ❑ *Sony has also led the way in shrinking the size of compact-disc players.*
PHRASE: V inflects, usu PHR *in* -ing/n

49 If you say that someone or something **has come a long way**, you mean that they have developed, progressed, or become very successful. ❑ *He has come a long way since the days he could only afford one meal a day.*
PHRASE: *have* inflects, oft PHR *since* n

50 You can use **by a long way** to emphasize that something is, for example, much better, worse, or bigger than any other thing of that kind. ❑ *It was, by a long way, the worst meeting I have ever attended.*
PHRASE: PHR with cl, compar/superl PHR [emphasis]

51 If you say that something is **a long way from** being true, you are emphasizing that it is definitely not true. ❑ *She is a long way from being the richest person in Britain.*
PHRASE: v-link PHR n/-ing [emphasis]

52 If you say that something **goes a long way towards** doing a particular thing, you mean that it is an important factor in achieving that thing. ❑ *Although by no means a cure, it goes a long way towards making the patient's life more tolerable.*
PHRASE: V inflects, usu PHR *towards/to* -ing/n

53 If you say that someone has **lost** their **way**, you are criticizing them because they do not have any good ideas any more, or seem to have become unsure about what to do. ❑ *Why has the White House lost its way on tax and budget policy?*
PHRASE: V inflects [disapproval]

54 When you **make** your **way** somewhere, you walk or travel there. ❑ *He made his way home at last.*
PHRASE: V inflects, PHR prep/adv

55 If one person or thing **makes way for** another, the first is replaced by the second. ❑ *He said he was prepared to make way for younger people in the party.*
PHRASE: V inflects, usu PHR *for* n

56 If you say **there's no way** that something will happen, you are emphasizing that you think it will definitely not happen. ❑ *There was absolutely no way that we were going to be able to retrieve it.*
PHRASE: V inflects, usu PHR that [emphasis]

57 You can say **no way** as an emphatic way of saying no. [INFORMAL] ❑ *Mike, no way am I playing cards with you for money.*
PHRASE [emphasis]

58 You use **in the way of** or **by way of** in order to specify the kind of thing you are talking about. ❑ *Latvia is a country without much in the way of natural resources... Meetings held today produced little in the way of an agreement... The man with whom she maintains a relationship provides nothing by way of support.*
PHRASE: PHR n, usu amount/n PHR n

59 If you **are on** your **way**, you have started your journey somewhere. ❑ *He has been allowed to leave the country and is on his way to Britain... By sunrise tomorrow we'll be on our way.*
PHRASE: V inflects, oft PHR prep/adv

60 If something happens **on the way** or **along the way**, it happens during the course of a particular event or process. ❑ *You may have to learn a few new skills along the way.*
PHRASE

61 If you are **on** your **way** or **well on** your **way to** something, you have made so much progress that you are almost certain to achieve that thing. ❑ *I am now out of hospital and well on the way to recovery.*
PHRASE: usu v-link PHR *to* n/-ing

62 If something is **on the way**, it will arrive soon. ❑ *The forecasters say more snow is on the way... She is married with twin sons and a third child on the way.*
PHRASE: v-link PHR, *with/have* n PHR

63 You can use **one way or another** or **one way or the other** when you want to say that something definitely happens, but without giving any details about how it happens. ❑ *You know pretty well everyone here, one way or the other.*
PHRASE: PHR after v, PHR with cl [vagueness]

64 You use **one way or the other** or **one way or another** to refer to two possible decisions or conclusions that have previously been mentioned, without stating which one is reached or preferred. ❑ *We've got to make our decision one way or the other... I didn't really care one way or another.*
PHRASE: PHR after v

65 You use **the other way around** or **the other way round** to refer to the opposite of what you have just said. ❑ *You'd think you were the one who did me the favor, and not the other way around.*
PHRASE

66 If something or someone is **on the way out** or **on** their **way out**, they are likely to disappear or to be replaced very soon. ❑ *There are encouraging signs that cold war attitudes are on the way out.*
PHRASE: usu v-link PHR

67 If you **go out of** your **way to** do something, for example to help someone, you make a special effort to do it. ❑ *He was very kind to me and seemed to go out of his way to help me.*
PHRASE: V inflects, usu PHR to-inf

68 If you **keep out of** someone's **way** or **stay out of** their **way**, you avoid them or do not get involved with them. ❑ *I'd kept out of his way as much as I could... He warned the army to stay out of the way of the relief effort.*
PHRASE: V inflects

69 When something is **out of the way**, it has finished or you have dealt with it, so that it is no longer a problem or needs no more time spent on it. ❑ *The plan has to remain confidential at least until the local elections are out of the way.*
PHRASE: v-link PHR, PHR after v

70 If you **go** your **own way**, you do what you want rather than what everyone else does or expects. ❑ *In school I was a loner. I went my own way.*
PHRASE: V inflects

71 You use **in the same way** to introduce a situation that you are comparing with one that you have just mentioned, because there is a strong similarity between them. ❑ *There is no reason why a gifted aircraft designer should also be a capable pilot. In the same way, a brilliant pilot can be a menace behind the wheel of a car.*
PHRASE: PHR with cl = *likewise*

72 You can use **that way** and **this way** to refer to a statement or comment that you have just made. ❑ *Some of us have habits few people know about and we keep it this way... We have a beautiful city and we pray it stays that way.*
PHRASE: PHR after v, adj PHR

73 You can use **that way** or **this way** to refer to an action or situation that you have just mentioned, when you go on to mention the likely consequence or effect of it. ❑ *Keep the soil moist. That way, the seedling will flourish.*
PHRASE: PHR with cl

74 If an activity or plan is **under way**, it has begun and is now taking place. ❑ *A full-scale security operation is now under way... The court case got under way last autumn.*
PHRASE: usu v-link PHR

75 **Every which way** and **any which way** are used to emphasize that something happens, or might happen, in a lot of different ways, or using a lot of different methods. [AM; also BRIT, INFORMAL] ❑ *He re-ran the experiment every which way he could.*
PHRASE: PHR after v, oft PHR cl [emphasis]

76 **Every which way** is used to emphasize that things move in a lot of different directions or are arranged in a lot of different positions. [AM; also BRIT, INFORMAL] ❑ *...cars parked every which way.*
PHRASE: PHR after v [emphasis]

77 to see **the error of** your **ways** → see **error**.

**-way** /-weɪ/ **-way** combines with numbers to form adjectives that describe a means of communication that functions or takes place between the stated number of people. ❑ *...a two-way radio. ...a system of three-way communication.* → See also **one-way, two-way**.
COMB in ADJ

**way|lay** /weɪleɪ, AM -leɪ/ **(waylays, waylaying, waylaid)** If someone **waylays** you, they stop you when you are going somewhere, for example in order to talk to you, to steal something from you, or to attack you. ❑ *The trucks are being waylaid by bandits... I'm sorry, Nick, I got waylaid.*
VERB
V n
*get* V-ed

**way of life** **(ways of life)** 1 A **way of life** is the behaviour and habits that are typical of a particular person or group, or that are chosen by them. ❑ *Mining activities have totally disrupted the traditional way of life of the Yanomami Indians.*
N-COUNT: usu sing, oft poss N, adj N

2 If you describe a particular activity as **a way of life** for someone, you mean that it has become a very important and regular thing in their life, rather than something they do or experience occasionally. ❑ *She likes it so much it's become a way of life for her.*
N-COUNT: usu sing

**way-out** If you describe someone or something as **way-out**, you are critical of them because they are very unusual, often in a way that is very modern or fashionable. [INFORMAL] ❑ *They will not allow your more way-out ideas to pass unchallenged.*
ADJ [disapproval] = *weird*

**way|side** /weɪsaɪd/ **(waysides)** 1 **The wayside** is the side of the road. [LITERARY]
N-COUNT: usu *the* N in sing

2 If a person or plan **falls by the wayside**, they fail or stop before they complete what they set out to do. ❑ *Amateurs fall by the wayside when the going gets tough.* PHRASE: V inflects

**way|sta|tion** **(way stations)** 1 A **way station** is a place where people stop to eat and rest when they are on a long journey. N-COUNT 2 A **way station** is a small station between two large stations on a railway. [AM] N-COUNT

**way|ward** /weɪwəʳd/ If you describe a person or their behaviour as **wayward**, you mean that they behave in a selfish, bad, or unpredictable way, and are difficult to control. ❑ *...wayward children with a history of severe emotional problems.* ADJ: usu ADJ n

**WC** /dʌbᵊljuː siː/ **(WCs)** A toilet is sometimes referred to as a **WC**, especially on signs or in advertisements for houses, flats, or hotels. **WC** is an abbreviation for 'water closet'. [BRIT] N-COUNT = toilet

**we** /wɪ, STRONG wiː/ ◆◆◆

> **We** is the first person plural pronoun. **We** is used as the subject of a verb.

1 A speaker or writer uses **we** to refer both to himself or herself and to one or more other people as a group. You can use **we** before a noun to make it clear which group of people you are referring to. ❑ *We ordered another bottle of champagne... We students outnumbered our teachers.* PRON 2 **We** is sometimes used to refer to people in general. ❑ *We need to take care of our bodies.* PRON 3 A speaker or writer may use **we** instead of 'I' in order to include the audience or reader in what they are saying, especially when discussing how a talk or book is organized. [FORMAL] ❑ *We will now consider the raw materials from which the body derives energy.* PRON

**weak** /wiːk/ **(weaker, weakest)** ◆◆◇ 1 If someone is **weak**, they are not healthy or do not have good muscles, so that they cannot move quickly or carry heavy things. ❑ *I was too weak to move or think or speak... His arms and legs were weak.* ADJ ≠ strong ♦ **weak|ly** *'I'm all right,' Max said weakly, but his breathing came in jagged gasps.* ADV: ADV with v ♦ **weak|ness** *Symptoms of anaemia include weakness, fatigue and iron deficiency.* N-UNCOUNT 2 If someone has an organ or sense that is **weak**, it is not very effective or powerful, or is likely to fail. ❑ *Until the beating, Cantanco's eyesight had been weak, but adequate... She tired easily and had a weak heart.* ADJ 3 If you describe someone as **weak**, you mean that they are not very confident or determined, so that they are often frightened or worried, or easily influenced by other people. ❑ *You have been conditioned to believe that it is weak to be scared.* ADJ ≠ strong ♦ **weak|ness** *Many people felt that admitting to stress was a sign of weakness.* N-UNCOUNT 4 If you describe someone's voice or smile as **weak**, you mean that it not very loud or big, suggesting that the person lacks confidence, enthusiasm, or physical strength. ❑ *His weak voice was almost inaudible.* ADJ = feeble ♦ **weak|ly** *He smiled weakly at reporters.* ADV: ADV after v 5 If an object or surface is **weak**, it breaks easily and cannot support a lot of weight or resist a lot of strain. ❑ *The owner said the bird may have escaped through a weak spot in the aviary... Swimming is helpful for bones that are porous and weak.* ADJ ≠ strong 6 A **weak** physical force does not have much power or intensity. ❑ *The molecules in regular liquids are held together by relatively weak bonds.* ADV ≠ strong ♦ **weak|ly** *The mineral is weakly magnetic.* ADV: ADV adj/-ed, ADV after v 7 If individuals or groups are **weak**, they do not have any power or influence. ❑ *The council was too weak to do anything about it.* ADJ = powerless ♦ **The weak** are people who are weak. ❑ *He voiced his solidarity with the weak and defenceless.* N-PLURAL: the N ♦ **weak|ness** *It made me feel patronised, in a position of weakness.* N-UNCOUNT = impotence 8 A **weak** government or leader does not have much control, and is not prepared or able to act firmly or severely. ❑ *The changes come after mounting criticism that the government is weak and indecisive... The chief editorial writer also blames weak leadership for the current crisis.* ADJ ≠ strong ♦ **weak|ly** *...the weakly-led movement for reform.* ADV ♦ **weak|ness** *Officials fear that he might interpret the emphasis on diplomacy as a sign of weakness.* N-UNCOUNT 9 If you describe something such a country's currency, economy, industry, or government as **weak**, you mean that it is not successful, and may be likely to fail or collapse. ❑ *The weak dollar means American goods are relative bargains for foreigners.* ADJ ≠ strong ♦ **weak|ness** *The weakness of his regime is showing more and more.* N-UNCOUNT: usu with poss 10 If something such as an argument or case is **weak**, it is not convincing or there is little evidence to support it. ❑ *Do you think the prosecution made any particular errors, or did they just have a weak case?* ADJ ≠ strong ♦ **weak|ly** *The doctor weakly puts the case that the mother-to-be has many relatives, so needs less support from the hospital.* ADV: ADV before v ♦ **weak|ness** **(weaknesses)** *...the strengths and weaknesses of the government's case.* N-VAR 11 A **weak** drink, chemical, or drug contains very little of a particular substance, for example because a lot of water has been added to it. ❑ *...a cup of weak tea. ...a very weak bleach solution.* ADJ ≠ strong 12 Your **weak** points are the qualities or talents you do not possess, or the things you are not very good at. ❑ *Geography was my weak subject... His short stories tend to be weak on plot.* ADJ: oft ADJ on n ≠ strong ♦ **weak|ness** *His only weakness is his temperament.* N-VAR 13 → See also **weakness**.

**weak|en** /wiːkən/ **(weakens, weakening, weakened)** ◆◇◇ 1 If you **weaken** something or if it **weakens**, it becomes less strong or less powerful. ❑ *The recession has weakened so many firms that many can no longer survive... Family structures are weakening and breaking up.* VERB ≠ strengthen V n V 2 If your resolve **weakens** or if something **weakens** it, you become less determined or less certain about taking a particular course of action that you had previously decided to take. ❑ *Jennie weakened, and finally relented... The verdict hasn't weakened his resolve to fight the charges against him.* VERB V V n 3 If something **weakens** you, it causes you to lose some of your physical strength. ❑ *Malnutrition obviously weakens the patient.* VERB V n 4 If something **weakens** an object, it does something to it which causes it to become less firm and more likely to break. ❑ *A bomb blast had weakened an area of brick on the back wall.* VERB V n

**weak-kneed** If you describe someone as **weak-kneed**, you mean that they are unable or unwilling to do anything because they are influenced by a strong emotion such as fear. [INFORMAL] ❑ *He would need all his authority to keep the weak-kneed volunteers from bolting.* ADJ

**weak|ling** /wiːklɪŋ/ **(weaklings)** If you describe a person or an animal as a **weakling**, you mean that they are physically weak. N-COUNT [disapproval]

**weak|ness** /wiːknəs/ **(weaknesses)** If you have a **weakness for** something, you like it very much, although this is perhaps surprising or undesirable. ❑ *Stephen himself had a weakness for cats... His one weakness, apart from aeroplanes, is ice cream.* N-COUNT: usu sing, oft N for n → See also **weak**.

**weal** /wiːl/ **(weals)** A **weal** is a swelling made on someone's skin by a blow, especially from something sharp or thin such as a sword or whip. [BRIT] N-COUNT = welt

> in AM, use **welt**

**wealth** /welθ/ ◆◇◇ 1 **Wealth** is the possession of a large amount of money, property, or other valuable things. You can also refer to a particular person's money or property as their **wealth**. ❑ *Economic reform has brought relative wealth to peasant farmers.* N-UNCOUNT = affluence 2 If you say that someone or something has **a wealth of** good qualities or things, you are emphasizing that they have a very large number or amount of them. [FORMAL] ❑ *...such a wealth of creative expertise.* N-SING: a N of n [emphasis] = abundance

**wealthy** /welθi/ **(wealthier, wealthiest)** Someone who is **wealthy** has a large amount of money, property, or valuable possessions. ❑ *...a wealthy international businessman.* ADJ = affluent, rich ♦ **The wealthy** are people who are wealthy. ❑ *...a measure to raise income taxes on the wealthy.* N-PLURAL: the N = the rich

**wean** /wiːn/ **(weans, weaning, weaned)**
1 When a baby or baby animal **is weaned**, its mother stops feeding it milk and starts giving it other food, especially solid food. ❑ *When would be the best time to start weaning my baby?... Phil took the labrador home and is weaning him off milk on to meat.* — VERB; V n; V n off/from n
2 If you **wean** someone **off** a habit or something they like, you gradually make them stop doing it or liking it, especially when you think is bad for them. ❑ *You are given pills with small quantities of nicotine to wean you from cigarettes.* — VERB; V n off/from n

**weap|on** /wepən/ **(weapons)** ◆◆◇
1 A **weapon** is an object such as a gun, a knife, or a missile, which is used to kill or hurt people in a fight or a war. ❑ *...nuclear weapons.* — N-COUNT
2 A **weapon** is something such as knowledge about a particular subject, which you can use to protect yourself or to get what you want in a difficult situation. ❑ *I attack politicians with the one weapon they don't have, a sense of humor.* — N-COUNT

**weap|on|ize** /wepənaɪz/ **(weaponizes, weaponizing, weaponized)**

in BRIT, also use **weaponise**

If a substance or material **is weaponized**, it is used as a weapon or made into a weapon. If an area **is weaponized**, it is used as a location for weapons. ❑ *They were close to weaponizing ricin - a lethal plant toxin. ...the plan to weaponize outer space.* — VERB; V n; V n

**wea|pon|ry** /wepənri/ **Weaponry** is all the weapons that a group or country has or that are available to it. ❑ *...rich nations, armed with superior weaponry.* — N-UNCOUNT

**weapons-grade** **Weapons-grade** substances such as uranium or plutonium are of a quality which makes them suitable for use in the manufacture of nuclear weapons. ❑ *...equipment which can produce weapons-grade uranium.* — ADJ: ADJ n

**wear** /weəʳ/ **(wears, wearing, wore, worn)** ◆◆◇
1 When you **wear** something such as clothes, shoes, or jewellery, you have them on your body or on part of your body. ❑ *He was wearing a brown uniform... I sometimes wear contact lenses... She can't make her mind up what to wear.* — VERB; V n
2 If you **wear** your hair or beard in a particular way, you have it cut or styled in that way. ❑ *She wore her hair in a long braid... He wore a full moustache.* — VERB; V n prep/adv; V n
3 If you **wear** a particular expression, that expression is on your face and shows the emotions that you are feeling. ❑ *When we drove through the gates, she wore a look of amazement.* — VERB; V n
4 You use **wear** to refer to clothes that are suitable for a certain time or place. For example, **evening wear** is clothes suitable for the evening. ❑ *The shop stocks an extensive range of beach wear.* — N-UNCOUNT: supp N
5 **Wear** is the amount or type of use that something has over a period of time. ❑ *You'll get more wear out of a hat if you choose one in a neutral colour.* — N-UNCOUNT = use
6 **Wear** is the damage or change that is caused by something being used a lot or for a long time. ❑ *...a large, well-upholstered armchair which showed signs of wear.* — N-UNCOUNT
7 If something **wears**, it becomes thinner or weaker because it is constantly being used over a long period of time. ❑ *The stone steps, dating back to 1855, are beginning to wear... Your horse needs new shoes if the shoe has worn thin or smooth.* — VERB; V; V adj
8 You can use **wear** to talk about how well something lasts over a period of time. For example, if something **wears well**, it still seems quite new or useful after a long time or a lot of use. ❑ *Ten years on, the original concept was wearing well.* — VERB; V adv

**PHRASES**
9 If one person in a couple, especially the woman, **wears the pants**, or in British English **wears the trousers**, they are the one who makes all the decisions. [INFORMAL] ❑ *She may give the impression that she wears the trousers but it's Tim who makes the final decisions.* — PHRASE: V inflects
10 If your patience or temper **is wearing thin**, you are becoming annoyed and are likely to get angry soon. ❑ *Her husband was sympathetic at first but his patience soon wore thin.* — PHRASE: V inflects, usu cont
11 If you say that something **is wearing thin**, you mean that people do not find it funny or interesting any more and are becoming annoyed with it, because they have seen or heard it so many times. ❑ *Some of Wilson's eccentricities are beginning to wear thin.* — PHRASE: V inflects, usu cont
12 If you say that someone is **the worse for wear**, you mean that they are tired, ill, or in a bad state because they have been very active, been through a difficult experience, or been drinking alcohol. [INFORMAL] ❑ *He arrived on January 9, disheveled and much the worse for wear.* — PHRASE: v-link PHR

♦ **wear away** If you **wear** something **away** or if it **wears away**, it becomes thin and eventually disappears because it is used a lot or rubbed a lot. ❑ *It had a saddle with springs sticking out, which wore away the seat of my pants... The softer rock wears away.* — PHRASAL VERB; V P n (not pron); V P; Also V n P

♦ **wear down**
1 If you **wear** something **down** or if it **wears down**, it becomes flatter or smoother as a result of constantly rubbing against something else. ❑ *Pipe smokers sometimes wear down the tips of their teeth where they grip their pipes... The machines start to wear down, they don't make as many nuts and bolts as they used to... Elephants wear the tusk down faster than they can grow it.* — PHRASAL VERB; V P n (not pron); V P; V n P
2 If you **wear** someone **down**, you make them gradually weaker or less determined until they eventually do what you want. ❑ *They hoped the waiting and the uncertainty would wear down my resistance... He believed that he could wear her down if he only asked often enough.* — PHRASAL VERB; V P n (not pron); V n P

♦ **wear off** If a sensation or feeling **wears off**, it disappears slowly until it no longer exists or has any effect. ❑ *For many the philosophy was merely a fashion, and the novelty soon wore off... Now that the initial shock was wearing off, he was in considerable pain.* — PHRASAL VERB; V P; V P

♦ **wear on** If you say that time **wears on**, you mean that it passes, especially when it seems to pass slowly. ❑ *As the day wore on Brand found himself increasingly impressed.* — PHRASAL VERB = go on; V P

♦ **wear out**
1 When something **wears out** or when you **wear** it **out**, it is used so much that it becomes thin or weak and unable to be used any more. ❑ *Every time she consulted her watch, she wondered if the batteries were wearing out... Horses used for long-distance riding tend to wear their shoes out more quickly... He wore out his shoes wandering around Mexico City.* — PHRASAL VERB; V P; V n P; V P n (not pron)
2 If something **wears** you **out**, it makes you feel extremely tired. [INFORMAL] ❑ *The past few days had really worn him out... The young people run around kicking a ball, wearing themselves out... The effect of the continuous attacks has been to wear out his troops.* — PHRASAL VERB; V n P; V pron-refl P; V P n (not pron)
3 → See also **worn out**.

**wear|able** /weərəbᵊl/ **Wearable** clothes are practical, comfortable, and suitable for ordinary people to wear, rather than being very unusual or extreme. ❑ *It's fashionable but wearable, and it's easy to look after.* — ADJ

**wear and tear** /weər ən teəʳ/ **Wear and tear** is the damage or change that is caused to something when it is being used normally. ❑ *...the problem of wear and tear on the equipment in the harsh desert conditions.* — N-UNCOUNT

**wear|er** /weərəʳ/ **(wearers)** You can use **wearer** to indicate that someone is wearing a certain thing on a particular occasion or that they often wear a certain thing. ❑ *These suits are designed to protect the wearer from cold shock as they enter the water... The mascara is suitable for contact lens wearers.* — N-COUNT: oft N of n, n N

**wear|ing** /weərɪŋ/ If you say that a situation or activity is **wearing**, you mean that it requires a lot of energy and makes you feel mentally or physically tired. ❑ *She finds the continual confrontation very wearing.* — ADJ: usu v-link ADJ = tiring, exhausting

**wea|ri|some** /wɪərɪsəm/ If you describe something as **wearisome**, you mean that it is — ADJ = tiresome very tiring and boring or frustrating. [FORMAL] ❑ *...a long and wearisome journey... Sympathising with him eventually becomes somewhat wearisome.*

**wea|ry** /wɪəri/ **(wearies, wearying, wearied, wearier, weariest)** [1] If you are **weary**, you are very tired. ❑ *Rachel looked pale and weary. ...a weary traveller.* [2] If you are **weary of** something, you have become tired of it and have lost your enthusiasm for it. ❑ *They're getting awfully weary of this silly war.* [3] If you **weary** of something or it **wearies** you, you become tired of it and lose your enthusiasm for it. [FORMAL] ❑ *The public had wearied of his repeated warnings of a revolution that never seemed to start... The political hysteria soon wearied him and he dropped the newspaper to the floor.*
ADJ = exhausted; ADJ: v-link ADJ *of* n/-ing = tired; VERB = tire; V *of* n/-ing; V n

**wea|sel** /wiːzᵊl/ **(weasels)** A **weasel** is a small wild animal with a long thin body, a tail, short legs, and reddish-brown fur. N-COUNT

**weath|er** /weðəʳ/ **(weathers, weathering, weathered)** ◆◆◇ [1] The **weather** is the condition of the atmosphere in one area at a particular time, for example if it is raining, hot, or windy. ❑ *The weather was bad... I like cold weather... Fishing is possible in virtually any weather. ...the weather conditions.* [2] If something such as wood or rock **weathers** or **is weathered**, it changes colour or shape as a result of the wind, sun, rain, or cold. ❑ *Unpainted wooden furniture weathers to a grey colour... This rock has been weathered and eroded.* ♦ **weath|ered** *The facade of the building was a little weathered... The man had a worn, weathered face.* [3] If you **weather** a difficult time or a difficult situation, you survive it and are able to continue normally after it has passed or ended. ❑ *The government has weathered its worst political crisis.* to **weather the storm** → see **storm**.
N-UNCOUNT; VERB; V; *be* V-ed; ADJ = weather-beaten; VERB; V n

**PHRASES** [4] If you say that someone **is making heavy weather of** a task, you are critical of them because they are doing it in an inefficient way and are making it seem more difficult than it really is. [BRIT] ❑ *Some of the riders in this section made heavy weather of the cross-country race.* [5] If you say that you are **under the weather**, you mean that you feel slightly ill. ❑ *I was still feeling a bit under the weather.*
PHRASE: V inflects, PHR n [disapproval]; PHRASE: v-link PHR = unwell

**weather-beaten** also **weatherbeaten.** [1] If your face or skin is **weather-beaten**, it is rough with deep lines because you have spent a lot of time outside in bad weather. ❑ *...a stout man with a ruddy, weather-beaten face.* [2] Something that is **weather-beaten** is rough and slightly damaged after being outside for a long time. ❑ *They would look out through the cracks of their weather-beaten door.*
ADJ: usu ADJ n = weathered; ADJ = weathered

**weath|er fore|cast** **(weather forecasts)** A **weather forecast** is a statement saying what the weather will be like the next day or for the next few days. N-COUNT

**weath|er fore|cast|er** **(weather forecasters)** A **weather forecaster** is a person whose job is to study weather conditions and make reports predicting what the weather will be like for the next few days. N-COUNT

**weath|er girl** **(weather girls)** A **weather girl** is a young woman who presents weather forecasts at regular times on television or radio. N-COUNT

**weather|man** /weðəʳmæn/ **(weathermen)** also **weather man.** A **weatherman** is a man who presents weather forecasts at regular times on television or radio. N-COUNT

**weather|proof** /weðəʳpruːf/ Something that is **weatherproof** is made of material which protects it from the weather or keeps out wind and rain. ❑ *Use a weatherproof rucksack to carry your camera and lenses around in.* ADJ

**weath|er sta|tion** **(weather stations)** A **weather station** is a place where facts about the weather are recorded and studied. N-COUNT

**weath|er vane** **(weather vanes)** A **weather vane** is a metal object on the roof of a building which turns round as the wind blows. It is used to show the direction of the wind. N-COUNT

**weather|woman** /weðəʳwʊmən/ **(weatherwomen)** also **weather woman.** A **weatherwoman** is a woman who presents weather forecasts at regular times on television or radio. N-COUNT

**weave** /wiːv/ **(weaves, weaving, wove, woven)**

> ✓ The form **weaved** is used for the past tense and past participle for meaning 4.

[1] If you **weave** cloth or a carpet, you make it by crossing threads over and under each other using a frame or machine called a loom. ❑ *They would spin and weave cloth, cook and attend to the domestic side of life... In one room, young mothers weave while babies doze in their laps.* ♦ **wo|ven** *...woven cotton fabrics.* ♦ **weav|ing** *When I studied weaving, I became intrigued with natural dyes.* [2] A particular **weave** is the way in which the threads are arranged in a cloth or carpet. ❑ *Fabrics with a close weave are ideal for painting.* [3] If you **weave** something such as a basket, you make it by crossing long plant stems or fibres over and under each other. ❑ *Jenny weaves baskets from willow she grows herself.* ♦ **wo|ven** *The floors are covered with woven straw mats.* [4] If you **weave** your **way** somewhere, you move between and around things as you go there. ❑ *The cars then weaved in and out of traffic at top speed... He weaves his way through a crowd.* [5] If you **weave** details into a story or design, you include them, so that they are closely linked together or become an important part of the story or design. [WRITTEN] ❑ *She weaves imaginative elements into her poems... Bragg weaves together the histories of his main characters.*
VERB; V n; V; ADJ: usu ADJ n; N-UNCOUNT; N-COUNT: usu supp N; VERB; V n; ADJ: usu ADJ n; VERB; V prep; V *way* prep/adv; VERB; V n *into* n; V pl-n with *together*

**weav|er** /wiːvəʳ/ **(weavers)** A **weaver** is a person who weaves cloth, carpets, or baskets. N-COUNT

**web** /web/ **(webs)** [1] A **web** is the thin net made by a spider from a sticky substance which it produces in its body. ❑ *...the spider's web in the window.* [2] A **web** is a complicated pattern of connections or relationships, sometimes considered as an obstacle or a danger. ❑ *He's forced to untangle a complex web of financial dealings... They accused him of weaving a web of lies and deceit.* [3] **The Web** is the same as the **World Wide Web**. [COMPUTING]
N-COUNT = cobweb; N-COUNT: usu sing, oft N *of* n; N-PROPER

**webbed** /webd/ **Webbed** feet or toes have a piece of skin between the toes. Water birds such as ducks have webbed feet. ADJ: ADJ n

**web|bing** /webɪŋ/ **Webbing** is strong material which is woven in strips and used to make belts or straps, or used in seats to support the springs. N-UNCOUNT

**web|cam** /webkæm/ **(webcams)** also **Webcam.** A **webcam** is a video camera that takes pictures which can be viewed on a website. The pictures are often of something that is happening while you watch. [COMPUTING] N-COUNT: usu sing

**web|cast** /webkɑːst, -kæst/ **(webcasts)** also **Webcast.** A **webcast** is an event such as a musical performance which you can listen to or watch on the Internet. [COMPUTING] N-COUNT

**web|master** /webmɑːstəʳ, -mæst-/ **(webmasters)** also **Webmaster.** A **webmaster** is someone who is in charge of a website, especially someone who does that as their job. [COMPUTING] N-COUNT: usu sing

**web page** **(web pages)** also **Web page.** A **web page** is a set of data or information which is designed to be viewed as part of a website. [COMPUTING] N-COUNT

**web ring** **(web rings)** also **Web ring, webring.** A **web ring** is a set of related websites that you can visit one after the other. [COMPUTING] ❑ *Log on to the Hammer Web ring, with 12 more sites devoted to macabre movies.* N-COUNT

**web|site** /websaɪt/ **(websites)** also **Web site, web site.** A **website** is a set of data and N-COUNT information about a particular subject which is available on the Internet. [COMPUTING]

**web|space** /wɛbspeɪs/ **Webspace** is computer memory that you can use to create web pages. [COMPUTING] ❑ *There's also 5Mb of webspace so that you can create your own personal web site.* N-UNCOUNT

**web|zine** /wɛbziːn/ **(webzines)** A **webzine** is a website which contains the kind of articles, pictures, and advertisements that you would find in a magazine. [COMPUTING] N-COUNT

**wed** /wɛd/ **(weds, wedded)**

> The form **wed** is used in the present tense and is the past tense. The past participle can be either **wed** or **wedded**.

If one person **weds** another or if two people **wed** or **are wed**, they get married. [JOURNALISM or OLD-FASHIONED] ❑ *In 1952 she wed film director Roger Vadim... The couple wed late at night in front of just nine guests.* ➔ See also **newlywed**, **wedded**. V-RECIP: no cont = marry; V n; pl-n V

**Wed.** also **Weds. Wed.** is a written abbreviation for **Wednesday**. ❑ *Our big task for tomorrow (Wed.) is to get them exit visas.*

**we'd** /wɪd, STRONG wiːd/ 1 **We'd** is the usual spoken form of 'we had', especially when 'had' is an auxiliary verb. ❑ *Come on, George, we'd better get back now... At the time we'd really nothing to tell the police.* 2 **We'd** is the usual spoken form of 'we would'. ❑ *I don't know how we'd have managed without her!*

**wed|ded** /wɛdɪd/ 1 If you are **wedded to** something such as an idea, you support it so strongly or like it so much that you are unable to give it up. [FORMAL] ❑ *Conservationists are mostly wedded to preserving diversity in nature.* ADJ: v-link ADJ *to* n = committed
2 **Wedded** means the same as **married**. [FORMAL] ❑ *He proposed she become his lawfully wedded wife.* ADJ: ADJ n

**wed|ding** /wɛdɪŋ/ **(weddings)** A **wedding** is a marriage ceremony and the party or special meal that often takes place after the ceremony. ❑ *Most Britons want a traditional wedding. ...a wedding present. ...the couple's 22nd wedding anniversary.* ◆◇◇ N-COUNT

**wed|ding band** **(wedding bands)** A **wedding band** is the same as a **wedding ring**. N-COUNT

**wed|ding cake** **(wedding cakes)** A **wedding cake** is a large cake, usually decorated with icing, that is served at a wedding reception. N-VAR

**wed|ding dress** **(wedding dresses)** A **wedding dress** is a special dress that a woman wears at her wedding. N-COUNT

**wed|ding ring** **(wedding rings)** A **wedding ring** is a ring that you wear to show that you are married. N-COUNT = wedding band

**wedge** /wɛdʒ/ **(wedges, wedging, wedged)**
1 If you **wedge** something, you force it to remain in a particular position by holding it there tightly or by fixing something next to it to prevent it from moving. ❑ *I shut the shed door and wedged it with a log of wood... We slammed the gate after them, wedging it shut with planks.* VERB; V n; V n adj
2 If you **wedge** something somewhere, you fit it there tightly. ❑ *Wedge the plug into the hole.* VERB; V n prep
3 A **wedge** is an object with one pointed edge and one thick edge, which you put under a door to keep it firmly in position. N-COUNT
4 A **wedge of** something such as fruit or cheese is a piece of it that has a thick triangular shape. N-COUNT: usu N *of* n
PHRASES 5 If someone **drives a wedge between** two people who are close, they cause ill feelings between them in order to weaken their relationship. ❑ *I started to feel Toby was driving a wedge between us.* PHRASE: V inflects, usu PHR *between* pl-n
6 If you say that something is **the thin end of the wedge**, you mean that it appears to be unimportant at the moment, but that it is the beginning of a bigger, more harmful development. [BRIT] ❑ *I think it's the thin end of the wedge when you have armed police permanently on patrol round a city.* PHRASE: v-link PHR, PHR after v

**wed|lock** /wɛdlɒk/ 1 **Wedlock** is the state of being married. [OLD-FASHIONED] N-UNCOUNT = marriage
2 If a baby is born **in wedlock**, it is born while its parents are married. If it is born **out of wedlock**, it is born at a time when its parents are not married. [FORMAL] PHRASE: PHR after v

**Wednes|day** /wɛnzdeɪ, -di/ **(Wednesdays)** **Wednesday** is the day after Tuesday and before Thursday. ❑ *Come and have supper with us on Wednesday, if you're free... Did you happen to see her leave last Wednesday?... David always collects Alistair from school on Wednesdays.* N-VAR

**wee** /wiː/ **(wees, weeing, weed)** 1 **Wee** means small in size or extent. [SCOTTISH, INFORMAL] ❑ *He just needs to calm down a wee bit.* ADJ: ADJ n = little
2 To **wee** means to urinate. **Wee** is an informal word used especially by children. [BRIT] ❑ *He said he wanted to wee.* ♦ **Wee** is also a noun. ❑ *The baby has done a wee in his potty.* VERB; V; N-VAR = pee

**weed** /wiːd/ **(weeds, weeding, weeded)** 1 A **weed** is a wild plant that grows in gardens or fields of crops and prevents the plants that you want from growing properly. ❑ *...a garden overgrown with weeds.* N-COUNT
2 **Weed** is a plant that grows in water and usually forms a thick floating mass. There are many different kinds of weed. ❑ *Large, clogging banks of weed are the only problem.* N-VAR
3 If you **weed** an area, you remove the weeds from it. ❑ *Caspar was weeding the garden... Try not to walk on the flower beds when weeding or hoeing.* VERB; V n; V
♦ **weed|ing** *She taught me to do the weeding.* N-UNCOUNT
♦ **weed out** If you **weed out** things or people that are useless or unwanted in a group, you find them and get rid of them. ❑ *He is keen to weed out the many applicants he believes may be frauds... A small group of neo-Nazis have infiltrated the ranks. We must weed them out as soon as possible.* PHRASAL VERB = root out; V P n (not pron); V n P

**weed|killer** /wiːdkɪləʳ/ **(weedkillers)** **Weedkiller** is a substance you put on your garden to kill weeds. N-MASS

**weedy** /wiːdi/ **(weedier, weediest)** 1 A **weedy** place is full of weeds. ADJ: usu ADJ n
2 If you describe someone as **weedy**, you are criticizing them because they are thin and physically weak. [mainly BRIT, INFORMAL] ADJ [disapproval] = puny

**week** /wiːk/ **(weeks)** 1 A **week** is a period of seven days. Some people consider that a week starts on Monday and ends on Sunday. ❑ *I had a letter from my mother last week... This has been on my mind all week... I know a wonderful restaurant where we can have lunch next week.* ◆◆◆ N-COUNT
2 A **week** is a period of about seven days. ❑ *Her mother stayed for another two weeks... Only 12 weeks ago he underwent major heart transplant surgery... Three million people will visit theatres in the annual six-week season.* N-COUNT
3 Your working **week** is the hours that you spend at work during a week. ❑ *It is not unusual for women to work a 40-hour week. ...workers on a three-day week.* N-COUNT: usu supp N
4 **The week** is the part of the week that does not include Saturday and Sunday. ❑ *...the hard work of looking after the children during the week.* N-SING: the N
5 You use **week** in expressions such as 'a week on Monday', 'a week next Tuesday', and 'tomorrow week' to mean exactly one week after the day that you mention. ❑ *The deadline to publish the document is a week tomorrow... The 800 metre final is on Monday week.* N-COUNT
6 You use **week** in expressions such as 'a week last Monday', 'a week ago this Tuesday', and 'a week ago yesterday' to mean exactly one week before the day that you mention. ❑ *'That's the time you weren't well, wasn't it?' — 'Yes, that's right, that was a week ago yesterday.'* N-COUNT
7 **weeks on end** ➔ see **end**.

**week|day** /wiːkdeɪ/ **(weekdays)** A **weekday** is any of the days of the week except Saturday and Sunday. ❑ *If you want to avoid the crowds, it's best to come on a weekday.* N-COUNT

**week|end** /wiːkɛnd/ **(weekends)** A **weekend** is Saturday and Sunday. ❑ *She had agreed to* ◆◆◇ N-COUNT *have dinner with him in town the following weekend... He told me to give you a call over the weekend.*

**week|end|er** /wiːkendəʳ, AM -endər/ **(weekenders)** A **weekender** is someone who goes to a place or lives at a place only at weekends. ❑ *He converted his barns into cottages for weekenders.* [N-COUNT: usu pl]

**week|ly** /wiːkli/ **(weeklies)** ◆◇◇ 1 A **weekly** event or publication happens or appears once a week or every week. ❑ *Each course comprises 10-12 informal weekly meetings... We go and do the weekly shopping every Thursday. ...a weekly newspaper.* [ADJ: ADJ n] ♦ **Weekly** is also an adverb. ❑ *The group meets weekly. ...a magazine published weekly since 2 January 1909.* [ADV: ADV after v] 2 **Weekly** quantities or rates relate to a period of one week. ❑ *In addition to my weekly wage, I got a lot of tips.* [ADJ: ADJ n] 3 A **weekly** is a newspaper or magazine that is published once a week. ❑ *Two of the four national daily papers are to become weeklies.* [N-COUNT]

**week|night** /wiːknaɪt/ **(weeknights)** A **weeknight** is the evening or night of a weekday. [mainly AUSTRALIAN] ❑ *...the half-hour weeknight show.* [N-COUNT: oft N n]

**wee|nie** /wiːni/ **(weenies)** → see **wienie**.

**weep** /wiːp/ **(weeps, weeping, wept)** 1 If someone **weeps**, they cry. [LITERARY] ❑ *She wanted to laugh and weep all at once... The weeping family hugged and comforted each other... She wept tears of joy.* [VERB: V, V-ing, V n] ♦ **Weep** is also a noun. ❑ *There are times when I sit down and have a good weep.* [N-SING: *a* N] 2 If a wound **weeps**, liquid or blood comes from it because it is not healing properly. ❑ *In severe cases, the skin can crack and weep. ...little blisters which develop into weeping sores.* [VERB: V, V-ing]

**weep|ing wil|low** **(weeping willows)** A **weeping willow** is a type of willow tree. It has long thin branches that hang down to the ground. [N-COUNT]

**weepy** /wiːpi/ **(weepies)** 1 Someone who is **weepy** is sad and likely to cry easily. ❑ *I suddenly felt very weepy. ...weepy moods.* [ADJ = tearful] 2 A **weepy** is a film or a story which is sentimental and makes you cry. [INFORMAL] [N-COUNT]

**wee|vil** /wiːvɪl/ **(weevils)** A **weevil** is a small insect which feeds on grain and seeds, and destroys crops. [N-COUNT]

**weft** /weft/ In weaving, **the weft** of a piece of cloth is the threads which are passed sideways across the other threads. Compare **warp**. [N-SING: usu *the* N]

**weigh** /weɪ/ **(weighs, weighing, weighed)** ◆◇◇ 1 If someone or something **weighs** a particular amount, this amount is how heavy they are. ❑ *It weighs nearly 27 kilos (about 65 pounds).* [VERB: no cont, V amount] 2 If you **weigh** something or someone, you measure how heavy they are. ❑ *The scales can be used to weigh other items such as parcels.* [VERB: V n] 3 If you **weigh** the facts about a situation, you consider them very carefully before you make a decision, especially by comparing the various facts involved. ❑ *He is weighing the possibility of filing criminal charges against the doctor... She spoke very slowly, weighing what she would say.* [VERB = consider: V n, V wh] ♦ **Weigh up** means the same as **weigh**. [mainly BRIT] ❑ *The company will be able to weigh up the environmental pros and cons of each site... You have to weigh up whether a human life is more important than an animal's life.* [PHRASAL VERB: V P n (not pron), V P wh, Also V n P]

♦ **weigh down** If something that you are wearing or carrying **weighs** you **down**, it stops you moving easily by making you heavier. ❑ *He took off his shoes. If they had to swim, he didn't want anything weighing him down... These nests increase in size each year, and can eventually weigh down the branch.* [PHRASAL VERB: V n P, V P n (not pron)]

♦ **weigh up** 1 → see **weigh 3**. 2 If you **weigh** someone **up**, you try and find out what they are like and form an opinion of them, especially when you are suspicious of them. [mainly BRIT] ❑ *My recruiting sergeant weighed me up when I first walked into his office.* [PHRASAL VERB = size up: V n P, Also V P n (not pron)]

**weigh-in** **(weigh-ins)** When there is a **weigh-in** on the day of a boxing match, each competitor is weighed to check their weight before the match. [N-COUNT: usu sing]

**weight** /weɪt/ **(weights, weighting, weighted)** ◆◆◇ 1 The **weight** of a person or thing is how heavy they are, measured in units such as kilograms, pounds, or tons. ❑ *What is your height and weight?... This reduced the weight of the load... Turkeys can reach enormous weights of up to 50 pounds.* [N-VAR: oft amount *in* N, with poss, N *of* amount] ● If someone **loses weight**, they become lighter. If they **gain weight** or **put on weight**, they become heavier. ❑ *I'm lucky really as I never put on weight... He lost two stone in weight during his time there.* [PHRASE: V inflects] 2 A person's or thing's **weight** is the fact that they are very heavy. ❑ *Despite the vehicle's size and weight it is not difficult to drive.* [N-UNCOUNT: with poss] 3 If you move your **weight**, you change position so that most of the pressure of your body is on a particular part of your body. ❑ *He shifted his weight from one foot to the other... He kept the weight from his left leg.* [N-SING: poss/*the* N] 4 **Weights** are objects which weigh a known amount and which people lift as a form of exercise. ❑ *I was in the gym lifting weights.* [N-COUNT: usu pl] 5 **Weights** are metal objects which weigh a known amount and which are used on a set of scales to weigh other things. [N-COUNT] 6 You can refer to a heavy object as a **weight**, especially when you have to lift it. ❑ *Straining to lift heavy weights can lead to a rise in blood pressure.* [N-COUNT] 7 If you **weight** something, you make it heavier by adding something to it, for example in order to stop it from moving easily. ❑ *It can be sewn into curtain hems to weight the curtain and so allow it to hang better.* [VERB: V n] 8 If you **weight** things, you give them different values according to how important or significant they are. ❑ *...a computer program which weights the different transitions according to their likelihood... This takes account of the number of countries in which a company wins approval for a new drug, weighted by the size of each country's market.* [VERB: V n, V-ed] 9 If something is given a particular **weight**, it is given a particular value according to how important or significant it is. ❑ *The scientists involved put different weight on the conclusions of different models.* [N-VAR = weighting] 10 If someone or something gives **weight** to what a person says, thinks, or does, they emphasize its significance. ❑ *The fact that he is gone has given more weight to fears that he may try to launch a civil war.* [N-UNCOUNT] 11 If you give something or someone **weight**, you consider them to be very important or influential in a particular situation. ❑ *Consumers generally place more weight on negative information than on the positive when deciding what to buy.* [N-UNCOUNT] 12 → See also **weighting, dead weight**.

PHRASES 13 If a person or their opinion **carries weight**, they are respected and are able to influence people. ❑ *That argument no longer carries as much weight... Senator Kerry carries considerable weight in Washington.* [PHRASE: V inflects] 14 If you say that someone or something is **worth** their **weight in gold**, you are emphasizing that they are so useful, helpful, or valuable that you feel you could not manage without them. ❑ *Any successful manager is worth his weight in gold.* [PHRASE: v-link PHR, emphasis] 15 If you **pull** your **weight**, you work as hard as everyone else who is involved in the same task or activity. ❑ *He accused the team of not pulling their weight.* [PHRASE: V inflects] 16 **a weight off** your **mind** → see **mind**.

♦ **weight down** If you **weight** something **down**, you put something heavy on it or in it in order to prevent it from moving easily. ❑ *Put some tins on top to weight it down.* [PHRASAL VERB: V n P]

**weight|ed** /weɪtɪd/ A system that is **weighted** in favour of a particular person or group is organized so that this person or group has an advantage. ❑ *The current electoral law is still heavily weighted in favour of the ruling party.* [ADJ: usu v-link ADJ prep = biased]

**weight|ing** /weɪtɪŋ/ **(weightings)** 1 A **weighting** is a value which is given to something according to how important or significant it is. ❑ *The tests and teacher assessments have equal weighting.* [N-COUNT] 2 A **weighting** is an advantage that a [N-COUNT:]

particular group of people receives in a system, especially an extra sum of money that people receive if they work in a city where the cost of living is very high. ❑ *I get an extra £2,700-a-year London weighting.* [3] → See also **weight**. — usu sing

**weight|less** /weɪtləs/ [1] Something that is **weightless** weighs nothing or seems to weigh nothing. ❑ *Photons have no mass – they are weightless. ...weightless silk curtains.* — ADJ [2] A person or object is **weightless** when they are in space and the earth's gravity does not affect them, so that they float around. ❑ *Helen described life in a weightless environment during her period in space.* — ADJ

**weight|lifter** /weɪtlɪftəʳ/ **(weightlifters)** A **weightlifter** is a person who does weightlifting. — N-COUNT

**weight|lifting** /weɪtlɪftɪŋ/ also **weight-lifting. Weightlifting** is a sport in which the competitor who can lift the heaviest weight wins. — N-UNCOUNT

**weight train|ing Weight training** is a kind of physical exercise in which people lift or push heavy weights with their arms and legs in order to strengthen their muscles. — N-UNCOUNT

**weighty** /weɪti/ **(weightier, weightiest)** [1] If you describe something such as an issue or a decision as **weighty**, you mean that it is serious or important. [FORMAL] ❑ *Surely such weighty matters merit a higher level of debate?* — ADJ: usu ADJ n = *serious, important* [2] You use **weighty** to describe something, especially a book, that is heavy or heavier than you would expect. [LITERARY] ❑ *Simon lifted a weighty volume from the shelf.* — ADJ = *hefty*

**weir** /wɪəʳ/ **(weirs)** [1] A **weir** is a low barrier which is built across a river in order to control or direct the flow of water. — N-COUNT [2] A **weir** is a wooden fence which is built across a stream in order to create a pool for catching fish. — N-COUNT

**weird** /wɪəʳd/ **(weirder, weirdest)** If you describe something or someone as **weird**, you mean that they are strange. [INFORMAL] ❑ *He's different. He's weird... Drugs can make you do all kinds of weird things... It must be really weird to be rich.* — ADJ: oft *it* v-link ADJ to-inf/-ing

**weir|do** /wɪəʳdoʊ/ **(weirdos)** If you describe someone as a **weirdo**, you disapprove of them because they behave in an unusual way which you find difficult to understand or accept. [INFORMAL, mainly SPOKEN] — N-COUNT disapproval = *crackpot*

**welch** /weltʃ/ **(welches, welching, welched)** also **welsh.** If someone **welches on** a deal or an agreement, they do not do the things they promised to do as part of that deal or agreement. [INFORMAL] ❑ *He welched on his agreement with the club that he would play for them in February.* — VERB; V *on* n

**wel|come** /welkəm/ **(welcomes, welcoming, welcomed)** ◆◆◇ [1] If you **welcome** someone, you greet them in a friendly way when they arrive somewhere. ❑ *Several people came by to welcome me... She was there to welcome him home from war... The delegates received a welcoming speech by the President.* — VERB; V n; V n adv/prep; V-ing ♦ **Welcome** is also a noun. ❑ *There would be a fantastic welcome awaiting him back here.* — N-COUNT: usu sing [2] You use **welcome** in expressions such as **welcome home, welcome to London**, and **welcome back** when you are greeting someone who has just arrived somewhere. ❑ *Welcome to Washington... Welcome back, Deborah – It's good to have you here.* — CONVENTION formulae [3] If you **welcome** an action, decision, or situation, you approve of it and are pleased that it has occurred. ❑ *She welcomed this move but said that overall the changes didn't go far enough.* — VERB; V n ♦ **Welcome** is also a noun. ❑ *Environmental groups have given a guarded welcome to the Prime Minister's proposal.* — N-COUNT: usu sing [4] If you describe something as **welcome**, you mean that people wanted it and are happy that it has occurred. ❑ *This was certainly a welcome change of fortune.* — ADJ [5] If you say that you **welcome** certain people or actions, you are inviting and encouraging people to do something, for example to come to a particular place. ❑ *We would welcome your views about the survey.* — VERB; V n [6] If you say that someone is **welcome** in a particular place, you are encouraging them to go there by telling them that they will be liked and accepted. ❑ *New members are always welcome... I told him he wasn't welcome in my home.* — ADJ: usu v-link ADJ [7] If you tell someone that they are **welcome to** do something, you are encouraging them to do it by telling them that they are allowed to do it. ❑ *You are welcome to visit the hospital at any time.* — ADJ: v-link ADJ, usu ADJ to-inf [8] If you say that someone is **welcome to** something, you mean that you do not want it yourself because you do not like it and you are very willing for them to have it. ❑ *If women want to take on the business world they are welcome to it as far as I'm concerned.* — ADJ: v-link ADJ *to* n [9] → See also **welcoming**.

PHRASES [10] If you **make** someone **welcome** or **make** them **feel** welcome, you make them feel happy and accepted in a new place. — PHRASE: *make* inflects [11] If you say that someone **outstays** their **welcome** or **overstays** their **welcome**, you mean that they stay somewhere longer than they are wanted or expected to. ❑ *After the kindness that had been shown to him, he didn't want to outstay his welcome.* — PHRASE: V inflects [12] You say **'You're welcome'** to someone who has thanked you for something in order to acknowledge their thanks in a polite way. ❑ *'Thank you for the information.' — 'You're welcome.'* — CONVENTION formulae

**wel|com|ing** /welkəmɪŋ/ If someone is **welcoming** or if they behave in a **welcoming** way, they are friendly to you when you arrive somewhere, so that you feel happy and accepted. ❑ *When we arrived at her house Susan was very welcoming.* — ADJ

**weld** /weld/ **(welds, welding, welded)** To **weld** one piece of metal to another means to join them by heating the edges and putting them together so that they cool and harden into one piece. ❑ *It's possible to weld stainless steel to ordinary steel... They will also be used on factory floors to weld things together... Where did Christopher learn to weld?* — VERB; V n *to* n; V n with *together*; V; Also V n ♦ **weld|ing** *All the welding had been done from inside the car. ...welding equipment.* — N-UNCOUNT

**weld|er** /weldəʳ/ **(welders)** A **welder** is a person whose job is welding metal. — N-COUNT

**wel|fare** /welfeəʳ/ ◆◇◇ [1] The **welfare** of a person or group is their health, comfort, and happiness. ❑ *I do not think he is considering Emma's welfare... He was the head of a charity for the welfare of children.* — N-UNCOUNT: usu with poss [2] **Welfare** services are provided to help with people's living conditions and financial problems. ❑ *Child welfare services are well established and comprehensive... He has urged complete reform of the welfare system.* — ADJ: usu ADJ n [3] In the United States, **welfare** is money that is paid by the government to people who are unemployed, poor, or sick. ❑ *States such as Michigan and Massachusetts are making deep cuts in welfare.* — N-UNCOUNT

**wel|fare state** In Britain and some other countries, the **welfare state** is a system in which the government provides free social services such as health and education and gives money to people when they are unable to work, for example because they are old, unemployed, or sick. — N-SING

**well**

① DISCOURSE USES
② ADVERB USES
③ PHRASES
④ ADJECTIVE USE
⑤ NOUN USES
⑥ VERB USES

① **well** /wel/ ◆◆◆

✓ **Well** is used mainly in spoken English.

⇛ Please look at category 13 to see if the expression you are looking for is shown under another headword. [1] You say **well** to indicate that you are about to say something. ❑ *Well, I don't like the look of that.* — ADV: ADV cl [2] You say **well** to indicate that you intend or want to carry on speaking. ❑ *The trouble with City is that they do not have enough quality players. Well, that can easily be rectified.* — ADV: ADV cl [3] You say — ADV: ADV cl

**well** to indicate that you are changing the topic, and are either going back to something that was being discussed earlier or are going on to something new. ❑ *Well, let's press on.* [= anyway, so]

4 You say **well** to indicate that you have reached the end of a conversation. ❑ *'I'm sure you will be an asset,' she finally added. 'Well, I see it's just about time for lunch.'.* [ADV: ADV cl]

5 You say **well** to make a suggestion, criticism, or correction seem less definite or rude. ❑ *Well, maybe it would be easier to start with a smaller problem... Well, let's wait and see.* [ADV: ADV cl]

6 You say **well** just before or after you pause, especially to give yourself time to think about what you are going to say. ❑ *Look, I'm really sorry I woke you, and, well, I just wanted to tell you I was all right.* [ADV: ADV cl]

7 You say **well** when you are correcting something that you have just said. ❑ *The comet is going to come back in 2061 and we are all going to be able to see it. Well, our offspring are, anyway.* [ADV: ADV cl/group]

8 You say **well** to express your doubt about something that someone has said. ❑ *'But finance is far more serious.' — 'Well I don't know really.'* [ADV: ADV cl] [feelings]

9 You say **well** to express your surprise or anger at something that someone has just said or done. ❑ *Well, honestly! They're like an old married couple at times.* [EXCLAM] [feelings]

10 You say **well** to indicate that you are waiting for someone to say something and often to express your irritation with them. ❑ *'Well?' asked Barry, 'what does it tell us?'... 'Well, why don't you ask me?' he said finally.* [CONVENTION] [feelings] [= so]

11 You use **well** to indicate that you are amused by something you have heard or seen, and often to introduce a comment on it. ❑ *Well, well, well, look at you. Ethel, look at this little fat girl.* [CONVENTION] [feelings]

12 You say **oh well** to indicate that you accept a situation or that someone else should accept it, even though you or they are not very happy about it, because it is not too bad and cannot be changed. ❑ *Oh well, it could be worse... 'I called her and she said no.' — 'Oh well.'* [CONVENTION] [feelings]

13 **very well** → see **very**.

## ②**well** /wel/ **(better, best)** ◆◆◆

1 If you do something **well**, you do it to a high standard or to a great extent. ❑ *All the Indian batsmen played well... He speaks English better than I do... It is a formula that worked very well indeed... I don't really know her very well.* [ADV: ADV after v]

2 If you do something **well**, you do it thoroughly and completely. ❑ *Mix all the ingredients well... Wash your hands well with soap.* [ADV: ADV after v] [= thoroughly]

3 If you speak or think **well of** someone, you say or think favourable things about them. ❑ *'He speaks well of you.' — 'I'm glad to hear that.'... It might help people think better of him.* [ADV: ADV after v]

4 **Well** is used in front of past participles to indicate that something is done to a high standard or to a great extent. ❑ *Helen is a very well-known novelist in Australia... People live longer nowadays, and they are better educated... British nurses were among the best trained in Europe.* [COMB in ADJ]

5 You use **well** to ask or talk about the extent or standard of something. ❑ *How well do you remember your mother, Franzi?... This new career doesn't pay nearly as well as the old one... He wasn't dressed any better than me.* [ADV: *how* ADV, *as* ADV *as*, ADV-compar *than*]

6 You use **well** in front of a prepositional phrase to emphasize it. For example, if you say that one thing happened **well before** another, you mean that it happened a long time before it. ❑ *Franklin did not turn up until well after midnight... There are well over a million Muslims in Britain.* [ADV: ADV prep] [emphasis]

7 You use **well** before certain adjectives to emphasize them. ❑ *She has a close group of friends who are very well aware of what she has suffered... The show is well worth a visit.* [ADV: ADV adj] [emphasis]

8 You use **well** after adverbs such as 'perfectly', 'jolly', or 'damn' in order to emphasize an opinion or the truth of what you are saying. ❑ *You know perfectly well I can't be blamed for the failure of that mission... I'd got myself into this marriage and I jolly well had to get myself out of it.* [ADV: adv ADV, ADV with v] [emphasis]

9 You use **well** after verbs such as 'may' and 'could' when you are saying what you think is likely to happen. ❑ *The murderer may well come from the estate... Ours could well be the last generation for which moviegoing has a sense of magic.* [ADV: modal ADV] [emphasis]

## ③**well** /wel/ ◆◆◆

⇛ Please look at category 11 to see if the expression you are looking for is shown under another headword.

1 You use **as well** when mentioning something which happens in the same way as something else already mentioned, or which should be considered at the same time as that thing. ❑ *It is most often diagnosed in women in their thirties and forties, although I've seen it in many younger women, as well... 'What do you like about it then?' — 'Erm, the history, the shops – people are quite friendly as well.'.* [PHRASE: cl PHR] [= too]

2 You use **as well as** when you want to mention another item connected with the subject you are discussing. ❑ *It is in his best interests as well as yours... As well as a good academic record I look for people who've climbed mountains or been captain of a team.* [PREP-PHRASE]

3 If you say that something that has happened **is just as well**, you mean that it is fortunate that it happened in the way it did. ❑ *Judging from everything you've said, it was just as well she wasn't there.* [PHRASE: V inflects, oft *it* PHR that]

4 You say **it is as well to** think or do something when you are advising someone to think in a particular way or to take a particular action. ❑ *It is as well to bear in mind that laughter is a great releaser of tension.* [PHRASE: V inflects, PHR inf]

5 If you say that someone **would do well to** do something, you mean that you advise or recommend that they do it. ❑ *He would do well to remember that, sooner or later, everyone's luck runs out... Investors would do well to take a look at the Swiss economy.* [PHRASE]

6 If you say that something, usually something bad, **might as well** be true or **may as well** be true, you mean that the situation is the same or almost the same as if it were true. ❑ *The couple might as well have been strangers... We might just as well be in prison for all the quality our lives have at present.* [PHRASE: PHR inf]

7 If you say that you **might as well** do something, or that you **may as well** do it, you mean that you will do it although you do not have a strong desire to do it and may even feel slightly unwilling to do it. ❑ *If I've got to go somewhere I may as well go to Birmingham... Anyway, you're here; you might as well stay... I'll come with you if you like. I might as well.* [PHRASE: usu PHR inf]

8 If you say that something is **all well and good**, you are suggesting that it has faults or disadvantages, although it may appear to be correct or reasonable. ❑ *It's all well and good for him to say he's sorry for dropping you, but has he told you why he did it?* [PHRASE: usu v-link PHR, oft PHR *for* n, PHR to-inf]

9 You say **well and good** or **all well and good** to indicate that you would be pleased if something happens but you are aware that it has some disadvantages. ❑ *If they arrive before I leave, well and good. If not, the responsibility will be mine... This is all well and good, but we have to look at the situation in the long term.* [PHRASE: usu PHR with cl, v-link PHR, *it* v-link PHR to-inf/-ing]

10 If you say that something is **well and truly** finished, gone, or done, you are emphasizing that it is completely finished or gone, or thoroughly done. [mainly BRIT] ❑ *The war is well and truly over.* [PHRASE: PHR group] [emphasis]

11 **all very well** → see **all**. **to know full well** → see **full**. **to mean well** → see **mean**. **pretty well** → see **pretty**.

## ④**well** /wel/ ◆◆◆

If you are **well**, you are healthy and not ill. ❑ *I'm not very well today, I can't come in... I hope you're well.* [ADJ: usu v-link ADJ] [≠ ill]

## ⑤**well** /wel/ **(wells)**

1 A **well** is a hole in the ground from which a supply of water is extracted. ❑ *I had to fetch water from the well.* [N-COUNT]

2 A **well** is an oil well. ❑ *About 650 wells are on fire.* [N-COUNT]

## ⑥**well** /wel/ **(wells, welling, welled)**

1 If liquids, for example tears, **well**, they come to the surface and form a pool. ❑ *Tears welled in her eyes... He fell back, blood welling from a gash in his thigh.* [VERB] [V] [V *from* n] ♦ **Well up** means the same as **well**. ❑ *Tears welled up in Anni's eyes.* [PHRASAL VERB] [V P]

2 If an emotion **wells** in you, it suddenly becomes stronger, to the point where you have to express it. ❑ *Gratitude welled in Chryssa... Her love for him welled stronger than ever.* [VERB] [V *in/inside* n] [V] ♦ **Well up** means the same as **well**. ❑ *He could feel the anger welling up inside him... Hope welled up.* [PHRASAL VERB] [V P *in/inside* n, V P]

**we'll** /wɪl, STRONG wiːl/ **We'll** is the usual spoken form of 'we shall' or 'we will'. ❑ *Whatever you want to chat about, we'll do it tonight... Will there be anything else? — If there is, we'll let you know.*

**well-adjusted** also **well adjusted.** A **well-adjusted** person has a mature personality and can control their emotions and deal with problems without becoming anxious. ❑ *...a happy, loving and well adjusted family.* ADJ ≠ maladjusted

**well ad|vised** also **well-advised.** If someone says that you would be **well advised to** do a particular thing, they are advising you to do it. ❑ *Moderates believe the party would be well advised to talk to the government.* ADJ: v-link ADJ to-inf = wise

**well-appointed** A **well-appointed** room or building has furniture or equipment of a high standard. [FORMAL] ADJ

**well-balanced** also **well balanced.** 1 If you describe someone as **well-balanced**, you mean that they are sensible and do not have many emotional problems. ❑ *...a fun-loving, well-balanced individual.* ADJ = stable 2 If you describe something that is made up of several parts as **well-balanced**, you mean that the way that the different parts are put together is good, because there is not too much or too little of any one part. ❑ *...a well balanced diet.* ADJ

**well-behaved** also **well behaved.** If you describe someone, especially a child, as **well-behaved**, you mean that they behave in a way that adults generally like and think is correct. ❑ *...well-behaved little boys.* ADJ

**well-being** also **wellbeing.** Someone's **well-being** is their health and happiness. ❑ *Singing can create a sense of wellbeing... His work emphasised the emotional as well as the physical well-being of children.* N-UNCOUNT: usu with supp

**well-born** Someone who is **well-born** belongs to an upper-class family. ADJ

**well-bred** also **well bred.** A **well-bred** person is very polite and has good manners. ❑ *She was too well bred to want to hurt the little boy's feelings.* ADJ = well-mannered

**well-brought-up** also **well brought up.** If you say that someone, especially a child, is **well-brought-up**, you mean that they are very polite because they have been taught good manners. ADJ

**well-built** also **well built.** A **well-built** person, especially a man, has quite a big body and quite large muscles. ❑ *Mitchell is well built, of medium height, with a dark complexion.* ADJ

**well-connected** also **well connected.** Someone who is **well-connected** has important or influential relatives or friends. ADJ

**well-defined** also **well defined.** Something that is **well-defined** is clear and precise and therefore easy to recognize or understand. ❑ *Today's pawnbrokers operate within well-defined financial regulations.* ADJ

**well dis|posed** also **well-disposed.** If you are **well disposed to** a person, plan, or activity, you are likely to agree with them or support them. ❑ *They are likely to be well disposed to an offer of a separate peace deal... He felt well disposed towards her.* ADJ: usu ADJ *to/towards* n

**well done** 1 You say **'Well done'** to indicate that you are pleased that someone has done something good. ❑ *'Daddy! I came second in history' — 'Well done, sweetheart!'* CONVENTION [feelings] 2 If something that you have cooked, especially meat, is **well done**, it has been cooked thoroughly. ❑ *Allow an extra 10-15 min if you prefer lamb well done.* ADJ

**well-dressed** also **well dressed.** Someone who is **well-dressed** is wearing smart or elegant clothes. ❑ *She's always well dressed.* ADJ = smart

**well-earned** also **well earned.** You can use **well-earned** to indicate that you think something is deserved, usually because the person who gets it has been working very hard. ❑ *Take a well-earned rest and go out and enjoy yourself. ...his well-earned win in Sunday's race.* ADJ: usu ADJ n

**well-endowed** 1 If someone says that a woman is **well-endowed**, they mean that she has large breasts. If someone says that a man is **well-endowed**, they mean that he has a large penis. People often use this expression if they are trying to be polite. ❑ *I spotted a well-endowed girl in the audience wearing a tight white T-shirt. ...the chalk figure of a well-endowed warrior.* ADJ 2 A **well-endowed** organization has a lot of money or resources. ❑ *In a large, well-endowed school, the opportunities for laboratory work are likely to be greater.* ADJ

**well-established** also **well established.** If you say that something is **well-established**, you mean that it has been in existence for quite a long time and is successful. ❑ *The University has a well-established tradition of welcoming postgraduate students from overseas. ...well-established companies such as Compaq and Olivetti.* ADJ

**well-fed** also **well fed.** If you say that someone is **well-fed**, you mean that they get good food regularly. ❑ *...his well-fed children.* ADJ

**well-founded** also **well founded.** If you say that a report, opinion, or feeling is **well-founded**, you mean that it is based on facts and can therefore be justified. ❑ *If the reports are well founded, the incident could seriously aggravate relations between the two nations.* ADJ

**well-groomed** also **well groomed.** A **well-groomed** person is very neat and tidy, and looks as if they have taken care over their appearance. ADJ

**well-heeled** Someone who is **well-heeled** is wealthy. ADJ = wealthy

**well-hung** If someone says that a man is **well-hung**, they are saying in a polite or humorous way that he has a large penis. ADJ

**well-informed** (better-informed) also **well informed.** If you say that someone is **well-informed**, you mean that they know a lot about many different subjects or about one particular subject. ❑ *...a lending library to encourage members to become as well informed as possible.* ADJ

**wel|ling|ton** /welɪŋtən/ (**wellingtons**) **Wellingtons** or **wellington boots** are long rubber boots which you wear to keep your feet dry. [mainly BRIT] N-COUNT: usu pl

✓ in AM, usually use **rubber boots**

**well-intentioned** also **well intentioned.** If you say that a person or their actions are **well-intentioned**, you mean that they intend to be helpful or kind but they are unsuccessful or cause problems. ❑ *He is well-intentioned but a poor administrator. ...rules that, however well-intentioned, are often hopelessly impractical.* ADJ = well-meaning

**well-kept** also **well kept.** 1 A **well-kept** building, street, garden, or other place is always neat and tidy because it is carefully looked after. ❑ *...two idyllic thatched cottages with well-kept gardens.* ADJ 2 A **well-kept** secret has not been told or made known to anyone, or has been told or made known to only a small number of people. ADJ: usu ADJ n

**well-known** also **well known.** 1 A **well-known** person or thing is known about by a lot of people and is therefore famous or familiar. If someone is **well-known for** a particular activity, a lot of people know about them because of their involvement with that activity. ❑ *He surrounds himself with attractive, intelligent, or well-known people... Hubbard was well known for his work in the field of drug rehabilitation.* ◆◇◇ ADJ 2 A **well-known** fact is a fact that is known by people in general. ❑ *It is well known that bamboo shoots are a panda's staple diet.* ADJ

**well-mannered** Someone who is **well-mannered** is polite and has good manners. ADJ

**well-meaning** also **well meaning.** If you say that a person or their actions are **well-meaning**, you mean that they intend to be helpful or kind but they are unsuccessful or cause problems. ❑ *He is a well-meaning but ineffectual leader... Even well-meaning attempts at conservation can bring problems.* ADJ = well-intentioned

**well-meant** also **well meant.** A **well-meant** decision, action, or comment is intended to be helpful or kind but is unsuccessful or causes problems. ❑ *Any decision taken by them now, however well meant, could complicate the peace process. ...a well-meant experiment gone wrong.* ADJ = well-intentioned

**well|ness** /welnəs/ Your **wellness** is how healthy you are, and how well and happy you feel. N-UNCOUNT

**well-nigh** also **well nigh. Well-nigh** means almost, but not completely or exactly. ❑ *Finding a rug that's just the colour, size and price you want can be well-nigh impossible.* ADV: ADV adj = practically

**well-off** also **well off.** Someone who is **well-off** is rich enough to be able to do and buy most of the things that they want. [INFORMAL] ❑ *My grandparents were quite well off.* ♦ **The well-off** are people who are well-off. ❑ *...higher tax rates on the well-off.* ADJ = well-to-do; N-PLURAL: the N

**well-oiled** Journalists sometimes refer to a system or organization that is operating very efficiently as a **well-oiled** machine. ❑ *...a well-oiled publicity machine.* ADJ: ADJ n

**well-paid** also **well paid.** If you say that a person or their job is **well-paid**, you mean that they receive a lot of money for the work that they do. ❑ *Kate was well paid and enjoyed her job... I have an interesting, well-paid job, with opportunities to travel.* ADJ

**well-preserved** also **well preserved.** 1 If you describe a middle-aged or old person as **well-preserved**, you mean that they look good for their age. ❑ *Annie is a well-preserved 50-year-old.* ADJ 2 A **well-preserved** object or building does not show any signs of its age. ❑ *...well-preserved fossils.* ADJ

**well-read** /wel red/ also **well read.** A **well-read** person has read a lot of books and has learned a lot from them. ❑ *He was clever, well-read and interested in the arts.* ADJ

**well-rounded** → see **rounded**.

**well-spoken** also **well spoken.** A **well-spoken** person speaks in a polite correct way and with an accent which is considered socially acceptable. ❑ *I remember her as a quiet, hard-working and well-spoken girl.* ADJ

**well-thumbed** A book or magazine that is **well-thumbed** is creased and marked because it has been read so often. ADJ

**well-timed** also **well timed.** A **well-timed** action or comment is done or made at the most appropriate or suitable time. ❑ *He built the company through a string of well-timed acquisitions... One well-timed word from you will be all it needs.* ADJ = timely

**well-to-do** A **well-to-do** person is rich enough to be able to do and buy most of the things that they want. ❑ *...a rather well-to-do family of diamond cutters. ...two well educated girls from well-to-do homes.* ♦ **The well-to-do** are people who are well-to-do. ❑ *...a firm that installed stereo equipment in homes of the well-to-do.* ADJ = well-off; N-PLURAL: the N

**well-travelled**

✔ in AM, use **well-traveled**

A **well-travelled** person has travelled a lot in foreign countries. ADJ = much-travelled

**well-tried** also **well tried.** A **well-tried** treatment, product, or method is one that has been used many times before and so is known to work well or to be successful. ❑ *There are a number of well-tried remedies which are perfectly safe to take.* ADJ = tried and tested

**well-trodden** 1 A **well-trodden** path is used regularly by a large number of people, and therefore looks worn and is easy to see. ❑ *He made his way along a well-trodden path towards the shed.* ADJ: usu ADJ n 2 You can use **well-trodden**, especially in expressions such as **a well-trodden path** and **well-trodden ground**, to indicate that a plan or course of action has been tried by a lot of people and so the result of it is easy to predict. ❑ *Political power has long been a well-trodden path to personal wealth... These working parties will be going over well-trodden ground.* ADJ: usu ADJ n

**well versed** also **well-versed.** If someone is **well versed in** a particular subject, they know a lot about it. ❑ *Page is well versed in many styles of jazz.* ADJ: usu v-link ADJ in n

**well-wisher** (**well-wishers**) also **wellwisher. Well-wishers** are people who hope that a particular person or thing will be successful, and who show this by their behaviour. ❑ *The main street was lined with well-wishers.* N-COUNT: usu pl

**well-worn** also **well worn.** 1 A **well-worn** expression, remark, or idea has been used so often that it no longer seems to have much meaning or to be interesting. ❑ *To use a well-worn cliche, it is packed with information.* ADJ = hackneyed 2 A **well-worn** object or piece of clothing has been worn or used so frequently that it looks rather old and untidy. ❑ *...well-worn brown shoes.* ADJ

**wel|ly** /weli/ (**wellies**) **Wellies** are long rubber boots which you wear to keep your feet dry. [BRIT, INFORMAL] N-COUNT: usu pl

**welsh** /welʃ/ → see **welch**.

**Welsh** 1 **Welsh** means belonging or relating to Wales, or to its people, language, or culture. ADJ ♦ **The Welsh** are the people of Wales. N-PLURAL: usu the N 2 **Welsh** is the language that is spoken in some parts of Wales. N-UNCOUNT

**Welsh|man** /welʃmən/ (**Welshmen**) A **Welshman** is a man who was born in Wales and considers himself to be Welsh. N-COUNT

**welt** /welt/ (**welts**) A **welt** is a mark which is made on someone's skin, usually by a blow from something such as a whip or sword. N-COUNT = weal

**wel|ter** /weltəʳ/ A **welter of** something is a large quantity of it which occurs suddenly or in a confusing way. [WRITTEN] ❑ *...patients with a welter of confusing symptoms. ...the welter of publicity that followed his engagement.* QUANT: QUANT of pl-n/n-uncount

**wench** /wentʃ/ (**wenches**) A **wench** was a girl or young woman who worked as a servant or served people food or drink. [OLD-FASHIONED] N-COUNT

**wend** /wend/ (**wends, wending, wended**) If you **wend** your **way** in a particular direction, you walk, especially slowly, casually, or carefully, in that direction. [LITERARY] ❑ *Sleepy-eyed commuters were wending their way to work.* PHRASE: V inflects, usu PHR prep/adv = make your way

**Wendy house** (**Wendy houses**) A **Wendy house** is a small toy house for a child to play in. [BRIT] N-COUNT

✔ in AM, use **playhouse**

**went** /went/ **Went** is the past tense of **go**.

**wept** /wept/ **Wept** is the past tense and past participle of **weep**.

**were** /wəʳ, STRONG wɜːʳ/ 1 **Were** is the plural and the second person singular of the past tense of **be**. 2 **Were** is sometimes used instead of 'was' in certain structures, for example in conditional clauses or after the verb 'wish'. [FORMAL] ❑ *He told a diplomat that he might withdraw if he were allowed to keep part of a disputed oil field.* 3 **as it were** → see **as**.

**we're** /wɪəʳ/ **We're** is the usual spoken form of 'we are'. ❑ *I'm married, but we're separated.*

**weren't** /wɜːʳnt/ **Weren't** is the usual spoken form of 'were not'.

**were|wolf** /weəʳwʊlf/ (**werewolves**) In stories and films, a **werewolf** is a person who changes into a wolf. N-COUNT

**west** /west/ also **West.** 1 The **west** is the direction which you look towards in the evening in order to see the sun set. ❑ *I pushed on towards* ◆◆◆ N-UNCOUNT: also the N

*Flagstaff, a hundred miles to the west... The sun crosses the sky from east to west.* [2] **The west of** a place, country, or region is the part of it which is in the west. ❑ *...physicists working at Bristol University in the west of England.* N-SING: usu the N, oft N of n [3] If you go **west**, you travel towards the west. ❑ *We are going West to California.* ADV: ADV after v [4] Something that is **west of** a place is positioned to the west of it. ❑ *...their home town of Paisley, several miles west of Glasgow.* ADV: usu ADV of n [5] The **west** part of a place, country, or region is the part which is towards the west. ❑ *...a small island off the west coast of South Korea.* ADJ: ADJ n [6] **West** is used in the names of some countries, states, and regions in the west of a larger area. ❑ *Mark has been working in West Africa for about six months. ...his West London home. ...Charleston, West Virginia.* ADJ: ADJ n [7] A **west** wind blows from the west. ADJ: ADJ n [8] **The West** is used to refer to the United States, Canada, and the countries of Western, Northern, and Southern Europe. ❑ *...relations between Iran and the West.* N-SING: the N

**west|bound** /we̱stbaʊnd/ **Westbound** roads or vehicles lead to the west or are travelling towards the west. ❑ *Traffic is slow on the westbound carriageway of the M4. ...the last westbound train to leave Chicago.* ADJ: ADJ n

**west|er|ly** /we̱stəʳli/ [1] A **westerly** point, area, or direction is to the west or towards the west. ❑ *...Finisterre, Spain's most westerly point.* ADJ: usu ADJ n [2] A **westerly** wind blows from the west. ❑ *...a prevailing westerly wind.* ADJ: usu ADJ n

**west|ern** /we̱stəʳn/ **(westerns)** also **Western.** ◆◆◇ [1] **Western** means in or from the west of a region, state, or country. ❑ *...hand-made rugs from Western and Central Asia. ...Moi University, in western Kenya.* ADJ: ADJ n [2] **Western** is used to describe things, people, ideas, or ways of life that come from or are associated with the United States, Canada, and the countries of Western, Northern, and Southern Europe. ❑ *Mexico had the support of the big western governments... Those statements have never been reported in the Western media.* ADJ: usu ADJ n [3] A **western** is a book or film about life in the west of America in the nineteenth century, especially the lives of cowboys. N-COUNT

**west|ern|er** /we̱stəʳnəʳ/ **(westerners)** also **Westerner.** A **westerner** is a person who was born in or lives in the United States, Canada, or Western, Northern, or Southern Europe. ❑ *No westerner could fly in without a visa.* N-COUNT

**west|erni|za|tion** /we̱stəʳnaɪzeɪʃᵊn/

> ✔ in BRIT, also use **westernisation**

The **westernization** of a country, place, or person is the process of them adopting ideas and behaviour that are typical of Europe and North America, rather than preserving the ideas and behaviour traditional in their culture. ❑ *...fundamentalists unhappy with the westernization of Afghan culture... The explosive growth in casinos is one of the most conspicuous signs of Westernisation.* N-UNCOUNT

**west|ern|ized** /we̱stəʳnaɪzd/

> ✔ in BRIT, also use **westernised**

A **westernized** country, place, or person has adopted ideas and behaviour typical of Europe and North America, rather than preserving the ideas and behaviour that are traditional in their culture. ❑ *...Africans educated in Europe, and thoroughly Westernized in their thinking.* ADJ

**west|ern|most** /we̱stəʳnmoʊst/ The **westernmost** part of an area or the **westernmost** place is the one that is farthest towards the west. ❑ *...the westernmost province of North Sudan.* ADJ: usu ADJ n

**West Ger|man** **(West Germans)** [1] **West German** means belonging or relating to the part of Germany that was known as the Federal Republic of Germany before the two parts of Germany were united in 1990. **West German** also means belonging or relating to the people or culture of this part of Germany. ADJ [2] A **West German** is someone who was a citizen of the Federal Republic of Germany, or a person of West German origin. N-COUNT

**West In|dian** **(West Indians)** [1] **West Indian** means belonging or relating to the West Indies, or to its people or culture. ADJ [2] A **West Indian** is a citizen of the West Indies or a person of West Indian origin. N-COUNT

**west|ward** /we̱stwəʳd/ also **westwards. Westward** means towards the west. ❑ *He sailed westward from Palos de la Frontera... Within hours, she was free to resume her journey westward.* ADV: usu ADV after v, also n ADV ♦ **Westward** is also an adjective. ❑ *...the one-hour westward flight over the Andes to Lima.* ADJ: ADJ n

**wet** /we̱t/ **(wetter, wettest, wets, wetting, wetted)** ◆◇◇

> ✔ The forms **wet** and **wetted** are both used as the past tense and past participle of the verb.

[1] If something is **wet**, it is covered in water, rain, sweat, tears, or another liquid. ❑ *He towelled his wet hair... I lowered myself to the water's edge, getting my feet wet... My gloves were soaking wet... I saw his face was wet with tears.* ADJ ≠ dry ♦ **wet|ly** *Her hair clung wetly to her head.* ADV: usu ADV after v ♦ **wet|ness** *Anti-perspirants stop wetness, deodorants stop odour.* N-UNCOUNT [2] To **wet** something means to get water or some other liquid over it. ❑ *When assembling the pie, wet the edges where the two crusts join... Fielding nervously wet his lips and tried to smile.* VERB V n V n [3] If the weather is **wet**, it is raining. ❑ *If the weather is wet or cold choose an indoor activity... It was a miserable wet day.* ADJ = rainy ≠ dry ♦ **The wet** is used to mean wet weather. ❑ *They had come in from the cold and the wet.* N-SING: the N [4] If something such as paint, ink, or cement is **wet**, it is not yet dry or solid. ❑ *I lay the painting flat to stop the wet paint running.* ADJ ≠ dry [5] If people, especially children, **wet** their beds or clothes or **wet themselves**, they urinate in their beds or in their clothes because they cannot stop themselves. ❑ *A quarter of 4-year-olds frequently wet the bed... To put it plainly, they wet themselves.* VERB V n V pron-refl [6] If you say that someone is still **wet behind the ears**, you mean that they have only recently arrived in a new place or job, and are therefore still not experienced. PHRASE: v-link PHR

**wet|back** /we̱tbæk/ **(wetbacks)** **Wetback** is sometimes used to refer to a Mexican or a Mexican-American who has entered the United States illegally in order to work or live there. [AM, INFORMAL, OFFENSIVE] N-COUNT

**wet blan|ket** **(wet blankets)** If you say that someone is a **wet blanket**, you are criticizing them because they refuse to join other people in an enjoyable activity or because they want to stop other people enjoying themselves. [INFORMAL] N-COUNT [disapproval] = spoilsport

**wet dream** **(wet dreams)** [1] If a man has a **wet dream**, he has a dream about sex which causes him to have an orgasm while he is asleep. N-COUNT [2] If someone says that a person or thing is a particular person's **wet dream**, they are saying in an unkind and mocking way that this person or thing would give that person a lot of pleasure. [INFORMAL, RUDE] N-COUNT: usu poss N

**wet|land** /we̱tlænd/ **(wetlands)** A **wetland** is an area of very wet, muddy land with wild plants growing in it. You can also refer to an area like this as **wetlands.** ❑ *...a scheme that aims to protect the wilderness of the wetlands... There are some areas of wetland which are of ancient origin.* N-VAR: oft N n

**wet nurse** **(wet nurses)** also **wet-nurse.** In former times, a **wet nurse** was a woman who was paid to breast-feed another woman's baby. N-COUNT

**wet suit** **(wet suits)** also **wetsuit.** A **wet suit** is a close-fitting rubber suit which an underwater swimmer wears in order to keep their body warm. N-COUNT

**we've** /wɪv, STRONG wiːv/ **We've** is the usual spoken form of 'we have', especially when 'have' is an auxiliary verb. ❑ *It's the first time we've been to the cinema together as a family.*

**whack** /ʰwæ̱k/ **(whacks, whacking, whacked)** [1] If you **whack** someone or something, you hit them hard. [INFORMAL] ❑ *You really have to whack* VERB V n *the ball... Someone whacked him on the head.* *V n prep* ♦ **Whack** is also a noun. *N-COUNT; SOUND* ❑ *He gave the donkey a whack across the back with his stick.* 2 *N-SING: oft poss N = share* Your **whack** of something is your share of it. [BRIT, INFORMAL] ❑ *The majority of people in this country pay their whack... We need to win a fair whack of the contracts.*

**whack|ing** /ʰwækɪŋ/ *ADJ: ADJ n* *emphasis* *= enormous* You can use **whacking** to emphasize how big something is. [BRIT, INFORMAL] ❑ *The supermarkets may be making whacking profits.* ♦ **Whacking** is also an adverb. *ADV: ADV adj* ❑ *...a whacking great hole.*

**whacky** /ʰwæki/ → see **wacky**.

**whale** /ʰweɪl/ **(whales)** 1 *N-COUNT* **Whales** are very large mammals that live in the sea. → See also **killer whale**, **sperm whale**. 2 *PHRASE: V inflects* If you say that someone **is having a whale of a time**, you mean that they are enjoying themselves very much. [INFORMAL] ❑ *I had a whale of a time in Birmingham.*

**whal|er** /ʰweɪləʳ/ **(whalers)** 1 *N-COUNT* A **whaler** is a ship which is used in hunting whales. 2 *N-COUNT* A **whaler** is someone who works on a ship which is used in hunting whales.

**whal|ing** /ʰweɪlɪŋ/ *N-UNCOUNT: oft N n* **Whaling** is the activity of hunting and killing whales. ❑ *...a ban on commercial whaling. ...the whaling industry.*

**wham** /ʰwæm/ *EXCLAM* You use **wham** to indicate that something happens suddenly or forcefully. [INFORMAL] ❑ *Then I met someone and wham, bam, I was completely in love.*

**wham|my** /ʰwæmi/ *N-SING: adj N* **Whammy** is used in expressions such as **double whammy** and **triple whammy** to indicate that two or three unpleasant or difficult situations occur at the same time, or occur one after the other. [mainly JOURNALISM] ❑ *This is a double whammy for public sector workers.*

**wharf** /ʰwɔːʳf/ **(wharves** or **wharfs)** *N-COUNT = jetty, quay* A **wharf** is a platform by a river or the sea where ships can be tied up.

**what** /ʰwɒt/ ◆◆◆

> Usually pronounced /ʰwɒt/ for meanings 2, 4 and 5.

1 *QUEST* You use **what** in questions when you ask for specific information about something that you do not know. ❑ *What do you want?... 'Has something happened?' — 'Indeed it has.' — 'What?'... Hey! What are you doing?* ♦ **What** is also a determiner. *DET* ❑ *What time is it?... 'The heater works.' — 'What heater?'... What kind of poetry does he like?* 2 *CONJ* You use **what** after certain words, especially verbs and adjectives, when you are referring to a situation that is unknown or has not been specified. ❑ *You can imagine what it would be like driving a car into a brick wall at 30 miles an hour... I want to know what happened to Norman... Do you know what those idiots have done?... We had never seen anything like it before and could not see what to do next... She turned scarlet from embarrassment, once she realized what she had done.* ♦ **What** is also a determiner. *DET* ❑ *I didn't know what college I wanted to go to... I didn't know what else to say. ...an inspection to ascertain to what extent colleges are responding to the needs of industry.*
3 *CONJ* *emphasis* You use **what** at the beginning of a clause in structures where you are changing the order of the information to give special emphasis to something. ❑ *What precisely triggered off yesterday's riot is still unclear... What I wanted, more than anything, was a few days' rest.* 4 *CONJ* You use **what** in expressions such as **what is called** and **what amounts to** when you are giving a description of something. ❑ *She had been in what doctors described as an irreversible vegetative state for five years.* 5 *CONJ* You use **what** to indicate that you are talking about the whole of an amount that is available to you. ❑ *He drinks what is left in his glass as if it were water.* ♦ **What** is also a determiner. *DET = whatever* ❑ *They had had to use what money they had.* 6 *CONVENTION* *formulae* You say **'What?'** to tell someone who has indicated that they want to speak to you that you have heard them and are inviting them to continue. [SPOKEN] ❑ *'Dad?' — 'What?' — 'Can I have the car tonight?'* 7 *CONVENTION* *formulae* You say **'What?'** when you ask someone to repeat the thing that they have just said because you did not hear or understand it properly. 'What?' is more informal and less polite than expressions such as 'Pardon?' and 'Excuse me?'. [SPOKEN] ❑ *'They could paint this place,' she said. 'What?' he asked.* 8 *CONVENTION* *feelings* You say **'What'** to express surprise. ❑ *'Adolphus Kelling, I arrest you on a charge of trafficking in narcotics.' — 'What?'* 9 *PREDET* *emphasis* You use **what** in exclamations to emphasize an opinion or reaction. ❑ *What a horrible thing to do... What a busy day.* ♦ **What** is also a determiner. *DET* ❑ *What ugly things; throw them away, throw them away... What great news, Jakki.* 10 *ADV: ADV n* You use **what** to indicate that you are making a guess about something such as an amount or value. ❑ *It's, what, eleven years or more since he's seen him.*
11 *CONVENTION* You say **guess what** or **do you know what** to introduce a piece of information which is surprising, which is not generally known, or which you want to emphasize. ❑ *Guess what? I'm going to dinner at Mrs. Combley's tonight.*

**PHRASES** 12 *PHRASE: cl PHR* *emphasis* In conversation, you say **or what?** after a question as a way of stating an opinion forcefully and showing that you expect other people to agree. ❑ *Look at that moon. Is that beautiful or what?... Am I wasting my time here, or what?*
13 *CONVENTION* *feelings* *= so* You say **so what?** or **what of it?** to indicate that the previous remark seems unimportant, uninteresting, or irrelevant to you. ❑ *'I skipped off school today,' — 'So what? What's so special about that?'... 'You're talking to yourself.' — 'Well, what of it?'* 14 *PHRASE: PHR cl* You say **'Tell you what'** to introduce a suggestion or offer. ❑ *Tell you what, let's stay here another day.* 15 *PHRASE: PHR n/-ing* You use **what about** at the beginning of a question when you make a suggestion, offer, or request. ❑ *What about going out with me tomorrow?* 16 *PHRASE: PHR group/cl* You use **what about** or **what of** when you introduce a new topic or a point which seems relevant to a previous remark. ❑ *Now you've talked about work on daffodils, what about other commercially important flowers, like roses?* 17 *PHRASE: PHR n* You say **what about** a particular person or thing when you ask someone to explain why they have asked you about that person or thing. ❑ *'This thing with the Corbett woman.' — 'Oh, yeah. What about her?'* 18 *PHRASE: n PHR, n and/or PHR* *vagueness* You say **what have you** at the end of a list in order to refer generally to other things of the same kind. ❑ *So many things are unsafe these days – milk, cranberry sauce, what have you... My great-grandfather made horseshoes and nails and what have you.* 19 *PHRASE: PHR cl* You say **what if** at the beginning of a question when you ask about the consequences of something happening, especially something undesirable. ❑ *What if this doesn't work out?* 20 *PHRASE: PHR after v* If you know **what's what**, you know the important things that need to be known about a situation. ❑ *You have to know what's what and when to draw the line... You should come across the river with us. Then you will really see what's what.*
21 **what's more** → see **more**.

**what|ev|er** /ʰwɒtevəʳ/ ◆◆◇ 1 *CONJ* You use **whatever** to refer to anything or everything of a particular type. ❑ *Franklin was free to do pretty much whatever he pleased... When you're older I think you're better equipped mentally to cope with whatever happens... He's good at whatever he does.* ♦ **Whatever** is also a determiner. *DET = any* ❑ *Whatever doubts he might have had about Ingrid were all over now.* 2 *CONJ* You use **whatever** to say that something is the case in all circumstances. ❑ *We shall love you whatever happens, Diana... People will judge you whatever you do... She runs about 15 miles a day every day, whatever the weather.* 3 *ADV: with brd-neg, n ADV* *emphasis* *= whatsoever* You use **whatever** after a noun group in order to emphasize a negative statement. ❑ *There is no evidence whatever that competition in broadcasting has ever reduced costs... I have nothing whatever to say.* 4 *QUEST* *emphasis* *= what* You use **whatever** to ask in an emphatic way about something which you are very surprised about. ❑ *Whatever can you mean?* 5 *CONJ* You use **whatever** when you are indicating that you do not know the precise identity, meaning, or value of the thing just mentioned. ❑ *I thought that my upbringing was 'normal', whatever that is.* [vagueness]

PHRASES [6] You say **or whatever** to refer generally to something else of the same kind as the thing or things that you have just mentioned. [INFORMAL] ❑ *You may like a Malt whisky that is peatier, or smokier, or sweeter, or whatever.* PHRASE: cl/group PHR [7] You say **'whatever you say'** to indicate that you accept what someone has said, even though you do not really believe them or do not think it is a good idea. ❑ *'We'll go in your car, Billy.' — 'Whatever you say.'* CONVENTION [feelings] [8] You say **whatever** you **do** when giving advice or warning someone about something. ❑ *Whatever you do, don't look for a pay increase when you know the company is going through some difficulty.* PHRASE: PHR cl [emphasis]

**what|not** /ʰwɒtnɒt/ People sometimes say **'and whatnot'** or **'or whatnot'** after mentioning one or more things, to refer in a vague way to other things which are similar. [INFORMAL, SPOKEN] ❑ *The women were there in their jeans and T-shirts and overalls and whatnot... The council can send messages or letters or whatnot in Spanish to their constituents.* PHRASE: cl/group PHR [vagueness] = whatever

**what's** /ʰwɒts/ **What's** is the usual spoken form of 'what is' or 'what has', especially when 'has' is an auxiliary verb.

**whats|her|name** /ʰwɒtsəʳneɪm/ also **whatsername.** You say **whatshername** instead of a woman's name when you cannot remember it or are trying to remember it. [SPOKEN] ❑ *That's the thing that whatshername gave me.* PRON

**whats|his|name** /ʰwɒtsɪzneɪm/ also **whatsisname.** You say **whatshisname** instead of a man's name when you cannot remember it or are trying to remember it. [SPOKEN] ❑ *...the new junior minister, whatsisname, Donald Sinclair.* PRON

**whats|it** /ʰwɒtsɪt/ **(whatsits)** You use **whatsit** instead of a noun or name which you cannot remember or which you do not want to say because it is rude. [SPOKEN] ❑ *We wanted to be here early in case the whatsit, maintenance supervisor had forgotten to deal with it.* N-VAR

**what|so|ev|er** /ʰwɒtsoʊevəʳ/ You use **whatsoever** after a noun group in order to emphasize a negative statement. ❑ *My school did nothing whatsoever in the way of athletics... I don't think they'll have any idea how I'm feeling. None whatsoever.* ADV: usu with brd-neg, n ADV [emphasis]

**wheat** /ʰwiːt/ **(wheats) Wheat** is a cereal crop grown for food. **Wheat** is also used to refer to the grain of this crop, which is usually ground into flour and used to make bread. ❑ *...farmers growing wheat, corn, or other crops. ...wheat flour.* to **separate the wheat from the chaff** → see **chaff.** N-MASS

**wheat|germ** /ʰwiːtdʒɜːʳm/ also **wheat germ. Wheatgerm** is the middle part of a grain of wheat which is rich in vitamins and is often added to other food. N-UNCOUNT

**whee|dle** /ʰwiːdᵊl/ **(wheedles, wheedling, wheedled)** If you say that someone **wheedles,** you mean that they try to persuade someone to do or give them what they want, for example by saying nice things that they do not mean. ❑ *Cross decided to beg and wheedle a bit... He managed to wheedle his way into the offices. ...an opportunity to wheedle more money out of Wilson.* VERB [disapproval] V; V *way* prep; V n *out of/from* n

**wheel** /ʰwiːl/ **(wheels, wheeling, wheeled)** ◆◇◇ [1] The **wheels** of a vehicle are the circular objects which are fixed underneath it and which enable it to move along the ground. ❑ *The car wheels spun and slipped on some oil on the road.* N-COUNT ● Something **on wheels** has wheels attached to the bottom, so that it can be moved easily. ❑ *...a trolley on wheels... The stove is on wheels so it can be shuffled around easily.* PHRASE: n PHR, v-link PHR [2] A **wheel** is a circular object which forms a part of a machine, usually a moving part. ❑ *...an eighteenth century mill with a water wheel.* N-COUNT [3] **The wheel** of a car or other vehicle is the circular object that is used to steer it. **The wheel** is used in expressions to talk about who is driving a vehicle. For example, if someone is **at the wheel** of a car, they are driving it. ❑ *My co-pilot suddenly grabbed the wheel... Curtis got behind the wheel and they started back toward the cottage... Roberto handed Flynn the keys and let him take the wheel.* N-COUNT: usu sing, the N = steering wheel [4] If you **wheel** an object that has wheels somewhere, you push it along. ❑ *He wheeled his bike into the alley at the side of the house... They wheeled her out on the stretcher.* VERB V n prep/adv [5] If something such as a group of animals or birds **wheels,** it moves in a circle. [LITERARY] ❑ *A flock of crows wheeled overhead.* VERB V [6] If you **wheel** around, you turn around suddenly where you are standing, often because you are surprised, shocked, or angry. ❑ *He wheeled around to face her.* VERB V adv [7] People talk about **the wheels of** an organization or system to mean the way in which it operates. ❑ *He knows the wheels of administration turn slowly.* N-PLURAL: the N *of* n to **oil the wheels** → see **oil.** [8] → See also **Catherine wheel, meals on wheels, potter's wheel, spare wheel, spinning wheel, steering wheel, water wheel.**

**wheel and deal (wheels and deals, wheeling and dealing, wheeled and dealed)** If you say that someone **wheels and deals,** you mean that they use a lot of different methods and contacts to achieve what they want in business or politics, often in a way which you consider dishonest. ❑ *He still wheels and deals all around the globe.* VERB V ♦ **wheel|ing and deal|ing** *He hates the wheeling and dealing associated with conventional political life.* N-UNCOUNT

**wheel|barrow** /ʰwiːlbæroʊ/ **(wheelbarrows)** A **wheelbarrow** is a small open cart with one wheel and handles that is used for carrying things, for example in the garden. N-COUNT

**wheel|base** /ʰwiːlbeɪs/ **(wheelbases)** The **wheelbase** of a car or other vehicle is the distance between its front and back wheels. N-COUNT: usu sing

**wheel|chair** /ʰwiːltʃeəʳ/ **(wheelchairs)** A **wheelchair** is a chair with wheels that you use in order to move about in if you cannot walk properly, for example because you are disabled or sick. N-COUNT

**wheel clamp (wheel clamps, wheel clamping, wheel clamped)** [1] A **wheel clamp** is a large metal device which is fitted to the wheel of an illegally parked car or other vehicle in order to prevent it from being driven away. The motorist has to pay to have the clamp removed. [BRIT] N-COUNT

☑ in AM, use **Denver boot**

[2] If a car **is wheel clamped,** a wheel clamp is fixed to one of its wheels so that it cannot be driven away. [BRIT] ❑ *Unauthorized vehicles will be wheel clamped or towed away.* VERB *be* V-ed

☑ in AM, use **boot**

♦ **wheel-clamping** *...drivers forced to pay wheel-clamping charges.* N-UNCOUNT

**wheeler-dealer (wheeler-dealers)** If you refer to someone, especially in business or politics, as a **wheeler-dealer,** you disapprove of the way that they try to succeed or to get what they want, often by dishonest or unfair methods. N-COUNT [disapproval]

**wheel|house** /ʰwiːlhaʊs/ **(wheelhouses)** A **wheelhouse** is a small room or shelter on a ship or boat, where the wheel used for steering the boat is situated. N-COUNT

**wheelie bin** /ʰwiːlibɪn/ **(wheelie bins)** A **wheelie bin** is a large, rectangular dustbin with a hinged lid and wheels on two of the corners. [BRIT, AUSTRALIAN] N-COUNT

**wheel|wright** /ʰwiːlraɪt/ **(wheelwrights)** A **wheelwright** is someone who makes and repairs wooden wheels and other wooden things such as carts, carriages, and gates. N-COUNT

**wheeze** /ʰwiːz/ **(wheezes, wheezing, wheezed)** If someone **wheezes,** they breathe with difficulty VERB and make a whistling sound. ❑ *He had quite serious problems with his chest and wheezed and coughed all the time... 'Boy,' wheezed old Pop Ryan.* V / V with quote

**wheezy** /ʰwiːzi/ A **wheezy** cough or laugh comes from someone who has difficulty breathing, so it makes a whistling sound. ADJ

**whelk** /ʰwelk/ **(whelks)** A **whelk** is a creature like a snail that is found in the sea near the shore. Whelks have hard shells, and soft bodies which can be eaten. N-COUNT

**whelp** /ʰwelp/ **(whelps)** A **whelp** is a young animal, especially a young dog or wolf. [OLD-FASHIONED] N-COUNT

**when** /ʰwen/ ◆◆◆ 1 You use **when** to ask questions about the time at which things happen. ❑ *When are you going home?... When is the press conference?... When were you in this house last?... 'I'll be there this afternoon.' — 'When?'* QUEST 2 If something happens **when** something else is happening, the two things are happening at the same time. ❑ *When eating a whole cooked fish, you should never turn it over to get at the flesh on the other side... Mustard is grown in the field when weeds are there, rather than when the growing crops are there.* CONJ 3 You use **when** to introduce a clause in which you mention something which happens at some point during an activity, event, or situation. ❑ *When I met the Gills, I had been gardening for nearly ten years.* CONJ 4 You use **when** to introduce a clause where you mention the circumstances under which the event in the main clause happened or will happen. ❑ *When he brought Imelda her drink she gave him a genuine, sweet smile of thanks... I'll start to think about it when I have to write my report.* CONJ 5 You use **when** after certain words, especially verbs and adjectives, to introduce a clause where you mention the time at which something happens. ❑ *I asked him when he'd be back to pick me up... I don't know when the decision was made.* CONJ 6 You use **when** to introduce a clause which specifies or refers to the time at which something happens. ❑ *He could remember a time when he had worked like that himself... In 1973, when he lived in Rome, his sixteen-year-old son was kidnapped.* PRON 7 You use **when** to introduce the reason for an opinion, comment, or question. ❑ *How can I love myself when I look like this?* CONJ 8 You use **when** in order to introduce a fact or comment which makes the other part of the sentence rather surprising or unlikely. ❑ *Our mothers sat us down to read and paint, when all we really wanted to do was to make a mess.* CONJ = *although*

**whence** /ʰwens/ **Whence** means from where. [LITERARY or OLD-FASHIONED] ❑ *No one ordered him back whence he came.* QUEST

**when|ever** /ʰwenevəʳ/ ◆◇◇ 1 You use **whenever** to refer to any time or every time that something happens or is true. ❑ *She always called at the vicarage whenever she was in the area... You can have my cottage whenever you like... I recommend that you avoid processed foods whenever possible.* CONJ 2 You use **whenever** to refer to a time that you do not know or are not sure about. ❑ *He married Miss Vancouver in 1963, or whenever it was.* CONJ

**where** /ʰweəʳ/ ◆◆◆

✔ Usually pronounced /ʰweəʳ/ for meanings 2 and 3.

1 You use **where** to ask questions about the place something is in, or is coming from or going to. ❑ *Where did you meet him?... Where's Anna?... Where are we going?... 'You'll never believe where Julie and I are going.' — 'Where?'* QUEST 2 You use **where** after certain words, especially verbs and adjectives, to introduce a clause in which you mention the place in which something is situated or happens. ❑ *He knew where Henry Carter had gone... If he's got something on his mind he knows where to find me... Ernest Brown lives about a dozen blocks from where the riots began.* CONJ ♦ **Where** is also a relative pronoun. ❑ *...available at the travel agency where you book your holiday... Wanchai boasts the Academy of Performing Arts, where everything from Chinese Opera to Shakespeare is performed.* PRON 3 You use **where** to ask questions about a situation, a stage in something, or an aspect of something. ❑ *If they get their way, where will it stop?... It's not so simple. They'll have to let the draft board know, and then where will we be?* QUEST 4 You use **where** after certain words, especially verbs and adjectives, to introduce a clause in which you mention a situation, a stage in something, or an aspect of something. ❑ *It's not hard to see where she got her feelings about herself... She had a feeling she already knew where this conversation was going to lead... I didn't know where to start.* CONJ ♦ **Where** is also a relative pronoun. ❑ *...that delicate situation where a friend's confidence can easily be betrayed... The government is at a stage where it is willing to talk to almost anyone.* PRON 5 You use **where** to introduce a clause that contrasts with the other parts of the sentence. ❑ *Sometimes a teacher will be listened to, where a parent might not.* CONJ = *whereas*

**where|abouts**

✔ Pronounced /ʰweərəbaʊts/ for meaning 1, and /ʰweərəbaʊts/ for meanings 2 and 3.

1 If you refer to the **whereabouts** of a particular person or thing, you mean the place where that person or thing may be found. ❑ *The police are anxious to hear from anyone who may know the whereabouts of the firearms.* N-SING-COLL: with poss 2 You use **whereabouts** in questions when you are asking precisely where something is. ❑ *Whereabouts in Liverpool are you from?... 'I actually live near Chester.' — 'Whereabouts?'* QUEST 3 You use **whereabouts** after certain words, especially verbs and adjectives, to introduce a clause in which you mention precisely where something is situated or happens. ❑ *I live in a village near to Germaine Greer and know whereabouts she lives.* CONJ

**where|as** /ʰweəræz/ ◆◇◇ You use **whereas** to introduce a comment which contrasts with what is said in the main clause. ❑ *Pensions are linked to inflation, whereas they should be linked to the cost of living.* CONJ = *while*

**where|by** /ʰweəʳbaɪ/ A system or action **whereby** something happens is one that makes that thing happen. [FORMAL] ❑ *...the system whereby Britons choose their family doctors and the government pays those doctors... They voted to accept a deal whereby the union will receive nearly three-quarters of a million pounds from the International Miners Organisation.* PRON

**where|fores** /ʰweəʳfɔːʳz/ **The whys and wherefores** of something are the reasons for it. ❑ *Even successful bosses need to be queried about the whys and wherefores of their actions.* PHRASE: usu PHR *of* n

**where|in** /ʰweərɪn/ 1 **Wherein** means in which place or thing. [FORMAL, LITERARY or OLD-FASHIONED] ❑ *...a riding school wherein we could learn the art of horsemanship.* PRON 2 **Wherein** means in which part or respect. [FORMAL] ❑ *Wherein lies the truth?* QUEST

**where|upon** /ʰweərəpɒn/ You use **whereupon** to say that one thing happens immediately after another thing, and usually as a result of it. [FORMAL] ❑ *Mr Muite refused to talk to them except in the company of his legal colleagues, whereupon the police officers departed.* CONJ

**wher|ever** /ʰweərevəʳ/ 1 You use **wherever** to indicate that something happens or is true in any place or situation. ❑ *Some people enjoy themselves wherever they are... Jack believed in finding happiness wherever possible.* CONJ 2 You use **wherever** when you indicate that you do not know where a person or place is. ❑ *I'd like to leave as soon as possible and join my children, wherever they are.* CONJ 3 You use **wherever** in questions as an emphatic form of 'where', usually when you are surprised about something. ❑ *Wherever did you get that idea?... Wherever have you been?* QUEST emphasis

**where|with|al** /ʰweəʳwɪðɔːl/ If you have **the wherewithal** for something, you have the N-SING: *the* N, oft N to-inf, means, especially the money, that you need for it. ❑ *She didn't have the financial wherewithal to do it.* N *for* n/-ing = *means*

**whet** /ʰwet/ **(whets, whetting, whetted)** If someone or something **whets** your **appetite for** a particular thing, they increase your desire to have it or know about it, especially by giving you an idea of what it is like. ❑ *A really good catalogue can also whet customers' appetites for merchandise.* PHRASE: V and N inflect, oft PHR *for* n

**wheth|er** /ʰweðəʳ/ ◆◆◆ 1 You use **whether** when you are talking about a choice or doubt between two or more alternatives. ❑ *To this day, it's unclear whether he shot himself or was murdered... They now have two weeks to decide whether or not to buy... I don't know whether they've found anybody yet.* CONJ 2 You use **whether** to say that something is true in any of the circumstances that you mention. ❑ *Whether they say it aloud or not, most men expect their wives to be faithful. ...beers and lagers of all kinds, whether bottled or draught.* CONJ

**whet|stone** /ʰwetstoʊn/ **(whetstones)** A **whetstone** is a stone which is used for sharpening knives or other tools that have a blade. N-COUNT: usu sing

**whew** **Whew** is used in writing to represent a sound that you make when you breathe out quickly, for example because you are very hot, very relieved, or very surprised. ❑ *'Whew,' he said. 'It's hot.'.* EXCLAM [feelings]

**whey** /ʰweɪ/ **Whey** is the watery part of sour milk that is separated from the thick part called curds, for example when you are making cheese. N-UNCOUNT

**which** /ʰwɪtʃ/ ◆◆◆

> Usually pronounced /ʰwɪtʃ/ for meanings 2, 3 and 4.

1 You use **which** in questions when there are two or more possible answers or alternatives. ❑ *Which do they want me to do, declare war or surrender?... Which are the ones you really like?... 'You go down that passageway over there.' — 'Which one?'... Which vitamin supplements are good value?* QUEST 2 You use **which** to refer to a choice between two or more possible answers or alternatives. ❑ *I wanted to know which school it was you went to... Scientists have long wondered which parts of the brain are involved in musical tasks.* DET ♦ **Which** is also a conjunction. ❑ *In her panic she couldn't remember which was Mr Grainger's cabin... There are so many diets on the market, how do you know which to choose?* CONJ 3 You use **which** at the beginning of a relative clause when specifying the thing that you are talking about or when giving more information about it. ❑ *Soldiers opened fire on a car which failed to stop at an army checkpoint... He's based in Banja Luka, which is the largest city in northern Bosnia... Colic describes a whole variety of conditions in which a horse suffers abdominal pain.* PRON 4 You use **which** to refer back to an idea or situation expressed in a previous sentence or sentences, especially when you want to give your opinion about it. ❑ *Since we started in September we have raised fifty thousand pounds, which is pretty good going.* PRON ♦ **Which** is also a determiner. ❑ *The chances are you haven't fully decided what you want from your career at the moment, in which case you're definitely not cut out to be a boss yet!* DET: DET sing-n 5 If you cannot tell the difference between two things, you can say that you do not know **which is which**. ❑ *They all look so alike to me that I'm never sure which is which.* PHRASE: V inflects 6 **any which way** → see **way**. **every which way** → see **way**.

**which|ever** /ʰwɪtʃevəʳ/ 1 You use **whichever** in order to indicate that it does not matter which of the possible alternatives happens or is chosen. ❑ *Israel offers automatic citizenship to all Jews who want it, whatever colour they are and whichever language they speak.* DET: DET sing-n = *whatever* ♦ **Whichever** is also a conjunction. ❑ *We will gladly exchange your goods, or refund your money, whichever you prefer.* CONJ = *whatever* 2 You use **whichever** to specify which of a number of possibilities is the right one or the one you mean. ❑ *...learning to relax by whichever method suits you best.* DET ♦ **Whichever** is also a conjunction. ❑ *Fishing is from 6 am to dusk or 10.30pm, whichever is sooner.* CONJ

**whiff** /ʰwɪf/ **(whiffs)** 1 If there is a **whiff of** a particular smell, you smell it only slightly or only for a brief period of time, for example as you walk past someone or something. ❑ *He caught a whiff of her perfume.* N-COUNT: usu sing, usu N *of* n 2 A **whiff of** something bad or harmful is a slight sign of it. ❑ *Not a whiff of scandal has ever tainted his private life.* N-COUNT: usu sing, usu N *of* n

**Whig** /ʰwɪg/ **(Whigs)** 1 A **Whig** was a member of a British political party in the 18th and 19th centuries that was in favour of political and social changes. [BRIT] N-COUNT 2 In the American Revolution, a **Whig** was an American who supported the revolution against the British. [AM] N-COUNT 3 A **Whig** was a member of an American political party in the 19th century that wanted to limit the powers of the President. [AM] N-COUNT

> **while**
> ① CONJUNCTION USES
> ② NOUN AND VERB USES

**① while** /ʰwaɪl/ ◆◆◆

> Usually pronounced /ʰwaɪl/ for meaning 4. The form **whilst** is also used in formal or literary English, especially British English.

1 If something happens **while** something else is happening, the two things are happening at the same time. ❑ *Racing was halted for an hour while the track was repaired... Her parents could help with child care while she works.* CONJ 2 If something happens **while** something else happens, the first thing happens at some point during the time that the second thing is happening. ❑ *The two ministers have yet to meet, but may do so while in New York... Never apply water to a burn from an electric shock while the casualty is still in contact with the electric current.* CONJ 3 You use **while** at the beginning of a clause to introduce information which contrasts with information in the main clause. ❑ *The first two services are free, while the third costs £35.00.* CONJ = *whereas* 4 You use **while**, before making a statement, in order to introduce information that partly conflicts with your statement. ❑ *While the numbers of such developments are relatively small, the potential market is large... While the news, so far, has been good, there may be days ahead when it is bad.* CONJ = *although*

**② while** /ʰwaɪl/ **(whiles, whiling, whiled)** ◆◆◇
⇒ Please look at category 3 to see if the expression you are looking for is shown under another headword. 1 **A while** is a period of time. ❑ *They walked on in silence for a while... He was married a little while ago... Working at low intensity means that you can continue to perform the activity for a long while.* N-SING: *a* N, usu adj 2 You use **all the while** in order to say that something happens continually or that it happens throughout the time when something else is happening. ❑ *All the while the people at the next table watched me eat.* PHRASE: PHR with cl 3 **once in a while** → see **once**. **worth your while** → see **worth**.
♦ **while away** If you **while away** the time in a particular way, you spend time in that way, because you are waiting for something else to happen, or because you have nothing else to do. ❑ *Miss Bennett whiled away the hours playing old films on her video-recorder.* PHRASAL VERB V P n (not pron) Also V n P

**whilst** /ʰwaɪlst/ ◆◇◇ **Whilst** means the same as the conjunction **while**. [mainly BRIT, FORMAL or LITERARY] CONJ

**whim** /ʰwɪm/ **(whims)** A **whim** is a wish to do or have something which seems to have no serious reason or purpose behind it, and often occurs suddenly. ❑ *We decided, more or less on a whim, to sail to Morocco... The premium can increase at the whim of the insurers.* N-VAR: oft *on/at* N

**whim|per** /ʰwɪmpəʳ/ **(whimpers, whimpering, whimpered)** 1 If someone **whimpers**, they make quiet unhappy or frightened sounds, as if they are about to start crying. ❑ *She lay at the bottom of the stairs, whimpering in pain... He made another pathetic* VERB V V-ing *whimpering sound.* ♦ **Whimper** is also a noun. N-COUNT ❑ *David's crying subsided to a whimper.* 2 If someone **whimpers** something, they say it in an unhappy or frightened way. VERB ❑ *'Let me go,' she whimpered. 'You're hurting me.'... She whimpered something inaudible.* V with quote / V n

**whim|si|cal** /ʰwɪmzɪkəl/ ADJ A **whimsical** person or idea is unusual, playful, and unpredictable, rather than serious and practical. ❑ *McGrath remembers his offbeat sense of humor, his whimsical side.*

**whim|sy** /ʰwɪmzi/ also **whimsey.** N-UNCOUNT **Whimsy** is behaviour which is unusual, playful, and unpredictable, rather than having any serious reason or purpose behind it.

**whine** /ʰwaɪn/ **(whines, whining, whined)** 1 VERB If something or someone **whines**, they make a long, high-pitched noise, especially one which sounds sad or unpleasant. ❑ *He could hear her dog barking and whining in the background... The engines whined.* V / V ♦ **Whine** is also a noun. N-COUNT: usu sing ❑ *...the whine of air-raid sirens.* 2 VERB [disapproval] If you say that someone **is whining**, you mean that they are complaining in an annoying way about something unimportant. ❑ *They come to me to whine about their troubles. ...children who whine that they are bored... 'Why can't you tell me?' I whined.* V *about* n/-ing / V that / V with quote

**whinge** /ʰwɪndʒ/ **(whinges, whingeing** or **whinging, whinged)** VERB [disapproval] = moan, whine If you say that someone **is whingeing**, you mean that they are complaining in an annoying way about something unimportant. [BRIT, INFORMAL] ❑ *All she ever does is whinge and complain.* V

**whing|er** /ʰwɪndʒəʳ/ **(whingers)** N-COUNT [disapproval] If you call someone a **whinger**, you are critical of them because they complain about unimportant things all the time. [BRIT, INFORMAL]

**whin|ny** /ʰwɪni/ **(whinnies, whinnying, whinnied)** VERB When a horse **whinnies**, it makes a series of high-pitched sounds, usually not very loudly. ❑ *The girl's horse whinnied.* V ♦ **Whinny** is also a noun. N-COUNT ❑ *With a terrified whinny the horse shied.*

**whip** /ʰwɪp/ **(whips, whipping, whipped)** ◆◇◇ 1 N-COUNT A **whip** is a long thin piece of material such as leather or rope, fastened to a stiff handle. It is used for hitting people or animals. 2 VERB If someone **whips** a person or animal, they beat them or hit them with a whip or something like a whip. ❑ *Eye-witnesses claimed Mr Melton whipped the horse up to 16 times.* V n ♦ **whip|ping (whippings)** N-COUNT = beating *He threatened to give her a whipping.* 3 VERB If something, for example the wind, **whips** something, it strikes it sharply. [LITERARY] ❑ *A terrible wind whipped our faces.* V n 4 VERB If someone **whips** something out or **whips** it off, they take it out or take it off very quickly and suddenly. ❑ *Bob whipped out his notebook... Players were whipping their shirts off.* V n with adv / V n with adv 5 VERB When you **whip** something liquid such as cream or an egg, you stir it very fast until it is thick or stiff. ❑ *Whip the cream until thick... Whip the eggs, oils and honey together. ...strawberries and whipped cream.* V n / V n adv/prep / V-ed 6 VERB If you **whip** people **into** an emotional state, you deliberately cause and encourage them to be in that state. ❑ *He could whip a crowd into hysteria.* V n *into* n 7 N-COUNT A **whip** is a member of a political party in a parliament or legislature who is responsible for making sure that party members are present to vote on important issues and that they vote in the appropriate way. ❑ *The Whips have the job of making sure MPs toe the line.* 8 PHRASE: PHR after v If you have **the whip hand**, you have power over someone else in a particular situation. ❑ *These days the shopper has the whip hand, and will not buy if stores fail to lower their prices.*

♦ **whip up** PHRASAL VERB = stir up If someone **whips up** an emotion, especially a dangerous one such as hatred, or if they **whip** people **up** into an emotional state, they deliberately cause and encourage people to feel that emotion. ❑ *He accused politicians of whipping up anti-foreign sentiments in order to win right-wing votes.* V P n (not pron) / Also V n P *into* n

**whip|lash** /ʰwɪplæʃ/ N-UNCOUNT: oft N n **Whiplash** is a neck injury caused by the head suddenly moving forwards and then back again, for example in a car accident. ❑ *His wife suffered whiplash and shock.*

**whip|per|snap|per** /ʰwɪpəʳsnæpəʳ/ **(whippersnappers)** N-COUNT [disapproval] If you refer to a young person as a **whippersnapper**, you disapprove of them because you think that they are behaving more confidently than they should. [INFORMAL, OLD-FASHIONED]

**whip|pet** /ʰwɪpɪt/ **(whippets)** N-COUNT A **whippet** is a small thin dog with long legs. Some whippets are used for racing.

**whip|ping boy** **(whipping boys)** N-COUNT = scapegoat If someone or something is a **whipping boy** for a particular situation, they get all the blame for it. ❑ *He has become a convenient whipping boy for the failures of the old regime.*

**whip|ping cream** N-UNCOUNT **Whipping cream** is cream that becomes stiff when it is stirred very fast.

**whip|poor|will** /wɪpʊəʳwɪl/ **(whippoorwills)** N-COUNT A **whippoorwill** is a North American bird that is active at night and has a call that sounds like 'whip poor will'.

**whip-round** N-SING When a group of people have a **whip-round**, money is collected from each person so that it can be used to buy something for all of them or for someone they all know. [INFORMAL]

**whir** /ʰwɜːʳ/ → see **whirr.**

**whirl** /ʰwɜːʳl/ **(whirls, whirling, whirled)** 1 VERB If something or someone **whirls** around or if you **whirl** them around, they move around or turn around very quickly. ❑ *Not receiving an answer, she whirled round... He was whirling Anne around the floor... The smoke began to whirl and grew into a monstrous column.* V adv/prep / V n adv/prep / V / Also V n ♦ **Whirl** is also a noun. N-COUNT ❑ *...the barely audible whirl of wheels.* 2 N-COUNT: usu sing, with supp You can refer to a lot of intense activity as a **whirl** of activity. ❑ *In half an hour's whirl of activity she does it all... Your life is such a social whirl.* 3 PHRASE: V inflects If you decide to **give** an activity **a whirl**, you do it even though it is something that you have never tried before. [INFORMAL] ❑ *Why not give acupuncture a whirl?... We decided to give it a whirl.*

**whirl|pool** /ʰwɜːʳlpuːl/ **(whirlpools)** N-COUNT A **whirlpool** is a small area in a river or the sea where the water is moving quickly round and round, so that objects floating near it are pulled into its centre.

**whirl|wind** /ʰwɜːʳlwɪnd/ **(whirlwinds)** 1 N-COUNT A **whirlwind** is a tall column of air which spins round and round very fast and moves across the land or sea. 2 N-COUNT: usu sing, with supp, usu N *of* n You can describe a situation in which a lot of things happen very quickly and are very difficult for someone to control as a **whirlwind**. ❑ *I had been running around southern England in a whirlwind of activity.* 3 ADJ: ADJ n A **whirlwind** event or action happens or is done much more quickly than normal. ❑ *He got married after a whirlwind romance. ... a whirlwind tour of France.*

**whirr** /ʰwɜːʳ/ **(whirrs, whirring, whirred)** also **whir.** VERB When something such as a machine or an insect's wing **whirrs**, it makes a series of low sounds so quickly that they seem like one continuous sound. ❑ *The camera whirred and clicked. ...the whirring sound of the film projector.* V / V-ing ♦ **Whirr** is also a noun. N-COUNT: usu sing; SOUND ❑ *He could hear the whirr of a vacuum cleaner.*

**whisk** /ʰwɪsk/ **(whisks, whisking, whisked)** 1 VERB If you **whisk** someone or something somewhere, you take them or move them there quickly. ❑ *He whisked her across the dance floor... I was whisked away in a police car.* V n prep/adv 2 VERB If you **whisk** something such as eggs or cream, you stir it very fast, often with an electric device, so that it becomes full of small bubbles. ❑ *Just before serving, whisk the cream... In a separate bowl, whisk together the remaining sugar and the yolks.* V n / V pl-n with *together* 3 N-COUNT A **whisk** is a kitchen tool used for whisking eggs or cream. → See picture on page 1710. ❑ *...an electric whisk.*

**whisk|er** /ʰwɪskəʳ/ **(whiskers)** 1 The **whiskers** of an animal such as a cat or a mouse are the long stiff hairs that grow near its mouth. N-COUNT: usu pl 2 You can refer to the hair on a man's face, especially on the sides of his face, as his **whiskers**. ❑ *...wild, savage-looking fellows, with large whiskers, unshaven beards, and dirty faces.* N-PLURAL 3 You can use **whisker** in expressions such as **by a whisker** or **within a whisker of** to indicate that something happened or is true, but only by a very small amount or degree. ❑ *A new pet census showed that cats now outnumber dogs by a whisker (7 million to 6.9 million)... She came within a whisker of taking a gold medal... Unemployment is now a whisker away from three million.* N-SING

**whisk|ery** /ʰwɪskəri/ If you describe someone as **whiskery**, you mean that they have lots of stiff little hairs on their face. ❑ *...a whiskery old man.* ADJ

**whis|key** /ʰwɪski/ **(whiskeys) Whiskey** is whisky that is made in Ireland or the United States. ❑ *...a tumbler with about an inch of whiskey in it.* N-MASS ♦ A **whiskey** is a glass of whiskey. N-COUNT

**whis|ky** /ʰwɪski/ **(whiskies) Whisky** is a strong alcoholic drink made, especially in Scotland, from grain such as barley or rye. ❑ *...a bottle of whisky. ...expensive whiskies and brandies.* N-MASS ♦ A **whisky** is a glass of whisky. ❑ *She handed him a whisky.* N-COUNT

**whis|per** /ʰwɪspəʳ/ **(whispers, whispering, whispered)** ◆◇◇ 1 When you **whisper**, you say something very quietly, using your breath rather than your throat, so that only one person can hear you. ❑ *'Keep your voice down,' I whispered... She sat on Rossi's knee as he whispered in her ear... He whispered the message to David... Somebody whispered that films like that were illegal... She whispered his name.* VERB V with quote V prep V n prep V that V n ♦ **Whisper** is also a noun. ❑ *Men were talking in whispers in every office.* N-COUNT 2 If people **whisper** about a piece of information, they talk about it, although it might not be true or accurate, or might be a secret. ❑ *Today, we no longer gasp when we hear a teenage girl is pregnant or whisper about unmarried couples who live together... It is whispered that he intended to resign... But don't whisper a word of that.* VERB V *about* wh/n *it be* V-ed that V n ♦ **Whisper** is also a noun. ❑ *I've heard a whisper that the Bishop intends to leave.* N-COUNT = *rumour*

**whist** /ʰwɪst/ **Whist** is a card game in which people play in pairs against each other. N-UNCOUNT

**whis|tle** /ʰwɪsəl/ **(whistles, whistling, whistled)** 1 When you **whistle** or when you **whistle** a tune, you make a series of musical notes by forcing your breath out between your lips, or your teeth. ❑ *He was whistling softly to himself... As he washed he whistled a tune.* VERB V V n 2 When someone **whistles**, they make a sound by forcing their breath out between their lips or their teeth. People sometimes whistle when they are surprised or shocked, or to call a dog, or to show that they are impressed. ❑ *He whistled, surprised but not shocked... Jenkins whistled through his teeth, impressed at last.* VERB V V prep ♦ **Whistle** is also a noun. ❑ *Jackson gave a low whistle.* → See also **wolf-whistle**. N-COUNT: oft supp N 3 If something such as a train or a kettle **whistles**, it makes a loud, high sound. ❑ *Somewhere a train whistled. ...the whistling car radio.* VERB V, V-ing ♦ **whis|tling** *...the whistling of the wind.* N-SING 4 If something such as the wind or a bullet **whistles** somewhere, it moves there, making a loud, high sound. ❑ *The wind was whistling through the building... As I stood up a bullet whistled past my back.* VERB V prep V prep 5 A **whistle** is a loud sound produced by air or steam being forced through a small opening, or by something moving quickly through the air. ❑ *Hugh listened to the whistle of a train. ...the whistle of the wind.* N-COUNT: oft N *of* n 6 A **whistle** is a small metal tube which you blow in order to produce a loud sound and attract someone's attention. ❑ *On the platform, the guard blew his whistle.* N-COUNT 7 A **whistle** is a simple musical instrument in the shape of a metal pipe with holes. → See also **tin whistle**. N-COUNT

PHRASES 8 If you **blow the whistle on** someone, or on something secret or illegal, you tell another person, especially a person in authority, what is happening. ❑ *Companies should protect employees who blow the whistle on dishonest workmates and work practices.* → See also **whistle-blower**. PHRASE: V inflects, usu PHR *on* n = *inform* 9 If you describe something as **clean as a whistle**, you mean that it is completely clean. PHRASE: v-link PHR

**whistle-blower** **(whistle-blowers)** also **whistleblower**. A **whistle-blower** is someone who finds out that the organization they are working for is doing something immoral or illegal and tells the authorities or the public about it. [JOURNALISM] ❑ *He has been a prominent victim of alleged witch-hunts against whistle-blowers in the NHS.* N-COUNT

**whistle-blowing** also **whistleblowing**. **Whistle-blowing** is the act of telling the authorities or the public that the organization you are working for is doing something immoral or illegal. ❑ *It took internal whistle-blowing and investigative journalism to uncover the rot.* N-UNCOUNT: oft N n

**whistle-stop** If someone, especially a politician, goes on a **whistle-stop** tour, they visit a lot of different places in a short time. ADJ: ADJ n

**whit** /ʰwɪt/ 1 You say **not a whit** or **not one whit** to emphasize that something is not the case at all. [mainly FORMAL or OLD-FASHIONED] ❑ *He cared not a whit for the social, political or moral aspects of literature.* PHRASE: with neg, PHR after v [emphasis] 2 **Whit** means the same as **Whitsun**. ❑ *The orchestra gave its first performance on Whit Monday.* N-UNCOUNT: usu N n

**white** /ʰwaɪt/ **(whiter, whitest, whites)** ◆◆◆ 1 Something that is **white** is the colour of snow or milk. ❑ *He had nice square white teeth... He was dressed in white from head to toe.* COLOUR ♦ **white|ness** *Her scarlet lipstick emphasized the whiteness of her teeth.* N-UNCOUNT 2 A **white** person has a pale skin and belongs to a race which is of European origin. ❑ *He was white, with brown shoulder-length hair and a moustache.* ADJ ♦ **Whites** are white people. ❑ *It's a school that's brought blacks and whites and Hispanics together.* N-COUNT: usu pl 3 If someone goes **white**, the skin on their face becomes very pale, for example because of fear, shock, anger, or illness. ❑ *Richard had gone very white, but he stood his ground... His face was white with fury.* ADJ: usu v-link ADJ ● If someone looks **white as a sheet** or **as white as a sheet**, they look very frightened, shocked, or ill. ❑ *He appeared in the doorway, white as a sheet, eyes wide with horror.* PHRASE: v-link PHR 4 **White** wine is pale yellow in colour. ❑ *Gregory poured another glass of white wine and went back to his bedroom.* ADJ ♦ You can refer to white wine as **white**. ❑ *I bought a bottle of Californian white.* N-MASS 5 **White** coffee has had milk or cream added to it. [BRIT] ❑ *Wayne has a large white coffee in front of him.* ADJ 6 **White** blood cells are the cells in your blood which your body uses to fight infection. ADJ: ADJ n 7 The **white** of an egg is the transparent liquid that surrounds the yellow part called the yolk. N-VAR 8 The **white** of someone's eye is the white part that surrounds the coloured part called the iris. N-COUNT: usu N *of* n

**white|board** /ʰwaɪtbɔːʳd/ **(whiteboards)** A **whiteboard** is a shiny white board on which people draw or write using special pens. Whiteboards are often used for teaching or giving talks. N-COUNT

**white Christ|mas** **(white Christmases)** A **white Christmas** is a Christmas when it snows. N-COUNT

**white-collar** also **white collar**. 1 **White-collar** workers work in offices rather than doing physical work such as making things in factories or building things. ❑ *White-collar workers now work longer hours.* ADJ: ADJ n ≠ *blue-collar* 2 **White-collar** crime is committed by people who work in offices, and involves stealing money secretly from companies or the government, or getting money in an illegal way. ADJ: ADJ n

**white el|ephant** **(white elephants)** If you describe something as a **white elephant**, you mean that it is a waste of money because it is complete- N-COUNT [disapproval] ly useless. ❑ *The pavilion has become a £14 million steel and glass white elephant.*

**white goods** People in business sometimes refer to fridges, washing machines, and other large pieces of electrical household equipment as **white goods**. Compare **brown goods**. N-PLURAL

**white-haired** Someone who is **white-haired** has white hair, usually because they are old. ADJ

**White|hall** /ʰwaɪthɔːl/ **Whitehall** is the name of a street in London in which there are many government offices. You can also use **Whitehall** to mean the British Government itself. ❑ *...people with banners marching down Whitehall... Whitehall said that it hoped to get the change through by the end of June.* ◆◇◇ N-PROPER

**white-hot** If something is **white-hot**, it is extremely hot. ❑ *It is important to get the coals white-hot before you start.* ADJ

**White House** **The White House** is the official home in Washington DC of the President of the United States. You can also use **the White House** to refer to the President of the United States and his or her officials. ❑ *He drove to the White House... The White House has not participated in any talks.* ◆◇◇ N-PROPER: *the* N, N n

**white knight** (**white knights**) A **white knight** is a person or an organization that rescues a company from difficulties such as financial problems or an unwelcome takeover bid. [BUSINESS] ❑ *...a white-knight bid.* N-COUNT

**white-knuckle** 1 In a fairground, a **white-knuckle** ride is any large machine that people ride on which is very exciting but also frightening. ❑ *...white-knuckle rides such as the rollercoaster.* ADJ: ADJ n 2 A **white-knuckle** experience is something that you find very exciting but also very frightening. ❑ *...a hellish white-knuckle ride through the heavy London traffic.* ADJ: ADJ n

**white lie** (**white lies**) If you refer to an untrue statement as a **white lie**, you mean that it is made to avoid hurting someone's feelings or to avoid trouble, and not for an evil purpose. N-COUNT

**white meat** (**white meats**) **White meat** is meat such as chicken and pork, which is pale in colour after it has been cooked. N-UNCOUNT: also N in pl

**whit|en** /ʰwaɪtᵊn/ (**whitens, whitening, whitened**) When something **whitens** or when you **whiten** it, it becomes whiter or paler in colour. ❑ *Her knuckles whiten as she clenches her hands harder. ...toothpastes that whiten teeth.* VERB V V n

**white noise** **White noise** is sound, especially of a loud, continuous, or unpleasant kind, that seems to have no pattern or rhythm. ❑ *They were made to listen to white noise, such as static of the sort you might pick up between radio stations.* N-UNCOUNT

**White Pages** **White Pages** is used to refer to the section of a telephone directory which lists names and telephone numbers in alphabetical order. Compare **Yellow Pages**. [AM] N-PLURAL

**White Pa|per** (**White Papers**) In Britain, Australia, Canada, and some other countries, a **White Paper** is an official report which describes the policy of the Government on a particular subject. N-COUNT

**white pep|per** **White pepper** is pepper which has been made from the dried insides of the fruits of the pepper plant. N-UNCOUNT

**white sauce** (**white sauces**) **White sauce** is a thick white sauce made from milk, flour, and butter. Meat, fish, or vegetables are often cooked in or served in white sauce. N-MASS

**white spir|it** **White spirit** is a colourless liquid that is made from petrol and is used, for example, to make paint thinner or to clean surfaces. [BRIT] N-UNCOUNT

☑ in AM, use **turpentine**

**white trash** Some people use **white trash** to refer to poor white people who they think are worthless. [AM, OFFENSIVE] ❑ *...a place peopled by illiterate poor white trash.* N-UNCOUNT-COLL disapproval

**white|wash** /ʰwaɪtwɒʃ/ (**whitewashes, whitewashing, whitewashed**) 1 **Whitewash** is a mixture of lime or chalk and water that is used for painting walls white. N-UNCOUNT 2 If a wall or building **has been whitewashed**, it has been painted white with whitewash. ❑ *The walls had been whitewashed. ...a town of picturesque whitewashed cottages.* VERB *be* V-ed V-ed 3 If you say that people **whitewash** something, you are accusing them of hiding the unpleasant facts or truth about it in order to make it acceptable. ❑ *The administration is whitewashing the regime's actions.* VERB disapproval = cover up V n 4 **Whitewash** is an attempt to hide the unpleasant facts or truth about someone or something. ❑ *He pledged that there would be no whitewash and that the police would carry out a full investigation.* N-UNCOUNT: also *a* N disapproval

**white-water raft|ing** **White-water rafting** is the activity of riding on a raft over rough, dangerous parts of a fast-flowing river. N-UNCOUNT

**white wed|ding** (**white weddings**) A **white wedding** is a wedding where the bride wears white and the ceremony takes place in a church. [mainly BRIT] N-COUNT

**whith|er** /ʰwɪðəʳ/ **Whither** means to where. [LITERARY or OLD-FASHIONED] ❑ *They knew not whither they went.* QUEST = where

**whit|ing** /ʰwaɪtɪŋ/ (**whitings** or **whiting**) A **whiting** is a black and silver fish that lives in the sea. ♦ **Whiting** is this fish eaten as food. ❑ *He ordered stuffed whiting.* N-VAR N-UNCOUNT

**whit|ish** /ʰwaɪtɪʃ/ **Whitish** means very pale and almost white in colour. ❑ *...a whitish dust.* COLOUR

**Whit|sun** /ʰwɪtsᵊn/ **Whitsun** is the seventh Sunday after Easter, and the week that follows that Sunday. [mainly BRIT] N-UNCOUNT

**Whit Sun|day** **Whit Sunday** is the seventh Sunday after Easter, when Christians celebrate the sending of the Holy Spirit to the first followers of Christ. N-UNCOUNT = Pentecost

**whit|tle** /ʰwɪtᵊl/ (**whittles, whittling, whittled**) If you **whittle** something from a piece of wood, you carve it by cutting pieces off the wood with a knife. ❑ *He whittled a new handle for his ax.* VERB V n

♦ **whittle away** To **whittle away** something or **whittle away at** it means to gradually make it smaller, weaker, or less effective. ❑ *I believe that the Government's general aim is to whittle away the Welfare State... Their approach is to whittle away at the evidence to show reasonable doubt.* PHRASAL VERB V P n (not pron) V P *at* n

♦ **whittle down** To **whittle down** a group or thing means to gradually make it smaller. ❑ *He had whittled eight interviewees down to two... The president has agreed to whittle down his proposal.* PHRASAL VERB V n P *to*/*from* num/n V P n (not pron)

**whizz** /ʰwɪz/ (**whizzes, whizzing, whizzed**) If something **whizzes** somewhere, it moves there very fast. [INFORMAL] ❑ *Stewart felt a bottle whizz past his head... A car whizzed past.* VERB V prep/adv V prep/adv

**whizz-kid** (**whizz-kids**) also **whizzkid, whizz kid.** If you refer to a young person as a **whizz-kid**, you mean that they have achieved success at a young age because they are very clever and very good at something, especially making money. [INFORMAL] ❑ *...a financial whizz kid. ...a whizz-kid physics student.* N-COUNT: usu with supp

**whizzy** /ʰwɪzi/ (**whizzier, whizziest**) **Whizzy** is used to describe products and activities that are new, exciting, and based on the latest technology. [INFORMAL] ❑ *Japanese camera makers continually introduce whizzy new electronic models.* ADJ

**who** /huː/ ◆◆◆

☑ Usually pronounced /huː/ for meanings 2 and 3.

**Who** is used as the subject or object of a verb. See entries at **whom** and **whose**.

1 You use **who** in questions when you ask about QUEST

the name or identity of a person or group of people. ❑ *Who's there?... Who is the least popular man around here?... Who do you work for?... Who do you suppose will replace her on the show?... 'You reminded me of somebody.' — 'Who?'* [2] You use **who** after certain words, especially verbs and adjectives, to introduce a clause where you talk about the identity of a person or a group of people. ❑ *Police have not been able to find out who was responsible for the forgeries... I went over to start up a conversation, asking her who she knew at the party... You know who these people are.* CONJ [3] You use **who** at the beginning of a relative clause when specifying the person or group of people you are talking about or when giving more information about them. ❑ *There are those who eat out for a special occasion, or treat themselves... The woman, who needs constant attention, is cared for by relatives.* PRON

**whoa** /ʰwoʊ/ [1] **Whoa** is a command that you give to a horse to slow down or stop. EXCLAM [2] You can say **whoa** to someone who is talking to you, to indicate that you think they are talking too fast or assuming things that may not be true. [INFORMAL] ❑ *Slow down! Whoa!* EXCLAM

**who'd** /huːd, huːd/ [1] **Who'd** is the usual spoken form of 'who had', especially when 'had' is an auxiliary verb. [2] **Who'd** is a spoken form of 'who would'.

**who|dun|nit** /huːdʌnɪt/ **(whodunnits)** also **whodunit.** A **whodunnit** is a novel, film, or play which is about a murder and which does not tell you who the murderer is until the end. [INFORMAL] N-COUNT

**who|ever** /huːevəʳ/ [1] You use **whoever** to refer to someone when their identity is not yet known. ❑ *Whoever wins the election is going to have a tough job getting the economy back on its feet... Ben, I want whoever's responsible to come forward.* CONJ
[2] You use **whoever** to indicate that the actual identity of the person who does something will not affect a situation. ❑ *You can have whoever you like to visit you... Everybody who goes into this region, whoever they are, is at risk of being taken hostage.* CONJ
[3] You use **whoever** in questions as an emphatic way of saying 'who', usually when you are surprised about something. ❑ *Ridiculous! Whoever suggested such a thing?* QUEST [emphasis] = who

**whole** /hoʊl/ **(wholes)** [1] If you refer to **the whole of** something, you mean all of it. ❑ *He has said he will make an apology to the whole of Asia for his country's past behaviour... I was cold throughout the whole of my body. ...the whole of August.* ◆◆◆ QUANT: QUANT *of* def-n ♦ **Whole** is also an adjective. ❑ *He'd been observing her the whole trip... We spent the whole summer in Italy that year.* ADJ: ADJ n = entire [2] A **whole** is a single thing which contains several different parts. ❑ *An atom itself is a complete whole, with its electrons, protons and neutrons and other elements.* N-COUNT: usu sing [3] If something is **whole**, it is in one piece and is not broken or damaged. ❑ *I struck the glass with my fist with all my might; yet it remained whole... Small bones should be avoided as the dog may swallow them whole and risk internal injury.* ADJ: v-link ADJ, v n ADJ = intact [4] You use **whole** to emphasize what you are saying. [INFORMAL] ❑ *It was like seeing a whole different side of somebody... His father had helped invent a whole new way of doing business.* ADV: ADV adj [emphasis] = totally ♦ **Whole** is also an adjective. ❑ *That saved me a whole bunch of money.* ADJ: ADJ n

**PHRASES** [5] If you refer to something **as a whole**, you are referring to it generally and as a single unit. ❑ *He described the move as a victory for the people of South Africa as a whole... As a whole we do not eat enough fibre in Britain.* PHRASE: n PHR, PHR with cl [6] You use **on the whole** to indicate that what you are saying is true in general but may not be true in every case, or that you are giving a general opinion or summary of something. ❑ *On the whole, people miss the opportunity to enjoy leisure.* PHRASE: PHR with cl = generally

**whole|food** /hoʊlfuːd/ **(wholefoods)** **Wholefoods** are foods which have not been processed much and which have not had artificial ingredients added. [mainly BRIT] ❑ *It pays to avoid food additives and eat only wholefoods.* N-MASS

**whole|grains** /hoʊlgreɪnz/ also **whole grains.**

✔ The forms **wholegrain** and **whole-grain** are used as modifiers.

**Wholegrains** are the grains of cereals such as wheat and maize that have not been processed. ❑ *Fruits, vegetables, and wholegrains are rich in potassium. ...crusty wholegrain bread.* N-PLURAL

**whole|hearted** /hoʊlhɑːʳtɪd/ also **whole-hearted.** If you support or agree to something in a **wholehearted** way, you support or agree to it enthusiastically and completely. ❑ *The Government deserves our wholehearted support for having taken a step in this direction.* ADJ [emphasis] ♦ **whole|hearted|ly** *That's exactly right. I agree wholeheartedly with you.* ADV: usu ADV with v

**whole|meal** /hoʊlmiːl/ [1] **Wholemeal** flour is made from the complete grain of the wheat plant, including the outer part. **Wholemeal** bread or pasta is made from wholemeal flour. [BRIT] ❑ *...a slice of wholemeal toast.* ADJ: usu ADJ n

✔ in AM, use **wholewheat**

[2] **Wholemeal** means wholemeal bread or wholemeal flour. [BRIT] ❑ *...one slice of white and one of wholemeal.* N-UNCOUNT

✔ in AM, use **wholewheat**

**whole|ness** /hoʊlnəs/ **Wholeness** is the quality of being complete or a single unit and not broken or divided into parts. ❑ *...the need for wholeness and harmony in mind, body and spirit.* N-UNCOUNT

**whole note** **(whole notes)** A **whole note** is a musical note that has a time value equal to two half notes. [AM] N-COUNT

✔ in BRIT, use **semibreve**

**whole num|ber** **(whole numbers)** A **whole number** is an exact number such as 1, 7, and 24, as opposed to a number with fractions or decimals. N-COUNT = integer

**whole|sale** /hoʊlseɪl/ [1] **Wholesale** is the activity of buying and selling goods in large quantities and therefore at cheaper prices, usually to shopkeepers who then sell them to the public. Compare **retail**. [BUSINESS] ❑ *Warehouse clubs allow members to buy goods at wholesale prices... I am in the wholesale trade.* N-UNCOUNT: usu N n [2] If something is sold **wholesale**, it is sold in large quantities and at cheaper prices, usually to shopkeepers. [BUSINESS] ❑ *The fabrics are sold wholesale to retailers, fashion houses, and other manufacturers.* ADV: ADV after v [3] You use **wholesale** to describe the destruction, removal, or changing of something when it affects a very large number of things or people. ❑ *They are only doing what is necessary to prevent wholesale destruction of vegetation.* ADJ: ADJ n [emphasis]

**whole|sal|er** /hoʊlseɪləʳ/ **(wholesalers)** A **wholesaler** is a person whose business is buying large quantities of goods and selling them in smaller amounts, for example to shops. [BUSINESS] N-COUNT

**whole|sal|ing** /hoʊlseɪlɪŋ/ **Wholesaling** is the activity of buying or selling goods in large amounts, especially in order to sell them in shops or supermarkets. Compare **retailing**. [BUSINESS] N-UNCOUNT

**whole|some** /hoʊlsəm/ [1] If you describe something as **wholesome**, you approve of it because you think it is likely to have a positive influence on people's behaviour or mental state, especially because it does not involve anything sexually immoral. ❑ *...good, wholesome fun.* ADJ [approval] [2] If you describe food as **wholesome**, you approve of it because you think it is good for your health. ❑ *...fresh, wholesome ingredients... The food is filling and wholesome.* ADJ [approval] = nutritious

**whole|wheat** /hoʊlʰwiːt/ also **whole wheat.** [1] **Wholewheat** flour is made from the complete grain of the wheat plant, including the outer part. **Wholewheat** bread or pasta is made from wholewheat flour. ❑ *...vegetables with* ADJ: usu ADJ n *wholewheat noodles.* [2] **Wholewheat** means wholewheat bread or wholewheat flour. ❑ *...a chicken salad sandwich on whole wheat.* N-UNCOUNT

**who'll** /huːl, huːl/ **Who'll** is a spoken form of 'who will' or 'who shall'.

**whol|ly** /hoʊlli/ You use **wholly** to emphasize the extent or degree to which something is the case. ❑ *While the two are only days apart in age they seem to belong to wholly different generations... For urban areas this approach was wholly inadequate.* ADV: ADV adj, ADV with cl/group [emphasis] = completely, entirely

**wholly-owned sub|sidi|ary** **(wholly-owned subsidiaries)** A **wholly-owned subsidiary** is a company whose shares are all owned by another company. [BUSINESS] ❑ *The Locomotive Construction Company Ltd is a wholly-owned subsidiary of the Trust.* N-COUNT

**whom** /huːm/ ◆◆◇

> ✔ **Whom** is used in formal or written English instead of 'who' when it is the object of a verb or preposition.

[1] You use **whom** in questions when you ask about the name or identity of a person or group of people. ❑ *'I want to send a telegram.' — 'Fine, to whom?'... Whom did he expect to answer his phone?* QUEST = who

[2] You use **whom** after certain words, especially verbs and adjectives, to introduce a clause where you talk about the name or identity of a person or a group of people. ❑ *He asked whom I'd told about his having been away.* CONJ = who

[3] You use **whom** at the beginning of a relative clause when specifying the person or group of people you are talking about or when giving more information about them. ❑ *One writer in whom I had taken an interest was Immanuel Velikovsky.* PRON: oft prep PRON

**whom|ever** /huːmevəʳ/ **Whomever** is a formal word for **whoever** when it is the object of a verb or preposition. CONJ = whoever

**whoop** /ʰwuːp, AM huːp/ **(whoops, whooping, whooped)** [1] If you **whoop**, you shout loudly in a very happy or excited way. [WRITTEN] ❑ *She whoops with delight at a promise of money.* VERB V ♦ **Whoop** is also a noun. ❑ *Scattered groans and whoops broke out in the crowd.* N-COUNT [2] → See also **whoops**.

**whoo|pee** /ʰwʊpiː/ People sometimes shout '**whoopee**' when they are very happy or excited. [INFORMAL] ❑ *I can have a lie in tomorrow. Whoopee!* EXCLAM [feelings] = hooray

**whoop|ing cough** /huːpɪŋ kɒf, AM - kɔːf/ **Whooping cough** is a serious infectious disease which causes people to cough and make a loud noise when they breathe in. N-UNCOUNT

**whoops** /ʰwʊps/ You say '**whoops**' to indicate that there has been a slight accident or mistake, or to apologize to someone for it. [INFORMAL] ❑ *Whoops, that was a mistake... Whoops, it's past 11, I'd better be off home.* EXCLAM [feelings] = oops

**whoosh** /ʰwʊʃ, AM hwuːʃ/ **(whooshes, whooshing, whooshed)** [1] People sometimes say '**whoosh**' when they are emphasizing the fact that something happens very suddenly or very fast. ❑ *Then came the riders amid even louder cheers and whoosh! It was all over.* EXCLAM [emphasis] [2] If something **whooshes** somewhere, it moves there quickly or suddenly. [INFORMAL] ❑ *Kites whooshed above the beach at intervals.* VERB V adv/prep

**whop|per** /ʰwɒpəʳ/ **(whoppers)** [1] If you describe a lie as a **whopper**, you mean that it is very far from the truth. [INFORMAL] ❑ *...the biggest whopper the president told.* N-COUNT [2] If you refer to something as a **whopper**, you mean that it is an unusually large example of the thing mentioned. [INFORMAL] ❑ *As comets go, it is a whopper.* N-COUNT

**whop|ping** /ʰwɒpɪŋ/ If you describe an amount as **whopping**, you are emphasizing that it is large. [INFORMAL] ❑ *The Russian leader won a whopping 89.9 percent yes vote.* ADJ: ADJ n, usu a ADJ amount [emphasis]

**whore** /hɔːʳ/ **(whores)** A **whore** is the same as a **prostitute**. N-COUNT

**who're** /huːəʳ, huːəʳ/ **Who're** is a spoken form of 'who are'. ❑ *I've got loads of friends who're unemployed... Who're you going to the pictures with?*

**whore|house** /hɔːʳhaʊs/ **(whorehouses)** A **whorehouse** is the same as a **brothel**. N-COUNT

**whorl** /ʰwɜːʳl, AM ʰwɔːʳl/ **(whorls)** A **whorl** is a spiral shape, for example the pattern on the tips of your fingers. [LITERARY] ❑ *He stared at the whorls and lines of her fingertips. ...dense whorls of red-purple flowers.* N-COUNT

**who's** /huːz, huːz/ **Who's** is the usual spoken form of 'who is' or 'who has', especially when 'has' is an auxiliary verb.

**whose** /huːz/ ◆◆◆

> ✔ Usually pronounced /huːz/ for meanings 2 and 3.

[1] You use **whose** at the beginning of a relative clause where you mention something that belongs to or is associated with the person or thing mentioned in the previous clause. ❑ *I saw a man shouting at a driver whose car was blocking the street. ...a speedboat, whose fifteen-strong crew claimed to belong to China's navy. ...tourists whose vacations included an unexpected adventure.* PRON

[2] You use **whose** in questions to ask about the person or thing that something belongs to or is associated with. ❑ *Whose was the better performance?... 'Whose is this?' — 'It's mine.'... 'It wasn't your fault, John.' — 'Whose, then?'... Whose car were they in?* QUEST

[3] You use **whose** after certain words, especially verbs and adjectives, to introduce a clause where you talk about the person or thing that something belongs to or is associated with. ❑ *I'm wondering whose mother she is then... I can't remember whose idea it was for us to meet again.* DET ♦ **Whose** is also a conjunction. ❑ *I wondered whose the coat was... That kind of person likes to spend money, it doesn't matter whose it is.* CONJ

**who|so|ever** /huːsoʊevəʳ/ **Whosoever** means the same as **whoever**. [LITERARY, OLD-FASHIONED] ❑ *They can transfer or share the contract with whosoever they choose.* CONJ = whoever

**who've** /huːv, huːv/ **Who've** is the usual spoken form of 'who have,' especially when 'have' is an auxiliary verb.

**why** /ʰwaɪ/ ◆◆◆

> ✔ The conjunction and the pronoun are usually pronounced /ʰwaɪ/.

[1] You use **why** in questions when you ask about the reasons for something. ❑ *Why hasn't he brought the whisky?... Why didn't he stop me?... 'I just want to see him.' — 'Why?'... Why should I leave?* QUEST

[2] You use **why** at the beginning of a clause in which you talk about the reasons for something. ❑ *He still could not throw any further light on why the elevator could have become jammed... Experts wonder why the US government is not taking similarly strong actions against AIDS in this country... I can't understand why they don't want us.* CONJ ♦ **Why** is also an adverb. ❑ *I don't know why... It's obvious why... Here's why.* ADV: ADV after v, be ADV

[3] You use **why** to introduce a relative clause after the word 'reason'. ❑ *There's a reason why women don't read this stuff; it's not funny... Unless you're ill, there's no reason why you can't get those 15 minutes of walking in daily.* PRON ♦ **Why** is also an adverb. ❑ *He confirmed that the city had been closed to foreigners, but gave no reason why.* ADV: n ADV

[4] You use **why** with 'not' in questions in order to introduce a suggestion. ❑ *Why not give Claire a call?... Why don't we talk it through?* QUEST

[5] You use **why** with 'not' in questions in order to express your annoyance or anger. ❑ *Why don't you look where you're going?... Why don't they just leave it alone?* QUEST [feelings]

[6] You say **why not** in order to agree with what someone has suggested. ❑ *'Want to spend the afternoon with me?' — 'Why not?'.* CONVENTION [formulae]

[7] People say '**Why!**' at the beginning of a sentence when they are surprised, shocked, or angry. [mainly AM] ❑ *Why hello,* EXCLAM [feelings]

*Tom.* [8] **the whys and wherefores** → see **wherefores**.

**Wic|ca** /wɪkə/ N-PROPER **Wicca** is a pagan religion that practises witchcraft.

**wick** /wɪk/ **(wicks)** [1] N-COUNT The **wick** of a candle is the piece of string in it which burns when it is lit. [2] N-COUNT The **wick** of a paraffin lamp or cigarette lighter is the part which supplies the fuel to the flame when it is lit.

**wick|ed** /wɪkɪd/ [1] ADJ = evil You use **wicked** to describe someone or something that is very bad and deliberately harmful to people. ❑ *She described the shooting as a wicked attack... She flew at me, shouting how wicked and evil I was.* [2] ADJ If you describe someone or something as **wicked**, you mean that they are rather naughty, but in a way that you find attractive or enjoyable. ❑ *She had a wicked sense of humour.*

**wick|er** /wɪkəʳ/ N-UNCOUNT: usu N n **Wicker** is long thin sticks, stems, or reeds that have been woven together to make things such as baskets and furniture. ❑ *...a wicker basket.*

**wicker|work** /wɪkəʳwɜːʳk/ N-UNCOUNT: usu N n **Wickerwork** is the same as **wicker**.

**wick|et** /wɪkɪt/ **(wickets)** ◆◇◇ [1] N-COUNT In cricket, a **wicket** is a set of three upright sticks with two small sticks on top of them at which the ball is bowled. There are two wickets on a cricket pitch. [2] N-COUNT In cricket, a **wicket** is the area of grass in between the two wickets on the pitch. [3] N-COUNT In cricket, when a **wicket** falls or is taken, a batsman is out.

**wicket|keeper** /wɪkɪtkiːpəʳ/ **(wicketkeepers)** also **wicket-keeper**. N-COUNT A **wicketkeeper** is the player in a cricket team who stands behind the wicket in order to stop balls that the batsman misses or to catch balls that the batsman hits.

**wide** /waɪd/ **(wider, widest)** ◆◆◆ [1] ADJ ≠ narrow Something that is **wide** measures a large distance from one side or edge to the other. ❑ *All worktops should be wide enough to allow plenty of space for food preparation. ...a wide-brimmed sunhat.* [2] ADJ: usu ADJ n = broad A **wide** smile is one in which your mouth is stretched because you are very pleased or amused. ❑ *It brought a wide smile to his face and laughter to his eyes.* ♦ **wide|ly** ADV: ADV after v *He was grinning widely, waving to her as he ran.* [3] ADJ: usu v n ADJ, v-link ADJ, also ADJ n If you open or spread something **wide**, you open or spread it as far as possible or to the fullest extent. ❑ *'It was huge,' he announced, spreading his arms wide... His eyes were wide in disbelief.* [4] ADJ: amount ADJ, *as* ADJ *as*, ADJ-compar *than*, *how* ADJ You use **wide** to talk or ask about how much something measures from one side or edge to the other. ❑ *...a corridor of land 10 kilometres wide... The road is only one track wide. ...a desk that was almost as wide as the room.* [5] ADJ: usu ADJ n = broad ≠ narrow You use **wide** to describe something that includes a large number of different things or people. ❑ *The brochure offers a wide choice of hotels, apartments and holiday homes... The proposed constitution gives him much wider powers than his predecessor.* ♦ **wide|ly** ADV: usu ADV after v *He published widely in scientific journals... He was widely travelled.* [6] ADJ: usu ADJ n = extensive You use **wide** to say that something is found, believed, known, or supported by many people or throughout a large area. ❑ *The case has attracted wide publicity... I suspect this book will have the widest appeal of all.* ♦ **wide|ly** ADV: ADV with v *At present, no widely approved vaccine exists for malaria.* [7] ADJ: usu ADJ n A **wide** difference or gap between two things, ideas, or qualities is a large difference or gap. ❑ *Research shows a wide difference in tastes around the country.* ♦ **wide|ly** ADV: ADV after v, ADV adj *The treatment regime may vary widely depending on the type of injury.* [8] ADJ: ADJ n **Wider** is used to describe something which relates to the most important or general parts of a situation, rather than to the smaller parts or to details. ❑ *He emphasised the wider issue of superpower cooperation.* [9] ADJ: usu v-link ADJ If something such as a shot or punch is **wide**, it does not hit its target but lands to the right or left of it. ❑ *Nearly half the missiles landed wide.* [10] **wide awake** → see **awake**. **far and wide** → see **far**. **wide of the mark** → see **mark**. **wide open** → see **open**.

**-wide** /-waɪd/ COMB in ADJ **-wide** combines with nouns to form adjectives which indicate that something exists or happens throughout the place or area that the noun refers to. ❑ *...a Europe-wide conference on security and cooperation... Is the problem one that's industry-wide?* ♦ COMB in ADV: n ADV, ADV with cl, ADV after v **-wide** also combines to form adverbs. ❑ *Employers want to be sure recruits understand business Europe-wide.*

**wide-angle lens** **(wide-angle lenses)** N-COUNT A **wide-angle lens** is a lens which allows you to photograph a wider view than a normal lens.

**wide awake** ADJ: usu v-link ADJ If you are **wide awake**, you are completely awake. ❑ *I could not relax and still felt wide awake.*

**wide boy** **(wide boys)** N-COUNT disapproval A **wide boy** is a man, especially a young man, who has a lot of money but who earns it in a dishonest or illegal way. [mainly BRIT, INFORMAL]

**wide-eyed** ADJ: usu ADJ n If you describe someone as **wide-eyed**, you mean that they are inexperienced and innocent, and may be easily impressed. ❑ *Her wide-eyed innocence soon exposes the pretensions of the art world.*

**wid|en** /waɪdᵊn/ **(widens, widening, widened)** [1] VERB If you **widen** something or if it **widens**, it becomes greater in measurement from one side or edge to the other. ❑ V n *He had an operation last year to widen a heart artery...* V *The river widens considerably as it begins to turn east.* [2] VERB If you **widen** something or if it **widens**, it becomes greater in range or it affects a larger number of people or things. ❑ V n *U.S. prosecutors have widened a securities-fraud investigation...* V *The search for my brother widened.* [3] VERB If your eyes **widen**, they open more. ❑ V *His eyes widened as he spoke the words.* [4] VERB If a difference or gap **widens** or if something **widens** it, it becomes greater. ❑ V *Wage differences in the two areas are widening.* V n *...policies that widen the gap between the rich and the poor.*

**wide-ranging** ADJ If you describe something as **wide-ranging**, you mean it deals with or affects a great variety of different things. ❑ *...a package of wide-ranging economic reforms.*

**wide|screen** /waɪdskriːn/ ADJ: usu ADJ n A **widescreen** television has a screen that is wide in relation to its height.

**wide|spread** /waɪdspred/ ◆◇◇ ADJ = extensive Something that is **widespread** exists or happens over a large area, or to a great extent. ❑ *There is widespread support for the new proposals... Food shortages are widespread.*

**widg|et** /wɪdʒɪt/ **(widgets)** N-COUNT You can refer to any small device as a **widget** when you do not know exactly what it is or how it works. [INFORMAL] ❑ *The secret is a little widget in the can.*

**wid|ow** /wɪdoʊ/ **(widows)** N-COUNT A **widow** is a woman whose husband has died and who has not married again.

**wid|owed** /wɪdoʊd/ V-PASSIVE If someone **is widowed**, their husband or wife dies. ❑ *be* V-ed *More and more young men are widowed by cancer...* V-ed *Imogen stayed with her widowed sister.*

**wid|ow|er** /wɪdoʊəʳ/ **(widowers)** N-COUNT A **widower** is a man whose wife has died and who has not married again.

**wid|ow|hood** /wɪdoʊhʊd/ N-UNCOUNT **Widowhood** is the state of being a widow or widower, or the period of time during which someone is a widow or widower. ❑ *Nothing can prepare you for the shock and grief of widowhood.*

**width** /wɪdθ/ **(widths)** [1] N-VAR: oft N *of* n The **width** of something is the distance it measures from one side or edge to the other. ❑ *Measure the full width of the window... The road was reduced to 18ft in width by adding parking bays... Saddles are made in a wide range of different widths.* [2] N-UNCOUNT: usu with poss The **width** of something is its quality of being wide. ❑ *The best utensil for steaming is a wok because its width easily accommodates a whole fish.* [3] N-COUNT A **width** is the distance from one side of a swimming pool to the other. ❑ *We swam several widths.*

**wield** /wiːld/ **(wields, wielding, wielded)** 1 If you **wield** a weapon, tool, or piece of equipment, you carry and use it. ❑ *...a lone assailant wielding a kitchen knife.* [VERB; V n] 2 If someone **wields** power, they have it and are able to use it. ❑ *He remains chairman, but wields little power at the company.* [VERB; V n]

**wie|nie** /wiːni/ **(wienies)** also **weenie. Wienies** are sausages made from smoked beef or pork. [AM] [N-COUNT; = hot dog, frankfurter]

**wife** /waɪf/ **(wives)** A man's **wife** is the woman he is married to. ❑ *He married his wife Jane 37 years ago... The woman was the wife of a film director.* → See also **old wives' tale.** [◆◆◆ N-COUNT: usu with poss]

**wife|ly** /waɪfli/ **Wifely** is used to describe things that are supposed to be typical of a good wife. ❑ *She strove to perform all her wifely functions perfectly. ...the ideology of wifely duty.* [ADJ: usu ADJ n]

**wig** /wɪg/ **(wigs)** A **wig** is a covering of false hair which you wear on your head, for example because you have little hair of your own or because you want to cover up your own hair. [N-COUNT]

**wig|gle** /wɪgᵊl/ **(wiggles, wiggling, wiggled)** If you **wiggle** something or if it **wiggles**, it moves up and down or from side to side in small quick movements. ❑ *She wiggled her finger... Your baby will try to shuffle or wiggle along the floor.* ♦ **Wiggle** is also a noun. ❑ *...a wiggle of the hips.* [VERB; V n; V prep/adv; N-COUNT]

**wig|wam** /wɪgwæm, AM -wɑːm/ **(wigwams)** A **wigwam** is the same as a **tepee**. [N-COUNT]

**wild** /waɪld/ **(wilds, wilder, wildest)** 1 **Wild** animals or plants live or grow in natural surroundings and are not looked after by people. ❑ *We saw two more wild cats creeping towards us in the darkness... The lane was lined with wild flowers.* [◆◆◇ ADJ: usu ADJ n] 2 **Wild** land is natural and is not used by people. ❑ *Elmley is one of the few wild areas remaining in the South East.* [ADJ: usu ADJ n] ♦ **wild|ness** *...the wildness of the mountains.* [N-UNCOUNT] 3 **The wilds** of a place are the natural areas that are far away from towns. ❑ *They went canoeing in the wilds of Canada.* [N-PLURAL: the N] 4 **Wild** is used to describe the weather or the sea when it is stormy. ❑ *The wild weather did not deter some people from swimming in the sea.* [ADJ: usu ADJ n = stormy] 5 **Wild** behaviour is uncontrolled, excited, or energetic. ❑ *The children are wild with joy... As George himself came on stage they went wild... They marched into town to the wild cheers of the inhabitants.* [ADJ: oft v-link ADJ with n] ♦ **wild|ly** *As she finished each song, the crowd clapped wildly.* [ADV: ADV with v] 6 If you describe someone or their behaviour as **wild**, you mean that they behave in a very uncontrolled way. ❑ *The house is in a mess after a wild party.* [ADJ] ♦ **wild|ly** *Five people were injured as Reynolds slashed out wildly with a kitchen knife.* [ADV: ADV with v] ♦ **wild|ness** *He had come to love the danger and the wildness of his life.* [N-UNCOUNT] 7 If someone is **wild**, they are very angry. [INFORMAL] ❑ *For a long time I daren't tell him I knew, and when I did he went wild.* [ADJ: usu v-link ADJ = mad, crazy] 8 A **wild** idea is unusual or extreme. A **wild** guess is one that you make without much thought. ❑ *Browning's prediction is no better than a wild guess.* [ADJ: ADJ n] ♦ **wild|ly** *'Thirteen?' he guessed wildly.* [ADV] 9 → See also **wildly, wild child.**

**PHRASES** 10 If you **are wild about** someone or something, you like them very much. [INFORMAL] ❑ *I'm just wild about Peter, and he's just wild about me.* [PHRASE: V inflects = be crazy about] 11 Animals that live **in the wild** live in a free and natural state and are not looked after by people. ❑ *Fewer than a thousand giant pandas still live in the wild.* [PHRASE: PHR after v, v-link PHR] 12 If something or someone, especially a child, **runs wild**, they behave in a natural, free, or uncontrolled way. ❑ *Everything that could grow was running wild for lack of attention.* [PHRASE: V inflects] 13 **beyond** your **wildest dreams** → see **dream. in** your **wildest dreams** → see **dream.** to **sow** your **wild oats** → see **oats.**

**wild boar** **(wild boar** or **wild boars)** A **wild boar** is a large fierce pig which has two long curved teeth and a hairy body, and lives in forests. [N-COUNT]

**wild card** **(wild cards)** also **wildcard.** 1 If you refer to someone or something as a **wild card** in a particular situation, you mean that they cause uncertainty because you do not know how they will behave. ❑ *The wild card in the picture is eastern Europe.* [N-COUNT: oft N in n] 2 If a sports player is given a **wild card** for a particular competition, they are allowed to play in it, although they have not qualified for it in the usual way. You can also use **wild card** to refer to a player who enters a competition in this way. [N-COUNT] 3 A **wildcard** is a symbol such as * or ? which is used in some computing commands or searches in order to represent any character or range of characters. [COMPUTING] [N-COUNT]

**wild|cat** /waɪldkæt/ **(wildcats)** 1 A **wildcat** is a cat which is very fierce and lives especially in mountains and forests. ❑ *A giant wildcat is being hunted after 58 lambs were butchered.* [N-COUNT] 2 A **wildcat** strike happens suddenly, as a result of a decision by a group of workers, and is not officially approved by a trade union. ❑ *Frustration, anger and desperation have led to a series of wildcat strikes.* [ADJ: ADJ n]

**wild child** Journalists sometimes use **wild child** to refer to a teenage girl who enjoys herself in an uncontrolled way, for example by going to a lot of parties. [BRIT] [N-SING]

**wil|de|beest** /wɪldɪbiːst, vɪl-/ **(wildebeest)** A **wildebeest** is a large African antelope which has a hairy tail, short curved horns, and long hair under its neck. Wildebeest usually live in large groups. [N-COUNT]

**wil|der|ness** /wɪldəʳnes/ **(wildernesses)** A **wilderness** is a desert or other area of natural land which is not used by people. ❑ *...the icy Canadian wilderness.* [N-COUNT: usu sing]

**wild|fire** /waɪldfaɪəʳ/ **(wildfires)** 1 A **wildfire** is a fire that starts, usually by itself, in a wild area such as a forest, and spreads rapidly, causing great damage. ❑ *...a wildfire in Montana that's already burned thousands of acres of rich grassland.* [N-COUNT] 2 If something, especially news or a rumour, **spreads like wildfire**, it spreads extremely quickly. ❑ *These stories are spreading like wildfire through the city.* [PHRASE: V inflects]

**wild flow|er** **(wild flowers)** also **wildflower. Wild flowers** are flowers which grow naturally in the countryside, rather than being grown by people in gardens. [N-COUNT]

**wild|fowl** /waɪldfaʊl/ also **wild fowl. Wildfowl** are birds such as ducks, swans, and geese that live close to lakes or rivers. [N-PLURAL]

**wild goose chase** **(wild goose chases)** also **wild-goose chase.** If you are on a **wild goose chase**, you waste a lot of time searching for something that you have little chance of finding, because you have been given incorrect information. ❑ *Harry wondered if Potts had deliberately sent him on a wild goose chase.* [N-COUNT: usu on N]

**wild|life** /waɪldlaɪf/ You can use **wildlife** to refer to the animals and other living things that live in the wild. ❑ *People were concerned that pets or wildlife could be affected by the pesticides.* [N-UNCOUNT]

**wild|ly** /waɪldli/ You use **wildly** to emphasize the degree, amount, or intensity of something. ❑ *Reports of his drinking have been wildly exaggerated... The island's hotels vary wildly.* → See also **wild.** [ADV: usu ADV adj, also ADV after v] [emphasis]

**Wild West** **The Wild West** is used to refer to the western part of the United States during the time when Europeans were first settling there. [N-SING: the N]

**wiles** /waɪlz/ **Wiles** are clever tricks that people, especially women, use to persuade other people to do something. ❑ *She claimed that women 'use their feminine wiles to get on.'* [N-PLURAL: usu supp N, N of n]

**wil|ful** /wɪlfʊl/

✓ in AM, use **willful**

1 If you describe actions or attitudes as **wilful**, you are critical of them because they are done or [ADJ: ADJ n] [disapproval]

expressed deliberately, especially with the intention of causing someone harm. ❑ *Wilful neglect of our manufacturing industry has caused this problem.*
2 If you describe someone as **wilful**, you mean that they are determined to do what they want to do, even if it is not sensible. ❑ *...as the beautiful Lara becomes ever more wilful and irresponsible.* ADJ = headstrong

**will**
① MODAL VERB USES
② WANTING SOMETHING TO HAPPEN

① **will** /wɪl/ ◆◆◆

**Will** is a modal verb. It is used with the base form of a verb. In spoken English and informal written English, the form **won't** is often used in negative statements.

1 You use **will** to indicate that you hope, think, or have evidence that something is going to happen or be the case in the future. ❑ *You will find a wide variety of choices available in school cafeterias... Representatives from across the horse industry will attend the meeting... 70 per cent of airports in the Far East will have to be upgraded... Will you ever feel at home here?... The ship will not be ready for a month.* MODAL
2 You use **will** in order to make statements about official arrangements in the future. ❑ *The show will be open to the public at 2pm; admission will be 50p... When will I be released, sir?* MODAL 3 You use **will** in order to make promises and threats about what is going to happen or be the case in the future. ❑ *I'll call you tonight... Price quotes on selected product categories will be sent on request... If she refuses to follow rules about car safety, she won't be allowed to use the car.* MODAL 4 You use **will** to indicate someone's intention to do something. ❑ *I will say no more on these matters, important though they are... In this section we will describe common myths about cigarettes, alcohol, and marijuana... 'Dinner's ready.' — 'Thanks, Carrie, but we'll have a drink first.'... What will you do next?... Will you be remaining in the city?* MODAL
5 You use **will** in questions in order to make polite invitations or offers. ❑ *Will you stay for supper?... Will you join me for a drink?... Won't you sit down?* MODAL politeness 6 You use **will** in questions in order to ask or tell someone to do something. ❑ *Will you drive me home?... Wipe the jam off my mouth, will you?* MODAL = would 7 You can use **will** in statements to give an order to someone. [FORMAL] ❑ *You will now maintain radio silence... You will not discuss this matter with anyone.* MODAL 8 You use **will** to say that someone is willing to do something. You use **will not** or **won't** to indicate that someone refuses to do something. ❑ *All right, I'll forgive you... He has insisted that his organisation will not negotiate with the government.* → See also **willing**. MODAL 9 You use **will** to say that a person or thing is able to do something in the future. ❑ *How the country will defend itself in the future has become increasingly important... How will I recognize you?* MODAL 10 You use **will** to indicate that an action usually happens in the particular way mentioned. ❑ *The thicker the material, the less susceptible the garment will be to wet conditions... There's no snake known that will habitually attack human beings unless threatened with its life.* MODAL 11 You use **will** in the main clause of some 'if' and 'unless' sentences to indicate something that you consider to be fairly likely to happen. ❑ *If you overcook the pancakes they will be difficult to roll.* MODAL
12 You use **will** to say that someone insists on behaving or doing something in a particular way and you cannot change them. You emphasize **will** when you use it in this way. ❑ *He will leave his socks lying all over the place and it drives me mad.* MODAL
13 You use **will have** with a past participle when you are saying that you are fairly certain that something will be true by a particular time in the future. ❑ *As many as ten-million children will have been infected with the virus by the end of the decade.* MODAL 14 You use **will have** with a past participle to indicate that you are fairly sure that something is the case. ❑ *The holiday will have done him the world of good.* MODAL

② **will** /wɪl/ **(wills, willing, willed)** ◆◆◇ 1 **Will** is the determination to do something. ❑ *He was said to have lost his will to live. ...the inevitable battle of wills as your child realises that he can't do or have everything he wants.* → See also **free will**. N-VAR: oft N to-inf 2 If something is **the will of** a person or group of people with authority, they want it to happen. ❑ *Democracy responds and adjusts to the will of the people.* N-SING: with poss 3 If you **will** something **to** happen, you try to make it happen by using mental effort rather than physical effort. ❑ *I looked at the telephone, willing it to ring.* VERB V n to-inf 4 A **will** is a document in which you declare what you want to happen to your money and property when you die. ❑ *Attached to his will was a letter he had written to his wife just days before his death.* N-COUNT
**PHRASES** 5 If something is done **against** your **will**, it is done even though you do not want it to be done. ❑ *No doubt he was forced to leave his family against his will.* PHRASE: PHR after v 6 If you can do something **at will**, you can do it when you want and as much as you want. ❑ *...scientists who can adjust their experiments at will.* PHRASE: PHR after v

**will|ful** /wɪlfʊl/ → see **wilful**.

**wil|lie** /wɪli/ → see **willy**.

**will|ing** /wɪlɪŋ/ ◆◆◇ 1 If someone is **willing to** do something, they are fairly happy about doing it and will do it if they are asked or required to do it. ❑ *The military now say they're willing to hold talks with the political parties... There are, of course, questions which she will not be willing to answer.* ADJ: v-link ADJ to-inf = prepared ≠ unwilling
2 **Willing** is used to describe someone who does something fairly enthusiastically and because they want to do it rather than because they are forced to do it. ❑ *Have the party on a Saturday, when you can get your partner and other willing adults to help.* ADJ: usu ADJ n ≠ unwilling, reluctant
3 **God willing** → see **god**.

**will-o'-the-wisp** /wɪl ə ðə wɪsp/ **(will-o'-the-wisps)** You can refer to someone or something that keeps disappearing or that is impossible to catch or reach as a **will-o'-the-wisp**. N-COUNT: usu sing

**wil|low** /wɪloʊ/ **(willows)** A **willow** or a **willow tree** is a type of tree with long branches and long narrow leaves that grows near water. N-COUNT ♦ **Willow** is the wood of this tree. ❑ *...willow furniture.* N-UNCOUNT: oft N n

**wil|lowy** /wɪloʊi/ A person who is **willowy** is tall, thin, and graceful. ADJ = slender

**will|power** /wɪlpaʊəʳ/ also **will-power, will power. Willpower** is a very strong determination to do something. ❑ *His attempts to stop smoking by willpower alone failed.* N-UNCOUNT

**wil|ly** /wɪli/ **(willies)** also **willie.** A boy's or man's **willy** is his penis. [BRIT, INFORMAL] N-COUNT

**willy-nilly** /wɪli nɪli/ also **willy nilly.**
1 If something happens to you **willy-nilly**, it happens whether you like it or not. ❑ *The government were dragged willy-nilly into the confrontation.* ADV: usu ADV with v, also ADV with cl
2 If someone does something **willy-nilly**, they do it in a careless and disorganized way, without planning it in advance. ❑ *Clerks bundled papers into files willy-nilly.* ADV: usu ADV after v, also ADV with cl

**wilt** /wɪlt/ **(wilts, wilting, wilted)** 1 If a plant **wilts**, it gradually bends downwards and becomes weak because it needs more water or is dying. ❑ *The roses wilted the day after she bought them.* VERB V
2 If someone **wilts**, they become weak or tired, or lose confidence. ❑ *She soon wilted in the morning heat... The government wilted in the face of such powerful pressure.* VERB V V

**wily** /waɪli/ **(wilier, wiliest)** If you describe someone or their behaviour as **wily**, you mean that they are clever at achieving what they want, especially by tricking people. ❑ *His appointment as prime minister owed much to the wily manoeuvring of the President.* ADJ = cunning

**wimp** /wɪmp/ **(wimps)** If you call someone a **wimp**, you disapprove of them because they lack confidence or determination, or because they are often afraid of things. [INFORMAL] N-COUNT disapproval

**wimp|ish** /wɪmpɪʃ/ **Wimpish** means the same as **wimpy**. [INFORMAL] ADJ disapproval

**wimpy** /wɪmpi/ If you describe a person or their behaviour as **wimpy**, you disapprove of them because they are weak and seem to lack confidence or determination. [INFORMAL] ❑ *...a wimpy unpopular schoolboy... This portrays her as wimpy, but she has a very strong character.* ADJ disapproval = drippy

**win** /wɪn/ **(wins, winning, won)** ◆◆◆ 1 If you **win** something such as a competition, battle, or argument, you defeat those people you are competing or fighting against, or you do better than everyone else involved. ❑ *He does not have any realistic chance of winning the election... The top four teams all won... Sanchez Vicario won 2-6, 6-4, 6-3.* VERB ≠ lose V n, V, V amount ♦ **Win** is also a noun. ❑ *...Arsenal's dismal league run of eight games without a win.* N-COUNT = victory ≠ defeat 2 If something **wins** you something such as an election, competition, battle, or argument, it causes you to defeat the people competing with you or fighting you, or to do better than everyone else involved. ❑ *That sort of gain for Labour is nothing like good enough to win them the general election.* VERB ≠ lose V n n 3 If you **win** something such as a prize or medal, you get it because you have defeated everyone else in something such as an election, competition, battle, or argument, or have done very well in it. ❑ *The first correct entry wins the prize... She won bronze for Great Britain in the European Championships.* VERB V n V n 4 If you **win** something that you want or need, you succeed in getting it. ❑ *...moves to win the support of the poor... British Aerospace has won an order worth 340 million dollars.* VERB = gain ≠ lose V n V n 5 If something **wins** you a prize or **wins** you something else that you want, it causes you to get it. ❑ *The feat won them a prize of £85,000.* VERB ≠ lose V n n 6 → See also **winning**. 7 to **lose the battle but win the war** → see **battle**. to **win the day** → see **day**. to **win hands down** → see **hand**.

♦ **win back** If you **win back** something that you have lost, you get it again, especially as a result of a great effort. ❑ *The Government will have to work hard to win back the confidence of the people... So he went and filed a suit and won his job back.* PHRASAL VERB V P n (not pron) V n P

♦ **win out** or **win through** If something or someone **wins out** or **wins through**, they are successful after a competition or struggle. ❑ *Sometimes perseverance does win out.* PHRASAL VERB V P

♦ **win over**

✓ in BRIT, also use **win round**

If you **win** someone **over** or **win** them **round**, you persuade them to support you or agree with you. ❑ *He has won over a significant number of the left-wing deputies... They still hope to win him round.* PHRASAL VERB V P n (not pron) V n P

♦ **win round** → see **win over**.

♦ **win through** → see **win out**.

**wince** /wɪns/ **(winces, wincing, winced)** If you **wince**, the muscles of your face tighten suddenly because you have felt a pain or because you have just seen, heard, or remembered something unpleasant. ❑ *Every time he put any weight on his left leg he winced in pain.* VERB V ♦ **Wince** is also a noun. ❑ *He suppressed a wince as motion renewed the pain.* N-COUNT: usu sing

**winch** /wɪntʃ/ **(winches, winching, winched)** 1 A **winch** is a machine which is used to lift heavy objects or people who need to be rescued. It consists of a drum around which a rope or chain is wound. N-COUNT 2 If you **winch** an object or person somewhere, you lift or lower them using a winch. ❑ *He would attach a cable around the chassis of the car and winch it up on to the canal bank.* VERB V n with adv/prep

| **wind** |
|---|
| ① AIR |
| ② TURNING OR WRAPPING |

**①wind** /wɪnd/ **(winds, winding, winded)** ◆◆◇ 1 A **wind** is a current of air that is moving across the earth's surface. ❑ *There was a strong wind blowing... The leaves rustled in the wind.* N-VAR 2 Journalists often refer to a trend or factor that influences events as a **wind of** a particular kind. ❑ *The winds of change are blowing across the country.* N-COUNT: N of n 3 If you **are winded** by something such as a blow, the air is suddenly knocked out of your lungs so that you have difficulty breathing for a short time. ❑ *He was winded and shaken... The cow stamped on his side, winding him.* VERB be V-ed V n 4 **Wind** is the air that you sometimes swallow with food or drink, or gas that is produced in your intestines, which causes an uncomfortable feeling. N-UNCOUNT 5 The **wind** section of an orchestra or band is the group of people who produce musical sounds by blowing into their instruments. ADJ: ADJ n

**PHRASES** 6 If someone **breaks wind**, they release gas from their intestines through their anus. PHRASE: V inflects 7 If you **get wind of** something, you hear about it, especially when someone else did not want you to know about it. [INFORMAL] ❑ *I don't want the public, and especially not the press, to get wind of it at this stage.* PHRASE: V inflects, PHR n 8 If you **sail close to the wind**, you take a risk by doing or saying something that may get you into trouble. ❑ *She was sailing dangerously close to the wind and risked prosecution.* PHRASE: V inflects 9 to **throw caution to the wind** → see **caution**.

**②wind** /waɪnd/ **(winds, winding, wound)** ◆◆◇ 1 If a road, river, or line of people **winds** in a particular direction, it goes in that direction with a lot of bends or twists in it. ❑ *The Moselle winds through some 160 miles of tranquil countryside... The convoy wound its way through the West Bank. ...a narrow winding road.* VERB V prep/adv V *way* prep/adv V-ing 2 When you **wind** something flexible around something else, you wrap it around it several times. ❑ *The horse jumped forwards and round her, winding the rope round her waist.* VERB V n prep/adv 3 When you **wind** a mechanical device, for example a watch or a clock, you turn a knob, key, or handle on it several times in order to make it operate. ❑ *I still hadn't wound my watch so I didn't know the time.* VERB V n ♦ **Wind up** means the same as **wind**. ❑ *I wound up the watch and listened to it tick... Frances took the tiny music box from her trunk and wound it up.* PHRASAL VERB V P n (not pron) V n P 4 To **wind** a tape or film **back** or **forward** means to make it move towards its starting or ending position. ❑ *The camcorder winds the tape back or forward at high speed.* VERB V n adv

♦ **wind down** 1 When you **wind down** something such as the window of a car, you make it move downwards by turning a handle. ❑ *Glass motioned to him to wind down the window... If a stranger stops you, just wind the window down a fraction.* PHRASAL VERB ≠ wind up V P n (not pron) V n P 2 If you **wind down**, you relax after doing something that has made you feel tired or tense. [INFORMAL] ❑ *I regularly have a drink to wind down.* PHRASAL VERB = unwind V P 3 If someone **winds down** a business or activity, they gradually reduce the amount of work that is done or the number of people that are involved, usually before closing or stopping it completely. ❑ *Foreign aid workers have already begun winding down their operation... In 1991 the Ada plant began to wind down.* PHRASAL VERB V P n (not pron) V P Also V n P

♦ **wind up** 1 When you **wind up** an activity, you finish it or stop doing it. ❑ *The President is about to wind up his visit to Somalia.* PHRASAL VERB V P n Also V n P 2 When someone **winds up** a business or other organization, they stop running it and close it down completely. [BUSINESS] ❑ *The Bank of England seems determined to wind up the company.* PHRASAL VERB V P n Also V n P 3 If you **wind up** in a particular place, situation, or state, you are in it at the end of a series of actions, events, or experiences, even though you did not originally intend to be. ❑ *He could wind up in gaol... Little did I know that I would actually wind up being on the staff... Both partners of the marriage wound up unhappy.* PHRASAL VERB = finish up, end up V P prep/adv V P -ing V P adj/n 4 When you **wind up** something such as the window of a car, you make it move upwards by turning a handle. ❑ *He started winding the window up but I grabbed the door and opened it.* PHRASAL VERB = roll up ≠ wind down V n P 5 If you **wind** someone **up**, you deliberately say PHRASAL VERB = annoy

things which annoy them. [BRIT, INFORMAL] ❑ *This woman really wound me up. She kept talking over me.* *V n P; Also V P n (not pron)*
6 If you **wind** someone **up**, you say untrue things in order to trick them. [BRIT, INFORMAL] ❑ *You're joking. Come on, you're winding me up.* *PHRASAL VERB = kid; V n P; Also V P n (not pron)*
7 → See also **wind 3**, **wind-up**, **wound up**.

**wind|bag** /wɪndbæg/ **(windbags)** If you call someone a **windbag**, you are saying in a fairly rude way that you think they talk a great deal in a boring way. [INFORMAL] *N-COUNT disapproval*

**wind-blown** /wɪnd bloʊn/ also **windblown.** 1 You can use **wind-blown** to indicate that something has been blown from one place to another by the wind. ❑ *...the wind-blown sand which forms the 60 ft dunes.* *ADJ* 2 If something such as someone's hair is **wind-blown**, it is untidy because it has been blown about by the wind. *ADJ*

**wind|break** /wɪndbreɪk/ **(windbreaks)** A **windbreak** is something such as a line of trees or a fence which gives protection against the wind. *N-COUNT*

**Wind|breaker** /wɪndbreɪkə^r/ **(Windbreakers)** A **Windbreaker** is a warm casual jacket. [mainly AM, TRADEMARK] *N-COUNT = anorak*

**wind|fall** /wɪndfɔːl/ **(windfalls)** 1 A **windfall** is a sum of money that you receive unexpectedly or by luck, for example if you win a lottery. *N-COUNT* 2 A **windfall** is a fruit, especially an apple, that has fallen from a tree. *N-COUNT*

**wind farm** /wɪnd fɑː^rm/ **(wind farms)** A **wind farm** is a place where windmills are used to convert the power of the wind into electricity. *N-COUNT*

**wind in|stru|ment** /wɪnd ɪnstrʊmənts/ **(wind instruments)** A **wind instrument** is a musical instrument that you blow into in order to produce sounds, such as a flute, a clarinet, or a recorder. *N-COUNT*

**wind|lass** /wɪndləs/ **(windlasses)** A **windlass** is a mechanical device for lifting heavy objects, which uses a motor to pull a rope or chain around a cylinder. *N-COUNT = winch*

**wind|less** /wɪndləs/ If the air is **windless**, or if it is a **windless** day, it is very calm and still. *ADJ ≠ windy*

**wind|mill** /wɪndmɪl/ **(windmills)** A **windmill** is a building with long pieces of wood on the outside which turn around as the wind blows and provide energy for a machine that crushes grain. A **windmill** is also a similar structure that is used to convert the power of the wind into electricity. *N-COUNT*

**win|dow** /wɪndoʊ/ **(windows)** ◆◆◇ 1 A **window** is a space in the wall of a building or in the side of a vehicle, which has glass in it so that light can come in and you can see out. → See pictures on pages 1705 and 1707. ❑ *He stood at the window, moodily staring out... The room felt very hot and she wondered why someone did not open a window. ...my car window.* *N-COUNT* 2 A **window** is a large piece of glass along the front of a shop, behind which some of the goods that the shop sells are displayed. ❑ *I stood for a few moments in front of the nearest shop window.* *N-COUNT* 3 A **window** is a glass-covered opening above a counter, for example in a bank, post office, railway station, or museum, which the person serving you sits behind. ❑ *The woman at the ticket window told me that the admission fee was $17.50.* *N-COUNT* 4 On a computer screen, a **window** is one of the work areas that the screen can be divided into. [COMPUTING] *N-COUNT* 5 If you have a **window** in your diary for something, or if you can make a **window** for it, you are free at a particular time and can do it then. ❑ *Tell her I've got a window in my diary later on this week.* *N-COUNT: usu sing* 6 → See also **French window**, **picture window**, **rose window**.

**PHRASES** 7 If you say that something such as a plan or a particular way of thinking or behaving **has gone out of the window** or **has flown out of the window**, you mean that it has disappeared completely. ❑ *By now all logic had gone out of the window.* *PHRASE: V inflects* 8 If you say that there is a **window of opportunity** for something, you mean that there is an opportunity to do something but that this opportunity will only last for a short time and so it needs to be taken advantage of quickly. [JOURNALISM] ❑ *The king said there was now a window of opportunity for peace.* *PHRASE: window inflects, oft PHR for n, PHR to-inf*

**win|dow box** **(window boxes)** A **window box** is a long narrow container on a shelf at the bottom of a window and is used for growing plants. *N-COUNT*

**window-dressing** also **window dressing.** 1 **Window-dressing** is the skill of arranging objects attractively in a window, especially a shop window, or the way in which they are arranged. *N-UNCOUNT* 2 If you refer to something as **window-dressing**, you are critical of it because it is done in order to create a good impression and to prevent people from realizing the real or more unpleasant nature of someone's activities. ❑ *The measures are little more than window dressing that will fade fast once investors take a hard look at them.* *N-UNCOUNT disapproval*

**win|dow frame** **(window frames)** A **window frame** is a frame around the edges of a window, which glass is fixed into. *N-COUNT*

**window|pane** /wɪndoʊpeɪn/ **(windowpanes)** also **window pane.** A **windowpane** is a piece of glass in the window of a building. *N-COUNT*

**win|dow seat** **(window seats)** 1 A **window seat** is a seat which is fixed to the wall underneath a window in a room. *N-COUNT* 2 On a train, bus, or aeroplane, a **window seat** is a seat next to a window. *N-COUNT*

**win|dow shade** **(window shades)** A **window shade** is a piece of stiff cloth or heavy paper that you can pull down over a window as a covering. [AM] *N-COUNT = shade*

☑ in BRIT, use **blind**

**win|dow shop|ping** also **window-shopping.** If you do some **window shopping**, you spend time looking at the goods in the windows of shops without intending to buy anything. *N-UNCOUNT*

**window|sill** /wɪndoʊsɪl/ **(windowsills)** also **window sill.** A **windowsill** is a shelf along the bottom of a window, either inside or outside a building. → See picture on page 1705. *N-COUNT*

**wind|pipe** /wɪndpaɪp/ **(windpipes)** Your **windpipe** is the tube in your body that carries air into your lungs when you breathe. *N-COUNT = trachea*

**wind|screen** /wɪndskriːn/ **(windscreens)** The **windscreen** of a car or other vehicle is the glass window at the front through which the driver looks. [BRIT] → See picture on page 1707. *N-COUNT*

☑ in AM, use **windshield**

**wind|screen wip|er** **(windscreen wipers)** A **windscreen wiper** is a device that wipes rain from a vehicle's windscreen. [BRIT] → See picture on page 1707. *N-COUNT: usu pl*

☑ in AM, use **windshield wiper**

**wind|shield** /wɪndʃiːld/ **(windshields)** The **windshield** of a car or other vehicle is the glass window at the front through which the driver looks. [AM] → See picture on page 1707. *N-COUNT*

☑ in BRIT, use **windscreen**

**wind|shield wip|er** **(windshield wipers)** A **windshield wiper** is the same as a **windscreen wiper**. [AM] → See picture on page 1707. *N-COUNT: usu pl*

**wind|surf|er** /wɪndsɜː^rfə^r/ **(windsurfers)** 1 A **windsurfer** is a long narrow board with a sail attached to it. You stand on a windsurfer in the sea or on a lake and are blown along by the wind. *N-COUNT* 2 A **windsurfer** is a person who rides on a windsurfer. *N-COUNT*

**wind|surf|ing** /wɪndsɜː^rfɪŋ/ **Windsurfing** is a sport in which you move along the surface of the sea or a lake on a long narrow board with a sail on it. *N-UNCOUNT*

**wind|swept** /wɪndswept/ A **windswept** place has no shelter and is not protected against strong winds. ❑ *...the remote and windswept hillside.* ADJ

**wind tun|nel** /wɪnd tʌnᵊl/ **(wind tunnels)** A **wind tunnel** is a room or passage through which air can be made to flow at controlled speeds. Wind tunnels are used to test new equipment or machinery, especially cars and aeroplanes. N-COUNT

**wind-up** /waɪnd ʌp/ **(wind-ups)** 1 A **wind-up** device is a mechanical device with a handle or key that you turn several times before you use it in order to make it work. ❑ *...an old-fashioned wind-up gramophone.* ADJ: ADJ n 2 A **wind-up** is a joke or trick in which someone deliberately tells you something untrue in order to annoy you. [BRIT, INFORMAL] ❑ *At first I couldn't believe it. I thought it was a wind-up by one of my mates.* N-COUNT: usu sing, usu *a* N

**wind|ward** /wɪndwəʳd/ **Windward** is used to describe the side of something, especially a ship, which is facing the wind. ❑ *...the windward side of the quarterdeck.* ADJ: ADJ n ≠ *leeward*

**windy** /wɪndi/ **(windier, windiest)** If it is **windy**, the wind is blowing a lot. ❑ *It was windy and Jake felt cold.* ADJ

**wine** /waɪn/ **(wines, wining, wined)** ◆◆◇ 1 **Wine** is an alcoholic drink which is made from grapes. You can also refer to alcoholic drinks made from other fruits or vegetables as **wine**. ❑ *...a bottle of white wine... This is a nice wine.* N-MASS 2 **Wine** is used to describe things that are very dark red in colour. ❑ *She wore her wine-coloured gaberdine raincoat.* COLOUR 3 If you **wine and dine**, or if someone **wines and dines** you, you go out, for example to expensive restaurants, and spend a lot of money. ❑ *Colleagues were furious at doing her work while she wined and dined... A lot of money went on wining and dining prospective clients.* PHRASE: Vs inflect

**wine bar** **(wine bars)** A **wine bar** is a place where people can buy and drink wine, and sometimes eat food as well. N-COUNT

**wine glass** **(wine glasses)** A **wine glass** is a glass, usually with a narrow stem, which you use for drinking wine. N-COUNT

**win|ery** /waɪnəri/ **(wineries)** A **winery** is a place where wine is made. [AM] N-COUNT

**wing** /wɪŋ/ **(wings)** ◆◆◇ 1 The **wings** of a bird or insect are the two parts of its body that it uses for flying. ❑ *The bird flapped its wings.* N-COUNT ♦ **-winged** *...black-winged birds.* COMB in ADJ 2 The **wings** of an aeroplane are the long flat parts sticking out of its side which support it while it is flying. N-COUNT ♦ **-winged** ❑ *...a wide-winged plane.* COMB in ADJ 3 A **wing** of a building is a part of it which sticks out from the main part. ❑ *We were given an office in the empty west wing.* N-COUNT: usu with supp 4 A **wing** of an organization, especially a political organization, is a group within it which has a particular function or particular beliefs. ❑ *...the military wing of the African National Congress.* ➔ See also **left-wing**, **right-wing**. N-COUNT: with supp, usu supp N 5 In a theatre, **the wings** are the sides of the stage which are hidden from the audience by curtains or scenery. ❑ *Most nights I watched the start of the play from the wings.* N-PLURAL: *the* N 6 In a game such as football or hockey, **the left wing** and **the right wing** are the areas on the far left and the far right of the pitch. You can also refer to the players who play in these positions as **the left wing** and **the right wing**. N-COUNT: usu supp N 7 A **wing** of a car is a part of it on the outside which is over one of the wheels. [BRIT] ➔ See picture on page 1707. N-COUNT

✓ in AM, use **fender**

8 If you say that something or someone **wings** their way somewhere or **wings** somewhere, you mean that they go there quickly, especially by plane. ❑ *A few moments later they were airborne and winging their way south... A cash bonanza will be winging its way to the 600,000 members of the scheme... The first of the airliners winged westwards and home.* VERB V *way* adv/prep V *way* adv/prep V adv/prep

PHRASES 9 If you say that someone is waiting **in the wings**, you mean that they are ready and waiting for an opportunity to take action. ❑ *There are now more than 20 big companies waiting in the wings to take over some of its business.* PHRASE: usu v PHR 10 If you **spread** your **wings**, you do something new and rather difficult or move to a new place, because you feel more confident in your abilities than you used to and you want to gain wider experience. ❑ *I led a very confined life in my village so I suppose that I wanted to spread my wings.* PHRASE: V inflects 11 If you **take** someone **under** your **wing**, you look after them, help them, and protect them. ❑ *Her boss took her under his wing after fully realising her potential.* PHRASE: V inflects

**wing back** **(wing backs)** also **wing-back.** In football, a **wing back** is a defender who also takes part in attacking play. N-COUNT

**wing com|mand|er** **(wing commanders)** A **wing commander** is a senior officer in the British air force. ❑ *...Wing Commander Christopher Moran.* N-COUNT; N-TITLE

**winged** /wɪŋd/ A **winged** insect or other creature has wings. ❑ *Flycatchers feed primarily on winged insects.* ADJ: usu ADJ n

**wing|er** /wɪŋəʳ/ **(wingers)** In a game such as football or hockey, a **winger** is an attacking player who plays mainly on the far left or the far right side of the pitch. N-COUNT

**wing mir|ror** **(wing mirrors)** The **wing mirrors** on a car are the mirrors on each side of the car on the outside. ➔ See picture on page 1707. N-COUNT

**wing|span** /wɪŋspæn/ **(wingspans)** also **wing span.** The **wingspan** of a bird, insect, or aeroplane is the distance from the end of one wing to the end of the other wing. ❑ *...a glider with an 18-foot wingspan.* N-COUNT: usu sing, usu with supp

**wink** /wɪŋk/ **(winks, winking, winked)** 1 When you **wink at** someone, you look towards them and close one eye very briefly, usually as a signal that something is a joke or a secret. ❑ *Brian winked at his bride-to-be.* VERB V *at* n ♦ **Wink** is also a noun. ❑ *I gave her a wink.* N-COUNT 2 If you say that you **did not sleep a wink** or **did not get a wink of sleep**, you mean that you tried to go to sleep but could not. [INFORMAL] ❑ *I didn't get a wink of sleep on the aeroplane.* PHRASE: V inflects

**win|kle** /wɪŋkᵊl/ **(winkles, winkling, winkled)** **Winkles** are small sea snails that can be eaten. [BRIT] N-COUNT = *periwinkle*

✓ in AM, use **periwinkles**

♦ **winkle out** 1 If you **winkle** information **out of** someone, you get it from them when they do not want to give it to you, often by tricking them. [BRIT, INFORMAL] ❑ *The security services will pretty well go to any lengths to winkle out information... The detective was trying to winkle information out of her.* PHRASAL VERB = *worm out* V P n (not pron) V n P *of* n 2 If you **winkle** someone **out of** a place where they are hiding or which they do not want to leave, you make them leave it. [BRIT, INFORMAL] ❑ *He somehow managed to winkle Picard out of his room... Political pressure finally winkled him out and on to a plane bound for Berlin... It will not be easy to winkle out the old guard and train replacements.* Also V n P PHRASAL VERB V n P *of* n V n P V P n (not pron)

**win|ner** /wɪnəʳ/ **(winners)** ◆◆◇ 1 The **winner** of a prize, race, or competition is the person, animal, or thing that wins it. ❑ *She will present the trophies to the award winners... The winner was a horse called Last Town.* N-COUNT ≠ *loser* 2 If you say that something or someone is **a winner**, you mean that they are popular and successful, or that they are likely to be popular and successful. [INFORMAL] ❑ *They think the appeal is a winner... Selling was my game and I intended to be a winner.* N-COUNT: usu sing, *a* N = *success*, *hit* ≠ *failure*

**win|ning** /wɪnɪŋ/ ◆◇◇ 1 You can use **winning** to describe a person or thing that wins something such as a competition, game, or election. ❑ *...the leader of the winning party... Donovan scored the winning goal.* ADJ: ADJ n 2 You can use **winning** to describe actions or qualities that please other people and make them feel friendly towards you. ❑ *She gave* ADJ: ADJ n = *engaging* *him another of her winning smiles.* 3 → See also **win**.

**win|nings** /wɪnɪŋz/ You can use **winnings** to refer to the money that someone wins in a competition or by gambling. ❑ *I have come to collect my winnings.* N-PLURAL: oft poss N

**win|now** /wɪnoʊ/ **(winnows, winnowing, winnowed)** If you **winnow** a group of things or people, you reduce its size by separating the ones that are useful or relevant from the ones that are not. [LITERARY] ❑ *Administration officials have winnowed the list of candidates to three.* VERB V n

♦ **winnow out** If you **winnow out** part of a group of things or people, you identify the part that is not useful or relevant and the part that is. [WRITTEN] ❑ *The committee will need to winnow out the nonsense and produce more practical proposals if it is to achieve results... Time has winnowed out certain of the essays as superior.* PHRASAL VERB V P n (not pron) V P n (not pron)

**wino** /waɪnoʊ/ **(winos)** Some people refer to alcoholics, especially homeless ones, as **winos**. [INFORMAL] N-COUNT

**win|some** /wɪnsəm/ If you describe a person or their actions or behaviour as **winsome**, you mean that they are attractive and charming. ❑ *She gave him her best winsome smile.* ADJ

**win|ter** /wɪntəʳ/ **(winters, wintering, wintered)** ◆◇◇ 1 **Winter** is the season between autumn and spring. In the winter the weather is usually cold. ❑ *In winter the nights are long and cold. ...the winter months. ...the late winter of 1941.* 2 If an animal or plant **winters** somewhere or **is wintered** there, it spends the winter there. ❑ *The birds will winter outside in an aviary... The young seedlings are usually wintered in a cold frame. ...one of the most important sites for wintering wildfowl.* 3 If you **winter** somewhere, you spend the winter there. [FORMAL] ❑ *The family decided to winter in Nice again.* N-VAR VERB V adv/prep be V-ed prep/adv V-ing VERB V prep/adv

**win|ter sports** **Winter sports** are sports that take place on ice or snow, for example skating and skiing. N-PLURAL

**winter|time** /wɪntəʳtaɪm/ also **winter time**. **Wintertime** is the period of time during which winter lasts. N-UNCOUNT

**win|try** /wɪntri/ **Wintry** weather is cold and has features that are typical of winter. ❑ *Wintry weather continues to sweep across Britain. ...a dark wintry day.* ADJ: usu ADJ n

**win-win** A **win-win** situation is one where you are certain to do well or be successful. ❑ *It is surprising that it has taken people so long to take advantage of what is a win-win opportunity.* ADJ: ADJ n ≠no-win

**wipe** /waɪp/ **(wipes, wiping, wiped)** 1 If you **wipe** something, you rub its surface to remove dirt or liquid from it. ❑ *I'll just wipe the table... When he had finished washing he began to wipe the basin clean... Lainey wiped her hands on the towel.* ♦ **Wipe** is also a noun. ❑ *She gave the table a quick wipe and disappeared behind the counter.* 2 If you **wipe** dirt or liquid from something, you remove it, for example by using a cloth or your hand. ❑ *Gleb wiped the sweat from his face... He shook his head and wiped his tears with a tissue.* 3 A **wipe** is a small moist cloth for cleaning things and is designed to be used only once. ❑ *...antiseptic wipes.* 4 to **wipe the floor with** someone → see **floor**. to **wipe the slate clean** → see **slate**. ◆◇◇ VERB V n V n with adj V n on n N-COUNT: usu sing VERB V n prep V n N-COUNT

♦ **wipe away** or **wipe off** If you **wipe away** or **wipe off** dirt or liquid from something, you remove it, for example by using a cloth or your hand. ❑ *He wiped away the blood with a paper napkin.* PHRASAL VERB V P n (not pron)

♦ **wipe off** → see **wipe away**.

♦ **wipe out** To **wipe out** something such as a place or a group of people or animals means to destroy them completely. ❑ *The spill could wipe out the Gulf's turtle population... The man is a fanatic who is determined to wipe out any opposition to the way he conducts himself.* PHRASAL VERB V P n (not pron) V P n (not pron) Also V n P

♦ **wipe up** If you **wipe up** dirt or liquid from something, you remove it using a cloth. ❑ *I spilled my coffee all over the table and Mom leaned across me to wipe it up... Wipe up spills immediately.* PHRASAL VERB V n P V P n (not pron)

**wip|er** /waɪpəʳ/ **(wipers)** A **wiper** is a device that wipes rain from a vehicle's windscreen. N-COUNT: usu pl

**wire** /waɪəʳ/ **(wires, wiring, wired)** 1 A **wire** is a long thin piece of metal that is used to fasten things or to carry electric current. ❑ *...fine copper wire. ...gadgets which detect electrical wires, pipes and timbers in walls.* 2 A **wire** is a cable which carries power or signals from one place to another. ❑ *I ripped out the telephone wire that ran through to his office. ...the voltage of the overhead wires.* 3 If you **wire** something such as a building or piece of equipment, you put wires inside it so that electricity or signals can pass into or through it. ❑ *...learning to wire and plumb the house herself... Each of the homes has a security system and is wired for cable television. ...a badly wired appliance.* ♦ **Wire up** means the same as **wire**. ❑ *He was helping wire up the Channel Tunnel last season... Wire the thermometers up to trigger off an alarm bell if the temperature drops.* 4 A **wire** is the same as a **telegram**. [mainly AM] 5 If you **wire** an amount of money to a person or place, you tell a bank to send it to the person or place using a telegram message. [mainly AM] ❑ *I'm wiring you some money... They arranged to wire the money from the United States.* 6 If something goes **to the wire**, it continues until the last possible moment. [mainly JOURNALISM] ❑ *Negotiators again worked right down to the wire to reach an agreement.* 7 → See also **barbed wire**, **high wire**, **hot-wire**, **live wire**. ◆◇◇ N-VAR N-COUNT: usu supp N = cable VERB V n be V-ed for n V-ed PHRASAL VERB V P n (not pron) V n P N-COUNT VERB V n n V n prep PHRASE

**wired** /waɪəʳd/ 1 If someone is **wired**, they are tense, nervous, and unable to relax. [mainly AM, INFORMAL] ❑ *Tonight he is manic, wired and uptight.* 2 A computer, organization, or person that is **wired** has the equipment that is necessary to use the Internet. [INFORMAL] ❑ *Once more people are wired, the potential to change the mainstream media will be huge.* 3 **Wired** is used to describe material or clothing that has wires sewn into it in order to keep it stiff. ❑ *...a length of wired ribbon.* ADJ: usu v-link ADJ = edgy, uptight ADJ ADJ: usu ADJ n

**wire|less** /waɪəʳləs/ **(wirelesses)** 1 **Wireless** technology uses radio waves rather than electricity and therefore does not require any wires. ❑ *...the fast-growing wireless communication market.* 2 A **wireless** or **wireless set** is a radio. [BRIT, OLD-FASHIONED] ADJ: ADJ n N-COUNT = radio

**Wire|less Ap|pli|ca|tion Proto|col** → see **WAP**.

**wire|tap** /waɪəʳtæp/ **(wiretaps, wiretapping, wiretapped)** also **wire-tap**. If someone **wiretaps** your telephone, they attach a special device to the line so that they can secretly listen to your conversations. [AM] ❑ *The coach said his club had wiretapped the hotel room of a player during a road trip.* ♦ **Wiretap** is also a noun. ❑ *...tapes of telephone conversations that can have been obtained only by illegal wiretaps.* VERB = bug V n N-COUNT

☑ in BRIT, use **tap**

♦ **wire|tapping** *...allegations of wiretapping.* N-UNCOUNT

**wire wool** **Wire wool** consists of very thin pieces of wire twisted together, often in the form of small pads. These are used to clean wooden and metal objects. [BRIT] N-UNCOUNT = steel wool

☑ in AM, use **steel wool**

**wir|ing** /waɪərɪŋ/ The **wiring** in a building or machine is the system of wires that supply electricity to the different parts of it. N-UNCOUNT

**wiry** /waɪəri/ 1 Someone who is **wiry** is rather thin but is also strong. ❑ *His body is wiry and athletic.* 2 Something such as hair or grass that is **wiry** is stiff and rough to touch. ❑ *Her wiry hair was pushed up on top of her head in an untidy bun.* ADJ ADJ = coarse ≠soft

**wis|dom** /wɪzdəm/ **(wisdoms)** 1 **Wisdom** is the ability to use your experience and knowledge N-UNCOUNT in order to make sensible decisions or judgments. ❑ *...the patience and wisdom that comes from old age. ...a great man, who spoke words of great wisdom.* [2] **Wisdom** is the store of knowledge that a society or culture has collected over a long period of time. ❑ *...this church's original Semitic wisdom, religion and faith.* [3] If you talk about **the wisdom of** a particular decision or action, you are talking about how sensible it is. ❑ *Many Lithuanians have expressed doubts about the wisdom of the decision.* [4] You can use **wisdom** to refer to ideas that are accepted by a large number of people. ❑ *Health education wisdom in the UK differs from that of the United States... Unchallenged wisdoms flow swiftly among the middle classes.* ● **The conventional wisdom** about something is the generally accepted view of it. ❑ *...the conventional wisdom that soccer is a minor sport in America.*

N-VAR; N-SING: *the* N *of* n/-ing; N-VAR: supp N; PHRASE: N *inflects*

**wis|dom tooth** **(wisdom teeth)** Your **wisdom teeth** are the four large teeth at the back of your mouth which usually grow much later than your other teeth. N-COUNT

**wise** /waɪz/ **(wises, wising, wised, wiser, wisest)** ◆◇◇ [1] A **wise** person is able to use their experience and knowledge in order to make sensible decisions and judgments. ❑ *She has the air of a wise woman.* ♦ **wise|ly** *The three of us stood around the machine nodding wisely.* [2] A **wise** action or decision is sensible. ❑ *She had made a very wise decision... It is wise to seek help and counsel as soon as possible.* ♦ **wise|ly** *They've invested their money wisely... Our man had wisely decided to be picked up at the farm.* [3] If you **get wise to** something, you find out about it, especially when someone has been trying to keep it secret. [INFORMAL] ❑ *Dealers have already got wise to the trend and increased their prices accordingly.*

ADJ ≠ *foolish*; ADV: ADV with v; ADJ: oft *it* v-link ADJ to-inf = *sensible*; ADV: usu ADV with v; PHRASE: V inflects, PHR n

♦ **wise up** If someone **wises up** to a situation or state of affairs, they become aware of it and take appropriate action. [INFORMAL] ❑ *Some insurers have wised up to the fact that their clients were getting very cheap insurance... It's time to wise up and tell those around you that enough is enough.*

PHRASAL VERB; V P *to* n; V P

**-wise** /-waɪz/ [1] **-wise** is added to nouns to form adverbs indicating that something is the case when considering the particular thing mentioned. ❑ *Career-wise, this illness couldn't have come at a worse time... It was a much better day weather-wise.* [2] **-wise** is added to nouns to form adverbs indicating that someone behaves in the same way as the person or thing that is mentioned. ❑ *We were housed student-wise in dormitory rooms.*

COMB in ADV: ADV with cl; COMB in ADV: ADV after v = *-like*

**wise|crack** /waɪzkræk/ **(wisecracks)** A **wisecrack** is a clever remark that is intended to be amusing, but is often rather unkind. N-COUNT = *quip*

**wise|crack|ing** /waɪzkrækɪŋ/ also **wise-cracking.** You can use **wisecracking** to describe someone who keeps making wisecracks. ❑ *...a wisecracking private eye.* ADJ: usu ADJ n

**wise guy** **(wise guys)** also **wiseguy.** [1] If you say that someone is a **wise guy**, you dislike the fact that they think they are very clever and always have an answer for everything. [INFORMAL] [2] A **wise guy** is a member of the Mafia. [mainly AM, INFORMAL]

N-COUNT [disapproval] = *smart alec*; N-COUNT

**wish** /wɪʃ/ **(wishes, wishing, wished)** ◆◆◇ [1] A **wish** is a desire or strong feeling that you want to have something or do something. ❑ *Clearly she had no wish for conversation... She wanted to go everywhere in the world. She soon got her wish... The decision was made against the wishes of the party leader.* ➔ See also **death wish.** [2] If you **wish to** do something or **to** have it done for you, you want to do it or have it done. [FORMAL] ❑ *If you wish to go away for the weekend, our office will be delighted to make hotel reservations... We can dress as we wish now... There were the collaborators, who wished for a German victory.* [3] If you **wish** something were true, you would like it to be true, even though you know that it is impossible or unlikely. ❑ *I wish I could do that... The world is not always what we wish it to be.* [4] If you **wish for** something, you express the desire for that thing silently to yourself. In fairy stories, when a person wishes for something, the thing they wish for often happens by magic. ❑ *We have all wished for men who are more considerate.* ♦ **Wish** is also a noun. ❑ *Blow out the candles and make a wish.* [5] If you say that you would not **wish** a particular thing **on** someone, you mean that the thing is so unpleasant that you would not want them to be forced to experience it. ❑ *It's a horrid experience and I wouldn't wish it on my worst enemy.* [6] If you **wish** someone something such as luck or happiness, you express the hope that they will be lucky or happy. ❑ *I wish you both a very good journey... Goodbye, Hanu. I wish you well.* [7] If you express your good **wishes** towards someone, you are politely expressing your friendly feelings towards them and your hope that they will be successful or happy. ❑ *I found George's story very sad. Please give him my best wishes.*

N-COUNT: oft with poss; VERB; V to-inf; V; V *for* n; VERB: no cont; V that; V n to-inf; VERB; V *for* n; N-COUNT; VERB: no cont, with brd-neg; V n *on* n; VERB; V n n; V n adv; N-PLURAL: adj N [politeness]

**wish|bone** /wɪʃboun/ **(wishbones)** A **wishbone** is a V-shaped bone in chickens, turkeys, and other birds. N-COUNT

**wish|ful think|ing** If you say that an idea, wish, or hope is **wishful thinking**, you mean that it has failed to come true or is unlikely to come true. ❑ *It is wishful thinking to expect deeper change under his leadership.* N-UNCOUNT

**wish list** **(wish lists)** If you refer to someone's **wish list**, you mean all the things which they would like to happen or be given, although these things may be unlikely. [INFORMAL] ❑ *...one special toy that tops the wish list of every child.* N-COUNT: oft with poss

**wishy-washy** /wɪʃi wɒʃi/ If you say that someone is **wishy-washy**, you are critical of them because their ideas are not firm or clear. [INFORMAL] ❑ *If there's anything I can't stand it's an indecisive, wishy-washy customer.* ADJ [disapproval]

**wisp** /wɪsp/ **(wisps)** [1] A **wisp of** hair is a small, thin, untidy bunch of it. ❑ *She smoothed away a wisp of hair from her eyes.* [2] A **wisp of** something such as smoke or cloud is an amount of it in a long thin shape. ❑ *A thin wisp of smoke straggled up through the trees.*

N-COUNT: usu N *of* n; N-COUNT: usu N *of* n

**wispy** /wɪspi/ [1] If someone has **wispy** hair, their hair does not grow thickly on their head. [2] A **wispy** cloud is thin or faint. ADJ; ADJ: usu ADJ n

**wis|te|ria** /wɪstɪəriə/ **Wisteria** is a type of climbing plant which has pale purple or white flowers. N-UNCOUNT

**wist|ful** /wɪstfʊl/ Someone who is **wistful** is rather sad because they want something and know that they cannot have it. ❑ *I can't help feeling slightly wistful about the perks I'm giving up.* ADJ

**wit** /wɪt/ **(wits)** [1] **Wit** is the ability to use words or ideas in an amusing, clever, and imaginative way. ❑ *Boulding was known for his biting wit.* [2] If you describe someone as a **wit**, you mean that they have the ability to use words or ideas in an amusing, clever, and imaginative way. ❑ *Holmes was gregarious, a great wit, a man of wide interests.* [3] If you say that someone has **the wit to** do something, you mean that they have the intelligence and understanding to make the right decision or take the right action in a particular situation. ❑ *The information is there and waiting to be accessed by anyone with the wit to use it.* [4] You can refer to your ability to think quickly and cleverly in a difficult situation as your **wits**. ❑ *She has used her wits to progress to the position she holds today.* [5] You can use **wits** in expressions such as **frighten** someone **out of their wits** and **scare the wits out of** someone to emphasize that a person or thing worries or frightens someone very much. ❑ *You scared us out of our wits. We heard you had an accident.*

N-UNCOUNT; N-COUNT; N-SING: *the* N to-inf = *sense*; N-PLURAL: usu poss N; N-PLURAL: usu *out of* poss N [emphasis]

**PHRASES** [6] If you **have** your **wits about** you or **keep** your **wits about** you, you are alert and ready to act in a difficult situation. ❑ *Travellers* PHRASE: V inflects *need to keep their wits about them.* 7 If you say that you are **at** your **wits' end**, you are emphasizing that you are so worried and exhausted by problems or difficulties that you do not know what to do next. ❑ *We row a lot and we never have time on our own. I'm at my wit's end.* PHRASE: usu v-link PHR [emphasis] 8 If you **pit** your **wits against** someone, you compete against them in a test of knowledge or intelligence. ❑ *He has to pit his wits against an adversary who is cool, clever and cunning.* PHRASE: V inflects, PHR n 9 **To wit** is used to indicate that you are about to state or describe something more precisely. [LITERARY] ❑ *He'd like 'happiness' to be given a new and more scientifically descriptive label, to wit 'Major affective disorder, pleasant type'.* PHRASE: PHR with cl, PHR n = *namely*

**witch** /wɪtʃ/ **(witches)** 1 In fairy stories, a **witch** is a woman, usually an old woman, who has evil magic powers. Witches often wear a pointed black hat, and have a pet black cat. N-COUNT 2 A **witch** is a man or woman who claims to have magic powers and to be able to use them for good or bad purposes. N-COUNT

**witch|craft** /wɪtʃkrɑːft, -kræft/ **Witchcraft** is the use of magic powers, especially evil ones. N-UNCOUNT

**witch doc|tor** **(witch doctors)** also **witch-doctor.** A **witch doctor** is a person in some societies, for example in Africa, who is thought to have magic powers which can be used to heal people. N-COUNT

**witch ha|zel** **Witch hazel** is a liquid that you put on your skin if it is sore or damaged, in order to help it to heal. N-UNCOUNT

**witch-hunt** **(witch-hunts)** A **witch-hunt** is an attempt to find and punish a particular group of people who are being blamed for something, often simply because of their opinions and not because they have actually done anything wrong. N-COUNT: oft N *against* n [disapproval]

**witchy** /wɪtʃi/ or **witch-like** A **witchy** person looks or behaves like a witch. **Witchy** things are associated with witches. ❑ *My great-grandmother was old and witchy looking.* ADJ

**with** /wɪð, wɪθ/ ◆◆◆

✓ Pronounced /wɪð/ for meanings 20 and 21.

> In addition to the uses shown below, **with** is used after some verbs, nouns and adjectives in order to introduce extra information. **With** is also used in most reciprocal verbs, such as 'agree' or 'fight', and in some phrasal verbs, such as 'deal with' and 'dispense with'.

1 If one person is **with** another, they are together in one place. ❑ *With her were her son and daughter-in-law... She is currently staying with her father at his home.* PREP 2 If something is put **with** or is **with** something else, they are used at the same time. ❑ *Serve hot, with pasta or rice and French beans... Cookies are just the thing to serve with tall glasses of real lemonade.* PREP 3 If you do something **with** someone else, you both do it together or are both involved in it. ❑ *Parents will be able to discuss their child's progress with their teacher... He walked with her to the front door.* PREP 4 If you fight, argue, or compete **with** someone, you oppose them. ❑ *About a thousand students fought with riot police in the capital... He was in an argument with his landlord downstairs.* PREP 5 If you do something **with** a particular tool, object, or substance, you do it using that tool, object, or substance. ❑ *Remove the meat with a fork and divide it among four plates... Doctors are treating him with the drug AZT.* PREP 6 If someone stands or goes somewhere **with** something, they are carrying it. ❑ *A man came round with a tray of chocolates.* PREP 7 Someone or something **with** a particular feature or possession has that feature or possession. ❑ *He was in his early forties, tall and blond with bright blue eyes... Someone with an income of $34,895 can afford this loan.* PREP 8 Someone **with** an illness has that illness. ❑ *I spent a week in bed with flu.* PREP 9 If something is filled or covered **with** a substance or **with** things, it has that substance or those things in it or on it. ❑ *His legs were caked with dried mud... They sat at a Formica table cluttered with dirty tea cups.* PREP 10 If you are, for example, pleased or annoyed **with** someone or something, you have that feeling towards them. ❑ *He was still a little angry with her... I am happy with that decision.* PREP: adj/n PREP n 11 You use **with** to indicate what a state, quality, or action relates to, involves, or affects. ❑ *Our aim is to allow student teachers to become familiar with the classroom... He still has a serious problem with money... Depression lowers the human ability to cope with disease.* PREP 12 You use **with** when indicating the way that something is done or the feeling that a person has when they do something. ❑ *...teaching her to read music with skill and sensitivity... He agreed, but with reluctance.* PREP 13 You use **with** when indicating a sound or gesture that is made when something is done, or an expression that a person has on their face when they do something. ❑ *With a sigh, she leant back and closed her eyes... The front door closed with a crash behind him.* PREP 14 You use **with** to indicate the feeling that makes someone have a particular appearance or type of behaviour. ❑ *Gil was white and trembling with anger... I felt sick to my stomach with sadness for them.* PREP 15 You use **with** when mentioning the position or appearance of a person or thing at the time that they do something, or what someone else is doing at that time. ❑ *Joanne stood with her hands on the sink, staring out the window... Michelle had fallen asleep with her head against his shoulder.* PREP: PREP n prep/-ing 16 You use **with** to introduce a current situation that is a factor affecting another situation. ❑ *With all the night school courses available, there is no excuse for not getting some sort of training... With the win, the US reclaimed the cup for the first time since 1985.* PREP 17 You use **with** when making a comparison or contrast between the situations of different people or things. ❑ *We're not like them. It's different with us... Sometimes I'm busy and sometimes I'm not. It's the same with most jobs.* PREP 18 If something increases or decreases **with** a particular factor, it changes as that factor changes. ❑ *The risk of developing heart disease increases with the number of cigarettes smoked... Blood pressure decreases with exercise.* PREP: v PREP n 19 If something moves **with** a wind or current, it moves in the same direction as the wind or current. ❑ *...a piece of driftwood carried down with the current.* PREP ≠ *against* 20 If someone says that they are **with** you, they mean that they understand what you are saying. [INFORMAL] ❑ *Yes, I know who you mean. Yes, now I'm with you... I'm not with you. Tell me what you mean.* PREP: v-link PREP n 21 If someone says that they are **with** you, they mean that they support or approve of what you are doing. ❑ *'I'm with you all the way.' — 'Thank you.'* PREP: v-link PREP n

**with|draw** /wɪðdrɔː/ **(withdraws, withdrawing, withdrew, withdrawn)** ◆◆◇ 1 If you **withdraw** something **from** a place, you remove it or take it away. [FORMAL] ❑ *He reached into his pocket and withdrew a sheet of notepaper... Cassandra withdrew her hand from Roger's.* VERB = *remove* V n V n *from* n 2 When groups of people such as troops **withdraw** or when someone **withdraws** them, they leave the place where they are fighting or where they are based and return nearer home. ❑ *He stated that all foreign forces would withdraw as soon as the crisis ended... Unless Hitler withdrew his troops from Poland by 11 o'clock that morning, a state of war would exist between Great Britain and Germany... Troops withdrew from the north east of the country last March.* VERB V V n *from* n V *from* n Also V *to* n 3 If you **withdraw** money **from** a bank account, you take it out of that account. ❑ *Open a savings account that does not charge ridiculous fees to withdraw money... They withdrew 100 dollars from a bank account after checking out of their hotel.* VERB V n V n *from* n 4 If you **withdraw from** an activity or organization, you stop taking part in it. ❑ *The African National Congress threatened to withdraw from the talks.* VERB V *from* n Also V 5 If you **withdraw** a remark or statement that you have made, you say that VERB = *retract* you want people to ignore it. [FORMAL] ❑ *He withdrew his remarks and explained what he had meant to say.* (V n)

**with|draw|al** /wɪðdrɔːəl/ **(withdrawals)** ◆◇◇
[1] (N-VAR: usu N *of* n) The **withdrawal of** something is the act or process of removing it, or ending it. [FORMAL] ❑ *If you experience any unusual symptoms after withdrawal of the treatment then contact your doctor.* [2] (N-UNCOUNT: usu with supp) Someone's **withdrawal from** an activity or an organization is their decision to stop taking part in it. ❑ *...his withdrawal from government in 1946.* [3] (N-COUNT ≠ *deposit*) A **withdrawal** is an amount of money that you take from your bank account. [4] (N-UNCOUNT) **Withdrawal** is the period during which someone feels ill after they have stopped taking a drug which they were addicted to. ❑ *Withdrawal from heroin is actually like a severe attack of gastric flu.*

**with|draw|al symp|toms** (N-PLURAL) When someone has **withdrawal symptoms**, they feel ill after they have stopped taking a drug which they were addicted to.

**with|drawn** /wɪðdrɔːn/ [1] **Withdrawn** is the past participle of **withdraw**. [2] (ADJ: v-link ADJ) Someone who is **withdrawn** is very quiet, and does not want to talk to other people. ❑ *Her husband had become withdrawn and moody.*

**with|drew** /wɪðdruː/ **Withdrew** is the past tense of **withdraw**.

**with|er** /wɪðəʳ/ **(withers, withering, withered)**
[1] (VERB) If someone or something **withers**, they become very weak. ❑ *When he went into retirement, he visibly withered... Industries unable to modernise have been left to wither.* (V) ♦ (PHRASAL VERB) **Wither away** means the same as **wither**. ❑ *To see my body literally wither away before my eyes was exasperating.* (V P) [2] (VERB) If a flower or plant **withers**, it dries up and dies. ❑ *The flowers in Isabel's room had withered.* (V)
♦ **wither away** → see **wither 1**.

**with|ered** /wɪðəʳd/ [1] (ADJ: usu ADJ n) If you describe a person or a part of their body as **withered**, you mean that they are thin and their skin looks old. ❑ *...her withered hands.* [2] (ADJ: usu ADJ n) **Withered** is used to describe someone's leg or arm when it is thin and weak because of disease or injury. ❑ *She has one slightly withered leg, noticeably thinner than the other.*

**with|er|ing** /wɪðərɪŋ/ (ADJ: usu ADJ n) A **withering** look or remark is very critical, and is intended to make someone feel ashamed or stupid. ❑ *Deborah Jane's mother gave her a withering look.*

**with|hold** /wɪðhoʊld/ **(withholds, withholding, withheld** /wɪðheld/**)** (VERB) If you **withhold** something that someone wants, you do not let them have it. [FORMAL] ❑ *Police withheld the dead boy's name yesterday until relatives could be told... Financial aid for Britain has been withheld.* (V n)

**with|hold|ing tax** **(withholding taxes)** (N-VAR) A **withholding tax** is an amount of money that is taken in advance from someone's income, in order to pay some of the tax they will owe. [mainly AM, BUSINESS]

**with|in** /wɪðɪn/ ◆◆◆ [1] (PREP ≠ *outside*) If something is **within** a place, area, or object, it is inside it or surrounded by it. [FORMAL] ❑ *Clients are entertained within private dining rooms. ...a 1987 agreement which would recognise Quebec as a distinct society within Canada.* ♦ (ADV: usu *from* ADV) **Within** is also an adverb. ❑ *A small voice called from within. 'Yes, just coming.'* [2] (PREP = *in*) Something that happens or exists **within** a society, organization, or system, happens or exists inside it. ❑ *...the spirit of self-sacrifice within an army... Within criminal law almost anything could be defined as 'crime'.* ♦ (ADV: usu *from* ADV, also ADV after v) **Within** is also an adverb. ❑ *The Church of England, with threats of split from within, has still to make up its mind.* [3] (PREP: PREP pron = *in*) If you experience a particular feeling, you can say that it is **within** you. [LITERARY] ❑ *He's coping much better within himself.* [4] (PREP) If something is **within** a particular limit or set of rules, it does not go beyond it or is not more than what is allowed. ❑ *Troops have agreed to stay within specific boundaries to avoid confrontations... Exercise within your comfortable limit.* [5] (PREP) If you are **within** a particular distance of a place, you are less than that distance from it. ❑ *The man was within a few feet of him... It was within easy walking distance of the hotel.* [6] (PREP: PREP amount) **Within** a particular length of time means before that length of time has passed. ❑ *About 40% of all students entering as freshmen graduate within 4 years... Within 24 hours the deal was completed.* [7] (PREP ≠ *out of*) If something is **within sight**, **within earshot**, or **within reach**, you can see it, hear it, or reach it. ❑ *His twenty-five-foot boat was moored within sight of West Church. ...her heels clicking on the tiled floor, probably an irritating noise to other people within earshot.* [8] **within reason** → see **reason**.

**with it** also **with-it.** [1] (ADJ) If you say that someone is **with it**, you mean that they are fashionable or know about new things, especially in culture. [INFORMAL, OLD-FASHIONED] [2] (ADJ: v-link ADJ, usu with brd-neg) If someone is not **with it**, they do not feel alert and therefore fail to understand things. [INFORMAL] ❑ *She wasn't really with it. She hadn't taken in the practical consequences.*

**with|out** /wɪðaʊt/ ◆◆◆

> In addition to the uses shown below, **without** is used in the phrasal verbs 'do without', 'go without', and 'reckon without'.

[1] (PREP ≠ *with*) You use **without** to indicate that someone or something does not have or use the thing mentioned. ❑ *I don't like myself without a beard... She wore a brown shirt pressed without a wrinkle.* [2] (PREP: PREP n/-ing) If one thing happens **without** another thing, or if you do something **without** doing something else, the second thing does not happen or occur. ❑ *He was offered a generous pension provided he left without a fuss... They worked without a break until about eight in the evening... Alex had done this without consulting her.* [3] (PREP ≠ *with*) If you do something **without** a particular feeling, you do not have that feeling when you do it. ❑ *Janet Magnusson watched his approach without enthusiasm... 'Hello, Swanson,' he said without surprise.* [4] (PREP ≠ *with*) If you do something **without** someone else, they are not in the same place as you are or are not involved in the same action as you. ❑ *I told Franklin he would have to start dinner without me... How can I rebuild my life without my husband?*

**with-profits** (ADJ: ADJ n) A **with-profits** savings scheme or financial plan is one in which the people who put money into the scheme receive extra money each year based on how successful the investment has been. [BUSINESS] ❑ *Returns on with-profits bonds have improved.*

**with|stand** /wɪðstænd/ **(withstands, withstanding, withstood** /wɪðstʊd/**)** (VERB = *stand up to*) If something or someone **withstands** a force or action, they survive it or do not give in to it. [FORMAL] ❑ *...armoured vehicles designed to withstand chemical attack.* (V n)

**wit|less** /wɪtləs/ (ADJ [disapproval] = *mindless, stupid*) If you describe something or someone as **witless**, you mean that they are very foolish or stupid. ❑ *...a witless, nasty piece of journalism.*

**wit|ness** /wɪtnəs/ **(witnesses, witnessing, witnessed)** ◆◇◇ [1] (N-COUNT: oft N *to* n) A **witness to** an event such as an accident or crime is a person who saw it. ❑ *Witnesses to the crash say they saw an explosion just before the disaster... No witnesses have come forward.* [2] (VERB = *see*) If you **witness** something, you see it happen. ❑ *Anyone who witnessed the attack should call the police.* (V n) [3] (N-COUNT: oft N *for* n) A **witness** is someone who appears in a court of law to say what they know about a crime or other event. ❑ *In the next three or four days, eleven witnesses will be called to testify.* [4] (N-COUNT) A **witness** is someone who writes their name on a document that you have signed, to confirm that it really is your signature. [5] (VERB) If someone **witnesses** your signature on a document, they write their name after it, to confirm that it really is your signature. ❑ *Ask a friend to witness your signature.* (V n) [6] (VERB = *see*) If you say that a place, period of time, or person **witnessed** a particular event or change, you mean that it happened in that place, during that period of time, or while that person was alive. ❑ *India has witnessed many political changes in recent years.* V n [7] If a person or thing **bears witness to** something, they show or say that it exists or happened. [FORMAL] ❑ *Many of these poems bear witness to his years spent in India and China.* PHRASE: V inflects, PHR n

**wit|ness box** The **witness box** in a court of law is the place where people stand or sit when they are giving evidence. [BRIT] N-SING: *the* N

☑ in AM, use **witness stand**

**wit|ness stand** The **witness stand** is the same as **the witness box**. [AM] N-SING: *the* N

**wit|ter** /wɪtəʳ/ **(witters, wittering, wittered)** If you say that someone **is wittering about** something, you mean that they are talking a lot about things that you think are silly and boring. [BRIT, INFORMAL] ❑ *They just sat there wittering about what lectures they had tomorrow.* ♦ **Witter on** means the same as **witter**. ❑ *They started wittering on about their last trip to Provence.* VERB [disapproval] = *prattle* V *about* n Also V PHRASAL VERB V P *about* n Also V P

**wit|ti|cism** /wɪtɪsɪzəm/ **(witticisms)** A **witticism** is a witty remark or joke. [FORMAL] N-COUNT

**wit|ting|ly** /wɪtɪŋli/ If you do something **wittingly**, you are fully aware of what you are doing and what its consequences will be. [FORMAL] ❑ *When she had an affair with her friend's husband, she wittingly set off a chain of crises.* ADV: usu ADV with v, also ADV adj ≠ *unwittingly*

**wit|ty** /wɪti/ **(wittier, wittiest)** Someone or something that is **witty** is amusing in a clever way. ❑ *His plays were very good, very witty... He is a very witty speaker.* ADJ

**wives** /waɪvz/ **Wives** is the plural of **wife**.

**wiz|ard** /wɪzəʳd/ **(wizards)** [1] In legends and fairy stories, a **wizard** is a man who has magic powers. N-COUNT [2] If you admire someone because they are very good at doing a particular thing, you can say that they are a **wizard**. ❑ *...a financial wizard.* N-COUNT: with supp [approval] [3] A **wizard** is a computer program that guides you through the stages of a particular task. [COMPUTING] ❑ *Wizards and templates can help you create brochures, calendars, and Web pages.* N-COUNT

**wiz|ard|ry** /wɪzəʳdri/ You can refer to a very clever achievement or piece of work as **wizardry**, especially when you do not understand how it is done. ❑ *...a piece of technical wizardry.* N-UNCOUNT

**wiz|ened** /wɪzənd/ A **wizened** person is old and has a lot of lines on their skin. ❑ *...a little wizened old fellow with no teeth.* ADJ

**wk** **(wks)** **wk** is a written abbreviation for **week**. ❑ *...6 wks holiday.*

**wob|ble** /wɒbəl/ **(wobbles, wobbling, wobbled)** If something or someone **wobbles**, they make small movements from side to side, for example because they are unsteady. ❑ *The table wobbled when I leaned on it... I narrowly missed a cyclist who wobbled into my path.* ♦ **Wobble** is also a noun. ❑ *We might look for a tiny wobble in the position of a star.* VERB V V prep/adv N-VAR

**wob|bly** /wɒbli/ [1] Something that is **wobbly** moves unsteadily from side to side. ❑ *I was sitting on a wobbly plastic chair. ...a wobbly green jelly. ...wobbly teeth.* ADJ [2] If you feel **wobbly** or if your legs feel **wobbly**, you feel weak and have difficulty standing up, especially because you are afraid, ill, or exhausted. ❑ *She could not maintain her balance and moved in a wobbly fashion.* ADJ

**wodge** /wɒdʒ/ **(wodges)** also **wadge**. A **wodge of** something is a large amount of it or a large piece of it. [BRIT, INFORMAL] ❑ *...a wodge of syrupy sponge.* N-COUNT: usu N *of* n

**woe** /woʊ/ **(woes)** [1] **Woe** is very great sadness. [LITERARY] ❑ *He listened to my tale of woe.* N-UNCOUNT ≠ *joy* [2] You can refer to someone's problems as their **woes**. [WRITTEN] ❑ *He did not tell his relatives and friends about his woes.* N-PLURAL: usu with poss [3] **woe betide** → see **betide**.

**woe|be|gone** /woʊbɪgɒn/ Someone who is **woebegone** is very sad. [WRITTEN] ❑ *She sniffed and looked woebegone.* ADJ = *miserable* ≠ *joyful*

**woe|ful** /woʊfʊl/ [1] If someone or something is **woeful**, they are very sad. ❑ *...a woeful ballad.* ♦ **woe|ful|ly** *He said woefully: 'I love my country, but it does not give a damn about me.'* ADJ ADV: ADV with v [2] You can use **woeful** to emphasize that something is very bad or undesirable. ❑ *...the woeful state of the economy.* ♦ **woe|ful|ly** *Public expenditure on the arts is woefully inadequate.* ADJ: usu ADJ n [emphasis] ADV: usu ADV adj

**wog** /wɒg/ **(wogs)** **Wog** is an extremely offensive word for anyone whose skin is not white. [BRIT, ⚠ VERY OFFENSIVE] N-COUNT

**wok** /wɒk/ **(woks)** A **wok** is a large bowl-shaped pan which is used for Chinese-style cooking. N-COUNT

**woke** /woʊk/ **Woke** is the past tense of **wake**.

**wok|en** /woʊkən/ **Woken** is the past participle of **wake**.

**wolf** /wʊlf/ **(wolves, wolfs, wolfing, wolfed)** [1] A **wolf** is a wild animal that looks like a large dog. N-COUNT [2] If someone **wolfs** their food, they eat it all very quickly and greedily. [INFORMAL] ❑ *I was back in the changing-room wolfing tea and sandwiches.* ♦ **Wolf down** means the same as **wolf**. ❑ *He wolfed down the rest of the biscuit and cheese... She bought a hot dog from a stand on a street corner and wolfed it down.* VERB V n PHRASAL VERB V P n (not pron) V n P [3] If someone **cries wolf**, they say that there is a problem when there is not, with the result that people do not believe them when there really is a problem. PHRASE: V inflects

♦ **wolf down** → see **wolf 2**.

**wolf|hound** /wʊlfhaʊnd/ **(wolfhounds)** A **wolfhound** is a type of very large dog. N-COUNT

**wolf-whistle** **(wolf-whistles, wolf-whistling, wolf-whistled)** also **wolf whistle.** If someone **wolf-whistles**, they make a whistling sound with a short rising note and a longer falling note. Some men wolf-whistle at a woman to show that they think she is attractive, and some women find this offensive. ❑ *They wolf-whistled at me, and I was so embarrassed I tripped up.* ♦ **Wolf whistle** is also a noun. ❑ *Her dancing brought loud cheers, wolf whistles and applause.* VERB V *at* n Also V N-COUNT

**wolves** /wʊlvz/ **Wolves** is the plural of **wolf**.

**wom|an** /wʊmən/ **(women)** [1] A **woman** is an adult female human being. ❑ *...a young Lithuanian woman named Dayva. ...men and women over 75 years old. ...a woman doctor.* ◆◆◆ N-COUNT [2] You can refer to women in general as **woman**. ❑ *...the oppression of woman.* N-UNCOUNT [3] → See also **career woman**. [4] **woman of the world** → see **world**.

**-woman** /-wʊmən/ **-woman** combines with numbers to indicate that something involves the number of women mentioned. ❑ *...a seven-woman team.* COMB in ADJ: ADJ n

**wom|an|hood** /wʊmənhʊd/ [1] **Womanhood** is the state of being a woman rather than a girl, or the period of a woman's adult life. ❑ *Pregnancy is a natural part of womanhood.* N-UNCOUNT [2] You can refer to women in general or the women of a particular country or community as **womanhood**. ❑ *She symbolised for me the best of Indian womanhood.* N-UNCOUNT

**wom|an|iz|er** /wʊmənaɪzəʳ/ **(womanizers)**

☑ in BRIT, also use **womaniser**

If you describe a man as a **womanizer**, you disapprove of him because he likes to have many short sexual relationships with women. N-COUNT [disapproval] = *philanderer*

**wom|an|iz|ing** /wʊmənaɪzɪŋ/

☑ in BRIT, also use **womanising**

[1] If you talk about a man's **womanizing**, you disapprove of him because he likes to have many short sexual relationships with women. N-UNCOUNT [disapproval] = *philandering* [2] A **womanizing** man likes to have many short sexual relationships with women. ADJ: ADJ n [disapproval] = *philandering*

**wom|an|kind** /wʊmənkaɪnd/ You can refer to all women as **womankind** when considering them as a group. [FORMAL] N-UNCOUNT

**wom|an|ly** /wʊmənli/ People describe a woman's behaviour, character, or appearance as **womanly** when they like it because they think it is typical of, or suitable for, a woman rather than a man or girl. ❑ *She had a classical, womanly shape. ...womanly tenderness.* ADJ approval

**woman-to-woman** also **woman to woman.** If you talk about a **woman-to-woman** conversation, you are talking about an honest and open discussion between two women. ADJ: ADJ n ♦ **Woman to woman** is also an adverb. ❑ *Maybe she would talk to her mother one day, woman to woman.* ADV: ADV after v

**womb** /wuːm/ **(wombs)** A woman's **womb** is the part inside her body where a baby grows before it is born. N-COUNT: oft *the* N, poss N = *uterus*

**wom|bat** /wɒmbæt/ **(wombats)** A **wombat** is a type of furry animal which has very short legs and eats plants. Wombats are found in Australia. N-COUNT

**wom|en** /wɪmɪn/ **Women** is the plural of **woman**.

**women|folk** /wɪmɪnfoʊk/ Some people refer to the women of a particular community as its **womenfolk**, especially when the community is ruled or organized by men. ❑ *Men never notice anything in a house run by their womenfolk.* N-PLURAL: oft poss N

**wom|en's group** **(women's groups)** A **women's group** is a group of women who meet regularly, usually in order to organize campaigns. N-COUNT

**Wom|en's Lib** **Women's Lib** is the same as **Women's Liberation**. [INFORMAL, OLD-FASHIONED] N-UNCOUNT

**Wom|en's Liber|ation** **Women's Liberation** is the belief and aim that women should have the same rights and opportunities in society as men. [OLD-FASHIONED] N-UNCOUNT: oft N n = *feminism*

**wom|en's move|ment** You use **the women's movement** to refer to groups of people and organizations that believe that women should have the same rights and opportunities in society as men. N-SING: usu *the* N

**women's room** **(women's rooms)** **The women's room** is a toilet for women in a public building. [mainly AM] N-COUNT: usu *the* N in sing

**won** /wʌn/ **Won** is the past tense and past participle of **win**.

**won|der** /wʌndəʳ/ **(wonders, wondering, wondered)** ♦♦◇ 1 If you **wonder about** something, you think about it, either because it interests you and you want to know more about it, or because you are worried or suspicious about it. ❑ *I wondered what that noise was... 'He claims to be her father,' said Max. 'We've been wondering about him.'... But there was something else, too. Not hard evidence, but it made me wonder.* VERB V wh V *about* n V 2 If you **wonder at** something, you are very surprised about it or think about it in a very surprised way. ❑ *Walk down Castle Street, admire our little jewel of a cathedral, then wonder at the castle... We all wonder you're still alive.* VERB V *at* n V that 3 If you say that it is a **wonder that** something happened, you mean that it is very surprising and unexpected. ❑ *It's a wonder that it took almost ten years... The wonder is that Olivier was not seriously hurt.* N-SING 4 **Wonder** is a feeling of great surprise and pleasure that you have, for example when you see something that is very beautiful, or when something happens that you thought was impossible. ❑ *'That's right!' Bobby exclaimed in wonder. 'How did you remember that?'.* N-UNCOUNT 5 A **wonder** is something that causes people to feel great surprise or admiration. ❑ *...a lecture on the wonders of space and space exploration. ...the wonder of seeing his name in print.* N-COUNT: usu *the* N *of* n/-ing 6 If you refer, for example, to a young man as a **wonder** boy, or to a new product as a **wonder** drug, you mean that they are believed by many people to be very good or very effective. ❑ *Mickelson was hailed as the wonder boy of American golf.* ADJ: ADJ n

PHRASES 7 You can say **'I wonder'** if you want to be very polite when you are asking someone to do something, or when you are asking them for their opinion or for information. ❑ *I was just wondering if you could help me.* PHRASE: V inflects, usu PHR wh politeness 8 If you say **'no wonder'**, **'little wonder'**, or **'small wonder'**, you mean that something is not surprising. ❑ *No wonder my brother wasn't feeling well... Under such circumstances, it is little wonder that they experience difficulties.* PHRASE: PHR that 9 You can say **'No wonder'** when you find out the reason for something that has been puzzling you for some time. ❑ *Brad was Jane's brother! No wonder he reminded me so much of her!* PHRASE: PHR that 10 If you say that a person or thing **works wonders** or **does wonders**, you mean that they have a very good effect on something. ❑ *A few moments of relaxation can work wonders.* PHRASE: V inflects, oft PHR *for* n/-ing, PHR *with/on* n

**won|der|ful** /wʌndəʳfʊl/ ♦♦◇ If you describe something or someone as **wonderful**, you think they are extremely good. ❑ *The cold, misty air felt wonderful on his face... It's wonderful to see you... I've always thought he was a wonderful actor.* ADJ: oft *it* v-link ADJ to-inf/that = *fantastic* ≠ *awful* ♦ **won|der|ful|ly** *It's a system that works wonderfully well.* ADV: usu ADV adv/adj/-ed

**wonder|land** /wʌndəʳlænd/ **Wonderland** is an imaginary world that exists in fairy stories. N-UNCOUNT

**won|der|ment** /wʌndəʳmənt/ **Wonderment** is a feeling of great surprise and pleasure. [LITERARY] ❑ *His big blue eyes opened wide in wonderment.* N-UNCOUNT: oft *in* N = astonishment

**won|drous** /wʌndrəs/ If you describe something as **wondrous**, you mean it is strange and beautiful or impressive. [LITERARY] ❑ *We were driven across this wondrous vast land of lakes and forests.* ADJ: usu ADJ n

**won|ky** /wɒŋki/ If something is **wonky**, it is not straight or level. [BRIT, INFORMAL] ❑ *The wheels keep going wonky.* ADJ

**wont** /woʊnt, AM wɔːnt/ 1 If someone is **wont to** do something, they often or regularly do it. [WRITTEN] ❑ *Both have committed their indiscretions, as human beings are wont to do.* ADJ: v-link ADJ to-inf = *inclined* 2 If someone does a particular thing **as is** their **wont**, they do that thing often or regularly. [WRITTEN] ❑ *Paul woke early, as was his wont.* PHRASE: V inflects

**won't** /woʊnt/ **Won't** is the usual spoken form of 'will not'. ❑ *His parents won't let him come.*

**woo** /wuː/ **(woos, wooing, wooed)** 1 If you **woo** people, you try to encourage them to help you, support you, or vote for you, for example by promising them things which they would like. ❑ *They wooed customers by offering low interest rates... They are trying to woo back electoral support.* VERB V n V n with adv ♦ **woo|ing** *This election has been marked so far by the candidates' wooing of each other's traditional political bases.* N-UNCOUNT: oft poss N, N *of* n 2 If a man **woos** a woman, he spends time with her and tries to persuade her to marry him. [OLD-FASHIONED] ❑ *The penniless author successfully wooed and married Fanny.* VERB = *court* V n ♦ **woo|ing** *...the hero's wooing of his beautiful cousin Roxanne.* N-UNCOUNT: oft poss N, N *of* n

**wood** /wʊd/ **(woods)** ♦♦◇ 1 **Wood** is the material which forms the trunks and branches of trees. ❑ *Their dishes were made of wood... There was a smell of damp wood and machine oil. ...a short piece of wood.* N-MASS 2 A **wood** is a fairly large area of trees growing near each other. You can refer to one or several of these areas as **woods**, and this is the usual form in American English. ❑ *After dinner Alice slipped away for a walk in the woods with Artie... About a mile to the west of town he came upon a large wood.* N-COUNT 3 → See also **dead wood**. 4 If something or someone is **not out of the woods** yet, they are still having difficulties or problems. [INFORMAL] ❑ *The nation's economy is not out of the woods yet.* PHRASE: v-link PHR 5 You can say **'touch wood'** in British English, or **'knock on wood'** in American English, to indicate that you hope to have good luck in something you are doing, usually after saying that you have been lucky with it so far. ❑ *She's never even been to the doctor's, touch wood... Touch wood, I've been lucky enough to avoid any other* CONVENTION serious injuries. [6] your **neck of the woods** → see **neck**. **can't see the wood for the trees** → see **tree**.

**wood-burning stove** (**wood-burning stoves**) A **wood-burning stove** is the same as a **wood stove**. N-COUNT

**wood carv|ing** (**wood carvings**) A **wood carving** is a decorative piece of wood that has been carved in an artistic way. N-VAR

**wood|chip** /wʊdtʃɪp/ (**woodchips**) [1] **Woodchip** is a type of wallpaper which has lots of small lumps on its surface that are formed by tiny pieces of wood glued to the underneath. N-UNCOUNT [2] **Woodchips** are very small pieces of wood, usually made from waste wood, which are used in processes such as making paper. ❑ *...the domestic market for woodchips. ...the Government's decision to cut woodchip exports by 20%.* N-VAR

**wood|cock** /wʊdkɒk/ (**woodcocks** or **woodcock**) A **woodcock** is a small brown bird with a long beak. Woodcock are sometimes shot for sport or food. N-COUNT

**wood|cutter** /wʊdkʌtəʳ/ (**woodcutters**) A **woodcutter** is someone who cuts down trees or who chops wood as their job. [OLD-FASHIONED] N-COUNT

**wood|ed** /wʊdɪd/ A **wooded** area is covered in trees. ❑ *...a wooded valley.* ADJ

**wood|en** /wʊdᵊn/ [1] **Wooden** objects are made of wood. ❑ *...the shop's bare brick walls and faded wooden floorboards.* ◆◇◇ ADJ: ADJ n [2] If you describe an actor as **wooden**, you are critical of them because their performance is not at all lively or natural. ADJ disapproval

**wooden spoon** (**wooden spoons**) [1] A **wooden spoon** is a spoon that is used for stirring sauces and for mixing ingredients in cooking. It is made of wood and has a long handle. N-COUNT [2] If someone gets **the wooden spoon**, they come last in a race or competition. [BRIT] ❑ *Jarvis took the wooden spoon in the first tournament.* N-COUNT: usu *the* N in sing

**wood|land** /wʊdlənd/ (**woodlands**) **Woodland** is land with a lot of trees. N-VAR

**wood|louse** /wʊdlaus/ (**woodlice** /wʊdlaɪs/) A **woodlouse** is a very small grey creature with a hard body and fourteen legs. Woodlice live in damp places. N-COUNT

**wood|pecker** /wʊdpekəʳ/ (**woodpeckers**) A **woodpecker** is a type of bird with a long sharp beak. Woodpeckers use their beaks to make holes in tree trunks. N-COUNT

**wood|pile** /wʊdpaɪl/ (**woodpiles**) A **woodpile** is a pile of wood that is intended to be burnt on a fire as fuel. N-COUNT: usu sing

**wood pulp** **Wood pulp** is wood that has been cut up into small pieces and crushed. Wood pulp is used to make paper. N-UNCOUNT

**wood|shed** /wʊdʃed/ (**woodsheds**) A **woodshed** is a small building which is used for storing wood for a fire. N-COUNT

**wood stove** (**wood stoves**)

> in AM, also use **woodstove**

A **wood stove** is a device that burns wood in order to heat a room. N-COUNT

**wood|wind** /wʊdwɪnd/ (**woodwinds**) **Woodwind** instruments are musical instruments such as flutes, clarinets, and recorders that you play by blowing into them. N-VAR: oft N n

**wood|work** /wʊdwɜːʳk/ [1] You can refer to the doors and other wooden parts of a house as the **woodwork**. ❑ *I love the living room, with its dark woodwork, oriental rugs, and chunky furniture... He could see the glimmer of fresh paint on the woodwork.* N-UNCOUNT [2] **Woodwork** is the activity or skill of making things out of wood. ❑ *I have done woodwork for many years.* N-UNCOUNT [3] If you say that people **are coming out of the woodwork**, you are criticizing them for suddenly appearing in public or revealing their opinions when previously they did not make themselves known. ❑ *When a song gets to the top, someone will come out of the woodwork and claim to have written it.* PHRASE: V inflects disapproval

**wood|worm** /wʊdwɜːʳm/ (**woodworms** or **woodworm**) [1] **Woodworm** are very small creatures which make holes in wood by eating it. N-COUNT [2] **Woodworm** is damage caused to wood, especially to the wooden parts of a house or to furniture, by woodworm making holes in the wood. ❑ *...treating the ground floor of a house for woodworm.* N-UNCOUNT

**woody** /wʊdi/ [1] **Woody** plants have very hard stems. ❑ *Care must be taken when trimming around woody plants like shrubs and trees.* ADJ: usu ADJ n [2] A **woody** area has a lot of trees in it. ❑ *...the wet and woody Vosges mountains.* ADJ: usu ADJ n

**woof** /wʊf/ **Woof** is the sound that a dog makes when it barks. [INFORMAL] ❑ *She started going 'woof woof'.* N-SING; SOUND

**wool** /wʊl/ (**wools**) [1] **Wool** is the hair that grows on sheep and on some other animals. N-UNCOUNT [2] **Wool** is a material made from animal's wool that is used to make things such as clothes, blankets, and carpets. ❑ *...a wool overcoat... The carpets are made in wool and nylon.* N-MASS [3] → See also **cotton wool**, **steel wool**, **wire wool**. [4] If you say that someone is **pulling the wool over** your **eyes**, you mean that they are trying to deceive you, in order to have an advantage over you. ❑ *Stop trying to pull the wool over my eyes! What were you two fighting about just now?* PHRASE: V inflects

**wool|len** /wʊlən/ (**woollens**)

> in AM, use **woolen**

[1] **Woollen** clothes or materials are made from wool or from a mixture of wool and artificial fibres. ❑ *...thick woollen socks.* ADJ: usu ADJ n [2] **Woollens** are clothes, especially sweaters, that are made of wool. ❑ *...winter woollens.* N-PLURAL

**wool|ly** /wʊli/ (**woollies**)

> in AM, also use **wooly**

[1] Something that is **woolly** is made of wool or looks like wool. ❑ *She wore this woolly hat with pompoms.* ADJ: usu ADJ n [2] A **woolly** is a woollen piece of clothing, especially a sweater. [BRIT, INFORMAL] N-COUNT [3] If you describe a person or their ideas as **woolly**, you are criticizing them for being confused or vague. ❑ *...a weak and woolly Government.* ADJ disapproval

**woozy** /wuːzi/ If you feel **woozy**, you feel rather weak and unsteady and cannot think clearly. [INFORMAL] ❑ *The fumes made them woozy.* ADJ: usu v-link ADJ ≠alert

**word** /wɜːʳd/ (**words, wording, worded**) [1] A **word** is a single unit of language that can be represented in writing or speech. In English, a word has a space on either side of it when it is written. ❑ *The words stood out clearly on the page... The word 'ginseng' comes from the Chinese word 'Shen-seng'. ...swear words.* ◆◆◆ N-COUNT [2] Someone's **words** are what they say or write. ❑ *I was devastated when her words came true... The words of the young woman doctor echoed in his ears.* N-PLURAL: oft with poss [3] **The words** of a song consist of the text that is sung, in contrast to the music that is played. ❑ *Can you hear the words on the album?* N-PLURAL: usu *the* N = *lyrics* [4] If you have **a word** with someone, you have a short conversation with them. [SPOKEN] ❑ *I think it's time you had a word with him... James, could I have a quiet word?* N-SING: *a* N [5] If you offer someone **a word of** something such as warning, advice, or praise, you warn, advise, or praise them. ❑ *A word of warning. Don't stick too precisely to what it says in the book.* N-COUNT: N *of* n [6] If you say that someone does **not** hear, understand, or say **a word**, you are emphasizing that they hear, understand, or say nothing at all. ❑ *I can't understand a word she says... Not a word was spoken.* N-SING: *a* N, with brd-neg emphasis [7] If there is **word** of something, people receive news or information about it. ❑ *There is no word from the authorities on the reported attack... Word has been spreading fast of the incidents on the streets.* N-UNCOUNT: also *the* N [8] If you give your **word**, you make a sincere promise to someone. ❑ *...an adult who gave his word the boy would be supervised...* N-SING: poss N

*He simply cannot be trusted to keep his word.* [9] If someone gives **the word** to do something, they give an order to do it. ❑ *I want nothing said about this until I give the word.* (N-SING: *the* N) [10] To **word** something in a particular way means to choose or use particular words to express it. ❑ *If I had written the letter, I might have worded it differently.* (VERB; V n adv/prep) ♦ **-worded** (COMB in ADJ) *...a strongly-worded statement. ...a carefully-worded speech.* [11] → See also **wording**, **code word**, **four-letter word**, **play on words**, **printed word**, **spoken word**, **written word**.

**PHRASES** [12] If you say that people consider something to be a **dirty word**, you mean that they disapprove of it. ❑ *So many people think feminism is a dirty word.* (PHRASE: usu v-link PHR) [13] If you do something **from the word go**, you do it from the very beginning of a period of time or situation. ❑ *It's essential you make the right decisions from the word go.* (PHRASE: PHR with cl) [14] You can use **in** their **words** or **in** their **own words** to indicate that you are reporting what someone said using the exact words that they used. ❑ *Even the Assistant Secretary of State had to admit that previous policy did not, in his words, produce results.* (PHRASE: PHR with cl) [15] You use **in a word** to indicate that you are giving a summary of what you have just been saying, or are giving a reply, in as brief a way as possible. ❑ *'Shouldn't he be given the leading role?' — 'In a word – No.'* (PHRASE: PHR with cl = *in short*) [16] If someone has **the last word** or **the final word** in a discussion, argument, or disagreement, they are the one who wins it or who makes the final decision. ❑ *She does like to have the last word in any discussion... The final word will still come from the Secretary of State.* (PHRASE) [17] If you say that something is **the last word in** luxury, comfort, or some other quality, you are emphasizing that it has a great deal of this quality. ❑ *The spa is the last word in luxury and efficiency.* (PHRASE: PHR n, usu v-link PHR [emphasis]) [18] If you say that someone has said something, but **not in so many words**, you mean that they said it or expressed it, but in a very indirect way. ❑ *'And has she agreed to go with you?' — 'Not in so many words. But I read her thoughts'.* (PHRASE: usu with brd-neg, usu PHR after v, PHR with cl) [19] If news or information passes by **word of mouth**, people tell it to each other rather than it being printed in written form. ❑ *The story has been passed down by word of mouth.* (PHRASE: oft *by/through* PHR) [20] You say **in other words** in order to introduce a different, and usually simpler, explanation or interpretation of something that has just been said. ❑ *The mobile library services have been reorganised – in other words, they visit fewer places.* (PHRASE: PHR with cl) [21] If you say something **in** your **own words**, you express it in your own way, without copying or repeating someone else's description. ❑ *Now tell us in your own words about the events of Saturday.* (PHRASE: PHR after v, PHR with cl) [22] If you say to someone **'take** my **word for it'**, you mean that they should believe you because you are telling the truth. ❑ *You'll buy nothing but trouble if you buy that house, take my word for it.* (PHRASE: V inflects) [23] If you repeat something **word for word**, you repeat it exactly as it was originally said or written. ❑ *I don't try to memorize speeches word for word.* (PHRASE: PHR after v = *verbatim*) [24] **not get a word in edgeways** → see **edgeways**. **not mince** your **words** → see **mince**. **the operative word** → see **operative**. **war of words** → see **war**.

**-word** /-wɜːʳd/ **(-words)** You can use **-word** after a letter of the alphabet to refer politely or humorously to a word beginning with that letter which people find offensive or are embarrassed to use. ❑ *It was the first show to use the F-word and show nudity on stage... Politicians began to use the dreaded R-word: recession.* (COMB in N-COUNT)

**word class** **(word classes)** A **word class** is a group of words that have the same basic behaviour, for example nouns, adjectives, or verbs. (N-COUNT)

**word|ing** /wɜːʳdɪŋ/ The **wording** of a piece of writing or a speech are the words used in it, especially when these are chosen to have a particular effect. ❑ *The two sides failed to agree on the wording of a final report... The wording is so vague that no one actually knows what it means.* (N-UNCOUNT: also *a* N)

**word|less** /wɜːʳdləs/ [1] You say that someone is **wordless** when they do not say anything, especially at a time when they are expected to say something. [LITERARY] ❑ *She stared back, now wordless... Here and there, husbands sit in wordless despair.* (ADJ = *silent*) ♦ **word|less|ly** *Gil downed his food wordlessly, his attention far away.* (ADV: ADV with v) [2] If someone makes a **wordless** sound, they make a sound that does not seem to contain any words. [LITERARY] ❑ *...a wordless chant... He shrieked a long, wordless cry.* (ADJ: usu ADJ n)

**word|play** /wɜːʳdpleɪ/ also **word play**. **Wordplay** involves making jokes by using the meanings of words in an amusing or clever way. (N-UNCOUNT)

**word pro|cess|ing** also **word-processing**. **Word processing** is the work or skill of producing printed documents using a computer. [COMPUTING] (N-UNCOUNT: oft N n)

**word pro|ces|sor** **(word processors)** A **word processor** is a computer program or a computer which is used to produce printed documents. [COMPUTING] (N-COUNT)

**word wrap|ping** In computing, **word wrapping** is a process by which a word which comes at the end of a line is automatically moved onto a new line in order to keep the text within the margins. [COMPUTING] (N-UNCOUNT)

**wordy** /wɜːʳdi/ If you describe a person's speech or something that they write as **wordy**, you disapprove of the fact that they use too many words, especially words which are very long, formal, or literary. ❑ *The chapter is mostly wordy rhetoric.* (ADJ [disapproval] = *verbose*)

**wore** /wɔːʳ/ **Wore** is the past tense of **wear**.

**work** /wɜːʳk/ **(works, working, worked)** ♦♦♦
[1] People who **work** have a job, usually one which they are paid to do. ❑ *Weiner works for the US Department of Transport... I started working in a recording studio... Where do you work?... He worked as a bricklayer's mate... I want to work, I don't want to be on welfare.* (VERB; V prep/adv; V prep/adv; V prep/adv; V *as* n; V) [2] People who have **work** or who are **in work** have a job, usually one which they are paid to do. ❑ *Fewer and fewer people are in work... I was out of work at the time... She'd have enough money to provide for her children until she could find work.* (N-UNCOUNT: oft *in/out of* N) [3] When you **work**, you do the things that you are paid or required to do in your job. ❑ *I can't talk to you right now – I'm working... He was working at his desk... Some firms expect the guards to work twelve hours a day.* (VERB; V; V; V n) [4] Your **work** consists of the things you are paid or required to do in your job. ❑ *We're supposed to be running a business here. I've got work to do... I used to take work home, but I don't do it any more... There have been days when I have finished work at 2pm.* (N-UNCOUNT) [5] When you **work**, you spend time and effort doing a task that needs to be done or trying to achieve something. ❑ *Linda spends all her time working on the garden... The most important reason for coming to university is to work for a degree... The government expressed hope that all the sides will work towards a political solution.* (VERB; V prep; V prep; V prep) ♦ **Work** is also a noun. ❑ *There was a lot of work to do on their house... We hadn't appreciated how much work was involved in organizing a wedding.* (N-UNCOUNT)
[6] **Work** is the place where you do your job. ❑ *Many people travel to work by car... She told her friends at work that she was trying to lose weight.* (N-UNCOUNT: usu *to/at* N)
[7] **Work** is something which you produce as a result of an activity or as a result of doing your job. ❑ *It can help to have an impartial third party look over your work... Tidiness in the workshop is really essential for producing good work.* (N-UNCOUNT: oft poss/adj N) [8] A **work** is something such as a painting, book, or piece of music produced by an artist, writer, or composer. ❑ *In my opinion, this is Rembrandt's greatest work.* (N-COUNT: usu with supp) [9] If someone **is working on** a particular subject or question, they are studying or researching it. ❑ *Professor Bonnet has been working for many years on molecules of this type.* (VERB; V *on* n) ♦ **Work** is also a noun. ❑ *Their work shows that one-year-olds are much more likely to have allergies if either parent smokes.* (N-UNCOUNT) [10] If you **work with** a person or a group of people, (VERB)

you spend time and effort trying to help them in some way. ❑ *She spent a period of time working with people dying of cancer.* ♦ **Work** is also a noun. ❑ *She became involved in social and relief work among the refugees.* (V *with/among* n; N-UNCOUNT: with supp)

11 If a machine or piece of equipment **works**, it operates and performs a particular function. ❑ *The pump doesn't work and we have no running water.* (VERB; V)

12 If an idea, system, or way of doing something **works**, it is successful, effective, or satisfactory. ❑ *95 per cent of these diets do not work... A methodical approach works best.* (VERB; V; V adv)

13 If a drug or medicine **works**, it produces a particular physical effect. ❑ *I wake at 6am as the sleeping pill doesn't work for more than nine hours... The drug works by increasing levels of serotonin in the brain.* (VERB; V; V prep/adv)

14 If something **works** in your favour, it helps you in some way. If something **works** to your disadvantage, it causes problems for you in some way. ❑ *One factor thought to have worked in his favour is his working class image.* (VERB; V prep)

15 If something or someone **works** their magic or **works** their charms **on** a person, they have a powerful positive effect on them. ❑ *Nevertheless, she is always optimistic about the possibilities and can work her charm on the disenchanted.* (VERB; V n *on* n)

16 If your mind or brain **is working**, you are thinking about something or trying to solve a problem. ❑ *My mind was working frantically, running over the events of the evening.* (VERB; V)

17 If you **work on** an assumption or idea, you act as if it were true or base other ideas on it, until you have more information. ❑ *We are working on the assumption that it was a gas explosion.* (VERB; V *on* n)

18 If you **work** a particular area or type of place, you travel around that area or work in those places as part of your job, for example trying to sell something there. ❑ *Brand has been working the clubs and the pubs since 1986, developing her comedy act.* (VERB; V n)

19 If you **work** someone, you make them spend time and effort doing a particular activity or job. ❑ *They're working me too hard. I'm too old for this.* (VERB; V n adv/prep)

20 If someone, often a politician or entertainer, **works** a crowd, they create a good relationship with the people in the crowd and get their support or interest. ❑ *The Prime Minister has an ability to work a crowd – some might even suggest it is a kind of charm.* (VERB; V n)

21 When people **work** the land, they do all the tasks involved in growing crops. ❑ *Farmers worked the fertile valleys.* (VERB; V n)

22 When a mine **is worked**, minerals such as coal or gold are removed from it. ❑ *The mines had first been worked in 1849, when gold was discovered in California.* (VERB; *be* V-ed)

23 If you **work** a machine or piece of equipment, you use or control it. ❑ *Many adults still depend on their children to work the video.* (VERB = operate; V n)

24 If something **works** into a particular state or condition, it gradually moves so that it is in that state or condition. ❑ *A screw had worked loose from my glasses.* (VERB; V adj)

25 If you **work** a substance such as dough or clay, you keep pressing it to make it have a particular texture. ❑ *Work the dough with the palm of your hand until it is very smooth.* (VERB; V n)

26 If you **work** a material such as metal, leather, or stone, you cut, sew, or shape it in order to make something or to create a design. ❑ *...the machines needed to extract and work the raw stone.* (VERB; V n)

27 If you **work** a part of your body, or if it **works**, you move it. ❑ *Each position will work the muscles in a different way... Her mouth was working in her sleep.* (VERB; V n; V)

28 A **works** is a place where something is manufactured or where an industrial process is carried out. **Works** is used to refer to one or to more than one of these places. ❑ *The steel works could be seen for miles.* (N-COUNT-COLL: usu n N, N n)

29 **Works** are activities such as digging the ground or building on a large scale. ❑ *...six years of disruptive building works, road construction and urban development.* (N-PLURAL: usu supp N)

30 → See also **working**.

**PHRASES**

31 If someone is **at work** they are doing their job or are busy doing a particular activity. ❑ *The salvage teams are already hard at work trying to deal with the spilled oil... Television cameras were invited in to film him at work.* (PHRASE: usu v-link PHR)

32 If a force or process is **at work**, it is having a particular influence or effect. ❑ *It is important to understand the powerful economic and social forces at work behind our own actions.* (PHRASE: usu v-link PHR)

33 If you say that you will **have** your **work cut out to** do something, you mean that it will be a very difficult task. ❑ *The new administration has its work cut out for it. Creating jobs in this kind of environment is not going to be easy... He will have his work cut out to get into the team.* (PHRASE: V inflects, oft PHR *for* n, PHR to-inf)

34 If something is **in the works**, it has already been planned or begun. [mainly AM] ❑ *He said there were dozens of economic plans in the works.* (PHRASE: usu n PHR, v-link PHR)

> ✓ in BRIT, usually use **in the pipeline**

35 You can use **work** to talk about how easily or quickly a particular task is done. For example, if a person or thing **makes** short **work of** doing something or **makes** light **work of** it, they do it quickly and easily. ❑ *An aerosol spray will make short work of painting awkward objects... This horse made light work of the cross-country course.* (PHRASE: V inflects, PHR -ing/n)

36 If you **put** someone **to work** or **set** them **to work**, you give them a job or task to do. ❑ *By stimulating the economy, we're going to put people to work... Instead of sending them to prison, we have set them to work helping the lemon growers.* (PHRASE: V inflects, oft PHR prep, PHR -ing)

37 If you **get to work**, **go to work**, or **set to work on** a job, task, or problem, you start doing it or dealing with it. ❑ *He promised to get to work on the state's massive deficit... He returned to America where he set to work on a new novel.* (PHRASE: V inflects, oft PHR *on* n)

38 If you **work** your **way** somewhere, you move or progress there slowly, and with a lot of effort or work. ❑ *Rescuers were still working their way towards the trapped men... Many personnel managers started as secretaries or personnel assistants and worked their way up.* (PHRASE: V inflects, PHR prep/adv)

39 to **throw a spanner in the works** → see **spanner**.

♦ **work in** or **work into** If you **work** one substance **into** another or **work** it **in**, you add it to the other substance and mix the two together thoroughly. ❑ *Gradually pour the liquid into the flour, working it in carefully with a wooden spoon... Work in the potato and milk until the mixture comes together... Work the oil gradually into the yolks with a wooden spoon.* (PHRASAL VERB; V n P; V P n (not pron); V n P n)

♦ **work off** 1 If you **work off** energy, stress, or anger, you get rid of it by doing something that requires a lot of physical effort. ❑ *She went for a brisk walk to work off her frustration... If I've had a bad day I'll work it off by cooking.* (PHRASAL VERB; V P n (not pron); V n P) 2 If you **work off** a debt, you repay it by working. ❑ *The report proposes that students be allowed to work off their debt through community service... There were heavy debts. It would take half Edward's lifetime to work them off.* (PHRASAL VERB; V P n (not pron); V n P)

♦ **work out** 1 If you **work out** a solution to a problem or mystery, you manage to find the solution by thinking or talking about it. ❑ *Negotiators are due to meet later today to work out a compromise... It took me some time to work out what was causing this... 'How will you contact me?' — 'We haven't worked that out yet.'* ● If you **have** something **all worked out**, you have thought about it carefully, and know exactly what you are going to do or exactly what you want. ❑ *I had the ideal man all worked out in my mind.* (PHRASAL VERB = figure out; V P n (not pron); V P wh; V n P; PHRASE: *have* inflects) 2 If you **work out** the answer to a mathematical problem, you calculate it. ❑ *It is proving hard to work out the value of bankrupt firms' assets... When asked what a £40.35 meal for five people would cost each diner, they were unable to work it out.* (PHRASAL VERB = calculate; V P n (not pron); V n P) 3 If something **works out at** a particular amount, it is calculated to be that amount after all the facts and figures have been considered. ❑ *The price per pound works out at £3.20... It will probably work out cheaper to hire a van and move your own things.* (PHRASAL VERB; V P *at* amount; V P adj) 4 If a situation **works out** well or **works out**, it happens or progresses in a satisfactory way. ❑ *Things just didn't work out as planned... One of the ways people experience loss is when relationships don't work out.* (PHRASAL VERB; V P prep/adv; V P) 5 If a process **works itself out**, it reaches a conclusion or satis- (PHRASAL VERB) factory end. ❑ *People involved in it think it's a nightmare, but I'm sure it will work itself out.* [6] If you **work out** your service or your notice, you continue to work at your job until you have completed a specified period of time. ❑ *There was an interim before her successor actually came because she had to work out her notice.* [7] If you **work out**, you do physical exercises in order to make your body fit and strong. ❑ *Work out at a gym or swim twice a week.* [8] → See also **workout**. V pron-refl P / PHRASAL VERB / V P n (not pron) Also V n P / PHRASAL VERB = exercise / V P

♦ **work up** [1] If you **work yourself up**, you make yourself feel very upset or angry about something. ❑ *She worked herself up into a bit of a state... Don't just lie there working yourself up, do something about it.* → See also **worked up**. [2] If you **work up** the enthusiasm or courage to do something, you succeed in making yourself feel it. ❑ *Your creative talents can also be put to good use, if you can work up the energy.* [3] If you **work up** a sweat or an appetite, you make yourself sweaty or hungry by doing exercise or hard work. ❑ *You can really work up a sweat doing housework.* [4] If you **work up** something such as a piece of writing, you spend time and effort preparing it. ❑ *I sketched the layout of a prototype store and worked up a business plan.* PHRASAL VERB / V pron-refl P *into/to* n / V pron-refl P / PHRASAL VERB / V P n (not pron) / PHRASAL VERB / V P n (not pron) / PHRASAL VERB / V P n (not pron)

**work|able** /wɜːʳkəbᵊl/ A **workable** idea or system is realistic and practical, and likely to be effective. ❑ *Investors can simply pay cash, but this isn't a workable solution in most cases.* ADJ = practicable ≠ unworkable

**worka|day** /wɜːʳkədeɪ/ **Workaday** means ordinary and not especially interesting or unusual. ❑ *Enough of fantasy, the workaday world awaited him.* ADJ: usu ADJ n = everyday

**worka|hol|ic** /wɜːkəhɒlɪk, AM -hɔːl-/ **(workaholics)** A **workaholic** is a person who works most of the time and finds it difficult to stop working in order to do other things. [INFORMAL] N-COUNT

**work|bench** /wɜːʳkbentʃ/ **(workbenches)** A **workbench** is a heavy wooden table on which people use tools such as a hammer and nails to make or repair things. N-COUNT

**work|book** /wɜːʳkbʊk/ **(workbooks)** A **workbook** is a book to help you learn a particular subject which has questions in it with spaces for the answers. N-COUNT

**work|day** /wɜːʳkdeɪ/ **(workdays)** also **work day.** [1] A **workday** is the amount of time during a day which you spend doing your job. [mainly AM] ❑ *His workday starts at 3.30 a.m. and lasts 12 hours.* N-COUNT: usu sing

☑ in BRIT, usually use **working day**

[2] A **workday** is a day on which people go to work. ❑ *What's he doing home on a workday?* N-COUNT

**worked up** If someone is **worked up**, they are angry or upset. ❑ *Steve shouted at her. He was really worked up now.* ADJ: v-link ADJ

**work|er** /wɜːʳkəʳ/ **(workers)** [1] A particular kind of **worker** does the kind of work mentioned. ❑ *...office workers... The society was looking for a capable research worker.* [2] **Workers** are people who are employed in industry or business and who are not managers. ❑ *Wages have been frozen and workers laid off.* [3] You can use **worker** to say how well or badly someone works. ❑ *He is a hard worker and a skilled gardener.* → See also **care worker**, **caseworker**, **dock worker**, **social worker**, **teleworker**, **youth worker**. ◆◆◆ N-COUNT: with supp, usu n N / N-COUNT: usu pl / N-COUNT: usu adj N

**work|fare** /wɜːʳkfeəʳ/ **Workfare** is a government scheme in which unemployed people have to do community work or learn new skills in order to receive welfare benefits. N-UNCOUNT

**work|force** /wɜːʳkfɔːʳs/ **(workforces)** [1] The **workforce** is the total number of people in a country or region who are physically able to do a job and are available for work. ❑ *...a country where half the workforce is unemployed.* [2] The **workforce** is the total number of people who are employed by a particular company. ❑ *...an employer of a very large workforce.* N-COUNT: usu sing / N-COUNT: usu sing = staff

**work|horse** /wɜːʳkhɔːʳs/ **(workhorses)** [1] A **workhorse** is a horse which is used to do a job, for example to pull a plough. [2] If you describe a person or a machine as a **workhorse**, you mean that they can be relied upon to do a large amount of work, especially work that is dull or routine. ❑ *...the Wellington bomber, the great workhorse of the war... My husband never even looked at me. I was just a workhorse bringing up three children.* N-COUNT / N-COUNT: usu with supp

**work|house** /wɜːʳkhaʊs/ **(workhouses)** In Britain, in the seventeenth to nineteenth centuries, a **workhouse** was a place where very poor people could live and do unpleasant jobs in return for food. People use **the workhouse** to refer to these places in general. ❑ *...a struggling Shropshire family which lived in fear of the workhouse.* N-COUNT = poorhouse

**work|ing** /wɜːʳkɪŋ/ **(workings)** [1] **Working** people have jobs which they are paid to do. ❑ *Like working women anywhere, Asian women are buying convenience foods.* [2] **Working** people are ordinary people who do not have professional or very highly paid jobs. ❑ *The needs and opinions of ordinary working people were ignored.* [3] A **working** day or week is the amount of time during a normal day or week which you spend doing your job. [mainly BRIT] ❑ *For doctors the working day often has no end... Automation would bring a shorter, more flexible working week.* ◆◆◆ ADJ: ADJ n / ADJ: ADJ n = working class / ADJ: ADJ n

☑ in AM, usually use **workday**, **work week**

[4] A **working** day is a day on which people go to work. [mainly BRIT] ❑ *The full effect will not be apparent until Tuesday, the first working day after the three day holiday weekend.* ADJ: ADJ n

☑ in AM, usually use **workday**

[5] Your **working** life is the period of your life in which you have a job or are of a suitable age to have a job. ❑ *He started his working life as a truck driver.* [6] The **working** population of an area consists of all the people in that area who have a job or who are of a suitable age to have a job. ❑ *Almost 13 per cent of the working population is already unemployed.* [7] **Working** conditions or practices are ones which you have in your job. ❑ *The strikers are demanding higher pay and better working conditions.* [8] **Working** clothes are designed for doing work in, and are intended to be practical rather than attractive. [9] A **working** relationship is the relationship you have with someone when you work with them. ❑ *The vice-president seems to have a good working relationship with the president.* [10] A **working** farm or business exists to do normal work and make a profit, and not only for tourists or as someone's hobby. [11] The **working** parts of a machine are the parts which move and operate the machine, in contrast to the outer case or container in which they are enclosed. [12] A **working** model is one that has parts that move. [13] A **working** knowledge or majority is not very great, but is enough to be useful. ❑ *This book was designed in order to provide a working knowledge of finance and accounts.* [14] A **working** title or definition is one which you use when starting to make or do something, but which you are likely to change or improve. ❑ *His working title for the script was 'Trust the People'.* [15] **The workings of** a piece of equipment, an organization, or a system are the ways in which it operates and the processes which are involved in it. ❑ *Neural networks are computer systems which mimic the workings of the brain.* [16] **in working order** → see **order**. ADJ: ADJ n / ADJ: ADJ n / ADJ: ADJ n / ADJ: ADJ n / ADJ: ADJ n / ADJ: ADJ n / ADJ: ADJ n / ADJ: ADJ n / ADJ: ADJ n / ADJ: ADJ n / N-PLURAL: usu N *of* n

**work|ing capi|tal** **Working capital** is money which is available for use immediately, rather than money which is invested in land or equipment. [BUSINESS] N-UNCOUNT

**work|ing class** **(working classes)** **The working class** or **the working classes** are the group of people in a society who do not own much N-COUNT-COLL: *the* N

property, who have low social status, and who do jobs which involve using physical skills rather than intellectual skills. ❑ *...increased levels of home ownership among the working classes.* ♦ **Working class** is also an adjective. ❑ *...a self-educated man from a working class background... The group is mainly black, mainly working-class.*
ADJ: usu ADJ n

**work|ing group** **(working groups)** A **working group** is the same as a **working party**. ❑ *There will be a working group on international issues.*
N-COUNT-COLL

**work|ing men's club** **(working men's clubs)** A **working men's club** is a place where working people, especially men, can go to relax, drink alcoholic drinks, and sometimes watch live entertainment.
N-COUNT

**work|ing par|ty** **(working parties)** A **working party** is a committee which is formed to investigate a particular situation or problem and to produce a report containing its opinions and suggestions. [mainly BRIT] ❑ *They set up a working party to look into the issue.*
N-COUNT-COLL = *working group*

☑ in AM, usually use **working group**

**work-in-pro|gress** In book-keeping, **work-in-progress** refers to the monetary value of work that has not yet been paid for because it has not yet been completed. [BUSINESS] ❑ *...five million pounds' worth of finished goods and two million pounds' worth of work-in-progress.*
N-UNCOUNT

**work-life bal|ance** Your **work-life balance** is how you organize your days, for example how many hours you spend at work, and how much time you spend with friends or doing things you enjoy. ❑ *Senior managers stipulated work-life balance as their main criterion when choosing jobs.*
N-UNCOUNT

**work|load** /wɜːʳkloʊd/ **(workloads)** also **work load.** The **workload** of a person or organization is the amount of work that has to be done by them. ❑ *The sudden cancellation of Mr Blair's trip was due to his heavy workload.*
N-COUNT: oft supp N

**work|man** /wɜːʳkmən/ **(workmen)** A **workman** is a man who works with his hands, for example building or repairing houses or roads. ❑ *In University Square workmen are building a steel fence.*
N-COUNT

**work|man|like** /wɜːʳkmənlaɪk/ If you describe something as **workmanlike**, you mean that it has been done quite well and sensibly, but not in a particularly imaginative or original way. ❑ *Really it's a workmanlike conference rather than a dramatic one... The script was workmanlike at best.*
ADJ

**work|man|ship** /wɜːʳkmənʃɪp/ **Workmanship** is the skill with which something is made and which affects the appearance and quality of the finished object. ❑ *The problem may be due to poor workmanship... The standard of workmanship is very high.*
N-UNCOUNT: oft supp N = *craftsmanship*

**work|mate** /wɜːʳkmeɪt/ **(workmates)** Your **workmates** are the people you work with. [mainly BRIT, INFORMAL] ❑ *My workmates, and, even more, the management, didn't want me to leave.*
N-COUNT: usu pl, usu supp N = *colleague*

**work of art** **(works of art)** 1 A **work of art** is a painting or piece of sculpture which is of high quality. ❑ *...a collection of works of art of international significance.*
N-COUNT
2 A **work of art** is something which is very complex or which has been skilfully made or produced. ❑ *The actual nest is a work of art.*
N-COUNT

**work|out** /wɜːʳkaʊt/ **(workouts)** A **workout** is a period of physical exercise or training. ❑ *Give your upper body a workout by using handweights. ...a 35-minute aerobic workout.*
N-COUNT

**work|place** /wɜːʳkpleɪs/ **(workplaces)** also **work place.** Your **workplace** is the place where you work. ❑ *...the difficulties facing women in the workplace.*
N-COUNT

**work|room** /wɜːʳkruːm/ **(workrooms)** A person's **workroom** is a room where they work, especially when their work involves making things.
N-COUNT

**work|sheet** /wɜːʳkʃiːt/ **(worksheets)** A **worksheet** is a specially prepared page of exercises designed to improve your knowledge or understanding of a particular subject.
N-COUNT

**work|shop** /wɜːʳkʃɒp/ **(workshops)** 1 A **workshop** is a period of discussion or practical work on a particular subject in which a group of people share their knowledge or experience. ❑ *Trumpeter Marcus Belgrave ran a jazz workshop for young artists.*
N-COUNT: oft supp N
2 A **workshop** is a building which contains tools or machinery for making or repairing things, especially using wood or metal. ❑ *...a modestly equipped workshop.*
N-COUNT

**work-shy** also **workshy.** If you describe someone as **work-shy**, you disapprove of them because you think they are lazy and do not want to work. [BRIT]
ADJ: usu ADJ n [disapproval] = *lazy*

**work|station** /wɜːʳksteɪʃᵊn/ **(workstations)** also **work station.** A **workstation** is a screen and keyboard that are part of an office computer system.
N-COUNT

**work sur|face** **(work surfaces)** also **worksurface.** A **work surface** is a flat surface, usually in a kitchen, which is easy to clean and on which you can do things such as prepare food.
N-COUNT

**work|top** /wɜːʳktɒp/ **(worktops)** A **worktop** is a flat surface in a kitchen which is easy to clean and on which you can prepare food. [BRIT]
N-COUNT

☑ in AM, usually use **countertop, counter**

**work week** **(work weeks)** A **work week** is the amount of time during a normal week which you spend doing your job. [mainly AM] ❑ *The union had sought a wage increase and a shorter work week.*
N-COUNT

☑ in BRIT, usually use **working week**

**world** /wɜːʳld/ **(worlds)** ◆◆◆
1 **The world** is the planet that we live on. ❑ *It's a beautiful part of the world... The satellite enables us to calculate their precise location anywhere in the world.*
N-SING: *the* N
2 **The world** refers to all the people who live on this planet, and our societies, institutions, and ways of life. ❑ *The world was, and remains, shocked... He wants to show the world that anyone can learn to be an ambassador. ...his personal contribution to world history.*
N-SING: *the* N, N n
3 You can use **world** to describe someone or something that is one of the most important or significant of its kind on earth. ❑ *Abroad, Mr Bush was seen as a world statesman... China has once again emerged as a world power.*
ADJ: ADJ n
4 You can use **world** in expressions such as **the Arab world, the western world**, and **the ancient world** to refer to a particular group of countries or a particular period in history. ❑ *Athens had strong ties to the Arab world. ...the developing world.*
N-SING: *the* supp N
5 Someone's **world** is the life they lead, the people they have contact with, and the things they experience. ❑ *His world seemed so different from mine... I lost my job and it was like my world collapsed.*
N-COUNT: oft poss N
6 You can use **world** to refer to a particular field of activity, and the people involved in it. ❑ *The publishing world had certainly never seen an event quite like this.*
N-SING: *the* N, with supp, oft N *of* n
7 You can use **world** to refer to a particular group of living things, for example **the animal world, the plant world**, and **the insect world**.
N-SING: *the* n N = *kingdom*
8 A **world** is a planet. ❑ *He looked like something from another world.*
N-COUNT
9 → See also **brave new world, New World, real world, Third World.**

**PHRASES**
10 If you say that two people or things are **worlds apart**, you are emphasizing that they are very different from each other. ❑ *Intellectually, this man and I are worlds apart.*
PHRASE: usu v-link PHR, oft PHR *from* n [emphasis]
11 If you say that someone has **the best of both worlds**, you mean that they have only the benefits of two things and none of the disadvantages. ❑ *Her living room provides the best of both worlds, with an office at one end and comfortable sofas at the other.*
PHRASE: PHR after v, v-link PHR
12 If you say that something **has done** someone **the world of good** or **a world of good**, you mean that it has made them feel better or improved their life. [INFORMAL] ❑ *A sleep will do you the world of good.*
PHRASE: V inflects
13 You use **in the world** to emphasize
PHRASE: oft

a statement that you are making. ❑ *The saddest thing in the world is a little baby nobody wants... He had no one in the world but her.* [14] You can use **in the world** in expressions such as **what in the world** and **who in the world** to emphasize a question, especially when expressing surprise or anger. ❑ *What in the world is he doing?* [15] You can use **in an ideal world** or **in a perfect world** when you are talking about things that you would like to happen, although you realize that they are not likely to happen. ❑ *In a perfect world, there would be the facilities and money to treat every sick person.* [16] If you say that someone is **a man of the world** or **a woman of the world**, you mean that they are experienced and know about the practical or social aspects of life, and are not easily shocked by immoral or dishonest actions. ❑ *Look, we are both men of the world, would anyone really mind? ...an elegant, clever and tough woman of the world.* [17] If you say that something is **out of this world**, you are emphasizing that it is extremely good or impressive. [INFORMAL] ❑ *These new trains are out of this world.* [18] You can use **the outside world** to refer to all the people who do not live in a particular place or who are not involved in a particular situation. ❑ *For many, the post office is the only link with the outside world.* [19] If you **think the world of** someone, you like them or care about them very much. ❑ *I think the world of him, but something tells me it's not love... We were really close. We thought the world of each other.* [20] **not be the end of the world** → see **end**. **the world is** your **oyster** → see **oyster**. **on top of the world** → see **top**.

PHR after superl [emphasis] / PHRASE: quest PHR [emphasis] / PHRASE: PHR with cl = *ideally* / PHRASE: *man/woman* inflects / PHRASE: v-link PHR [emphasis] / PHRASE / PHRASE: V inflects, PHR n

**world beat|er** **(world beaters)** also **world-beater.** If you describe a person or thing as a **world beater**, you mean that they are better than most other people or things of their kind. [BRIT] — N-COUNT

**world-class** A **world-class** sports player, performer, or organization is one of the best in the world. [JOURNALISM] ❑ *He was determined to become a world-class player.* — ADJ: usu ADJ n

**world-famous** Someone or something that is **world-famous** is known about by people all over the world. ❑ *...the world-famous Hollywood Bowl.* — ADJ

**world lead|er** **(world leaders)** [1] A **world leader** is someone who is the leader of a country, especially an economically powerful country. — N-COUNT [2] A product, company, organization, or person that is a **world leader** is the most successful or advanced one in a particular area of activity. [JOURNALISM] ❑ *In the field of consumer electronics, Philips is determined to remain a world leader.* — N-COUNT

**world|ly** /wɜːʳldli/ [1] **Worldly** is used to describe things relating to the ordinary activities of life, rather than to spiritual things. [LITERARY] ❑ *I think it is time you woke up and focused your thoughts on more worldly matters.* — ADJ [2] Someone who is **worldly** is experienced and knows about the practical or social aspects of life. ❑ *He was different from anyone I had known, very worldly, everything that Dermot was not.* — ADJ: usu v-link ADJ [3] **Worldly** is used to describe things relating to success, wealth, and possessions. [mainly LITERARY] ❑ *Today the media drive athletes to the view that the important thing is to gain worldly success.* — ADJ: ADJ n [4] You can refer to someone's possessions as their **worldly** goods or possessions. [LITERARY] ❑ *...a man who had given up all his worldly goods.* — ADJ: ADJ n

**worldly-wise** If you describe someone as **worldly-wise**, you mean they are experienced and know about the practical or social aspects of life, and are not easily shocked or impressed. — ADJ

**World Trade Or|gani|za|tion** **The World Trade Organization** is an international organization that encourages and regulates trade between its member states. The abbreviation **WTO** is also used. — N-PROPER

**world view** **(world views)** also **world-view.** A person's **world view** is the way they see and understand the world, especially regarding issues such as politics, philosophy, and religion. ❑ *Many artists express their world view in their work.* — N-COUNT: with supp

**world war** **(world wars)** A **world war** is a war that involves countries all over the world. ❑ *Many senior citizens have been though two world wars... At the end of the second world war he was working as a docker.* — ◆◇◇ N-VAR

**world-weary** A **world-weary** person no longer feels excited or enthusiastic about anything. — ADJ = *jaded*

**world|wide** /wɜːʳldwaɪd/ also **world-wide.** If something exists or happens **worldwide**, it exists or happens throughout the world. ❑ *His books have sold more than 20 million copies worldwide... Worldwide, an enormous amount of research effort goes into military technology.* ♦ **Worldwide** is also an adjective. ❑ *Today, doctors are fearing a worldwide epidemic.* — ◆◇◇ ADV: ADV after v, n ADV, ADV with cl / ADJ: usu ADJ n

**World Wide Web** **The World Wide Web** is a computer system which links documents and pictures into a database that is stored in computers in many different parts of the world and that people everywhere can use. The abbreviations **WWW** and the **Web** are often used. [COMPUTING] — N-PROPER: *the* N

**worm** /wɜːʳm/ **(worms, worming, wormed)** [1] A **worm** is a small animal with a long thin body, no bones and no legs. — N-COUNT [2] If animals or people have **worms**, worms are living in their intestines. — N-PLURAL [3] If you **worm** an animal, you give it medicine in order to kill the worms that are living in its intestines. ❑ *I worm all my birds in early spring... All adult dogs are routinely wormed at least every six months.* — VERB: V n, *be* V-ed [4] If you say that someone **is worming** their **way** to success, or **is worming** their **way** into someone else's affection, you disapprove of the way that they are gradually making someone trust them or like them, often in order to deceive them or gain some advantage. ❑ *She never misses a chance to worm her way into the public's hearts.* — VERB [disapproval] V *way* prep/adv [5] A **worm** is a computer program that contains a virus which duplicates itself many times in a network. [COMPUTING] — N-COUNT [6] If you say that someone is opening **a can of worms**, you are warning them that they are planning to do or talk about something which is much more complicated, unpleasant, or difficult than they realize and which might be better left alone. ❑ *You've opened up a whole new can of worms here I think. We could have a whole debate on student loans and grants.* — PHRASE: PHR after v, v-link PHR

**worm|wood** /wɜːʳmwʊd/ **Wormwood** is a plant that has a very bitter taste and is used in making medicines and alcoholic drinks. — N-UNCOUNT

**worn** /wɔːʳn/ [1] **Worn** is the past participle of **wear**. [2] **Worn** is used to describe something that is damaged or thin because it is old and has been used a lot. ❑ *Worn rugs increase the danger of tripping.* — ADJ: usu ADJ n [3] If someone looks **worn**, they look tired and old. ❑ *She was looking very haggard and worn.* — ADJ: v-link ADJ [4] → See also **well-worn**.

**worn out** also **worn-out.** [1] Something that is **worn out** is so old, damaged, or thin from use that it cannot be used any more. ❑ *...the car's worn out tyres. ...faded bits of worn-out clothing.* — ADJ [2] Someone who is **worn out** is extremely tired after hard work or a difficult or unpleasant experience. ❑ *Before the race, he is fine. But afterwards he is worn out.* — ADJ: usu v-link ADJ = *exhausted*

**wor|ried** /wʌrid, AM wɜːrid/ When you are **worried**, you are unhappy because you keep thinking about problems that you have or about unpleasant things that might happen in the future. ❑ *He seemed very worried... If you're at all worried about his progress, do discuss it with one of his teachers.* ♦ **wor|ried|ly** *'You don't have to go, you know,' she said worriedly.* — ◆◇◇ ADJ: oft ADJ *about* n, ADJ that = *anxious* / ADV: usu ADV with v

**wor|ri|er** /wʌriəʳ, AM wɜːriər/ **(worriers)** If you describe someone as a **worrier**, you mean that they spend a lot of time thinking about problems that they have or unpleasant things that might happen. N-COUNT

**wor|ri|some** /wʌrɪsəm, AM wɜːr-/ Something that is **worrisome** causes people to worry. [mainly AM] ADJ

in BRIT, usually use **worrying**

**wor|ry** /wʌri, AM wɜːri/ **(worries, worrying, worried)** ◆◆◇ [1] If you **worry**, you keep thinking about problems that you have or about unpleasant things that might happen. ❑ *Don't worry, your luggage will come on afterwards by taxi... I worry about her constantly... They worry that extremists might gain control.* VERB V V about n/-ing V that [2] If someone or something **worries** you, they make you anxious because you keep thinking about problems or unpleasant things that might be connected with them. ❑ *I'm still in the early days of my recovery and that worries me... 'Why didn't you tell us?' — 'I didn't want to worry you.'.* VERB V n V n [3] If someone or something does not **worry** you, you do not dislike them or you are not annoyed by them. [SPOKEN] ❑ *The cold doesn't worry me.* VERB: oft with neg = bother V n [4] **Worry** is the state or feeling of anxiety and unhappiness caused by the problems that you have or by thinking about unpleasant things that might happen. ❑ *His last years were overshadowed by financial worry.* N-UNCOUNT [5] A **worry** is a problem that you keep thinking about and that makes you unhappy. ❑ *My main worry was that Madeleine Johnson would still be there... His wife Cheryl said she had no worries about his health.* N-COUNT

**wor|ry|ing** /wʌriɪŋ, AM wɜːriɪŋ/ If something is **worrying**, it causes people to worry. [mainly BRIT] ❑ *It's worrying that they're doing things without training. ...a new and worrying report about smoking.* ADJ: oft it v-link ADJ that

in AM, usually use **worrisome**

♦ **wor|ry|ing|ly** *The rate of assaults was worryingly high.* ADV: ADV adj, ADV with cl

**worse** /wɜːʳs/ ◆◇◇ [1] **Worse** is the comparative of **bad**. [2] **Worse** is the comparative of **badly**. [3] **Worse** is used to form the comparative of compound adjectives beginning with 'bad' and 'badly.' For example, the comparative of 'badly off' is 'worse off'.

**PHRASES** [4] If a situation **goes from bad to worse**, it becomes even more unpleasant or unsatisfactory. ❑ *For the past couple of years my life has gone from bad to worse.* PHRASE: V inflects [5] If a situation changes **for the worse**, it becomes more unpleasant or more difficult. ❑ *The grandparents sigh and say how things have changed for the worse.* PHRASE: PHR after v [6] If a person or thing is **the worse for** something, they have been harmed or badly affected by it. If they are **none the worse for** it, they have not been harmed or badly affected by it. ❑ *Father came home from the pub very much the worse for drink... They are all apparently fit and well and none the worse for the fifteen hour journey.* PHRASE: PHR after v, PHR n [7] **for better or worse** → see **better**.

**wors|en** /wɜːʳsən/ **(worsens, worsening, worsened)** If a bad situation **worsens** or if something **worsens** it, it becomes more difficult, unpleasant, or unacceptable. ❑ *The security forces had to intervene to prevent the situation worsening... These options would actually worsen the economy and add to the deficit... They remain stranded in freezing weather and rapidly worsening conditions.* VERB ≠ improve V V n V-ing

**wor|ship** /wɜːʳʃɪp/ **(worships, worshipping, worshipped)**

in AM, use **worshiping, worshiped**

[1] If you **worship** a god, you show your respect to the god, for example by saying prayers. ❑ *I enjoy going to church and worshipping God. ...Jews worshipping at the Wailing Wall.* ♦ **Worship** is also a noun. ❑ *St Jude's church is a public place of worship.* VERB V n V N-UNCOUNT ♦ **wor|ship|per (worshippers)** *At the end of the service, scores of worshippers streamed down to the altar.* N-COUNT [2] If you **worship** someone or something, you love them or admire them very much. ❑ *She had worshipped him for years.* VERB V n

**wor|ship|ful** /wɜːʳʃɪpfʊl/ If someone has a **worshipful** attitude to a person or thing, they show great respect and admiration for them. ❑ *...Franklin's almost worshipful imitation of his cousin.* ADJ: ADJ n = reverential

**worst** /wɜːʳst/ ◆◇◇ [1] **Worst** is the superlative of **bad**. [2] **Worst** is the superlative of **badly**. [3] **The worst** is the most unpleasant or unfavourable thing that could happen or does happen. ❑ *Though mine safety has much improved, miners' families still fear the worst... The country had come through the worst of the recession.* N-SING: the N, oft N of n ≠ best [4] **Worst** is used to form the superlative of compound adjectives beginning with 'bad' and 'badly'. For example, the superlative of 'badly-affected' is 'worst-affected'.

**PHRASES** [5] You say **worst of all** to indicate that what you are about to mention is the most unpleasant or has the most disadvantages out of all the things you are mentioning. ❑ *The people most closely affected are the passengers who were injured and, worst of all, those who lost relatives.* PHRASE: PHR with cl [6] You use **at worst** or **at the worst** to indicate that you are mentioning the worst thing that might happen in a situation. ❑ *At best Nella would be an invalid; at worst she would die.* PHRASE: PHR with cl/group [7] When someone is **at their worst**, they are as unpleasant, bad, or unsuccessful as it is possible for them to be. ❑ *This was their mother at her worst. Her voice was strident, she was ready to be angry at anyone.* PHRASE: n PHR, PHR after v, v-link PHR [8] You use **if the worst comes to the worst** to say what you might do if a situation develops in the most unfavourable way possible. The form **if worst comes to worst** is also used, mainly in American English. ❑ *If the worst comes to the worst I guess I can always ring Jean... He was asked whether he would walk out if the worst came to the worst.* PHRASE: V inflects, PHR with cl

**wor|sted** /wʊstɪd/ **(worsteds) Worsted** is a kind of woollen cloth. N-MASS

**worth** /wɜːʳθ/ ◆◆◇ [1] If something is **worth** a particular amount of money, it can be sold for that amount or is considered to have that value. ❑ *These books might be worth £80 or £90 or more to a collector... The contract was worth £25 million a year.* v-link worth amount [2] **Worth** combines with amounts of money, so that when you talk about a particular amount of money**'s worth of** something, you mean the quantity of it that you can buy for that amount of money. ❑ *I went and bought about six dollars' worth of potato chips.* ♦ **Worth** is also a pronoun. ❑ *'How many do you want?' — 'I'll have a pound's worth.'* COMB in QUANT: QUANT of n PRON [3] **Worth** combines with time expressions, so you can use **worth** when you are saying how long an amount of something will last. For example, a week's **worth of** food is the amount of food that will last you for a week. ❑ *You've got three years' worth of research money to do what you want with.* ♦ **Worth** is also a pronoun. ❑ *There's really not very much food down there. About two weeks' worth.* COMB in QUANT: QUANT of n PRON [4] If you say that something is **worth** having, you mean that it is pleasant or useful, and therefore a good thing to have. ❑ *He's decided to get a look at the house and see if it might be worth buying... Most things worth having never come easy.* v-link worth -ing [5] If something is **worth** a particular action, or if an action is **worth** doing, it is considered to be important enough for that action. ❑ *I am spending a lot of money and time on this boat, but it is worth it... This restaurant is well worth a visit... It is worth pausing to consider these statements from Mr Davies.* v-link worth n/-ing [6] Someone's **worth** is the value, usefulness, or importance that they are considered to have. [FORMAL] ❑ *He had never had a woman of her worth as a friend.* N-UNCOUNT: usu with poss

**PHRASES** [7] If you do something **for all** you **are worth**, you do it with a lot of energy and enthusiasm. ❑ *We both began waving to the crowd for all we were worth... Push for all you're worth!* PHRASE: V inflects [8] If you add **for what it's worth** to something that you PHRASE: PHR with cl say, you are suggesting that what you are saying or referring to may not be very valuable or helpful, especially because you do not want to appear arrogant. ❑ *I've brought my notes, for what it's worth.* 9 If an action or activity is **worth** someone's **while**, it will be helpful, useful, or enjoyable for them if they do it, even though it requires some effort. ❑ *It might be worth your while to go to court and ask for the agreement to be changed.* 10 **worth** your **weight in gold** → see **weight**. PHRASE: v-link PHR = *worthwhile*

**worth|less** /wɜːʳθləs/ 1 Something that is **worthless** is of no real value or use. ❑ *The guarantee could be worthless if the firm goes out of business... Training is worthless unless there is proof that it works. ...a worthless piece of old junk.* 2 Someone who is described as **worthless** is considered to have no good qualities or skills. ❑ *You feel you really are completely worthless and unlovable.* ADJ = *useless*; ADJ: usu v-link ADJ

**worth|while** /wɜːʳθʰwaɪl/ If something is **worthwhile**, it is enjoyable or useful, and worth the time, money, or effort that is spent on it. ❑ *The President's trip to Washington this week seems to have been worthwhile... It might be worthwhile to consider your attitude to an insurance policy.* ADJ: oft *it* v-link ADJ to-inf

**wor|thy** /wɜːʳði/ **(worthier, worthiest)** 1 If a person or thing is **worthy of** something, they deserve it because they have the qualities or abilities required. [FORMAL] ❑ *The bank might think you're worthy of a loan... The Minister says the idea is worthy of consideration.* 2 A **worthy** person or thing is approved of by most people in society and considered to be morally respectable or correct. [FORMAL] ❑ *...worthy members of the community.* ADJ: usu v-link ADJ, usu ADJ *of* n ≠ *unworthy*; ADJ

**-worthy** /-wɜːʳði/ **-worthy** can be added to words to form adjectives which indicate that someone or something deserves a particular thing or action. For example, if a remark or person is **quote-worthy**, they are worth quoting. ❑ *...a few newsworthy events... You may see yourself as useless, incompetent and blameworthy.* → See also **airworthy, creditworthy, newsworthy, noteworthy, praiseworthy, seaworthy, trustworthy.** COMB in ADJ

**wot** **Wot** is sometimes used in writing to represent **'what'**, to show that someone is speaking very informally or that they are being humorous. [BRIT, INFORMAL] ❑ *'Cor, wot brilliant prizes!'*

**would** /wəd STRONG wʊd/ ◆◆◆

> **Would** is a modal verb. It is used with the base form of a verb. In spoken English, **would** is often abbreviated to **'d**.

1 You use **would** when you are saying what someone believed, hoped, or expected to happen or be the case. ❑ *No one believed he would actually kill himself... Would he always be like this?... He expressed the hope that on Monday elementary schools would be reopened... A report yesterday that said British unemployment would continue to rise.* MODAL 2 You use **would** when saying what someone intended to do. ❑ *The statement added that although there were a number of differing views, these would be discussed by both sides... George decided it was such a rare car that he would only use it for a few shows.* MODAL 3 You use **would** when you are referring to the result or effect of a possible situation. ❑ *Ordinarily it would be fun to be taken to fabulous restaurants... It would be wrong to suggest that police officers were not annoyed by acts of indecency... It would cost very much more for the four of us to go from Italy.* MODAL 4 You use **would**, or **would have** with a past participle, to indicate that you are assuming or guessing that something is true, because you have good reasons for thinking it. ❑ *You wouldn't know him... His fans would already be familiar with Caroline... It was half seven; her mother would be annoyed because he was so late.* MODAL 5 You use **would** in the main clause of some 'if' and 'unless' sentences to indicate something you consider to be fairly unlikely to happen. ❑ *If only I could get some sleep, I would be able to cope... A policeman would not live one year if he obeyed these regulations.* MODAL 6 You use **would** to say that someone was willing to do something. You use **would not** to indicate that they refused to do something. ❑ *They said they would give the police their full cooperation... She indicated that she would help her husband... He wouldn't say where he had picked up the information.* MODAL 7 You use **would not** to indicate that something did not happen, often in spite of a lot of effort. ❑ *He kicked, pushed, and hurled his shoulder at the door. It wouldn't open... He kept trying to start the car and the battery got flatter and flatter, until it wouldn't turn the engine at all.* MODAL 8 You use **would**, especially with 'like', 'love', and 'wish', when saying that someone wants to do or have a particular thing or wants a particular thing to happen. ❑ *Right now, your mom would like a cup of coffee... Ideally, she would love to become pregnant again... He wished it would end.* **would rather** → see **rather**. MODAL 9 You use **would** with 'if' clauses in questions when you are asking for permission to do something. ❑ *Do you think it would be all right if I smoked?... Mr. Cutler, would you mind if I asked a question?* MODAL 10 You use **would**, usually in questions with 'like', when you are making a polite offer or invitation. ❑ *Would you like a drink?... Perhaps you would like to pay a visit to London.* MODAL politeness 11 You use **would**, usually in questions, when you are politely asking someone to do something. ❑ *Would you come in here a moment, please?... Oh dear, there's the doorbell. See who it is, would you, darling.* MODAL politeness = *could* 12 You say that someone **would** do something when it is typical of them and you are critical of it. You emphasize the word **would** when you use it in this way. ❑ *Well, you would say that: you're a man.* MODAL disapproval 13 You use **would**, or sometimes **would have** with a past participle, when you are expressing your opinion about something or seeing if people agree with you, especially when you are uncertain about what you are saying. ❑ *I think you'd agree he's a very respected columnist... I would have thought it a proper job for the Army to fight rebellion... I would imagine she's quite lonely living on her own.* MODAL vagueness 14 You use **I would** when you are giving someone advice in an informal way. ❑ *If I were you I would simply ring your friend's bell and ask for your bike back... There could be more unrest, but I wouldn't exaggerate the problems.* MODAL 15 You use **you would** in negative sentences with verbs such as 'guess' and 'know' when you want to say that something is not obvious, especially something surprising. ❑ *Chris is so full of artistic temperament you'd never think she was the daughter of a banker.* MODAL 16 You use **would** to talk about something which happened regularly in the past but which no longer happens. ❑ *Sunday mornings my mother would bake. I'd stand by the fridge and help.* MODAL = *used to* 17 You use **would have** with a past participle when you are saying what was likely to have happened by a particular time. ❑ *Within ten weeks of the introduction, 34 million people would have been reached by our television commercials.* MODAL 18 You use **would have** with a past participle when you are referring to the result or effect of a possible event in the past. ❑ *My daughter would have been 17 this week if she had lived... If I had known how he felt, I would never have let him adopt those children.* MODAL 19 If you say that someone **would have** liked or preferred something, you mean that they wanted to do it or have it but were unable to. ❑ *I would have liked a life in politics... She would have liked to ask questions, but he had moved on to another topic.* MODAL

**would-be** You can use **would-be** to describe someone who wants or attempts to do a particular thing. For example, a **would-be** writer is someone who wants to be a writer. ❑ *...a book that provides encouragement for would-be writers who cannot get their novel into print.* ADJ: ADJ n

**wouldn't** /wʊdᵊnt/ **Wouldn't** is the usual spoken form of 'would not'. ❑ *They wouldn't allow me to smoke.*

**would've** /wʊdəv/ **Would've** is a spoken form of 'would have', when 'have' is an auxiliary verb. ❑ *My mum would've loved one of us to go to college.*

**wound**
① VERB FORM OF 'WIND'
② INJURY

① **wound** /waʊnd/ **Wound** is the past tense and past participle of **wind** 2.

② **wound** /wuːnd/ **(wounds, wounding, wounded)** ◆◆◇ 1 A **wound** is damage to part of your body, especially a cut or a hole in your flesh, which is caused by a gun, knife, or other weapon. N-COUNT ❑ *The wound is healing nicely... Six soldiers are reported to have died from their wounds.* 2 If a weapon or something sharp **wounds** you, it damages your body. VERB ❑ *A bomb exploded, killing six people and wounding another five...* V n *The two wounded men were taken to a nearby hospital.* V-ed ♦ **The wounded** are people who are wounded. N-PLURAL ❑ *Hospitals said they could not cope with the wounded.* 3 A **wound** is a lasting bad effect on someone's mind or feelings caused by a very upsetting experience. N-COUNT [LITERARY] ❑ *She has been so deeply hurt it may take forever for the wounds to heal.* 4 If you **are wounded** by what someone says or does, your feelings are deeply hurt. VERB = hurt ❑ *He was deeply wounded by the treachery of close aides.* be V-ed 5 to **rub salt into the wound** → see **salt**.

**wound up** /waʊnd ʌp/ If someone is **wound up**, they are very tense and nervous or angry. ADJ: usu v-link ADJ

**wove** /woʊv/ **Wove** is the past tense of **weave**.

**wo|ven** /woʊvᵊn/ **Woven** is a past participle of **weave**.

**wow** /waʊ/ **(wows, wowing, wowed)** 1 You can say '**wow**' when you are very impressed, surprised, or pleased. EXCLAM feelings [INFORMAL] ❑ *I thought, 'Wow, what a good idea'.* 2 You say that someone **wows** people when they give an impressive performance and fill people with enthusiasm and admiration. VERB [INFORMAL] ❑ *Ben Tankard wowed the crowd with his jazz.* V n

**WPC** /dʌbᵊljuː piː siː/ **(WPCs)** In Britain, a **WPC** is a female police officer of the lowest rank. N-COUNT; N-TITLE **WPC** is an abbreviation for 'woman police constable'.

**wraith** /reɪθ/ **(wraiths)** A **wraith** is a ghost. N-COUNT [LITERARY] ❑ *That child flits about like a wraith.*

**wran|gle** /ræŋgᵊl/ **(wrangles, wrangling, wrangled)** If you say that someone **is wrangling with** someone **over** a question or issue, you mean that they have been arguing angrily for quite a long time about it. V-RECIP ❑ *The two sides have spent most of their time wrangling over procedural problems...* pl-n V over n *A group of MPs is still wrangling with the government over the timing of elections.* V with n over n

**wran|gler** /ræŋgləʳ/ **(wranglers)** A **wrangler** is a cowboy who works with cattle and horses. N-COUNT [AM]

**wrap** /ræp/ **(wraps, wrapping, wrapped)** ◆◇◇ 1 When you **wrap** something, you fold paper or cloth tightly round it to cover it completely, for example in order to protect it or so that you can give it to someone as a present. VERB ≠ unwrap ❑ *Harry had carefully bought and wrapped presents for Mark to give them...* V n *Mexican Indians used to wrap tough meat in leaves from the papaya tree.* V n in n ♦ **Wrap up** means the same as **wrap**. PHRASAL VERB ❑ *Diana is taking the opportunity to wrap up the family presents.* V P n Also V n P 2 **Wrap** is the material that something is wrapped in. N-UNCOUNT: usu supp N ❑ *I tucked some plastic wrap around the sandwiches to keep them from getting stale. ...gift wrap.* 3 When you **wrap** something such as a piece of paper or cloth round another thing, you put it around it. VERB ❑ *She wrapped a handkerchief around her bleeding palm.* V n around/over n 4 If someone **wraps** their arms, fingers, or legs around something, they put them firmly around it. VERB ❑ *He wrapped his arms around her.* V n around n 5 → See also **wrapping**. 6 If you keep something **under wraps**, you keep it secret, often until you are ready to announce it at some time in the future. PHRASE: v-link PHR, PHR after v ❑ *The bids were submitted in May and were meant to have been kept under wraps until October.*

♦ **wrap up** 1 If you **wrap up**, you put warm clothes on. PHRASAL VERB ❑ *Markus has wrapped up warmly in a woolly hat.* V P adv/adj/prep, Also V P 2 If you **wrap up** something such as a job or an agreement, you complete it in a satisfactory way. PHRASAL VERB ❑ *NATO defense ministers wrap up their meeting in Brussels today...* V P n (not pron) *Seeing Sticht was keeping him from his golf game, and he hoped they could wrap it up quickly.* V n P 3 → See also **wrap 1**, **wrapped up**.

**wrapped up** If someone is **wrapped up in** a particular person or thing, they spend nearly all their time thinking about them, so that they forget about other things which may be important. ADJ: v-link ADJ in/with n ❑ *He's too serious and dedicated, wrapped up in his career.*

**wrap|per** /ræpəʳ/ **(wrappers)** A **wrapper** is a piece of paper, plastic, or thin metal which covers and protects something that you buy, especially food. N-COUNT: oft supp N ❑ *I emptied the sweet wrappers from the ashtray.*

**wrap|ping** /ræpɪŋ/ **(wrappings) Wrapping** is something such as paper or plastic which is used to cover and protect something. N-VAR ❑ *...food wrapping.*

**wrap|ping pa|per** **(wrapping papers) Wrapping paper** is special paper which is used for wrapping presents. N-MASS

**wrath** /rɒθ, AM ræθ/ **Wrath** means the same as anger. N-UNCOUNT: oft with poss [LITERARY] ❑ *He incurred the wrath of the authorities in speaking out against government injustices.*

**wreak** /riːk/ **(wreaks, wreaking, wreaked)**

☑ The form **wrought** can also be used as the past participle.

1 Something or someone that **wreaks** havoc or destruction causes a great amount of disorder or damage. VERB [JOURNALISM or LITERARY] ❑ *Violent storms wreaked havoc on the French Riviera, leaving three people dead and dozens injured.* V n 2 If you **wreak** revenge or vengeance on someone, you do something that will harm them very much to punish them for the harm they have done to you. VERB [JOURNALISM or LITERARY] ❑ *He threatened to wreak vengeance on the men who toppled him a year ago.* V n 3 → See also **wrought**.

**wreath** /riːθ/ **(wreaths)** 1 A **wreath** is an arrangement of flowers and leaves, usually in the shape of a circle, which you put on a grave or by a statue to show that you remember a person who has died or people who have died. N-COUNT ❑ *The coffin lying before the altar was bare, except for a single wreath of white roses.* 2 A **wreath** is a circle of leaves or flowers which someone wears around their head. N-COUNT 3 A **wreath** is a circle of leaves which some people hang on the front door of their house at Christmas. N-COUNT

**wreathe** /riːð/ **(wreathes, wreathing, wreathed)** 1 If something **is wreathed in** smoke or mist, it is surrounded by it. VERB = shroud [LITERARY] ❑ *The ship was wreathed in smoke...* be V-ed in n *Fog wreathes the temples.* V n 2 If something **is wreathed with** flowers or leaves, it has a circle or chain of flowers or leaves put round it. VERB: usu passive ❑ *Its huge columns were wreathed with laurel and magnolia.* be V-ed with/in n

**wreck** /rek/ **(wrecks, wrecking, wrecked)** 1 To **wreck** something means to completely destroy or ruin it. VERB ❑ *A coalition could have defeated the government and wrecked the treaty...* V n *His life has been wrecked by the tragedy.* V n *...missed promotions, lost jobs, wrecked marriages.* V-ed 2 If a ship **is wrecked**, it is damaged so much that it sinks or can no longer sail. VERB: usu passive ❑ *The ship was wrecked by an explosion.* be V-ed *...a wrecked cargo ship.* V-ed 3 A **wreck** is something such as a ship, car, plane, or building which has been destroyed, usually in an accident. N-COUNT ❑ *...the wreck of* *a sailing ship... The car was a total wreck... We thought of buying the house as a wreck, doing it up, then selling it.* [4] A **wreck** is an accident in which a moving vehicle hits something and is damaged or destroyed. [mainly AM] ❑ *He was killed in a car wreck.* N-COUNT: usu supp N

✔ in BRIT, usually use **crash**

[5] If you say that someone is a **wreck**, you mean that they are very exhausted or unhealthy. [INFORMAL] ❑ *You look a wreck.* ➔ See also **nervous wreck**. N-COUNT: usu sing

**wreck|age** /rekɪdʒ/ When something such as a plane, car, or building has been destroyed, you can refer to what remains as **wreckage** or **the wreckage**. ❑ *Mark was dragged from the burning wreckage of his car.* N-UNCOUNT: also *the* N

**wreck|er** /rekəʳ/ **(wreckers)** [1] A **wrecker** is a motor vehicle which is used to pull broken or damaged vehicles to a place where they can be repaired or broken up, for example after an accident. [mainly AM] N-COUNT [2] **Wreckers** are people whose job involves destroying old, unwanted, or damaged buildings. [mainly AM] N-COUNT

**wren** /ren/ **(wrens)** A **wren** is a very small brown bird. There are several kinds of wren. N-COUNT

**wrench** /rentʃ/ **(wrenches, wrenching, wrenched)** [1] If you **wrench** something that is fixed in a particular position, you pull or twist it violently, in order to move or remove it. ❑ *He felt two men wrench the suitcase from his hand... They wrenched open the passenger doors and jumped into her car.* VERB; V n prep; V n with adj [2] If you **wrench** yourself free from someone who is holding you, you get away from them by suddenly twisting the part of your body that is being held. ❑ *She wrenched herself from his grasp... He wrenched his arm free... She tore at one man's face as she tried to wrench free.* VERB; V pron-refl prep; V n adj; V adj [3] If you **wrench** one of your joints, you twist it and injure it. ❑ *He had wrenched his ankle badly from the force of the fall.* VERB; V n [4] If you say that leaving someone or something is **a wrench**, you feel very sad about it. [BRIT] ❑ *I always knew it would be a wrench to leave Essex after all these years... Although it would be a wrench, we would all accept the challenge of moving abroad.* N-SING: usu *a* N to-inf/-ing [5] A **wrench** or a **monkey wrench** is an adjustable metal tool used for tightening or loosening metal nuts of different sizes. ➔ See picture on page 1709. N-COUNT [6] If someone **throws a wrench** or **throws a monkey wrench** into a process, they prevent something happening smoothly by deliberately causing a problem. [AM] ❑ *Their delegation threw a giant monkey wrench into the process this week by raising all sorts of petty objections.* PHRASE: V inflects, PHR *in/into* n

✔ in BRIT, use **throw a spanner in the works**

**wrest** /rest/ **(wrests, wresting, wrested)** [1] If you **wrest** something **from** someone else, you take it from them, especially when this is difficult or illegal. [JOURNALISM or LITERARY] ❑ *For the past year he has been trying to wrest control from the central government... The men had returned to wrest back power.* VERB = seize; V n *from* n; V n with *away/back* [2] If you **wrest** something **from** someone who is holding it, you take it from them by pulling or twisting it violently. [LITERARY] ❑ *He wrested the suitcase from the chauffeur... He was attacked by a security man who tried to wrest away a gas cartridge.* VERB; V n *from* n; V n with *away*

**wres|tle** /resəl/ **(wrestles, wrestling, wrestled)** [1] When you **wrestle with** a difficult problem, you try to deal with it. ❑ *Delegates wrestled with the problems of violence and sanctions.* VERB; V *with* n [2] If you **wrestle** with someone, you fight them by forcing them into painful positions or throwing them to the ground, rather than by hitting them. Some people wrestle as a sport. ❑ *They taught me to wrestle.* VERB; V [3] If you **wrestle** a person or thing somewhere, you move them there using a lot of force, for example by twisting a part of someone's body into a painful position. ❑ *We had to physically wrestle the child from the man's arms.* VERB; V n prep [4] ➔ See also **wrestling**.

**wres|tler** /resləʳ/ **(wrestlers)** A **wrestler** is someone who wrestles as a sport, usually for money. N-COUNT

**wres|tling** /reslɪŋ/ **Wrestling** is a sport in which two people wrestle and try to throw each other to the ground. ❑ *...a championship wrestling match.* N-UNCOUNT

**wretch** /retʃ/ **(wretches)** [1] You can refer to someone as a **wretch** when you feel sorry for them because they are unhappy or unfortunate. [LITERARY] ❑ *Before the poor wretch had time to speak, he was shot.* N-COUNT [2] You can refer to someone as a **wretch** when you think that they are wicked or if they have done something you are angry about. [LITERARY] ❑ *Oh, what have you done, you wretch!* N-COUNT disapproval

**wretch|ed** /retʃɪd/ [1] You describe someone as **wretched** when you feel sorry for them because they are in an unpleasant situation or have suffered unpleasant experiences. [FORMAL] ❑ *You have built up a huge property empire by buying from wretched people who had to sell or starve.* ADJ [2] You use **wretched** to describe someone or something that you dislike or feel angry with. [INFORMAL] ❑ *Wretched woman, he thought, why the hell can't she wait?* ADJ: ADJ n feelings [3] Someone who feels **wretched** feels very unhappy. [FORMAL] ❑ *I feel really confused and wretched.* ADJ = miserable

**wrig|gle** /rɪgəl/ **(wriggles, wriggling, wriggled)** [1] If you **wriggle** or **wriggle** part of your body, you twist and turn with quick movements, for example because you are uncomfortable. ❑ *The babies are wriggling on their tummies... She pulled off her shoes and stockings and wriggled her toes.* VERB; V; V n [2] If you **wriggle** somewhere, for example through a small gap, you move there by twisting and turning your body. ❑ *He clutched the child tightly as she again tried to wriggle free... Bauman wriggled into the damp coverall.* VERB; V adv/prep; V adv/prep

♦ **wriggle out of** If you say that someone **has wriggled out of** doing something, you disapprove of the fact that they have managed to avoid doing it, although they should have done it. ❑ *The Government has tried to wriggle out of any responsibility for providing childcare for working parents.* PHRASAL VERB disapproval = get out of; V P P n/-ing

**wring** /rɪŋ/ **(wrings, wringing, wrung)** [1] If you **wring** something **out of** someone, you manage to make them give it to you even though they do not want to. ❑ *Buyers use different ruses to wring free credit out of their suppliers.* VERB = squeeze; V n *out of/from* n [2] If someone **wrings** their **hands**, they hold them together and twist and turn them, usually because they are very worried or upset about something. You can also say that someone is **wringing** their **hands** when they are expressing sorrow that a situation is so bad but are saying that they are unable to change it. ❑ *The Government has got to get a grip. Wringing its hands and saying it is a world problem just isn't good enough.* PHRASE: V inflects

♦ **wring out** When you **wring out** a wet cloth or a wet piece of clothing, you squeeze the water out of it by twisting it strongly. ❑ *He turned away to wring out the wet shirt... Soak a small towel in the liquid, wring it out, then apply to the abdomen.* PHRASAL VERB; V P n (not pron); V n P

**wring|er** /rɪŋəʳ/ If you say that someone **has been put through the wringer** or **has gone through the wringer**, you mean that they have suffered a very difficult or unpleasant experience. [INFORMAL] PHRASE: V inflects

**wrin|kle** /rɪŋkəl/ **(wrinkles, wrinkling, wrinkled)** [1] **Wrinkles** are lines which form on someone's face as they grow old. ❑ *His face was covered with wrinkles.* N-COUNT: usu pl [2] When someone's skin **wrinkles** or when something **wrinkles** it, lines start to form in it because the skin is getting old or damaged. ❑ *The skin on her cheeks and around her eyes was beginning to wrinkle. ...protection against the sun's rays that age and wrinkle the skin.* VERB; V; V n

♦ **wrin|kled** *I did indeed look older and more wrinkled than ever.* ADJ

3 A **wrinkle** is a raised fold in a piece of cloth or paper that spoils its appearance. ❑ *He noticed a wrinkle in her stocking.* N-COUNT

4 If cloth **wrinkles**, or if someone or something **wrinkles** it, it gets folds or lines in it. ❑ *Her stockings wrinkled at the ankles... I wrinkled the velvet.* VERB V V n

♦ **wrin|kled** *His suit was wrinkled and he looked very tired.* ADJ = crumpled

5 When you **wrinkle** your nose or forehead, or when it **wrinkles**, you tighten the muscles in your face so that the skin folds. ❑ *Frannie wrinkled her nose at her daughter... Ellen's face wrinkles as if she is about to sneeze.* VERB V n V

**wrin|kly** /rɪŋkli/ A **wrinkly** surface has a lot of wrinkles on it. ❑ *...wrinkly cotton and wool stockings.* usu ADJ n

**wrist** /rɪst/ **(wrists)** Your **wrist** is the part of your body between your hand and your arm which bends when you move your hand. N-COUNT

**wrist|watch** /rɪstwɒtʃ/ **(wristwatches)** A **wristwatch** is a watch with a strap which you wear round your wrist. N-COUNT

**writ** /rɪt/ **(writs)** A **writ** is a legal document that orders a person to do a particular thing. ❑ *He issued a writ against one of his accusers.* N-COUNT: oft N *for/against* n

**write** /raɪt/ **(writes, writing, wrote, written)** ◆◆◆

1 When you **write** something on a surface, you use something such as a pen or pencil to produce words, letters, or numbers on the surface. ❑ *If you'd like one, simply write your name and address on a postcard and send it to us... They were still trying to teach her to read and write... He wrote the word 'pride' in huge letters on the blackboard.* VERB V n adv/prep V V n

2 If you **write** something such as a book, a poem, or a piece of music, you create it and record it on paper or perhaps on a computer. ❑ *I had written quite a lot of orchestral music in my student days... Finding a volunteer to write the computer program isn't a problem... Thereafter she wrote articles for papers and magazines in Paris... Jung Lu wrote me a poem once.* VERB V n V n V n *for* n V n n

3 Someone who **writes** creates books, stories, or articles, usually for publication. ❑ *Jay wanted to write... She writes for many papers, including the Sunday Times.* VERB V V *for* n

4 When you **write to** someone or **write** them a letter, you give them information, ask them something, or express your feelings in a letter. In American English, you can also **write** someone. ❑ *Many people have written to me on this subject... She had written him a note a couple of weeks earlier... I wrote a letter to the car rental agency, explaining what had happened... Why didn't you write, call, anything?... He had written her in Italy but received no reply.* **nothing to write home about** → see **home**. VERB V *to* n V n n V n *to* n V V n

5 When someone **writes** something such as a cheque, receipt, or prescription, they put the necessary information on it and usually sign it. ❑ *Snape wrote a receipt with a gold fountain pen... I'll write you a cheque in a moment.* VERB V n V n n

♦ **Write out** means the same as **write**. ❑ *We went straight to the estate agent and wrote out a cheque... Get my wife to write you out a receipt before you leave.* PHRASAL VERB V P n V n P n Also V n P

6 If you **write to** a computer or a disk, you record data on it. [COMPUTING] ❑ *You should write-protect all disks that you do not usually need to write to.* VERB V *to/onto* n

7 → See also **writing**, **written**.

♦ **write back** If you **write back** to someone who has sent you a letter, you write them a letter in reply. ❑ *Macmillan wrote back saying that he could certainly help... I wrote back to Meudon at once to fix up a meeting.* PHRASAL VERB V P V P *to* n

♦ **write down** When you **write** something **down**, you record it on a piece of paper using a pen or pencil. ❑ *On the morning before starting the fast, write down your starting weight... Only by writing things down could I bring some sort of order to the confusion.* PHRASAL VERB V P n (not pron) V n P

♦ **write in** 1 If you **write in** to an organization, you send them a letter. ❑ *What's the point in writing in when you only print half the letter anyway?... So there's another thing that you might like to write in to this programme about.* PHRASAL VERB V P V P *to* n

2 In the United States, if someone who is voting in an election **writes in** a person whose name is not on the list of candidates, they write that person's name on the voting paper and vote for him or her. ❑ *I think I'll write in Pat Wilson... I'm going to write him in on my ballot next year.* PHRASAL VERB V P n (not pron) V n P

3 → See also **write-in**.

♦ **write into** If a rule or detail **is written into** a contract, law, or agreement, it is included in it when the contract, law, or agreement is made. ❑ *They insisted that a guaranteed supply of Chinese food was written into their contracts... I didn't write that into the rules but I don't think it's a bad idea.* PHRASAL VERB *be* V-ed P n V n P n

♦ **write off** 1 If you **write off** to a company or organization, you send them a letter, usually asking for something. ❑ *He wrote off to the New Zealand Government for these pamphlets about life in New Zealand.* PHRASAL VERB = write V P *to* n Also V P

2 If someone **writes off** a debt or an amount of money that has been spent on a project, they accept that they are never going to get the money back. [BUSINESS] ❑ *The president persuaded the West to write off Polish debts.* PHRASAL VERB V P n Also V n P

3 If you **write** someone or something **off**, you decide that they are unimportant or useless and that they are not worth further serious attention. ❑ *He is fed up with people writing him off because of his age... His critics write him off as too cautious to succeed... These people are difficult to write off as malingering employees.* PHRASAL VERB = dismiss V n P V n P *as* n/adj V P n (not pron) *as* n/adj

4 If someone **writes off** a vehicle, they have a crash in it and it is so badly damaged that it is not worth repairing. [BRIT] ❑ *John's written off four cars. Now he sticks to public transport... One of Pete's friends wrote his car off there.* PHRASAL VERB V P n (not pron) V n P

5 If you **write off** a plan or project, you accept that it is not going to be successful and do not continue with it. ❑ *We decided to write off the rest of the day and go shopping... The prices were much higher. So we decided to write that off.* PHRASAL VERB V P n (not pron) V n P

6 → See also **write-off**.

♦ **write out** 1 When you **write out** something fairly long such as a report or a list, you write it on paper. ❑ *We had to write out a list of ten jobs we'd like to do... The application form is important. Sit down and write it out properly.* PHRASAL VERB V P n (not pron) V n P

2 If a character in a drama series **is written out**, he or she is taken out of the series. ❑ *When Angie was written out of 'Eastenders' her character went to Spain to open a bar.* PHRASAL VERB *be* V-ed P *of* n Also V n P

3 → see **write 5**.

♦ **write up** If you **write up** something that has been done or said, you record it on paper in a neat and complete form, usually using notes that you have made. ❑ *He wrote up his visit in a report of over 600 pages... Mr Sadler conducted interviews, and his girlfriend wrote them up.* → See also **write-up**. PHRASAL VERB V P n (not pron) V n P

**write-in (write-ins)** In the US, a **write-in** is a vote that you make by writing the candidate's name on the ballot paper. ❑ *When Republican write-ins were included, Johnson's margin of victory was only 330 votes.* N-COUNT: also N n

**write-off (write-offs)** 1 Something such as a vehicle that is a **write-off** has been so badly damaged in an accident that it is not worth repairing. [BRIT] ❑ *The car was a write-off, but everyone escaped unharmed.* N-COUNT

2 A **write-off** is the decision by a company or government to accept that they will never recover a debt or an amount of money that has been spent on something. ❑ *Mr James persuaded the banks to accept a large write-off of debt.* N-COUNT

3 If you describe a plan or period of time as a **write-off**, you mean that it has been a failure and you have achieved nothing. [INFORMAL] ❑ *Today was really a bit of a write-off for me.* N-SING

**writ|er** /raɪtəʳ/ **(writers)** ◆◆◇ 1 A **writer** is a person who writes books, stories, or articles as a job. ❑ *Turner is a writer and critic. ...detective stories by American writers. ...novelist and travel writer Paul Theroux.* N-COUNT: oft supp N

2 The **writer** of a particular article, report, letter, or story is the person who wrote it. ❑ *No-one is to see the document without the permission of the writer of the report.* N-COUNT: usu with supp

**write-up (write-ups)** A **write-up** is an article in a newspaper or magazine, in which someone N-COUNT: usu with supp = review gives their opinion of something such as a film, restaurant, or new product. ❑ *The show received a good write-up... The guide book contains a short write-up of each hotel.*

**writhe** /raɪð/ **(writhes, writhing, writhed)** VERB If you **writhe**, your body twists and turns violently backwards and forwards, usually because you are in great pain or discomfort. ❑ V *He was writhing in agony...* V adv/prep *The shark was writhing around wildly, trying to get free.*

**writ|ing** /raɪtɪŋ/ **(writings)** ◆◆◇ 1 N-UNCOUNT **Writing** is something that has been written or printed. ❑ *'It's from a notebook,' the sheriff said, 'And there's writing on it.'... If you have a complaint about your holiday, please inform us in writing.* 2 N-UNCOUNT You can refer to any piece of written work as **writing**, especially when you are considering the style of language used in it. ❑ *The writing is brutally tough and savagely humorous... It was such a brilliant piece of writing.* 3 N-UNCOUNT **Writing** is the activity of writing, especially of writing books for money. ❑ *She had begun to be a little bored with novel writing. ...activities to help prepare children for writing.* 4 N-UNCOUNT: usu poss N = handwriting Your **writing** is the way that you write with a pen or pencil, which can usually be recognized as belonging to you. ❑ *It was a little difficult to read your writing... I think it's due to being left handed that he's got terrible writing.* 5 N-PLURAL: usu with poss An author's **writings** are all the things that he or she has written, especially on a particular subject. ❑ *Althusser's writings are focused mainly on France... The pieces he is reading are adapted from the writings of Michael Frayn.* 6 PHRASE: V inflects If you say that **the writing is on the wall**, you mean that there are clear signs that a situation is going to become very difficult or unpleasant. ❑ *The writing is clearly on the wall. If we do nothing about it, we shall only have ourselves to blame.*

**writ|ing desk (writing desks)** N-COUNT A **writing desk** is a piece of furniture with drawers, an area for keeping writing materials, and a surface on which you can rest your paper while writing.

**writ|ing pa|per (writing papers)** N-MASS **Writing paper** is paper for writing letters on. It is usually of good, smooth quality.

**writ|ten** /rɪtᵊn/ ◆◇◇ 1 **Written** is the past participle of **write**. 2 ADJ: usu ADJ n A **written** test or piece of work is one which involves writing rather than doing something practical or giving spoken answers. ❑ *Learners may have to take a written exam before they pass their driving test.* 3 ADJ: ADJ n ≠ unwritten A **written** agreement, rule, or law has been officially written down. ❑ *The newspaper broke a written agreement not to sell certain photographs.* 4 to **be written all over** someone's **face** → see **face**.

**writ|ten word** N-SING: usu *the* N You use **the written word** to refer to language expressed in writing, especially when contrasted with speech or with other forms of expression such as painting or film. ❑ *Even in the 18th century scholars continued to give primacy to the written word.*

**wrong** /rɒŋ, AM rɔːŋ/ **(wrongs, wronging, wronged)** ◆◆◇ 1 ADJ: v-link ADJ, oft ADJ *with* n ≠ right If you say there is something **wrong**, you mean there is something unsatisfactory about the situation, person, or thing you are talking about. ❑ *Pain is the body's way of telling us that something is wrong... Nobody seemed to notice anything wrong... What's wrong with him?* 2 ADJ: usu ADJ n ≠ right If you choose the **wrong** thing, person, or method, you make a mistake and do not choose the one that you really want. ❑ *He went to the wrong house... The wrong man had been punished... Could you have given them the wrong drug by mistake?... There is no right or wrong way to do these exercises.* ♦ ADV: ADV after v ≠ right **Wrong** is also an adverb. ❑ *You've done it wrong... I must have dialed wrong.* 3 ADJ: ADJ n ≠ right If something such as a decision, choice, or action is **the wrong** one, it is not the best or most suitable one. ❑ *I really made the wrong decision there... The wrong choice of club might limit your chances of success... We got married when I was 30 for all the wrong reasons.* 4 ADJ ≠ right If something is **wrong**, it is incorrect and not in accordance with the facts. ❑ *How do you know that this explanation is wrong?... 20 per cent of the calculations are wrong. ...a clock which showed the wrong time... Lots of people got the questions wrong.* ♦ ADV: ADV after v **Wrong** is also an adverb. ❑ *I must have added it up wrong, then... It looks like it's spelled wrong... I can see exactly where he went wrong.* ♦ ADV: ADV with v **wrong|ly** *A child was wrongly diagnosed as having a bone tumour... Civilians assume, wrongly, that everything in the military runs smoothly.* 5 ADJ: v-link ADJ, usu ADJ *with* n If something is **wrong** or goes **wrong with** a machine or piece of equipment, it stops working properly. ❑ *We think there's something wrong with the computer... Something must have gone wrong with the satellite link.* 6 ADJ: v-link ADJ, oft ADJ *about* n, ADJ *in* -ing, *it* v-link ADJ to-inf, ADJ to-inf ≠ right If you are **wrong** about something, what you say or think about it is not correct. ❑ *I was wrong about it being a casual meeting... It would be wrong to assume that rich countries will always be able to insulate themselves with drugs against the ravages of new diseases... I'm sure you've got it wrong. Kate isn't like that... It's been very nice to prove them wrong.* 7 ADJ: ADJ to-inf ≠ right If you think that someone was **wrong to** do something, you think that they should not have done it because it was bad or immoral. ❑ *She was wrong to leave her child alone... We don't consider we did anything wrong.* ♦ N-UNCOUNT **Wrong** is also a noun. ❑ *...a man who believes that he has done no wrong.* 8 ADJ: v-link ADJ, oft *it* v-link ADJ to-inf/that **Wrong** is used to refer to activities or actions that are considered to be morally bad and unacceptable. ❑ *Is it wrong to try to save the life of someone you love?... They thought slavery was morally wrong... The only thing I consider wrong is when you hurt someone... There is nothing wrong with journalists commenting on the attractiveness of artists.* ♦ N-UNCOUNT ≠ right **Wrong** is also a noun. ❑ *Johnson didn't seem to be able to tell the difference between right and wrong.* 9 N-COUNT A **wrong** is an unfair or immoral action. ❑ *I intend to right that wrong... The insurance company should not be held liable for the wrongs of one of its agents.* 10 VERB If someone **wrongs** you, they treat you in an unfair way. ❑ V n *You have wronged my mother...* V n *She felt she'd been wronged...* V *Those who have wronged must be ready to say: 'We have hurt you by this injustice.'* 11 ADJ: ADJ n You use **wrong** to describe something which is not thought to be socially acceptable or desirable. ❑ *If you went to the wrong school, you won't get the job.*

PHRASES 12 PHRASE: V inflects If a situation **goes wrong**, it stops progressing in the way that you expected or intended, and becomes much worse. ❑ *It all went horribly wrong.* 13 PHRASE: usu v-link PHR If someone who is involved in an argument or dispute has behaved in a way which is morally or legally wrong, you can say that they are **in the wrong**. ❑ *He didn't press charges because he was in the wrong.* 14 **not far wrong** → see **far**. to **get off on the wrong foot** → see **foot**. to **get hold of the wrong end of the stick** → see **stick**. to **be barking up the wrong tree** → see **tree**.

**wrong|doer** /rɒŋduːəʳ, AM rɔːŋ-/ **(wrongdoers)** N-COUNT A **wrongdoer** is a person who does things that are immoral or illegal. [JOURNALISM]

**wrong|doing** /rɒŋduːɪŋ, AM rɔːŋ-/ **(wrongdoings)** N-VAR **Wrongdoing** is behaviour that is illegal or immoral. ❑ *The city attorney's office hasn't found any evidence of criminal wrongdoing.*

**wrong-foot (wrong-foots, wrong-footing, wrong-footed)** also **wrong foot.** VERB If you **wrong-foot** someone, you surprise them by putting them into an unexpected or difficult situation. [mainly BRIT] ❑ V n *He has surprised his supporters and wrong-footed his opponents with his latest announcement.*

**wrong|ful** /rɒŋfʊl, AM rɔːŋ-/ ADJ: usu ADJ n A **wrongful** act is one that is illegal, immoral, or unjust. ❑ *He is on hunger strike in protest at what he claims is his wrongful conviction for murder... One of her employees sued her for wrongful dismissal.* ♦ ADV: ADV with v = unjustly **wrong|ful|ly** *The criminal justice system is in need of urgent reform to prevent more people being wrongfully imprisoned.*

**wrong-headed** If you describe someone as **wrong-headed**, you mean that although they act in a determined way, their actions and ideas are based on wrong judgments. ADJ

**wrote** /rout/ **Wrote** is the past tense of **write**.

**wrought** /rɔːt/ 1 If something has **wrought** a change, it has made it happen. [JOURNALISM or LITERARY] ❑ *Events in Paris wrought a change in British opinion towards France and Germany.* VERB: only past V n
2 → See also **wreak**.

**wrought iron** also **wrought-iron**. **Wrought iron** is a type of iron that is easily formed into shapes and is used especially for making gates, fences, and furniture. N-UNCOUNT

**wrung** /rʌŋ/ **Wrung** is the past tense of **wring**.

**wry** /raɪ/ 1 If someone has a **wry** expression, it shows that they find a bad situation or a change in a situation slightly amusing. ❑ *Matthew allowed himself a wry smile.* ADJ: usu ADJ n
2 A **wry** remark or piece of writing refers to a bad situation or a change in a situation in an amusing way. ❑ *There is a wry sense of humour in his work.* ADJ: usu ADJ n

**wt** also **wt.** **Wt** is a written abbreviation for **weight**.

**WTO** /dʌbᵊljuː tiː oʊ/ **WTO** is an abbreviation for **World Trade Organization**. ❑ *The world desperately needs an effective WTO.* N-PROPER

**wuss** /wʊs/ **(wusses)** If you call someone a **wuss**, you are criticizing them for being afraid. [INFORMAL] N-COUNT: usu *a* N disapproval

**WWW** /dʌbljuː dʌbljuː dʌbljuː/ **WWW** is an abbreviation for 'World Wide Web'. It appears at the beginning of website addresses in the form **www.** [COMPUTING] ❑ *Check out our website at www.cobuild.collins.co.uk.*

**WYSIWYG** /wɪziwɪg/ **WYSIWYG** is used to refer to a computer screen display which exactly matches the way that a document will appear when it it is printed. **WYSIWYG** is an abbreviation for 'what you see is what you get'. [COMPUTING] ❑ *...the first WYSIWYG application for creating documents on the Web.*

# Xx Yy Zz

**X, x** /eks/ **(X's, x's)** 1 **X** is the twenty-fourth letter of the English alphabet. 2 When writing down the size of something, you can use **x** in between the measurements to mean 'by'. ❑ *The conservatory measures approximately 13ft x 16ft.* N-VAR

**X chro|mo|some** **(X chromosomes)** An **X chromosome** is one of an identical pair of chromosomes found in a woman's cells, or one of a non-identical pair found in a man's cells. X chromosomes are associated with female characteristics. Compare **Y chromosome**. N-COUNT

**xeno|pho|bia** /zenəfoʊbiə/ **Xenophobia** is strong and unreasonable dislike or fear of people from other countries. [FORMAL] N-UNCOUNT

**xeno|pho|bic** /zenəfoʊbɪk/ If you describe someone as **xenophobic**, you disapprove of them because they show strong dislike or fear of people from other countries. [FORMAL] ❑ *Xenophobic nationalism is on the rise in some West European countries... Stalin was obsessively xenophobic.* ADJ disapproval

**Xer|ox** /zɪərɒks/ **(Xeroxes, Xeroxing, Xeroxed)** 1 A **Xerox** is a machine that can make copies of pieces of paper which have writing or other marks on them. [TRADEMARK] ❑ *The rooms are crammed with humming Xerox machines.* 2 A **Xerox** is a copy of something written or printed on a piece of paper, which has been made using a Xerox machine. 3 If you **Xerox** a document, you make a copy of it using a Xerox machine. ❑ *I should have simply Xeroxed this sheet for you.* N-COUNT: usu N n; N-COUNT; VERB; V n

**Xmas** **Xmas** is used in informal written English to represent the word Christmas. ❑ *Merry Xmas!*

**X-ray** **(X-rays, X-raying, X-rayed)** also **x-ray**. 1 **X-rays** are a type of radiation that can pass through most solid materials. X-rays are used by doctors to examine the bones or organs inside your body and are also used at airports to see inside people's luggage. 2 An **X-ray** is a picture made by sending X-rays through something, usually someone's body. ❑ *She was advised to have an abdominal X-ray.* 3 If someone or something **is X-rayed**, an X-ray picture is taken of them. ❑ *All hand baggage would be x-rayed... They took my pulse, took my blood pressure, and X-rayed my jaw.* N-COUNT: usu pl; N-COUNT; VERB; be V-ed; V n

**xy|lo|phone** /zaɪləfoʊn/ **(xylophones)** A **xylophone** is a musical instrument which consists of a row of wooden bars of different lengths. You play the xylophone by hitting the bars with special hammers. N-COUNT: oft *the* N

**Y, y** /waɪ/ **(Y's, y's)** 1 **Y** is the twenty-fifth letter of the English alphabet. 2 A YMCA or YWCA hostel is sometimes referred to as **the Y**. [AM, INFORMAL] ❑ *I took him to the Y.* N-VAR; N-SING: *the* N

**-y** /-i/ **(-ies, -ier, -iest)** 1 **-y** is added to nouns in order to form adjectives that describe something or someone as having the characteristics of what the noun refers to. ❑ *...a smoky pub. ...juicy red berries... The process results in a much fruitier wine.* 2 **-y** is added to colours in order to form adjectives that describe something as being roughly that colour or having some of that colour in it. ❑ *...a rich, reddy, brown wood... Her eyes were a bluey-green colour.* 3 **-y** is added to a name or a noun in order to give it a more affectionate or familiar form. ❑ *'Hello, Mikey?'. ...a little doggy.* SUFFIX; SUFFIX; SUFFIX

**yacht** /jɒt/ **(yachts)** A **yacht** is a large boat with sails or a motor, used for racing or pleasure trips. ❑ *...a round-the-world yacht race.* ◆◇◇ N-COUNT

**yacht|ing** /jɒtɪŋ/ **Yachting** is the sport or activity of sailing a yacht. ❑ *...the Olympic yachting regatta.* N-UNCOUNT

**yachts|man** /jɒtsmən/ **(yachtsmen)** A **yachtsman** is a man who sails a yacht. N-COUNT

**yachts|woman** /jɒtswʊmən/ **(yachtswomen)** A **yachtswoman** is a woman who sails a yacht. N-COUNT

**ya|hoo** **(yahoos)**

> ✔ Pronounced /jɑːhuː/ for meaning 1, and /jɑːhuː/ for meaning 2.

1 People sometimes shout **'yahoo!'** when they are very happy or excited about something. 2 Some people refer to young rich people as **yahoos** when they disapprove of them because they behave in a noisy, extravagant, and unpleasant way. [BRIT, INFORMAL] EXCLAM; N-COUNT disapproval

**yak** /jæk/ **(yaks** or **yak)** A **yak** is a type of cattle that has long hair and long horns. Yaks live mainly in the Himalayan mountains and in Tibet. N-COUNT

**yam** /jæm/ **(yams)** 1 A **yam** is a root vegetable which is like a potato, and grows in tropical regions. 2 **Yams** are the same as **sweet potatoes**. [AM] N-VAR; N-VAR

**yank** /jæŋk/ **(yanks, yanking, yanked)** If you **yank** someone or something somewhere, you pull them there suddenly and with a lot of force. ❑ *She yanked open the drawer... A quick-thinking ticket inspector yanked an emergency cord.* ♦ **Yank** is also a noun. ❑ *Grabbing his ponytail, Shirley gave it a yank.* VERB; V n with adj; V n; N-COUNT

**Yank** **(Yanks)** Some people refer to people from the United States of America as **Yanks**. This use could cause offence. [INFORMAL] N-COUNT

**Yan|kee** /jæŋki/ **(Yankees)** 1 A **Yankee** is a person from a northern or north-eastern state of the United States. [mainly AM] 2 Some speakers of British English refer to anyone from the United States as a **Yankee**. This use could cause offence. [INFORMAL] N-COUNT; N-COUNT

**yap** /jæp/ **(yaps, yapping, yapped)** If a small dog **yaps**, it makes short loud sounds in an excited way. ❑ *The little dog yapped frantically.* VERB; V

**yard** /jɑːʳd/ **(yards)** 1 A **yard** is a unit of length equal to thirty-six inches or approximately 91.4 centimetres. ❑ *The incident took place about 500 yards from where he was standing. ...a long narrow strip of linen two or three yards long. ...a yard of silk.* 2 A **yard** is a flat area of concrete or stone that is next to a building and often has a wall around it. ❑ *I saw him standing in the yard.* 3 You can refer to a large open area where a particular type of work is done as a **yard**. ❑ *...a railway yard. ...a ship repair yard.* 4 A **yard** is a piece of land next to someone's house, with grass and plants growing in it. [AM] ❑ *He dug a hole in our yard to plant a maple tree when I was born.* ◆◆◇ N-COUNT: num N, oft N *of* n; N-COUNT = courtyard; N-COUNT: usu supp N; N-COUNT

> ✔ in BRIT, use **garden**

**Yar|die** /jɑːʳdi/ **(Yardies)** A **Yardie** is a member of a secret criminal organization, based in Jamaica, which is especially associated with drug dealing. [BRIT] N-COUNT

**yard sale** **(yard sales)** A **yard sale** is a sale where people sell things they no longer want from a table outside their house. [AM] N-COUNT

**yard|stick** /jɑːʳdstɪk/ **(yardsticks)** If you use someone or something as a **yardstick**, you use them as a standard for comparison when you are judging other people or things. ❑ *There has been no yardstick by which potential students can assess individual schools before signing up for a course.* N-COUNT

**yarn** /jɑːʳn/ **(yarns)** [1] **Yarn** is thread used for knitting or making cloth. ❑ *She still spins the yarn and knits sweaters for her family. ...vegetable-dyed yarns.* N-MASS [2] A **yarn** is a story that someone tells, often a true story with invented details which make it more interesting. ❑ *Doug has a yarn or two to tell me about his trips into the bush.* N-COUNT

**yaw** /jɔː/ **(yaws, yawing, yawed)** If an aircraft or a ship **yaws**, it turns to one side so that it changes the direction in which it is moving. [TECHNICAL] ❑ *As the plane climbed to 370 feet, it started yawing... He spun the steering-wheel so that we yawed from side to side.* VERB V V prep/adv

**yawn** /jɔːn/ **(yawns, yawning, yawned)** [1] If you **yawn**, you open your mouth very wide and breathe in more air than usual, often when you are tired or when you are not interested in something. ❑ *She yawned, and stretched lazily.* ♦ **Yawn** is also a noun. ❑ *Rosanna stifled a huge yawn.* VERB V N-COUNT [2] If you describe something such as a book or a film as **a yawn**, you think it is very boring. [INFORMAL] ❑ *The debate was a mockery. A big yawn... The concert was a predictable yawn.* N-SING: *a* N = *bore* [3] A gap or an opening that **yawns** is large and wide, and often frightening. [LITERARY] ❑ *The gulf between them yawned wider than ever.* VERB V

**Y chro|mo|some** **(Y chromosomes)** A **Y chromosome** is the chromosome in a man's cells which will produce a male baby if it joins with a female's X chromosome. Y chromosomes are associated with male characteristics. Compare **X chromosome**. N-COUNT

**yd** **(yds)** also **yd. yd** is a written abbreviation for **yard**. ❑ *The entrance is on the left 200 yds further on up the road.*

**ye** /jiː/ [1] **Ye** is an old-fashioned, poetic, or religious word for **you** when you are talking to more than one person. ❑ *Abandon hope all ye who enter here.* PRON [2] **Ye** is sometimes used in imitation of an old written form of the word 'the'. DET

**yea** /jeɪ/ [1] **Yea** is an old-fashioned, poetic, or religious word for 'yes'. CONVENTION [2] **Yea** is sometimes used to mean 'yes' when people are talking about voting for or agreeing to do something. ❑ *The House of Commons can merely say yea or nay to the executive judgment.* CONVENTION

**yeah** /jeə/ **Yeah** means yes. [INFORMAL, SPOKEN] ❑ *'Bring us something to drink.' — 'Yeah, yeah.'* ➔ See also **yes**. ◆◆◆ CONVENTION

**year** /jɪəʳ/ **(years)** [1] A **year** is a period of twelve months or 365 or 366 days, beginning on the first of January and ending on the thirty-first of December. ❑ *The year was 1840... We had an election last year. ...the number of people on the planet by the year 2050.* ➔ See also **leap year**. ◆◆◆ N-COUNT [2] A **year** is any period of twelve months. ❑ *The museums attract more than two and a half million visitors a year... She's done quite a bit of work this past year... The school has been empty for ten years.* N-COUNT [3] **Year** is used to refer to the age of a person. For example, if someone or something is twenty **years** old or twenty **years** of age, they have lived or existed for twenty years. ❑ *He's 58 years old... I've been in trouble since I was eleven years of age... This column is ten years old today.* N-COUNT: num N adj/prep [4] A school **year** or academic **year** is the period of time in each twelve months when schools or universities are open and students are studying there. In Britain and the United States, the school year starts in September. ❑ *...the 1990/91 academic year... The twins didn't have to repeat their second year at school.* N-COUNT: usu adj/ord N [5] You can refer to someone who is, for example, in their first year at school or university as a first **year**. [BRIT] ❑ *The first years and second years got a choice of French, German and Spanish.* N-COUNT: ord N [6] A financial or business **year** is an exact period of twelve months which businesses or institutions use as a basis for organizing their finances. [BUSINESS] ❑ *He announced big tax increases for the next two financial years... The company admits it will make a loss for the year ending September.* N-COUNT: with supp [7] You can use **years** to emphasize that you are referring to a long time. ❑ *I haven't laughed so much in years... It took me years to fully recover.* N-PLURAL [emphasis] = *age* [8] ➔ See also **calendar year**, **fiscal year**.

PHRASES [9] If something happens **year after year**, it happens regularly every year. ❑ *Regulars return year after year.* PHRASE: PHR after v [10] If something changes **year by year**, it changes gradually each year. ❑ *This problem has increased year by year... The department has been shrinking year by year because of budget cuts.* PHRASE: PHR after v [11] If you say something happens **all year round** or **all the year round**, it happens continually throughout the year. ❑ *Town gardens are ideal because they produce flowers nearly all year round... Drinking and driving is a problem all the year round.* PHRASE: PHR after v, PHR with cl [12] **donkey's years** ➔ see **donkey**.

**year|book** /jɪəʳbʊk/ **(yearbooks)** A **yearbook** is a book that is published once a year and that contains information about the events and achievements of the previous year, usually concerning a particular place or organization. ❑ *...an American college yearbook for 1955.* N-COUNT

**year-long** **Year-long** is used to describe something that lasts for a year. ❑ *The miners ended their year-long strike in March 1985.* ADJ: ADJ n

**year|ly** /jɪəʳli/ [1] A **yearly** event happens once a year or every year. ❑ *The seven major industrial countries will have their yearly meeting in London.* ♦ **Yearly** is also an adverb. ❑ *Clients normally pay fees in advance, monthly, quarterly, or yearly.* ADJ: ADJ n = *annual* ADV: ADV after v [2] You use **yearly** to describe something such as an amount that relates to a period of one year. ❑ *In Holland, the government sets a yearly budget for health care.* ♦ **Yearly** is also an adverb. ❑ *Novello says college students will spend $4.2 billion yearly on alcoholic beverages.* ADJ: ADJ n = *annual* ADV: ADV after v = *annually*

**yearn** /jɜːʳn/ **(yearns, yearning, yearned)** If someone **yearns for** something that they are unlikely to get, they want it very much. ❑ *He yearned for freedom... I yearned to be a movie actor.* VERB = *long* V *for* n V to-inf

**yearn|ing** /jɜːʳnɪŋ/ **(yearnings)** A **yearning for** something is a very strong desire for it. ❑ *He spoke of his yearning for another child... He always had a yearning to be a schoolteacher.* N-VAR: oft N *for* n, N to-inf = *longing*

**-year-old** /-jɪər-oʊld/ **(-year-olds)** **-year-old** combines with numbers to describe the age of people or things. ❑ *She has a six-year-old daughter. ...their 200-year-old farmhouse in Ohio.* ♦ **-year-old** also combines to form nouns. ❑ *Snow Puppies is a ski school for 3 to 6-year-olds.* COMB in ADJ: ADJ n COMB in N-COUNT

**year-round** **Year-round** is used to describe something that happens, exists, or is done throughout the year. ❑ *Cuba has a tropical climate with year-round sunshine.* ♦ **Year-round** is also an adverb. ❑ *They work 7 days a week year-round.* ADJ: ADJ n ADV: ADV with cl

**yeast** /jiːst/ **(yeasts)** **Yeast** is a kind of fungus which is used to make bread rise, and in making alcoholic drinks such as beer. N-MASS

**yeast ex|tract** **(yeast extracts)** **Yeast extract** is a brown sticky food that is obtained from yeast. It can be used in cooking or spread on bread. N-MASS

**yeasty** /jiːsti/ Something that is **yeasty** tastes or smells strongly of yeast. ADJ

**yell** /jel/ **(yells, yelling, yelled)** [1] If you **yell**, you shout loudly, usually because you are excited, angry, or in pain. ❑ *'Eva!' he yelled... I'm sorry I yelled at you last night... Christian pushed him away, yelling abuse.* ♦ **Yell out** means the same as **yell**. ❑ *'Are you coming or not?' they yelled out after him.* VERB V with quote V *at* n V n PHRASAL VERB V P [2] A **yell** is a loud shout given by someone who is N-COUNT afraid or in pain. ❑ *Something brushed past Bob's face and he let out a yell.* = cry

♦ **yell out** → see **yell 1**.

**yel|low** /jeloʊ/ **(yellows, yellowing, yellowed)** ♦♦♦ 1 Something that is **yellow** is the colour of lemons, butter, or the middle part of an egg. ❑ *The walls have been painted bright yellow.* COLOUR 2 If something **yellows**, it becomes yellow in colour, often because it is old. ❑ *The flesh of his cheeks seemed to have yellowed... She sat scanning the yellowing pages.* VERB V V-ing

**yel|low card (yellow cards)** In football or rugby, if a player is shown the **yellow card**, the referee holds up a yellow card to indicate that the player has broken the rules, and that if they do so again, they will be ordered to leave the pitch. N-COUNT: usu sing

**yel|low fe|ver** **Yellow fever** is a serious infectious disease that people can catch in tropical countries. N-UNCOUNT

**yel|low|ish** /jeloʊɪʃ/ Something that is **yellowish** is slightly yellow in colour. ❑ *...a small yellowish cauliflower.* ADJ

**yel|low line (yellow lines)** A **yellow line** is a narrow yellow line painted at the edge of a road to warn drivers that parking is not allowed there, or is only allowed at certain times. N-COUNT

**Yel|low Pages** **Yellow Pages** is a book that contains advertisements and telephone numbers for businesses and organizations in a particular area, grouped according to the type of business they do. Compare **White Pages**. [TRADEMARK] N-UNCOUNT: also *a* N

**yel|lowy** /jeloʊi/ Something that is **yellowy** is slightly yellow in colour. ♦ **Yellowy** is also a combining form. ❑ *...black ink, fading now to a yellowy brown.* ADJ COMB in COLOUR

**yelp** /jelp/ **(yelps, yelping, yelped)** If a person or dog **yelps**, they give a sudden short cry, often because of fear or pain. ❑ *Her dog yelped and came to heel.* ♦ **Yelp** is also a noun. ❑ *I had to bite back a yelp of surprise.* VERB V N-COUNT: oft N *of* n

**Yem|eni** /jemɪni/ **(Yemenis)** 1 **Yemeni** means belonging or relating to the Yemen, or to its people or culture. ADJ 2 A **Yemeni** is a Yemeni citizen, or a person of Yemeni origin. N-COUNT

**yen** /jen/ **(yen)** ♦◇◇ 1 The **yen** is the unit of currency used in Japan. ❑ *She's got a part-time job for which she earns 2,000 yen a month.* ♦ **The yen** is also used to refer to the Japanese currency system. ❑ *...sterling's devaluation against the yen.* N-COUNT: usu num N N-SING: *the* N 2 If you have a **yen to** do something, you have a strong desire to do it. ❑ *Mike had a yen to try cycling.* N-SING: usu *a* N, N to-inf, N *for* n

**yeo|man** /joʊmən/ **(yeomen)** In former times, a **yeoman** was a man who was free and not a servant, and who owned and worked on his own land. N-COUNT

**yep** /jep/ **Yep** means yes. [INFORMAL, SPOKEN] ❑ *'Did you like it?' — 'Yep.'.* CONVENTION

**yer** /jɜːʳ/ 1 **Yer** is used in written English to represent the word 'your' when it is pronounced informally. [BRIT] ❑ *Mister, can we 'elp to carry yer stuff in?* 2 **Yer** is used in written English to represent the word 'you' when it is pronounced informally. [BRIT] ❑ *I bloody told yer it would sell.*

**yes** /jes/ ♦♦♦

> In informal English, **yes** is often pronounced in a casual way that is usually written as **yeah**.

1 You use **yes** to give a positive response to a question. ❑ *'Are you a friend of Nick's?' — 'Yes.'... 'You actually wrote it down, didn't you?' — 'Yes.'... Will she say yes when I ask her out?* CONVENTION ≠ no 2 You use **yes** to accept an offer or request, or to give permission. ❑ *'More wine?' — 'Yes please.'... 'Will you take me there?' — 'Yes, I will.'... 'Can I ask you something?' — 'Yes, of course.'* CONVENTION ≠ no 3 You use **yes** to tell someone that what they have said is correct. ❑ *'Well I suppose it is based on the old lunar months isn't it.' — 'Yes that's right.'... 'That's a type of whitefly, is it?' — 'Yes, it is a whitefly.'* CONVENTION ≠ no 4 You use **yes** to show that you are ready or willing to speak to the person who wants to speak to you, for example when you are answering a telephone or a knock at your door. ❑ *He pushed a button on the intercom. 'Yes?' came a voice... Yes, can I help you?* CONVENTION 5 You use **yes** to indicate that you agree with, accept, or understand what the previous speaker has said. ❑ *'A lot of people find it very difficult indeed to give up smoking.' — 'Oh yes. I used to smoke nearly sixty a day.'... 'It's a fabulous opportunity.' — 'Yeah. I know.'* CONVENTION 6 You use **yes** to encourage someone to continue speaking. ❑ *'I remembered something funny today.' — 'Yeah?'* CONVENTION 7 You use **yes**, usually followed by 'but', as a polite way of introducing what you want to say when you disagree with something the previous speaker has just said. ❑ *'She is entitled to her personal allowance which is three thousand pounds of income.' — 'Yes, but she doesn't earn any money.'.* CONVENTION [politeness] 8 You use **yes** to say that a negative statement or question that the previous speaker has made is wrong or untrue. ❑ *'That is not possible,' she said. 'Oh, yes, it is!' Mrs Gruen insisted... 'I don't know what you're talking about.' — 'Yes, you do.'* CONVENTION 9 You can use **yes** to suggest that you do not believe or agree with what the previous speaker has said, especially when you want to express your annoyance about it. ❑ *'There was no way to stop it.' — 'Oh yes? Well, here's something else you won't be able to stop.'* CONVENTION [feelings] 10 You use **yes** to indicate that you had forgotten something and have just remembered it. ❑ *What was I going to say. Oh yeah, we've finally got our second computer.* CONVENTION 11 You use **yes** to emphasize and confirm a statement that you are making. ❑ *He collected the £10,000 first prize. Yes, £10,000.* CONVENTION [emphasis] 12 You say **yes and no** in reply to a question when you cannot give a definite answer, because in some ways the answer is yes and in other ways the answer is no. ❑ *'Was it strange for you, going back after such a long absence?' — 'Yes and no.'* CONVENTION [vagueness]

**yes-man (yes-men)** If you describe a man as a **yes-man**, you dislike the fact that he seems always to agree with people who have authority over him, in order to gain favour. N-COUNT [disapproval]

**yes|ter|day** /jestəʳdeɪ, -di/ **(yesterdays)** ♦♦♦ 1 You use **yesterday** to refer to the day before today. ❑ *She left yesterday... Yesterday she announced that she is quitting her job.* ♦ **Yesterday** is also a noun. ❑ *In yesterday's games, Switzerland beat the United States.* ADV: ADV with cl N-UNCOUNT 2 You can refer to the past, especially the recent past, as **yesterday**. ❑ *The worker of today is different from the worker of yesterday.* N-UNCOUNT: also N in pl

**yes|ter|year** /jestəʳjɪəʳ/ You use **yesteryear** to refer to the past, often a period in the past with a set of values or a way of life that no longer exists. [LITERARY] ❑ *The modern-day sex symbol has now taken the place of the old-fashioned hero of yesteryear.* N-UNCOUNT

**yet** /jet/ ♦♦♦ 1 You use **yet** in negative statements to indicate that something has not happened up to the present time, although it probably will happen. You can also use **yet** in questions to ask if something has happened up to the present time. In British English the simple past tense is not normally used with this meaning of 'yet'. ❑ *They haven't finished yet... No decision has yet been made... She hasn't yet set a date for her marriage... 'Has the murderer been caught?' — 'Not yet.'... Have you met my husband yet?... Hammer-throwing for women is not yet a major event.* ADV: usu with brd-neg, ADV with v, ADV group 2 You use **yet** with a negative statement when you are talking about the past, to report something that was not the case then, although it became the case later. ❑ *There was so much that Sam didn't know yet... He had asked around and learned that Billy was not yet here.* ADV: usu with brd-neg, ADV with v, ADV group 3 If you say that something should not or cannot be done **yet**, you mean that it should not or cannot be done now, although it will have to be done at a later time. ❑ *Don't get up yet... The hostages cannot go home just yet... We should not yet abandon this option for the disposal of highly radioactive waste.* ADV: with brd-neg, ADV with v 4 You use **yet** after a superlative to in- ADV: n ADV, dicate, for example, that something is the worst or the best of its kind up to the present time. ADV adv/-ed, ADV after superl ❑ *This is the BBC's worst idea yet... Her latest novel is her best yet. ...one of the toughest warnings yet delivered.* 5 You can use **yet** to say that there is still a possibility that something will happen. ADV: ADV before v = still ❑ *A negotiated settlement might yet be possible.* 6 You can use **yet** after expressions which refer to a period of time, when you want to say how much longer a situation will continue for. ADV: n ADV ❑ *Unemployment will go on rising for some time yet... Nothing will happen for a few years yet... They'll be ages yet.* 7 If you say that you have **yet to** do something, you mean that you have never done it, especially when this is surprising or bad. ADV: ADV to-inf ❑ *She has yet to spend a Christmas with her husband... He has been nominated three times for the Oscar but has yet to win.* 8 You can use **yet** to introduce a fact which is rather surprising after the previous fact you have just mentioned. CONJ = but ❑ *I don't eat much, yet I am a size 16... It is completely waterproof, yet light and comfortable.*

9 You can use **yet** to emphasize a word, especially when you are saying that something is surprising because it is more extreme than previous things of its kind, or a further case of them. ADV: ADV with adj/n/adv, usu ADV with compar [emphasis] ❑ *I saw yet another doctor... They would criticize me, or worse yet, pay me no attention... It is plain to see we will not have anything to eat yet again.* 10 You use **as yet** with negative statements to describe a situation that has existed up until the present time. PHRASE: PHR with cl [FORMAL] ❑ *As yet it is not known whether the crash was the result of an accident.*

**yew** /juː/ **(yews)** A **yew** or a **yew tree** is an evergreen tree. It has sharp leaves which are broad and flat, and red berries. N-VAR ♦ **Yew** is the wood of this tree. N-UNCOUNT

**Y-fronts** **Y-fronts** are men's or boys' underwear with an opening at the front. N-PLURAL [BRIT, TRADEMARK]

**Yid|dish** /jɪdɪʃ/ **Yiddish** is a language which comes mainly from German and is spoken by many Jewish people of European origin. N-UNCOUNT

**yield** /jiːld/ **(yields, yielding, yielded)** ♦◇◇ 1 If you **yield to** someone or something, you stop resisting them. VERB = give in V to n [FORMAL] ❑ *Will she yield to growing pressure for her to retire?... If the government does not yield, it should face sufficient military force to ensure its certain and swift defeat.* V 2 If you **yield** something that you have control of or responsibility for, you allow someone else to have control or responsibility for it. VERB = surrender [FORMAL] ❑ *He may yield control.* V n 3 If a moving person or a vehicle **yields**, they slow down or stop in order to allow other people or vehicles to pass in front of them. VERB [AM] ❑ *When entering a trail or starting a descent, yield to other skiers.* V to n *...examples of common signs like No Smoking or Yield.* V

✔ in BRIT, usually use **give way**

4 If something **yields**, it breaks or moves position because force or pressure has been put on it. VERB ❑ *The door yielded easily when he pushed it.* V 5 If an area of land **yields** a particular amount of a crop, this is the amount that is produced. You can also say that a number of animals **yield** a particular amount of meat. VERB = produce ❑ *Last year 400,000 acres of land yielded a crop worth $1.75 billion.* V n 6 A **yield** is the amount of food produced on an area of land or by a number of animals. N-COUNT: with supp ❑ *Polluted water lessens crop yields.* 7 If a tax or investment **yields** an amount of money or profit, this money or profit is obtained from it. VERB [BUSINESS] ❑ *It yielded a profit of at least $36 million.* V n 8 A **yield** is the amount of money or profit produced by an investment. N-COUNT: with supp, oft N of amount, N on n [BUSINESS] ❑ *The high yields available on the dividend shares made them attractive to private investors. ...the yield on a bank's investments.* 9 If something **yields** a result or piece of information, it produces it. VERB ❑ *This research has been in progress since 1961 and has yielded positive results.* V n

**yield|ing** /jiːldɪŋ/ A **yielding** surface or object is quite soft and will move or bend rather than staying stiff if you put pressure on it. ADJ ❑ *...the yielding ground. ...the soft yielding cushions.*

**yip** /jɪp/ **(yips, yipping, yipped)** If a dog or other animal **yips**, it gives a sudden short cry, often because of fear or pain. VERB = yelp [mainly AM] ❑ *Far up the west rim of the canyon, a coyote yipped twice.* V ♦ **Yip** is also a noun. N-COUNT: oft N of n ❑ *...a yip of pain.*

**yip|pee** /jɪpiː/ People sometimes shout **yippee** when they are very pleased or excited. EXCLAM

**YMCA** /waɪ em siː eɪ/ **(YMCAs)** **The YMCA** is a place where men can stay cheaply, which is run by the YMCA organization. N-COUNT: usu the N in sing **YMCA** is an abbreviation for 'Young Men's Christian Association'.

**yo** /joʊ/ People sometimes say **'yo'** to greet other people or to get their attention. CONVENTION [INFORMAL, SPOKEN] ❑ *Yo, Carl, great outfit man!*

**yob** /jɒb/ **(yobs)** If you call a boy or a man a **yob**, you disapprove of him because he behaves in a noisy, rude, and perhaps violent way in public. N-COUNT: usu with supp [disapproval] = lout [BRIT, INFORMAL] ❑ *Violent and dangerous yobs deserve to be locked up.*

**yob|bish** /jɒbɪʃ/ If you describe a boy or a man as **yobbish**, you disapprove of him because he behaves in a noisy, rude, and perhaps violent way in public. ADJ [disapproval] = loutish [BRIT, INFORMAL] ❑ *...yobbish football supporters.*

**yob|bo** /jɒboʊ/ **(yobbos)** A **yobbo** is the same as a **yob**. N-COUNT [BRIT, INFORMAL]

**yo|del** /joʊdᵊl/ **(yodels, yodelling, yodelled)**

✔ in AM, use **yodeling, yodeled**

When someone **yodels**, they sing normal notes with very high quick notes in between. VERB ❑ *You haven't lived till you've learned how to yodel at a tea dance in a mountain hut!* V ♦ **yo|del|ling** *Switzerland isn't all cow bells and yodelling, you know.* N-UNCOUNT

**yoga** /joʊgə/ 1 **Yoga** is a type of exercise in which you move your body into various positions in order to become more fit or flexible, to improve your breathing, and to relax your mind. N-UNCOUNT 2 **Yoga** is a philosophy which first developed in India, in which physical exercises and meditation are believed to help people to become calmer and united in spirit with God. N-UNCOUNT

**yo|ghurt** /jɒgəʳt, AM joʊ-/ → see **yogurt**.

**yogi** /joʊgi/ **(yogis)** A **yogi** is a person who has spent many years practising the philosophy of yoga, and is considered to have reached an advanced spiritual state. N-COUNT

**yo|gurt** /jɒgəʳt, AM joʊ-/ **(yogurts)** also **yoghurt**. **Yogurt** is a food in the form of a thick, slightly sour liquid that is made by adding bacteria to milk. N-VAR A **yogurt** is a small pot of yogurt.

**yoke** /joʊk/ **(yokes, yoking, yoked)** 1 If you say that people are under the **yoke of** a bad thing or person, you mean they are forced to live in a difficult or unhappy state because of that thing or person. N-SING: usu N of n, adj N [LITERARY] ❑ *People are still suffering under the yoke of slavery.* 2 A **yoke** is a long piece of wood which is tied across the necks of two animals such as oxen, in order to make them walk close together when they are pulling a plough. N-COUNT

3 If two or more people or things **are yoked together**, they are forced to be closely linked with each other. VERB ❑ *The introduction attempts to yoke the pieces together... The Auto Pact yoked Ontario into the United States economy... Farmers and politicians are yoked by money and votes.* V pl-n together, V n to/into n, be V-ed

**yo|kel** /joʊkᵊl/ **(yokels)** If you refer to someone as a **yokel**, you think they are uneducated and stupid because they come from the countryside. N-COUNT [disapproval] = bumpkin

**yolk** /joʊk/ **(yolks)** The **yolk** of an egg is the yellow part in the middle. N-VAR ❑ *Only the yolk contains cholesterol. ...buttered toast dipped in egg yolk.*

**Yom Kip|pur** /jɒm kɪpʊəʳ/ **Yom Kippur** is the religious holiday when Jewish people do not eat, but say prayers asking to be forgiven for the things they have done wrong. It is in September or October. N-UNCOUNT

**yon** /jɒn/ **Yon** is an old-fashioned or dialect word for 'that' or 'those'. ❑ *Don't let yon dog nod off.* **hither and yon** → see **hither**. DET

**yon|der** /jɒndəʳ/ **Yonder** is an old-fashioned or dialect word for 'over there'. ❑ *Now look yonder, just beyond the wooden post there.* ADV: ADV with v

**yonks** /jɒŋks/ **Yonks** means a very long time. [BRIT, INFORMAL] ❑ *...the most wonderful club I've been to for yonks.* N-PLURAL = *ages*

**yore** /jɔːʳ/ **Of yore** is used to refer to a period of time in the past. [JOURNALISM or LITERARY] ❑ *The images provoked nostalgia for the days of yore.* PHRASE: n PHR, *than* PHR = *of old*

**York|shire pud|ding** /jɔːʳkʃəʳ pʊdɪŋ/ **(Yorkshire puddings)** **Yorkshire pudding** is a British food which is made by baking a thick liquid mixture of flour, milk, and eggs. It is often eaten with roast beef. N-VAR

**you** /juː/ ◆◆◆

> **You** is the second person pronoun. **You** can refer to one or more people and is used as the subject of a verb or the object of a verb or preposition.

1 A speaker or writer uses **you** to refer to the person or people that they are talking or writing to. It is possible to use **you** before a noun to make it clear which group of people you are talking to. ❑ *When I saw you across the room I knew I'd met you before... You two seem very different to me... I could always talk to you about anything in the world... What is alternative health care? What can it do for you?... What you kids need is more exercise.* PRON 2 In spoken English and informal written English, **you** is sometimes used to refer to people in general. ❑ *Getting good results gives you confidence... In those days you did what you were told.* PRON

**you'd** /juːd/ 1 **You'd** is the usual spoken form of 'you had', especially when 'had' is an auxiliary verb. ❑ *I think you'd better tell us why you're asking these questions.* 2 **You'd** is the usual spoken form of 'you would'. ❑ *With your hair and your beautiful skin, you'd look good in bright colors.*

**you'll** /juːl/ **You'll** is the usual spoken form of 'you will'. ❑ *Promise me you'll take care of yourself... I think you'll find everything you need here.*

**young** /jʌŋ/ **(younger** /jʌŋgəʳ/, **youngest** /jʌŋgəst/**)** ◆◆◆ 1 A **young** person, animal, or plant has not lived or existed for very long and is not yet mature. ❑ *In Scotland, young people can marry at 16. ...a field of young barley... He played with his younger brother.* ADJ ≠ *old* ♦ **The young** are people who are young. ❑ *The association is advising pregnant women, the very young and the elderly to avoid such foods.* N-PLURAL: *the* N 2 You use **young** to describe a time when a person or thing was young. ❑ *In her younger days my mother had been a successful fashionwear saleswoman.* ADJ: ADJ n 3 Someone who is **young** in appearance or behaviour looks or behaves as if they are young. ❑ *I was twenty-three, I suppose, and young for my age.* ADJ 4 The **young** of an animal are its babies. ❑ *The hen was unable to feed its young.* N-PLURAL

**young gun** **(young guns)** You can use **young guns** to talk about people, especially young men, who have lots of energy and talent, and are becoming very successful. [JOURNALISM] ❑ *He may have been eclipsed by the young guns, but his films are still very popular.* N-COUNT: oft plural

**young|ish** /jʌŋɪʃ/ A **youngish** person is fairly young. ❑ *...a smart, dark-haired, youngish man.* ADJ

**young|ster** /jʌŋstəʳ/ **(youngsters)** Young people, especially children, are sometimes referred to as **youngsters**. ❑ *Other youngsters are not so lucky... I was only a youngster in 1935.* ◆◇◇ N-COUNT

**your** /jɔːʳ, jʊəʳ/ ◆◆◆

> **Your** is the second person possessive determiner. **Your** can refer to one or more people.

1 A speaker or writer uses **your** to indicate that something belongs or relates to the person or people that they are talking or writing to. ❑ *Emma, I trust your opinion a great deal... I left all of your messages on your desk... If you are unable to obtain the information you require, consult your telephone directory.* DET 2 In spoken English and informal written English, **your** is sometimes used to indicate that something belongs to or relates to people in general. ❑ *Pain-killers are very useful in small amounts to bring your temperature down... I then realized how possible it was to overcome your limitations.* DET 3 In spoken English, a speaker sometimes uses **your** before an adjective such as 'typical' or 'normal' to indicate that the thing referred to is a typical example of its type. ❑ *Stan Reilly is not really one of your typical Brighton Boys.* DET

**you're** /jɔːʳ, jʊəʳ/ **You're** is the usual spoken form of 'you are'. ❑ *Go to him, tell him you're sorry... I think you're expecting too much of me.*

**yours** /jɔːʳz, jʊəʳz/ ◆◇◇

> **Yours** is the second person possessive pronoun. **Yours** can refer to one or more people.

1 A speaker or writer uses **yours** to refer to something that belongs or relates to the person or people that they are talking or writing to. ❑ *I'll take my coat upstairs. Shall I take yours, Roberta?... I believe Paul was a friend of yours... If yours is a high-stress job, it is important that you learn how to cope.* PRON 2 People write **yours**, **yours sincerely**, or **yours faithfully** at the end of a letter before they sign their name. ❑ *With best regards, Yours, George... Yours faithfully, Michael Moore, London Business School.* CONVENTION **yours truly** → see **truly**.

**your|self** /jɔːʳself, jʊəʳ-/ **(yourselves)** ◆◆◇

> **Yourself** is the second person reflexive pronoun.

1 A speaker or writer uses **yourself** to refer to the person that they are talking or writing to. **Yourself** is used when the object of a verb or preposition refers to the same person as the subject of the verb. ❑ *Have the courage to be honest with yourself and about yourself... Your baby depends on you to look after yourself properly while you are pregnant... Treat yourselves to a glass of wine to help you relax at the end of the day.* PRON: v PRON, prep PRON 2 You use **yourself** to emphasize the person that you are referring to. ❑ *They mean to share the business between them, after you yourself are gone, Sir... I've been wondering if you yourselves have any idea why she came.* PRON [emphasis] 3 You use **yourself** instead of 'you' for emphasis or in order to be more polite when 'you' is the object of a verb or preposition. ❑ *A wealthy man like yourself is bound to make an enemy or two along the way.* PRON: v PRON, prep PRON [politeness] **by yourself** → see **by**.

**youth** /juːθ/ **(youths** /juːðz/**)** ◆◆◇ 1 Someone's **youth** is the period of their life during which they are a child, before they are a fully mature adult. ❑ *In my youth my ambition had been to be an inventor. ...the comic books of my youth.* N-UNCOUNT: usu poss N 2 **Youth** is the quality or state of being young. ❑ *Gregory was still enchanted with Shannon's youth and joy and beauty... The team is now a good mixture of experience and youth.* N-UNCOUNT 3 Journalists often refer to young men as **youths**, especially when they are reporting that the young men have caused trouble. ❑ *...gangs of youths who broke windows and looted shops.* N-COUNT 4 **The youth** are young people considered as a group. ❑ *He represents the opinions of the youth of today.* N-PLURAL: usu with poss

**youth club** **(youth clubs)** A **youth club** is a club where young people can go to meet each other and take part in various leisure activities. Youth clubs are often run by a church or local authority. ❑ *...the youth club disco.* N-COUNT

**youth|ful** /juːθfʊl/ Someone who is **youthful** behaves as if they are young or younger than they really are. ❑ *I'm a very youthful 50. ...youthful enthusiasm and high spirits.* ADJ

**youth hos|tel** **(youth hostels)** A **youth hostel** is a place where people can stay cheaply when they are travelling. N-COUNT

**you|th work|er** **(youth workers)** A **youth worker** is a person whose job involves providing support and social activities for young people, especially young people from poor backgrounds. [mainly BRIT] N-COUNT

**you've** /juːv/ **You've** is the usual spoken form of 'you have', especially when 'have' is an auxiliary verb. ❑ *Now you've got your degree, what will you do?... Many of the fruits you've tasted on your holidays can be found in supermarkets.*

**yowl** /jaʊl/ **(yowls, yowling, yowled)** If a person or an animal **yowls**, they make a long loud cry, especially because they are sad or in pain. ❑ *The dog began to yowl.* ♦ **Yowl** is also a noun. ❑ *Patsy could hardly be heard above the baby's yowls.* ♦ **yowl|ing** *I couldn't stand that yowling.* VERB; V; N-COUNT; N-UNCOUNT

**yo-yo** /joʊ joʊ/ **(yo-yos)** A **yo-yo** is a toy made of a round piece of wood or plastic attached to a piece of string. You play with the yo-yo by letting it rise and fall on the string. N-COUNT

**yr** **(yrs)** also **yr.** **yr** is a written abbreviation for **year**. ❑ *They are quite something for 2 yr olds.*

**yuan** /juːæn, AM -ɑːn/ **(yuan)** The **yuan** is the unit of money used in the People's Republic of China. ❑ *For most events, tickets cost one, two or three yuan.* ♦ **The yuan** is also used to refer to the Chinese currency system. ❑ *The yuan recovered a little; it now hovers around 8.2 to the dollar.* N-COUNT: num N; N-SING: *the* N

**Yu|go|slav** /juːgəslɑːv/ **(Yugoslavs)** **Yugoslav** means belonging or relating to the former Yugoslavia, or to its people or culture. ♦ A **Yugoslav** was a Yugoslav citizen, or a person of Yugoslav origin. ADJ; N-COUNT

**Yu|go|sla|vian** /juːgəslɑːviən/ **Yugoslavian** means the same as **Yugoslav**. ADJ

**yuk** /jʌk/ Some people say **'yuk'** when they think something is very unpleasant or disgusting. [INFORMAL] ❑ *'It's corned beef and cabbage,' said Malone. 'Yuk,' said Maureen.* EXCLAM

**Yule** /juːl/ **Yule** is an old-fashioned word for **Christmas**. N-UNCOUNT

**Yule|tide** /juːltaɪd/ **Yuletide** is the period of several days around and including Christmas Day. ❑ *...ideas for Yuletide food, drink and decorations.* N-UNCOUNT: oft N n

**yum** /jʌm/ People sometimes say **'yum'** or **'yum yum'** to show that they think something tastes or smells very good. [INFORMAL] EXCLAM

**yum|my** /jʌmi/ **Yummy** food tastes very good. [INFORMAL] ❑ *I'll bet they have yummy ice cream... It smells yummy.* ADJ

**yup|pie** /jʌpi/ **(yuppies)** A **yuppie** is a young person who has a well-paid job and likes to show that they have a lot of money by buying expensive things and living in an expensive way. ❑ *The Porsche 911 reminds me of the yuppie era.* N-COUNT [disapproval]

**YWCA** /waɪ dʌbəljuː siː eɪ/ **(YWCAs)** **The YWCA** is a place where women can stay cheaply, which is run by the YWCA organization. **YWCA** is an abbreviation for 'Young Women's Christian Association'. N-COUNT: usu *the* N in sing

**Z, z** /zed, AM ziː/ **(Z's, z's)** **Z** is the twenty-sixth and last letter of the English alphabet. N-VAR

**zany** /zeɪni/ **(zanier, zaniest)** **Zany** humour or a **zany** person is strange or eccentric in an amusing way. [INFORMAL] ❑ *...the zany humour of the Marx Brothers.* ADJ: usu ADJ n = wacky

**zap** /zæp/ **(zaps, zapping, zapped)** 1 To **zap** someone or something means to kill, destroy, or hit them, for example with a gun or in a computer game. [INFORMAL] ❑ *A guard zapped him with the stun gun.* 2 If you **zap** channels while watching television, you change channels using the remote control. [INFORMAL] ❑ *Men like to zap the TV channels, something that can drive certain women berserk.* 3 To **zap** something such as a computer file or document means to to delete it from the computer memory or to clear it from the screen. [COMPUTING, INFORMAL] VERB; V n; VERB; V n; VERB

**zap|per** /zæpəʳ/ **(zappers)** A **zapper** is a small device that you use to control a television, video, or stereo from a distance. [INFORMAL] N-COUNT = remote control

**zeal** /ziːl/ **Zeal** is great enthusiasm, especially in connection with work, religion, or politics. ❑ *...his zeal for teaching... Mr Lopez approached his task with a religious zeal.* N-UNCOUNT

**zeal|ot** /zelət/ **(zealots)** If you describe someone as a **zealot**, you think that their views and actions are very extreme, especially in following a particular political or religious belief. ❑ *He was forceful, but by no means a zealot.* N-COUNT [disapproval]

**zeal|ous** /zeləs/ Someone who is **zealous** spends a lot of time or energy in supporting something that they believe in very strongly, especially a political or religious ideal. ❑ *She was a zealous worker for charitable bodies.* ADJ

**zeb|ra** /zebrə, ziː-/ **(zebras** or **zebra)** A **zebra** is an African wild horse which has black and white stripes. N-COUNT

**zeb|ra cross|ing** **(zebra crossings)** In Britain, a **zebra crossing** is a place on the road that is marked with black and white stripes, where vehicles are supposed to stop so that people can walk across. N-COUNT

**zeit|geist** /zaɪtgaɪst/ The **zeitgeist** of a particular place during a particular period in history is the attitudes and ideas that are generally common there at that time, especially the attitudes and ideas shown in literature, philosophy, and politics. ❑ *He has caught the zeitgeist of rural life in the 1980s very well indeed.* N-SING

**Zen** /zen/ **Zen** or **Zen Buddhism** is a form of the Buddhist religion that concentrates on meditation rather than on studying religious writings. N-UNCOUNT

**zen|ith** /zenɪθ, AM ziː-/ The **zenith** of something is the time when it is most successful or powerful. ❑ *His career is now at its zenith.* N-SING: usu with poss = peak

**zero** /zɪəroʊ/ **(zeros** or **zeroes, zeroing, zeroed)** ◆◆◆ 1 **Zero** is the number 0. ❑ *Visibility at the city's airport came down to zero, bringing air traffic to a standstill. ...a scale ranging from zero to seven.* 2 **Zero** is a temperature of 0°. It is freezing point on the Centigrade and Celsius scales, and 32° below freezing point on the Fahrenheit scale. ❑ *It's a sunny late winter day, just a few degrees above zero... That night the mercury fell to thirty degrees below zero.* 3 You can use **zero** to say that there is none at all of the thing mentioned. ❑ *This new ministry was being created with zero assets.* NUM = nought; N-UNCOUNT; ADJ
♦ **zero in on** 1 To **zero in on** a target means to aim at it or move towards it. ❑ *He raised the binoculars again and zeroed in on an eleventh-floor room.* 2 If you **zero in on** a problem or subject, you give it your full attention. ❑ *Many of the other newspapers have not zeroed in on the problem.* PHRASAL VERB = home in on; V P P n; PHRASAL VERB = home in on; V P P n

**zero-emission** A **zero-emission** vehicle does not produce any dangerous gases. ❑ *...zero-emission electric cars.* ADJ: ADJ n

**zero-sum game** If you refer to a situation as a **zero-sum game**, you mean that if one person gains an advantage from it, someone else involved must suffer an equivalent disadvantage. ❑ *They believe they're playing a zero-sum game, where both compete for the same resources.* N-SING

**zero tol|er|ance** If a government or organization has a policy of **zero tolerance** of a particular type of behaviour or activity, they will not tolerate it at all. ❑ *They have a policy of zero tolerance for sexual harassment.* N-UNCOUNT: oft N prep

**zest** /zest/ **(zests)** 1 **Zest** is a feeling of pleasure and enthusiasm. ❑ *He has a zest for life and a quick intellect.* 2 **Zest** is a quality in an activity or situation which you find exciting. ❑ *Live interviews add zest and a touch of the unexpected to any piece of research.* 3 The **zest of** a lemon, orange, or lime is the outer skin when it is used to give flavour to something such as a cake or a drink. N-UNCOUNT: also *a* N, oft N *for* n; N-UNCOUNT; N-UNCOUNT: also N in pl, usu N *of* n, n N

**zig|zag** /zɪgzæg/ **(zigzags, zigzagging, zigzagged)** also **zig-zag.** 1 A **zigzag** is a line N-COUNT which has a series of angles in it like a continuous series of 'W's. ❑ *They staggered in a zigzag across the tarmac. ...a zigzag pattern.* [2] If you **zigzag**, you move forward by going at an angle first to one side then to the other. ❑ *I zigzagged down a labyrinth of alleys... Expertly he zigzagged his way across the field, avoiding the deeper gullies.* VERB V prep V *way* prep Also V

**zilch** /zɪltʃ/ **Zilch** means nothing. [INFORMAL] ❑ *At the moment these shares are worth zilch.* PRON = nothing

**zil|lion** /zɪljən/ **(zillions)** If you talk about a **zillion** people or things, you are emphasizing that there is an extremely large number of them. [INFORMAL] ❑ *It's been a zillion years since I've seen her.* NUM emphasis

**Zim|mer frame** /zɪmə^r freɪm/ **(Zimmer frames)** A **Zimmer frame** or a **Zimmer** is a frame that old or ill people sometimes use to help them walk. [BRIT, TRADEMARK] N-COUNT

✔ in AM, use **walker**

**zinc** /zɪŋk/ **Zinc** is a bluish-white metal which is used to make other metals such as brass, or to cover other metals such as iron to stop a brown substance called rust from forming. N-UNCOUNT

**zine** /ziːn/ **(zines)** A **zine** is a magazine about a particular subject, written by people who are interested in that subject rather than by professional journalists. N-COUNT = fanzine

**zing** /zɪŋ/ If you refer to the **zing** in someone or something, you mean the quality that makes them lively or interesting. [INFORMAL] ❑ *He just lacked that extra zing... There's nothing like fresh basil to put a zing into a tomato sauce.* N-UNCOUNT: also *a* N

**zing|er** /zɪŋə^r/ **(zingers)** A **zinger** is a witty remark, or something that is lively, interesting, amusing, or impressive. [AM, INFORMAL] ❑ *The panelists are left to compress their inquiries into one good zinger of a question... I thought it looked like a zinger.* N-COUNT

**Zi|on|ism** /zaɪənɪzəm/ **Zionism** is a movement which was originally concerned with establishing a political and religious state in Palestine for Jewish people, and is now concerned with the development of Israel. N-UNCOUNT

**Zi|on|ist** /zaɪənɪst/ **(Zionists)** [1] A **Zionist** is someone who believes in Zionism. ❑ *He was an ardent Zionist.* [2] **Zionist** means relating to Zionism. ❑ *...the Zionist movement.* N-COUNT ADJ: usu ADJ n

**zip** /zɪp/ **(zips, zipping, zipped)** [1] A **zip** or **zip fastener** is a device used to open and close parts of clothes and bags. It consists of two rows of metal or plastic teeth which separate or fasten together as you pull a small tag along them. [mainly BRIT] ❑ *He pulled the zip of his jacket down slightly.* N-COUNT

✔ in AM, usually use **zipper**

[2] When you **zip** something, you fasten it using a zip. ❑ *She zipped her jeans... I slowly zipped and locked the heavy black nylon bags.* VERB V n V n

♦ **zip up** [1] If you **zip up** something such as a piece of clothing or if it **zips up**, you are able to fasten it using its zip. ❑ *He zipped up his jeans... My jeans wouldn't zip up.* [2] To **zip up** a computer file means to compress it so that it needs less space for storage on disk and can be transmitted more quickly. [COMPUTING] ❑ *These files have been zipped up to take up less disk space so they take less time to download.* PHRASAL VERB V P n (not pron) V P PHRASAL VERB V P Also V P n

**zip code** **(zip codes)** Your **zip code** is a short sequence of letters and numbers at the end of your address, which helps the post office to sort the mail. [AM] N-COUNT

✔ in BRIT, use **postcode**

**zip disk** **(zip disks)** A **zip disk** is a computer disk, similar to a floppy disk but capable of storing greater amounts of data. [COMPUTING] ❑ *Zip disks can store the equivalent of three music CDs.* N-COUNT

**zip drive** **(zip drives)** A **zip drive** is a piece of computer equipment that you use for storing large amounts of data. [COMPUTING] ❑ *Zip drives help people to organise their important information.* N-COUNT

**zip file** **(zip files)** A **zip file** is a computer file containing data that has been compressed. [COMPUTING] ❑ *When you download the font it may be in a compressed format, such as a zip file.* N-COUNT

**zip|per** /zɪpə^r/ **(zippers)** A **zipper** is a device used to open and close parts of clothes and bags. It consists of two rows of metal or plastic teeth which separate or fasten together as you pull a small tag along them. [mainly AM] N-COUNT

✔ in BRIT, usually use **zip**

**zit** /zɪt/ **(zits)** **Zits** are spots on someone's skin, especially a young person's. [INFORMAL] N-COUNT = spot

**zith|er** /zɪðə^r/ **(zithers)** A **zither** is a musical instrument which consists of two sets of strings stretched over a flat box. You play the zither by pulling the strings with both hands. N-COUNT

**zo|di|ac** /zoʊdiæk/ **The zodiac** is a diagram used by astrologers to represent the positions of the planets and stars. It is divided into twelve sections, each of which has its own name and symbol. The zodiac is used to try to calculate the influence of the planets, especially on someone's life. ❑ *...the twelve signs of the zodiac.* N-SING: *the* N

**zom|bie** /zɒmbi/ **(zombies)** [1] You can describe someone as a **zombie** if their face or behaviour shows no feeling, understanding, or interest in what is going on around them. ❑ *Without sleep you will become a zombie at work.* [2] In horror stories and some religions, a **zombie** is a dead person who has been brought back to life. N-COUNT N-COUNT

**zone** /zoʊn/ **(zones, zoning, zoned)** [1] A **zone** is an area that has particular features or characteristics. ❑ *Many people have stayed behind in the potential war zone... The area has been declared a disaster zone. ...time zones.* [2] If an area of land **is zoned**, it is formally set aside for a particular purpose. ❑ *The land was not zoned for commercial purposes.* ♦ **zon|ing** *...the use of zoning to preserve agricultural land.* ◆◇◇ N-COUNT: oft n N VERB: usu passive *be* V-ed N-UNCOUNT

**zonked** /zɒŋkt/ If someone is **zonked** or **zonked out**, they are not capable of doing anything because they are very tired, drunk, or drugged. [INFORMAL] ADJ

**zoo** /zuː/ **(zoos)** A **zoo** is a park where live animals are kept so that people can look at them. ❑ *He took his son Christopher to the zoo. ...the penguin pool at London Zoo.* N-COUNT; N-IN-NAMES

**zo|ol|ogy** /zuːɒlədʒi, zoʊ-/ **Zoology** is the scientific study of animals. ♦ **zoo|logi|cal** ❑ *...zoological specimens.* ♦ **zo|olo|gist** /zuːɒlədʒɪst, zoʊ-/ **(zoologists)** *...a renowned zoologist and writer.* N-UNCOUNT ADJ: ADJ n N-COUNT

**zoom** /zuːm/ **(zooms, zooming, zoomed)** [1] If you **zoom** somewhere, you go there very quickly. [INFORMAL] ❑ *We zoomed through the gallery.* [2] If prices or sales **zoom**, they increase greatly in a very short time. ❑ *The economy shrank and inflation zoomed.* [3] A **zoom** is the same as a **zoom lens**. VERB = speed V prep/adv VERB = soar V N-COUNT

♦ **zoom in** If a camera **zooms in on** something that is being filmed or photographed, it gives a close-up picture of it. ❑ *...a tracking system which can follow a burglar round a building and zoom in on his face.* PHRASAL VERB V P *on* n

**zoom lens** **(zoom lenses)** A **zoom lens** is a lens that you can attach to a camera, which allows you to make the details larger or smaller while always keeping the picture clear. N-COUNT

**zuc|chi|ni** /zuːkiːni/ **(zucchini** or **zucchinis)** **Zucchini** are long thin vegetables with a dark green skin. [mainly AM] ➔ See picture on page 1712. N-VAR

✔ in BRIT, usually use **courgette**

**Zulu** /zuːluː/ **(Zulus)** [1] A **Zulu** is a member of a race of black people who live in Southern Africa. [2] **Zulu** is the language spoken by Zulus and also by many other black South Africans. N-COUNT N-UNCOUNT

**zy|gote** /zaɪgoʊt/ **(zygotes)** A **zygote** is an egg that has been fertilized by sperm, and which could develop into an embryo. [TECHNICAL] N-COUNT

# IRREGULAR VERBS

| INFINITIVE | PAST FORM (PRETERITE) | PAST PARTICIPLE | INFINITIVE | PAST FORM (PRETERITE) | PAST PARTICIPLE |
|---|---|---|---|---|---|
| **arise** | arose | arisen | **eat** | ate | eaten |
| **awake** | awoke | awoken | **fall** | fell | fallen |
| **be** | was, were | been | **feed** | fed | fed |
| **beat** | beat | beaten | **feel** | felt | felt |
| **become** | became | become | **fight** | fought | fought |
| **begin** | began | begun | **find** | found | found |
| **bend** | bent | bent | **fly** | flew | flown |
| **bet** | bet | bet | **forbid** | forbade | forbidden |
| **bind** | bound | bound | **forget** | forgot | forgotten |
| **bite** | bit | bitten | **freeze** | froze | frozen |
| **bleed** | bled | bled | **get** | got | got, |
| **blow** | blew | blown | | | *(AM)* gotten |
| **break** | broke | broken | **give** | gave | given |
| **bring** | brought | brought | **go** | went | gone |
| **build** | built | built | **grind** | ground | ground |
| **burn** | burned *or* | burned *or* | **grow** | grew | grown |
| | burnt | burnt | **hang** | hung *or* | hung *or* |
| **burst** | burst | burst | | hanged | hanged |
| **buy** | bought | bought | **have** | had | had |
| **can**[1] | could | – | **hear** | heard | heard |
| **cast** | cast | cast | **hide** | hid | hidden |
| **catch** | caught | caught | **hit** | hit | hit |
| **choose** | chose | chosen | **hold** | held | held |
| **cling** | clung | clung | **hurt** | hurt | hurt |
| **come** | came | come | **keep** | kept | kept |
| **cost** | cost *or* | cost *or* | **kneel** | knelt *or* | knelt *or* |
| | costed | costed | | kneeled | kneeled |
| **creep** | crept | crept | **know** | knew | known |
| **cut** | cut | cut | **lay** | laid | laid |
| **deal** | dealt | dealt | **lead**[1] | led | led |
| **dig** | dug | dug | **lean** | leaned *or* | leaned *or* |
| **dive** | dived, | dived | | leant | leant |
| | *(AM)* dove | | **leap** | leaped *or* | leaped *or* |
| **do** | did | done | | leapt | leapt |
| **draw** | drew | drawn | **learn** | learned *or* | learned *or* |
| **dream** | dreamed *or* | dreamed *or* | | learnt | learnt |
| | dreamt | dreamt | **leave** | left | left |
| **drink** | drank | drunk | **lend** | lent | lent |
| **drive** | drove | driven | **let** | let | let |

Numbers relate to superheadword numbers in the main dictionary text.

| INFINITIVE | PAST FORM (PRETERITE) | PAST PARTICIPLE |
|---|---|---|
| **lie**[1] | lay | lain |
| **light** | lit *or* lighted | lit *or* lighted |
| **lose** | lost | lost |
| **make** | made | made |
| **may** | might | – |
| **mean**[1] | meant | meant |
| **meet** | met | met |
| **pay** | paid | paid |
| **put** | put | put |
| **quit** | quit | quit |
| **read** | read | read |
| **rid** | rid | rid |
| **ride** | rode | ridden |
| **ring**[1] | rang | rung |
| **rise** | rose | risen |
| **run** | ran | run |
| **say** | said | said |
| **see** | saw | seen |
| **seek** | sought | sought |
| **sell** | sold | sold |
| **send** | sent | sent |
| **set**[2] | set | set |
| **shake** | shook | shaken |
| **shed** | shed | shed |
| **shine** | shone *or* shined | shone *or* shined |
| **shoe** | shod | shod |
| **shoot** | shot | shot |
| **show** | showed | shown |
| **shrink** | shrank | shrunk |
| **shut** | shut | shut |
| **sing** | sang | sung |
| **sink** | sank | sunk |
| **sit** | sat | sat |
| **sleep** | slept | slept |
| **slide** | slid | slid |
| **smell** | smelled *or* smelt | smelled *or* smelt |

| INFINITIVE | PAST FORM (PRETERITE) | PAST PARTICIPLE |
|---|---|---|
| **speak** | spoke | spoken |
| **speed** | speeded *or* sped | speeded *or* sped |
| **spell** | spelled *or* spelt | spelled *or* spelt |
| **spend** | spent | spent |
| **spill** | spilled *or* spilt | spilled *or* spilt |
| **spit** | spat, *(AM)* spit | spat, *(AM)* spit |
| **spoil** | spoiled *or* spoilt | spoiled *or* spoilt |
| **spread** | spread | spread |
| **spring** | sprang | sprung |
| **stand** | stood | stood |
| **steal** | stole | stolen |
| **stick**[2] | stuck | stuck |
| **sting** | stung | stung |
| **stink** | stank | stunk |
| **strike** | struck | struck *or* stricken |
| **swear** | swore | sworn |
| **sweep** | swept | swept |
| **swell** | swelled | swollen |
| **swim** | swam | swum |
| **swing** | swung | swung |
| **take** | took | taken |
| **teach** | taught | taught |
| **tear**[2] | tore | torn |
| **tell** | told | told |
| **think** | thought | thought |
| **throw** | threw | thrown |
| **wake** | woke, (*AM*) waked | woken |
| **wear** | wore | worn |
| **weep** | wept | wept |
| **win** | won | won |
| **wind**[2] | wound | wound |
| **write** | wrote | written |

Numbers relate to superheadword numbers in the main dictionary text.

# PREFIXES AND SUFFIXES

Prefixes are beginnings of words, which have a regular and predictable meaning. Suffixes are word endings which can be added to words, usually to make a new word with a similar meaning but different part of speech. Listed here are the most frequent prefixes, followed by the most frequent suffixes.

## Prefixes

**a-** forms adjectives which have 'not', 'without', or 'opposite' in their meaning. For example, *atypical* behaviour is not typical of someone.

**aero-** forms words, especially nouns, that refer to things or activities connected with air or movement through the air. For example, an *aeroplane* is a vehicle which flies through the air.

**astro-** is used to form words which refer to things relating to the stars or to outer space. For example, an *astronaut* is a person who travels in space.

**anti-** forms nouns and adjectives which refer to some sort of opposition. For example, an *anti-government* demonstration is a demonstration against the government.

**auto-** forms words which refer to someone doing something to, for, or about themselves. For example, your *autobiography* is an account of your life, which you write yourself.

**be-** can be added to a noun followed by an '-ed' suffix to form an adjective that indicates that a person is covered with or wearing the thing named. For example, a person who is *bespectacled* is wearing spectacles.

**bi-** forms nouns and adjectives which have 'two' as part of their meaning. For example, if someone is *bilingual*, they speak two languages.

**bi-** also forms adjectives and adverbs which refer to something happening twice in a period of time, or once in two consecutive periods of time. A *bimonthly* event happens twice a month, or once every two months.

**bio-** is used at the beginning of nouns and adjectives that refer to life or to the study of living things. For example, a *biography* is a book about someone's life.

**co-** forms verbs and nouns which refer to people sharing things or doing things together. For example, if two people *co-write* a book, they write it together. The *co-author* of a book is one of the people who has written it.

**counter-** forms words which refer to actions or activities that oppose another action or activity. For example, a *counter-measure* is an action you take to weaken the effect of another action or situation.

**de-** is added to some verbs to make verbs which mean the opposite. For example, to *deactivate* a mechanism means to switch it off so that it cannot work.

**demi-** is used at the beginning of some words to refer to something equivalent to half of the object or amount indicated by the rest of the word. For example, a *demigod* is a god which is half god and half human.

**dis-** can be added to some words to form words which have the opposite meaning. For example, if someone is *dishonest*, they are not honest.

**e-** is used to form words that indicate that something happens on or uses the Internet. 'e-' is an abbreviation for 'electronic'. For example, *e-business* is the buying, selling, and ordering of goods and services using the Internet.

**eco-** forms nouns and adjectives which refer to something related to the environment. For example, *eco-friendly* products do not harm the environment.

**em-** is a form of 'en-' that is used before 'b-', 'm-' and 'p-'. See **en-**.

**en-** is added to words to form verbs that describe the process of putting someone into a particular state, condition or place, or to form adjectives and nouns that describe that process or those states and conditions. For example, if you *endanger* someone or something, you put them in a situation where they might be harmed or destroyed.

**Euro-** is used to form words that describe or refer to something which is connected with Europe or with the European Union. For example, If you describe something as *Eurocentric*, you disapprove of it because it focuses on Europe and the needs of European people, often with the result that people in other parts of the world suffer in some way.

**ex-** forms words which refer to people who are no longer a particular thing. For example, an *ex-policeman* is someone who is no longer a policeman.

**extra-** forms adjectives which refer to something being outside or beyond something else. For example, Britain's *extra-European* commitments are its commitments outside Europe.

**extra-** also forms adjectives which refer to something having a large amount of a particular quality. For example, if something is *extra-strong*, it is very strong.

**geo-** is used at the beginning of words that refer to the whole of the world or to the Earth's surface. For example, *geology* is the study of the Earth's structure, surface, and origins.

**great-** is used before some nouns that refer to relatives. Nouns formed in this way refer to a relative who is a further generation away from you. For example, your *great-aunt* is the aunt of one of your parents.

**hyper-** forms adjectives which refer to people or things which have a large amount of, or too much of a particular quality. For example, *hyperinflation* is very extreme inflation.

**il-**, **im-**, **in-**, and **ir-** can be added to some words to form words which have the opposite meaning. For example, if an activity is *illegal*, it is not legal. If someone is *impatient*, they are not patient.

**inter-** forms adjectives which refer to things that move, exist, or happen between two or more people or things. For example, *inter-city* trains travel between cities.

**ir-**. See **il-**.

**kilo-** forms words which refer to things which have a thousand parts. For example, a *kilometre* is a thousand metres.

**macro-** is added to words in order to form new words that are technical and that refer to things which are large or involve the whole of something. For example *macroeconomic* means relating to the major, general features of a country's economy, such as the level of inflation or unemployment.

**mal-** forms words which refer to things that are bad or unpleasant, or that are unsuccessful or imperfect. For example, if a machine *malfunctions*, it does not work properly.

**mega-** forms words which refer to units which are a million times bigger. For example, a *megawatt* is a million watts.

**micro-** forms nouns which have 'small' as part of their meaning. For example, a *micro-organism* is a very small living thing that you cannot see with the naked eye.

**mid-** forms nouns and adjectives which refer to the middle part of a particular period of time, or the middle part of a particular place. For example, *mid-June* is the middle of June.

**milli-** forms nouns which refer to units which are a thousand times smaller. For example, a *millimetre* is a thousandth of a metre.

**mini-** forms nouns which refer to things which are a smaller version of something else. For example, a *minibus* is a small bus.

**mis-** forms verbs and nouns which refer to something being done badly or wrongly. For example, if you *miscalculate* a figure, you wrongly calculate it.

**mono-** forms nouns and adjectives which have 'one' or 'single' as part of their meaning. For example, *monogamy* is the custom of being married to only one person.

**multi-** forms adjectives which refer to something that consists of many things of a particular kind. For example, a *multi-coloured* object has many different colours.

**narco-** is added to words to form new words that relate to illegal narcotics. For example, a *narco-trafficker* is a person who illegally buys or sells narcotics.

**neo-** forms nouns and adjectives which refer to modern versions or styles and particular groups of the past. For example, *neo-classical* architecture is based on ancient Greek or Roman architecture.

**neuro-** is used to form words that refer to or relate to a nerve or the nervous system. For example, *neurology* is the study of the structure, function, and diseases of the nervous system.

**non-** forms nouns and adjectives which refer to people or things that do not have a particular quality or characteristic. For example, a *non-smoker* does not smoke. A *non-fatal* accident is not fatal.

**non-** also forms nouns which refer to situations where a particular action has not taken place. For example, someone's *non-attendance* at a meeting is the fact of their not having attended the meeting.

**out-** forms verbs which refer to an action as being done better by one person than by another. For example, if you can *outswim* someone, you can swim further or faster than they can.

**over-** forms words which refer to a quality of action that exists or is done to too great an extent. For example, if someone is being *over-cautious*, they are being too cautious.

**pan-** is added to the beginning of adjectives and nouns to form other adjectives and nouns that describe something as being connected with all places or people of a particular kind. For example, a *pandemic* is an occurrence of a disease that affects many people over a very wide area.

**para-** forms nouns and adjectives which refer to people or things which are similar to other things. For example, a *paramilitary* organization is organized like an army. A *paramedic* is a person whose training is similar to that of a nurse and who helps to do medical work.

**para-** also forms nouns and adjectives which refer to situations which are unusual or more important than normal. For example, a *paranormal* event cannot be explained by scientific laws and is thought to involve strange, unknown forces.

**part-** forms words which refer to something that is partly but not completely a particular thing. For example, *part-baked* bread is only partly baked.

**poly-** forms nouns and adjectives which have 'many' as part of their meaning. For example, a *polysyllabic* word contains many syllables.

**post-** forms words that refer to something that takes place after a particular date, period, or event. For example, a *post-Christmas* sale takes place just after Christmas.

**pre-** forms words that refer to something that takes place before a particular date, period, or event. For example, a *pre-election* rally takes place just before an election.

**pro-** forms adjectives which refer to people who strongly support a particular person or thing. For example, if you are *pro-democracy*, you support democracy.

**proto-** is used to form adjectives and nouns which indicate that something is in the early stages of its development. For example, a *prototype* is a new type of machine or device which is not yet ready to be made in large numbers and sold.

**pseudo-** forms nouns and adjectives which refer to something which is not really what is seems or claims to be. For example, a *pseudo-science* is something that claims to be a science, but is not.

**psycho-** is added to words in order to form other words which describe or refer to things connected with the mind or with mental processes. For example, a *psychoanalyst* is someone who treats people who have mental problems.

**re-** forms verbs and nouns which refer to an action or process being repeated. For example, if you *re-read* something, you read it again.

**semi-** forms nouns and adjectives which refer to people and things that are partly, but not completely, in a particular state. For example, if you are *semi-conscious*, you are partly, but not wholly, conscious.

**sub-** forms nouns which refer to things that are part of a larger thing. For example, a *subcommittee* is a small committee made up of members of a larger committee.

**sub-** also forms adjectives which refer to people or things that are inferior. For example, *substandard* living conditions are inferior to normal living conditions.

**super-** forms nouns and adjectives which refer to people and things that are larger, better, or more advanced than others. For example, a *super-fit* athlete is extremely fit, and a *supertanker* is a very large tanker.

**techno-** is used at the beginning of words that refer to technology. For example, if you refer to someone as a *technophobe*, you mean that they do not like new technology, such as computers or mobile telephones, and are afraid to use it.

**trans-** is used to form adjectives which indicate that something moves or enables travel from one side of an area to another. For example, *transatlantic* flights go across the Atlantic.

**trans-** is also used to form words which indicate that someone or something moves from one group, thing, state or place to another. For example, a *blood transfusion* is a process in which blood is injected into the body of a person who is badly injured or ill.

**tri-** forms nouns and adjectives which have 'three' as part of their meaning. For example, a *tricycle* is a cycle with three wheels.

**ultra-** forms adjectives which refer to people and things that possess a quality to a very large degree. For example, an *ultra-light* fabric is extremely light.

**un-** can be added to some words to form words which have the opposite meaning. For example, if something is *unacceptable*, it is not acceptable.

**under-** forms words which refer to an amount or value being too low or not enough. For example, if someone is *underweight*, their weight is lower than it should be.

**vice-** is used before a rank or title to indicate that someone is next in importance to the person who holds the rank or title mentioned. For example, a *vice-president* is next in importance to the president.

## Suffixes

**-ability** and **-ibility** replace '-able' and '-ible' at the end of adjectives to form nouns which refer to a particular state or quality. For example, *reliability* is the state or quality of being reliable.

**-able** and **-ible** forms adjectives which indicate what someone or something can have done to them. For example, if something is *readable*, it can be read.

**-al** forms adjectives which indicate what something is connected with. For example, *environmental* problems are problems connected with the environment.

**-ally** is added to adjectives ending in '-ic' to form adverbs which indicate how something is done or what something relates to. For example, if something is done *enthusiastically*, it is done in an enthusiastic way.

**-ance**, **-ence**, **-ancy** and **-ency** form nouns which refer to a particular action, state, or quality. For example, *brilliance* is the state or quality of being brilliant, and *reappearance* is the action of reappearing.

**-ancy**. See **-ance**.

**-ation**, **-ication**, **-sion** and **-tion** form nouns which refer to a state or process, or to an instance of that process. For example, the *protection* of the environment is the process of protecting it.

**-cy** forms nouns which refer to a particular state or quality. For example, *accuracy* is the state or quality of being accurate.

**-ed** is added to verbs to make the past tense and past participle. Past participles formed are often used as adjectives which indicate that something has been affected in some way. For example, *cooked* food is food that has been cooked.

**-ence**. See **-ance**.

**-ency**. See **-ancy**.

**-er** and **-or** form nouns which refer to a person who performs a particular action, often because it is their job. For example, a *teacher* is someone who teaches.
**-er** and **-or** also form nouns which refer to tools and machines that perform a particular action. For example, a *mixer* is a machine that mixes things.

**-er** is also added to many short adjectives to form comparatives. For example, the comparative of 'nice' is *nicer* and the comparative of 'happy' is *happier.* You also add it to some adverbs that do not end in '-ly'. For example, the comparative of 'soon' is *sooner.*

**-est** is added to many short adjectives to form superlatives. For example, the superlative of 'nice' is *nicest*, and the superlative of 'happy' is *happiest.* You also add it to some adverbs that do not end in '-ly'. For example, the superlative of 'soon' is *soonest.*

**-fold** combines with numbers to form adverbs which say how much an amount has increased by. For example, if an amount increases *fourfold*, it is four times greater than it was originally.

**-ful** forms nouns which refer to the amount of a substance that something contains or can contain. For example, a *handful* of sand is the amount of sand that you can hold in your hand.

**-ibility**. See **-ability**.

**-ible**. See **-able**.

**-ic** forms adjectives which indicate that something or someone is connected with a particular thing. For example, *photographic* equipment is equipment connected with photography.

**-ication**. See **-ation**.

**-icity** replaces **-ic** at the end of adjectives to form nouns referring to the state, quality, or behaviour described by the adjective. For example, *authenticity* refers to the quality of being authentic.

**-ify** is used at the end of verbs that refer to making something or someone different in some way. For example, if you *simplify* something, you make it easier to understand or you remove the things which make it complex.

**-ing** is added to verbs to make the **-ing** form, or present participle. Present participle forms are often used as adjectives describing a person or thing who is doing something. For example, a *sleeping* baby is a baby that is sleeping, and an *amusing* joke is a joke that amuses people. Present participle forms are also used as nouns which refer to activities. For example, if you say you like *dancing*, you mean that you like to dance.

**-ise**. See **-ize**.

**-ish** forms adjectives which indicate that someone or something has a quality to a small extent. For example, if you say that something is *largish*, you mean it is fairly large, and something that is *yellowish* is slightly yellow in colour.

**-ish** also forms words that indicate that a particular time or age mentioned is approximate. For example, if someone is *fortyish*, they are about forty years old.

**-ism** forms nouns which refer to particular beliefs, or to behaviour based on these beliefs. For example, *professionalism* is behaviour that is professional, and *racism* is the beliefs and behaviour of a racist.

**-ist** replaces '-ism' at the end of nouns to form nouns and adjectives. The nouns refer to the people who have particular beliefs. For example, a *fascist* is someone who supports fascism. The adjectives indicate that something is related to or is based on particular beliefs.

**-ist** also forms nouns which refer to people who do a particular kind of work. For example, a *geologist* is someone who works in the field of geology.

**-ist** also forms nouns which refer to people who play a particular musical instrument, often as their job. For example, a *violinist* is someone who plays the violin.

**-ity** forms nouns which refer to a particular state or quality. For example, *solidity* is the state or quality of being solid.

**-ize** is used at the end of many verbs to describe processes by which things or people are brought into a new state. For example, to *standardize* things means to change them so that they all have the same features. The spelling **-ise** is also used, especially in British English.

**-less** forms adjectives which indicate that someone or something does not have a particular thing. For example, someone who is *childless* does not have any children.

**-logical**. See **-ological**.

**-logist**. See **-ologist**.

**-logy**. See **-ology**.

**-ly** forms adverbs which indicate how something is done. For example, if someone whistles *cheerfully*, they whistle in a cheerful way.

**-ment** forms nouns which refer to the process of making or doing something, or to the result of this process. For example, *assessment* is the process of assessing something or the judgment made as a result of assessing it.

**-nd** is added to written numbers ending in 2, except for numbers ending in 12, in order to form ordinal numbers, for example, *22nd February, 2nd edition.*

**-ness** forms nouns which refer to a particular state or quality. For example, *gentleness* is the state or quality of being gentle.

**-ological** or **-logical** is used to replace **-ology** or **-logy** at the end of nouns in order to form adjectives that describe something as relating to a particular science or subject. For example, *biological* means relating to biology.

**-ologist** or **-logist** is used to replace **-ology** or **-logy** at the end of nouns in order to form other nouns that refer to people who are concerned with a particular science or subject. For example, a *biologist* is concerned with biology.

**-ology** or **-logy** is used at the end of some nouns that refer to a particular science or subject. For example, *biology* is the science which is concerned with the study of living things.

**-or**. See **-er**.

**-ous** forms adjectives which indicate that someone or something has a particular quality. For example, someone who is *courageous* shows courage.

**-phile** occurs at the end of words which refer to someone who has a very strong liking for people or things of a particular kind. For example, if you describe a non-British person as an *Anglophile*, you mean that they admire Britain and British culture.

**-phobe** occurs at the end of words which refer to someone who has a very strong irrational fear or hatred of people or things of a particular kind. For example, if you refer to someone as a *technophobe*, you mean that they do not like new technology, such as computers or mobile telephones, and are afraid to use it.

**-phobia** occurs at the end of words which refer to a very strong irrational fear or hatred of something. For example, someone who suffers from *claustrophobia* feels very uncomfortable or anxious when they are in small or enclosed places.

**-phobic** occurs at the end of words which describe something relating to a strong, irrational fear or hatred of people or things of a particular kind. For example, you describe a place or situation as *claustrophobic* when it makes you feel uncomfortable and unhappy because you are enclosed or restricted.

**-rd** is added to written numbers ending in 3, except for numbers ending in 13, in order to form ordinal numbers, for example, *September 3rd, the 33rd Boston Marathon.*

**-sion**. See **-ation**.

**-st** is added to written numbers ending in 1 except for numbers ending in 11, in order to form ordinal numbers, for example, *1st August 1993, the 101st Airborne Division.*

**-th** is added to written numbers ending in 4, 5, 6, 7, 8, 9, 10, 11, 12 or 13 in order to form ordinal numbers, for example, *6th Avenue, the 25th amendment to the American Constitution.*

**-tion**. See **-ation**.

**-y** forms adjectives which indicate that something is full of something else or covered in it. For example, if something is *dirty*, it is covered with dirt.

**-y** also forms adjectives which mean that something is like something else. For example, if something tastes *chocolatey*, it tastes like chocolate, although it is not actually chocolate.

# FREQUENCY BANDS

Information on the frequency of words in COBUILD is uniquely given using three frequency bands, shown by blue diamonds in the Extra Column, so that you can see immediately how important a word is. The most frequent words have three diamonds, the next most frequent two, and the ones which are less frequent have one diamond. Words which occur less frequently still, but which deserve an entry in the dictionary, do not have any blue diamonds.

The words in the top frequency band are of immense importance to learners because many of them are the common grammar words such as **the**, **and**, **of** and **to**, which are an essential part of the way we put words together. Also, in this band are the very frequent vocabulary items, such as **like**, **go**, **paper**, **return**, and so on. In order to help you become familiar with all of these core words, we have listed the words in the top band on the following pages.

a
able
about
accept
accord
according to
account
across
act
action
actually
add
after
again
against
age
ago
agree
aid
air
all
allow
almost
along
already
also
although
always
among
and
announce
another
answer
any
anything
appear
area
arm
army
around
art
as
ask
at
attack
attempt
authority
available
away
back
bad
bank
base
based
be
beat
because
become
before
begin
behind
believe
best
better
between
big
billion
bit
bite
black
blue
body
book
both
boy
break
bring
brother
brown
build
building
business
but
buy
by
call
campaign
can
capital
car
care
carry
case
cause
central
centre
century
chance
change
charge
chief
child
city
claim
class
clear
close
club
colour
come
coming
committee
common
community
company
complete
concern
condition
conference
consider
continue
control
cost
could
council
country
course
court
cover
create
cup
current
cut
daughter
day
deal
decide
decision
demand
department
describe
design
develop
development
die
different
difficult
direct
director
do
dollar
door
down
draw
drive
drug
during
each
early
east
easy
economic
economy
effect
effort
eight
eighteen
eighty
either
election
eleven
else
end
enough
even
event
ever
every
everything
example
expect
experience
eye
face
fact
fail
fall
family
far
father
fear
feel
few
fifteen
fifty
fight
figure
film
final
financial
find
firm
first
five
fly
follow
food
foot
for
force
foreign
form
former
forty
four
fourteen
free
friend
from
front
full
fund
further
future
game
general
get
girl
give
go
going
good
got
government
great
green
ground
group
grow
half
hand
happen
hard
have
he
head
health
hear
help
her
here
herself
high
him
himself
his
history
hit
hold
home
hope
hospital
host
hour
house
how
however
human
hundred
husband
I
idea
if
important
in
include
including
increase
independent
industry
information
interest
international
into
issue
it
its
itself

job
join
just
keep
kill
kind
know
labour
land
large
last
late
later
laugh
law
lead
leader
learn
least
leave
left
less
let
letter
level
life
like
likely
line
list
little
live
local
long
look
lose
lot
love
low
main
major
make
man
many
market
match
matter
may
me
mean
meet
meeting
member
middle
might
military
million
mind
mine
minister
minute

miss
moment
money
month
more
morning
most
mother
move
much
music
must
my
name
nation
national
near
need
never
new
news
next
night
nine
nineteen
ninety
no
north
not
nothing
now
number
of
of course
off
offer
office
officer
official
often
oil
old
on
once
one
only
open
operate
operation
or
order
other
our
out
outside
over
own
page
paper
parent
part

party
pass
past
pay
peace
people
per cent
perhaps
person
photo
place
plan
plant
play
player
point
police
policy
political
position
possible
pound
power
president
press
pressure
price
Prime Minister
probably
problem
process
produce
product
programme
provide
public
put
question
quick
quite
race
radio
raise
rate
rather
reach
read
real
really
reason
receive
recent
record
red
release
remain
remember
report
research
result
return

right
rise
road
role
room
rule
run
sale
same
say
school
season
second
secretary
security
see
seem
sell
send
sense
serious
service
set
seven
seventeen
seventy
several
share
she
short
should
show
side
sign
since
single
sister
sit
situation
six
sixteen
sixty
small
so
social
society
some
something
son
soon
sort
sound
south
speak
special
spend
staff
stage
stand
star
start

state
stay
step
still
stop
story
street
strong
student
study
such
suggest
support
sure
system
take
talk
tax
team
tell
ten
term
test
than
thank
that
the
their
them
themselves
then
there
these
they
thing
think
thirteen
thirty
this
those
though
thought
thousand
three
through
time
to
today
together
too
top
total
towards
town
trade
try
turn
twelve
twenty
twice
two

under
understand
union
university
until
up
us
use
value
very
view
visit
vote
wait
walk
wall
want
war
watch
water
way
we
week
well
west
what
when
where
whether
which
while
white
who
whole
whose
why
wide
wife
will
win
with
within
without
woman
word
work
worker
working
world
would
write
yeah
year
yellow
yes
yesterday
yet
you
young
your
zero

# Housing

aerial [BRIT]/antenna [AM]
chimney pot
tiles
roof
chimney
chimney stack
wall
gable
lintel
gutter
eaves
sash window
drainpipe
windowsill
bricks
porch
front door
garage
door bell
letterbox
dustbin [BRIT]/
garbage can [AM]
doorstep
bay window
path
flowerbed
hedge
gate
lawn
fence

# Housing

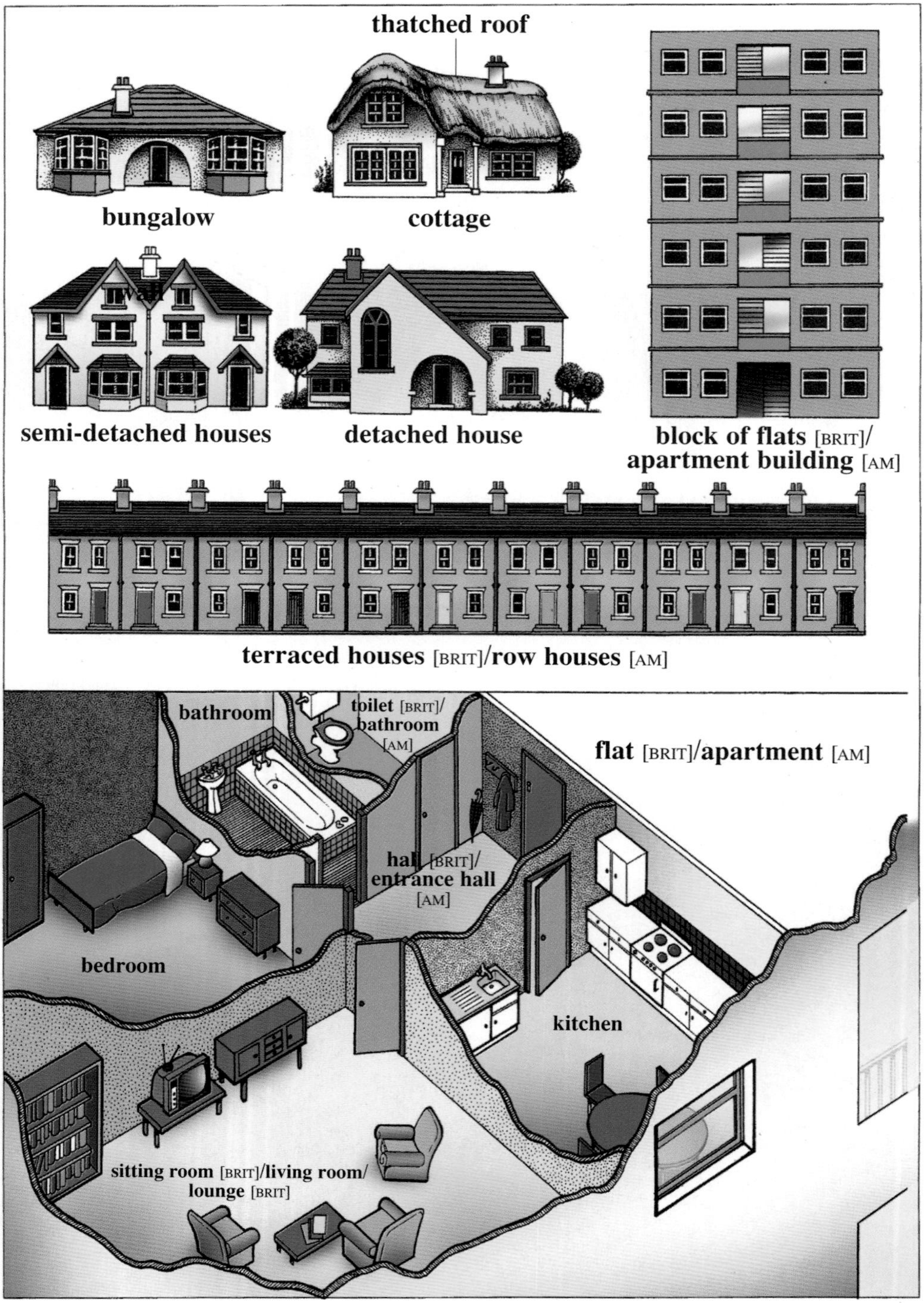
thatched roof
bungalow
cottage
semi-detached houses
wall
detached house
block of flats [BRIT]/
apartment building [AM]
terraced houses [BRIT]/row houses [AM]
bathroom
toilet [BRIT]/
bathroom
[AM]
flat [BRIT]/apartment [AM]
hall [BRIT]/
entrance hall
[AM]
bedroom
kitchen
sitting room [BRIT]/living room/
lounge [BRIT]

# Car

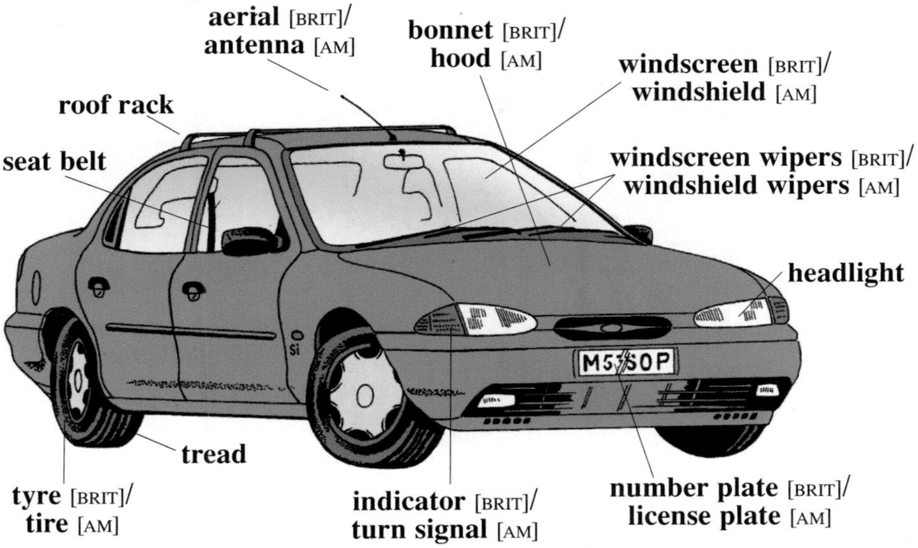

aerial [BRIT]/
antenna [AM]
bonnet [BRIT]/
hood [AM]
windscreen [BRIT]/
windshield [AM]
roof rack
seat belt
windscreen wipers [BRIT]/
windshield wipers [AM]
headlight
M53SOP
tread
tyre [BRIT]/
tire [AM]
indicator [BRIT]/
turn signal [AM]
number plate [BRIT]/
license plate [AM]


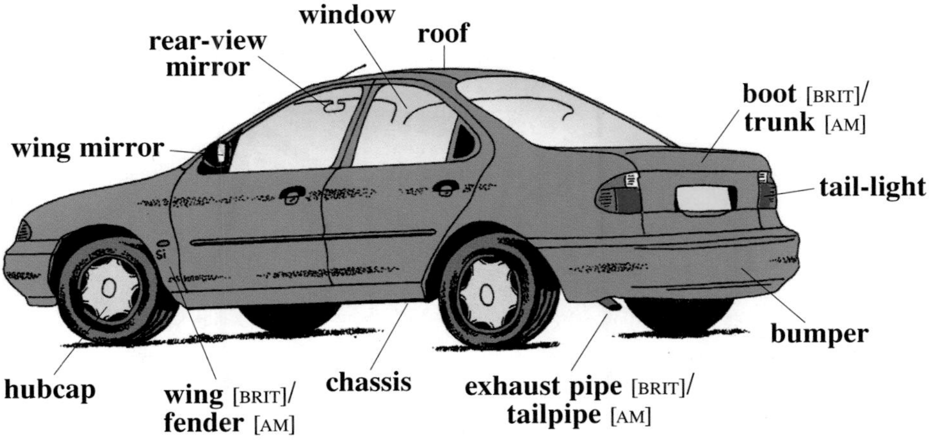

window
rear-view
mirror
roof
boot [BRIT]/
trunk [AM]
wing mirror
tail-light
bumper
hubcap
wing [BRIT]/
fender [AM]
chassis
exhaust pipe [BRIT]/
tailpipe [AM]

# Car and Bicycle

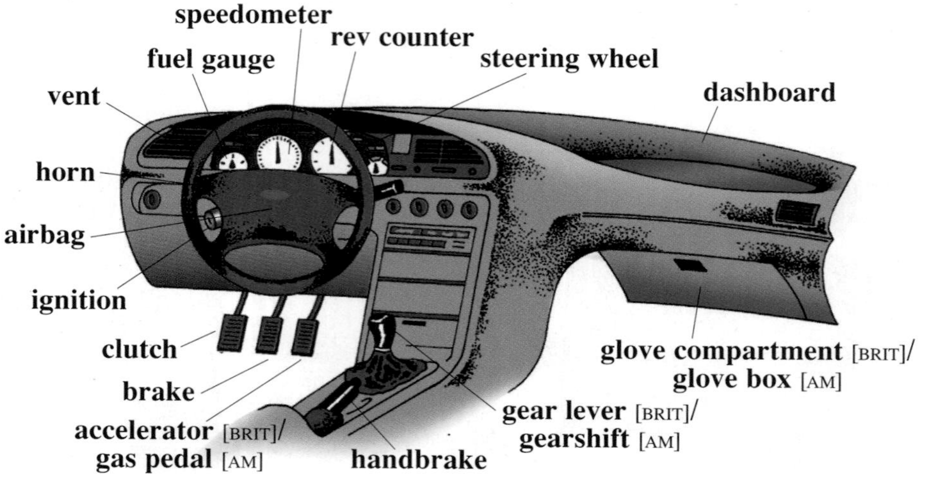
speedometer
rev counter
fuel gauge
steering wheel
vent
dashboard
horn
airbag
ignition
clutch
brake
accelerator [BRIT]/
gas pedal [AM]
handbrake
gear lever [BRIT]/
gearshift [AM]
glove compartment [BRIT]/
glove box [AM]

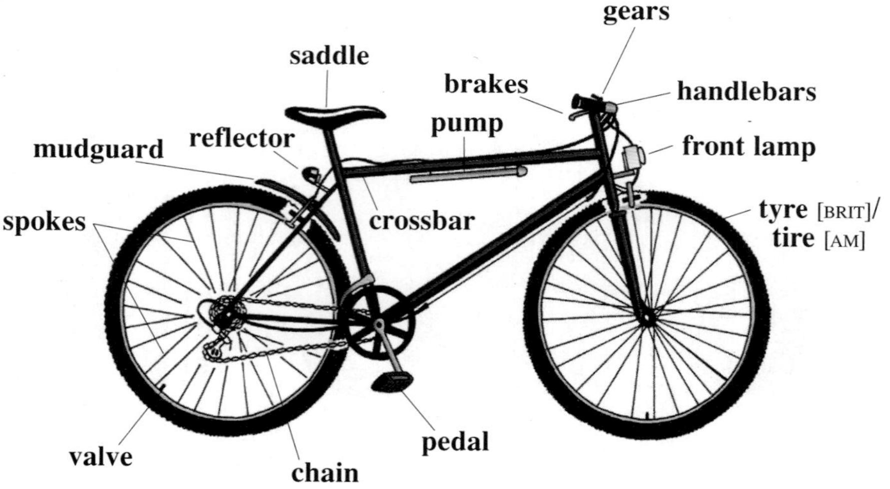
gears
saddle
brakes
handlebars
pump
reflector
mudguard
front lamp
spokes
crossbar
tyre [BRIT]/
tire [AM]
valve
chain
pedal

# Tools

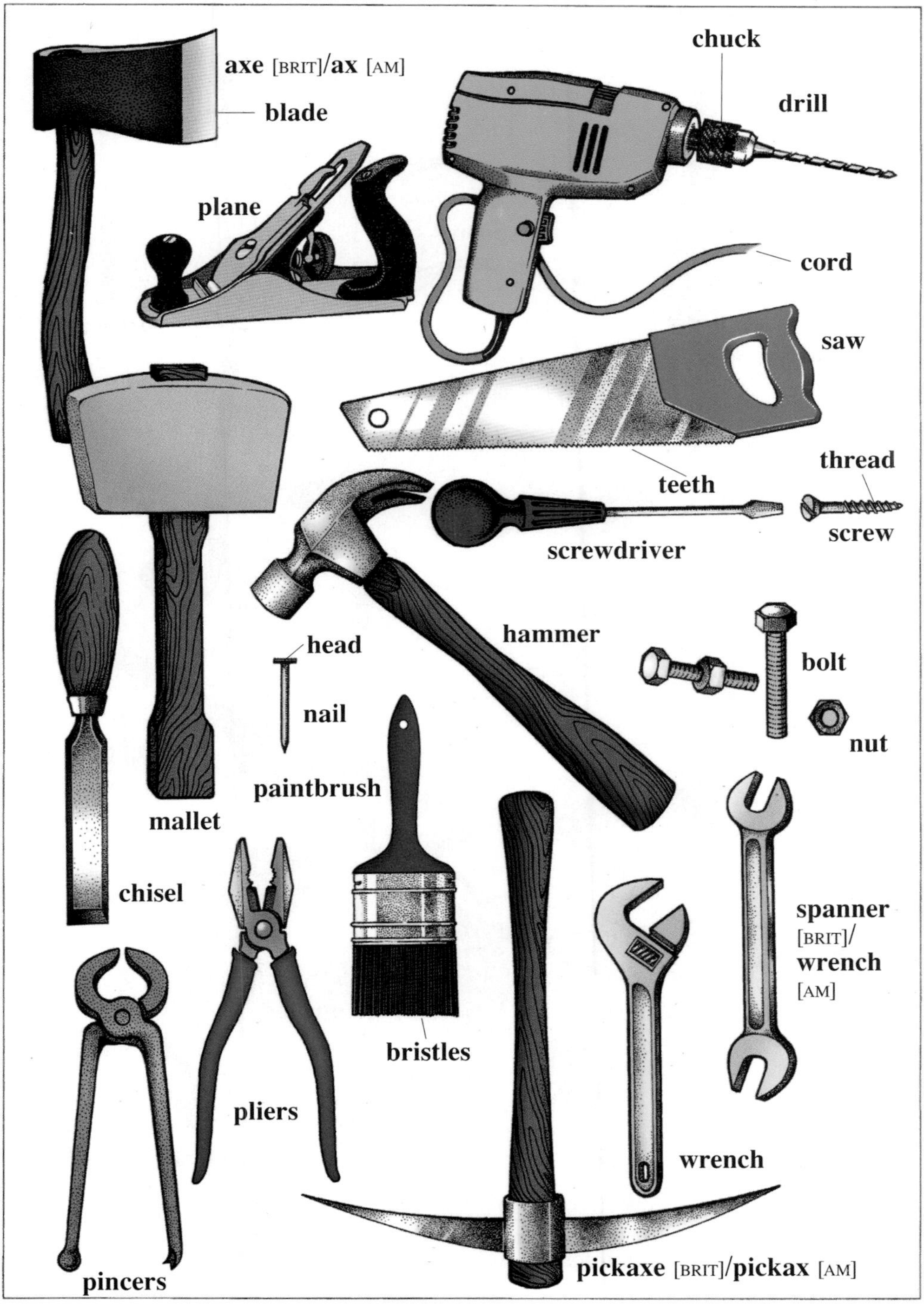
axe [BRIT]/ax [AM]
blade
chuck
drill
plane
cord
saw
thread
teeth
screw
screwdriver
hammer
head
bolt
nail
nut
paintbrush
mallet
chisel
spanner [BRIT]/ wrench [AM]
bristles
pliers
wrench
pincers
pickaxe [BRIT]/pickax [AM]

# Kitchen Utensils

whisk
spatula
fork
spoon
funnel
corkscrew
lid
potato peeler
ladle
handle
saucepan
pressure cooker
frying pan
sieve
bowl
fish slice
grater
knives
tin opener [BRIT]/ can opener [AM]
scissors

# Fruit

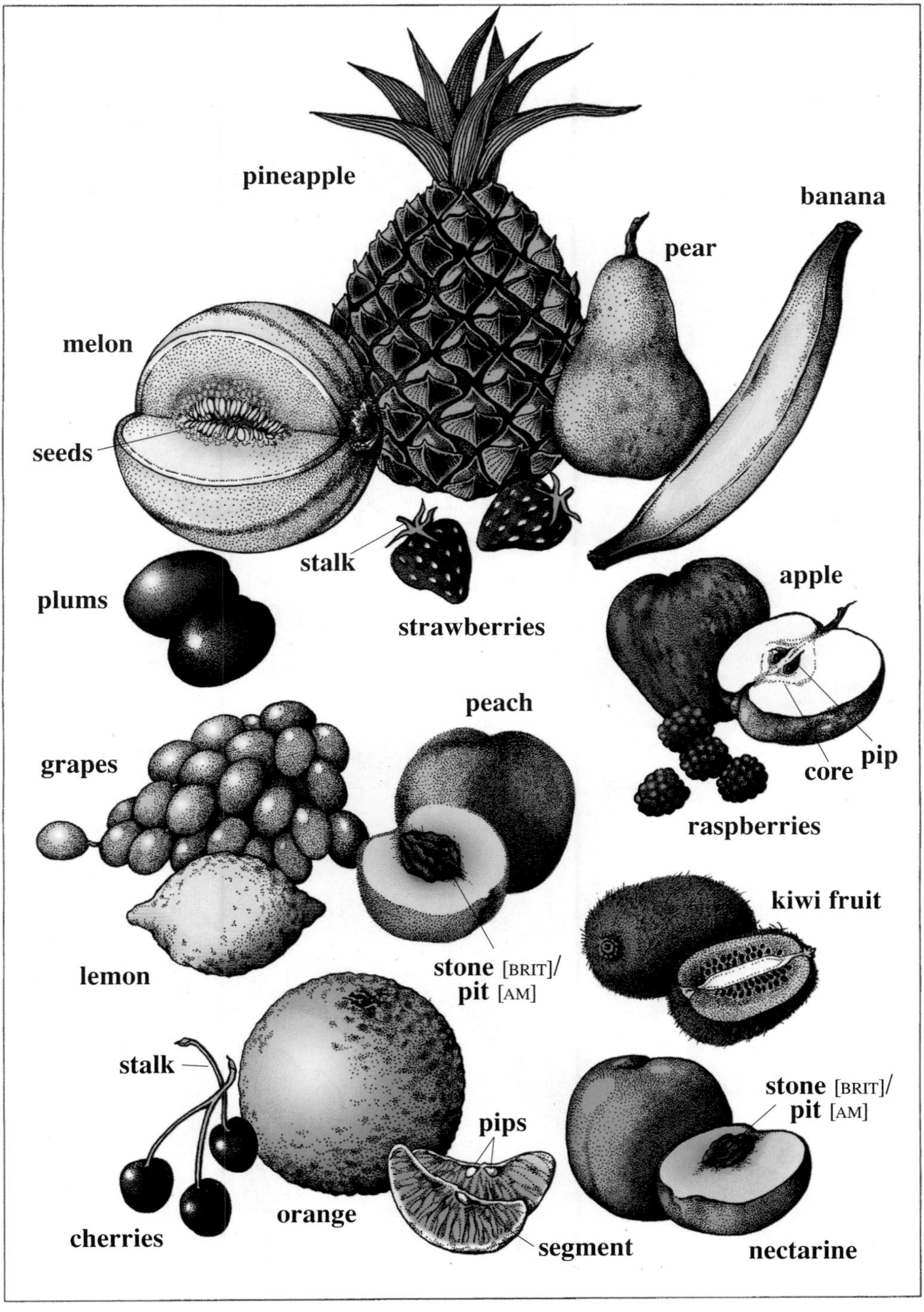
pineapple
banana
pear
melon
seeds
stalk
plums
strawberries
apple
peach
grapes
pip
core
raspberries
kiwi fruit
lemon
stone [BRIT]/
pit [AM]
stalk
stone [BRIT]/
pit [AM]
pips
orange
cherries
segment
nectarine

# Vegetables

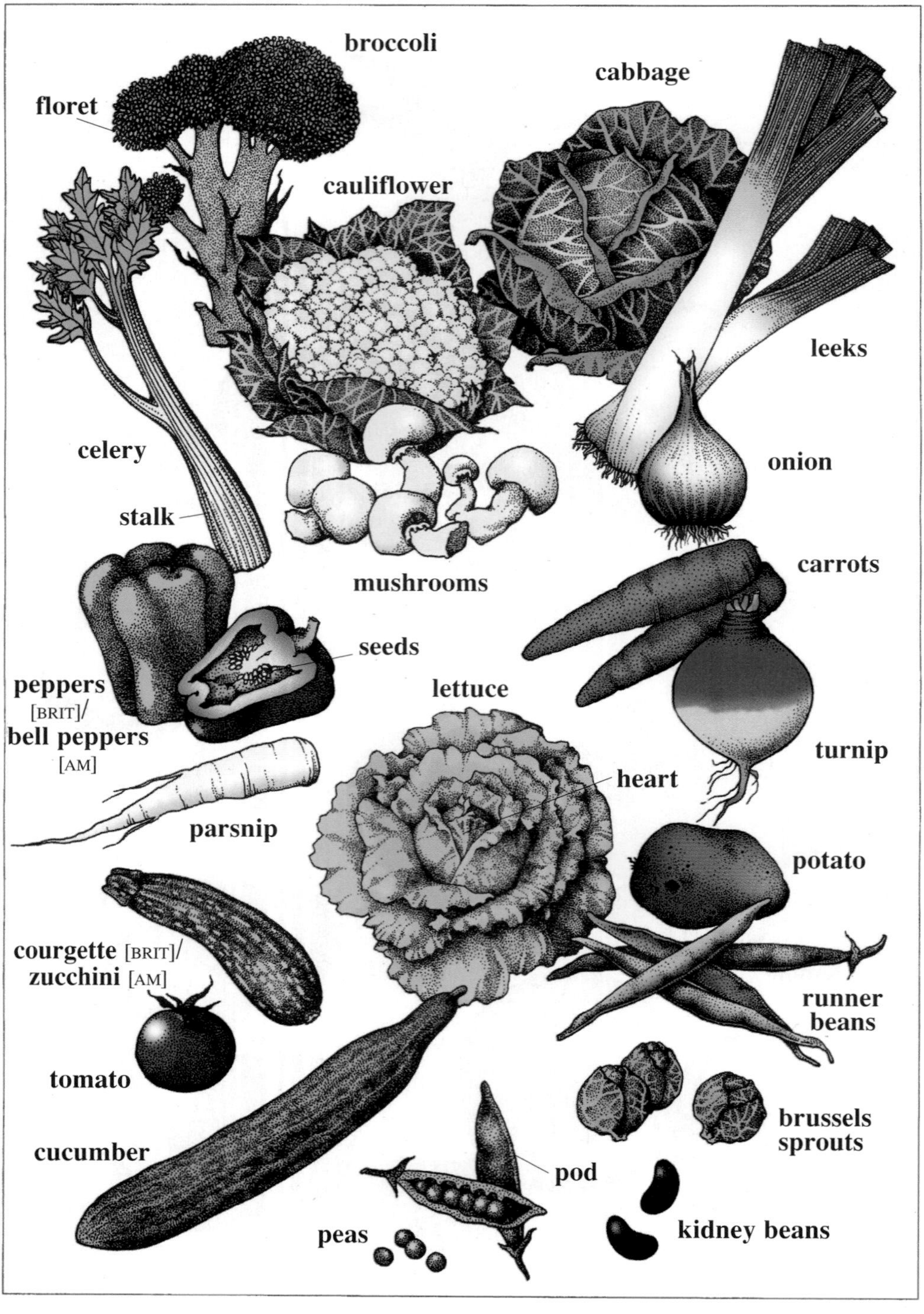
broccoli
floret
cabbage
cauliflower
leeks
celery
onion
stalk
carrots
mushrooms
seeds
peppers [BRIT]/ bell peppers [AM]
lettuce
turnip
heart
parsnip
potato
courgette [BRIT]/ zucchini [AM]
runner beans
tomato
brussels sprouts
cucumber
pod
peas
kidney beans

# Access to English

## Introduction

In this practical language section, you will find a large number of phrases which will help you to express yourself in natural English in numerous different situations. The first section, 'Essay Writing', includes useful phrases for academic writing. The following sections provide help with the language of presentations, telephoning and business correspondence, e-mail and job applications. All the examples are taken from the *Bank of English* corpus, so you can be sure that they are phrases that are really used in written English. Underlined words show at which entry in the dictionary you can find further information.

## Contents

# ESSAY WRITING

*Be careful with some of these expressions. In formal academic style, it is considered inappropriate in writing to use the first person ('I'), and other expressions which refer to the writer. This is beginning to change, especially in the USA, but if you are unsure, check with a teacher.*

## 1 Introductions

### 1.1 Introducing the subject of an essay

**It is often said/asserted/claimed that ...**

*It is often said that John Wesley saved England from a French-style revolution.*
*It is often asserted that America has traded higher inequality for faster growth.*
*Although it is often claimed that retiring from a lifelong job can lead to depression and poor physical health, there is no evidence that this is the case.*

**It is sometimes forgotten that ...**

*It's sometimes forgotten that what we're talking about is only the northern half of the country.*

**The concept of ...**

*The concept of animal rights is founded theologically on the belief that God has a right to have his creatures treated with respect.*

**The idea of ...**

*The idea of creating a powerful financial regulator is finding growing support.*

**The question of whether ...**

*The question of whether the economy is capable of sustained growth is still very much an open one.*

**... is much debated ...**

*This is much debated at present in both Britain and New Zealand.*
*The success of their attempts has been much debated.*

**... the most interesting features of ...**

*One of the most interesting features of the British economy in recent years has been the surprising strength of consumer spending.*
*The two most striking features of the elections to the European Parliament were a shift to the right and a huge abstention from voting.*

### 1.2 How the essay is to be organized

**The first thing that needs to be done is ...**

*The first thing that needs to be done is to identify those areas where you have, or could potentially have, some problems.*
*The first thing to understand when trying to improve communication and social skills is how you perceive others.*

**It is important to try to understand ...**

*To answer this question it is important to understand first why people are still fleeing the country.*
*However, it is essential to understand that technology is implemented to reflect common business practice but does not fundamentally change business practice.*

**... at the outset ...**

*I should say right at the outset that this chapter is not going to be an exhaustive survey of all the contending resolutions – or attempted resolutions – of the problem.*
*The first question we need to address, however, is the one we posed at the very outset.*

**I would like to start with ...**

*I would like to start with a very sweeping statement which can be easily challenged.*

**I/We will begin/start by ...**

*In order to do this, we will begin by examining some general theories about the nature of romantic love.*
*I shall start by briefly examining some of the Report's key comments and criticisms.*
*We will begin by looking at what interest is, how interest rates are determined, and how they are measured.*

**This essay/paper/project will begin by ...**

*The project will begin by identifying the primary players within a VAS.*
*The essay begins with a brief narrative.*

**I would like to summarize ...**

*I would like to summarize some of those points here.*
*In this chapter I shall summarize three such arguments.*
*Here let me simply summarize Freud's and Erikson's views:*

**I would like to outline ...**

*I would like to outline briefly some of the major developments over the past 30 years which have had far-reaching effects on the careers, aspirations and the lifestyle of women.*

**Let us look at ...**

*Now let us look at another way cost accounting might operate.*
*Let us look at the concrete example of Thatcher government policies between 1979 and 1988.*

**Let us begin/start by/with ...**

*Let us begin with what we now know about cognition in infancy.*
*We need to begin by identifying what or where the problems are.*
*To start with we must address the question: How important is it to rotate crops?*

**First of all, let us ...**

*First of all let us look at what is required of employers by law.*
*Let us first review this problem, and discuss the various arguments.*

**There are a number of issues ...**

*There are a number of issues to look at here.*

**We shall see how ...**

*In the next chapter we shall see how the revenue from this trade found its way into the coffers of the ruling party.*

## 1.3 Limiting the scope of the essay

**I will deal with the question of ...**

*I will then deal with the question of whether or not these requirements are compatible with criminal procedure.*
*In this chapter we do not deal with the issue of whether abortion is always wrong or the circumstances under which it is ethically justifiable.*

**I will confine myself to ...**

*I will confine myself to a few points.*
*In this chapter, I shall largely confine myself to a consideration of these methods.*

**It is beyond the scope of ...**

*Techniques such as job analysis, time management, role analysis and personal effectiveness at work are beyond the scope of this book.*
*It is beyond the scope of this book to discuss every aspect of this large problem.*

## 2 Building an argument

### 2.1 Introducing a topic

**The main issue is ...**

*The main issue in this case is the effect the proposal would have on the character and appearance of the countryside.*

*One of the issues under discussion will be land degradation.*

**The issue at stake here is ...**

*The issue at stake is an absolutely vital one for the future course of Scottish politics.*

**An important aspect of ... is ...**

*An essential aspect of knowledge is its ambiguity and constant change.*

*The most significant aspect of this type of accident is shock.*

**It is worth mentioning that ...**

*It is probably worth mentioning, in this context, that – as reported in the Scottish Medical Journal – middle-aged Scottish men eat very little fruit and green vegetables.*

**It is interesting to consider ...**

*It is interesting to consider what the ocean would be like if water properties were different.*

*It is useful to consider human impacts in the above perspective.*

**On the question of ...**

*Economists are divided on the question of whether we're already in a recession.*

**We are faced with the choice between ... and ...**

*The country is faced with a choice between opting out and helping to foot the bill.*

**It is argued ...**

*It is, however, widely argued that the current proposals will, for the first time, allow unilateral access to divorce by either partner without any objective proof of breakdown.*

**There is the argument that ...**

*There is the argument that some employers might substitute volunteers for paid workers and thus cut back further on employment.*

*Whether we women like the idea or not, there is an argument that male handbags are long overdue in this country.*

*In addition to the pain and suffering, there is an economic argument to take into consideration.*

### 2.2 Making a generalization

**... tend to believe that ...**

*Politicians have far too much tended to believe that television and newspapers were the main game.*

**... a tendency to ...**

*Enterprise bargaining based on productivity alone has a tendency to result in longer shifts for workers.*

*There is a tendency for people to divorce around the fourth year of marriage.*

**It is generally/widely accepted/believed that ...**

*Following extensive studies it is now widely accepted that most children with a family history of epilepsy can be safely immunised against whooping cough.*

*It is widely believed that the cuts by the two largest mortgage lenders will prompt other lenders to take similar action this week.*

*It is generally accepted that many of us consume far less than we need to stay healthy.*

**In the (vast) majority of cases ...**

*Even when the pregnant woman suffers from poor health, in the vast majority of cases her baby is born healthy.*

*She also found that in the majority of cases dreams decrease in number as old age comes on.*

**For most of us ...**

*For most of us the mobile office will be more straightforward – a notebook computer and a mobile phone.*

*Working five hours a day is well and good, but for most of us the reality can be different.*

**There are numerous examples/instances of ...**

*History shows numerous examples in which strong leadership has mastered the most difficult, even apparently hopeless situations.*

*There have been numerous instances over the years of anti-English sentiment in letters to the press.*

**In many cases ...**

*In many cases, these people may be working full time at low-paying jobs that provide no health care benefits.*

*The end result can be devastating in many cases.*

**In most cases ...**

*They also know that in most cases the people they are meeting will be free to start work straightaway.*

*In most cases, the only long-term solution will be to close down or privatise these state-owned banks.*

**On the whole ...**

*On the whole children today are far healthier, safer and better educated than they were in 1900.*

*This generation grew up using a PC, but not the Internet, and are, on the whole, comfortable with technology.*

**For the most part ...**

*For the most part, these American problems are commercial.*

*The curriculum is for the most part broad, balanced and effectively delivered.*

**As a rule ...**

*As a rule, we spend at least 30 per cent of any project's effort and time in testing.*

*Foundations did not, as a rule, pay large salaries to any but a few top executives.*

**In general ...**

*In general, Americans are poorly informed about politics and government.*

*Do great people in general have limited power to change the directions of a society?*

**Usually ...**

*She adds that the product is usually sold by staff who do not have any training or understanding of insurance.*

*Usually a broadcaster has two ways to exert at least some control over a star: money and exposure.*

## 2.3 Being more precise

**In particular ...**

*Rural commodity prices, in particular, had dragged down the index.*

*Linguists, in particular, have remained sceptical.*

*So when you talk about technology or when you think about technology, what in particular are you thinking of?*

**... particularly ...**

*What has happened in western Europe and particularly the UK will affect the global market.*
*The government believes it is particularly important to encourage young people to get involved.*

**More specifically, ...**

*More specifically, such tests are said to underestimate the true ability of the disadvantaged.*
*Some people have also expressed the opinion that the government has given in to foreign, or more specifically American, pressure to liberalise the economy.*
*My topic will be the future of punishment and, more specifically, the necessity of punishment in a just social order.*

**... and especially ...**

*Even though parents, and especially mothers, may be busier than ever, many seem to be managing to fit in more time with their children than an earlier generation of parents did.*
*The team says much more is needed, particularly in terms of outdoor activities and especially in deprived communities.*

**... mainly ...**

*Britain's industrial output rose by 0.9% in September, mainly because of increased energy production.*
*About 350,000 general anaesthetics are administered in dentistry every year, resulting in an average of three deaths annually, mainly in children.*

## 3 Dealing with sources and supporting an argument

### 3.1 Introducing a quotation or paraphrase

***Plagiarism***

*Please note that you should always acknowledge other people's work when you use it in your writing. Failure to do so is considered to be plagiarism, or cheating, and is punished severely in English-speaking universities. If you are unsure about how to acknowledge work correctly, check with a teacher or look at the work of other writers in English.*

**As ... claims/points out/remarks/suggests, ...**

*As Betts rightly claims, this class has grown very rapidly.*
*But, as Mr Dampier points out, investing small sums on a monthly basis is the best way to spread your risk.*
*Food is intimately related to identity, as Suzanne Moore points out.*
*As Jacob remarks, 'The whole truth needs to be told. Nothing should be kept secret.'*
*There is some data indicating, as Professor Miles suggests, that countries with high benefits levels have slightly higher levels of unemployment.*

**According to ...**

*According to Professor Florey, the evidence against women smoking during pregnancy has remained consistent.*

**In the words of ...**

*In the words of one worried UN official, 'The fighting today may show that events are slipping away from us again.'*

## 3.2 Paraphrasing and reformulating

**What he is saying is that ...**

*What he is saying is continuity is important because that is one of the key ingredients of success.*

**According to ...**

*According to textbooks, Napoleon died from stomach cancer.*

**In other words ...**

*The evaluation showed she was making 'sub-maximal effort', or, in other words, wasn't trying as hard as she could be.*

*The new ways of working are all about communication, flexibility, team-work and the ability to do several things at the same time. The world of modern employment requires men, in other words, to behave more like women.*

**What this means ...**

*You can have different sets of genes coming together. What this means is that every plant produced from those seeds can be a little bit different to every other seed.*

**To put it another way ...**

*It may only mean that the mentally ill are more likely to be admitted to a mental hospital if they live in a city than in the country. To put it another way, if there are no mental hospitals in a rural area we cannot conclude that there are no mentally ill people in that area.*

*The club celebrates its 25th birthday this year. Or, to put it another way, its silver anniversary.*

**That is to say ...**

*This is equal to the annual income of the poorest 47 per cent of the world's people, (that is to say, 2.5 billion individuals).*

*It is a good thing to spell out that the future belongs to private and public, that is to say, mixed economies.*

**... or rather ...**

*Bly explores what he believes is happening, or rather, not happening to men in society in the United States.*

*Their approach is to start by studying the locust itself. Or rather, they are looking back through all research results to try to get a better understanding of the insect's behaviour and habits.*

## 3.3 Introducing examples

**To take another example ...**

*To take another example, changes in the economy often affect the ideas Americans have about what government should do.*

*So let us take another example, a little less straightforward.*

**... for example ...**

*Consider, for example, the fictional works of the offbeat British writer David Lindsay.*

*Take, for example, Glasgow's Year of Architecture and Design in 1999.*

**... for instance ...**

*Consider for instance the intense debate provoked in 1908 by the proposal to restore the inscription 'In God We Trust' on United States gold coins.*

**... serves to illustrate ...**

*A bitter struggle between the Labour Party and one of its own local authorities has served to illustrate how the political landscape, even at local level, has changed.*

**By way of illustration ...**

*By way of illustration, one can point to Peggy Sue Got Married, the stage musical of the 1986 film.*

**A case in point is ...**

*A case in point is the work that's going on at the moment.*

**... if we take the case of ...**

*If we take the case of India, regional inequalities have been reinforced.*
*If you take the case of Japan, industry is the only way to survive.*
*For example, let's take the case of someone who is not doing well at work.*

**... as follows: ...**

*... one example of the many supportive studies is as follows:*

## 3.4 Evaluating an argument

**... could be interpreted as ...**

*The reductions could also be interpreted as a defensive move.*
*This should not be interpreted as symptomatic of a national decline.*

**Could be taken to mean that ...**

*This was higher than expected and could be taken to mean that inflationary pressures remain strong.*

**This leads one to suppose that ...**

*A number of aspects of military technology might lead one to suppose that technical innovations would be readily agreed.*
*We are led to suppose that the same principles apply from one case to the next.*

**It is reasonable to assume that ...**

*From what we know of other star systems and other galaxies, it seems reasonable to assume that there are Earth-like planets throughout the universe.*

**... weigh up the pros and cons ...**

*As firms weigh up the pros and cons of the single currency, this will be one of their biggest concerns.*
*Weighing up the pros and cons, then, how does ecstasy fare in the league table of recreational drugs?*

**... a convincing explanation**

*However, there is a more convincing explanation. The government is running out of cash.*

**The truth of the matter is that ...**

*The truth of the matter is that we have one of the most efficient, competitive agricultural sectors in the world.*

**The truth is that ...**

*The truth is that all cultures are equal, and no single one of them has the right to judge and interpret the others in its own terms.*
*The unpalatable truth is that relative decline in the future is unavoidable.*

**This raises the question of ...**

*This raises the question of whether they can really be called soldiers at all.*
*This raises the whole question as to the status of the Council.*

**This is true up to a point ...**

*It is true up to a point that we wanted to write about improved conditions in the country's west.*
*All this is true only up to a point.*

**... is somewhat misleading ...**

*Having said that, I need to add a caution: it is somewhat misleading to talk about 'male' and 'female' hormones.*

**... the wrong approach ...**

*Others, however, suspect that focusing on individual genes is the wrong approach.*

**... considerable advantages ...**

*Unit trusts are perfect for such people while also having considerable advantages for larger investors as well.*

**It would make sense to ...**

*In my opinion it would make sense to introduce some sort of sliding scale of deductions.*

**The advantages outweigh the disadvantages**

*There was no doubt that the advantages outweighed the disadvantages.*
*The long-term benefits of a single currency far outweigh the drawbacks.*

### 3.5 Agreeing

**... agree wholeheartedly with ...**

*My first reaction is to agree wholeheartedly with these statements.*
*I fully agree with Richard Littlejohn about the doubts of CJD being linked to beef.*

**It is hard to disagree with ...**

*Now most people would find it hard to disagree with these pronouncements.*

**One must acknowledge that ...**

*One has to acknowledge the importance of new standards of care and more stringent Commonwealth regulations.*

**It is quite right to ...**

*It is quite right to set a ceiling on such spending. But the proposed limit of £20 million is far too high.*
*But at the same time it is quite right to recognise that the situation is so serious that there can be no room for complacency.*

**... support this claim ...**

*There is evidence to support this claim.*

**In support of this theory ...**

*In support of the theory, she is forced to resort to statements which are entirely without foundation.*

**... argument in favour of ...**

*The minister presented a further strong argument in favour of the independent sector.*

**... deserves support**

*This is a great campaign and deserves support.*
*This is the one Government motoring campaign of the past couple of decades which is working and which deserves unqualified support.*

**... viewed favourably ...**

*We expect recent changes at Coles Myer to be viewed favourably by the market and will contribute to a higher share price.*

### 3.6 Disagreeing

**I must disagree with ...**

*The senator says there is no international crisis; I have to disagree with him very strongly.*
*I would totally disagree with that assertion.*

**I cannot agree with ...**

*I cannot agree with that view.*

**I do not share the view that ...**

*I do not share her view that the campaign on her behalf has become a personal vendetta against Gus John.*

**This is far from the truth**

*It is sometimes assumed that the Trust is a wealthy organisation. This is very far from the truth.*

**It is simply not true**

*It is simply not true that massive savings are waiting to be made through the elimination of 'waste'.*

**It is quite wrong to ...**

*It is quite wrong to suggest that someone with cancer has personal control over the disease process.*
*But it would be quite wrong to assume that such behaviour is unique to this country.*

**... out of the question ...**

*Military action and economic embargoes would be out of the question.*
*Many Evangelicals today wish that this issue could be dealt with in a General Council of the Church. However, this is out of the question in the foreseeable future.*

**... is untenable**

*To assert that what people think, believe and act upon is of no consequence, is a position which, for any sociologist, is surely untenable.*

**The opposite is true**

*I gave the impression that the effort to understand the parents' point of view should be part of any therapy. The opposite is in fact true.*

**It is difficult to share the opinion that ...**

*In view of the results, it is difficult for us to share such an opinion.*

**This argument does not hold water**

*But when everything is considered, neither argument holds water.*
*But do these objections hold water?*

**This argument does not stand up**

*The monopoly argument does not stand up.*
*Legal advisers said their argument wouldn't stand up in court.*

**... not ..., ... but rather that ...**

*The problem is not so much that average university pay is too low because of stingy governments, but rather that there is no genuine competition in the academic job market.*

**The problem with ...**

*The problem with this view is that any significant health problem occurring when we are younger is labeled non-normative because it is untimely.*

**... unjustified ...**

*To continue the war is absolutely unjustified from any point of view.*

## 3.7 Introducing your own point of view

**In my opinion ...**

*In my opinion the problem is not lack of money, but the belief that people should work all hours without complaining.*
*Any general enquiry would therefore, in my opinion, be unproductive.*

**My personal <u>opinion</u> is that ...**

*My personal opinion is that the world community is not addressing the problems that need to be addressed with a level of urgency that they require.*

**Speaking <u>personally</u> ...**

*Speaking personally, I have no problem with this idea.*
*Personally speaking I think the council waste a lot of money.*

**<u>Personally</u> ...**

*Personally, I believe that the European economy ought to be perfectly capable of achieving sustained 4 per cent growth without inflation.*
*I personally am not in favour of church schools, but if they exist what purpose do they serve if they don't give priority to committed church attenders?*

**My own <u>view</u> is that ...**

*My own view is that no good can come from encouraging the public to believe that a nineteenth-century attitude to freedom is relevant to the current difficulties.*

**In my <u>view</u> ...**

*In my view the market has got considerably further to fall and will only bottom out at the point at which the price becomes attractive to the venture-capital market.*
*That would, in my view, be a retrograde step for our democracy.*

**From my <u>point of view</u> ...**

*The irony, from my point of view, is that the church requires its employees to work unsociable hours.*
*From my point of view the business was a worthwhile investment.*

**It is my <u>belief</u> that ...**

*It is my belief that manufacturers will play a small part in the overall scheme of things.*

**I <u>feel</u> that ...**

*I feel that the financial situation for students is rapidly getting worse.*

**I am <u>convinced</u> that ...**

*I am convinced that our research into cost accounting and other forms of contractual relationship are all moves in the right direction.*
*I am not convinced that global warming is all man-made.*

**As far as I'm <u>concerned</u> ...**

*As far as I'm concerned the officials incited the fight.*
*It has been said by members of Alison's family that she may have known her killers. But as far as I'm concerned, there is no evidence of that.*

**It <u>seems</u> to me that ...**

*It seems to me that this is a better long-term economic strategy for the future.*
*It seems to me that what is under way in this country is a systematic attempt to broaden the divisions.*

**As I <u>see</u> it ...**

*As I see it, centrally fixed prices will constitute 60 to 70 per cent of all prices.*
*The main thing, as I see it, is now to ensure the withdrawal of troops.*

**I <u>believe</u> that ...**

*I believe that the referendum will be defeated very decisively.*
*I believe that this is not just South Africa's problem.*

### 3.8 Proposing an alternative and introducing a counter-argument

**Another approach ...**

*Still another approach would allow parents to send their child to any district school they chose.*

**Another way of looking at this ...**

*Another way at looking at this is that in terms of a closed economy everybody's expenditure is someone else's income.*

*Another way of looking at the risk from secondhand smoke is to ask, how much does it increase your individual risk of getting lung cancer?*

**On the other hand ...**

*On the other hand, there is evidence that sleep deprivation has a bad effect on children as well as on their parents.*

**The other side of the coin is ...**

*Share prices do go up and down, so there's bound to be an element of risk. But as most professional investors know well – the other side of the coin is the real potential for significant rewards.*

**It is more accurate to speak of ...**

*It would be more accurate to speak of a criticism of Western development studies in its two branches of economy and sociology.*

## 4 Referring to data

**From the table/chart/data/diagram/graph it can be seen that ...**

*From this table it can be seen that scientific, technical and related workers are very numerous.*

*From Figures 1 and 2 it can be seen that increasing density up to point 'a' will increase total yield without affecting plant size.*

*The heart, as can be seen from the diagram, has four distinct chambers, two upper collecting chambers and two lower pumping chambers.*

**As you can see from the table/chart/data/diagram/graph ...**

*As you can see from Table 15-3, foreign banks are major players in this market.*

*The results look impressive, as you can see from this picture.*

*We did a market test in Salt Lake City and Indianapolis last Fall, and as you can see from this chart, we had a very high customer satisfaction rating.*

**The chart/data/diagram/graph/table shows that ...**

*This table clearly shows the rising importance of education in people's lives.*

*This survey clearly shows that business is strongly committed to Europe, but to a Europe that works.*

**According to the chart/data/diagram/graph/table ...**

*House prices are now rising at their fastest rate for six years, according to the latest data from the Nationwide Building Society.*

*According to ONS figures, clothing and footwear sales were up 0.5 per cent last month.*

**... figures show that ...**

*Government figures show that two thirds of rural parishes do not have a village shop any more and 83 per cent do not have a daily bus service.*

*Government figures show clearly that earnings are outpacing improvements in efficiency.*

**It seems/appears from the chart/data/diagram/graph/table that ...**

*It seems from the studies that, broadly speaking, scientists are creative in a different way from those working in humanities and the arts.*

*It appears from the figures that recent activity in these regions has been absorbed by the local markets.*

*It appears from the trends to date that the larger fish are more mobile.*

*It would appear from the chart that good health always has to be fought for.*

## 5 Stages in the argument

### 5.1 Transition markers

**<u>First</u> of all ...**

*First of all, let's recap on just a few of the past misdeeds of the paper-pushers of Brussels.*

*So he is proposing, first of all, to bring forward the tax cuts that Congress has already approved for later years.*

**<u>Firstly</u> ...**

*Firstly, the battle of Waterloo was actually two separate battles. One at Waterloo itself and another at a small, remote farmhouse at Hougomont.*

*The raid's objectives were twofold: firstly to destroy the Gestapo's intelligence on Norwegian resistance units and secondly to wreck a Fascist rally being held by the country's leader.*

**First and <u>foremost</u> ...**

*In terms of symptoms, schizophrenia is first and foremost a disorder of thinking.*

*First and foremost is the economic argument.*

**In the first <u>place</u> ...**

*In the first place, it is hard to see what Holt adds to Edmund Dell's more comprehensive recent work on post-war Chancellors.*

**<u>Secondly</u> ...**

*Secondly, it is important to establish lines of responsibility and accountability.*

*The raid's objectives were twofold: firstly to destroy the Gestapo's intelligence on Norwegian resistance units and secondly to wreck a Fascist rally being held by the country's leader.*

**A second <u>problem</u> is that ...**

*A second problem is that a Bill of Rights would further enhance the powers of the courts, at the expense of politicians.*

*Another problem is that many industries aren't required to monitor their toxic emissions at all.*

**<u>Thirdly</u> ...**

*The amount of money that a member can borrow depends firstly on the amount of money in the 'common pool', secondly on the amount that particular member has saved and thirdly on his/her ability to repay the loan.*

**Let us now <u>consider</u> ...**

*Let us now consider the case where the demand for investment capital falls.*

*Given that assumption, we can now consider particular cases.*

**Let us now <u>look</u> at ...**

*Let us now look a little more closely at some specific examples of the problem.*

*Let us now look at each of these reasons in more detail.*

**Let us now <u>turn to</u> ...**

*Let us now turn to the problem of compensating the population for higher food prices.*

*Let me now turn to my two final questions.*

**<u>Finally</u> ...**

*Finally, it must be recognized that most of the research reported on here was done with relatively young, well-educated, predominantly white men.*

*Finally, we need to summarize where we wanted our operation to be in the terms of the market life cycle.*

**<u>Lastly</u> ...**

*Lastly, there is a question of money.*

*The world's farm policies ripple through consumers, producers, exporters, developing countries, and lastly, the non-farm economy.*

**To conclude this section ...**

*It would be appropriate to conclude this section of our discussion with closer clarification of these issues.*

**This merits closer examination ...**

*The situation will deserve much closer examination.*
*The example it provides of how even a disease may be politicized and recruited to serve the cause of radical politics merits careful attention.*

### 5.2 Addition markers

**In addition, ...**

*In addition, there is evidence to suggest that genetics and hormonal factors play a part.*

**In addition to ...**

*In addition to being the murder capital of the world, Washington also has the highest rate of infant mortality in the country.*

**Added to this ...**

*Added to this is the problem that MI5 is not accountable to Parliament.*

**An added ... is ...**

*An added consideration is the human geography of the minorities.*
*An added difficulty for many women after the birth of a child is a period of depressed mood, often called the 'maternity blues' or 'postpartum blues'.*

**As well as ...**

*As well as being subject to Government legislation, the disposal of radioactive wastes is overseen by various authorising departments.*
*Most of the cash will now go to help organic farming, as well as the setting up of new rural enterprises.*

**Over and above that ...**

*Over and above that, we return to a more fundamental point. As the IFS has pointed out, sustaining big increases in education and health spending beyond 2003 was always likely to require increased taxation.*

**Furthermore ...**

*Approximately 2 million people work in the new co-operatives or are self-employed. Furthermore, we constantly review the new economic conditions and change our planning ideas as a result.*
*Furthermore, recent studies in Europe have found that the duration of AZT's benefits may be limited and that it may not actually prolong life to a meaningful extent.*

**Moreover ...**

*I like him and moreover, I like his work.*
*An even greater increase can be seen among mothers who have children aged 0-4; only 25% were working mums in 1973 compared to 49% in 1996. Moreover, women are waiting until they are older to start a family.*

**In the same way ...**

*This is why it is hard for people to tell you consciously you how they do things well, they have forgotten the learning stages. In the same way it is hard to see how a building was constructed once the scaffolding has been dismantled.*

**Not only ... but also ...**

*Not only do I think that it is important to share friendships with people of different ages, but also of different backgrounds.*

*There are no reliable population figures, not only because of the size of the country but also because of the political sensitivity involved in counting its ethnic and religious groups.*

**What is more ...**

*By 2050, the Census Bureau estimates, about 80m people, one American in five, will be 65 or over. What is more, the elderly are on average no longer poor.*
*He has done everything, and what is more, he has given everything.*

**In the same way ...**

*If you have a weak chest, catching a chill or getting over-tired could result in bronchitis. In the same way, if your nerves are over-strained, an unexpected gas bill may make you feel ill.*

## 6 Degrees of certainty

### 6.1 Expressing certainty

**It is clear that ...**

*It is clear that business organisations are becoming increasingly unhappy about the revaluation.*
*I think this makes it clear that this is a national issue that must be addressed nationally.*

**Indisputably ...**

*Paris is indisputably one of the world's cultural capitals.*
*The law and order situation in the state was deteriorating. This is indisputably true.*

**Undeniably ...**

*These children are able to debate among themselves in language that is undeniably more mature than most other groups of their age.*
*Undeniably, however, over the past few years fiction has been through a bad patch.*

**There can be no doubt that ...**

*There can be no doubt either that Nato is acting within international law.*

**It is undoubtedly true that ...**

*It is undoubtedly true that Labor faced a protest vote at the polls on Saturday.*

**As we all know, ...**

*As we all know, economic reforms have been carried out since 1978.*

**One thing is certain ...**

*One thing is certain, we will be living in interesting times in the twenty-first century.*

**It is certain that ...**

*It is certain that the more cars are planned and built by computers, the less scope there is for style.*
*But one thing is quite certain: no kid should have to live the way children in our inner cities do.*

**It is true that ...**

*It is true that there is an increasing awareness of this particular problem among UK-based specialists.*

**It is noticeable that ...**

*It is noticeable that mature students generally obtain better degree results than younger students.*

**It can be observed ...**

*This tendency can be observed worldwide.*

**It can be seen that ...**

*In much the same way, it can be seen that children apply rules to learning to read and write.*

## 6.2 Emphasizing a point

**It is significant that ...**

*It is significant that even this powerful body of people was quite unable to remove all knowledge of the trail from the historical record.*

**It should not be forgotten that ...**

*It should never be forgotten that Marx's overriding aim was the practical emancipation of the people from oppression.*

**It should be stressed that ...**

*It should be stressed that today's findings relate only to the position that applies at the moment.*

**The important point ...**

*The important point to remember is that these are only trends.*
*The important point is that people should remember the need to reduce pollution after the hot weather has ended.*

## 6.3 Expressing doubt and qualifying an argument

**It is doubtful whether ...**

*It is doubtful whether the report will be acceptable to the United Nations or the United States.*

**It remains to be seen whether ...**

*It remains to be seen whether this book will help more psychologists to evaluate their approaches to teaching, learning and the training of teachers.*

**I wonder whether ...**

*I do begin to wonder whether this will ever really happen.*

**I have reservations about ...**

*I do have reservations about his views, notably about his anti-American attitude.*

**It is by no means certain that ...**

*It is by no means certain that this system will now disappear.*
*But the change is by no means certain to be adopted.*

**It's difficult to say whether ...**

*The extra material was shot but not used in the final film, and it is difficult to say whether it would have made any improvement in practice.*

**It is questionable whether ...**

*It's questionable whether the university even has jurisdiction off campus.*

**Is there any real substance ...**

*We need to find out if there really is substance behind the hype.*
*I do not know if there is any actual substance in the allegation.*

**This poses/raises fundamental questions ...**

*This issue poses fundamental questions for each director of the company individually.*
*The declaration also poses a number of questions about the future relationship between the two states.*
*The analysis raises fundamental questions about how the talents of Britain's able children can be fulfilled.*

**This raises again the question of ...**

*Her work raises again the question of whether animals are capable of abstract thought.*
*This raises once again the issue of who really runs the economy.*

**... may well be true but ...**

*This may be true, but does it signify that student intake should be reduced again?*

**It is hard to believe that ...**

*It is hard to believe that cities have grown simply because of these policies.*

*GNP growth is still on target at 6.1%, but it is hard to believe that growth can continue in spite of the disruptions to both agriculture and industry caused by the flooding.*

## 7 Making comparisons and contrasts

### 7.1 Objective comparisons

**... compared with ...**

*The cost of living is relatively low compared with other European countries.*

*Compared with the past, rates are amazingly stable at the moment.*

**In/by comparison with ...**

*In comparison with other EU countries, Britain had one of the lowest unemployment rates.*

*They are convinced that they are underpaid in comparison with other professions.*

*Drug-related crime rates are low by comparison with the number of addicts.*

**The former ... the latter ...**

*There is a difference between knowing exactly what it is you want done and how it should be done and allowing someone to make their own decisions and do it their way. The latter is delegation, the former simply carrying out your instructions.*

**Similarly ...**

*Similarly, the Australian controlling body is also going further to invoke safety measures.*

**Likewise ...**

*The first tape of a Hollywood film costs a great deal more to produce than the second. Likewise, a new drug may cost millions of pounds to develop but only a few pence per unit to produce.*

**Equally ...**

*The increase in deafness is only partly explained by an ageing population. Equally important is the increasing noisiness of leisure activities.*

*If it is true that history turns our gaze towards the past, it is equally true that history reveals the present more than the past.*

**There is a fundamental difference between ...**

*Europe is one issue on which there is a fundamental difference between the parties.*

*There is one fundamental difference: Western society as a whole is becoming a unisex society.*

### 7.2 Favourable comparisons

**Far superior to ...**

*I found the newspaper technology was far superior to my own paper and I also learnt a great deal about organising and administration in newspapers.*

**... have the edge over ...**

*CD-ROM encyclopaedias do have a definite edge over their printed counterparts when it comes to cross-referencing, instant access to information and multimedia facilities.*

### 7.3 Unfavourable comparisons

**... cannot compete with ...**

*Most have abandoned in-house component manufacturing because they cannot compete with specialists.*

**... nowhere near as ... as ...**

*Export growth is still positive, but it's nowhere near as strong as it was a few years ago.*
*Part of the reason for this is that the decision to go to war against Vietnam was nowhere near as clear-cut as the decision to fight Japan a generation earlier.*

**... no match for ...**

*A report published by the French Senate said that Air France is hugely inefficient and no match for leaner competitors.*

**... not measure up to ...**

*Shell executives concede that Nigeria does not measure up to the environmental standards in other countries, although Shell is spending $100m this year.*

**... cannot compare with ...**

*All the riches in the world can't compare with the joys of motherhood.*

**There's no comparison between ... and ...**

*But John Pike, a space expert at the Federation of American Scientists, says there's no comparison between the quality of these commercially available pictures and the secret images that American spy satellites gather.*

## 7.4 Comparing similar things

**... much/almost/virtually the same as ...**

*Direct wage costs in Britain are much the same as in France and considerably lower than in Germany.*
*Profits were virtually the same as last year, at £341m.*

**... not much to choose between ...**

*It accepts that there's not much to choose between public relations agencies of its size, but invests in human resources initiatives to give it the edge.*

**There is no difference between ...**

*In legal terms however there is no difference between unofficial and official strikes.*
*Results of the Concorde trial showed no difference between a sample who took the drug and those administered a placebo.*

**... equivalent to ...**

*Turn your attention to debit cards, the modern equivalent to paying by cheque.*
*The cost of buying a new sofa can be equivalent to buying a secondhand car.*

**... on a par with ...**

*Parts of Glasgow are on a par with the worst areas of London for burglaries.*
*British food, if it is properly prepared, is on a par with any cuisine, anywhere.*

**... corresponds to ...**

*Research shows that national policy corresponds to public attitudes about two-thirds of the time.*
*The results of these barbaric tests may not offer any medical benefit to humans because, in so many highly significant respects, our biological make-up does not correspond to that of monkeys.*

**... can be likened to ...**

*In many ways, the process of addiction can be likened to a developing relationship.*
*This approach to economic reform has been likened to deciding to move driving from one side of the road to the other.*

## 7.5 Comparing dissimilar things

**... have little/nothing in common with ...**

*It would be foolish to ditch our special relationship with the United States and merge our foreign policy with countries that have little in common with us.*

*Conglomerates tend to believe they can apply their management skills to industries that apparently have nothing in common.*

**... bear little resemblance to ...**

*This is all the more remarkable given the fact that Greek cosmology, and other early models of the universe, bear little resemblance to the modern scientific picture of the universe.*

**... is completely/entirely/quite/totally different from ...**

*Efficient processing by a computer may be quite different from what human beings do.*

*The present slowdown is totally different from the cycles of the past 60 years.*

## 7.6 Contrast

**... but in reality ...**

*Property was supposed to belong to the people but in reality belonged to the state.*

*These people will always moan and groan about their cares but in reality they know how lucky they are.*

**In contrast to ...**

*In contrast to so many American inner-city schools, which are sites of violent unruliness, Golden Door is notably orderly.*

*His views are in direct contrast to the Prime Minister's.*

*Their performance was in stark contrast to the rest of the England team.*

**... as opposed to ...**

*The primary emphasis fell upon practical as opposed to theoretical skills.*

**Unlike ...**

*Unlike most other lenders, we arrange our loans over the telephone.*

*CDs, unlike VHS tape, do not degenerate.*

**Whereas ...**

*Whereas they see driving aggressively and speeding as unacceptable in others, they believe their own skill will keep them safe when they drive.*

**... differentiate ... from ...**

*Success is often the result of staying power and determination, factors that differentiate true entrepreneurs from also-rans.*

*It is important to differentiate between political and social differences.*

**On the one hand, ... on the other hand ...**

*On the one hand you reduce inflation. On the other hand you raise the rate of economic growth.*

*Once they are online, women are more likely than men to buy books and clothes. Men, on the other hand, are more likely to view the Web as a tool for handling personal finance.*

**Conversely ...**

*'We have to factor in all these variations when we're developing a website,' Mr Richardson says. 'Conversely, there are very few variations to consider when developing an intranet site.'*

**... on the contrary ...**

*We Britons are not against marriage – on the contrary, we like it so much that we do it again and again – because we are incredibly romantic.*

*The problem with believing we are all born equal is that it blames the poor and ignorant for their own predicament. Class and privilege, on the contrary, show this is nonsense.*

**In actual fact ...**

*In actual fact, most people are well aware that feeding the world is a matter of distribution and production methods rather than sophisticated bioengineering.*

## 8 Expressing cause and effect

**The fundamental reason for ...**

*The fundamental reason for its failures lay in the discrepancy of the American experience.*

*The main reason for the change is that consumers are more concerned about what they eat.*

**As a result/consequence ...**

*'People are spending money on mobile phones and eating out, television, nightclubbing, wine bars' he says. 'As a result, they're spending less money on food and clothes.'*

*Could low levels of radiation cause the mice to lose their appetite, eat less food, and live longer as a result?*

*This, it was observed, often happened as a consequence of foreign journeys.*

**... because of this ...**

*The number of couples marrying has fallen by more than 20 per cent in the past two decades. Because of this, the Government predicts that for the first time the married will soon form a minority of the adult population.*

*You come to like people you know because you can predict their behavior, and perhaps because of this they seem less frightening than complete strangers do.*

**Therefore ...**

*The process is said to be much quicker and therefore cheaper.*

*'This event reminds us that if a comet collides with Jupiter, one may also collide with the earth. Therefore, the study of the collision is of great significance,' he explained.*

**Thus ...**

*Five of the vessel's five safety doors hadn't worked, thus allowing the fire to be fed with oxygen.*

*Immunology has demonstrated the link between the brain/nervous system and the defence systems of the body. Thus, a stressed person will have lower resistance to disease than a relaxed person.*

**Consequently ...**

*Current technical staff will find themselves moving into middle management roles to fill the gaps. Consequently, this will leave a huge technical skills shortage at the lower end of the jobs market.*

*Wealthy American universities can afford to pay their academics much more than their British counterparts, making it easier for them to attract renowned professors and, consequently, more able students.*

**... in order to ...**

*I know what I want and I'll go as far as I have to in order to be successful.*

*In order to make training more attractive to employers and employees alike the format of courses offered needs careful consideration.*

**For this reason ...**

*We must ensure that one of the greatest classical theatre companies in the world is always alive and constantly changing. For this reason I find these developments fantastically liberating.*

*It's a very substantial sum, and for this reason part of the investment process is knowing how much you can afford in monthly losses.*

**... so that ...**

*The state often monopolises markets, so that, for instance, people with low incomes should have access to high standards of education.*

*A program is being written so that the hospital computer can spot and highlight trends such as rising blood pressure.*

**... leads to ...**

*If raising fines leads to a reduction in deaths, that is a good thing.*
*Increases in global travel and population mixing have led to worldwide exposure to the virus.*

**The consequence of this is ...**

*Competition for the decreasing number of homes becoming available in these areas is intense. The consequence of this is that hundreds of families face years of waiting.*
*The generally low tone and quality of public Internet communication is a consequence of the fact that it is casual, direct, and private, unedited and uncensored.*

**On this basis ...**

*The price of houses is rising because, by the usual historical yardsticks, they are cheap. On this basis, they might have a considerable way to rise yet.*

## 9 Conclusions

### 9.1 Summarizing the arguments

**I have demonstrated/shown that ...**

*I have demonstrated how changes in policy and practice could be traced to the highest level of political activity.*
*I have shown here just a few examples of the process.*

**This shows how ...**

*This shows how far rail operators still have to go to meet passenger expectations.*

**So it would appear that ...**

*So really it would appear that the military option is now becoming increasingly likely.*

**This goes to show that ...**

*This goes to show that the world's third most populous democracy is not an easy country to govern democratically.*
*All of which goes to show that people still wrestle with the same big questions.*

**To sum up ...**

*To sum up: France's recent economic management has been impressive.*
*One way to sum up its dilemma is this. To survive, it must deliver growth.*

**To summarize, ...**

*To summarize, an addiction is a behavior we choose that we can do easily, that does not depend on others, and that consistently gives us immediate pleasure or, we believe, will soon give us pleasure.*
*To summarize: the sociology of modernization and development is that branch of sociology which examines the processes of modernization and development.*

**In a nutshell, ...**

*To put it in a nutshell, and as G. Lichtheim expressed it, social Darwinism is the proposition that the weak deserve their fate.*

**The key to the argument is ...**

*The key to Wolf's argument is that all goods and services that are bought on price alone (books, for example, or compact discs), will eventually be sold on the Internet.*
*The key to this argument is an understanding of what is meant by fats and carbohydrates, and what would be considered a natural balance between the two.*

**In any case ...**

*In any case, the final few results will make no significant difference to the election outcome.*

**Basically ...**

*Basically I think the structure's going to be a little bit tighter.*

**In brief ...**

*In brief, health education is most effective when it promotes activities rather than condemning unsafe behaviour.*

**In short ...**

*In short, it is a political system markedly similar to the social democracies of Western Europe and North America.*

## 9.2 Drawing conclusions

**On balance ...**

*On balance, he did far more good than harm to the British monarchy.*

**We have to conclude that ...**

*We have to conclude that, theoretically, economic development for the Third World is possible and likely.*

*In fact, one has to conclude that there is just one major way of arresting the declines in our butterfly population – and that is the protection of the size and variety of the countryside itself.*

**This leads to the conclusion that ...**

*This model leads to the conclusion that even the most 'vulnerable' child can show improvement if her environment improves markedly.*

*From this we have drawn the inevitable conclusion that we must become more involved in the international division of labour, in the system of world economic relations.*

**In conclusion ...**

*In conclusion, the transformation of the French party system during the first thirty years of the Fifth Republic was the result of a series of complex, interrelated factors.*

**Ultimately, ...**

*Ultimately, then, this will undoubtedly be one of the important discoveries of the year.*

**On the whole ...**

*It delivers directly to Europe, or will arrange shipping to anywhere except Albania and South Africa. On the whole, though, Britons are not terribly good at buying by post.*

*On the whole the German company has been allowed to maintain its sense of independence.*

**There is a need for further investigation/research/study ...**

*It also emphasizes the need for further research.*

*The results clearly point to the need for further study.*

# GIVING PRESENTATIONS

## 1 Introductions

| | | |
|---|---|---|
| Good | morning<br>afternoon<br>evening | and thank you for coming. |

Let me introduce myself. My name is … and I am …

| | | |
|---|---|---|
| The | subject<br>topic | of my talk today is … |

| | |
|---|---|
| Today,<br>In this presentation, | I'd like to look at … |

## 2 Outlining the structure of the talk

| | | | |
|---|---|---|---|
| Today | I'm going to<br>I'd like to | look at<br>consider<br>discuss<br>talk about | three main areas … |

I'm going to divide this presentation into three main sections …

| | | |
|---|---|---|
| First, …<br>Firstly, …<br>To start with, … | Second, …<br>Secondly, …<br>Next, …<br>Then …<br>Following this, … | Third, …<br>Thirdly, …<br>Finally, …<br>Lastly, … |

If you have any questions, I'll be glad to answer them at the end of the presentation.

## 3 Introducing a new point/section

| | |
|---|---|
| Moving on now to | look at …<br>consider …<br>my next point … |
| Having looked at …, | I'd now like to move on to …<br>let's now consider … |

## 4 Concluding a point/section

So, you can see that …

To summarize my point, …

## 5 Changing focus

Moving away from … to consider …

| | |
|---|---|
| Let's now look at a different | example.<br>topic.<br>subject. |

To digress for a moment, …

## 6 Introducing an example

For example, …

For instance, …

To take (just) one example, …

| | | |
|---|---|---|
| By way of example, | think of<br>look at<br>consider | … |

## 7 Referring to visual aids

| | | |
|---|---|---|
| If you look at this | OHT<br>slide<br>graph<br>table<br>picture | now, you can see … |

| | |
|---|---|
| To illustrate this point, have a look at this | table<br>chart<br>diagram |

| | | |
|---|---|---|
| You can see from this | chart<br>table<br>diagram | that … |

| | | |
|---|---|---|
| In this<br>Looking at this | chart<br>table<br>diagram | you can see …<br>it is clear that … |

## 8 Concluding and summarizing

In summary, …

In conclusion, …

To summarize, …

| | |
|---|---|
| To sum up<br>To conclude | what I've been saying … |

By way of conclusion, I'd like to …

So, …

| | | |
|---|---|---|
| I hope this presentation has | provided<br>given you | some useful information<br>some issues to think about<br>some help with …<br>an insight into … |

I'd like to conclude by…

| | |
|---|---|
| Thank you for | your attention.<br>listening.<br>your time. |

## 9 Inviting questions

Now, if anyone has any questions, I'd be pleased to answer them.

| | |
|---|---|
| Does anyone have any | questions?<br>comments? |

What questions do you have?

## 10 Dealing with questions

| | |
|---|---|
| Perhaps I can answer that by | referring to …<br>looking at … |

I'm not quite sure about that, but I'll think about it and get back to you.

What does everyone else think?

# THE TELEPHONE

## 1 Getting a number

### 1.1 Generally

*The number's not in the phone book.*
*He's not in the phone book.*
*Are you in the phone book?*
*You omit the zero when dialling France from England.*
*In America, you dial nine one one to get the police station.*

### 1.2 From directory enquiries [BRIT]/ directory assistance [AM]

*Could you get me the number for …*
*What is the dialling code for Liverpool? [BRIT]*
*What is the area code for Los Angeles? [AM]*

### 1.3 From the operator

*I want to make a reverse-charge call to a London number. [BRIT]*
*I want to make a collect call to London. [AM]*
*I want to make an international call.*

### 1.4 In a hotel

*How do I get an outside line?*
*What number do I dial to get room service?*
*I'd like a wake-up call for 7.30 tomorrow (morning).*

## 2 When your number answers

### 2.1 Getting through

*Could I have extension 3179 please?*
*Could you put me through to Dr. Henderson, please?*
*Could I speak to Mr. Smith, please?*
*Is this Mr. Smith's line?*
*Who's speaking?*
*I'm ringing from a callbox. [BRIT]*
*I'm calling from a phone booth. [AM]*
*I'm phoning from England.*

### 2.2 Leaving a message

*Could I leave a message, please?*
*Would you take a message for me, please?*
*I'll call back in half an hour.*
*Could I leave/give you my number for her to call me back?*
*Shall I give you my phone number?*
*Would you ask him to call me when he gets back?*

## 3 Answering the telephone

### 3.1 Generally

*Hello, this is Anne speaking.*
*(Is that Anne?) Speaking.*
*Hello, eight six nine two three five seven.*

### 3.2 The operator speaks

*Which name, please?*
*Which town, please?*
*Where are you calling from?*
*Would you repeat the number, please?*
*Here's the number for you now.*
*There's no listing under that name.*
*They're ex-directory. [BRIT]*
*They have an unlisted number. [AM]*
*All international lines are busy, please try later.*
*I'm trying it for you now.*
*Calling for you now.*
*There's a Mr. Campbell calling you from Brussels. He wishes to reverse the charges. Will you accept?*

### 3.3 The receptionist speaks

*Good morning, Swallow Hotel, can I help you?*
*You've reached our Sales Department.*
*Who's calling, please?*
*Who shall I say is calling?*
*Do you know his extension number?*
*Hold the line, please.*
*Please hold.*
*I'm connecting you/putting you through now.*
*There's no reply.*

### 3.4 The secretary speaks

*I have a call from Tokyo for Mrs. Thomson.*
*I've got Ms. Brown on the line for you.*
*Dr. Roberts is on the other line.*
*Would you like to leave a message?*
*Can I take a message for him?*

## 4 In case of difficulty

### 4.1 Generally

*I've called them several times with no reply.*
*I can't get through (at all).*
*Their phone is out of order.*
*We were cut off.*
*We've got a crossed line.*
*This is a very bad line.*
*I must have dialled the wrong number.*
*You gave me the wrong number.*
*I got the wrong extension.*

### 4.2 On a mobile phone

*The phone line is breaking up.*
*My battery is low.*
*I can't get a signal here.*
*I haven't got any credit on my phone.*

## 5 Recorded messages

*This is a recorded message.*
*Please speak after the tone [BRIT]/after the beep.*
*Please press the hash key [BRIT]/number sign [AM] after the beep.*
*Press the star (*) key twice now.*
*The following options are available from the main menu.*
*If you would like to speak to a Customer Services advisor, please press one.*
*Please replace the handset and try again.*
*The number you are calling knows you are waiting. Please hold the line while we try to connect you.*
*The number you are calling is engaged [BRIT]/busy [AM]. Please try again later.*
*The number you have dialled has been changed. Please redial using the area code/number 0208.*
*The number you have dialled has not been recognized.*
*The number you have dialled no longer exists.*
*Your call is in a queue and will be answered shortly.*

# CORRESPONDENCE

## 1 Business correspondence

### 1.1 E-mail

New message

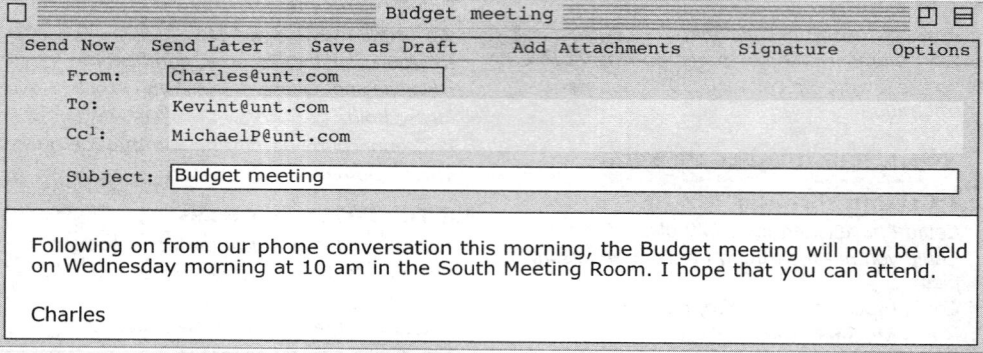

Budget meeting

Send Now | Send Later | Save as Draft | Add Attachments | Signature | Options

From: Charles@unt.com
To: Kevint@unt.com
Cc[1]: MichaelP@unt.com

Subject: Budget meeting

Following on from our phone conversation this morning, the Budget meeting will now be held on Wednesday morning at 10 am in the South Meeting Room. I hope that you can attend.

Charles

[1]carbon copy = copy of message also sent to this address

Received message

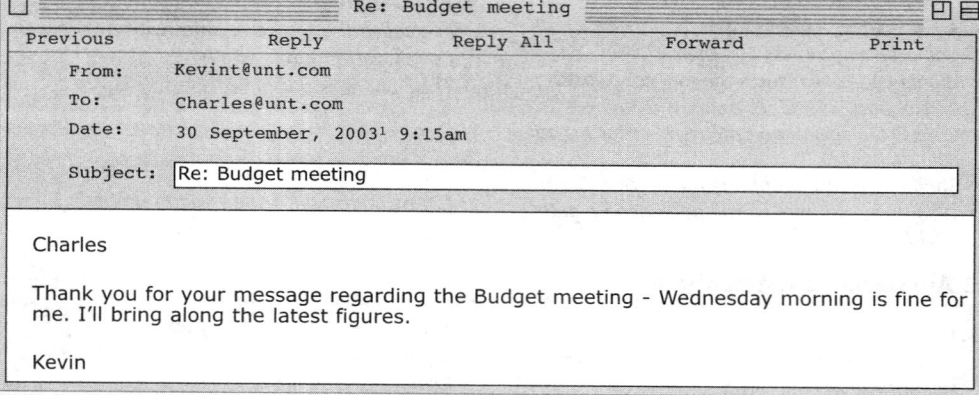

Re: Budget meeting

Previous | Reply | Reply All | Forward | Print

From: Kevint@unt.com
To: Charles@unt.com
Date: 30 September, 2003[1] 9:15am

Subject: Re: Budget meeting

Charles

Thank you for your message regarding the Budget meeting - Wednesday morning is fine for me. I'll bring along the latest figures.

Kevin

[1]In American English, the date is written September 30, 2003.

### 1.2 Memo

**MEMORANDUM**

***TO:*** All staff
***FROM:*** Michael Rivers

***DATE:*** 12 December 2003[1]
***CC:*** Charles Perkins

***SUBJECT:*** Announcement

I am delighted to announce that Kevin Tomms has been promoted to the post of Senior Financial Supervisor with immediate effect. I am sure that you will all join me in wishing him well in his new position.

[1]In American English, the date is written December 12, 2003.

### 1.3 Fax

**FAX MESSAGE**

from **United Signs**

***To:*** Brian Cameron
***From:*** Charles Perkins
***Date:*** 28 November 2003[1]
***Subject:*** December order

***Fax number:*** 0116 423977
***No. of pages (incl. this one):*** 2

Dear Brian,

Please find attached our order for December. Could you please arrange for the goods to be supplied to our warehouse by December 5.

Regards,

Charles

[1]In American English, the date is written November 28, 2003.

## 2 Commercial correspondence

### 2.1 Requesting information

I would be grateful if you would send me …
Please send me details of …
Please advise whether …
Please let me know by return [BRIT]/by return mail [AM] if …

### 2.2 Sending information

Thank you for your enquiry about …
In response to your enquiry of (+*date*) …
We would be delighted to …
We have pleasure in enclosing details of …
I have enclosed …

### 2.3 Reservations

I would like to reserve …
Please consider this a firm reservation.
Please confirm the reservation by fax.
Could I ask you to alter my reservation from … to …
I am afraid I must cancel the reservation.

### 2.3 Placing an order

I would like to place an order for …
Please find enclosed our order no. 623BTX…

### 2.4 Acknowledging an order

Thank you for your order of …
We acknowledge receipt of your order no. 623BTX …
We regret that the goods you have ordered are temporarily out of stock.
Please allow 28 days for delivery.

### 2.5 Delivery

Our delivery time is …
We await confirmation of your order before delivery can be arranged.
We confirm that the goods were dispatched/sent on …
We cannot accept responsibility for goods damaged in transit.

### 2.6 Complaints

We have not yet received …
We wish to draw your attention to …
The goods received differ significantly from the description in your catalogue [BRIT]/catalog [AM].
We shall have to cancel our order.

### 2.7 Payment

The total amount outstanding/due is …
We would be grateful if you would pay immediately.
Please send payment by return [BRIT]/by return mail [AM].
Payment due within 30 days.
I enclose a cheque [BRIT]/check [AM] for … to settle our invoice.
I enclose … as payment for invoice no. …
I would be grateful if you could adjust your invoice accordingly.
We enclose a credit note for …
Thank you for your cheque [BRIT]/check [AM] for …
We look forward to doing further business with you in the near future.

## 3 Standard opening and closing lines

### 3.1 Writing to a firm or institution

| OPENING LINE | CLOSING LINE |
|---|---|
| Dear Sir, | Yours faithfully, |
| Dear Sirs, | |
| Dear Madam, | |
| Dear Sir or Madam, | |

### 3.2 When the person is known to you

| OPENING LINE | CLOSING LINE |
|---|---|
| Dear Professor Brown, | Yours sincerely, |
| Dear Dr Jones, | Sincerely, |
| Dear Mrs Newman, | With kindest regards, |
| Dear Mr and Mrs Jones, | Best wishes, |
| Dear Ms Jackson, | Kind regards, |
| Dear Alison, | All the best, |

In American English, Dr., Mrs., Mr. and Ms. are used.

# CORRESPONDENCE

18 Newton Lane
Oak Ridge, TN
18730

March 23, 2003

Cosy Clothes
36 Bath Street
Liverpool
L23 4JX

Dear Sir or Madam,

I would like to place an order for a ladies' cardigan (ref no. 223-071) from your Winter catalog, and enclose a check for $25.99. Please could you inform me by return letter if this item is not currently in stock.

I would also be grateful if you would send me your latest catalog and price list, and details of the stores in my area which stock your products.

I look forward to hearing from you shortly.

Yours faithfully,

***Margaret Camson***

Margaret Camson

Cosy Clothes
36 Bath Street
Liverpool
L23 4JX

4 April 2003

18 Newton Lane
Oak Ridge, TN
18730

Dear Ms Camson,

Order No: 094512/mxc

Thank you for your order of a ladies' cardigan - the item is currently in stock, and your order will be dispatched within 14 days. We also gratefully acknowledge receipt of your cheque for $25.99.

We have pleasure in enclosing a copy of our new catalogue and price list, and a list of stores in which our products are sold. If you require any further information, please do not hesitate to contact us again. We look forward to doing business with you in the future.

Yours sincerely,

***Moira Smith***

Moira Smith
Manager

## 1 In Britain

17 Alder Avenue
Fintry
Glasgow G63 0BB

27 January 2003

The Personnel Director
Thomas International
Westside Industrial Park
Glasgow G64 4EL

Dear Sir or Madam

Re: Job Reference 685Z

With reference to your advertisement in the Guardian of 25 January 2003, I wish to apply for the post of Export Sales Manager in your company.

I am currently employed as an Export Sales Co-ordinator with Sportswear Ltd, have over ten years' experience in sales and marketing, and am responsible for the sales to the German market. I speak fluent German, and have a working knowledge of French, Spanish and Italian. I feel that my skills and experience could be of great benefit to your company in this post.

I enclose my curriculum vitae for your consideration, and am available for interview at any time. Please feel free to contact me should you require any further information.

Yours faithfully,

Lisa Brown

## *CURRICULUM VITAE*

| | |
|---|---|
| **NAME:** | Lisa Brown |
| **ADDRESS:** | 17 Alder Avenue, Fintry, Glasgow G63 0BB |
| **TELEPHONE:** | 01332 654654 |
| **E-MAIL:** | lisa.brown@skynet.com |
| **DATE OF BIRTH:** | 12.12.67 |
| **NATIONALITY:** | British |
| **QUALIFICATIONS:** | MA Honours in German (First class), Edinburgh University, 1989<br>3 A-levels: German, French, English (all A)<br>8 GCSEs: (all A) |
| **EMPLOYMENT:** | 1992-present: Export Sales, Sportswear Ltd<br>1989-1992: Sales representative, United Confectionery Ltd |
| **HOBBIES:** | I enjoy skiing, running, DIY and travel. |
| **OTHER INFORMATION:** | I speak fluent German, and have a working knowledge of French, Spanish, and Italian<br>I am computer literate<br>I hold a full, clean driving licence |
| **REFEREES:** | I can supply details of two referees on request |

## 2 In the United States

110 West 92nd Street
New York, New York
10025

January 27, 2003

Mr. John Smith
Personnel Director
Thomas International Corporation
53 Madison Avenue
New York, New York
10016

Dear Mr. Smith,

Re: Export Sales Manager Position

With reference to your advertisement in the New York Times of January 25, I wish to apply for the position of Export Sales Manager in your company.

I am currently employed as an Export Sales Co-ordinator with General Sportswear Company, have more than ten years of experience in sales and marketing, and am responsible for all sales to the German market. I speak fluent German, and have a working knowledge of French, Spanish, and Italian. I feel that my skills and experience would be great assets for your company in this position.

I enclose my résumé for your reference, and am available for an interview at any time. Please feel free to contact me if you require any further information.

Thank you for your time and consideration.

Sincerely,

Lisa Brown

### *RÉSUMÉ*

| | |
|---|---|
| **NAME:** | Lisa Brown |
| **ADDRESS:** | 110 West 92nd Street, New York, New York 10025 |
| **TELEPHONE:** | 1-212-873-4150 |
| **E-MAIL:** | lisa.brown@skynet.com |
| **EDUCATION:** | University of Pennsylvania, 1992-1994<br>Master of Arts in Business<br><br>Cornell University, 1987-1991<br>Bachelor of Arts in History, Magna Cum Laude |
| **EMPLOYMENT:** | 1997-Present: General Sportswear Company, New York, New York: Export Sales Co-ordinator:<br>Sell the entire range of sportswear products to all key German accounts. Negotiate terms with all German customers, and conduct regular sales trips to Germany.<br><br>1994-1997: Brooklyn Candy Company, Brooklyn, New York: Sales Representative:<br>Sold the entire range of products to all key national and French accounts. Increased domestic sales by 24% in the fiscal year 1997. |
| **SKILLS:** | Fluent German. Working knowledge of French, Spanish, and Italian. Negotiating. Selling. Familiarity with many computer programs. Typing at 65 words per minute. |
| **REFERENCES:** | References available upon request. |

## 3 Writing a covering letter [BRIT]/cover letter [AM]

### 3.1 Beginning the letter

In reply to your advertisement …
With reference to your advertisement in ….
I wish to apply for the post of ….
I am writing to enquire about the possibility of …

### 3.2 Talking about experience

I am currently working as …
I have a lot of experience in …
I am familiar with …
I am responsible for …
I have a working knowledge of …
I have a reading knowledge of …
My current salary is …

### 3.3 Closing the letter

I enclose my curriculum vitae [BRIT]/résumé [AM] for your consideration.
I am available for interview at any time.
Please do not hesitate to contact me if you require further information.

### 3.4 Accepting/declining an offer

I will be pleased to attend for interview on …
I would like to confirm my acceptance of the post of …
I am delighted to accept your offer of the post of …
I would be delighted to accept this post. However, …
I regret that I am unable to accept your offer of the post of …